大韓每日申報
대한미일신보

1

1904. 8 ～ 1905. 3

한국학자료원

The Korea Daily News.

全帙目次

The Korean Press Institute

대한매일신보
[大韓每日申報]

1904년부터 국권피탈 때까지 발간되었던 일간신문이다. 2012년 10월 17일 국가등록문화재로 지정되었다.

1904년 2월에 일어난 러일전쟁을 취재하기 위해 한국에 왔던 영국인 배설(裵說, 베델:Ernest Thomas Bethell)이 양기탁(梁起鐸) 등 민족진영 인사들의 도움을 받아 7월 18일에 창간하였다.

《대한매일신보》가 창간되던 무렵은 일본측이 한국 언론에 대해 검열을 실시하고 직접적인 탄압을 가하기 시작한 때였다. 그러나 《대한매일신보》는 발행인이 영국인이었기 때문에 주한 일본 헌병사령부의 검열을 받지 않고 민족진영의 대변자 역할을 다할 수 있었다. 사세(社勢)가 확장되고 독자수도 늘어나면서, 통감부(統監府)가 설치된 이후에는 민족진영의 가장 영향력 있는 대표적인 언론기관이 되었다.

《대한매일신보》는 창간 당시에는 타블로이드판(版) 6페이지로서 그 중에서 2페이지가 한글전용이었고, 4페이지는 영문판이었다. 창간 다음해인 1905년 8월 11일부터는 영문판과 국한문신문을 따로 분리하여 두 가지 신문을 발간하였다. 영문판의 제호는 《The Korea Daily News》였고, 창간 당시는 순한글로 만들었던 국문판은 국한문을 혼용하여 발간하였다. 그러나 국한문판을 이해하지 못하는 독자들을 대상으로 하는 한글전용 신문의 필요성을 다시 느끼게 되어 1907년 5월 23일부터는 따로 한글판을 창간하여 대한매일신보사(社)는 국한문 · 한글 · 영문판 3종의 신문을 발행하였으며, 발행부수도 세 신문을 합쳐 1만 부를 넘어 당시로서는 최대의 신문이 되었다. 논설진으로는 양기탁 외에 박은식(朴殷植) · 신채호(申采浩) 등이 있었다.

이와 같이 큰 영향력을 가진 신문이 일제의 한국침략정책을 정면으로 반박하고 나서자 일제는 이 신문에 대해 여러 가지 탄압을 가하게 되었다. 일본측은 외교경로를 통해 소송을 제기하여 발행인 배설은 1907년과 1908년 2차례에 걸쳐 재판에 회부되었고, 양기탁도 국채보상의연금(國債報償義捐金)을 횡령했다는 혐의로 체포되어 재판에 회부되었으나 무죄로 석방되었다. 배설은 이러한 탄압과 싸우는 가운데 1908년 5월 27일부터 발행인 명의를 영국인 만함(萬咸:Alfred Marnham)으로 바꾸었다.

그러나 1909년 5월 1일 배설이 죽고 난 후, 1910년 6월 1일부터는 발행인이 이장훈(李章薰)으로 바뀌었고, 국권피탈이 되면서 조선 총독부의 기관지로 전락했다.

2012년 10월 17일 국가등록문화재로 지정되었으며, 대한매일신보(2012-1)은 서울 서초구 국립중앙도서관에, 대한매일신보(2012-2)는 서울 종로구 국립고궁박물관에, 대한매일신보(2012-3)은 서울 관악구 서울대 중앙도서관에 각각 소장되어 있다.

대한매일신보 [大韓每日申報] (두산백과 두피디아)

大韓每日申報 題号의 변천

報申日每韓大
보신일미한대

창간 당시 題号, 1904년 7월 18일부터

The Korea Daily News.

英文版 The Korea Daily News 題号

報申日每韓大
보신일미한대

国漢文版 1905년 8월 11일(제 3 권 1호)부터

報申日每韓大
보신일미한대

国漢文版 1906년 12월 19일(제400호) 부터
한글판은 1907년 5월23일자 창간호부터 이 제호를사용

報申日每韓大

国漢文版 1907년 4월 16일(제487호)부터

報申日每韓大

国漢文版 1909년 11월 9일(제1237호)부터

보신일미한대
報申日每韓大

한글판 1909년11월 9일(제714호)부터 1910년 8월까지

호외
목요일
ㅣ 십이시까지
숑홈으로 당도시ᄂᆞᆫ
어보를 치실일이오
하며 사파ᄒᆞᆯ실일
보셧다더라
친을 임명ᄒᆞ엿더라
평화회의에 한국 파견원으
동경면보를 거ᄒᆞᆫ즉 해씨가
신압에 피를뿌려서 만국을
인 비셜
삼총약에
일신보사

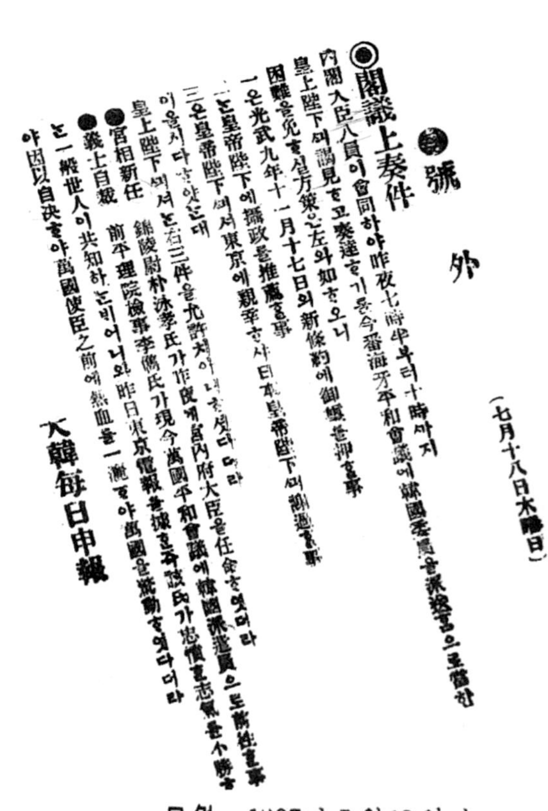

(七月十八日木曜日)

號外

◉閣議上奏件
內閣大臣八員이會同하야昨夜七時半부터十時까지
皇上陛下씌謁見ᄒᆞ고奏達ᄒᆞᆫ기로今番海牙平和會議에韓國委員을派送ᄒᆞᆷ으로由ᄒᆞᆫ
困難을免ᄒᆞᆯ方策은左와如ᄒᆞ오니
一은光武九年十一月十七日의新條約에御璽를押ᄒᆞᆯ事
二ᄂᆞᆫ皇帝陛下에攝政을推薦ᄒᆞᆯ事
三은皇帝陛下씌서東京에親幸ᄒᆞ사日本皇帝陛下씌謝過ᄒᆞᆯ事
이올시다ᄒᆞ얏ᄂᆞᆫ대
皇上陛下씌서ᄂᆞᆫ右三件을允許치아니ᄒᆞ셧다더라

◉宮相新任 錦陵尉朴泳孝氏가昨夜에宮內府大臣을任命ᄒᆞ엿더라

◉義士自殺 前平理院檢事李儁氏가現今萬國平和會議에韓國派遣員으로赴往ᄒᆞᆫ事
ᄂᆞᆫ一般世人이共知하ᄂᆞᆫ비어니와昨日東京電報를據ᄒᆞᆫ즉該氏가忠憤ᄒᆞᆫ志氣를不勝ᄒᆞ
야因以自決ᄒᆞ야萬國使臣之前에熱血을一灑ᄒᆞ야萬國을聳動ᄒᆞ엿다더라

大韓每日申報

号外. 1907년 7월 18일자

大韓每日申報편집국 志士風의 갓쓴 기자들이 붓을 들고 기사를 쓰고 있다.

第七卷第 號

領收證

一金參十錢也

右と 自隆熙三年五月一日 至同年五月卅一日 代金으로 領收홈

隆熙三年五月卅一日

京城南部石井洞大韓每日申報社

收取人

白時鏞 座下

大韓每日申報구독자領收證
1909년 5월분으로 구독한 사람은 白時鏞, 구독료는 30錢이다.

大韓每日申報사장 英国人 裵說 그는 1904년에 来韓하여 국한문판, 영문판, 한글판등 3종의 신문을 발간했다.

裵說의 墓 裵說은 合邦한해 전인 1909년5월1일 이땅에서 죽었다.
이듬해 梁起鐸、張志淵등이 墓碑를 세웠으나(왼쪽) 日人 들이 그 碑文을 깎아 없앴으므로 1964년 언론인들이 새로 작은 碑를 세우고(오른쪽) 그 碑文을 새겼다.

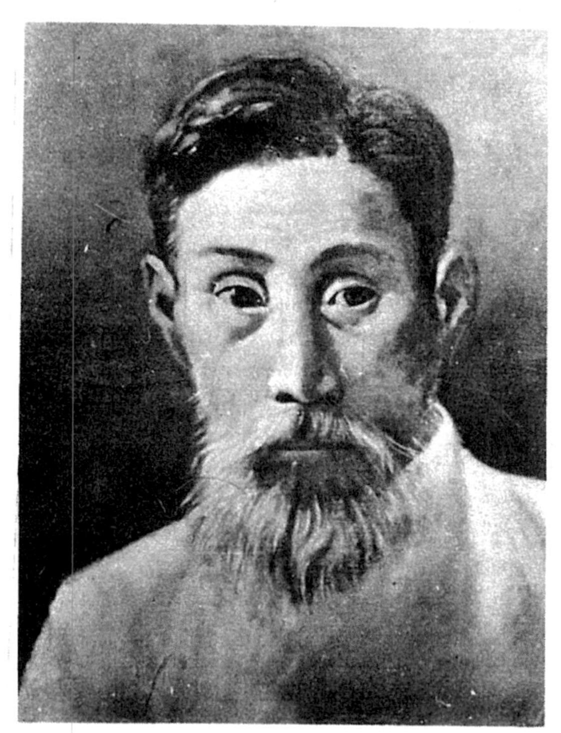

大韓每日申報主筆 梁起鐸 실질적 제작 책임자로서 강경한 抗日論說을 집필하여 자주독립사상을 고취하고 日帝와 싸웠다.

論說委員

朴 殷 植

申 采 浩

大韓每日申報工務局 상투틀고 짚신신은 文選工들 오른쪽에 활자케이스가 보인다.

駐韓英国総領事館건물 1891년에 건립되어 1907년과 1908년 두차례에 걸쳐 裵説에 대한 裁判이 진행되었다.

明治四十年一月改正 同文館發行教育及家庭書類一覽

倫理及修養書類 / 教育學及教育史類 / 心理學及論理學 / 國語及算術書 / 教授法書類

同文館發行商業經濟財政書目は御申越次第無代進呈仕候

이곳치ᄂᆞᆫ광고

경계자ᄂᆞᆫ 본인이귀국에나온지수삼년간
에귀국동포남녀로쇼의츙치、절치、소락치、
전락치、와각죵병치를다수히치료ᄒᆞ얏ᄉᆞᆫ
터청년동포의게ᄂᆞᆫ치의뎨근을젼달ᄒᆞ고고치
의묘법을ᄌᆞ세히졀뎡ᄒᆞ야연헌ᄒᆞᆫ졍ᄆᆞᆫ을공급
ᄒᆞ고특별히소락치와젼락치ᄂᆞᆫ모ᄒᆞᆫ도ᄒᆞ며
물을ᄡᅦ고ᄊᆞᆫ뎨긴ᄒᆞᆫ
ᄒᆞ시게ᄒᆞ야도건의무ᄒᆞᆫ
니와ᄌᆞ금위ᄒᆞ야
료홀터이오니
다수광림ᄒᆞ심을경망
시간은미쳐상오八시
서브터
月 日
공쳐다의셥쥬
ᄃᆡ한대위 근ᄇᆡᆨ

大韓每日申報에끼워 배포되었던 伝単広告들
上은 서적광고, 下는 치과광고

西曆一千九百七年二月一日 金曜日

大韓每日申報

대한매일신보

第五卷 第四百五十一號

月曜及慶節 休刊

論說

한인忠愛

官報

敍任及辭令

部令

外報

雜報

第四百八十二號

報 보

6段制와 7段制의 紙面크기 비교 창간호부터 1907년 4월 6일(제479호)까지는 현재의 타블로이드판보다 약간 넓은 26.5㎝×40㎝에 6段 조판이었으나 4월 7일자 부터는 30.5㎝×46 ㎝로 지폭을 확장하여 7段 조판으로 제작되었다.

約7、000페이지에 달하는 이 尨大한 影印本은 今年에 一次로 3卷을 발행하고 나머지 3卷은 明年初에 發行될것이다。

이 影印本中 後期分에 印刷가 鮮明치 못한 부분은 当時는 오늘날과 같이 活字를 매일 鑄造하지 못하고 한번만든 活字로 一年내지 数年동안 印刷를 했기 때문에 原本자체가 희미한데다가 이것을 다시 影印을 하자니 印刷効果가 나지 않았음을 밝힌다。

本 大韓每日申報 影印本은 韓国文化芸術振興院의 支援으로 刊行된 것입니다.

大韓每日申報
대한매일신보

(뎨십륙호) (목요일) 일쳔구빅사년팔월사일

본사고ᄇᆡᆨ

이 신보는 영어와 한어로셔 ᄆᆡ일 츌판ᄒᆞᆷ

신문가

ᄒᆞᆫ 쟝 엽두돈 오푼

일삭됴 엽두량 닷돈 맛돈으로 밧숩

광고료는

긔한의 쟝단과 ᄌᆞ항의 다쇼로 ᄎᆞ등감ᄒᆞ되 ᄒᆞᆫ가로 밧을터이오며 오릭지 아녀 대한사람마다 다 이 신문을 보실터이니 광고내시기를 원ᄒᆞ시는 이들은 우리 신문사에 와서 변약ᄒᆞ심을 희망ᄒᆞᆸ

발행소 (사쟝 영국인 비셜)

박동 대한ᄆᆡ일신보사 ᄇᆡᆨ어학교 앞희 젼 영국인 설패림 집자리오 인쳔항 교젼동 신지명씨로 우리 대한ᄆᆡ일신보사 인쳔지뎜쟝을 택졍ᄒᆞ엿ᄉᆞ오니 인쳔항에 계신 구람코쟈 ᄒᆞ시는 쳠군ᄌᆞ는 해지뎜에 왕림면의ᄒᆞ시옵

사고

○우리 대한ᄆᆡ일신보의 목뎍은 대한의 안녕질셔에 관한 모든 뎨목에 ᄃᆡᄒᆞ야 논공평한 변론을 주장ᄒᆞᆷ이라 우리 동신원의 뎌보는 신문보시는 쳠군ᄌᆞ의 계ᄒᆞᆼ샹보도ᄒᆞ려며 편지를 긔셔ᄒᆞ여주시는 이 논셜명과 번디를 쳐어붓쳐시기를 희망ᄒᆞ오니 비거슨 신문상에 긔재ᄒᆞ란는 거시 아니오 다만 극히 신용ᄒᆞ는 증거를 숨고자 ᄒᆞᆷ이라 긔쟈는 아모 긔서던지 긔재ᄒᆞᆷ을 뢰각ᄒᆞ는 권리를 가졋소나 뢰각ᄒᆞ는 리유를 말ᄒᆞᆯ터이오며 공중평화를 문란케 ᄒᆞ는 듯ᄒᆞᆫ 긔서는 의례히 밧지 아니ᄒᆞ겟ᄉᆞᆸ나이다

논셜

대한에 잇는 일본반뒤당의 감졍

이 아래 잇는 말은 칠월이십이일에 츌판한 일본영ᄌᆞ시ᄉᆞ보에셔 긔재ᄒᆞᆫ 거시니 운ᄒᆞ되

한셩에 잇는 일본신문 통신원이 지금 대한에 쳔츌ᄒᆞᆫ 일본반뒤당의 긴요ᄒᆞᆫ 소식중에 ᄒᆞᆫ가지 확실ᄒᆞᆫ 원인을 알고 긔재ᄒᆞ여 보내는 뒤항자에 디한셔 북편도 감동반 국인피패버써와너부교본판비 국인 디일광써가 반쥬행편을 시찰ᄒᆞ러 북경으로 파견ᄒᆞ엿더니 칠월십칠일에 도라와 져희 연구ᄒᆞᆫ 거슬 대한공ᄉᆞᆼ에 보고ᄒᆞ엿는디 그 ᄉᆞ실 ᄇᆡ아인의 세민우편당ᄒᆞ여 말ᄒᆞ엿고 쳥금란솜구에 아병ᄉᆞ 만여명이 잇고 랑식은 가히 일년이나 넉넉히 지탱ᄒᆞ겟다ᄒᆞ며 산란솜구에 모든 방어지척을 ᄎᆡ용ᄒᆞ야슴으로 일인이 아무리 맹렬ᄒᆞᆫ 공격을 ᄒᆞ드리도 맛ᄎᆞᆷ내 ᄲᅢ앗기가 어려올 거시라 ᄒᆞ엿다 ᄒᆞ니

반일본일신문통신원이 일본반뒤당을 비양시비는 듯ᄒᆞᆫ 비샹보고를 론급ᄒᆞ올진디 반뒤당을 권면되게 ᄒᆞ며 증비라이니 아기예시 소문펼게스ᄂᆞᆫ영는 거시 이와 굿ᄒᆞᆫ 보고들이 련속ᄒᆞ여 출판이 되엿는디 더러 신문에 이우회난 말보다 며 만히 로국편당들을 긔재ᄒᆞ엿는지라 모든 이런 소문을 ᄒᆞᆯ수 잇는 디로 말ᄒᆞ는 거시 도로혀 이왕 로국편당 되엿든 대한사름들의게 위로ᄒᆞ며 증이라 일본을 반뒤ᄒᆞ는 감졍을 부동식힌다고 말ᄒᆞ는 거슨 부당ᄒᆞ고 우리가 이샹예 엇른ᄒᆞ는 두량반을 위ᄒᆞ야 두돈ᄒᆞ는 거슨 아니로되 일일신문 동신원이 그 동신을 보낼 때에 소문에는 ᄎᆔ우러흠이라 ᄒᆞ노라

잡보

○셩갑일셩 셩진젼감리 심후퇴씨가 궤귀ᄒᆞ야 일젼에 양셩ᄒᆞ엿다더라

○외뷔부진 외부대신 리하영씨가 산림원야 수권으로 오리ᄉᆞ진치 아니ᄒᆞ엿더니 이제 드른즉 ᄒᆞᆫ수간이 겨ᄅᆞᆯ 되기젼에는 일향 시무치 아니ᄒᆞᆫ다더라

○젼조상명 철도원에서 외부로 조회ᄒᆞ기를 젼의군슈 보고니에 칠월구일에 본군 쟝거장에서 일본인이 공영비가 츙을 노와 본국인 리재관이 가츙을 마저 중상ᄒᆞᆫ지라 방포ᄒᆞᆫ 리유를 무른즉 일인의 말이 우연이 방포ᄒᆞᆫ 거시오 사름을 맛치란고 방포ᄒᆞᆷ이 아니라ᄒᆞ고 리재관의 말은 맛참 지음을 지라ᄒᆞᆯ 즈음에 ᄒᆞᆫ지에 탄환을 마저 괴상ᄒᆞ엿다 ᄒᆞᄂᆞᆫ디 그ᄯᅢ에 일본슌ᄉᆞ가 그 방포ᄒᆞᆫ 일인을 잡아셔울 일본령ᄉᆞ관으로 보니엿다ᄒᆞ엿는디 츄후로 산힌군 보고를 졉ᄒᆞᆫ즉 리재관이가 불과긔일에 치명ᄒᆞ엿ᄉᆞ니 샹히 ᄎᆞᆷ흑ᄒᆞ다ᄒᆞ엿기로 이에 조회ᄒᆞ니 일공관으로 조회ᄒᆞ야 뒤샹케 ᄒᆞ라 ᄒᆞ엿더라

졍오

○본월삼일 쟝보니 풍부회ᄉᆞ권으로 희수원 박필원씨가 본사에 리ᄒᆞ야 좌와 굿치 쟝오를 쳥ᄒᆞ는 고로 그디로 긔재ᄒᆞ노라

풍부회사는 쟉년구월에 셜립ᄒᆞ엿고 회사목적은 셕탄광 셕유광 금광 단산 슈긔엽ᄉᆞ 등건이오 회ᄉᆞ는 황실소관이오 ᄉᆞ쟝은 민영철씨오 총무는 박필원 반문교카씨 등이오 고용ᄒᆞᆫ 광ᄉᆞ는 미국인 박비노요 발괴ᄒᆞ기는 민영철씨 박필원씨 아쟝카바노써오 기간소요간 뎡인ᄒᆞ야 쟝시 졍역ᄒᆞ엿다가 일다시셔ᄒᆞᆫ다더라

○민샹의·아 일본헌병이 대한관인 쳑거ᄒᆞᆫ 사건은 쟉보에 긔재ᄒᆞ엿거니와 갱문ᄒᆞᆫ즉 히관인은 보안회 회쟝 원세셩씨와 회원 신형균 리범셕 샹쎼라는 뒤고양으로 쳑거ᄒᆞᆫ 리유는 아직 알수 업스나 민샹이 뫼우위ᄒᆞ다더라

○뒤부죠수 궤병뒤참령셔리 부령 권퇴릭씨는 무승불션ᄒᆞᆫ수가 잇섯는지 칙령으로 급속히 치즁뒤분부를 조수ᄒᆞ는디 만약 ᄎᆡᆼ졀이 잇스면 위션 면관되리라ᄒᆞ며 그후로는 다시에 궐얼시 틀이 젼못ᄒᆞᆫ다더라

○각부유력 일본중의원의원 법학ᄉᆞ 소촌평길씨가 본월삼일에 각부귀쳥을 유력ᄒᆞ겟다고 일본공ᄉᆞ가 외부로 공문ᄒᆞᆫ고로 외부에셔 각부에 통지ᄒᆞ엿더라

○금칙긔간 궁내부에셔 경무쳥으로 조회ᄒᆞᆫ긔에 하도감압 젼쳥진긔지는 곳 슈ᄉᆞᆼ년젼에 좌련ᄒᆞ던 ᄎᆡ소라 비록 ᄒᆞᆫ백ᄒᆞᆫ셔이나 소중이 쳥별ᄒᆞ거늘 흑인리틀 어덧다 ᄎᆞ탁ᄒᆞ고 긔간ᄒᆞ야 밧갈기를 무란이ᄒᆞ니 심히 경히ᄒᆞᆫ지라 붇가불 엄칙금단이니 츙슌파 슌검을 파숑ᄒᆞ야 져간ᄒᆞᆫ 후에 황실과지로 쟝계ᄒᆞ야 표목을 세우고 영구히 보호ᄒᆞ되 만약 범경ᄒᆞᄂᆞᆫ 수름 잇거든 착슈ᄒᆞ고 조시 보고ᄒᆞ야 엄징케 ᄒᆞ라 ᄒᆞ엿더라

○가츙인휘 젼하도감귀지에 ·본인 중림비가 궁내부인리를 득ᄒᆞ엿다 자탁ᄒᆞ고 파목원을 삭미ᄒᆞᄂᆞᆫ 고로 경무쳥에셔 엄히 금지ᄒᆞᄂᆞᆫ 고로 일인비 쟝역ᄒᆞ엿더라

○ᄉᆞ관쳥악 본월일일 하오시에 일본ᄉᆞ관들이 대관쟝에 계회ᄒᆞ야 대한군악뒤ᄉᆞ관 이인으로 더부러 대한군악뒤 샹십오며을 불너 군악을 듯고 샹시ᄒᆞᆼ에 파귀ᄒᆞ엿더라

○범쳥제결 법공ᄉᆞ가 외부로 조회ᄒᆞ기를 한영슈와 의양군 카치칼의 젼답송ᄉᆞ는 광무륙년구월ᄂᆞ리 임의 샹차지관들ᄒᆞ엿ᄉᆞ되 의양군비 ᄌᆞ긔세력을 밋고 종시 ᄌᆞ복지 아니ᄒᆞ니 청컨디 귀대신은 귀법부에 조회ᄒᆞ야 즉시 지관공겨ᄒᆞ야 한영슈로 ᄒᆞ여곰 원억ᄒᆞᆷ이 업게 ᄒᆞ라 ᄒᆞ엿더라

○함챵젼보 함흥관찰ᄉᆞ가 외부로 젼보ᄒᆞ엿스되 북쳥참령의 보고를 졉ᄒᆞᆫ즉 아병 삼ᄇᆡᆨ명이 음력 본월십팔일에 이원으로븟터 북쳥지방에 젼진ᄒᆞ엿다 ᄒᆞ엿더라

뎐보

●탁목셩젼령 본월일일 동경뎐보에 ᄒᆞ기를 거월삼십일일에 일본긔병이 아국긔스단을 격퇴ᄒᆞ야 탁목셩을 졈령ᄒᆞ엿다 ᄒᆞ엿더라

○송슈구졈령 이일 샹오십이시 발젼보에 ᄒᆞ기를 일본군은 거월삼십일븜티 송슈구를 공격ᄒᆞ엿다가 삼십일일에 맛ᄎᆞᆷ내 졈령ᄒᆞ엿다 ᄒᆞ엿더라

흑목대쟝공보 팔월이일 오후팔시공수파착젼

○유슈림격젼 우리 군ᄉᆞ는 유슈림(세하연안셔편샹오리)와 믹사 [illegible] 쳔령에셔 이십오리샹 [illegible] 은다로양에셔 빅리샹) [illegible] 히 졈령ᄒᆞᆫ 젹군을 티ᄒᆞ야 [illegible] 일시 벽브티 공격ᄒᆞ는 [illegible] 엿는디 유슈림방면을 공격ᄒᆞ운돈ᄋᆞ은 그날 황혼에 미리 졈ᄒᆞᆷ과 굿치 젼진ᄒᆞ야 젹군 좌우익을 격파ᄒᆞ엿스나 젹군의 방어비 강ᄒᆞ야ᄒᆞ고 진리가 젼코ᄒᆞᆷ으로 인ᄒᆞ야 밤드도록 격퇴ᄒᆞᆷ을 엇지 못ᄒᆞ엿

일미명에다시
아정오에니르러
로학령(유슈림
습오리)ᄭᆞ지츄격
조령방면을공격홈도
점점실효가잇셔칠월삼십일일
오후한시지나셔브터담만파마
군면산방면에셔브터보병과훈
가지로공격ᄒᆞ며젼진ᄒᆞ여황혼
젼에적진의큰진터를탈취ᄒᆞ엿
ᄉᆞ나적군의일부는가쟝강경ᄒᆞᆫ
게항거ᄒᆞ미밤들기ᄭᆞ지도퇴각
ᄒᆞ지못ᄒᆞ엿고공격ᄒᆞᄂᆞᆫ각군단
온져투ᄒᆞᄂᆞᆫ형셰로밤을지니고
팔월일일미명에다시공격을시
작ᄒᆞ여오젼팔시에양조령부근
일ᄃᆡ의놉흔쌍이온젼히우리군
ᄉᆞ의게도라왓고싸홈이길게되
지못ᄒᆞᆯ거ᄉᆞᆫ지형이험슌ᄒᆞ여공
격ᄒᆞᄂᆞᆫᄃᆡ불편ᄒᆞ고포병의죠흔
진터가업고한셔표가빅도이샹
에달ᄒᆞᆫ이런염텬을당ᄒᆞ야군ᄃᆡ
의로고홈이심홈을인홈이라아
군을ᄃᆡ적ᄒᆞ든양조령부근에잇
든적군은조격보병이ᄉᆞ단반과
포병ᄉᆞ즁ᄃᆡ인데탕하원방면으
로퇴각ᄒᆞ엿고ᄯᅩ유슈림부근에
잇든거ᄉᆞᆫ적어도이ᄀᆡᄉᆞ단과밋
거긔속ᄒᆞᆫ포병인ᄃᆡ그ᄃᆡ부은안
평방면으로퇴각ᄒᆞ엿더라피아
잔ᄉᆞ샹은됴ᄉᆞ즁이오포획ᄒᆞᆫ거
ᄉᆞᆫ야포약잔이더라

외보

○려슌졍황 거월이십륙일에
영국륜선에온보고데알려슌에
괴질은점점만연ᄒᆞ게되처ᄒᆞᄂᆞᆫ
ᄃᆡ처음붓터ᄉᆞ망이삼빅명이나
되고려슌의아군젼투ᄒᆞᄂᆞᆫ군인
은족히말ᄒᆞᆯ잘것업ᄉᆞ나이만가
량에넘지못홈이적실ᄒᆞ고ᄯᅩ모
쳐에셔항복을권ᄒᆞᄂᆞᆫᄃᆡ아군즁
고등참모에지식잇고근리젼술
을빈운ᄌᆞ들은만히항복홈을찬
셩ᄒᆞᄂᆞᆫ모양이잇스ᄂᆞ려슌ᄀᆡ쳑
시붓터잇든참모들은불가타ᄒᆞ
ᄂᆞᆫ고로아직의론이귀일치못ᄒᆞ
고모쳐에회답홀긔한은거월이
십ᄉᆞ일이더니그져회답이이르
지아니ᄒᆞ엿고ᄯᅩ아국관동보ᄂᆞᆫ
금월(양칠월)로한졍ᄒᆞ고졍간
치아니ᄒᆞ면쓸됴회가결핍ᄒᆞ겟
고ᄯᅩ동신은젼셔구라ᄒᆞᄂᆞᆫ비둘
가로써료양ᄭᆞ지간신이통신ᄒᆞᆫ
다더라

○구축아인 미국오리곤시엿
도라인철노에셔ᄂᆞᆫ젼붓터아국
인역부를만히부리더니근일에
다히고ᄒᆞ엿다더라

○여론일변 빅림젼보에왈덕
국신문즁에ᄌᆞ리로아국에ᄃᆡ단
호졍을가지든것도즉금은아국
ᄒᆡᆼ동에ᄃᆡᄒᆞ야미우격앙ᄒᆞ고번
연ᄒᆞ게일본를찬셩ᄒᆞ야일잔은
일본칭찬ᄒᆞᄂᆞᆫ말놀긔지ᄒᆞ게되
엿다더라

관보

○의원면본관 셔북철도국주
ᄉᆞ 송민회 허유 오지슌
김진규 원셰학 리용묵 죠
경묘참봉 송죵학 경긔젼참
봉 우죵민 긔ᄌᆞ릉참봉 리
우교 임셔북철도국주ᄉᆞ셔관
임관륙등 륙품 용셔유
학 홍우긔 김명션 리샹직
김동진 하종호 리근명 김
틱쥰 룡영쥬 리응렬 입죠
경묘참봉셔관임관팔등구품
졍ᄌᆡ셩 임경긔젼참봉셔관임
관팔등 륙품 송대진 임긔
ᄌᆞ릉참봉 셔관임관팔등 임동명
왕릉참봉 강희린 임동명왕
릉참봉셔관임관팔등 윤틱진
승셔관임관칠등 규쟝각쥬ᄉᆞ
윤우영

○궁졍록ᄉᆞ
죠왈죵이픔리명샹으로위비셔
원승ᄒᆞ라 칠월삼십일
궁닉부대신셔리박용화근쥬
ᄒᆞ되쟝례원긔록과쟝엄건영현
지명우ᄒᆞ니난부싱슈ᄒᆞ온자라
긔북시무ᄒᆞ옴이하여ᄒᆞ올지샹
쥬ᄒᆞ와봉 지의쥬ᄒᆞ다○의졈
부참졈홍슌형ᄉᆞ직소 비지닉
에병을엇지말ᄒᆞ리오ᄉᆞ양말고
ᄒᆡᆼ공ᄒᆞ라○농샹공부협관리군
샹ᄉᆞ직소 비지닉에ᄉᆞ양말고
ᄒᆡᆼ공ᄒᆞ라○황히도관찰ᄉᆞ김학
슈ᄉᆞ직소 비지닉에고집홀의
리가업거놀일향굿게ᄉᆞ양ᄒᆞ니
이엇지훈도리뇨경인즉보외로
시ᄒᆡᆼᄒᆞ리라 어샹칠월삼십일
포달
포달뎨일빅이십일호
뎨이십륙죠 궁닉부소속 직
원즁 어공원관졔를산거홈이
라
뎨에팔쳔빅구십오호 광무
팔년팔월삼일
○셔임급사령
○셔훈ᄉᆞ등ᄉᆞ팔패쟝 졍삼픔
한억길 셔훈오등ᄉᆞ팔패쟝
농샹공부기ᄉᆞ 졍룡환 시죵
원시죵 박용슉
○의원면본관 황히도관찰부
쥬ᄉᆞ 하계호 츙쳥남도관찰
부쥬ᄉᆞ 김룡셔 임황히도관찰
찰부쥬ᄉᆞ셔관임관륙등 리졍
구 임츙쳥남도관찰부쥬ᄉᆞ셔
관임관륙등 빅지화 이샹칠
월삼십일
○의원면본관 규쟝각직학ᄉᆞ
김셕규 졍통참봉 리병억
닉쟝원공업과쥬ᄉᆞ 윤승슈
김은길 동신ᄉᆞ젼화과쥬ᄉᆞ
송슈영 오호영 김동만 김
지홍 윤지철 곽종ᄃᆡ 윤경
의 김영필 법관양셩소박ᄉᆞ
심종ᄃᆡ 로종빈 구승회 셩
기영 박쥰영 류룡균 윤달
영 비영균○히 겸임닉쟝원
소관경샹북도봉셰감리 샹쥬
군슈 안학쥬 ○명 닉쟝원
경셔칙임관삼등 졍이픔오졍
션 임규쟝각직학ᄉᆞ셔쥬임관
오뜽 졍삼픔 홍슌구 임닉
쟝원봉셰관셔쥬임관륙등 륙
픔 김동두 ○명 한미젼긔
회ᄉᆞ금찰쟝 농샹공부협관
리근샹 명 한미젼긔회ᄉᆞ금
찰관 례식원참리관 남졍규
학부농샹공학교쟝 홍우관
입닉쟝원공업과쥬ᄉᆞ셔관임관
팔등 허 현 안병규 임영
릉령셔관임관칠등 졍릉령
임빅션 임졍릉령셔관임관칠
등 션릉령 한창리 임션릉
령셔관임관칠등 틱릉참봉김
직형 임졍릉참봉셔관임관팔
등틱릉참봉 민영욱 명 닉
쟝원봉셰위원 륙픔 최진우
승셔관임관오등 돈령원쥬ᄉᆞ
오규환 승셔판임관ᄉᆞ등 법
부쥬ᄉᆞ 류갑슈 임법관양셩
소박ᄉᆞ셔관임관륙등 구픔
졍홍우 유학 권틱졍 신졍
식 남보원 죠동슉 권중근
리한구 이샹팔월일일

○궁졍록ᄉᆞ
○죠왈졍삼픔한억길이왕년에
특이한공로가잇스니특별이ᄉᆞ
등훈에셔훈ᄒᆞ야팔괘쟝을쥬고
농샹공부기ᄉᆞ졍룡환과시죵원
시죵박용슉이ᄯᅩ한왕년에긔렴
할만훈효로가잇스니특별이오
등에셔훈ᄒᆞ야팔괘쟝을쥬라
광무팔년칠월삼십일
죠왈졍이픔오졍션으로위쟝
례원경ᄒᆞ라 팔월일일
○즁츄원의쟝신민영소근쥬
본원의관신히영이광무삼년일
월삼일에망명죄인을혼거ᄒᆞ자
고회의홀때에가훈번으로거슈
훈ᄉᆞ로의정부에셔봉현고상
쥬ᄒᆞ와면본관ᄒᆞ엿숩더니일
년구ᄒᆞ야임의경감ᄒᆞ엿시니특
별이면징계ᄒᆞ옴이하ᄒᆞ올는
지 상 쥬ᄒᆞ와봉 지의쥬
ᄒᆞ라
○닉장원경최병쥬ᄉᆞ직소
비지닉에소청ᄃᆡ로의시ᄒᆞ라ᄒᆞ
셧더라

잡보

○슉시슉비 대안문젼일인의
집근쳐에한ᄃᆡ뒷간이잇ᄂᆞᆫᄃᆡ평
양병졍이뒤보고나올조음에일
인이총집우에셔소리지르며
나려와병졍더러ᄌᆞ긔집이셔시
계를ᄯᅥ여가다가니소리를듯고
ᄶᅡ에ᄶᅥ졋다ᄒᆞ고잡아가지고힐
난ᄒᆞᆯᄌᆞ음에헌병이보고잡아간
고로병졍들이말ᄒᆞ되대한사ᄅᆞᆷ
온ᄯᅩᆼ도눌슈업다ᄒᆞ고ᄀᆡ탄불이ᄒᆞ
더라더라
○군인셩칙 원슈부금ᄉᆞ국총
쟝현영운씨가각ᄃᆡ로훈령ᄒᆞ되
령위긴과병졸이년본거쥬와부
며파군인의참례ᄒᆞᆫ년월일ᄌᆞ를
셩칙ᄒᆞ여드리라고신칙ᄒᆞ엿다
더라
○지쟝셔리 작야에 대닉쳐
분이계옵셔법부로젼화ᄒᆞ옵시
되평리원지관쟝셔력를슈반관
ᄉᆞ로내젼례가잇나냐ᄒᆞ옵셧ᄂᆞᆫ
되젼례가잇슴으로샹 쥬ᄒᆞ엿
손즉슈반관ᄉᆞ허쉬씨가광리원
지관쟝셔리가되리라더라
○가ᄃᆡ환되 동ᄃᆡ문밧마쟝리
리병찬의가ᄃᆡ를일본사람이오
빅원에ᄉᆞ셔일변가ᄉᆞ를건축ᄒᆞ
며과목과포도등물을시무ᄂᆞᆫ고
로한셩부에셔관사람과산얼인
을합셔ᄒᆞ고소윤박승됴씨가재
작이일에지화륙쳔원을환퇴ᄒᆞ
기로계약ᄒᆞ고일인이다시ᄂᆞᆫ과
목죵벌에착슈아니ᄒᆞ고실과가,,
다셩실ᄒᆞᆫ후음력구월후에영의
리병찬의게환급ᄒᆞ기로확졍ᄒᆞ
엿더라
○함젼아병 함경남도젼유ᄉᆞ
리교영씨가닉부로젼보ᄒᆞ되아
병일빅오십긔가북청에닉도ᄒᆞ
야방금함흥을향ᄒᆞᆫ다는급보
가잇ᄂᆞᆫ고로빅셩이다경황ᄒᆞ야
만히환산ᄒᆞᆫ다ᄒᆞ엿더라
○연안적보 연안군슈민영원
씨가닉부로보고ᄒᆞ되음력륙월
십ᄉᆞ일에본군라포동거민이급
보ᄒᆞ되즉금병복ᄒᆞᆫ적ᄒᆞᆫ일명파
빅의적십륙명이다양총을가지
고본동에돌입ᄒᆞ야젼지와의복
등물을탈취ᄒᆞ고평명에슈로로
츌포ᄒᆞᆫ다ᄒᆞ오니여간교졸노ᄂᆞᆫ
형착ᄒᆞ기어렵고적슈공권으로
ᄂᆞᆫ집포ᄒᆞᆯ슈업쓰니양총오십병
과탄환오쳔기를하송ᄒᆞ야방어
케ᄒᆞ라ᄒᆞ엿더라
○일ᄉᆞ죠회 일본공ᄉᆞ가외부
에죠회ᄒᆞ기를안쥬군슈가부임
치아니홈으로군ᄉᆞ샹에구익됨
이만코셩진감리ᄂᆞᆫ원산항에체
류ᄒᆞ야부임치아니ᄒᆞᄂᆞᆫ고로군
ᄉᆞ샹에ᄯᅩᄒᆞᆫ구익가만으니일체
훈령ᄒᆞ야군슈와감리를속히부
임케ᄒᆞ라ᄒᆞ엿더라

TELEGRAMS.

REPORT FROM KUROKI.

HEAVY FIGHTING.

Tokyo, August 2nd, 8 P. M.

Our troops commenced to attack the enemy at daybreak on the 31st July. They occupied a strong position in the vicinity of Yusulintze (15 *li* west of Seiho) and Yangtzeling, (25 *li* from Motienling) both places situated about 100 *li* from Liaoyang. We succeeded in attacking the left and right wings of the enemy's force at dusk on the same day as previously resolved, but we were unable to drive them from their strong position. At daybreak on the 1st we again attacked and at noon succeeded in driving them from their position and pursuing them as far as Laoholing, 15 *li* west of Yusulintze. Also we did well in our attack at Yangtzeling. At 1 P. M. on the 31st we moved forward to the attack and occupied a strong position, but owing to the stubborn resistance of the enemy we were unable to dislodge them and fighting continued all night.

At daybreak we again commenced a strong attack and at 8 A. M. succeeded in occupying all the heights in the vicinity of Yangtzeling. The battle could not have continued longer on account of the dangerous positions of the artillery and the excessive heat, the thermometer registering over 100 degrees, causing great hardship to the troops. The enemy engaged in the attack were 2½ divisions of sharp shooting infantry and 4 batteries of artillery. These retreated in the direction of Tang-ho-wan. The enemy who were engaged at Yusulintze were probably two divisions and some artillery. Most of these retreated in the direction of Anping. We are now engaged in counting the casualties. We have captured a few field guns.

Tokyo August 1st.

On July 31st, Japanese cavalry drove one division of Russian infantry from Semuchŏng.

Tokyo Aug 2nd.

On the 30th July, commenced the attack on Sungsukow and occupied that place next day. (Sungsukow is north of Motienling and east of Liaoyang.)

THE DEATH OF JAPANESE SPIES.

The following is translated from a pathetic account of the execution of two Japanese officers, appearing in the columns of Le Petit Temps.

I have from a Russian Marine, who has returned from Kharbin, the unpublished details of the death of the two Japanese spies, whom the Russian Cossacks arrested when they were just about to blow up a railway bridge in Manchuria.

My interlocutor, quite a young man, was severely wounded during the first bombardment of Port Arthur. He obtained leave to visit Italy, but enroute, went to Kharbin where he arrived at the moment when the two Japanese were caught in the act, tried and arrested. "You assisted at the execution of the two Japanese?" I asked him, "Alas! I saw them die," replied the young marine. And as I regarded him with astonishment, he hastily added, "Do not take me for an anarchist I am on the the contrary, patriotic to the soul. I ardently wished for war with Japan, wished to see the Japanese exterminated and to be able to dictate other terms of peace than at Tokyo, but, like all my comrades, when I saw these two officers, who have given their life so courageously for their country, fall before the bullets of our soldiers, I could not help but think the execution cruel.

"You were present at the trial?"

I saw the two spies arrested and I was present at their trial and execution. I will relate everything to you in detail. The horrible spectacle haunts me and I shall never forget it.

The formalities of the trial were very simple, the indictment without interest, the prisoners from the very first acknowledging full responsibility for their actions.

They declared their names and rank without the vestige of tremor in their voices.

"Tchomo Jokoka, 41 years of age, Colonel in his Imperial Majesty's army, graduate of the military school of Yeddo." "Teisko Jokki, 31 years of age, Captain in his Imperial Majesty's army," said his companion, a man of swarthy face and prominent features. "Buddhist," he added after an instant.

"And you Colonel," asked the President of the Court of Justice, "are you of the same religion as your companion?"

"No, President, I am a Christian," and remarking the astonishment produced by this declaration, he hastened to add, "I am all the same a true Japanese, born of Japanese parents, only during my youth I was drawn by the sweet word of Christ and I am converted to Lutheranism."

Colonel Jokoka spoke English, and a British subject, an employé of the Russo-Japanese bank acted as translator. Captain Jokki was interrogated through the intermediary of a Chinese interpreter. I observed the faces of the two men, when the sentence of death was passed upon them, and I could not discern the slightest trace of fear in either. They were absolutely impassive, the sorrowful trend of their thoughts was not betrayed by sign. The trial lasted half an hour and the tribunal condemned them to the maximum punishment, hanging.

The sentence was to be executed at dawn the following day. They only awaited a confirmatory telegram from General Kuropatkin. The telegram arrived promptly, the general approved their condemnation, but wished them to be spared the humiliation of hanging and ordered them instead to be shot, as a tribute to their rank and bravery.

I was present when the commandant read the message to the prisoners.

"It is well," said Colonel Jokoka, "I am ready." The Captain said nothing.

The Colouel asked for permission to write to his family, afterwards he embraced the Captain. "I shall die more quietly than you, Colonel," said the latter.

"How is that"?

"I have fulfilled my duty to my sountry and my Gods. You have only done your duty to your country."

"Why so"?

"I have reflected much, Colonel, on what you have told me of Christianity, you are always vaunting its superiority. And now I find you are not in sympathy with Christ. I have nothing to reproach myself with."

"You are quite right Captain. And now I have a favor to beg of you.

"Give me authorisation to perform the one truly Christian act I shall have done in my life. You know that I still possess a number of bank notes. I have a thousand Russian roubles. And now I desire to present this money to the Russian commandant for donation to the Russian Red Cross Society, for the benefit of our wounded enemies."

Jokki after reflecting for an instant replied, "I have always had great affection Colonel, and if it would give you pleasure, you can present this money to our enemies."

When the Commandant came to find the prisoners, Colonel Jokoka gave him the notes. "Here are about a thousand roubles, we beg you to give them to the Red Cross." "But wouldn't it be better if I were to send the money to your families?" "asked the Colonel. "No, no, they cried together, "our Emperor will not forget our wives and children." "Do not refuse us this satisfaction," said Jokoka, "distribute this money among the Russian wounded."

The Russian commandant at length agreed and asked the prisoners if he could do anything for them.

"I would like to take a bath if it is possible," said the Buddhist, "after that we are at your disposal."

A bath-room being a luxury unknown at Kharbin, the commandant gave orders to the sentries to fetch buckets of water and leave the prisoners to their ablutions.

The Colonel's desire was to see a priest. As there was no Lutheran pastor the regimental priest was brought to him and together they read The Sermon on the Mount, the priest reading in Slav and the Colonel following the words from his Japanese bible.

"Jokki," said the Colonel, "you are right you will die more tranquilly than I for I have never more vividly realised how entirely in disaccord with Christ my life has been."

The carriage which was to convey them to the execution ground was waiting.

The two Japanese arrived, as impassive as ever, but one could see that the Colonel was engrossed in sorrowful thoughts. They both lit cigarettes and asked not to be tied up to posts.

The Commandant prepared two pocket handkerchiefs and tendered them to the prisoners.

The Colonel bandaged his eyes himself. The Captain refused the proferred handkerchief disdainfully, remarking that he would like to see how an execution was carried out.

A dozen soldiers were posted facing the Colonel, a dozen in front of the Captain. "If you have pity on these unfortunate men, "said the Colonel," aim straight at the heart. Death with be instantaneous." A volley was fired. The Colonel fell on his left side, the Captain straight forward on his face.

Both had been immediately killed. Our soldiers had pity on them.

JAMES McNEIL WHISTLER.

THREE EXTRACTS.

It has been said and said again within the past month that James McNeill Whistler was an artist in words as well as a poet in colours. It is pleasant to turn to his famous "Ten o'clock" to find there proof upon proof of the statement. As for instance this ethereal account of the beginning of art:—

"In the beginning, man went forth each day—some to do battle, some to the chase; others, again, to dig and to delve in the field—all that they might gain and live or lose and die. Until there was found among them one differing from the rest, whose pursuits attracted him not, and so he stayed by the tents with the women and traced strange devices with a burned stick upon a gourd.

"This man, who took no joy in the ways of his brethren, who cared not for conquest, and fretted in the field; this designer of quaint patterns, this deviser of the beautiful, who perceived in nature about him curious curvings, as faces are seen in the fire; this dreamer apart, was the first artist."

Or this:—

"Seldom does nature succeed in producing a picture. The sun blares, the wind blows from the east, the sky is bereft of cloud, and without all is of iron. The windows of the Crystal Palace are seen from all points of London. The holiday-maker rejoices in the glorious day, and the painter turns aside to shut his eyes."

Or, finally, take the following embroidery on Mr. Whistler's doctrine that Art is the most exclusive of all teachers:—

"With the man, then, and not with the multitude, are her intimacies; and in the book of her life the names inscribed are few—scant, indeed, the list of those who have helped to write her story of love and beauty.

"We have then but to wait until, with the mark of the Gods upon him, there come among us again the chosen—who shall continue what has gone before. Satisfied that, even were he never to appear, the story of the beautiful is already complete, hewn in the marbles of the Parthenon, and broidered, with the birds, upon the fan of Hokusai, at the foot of Fusiyama."

Signor Nicola
gineer, has just
appliance for the d.
accidents. It is an
which Signor Stea n
Warning." Its actio
such that no two trains
selves on the same line of rails within a danger area, without the guards of both receiving warning. In the case of two trains following each other, the rear train would only receive warning in case of the stoppage of the train in front, or of a portion of it. The fall of a bridge, or a landslip, would also cause the warning apparatus of an approaching train to act.

Mr. Song Su-man, while in the Korean prison, suffered greatly from the oppression of the jailers, who refused to give him proper food without a substantial bribe. His cousin came to the rescue with funds and ensured his proper treatment.

We learn that the three Koreans, who were taken by the Japanese outside the city as reported in our issue yesterday, are Messrs. Won Se-sung, Sin Hyong-kiune and Yi Pom-sok. They were "wanted" in connection with the Po-an-hoi meetings.

A Korean named Yi Chai Kwan was recently shot by a Japanese coolie on the railway line at Chon Eui. The victim has since died and the Magistrate prays for capital punishment of the offender.

The resignation of the Minister of Foreign Affairs has been refused until the Waste Land concern is finished.

The Korea Daily News.

To be published daily except Sundays.

Rate of Subscription:—

Per Year,	Yen 25.
Per Quarter,	Yen 7.
Per Month	Yen 2.50

Postage in Korea not charged extra.
Postage abroad charged extra.

Advertisements, 50 sen per day for 1 inch or less.
5 yen per month per inch.
50 yen per year per inch.

All communications to

E. T. BETHELL,
Editor and Publisher.
Pak-tong, Seoul.

PROTECTING KOREA.

The "Kobe Chronicle" of July 18th in a long editorial article dealing with the Waste Lands scheme, and some remarks made by Mr. Nagamori in connection therewith, says:—

It is melancholy to reflect that the nation which a few years ago was fiercely indignant at the restrictions imposed on its fiscal policy and its judicial jurisdiction by means of treaties, should now be so indifferent to the right of a neighbouring state to decide adversely to the Japanese proposal on a matter which, according to former Japanese contentions, lies at the very foundations of national existence. In Japan, foreigners are not permitted to own land, and a proposal on the part of the government to grant a charter to foreigners to cultivate the unoccupied land even of the Hokkaido would result in a national outburst of indignation that would drive the minister responsible from power. In the course of the negotiations on the revision of the Anglo-Japanese Treaty, Viscount Aoki said the ownership of real estate by foreigners in Japan was a question which his Government were of opinion should not be regulated by treaty, but should be reserved for treatment by autonomic legislation. He himself, he added, and many of his official friends, were in favour of granting to foreigners the right to own real estate, but public opinion was not yet on their side.

Yet a scheme which would be bitterly resented in Japan is to be forced on the Koreans because they are helpless to prevent their protector from paying himself for their protection. "Treat a fool as a fool," says Mr. Nagamori with a courtesy that we should not like to describe as Japanese, "and we shall succeed in our work." And if the scheme fails Mr. Nagamori thinks it will be better for the Japanese to withdraw from Korea altogether. The interests of the Koreans in the matter are absolutely ignored. They are "fools" who are not worth consideration. The waste land is to be cultivated by Japanese, who are to be sent to the peninsula in large numbers—Mr. Nagamori talks of millions in connection with the abortive Siam scheme—and the twenty millions which are to be realized by the import of the rice from the reclaimed land are to go into the pockets of Japanese colonists. In return for providing Japan with rice, the Japanese in Korea are apparently expected to take Japanese goods, which may raise the inquiry as to whether the rice imported into Japan is not already paid for in this way rather than in specie. But the important and interesting feature of the incident is its disclosure of the fashion in which some influential Japanese would treat a subject nation, so soon after the recovery by Japan herself of judicial jurisdiction and fiscal control,—efforts that covered some thirty years during which full use was made of the right of a governing state to demand equality of treatment. We ourselves strongly supported that claim as a matter of justice and we regret to find eminent Japanese refusing to extend to others the rights so insistently claimed for themselves.

It is hard to see what reply Japan can make to the "Kobe Chronicle's" able indictment. True we are told that Nagamori's scheme—and Nagamori himself—have been abandoned by the Japanese Government and we are promised that the demand which is now being formulated is of a greatly modified character, but we very much doubt whether a scheme can be devised, satisfactory to this newly developed land grabbing instinct of the Japanese, to which the "Chronicle's" arguments will not apply with equal force.

MRS. LONDON SUES FOR DIVORCE.

San Francisco, June 28th.

Mrs. London, wife of Jack London, the novelist, to-day filed a suit for divorce, basing her petition on the grounds of cruelty.

Mrs. London asserts that her husband brought to their home in Oakland a young woman graduate of Stanford, Miss Anna Strunsky, who collaborated with him in a series of papers called he "Kempton-Wace Letters." Miss Strunsky was installed in the London household for several weeks, and remained despite Mrs. London's protests.

Mrs. London further states that her husband frankly told her he cared for another. They were married in 1900.

WONDERFUL COMBINATION OF MINERALS.

We are given to understand that a company named the Pung Bu Hoi Sa will shortly be established and capitalised at the expense of the Government. The originators of the concern are three men, General Min Yong Chul, an American miner, and Mr. Pak Pil-yun, who is known to many residents under an English soubriquet.

These gentlemen have discovered a veritable mine of wealth, comprising gold and coal mines, kerosene and mineral water springs in the neighborhood of Pyeng Yang. For the benefit of those who may wish to try Korean Tansan, we trust that the springs are not too closely situated.

A GARDEN ON THE BLUFF.

Dispensing with all tiresome details, such as the trivial item of purchasing the property, a man named Nakahayashi, a Japanese subject, found some ground to his liking in the neighbourhood of Ha-Do-Kam. His primeval instincts once asserted in this manner, he commenced building a sylvan retreat of fruit trees, their product of course not destined for the market! Whether Mrs. Eve Nagahayashi was concerned in the deal has not transpired, but unfortunately for the gentleman's plans, police departments and sundry other nuisances have developed since the days of Adam and he no onger enjoys the delights of stolen fruit.

SUSPECTED COMMISARIAT FRAUDS.

His Majesty has ordered an enquiry into the transactions and affairs of Major Yi-Tai-Rai, chief of the commisariat department, who is suspected of fraudulent dealings in connection with the department under his care.

Mr. Kogawa, a member of the Japanese House of Commons, has expressed a desire to visit all Korean Government Departments.

MANCHURIAN VEGETABLES AND FRUITS.

Mr. Hosil in his interesting book on Manchuria enumerates its vegetables and fruits. The armies campaigning there should be fairly supplied in these respects. There are several varieties of potato of excellent quality, turnips, radish, carrot, garlic, onion, leek, celery, brinjals, and, most important of all, Shantung cabbage. The last named enters largely into the diet of the people, and is universally cultivated, not merely in gardens, but in fields. In the Sanking province, more especially in the Laichou prefecture, it developes tremendous proportions. A gentleman in Chefoo received a letter from a friend in Laichou announcing that he was sending him a present of a cabbage. The recipient was somewhat surprised at what he considered the insignificance of the gift. He tossed the letter aside, and thought nothing more of the matter until a day or two afterwards, when his servant reported to him that a cabbage had arrived, and that the carter evidently expected a "pour-boire." "Carter!" said the gentleman, "what do you mean? Has the cabbage come by cart?" "Yes," replied the servant, "the cart is now at the gate." Determined to get to the bottom of the matter, he went to the gate, and there lay a huge cabbage, about 400 pounds in weight, occupying the whole of the cart! "That cabbage," said the gentlemen, "lasted me a whole winter." White heart weighing 20 pounds and upwards from Shantung are frequently to be seen in the market at Niuchwang. There are also many forms and varieties of melon, pumpkin, squash, vegetable marrow, cucumbers, and gourds. Another important vegetable in Manchuria is "kait'sai." It developes a bulk inferior in size to a turnip, and has numerous long broad finely scalloped leaves. Both bulb and leaves are salted in jars and eaten as a pickle. The seeds of sunflower are also roasted and found principally in the east of Kerin province. Foreign vegetables such as tomato, lettuce, cabbage, and Jerusalem artichoke, grow well in Manchuria.

There are several varieties of excellent grapes, both green and purple. Pears except one kind are hard and insipid. The best kind are so soft as not readily to bear transit in a fresh state. It is preserved and packed in boxes like figs. Apples are most poor but there are two good varieties of chestnut, while walnut, peaches, plums, apricots, and a kind of cherry are plentiful. Strawberries, bilberries, gooseberries, and currants grow wild, and are only cultivated in the gardens of a few foreign residents.—Rangoon Times.

Cronje, the redoubtable soldier of Laing's Nek, Modder River, Maggersfontein, and Paardeburg, reduced to the level of circus exhibit, remarks the *Globe*, is a thought many would wish to banish. But such is the fact. All his dogged struggles among the kopjes, and the trenches, and the deadly Boer marksmen, are all to be reproduced in pasteboard make-believe for the sightseers of St. Louis Exhibition, with Cronje himself as chief "draw." The old Commander's self-justification for accepting such a position, as explained by himself in a Paris newspaper to-day, speaks for itself. Unlike some others of the old ruling Transvaal caste, he had no Rand gold, but was simply an agriculturist, and with lands devastated, buildings wrecked, and stock swept away in the war, he is literally a beggar, on the brink of old age, with nothing but the showman's offer to save him from destitution.

The Education Department are in receipt of an Imperial order to provide the names of sons and relatives of high officials with a view to sending them to Japan to study. They are unable to furnish this list however as the sons and relatives referred to show a great disinclination to come forward.

Three hundred Russians are reported to be marching from Yi Won southward to Puk Chong.

The Korea Daily News

VOL. I, THURSDAY, AUGUST 4, 1904.

HONGKONG & SHANGHAI BANKING CORPORATION.

Paid-up Capital	$10,000,000
Reserve Fund:—Sterling Reserve	10,000,000
Silver Reserve	6,500,000
	26,500,000
Reserve Liability of Proprietors	10,000,000

HEAD OFFICE, HONGKONG.

London Bankers, London and County Banking Company Limited.

Branches and Agencies,

London.

Amoy,	Hankow	Penang,
Bangkok,	Hiogo,	Rangoon,
Batavia,	Iloilo,	Saigon,
Bombay,	Lyons,	San Francisco,
Calcutta,	Manila,	Singapore,
Colombo,	Nagasaki,	Sourabaya,
Foochow,	New York,	Tientsin,
Hamburg,	Peking,	Yokohama,

Credits granted on approved Securities, and every description of Banking and Exchange business transacted.

Drafts granted on London and the chief Commercial places in Europe, India, Australia, America, China and Japan.

HOLME RINGER & CO., AGENTS, CHEMULPO.

ON CHEONG & CO.,
SEOUL.

GENERAL STORE KEEPERS.

Imported provisions, Cooking Utensils Crockery, etc.

FRESH BREAD DAILY.

MITSU BISHI DOCKYARD & ENGINE WORKS,

NAGASAKI.

CODE WORD, "DOCK."

A. 1, A. B. C., and Engineering Codes used.

DOCK No. 1 (at Tategami).

Extreme Length	523 feet
Length on blocks	513 ,,
Width of Entrance on Top	89 ,,
,, ,, Bottom	77 ,,
Water on Blocks at Spring Tide	26½ ,,

DOCK No. 2 (Mukaijima).

Extreme Length	371 feet
Length on Blocks	360 ,,
Width of Entrance on Top	66 ,,
,, ,, Bottom	53 ,,
Water on Blocks at Spring Tide	22 ,,

PATENT SLIP (at Kosuge).

Can take vessels up to 1,000 tons gross.

THE WORKS are well equipped with the LATEST IMPROVEMENTS, and can execute any kind of work in SHIPBUILDING and MARINE ENGINEERING, as well as in REPAIRING of SHIPS.

The COMPANY'S new powerful steamer OURA-MARU (712 tons, 700 I.H.P.), specially built for SALVAGE PURPOSES, and equipped with necessary gear, is always READY at SHORT NOTICE.

CHARTERED BANK OF INDIA AUSTRALIA & CHINA.

INCORPORATED BY ROYAL CHARTER 1853

HEAD OFFICES:—LONDON.

Paid-up Capital	£800,000
Reserve Liability of Shareholders	800,000
Reserve Fund	725,000

Drafts granted upon all the principal places in the world and every description of Exchange and banking business transacted.

E. MEYER & Co., Agents, Chemulpo.

JUHACHI GINKO, LD.

Eighteen Bank.

CAPITAL .... Y. 2,000,000.

HEAD OFFICE NAGASAKI.

BRANCHES AND AGENCIES.

OSAKA	SASEBO	IDSUHARA
KUMAMOTO	CHEMULPO	YUENSAN
FUSAN	BUSHŌDSW	FUKUYE.

Chemulpo Branch.

TAKIJIRO ADACHI. Manager.

E. MEYER & CO.
Chemulpo.

SOLE AGENTS IN KOREA FOR:

A. T. Morse, Sons & Co's "Fresco" Distemper

In all colours ready for use on walls, Ceilings etc.

and

AVENARIUS CARBOLINEUM

A wood-preserving and antiseptic oil preparation

Against decay, dry-rot, fungus and wood-destroying insects.

A large supply always in Stock. Prices upon application.

E. MEYER & Co., Chemulpo.

DAI-ICHI GINKO.

LIMITED.

(Formerly the First National Bank)

ESTABLISHED 1873

INCORPORATED UNDER PRESENT LAW 1896

Capital	Yen 5,000,000
Reserve Fund	" 1,350,000

HEAD OFFICE:—TOKIO.

President: Baron SHIBUSAWA.

BRANCHES AND CORRESPONDENTS

In the Principal Cities and Towns of Japan.

Interest Allowed on

Fixed deposits	1 year	6½ per cent
" "	6 months	6 per cent

Special current accounts 1½ sen daily per Y 100

General " " 1 " " " 100

M. TANAKA, Manager, Chemulpo.

HOLME, RINGER & CO.,
JAPAN AND KOREA.

Merchants, Importers and Exporters, Government and General Contractors.

Shipping and Insurance Agents. Special Agencies:—

Taikoo Sugar Refinery Co., Hongkong.
Brunner; Mond & Co., Alkali merchants, London.

W. G. BENNETT, Manager, Chemulpo.

ROYAL EXCHANGE ASSURANCE CORPORATION.

FIRE DEPARTMENT.

The undersigned are prepared to issue policies on approved risks at current rates.

HOLME RINGER & Co., Agents, Chemulpo.

LAW UNION & CROWN INS. CO.

Fire risks accepted at Current rates, on godowns, merchandise, dwellings, and other property, subject to usual conditions.

HOLME RINGER & Co., Agents, Chemulpo

THE METHODIST PUBLISHING HOUSE,

Little West Gate, Seoul.

JOB PRINTING, TYPEWRITER PAPER
CARBON PAPER, VISITING CARDS
STATIONERY, BOOK BINDING
BOOK PUBLISHERS
AMERICAN SCHOOL BOOKS
SPENCERIAN COPY BOOKS
PEN CARBON LETTER AND BILL BOOKS

S. A. BECK, Manager.

KAMEYA & CO.

GENERAL STOREKEEPERS

Chinkokai - - Seoul

(Established 1895, Tokyo)

Confectionery, Hams, Canned Goods, Cutlery, Hirano & Tansan Water. Provisions, Gents, Furnishing goods, Toilet Articles, Travelling Bags, Tobacco, Cigars & Cigarettes Kitchen Utensils. Coffee, Biscuits.

Fresh Goods always kept in Stock.

Prices Moderate

Please come and insbect our goods.

NIPPON YUSEN KAISHA.

JAPANESE MAIL STEAMSHIP CO.

DER MAIL CONTRACT WITH THE IMPERIAL JAPANESE GOVERNMENT.

European Line

Regular Fortnightly Service between Yokohama, Kobe, Moji, Shanghai, Hongkong, Singapore, Penang Colombo, Port Said, Marseilles, London and Antwerp

American Line

Regular Fortnightly Service between Hongkong and Seattle, calling at Shanghai, Moji, Kobe, Yokohama and Victoria, B. C.

Australian Line

Regular weekly Service betwen Japan Ports and Australia, calling at Hongkong and Manila.

(Above Three Lines Suspended until further notice).

Shanghai Line

Weekly Service between Shanghai and Japan Ports

Korea Line

Service Kobe, Moji, Nagasaki, Fusan, Chemulpo, Chefoo, Taiku.

S. S. Babelsberg, 2181 tons.

Service Kobe, Moji, Fusan, Chemulpo, Chinnampo

S. S ARGO, S. S. Ohio.

BORDEN'S CONDENSED MILK CO.

New York, U. S. A.

ALWAYS IN STOCK

Eagle Brand Condensed Milk.

Gold Seal Condensed Milk.

Peerless (Family) Evaporated Cream.

Borden's Malted Milk.

E. MEYER & CO.
Chemulpo, Korea,
Sole Agents

ROYAL INSURANCE COMPANY,

Funds exceed £10,000,000

FIRE

AT CURRENT RATES.

LIFE

REDUCED PREMIUM.

HOLME RINGER & Co., Agents, Chemulpo.

HOTEL DU PALAIS

SEOUL.

The only first class Hotel in Seoul. Situated in the centre of the city opposite the palace.

Cuisine under the supervision of an experienced French Chef.

Well ventilated and furnished throughout.

TARIFF UPON APPLICATION

L. MARTIN,
Proprietor and Manager.

大韓每日申報
대한ᄆᆡ일신보

(뎨이십호) (화요일) 일쳔구빅사년팔월구일

본샤고빅

이 신보는 영어와 한어로 셔계 ᄆᆡ일 츌판ᄒᆞᆸ

신문가

ᄒᆞᆫ쟝 엽두돈오푼

일삭료 엽두량닷돈 맛돈으로 밧ᄉᆞᆸ

광고료는

귀한의 쟝단과 ᄌᆞ항의 다쇼로 ᄎᆞ감ᄒᆞ되 렴가로 밧을터이오며 오ᄅᆡ지 아녀 대한 사람마다 다 이 신문을 보실터이니 광고 내시기를 원ᄒᆞ시는이들은 우리 신문샤에 와셔 면약ᄒᆞ심을 ᄇᆞ라ᄋᆞᆸ

○대한ᄆᆡ일신보 [illegible]

사쟝 영국인 (비셜)

본샤지졈

[illegible]

샤고

[illegible]

론셜

[illegible]

관보

[illegible]

잡보

[illegible]

가전보ᄒᆞ되루차전보를ᄒᆞᄂᆞ토회복업스니민을ᄒᆞᆫ지라본ᄉᆞ가외국에쥬차ᄒᆞᆫ지오년이오니각국전례을의지ᄒᆞ야쳥유를시힝ᄒᆞ라ᄒᆞ엿더라

○고셩역비 강원도고셩군슈리명리씨가닉부에보고ᄒᆞ되본군군니면창ᄒᆞ가장마에사루되야동되셔북ᄒᆞ여셔방장기축코저ᄒᆞ오니역비를지발ᄒᆞ라ᄒᆞ엿더라

○히찰보고 희쥬관찰ᄉᆞ셔리신천군슈리용필씨가닉부에보고ᄒᆞ엿ᄂᆞᆫ디신계군민요ᄉᆞ건에디ᄒᆞ야곡산군슈로졍ᄉᆞ관ᄒᆞ야ᄉᆞ힉ᄒᆞᆫ즉화젼도죠ᄂᆞᆫ오랜졍규온디무업ᄒᆞᆫ백셩들이쟉요ᄒᆞᆫ고로쟝두등은위션압샹ᄒᆞ고죄명은법부로보흘터이옵고어형지를위션보고ᄒᆞᆫ다ᄒᆞ엿더라

○힉실전복 외부에셔닉부로죠복ᄒᆞᆫ기를일본셔슈증아심틱랑이힝흉ᄒᆞᆫᄉᆞ건으로동니감리의게훈칙ᄒᆞ야ᄉᆞ실케ᄒᆞ엿더니히범은일슌ᄉᆞ의게압교라ᄒᆞ엿더라

○역부모집 평남관찰ᄉᆞ리즁하씨가닉부로보고ᄒᆞᆫ기를즁화평양간에철로공역역부를이삼빅ᄉᆞ오빅명식모집ᄒᆞᄂᆞᆫ즁에삼화강셔룡강즁화사읍에셔ᄂᆞᆫ역부합이천명가량을모집ᄒᆞᆫ고로읍촌이소요ᄒᆞ야폐농홀지경이되ᄂᆞᆫ디또역부들쳥국지경으로더려잔다ᄒᆞᄂᆞᆫ고로인심이황황ᄒᆞ고일본인이례로공역은날노독ᄒᆞ오니장차엇지죠쳐ᄒᆞ올는지ᄒᆞ엿더라

○보쳥셜티 평안북도관찰사리용관씨의보고를거ᄒᆞᆫ즉관하연변각군에쳥비작경이자젼으로잔간잇섯더니일아기쟝후로쳥아양국비도무시로츌몰하소과ᄒᆞᄂᆞᆫ곳에부녀겁욕과재산야겁략이종종잇ᄉᆞ오니방어ᄒᆞᄂᆞᆫ방략이잇ᄉᆞᆫ연후에야빅셩이가히지보홀터인ᄃᆡᄉᆞᄉᆞ로약잔포군을셜치ᄒᆞ엿ᄉᆞ나경비지츌이말유ᄒᆞᆯ쁜아니라쳐소가업고각기동리에흣터잇셔젹경이잇셔급ᄒᆞᆫ지경에ᄂᆞᆫ민양취군에미급지란이잇셔유명무실이라의쥬강계에ᄂᆞᆫ임의지방대가잇거니와벽동초산위원삼군에ᄂᆞᆫ각기이빅명식두고삭쥬창셩자셩후창ᄉᆞ군에ᄂᆞᆫ각기일빅명식두어지방디를편제ᄒᆞ되각기그고을빅셩즁건장ᄒᆞᆫ쟈로션택ᄒᆞ야기에련습ᄒᆞ면외구와니란을가이방어ᄒᆞ겟다ᄒᆞ엿더라

○길씨구초 일젼에일병의게피착된길영슈씨구초니에부샹갱과ᄉᆞ와또무숨비밀ᄉᆞ건이란로가되엿ᄂᆞᆫ디모대신파모모위관이역지기죵ᄒᆞᆫ지라일본헌병이방금괴포즁이라더라리씨거의 근일리근틱씨샹경ᄒᆞ엿ᄃᆞ가가길씨구초소문을듯고즉시되거ᄒᆞ엿ᄂᆞᆫ디일병이츄포차로파천으로하거ᄒᆞ엿더니발셔부지거쳐라더라

○일병츌분 본월오일샹오팔시량에일본ᄉᆞ관삼인이병졍일빅칠십오명과복티십필를영솔ᄒᆞ고혜화문으로츌거ᄒᆞ고동일정오에ᄉᆞ관일인이병졍삼명파복티삼십칠팔과탄환궤를영솔ᄒᆞ야또츌거ᄒᆞ고하오ᄉᆞ시량에병졍십팔명이복티삼십칠필을영솔ᄒᆞ고츌거ᄒᆞ엿더라

○비관축지 회동비국령ᄉᆞ관을방쟝건축ᄒᆞᄂᆞᆫ디소용에셕지틀장동병문에젹치ᄒᆞ엿ᄂᆞᆫ디인마리왕에방히가되ᄂᆞᆫ고로토목회샤에셔밤마다등불을권다더라

○샹셔정부 일젼에평남북도신ᄉᆞ최당헌김병도최익환졔씨가박동오승티집에모야셔풍부회ᄉᆞ시건을회의ᄒᆞ엿ᄂᆞᆫ디당일경위원별슌검이젹간ᄉᆞ지ᄒᆞ엿다ᄒᆞ며정부에샹셔ᄒᆞ엿스되즉금셔경 풍경궁공역이쥰공치못ᄒᆞ엿고 향결전이왕바든것과아직미봉ᄒᆞᆫ것시빅여만량이되오니이걸노써 궁역을필역흠도가ᄒᆞ고 본궁경용에쓰ᄂᆞᆫ거시가ᄒᆞ거놀즉금드르니전평양ᄉᆞ령무부관박문교가풍부회ᄉᆞ를셜시ᄒᆞᆫ다칭탁ᄒᆞ고히공젼을라용ᄒᆞ야훈자본을삼ᄂᆞᆫ다ᄒᆞ니ᄉᆞ리에부당ᄒᆞᆫ지라만일박문교가회ᄉᆞ롤부ᄒᆞ랴ᄒᆞ면히회ᄉᆞ원즁으로합조ᄒᆞᄂᆞᆫ거시회ᄉᆞ규칙이어날이제 궁역소용으로민간에슈렴ᄒᆞᆫ공젼을회ᄉᆞ자본에쓰ᄂᆞᆫ거시근리치안싸오며또박문교가ᄉᆞ령부에잇슬때에그힝위범빅이본도인이목에란로ᄒᆞᆫ지라만약불소ᄒᆞᆫ지졍이그슈즁에드러간즉필경그ᄉᆞ락에도라가한만이허비될거시니쟝차궁역에ᄂᆞᆫ무어스로쓰올잇가또빅셩의게ᄂᆞᆫ지졍ᄒᆞ리잇가이게실노심등의스려운비라원컨ᄃᆡ각하ᄂᆞᆫ이ᄉᆞ샹을 텬폐의샹 쥬ᄒᆞ와즉시귀정ᄒᆞ야빅셩의려졍온위로ᄒᆞ심을복망ᄒᆞᆫ다ᄒᆞ엿고또쟝차샹소ᄉᆞ지ᄒᆞᆫ다더라

○립복톡셔 일본인이전션혜쳥문전에표목을세우고쓰기를지급히한국역부를모집ᄒᆞᄂᆞᆫ경셩병참졍령부니티창조파츌소리특셔ᄒᆞ고인부를모집ᄒᆞᆫ다더라

○일병리왕 지작일에일본ᄉᆞ관이인이병졍륙십륙명과말륙십륙필과대포륙좌를령솔ᄒᆞ고모화관으로ᄂᆞ가다가도루립셩ᄒᆞ더니희ᄉᆞ관삼인과포병삼십오명이대포이좌를령솔ᄒᆞ고황단압ᄒᆞ로셔대안문젼으로지ᄂᆞ갓다더라

○광고의휼 원세셩리범셕신형균삼씨가진항지ᄉᆞ건으로의거를힝ᄒᆞ다가일본ᄉᆞ령부에잡피여어되ᄶᅥ지간지거처를모로오니희등삼씨가국민을위ᄒᆞ야쥬ᄉᆞᄒᆞ다가이런경위밧고쵸를당ᄒᆞ니그ᄉᆞ롭인즉ᄉᆞ지에ᄶᅡ져도오히려영광되고유한이업스려니와각기그집ᄉᆞ세가궁박ᄒᆞᆫ처지에겸ᄒᆞ여외무쥬간ᄒᆞᆫ온즉전학지화를면치못홀지라우리동포쳠군ᄌᆞᄂᆞᆫ엇지측연히동심치아니ᄒᆞ리요구졔ᄒᆞ기위ᄒᆞ야광포ᄒᆞ오니원컨ᄃᆡ쳠군ᄌᆞᄂᆞᆫ다소를불계ᄒᆞ시고의금을니여무리힘을합ᄒᆞ야이셰집의사경에이른인명구졔ᄒᆞ기를바란다ᄒᆞ고유지ᄒᆞᆫ군ᄌᆞ들이각쳐에광고ᄒᆞ엿더라

○리씨보방 젼젼라어사리승욱과젼젼라관찰사리완용양씨가공전이십여만량사건으로평리원에셔다년지관ᄒᆞ엿더니리완용씨ᄂᆞᆫ방면이되고리승욱씨ᄂᆞᆫ상금구슈ᄒᆞ엿더니리승욱씨그천상삼년에분곽도못ᄒᆞ엿ᄂᆞᆫ디즉금히샹ᄒᆞ고환슈ᄒᆞ겟다ᄒᆞ고법부에쳥원ᄒᆞ엿더나지령내에권리가히원에잇다흠으로셔리지관쟝허위셋가리씨를보방ᄒᆞᆫ즉겁사홍종억씨가도타홀넘녀가잇다고만단져회ᄒᆞ미허위씨가담당ᄒᆞ마ᄒᆞ고보방ᄒᆞ엿더니홍금ᄉᆞ가대단반대ᄒᆞ야경무쳥에지휘ᄒᆞ야리씨를다시착슈ᄒᆞ라ᄒᆞ미재장과검ᄉᆞ가셔로규각나셔량씨가다ᄉᆞ직ᄒᆞ기로작정ᄒᆞᆫ다더라

●방셕근쳐 지작일요일에ᄉᆞ젼 쥬본이 지하됨으로법부관인과한셩지관소슈관ᄉᆞ이하가감옥셔에회동젼왕ᄒᆞ야죠칙을랑독ᄒᆞ고죄슈를병방ᄒᆞᄂᆞᆫ디평리원검ᄉᆞᄂᆞᆫ공일이라고ᄉᆞ진아니ᄒᆞᆫ고로히원소관죄슈ᄂᆞᆫ그익일에야방송이되엿ᄒᆞ니광대ᄒᆞᆫ신던은으로방송되ᄂᆞᆫ죄슈를일야라도옥즁에구류ᄒᆞ니법관의용심을가지라고들ᄒᆞᆫ다더라

뎐보

동경팔월칠일발

오대쟝공보

○우쟝졈령 우리군ᄉᆞᄂᆞᆫ팔월일일에대셕교부근의진터를ᄯᅡ난거시다셧종티인티각종티ᄂᆞᆫ각기방면에당ᄒᆞᆫ다쇼의뎍군과ᄡᅡ홈ᄒᆞ면셔젼진홀셰각각졍오젼후에히셩남방과밋셔남방에셔삼십ᄉᆞ리즘되ᄂᆞᆫ모든놉흔ᄯᅡᆼ을졈령ᄒᆞ엿ᄂᆞᆫ디뎍군은대단히항거치아니ᄒᆞ고오젼열시젼후브터졈졈히셩방향으로퇴각ᄒᆞᆫ지라우리외계티뎍ᄒᆞ든뎍군은총계가일ᄉᆞ단즘되고우리군ᄉᆞᄂᆞᆫ팔월이일에히셩에셔남으로일리즘되ᄂᆞᆫ팔리가에젼진ᄒᆞ엿고익일삼익졍오즘에히셩에셔우쟝ᄉᆞ지련ᄒᆞᆫ도록졈령ᄒᆞ엿고이날에히셩에셔동북으로퇴각ᄒᆞᆫ뎍군은이ᄉᆞ단즘된다ᄒᆞ엿더라

동일동뎐

동향보고

●션싱각함투 팔월오일하오오시량에구축함셔호아밋대황량호가뎍군의경샹을졍찰ᄒᆞ기를위ᄒᆞ야려슌구박긔니론즉뎍의구축함십ᄉᆞ쳑이급히우리를향ᄒᆞ야돌연히오미ᄉᆞ쳑은셔남으로ᄒᆞ고칠쳑은직남으로ᄒᆞ고삼쳑은션싱각방면으로진로를취ᄒᆞ야우리를에워싸고져ᄒᆞᄂᆞᆫ지라우리량함이오후네시ᄉᆞ십분에샹거가오쳔미돌즘되ᄂᆞᆫ디셔뎍군의밍렬ᄒᆞᆫ포화무릅쓰고진로를동북으로취ᄒᆞ야션셩각방면으로젼진ᄒᆞ야뎍의구축함삼쳑의젼면으로나아가갓가히다질녀핍박ᄒᆞ며밍렬히공격ᄒᆞᆫ즉뎍이즉시빈머리를도로혀항구로도주ᄒᆞ미이거슬츄격ᄒᆞ엿고오후다셧시가지내미구축함이가쥬지호가와셔합ᄒᆞ야삼함이일디가되여다시남방으로분리ᄒᆞᆫ뎍의구축함십일쳑을갓가히다질녀핍박ᄒᆞᆫ즉그도또ᄒᆞᆫ항구로향홈으로젼투를뎡지ᄒᆞ엿고우리삼함은ᄒᆞᆫ나토손샹홈이업고뎍의구축함은오후륙시량에좌다항니로드러갓ᄂᆞᆫ디뎍의손히ᄂᆞᆫ미샹이라ᄒᆞ엿더라

동일동뎐

오대쟝공보

○로합파손 뎍군의포함이파쟝ᄒᆞᆫ되로요가에셔져절노ᄶᅡ손ᄒᆞ엿다더라

동일동뎐

흑목대쟝보고

○포로와ᄉᆞ샹 유슈립자와양조령부근젼투에포로된쟈즁에건강ᄒᆞᆫ쟝교가오명이오하사와병졸이일빅ᄉᆞ십팔이오부샹ᄒᆞᆫ쟝교가삼명이오하사와병졸이일빅십이명이니합계가이빅륙십팔명이오미쟝ᄒᆞᆫ뎍군의시례ᄂᆞᆫ쟝교가륙명이오하사와병졸이오빅륙명이라ᄒᆞ엿더라

○권유항복 팔월륙일연틱찰지부발젼을거ᄒᆞᆫ즉일본군이거월이십륙일에로산을졈령ᄒᆞ엿ᄂᆞᆫ디아병의ᄉᆞ샹은오천이오일본군이려슌구에동셔양편아국리슈오리되ᄂᆞᆫᄯᅡ에핍박ᄒᆞ야이십팔일에이룡산을졈령ᄒᆞ엿ᄂᆞᆫ디일본군은아병의게항복ᄒᆞ라고권ᄒᆞ엿다더라

TELEGRAMS.

GENERAL OKU'S REPORT.

Tokyo Aug. 7th.

On the 1st August 5 columns of our troops advancsd from Tachichao, driving the enemy before us. We occupied some high positions 34 *li* southwest of Haickeng at noon, the enemy retreating in the direction of Haicheng.

On the 2nd our troops advanced to Balicha, one *li* south of Haicheng. The next day, 3rd, we occupied the line between Newchwang and Haicheng and the enemy, about 2 divisions, retreated to the northeast.

RUSSIAN REPORT.

Tokyo Aug. 6th.

General Kuropatkin in his official report to St. Petersburg states that during the recent series of battles, he suffered great casualties and has retreated to his base. The weather is terribly hot, many of the men being down with sunstroke in consequence.

KUROKI'S REPORT.

Tokyo Aug. 7th.

General Kuroki reports that in the battles at Yasnliutze and Yangtzeling many prisoners were taken. He appends a list. Unwounded 5 officers and 148 Non-coms and men.

Wounded 3 officers and 112 men. They have buried 6 Russian officers and 566 men.

NAVAL REPORT.

Tokyo Aug. 7th.

Admiral Tago reports that at 5 P. M. on the 5th inst. the destroyers Asatsuki and Obaru were despatched to Port Arthur to reconnoitre. The enemy's destroyers 14 in number came out to meet them and spread out in different directions. Four went to the southwest, seven due south and three steamed in the direction of Sunsingko, evidently attempting to surround us.

Our two boats were about 5000 meters from the enemy and were under heavy fire but they managed to steam to Sung Singko and there attacked the enemy's three destroyers, but these turned back and ran for the harbour. At 5 P. M. another destroyer the I Kajuge came up to assist and the three together attacked the whole body of the enemy, but these also retired into the harbour. We had no casualties.

COOLIES WANTED.

The Japanese demand for coolies seems increasing in all directions. Complaints come from the Governor of Pyeng-yang that thousands of coolies are being commandeered to assist on the railway. The people of all dtstricts are terrified lest their turn should come to be taken away from the cultivation of the fields.

In Seoul an office has been started, the former Government granary having been occupied for that purpose.

RUSSIAN OCCUPATION OF HAMHEUNG.

On the evening of the 2nd inst. 300 Russians with 400 horses and 2 field-guns entered Hamheung and occupied the town. They have taken charge of the telegraph office but have not destroyed communication to the south. Their conduct is described as orderly and they are paying good prices for provisions and fodder.

A telegram, which originates in Chefoo and reaches via Tokyo and through the medium of a local Japanese newspaper, states that Japanese troops occupied Lastesan on the 26th ult., and later advanced to within 5 Russian miles of Port Arthur. They then advised the Russians to surrender.

Mr. Yi Chong-il, editor of the Che Kuk-sinmun whose crime seems to have been illegal filching of a contemporary's editorial leader, has been released after 4 months' imprisonment.

THE DARDANELLES QUESTION AND THE TOKYO PRESS.

The editors of the metropolitan papers met some days ago at the Press Club in the compound of the House of Representatives and unanimously passed a resolution on the question of the passage of the Russian Volunteer Fleet steamers through the Dardanelles. The substance of the resolution may be translated as follows:—

"We consider the passage through the Dardanelles of the Russian Volunteer Fleet steamers under disguise of mercantile vessels as a violation of the Treaty of London and the Declaration of Paris and also an insult to the Powers.

"We consider the seizure and search of the English and German mail steamers by the Russians as an outrageous action, directly injuring the interests of those two countries and indirectly jeopardizing the interests of all neutral Powers.

"Considering as we do that acting in this way Russia has deliberately ignored the rules of International Law and set aside the dictates of international morality and has thereby endangered the peace of the world, we hereby resolve that we should persevere and not rest till we shall have vanquished the common enemy of the Powers and thus secured the permanent peace of the world."

"LURING THEM ON."

"I see that some of the Russian editors are explaining that Kuropatkin's plan is to lure the Japanese to Manchuria," said an old army officer. "It reminds me of a country editor out West, whom I knew during the Franco-Prussian war.

"The editor's sympathies were with the French. He wrote editorials by the yard showing how France was luring the Dutch, as he called them, to destruction.

"His paper came out once a week, so that he had ample time to work out the French plans. He had a map in a window of his office, and the yeomanry from the country rounded up as they came in to hear the news.

"The editor stood without and indicated the strategic points on the map by pointing to them with a piece of fishing rod. Weissenburg, Worth, Saarbruck, Gravelotte and Sedan were plotted as the engagements took place from time to time. You will remember that the French were defeated in every instance.

"Occasionally some hayseed would ask from his wagonload or track how it was that the French were falling back, or, how it was that they had been defeated.

"That's where the French strategy comes in,' the editor would explain.

"They are too much for the Dutch. You farmers are not on to this game of war!'

"Then he would tell them to see the next issue of the paper, in which it would be further explained. He was a foxy editor, after all. By this means he increased his circulation.

"His editorials explained how the farther any army got from its base the nearer it got to defeat. There were some officers in the civil war who operated, or tried to operate, on the same hypothesis. I think General Sherman knocked that idea into a cocked hat.

"When Bazine surrended 176,000 men at Metz the editor explained that France could afford to give up that number in order to get the Dutch under the walls of Paris.

"When the news of the end of the war came the editor explained in a brief paragraph—his edttorials had been dwindling week after week—that if the French had done more fighting and less luring the result might have been different. In winding up his paragraph the editor said:

"And besides, it's none of our damned business, anyway.'

"From that time on he confined his editorials to a discusson of the tariff until the Sheriff closed up his shop. If you ask me if history is liable to repeat itself I can only say that it has done so on several occasions.—"New York Sun.

SOME STORIES OF THE KAISER.

FRANK BIOGRAPHY WHICH ENTERS INTO THE INTIMATE PERSONAL LIFE OF THE EMPEROR.

Some excellent pen-portraits of the Kaiser are given in M. Heuri de Noussanne's book, which has just been published in Paris under the title of "The Real William II."

It is certainly not written with any bias in favour of the Kaiser. Nor is it wholly prejudiced against him. Its sting lies in its frankness—in the manner in which it takes the Kaiser's life day by day, hour by hour, and lays it bare to the world.

No one in this country has any desire to reproduce many of the details given in this surgical biography. It is more pleasant and also more entertaining to quote a few of the many pictures with which it abounds.

The Kaiser, it is well known, delights in occasionally throwing off the mask of royalty, and dining with favoured subjects. On one occasion he came to the house of the Prince of Pless somewhat unexpectedly.

His first words after his arrival were, "Do not forget that I put away my sceptre and my crown when I entered your door."

He was placed at the head of the table, but rose, saying, "Pless, take the place that you occupy on ordinary occasions. I willingly renounce my prerogative as your Sovereign for the pleasure of sitting between two beautiful women."

With these words the Emperor took his seat between the Princess of Pless and the Dutchess of Ratibor.

THE KAISER'S SURPRISE BOX.

Again, at another surprise dinner, the Emperor undertook the entertainment of the guests. "I have a surprise for you," he said. Therewith he had a box brought into the drawing-room. It was opened, while every one waited, some eagerly, some with apprehension. A ping-pong outfit was produced, and as the Emperor proceeded to put it in position on a table, he explained that it was a present which his uncle Edward had sent him.

The Kaiser's taste in wines inclines to the sweet. He is an inveterate foe to champagne, and shows a marked preference for Tokay. As in duty bound, he also favours the varieties of wine that are produced in Germany. To test the sincerity of his preferences, a bottle of French champagne was one day placed before him at table under a German mark. He detected the trick in a moment, and was furious at the suggestion that he could not tell the difference between the two wines. Beer is his great drink, and etiquette demands that whenever the Kaiser takes a fresh draught a glass that has never previously been used shall be set before him.

William II. occasionally is fond of a little horseplay. M. de Noussanne relates that one evening after dinner on the royal yacht "Hohenzollern" the Kaiser produced a mirror. He then made his guests open their mouths very wide, and took the mirror round to each of them that they might see what they looked like in such an attitude. A tactful officer pocketed the mirror when it came to him, saying that he wished to preserve it as a souvenir of such a memorable incident.

Humour is not one of the Kaiser's strong points. He wanted to cut a cigar one evening, but could not find his penknife. A member of his suite hastened to proffer one. The Emperor took it, solemnly cut his cigar, and then returned the knife to its owner, with the remark:—"Keep it, and guard it well. One of these days it will be historic."

The Korean Minister to Japan has applied for leave. He complains bitterly that he has been five years at Tokyo without one single holiday, whereas Ministers of other nations are frequently permitted to take vacations.

The new Korean Mining and Cultiavtion Co. is regarded as a danger at the Japanese Legation. In a despatch to the Foreign Office, the Minister begs that it be abolished on the grounds that foreign capital will surely be requisitioned.

The Dai Han Shimpo learns that Mr. Paik Si Yong, translator in the Ceremonial Department, who is suspected of having communicated secretly with Messrs. Hyon Sang-keun and Yi Hak-kiune at Shanghai, has disappeared and is presumed to be in hiding. What with the number of arrests recently made and the dire threats of martial law made by the Japanese, we tare not surprised to hear of officials secreting themselves.

Major Yi Tai-rai, who is under suspicion in connection with the commissariat frauds had been forbidden entrance to the Palace until his documents had passed inspection. However he recently pushed his way past the guard at the entrance and had to be forcibly ejected. The poor gendarme, who was not strong enough to prevent him entering has lost his billet.

The Korea Daily News.

To be published daily except Sundays.
Rate of Subscription:—
Per Year, Yen 25.
Per Quarter, Yen 7.
Per Month Yen 2.50

Postage in Korea not charged extra.
Postage abroad charged extra.

Advertisements, 50 sen per day for 1 inch or less.
5 yen per month per inch.
50 yen per year per inch.

All communications to

E. T. BETHELL,
Editor and Publisher.
Pak-tong, Seoul.

PROGRESS OF THE WAR.

The war has now reached a stage where the movements of the various armies for the next few weeks will be watched with very great interest. On both sides the censorship is very rigorous and the reports that reach us are therefore far from impartial. General Kuroki's reports are meagre, confined as they are to a few dry details of the various engagements with reports of his own losses and an estimate of the casualties suffered by the enemy. The foreign correspondents who are with his staff do not go much further. Until quite recently they were not apparently allowed to witness any of the fighting and their reports therefore were much the same as the official ones with the addition of such "colour" as a subsequent visit to the battlefield enabled them to surround their story with. They seem however to have been allowed to witness the latest engagements and their reports are of more interest, but of course the censor is as busy as ever and nothing to contradict the impression that the progress of the first army is one unbroken chain of successes ever reaches us from them. Sickness, which is always resposible for far more loss to an army than powder and shot, has not been mentioned, neither has the suggestion of a reverse, however trifling.

The despatches of the correspondents with the Russian forces are also full of a buoyant optimism, they send no stories of defeats or defects in the army and are confident that they are on the winning side. Although a comparison of the reports of the correspondents with the opposing armies leads to nought but bewilderment it would be wrong to conclude that they are not telling the truth—as they see it. The men who have been sent to the front as correspondents for the various newspapers are men of eminence in their calling, having a proper sense of responsibility and alive to the duty which they owe to the public of providing true and unbiassed accounts of the events which transpire within their purview. Still it is easy to see how, living with an army, and to some extent sharing its lot, their sympathies unconsciously come into line with those who surround them and even if they have the opportunity they gradually lose the desire to transmit any news unfavorable to the cause of the army which they are with.

Very conflicting reports reach us as to the strength and composition of Kuropatkin's army, and his intentions are unknown. He has now two armies marching upon him. From the South the Takushan army is approaching Liaoyang along the railway, while from the West General Kuroki's victorious army is threatening to advance and attack his flank or rear. From such information as we possess, General Kuropatkin's position at Liaoyang seems a precarious one—but some weeks must elapse before a decisive engagement is fought. Whatever the result of the battle either side will have great difficulty in following up a victory so that future movements in this region are purely a matter of speculation.

The operations in the neighbourhood of Port Arthur are still shrouded in mystery. The theory has been advanced that the Japanese are hoping to starve the Russians into submission, but this we look upon as improbable. We incline to the view that the Japanese greatly under-estimated their task and are now making preparations for an attack on a more formidable scale.

Raids from Vladivostock, by sea and land, will continue so long as Port Arthur remains untaken. Until the operations in the Liaotung peninsula have met with success, Japan can spare neither ships nor men for offence or defence in this direction.

MERCHANT SHIPPING AND INTERNATIONAL LAW.

The Russian Press has been urging that the best means of inflicting heavy loss on Japan is to employ fast cruisers and destroy Japanese merchant vessels. The Vladivostok squadron, which has frequently appeared in Japanese waters, has been putting into practice the plan suggested by the Russian Press, and has destroyed foreign steamers as well as Japanese vessels. The Japanese, says a vernacular contemporary, are quite inexperienced in warfare as far as the destruction of merchant shipping goes, and do not place much importance on those operations of the Russian squadron, but in Europe the destruction of merchant shipping is more dreaded than either military or naval fighting. Some of the vernacular journals publish an interesting epitome of the views expressed by an authority on the law of nations in regard to the destruction of merchant shipping. This authority says:—The Paris declaration of 1856 provides that goods belonging to hostile States carried by a vessel under the flag of a neutral State, and goods belonging to a neutral State carried by a vessel under the flag of a belligerent State, except contraband of war, cannot be seized. According to this arrangement merchant vessels of hostile States and the goods of belligerents carried by neutral vessels can only be seized. Opinion varies in Europe as to the interpretation to be given the phrases "vessels and goods belonging to hostile States." Great Britain regards vessels of a neutral State as vessels of a belligerent when they are under a belligerent's flag. On the other hand, France would refrain from seizing the vessel when she is owned by the subject of a neutral State, even if navigating under the flag of a belligerent country. In regard to the ownership of vessels, Great Britain would deal with a vessel according to the domicile of her owner, and would regard as the vessel of a belligerent a ship owned by the subject of a neutral State who resides in the dominion of a belligerent. France would treat the vessel according to the nationality of her owner, irrespective of his place of residence. If Russia follows the French principle, she would seize a vessel owned by a Japanese residing at Shanghai. The principles followed by Great Britain and France in regard to cargo are the same as in regard to shipping. The French principle is generally followed in Europe, and it may be understood that Russia follows that principle. What principle the Japanese Government pursues in the present war, the authority quoted is not in a position to say, but in the Japan-China War the Japanese Government adopted the British principle.—Kobe Chronicle.

On the 5th inst. about 200 Japanese soldiers in charge of a train of pack ponies, carrying ammunition and supplies, left the city by the East Gate.

THE SINKING OF THE "KNIGHT COMMANDER."

CAPTAIN BROWN'S STATEMENT.

Regarding the sinking by the Russians of the British steamer "Knight Commander," according to the "Japan Gazette" Captain Brown reported that at 3:30 on Sunday afternoon, at a point about sixty miles south of Rock Island, he was stopped by the Vladivostok Squadron, but was allowed to proceed at about five o'clock. A boat's crew in charge of an officer was sent from the "Rossia" to examine the manifest. As each item on the manifest was read it was semaphored to the admiral, and when this task was completed the officer signalled to ask if the admiral was going to send a prize crew on board, but the reply was that the "Tsinan" should be allowed to proceed. The Russians said they wanted her to take 21 Lascars on board from the "Knight Commander," and these men were accordingly sent.

The officers of the "Knight Commander" were retained as prisoners of war. There did not appear to have been any fatalities in connection with the sinking of the ill-fated steamer.

Captain Brown further reported that the officer from the "Rossia" was particularly gentlemanly in his behaviour and general treatment. He was also very communicative, and said they had had telegraghic instructions from St. Petersburg to treat the British flag with great repect. He added, however, that if they had any railway material or anything connected with railway material on board they would have been either seized or sunk, British flag or no British flag. The officers also mentioned that they had received a very severe reprimand from St. Petersburg for sinking the "Sado-maru" without making sure there were no lives on board the ship.

Speaking with regard to the sinking of the "Knight Commander," he said the Captain had himself to blame because he took no notice of the customary shot and did not heave to until three or four shots had been fired. The Russian officer, who spoke excellent English, rallied Captain Brown, and said: "They say we are beaten, yet here we are within a few miles of Tokyo."

Subsequently Captain Brown asked his uninvited visitor if he would have a drink. The officer, who certainly seemed to have acquired some Anglo-Saxon habits with the Angle-Saxon language, replied: "Yes, rather, if you have a whisky and soda." This refreshment having been disposed of, he asked if the Captain could sell him any whisky. Receiving a reply in the affirmative, he semaphored to the fleet asking if they had any English money on board. The answer was in the negative, and the officer regretted that he was unable to make the purchase. He was consoled, however, with the offer of a few bottles, a gift which he accepted.

A rumour is current to the effect that Mr. Yi Yong-ik will return from Japan in October.

A band of insurgents in Northern Korea, calling themselves the righteous army, are creating disturbances.

Twenty-one houses on Roze Island have been bought by the Japanese, who require the ground for military operations.

News of the Japanese victory at Tachichao is being given publicity through the medium of notice-boards placed in prominent positions throughout the city.

The house of one Yi Chun-woo at the West Gate has been commandeered for use as a guard house for the Japanese sentries now stationed day and night at that place.

The Governor of North Pyeng-An lays an urgent request before the Home Office for military guards for several districts in his province. He asserts that since the beginning of the war Chinese robbers have been allowed to carry on depredations unchecked in all the districts near the coast-line.

The Korea Daily News.

VOL. I, TUESDAY, AUGUST 9, 1904. No. 20

大韓每日申報
대한ᄆᆡ일신보

(뎨이십일호) (슈요일) 일쳔구빅사년팔월십일

본샤고빅

이신보는영어와한국문셔계ᄆᆡ
일츌판ᄒᆞᆸ

신문가

ᄒᆞᆫ쟝 엽젼두돈오푼
일삭됴엽두량닷돈 밋돈으로
밧ᄉᆞᆸ

광고료는

귀한의쟝단과ᄌᆞ항의다쇼로증
감ᄒᆞ되혐가로밧을터이오며오
리지아니ᄒᆞ매대한사람마다이신
문을보실터이니광고내시기를
원ᄒᆞ시는이들은우리신문사에
와서면약ᄒᆞ심을희망ᄒᆞᆸ

○발행소 대한ᄆᆡ일신보
사발어학교앞회젼영국인셜필
림집자리오
사쟝 영국인 (배셜)

본샤지졈

인쳔항교젼동신지쟝에셔로우리
대한ᄆᆡ일신보사인항지졈쟝을
확졍ᄒᆞ엿ᄉᆞ오니인쳔항에계신
구람코자ᄒᆞ시는쳠군ᄌᆞ는해지
졈에왕림면의ᄒᆞ시ᄋᆞᆸ

사고

○우리대한ᄆᆡ일신보의목뎍은
대한의안녕질셔에관한모든대
목에되ᄒᆞ야는공평한번론을쥬
쟝ᄒᆞᆯ이라우리ᄂᆞᆫ신원회담보는
신문보시는쳠군ᄌᆞ의게ᄒᆞᆼ상보
도ᄒᆞ리며편지ᄅᆞᆯ긔셔ᄒᆞ여주시
는이는셩명과번디ᄅᆞᆯ계어붓치
시기ᄅᆞᆯ희망ᄒᆞ오니미거ᄒᆞᆫ신문
샹에긔재ᄒᆞ랴는거시아니오다
만극히신용ᄒᆞ는증거ᄅᆞᆯ숨고자
ᄒᆞᆷ이라긔자ᄂᆞᆫ아모긔셔던지긔
재ᄒᆞᆷ을퇴각ᄒᆞ는권리ᄅᆞᆯ가졋소
나퇴각ᄒᆞ는리유ᄅᆞᆯ말ᄒᆞᆯ터이오
며공중광화ᄅᆞᆯ문란케ᄒᆞᄂᆞᆫ듯ᄒᆞᆫ
긔서는의례히밧지안케ᄉᆞᆸ나이
다

론셜

○금제품과중립권

대개교젼ᄒᆞᄂᆞᆫ나라이셔로젼시
금물된에실은거슬분명히주의
ᄒᆞᄂᆞᆫ거시ᄒᆞᆫ조ᄒᆞᆫ일인거시로되
으로셔다른ᄒᆞᆫ대에발ᄒᆞᆫ면보를
본즉나이르ᄉᆞ형관이히ᄒᆞᆫ샴위ᄒᆞᆷ
대의계경쳠됨에티ᄒᆞ야공박ᄒᆞᆫ샹
에대단히위약ᄒᆞᆫ일이라고말ᄒᆞᆷ
이로영국정부로셔근론헤이
ᄒᆞ며나는조음에도리쳐오날우리
신문에츌판ᄒᆞᆫ거와갓치아라
사수사대뎡ᄉᆞ크리노프씨가모
처에서무싱교발ᄒᆞᆫ기를영국수
병관나이르씨가젼시검문ᄒᆞᆯ빈
에시섯교횡빈으로향ᄒᆞ되고빈
셜은셕탄인족ᄒᆞᆫ샹위에서지ᄒᆞᆼ션
ᄒᆞᆫ기에는보지못ᄒᆞᆫ겟더라ᄒᆞᆫ
엿슨즉이란ᄒᆞᆫ횡졔비히대ᄃᆞᆼ즈
귀양으로발셜ᄒᆞᄂᆞᆫ되드리낫는
지라이왕에도비쟝ᄒᆞᆫ셔록으로
공론ᄒᆞᄂᆞᆫ거시외면샹으로반ᄊᆡ
연중지가되엿ᄉᆞ나그리ᄂᆞᆫ미계
당ᄒᆞ여셔는재확실ᄒᆞᆫ증거를미
투어봄됴건진티영항격쳠된티
티ᄒᆞ야됴리를분쳐번명ᄒᆞᆯᄒᆞᆫ지
라아라사이쌍아비만나ᄂᆞᆫ티과
연데일이라고ᄒᆞᆯ반ᄒᆞ도다가평
여귀를진실은비ᄒᆞ는이잇스면
이벼ᄂᆞᆫ엇던빈던지외레히격병
을도아주며쇼반일이빈가셕란
실은게엿시쟈의ᄒᆞᆼ구에도박ᄒᆞ
면응당아국함대에서셕탄즁결
을도엿ᄉᆞᆯ게시오필경항당히낙
일년지도모르겟ᄉᆞᆫ쥬우리군항
ᄂᆞᆫ다격쳠식인거ᄉᆞᆫ쏘ᄒᆞᆫ능멸히
여여고리ᄒᆞᆷ이요ᄌᆞ연그리되엿
다교롯ᄒᆞᆯ일인즉이거ᄉᆞᆫ정진아
라사이무슨학술노아라서이왕
ᄒᆞᆫ힘에ᄒᆞᆫ번서ᄊᆡ본후에ᄯᅩᄒᆞᆷ당
ᄒᆞᆫ게ᄂᆡ이ᄂᆞᆫ마음으로비번에이
일에ᄎᆡ지ᄅᆞ이ᄒᆞᆫ엿더라

잡보

○졍ᄊᆡ쳔샹 일젼에감옥셔죄
슈등을방숑하ᄂᆞᆫ티쟝졍일빅이
십슈명을방츌ᄒᆞᆫ세에그쳥의ᄅᆞᆯ
빗기교방숑ᄒᆞᄂᆞᆫ고로슈다쟝졍
이젹신으로감옥셔문젼에죠좌
ᄒᆞᆷ을보교횡로지인비다쳠ᄒᆞᆫ이
니ᄒᆞ기더니쟝규환ᄊᆡ가의귀등니
여고계인을일졔로ᄌᆞ귀소랑으
로술게ᄒᆞ야쟝차의복을낫낫치
지여의판단ᄒᆞ니세샹ᄉᆞ룸이대
단칭숑ᄒᆞ더라

○류쳔모군 샹화갑리가외부
로보교ᄒᆞ되본항에주차ᄒᆞᆫ일본
영ᄉᆞ엄공성쟝의죠회ᄅᆞᆯ게ᄒᆞᆫ즉
봉황셩에서긴급히쓸역부가류
쳔명이ᄂᆞ되여야ᄒᆞ겟ᄉᆞᆫ즉쳥쳔
티룡강갑서샴화안악신쳔문화
은률쟝련등팔군에서모집ᄒᆞ야
보내며샤젼ᄂᆞ죄와갓치시ᄒᆡᆼᄒᆞᆫ
다교ᄒᆞ엿기로각히군으로신칙
ᄒᆞ엿ᄂᆞᆫ티모군사젼인즉본항에
내회ᄉᆞ에ᄂᆞᆫ날불리류련비ᄅᆞᆯ용달
회ᄉᆞ에서담당ᄒᆞᆫ는티모군에사
젼은미샤한회샹실를원시이오
모군들이쳥국안동현으로가ᄂᆞᆫ
션가와셕비ᄂᆞᆫ본항ᄉᆞ가출급ᄒᆞ
교모군들은각각지게ᄅᆞᆯ지교오
되만일지게가업거든길방을가
지교오라ᄒᆞ엿더라

○ᄉᆞ진규칙 외부에셔ᄉᆞ진규
칙을세로뎡ᄒᆞ엿ᄂᆞᆫ티본일노부
터샹오열시에ᄉᆞ진ᄒᆞ교하오두
시에ᄉᆞ퇴ᄒᆞᆫ다더라

●텬도립표 가산군슈가외부
에보교ᄒᆞᆫ니기에서남랑면장
의보고를게ᄒᆞᆫ즉본랑면이철학
산동편과밋쟝슈랑북편에잇서
인민이다못ᄂᆞ업으로만힘쓰며
니ᄒᆞᆯ티에일인등이텰도를시벽
ᄒᆞᆫ다ᄒᆞ고본면에뢰도ᄒᆞ야수변
에립표ᄒᆞᆫ거시샴수십리가되오
니츄슈ᄒᆞᆯ가망이지금업서졋ᄉᆞ
와젼면이통곡ᄒᆞ오며빈이구가
비등ᄒᆞᆫ다ᄂᆞᆫ등졍이오미민졍ᄉᆞ
을게ᄒᆞᆫ즉ᄒᆞᆫ샹ᄒᆞ기가측량업ᄉᆞ
와못병참부에가서가을기ᄃᆞ
려시명ᄒᆞᆷ을면탁ᄒᆞᆫ즉티답ᄒᆞ티
우리ᄉᆞ령관의지휘ᄅᆞᆯ니감히젼편
치못ᄒᆞ겟노라ᄒᆞ미보라가대못
일본공ᄉᆞ의게죠회ᄒᆞ야가을을
기ᄃᆞ려벽ᄉᆞ를시작ᄒᆞ야ᄊᆡ츄수
를온젼케ᄒᆞᆷ을복망이라ᄒᆞ
엿더라

○린쎄귀셜 일본동경에유ᄒᆞ
ᄂᆞᆫ린용익씨ᄂᆞᆫ신월샹슌귀국ᄒᆞᆫ다
ᄂᆞᆫ말이잇다더라

○교문리한 농샹공부교문관
가등졍웅씨가본월륙일에동경
에셔발졍ᄒᆞ야한국으로향ᄒᆞ야
온다더라

○향복의당 근일동셜에황경
북도에비도등이자칭의당이라
ᄒᆞ교작괴가티단ᄒᆞ야민졍이샹
히곤란ᄒᆞ다더라

○회의하ᄉᆞ 근일에한국각티
병졍의익슈ᄅᆞᆯ쥴인다ᄂᆞᆫ말이랑
ᄌᆞᄒᆞᆫ티졔작ᄒᆞᆯ하오ᄉᆞ시에각대
티령관들이위ᄉᆞ로회동ᄒᆞ야
무샹ᄉᆞ항을샹의ᄒᆞ엿다더라

○거류망망 근일풍셜에일본병
의계교ᄒᆞ야셔편으로느려가
ᄂᆞᆫ원셰셩신쳥군ᄊᆡ등이과쥬ᄒᆞᆷ
진강에셔죽엇다ᄒᆞ더니화셜ᄒᆞᆫ
ᄉᆞ문을들은니젼졈셔편으로ᄂᆞ
려갓다ᄒᆞ엿더라

○역부청발 일본ᄉᆞ령부관인
이니부대신을방문ᄒᆞ고셜명ᄒᆞ
되쳥국안동현디방공역에슈용
ᄒᆞᆯ차로역부ᄅᆞᆯ모집ᄒᆞᄂᆞᆫ중이니
귀부에셔경긔충쳥경샹젼라각
도에훈칙ᄒᆞ야역부ᄅᆞᆯ한이쳔명
ᄒᆞ교모집ᄒᆞ야보내게ᄒᆞ라ᄒᆞ엿
더라

○죠칭압부 김영슈리진화씨
등ᄉᆞ건에티ᄒᆞ야외부에셔일공
관에죠회ᄒᆞ되귀ᄉᆞ령부에젼칙
ᄒᆞ야희인등을본경부로압부ᄒᆞ
면의률엄징ᄒᆞᆯ터이라ᄒᆞ엿다더
라

○젼관모집 일본헌병ᄉᆞ령부
에셔죵로에교시ᄒᆞ되한인역부
들다슈로모집ᄒᆞ야안동현지방
으로보내ᄂᆞᆫ티매쳥조셕무계가
젼관ᄒᆞ야모집ᄒᆞ니타인이미역부
들모집ᄒᆞ라면본ᄉᆞ령부허리가
잇슨후에야힝ᄒᆞ교반ᄃᆞ시역부모
집ᄒᆞᄂᆞᆫ티방해ᄒᆞᄂᆞᆫ자ᄂᆞᆫ군률로
시행ᄒᆞᆯ터이라ᄒᆞ엿더라

○황실흉변

대한국황실에셔대일본군츌졍
군인과그가속의경경을흉변히
하렴ᄒᆞ수일본흉병부로금위을
하ᄉᆞᄒᆞ옵셧ᄂᆞᆫ티
대황뎨폐하계셔오쳔원
황태ᄌᆞ젼하와
황태ᄌᆞ비젼하계셔각삼쳔원
슌비젼하와
영친왕젼하계셔각이쳔원이라
더라

○공대흉금 일젼에궁내대신
민병셕씨ᄂᆞᆫ
황명을봉승ᄒᆞ야이샹흉병금을
일본공관에죵숑ᄒᆞ교ᄯᅩ셰도흉
금빅원을죵숑ᄒᆞ엿더라

●죠칭쳘병 일젼에일본군ᄉᆞ
령부에셔군부로죠회ᄒᆞ기를
경셩과의쥬ᄉᆞ이연로에일본병
참이쳐쳐에잇스니티방은자연
안연ᄒᆞ야만료ᄂᆞᆷ녀가업스니귀
국병졍은일병쳘환ᄒᆞᆷ이가ᄒᆞ다
ᄒᆞ엿다ᄂᆞᆫ소문이잇더라

○하교퇴관 근일에벼항소문
을드른즉오서니귀구잇ᄂᆞᆫ졍ᄋᆡ
셔들은만히근거디방으로ᄂᆡ힝
을보내라ᄒᆞ야항계를쟝만ᄒᆞᆷ으

UNION INSURANCE SOCIETY OF CANTON.

Head office Hongkong.
Marine risks underwritten at current rates.
Agents in Chemulpo,
MEYER & Co.

OCEAN S. S. CO., L'T'D.,
CHINA MUTUAL S. N. CO., L'T'D.,

Combined Services.

Japan to London and Antwerp fortnightly service.
S. S. KINTUCK leaves Kobe 8th July.

Japan to Liverpool direct,
S. S. KEEMUN leaves Kobe 14th July.

Japan to Seattle, U. S. A.
taking cargo for all Pacific coast ports.

CHINA NAVIGATION CO., L'T'D.

Japan to Australia
regular mail contract service.
S. S. TAIYUAN leaves Kobe July 22.

For particulars apply to
HOLME RINGER & Co.,
Agents, Chemulpo.

HAYASHIDA & CO.

16 MYENG DONG, CHING KO KAI, SEOUL.
BRANCH OFFICE AT CHEMULPO.

Money changers, Coal and Wood Merchants, Express Agents.

We are agents for the Pyeng-yang Coal Company and the Karazu Coal Company of Japan. We have the best quality of both anthracite and bituminous coal, and prompt execution of orders is our speciality. Firewood of all kinds kept in stock. Full weight guaranteed. Money of all denominations exchange, at current rates. Parcels received for all parts

---

CHINA MUTUAL LIFE INS. CO.

Most favourable terms to policy holders.

Benefit system unsurpassed.

HOLME RINGER & Co.
Agents, Chemulpo.

C. P. R.

CANADIAN PACIFIC RAILWAY COMPANY'S ROYAL MAIL STEAMSHIP LINE.

THE FAST ROUTE BETWEEN CHINA, JAPAN, AND EUROPE VIA CANADA AND THE UNITED STATES.

Route from Hongkong via Shanghai, Nagasaki (Inland Sea of Japan) Kobe, Yokohama, Victoria and Vancouver.

Twin Screw Empress Steamships—6,000 Tons—Speed 19 knots.

PROPOSED SAILINGS FROM YOKOHAMA.

R. M. S. Empress of India - - - - - 1st July 1904
R. M. S. Empress of Japan - - - - 22nd July 1904
R. M. S. Athenian - - - - - - - 29th July 1904
R. M. S. Empress of China - - - - 12th Aug. 1904

Special reduction (first class only) granted to members of the Military, Naval, Diplomatic and Civil Services and to Missionaries.

Passengers have choice of ten routes across the Continent of America and have privilege of travelling by any Atlantic Steamship Line.

Round the World passage tickets in connection with the P. and O. S. N., North German Lloyd and Messageries Co.'s £125.

All rates payable at current rate of exchange.

For further information, Tickets, Guide Books, etc., apply to

HOLME, RINGER & Co., AGENTS,
Chemulpo.

Grand Hotel,

(Formerly the Station Hotel)

Near the Railway Terminus,

West Gate, Seoul.

The Best Hotel in Korea.
Handsome new Building.
Fine airy Rooms
Excellent Cuisine.
Terms Moderate.
Special terms to Missionaries and to permanent boarders.

Electric cars within 2 minutes' walk.

W. H. EMBERLEY,
Proprietor.

EVERY FACILITY

In connection with Life Assurance Business is afforded by

The Standard Life Assurance Co.,

One of the largest and wealthiest of the Provident Institutions of the United Kingdom. Forms of Application and all information will be promptly afforded on application.

10 CENTS A DAY.

Not a very large expenditure is it? But it is sufficient to secure for a man of 30 a policy with the STANDARD LIFE OFFICE for

$1323.

For all particular of rates, etc., apply to

Holme, Ringer & Co.,
Agents, Chemulpo.

THE NEW YORK LIFE INSURANCE COMPANY.

Have you ever been declined by and Company?

Are you engaged in as pecially hazardous occupation?

Have you heard of the New York Life Insurance Company's New Classifications for this class of Risks?

If not, send your date of birth, occupation and particulars of rejection, if any to

E. MEYER & Co., Agents, Chemulpo.

MITSUI BUSSAN KAISHA.
(MITSUI & Co.)
MITSUI GINKO.
(MITSUI BANK.)

The Bank is owned by the members of the Mitsui Family, who, as partners, assume an unlimited responsibility for all liabilities of the Bank:—

Capital.......................Yen 5,000,000
Reserve Fund................. " 5,600,000

HEAD OFFICE, TOKYO.
LONDON OFFICE, 34 LIME ST., E. C.

BRANCHES AND AGENCIES:—

New York, San Francisco, Hamburg, Bombay, Singapore, Manila, Hongkong, Amoy, Chefoo, Tientsin.

Kobe, Hakodate, Yokohama, Kure, Yokosuka, Moji, Shimonoseki, Miike, Wakamatsu Nagasaki, Kuchinotsu, Karatsu, Sasebo, Misume, Taipeh, &c.

Telegraphic Address for all the Offices:
"MITSUI."
A. B. C. AND A. 1 CODES USED.

Contractors of Coal
To the Imperial Japanese Navy. Arsenals and Railway Bureau, Principal Railway Companies and Industrial Works, Home and Foreign Mail and Freight Steamers.

Sole Proprietors
Of the famous Miike, Tagawa and Yamano Coal Mines.

Sole Agents
For the sale of Fukumo, Hokoku, Ichimura, Kanoda, Mannoura, Onoura, Ostuji, Sonoda, Tsubaruro, Yoshinotani, Yoshio, Yurokibura and other coals.

YANGTSE INSURANCE ASSOCIATION, LTD.

The undersigned, having been appointed agents for the above company, are prepared to issue policies and pay losses on marine risks at regular rates.

E. MEYER & Co.,
Agents, Chemulpo.

AMERICAN KOREAN ELECTRIC COMPANY.

Light and Power.

Main Office: Electric Building, Chong No.

RAILWAY DEPARTMENT.

OPERATING CARS BETWEEN EAST AND WEST GATE, EVERY TEN MINUTES:—

First Car leaves East Gate at 6:30 A. M. First Car leaves West Gate at 6:55 A. M.
Last Car " East Gate at 10:40 P. M. Last " " West Gate at 11:00 P. M.

OPERATING CARS BETWEEN EAST GATE AND IMPERIAL TOMB TERMINUS, EVERY TWENTY MINUTES:—

CONNECTING WITH EVERY ALTERNATE CAR ARRIVING AT EAST GATE FROM CHONG NO.

First Car leaves East Gate for Tomb at 6:50 A. M.
" " " Tomb for East Gate at 7:10 A. M.
Last " " East Gate for Tomb at 9:50 P. M.
" " " Tomb for East Gate at 10:10 P. M.

OPERATING CARS BETWEEN CHONG NO AND YUNG SAN (RIVER) EVERY TWELVE MINUTES:—

First Car leaves Chong No for South Gate at 6:48 A. M.
" " " Chong No for Yung San at 7:24 A. M.
" " " South Gate for Chong No at 6:56 A. M.
" " " Yung San for Chong No at 7:57 A. M.
Last " " South Gate for Chong No 11:00 P. M.
" " " Yung San for Chong No at 10:11 P. M.

SPECIAL PRIVATE CARS FURNISHED TO SUIT CONVENIENCE OF PATRONS. PRICES ON APPLICATION AT HEAD OFFICE.

LIGHTING DEPARTMENT.

Where less than 250 candle power of light is used, the rate per month will be. Per 16 candle power incandescent lamp. All night.—Yen 2.50. Per 32 candle power incandescent lamp:—All night:—Yen 4.00. Per 50 candle power incandescent lamp:—All night:—Yen 6.00. " 150 " " " " — " " 10.00. " 1200 " " enclosed arc " " " " 20.00.

Where more than 250 candle power of light is used, a Meter will be installed, if requested:—Rent of Meter Yen 2.00 per month. Rate of charges by meter reading:—Two Sen per Ampere per hour. (Approximately this is equal to about One Sen per 16 c. p. lamp per hour) Minimum monthly charge where meter is installed, Yen 20.00 per month, which includes rental of meter.

Estimates for installing lights furnished on application. An assortment of chandeliers always on hand.

AMUSEMENT DEPARTMENT.

ANIMATED PICTURES AT EAST GATE.
Every evening - - - Except Sunday.
From 8 to 10 P. M.

10 Cents:—Gen. Admission:—10 Cents. Seats in First Class Section. 15 Cents Extra.

Change of program each week. Pictures from Foreign Lands. Pictures of Local Scenes:—Amusing and Instructive.

An entertaining evening for a reasonable price.

MERRY-GO-ROUND:—At East Gate.
From 10:00 A. M. till 11:00 P. M.

5 Cents a Ride.

Take your Exercise on The Galloping Horses.

Comfortable seats in the Chariots.

한셩뎐긔회샤

미국뎐긔회샤 고불안 보사뎍 고빅
도ᄒᆞ옵나이다
샹활동사진젼■소와목마운동쟝량셔로연
여ᄂᆞᆫ뎐차가온쟝안으로통힝ᄒᆞ여ᄃᆞ니여이
습
ᄯᅩ이긔계에ᄀᆞᆺ치노힌편ᄒᆞ고됴흔마차도잇
습
코ᄆᆡ우편ᄒᆞ고ᄯᅩ조미잇ᄂᆞᆫ됴흔운동이되겟
어됴흔모형ᄒᆞᆫ달나아논물을ᄐᆞ고위티치안
ᄃᆡ가ᄂᆞᆫᄒᆞᆫ번ᄐᆞᄂᆞᆫ데오젼식이오
ᄆᆡ일샹오열시브러하오열ᄒᆞᆫ시ᄭᆞ지ᄒᆞ옵고
목마운동쟝은동대문안에잇습고
가되겟습
쳡군조의게갑도싸고저녁에됴흔쇼일거리
잇고구경ᄒᆞᆯ만ᄒᆞᆫ거시오니
셔양사진과대한과온동양사진인ᄃᆡᄃᆡ로ᄂᆞ미ᄒᆞ
ᄂᆞᆫᄃᆡ
젼이옵고ᄆᆡ쥬일에사진을삼것스로다밧고
고젼ᄒᆞᄂᆞᆫᄃᆡ금은하등에십젼이오상등에이십
일외에ᄂᆞᆫᄆᆡ야에여덜시브터열시ᄭᆞ지ᄒᆞ옵
활동사진젼람소ᄂᆞᆫ동대문안에잇습고일요
회락부

All Cars Run Direct to the Animated Pictures and Merry-Go-Round.

로파쥬양쥬광쥬과쳔시흥고양등디ᄂᆞᆫ집갑시고등ᄒᆞ다ᄒᆞ니아병이ᄂᆞ온다ᄂᆞᆫ풍셜을곳이듯고그런지일본에대포오ᄂᆞᆫ거슬보고공동ᄒᆞ야그런지알슈업다ᄒᆞ더라

○문셜양양 근일젼셜에ᄒᆞ기를슈다ᄒᆞᆫ아병이점점남으로온다ᄂᆞᆫ소문을듯고아어졸업싱덜아득외ᄒᆞᆯ때가당ᄒᆞ온다ᄒᆞ고의긔가양양ᄒᆞ다더라

○초가여금 금년남초갑시고등ᄒᆞ되목쳔등디로셔상리ᄒᆞᆫ쳔구에소젼을드른즉엽초일파갑시엽젼십일량ᄉᆞ젼ᄉᆞ지고등ᄒᆞ야빅미일두오승으로엽초일파를상환ᄒᆞᆫ다더라

○평북농형 평안북도농형을드른즉금년장마가미우지리ᄒᆞ야모믹이잘되지못ᄒᆞ엿고화곡에풍흉은아직료량처못ᄒᆞᆫ다더라

○가역평장 근일에파쳔군거ᄒᆞᄂᆞᆫ어ᄂᆞ셰력잇ᄂᆞᆫ집의셔역ᄉᆞ를되단히ᄒᆞᄂᆞᆫ디모군부역식임이평장ᄒᆞ다더라

●박가슈탐 여경방신쟝로쟝응옥집에본월팔일에일본헌병일명파평북일인이명이돌립ᄒᆞ야가장즙물을세세히슈탐ᄒᆞ고문셔쟝파휴지를다슈습ᄒᆞᆫ후에박유티를차져노으라ᄒᆞᆫ즉쟝가쳡의말이이왕에ᄂᆞᆫ박씨와작비ᄒᆞ야사랏거니와피차파의ᄒᆞᆫ후에즉금은상관이업노라ᄒᆞᆫ즉히일안야쟝가의쳡을다라고다동박유티집에잔즉박씨ᄂᆞᆫ입의솔권ᄒᆞ야시플노철귀ᄒᆞᆫ고로박씨의동싱유풍의집에가셔돌립ᄒᆞ야슈지문셔를낫낫치슈습ᄒᆞ야갓다더라

○강도오한 본월구일축시에공덕리홍례동박용티집에적ᄒᆞᆫ오명이방포ᄒᆞ며돌립ᄒᆞ야고용인리셩룡을군도로란타ᄒᆞ야ᄉᆞ경에이르고기타지산을몰슈히탈취ᄒᆞ야갓다더라

○죄슈샹다 금번ᄉᆞ젼에각죄슈방송ᄒᆞᆫ후에현금감옥셔에슈도를죠ᄉᆞᄒᆞᆫ즉징정ᄉᆞ십구명파경무청좌슈구명파평리원좌슈륙십삼명파한셩지관소좌인삼삽이명이니합일빅오십삼인이더라

○민요장긔 저작일에평양관찰ᄉᆞ리중하씨가젼보ᄒᆞᆫ기를일본병참소에셔삼화룡강등ᄉᆞ군에청국보벌역부를억지로륵청ᄒᆞᄂᆞᆫ고로상지ᄒᆞᆫ지루일에민요가일려날념녀가잇스니즉각으로일본공관에죠회ᄒᆞ야무ᄉᆞ케라렵되도록ᄒᆞᆫ후에급젼으로회시ᄒᆞ라ᄒᆞ엿더라

○일본류학 학부에셔각부부원쳥의론죠ᄒᆞ엿스되쟈일경부전화를접ᄒᆞᆫ즉일본에류학싱쳔ᄒᆞᄂᆞᆫ단ᄌᆞ를금월십오일너로슈랍ᄒᆞ라신 셔분를봉승ᄒᆞ야통지ᄒᆞᆫ다ᄒᆞ엿시니긔어하졍ᄒᆞᆫ일안으로각기거천ᄒᆞ라ᄒᆞ엿ᄂᆞᆫ디ᄌᆞ이왕거천된의슈가팔명이라더라

○외인긔셔 수일젼에황셩에지류ᄒᆞᆫ외국인이본샤샤쟝의게긔셔ᄒᆞᆫᄉᆞ의를본즉말ᄒᆞ엿스되지난토료에귀신문에계지ᄒᆞᆫ크로늬클신문을안중ᄒᆞ야론셜ᄒᆞᆫ거슬닑으미우리의게얼마큼샹쾌ᄒᆞ엿ᄂᆞᆫ지족하ᄂᆞᆫ알지못ᄒᆞ려니와대져일본이대한의독립과안령질셔를쥬의ᄒᆞᄂᆞᆫ죠약의의무를담부ᄒᆞ엿스미그직분을다ᄒᆞᆷ으로류의ᄒᆞᆯ지니만일신의를져바릴지경이면세계의셔존즁히넉이며동졍을표ᄒᆞ던거슬일허ᄇᆞ릴줄노확실히말ᄒᆞ리로다자금에족하ᄂᆞᆫ대한에되ᄒᆞ야긴요ᄒᆞᆫᄉᆞ건과공졍ᄒᆞᆫ리유로써쥬장ᄒᆞᆯ지어다족하ᄂᆞᆫ아모죠록ᄒᆞᆫ갈ᄀᆞᆺ치ᄒᆞ여ᄒᆞᆯ만ᄒᆞᆫ일에당ᄒᆞ야쥬져치말며이런간우지시를당ᄒᆞ여대한을위ᄒᆞ야변호ᄒᆞ여주기를쳔만힝심이오며또그런족족하의공졍ᄒᆞᆫ량식파모든정직ᄒᆞᆫ동지쟈들의우익를가히나타낼지로다

○아병거향 향남ᄒᆞᄂᆞᆫ아병의수효와졍황에되ᄒᆞ야그보고가귀일치안터니즉금이야그확실ᄒᆞᆫ소문을드른즉아국긔병어ᄉᆞ빅명가량인디금월이일에함흥에이르고ᄉᆞ일에졍평에이르고오일에영흥에이르러륙일은히다에쥬둔ᄒᆞ엿스니삼작일쯤고원이나문천에다다랏ᄂᆞᆫ지모로겟스며그군죵에긔관포인좌ᄂᆞᆫ적실히잇고또후진이함흥북편에잇다ᄒᆞᄂᆞᆫ젼셜인즉밋업자안코히아병이영흥에셔한국인오명을살히ᄒᆞ엿다더라

외보

○법병피살 청국산히관근디에셔법국병졍이술을먹고술집에셔힝악ᄒᆞ거ᄂᆞᆯ일본헌병이금지ᄒᆞᆫ즉법병이일본헌병을씨르ᄂᆞᆫ지라일병파히더근쳐삼인이합력ᄒᆞ야법병ᄉᆞ명을다살ᄒᆞ엿ᄂᆞᆫ디일본군디와법국군디가각기리도ᄒᆞ야일차죠ᄉᆞᄒᆞᆫ후에무ᄉᆞ히타쳡되엿슨즉필경국제샹문제ᄂᆞᆫ일어ᄂᆞ지안으리라고데군신문에긔지ᄒᆞ엿더라

뎐보

○일ᄉᆞ병대치
동일동지찰
아쟝[구로팟긴]의공보를거ᄒᆞᆫ즉아군이비샹히손히를바다근거지로되각ᄒᆞ엿스ᄂᆞ감경ᄒᆞᆫ적군에되ᄒᆞ야그짜를굿게직힐거시오더위ᄒᆞ독ᄒᆞᆷ으로군ᄉᆞ에일ᄉᆞ병알ᄂᆞᆫ자만타더라

동일동뎐
로함우출 본월ᄉᆞ일에국후히협에셔로국가장함일척이현출ᄒᆞ엿다ᄂᆞᆫ보고가잇다ᄒᆞ엿더라

관보

뎨이천구빅호 광무팔년팔월구일

○셔임급ᄉᆞ령

명 셔리평리원지판쟝ᄉᆞ무 평리원판ᄉᆞ 허위 팔월삼일 ○의원면본관 비셔원승셔궁슌 화룽참봉 김쥬영 경룽령 홍진표 자룽참봉 셩원식 효룽참봉 윤교셩 임 비셔원승 셔쥬임관륙등 사종원시종 졍환덕 암시종원시종 셔쥬임관륙등 졍삼품 오환영 임지룽참봉 셔관임관팔등 슌룽참봉 유명자 임슌룽참봉 셔관임관팔등 로창셔 임화룽참봉 셔관임관팔등 죠철호 임경룽령 셔관임관칠등 슌룽령 리응직 임슌룽령 셔관임관칠등 [illegible] 관 심룽우 임슌강원슈봉관 셔관임관팔등 돈령원쥬ᄉᆞ 로셩삼 임돈령원쥬ᄉᆞ 셔관임관칠등 륙품 홍진표 임효룽참봉셔관임관팔등 리샹립 임광쥬군공립쇼학교교원셔관임관륙등 셔샹휘 이샹팔월륙일

○의원면본관 비셔원승 리민영 원구단ᄉᆞ졔셔참봉 리윤슈 ○히 겸임함경남북도각광감리 함경북도관찰ᄉᆞ 리윤지 ○명 궁니부특진관 셔칙임관삼등 종이품 김셕규 임비셔원승 셔쥬임관륙등 시종원시종 김병욱 임시종원시종셔쥬임관륙등 륙품 리과셩 겸임쟝례원쟝례 비셔원승 홍승두 임통신ᄉᆞ젼화과쥬ᄉᆞ 셔관임관팔등 ᄉᆞ직셔참봉 리병철 임ᄉᆞ직셔참봉셔관임관륙등 허정 임권구단ᄉᆞ졔셔참봉셔관임관팔등 홍룽참봉 윤쥰구 임홍룽참봉셔관임관팔등 소경원참봉 리긔티 임소경원참봉셔관임관팔등 륙품 리윤슈 ○명 함경남북도금광감리 졍삼품 렴홍진 이샹팔월칠일

○궁졍록ᄉᆞ

젼라남도관찰ᄉᆞ 김세긔ᄉᆞ직소
비지니에다사번거이ᄉᆞ양치말고ᄉᆞ속히등졍ᄒᆞ고종편ᄒᆞ야왕리ᄒᆞ라

즁츄원의관죠병승ᄉᆞ직소
비지니에소청디로의시ᄒᆞ라
이샹팔월륙일

니쟝원경민치쥰ᄉᆞ직소
비지니에소청디로의시ᄒᆞ라
팔월칠일

일쥬일감봉 한셩지관소젼슈반관ᄉᆞ 윤시영○젼칙 한셩지관소슈반관ᄉᆞ김연식 한셩지관소관ᄉᆞ 하규일 한셩지관소젼검ᄉᆞ리풍의○삼ᄀᆡ월감봉 인천우체ᄉᆞ쥬ᄉᆞ 박지슌 셔윤창○삼ᄀᆡ일감봉 시흥우체ᄉᆞ쥬ᄉᆞ 리쥰영

광고

TELEGRAMS.

Gensan, Aug. 6th.

Two field guns have been brought to Tangchaen enroute to Hamheung by the Russians.

A former officer of the Korean army is with the invading force at Hamheung.

It is reported that 800 more soldiers are on their way to join this advance guard.

Gensan, Aug. 7th.

Russian advance continues. Yesterday 24 scouts came within 50 *li* of Gensan, reconnoitered and returned. It is estimated that now there are seven hundred Russians south of the Yengheung river. Yesterday five Korean spies were shot at Hamheung. The Machierien pass, the highest road of travel on the East Coast and situated close to Songchin, is being fortified. The force at Hamheung has now been increased to 500.

RUSSIAN ADVANCE INTO KOREA.

Gensan Aug. 5th.

On the 2nd inst. information of the arrival of the Russian force was brought to Hamheung. The governor rode 30 *li* outside the city to welcome the troops who arrived at six P. M. One official who failed to supply fodder was beaten by order of the Governor. The force consisted of 150 cavalry 200 pack ponies and five ox-carts. Each house in the towns of Tiengpieng, Yengheung and Koonen furnish one bundle of grass and one measure of barley. These are for storage.

On the 3rd inst. three Russians were shot by the order of their officers for outrages committed on Korean women.

THE EXODUS OF COOLIES.

On the 8th instant the Governor of Ping Yang telegraphed that the compulsory collection of coolies from Yongkang, Samwha, etc., for service with the Japanese army is causing much ill feeling and is likely to give rise to riots. Therefore he asks that the Japanese authorities be requested to desist from this recruiting.

STUDENTS FOR JAPAN.

It seems that only eight students have signified their desire to go to Japan to study. The Department of Education has issued a circular asking for more nominations and states that the list will close on the 15th of this month.

The Foreign Office have requested the Japanese military authorities to hand over the officers recently arrested for their supposed connection with an Anti-Japanese plot.

Fifteen thousand dollars has been contributed by the members of the Korean Royal family to the fund for the relief of families of Japanese soldiers in the field.

The Japanese Army Headquarters have requested the War Office to withdraw all Korean troops stationed at any place on the road between Seoul and Wiju.

The Magistrate of Taichon has contributed 500 dollars to the Japanese relief fund.

THE ASSASSINATION OF M. VON PLEHVE.

By George Kennan in the Japan Times.

The assassination of M. von Plehve, the Russian Minister of the Inrerior, has removed from the stage of public life one of the most powerful and influential leaders of the Russian reactionary party, and one of the bitterest enemies that free thought, liberal institutions, and progressive tendencies have had in Russia since the accession to the throne of Alexander III. No single man, with the possible exception of Pobyedonostseff has done more than he to sustain the Russian bureaucracy, to restrict freedom of speech, to gag the press, to crush individual liberty and to keep the people of the Empire in a state of mediaeval ignorance and poverty. He, more than any other man, was responsible for the barbarous treatment of the Jews in Russia, and particularly for the bloody massacre of the people of that unfortunate race in Kishineff last year, and it was he who encouraged and supported, even if he did not instigate, the policy that the Tsar pursued in Finland. Since he first came into power as the director of the Department of Imperial Police in 1881, he has used all his influence and employed all his faculties in the work of crushing the aspirations of the Russian people for freedom, and in a persistent effort to cripple or render ineffective the reforms granted by Alexander II. In carrying out this policy he has put a large part of European Russia under martial law, even in time of profound peace; he has suspended or suppressed almost every newspaper or magazine that criticized his actions or condemned his methods; and he has resorted, on the most extensive scale, to house-searches, arrests, and administrative exile as a means of intimidating or punishing not only liberals and members of the revolutionary party, but even private citizens who incurred his displeasure on account of their political opinions. Under his regime there were no less than 11,000 arrests in Russia for political offences last year, and hundreds of men and women were exiled to Siberia or to the northern part of European Russia for periods of from one to five years without trial and without even a hearing. Unjust and arbitrary measures of this kind greatly embittered, of course, the people who suffered from them, and as there was no redress in the courts some aggrieved person finally took the law into his own hands, and killed the man who was regarded as responsible for them. M. von Plehve is the second Minister of the Interior who has met deat in Russia at the hands of an assassin within the last three years. His predecessor M. Sipiagin was killed in the same way about two years ago.

The salient features of M. von Plehve's career are briefly as follows. He was born in 1846. After his graduation from the Moscow University in 1867 he entered the Government service as an assistant to the *procureur* of the Moscow Circuit Court and served in the Ministry of Justice for a period of 14 years. In 1881, shortly after the assassination of Alexander II. he was made Director of the Department of Imperial Police, and held that position until 1884. He then becime a Senator and was appointed Assistant Minister of the Interior, and in 1902, when Mr. Sipiagin was assassinated, he took full charge of the Ministry in the latter's place.

M. von Plehve was a man of strong character and great ability, and he has had more influence over the Tsar in the past two years than any other of the latter's councillors.

The method of his removal is greatly to be regretted, and condemned; but tens of thousands of Russians will breathe more freely when his body is laid away in the grave.

LORD DUNDONALD AND THE CANADIAN MILITIA.

THE STATE OF CANADA'S DEFENSIVE FORCE.

Lord Dundonald, who, it will be remembered, was recently relieved from the command of the Canadian Militia for criticising the acts of the Minister of Agriculture, has since communicated a lengthy statement to the Ottawa Press. The statement is a five-column summary of grievances which have existed since Lord Dundonald first went to Canada. The late Commander-in-Chief declares he sedulously kept out of politics and sought only to improve the force. He had not endeavoured to impose his policy on the Minister of Militia or the Government, but had sought to carry out the plans approved by the Government. His claim for freedom extended only to the "technical" side of the work. But he asserts that his efforts were constantly hampered by interference with that particular part.

"This interference," Lord Dundonald claims, "began very soon after my arrival. It has continued incessantly ever since. The Hon. Mr. Fisher's interest in the affairs of the Scottish Light Dragoons was simply a final incident in a long list of various phases of obstruction. My only reason for remaining in my positton was to benefit the Militia of Canada, but my efforts were so persistently blocked that I came to look upon the case as a hopeless one. It seemed to me that the best way to help the Militia was to let daylight into the working of the system."

He realised, moreover, that the new Militia Bill would soon be discussed in Parliament, and that it was his duty to give warning of certain dangerous items before it was too late. It seemed better to make a public protest and leave with the Government the option of heeding it or of opposing a system which is destructive to the efficiency of national defence.

He was in this frame of mind when the Hon. Mr. Fisher "interfered," as Lord Dundonald puts it, with the Scottish Light Dragoons. This brought matters to a head. It precipitated his resolution to speak out, no matter what the consequence.

Proceeding, the officer charges Sir Frederick Borden with suppressing a portion of his report and of characterising it as "private and confidential," when he expressly told the Minister he desired it should be published. In the 1903 report Sir Frederick Borden, he claims, struck out whole pages without reference to the General.

"Among the portions so eliminated were references to the condition of the Permanent Corps, which I pronounced in many respects unsatisfactory. Last year, for instance, the Permanent Corps, with an establishment of 995, was 207 under strength and had 277 enlistments and 154 desertions. Two small instruction batteries at Kingston were practically reduced to one. Dissatisfaction in the Permanent Corps and its urgent requirements had been pointed out by me to the Minister ever since I came to the country.

"A more recent instance occurred in connection with the organisation of the Ordnance Corps. The establishment of this corps was fixed at a Colonel, Second-in-command, with the rank of Lieutenant-Colonel, and three Lieutenant-Colonels. This was a larger establishment than I would have recommended had I been unhampered, but Sir Frederick Borden was anxious to have a number of senior and highly-paid posts, and the scheme which he desired was carried out. Soon after this I went to the Northwest. As soon as I had left Ottawa the Minister of Militia ordered the Adjutant-General to prepare an order increasing the number of Lieutenant-Colonels to five, thus giving seven officers of the rank of Lieutenant-Colonel to a corps of about one hundred men. In this connection it must be remembered that the most elementary requirements of the Militia were neglected for want of money."

The General then deals at length with cases of what he calls "political interference" in the Second Dragoons and the Scottish Light Dragoons. He complains that his educational scheme for the promotion of officers was side-tracke, that nothing was done to procure suitable training grounds, and that many other suggestions were pigeonholed. Proceeding, Lord Dundonald says:—

"It may be a matter of indifference to some whether the Militia lacks guns, rifles, ammunition, equipment and all that is necessary to make this fighting force efficient; it may be a matter of indifference whether the great Northwest, with its splendid fighting material, is to be left in a defenceless state, without a gun and with patriotic offers to organise urgently-needed corps ignored; above all, it may be matter of indifference whether other considerations beside military considerations influence the chaice and advancement of the military leaders of the people, but as I am now free to speak more openly on matters I have often referred to in public, I desire here emphatically to warn the people of Canada that, though they may be indebted for the integrity of their territory, and, indeed, their national existence, to the forbearance of others, they are, as regards their preparations for war and their belief in readiness to successfully resist aggression, living in a fool's paradise."

Lord Dundonald concludes: "I take leave of the Canadian Militia with regret. My relations with the officers and men have been exceedingly pleasant. My observations of the force have confirmed the high regard which I formed in South Africa of the soldierly qualities of Canadians. From my brother officers and fellow-soldiers of the rank and file I have received loyal, ungrudging support, which I can never forget. Had I been able to help to place these troops of such fine, natural qualities in that thorough state of preparedness which is their due and which the nation desires, it would have been an achievement of which I should ever have bean proud."—Kobe Chronicle.

The Korea Daily News.

To be published daily except Sundays.

Rate of Subscription:—

Per Year, Yen 25.
Per Quarter, Yen 7.
Per Month Yen 2.50

Postage in Korea not charged extra.
Postage abroad charged extra.

Advertisements, 50 sen per day for 1 inch or less.
5 yen per month per inch.
50 yen per year per inch.

All communications to E. T. BETHELL, Editor and Publisher. Pak-tong, Seoul.

A REIGN OF TERROR.

Being arrested under martial law is a fate desired by no one. The charge may be of the vaguest and the subsequent trial is conducted "in camera." Therefore it is a matter of no wonder that the recent arrests, by Japanese gendarmerie, of a number of influential Koreans, have spread dismay and consternation throughout the country. The reasons for the arrests are apparently of the flimsiest. WE only know what the Japanese authorities choose to make public, and that is very little. If more information were vouchsafed we might be in a position to criticise less harshly but in the meantime it appears to those not "in the know" that Korea is being hardly dealt by.

Men have been arrested on such slight grounds, and so many rumours are current of this and that man being "wanted" on one charge or another, that it is not to be marvelled at that all Koreans of any prominence and influence who are not avowed friends of the Japanese are in a state of some concern.

If the accused were assured of a fair and open trial, fear could be construed as a sign of guilt, but while the proceedings subsequent to arrest retain their present vague character, it is only natural that those who are threatened do their best to avoid being arrested in the first place.

We say this because there is a possibility of the feeling getting abroad that because Koreans, being threatened with arrest, go into hiding they are necessarily guilty of acts contrary to the spirit of the treaty which exists between this country and Japan.

It appears to us that the action which the Japanese are taking is hardly that which was contemplated by Korea when the protocol was signed and it is calculated to unnecessarily irritate and antagonize the Koreans.

The war is not yet over, some of Japan's most important lines of communication lie in this country, and apart from all questions of right or wrong a policy of pacification would seem the wisest for her to pursue.

RUSSIAN MOVEMENTS ON THE NORTHEAST COAST.

The operations of the Russians in Northeast Korea would appear, from the Gensan telegrams appearing in our columns, to be assuming larger proportions. In April when the first party made their swoop down upon Songchin and destroyed the town, it was regarded merely as a freak and an act of brutality on a defenceless township. However, seen in the light of recent events, it would seem to be the first move towards obtaining ascendance over the whole coast line north of Gensan. The systematic repairing of roads and the fortifying of the Machierien pass surely denote that they have some large object in view, at any rate their proximity to the Japanese line of communication between Pyeng Yang and Wiju is a serious danger.

RUSSIAN ARTILLERY WEAKNESS.

Paris, June 24.—The special correspondent of the "Petit Parisien" in St. Petersburg, explaining the delay in furnishing the Russian artillery with modern quick-firing guns, says:—

"Thus, when the war broke out in February last, the Russian artillery found itself in the midst of the work of transformation, and consequently by no means in a position effectively to resist the Japanese artillery with its ultra-modern, quick-firing, long-range guns, whose crushing superiority was but too well proved at the battle of the Ya-lu . . The Russians were, there, therefore, obliged to despatch to Manchuria the greater part of the quick-firing batteries with which the European regiments were provided. The foundries and workshops are now engaged day and night, yet they hardly succeed in turning out more than 60 pieces with their corresponding gun carriages per month. On the other hand, the large guns from Kronstadt and those from the fortress at Warsaw are at Port Arthur. In a word, the Russian artillery is in a critical state . . . . It is almost certain that at this moment General Kuropatkin has not more than 350 guns at his disposal, while the centres for the supply of ammunition are at a terrible distance from the seat of war."—London Times.

WALK UP, COOLIES!

The Kamni of Chinnampo reports that acting under instructions received from the Japanese Consul at that port, he has given orders for the collection of 6,000 coolies from neighbouring districts. He says that they are wanted urgently in connection with military operations at Feaghwancheng and will receive pay and be subject to rules as follows.

1. On the arrival of the coolies at Chinnampo, the Japanese Commisariat Department will be responsible for their keep.

2. Each coolie will receive 36 dollars a month wages.

3. Expenses of transit to Antung China will be paid by the Japanese.

The coolies are to supply their own packs.

The Foreign Office in Seoul have also received a request for 2,000 coolies for the same purpose.

A PROTEST.

Some delegates from the Pyeng An province are in Seoul with the object of protesting against the manner in which the Government is about to use funds subscribed in the Pyeng An district expressly for the purpose of building the Palace at Pyeng Yang.

It appears that the money, 40,000 dollars in all, will now be appropriated for the establishment of the new Mining Co. near Pyeng Yang.

If the facts are as given, the people of Pyeng Yang certainly seem to have a genuine grievance.

The "Japan Daily Herald" quotes a French correspondent of the "Russki Viedomisti" as to the difficulty of attacking Vladivostok from the sea. He explains that there are twenty-two forts and batteries on which are placed 100 heavy guns and sixty light guns with calibres ranging from six inches to eleven inches. There are also four ironclad cruisers (one of which has been wrecked, however), several transports (the largest one of which is the Lena), several secondclass torpedo-boats (which are from 100 to 200 tons in displacement and from nineteen to twenty-one knots in speed), and ten small torpedo-boats of an old type. Under the circumstances, the Japanese squadron can only attack Vladivostok by torpedo-boats. Small torpedo-boats cannot steam with the main squadron for the distance of 10,000 nautical miles, so the six destroyers of from 280 to 350 tons' displacement must be sent out from Japan. The Japanese squadron would incur a great loss in passing through the straits to the entrance to Vladivostok, since the east and west channels of the straits are strongly defended.

SHANGHAI HEALTH REPORT.

The North China Herald, commenting upon the report of the Shanghai health officer says:—

Of the two papers by Dr. Stanley appended to his official report the one on "Sudden Heart Failure in Toxæmic Condition" is, from its technical character, principally interesting to medical students. The other on "Chinese Hygiene" is, however, of a more popular character, and the conclusions Dr. Stanley has arrived at have a readable air of audacity for those who have, perhaps thoughtlessly, made up their minds that everything Chinese is as bad as it can be. In few words, Dr. Stanley makes the assertion that the Chinese have very sound ideas on sanitation, more sound indeed than those of Western nations. And in main proof of his contention he points out that among the peoples of the earth none has enjoyed a more prolonged national life, while the individual health of the Chinese is also above the average. He quotes their two main laws of health, and makes us wonder whether they do really follow them—in Shanghai at all events. They sound so simple, and so "un-Chinese," though that is probably our mistake; (1) Restraint of all the appetites, (2) Cleanliness in house and person. The following paragraph is worth studying for its lessons:—

"The Chinaman eats and drinks little that has not been subjected to the temperature of boiling water or boiling oil, and is therefore largely preserved from typhoid fever, cholera, and other diseases which are caused by infected food. The Chinaman is not a great fruit eater. He is such an excellent cook that he prefers foods in which nature has been improved by art. He abhors raw things as a rule. Raw oysters, for example, the Chinese will not eat, considering them 'too cold for the stomach.' Except under great stress he drinks no cold water but always tea made with boiled water and thus avoids water-borne disease."

It is almost startling to find Dr. Stanley commending the close aggregation of Chinese houses, which by tending to warmth in winter and coolness in summer, co-operates with the warm, light clothing worn, to diminish catarrhs, bronchitis and rheumatisms. "The Chinese dwelling has plenty of natural ventilation. With regard to sleeping accommodation the Chinese closely resemble most of the rest of animal creation in getting into a small, close, warm place for sleep. It is probable, however, that impure warm air is less injurious than cold pure air, and during sleep less air is required than at other times; while the body during sleep is more subject to chills. Although bad smells abound near Chinese houses, smells are not a perfect test of unhealthy environment." Verily, unless Dr. Stanley is perpetrating some Chinese topsy-turvey sort of joke on his unsuspecting readers, whole volumes of theories must go by the board. We are not surprised, after this, to find him giving good words to the Chinese method of disposing of the dead, and the polygamous marriage system as preferable to the social irregularities of the West. It would not be fair to press all these points without saying that Dr. Stanley indicates directions in which modern science can effect improvements even in this empire of all the ideals. But that makes far less striking reading.

A notice from the Japanese Headquarters of Gendarmes has been posted at Chong No. It reads to the effect that while the Japanese are collecting coolies, no individuals may indulge in the same pursuit without their permission, and any one putting any trouble in the way or otherwise hindering the Japanese in their task will be punished by martial law.

The "Dai-han-il-po" frequently contains paragraphs to the effect that various Koreans are to be "dealt with" for alleged pro-Russian sympathies. It would be interesting to know where the "Dai-han-il-po gets its information from. Presently we propose investigating some of its charges.

The Korea Daily News.

VOL. I, WEDNESDAY, AUGUST 10, 1904. No. 21

大韓每日申報
대한매일신보

(호이십이뎨)　　　　(일요목)　　　　일일십월팔년사빅구쳔일

본샤고빅

이신보는영어와한국문셔계믹
일출판홈
　　신문가
흔쟝　엽뎐두푼오리
일삭됴엽뎐두량닷돈　　밧돈이로
밧숩
　　광고료는
귀한의쟝단과조힝의다쇼로죵
갑홍되뎡가로밧을터이오며오
리지아녀대한사람마다다이신
문을보실터이니광고버시기를
원흥시는이들은우리신문사에
와셔뎡약홍셔을회망흥숩
○발힝소　대한박동미일신보
샤발힝부교셥홈젼영국인셜필
림쳥자라오
　샤쟝영국인(비셜)

본샤지졍

일원한만교젼동서쟝명례로우리
대한미일신보샤가인항지셔양울
귀경흥엿슨오니인원항에계신
구람자흥시는쳥로(?)에진흥는
졍예와뎡일의흥시웁

샤고

○우리미한미일신보의목뎍은
대한의이길면셔빛한원모든폐
묵에관흥야는공평흥번론을쥬
쟝흥여다우리동신의원한맑아보는
도리오보시는범로조의계흥셔보
는흥는리려흥지를레서흥며주서
이논민셔럼과비대뎜쳔이셧계
사기들의광우오나이기슬신문
샹에게흥라는거시아니오다
쥰국히실오흥는즁거든을숩고자
죵이라괴자는아모지셔면지괴
지흥을퇴자흥는리리들가젓스
니퇴자흥는리이드를밝흉터이오
뮈곡중명화요를문관케흥는듯흔
거셔눈의피희벗지안계술나이
다

론셜

　전두예진보
이제일안일거긔현국현요률의
정홍흥이오리라아나홍여미우
크게진보되라유위흥겨슬가히
흠밧흔개시일안영지에서짐작
흥는고라힘들이국히엉뎡흥야흥
신과보고거지라도성히교정졔

흥는거시앙본흥목며쟝의보고
틀보본죽조리의며봉을이젹병의계
샤샹되거시며과젼흥예순샹흥
것게지라도다조셰히화아레보
고흥는지금에외국흥신원들이
이일노잣가히알거시영시되고
쇼군일영지지리도도모지관젼흥
을보면히리라지아니흥는고료로
등진령들의보교들도흥목며쟝
외보교와갓혼거시면교또젼쟝
으로가셔보긔도지들의등을너
셔셔수작흥는소리들드듸동수가
엄스티벌명는그젼쟝이엇더
케결쟝되긔슬텁옥조셔흥교쟝
면흥계보고흥나그러흥나고로쥬
쟝흥야직젼흥는관리들은이미
예보만흥야조표도펼벽피이오
론흥이영시흥며최쳔솜반훈군
수가졍졍진보흥야가다는보고
가도달흥는터밀당수출운응당
총환에며착죽은이보다며훈옺
흥나도모지크계일이나흥는거슨쳔
례은일인셔흥에그리흥는듯흥
며아국사흥진령을은것쳐된젼쥬
교를승졍흥는나서들이님솔에서조
긔나라군사가졍흥였다타지계
못흥다는말은나지아니흥고다
만제희가셩치훗을도보면버느믈
라그런교로라다사흥신원들은
조긔의군은고노흥며봄아모것도
아지못흥고다만은미계흥야조
귀들의분발하였지엇졍은말흥
지아니흥며따각종심문통신원
중에위교한지들을볼니보니계
되변조리여병위드는다티로셩각
흥다구이의희가아니흥스쟝이로
벌졍부에보고흥며보고그병졍틀노
도가지지피여조교마흔게시라
도자지는아니흥는계볼으로흥일
별의계흐며신혼빈것만되면지흥
분진흥는소문이들이도티도일선
주지아니흥며
쇼젼쥬흥는보교가우리의계오
는종아마수가로피드긔진쟝군의
근며평소흔것도며보동셔의의힝
을영더흔지도모지일수엽는기
시지금에는고부좌에다만이며
병졍만엇셔남방에구쳔예엇는
병졍온수쥬으얘졍도부근으로
나오는티그셔남이으로보터드러
가는일본흥목며쟝의군사의의서
로맛는디진영의와우졍톤흔흥야
병의젼후며등화젹흥연다는티

우리이드르말파잇다시는이써
흥예구조파도긴의요양근티가
괴졔자가웅을거로기젼예태쳔흥
엿슬듯흥티이써흥여계넌은어
느편이던지죡승승흥양이면근편
을티리라흥티인이속후운논음
한인우것치성각흥엿던이오이제
쇼흥구로지과히긴요흥미아소주
이예엇지될넌지아슬수업는이이
는편엇일본이하변이긔긴을보편
대지못흥야쥰봉을영은보려흥는
뜻이오로티우리의보는바에도더
단히어려울듯흥고또한일남흥며
논티이아라계힘을드티고평쟝이
쥬퇴흥는이쉬는티우셩각흥는바
흔이오도티보　군시을수통변
진흥야히셩위글보티쇼흥돈은엇
슬지쟝이브며쇼흥남은엇지못
흥엿슬이오기엉요앙써예셔셔
계승리흥엿슨죽일본이흥막셩
권자엇지옵으미오흥노라

잡보

○영수히운　외부에서쥬원영
관에관보홍기를영수는쥬우를
권히흥교영수관졍셔관힘보은써
로되리영수를보흥다흥엿더라
○쳥죠외부　경무수가외부로
조회흥기를일병이각셩문예쥬
야로파슈흥나일인이미상흥지라
일슈이에조회흥야즉시다관흥
라흥엿더라
○지졍교셥은볼영수가외부로
조회흥기를우리공쥬차군수혐부
에셔군신샹쇼관흔안건이잇셔
귀졍부에쳥흥야각처괸부에지
졍이로교셥흔이너각관부에
지조흥야보흥수슉히관리케
흠을티란다흥엿더라
○뎡남정평　평안북도관찰사
운쳔세보고니에도나졍졍이대
치흥야소출흥에무상흥고너입딕
수흥이셩승흥업을이젹당당셤성의
멍이흥홍유그니며조슝지남저의
쳥산을구흥은승도로훈을가지가
며드셔흥아전지들로셔흥엿교
이셥쳥흥의외셔셔변졍흥속이외부
가외흥팀흥야봉졍도져켠흥조
음에도군관교가교가포셕교셔흥속
쵸졔이방도흥며관노교즁발순
오들셩니대졍셔수흥며졔당이
의병문졍안진일이졍에돈팀흥야
흥젹샹을흥교교음소셔이엇에하

쌍의춘예과당오빅심며많다총결
을소가지고도팀흥야면가로조를
흥쳥확흥교빅성이며엉울살히흥교
조으인군삼거라등지에서화확쳔이
쳥졍흥야은인이명이외과리흥야
십셩흥는셩지오흥엿수오니면쳥울흥
셔볼쳥흥야외도나유형즁흥엿쌍도조
로우관평흥야유좌교락서졍흥야도
권쳥왕교흥는티수지흥이오셔는학
흥엿더라
○교수불응　일병수가외부로
조회흥기를일인이교수쳑졍쥬청
의목쳥흥야샤불흥은이뵈원샤딥
경빅상헝원병이빅원쥭씨원을셕헝
부에셔샹금은지불치아니흥으로
귀졍부에셔데일은졍엉병이얻지흔
경부쳐도남은일외려귀셔가귀일
이한스쳐경나에치겨흥아취교
수의계츙곰결티이니조당흥라
흥엿더라
○한병차로　헌병셰명영국공소
가조회흥도로는수가일졍예셔원
외에는뎡시소민동에셔거곡과
슈병졍이성이엽졍믈민는교로셔
보수가보고국공소로셔결명흥야
도병졍김은에관조가일형흥지
아교순이도피리로쳥명나가지
못흥엿는티분보면리로드이건지
경이셩차가되는교로화병졍흥
성운즁관빅윤민과병졍김은에
김은승을계록흥야슈졍흥니원
쥬부에젼조흥야히젼쟝을영쥬흥
히치판흥야습을졍케흥라
흥엿더라
○조흥폐사　외부대신이공쇼니
부와흥샹롱부에조회흥되로분
공소가조회흥기를항열에귀티
선과샹졀쟝이회무지관계수졍
으로귀국대화의폐하
샤쳥면을봉승흥야관비희관빙흥
수률셩의흥계이노쇼회수폐지홈
히회수계주분일외국으로셔각
관흔다흥니한일그리흥면귀정
부가쟝관위당흥계흥야을번지못
흥계시오본수의가라에도볼형
흥니히회수폐지며부를시명흥오니
라흥교로동일흥야조회흥오니
샹쇽히관리흥교조불흥라흥엿
더라
김새롱빈　이완용국경필이
로탕외가잇든쟝명긔금일인슈세는
지금교원에가두흔로빙종에잇

UNION INSURANCE SOCIETY OF CANTON.

Head office Hongkong.
Marine risks underwritten at current rates.
Agents in Chemulpo,
MEYER & Co.

OCEAN S. S. CO., L'T'D.,

CHINA MUTUAL S. N. CO., L'T'D.,

Combined Services.

Japan to London and Antwerp fortnightly service.
S. S. KINTUCK leaves Kobe 8th July.

Japan to Liverpool direct,
S. S. KEEMUN leaves Kobe 14th July.

Japan to Seattle, U. S. A.
taking cargo for all Pacific coast ports.

CHINA NAVIGATION CO., L'T'D.

Japan to Australia
regular mail contract service.
S. S. TAIYUAN leaves Kobe July 22.

For particulars apply to
HOLME RINGER & Co.,
Agents, Chemulpo.

HAYASHIDA & CO.

16 MYENG DONG, CHING KO KAI, SEOUL.
BRANCH OFFICE AT CHEMULPO.

Money changers, Coal and Wood Merchants, Express Agents.

We are agents for the Pyeng-yang Coal Company and the Karazu Coal Company of Japan. We have the best quality of both anthracite and bituminous coal, and prompt execution of orders is our speciality. Firewood of all kinds kept in stock. Full weight guaranteed. Money of all denominations exchange, at current rates. Parcels received for all parts

---

CHINA MUTUAL LIFE INS. CO.

Most favourable terms to policy holders.

Benefit system unsurpassed.

HOLME RINGER & Co.
Agents, Chemulpo.

C. P. R.

CANADIAN PACIFIC RAILWAY COMPANY'S ROYAL MAIL STEAMSHIP LINE.

THE FAST ROUTE BETWEEN CHINA, JAPAN, AND EUROPE VIA CANADA AND THE UNITED STATES.

Route from Hongkong via Shanghai, Nagasaki (Inland Sea of Japan) Kobe, Yokohama, Victoria and Vancouver.

Twin Screw Empress Steamships—6,000 Tons—Speed 19 knots.

PROPOSED SAILINGS FROM YOKOHAMA.

R. M. S. Empress of India	1st July 1904
R. M. S. Empress of Japan	22nd July 1904
R. M. S. Athenian	29th July 1904
R. M. S. Empress of China	12th Aug. 1904

Special reduction (first class only) granted to members of the Military, Naval, Diplomatic and Civil Services and to Missionaries.
Passengers have choice of ten routes across the Continent of America and have privilege of travelling by any Atlantic Steamship Line.
Round the World passage tickets in connection with the P. and O. S. N., North German Lloyd and Messageries Co.'s £125.
All rates payable at current rate of exchange.
For further information, Tickets, Guide Books, etc., apply to
HOLME, RINGER & Co., AGENTS, Chemulpo.

Grand Hotel,

(Formerly the Station Hotel)

Near the Railway Terminus

West Gate, Seoul.

The Best Hotel in Korea.
Handsome new Building.
Fine airy Rooms
Excellent Cuisine.
Terms Moderate.
Special terms to Missionaries and to permanent boarders.

Electric cars within 2 minutes' walk.

W. H. EMBERLEY,
Proprietor.

EVERY FACILITY

In connection with Life Assurance Business is afforded by

The Standard Life Assurance Co.,

One of the largest and wealthiest of the Provident Institutions of the United Kingdom. Forms of Application and all information will be promptly afforded on application.

10 CENTS A DAY.

Not a very large expenditure is it? But it is sufficient to secure for a man of 30 a policy with the STANDARD LIFE OFFICE for

$1323.

For all particular of rates, etc., apply to

Holme, Ringer & Co.,
Agents, Chemulpo.

THE NEW YORK LIFE INSURANCE COMPANY.

Have you ever been declined by and Company?

Are you engaged in as pecially hazardous occupation?

Have you heard of the New York Life Insurance Company's New Classifications for this class of Risks?

If not, send your date of birth, occupation and particulars of rejection, if any to

E. MEYER & Co., Agents, Chemulpo.

MITSUI BUSSAN KAISHA.
(MITSUI & Co.)

MITSUI GINKO.
(MITSUI BANK.)

The Bank is owned by the members of the Mitsui Family, who, as partners, assume an unlimited responsibility for all liabilities of the Bank:—

Capital.................... .....Yen 5,000,000
Reserve Fund.................. " 5,600,000

HEAD OFFICE, TOKYO.

LONDON OFFICE, 34 LIME ST., E. C.

BRANCHES AND AGENCIES:—

New York, San Francisco, Hamburg, Bombay, Singapore, Manila, Hongkong, Amoy, Chefoo, Tientsin.

Kobe, Hakodate, Yokohama, Kure, Yokosuka, Moji, Shimonoseki, Miike, Wakamatsu Nagasaki, Kuchinotsu, Karatsu, Sasebo, Misume, Taipeh, &c.

Telegraphic Address for all the Offices:
"MITSUI."

A. B. C. AND A. I CODES USED.

Contractors of Coal
To the Imperial Japanese Navy. Arsenals and Railway Bureau, Principal Railway Companies and Industrial Works, Home and Foreign Mail and Freight Steamers.

Sole Proprietors
Of the famous Miike, Tagawa and Yamano Coal Mines.

Sole Agents
For the sale of Fukumo, Hokoku, Ichimura, Kanoda, Mannoura, Onoura, Ostuji, Sonoda, Tsubaruro, Yoshinotani, Yoshio, Yurokiburu and other coals.

YANGTSE INSURANCE ASSOCIATION, LTD.

The undersigned, having been appointed agents for the above company, are prepared to issue policies and pay losses on marine risks at regular rates.

E. MEYER & Co.,
Agents, Chemulpo.

AMERICAN KOREAN ELECTRIC COMPANY.

Light and Power.

Main Office: Electric Building, Chong No.

RAILWAY DEPARTMENT.

OPERATING CARS BETWEEN EAST AND WEST GATE, EVERY TEN MINUTES:—

First Car leaves East Gate at 6:30 A. M. First Car leaves West Gate at 6:55 A. M.
Last Car " East Gate at 10:40 P. M. Last " " West Gate at 11:00 P. M.

OPERATING CARS BETWEEN EAST GATE AND IMPERIAL TOMB TERMINUS, EVERY TWENTY MINUTES:—

CONNECTING WITH EVERY ALTERNATE CAR ARRIVING AT EAST GATE FROM CHONG NO.

First Car leaves East Gate for Tomb at 6:50 A. M.
" " " Tomb for East Gate at 7:10 A. M.
Last " " East Gate for Tomb at 9:50 P. M.
" " " Tomb for East Gate at 10:10 P. M.

OPERATING CARS BETWEEN CHONG NO AND YUNG SAN (RIVER) EVERY TWELVE MINUTES:—

First Car leaves Chong No for South Gate at 6:48 A. M.
" " " Chong No for Yung San at 7:24 A. M.
" " " South Gate for Chong No at 6:56 A. M.
" " " Yung San for Chong No at 7:57 A. M.
Last " " South Gate for Chong No 11:00 P. M.
" " " Yung San for Chong No at 10:11 P. M.

SPECIAL PRIVATE CARS FURNISHED TO SUIT CONVENIENCE OF PATRONS. PRICES ON APPLICATION AT HEAD OFFICE.

LIGHTING DEPARTMENT.

Where less than 250 candle power of light is used, the rate per month will be. Per 16 candle power incandescent lamp. All night.—Yen 2.50
Per 32 candle power incandescent lamp:—All night:—Yen 4.00. Per 50 candle power incandescent lamp:—All night:—Yen 6.00.
" 150 " " " " " — " " " 10.00. " 1200 " " enclosed arc " " " " 20.00.

Where more than 250 candle power of light is used, a Meter will be installed, if requested:—Rent of Meter Yen 2.00 per month. Rate of charges by meter reading:—Two Sen per Ampere per hour. (Approximately this is equal to about One Sen per 16 c. p. lamp per hour) Minimum monthly charge where meter is installed, Yen 20.00 per month, which includes rental of meter.

Estimates for installing lights furnished on application. An assortment of chandeliers always on hand.

AMUSEMENT DEPARTMENT.

ANIMATED PICTURES AT EAST GATE.
Every evening - - - Except Sunday.
From 8 to 10 P. M.

10 Cents:—Gen. Admission:—10 Cents. Seats in First Class Section. 15 Cents Extra.

Change of program each week. Pictures from Foreign Lands. Pictures of Local Scenes:—Amusing and Instructive.

An entertaining evening for a reasonable price.
MERRY-GO-ROUND:—At East Gate.
From 10:00 A. M. till 11:00 P. M.

5 Cents a Ride.

Take your Exercise on The Galloping Horses.

Comfortable seats in the Chariots.

한셩뎐긔회사

미국뎐긔회사 고불안 보사뎨 고빅
도ᄒᆞ옵나이다
상활동사진젼람소와목마운동쟝량쳐로연
여러면차가오쟝안으로통힝ᄒᆞ여ᄃᆞᆫ니여이
습
또이긔계에ᄀᆞᆺ치노힌편ᄒᆞ고됴흔마차도잇
습
코미우편ᄒᆞ고또ᄌᆞ미잇ᄂᆞᆫ됴흔운동이되겟
셔됴흔모형ᄒᆞᆫ달나아ᄂᆞᆫ물을ᄐᆞ고위티치안
되가ᄂᆞᆫᄒᆞᆫ번ᄐᆞᄂᆞᆫ데오젼ᄉᆡ이오
미일샹오열시브터하오열ᄒᆞᆫ시ᄭᆞ지ᄒᆞ옵고
목마운동쟝은동대문안에잇습고
가되겟습
쳡군조의게갑도싸고저녁에됴흔쇼일거리
잇고구경ᄒᆞᆯ만ᄒᆞᆫ거시오니
셔양사진과대한과온동양사진언네대ᄌᆞ미
ᄂᆞᆫ되
젼이옵고미쥬일에사진을션것스로다밧고
고젼람되금은하등에십젼이오상등에이십
일외에ᄂᆞᆫ미야에여덟시브터열시ᄭᆞ지ᄒᆞ옵
활동사진젼람소ᄂᆞᆫ동대문안에잇습고일요
회락부

All Cars Run Direct to the Animated Pictures and Merry-Go-Round.

서등번ᄒᆞ여준다고죠션신보에 귀지ᄒᆞ엿더라

○일인어업 일본강산현에 사ᄂᆞᆫ 어업ᄒᆞᄂᆞᆫ 촌상쇼반쎄 등이 ᄒᆡᆼ 운거월하순에 어션이 십쳑을 거ᄂᆞ리고 먼저 츌발ᄒᆞ엿ᄂᆞᆫᄃᆡ 젼일 에 쟝ᄎᆔ후로 오ᄂᆞᆫ 비일쳑이 인쳔 항에 도박ᄒᆞ야 ᄯᅥ러저 잇던 영무 ᄊᆡ 등이 셔도 연히로 ᄯᅥ낫다 더라

○쳥어통ᄉᆞ 반쥬젼진군에셔 쳥어통ᄉᆞ를 만히 슈용이 되ᄂᆞᆫ고 로 한셩에 잇ᄂᆞᆫ 일본쥬차군ᄉᆞ령 부에셔 쳥어통ᄉᆞ로 가기를 원ᄒᆞ ᄂᆞᆫ 사ᄅᆞᆷ들을 모집ᄒᆞᆫ다 더라

○박민쳑거 미동거ᄒᆞᄂᆞᆫ 박쳔 근이 가ᄅᆞᆷ번 모군에 역부로 ᄲᅩᆸ펴 빈진 여왼 일병 등ᄉᆞ 이에 시비 가 되엿ᄂᆞᆫᄃᆡ 일본헌병이 박원근을 헌병파쥬소로 챡거ᄒᆞ엿더라

○농부조복 농광회사 ᄉᆞ건으 로 농부에셔 외부로 조복ᄒᆞ기를 히회사를 폐지ᄒᆞ게 ᄒᆞ라ᄒᆞ엿다 더라

○쟝ᄃᆡ변통 호위병ᄉᆞ 건을 ᄌᆞ 셰히 드른즉 쟝ᄃᆡ방젼위ᄃᆡᄂᆞᆫ 아 직 잉존ᄒᆞ고 시위 진위 쟝ᄃᆡᄂᆞᆫ 갈셩ᄒᆞ고 ᄒᆞᆫ셩호위차로 근위 병일쳔오ᄇᆡᆨ명만 셜치ᄒᆞ게 된고 로 쟝ᄃᆡ령위관들이 미리 자퇴ᄒᆞᆫ 다더라

○국폐림원 셔북텰도국을 폐 지ᄒᆞ야 텰도원에 합셜ᄒᆞᆫ지라 총 재ᄂᆞᆫ 몰시ᄒᆞ고 국쟝만 잉존ᄒᆞᆫ다 더라

○참졍힝용 참졍 셔리 박졔순 씨가 루조ᄉᆞ직 상소ᄒᆞ엿더니 일젼에 수직ᄒᆞ고 힝공ᄒᆞᆫ다더라

○수유환국 주일공사 조민희 씨가 수유ᄒᆞ야 잠시 환국ᄒᆞᆫ다 더 라

○참졍면세 동양협ᄌᆞ금광회 사에셔 수용차로 쭁ᄇᆞᆫ약을 인항 으로 수입ᄒᆞᆯ터이니 허판에 지쵸 ᄒᆞ야 면세케ᄒᆞ라고 미국공사가 외부로 조회ᄒᆞ엿더라

○요구불쳥 인쳔상보를 거ᄒᆞᆫ 즉 일본 당국자가 공언ᄒᆞ되 한국 황무디 기간 문제의 요구를 단졍 코 쳘회치아니ᄒᆞᆫ다ᄒᆞ엿더라

○국민학교 련동에 소교회인 들리 자본을 구취ᄒᆞ야 학교계를 조직ᄒᆞ되 원계원의 계젼은 이원 식이오 비외국을 분ᄅᆞᆫᄒᆞ고 유지 ᄒᆞᆫ 쳠셩계원의 의연금은 다과를 블계ᄒᆞ고 그 계젼으로 국민학교 를 셜립ᄒᆞ야 후진을 교육ᄒᆞ야 문 명에 진보코자ᄒᆞᄂᆞᆫᄃᆡ 그 취지와 규칙을 각관ᄒᆞ여 각쳐에 젼파ᄒᆞ 엿더라

○이ᄅᆞᆷ쟝죨셔 일본 흥군ᄃᆡ쟝ᄌᆞ 작산구소신 씨가 일젼밤에 동병 에셔 죨셔ᄒᆞ엿다더라

○일병동츌 본월 구일샹오 십 시량에 일본수관 오ᄇᆡᆨ명이 빅쟝이 빌령을 거ᄂᆞ리고 동소문으로 츌 거ᄒᆞ엿더라

○공셩위병 자젼으로 공셩 호위병은 시위 ᄃᆡ가 그 호위ᄒᆞᄂᆞᆫ 직무에 쥬관ᄒᆞ 되ᄃᆡ 너ᄌᆞ금 이후 에ᄂᆞᆫ 쟝ᄃᆡ 중으로 병쟝을 ᄲᅡᆸ틱ᄒᆞ 야 일ᄃᆡ ᄃᆡ가 평에 호위병을 셜치 ᄒᆞ되 복쟝 갓ᄒᆞᆫ 계도 다ᄅᆞᆫ 군ᄃᆡ와 룩별이 표나 게 마련ᄒᆞᆫ다 더라

○소쳥셔임 찬졍 권지형 씨가 현금 궐 잇ᄂᆞᆫ 슈평을 ᄉᆞ기셔 임ᄒᆞᆯ ᄉᆞ로 상소ᄒᆞ엿더라

○ᄉᆞ직운운 졍부 ᄃᆡ관을 평졀 조직ᄒᆞᆫ다ᄂᆞᆫ 소문이 잇슴으로 각 ᄃᆡ관이 일졔로 ᄉᆞ직 상조ᄒᆞᆫ다ᄂᆞᆫ 말이 잇더라

○김써괴신 일본군에 군ᄉᆞ상 경찬이시 힝된 이후로 젼북리 아 국간텹된자와 일본 비쳑에 운동 ᄒᆞ든 무리 ᄃᆞ리 급급히 도쥬ᄒᆞᄂᆞᆫ 거슨 세상이 다 아ᄂᆞᆫ 바어니와 뢰 식원 참서관 김도일 씨도 ᄯᅩ 한 종 젹을 감초왓다 더라

관보

뎨이쳔구ᄇᆡᆨ일호 광무팔년 팔월 십일

셔 임 급 ᄉᆞ 령

○의원 면본관 중추원 의관 신셕영 빈 젼 ○임중추원 의관 셔쥬임관 륙등 젼라북도 관찰부 총순 리계원 강원도 관찰부 총순 김광욱 이상 팔 월 륙일

○의원 면본관 시종원 시종 리 귀셩 ○임시종원 시종 셔쥬임 관 륙등 룩품 신영틔 이상 팔월 칠일 ○의원 면본관 비셔 원승 경환덕 김병욱 셔북 쳘도국 주ᄉᆞ 홍우괴 리근영 김명션 리용션 리상직 김 퇴준 김동진 룡명쥬 하종 린호 리응렬 효룡쳠봉 리상 비셔 원승 셔쥬임관 륙등 젼환국 주ᄉᆞ 졍규일 임 귀븜 셔공순 리빈영 ○경성 퇴의원소경 비셔원승 셔공 쥰 임효룡 쳠봉 셔관임관 팔등 룩품 윤교셕 임한셩부공립 소학교교원 셔관임관 륙등 젼 교원 신승덕 임농상공부 주 ᄉᆞ 셔관임관 륙등 리광우

○면본관 경무쳥 총순 륙귀 량 힘원이 거조히 망ᄒᆞᆷ이 잇기로 면본관ᄒᆞᆷ이라

○임경무쳥 총순 셔관임관 륙등 길ᄐᆡᆼ 임젼환국 주ᄉᆞ 셔관임 관 륙등 김학리 이상 팔월팔 일

○셔임 의원 변봉 경무쳥 총순 리셕구 고명환

○궁졍록ᄉᆞ

○의정부 찬정 홍순형 ᄉᆞ직 소 비지 너 에 ᄉᆞ양 말고 힝공ᄒᆞ라 ○의정부 찬정 권중현 ᄉᆞ직 인ᄉᆞ 소 비지 너에 의론ᄒᆞᆫ ᄇᆡ가 심히 간졀 ᄒᆞ고 셜샹 된 지 라이 세에 엇지 가 히 기졀 말 ᄒᆞᄂᆞ뇨 ᄉᆞ양 말고 힝공ᄒᆞ 라

○중추원의관 김지션 ᄉᆞ직소 비지 너에 본직을 허ᄒᆞ노라

이상 팔월 팔일

학ᄉᆞ

경진향공립소학교 부교원은 쟝 두남으로 포쳔군공립소학교 부 교원은 홍종헌으로 임용ᄒᆞ고 김 희근공립소학교부교원최탁현 은 희임ᄉᆞ

뎐보

원산발

○원산통보 구일샹오 구시 챡 로국긔병 오ᄇᆡᆨ명가량이 팔일하 오이시에 문쳔을 지나 덕원 〔원 산샹거 십리〕근쳐에 쳔로ᄒᆞᆫ고 로 일본보병이 충돌ᄒᆞ야 즉시로 병을 격퇴ᄒᆞ엿더라

●아병경계 동일동시 챡 본월팔일에 아병 샹ᄇᆡᆨ 오십여긔 가 단시교원 ᄃᆡ방에 이로 나귀관 포비좌를 가진 지라 힝인을 엄ᄒᆞᆫ 중 히 겸슉ᄒᆞ고 엄의 한인 ᄉᆞ 오명을 의샹 된 ᄌᆞ로 지목ᄒᆞ야 포살ᄒᆞ엿 다더라

○아병후숙 동일동시 챡 금월 구일에 아국 졍탐군 ᄉᆞ십여 긔 가 원산 후면에 쳔로ᄒᆞ고 ᄯᅩ 이십 여긔가 덕원가로샹에 쳔로ᄒᆞ엿 더라

○충돌속보 구일하오 챡 아국 졍탐군은 쳐음에 이십여긔 가 문쳔 리에 셔 쳔안을 연ᄒᆞ야 하 오일시 ᄉᆞ십분에 원산항에 셔북 으로 오리되ᄂᆞᆫ ᄃᆡ방에 쳔로ᄒᆞ엿 스나 일본군의 게 격퇴ᄒᆞᆫ비되고 아병의 ᄉᆞ샹은 군마 일필을 비 로 리 교퇴 쟝ᄒᆞ엿고 샹금원산 ᄃᆡ로 샹 샹에 셔 귀가 하 오 샹시 량 에 본 항 한샹 거 칠리 지 지 츌 현 ᄒᆞ엿 스나 ᄯᅩ 병 중 에 일 병 의 게 격 퇴 ᄒᆞᆫ비 되 엿 고 아 교 히 거 두 위 ᄎᆞᆺ 고 ᄯᅩ 숙 후 병 도 퇴 각 ᄒᆞ 엿 ᄂᆞᆫᄃᆡ 그 후 동 졍 은 미 샹 ᄒᆞ 고 일 본 군 은 손 히 가 엽 셧 더 라

○덕원포젼 동일동시 챡 로병은 금월구일샹오 칠시 이 샹 분에 ᄋᆡᆼ일 등의 놉ᄒᆞᆫ 곳 과 덕원부 근에 놉ᄒᆞᆫ 곳 슬 웅 거 ᄒᆞ 야 일 본 군 과 방 포 격 젼 ᄒᆞ 야 팔 시 가 지 넌 지 란 ᄋᆡᆼ 일 등 놉 ᄒᆞᆫ 곳 에 웅 거 ᄒᆞ 엿 든 로병은 ᄉᆞ ᄇᆡᆨ 긔 가 량 이 나 ᄒᆞ 엿 지 가 이 스 긔 판 포 를 가 졋 고 원 산 부 근 놉 ᄒᆞᆫ 곳 에 웅 거 ᄒᆞᆫ 로 병 은 ᄇᆡᆨ 여 긔 나 되 ᄂᆞᆫ 둣 ᄒᆞ 고 로 병 의 손 히 ᄂᆞᆫ 미 샹 ᄒᆞ 고 일 병 은 손 히 가 엽 고 로 병 을 은 초 쵸 퇴 각 ᄒᆞᄂᆞᆫ 모 양 이 나 방 금 경 탐 중 이 라 더 라

외보

○련순난파 팔월ᄉᆞ일에 발간 ᄒᆞᆫ 지부런 일신문 영ᄌᆞ보를 거ᄒᆞᆫ 즉 련 순 구 에 셔 괴 란 군 들 이 쳥 셥 ᄒᆞ 엿 ᄂᆞᆫ ᄃᆡ 그 젼 ᄒᆞᄂᆞᆫ 말 을 드 른 즉 쳔 월 이 상 륙 일 아 츔 브 ᄃᆡ 시 가 근 디 에 셔 젼 투 가 평 쟝 히 되 엿 ᄂᆞᆫ ᄃᆡ 이 괴 란 군 들 은 괄 월 이 일 아 츔 에 련 순 구 를 ᄯᅥ 낫 고 ᄊᆡ 흠 은 칠 월 이 십 팔 일 에 거 우 칭 식 이 되 엿 스 나 그 동 안 에 ᄂᆞᆫ 련 속 부 졀 ᄒᆞ 여 평 쟝 히 되 엿 스 며 란 환 이 비 오 듯 ᄒᆞᄂᆞᆫ 디 셔 잇 기 가 불 편 ᄒᆞ 여 견 ᄃᆡᆯ 수 업 서 셔 일 노 ᄡᅥ 비 젼 투 원 들 이 만 히 ᄯᅥ 나 며 엇 던 이 들 은 병 괴 들 나 고 의 지 로 셔 이 ᄂᆞᆫ 거 슬 쳥 죵 ᄒᆞ 기 슬 혀 셔 ᄯᅥ 나 오 ᄂᆞᆫ 이 도 만 터 라 련 슌 구 로 셔 오 ᄂᆞᆫ ᄉᆞ 름 마 다 그 쇼 견 틔 구 로 말 ᄒᆞ 기 를 일 군 이 비 록 련 슌 구 를 졈 령 코 져 ᄒᆞ 야 ᄂᆞᆫ 죵 시 지 블 앗 고 ᄉᆞ 징 ᄒᆞ 고 ᄊᆡ 호 ᄃᆞ 리 도 아 조 셰 운 슈 가 업 다 고 들 ᄒᆞ 더 라 어 제 에 괴 란 군 들 중 에 이 왕 에 쳥 니 와 사 에 셔 샹 업 ᄒᆞ 든 동 쳥 탈 도 귀 셤 회 에 ᄉᆞ 무 원 고 런 셰 고 ᄊᆡ 와 련 순 구 모 든 ᄃᆡ 퇴 포 를 부 셜 ᄒᆞᄂᆞᆫ ᄃᆡ 감 독 ᄒᆞ 든 귀 ᄉᆞ 이 ᄅᆞᆷ 명 이 왓 다 ᄒᆞ 엿 더 라

○신랑산격젼 등일동보를 거 ᄒᆞᆫ즉 련순구에셔 로국 비를 타고 작일에 도챡ᄒᆞᆫ 션ᄀᆡᆨ의 말을 드른 즉 항구 북편에 잇ᄂᆞᆫ 신랑산에서 대젼이 되엿ᄂᆞᆫᄃᆡ 여러 셔 더 일 군 ᄉᆡᆨ 흠이 되 라 고 ᄃᆞᆯ 이 미 리 말 ᄒᆞ 든 곳 에 련 순 구 근 디 젼 투 의 ᄉᆞ 실 귀 역 ᄒᆞ 여 ᄇᆡᆨ 이 ᄯᅩ ᄉᆞ ᄅᆞᆷ 들 의 편 ᄇᆡᆨ 되 이 종 ᄉᆞ ᄒᆞᆫ 배 라 그 ᄲᅦ 에 고 이 들 은 신 당 산 너 머 잇 ᄂᆞᆫ 련 도 를 졔 명 거 쟝 근 디 에 잇 셧 ᄂᆞᆫ ᄃᆡ 칠 월 이 십 륙 일 조 죠 비 시 ᄶᅵᆨ 음 에 일 군 이 젼 진 ᄒᆞ 야 공 격 ᄒᆞ 야 이 곳 을 탈 샹 취 ᄒᆞ 란 ᄒᆞ 다 가 도 로 허 퇴 ᄒᆞ 야 ᄉᆞ 가 량 이 아 인 의 묘 탕 에 일 만 오 쳔 명 오 드 른 즉 이 젼 투 에 로 군 의 ᄉᆞ 샹 은 일 쳔 오 ᄇᆡᆨ 명 이 라 ᄒᆞ 고 괴 란 군 들 의 말 을 월 이 샹 북 일 경 에 루 거 괄 좌 가 오 쳔 명 이 라 고 도 ᄒᆞ 며 후 은 블 과 ᄒᆞ ᄂᆞᆫ 티 쳘 군 의 ᄐᆞᆨ 니 리 딕 룡 과 ᄒᆞ 야 일 본 공 격 ᄒᆞᆫ 려 순 구 로 시 리 드 리 간 계 시 아 마 ᄃᆡ 단 히 만 ᄒᆞᆫ 모 양 이 라 ᄒᆞ 엿 더 라

○려순ᄃᆡ퇴 동일동보를 거ᄒᆞᆫ 즉 아라ᄉᆞ에셔 려순항구를 지 퇴 포 무 ᄃᆡ 다 ᄂᆞᆫ 말 이 파 다 ᄒᆞ 야 ᄒᆞ 야 셜 에 면 빗 기 를 무 더 드 라 고 ᄒᆞ 며 ᄒᆞᆨ 셜 에 ᄂᆞᆫ 면 긔 가 아 니 되 드 라 고 ᄒᆞ 야 도 ᄆᆡ 흉 은 통 히 엽 드 라 고 도 ᄒᆞ 야 도 쳥 도 셜 이 되 여 도 모 지 고 젹 보 를 ᄎᆞ 보 고 온 양 반 의 ᄒᆞ 란 슌 으 로 좃 ᄎᆞ 사 원 이 드 ᄅᆞᆫ 바 젼 셜 을 거 ᄒᆞᆫ 즉 련 슌 항 방 어 ᄒᆞᄂᆞᆫ 등 에 ᄂᆞᆫ 맛 치 련 슌 졈 령 ᄒᆞ 기 가 련 ᄒᆞ 나 간 구 면 이 별 동 갓 티 슌 즉 필 경 공 격 되 여 ᄡᅡᆯ ᄯᅢ 에 ᄂᆞᆫ 티 단 히 무 셥 고 손 히 가 만 히 되 여 ᄡᅡᆯ 듯 ᄒᆞ 드 라 ᄒᆞ 엿 더 라

TELEGRAMS

Tokyo Aug. 8th.

The German steamer "Arabia," after discharging her cargo of flour and railway material at Vladivostok, has been released.

IN THE GERMAN CONSULAR COURT.

CROWN *v.* FRAU KALITZKY.

This much-discussed case came up for trial yesterday before Dr. Ney, H. I. G. M's Consul with Messrs. Wolter, Eckert, Schirbaum and Dr. Wunsch as assessors.

Herr Kalitzky, husband of the defendant, conducted the case on her behalf. Prior to the opening of the case he lodged a complaint against two of the assessors, Dr. Wunsch and Mr. Eckert, alleging that as employes of the Korean Government they were not fit and proper persons to assist in adjudicating upon the weighty issues involved. The members of the Tribunal retired and after a short interval returned and announced that the objection was disruled. The charge against the accused was of assault and forcible detention on the person of one Ku Yong-sik, soldier of the 4th company, 3rd batallion of Seoul troops.

Mr. Wolter, acting as spokesman, requested the defendant, who apparently speaks German indifferently, to make a plain statement of the occurrence of events in the English language.

Frau Kalitzky, sworn, then stepped forward and stated that on the occasion in question she was leaving her house when she found herself amongst some Korean soldiers, who passed some highly insulting remarks upon her. Mortified and angered at this, she turned on the principal offender who immediately took to his heels. She, in her excitement, started in pursuit. Failing to overtake him, she seized one of his comrades (presumably as a hostage) and took him to her house until such time as the real offender should be identified. This was not the first time she had been insulted by the soldiers.

The Captain of the 3rd company, 4th Batallion was then examined and deposed that on the day in question, he went to the house of defendant to demand the return of her prisoner. During the course of his conversation with Frau Kalitzky.

When he could glean nothing, she became violent and seized him by the arm. He did not see the circumstances of the soldier's seizure by the defendant. Mr. Kalitzky here intervened. "Did the Captain see the uniform of the soldier torn, as deposed in the charge"? The Captain had not seen it.

Ku Yong-sik was then called and deposed that while on duty at the sentry post near the south-west gate of the palace, he was violently seized and beaten by the defendant. Asked how many times and where he was struck, replied immediately, "fifteen times on the face." Questioned as to his remarkable faculty for lightning calculation, became confused. Further stated several persons witnessed the assault, after which he was taken by scruff of neck and arm and dragged to the house of a Chinese tailor in the same compound as the defendant's house.

Asked for apparent reason of assault, he replied that it seemed to be because he could not understand the language in which the defendant first spoke to him.

The other witnesses were Kim Sung Hun 20 years of age "boy" in the Palace and a Chinese tailor in whose house Ku Yong-sik had been detained. The former's evidence was immaterial. The latter, cross-examined by Mr. Wolter, who showed a great command of "Pidjin" English, deposed that the defendant appeared at his house, accompanied by the prisoner, whom he was grasping by the arm.

He asked her "What's the matter?" She replied that here was a soldier that she was going to keep until one of his comrades, who had insulted her, should be apprehended.

The court after further cross-examination of the witness which led to much contradictory evidence, then adjourned for their decision.

After 35 minutes' absence they returned and Dr. Ney, after reading the accepted evidence of the witnesses, pronounced that the defendant would be fined 50 marks, but would be given one week's grace in which to appeal to the Supreme Court of Leippzig.

AN EVENING GOWN

"An invitation to dinner from the Clarks," says Charles at breakfast, handing me the note across the table. "We accept, of course."

"Yes, dear, if you like; but I really have nothing fit to wear at a dinner party."

"Nothing to wear?" repeats Charles; "why, your wardrobe is stuffed with things."

"Oh, yes; all old gowns. Still perhaps my black chiffon—"

"I won't have you in that hearse," says Charles with brutal decision. "If you really haven't a dress you must get a new one for the occasion. You must look nice, you know; this is the first time they have asked us, and it's important, as you know."

Yes, I knew it was important. Mr. Clark is a partner in a large firm of solicitors, and my husband is a barrister—a rising one, I think—and Mr. Clark has put a good deal of work in his way.

Charles takes out his cheque book and passes a cheque over to me..

"Nine guineas! Oh, Charlie, you are a dear," I say as I look at it.

"Well, you've a fortnight's notice; so you ought to be able to get a decent dress."

When I go out I buy various fashion journals and cash the cheque. On returning home I lock up five pounds of it in my dressing-case and deposit the rest in the chocolate box where I usually keep my money.

I look through the fashion plates; decide I don't much care for anything.

I spend a whole day—at intervals—in examining patterns and materials. I try the different colours against my face; find they make me look green and sickly; go to bed regretting the days when I could wear anything.

Next day I decide that nine guineas is too much to spend on an evening dress; surely I can get one good enough for five or six. Tom needs a new suit, Mollie wants flannel nightdresses, both children ought to have new boots. In the drawing-room that morning I am afflicted with an aching longing for different cushion covers. I write for more patterns, buy more books—spend the next few days considering them; meanwhile a pound goes on the housekeeping.

Charles informs me that he believes the dinner is going to be a very large affair; he hopes I am getting myself a nice frock. I dare not say I have not set about it yet.

I decide there will be nothing for it but to go to town. As I am going up I may as well do everything under one head, I tell myself. Everything in the house seems to want attention. The dress has fallen quite into the background.

Three days before the dinner I boldly take my courage in my hands and inform Charles that I have not yet got the evening gown and contemplate going up to London by the 8:45 with him next morning to buy it. Charles, when he has got over his astonishment, willingly consents to my accompanying him. So far, good.

As the day goes on I realise what an awful thing I have undertaken. Shall I ever catch that early train? I doubt it.

I spend the rest of the day making arrangements for what is to be done during my absence on the morrow. I am so worried I hardly know what I'm doing. In spite of the tried trustworthiness of my servants, I cannot bring myself to believe that things will go right while I am away. I have a long discussion with Marcelline, my French nurse, as to what I had better get for the children in the way of clothes. I mend my best petticoat, and discover to my great delight, that there is a pocket in the foot of it. Get to bed very late, and have nightmare whenever I do fall asleep, being haunted and with a vision of the 8:45 going out of the station leaving me on the platform.

I have given orders that my early tea is to be brought at six. I hear the household astir by half-past five; get up and light the gas, drinking my tea as I walk about the room getting my things together. Under infinite difficulties I manage to get dressed; tear my skirt lining as I put it on, Marcelline has to come with needle and thread. Cook runs messages while I am being put to rights, and I give last instructions as to meals at intervals. Cook comes up with my shoes, and brings a message from Charles, wishing to know if I am coming down to breakfast. Breakfast! As if one had time to think of eating when catching the 8.45 train.

(To be continued).

The former major of the Korean army, who, as reported in our telegram column yesterday, is with the Russian troops at Hamheung, is named Kim Insu and is acting as scout and interpreter to the Russians.

The Korea Daily News.

To be published daily except Sundays.

Rate of Subscription:—

Per Year, Yen 25.
Per Quarter, Yen 7.
Per Month Yen 2.50

Postage in Korea not charged extra.
Postage abroad charged extra.

Advertisements, 50 sen per day for 1 inch or less.
5 yen per month per inch.
50 yen per year per inch.

All communications to

E. T. BETHELL,
Editor and Publisher.
Pak-tong, Seoul.

THE SITUATION AT PORT ARTHUR.

The news as to the situation at Port Arthur which we publish today is indeed portentous. It indicates that the prophesies as to the speedy fall of Port Arthur have all been too "previous" and that even if the Japanese succeed in taking the stronghold it will only be at the cost of an appalling number of lives. The actual loss of life will, from a sentimental point of view, weigh little with the Japa ese. They are a nation of warriors and the patriotism of the soldiers amounts almost to fanaticism. Therefore if Port Arthur be successfully stormed and taken, the inevitable heavy mortality will be looked upon as a means to an end and no reproach to the attacking generals.

On the other hand it will be evident that Japan cannot afford to be continually throwing away thousands of men in unsuccessful attempts to reduce the fortress. The garrison seems to be in a position to defend Port Arthur for at any rate some weeks to come. Junks arrive and depart with comparative freedom and there is therefore little reason to believe that Port Arthur can be starved into submission.

On the other hand the public in Japan insists that Port Arthur must be taken at all cost. At the close of the last war Japan was ousted from the fortress by "diplomacy" and by "diplomacy" Russia stepped in. Japan has never forgiven this injury, and the feeling throughout the country that Port Arthur must be her's is so strong, that brave as they are we do not think there is a general brave enough to raise the siege and confess himself beaten.

Under these circumstances continued fighting seems to be the only thing to expect. Russia will hold out for some time yet, the Japanese soldiers will slowly creep forward over the dead bodies of thousands of fallen comrades, and unless Port Arthur receives assistance from without, an ultimate Japanese victory is only a matter of time and men.

We know so little of Japan's intentions that it is quite conceivable that she has "up her sleeve" a plan of overwhelming assault or strategy which will bring the fortress into her hands. On the other hand the reports which reach us from Port Arthur are so circumstantial as to carry conviction and it becomes apparent that two factors which were expected to materially contribute to the downfall of the fortress—the destruction of the navy and lack of provisions—are absent.

PORT ARTHUR NEWS.

(From the Chefoo Daily News of August 4th.)

Quite a number of refugees arrived from Port Arthur yesterday by junk. They report that the fighting about the city has been very severe since the morning of July 26th. These people left Port Arthur on the morning of August 2nd. The fighting had somewhat abated on July 28th, but during the time it continued was very severe. It is stated that life in Port Arthur is becoming unbearable on account of the uncertainty as to where missiles are going to drop next. This has induced many of the non-combatants to leave. Others have come away on account of their unwillingness to comply with the request to bear arms. All persons coming from Port Arthur express the opinion that the place will never be taken by the Japanese, though they admit that the latter are fighting desperately for its possession.

Among the people arriving yesterday is an official of the Chinese Eastern Railway Steamship service, Mr. Grunberg, formerly in business in Dalny and the engineer who is said to have superintended the laying of so many land mines about Port Arthur.

The Russian junk passengers who arrived from Port Arthur yesterday report a very severe engagement at Wolf Mountain, to the North of the city. It will be remembered by those who have followed the trend of events in the operations about Port Arthur, that this is the place at which it was predicted the heaviest fighting would take place. The Russians were at that time in possession of the second station on the railway beyond Wolf Mountain.

It is said that about 4 o'clock on the morning of July 26th the Japanese in force attempted to take the place by storm, but were repulsed with a loss which is estimated by. the Russians at fifteen thousand. Some of the refugees stated the Russian losses in this engagement at five thousand, while others reduced it to fifteen hundred. It was probably comparatively heavy as eight trains passed up and down the line during the day of July 26th, carrying into Port Arthur those who fell under the heavy storming fire of the attacking troops.

Much has been said about land mines laid about Port Arthur by the Russians, many persons asserting that there are myriads of them, others stating that there are a few, and still others that there are none at all. The truth probably is not generally known.

Among the passengers arriving on yesterday's junks is a gentleman who is said to have superintended the placing of a good many of these mines, and in an indirect way a "Daily News" man was informed that he positively says the destructive explosives honeycomb the ground about the city's defenses, and that when they are touched off, the result must be a tremendous loss to the attacking troops.

The Russian fleet is reported to be shelling Japanese positions from its anchorage in Port Arthur harbour. The report indicates that the Japanese troops, in one direction at least, are getting close to the city. It is said by those who have stated the location of the attacking forces that they are now within four miles on the Northeast side. Japanese artillery is getting some of its shells into the city which is beginning to make the safety of the non-combatants somewhat uncertain, and many are making preparations to leave as soon as possible.

A KOREAN SHERLOCK HOLMES.

The lynx-eyed police of Seoul have, with wonderful perspicacity, just discovered that the gates of the city are guarded day and night by Japanese soldiers. They have now made a complaint about the matter to the Japanese Legation.

YELLOW JOURNALISM.

We regret to find that the intolerable system of personal espionage which is such an undesirable feature of some of the lower class journals in Japan is beginning to be practised in this country. Some time ago two foreigners were accused of fostering anti-Japanese feeling in Seoul because on their return from Chefoo they repeated news which was current there to the effect that Port Arthur was not in the parlous condition it had been imagined to be! We now see that the "Dai-han il-po," arrogating to itself privileges which are quite outside of its scope, arraigns a Korean for speaking French, visiting the French Legation and being on friendly terms with the French. On these grounds the "Dai-han-il-po" concludes that the man is an enemy to Japan and a friend of Russia and finally passes judgment, saying portentously that something will "certainly be decided about him." This is intolerable. Unless the article is inspired it is none of the "Dai-han-il-po's" business. If the article has official sanction it is still more intolerable. To threaten in this way is grossly unfair. Even if no further action ensues, a great deal of harm is already done, on the principle that if enough mud be thrown some of it is pretty sure to stick.

THE OPERATIONS IN THE NORTHEAST.

The object of the Russian descent on Gensan is obscure. As an isolated movement it seems destined to accomplish practically nothing and should a success at Port Arthur enable the Japanese Navy to turn its attention to this district, their situation would be a precarious one. Their line of communications closely follows the sea coast and it they advance far into Korea they run a serious risk of having their retreat cut off and being caught in a trap.

In concert with another army advancing from the westward they could accomplish much more as they would then be a serious menace to Japanese communications in this country.

Having occupied Ham-heung, an advance guard of some 500 cavalry with Hotchkiss guns seems to have advanced on Gensan, arriving there on the 9th. They appear to have come for purely scouting purposes, as directly they met with opposition from the Japanese garrison they retired without giving battle. There do not appear to have been any casualties, neither did the Japanese pursue the retreating Russians.

THE KOREAN MINING AND CULTIVATING COMPANY.

The Minister for Foreign Affairs forwards to the Imperial Household Department and Department of Agriculture a despatch which he has received from the Japanese Minister. His Excellency Mr. Hayashi says that when by order of the Emperor, the Minister for Foreign Affairs and the Vice-President of State visited him to discuss the Waste Land scheme, he received an assurance that the Korean Mining and Cultivating Company would be abolished. He has now heard that the Company intends to raise foreign capital and proceed with its work. Mr. Hayashi protests that such a course will afterwards place the Government in a dangerous position and asks for information as to the truth or otherwise of the story.

REPORTED SUICIDE OF RUSSIAN GENERAL.

A telegram coming from Chefoo via Tokyo states that General Stoessel committed suicide at Port Arthur on the 10th inst. This should be accepted with some reserve.

Chinese interpreters are in demand with the Japanese army. Good billets are being offered to Koreans conversant with the language by the army Headquarters in Seoul.

The Korean Minister to Tokyo has obtained his coveted leave of absence. His secretary will be appointed Chargé d'Affaires

The Korea Daily News.

VOL. I, THURSDAY, AUGUST 11, 1904. No. 22

大韓每日申報
대한ᄆᆡ일신보

(뎨이십삼호) (금요일) 일천구ᄇᆡᆨ사년팔월십이일

본사고ᄇᆡᆨ

이신보는영어와한국어로셔계ᄆᆡ일발ᄒᆡᆼᄒᆞ옵

일쥬[illegible]

션금가

ᄒᆞᆫᄌᆞᆼ 엽젼두돈오푼

일삭됴 엽젼두량닷돈 ᄇᆡᆨ돈으로 밧숩

광고료는

긔한의쟝단과ᄌᆞ힝의다쇼로ᄌᆞᆼ감ᄒᆞ되헐가로밧을터이오며오리지아녀대한사람마다다이신문을보실터이니광고버시기를원ᄒᆞ시는이들은우리신문사에와서편약ᄒᆞ심을희망ᄒᆞ옵

○발ᄒᆡᆼ소 대한ᄆᆡ일신보사발ᄒᆡᆼ이항교헐해져영국인셜필림쟝자리오

사쟝 영국인 (ᄇᆡ셜)

본사자ᄇᆡᆨ

인쳔항교젼동신지평씨로우리대한ᄆᆡ일신보사인쳔지졈쟝을퇴졍ᄒᆞ엿ᄉᆞ오니인쳔항에계신구람코자ᄒᆞ시는쳠군ᄌᆞ는최지졍에왕림편의ᄒᆞ시옵

사고

○우리대한ᄆᆡ일신보의목뎍은대한의안녕질셔에관한모든뎨목에대ᄒᆞ야는공평한번론을주쟝ᄒᆞ이라우리동신원의답보는신문보시는쳠군ᄌᆞ의게ᄒᆞᆼ상보도ᄒᆞ리며편지를긔셔ᄒᆞ여주시는이는셩명과번디를젹어붓치시기를희망ᄒᆞ오나하긔슨신문상에긔쟤ᄒᆞ라는거시아니오다만극히신용ᄒᆞ는증거를숨고자홈이라긔쟈는아모긔셔던지과지ᄒᆞᆷ을뫼쟉ᄒᆞ는권리를가졋스나뫼쟉ᄒᆞ는리유는말ᄒᆞᆯ터이오며공즁광회를문란케ᄒᆞ는듯ᄒᆞᆫ긔셔는일졀게ᄌᆡ치아니ᄒᆞ겟ᄉᆞᆸ나이다

론셜

국권의위ᄐᆡᄒᆞᆷ이라

○무릇사ᄅᆞᆷ마다시러ᄒᆞ고크게관계되는거슨병력으로사ᄅᆞᆷ잡을운ᄒᆞᆫ일과비리ᄒᆞᆫ일을ᄒᆞᆼ상소활ᄒᆞ게ᄒᆞᆷ은심히그른거시근일에일본헌병으로ᄒᆞ여곰돈목히지나는대한빅셩들을잡아가는거시변노ᄒᆞ괴이ᄒᆞᆫ것도업고다만이나라로ᄒᆞ여곰공동케ᄒᆞ는거시요연약ᄒᆞ게아라그리ᄒᆞᆷ이로되우리의소견갓타서는아모ᄅᆞᆯ용졍히일을ᄒᆡᆼᄒᆞ고이러ᄒᆞᆫ[illegible]ᄒᆡᆼᄒᆞ거[illegible]아라노라만일우리의평론ᄒᆞ야셜명ᄒᆞᆷ을남ᄒᆞ셜진ᄃᆡᆫ대강더ᄒᆞᆯ말이잇는거시대한의일본에게셩히관곡히ᄒᆞ는조리에이티되를ᄒᆞ는거시셩취아니ᄒᆞᆫ지모르겟고또ᄒᆞᆫ지에괴착ᄒᆞ야간사ᄅᆞᆷ들과련항소문을드른즉우리나라이일본으로특별히동졍을표ᄒᆞ는사이에이러케강박히ᄒᆞᆯ슈은모른거시라고들ᄒᆞ니이말이과연란복ᄒᆞᆯ만ᄒᆞ도다

만일대한빅셩의취몰을분명히드러번스를걋갓드면조귀들의죄를면져ᄌᆡ닷고필경처음에도죄ᄒᆞ야쟝히지아니ᄒᆞ엿슬터이로되이엇지횟도이포착ᄒᆞᆷ을아라쓰리요

우리가이말ᄒᆞ는거슨대한도우리의게방ᄒᆞ여서는ᄆᆡ시외국인지라아모조록외국사ᄅᆞᆷ을셰다라알게ᄒᆞ란는목젹으로이리ᄒᆞᆷ이니이공연히포착ᄒᆞ야경동케ᄒᆞᆷ은일한량국에조약ᄒᆞᆫ바일후범죄필례로ᄒᆞ게만드는거시라일본서ᄒᆡᆼᄒᆞ는일이맛치대한빅셩들을공연히경동ᄒᆞ고저항ᄒᆞ시라는뜻을두고조약홈과갓튼거아시즈쥰졍이숏케아니낫고또일본의최긴ᄒᆞᆫ동셔면셤은한국ᄆᆡᆫ엿는티셔시비찬에졍최들에권히ᄒᆞ야ᄌᆞ긔의요ᄒᆞᆫ방침으로숏계시리ᄒᆞ는목젹과는티단히어그러젓도다

잡보

○원항졉젼 덕원감리가외부로젼보ᄒᆞ엿스되아병이다슈로항외에리도ᄒᆞ야일병과교젼ᄒᆞ엿는티아병편명이중온후에퇴거ᄒᆞ엿는티항구상거이십리외의서쏘졉젼ᄒᆞᆫ듯ᄒᆞ다고ᄒᆞ엿더라

○양ᄉᆞ폐쳥 졔작일하오셰시에는외티리국공ᄉᆞ가친셔를봉정ᄒᆞ야 폐현ᄒᆞ고하오오시에는비리시국령ᄉᆞ가친셔를봉졍ᄒᆞ야 폐현ᄒᆞ엿더라

○죠쳥호죠 영국공ᄉᆞ가외부로죠회ᄒᆞ되본국룩군부령빅리등이빅두산에유람코자ᄒᆞ니호죠와런로보호ᄒᆞᆫ령을너보니기로바란다ᄒᆞ엿더라

○법쳥호죠 법국공ᄉᆞ가외부에죠회ᄒᆞ기를회랍국인에변명이경과강원도로유람코자ᄒᆞᆫ다니호죠를너보너기로위ᄒᆞ야쳥ᄒᆞ엿더라

○티권쳥금 외부에서일본공ᄉᆞ의게죠회ᄒᆞ되귀국인아요위ᄒᆞ야귀국출젼군인을위ᄒᆞ야금을쳥구ᄒᆞᆫᄉᆞ건은귀졍부에승인ᄒᆞᆷ이나시명ᄒᆞ라ᄒᆞ엿더니일공ᄉᆞ가답ᄒᆞ되휘쇼건을귀룽할졉ᄒᆞᆫ후에비로소아랏노라ᄒᆞ손건면말을쇼상셰명ᄒᆞ라ᄒᆞ엿더라

○경쳥금츤 경무쳥에서각방곡에게시ᄒᆞᆫ춘ᄒᆞᆫ에ᄒᆞ엿스되근빅셩리황셩니외각방곡에우리ᄒᆞᆫ목젼에란의쇼ᄉᆞ중을모로고다만지티와금산에졍을짓는디키잔을ᄒᆞᆫ다칭탁ᄒᆞ는티인하를밧고다코빙자ᄒᆞ며또ᄒᆞᆫ졔지으며벗도졍탁ᄒᆞ야편간졍도지가금기종이랑밧ᄒᆞᆫ기찬ᄒᆞ엿다가당면이벌에는을날리도ᄒᆞ야수단을쳐계ᄒᆞ며팔기도ᄒᆞ는일니되어가ᄒᆞᆯ수가업게되엿스니그쟝흔ᄇᆡ논이무가론이어니와진실노고일을연구ᄒᆞᆯ진댄실노심상ᄒᆞᆫ곤생이아니라일노써ᄒᆞ는칙ᄒᆞ니조금이후로는쟝님각방곡과금산근디에인민들이괴디를파거나쟝을짓게나혹세ᄒᆞᆫ쟝이던가ᄒᆞᆫ는중일지라도과서가는일이잇스면도저히셜폐써쟉간ᄒᆞ야범죄치안토록ᄒᆞ며또ᄒᆞᆫ곳저져히신칙ᄒᆞ야쇼유ᄒᆞ되만일ᄒᆞᆫ반히냐여살피지못ᄒᆞ는폐단이잇스면고칙망이도로혀ᄒᆞᆯ터가잇너대단히착념ᄒᆞ이가ᄒᆞ다ᄒᆞ엿더라

○일ᄉᆞ쇼졉 금일하오삼시반에일본공ᄉᆞ가 폐현ᄒᆞᆫ다더라

○금평교시 경무쳥에서셰샹에과되ᄒᆞ는자와졍치는자를금단ᄒᆞ기위ᄒᆞ야작일가방곡에게방교시ᄒᆞ엿스되금번교시ᄒᆞᆫ후에번일범과ᄒᆞ는자잇스면귀쳔을불논ᄒᆞ고괴착되는티로증벌ᄒᆞᆫ다ᄒᆞ엿더라

○일ᄉᆞ샹쥬 향자일공ᄉᆞ폐현시에샹 쥬ᄒᆞᆫᄉᆞ건을등문ᄒᆞᆫ즉즉셤샹도관찰부에일본인으로시찰ᄉᆞ를파송ᄒᆞᆫᄉᆞ와궁니에최고등고문관을일인으로고빙ᄒᆞᆯᄉᆞ와긴급치아니ᄒᆞᆫ관제를폐지ᄒᆞᆯᄉᆞ건을샹 쥬ᄒᆞ엿다더라

○졍부회향 졍부에서일본공ᄉᆞ 폐현시 샹쥬ᄒᆞᆫ계ᄉᆞ건셜시ᄒᆞ기젼에먼져교졍쳥을셜시ᄒᆞ야용관ᄒᆞᆯ시ᄒᆞ고인지를퇴용ᄒᆞᆫ다[illegible]

○비대불ᄉᆞ 일본ᄉᆞ[illegible]셔역부로졉ᄉᆞ건으로니부에티ᄒᆞ야연일독촉ᄒᆞ미비샹ᄒᆞ고로니부대신조병필씨가티답ᄒᆞ기극난ᄒᆞ야연일ᄉᆞ진ᄒᆞ야니ᄒᆞᆫ다더라

○직졍폐현 일본ᄉᆞ령부에서공니형관박용화씨를쳥ᄒᆞ야발ᄒᆞ되리국공ᄉᆞ는 폐현시에외부로죠회도ᄒᆞ고궁ᄂᆡ쇼원으로통지ᄒᆞᆫ후에폐현을ᄒᆞ거니와우리ᄉᆞ령부는일의동맹국시인즉비록하졀ᄒᆞᆫ이라도곳바로 폐현ᄒᆞᆯᄉᆞ로 샹쥬ᄒᆞ라ᄒᆞ엿더라

○리하령관 평리원판ᄉᆞ리위셔는의졍부참찬으로젼임ᄒᆞ고젼의관리상텬씨는평리원졔판쟝을ᄒᆞᆫ다더라

○가등향경 일본가등고문관과갑부ᄌᆞ쟉과엥쟝쥰씨가본월구일에부산서지츌발ᄒᆞ야경셩으로향ᄒᆞ엿다더라

○민씨연금 보국영환씨가일작에일본출젼군인유족의휼금금화일ᄇᆡᆨ원을증송ᄒᆞ엿다더라

○슌ᄉᆞ리한 한셩에쥬차ᄒᆞᆫ일본영ᄉᆞ관ᄉᆞ무보기로신임ᄒᆞᆫ일본외무셩슌ᄉᆞ룩명이일젼에리도ᄒᆞ엿다더라

○영협립향 영국군함회이스호가졔작일오후일시에위히위로서인항에리도ᄒᆞᆫ다더라

○소쳥쳥원 남촌소쳥에서을ᄉᆞ병씨가평리원에지ᄎᆞ쳥원ᄒᆞᆫ니기셔지에국졔권즁셕과지관을엿ᄒᆡ지라ᄊᆞᆨᄒᆞᆫ졔관ᄒᆞᆫ아개글말ᄒᆞᆫ가ᄒᆞ엿더라

UNION INSURANCE SOCIETY OF CANTON.

Head offiice Hongkong.
Marine risks un'erwritten at current rates.
Agents in Chemulpo,
MEYER & Co.

OCEAN S. S. CO., L'T'D.,
CHINA MUTUAL S. N. CO., L'T'D.,

Combined Services.

Japan to London and Antwerp fortnightly service.
S. S. KINTUCK leaves Kobe 8th July.

Japan to Liverpool direct,
S. S. KEEMUN leaves Kobe 14th July.

Japan to Seattle, U. S. A. taking cargo for all Pacific coast ports.

CHINA NAVIGATION CO., L'T'D.

Japan to Australia regular mail contract service.
S. S. TAIYUAN leaves Kobe July 22.

For particulars apply to
HOLME RINGER & Co.,
Agents, Chemulpo.

HAYASHIDA & CO.

16 MYENG DONG, CHING KO KAI, SEOUL.
BRANCH OFFICE AT CHEMULPO.

Money changers, Coal and Wood Merchants, Express Agents.

We are agents for the Pyeng-yang Coal Company and the Karazu Coal Company of Japan. We have the best quality of both anthracite and bituminous coal, and prompt execution of orders is our speciality. Firewood of all kinds kept in stock. Full weight guaranteed. Money of all denominations exchange, at current rates. Parcels received for all parts

---

CHINA MUTUAL LIFE INS- CO.

Most favourable terms to policy holders.

Benefit system unsurpassed.

HOLME RINGER & Co.
Agents, Chemulpo.

C. P. R.

CANADIAN PACIFIC RAILWAY COMPANY'S ROYAL MAIL STEAMSHIP LINE.

THE FAST ROUTE BETWEEN CHINA, JAPAN, AND EUROPE VIA CANADA AND THE UNITED STATES.

Route from Hongkong via Shanghai, Nagasaki (Inland Sea of Japan) Kobe, Yokohama, Victoria and Vancouver.

Twin Screw Empress Steamships—6,000 Tons—Speed 19 knots.

PROPOSED SAILINGS FROM YOKOHAMA.

R. M. S. Empress of India - - - - 1st July 1904
R. M. S. Empress of Japan - - - 22nd July 1904
R. M. S. Athenian - - - - - 29th July 1904
R. M. S. Empress of China - - - 12th Aug. 1904

Special reduction (first class only) granted to members of the Military, Naval, Diplomatic and Civil Services and to Missionaries.

Passengers have choice of ten routes across the Continent of America and have privilege of travelling by any Atlantic Steamship Line.

Round the World passage tickets in connection with the P. and O. S. N., North German Lloyd and Messageries Co.'s £125.

All rates payable at current rate of exchange.

For further information, Tickets, Guide Books, etc., apply to

HOLME, RINGER & Co., AGENTS,
Chemulpo.

Grand Hotel,

(Formerly the Station Hotel)

Near the Railway Terminus,

West Gate, Seoul.

The Best Hotel in Korea.
Handsome new Building.
Fine airy Rooms
Excellent Cuisine.
Terms Moderate.
Special terms to Missionaries and to permanent boarders.

Electric cars within 2 minutes' walk.

W. H. EMBERLEY,
Proprietor.

EVERY FACILITY

In connection with Life Assurance Business is afforded by

The Standard Life Assurance Co.,

One of the largest and wealthiest of the Provident Institutions of the United Kingdom. Forms of Application and all information will be promptly afforded on application.

10 CENTS A DAY.

Not a very large expenditure is it? But it is sufficient to secure for a man of 30 a policy with the STANDARD LIFE OFFICE for

$1323.

For all particular of rates, etc., apply to

Holme, Ringer & Co.,
Agents, Chemulpo.

THE NEW YORK LIFE INSURANCE COMPANY.

Have you ever been declined by and Company?

Are you engaged in as pecially hazardous occupation?

Have you heard of the New York Life Insurance Company's New Classifications for this class of Risks?

If not, send your date of birth, occupation and particulars of rejection, if any to

E. MEYER & Co., Agents, Chemulpo.

MITSUI BUSSAN KAISHA.
(MITSUI & Co.)

MITSUI GINKO.
(MITSUI BANK.)

The Bank is owned by the members of the Mitsui Family, who, as partners, assume an unlimited responsibility for all liabilities of the Bank:—

Capital..................Yen 5,000,000
Reserve Fund............. " 5,600,000

HEAD OFFICE, TOKYO.

LONDON OFFICE, 34 LIME ST., E. C.

BRANCHES AND AGENCIES:—

New York, San Francisco, Hamburg, Bombay, Singapore, Manila, Hongkong, Amoy, Chefoo, Tientsin.

Kobe, Hakodate, Yokohama, Kure, Yokosuka, Moji, Shimonoseki, Miike, Wakamatsu Nagasaki, Kuchinotsu, Karatsu, Sasebo, Misumi, Taipeh, &c.

Telegraphic Address for all the Office.
"MITSUI."

A. B. C. AND A. I CODES USED.

Contractors of Coal
To the Imperial Japanese Navy. Arsenals and Railway Bureau, Principal Railway Companies and Industrial Works, Home and Foreign Mail and Freight Steamers.

Sole Proprietors
Of the famous Miike, Tagawa and Yamano Coal Mines.

Sole Agents
For the sale of Fukumo, Hokoku, Ichimura, Kanoda, Mannoura, Onoura, Ostuji, Sonoda, Tsubaruro, Yoshinotani, Yoshio, Yurokibura and other coals.

YANGTSE INSURANCE ASSOCIATION, LTD.

The undersigned, having been appointed agents for the above company, are prepared to issue policies and pay losses on marine risks at regular rates.

E. MEYER & Co.,
Agents, Chemulpo.

AMERICAN KOREAN ELECTRIC COMPANY.

Light and Power.

Main Office: Electric Building, Chong No.

RAILWAY DEPARTMENT.

OPERATING CARS BETWEEN EAST AND WEST GATE, EVERY TEN MINUTES:—

First Car leaves East Gate at 6:30 A. M. First Car leaves West Gate at 6:55 A. M.
Last Car " East Gate at 10:40 P. M. Last " " West Gate at 11:00 P. M.

OPERATING CARS BETWEEN EAST GATE AND IMPERIAL TOMB TERMINUS, EVERY TWENTY MINUTES:—

CONNECTING WITH EVERY ALTERNATE CAR ARRIVING AT EAST GATE FROM CHONG NO.

First Car leaves East Gate for Tomb at 6:50 A. M.
" " " Tomb for East Gate at 7:10 A. M.
Last " " East Gate for Tomb at 9:50 P. M.
" " " Tomb for East Gate at 10:10 P. M.

OPERATING CARS BETWEEN CHONG NO AND YUNG SAN (RIVER) EVERY TWELVE MINUTES:—

First Car leaves Chong No for South Gate at 6:48 A. M.
" " " Chong No for Yung San at 7:24 A. M.
" " " South Gate for Chong No at 6:56 A. M.
" " " Yung San for Chong No at 7:57 A. M.
Last " " South Gate for Chong No 11:00 P. M.
" " " Yung San for Chong No at 10:11 P. M.

SPECIAL PRIVATE CARS FURNISHED TO SUIT CONVENIENCE OF PATRONS. PRICES ON APPLICATION AT HEAD OFFICE.

LIGHTING DEPARTMENT.

Where less than 250 candle power of light is used, the rate per month will be. Per 16 candle power incandescent lamp. All night.—Yen 2.50.
Per 32 candle power incandescent lamp:—All night:—Yen 4.00. Per 50 candle power incandescent lamp:—All night:—Yen 6.00.
" 150 " " " " " " 10.00. " 1200 " " enclosed arc " " " " 20.00.

Where more than 250 candle power of light is used, a Meter will be installed, if requested:—Rent of Meter Yen 2.00 per month. Rate of charges by meter reading:—Two Sen per Ampere per hour. (Approximately this is equal to about One Sen per 16 c. p. lamp per hour) Minimum monthly charge where meter is installed, Yen 20.00 per month, which includes rental of meter.

Estimates for installing lights furnished on application. An assortment of chandeliers always on hand.

AMUSEMENT DEPARTMENT.

ANIMATED PICTURES AT EAST GATE.
Every evening - - - Except Sunday.
From 8 to 10 P. M.

10 Cents:—Gen. Admission:—10 Cents. Seats in Firs Class Section. 15 Cents Extra.

Change of program each week. Pictures from Foreign Lands. Pictures of Local Scenes:—Amusing and Instructive.

An entertaining evening for a reasonable price.
MERRY-GO-ROUND:—At East Gate.
From 10:00 A. M. till 11:00 P. M.

5 Cents a Ride.

Take your Exercise on The Galloping Horses.

Comfortable seats in the Chariots.

한셩뎐긔회사

미국뎐긔회사 고불안 보사ᄇᆡᆨ 고ᄇᆡᆨ
도ᄒᆞ옵나이다
상활동사진뎐람소와목마운동쟝량쳐로연
여뎐차가온쟝안으로통힝ᄒᆞ여ᄃᆞ니여이
습
또이긔계에ᄀᆞᆺ치노힌편ᄒᆞ고ᄆᆞᆷ혼마차도잇
습
코ᄆᆡ우편ᄒᆞ고또조미잇는ᄆᆞᆷ혼운동이되겟
어ᄆᆞᆷ혼모형ᄒᆞᆫ달나아는물을ᄐᆞ고위ᄅᆡ치안
되가는ᄒᆞᆫ번ᄐᆞ는데오젼식이오
ᄆᆡ일샹오열시브터하오열ᄒᆞᆫ시ᄭᆞ지ᄒᆞ옵고
목마운동쟝은동대문안에잇숩고
가되겟습
쳠군조의게갑도싸고저녁에ᄆᆞᆷ혼쇼일거리
잇고구경ᄒᆞᆯ만ᄒᆞᆫ거시오니
셔양사진과대한과온동양사진인네ᄃᆡ조미
는ᄃᆡ
뎐이옵고ᄆᆡ쥬일에사진을ᄉᆡᆫ것스로다밧고
고뎐람되금은하등에십젼이오샹등에이십
일외에는ᄆᆡ야에여덜시브터열시ᄭᆞ지ᄒᆞ옵
활동사진뎐람소는동대문안에잇숩고일요
희락부

All Cars Run Direct to the Animated Pictures and Merry-Go-Round.

○압씨작셜 공셔호씨가슈원
지방에셔일본공관의계착거ᄒᆞᆫ
비되엿다표대등신보에긔저ᄒᆞ
엿더라
○싱션산쇼 금월십ᄉᆞ일에일
본으로셔한국에져음오ᄂᆞᆫ륜션
의쥬환은금번에상션회ᄉᆞ에셔
한일량국간에항히왕릭ᄒᆞᆯ기위
ᄒᆞ야셔로제죠ᄒᆞᆫ륜션인ᄃᆡ돈슈
ᄂᆞᆫ팔빅돈이라더라
○난화지령 호대ᄒᆞᆫ신 련은
으로감옥셔외죄슈외졀도ᄭᆞ지
라도금번ᄉᆞ면에방셕이되엿ᄂᆞᆫ
자라방셕되엿든졀도동이슈일
나에숨ᄉᆞ명이또도젹질ᄒᆞ다가
피착이되엿다니춤산화라고할
만ᄒᆞ다고들ᄒᆞ더라
○셔긔도관 황셩쥬차일본령
ᄉᆞ관외무셔긔싱으로신임ᄒᆞᆫ면
구묘삼남씨가삼작일에일본령
ᄉᆞ관으로리도ᄒᆞ엿다더라
○도변귀국 일본경찰셔경부
도변씨가그친환에근친ᄒᆞᆯ차로
삼작일에슈유ᄒᆞ고일본으로젼
왕ᄒᆞ엿더라
○윤씨헌의 젼비셔승윤병씨
와그외에제씨가원슈부에헌의
ᄒᆞ되현금일본이동양에평화롤
위ᄒᆞ야젼국에동병ᄒᆞ고지졍을
탕갈ᄒᆞ야만리허륙에젼투를진
력ᄒᆞ되한청양국은력업시승평
을누리나일본어아모리말ᄒᆞ지
아니ᄒᆞᆯ들우리마음에붓그럽지
아니리오맛당히원슈부로셔문
음무죠신즁에지력잇ᄂᆞᆫ쟈를턱
취ᄒᆞ고병졸은각ᄃᆡ즁쟈원쟈와
셔북간도등디의용병을뽑고군
비ᄂᆞᆫ모든귀척의게와모든부쟈
의게연금ᄒᆞ야보죠케ᄒᆞ고또이
왕관리즁담학ᄒᆞ든쟈의쟝젼을
거두고또경향간에범죄ᄒᆞᆫ쟈징
역ᄒᆞᄂᆞᆫ쟈의허다ᄒᆞᆫ속젼으로치
와쓰게ᄒᆞ고[illegible]
식켜일병으[illegible]
아국을공격ᄒᆞ면대공을일울거
[illegible]잇스니
대일ᄂᆞᆫ셔북비셩이아병의로략
을면ᄒᆞᆯ거시오데이ᄂᆞᆫ간도에국
계롤졍ᄒᆞᆯ거시오데삼은강ᄒᆞᆫ린
국의게후일척망을면ᄒᆞᆯ거시오
데ᄉᆞᄂᆞᆫ근일병졍감익ᄒᆞᆫ다ᄂᆞᆫ의
논이잇스니곳각ᄃᆡ병졸긔천명
을셔북으로하송ᄒᆞ면아라셔ᄂᆞᆫ
무고히ᄅᆡ거당ᄒᆞᆫ원망이업쓸거
시오우쾌셔ᄂᆞᆫ슈용ᄒᆞᆯᄂᆞᆫ지효험이
잇슬이이다ᄒᆞ엿더라

외보

파ᄉᆞ위문 인쳔샹보에동경
면을거ᄒᆞᆫ즉일본 대원슈폐하
셔셔ᄂᆞᆫ출젼군ᄃᆡ가셩셔를무릅
쓰고젼디에셔로ᄊᆞ홈을하렴ᄒᆞ
샤웅ᄉᆞ시종무관을파견ᄒᆞ야만
쥬와요동군ᄃᆡ들위문ᄒᆞᆫ다ᄒᆞ엿
더라
○휘긔위신 항일에긔평젼징
에일아라국군이핑쟝히방포악
전ᄒᆞᆯ새에란환이공즁에비오듯
ᄒᆞᆯ젹에셩북편코도구라ᄒᆞᄂᆞᆫ근
쳐언덕우헤청인슈명이셔셔란
환맛고아니맛ᄂᆞᆫ여부롤아인의
게져시ᄒᆞ되슈즁에든긔를좌우
로둘너가부를지시ᄒᆞ다가일군
의게피착되여괄명을쥭더에포
살ᄒᆞ엿다더라
로함포격 동일동보를거ᄒᆞᆫ
즉아라ᄉᆞ함대가려쇼항구졈박
쳐에셔일본군ᄉᆞ를포격ᄒᆞ엿다
ᄂᆞᆫᄃᆡ엇지던지일병이그여히이
번에ᄂᆞᆫ아병을모라넛코함낙ᄒᆞ
라ᄂᆞᆫᄃᆡ일병들온려쇼동북방사
영리안에잇다ᄒᆞ엿고또일본포
병들은히항구포격ᄒᆞᆷ을시작ᄒᆞ
엿ᄂᆞᆫᄃᆡ무죄ᄒᆞᆫ빅셩들을아모조
록편안케ᄒᆞ려ᄒᆞ되피란ᄒᆞ야리
산ᄒᆞᄂᆞᆫ재만타더라

관보

대어쳔구빅이호 광무팔년
팔월십일일
○셔임급ᄉᆞ령
○의원면본관〃삼화항총순
김룡진 임삼화항총순셔관입
관륙등 구픔 젼긔완 이샹
팔월륙일
○의원면본관 슝령젼참봉
김쟝욱 임동션ᄉᆞ젼화과쥬ᄉᆞ
셔관임관팔등 리병지 리문
피 송연학 김셩윤 죠셩찬
리쥬단○임슝령젼참봉셔판관
팔등리유진
이샹팔월팔일
○의원면본관 비셔원승 김
연회 시죵원시죵 신영틱
니쟝원봉세관 지셩희 한창
졍 겸임니쟝원봉세관 김갑
슌○명니쟝원셔칙임관삼등
군부대신관방쟝 한진창
●명궁니부흑진관셔칙임관일
등 졍이픔 민형식 ○임비
셔원승셔쥬임관오등 졍삼픔
김교덕 ○임시종원시종셔쥬
임관륙등 륙픔 김병관
○임니쟝원봉세관셔쥬임관륙
등 륙픔 류승회 김학제
○명니쟝원봉세위원 륙픔
리교승 밍덕민
이샹팔월구일
○견칙 궁신원쥬ᄉᆞ 김용익

공보

일본쥬차군ᄉᆞ령부착
원산츙돌속보
○로병ᄉᆞ샹 거구일미명에로
국긔병부ᄃᆡ가지ᄎᆞ일본젼초압
헤현출ᄒᆞ야ᄃᆡ그포병온대포를양
일리놉흔곳에놋ᄂᆞᆫ고로일군젼
초부ᄃᆡᄂᆞᆫ이거슬ᄃᆡᄒᆞ야밍렬ᄒᆞᆫ
샤격을힝ᄒᆞ더니오젼팔시삼십
분에니르러로병이졈졈문평리
북방으로퇴각ᄒᆞᆫ지라로병의쥭
은쟈ᄂᆞᆫ병졸삼명의시톄를버리
고갓고부샹ᄒᆞᆫ쟈ᄂᆞᆫ쟝교일명과
그외륙명을운송ᄒᆞ여감을보앗
고일병에ᄂᆞᆫᄉᆞ상이업고소총과
군도가각샹긔요대포란환이얼
빅괄십긔요소총탄환이일빅긔
들엇엇다ᄒᆞ엿더라

잡보

○시졍긔션 의졍셔리박제슌
씨가출셕ᄒᆞ야금일하오삼졈죵
에회의ᄒᆞᆯᄎᆞ로각부부에통쳡ᄒᆞ
엿ᄂᆞᆫᄃᆡ그안건은시졍긔션에관
ᄒᆞᆫ대문뎨라더라
○한인피착 작일샹오두시에
명부지달명ᄒᆞᆫ한인일인을남셔
방니에셔일본헌병이포착ᄒᆞ야
미동잇ᄂᆞᆫ헌병류쥬소로압거ᄒᆞ
엿다더라
○일병우출 지작십일인시량
에일본ᄉᆞ관십인이담총ᄒᆞᆫ병졍
이빅구십ᄉᆞ명과복ᄐᆡᄉᆞ십필을
령솔ᄒᆞ고동소문으로나갓더라
○경안치도 일공ᄉᆞ가외부로
죠회ᄒᆞ야경셩에셔안쥬ᄭᆞ지도
로슈츅ᄒᆞᆯ을권ᄒᆞ고ᄒᆞ더니현금
셩부로셔쥬관ᄒᆞ야박셕고ᄀᆡ에한
셔치도를시역ᄒᆞ엿더라
○죠회빈반 일병이셩문에파
슈ᄒᆞᄂᆞᆫ셔닭으로경무쳥에셔한
셩부로공문ᄒᆞᆫ다더니작일에또
외부로죠회ᄒᆞ기를폐쳥인즉교
지상에몽미ᄒᆞ야엇더ᄒᆞᆫᄉᆞ건이
귀부소관이며엇더ᄒᆞᆫᄉᆞ건이한
셩부소관인지젼허아지못ᄒᆞᆫ
나평일소견으로말ᄒᆞᆯ이진ᄃᆡ한셩
부ᄂᆞᆫ외국령ᄉᆞ와교섭관단ᄒᆞᄂᆞᆫ
일은상민의일과평민의치송과
가ᄉᆞ매ᄆᆡᄒᆞᄂᆞᆫ일과긔디상관되
ᄂᆞᆫ일파인민의징투ᄒᆞᄂᆞᆫ등ᄉᆞ만
관리ᄒᆞᄂᆞᆫ줄알엇더니지금귀죠
회를본즉차등ᄉᆞ항도히부에셔
교섭ᄒᆞᆯ일이라ᄒᆞ니다시말ᄒᆞᆯ것
손업스나일병이표목세우ᄂᆞᆫ것
스로만말ᄒᆞᆯ지라도이것시그나
라병참부군ᄉᆞ샹소관이오상민
이나평민의일에ᄒᆞᆯ것순아닌즉
ᄒᆞᆫ긔표목을세우ᄂᆞᆫ것시혹등한
ᄒᆞᆫ일갓흐나그것도또ᄒᆞᆫ긴즁ᄒᆞᆫ
일인즉응당귀부로셔일공관에
죠회ᄒᆞ야그병참부로긔별케ᄒᆞ
야충불충은고ᄉᆞᄒᆞ고ᄒᆞᆫ번협의
ᄒᆞ야관리ᄒᆞᆷ이가ᄒᆞ며또외국인
의이상ᄒᆞᆫ힝동을보ᄂᆞᆫᄃᆡ로귀부
로조회ᄒᆞᆷ은본쳥경찰상직칙이
오그ᄉᆞ건ᄃᆡ로량의죠쳐ᄒᆞᆷ은귀
부권한에잇ᄂᆞᆫᄃᆡ이갓치범홀이
ᄃᆡ답ᄒᆞᆷ은귀부의실칙인듯ᄒᆞ기
로죠복ᄒᆞ오니죠량관리ᄒᆞ라ᄒᆞ
엿더라
○량찰급면 황히관찰ᄉᆞ가외
부로젼보ᄒᆞᆫ바를거ᄒᆞᆫ즉일인이
역부들긔송ᄒᆞ라ᄒᆞ고최촉ᄒᆞᄂᆞᆫᄭᅵ
달게민심이소료ᄒᆞ야시각이민
망ᄒᆞ니일관에조회ᄒᆞ야히병참
소에지휘ᄒᆞ야완독케ᄒᆞ라ᄒᆞ엿
고평양관찰ᄉᆞ의외부로ᄒᆞᆫ젼보
ᄉᆞ의도역부ᄉᆞ건으로통감샹화
등지에민료날념녀가급급ᄒᆞ다
고일ᄉᆞ의게죠쳥ᄒᆞ야히병참에
지휘케ᄒᆞ야완독케ᄒᆞ라ᄒᆞ엿시
니셩각건ᄃᆡ양셔디방은역부ᄉᆞ
건으로ᄃᆡ단소요ᄒᆞᆫ가보더라
○훈장리도 향쟈에이등대ᄉᆞ
가한국에왓슬때에영졉위원셔
훈즁에ᄲᅡ젓든례식원회계과쟝
빅시용과쥬ᄉᆞ한셩동과동쥬ᄉᆞ
일인과경위원총슌의게훈장이
본관에리도ᄒᆞ엿스니히원등을
긔송ᄒᆞ야훈장을바드라ᄒᆞ엿더
라 훈오등욱일장 빅시용
훈륙등셔보장 한셩동 우쥬
ᄉᆞ일인 총슌 리긍슌
○농광폐렬 외부에셔일본공
관에복함ᄒᆞ기를농광회샤렬폐
ᄒᆞᄂᆞᆫ일ᄉᆞᄂᆞᆫ귀공함ᄉᆞ의를빙거
ᄒᆞᆯᄒᆞ야궁니부와농샹공부에죠
회ᄒᆞ엿더니양부답죠를졉ᄒᆞᆫ즉
임의폐렬ᄒᆞ엿노라ᄒᆞ엿스니회
ᄉᆞ를임의폐렬ᄒᆞ엿슨즉외국인
의게자본차관ᄒᆞᄂᆞᆫᄉᆞᄂᆞᆫ다시변
명ᄒᆞᆯ거시업다ᄒᆞ엿더라
○죄슈언졀 ᄉᆞ죄이하병방ᄒᆞ
라신 죠칙이나리신후로죄슈
들이회희락닥ᄒᆞ야평싱에처음
당ᄒᆞᆫᄂᆞᆫ경ᄉᆞ라ᄒᆞ면셔
대황제폐하의지극히인익ᄒᆞ신
셩덕을감격ᄒᆞ고롱긔되기를날
마다갈망ᄒᆞ더니일젼에그ᄉᆞ샹
을드른즉평리원죄슈방쪌에어
결슈십삼인에오미결슈십ᄉᆞ인
이니합이십칠인이오한셩부죄
슈방쪌에쳐교죄인십오인이죄
결슈일빅이십ᄉᆞ인이오오미결슈
이십오인이니합일빅오십구인
을법부법무국과ᄉᆞ리국쟝이
죠칙을반포ᄒᆞᆫ후방송ᄒᆞ엿고감
등쪌평리원에팔인이오한셩
부에쳐교십팔인이오이결십일
인을감등ᄒᆞᆯ때에그즁에죄슈ᄒᆞᆫ
ᄉᆞ롬이법관의게향ᄒᆞ야말ᄒᆞ되
의신은일영협샹을담론ᄒᆞᆫ일노
십년징역에쳐ᄒᆞ엿다가금번
ᄉᆞ젼에감일등ᄒᆞ야칠년이되엿
ᄉᆞ니실노감격ᄒᆞᆫ비어니와금번
에졀도강도즁삼ᄉᆞ차범죄ᄒᆞ야
쳐교ᄭᆞ지ᄒᆞᆫ자를만히방셕ᄒᆞ심
은ᄉᆞ죄이하병방ᄒᆞ라신 죠칙
을봉승ᄒᆞᆷ이어니와산송과협잡
등죄ᄂᆞᆫ겨우감등만되옵고또졀
도에도일이삼년징역에방셕되
지못ᄒᆞ고감등ᄭᆞ지못된자가잇
스니경죄인를쳐교ᄒᆞ고즁죄인
을도로혀징역일이년에쳐ᄒᆞ옵
ᄂᆞᆫ지실노아혹ᄒᆞᆯ일이옵고또일
본에류학ᄒᆞ며혹유람ᄒᆞᆫᄉᆞ로ᄉᆞ
오년쳬슈미결자ᄂᆞᆫ젼혀뭇지도
아니ᄒᆞ오니하날갓ᄒᆞ신 셩의
를ᄃᆡ양ᄒᆞᆷ이엇지이러ᄒᆞ온잇가
ᄒᆞ고언ᄉᆞ가격졀ᄒᆞ니법관이ᄃᆡ
답ᄒᆞᆯ기를너ᄂᆞᆫ엿지광륙ᄒᆞ뇨ᄌᆞ
긔ᄉᆞ나말ᄒᆞᆯ거시지타인의일을
말ᄒᆞᄂᆞ냐ᄒᆞ고ᄉᆞ지져물너니쳣
다더라

TELEGRAMS.

Gensan, Aug. 9th.

The enemy again appeared today at daybreak and opened fire with one machine gun. Our troops advanced to the attack and drove the enemy away.

Russian casualties were 3 killed and seven wounded, including one officer. We secured one rifle, three swords and 200 cartridges.

THE RELATIONS OF ENGLAND AND EUROPE.

Mr. Frederick Greenwood writes in the "Westminster Gazette:—

If uninterrupted, which we may begin to doubt, the war may still be a long war, notwithstanding the sweep and celerity of the Japanese victories. Already however, these startling triumphs compel the European Governments to think of consequences which were supposed to lie at a distance measured by years, and therefore, so open to modifying incidents and events that it was enough to await their approach watchfully. One consequence, indeed, was everywhere believed to be certain. If left alone together to fight it out (and that was the original proposal) either Japan or Russia must undergo absolute defeat. The conditions were such that the two nations could not live together in the East either as friend or enemies. Victory would be worthless for Japan if it failed to break down the Russian power once for all. There could be no victory for Russia short of the absolute crushing of Japan.

So much was commonly understood before the war began; but very little attention was allowed to what followed from this state of things. Yet it was nothing less than that a resounding triumph for either combatant would give him, if uninterfered with, the complete mastery of Eastern Asia; which was never intended. In any event that result could be endured by none of the great commercial nations: at the same time, however, no applied intelligence could fail to understand that though the Far Eastern domination of Russia, of Japan, would be alike intolerable it would be so in different degrees. Plainly, the "crumpling up" of Russia by Japan must have far more formidable consequences for Europe than would the disarming of Japan by Russia. The disarming of Japan by Russia may be fairly said to have none but local consequences; while as for the domination of Russia, the interests and ambitions of Germany, France, the United States, Great Britain are so imperative that they would certainly limit it. Without necessarily working together they would work to the same end upon a war-worn Power too fatigued to defy them; unless, indeed, by circular. But now take the case of the crumpling up of Russia by Japan, the likelihood of which so many of us are rejoicing over. That cannot be done without extreme risk of universal upset. Ruined in Asia as by the breath of a newly risen Asiatic people—a people already on the way to be thought Redemptionist and endowed with mystic powers—Russia may expect insurrection throughout her Asiatic provinces. What is next to be expected is such a fall from her high place in Europe as would derange the whole Continental system; and it would be strange if at the same time far worse derangements did not ensue from a general revolt of those Far Eastern races against European proprietorship.

Such is the difference between the natural consequences of the smashing of Japan by Russia and the smashing of Russia by Japan. A difference, this, which was not much considered where and when the end of the war was thought to be two or three years off, and that the last blow would be Russia's; while with us it was ejected from consideration by an enthusiasm for Japan passionate as young love. Abroad, it seemed too soon to calculate: at home, too execrably sordid.

But the merits of the Japanese as a conquering people have now been so magnificently displayed, at all points, in all ways, and with a quickness in itself so significant, that Europe begins to stir regardless of the Russian circular. The Japanese demonstration may not be complete even yet, but it is complete enough. Effects so decisive in appearance were not expected on either side for many a month, to say the least; and by the surprise of them in Europe, the sensation they create in Asia far and near [illegible] may be judged. That is a point which only a very romantic or helpless partisanship will belittle; for what it signifies is that, starting in immense strength, the ferment spreading throughout the East from Manchuria will take no check till—when? Not at any rate till Russia has had time to gather her forces and strike a heavy return blow; which is not expected soon. We may be sure that for Germany and France who have great possessions and greater ambitions in the Far East, this alone is enough to quicken their interest in the war, to bring up before them the differing consequences of an Asian triumph for Russia or Japan, and to teach them already to consider what action they should take and what oppose. Though its interests are not primarily in Eastern Asia, the same thing may be said of the Austrian Government, which was the first to declare its belief in a real danger to Europe from the Anglo-American-Japanese coalition

There is not much doubt anywhere, I suppose, that this is a true account of the present situation. And if it be so, we should ask ourselves betimes whether the Continental nations are not entering into one drift, England being set in another. As to the first point we may make up our minds at once. France?—It is believed that an agreement lately concluded has changed our relations with that country very much for the better. Yes; but on this subject how stand the interests of France and her more delicate relations with other countries? Let us remember how large a stake she has in Indo-China and her long-cherished hope of substantial acquisition of the southernmost province of China itself. Her immense financial interest in the stability of the Russian Empire is to the purposes, and it is something that an alliance which has been so greatly serviceable to her should suddenly become a broken reed. Russia interposed at a well-remembered moment to save her from destruction. If that was done on calculation, as I do not dispute it, it was calculation friendly to France, and it was based on balance-of-power considerations, which comes into question now. Lastly, there is the yet standing alliance with Russia, and the particular obligations to that country which were entered into when the Anglo-Japanese alliance became known. The German Government was to all intents and purposes a partner in that understanding. In case of a blazing Japanese success as it is so far, Germany stands to lose one of the richest provinces in China. No Government is so avowedly alarmed at the prospect of more Mongolian "awakening;" and though it is likely enough that a weakened Russia would not be displeasing to the German States, its precipitate destruction can by no means be desired. Of Austria no more can be said for want of space to say it in; but, reminding the reader that there is such a thing as a European sentiment which England is often accused of being treacherous to, I suggest that there are good and sound reasons for believing that the whole of Continental Europe is in a drift of helpfulness to Russia.

In what drift are we? I doubt whether many foreigners living in England would hesitate to answer that they can at least see what is wished for—even confidently wished for: alliance of Great Britain, the United States, and Japan against the world. And, indeed, for my own part I can make nothing else of a great deal that I hear and read, on the supposition that it has meaning and intention. Of course I do not speak of the Government, for no Englishman has the faintest inkling of what the Government may think, or hope, or fear, or dream of contriving in this transcendently important matter. But, as for the country, we have named the policy which is its impassioned ideal: alliance of Great Britain, Japan, and the United States. That is the drift in which we stand; and by every sign and token to this hour visible it cannot be continued without leading England into collision with Europe. In itself, too, it is most probably a complete illusion. For what is the likelihood that the United States will enter a compact which would either be a fighting coalition or practically of no account? Do they see [illegible]sition so much to covet that is our posi[illegible] [illegible] case is they would fain partake? [illegible] that we stand from to-day in danger of being compelled—by accident, by hostile contrivance—to take arms with Japan and the Mongol Revolution against Europe; and the American Government is supposed to be willing to share this liability! I refuse to believe it. Intent as the American Republic may be upon a world-power career, it will not do business in that way. It is a dream, this fighting coalition of Great Britian, Japan, and the United States. But its dissolution leaves us another alliance—the alliance with Japan. In the present state of things that alliance and the vaunting of it may be enough to hasten the ranging up of the Continental Powers; is it enough to see us through an opposed line of policy extending into war? To put another question, are we excused for averting the Mongol Revolution by the bravery, the ingenuity, the heroic devotion, the every virtue and accomplishment of our allies? And is it again so very clear that the eviction of European authority from Eastern Asia does not mean the eviction of English authority there and cannot go on to it? These are questions which a practical people should ask first, and, if possible, be enthusiastic afterwards. But we are a changed people, and pride ourselves on the excess of our uncalculating emotions. We are enthusiastic first, considerate afterwards.

But, too much is unconsidered when, sweeping aside all such questions as are sampled above, the country dashes into a course of policy which can neither be dropped without humiliation nor continued without risk of being forced into a perilous anti-European war. True, we are not yet actually and visibly in that plight. But we are on the verge of it. The war has only to go on upon its present course a little farther, and our joy at its victories to rise accordingly, and we shall find that we have drifted into a very undesirable position of antagonism.

The police department have issued an edict forbidding the practice of fortune-telling. Any wizards found after this are to expect a bad time.

Autograph letters to His Majesty from their rulers were presented by the Italian and Belgian Ministers at an audience held on the 10th inst.

The Japanese Minister will be received in audience by His Majesty today.

The Japanese Gendarme service of Seoul is to be augmented.

The Korea Daily News.

To be published daily except Sundays.

Rate of Subscription:—

Per Year,	Yen 25.
Per Quarter,	Yen 7.
Per Month	Yen 2.50

Postage in Korea not charged extra.
Postage abroad charged extra.

Advertisements, 50 sen per day for 1 inch or less.
5 yen per month per inch.
50 yen per year per inch.

All communications to
E. T. BETHELL,
Editor and Publisher.
Pak-tong, Seoul.

KUROKI'S ADVANCE ON LIAOYANG.

Slowly but surely General Kuroki's victorious army pursues its march towards Liaoyang. Particulars are now to hand of the engagements of July 31st and August 1st which culminated in the Japanese occupation of Yusulintze and Yangtzeling, points some six miles from Motienling on the road to Liaoyang.

Operations in this neighbourhood are extremely difficult. The country is mountainous and thickly wooded and the heat is awful, the thermometer frequently reaching 100°.

Kuropatkin's positions were especially strong and roads had been made connecting the positions so that infantry could be hurried to any threatened point with great facility. All the Russian artillery positions were well chosen, they were skilfully masked and so situated as to be only assailable from the front. Dummy guns were mounted here and there upon which the Japanese wasted their attack until their real nature was discovered. The Russian infantry was also exceptionally well placed. Entrenched in three tiers on the side of a thickly wooded hill with their trenches masked with brushwood they were for a long time secure from the Japanese attack and were able to do most effective work. The Russian artillery was extremely well served, the ranges had evidently been previously carefully ascertained, and their fire was characterized by much more precision than has been the case in previous battles.

On the night July 30th with all these odds against him, General Kuroki with characteristic nerve advanced to the attack. The whole weight of his centre and left wing was thrown against the Russian positions in the neighbourhood of Yangtzeling and the morning of the 31st found the Japanese batteries in position about 4,000 yards from the enemy. An artillery duel continued all day and in the afternoon the Japanese infantry advanced on the Russian trenches. Here the conditions seem to have been horrible. Exhausted, famished with thirst, and suffering terribly from the heat the Japanese infantry left its cover and under a decimating hail of shrapnel and bullets hurled itself time after time against the Russian defences. When night fell and fighting had to cease the Japanese third and fourth regiments had occupied the outermost of the Russian trenches and bivouacked there.

In the meantime the Japanese right wing, making a detour, was advancing on the Russian rear, and finding this, the Russians under cover of darkness withdrew their whole army and retreated towards Anping leaving the Japanese free to occupy the positions in the morning. The Japanese and Russian artillery seem to have been evenly matched, both sides making excellent practise. General Kuroki's victory although a great one was somewhat of a disappointment, as he had hoped with his right wing to take the Russians in the rear and thus secure a really decisive victory.

It is stated that the newly formed Mining and Cultivation Co. will be abolished.

The Hang-sung Shimpo states that Viscount Yamaguchi, a general of the Japanese army, died at his home in Tokyo on the 8th inst.

According to the Iuchŏn Sang-po the Japanese have not withdrawn their application for waste lands.

The Kamni of Gensan reports that in the fight on the 7th inst. near Gensan eight Russians were killed.

The numbers of the Imperial Guard are to be reduced. Several officers have sent in their resignations.

AN EVENING GOWN.

CONCLUDED.

Towards Paddington I begin to wonder if I really brought the remaining £5 after all, feel for it—yes, it is safe. Where is my list? I look everywhere, in my sleeves, in my handbag, in my gloves. Have I left it behind? I remember the pocket in my underskirt, yes, there it is. I feel tired out already; and all the day's work to do yet.

I take a hansom and drive to Westbourne Grove. I am not thinking of the dress at all, there are so many other things to be done. I get along pretty well; by three o'clock most of the shopping is done. I have chosen charming stuff for the drawing-room, nice little things for the children, a present for a friend, and I have done all the household business. I can now put my mind to the dress. But the note has been broken into; I have but four pounds left.

I look in different shop windows, nothing pleases me. I come to a place where a sale of costumes is going on; I am badly in want of one. Suppose I try one on. I don't mean to buy it, of course, but still there is one in the window that does look very attractive.

I go in and am taken immediate possession of by an elegant young lady in an ultra-fashionable gown, who rather alarms me by her decisive manner. I try on the dress that I liked in the window; am relieved to find I don't like it on myself. I am about to make my escape when she produces another, and I turn round to find a second young woman bearing at least half-a-dozen on her arm. I feel I am caught in a trap. They try on one after the other, with the occaional remark, "That suits you beautifully, madam," varied by the statement, "That does set off madam's figure." Madam herself does not usually share these opinions: and decides not to waste any more time, when a costume of pink frieze is brought.

It looks fascinating. I consent to try it on. The gown does suit me. Pink always does. Not very serviceable, I tell myself, but I never had a dress that suited me so well. So cheap, too, and I do want a smart walking gown. I really have nothing to wear when I call on the Clarks after the dinner party.

Meanwhile the questtion must be decided. Shall I, or shall I not? Three guineas. There will be still a pound left. I can get an over-dress with that.

It ends in my taking the costume. A new difficulty arises. I must have a hat to go with it. I arrange to have a toque of the same stuff; and my funds are reduced to ten shillings.

I must go to a place where I have credit to get the over-dress. But behold, in this establishment, they have no such thing just then. I daren't leave it to their discretion to get it, and decide I will try in the little town where I live. Marcelline will be able to help me.

I get into the train to go home. I am seized with awful qualms as I think of my conduct. Charles, the kindest possible husband, gives me nine guineas to buy a dress so as to do him credit, and I've spent it on all sorts of other things. It is wicked, ungrateful, dishonest. I am a bad, selfish woman, I tell myself. I could cry if it were not for the presence of the other passengers.

Tired to death and very miserable, I set to work to find the over-dress in the town. There does not seem to be one to be had. I arrive home late and desperate; rush up to Marcelline and put the case before her. Luckily Charles has said he will be late this evening.

Marcelline is a woman of resource.

"If madame will leave it to me," she says, "I will see that madame's toilette is all she can desire."

"Of course, I'll leave it to you, Marcelline; what do you want?"

"Madame will let me have her wedding dress?"

"Yes, but it's ten years old," I say.

"That matters not so far as madame is concerned, madame has still a beautiful figure. And the Brussels lace veil; can I——" She waved her hands to express her meaning—"manipulate that?"

"Yes, but don't cut it; anything else?"

"Madame has in one trunk a corsage trimmed with silver garniture; if I could have that, and ten yards of white chiffon, I will undertake monsieur shall not be disappointed when he see her."

I procure her the things she wants, go out myself and buy the chiffon. When I get in I find my old dress is already ripped. Till late at night we sit and sew, I following Marcelline's directions. She soon has the dress altered to fit me, and then it is wonderful to watch the transformation thereof. Half way up the skirt and train are tiny flounces of chiffon, effectually hiding the grubby state of the satin; the Brussels lace veil is draped in some wonderful way from the shoulders and hangs down straight to the feet; tiny little chiffon sleeves are put in and round the neck is fixed the broad silver trimming, which comes to a deep point in front. It was not till late the following afternoon that this result was achieved; but at the end of our labours I had a dress that would have fetched twenty guineas if I had had to buy it outright.

I get into it with Marcelline's assistance, and look at myself in the glass. No it does not look a makeshift—a thing of which Charles has a horror. I go downstairs, Marcelline carries my cloak; Charles is waiting in the hall.

"Humph, you'll do," he says.

Tremendous praise from Charles; I feel quite elated.

The dinner goes off well; and in the cab going home Charles compliments me on my success. "There wasn't a woman in the room to touch you," he says. "A wife like you does help a fellow to get on."

I am so pleased I decide to risk confession.

"Marcelline and I made it ourselves," I say, "out of my wedding-dress and veil and ten yards of Chiffon."

"Oh! And the nine guineas?"

"I've spent them, dear."

"Upon what, may I ask?"

I lean back in the cab and arrange my cloak over my knees.

"I bought two pairs of boots for the children," I begin, "a winter suit for Tom, under things for Mollie, a new sweeper, three remnants of stuff to do the drawing-room cushions, a curtain for the study door, a housemaid's box, a kitchen coal scuttle, a thing to open the dining-room door—which you are always saying you ought to have—a present for Aunt Maria—it's her birthday on Wednesday and you always forget it—paid Smith's bill and the newspaper bill, bought myself a new frieze coat and skirt (you will like it, Charlie!) a hat to match, a long-handled broom, a dustpan, and a new kind of kettle that doesn't boil over, ten yards of chiffon, and—that's all, I think."

"Um," says Charles, "Anything over, may I ask?"

"Yes, five shillings to the good. I'm going to give it to Marcelline with my second best coat and skirt."

"My dear," says Charles after a moment's reflection, "you ought to be Chancellor of the Exchequer!"—Lady's Magazine.

The Korea Daily News.

VOL. I, FRIDAY, AUGUST 12, 1904. No. 23

HONGKONG & SHANGHAI BANKING CORPORATION.

Paid-up Capital..... ....$10,000,000
Reserve Fund:—Sterling Reserve... 10,000,000
Silver Reserve..... 6,500,000

$6,500,000
Reserve Liability of Proprietors... 10,000,000

HEAD OFFICE, HONGKONG.

London Bankers, London and County Banking Company Limited.

Branches and Agencies, London.

Amoy,	Hankow	Penang,
Bangkok,	Hiogo,	Rangoon,
Batavia,	Iloilo,	Saigon,
Bombay,	Lyons,	San Francisco,
Calcutta,	Manila,	Singapore,
Colombo,	Nagasaki,	Sourabaya,
Foochow,	New York,	Tientsin,
Hamburg,	Peking,	Yokohama,

Credits granted on approved Securities, and every description of Banking and Exchange business transacted.

Drafts granted on London and the chief Commercial places in Europe, India, Australia, America, China and Japan.

HOLME RINGER & Co., AGENTS, CHEMULPO.

ON CHEONG & CO., SEOUL.

GENERAL STORE KEEPERS.
Imported provisions, Cooking Utensils Crockery, etc.
FRESH BREAD DAILY.

MITSU BISHI DOCKYARD & ENGINE WORKS,
NAGASAKI.

CODE WORD, "DOCK."

A. 1, A. B. C., and Engineering Codes used.

DOCK No. 1 (at Tategami)

Extreme Length..............523 feet
Length on blocks .... 513 ,,
Width of Entrance on Top......89 ,,
,, ,, Bottom....77 ,,
Water on Blocks at Spring Tide 26½ ,,

DOCK No. 2 (Mukaijima).

Extreme Length..............371 feet
Length on Blocks.............360 ,,
Width of Entrance on Top......66 ,,
,, ,, Bottom 53 ,,
Water on Blocks at Spring Tide 22 ,,

PATENT SLIP (at Kosuge).

Can take vessels up to 1,000 tons gross.

THE WORKS are well equipped with the LATEST IMPROVEMENTS, and can execute any kind of MARINE in SHIPBUILDING and MARINE ENGINEERING, as well as in REPAIRING of SHIPS.

The COMPANY'S new powerful steamer OURA-MARU (712 tons, 700 I.H.P.), specially built for SALVAGE PURPOSES, and equipped with necessary gear, is always READY at SHORT NOTICE.

CHARTERED BANK OF INDIA AUSTRALIA & CHINA.

INCORPORATED BY ROYAL CHARTER 1853

HEAD OFFICES:—LONDON.

Paid-up Capital £800,000
Reserve Liability of Shareholders 800,000
Reserve Fund 725,000

Drafts granted upon all the principal places in the world and every description of Exchange and banking business transacted.

E. MEYER & Co., Agents, Chemulpo.

E. MEYER & CO.
Chemulpo.

SOLE AGENTS IN KOREA FOR:
A. T. Morse, Sons & Co's "Fresco" Distemper

In all colours ready for use on walls, Ceilings etc.
and
AVENARIUS CARBOLINEUM

A wood-preserving and antiseptic oil preparation

Against decay, dry-rot, fungus and wood-destroying insects.

A large supply always in Stock.
Prices upon application.

E. MEYER & Co., Chemulpo.

LAW UNION & CROWN INS. CO.

Fire risks accepted at Current rates, on go downs, merchandise, dwellings, and other property, subject to usual conditions.

HOLME RINGER & Co., Agents, Chemulpo

THE METHODIST PUBLISHING HOUSE,
Little West Gate, Seoul.

JOB PRINTING, TYPEWRITER PAPER
CARBON PAPER, VISITING CARDS
STATIONERY, BOOK BINDING
BOOK PUBLISHERS
AMERICAN SCHOOL BOOKS
SPENCERIAN COPY BOOKS
PEN CARBON LETTER AND BILL BOOKS

S. A. BECK, Manager.

DAI-ICHI GINKO.
LIMITED.
(Formerly the First National Bank)

ESTABLISHED 1873

INCORPORATED UNDER PRESENT LAW 1896

Capital - - - - - - - - - Yen 5,000,000
Reserve Fund - - - - - - " 1,350,000

HEAD OFFICE:—TOKIO.

President: Baron SHIBUSAWA.

BRANCHES AND CORRESPONDENTS
In the Principal Cities and Towns of Japan.

Interest Allowed on
Fixed deposits 1 year - - - 6½ per cent
" " 6 months - - - 6 per cent

Special current accounts 1½ sen daily per Y 100
General " " 1 " " " 100

M. TANAKA, Manager, Chemulpo.

HOLME RINGER & Co.
Chemulpo.

General Merchants and Government Contractors.

Agents for the leading
Banks
Steamship Companies
and
Insurance Companies

Importers of Merchandise of every description.

KAMEYA & CO.

GENERAL STOREKEEPERS
Chinkokai - - Seoul
(Established 1895, Tokyo)

Confectionery, Hams, Canned Goods, Cutlery, Hirano & Tansan Water. Provisions, Gents, Furnishing goods, Toilet Articles, Travelling Bags, Tobacco, Cigars & Cigarettes Kitchen Utensils. Coffee, Biscuits.

Fresh Goods always kept in Stock.
Prices Moderate
Please come and inspect our goods.

NIPPON YUSEN KAISHA.
JAPANESE MAIL STEAMSHIP CO.

DER MAIL CONTRACT WITH THE IMPERIAL JAPANESE GOVERNMENT.

European Line

Regular Fortnightly Service between Yokohama, Kobe, Moji, Shanghai, Hongkong, Singapore, Penang Colombo, Port Said, Marseilles, London and Antwerp

American Line

Regular Fortnightly Service between Hongkong and Seattle, calling at Shanghai, Moji, Kobe, Yokohama and Victoria, B. C.

Australian Line

Regular weekly Service betwen Japan Ports and Australia, calling at Hongkong and Manila.

(Above Three Lines Suspended until further notice).

Shanghai Line

Weekly Service between Shanghai and Japan Ports

Korea Line

Service Kobe. Moji, Nagasaki, Fusan, Chemulpo, Chfoo, Taiku.
S. S. Bahelsberg, 2181 tons.
Service Kobe. Moji, Fusan, Chemulpo, Chinnampo
S. S Argo, S. S. Ohio.

BORDEN'S CONDENSED MILK CO.
New York, U. S. A.

ALWAYS IN STOCK
Eagle Brand Condensed Milk.
Gold Seal Condensed Milk.
Peerless (Family) Evaporated Cream.
Borden's Malted Milk.

E. MEYER & CO.
Chemulpo, Korea,
Sole Agents

ROYAL INSURANCE COMPANY,
Funds exceed £10,000,000
FIRE
AT CURRENT RATES.
LIFE
REDUCED PREMIUM.
HOLME RINGER & Co., Agents, Chemulpo.

HOTEL DU PALAIS
SEOUL.

The only first class Hotel in Seoul. Situated in the centre of the city opposite the palace.

Cuisine under the supervision of an experienced French Chef.

Well ventilated and furnished throughout.

TARIFF UPON APPLICATION

L. MARTIN,
Proprietor and Manager

大韓每日申報
대한매일신보

(뎨이십ᄉᆞ호) (토요일) 일쳔구빅사년팔월십삼일

본샤고빅

이신보ᄂᆞᆫ영어와한어로셕거ᄆᆡ일츌판ᄒᆞᆸ

신문가

ᄒᆞᆫ장 엽두돈오푼

일삭됴엽두량닷돈 맛돈으로 밧ᄉᆞᆸ

광고료ᄂᆞᆫ

긔한의장단과ᄌᆞ힝의다쇼로증감ᄒᆞ되렴가로밧을터이오며오리지아녀대한사람마다다이신문을보실터이니광고내시기를원ᄒᆞ시ᄂᆞᆫ이들은우리신문샤에와셔면약ᄒᆞ심을희망ᄒᆞᆸ

○발힝소 대한박동ᄆᆡ일신보샤법어학교압혜젼영국인셜필림집자리오

샤장 영국인 (비셜)

본샤지점

인쳔항고잔동신지명씨로우리대한ᄆᆡ일신보샤인쳔항지점쟝을뎡ᄒᆞ엿ᄉᆞ오니인쳔항에계신구람코쟈ᄒᆞ시ᄂᆞᆫ쳠군ᄌᆞᄂᆞᆫ히지점에왕림면의ᄒᆞ시ᄋᆞᆸ

샤고

○우리대한ᄆᆡ일신보의목덕은대한의안녕질셔에관ᄒᆞᆫ모든뎨목에ᄃᆡᄒᆞ야ᄂᆞᆫ공평ᄒᆞᆫ변론을쥬쟝홈이라우리통신원의담보ᄂᆞᆫ신문보시ᄂᆞᆫ쳠군ᄌᆞ의게ᄒᆞᆼ상보도ᄒᆞ리며편지를긔셔ᄒᆞ여주시ᄂᆞᆫ이ᄂᆞᆫ셩명과반ᄃᆡ를적어붓치시기를희망ᄒᆞ오니이거슨신문샹에긔ᄌᆡᄒᆞ랴ᄂᆞᆫ거시아니오다만극히신용ᄒᆞᄂᆞᆫ증거를숨고쟈홈이라긔쟈ᄂᆞᆫ아모긔셔던지긔ᄌᆡ홈을되각ᄒᆞᄂᆞᆫ권리를가졋ᄉᆞ나되각ᄒᆞᄂᆞᆫ리유를말ᄒᆞᆯ터이오며공즁평화를문란케ᄒᆞᄂᆞᆫ듯ᄒᆞᆫ긔셔ᄂᆞᆫ의례히밧지안켓ᄉᆞᆸ나이다

론셜

여순구위치라

○오날우리신문에여순구위치가실노좃치아니ᄒᆞᆫ즁조가잇다고미리말ᄒᆞᆫ거슨이왕에도여순셔속히결단나미잇고또이번에일본이비록싸홈을이기여셔쳑을졈령ᄒᆞ드ᄅᆡ도필연수다싱명이죽을터인즉그싱명손상으로말ᄒᆞᆯ진ᄃᆡ우리의동정ᄒᆞᄂᆞᆫ마음으로보ᄂᆞᆫ바에일본을위ᄒᆞ야대단히싱각ᄒᆞᆯ거시이나라군ᄉᆞ들은모도츙군ᄋᆡ국ᄒᆞᄂᆞᆫ마음을렬심으로ᄒᆞᄂᆞᆫ서닭에분명히여순을공격ᄒᆞ야졈령ᄒᆞᆯ늣ᄒᆞ나그러나인명은필경에대단히멸망ᄒᆞ여싸홈ᄒᆞᆫ쟝관이라도쳑망ᄒᆞᆯ수업슬터이요

또달니말ᄒᆞᆯ진댄일본으로셔속히셩취아니되ᄂᆞᆫ일에몃쳔명식니로발병치도못ᄒᆞᆯ듯ᄒᆞ되지금으로볼진ᄃᆡ미구에일본군사들은여순를긴밀히막아셔조긔나라병합들노임의왕리케ᄒᆞ고그안에잇ᄂᆞᆫ아라샤군병들은모도굴머조진ᄒᆞ야조연이복죵케홈이요

또일본셔ᄂᆞᆫ빅셩들이다쥭드ᄅᆡ도긔여히여순을굿게직히려ᄒᆞᄂᆞᆫᄃᆡ요젼번싸홈결국은일본이진첫ᄃᆞᆫ조리로브러집짓되보ᄒᆞᆫ것슨외교샹과계로아병을유인ᄒᆞ여드리라홈인ᄃᆡ일본셔ᄂᆞᆫ이러케손히됨을싱각지안코엇지던지여순을취ᄒᆞ려홈이나우리의싱각에ᄂᆞᆫ져림젼ᄒᆞᆫ쟝관의굿센마음이능히죽드ᄅᆡ도긔여히에워싸셔격젼ᄒᆞᆯ넌지알수업스되

이여러가지로놋코보면일본셔런속ᄒᆞ야싸호ᄂᆞᆫ거시긔여히ᄒᆞ려홈인즉아라샤이여간쥰비ᄒᆞᆫ드ᄅᆡ도일본군사들은여러쳔명식죽은우ᄒᆞ로밟쇼졈졈련속ᄒᆞ야나간즉만일여슌을엇지못ᄒᆞᄂᆞᆫ경우라도일본에셔ᄂᆞᆫ승쳡ᄒᆞ랴면아쥭도사룸과ᄯᅢ가넉넉히잇게역임이라

우리알기에ᄂᆞᆫ일본의의향이졍령솜의속에다모도잡아넛코또긔묘ᄒᆞᆫ묘계로쳐셔ᄶᅥ트려조긔의손아귀에잡아녀ᄒᆞ려홈인듯ᄒᆞ나우리의여슌소문듯기에ᄂᆞᆫ두나라에셔셔로병진을ᄶᅥ트려군사를다죽이고식료가업셔지기를바라셔그리홈이라더라

잡보

○쳥결불결 근일에한셩니외에방방곡곡이오예지물이가득ᄒᆞ되가가호호이ᄯᅩᆼ니음시가쵹비ᄒᆞ야지나가ᄂᆞᆫ힝인들도그악취를견댈수업거든하물며그집안사룸들이야여북난감ᄒᆞ리오대져쳥결법실시이리로거의의돈을쇼비ᄒᆞ야길을닥ᄂᆞᆫ다ᄀᆡ쳔을친다ᄯᅩᆼ통을신비ᄒᆞ야쳥결ᄉᆞ업에극진ᄒᆞᆫ방법이쾌히시힝이되ᄂᆞᆫ줄노알앗더니길도이젼모양ᄀᆡ쳔도더욱우심지어ᄯᅩᆼ통ᄒᆞ야ᄂᆞᆫ이왕에ᄂᆞᆫ지취가업서도거름쟝ᄉᆞ가감지덕지ᄒᆞ야ᄯᅩᆼ이모힐시업시말가케쳐가셔뒤보기ᄂᆞᆫ편리ᄒᆞ더니지금에쳥결법결과로인ᄒᆞ야내음서ᄂᆞᆫ고샤물론ᄒᆞ고ᄯᅩᆼ통에ᄯᅩᆼ이젹여구산ᄒᆞ야가위분산이라사룸마다ᄯᅩᆼ눌걱정ᄲᅮᆫ이니당초에셜시ᄒᆞᆫᄯᅩᆼ치ᄂᆞᆫ구루마ᄂᆞᆫ어ᄃᆡ로다갓ᄂᆞᆫ지쳥결위원제ᄃᆡᆨ에만둔니며쳐가ᄂᆞᆫ지아마그러가보아그러치아니면쳥결위원제공이모들리가업슬걸본시쳥결법실시ᄒᆞᄂᆞᆫ본의ᄂᆞᆫ질소를제어홈이오질소를제어홈은류힝병을레방홈이요류힝병레방홈은위싱상에데일최긴ᄒᆞᆫ일이라지금에혹드른즉류힝병이각금발현ᄒᆞᆫ다ᄒᆞ니척임맛혼졔룡은아마선후방칙이잇슬여니와빅셩들은시각이밧비넉이며쳥결이불결이라고원셩이랑쟈ᄒᆞ더라

○면쳥역부 일본ᄉᆞ령부에셔니부에역부모집ᄉᆞ로각도에훈령홈을쳥ᄒᆞ더니지작일샹오십일시에ᄉᆞ령부참모관제등력삼랑씨가니부에리도ᄒᆞ야협관리봉리씨와샹의ᄒᆞ엿다더라

○통변팔인 지작일학부에셔일본군접응소공합놀거ᄒᆞ야일어졸업싱팔인을히소로긔송ᄒᆞ엿ᄂᆞᆫᄃᆡ쟝차한인역부를다슈로모집ᄒᆞ야쳥국안동현등디로슈송ᄒᆞᄂᆞᆫᄃᆡ통ᄉᆞ로슈용ᄒᆞᆫ다더라

○일관예겹 지작일샹오십일에일본ᄉᆞ관ᄉᆞ명과평복ᄒᆞᆫ일인일명이포덕문으로예겹ᄒᆞ엿다가십이시에퇴거ᄒᆞ엿다더라

○농대례임 농샹대신김가진씨ᄂᆞᆫ치작야에례임되엿더라

○각ᄃᆡ폐셜 원슈부에셔결졍ᄒᆞ되각ᄃᆡᄃᆡᄂᆞᆫ일일혁파ᄒᆞ고황셩에병졍삼쳔명만셜치ᄒᆞ되위관은총슌를례겸ᄒᆞ고병졍은슌검을례겸ᄒᆞ되슌검의슈를즁가ᄒᆞ며각도진위ᄃᆡᄂᆞᆫ일병혁파ᄒᆞᆫ다더라

○졍탐오보 일본군원산졍탐병이한셩ᄉᆞ령부에보고ᄒᆞ기를금번면두에아병의후진이평쟝ᄒᆞ다고ᄒᆞᆫ고로한셩쥬ᄃᆡ병이만히원산에하거ᄒᆞ엿ᄂᆞᆫᄃᆡ실샹인즉오보을면치못ᄒᆞᆫ지라군ᄉᆞ샹졍탐오보ᄒᆞᆫ죄로히탐달병을포살ᄒᆞ기로ᄉᆞ령부에셔결졍ᄒᆞ엿다더라

○경훈각항 경위원에셔각항구로훈령ᄒᆞ되일본군ᄉᆞ령부에셔역부를쳥구ᄒᆞᄂᆞᆫᄃᆡ로모집ᄒᆞ야시힝ᄒᆞ라고ᄒᆞ엿다더라

○훈칙각도 ᄂᆡ외량부에셔도십삼부에훈령ᄒᆞ기를일본군ᄉᆞ령부에셔역부를모집ᄒᆞᆯ터이니쳥구ᄒᆞᄂᆞᆫᄃᆡ로츄응ᄒᆞ라ᄒᆞ엿더라

○쳥원쥬병 경샹북도문경등디에근일젹경이심ᄒᆞᆫ고로문경빅셩등이원슈부에쳥원ᄒᆞ야안동ᄃᆡ병졍오명을본군농암쟝에츌쥬케ᄒᆞ엿더니히병졍이힝위가단졍ᄒᆞ야일절작폐가업ᄂᆞᆫ고로빅셩이안도ᄒᆞ더니그후에히군슈가무삼ᄉᆞ단이잇던지원슈부로보고ᄒᆞ야병졍을렬환ᄒᆞᆫ후로도젹이ᄃᆡ치ᄒᆞᄂᆞᆫ고로ᄯᅩ빅셩의쳥원으로안동ᄃᆡ병졍오명을농암쟝에다시츌쥬ᄒᆞ엿ᄂᆞᆫᄃᆡ본군슈가ᄯᅩ원슈부에보고ᄒᆞ야병졍을렬환케된지라히군빅셩삼인이샹경ᄒᆞ야농알쟝츌쥬병졍을렬환치말아달나고원슈부에쳥원ᄒᆞᆫ다더라

○긔욕포착 젼호에도이왕긔ᄌᆡᄒᆞ엿거니와다동박참령유티씨를포착ᄒᆞᆫ량으로지작야에일본헌병수십명이히가를포위ᄒᆞ고니졍애돌입ᄒᆞ야수식ᄒᆞ엿다더라

○죄슈억울 작년겨울게경무쳥에피착된공쥬거ᄒᆞᄂᆞᆫ박희졍이다월례슈되여훈번도신문ᄒᆞ지아니ᄒᆞ고엿ᄒᆡᄉᆞ지죄명도알지못ᄒᆞᆫ고옥즁귀신을면치못ᄒᆞ겟다고향쟈에경무쳥에쳥원ᄒᆞ엿더니빅퇴ᄒᆞᆫ미부득이ᄒᆞᆫ야지슈ᄒᆞ여잇스나이런복염을당ᄒᆞ야필ᄉᆞ니이라고경무쳥에호소

ᄒᆞ라ᄂᆞᆫᄃᆡ무삼죄목인지알기나ᄒᆞ면됴켓다고ᄒᆞᆫ다더라

○도로간심 ᄂᆡ부에셔경셩으로븟터김화군ᄭᆞ지가ᄂᆞᆫ연로각군에훈령ᄒᆞ기를지금한셩에쥬차ᄒᆞᆫ일본병참소감부륙군공병소좌도변셩일이가군용상도로를잔심차로벽경여십명을령솔ᄒᆞ고방금한셩을ᄯᅥ나김화등디로향ᄒᆞᆫ다ᄒᆞ니이르ᄂᆞᆫ곳마다지슈쳐소에특별이슌검을파송ᄒᆞ야미리그쥬막쥬인의게신칙ᄒᆞ고각별보호ᄒᆞ되만일무ᄉᆞᆷ물픔을쳥구ᄒᆞ거든갑슬뎡ᄒᆞ야슈응ᄒᆞ되혹쇼홀ᄒᆞ고지완ᄒᆞᆫ폐단이업도록ᄒᆞ라ᄒᆞ엿ᄂᆞᆫᄃᆡ본월구일에발셔그일힝이연쳔등디를지나갓다더라

○단발건의 근일에엇더ᄒᆞᆫ사ᄅᆞᆷ이일본공ᄉᆞ의게건의셔를지에보ᄂᆡ되단발령반포ᄒᆞᆯᄉᆞ를대한졍부에권고ᄒᆞ라고ᄒᆞ엿다더라

○치도시역 일본공ᄉᆞ가외부로죠회ᄒᆞ야한셩안쥬가도로슈츅ᄒᆞᆯᄉᆞ를권고ᄒᆞ엿더니현금한셩부에셔쥬관ᄒᆞ야박셕이에붓터시역ᄒᆞᆫ다더라

○삼남각당 근일젼셜을득문ᄒᆞᆫ즉삼남등디에여러가지모힌당이만히이러나셔민심이대단소동된다고ᄒᆞᄂᆞᆫᄃᆡ화젹파교동한당파교당파아젼의당이더욱셩ᄒᆞᆫ다더라

○슌검불검 일젼에진골아모대관가에셔리모와또ᄉᆞ오명관인이잡기를ᄒᆞᄂᆞᆫᄃᆡ슌검이삼인이돌입ᄒᆞᆫ지라잡기관인이졈잔은소리로ᄭᆞ지져가ᄅᆞᄃᆡ너의등이예가어ᄃᆡ라고감히드러왓나냐ᄒᆞᆫ즉슌검등의ᄃᆡ답이과연모로고드러왓슴니다ᄒᆞ고고ᄀᆡ를숙이고황송무디ᄒᆞ야나왓다더라

○룬거면복 남문외쳥파빅다희에셔작일대이ᄶᆡ룬거가샹결ᄒᆞ다가하등한간이면복ᄒᆞ야승킥즁에일본인이명이피샹ᄒᆞ엿다더라

관보

메이천구빅삼호 광무팔년팔월십이일

○셔임급ᄉᆞ령

○히림시사리셔북럴도국총지ᄉᆞ무 렬도원감독 강홍대

팔월구일

○의원면본관 비셔원승 홍승두 시종원시종 김병관 의종령 류인철

○임비셔원승셔쥬임관륙등 졍삼픔 김광현 ○겸임쟝례원쟝례 비셔원승 김교덕 임시종권시종셔쥬임관삼등 례식원참리관 리괴현 임례식원참리관셔쥬임관삼등 종원좌시어 오한영 임시종원좌시어셔관임관팔등 구픔 리희신 임의룽참봉셔관임관팔등 젼홍우 임의졍부참찬셔칙임관이등 평리원관ᄉᆞ 허위

○궁졍록ᄉᆞ

○의졍부참찬리셩렬ᄉᆞ직소 비지ᄂᆡ에소쳥ᄃᆡ로의시ᄒᆞ노라

○ᄂᆡ부대신죠병필ᄉᆞ힉소 비지ᄂᆡ에경은ᄉᆞ양말고힝공ᄒᆞ라

팔월십일

뎐보

팔월십일일공ᄉᆞ관착뎐

○려슌격젼 대련만외방면으로온모든보고를거ᄒᆞᆫ즉려슌의뎍군함ᄃᆡᄂᆞᆫ팔월십일조죠에ᄲᆞ져나가기를시험ᄒᆞ다가일본련합함ᄃᆡ와충돌ᄒᆞ고져믈기ᄭᆞ지피ᄎᆞ함ᄃᆡ간에격젼을ᄒᆞ야밤에니르러ᄂᆞᆫ일본구축ᄃᆡᄂᆞᆫ뎍군의함ᄃᆡ를습격ᄒᆞᆫ듯ᄒᆞ고또어늘아츰에밧은바엇던망루에셔ᄒᆞᆫ뎐보를거ᄒᆞᆫ즉로함리도위싼호와보위에다ᄀᆞᆺᄒᆞᆫ혼쳑이팔월십일일미명에려슌히면으로도주ᄒᆞ여간듯ᄒᆞ다ᄒᆞ엿더라

원산뎐보

○합경로병 거구일원산에셔일본젼초부ᄃᆡ의격퇴ᄒᆞᆫ로국긔병부ᄃᆡᄂᆞᆫ그날밤에문쳔ᄭᆞ지물너가진치고십일에다시퇴각ᄒᆞ야야고원에니르럿더라 표원과영흥에ᄂᆞᆫ이긔병부ᄃᆡ외에또긔병오빅명이잇다더라 문평리에사ᄂᆞᆫ토민의말을드른즉뎍군은구일에시례다섯파죡은쟈열명을복방으로운송ᄒᆞ엿다더라 셩진과영흥간에ᄂᆞᆫ대부ᄃᆡ가잇다ᄒᆞ고또뎍군은셩진이남의도로를슈츅ᄒᆞ지아니ᄒᆞ고면션도가셜ᄒᆞ지아니ᄒᆞ엿다더라

외보

○쳔왕죵군 셔반아국쳔왕하나히로국황뎨ᄭᅴ셔비알ᄒᆞ고일아젼징에죵군ᄒᆞ기를원ᄒᆞᆫᄃᆡ로국황뎨ᄭᅴ셔허가ᄒᆞ신고로히쳔왕이현금구로팟긴쟝군군즁에머문다더라

○이동이동 근쟈에이동후작이다시도한ᄒᆞᆫ다ᄂᆞᆫ풍셜이만터니후ᄂᆞᆫ오지아니ᄒᆞ고그ᄃᆡ에이동남작이도한ᄒᆞᆫ다ᄂᆞᆫᄃᆡ동남작은목하에데실뎨도죠ᄉᆞ국부총저요중왕에ᄂᆞᆫ어등후가ᄂᆡ각총리대신으로잇슬때에이동남작은ᄂᆡ각서리관쟝으로잇셔각금후를ᄃᆡ표ᄒᆞ야흔일이만다더라

○퇴각쥰비 죠션신보에팔월십일동경발뎐에운ᄒᆞ되지부발뎐을거ᄒᆞᆫ즉료양에ᄂᆞᆫ인심이대단져샹ᄒᆞ야량식에일부분ᄂᆞᆫ텰령으로환송ᄒᆞᄂᆞᆫ즁이라ᄒᆞ니필시퇴각ᄒᆞ기를쥰비홈이라ᄒᆞ엿더라

○려슌화염 동보동뎐을거ᄒᆞᆫ즉려슌시가에셔화염이대단히니러남을보앗ᄂᆞᆫᄃᆡ일본군이공격ᄒᆞᆫ결과인줄노짐작ᄒᆞᆫ다더라

○려슌함락 긔동보동뎐을거ᄒᆞᆫ즉쳥니와에셔도라온자의말을드른즉작야에려슌히면에셔비샹ᄒᆞᆫ포셩이들엿ᄂᆞᆫᄃᆡ려슌은릭십팔일ᄭᅳᆷ함락될ᄯᅳᆺᄒᆞ다고ᄒᆞ더라더라

○직공파업 동일동뎐을거ᄒᆞᆫ즉려슌션거에잇ᄂᆞᆫ공쟝등이파업ᄒᆞ자고동밍홈으로구라파사룸들의직공ᄒᆞᄂᆞᆫ삭뎐을더올녀쥰다더라

○젹함도쥬 동보동뎐을거ᄒᆞᆫ즉십일일지부발뎐에운ᄒᆞ되로국구축함일척이오날아참에당디에도망ᄒᆞ야왓다ᄒᆞ엿더라

○아병도타 동일동뎐을거ᄒᆞᆫ즉복경발뎐에운ᄒᆞ엿스되아병이금쥬로도망ᄒᆞ야온고로그병복을벳기고텬진으로호송ᄒᆞ엿다ᄒᆞ엿더라

○아군호의 동일동뎐을거ᄒᆞᆫ즉아군이마젹즁에일본인이은복ᄒᆞ야잇ᄂᆞᆫ가의심ᄒᆞ야포박ᄒᆞᆯ차로향평현신민둔부근으로군ᄃᆡ를파송ᄒᆞ야뒤진다ᄒᆞ엿더라

광고

TELEGRAMS.

OPERATIONS AT PORT ARTHUR.

A message received at the Japanese Legation says:—

According to reports from Dalny, the Russian Squadron at dawn on the 10th inst. made its way out of Port Arthur. They were met by Admiral Togo's fleet and fighting continued until night fell. The result is not known and it is believed that a night attack was also made by the Japanese torpedo craft. On the morning of the 11th two Russian battleships were seen re-entering Port Arthur. One of them appeared to be the "Retvisan."

London, August 4, 8.05 P. M.

Four cruisers and four torpedo boats are reported to have left Cronstadt yesterday for the Far East.—Kobe Herald.

London, August 4, 8.05 P. M.

Very pessimistic reports on the situation of General Kuropatkin's army at Liaoyang have just been published in Paris.—Kobe Herald.

The following are from the Nagasaki press.—

London, August 5th.

An official despatch received in St. Petersburg from General Kuropatkin states that he hopes that the Russian troops, having retreated on their main position after heavy losses, will be able to maintain it against the enemy, although the latter are numerically superior.

The troops withdrew from Haicheng, unmolested, by the Anshientien road. Though carts were provided to carry their kits and coats, the men suffered terribly from the heat, considerable numbers having sunstrokes.

London, August 5th.

Viceroy Alexeieff has gone to Harbin, from whence he will proceed to Vladivostock.

London, August 5th.

The United States Government has been corresponding with the Russian and other Governments, relative to the seizures of shipping, and state that under no circumstances will America recede from the doctrine that foodstuffs, not directly intended for a belligerent's army or navy, cannot be regarded as contraband of war.

London, August 7th.

The Russian despatches, while admitting considerable Russian losses, including six guns, declare that the operations of July 31st were indecisive.

The battle began under favourable auspices but eventually the Japanese succeeded in enfilading the Russian position.

London, August 7th.

The cargo of the Hamburg-America Line s. s. "Arabia," which was recently captured by the Russian Vladivostock squadron, has been released with the exception of the railway materials and flour, which have been removed.

London, August 7th.

The Peninsular and Oriental Steam Navigation Company announce that, owing to the uncertainty regarding contraband, their steamers will cease to carry passengers and cargo beyond Shanghai. The steamers will still, however, carry passengers and cargo from Japan.

London, August 7th.

Russia has notified the Porte that two coal laden steamers, belonging to the Volunteer Fleet, are about to pass the Dardanelles.

The notification states that Russia guarantees that the vessels will retain their character as merchantmen.

London, August 9th.

The Secretary of the Peninsular and Oriental Steam Navigation Company has written a letter to the "Times" denying the Russian official declaration that the "Malacca" was seized because the Captain refused to show the ship's papers. Not only were the manifests given but a number of the ship's people, who were sent on board the Volunteer Fleet steamer "Petersburg," were offered inducements to give information justifying the seizure.

THE FOREIGN OFFICERS OF THE "HITACHI MARU."

We learn from the "Kobe Chronicle" that the Japanese Government, with the Imperial approval, has expressed its great regret regarding the loss of the foreign officers of the "Hitachi Maru," and has awarded the next-of-kin of the officers grants in money. In making this grant the Government declares that the deceased rendered useful and praiseworthy service to the maritime transport, and sacrificed their lives to their duty. On the 4th inst. General Baron Terauchi, the Minister for War, with the Emperor's approval, granted as a token of condolence with the relatives of the deceased officers the following sums:—In respect of the death of Captain Campbell, Y5,000; Chief Engineer Glass, Y4,500; and Chief Officer Bishop, Y4,000.

THE SETTLEMENT OF THE ETZEL MURDER.

The "Universal Gazette" has the following concerning the settlement with reference to the murder of the late Mr. Etzel by Chinese soldiers, near Newchwang:—The Commandant of the delinquent soldiers, the expectant prefect Chu, whose brigade is stationed at Tienchuangtai, has been cashiered; the officer commanding the detachment which fired the fatal shots, has been condemned to five years' imprisonment and the sum of Tls. 25,000 is to be paid to the family of the late Mr. Etzel as indemnity for his murder.

THE NORTHEAST.

There is no news of any note from Gensan up to the time of going to press. It seems that the squadron of Russian cavalry which approached Gensan has retired back on the main army in the neighbourhood of Yŏng Hung. There is a good deal of Japanese military activity observable in Seoul—probably due to measures being taken to check a Russian descent.

THE SALT MONOPOLY.

It is said that the Japanese Government has the salt monopoly law draft prepared to introduce to the next (21st) session of the Diet, the substance of the draft being the same as that placed before the former session. The Anti-Salt Monopoly Association has lately addressed a memorial to the Premier and the Minister of Finance, pointing out eleven different defects in this resource.—Japan Gazette.

THE UN-PACIFIC ROUTE.

From the Japan Mail we learn that the Foreign Office has received a telegram stating that the P. M. S. S. Company and the O. & O. Company have decided not to take any freight for Japan in view of the uncertainty existing as to what constitutes contraband of war in Russia's eyes.

JAPANESE BONDS.

According to a telegram received in Yokohama, on the 1st inst., Japanese bonds have risen in London. The four per cents. are quoted at £74¼; the five per cents. and war bonds at £90 1s. 9d. The premium on the new bonds is £2¼.

The Kamni (superintendent of foreign trade) of Pyeng Yang telegraphs for permission to come to Seoul. Some questions of urgency having arisen, and he wishes to consult with the Emperor himself.

According to the 'Chosen Shimpo" a Chefoo telegram received in Tokyo states that a Russian destroyer entered that port on the 11th inst.

AN UNDERGROUND TRAMWAY IN LONDON.

Londoners who have watched for some years the slow progress of the works which will one day give them two noble thoroughfares in Kingsway and Aldwych, may not all be aware that in addition to these broad and open ways the London County Council are constructing an underground electric tramway from Holborn to the Strand. This undertaking, of which details as given by the "Tramway & Railway World" in its issue of June 9th, is a new departure in Great Britain, being to some extent modelled on train subways in Boston, U.S.A. The line now in course of construction is really part of a truncated scheme. Originally the municipal authorities had proposed to connect the north and south of London tram lines by a service running along the Thames Embankment and over Westminster Bridge, but Parliamentary opposition was against this project.

The new subway will run from Theobalds Road to a point south of the Strand, not far from the Gaiety Theatre. The subway will be rather shallow, so shallow that only singledeck cars can be used. A deeper tunnel would, of course, have meant a greater initial outlay, but it is pointed out that an additional depth of 3½ ft. would have accommodated the top-seat tramcars used on the county Council's lines. The subway will not be completed for some years yet. The cost of its construction has been estimated at £282,000 per mile, exclusive of what may be required for the purchase of vaults, cellars, and other property, and also exclusive of the cost of pipe galleries.

WITHOUT MONEY.

The Marquis of Anglesey, whose private theatre, amateur acting, and great eccentricities made him one of the most prominent social figures in Great Britain, has been declared bankrupt. A correspondent says scarcely any event in recent years has startled Society like the revelation of the hopeless bankruptcy of the Marquis as revealed at the first meeting of the creditors. "Hiding in some shabby hotel on the Continent, bereft of income, drifting near the line of actual poverty and slowly dying of an incurable disease, the Marquis is today the most pitiable of all figures." His liabilities, it was shown, reach £500,000. Against this sum he had life insurance of £200,000, and the insurance company refused to accept any further risks even at a premium of 30 per cent. The Anglesey estates yield nominally an income of a little more than £100,000, but when mortgages and jointures, including one of £10,000 per annum, have been deducted, there remains an income of only £10,000 a year. The decision of the creditors to throw the whole estate into bankruptcy will deny the Marquis this income for twenty-five years. Creditors and friends are asking what has become of the proceeds of the great sale of jewelry held recently, before the Marquis went abroad. One passage in the bankruptcy proceedings is full of a grim truth of the position into which the Marquis' extravagances and unspeakable eccentricities have led him. "Has the Marquis any friends who will assist him?" asked a creditor. "The Marquis has no friends," was the laconic reply of his attorney.

In accordance to the Japanese request to have the road between Seoul and Anju put in repairs, the Seoul district office has commenced operations on the 20 miles of road between here and Pak Sŏkhyŏn.

The Eastern world of July 30th says, "A Korean refugee and his son have been arrested at Shimonoseki. They are reported to be leaders of the Anti-Japanese party in Seoul."

A somewhat prolonged shock of earthquake was experienced in Yokohama about 9.45 p.m. on Thursday.

The Korea Daily News.

To be published daily except Sundays.
ate of Subscription:—

Per Year.	Yen 25.
Per Quarter.	Yen 7.
Per Month	Yen 2.50

Postage in Korea not charged extra.
Postage abroad charged extra.

Advertisements, 50 sen per day for 1 inch or less.
5 yen per month per inch.
50 yen per year per inch.

All communications to

E. T. BETHELL,
Editor and Publisher.
Pak-tong, Seoul.

WAR v. AGRICULTURE.

From the provinces reports are continually reaching 'us of the protests from governors and magistrates of the difficulty of complying at this season of the year with the Japanese demand for coolie labour. Undoubtedly this is a busy time with farmers, the growing rice requires a great deal of attention and there are many other crops coming on which must soon be harvested. Time waits for no man and in agriculture this is especially true. It is well known that even in normal times, at this season of the year, labour is at a premium in all agricultural countries. Throughout the Orient in late Summer and Autumn all industries suffer severely from the diversion of their labour to the needs of the harvest.

Therefore it is not a matter of surprise that the farmers are complaining loudly at the prospect of being deprived of labour during the coming season.

Still it must be borne in mind that if the demands of agriculture are important, the demands of war are imperative. Korea has agreed to render to Japan all possible assistance to bring this war to a successful issue, and she must not go back on her promise. A steady supply of labourers for transport and construction work is of the utmost importance to an army, and to see that these men are forthcoming is the least that Korea can do in fulfilment of her promises to render all possible assistance to Japan.

There is no scarcity of the raw material. Korea abounds in examples of laziness and mis-directed energy. The first thing remarked by a visitor to this country is the preponderance of men lounging or aimlessly strolling about, over those who are engaged in productive work. The spade with four men to do work that could easily be done by one, the chair with six or eight coolies, and the absurdly large proportion of overseers to labourers in all undertakings are examples, which could be endlessly added to, of mis-directed "energy." In conclusion, there are the soldiers. Korea has no need for an army, the largest army she could raise would be insignificant and useless in comparison to that of either of her neighbours, and a small body of picked men to act as gendarmerie or mounted police to maintain order in the country, would be quite sufficient for all her needs. In the meantime we have the spectacle of some fifteen or twenty thousand young men with nothing to do most of their time but loaf about. They do not even acquire habits of tidiness and cleanliness and are nuisances in more ways than one. A Korean is often a born loafer and a military life is a post-graduate course serving to confirm his natural tendency to idleness.

We have shown that there is no scarcity of labour in this country, and if those who habitually do nothing are "rounded up" and sent to assist the Japanese, the needs of Agriculture will not be interfered. Probably every man who could be spared from Japan has already been sent to the seat of war, and now is Korea's opportunity to step in and vindicate her promise to assist Japan to the best of her ability. We venture to suggest that an Imperial proclamation, pointing out the justice of Japan's demand and calling upon the people in the name of the national honour to volunteer for the work, would have an immediate effect, and protests from the country would no longer be heard.

MILITARY ROADS.

Major Watanabe of the Japanese army is going on a visit of inspection of the roads in the vicinity of Kimwha, accompanied by 20 soldiers. The Home Department has issued instructions that the water supply en route must receive attention and that everything possible be done for the comfort of the expedition. This visit to Kimwha appears to be purely a precautionary measure, as the town does not lie on the road to Gensan.

DEMISE OF THE KOREAN MINING & CULTIVATING COMPANY.

This concern, which came forth with such a flourish of trumpets, is no more. In response to a protest from the Japanese Legation against the company working on foreign capital, the Foreign Office replies that the company has ceased to exist and that the money side of the question dies with it.

ACCIDENT ON THE RAILWAY.

On the 11th instant as the train which left Chemulpo at 8:30 a. m. was approaching South Gate station the speed at which the curve was taken caused the last car to leave the track. No injury was sustained by the inmates but the track was torn up for some distance, the car was overturned, and traffic was disorganized for some hours.

REFORM IN THE AIR.

With the object of effecting reforms in the present procedure in the various Government departments, Mr. Pak Cheesoon the acting president of state called a meeting at 3 p. m. yesterday to which the heads of all departments were requested to attend.

THE "SUNGARI."

We learn that it has been decided that the "Oura Maru" shall tow the "Sungari" to Nagasaki. The two vessels will start as soon as they have been cleared of the accumulations of weeds and barnacles with which they are now covered.

THE COOLIE QUESTION AGAIN.

The Governor of Whanghai province telegraphs that the popular feeling against the Japanese demand for coolies is very strong and that he fears a riot. He asks for instructions how to proceed.

MARTIAL LAW.

The Japanese gendarmes continue to make arrests of Koreans. The latest victim, whose name is not given, was captured in Chinkokai at 2 a. m. on the 11th instant.

Messrs. Paik Si-yong, Ham Sung-dong and Yi Kung-sun, the officers who went to meet Marquis Ito when he visited this country, have been decorated by the Emperor of Japan. The Japanese Minister notifies the Foreign Office that the insignia has arrived and asks that these gentlemen be requested to attend his Legation to receive it.

The Governor of Pyeng Yang again telegraphs that attempts to collect coolies for the Japanese only cause ill-feeling and that the people threaten to become violent.

THE GROWTH OF SHANGHAI.

The promised demolition of the "Central Hotel" and the erection on its site, and on the site already vacant immediately behind it of the proposed "New Palace Hotel," will add another to the imposing hotels of Shanghai and give us on the Bund a handsome building, worthy of its position in the very heart of the Model Settlement, says the "North China Herald." The designs prepared by Messrs. Scott and Carter for the Company are now on exhibition. The plans contemplate the widening of the Nanking Road and on this thoroughfare will be the chief or grand entrance to the hotel. The Nanking Road face of the building will be more than double that of the present structure, many shops having been demolished to make room for the sky-scraper. The ground floor is to be chiefly used for shops, hotel entrances, and hotel bar, and will be built of cut, mottled, volcanic agglomerate, which beautifies so many of Shanghai's best buildings and in particular the Russo-Chinese Bank. This same stone, carved into various devices known to architectural skill, will be untilised in the chief facings of the upper structure of this six-storied building. the rest of which will, however, be of red and terracotta brick. The size of the building will be appreciated when it is understood that the Nanking Road frontage will cover 284 feet, while that on the Bund will be 59 feet. Besides having 196 bedrooms, both double and single (varying in size from 13 feet by 15 feet to 15 feet by 20 feet), each with bathroom, there will be four private dining rooms, ladies' room, banqueting hall (49 feet by 63 feet), and large buffet rooms leading off an extensive lounge. The upper stories will all have 4½ foot wide iron balconies running the length of the building on the Southern side, fitted with fire-escape arrangements.

The various dining rooms, ladies' room, lounge, etc., will be situated in the top storey, which can be approached by a beautiful broad stairway, in carved wood, or by means of lifts, two of which will be continuously operating. Surmounting the Bund half of the structure will be a roof garden measuring 115 feet by 54 feet, on which a band will play to the guests during the hot Summer evenings after dinner hour. Wherever fire-proof material can be possibly used it will be put into this building, and everything will be arranged to minimise the danger from fire.

RULES FOR RICSHA COOLIES.

The following rules should, it is suggested, be printed on the backs of the ricsha licenses in order to train up the ricsha coolie in the way he should go.

1.—Always run along with your head down and your eyes closed. If a shock should come it should, as the poet said, like great feelings come unawares.

2.—Foreigners have a great liking for garlic. If therefore you wish to ingratiate yourself with your fares and thus obtain handsome cumshaws from them, always take plenty of this inspiriting vegetable before you take your place on the stand.

3.—If you hear the fire trucks coming, drop the ricsha in the middle of the road and dart into the nearest shop. If your fare is not injured when the trucks have passed, it is well to approach him with caution.

4.—If a globe-trotting fare unwisely gives you $1 instead of 10 cents, it is advisable not to bobbery for more as the foreign policemen are apt to interfere and deduct 90 per cent from the proffered fare.

5.—Remember that when a Sikh policeman waves his arms it is simply to signal some private message to a comrade up the street. When you pass him beware lest he signal something into your ear.—North China Herald.

Hitherto the palace has been guarded by the Imperial Guard. It is now announced that a picked Palace Guard will be raised from all branches of the service and that a new uniform will be provided for them.

The Korea Daily News.

VOL. I, SATURDAY, AUGUST 13, 1904. No. 24

大韓每日申報
대한ᄆᆡ일신보

(뎨이십륙호) (화요일) 일쳔구ᄇᆡᆨ사년팔월십륙일

본사고ᄇᆡᆨ

이신보ᄂᆞᆫ영어와한어로셔계ᄆᆡ일츌판ᄒᆞᆸ

신문가

ᄒᆞᆫ쟝 엽두돈오푼

일삭도엽두량닷돈 맛돈으로 밧ᄉᆞᆸ

광고료ᄂᆞᆫ

긔한의쟝단과ᄌᆞ형의다쇼로즁감ᄒᆞ되몃가로밧을터이오매오림지아녀대한사ᄅᆞᆷ마다다이신문을보실터이니광고ᄇᆡ시기를원ᄒᆞ시ᄂᆞᆫ이들은우리신문사에와서면약ᄒᆞ심을희망ᄒᆞᆸ

○발힝소 대한ᄆᆡ일신보사범어학교압희 젼영국인셜필림집자리오

사쟝 영국인 (ᄇᆡ셜)

본사지졈

인쳔항교젼동신지명씨로우리대한ᄆᆡ일신보사인쳔항지졈장을튁졍ᄒᆞ엿ᄉᆞ오니인쳔항에계신구람코자ᄒᆞ시ᄂᆞᆫ쳠군ᄌᆞᄂᆞᆫ히지졈에왕림편의ᄒᆞ시ᄋᆞᆸ

사고

○우리대한ᄆᆡ일신보의목뎍은대한의안녕질셔에관한모든뎨목에디ᄒᆞ야ᄂᆞᆫ공평한번론을주쟝홈이라우리등신원의탐보ᄂᆞᆫ신문보시ᄂᆞᆫ쳠군ᄌᆞ의게ᄒᆞᆼ상보도ᄒᆞ려며편지를긔서ᄒᆞ여주시ᄂᆞᆫ이ᄂᆞᆫ셩명과반ᄃᆡ를젹어붓치시기를희망ᄒᆞ오니이거슨신문샹에긔ᄌᆡᄒᆞ란ᄂᆞᆫ거시아니오다만구히신용ᄒᆞᄂᆞᆫ즁거를삼고자ᄒᆞᆷ이라긔자ᄂᆞᆫ아모긔서던지과지ᄒᆞᆷ을되각ᄒᆞᄂᆞᆫ권리를가졋ᄉᆞ오나되각ᄒᆞᄂᆞᆫ리유를말ᄒᆞᆯ터이오며공즁평화를문란케ᄒᆞᄂᆞᆫ듯ᄒᆞᆫ긔서ᄂᆞᆫ의례히밧지안켓ᄉᆞᆸ나이다

론셜

젼쟝이농ᄉᆞ에샹좌됨이라

○근일소문을드른즉일본셔각도각군에역부모집ᄒᆞ라ᄂᆞᆫᄉᆞ건에대ᄒᆞ여관찰사와군슈들이시힝ᄒᆞ기가대단히어렵다고번로ᄒᆞᄂᆞᆫ거시ᄇᆡᆨ곡이졈졈이거간즉가을일이장ᄎᆞ발ᄉᆡᆼᄒᆞᆯ터이라농ᄉᆞᄒᆞᄂᆞᆫ사ᄅᆞᆷ들에셔ᄂᆞᆫ추셩ᄒᆞᆯ시를당ᄒᆞ면오히려사ᄅᆞᆷ이부족ᄒᆞᆯ을한ᄒᆞ고품군을ᄉᆞ셔쓰ᄂᆞᆫᄃᆡ동방졔국에셔야더욱근농ᄒᆞᄂᆞᆫ사ᄅᆞᆷ들은추수를밋고하추지간에농량드린것과수고ᄒᆞᆫ거시엇더ᄒᆞ리요

이추셩ᄒᆞᆯ지음에농민들의역군모집ᄒᆞᆫ다고ᄒᆞ소ᄒᆞᄂᆞᆫ거시용혹무괴ᄒᆞ거시와반일ᄌᆡ빅셩들노ᄒᆞ여곰농ᄉᆞ에힘을쓰라ᄒᆞ면ᄆᆡ우긴ᄒᆞᆫ게드ᄂᆞᆫᄃᆡ니ᄭᆡ와ᄯᆞᆷ에당ᄒᆞ여셔ᄂᆞᆫᄃᆡ단히관계되게싱각ᄒᆞᆯ거시로ᄃᆡ대한셔긔왕에일본젼쟁에대ᄒᆞ야방조ᄒᆞᆯ밧한일에ᄂᆞᆫ진션진미ᄒᆞᆫ게청죵ᄒᆞ엿슨즉지금일에도응당시힝ᄒᆞᆯ듯ᄒᆞᆫ거시일본셔역군을모집ᄒᆞ야긔송ᄒᆞ란ᄂᆞᆫ평영이ᄌᆞ긔의군수상에ᄂᆞᆫ대단ᄒᆞ긴ᄒᆞᆫᄉᆞ진인ᄃᆡ청구ᄒᆞᄂᆞᆫ역군수ᄒᆞᆫ도만치아니ᄒᆞᆫ즉대한방죠ᄒᆞᄂᆞᆫ마음에능히시힝ᄒᆞ기셔로하탁ᄒᆞᆯ듯ᄒᆞᆫᄃᆡ

대한에이러ᄒᆞᆫ혜싱기ᄂᆞᆫ거시어렵지아니ᄒᆞᆯ듯ᄒᆞᆫ거시근본빅셩들을위ᄒᆞ라ᄒᆞ고방향업시가르쳐서누구던지이나라에와서보ᄂᆞᆫ사ᄅᆞᆷ들은가히일ᄒᆞᆯ만ᄒᆞᆫ빅셩들이세월을탕도ᄒᆞ야동연히비리ᄌᆞ려왕리ᄒᆞ며가뢰질ᄒᆞᆯ배라도ᄒᆞᆫᄌᆞ가히ᄒᆞᆯ법ᄒᆞᆫ거슬비명식이ᄂᆞᆫ봇리ᄒᆞ고ᄑᆞᆯ군타ᄂᆞᆫᄃᆡ도빗식여뎐셰이ᄂᆞᆫ쌀ᄒᆞ여단미며역군노괴쟝이라ᄂᆞᆫ겻도일이아니ᄒᆞᄂᆞᆫ길셩습이되엿슨즉이리케방향업시교민ᄒᆞᄂᆞᆫᄃᆡ쳐지히ᄅᆞᆫ셔필경에ᄂᆞᆫ군ᄉᆞ쳐지잇스되실샹인즉양병도만히ᄒᆞᆯ겨엽고양문도평쟝히긴츅ᄒᆞᆯ거시엽ᄂᆞᆫ거신즉여간병쟝밋소ᄃᆡ와헌병순검약간만두드ᄃᆡ도나라유지ᄒᆞᄂᆞᆫᄃᆡ필요ᄒᆞᆫ거시우리보기에ᄂᆞᆫ모도함ᄒᆞ야게위이반명이ᄂᆞᆫ되ᄂᆞᆫ순검병정들이아모것도아지못ᄒᆞ야싱지이몸을도쟝ᄒᆞ게못ᄒᆞᆫ즉이거슨맛치ᄒᆞᆫ벽무취갓튼지라흉유ᄉᆞ지시를당ᄒᆞ드ᄅᆡ도ᄒᆞ나도방어ᄒᆞ지못ᄒᆞᆯ듯ᄒᆞᆫ거시ᄃᆡ한셔ᄂᆞᆫ사ᄅᆞᆷ을나아서능히군인조격이되드ᄅᆡ도우례졸업을식이ᄂᆞᆫ거ᄉᆞᆫ확실히ᄒᆞᆯ타ᄒᆞᆫᄃᆡ셩습이되여그리ᄒᆞᆷ인즉

우리보기에ᄂᆞᆫ이나라에서역군모집ᄒᆞ기가용이ᄒᆞᆯ듯ᄒᆞᆫ거시무항산ᄒᆞᆫ유산ᄒᆞᆫ빅셩들을보니게되면ᄒᆞᆫ수에도방ᄒᆡ됨이업슬거신즉미리ᄒᆞᆯ지경이면일본셔젼쟝에보ᄂᆡ라고청구ᄒᆞᄂᆞᆫ빅셩들노ᄒᆞ여곰악기ᄂᆞᆫ거시요시힝ᄒᆞᄂᆞᆫᄃᆡ대ᄒᆞ여셔도이맛금묘ᄒᆞᆫ방칙이업슬터인즉우리싱각에ᄂᆞᆫ졍부로셔일본역부쳥구ᄒᆞᄂᆞᆫ수진에ᄃᆡᄒᆞ야나라를위ᄒᆞ여셔이일에소모ᄒᆞ게ᄒᆞ라ᄂᆞᆫᄒᆞᆫ령을발ᄒᆞᆫ진ᄃᆡᆫ모집ᄒᆞ기도심히속ᄒᆞᆯ듯ᄒᆞ고각도각군에빅셩들의오오ᄒᆞᄂᆞᆫ쳥문도업슬듯ᄒᆞ더라

잡보

○폐졍후문 샹쟉일하오셥시일공ᄉᆞ 폐졍이두시간쯤되엿스며ᄇᆡᆨ작우ᄒᆞ엿ᄂᆞᆫᄃᆡ외대와레식원쟝만시립ᄒᆞ엿다ᄒᆞ며무삼비밀히 샹쥬ᄒᆞᆷ이잇다더라

○회의중지 일젼에외졍부에서회의ᄒᆞᆯ쟈로각부에쳥쳡ᄒᆞ엿더니의정셔리대신이샹소ᄒᆞᆫ고로긔회치못ᄒᆞ엿다더라

○졔관불가 평남거ᄒᆞᄂᆞᆫ오신평모가류경ᄒᆞ 즁인ᄃᆡ순검과무샹관이잇셧든지뢰차슈작ᄒᆞ다가반말을ᄒᆞ엿다고순검이지고관ᄒᆞᆫ자ᄒᆞ야경무남서로다리고챳ᄂᆞᆫᄃᆡ셔쟝이죠케말ᄒᆞ야오씨를환송ᄒᆞ고희숑은ᄌᆞᆷ은희망ᄒᆞ엿다ᄂᆞᆫᄃᆡ오씨ᄂᆞᆫ곳직픔이졍샹이등에죵경슈령이요샹칙성노인고나순검보고반말ᄒᆞ엿기로무샹관계가잇스리오ᄒᆞ고그슌검을미오시ᄇᆡ들ᄒᆞᆫ다더라

○대관탁용 려항젼셜을듯문ᄒᆞᆫ즉참졍신샹훈씨ᄂᆞᆫ외졍대신으로승임되고일본에두류ᄒᆞᆫ다가환국ᄒᆞᆫ송병쥰씨가참졍을ᄒᆞᆫ리라고들ᄒᆞ더라

○란민발현 경샹도랍동강불자당장쳔하류슈현동에셔두골틔셕탄광ᄆᆡᆨ을발견ᄒᆞ엿ᄂᆞᆫᄃᆡ일본엇던ᄒᆞᆫ기ᄉᆞ의말이그탄광이무궁에연탁ᄒᆞᆫ것신ᄃᆡ상거가빅리나연ᄒᆞ야광ᄃᆡᄒᆞᆫ탄광인ᄃᆡ셕탄품질의호불호와산츌의다소ᄂᆞᆫ아즉알수업스나방금조ᄉᆞᄒᆞᄂᆞᆫ즁이라더라

○쳥방죄인 희쥬관찰ᄉᆞ셔리가쳥원ᄒᆞ엿스되강령군창암포쳠부를쳔단이얼인에게방미ᄒᆞᆫ죄인을금번ᄉᆞ면을의쥰ᄒᆞ야특별이방면ᄒᆞ게다ᄒᆞ엿더라

○송가리호 인쳔항에셔침몰된로국긔선송가리호ᄂᆞᆫ일의진져비여고빈에격퇴ᄒᆞ여잇ᄂᆞᆫ휘초와모든거슨간쳥히ᄒᆞ고빈슈ᄒᆞᆯ역ᄉᆞ를필ᄒᆞᄂᆞᆫᄃᆡ로대포환이신을고쟝긔로회항ᄒᆞ여가기로결졍ᄒᆞ엿다더라

○샹록환원 고베크로니클신문을거ᄒᆞᆫ즉일본졍부에셔청명지가를붕숭ᄒᆞ야미왕로항의게격침된샹록환의승조원외국인의ᄉᆞ망홈을대단히유감히넉여그유족의게ᄒᆞᆫ금하ᄉᆞᄒᆞᆷ을셜명ᄒᆞ엿스니하ᄉᆞ금을버림은희ᄉᆞ망인들이희군의슈운ᄒᆞᄂᆞᆫᄉᆞ업에ᄆᆡ우유익ᄒᆞ고친송ᄒᆞᆯ빈ᄒᆞ게일을ᄒᆞ엿고쏘저회ᄌᆡ분에당ᄒᆞᆫ아셩명을밧쳐다고졍부에셔포양ᄒᆞᆷ이라금월ᄉᆞ일에남쟉ᄉᆞ포대쟝ᄌᆞᆫ군대신이칙지를무루위수망ᄌᆞᆫ승조원의족쳑의게위흘금으로하ᄉᆞᄒᆞᆫ거시여좌ᄒᆞ니

함쟝킹쎄ᄅᆞᆯ씨의게ᄂᆞᆫ오빅원이오

일등긔관슈조버쓰씨의게ᄂᆞᆫᄉᆞ쳔오빅원이오

일등ᄉᆞ무원셰승씨의게ᄂᆞᆫᄉᆞ쳔원이라ᄒᆞ엿더라

○민영즁권 일본관보를거ᄒᆞᆫ즉일본졍부에셔소금을젼민ᄒᆞᄂᆞᆫ특허권법령의긔초ᄒᆞᆫ안건을이다음이삼일국회기회일에데출ᄒᆞ기로ᄒᆞ엿ᄂᆞᆫᄃᆡ긔초의본의ᄂᆞᆫ젼번긔회일에버엿든것과굿고민영즁회권반ᄃᆡ동밍회에셔ᄂᆞᆫ근자에ᄎᆞᆼ리대신과대쟝대신계건의셔를드리이계칙에티ᄒᆞ야엽ᄒᆞᆫ가지부당ᄒᆞᆫ일을지목ᄒᆞ엿더라

●망명괴착 칠월샴십일의동방에소문을드른즉대한망명긱부ᄌᆞ가마관에셔잡혓다ᄒᆞᄂᆞᆫᄃᆡ그량인은헌셩에잇ᄂᆞᆫ일본ᄇᆡᆫᄃᆡ장의평슈라ᄒᆞ더라

○셜치호소 진고기거ᄒᆞᄂᆞᆫ김덕현이라ᄒᆞᄂᆞᆫ자가원리반찬가가를ᄒᆞᄂᆞᆫᄃᆡ그동리거ᄒᆞᄂᆞᆫ쳔위ᄃᆡ병졍리운셕의쳐가ᄂᆞᆫ반찬ᄒᆞᆯ경을ᄒᆞ기로샹죵ᄒᆞᆫ번이ᄒᆞ더니김가와등간이되지라가반연ᄒᆞ야김가가린가의방쟝을어드라ᄒᆞᄂᆞᆫ돈오빅량을간몰셕짐ᄒᆞ

엿더라 근일리가번졍이 출번훈 쥬계쳐가 가산운동훈제며가지 교도망훈자 리가 가본리자과 쳐가김가와 쟝동훈 간샹을안교 로김가를 거리중에 천병과 쥬소 예호소훈엿다더라

○셔로참샹 평안남도로셔 샹리훈사룸의 말을드른즉 히 각군에서 인부를 징발훈야 치도ᄒᆞ는역부에 쓰는디 미일공가는 샹냥오젼식 출급ᄒᆞ나 졍이 번수를 운번테와 일훈고 명일에 쓰쌀 쳠오면리왕부비 가식네 량식뒤즉 농수방은훈버에 ᄒᆞ수에 젼긔ᄒᆞ지못훈고 잔민의 수세에 부비 ㅂ티더 ᄒᆞ니 못살지 경이라 고방방곡곡이 소요ᄒᆞ고 쓰리로 역수ᄒᆞ는도로에 방쟝부셩훈곡식을 치도ᄒᆞ기위ᄒᆞ야 마우죵이는고로 농수ᄒᆞ는인민드리 젼답으로 비회ᄒᆞ며 도로로 방황ᄒᆞ야 호곡ᄒᆞ는 형샹이 참불인견이라ᄒᆞ더라

○싱쳔군보 싱쳔군수리용필씨가 나부로 보고ᄒᆞ기를 본군이 히쥬와 지경이 인접훈 요로에 잇셔 서봄부터 너름ᄭᆞ지 역부수응에 빅셩이 곤난ᄒᆞ엿고 또 일젼부터 히쥬 봉산 량군도 역ᄉᆞ에 쓰 부역ᄒᆞ노라고 이 ᄯᅢ셔시ᄒᆞ엿는ᄃᆡ 농무가 방쟝공극훈ᄃᆡ 샹화 감리의 역부를 빅명모집ᄒᆞ라는 훈령이 오후로 빅셩이 다 의구지 심을 품어 농민의 환산은 아무가론이어니와 샹고 셔지도 본군 경니에 드리오지 안코 기민은 다 이졍ᄒᆞ기를 싱각ᄒᆞ야 흉흉훈 민졍이 란리를 맛는듯ᄒᆞ니 목하ᄉᆞ샹으로 보면 단순셕명도 모집ᄒᆞᆯ수 업거든 하물며 류빅명인부를 엇지 쳔리타국에 출발ᄒᆞ리가 ᄒᆞ릇 반이 반반ᄒᆞ라 처분을 ᄂᆞ리와 빅셩을 안도케ᄒᆞ라 ᄒᆞ엿더라

○대포쇄공 본월십이일에 일본병졍십팔명이 와 쟝터에 셜치ᄒᆞ엿던 대포루문을 쇄공ᄒᆞᆫ다ᄒᆞ고 광희문 안으로 실고 갓다가 즉시 도로 와 도로 왜쟝터에 두엇다더라

○일파죵병 이왕에는 각문에 일병이 명식 파슈ᄒᆞ더니 본월십이일붓터는 서문 남문 서소문에 만 병이 명과 남ᄒᆞ병칠명식 파슈훈다더라

○일관연회 작일하오팔시에 일공ᄉᆞ관에서 만찬회를 ᄒᆞ는ᄃᆡ 한국대관에 샹훈리지용 박제순 리하영 제씨를 청요ᄒᆞ야 연ᄒᆞ엿다더라

○민씨피셔 근일에 민보국영환씨는 피셔ᄒᆞᆯ 차로 신문외 산정에 나가셔 한양훈다더라

○가련아귀 죄착일인창에서 한인역부 수빅여명을 훈련에 탑승ᄒᆞ고 발션훈지 을마 만에 히상에서 일제히 단발ᄒᆞ는ᄃᆡ 남디문 안수교 남의 집교용ᄒᆞ던 병어리 아희가 산발을 반티ᄒᆞ야 향가훈 죽여 쓴이 죽더에 고아회을 참형ᄒᆞ엿다고 젼셜이 분분ᄒᆞ는ᄃᆡ 사룸마다 가긍ᄒᆞ다고 ᄒᆞ더라

리방일관 이신호에 귀쥐훈 리씨거의 대목에 리근틱씨가 부지거쳐ᄒᆞ엿더니 후문을 조세히 드른즉 동씨는 일젼에 샹경ᄒᆞ야 일본공ᄉᆞ을 방문ᄒᆞ고 각신문샹에 오른 과장의 된 일을 변명ᄒᆞ야 과흥ᄒᆞ엿다ᄒᆞ며 과천으로 다시 내려 갓다더라

○샹쥬귀젼 일젼에 일공ᄉᆞ의 폐현훈 소식을 샹문훈즉 일공ᄉᆞ가 시졍개션에 셜시ᄒᆞᆯ 은죵 고ᄒᆞ기를 지졍을 불가불 졍리훌지니 탁지부에 감독을 두되 일본인으로 고빙ᄒᆞ고 외부에는 미국인으로 고문관을 고빙ᄒᆞ고 군티는 감셩ᄒᆞ야 일쳔오빅명만 셜치ᄒᆞ고 인지를 퇴용ᄒᆞ고 쳔명은 갓가이 마시고 쥬외공ᄉᆞ를 소환ᄒᆞᆯ시ᄉᆞᄒᆞ고 그 후에는 등별히 샹쥬ᄒᆞᆯ 수건이 잇서 즉티ᄒᆞ야 샹쥬ᄒᆞ엿다는ᄃᆡ 일공ᄉᆞ를 공녀부에서 연졉ᄒᆞ엿더라

○참령삭직 참령김인슈가 현금북도에 하거ᄒᆞ야 아병의 션봉이 되야 남출ᄒᆞ야 기젼훈다ᄒᆞ니 일젼에 원슈부에서 샹쥬ᄒᆞ야 면관삭직ᄒᆞ엿더라

○한부계방 일군병참소에서 역부모집수로 한셩 대단소동되는지라 일젼에 한셩부에서 각부에 고시ᄒᆞ기를 일아개젼 이리로 치즁왕리가 자연 호번훈즉 역부모집은 부득이훈일이어늘 인민이 로 와언을 젼파ᄒᆞ야 소요를일으는고로 이에 고시ᄒᆞ니 인민은 지실ᄒᆞ야 각각 안업ᄒᆞ라ᄒᆞ엿더라

○대관회의 일젼에 일공ᄉᆞ 폐현시 샹쥬훈일로 십삼일에 고수 긴샹의ᄒᆞ기 위ᄒᆞ야 외대와 기타 관인이 샹참졍가로 모히의론ᄒᆞ엿다더라

○출송본국 일본인 삼본구헌과 협곡안쟝이 명이 근일에 대한에 와셔 군인유죠보금이라 칭ᄒᆞ고 돈 일쳔이빅수십원을 거두엇다가 그 일이 탄로되야 그 돈은 차저셔 본처로 환송ᄒᆞ고 히 량인은 본국으로 쏫차 보니엿다더라.

○부외조회 외부에서 덕국공관에 조복ᄒᆞ되 향일 귀조회니에 귀국인 수건에 ᄃᆡᄒᆞ야 조사ᄒᆞᆯᄉᆞ로 부위 김병도를 일젼 발일 하오이시에 귀국령ᄉᆞ관으로 귀송케ᄒᆞ라 훈샹을 듯인ᄒᆞ야 원슈부에 공함ᄒᆞ엿더니 함복니에 부위 김병도를 시명훈신 날에 귀송ᄒᆞ마 ᄒᆞ옴을 듯인ᄒᆞ야 조복ᄒᆞ노라ᄒᆞ엿더라

○공부개조 공납부에서 외부로 조회ᄒᆞ되 향일 조복에 일공ᄉᆞ의 소청훈 인쳔 텬시관 즉소 귀지 일ᄉᆞ를 찰셜에 소유귀지라고 조복ᄒᆞ엿더니 추후 샹탐훈즉 청금일인의 슈츅훈바 되단이 실샹 횡셜의 소유 티 단이 아니고로 곳처조회ᄒᆞ노라ᄒᆞ엿더라

○조ᄉᆞ난퇴 쥬일공ᄉᆞ 조민희씨가 면보ᄒᆞ되 본공ᄉᆞ가 리식구일에 발환ᄒᆞᆯ터이니 려본운으로 공ᄉᆞ소무를 티귀케ᄒᆞ라고 면칙ᄒᆞ심을 복망이라ᄒᆞ엿더라

○진리퇴렴 일젼 일공ᄉᆞ 폐현시에 샹쥬ᄒᆞ되 리용익을 쟝차 환국케ᄒᆞ야 셔용ᄒᆞ는 거시 좃소이다ᄒᆞ고 쳔령은 쓸쓰는 거시 손비유ᄒᆞ야 말슴ᄒᆞ오면 게더리 나무우회 올나 가라는 것과 갓소오니 고양이는 쥬제비가 안이면 엇지을는가릿가ᄒᆞ엿다더라

○고빙계약 샹작일 아에 참졍 신샹훈씨가 여각대관이 제회ᄒᆞ야 회의ᄒᆞ엿는ᄃᆡ 젼셜을 듯무론훈즉 일본인 목하면 죵티랑을 탁지부 고문관으로 고빙ᄒᆞ고 미국인 모씨로 외부 고문관 고빙ᄒᆞᆯ수로 합동계약셔를 위젼 초본ᄒᆞ엿다더라

관보

대비 젼구빅오호 광무팔년팔월십오일

서임급사령

임륙군졍위 륙군부위 구의조 팔월팔일

○임평리원판ᄉᆞ 서칙임판ᄉᆞ등 정삼품 리샹텬 의원면본관 중추원의관 김광옥 리승조 리두하 김광식 김대수 최휴철 리계원 리문화 오상영 박대셩 박규희 곽덕녀 중추원참서관 송인회

임중추원의관 서쥬임관륙등 정삼품 안교민 륙품 박남현 김우식 최학영 리틱영 김상연 쟝윤원 리승범 김긔셕 젼영긔 구품 신용휴 구연명

○임중추원참서관 서쥬임관륙등 륙품 리원화

○승서판임관수등 경무청총순 박희옥 이상팔월십일일

○의원면본관 비서원승 임봉호 사종원시종 리귀현 홍문관시독 신응우 평도원쥬ᄉᆞ 김종연 친릉령 리종석 릉신ᄉᆞ 면회과쥬ᄉᆞ 리병지 김셩운 리문피 조셩찬 송연학 리쥬텬

○명궁나부를진관 서칙임판ᄉᆞ등 종이품 김종근 리호셕

○임비서원승 서쥬임관오등 정삼품 홍승무

○임시종원시종 서쥬임관삼등 례식원참리관 오한영

○임례식원쟝리관 서쥬임관삼등 륙품 리귀현

○임홍문관시독 서관임관륙등 륙품 리 현

○임친릉령 서관임관칠등 젼능령 김진형

○임진릉령 서관임관칠등 졍능령 한창리

○임경릉령 서관임관칠등 륙품 리종셕

○임중추원의관 서칙임판ᄉᆞ등 정삼품 김익승

이상팔월십이일

○견칙 한셩재판소쥬ᄉᆞ 김쥰명

서리대신ᄉᆞ무 농상공부협판 리근상

팔월십삼일

궁졍륙ᄉᆞ

○법부대신의졍부의졍 서리 박제순 수직소 비지니에 번거ᄒᆞ수 양 말고 시무ᄒᆞ라

팔월십이일

외보

●리순대승 대한일보 동경젼에 ᄒᆞ엿스되 지부 발젼을 거훈즉 본월십일에 리순항외에서 일아 량국함티가 크게 충돌ᄒᆞ엿다는 말이 잇다ᄒᆞ엿더라

●취륙대젼 동보 동젼에 왈위히위와 지부에서 발훈 면보를 거훈즉 본월팔일에 리순에서 히륙대격젼이 되엿스되 기젼이 티로 결졍이 잇지 안는 일명훈 조션을 드럿는대 겸 운연귀가 연속히 충텬훈다ᄒᆞ엿더라

○마적후린 칠월십구일에 산히관에서 발훈 동신을 거훈즉 십구일에 마적 오쳔명이 발충에 안기가 대단이 쉬인 배을 승구ᄒᆞ야 봉천북방셔 평가에 ᄒᆞ티져 잇는 아병을 겨습ᄒᆞ야 면젼파ᄒᆞᆯ도를 파피ᄒᆞ고 또 소총과 대포탄약과 량식등물을 탈취ᄒᆞ야 갓는ᄃᆡ 다시 탐문훈바를 거훈즉 그 마적등이 진조의 계반운동을 시ᄒᆞᆷ으로 아군은 티단이 념려훈다더라

광고

TELEGRAMS.

THE NAVAL BATTLE.

TOGO'S REPORT.

Tokyo, Aug. 12th.

In the battle on the 10th inst. five or six of the enemy's ships were badly damaged. The two masts of the "Pobieda" were shot away, preventing the use of her big guns. We shelled the flagship (Csarevitch) at a range of 3.500 metres, inflicting severe damage on her. The enemy's cruisers did not appear to be injured.

The repairs to our ships are about completed.

NAVAL ENGAGEMENT NEAR TSUSHIMA.

Tokyo August 14th.

This morning the Russian Cruiser Rurik was discovered by Admiral Kamimura's fleet to the north of Tsushima and after a spirited engagement lasting half an hour was sunk.

The cruiser Terrible, says the Pall Mall Gazette, will live in history as one of the biggest white elephants ever known in the British Navy. From the time she went on trials as an absolutely new ship to the present day, this huge cruiser has been a constant source of expense to the country. Belleville boilers had much to do with her deficiencies. Since she paid off from her last commission in China waters a fortune has been spent on refitting the vessel for future service.

THE JAPANESE PRESS.

HOW IT WAS FOUNDED AND IS PRINTED.

In no other country is the history of the Press so closely associated with the national development as it is in Japan, says the "Globe." The remarkable vitality and elasticity of the national character is nowhere more strikingly exemplified than in the amazing growth of popular literature during the last half-century of the nation's life. The reflection must be a pleasurable one to our countrymen that it is to the initiative of an Englishman that our brave ally owes her present progressive newspaper Press. For it was a certain Mr. Black, an English resident in Yokohama, who in the late sixties published the "Nisshin Shingisha," the first newspaper issued in Japan that was at all worthy of the name. It was a modest sheet, containing a leading article and a number of crisp paragraphs commenting in a chatty way on the news of the day. Now, there is a regular issue of over 1,500 dailies, weeklies, and monthly magazines, about 30 dailies being published in Tokio alone.

Before Mr. Black's time small sheets had been issued from time to time as the occasion arose, these papers being hawked about the streets by a vendor who announced his progress by means of a little bell which was attached to his waistband. Mr. Black's venture having met with fair success, he was soon followed by an enterprising Japanese, a Mr. Kido, who started the "Shimbun Zashi," or New Budget, in Tokio, an enterprise in which he was financially assisted by the Empress, who has ever since given proof of an admirable devotion in the cause of popular education, especially among women and girls. Other and smaller papers soon after made their appearance. But for years Japanese journalism was a most risky business, and one full of vicissitudes. The ranks of the Press writers were mostly filled from the families of the ancient feudal nobles—the Samurai class—and these carried the boldness and dash that had characterised their actions in the days when, armed with two huge swords, they swaggered about among the people, into their new career. The time was not yet ripe for their audacious outspokenness, and the result was that more than 30 per cent. of the journalists were constantly languishing in gaol. But the journalists rose to the occasion, and rather than abandon their criticism of the Government, the newspaper men included on their staffs persons who became known as prison editors. These became the scapegoats for all transgressions of the stringent Press laws, and for a consideration they would readily serve their time in gaol, thus giving the actual writers a free field to indulge in their attacks on the authorities. Nowadays all this is changed, and the Japanese Press at present enjoys a considerable freedom, much more so, indeed, than is the case in certain European countries. To the Western mind a Japanese paper, both in style and preparation, must appear a veritable curiosity of literature.

To begin with, what would be the last page in an English journal is the first in a Japanese one, and the headlines and titles of articles, instead of appearing at the top of a column, are run alongside of it. Now, let us take a glance at the composing-room of a Japanese newspaper. An English typesetter should thank his stars that his lines have fallen in pleasant places. For, see what his brothers in craft in the Land of the Rising Sun have to put up with. The Japanese, like the Chinese, employ a written language—a kind of literary dialect—that is considerably removed from the colloquial. They do not, as we do, write as they speak. This necessitates the papers being printed to an extent in two languages—the "Kana" and the square characters, one acting as a key to the other. The square characters are modelled on the Chinese ideographs, a terrible jumble of geometrical figures, crosses, and zig-zags, the whole effect presenting the appearance of the trial of innumerable inky footprints of drunken flies. Of these ideographs, at least 4,000 to 5,000 are in every day use. So that the compositor must needs be a scholarly man to recognise characters at sight, the strain on the eyes being terrible. In order to facilitate the type-setter's task as much as possible, the composing-room is arranged in the following manner. The compositor is seated at a little table, on which are spread 47 "Kana" characters. On receiving his copy, he cuts it into small strips, and hands each strip to a boy. The latter marches along the room with this strip until finally he has been able to collect from a number of cases the different ideographs. Half-a-dozen boys are thus running hither and thither searching for ideographs, all the time keeping up a dirge-like chant, in which they sing the name of the character they want, as in order to recognise it he has to hear its sound first, no Japanese of the lower classes being even able to read a paper or book unless he reads it aloud. The writer of this article recalls to mind his first night's engagement on a newspaper in Tokio. Hearing a continual babel of voices and sounds of melancholy attempts at vocalisation rising upward from the room below his, he, at a loss to account for the queer noises, asked the Japanese manager whether he conducted a singing class for his compositors. He was at once informed that such was the indispensable accompaniment to a Japanese compositor's work. When the boys have collected all their ideographs, they place them before the compositor, who then has to have recourse to a pair of goggles in order to decipher the characters, fish out the corresponding types in the "Kana" character, and, finally, set up the whole in proof. These proofs, again, are sung out aloud by one proof-reader to another, adding more noise to the bustle and confusion of weird sounds already reigning in the room.

The oldest newspaper is Tokyo is the "Nichi Nichi Shimbun." Its editor, Mr. Seki, has been educated in England and is an expert writer on political subjects. His paper wields a great influence over the educated young Japan party. The most interesting personality, however, in vernacular journalism, was that of Mr. Fukuzawa, lately deceased. This gentlemen, indeed, stood for all that is lofty and ennobling in the spirit of modern Japan. An idealist among an idealist people, he was, however, in no sense a dreamer. One of the first of his nation to recognise the necessity of adding a superstructure of Western culture and science to the ancient strata of Japanese civilisation, he gave the first impetus to the translation into the vernacular of standard foreign works on history, philosophy, science, political economy, &c. To encourage young Japan to study these works he founded in Tokio a private university college, which is now attended by over 1,000 students. He instituted scholarships for languages, history, political economy, &c., and last, but not least, started the "Jiji Shimpo," or "Times"—a journal of broad and independent views, which has been, and still is, a mighty factor in the wonderful advancement of the Era of Enlightenment, as the Japanese have appropriately styled the years of national progress, dating from the Restoration.

Among the rest of the Japanese journals, foremost places must be ascribed to the "Hochi Shimbun," the organ of Count Okuma, the "Mainichi Shimbun," owned by the Speaker of the House of Representatives, the "Tokyo Dempo," a Conservative organ, the "Kokumin," independent, the "Rikogu Zasshi," the mouthpiece of the Christian party, and the "Maru-Maru Shimbun," which is the Japanese "Punch." Mention must also be made of the "Japan Times," an important daily published in English, and inspired by Marquis Ito, the staff of which is entirely composed of Japanese who have been educated in England or the United States.

IMPROVEMENT IN WIRELESS TELEGRAPHY.

Washington, July 17th.—The closing of a contract between the United States government and the De Forest Wireless Telegraph Company for service in the West Indies and at Panama has had the effect of strengthening the claim of that company that a wireless service will be established between the North Pacific coast and China. The company has reiterated its declaration that communication with the Orient will soon be established through a chain of stations at Seattle, Cape Flattery, Dutch Harbour, Kamchatka, Japan and Weihaiwei.

At Panama the highest mast in the world for wireless telegraphy is being erected, while at Cape Flattery the largest station in the world, according to the claims of the De Forest company, is to be established. The station at Dutch Harbour is to be made the key to all Alaska and the Orient.

If the DeForest carries out its plans, which are now largely on paper, a long step forward will soon be taken in wireless communication. It will be possible to send a wireless message from a ship at sea off the New England coast through a chain of stations extending to Japan, China or the Philippines.

The contract just made with the government is especially notable as the largest of its kind ever executed, and the guarantee of the company to maintain at all times communications between stations one thousand miles apart gives assurance that obstacles which have hitherto stood in the way have been surmounted.

There is still a good deal of scepticism, however, about the ability of the company to carry out ambitious plans, but the government stands to lose nothing in the contract, which was executed last week.

The Korea Daily News.

To be published daily except Sundays.
ate of Subscription:—

Per Year,	Yen 25.
Per Quarter,	Yen 7.
Per Month	Yen 2.50

Postage in Korea not charged extra.
Postage abroad charged extra.

Advertisements, 50 sen per day for 1 inch or less.
5 yen per month per inch.
50 yen per year per inch.

All communications to

E. T. BETHELL,
Editor and Publisher.
Pak-tong, Seoul.

NAGAMORI AGAIN.

We could not have asked for a more complete vindication of our condemnation of the Nagamori Scheme than is provided by the defence of it by the "Jiji Shimpo" a leading Tokio newspaper and a staunch supporter of the Japanese Government. The whole tone of the article in the "Jiji" is one of regret that the waste lands scheme was ever put forward but it insists that now it has once been presented, Japanese honour and prestige will suffer a severe blow if it be withdrawn.

If this is the best the "Jiji" can say for the scheme then it stands condemned out of the mouths of its own supporters or those who would be expected to support it if anybody did. It is bad enough to make a mistake of the magnitude of the Nagamori Scheme but it is infinitely worse to persevere in the mistake after its defects have become apparent.

The conclusion of the "Jiji" article is as follows:—

"Our Government cannot be acquitted of the reproach of not having fully thought of the consequences when it supported the Nagamori scheme before setting the main lines of our policy towards Korea. But as our Government, through our Minister in Seoul, has repeatedly pressed the Korean Government to grant the required concession and explained it would be to the common advantage of the two countries, it can no longer be withdrawn even if Korea objects to it. The Koreans have no measure, no gratitude, no sense of right. If they once get an advantage they get puffed up and don't know where to stop. If we withdraw the scheme on account of Korea's objections to it, Japan will lose face in the eyes of the Koreans and our prestige will be lowered. Korea will likewise refuse any demands we may make in the future, and the rights we have in virtue of the treaty of alliance will remain a dead letter. Such a result would be most unfortunate. So we must appoint at once a strong man as adviser to the Korean Court; the judicial administration must be reformed at once, and measures must be devised to enforce the new laws on all who wish to live in the interior and own land, whether Japanese or foreigners. At the same time, we must bring pressure to bear on the Korean Court and push through the Nagamori scheme (even if its operation is to be deferred). We cannot agree with the attacks on the character of Nagamori which only furnish the Koreans with pretexts for opposition and injure our national prestige."

It will be seen that in effect the "Jiji" says the Koreans have "no measure, no gratitude and no sense of right" because they object to a scheme of which it also says the government is not free from reproach for not having fully thought out the consequences of, before it supported it at the present juncture.

The "Jiji" also, apparently not including its own country, makes some sweeping charges against "foreigners" in Korea which would be all the better for a few facts to support them. It says:—

"Not all of them (foreigners), however, are satisfied with enjoying the advantages of peace. Some of them under cover of industrial undertakings are pursuing quite a different object. Such was the Russian timber concession on the Yalu."

So it might have been, but who are the other foreigners that the "Jiji" would persuade its readers are developing sinister designs under cover of commercial enterprise?

All that we have seen written in defence of this waste land scheme is very weak and unconvincing. No one denies that by virtue of the trouble the country has given her Japan is entitled to the lion's share of what good things are going, but a better way of obtaining privileges can surely be found by her statesmen.

ADVICE TO THE GOVERNMENT.

The Japanese Minister has made one or two new suggestions for the bettering of the Korean Government service. He proposes that a Japanese adviser shall be appointed to the Financial department and a foreigner to the Foreign Office, also that the number of troops be further reduced to 1500 and only capable officers be retained. Mr. Hayashi was also received in private audience by His Majesty when a lengthy conversation in secret took place. The result of the discussion has not transpired but His Majesty did not afterwards appear to be greatly perturbed.

By entering into an agreement with England and receiving from her, in exchange for real concessions, the great but dangerous task of clearing up the Morocco muddle, France has undoubtedly played into the hands of the British Foreign Office—"Novoe Vremya," St. Petersburg.

Two Japanese adventurers, posing as delegates of the Relief Society, have been receiving contributions to the fund for the relief of the families of soldiers in the field. Before their swindle was discovered they had collected Y1,440 from gullible citizens of Seoul.

The vessels which were formerly sunk by the Russians at Dalny for the purpose of blockading the port have almost all been refloated. The vessels were painted with some waterproof paint, so that the Russians apparently intended to use them again.

The bodies of three Russians left dead on the field outside Gensan were interred by the Japanese with due ceremony on the 11th inst. Representatives of the Military and Consular bodies as well as many foreigners assisted at the burial.

It appears that the Japanese scouts at Gensan made a numercial error in their report on the Russian advance, causing many troops from Seoul to be sent to the east coast needlessly. It is said that they will be court-martialed.

On the scene of the new railway operations at Woosuhyon on the 11th while a gang of coolies were at work, part of a rocky cutting slid down, killing one Japanese and crushing a Korean badly.

In addition to the Japanese guard at the South and West Gates the Korean gendarme guards there have been augmented by an addition of seven soldiers.

The Korean Minister to Japan leaves Tokyo for a visit to Seoul on the 19th inst.

BALL BEARING GUN.

If all that is claimed for the new "ball-bearing rifled gun," be true, says a rather sceptical expert at home, its introduction would mark the epoch of a revolution in ordnance construction. By the use of "a cylindrical projectile of smooth, hard steel, travelling upon the smooth and almost frictionless path afforded by hard steel ballbearings," Mr. Orlan C. Cullen (it is hardly necessary to add, an American inventor) has introduced a gun that outdoes in velocity, penetration, and range all weapons rifled on the present system. Recoil is done away with, "the tendency of the bullet being rather to drag the gun after it than to kick it away behind it."

The steel balls which fill the rifling grooves are so arranged that when the breech is closed the projectile lies with its head just engaging the first ball in each groove, and thus travels upon a rolling bed offering "the least possible resistance to both its forward and its rotary motions." Mr. Cullen's gun of 303 calibre has a muzzle velocity of 8,200 foot-seconds, and a point blank range of 650 yards. Our new short Lee-Enfield rifle of the same calibre has a muzzle velocity of 2,025 foot-seconds, and a point blank range of about 500 yards. Our service rifle can put its projectile through 72 one-inch boards. The Cullen gun, using the same charge, can penetrate 116 boards of similar thickness. The balls can be easily renewed, and if made of properly hardened steel seldom break. For artillery of heavy calibre the new method will enormously reduce the wear and tear to guns caused by erosion, and the absence of recoil should enormously simplify the question of mounting. Japan, we are told, has contracted to take the whole output of Mr. Cullen's works for two years, and has at present in use twenty 6 pounders and a 4in. gun rifled on Mr. Cullen's system. Altogether, the description is what Americans describe as "tall."

ARRIVAL OF HIPSANG'S CREW AT CHEFOO.

The Captain of the steamer Hipsang, and twenty-three others who were on board the Hipsang when she was sunk by a Russian torpedo boat, arrived at Chefoo on August 8th from Port Arthur. The Mainichi correspondent has succeeded in getting an account of their experiences which he has wired across. The Hipsang, he learns, was stopped by the Russian torpedo destroyer thirteen miles off Iron Island on July 16 .t 5 a.m. The Russians suddenly torpedoed her with the result that, of the crew, five men were killed on the spot, and seven others severely wounded. The wounded and thirty others were conveyed to Port Arthur. On arrival there the wounded were taken to a hospital, while the rest were confined in prison. When the Russians were ordered to send all non-combatants out of the fortress, the Hipsang's people were put in a junk, and told they could sail away, but no food was given them. On the way across the junk met a Japanese torpedo boat, the Commander of which did what he could to relieve her passengers' wants, and a short time afterwards the German steamer Sulberg, under charter to the N. Y. K., came up and took every one on board and conveyed them to Chefoo.

A PRODIGAL KAMNI.

The former Kamni of Chemulpo Mr. So Sang Chip, who recently fled to Shanghai to escape punishment for embezzling 50,000 dollars of Government funds, has returned bringing with him the exact amount of his defalcations. He has been forgiven by the Emperor and it is said he will be reinstated in office.

The Magistrate of Sinchon sends a pitiful wail to the Foreign Office complaining of the desolation of his district, owing to the coolies running away in all directions on hearing of the Japanese demand for labour. He questions them sorrowfully. "How can I supply the Kamni of Chinnampo with 600 coolies, as he requests? I havn't got 6, let alone 600.

The Korea Daily News.

VOL. I, TUESDAY, AUGUST 16, 1904. No. 26

大韓每日申報
대한ᄆᆡ일신보

(뎨이십칠호) (슈요일) 일쳔구ᄇᆡᆨ사년팔월십칠일

본샤고ᄇᆡᆨ

이신보는영어와한어로셔계ᄆᆡ일출판ᄒᆞᄋᆞᆸ

신문가

ᄒᆞᆫ쟝 엽두돈오푼

일삭됴 엽두량닷돈 ᄆᆡᆺ돈으로 밧ᄉᆞᆸ

광고료는

긔한의쟝단과ᄌᆞ항의다쇼로죵갑ᄒᆞ되렴가로밧을터이오며오리지아녀대한사람마다다이신문을보실터이니광고내시기를원ᄒᆞ시ᄂᆞᆫ이들은우리신문사에와서뎡약ᄒᆞ심을희망ᄒᆞᄋᆞᆸ

○발ᄒᆡᆼ소 대한ᄆᆡ일신보사범어학교압헤젼영국인셜필림집자리오

사쟝 영국인 (ᄇᆡ셜)

본샤지뎜

인쳔항교젼동신지명씨로우리대한ᄆᆡ일신보사인항지뎜쟝을ᄐᆡᆨ졍ᄒᆞ엿ᄉᆞ오니인쳔항에계신구람코자ᄒᆞ시ᄂᆞᆫ쳠군ᄌᆞᄂᆞᆫ히지뎜에왕림면의ᄒᆞ시ᄋᆞᆸ

샤고

○우리대한ᄆᆡ일신보의목뎍은대한의안녕질셔에관한모든뎨목에대ᄒᆞ야는공평한변론을쥬쟝흠이라우리동신원의탐보ᄂᆞᆫ신문보시ᄂᆞᆫ쳠군ᄌᆞ의게흥상보도ᄒᆞ려니와편지를긔서ᄒᆞ여주시ᄂᆞᆫ이ᄂᆞᆫ셩명과반ᄃᆡ를젹어붓치시기를희망ᄒᆞ오니이거ᄉᆞᆫ신문상에긔졔ᄒᆞ랴ᄂᆞᆫ거시아니오다만그ᄒᆞᆫ신용ᄒᆞᄂᆞᆫ증거를삼고자흠이라긔자ᄂᆞᆫ아모긔서던지과지흠을퇴각ᄒᆞᄂᆞᆫ권리를가젓ᄉᆞ오나퇴각ᄒᆞᄂᆞᆫ리유를말ᄒᆞᆯ터이오며공중평화를문란케ᄒᆞᄂᆞᆫ듯ᄒᆞᆫ긔서ᄂᆞᆫ의례히밧지안켓ᄉᆞᆸ나이다

론셜

폐막에한로진ᄒᆞᆫ방문

○대저나라의부요흠은쳔리와ᄌᆞ못ᄇᆡᆨ셩의ᄉᆡᆼ근에잇ᄂᆞ니쳔하만국중에쳔리로부요ᄒᆞᆫ나라ᄂᆞᆫ대한이되오자빈평흠은ᄇᆡᆨ셩들이ᄉᆞ업에불근ᄒᆞᆫ연고인데셰계ᄇᆡᆨ셩중에쳔픔으로희ᄐᆡᄒᆞᆷ과흑히ᄐᆡᄒᆞ게될ᄇᆡᆨ셩은대한에셔더심ᄒᆞᆯ나라가엽ᄂᆞᆫ거시이졔불진뎐가히수엽ᄒᆞᆫ만ᄒᆞᆫᄇᆡᆨ셩들노ᄒᆞ여곰신례를보존ᄒᆞ고ᄉᆡᆼ신을졍려ᄒᆞ야편리ᄒᆞ도록ᄒᆞ고ᄒᆞᆫᄒᆞ지못ᄒᆞᆫ셔ᄃᆡ의이요대한에소위대소관리들은남의재물을ᄲᆡ아서비과흠으로주쟝을삼아서필경도식ᄒᆞ야느탈ᄒᆞᄂᆞᆫ밧ᄌᆞ에ᄂᆞᆫ근엽ᄒᆞ고졈박ᄒᆞ야당쵸에마음도먹지아니ᄒᆞ엿든ᄇᆡᆨ셩의게맛친죽이일은졈졈힝ᄒᆞᆯ진데셰계에ᄃᆡ단ᄒᆡ면을이를거시쳥국ᄒᆞᆫ괴ᄌᆞ의말을드른즉히나라이만일유신ᄒᆞ야긔명ᄒᆞ랴ᄒᆞᆯ진데졍법지관이던지자목지임서지라도가히감엽ᄒᆞ야관리ᄒᆞᆯ만ᄒᆞᆫ사ᄅᆞᆷ도잇고ᄇᆡᆨ셩들도명령ᄒᆞᄂᆞᆫ바를응당복죵ᄒᆞᆯ듯ᄒᆞ다고ᄒᆞᄂᆞ우리ᄉᆡᆼ각ᄒᆞ에ᄂᆞᆫ어려울ᄂᆞᆺᄒᆞᆫ거시쳣ᄌᆡ탐학ᄒᆞᄂᆞᆫ악습파남뵈ᄒᆞᄂᆞᆫ폐단이며ᄉᆡᆼ지어죄인빈의쳥젼명식이지라도일졀엄검ᄒᆞᆯ거신계시이려ᄒᆞᆫ셔담으로각부ᄉᆞ무에도취서ᄂᆞᆫ되지안코졈졈갈ᄉᆞ록분경만더ᄉᆡᆼ기며또누구던지ᄉᆞ무에막ᄆᆡᄒᆞ든리도돈만되리면ᄒᆞᄂᆞᆫ엽유들대한셔ᄂᆞᆫ한요ᄒᆞᆫ방침으로아라셔ᄎᆞᄎᆞ로지방관들에셔지폐젓ᄉᆞᆫ즉만일폐지가되ᄂᆞᆫ지경이면자갓흔관리들은비록올경이아니일노명일든ᄒᆞ나우리싱각에ᄂᆞᆫ반다시계칙ᄒᆞᆯ배에ᄌᆞ본되리거ᄉᆞᆯ습ᄒᆞ고ᄒᆞᄂᆞᆫ듯ᄒᆞ고ᄯᅩ이일우힝ᄒᆞ기가ᄉᆡᆼ히어란을듯ᄒᆞᆫ거서당쵸에그사ᄅᆞᆷ들이탐학ᄒᆞᄂᆞᆫ일노비긔ᄒᆞᆫ편든바에실망이되여그런ᄒᆞᆯ듯ᄒᆞ나이런ᄒᆞᆫ일은폐노코힝ᄒᆞ건ᄒᆞ호티남뢰등ᄉᆞ와불법힝위ᄂᆞᆫᄌᆞ괴들도그런즁로아라비밀히ᄉᆞᆷ기ᄂᆞᆫ바ᄂᆞᆫ죠ᄉᆡ로법률을반포ᄒᆞ야법과ᄒᆞᄂᆞᆫᄌᆞ를져관ᄒᆞ야엄ᄌᆞᆼᄒᆞᆯ지경이면이후에ᄂᆞᆫ이일에젹당ᄒᆞ야나며일사ᄅᆞᆷ도엽슬거시요ᄯᅩ졍부에셔도ᄂᆞᆼ히비런ᄒᆞᆫ사ᄅᆞᆷ은파출ᄒᆞ고라도가엽ᄒᆞᆫ사ᄅᆞᆷ을어들만ᄒᆞᆫ죽ᄇᆡᆫ일탐학남뢰등ᄉᆞ을일병엄시ᄒᆞ고유신ᄒᆞ게긔명ᄒᆞᆯ지경이면젼국진보ᄒᆞᄂᆞᆫ티ᄉᆡᆼ히유익ᄒᆞᆯ거시ᄇᆡᆨ셩들의ᄌᆞ유와ᄉᆡᆼ명을보젼ᄒᆞ며국고에셰입이쳥징ᄒᆞ야대한에셔로은시티를불만ᄒᆞ도다

관보

뎨이쳔구ᄇᆡᆨ륙호 광무팔년팔월십륙일

○셔임급ᄉᆞ령

○의원면본관 셩진항경무관 젼계익

○임셩진항경무관셔쥬임관륙등 륙품 졍두남 이샹팔월십이일

○보군부대신관방쟝 륙군부령 한진창 팔월십이일

○의원면본관 비서원승 홍승두 영희뎐령 리기종 령 홍승태 진 ᄉᆞ덕뎐참봉 박영쥰

○비서원승셔쥬임관륙등 궁닉부참셔관 윤쳥구 임뎡부원주ᄉᆞ 셔관임관륙등 류쥬봉 규병완 ᄉᆞ제학 쟝샹학 권명쥬 홍경후 임동호 최경린 박헌동 리근하 박리셩 남졍진 임경긔뎐참봉셔관임관팔등 리졍화 박인승덕뎐참봉셔관임관팔등 박인순 원릉참봉 경릉령셔관임관칠등 리충용 임원릉참봉셔관임관팔등 신현갑 임영희뎐령셔관임관칠등 수직셔령 졍직덕 임수직셔령셔관임관칠등 리봉슈 김봉규 임티복ᄉᆞ주ᄉᆞ셔관임관칠등 최룡현 홍승범 임휘릉령셔관임관칠등 리룡현 윤종섭 임티릉령셔관임관칠등 륙품 리기종 이샹팔월십삼일

○명녀쟝원경셔칙임관삼등 죵이품 홍병진 팔월십ᄉᆞ일

○반기월갑봉 평도원기수 리병철

○일주일즁근신 친위뎨일련ᄃᆡ뎨일ᄃᆡᄃᆡ부소ᄃᆡ쟝륙군보병부위 리졍한 팔월십이일

○희궁리ᄃᆡ신ᄉᆞ무 국부졍관 엄쥬익

○명림시셔리군부대신ᄉᆞ무 ᄒᆞ호위ᄃᆡ총관 민영긔 이샹팔월십ᄉᆞ일

○궁졍록ᄉᆞ

○관도령원ᄉᆞ셔졍순ᄉᆞ직쇼비지닉에쇼쳥ᄃᆡ로의시ᄒᆞ노라

○한셩부관윤김규희언ᄉᆞ쇼비지닉에샹쇼ᄉᆞ연은졍부에셔품쳐ᄒᆞ라

○비쟝원경신경균ᄉᆞ직쇼비지닉에쇼쳥ᄃᆡ로의시ᄒᆞ노라 팔월십ᄉᆞ일

뎐보

논돈팔월구일발

○사원반셜 영국폐난순나와오리엔탈과션항회사사원이타임쓰신문에편지를보내여로국공보에셜명ᄒᆞ기를거션말락카호ᄂᆞᆫ그션쟝이반에실은물목표를보이지아니ᄒᆞᆫ셰문에디ᄒᆞ야반ᄐᆡ이되엿다ᄒᆞᄂᆞᆫ말에ᄃᆡᄒᆞ야반ᄐᆡᄒᆞ여말ᄒᆞ기를그물목표를보앗스나ᄒᆞᆫ고빗사ᄅᆞᆷ들이의용함ᄃᆡ의속ᄒᆞᆫ그션과리쓰ᄇᆡᆨ호에올거셔은여러사ᄅᆞᆷ들도피착된일을벋명ᄒᆞ여둥보ᄒᆞᆫ문서도보변거시잇다ᄒᆞ엿더라

진남포발뎐팔월십이일

○로병남하 로병삼쳔명이남으로버려와지금평양서동북으로일ᄇᆡᆨ오십리되ᄂᆞᆫ(아바은산디경)곳에두류ᄒᆞ엿고평양티대동낭에주교를건너노케다고ᄒᆞᆫ다ᄒᆞ엿더라

동경발뎐팔월십이일 동양수평관보고

○려슌젼격샹보 런합함ᄃᆡᄂᆞᆫ십일에우암부근에뎍군의함ᄃᆡ거를맛나공격ᄒᆞ고그다음에ᄃᆡᆼ합ᄒᆞᆫ슐둥방에츄격ᄒᆞ야오후에시보ᄅᆞᆫ리히지기ᄉᆞ지격젼ᄒᆞ야뎍군의젼투력이대단히만흔지라이젼쟁에가하ᄂᆞᆫ뎍군이온젼히그진형세가착란ᄒᆞ고그포화가대단히쇠ᄒᆞ야각ᄐᆡ가기히리산ᄒᆞ야스ᄭᅩ럿드호와노오빅코호와주아렌비쟈호와팔파ᄡᅡ호와밋구축평수젹은남방으로도망ᄒᆞ고기타모든군함은싱일아층에런슌구로도망ᄒᆞ여드리간듯ᄒᆞᆫ고로그날밤에우리구축뎡ᄃᆡ와밋슈뢰뎡ᄃᆡ의진격흠은지샹보를밋슈퇴지못ᄒᆞ엿고주아렌비쟈호의구축ᄒᆞᆫ죠ᄒᆞᆫ인원과밋부속ᄒᆞᆫ긔구ᄂᆞᆫ횡샹에부동ᄒᆞ며우리함ᄃᆡᄂᆞᆫ대단ᄒᆞᆫ손히ᄂᆞᆫ엽고ᄉᆞ샹ᄒᆞᆫ쟈ᄂᆞᆫ쟝교이하일ᄇᆡᆨ칠십명즘이라ᄒᆞ엿더라

팔월십삼일 공ᄉᆞ관챠뎐

○려순젼격속보 동항ᄉᆞ령쟝관보고ᄅᆞᆯ졉ᄒᆞᆫ즉지작십일젼투에젹의젼함은비샹ᄒᆞᆫ손히ᄅᆞᆯ당흠을아랏고(보빈와)갓ᄒᆞᆫ빈ᄂᆞᆫ돗ᄃᆡ두ᄀᆡ가다부러졋고젹의ᄃᆡ포ᄂᆞᆫ능히쳐ᄅᆞᆫ듯ᄒᆞ게되엿고뎌의긔함도우이젼ᄂᆞᆫ샹쳐오ᄇᆡᆨ미돌

의샹거에셔일군의탄환을마자셔그손히가되단ᄒᆞ엿고져의숀양함은손히가되단치아니ᄒᆞ고다만바야ᄂᆞ은당초에출리치아고일함의손샹ᄒᆞᆫ거ᄉᆞᆫ급히슈리ᄒᆞᆷ을맛쳣다더라

동경십이일발뎐

○지부각국군함 현금지부에졍박ᄒᆞᆫ군함은쳥국군함삼쳑미국군함이쳑법국군함일쳑덕국군함일쳑인ᄃᆡ본일에또덕국군함일쳑이립항ᄒᆞ엿다더라

동경동일발뎐

○엄슈즁립 쳥국졍부에셔지부도ᄃᆡ의게아합을되거케ᄒᆞ고즁립을엄즁히직힐ᄉᆞ의로엄ᄒᆞᆫᄒᆞᆫ다더라

동경십ᄉᆞ일발뎐

○로함격침 샹촌함ᄃᆡᄉᆞ령관의보고를거ᄒᆞᆫ즉로국히삼위함ᄃᆡ삼쳑을ᄃᆡ마도북방에셔맛나류릭크호ᄂᆞᆫ침몰이되고기외이쳑은대손히를당ᄒᆞ고북방으로도쥬ᄒᆞ엿다ᄒᆞ엿더라

십이일원산발뎐

○로병경황 팔월구일원산을음습ᄒᆞᆫ로국긔병부ᄃᆡᄂᆞᆫ되각할시에도로부근민가에돌립ᄒᆞ야지산약탈과부녀겁잔ᄒᆞᄂᆞᆫ포악ᄒᆞᆫ힝위가빈빈ᄒᆞ엿고로병의젼ᄉᆞᄒᆞᆫ시톄ᄂᆞᆫ원산북편삼십리ᄶᅡ에미장ᄒᆞ고륙칠명샹ᄒᆞᆫ쟈ᄂᆞᆫ시려셔로국으로가져갓고로군이버리고간병졍삼인시톄ᄂᆞᆫ십이일에일본군원산슈비ᄃᆡ의손으로미장ᄒᆞᄂᆞᆫᄃᆡ그쟝ᄉᆞ시에일본쟝교하ᄉᆞ병졸과령ᄉᆞ관원과세관관리와외국거류디에잇ᄂᆞᆫ외국션교ᄉᆞ와일본각파즁들이평쟝이회쟝ᄒᆞ엿다ᄒᆞ고또마뎐령을넘어합홍에드러온로병은총슈가일쳔이삼빅명이된다ᄒᆞ며또원산방면에셔되각ᄒᆞᆫ로국긔병은영홍에되각ᄒᆞ야동디에잇든부ᄃᆡ와합ᄒᆞ야일쳔명니외나된다ᄒᆞ며길쥬와셩진에ᄂᆞᆫ오백여명되ᄂᆞᆫ로병이잇고종셩에도오빅명이샹에로병이현로되엿다ᄒᆞ엿더라

잡보

○보쳥역비 기셩권ᄐᆡ익씨가ᄂᆡ부에보고ᄒᆞ되기셩금쳔잔도로슈츅ᄒᆞᄂᆞᆫ역부가일쳔삼빅ᄉᆞ십구인인ᄃᆡ역부고가와목셕지료을본부에쥬차ᄒᆞᄂᆞᆫ일본ᄉᆞ령관의게샹의ᄒᆞᆫ즉ᄃᆡ답이이역ᄉᆞ가귀국도로슈츅인즉역비ᄂᆞᆫ귀국에셔담당ᄒᆞᆷ이가ᄒᆞ다ᄒᆞ오니이역비를즉시획하ᄒᆞ야달나ᄒᆞ엿더라

○리씨가샹 공쥬관찰ᄉᆞ보고ᄂᆡ에경부털도ᄉᆞ원리철영이가연로각군에폐막금단ᄒᆞᆫ일ᄉᆞᄂᆞᆫ임의보고ᄒᆞ엿거니와향일연산군슈가일인의게피타ᄒᆞᆯᄯᅢ에히원의보호를힘닙어셩명을보젼ᄒᆞ엿고또강경포에셔한일량국역부가샹징ᄒᆞ야일쟝젼국이되엿더니히원이불가언번으로효유ᄒᆞ야맛참ᄂᆡ평화케ᄒᆞ엿스니이러ᄒᆞᆫ사ᄅᆞᆷ은샹ᄂᆞᆼᄒᆞᆫ직무를맷겨셔즁인의소망에맛게ᄒᆞ기를바란다ᄒᆞ엿더라

○가평군보 가평군슈가외부에보고ᄒᆞ되일헌병이본군에리도ᄒᆞ야인부를모집ᄒᆞᄂᆞᆫᄃᆡ빅셩이다불원ᄒᆞᆫ즉헌병의말이우리쳥구를시힝시가니ᄒᆞ면반다시아라ᄉᆞ쳥구를좃치랴느냐ᄒᆞ고독촉ᄒᆞ오니이농무방은ᄒᆞᆫᄯᅢ를당ᄒᆞ와자원ᄒᆞᄂᆞᆫ빅셩은ᄒᆞ나도업ᄉᆞ오니엇지억륵으로모집ᄒᆞ올잇가민졍을싱각ᄒᆞ오면극히한심ᄒᆞ다ᄒᆞ엿더라

○울진일인 츈쳔관찰ᄉᆞ쥬셕면씨가외부로보고ᄒᆞ기를울진군슈보고ᄂᆡ에본군죽변포에일인이와셔가옥을결구ᄒᆞᄂᆞᆫᄉᆞᄂᆞᆫ임의치보ᄒᆞ엿거니와음력륙월륙일에일함쳥룡환에벽긔를싯고본포에리박ᄒᆞ야슈십명이하륙ᄒᆞ엿ᄂᆞᆫᄃᆡ그즁에이명은히군일등병조라말ᄒᆞ기를츄후로몃만명이또올터이라ᄒᆞ고그젼에와잇든륙칠십명은다ᄯᅥ나갓다ᄒᆞ엿더라

○한관소비 한셩관윤김규희씨가샹소ᄒᆞᆫ대개를거ᄒᆞᆫ즉한셩부ᄂᆞᆫ즉젼일경죠부라지금도소쟝이호구됴샤와권샹환과민간에ᄉᆞ향시와도로슈축과외인교섭등ᄉᆞ이즁대ᄒᆞᆫ아문이아니라할슈업ᄂᆞᆫᄃᆡ그권리샹당치못ᄒᆞ야직칙을다ᄒᆞᆯ수업ᄂᆞᆫ지라한셩부가ᄂᆡ부에졀제ᄂᆞᆫ의례밧으련니와각원쳥에평등이못되고훈령을밧ᄂᆞᆫ고로ᄉᆞ무가만이구인되ᄂᆞᆫᄃᆡ한셩부가경무쳥과권리가갓지아니ᄒᆞ고로각셔쟝과경찰관리에게능이지휘를힝치못ᄒᆞᄂᆞᆫ고로민졍을담지ᄒᆞᆯ슈업셔ᄉᆞ무가젹체되고또외국인의송ᄉᆞ가한셩부에관계인ᄃᆡ한셩지관소가각셜이되야교졔샹에폐단이충싱쳡츌ᄒᆞ니관계를속히기졍ᄒᆞ야ᄉᆞ무의간격이업게ᄒᆞ소셔ᄒᆞ엿더니비지ᄂᆡ에샹소ᄉᆞ연은졍부에셔픔쳐ᄒᆞ라ᄒᆞ옵셧더라

○죠쳥치도 일본공ᄉᆞ가외부로죠회ᄒᆞ되안쥬의쥬간도로슈축을곳거힝ᄒᆞᆯ터인ᄃᆡ인부와셕공등이불과만여명이니쳥컨ᄃᆡ즉시시힝ᄒᆞ라

○살인방셕 일공ᄉᆞ가외부로죠회ᄒᆞ되일병이졍쥬에셔홍대형자살ᄒᆞᆫᄉᆞ건으로ᄉᆞ령부에동지ᄒᆞ야ᄉᆞ획ᄒᆞᆫ즉그병졍등이기시에피치못ᄒᆞᆯ위급ᄒᆞᆫ경우를당ᄒᆞ야자긔몸을보호ᄒᆞᆫ졍당ᄒᆞᆫ슈단으로ᄒᆞᆫ일인고로임의방셕ᄒᆞ엿노라ᄒᆞ엿다고ᄒᆞ엿다더라

○겸겁도타 황히도관찰ᄉᆞ셔리의뎐보를거ᄒᆞᆫ즉안악신쳔문화은눌쟝련등오군에셔역부를모집ᄒᆞᄂᆞᆫᄉᆞ로민심이경겁ᄒᆞ야거ᄀᆡ도타ᄒᆞᆫ즉모집ᄒᆞᆯ도가만무ᄒᆞ다ᄒᆞ엿더라

○롱증무망 일공ᄉᆞ가일젼 폐현ᄒᆞ기젼에리지용씨를쳥ᄒᆞ야다가말ᄒᆞ되본ᄉᆞ가시졍개션ᄒᆞᆯ모ᄉᆞ건를샹쥬ᄒᆞᆯ터이니속히 폐현케ᄒᆞ라ᄒᆞ고위협ᄒᆞ거ᄂᆞᆯ동씨가일ᄉᆞ의말ᄂᆞᆫ미리샹쥬ᄒᆞ엿더니급기 폐현시에일ᄉᆞ가리씨ᄃᆡᄒᆞ야셜명ᄒᆞ든ᄉᆞ건을 샹쥬치아니ᄒᆞᆫ지라자샹으로리씨의무망ᄒᆞᆷ을통증이녀기신다더라

○보관연회 지작일요일에황셩신문사에셔각부대관을쳥요ᄒᆞ야연ᄃᆡᄒᆞ엿다더라

○쇼환공ᄉᆞ 젼셜을득문ᄒᆞᆫ즉젼국지졍을졍리ᄒᆞᄂᆞᆫᄃᆡ경비감싱ᄒᆞ기위ᄒᆞ야각국의쥬차ᄒᆞᆫ대한공ᄉᆞ를일졔히소환ᄒᆞᆫ다고들ᄒᆞ더라더라

○형졔형졔 마동사ᄂᆞᆫ젼봉산군슈졍시화씨가져자ᄂᆡ에감옥셔에피슈ᄒᆞ엿다가일젼에몽방이되야그집에나온즉그쳡이다른사ᄅᆞᆷ과사ᄂᆞᆫ지라그리유를담지ᄒᆞᆫ즉쳡동셔채쥬ᄉᆞ규록이가졍씨의체슈ᄒᆞᆷ을승시ᄒᆞ야쳡졔를ᄶᅦ여제아오규방을쥬어쳡을삼엇다ᄒᆞ니가위외형졔ᄂᆡ형졔라고들말ᄒᆞ며채씨가남의불힝ᄒᆞᆫᄯᅢ를승시ᄒᆞ야그사ᄂᆞᆼ의가속을유인ᄒᆞ니자긔ᄂᆞᆫ능소로여기ᄂᆞᆫ지모로거니와남들와채씨의힝위를엇더다ᄒᆞᆯᄂᆞᆫ지

○참령자현 참령박유ᄐᆡ씨집에일헌병이슈탐ᄒᆞ거ᄉᆞᆫ본신문에지차긔저ᄒᆞ엿거니와박씨가함경남도안변군셕왕ᄉᆞ에피셔차로가잇다가그집슈탐ᄒᆞᆷ을듯고원산감리셔에가셔일본령ᄉᆞ관으로긔별ᄒᆞ기를나를잡으라ᄒᆞ다니무삼연고가잇ᄂᆞ냐ᄒᆞ고동긔ᄒᆞ엿더니일헌병이와셔착거ᄒᆞᄂᆞᆫᄃᆡ박씨의말이ᄂᆡ가김인슈와의형졔ᄒᆞ엿다ᄒᆞ고잡아가되나ᄂᆞᆫ과연김인슈와상동이업다고셜명ᄒᆞ엿다더라

○회샤쟈본 외부에셔일공관으로공함ᄒᆞ기를농광회샤쳘폐ᄒᆞᆫ일은이미공문ᄒᆞ엿거니와그회샤가창셜초에문자본금을구집ᄒᆞ엿거ᄂᆞᆯ귀함ᄂᆡ에곳쳐를엇어자본ᄒᆞᆫ다고셩언ᄒᆞ엿고또각신문에관츌되엿스니그외쳐엇ᄂᆞᆫ다ᄂᆞᆫ일은당초에언론치도아니ᄒᆞ엿ᄂᆞᆫᄃᆡ어ᄃᆡ셔그말을드럿ᄂᆞ냐ᄒᆞ엿더라

○경ᄉᆞ담관 경무ᄉᆞ신ᄐᆡ휴씨가일본군ᄉᆞ샹일을반ᄃᆡᄒᆞᆫ다ᄒᆞ고일공령ᄉᆞ와ᄉᆞ령관이탄희ᄒᆞᄂᆞᆫ고로일젼에신경무ᄉᆞ가일본령ᄉᆞ를심방ᄒᆞᆫ즉령ᄉᆞ가업ᄂᆞᆫ고로일본ᄉᆞ령관을샹봉ᄒᆞ야담관ᄒᆞ기를관유민우ᄃᆡ를물론ᄒᆞ고우미ᄒᆞᆫ빅셩들이일인의게압미ᄒᆞᄂᆞᆫ고로ᄂᆡ빅셩을착징ᄒᆞ엿고황셩ᄂᆡ에표목을세우며각문에일슌ᄉᆞ로파슈ᄒᆞᄂᆞᆫ고로경찰직칙을의ᄒᆞ야쳘환ᄒᆞᆷ을쳥ᄒᆞ엿슨즉이ᄉᆞ건이무슴반ᄃᆡ냐ᄒᆞ엿더니ᄉᆞ령관이말ᄒᆞ기를일본을비쳑ᄒᆞᄂᆞᆫ보안회원을압송ᄒᆞ엿더니즉시방송ᄒᆞ엿다ᄒᆞᄂᆞᆫ지라신경무ᄉᆞ가말ᄒᆞ기를산림쳔ᄐᆡᆨ문뎨로즁의를취용ᄒᆞ야샹소ᄒᆞᆫ차로회의ᄒᆞᆫ사ᄅᆞᆷ을무슴죄가잇다고시형ᄒᆞ며또지관소로이슈ᄒᆞᆫ후에방송여부ᄂᆞᆫ내가알것아니라각항경찰은일층엄명이ᄒᆞᆯ터이니각문파슈헌병을것어가라ᄒᆞᆫ즉본ᄉᆞ령부훈령이잇슨즉것어갈슈업다ᄒᆞ엿다더라

○일축경관 일본령ᄉᆞ가경위원총관의게죠회ᄒᆞ기를원산항경무관홍슌국ᄃᆡ에박ᄐᆡ호로셔임ᄒᆞ라ᄒᆞ엿더라

○일포최민 지작일에젼쥬거ᄒᆞᄂᆞᆫ최홍여라ᄒᆞᄂᆞᆫ사ᄅᆞᆷ을일헌병이포착ᄒᆞ야남문으로드러와셔ᄉᆞ령부로잡아가드라더라

○슌슈부지 본월십오일에리지용씨집ᄂᆡ힝이동문외에출거ᄒᆞ야물맛ᄂᆞᆫᄃᆡ죠흔산슈를구ᄒᆞ고자ᄒᆞ야리대신이동셔에긔별ᄒᆞ되슌산슌검의게지휘ᄒᆞ야죠흔산슈를지시ᄒᆞᆫ즉셔쟝이대답ᄒᆞ되슌산슌검이슌산은ᄒᆞ엿거니와슌슈ᄂᆞᆫ부지라ᄒᆞ엿다더라

○쥬본쳐분 일젼에 대ᄂᆡ에셔ᄂᆡ부대신을명초ᄒᆞ샤현과된슈령을셔임ᄒᆞ라ᄒᆞ셧고현쳡군슈를ᄒᆞ의쥬본ᄒᆞ라신쳐분이루차계셧ᄂᆞᆫᄃᆡ현영운씨가쥬권ᄒᆞ야공평치안니ᄒᆞᆫ죠짐이잇ᄂᆞᆫ고로의졍셔리박졔슌씨ᄂᆞᆫ그ᄉᆞ샹을료량ᄒᆞ야누문ᄉᆞ긱ᄒᆞ고져차ᄉᆞ직샹소ᄒᆞ엿더라

○보감역부 경긔관찰ᄉᆞ가보고ᄒᆞ기를일인소쳥역부을쳔이빅명ᄂᆡ에칠빅명을특별이감익ᄒᆞ야빅셩을안도케ᄒᆞ라ᄒᆞ엿더라

○량군소요 김포군에역부삼빅명을모집ᄒᆞᄂᆞᆫᄃᆡ당초에자원ᄒᆞᄂᆞᆫ자업고민요가대긔ᄒᆞ엿다ᄒᆞ고과쥬군에도역부모집ᄉᆞ로대단소요ᄒᆞ다ᄒᆞ더라

○미음회샤 일본인이하남촌에미음ᄒᆞᄂᆞᆫ계집회샤를셜시ᄒᆞᆯ차로가옥을미슈ᄒᆞᄂᆞᆫ즁이라더

TELEGRAMS.

BATTLE BETWEEN DESTROYERS IN CHEFOO HARBOUR.

Tokyo, Aug. 14th.

On the night of Aug. 10th as our destroyers Asahio and Tsuyu were cruising in search of the enemy's squadron, they sighted a Russian destroyer steaming full-speed westward. They started in pursuit but lost sight of her in the darkness. On the next morning they found her in Chefoo harbour and after waiting some time to see if she would come out Commander Fujimoto took our destroyers inside the harbour. Lieutenant Terashima was sent to request the enemy to come out and give battle or surrender. As soon as his message was delivered the Russian commander gave the order to fire on the destroyers and at the same time picked up Lieutenant Terashima and threw him into the sea. The official interpreter was likewise dealt with by one of the Russian crew. After a short engagement we overcame and captured the enemy's vessel.

Our casualties were 1 non commissioned officer killed and 13 men wounded.

RUSSIAN DESTROYERS WRECKED.

Tokyo, Aug. 14th

On the 11th inst. two Russian destroyers ran aground to the East of Weihaiwei. Their captains landed and after walking for 20 hours succeeded in obtaining the assistance of a British gunboat, which went to the assistance of the shipwrecked crews of the destroyers.

CSAREWITCH OUT OF ACTION.

Tokyo August 14th.

The Russian battleship Csarewitch is anchored off Kiauchao and is disarming.

Tokyo August 14th

One Russian destroyer which ran ashore near Weihaiwei has been rescued by a British steamer and will be taken to Hongkong.

PORT ARTHUR.

TIT-BITS OF NEWS.

Tokyo, Aug. 15th.

The Kasuga, recently reported sunk, is undamaged. It is said that the Diana has run up the Yangtse for safety. It is considered that Port Arthur cannot now hold out for longer than four days.

THE SALVATION ARMY CONGRESS.

A PATRIOTIC JAPANESE OFFICER.

London, July 1st.

The International Salvationist Congress that is being held this week, with its picturesquely-clad delegates from every quarter of the globe, its banners, its processions, and its daily audiences of enthusiastic thousands, demonstrates to the world in a concrete and unmistakable fashion the extraordinary results achieved by General Booth's organization. The Japanese contingent, which includes "Staff Captain" Yamamura, editor of the Japanese "War Cry," met with a rousing reception.

At the conclusion of the proceedings on the 25th, Staff-Captain Yamamura wound up the gathering in an amusing manner. The little man, says the "Daily News" reporters, could not keep the Russian war out of his remarks, in spite of several good-humoured warnings from the General. "Never mind, I pray every morning for Russia as well as for Japan," he said. He was getting on very well until a fatal reference to the war made the General push him back to his seat amid much laughter. This is how it happened. "We want to grow in education and religion in Japan," he said. "Japan does not close its heart to anything; we only close Port Arthur." Here the little man was overwhelmed. But somebody cried "God bless Japan!" He responded with "Alleluia!"

A meeting at Exeter Hall on 27th ult. was styled on the programme, "The Salvation of Asia." "Colonel" Bullard, the "Commanding Officer" in Japan, said that the Japanese were a small people, but they were capable of great achievements. The Salvation Army's work in that land was fairly satisfactory. They had 13 corps in Tokyo, and though they had only been engaged in the country eight years, they had won the confidence of the people from the highest to the lowest. Their leading men had expressed a very high appreciation of the work done by the Army amongst the natives. They maintained a Prison Gate Mission and other Missions amongst the poor, and they were now regarded by the masses as their special friends. All the doctors in Tokyo attended their members free of charge. "Staff Captain" Yamamura, of Tokyo, also gave an interesting account of the work carried on by the Army in his country.

THE POPE AND JAPAN.

London, July 1st.

The Pope on 26th ult. received in private audience Monsignor Mugabure, Coadjutor of the Roman Catholic Archbishop of Tokyo. His Holiness discussed the situation in Japan and the events of the War, expressing his satisfaction at the complete liberty which Roman Catholics enjoy in Japan. According to the "Petit Parisien," Pius X. confirmed the announcement that a few days before the outbreak of the war he had done all in his power to induce the Czar to maintain peace in the spirit of The Hague Conference, of which he had been the promoter. The Czar replied courteously, but in terms showing that war had become inevitable. In Mgr. Mugabure's opinion the Japanese upper classes are more and more inclined to favour the Christianization of their country. The Pope was deeply moved on learning that many soldiers in the Japanese army had fulfilled their religious duties as good Roman Catholics before starting for the war. His Holiness promised shortly to transform the present Bishopric of Tokyo into an Archbishopric, and commissioned Mgr. Mugabure to present to the Mikado his thanks for the great tolerance shown to Roman Catholics.

An Eastern inventor has produced a submarine sound receiver which he expects will meet all the requirements of the case. A test has been made with it in a mackerel smack off the Massachusetts coast which proved eminently successful so far as the detection of an in visible paddle-wheel steamer's presence was concerned. By the end of the submerged receiver the captain of the fishing craft equipped with the apparatus heard plainly the noise of the paddle wheels of an approaching steamer at night while she was three miles off. At the time she was invisible, and the noise of her paddle wheels was indistinguishable from the deck. But in the case of a paddle wheel steamer the noise is created by the pounding of the surface of the water and the explosion of an air cushion. The utility of the device as a submarine detector depends upon whether or not the submarine boat makes any noise with her propeller when moving through the water submerged. If her propeller works noiselessly the new device will be no safeguard against her insidious method of attacking.

Mr. Hall Caine has gone to Iceland for the background of the new play upon which he is now engaged. "The Prodigal Son," as it is called, will first be published in serial form as a story. The theme handled is the misdeeds of a younger son who brings ruin and disgrace upon his family and then leaves home to try to recover their lost honour and fortunes. By the love of a good woman he is stimulated to worthy endeavour and becomes a wealthy and prosperous man. Then after many years he returns to his old home to find his father dead and poverty and desolation in the household. Being unrecognised, he begs for shelter, and in the home he had wrecked is invited to pass the night. Then a terrible temptation comes to the impoverished family to rob this supposed stranger, and in a fight that ensues between the two brothers the prodigal is killed. It will make a play of strong emotions. and the setting of the Iceland scenes promises to reveal some new stage effects.

Popular favour came to the late George Gissing too late to enable him to make adequate provision for children, and a small pension has been bestowed upon the sons of the novelist from the Royal Civil List "in consideration of the services to literature of their father, and of their straitened circumstances." The name of Sir W. Laird Clowes, "in recognition of his services to naval literature," also appears in this list, as does that of Mrs. Charlotte Stopes; while there is a remembrance of Crimean days in the Civil List as well as in the Birthday Honours, in the pension given to Mrs. Lucy Allen. It comes as a recognition of the services of her late husband, Mr. R. Roberts, Master R. N., in connection with the disembarkation of troops during the Crimean War. The wife of the late Phil May, the black-and-white artist, receives a pension.

Another advice of the Japanese government is that Yi Yong-ik, at present in Japan, should be recalled and given a good post in the government, while the services of Mr. Hyon Yong-woon do not seem to be regarded with much favour.

The Japanese Government has issued a demand to the Foreign Office for the repair of the Anju-Wiju road. Ten thousand coolies and stone-masons must be employed.

On the 15th inst the Japanese Minister entertained the Minister for Foreign Affairs, and the chief of Korean gendarmes at dinner at the Legation.

Three sorcerers, wizards of exil fame, have been arrested under the new prohibition act.

By late advices we learn that Mr. Yi Yong Ik will return to Korea about the 20th inst.

The Korea Daily News.

To be published daily except Sundays.

Rate of Subscription:—

Per Year,	Yen 25.
Per Quarter,	Yen 7.
Per Month	Yen 2.50

Postage in Korea not charged extra.
Postage abroad charged extra.

Advertisements, 50 sen per day for 1 inch or less.
5 yen per month per inch.
50 yen per year per inch.

All communications to

E. T. BETHELL,
Editor and Publisher,
Pak-tong, Seoul.

THE COOLIE QUESTION.

The difficulties which the Japanese are experiencing in collecting the coolies which they so urgently require for purposes in connection with the war are evidence that their contention that the Koreans are difficult people to deal with is not without justification.

As we have said before we consider the request a perfectly reasonable one and the Korean Government should leave no stone unturned to ensure its being complied with. And yet, from the reports which come in from the country it would appear that the various local authorities are treating the request in anything but a complaisant spirit. From the tone of their despatches it is impossible to believe that they are doing their best to collect the coolies they have been asked for. The unanimity with which they reply that all the coolies are engaged in agriculture at this season and cannot be dispensed with is a little suspicious. Their immediate object is probably to save themselves trouble but it is possible that they are also actuated by vague motives of hostility to Japan.

Whatever their motives may be there is every indication that they are not doing their best and a message from their Government that the request is not to be trifled with would probably have a salutary effect.

REFORM.

There is a prospect that some of the reforms which it is announced that the government will institute upon the advice of the Japanese Minister will lead to a better state of things in this country. The recall of Mr. Yi Y[illegible]ik we look upon as a happy [illegible] future. Stability and fixit[illegible] are not characteristic of the Ko[illegible]nd a man of his strength of character and integrity should be of great assistance. With a few strong men at the head of the government reforms which are at present impossible would come within the range of practical politics.

Corruption has been such an accepted fact here and is so firmly rooted that it is difficult to say where the first blow should be struck. It seems probable that any attempt at radical interference with various local officials would not be properly understood and would cause a great deal of discontent—or worse. If the reform commences from the head of the government it may be possible to institute a gradual improvement in the service and we sincerely hope it may prove to be so.

The apparently impossible is often accomplished, and a few strong men, bent on reform, with the power to put their proposals into effect, would soon work a wonderful improvement in the condition of Korea.

A HIGH OLD KETTLE OF FISH.

The following is from a report of a "Daily Mail" correspondent's alleged interview with an alleged Russian Prince at St. Petersburg:—

"The Japanese," he drawled, "the more they make war, the more they are European. But we, the longer we fight, the more we are Easterns, and some day we will be—how is it?—seriously annoyed. With her back against the wall of a partisan Europe, rearing, however to chip in, Russia will—er—come out wonderfully. Like a rat in a corner. It is our way. These etiquettes of fighting, these punctilios of making dead people, they cramp our style. But when we get our shirt out, as Rudyard Shakespeare says, then there will be a high old kettle of fish. There will be such a war as is not written of, a devastation, a fight to a finish, with nobody to say, "Oh, fie!" when there is a hit under the zone, and nobody shout, "Please come out of it," when one is down and the other is engorging him. Think, only!"

He shook his head meditatively.

"There has not been a war," he declared. "No in verity, a war of the true actual. War is the end of law, and it is proper to kill wounded and hang prisoners and torture spies and poison water. It is the real thing, but uneasy to do. Yet conceive a great people of Easterns fighting for very life, what shall they stop at? What can you forbid, with all to lose—life, credit, power, an' all an'all? And fighting you must cogitate, not with a people like them, but with a race they regard like yellow niggers, impertinents, insolents, with a blooming cheek, coming out of the East to be cock of the walk. Ah, but Russia will engage herself. She will take off her coat, and gird up her groins, and tuck in her tuppenny—all Russia, the people and the Government fighting together with money and blood and brains, like the boys of the old brigade. But not yet, mark! Not simply for the Petropavlovsk and Port Arthur. No! she will take a hand when there is danger, so near that it can kindle what is not easy to find in the Russian—his imagination. Ah, but once that is done, we shall be busy, and there will be wigs on the lawn."

"Oh! it is no end of game to be an Eastern," he concluded. "When you have come to the conclusion of your humanity, you have a fine animal left. It is not only the Western that can make a hog of himself, but you will find that when Russia is forced to it she can be simply beast."

REDUCTION OF EXPENSES.

MINISTERS TO BE RECALLED.

The Government in order to reduce expenses, has, at the advice of the Japanese Government, decided to recall her Ministers from all foreign countries. It is further said that the staff of foreign employés in various departments will be reduced.

The Japanese have advised that an American subject at present connected with their Embassy in Washington, be appointed as adviser to the Foreign Office.

PROPOSED CELEBRATION OF THE FALL OF PORT ARTHUR.

On the 13th inst. a meeting of prominent Japanese residents was held in their club with the object of deciding in what manner the occupation of Port Arthur by their troops, an event which they consider to be imminent, shall be celebrated.

The usual lantern procession has of course been agreed upon but this time it has been arranged upon an organised plan. Led by the entertaining committee and with the Korean band in attendance the whole population of the Japanese settlement will march through Chinkokai to the Palace, thence proceeding to the old Palace and returning to the hillside near the Japanese Legation when they will partake of an "at fresco" supper with its accompaniment of much beer and "sake." A feature of the procession will be dummy artillery which will give a Martial aspect, symbolic of the occasion celebrated.

ASSASSIN'S LETTER.

The Stockholm "Aftonblad" publishes a copy of a letter to the Emperor of Russia, the original of which was found on the body of Herr Schaumann after the murder of Gen. Bobrikoff. The letter is as follows:—

"Sir,—Through the Senate, which is obedient to Gen. Bobrikoff, the latter has succeeded in creating lawlessness in Finland. Through lies and false representations, Gen. Bobrikoff and M. von Plehwe have induced your Majesty to issue ordinances incompatible with the Finnish laws which at your accession to the Crown you promised to guard firm and unshaken. The best officials of the State are removed without trial, to give place to fortune-hunters and persons to whom the laws of Finland give no right to occupy State offices. The most intelligent and the truest subjects are banished. M. von Plehwe, whose duty it is to report to your Majesty on all matter concerning the Grand Duchy of Finland, is not a Finlander, and has no knowledge of Finland's laws and customs, and he has common interests with Gen. Bobrikoff. Therefore, your Majesty will never get true knowledge of the real situation. As it is not probable that the real situation will be known to you in the near future, unless Gen. Bobrikoff can be removed, there is only one way to take in self-defence for rendering him innocuous. The remedy is violent, but it is the only one. Your Majesty, I have done my deed alone, after mature deliberation. In the moment of death I swear by God there is no conspiracy. Knowing the good heart and noble intentions of your Majesty, I implore you solely to seek information regarding the real situation in the whole empire, including Finland, Poland, and Baltic provinces. I am, with deepest veneration, your Majesty's most humble and truest subject.—(Signed), EUGEN SCHAUMANN."

SUBMARINE SIGNALING.

The introduction of submarine boats into naval warfare has created a demand for something that will reveal their presence in the neighbourhood of the vessels they contemplate attacking. Battleships and cruisers are able fairly well to protect themselves against the assault of invisible torpedoes by the use of submerged netting suspended to the depth of their keels by outstanding booms. It has been suggested that a submerged searchlight might be effectively used to ward off night attacks of submarines, but the objection to their use is that they would serve as a sure guide for the attacking craft to find her intended prey. But, however, effective a searchlight might prove in the night, it would manifestly be of no value in the daytime.

The Prefect of Kai Sung reports that having received instructions to repair the road between Kai Sung and Keunchon he applied for funds, to the Japanese military authorities, wherewith to buy materials and pay the 1,300 coolies who will be employed. They replied that the payment was the duty of the Korean Government.

At the last General Meeting of the Dai Ichi Ginko it was decided to increase the reserve fund by Y150,000, thus making a total reserve of Y1,500,000.

The warships anchored in Chefoo on the 12th inst. were 3 Chinese, 2 American, 1 French and 1 German.

A Korean named Choi Hong Yo, who resides at Djou-Chu was, arrested at at his home by Japanese gendarmes and conducted to the army headquarters on the 15th inst.

A Japanese soldier, who was tried for the murder of one Hong Dai Hyong at Djengchu has been acquitted. His justification of the act lay in self-defence.

The Russian telegraph line on the east coast now reaches south to Songchin in direct communication with Vladivostok.

Complaints of the difficulty of collecting coolies still pour in from magistrates of all districts.

The Korea Daily News.

VOL. I, WEDNESDAY, AUGUST 17, 1904. No. 27

HONGKONG & SHANGHAI BANKING CORPORATION.

Paid-up Capital..... ....$10,000,000
Reserve Fund:—Sterling Reserve... 10,000,000
Silver Reserve..... 6,500,000

26,500,000
Reserve Liability of Proprietors... 10,000,000

HEAD OFFICE, HONGKONG.

London Bankers, London and County Banking Company Limited.
Branches and Agencies, London.

Amoy,	Hankow	Penang,
Bangkok,	Hiogo,	Rangoon,
Batavia,	Iloilo,	Saigon,
Bombay,	Lyons,	San Francisco,
Calcutta,	Manila,	Singapore,
Colombo,	Nagasaki,	Sourabaya,
Foochow,	New York,	Tientsin,
Hamburg,	Peking,	Yokohama,

Credits granted on approved Securities, and every description of Banking and Exchange business transacted.

Drafts granted on London and the chief Commercial places in Europe, India, Australia, America, China and Japan.

HOLME RINGER & Co., AGENTS, CHEMULPO.

ON CHEONG & CO., SEOUL.
GENERAL STORE KEEPERS.
Imported provisions, Cooking Utensils Crockery, etc.
FRESH BREAD DAILY.

MITSU BISHI DOCKYARD & ENGINE WORKS,
NAGASAKI.

CODE WORD, "DOCK."

A. 1, A. B. C., and Engineering Codes used.

DOCK No. 1 (at Tategami).

Extreme Length..............523 feet
Length on blocks .... 513 ,,
Width of Entrance on Top......89 ,,
,, ,, Bottom....77 ,,
Water on Blocks at Spring Tide 26½ ,,

DOCK No. 2 (Mukaijima).

Extreme Length..............371 feet
Length on Blocks.............360 ,,
Width of Entrance on Top......66 ,,
,, ,, Bottom 53 ,,
Water on Blocks at Spring Tide 22 ,,

PATENT SLIP (at Kosuge).

Can take vessels up to 1,000 tons gross.

THE WORKS are well equipped with the LATEST IMPROVEMENTS, and can execute any kind of work in SHIPBUILDING and MARINE ENGINEERING, as well as in REPAIRING of SHIPS.

The COMPANY'S new powerful steamer OURA-MARU (712 tons, 700 I.H.P.), specially built for SALVAGE PURPOSES, and equipped with necessary gear, is always READY at SHORT NOTICE.

CHARTERED BANK OF INDIA AUSTRALIA & CHINA.

INCORPORATED BY ROYAL CHARTER 1853

HEAD OFFICES:—LONDON.

Paid-up Capital £800,000
Reserve Liability of Shareholders 800,000
Reserve Fund 725,000

Drafts granted upon all the principal places in the world and every description of Exchange and banking business transacted.

E. MEYER & Co., Agents, Chemulpo.

E. MEYER & CO.
Chemulpo.

SOLE AGENTS IN KOREA FOR:
A. T. Morse, Sons & Co's "Fresco" Distemper

In all colours ready for use on walls, Ceilings etc.
and
AVENARIUS CARBOLINEUM

A wood-preserving and antiseptic oil preparation

Against decay, dry-rot, fungus and wood-destroying insects.

A large supply always in Stock.
Prices upon application.

E. MEYER & Co., Chemulpo.

LAW UNION & CROWN INS. CO.
Fire risks accepted at Current rates, on go downs, merchandise, dwellings, and other property, subject to usual conditions.
HOLME RINGER & Co., Agents, Chemulpo

THE METHODIST PUBLISHING HOUSE,
Little West Gate, Seoul.

JOB PRINTING, TYPEWRITER PAPER
CARBON PAPER, VISITING CARDS
STATIONERY, BOOK BINDING
BOOK PUBLISHERS
AMERICAN SCHOOL BOOKS
SPENCERIAN COPY BOOKS
PEN CARBON LETTER AND BILL BOOKS

S. A. BECK, Manager

DAI-ICHI GINKO.
LIMITED.
(Formerly the First National Bank)

ESTABLISHED 1873

INCORPORATED UNDER PRESENT LAW 1896

Capital - - - - - - - - - Yen 5,000,000
Reserve Fund - . - - - - - " 1,500,000

HEAD OFFICE:—TOKIO.

President: Baron SHIBUSAWA.

BRANCHES AND CORRESPONDENTS
In the Principal Cities and Towns of Japan.
Interest Allowed on
Fixed deposits 1 year - - - 6½ per cent
" " 6 months - - - 6 per cent

Special current accounts 1½ sen daily per Y 100
General " " 1 " " " 100

M. TANAKA, Manager, Chemulpo.

HOLME RINGER & Co.
Chemulpo.

General Merchants and Government Contractors.

Agents for the leading
Banks
SteamshipCompanies
and
Insurance Companies

Importers of Merchandise of every description.

KAMEYA & CO.
GENERAL STOREKEEPERS
Chinkokai - - Seoul
(*Established 1895, Tokyo*)

Confectionery, Hams, Canned Goods, Cutlery, Hirano & Tansan Water. Provisions, Gents, Furnishing goods, Toilet Articles, Travelling Bags, Tobacco, Cigars & Cigarettes Kitchen Utensils. Coffee, Biscuits

Fresh Goods always kept in Stock.
Prices Moderate
Please come and inspect our goods.

NIPPON YUSEN KAISHA.
JAPANESE MAIL STEAMSHIP CO.
DER MAIL CONTRACT WITH THE IMPERIAL JAPANESE GOVERNMENT.

European Line
Regular Fortnightly Service between Yokohama, Kobe, Moji, Shanghai, Hongkong, Singapore, Penang Colombo, Port Said, Marseilles, London and Antwerp

American Line
Regular Fortnightly Service between Hongkong and Seattle, calling at Shanghai, Moji, Kobe, Yokohama and Victoria, B. C.

Australian Line
Regular weekly Service betwen Japan Ports and Australia, calling at Hongkong and Manila.
(Above Three Lines Suspended until further notice).

Shanghai Line
Weekly Service between Shanghai and Japan Ports

Korea Line
Service Kobe, Moji, Nagasaki, Fusan, Chemulpo, Choo, Taiku.
S. S. Bahelsberg, 2181 tons.
Service Kobe, Moji, Fusan, Chemulpo, Chinnampo
S. S ARGO. S. S. Ohio.

BORDEN'S CONDENSED MILK CO.
New York, U. S. A.

ALWAYS IN STOCK
Eagle Brand Condensed Milk.
Gold Seal Condensed Milk.
Peerless (Family) Evaporated Cream.
Borden's Malted Milk.

E. MEYER & CO.
Chemulpo, Korea,
Sole Agents

ROYAL INSURANCE COMPANY,
Funds exceed £10,000,000
FIRE
AT CURRENT RATES.
LIFE
REDUCED PREMIUM.
HOLME RINGER & Co., Agents, Chemulpo.

HOTEL DU PALAIS
SEOUL.

The only first class Hotel in Seoul. Situated in the centre of the city opposite the palace.

Cuisine under the supervision of an experienced French Chef.

Well ventilated and furnished throughout.

TARIFF UPON APPLICATION

L. MARTIN,
Proprietor and Manager

大韓每日申報
대한미일신보

(뎨이십팔호)　(목요일)　일쳔구빅사년팔월십팔일

본사고빅

이신보는영어와한어로셔계미일츌판ᄒᆞ옵

신문가

ᄒᆞᆫ쟝 엽두돈오푼

일삭됴엽두량닷돈 맛돈으로밧ᄉᆞᆸ

광고료는

긔한의쟝단과ᄌᆞ힝의다쇼로쥬감ᄒᆞ되련가로밧을터이오며오릭지아녀대한사ᄅᆞᆷ마다다이신문을보실터이니광고버서기를원ᄒᆞ시는이들은우리신문사에와셔면약ᄒᆞ심을희망ᄒᆞ옵

○발힝소 대한반동미일신보사발어하교엽헤 젼영국인셜필립졍자리오

사쟝 영국인 (비셜)

본사지졈

인쳔항교쟝동신지명씨로우리대한미일신보사인쳔항지졈쟝을틱졍ᄒᆞ엿ᄉᆞ오니인쳔항에계신구람ᄒᆞ코자ᄒᆞ시는쳠군ᄌᆞ는히지졈에왕림면의ᄒᆞ시옵

사고

○우리대한미일신보의목뎍은대한의안녕질서에관한모든데목에ᄃᆡᄒᆞ야는공평한번론을쥬쟝ᄒᆞᆷ이라우리ᄒᆞᆫ신원의힘보는신문보시는쳠군ᄌᆞ의게ᄒᆞᆼ상보도ᄒᆞ려니와편지를긔셔ᄒᆞ여주시는이는셩명과번디를젹어붓치시기를희망ᄒᆞ오니이거슨신문상에긔졔ᄒᆞ라는거시아니오다만구히신용ᄒᆞ는증거를숨고자ᄒᆞᆷ이라긔쟈는아모긔셔던지긔지ᄒᆞᆯ퇴각ᄒᆞᆯ권리를가졋ᄉᆞ오나긔각ᄒᆞ는리유를말ᄒᆞᆯ터이오며공즁평화를문란케ᄒᆞ는듯ᄒᆞᆫ긔셔는외례히밧지안켓ᄉᆞᆸ나이다

론셜

쟝삼씨의문뎨긧론이라

○우리는쟝삼씨의황무지긔간ᄉᆞ건에ᄃᆡᄒᆞ야대강말ᄒᆞ코ᄒᆞ분을밝히졍문치아니ᄒᆞᆷ은일본으로셔발간ᄒᆞ는바시ᄉᆞ신보는동경한신보이기로쟝삼씨ᄉᆞ건갓롤깃도응당거졀ᄒᆞ야셜명ᄒᆞᆯ줄노알엿더니이제시ᄉᆞ신보에젼폭계지ᄒᆞᆫ주의를보존ᄒᆞᆫ황무지ᄉᆞ건을유익ᄒᆞᆷ은안된일노빗우ᄒᆞᆫ것스느고려ᄒᆞ는고주장ᄒᆞ야말ᄒᆞᆷ인즉만일이일이못되는지경이면일본에병폐와권세가대단히감손이되겟다고ᄒᆞ엿슨즉

만일이신보가일본각신문중에미우낫다고ᄒᆞᆯ것갓트면이러ᄒᆞᆫ일에던지무론누구라도잘못ᄒᆞ는일이잇슬진댄아못조록그사ᄅᆞᆷ의리론을말ᄒᆞ야권도ᄒᆞ고유지ᄒᆞ게ᄒᆞᆯ만ᄒᆞ거늘쟝삼씨의요구ᄒᆞ는바쟝대ᄒᆞᆫ일과그릉을셰닷지못ᄒᆞ고요악ᄒᆞ게고집ᄒᆞ는거시성히그르거늘셰수신보에긔재ᄒᆞᆫ젼문이며죄ᄒᆞ기로등지ᄒᆞ니대한빅셩들은아모조록이글을자셰히보고깁히싱각ᄒᆞ시오

우리나라로셔한국에졍권을설힝ᄒᆞ기젼에라도ᄒᆞᆷ즉지못ᄒᆞᆫ바이리ᄒᆞᆫ쟝삼씨의황무지ᄉᆞ건갓튼거슬노아둘수엽는거시과왕우리졍부로셔한국에주차ᄒᆞᆫ공사의게문ᄒᆞ여금에린번한국졍부에문즈왕복도되고일한량국셰에젹당ᄒᆞᆫ리익을ᄒᆞ기위ᄒᆞ야조약을인허ᄒᆞᆷ을노셜명도ᄒᆞ엿스즉비록한국으로서블긍ᄒᆞ드ᄅᆡ도오리신을지못ᄒᆞ는거시한국빅셩들은아모방침도업고조하ᄒᆞ는마음과을케역이는싱각이업슨주만일한리뭇을보면빅우조하ᄒᆞᆯ터이오또이요구ᄒᆞ는바를한국에서반ᄃᆡᄒᆞᆷ으로중지ᄒᆞ는경우에는일본이한국빅셩들의게대단히수치가될터이요우리들의권리도ᄎᆞᄎᆞ느ᄌᆞ질터이미요이후라도우리의쳥구ᄒᆞ는바를한국에서외례히반ᄃᆡᄒᆞ야거졀ᄒᆞᆯ터인즉이런지경이면일한량국에동맹약조ᄒᆞᆫ것도필경문구가될터이요느즁일이다숫치아니ᄒᆞᆯ터인즉우리는아모조록속히일ᄒᆞᆯ만ᄒᆞᆫ사ᄅᆞᆷ을쌥아한국졍부에고문관으로쳐임ᄒᆞ야사법과힝졍등ᄉᆞ를일병기신ᄒᆞ고지이로디츄광셕지라도ᄌᆞ셔히답사ᄒᆞ야신식으로만다도지일본빅셩과외국인종이나와디방에셔거주ᄒᆞ라고원ᄒᆞ는티로외간쳥ᄒᆞ고또쟝삼씨의황무지긔로들거시아니요한국졍부를위ᄒᆞᆷ으로협졔ᄒᆞ기라도ᄒᆞᆯ거시쟝삼씨요구ᄒᆞᆷ에ᄃᆡᄒᆞ야한국빅셩들이반ᄃᆡᄒᆞᆫ다ᄒᆞ고일본명예를손상ᄒᆞ는거시대단히올치아니ᄒᆞ다ᄒᆞ엿스니

그신보에한국빅셩들은아모방칙도업고조아ᄒᆞ는마음과을케녁이는싱각이업다고ᄒᆞᆷ은저희의요구ᄒᆞᆷ을반ᄃᆡᄒᆞᆫ셔듦에그리ᄒᆞᆷ이오또일본졍부로셔이버싱각에ᄒᆞᆷ즉ᄒᆞ도록조유로힝ᄒᆞ지못ᄒᆞᆫ다고ᄒᆞ엿스니그셔스신보도쏘ᄒᆞᆫ분명히이나라에잇지아니ᄒᆞᆫ데한국에잇는외국사ᄅᆞᆷ의게셔지도무어지ᄒᆞ게ᄒᆞ는일이단을ᄒᆞᆫ날지를ᄀᆞ시외국사ᄅᆞᆷ즁에도ᄒᆞ조긔의계힝당ᄒᆞ야싱지를나평케지빌사ᄅᆞᆷ도잇고혹은조과사엽상에죵ᄉᆞᄒᆞ야무의ᄒᆞ게지사ᄅᆞᆷ도잇스즈이왕와갓치사ᄅᆞᆷ의화흥인듯ᄒᆞ디와외국사ᄅᆞᆷ이나누가동상보호ᄒᆞ는조리에그르케권ᄒᆞ야셜계ᄒᆞᆷ을ᄌᆞ닷치리오

우리가황무지ᄉᆞ건에ᄃᆡᄒᆞ야일언반ᄉᆞ도업고또일본셔ᄌᆞ긔의조ᄒᆞᆯ티로ᄒᆞ게권리를주어미나라에분경싱진것도반ᄃᆡ치아ᄒᆞ엿스나그러ᄒᆞ나장리리익은일본졍부에향ᄒᆞ야군쳥ᄒᆞᆯ닷ᄒᆞ노라

잡보

○술김파착 근일경무쳥에셔잡술긴ᄉᆞᆷ명을포착ᄒᆞ야엄슈ᄒᆞ엿다더라

○잡술힝챡 경무쳥에셔작일셕지한ᄒᆞ야경셩니에잇는무녀눈등문외가ᄉᆞ와셔문외로돌등디로츅송ᄒᆞ고잡술긴은일병힝챡ᄒᆞ엿더라

○졔등방니 쥐쟉일하오이시에일본ᄉᆞ령부참모쟝졔등씨가나부대신을방문ᄒᆞ엿더라

○량셔면훈 일본ᄉᆞ령관원구경계씨가너부로공함ᄒᆞ기를역부모집ᄉᆞ로경긔와충쳥젼라경상각도에는임의훈령ᄒᆞ엿거니와황ᄒᆡ평안량도에는훈령안이ᄒᆞᆫ고로모집ᄒᆞ는틔구 ᄀᆡ니일체에셔황ᄒᆡ평안량도에면훈ᄒᆞ엿더라

○일병교련 근이일병군긔병과포병이츌이ᄒᆞᆫ련원에가서련조ᄒᆞ엿다더라

○대동졍보 대동신보사에서ᄉᆞ령부에ᄃᆡᄒᆞ야무샹ᄉᆞ건을긔지ᄒᆞ엿던지ᄒᆞᆨᄉᆞ령부에셔신문사쟝국지경양씨를쳥요ᄒᆞ야슈샴일졍보케ᄒᆞ엿더라

○포쳔군보 포쳔군보를거ᄒᆞᆫ즉본월삼일봇터롱일셔지이일병이뎌류슉ᄒᆞ고나려갓는ᄃᆡ젼후병수가이쳔여명이요복리가항이ᄉᆞ빅여필이라ᄒᆞ엿더라

○운세립셩 셩북동에괴셔한양ᄒᆞ는병리원지퇴쟝운덕명씨는일젼에립셩ᄒᆞ야경계샹동졍을구경ᄒᆞᆫ다더라

○불소불수 평리원검ᄉᆞᄒᆞ종억씨는젼젼라어ᄉᆞ리승욱씨를방송치아니ᄒᆞᆫ다ᄒᆞᆷ으로젼지관쟝뢰위씨와상힐ᄒᆞ고상소퇴거ᄒᆞᆫ다니ᄀᆡᆼ문ᄒᆞᆫ즉상소도아니ᄒᆞ고ᄉᆞ진도아니ᄒᆞᆫ다더라

○현티불학 현병티참평운원구씨가티무에열심ᄒᆞ야위관이ᄒᆞ로대명을항파를셜ᄒᆞ야법률을알아헌다더라

○동거하좌 셔산군거ᄒᆞ는신틔경이가다년홀거ᄒᆞ다가본년삼월에우연이ᄒᆞᆫ과부를엇어동거ᄒᆞ더니거월에더산거죠죵호락ᄒᆞ는자이취당유실명ᄒᆞ고신쎄징에리도ᄒᆞ야신쎄를겁박ᄒᆞ탈ᄒᆞᆫ더니유위가장죵런지신쎄사측의집으로병쟝을보니여니졍돌텁ᄒᆞ고즁산과보리등물을탈취ᄒᆞ여가교셰무이시부죵ᄒᆞ야며찬군슈에게쳥송ᄒᆞ고신쎄는엇지ᄒᆞ야그자커ᄅᆞᆯ그리ᄒᆞ는지곡졀도모르고자기갓치ᄒᆞᆫ셰처잇서동분이을ᄒᆞᆫ졍형이비ᄒᆞᆷ데엿다더라

○츙량하의 직쟉일에일본ᄉᆞ관일인과병졍팔명이남셔이티쳔등디에나가서그전쳐를츙량조사ᄒᆞ엿다더라

○롱셤만병 대한일보를거ᄒᆞᆫ즉소환봉ᄒᆞ라는병명을죠징키인코샹금아라스경셩에귀류ᄒᆞᆫ리병진은공즁에써보ᄒᆞ되아병룩삼만명이쟝츳참경북도로향ᄒᆞᆫ

다ᄂᆞᆫᄉᆞ와 한일량국간에 중요ᄒᆞᆫ ᄉᆞ건에 ᄃᆡᄒᆞ야 면의ᄒᆞ엿다더라 ᄒᆞ엿더라

○부인출발 동경에 체류ᄒᆞᄂᆞᆫ 현영운씨의 부인이 ᄉᆞᆷ작일에 출발ᄒᆞ야 귀국ᄒᆞᆫ다고 궁ᄂᆡ부에 뎐보가 왓다더라

○바문령ᄉᆞ 굿ᄃᆡ민 병셕씨가 ᄉᆞᆷ작일에 인항일령ᄉᆞ를 방문ᄒᆞ엿더라

○잡술시벌 재작일 경무쳥에셔 잡술ᄭᆡᆨ을 포착ᄒᆞ엿ᄂᆞᆫᄃᆡ 그 잡술칙을 제등어리에 지우고 ᄃᆡ로즁으로 조리돌니고 도로 경쳥에 가두엇다더라

○가등류탐 농부고문관 가등중웅씨가 본월 십륙일 상오 십일시에 옥류쳔을 유람ᄒᆞᄂᆞᆫᄃᆡ 궁ᄂᆡ부대신 이하 졔관원이 동졉ᄂᆡ에 오찬을 비셜ᄒᆞ야 연ᄃᆡᄒᆞ엿더라

○근일풍셜 근일 풍셜을 득문ᄒᆞᆫ즉 일헌병ᄉᆞ령부를 궐ᄂᆡ에 셜치ᄒᆞᆫ다ᄒᆞ더니 지작일에 일헌병 이명이 평셩문으로 드러가셔 돈덕뎐을 죠ᄉᆞᄒᆞ고 갓다더라

○외대부진 외부대신 리하영씨가 무ᄉᆞᆷ ᄉᆞ고가 잇ᄂᆞᆫ지 작일에 ᄉᆞ진 아니ᄒᆞ엿다더라

○미고긴셜 외부고문관을 미국인으로 고빙ᄒᆞᆫ다ᄂᆞᆫ 소문이 ᄆᆡ우 긴착ᄒᆞ더라

○젹셩군보 젹셩군슈가 외부로 보고ᄒᆞ되 일헌병 이명이 역부로 모집ᄒᆞᆯ ᄉᆞ로 광고를 가지고 본군에 ᄅᆡ도ᄒᆞ야 인부를 청구ᄒᆞᄂᆞᆫᄃᆡ 농치를 당ᄒᆞ야 자원지민이 졀무ᄒᆞᆫ고로 일헌병의 말이 고을 지경 안에 ᄉᆞᆫ힝ᄒᆞ야 억지로 압령ᄒᆞ야 가겟다ᄒᆞᄂᆞᆫ고로 민졍이 ᄃᆡ단 소동ᄒᆞ오니 일공관에 죠회ᄒᆞ야 죠계ᄒᆞ라ᄒᆞ야 민심을 안졍케ᄒᆞ심을 복망ᄒᆞᆫ다 ᄒᆞ엿더라

가등소졉 재작일 하오 시에 농부고문관 가등중웅씨가 대ᄂᆡ에 소졉이 되엿더라

○공ᄉᆞᄃᆡ리 쥬일대한공ᄉᆞ 죠민희씨가 발졍환국되ᄂᆞᆫ고로 참서관 현보운으로 공ᄉᆞ ᄉᆞ무를 ᄃᆡ리ᄒᆞ라고 외부에셔 쥬일공관에 뎐보ᄒᆞ엿더라

○법함출항 재작일 인쳔감리 하샹긔씨가 외부로 뎐보ᄒᆞ되 법국군함 일쳑이 작셕에 출항ᄒᆞ엿다 ᄒᆞ엿더라

○직졉교섭 외부에셔 각부부원쳥에 죠회ᄒᆞ되 일본공ᄉᆞ 죠회ᄂᆡ에 우리 군ᄉᆞ상에 급속히 상관될 안건이 잇ᄂᆞᆫ ᄯᆡ를 당ᄒᆞ여셔ᄂᆞᆫ 쥬차군ᄉᆞ령부에셔 그 ᄉᆞ건 당ᄒᆞᆫ 그 관부에 향ᄒᆞ야 직졉으로 교섭ᄒᆞ야 편의케 ᄒᆞᆯ터이니 이 ᄯᅳᆺ스로 각관부에 젼포ᄒᆞ야 민속죠쳐케 ᄒᆞ기를 ᄇᆞ란다ᄒᆞᆷ을 등인ᄒᆞ야 죠회ᄒᆞ노라 ᄒᆞ엿더라

○일병효로 평안북도관찰ᄉᆞ가 외부로 죠회ᄒᆞ되 션쳔군슈의 보고를 거ᄒᆞᆫ즉 쳥국비도가 본군에 드러와 지산촌을 노략ᄒᆞ고 박림쳥을 착거ᄒᆞᆯ시에 본군쥬차일병 십ᄉᆞ명이 ᄯᅩ 차가셔 박가의 지산을 다 도로 차져올ᄲᅮᆫ아니라 ᄯᅩ 비도 일명ᄭᆞ지 착리ᄒᆞ엿다ᄒᆞ니 싱각건ᄃᆡ 그 일병 등의 효로가 극히 가샹ᄒᆞᆫ지라 히병 등을 포즁쟝을 주ᄂᆞᆫ거시 타당ᄒᆞ다 ᄒᆞ엿더라

○부인귀국 현영운씨의 부인이 슈일젼에 동경셔 출발ᄒᆞ야 지작일 부산에 도착ᄒᆞ엿ᄂᆞᆫᄃᆡ 명일 입경ᄒᆞ기로 예졍이라더라

관보

뎨이쳔구빅칠호 광무팔년팔월십칠일

○셔임급ᄉᆞ령

○의원면본관 젼라남도관찰부쥬ᄉᆞ 박긔오 ○임젼라남도관찰부쥬ᄉᆞ 서판임관륙등 김샹두

이샹팔월십삼일

○의원본관 텰도원쥬ᄉᆞ 임동호 류병완 최경린 송지혁 박인동 공샹혁 리근하 권명규 박린셥 홍경후 남졍진 의릉참봉 젼홍우 후릉참봉 홍덕쥬 경긔면참봉 리졍화 목쳥면참봉 리규영 조릉참봉 강희린 슌창원참긔봉 리두로 희릉참봉 리은필 졔릉참봉 김진슈 ○궁ᄂᆡ부참서관겸임대신관방비서관 쥬임관륙등 비서원승 윤형구 ○임텰도원쥬ᄉᆞ서판임관륙등 리병운 김졍옥 박졍참 김병용 안식 리쥬익 ○임의릉참봉서판임관팔등 최영렬 ○임후릉참봉서판임관팔등 김처연 ○임경긔면참봉서판임관팔등 륙품 송대진 ○임목쳥면참봉서판임관팔등 리시우 ○임과조릉참봉서판임관팔등 최셩항 ○임슌창원참봉서판임관팔등 문원국 ○임희릉참봉서판임관팔등 남졍셥 ○임졔릉참봉서판임관팔등 김학진 ○면본관 삼화감리서쥬ᄉᆞ 경희운

이샹팔월십오일

궁졍록ᄉᆞ

●법부대신의졍부의졍림시셔리박졔슌ᄉᆞ직소 비지ᄂᆡ에 다시ᄉᆞ양말고 곳시무ᄒᆞ라

팔월십오일

뎐보

동경팔월십ᄉᆞ일발 공ᄉᆞ관착뎐

○무쟝히졔 덕함조에자레우잇지호ᄂᆞᆫ 교쥬만의 잔교에ᄆᆡ여두ᄆᆞ 무쟝은 다 ᄃᆞᆯ히ᄒᆞ엿다더라

○ᄉᆞ령관ᄉᆞ망 쳥모병원에 드러가 잇든 로국ᄉᆞ령관 시스잇지인뎟은 죽엇다더라

○로함각안 지부리뎐을 거ᄒᆞᆫ즉 팔월십이일에 로국구축졍이 ᄎᆡᆨ이 위히위에셔 동방으로 이십리즘되ᄂᆞᆫ 곳에 걸니여 함쟝 등은 륙노로 쥬야비도ᄒᆞ야 십이일에 위히위에 니르러 구조ᄒᆞᆷ을 인걸ᄒᆞ고 승죠원 륙십명은 영국 슈뢰졍에셔 구조ᄒᆞ엿다더라

○구축함구조 위히위부근에 걸닌 로국구축함 일쳑은 무ᄉᆞ히 구조ᄒᆞ엿ᄂᆞᆫᄃᆡ 영국병함 찬빠호로 향항에 보낸다더라

동일동뎐

○덕함포획 뎨일구축함의 죠호와 하호 이쳑이 팔월십일야에 덕의 합ᄃᆡ를 수식ᄒᆞ기 위ᄒᆞ야 슌힝ᄒᆞᄂᆞᆫ 즁에 멀니 보미 덕의 구축함 ᄀᆞᆺ흔 비가 셔방으로 급히 힝홈을 알고 츄격ᄒᆞ다가 밤이 깁허 죵젹을 일코 익일 십일일 ᄭᆞ지련 속히 슈식ᄒᆞ야 덕함이 지부에 잠입홈을 알고 그 부근히면 밧긔 표박ᄒᆞ야 그 출항ᄒᆞ기를 기ᄃᆞ리되 히진후ᄭᆞ지도 ᄂᆞ오지 아니ᄒᆞ거ᄂᆞᆯ 등본ᄉᆞ령관은 덕함이 혹 야반에 잠출ᄒᆞ야 우리 함ᄃᆡᄂᆞᆫ 혹샹션에 가히 홀념려 기잇기로 죠죠호와 하호를 거ᄂᆞ리고 지부항구에 드러가니 덕함은 ᄯᅥ시렐늬이호인ᄃᆡ 안직 그 무쟝을 그르지 안인 형젹이 잇거로 히군즁위ᄉᆞ도우차미를 보니여 덕함쟝의게 ᄃᆡᄒᆞ야 왈 명일 미명에 항구밧그로 ᄂᆞ오라ᄂᆞ냐 항복을 ᄒᆞᆯ라ᄂᆞ냐 ᄒᆞ고 직졉으로 교졉ᄒᆞᄂᆞ 덕함쟝은 응답지 아니ᄒᆞᆫ고로 문답ᄒᆞᄂᆞᆫ 즁에 부하의게 향ᄒᆞ야 계를 파ᄒᆞ기로 대포를 노흐라고 명령ᄒᆞ더니 홀연 ᄉᆞ도즁위를 ᄯᅳ러안코 혁슈즁으로 ᄯᅥ러가다ᄂᆞᆫ 덕병 일명은 우리 즁광을 돌연이 ᄯᅳᆷ러안교 ᄀᆞᆺ치 혁슈즁으로 ᄯᅥ러가고 기다 덕병도 우리의 배로 드러향거ᄒᆞᄂᆞᆫ 힝위를 시작ᄒᆞ엿ᄂᆞᆫᄃᆡ 그잔에 ᄒᆞᆫ 덕함의 젼부단약고 부근에셔 화약이 폭발ᄒᆞ야 우리 파견ᄒᆞ엿든 군ᄉᆞ가 ᄉᆞ샹ᄒᆞᆫ 자가 잇스ᄂᆞ 맛ᄎᆞᆷ니 덕함을 포획ᄒᆞ여 ᄭᅳᆯ고 도라왓더라 우리 ᄉᆞ샹은 젼ᄉᆞᄒᆞᆫ쟈 하ᄉᆞ 일명이요 즁샹ᄒᆞᆫ쟈 하ᄉᆞ 이하ᄉᆞ 명이요 경샹ᄒᆞᆫ쟈 죠호에 승조원ᄉᆞ 도즁위와 동력관과 밋 하ᄉᆞ 이하 구명이더라

원산뎐보

○함흥로병 원산에 습래ᄒᆞ엿든 덕병이 함흥으로 퇴각ᄒᆞ엿ᄂᆞᆫᄃᆡ 그후 속병과 합ᄒᆞ야 동ᄃᆡ현지ᄒᆞᆫ 병력이 보긔포병을 병ᄒᆞ야 삼쳔여명이더라

함흥에셔 남으로 원산ᄭᆞ지 뎐션은 로병이 다 ᄭᅳᆫ어버리고 한인이 함흥에 드러가ᄂᆞᆫ쟈를 엄즁히 ᄉᆞ찰ᄒᆞᆫ다더라

함흥에 지ᄒᆞᆫ 보병부ᄃᆡ 즁약 오십명은 일젼에 ᄯᅥᄂᆞᆫ 쟝진과 강계를 지나서 초산으로 향ᄒᆞ엿다더라

로국정탐이 원산에 드러온 자가 근일에 더욱 만은ᄃᆡ 지작일 한인 ᄉᆞ명은 로국을 위ᄒᆞ야 정탐ᄒᆞᄂᆞᆫ 형젹이 드러나셔 우리 군즁에셔 포살ᄒᆞ엿더라

함흥에 로병이 획쳑을 니여 삼면으로 에워싸셔 원산을 두러ᄶᅡᆯ게 획인ᄃᆡ 일ᄃᆡᄂᆞᆫ 원산원길로 좃차 남으로 ᄂᆞ리고 일ᄃᆡᄂᆞᆫ 히변길노 좃차 남으로 ᄂᆞ리고 일ᄃᆡᄂᆞᆫ 히로로 좃차 안변에 하륙ᄒᆞ야 삼ᄃᆡ가 일시에 원산을 두려ᄶᅡᆯ 슈단이라더라

동경팔월십륙일발

○샹촌샹보 샹촌뎨이합ᄃᆡᄉᆞ령쟝관보고요령

십ᄉᆞ일련명에 뎨이함ᄃᆡ의 출운과 오처와 샹반과 반슈ᄉᆞ함이 한국 울산 히면에셔 덕함을 수색ᄒᆞᄂᆞᆫ 즁에 히삼위함ᄃᆡ 삼쳑이 남으로 향히홈을 발현ᄒᆞ엿ᄂᆞᆫᄃᆡ 덕함은 우리 함ᄃᆡ를 보고 북방으로 향ᄒᆞ야 도주ᄒᆞ미 곳 그 압길을 막고 오젼 다섯시 이십삼분에 니르러 젼투를 시작ᄒᆞ엿ᄂᆞᆫ지라 덕의 뒤에 잇ᄂᆞᆫ 군함 류릭크호ᄂᆞᆫ 흉샹뫼 뒤에 잇셔 밍렬ᄒᆞᆫ 포화를 밧앗고 압헤 잇ᄂᆞᆫ 량함은 루루히 이거슬 구리워 보호ᄒᆞ야 샹거가 초원ᄒᆞ면 도로 도라와 곳가히 졉착ᄒᆞ야 감히 마리위 구원ᄒᆞ기로 우리 함ᄃᆡᄂᆞᆫ 루루히 뎜ᄌᆞ형으로 버려 덕함을 향ᄒᆞ야 단발의 편리를 얻으니 그 결과ᄂᆞᆫ 덕함 삼쳑이 슈차 큰 화재를 당ᄒᆞ야 손히를 대단히 밧이 보잇ᄂᆞᆫᄃᆡ 그즁에 류릭크호ᄂᆞᆫ 지톄에 자유를 일코 ᄯᅩ 포화도 아쥬 감ᄒᆞ야 잇다금ᄂᆞᆫ 손히 발샤ᄒᆞᆯᄲᅮᆫ이더니 그ᄂᆞᆫ 쇠리가 현저이 침몰ᄒᆞ교 ᄯᅩ 그 좌편뎐이 기우러짐을 보고 덕이 군함을 버리고 도망ᄒᆞ미라 맛ᄎᆞᆷ 그ᄯᆡ에 대ᄉᆞ함ᄃᆡ의 당속과 교텬슈가 젼장에 졉근ᄒᆞ야 류릭크를 공격ᄒᆞᆷ을 보고 본ᄃᆡᄂᆞᆫ 보시야와 구론보이를 츄격ᄒᆞ엿더라 이동안 격젼ᄒᆞᆫ지 오시간에 덕함 이쳑이 젼속력으로 도쥬ᄒᆞ엿더라 오젼 십시 구십분에 우리 함ᄃᆡ가 우편비젼에 회두ᄒᆞ야 류릭크호를 슈탐차로 남으로 향히ᄒᆞ다가 히함의 침몰함을 듯고 젼합ᄃᆡ를 집합ᄒᆞ야 류릭크호 침몰ᄒᆞᆫ 히면에 니르러 히슈샹에셔 허염치ᄂᆞᆫ 인원 륙빅명가량을 구졔ᄒᆞ엿다더라 우리 함ᄃᆡᄂᆞᆫ 다소간 손히를 바닷스ᄂᆞ 대단치ᄂᆞᆫ 아니ᄒᆞ고 사긔가 극히 왕셩ᄒᆞ더라

TELEGRAMS.

SINKING OF THE "RURIK."

KAMIMURA'S REPORT.

Tokyo, Aug. 16th.

On the 14th inst. at daybreak 4 vessels of our 2nd squadron, the "Izume," "Tokiwa," "Iwate" and "Wakasa" were cruising off the Korean coast when they discovered three Russian cruisers steaming southward. On sighting our fleet they turned tail and ran northward but our ships catching up with them forced them to give battle. The "Rurik" was in the rear of the three when they started to fly and consequently bore the brunt of the fight. After five hours' fighting it was seen that the "Rurik" was sinking by the stern and the "Naniwa" and "Takachiho" of the 4th squadron, arriving at this time, the two remaining ships of the enemy steamed away at full speed to the north. We followed in pursuit but they outdistanced us and so we returned to the scene of the battle and managed to rescue 600 of the crew of the "Rurik," which had then sunk. Our squadron suffered some damage but nothing very serious and the fight was a good experience for our seamen.

REPORTED SINKING OF RUSSIAN CRUISER.

Tokyo, August 16th.

It is reported that the Russian Cruiser Pallada was sunk during the engagement outside Port Arthur on the night of the 10th inst.

RUSSIAN REPORTS OF FIGHTING AT PORT ARTHUR.

London, August 8.

According to a St. Petersburg telegram, a fierce battle took place on the land side of Port Arthur on the 5th inst. The Japanese are reported to have been repulsed with great loss, the killed alone being estimated at en thousand. The Russians lost about one thousand.

General Stoessel telegraphs that the Japanese attacks on Port Arthur from the 26th to the 28th ult. were repulsed with enormous losses. The Russian losses during the three days' fighting were forty officers and 1,500 men.

ROM JAPAN PAPERS.

The following telegrams are taken from Japan papers.

Chefoo, Aug. 4.—Most of the Russians who have arrived here from Port Arthur since yesterday are labourers at the dock there. The Russian Consul sent them to Tientsin to-day by steamer. The Russians also arrived here to-day. —"Asahi."

London, Aug. 5.—Viceroy Alexieff has gone to Harbin, thence he proceeds to Vladivostock.—"Reuter."—"Japan Mail."

London, Aug. 6th.

The Russian Volunteer Fleet steamer "Petersburg," which recently captured the "Malacca" and other vessels in the Red Sea, has passed Aden going eastward.

London, August 6, 2:20 p. m.—It is reported from St. Petersburg that the Czar has asked Kuropatkin for explanation of the continual retreats. General Kuropatkin has answered that the men are over fatigued and that the Siberian Corps are not accustomed to mountain warfare.

Later.

General Kuropatkin, Commander-in-Chief of the Russian troops in Manchuria, is likely to be recalled. The idea is that he will be appointed Minister of the Interior.—"Mainichi.

Berlin, Aug. 7th.

The case of the German steamer "Thea," sunk by the Russians at Vladivostok, is very complicated owing to the fact that the vessel has been chartered and re-chartered.

London, Aug. 7th.

The P. & O. steamship "Malacca," which was recently captured by the Russians in the Red Sea and taken to Algiers in order that her cargo might be examined, has left for Port Said.

SINKING OF THE "KNIGHT COMMANDER."

ACTION JUSTIFIED BY PRIZE COURT.

London Aug. 7.

The Russian Prize Court at Vladivostok justifies the sinking of the British steamer "Knight Commander" by the Vladivostok Squadron on the ground that the vessel with cargo was considered a lawful prize owing to the fact that she carried railway material destined for Chemulpo, viâ Japan.

STATEMENT BY MR. BALFOUR.

London, Aug. 8.

Mr. A. J. Balfour, the Premier, in a statement in the House of Commons on Russia's attitude with regard to the searching of neutral vessels, pointed out that the case of the "Malacca" was the first of its kind that had arisen since the signing of the Treaty of Paris, and any settlement must be of the nature of a compromise. Russia had shown a desire to meet Great Britain in the matter; his (the Premier's) object was to prevent the incident causing a great strain in the relations between the two countries.

Mr. Balfour added that he in nowise regretted that the Government had done its best to meet Russia, who had made no impracticable suggestions. Great Britain adhered to the opinion that the grounds advanced by Russia for sinking the "Knight Commander," whether true or not, did not justify the sinking of the vessel, and the Government had not abandoned in the smallest degree the position taken up on the question.

OPINON IN BERLIN.

Berlin, Aug. 8.

In authoritative circles here it is believed that Japan's military strength and financial resources are far from being exhausted by the present campaign.

Berlin, Aug. 9.

As the result of the collapse of a railway bridge in Missouri 125 men have lost their lives.

Berlin, Aug. 9.

The United States Government, which was reported to be sending its European Squadorn to Smyrna to obtain recognition of certain claims, has declared that it does not intend a permanent occupation, but only a naval demonstration.

LORD ROBERTS ON WAR.

Mr. Harold Begbie's new "Master Worker" in the July number of the "Pall Mall Magazine" is Lord Roberts, of whom a spirited sketch is given. 'I asked him," says Mr. Begbie, "if he had ever experienced that sensuous intoxication in battle which Lord Wolseley has described so graphically in his book. No, he could remember nothing of such a sensation; the nearest to it, perhaps, was the joy he experienced on riding a sweating horse into Delhi and finding that he was in time for the siege. In actual fighting he could recall no exaltation of the senses; there was excitement, no doubt, tremendous excitement, but he had always studied, from the very first, to fight against that excitement, in order to preserve an absolutely unclouded intellect. 'The first virtue of an officer,' he said, 'is calmness.'

"I spoke about the shock which many people feel in reading of this joy and delight in battle, and asked Lord Roberts whether he himself did not regard war as something barbarous, and whether he did not look forward to a millennium of universal peace.

"He shook his head and smiled. 'I think,' he said, with measured, clean-cut words, 'that there is a purpose in war. It is true that fighting is a stern remedy, but are we quite sure that frail humanity does not need stern remedies? A war is a wicked war when it is needlessly waged, or when it is waged for greed; but even in these cases it may have its benefits for a nation. Without war—at any rate without the vigilance and discipline which prepare for that stern emergency—a nation is in risk of running to seed. And where a war is a just one— where it is waged as an act of self-defence, as in the case of the Japanese, who are now fighting for their very life—its benefit to the nation is great. It is an appeal to the manhood and the virtue of a people. It prevents decadence and effeminacy. It corrects the selfishness and querulousness which are inevitably bred by a long peace. Without the preparation for an armed defence of its boundaries or the vindication of its honour, an empire would slip into habits dangerous for itself and dangerous for the whole of humanity.

"'Even in the Anglo-Saxon race, which is as vigorous as any in the world, we find that a long peace breeds a complaining and luxurious spirit, to which every hardship and every little inconvenience becomes an intolerable injustice. Fortitude and the cheerful bearing of adversity are apt to fall out of the category of human duties in a long and luxurious peace. And since character is tried by sorrow and affliction, this querulous antipathy to hardship and exertion is bad for the individual, and consequently for the State. We are all tried by fire, are we not? And the test of a man's character is his ability to bear gallantly the sorrows and afflictions of his life; so too, I think, a nation needs to be tried by fire—needs to be put upon its trial every now and then, and tested by the laws which govern this planet— the law, I mean particularly, that only the efficient survive.'"

The wages offered to coolies by the Japanese military authorities, have been raised from $1.10 to $1.50.

Lady Hyon, who has been creating such a sensation in Tokyo, has left Japan on her return home.

Sir William MacGregor, the Governor of Lagos, has been appointed to be Governor of Newfoundland.

Japanese cavalry and artillery now undergo a daily course of drill near the East Gate.

The Korea Daily News.

To be published daily except Sundays.

Rate of Subscription:—

Per Year,	Yen 25.
Per Quarter,	Yen 7.
Per Month	Yen 2.50

Postage in Korea not charged extra.
Postage abroad charged extra.

Advertisements, 50 sen per day for 1 inch or less.
5 yen per month per inch.
50 yen per year per inch.

All communications to

E. T. BETHELL,
Editor and Publisher.
Pak-tong, Seoul.

PORT ARTHUR.

FALL IMMINENT.

ALL AUTHORITIES AGREE THAT ITS CAPTURE IS ONLY A MATTER OF A FEW DAYS.

The news which has reached us by the latest mails to hand leaves no room for doubt that Port Arthur cannot hold out much longer. Its capitulation is said to be only a matter of a few days. Apart from the steady drawing in of the Japanese attack and the consequent untenability of the town owing to the hail of Japanese shell which is continually falling, the conditions within the town appear to be of the worst. The defenders seem to be demoralized and the return of part of their fleet after the engagement of August 10th cannot fail to be disheartening, especially in view of the fact that the escape of the remainder is probably unknown to them.

It is difficult to arrive at anything like an accurate estimate of the situation. Optimistic reports still emanate from Chefoo. Japanese official reports there are none at present and all the newspapers in the East refuse to accept the Russian official reports, declaring them to be obviously exaggerated or untrue. Of the Japanese newspaper telegrams little need be said. The Japanese public is hungry for news of Port Arthur, stories of any kind find a ready market, the Chefoo correspondents are equal to the occasion and the supply keeps pace with the demand.

It seems that the refugees who have arrived at Chefoo by junk lately are much more reticent than their predecessors and that little information is obtainable from them. It is very likely that most of the people in Port Arthur itself have as little idea of what is going on in its immediate neighbourhood as we have here in Seoul. A soldier may even go into battle and fight the whole day through and still not know with which side the victory rested.

Therefore until the official reports come to hand it is necessary to treat all statements with regard to the condition of either army with great reserve. From the attempted escape of the Russian squadron on August 10th it is safe to assume that the Russian position is becoming desperate. A rumour that the discontent among the dockyard workmen there has culminated in a strike seems well founded while the report that the Russian ammunition is becoming exhausted begins to command credence on account of its very peristency. No more messages alleging the shortness of supplies have reached us lately, so we think the factor of starvation may be left out of the question.

The Japanese freely admit that the Russian defenses are very complete and formidable but if it proves to be true, as alleged, that their ammunition is giving out, these defenses are robbed of the greater part of their potentialities and terrors. Furthermore as the outer defenses are evacuated by the Russians and fall into the hands of the Japanese they become in succession serious menaces to the neighbouring positions.

We have been told that the land approaches to Port Arthur are protected by a perfect labyrinth of mines and that trenches to protect the defenders abound everywhere.

On the other hand the quiet confidence in the impending capture of the stronghold displayed by well informed Japanese carries conviction with it and inspires confidence in others. We think it is safe to assume that Port Arthur is doomed and that in the course of a few days we shall be able to congratulate a heroic army upon an achievement for which there is no parallel in history, but the victory will only have been achieved at the cost of many, many, heroic lives, and we must be prepared for a casualty list, on both sides, of appalling magnitude. The Japanese probably measured the cost before embarking upon the enterprise, and had it been twice as great they would still, if assured of ultimate victory, have pursued the same course.

Warfare as an exact science, has been studied and practised by the Japanese with a diligence, minuteness and completeness unequaled in the history of the world, and it is safe to say that any enterprise, such as the present one, is practically assured of success before it is undertaken.

RESULT OF THE VLADIVOSTOK SQUADRON'S CRUISE.

JAPAN TRADE SERIOUSLY AFFECTED.

By latest telegraphic and mail advices we learn that nearly every shipping company trading from Europe to the far east has placed a taboo on cargoes for Japan.

The P. & O. company set the ball rolling by refusing to book cargo for ports north of Shanghai. Messrs. Holt and Co. Ltd., followed suit, announcing that, owing to the uncertain definition of contraband goods, no bookings of cargo for Japan will be made by either of their lines, viz., The Ocean Steamship Co., Ltd., and the China Mutual Steam Navigation Co., Ltd. The Glen and Ben line of steamers have also taken the same action, the combination thus formed being a large section of the far eastern traders.

A critic on the war, writing recently in a leading London journal, remarked that whereas, in Europe, the opinion of naval experts was that the commerce destroyer was to be feared every bit as much as its fighting brethren, the Japanese did not seem to attach much importance to the cruise of the Vladivostok squadron.

If, as it would seem, *all* shipping companies are going to take the same action, the European opinion would appear to be the more correct.

Could it be assumed that the scare is only temporary, owing to the possibility of a better arrangement being made with Russia, or by the Japanese regaining absolute command of the sea, the situation would not be so serious. But, bearing in mind that the Baltic Squadron appears really to be on its way out, this same commerce destroying will, if continued indefinitely, prove a serious menace to Japan in her loss of trade.

FOODSTUFFS AS CONTRABAND.

The American and Russian Governments seem to have come to a deadlock as to what constitutes contraband of war. The recent seizures of shipping have led to the American declaration that under no circumstances will she recede from the doctrine that foodstuffs not directly intended for a belligerent army or navy cannot be regarded as contraband to which the Russian Government replies that the question as to whether foodstuffs are to be regarded as contraband, of war must be decided on the merits of each case. The captain of each vessel suspected must furnish evidence to show that any provisions comprised in his cargo were not intended for the enemy, and the case must be settled on consideration of such evidence.

THE PASSAGE OF THE DARDANELLES.

According to telegrams form London on the 6th inst. Russia notified the Porte at Constantinople that two coal-laden Volunteer Fleet steamers would pass through the Dardanelles and would retain their character as merchantmen. The Porte, however, replied that a written guarantee to that effect must be given before they would be allowed to make the passage, a verbal assurance being insufficient.

REFRACTORY MINISTER.

The Daihan-ilpo learns that Mr. Yi Pom Chin, the Korean Minister to St. Petersburg, refuses to leave his post, although he has been several times recalled. He gives as an excuse the statement that important diplomatic communications between Russia and Korea will shortly be commenced and he further states that 600,000 Russian soldiers are immediately being despatched to Korea. Oh, Mr. Yi, who told you that fairy tale?

Mayor Pak Yu Tai complained that while absent on a visit to the country, his house in Seoul was broken into by Japanese gendarmes and all his papers seized. He was, shortly after this complaint was made, arrested and when apprehended remarked, "I suppose you arrest me because I am the adopted brother of Kim In-su, but I have not communicated with him."

King Menelik of Abyssinia has decided to have his country represented by a minister at Washington. The recent visit of a special commission from the United States to Abyssinia has resulted in a desire for better trade with Uncle Sam and the appointment of a minister indicates a desire for closer relations.

"The Times" and the "Standard," commenting on the finding of the Vladivostock Prize Court in the case of the "Knight Commander," say that such procedure does not differ from executing a man first and then sitting in judgment to determine whether he had been guilty of a capital crime.

Several hundred Korean soldiers were recently sent from Pyeng Yang to assist in repelling the Russians at Gensan. On arrival in the neighbourhood, however, the sound of rifle shots was too much for their nerves, and they retreated to Byong An, whence they refuse to budge.

The people of Pyeng Yang complain bitterly of their magistrate, Paing Hanchu, who they assert grinds them down and takes all their earnings. He has now made the collection of coolies an excuse for a further squeeze.

The Editor of the Daito Shinpo, a Japanese daily, has been forbidden by the military authorites to issue his journal for one week.

On the 16th inst. Mr. Kato, adviser to the Agricultural Department, was received in private audience by His Majesty.

The Korea Daily News.

VOL. I, THURSDAY, AUGUST 18, 1904. No. 28

HONGKONG & SHANGHAI BANKING CORPORATION.

Paid-up Capital..... ....$10,000,000
Reserve Fund:—Sterling Reserve... 10,000,000
Silver Reserve..... 6,500,000

26,500,000
Reserve Liability of Proprietors... 10,000,000

HEAD OFFICE, HONGKONG.

London Bankers, London and County Banking Company Limited
Branches and Agencies, London.

Amoy,	Hankow	Penang,
Bangkok,	Hiogo,	Rangoon,
Batavia,	Iloilo,	Saigon,
Bombay,	Lyons,	San Francisco,
Calcutta,	Manila,	Singapore,
Colombo,	Nagasaki,	Sourabaya,
Foochow,	New York,	Tientsin,
Hamburg,	Peking,	Yokohama,

Credits granted on approved Securities, and every description of Banking and Exchange business transacted.

Drafts granted on London and the chief Commercial places in Europe, India, Australia, America, China and Japan.

HOLME RINGER & CO., AGENTS, CHEMULPO

CHARTERED BANK OF INDIA AUSTRALIA & CHINA.

INCORPORATED BY ROYAL CHARTER 1853

HEAD OFFICES:—LONDON.

Paid-up Capital £800,000
Reserve Liability of Shareholders 800,000
Reserve Fund 725,000

Drafts granted upon all the principal places in the world and every description of Exchange and banking business transacted.

E. MEYER & Co., Agents, Chemulpo.

DAI-ICHI GINKO.

LIMITED.

(Formerly the First National Bank)

ESTABLISHED 1873

INCORPORATED UNDER PRESENT LAW 1896

Capital - - - - - - - - Yen 5,000,000
Reserve Fund - . - - - - " 1,500 000

HEAD OFFICE:—TOKIO.

President: Baron SHIBUSAWA.

BRANCHES AND CORRESPONDENTS In the Principal Cities and Towns of Japan.

Interest Allowed on
Fixed deposits 1 year - - - 6½ per cent
" " 6 months - - - 6 per cent
Special current accounts 1½ sen daily per Y 100
General " " 1 " " " 100

M. TANAKA, Manager, Chemulpo

NIPPON YUSEN KAISHA.

JAPANESE MAIL STEAMSHIP CO.

DER MAIL CONTRACT WITH THE IMPERIAL JAPANESE GOVERNMENT.

European Line

Regular Fortnightly Service between Yokohama, Kobe, Moji, Shanghai, Hongkong, Singapore, Penang Colombo, Port Said, Marseilles, London and Antwerp

American Line

Regular Fortnightly Service between Hongkong and Seattle, calling at Shanghai, Moji, Kobe, Yokohama and Victoria, B. C.

Australian Line

Regular weekly Service betwen Japan Ports and Australia, calling at Hongkong and Manila.

(Above Three Lines Suspended until further notice)

Shanghai Line

Weekly Service between Shanghai and Japan Ports

Korea Line

Service Kobe, Moji, Nagasaki, Fusan, Chemulpo, Choo, Taiku.
S. S. Bahelsberg, 2181 tons.
Service Kobe, Moji, Fusan, Chemulpo, Chinnampo
S. S Argo, S. S. Ohio.

ON CHEONG & CO., SEOUL.

GENERAL STORE KEEPERS. Imported provisions, Cooking Utensils Crockery, etc.

FRESH BREAD DAILY.

MITSU BISHI DOCKYARD & ENGINE WORKS, NAGASAKI.

CODE WORD, "DOCK."

A. 1, A. B. C., and Engineering Codes used.

DOCK No. 1 (at Tategami).

Extreme Length..............523 feet
Length on blocks .... 513 ,,
Width of Entrance on Top......89 ,,
,, ,, Bottom....77 ,,
Water on Blocks at Spring Tide 26½ ,,

DOCK No. 2 (Mukaijima).

Extreme Length..............371 feet
Length on Blocks.............360 ,,
Width of Entrance on Top......66 ,,
,, ,, Bottom . 53 ,,
Water on Blocks at Spring Tide 22 ,,

PATENT SLIP (at Kosuge).

Can take vessels up to 1,000 tons gross.

THE WORKS are well equipped with the LATEST IMPROVEMENTS, and can execute any kind of work in SHIPBUILDING and MARINE ENGINEERING, as well as in REPAIRING of SHIPS.

The COMPANY'S new powerful steamer OURA-MARU (712 tons, 700 I.H.P.), specially built for SALVAGE PURPOSES, and equipped with necessary gear, is always READY at SHORT NOTICE.

E. MEYER & CO. Chemulpo.

SOLE AGENTS IN KOREA FOR:
A. T. Morse, Sons & Co's "Fresco" Distemper

In all colours ready for use on walls, Ceilings etc.

and

AVENARIUS CARBOLINEUM

A wood-preserving and antiseptic oil preparation

Against decay, dry-rot, fungus and wood-destroying insects.

A large supply always in Stock. Prices upon application.

E. MEYER & Co., Chemulpo.

LAW UNION & CROWN INS. CO.

Fire risks accepted at Current rates, on go downs, merchandise, dwellings, and other property, subject to usual conditions.

HOLME RINGER & Co., Agents, Chemulpo

THE METHODIST PUBLISHING HOUSE, Little West Gate, Seoul.

JOB PRINTING, TYPEWRITER PAPER
CARBON PAPER, VISITING CARDS
STATIONERY, BOOK BINDING
BOOK PUBLISHERS
AMERICAN SCHOOL BOOKS
SPENCERIAN COPY BOOKS
PEN CARBON LETTER AND BILL BOOKS

S. A. BECK, Manager

HOLME RINGER & Co. Chemulpo.

General Merchants and Government Contractors.

Agents for the leading Banks SteamshipCompanies and Insurance Companies

Importers of Merchandise of every description.

KAMEYA & CO.

GENERAL STOREKEEPERS
Chinkokai - - Seoul
(Established 1895, Tokyo)

Confectionery, Hams, Canned Goods, Cutlery, Hirano & Tansan Water. Provisions, Gents, Furnishing goods, Toilet Articles, Travelling Bags, Tobacco, Cigars & Cigarettes Kitchen Utensils. Coffee. Biscuits.

Fresh Goods always kept in Stock.

Prices Moderate

Please come and inspect our goods.

BORDEN'S CONDENSED MILK CO.

New York, U. S. A.

ALWAYS IN STOCK
Eagle Brand Condensed Milk.
Gold Seal Condensed Milk.
Peerless (Family) Evaporated Cream.
Borden's Malted Milk.

E. MEYER & CO. Chemulpo, Korea, Sole Agents

ROYAL INSURANCE COMPANY,
Funds exceed £10,000,000
FIRE
AT CURRENT RATES.
LIFE
REDUCED PREMIUM.
HOLME RINGER & Co., Agents, Chemulpo.

HOTEL DU PALAIS SEOUL.

The only first class Hotel in Seoul. Situated in the centre of the city opposite the palace.

Cuisine under the supervision of an experienced French Chef.

Well ventilated and furnished throughout.

TARIFF UPON APPLICATION

L. MARTIN, Proprietor and Manager

大韓每日申報
대한미일신보

(뎨삼십호)　(토요일)　일쳔구빅사년팔월이십일일

본사고빅

이신보는영어와한어로셔거리일출판ᄒᆞ옵

신문가

ᄒᆞᆫ쟝 엽두돈오푼

일삭됴엽두량닷돈 미리돈이로밧ᄉᆞᆸ

광고료는

귀한의쟝단과ᄌᆞ힝의다쇼로즁감ᄒᆞ되뎡가로밧을터이오며오릭거ᄒᆞ녀대한사람마다다이신문을보실터이니광고버시기를원ᄒᆞ시는이들은우리신문사에와셔뎡약ᄒᆞ심을희망ᄒᆞ옵

○발힝소 박동대한미일신보사뎡이향교뎡해뎐영국인셜셀발힝쟈리오

사쟝 영국인 (베셜)

본사지졈

인쳔항교쟝동션지명셰로우리대한미일신보사인쳔지졈쟝을뎡ᄒᆞᆫ엿ᄉᆞ오니인쳔항에계신구람코쟈ᄒᆞ시는쳠군ᄌᆞ는히지졈에왕림ᄒᆞ시ᄋᆞᆸ

사고

○우리대한미일신보의목뎍은대한의안녕질셔에관ᄒᆞᆫ모든대목에딕ᄒᆞ야는공평ᄒᆞᆫ법률을쥬쟝홈이라우리등신원외임보는신문보시는쳠군ᄌᆞ의게ᄒᆞᆼ상보도ᄒᆞ려며편지를귀셔ᄒᆞ여주시논이논셩명과번디를쳑어붓치시기를희망ᄒᆞ오니이거슨신문샹에긔ᄌᆡᄒᆞ란는거시아니오다만극히신용ᄒᆞ논증거를숨코쟈홈이라귀쟈는아모귀셔던지긔ᄌᆡ홈을되갸ᄒᆞ는권리를가졋스나되갸ᄒᆞ는리유를말ᄒᆞᆯ터이오며공즁쟁화를문란케ᄒᆞ는듯ᄒᆞᆫ귀셔는의례히밧지안켓ᄉᆞᆸ나이다

론셜

흥복대쟝의젼진

○팔월삼이일우리신문론셜에말ᄒᆞᆫ바와ᄀᆞᆺ치유수란시와양ᄌᆞ평에셔젼쟁을ᄒᆞᆫ둥이일본흥복대쟝의소망과계획ᄒᆞᆫ되로다못되엿는디근일오일대련만일신문에론ᄒᆞᆫ면보ᄅᆞᆯ계ᄒᆞᆫ거슬보ᄂᆞᆫ즉팔월삼십신문등신원이쳘일삼십이일에흥복대쟝의젼졍ᄒᆞᆫ보고에져병이군졍샹필요ᄒᆞᆫ방법이진취가되여광편군병의방ᄎᆞᆼᄒᆞᆯ파쟁을과셔운신ᄒᆞᄂᆞᆫ계교쌈이되ᄎᆞ흥사ᄒᆞ야일병나가ᄂᆞᆫ디방이가되엿다ᄂᆞᆫ디

흥복대쟝과그부하쟝졸들의담대ᄒᆞᆫ힘은너ᄂᆞ나ᄂᆞ나그러나우리싱각에ᄂᆞᆫ졍평쳘월삼십일에파팔월일일에싸홈에아병들의디젹ᄒᆞᄂᆞᆫ힘이ᄆᆡ우건강ᄒᆞ야처음싸호든군ᄉᆞ들버텨셔옥조심ᄒᆞ고진혁ᄒᆞᆫ쳐담에그러ᄒᆞᆫ듯ᄒᆞᆫ디아라ᄉᆞ군ᄉᆞ들의승젼ᄒᆞ란ᄂᆞᆫ마음인즉우리가리왕면보에셔본바와ᄀᆞᆺ치아라사황뎨계셔구로파트킨쟝군의게뎐졍권리ᄒᆞᆫ리유를하숨ᄒᆞ시ᄂᆞᆫ디엇지ᄒᆞᆯ수업셔그러ᄒᆞᆫᄉᆞ졍을카뎐ᄒᆞ계ᄒᆞᆫ외운연고라ᄂᆞᆫ디

이러케그계획계되ᄂᆞᆫ일은필경일본으로더부러동맹ᄒᆞ야방조ᄒᆞᆫ령인듯ᄒᆞᆫ증비구에쟈흥복대쟝이젹병의계획ᄒᆞ야쟉죄ᄒᆞᆫ너버ᄐᆡᆫ터ᄒᆞ바구로파트킨쟝군으로ᄒᆞ여곰소명이잇셔셔너쟉대신식비ᄂᆞᆫ구라파소문을드를터인거시구로파트킨의대신ᄉᆞ무ᄒᆞᆫ거시반주셔일ᄒᆞ니버텨불만ᄒᆞ고광론이잇쓸터이나그러나반일아라사에셔쾌연그러ᄒᆞᆯ진댄챵문듯ᄒᆞ일인거시

구로파트킨의지휘은나라로ᄒᆞ여곰동쟁을로ᄒᆞ야위ᄒᆞᄂᆞᆫᄌᆞ리에잇셔셔필경도로젼ᄉᆞ를츙찰ᄒᆞᆫ다빙ᄌᆞᆺᄒᆞ고하모일토ᄒᆞ거영시그사름의형젹반되ᄒᆞ기조ᄒᆞᆫ너쟈대신ᄌᆞ희로불너드리ᄂᆞᆫ거시싱각ᄒᆞ여불만ᄒᆞᆫ거시

일본흥복대쟝은어느싸홈에던지ᄌᆞ긔의힘디로구로파트킨을공격ᄒᆞ엿고ᄯᅩ그사름의용계디로명령ᄒᆞ여볼이쳐셔대쟝된직칙반나란너ᄂᆞᆫ디잇ᄂᆞᆫ디

요양에셔지ᄎᆞ싸홈에젹병이ᄌᆞ연이디젹ᄒᆞ야방어ᄒᆞ기가조ᄒᆞᆯ듯ᄒᆞᆫ거시그싸지힝이대젹기우러놈과ᄒᆞᆼᄉᆞᄒᆞ야산밋누로도ᄎᆞ가면셔광지로둘녀잇ᄉᆞᆫ증지형숭괴얄거도대단이어려운디로병들노ᄒᆞ여곰빈치ᄒᆞ야누구던지왕리ᄒᆞᄂᆞᆫ거슬승리케ᄒᆞ엿ᄉᆞᆫ즉그곳문쳐ᄒᆞ기가싱하워헝ᄒᆞᆯ일이로되하깃헝당치못ᄒᆞᆯ거시ᄉᆞᆫ등ᄒᆞᆫ길이더만ᄒᆞ나취잇셔셔퇴ᄒᆞᄂᆞᆫ경우에ᄂᆞᆫ다나라기가대단히어려올샌인터아라사구로파트킨이ᄌᆞ긔의군디를싱양으로퇴거케ᄒᆞ랴고ᄒᆞᆫ바흥복대쟝의모둥이로음숭ᄒᆞ야운동ᄒᆞ기가ᄆᆡ우어려우되요량셔ᄂᆞᆫ다수ᄒᆞᆫ군병이라도운동ᄒᆞ기가됴ᄒᆞᆫ요지인즉

요양셔한번싸화졍평만ᄒᆞᄂᆞᆫ지경이면군ᄉᆞ로ᄒᆞ여곰ᄯᆞᆺ기리도ᄒᆞᆫ용ᄒᆞᆯ터이되아라사에셔한번힘쓸만ᄒᆞᆯ터인즉흥복대쟝도잘히싱각ᄒᆞ야운동ᄒᆞᆯ일이로다

잡보

○쟝샹의병 쟝샹등쳘량에ᄂᆞᆫ곽셔편에셔쳐류ᄒᆞᄂᆞᆫ디근일에병이즁ᄒᆞ야병셰가누허잇셔쾌치을수젼ᄒᆞ다더라

○군용디역 일궁수가황셩부에조회ᄒᆞ기를우리군용디역을슈용ᄒᆞᄂᆞᆫ디관ᄒᆞ야쟉기ᄒᆞᆫ과ᄀᆞᆺ치고시를발포ᄒᆞ엿ᄉᆞ니하량ᄒᆞᆫ시고분일너로히디역을조슈ᄒᆞᆫ기위ᄒᆞ야용수관원일과젼ᄒᆞᆯ평우에는귀부관리로회동ᄒᆞ라ᄒᆞᆫ엿ᄉᆞ며고시문에왈군용진츅에목젹으로경셩남대문외에셔한강ᄭᆞ지디역을아군에수용ᄒᆞ고히디역닉에셔ᄂᆞᆫ좌기ᄒᆞᆫ군령을시힝ᄒᆞᆯ뜻스로본월삼오일에한국쥬차군ᄉᆞ령관의통쳡이잇ᄂᆞᆫ디일은군용디역닉에잇ᄂᆞᆫ토디와가옥은일졀ᄆᆡ리ᄒᆞ며양여ᄒᆞ며젼당ᄒᆞ기부득ᄒᆞᆯᄉᆞ 이ᄂᆞᆫ군용디역닉에ᄂᆞᆫ수렵부헤인가를엇지못ᄒᆞᆫ쟈ᄂᆞᆫ집을짓거나디형을변쟉ᄒᆞᆷ이불가ᄒᆞᆯᄉᆞ 삼은이샹졈령을범ᄒᆞᄂᆞᆫ쟈ᄂᆞᆫ군률노쳐벌ᄒᆞᆯᄉᆞ 군용디역은표목을셰워구역을시명ᄒᆞᆷ이라ᄒᆞ엿더라

○쳐도역부 일본공ᄉᆞ가외부에조회ᄒᆞ되경셩셔한쥬ᄭᆞ지도로를슈츅ᄒᆞᄂᆞᆫ거ᄉᆞᆫ일젼에조회ᄒᆞᆫ바어니와지금쥬차군ᄉᆞ령관이셩명ᄒᆞᆫ바를거ᄒᆞᆫ즉ᄯᅩ안쥬셔의쥬ᄭᆞ지도로를슈츅ᄒᆞ미먼당ᄒᆞ다ᄒᆞᆫ엿ᄉᆞ니그도로슈츅에디ᄒᆞ여역부와죵약을회기ᄒᆞᆫ디로공급ᄒᆞ되일과에쟝발ᄒᆞ기시아니라즁용되기셔지공급ᄒᆞ되의쥬셩너에셔본읍비취면쟝거리셔지역부가구싱비ᄒᆞᆫ냥에셕공이싱인인데쪽야비싱근이오비쳔며쟝거리에셔차연관셔지역부가비쳔오빅명이오차연관에셔션쳔셔지역부가이쳔샹빅오싱인이오션쳔에셔쟝쥬셔지역부가일쳔구빅삼싱인이오쟝쥬에셔가산셔지역부기룡빅수싱인이오가산에셔안쥬셔지역부가수쳔이빅이싱인가량이나이것슨대강슈효인즉추후로ᄒᆞ증감이될뜻ᄒᆞ다ᄒᆞ엿더라

○용쳔일인 평샹남도용쳔군쥬와도라ᄒᆞᄂᆞᆫ셤에일본인수빅명이래쥬ᄒᆞ고ᄯᅩ계도에도슈빅명이래도ᄒᆞ엿다더라

○거졔일병 거졔군숑진포부근쳐리에일병이래도ᄒᆞ여뎐션을가셜ᄒᆞ고조디를싸코가옥을짓ᄂᆞᆫ다더라

○사와셜치 향쟈에본울ᄒᆞ든샨림쳔뎍문뎨가다시이러나셔일본공ᄉᆞ와외부대신ᄉᆞ이에쳔금교셥즁이라더라

○오셩동학 원쳔붓티일본에파견ᄒᆞᆫ학도를쳥ᄒᆞᆫ관쳔슉으로오셩명을거쳔ᄒᆞᆫ다더니쳔된쟈가이셩명이못되고로디시 쳐분이나리사쳔디주임관의쳔슉으로거쳔ᄒᆞ되본월이십오일너로여수히거쳔ᄒᆞ라ᄒᆞ음셧다고계쟉일학부에셔각부원쳥에훈조ᄒᆞ엿다더라

○츈보난모 츈쳔관찰ᄉᆞ가외부로보고ᄒᆞ되일본헌병이헝인일명과통ᄉᆞ일명을거ᄂᆞ리고츈부에리도ᄒᆞ야말ᄒᆞ기를티단공ᄒᆞᆫ일이나금월이십일브로역부를모집ᄒᆞ여달나ᄒᆞᄂᆞᆫ디샹부에셔ᄒᆞᆫ쳑이엄셧ᄉᆞ니쳔편ᄒᆞ기어렵고ᄯᅩ본도가공ᄇᆡᆨᄒᆞᆫ샨쳥에쳐ᄒᆞ야본리모군이엄ᄉᆞᆫ즉만일ᄇᆡᆨ셩을모집ᄒᆞ란ᄒᆞᆫ즉ᄂᆞᆼ시를당ᄒᆞ야며윽모집ᄒᆞᆯ슈엄ᄂᆞᆫ고로쳐보ᄒᆞ오니속히훈령을ᄂᆞ리ᄉᆞ미ᄇᆡᆨ셩을안졍케ᄒᆞ라ᄒᆞ엿더라

○쳥의슈로 외부에셔경부에쳥의ᄒᆞ기를향일공ᄉᆞ관찰ᄉᆞ의보고를거ᄒᆞᆫ즉ᄒᆞ엿스되경부텰도회ᄉᆞ원리쳘명이가평도엄로에일인과밋역부등의작폐를엄일히ᄒᆞᆫ금ᄒᆞᆫ엿고ᄯᅩ연산군슈가일인의게피상ᄒᆞᆫ셰에히원이향

UNION INSURANCE SOCIETY OF CANTON.

Head office Hongkong.
Marine risks underwritten at current rates.
Agents in Chemulpo,
MEYER & Co.

COMPAGNIE DES MESSAGERIES MARITIMES.

Fortnightly Direct Service.

For Marseilles
Via Ports.
Sailing from Yokohama
Calling at Kobe,
Shanghai, Hongkong, Saigon, Singapore,
Colombo, Djibonti, Suez, Port Said
and Marseilles.

For particulars apply to
HOLME RINGER & Co.,
Chemulpo

HAYASHIDA & CO.

16 MYENG DONG, CHING KO KAI, SEOUL.
BRANCH OFFICE AT CHEMULPO.

Money changers, Coal and Wood Merchants, Express Agents.

We are agents for the Pyeng-yang Coal Company and the Karazu Coal Company of Japan. We have the best quality of both anthracite and bituminous coal, and prompt execution of orders is our speciality. Firewood of all kinds kept in stock. Full weight guaranteed. Money of all denominations exchange, to current rates. Parcels received for all parts

---

CHINA MUTUAL LIFE INS- CO.

Most favourable terms to policy holders.

Benefit system unsurpassed.

HOLME RINGER & Co.
Agents, Chemulpo.

C. P. R.

CANADIAN PACIFIC RAILWAY COMPANY'S ROYAL MAIL STEAMSHIP LINE.

THE FAST ROUTE BETWEEN CHINA, JAPAN, AND EUROPE VIA CANADA AND THE UNITED STATES.

Route from Hongkong via Shanghai, Nagasaki (Inland Sea of Japan) Kobe, Yokohama, Victoria and Vancouver.

Twin Screw Empress Steamships—6,000 Tons—Speed 19 knots.

PROPOSED SAILINGS FROM YOKOHAMA.

R. M. S. Empress of India.
R. M. S. Empress of Japan.
R. M. S. Empress of China.
R. M. S. Athenian.
R. M. S. Tartar.

Special reduction (first class only) granted to members of the Military, Naval, Diplomatic and Civil Services and to Missionaries.

Passengers have choice of ten routes across the Continent of America and have privilege of travelling by any Atlantic Steamship Line.

Round the World passage tickets in connection with the P. and O. S. N., North German Lloyd and Messageries Co.'s £125.

All rates payable at current rate of exchange.

For further information, Tickets, Guide Books, etc., apply to

HOLME, RINGER & Co., AGENTS,
Chemulpo.

Grand Hotel,

(Formerly the Station Hotel)

Near the Railway Terminus, West Gate, Seoul.

The Best Hotel in Korea.
Handsome new Building.
Fine airy Rooms
Excellent Cuisine.
Terms Moderate.
Special terms to Missionaries
and to permanent boarders.

Electric cars within 2 minutes' walk.

W. H. EMBERLEY,
Proprietor.

EVERY FACILITY

In connection with Life Assurance Business is afforded by

The Standard Life Assurance o.,

One of the largest and wealthiest of the Provident Institutions of the United Kingdom. Forms of Application and all information will be promptly afforded on application.

10 CENTS A DAY.

Not a very large expenditure is it? But it is sufficient to secure for a man of 30 a policy with the STANDARD LIFE OFFICE for

$1323.

For all particular of rates, etc., apply to

Holme, Ringer & Co.,
Agents, Chemulpo.

THE NEW YORK LIFE INSURANCE COMPANY.

Have you ever been declined by and Company?

Are you engaged in as pecially hazardous occupation?

Have you heard of the New York Life Insurance Company's New Classifications for this class of Risks?

If not, send your date of birth, occupation and particulars of rejection, if any to

E. MEYER & Co., Agents, Chemulpo.

MITSUI BUSSAN KAISHA.
(MITSUI & Co.)

MITSUI GINKO
(MITSUI BANK.)

The Bank is owned by the members of the Mitsui Family, who, as partners, assume an unlimited responsibility for all liabilities of the Bank:—

Capital.......................Yen 5,000,000
Reserve Fund.................. " 5,600,000

HEAD OFFICE, TOKYO.
LONDON OFFICE, 34 LIME St., E. C.

BRANCHES AND AGENCIES:—

New York, San Francisco, Hamburg, Bombay, Singapore, Manila, Hongkong, Amoy, Chefoo, Tientsin.

Kobe, Hakodate, Yokohama, Kure, Yokosuka, Moji, Shimonoseki, Miike, Wakamatsu, Nagasaki, Kuchinotsu, Karatsu, Sasebo, Misume, Taipeh, &c.

Telegraphic Address for all the Offices:
"MITSUI"
A. B. C. AND A. 1 CODES USED.

Contractors of Coal
To the Imperial Japanese Navy. Arsenals and Railway Bureau, Principal Railway Companies and Industrial Works, Home and Foreign Mail and Freight Steamers.

Sole Proprietors
Of the famous Miike, Tagawa and Yamano Coal Mines.

Sole Agents
For the sale of Fukumo, Hokoku, Ichimura, Kanoda, Mannoura, Onoura, Ostuji, Sonoda, Tsubaruro, Yoshinotani, Yoshio, Yurokibura and other coals.

YANGTSE INSURANCE ASSOCIATION, LTD.

The undersigned, having been appointed agents for the above company, are prepared to issue policies and pay losses on marine risks at regular rates.

E. MEYER & Co.,
Agents, Chemulpo.

AMERICAN KOREAN ELECTRIC COMPANY.

Light and Power.

Main Office: Electric Building, Chong No.

RAILWAY DEPARTMENT.

OPERATING CARS BETWEEN EAST AND WEST GATE, EVERY TEN MINUTES:—

First Car leaves East Gate at 6:30 A. M. First Car leaves West Gate at 6:55 A. M.
Last Car " East Gate at 10:40 P. M. Last " " West Gate at 11:00 P. M.

OPERATING CARS BETWEEN EAST GATE AND IMPERIAL TOMB TERMINUS, EVERY TWENTY MINUTES:—

CONNECTING WITH EVERY ALTERNATE CAR ARRIVING AT EAST GATE FROM CHONG NO.

First Car leaves East Gate for Tomb at 6:50 A. M.
" " " Tomb for East Gate at 7:10 A. M.
Last " " East Gate for Tomb at 9:50 P. M.
" " " Tomb for East Gate at 10:10 P. M.

OPERATING CARS BETWEEN CHONG NO AND YUNG SAN (RIVER EVERY TWELVE MINUTES:—

First Car leaves Chong No for South Gate at 6:48 A. M.
" " " Chong No for Yung San at 7:24 A. M.
" " " South Gate for Chong No at 6:56 A. M.
" " " Yung San for Chong No at 7:57 A. M.
Last " " South Gate for Chong No 11:00 P. M.
" " " Yung San for Chong No at 10:11 P. M.

SPECIAL PRIVATE CARS FURNISHED TO SUIT CONVENIENCE OF PATRONS. PRICES ON APPLICATION AT HEAD OFFICE.

LIGHTING DEPARTMENT.

Where less than 250 candle power of light is used, the rate per month will be. Per 16 candle power incandescent lamp. All night.—Yen 2.50.
Per 32 candle power incandescent lamp:—All night:—Yen 4.00. Per 50 candle power incandescent lamp:—All night:—Yen 6.00.
" 150 " " " " — " " 10.00. " 1200 " " enclosed arc " " 20.00.

Where more than 250 candle power of light is used, a Meter will be installed, if requested:—Rent of Meter Yen 2.00 per month. Rate of charges by meter reading:—Two Sen per Ampere per hour. (Approximately this is equal to about One Sen per 16 c. p. lamp per hour) Minimum monthly charge where meter is installed, Yen 20.00 per month, which includes rental of meter.

Estimates for installing lights furnished on application. An assortment of chandeliers always on hand.

AMUSEMENT DEPARTMENT.

ANIMATED PICTURES AT EAST GATE.
Every evening - - - Except Sunday.
From 8 to 10 P. M.

10 Cents:—Gen. Admission:—10 Cents. Seats in First Class Section. 15 Cents Extra.

Change of program each week. Pictures from Foreign Lands. Pictures of Local Scenes:—Amusing and Instructive.

An entertaining evening for a reasonable price.
MERRY-GO-ROUND:—At East Gate.
From 10:00 A. M. till 11:00 P. M.

5 Cents a Ride.

Take your Exercise on The Galloping Horses.

Comfortable seats in the Chariots.

한셩뎐긔회사

미국뎐긔회사 고뵬안 보사백 고빅
도ᄒ옵나이다
상활동사진관ᄉ소와목마운동장량쳐로연
여叫면차가온장안으로통힝ᄒ여ᄃ니여이
습
또아긔계에곳치노힌편ᄒ고됴흔마차도잇
습
코마우편ᄒ고또조미잇는됴흔운동이되겟
어됴흔모형흘달나아는물을ᄒ고워ᄐ치안
ᄃ카는ᄒ번ᄐ는데오젼식이오
미일상오열시브터하오열ᄒ시ᄭ지ᄒ옵고
목마운동장은동대문안에잇습고
가되겟습
쳠군조외게갑도싸고저녁에됴흔쇼일거리
잇고구경흘만ᄒ거시오니
셔양사진과대한과온동양사진션비대ᄌ미
는ᄃ
젼에옵고빅쥬일에사진을싼것스로다밧고
고젼랑ᄃ금은하등에십젼이오상등에이십
일외에는미야에여덟시브터열시ᄭ지ᄒ옵
활동사진젼람소는동대문안에잇습고일요
회락부

All Cars Run Direct to the Animated Pictures and Merry-Go-Round.

동경팔월십칠일발

대본영공보

송권향서 어제아춤에우리

산길츙모는군중수신을숨아려

순구에잇는뎍군젼초에차편ᄒᆞ

야우리텬황폐하의셩지와항복

ᄒᆞ기를권고ᄒᆞ는문서를뎍군쟝

모장의게보내엿는ᄃᆡ뎍군에서

는십칠일아춤에회답이올터이

라ᄒᆞ엿더라

동경발 팔월십팔일

공수관착

○거졀항복 려순을에워싼일

[illegible]

동군공보 동일

공수관착

[illegible]

광고

[illegible]

뎐보

[illegible]

뎐보

[illegible]

[illegible]

TELEGRAMS.

RUSSIANS AT PORT ARTHUR REFUSE TO SURRENDER.

Tokyo, Aug. 18.

The Commander-in-Chief of the attacking force at Port Arthur reported that after a short deliberation on the Japanese demands of surrender, the Russian General replied that be refused to surrender and did not even desire to send away non-combatants.

NAVAL NEWS.

Tokyo, Aug. 17th.

It is rumoured that the Rossia after her return to Vladivostock sank in the harbour, owing to the severe damage received in the battle.

FURTHER DETAILS FROM TOGO.

Tokyo, Aug. 18th.

On 11th inst. our two gunboats Maya and Akagi while scouting in the vicinity of Port Arthur discovered two Russian gunboats near Sunsangko, engaged in shelling the Japanese land forces. Our gunboats steamed to attack them and opened fire, one shell taking effect on the gunboat Kiriak. The enemy then retreated to Port Arthur.

During the battle on the 10th inst. one of our destroyers, the Murakamo, approached within 400 metres of a cruiser, which appeared to be the Pallada. She discharged a torpedo which appeared to take effect.

BRITAIN AND WEI-HAI-WEI.

RUMOURED PERPETUAL OCCUPATION.

We are indebted to a correspondent in America for the following important statement repecting Wei-hai-wei, by the London correspondent of the Cleveland Plain Dealer, under date July 16th:—

It is rumoured in political circles that Great Britain, in view of the predicted early fall of Port Arthur, is on the point of concluding negotiations with China for the occupation in perpetuity of Wei-hai-wei. The exact nature of the reported transaction is not definitely stated, but it is thought that it will take the form either of a purchase of the port and the adjacent land or their acquisition by a ninety-nine year lease, renewable forever.

This report is credited by those especially well informed in East-Asiatic affairs. They point out that by the terms of Britain's tenure Wei-hai-wei reverts to China the moment Russian occupation of Port Arthur and the Liaoting peninsula ceases. That Lord Lansdowne, who will be compelled to deal with the situation, will do his utmost to prevent British evacuation of the port is considered certain. He is a tenacious imperialist and disapproves of surrender of political advantages in any part of the world, particularly where the interests of Britain and Russia or the interests of Britain and Germany are in juxtaposition.

Sir Ernest Satow, British Minister to China, who is an aggressive defender of British possessions and prestige in the Far East, is likely to favour the retention of Wei-hai-wei at any cost. His influence is great with Downing Street, because weight is attached to his judgment with regard to everything that concerns the West Pacific. Above all, Japan is determined to keep Britain in Whi-hai-wei. Mr. Uchida, Japanese Minister in China, is devoting all his power to strengthening Sir Ernest Satow's purpose to retain the stronghold. It is understood that he has gone so far as to declare that if Britain goes out Japan will go in.

Tokio is afraid of Germany, whose occupation of Kiaochao bay has caused deep distrust, and does not intend to permit Wei-hai-wei to pass into German hands or any other hands regarded as hostile to the Island State. The Japanese argue that to allow such a thing would be equivalent to relinquishing the chief value of Port Arthur to Japan, since the present Russian fortress would thereby be strategically neutralized.—Kobe Herald.

General Oku reports the enemy's gunboat "Sivoutch" blew herself up in the river Liao without having been disarmed beforehand.

The Yungtung River has overflowed its banks in Chihli, causing great destruction of property. It is believed many lives were lost.

We learn that the Waste Land scheme has again come up for discussion but whether it is in its original or an amended form has not transpired.

General Kuropatkin has ordered the useless civil elements to be removed from Harbin, where winter quarters for the army are to be prepared.

Reuter's correspondent at St. Petersburg states on good authority that there were at least 4,000 Russian casualties in the last battles in the Haicheng district.

Special instructions to the Government as to the best manner in which to repair the northern roads have been issued by the Japanese Military Headquarters.

It is reported that His Majesty's interests in the American Korean Electric Co. are represented by a committee, the chief of which is the Vice Minister of the Agriculture Department.

The Governor of Pyeng Yang telegraphs Seoul requesting permission to make some changes in the magistracies of certain districts in order to facilitate the work of rendering assistance to the Japanese military authorities.

Difficulty seems to be experienced in finding sufficient candidates to fill the number of 50 sons of high officials to be educated in Japan, as recently ordered by His Majesty. Only so have so far responded to the invitation, which consequently has been extended to relatives of middle grade officials.

From London papers we learn that there will be no attempt at present to settle all the questions pending between Russia and Great Britain. The Foreign Office has received from Sir Charles Hardinge the British Ambassadorto Russia, the Russian answer to its representations in which the St. Petersburg Government regrets its inability, while the war with Japan is in progress, to undertake such important negotiations but when peace is restored it will be willing to, provided circumstances permit.

Speaking in London on July 22nd, Mr. Chamberlain, referring to the preference shown for Chinese over Indian labour in the Transvaal, said that when he proposed a large emigration of coolies the Indian Government was unreasonable and ignored evey interest except those of India. He sympathised with the apprehension of the Transvaal whites that Indian immigration was overwhelming them. Mr. Lyttleton said that with regard to future Indian immigration into the Transvaal, they might urge that a certain policy was short-sighted and inhuman, but to coerce the colony was impossible. The case of the Indians in the Transvaal under the Boers was far different, the honour and dignity of the British name demanded that the decision of May 12 should be upheld. He had put the matter clearly to the Transvaal and he was confident as to the result.

THE MOUJIK.

Writing from St. Petersburg to the "Daily Mail," Mr. Perceval Gibbons says:—

He was like a piece of the brown land he stood on—stale, overworked, unprofitable.

Bowed somewhat, and cowering uncouthly at the shoulders, with his greasy garments belted about his middle by an end of rope, he was hardly a human figure, scarcely a thing to claim kin with on any plane of philanthropy or tolerance. His eyes glowered dully amid the hair that sprouted rankly on his face, and they were the hostile ominous eyes of an animal, a plagued and cornered beast—never of a man. Even his walk was less than human, for he dragged one great foot after another without alertness or seeming volition. The dust he was made of was only half-translated; there was yet raw earth in it.

He lurched on, through the sparse young green of his field, and so about the clump of dark firs to the hut that stood at the hub of his existence. He glanced neither to the right nor left as he went, but drove onward with drooped head and forethrust chin that proclaimed the whole world his enemy. His great red hands swung idly athwart ships as he went, crooked to the shape of the spade handle they belonged to; and the little eyes in the flat hairy face glared swiftly and unwinkingly at the narrow path he traversed. As he rounded the corner of the road he came in sight of his home. There were people about it, and he went slower as he gazed, with parted lips, at them. A woman was there, a woman unsexed, worn, like himself, to the bone with toil, and a man—a man in uniform.

THE TAX-GATHERER.

What the words hide, the eyes betray. At the bottom of the dull eyes there grew a red speck, a small angry gleam that lent for a moment life and some quality of terror to the huge loutish frame of the moujik. He had recognized the tax-gatherer, the publican of the New Testament, and there awoke in him a sudden old hatred of the authority which takes the bread of the poor man. At that instant he might have been a man; there was devil in him, just that touch of animal fury blended with a sense of wrong which makes great demagogues. It was murder that showed through, passionate resentment, fiery self-protection—anything awful, elemental, and irresistible. And then, as the tide of long oppression and generations of serfdom reasserted itself, he was a moujik again, bestial, obsequious, incoherent, dropping nervously a ceremonial cap to the smile of the taxgatherer.

The woman, wife of the moujik, turned dull eyes from the one to the other as the tax-gatherer, stretching forth his legs, talked patronisingly. She, too, was just a beast, the frame of a woman from which hardship, never-ending toil, sterile hope, abortive desires, had expelled the woman's soul. Flat-breasted, red-armed, she slouched like a weary man and listened mechanically to the patter of the tax-gatherer. She should have been at work, but death and taxes interrupt business in Russia as elsewhere.

A LITTLE DEBT.

"It is the little debt," explained the tax-gatherer. "Not a tax at all, moujik, but the little debt. Eleven years now that there has not been enough to pay the district-tax. The Tsar, you know—God keep him—cannot wait for ever. There is the war, and that costs —Lord, you could never guess how it costs! So there must be money. You see, the Little Father must have money."

"God keep him," mumbled the moujik. "But there is no money here. None at all!"

The tax-gatherer pulled down the cuffs of his long coat.

"I grieve," he said, lightly. "Truly, I grieve. I would rather take money. But you cannot give it if you have none. Still, there is always the cow."

"Now, what the devil!" he added, turning sharply.

It was only the woman. She had moaned, strickenly, and now trembled under the official's eyes.

"But—but," the moujik stammered, 'I have only the one, Excellency. Only the one, by St. Nicholas and all the kind saints."

He was putting forward the extreme plea. In Russia they strip you of your goods down to the cow. They must leave you the one cow.

(To be continued.)

The Korea Daily News.

To be published daily except Sundays.
Rate of Subscription:—
Per Year, Yen 25.
Per Quarter, Yen 7.
Per Month Yen 2.50

Postage in Korea not charged extra.
Postage abroad charged extra.

Advertisements, 50 sen per day for 1 inch or less.
5 yen per month per inch.
50 yen per year per inch.

All communications to
E. T. BETHELL,
Editor and Publisher.
Pak-tong, Seoul.

THE STAUS OF THE FINANCIAL ADVISOR.

There seems to have been a difference of opinion between the Japanese Minister and the Korean Minister for Foreign Affairs.

A report reaches us to the effect that on the 16th at the Japanese Legation, Mr. Hayashi handed Mr. Yi Ya yŏng a a document for the appointment of a Japanese supervisor to the Finance Department and asked for his assent to it. Finding that the document gave the "advisor" complete control over the Finance Department Mr. Yi Ya-yŏng very warmly declined to endorse it. Mr. Hayashi as warmly pressed it and the result was a deadlock for some time.

Finally an agreement seems to have been reached to the effect that although nominally under the commands of the Minister for Finance, the advisor shall have full executive control of the Department. Precisely what the scope of the arrangement is, it is difficult to determine. It appears to give the "advisor" a free hand so long as he retains his appointment, but appears to give the Minister for Finance power to dispense with his services should he so desire.

If this version of the interview be correct, a fairly satisfactory conclusion seems to have been arrived at. If the powers of the new "advisor" were to be purely and simply advisory his efforts would be as much of a dead letter as have been those of other foreigners who have at different times acted as advisors to the various government departments.

Of course a good deal will depend upon Mr. Kinoshita himself. If he can conduct his department without friction, he will be able to achieve important reforms. If on the other hand he raises a storm of opposition, very little improvement in the existing state of things need be looked for. If the finances of the country were properly looked after a very important advance would be made in the direction of the suppression of the bribery and corruption which are now so rampant.

If the arrangement is as given above, and the new "advisor" proves to be a gentleman of honesty, tact and ability we think Korea will have taken a step in the right direction without the sacrifice of any of the rights and privileges which belong to her as a nation.

GERMANY AND RUSSIA.

Telegrams from Berlin state that the new Russo-German Commercial Treaty will be put into force on Jan. 1st 1906 and will remain in force for twelve years.

The rumours prevalent that as a result of the satisfactory conclusion of this Treaty, Germany has agreed to take charge of the raising of Russian loans, are without foundation, as are also the reports circulated that Germany is likely to mediate between Japan and Russia in the present dispute.

THE CZAR AND HIS MONEY.

The fact that the Czar has just made a little contribution of $100,000,000 from his private purse to the Russian war funds reminds us that Mr. Rockefeller is not the only rich man in the world. There are a few others, and there is hardly a doubt that the Russian monarch overtops the Standard Oil emperor, not only as the first of autocrats, but as the first of plutocrats, says a writer in the Philadelphia "Saturday Evening Post."

Most royalties are very small potatoes financially compared with anyone of several American millionaries. Mr. Rockefeller could put all the sovereigns of Europe, except the Czar, on his payroll at their present wages without depriving himself of a single bowl of crackers and milk or even lacking a quarter to drop into the contribution box on Sunday. He could pay the salary of King Edward or the Kaiser for a year out of a month's income, and have something left for carfare.

But the Russian Emperor is in a different class. In the imperial budget the allowance for his household is figured at the meagre rate of about $8,000,000 a year, but that is merely the beginning of his resources. He owns a great part of Russia as his private property—mines, forests, and illimitable stretches of arable lands. In European Russia alone the strictly private domains of the imperial family are as large as Indiana. The state owns twenty times as much more, and the Czar is the state. In Siberia the imperial resources are still more opulent. Most of the rich mines of gold, platinum, and precious stones are worked for the benefit of the Czar and his family.

But beyond all this, the Emperor is the absolute master of the National Treasury and all its varied sources of income. In England the king talks in his speeches of "my army," "my navy," and "my exchequer," but all this is understood to be a legal fiction. Everything is regulated by parliament and the king cannot touch a penny that is not appropriated to his use. But in Russia the Czar can speak of "my army" and "my navy" in literal fact. He could disband the whole outfit if he chose, and pocket the money saved by the operation. His civil list is simply the amount that he sees fit to dip out of the treasury. He could double or triple it without asking anybody's permission. The whole treasury is his, and all the taxing power of the empire, to the limit of the ability of his subjects to pay. Is it not clear that the diffident young Nicholas is the richest man in the world?

M. WALDECK-ROUSSEAU.

The Kobe Herald of August 12th has the following biography of the late Y. Waldeck-Rousseau.

[M. Pierre Marie Waldeck-Rousseau, French statesman and lawyer, was born December 2, 1846. He followed his father in choosing the profession of the law, and in 1879 was elected a member of the Chamber of Deputies of Rennes. After introducing a bill for the Reform of the Judiciary, he was re-elected in 1881, and joined the Gambetta Ministry as Minister of the Interior. In Men and Women of the Time it is said of him that he endeavoured to keep the administration of the country free from political interferance. He resigned with the rest of the Ministry in January, 1882, but accepted the same post in Jules Ferry's Cabinet of the following year, retaining it until March, 1885. In 1886 he joined the Paris Bar, and there achieved a great success, notably in the defence of M. De Lesseps in the famous case arising out of the Panama Canal scandals. So great was his legal work that in 1889 he did not stand as a Parliamentary candidate. He was elected a Senator a few years later. Some time later he completely severed himself from political life but in June 1899, after the fall of the Dupuy Cabinet, he consented to form a Coalition Ministry (at the earnest solicitation of President Loubet) to see the Dreyfus rehabilitation through. After one failure, he succeeded in his enormous task, thanks in some measure to the presence in the Cabinet of the former Imperialist, General de Galifet, as Minister of War, and the Socialist, M. Millerand, as Minister of Commerce. To M. Waldeck-Rousseau belongs the credit of having remained longer in office as Premier than any of his contemporaries, and when he retired from office he carried with him the respect and esteem of all right-thinking Frenchmen. The deceased statesman was only in his fifty-eighth year.]

TRANSPORT CREWS AT TOMSK.

The head office of the Nippon Yusen Kaisha is in receipt of a telegram from Captain Higo, who commanded the transport "Idzumi-maru," sunk in June by the Vladivostok squadron. Captain Higo's message is from the Siberian city of Tomsk, and states that all the crew of the "Idzumi" were saved, consisting of fourteen officers and fifty-two men, and are at present in good health. The telegram also mentions that thirteen officers and sixty-six men of the "Sado-maru" are also at Tomsk and are well. The officers include Captain Anderson, Chief Engineer Willian Keer, Chief Officer Dring, and Second Engineer A. Carmichael. There were eighteen officers althgether on the "Sado"—four escaped being taken to the Russian ships and were afterwards rescued, while one was drowned.

THE CALCHAS

Reuter having wired out that the Blue Funnel steamer Calchas had been captured by the Russians, during the recent raid of the Vladivostock cruisers, considerable anxiety has been felt in several quarters as to the fate of the steamer. The idea that she had been captured was dispelled some days ago, no confirmation of any kind having been received from London. It now appears that the steamer Lyra had instructions when she left Yokohama to warn the Calchas, if she sighted her, to proceed to Hongkong instead of Yokohama. The Lyra was evidently successful in meeting the incoming steamer, as the Calchas (we learn from the Japanese Herald) has since been sighted steaming slowly (perhaps short of coal) for the southern British port.

FRICTION AT NEWCHWANG.

According to a Chefoo message of August 6th. the Japanese Military Administrative Commissioners have applied to the French Consul to remove the French flag on the Russian consulate at Inkao. The French Consul appears to have claimed the right of flying his flag on the building on the plea that he had been appointed Honorary Consul for Russia. The question is still unsettled. On August 4 a Russian woman arrived at Inkao from Tientsin. The Japanese refused to permit her to live in the city for reasons which they made known to her. It is alleged that the French Consul tried to take her away with him, whereupon both are said to have been detained.—Japan Advertiser.

MILITARY REQUIREMENTS.

The Japanese military authorities have issued a proclamation stating that all the ground between the South Gate of the city and the Han River will be required for military purposes. The land will be staked out and anybody buying or selling land or otherwise interfering with the property within the mark poles will be liable to punishment by martial law.

On the 17th inst. H. E. Mr. Hayashi, accompanied by his interpreter, Mr. Kokubo, was received in audience by His Majesty.

A Melbourne despatch states that both the Senate and the House of Representatives have selected Dalgety, New South Wales, to be the Federal Capital.

Lieutenant Wilton, the Australian officer who was sentenced to life imprisonment for killing unarmed Boers during the South African War, has been released.

The Korea Daily News.

VOL. I, SATURDAY, AUGUST 20, 1904. No. 30

大韓每日申報
대한ᄆᆡ일신보

일쳔구ᄇᆡᆨ사년팔월이십삼일 (화요일) (뎨삼십이호)

본샤고ᄇᆡᆨ

이신보는영어와한어로셔거ᄆᆡ일츌판ᄒᆞᆸ

신문가

ᄒᆞᆫ쟝 엽두돈오푼

일삭됴엽두량닷돈 맛돈으로밧숩

광고료는

긔한의쟝단과ᄌᆞ힝의다쇼로즁감ᄒᆞ되렴가로밧을터이오며오릐지아녀대한사람마다다이신문을보실터이니광고내시기를원ᄒᆞ시는이들은우리신문샤에와셔면약ᄒᆞ심을희망ᄒᆞᆸ

○발힝소 박동대한ᄆᆡ일신보샤법어학교압헤젼영국인셜필림집자리오

샤쟝 영국인 (비셜)

본샤지뎜

인쳔항고잔동셰지명씨로우리대한ᄆᆡ일신보샤인쳔지뎜쟝을뎡ᄒᆞ엿ᄉᆞ오니인쳔항에계신구람코쟈ᄒᆞ시는쳠군ᄌᆞ는히지뎜에왕림면의ᄒᆞ시옵

사고

○우리대한ᄆᆡ일신보의목뎍은대한의안녕질셔에관한모든폐목에ᄃᆡᄒᆞ야는공평한변론을쥬장ᄒᆞᆷ이라우리동신원의탐보는신문보셔는쳠군ᄌᆞ의계ᄒᆞᆼ상보도ᄒᆞ리며편지를긔셔ᄒᆞ여주시는이는셩명과반디를젹어붓쳐시기를희망ᄒᆞ오니이거슬신문샹에긔지ᄒᆞ라는거시아니오다만극히신용ᄒᆞ는증거를삼고쟈ᄒᆞᆷ이라긔쟈는아모긔셔던지긔지ᄒᆞᆷ을되각ᄒᆞ는권리를가졋스나되각ᄒᆞ는리유를말ᄒᆞᆯ터이오며공즁평화를문란케ᄒᆞ는듯ᄒᆞᆫ긔셔는의례히밧지안켓숩나이다

론셜

려순함복에거졀이라

합즁국부령싸비쓰씨의만국공법샹대례의변론

려순항공격에ᄃᆡᄒᆞ야죵말에비들ᄒᆞ엿는ᄃᆡ일본셔아라사진에향ᄒᆞ야항복ᄒᆞ라ᄒᆞᆫ즉아라사이거졀ᄒᆞ엿더니ᄯᅩ아진쟝군의게말ᄒᆞ기를이거졀ᄒᆞᆷ으로셔로싸ᄒᆞᆯ터인즉군인아닌사ᄅᆞᆷ은다니여보니라ᄒᆞ엿더니일본셔이러ᄒᆞᆫᄉᆞ건에ᄃᆡᄒᆞ야군법샹졍ᄒᆞᆫ조관ᄃᆡ로직혀시힝ᄒᆞ는쟝관의말이가감동ᄒᆞ야긔록ᄒᆞᆯ만ᄒᆞ노라려슌을지금ᄭᅡ지굿게직혀잇슴은불시에군인아니사ᄅᆞᆷ들노ᄒᆞ야곰조직ᄒᆞᆷ은아니로ᄃᆡ그여러사ᄅᆞᆷ의ᄉᆞ졍인즉져히들의처소를ᄯᅥ나지못ᄒᆞ게ᄒᆞᆷ이니

이사실을깁히싱각ᄒᆞ건ᄃᆡ그셩책요히처와밋산ᄆᆡᆨ에다모도포병으로둘너셰워방비ᄒᆞ게ᄒᆞ엿고ᄯᅩ능히방비치못ᄒᆞᆯᄇᆡᆨ셩들은억제로잡아두어셩직히는군사들노ᄒᆞ여곰조력ᄒᆞ야ᄃᆡ젹ᄒᆞ게ᄒᆞ라는마음이잇셔셔그리ᄒᆞᆷ인듯ᄒᆞ되군사들의둘너셰운ᄃᆡ는방형업시측량ᄒᆞ야졍당치아니ᄒᆞ고군사들은수효만츙수ᄒᆞ야느리는거시긴치아니ᄒᆞᆫ일인ᄃᆡ이런거슬모르고져히들의로력ᄒᆞ야쥰비ᄒᆞ는거시실노가련ᄒᆞᆫ거시만일지휘ᄒᆞ는관리가군졍을진보케ᄒᆞᆯ진ᄃᆡᆫ환위ᄒᆞ리도긴밀히만드러실심으로운동ᄒᆞ며ᄯᅩ공격을방비ᄒᆞ는ᄃᆡ도가히ᄒᆞᆯ만ᄒᆞᆫ군사외에는모도감싱ᄒᆞ야도져희단속ᄒᆞ는거시올커놀셩책에셔지휘ᄒᆞ는관리들은조리업시다만방어ᄒᆞ기만주장ᄒᆞ며방비ᄒᆞᆫᄃᆡ쓸짐를은죽게된바ᄊᆞ홈아니ᄒᆞ는ᄇᆡᆨ셩들노억제로담부ᄒᆞ야수운ᄒᆞ게ᄒᆞ며ᄯᅩ이왕붓터지휘관이방어ᄒᆞᆷ을지체ᄒᆞ야미급ᄒᆞ면벌금을척즁ᄒᆞᆷ이젼례가되여셔이러ᄒᆞᆫᄯᅢ에도이법쓰는거시엇지셩취ᄒᆞᆯ긔회를싱각ᄒᆞ야유지ᄒᆞ라는마음이리오이거시다쟝구치못ᄒᆞᆯ일인즉소위방비ᄒᆞᆫ다ᄒᆞᆷ에도관활ᄒᆞᆯ사ᄅᆞᆷ이업스며ᄃᆡ젹ᄒᆞ야ᄊᆞ홀것도이러케오릭지체ᄒᆞᆷ은약ᄎᆞᄒᆞᆫ일에졍부에리익을취ᄒᆞ야그리ᄒᆞᆷ이느그러느이러ᄒᆞᆫ의견은히셕ᄒᆞ기가어렵지아니ᄒᆞᆫ거시사령관되는사ᄅᆞᆷ이방어ᄒᆞ기로쟉졍ᄒᆞ야졍당ᄒᆞ게ᄒᆞ련다ᄒᆞ면필경셩취될소망이잇스되만일이러케오릭만ᄉᆞ으러가면점점싱명만손히ᄒᆞ야부지ᄒᆞ지못ᄒᆞᆯ터이요종말에는항복밧게ᄒᆞᆯ수업슬터이느그러ᄒᆞ느조긔는긔왕위로나라를도으고아릭로즁인의게명령ᄒᆞ는직권을잡아손즉이일ᄒᆞ는ᄃᆡ조긔의힝호시령ᄒᆞ기가넉넉ᄒᆞᆯ진ᄃᆡᆫ아모조록길을헤치고ᄃᆡ젹ᄒᆞ야느오랴ᄒᆞᆯ터인거시일본셔어느ᄯᅢ지든지조긔의항복ᄒᆞᆯᄯᅢ와명령ᄒᆞ는ᄃᆡ로든지군즁의갓처잇는사ᄅᆞᆷ들의마음ᄃᆡ로와ᄯᅩ항복ᄒᆞ라ᄒᆞᆷ에거졀ᄒᆞ는ᄃᆡ로둘리가만무ᄒᆞ고이러케약잔공동만식일리가업슬터이며ᄯᅩᄒᆞᆫ이러케오릭도록방어치못ᄒᆞ고다만구차히항복만거졀ᄒᆞ야일병의공격ᄒᆞ라ᄒᆞᆷ을핍박ᄒᆞᆯ지경이면필경에는인명만만히죽이고견ᄃᆡ지못ᄒᆞ야항복ᄒᆞᆫ뒤에는호원ᄒᆞᆯ곳도업슬터인즉

이거슬츄탁ᄒᆞᆯ진ᄃᆡᆫ아라사사령관의항복거절ᄒᆞ는거시두어가지료량이잇셔그리ᄒᆞᆷ인듯ᄒᆞᆫᄃᆡ쳣지는날ᄌᆞ를ᄭᅳ으러조긔졍부에셔구완병보내기를기다림인듯ᄒᆞ고둘지는방어ᄒᆞ는거시필경셩취가될줄로싱각ᄒᆞᆷ인듯ᄒᆞ느둘지싱각은조곰도건리치아니ᄒᆞᆫ일이요쳣지의사는쟝ᄎᆞ종말ᄃᆡ젹ᄒᆞ야항거ᄒᆞᆯᄯᅢ에우리가가히볼만ᄒᆞᆯ거시되

려슌항진즁에잇는아라사군사가모도합ᄒᆞ야이만오쳔명이라ᄒᆞᆫ즉일본히군이아국함ᄃᆡ침노ᄒᆞ는바목아쇼쟝부하에잇는군사륙칠만명으로엇지ᄒᆞᆫ바다목쟝이느직히기를료량ᄒᆞ리요만일려슌을취ᄒᆞ야공훈세움을말ᄒᆞᆯ진ᄃᆡᆫ일병을두관으로난호와요양ᄊᆞ홈을ᄌᆞ유로련속ᄒᆞ게ᄒᆞ며히ᄊᆞ위로파견ᄒᆞᆫ군졸은셩공치못ᄒᆞᆷ을후회ᄒᆞᆯ지니려슌함낙을날노참아구로파트킨의진세만점점견확ᄒᆞ게ᄒᆞ며ᄯᅩ지휘관의히셕키어려운일을싱각ᄒᆞ야항복ᄒᆞ라고ᄒᆞᆷ을거절ᄒᆞ도록ᄒᆞᆷ인즉만일담대ᄒᆞᆫ사ᄅᆞᆷ갓틀진ᄃᆡ엇지용납ᄒᆞ야힘동쳐아니리요이러케오릭려슌을참아잇기로만합당히넉여그리ᄒᆞᆷ이나셜혹그나마지군사들노더부러굿세게ᄃᆡ젹ᄒᆞ드ᄅᆡ도저희의변심되는ᄭᅡ닭에일본셔능히방비ᄒᆞ야물니칠만ᄒᆞ도다

잡보

○신문검열 본월이십일에일본ᄉᆞ령부에셔졔국황셩량신문샤쥬무원을초치ᄒᆞ야말ᄒᆞ되군ᄉᆞ상ᄉᆞ항을신문상에일졀긔지ᄒᆞ지말느ᄒᆞ고ᄯᅩ신문을긔여히검열ᄒᆞ겟다ᄒᆞ엿다더라

○면샤협졍 한미면긔회샤ᄉᆞ무를ᄃᆡ강협졍ᄒᆞᆫ후에졍부에셔검찰위원을파송ᄒᆞ엿는ᄃᆡ츌립문부를피ᄎᆞ긔록ᄒᆞᆫ다더라

○신회검지 본보젼호에긔지ᄒᆞᆫ바유신회ᄉᆞ건을깁문ᄒᆞᆫ즉본월이십일에유신회가죵로지젼도가로회동ᄒᆞ엿더니경무청에셔슌검오십명을파송ᄒᆞ야훈칙ᄒᆞ기를무론모인ᄒᆞ고오인이상이회집ᄒᆞᆫ자는그ᄉᆞ항을담문ᄒᆞ고즉시효유ᄒᆞ야히산케ᄒᆞ되완거ᄒᆞ야슌죵치아니ᄒᆞ는자는즉각에착리ᄒᆞ라ᄒᆞ엿다더라

○쥬본지설 각군슈과궐이현금십팔군인ᄃᆡ일간쥬본이된다더라

○롱금잡술 경무청에셔오ᄂᆡ무당과잡술ᄒᆞ는남녀와ᄉᆞ가에관공뫼신자를낫낫치죠사ᄒᆞ야슈탐ᄒᆞᆫ즉ᄒᆞᆫ셩ᄂᆡ거ᄒᆞᆫ자가오ᄇᆡᆨ여명인ᄃᆡ그즁에 명셩황후ᄭᅴ셔의신ᄒᆞ엿다ᄒᆞ는녀인이명인ᄃᆡᄒᆞᆫ녀인만위션착슈ᄒᆞ고하나는방금형착즁이오ᄐᆡ조고황제ᄭᅴ셔와졔갈공명과디쟝보살이와신ᄒᆞ엿다ᄒᆞ는자의뫼신화상은일일히소화ᄒᆞ고범죄인은경자는방송ᄒᆞ고즁자는즁률에쳐ᄒᆞᆫ다더라

○명초회의 일젼에 대ᄂᆡ에셔탁지대신박졍양씨를 명초ᄒᆞ사명일에는단당회의ᄒᆞ라ᄒᆞ신 쳐분이느리셧는ᄃᆡ그익일을당ᄒᆞ야박대신이병와ᄒᆞᆫ고로회의가못되엿다더라

○시무옹망 려항젼셜을독문ᄒᆞᆫ즉평리원에셔셔를당ᄒᆞ야의례졍송ᄒᆞ엿스나무죄히획리ᄒᆞᆫ자들은다일지관을못ᄒᆞ야곤고가자심ᄒᆞ야셔시무되기를쥬야로옹망ᄒᆞᆫ다더라

○쟝시협잡 슈원셩ᄂᆡᄇᆡᆨ셩들이싱계가끌칙ᄒᆞ야셩밧쟝시를셩ᄂᆡ에옴기라ᄒᆞᆸ신 쳐분을봉승ᄒᆞ야셩ᄂᆡ거민이젹이소셩

UNION INSURANCE SOCIETY OF CANTON.

Head office Hongkong.
Marine risks underwritten at current rates.
Agents in Chemulpo,
MEYER & Co.

COMPAGNIE DES MESSAGERIES MARITIMES.

Fortnightly Direct Service.

For Marseilles
Via Ports.
Sailing from Yokohama
Calling at Kobe,
Shanghai, Hongkong, Saigon, Singapore,
Colombo, Djibouti, Suez, Port Said
and Marseilles.

For particulars apply to
HOLME RINGER & Co.,
Chemulpo

HAYASHIDA & CO.

16 MYENG DONG, CHING KO KAI, SEOUL.
BRANCH OFFICE AT CHEMULPO.

Money changers, Coal and Wood Merchants, Express Agents.

We are agents for the Pyeng-yang Coal Company and the Karazu Coal Company of Japan. We have the best quality of both anthracite and bituminous coal, and prompt execution of orders is our speciality. Firewood of all kinds kept in stock. Full weight guaranteed. Money of all denominations exchange, to current rates. Parcels received for all parts

CHINA MUTUAL LIFE INS. CO.

Most favourable terms to policy holders.

Benefit system unsurpassed.

HOLME RINGER & Co.
Agents, Chemulpo.

C. P. R.

CANADIAN PACIFIC RAILWAY COMPANY'S ROYAL MAIL STEAMSHIP LINE.

THE FAST ROUTE BETWEEN CHINA, JAPAN, AND EUROPE VIA CANADA AND THE UNITED STATES.

Route from Hongkong via Shanghai, Nagasaki (Inland Sea of Japan) Kobe, Yokohama, Victoria and Vancouver.

Twin Screw Empress Steamships—6,000 Tons—Speed 19 knots.

PROPOSED SAILINGS FROM YOKOHAMA.

R. M. S. Empress of India.
R. M. S. Empress of Japan.
R. M. S. Empress of China.
R. M. S. Athenian.
R. M. S. Tartar.

Special reduction (first class only) granted to members of the Military, Naval, Diplomatic and Civil Services and to Missionaries.
Passengers have choice of ten routes across the Continent of America and have privilege of travelling by any Atlantic Steamship Line.
Round the World passage tickets in connection with the P. and O. S. N., North German Lloyd and Messageries Co.'s £125.
All rates payable at current rate of exchange.
For further information, Tickets, Guide Books, etc., apply to
HOLME, RINGER & Co., AGENTS, Chemulpo.

Grand Hotel,

(Formerly the Station Hotel)

Near the Railway Terminus,

West Gate, Seoul.

The Best Hotel in Korea.
Handsome new Building.
Fine airy Rooms
Excellent Cuisine.
Terms Moderate.
Special terms to Missionaries and to permanent boarders.

Electric cars within 2 minutes' walk.

W. H. EMBERLEY,
Proprietor.

EVERY FACILITY

In connection with Life Assurance Business is afforded by

The Standard Life Assurance Co.,

One of the largest and wealthiest of the Provident Institutions of the United Kingdom. Forms of Application and all information will be promptly afforded on application.

10 CENTS A DAY.

Not a very large expenditure is it? But it is sufficient to secure for a man of 30 a policy with the STANDARD LIFE OFFICE for

$1323.

For all particular of rates, etc., apply to

Holme, Ringer & Co.,
Agents, Chemulpo.

THE NEW YORK LIFE INSURANCE COMPANY.

Have you ever been declined by and Company?

Are you engaged in as pecially hazardous occupation?

Have you heard of the New York Life Insurance Company's New Classifications for this class of Risks?

If not, send your date of birth, occupation and particulars of rejection, if any to

E. MEYER & Co., Agents, Chemulpo.

MITSUI BUSSAN KAISHA.
(MITSUI & Co.)

MITSUI GINKO.
(MITSUI BANK.)

The Bank is owned by the members of the Mitsui Family, who, as partners, assume an unlimited responsibility for all liabilities of the Bank:—

Capital.......................Yen 5,000,000
Reserve Fund.......................“ 5,600,000

HEAD OFFICE, TOKYO.

LONDON OFFICE, 34, LIME ST., E. C.

BRANCHES AND AGENCIES:—

New York, San Francisco, Hamburg, Bombay, Singapore, Manila, Hongkong, Amoy, Chefoo, Tientsin.

Kobe, Hakodate, Yokohama, Kure, Yokosuka, Moji, Shimonoseki, Miike, Wakamatsu, Nagasaki, Kuchinotsu, Karatsu, Sasebo, Misume, Taipeh, &c.

Telegraphic Address for all the Offices:
"MITSUI"

A. B. C. AND A. 1 CODES USED.

Contractors of Coal
To the Imperial Japanese Navy. Arsenals and Railway Bureau, Principal Railway Companies and Industrial Works, Home and Foreign Mail and Freight Steamers.

Sole Proprietors
Of the famous Miike, Tagawa and Yamano Coal Mines.

Sole Agents
For the sale of Fukumo, Hokoku, Ichimura, Kanoda, Mannoura, Onoura, Ostuji, Sonoda, Tsubaruro, Yoshinotani, Yoshio, Yurokibura and other coals.

YANGTSE INSURANCE ASSOCIATION, LTD.

The undersigned, having been appointed agents for the above company, are prepared to issue policies and pay losses on marine risks at regular rates.

E. MEYER & Co.,
Agents, Chemulpo.

AMERICAN KOREAN ELECTRIC COMPANY.

Light and Power.

Main Office: Electric Building, Chong No.

RAILWAY DEPARTMENT.

OPERATING CARS BETWEEN EAST AND WEST GATE, EVERY TEN MINUTES:—

First Car leaves East Gate at 6:30 A. M. First Car leaves West Gate at 6:55 A. M.
Last Car " East Gate at 10:40 P. M. Last " " West Gate at 11:00 P. M.

OPERATING CARS BETWEEN EAST GATE AND IMPERIAL TOMB TERMINUS, EVERY TWENTY MINUTES:—

CONNECTING WITH EVERY ALTERNATE CAR ARRIVING AT EAST GATE FROM CHONG NO.

First Car leaves East Gate for Tomb at 6:50 A. M.
" " " Tomb for East Gate at 7:10 A. M.
Last " " East Gate for Tomb at 9:50 P. M.
" " " Tomb for East Gate at 10:10 P. M.

OPERATING CARS BETWEEN CHONG NO AND YUNG SAN (RIVER) EVERY TWELVE MINUTES:—

First Car leaves Chong No for South Gate at 6:48 A. M.
" " " Chong No for Yung San at 7:24 A. M.
" " " South Gate for Chong No at 6:56 A. M.
" " " Yung San for Chong No at 7:57 A. M.
Last " " South Gate for Chong No 11:00 P. M.
" " " Yung San for Chong No at 10:11 P. M.

SPECIAL PRIVATE CARS FURNISHED TO SUIT CONVENIENCE OF PATRONS. PRICES ON APPLICATION AT HEAD OFFICE.

LIGHTING DEPARTMENT.

Where less than 250 candle power of light is used, the rate per month will be. Per 16 candle power incandescent lamp. All night.—Yen 2.50.
Per 32 candle power incandescent lamp:—All night:—Yen 4.00. Per 50 candle power incandescent lamp:—All night:—Yen 6.00.
" 150 " " " " " " 10.00. " 1200 " " enclosed arc " " " 20.00.

Where more than 250 candle power of light is used, a Meter will be installed, if requested:—Rent of Meter Yen 2.00 per mouth. Rate of charges by meter reading:—Two Sen per Ampere per hour. (Approximately this is equal to about One Sen per 16 c. p. lamp per hour) Minimum monthly charge where meter is installed, Yen 20.00 per month, which includes rental of meter.

Estimates for installing lights furnished on application. An assortment of chandeliers always on hand.

AMUSEMENT DEPARTMENT.

ANIMATED PICTURES AT EAST GATE.
Every evening - - - Except Sunday.
From 8 to 10 P. M.

10 Cents:—Gen. Admission:—10 Cents. Seats in Firs Class Section. 15 Cents Extra.

Change of program each week. Pictures from Foreign Lands. Pictures of Local Scenes:—Amusing and Instructive.

An entertaining evening for a reasonable price.
MERRY-GO-ROUND:—At East Gate.
From 10:00 A. M. till 11:00 P. M.

5 Cents a Ride.

Take your Exercise on The Galloping Horses.

Comfortable seats in the Chariots.

한셩뎐긔회샤

미국뎐긔회사 고문안 보사뎨 고ᄇᆡᆨ
토ᄒᆞ옵나이다
샹활동사진뎐ᄂᆞᆫ소와목마운동쟝량쳐로연
여ᄃᆡ뎐차가운쟝안으로통힝ᄒᆞ여ᄃᆞ니ᄋᆞ이
습
또이긔계에ᄀᆞᆺ쳐노힌편ᄒᆞ고 됴흔마차도잇
습
코미우편ᄒᆞ고또조미잇ᄂᆞᆫ됴흔운동이되겟
어됴흔모형흘달나아ᄂᆞᆫ몸을ᄐᆞ고위ᄐᆡ치안
디가ᄂᆞᆫ흘번ᄯᅳᄂᆞᆫ데오젼시이오
비입샹오열시브터하오열흘시ᄭᆞ지ᄒᆞ옵고
목마운동쟝은동대문안에잇습고
가되겟습
쳡군조의게감도싸고져ᄒᆞ에됴흔쇼일거리
잇고구경흘만ᄒᆞᆫ거시오니
셔양사진과대한과운동ᄒᆞ사진언네ᄃᆡ조미
논ᄃᆡ
젼이옵고미쥬일에사진을ᄇᆞ긘것스로다밧고
고젼ᄅᆞᆫ되금은하동에십젼이오상동에이십
일외에ᄂᆞᆫ미야에여덟시브터열시ᄭᆞ지ᄒᆞ옵
활동사진뎐람소ᄂᆞᆫ동대문안에잇습고입료
회판부

All Cars Run Direct to the Animated Pictures and Merry-Go-Round.

ᄒᆞᆯ가망이잇더니셩외에ᄉᆞᄂᆞᆫ김윤환선윤삼등이감히체긔ᄒᆞᆯ욕심으로슈다ᄒᆞᆫ젼지를도득ᄒᆞ야히쟝들셩외에도로옴기랴고경향에출몰ᄒᆞ야몽문도독ᄒᆞᆯ셰쳥젼파슌검소비젼이합ᄉᆞ만여량이라ᄒᆞ고그돈을긔쥬두사ᄅᆞᆷ의계팔쳔량식록봉ᄒᆞ고여잔잔피ᄒᆞᆫ쥬식상의개도열이쳔량식억륵으로비령ᄒᆞᆫ죽진극히빈잔ᄒᆞᆫ상민아집파라넛키외에ᄂᆞᆫ죠희ᄒᆞᆯ도리가만무ᄒᆞ야원셩이랑자ᄒᆞ다더라

○허민도탁 황히판철ᄉᆞ가내부에면보ᄒᆞ되인부모집ᄉᆞ로빈셩이만히도타ᄒᆞ야망죠ᄒᆞᆫ지라엇지ᄒᆞ올지회면하시ᄒᆞ라ᄒᆞ엿더라

○가평군보 가평군슈가외부로보고ᄒᆞ엿스되인부모집ᄉᆞ로본군두메ᄇᆡᆨ셩들이일헌병의공갈ᄒᆞᄂᆞᆫ데경겁ᄒᆞ야ᄒᆞᄂᆞᆫ말들이ᄉᆞ러가셔죽어도라오리라ᄒᆞ고면면이ᄉᆞ발동문을돌리고합ᄉᆡᆨ읍즁으로모히니어ᄂᆞ지경에일울지모른다ᄒᆞ엿더라

○됴약됴연 일젼에락지대신박졍양씨와외부대신리하영씨가합셕ᄒᆞ야졍부에셔한일간됴약셔를졍졍ᄒᆞ고됴인ᄒᆞᆫ여좌와곳ᄒᆞ니 일은대한졍부ᄂᆞᆫ대일본졍부에셔쳔거ᄒᆞᆫ일인일명을재무고문관으로고빙ᄒᆞ야재무에관ᄒᆞᆫᄉᆞ항은일졀그의권을무러시힝ᄒᆞᆯᄉᆞ 일은대한졍부ᄂᆞᆫ대일본졍부에셔쳔거ᄒᆞᆫ외국인일명을외교고문관으로고빙ᄒᆞ야외교에관ᄒᆞᆫ요긴ᄒᆞᆫᄉᆞ무ᄂᆞᆫ일졀그의견을무러셰힝ᄒᆞᆯᄉᆞ 대일본젼권공ᄉᆞ림권조 대한외부대신리하영댱지ᄒᆞᆫ대신박졍양도일

○일ᄉᆞ쳥폐 본월이십일에외부에셔래셕원으로죠회ᄒᆞᆫ거ᄂᆞᆯ일본공ᄉᆞ림권조씨가긴급폐샹쥬ᄒᆞᆯᄉᆞ가잇셔셔본일하오ᄉᆞ시에폐현ᄒᆞ겟다ᄒᆞ엿ᄂᆞᆫ데대황뎨폐하셰셔ᄂᆞᆫ요ᄉᆞ이 옥톄가미령ᄒᆞ샤폐ᄉᆞ를졍권ᄒᆞ실슈업ᄂᆞᆫ지라림공ᄉᆞ가래셕원으로공함ᄒᆞ기를동일하오ᄉᆞ시에긔어히컬니에드러가아모셰셔지라도 폐현ᄒᆞ고셔야ᄂᆞ오겟노라ᄒᆞᆫ지라래셕원에셔회답ᄒᆞ기를외부대신이귀공관에방문ᄒᆞ야샹의ᄒᆞᆯ터이니 폐현은ᄒᆞᆯ슈업다고ᄒᆞ엿ᄂᆞᆫ데맛춤외대ᄂᆞᆫ신병으로자지못ᄒᆞ고외부협판윤치호씨가더힝ᄒᆞ엿더니아모ᄉᆞ건도샹의ᄒᆞ지못ᄒᆞ엿고림공ᄉᆞ가또래셕원으로공함ᄒᆞ기를이십이일하오ᄉᆞ점종에ᄂᆞᆫ긔어히폐현ᄒᆞᆯ터이라ᄒᆞ엿ᄂᆞᆫ데작일에ᄂᆞᆫ아마 폐현이되엿슬듯ᄒᆞ다더라

○영ᄉᆞ청폐 영국공ᄉᆞ쥬어면씨가외부로죠회ᄒᆞ엿스되명헌태후폐하승하ᄒᆞ옵신후위문ᄒᆞ옵신영국 황대폐하의친셔를봉정ᄒᆞᆯ차로 폐현ᄒᆞᆯ을청ᄒᆞ노라ᄒᆞ엿더라

○덕쳥즁셔 덕국공ᄉᆞ가외부로죠회ᄒᆞ기에왈덕국샹고셰창양힝에셔쌀ᄉᆞ냥질소용화약수십궤와탄환ᄒᆞᆫ샹조를덕국한보로말미암아향항에셔지도착ᄒᆞ엿더니허항에셔ᄒᆞ기를허항이즁립디라ᄒᆞᆫ고화약과탄환을집류ᄒᆞ고쥬지아니ᄒᆞᄂᆞᆫ고로죠쳥ᄒᆞ니귀대신은사죠ᄒᆞᆫ신후에슈입즁셔를써보니여히항영국관원의게교부ᄒᆞ야히량건물을무란이출구케ᄒᆞ심을바란다ᄒᆞ엿더라

○잡기착슈 지작야에원동헌병더ᄉᆞ령관리재용씨가에셔잡기군을슌검이경무쳥으로착거ᄒᆞ엿다ᄒᆞᄂᆞᆫ풍셜이잇ᄂᆞᆫ데 그들셩명은안직알수업다더라

○탁지고문 탁지고문관고빙ᄒᆞᄂᆞᆫ계약은멀지아녀셔결졍ᄒᆞᆯ모양이오이계약을셩립ᄒᆞᄂᆞᆫ데로일본대쟝셩의목하면죵태랑씨ᄂᆞᆫ력ᄒᆞᆫᄒᆞᆯ터이라더라

○창고회사 경셩에잇ᄂᆞᆫ일본인들이보셰창고와창고쥬식회샤를셜립ᄒᆞᆯ계획이라더라

○리씨샹소 죵어픔리돈형씨가박의병송규헌량씨의샹소ᄉᆞ의에더ᄒᆞ야단히소를봉졍ᄒᆞ엿ᄂᆞᆫ데그ᄉᆞ의ᄂᆞᆫ박송량씨구라ᄒᆞ야무엄ᄒᆞᆫ죄를징치ᄒᆞᆯ을쳥ᄒᆞ엿더라

외보

●아ᄉᆞ힐문 죠션신보에동경면을거ᄒᆞᆫ즉쥬쳥아공ᄉᆞ가쳥졍예힐문ᄒᆞ되청국졍부에일본에즁립권침허ᄒᆞᆯ을용납ᄒᆞᆫ연지일본을엄ᄒᆞ호ᄂᆞᆫ듯션지혹그즁립ᄒᆞᆯ슈업슴을스ᄉᆞ로써다름인지ᄒᆞ엿더라

●청졍요구 동보동면을거ᄒᆞᆫ즉청국졍부에셔ᄂᆞᆫ쥬쳥일공의게더ᄒᆞ야쳥구ᄒᆞ기를일함어연터에셔포획ᄒᆞᆫ아함레시톄레누어호를환부ᄒᆞ라ᄒᆞ엿다더라

●구입슌양함 아국어아연명공화국에셔구립ᄒᆞᆫ슌양함이쳑을히삼위협티에합동케ᄒᆞᆫ기위ᄒᆞ야향일히삼위항티가일본동경히에유익ᄒᆞ야권제운동을힝ᄒᆞ엿ᄂᆞᆫ데히함이쳑이무익히죵곡히협을지ᄂᆞ히삼위에도착ᄒᆞ엿단말이잇더라

○급쥬션발명 미국인후언도씨가십이년간에칠만원을허비ᄒᆞ야삼일간에쵹육화리파간에항힝ᄒᆞᄂᆞᆫ급쥬션을발명ᄒᆞᆫ또며이일반에텨셔양에횡단ᄒᆞᄂᆞᆫ급쥬션을제죠ᄒᆞᆯ차로준비즁이라더라

○로합거취 지부에셔온뎐보를거ᄒᆞᆫ즉본월십일오후에교쥬만으로도쥬ᄒᆞᆫ로국슌양함노ㅣ우치구호와아수콜드호이쳑은동디에셔셕탄을만재ᄒᆞ고그밤에출항ᄒᆞ야힝위가분명치아니ᄒᆞᆫ데십이일오후셰셔쯤에샹히바다밧긔잇ᄂᆞᆫ슈명도부근에셔십삼일아ᄎᆞᆷ셔지뎡박ᄒᆞ야잇섯다ᄒᆞ엿더라

○로쟝부인 려슌에셔연텩로도주ᄒᆞᆫ로함레시레리누이호를ᄐᆞ고간부인ᄒᆞᆫ나혼나히삼십오륙셰쯤되엿ᄂᆞᆫ데쓰렛셀즁쟝의부인이오기타부인들도그즁에만히잇다ᄒᆞ더라

○로쟝젼ᄉᆞ 샹히셔온뎐보를거ᄒᆞᆫ즉교쥬만에도주ᄒᆞ엿든스테라잇지ᄉᆞ관의담화를드른즉쎄얀호ᄂᆞᆫ출항ᄒᆞᆯ즈음에포셜ᄒᆞᆫ슈뢰에걸녀항구안으로도로드러가고다른군함은산동각방면에셔일본함티와격젼ᄒᆞ여ᄉᆞ령쟝관위드쎄우트쇼장은대포탄환을맛져신체젼부를일코발만남아참모와ᄒᆞᆫ가지로젼ᄉᆞᄒᆞ엿고맛세윗지쇼장과밋함쟝도부샹ᄒᆞ여간션이청도로그망ᄒᆞ엿고함재의손샹은대단히심ᄒᆞᆫ데슈리ᄒᆞᆫ후에출항ᄒᆞᆯ엿ᄂᆞᆫ지아니ᄒᆞ엿ᄂᆞᆫ지알수업다ᄒᆞ더라ᄒᆞ엿

관보

뎨이쳔구빅십일호

광무팔년팔월이십이일

○셔임급ᄉᆞ령

○면본직 시위뎨일련대뎨이대대부관륙군보병부위 라호쳔 위뎨일련대뎨일대대부륙군보병부위 리즁완 진위뎨일련대뎨이대대부륙군보병참위 리졔뎡 진위뎨일련대뎨삼대대부륙군보병참위 셔병억 진위뎨ᄉᆞ련대뎨일대대부륙군보병참위 려슌근

○보시위뎨일련대뎨이대대부관 륙군보병부위 리쥬완

보천위뎨일련대뎨일대대부 륙군보병부위 라호

○관륙군보병부위 라호

○보진위뎨일련대뎨일대대부 륙군보병참위 셔병익

○보진위뎨일련대뎨삼대대부 륙군보병참위 려슌근

○보진위뎨ᄉᆞ련대뎨일대대부 륙군보병참위 리졔뎡

이샹팔월십륙일

○승셔관임관오등 남양군공립소학교교원 정운호

○의원면본관 즁츄원의관 장윤원 젼영긔 최학여 남양군공립소학교교원 정운호 과산군공립소학교교원 윤대션

○임즁츄원의관셔쥬임관륙등

울산군슈 김우식 샹의ᄉᆞ쥬ᄉᆞ 리희영 경긔면령 죠영년

○임남양군공립쇼학교교원서관임관오등 삼화항공립소학교교원 리필구

○임파산군공립쇼학교교원서관임관륙등 공쥬군공립쇼학교교원 김인형

○임삼화항공립쇼학교교원서관임관오등 김포군공립소학교교원 엄관셥

임홍쥬군공립소학교교원서관임관오등 양천군공립소학교교원 박졔현

이샹팔월십팔일

○의원면본관 비서원승 김경즁 경릉령 리츙용

○명홍문관학ᄉᆞ셔칙임관삼등 졍이품 남정철

○명니쟝원경셔칙임관삼등 렬도원감독 강홍대

○임비셔원승셔쥬임관오등 졍삼품 홍승두

○임경긔면령셔관임관칠등 영희면령 정지덕

○임영희면령셔관임관ᄉᆞ등 원구단ᄉᆞ제셔령 장길샹

○임원구단ᄉᆞ제셔령셔판임관륙등 릉신ᄉᆞ면화과쥬ᄉᆞ 정철영

○샹의ᄉᆞ쥬ᄉᆞ서관임관ᄉᆞ등 릉신ᄉᆞ면화과쥬ᄉᆞ 김창진

○임릉션ᄉᆞ면화과쥬ᄉᆞ서관임관륙등 윤긔익

○임경릉령서관임관칠등 창릉령 한즁교

○임창릉령서관임관칠등 익릉령 김히슈

○임익릉령서관임관칠등 륙픔 리츙용

이샹팔월십구일

○임삼화감리서쥬ᄉᆞ서관임관일등 옥구감리서쥬ᄉᆞ 면록훈

○임옥구감리서쥬ᄉᆞ서관임관륙등 리종인

이샹팔월이십일

○임쥬일법봉 인쳔면보ᄉᆞ쥬ᄉᆞ 박경환

팔월십팔일

○허림시셔리의정부의정ᄉᆞ무 법부대신 박졔슌

팔월이십일

○궁졍록ᄉᆞ

○니쟝원경리근형ᄉᆞ직소 비지니에소청더토의시ᄒᆞ라

팔월십구일

탁지부대신박정양ᄉᆞ직ᄉᆞ 비지니에다시번거이말고즉시시무ᄒᆞ라

○의정부찬정홍슌형ᄉᆞ직소 비지니에ᄉᆞ양ᄒᆞᆫ즁에홍문학ᄉᆞ져임은의시ᄒᆞ라

팔월십구일

companion, communicate the Admiral's message and get her to return. She then steamed ahead and in company with the other boat and the tow, proceeded directly to sea.

"The Admiral intended to enforce his order, but was deceived by the lying statement of the second torpedo boat. He was also afraid that if he fired unnecessarily, he might injure merchant shipping.

"Undoubtedly the Japanese were fully cognizant of the dismantling of the Russian vessel, because the Admiral advised them twice early in the evening, and also advised the Japanese consul several times about the matter. The dismantling was completed and the guns loaded in my launch at 4:30 P. M. on the preceding afternoon. Unquestiona bly the Japanese have committed a grave error."

* * *

The departure of the torpedo boats with the Russian was witnessed aboard the U. S. cruiser "Cincinnati," and the statement of persons aboard that ship are about as follows:

At roll call they saw a torpedo boat with another in tow. The boats were not recognized but when they got opposite the Chinese flagship the Japanese colours were hoisted. The flagship was observed to run up international signals and at the same time her bugles sounded the call to clear for action which was apparently accomplished in five minutes. The torpedo boat was steaming slowly.

The flagship manned and trained her guns on the passing vessel. Meantime another Japanese torpedo-boat a mile away near shore landed several persons, then steamed in the direction of the flagship, stopping a short distance away while the first boat with her tow proceeded. The second torpedo boat remained until the first one was well out then steamed ahead full speed and joined her, proceeding to sea.

It was impossible to see Admiral Sah yesterday, it being stated on the flagship that he was sick and could receive no one. Some of the officers stated that the admiral felt keenly the successful deception that had been practiced on him by the Japanese, and that he had reported the entire affair to higher authority.

The general expression yesterday both among Chinese and foreigners, was that of regret that the commanding officer of the Chinese squadron did not take advantage of his opportunity to decide the affair quickly and let the raiders know that they are not to be allowed to disobey lawful orders and carry things with a high hand, even in a Chinese port. Admiral Sah is a highly respected official, among his own countrymen and among foreigners, a man of character, who has demonstrated his ability to handle trying situations, and it is generally deplored that his cautiousness and honesty of purpose should have been taken advantage of and led him to be hoodwinked into failing to mete out a punishment richly deserved by unlawful acts in disrespect of his orders.

PRESS CENSORSHIP.

We note that all our contemporaries, Japanese and Korean, have received instructions from the Army Headquarters to refrain from publishing information of military movements, and to submit their issues to the censor before putting them into circulation. So far we have received no request of the kind but it has been our practise to voluntarily submit any item the publication of which might in any way affect military interests. We note that in Japan the censorship is still very rigorous and it is a common thing for an apparently harmless article to go the rounds of the press and lead to the wholesable infliction of fines.

THE FOREIGN ADVISORS.

On the 19th instant agreements were signed by Mr. Hayashi and the Ministers for Finance and Foreign Affairs relating to the appointment of foreign advisors to these two departments. The two principal clauses provide that: (1) The advisors shall be recommended by the Japanese Government. (2) They shall have full executive control in their respective departments.

IMPORTANT CORRECTIONS.

1. Referring to a paragraph, which appeared in yesterday's issue, it was not an ox but an axe that Mr. Choi Ik-hyon carried with him as an argument in favor of his memorial to the throne.

2. In reply to several enquiries, we are unable to say what Throne ordered viceroy Yuan Shih-kai (whoever he may be) to repair what embankment and how that will relieve sufferers.

The article came from an exchange, was cut out and pasted in the midst of some carefully gleaned explanatory information. The paste preved too seductive to the office rat, and all our work was wasted, so we ask our readers to be patient while we try and find out what the Throne is, what the embankment is, who the viceroy is, and how the repairs to the embankment will relieve the sufferers. This will take weeks, unless we can catch the rat.

THE END OF A SPY.

A Korean named Pak Kye-hyŏk, who was for many years domiciled in Vladivostok, has been shot by the Japanese gendarmes at Wiju. Suspected of being in Russian employ he was arrested near Wiju on July 27th and subsequent investigations and his own comfession convicted him of having given information to the Russians as late as February 15th. He was accordingly sentenced to death. Northern Korea abounds in natives with pro-Russian tendencies, so it is surprising that we do not hear of more of these captures.

ANOTHER SOCIETY.

A new political society has come into existence. It is called Yu Shin or Il Sing, and meetings are held daily near the big bell. The Japanese gendarmes do not interfere, and whether this or something else is the reason we cannot say, but the Koreans believe the speakers to be in Japanese employ and consequently do not manifest much interest in the proceeedings.

COOLIE AGITATOR EXECUTED.

Yesterday morning, a Korean coolie malcontent at Pyeng Yang was discovered in "flagrante delicto," destroying railway works, and was publicly shot by the Japanese in the presence of some thousands of spectators as a warning to others.

A Shanghai telegram states that many Russians are leaving Liayoang in the direction of Mukden.

A man can be a poet without living in an attic, but not long, if he depends upon the poetry for a living.

Some men become famous by having five cent cigars named after them and others deserve fame for smoking them.

A telegram from Ninkow states that a general attack, which is believed the final one, commenced on Port Arthur on the night of the 17th inst.

The "Resitelnai" is reported to be the destroyer, which conveyed Madame General Stoessel and a party of officers' wives in safety to Chefoo.

Mr. Yi Yu-hyong, a Korean gentleman, has made the sensible proposal to the govement that the disbanded soldiers should fill the much-felt want of coolies.

A sorcerer by the name of Sul was recently arrested and offered his captor $40.00 as a bribe for his release. With commendable honesty the policeman refused it and carried out his duty.

The brave defenders of their country recently despatched to assist in repelling the Russian invasion have taken up their quarters in the Chol Won district, where they complain, food is very scarce.

Never mind, they are safe there.

The British Minister has applied for an audience with H. M. the Emperor in order to present an autograph letter of condolence on the death of the Empress Dowager which has been received from the King of England.

THE SPELLING OF WAR NAMES.

Our worst anticipations nave been fulfilled and something more, remarks the New York Weekly Tribune. The Manchurian war has resulted in a confusion of nomenclatures worse coufounded than even in a pessimistic mood we feared. Chinese names have been Japanned, Korean names have been Russianized, and inconsistency has run riot. We have been daily confronted with Feng-Wang-Cheng divided into syllables, and with Wafangtien undivided, though assuredly if Feng-Wang-Cheng is correct, we should write Wa-Fang-Tien, and if Wafangtien is the true form, then we should adopt Fengwangcheng. For the thousand cases of such inconsistency it is easy to blame correspondents and editors, though it may not be as just as it is easy. Certainly the professional geographers are not entitled to cast the first stone. The most hurried "stop press" despatches in the morning papers are as consistent in their use of names as the most carefully drawn and engraved maps of the standard atlases. Note, for example, how such a work deals with names not only in Manchuria, but elsewhere. The work before us, one of the best extant, puts down Jaipur and Bhartur for our oldtime Jeypore and Bhurtpore—that "pur" has so smart an air of superior learning!—yet it leaves Cawnpore and Lahore unchanged. It transforms Bangalore into Bangalur, but spares Mysore. It insists upon putting the German K. in what we used to spell Congo, but does not change Africa to Afrika. Why not? It changes the familiar Kowloon into Kaulun, but lets Rangoon remain as of old. It alters Cameroon to Kamerun, but fails to turn Karoo into Karu. The map is published by those who insist upon the old spelling of "colour" and "honour," yet it makes "Mush" of Moush and "Batum" of Batoum.

Nor is the work more consistent when it turns from alien lands to Europe itself. Cracow is changed to Krakau, but on the same map Tarnow and Moscow remain unchanged. Courland and Cronstadt are printed Kurland and Kronstadt. but Crimea and Carpathian retain their ancient forms. On one map we find Kattegat and Cattegat side by side. Coblentz is Koblenz, but Cologne is not turned into Köln. Aix la-Chapelle is Germanized into Aachen, but Lorraine is not changed to Lothringen. Elsewhere are the Bay of St. Michael and the Baie de la Seine.

We submit that such eclecticism run mad is worse then anything our news-papers have ever done. If at half-past 1 in the morning the night editor should take time to refer to the atlases for the approved spelling of every outlandish name that comes to him, the result would be about eleven times worse than the present state of affairs. We wish there might be some improvement. Perhaps there will be. We shall keep on working for it. But if it comes, it will more probably begin with the newspapers and extend thence to atlases and gazetteers than in the reverse order.

THE MOUJIK.

CONCLUDED.

The tax-gatherer joined his fingertips and shook his head.

"Eleven years," he said deprecatingly, "and the district-tax never once paid in full! Yet a cow has always been exempted. Moujik, that makes eleven cows the Little Father has spared you. Eleven! By St. Izak, one would think you were a baron! And now you would make it twelve."

"God keep him," the moujik murmured. "I have only the one."

THE TSAR'S COW.

You cannot cheat a beast. Honest and dishonest are distressingly clear to him. The tax-gatherer was annoyed, and proceeded to hurry up the cow.

"Two hundred and eleven roubles you owe," he said impressively, "and the Tsar is at war. Have you no share? The cow will make, say, twenty-five roubles. Yes we will be generous. Our Lady be merciful to those that show mercy. Twenty-five roubles, and the rest can wait. That is, if you bring the cow forthwith."

"But I have only the one," pleaded the moujik. He could only urge the law; his grief constituted no kind of claim. But the woman moaned again.

"But bring the cow," urged the tax-gatherer. "Let us see this cow. Twenty-five roubles is no trifle—and there is the war. The cow, then. Why does your wife not bring the cow, the Tsar's cow?"

"God keep him! Bring the cow," said the moujik.

It was then the woman fell on her knees, as though she were to be considered. But sweat a woman as you will, wear her, wrench her with labour, bedraggle and unsex her as you may, she will still fall on her knees in extremity and urge that she is a woman.

"Excellency, Excellency," she gasped hoarsely, "it is our last. It is our last. And the children—the children——"

It was amazing, but it did not last long. Her husband struck her savagely, and off she went, slowly and heavily, and brought the cow, while the tax-gatherer twisted his moustache and the moujik blinked apologetically.

"OF THE PEOPLE."

"This, then is the Tsar's cow!" The tax-gatherer looked critically at the beast, which turned pointedly away from him. "It has not that appearance, but we must be considerate for the poor. Twenty-five roubles we said? It shall be so. The rest shall remain. Moujik good-day."

"Good-day, Excellence!" and away went the official, warily driving the Tsar's cow, while the peasant stood staring dumbly after him.

The woman moaned again, and the man turned and glared at her fiercely.

"Be silent!" he rumbled.

"The last one," she wept. "The last one. The Tsar takes all!"

He would have struck her again, but she stepped away, and he left her and entered the hut. It had but one room, and in a corner hung its only ornaments, a picture of St. Nicholas and one of the Emperor, the latter, a gaudy print, surveyed the tragic squalor of the apartment with a fixed simper. The moujik paused before the two pictures and dragged off his cap. He proceeded to cross himself in the lengthy, intricate form of the Greek Church, clumsily and slowly.

The woman entered ere he had done, and as he finished he looked at her.

"After all, it is the Tsar, the Little Father. He—he needs the cow,"

As he turned away to sit down the woman raised a passionate hand, and shook her fist behind her husband's back in the face of the Emperor and saint of Russia.

"And we are of the people of Russia," added the moujik, drowsily.

But the woman moaned again.

PERCEVAL GIBBON

The Korea Daily News.

To be published daily except Sundays.
Rate of Subscription:—

Per Year,	Yen 25.
Per Quarter,	Yen 7.
Per Month	Yen 2.50

Postage in Korea not charged extra.
Postage abroad charged extra.

Advertisements, 50 sen per day for 1 inch or less.
5 yen per month per inch.
50 yen per year per inch.

All communications to

E. T. BETHELL,
Editor and Publisher.
Pak-tong, Seoul.

THE COOLIE QUESTION.

The difficulties which the Japanese authorities are experiencing in obtaining the requisite number of Korean coolies for military works in Manchuria is a far from healthy sign of the times.

The excuse that all available labour is at this season required for Agriculture is all rubbish. Loafers abound on all sides and they will continue to abound right through the rice season. The difficulty is partly explainable by the rooted antipathy of the Korean for hard work in anything but homeopathic doses, but we believe an investigation would show that there are other influences at work. The protests—some of them couched in very inflammatory language—against the Nagamori scheme which were recently circulated through the country, have very likely had some influence in predisposing the ignorant country people against any and all Japanese proposals, but the frequency with which reports of the difficulty of obtaining coolies come from all parts of the country indicate that organized opposition is being met with.

From Pyeng Yang we hear that the only coolies obtainable are those who owe money. These are threatened with imprisonment for debt unless they volunteer, and similar stories come from other parts of the country. Someone has put into circulation a story to the effect that Manchuria is full of explosive mines laid by the Russians and that thousands of Korean coolies have already been killed by them.

With the people in their present frame of mind it seems hopeless for the authorities to persevere in their quest for volunteers. Some means must be found of restoring confidence among the people and an authoritative statement of the true state of affairs would probably greatly assist in accomplishing this.

THE REAL STORY OF THE CHEFOO INCIDENT.

(Continued from No. 31.)

We rescued one officer and two men with our life boat.

At 4.20 a Japanese torpedo boat towing the Russian torpedo boat got under way. The second Japanese torpedo boat went in the direction of the Russian consulate. A boat was sent ashore four hundred yards from the Beach Hotel and returned in twenty minutes. The torpedo boats went out to sea.

The Russian was anchored within two hundred feet of the lightship; so close in fact that Captain Nielsen, earlier in the evening had requested Admiral Sah to remove her to a greater distance, as he feared in case of her swinging round she might foul the "Newchwang." The lightship officers were therefore in position to observe very closely what was going on after they sighted the Japanese. The latter, however, had been at anchor for some hours before they were observed and their movements marked by the officers of the "Newchwang." The Japanese in the boats sent off to the Russian lost no time in getting down to business. Their defiance of the orders of Admiral Sah in their every move sticks out with an annoying prominence, and if the story of the captain of the dismantled destroyer is correct, and there is absolutely no reason to believe otherwise, their acts were simply those of bandits and piratical raiders, and they should have been subsequently saluted with the six-pounders of the "Hai Che" and blown to atoms while attempting to get out of the harbour.

A Daily News man visited the cruiser "Hai Yung" yesterday, where he was most courteously received by the commanding officer and ushered into the presence of the Russian captain, who had received a bullet wound in the hip and was lying contentedly awaiting his transfer to the hospital for the probing of the wound and removal of the missile. The Captain stated:

"About one o'clock in the morning several boats with a Japanese officer and about thirty armed men approached my vessel. The officer came alongside and asked me if he might come aboard. I replied that I did not think that officers of nations which were fighting each other paid social visits, and asked him if he would be kind enough to tell me his business. He answered that he was under orders from the Japanese naval authorities to engage my vessel in a fight outside the harbor, or seize my ship and take my officers and men prisoner inside the harbor.

I told him that we could not fight, as our vessel had been totally dismantled the preceding evening by the Chinese authorities, that all small arms and the breech blocks of our armament were in their possession, that our engines were disabled; and that we had placed ourselves under the orders of the Chinese Admiral; we were noncombatants and were under his protection. That we had signed an agreement not to take up arms again.

"The conversation continued about an hour, my statement that we were in the hands of the Chinese being reiterated.

"There was also alongside a boat with armed Chinese marines who were acting as a guard over us. The Japanese officer insisted that we would have to fight or be taken prisoners, and I finally told him that we could not fight, but that we would not be taken prisoners. With that I struck him in the face with my fist. He grabbed at me and we grappled, and a moment afterward we went overboard together. At the same time I shouted to my men to throw overboard anyone who might get on board. Immediately the Japanese in the boats started firing and many of them clambered aboard, where the firing continued, together with hand to hand encounters.

"I continued to struggle with the officer in the water and made an effort to get on board. Japanese who had gained the deck shot at me and a bullet pierced my thigh. I realized that I would soon be too weak to attempt to regain my vessel in the face of the fire directed at me, but being a strong swimmer, I turned about and made for some junks a short distance away.

"I reached the junks all right, but the Chinese on board, apparently frightened by the firing, struck at me with poles and prevented me from getting out of the water.

"I then turned toward a steamer nearby, which afterward proved to be a British merchant ship, and succeeded in getting on board, whence I was later removed to the Chinese cruiser.

"While I was swimming in the water the Japanese in their boats came after me and fired at me.

"At the time the Japanese first approached my ship, I gave orders to one of my officers to go below and prepare to explode charges which would blow up the ship. He succeeded in placing two charges in the engine room and one in the magazine and an explosion occurred about the time of my encounter with the Japanese officer, causing considerable damage. I don't think that the vessel will prove of much value to the Japanese as I think the explosion caused sufficient damage to prevent her being towed very far.

"The boat from the Chinese man-of-war had been alongside with an armed guard since four o'clock the previous afternoon, the time when the dismantlement of my vessel was completed. This guard attempted to prevent the Japanese from molesting my ship but the Japanese paid no attention to them, and they were absolutely powerless to stop them from boarding the ship.

"When the Japanese came aboard they thoroughly understood that the ship had been dismantled hours before, as they were so notified by me at the time of their approach, and also by the Chinese admiral previously.

"Including myself, there were fifty-one persons on board my vessel, forty-seven men and four officers. Fifteen men are missing to-day. I think the explosion killed some of my men, and also some of the Japanese.

"This is a humiliating affair for me and after I was wounded in the water, if I had had a gun I would have killed myself."

* * *

Some of the escaping Russian crew were picked up by the newspaper men and one officer and two men, as above stated, by the lightship boat.

At a late hour last night it could not be ascertained whether the Captain's statement as to the number of missing men still held good. The probability is that some of those who were reported as missing earlier in the day have turned up later, and that the first list will be somewhat reduced.

After the encounter above described one of the torpedo boats attached a tow line to the destroyer and began to move off. The other took the course indicated in Captain Nielsen's report. Shortly after getting under way between four and five o'clock they passed the Chinese squadron. What took place at this time is best stated by the commanding officer of the "Hai Yung," whose version is as follows:

STATEMENT OF COMMANDING OFFICER OF THE "HAI YUNG."

"About dark we noticed two torpedo boats entering the harbor; on their coming closer we identified them as Japanese. Admiral Sah sent his flag lieutenant to advise them to depart, but they failed to comply within a reasonable time. The Admiral half an hour later went personally to communicate with them and insure an understanding and fulfillment of his order. They again consented to obey, but steamed in the direction of the Russian ship, where they anchored. A launch was sent from the flagship to investigate. A boat with an armed guard had been stationed at the dismantled vessel since four o'clock the previous evening. The Japanese made no move to get out of the harbour and at about 3 o'clock in the morning sent several boats with armed men and one officer who approached the Russian. The Chinese guard informed the Japanese that they could not board the vessel, as she had been dismantled and was now under Chinese protection They paid no attention to this warning, but engaged in conversation with the Russian commanding officer, asking permission to go aboard. The Chinese officer again interfered but the Japanese ignored the guard.

"They then boarded the vessel, and the Japanese officer had a scuffle with the Russian captain, and both went overboard. The Chinese guard was powerless to do anything, and the Japanese then clambered on deck and commenced firing. There was a general fight followed by a loud explosion.

"The Chinese guard, unable to do anything, moved away and assisted in picking up members of the Russian crew from the water. I saw the captain of the Russian ship swimming toward the junks with the Japanese boats pursuing and firing at him.

"One torpedo boat then attached a tow-rope to the Russian ship and started off. The flagship was informed and when the torpedo boat and her tow passed, she was signalled to stop. The other torpedo boat circled around the Chinese cruisers, and ran alongside the flagship. They were then signalled that they must not leave the harbor with the Russian, at the same time the flagship being cleared for action, and the guns trained on the second torpedo boat. The latter replied that if she was fired on she would torpedo every Chinese cruiser in the harbor. The flagships answered that if she would endeavor to overtake her

The Korea Daily News.

VOL. I, TUESDAY, AUGUST 23, 1904. No. 32

大韓每日申報
대한매일신보

뎨삼십삼호　　수요일　　일쳔구ᄇᆡᆨ사년팔월이십사일

본샤고ᄇᆡᆨ

이신보ᄂᆞᆫ영어와한ᄀ문으로셕거ᄆᆡ
일츌판ᄒᆞᆸ

신문가

ᄒᆞᆫ쟝　엽두돈오푼
일삭됴엽두량닷돈　　맛돈으로
밧ᄉᆞᆸ

광고료ᄂᆞᆫ

귀ᄒᆞᆫ의쟝단과ᄌᆞ항의다쇼로죵
감ᄒᆞ되렴가로밧을터이오며오
ᄅᆡ지아녀대한사람마다이신
문을보실터이니광고버시기를
원ᄒᆞ시ᄂᆞᆫ이들은우리신문샤에
와셔뎡약ᄒᆞ시믈희망ᄒᆞᆸ

○발힝소　　남셔대한ᄆᆡ일신보
샤발ᄒᆡᆼ소쇼교동ᄒᆡ젼영국인셜필
림쟝자리오
　사쟝　영국인　(ᄇᆡ셜)

본샤지뎜

인쳔항교쟝동신지방쎄로우리
대한ᄆᆡ일신보사인항지뎜쟝을
ᄐᆡᆨ뎡ᄒᆞ엿ᄉᆞ오니인쳔항에계신
구람코자ᄒᆞ시ᄂᆞᆫ쳠군ᄌᆞᄂᆞᆫ히지
뎜에왕림벌의ᄒᆞ시ᄋᆞᆸ

샤고

○우리대한ᄆᆡ일신보의목뎍은
대한의인녕진셔에관한모든대
목에ᄃᆡᄒᆞ야ᄂᆞᆫ공평한변론을쥬
쟝홈이라우리동신원의탐보ᄂᆞᆫ
신문보시ᄂᆞᆫ쳠군ᄌᆞ의계ᄒᆞᆼ샹보
도ᄒᆞ리며폐지를귀셔ᄒᆞ며주시
ᄂᆞᆫ이ᄂᆞᆫ셩명과번디를젹어붓쳐
시기를희망ᄒᆞ오나이제승신문
샹에긔쟈ᄒᆞᆫ다ᄂᆞᆫ거시아니오다
만국히신용ᄒᆞᄂᆞᆫ죵거를숨고자
홈이라긔쟈ᄂᆞᆫ아모긔셔던지긔
지ᄒᆞᆷ을되각ᄒᆞᄂᆞᆫ권리를가젓스
나뢰쟉ᄒᆞᄂᆞᆫ리유를말ᄒᆞᆯ터이오
며공즁평화를문란케ᄒᆞᄂᆞᆫ듯ᄒᆞᆫ
긔셔ᄂᆞᆫ의뢰히밧지안켓슴나이
다

론셜

역부문제라

⊙이번에일본으로셰겨원ᄒᆞᆫ바
주써에ᄌᆞ긔의군ᄉᆞ샹필요한일
이라ᄒᆞ고한국에ᄃᆡᄒᆞ야다수외
ᄇᆡᆨ셩으로역부쳥구ᄒᆞᄂᆞᆫ거시호
어려운일인거시맛츰츄셩지시
를당ᄒᆞ야가히쓸바ᄒᆞᆫ사ᄅᆞᆷ미엿
계되면ᄉᆞ어디던지사ᄅᆞᆷ들만엽

히면년사룸들홉을말ᄒᆞ고쏘홍
엇던사ᄅᆞᆷ들은일본셔한국ᄇᆡᆨ셩
들을피ᄒᆞ야ᄌᆞ긔의일만될것
갓흐면무ᄉᆞᆫ어려운일에던지식
이랴ᄒᆞᆫ다고들말ᄒᆞᄂᆞᆫ거시우리
셩각에ᄂᆞᆫ필경다른일에위ᄒᆞᆷ으
로ᄒᆞᆫᄌᆞ답에그리홈인듯ᄒᆞᆫ거시
근일쟝셩써의힝무지기간ᄉᆞ건
에ᄃᆡᄒᆞ야몃사ᄅᆞᆷ이분격ᄒᆞ게말
을ᄒᆞᆫ다ᄂᆞᆫ대로박ᄒᆞᆫ거시젼국에젼
파ᄒᆞ엿ᄉᆞᆫ즉시골무식ᄒᆞᆫᄇᆡᆨ셩들
은일본셔무어슬말ᄒᆞ엿던지반
ᄃᆡ홈의ᄉᆞ가잇셔셔역부쳥구ᄒᆞᆫ
ᄂᆞᆫᄃᆡ모도다못ᄒᆞ겟다고각도에
셔오ᄂᆞᆫ보고에ᄒᆞ엿ᄉᆞᆫ즉이런거
시필경반ᄃᆡᄒᆞ기로작쟝ᄒᆞᆫ거신
듯ᄒᆞᆫᄃᆡ다만광양셔만역부를구
처ᄒᆞ엿다ᄂᆞᆫᄃᆡ이ᄇᆡᆨ셩들은남의
계부치가잇셔반일ᄌᆞ원치아니
ᄒᆞ면죄수되여잇슬일을두려워
ᄒᆞ며고리홈이라ᄂᆞᆫᄃᆡ이ᄉᆞ분인
즉다른ᄃᆡ셔들이ᄂᆞᆫ바요또엇던
사ᄅᆞᆷ들은말ᄒᆞ기를아라사사ᄅᆞᆷ
들이만쥬의다지뢰포을뭇어셔
한국ᄇᆡᆨ셩수쳔명으로ᄒᆡᆺ드러죽
이라고ᄒᆞᆫ다ᄒᆞᆫ즉
한국ᄇᆡᆨ셩들의이마음두ᄂᆞᆫ거슬
관찰사와군수들도이제로ᄒᆞ라
고시일수업ᄉᆞᆫ즉아모조록ᄇᆡᆨ셩
들노ᄒᆞ여곰실샹쳥편을말ᄒᆞ야
밋게ᄒᆞ고이일이되도록방조ᄒᆞ야
아도리키게ᄒᆞ기를싱각ᄒᆞᆯ수밧
게엽노라

관보

○외부대신리하영씨직소
ᄇᆡ지난에셜병이이런ᄒᆞ니조리
힝공ᄒᆞ라
○평리원재판쇼쟝ᄉᆞ
무 의졍부찬졍　권즁현
○명셔리대신ᄉᆞ무　외부협판
윤치호　　이샹팔월이십일
　대이쳔구ᄇᆡᆨ십이호
　광무팔년팔월이십삼일
○셔임ᄒᆞᆷ수령
○임김포군공립쇼학교교원셔
판임관ᄉᆞ등　진위군공립쇼학
교교원　김현키
○임양쳔군공립쇼학교교원셔
판임관오등　젼교원　정운호
○임진위군공립쇼학교교원셔
판임관ᄉᆞᆷ등　젼교원　윤대션
　이샹팔월십팔일

○봉시위대일련대쟝　륙군보
병부령　리근형
　팔월십구일
○의원면본관　내쟝원봉세관
김형날　졍인흥
○힝평안남북도각광위원　구
품　지귀영　김봉훈
○명련토원감독셔칙임관삼등
내쟝원경　강홍대
○명내쟝원경셔칙임관삼등
종이픔　셩면호
○임내쟝원봉세관셔주임륙등
즁추원의관김션용　쟝용급
○명내쟝원봉세위원　됴죵범
박승렬
○명평안남북도각광위원　한
병회　림병쥬
○면본관　경무쳥주ᄉᆞ　면직
현
○임기원별봉　경무쳥경무관
강즁우
　이샹팔월이십일
○삼쥬일죵군선　시위긔병대
대죵티쟝륙군긔병졍위　황영
슈　박문병
　팔월이십일일
○임외졍부찬졍셔칙임관일등
궁내부특진관　최익현　군부
대신　윤웅렬
○임군부대신셔칙임관일등
호위대총관　민영긔
○임농상공부대신셔칙임관일
등　륙군부쟝　리도지
　이샹팔월이십일일
○궁졍륙소
○죠의륙군부쟝　리죵건으로
호위총관ᄒᆞ라
　팔월이십일일

잡보

○쟝술ᄅᆡ착　일젼에남교동셔
쟝술키셥쳠봉이라ᄒᆞᄂᆞᆫ자가교
계쳔금됴지로인졍을삼은즉순검의
게착되엿ᄂᆞᆫᄃᆡ셥씨가소착순검의
의말이엄평지하에진말말나ᄒᆞ
교쳔금을ᄌᆞ지ᄒᆞ고착게ᄒᆞ엿ᄂᆞᆫᄃᆡ
ᄃᆡ경무쳥에셔신문홈에에　대
내에셔엄ᄒᆞ면쳐이나리셧ᄂᆞᆫ
ᄃᆡ경무ᄉᆞ가그릇치아니ᄒᆞᆫ리유
를회쥬ᄒᆞ고신문ᄒᆞ야등졍셔
지ᄒᆞ엿더라
○쟝긔지교　수동거ᄒᆞᄂᆞᆫ너부
참셔관죠남승씨집에셔박로항
이란자가계인과곳쳐ᄂᆞᆫ삼원을
가지고쟝외니기소ᄋᆞᆯ을ᄒᆞᆫᄂᆞᆫᄃᆡ

순검이포착ᄒᆞ로드리간죠계인
이안방으로되신ᄒᆞᆫ거ᄂᆞᆫ순검이
쎵ᄎᆞ드리가계인을포박ᄒᆞᆫ조ᄋᆞᆷ
에조씨쇼실의손을잇셔리손이
셰엿ᄂᆞᆫ지라박로항이순검을구
타ᄒᆞ엿더니조곰잇다가ᄉᆞ오명
순검이돌닙ᄒᆞ야박씨등과녀인
가ᄒᆞᆯ경무쳥으로착거ᄒᆞᆫ지라조씨
가희ᄉᆞ실을　대니의탑　쥬ᄒᆞ
온즉자연구별이잇ᄉᆞ리라ᄒᆞ고
쳐분이나리셧다더라
○윤쥬불방　감옥셔에지슈ᄒᆞᆫ
강도윤인식을평리원에셔징사
ᄒᆞ야그무죄ᄒᆞᆷ을번ᄇᆡᆨᄒᆞ고금번
ᄉᆞ젼에여위방송ᄒᆞ라ᄂᆞᆫ　지가
를ᄂᆞ등보ᄒᆞ엿ᄂᆞᆫ지라법부에셔다
시사실ᄒᆞ고히법을방송치못ᄒᆞ
ᄅᆞᆼ으로부록ᄒᆞ야샹쥬ᄒᆞ엿더니
회원검ᄉᆞᄂᆞᆫ관계를분명치못ᄒᆞ
게ᄒᆞ엿슴으로미안ᄒᆞ신　쳐분
이나리셧다더라
●이진션기죠　영평군수리민식
씨가ᄇᆡ부로보교ᄒᆞ기를본군나
루빈틀다시슈비ᄒᆞ엿ᄂᆞᆫᄃᆡ그슈
리비가합구십쳘원오십젼이오
나탁지부로이죠ᄒᆞ와곳지밧게
ᄒᆞ라ᄒᆞ엿더라
○룡쳔희망　각도에갓잇ᄂᆞᆫ군
슈주본이불구에되다ᄒᆞᄂᆞᆫᄃᆡ평
일학문과힝위가쓸만ᄒᆞᆫ인지를
튁용ᄒᆞᆫ다ᄒᆞᆷ으로젼일에젼지로
슈령을도등ᄒᆞ라던자들은탐학
ᄒᆞ야ᄇᆡ랑퓌를당ᄒᆞ엿고공쳔을
라이바라던사ᄅᆞᆷ들은사ᄅᆞᆷ마다희망
간졀ᄒᆞ다고풍셜이분분ᄒᆞ더
○일진긔회　일젼본보에긔재
ᄒᆞ엿던유신회ᄂᆞᆫ일진회로기쟝
ᄒᆞ엿ᄂᆞᆫᄃᆡ그취지인즉　일은
대실을안녕케홀ᄉᆞ　이ᄂᆞᆫ졍부
를기혁ᄒᆞᆯᄉᆞ　삼은인민의싱명
과지산을보호홀ᄉᆞ　ᄉᆞᄂᆞᆫ군졍
과지졍을졍리ᄒᆞᆯᄉᆞ이라ᄒᆞ고지
작일하오이시에죵로지젼도가
로긔회ᄒᆞᄂᆞᆫᄃᆡ병정일쇼ᄃᆡ와슌
검삼십여명이ᄇᆡ리파송되야힝
인을금지ᄒᆞ더니거미구에일본
헌병삼ᄉᆞ명이리도ᄒᆞ야금케ᄒᆞ
지ᄂᆞᆫ고샹지ᄒᆞ다가자여동로가된
ᄃᆡ회원이인ᄒᆞ야회동ᄒᆞ엿ᄂᆞᆫ
즉쳐소가쳥착ᄒᆞ야빗몽ᄒᆞᆫ도가
로을마긔회ᄒᆞ엿ᄂᆞᆫᄃᆡ회쟝윤시
병씨가츌셕ᄒᆞ야젼회의에우신

회를일진회로지칭ᄒᆞ야졍부에롱고ᄒᆞ소를공포ᄒᆞ고규칙을랑독ᄒᆞ엿는ᄃᆡ회원은이십일세이샹으로허입ᄒᆞ되쥬임관이샹에현ᄃᆡ훈관인은밧지안코찬셩권은니외국인을물론ᄒᆞ고참셕ᄒᆞ되이십인이샹으로작졍ᄒᆞ고룽샹회는미토요일하오두시로결졍ᄒᆞ고특별회는아한에잇지아니ᄒᆞ고아모ᄯᅢ던지모히게ᄒᆞ엿다ᄒᆞ며일헌병은폐회ᄒᆞ기ᄅᆞᆯ지문구에파유ᄒᆞ엿더라

○공찰뎐보　공쥬관찰ᄉᆞ부에보고ᄒᆞ되역부모집ᄒᆞ는ᄃᆡ하나토조원ᄒᆞ는쟈는업고ᄉᆞ방으로분쥬히도망ᄒᆞ야도로에셔호곡ᄒᆞ오니자연농ᄉᆞ를젼폐ᄒᆞᆯ지라대단송민ᄒᆞ다ᄒᆞ엿더라

○졍부긔의　지작일하오삼시에의졍부에셔무삼ᄉᆞ고인지회의ᄒᆞ엿다더라

○후원지셜　항셜을드른즉일진회경비는일본인이슈응ᄒᆞᆫ다ᄒᆞ며ᄯᅩ일본긔진당슈령신편지샹씨가히회에후원이되야운동ᄒᆞᆫ다는풍셜이분분ᄒᆞ다더라

○외협셔리　본월이십일에외부에셔각공관에죠회ᄒᆞ되본부대신리하영이상소ᄒᆞ고묘리힝공ᄒᆞ는ᄉᆞ이에일졀교셥ᄉᆞ무를본협판이승　명ᄒᆞ야본일붓터시무ᄒᆞ노라ᄒᆞ엿더라

○폭약파벽　일본공관에셔외부에죠회ᄒᆞ되경의텰도놋는길에텰산차연관뒤끌자이고셩벽에는별노히갈을돌녀낼수업ᄂᆞᆫ고로불가불본월하슌에폭약으로고셩벽을훼파ᄒᆞᆯ터인즉히ᄃᆡ방관에훈칙ᄒᆞ야빅셩이미리통지ᄒᆞ야경동ᄒᆞᄂᆞᆫ폐가업게ᄒᆞ라ᄒᆞ엿더라

○대관젼임　호위ᄃᆡ총관민영긔씨는군부대신을피임ᄒᆞ고부쟝리도직씨는농상공부대신을피임ᄒᆞ고부쟝리죵근씨는호위ᄃᆡ총관을피임ᄒᆞ고윤웅렬씨는찬졍을피임ᄒᆞ엿더라

○히찰보고　황해관찰ᄉᆞ가외부에보고ᄒᆞ되향일에역부모집ᄉᆞ로귀부면칙을연ᄒᆞ야그인부수효를감ᄒᆞ고삭긔을후이ᄒᆞᆯ뜻스로십화감리게로일본령ᄉᆞ의게교셥ᄒᆞ다가가감을엇지못ᄒᆞᆫ고로그ᄃᆡ로죵인을효유ᄒᆞᆫ즉빅셩이다의혹ᄒᆞ고겁니여만히도쥬ᄒᆞ는ᄃᆡ혹젼답ᄉᆞ이에잇다가도힝인을보면관속인가의심ᄒᆞ야농긔를바리고도망ᄒᆞ는쟈가불가승수이오ᄂᆡ빅셩은다살농만되고역부는모집ᄒᆞᆯ도가만무ᄒᆞ다ᄒᆞ엿더라

○죠청철표　젼에외부에셔일공관으로죠회ᄒᆞ기를일본의작젼진요디는곳압록강이셔와려슌구이남이라한국경셩에군용디를뎡ᄒᆞᆯ것시업스니남문외군용디로립표ᄒᆞᆫ것슨곳것으라ᄒᆞ엿더라

○술직유산　근일에경부ᄉᆞ가제반술직파잡류비를엄령금집ᄒᆞᆷ으로각죵술직들이모다피착될가공겁ᄒᆞ야유산직모양으로쥭장망혜에단출ᄒᆞᆫ힝쟝으로산천경긔구경ᄒᆞ며각쳐절을차져다니며류숙ᄒᆞᆫ다더라

○민ᄉᆞ보고　쥬쳥공ᄉᆞ민영철씨가외부에보고ᄒᆞ되향일본부훈령ᄉᆞ의ᄃᆡ로일본쥬진총령ᄉᆞ이집원언길의게대한국민천진에거류ᄒᆞ는쟈보호ᄒᆞᆯ일ᄉᆞ는쳥국외부에셩명ᄒᆞ고히령ᄉᆞ의게함칙ᄒᆞ엿다ᄒᆞ엿더라

○진위민요　인부모집ᄉᆞ로일인이진위군슈더러미호에일인식ᄲᅩᆸ아달ᄂᆞᆫᄒᆞ거ᄂᆞᆯ군슈ᄃᆡ답이본군은이왕텰로역부로모군을만이ᄒᆞ엿스니한빅명ᄒᆞ고모집ᄒᆞ마ᄒᆞ야허락ᄒᆞᆫ뒤에리방을불너지휘ᄒᆞ라ᄒᆞᆫ즉리방의말이이ᄉᆞ요즁에모군을ᄒᆞ라ᄒᆞ면이빅명이ᄂᆞ지휘ᄒᆞ여야빅명츙슈가된다ᄒᆞ고이빅명으로각면에분비ᄒᆞ야지휘ᄒᆞ엿는ᄃᆡ리방이즁간에셔협잡이잇는고로빅셩이작당ᄒᆞ여향쳥과작쳥과민가칠호를부쉿다더라

○션산불치　남즁으로셔샹리ᄒᆞᆫ친구의말을드른즉션산젼젼군슈졍우묵씨는학졍이파다ᄒᆞᆫ고로빅셩이환산지경에이르럿더니다힝이민병셩씨ᄀᆞᆺᄒᆞᆫ명관을만나셔쥭게된빅셩이안도가되엿는ᄃᆡ민군슈의치적을평론ᄒᆞ자ᄒᆞ면겸뎐을당ᄒᆞ야반방략으로진휼ᄒᆞ야빅셩이아표를면ᄒᆞ엿스며송ᄉᆞ결처를공평케ᄒᆞ고신속케ᄒᆞ며졍령이엄명ᄒᆞ고이민ᄒᆞ는고로촌민이쟝차를보지못ᄒᆞᆫ다고송셩이근읍에파젼ᄒᆞ더니불과수삭에례임된고로일읍빅셩이공론ᄒᆞ고히관찰부와ᄂᆡ부에원류ᄒᆞ다가못되고신군슈송영대씨도임후로션치ᄒᆞᆯ마음은잇는듯ᄒᆞᄂᆞ간리비의게속아셔일읍폐막은이로형언ᄒᆞᆯ수업거니와데일악습은혹결젼미슈ᄉᆞ라혹호포밧는다ᄒᆞ고궁츈빅셩을일일착슈ᄒᆞ야일량미슈에쟝차주는예채와온즁부비가수십량식되니빅셩이지보ᄒᆞᆯ수업는지라빅셩들의말이이려ᄒᆞᆫ군슈는틱차가도로혀불치ᄅᆞᆯ만낫고민군슈의례귀ᄒᆞᆫ거슨어린ᄋᆞ히가사랑ᄒᆞ는부모일은것과갓다고들ᄒᆞ더라더라

○틱안슈젹　호즁으로셔온사름의소젼을드른즉월젼에슈젹십ᄂᆞ명이틱안군관가에돌입ᄒᆞ엿는ᄃᆡ본군슈가쥬효로관ᄃᆡᄒᆞ고젼삼빅량을쥰즉젹다ᄒᆞ야모도헛쳐니ᄲᅢ리고히읍손과부가의가셔젼삼쳔량을창탈ᄒᆞ고본군고리ᄲᅳᆯ젼군슈리기셕가에가셔젼오쳔량을토식ᄒᆞ되본군포구로가져오라ᄒᆞ고갓는ᄃᆡ그져녁에그집에셔젼오쳔량을보낸더니도젹의비가발셔ᄯᅥ낫더라츄후로히젹당의소문을드른즉기시에안흥포변으로가다가졔쥬샹션일쳑을맛난즉히션은시로지은빈ᄃᆡ라도젹등이져의빈와샹환ᄒᆞ야도젹ᄒᆞᆫ물건을시비에옴겨실고도셕일인이슈직ᄒᆞ고여당은쥬졈에잔ᄉᆞ이에순풍이부러힝션ᄒᆞᆯ만ᄒᆞᆫ지라졔쥬션인이즈긔힝쟝을졔비에실고젹당의젼량ᄭᆞ지가지고순풍힝션ᄒᆞ야갓다ᄒᆞᄂᆞᆫᄃᆡ본군슈가면쳔거ᄒᆞᄂᆞᆫ부직인고로즈긔집의후환이잇슬ᄭᆞ염녀ᄒᆞ야도젹을강박히잡지아니ᄒᆞᄂᆞᆫ고로도젹이셩ᄒᆞᆫ다고ᄒᆞ더라

○우자통신　건일에한어리셕은통신원의보ᄒᆞᆷ을거ᄒᆞᆫ즉진교ᄀᆡ에셔축하연에각항쥰비가다되ᄂᆞᆫᄃᆡ로려슌구ᄂᆞᆫ포획이되리라고ᄒᆞ엿더라

○졍부쥬픔　건일일본군ᄉᆞ령부의청구ᄒᆞᆫ바역부모집에ᄃᆡᄒᆞ야내부대신죠병필씨가무ᄉᆞᆷ잘못ᄒᆞᆫ일이잇다ᄒᆞ야작일졍부에셔그사실을쥬픔ᄒᆞ엿다더라

뎐보

진남포팔월이십이일하오일시발

○한인쳐률　한인역부ᄒᆞ나이경의텰도역ᄉᆞ에방히ᄒᆞᆫ죄로일본헌병의게포착되야오날아츰에군률에쳐ᄒᆞ야단방에포살ᄒᆞ엿ᄂᆞᆫᄃᆡ구경군은산샹에여러쳔명이둘너잇셧더라

대본영동월동일발
공ᄉᆞ관착뎐

○젹함손샹　히삼위함ᄃᆡ의히젼에관ᄒᆞ야아력시후대쟝의보고즁긔ᄉᆞ가좌갓ᄒᆞ니　일본함ᄃᆡ와긔젼후로국함ᄃᆡᄂᆞᆫ쟝ᄎᆞ북방으로ᄲᅢ져다라놀ᄯᅢ에（리우릭구）는긔계를손샹ᄒᆞ엿다ᄂᆞᆫ동긔가잇스무로우리함ᄃᆡ가극력히구원ᄒᆞ기에로력ᄒᆞ엿스나효흠무망ᄒᆞᆯ줄노넉엿고히함ᄃᆡ졔독지옛샌은히삼위를향ᄒᆞ야힝션ᄒᆞ라고명ᄒᆞ야로함）구론보이）와밋（로시야）두군함은셔북으로진항ᄒᆞ면셔젼투를계속ᄒᆞᆯ시다라나ᄂᆞᆫ즁에일본군과교젼은이시잔이ᄂᆞ되엿ᄂᆞᆫᄃᆡ로함에쳑이일반으로손히를밧아스되특이（구론보이）ᄂᆞᆫ그긔계와연통에큰손샹을밧앗ᄂᆞᆫ비ᄭᅥᆺ과비젼의탄환을맛기ᄂᆞᆫ（로시야）호ᄂᆞᆫ십일ᄎᆞ요（구런보이）호ᄂᆞᆫ륙ᄎᆞ요샹합ᄒᆞᆫ소샹쟝교ᄂᆞᆫ함니인원즁ᄂᆡ반이되고하ᄉᆞ졸은ᄉᆞ분지일이되ᄂᆞᆫ지라하ᄉᆞ졸수를확실이말ᄒᆞ면쥭은자가일빅삼십오명이며부샹ᄒᆞᆫ자ᄂᆞᆫ삼빅칠명이라량군함은급히슈리ᄒᆞ고힝ᄒᆞ야팔월십륙일에히삼위에도착ᄒᆞ엿노라ᄒᆞ엿더라

쳔셰호함쟝도목씨의보고

○아함격침　동일동면을거ᄒᆞᆫ즉쳔셰호와대마호가이십일오후와이십일일오젼에회ᄐᆡ도（뮬사코푸항구）에셔젹함노우익호를포격ᄒᆞ야크게손히되게ᄒᆞ엿ᄂᆞᆫᄃᆡ필경은그비가여울목에걸니여반침반몰ᄒᆞ엿ᄂᆞᆫᄃᆡ대마호ᄂᆞᆫ셕탄고에손히를밧엇스나급히슈리ᄒᆞ야전투에나항히ᄒᆞᄂᆞᆫᄃᆡ샤용ᄒᆞ기에관계치안코다른것슨우리게손히도업고사샹은일명도업다ᄒᆞ엿더라

외보

●려슌쟝함　동경셔온여러보고를거ᄒᆞᆫ즉려슌이쟉일쯤은함락이될듯ᄒᆞ다ᄒᆞ엿더라

●로함입항　일젼에샹히에잇ᄂᆞᆫ일본령ᄉᆞ관에셔일본외부대신의게달ᄒᆞᆫ뎐보를거ᄒᆞᆫ즉로국슈뢰구축뎡일쳑이금십이일오후열두시반에오송항에드러와샹히로올예졍이라ᄒᆞ며이외에ᄯᅩ로국슌양함일쳑이동일하오세시지나셔동항에왓다ᄒᆞ엿더라

○동병령발포　동경뎐보를거ᄒᆞᆫ즉칠월오일로국도셩셩피득보발뎐에왈이번에로국은다시동병령을발포ᄒᆞ야좌긔ᄒᆞᆫ각ᄃᆡ방에셔후비병을취합ᄒᆞᆫ다ᄒᆞ엿더라

일은　피텰부루이관하이십현（에스트란드와리브란드와푸레스카우와노오고와로드등현）
이는　막ᄉᆞ과
삼은　로벨
ᄉᆞ는　토라관하삼현
오는　가산관하
륙은　기와현하
칠은　폴타와현하라더라

○포ᄃᆡ파피　려슌비면에포ᄃᆡᄂᆞᆫ큰화직가나셔졀노파피ᄒᆞ엿다ᄂᆞᆫ보고가공ᄉᆞ관에도착ᄒᆞ엿스나그화직난일은아직알수업묘이거시공보가안인즉잠간긔직ᄒᆞ오나츄후샹보를기다려다시보도ᄒᆞ리다

○장졸부동　법국군인하나히봉쳔부와료동에쥬둔ᄒᆞᆫ로국군의군즁을목도ᄒᆞ고발ᄒᆞ되로국군ᄃᆡ의량식이거의부족ᄒᆞ야병졸의계쥬ᄂᆞᆫ면보ᄂᆞᆫ젼일보다삼분에일을감ᄒᆞᆯ뿐더러군ᄉᆞ먹이ᄂᆞᆫᄃᆡ우육을ᄃᆡ신ᄒᆞ야마육으로쥬되장교ᄂᆞᆫ항샹삼판쥬를먹은즉장졸간에동고ᄒᆞ지안아ᄒᆞ니로국병의싸홈ᄭᆞ다핑ᄒᆞᆷ이당연ᄒᆞ다ᄒᆞ엿더라

TELEGRAMS.

ALEXIEFF'S REPORT OF VLADIVOSTOCK SQUADRON'S BATTLES.

Tokyo, Aug. 22nd.

Viceroy Alexieff's official report of the naval engagement off Tsushima is as follows:—After the marine battle in which the "Rurik," "Rossia" and "Gromoboi" were engaged, our ships attempted to escape in a northerly direction, when the "Rurik" signalled that her engines were entirely disabled. Our two other steamers endeavoured to save her, but without effect, so they steamed for Vladivostock, still fighting as they went. After two hours the Japanese gave up the chase. Both ships were much damaged, the "Rossia" being struck with large shells 11 times, the "Gromoboi" 6. The engines of the latter ship were damaged. Of their crews, half the total number of officers and one third of the men were killed and wounded, the number of casualties in all being killed 135 and wounded 307.

Both ships are now being repaired in Vladivostock.

NOVIK IN ACTION NEAR SAGHALIEN.

Tokyo, Aug. 22nd.

Captain Takagi of the Chitose reports that on the afternoon of the 20th the Chitose in company with the Sushima discovered the Russian cruiser Novik in the neighbourhood of Saghalien and on the morning of the 21st forced her to give battle at Port Kolsakoff, inflicting heavy damage on her.

The Sushima received a shell through her coal bunkers but the damage was quickly repaired. The Chitose was undamaged and without any casualties.

Prince Yorihito was second in command on the Chitose.

[This report is rather vague as it gives no subsequent details as to whether the Novik got away or was captured.]

THE ARMY.

From the "Japan Times" we learn that the "Asahi" is one of the journals which attach but little importance to the "Nagamori affair," which for a time provoked more or less animated comments both at Tokyo and Seoul, and does not seem to be concerned about its fate. But the question of abolishing the standing army of Korea having lately been mentioned in connection with the "affair," the journal has eagerly taken up that phase of the question. In short, it strongly advocates the abolition. It was in 1879 that, by the request of the Korean Government, Captain Horimoto of our Army began the training of Korean soldiers under the new modern system. The training has been maintained, with more or less vicissitude, it is true, for twenty-five years, with the only result that the Korean Imperial army is not efficient enough to put down even a small provincial uprising! Owing to the Japan-Korea Agreement we are now obliged to maintain our garrisons in the peninsula and if the cooperation of the Korean army could be of any service, it is only natural that we should desire its preservation. But that its existence is worse than useless is plain from the above fact, and it can only constitute a wasteful drain on the not over-strong Treasury of Korea; and as such the "Asahi" urges its immediate dissolution and abolition.

THE GERMAN STEAMER "GERMANICUS."

In connection with the arrival of the German steamer "Germanicus" at Muroran with Japanese prisoners and refugees from Vladivostock, the "Jiji" states that judging from the fact that she has never before plied in the Far East, it seems possible that she has recently brought munitions of war to Vladivostock. After her arrival at Muroran, the Captain at first stated that the ship was to carry coal to Batavia, but later he refussed to take any coal beyond that required for the vessel's own use.

NARROW ESCAPE OF THE TRANSPORT "GENKAI MARU."

A report which reaches the "Japan Times" states that at 2 p.m. on the 11th inst. the transport "Genkai Maru" whilst off the coast of Hwang-hai-do, Korea, encountered two Russian torpedo-boats which were steaming westward from the east, the distance separating the transport from the enemy being only one-quarter of a nautical mile.

The torpedo-boats at first showed no signs of hostility, but after the transport had proceeded a distance of some five miles, the enemy suddenly turned round, with the intention apparently of pursuing the transport. The latter then steamed off at full speed for about 20 minutes, with the object of beaching herself at the nearest shore. Greatly to the relief of the transport, the enemy shortly after gave up the pursuit and again turned to the west. The transport accordingly effected her escape and subsequently reached her destination in safety.

THE CHEFOO INCIDENT.

We note that the "Tokio Asahi" in referring to the reported escape of some of the Russian warships into Chefoo Kiaochao, advanced the view that Japan should immediately despatch the neccessary ships to the two ports in order to capture the refugees vessels even though the act should result in establishing a new international precedent.

The millions of the late Lloyd Tevis, banker and stock raiser, will establish in San Francisco the finest aquarium in the world. Dr. Harry Tevis has determined to build this unique monument to his father, and he will spend between $3,000,000, and $4,000,000 to bring to it a most complete and wonderful collection of fish from all over the world. The Tevis aquarium will be built in Golden Gate Park and John Galen Howard, supervising architec of the University of California, is prepraing the plans.

The explanation of the reported destruction of the 28,000 men of the Japanese Army investing Port Arthur is now thought to be as follows:—General Nogi was not satisfied with the progress that was being made towards the reduction of the fortress, and spoke in very forcible terms to his men. A Russian spy overheard the remarks and reported to headquarters that the whole Japanese army had been "blown up" (!)

The colored population of Baltimore positively refuse to patronize the street railways since the introduction of the "Jim Crow" cars, which separate the passengers according to race. Meantime the railway companies' revenues are falling off so rapidly that the objectionable cars will probably have to be withdrawn to stop further losses.

The Foreign Office have dispatched a note to the Japanese Legation informing them that the country in use for military operations stretches from the Yalu river Port Arthur and not from the South Gate of the city of Seoul to the Han river, consequently that the poles used for marking out that stretch be removed at an early opportunity.

Reuter's correspondent at St. Petersburg wires that it is expected that the railway round Laike Baikal will be opened by the middle of September. The intended doubling of the Siberian railway has been postponed, and favourable tenders from foreign contractors have therefore been declined.

According to Peking despatches the Japanese forces are marching on Liaoyang from five different directions and the Russians will shortly be compelled to evacuate that place. Another report announces that the Japanese outposts have already reached Shanwanchai, about four miles from Mukden.

PESSIMISM IN GREAT BRITAIN.

The British croaker is not likely to starve for lack of woful tidings. Almost any morning, remarks "Traction and Transmission" he can buy for a halfpenny enough national trouble to depress his day's conversation below freezing-point; and if by a synthetic process we construct the state of the country from these printed materials we may well be appalled at the dismal prospect. Take such items as an alarming decline in the birth rate, which we are told is indicative of an early arrest or even decline of population. Add to that the frequent dissertations upon the alleged flimsy feebleness of the national physique; the recruiting returns, that suggest that we have no raw material for our Army save the undersized and unsound adolescents of the gutter, and even they will have to be taken by compulsion. Next let us give heed to the plausible tale that our few remaining stalwart descendants of the English country stock are joining the ranks of the £2 emigrants, ousted from their birthright by the inrush of the cunning and tenacious alien. That probably will be sufficient, even if we omit the warning of infant mortality and the ominous lunacy statistics, to disturb the patriotic citizen from his complacency so far as the bodily welfare of the nation is concerned.

AN EDITOR'S WOES.

Editing a paper is a pleasant business —if you like it.

If it contains much political matter people won't have it.

If the type is large it doesn't contain much reading matter.

If we omit jokes folks say we are nothing but fossils.

If we publish original matter they blame us for not giving selections.

If we give selections people say we are lazy for not writing more and giving them what they have not read in some other paper.

If we give a complimentary notice we are censured for being partial.

If we don't, everyone says we are unjust.

If we insert an article which pleases the ladies the men snort, and vice versa.

If we remain in our office attending to our business, folks say we are too proud to mingle with other fellows.

If we go out they say we don't attend to our business.

If we attend church they say it is all for show.—Ex.

It would serve the Russians and Japanese only right were the newspapers to quit them and take on the Macedonians, who are willing to fight in print.—Puck.

COOKERY IN THE FUTURE.

Give me a spoon of oleo, ma,
And the sodium alkali,
For I'm going to make a pie, mamma,
I'm going to make a pie;
For John will be hungry and tired ma,
And his tissues will decompose,
So give me a gramme of phosphate,
And the carbon and cellulose.
Now give me a chunk of caseine, ma,
To shorten the thermic fat,
And give me the oxygen bottle, ma,
And look at the thermostat;
And if the electric oven is cold,
Just turn it on half an ohm,
For I want to have the supper ready
As soon as John comes home.

We have been courteously informed that the French despatch boat "Kersaint" will leave Shanghai for Chemulpo immediately on the arrival of the European mail. She is due here on the 28th and will bring European dates up to July 24th.

In addition to the distinguished orders, which he already holds, His Excellency Herr von Saldern, the German Minister to Seoul is now the recipient of the Knight Commandership of the Prussian Red Eagle. This is a signal mark of distinction, there be ng only one Prussian order of higher rank. It is therefore with great pleasure that we beg to add our congratulations to the many, which will doubtless have been already tendered to His Excellecy.

Deibler, the elder, who some years ago retired from business as public executioner, is about to publish his memoirs. "Much of my book," he says, "will read like a novel, but I shall have to kill off one of my characters at the end of each chapter."

An unofficial report to the effect that one of the land defences outside Port Arthur has been destroyed by heavy shell fire, has been received at the Japanese Legation. No details or official confirmation have arrived.

The Official Gazette published the following appointments:—Messrs. Choi Ikhyon and Yun Woong-yul to be Councillors of State, Min Yong-ki to be Minister of War and Yi Do-chai Minister of Agriculture, Commerce and Industry.

A London telegram of Aug. 10th states that although great importance is attached to the capture of Laoshan (Wolf Hill) by the Japanese, St. Petersburg is strangely optimistic as to the fate of Port Arthur.

"Say, waiter, how do you pronounce C-a-m-e-m-b-e-r-t cheese?"

"It is largely a personal matter, sir. A gentleman who was in here last night pronounced it the worst he ever saw."

According to a frivolous correspondent Port Arthur will be captured as soon as the decorations in Chinkokai are completed.

The Korea Daily News.

To be published daily except Sundays.
Rate of Subscription:—
Per Year, Yen 25.
Per Quarter, Yen 7.
Per Month Yen 2.50

Postage in Korea not charged extra.
Postage abroad charged extra.

Advertisements, 50 sen per day for 1 inch or less.
5 yen per month per inch.
50 yen per year per inch.

All communications to
E. T. BETHELL,
Editor and Publisher.
Pak-tong, Seoul.

AN EXPLANATION.

The "Japan Daily Mail" of August 13th in noting an article which we reproduced from the "Kobe Chronicle" dealing with the Nagamori scheme, enters the lists in defense. It sould be borne in mind that there is no love lost between these two papers and that whatever attitude the "Chronicle" may assume on a subject it is generally safe to say that the "Mail" will, if an opportunity presents itself, oppose it.

The "Mail" says;—"In the "Korea Daily News" we read an article reproduced from the "Kobe Chronicle" on the subject of the Nagamori waste-lands scheme. The article is written with all that insidious show of moderation under which the Kobe journal seeks to shelter the assaults it makes from time to time on the Japanese. To the meanest intelligence it must be perfectly obvious that no comparison whatever exists between the Japan of a few years ago and the Korea of to-day. Japan, from the very beginning of the "Meiji" era, 38 years back, worked strenuously and earnestly to qualify for the recovery of judicial and tariff autonomy, and her work was of such a nature as to elicit the strong approval of the world. Korea has done nothing whatever of the kind. Her resources are just as undeveloped, her institutions just as faulty, her systems of government just as benighted as they were when, by Japan's good offices, she first acquired a title to independence. Could anything be more unjust than to blame Japan for not now recognizing Korea's judicial and fiscal autonomy? Besides, what has judicial autonomy to do with the reclamation of waste land? It would be a fair criticism to say that Japan is unfortunate in having to press upon the Koreans a measure which she would not suffer to have pressed upon herself. She withholds from aliens the privilege of owning real estate within her own territories, yet she asks Korea to allow Japanese subjects to undertake the reclamation of waste lands within the peninsular empire. That contrast can be adduced with some effect, though no critic possessing any desire to be honest or fair would adduce it without noting the radical differences between Japan's condition and Korea's and without duly allowing for the difficult position occupied by this country towards its hopelessly lethargic and corrupt neighbour. But the "Kobe Chronicle" neither notes nor allows. It condemns Japan unreservedly, and it accentuates the condemnation by dragging in the question of jurisdiction, which has no legitimate place whatever in the discussion."

Precisely what the "Japan Mail" means when it says that the question of jurisdiction has no "legitimate" place in the discussion we cannot say. It certainly has a place in the discussion, such an important place that the scheme practically depends upon it. The whole world over, farming rights are more vague and indefinite than any other vested interests and disputes are largely settled upon the bases of tradition and custom. Disputes would most assuredly arise between Japanese settlers and their Korean neighbours, questions of water supply and throughfare immediately present themselves as fruitful sources of trouble, and tribunals for settlement of these disputes would have to be established all over the country. The Nagamori scheme was sent forth in such an unfinished state that we have no means of knowing how it is proposed to accomplish this, but in the absence of any provision to the contrary, it is to be presumed that as heretofore Koreans having grievances against Japanese must seek redress in the Japanese consular courts. Newcomers are bound to disturb the existing order of things and thus we shall have the anomaly of Koreans continually appealing to an alien tribunal for protection against what they may consider infringements of their rights. We think this answers the "Japan Mail's" question as to the connection between judicial autonomy and the reclamation of waste lands, and its statement that the question of jurisdiction has no place in the discussion.

One more word. After "sailing into" the "Chronicle" the "Mail" concludes as follows:

"In one thing at all events the Japanese show that magnanimity. They allow these mischievous articles to be reproduced by a British journal published in Seoul at a time when a foolish anti-Japanese agitation prevails in that city. It is prudent license. For all things offensive the free atmosphere of heaven is the best corrective."

If the course is a prudent one wherein lies the magnanimity?

THE PRESERVATION OF NEUTRALITY.

The English were very friendly to the United States when we were quarreling with the Spaniards. Whenever they could strain a point on the question of neutrality they usually did so. A few days before war was declared the American fleet lay in the harbour of Hongkong. Somewhere on the China Sea the cruiser "Baltimore" was running down with ammunition and extra men which were necessary before Dewey could go after the Spaniards. Over in the Atlantic the "Nashville" had captured the "Buenaventura" and England considered that war, though not actually declared, was then a fact. The Governor of Hongkong was ordered to notify the American fleet to leave the port. Now, the Governor was a scholar and a gentleman, and he knew that the "Baltimore" had not come and that Dewey could not well leave before that ship arrived. The "Baltimore" would also need to be docked. So the Governor reasoned as follows: Supposing she came the following morning, when she was due, and supposing twenty-four hours would be required for docking—that made forty-eight hours. So he issued an order requiring the American fleet to leave in forty-eight hours. At the expiration of that time the "Baltimore" had been docked; and everybody blessed good Governor Blake, of Hongkong.

Coal is an important commodity in times of war, but according to the polite rules of neutrality, a neutral port must not sell coal to a belligerent except in quantities sufficient to enable the warring ship to reach the next port. Consequently, coal was a source of much worry to Admiral Dewey when his fleet lay in Manila Bay during the blockade. Fortunately, there are more ways of skinning a cat than one, as some resourceful sage has remarked. Though a neutral nation may not sell coal there is nothing to prevent its vessels from being captured and the coal confiscated at a good fat price. This is what frequently happened in Manila Bay. It was remarkable how many coal-laden ships drifted in to be captured and their coal seized at thirty shillings a ton. The first of the "unfortunates" was the good ship "Ellen A. Reed," with 2,600 tons of coal from Australia. The "Ellen," of course, didn't dream that Dewey wanted coal, and the presumption is that she drifted out of her course right into Manila Bay. At any rate, Dewey soon had 2,600 tons of good coal and the skipper of the "Ellen" had £3,900; and the glorious institution of neutrality had not been violated.—"Phila. Evening Post."

THE DARDANELLES QUESTION.

The following report has been received at the Foreign Office in Tokio:—

The Constantinople correspondent of the London "Times" telegraphs to his paper under date of the 9th inst. to the following effect:—

The Turkish Government has given its consent to the Russian passage of the remainder of the Russian Volunteer Fleet steamers through the Dardanelles. The Russian Ambassador at Constantinople has given a verbal guarantee that the Fleet steamers will henceforth continue flying the commercial flag and that they will not again be used as cruisers. In this connection, Turkey had definitely announced that she would not give her consent to the Russian proposal without the above guarantee.

A Reuter's telegram regarding this question says that the Russians' guarantee contains a statement that the Fleet steamers shall not carry arms and munitions and that the steamers shall only pass the Straits in single order at certain intervals of time. The telegram adds that the first passage of the steamers through the Dardanelles in consequence of the said guarantee was expected to take place on August 12.

NEW MAIL SERVICE.

It is reported that the Mitsu Bishi Dockyard and Engine Works signed a contract, a few days ago, to construct two ferry boats of some 1,500 tons each for the Sanyo Railway Company's steamship intermediary between the company's western terminus at Shimonoseki and the Seoul-Fusan Railway's terminus at Fusan. The completion of these steamers will take place next spring.

THE "BLACK ART" IN DISGRACE.

Fortune-tellers, wizards, sorcerers and other exponents, male and female, of the occult sciences, are having a hard time of it. It seems that the police has a list of some 500 of these gentry whom it is proposed to arrest and examine. It is not intended to punish them all but there are said to be pretty severe sentences in store for some of them.

The Korean Minister to China has requested the Japanese consul at Tientsin to look after the interests of Koreans in that city.

The Governor of Whanghai reports that his province is rapidly becoming depopulated, owing to the scare the demand for coolies has raised among the inhabitants.

It is reported that while on her way to Sasebo a Japanese steamer, which left a certain naval base on the 13th inst. was chased by a Russian torpedo-boat, from which she narrowly escaped.

It is officially reported in St. Petersburg that the Baltic Squadron will leave on Aug. 16th and is expected to arrive in the Far East about the middle of October. The fleet consists of sixty ships.

We have received from Mous. Laurent Crémazy, the compiler, a copy of "Le code penal de La Corée." A monument of labour and industry this work is a translation into the French language of all the ancient and modern penal laws of Korea. The author is to be congratulated on his highly interesting and instructive work.

The Korea Daily News.

VOL. I, WEDNESDAY, AUGUST 24, 1904. No. 33

HONGKONG & SHANGHAI BANKING CORPORATION.

Paid-up Capital..... ....$10,000,000
Reserve Fund:—Sterling Reserve... 10,000,000
Silver Reserve..... 6,500,000

26,500,000

Reserve Liability of Proprietors... 10,000,000

HEAD OFFICE, HONGKONG.

London Bankers, London and County Banking Company Limited.
Branches and Agencies, London.

Amoy,	Hankow	Penang,
Bangkok,	Hiogo,	Rangoon,
Batavia,	Iloilo,	Saigon,
Bombay,	Lyons,	San Francisco,
Calcutta,	Manila,	Singapore,
Colombo,	Nagasaki,	Sourabaya,
Foochow,	New York,	Tientsin,
Hamburg,	Peking,	Yokohama,

Credits granted on approved Securities, and every description of Banking and Exchange business transacted.

Drafts granted on London and the chief Commercial places in Europe, India, Australia, America, China and Japan.

HOLME RINGER & Co., AGENTS, CHEMULPO.

ON CHEONG & CO., SEOUL.
GENERAL STORE KEEPERS.
Imported provisions, Cooking Utensils Crockery, etc.
FRESH BREAD DAILY.

MITSU BISHI DOCKYARD & ENGINE WORKS,
NAGASAKI.

CODE WORD, "DOCK."

A. 1, A. B. C., and Engineering Codes used.

DOCK No. 1 (at Tategami).

Extreme Length..............523 feet
Length on blocks............ 513 ,,
Width of Entrance on Top...... 89 ,,
,, ,, Bottom.... 77 ,,
Water on Blocks at Spring Tide 26½ ,,

DOCK No. 2 (Mukaijima).

Extreme Length..............371 feet
Length on Blocks.............360 ,,
Width of Entrance on Top...... 66 ,,
,, ,, Bottom 53 ,,
Water on Blocks at Spring Tide 22 ,,

PATENT SLIP (at Kosuge).

Can take vessels up to 1,000 tons gross.

THE WORKS are well equipped with the LATEST IMPROVEMENTS, and can execute any kind of work in SHIPBUILDING and MARINE ENGINEERING, as well as in REPAIRING of SHIPS.

The COMPANY'S new powerful steamer OURA-MARU (712 tons, 700 I.H.P.), specially built for SALVAGE PURPOSES, and equipped with necessary gear, is always READY at SHORT NOTICE.

CHARTERED BANK OF INDIA AUSTRALIA & CHINA.

INCORPORATED BY ROYAL CHARTER 1853

HEAD OFFICES:—LONDON.

Paid-up Capital £800,000

Reserve Liability of Shareholders 800,000

Reserve Fund 725,000

Drafts granted upon all the principal places in the world and every description of Exchange and banking business transacted.

E. MEYER & Co., Agents, Chemulpo.

E. MEYER & CO.
Chemulpo.

SOLE AGENTS IN KOREA FOR:
A. T. Morse, Sons & Co's "Fresco" Distemper

In all colours ready for use on walls, Ceilings etc.
and
AVENARIUS CARBOLINEUM

A wood-preserving and antiseptic oil preparation

Against decay, dry-rot, fungus and wood-destroying insects.

A large supply always in Stock.
Prices upon application.

E. MEYER & Co., Chemulpo.

LAW UNION & CROWN INS. CO.

Fire risks accepted at Current rates, on go downs, merchandise, dwellings, and other property, subject to usual conditions.

HOLME RINGER & Co., Agents, Chemulpo

THE METHODIST PUBLISHING HOUSE,
Little West Gate, Seoul.

JOB PRINTING, TYPEWRITER PAPER
CARBON PAPER, VISITING CARDS
STATIONERY, BOOK BINDING
BOOK PUBLISHERS
AMERICAN SCHOOL BOOKS
SPENCERIAN COPY BOOKS
PEN CARBON LETTER AND BILL BOOKS

S. A BECK, Manager

DAI-ICHI GINKO.
LIMITED.
(Formerly the First National Bank)
ESTABLISHED 1873
INCORPORATED UNDER PRESENT LAW 1896

Capital - - - - - - - - Yen 5,000,000
Reserve Fund - - - - - 1,500,000

HEAD OFFICE:—TOKIO.

President: Baron SHIBUSAWA.

BRANCHES AND CORRESPONDENTS
In the Principal Cities and Towns of Japan.
Interest Allowed on
Fixed deposits 1 year - - - 6½ per cent
" " 6 months - - - 6 per cent

Special current accounts 1½ sen daily per Y 100
General " " 1 " " " 100

M. TANAKA, Manager, Chemulpo

HOLME RINGER & Co.
Chemulpo.

General Merchants and Government Contractors.

Agents for the leading
Banks
Steamship Companies
and
Insurance Companies

Importers of Merchandise of every description.

KAMEYA & CO.
GENERAL STOREKEEPERS
Chinkokai - - Seoul
(*Established 1895, Tokyo*)

Confectionery, Hams, Canned Goods, Cutlery, Hirano & Tansan Water, Provisions, Gents, Furnishing goods, Toilet Articles, Travelling Bags, Tobacco, Cigars & Cigarettes Kitchen Utensils. Coffee, Biscuits.

Fresh Goods always kept in Stock.
Prices Moderate
Please come and inspect our goods.

NIPPON YUSEN KAISHA.
JAPANESE MAIL STEAMSHIP CO.
DER MAIL CONTRACT WITH THE IMPERIAL JAPANESE GOVERNMENT.

European Line

Regular Fortnightly Service between Yokohama Kobe, Moji, Shanghai, Hongkong, Singapore, Penang Colombo, Port Said, Marseilles, London and Antwerp

American Line

Regular Fortnightly Service between Hongkong and Seattle, calling at Shanghai, Moji, Kobe, Yokohama and Victoria, B. C.

Australian Line

Regular weekly Service betwen Japan Ports and Australia, callingat Hongkong and Manila.
(Above Three Lines Suspended until further notice).

Shanghai Line

Weekly Service between Shanghai and Japan Ports

Korea Line

Service Kobe, Moji, Nagasaki, Fusan, Chemulpo, Chioo, Taiku.
S. S. Babelsberg, 2181 tons.
Service Kobe, Moji, Fusan, Chemulpo, Chinnampo
S. S ARGO. S. S. Ohio.

BORDEN'S CONDENSED MILK CO.
New York, U. S. A.

ALWAYS IN STOCK
Eagle Brand Condensed Milk.
Gold Seal Condensed Milk.
Peerless (Family) Evaporated Cream.
Borden's Malted Milk.

E. MEYER & CO.
Chemulpo, Korea,
Sole Agents

ROYAL INSURANCE COMPANY,
Funds exceed £10,000,000
FIRE
AT CURRENT RATES.
LIFE
REDUCED PREMIUM.
HOLME RINGER & Co., Agents, Chemulpo.

HOTEL DU PALAIS
SEOUL.

The only first class Hotel in Seoul. Situated in the centre of the city opposite the palace.

Cuisine under the supervision of an experienced French Chef.

Well ventilated and furnished throughout.

TARIFF UPON APPLICATION

L. MARTIN,
Proprietor and Manager.

大韓每日申報
대한ᄆᆡ일신보

일쳔구ᄇᆡᆨ사년팔월이십오일 (목요일) (뎨삼십사호)

본샤고ᄇᆡᆨ

이신보는영어와한어로셕거ᄆᆡ일츌판ᄒᆞ옵

신문가

ᄒᆞᆫ쟝 엽두돈오푼

일삭됴엽두량닷돈 맛돈으로 밧ᄉᆞᆸ

광고료는

긔한의쟝단과ᄌᆞ힝의다쇼로쥬감ᄒᆞ되렴가로밧을터이오며오ᄅᆡ지아녀대한사람마다다이신문을보실터이니광고내시기를원ᄒᆞ시는이들은우리신문샤에와셔면약ᄒᆞ심을희망ᄒᆞ옵

○발힝소 박동대한ᄆᆡ일신보샤법어학교압헤젼영국인셜필림집자리오

샤쟝 영국인 (비셜)

본샤지점

인쳔항고잔동신지명씨로우리대한ᄆᆡ일신보샤인쳔항지점쟝을퇴졍ᄒᆞ엿ᄉᆞ오니인쳔항에계신구람코쟈ᄒᆞ시는쳠군ᄌᆞ는히지점에왕림면의ᄒᆞ시옵

샤고

○우리대한ᄆᆡ일신보의목뎍은대한의안녕질셔에관한모든뎨목에ᄃᆡᄒᆞ야는공평한변론을쥬쟝홈이라우리동신원의담보는신문보시는쳠군ᄌᆞ의게홍상보도ᄒᆞ리며편지를긔셔ᄒᆞ여주시는이는셩명과반ᄃᆡ를젹어붓치시기를희망ᄒᆞ오니이거슬신문샹에긔지ᄒᆞ라는거시아니오다만극히신용ᄒᆞ는증거를숨고쟈홈이라긔쟈는아모긔셔던지긔지홈을퇴각ᄒᆞ는권리를가졋스나퇴각ᄒᆞᆫ리유를말ᄒᆞᆯ터이오며공즁평화를문란케ᄒᆞ는듯ᄒᆞᆫ긔셔는의례히밧지안켓ᄉᆞᆸ나이다

론셜

한셜명홈이라

○이왕신조크로뇌클영ᄌᆞ신문에쟝삼씨의황무지ᄀᆡ간ᄉᆞ건에셜명ᄒᆞᆫ바에ᄃᆡᄒᆞ야우리신보론셜에ᄀᆡ론등ᄌᆡᄒᆞ엿더니금월십팔일일본ᄆᆡ일신문에변론ᄒᆞ야ᄃᆡ답ᄒᆞᆫ거슬본즉이두신문셔이에셔로사랑홈을일치아니ᄒᆞ려는마음이잇셔셔크로뇌클신문뎨에무어슬말ᄒᆞ엿든지항샹위ᄒᆞ야말ᄒᆞ기는호ᄃᆡᄆᆡ일신문이만일한긔회만잇슬지경이면곳반ᄃᆡᄒᆞᆯ듯ᄒᆞ느그ᄆᆡ일신문에계ᄌᆡ홈이여좌ᄒᆞ니

크로뇌클신문에쟝삼씨의황무지ᄀᆡ간ᄉᆞ건등ᄌᆡ홈으로대한ᄆᆡ일신보론셜에ᄀᆡ론홈을본즉크로뇌클신문게ᄌᆡᄒᆞᆫ바일본사ᄅᆞᆷ이젼후로한국을위ᄒᆞ야아모ᄯᅩ록두호ᄒᆞ라고듯기좃치안케말ᄒᆞᆫ바에ᄃᆡᄒᆞ야교사ᄒᆞ게점잔ᄒᆞᆫᄃᆡ도로말ᄒᆞ엿스나그러나일본의수년젼과한국에오날날을엇지셔로비교ᄒᆞ리요일본셔는사법상과졍상에ᄌᆞ유ᄒᆞ는권리를회복ᄒᆞᆯ마음으로수업들에렬심ᄒᆞ야명치삼십칠년동안에셰계에평등지국이되엿는ᄃᆡ한국에셔는아모수업도ᄒᆞᆫ거시업슬ᄲᅮᆫ더러수단부린다는거슨발달되지못ᄒᆞᆯ일만힝ᄒᆞ며졍부에셔들은모도몽롱ᄒᆞ야우리일본셔이러케진보홈을안에무어슬ᄒᆞ엿는지모르겟고ᄯᅩ일본버뎜면져독립국이라고칭호ᄒᆞ고미ᄉᆞ에부졍이ᄒᆞ야사법샹과졍상에ᄌᆞ유ᄒᆞ는권리가무어신지도ᄶᅵ닷지못ᄒᆞ면셔황무지ᄀᆡ간ᄒᆞ라ᄒᆞ는ᄃᆡ는사법샹에ᄌᆞ유ᄒᆞ는권리가잇다홈이엇지붓그럽지아니ᄒᆞᆯ넌지모르겟고응당셰샹공론에도한국셔의례히ᄒᆞᆯ일을일본셔불힝이수고ᄒᆞᆫ다고ᄒᆞᆯ터이요ᄯᅩ한국반도로ᄃᆡ리익을일본사ᄅᆞᆷ을주어착수ᄒᆞ게ᄒᆞᆯ다는반ᄃᆡ는필경결국되는날에드러나알듯ᄒᆞᆫ거시일한량국간형편이조곰도다를거시업슨즉이웃나라에셔아즉도잠을ᄶᅢ지못ᄒᆞ야폐단만싱기는ᄃᆡ엇지안연히보고만잇스리요그러ᄒᆞ나크로뇌클신문에는이왕에이러ᄒᆞᆫ말은긔지치아니ᄒᆞ엿슨즉일본에허물을드러ᄂᆡ고아모ᄯᅩ녹셩언ᄒᆞ야지관셔지ᄒᆞ드리도변론ᄒᆞ야죠률ᄒᆞᆯ거슨업다ᄒᆞ엿스되우리싱각에는지관을ᄒᆞ엿드리도변론ᄒᆞ야조률ᄒᆞᆯ거시업다고말ᄒᆞᆫ지못ᄒᆞᆯ듯ᄒᆞᆫ거시세계샹에어느나라든지농업홈이번번치아니ᄒᆞ고방한이업드릭도남의게양도ᄒᆞ야리익을옴겨오는ᄌᆞ리에는변론을무수히ᄒᆞ야법ᄃᆡ로작졍홈이어늘근일에소위도로를통ᄒᆞᆫ다는것과국닉수도놋는다는거슬일한량국에일ᄒᆞ는사ᄅᆞᆷ들이ᄌᆞ의로시작ᄒᆞ와되기는ᄒᆞ엿스되의례히각국에셔변론이잇셔셔작졍ᄒᆞᆯ터인ᄃᆡ

이번에장삼씨의황무지ᄀᆡ간ᄉᆞ건은엇더케시작이되여결말이되엿는지알수업는바귀졍아니된일을졔츌ᄒᆞ야ᄒᆞ드리도반ᄃᆡ아니홈은일본사ᄅᆞᆷ으로더부러괴롭게반ᄃᆡᄒᆞᆯ거시아니라일본령ᄉᆞ관에호소ᄒᆞ야도로회복ᄒᆞ랴홈이요우리가이일에소요ᄒᆞ게말ᄒᆞ는거슨한국사ᄅᆞᆷ들이ᄌᆞ긔의올흔일노반ᄃᆡᄒᆞ는ᄃᆡ도아주기를간청ᄒᆞ는ᄭᆞ닭인즉우리ᄉᆡᆼ각에는일본ᄆᆡ일신문에계지ᄒᆞ야사법샹ᄌᆞ유ᄒᆞ는권리와황무지ᄀᆡ척ᄒᆞᆫ다홈과밋지관ᄒᆞᆫ드리도변론ᄒᆞᆯ거시업스리라ᄒᆞ고질문ᄒᆞᆫ거슬답언ᄒᆞᆯ만홈이이러홈으로잇도다

ᄯᅩ크로뇌클신문을위ᄒᆞ야말ᄒᆞᆫ후에다시등ᄌᆡ홈이여좌ᄒᆞ기에긔ᄌᆡᄒᆞ며이말에ᄃᆡᄒᆞ야수답ᄒᆞ엿스니

일본셔활달대도로ᄆᆡ사에힝ᄒᆞ거놀일본을반ᄃᆡᄒᆞ는우ᄆᆡᄒᆞᆫ한국에셔는서울에다영국신문을간힝ᄒᆞ야교약ᄒᆞᆫ론셜놀만달게가만히두는지알수업슨즉이거ᄉᆞᆫ죠심ᄒᆞ여인허ᄒᆞᆯ거신거시ᄆᆡ사에ᄌᆞ유로힝동홈을쳑지ᄀᆡ졍ᄒᆞᆯ일이라ᄒᆞ엿스니

만일말ᄒᆞᆫ바와갓치조심만ᄒᆞ야인허ᄒᆞᆫ면소위활달대도라거는슬어ᄃᆡ다가쓸라고ᄒᆞ는지

관보

뎨이쳔구ᄇᆡᆨ십삼호 광무팔년팔월이십ᄉᆞ일

○셔임급ᄉᆞ령

○희평리원지관쟝셔리ᄉᆞ무 평리원젼관ᄉᆞ 허위

팔월십구일

○면겸임츙청남도지관소관ᄉᆞ 츙청남도젼관찰ᄉᆞ 리항의

○면겸임젼라남도지관소관ᄉᆞ 젼라남도젼관찰ᄉᆞ 리윤용

○겸임츙청남도지관소관ᄉᆞ 츙청남도관찰ᄉᆞ 심건틱

○겸임젼라남도지관소관ᄉᆞ 젼라남도관찰ᄉᆞ 김셰긔

이샹팔월이십일

○권칙 관립소학교교원 리원규 팔월이십이일

○궁졍록ᄉᆞ

○의졍부참졍신심샹훈근쥬호ᄃᆡ이간우ᄒᆞᆫ셰를당ᄒᆞ야싱민을안업케ᄒᆞ고린국에청구를슈응ᄒᆞᆫ드ᄃᆡ슈령틱ᄎᆞ홈이데일이어놀겁잇는수령을셔임치아니ᄒᆞ야허구히광관ᄒᆞ오니민국ᄉᆞ셰를념녀ᄒᆞ야민읽ᄒᆞᆫ온지라신부로셔닉부에엄칙ᄒᆞ야즉시쥬차ᄒᆞ야불일노하송케ᄒᆞ고슈유ᄒᆞ고환관치아니홈과밋서임ᄒᆞ고도임치아니ᄒᆞᆫ온각군슈도일례로최촉하송ᄒᆞ옴이하여ᄒᆞ올지근샹 쥬ᄒᆞ와봉 지의쥬ᄒᆞ다ᄒᆞ시다

팔월이십이일

○식졍부참졍신심샹훈근쥬호ᄃᆡ신부에셔회의ᄉᆞ로루ᄎᆞ뎡긔ᄒᆞ왓스되젼혀칭탁ᄒᆞ야인원이갓초지못ᄒᆞ야묘당ᄉᆞ무를건체케ᄒᆞ엿스니진실노ᄀᆡ탄ᄒᆞ온지라회의에참셕지아니ᄒᆞ온닉부대선죠병필과군부대신민영긔와농샹공부대신셔리근샹은다경계아니ᄒᆞᆯ수업고찬졍김가진은졔빈ᄒᆞᆫ지일구ᄒᆞᆫᄃᆡ슈칙을아니ᄒᆞ오니ᄉᆞ례에극히미안ᄒᆞᆫ온지라다죵젼칙ᄒᆞ옴이하여ᄒᆞ올지근샹 쥬ᄒᆞ와봉 지의쥬ᄒᆞ라ᄒᆞ셔다

팔월이십이일

○경효뎐졔쥬윤용식ᄉᆞ직소비지닉에소청ᄃᆡ로의시ᄒᆞ노라

팔월이십이일

잡보

○진회공함 작일에일진회에셔졍부로공함ᄒᆞ기를작일본회에셔좌긔ᄒᆞᆫᄉᆞ항을졍부에불일닉로권고ᄒᆞᆯ뜻스로취결이온바이에앙포ᄒᆞ오니죠량ᄒᆞ오셔일일히속히실시ᄒᆞ심을복망홈

광무팔년팔월이십삼일

일진회쟝 윤시병

의졍부참졍심샹훈 각하

일은 황실을존중케ᄒ고국가
긔초를공고케ᄒᆯᄉ
총대위원 셔상춘
일은인민의성명과재산을보호
케ᄒᆯᄉ
총대위원 량재익
일은졍부의 기젼졍치를실시케
ᄒᆯᄉ
총대위원 [illegible]균
일은군졍과재졍을[illegible]케ᄒᆯᄉ
총대위원 범흥모
이상총대위원수인들졍부로파
송ᄒᆫ후상시에폐회ᄒ고금일하
오이시에개회ᄒ기로가결ᄒ엿
더라

○대관결혹 졔작일에인원이
미비ᄒ야졍부에셔ᄀ회치못ᄒᆫ
연고로참졍이하모모대신을견
칙ᄒ엿다더라

○대관면파 졔작야에참졍심
상훈씨가 상쥬ᄒ야원수부검
수국장현영운는외국인들의로
ᄒ야국권롱락ᄒᆫ수로면관ᄒ고
시부장리근틱은경위원총관재임
구에빅셩의재산을륵탈ᄒᆫ수로
파면ᄒ고녀부대신조병필과쳥
판리봉뤼는여부모졍수로간도
에ᄎᆫ령ᄒ논ᄃ착오홈이잇서읍
음이민요논수로면관ᄒ엿다라

○일ᄉ진궁 졔작일하오ᄉ시
에일본공ᄉ림권조씨가셔괴평
츄원슈헌과동헌관ᄀ분상티탕
방셰롱리동ᄒ고
궐문에와셔진 궁ᄒ기를쳥ᄒ
텍인도ᄒ야돈덕뎐으로드러가
셔일ᄉ가말ᄒ기를여긔셔슈옥
쳔이상계가쵸쳥ᄒ여디향왕리
ᄒ며 쥬품ᄒ기가난편ᄒ다ᄒ
논고로이셧스로 주ᄒ고인ᄒ
여슈옥헌으로옴마가좌졍ᄒ후
에힝공ᄉ가다시말ᄒ기를 폐
하의신용ᄒ시논대신으로졍용
케ᄒ라ᄒ며다시 상쥬ᄒ여
ᄌ 상으로참졍심상훈씨와궁
니대신민병셕씨와헌병ᄉ령관
리지용씨를 명ᄒ샤졍용ᄒ고
상의ᄒ야립품ᄒ라ᄒ셧ᄂᆫ뎨
식원쟝민종묵씨와외대셔리윤
치호씨도참셕ᄒ엿고하오팔시
에공관으로퇴거ᄒ엿더라

○회의상진 졔작일에외졍부
에셔회의ᄀ되엿ᄂᆫ뎨그안건이
좌와ᄀᆺ더라
일은녀부소관각군슈의청원면
관관에ᄒᆞᆫᄉ
이ᄂᆫ고문관항동을경의ᄒᆯᄉ
삼은각항세산외지출ᄒᄂᆫᄉ라
ᄒ더라

○로문일병 일본출쥬군을로
문ᄒ기위ᄒ야로문ᄉ이인이낫
ᄂᆫ뎨원슈부부령신셩균씨와시
위련뒤쟝관셩환씨라ᄂᆫ뎨쟝춧
샹션세논의쥬로향ᄒ고량씨ᄂ원
산으로향ᄒᆫ다더라

○슈부발훈 원슈부에셔각도
에ᄒ논평ᄒ되각뎌병정이민일쟉
폐ᄒ논쟈가잇거든즉시사힉ᄒ야
야셜범잇논쟈논위젼히뎌에통
보ᄒ며본군에셔엄슈ᄒ고즉시치
보ᄒ라ᄒ엿더라

○룡인민요 룡인군슈현챵봉
씨의보고를거ᄒ즉본도관찰부
훈령니에본군에ᄆ부필셩명을
빈졍ᄒ엿ᄂ데음력칠월초삼일
에일헌병이명이본군에리도ᄒ
야초십일니로히녀부를등뎌ᄒ
라말ᄒ더니십일일오후에일인이
위챵ᄒ야군슈와셔긔를뎌통ᄒ
고십여리허에젼진ᄒ야삼인을
착득ᄒ고다시양갈노나찬즉지
니논바쥬막이낫낫치뷔엿ᄂ지
라거우수인을잡아가지고환읍
ᄒ엿더니그날밤에인민수오쳔
명이관졍에돌립ᄒ며일인이툭
쳘포를노은즉인심이대단소요
ᄒ야룡동이외돌등이로창문을
파쇄ᄒ고외치왈빅셩을죽일뜻
으로구함ᄒᆫ다ᄒ고쟝앗든수인
을히방ᄒ며본군슈를셰리ᄒ니
거죠가황급ᄒ지라일인은본군
슈가셔오리밧그로호송ᄒ고인
민을효유ᄒ니수일후에모혓든
빅셩다흐산ᄒ엿다ᄒ엿더라

○룡뎌됴ᄉ 궁니부에셔각도
에훈령ᄒ기를공헌지뎌와산림
과황쾌지뎌와논쫙을슈츌ᄒᆯ뜻
펴쟁너모든가히번식케ᄒ며이
업의뎌당ᄒᆫ뜻을됴ᄉᄒ야쳐보
ᄒ라ᄒ엿더라

○취혁주본 법부에셔법률을
귀졍ᄒ야포흠군슈는못그군에
가셔징역ᄒ게ᄒᆫ지라김동빈은
셩쥬에가징역ᄒ고엄쥬영은진
쥬에징역ᄒ고쟝교준강ᄒ형쟝
뎍괴논구류ᄒ기로주본을녈ᄂ
다더라

●비셔일시 요수이일본셔귀
국ᄒᆫ현영운씨 부인빈씨논이심
일일야에
태황뎨폐하게알시ᄒ야이시로
록 상쥬ᄒᆫ일이잇다더라

○각관조복 각공ᄉ관에셔외
부로조복ᄒ기를귀부조회를졉
쥰ᄒ즉귀청관이대신셔리ᄒᆫ줄
을지실ᄒᆫᄉ라ᄒ엿더라

○일ᄉ청약 일본공ᄉ가ᄒ야
됴들어지로쳥ᄒ엿ᄂ뎨향일에
외부와탁지부랑부고문관을추
쳔ᄒ여고빙ᄒ는외에대한졍부
ᄂ다른외국으로더브러헤약ᄒ
며혹고빙ᄒᆯ경우에는일본졍부
뎌포쟈와미리샹의ᄒᆯᄉ라ᄒ더
라

○법ᄉ방외 법국공ᄉ가외부
로공함ᄒ기를작일슈요일에본
ᄉ가귀부에방문ᄒ야담화코져
ᄒ며졍권여부를시명ᄒ라ᄒ엿
더라

○챵리선남 함평도사름ᄒ나
히샹경ᄒ야부츈ᄒᆷ젼두직에와
셔쳥호에샹뎌니그인힝가월젼
에초산으로싱남ᄒ엿ᄂ뎨영악
리가핏뒤밋ᄒ로나온지라힝산
은ᄒ엿ᄂ뒤뎌도엽고괴도엽ᄂ
ㄱ로쥬인졉에셔의싱ᄒ고탐지
ᄒ야본즉ᄋ연젹실ᄒ지라그소
문이경무쳥에탐문되야일젼에
착거ᄒ야현금감옥셔에제슈ᄒ
엿ᄂ뒤문초ᄒᆯ시에공ᄉ에도과
연쳥뒤싱이라ᄒ엿다ᄒ며그남
ᄌ논이십세요부녀논이십이세
가되엿다ᄒ고아희논형톄가미
우쟝대ᄒ다더라

○유월괴슈 충쳥남도홍산군
김셩날가에이상ᄒᆫ즘싱ᄒ나히
잇ᄂ뒤원리산도야지와말이셔
로교합ᄒ야나은거시라ᄒ야그
일은도야지엉갓고그뎔은바늘
과갓고그소리ᄂ피이ᄒ야비ᄒᆯ
데업스며졍을시르면수쳔근을
쟝지ᄒ고도그날니기가날즘싱
과갓ᄒ며대단ᄉ노와셔부리기
가극난ᄒ다더라

○쳑젼면화 문쳔으로셔샹리
ᄒᆫ사름의소젼을드른즉향일에
일본쳑후병이원산에셔문쳔젹
지젼진ᄒ엿다가ᄒᆫ아병을봉착
ᄒ여셔로츙돌ᄒ다가아병이퇴
거ᄒ거놀일병이추후ᄒ더니별
안간에다수아병이돌출ᄒ야화
셕이비발두ᄒ지라일병이은젼심
력원을로샹에ᄆ리고다리온즉
야병이그돈을쥬을ᄉ어예혈병
이급ᄒ다ᄒ와셔면화ᄒ엿다
더라

○공뎌즁병 원슈부에셔공쥬
부로면훈ᄒ되히뎌방진위뒤에
병졍이빅명을즁셜ᄒ리이니속
속히모집ᄒ고복쟝ᄂ리가라고
ᄒ고로흿부에셔방쟝병명을모
집ᄒ논중이라더라

○리현랑씨 일작에참졍심상
훈씨가상 쥬ᄒ고면관구라ᄒ
논중현영운씨와리근틱씨수논
후지부지ᄒᆫ다더라

●면사리의 한셩면과회사를
한미과엉회사로귀쳥ᄒ고졍부
에셔감찰원을히회사에파견ᄒ
야미국인과갓치사무를본다논
수논본보에이왕게ᄌ홈과갓치
되논뒤히사문부를됴사ᄒᆫ즉일
긔월동안에면과회사에셔팔니
논차표갑만계산ᄒ야도금화로
표환ᄒ야일만원이상이된즉히
회사관원봉급과기타경비를지
발ᄒᆫ외에이천여원리익은회셜
이잇다더라

○황셩가면 작보뒤일본공관
에셔이하젼정의공보가도착ᄒ
논시에논낫낫치쟝셔ᄒ야 황
샹폐하의 을람이되엿ᄂ뒤그
휘케ᄒᄌ면ᄒ마시간이희비되
고또시경기셔를작슈ᄒ후면진
금ᄉ진이번다ᄒ겟기로 대넘
와일본공관ᄉ이에면화를가셜
ᄒ기로작뎡ᄒ엿다더라

○죠ᄉ도착 주일공ᄉ죠빈회
씨가금월인항에도박ᄒᆫ다논뎌
로대ᄉ관인이여젼ᄒ로친향에
만히ᄒ거ᄒ엿다더라

○샹됴문답 작일에일진회에
셔총대위원수인을졍부에파송
ᄒ엿더니그위원이회중에회보
ᄒ되샹참졍이무러왈회논어느
곳에셔인허ᄒ엿스며회중규칙
은엇더ᄒ며외국방이보호ᄒ기
논무슨뜻이냐ᄒ거놀위원이대
답ᄒ라그회답을본후에나도회
답을붓치라ᄒ라ᄒ더라ᄒ거놀회
회에셔쟝셔를지어졍부에셔젼
문ᄒᆫ샹됴건을티답ᄒ며왈대져
교인민의셜회홈이다만동교만잇
ᄒ논규례오며본회규칙은일본의
타졍ᄒᄂᆫ일엿ᄉ오ᄆ외국병이보호
경찰ᄒ논약조가잇ᄂ지라일병의
즁에셔후군ᄉ샹방히ᄒ며내가
족이방게논달니고훈졋ᄉ온영단
ᄒ엿ᄂᆫ디기시총대위원은정틔
용세더라

외보

○연셜샹졍 론돈에ᄂ신보를
거ᄒᆫ즉아국구로팟긴쟝군이국
동으로발힝ᄒᆯ때에누구보고말
ᄒ되현국에하류ᄒᆫ일본인을한
나도사ᄅᆫ가지못ᄒ게ᄒ고귀이
히동경에니르러셩하명을엇게
ᄒ게ᄒ리라ᄒ엿고아국에모든
신문에도민심을격려케ᄒ야크
게셩공ᄒᆷ을즁노앗더니동쟝군이
도금ᄒ야형세이불미ᄒᆷ을보고
빅셩들이가로샹에셔셔로평론
ᄒ고며밀히불평ᄒᆫ말ᄒ논자가
죵죵잇스니즉발야졍부에서동쟝
군을십분원조ᄒ야후환이엄케
ᄒ지아니ᄒ면고민간에셔밋치
논희가젼과ᄒᆫ것보다우심ᄒᆯ지
라이럼으로아국졍부에셔속마
음에논셰릭릉과권고져ᄒ야
니ᄒᆯ지라도그외세를성각ᄒ야
부득불파권ᄒᆯ경우에니르럿다
ᄒ엿더라

○즁립엄칙 거십샹일에원총
통이샨히관황총병의게면훈ᄒ
기를총후에일아량국병을분로
ᄒ고로하즁립디에도망ᄒ야오
논쟈잇거든즉시그무쟝을셕고
고관게잇논셩으로호송ᄒ되평
슝히ᄉ단을니르키논힝위논엄
게ᄒ라ᄒ엿더라

○청이빈방비 청이빈에셔온
사롬의말을드른즉그쥬위의히
ᄌ논샹금여수중이며동방산샹
에츅조ᄒᆫ쳡관과포뒤논진졍쥰
공이되엿고동디에논슈비병만
조곰쥬둔ᄒ여잇슬ᄲᅮᆫ이오인부
쳔여명은부샹병을운반ᄒ과쥭
은쟈를미쟝ᄒ과셔로공을셰노
티미우분쥬ᄒ다더라

TELEGRAMS.

Berlin, July 2.—The Lokal Anzeiger's Lisbon correspondent telegraphs that a report has been going about of the sudden death of King Carlos on board his yacht. The truth appears to be that the King, when in a heated condition, drank two glasses of ice-cold beer, causing a rush of blood to the head, in consequence of which he remained some time unconscious.

ADMIRAL KAMIMURA DEFENDED.

"C.B," a naval expert, writes thus in the "Daily Graphic:"—

The Vladivostock cruisers "Gromoboi, Rossia," and "Rurik," under Admiral Skrydloff, have made a raid on the Japanese sea communications, and penetrated as far as Iki Island, in the narrow part of the Straits of Korea. They have sunk two large transports, while the fate of a third one is unknown. The Japanese loss of life and stores must have been considerable. A London morning paper lectures Admiral Kamimura, but if the writer of the article could explain how the inadequate naval forces with which the Japanese have been conducting this war are to keep all Russian vessels from escaping it would certainly be a novel piece of instruction. The raid in ordinary circumstances would mean nothing, for, as I have pointed out before, there is no victory in evasion. The campaign has, however, forced the Japanese to hazard upon the sea, within two day's steaming of Vladivostock, a number of transports. No passive defences on shore are of the slightest avail for their protection, in spite of the ridiculous talk at the outset of the war about fortified positions conferring the command of the Korean Strait. One can only say that if a number of transports had been in one mass under convoy the opportunities of attack would have been much greater. As I pointed out once before, if raiding cruisers would be so accommodating as to fight the defending convoy, the protection of an invading force might be arranged, but that is the last thing in the world they would do. They would make for the helpless transports, firing common shell and torpedoes into "the brown of them."

The "Times" military critic has resumed his singularly unjust criticism of Admiral Kamimura for the escape of the Vladivostock squadron. He appears to be quite oblivious of the inadequate naval force at that officer's command, and he disregards the very dangerous nature of the currents, fogs, and coast off which Kamimura has to attempt to blockade one of the most difficult harbours to seal in the world. I freely attacked the plan of campaign under which Kamimura bombarded Vladivostock, and the "pre-arranged plan" has never been repeated. Justice compels me to support as strenuously as I previously condemned an officer's actions when he is now suffering under criticisms made by those unacquainted with the difficulties of sea work. To criticise Kamimura because the Japanese run the risks of hazarding transports at sea, and to compare him with Nelson, is to provoke the retort that Nelson allowed Villeneuve to escape from Toulon with a great fleet and two weeks' start. It was not, however, necessary to have made so silly a comparison. It is unlikely that Kamimura is a Nelson, but he cannot prove it one way or the other until he has had the opportunity. It is not at all certain that Kamimura may not yet bring the "Rurik," "Rossia," and "Gromoboi" to action if he remains off Vladivostock. The most futile strategy is to look for the cruisers in the last place at which they were seen. That is the function of a home, or reserve division of ships, which, unfortunately, the Japanese, with their inadequate naval forces, do not possess.

I stated that Kamimura should make for Vladivostok to intercept the Vladivostok cruisers. It does not at all follow that he was wrong not to have done so. He is handicapped beyond measures through the absence of any home squadron in the Straits of Korea, and with a number of valuable transports there, he could not leave those straits exposed to fresh attacks in the absence of any certain information as to the whereabouts of the raiders. The utter futility of the numerous fortified positions in the Straits of Korea needs no comment. There are some people who imagine that with forts and a great home defence army we can leave the Channel without a single fleet in its vicinity. Considering it is our Straits of Korea with an infinitely greater stakes upon it, I hope that this episode makes them wiser. I have all along pointed out the Japanese naval force is quite inadequate, though the Russians, by their passive reliance on their fortified ports, have hitherto atoned for this inadequacy.

THE FUNERAL OF VISCOUNT YAMAGUCHI.

The funeral service of the late General Viscount Yamaguchi, writes the "Japan Herald," was held according to Buddhist rites at Aoyama Cemetery on Tuesday morning.

The cortége, reports the "Japan Times," left the residence of the deceased at Kitamachi, Aoyama, at 7 a. m., the coffin being placed on a gun carriage and escorted by a military guard. On each side of the coffin walked Lieut. General Terauchi, Minister of War, Major-General Ishimoto, Vice-Minister of War, Major-General Nagaoka, Assistant-Chief of the General Staff, and the aides-de-camp to the late General. Then came the chief mourner, Mr. Sotaro Yamaguchi, brother of the deceased, followed by the members of the bereaved family. The ladies were in carriages, while most of the gentlemen were on foot. The roads near the cemetery ground, through which the procession passed, were furnished with a guard of honour, the troops numbering in all about two battalions.

The procession arrived at the cemetery at 7:30 a. m., where many people had already assembled to pay their last homage to the dead soldier. The coffin was borne to the building attached to the cemetery, where the the ceremony began exactly at 8 a. m. Among those who attended the service, we noticed Count Katsura, the Premier, and other Ministers of State, Sir Claude Macdonald, F[illegible] Minister, Count von Arco-Valman Minister, and other mem[illegible] the diplomatic body, together [illegible]he military and naval attachés; [illegible]bers of the Privy Council; several dignitaries in the Army and Navy; and many of the principal figures in official and private circles. Most of the Princes of the Blood, as well as Marquis Ito and other genros, were represented at the funeral.

The ceremony terminated at about 10 a. m.

WHAT IS IT?

Wonders will never cease—in Korea. A notive reporter writes us as follows. There is a serious beast in the house of the man named Kim in Hongsan district of Choong Chong province, that was born which between wild pig and horse. It's hair is like pins and it's mouth is like pig's mouth. It make a very curious noise, many catties of things can be loaded on its back and it can run very fast like the fowls do.

The Occidental and Oriental steamship "Gaelic" for years past plying between San Francisco and the Asiatic coast, is to be sent back to England to her owner, the White Star company, the first of the coming year. Of all the liners running across the Pacific the "Gaelic" is the oldest, with the greatest number of voyages to her credit, now closely approaching the hundred mark. Captain William Finch has been her commander for years past. The "Gaelic," while still a good and reliable steamer, is the slowest of all the Oriental liners running out of San Francisco, and the schedule of all the liners is made to suit her speed, to prevent inconvenience anywhere along the route. But before she is sent home the "Gaelic" may make two more voyages to the Orient. —Japan Herald.

THE OLDEST CITY IN THE WORLD.

According to a dispatch of the 18th ult. Udnunki, ancient Adab, perhaps the oldest city in the world, has been discovered by the University of Chicago's excavating expedition in Babylonia. This city has for many years been the object of search by Orientalists. It is mentioned in the code of Hammurabi, an early King of Babylon, which document was translated recently by Professor Robert A. Harper of Midway University, director of the expedition. He received news here to-day in a cablegram from Professor E. J. Banks, field director of the expedition, who since leaving this country last winter for Dislya, in Babylonia, has announced many important discoveries. The uncovering of the ancient city is a great triumph of the expedition and one of the most important archaeological achievements of recent years.

Dr. Banks informed Professor Harper that he had found bricks bearing the syllables "Ud-nun-ki" at the lowest level of the ruins. He is certain that these bricks identify the city of Adab. With a force of 120 men he excavated the ruins at Bismaya and found the remains of four temples, built one above the other, which he named according to the kings who built them. The dates became earlier, until finally the bricks bearing "Udnunki" were found.

Among other articles which Dr. Banks found were marble statues, onyx and sandstone lamps and many bronze objects. He denied the report that there had been a theft of valuables.

"The discoveries are of the greatest importance to science," said Professor Harper. "The site, which is being excavated by our expedition under the present name of Bismaya, undoubtedly had the ancient name of Udnunki. Work on the ruins of Udnunki will be discontinued for the present, as the excavators are spending the heated term in Bagdad."

Three Korean gentlemen, Messrs. Yi Chai-wan, Min Yong-sa and Yi Chai-kou have subscribed Y250.00 to the Japanese Army fund.

It is rumoured that Russia is negotiating with Great Britain and America as to whether kerosene oil is contraband of war or not. The latter countries are of the opinion that the oil is not contraband. Messrs. Samuel & Co. of Japan are reported to have suspended the sale of kerosene oil till furthur notice.

A nasty trick has been played on a gentleman of Paris whose walk in life seems to have been the draining of the festive beaker. After a glass or two the other day, he lay down, as was his custom, to enjoy a refreshing sleep on the pavement. When getting-up time arrived he tried to rise, but failed. Remembering the adage, he tried, and tried, and tried again, but without result. Then he began to examine into the matter, and found that both his legs had been removed at the knee. He had suffered no pain—this, perhaps, because of the fact that the legs were both wooden; but his mortification on discovering that it was his wife who had taken such a mean advantage of him quite spoiled his stay in the local gaol.

A wonderful story somewhat akin to that of the man, who, pursued by wolves, threw his child to them and thus managed to escape, comes from Munchon. A resident of that discrict tells a story to the effect that a few days ago some Japanese scouts, while on a jaunt near Munchon suddenly came upon a Russian cossack, who turned tail and fled, the Japanese pursuing. They had not gone far when a large body of cossacks hove in sight. The Japanese outnumbered and the enemies' mounts being fresher and swifter than theirs, what should they do? They turned out their pockets and strewed the roadway with silver money and then rode off at full speed. The flock of wolves (I mean the cossacks) arrived at the silver mine and throwing themselves from their horses, grabbed and fought for the nickels and ten cent bits while their enemy got safely away.

DIED:—On Wednesday August 24th, at the age of 5 months, LETITIA PAULINE, the beloved daughter of Thos. Garnier.

The funeral service will be held at the French cathedral at 4 p.m. today, after which the cortége will proceed to the foreign cemetery.

Friends are invited to attend.

It is understood that the Japanese Government has requested the Foreign Office to consult with them in future before giving employment to any foreigner in the Korean Government service.

The South African "Owl" publishes a letter from a Press correspondent at Tokyo stating that the Transvaal Labour Association, being unable to secure sufficient Chinese, has made unsuccessful endeavours to obtain Japanese labourers.

The Korea Daily News.

To be published daily except Sundays.

Rate of Subscription:—

Per Year,	Yen 25.
Per Quarter,	Yen 7.
Per Month	Yen 2.50

Postage in Korea not charged extra.
Postage abroad charged extra.

Advertisements, 50 sen per day for 1 inch or less.
5 yen per month per inch.
50 yen per year per inch.

All communications to

E. T. BETHELL,
Editor and Publisher.
Pak-tong, Seoul.

RECRUITING.

The feeling of distrust with which the Japanese demand for coolie labour is regarded in the provinces is exemplified by a report which has reached the Home Office from the magistrate of Young-in, a district about 20 miles South of Seoul.

It appears that the Government had notified him that he would be expected to provide 80 coolies from his district and that up to the 17th instant he had not succeeded in recruiting a single volunteer. On that date two Japanese gendarmes arrived, and installing themselves in his office, urged him to collect the neccessary coolies by the 20th instant. That date having arrived without any coolies being forthcoming, the magistrate says the gendarmes forced him and his secretary to accompany them on a raiding expedition to a village some three miles away. Three men were found and captured but as the party proceeded, all the houses were found to be deserted and no coolies were anywhere in sight and one more capture was all they were able to effect before returning to the magistrate's office.

That there was no dearth of coolies in the neighbourhood was shortly afterwards demonstrated, as when night fell the office was besieged by thousands of people who demanded the release of the captives. A free fight ensued, the Japanese gendarmes using their revolvers and the mob retaliating with sticks and stones. The office was smashed up and the magistrate was dragged out and accused of conniving at sending the people to certain death. The magistrate reports that the populace rescued their four fellow-villagers and assumed a very threatening attitude toward the gendarmes, whom he finally succeeded in smuggling out of the place. He says that at one time things looked very serious but that the people afterwards calmed down and dispersed.

This is an official's report and as it is apparently quite true it only shows the undesirability of the Japanese persisting in their quest for coolies with the people in their present frame of mind. It is not easy to suggest a remedy, but it is evident that a "fracas" of this description only adds fuel to the opposition fire and invests their arguments with plausibility.

KUROPATKIN'S MOVEMENTS.

The Taihan Il Po learns from a special report, that the majority of the Russian troops at Liaoyang have been withdrawn to Silipo 20 miles norteast of Liaoyang and their provisions removed to Teiling. On the 9th inst. they burnt the railway station at Liaoyang.

The Imperial Household Department are making researches in the country, with the purpose of discovering uncultivated ground, suitable for the raising of mulberry trees. Fisheries also are receiving their attention, the authorities of seaport districts having been told to furnish detailed reports of the places most favourable for this industry.

RUSSIA'S ARGUMENTS.

The St. Petersburg paper, "The Russ," published an editorial article on July 20th reagarding Russia's position relative to the stopping of neutral ships in the Red Sea by vessels of the Volunteer fleet. The statement possesses interest because it is believed to reflect directly the views of the Russian Foreign Office. It runs as follows:

"The operations of the converted cruisers "Smolensk" and "St. Petersburg" are causing tremendous excitement in England. Questions are being asked in Parliament, the newspapers are appealing to the public, and there is a panic among shipowners. There also is a good deal of talk in Germany because of the seizure of mails on the steamer "Prinz Heinrich," but the most noise there is being made by extremist organs, the others treating the matter coolly.

"It is a pity the English do not display the same Tuetonic coldness.

"It is easy to understand that the British merchant marine feels these restrictions severely. As a result of the stopping and searching of vessels, English ships either must give up transporting contraband or continue at their own risk and peril in time of war between the two powers. Others are bound to suffer more or less, as it is impossible to check contraband traffic without seizing.

"In regard to the detention of the "Prinz Heinrich's" mails, details have not yet reached St. Petersburg. Comprehensive discussion of this incident is therefore impossible. But, it must be pointed out, the official correspondence of a belligerent is contraband. Consequently if the "Prinz Heinrich" carried Japanese diplomatic and consular reports, she was liable to seizure. Of course whether she did or not, the correspondence can be inspected to determine this fact.

"The English, in their examination, even raised the question as to whether we were justified in converting the Volunteer fleet steamers into warships after they had passed the Dardanelles, under the commercial flag. This is strange. Every Government has a right to build warships in its own yards, order them abroad, buy them already built, and finally to convert them into warships. The war volunteer, at its very inception, was intended to be converted into a military fleet upon the declaration of war.

The English should not be incensed at the passage of the "St. Petersburg" and "Smolensk" through the Dardanelles. The British Embassy at Constantinople hands in a protest to the Turkish Government every time a Volunteer fleet passes the Strait. For many years these protests have been entirely disregarded, and therefore long ago lost their importance. Before the war, the Dardanelles were repeatedly passed by Volunteer ships on the way to the Far East, even with troops, arms and munitions aboard.

"If this was possible before the war, it is possible now, as there has been no change in our relations with Turkey as a result of the war with Japan. When the "St. Petersburg" and "Smolensk" passed through the Strait under the merchant flag, their destinuation was correctly given as being the Far East.

"In fact the vessels, upon entering the Red Sea, armed, hoisted the military flag. A fundamental principle of international law that a neutral flag covers neutral goods will not of course be violated by our cruisers, consequently cargoes aboard the ships of neutral Powers containing no contraband of war will remain as free as ever."

On the 22nd inst. the government session had to be abandoned, owing to the failure of several ministers to appear. His Majesty has addressed a note of censure to the Vice President of State and several other ministers.

The Osaka Shosen Kaisha has decided to open navigation to the ports occupied by the Japanese as far as there is no military objection. Two officials of the company are to be despatched to inspect Yingkau and the vicinity.

All Legations have acknowledged the appointment of the Vice Minister for Foreign Affairs to be Acting Minister.

Lady Hyon, who has returned from Japan, had a long interview with His Majesty on the evening of the 21st inst.

Order at Dalny has now been entirely restored and it is reported that the Osaka Shosen Kai-ha will commence a service to that place within a few days.

The Korean Military staff have ordered all provinces to arrest and punish soldiers, who may cause disturbances in the country. This order is probably made with the idea that the disbanding of the larger portion of the army may cause some of the ex-soldiers to give trouble.

Liuetenant Sin Sung-kiune and Captain Yang Sung-whang of the Imperial Guard have been despatched as envoys respectively to Wiju and Gensan, to enquire after the health of the Japanese troops at these places. Why not use the telegraph line instead, or even a postcard might have answered the purpose?

The authorities of the Judicial Department have altered their laws regarding the punishment of magistrates who have appropriated public monies Under the new law, any of these gentry will be liable to imprisonment with hard labor in the districts in which they previously acted in their judicial capacity. The Department have already pointed out offenders and Kim Doug Man and Om Chu Yong have requested the Government to send them to serve their term in their respective districts viz. Song Chu and Chinchu. Three other magistrates, Chang Kio Chun, Kang Man Hyong and Chang Han Ki are to be arrested and tried in the same connection.

The result of the Japanese Minister's several applications for an Imperial Audience was a refusal, but on Monday at 4 P. M., he, together with Mr. Hagiwara, Colonel Saito and his official interpreter arrived at the Palace. They were conducted to the Dondok temple, but after a few minutes, Mr. Hayashi complained that they were too distant from His Majesty's place of residence. His Majesty sent for them to be conducted to the So-ok-hon temple, where, after Mr. Hayashi had requested that some responsible person be sent to converse with him, the Vice President of State, the Minister of the Imperial Household and the Chief of Gendarmes were despatched to confer with him and report the discussion to the Throne. The conference, at which the Chief of the Ceremonial Department and the Acting Minister of Foreign Affairs were also present, lasted until 8 P. M.

M. Souvrin, Manager of the "Novoe Vremya" in a leading article in that paper which is attracting much attention, declares that it is not Manchuria nor Korea for which Russia is fighting, but it is her future position in the Far East, where covetous hands are stretched out, not only by Japan, but by the United States and Great Britain, which is the cause of the American and English sympathy with Japan. Russia, he continues, has been spoiled by easy, bloodless victories in the Far East, and consequently was not prepared for the struggle which was only avoidable by following Tolstoi's teachings and letting the Japanese take what they wanted, with the result that Russia would again be placed under the Mongol, destroying the national spirit and the unity of the empire. The contest, therefore, was accepted under unfavourable conditions. The Russians, as plainsmen, are out of their element in the mountains. The Japanese were able at the outset to put in the field twice as many men as was Russia, and they have displayed marvellous skill, but these advantages are being overcome. Still the event of the Russian victory on land will be barren so long as the Japanese hold the sea. This is why the Baltic squadron acquires such enormous importance in the destinies of Russia and why the ardent wish of the majority of the people is to see the last division start out to re-enforce the Pacific fleet.

The Korea Daily News.

VOL. I, THURSDAY, AUGUST 25, 1904. No. 34

HONGKONG & SHANGHAI BANKING CORPORATION.

Paid-up Capital	$10,000,000
Reserve Fund:—Sterling Reserve	10,000,000
Silver Reserve	6,500,000
	26,500,000
Reserve Liability of Proprietors	10,000,000

HEAD OFFICE, HONGKONG.

London Bankers, London and County Banking Company Limited.

Branches and Agencies, London.

Amoy,	Hankow	Penang,
Bangkok,	Hiogo,	Rangoon,
Batavia,	Iloilo,	Saigon,
Bombay,	Lyons,	San Francisco,
Calcutta,	Manila,	Singapore,
Colombo,	Nagasaki,	Sourabaya,
Foochow,	New York,	Tientsin,
Hamburg,	Peking,	Yokohama,

Credits granted on approved Securities, and every description of Banking and Exchange business transacted.

Drafts granted on London and the chief Commercial places in Europe, India, Australia, America, China and Japan.

HOLME RINGER & Co., AGENTS, CHEMULPO.

ON CHEONG & CO., SEOUL.

GENERAL STORE KEEPERS.
Imported provisions, Cooking Utensils Crockery, etc.
FRESH BREAD DAILY.

MITSU BISHI DOCKYARD & ENGINE WORKS, NAGASAKI.

CODE WORD, "DOCK."

A. 1, A. B. C., and Engineering Codes used.

DOCK No. 1 (at Tategami).

Extreme Length	523 feet
Length on blocks	513 ,,
Width of Entrance on Top	89 ,,
,, ,, Bottom	77 ,,
Water on Blocks at Spring Tide	26½ ,,

DOCK No. 2 (Mukaijima).

Extreme Length	371 feet
Length on Blocks	360 ,,
Width of Entrance on Top	66 ,,
,, ,, Bottom	53 ,,
Water on Blocks at Spring Tide	22 ,,

PATENT SLIP (at Kosuge).

Can take vessels up to 1,000 tons gross.

THE WORKS are well equipped with the LATEST IMPROVEMENTS, and can execute any kind of work in SHIPBUILDING and MARINE ENGINEERING, as well as in REPAIRING of SHIPS.

The COMPANY'S new powerful steamer OURA-MARU (712 tons, 700 I.H.P.), specially built for SALVAGE PURPOSES, and equipped with necessary gear, is always READY at SHORT NOTICE.

CHARTERED BANK OF INDIA AUSTRALIA & CHINA.

INCORPORATED BY ROYAL CHARTER 1853

HEAD OFFICES:—LONDON.

Paid-up Capital	£800,000
Reserve Liability of Shareholders	800,000
Reserve Fund	725,000

Drafts granted upon all the principal places in the world and every description of Exchange and banking business transacted.

E. MEYER & Co., Agents, Chemulpo.

E. MEYER & CO.

Chemulpo.

SOLE AGENTS IN KOREA FOR:

A. T. Morse, Sons & Co's "Fresco" Distemper

In all colours ready for use on walls, Ceilings etc.

and

AVENARIUS CARBOLINEUM

A wood-preserving and antiseptic oil preparation

Against decay, dry-rot, fungus and wood-destroying insects.

A large supply always in Stock. Prices upon application.

E. MEYER & Co., Chemulpo.

LAW UNION & CROWN INS. CO.

Fire risks accepted at Current rates, on godowns, merchandise, dwellings, and other property, subject to usual conditions.

HOLME RINGER & Co., Agents, Chemulpo

THE METHODIST PUBLISHING HOUSE,

Little West Gate, Seoul.

JOB PRINTING, TYPEWRITER PAPER
CARBON PAPER, VISITING CARDS
STATIONERY, BOOK BINDING
BOOK PUBLISHERS
AMERICAN SCHOOL BOOKS
SPENCERIAN COPY BOOKS
PEN CARBON LETTER AND BILL BOOKS

S. A BECK, Manager

DAI-ICHI GINKO.

LIMITED.

(Formerly the First National Bank)

ESTABLISHED 1873

INCORPORATED UNDER PRESENT LAW 1896

Capital	Yen 5,000,000
Reserve Fund	1,500,000

HEAD OFFICE:—TOKIO.

President: Baron SHIBUSAWA.

BRANCHES AND CORRESPONDENTS
In the Principal Cities and Towns of Japan.

Interest Allowed on

Fixed deposits	1 year	6½ per cent
" "	6 months	6 per cent

Special current accounts 1½ sen daily per Y 100
General " " 1 " " " 100

M. TANAKA, Manager, Chemulpo

HOLME RINGER & Co.

Chemulpo.

General Merchants and Government Contractors.

Agents for the leading

Banks

SteamshipCompanies

and

Insurance Companies

Importers of Merchandise of every description.

KAMEYA & CO.

GENERAL STOREKEEPERS

Chinkokai - - Seoul

(Established 1895, Tokyo)

Confectionery, Hams, Canned Goods, Cutlery, Hirano & Tansan Water. Provisions, Gents, Furnishing goods, Toilet Articles, Travelling Bags. Tobacco, Cigars & Cigarettes Kitchen Utensils. Coffee, Biscuits.

Fresh Goods always kept in Stock.

Prices Moderate

Please come and inspect our goods.

NIPPON YUSEN KAISHA.

JAPANESE MAIL STEAMSHIP CO.

DER MAIL CONTRACT WITH THE IMPERIAL JAPANESE GOVERNMENT.

European Line

Regular Fortnightly Service between Yokohama Kobe, Moji, Shanghai, Hongkong, Singapore, Penang Colombo, Port Said, Marseilles, London and Antwerp

American Line

Regular Fortnightly Service between Hongkong and Seattle, calling at Shanghai, Moji, Kobe, Yokohama and Victoria, B. C.

Australian Line

Regular weekly Service betwen Japan Ports and Australia, calling at Hongkong and Manila.
(Above Three Lines Suspended until further notice).

Shanghai Line.

Weekly Service between Shanghai and Japan Ports

Korea Line

Service Kobe, Moji, Nagasaki, Fusan, Chemulpo, Chioo, Taiku.
S. S. Bahelsberg, 2181 tons.
Service Kobe, Moji, Fusan, Chemulpo, Chinnampo
S. S Argo, S. S. Ohio.

BORDEN'S CONDENSED MILK CO.

New York, U. S. A.

ALWAYS IN STOCK

Eagle Brand Condensed Milk.

Gold Seal Condensed Milk.

Peerless (Family) Evaporated Cream.

Borden's Malted Milk.

E. MEYER & CO.
Chemulpo, Korea,
Sole Agents

ROYAL INSURANCE COMPANY,
Funds exceed £10,000,000
FIRE
AT CURRENT RATES.
LIFE
REDUCED PREMIUM.
HOLME RINGER & Co., Agents, Chemulpo.

HOTEL DU PALAIS

SEOUL.

The only first class Hotel in Seoul. Situated in the centre of the city opposite the palace.

Cuisine under the supervision of an experienced French Chef.

Well ventilated and furnished throughout.

TARIFF UPON APPLICATION

L. MARTIN,
Proprietor and Manager.

大韓每日申報
대한미일신보

(뎨삼십륙호) (토요일) 일천구빅사년팔월이십칠일

본샤고빅

이신보는영어와한국문셔계리
일츌판ᄒᆞᆸ

쳔문가

ᄒᆞᆫ쟝 엽두돈오푼
일삭됴엽두량닷돈 맛돈으로
밧ᄉᆞᆸ

광고료는

긔한의쟝단과ᄌᆞ항의다쇼로즁
감ᄒᆞ되헝가로밧을터이오매오
림지아녀매ᄒᆞᆫ사ᄅᆞᆷ마다다이신
문을보실터이니광고내시기를
원ᄒᆞ시는이들은우리신문사에
와셔편약ᄒᆞ심을희망ᄒᆞᆸ

○발ᄒᆡᆼ소 박동대한ᄆᆡ일신보
사 발ᄒᆡᆼ겸 편즙인 영국인 셜필
림 쟝지리오

사쟝 영국인 (빈셜)

본사지졈

인쳔항교쟝동신지명씨로우리
대한ᄆᆡ일신보사인쳔항지졈쟝을
턱졍ᄒᆞ엿ᄉᆞ오니인쳔항에계신
구람코쟈ᄒᆞ시는쳠군ᄌᆞ는허졔
졍에왕림편의ᄒᆞ시ᄋᆞᆸ

사고

○우리대한ᄆᆡ일신보의목뎍은
대한의안녕질셔에관한모든대
목에되ᄒᆞ야는공평한변론을주
쟝ᄒᆞᆷ이라우리동신원의담보는
신문보시는쳠군ᄌᆞ의게ᄒᆞᆼ상보
도ᄒᆞ리며편지를긔셔ᄒᆞ여주시
는이는셩명과번디를젹어붓치
시기를희망ᄒᆞ오니이거슨신문
샹에긔진ᄒᆞ란는거시아니오다
만극히신용ᄒᆞ는증거를숨고쟈
ᄒᆞᆷ이라긔쟈는아모긔셔던지긔
진ᄒᆞᆷ을퇴각ᄒᆞ는권리를가젓ᄉᆞ오
나퇴각ᄒᆞ는리유를말ᄒᆞᆯ터이오
며공즁평화를문란케ᄒᆞ는듯ᄒᆞᆫ
긔셔는의례히밧지안켓ᄉᆞᆸ나이
다

사고

●본사에셔신문갑ᄉᆞᆫ뒤월에맛
ᄎᆞᆫ으로밧ᄉᆞ오니리월초싱에는
시로신문갑슬미리보내주시기
를쳔만바라오며
본사에셔아직긔계를쟝만치못
ᄒᆞ와다른디셔박여오는고로미
안ᄒᆞᆫ월요일에는츌판이대단히늣
게되는듯ᄉᆞ오니우리신문을구람
ᄒᆞ시는쳠군ᄌᆞ의게붑젼이뒤우
늣게되는거슬 용셔ᄒᆞ여주심
을희망ᄒᆞᆸ나이다

론셜

한등변ᄒᆞᆫ회라

근일에유지ᄒᆞᆫ군ᄌᆞ들이국사에
진급ᄒᆞᆷ을명ᄒᆞ고ᄒᆞᆫ목젹으로일진
회를창셜ᄒᆞ고각각총대위원을
션뎡ᄒᆞ야졍부에ᄀᆞ초의를쟝셔
ᄒᆞ엿는디
이른ᄇᆞᆫ 황실을존숭ᄒᆞ며나라긔
초를공고케ᄒᆞ자는위원 서상
춘
이는 인민의싱명지산을보호
케ᄒᆞ자는위원 랑졔익
삼은 졍부를기혁케ᄒᆞ자는위
원 김병쥰
사는 군졍과지졍을졍리케ᄒᆞ
자는위원 엄즁모졔써인디이
번가지취의가나라를아모쬬록
광안케ᄒᆞ자는목젹으로주의ᄒᆞ
야셩언ᄒᆞᆫ듯ᄒᆞ되우리가싱각에
는비사ᄅᆞᆷ들이ᄆᆡ일긔회ᄒᆞ야론
사가겻ᄒᆞᆫ다는거시조곰도나라
에유익ᄒᆞᆷ이업슬뿐ᄒᆞᆫ거시괴
왕쟝삼씨의황무지쳥간ᄉᆞ건에
티ᄒᆞ야렬심으로반티ᄒᆞ든보안
회는환샨케ᄒᆞ고일진회라셜시
ᄒᆞ야일본헌병으로ᄒᆞ여곰보호
세지ᄒᆞᆫ다ᄒᆞᆫ즉필경일본셔긴졀
이요구ᄒᆞᆫ라는주의가잇셔그리
ᄒᆞ는듯ᄒᆞ며
쏘ᄒᆞᆫ셩신보에말ᄒᆞ기를이왕보
안회라ᄒᆞ는거ᄉᆞᆫ고약ᄒᆞᆫ목젹으
로쟝리에분경을싱기게ᄒᆞᆫ셔닭
에셩취가못되엿스되일진회에
셔는셜회ᄒᆞ는리유와긔회ᄒᆞ는
시간이며주의ᄒᆞ는목젹에일본
을반티ᄒᆞᆷ이업슴을일본사ᄅᆞᆷ이
게번져공포ᄒᆞᆷ으로병졸셔지파
송ᄒᆞ야한국순검과졍ᄒᆞᆷ에구인
됨이업도록극진히보호ᄒᆞᆫ다ᄒᆞ
엿는디
쟈과연일본헌병의게보호밧음을
자세하고히회총디위원들이챰
졍싱샹ᄒᆞᆫ씨의게와셔셜회ᄒᆞᆫ목
젹을말ᄒᆞᆯ때에도과샹ᄒᆞᆫ일이잇
ᄃᆞ라하며쏘ᄌᆞ긔들의일의티로
ᄒᆞ는게업시티사ᄅᆞᆷ일본헌병의
게문의ᄒᆞ여일본에관계되지안
ᄐᆞ록ᄒᆞᄃᆞ라ᄒᆞᆫ즉
이회는분명히일본에계휘밧은
리도엽고다만이혹싱기
라에손히됨은잇스되조곰도유나
익ᄒᆞᆯ는지는맛을수업는거시
근일갓티셔는뮈우을ᄒᆞᆫ목젹으
로일을힝ᄒᆞ는듯ᄒᆞ되ᄎᆞᄎᆞ오리
되드리도다론의결이업시어일
ᄒᆞ게갈는지알수업스며이거손
후진보가되드리도ᄒᆞᆫ어리셕은
일인거시비컨티셔양에우미ᄒᆞᆫ
사ᄅᆞᆷ은집안에셔고양이나기르
고남방셤에셔거싱ᄒᆞ는사ᄅᆞᆷ들
은하졀에도외복을두텁게입는
것갓도다이번번취못ᄒᆞᆫ일에군
병으로시위ᄒᆞ는것과한셩신보
에쟝황이셜명ᄒᆞᆫ거시셜노이샹
ᄒᆞ야경아ᄒᆞᆷ을만ᄒᆞ도다

관보

뎨이쳔구빅십오호 광무팔
년팔월이십륙일

셔임급ᄉᆞ령

명쥰도원참령셔칙임관삼등
통신원회판 김인규
팔월이십삼일
명중ᄂᆡ부특진관셔칙임관일등
경흥오젼졔쥬 조동희
명경흥오젼졔쥬셔칙임관이등
졍이품 리헌영 임셩진면보
ᄉᆞ쥬ᄉᆞ셔쥬임관륙등 윤졍힝
금삼급봉 셩진면보ᄉᆞ쥬ᄉᆞ
윤셩협
승ᄋᆞᆫ급봉 외국어학교부교관
최항셕 류 면 관립소학교
교원 윤보영
승이급봉 외국어학교부교관
최지익 졍일범 즁학교교관
김한규 의학교교관 면등규
관립소학교교원 박희명
이샹팔월이십ᄉᆞ일

궁졍록ᄉᆞ

의졍부참졍신셩샹ᄒᆞᆫ근 쥬ᄒᆞᆫ
티한셩부관윤김규희샹소ᄉᆞ의
를졍부로ᄒᆞ야곰품쳐ᄒᆞᆯᄉᆞ로
명하옵신지라칙부관졔가텬이
됨이만하셔변통하음이합당하
겟는고로니부와법부로ᄒᆞ야곰
시의를참작ᄒᆞ야안건을갓추와
신부에졔의ᄒᆞ야귀졍ᄒᆞ는티
쥐가ᄒᆞᆷ이ᄉᆞᆷ하ᄒᆞ여ᄒᆞᆯ을지근샹
쥬ᄒᆞ와봉 지의쥬ᄒᆞ시다
호위티총관 리즁진ᄉᆞ식소
비지니에수앙말고힝공ᄒᆞ라
협령부도관찬ᄉᆞ 리응진ᄉᆞ직
소 비지니에소쳥티로의시ᄒᆞ
노라
군부대신 민영긔ᄌᆞ명소 비
지니에이곳치말ᄒᆞᆫ거시아니라
ᄒᆞ시다
법부대신 박졔순ᄉᆞ직소 비
지니에됴리힝공ᄒᆞ라
농샹공부대신셔리농샹공부협
판리근샹ᄌᆞ현소 비지니에
이곳치말ᄒᆞᆫ거시아니라ᄒᆞ시다
이샹팔월이십ᄉᆞ일

잡보

○총티가탑 샹쟈이른진회에
셔졍부에쟝셔홈으로총티위원
졍티용씨가쟝서를휴티ᄒᆞ고졍
부에간즉참졍신샹ᄒᆞᆫ씨가졍부
에불입ᄒᆞᆫ지라루합ᄒᆞ고도라왓
더라쟈작이ᄅᆞᆫ하오이시에일진회
가쏘긔회ᄒᆞ고의견ᄒᆞ여왈참졍
외하문ᄒᆞᆫ스돌입의ᄒᆞᆷ으로셜
병ᄒᆞ엿ᄉᆞᆫ죠등츙ᄒᆞ엿슬지라ᄉᆞ
도건셜시ᄒᆞ기를지츙ᄒᆞᄌᆞᄒᆞ고
총티위원ᄉᆞ명을더튁ᄒᆞ엿는
티림진슈죠병우윤갑병류진호
ᄉᆞ인이라젼총티황희원외에방졍부
자는즁립ᄒᆞ지못ᄒᆞ게ᄒᆞ고일헌
병은어젼히과슈ᄒᆞ엿ᄉᆞ며졍일본
은귀국귀원졍인고로회원이보
호병츌ᄒᆞ엿다ᄒᆞ더라

○일산광ᄒᆞᆫ 금쳔금슈김현티
써가니부에보고ᄒᆞ되향자에
산림쳔리진황디를거ᄂᆞᆫ단코티국
에차여치아니ᄒᆞᆫ츳로임의ᄒᆞᆫ령
이잇수왓고공ᄂᆡ부ᄒᆞᆫ령ᄂᆡ에본
군소지대드산과구봉산은본리
관유디란영셧금양ᄒᆞᆫ지ᄂᆡ표목
을세우고경계를졍ᄒᆞ고산직이
를틱졍ᄒᆞ야별반슈호하라하엿
더니관찰부ᄒᆞᆫ령ᄂᆡ에의졍부훈
수김인영이가소구하되본인이
황셩명동원임의졍운대신지교
를봉ᄒᆞ야와금쳔소지구봉산샹
하수방젼즉을졍계립표ᄒᆞ야운
의졍원하기로이에발ᄒᆞᆫᄒᆞᆫ츳로
쳥치보ᄒᆞ라ᄒᆞ엿수오니산졍계
산이온티ᄒᆞᆫ령인즉두곳이오니
엇지거힝ᄒᆞ올지지령ᄒᆞ라ᄒᆞ엿
더라

○류목졍류 의쥬군구룡포에
류하ᄒᆞ는셰목은한쳥량국목상

UNION INSURANCE SOCIETY OF CANTON.

Head office Hongkong.
Marine risks underwritten at current rates.
Agents in Chemulpo,
MEYER & Co.

COMPAGNIE DES MESSAGERIES MARITIMES.

Fortnightly Direct Service.

For Marseilles
Via Ports.
Sailing from Yokohama
Calling at Kobe,
Shanghai, Hongkong, Saigon, Singapore,
Colombo, Djibonti, Suez, Port Said
and Marseilles.

For particulars apply to
HOLME RINGER & Co.,
Chemulp

HAYASHIDA & CO.

16 MYENG DONG, CHING KO KAI, SEOUL.
BRANCH OFFICE AT CHEMULPO.

Money changers, Coal and Wood Merchants, Express Agents.

We are agents for the Pyeng-yang Coal Company and the Karazu Coal Company of Japan. We have the best quality of both anthracite and bituminous coal, and prompt execution of orders is our speciality. Firewood of all kinds kept in stock. Full weight guaranteed. Money of all denominations exchange, at current rates. Parcels received for all parts

CHINA MUTUAL LIFE INS. CO.

Most favourable terms to policy holders.

Benefit system unsurpassed.

HOLME RINGER & Co.
Agents, Chemulpo.

C. P. R.

CANADIAN PACIFIC RAILWAY COMPANY'S ROYAL MAIL STEAMSHIP LINE.

THE FAST ROUTE BETWEEN CHINA, JAPAN, AND EUROPE VIA CANADA AND THE UNITED STATES.

Route from Hongkong via Shanghai, Nagasaki (Inland Sea of Japan) Kobe, Yokohama, Victoria and Vancouver.

Twin Screw Empress Steamships—6,000 Tons—Speed 19 knots.

PROPOSED SAILINGS FROM YOKOHAMA.

R. M. S. Empress of India.
R. M. S. Empress of Japan.
R. M. S. Empress of China.
R. M. S. Athenian.
R. M. S. Tartar.

Special reduction (first class only) granted to members of the Military, Naval, Diplomatic and Civil Services and to Missionaries.
Passengers have choice of ten routes across the Continent of America and have privilege of travelling by any Atlantic Steamship Line.
Round the World passage tickets in connection with the P. and O. S. N., North German Lloyd and Messageries Co.'s £125.
All rates payable at current rate of exchange.
For further information, Tickets, Guide Books, etc., apply to
HOLME, RINGER & Co., AGENTS, Chemulpo.

Grand Hotel,

(Formerly the Station Hotel)

Near the Railway Terminus,

West Gate, Seoul.

The Best Hotel in Korea.
Handsome new Building.
Fine airy Rooms
Excellent Cuisine.
Terms Moderate.
Special terms to Missionaries and to permanent boarders.

Electric cars within 2 minutes' walk.

W. H. EMBERLEY,
Proprietor.

EVERY FACILITY

In connection with Life Assurance Business is afforded by

The Standard Life Assurance Co.,

One of the largest and wealthiest of the Provident Institutions of the United Kingdom. Forms of Application and all information will be promptly afforded on application.

10 CENTS A DAY.

Not a very large expenditure is it? But it is sufficient to secure for a man of 30 a policy with the STANDARD LIFE OFFICE for

$1323.

For all particular of rates, etc., apply to

Holme, Ringer & Co.,
Agents, Chemulpo.

THE NEW YORK LIFE INSURANCE COMPANY.

Have you ever been declined by and Company?

Are you engaged in as pecially hazardous occupation?

Have you heard of the New York Life Insurance Company's New Classifications for this class of Risks?

If not, send your date of birth, occupation and particulars of rejection, if any to

E. MEYER & Co., Agents, Chemulpo.

MITSUI BUSSAN KAISHA.
(MITSUI & Co.)

MITSUI GINKO.
(MITSUI BANK.)

The Bank is owned by the members of the Mitsui Family, who, as partners, assume an unlimited responsibility for all liabilities of the Bank:—
Capital.......................Yen 5,000,000
Reserve Fund...................." 5,600,000

HEAD OFFICE, TOKYO.
LONDON OFFICE, 34 LIME ST., E. C.

BRANCHES AND AGENCIES:—
New York, San Francisco, Hamburg, Bombay, Singapore, Manila, Hongkong, Amoy, Chefoo, Tientsin.
Kobe, Hakodate, Yokohama, Kure, Yokosuka, Moji, Shimonoseki, Miike, Wakamatsu, Nagasaki, Kuchinotsu, Karatsu, Sasebo, Misume, Taipeh, &c.

Telegraphic Address for all the Offices:
"MITSUI."
A. B. C. AND A. I CODES USED.

Contractors of Coal
To the Imperial Japanese Navy. Arsenals and Railway Bureau, Principal Railway Companies and Industrial Works, Home and Foreign Mail and Freight Steamers.
Sole Proprietors
Of the famous Miike, Tagawa and Yamano Coal Mines.
Sole Agents
For the sale of Fukumo, Hokoku, Ichimura, Kanoda, Mannoura, Onoura, Ostuji, Sonoda, Tsubaruro, Yoshinotani, Yoshio, Yurokibura and other coals.

YANGTSE INSURANCE ASSOCIATION, LTD.

The undersigned, having been appointed agents for the above company, are prepared to issue policies and pay losses on marine risks at regular rates.

E. MEYER & Co.,
Agents, Chemulpo.

AMERICAN KOREAN ELECTRIC COMPANY.
Light and Power.
Main Office: Electric Building, Chong No.

RAILWAY DEPARTMENT.

OPERATING CARS BETWEEN EAST AND WEST GATE, EVERY TEN MINUTES:—
First Car leaves East Gate at 6:30 A. M. First Car leaves West Gate at 6:55 A. M.
Last Car " East Gate at 10:40 P. M. Last " " West Gate at 11:00 P. M.

OPERATING CARS BETWEEN EAST GATE AND IMPERIAL TOMB TERMINUS, EVERY TWENTY MINUTES:—
CONNECTING WITH EVERY ALTERNATE CAR ARRIVING AT EAST GATE FROM CHONG NO.
First Car leaves East Gate for Tomb at 6:50 A. M.
" " " Tomb for East Gate at 7:10 A. M.
Last " " East Gate for Tomb at 9:50 P. M.
" " " Tomb for East Gate at 10:10 P. M.

OPERATING CARS BETWEEN CHONG NO AND YUNG SAN (RIVER) EVERY TWELVE MINUTES:—
First Car leaves Chong No for South Gate at 6:48 A. M.
" " " Chong No for Yung San at 7:24 A. M.
" " " South Gate for Chong No at 6:56 A. M.
" " " Yung San for Chong No at 7:57 A. M.
Last " " South Gate for Chong No 11:00 P. M.
" " " Yung San for Chong No at 10:11 P. M.

SPECIAL PRIVATE CARS FURNISHED TO SUIT CONVENIENCE OF PATRONS. PRICES ON APPLICATION AT HEAD OFFICE.

LIGHTING DEPARTMENT.

Where less than 250 candle power of light is used, the rate per month will be. Per 16 candle power incandescent lamp. All night.—Yen 2.50.
Per 32 candle power incandescent lamp:—All night:—Yen 4.00. Per 50 candle power incandescent lamp:—All night:—Yen 6.00.
" 150 " " " " — " " " 10.00. " 1200 " " enclosed arc " " " 20.00.
Where more than 250 candle power of light is used, a Meter will be installed, if requested:—Rent of Meter Yen 2.00 per month. Rate of charges by meter reading:—Two Sen per Ampere per hour. (Approximately this is equal to about One Sen per 16 c. p. lamp per hour) Minimum monthly charge where meter is installed, Yen 20.00 per month, which includes rental of meter.
Estimates for installing lights furnished on application. An assortment of chandeliers always on hand.

AMUSEMENT DEPARTMENT.

ANIMATED PICTURES AT EAST GATE.
Every evening - - - Except Sunday.
From 8 to 10 P. M.

10 Cents:—Gen. Admission:—10 Cents. Seats in Firs Class Section. 15 Cents Extra.

Change of program each week. Pictures from Foreign Lands. Pictures of Local Scenes:—Amusing and Instructive.

An entertaining evening for a reasonable price.
MERRY-GO-ROUND:—At East Gate.
From 10:00 A. M. till 11:00 P. M.

5 Cents a Ride.

Take your Exercise on The Galloping Horses.

Comfortable seats in the Chariots.

한셩뎐긔회사

미국뎐긔회사 고보안 보사며 고빅
또ᄒᆞ옵나이다
상활동사진뎐람소와목마운동쟝량쳐로언
여러뎐차가온쟝안으로통힝ᄒᆞ여ᄃᆞ니여이
습
또이긔계에굿처노힌편ᄒᆞ고됴흔마차도잇
습
코미우편ᄒᆞ고또조미잇는됴흔운동이되겟
어됴흔모형ᄒᆞᆫ달나아는몰을ᄐᆞ고위티치안
틔가는ᄒᆞᆫ번ᄐᆞ는데오젼식이오
미일샹오열시브터하오열ᄒᆞᆫ시ᄭᆞ지ᄒᆞ옵고
목마운동쟝은동대문안에잇습고
가되겟습
쳠군조의계갑도싸고저녁에됴흔쇼일거리
잇고구경ᄒᆞᆯ만ᄒᆞᆫ거시오니
셔양사진과대한과온동양사진인데대조미
는딕
젼이옵고미쥬일에사진을싼것스로다밧고
고젼랑듸금은하등에십젼이오상등에이십
일외에는미야에여덟시브터열시ᄭᆞ지ᄒᆞ옵
활동사진뎐람소는동대문안에잇습고일요
희락부

All Cars Run Direct to the Animated Pictures and Merry-Go-Round.

의붙진인ᄃᆡ근일에일본사ᄅᆞᆷ이졍류ᄒᆞ야ᄒᆡᆼ동치못ᄒᆞ게ᄒᆞᆫ다더라

○가련셔민 희쥬군슈구완회씨의보고를거ᄒᆞᆫ즉ᄒᆞ엿스되각군인부를쳥국ᄃᆡ경으로모집ᄒᆞ야보너는졍랑을됴사ᄒᆞᆫ즉룡쳔과쳘산에셔각쳔여명식이오션쳔에셔일쳔오빅명이오가산에셔이쳔명이오곽산졍쥬량군에셔각쳔명식인ᄃᆡ도로가추원ᄒᆞᆫ즉쌩혀가는모군매명하동즁으로셔돈을관비ᄒᆞ야그도로원근ᄃᆡ로오빅량식흑쳔량식주는ᄃᆡ령세구ᄎᆞᄒᆞᆫ즁평민무관인들은모군벌수도업고돈벌수도업스니그참혹ᄒᆞᆫ졍샹을참아보지못ᄒᆞ겟노라ᄒᆞ엿더라

○군ᄃᆡ됴사 일젼에한셩순운박승조와너부참셔관오지룡량씨가남문외로한강ᄭᆞ지일본군용디뎜으로표목세운곳을됴사ᄒᆞᆫ즉표목세운거시구십팔기인ᄃᆡ그주회가일만팔쳔보가량이논되엿더라

○희쥬군보 희쥬군수구완회씨보고에ᄒᆞ엿스되인부를빙일쳔빅명식모집ᄒᆞ야보니는ᄃᆡ그즁에즁평문음무관인비왕왕이셕진거슬블블헌젼이라ᄒᆞ엿더라

○등ᄌᆞᆼ포쟝 일본순사면하좌ᄃᆡ랑이희쥬군슈구완회씨를ᄯᅢ라희군에하거ᄒᆞ야빅셩의게ᄃᆡᄒᆞ야쳐ᄉᆞ를공평케ᄒᆞ셔코계ᄒᆞ고로가잇셔셔본군빅셩외원류가잇는고로외부에셔희일인의게포증쟝을주엇더라

○례포셩명 일젼에외부에셔각국공관에공함ᄒᆞ되원슈부공함을졉ᄒᆞᆫ즉음력칠월십삼일긔국긔원졀과동월이십오일만슈셩졀과ᄯᅩ다른령시축례일에포병ᄃᆡ에셔례포를거ᄒᆡᆼᄒᆞᆯ터이니각공관에셩명ᄒᆞ라ᄒᆞ엿기로함교ᄒᆞ니죠량ᄒᆞ라ᄒᆞ엿더라

○평양란신 평양소식을거ᄒᆞᆫ즉함흥원산등디에쥬둔ᄒᆞᆫ로국병이셩쳔강동등디에범히리도ᄒᆞ는고로인심이민우소요ᄒᆞ다더라

○량폐현 금일하오세시반에는일본공ᄉᆞ림권조씨가 폐현ᄒᆞ고하오다섯시에는영국공ᄉᆞ주이뎐씨가 폐현ᄒᆞᆫ뒤후분셔ᄒᆞ신ᄃᆡᄃᆡᄒᆞ야영국대황뎨폐하의친셔를봉정ᄒᆞ고 폐현ᄒᆞᆫ다더라

○룡강민쇼 평안도룡강사ᄅᆞᆷ의말을드른즉룡강읍에서는역부모집ᄒᆞ는ᄉᆞ건에ᄃᆡᄒᆞ야우리ᄒᆞᆫ빅셩들이미병을쌜는다고외언을류ᄒᆡᆼᄒᆞ며민료을이르키엿다ᄒᆞ는ᄃᆡ그즁에괴란ᄒᆞ며너가는자도만코비른다고괴란ᄒᆞ여가든자들이과젼에되여인명이만히샹수ᄒᆞ엿다더라

○죠ᄉᆞ양샹 쥬일공ᄉᆞ조민희씨와참셔관현긔우씨가지작일경오에인항에도착ᄒᆞ야하오삼시랑에입셩ᄒᆞ야즉시 폐현ᄒᆞ엿더라

○부인샤기 리항공셜은통문ᄒᆞᆫ즉총쟝현영운씨부인이환가이후로무샹연고가잇는지칭병ᄒᆞ야리직을사졀ᄒᆞ고ᄒᆞᆫ번도출근치아니ᄒᆞ엿다더라

○충효쌍젼 양쥬군슈홍틔윤씨가치적이렴명ᄒᆞ고곡정ᄒᆞ며예들일세인이칭찬ᄒᆞ는ᄃᆡ그가풍블득문ᄒᆞᆫ즉그부친이항샹고ᄌᆞᄃᆡ를ᄒᆞᆫ게ᄒᆞ야곤으ᄃᆡ세샹사ᄅᆞᆷ들이만히젼셩지방을조티ᄒᆞᄂᆞ니이거시효도가아니라관ᄒᆡᆼ즁남어지돈이ᄉᆞ가에드러오는거시너몸에블안ᄒᆞᆫ지라미상월봉으로일비가부족ᄒᆞ거든본집젼랑으로보용ᄒᆞ라ᄒᆞᆫ다더니홍씨가그부교를봉ᄒᆡᆼᄒᆞ야치민ᄒᆞ는ᄃᆡ극히쳥렴홈으로이런소요ᄒᆞᆫ때를당ᄒᆞ며도홍노셩명이현저ᄒᆞ니가위립신양명ᄒᆞ야이현부모라ᄒᆞ고흠만ᄒᆞ더라

○김슈션정 함창군슈김괴슈씨가리임ᄒᆞᆫ지수삭에일신으로공ᄉᆞ를ᄒᆞ며폐읍이다시소셩ᄒᆞ고흰산ᄒᆞ엿든빅셩이곳처환집ᄒᆞ며인민의송셩이디작ᄒᆞᆫ다더라

○교육회의 삼작일에동대문안련동에서국민교육회의정후교인들이회합ᄒᆞ야연셜ᄒᆞ엿단말은본보에임의긔ᄌᆡᄒᆞ엿거니와당일회회에윤치호여운명리원긍졔씨가참회ᄒᆞ엿는ᄃᆡ하회ᄎᆞ빈세가이거슬부리발을문드리고공증에무교ᄒᆞ기를이젼동아회동ᄒᆞ니회쟝이셜회ᄒᆞ스리라ᄒᆞᆫ지라 쳐분이나리라는데첫회회원등을포라ᄒᆞ리라는데ᄋᆡ번김명근씨가돌연이경무ᄉᆞ를피임ᄒᆞᆫ거시그ᄉᆞ롬인지

○윤어량씨 젼향곳치교육회가ᄎᆡ의를밧아회원들을장찻포라ᄒᆞᆫ다는항셜이잇는ᄃᆡ윤치호씨와어운뎍씨는본시회원도아니오그시에구경으로갓다고셜명ᄒᆞ엿다더라

○량씨셔리 찬정윤용렬씨는농상공부대신셔리를피명ᄒᆞ고김가진씨는법부대신셔리를피명ᄒᆞ엿더라

○쥬본미하 참정신셩훈씨가일젼에너부대신조병필씨와졍관리봉릭씨와륭진관리근틱씨와겸수총쟝현영운씨를면관ᄒᆞ구라 쥬본을드럿ᄂᆞᆫ대발은젼호에괴치ᄒᆞ엿거니와한칙을괴ᄒᆞᆫ즉에조너대는일기로대관으로너정의다ᄉᆞᄒᆞᆷ을블감ᄒᆞᆫ셴이오니쳥리봉릭씨의죄안도과중치아니ᄒᆞ고리근틱씨는불과지변일노지금문죄ᄒᆞᆷ인즉시괴에진졍ᄒᆞᆫ일이아니즉희쥬분의복덕은젼희현영운씨의죄안을넘음이라현씨가오리권세를잡아국가대ᄉᆞ를만히주무ᄒᆞ며너신참졍이그권세티종ᄒᆞᆷ으로면관구라 쥬본을샹ᄒᆞ엿는ᄃᆡ동씨와그부인빈씨가궁중에잇셔서만단으로운동ᄒᆞ야식참정을과희ᄒᆞ이축출ᄒᆞᆫ라ᄒᆞᆫ다ᄒᆞ는ᄃᆡ희 쥬본이류중ᄒᆞ쳔졔거가비리시지아니ᄒᆞᆷ으로관정이ᄉᆞ진치아니ᄒᆞ니다른대관도ᄯᅩᄒᆞᆫ능히시무치못ᄒᆞ야정부가일공이되엿다더라

갱위기정 정부에서너부로조회ᄒᆞ기를한성부관졔기정ᄒᆞᆫ안긴을ᄯᅩ곳쳐기정ᄒᆞ야대의ᄒᆞ라ᄒᆞ엿더라

○역부교가 대구관찰ᄉᆞ윤헌씨가작일에너부로면보ᄒᆞ기를일본군용역부교가를원일오십젼식작정ᄒᆞ엿다ᄒᆞ오니한화와일화를지명ᄒᆞ야죠시회면ᄒᆞ라ᄒᆞ엿더라

○박종적묘 룡쥬관찰ᄉᆞ가작일에너부로면보ᄒᆞ기를본군포리박모를룡남둥츅ᄒᆞᆫᄎᆞ로이닷여도들ᄃᆡ별ᄒᆞ여척슈ᄒᆞ엿더니수일만에귀ᄉᆞᄒᆞᆫ지라박가의게죽이관문도릉ᄒᆞ야군슈들구타ᄒᆞᆫ뒤순교와ᄉᆞ령등이일제이보호ᄒᆞ야군슈는관찰부로피ᄒᆞ엿아위경을면ᄒᆞ엿는ᄃᆡ안군슈로ᄉᆞ슈는착슈ᄒᆞ엿고티안군슈로ᄉᆞ검관을경ᄒᆞ야ᄉᆞ회케ᄒᆞ고괴란ᄒᆞᆫ군슈는ᄃᆡ에류ᄒᆞ야보호ᄒᆞᆫ다ᄒᆞ엿더라

○잔리불법 삼화거ᄒᆞᄂᆞᆫ한평욱이가평리원에정소ᄒᆞᆫ기의를들은즉동군간리빈영탁이가본인의소유를임의로작별ᄒᆞ고ᄯᅩ종징젼이란칭탁ᄒᆞ고관련을청세ᄒᆞ야분인의돈쳔여량을륵탈ᄒᆞ엿스ᄆᆡ죵량합이쳔오빅칠십여량이온ᄃᆡ무ᄎᆞ부군에정ᄒᆞ야빈가라송ᄒᆞ야탐교표에감리의인쟝을써여셩급ᄒᆞ여주엇는ᄃᆡ한이지너도록돈을안이너는고로광리원에정소ᄒᆞ야엄훈ᄒᆞᆫ평을감리평으로ᄒᆞ엿는ᄃᆡᄒᆡᆼ감리교영쳘씨가도리여셩너에수평용식여한씨의쌩을져관문밧케츌츌ᄒᆞ엿는ᄃᆡ한씨의억음너가새지고ᄯᅩ빈가의ᄌᆞ식이관문밧케은신ᄒᆞ엿다가한씨의는옴을보고달녀드러의관을렬파ᄒᆞ고소장츅을들탐ᄒᆞᆫ지라한씨가분을ᄒᆞ야감리의게말ᄒᆞ되샹부ᄒᆞᆫ평을거여ᄒᆞ고돈도아니밧아쥬고도리여압제ᄒᆞᄂᆞ니교ᄒᆞ엿더니ᄒᆡᆼ감리가관문발악이라말ᄒᆞ고일변착슈ᄒᆞ며일년반징역에쳐ᄒᆞ엿다ᄒᆞ더니멋날후에한씨를불너분부ᄒᆞ되징역슈젼밧치라ᄒᆞ고등츅ᄒᆞ엿는ᄃᆡ슈쾌ᄒᆞᆫ지일삭후에아모말도업시방송ᄒᆞ엿스니등츅ᄒᆞ신후돈을추쥐달는ᄒᆞᆫ시라평리원에서ᄒᆡᆼ감리셔예ᄒᆞᆫ령ᄒᆞ되괴교빈룡탁을착슈ᄒᆡ압샹ᄒᆞ야지겸케ᄒᆞ라ᄒᆞ엿다더라

○시비난변 평도원기수는월봉이싱원외에는란비등도지발치안니ᄒᆞ는ᄃᆡ평도에ᄉᆞ역ᄒᆞ는자들관할ᄒᆞ는직권을잡고경부평도에서역부에샤쳔ᄌᆞ는것과평도소용으로미슈ᄒᆞ는토디갑슬지발ᄒᆞᆯ때에는기ᄉᆞ들이맛ᄒᆞ셔주는고로희기ᄉᆞ는그평슈ᄒᆞᆫ금액을ᄃᆡ반이나범용ᄒᆞ고그남어지를본인의게주는ᄃᆡ근간에부산감리가경부텰도에셔슈용ᄒᆞᆫ토디갑슬평슈ᄒᆞ야토디본쥬의게츌급ᄒᆞᆫ일에부산감리가토디본쥬의게슈뇌흠이라ᄒᆞ고텰도원기ᄉᆞ들이희감리를박론ᄒᆞ야대풍파를일희켯다ᄒᆞ고대한일본에괴치ᄒᆞ엿더라

○박씨양샹 원산셔일본헌병의게피착된참령박유ᄃᆡ씨는일젼경셩으로압샹되야일본병참에구슈되엿더라

○형뎨광관 괴쥬군슈신석호씨와그계씨진위군슈신셕현씨는경셩에오래두류ᄒᆞᆷ으로희량씨읍민졍이발못되다ᄒᆞ니희량씨는목민지관이되야민졍을교겸치안이ᄒᆞᆷ리가업무ᄒᆞᆫ즉아마젼지자오인듯ᄒᆞ더라

○기국귀원젼 작일은대한긔국귀원졀인고로각부에서휴가ᄒᆞ고경축ᄒᆞ엿더라

공보

동경팔월이십오일발 공ᄉᆞ관착뎐

로한젼쟁은 셰곡ᄉᆞ평관보고에왈려순방면의모든망루와포상의보고충합ᄒᆞᆫ거ᄉᆞᆯ거ᄒᆞᆫ즉금이십ᄉᆞ일오후륙시삼십분에로텬산에셔동으로이희리즘되는곳에셔적의구츅함일쳑이괴계슈뢰에걸녀진즁침몰ᄒᆞ엿고동륙시삼십분에뎌의다른구츅뎡ᄒᆞᆫ쳑도ᄯᅩᄒᆞᆫ슈뢰에걸녓는ᄃᆡ뎌의군함이구조ᄒᆞ야려순항구안으로드러갓더라젼거ᄉᆞᆫ셰굴둑박이요ᄒᆞᆫ거ᄉᆞᆫ비굴둑박인데오날아츰에뎌의항외에나아온거ᄉᆞᆫ소흠뎡이오쳑이오구츅뎡이삼쳑인ᄃᆡ그두빈가나리를맛나그후ᄯᅦ에다항구안으로도망ᄒᆞ여도라갓다ᄒᆞ엿더라

광고

뎨십팔은ᄒᆡᆼ
본졈은일본쟝긔에잇고
지졈은인쳔부산원산에잇슴
경셩십팔은ᄒᆡᆼ

TELEGRAMS.

NAVAL REPORT ON THE PORT ARTHUR SITUATION.

Tokyo, Aug. 25th.

Captain Hosatain of the 3rd naval squadron states that he received reports from the ship Hashitashi, which assert that at 6:20 p. m. on the 24th inst., one of the enemy's destroyers was sunk by a mine 2 miles east of Laotisan and sunk. At 6:25 another destroyer struck a mine but was assisted into the harbour by another ship.

Berlin, Aug. 16.

Russia has issued a Circular announcing the steps taken by Russia and France regarding the seizure of the "Retshitelny" at Chefoo, but the receipt of the Circular has only been noted in Berlin, as Germany does not intend to join in the protest.

The London "Daily News" "Daily Chronicle," "Times," and "Standard" express the opinion that Japan by her action in seizing the vessel has violated the principles of international law.

In official circles in Berlin the hope is expressed that the matter will be settled amicably.

FROM JAPAN PAPERS.

London, Aug. 17.

The correspondent of the "Daily Telegraph" at St. Petersburg states that the protest forwarded by Great Britain to the Russian Government reviews, firstly, the claim of the Russians to treat as contraband articles recognised by international law as legitimate cargo; secondly, the refusal to limit the zone wherein alleged contraband may be pursued by belligerent war-ships, thus involving the right to hamper even the coasting trade; and thirdly, the sinking of neutral vessels. Lastly, the Note demands that compensation be paid for the heavy losses inflicted on British shipping, including the confiscation of cargoes and the sinking of steamers.

The language of the protest, though courteous, is emphatic.

The United States simultaneously presented an energetic protest similar to the first section of the British Note, and points out that Russia implicitly claims the right to forbid all trade by neutrals with an enemy's country without effectually blockading the coasts.

London, Aug. 18.

The Russian cruiser "Ural," formerly the German liner "Kaiserin Maria Theresa," has stopped a British collier west of the Straits of Gibraltar.

The commander of the cruiser stated that he was searching for two hundred steamers carrying contraband cargo(!).

London, Aug. 18.

The Hamburg-Amerika and Norddeutscher Lloyd are doubling their service to Japan mainly for the purpose of providing for the transit of freight refused by the British steamship companies.

[Several of the British lines recently refused to book cargoes for Japan in consequence of the treatment of neutral vessels by Russian war-ships.]

In the debate in the House of Commons on the new tobacco duty, Mr. Labouchere, M.P., said the foreign cigarette was more a necessity than a luxury. "It produced a similar effect to that produced by reading the Bible—laughter—it soothed and calmed the nerves and caused evil passions to fade away. He did not know which way he should vote on the amendment. Perhaps the best thing would be not to vote at all, but to leave the House and go and have a cigarette." So saying Mr. Labouchere, amid roars of laughter, turned his back on the assembly, and gravely strode away in the direction of the smoking room.

THE LATE M. DE PLEHWE ON THE CONDITION OF RUSSIA.

In view of the tragic fate which shortly afterwards overtook him, the following report from "The Times" of an interview with M. de Plehwe will be read with interest:—

Paris, June 27th.—The St. Petersburg correspondent of the "Matin" has interviewed M. de Plehwe, who made certain remarks to him that are by no means uninteresting. The correspondent was struck by the contrast between his emphatic and sharp statements and the suave courtesy of his manner, together with the almost unctuous gentleness of his gesticulations. "It donne l'impression d'un homme quievent des choses terribles avec tranquillité," says the representative of the "Matin," but he thinks that M. de Plehwe is not quite so terrible as people imagine. As to the affairs of Finland, for instance, he is authorized by M. de Plehwe to contradict the rumors respecting the uncompromising attitude of the Tsar's Government and the suppression of all kinds of privileges. This is however, hardly consistent with what follows. For example, referring to the murder of General Bobrikoff, M. de Plehwe observed:—"The assassin had accomplices and the plot was hatched in Sweden. All the guilty will be punished." The correspondent adds that one should have heard M de Plehwe say in his quiet voice:—"All the guilty will be punished." It left the rather uncomfortable impression that not a single one would escape.

M. de Plehwe described the domestic peace of the Empire as being "perfect." The agrarian disturbances had not been renewed. Crops were excellent. The first of the Imperial ukases concerning the new conditions of existence for the Jews had just been issued. War, which in all countries had such a disastrous effect upon the labour question, had not had that result in Russia. Speaking of the war, he said that from the despatches he had read yesterday morning the next battle did not seem to be as imminent as was expected. "In consequence of certain circumstances we shall be obliged to retreat even as far as Harbin, but that move, instead of being prejudicial for us, can only be of advantage. The army of to-day will thus find itself united with the army of tomorrow, which during the rainy season will roll uninterruptedly along the Trans-Siberian Railway. . . . Believe me," said his Excellency, "any proposal for peace would at the present moment be altogether unpopular in our country. I will even go so far as to say that to mention it is to insult the nation."

It is instructive to read M. de Plehwe's categorical statements in the light of a letter from the Russian correspondent of the "Aurose." "One of the principal representatives of the "régime" against which Schaumann's revolver was directed," in conversation with this correspondent, contended that the Liberal European Press largely contributed to create in Finland the frame of mind of which Schaumann's deed was a consequence. It was the foreigner, he said, who was to blame for everything—the foreigner abroad and the foreigner resident in Russia; that is to say, the Jew, the Finn, the Pole, the Armenian, and even the Little Russian. He added that, of course, there was solidarity between these two categories of foreigners. That was M. de Plehwe's theory and, says the correspondent of the "Aurore," "from his own standpoint it must be admitted that it is in accordance with facts. But the Grand Master of the Russian Empire forgets just one detail, which he regards as insignificant. It is that the solidarity of the opponents of the autocracy is the solidarity of civilized human beings against the survival of a primitive system." This authority goes on to say that, just as Anti Semitism was invented after the violent death of Alexander II. as a diversion against Nihilism, so, on the present occasion, and particularly during a war characterized by disaster, hatred of the foreigner seems likely to be cultivated as an antidote to the general discontent.

The correspondent goes on to say that for the small group of personages who incarnate the existing "regime" the recent assassination was formidable. M. de Plehwe felt that it affected himself in particular. For a long time his enemies at Court and in certain Government departments had endeavoured to convince the Tsar of the danger of the policy of repression, and some of them had even predicted months ago the catastrophe which had eventually occurred. The correspondent inquires whether the confidence of the Tsar in the efficacy of a policy which culminated in the events at Kishineff, Taganrog, Etchmiadzin, and Helsingfors will not at length be shaken. Two officials have refused the honour of succeeding General Bobrikoff in Finland, and he thinks that the Tsar must have vaguely felt that the event was of a graver character than he had imagined. For the last three months the Government's sole pre-occupation has been to save appearances, but that has not improved its position. "Up to the present M. de Plehwe has succeeded in concealing the serious flaws of this Empire, one and indivisible. . . . He has succeeded in making the most of the patriotic funds provided by the so-called foreigners resident in Russia and in ordering by telegram the declaration of bellicose Chauvinism from the Finnish Senate, the Armenian Synod and the Polish upper classes. He has been able to inspire the Tsar with illusion that there is a universal outburst of patriotism. Mais le château de, cartes s'est écroulé.

CASUALTIES TO KAMIMURA SQUADRON.

The casualties to the Kamimura Squadron in the recent naval battle off Tsushima have so far been reported as follows:—

CRUISER "IWATE."

Killed: Lieutenant Haraguchi, and Second Sub Lieutenant M. Noda.

Wounded: Lieut. Commanders F. Nomura and Y. Sugano, Lieutenant T. Kanesaka, Midshipman W. Matsumura, and Warrant Officer T. Yoshitomi.

CRUISER "TAKACHIHO."

Wounded: Lieutenant H. Asakawa, Doctor H. Issen and Warrant Officer S. Horio.

In addition to the above, there were 100 men killed and wounded throughout the whole squadron.

The friends of Mr. Norman Cullen, who came to Japan some months ago as the correspondent of the London "Daily Mail," are much concerned by his sudden disappearance. He had lately been suffering from a severe illness, and was about to return to England, when, on the 4th inst, he left his quarters at the Bluff Hotel, and after spending the night at a friend's house in Tsukiji, departed thence in a jinrikisha. He was traced afterwards as far as the Uyeno Station, but from there no clue to his whereabouts has been found, though every effort has been made by the British Consul through the authorities. As he was in a very weak and depressed condition, occasioned by his illness, his disappearance gives great anxiety to his many friends in Yokohama.

The state of health of the Czarina, after the birth of her son, the crown prince, is satisfactory.—"Deutsche Japan-Post" service.

The whereabouts of the missing steamer "Calchas" are rather doubtful. By the latest Japan papers we see that she is reported to have been captured by the Russians and sent to Saghalien, but what then of the report that she had been warned by another steamer and has put back to Hongkong?

The Korea Daily News.

To be published daily except Sundays.
Rate of Subscription:—
Per Year, Yen 25.
Per Quarter, Yen 7.
Per Month Yen 2.50

Postage in Korea not charged extra.
Postage abroad charged extra.

Advertisements, 50 sen per day for 1 inch or less.
5 yen per month per inch.
50 yen per year per inch.

All communications to
E. T. BETHELL,
Editor and Publisher.
Pak-tong, Seoul.

JAPAN'S NEED OF FOREIGN CAPITAL.

In the "Jiji Shimpo" of August 8th, says the "Kobe Herald," we find a leading article on the "Necessity of Importing Foreign Capital." As will be seen by the translation here given, it is an interesting contribution on an important subject. This need of additional foreign capital for the development of the state is frankly recognised, and two suggestions are thrown out for the advancement of this end. On the one hand, we understand the "Jiji" to say, avail of the widespread interest now shown in Japan (by reason of the war) and, by a judicious use of the various organs of publicity, attract attention abroad to the advantages which Japan is in a position to offer (industrially, commercially, financially): and, on the other hand, reform the country's laws so that foreigners may own land and other property such as mines, railways, etc. We are glad to see a journal of the "Jiji's" weight and position taking this question up in this way. Here is the article:—

Our financial condition at this critical juncture is fortunately very good. Many subscribers to the national loans are reported to have paid the whole amount in advance. This may be the result of the Japanese being extremely patriotic. Indeed that is no doubt the explanation up to a certain point, but the circumstance also shows that the people are rich enough to manifest their patriotic feelings in a material way. Such being the case, there can never be any need for our soldiers at the front to be anxious about the nation's finances. But we must not forget that we are fighting against one of the strongest countries in the world, and that it would be perilous not to be careful in every respect. However long the war may last, and even should our financial position become less favourable than may be anticipated, we must never allow ourselves to be flurried, but must always try to be prepared for the worst, by having always a monetary reserve. If the floating of foreign loans be the only means to effect our purpose, we must raise money in this way whenever there is a proper opportunity for doing so. If peace should be restored sooner than is expected, owing to the enemy surrendering, the floating of a foreign loan would still be necessary. We shall have numberless things to undertake when the war is over, and we have to consider how we shall meet the expenditure. The navy alone involves a monetary responsibility which is very far from being light even at the present time. According to Admiral Colomb, in 1901 Russia had the heaviest naval burden in proportion to her commerce, and Japan comes next. Since then it has been said that our navy has outgrown our commerce. It is certainly a serious question with us how our ever-increasing military expenditure is to be maintained. Fortunately, Japanese labour is very cheap compared with that of Europe, while its efficiency is generally greater. For instance, the Japanese troops, who can be supported on a comparatively small amount of money, have constantly defeated the Russian soldiers, who are much more expensive. Moreover, not only our own country, but also Korea, Manchuria, and China proper, abound in natural resources which may be developed by the Japanese. The only difficulty is as to how the necessary capital can be obtained. As everybody knows very well, America is outdoing Europe industrially, even though she is short of labour, simply because much European capital has been invested in the working of her natural resources. The case of this country is similar. Japan is rich in natural resources and, in addition, labour is cheap. Consequently, if foreign capital be imported successfully Japanese industries will no doubt undergo a wonderful development. But there are two obstacles which keep foreign capital out of our country. In the first place, Japan's advantages are not fully known to foreign countries, and in the second place, foreigners are not allowed to enjoy the same rights regarding land, mines, railways and such things as the Japanese do. We had thought the first mentioned difficulty would be the least easy to get rid of, but we find, to our great pleasure, that most of the leading papers and magazines in the world have been publishing not only the war news but also every item concerning our country. We should take advantage of this world-wide interest and advertise our country in order to let foreigners know its true condition and with a view to the floating of future loans abroad.

THE "RURIK."

The Russian armoured cruiser "Rurik," which was sunk by the Kamimura Squadron on Sunday, had an interesting history. She was the flagship of the Russian Pacific Squadron when the Northern Power, allied with France and Germany, coerced Japan and made her relinquish the Liaotung Peninsula, the hardearned gain of the Japan-China War. It was the "Rurik" that at the head of the Russian Squadron ran out her guns and assumed an intimidating attitude against the Japanese envoy, Baron Ito, when the latter entered Chefoo in order to exchange the ratifications of the treaty of peace with China. This incident occurred about 10 years ago. Our flagship then was the "Matsushima," of only 4,277 tons displacement. The "Rurik" was successful in carrying Russia's point of intervention, but at the same time the action of Russia gave a beneficial stimulus to our navy and caused its advancement to the present state. Thus the report of her destruction has been received by every Japanese with feelings of satisfaction.

The "Rurik" was of 10,923 tons displacement, built in 1892. At that time, the naval policy of Russia required the construction of ships of great coal capacity, or in order words, ships that would be able to minimize the necessity of frequently coaling in their voyage from the Baltic to the Far East. The plan of the "Rurik" was made with this object in view, but the question was whether the Russian naval architects would be able to construct her or not. The Russian authorities, however, decided to build the ship at the Baltic Shipbuilding yard, which successfully completed the work in 1895. The "Rurik" and "Gromoboi" were also built by the same dockyard. The "Rurik" first hoisted her naval flag 9 years and 9 months ago, and her cost was 7,435,112 roubles. Her armament consisted of 4 8-in., 16 6in. 6 4.7in., and 18 small quickfirers and maxims.—Japan Times.

THE SEOUL-FUSAN RAILWAY

In order to complete the construction of the Seoul-Fusan Railway, the sum of 2,300,000 yen is still required. As the result of investigations made by the Communications Department, reports the "Tokyo Asahi," the Government has decided to grant the Railway Company the sum of 1,580,000 yen as a grant-in-aid for the prosecution of the work, this decision being approved at the recent meeting of the Cabinet Ministers. On the 13th inst, the Railway Company was informed to the above effect, together with necessary instructions relating thereto. The difference between the two sums is to be made good by the curtailment of expenditure on the part of the Company. With regard to the method of redemption, it is stated that no payments are to be made for full five years, and during this period no interest is to be paid. From the fifth year and onward, the subsidy is to be repaid in yearly instalments of 50,000 yen or thereabouts, provided that this does not interfere with the payment by the Company of a dividend of eight per cent. per annum. It will therefore be easily seen, says the journal, that in case the Company fails to declare the abovementioned dividend the period of redemption will be prolonged.—Japan Times.

Mr. Cho Min Hi, Minister to Tokyo, arrived in Chemulpo at noon on the 25th.

Yesterday was celebeated as the anniversary of the foundation of the present dynasty.

The Japanese Minister was granted an audience yesterday at 3:30 p. m., and Sir John Jordan was received at 5 p. m.

The 4th of September, the Emperor's birthday is to be the occasion of great jubilation. A salvo will be fired at noon.

The Ilchin Hoi desisted from their speechifying yesterday, taking a holiday in celebration of the foundation of the present dynasty.

An educational society has been formed with it's headquarters in You Dong. Foreigners as well as natives are invited to attend, but only those who are earnest in their endeavours to assist Koreans in intellectual pursuits.

The Magistrate of Wiju states that among the coolies now used by the Japanese in their transport service, are many military officers, who, by the disbanding of the army, are reduced to this employment for a living.

The Reuter report, dated Tokyo, that the Japanese military attache in Berlin complained that he was neglected by Kaiser Wilhelm, is a lie. Contrarily, the Kaiser showed marked respect to the military attache of Japan several times.

A new arrival from the Pyong An province states that a riot, in connection with the coolie question, arose in the Yong Kang district. A boat loaded with refugees, attempting to evade trouble, was upset and most of the occupants drowned.

A gentleman from Suwon reports that the natives there are extremely incensed at the idea of being included in the ranks of the coolie *volunteers*. They are taking measures to defend themselves by laying up a stock of stones and cutting sticks suitable for an Irish argument; so many of the latter instruments have been collected that the hills for many miles around are quite bare of the beautiful foliage they displayed a month ago.

The Korea Daily News.

VOL. I, SATURDAY, AUGUST 27, 1904. No. 36

HONGKONG & SHANGHAI BANKING CORPORATION.

Paid-up Capital.................$10,000,000
Reserve Fund:—Sterling Reserve... 10,000,000
Silver Reserve..... 6,500,000

26,500,000
Reserve Liability of Proprietors... 10,000,000

HEAD OFFICE, HONGKONG.

London Bankers, London and County Banking Company Limited.

Branches and Agencies, London.

Amoy,	Hankow	Penang,
Bangkok,	Hiogo,	Rangoon,
Batavia,	Iloilo,	Saigon,
Bombay,	Lyons,	San Francisco,
Calcutta,	Manila,	Singapore,
Colombo,	Nagasaki,	Sourabaya,
Foochow,	New York,	Tientsin,
Hamburg,	Peking,	Yokohama,

Credits granted on approved Securities, and every description of Banking and Exchange business transacted.

Drafts granted on London and the chief Commercial places in Europe, India, Australia, America, China and Japan.

HOLME RINGER & Co., AGENTS, CHEMULPO.

ON CHEONG & CO., SEOUL.

GENERAL STORE KEEPERS.
Imported provisions, Cooking Utensils Crockery, etc.
FRESH BREAD DAILY.

MITSU BISHI DOCKYARD & ENGINE WORKS,
NAGASAKI.

CODE WORD, "DOCK."

A. 1, A. B. C., and Engineering Codes used,

DOCK No. 1 (at Tategami).

Extreme Length..............523 feet
Length on blocks.............513 ,,
Width of Entrance on Top........89 ,,
,, ,, Bottom....77 ,,
Water on Blocks at Spring Tide 26½ ,,

DOCK No. 2 (Mukaijima).

Extreme Length..............371 feet
Length on Blocks.............360 ,,
Width of Entrance on Top......66 ,,
,, ,, Bottom 53 ,,
Water on Blocks at Spring Tide 22 ,,

PATENT SLIP (at Kosuge).

Can take vessels up to 1,000 tons gross.

THE WORKS are well equipped with the LATEST IMPROVEMENTS, and can execute any kind of work in SHIPBUILDING and MARINE ENGINEERING, as well as in REPAIRING of SHIPS.

The COMPANY'S new powerful steamer OURA-MARU (712 tons, 700 I.H.P.), specially built for SALVAGE PURPOSES, and equipped with necessary gear, is always READY at SHORT NOTICE.

CHARTERED BANK OF INDIA AUSTRALIA & CHINA.

INCORPORATED BY ROYAL CHARTER 1853

HEAD OFFICES:—LONDON.

Paid-up Capital £800,000

Reserve Liability of Shareholders 800,000

Reserve Fund 725,000

Drafts granted upon all the principal places in the world and every description of Exchange and banking business transacted.

E. MEYER & Co., Agents, Chemulpo.

E. MEYER & CO.
Chemulpo.

SOLE AGENTS IN KOREA FOR:
A. T. Morse, Sons & Co's "Fresco" Distemper

In all colours ready for use on walls, Ceilings etc.

and

AVENARIUS CARBOLINEUM

A wood-preserving and antiseptic oil preparation

Against decay, dry-rot, fungus and wood-destroying insects.

A large supply always in Stock. Prices upon application.

E. MEYER & Co., Chemulpo.

LAW UNION & CROWN INS. CO.

Fire risks accepted at Current rates, on godowns, merchandise, dwellings, and other property, subject to usual conditions.

HOLME RINGER & Co., Agents, Chemulpo

THE METHODIST PUBLISHING HOUSE,
Little West Gate, Seoul.

JOB PRINTING, TYPEWRITER PAPER
CARBON PAPER, VISITING CARDS
STATIONERY, BOOK BINDING
BOOK PUBLISHERS
AMERICAN SCHOOL BOOKS
SPENCERIAN COPY BOOKS
PEN CARBON LETTER AND BILL BOOKS

S A BECK, Manager

DAI-ICHI GINKO.

LIMITED.

(Formerly the First National Bank)

ESTABLISHED 1873

INCORPORATED UNDER PRESENT LAW 1896

Capital - - - - - - - - Yen 5,000,000
Reserve Fund - - - - - 1,500,000

HEAD OFFICE:—TOKIO.

President: Baron SHIBUSAWA.

BRANCHES AND CORRESPONDENTS
In the Principal Cities and Towns of Japan.

Interest Allowed on
Fixed deposits 1 year - - - 6½ per cent
" " 6 months - - - 6 per cent

Special current accounts 1½ sen daily per Y 100
General " " 1 " " " 100

M. TANAKA, Manager, Chemulpo

HOLME RINGER & Co.
Chemulpo.

General Merchants and Government Contractors.

Agents for the leading Banks SteamshipCompanies and Insurance Companies

Importers of Merchandise of every description.

KAMEYA & CO.
GENERAL STOREKEEPERS
Chinkokai - - Seoul
(*Established 1895, Tokyo*)

Confectionery, Hams, Canned Goods, Cutlery, Hirano & Tansan Water, Provisions, Gents, Furnishing goods, Toilet Articles, Travelling Bags, Tobacco, Cigars & Cigarettes Kitchen Utensils. Coffee, Biscuits.

Fresh Goods always kept in Stock.
Prices Moderate
Please come and inspect our goods.

NIPPON YUSEN KAISHA.

JAPANESE MAIL STEAMSHIP CO.

DER MAIL CONTRACT WITH THE IMPERIAL JAPANESE GOVERNMENT.

European Line

Regular Fortnightly Service between Yokohama Kobe, Moji, Shanghai, Hongkong, Singapore, Penang Colombo, Port Said, Marseilles, London and Antwerp

American Line

Regular Fortnightly Service between Hongkong and Seattle, calling at Shanghai, Moji, Kobe, Yokohama and Victoria, B. C.

Australian Line

Regular weekly Service betwen Japan Ports and Australia, calling at Hongkong and Manila.
(Above Three Lines Suspended until further notice).

Shanghai Line

Weekly Service between Shanghai and Japan Ports

Korea Line

Service Kobe, Moji, Nagasaki, Fusan, Chemulpo, Chioo, Taiku.
S. S. Bahelsberg, 2181 tons.
Service Kobe, Moji, Fusan, Chemulpo, Chinnampo
S. S ARGO, S. S. Ohio.

BORDEN'S CONDENSED MILK CO.
New York, U. S. A.

ALWAYS IN STOCK
Eagle Brand Condensed Milk.
Gold Seal Condensed Milk.
Peerless (Family) Evaporated Cream.
Borden's Malted Milk.

E. MEYER & CO.
Chemulpo, Korea,
Sole Agents

ROYAL INSURANCE COMPANY,
Funds exceed £10,000,000
FIRE
AT CURRENT RATES.
LIFE
REDUCED PREMIUM.
HOLME RINGER & Co., Agents, Chemulpo.

HOTEL DU PALAIS
SEOUL.

The only first class Hotel in Seoul. Situated in the centre of the city opposite the palace.

Cuisine under the supervision of an experienced French Chef.

Well ventilated and furnished throughout.

TARIFF UPON APPLICATION

L. MARTIN,
Proprietor and Manager.

大韓每日申報
대한미일신보

(뎨삼십팔호) (화요일) 일쳔구빅사년팔월삼십일

본샤고빅

이신보는영어와한어로셔계미일출판ᄒᆞᆸ

신문가

ᄒᆞᆫ장 엽두돈오푼

일삭도엽두량닷돈 맛돈이로 밧ᄉᆞᆸ

광고료는

긔한의쟝단과ᄌᆞ힝의다쇼로죵감ᄒᆞ되렴가로밧을터이오며오리지아니ᄒᆞ야대한사람마다다이신문을보실터이니광고내시기를원ᄒᆞ시는이들은우리신문사에와셔편의ᄒᆞ심을희망ᄒᆞᆸ

○발힝소 박동대한미일신보사범어학교압헤젼영국인셜필림쟝자리오

사쟝 영국인 (배셜)

본사지졈

인쳔항교쟝동신지명씨로우리대한미일신보사인항지졈쟝을택졍ᄒᆞ엿사오니인쳔항에계신구람코쟈ᄒᆞ시는쳠군ᄌᆞ는히지졈에왕림편의ᄒᆞ시옵

사고

○우리대한미일신보의목뎍은대한의안녕질서에관한모든대목에ᄃᆡᄒᆞ야는공평한변론을쥬쟝홈이라우리통신원의탐보는신문보시는쳠군ᄌᆞ의게ᄒᆞᆼ샹보도ᄒᆞ리며편지를긔셔ᄒᆞ여주시는이는셩명과반디를젹어붓치시기를희망ᄒᆞ오나이거슨신문샹에긔재ᄒᆞ란ᄂᆞᆫ거시아니오다만극히신용ᄒᆞᄂᆞᆫ증거를삼고쟈홈이라긔쟈는아모긔서던지긔직ᄒᆞᆯ을퇴각ᄒᆞ는권리를가졋스나퇴각ᄒᆞ는리유를말ᄒᆞᆯ터이오며공중쟝회를문란케ᄒᆞ는듯ᄒᆞᆫ긔서는의례히밧지안켓ᄉᆞᆸ나이다

사고

○본샤에셔는신문갑슨미월에션금으로밧ᄉᆞ오며본신문은우톄로붓치는고로본샤에셔는다른신문사처럼금액을거두러돈니지안ᄉᆞ오니우리신문을ᄉᆞ랑ᄒᆞ야구람ᄒᆞ시는쳠군ᄌᆞ는양력미월쵸승에리월됴션금과거쥬셩명통호수를ᄌᆞ셰히젹어셔박동본샤로보내시기를ᄇᆞ라오며양력금월회일니로션금을아니보내시는곳에는리월일일부터신문을아니보낼터이오니죠량ᄒᆞ옵소셔

론셜

연터에우연ᄒᆞᆫ일

○연터에셔일본군함죠죠환과밋한쳥량쳑이아라사군함우터쉬를령예계교히홈으로인ᄒᆞ야긔셔히포회ᄒᆞ랴고주의ᄒᆞ는일본터도를실로료량키어려운거시일본졍부에셔즁립셩명ᄒᆞᆫ쳥국연터에셔적국병함젼쵸되엿다고연터에잇는쳥국수사데독의게힐칙ᄒᆞ는거시당연ᄒᆞᆫ일인듯ᄒᆞ나히데독은ᄌᆞ긔의즁립ᄒᆞ는의무를확실히직힘ᄒᆞ이되일본셔공교히그곳으로군함과견ᄒᆞ기에그리됨인ᄌᆞ무어시라고쟝담ᄒᆞ야말ᄒᆞ리요

일젼우리신보에연터졍항계졔ᄒᆞᆫ기를아라사군함우리쉬를령은포격ᄒᆞᆯ에비를운동ᄒᆞ야군물을옴겨가려우ᄒᆞ로다니다노ᄒᆞ사되쳥국셔는사령관이ᄌᆞ긔의군사들노ᄒᆞ여곰방쵸에군긔를손에쟝지못ᄒᆞ게명령ᄒᆞ엿다고ᄒᆞ엿더니추후샹보를거ᄒᆞᆫ즉젹국들이셔로라샹홀이잇스면군함에을나가의론홀배에이심샤시잔동안놉히금ᄒᆞᄂᆞᆫ거슨만국공법샹졍셕ᄒᆞᆫ일이어놀일본사름이아함에오른거슨옹남지아니ᄒᆞ고론박ᄒᆞᄂᆞᆫ거슨아국사령관의무식ᄒᆞᆫ허믈이오또쳥국수사데독이아합일항홈에ᄃᆡᄒᆞ야치ᄶᅦ를문ᄒᆞᆫ거슨옹호무피인거시가령영국수사데독이이러ᄒᆞᆫᄶᅢ를당ᄒᆞ엿드리도쟝령피ᄎᆞ싸홈ᄒᆞ기젼에는적국의슌양함이던지무슨물건이던지즁립ᄒᆞᆫ나라항구동모에힝션ᄒᆞᄂᆞᆫ거슬합쟝의계ᄒᆞᆫ령ᄒᆞ야직희지아니ᄒᆞ고보존ᄒᆞ게만ᄒᆞᆯ터인즉비록일본이용ᄒᆞ엿ᄂᆞᆫ터로쥿ᄎᆞ쳐사를온당이ᄒᆞ엿ᄂᆞᆫ티아라사군함에셔병긔를갓초아싸고시비ᄒᆞᆯ지라도슬터엽ᄂᆞᆫ말인거시아라사령관의ᄉᆡᆼ각에는공법이ᄌᆞ파약되ᄂᆞᆫ것ᄎᆞᆫ불계ᄒᆞ고용감가지ᄀᆞ온군사를파송ᄒᆞ계쟝ᄂᆞᆫ것만을키고리ᄒᆞᆷ이라 ᄒᆞᆫ즉즁와쳥국함에셔하샹일본사름들은아국군함으로셰러다듄거시아니죡지금쳥국에계ᄒᆞ여ᄀᆞ르다고엇지말ᄒᆞ리요가령ᄌᆞ긔의힘티로아라사를향ᄒᆞ야론박ᄒᆞᆫ다던지셜치ᄒᆞᄂᆞᆫ거슨당연ᄒᆞᆫ일이로되일본셔쳥국다려용숙ᄒᆞ다고ᄒᆞᄂᆞᆫ거슨경위에ᄃᆡ단히올치아니ᄒᆞᆫ일이요쏘쳥국에셔엄졍즁립ᄒᆞᆫ셕닭에아모것도샹관아니ᄒᆞᆫ거슬무어시라고발ᄒᆞ리오ᄒᆞ노라

잡보

○가쳥시찰 공쥬관찰ᄉᆞ가닉부로보고ᄒᆞ되명부지하히쟝규가죵인수실인을거느리고졍산부여랑군에리ᄒᆞ야시찰이라ᄌᆞ칭ᄒᆞ고빅셩의지물을토식ᄒᆞ야힝패를무수히ᄒᆞ고로히군민인등이부군에호소ᄒᆞ오니졍부에셔과연시찰을하송ᄒᆞ엿ᄂᆞᆫ지회면ᄒᆞ라ᄒᆞᆫ지라니부에셔면ᄒᆞᆫ즉ᄒᆞ기를소위시찰과그죵인비를낫낫치잡아부옥에가듀후에볼회면ᄒᆞ라ᄒᆞ엿다더라

○소쳥치소 츙쳥도소쳥에셔죵이품박졔빈씨가소슈가되고오빅구십여인이련명ᄒᆞ야 샹소ᄒᆞ엿ᄂᆞᆫ티그스의인즉진즁셩을수범에붓쳐곳처광ᄒᆞ고일젼싱창졍의샹 쥬진을 지하ᄒᆞ옵소셔ᄒᆞ엿더라

○보회긔셩 황용셩리진셕등제씨가교시ᄒᆞ되음력본월십칠일에보안회를다시긔회ᄒᆞᆫ다ᄒᆞ더니무슨미비ᄒᆞᆫᄉᆞ건이잇다ᄒᆞ야십구일하오이시로회긔를퇴졍ᄒᆞ엿ᄂᆞᆫ티그목젹은여좌ᄒᆞ니 일은 황실을안녕케ᄒᆞᆯ수 일은국례를존즁케ᄒᆞᆯ수 일은독립을공고케ᄒᆞᆯ수 일은민지를발달케ᄒᆞᆯ수 일은졍치샹방침을쳥고ᄒᆞᆯ수 일은인민의싱명과지산을보호ᄒᆞᆯ수 일은언로를광기ᄒᆞ야민졍을샹달케ᄒᆞᆯ수인되회소ᄂᆞᆫ죵로션면도가라더라

○롱탐민담 포쳔사ᄂᆞᆫ젼쥬ᄉᆞ리필용씨가영평셔에잇ᄂᆞᆫ진답쳐에보ᄂᆞᆫ막아농업을흥왕케ᄒᆞᆯᄎᆞ로ᄌᆞ본슈만냥을버혀거의쥰공이되엿더니관의감지수한죵셰를탐ᄒᆞ야하ᄒᆞᆫ일을다발ᄒᆞ야역ᄉᆞ를뎡지케ᄒᆞ고빅반저희ᄒᆞ니리씨의게만여금을쎗이아니라ᄒᆞ민들도원셩이대단ᄒᆞ다더라

○연명렴보 진쥬관찰ᄉᆞ셩기운씨ᄂᆞᆫ도임이후로각군슈가연명ᄎᆞ로리도ᄒᆞ면쟝젼ᄒᆞ기젼에미리싱목이을보내여탐리홈을쳥ᄒᆞ여밧은후에연명홈을허락ᄒᆞᄂᆞᆫ티리물을예비치못ᄒᆞᆫ슈령들은죵ᄂᆡ에관비ᄒᆞ노라고극히곤난ᄒᆞ다ᄒᆞ며창원군슈진익샹씨와기타모모슈령이연명ᄎᆞ로ᄒᆡ관찰부에몽슈로깃다가무한구ᄎᆞ를당ᄒᆞᆫ후에야연명ᄒᆞ엿다더라

○쟝진샹지 쟝진군슈리종셜씨의보고를거ᄒᆞᆫ즉ᄒᆞ엿스되본군디경에랑ᄎᆞ로국병이지ᄂᆞᆫ간리유는본도관찰부에셔잉의보고ᄒᆞ엿거니와본군슈가도임후에몽소서찰ᄒᆞ즉무ᄎᆞ병화를당ᄒᆞ야연로이빅여리사이에가옥즙물과셰간우마셕지소여ᄒᆞ야에남ᄌᆞ수명과너인비ᄐᆡ명이피살되엿고빅여명이쟝ᄒᆡ여차ᄃᆞ가일변피샬ᄒᆞᆫ외의ᄂᆞᆫ다다힝이노희도라왓고피란ᄒᆞ엿던빅셩이며리환귀ᄒᆞ엿스나민간ᄉᆞ산은틀수히로병의게로란된고로싱활ᄒᆞᆯ길이츄ᄉᆡᆼ됨을바랄ᄉᆡᆼ업너니의외음력류월쵸일이삼일에밥마다셔리가온고로들에푸른빗치업ᄉᆞ니이러ᄒᆞᆫ지변은고금에엽ᄂᆞᆫ바라빅셩이쟝ᄎᆞ구학에젼연ᄒᆞᆯ디경이라ᄒᆞ엿더라

○면블루모 외부에셔쟝항구와기시쟝간리의게면칙ᄒᆞ되역부을빅셩의ᄌᆞ원을좃ᄎᆞ로징ᄒᆞᄂᆞᆫ거슨일본수령부의주의어ᄂᆞᆯ

관보

○리윤화 김쳘영 범송죄 역삼년○심진틱 졀도죄역삼년○차순거 졀도죄 역칠년○림치셩 박창하 ᄉᆞ쥬죄 역십년○금죵빈 찬탈죄 역십년○김명옥 김영두 졀도죄 역죵신○최셩훈 윤원춘 ᄉᆞ쥬죄 역죵신○리판유 졀도죄 역이년반○윤태복 졀도죄 역오년○빈셔봉 도창고문죄 역팔기월○오셩삼

도가장지죄 역일년(리윤여 박종남 차운식 리종호 흡아편연죄 감금삼년(송의슈 홍재영 송표현 김홍규 강준명 흡아편연죄 감금이년(조셩춘 사가관총죄 역종신(서원용 흡아편연죄 감금이년(박룡운 오소죄 역십오년(리지근 절도죄 역십년(박셩화 절도죄 역이년반(김복셩 절도죄 역일년 이셩합일빅이십칠명

데이천구빅십칠호 광무팔년팔월이십구일

서임급사령

○입경무사서칙임판삼등 륙군참장 김졍근

○면장계 젼총슌 류지렬

이상팔월이십오일

○명궁니부특진관서칙임관ᄉ등 종묘서제쥬 박재번

○명종묘서제쥬서칙임관ᄉ등 사직서제쥬 리지덕

○경샤뎌서제쥬서칙임관ᄉ등 종이픔 종병의

○명녀장원경여칙엄관삼등 종이픔 윤승구

○명협천군금광위원 륙군부장 김교현

○명군제의정관 륙군부장 민영환 리지용 리윤용 민영괴 권중현 륙군참장 박제슌 구영조 엄준원 현영운 군부교문관 야진진무 륙군참령 피병무 리희두

○면본직 천위데일련디데일대디부관륙군보병부위 라호 진위데삼련디데일대디부관륙군보병부위 빅남규

○보천위데일련디데일대디부관 륙군보병부위 빅남규

○보진위데삼련디데일대디부관 륙군보병부위 라호

이상팔월이십륙일

○견칙 충쳥북도파찰부총쥰리근비

궁뎌륙ᄉ

○죠왈궁니부대신민병셕으로졉임장례원경ᄒ라

○니장원경한용위ᄉ직소 비지니에소쳥되로의시ᄒ노라

이상팔월이십륙일

잡보

●잡보중(면물륙모)란제목아래말이연속이못된고로관보하에련속긔재ᄒ노라

드로니륙모를만히ᄒ야민간이소요케ᄒ얏다ᄒ니엇지놀납지아니리오추후에는민인놀기유ᄒ여조원ᄒ는조만발송ᄒ되만일여전히륙모ᄒ다가두나라교제에화평이손상케됨이잇스면단당즁감ᄒ리라ᄒ엿더라

○길쥬군보 길쥬군슈가외부로보고ᄒ되음력륙월십팔일에아병오빅명이명쳔으로죠ᄎ본군에와조고셩진으로향ᄒ엿다ᄒ엿더라

○무쥬군보 무쥬군슈가외부에보고ᄒ기를금산거ᄒ는김참봉위명인이일본인일명과함ᄭ본군에리도ᄒ야채젼밧을거시잇다칭탁ᄒ고본군거ᄒ는도한에박광슌을착거ᄒ야젼ᄉ천여량을륵탈ᄒ엿스니곳일공관에이죠ᄒ야히일인을착ᄒ야히륵탈젼을젼쥬의게로환급케ᄒ고또그악습을징즙케ᄒ라ᄒ엿더라

○경효뎐이봉 작일묘시에경효뎐을유풍궁으로이봉ᄒ옵신후에대황제폐하ᄭ셔와 황태ᄌ뎐하ᄭ셔 별다례를친힝ᄒ옵섯는디범관이입참되엿더라

○위문발졍 향일본보에긔지ᄒ엿거니와일본출진군위문ᄎ로시위삼디참령민용긔씨는어왕일본군에죵군ᄒ엿든위관를부관으로디동ᄒ고의쥬로향ᄒ여발졍ᄒ엿고시위련디쟝량셩환씨는원산을향ᄒ고발졍ᄒ엿는디각가 칙셔를밧들고젼파ᄒ엿다더라

○참찬담화 일작에참찬허뒤씨가일군ᄉ령관을방문ᄒ여왈역부모집ᄉ로륵모ᄒ는폐단이잇는고로규모업는빅셩이경겁ᄒ야대단쇼요ᄒ즉념려들츅량치못ᄒ지라심량ᄒ여보라조금이후로는조원쟈외에는일졀샙지말나고면칙ᄒ터이니귀ᄉ령부에서도각디병참소에면보ᄒ여륵모소요지폐를업게ᄒ라훈즉그리ᄒ기로응답ᄒ엿다더라

○니훈각도 니부에서십삼도관찰부에면훈ᄒ되인부모집ᄉ를조원응모쟈로ᄲ고일졀륵모ᄒ는폐단을엄금ᄒ라ᄒ엿더라

○오회병긔 일진회는여젼히긔회ᄒ며져잔파회ᄒ엿던보안회가갱긔되는디리셩로씨가쥬장ᄒ다ᄒ고원세셩씨는금명간입셩ᄒ다ᄒ며국민교육회는미토요일에긔회ᄒ다ᄒ며또친목회라ᄒ는회가설립된다ᄒ며또일진회반뎌ᄒ라는회가취회훈다고소문이분분ᄒ다더라

○윤씨샹소 의정부찬정윤웅렬씨가일젼에샹소ᄒ엿는디그긔의에왈대져님군의군권우샹벌에강령만잡고그아리빅반ᄉ무는각각유ᄉ가잇셔셔인쥬의천집ᄒ빋아니오니이제폐하ᄭ옵셔군권에대강령만잡으샤셰무를친찰치마옵시고유ᄉ의게각기직무를칙임ᄒ옵쇼셔샹벌를베푸시면궁금이ᄌ연청슉ᄒ거시오정치샹폐단이ᄌ연긔혁될거시오정부관제가ᄌ연정제ᄒ거시오니엇지군권이존즁치못ᄒ오며던하가다소리지못ᄒ옴늘근심ᄒ리잇가찰랍ᄒ옵심을복망ᄒ노이다ᄒ더라

○일진회보 거토요일하오이시에일진회에셔긔회ᄒ고김규창리승언김윤오송석창소씨를별턱ᄒ야젼총디팔인과함심이명총디위운*정부에파송ᄒ야젼일제정ᄒ네됴건을즉시실시ᄒ라고독촉ᄒ엿고또ᄒ원즁에송병쥰놀치의ᄒ는쟈가만흔고로회장윤시병씨와회원한셕진유학쥬제씨가송씨의리력을셜명ᄒ야즁인의의혹을히혹ᄒ게ᄒ엿더라

외보

○마도분쟁히결 본월십오일빅림발면을거ᄒ즉미묵파토이괴국간에분쟁ᄒ는ᄉ건이나려낫더니임의히결이되엿는고로미국군함은근일에스밀나항구에셔떠거ᄒ다더라

○료양도주 구로팟기쟝군은료양을도져히부지ᄒ수업는줄을알고임의봉텬으로도주ᄒ엿다는풍셜이잇더라

○샹촌합디ᄉ샹 본월십ᄉ일에디마도북방에셔로국함디와교전ᄒ제ᄉ샹ᄒ쟈가좌와ᄀᆺ흔지라

반슈함승원의전ᄉ쟈는 히군대위원구학ᄎ와 히군쇼위야면삼부요 즁샹쟈는 히군대위경관륭이오 경샹쟈는 히군군쇼좌야촌언ᄎ랑과 히군대쇼좌관야용칠과 쇼위후보싱송촌회거와 샹등필긔길누텰이오

고천슈합승원의경샹ᄒ쟈는 히군대위쳔천범려 히군군의일천일 샹등긔관병조굴미문옹 이외에하ᄉ와병졸ᄉ샹이일빅명이라더라

○려슌교전ᄉ상 본월십일에려슌구밧ᄭ셔로국함디와교젼ᄒ제ᄉ샹쟈를츄가ᄒ수효가여좌홈

일진합승원의즁샹쟈는병졸이ᄉ명이오 경샹ᄒ쟈는병조와병졸합이구명이오

춘일합승원의경샹ᄒ쟈는병졸이일명이오 진원함승원의경샹쟈는 병졸이오명이오 화천함승원의경샹쟈는 병졸이일명이오 죠일함승원의경샹쟈는 히군쇼좌화면힝ᄎ랑과병졸일명이오

죠무함승원의전ᄉ쟈는 병조와병졸이팔명이라더라

○유끌도박 일로긔젼이리로일군대일ᄉ단에속ᄒ오월륙월칠월석둘동안에젼망ᄒ장졸의유끌과유물등륙박륙십긔가거십오일에일본동경신교에도착ᄒ엿는디그익일에동ᄉ단병참긔지ᄉ령부에셔분비식을거힝ᄒ엿다더라

뎐보

동경팔월이십칠일발

로합쳐치 샹히로도망ᄒ여드러간로국군함은본월이십ᄉ일브터무장을히제ᄒ기를착슈ᄒ야이십륙일에맛ᄎ기로예정ᄒ야청국정부는승락ᄒ엿는디최후일에니르러는로국이다시이〃팔일ᄭ지연긔ᄒ기를요구ᄒ미청국정부에셔이거슬마시허락ᄒ엿는지라인ᄒ야일본정부는로국군함이샹히에도입ᄒ이후로강경ᄒ쥬장으로써청국정부가단연이중립규례를덕용ᄒ기를요구ᄒ엿스나이우회말ᄒ것과ᄀᆺ치청국로국ᄉ이에는수ᄎ긔한을쳔연ᄒ고지금또이십팔일ᄭ지연긔를승락ᄒ엿기로만일청국정부가즁립을능히유지치못ᄒ면일본은부득이ᄒ야교젼국의권리에의거ᄒ야단연ᄒ슈단을쓰기로통고ᄒ야갈경ᄒ게항의ᄒ엿다더라

동일동뎐

○무장히제 ᄉ국이승대히되랴ᄒ미로국황데는칙명으로샹히에잇는로함의무장을철거ᄒ을명ᄒ엿는디작이십륙일하오다섯시브터국긔를철거ᄒ고본이십칠일브터무장히제ᄒ기를착슈ᄒ엿더라

동일동뎐

○로함원주 교쥬만으로브터샹히에도주ᄒ엿다가다시샹히를ᄯ나거취가분명치안튼로국군함디아나호는본월이십륙일에법국령토안남에잇는항구셔공항에도착ᄒ엿더라

팔월이십팔일공ᄉ관착뎐

데일군공보

○료양방면승젼 흑목대장보고를거ᄒ즉아군의공격은이십오일야반에젹진즁앙을향ᄒ야총과검으로ᄡ돌겨ᄒ을시작ᄒ엿는디작이십칠일져녁ᄭ지격전ᄒ후에덕의메일션되는고사령예셔브터손가시남방에잇는놉흔ᄊᆡᆼ을지나고ㅣ호ㅣ디방의놉흔ᄊᆡᆼᄭ지점령ᄒ엿는지라덕군은조격되가데삼네륙ᄉ단이오젼렬에는데구데삼십일ᄉ단이오대포가일빅여문인디그본부되는료양방면으로퇴각ᄒ엿고이전투에는덕은수월젼브터공교ᄒ게장산우헤건축ᄒ견고ᄒ진디에셔ᄀ장용감ᄒ게교젼ᄒ엿더라동일전투에우리ᄉ상은쟝교이하이천여명이오엇은물건은대포팔문파탄약파밋기타물건의다수요덕의ᄉ상은미샹ᄒ다ᄒ엿더라

TELEGRAMS.

KUROKI'S ADVANCE.

BATTLE IN VICINITY OF LIAO-YANG.

Tokyo, Aug. 28th.

General Kuroki reports that our troops made a concentrated attack on the centre of the enemy's position at midnight on the 25th inst., the fighting lasted till the evening of the 27th, when we succeeded in occupying the 1st line of positions, stretching from Kaoshaling to the hilly country between Koho to Sun chase (Directly south of Anping). The positions were shelled by our artillery and finally rushed at the point of the bayonet. The enemy's troops were the 3rd and 6th divisions of sharp-shooters and the 9th and 31st divisions of infantry. The Russians, who fought and defended their positions with the utmost bravery, retreated in the direction of Liaoyang.

We captured 8 guns and a large quantity of powder and ammunition. Our casualties were over 2,000 killed and wounded. The enemy's losses are unknown.

PO-AN-HOI MEETING DISPERSED.

This society which as we stated in yesterday's issue, has just recommenced meeting, was broken up by Japanese gendarmes and the leader Mr. Yi Kun Suk was arrested.

THE S. S. "MALACCA."

ARRIVAL OF PASSENGERS AT HONGKONG.

After a somewhat eventful journey, lasting about forty-seven days in all, the passengers who originally left London for Hongkong by the P. and O. S. N. Co.'s s.s. "Malacca" arrived here yesterday morning (reports the "S. C. Morning Post" of the 12th inst.) on the P. and O. S. N. Co.'s mail steamer "Coromandel." Amongst these passengers was Major C. L. Gosling, who very kindly related to a "Morning Post" representative the story of the seizure of the "Malacca" by the Russian Volunteer Fleet cruisers, a portion of which we reproduce.

To take charge of the "Malacca" during her voyage back to Suez the Russians sent aboard two executive officers, three engineers, and fifty or sixty men, who assumed complete control. None of the "Malacca's" officers were allowed any say in the navigation of the vessel. They were kept from the bridge and from the engine room, Russian guards being placed on duty for this purpose. It is questionable whether or not the crew enjoyed this cessation from work. It must have been annoying to be made into subordinates on their own vessel. When any other vessel hove in sight extra guards were stationed on deck to see that nobody signalled; and when Suez was reached, armed sentries held the gangway, and no one was allowed to leave or join the vessel. Even the British Consul was refused permission to come aboard; likewise the P. and O. agent. The strictest measures were taken to prevent the captain sending any despatches ashore. For some reason or other the "Malacca" left Suez and proceeded through the Canal to Port Said, where she arrived on July 20th. Here the adventures of the passengers ceased, for they transshipped to the P. and O. s.s. "Marmora," which took them to Colombo, at which port they again transshipped to the "Coromandel, which brought them to their Far Eastern destinations. At Port Said the original crew of the "Malacca" had to leave the vessel, and Captain Andrews proceeded at once to London by the fast mail route.

Major Gosling added that when the "Petersburg" held up the "Malacca" she had no bags of coal on deck, as was reported when she passed the Dardanelles. During the return journey to Port Said the Russian officers were pleasing enough, though there were some very underhand dealings tried with the "Malacca's" original crew. The Russians tried to obtain information which they could use to justify the seizure by bribing the men—at least, so the passengers heard from the captain. Before the Russians decided to seize the vessel three or four European members of the crew were sent for by the officers on the "Petersburg," who tried to extract from them information about the cargo, offering bribes as inducement. The officer who was given the command of the "Malacca" was a junior of the Imperial service; the other officers and the prize crew were all reserve men of the Volunteer Fleet. This junior could not speak English, but one or two of the other officers could, and Major Gosling had several interesting conversations with them, one of them being rather an obliging fellow. They seemed very confident of their position with regard to the seizure, and were not of the opinion that the British Government would interfere in the matter. The "Malacca" was, they said, to be taken to Libau, in the Baltic, where she would be unloaded and her future would then be in the hands of the Prize Court. They did not show any animosity towards the British, and were quite civil enough with the passengers, but very high-handed indeed in their dealings with the captain. They threatened to put him under arrest in his own cabin if he persisted with his protests. The captain felt his position very keenly. He was not allowed on the bridge, and, so far as holding communication with anyone as Suez or Port Said was concerned, was treated much as a prisoner. The stewards and cooks were fortunately not interfered with, and meals were forthcoming as usual. The Russians, of course, used the ship's stores, and had a table in the saloon, making use of everything they wanted.

The passengers were put to much expense by the seizure, and it is understood that application for compensation is to be made to St. Petersburg. We should think the British Government will support the passengters in this matter.

EXERCISE FOR LADIES.

[According to Chic, housework is by far the healthiest exercise that a lady can indulge in.]

If the world seems dark, dear madam,
and you don't feel very well,
If your enervated system needs
correction,
If a mouth or two of dances has at last
begun to tell,
On the freshness of your exquisite
complexion;
Oh! seek not on the cricket fields to
drive the ball for four,
Oh! sport not on the tennis court or
river!
It's far more healthy exercise to scrub
the kitchen floor;
And extremely beneficial to the liver.
It will seem a little odd at first if Lady
Clara Jones,
On calling, asks "Is Mrs. Verrey
Ritch in?"
And your grave and stately butler says
in supercilious tones,
"She's shining up the saucepans in
the kitchen."
But never mind appearances. In this
the matter ends,
While cleaning up the house is your
vocation,
The Lady Clara spends her time in
cleaning out her friends,
And yours is far the healthier
occupation.

—Bystander.

Probate has been granted of the will of the late Sir H. M. Stanley, G. C. R., the famous explorer, the estate being valued at the gross amount of £155,151.

AN AMUSING LETTER FROM RUSKIN.

The following amusing and characteristic passage is from a Ruskin letter published in the Atlantic Monthly:—

Indeed, I rather want good wishes just now, for I am tormented by what I cannot get said, nor done. I want to get all the Titians, Tintorets, Paul Veroneses, Turners, and Sir Joshuas in the world into one great fireproof Gothic gallery of marble and serpentine. I want to get them all perfectly engraved. I want to go and draw all the subjects of Turner's 19,000 sketches in Switzerland and Italy elaborated by myself. I want to get everybody a dinner who hasn't got one. I want to macadamise some new road to Heaven with broken fools' heads; I want to hang up some knaves out of the way, not that I've any dislike to them, but I think it would be wholesome for them, and for other people, and that they would make good crow's meat. I want to play all day long and arrange my cabinet of minerals with new white wool; I want somebody to amuse me when I'm tired; I want Turner's pictures not to fade; I want to be able to draw clouds, and to understand how they go—and can't make them stand still, nor understand them—they all go sideways; (what a fellow that Aristophanes was! and yet to be always wrong in the main, except in his love for Æschylus and the country. Did ever a worthy man do so much mischief on the face of the Earth?) Farther, I want to make the Italians industrious, the Americans quiet, the Swiss romantic, the Roman Catholics rational, and the English Parliament honest—and I can't do anything and don't understand what I was born for. I get melancholy—overeat myself, over-sleep myself—get pains in the back—don't know what to do in anywise. What with that infernal invention of steam, and gunpowder, I think the fools may be a puff or barrel or two too many for us. Nevertheless, the gunpowder has been doing some work in China and India."

The notice which has lately been seen over a shop in Cairo, "I speak English, and understand American," recalls a story which was going round New York society last winter. It was said that the daughter of a certain Chicago millionaire, for her first season in London, devoted herself to studying Welsh so that she might be ready to do the correct thing when conversing with the Prince of Wales. We do not know whether that conversation ever began.

Count Tolstoi's recent pamphlet on the war is being secretly circulated in Russia by hundreds of thousands of copies. On the other hand, it has sown discord of the most acute nature in the Count's own family. His son Andrea is at the front with his regiment, and the younger son Leo, as a military correspondent. Countess Tolstoi is also on the side of her two sons against her husband's anti-national theories. Tolstoi devoted two whole months to the preparation of his pamphlet. During that period he suspended all other work.

The Korea Daily News.

To be published daily except Sundays.
Rate of Subcription:—
Per Year, Yen 25.
Per Quarter, Yen 7.
Per Month Yen 2.50

Postage in Korea not charged extra.
Postage abroad charged extra.

Advertisements, 50 sen per day for 1 inch or less.
5 yen per month per inch.
50 yen per year per inch.

All communications to
E. T. BETHELL,
Editor and Publisher.
Pak-tong, Seoul

LIAOYANG.

It is extremely difficult to judge of the real state of affairs at Liaoyang. From both Russian and Japanese sources we learn that heavy fighting is imminent but there seems to be a good deal of preliminary manoeuvering for position. General Kuroki is trying to dispose his army for an attack on the Russian flank so that their retreat will lie parallel with their fighting line. It also appears that there is an army advancing on Kuropatkin's right flank which he seems to be harassing pretty effectively with a strong force of cavalry.

That the battle will not be long delayed there is little reason to doubt as provision has to be made for winter quarters and until Liaoyang is taken there is nowhere suitable for the concentration of the several Japanese armies now pushing northwards.

It is safe to assume that Liaoyang will be eventually captured by the Japanese, but so many conflicting reports reach us as to Kuropatkin's intentions and the disposition of his troops that it is impossible to estimate the magnitude of the struggle which will take place.

His line of communications must be a great source of anxiety to Kuropatkin and this has probably given rise to the rumours that he is withdrawing the greater part of his army to Mukden, leaving only some six divisions to oppose the Japanese at Liaoyang. The Japanese newspapers do not credit this and Kuropatkin's telegram to the Czar that a decisive battle was imminent also does not fit in with the report.

The field of battle will apparently be a very extended one. A telegram to the "Jiji" states that the Japanese commenced their attack at Aushantien, some twenty miles south of Liaoyang, on the 20th, and it is generally considered that Kuroki will bring his attack to bear somewhere to the east or northeast of Liaoyang. The extreme left and extreme right of the Japanese army are probably at present some 25 miles apart.

Both sides will have enormous difficulties to contend with. North of Haicheng the country is almost absolutely flat, and recent reports said that owing to the heavy rains the roads were over knee-deep in mud. Again it is said that the Japanese are not obtaining reports of the Russian strength and positions with their usual facility. The level nature of the ground probably renders reconnoitering difficult.

On the other hand the Russian trenches are reported to be full of water and the necessity for protecting his lines of communications and retreat will greatly hamper Kuropatkin's movements.

So far as can be learned, the opposing armies are about equally matched in point of numbers and south and southeast Kuropatkin has the best of the position.

A number of factors which have been put forth in explanation of the Russian defeats hitherto, will be absent in this battle. It has been said that until recently Kuropatkin had only inferior soldiers at his disposal, and that the hilly nature of the country in which previous battles have been fought has been all in favour of the Japanese against their heavy and slow-moving opponents. As the Liaoyang battlefield will be a comparatively flat one and the last battles showed that Kuropatkin had been re-inforced by several divisions of Russia's best fighitng material, these conditions no longer exist and if an advantage lies with either side, the Russians would appear to have it. A victory will be an important one for either side but a defeat for Kuropatkin will probably turn his retreat into a rout.

TYPHOON IN THE KOREAN SEA.

SEOUL-FUSAN RAILWAY DAMAGED.

The earlier reports of the typhoon which raged off the southern coast of Korea on the 20th inst. did not give any idea of the severity of the storm, such as the detailed story brings forth. In Fusan harbor sixty Japanese schooners, whose value is estimated at $20,000, were sunk at their anchorage. Many houses were wrecked and some of the occupants killed. Great damage was done the Seoul-Fusan railway works. Rough estimates give the loss as $100,-000. Many fishing boats, which were at sea, are missing and presumably were sunk.

The oldest inhabitants state that it was the roughest weather and strongest gale experienced since Fusan was opened as a treaty port.

EVERY MAN HIS PRICE.

A correspondent of the "Independent" says:

I have spoken of Mr. Hearst's lack of faith in others. This manifests itself in his assurance that money will buy the fruit of any man's effort, and that the sole consideration with most men is the amount they can command. Some time ago a young writer applied to him for employment on his New York newspaper and was engaged to fill a position which would become vacant at the end of a week, but in the interval the fact came to the attention of a university professor who had always taken an interest in his advancement.

"I am sorry," said the good man, "that you should have chosen that particular school of journalism for your professional start." And he proceeded to descant upon the responsibility a journalist owed to society, the influence of one educated youth's example upon others of his class, the tone a writer inevitably took from the character of the journals he worked for, etc. "And your untarnished sense of self-respect," he concluded, "will be worth more to you, when you reach my time of life, than all the salaries an unprincipled employer can pour into your purse."

So impressed was the neophyte with this lecture in morals that he called upon Mr. Hearst the next morning and announced that he had changed his mind about accepting the proffered position. The editor scanned his face shrewdly, and then inquired the reason. After much hesitancy the young man told him the whole story, and started to leave.

"Ah!" said Mr. Hearst. "Be seated a moment, please." And turning to his secretary, he added: "Write a letter at once to Professor X.Y., present my compliments, and say that I should be pleased to receive from him a signed article of 500 words—subject and treatment to be of his own choosing—for the editorial page of next Sunday's paper. Enclose check for $250.

"Now," he remarked, with a cynical smile, as he bade his caller good-by, "you can see for yourself what comes of that."

He did. The Sunday issue contained a signed article, which gave the paper the reflection of a good man's fame, and spread the influence of his example among other university professors—and did what to his selfrespect?—all at the net rate of fifty cents per word!

Is it wonderful that Mr. Hearst catalogues humanity by its price-marks?

THE RUSSIANS IN KOREA.

A report from the Ham Kyeng province states that Major Kim In Su, who is with the Russians at Ham-heung has spread a report that 500,000 Russians are on their way to Korea, and has ordered the authorities under threats of punishments by martial-law, to repair the roads, lay up stocks of provisions and collect coolies to assist in transport.

It is proposed to establish a Korean-Japanese Club in the city, for the benefit of civil and military officials of both nations.

The private effects, numbering 660 packages in all, of Japanese soldiers of the 1st division killed in battle during May, June and July, arrived in Tokyo on the 15th.

The Financial Department are busy preparing for the advent of their new adviser. Besides overhauling documents, they are building a spacious office, for his use, in their quarters.

The Il Chin Hoi seems to have a sort of progressive game on hand. Each time they send delegates to the Government, the committee is increased by 4 men. In their last visit, they numbered 12.

The "Ohio" is once more in these waters, having completed her repairs at Nagasaki. Among the passengers on her return trip were Mr. D. W. Deshler, owner of the vessel, and Mr. Harris, U. S. Consul at Nagaski.

A report of a riot in Ko Yang has reached the Home Office. It appears that the people, excited about the coolie question, suddenly rose and stoned the magistrate's office. The Japanese gendarmes, only a few in number, were powerless to quell the disturbance.

Who said that Port Arthur is on the Liaotung promontory? It's false. The real Port Arthur is situated under the wall near the West Gate. When that sham fortress at Lioatung falls, the residents of Seoul may witness the storming of the real thing at their very gates. It is a formidable looking structure and is worth a visit of inspection.

The Magistrate of Muchu reports a barefaced robbery on the part of a Korean named Kim and a Japanese confederate. These worthies visited the house of an opulent butcher named Pak and forcibly seized upon $800.00, which were secreted under his roof. They made good their escape, but the Magistrate prays the Japanese Legation to take steps for their arrest.

According to information which has reached an official quarter here from St. Petersburg, says the London correspondent of the Birmingham-Post, it is understood that a Russian political officer, with a small escort, will be sent to Lhassa immediately the British expedition arrives there, to be present at, though not to take any part in, the negotiations for a peaceful settlement of the present difficulty between Great Britain and Thibet. As to whether the officer will join in the British expedition on the way, or, with his escort, will make his own way to Lhassa, is not yet clear; but the step is not without interest as showing Russian anxiety to maintain its influence in Thibet.

The Korea Daily News.

VOL. I, TUESDAY, AUGUST 30, 1904. No. 38

HONGKONG & SHANGHAI BANKING CORPORATION.

Paid-up Capital.... ....$10,000,000
Reserve Fund:—Sterling Reserve... 10,000,000
Silver Reserve..... 6,500,000

26,500,000
Reserve Liability of Proprietors... 10,000,000

HEAD OFFICE, HONGKONG.

London Bankers, London and County Banking Company Limited.
Branches and Agencies,
London.

Amoy,	Hankow	Penang,
Bangkok,	Hiogo,	Rangoon,
Batavia,	Iloilo,	Saigon,
Bombay,	Lyons,	San Francisco,
Calcutta,	Manila,	Singapore,
Colombo,	Nagasaki,	Sourabaya,
Foochow,	New York,	Tientsin,
Hamburg,	Peking,	Yokohama,

Credits granted on approved Securities, and every description of Banking and Exchange business transacted.

Drafts granted on London and the chief Commercial places in Europe, India, Australia, America, China and Japan.

HOLME RINGER & CO., AGENTS,
CHEMULPO.

ON CHEONG & CO.,
SEOUL.

GENERAL STORE KEEPERS.
Imported provisions, Cooking Utensils Crockery, etc.
FRESH BREAD DAILY.

MITSU BISHI DOCKYARD & ENGINE WORKS,
NAGASAKI.

CODE WORD, "DOCK."

A. 1, A. B. C., and Engineering Codes used.

DOCK No. 1 (at Tategami).

Extreme Length..............523 feet
Length on blocks .... 513 ,,
Width of Entrance on Top......89 ,,
,, ,, Bottom....77 ,,
Water on Blocks at Spring Tide 26½ ,,

DOCK No. 2 (Mukaijima).

Extreme Length..............371 feet
Length on Blocks.............360 ,,
Width of Entrance on Top......66 ,,
,, ,, Bottom 53 ,,
Water on Blocks at Spring Tide 22 ,,

PATENT SLIP (at Kosuge).

Can take vessels up to 1,000 tons gross.

THE WORKS are well equipped with the LATEST IMPROVEMENTS, and can execute any kind of work in SHIPBUILDING and MARINE ENGINEERING, as well as in REPAIRING of SHIPS.

The COMPANY'S new powerful Steamer OURA-MARU (712 tons, 700 I.H.P.), specially built for SALVAGE PURPOSES, and equipped with necessary gear, is always READY at SHORT NOTICE.

CHARTERED BANK OF INDIA AUSTRALIA & CHINA.

INCORPORATED BY ROYAL CHARTER 1853

HEAD OFFICES:—LONDON.

Paid-up Capital £800,000
Reserve Liability of Shareholders 800,000
Reserve Fund 725,000

Drafts granted upon all the principal places in the world and every description of Exchange and banking business transacted.

E. MEYER & Co., Agents,
Chemulpo.

E. MEYER & CO.
Chemulpo.

SOLE AGENTS IN KOREA FOR:
A. T. Morse, Sons & Co's "Fresco" Distemper

In all colours ready for use on walls, Ceilings etc.
and
AVENARIUS CARBOLINEUM

A wood-preserving and antiseptic oil preparation

Against decay, dry-rot, fungus and wood-destroying insects.

A large supply always in Stock.
Prices upon application.

E. MEYER & Co.,
Chemulpo.

LAW UNION & CROWN INS. CO.

Fire risks accepted at Current rates, on godowns, merchandise, dwellings, and other property, subject to usual conditions.

HOLME RINGER & Co.,
Agents, Chemulpo

THE METHODIST PUBLISHING HOUSE,
Little West Gate, Seoul.

JOB PRINTING, TYPEWRITER PAPER
CARBON PAPER, VISITING CARDS
STATIONERY, BOOK BINDING
BOOK PUBLISHERS
AMERICAN SCHOOL BOOKS
SPENCERIAN COPY BOOKS
PEN CARBON LETTER AND BILL BOOKS

S A BECK, Manager

DAI-ICHI GINKO.
LIMITED.
(Formerly the First National Bank)

ESTABLISHED 1873

INCORPORATED UNDER PRESENT LAW 1896

Capital - - - - - - - - Yen 5,000,000
Reserve Fund - - - - - 1,500,000

HEAD OFFICE:—TOKIO.

President: Baron SHIBUSAWA.

BRANCHES AND CORRESPONDENTS
In the Principal Cities and Towns of Japan.
Interest Allowed on
Fixed deposits 1 year - - - 6½ per cent
" " 6 months - - - 6 per cent

Special current accounts 1½ sen daily per Y 100
General " " 1 " " " 100

M. TANAKA,
Manager, Chemulpo

HOLME RINGER & Co.
Chemulpo.

General Merchants and Government Contractors.

Agents for the leading Banks SteamshipCompanies and Insurance Companies

Importers of Merchandise of every description.

KAMEYA & CO.
GENERAL STOREKEEPERS
Chinkokai - - Seoul
(*Established 1895, Tokyo*)

Confectionery, Hams, Canned Goods, Cutlery, Hirano & Tansan Water. Provisions, Gents, Furnishing goods, Toilet Articles, Travelling Bags, Tobacco, Cigars & Cigarettes Kitchen Utensils. Coffee, Biscuits

Fresh Goods always kept in Stock.
Prices Moderate
Please come and inspect our goods.

NIPPON YUSEN KAISHA.
JAPANESE MAIL STEAMSHIP CO.
DER MAIL CONTRACT WITH THE IMPERIAL JAPANESE GOVERNMENT.

European Line
Regular Fortnightly Service between Yokohama Kobe, Moji, Shanghai, Hongkong, Singapore, Penang Colombo, Port Said, Marseilles, London and Antwerp

American Line
Regular Fortnightly Service between Hongkong and Seattle, calling at Shanghai, Moji, Kobe, Yokohama and Victoria, B. C.

Australian Line
Regular weekly Service betwen Japan Ports and Australia, calling at Hongkong and Manila.
(Above Three Lines Suspended until further notice)

Shanghai Line
Weekly Service between Shanghai and Japan Ports

Korea Line
Service Kobe, Moji, Nagasaki, Fusan, Chemulpo, Chioo, Taiku.
S. S. Bahelsberg, 2181 tons.
Service Kobe, Moji, Fusan, Chemulpo, Chinnampo
S.S ARGO, S. S. Ohio.

BORDEN'S CONDENSED MILK CO.
New York, U. S. A.

ALWAYS IN STOCK
Eagle Brand Condensed Milk.
Gold Seal Condensed Milk.
Peerless (Family) Evaporated Cream.
Borden's Malted Milk.

**E. MEYER & CO.
Chemulpo, Korea,**
Sole Agents

ROYAL INSURANCE COMPANY,
Funds exceed £10,000,000
FIRE
AT CURRENT RATES.
LIFE
REDUCED PREMIUM.
HOLME RINGER & Co.,
Agents, Chemulpo.

HOTEL DU PALAIS
SEOUL.

The only first class Hotel in Seoul.
Situated in the centre of the city opposite the palace.
Cuisine under the supervision of an experienced French Chef.
Well ventilated and furnished throughout.

TARIFF UPON APPLICATION

L. MARTIN,
Proprietor and Manager.

大韓每日申報

대한매일신보

(뎨삼십구호) (슈요일) 일쳔구빅사년팔월삼십일일

본샤고빅

이신보는영어와한국문셔계리일출판하옵

신문가

한장 엽두돈오푼

일삭도엽두량닷돈 맛돈으로밧숩

광고료는

귀한의장단과주항의다쇼로죵갈하되명가로밧을터이오며오릭지아녀대한사람마다다이신문을보실터이니광고내시기를원하시는이들은우리신문샤에와셔뎡약하심을희망하옵

○발행소 박동대한매일신보샤법어학교압헤젼영국인셜필림졍자리오

사쟝 영국인 (빅셜)

본샤지졈

인쳔항교쟝동셰지명씨로우리대한매일신보사인쳔항지졈쟝을뢰뎡하엿사오니인쳔항에계신구람코자하시는쳠군자는히지졈에왕림뎐의하시옵

사고

○우리대한매일신보의목뎍은대한의안녕질서에관한모든대목에되하야는공평한변론을주쟝할이라우리동신원의담보는신문보시는쳠군즈의게하샹보도하리며편지들귀셔하여주시는이는셩명과번디를젹어보치시기를희망하오니이거슨신문샹에긔재하란는거시아니오다만극히신용하는죵거를숨고쟈함이라긔쟈는아모긔셔던지긔지할을되쟉하는권리를가졋스나되쟉하는리유를말할터이오며공즁광화를문란케하는듯한긔셔는의례히밧지안켓삽나이다

사고

○본샤에셔는신문갑슨빅월에셤금으로밧사오며본신문은우톄로붓치는고로본샤에셔는다른신문샤처럼금햅을거두러드니지안사오니우리신문을구람하야구람하시는쳠군주는양력미월쵸죵에리월도션금과거쥬셩명통호수를존세히젹어셔박동본샤로보내시기를바라오며양력금월회일나로션금을아니보내시는곳에는리월일브터신문을아니보낼터이오니죠량하옵소셔

●본샤에셔아직긔계를쟝만치못하와다른되셔박여오는고로민양월요일에는출판이대단히늣게되는듯스로본젼이미우늣는게되오니우리신문을구람하서는쳠군즈는 용셔하여쥬심을희망하옵나이다

론셜

요양싸홈관측이라

○우리는귀왕에일아량국이게싸와피추위형호ㅅ경에이로즁노아라며너이금소문으로아죡도진리졍평하기위하야군병의진퇴와기타에비가대단한듯한거시엘본흥목데쟝은부하로하여곰아방을공계하라고분빈하는중에요쟝시되게ᄒ엿든아병들은아죡도셔로응젹하야싸홈하던겻헤잇다하나일병은뒤가아라사구로파트킨쟝군의군되우익을향하야젼진혼다혼즉필경포병들로더부러곤핍한듯하쇗더라요양싸홈에젼국이장차엇더케되리라고환셜이만하기가심히어려우되그젼쟁이오리신을지못할듯한거시아라사에서거울삼삭군량을준비치도못하엿슬터이요또일병들이북으로향하야모라드러가는조리에응당요양셔에서는모히잇슬밧한곳이업는즉필경에는요양셔일병의게포회이되고말듯하며또우리듯기에는구로파트킨회의소외군되정리흠이아모리하여도그곳을부지하지못할듯하며

또아라사로련혼동신에는구로파트킨쟝군의가ㄱ졍만되게하는거시퐁셜에들이기를히쟝군이고병졸로더부러봉쳔셔으로퇴거하야다만룩긔티병으로하여곰일병을티젹혼다는티일본신문들은이말을밋지아니하며히쟝군이ᄌ긔나라황뎨의게뎐보하기를요양에셔크게싸와ᄌ용을결단하라하엿다고하엿스나이러한보고도여시험이여이지아니하되

엇지던지아젼은분명히한번크게될듯한거시샤실문에뎐보등지혼거슨본죠금월이십일에요양남방이십영리되는안산졈이라하는데셔싸홈시작이되엿슨즉하루태쟝은응당요양싸동방이나흑동북간방에느런셔싸흠듯하다하엿는되이러하지경이면일본군병좌우량되후진은필경이십오영리샹거밧게아니되겟다고하엿는지라

이번젼쟁에량편이셔로대단히어려울듯한거시요양북방히창이라하는곳은산젼한평원광야인되또근일소문을드른즉대가쪽쥬하야모든진흙길이사롬의무릅ㅅ지닉게빠진다하며또지형이평탄한쳐닭에일본셔아라사의병력과진셰를혐셰탐아흘거시엽다하며

단비아병의진퇴허존관계쳔에는무이죵케되엿고또셔등신쳠보호하기가리로되ㅅ고곳으로가로대뭇거흔거시만ㅅ치광주린속드린안죤긷갓다혼즉

만일고러하진되군수를모라방과및동남간방으로나왓슬지경이면구로파트킨쟝군이미우조혼곳을차지하엿슬듯하되만약일본이곳칭펀에아병퇴흘즁을얼고츙돌하야나왓슬진티이러한싸홈도엽셔슬터이요우리듯기에는구로파트킨의쟝계하지못혼군수로하여곰이왕에도여러번싸와쓰되지리를엇어산셰들의지하야더헝이일병은동의지완이되젹혼뎍일입엿스나그러하나요양젼쟝은특별이넘나한광탄혼싸인죽종말싸홈하량으로에산하야젼일과하엿든군수를노하여곰극력하야싸호게되면량진이셔로밧ᄃ블하드리도아라사에셔쟝병샹호가잇슬듯하며이번젼쟁이피ᄎ미우긴요혼즉구로파트킨쟝군의괴산하엿던군수가흥다시회복하여볼듯하노라

잡보

○회장괴차 작일에보안회를셩젼도가에기회하엿더니일본헌병펄명이리로ᄒ야회쟝리건셕씨를잡아가고회중문부와규칙방망이틀을슈히슈탐하여가고셩젼도가젼후문을파슈하되라

○함흥로병 원산이북의로병은샹금함흥에취집하야남으로나아오는모양도뵈이지안코또북으로퇴거하는형젹도업고함흥부근의면셔은로병이일의다슌히젹고면셔와밋모든괴게물모도다파샹하엿기로쟉금에로병이다시가셜하기를착슈하는되목뎍이가흡펀홈으로군란하야항도판징인슈로하야금면보수를위쳥하야거긔잇는물품을수샥하는되죵슈하다더라

○김최향도 젼참령김인슈씨가함북로군중의향도관으로빗단말은이왕다아는바이어니와동씨는로군의쟝봉이되여귀우에대쟝김인슈라크게써셔세우고문중에닛며젼군슈최회헌쥬씨도고군을따랏다하더라

○슈분슈괴 일젼에본보에긔재혼바련동교육회에셔무고를맛나포라혼린라는풍셜이잇는뒤그스괴를조셰히드른즉그런쳐안교고닙게회혼졔쇼졈이와셔회의수연을알녀하미분회의국민학교셜립하는추지셔를뵈이고셜명하즉슌검도보고당쏘연이흠일이란고을케알교갓교는츄지를대신도그학교를셜립하셔른조셰히가샹혀ㅅ여그츄지셔흔라라히젹어 다니엔일 감라더라

○교양민요 혁부모집수로교양군에민요가나셔대소인민이일졔히관수에도립하야돌을뵈분하던지미판슉은일병도피하고일본병도와신하는금보가나부에리도ᄒ민괴로하는인민을효유안졉추로나부시찰관병의에가지쟉일에교양으로나려갓다더라

○일인횡악 지나간토요일오후에셔에일인들이횡쥬나외샹하동에도립하야담과계란등을을투탁하는고로인민들이그일인과샹지하엿더니그날밤에일인십여명이각기칼을가지고사룸을맛나는되로구타하미남녀로소가수방으로되란하야산중에셔경야하고그이튼날슈방으로환샹하엿는되한가지로과외인민중에자죵칼을갈로치셔긔

지수경인티고일인들이합병ㅎ야가지고뵈지게챠라고일인들와힝악은다시 비흘곳시엽다더라

○우도피착 저작일에 로들근티에셔엇던흔병뎡이소한필을몰고오논티젼일에별헌병단이는사름ㅎ나히맛츙만나본즉병뎡의힝식이슈상ㅎ더니뒤로슈다흔사름이각각몽동이들가지코도젹을웨이며쏫츠오거놀도젹인줄알고그젼별헌병단이든사름이착거ㅎ엿다더라

○가쟉려승 신문외뎡거쟝위셩밋헤다가일본인들이긴츅ㅎ야포티모양을민드러놋코칭호를려승구라ㅎ고수번으로아국국괴을민드러쏫고슈십간동안위언덕에는일본군함이류진ㅎ모양으로민드러긴츅ㅎ엿는티련일에려순구을층으로합락ㅎ는날은이가쟉흔려승포티서지파쇄흔다더라

○경스록룩 경무수김졍근씨가수진ㅎ야청즁에단속ㅎ야젼경무수의제반힝졍을게속실시코자흔즉모든경관등이말ㅎ되젼경무수가무겨을금지ㅎ미셜창병을착슈ㅎ고무녀슈연을귀레포ㅎ다가아져쳑즁지못ㅎ고경계속ㅎ여ㅎ실렷가흔티경무수가난처ㅎ여거무부답ㅎ엿다더라

○표목하다 향일물티일본인이쥬동병참소로셔감찰당서지표목을세웟더니본월이십칠일에쏘감찰당으로셔일공관뒤문서지향ㅎ야련락ㅎ게표목을세웟는티표목이합삼십칠기라더라

○헌제우기 의정부에셔내부로조회ㅎ기를한셩부관제를량의ㅎ야기정ㅎ기로데의ㅎ라ㅎ엿논티히부관제가향일에기정이되엿스나오히려미흡흠이잇셔셔다시기정흔다더라

○ㅊ의죽표 남셔마메교들일본인이ㅊ의로슈축ㅎ는고로경무청에셔금지흔즉디답ㅎ되귀국셔마메교를슈축흔단말만ㅎ변창슈치아니ㅎ는고로우리가슈축ㅎ노라ㅎ더라더라

○로병도강 평ㅎ군수긴창수씨가빅부로보고ㅎ되칠월신팔일에로국괴병롯빅명가량이일보시에두만강안에도달ㅎ엿는티그잇흔날경셩방면으로향ㅎ야갓다ㅎ엿다더라

○온궁립표 온양군수권중억씨보고를거흔즉음력칠초스일에일본인심상명이본군온쳔동리에리도ㅎ야표목팔기를온궁과고동리에통녀세우고표목진면에다가온현궁괴디라씨고소중흔힝궁안장원때문에다가심ㅈ횡목을지르고펄쇄ㅎ엿다ㅎ엿더라

○북니흉신 원산으로셔보쳐에도달흔셔신니에ㅎ엿스되본월십구일에일아량군이기젼되엿논티그후로는병비가대단ㅎ다ㅎ엿고젼쟁승픽는말아니라ㅎ엿다더라

○외형ㅅ소 외부대신서리형관윤치호씨가작일에ㅅ직샹소흔고로당일ㅅ진을아니ㅎ엿다더라

○강씨귀국 주영공관셔리쟉강괴승씨가신병을인ㅎ야일작에귀국ㅎ엿더라

○텬진분포 과주텬진에셔경의텰도부설ㅎ는티관ㅎ야분포가대단히니러낫더니일본병참소에셔즉시파병ㅎ야히산ㅎ엿다더라

○룡소무비 초동청에셔대룡ㅊ상소셔지ㅎ엿스되 비지들무근지못흔고로소슈비하소청계인이대안문젼에진복티명흠이가ㅎ다고외론이분운ㅎ다더라

○조처특당 참찬취위씨가일본용ㅅ림권조도를구츌방면ㅎ고말ㅎ여왈갈도쟉향에역부빈졍수들을시ㅎ며아루모지회가엉셔지고빈요가졈식되야조원조가만리셔귀군슈를풍슈운이편리ㅎ라라ㅎ되림용ㅅ가가타ㅎ아일공ㅅ는감처ㅅ평부와병참소에면척ㅎ고니외부에셔는각관찰부와감리셔에면훈ㅎ엿더니지작일에림용ㅅ가리참찬을청ㅎ야말ㅎ되역부빈졍을가잉ㅎ야각도에다시면보ㅎ라ㅎ거눈참찬이티답ㅎ되이제ㅎ면보를오놀곳치는거시블가ㅎ고ㅎ시며부는ㅊㅊ조원조가만을거시니파히제츌말나ㅎ엿다더라

○북리쇼식 북도로셔상리흔사름의젼셜을드른즉아국병이리원서지면간목을세웟는티한인을봉착ㅎ는대로만집ㅎ야못가게ㅎ는고로도로에힝인이조졀ㅎ엿다ㅎ더라

○팔흥로병 세작일원산셔발흔면보를거흔즉지금함흥에잇는아병은그근처한국빅셩의집으로셔량식을증발ㅎ고또한인을위협ㅎ야도로를슈축케ㅎ고후슈티라칭ㅎ고빈아병이수오십명식로리도ㅎ는티금넌보츄슈후에운동을시작ㅎ라는모양이라ㅎ엿더라

○일군로페 본월십삼일에원산항일본군수부에셔군령을반포ㅎ엿스되원산과히항부근디에셔로국지페교환ㅎ는것과통용ㅎ는거슬엄금ㅎ되이금령을범ㅎ논자는군률노시힝흔다ㅎ엿더라

○법ㅅ인셩 일젼에분린셔ㅅ판오인이인셩ㅎ엿더라

○뎡리분공 한셩저판소뎡리가송민늬소장을밧을젹에친소를싸라니중에분별이잇는고로뎡리의계반연이업는자는정소ㅎ기가입의롭지못ㅎ고쏘밧는바소장을긴칠을분등ㅎ야친소의분별이잇는고로송민의리히가불소ㅎ다고원성이자자ㅎ다더라

○진주군보 진주군슈리익호씨가너부에보고ㅎ되음력륙월십수일오시량에로국괴병ㅅ빅명이명천군으로좃차본군서문외에리도ㅎ야몽한지디에셔ㅅ로범ㅈ고그잇흔날진시에셩진으로향ㅎ엿다ㅎ엿더라

○길군우보 길쥬군슈가또보고ㅎ되음력륙월심륙일신시량에로국괴병이빅여명이명천으로좃차와본군에셔졈시머물고유시량에셩진으로발힝ㅎ엿고십칠일진시량에쏘로국병칠십명이쏘한명천으로좃차와본군을지나며셩진으로향ㅎ야힝군ㅎ엿다ㅎ엿더라

○공조외부 궁니부에셔외부에조회ㅎ되동리젼영도교쿠논본리 황실에셔관할ㅎ는연창괴지란본부에셔인원을파송ㅎ야됴사흔즉히항감리가보고ㅎ되교쿠를외부에셔임의조젼회사에히금ㅎ엿다ㅎ고방보ㅎ엿시니귀부에셔히도를칙히ㅎ거든히인허쟝을곳환슈ㅎ라ㅎ엿더라

○일진회황 재작일하오이시에일진회에셔기회ㅎ엿는티렴중모씨가졔의ㅎ며왈졍부에셔수도건셜ㅅㅎ기젼에는언제서지지면지ㅎ티우원을가퇴ㅎ야파송ㅎ자ㅎ엿더니신엄흔참정이아직수진치안니흔즉수세소치로ㅎ티파송흠을괴이흔간류안ㅎㅎ고기간은용귀연셜ㅎ기로동의ㅎ야가결되고일조는제명구월일일하오이시로수시셔저정ㅎ고연셜쟝은탑골공원쟝으로정ㅎ엿더라

○군제기셜 군제기정ㅎ기위ㅎ야의졍관심이인을차하흠은본보에임의긔지ㅎ엿거니와긔문흔즉시위와진위뎨를감ㅎ고아군위병삼쳔오빅명을셜치ㅎ고진위티는일병참과흔다는말이잇다더라

○공찰부임 공쥬관찰ㅅ심진틱씨가도임츳로작일발졍ㅎ엿더라

○개탄회명 재작일에일본헌병이보안회회쟝리건ㅅ씨를ㅅ평부로거착ㅎ더니쟝관이그회의목뎍을무르미셜샹으로디답흔즉쟝관말이이회의주의가젼회보다티승ㅎ지라목뎍이과연이려흉흔진틔우리도쏘흔친셩흔려인더하펼젼일란민의보안회일흔흥을련속ㅎ야회명을지엇는가회녜을다시곳치표셜시ㅎ되본수령부인회를맛하가교ㅎ미티념ㅎ기를다론회는비록인취를박앗ㅅ나우리는주유힝동흥껏다ㅎ녕이도라와회명을곳치기로평의중인데일진회회가셜시ㅎ노다더라

○식욕구진 대한일보를거흔즉샹회위명인이구슈중에잇는길영슈를구ㅎ여니자고셩언ㅎ고려주디방에셔슈다흔부샹등을소집ㅎ란다고운동중이라ㅎ엿더라

○청원퇴각 근조에신림철퇴황무디기간흔ㅅ로한인모씨가농샹공부에청원ㅎ엿더니히부에셔그청원을퇴각ㅎ엿다더라

○금회관난 근일에일진회보안회교육회등각회가처처에봉기ㅎ는고로김정근씨가이과회를승시ㅎ야경무수를도득ㅎ엿더니션흔계회 금지ㅎ는방침이엽셔셔관난흔중이라더라

관보

데이쳔구빅십팔호 광무팔년팔월삼십일

서임급ㅅ령

○의원면본관 원구단ㅅ제셔참봉 윤춘구 동션ㅅ면화파주ㅅ 윤긔익

○임원구단ㅅ제셔참봉셔관임관팔등 희릉참봉 리은필

○임희릉참봉셔관임관팔등 구표윤춘구 임동신ㅅ면화과쟝ㅅ셔관임관륙등 륙표음 신셕용 이상팔월이십칠일

○명텰도원총재셔칙임관이등 궁니부특진관 심상훈 ○임중추원의관셔칙임관ㅅ등 군슈 윤필 ○임의졍부참정 신긔션 셔칙임관일등 텰도원총재 이상팔월이십팔일

외보

○션거파손 본월이십삼일루터발면을거흔즉로국부션거흔기가셩괴등보에셔리쌘항구로회항ㅎ다가반이결나져아주파손이되엿다더라

○남아로함 동일동뎐에왈남아비리가에잇는셔ㅣ쎈항구에셔온로션이리젼ㅎ기를거목에셔일에셴드프렌싸쓰갑각히외에셔로국군함곳흔거슬보앗다더라

○홍히로함 동일동뎐에왈로국슌양함셰렛즈호와밋슈리뎡이젹은홍히해셔상션을검열ㅎ기위ㅎ야거미신일에단국에잇는선리엇드쌘드힝쟝을동파ㅎ엿다더라

TELEGRAMS.

FROM JAPAN AND SHANGHAI PAPERS.

Chefoo, 19th August—At 5:30 a. m. several Japanese destroyers entered the harbour. Four left for Port Arthur almost immediately and three sailed in an easterly direction.

Berlin, August 21st.

A Press telegram reaching Paris states that General Kuropatkin is about to proceed to Mukden.

Russia is about to call out her reserves in forty-seven provinces, and all reserve officers throughout the whole of the Empire.

Berlin, August 21st.

The Russian Government has requested the Norddeutscher Lloyd to supply the Baltic Suadron with coal during the voyage to the Far East.

The Company has declined to do so, on the ground that it would be incompatible with the policy of neutrality adopted by Germany.

The Russian cruiser "Ural" has put into Lisbon for the purpose of repairing her screw. On completing repairs the vessel took on board sufficient coal to enable her to make the run to Malta.

At Malta the Governor has forbidden coal to be supplied to Russian warships except in cases of special need.

London, August 24th.

It is stated that the cruiser sighted off Cape Colony is the Russian Volunteer Fleet steamer "Smolensk," but it is possibly one of the converted German liners.

London, August 24th.

The Liverpool Chamber of Commerce has forwarded to the Marquess of Lansdowne, Secretary of State for Foreign Affairs, a resolution earnestly hoping that arrangements will be speedily concluded to remedy the grave detriment to British commerce resulting from Russia's proceedings with respect to contraband of war.

The Liverpool Chamber of Commerce is soliciting the co-operation of all other Chambers throughout the country.

RUSSIA'S WEALTH OF PUMICE.

The mineral wealth of Russia is hardly appreciated, and new industries are from time to time being developed, though the effect of the present war may be felt in many new schemes. A recent proposition is the development of the pumice stone, which has been found in the provinces of Erivan and Kars, in Trans caucasia. The deposits in Kars, at Ma ayakutma, are near the surface in horizo ntal strata, and occasionally run over t wo and a half feet thick, furnishing a high-grade mineral that is used for polishing, and poorer quality from which hydraulic cement can be made. The material is convenient to Kars, from which place it will be shipped by rail to Poti, on the Black Sea, and thence conveyed by steamer to Odessa. When the works are operating to their full capacity several million pounds a year of the material will be produced. The world's supply of pumice is now largely derived from the Lipari Islands near Sicily.

The Japan Times states that a Yingkow despatch dated the 22nd states that our administrative office at that port dispatched on the evening of the 20th an expeditionary force, consisting of a number of Japanese gendarmerie and Chinese police, to a place some 20 miles off the mouth of the Liao, where a body of pirates with eight vessels was then stationed. After a fierce fight between the opposing parties one of the pirates was killed and four others were wounded, while the eight vessels were captured, together with fire-arms and ammunition. According to the statement of the captured pirates, they made the mouth of the Liao their headquarters and also possessed a number of sailing-vessels and junks. It appears that these pirates had obtained their ammunition supplies from foreign merchants at Yingkow.

RESTAURANTS AT SEA.

The Hamburg-American Line is about to add two more immense steamers to its fleet, one of 25,000 tons to be built at Stettin, and one of 22,000 tons which Messrs. Harland and Wolff are to build.

The larger of the two boats is to be fitted with a restaurant, where travellers who do not care for the table d'hôte meals of the ship may order their own repasts à la carte at what hour they please. The arrangements will probably be undertaken by the Ritz Hotel Company.

"This plan will never be adopted on an English vessel," said the manager of a leading Liverpool and New York line. "Neither English nor American passengers want it." The manager of the White Star Line and a director of a Canadian line agreed.

There are many reasons why Liverpool shipowners are opposed to the idea. It would not do to split the passage money. If a saloon passenger were to pay separately for his passage and buy his meals as he required them aboard, he would eventually discover that it would have been cheaper in the end to book at inclusive rates.

A passenger on a palatial Atlantic liner knows that what he pays for is not so much the food he eats as the security and speed, general comfort, and a large well-disciplined staff. All these things have to be maintained whether the passenger sits down to a twelve-course dinner or a grilled steak.

No hotel on the Continent can serve a better dinner in better style than that on board a first-class liner. Notwithstanding oyster patties and game courses at dinner, the sumptuous breakfast, the luxurious lunch, the intermediate bowl of soup on deck, and the afternoon cup of tea, the actual cost of feeding a saloon diner is estimated at not more than 5s. 6d. per day.

Though the passenger may be eating all the time he is aboard, he is actually paying not more than half as much for his food as for his share of the coal that an army of sweltering firemen are shovelling down beneath him somewhere, and many other things he never dreams of.

A man desiring to dine à la carte cannot expect a rebate of more than 30s. on his fare.

"If people do not desire or cannot afford all the epicurean delights of the saloon their alternative is the second cabin," declared the passenger superintendent of an Atlantic line. "If we split the fares an avenue would be opened for an undesirable and stingy class. I have no doubt that even the restaurant would be neglected, for the mean class of travellers would feed themselves on tinned meats and other food carried in their trunks."—Japan Gazette.

ANOTHER UNIVERSAL LANGUAGE.

Never do six months pass by without some attempt being made to do away with the disadvantages of the diversity of tongues, but so far success has not attended any one of them. Volapuk and all the rest of them have disappeared, and a recent suggestion, Commercial Latin, or the language of the old traders of the world, has not been heard of for at least a year. Struggle as they may, the inventors of universal languages cannot get away from Latin, and the latest attempt, that by Professor Peame, of Turin, resolves itself into Latin without inflections. The Professor proposes to do away with cases, numbers, genders, and persons, and also with tenses and voices, using the ablative in the case of substantives, and the infinitive minus -re or -ri for the verbs. In fact, his system is the evolution of the Italian tongue carried to its logical conclusion. The grammar is to be simpler even than English, though what the Professor does to make up for the absence of the article, which is absolutely necessary in a modern language, we are not told. His new Latin seems to be a sort of "pidgin," for which life can neither be expected nor desired. Nearly everyone learns Latin more or less, and it is difficult to see why the simple Latin of the Middle Ages, without any straining after Ciceronian elegancies, should not suffice for all our international needs, during the few years which must pass before all the world speaks English.—The Globe.

A NEW TYPE OF TORPEDO BOAT.

Francis Herreshoff, a nephew of Capt. "Nat" Herreshoff, has suggested to the United States Government that an improvement might be made on the present system of torpedo warfare, and is said to be constructing a model to illustrate the idea. Instead of building a costly and elaborate boat for the purpose of launching a missile, he would combine the latter with a light, inexpensive craft. The charge would be carried in the bow, just it is in the head of a self-propelled Whitehead torpedo. When this exploded, of course, the whole thing would be destroyed.

Only two men would be required to manage such a boat, and the inventor thinks that it might not be necessary to sacrifice their lives. When the boat had approached close enough to the enemy's ship to leave no doubt about the result they could lock the steering gear, don life-belts and jump overboard. There would then be a chance that they might be picked up and be able to join the fleet to which they were attached. Boats of this description might be easily carried on battleships and cruisers, especially if built of aluminum. They should not involve an expenditure much greater than that now needed for a first-class torpedo, the largest share being the outlay for machinery.

FINE STATUE FOR PRINCE BISMARCK.

Bremen, July 23.—There are rules of etiquette in Germany with regard to representing rulers and other men of prominence in bronze. It is an unwritten law that rulers alone shall have the privilege of appearing on horseback. Quite a stir was caused, therefore, in art circles and among those who regard it their duty jealously to guard monarchial traditions and prerogatives when Bremen, through its city mayor, announced its intention to depart from this rule and to give Bismarck, the real maker of the German Empire, an equestrian statue.

The proposed monument is the first one in Germany representing a statesman on horseback, but the Bremen monument committee thinks that Bismarck deserves to be placed in bronze on equal footing with rulers, however great they may have been. The choice of an equestrian statue was due not only to a desire to honour the great statesman in a special way, quite out of the ordinary manner, but also to create a monument that will be able to rival in uniqueness the proposed Bismarck monument at Hamburg, which is to be a colossal statue with the principal figure represented as a Roland.

A DENIAL BY A GERMAN STEAMSHIP COMPANY.

A telegram received at the Foreign Office states that the report made public in a recent issue of the London "Times" and Laffan's Telegraph Agency to the effect that the Norddeutscher Lloyd Steamship Company, Bremen, Germany, has undertaken to supply coal to the Baltic fleet, is absolutely contradicted by that company. The latter has not entered into any such contract either directly or indirectly, nor has it received any such order or been entrusted with such mission. It is true that some time ago the company was approached by the Russian Government for the engagement of its vessels for the abovementioned purpose, but this request was declined at the time.

The transport "Ni-Yoshino Maru," which left Ujina on the 18th inst. for the front, encountered a storm in the Korean channel, during which she sprang a leak, with the result that her bunkers were filled with water. Thanks to the prompt action of the crew, the steamer was enabled to put back to Moji on the 20th inst., whence she returned to Ujina on the morning of the 22nd.

EUROPE'S LARGEST HOSPITAL

On the banks of the "beautiful blue Danube" medical men are busy to good purpose. The largest hospital in Europe is to be built in Vienna, with forty pavilions, and the Austrian Emperor, Francis Joseph, recently laid the cornerstone. In each operating amphitheater there will be space for two hundred and fifty students. One of the novel features will be the separation, by glass screens, in the clinical institutes of patients afflicted with infectious disease from the young men who are studying medicine and surgery.

The new hospital, with its grounds, will include sixty acres, and $10,000,000 will be spent upon it. A match for it would be hard to find. For generations Vienna has been a famous center and headquarters for medical and surgical research and experiment, for splendid achievements in the benefit of the sick and suffering and for education in healing and relief. It certainly is not falling backward, but is making giant strides ahead.

The funeral of the four Russian blue jackets formerly on the "Rurik" was held at the Russian cathedral at Inasa, Nagasaki, in the forenoon of the 21st inst. The coffins covered with the Russian naval flag were brought there from Saseho that morning. A body of bluejackets from a Japanese guardship in the harbour acted as a guard of honour. The procession consisted of the local Governor, the French Consul and many other mourners preceded by bearers of four wreaths sent by Admiral Samejima, Commander of the Saseho Admiralty. The Russian Chaplain, who was released from the rest of the "Rurik" prisoners, conducted the burial service. In the course of his address the Chaplain thanked the Japanese for their courteous action and emphasized the fact that he would have the pleasure of informing the Russian nation of the Japanese kindness when he returned home. The Chaplain was to leave for Shanghai to day.

A giant horse, which was bred in America, is on exhibition and attracting large crowds in Berlin. It measures 9ft. 10in. from the ground to the tips of the ears. Its other measurements are: Length of back, 6ft. 6in.; head to tail, 11ft. 9in.; girth, 10ft. 10 inch.; girth of top of fore-legs, 3ft.; girth of fore-hoof, 2ft, 10in.

Ibsen began to earn his own living at the age of 16, and for five or six years worked in an apothecary's shop, amusing himself during the time by reading curious books and writing weird verses. Only 23 copies of his first book were sold; the rest were disposed of as waste paper to buy him food.

The Korea Daily News.

To be published daily except Sundays.

Rate of Subscription:—

Per Year,	Yen 25.
Per Quarter,	Yen 7.
Per Month	Yen 2.50

Postage in Korea not charged extra.
Postage abroad charged extra.

Advertisements, 50 sen per day for 1 inch or less.
5 yen per month per inch.
50 yen per year per inch.

All communications to

E. T. BETHELL,
Editor and Publisher.
Pak-tong, Seoul

THE RUSSIAN TROOPS IN MANCHURIA.

VIEWS OF A CORRESPONDENT.

A correspondent, attached to the Staff of General Kuropatkin for the past three months, has stated in an interview at Shanghai some particulars of the situation.

General Kuropatkin's position he considers a strong one, the Japanese having to take great precautions to keep from falling into ambushes.

General Kuropatkin, General Sahaloff, Chief of the Staff, and General Chalketitch (?), Superintendent of the Line of Communications, are training newly arrived troops and will not make any active movement until the training is completed.

The main object of General Kuropatkin is to obtain a large store of materials necessary for a great army. Accordingly 90 per cent. of the trains from Europe have been carrying provisions, ammunition, clothing, and hospital materials, so that those articles are plentiful at present. Food is not so necessary, since Manchuria itself supplies all kinds of nourishing food necessary for the Russians.

Trains arrive from Europe over eleven times a day. Nine or ten of them are filled with military necessities, only one or two transporting troops and officials. The 10th Army Corps arrived at the rate of 3,000 troops a day but the general average is less.

If Russia would adopt the American system, thinks the correspondent, or use a few American managers and 200 skilled assistants the utility of the railway would be doubled. At present, the railway loses half its true value by the confusion and delay owing to the up and down trains on the various branch lines. The situation chiefly depends not upon whether the commander at the front is good or bad, but upon how the railway is managed.

Over 125,000 Russian troops, under the command of General Kuropatkin, are stationed at a place not far from Liaoyang, and not more than 20,000 were in the town at the time the correspondent left. Numerous reinforcements are expected to arrive from home this month or next, since military necessities sufficient for a greater force than is at present assembled have all arrived from Russia.

The artillery all have guns of a new type and are more efficient than the other troops. The hospitals and surgeons are very efficient and the correspondent praises the arrangements warmly. A great number of the casualties are among the Russian officers who expose themselves more than the privates.

The correspondent was with General Kellor in the battle at Motienling. He decribes the General as one of the best the Russians have, his death being greatly felt.

RUSSIANS AND JAPANESE AT SHANGHAI.

Under the heading of "War in Boone Road," the Shanghai "Times" publishes the following account of a "fracas" between Russians and Japanese at Shanghai.

During the past week there have been signs that perhaps Shanghai would be included in the war zone. This became an absolute fact on Saturday night. A party of Russian and French sailors were "doing" the town and were drawn into an encounter with Japanese in the Boone Road.

The fracas started by a French sailor leaving the Concordia Hotel and turning into a dark alley. He was followed by a Japanese who removed his thick wooden sandal and hit him on the head from behind. The sailor stumbled and fell on to his knees but soon got up crying for assistance. His comrades upon seeing him bleeding and hearing his story rushed out to avenge him.

A number of Japanese were sitting outside their houses on the opposite side of the road, and were immediately attacked, but they defended themselves and being reinforced by a number of others soon put their assailants to rout. Four Japanese were badly bruised, one had to be sent to hospital to have his wounds dressed.

The Japanese appeared to be greatly excited and started to hunt for the sailors, and it was not until after 1 A. M. yesterday that they gave up their search for the men who had attacked them. The man who was the origin and cause of the trouble cannot be traced, but four men—Japanese—are known as having taken a prominent part in the fight.

While the row was in progress a Sikh policeman came upon the scene and blew his whistle for assistance, which to a certain extent was a factor in making the Europeans take to their heels and in the chase after them by the Japanese, one of the latter was caught.

The Europeans ran to a launch which was in waiting for them near the Old Dock, which they boarded at once and steamed away.

ATTEMPTED SEIZURE OF SULPHUR SPRING.

An official report from Ouyang, w[illegible] some excellent sulphur springs [illegible] states that a few days ago 13 Japan[illegible], with a train of pack-ponies carr[illegible]g poles and boards, arrived at Ou[illegible]g. They proceeded to stake out [illegible] nd and to board up the va[illegible]gs. The gates of the buildi[illegible] enclosing some of this val[illegible]erty were nailed up by these enterprising gentry, who apparently have an eye to the future, and seem to think that they are as much at liberty to stake out property and claim ownership thereof, as were the miners in the early Australian gold-fields rush.

PILLAGE AT HANGCHU.

On the afternoon of Saturday last, some Japanese entered the village of Hangchu (some 2 or 3 miles from Yongsan) and attempted to steal chickens and eggs from the villagers, who however made the situation too hot for them.

At night time 10 of the marauders, armed with swords, returned and commenced to terrorize the populace, most of whom fled to the hills. One old woman and one man, named Chong chung-sun, whom they struck down, were carried off by these gentle robbers.

RUSSIAN ACTIVITY IN KOREA.

The Magistrate of Kyong Heung reports that a further batch of 600 Russian cavalry crossed the Tumen river on the 10th inst. on their way south. A despatch from Ham Heung states that the force there is augmented by 40 or 50 arrivals daily.

The secretary of the Korean Legation in London returned to Seoul on the 28th inst.

The Magistrate of Song-chin reports the passage of 270 Russian cavalry through his district on their way to Ham-heung.

Two official representatives of His Majesty have left for Wiju and Gensan bearing letters enquiring after the health of the Japanese troops at those places.

It is said the 12 members of the Military Committee have finally decided to abolish the whole army, with the exception of 3,500 men for an imperial body-guard.

The Independence celebrations in America were a great success this year. But the roll of killed and injured—roughly 1,400— is considered small for so free a country.

The Japanese military authorities have forbidden the Korean inhabitants of Gensan and northwards to accept Russian roubles in payment of merchandise or labour.

Mr. Sim Sang-hun has been transferred to the Railroad Department as superintendent and Mr. Sim Ki-son has been appointed to the vacated Vice Presidency of State.

The Dai Han Il Po learns that a Korean, named Sing Sang Heui, has pledged himself, with the aid of peddlers, to rescue Colonel Kil Yung-su, from his imprisonment by the Japanese.

An American Judge has held that insanity is not a ground for divorce. He will be supported by a great weight of opinion among those who contend that marriage is originally impossible without insanity in at least one of the parties.

Mr. Yi Kum-sok, chief of the Po An Hoi meeting, who, as reported yesterday, was arrested by Japanese gendarmes, has been released, as nothing libellous was discussed at the meeting. He has been instructed to have the name of the society altered.

Mr. Kim Dyung-kun, the lately appointed Chief of Police, is said to be suffering from a fit of remorse. "It appears he took an oath to stop the Il Chin Hoi and Po An Hoi meetings but in the words of our reporter, "He is quite sad lately on account that he can not think out any single idea to prohibit them meetings."

A concern called the "Mankan Baiyaku Shokai," or a company to sell patent medicines in Korea and Manchuria, has been organized by Mr. Otomatsu Arita, at Tamondori Shichome, Kobe. Branch offices have been established at Taiku, and Pyeng-yang, Korea, and will also be opened at Seoul, Chinnampo, Mokpo, Kunsan, Fusan, etc.

The "Tokyo Asahi's" Chefoo correspondent, wiring under date of the 22nd inst., states that, according to Lieutenant-Commander Hopman, German naval attaché who was recently taken to Tsingtao from Port Arthur by the Japanese warship "Yaeyama," there were at one time in Port Arthur four foreign attchés namely, an American, a French and two Germans, but on the 14th inst., the French officer and one of the Germans left Pigeon Bay for Shanhaikwan in a junk and on the 17th the American officer also quitted Port Arthur for Shanhaikwan. On the 18th Lieutenant-Commander Hopman left Port Arthur by a junk, which met our destroyers outside that port. After examination, the German officer was courteously received by the Commander of our destroyers and then taken on board the flagship "Mikasa," where he was introduced to Admiral Togo, and was afterwards sent to Tsingtao in the "Yaeyama." In conclusion, Lieutenant-Commander Hopman said that he had received the kindest treatment from our officers and men.

The Korea Daily News.

VOL. I, WEDNESDAY, AUGUST 31, 1904. No. 39

HONGKONG & SHANGHAI BANKING CORPORATION.

Paid-up Capital..... ....$10,000,000
Reserve Fund:—Sterling Reserve... 10,000,000
Silver Reserve..... 6,500,000

26,500,000
Reserve Liability of Proprietors... 10,000,000

HEAD OFFICE, HONGKONG.

London Bankers, London and County Banking Company Limited.

Branches and Agencies,
London.

Amoy,	Hankow	Penang,
Bangkok,	Hiogo,	Rangoon,
Batavia,	Iloilo,	Saigon,
Bombay,	Lyons,	San Francisco,
Calcutta,	Manila,	Singapore,
Colombo,	Nagasaki,	Sourabaya,
Foochow,	New York,	Tientsin,
Hamburg,	Peking,	Yokohama,

Credits granted on approved Securities, and every description of Banking and Exchange business transacted.

Drafts granted on London and the chief Commercial places in Europe, India, Australia, America, China and Japan.

HOLME RINGER & Co., AGENTS,
CHEMULPO.

ON CHEONG & CO.,
SEOUL.

GENERAL STORE KEEPERS.
Imported provisions, Cooking Utensils
Crockery, etc.
FRESH BREAD DAILY.

MITSU BISHI DOCKYARD & ENGINE WORKS,
NAGASAKI.

CODE WORD, "DOCK."

A. 1, A. B. C., and Engineering Codes used.

DOCK No. 1 (at Tategami).

Extreme Length..............523 feet
Length on blocks .... 513 ,,
Width of Entrance on Top......89 ,,
,, ,, Bottom....77 ,,
Water on Blocks at Spring Tide 26½ ,,

DOCK No. 2 (Mukaijima).

Extreme Length..............371 feet
Length on Blocks..............360 ,,
Width of Entrance on Top......66 ,,
,, ,, Bottom 53 ,,
Water on Blocks at Spring Tide 22 ,,

PATENT SLIP (at Kosuge).

Can take vessels up to 1,000 tons gross.

THE WORKS are well equipped with the LATEST IMPROVEMENTS, and can execute any kind of work in SHIPBUILDING and MARINE ENGINEERING, as well as in REPAIRING of SHIPS.

The COMPANY'S new powerful steamer OURA-MARU (712 tons, 700 I.H.P.), specially built for SALVAGE PURPOSES, and equipped with necessary gear, is always READY at SHORT NOTICE.

CHARTERED BANK OF INDIA AUSTRALIA & CHINA.

INCORPORATED BY ROYAL CHARTER 1853

HEAD OFFICES:—LONDON.

Paid-up Capital £800,000
Reserve Liability of Shareholders 800,000
Reserve Fund 725,000

Drafts granted upon all the principal places in the world and every description of Exchange and banking business transacted.

E. MEYER & Co., Agents,
Chemulpo.

E. MEYER & CO.
Chemulpo.

SOLE AGENTS IN KOREA FOR:

A. T. Morse, Sons & Co's "Fresco" Distemper

In all colours ready for use on walls, Ceilings etc.

and

AVENARIUS CARBOLINEUM

A wood-preserving and antiseptic oil preparation

Against decay, dry-rot, fungus and wood-destroying insects.

A large supply always in Stock.
Prices upon application.

E. MEYER & Co.,
Chemulpo.

LAW UNION & CROWN INS. CO.

Fire risks accepted at Current rates, on go downs, merchandise, dwellings, and other property, subject to usual conditions.

HOLME RINGER & Co.,
Agents, Chemulpo

THE METHODIST PUBLISHING HOUSE,
Little West Gate, Seoul.

JOB PRINTING, TYPEWRITER PAPER
CARBON PAPER, VISITING CARDS
STATIONERY, BOOK BINDING
BOOK PUBLISHERS
AMERICAN SCHOOL BOOKS
SPENCERIAN COPY BOOKS
PEN CARBON LETTER AND BILL BOOKS

S A BECK, Manager

DAI-ICHI GINKO.
LIMITED.

(Formerly the First National Bank)

ESTABLISHED 1873

INCORPORATED UNDER PRESENT LAW 1896

Capital - - - - - - - - - Yen 5,000,000
Reserve Fund - - - - - 1,500,000

HEAD OFFICE:—TOKIO.

President: Baron SHIBUSAWA.

BRANCHES AND CORRESPONDENTS
In the Principal Cities and Towns of Japan.

Interest Allowed on
Fixed deposits 1 year - - - 6½ per cent
" " 6 months - - - 6 per cent

Special current accounts 1½ sen daily per Y 100
General " " 1 " " " 100

M. TANAKA,
Manager, Chemulpo

HOLME RINGER & Co.
Chemulpo.

General Merchants and Government Contractors.

Agents for the leading

Banks

SteamshipCompanies

and

Insurance Companies

Importers of Merchandise of every description.

KAMEYA & CO.
GENERAL STOREKEEPERS
Chinkokai - - Seoul

(*Established 1895, Tokyo*)

Confectionery, Hams, Canned Goods, Cutlery, Hirano & Tansan Water. Provisions, Gents, Furnishing goods, Toilet Articles, Travelling Bags, Tobacco, Cigars & Cigarettes Kitchen Utensils. Coffee, Biscuits.

Fresh Goods always kept in Stock.

Prices Moderate

Please come and inspect our goods.

NIPPON YUSEN KAISHA.
JAPANESE MAIL STEAMSHIP CO.

DER MAIL CONTRACT WITH THE IMPERIAL JAPANESE GOVERNMENT.

European Line

Regular Fortnightly Service between Yokohama Kobe, Moji, Shanghai, Hongkong, Singapore, Penang Colombo, Port Said, Marseilles, London and Antwerp

American Line

Regular Fortnightly Service between Hongkong and Seattle, calling at Shanghai, Moji, Kobe, Yokohama and Victoria, B. C.

Australian Line

Regular weekly Service betwen Japan Ports and Australia, calling at Hongkong and Manila.

(Above Three Lines Suspended until further notice).

Shanghai Line

Weekly Service between Shanghai and Japan Ports

Korea Line

Service Kobe, Moji, Nagasaki, Fusan, Chemulpo, Chioo, Taiku.
S. S. Bahelsberg, 2181 tons.
Service, Kobe, Moji, Fusan, Chemulpo, Chinnampo
S. S ARGO, S. S. Ohio.

BORDEN'S CONDENSED MILK CO.
New York, U. S. A.

ALWAYS IN STOCK

Eagle Brand Condensed Milk.

Gold Seal Condensed Milk.

Peerless (Family) Evaporated Cream.

Borden's Malted Milk.

E. MEYER & CO.
Chemulpo, Korea,
Sole Agents

ROYAL INSURANCE COMPANY,
Funds exceed £10,000,000

FIRE
AT CURRENT RATES.
LIFE
REDUCED PREMIUM.

HOLME RINGER & Co.,
Agents, Chemulpo.

HOTEL DU PALAIS
SEOUL.

The only first class Hotel in Seoul. Situated in the centre of the city opposite the palace.

Cuisine under the supervision of an experienced French Chef.

Well ventilated and furnished throughout.

TARIFF UPON APPLICATION

L. MARTIN,
Proprietor and Manager.

大韓每日申報
대한미일신보

일쳔구빅사년구월일일 (목요일) (뎨사십호)

본사고빅

이신보는영어와한어로셔계민
일츌판ᄒᆞᆸ

신문가

ᄒᆞᆫ쟝 엽두돈오푼
일삭됴엽두량닷돈 맛돈으로
밧ᄉᆞᆸ

광고료는

귀한의쟝단과ᄌᆞ졍의다쇼로ᄌᆞᆼ
감ᄒᆞ되면가로밧을터이오며
뒤지아녀대한사람마다이신
문을보실터이니광고버시기를
원ᄒᆞ시는이들은우리신문사에
와셔면약ᄒᆞ심을희망ᄒᆞᆸ

○발힝소 박동대한미일신보
사별어학교압해젼영국인셜필
림졍자리오

사쟝 영국인 (베셜)

본사지졈

인쳔항교쟝동신지명씨로우리
대한미일신보사인쳔항지졈쟝을
틱졍ᄒᆞ엿스오니인쳔항에계신
구람코자ᄒᆞ시는쳠군ᄌᆞ는희지
졈에왕림편의ᄒᆞ심을

사고

○우리대한미일신보의목뎍은
대한의인녕질셔에관한모든데
목에티ᄒᆞ야는공평한번론을쥬
쟝ᄒᆞᆷ이라우리등신원의람보는
신문보시는쳠군ᄌᆞ의게ᄒᆞᆫ상보
도ᄒᆞ려며편지를거셔ᄒᆞ며주시
는이는셩명과번디를쟈어붓치
시기를희망ᄒᆞ오니이거슨신문
샹에긔쟤ᄒᆞ란는거시아니오다
만구ᄒᆞ신용ᄒᆞ는즁거를숨고자
ᄒᆞᆷ이라긔쟈는아모긔셔던지과
져ᄒᆞᆯ뢰쟈ᄒᆞ는권리를가졋스오
나뢰쟈ᄒᆞ는리유를말ᄒᆞᆯ터이오
며공즁평화를문란케ᄒᆞ는듯ᄒᆞᆫ
긔셔는의뢰ᄒᆞ박지안켓ᄉᆞᆸ나이
다

사고

○본사에셔는신문갑슨미월에
션금으로밧ᄉᆞ오며본신문은우
톄로붓치는고로본사에셔는다
른신문사쳐름금액을거두러ᄃᆞᆫ
니지안ᄉᆞ오니우리신문을ᄉᆞ랑
ᄒᆞ야구람ᄒᆞ시는쳠군ᄌᆞ는양력
미월쵸에리월됴션금과거쥬
셩명등호수를ᄌᆞ세히젹어셔박
동본사로보내시기를바라오며
양력금월회일니로션금을아니
보내시는곳에는릭월일일부터
신문을아니보내리이오니죠량
ᄒᆞ옵소셔

●본사에셔아직긔계를쟝만치
못ᄒᆞ와다른티셔박여오는고로
미양월요일에는출판이대단히
늣게되는듯스로분젼이미우늣
게되오니우리신문을구람ᄒᆞ시
는쳠군ᄌᆞ는 용셔ᄒᆞ여주시심
을희망ᄒᆞᆸᄂᆞ이다

론셜

참졍평결

○향일에참졍신샹ᄒᆞᆫ씨가졈사
총쟝쳥양운닉부대신조병필닉
부쳥판리봉리젼경위총판리근
틱수씨를탄힉ᄒᆞ야상 주ᄒᆞᆷ
에티ᄒᆞ야제가를무르지못ᄒᆞ고
그주본이즁지가되는고로참졍
미시무치아니ᄒᆞ는지라이럼으
로여항론에빌이심참졍이쟝
차사직소를밧친다고도ᄒᆞ며ᄒᆞ
은벼슬을갈이고시골로가리라
고들ᄒᆞ야도쳥도셜이분운ᄒᆞ더
니작일은관보를본즉ᄒᆞᆫ연신씨가
참졍지임을갈이고등진관이되
엿다가또단시쳥도원총졔로이
일이되엿고쳥도원총졔신기션
씨는참졍을슈임ᄒᆞ엿스니
우리는졍부에엇더ᄒᆞᆫ사름이던
지임히되는거슨상관ᄒᆞᆯ거시업
고다만오날시국에티ᄒᆞ야시가
히시졍기션ᄒᆞᆯ제릉이잇는자가
졍사를쟝케되면진셜노
죵ᄉᆞ와민국의힝복인고로오리
로옹쥬ᄒᆞᆷ이미밧게엇거니와근
일문론을듯게되면금번참졍기
체됨에티ᄒᆞ야조야인심이대단
히셥망지탄이잇스즉이거슨엇
젼셔담힌고ᄒᆞ면사름마다말ᄒᆞ
기를신참졍의셩힝이능히 젼
싱을감격지못ᄒᆞᆷ으로참졍의지
위를비럿다고도ᄒᆞ며또ᄒᆞᆫ자는
신참졍혜ᄒᆞᆯ의참졍구귀로인ᄒᆞ
야에 괸치못ᄒᆞ는셕담에버슬
을갈게ᄒᆞ고ᄒᆞᆫ양ᄒᆞ는뜻이잇서고
린ᄒᆞᆷ이라도말ᄒᆞ니귀쟈는이두
사름의말이엿던케가ᄒᆞ믜을만
ᄒᆞᆫ지알수업스되만일ᄒᆞ나라도
이와굿흔진뎐엇지국가의복이
라ᄒᆞ리요

대기참졍은귀위 대황졔폐
하의신용ᄒᆞ시는소즁이잇고나
라로ᄒᆞ여곰후젹ᄒᆞ는의분을담
부ᄒᆞ엿슨즉맛당이조고마ᄒᆞᆫ일
로구괴ᄒᆞᆯ거시업고아모조록몸
고싱ᄒᆞᆯ셩으로나라를위ᄒᆞ야몸
이곤ᄎᆡᄒᆞ드리도위엄ᄒᆞ신 은
혜를보답ᄒᆞᆷ이가ᄒᆞ거늘엇지ᄒᆞᆫ
번 샹소에승비치못ᄒᆞᆷ으로거
연이가기를구ᄒᆞ고져ᄒᆞ며또구
귀ᄒᆞᆫ다는말은더욱말ᄒᆞᆯ거시업
는지라이런위급존망지츄를당
ᄒᆞ야오히려소쇼ᄒᆞᆫ구귀의혐의
가잇다고이에벼슬을버리고한
가ᄒᆞᆫ데나아가려ᄒᆞ리오이는다
불론의쥬목ᄒᆞ는바요실망ᄒᆞᆷ이
라도라보건티시국이엄마금졀
박ᄒᆞ진티오호라우리는신참졍
비능히광셰제민ᄒᆞᆯ망을갑당
치못ᄒᆞ겟다ᄒᆞᆷ이아니로티특별
히싱참졍을위ᄒᆞ야고위를버림
을가셕히너여봇슬장으민능히
긔탄ᄒᆞᆷ이업지못ᄒᆞ미어니와오
적원컨티신참졍은블일노분발
려졍ᄒᆞ야써광셰제민ᄒᆞ는칙임
을담보ᄒᆞ기를우리의간졀
히희망ᄒᆞ는바라ᄒᆞ노라
본과쟈가신참졍이샹소씨를
탄힉ᄒᆞ야샹 주ᄒᆞᆫ후에하회의
엇지됨을보려기드리더니그
주본이중지가되며블론에참졍
이스졔ᄒᆞ고탁향ᄒᆞᆫ다고들ᄒᆞ미
의아히지내다가수일젼죠지에
신참졍이맛ᄎᆞᆷ버졔임이됨을보
고비단블론의혀ᄒᆞᆫ의아지생
이업슬수업슬ᄲᆞᆫ아니라본긔쟈
도미샹블긔히녀ᄒᆞ는마티말
을붓쳐귀계코져ᄒᆞ엿더니맛ᄎᆞᆷ
ᄒᆞᆼ셩신문론셜을보민의가딕합
ᄒᆞ기로그티로등진ᄒᆞ노라

잡보

○대관방송 송병쥰씨가츌티
ᄒᆞᆫ이후로일본수령부에잇서국
파유세령ᄒᆞᆫ지라박보국죠보국
모씨가방문ᄒᆞ엿다더라

○강셔원류 셔창보씨가평남
강셔군ᄉᆞ로재임시에향교를슈리
며궁민을구휼ᄒᆞ며학교를ᄒᆞ괴
ᄒᆞ며부로를후티ᄒᆞ야빅폐가잉
셔지고은군이소복되는고로인
민이칭송ᄒᆞ되벗헌나라배소부
두모룸금세상에다시본다ᄒᆞ더
닉불의에취임ᄒᆞᆯ지라일군인민
등이동심으로상의ᄒᆞ고셔군슈
를원류ᄎᆞ로경부에호소ᄒᆞ지ᄒᆞ
엿다더라

○한일구락부 한일량국교졍
이졈졈친밀ᄒᆞ고시졍기션ᄒᆞ는
데도유조ᄒᆞᆯ일이잇다ᄒᆞ야졍부
에셔는한국에주차ᄒᆞᆫ일본문무
관졔씨의게한일구락부셜립ᄒᆞᆯ
수를교셥즁이라는일은거월비
리로젼파ᄒᆞ는티일본문무관졔
씨도찬셩ᄒᆞ는자가불소ᄒᆞ며졍
부에셔는기위 황샹폐하의비
의를봉승ᄒᆞ엿다ᄒᆞᆫ즉그셜립ᄒᆞ
는긔한도불원ᄒᆞ리라ᄒᆞ며그구
락부는졍부각대신과관리즁
쥬임관과기타초아에잇는어리
명수를을합동ᄒᆞ고일본관리즁
에는공ᄉᆞ령ᄉᆞ와공평관소속관
원들과기타찬셩자를합동ᄒᆞ고
그경비금은량국인즁으로셔비
비ᄒᆞ여낸다더라

○포살한민 샹화갑리교영쳘
씨가외부에보고ᄒᆞᆫ되양쥬사ᄅᆞᆷ
김빅조를일본병참소에서장아
다가수죄ᄒᆞᆫ말이군령을메시
ᄒᆞ야텬도를방히ᄒᆞᆫ나군수상형
동에구인된다ᄒᆞ고본월이십이
일샹오십시에항구밧지동에서
포살ᄒᆞ엿다ᄒᆞ엿더라

○쾌셜보교 평안남도관찰ᄉᆞ
리중하씨가내부로보고ᄒᆞ기를
평양외성에일본텬도티에서오
월망간에대위도면씨가하빈ᄒᆞ
야명거쟝셩계에표목을세운일
은이왕보고ᄒᆞ온바저금ᄒᆞᆫ일미
졍케밧게남부으로디단을면광
졈ᄒᆞ야다시립표ᄒᆞ거시그쟝이
일쳔이빅여보요광이수빅보이
온티빈가빅여호와밧메쳔이랑
과외셩젼쭉이다고중에드럿수
오닉교제샹레면에반다시이런
리치가업슬리인티젼의일의경
계를확실히닉ᄒᆞ고빈호를쥐쳘
ᄒᆞ야옹겻는티지금에엇지ᄒᆞ야
티방관에게문의치아니ᄒᆞ고ᄌᆞ
의로광졍ᄒᆞ는거시일미성히아
ᄒᆞᆼᄒᆞ기로병참부에힐문ᄒᆞᆫ즉팔
도텩로밀이칭탁ᄒᆞ미텬도의간
수ᄒᆞ는일본리ᄉᆞ의게무론즉말
ᄒᆞ기를인쳔텬도감부에서명령
ᄒᆞ여티계를넘히라ᄒᆞ엿다ᄒᆞ논
고로티답ᄒᆞ기를원졍폐ᄒᆞᆫ이외

에ᄂᆞᆫ계셔존지ᄒᆞᆯ디라도우리정부의명령이업스면가히ᄒᆡᆼ시치못ᄒᆞ겟노라ᄒᆞᆫ즉말ᄒᆞ기를인쳔리도감부에셔귀졍부와교셥ᄒᆞᆷ이잇다ᄒᆞ고ᄒᆞ오니아지못게라과연이런쳥구가잇ᄉᆞ온지당초의졍계가엄의극히광졈ᄒᆞ엿ᄂᆞᆫ디지금또더광활이졈거ᄒᆞᄂᆞᆫ거시신의의셔로밋ᄂᆞᆫ도리가아니오며만일또더광졈ᄒᆞᄂᆞᆫ거슬허시ᄒᆞ면존쥬의셩젼북니에오직청ᄒᆞᆫ공과지외에ᄂᆞᆫ거진업디기업슬터이오거니와젼예임의가옥을ᄆᆡ과ᄒᆞ야경외로이거ᄒᆞ엿ᄂᆞᆫ디지금또다시이거ᄒᆞ라ᄒᆞ면ᄇᆡᆨ셩이밋을곳이업슬지라급히일공관과텬도감부에교셥ᄒᆞ와더광졈치못ᄒᆞ게ᄒᆞ라ᄒᆞ엿더라

○위ᄃᆡ하향 위부경임ᄃᆡ신리하영씨ᄂᆞᆫ경로소에셔동문외로신병에됴리ᄎᆞ로츌거ᄒᆞ엿더니거이십구일에입경본ᄃᆡ로ᄒᆞᆫ왕ᄒᆞ엿다더라

○강민등소 응친왕부에셔오강에어염수세을탐봉ᄒᆞᆫ다ᄒᆞ고오강동두민샹실여명이회동ᄒᆞ야거이십구일에영친왕부에등소ᄒᆞ엿다더라

○경부이셜 의정부가원리결문외에잇더니슈옥헌안에쳐소를신건ᄒᆞ야즁용이된지라저작일하오쳘시에의졍부를그리로이셜ᄒᆞ고각부원청에동쳡ᄒᆞ엿더라

○공원불허 ᄒᆡ진회에셔공동연셜장을탑골공원장으로졍ᄒᆞᆫ다더니취공원관할인빅탁안씨가불허ᄒᆞᄂᆞᆫ고로본ᄉᆞ무소에셔최동연셜ᄒᆞᆫ다더라

○류민청휼 외부에셔니부로조회ᄒᆞ되창원감리보고를거ᄒᆞᆫ즉본월이십일에풍우가ᄃᆡ작ᄒᆞ야본항민호삼ᄇᆡᆨ칠십륙호가표퇴ᄒᆞ고녀인칠명이수즁에ᄲᆡ져죽고빈산샹쳑이표몰되야부지거쳐되고가산즙물의표류된거슨부지기수요수쳔인명이도로에방황ᄒᆞ며호곡ᄒᆞᄂᆞᆫ졍경이비우슈참ᄒᆞ다ᄒᆞ엿스니상갈진퇴허청구가하로ᄉᆞ이에창상지변을당ᄒᆞ엿슨즉됴가에셔구휼지젼이업지못ᄒᆞᆯ지라청컨ᄃᆡ이수의들탁지부에이조ᄒᆞ야휼금을특하ᄒᆞ야류리ᄒᆞᄂᆞᆫᄇᆡᆨ셩을면졍케ᄒᆞ라ᄒᆞ엿더라

○일ᄉᆞ함쳥 일본공ᄉᆞ가공함ᄒᆞ고등신원총관민샹호씨와외부협판윤치호씨를작일하오에본공관으로왕림ᄒᆞ라고청ᄒᆞ엿다더라

○쳥발경비 죠공수민희셰가외부로공함ᄒᆞ되주일공관금년도경비를칠쳔여원을취관에셔지발치아니ᄒᆞ엿스니탁지부에이죠ᄒᆞ야즉시지발케ᄒᆞ라ᄒᆞ엿더라

○인부담판 경셩주차일본ᄉᆞ령관원구와직등씨가작일에회위씨를방문ᄒᆞ고인부ᄉᆞ건으로수시간을담판ᄒᆞ엿더라

○지쟝원계 평리원지판쟝셔리권즁현씨가ᄉᆞ지ᄒᆞᆫ이후에모든죄슈를쳐결ᄒᆞ야법부로보고ᄒᆞ엿더니법부에셔엇던거슨ᄲᆡ여버리고엇던거슨쳠입ᄒᆞ엿ᄂᆞᆫ지라권지쟝이과히이케임ᄒᆞ기를원ᄒᆞᆫ다더라

○봉방미방 수죄이하방셕ᄒᆞ란신샤면죠칙이나린신이후에평리원과한셩재판소죄인은주원ᄒᆞ며방송ᄒᆞ엿거니와싱샹도각재판소죄슈의방송ᄒᆞᆯ자와감등ᄒᆞᆯ자를성칙ᄒᆞ야법부에보고ᄒᆞᆫ지임의삼십여일이지낫ᄂᆞᆫ디법부대신유비동이 만슈셩졀인즉 주본을드릴슈엽다ᄒᆞ고젹치ᄒᆞ며두민이린주본은ᄒᆞ오셩ᄒᆞᄂᆞᆫ졍령인디무슴구괴ᄒᆞᆷ이잇스리며임의노헌죄인을수례슈케ᄒᆞ니엇지이진사름의정수란ᄇᆞ리오ᄒᆞ며법부로정소ᄒᆞᄂᆞᆫ자가답지ᄒᆞᆫ다더라

○하우창발 일진회ᄂᆞᆫ일인을의뢰ᄒᆞ야셜립ᄒᆞᆫ자오보안회ᄂᆞᆫ충분을격동ᄒᆞ야나오ᄂᆞᆫ자인디일병이일진회ᄂᆞᆫ보호ᄒᆞ며보안회ᄂᆞᆫ무어시방히가될가의려ᄒᆞᆷ인지회동ᄒᆞᄂᆞᆫ디로금지ᄒᆞ더라

○면쳥인암 덕원감리가외부에면보ᄒᆞ엿스되본서쥬슈싱원명이수무에헌슈ᄒᆞ야이사름이니면가함ᄒᆞ리엿더니드른즉히원이광양으로이임되엿다ᄒᆞ니이유수ᄒᆞᆫ배를당ᄒᆞ야본셔수무가더욱번극ᄒᆞ오니히쥬슈를인임ᄒᆞ기를복망이라ᄒᆞ엿더라

○군제의정 군제의정관계씨가군부에회동ᄒᆞ야군제를의정ᄒᆞ엿ᄂᆞᆫ디위관수오십셰이샹과ᄉᆞ졸이삼오셰이샹에인원을다로퇴케ᄒᆞ야군인을감셩ᄒᆞᆫ다ᄒᆞ더라

○외숙기학 지작일하오팔시에어의동해진의숙에셔츄긔시험을힝ᄒᆞᄂᆞᆫ디숙쟝은찬졍권즁현씨요학원은범빅여명이라더라

○셜치호소 과쳔거ᄒᆞᄂᆞᆫ안종호란자가경무쳥에고소ᄒᆞ엿ᄉᆞ되본인의쳐가도라ᄒᆞ야경셩에은신ᄒᆞ엿스니탐쳑ᄒᆞ야달나ᄒᆞ엿다더라

○민욕타살 양쥬군에서샹리한사름의소젼을드른즉히군사름로인과쇼년간에일인이부모집수에즈원ᄒᆞ엿더니히군인민들이작당ᄒᆞ야그두사름을타살ᄒᆞᆫ다ᄒᆞᄂᆞᆫ고로두사름을본군옥에게가두엇다더라

○외대죵젹 외부대신리하영씨가일젼에인쳔으로하계ᄒᆞ엿

다고본보에괴직ᄒᆞ엿거니와ᄯᅢ문즁노씨가ᄒᆞ셜을한양ᄎᆞ로동문외엇던ᄒᆞᆫ졀에가잇다ᄒᆞ며후셜은황부디기잔수를조직ᄒᆞ노라고신문외시젼에나가잇다ᄒᆞ고도ᄒᆞ며혹은남문니에셔보앗다ᄒᆞᆫ다ᄂᆞᆫ디취부비셔관원들도히대신의거쳐를부지ᄒᆞᆫ다더라

셜취초모 강화로셔샹리ᄒᆞᆫ사름의말을드른즉히부윤윤쳘규씨가년부모집수에괴이ᄒᆞᆫ계칙으로모집을별방ᄒᆞ엿다ᄂᆞᆫ디그수실을드른즉히군남문니외에젼왕ᄒᆞ야연셜ᄒᆞ기를너가며괴지잇스니너의에디졉은되엿ᄂᆞᆫ지라너의등은청국을가면유탐도잘ᄒᆞᆯ셴아니라이년에샤젼을계ᄒᆞ야본즉만여량이란너의등은이셔즈원ᄒᆞ면가라ᄒᆞᆫ빅가면에서삼수인시민명에수쳔란식주고수셔초모ᄒᆞ야발졍ᄒᆞᆫ자가비샹오인이라더라

관보

관보 뎨이쳔구빅삼구호
광무팔년팔월삼십일일
셔임급ᄉᆞ령
의원면본관 시종우례수주수
리쥰영 임시종우례수주수서관임관오등 부산우례수주수 유궁진○면본관 광주우례수주수 서병희 임광주우례수주수서관임관이등 원산우례수주수 김용빈 임원산우례수주수서관임관오등 젼주우례수주수 진희셩
이샹팔월이십칠일
○임농상공학교교관서관임관륙등 송지관 임외국어학교부교관서관임관륙등 김원셩 최영휘
이샹팔월이십구일
○견칙 학부주ᄉᆞ 김정운
팔월이십구일
공명록수
○의정부참졍 신긔션수직소비지비에이간우ᄒᆞᆫ괴회에엿지수양ᄒᆞ리오못힝공ᄒᆞ라
○농상공부대신 권도쥐수직소 비지비계ᄉᆞ양말고곳힝공ᄒᆞ라
○외부대신셔리외부협판 윤치호수작소 비지비에번거이수양말고곳시무ᄒᆞ라
이샹팔월이십구일

광고

○관립중학교학원모집광고
○현금에관립중학교학원을모집ᄒᆞᆯ터이니입학ᄒᆞ기원ᄒᆞᄂᆞᆫ자ᄂᆞᆫ구월구일(음력칠월삼십일)너로품쳥ᄒᆞᆫ줄본부로구쳥ᄒᆞ고당일에본부로리도ᄒᆞ야입학시험에응ᄒᆞᆯ수
광무팔년팔월이일 학부

중학교학원시험과목
일은 국문독셔 작문사조
이ᄂᆞᆫ 산술문ᄃᆡ 필수문ᄃᆡ
삼은 한문독셔 작문사조
ᄉᆞᄂᆞᆫ 디지문ᄃᆡ
오ᄂᆞᆫ 입학자의년령은십칠세이샹으로 이십오세ᄭᆞ지
품쳥즁지ᄂᆞᆫ본부로리도ᄒᆞ야구용ᄒᆞᆯ수

각외국어학교학원모집광고
각외국어학교(일영법한덕)학원을가취ᄒᆞᆯ터이니입학ᄒᆞ기원ᄒᆞᄂᆞᆫ자ᄂᆞᆫ본월삼십일일〔음력칠월이십일일〕너로품쳥즁을본부로구쳥ᄒᆞ고당일에본부로리도ᄒᆞ야입학시험에응ᄒᆞᆯ수
광무팔년팔월이십이일
학부

○각외국어학교학원시험과목
일은 국문독셔 작문
이ᄂᆞᆫ 한문독셔 작문
삼은 년령십오세이샹이십삼세이하
품쳥즁지ᄂᆞᆫ본부로리도ᄒᆞ야구용ᄒᆞᆯ수

○관립농상공학교학원모집광고
○현금에농상공학교를신셜ᄒᆞ고공업과를위션교슈ᄒᆞᆯ터이니입학ᄒᆞ기원ᄒᆞᄂᆞᆫ자ᄂᆞᆫ구월이십이일(음력팔월십삼일)너로품쳥즁을본부에구쳥ᄒᆞ고당일샹오십이시에본부로리도ᄒᆞ야입학시험에응ᄒᆞᆯ수
광무팔년팔월이십이일

외보

○로황티ᄌᆞ 동일통신에왈로국황티ᄌᆞ세례식에참예ᄒᆞᄂᆞᆫ교부들즁에덕국황뎨와영국황뎨와밋단국왕이드럿다더라

○포로호송 본월이십삼일광도발뎐을거ᄒᆞᆫ즉로항루텍크호의포로수빅이십ᄉᆞ명과기타히륙젼의포로일빅삼십이명ᄭᆞ지작야에우픔에드러왓고오늘아참에두번에분ᄒᆞ야히로로호송ᄒᆞ엿다더라

○무션뎐신 마드릿드에셔온보고를거ᄒᆞᆫ즉셔반아국통군은이수히에무션뎐신에쇼용ᄒᆞᄂᆞᆫ밧면신귀계를슈린에시험ᄒᆞᆯ터ᄋᆞᆫ유동ᄒᆞ엿ᄂᆞᆫ디샹거가일빅삼십리로미돌되ᄂᆞᆫ곳사우히셔셔로통신이쾌히되ᄂᆞᆫ지라이시험에ᄂᆞᆫ셰리롬친의형식과계를쎳고또그리ᄒᆞᆫ터에일발면소ᄂᆞᆫ마드릿드에두고대에이발면소ᄂᆞᆫ쎌나--괴ㅣ답나마ㅣ를지나아렛조로썽에이동ᄒᆞ엿ᄂᆞᆫ디그샹거ᄂᆞᆫ일빅삼십칠리로미돌이오그즁간에ᄂᆞᆫ이천미돌되ᄂᆞᆫ슈림이무셩ᄒᆞᆫ산이잇셔도오히려뎐보를셔로교환ᄒᆞ엿다ᄒᆞ며이시험ᄒᆞᆯ제덕국황뎨와포르투갈왕이참셕ᄒᆞ엿다더라

KOREA.

FROM THE N. C. HERALD'S CORRESPONDENT.

Seoul, 1st August.

Korea's fraternal relations with Japan are almost at the breaking point. This "waste land" has indeed turned itself into a howling wilderness, and we hear threatenings from all quarters. The following translation of a placard will show something of the attitude of Korea's mind :—

ASSOCIATION TO PRESERVE PEACE.

We respectfully call attention to the fact that our country (Korea), is confronted by a demand of the Japanese for its hills, forests, streams, lakes, unoccupied and waste lands. This fact is already known to the people. If, we ask, our standing as an Empire? If our Empire be lost to us, how about our people, where will they be? On this account our fraternity including the great and the small has formed itself into an association to resist these demands. The byelaws, etc., were not yet fully drawn up, when yesterday at noon, two unknown Japanese broke up the meeting saying they were sent from the Legation with orders to arrest our leader. Into the crowded square they came with violence, firing off their revolvers, and in the tumult that followed they carried away our chairman and we know not where he is. Alas, brethren, will you put up with this sort of thing? Will you sit by quietly at such a time? If you regard this with indifference to-day and tomorrow, it will not be a question of our land but our people themselves will be but fish and flesh, and there will be no help for it. For this reason let the few members left us step on after our leader, and today, at 10 a.m., hold another meeting. All you brethren who have the spirit of life in you come, and give vent to your loyal anger. Let us meet and if but the ten thousand weaklings (hairs) join forces, and the "ten thousand horses roar," we will save our land and perhaps save our brethren from becoming flesh and fish.

CHEUNG IN-HO,
Chairman.

This was printed and scattered broadcast on the 16th July and since that time a strong anti-Japanese feeling has been fermenting. Other arrests have been made with no end of wild rumour of shooting and beheading. Koreans and Japanese cannot mix, I fear, any more than oil and water. With Japan it is twentieth-century methods that count for everything; with Korea it is the five original elements, metal, wood, water, fire, and earth. Whether it be an international treaty or only a common everyday marriage, the symbolical elements of the contracting parties must agree or disaster will immediately proceed to follow. There is no room as yet for the twentieth century in the soul of the Korean where these Oh-h'ang (Five Elements) are so deeply ingrained. Where the husband and wife quarrel, or there is a sudden death, or a land slide overtakes the town, or a flood, there has been some bad matching of the Oh-h'ang that has had to do with it.

On the walls of the room where I write I see posted up what translated means, "1869—Trees of the Forest, 1872—Metal of the Sword Blade, 1887—Water of the River, 1893—Word of the Willow, 1904—Water of the Well, 1908 Fire of the Lightning Flash," etc., etc. The years are all tabulated and men, women, and nations, fall under their fates as surely as the sun goes round the earth.

The master of the house where I now reside is a professional at astrology and fortune-telling.

"What do you think about Japan?" I asked.

"Japan? I understand that she is being licked by the Russians," was the reply.

"Yes," I replied, "that's all right, but what's Japan's natural element?"

At once he answered "Fire, Japan is Fire, consuming and rising; as long as she lasts she'll try to mount up to heaven.

"What is Korea?"

"Water. Runs anywhere that someone happens to lead the way."

"Will they agree?" I asked.

"Never," was the answer, "How can fire and water agree; they are diametrically opposed and will fight to the death."

There is more truth than imagination in the fortune-teller's view. Japan and Korea cannot agree, and there must come about some similarity of thought before they ever can.

The present movement against the Japanese will add to Korea's misery and only heap up sorrows on her hoary head.

It is said that, when the Japanese gendarmes arrested the leader of the Peace Society in the public square of the city, one of them, who spoke Korean fluently, said "You people think you are in a tight box these days, but so are we all, I want this man," and he marched off the leader.

Korea and Japan hitched together will never make a team. Balaam's ass and the Flying Scotchman could not hit it off worse. The Scotchman had better take the ass on board and teach him how to read a just his stomach and lungs so that they may be able by-and-by to work by steam and electricity.

ESSON THIRD.

VON PLEHVE'S SUCCESSOR.

London, July 30.—A special from St. Petersburg to the "Agencie Russe says that Count Ignatieff will succeed the late M. von Plehve as Minister of the Interior.

Nicholas Pavlovitch Ignatieff is over seventy-two years of ago. Twenty years ago he was the most prominent man in Russia, with the single exception of the Emperor. He fought in the Crimean war and shortly after its close entered the diplomatic corps. In this work he was destined to gain a great name for himself.

He was a leader in Russia's Asiatic expansion policy and in 1860 arranged the treaty with China by which Russia, without having fired a shot, received the whole basin of the Amur, over 1,000 miles of coast and twenty-two ports, and the boundaries of the empire of the Czar were extented to the Celestial mountains.

Previously he had been sent on a special mission to Khiva and Bokhara, where he drew up commercial treaties favourable to Russia.

In 1864 he was appointed Minister at Constantinople, where his legation was afterward (1867) raised to the rank of an embassy. Apart from his rank as Ambassador he was a Lieutenant-General and general aide-de-camp to the Emperor. The object which General Ignatieff steadily pursued at Constantinople was to secure for Russia powerful influence over Turkey. He completely reassured Sultan Abdul Aziz as to the intentions of the Government of St. Petersburg, while on the other hand he gained the good will of the Christian subjects of the Porte by his courteous behaviour and his simulated anxiety to protect them.

In the negotiations between the various European powers prior and subsequent to the war between Russia and Turkey General Ignatieff took a very prominent part. He was recalled from the embassy at Constantinople and was appointed Minister of the Interior, from which post he was dismissed in June, 1882. He remained, however, a member of the Council of the Empire, and was appointed a Senator and President of the Academy.

The vast power which became his after his great diplomatic success in China grew with each succeeding triumph until the cash in 1882, when he fell from his high position.

Ignatieff is not an unfamiliar type of the Russian diplomat. He is amiable, affable and audacious, yet at the same time wily and deceitful. He can see far ahead, and has the skill to bring all his plans to converge to the desired focus. Like some other clever men, it has been said of him that he thinks cleverness can dispense with straightforward honesty. Accustomed to deal with the crafty races of effete Turkey and to wield the arms of a tortuous diplomacy, Ignatieff will find himself face to face with problems which require other methods than those he has been accustomed to practice.

JAPANESE SOLDIER'S LAST SKETCH.

A letter from a Russian officer named Prosiekin shows that the Japanese are artists even in death. "During our retirement," reads the letter, "we passed a number of wounded Japanese belonging to the force outflanking us. Seeing one of the these, apparently writing a letter, I went over to him. He was sitting in a pool of blood with a badly-arranged bandage on his left arm, and a look of suppressed agony on his face. Across his knee, face downwards, was a tattered map, and on this, with a stick dipped in blood, he was laboriously sketching a field gun on the top of a hill, with a little Japanese infantryman running straight at the muzzle .... I gave the artist a drink of water."

The financial troubles of Young Marques of Anglesey have caused something of a sensation in England. His quaint customs are the subject of some notes in Vanity Fair. He would dine, for instance, in dress clothes of varying colours. Blue or pink were his favourites. His collection of walking-sticks numbered over a thousand. His overcoats were another remarkable assortment. Persian lamb, sealskin, Russian sables—all were represented. In number over a hundred, they hung in ordered rows, special care of his valets, four in number. His taste in morning suits was certiainly unusual. He preferred striking patterns, and would often top a flaring check with a red tam o' shanter or other strange headgear. As for his jewels, he was a "crank on pearls." He had many necklaces of pearls, which were a favourite hobby. For one black pearl he gave £10,000.

Reports regarding the whereabouts of Mr. Yi Ha Yong, the Minister of Foreign Affairs who recently has been too ill to attend office, are rather vague. Some say that he is staying at a monastery for his health's sake, others that he has gone down to Chemulpo to obtain the benefit of sea-air, and again others say that he has city, while another party declare that he has gone to a private place to sign the Waste Land contract.

The people of Kang Wha district are more amenable to the coolie demand than in other townships. Already 25 volunteers have presented themselves at the magistracy. The Yangchun people, on the other hand, recently attempted to kill two of their fellow townsmen, who volunteered in the same cause, and their prospective victims had to seek sanctuary in the local jail.

The magistrate of Chong Cheoi, scared at the large dimensions, of a riot probably to be adopted by the inhabitants of his district as a protest against the coolie collection, has fled to a neighbouring magistracy for safety.

The Korea Daily News.

To be published daily except Sundays.
Rate of Subscription:—
Per Year, Yen 25.
Per Quarter, Yen 7.
Per Month Yen 2.50

Postage in Korea not charged extra.
Postage abroad charged extra.

Advertisements, 50 sen per day for 1 inch or less.
5 yen per month per inch.
50 yen per year per inch.

All communications to

E. T. BETHELL,
Editor and Publisher.
Pak-tong, Seou

JAPAN'S IVFLUENCE IN KOREA.

In a resent issue of the "Kobe Herald" we are accused of adoping an anti-Japanese policy and of fostering ill feeling between the two nations.

That this view is wholly erroneous we shall presently prove, but as most of the news about Korea which reaches Japan comes from Japanese correspondents in this city, it is naturally enough of a very pro-Japanese character, and by contrast our views as published in the "Korea Daily News" appear to be anti-Japanese. The "Kobe Herald" can therefore hardly be blamed for having fallen into the error.

True, we opposed, tooth and nail, the Nagamori land scheme, being firmly convinced that dissatisfaction and anarchy would be its inevitable accompaniments. We protested against the Japanese arrests of the leaders of Po An Hoi movement as we considered this action an abuse of the powers which were conferred on the Japanese by the protocol which was signed by the Emperor on the outbreak of war.

Our readers may remember that we opposed the Japanese actions principally on the ground of their inexpediency. We considered them calculated to foster ill feeling between the two countries and that at a most unpropitious time. What the attitude of the Government of Korea will be, it is impossible to say from one day to another, but the sentiments of the people are unmistakeable. The people do not like the Japanese. The ill-feeling dates from many years back but received a great impetus in 1895 when the Queen was murdered. In this lamentable affair the Japanese were undoubtedly implicated. Immediately following this, on the same day in fact, the Japanese Minister was received in audience by the Emperor and what followed we take from the official report of the proceedings as published in the "Korean Repository" for March 1896:

"At this audience, not only Mr. Sugimura and the interpreter accompanied Viscount Miura and were present, but also a certain Japanese who had come to the palace with the "Soshi" and had apparently been their leader and had been seen by His Majesty as an active participant in their work. The Tai-won-kun, who had come to the palace with the Japanese troops, was also present. Here at this audience three documents were prepared by those present and presented to His Majesty for signature, one of them being, in substance, that the Cabinet should thereafter manage the affairs of the country, another, appointing Prince Yi Chai-miun, who had accompanied the Tai-won-kun on his entrance into the palace, Minister of the Royal Household in place of Yi, who had been killed scarcely more than an hour before, and the other appointing a Vice-Minister of the Royal Household.

"His Majesty signed all these documents. Later in the day, the Ministers of the War and Police Departments were dismissed, and Cho Hui Yen was made Minister of War and Acting Minister of Police and on the 10th, Kwan Yung Chin was made full Minister of Police. Both of these men were and are supposed to be privy to the plot to attack the palace, and both were recently denounced (on February 11th) by the Proclamation of His Majesty and have fled to parts unknown. In this way, all the armed forces of the Korean Government, and even the personal attendants of His Majesty, were put under the control and orders of officials who had been more or less connected with the attack on the palace."

These appointments formed the nucleus of the detested Kim Hong Chip cabinet. This cabinet was said by the people to owe its existence to Japanese support and influence. This alone was sufficient to make it most unacceptable, but its subsequent performances did more to bring unanimous execration upon itself and its Japanese supporters.

A number of incredibly silly laws were promulgated. A Korean dearly loves a long pipe. The length of this was limited. Restrictions were placed on the size of the hat-brim and the width of the sleeves and the colours of cloths. And as a crowning piece of tyranny the people were ordered to cut off their topknots.

Had these arrogant laws apparently served any useful end, there might have been some excuse for them, but appearing to be uselessly vexatious and aiming as they did at the ancient traditions of a particularly conservative people, they aroused deep resentment which was only increased by the harshness with which the measures were enforced. The Japanese disclaimed any responsibility for these laws but the people remember that the cabinet which promulgated them was one which the Japanese were largely, if not wholly, instrumental in putting in office.

(To be continued).

THE "HITACHI-MARU" DISASTER.

FUNERAL OF THE VICTIMS.

The funeral of 635 of the Imperial guards, who were killed in the "Hitachi-maru" disaster, was held on Saturday morning at the Aoyama Cemetery, reports the "Japan Times," the cortege leaving the quarters of the Imperial guards division from the Kudan gate at 7 a.m. The remains of the unfortunate soldiers were carried in 635 separate small coffins, each being borne by the members of the divison. The first battalion of the reserve regiment followed the procession as a guard of honour, the remainder of the division lining the streets from Ichibancho to Aoyama Oyokomachi. The funeral was attended by tens of thousands from all walks in life.

There were present some 500 Shinto and Buddhist priests, and the service was conducted according to the former rites. The monument, which is erected on the slope of the cemetery facing Kasumicho, is a hewn stone 27 feet high and bears the inscription, "Tomb of the officers and men of the Second Reserve of the Imperial Guards Division killed in the "Hitachi-maru" disaster." These words have been inscribed from an autograph of Marshal Marquis Yamagata.

The Il Chin Hoi recently declared their intention of holding a meeting in the public park on September 1st, but permission to do so was refused by Mr. McLeavy Brown, who controls the property.

On the 30th inst. the members of the Po An Hoi society again met and also made a proposal to change the name of the gathering as requested by the Japanese. However they were again dispersed by Japanese gendarmes.

The military surgeons at Matsuyama have watched with great interest, states the S. C. Morning Post, the case of a prisoner of war who was wounded in the stomach at the battle of Kiuliencheng. The injury was at first thought to be nothing more than a surface wound caused by a fragment of shell, and was treated as such. Some days passed by, and the wound, instead of healing, suppurated. An operation was decided upon, when pieces of a boat and shirt were extracted. It was thought this caused the suppuration, and that the wound, being now free, would heal, but another month passed by with scarcely any improvement. Again an operation was found necessary, and some days ago Dr. Yamanaka, a military surgeon, opened the stomach. Ho probed the wound with his hand, and to his astonishment extracted a round piece of shell over an inch in diameter and two-fifths of an inch thick, weighing about a pound. The surgeons were surprised that such an obstruction could remain in so sensitive a part of the body for over two months without proving fatal. The patient is now progressing favourably.

Col. Grandprey, once French military attache in Peking, gives some, very interesting information regarding the Chinese army, in the May number of the "Revue de Paris." He says that few countries have such excellent material as China for an army, where the whole population of 420 millions consist, so to speak, of one people, displaying the same racial qualities. The Chinese is long-lived and tenacious of life. He thrives in every climate, in spite of heat or cold, is extremely thrifty, and therefore easily supported. He has nerves of steel, he can sleep in any position and in any place, and can do with a minimum of sleep. He seldom needs a doctor, and bears pain with the greatest stoicism. The Chinese is very teachable, and what he has once been taught he never forgets.

It appears that once before the late Russian painter, Vassili Verestschagin, drowned with the Petropavlovsk, very nearly came by his death on the water. For, in the earnest quest for artistic "copy," he was on board a gunboat which assisted in the crossing of the Danube at Simritza by the Russians in 1877, as described by his friend Archibald Forbes. The same desire to see his subject at first hand sent him on board the Petropavlovsk. "My first desire is to paint the truth—to paint things as they strike me"—so said Verestschagin in a long interview once, adding that "war is stupid—a stupid sport...... A battlefield is the stupidest place in the world."

The army committee have decided to dispense with the services of all soldiers over 25 and all officers over 45 years of age.

The Governor of Ping-yang complains of the excessive quantity of ground staked out for the use of the railroad.

The Foreign Office are agitating the Home Department to order the payment of a relief fund to the sufferers, by the typhoon, at Masanpo.

Mr. Cho Min Hi, who recently returned from Japan, claims $6,000 from the Foreign Office for expenses, which are orverdue to the Legation in Tokyo.

It has been finally resolved that the billets of advisers to the Foreign Office and Finance Department will be filled by Mr. Stephens (American) and Mr. Megata (Japanese).

Their "bête-noir" in the shape of the lately resigned Chief of Police, being out of the way, sorceresses and wizards are reported to have come back to their old haunts and practices.

The Chinese Government has at last decided to conform to the practice of other Governments in sending military and naval officers as attaches' to their various embassies.

The Korea Daily News.

VOL. I, THURSDAY, SEPTEMBER 1, 1904. No. 40

大韓每日申報

보신일미한대

(호일십사뎨)　(일요금)　일이월구년사ᄇᆡᆨ구쳔일

본샤고ᄇᆡᆨ

이신보는영국과한어로셔계ᄃᆡ
일츌판ᄒᆞᆸ

신문가

ᄒᆞᆫ쟝　엽두돈오푼
일삭료엽두량닷돈　ᄆᆡᆨ돈으로
밧ᄉᆞᆸ

광고료는
귀한의쟝단과ᄌᆞᄒᆡᆼ의다쇼로ᄌᆞ
감ᄒᆞ되렴가로밧을터이오며오
ᄅᆡ지아녀대한사람마다다이신
문을보실터이니광고버시기를
원ᄒᆞ시는이들은우리신문샤에
와서면약ᄒᆞ심을희망ᄒᆞᆸ
○발ᄒᆡᆼ소　박동대한ᄆᆡ일신보
사발ᄒᆡᆼ겸편집인영국인셜ᄇᆡᆯ
ᄅᆡᆼ쟈리오
사쟝　영국인 (ᄇᆡ셜)

본사지졈

인쳔항고젼동신지멍씨로우리
대한ᄆᆡ일신보사인항지졈쟝을
ᄐᆡᆨ졍ᄒᆞ엿ᄉᆞ오니인쳔항에계신
구람코자ᄒᆞ시는쳠군ᄌᆞ는힝지
졈에왕림면의ᄒᆞ시ᄋᆞᆸ

사고

○우리대한ᄆᆡ일신보의목뎍은
대한의안녕질서에관ᄒᆞᆫ모든데
목에ᄃᆡᄒᆞ야는공평한변론을주
쟝ᄒᆞᆯ이라우리동신원의탐보는
신문보시는쳠군ᄌᆞ의게ᄒᆞᆼ샹보
도ᄒᆞ리며편지를귀서ᄒᆞ여주시
는이는셩명과번디를젹어붓치
시기를희망ᄒᆞ오니이거ᄉᆞᆯ신문
샹에긔ᄌᆡᄒᆞᆫ다는거시아니오다
만극히신용ᄒᆞ는증거를숨고자
ᄒᆞᆷ이라긔쟈는아모귀서던지과
지ᄒᆞᆷ을피ᄌᆞᆨᄒᆞ는권리를가졋ᄉᆞ
나피ᄌᆞᆨᄒᆞ는리유를말ᄒᆞᆯ터비오
며공중평화를문란케ᄒᆞ는듯ᄒᆞᆫ
귀서는의례히밧지안켓ᄉᆞᆸ나이
다

사고

○본사에서는신문갑ᄉᆞᆯᄆᆡ월에
션금으로밧ᄉᆞ오며본신문은우
체로붓치는고로본사에서는다
른신문사처름금액을거두러ᄃᆞᆫ
니지안ᄉᆞ오니우리신문을ᄉᆞ랑
ᄒᆞ야구람ᄒᆞ시는쳠군ᄌᆞ는양력
ᄆᆡ월쵸승에ᄅᆡ월됴션금과거쥬
셩명통호수를ᄌᆞ세히젹어셔박
동본사로보내시기를바라오며

양력금월회일니로션금을아니
보내시는곳에는ᄅᆡ월일일부터
신문을아니보낼터이오니죠량
ᄒᆞᆸ소서

●본사에셔아직귀게를쟝만치
못ᄒᆞ와다른ᄃᆡ셔박여오는고로
ᄆᆡ양월요일에는츌판이대단히
늣게되는듯스로분젼이ᄆᆡ우늣
게되오니우리신문을구람ᄒᆞ시
는쳠군ᄌᆞ는용서ᄒᆞ여주심
을희망ᄒᆞᆸ나이다

론셜

한국에일본위력이라
일본신호하라는신문에우리의
일본졍권을반ᄃᆡᄒᆞᆷ과일한량국
간되병는일을말ᄒᆞᆷ에ᄃᆡᄒᆞ야ᄒᆡᆼ
을을드러발표ᄒᆞ엿스니죡
이거서모도잘못ᄒᆞ는일이기에
우리가불가불증거ᄒᆞ야셜명ᄒᆞᆯ
반ᄒᆞᆫ거시일본셔는한셩에잇는
일본통신원들로ᄒᆞ여곰한국에
최요ᄒᆞᆫ소문을만히탐보ᄒᆞ여간
죡우리대한ᄆᆡ일신보에셔일본
을반ᄃᆡᄒᆞ야발간ᄒᆞ는것도듯고
ᄌᆞ긔의마음ᄃᆡ로녀녀히셜명ᄒᆞᆫ
듯ᄒᆞ되번연이그론죠알고이런
케말ᄒᆞ는거시졍령붓그럽지아
니ᄒᆞᆫ는지
우리는과연렬심이로반ᄃᆡᄒᆞᆷ은
다름이아니라졍강이문란ᄒᆞ다
는말을면ᄒᆞ기어려운바졍당치
못ᄒᆞᆫ쟝샹씨의황무지긔간쳥구
ᄒᆞᆷ에ᄃᆡᄒᆞ야분쟁소발에렬심으
로론박ᄒᆞ든보안회회원들을경
계ᄒᆞᆸ시ᄀᆡᆨ쳥ᄒᆞ는일과쇼일번이
로젼쟁이미식ᄒᆞᆫ이ᄯᆡ를당ᄒᆞ야
소위계약서등건에도남의나라
황뎨폐하외게셔양ᄒᆞ시기를억
졔로쳥ᄒᆞ는바약조ᄒᆞᆫ범람ᄒᆞᆫ권
리를부란ᄂᆞᆫ거시대단히불법ᄒᆞᆫ
ᄒᆡᆼ위이죡
우리신문구람ᄒᆞ시는쳠군ᄌᆞ는
아모조록일본사름이ᄌᆞ의로ᄒᆡᆼ
ᄒᆞᆷ에ᄃᆡᄒᆞ야우리의반ᄃᆡᄒᆞᆷ을ᄎᆞ
세이보고과히ᄒᆞ시오일한량국
간에다만병만드리고도모지사
랑ᄒᆞ지아니ᄒᆞ는일본사름을ᄒᆡ도
아리집히싱각ᄒᆞᆯ거시졍부ᄃᆡ로
는엇더케ᄒᆞᆯ는지당쟈말ᄒᆞᆯ수업
스되ᄇᆡᆨ셩들은일본사름이라면
대단히조케아니역이는거ᄉᆞᆫ갑
졍샹으로ᄌᆞ연이소ᄉᆞ나는바음
인ᄃᆡ고중민심으로항원ᄒᆞ게만

드기는을마사번에　죤졍샹히
ᄒᆞᆷ으로그ᄇᆡ불리더욱심ᄒᆞ야슬
펴ᄒᆞ며ᄎᆞ무모ᄒᆞ는마음이싱기ᄉᆡᆨ
닭에일본사름의게는이거시ᄒᆞᆫ
큰ᄒᆞᆷ졍이되엿는증쟈그날에일
본공ᄉᆞ의　폐현ᄒᆞᆫ리유와슬미
이후젼후수졉을병신년사월에
소샹이편셤ᄒᆞᆫ칙ᄌᆞ되로그리됨
이기에그불평지수ᄒᆡᆼᄒᆞᆷ을죄에
게져ᄒᆞ노니
기시　폐현에다만일본샹포공
수와삼촌서귀관과밋통역관만
참예ᄒᆞ엿슬ᄲᅮᆫ아니라ᄇᆡ왕에
폐하의룡안을잠ᄒᆞ엿든ᄌᆞ와
ᄭᅵ니ᄯᅡ라는표약ᄒᆞᆫ무리들로ᄇᆡ
부리져ᄒᆞᆫ회외일ᄒᆞ기만위ᄒᆞ야무
관ᄒᆞᆫ셰을지어드리편갈셰에ᄂᆡ원
군을일병들로응위ᄒᆞ야입　젼
ᄒᆞ엿는ᄃᆡ이ᄇᆡ에세가지조목을
예비ᄒᆞ야가지고드리가서　시
압ᄒᆞ시기를쳥ᄒᆞ기를젼국수무
는ᄂᆡ각에서통할감독케ᄒᆞᆫ일과
궁ᄂᆡ대신리경직씨샹히ᄒᆞᆫᄃᆡ에
리지면씨로입명ᄒᆞᆫ일과궁ᄂᆡ칭
관입명ᄒᆞᆫ조건인ᄃᆡ　폐하계옵
서이세조관에다모도식압ᄒᆞ셧
는지라이날젼역셰군부대신과
무수ᄒᆞᆫ다길표조희연으로ᄒᆞ
야공군부대신경입평무수ᄒᆞᆫ졔
수ᄒᆞ엿다가ᄇᆡ당싱일에진영진
으로경무수쟝입을셔이엿는ᄃᆡ
이두사름이동모ᄒᆞ야범궐ᄒᆞᆫ피
게를품어동월싱ᄇᆡ일에범남히
폐하를위협ᄒᆞ야　칙령을반포
ᄒᆞᆷ으로필경도주ᄒᆞ여종젹을
을숨기엿는ᄃᆡ가련ᄒᆞᆫ음모지수
로졍부를병력으로위협ᄒᆞ고싱
지어관리출쳑과각항졍령을쳔
단이입궤ᄒᆞ야일외로조종ᄒᆞ는
지라
이렴으로니각총리대신김홍집
은젼국인민의게큰령의가되며
만구일담이모도일본세력을밋
고아모조록일본만도으는지라
고지못ᄒᆞ는ᄃᆡᄎᆞᄎᆞ로ᄒᆞ는일은
폐하의불윤ᄒᆞ신은불계ᄒᆞ고다
만일인으로ᄒᆞ여곰졔갈ᄒᆞ야방
ᄌᆞ이피샹ᄒᆞᆫ병평을인민의게고
시ᄒᆞ는ᄃᆡ
쳣ᄌᆡ빗셩들의담ᄇᆡᄃᆡ긴것과ᄎᆞᆺ
양ᄂᆡ른것과의복소ᄆᆡ큰거ᄉᆞᆯ주
리게ᄒᆞᆷ과분ᄉᆡᆨ긋치는거시며ᄯᅩ
양계로신민들상ᄉᆡᆼ이는ᄃᆡ셔
지이로지라

폐경에위혁으로이리ᄒᆞᆫ구약ᄒᆞᆫ
법률을힝ᄒᆞ야ᄇᆡᆨ셩들로ᄒᆞ여곰
피ᄒᆞ게만드는ᄯᅡ닭에분격ᄒᆞᆫ마음
들이싱겨서머ᄯᅩ오렌수구당들
은틈으로ᄒᆞᆯ더욱비기지못ᄒᆞ야
불ᄒᆞ등ᄒᆞ는ᄯᅡ닭에일도되지못
ᄒᆞ고공연ᄒᆞᆫ로귀만ᄒᆞᆼ발이되엿
는지라　미완

잡보

○츄념관난　지쟉일에참졍신
귀션씨가슈칙ᄒᆞ고힝공ᄒᆞᆯ지라
인진회에서ᄎᆞᄐᆡ위원을파송ᄒᆞ
란ᄒᆞ는ᄃᆡ의졍부가　권ᄂᆡ에잇
는고로츄념이미우곤난ᄒᆞ엿다
더라
○덕수죠회　덕국공ᄉᆞ가외부
에죠회ᄒᆞ되졔물포덕국쟝ᄉᆞ세
찬양ᄒᆡᆼ에ᄉᆞ남젼소용화약과ᄇᆞᆫ
ᄭᅥ미향ᄒᆡᆼ에졍류된것슈입ᄒᆞᆫᄎᆞ
로귀대신은향ᄒᆞ야슈입조서를
쳥ᄒᆞ녀ᄉᆞᄂᆞᆫ디샹금업ᄃᆡ라는회죠
미업스니싱히아흥ᄒᆞᆫ지리쟈시
시복ᄒᆞ라ᄒᆞ엿더라
○교하군보　교하군슈서리교
양군슈리쥬현씨가ᄂᆡ부에보고
ᄒᆞ되음력금월신륙일ᄭᅦ본군금
셩리에젼왕ᄒᆞᆫ죵일본쟝관이ᄇᆡᆨ
부모집수들만시금ᄒᆞ다ᄒᆞ여
둥츅비경화ᄀᆞᆺ고향쟝을잡아오
라ᄒᆞ는고로부등이ᄒᆞ야향쟝을
초치ᄒᆞ엿더니빗셩들이경겁ᄒᆞ
야도피ᄒᆞ는지라본관이곳희군
에젼왕ᄒᆞ야각동집강을리ᄃᆡᄒᆞ
라고반령ᄒᆞ엿더니싱쳘일죠료
에히군팔면삼십오동ᄇᆡᆨ셩수삼
쳔명이일졔히리회ᄒᆞ야호소ᄒᆞ
되인부는응모ᄒᆞᆯ수업스니모질
ᄃᆡᆼ을몰서ᄒᆞ야냐는고이길ᄒᆞ는
ᄃᆡ일본쟝관이병쟝쳘십여명을
휘동ᄒᆞ야수면으로에워싸고각
동집강을쇠노치고공갈ᄒᆞ야
왈인부일이신명을당쟝ᄉᆡᆼ아니
라만약일향완거ᄒᆞ면포살ᄒᆞ리
라ᄒᆞ고총ᄭᅦ칸환을ᄇᆡᆨ어가지고
두루는고로본군슈가몸을ᄇᆞᆯ발
ᄒᆞ여몸에칼반기를ᄌᆞ원ᄒᆞ엿더
니일헌병이집강구명을일변결
박ᄒᆞ고형벌ᄒᆞ니이일을엇지조
쳐ᄒᆞ올지등ᄇᆡᆯ히처분ᄒᆞ라ᄒᆞ엿
더라
○일인충량　일본쟝교이명과
병뎡십명이듀지미등디에젼왕ᄒᆞ
야산에올나괴물셜자쳑량ᄒᆞ

고도형셔지ᄒᆞ여가고한강연로에도쳑량ᄒᆞ엿다더라

○ᄉᆞ무원가셜 군제의정관졔씨가회동ᄒᆞ야군제의졍ᄒᆞᆫ다는말은작보에긔지ᄒᆞ엿거니와작일하오삼시에지초의졍ᄒᆞ엿는ᄃᆡᄉᆞ무원을가셜ᄒᆞ기로공론죡이라더라

○학도시취 지작일학부에셔일영법덕ᄒᆞ각어학교학도를시취ᄒᆞ엿더라

○평양긔문 평양빅셩삼ᄉᆞ십명이샹경ᄒᆞ야경부와평리원에호소ᄒᆞᆫ다는ᄃᆡ그ᄀᆡ의를득문ᄒᆞᆫ즉평양군슈팽한쥬씨가소위가하젼과무명식ᄒᆞᆫ돈과인부뎐젼등을임의비렴ᄒᆞᆫ거시일빅삼십여만량이라빅셩들이그담학홈을견ᄃᆡ다못ᄒᆞ야일군이소동ᄒᆞ야평양셩닉로둔취하고팽씨를뒤ᄒᆞ야말ᄒᆞ기를빅셩의계륵탈ᄒᆞᆫ돈을다무어세썻는냐ᄒᆞ고됴목을무른즉팔십만량은둔ᄉᆞ로ᄋᆞ리져리지목ᄒᆞ고오십여만량은빙거ᄒᆞᆯ곳이업셔셔조긔흠포라ᄒᆞᆫ지라여러빅셩들이온슌ᄒᆞᆫ말노써평양이갑오란리를지닉고소셩이못되여셔ᄯᅩ금번젼징을당ᄒᆞ여부즁빅셩들은부로휴유ᄒᆞ고류리도로ᄒᆞ야풍찬로숙을면치못ᄒᆞ엿스며촌민들은수세경년을당ᄒᆞ야거한을면치못ᄒᆞ는ᄃᆡ셩쥬ᄭᅦ셔우리의이가궁홈을싱각지아니ᄒᆞ시고빅셩의ᄢᅢ을글어기름을ᄲᆡ시니우리는다죽을지라지목못ᄒᆞᆫ오십여만량은우리를닉쥬셔셔원통홈이업게ᄒᆞ라ᄒᆞ며그즁에예수교도들은 하ᄂᆞ님ᄭᅴ도ᄒᆞ기를우리여러빅셩을불샹이여겨사도탄을면케ᄒᆞ시며히군슈의악심을버리게ᄒᆞ사우리의게어진졍ᄉᆞ를힝케ᄒᆞ소셔ᄒᆞ고눈물이흘너옷슬젹시더라ᄒᆞ며츄후ᄒᆞ야빅셩이륙속샹경ᄒᆞᆫ다는ᄃᆡ히군슈는동헌을ᄯᅥ나ᄉᆞ처를졍ᄒᆞ고잇다더라

○공ᄉᆞ면관 쥬아공ᄉᆞ리범진씨는소환ᄒᆞ기로루ᄎᆞ뎐보ᄒᆞ되환국아니ᄒᆞᄂᆞᆫ고로위션면관되엿다더라

○긔표쳥발 일젼에일본인이한강등디에립표ᄒᆞ엿고쥬동셔일본공관뒤셔지립표ᄒᆞ고ᄯᅩ남산봉두에는긔를세운고로외부에셔일관에죠회ᄒᆞ여왈모모등디가군용샹필요지디가될니만무ᄒᆞ거늘공연히립표ᄒᆞ야인심을소동ᄒᆞ고국톄를손샹케ᄒᆞ니냐ᄒᆞ고모모쳐긔ᄃᆡ와표목을다거두기를쳥ᄒᆞ노라ᄒᆞ엿다더라

○민망환임 신경부ᄉᆞ지임시에는죵로각젼에셔샹로거리에미양직젼으로통화를만히ᄒᆞ는고로샹황에편리홈이만터니톄임후에는여젼히어음으로돌니는고로샹로에방히가만타ᄒᆞ야샹민들이션씨가다시경무ᄒᆞᆫ를옹망ᄒᆞᆫ다더라

○신샹회샤 전라남도함열룡안림피등각군각포구에신샹회샤를셜립ᄒᆞ고각쳐직쥬에셔구문을슈입ᄒᆞ기로ᄒᆞᆫ다ᄒᆞ는ᄃᆡ궁닉부로셔발셔인허ᄒᆞ엿더라

○홍씨샹소 의관홍우셕씨가샹소ᄒᆞ엿다는ᄃᆡ그ᄀᆡ의를득문ᄒᆞᆫ즉ᄒᆞ엿스되공쥬관찰ᄉᆞ심건택광쥬관찰ᄉᆞ김셰긔씨는힝되ᄒᆞ고ᄒᆞᆫ거시라ᄒᆞ고물론이랏쟈ᄒᆞ야각신보에셔지긔되엿스니청컨ᄃᆡ이피당ᄒᆞ옵고슉청ᄒᆞ금ᄒᆞ랍신 칙교가절엄ᄒᆞ신뒤샹금강홍대졍환덕등이 궁즁에출입ᄒᆞ야 교훈말노 련총을옹폐케ᄒᆞ니급히엄금ᄒᆞ실거시요젼참졍심샹훈의샹 쥬ᄒᆞ온모모네신하의일은의쥬ᄒᆞ시와안법ᄒᆞ옵시ᄉᆞᄒᆞ는제ᄉᆞ건이라ᄒᆞ더라

○부진하다 닉부에는대신과협판이탄힉을당ᄒᆞᆫ고로사진치안코외부대신은치료차로동셔분쥬ᄒᆞ고학부와탁지부에는사진ᄒᆞ되농부에는졍임대신과셔리대신이서로미루며사진치안코법부에는졍임대신은참척을본고로사진치못ᄒᆞ고셔리대신은무고이사진치안코군부대신은회의쟈겹ᄒᆞ고의졍부는참졍과찬졍이칠령팔락ᄒᆞ며일국졍부가무이공허ᄒᆞᆫ모양이라더라

○기역피금 보안회를협회로긔졍ᄒᆞ야그취지셔를졍부에쟝셔ᄒᆞ고긔회ᄒᆞᆫ라ᄒᆞᆫ는ᄃᆡ일본헌병사령부에셔히회의셰칙셔를슈담ᄒᆞ야가고무삼불미ᄒᆞᆫ귀졀이잇든지군략상에방히가되겟다ᄒᆞ고회동홈을금지ᄒᆞᆫ다더라

○죠쳥쳘표 궁닉부에셔외부로죠회ᄒᆞᆫ긔에온양군슈보고를거ᄒᆞᆫ즉일인이본군온궁에와셔운현궁과지라칭ᄒᆞ고표목을세운외에ᄯᅩ궁문에횡목을세워박쳘ᄒᆞ고갓다ᄒᆞ니막즁ᄒᆞᆫ힝궁에외국인이립표ᄒᆞᆫ거시심히피샹ᄒᆞᆫ지라일관에교셥ᄒᆞ야급히것어가게ᄒᆞ라ᄒᆞ엿더라

○쳥물광졈 외부에셔일본공관에죠회ᄒᆞ되평양관찰ᄉᆞ의보고를거ᄒᆞᆫ즉부외셩졍거쟝과지외에일본인이디방관의게교셥아니ᄒᆞ고조의로더광졈ᄒᆞᆫ디단이기리가일쳔이빅더광이ᄉᆞ빅보에한가빅여호와보요수쳔묘가범입ᄒᆞᆫ즉외셩젼폭와다드러간지라이왕뎡거쟝긔디에셔외셩으로이거식킨빅셩을ᄯᅩ지금두번이로거케ᄒᆞ면그졍경이참혹ᄒᆞ다ᄒᆞ엿스니싱각건ᄃᆡ이왕뎡거쟝긔디졍ᄒᆞᆯ시에그소용을량ᄒᆞ엿슬터인ᄃᆡ이졔ᄯᅩ더광졈축ᄒᆞ는거시심히아혹ᄒᆞᆫ지라히털도ᄃᆡ에면칙ᄒᆞ야광졈디단일수를물시케ᄒᆞ라ᄒᆞ엿더라

○축보샹지 김지ᄉᆞ한죵씨가영평써에축보ᄎᆞ로작년봄에핑를쇼조ᄯᅥ니포천거ᄒᆞ는리지만씨의조뎨쥬ᄉᆞ필용씨가금년오월분에그쇠쇼진긔디에다가축보를ᄒᆞᆫ다기로김씨가에셔인ᄒᆞ나를보닉여션후지별을말ᄒᆞᆫ즉비단리씨가리굴ᄒᆞᆫ줄을조각ᄒᆞᆯᄲᅮᆫ아니라일동빅셩의공론으로즉시졍역ᄒᆞ엿는ᄃᆡ리씨가ᄯᅩ축보ᄒᆞ던소비를김씨의게징츌코져말ᄒᆞ거놀김씨가에셔그경위에부당ᄒᆞᆫ리유를셜명ᄒᆞ여되답ᄒᆞ엿더니리씨가와언류ᄒᆞ여젼ᄒᆞ야왈김씨가에셔륵탈민탑이라고ᄒᆞ며장ᄎᆞᆺ지관셔지ᄒᆞᆫ다더라

○연향물셜 외부에셔각항구감리의게됴회ᄒᆞ되음력금월이십오일 만슈셩졀에연향을셜힝치말나ᄒᆞ엿다더라

○아교무인 일아긔젼이후로아어학교는조연폐지되엿는ᄃᆡᄯᅩ일인의치의홀쌔ᄒᆞ야일작각어학교시취시에도아어학교에는원입하는쟈가일긔도업셧다더라

○외죠법관 외부에셔법국공관에죠복ᄒᆞ되귀죠회를졉쥰ᄒᆞᆫ즉긔계창기ᄉᆞ비요을과로이의히고ᄒᆞᆫ일ᄉᆞ는귀공ᄉᆞ의타파홈이되단감격ᄒᆞ다ᄒᆞ엿더라

○등소후됴 황히도지령봉산셔흥삼군빅셩이등소ᄒᆞ되금년졍월붓터일본군의군용물품을슈운ᄒᆞ노라고빅셩이다곤췌ᄒᆞ엿고ᄯᅩ오월노붓터도역ᄉᆞ에츅호ᄒᆞ야부역ᄒᆞ기로농ᄉᆞ를실시ᄒᆞ야츄셩은아죠단망이온ᄃᆡ더구ᄂᆞᆫ털도역가를불일ᄒᆞ게쥬는ᄃᆡ혹삼량혹일량이젼혹일량식을불일ᄒᆞ게쥰즉조곰면ᄃᆡᄉᆞ는빅셩은왕리로조와당일조싱이못되는고로가가호호이수빅량식부쳬ᄒᆞᆫ온지라대져농민의ᄒᆞᆫ집산이불파수빅금이온즉장ᄎᆞᆺ지지보ᄒᆞ오릿가곳일본공관에조회ᄒᆞ야털도로젼칙ᄒᆞ야삭젼을후급ᄒᆞ게ᄒᆞ라고호소ᄒᆞ엿다더라

○리씨후쥬 삼작야에젼승지리즁옥씨가소친ᄒᆞ던슌검으로더부러ᄃᆡ작ᄒᆞ야술먹는ᄃᆡ쥬졍을과히ᄒᆞ야큰소리가밧게들니거놀힝슌슌검이그슌검을착거ᄒᆞᆫ지라리씨가그슌검을엇지그닥져의호ᄒᆞ던지북셔와경무쳥으로왕리ᄒᆞ면셔야료ᄒᆞ야왈슌검욕방송ᄒᆞ던지그렷치아니ᄒᆞ면닉가즉금리복ᄉᆞ쟝에라슌겁고갓치착슈ᄒᆞ라ᄒᆞ고밤시도록쥬졍ᄒᆞ엿다더라

뎐보

동경팔월삼십일일 공ᄉᆞ관착뎐

○료양방면격젼 이십오일로브터이십팔일ᄭᆞ지그동안에일본뎨일군은격젼ᄒᆞᆫ후에안평과탕하방면의여러긴요ᄒᆞᆫ싸흘탈취ᄒᆞ고ᄯᅩ힝셩과료양의길을연ᄒᆞ야젼진ᄒᆞ고여러다른군ᄉᆞ들은안산점과사하진방면일ᄃᆡ를졈령ᄒᆞ야써뎍병을료양부근에다진ᄂᆞᆫ뎨일군의젼투ᄂᆞᆫ극히격렬ᄒᆞ고그ᄉᆞ샹이쳔명가량인ᄃᆡ대포팔문과탄약등여러가지물픔을포획ᄒᆞ엿스며그ᄌᆞ세ᄒᆞᆫ거슨츄후로뎐보ᄒᆞ겟다ᄒᆞᄂᆞᆫᄃᆡ힝셩과료양길로연ᄒᆞ야젼진ᄒᆞᆫ여러군ᄉᆞᄂᆞᆫ즁도에약간뎍병을구축ᄒᆞ엿고팔월이십팔일아참에안산점부근에셔젼고ᄒᆞᆫ뎍병의진을공격ᄒᆞ기에착슈ᄒᆞ엿는ᄃᆡ뎍병은항거치안코북방으로퇴각ᄒᆞᄂᆞᆫ죠즁이잇셔셔우리군ᄉᆞ는즉시그것을ᄯᆞ라가쳣고각종ᄃᆡ와포병단은다팔월이십팔일오젼십시에ᄉᆞ하진부근에셔혼잡히퇴각ᄒᆞᄂᆞᆫ뎍병을ᄯᆞ라가맹렬ᄒᆞᆫ포격을ᄒᆞ야몰슈이ᄉᆞ하이북으로격퇴ᄒᆞ엿고이방면에셔도대포팔문과탄약거쳐ᄌᆞ거등물을만히포획ᄒᆞ엿더라

관보

학부

시험과목

일은 국문 독셔 작문

일은 한문 독셔 작문

일은 학자의 년령은 십칠세이샹으로 이십오세ᄭᆞ지

품청증지ᄂᆞᆫ 본부로ᄅᆡ도ᄒᆞ야구용ᄒᆞᆯᄉᆞ

메이쳔구빅이십호

광무팔년구월일일

○셔임급ᄉᆞ령

급일급봉 광쥬우톄ᄉᆞ쥬ᄉᆞ 김용빈

급삼급봉 시흥우톄ᄉᆞ쥬ᄉᆞ 유궁진 원산우톄ᄉᆞ쥬ᄉᆞ 진희셩

이샹팔월이십칠일

○승셔판임관ᄉᆞ등 인쳔감리셔쥬ᄉᆞ 죠남직

팔월이십구일

○명닉장원경셔칙임관삼등 시종원좌시어 김응모

○명겸임닉장원문부리졍위원 한셩지판소판ᄉᆞ 하규일 탁지부량디국기ᄉᆞ 김용제

○명닉장원문부리졍위원 졍삼품 윤용셩

이샹팔월삼십일

○궁뎐록ᄉᆞ

○닉장원경윤승구ᄉᆞ직소 비지닉에소청ᄃᆡ로의시ᄒᆞ노라

TELEGRAMS.

JAPANESE OFFICIAL REPORT.

Tokio, Aug. 31st.

On the 25th our first army attacked the Russian positions near Anping. The fighting was very severe, lasting until the 28th, when we succeeded in driving the enemy back in the directions of Liao Yang and Hai Cheng. Our casualties were about 2,000 and we captured 8 guns and large quantities of ammunition.

Our army advancing from Hai Cheng made preparations to attack the Russian position at Anshantien but on the 28th when we arrived it was found that the Russians were in retreat. We followed and drove them as far north as Shaochien. We captured 8 cannons, ammunition and supplies.

COOLIE VOLUNTEERS.

The acting magistrate of Kioha, Mr. Yi Chai Kyong reports officially that on the 23rd ult he received a visit from the Japanese military authorities, who urged the necessity of the immediate collection of coolies and asked him to call on the vice-magistrate to commence the work at once. Mr. Yi then went to the principal town of the district and called out the head men, telling them to bring together volunteers for coolie work and report at the magistracy on the following day. Next day his office was besieged by many hundreds of people, who implored him to intercede on their behalf with the Japanese and inform them that no volunteers could be found. Thereupon 70 soldiers were sent by the Japanese commanding officer and the head men of the villages were surrounded and threatened with immediate death by Japanese bullets unless each immediately produced 20 coolies.

Mr. Yi Chu-hyon asks for special instructions as to how this extraordinary case is to be dealt with.

THE STREET CAR SYSTEM.

The month of August, just closed, has proved a record for the Street Car system of the American Korean Electric Co. The following are the results as shown by the Company's traffic report.

Total number of passengers carried, 355,577, constituting an average of 11,470 per day.

Total number of miles covered by the Company's cars, 30,865.

During the month the company handled 171 carloads of freight, mostly from the river to the city. The increase in traffic during August of this year, over the corresponding month last year, is 60.2%.

It is very satisfactory to be able to report the progress this excellent service is making. In this city, where means of conveyance are so limited and undesirable, the street car fills a much-felt want, and it only seems a pity that the system is not extended to a larger radius.

REAR-ADMIRAL WITGEFT.

Rear-Admiral Witgeft, the late Commander-in-Chief of the Port Arthur Squadron, was of German descent. On the precipitous flight of Admiral Alexieff from Port Arthur at the beginning of May, Admiral Witgeft was appointed naval commander, but his talents were, it is reported, more conspicuous in naval administration and organization than in actual fighting. From 1899 to 1904 he was the Chief of the Naval Staff of Viceroy Alexieff. He was chiefly responsible for the repairs and the general rehabilitation of the shattered fleet at Port Arthur, and for its bold sorties from the blockaded harbour. Prior to his promotion to the rank of Rear-Admiral in 1899, he was captain of the "Dmitri Donskoi," 1895-8, and of the battleship "Oslabya," 1898-9.

At another meeting of the army reorganisation committee it was decided that their number must be increased, 12 being considered insufficient to deal with the weighty problem.

The Education Department, on the 30th ult., held an examination of candidates for scholarships in the various foreign schools.

The burden to be placed on the shoulders of the new Financial Adviser is likely to be heavy. In addition to his actual duties, we understand that the military reorganization committee intend to take advantage of his experience and ask him to assist them in their work of army reform.

The Magistrate of Ping-yang has squeezed $300,000 during the last few years out of his people, who at last have determined to resist his oppression. They recently surrounded his house and demanded the return of their money, but of course, met with no success. They are now appealing to the Government for assistance.

THE SUPERNATURAL.

BY MRS NEISH.

"Majorie," said Lady Isabel, "do you believe in the supernatural?"

"Do you mean religion, Isabel?"

"Of course not," she answered, looking rather shocked. "I mean white heather bringing luck and palmists telling you your future, and presentiments, and crystal gazing, and all that sort of thing."

"Oh! I see, you mean superstition—"

"Well, if you like to call it that."

"No, I don't."

"Well, you're going tc—"

"Am I?"

"Yes; don't sniff, it's vulgar and inopportune. I've found a really successful one."

"A what?"

"A clairvoyante," she answered, "and she lives in— —street, you know, just off New Bond street."

"What does she do?"

She puts herself into a trance and tells you your past and your future."

"Have you asked her to tell you how to make an income?" I said, pleasantly.

"My dear girl, I am not always thinking of money," said Lady Isabel, severely—"besides, I don't suppose she dreams of anything so sordid. Lady Massingham is going to her to-day, and I am going to meet her there, and Evelina too, you know, the dark one, who is so pretty, and dresses so well. Do come and let her tell your future?"

I scoffed—but she insisted, and an hour later we were driving down to Madame Fanfare's rooms.

The light was so dim that for a moment I did not recognise Miss Elvaston, but I noticed a slight trembling in the voice that greeted Lady Isabel. "She's awful—perfectly uncanny, Isabel"—Miss Elvaston was almost in tears.

"What did she tell you, Mona? I do hope you haven't been a naughty girl."

I was growing more accustomed to the dimly-lighted ante-room, and saw Mona Elvaston flush and bite her lip.

"Of course not," she said hotly and with much haste.

"Has your mother been yet?—I must tell her to come."

"Mamma? Oh! no, please don't" said Mona, in a horrified voice. "She'd only ask hateful questions about me, and, at least, I mean she'd want to know how much I owe——"

"All right, I'll put her off," laughed Lady Isabel, who is always kind to and is adored by unmarried girls. "Don't take what she says too much to heart, my dear girl," she added, airily, "and take my advice, drop Lord Massingham or you'll get into a mess," and she had rustled away before Miss Elvaston had recovered her voice or lost her colour.

"Hullo! Evelina," I heard her say a moment later.

A tall, handsome girl was coming towards us, with laughing eyes that were full of mischief.

"Caught," she said, gaily, "My dear Isabel, you've sent me either to a fraud or a wonder—she has told me everything excepting how much I owe at Bridge, and she even knew I'd given Bertie up,"

"Marjorie has come to have her future told" said Lady Isabel.

"Indeed, I haven't," I said indignantly. "I came to hear yours, Isabel,"

Lady Isabel laughed. "Oh, she told me mine quite long ago; but she is very wonderful," she added, turning to Lady Evelina, "I met poor little Mona Elvaston just now, and she was almost in tears."

"H'm, she'll do some good with her rubbish if she advises Mona to give up Massingham. Lady Massingham is in there now. It's a pity Mona has taken such a fancy to him, because he's an awful humbug, Isabel; but she—well, really, Lady Masingham is his excuse, isn't she?—such a woman—ye gods, how do they ever get the men to marry them? Ta-ta, chérie, I have a party on at the Vernons, and I'm late already. Il faut que je me sauve."

Lady Isabel and I waited in the ante-room that led to the "Chamber of Futurity," as Madame Fanfare called her room of consultation. There was a heavy odour of some sickly scent that came even through the thick curtains that hung between the rooms, and I was beginning to feel quite faint and sleepy, and the hot room was filling more and more with people, when Lady Isabel exclaimed in a whisper, "Here, I've had enough of this. I feel as though we were at the dentist's. Let's go in; she knows me, and won't mind; besides, I believe something has happened—perhaps she can't come to, or Lady Massingham has strangled her." She pushed open the curtains and I followed her mechanically.

In the even dimmer light I discerned a feminine figure dressed in flowing white, leaning back with closed eyes and a deathlike face, and very dark, untidy hair. Lady Massingham's back was turned, and she seemed as though she was sitting very rigid.

"Wait—I—see—no—wait, it is all dark," the voice murmured. "Ah! Yes—your question—your husband. I see him now—he is with a fair girl—her name is Mona—be careful—watch him, be more amiable to him, more loving—more gentle, or he will leave you and go with her—it lies in your hands."

With a half-suppressed scream of rage, Lady Massingham jumped up, and Lady Isabel drew me quickly back and into the little ante-room again.

"Well, she's doing poor old Massingham a good turn, anyway, but she'll never make that cat amiable."

A moment later Lady Massingham came out, looking very flushed and very angry, and, without even seeing us, passed out and down stairs.

"Now, Marjorie, it's your turn," said Lady Isabel. But for once I ignored the compelling hand, and, running down the stairs, got into the automobile and drew a deep, glad breath of London air.

"Of all the rubbish——"

"Marjorie, don't you believe in it?"

"My dear Isabel," I said, crossly, "please don't think I am such an absolute fool. The sickly scent, the woman's ridiculous pose and voice, the whole thing is such a and obvious fraud"

"Unbeliever," she said, "go yourself and see how soon you'll be converted."

In the Park we ran across Lady Massingham.

"I saw you at Fanfare's," said Lady Isabel. "Isn't she a marvel? She told such wonderful, wonderful things."

"She is very uncanny," said Lady Massingham, with a slight shudder. "I would rather not talk about her, please."

Lady Isabel deftly changed the conversation, and soon afterwards we drove on.

"What does that fraud charge you, Isabel?"

"Me? Oh! nothing."

"When I say you, I mean her clients," I said, crossly. "What does she charge the silly women that go to her?"

"Three guineas."

"Three guineas!" I echoed. "Why, I thought the worst of them only charged a guinea."

"Well," said Lady Isabel, "you see this isn't real clairvoyance, so there's my share, too, to pay."

"Your share, Isabel—where do you come in?"

"Oh! I don't come in," she said, as she bowed gracefully to a passing man—"I only give her all the information."—London Mail.

The Korea Daily News.

To be published daily except Sundays.

Rate of Subscription:—

Per Year,	Yen 25.
Per Quarter,	Yen 7.
Per Month	Yen 2.50

Postage in Korea not charged extra.
Postage abroad charged extra.

Advertisements, 50 sen per day for 1 inch or less.
5 yen per month per inch.
50 yen per year per inch.

All communications to

E. T. BETHELL,
Editor and Publisher.
Pak-toug, Seou

JAPAN'S INFLUENCE IN KOREA.

PART. II.

These laws were subsequently repealed when the Emperor got out of the reach of his cabinet by taking refuge in the Russian Legation but not until a great deal of harm had been done.

In themselves the innovations, although obnoxious were not matters of life and death and we have no absolute proof that the Japanese friends of the cabinet were directly responsible for them.

There is however evidence that other causes were at work promoting ill-feeling between the two races. The "Japan Gazette" of June 29th 1895 translates a speech by Count Inouye on Korea. Among other things he said, "Japanese residents in Korea must be reformed." The count made three charges against his fellow countrymen in this country, lack of coöperation, arrogance and extravagance. Each charge was backed by forcible illustration. Under the second charge His Excellency said:

"The Japanese are not only impolite but often insult the Koreans. They are rude in their treatment of Korean customers, and when there is some slight misunderstanding they do not hesitate to appeal to fists and even go so far as to throw Koreans into rivers as to use weapons. Merchants thus frequently become rowdies and many of them are consequently convicted. Those who are not merchants are still more rude and violent They say they have made Korea independent, they have suppressed the Tong Haks and those Koreans who dare oppose them, who dare disobey them, are ungrateful fellows. How can the Koreans help being frightened by the Japanese? But flight follows fright and hatred follows dislike. Then it is only natural for Koreans to seek friendship with other foreigners. With restoration of peace, many Chinese are coming again to Korea; and if the Japanese continue in their arrogance and rudeness, all the respect and love due to them will be lost and there will remain hatred and enmity against them."

Count Inouye was evidently speaking from the political point of view as the increasing influence of Russia in Korea was causing grave concern among Japanese statesmen.

About a year and a half later, on November 6th 1896, we have an important speech by Count Okuma on the commercial relations between the two countries. The occasion was a deputation from the Japanese Korean Trading association, an organization presided over by Mr. Otori, who was previously Japanese Minister to the Korean Court. The report of the speech, which follows, appeared in the Japan Herald Mail Summary of November 16th, 1896. Count Okuma said:—

"The public are apt to call Korea a poor country but this is a great mistake. There was little or no difference between Japan of forty years ago and Korea of twenty years ago, in the scale of civilization. The progress of Korea since then had been comparatively rapid. Forty years ago the Japanese people had entertained strong feelings against and acted violently against foreign ministers and foreign residents. So the feeling of the Kroeans against the Japanese is not to be wondered at if compared with how the Japanese treated foreigners in the old days. The Japanese, who attained the predominant place in the trade of Korea as a result of the war, are being again driven out of the market by the Chinese now that peace is restored. This is attributed by some to the failure of the diplomatic policy, but that was not for him to decide although it might be true. There are over 10,000 Japanese in various parts of Korea besides over 10,000 engaged in the fisheries on her coasts. But it is open to question whether they are as kind to the Koreans as they should be, and he doubted whether the people themselves might not have merited cold treatment from Koreans and foreigners, as well as the loss of ground in trade in Korea. The relation of Japan with Korea is 3,000 years old, and at the present time, not only in trade, but also in her political relations, Korea is a very important factor and her independence or not has a very close relation to the balance of power of Japan, This is why Japan introduced Korea into the comity of nations. For Korea the time is now ripe to undergo a change. This is owing to her independence having been secured by the war with China. The Imperor felt sympathy with the difficulty of Korea and desired to help her out of the same, because His Majesty thought also that Korean civilization would give great profit to Japan, and the cabinet has acted according to the Imperial will. But the 10,000 Japanese in Korea are acting in such a way as to injure the honor of Japanese and they deserve the loss they suffer. An association such as this one must make an effort to root out such evil practices in the Korean settlement and if an effort be made, he felt certain that the trade would not be usurped by Chinese, as machinery could not be made by Chinese, and Japan is more generally advanced in her industries,

"Further than that, her military power must also be depended upon. But they must understand that he had no thought of threatening Korea because she is weak or of plotting intrigues. The policy towards Korea should be shaped after that of the Declaration of War in 1894. Japan must strongly oppose any obstruction of the independence of Korea. He would not think of advocating an invasion of Korea, because Korean politics are opposed to Japanese. What Japan should be towards Korea should be like a father to his son, or an elder to a younger brother. Japan may act like a father chiding his son, but should assuage his grief on the other hand. Considering this, the Koreans should be led towards enlightenment white trading with Japanese. If the Koreans were roused to activity, considerable profits would be realized in trade. The result of victory has been great as will be seen from the fact that the Chinese power, which continued for twenty or thirty years in Korea has been broken. But the ultimate profit is not so great as expected. Among the 10,000 Japanese residents there are descendants of those who have been engaged in trade in Korea since Taiko invaded the country 300 years ago. They regard the Koreans as an inferior race, while the latter consider the Japanese over-bearing and oppressive. Now if the Japanese residents in Korea would make an effort to banish these ill-feelings with a view to promote the honor of Japan, it is certain that the trade between the two countries would become prosperous. The conduct of Japanese in Korea is observed now by all the world, and so it is to be wished that still more care should be exercised. The present enterprise might confer greater benefits on the world than the subjugation of the enemy by a large army. The only thing to be feared is the ill-feeling generated among the Koreans since the time of the invasion by Taiko: once let this be rooted out, and there is no doubt tkat the trade of Japan in Korea would be greatly improved."

(To be continued).

CHINA'S EMPRESS DOWAGER.

If we endeavour, as we naturally do, to find in the record of her life a clue to the heart and character of the Empress Dowager, remarks a writer in "The National Review," our attention is at once arrested by the two characteristics which chiefly distinguish her, namely, her extraordinary force of will and her love of power, and we realize that these have made her what she is, an opportunist. Our attention is also inevitably drawn to the fact of her extreme unscrupulousness in attaining her ends and to her innate cruelty. Nothing comes amiss to her which can further her ambitions; she stops at nothing and is afraid of no one. This was proved beyond doubt during the troubles of 1900. It is evident that she recognized in the presence of foreigners in China an element of danger to herself. She therefore determined to be rid of them. Whether the Boxer movement was actually originated by her to that end, or whether, detecting in it the seeds of a revolution against herself and her dynasty, she cleverly contrived to turn its anger against the foreigner, will never be clearly known. All that seems certain is that she ended by deliberately encouraging the dastardly attack made by them, in defiance of all civilized nations, upon envoys accredited to the Chinese Court by friendly Powers. When, however, she realized that the game had failed, and that the foreigner could not be wiped out, she began to see the folly of her policy, and being equally comfortable on whichever side of the fence she sat, provided it was on the throne, she veered round and sent presents of rice and watermelons to the very people she had sought to destroy! Good luck has attended her always. Although when the allies entered Peking she was obliged to flee, yet anon she returned, her position apparently undamaged, owing to the simple fact that the Foreign Ministers could not agree as to what was the best thing to do with her should she be deposed. A figurehead was wanted with whom they could treat; she would serve as well as another. The Empress Dowager accepted the situation as it was. Being, before all things, an opportunist, it came easy to her to return to Peking and reopen relations with the hated foreigner. She simply bided her time.

San Francisco, July 26.—Naval officers and Union Iron Works officials are so enthusiastic over the showing made by the new battleship Ohio during her unofficial builders' trial to-day that they expect her to make nearly nineteen knots on her official trial at Santa Barbara, though the Government contract calls for only eighteen knots. During several runs over the measured mile to-day, the Ohio averaged 17.6 knots without any special effort, steam being carried at a moderate pressure. The fires were also not tended with the zeal that marks an official trial. The Ohio was under the general supervision of Engineer-in-Chief Forsythe of the Union Iron Works. Capt. L. C. Logan, who is to command her when she goes into commission, was on board.

Sixty fishing-boats, which were at sea off the coast near Kang Nung, are said to have been lost during the recent typhoon.

The Foreign Office have made a complaint to the Japanese Legation relative to the excessive demands of the Railway authorities for land near Pyengyang.

The Foreign Office have issued instructions to the Kamnis of treaty ports to dispense for this year with the usual feast, given at their offices, on the occasion of His Majesty's birthday.

We are pleased to be able to state that the rumour that Mr. Yun Chi Ho had resigned his position as acting Minister of Foreign Affairs, is untrue. A preliminary resignation was sent in but was refused by His Majesty and Mr. Yun has not left his post.

The Korea Daily News.

VOL. I, FRIDAY, SEPTEMBER 2, 1904. No. 41

HONGKONG & SHANGHAI BANKING CORPORATION.

Paid-up Capital..... ....$10,000,000
Reserve Fund:—Sterling Reserve... 10,000,000
Silver Reserve..... 6,500,000

26,500,000
Reserve Liability of Proprietors... 10,000,000

HEAD OFFICE, HONGKONG.

London Bankers, London and County Banking Company Limited.
Branches and Agencies,
London.

Amoy,	Hankow	Penang,
Bangkok,	Hiogo,	Rangoon,
Batavia,	Iloilo,	Saigon,
Bombay,	Lyons,	San Francisco,
Calcutta,	Manila,	Singapore,
Colombo,	Nagasaki,	Sourabaya,
Foochow,	New York,	Tientsin,
Hamburg,	Peking,	Yokohama,

Credits granted on approved Securities, and every description of Banking and Exchange business transacted.

Drafts granted on London and the chief Commercial places in Europe, India, Australia, America, China and Japan.

HOLME RINGER & CO., AGENTS,
CHEMULPO.

ON CHEONG & CO.,
SEOUL.
GENERAL STORE KEEPERS.
Imported provisions, Cooking Utensils Crockery, etc.
FRESH BREAD DAILY.

MITSU BISHI DOCKYARD & ENGINE WORKS,
NAGASAKI.

CODE WORD, "DOCK."

A. 1, A. B. C., and Engineering Codes used.

DOCK No. 1 (at Tategami).

Extreme Length..............523 feet
Length on blocks .... 513 ,,
Width of Entrance on Top......89 ,,
,, ,, Bottom....77 ,,
Water on Blocks at Spring Tide 26½ ,,

DOCK No. 2 (Mukaijima).

Extreme Length..............371 feet
Length on Blocks..............360 ,,
Width of Entrance on Top......66 ,,
,, ,, Bottom 53 ,,
Water on Blocks at Spring Tide 22 ,,

PATENT SLIP (at Kosuge).

Can take vessels up to 1,000 tons gross.

THE WORKS are well equipped with the LATEST IMPROVEMENTS, and can execute any kind of work in SHIPBUILDING and MARINE ENGINEERING, as well as in REPAIRING of SHIPS.

The COMPANY'S new powerful steamer OURA-MARU (712 tons, 700 I.H.P.), specially built for SALVAGE PURPOSES, and equipped with necessary gear, is always READY at SHORT NOTICE.

CHARTERED BANK OF INDIA AUSTRALIA & CHINA.

INCORPORATED BY ROYAL CHARTER 1853

HEAD OFFICES:—LONDON.

Paid-up Capital £800,000
Reserve Liability of Shareholders 800,000
Reserve Fund 800,000

Drafts granted upon all the principal places in the world and every description of Exchange and banking business transacted.

E. MEYER & Co., Agents,
Chemulpo.

E. MEYER & CO.
Chemulpo.

SOLE AGENTS IN KOREA FOR:
A. T. Morse, Sons & Co's "Fresco" Distemper

In all colours ready for use on walls, Ceilings etc.
and
AVENARIUS CARBOLINEUM

A wood-preserving and antiseptic oil preparation

Against decay, dry-rot, fungus and wood-destroying insects.

A large supply always in Stock.
Prices upon application.

E. MEYER & Co.,
Chemulpo.

LAW UNION & CROWN INS. CO.

Fire risks accepted at Current rates, on go downs, merchandise, dwellings, and other property, subject to usual conditions.

HOLME RINGER & Co.,
Agents, Chemulpo

THE METHODIST PUBLISHING HOUSE,
Little West Gate, Seoul.

JOB PRINTING, TYPEWRITER PAPER
CARBON PAPER, VISITING CARDS
STATIONERY, BOOK BINDING
BOOK PUBLISHERS
AMERICAN SCHOOL BOOKS
SPENCERIAN COPY BOOKS
PEN CARBON LETTER AND BILL BOOKS

S A BECK, Manager

DAI-ICHI GINKO.
LIMITED.
(Formerly the First National Bank)

ESTABLISHED 1873

INCORPORATED UNDER PRESENT LAW 1896

Capital - - - - - - - - - Yen 5,000,000
Reserve Fund - . - - - 1,500,000

HEAD OFFICE:—TOKIO.

President: Baron SHIBUSAWA.

BRANCHES AND CORRESPONDENTS
In the Principal Cities and Towns of Japan.
Interest Allowed on
Fixed deposits 1 year - - - 6½ per cent
" " 6 months - - - 6 per cent

Special current accounts 1½ sen daily per Y 100
General " " 1 " " " 100

M. TANAKA,
Manager, Chemulpo

HOLME RINGER & Co.
Chemulpo.

General Merchants and Government Contractors.

Agents for the leading
Banks
SteamshipCompanies
and
Insurance Companies

Importers of Merchandise of every description.

KAMEYA & CO.
GENERAL STOREKEEPERS
Chinkokai - - Seoul
(*Established 1895, Tokyo*)

Confectionery, Hams, Canned Goods, Cutlery, Hirano & Tansan Water. Provisions, Gents, Furnishing goods, Toilet Articles, Travelling Bags, Tobacco, Cigars & Cigarettes Kitchen Utensils. Coffee, Biscuits.

Fresh Goods always kept in Stock.
Prices Moderate
Please come and inspect our goods.

NIPPON YUSEN KAISHA.
JAPANESE MAIL STEAMSHIP CO.
DER MAIL CONTRACT WITH THE IMPERIAL JAPANESE GOVERNMENT.

European Line

Regular Fortnightly Service between Yokohama Kobe, Moji, Shanghai, Hongkong, Singapore, Penang Colombo, Port Said, Marseilles, London and Antwerp

American Line

Regular Fortnightly Service between Hongkong and Seattle, calling at Shanghai, Moji, Kobe, Yokohama and Victoria, B. C.

Australian Line

Regular weekly Service betwen Japan Ports and Australia, calling at Hongkong and Manila.
(Above Three Lines Suspended until further notice).

Sharghai Line

Weekly Service between Shanghai and Japan Ports

Korea Line

Service Kobe, Moji, Nagasaki, Fusan, Chemulpo, Chioo, Taiku.
S. S. Bahelsberg, 2181 tons.
Service Kobe, Moji, Fusan, Chemulpo, Chinnampo
S. S ARGO, S. S. Ohio.

BORDEN'S CONDENSED MILK CO.
New York, U. S. A.

ALWAYS IN STOCK
Eagle Brand Condensed Milk.
Gold Seal Condensed Milk.
Peerless (Family) Evaporated Cream.
Borden's Malted Milk.

E. MEYER & CO.
Chemulpo, Korea,
Sole Agents

ROYAL INSURANCE COMPANY,
Funds exceed £10,000,000
FIRE
AT CURRENT RATES.
LIFE
REDUCED PREMIUM.
HOLME RINGER & Co.,
Agents, Chemulpo.

HOTEL DU PALAIS
SEOUL.

The only first class Hotel in Seoul. Situated in the centre of the city opposite the palace.

Cuisine under the supervision of an experienced French Chef.

Well ventilated and furnished throughout.

TARIFF UPON APPLICATION

L. MARTIN,
Proprietor and Manager.

大韓每日申報

대한미일신보

(뎨사십이호) (토요일) 일쳔구빅사년구월삼일

본샤고ᄇᆡᆨ

이신보는영어와한국문으로셔계ᄆᆡ일출판ᄒᆞᆸ

신문가

ᄒᆞᆫ쟝 엽두돈오푼

일삭료엽두량닷돈 맛돈으로 밧ᄉᆞᆸ

광고료는

귀한의쟝단과ᄌᆞ힝의다쇼로즁감ᄒᆞ되렴가로밧을터이오며오릭지아녀대한사람마다이신문을보실터이니광고내시기를원ᄒᆞ시는이들은우리신문사에와셔면약ᄒᆞ심을희망ᄒᆞᆸ

○발힝소 발동대한ᄆᆡ일신보사발어학교압희 젼영국인셜필림쟝자리오

사쟝 영국인 (베셜)

본사지졈

인쳔항교쟝동신쥐평씨로우리대한ᄆᆡ일신보사인쳔지졈쟝을퇴졍ᄒᆞ엿ᄉᆞ오니인쳔항에계신구람코자ᄒᆞ시는쳠군ᄌᆞ는해지졈에왕림편의ᄒᆞ시ᄋᆞᆸ

사고

○우리대한ᄆᆡ일신보의목뎍은대한의인녕졀서에관ᄒᆞᆫ모든데목에ᄃᆡᄒᆞ야는공평ᄒᆞᆫ번론을쥬쟝ᄒᆞᆷ이라우리동신원의탐보는신문보시는쳠군ᄌᆞ의계ᄒᆞ샹보도ᄒᆞ리며편지들과셔ᄒᆞ며주시는이는셩명과번디를젹어붓치시기를희망ᄒᆞ오니이거슨신문샹에괴계ᄒᆞ란는거시아니오다만구히신용ᄒᆞ는증거를숨고자ᄒᆞᆷ이라귀자는아모귀셔던지과지ᄒᆞᆷ을퇴각ᄒᆞ는권리를가젓스오나퇴각ᄒᆞ는리유를말ᄒᆞᆯ터이오며공중평화를문란케ᄒᆞ는듯ᄒᆞᆫ귀셔는의레히밧지안켓ᄉᆞᆸᄂᆞ이다

사고

○본사에셔는신문갑슨ᄆᆡ월에션금으로밧ᄉᆞ오며본신문은우체로붓치는고로본사에셔는다른신문사처럼금액을게두리는니져안ᄉᆞ오니우리신문을ᄉᆞ량ᄒᆞ야구람ᄒᆞ시는쳠군ᄌᆞ는향혀ᄆᆡ월초에리월도션금과거쥬셩명통호수를조셰히기ᄌᆡᄒᆞ야본샤로보내시기를바라오며양력금월회일노션금을아니보내시는곳에는리월일일부터신문을아니보낼터이오니죠량ᄒᆞᆸ소셔

●본사에셔아직귀게를장만치못ᄒᆞ와다른데셔박여오는고로ᄆᆡ양월요일에는출판이대단히늣게되는ᄃᆞᆺ스로분젼이ᄆᆡ우늣게되오니우리신문을구람ᄒᆞ시는 쳠군ᄌᆞ는 용셔ᄒᆞ여주시심을희망ᄒᆞᆸᄂᆞ이다

론셜

젼호련쇽

아모리일본셔이러ᄒᆞᆫ법률은못ᄒᆞ게ᄒᆞ엿드리도빅셩들은시장졍코시ᄒᆞᆫ거슬보게되면모도일본서식인줄노아랏슨즉만일이러케공평이로만ᄒᆞ시힝케아니ᄒᆞ엿드면그중에되는일도잇서슬듯ᄒᆞᆫ지라

대황뎨페하게옵서국권을자힝ᄒᆞ는왕망동탁의류를피ᄒᆞ사대우히국ᄒᆞ기젼에아국공관으로파쳔ᄒᆞ신후로약초ᄒᆞᆫ법률이초초로폐지가되엿는티

비소위닉각대신들의거ᄒᆡᆼᄒᆞᆫ일은결본국사ᄅᆞᆷ관계ᄒᆞᆫ거슨엽고다만오국지사ᄅᆞᆷ으로며부러친결ᄒᆞ야확실이증거ᄒᆞᆯ거슨업스되

일청량국간에병되는일을졈졈이르긴다고분명이말ᄒᆞᆯ조건은잇는거시일쳔팔빅구십오년이십구일에(음력병신)일본졍샹이빅작이한국에ᄃᆡᄒᆞ야연셜ᄒᆞᆫ바신문에게지ᄒᆞ기를한국에주차ᄒᆞᆫ관리들을불가불기차ᄒᆞᆯ거시소위공사이한샹인이교만방자ᄒᆞ야광픽ᄒᆞᆫ힝실에동심협력ᄒᆞ엿슨즉이리ᄒᆞ고는힝졍이업다ᄒᆞᆷ으로차계로졔귀가되고그후임으로나오는졔원외계이근기를일본사ᄅᆞᆷ들이무례히아니ᄒᆞ는티한국사ᄅᆞᆷ들의능욕ᄒᆞ는거슨주권지의로티졉ᄒᆞᆷ이망미ᄒᆞ야그리ᄒᆞᆷ인즉만일평슈히이를ᄒᆞ야는일이잇거든주먹으로라도셰닷리되고리ᄒᆞ여도평의ᄒᆞ야세닷지못ᄒᆞ거든깃블에다장아보린이지퐌노라도배히라고ᄒᆞᆫ지라이랑으로샹고ᄒᆞ면도갈수록무퇴잇빈가되고여왕이겹탄ᄒᆞ는일ᄯᅩ샹교외에일이라도용렴ᄒᆞᆫ무

식ᄒᆞᆫ자들은더욱시ᄒᆞᆫ일이만은중ᄒᆞᆫ이언두에을니기를한국동림도일본셔식엿고동학들도일본셔진양ᄒᆞ엿슨즉갑히우리를빈티ᄒᆞ며우리를블복ᄒᆞ는ᄌᆞ들은대단히블공ᄒᆞᆫ놈이라ᄒᆞ며져희들이엇지우리일본사ᄅᆞᆷ들을용졉ᄒᆞ게ᄒᆞ리오ᄒᆞ는지라그러나한국사ᄅᆞᆷ싱각에는ᄯᅢᆼ은더러워피ᄒᆞ고도망은부셔워ᄒᆞᆫ다는거슬싱각ᄒᆞ야다른외국사ᄅᆞᆷ들보다더욱우의가잇는것갓치화목ᄒᆞ게지니다가청인이한국에다시나온이후에도일청교만ᄒᆞ교용ᄒᆞᆫ일을힝ᄒᆞ는고로련이지졍은업셔지고구수지심만싱겻는지라

졍샹빅작의괴왕ᄒᆞᆫ말은일본졍부에셔진중ᄒᆞ게샹관ᄒᆞ란졍은일을아라사에셔졉졉헤아셔졍권지라도권리를부리는것갓치ᄒᆞ야고리ᄒᆞᆷ이분명ᄒᆞ며ᄯᅩ그후일쳔팔빅구십륙년신일월륙일(음력정유년)에대외박작이일한량국간동샹ᄉᆞ건에ᄃᆡᄒᆞ야연셜ᄒᆞᆫ거슬본즉이왕에우리나라용수미조씨로써한국정부에고셜과ᄒᆞ야통샹약조를쳬결ᄒᆞ엿스나림ᄒᆞ엿다ᄒᆞ엿ᄂᆞᆫ티일본졍샹빅작이일쳔팔빅구십륙년샹비원시룸일에연셜ᄒᆞᆫ거슬일본히란신문에게지ᄒᆞᆫ젼문이여좌ᄒᆞ니라

우리나라빅셩들이한국을가련ᄒᆞᆫ나라이라고의례히말ᄒᆞ는거슨크게잘못ᄒᆞ는듯ᄒᆞᆫ거시일본에수십년젼과한국에이십도년젼의경이면한국에셔진보됨이홈지경이면한국에셔진보됨이ᄆᆡ오속ᄒᆞᆫ거시일본빅셩들이수십년젼에는겸화ᄒᆞᆫ주의로위티ᄒᆞᆫ일을힝ᄒᆞ야외국공수의게던지외국인의거싱ᄒᆞ는자들의게평악히빈티ᄒᆞᆫ일이잇섯슨즉귀왕일본셔도외국사ᄅᆞᆷ티졉ᄒᆞᆫ거슬본진티한국셔일본빅티ᄒᆞ지는거시실노이샹ᄒᆞᆫ거시업는지국샹엽에의ᄒᆞ야오조ᄒᆞᆫ곳을차지ᄒᆞ엿다가졍인의게블이여나왓더니지금은다시평화ᄒᆞ야회복ᄒᆞᆫ지라외국이란ᄒᆞᆫ일은말ᄒᆞᆯ진티

교샹에셜계됨이라고ᄒᆞᆫ듯ᄒᆞ나비록ᄌᆞ긔의마음대로진졍그리ᄒᆞ엿드리도무엇시라고분명이작졍ᄒᆞ여말ᄒᆞᆯ수는업스며한국이경되방에일본빅셩이거우만명디남게셔싱ᄒᆞ는중모도연히등조에셔어럽으로위ᄒᆞᆫ즉아모사록한국빅셩의게ᄃᆡᄒᆞ야가히도랑ᄒᆞᆯ만ᄒᆞᆫ일이잇거든진실노국아줄거시만일져빅셩들이외모사ᄅᆞᆷ을노ᄒᆞ며곰와ᄒᆞᆫᄒᆞ야에경도주지아니ᄒᆞ엿더면한국ᄯᅩ샹엽디라도엇지ᄒᆞ엿스리요일본이한국으로더브러상관ᄒᆞᆫ지가우금삼쳔년이되엿슨즉비단오ᄂᆞᆯ날샹업샹리익으로만말ᄒᆞᆯᄲᅮᆫ아니라졍약상관계로말ᄒᆞᆯ지라도일본은힘으로독립ᄒᆞ엿던지아니ᄒᆞ엿던지ᄆᆡ오중요ᄒᆞᆫ나라인즉엇던셔아모조록인도ᄒᆞ야례법에잇게지니야ᄒᆞᆯ거시한국이독립이되며졍졍ᄒᆞ게명ᄒᆞ야가는셔담에일쳥교전이되엿슨즉일황폐하게셔도아모조록동졍샹의리를베프셔한국으로ᄒᆞ여곰방조ᄒᆞ야기명진보케ᄒᆞ시고니각대신들도황칙을봉승ᄒᆞ야져수ᄒᆞᄂᆞᆫ거시일본에큰유익ᄒᆞᆷ이될터이되만일한국에잇는일본빅셩들이우리나라에셔공평ᄒᆞ는마음을조곰이라도샹ᄒᆞᆯ지경이면당연이순히되미잇슬터인즉아모조록무ᄉᆞ히에던지친졀히ᄒᆞ야교약ᄒᆞᆫ일을힝ᄒᆞ지아니ᄒᆞ게되면샹업샹과조블샹에도졍인의게셰잇기지아니ᄒᆞ고졈졈크게진보가될터이라고ᄒᆞ엿는지라

갑오년란리들이르킨후에이린말ᄒᆞ는거슨한국독립에일본셔방히ᄒᆞᆷ과한국을침노ᄒᆞᆷ에ᄃᆡᄒᆞ야변론ᄒᆞᆷ이아니라한국빅셩들노ᄒᆞ여곰일본사ᄅᆞᆷ을두려워ᄒᆞ야음모간계를힝ᄒᆞ는티슈도록ᄒᆞᆫ거신거시일본셔한국에ᄃᆡᄒᆞ무아부조청에간과곳치말ᄒᆞ거시계무어시뇨일본셔이러케관곡ᄒᆞ시밤ᄒᆞ는거슨한국빅셩들의슬픈마음을화ᄒᆞ게ᄒᆞ야조긔의샹업상진보가되도록ᄒᆞ리ᄒᆞᆷ인즉만일한국빅셩들이이청교전ᄒᆞᆫ원인ᄒᆞ야수십년에박은졍국권리가엿셔졋슨즉이년등을파라

운동ᄒᆞ엿더면상업상에유익홈이만핫슬터이요한민의소망과곳치모든일이다셩취가되엿슬터이요또도리여삼빅년젼에한국대구싸으로침노ᄒᆞ야드러오려ᄒᆞ든일본빅셩들의후예들이한국사름들을하등지인으로싱각ᄒᆞ야필경에는압제ᄒᆞ야젼디지못ᄒᆞ게ᄒᆞ량으로싱각ᄒᆞ엿다ᄒᆞ나그러ᄒᆞ나지금에이러ᄒᆞᆫ못된싱각을다업시ᄒᆞ고아모조록일본에진보케ᄒᆞ랴면량국간셔로공경ᄒᆞ여야상업에대단이흥왕ᄒᆞᆯ터이요또일본셔한국에ᄃᆡᄒᆞ야ᄒᆡᆼᄒᆞ는일을세계에셔따주목ᄒᆞ야보는바인즉미우조심ᄒᆞ야운동ᄒᆞᆯ거시지금에군ᄉᆞ들을이르케ᄃᆡ젹ᄒᆞ야항복바든이보다쟝ᄅᆡ큰리익이잇슬터이요또젼자에대구로드러오려ᄒᆞ다가못된바그일로병되도록깁히싱각ᄒᆞᆯ거시아닌즉다만한국에통상만잘ᄒᆞᆯ진ᄃᆡ크게진보됨도만히잇슬터이요 (미완)

관보

뎨이쳔구빅이십일호
광무팔년구월이일

○셔임급ᄉᆞ령
○임강원도관찰부쥬ᄉᆞ셔관임관륙등 경긔관찰부쥬ᄉᆞ 박창실
○임경긔관찰부쥬ᄉᆞ셔관임관륙등 차희균
이상팔월십이일
○명궁ᄂᆡ부특진관셔칙임관일등 홍문관학ᄉᆞ 남뎡철 졍이픔 리근호
○명궁ᄂᆡ부특진관셔칙임관삼등 종이픔 죠한국
○명홍문관학ᄉᆞ셔칙임관삼등 졍이픔 윤덕영
○급삼급봉 농상공학교 교관 송직관
이상팔월삼십일일
○죵견칙 즁추원쥬ᄉᆞ 빅남규 윤영권 림학슈
○일쥬일감봉 한셩지판소쥬ᄉᆞ 김창형
○견칙 법부쥬ᄉᆞ 류원셩 궁뎡록ᄉᆞ
이상팔월삼십일일
○의졍부찬졍권즁현ᄉᆞ직소비지ᄂᆡ에ᄉᆞ양ᄒᆞᆫ즁지관장셔리지임만의시ᄒᆞ노라
○평리원지관장윤덕영ᄉᆞ직소비지ᄂᆡ에소쳥ᄃᆡ로의시ᄒᆞ노라
이상팔월삼십일일

잡보

○지장임체 평리원지판장셔리권즁현씨는히셔리ᄒᆞ고졍임지판장윤덕영씨는체임되고그ᄃᆡ에는젼협판민병한씨가피임ᄒᆞ엿다더라

○군졔회의 군졔의졍관이연일회의ᄒᆞ는ᄃᆡ그의안의권한을고문관야진씨의가부를의ᄒᆞ야ᄒᆞ는ᄃᆡ탁지부고문관이리도ᄒᆞᆫ후에야지졍의족부족을예산ᄒᆞ야군익을감ᄒᆞᆯ터이라더라

○츄긔기학 하긔방학되엿든각학교에셔본월일일붓터기학ᄒᆞ엿더라

○공긔연셜 지작일하오이시에일진회에셔긔회ᄒᆞ고공긔연셜을ᄒᆞ엿는ᄃᆡ각각구별을졍ᄒᆞ야연셜위원ᄉᆞ인을ᄅᆡᆨ취ᄒᆞ야가지고연셜을ᄒᆞ엿는ᄃᆡ 황실을존즁히ᄒᆞ며국가긔초를공고케ᄒᆞᆯ연셜위원은김명쥰씨요인민의ᄉᆡᆼ명재산을보호ᄒᆞᆯ연셜위원은윤길병씨요졍부시졍긔션의연셜위원은홍셕후씨요군졍지졍을졍리의연셜위원은렴즁모씨더라

○진복운동 초동소쳥에셔셔고각ᄂᆡ로이셜ᄒᆞ고장ᄎᆞ뎨칠ᄎᆞ샹소를ᄒᆞ는ᄃᆡᄉᆞ의는대긔젼ᄎᆞ샹소와방불ᄒᆞ고소슈는젼참관윤샹학씨가된다ᄒᆞ며각시면을합동ᄒᆞ야 권문외로진복ᄒᆞ기로운동즁이라ᄒᆞ더라

○슈도즁지 궁ᄂᆡ부소관으로일본인과계약ᄒᆞ고삼청동에슈도를시역ᄒᆞ다가무삼연고인지즁지ᄒᆞ엿는ᄃᆡ히일인등은금일즘쳘거ᄒᆞ고파슈보는슌검은일쳘귀ᄒᆞᆫ다더라

○양쥬군보 양쥬군슈홍티윤씨의보고를거ᄒᆞᆫ즉일본ᄉᆞ령관길영승삼랑의죠회를쥰ᄒᆡᆼᄒᆞ야본군신쳘면구타발쥬막아리협착ᄒᆞᆫ길을삭쥬고치도ᄒᆞ엿는ᄃᆡ치도비가일빅이십오량ᄉᆞ젼이오니공젼즁으로계감ᄒᆞ라ᄒᆞ엿더라

○삼포셜슌 긔셩부에셔남문외에경무지셔를셜치ᄒᆞ고삼포에도적을경찰ᄒᆞᆯᄎᆞ로슌검이파슈ᄒᆞ더니일본ᄉᆞ령관우강졍슌씨가부윤을젼견ᄒᆞ고히지셔를쳘거ᄒᆞ라ᄒᆞ엿다더라

○위츅작폐 경샹북도인민등이ᄂᆡ부에면보ᄒᆞ되신령권마마가영쳔은히ᄉᆞ위츅을맛핫다ᄒᆞ고대구신령영쳔등디로왕ᄅᆡᄒᆞ며작폐가무쌍ᄒᆞ야빅셩의토디와젼지를무수히륵탈ᄒᆞ는고로민원이자쟈ᄒᆞ오니동촉ᄒᆞ사엄금ᄒᆞ심을복망이라ᄒᆞ엿더라

○의아일치 군무총장구영죠씨가ᄂᆡ부에면보ᄒᆞ되의쥬쥬ᄎᆞ일본병참ᄉᆞ령관면보에ᄒᆞ엿스되의쥬진위ᄃᆡ대ᄃᆡ장구완희의게본ᄉᆞ령부에셔군ᄉᆞ샹필요로요구홈을좌긋치인허홈을언ᄒᆞ야진위ᄃᆡ영문을차용ᄒᆞ엿고관사에는야젼우편국이이접ᄒᆞ엿고병졸은근방민가에차거ᄒᆞ엿다ᄒᆞ엿스니죠량ᄒᆞ라ᄒᆞ엿더라

○마면환퇴 평안남도관찰ᄉᆞ리즁하씨가외부에면보ᄒᆞ엿스되시민리일영이가즁셩에잇는삼밧륙심니랑을미국인의게방믹ᄒᆞᆫ고로방금리일영을착슈ᄒᆞ고환퇴ᄒᆞ기를녹촉ᄒᆞᆫ다ᄒᆞ엿다라

○일청훈령 동ᄅᆡ감리가외부로면보ᄒᆞ엿스되일본례신셩에셔파송ᄒᆞᆫ인원이본항에셔붓터울산에일으기ᄭᆞ지군용뎐긔션을가셜ᄒᆞ기위ᄒᆞ야긔지를답사ᄒᆞᆯᄎᆞ로연로에보호훈령을쳥ᄒᆞ엿다ᄒᆞ엿더라

○공ᄉᆞ면쥬 외부에셔쥬아공ᄉᆞ리범진씨를면관ᄒᆞ기로샹쥬ᄒᆞ엿는ᄃᆡ쥬본ᄉᆞ의를드른즉쥬아공ᄉᆞ리범진의게회국홈을루ᄎᆞ신칙ᄒᆞ엿스되상금불환ᄒᆞ오니심히히연ᄒᆞᆫ일이라면본관ᄒᆞ옴이하여ᄒᆞ올지ᄒᆞ엿다더라

○연셜소문 지작일하오이시에일진회에셔공긔연셜ᄒᆞᆫᄉᆞ를긔문ᄒᆞᆫ즉방쳥ᄒᆞ는인민이환잡ᄒᆞᆫ즁에회원김명쥰씨가일병파슈ᄉᆞ를발명ᄎᆞ로만단셜명ᄒᆞ여왈일아긔젼에일본이대한경셩을작젼요디로졍ᄒᆞ야군ᄉᆞ샹에조ᄒᆡᆼ경찰ᄒᆞ는거슬졍부에셔계약ᄒᆞᆫ고로일병이경찰샹ᄉᆞ무로본회에도와파슈홈이오보호ᄒᆞᆯ리치는만무ᄒᆞ다고일장연셜을쟝황이ᄒᆞ엿는ᄃᆡ방쳥인즁유지자가반ᄃᆡᄒᆞ기를우리경셩이무삼연고로일아젼징작젼요디가되리오언으ᄯᅢ에계약ᄒᆞ엿ᄂᆞ냐향일에의부에셔일공관에죠회ᄒᆞ기를현금쳥국디방에셔교젼ᄒᆞᆫ즉입녹강이셔와려슌구이남이ᄭᆞ지작젼요디어늘한셩ᄯᅩ작젼요디라ᄒᆞ는거시리외지언이라군용디로립표ᄒᆞᆫ거슬쳘거ᄒᆞ라ᄒᆞ엿스니본ᄅᆡ계약이잇셧스면이죠회를ᄒᆞ엿겟ᄂᆞ냐ᄉᆞ실이이러ᄒᆞᆫ즉아모리의뢰ᄒᆞ야보호를밧기로엇지이ᄀᆞᆺ치스ᄉᆞ로자젼디라ᄒᆞ고셩언ᄒᆞ야써일인의게붓치ᄂᆞᆫ고ᄒᆞ고방쳥인이일층격분ᄒᆞ야모도뢰귀ᄒᆞ엿다더라

○민요속문 교하민요ᄉᆞ는작보에긔재ᄒᆞ엿거니와ᄉᆞ실을속문ᄒᆞᆫ즉히군팔면두민은일병의게피형ᄒᆞ야긔지ᄉᆞ경인ᄃᆡ모라가는위풍에빅셩이몰니여일명은다리가졀샹ᄒᆞ야죽고이명은ᄂᆡ에ᄲᅡ져죽엇다더라

○의금칭송 평양에유지ᄒᆞᆫ군조와의리잇는부인들이의연금을구취ᄒᆞ야지폐삼십칠원을뎨국신문사로보ᄂᆡ면서편지ᄒᆞ기를우리대한젼국토디보호ᄒᆞ기위ᄒᆞ야보안회를열심으로ᄒᆞ다가외국인의게피착ᄒᆞ여간원셰셩씨가권의계송교ᄒᆞ야달나고ᄒᆞ엿다ᄒᆞ니평양쳠군ᄌᆞ제부인의ᄋᆡ국ᄒᆞ는열심을사름마다칭송ᄒᆞᆫ다더라

○지화신본 쥬식회샤뎨일은ᄒᆡᆼ지점에셔지비인쳥슈티길씨가외부와탁지부에공함ᄒᆞ고지화삼원식보낸는대지화안팟게견보이라두ᄌᆞ를쓰고구녕네슬둥굴게뚤엇는ᄃᆡ못할ᄉᆞ의에말ᄒᆞ기를조금이후로는이모양으로제조ᄒᆞᆫ지젼을ᄒᆡᆼ용ᄒᆞᆫ다ᄒᆞ엿다더라

○환화피착 남문외거ᄒᆞ는미샹ᄒᆞ나히진고긔가셔지화를교환ᄒᆞ는ᄃᆡ일본슌사가ᄉᆞ젼이라ᄒᆞ야낫낫치검사ᄒᆞᆫ즉그즁에ᄉᆞ지화일원이잇는지라츌쳐를무론즉미샹ᄃᆡ답이남문외리쥬ᄉᆞ의게셔ᄎᆞ진거시라ᄒᆞ기로리씨를경쳥에셔착거ᄒᆞ야심문ᄒᆞᆫ즉본ᄅᆡᆨ령남인의게셔온거시라ᄒᆞ더라더라

뎐보

동경구월일일발
론돈발뎐보

○료양젼황 구로팟킨장군의보고를거ᄒᆞᆫ즉일본군은료양동남방면에다다라셔이십ᄉᆞ일브터이십오일ᄭᆞ지격젼ᄒᆞᆫ후에로국군에젼디를탈취ᄒᆞ엿다ᄒᆞ엿더라

동일동경발
쳔진발뎐보

○덕군퇴로단졀 일본뎨일군은료양봉텬간텰도다리를파피ᄒᆞ엿더라

동일동경발
모쳐착뎐

○덕군궤쥬 료양에쥬둔ᄒᆞᆫ덕병은일본군의ᄆᆡᆼ렬ᄒᆞᆫ젼진를져항치못ᄒᆞ야젼군이환산ᄒᆞ야다라나기를시작ᄒᆞ엿다ᄒᆞ엿고일본군이료양을졈령ᄒᆞ기는금명간에될줄노밋는다ᄒᆞ엿더라

외보

○실난증병 려슌에셔발ᄒᆡᆼᄒᆞᆫ논최근(관동보)의보도ᄒᆞᆫ바를거ᄒᆞᆫ즉「구로팟긴」장군이극동에ᄉᆞ십만병더파송ᄒᆞᆯᄉᆞ를히국졍부에요구ᄒᆞ엿스나아국졍부에셔는만약이ᄀᆞᆺ치수다ᄒᆞᆫ병ᄉᆞ를즁파ᄒᆞ면일일에불가불일쳔륙빅돈뭇게의량식을쥰비ᄒᆞ겟기로대병를즁파ᄒᆞ기극난ᄒᆞᄂᆞ「구로팟긴 장군이젼ᄃᆡ에셔군량쥰비ᄒᆞᆯ방략이잇스면삼십만병은즉시파송ᄒᆞ겟다ᄒᆞ고회답ᄒᆞ엿다더라

광고

TELEGRAMS.

KUROKI OCCUPIES LIAO-YANG

HEAVY FIGHTING RESULTS IN SUCCESS.

RUSSIAN ARMY RETIRES NORTHWARDS.

Tokyo, 4.35 p.m. Aug. 31st.

While our first army is operating at Tangchayuen in the vicinity of Liaoyang and attacking the enemy's line of defences stretching from Shitou to Shemunling, the other armies are converging from left and right on the enemy's central position.

Tokyo, Sep. 1st. 12.15 a.m.

Our armies advancing on Liaoyang are in communication with each other and have forced the enemy back. We have occupied, with hardly any effort, all positions as far as the heights of Paouchunfung, Maouchafung (north of Paouchoosan). From the early morning of Aug. 30th, our armies opened a heavy artillery attack on the Russian positions but success was not assured until the afternoon of the 31st, when the enemy commenced to retire.

The enemy's force appears to consist of about 12 divisions.

Tokyo, Sep. 1st 9.30 a.m.

At dawn on the 1st our troops occupied the heights in the direction of Shinmintoon and Choosanpoon and the enemy engaged by our center and left armies commenced to retire, our troops hotly following up their advantage.

Tokyo Sep. 2nd 6.00 a.m.

Our armies have occupied Liaoyang after a series of brilliant victories.

KUROKI'S ADVANCE. RAILWAY BRIDGE DESTROYED.

Tokyo, Sept. 1st.

A telegram from Tientsin reports that a section of Kuroki's army succeeded in destroying a railway bridge between Liaoyang and Mukden.

ANOTHER VICTORY.

The news of the Japanese occupation of Liaoyyang which we publish today is another monument to Japanese strategy.

Starting from Seoul, in Korea, the Japanese army has gradually made its way northward and westward. The first serious opposition was met on the Yalu River. There the Japanese were victorious. Superior strategy and organization had a good deal to do with it but weight of numbers largely aided the Japanese. Since then the Japanese advance has been opposed by the Russians in increasing force and yet there has not been a single engagement where Russia was able to claim a victory.

With almost mathematical precision, the Japanese army advances, and with the same mathematical precision, the Russian army retreats.

We have yet to learn the details of the latest Russian "strategic movement to the rear," but if Kuropatkin has conducted it as ably as he has his previous retreats he is to be congratulated upon it.

With relentless exactiude the Japanese army advances, all loopholes for escape are traps, and the harassed Russians have no option but to retreat.

It had been said that Kuropatkin would make a stand at Liaoyang, but it is evident that the vulnerability of his line of communications (and retreat) has caused him to alter his mind.

The future Japanese operations are doubtful. Massed as their armies are now at Liaoyang, a movement towards the northeast seems the only sequence and we now expect to hear of a determined attack upon the Russian communications between Moukden and Vladivostok.

THE LATE PAUL KRUGER.

"TIMES" OBITUARY NOTICE.

The following is the conclusion of a long and, on the whole, sympathetic account of the life of the late Mr. Paul Kruger, ex-President of the Boer Republic, printed in the "Times" of July 15th:—

The total collapse which characterizes the last act in the drama of his life must of necessity prevent his figure from living in the annals of history with that halo of the heroic about it which is readily accorded by a generous posterity to the unfortunate. His claim for public sympathy and repect was based on strength and simplicity of character. It was believed that if ignoraut he was prepared to take all the consequences of his ignorance that he would stand or fall by his own flag, that the people who had trusted him would be led by him to the end, that the last man to surrender and the last man to leave the country would be the man who had not feared to take the responsibility of plunging it into war. But in that darkest hour when patriots arise Paul Kruger could find no higher sentiment by which to guide his actions than the sentiment of self-interest. His old fighting experience served to tell him when the fortune of the war was lost. He was able to secure a safe retreat, and with the faint gloss for his conscience that he meant to plead the Boer cause in Europe he took the opportunity which presented itself. It was an unworthy end of a career which might more fitly have terminated as it began, "fighting against fearful odds."

His absence from the battlefield was, no doubt, to be attributed in part to age. In other respects, the insensitiveness which he displayed towards his country's misfortunes was not inconistent with his previous career. President Kruger was not a hero. He had allowed himself to become for selfish ends a power for evil in the world. Had he triumphed, oppression, ignorance, and injustice must have triumphed at his side. But the last chapters of his life from the time when the Transvarl came prominently before the world, were but the sequel of the early and less known chapters of which the outline has been briefly summarized. Circumstances changed around him, but he changed nothing in himself. He learned nothing from experience. The man who defended the impossible system of Pretorian corruption against the world was the same who as a child had helped to defend the Vetchkop laager against the enveloping hordes of the Matabele. Odds had no terrors for him. He meant to succeed. Up to the last moment he thought he could succeed. Rightly and justly, Great Britain prevented him from succeeding. But we may permit ourselves, in presence of the peace which ends all strife, to recognize the pathos of the delusion which led him to the final catastrophe of his career.

SIR ROBERT HART.

This is how the leading Republican paper of America, the Springfield "Republican" speaks of Sir Robert Hart:—

Sir Robert Hart, the Englishman who has been in China 50 years and who has long been the Chinese Inspector-General of Customs, is as genuine and unselfish a friend as China can find among alien peoples. By "unselfish" is meant that his views concerning the policy of China are not coloured by patriotic or commercial prepossessions in favour of the interests of other countries. Foreign states men, whether European or American, always base their Chinese policy upon the assumed interests of their own people. If the German Emperor is indifferent to the open door policy and the preservation of China's territorial integrity, that is because he thinks Germany's interests would be advancad by opposite principles of development. And if the English and Amarican Governmdnts labour to sustain China's territorial integrity and the policy of the open door in trade, that is because English and American interests can be best subserved thereby. No one anywhere will work primarily for China, unless it be a Chinaman or an exceptional foreign resident like Sir Robert Hart.

In a recent discussion on naval matters, Admiral Sir E. R. Fremantle remarked it had been found that our percentage of loss due to the enemy in the past had been about 5 per cent. He did not think that steamers had increased the risk, and he could not understand why the Government, so as to prevent a panic, as insurance would go up unreasonably at first, should not have a small official department with Lloyd's, and arrange that Lloyd's should carry on operations as before in connection with the Government and that the Government should take the war risks. If there was no greater loss than 5 per cent. the Government would sustain no loss; if it happened to be much greater, the country would benefit, because there would be more ships running, the cargoes of which would be essential to our existence. He agreed that it would be of the utmost value to increase the intelligence of mail ships; we were inclined to deprecate intelligence in times of peace. He was able in the China war to give the Admiralty information as to what was going on.

An enormous floating coal depôt, the largest in the world, arrived at Portsmouth recently from the Tyne. The depot will hold 12,000 tons, and is to be moored in Portsmouth Harbour. It will be fitted with machinery that will enable the biggest warships to fill their bunkers alongside it. Being over 400 feet long, the depôt will accommodate the largest cruisers afloat. It is understood that Admiralty intend to have built floating depôts that will hold as much as 20,000 tons of coal.

The Emperor of Russia has presented to the Grand Duke Cyril a gold sword with the inscription "For Valour," in recognition of his gallant behaviour when the Petropavlovsk was sunk at Port Arthur.

The Sultan of Morocco, though only 23 years old, is already quite portly. Notwithstanding the opposition of his subjects, he persists in his preference for everything that is foreign and ultra modern. Automobiles, bicycles, photography, take up much of his time. He has formed a band of over one hundred musicians and has a piano, which had to be transported from Larrash to Fez on the back of a camel.

TENNIS.

The final game in the tennis singles handicap was played yesterday between Mr. Hulbert (handicap-30) and Mr. Porter (scratch). Two sets sufficed to determine the result, Mr. Porter winning with scores 6-3, 7-5. In the second set the score at one time stood 5-2 in favor of Mr. Hulbert, but his opponent managed to win 5 consecutive games thus, securing the match and the 1st prize.

The Korea Daily News.

To be published daily except Sundays.

Rate of Subscription:—

Per Year,	Yen 25.
Per Quarter,	Yen 7.
Per Month	Yen 2.50

Postage in Korea not charged extra.
Postage abroad charged extra.

Advertisements, 50 sen per day for 1 inch or less.
5 yen per month per inch.
50 yen per year per inch.

All communications to
E. T. BETHELL,
Editor and Publisher.
Pak-tong, Seou

JAPAN'S INFLUENCE IN KOREA.

PART III.

Between the year 1895 and the outbreak of the present war Japan or her diplomatic representatives have had little influence in this country, so that her political operations, for good or bad, have counted for litttle. During this time, however, Japan has had an opportunity of improving the social relations between the two countries, and of impressing upon her nationals residing in Korea the necessity of following the advice so strenuously set forth by Counts Inouye and Okuma. We cannot say that there are any signs of this having been done. The Koreans still come in for a lot of ill-treatment at the hands of the Japanese, and we think the worst offenders are those born and bred in this country. Personal violence is common, but an attitude of contemptuous superiority is still more common, and we should think, quite as maddening to the Koreans. This contemptuous superiority is the keynote of the position taken up by the Japanese in Korea, not only by the merchants and lower classes but by officials and men of education.

In fairness it must be said that there is some justification for the Japanese point of view. The man who is sent abroad is generally selected from many for his superior attainments, and the man who voluntarily emigrates has at least more than the average amount of enterprise. But the same thing applies equally in Japan itself and yet the foreigners there have not adopted the attitude of violence and contempt which has commended itself to the Japanese in Korea. Let the Japanese think how little they would like to be the victims of such proceedings, and they will realize the state of exasperation into which the Koreans are being driven.

The system of government in this country, which robs the Korean of all ambition, certainly tends to make a ne'er-do-well of him, but we do not for a moment believe that, given equal opportunities, the average Korean is in any way inferior to the average Japanese.

Since the outbreak of the war, and the disappearance of Russian influence from Korea, the Japanese have again become diplomatically powerful. Here was an opportunity for Japan to restore the confidence of the Koreans in her protests of disinterestedness, and recover the prestige which Counts Inouye and Okuma saw so plainly 8 or 9 years ago was slipping from her.

And what did the Japanese do? There were one or two incidents of minor importance such as the exile of three prominent Korean politicians but it cannot be shown that the Japanese were responsible for this, and anyhow one of them, at all events, was not greatly regretted. But he was a strong man and had great influence with the Emperor.

The next item on the programme was the celebrated Nagamori scheme. Its details are well known, it aimed at the grant to Japanese of all the waste lands in Korea. (It should be understood in this connection that the term "Waste Lands" was only a figure of speech and that a lot of the land was by no means of the bleak and barren description which the name conveyed). This demand was first of all made by one Nagamori in his capacity of a private Japanese citizen, but was subsequently adopted by the Japanese government, and her representatives in Seoul did all they could to obtain the Korean government's assent to the measure. It was frankly enough an application for the concession of about half of the Empire, and far from being a step towards the amelioration of the condition of the people, it appeared to be a distinct menace to the "Independence and integrity" which Japan had promised Korea, and a scheme which if put into practice, would from its very nature cause endless dissention and ill-feeling throughout the country. Korean statesmen strenuously resisted the proposal and it is to be hoped that it has now died a natural death. Still it was an ill-judged proposal. The most its supporters could say for it was that if Korea would not develop her own resources Japan must do it for her, and that once the proposal had been made Japan would lose prestige by withdrawing it. However it seems likely that we have now heard the last of it and it is much to be regretted that it was ever made. It has done a great deal to awaken distrust of Japan's intentions with regard to this country, and re-open old wounds which time alone will heal.

(To be continued).

APPEARANCE OF A LONG EXPECTED GOD.

A Reuter despatch from Bijsk, Tomsk, Siberia, states that unrest prevails among the Mongols in the Altai Mountains. They believe that their god, Airot, will shortly appear, and after delivering them from the foreign yoke, well help them to found an independent kingdom. The Mongols have assembled in thousands, under the leadership of three unknown persons, who employ every artifice, including the use of electric apparatus, to influence the ignorant peasants. Travellers arrived from the Altai Mountains narrate that a man has already made his appearance in the neigebourhood of Ustjnana, who declares that he is Airot, the long expected God of the Mongols and Kalmucks. This man is at present living in a Mongol "yurt," or tent, and will not show himself to the people. He is waited on by an old man robed in white, and a young girl, whom he employs as intermediaries for his messages to the Mongols. The travellers add that it is difficult to discover the purport of these messages, as the Mongols and Kalmucks, who were formerly very communicative to the Russians, now keep everything secret. What is, however, known is that by the doctrine of this man no one is allowed to possess any money except gold or silver, and that, consequently, the Mongols who possess paper money are seeking to get rid of it at any price.

THE EMPEROR'S BRITHDAY.

In consequence of the country being in mourning for the late Empress Dowager, His Majesty's birthday will this year be celebrated in a less ostentatious manner than usual. At the reception given all members of the Foreign Diplomatic corps and foreign employes of the Government will be present.

In the July number of the Pall Mall Magazine appears a personal sketch of, and a conversation with, Sir Edmund Monson, British Ambassador to the French Republic. In the course of this occurs the following passage:—"The condition of life in these days are such," said Sir Edmund, "that secret diplomacy is practically out of the question. The journalists render it so. They have the courage of their opinions, and they rush in everywhere. I confess I think people are too ready to talk nowadays. Diplomatic events come out before they are intended to. The Ambassador, is not the mysterious person that he once was—supposed to be the repository of State secrets. There are now comparatively few State secrets. You cannot conclude a secret treaty with a nation." "I gathered," says the writer, Mr. C. Dawbarn, "that in general diplomacy had become a less romantic calling. The despatches an Ambassador sends to his Foreign Office are short and dry and to the point. They are no longer expanded with political and social details. That is left to the professional correspondent of the newspapers."

King Humbert has now been dead just four years, yet so well was his body embalmed, at the time of his murder, that his appearance has remained almost unchanged. King Victor Emmanuel was able to assure himself of this recently, when the corpse of Humbert was transferred from the temporary tomb in the Pantheon to the magnificent sarcophagus in which he is henceforth to lie. After the celebration of mass, the service for the dead was recited by the clergy, and then the coffin, which had been brought into the centre of the Pantheon, was opened, in order that the Prime Minister, Signor Giolitti, as Crown Notary, might certify to the identity of the defunct monarch. Victor Emmanuel remained immovable for a long time, gazing on the body of his father, the royal bodyguard of cuirassiers saluting in the meantime with their sabres. Then the priest pronounced the benediction, the coffin was reclosed and resealed and placed by twelve non-commissioned officers of the bodyguard in its new and final resting place.

Mr. Kim Yong-chin, chief of the Household Bureau, visited the Japanese Legation on the 1st inst.

The Korean Police Station, which guards the ginseng fields outside the South Gate, is to be removed at the request of the Japanese military authorities.

The Kamni of Fusan telegraphs that a Japanese has applied for a passport to travel in the interior, in order to survey the country with the prospect of constructing a military telegraph line from Fusan to Woolsan.

On the 26th inst. a soldier of the Japanese telegraph corps, while patrolling the line near Chodong in a northern province, suddenly encountered 80 robbers, who attacked him and inflicted severe injuries on his person.

The Kanjo Shimpo learns that the Po An Hoi society have been secretly communicating with members of the Peddler's Guild and influential country residents with the object of bringing them up to Seoul to attend the meetings.

The Japanese are using twenty of Orlan Cullen's American 6-pounder ball-bearing rifled guns and one 4 inch cannon with ball-bearings. With these guns they secure 40 per cent. greater velocity, penetration, and range than under the old system. The United States and Great Britain are negotiating for the adoption of the new gun.

KOREAN MINISTER TO RUSSIA.

The Foreign Office have requested His Majesty to decide whether Mr. Yi Pomchin, the Korean Minister to Russia, has not, by his disobedience to their commands of recall, forfeited his position. They consider that he should be dismissed from the service.

The Korea Daily News.

VOL. I, SATURDAY, SEPTEMBER 3, 1904. No. 42

HONGKONG & SHANGHAI BANKING CORPORATION.

Paid-up Capital.................$10,000,000
Reserve Fund:—Sterling Reserve... 10,000,000
Silver Reserve..... 6,500,000

26,500,000
Reserve Liability of Proprietors... 10,000,000

HEAD OFFICE, HONGKONG.

London Bankers, London and County Banking Company Limited.
Branches and Agencies, London.

Amoy,	Hankow	Penang,
Bangkok,	Hiogo,	Rangoon,
Batavia,	Iloilo,	Saigon,
Bombay,	Lyons,	San Francisco,
Calcutta,	Manila,	Singapore,
Colombo,	Nagasaki,	Sourabaya,
Foochow,	New York,	Tientsin,
Hamburg,	Peking,	Yokohama,

Credits granted on approved Securities, and every description of Banking and Exchange business transacted.

Drafts granted on London and the chief Commercial places in Europe, India, Australia, America, China and Japan.

HOLME RINGER & Co., AGENTS, CHEMULPO.

ON CHEONG & CO., SEOUL.
GENERAL STORE KEEPERS.
Imported provisions, Cooking Utensils Crockery, etc.
FRESH BREAD DAILY.

MITSU BISHI DOCKYARD & ENGINE WORKS,
NAGASAKI.

CODE WORD, "DOCK."

A. 1, A. B. C., and Engineering Codes used.

DOCK No. 1 (at Tategami).

Extreme Length..............523 feet
Length on blocks............ 513 ,,
Width of Entrance on Top......89 ,,
,, ,, Bottom....77 ,,
Water on Blocks at Spring Tide 26½ ,,

DOCK No. 2 (Mukaijima).

Extreme Length..............371 feet
Length on Blocks.............360 ,,
Width of Entrance on Top......66 ,,
,, ,, Bottom 53 ,,
Water on Blocks at Spring Tide 22 ,,

PATENT SLIP (at Kosuge).

Can take vessels up to 1,000 tons gross.

THE WORKS are well equipped with the LATEST IMPROVEMENTS, and can execute any kind of work in SHIPBUILDING and MARINE ENGINEERING, as well as in REPAIRING of SHIPS.

The COMPANY'S new powerful steamer OURA-MARU (712 tons, 700 I.H.P.), specially built for SALVAGE PURPOSES, and equipped with necessary gear, is always READY at SHORT NOTICE.

CHARTERED BANK OF INDIA AUSTRALIA & CHINA.

INCORPORATED BY ROYAL CHARTER 1853

HEAD OFFICES:—LONDON.

Paid-up Capital £800,000

Reserve Liability of Shareholders 800,000

Reserve Fund 800,000

Drafts granted upon all the principal places in the world and every description of Exchange and banking business transacted.

E. MEYER & Co., Agents, Chemulpo.

E. MEYER & CO.
Chemulpo.

SOLE AGENTS IN KOREA FOR:
A. T. Morse, Sons & Co's "Fresco" Distemper

In all colours ready for use on walls, Ceilings etc.
and
AVENARIUS CARBOLINEUM

A wood-preserving and antiseptic oil preparation

Against decay, dry-rot, fungus and wood-destroying insects.

A large supply always in Stock. Prices upon application.

E. MEYER & Co., Chemulpo.

LAW UNION & CROWN INS. CO.

Fire risks accepted at Current rates, on godowns, merchandise, dwellings, and other property, subject to usual conditions.

HOLME RINGER & Co., Agents, Chemulpo

THE METHODIST PUBLISHING HOUSE,
Little West Gate, Seoul.

JOB PRINTING, TYPEWRITER PAPER
CARBON PAPER, VISITING CARDS
STATIONERY, BOOK BINDING
BOOK PUBLISHERS
AMERICAN SCHOOL BOOKS
SPENCERIAN COPY BOOKS
PEN CARBON LETTER AND BILL BOOKS

S A BECK, Manager

DAI-ICHI GINKO.
LIMITED.
(Formerly the First National Bank)
ESTABLISHED 1873

INCORPORATED UNDER PRESENT LAW 1896

Capital - - - - - - - - Yen 5,000,000
Reserve Fund - - - - - 1,500,000

HEAD OFFICE:—TOKIO.

President: Baron SHIBUSAWA.

BRANCHES AND CORRESPONDENTS
In the Principal Cities and Towns of Japan.
Interest Allowed on
Fixed deposits 1 year - - - 6½ per cent
" " 6 months - - - 6 per cent

Special current accounts 1½ sen daily per Y 100
General " " 1 " " " 100

M. TANAKA, Manager, Chemulpo

HOLME RINGER & Co.
Chemulpo.

General Merchants and Government Contractors.

Agents for the leading Banks SteamshipCompanies and Insurance Companies

Importers of Merchandise of every description.

KAMEYA & CO.
GENERAL STOREKEEPERS
Chinkokai - - Seoul
(*Established 1895, Tokyo*)

Confectionery, Hams, Canned Goods, Cutlery, Hirano & Tansan Water. Provisions, Gents, Furnishing goods, Toilet Articles, Travelling Bags, Tobacco, Cigars & Cigarettes Kitchen Utensils. Coffee, Biscuits.

Fresh Goods always kept in Stock.
Prices Moderate
Please come and inspect our goods.

NIPPON YUSEN KAISHA.
JAPANESE MAIL STEAMSHIP CO.
UNDER MAIL CONTRACT WITH THE IMPERIAL JAPANESE GOVERNMENT.

European Line

Regular Fortnightly Service between Yokohama Kobe, Moji, Shanghai, Hongkong, Singapore, Penang Colombo, Port Said, Marseilles, London and Antwerp

American Line

Regular Fortnightly Service between Hongkong and Seattle, calling at Shanghai, Moji, Kobe, Yokohama and Victoria, B. C.

Australian Line

Regular weekly Service betwen Japan Ports and Australia, calling at Hongkong and Manila.
(Above Three Lines Suspended until further notice).

Shanghai Line

Weekly Service between Shanghai and Japan Ports

Korea Line

Service Kobe, Moji, Nagasaki, Fusan, Chemulpo, Chefoo, Taiku.
S. S. Bahelsberg, 2181 tons.
Service Kobe, Moji, Fusan, Chemulpo, Chinnampo
S. S ARGO, S. S. Ohio.

BORDEN'S CONDENSED MILK CO.
New York, U. S. A.

ALWAYS IN STOCK
Eagle Brand Condensed Milk.
Gold Seal Condensed Milk.
Peerless (Family) Evaporated Cream.
Borden's Malted Milk.

E. MEYER & CO.
Chemulpo, Korea,
Sole Agents

ROYAL INSURANCE COMPANY,
Funds exceed £10,000,000
FIRE
AT CURRENT RATES.
LIFE
REDUCED PREMIUM.
HOLME RINGER & Co., Agents, Chemulpo.

HOTEL DU PALAIS
SEOUL.

The only first class Hotel in Seoul. Situated in the centre of the city opposite the palace.

Cuisine under the supervision of an experienced French Chef.

Well ventilated and furnished throughout.

TARIFF UPON APPLICATION

L. MARTIN,
Proprietor and Manager.

大韓每日申報
대한ᄆᆡ일신보

천구ᄇᆡᆨ사년구월오일　(월요일)　(뎨사십삼호)

본사고ᄇᆡᆨ

이신보는영어와한어로셕거ᄆᆡ일출판ᄒᆞ옵

신문가

ᄒᆞᆫ장 엽두돈오푼

일삭됴엽두량닷돈　ᄆᆡᆺ돈으로 밧숩

광고료는

긔한의장단과ᄌᆞ힝의다쇼로좃차ᄒᆞ되렴가로밧을터이오며오리지아녀대한사ᄅᆞᆷ마다이신문을보실터이니광고내시기를원ᄒᆞ시는이들은우리신문사에와셔면약ᄒᆞ심을희망ᄒᆞ옵

○발ᄒᆡᆼ소　박동대한ᄆᆡ일신보사범어학교압헤젼영국인셜필림졍자리오

사쟝 영국인 (빈셜)

본사지졈

인천항교젼동신치명씨로우리대한ᄆᆡ일신보사인천지졈쟝을퇴졍ᄒᆞ엿ᄉᆞ오니인천항에계신구람코자ᄒᆞ시는쳠군ᄌᆞ는히지졈에왕림면의ᄒᆞ시옵

사고

○우리대한ᄆᆡ일신보의목뎍은대한의인녕졀셔에관ᄒᆞᆫ모든뎨목에되ᄒᆞ야는공평ᄒᆞᆫ변론을주쟝ᄒᆞᆷ이라우리통신원의탐보는신문보시는쳠군ᄌᆞ의게ᄒᆞ샹보도ᄒᆞ려ᄒᆞ며편지를긔셔ᄒᆞ여주시는이는셩명과번디를젹어붓치시기를희망ᄒᆞ오나이거슨신문샹에긔지ᄒᆞ라는거시아니오다만극히신용ᄒᆞ는증거를숨고자ᄒᆞᆷ이라긔자는아모긔셔던지긔지ᄒᆞᆷ을퇴각ᄒᆞ는권리를가졋ᄉᆞ오나퇴각ᄒᆞ는리유를말ᄒᆞᆯ터이오며공중평화를문란케ᄒᆞ는듯ᄒᆞᆫ긔셔는의례히밧지안켓ᄉᆞᆸ나이다

사고

○본사에셔는신문갑슬ᄆᆡ월에션금으로밧ᄉᆞ오며본신문은우톄로붓치는고로본사에셔는다른신문사쳐럼금액을거두러ᄃᆞᆫ니지안ᄉᆞ오니우리신문을ᄉᆞ랑ᄒᆞ야구람ᄒᆞ시는쳠군ᄌᆞ는양력ᄆᆡ월쵸ᄉᆞ흘ᄂᆡ에리월됴션금과거쥬셩명등ᄒᆞ오수를ᄌᆞ셰히젹어셔박동본사로보ᄂᆡ시기를바라오며양력금월회일ᄂᆡ로션금을아니보ᄂᆡ시는곳에는ᄅᆡ월일일부터신문을아니보낼터이오니죠량ᄒᆞ옵소셔

●본사에셔아직긔계를쟝만치못ᄒᆞ와다른ᄃᆡ셔박여오는고로ᄆᆡ양월요일에는츌판이ᄆᆡ우늣게되는듯ᄉᆞ오로분젼이ᄆᆡ우늣게되오니우리신문을구람ᄒᆞ시는쳠군ᄌᆞ는 용셔ᄒᆞ여주심을희망ᄒᆞ옵나이다

론셜

젼호련쇽

병신년브터금번ᄭᆞ지젼된동안에일본셔와밋일본외교관들이한국에권력을부려졍치샹운동도션약간ᄒᆡᆼᄒᆞ야엇지던지일한량국간교제친밀ᄒᆞᆷ과회도엇엇고ᄯᅩ한국에거류ᄒᆞ는ᄌᆞ긔나라빅셩들의게도대단히유익ᄒᆞᆫ게되엿는고로젼자에졍샹ᄇᆡᆨ작ᄒᆞᆫ과대외ᄇᆡᆨ작의권도ᄒᆞᆫ되로ᄒᆡᆼᄒᆞ려ᄒᆞ는듯ᄒᆞᆫ즉우리는엇더케ᄒᆞ리라고말ᄒᆞᆯ수업는거시지금한국사ᄅᆞᆷ의고젼된병고치여벌일이일본사ᄅᆞᆷ슈단에달녀슨즉이사ᄅᆞᆷ들은졍풍의피샹ᄒᆞ게셩기여모도하등지류인되고중에샹등인물이라는거슨공연이ᄌᆞ공하ᄒᆞ고등명ᄒᆞ는되도만잇셔셔하등지인버럼며옥고악ᄒᆞᆫ즉일본셔이사ᄅᆞᆷ들로ᄒᆞ여곰더도ᄒᆞ라면필경밋치게될듯ᄒᆞᆫ거시소위샹등인의ᄒᆞ야ᄒᆞᆫ거시요시졍비와샹옥ᄒᆞᆫ들의게만어려올ᄲᅮᆫ이아니라소위고흉바다ᄡᅥ는사ᄅᆞᆷ이며관리들도이를반일터인즉이사ᄅᆞᆷ들로ᄒᆞ야곰일본에쥬의ᄒᆞ는형편퇴로ᄒᆞ란면ᄒᆞᆫ조ᄒᆞᆫ도리가잇는거시외국에보니엿든관비셩중ᄒᆞᆫ편이쵸등ᄒᆞᆫ사ᄅᆞᆷ으로퇴츌ᄒᆞ면지흥사비셩이라도공부를도져히ᄒᆞ고ᄇᆡᆫ스에경험만ᄒᆞᆫ사ᄅᆞᆷ을ᄲᅢᆸ아셔일을ᄒᆞ게ᄒᆞ엿스면되오조흘듯ᄒᆞ나그러나한일아모일본사ᄅᆞᆷ이거나흑외국사ᄅᆞᆷ의게라도졈잔ᄒᆞ고헐긔잇게교훈밧지못ᄒᆞᆫ사ᄅᆞᆷ으로ᄡᅳᆯ지경이면역시일반일터인즉일본사ᄅᆞᆷ은이일ᄒᆞ는ᄃᆡ엇더케방침을ᄉᆡᆼ각ᄒᆞ는지모르게스되한국사ᄅᆞᆷ들로ᄒᆞ야곰ᄀᆞᆫ숙히ᄒᆡᆼᄒᆞ야분격ᄒᆞ케될지라도아모조록셩취만되엿스면좃케는지라

한국졍부에셔ᄒᆞ는이들은단지환욕에만ᄲᅡ져잇셔아모조록다른사ᄅᆞᆷ버덤낫게ᄒᆞᆯ샹각인즉이거슨일본이나한국이나하등인물을조곰도다르게시업셔고리ᄒᆞᆷ이되우리ᄉᆡᆼ각에는이런것도치지물론ᄒᆞᆯ리가업ᄉᆞᆯ듯ᄒᆞᆫ거시일아기젼되여아인의셰력업셔진이후로일본사ᄅᆞᆷ의게로외교권리가도라왓스니이런과회에아모조록한국빅셩들의게밋부케ᄒᆞ야불리ᄒᆞᆫ일로좌론ᄒᆞᆷ이업시ᄒᆞ고팔구년젼에경샹대외량ᄇᆡᆨ작의말ᄒᆞᆫ바를참쟉ᄒᆞ야명망이나도록ᄒᆞ는거시조흘듯ᄒᆞ며 일본셔긔왕에ᄒᆞᆫ일비무어시됴ᄒᆞ면한국에소위탁월ᄒᆞᆫ졍치가락ᄒᆞ는피셩넌된ᄌᆞ들이국사범이되여일본으로도주ᄒᆞ엿스되죽시히사ᄅᆞᆷ들을살퇴여드리니지아니ᄒᆞ엿슨즉이리ᄒᆞᆫ여도ᄒᆞᆫ명도쎄다라후회ᄒᆞᆫ쟈업는지라그런고로이거슨 황뎨의온당치아니ᄒᆞ여도말ᄒᆞᆯ것업고황무디기잔일스로말ᄒᆞᆯ진대한국에잇논황폐지디를일본의계획ᄒᆞ여케ᄒᆞᆯᄯᅳᆺ이다만잇셔그리ᄒᆞᆷ은다ᄌᆞ셰히아는바이로되이거슨공연히말ᄒᆞᆯ만ᄒᆞᆫ고로되지도못ᄒᆞᆯ일을졔츌ᄒᆞᆷ인ᄃᆡ당초에는쟝샹셰의자유로쳥구ᄒᆞ는것ᄀᆞᆺ치ᄒᆞ더니필경에는공ᄉᆞ가한국졍부에되ᄒᆞ야쳥구ᄒᆞᆫ즉셜ᄒᆞ되시드리도한국젼토에반밧게쓸거시업슬터이니거슨일본에셔한국에등림과자유ᄒᆞ는권리를억졔ᄒᆞ란는것ᄀᆞᆺᄒᆞ셔말ᄒᆞᆯ수록반디만셩기고젼국에병반되게ᄒᆞ는일이죽되지도못ᄒᆞᆯ터이ᄲᅮᆫ더러한국대관들은지금ᄭᅡ지ᄒᆞ여셔는렴치으로보존ᄒᆞ란논마음이잇ᄉᆞ되필경에ᄌᆞ연이엿셔젼리이요ᄉᆡᆼ이사ᄅᆞᆷ들의말은우리나라이만일반ᄃᆞᆯ이되지못ᄒᆞᆯ졔경이면일본셔차지ᄒᆞᆯ터이라ᄒᆞ고ᄒᆞᆫ즉명에만손샹이될터이니우리듯는바로보드리도긔경에아일로ᄒᆞ여후회ᄒᆞᆯ터인즉죵금이후로는한국에되ᄒᆞ야ᄒᆞ란는거슬밋지아니ᄒᆞ고의흥ᄒᆞ는마음을써치ᄒᆞ오리된병만낫치셔쾌복ᄒᆞ게ᄒᆞᆯ거시오 (미완)

잡보

○장관졍임　ᄂᆡ부ᄃᆡ방국쟝김용진씨소톄ᄒᆞᆫ되에학부편집국쟝리규환씨가긔임되엿는되그되에는참셔관신퇴유죠현볍량씨중에승임ᄒᆞᆫ다ᄒᆞ고그되에는주ᄉᆞ김영진씨가승임ᄒᆞᆫ다더라

○파송ᄉᆞ뎨　지작일진회에셔긔회ᄒᆞ엿는되ᄃᆡ광진의씨가동의ᄒᆞ기를묘진실시ᄒᆞᆯ수로총ᄃᆡ위원을루ᄎᆞ파송ᄒᆞ엿스되긔시경부가의공ᄒᆞ엿고지금은경부가권닉로이졉ᄒᆞ엿ᄉᆞ나츌입ᄒᆞᆯ수업슨즉신참졍ᄉᆞ뎨로파송ᄒᆞᆫ는거시가타ᄒᆞ야가결되엿기로김초ᄉᆞ총ᄃᆡ위원에셔샹훈량지의명쥰평중보수씨를파송ᄒᆞ엿더라

○팔민쳥거　희천군슈의보고를거ᄒᆞᆫ즉일본헌병조쟝중졍호지ᄀᆞ가본월삼륙일에본군에리도ᄒᆞ야마젼리거ᄒᆞ는량회두라희졍랑의과롱김증록최수졍리경화김준흥리응모등이각군에비민이왕리ᄒᆞ며일본군수샹일을곳시졍탐ᄒᆞᆫ다ᄒᆞ고잉의로장아셔안쥬병참소로잡다고ᄒᆞ엿더라

○손가젹심　샹쥬거젼의관차일룡의손ᄌᆞ명한이가샹경ᄒᆞ야두루류ᄒᆞ더니작년에경거인손셩환이가차씨가에가셔차의관을보고그손ᄌᆞ명한이가셔울셔부최ᄒᆞᆫ돈십여만량을당쟝ᄂᆡ라고독촉ᄒᆞ거늘차씨가샹경ᄒᆞ야탐문ᄒᆞᆫ즉차명한이가긔주김문원의계돈도쓰기젼에표반ᄒᆞ여쥰거시라중간에음최샹쳔량만보나ᄒᆞ는고로손셩환의게로젼오ᄇᆡᆨ량을이음최로주고타렵ᄒᆞ엿스나샹쳔량표는쇼ᄃᆡ는사ᄅᆞᆷ의계잇다ᄒᆞ는고로주시ᄎᆞᆺ지못ᄒᆞ엿더니붐쥭ᄒᆞᆫ쇼가가대구거ᄒᆞ는김영갑을부동ᄒᆞ야금년졍월분에젼션산군슈모씨가샹쥬군슈로겸임ᄒᆞ엿슬ᄯᅢ에회군슈의계쳥촉ᄒᆞ야차의관을본음에착슈ᄒᆞ고관차가차의관가에싱야에리도ᄒᆞ야ᄂᆡ졍에도둡ᄒᆞ야등ᄡᅢᆨ을파쇄ᄒᆞ고오셔여두지기는문

셔울특달ᄒᆞ야간지라차씨의가권이도로에셔호곡ᄒᆞᆫ다더라·

○아비만여 령변관찰ᄉᆞ리용관씨의보고를거ᄒᆞᆫ즉음력칠월일일에아병오십여명이청국쌍분구에리도ᄒᆞᆫ일은이왕보고ᄒᆞ엿거니와기시일즁ᄃᆡ병졍과입번포군으로써방슈ᄒᆞ엿더니아병이월강을못ᄒᆞ고청국ᄃᆡ경삼십리허파발산으로되거ᄒᆞ엿고젼셜에아국비류만여명이분구에둔취ᄒᆞ엿다ᄒᆞ는고로ᄇᆡᆨ셩이경겁ᄒᆞ야황황히환산ᄒᆞ니심히슈참ᄒᆞ다ᄒᆞ엿더라

○보쳥후고 신계군슈가외부로보고ᄒᆞ되평산렬도역ᄉᆞ에본군에비졍ᄒᆞᆫ역부칠ᄇᆡᆨ명을농민즁모집ᄒᆞ야부역식엿더니그삭젼이당일식비도못되는고로각면각리에셔징ᄒᆞ야비렴ᄒᆞᆫ돈이ᄉᆞ오쳔량이어놀현금감독부에셔 칠ᄇᆡᆨ명을쳥구ᄒᆞ고로겨우모집ᄒᆞᆫ거시오ᄇᆡᆨ명인ᄃᆡ그삭젼이미우박ᄒᆞᆫ즉역부에당일식비부족ᄒᆞᆫ거슬구쳐ᄒᆞᆯ방략이업스니곳일공관에이죠ᄒᆞ야삭젼을후이쥬게ᄒᆞ라ᄒᆞ엿더라

○만슈셩졀 작일은 대황뎨폐하만슈셩졀이라샹오십시에돈덕뎐에 친어ᄒᆞ샤각국공령ᄉᆞ츅하를밧으시고십시반에고용된각외국인원들도입참ᄒᆞ엿더라

●광구소슈 광션문안소쳥에셔각군향교에임원을렬명ᄒᆞ야뎨칠ᄎᆞ샹소를ᄒᆞᆯ터인ᄃᆡ칙임관즁에소슈원ᄒᆞ는사람이ᄒᆞ나도업는고로현금광구즁이라더라

○량티ᄉᆞ씨 향일심참졍이모모사씨를 쥬면ᄒᆞᆫᄉᆞ는원동뎐동량ᄐᆡ의바밀이찬조ᄒᆞᆫ바일녀니본식이현로ᄒᆞ야픠힉ᄒᆞᆫ모모씨가동셩탄힉ᄒᆞ는고로모쳐세력이졈졈무령ᄒᆞ다더라

○우쟝소 일젼에ᄂᆡ부대신과협판이상소승 비ᄒᆞ엿스ᄂᆞ우비가아닌줄노싱각ᄒᆞ야힝공치아니ᄒᆞ고쟝ᄎᆞ또샹소ᄒᆞᆫ다ᄒᆞ더라

○단속쳔필 향일에경무쳥에셔산림동큰부당의집을슈탐ᄒᆞ야그신위의물품을거둔거시수쳔량어치오은괴반샹이ᄒᆞᆫ벌이잇는ᄃᆡ그비단명식은다소화ᄒᆞ엿더라

○작목난검 덕원군슈가ᄂᆡ부로보고ᄒᆞ기를일본ᄉᆞ령부에셔쳘령과원산간에뎐션을셜시ᄎᆞ로뎐한목ᄒᆞᆯ나무를작벌ᄒᆞ기를독촉ᄒᆞ기에외부로뎐보ᄒᆞ엿더니회뎐내에원산과쳘령간에뎐보셜시홈을일공ᄉᆞ가당초에쳥ᄒᆞᆫ일이업스니뎐한목을쥰비ᄒᆞ야쥬난것시가치안타ᄒᆞ엿기로일본ᄉᆞ령부에가셔뎐한목을관비치못ᄒᆞᆯ일을타관ᄒᆞ엿더니지금ᄉᆞ령부로셔통긔도업시각군으로편힝ᄒᆞ며검산나무를무란작벌ᄒᆞ는ᄃᆡ능히검집ᄒᆞᆯ수업다ᄒᆞ엿더라

○인민호곡 일젼에황히관찰ᄉᆞ가외부로또보고ᄒᆞ엿는ᄃᆡ관하각군의인부ᄉᆞ건에ᄃᆡᄒᆞ야인민이길노호곡ᄒᆞ며둔난다고ᄒᆞ엿더라

○고문ᄐᆡ다 탁지부에길인고문관이나온후에는각관찰부에고문관도파송ᄒᆞ고각ᄃᆡ방관에도고문관을보낸다ᄒᆞ며각군봉세관도일인이나간다ᄒᆞ며셔군부관제도탁지고문관이와셔지졍을졍리ᄒᆞᆫ후에야귀졍이된다더라

○아병소문 셩진감리가외부로보고ᄒᆞ기를칠월삼일이리로아국긔병과보병이혹삼ᄉᆞᄇᆡᆨ명오륙ᄇᆡᆨ명식연일도강ᄒᆞ야젼진ᄒᆞ는ᄃᆡ군인즁우리ᄇᆡᆨ셩이ᄐᆡ반이셕긴고로그군졍을무른즉ᄒᆞ기를이번동병이합십륙만명인ᄃᆡ슈륙병진ᄒᆞᆫ다ᄒᆞ며이길노나올것도오만명가량이나되난ᄃᆡ황셩으로직향ᄒᆞᆫ다ᄒᆞ며또뎐션을가셜ᄒᆞ며도로를슈츅ᄒᆞ야현금본항々지일을엇는ᄃᆡ아인의말인즉한국인민을보호ᄒᆞᆫ다ᄒᆞ나지ᄂᆡ는곳마다졔반슈응ᄒᆞᆯ방략이업ᄊᆞ니보호밧기는고샤ᄒᆞ고교을과ᄇᆡᆨ셩이먼져피폐ᄒᆞ니한심ᄒᆞᆫ일이라ᄒᆞ엿는ᄃᆡ팔월삼일에츌발ᄒᆞᆫ보고라더라

○구협신지 신임ᄒᆞᆫ평리원지관쟝민병한씨는젼일ᄂᆡ부협관지임시에힝위가괴당ᄒᆞ야면관되야오리ᄒᆞᆫ젼이냉락ᄒᆞ더니금번에지관쟝ᄀᆞᆺᄒᆞᆫ즁임을ᄒᆞ미젼일문싱고리도다시문젼에운집ᄒᆞᆯ거시오동씨도필경십분공심을다ᄒᆞ야영어에원억ᄒᆞᆫ죄슈가업슬쯧ᄒᆞ더라

○쳥벌역부 텰도원에셔외부로죠회ᄒᆞ기를김산군슈가텰도역부비의게봉욕ᄒᆞ야피타ᄒᆞᆫᄉᆞ는즉금히군지ᄎᆞ보고를졉ᄒᆞᆫ즉본군슈가칠곡을지나갈때에역부픽쟝홍명션이가횡죽ᄒᆞ고로변에누어셔눈을흙겨여시ᄒᆞ는고로본군관례가그무례ᄒᆞᆷ을칙망ᄒᆞᆫ즉홍가대로ᄒᆞ야군슈를교ᄌᆞ밧게쯔러ᄂᆡ여교ᄌᆞ와의관을타파ᄒᆞ고일인역부가합력ᄒᆞ야큰몽동이로란타ᄒᆞ더니오리지아니ᄒᆞ야엇던일인이명함을드리고보기를쳥ᄒᆞ거늘연졉ᄒᆞ야본즉군슈구타ᄒᆞ든일인인ᄃᆡ그일홈은진등졍일이라ᄉᆞ실이이ᄀᆞᆺ치명ᄇᆡᆨᄒᆞᆫ즉하량조쳐ᄒᆞ라ᄒᆞ엿고향일일본ᄃᆡ리공ᄉᆞ의죠회에김산군슈의보고를괴망ᄒᆞᆷ이라ᄒᆞ엿스니일이심히무리ᄒᆞᆫ지라곳쳐일관에죠회ᄒᆞ야진등과홍가등을압상ᄒᆞ고히군슈를불너올녀량국관원이회동심사ᄒᆞ야히범등을의률ᄒᆞ야징쇄케ᄒᆞ라ᄒᆞ엿더라

○츄쳔박씨 츙쳥남도관찰ᄉᆞ리항의씨가례귀ᄒᆞ면셔ᄂᆡ부로보고ᄒᆞ기를목쳔군슈박졍빈은츙치가리락ᄒᆞ고강명졍직ᄒᆞ야도임ᄒᆞᆫ후에일경이안연ᄒᆞ온바이번공쥬포리가치폐ᄒᆞ야관쟝의게범슈ᄒᆞᆫᄉᆞ로목쳔군슈로사관을졍ᄒᆞ엿더니법으로써죵ᄉᆞᄒᆞ고리로써결쳐ᄒᆞ야인인이칭송ᄒᆞ니물즁ᄃᆡ대ᄒᆞᆫ고을에이사룸이아니면진압ᄒᆞᆯ슈업ᄊᆞ니박군슈를공쥬로이임ᄒᆞ야인심은안졍케ᄒᆞ라ᄒᆞ엿더라

○쟝유대용 특진관리근호씨는쟝ᄎᆞᄂᆡ부대신을ᄒᆞ고민영환리도지박졔슌리하영졔씨가다시졍ᄀᆡ션ᄒᆞ는ᄃᆡ참예ᄒᆞᆫ다ᄒᆞ며일진회원모모씨도다슈용된다ᄒᆞ더라

○셩졀문안 일작에의졍부에셔각부부원쳥에통텹ᄒᆞ기를음력본월이십오일 만슈셩졀에ᄇᆡᆨ관문안이되니죠량ᄒᆞ라ᄒᆞ엿더니작일 탄신문안에ᄇᆡᆨ관이입참되엿더라

○죵편왕리 옹진군슈긴홍쥬씨가ᄂᆡ부에보고ᄒᆞ되본군슈가탄신문안에슈유샹경ᄒᆞ거니와이왕죵편왕리ᄒᆞ라ᄒᆞᆫ신쳐분을무루엇시니부이히왕리ᄒᆞ노라ᄒᆞ엿더라

관보

뎨이쳔구ᄇᆡᆨ이십이호

광무팔년구월삼일

○셔임급ᄉᆞ령

○익부산우톄ᄉᆞ쥬ᄉᆞ셔판임관륙등 셔홍우톄ᄉᆞ쥬ᄉᆞ 권즁목

○임셔홍우톄ᄉᆞ쥬ᄉᆞ셔판임관륙등 셔샹룡

○의원면본관 벽동우톄ᄉᆞ쥬ᄉᆞ 신용우

○임벽동우톄ᄉᆞ쥬ᄉᆞ셔판임관륙등 량지쇼

이상팔월삼십일일

○임평리원지관쟝셔칙임관이등 죵이픔 민병한

○명셩쥬군림시우톄쥬ᄉᆞ 리승쳘

○명협곡군림시우톄쥬ᄉᆞ 리후긔

○명은산군림시우톄쥬ᄉᆞ 리건응

○명오쳔군림시우톄쥬ᄉᆞ 최쥬영

이상구월일일

○이쥬일감봉 탁지부량디국기슈 변지샹

○즁견칙 시종원봉시 양쥰긔

구월이일

구월이일

궁뎡록ᄉᆞ

○ᄂᆡ장원경김응모ᄉᆞ직소비지ᄂᆡ에소쳥ᄃᆡ로이[illegible]

광고

○법관양셩소학원모[illegible]고

현금에법관양셩소학원을가취ᄒᆞᆯ터이니입학ᄒᆞ기원ᄒᆞ는사룸은구월십이일［음력팔월초삼일］ᄂᆡ로품쳥쟝을본소로구졍ᄒᆞ고당일에본소로리도ᄒᆞ야입학시험에응ᄒᆞᆯᄉᆞ

광무팔년팔월삼십일일

일은국문 독셔 작문

일은한문 독셔 작문

일은본국 디지 문ᄃᆡ

일은본국 력ᄉᆞ 문ᄃᆡ

일은년령이십세이샹삼십오세이하

품쳥즁지는본소로리도ᄒᆞ야구용ᄒᆞᆯᄉᆞ

뎐보

셰곡뎨삼함ᄃᆡᄉᆞ령관보고

칠월이일오젼구시십분동경대본영착뎐

○군량션피착 거이십오일에려슌구로량식을운송ᄎᆞ로위히위를발ᄒᆞᆫ아국군용풍범션이십륙쳑은이십팔구량일에단도와남삼도부근에셔우리봉쇄함이포획ᄒᆞ고대렵만으로보ᄂᆡ엿는ᄃᆡ연합ᄃᆡᄉᆞ령관의훈령을봉승ᄒᆞ야죠ᄉᆞᄒᆞᆫ후에그비와실은물품은모다속공ᄒᆞ고비랏든사룸들은청국풍범션삼쳑에분비ᄒᆞ야옴겨ᄐᆡ우고히방식혓다ᄒᆞ엿더라

동경발팔월삼십일일

○료양점령형편 료양부근당가원방면의우리군ᄉᆞ는다시셕두에셔셕문령에연ᄒᆞ는덕국을공격ᄒᆞ는즁인ᄃᆡ다른여러군ᄃᆡ도또ᄒᆞᆫ동ᄒᆞ기를시작ᄒᆞ엿더라

구월일일오후발

료양방면의우리각군ᄃᆡ는연락을통ᄒᆞ야이십팔일이릭로밍렬히츄격ᄒᆞᆫ결과인즉덕군은되각치못ᄒᆞ고모가봉보쥬산보촌봉놉흔짜에연ᄒᆞᆫ진터를죽기로써직히고우리군ᄉᆞ는삼십일미명에젼력ᄒᆞ야공격을시작ᄒᆞ야격렬히싸왓는ᄃᆡ작일오후ᄭᆞ지는싸홈긔미이쎄치는것을보지못ᄒᆞ고싸호는즁인ᄃᆡ덕의군ᄉᆞ는십삼ᄉᆞ단씀되는모양이오

일일오후구시삼십분발

구월일일미명에우리좌익군은신민둔쥬산보방면놉흔곳을졈령ᄒᆞ고즁앙군과좌익군전면에덕군은괴시되각ᄒᆞ엿는ᄃᆡ량군은츄격즁이오

이일오젼륙시발

우리군ᄉᆞ는료양을크게공경ᄒᆞᆫ후에젼혀졈령ᄒᆞ엿다더라

TELEGRAMS.

(FROM JAPAN PAPERS.)

Berlin, Aug. 28.

At Hoboken (New York) all the kerosene tanks have been destroyed by fire, the damage being estimated at seven million dollars.

ADMIRAL SKRYDLOFF DISMISSED.

A despatch has been received in Tokyo from London stating that, according to a telegram from St. Petersburg, Vice-Admiral Skrydloff, commanding the Russian naval forces in East Asia, has been dismissed from the service.

Berlin, Aug. 25.

An apparently inspired article appearing in the "Petit Parisien" intimates that Great Britain the United States, France, and Germany will offer their services to the belligerents with a view to the conclusion of peace.

In Berlin no notice has been taken of this suggestion.

London, Aug. 25.

The christening of the Tsesarevitch has taken place amid a most gorgeous ceremonial.

A salutes of 301 guns was fired, while the capital was most lavishly decorated in honour of the occasion.

London, Aug. 25.

Much dissatisfaction is expressed in St. Petersburg at the proclamation issued by the Governor of Malta, which forbids the coaling of ships proceeding to the seat of war or anywhere on the line of route with the object of intercepting neutral ships suspected of carrying contraband. The "Novoye Vremya" describes this as an act of hostility to Russia, since it cannot possibly affect Japan.

Later.

The Capetown correspondent of the "Daily Telegraph" states that orders have been given that no Russian warships are to be allowed to coal at Cape ports without reference to headquarters.

It is stated at St. Petersburg that before dismantling her warships now lying in neutral ports, Russia insists on Japan giving an assurance that she will not repeat the "Retshitelny" incident.

A hastily summoned meeting of the India and China section of the London Chamber of Commerce was held on the 25th instant in order to consider the present situation as affected by Russia's action in dealing with vessels carrying cargo regarded by her as contraband.

London, Aug. 26th.

Mr. Balfour, replying to the deputation from the London Chamber of Commerce, said the Government recently directed that urgent inquiries be made of the Russian Government regarding the appearance of the "Smolensk" in South African waters. It appeared that the Russian Government had hitherto been unable to communicate instructions to the Volunteer steamers; hence the recent incidents. Thereupon the two Governments agreed that cruisers be sent from the Cape Station to find the Volunteer steamers, and Great Britain consequently ordered two of the Cape cruisers to be immediately dispatched to seek the "Smolensk" and "Petersburg" and convey to them the instructions from the Russian Government to desist searching neutral vessels. He (Mr. Balfour) hoped, therefore, that the incidents of which complaint had been made were now ended.

The Premier added that the deputation might rely on the fact that the declaration made in the King's Speech on the occasion of the prorogation of Parliament (that full protection would be given to all British subjects in exercising the rights of neutrals under the law of nations) was not mere vague language. The British Government meant exactly what was said in the Speech, and the rights of the great shipping trade would not be ignored by the Government or by any Government to whom British interests were confided.

Berlin, Aug. 27.

The Chinese Government has communicated to the Russian Minister at Peking the information that the Chinese Admiral in command at Chefoo is to be court-martialed because he took no steps to prevent the Japanese from capturing the Russian destroyer "Retshitelny" and thereby violating the neutrality of China.

London, Aug. 27.

Two Russian ships carrying coal and water for the Baltic Squadron have passed the Bosphorous.

BERLIN, Aug. 28.

The departure of the Baltic squadron for the Far East has again been postponed, and it is now stated the squadron will not leave till the end of December.

The authorities here doubt whether the squadron will ever reach the East.

The Paris correspondent of the "Daily Chronicle" sends a report that Russia intends to buy war-ships from Chile and Argentina. These war-ships, it is stated, will leave American waters under the French flag, and hoist the Russian naval flag on reaching the Far East.

[Similar statements have been repeatedly made, only to be as often denied.]

BERLIN, Aug. 28.

The Paris correspondent of the "Berliner Tageblatt" wires the information that a Russian Second Army Corps will be formed, to be concentrated at Mukden.

LIAOYANG.

Although we have already received news from Tokio that Liaoyang has been occupied by Japanese troops, there is now reason to doubt its accuracy. Although we have been of opinion that general Kuropatkin would find Liaoyang untenable on account of the vulnerability of his lines of communication we must confess that the news of the Japanese occupation of Liaoyang which we published on Saturday came to us as a very considerable surprise.

It now appears (although the second report carries no better credentials than the first) that Liaoyang, although seriously menaced, has not yet been taken. The Japanese army seems to be advancing with a view to surrounding the Russian position but there is nothing to show how Kuropatkin intends meeting them. He may be retreating, he may be making counter-movements or he may be "sitting tight."

That the Japanese attach great importance to the position is evidenced by the news that their losses in attacking have so far exceeded 10,000.

Probably part of Kuropatkin's army will be driven into Chinese territory, when we may expect to hear of another batch of war-lawyer disputes.

BIRTHDAY CELEBRATIONS.

A reception was held yesterday morning in the Palace in honor of His Majesty's fifty-third birthday. Members of the Foreign Diplomatic Corps and nearly all Foreign Employees of the Government were present. More extensive celebrations were dispensed with owing to the nation still being in mourning for the late Empress Dowager.

The Imperial Marine Association has, a Tokyo despatch to the "Osaka Mainichi" says, decided, at a meeting of its chief officials held a few days ago, to construct a volunteer fleet, composed of about 10 commercial destroyers of several thousand tons each. The building programme and other particulars for the enterprise were to have been discussed at another meeting of the association held at Tokyo yesterday morning.

On Friday last the Il-chin-hoi despatched a portion of their delegates Messrs. So Saug-yun, Yang Chai-ik, Kim Myong-chun and Yom Chung-mo, to the residence of the Vice President of State urging a recognition of their first despatch with its 4 clauses of advice.

NEW BRITISH DIPLOMATIC GRADE.

A recent issue of the London "Official Gazette" contains the announcement of the creation of a new grade in the diplomatic service of the British Crown, namely, that of Councillor of Embassy, a rank which, while superior to that of first secretary of embassy, is inferior to that of minister resident or plenipotentiary. It is a grade that has existed for a number of years past in the diplomatic services of Germany, Austria and France, but not in that of England. Among those thus promoted are the Hon. Alan Johnstone, who married the sister of Gifford Pichot, of New York and Washington; Arthur Herbert, whose wife was Miss Helen Gammell, of New York and Newport; Arthur Raikes, until recently First Secretary of the Embassy at Washington; Cecil Spring Rice, now First Secretary at St. Petersburg, and lately married to the daughter of Sir Frank Lascelles, British Ambassador at Berlin, and Charles Fox Adam, whose wife is a daughter of Dr. J. Croxhall Palmer, formerly of the United States navy. At the same time Percy Wyndham, of the British Embassy at Washington, and Wilhelm Max Muller, are promoted to be first secretaries of embassy.

"My breakfast is a cereal story," declared the dyspeptic.

Complainst are received of the small wages paid to coolies, working on the railroad. The Magistrate of Sinkyeh states that 700 coolies he has supplied to the authorities receives insufficient pay for their food.

A picture by the late M. Verestchagin, representing Admiral Makaroff holding a council of War, is reported in Berlin to hare been recovered from the floating débris of the Petropavlovsk, on board of which it was painted.

The Daito Shimpo states that "secret correspondence finds its way into Russia via the northeastern provinces and Vladivostock." It would be interesting to know how our Japanese contemporary is cognizant of this if the correspondence is conducted secrettly.

Mr. Brindle, the Special Correspondent of the "Daily Mail" at Newchwang, was thrown from his horse at Karpangtse recently and wss so badly knocked about that he had to be removed to Newchwang hospital by spebial train. Mr. Brindle is the correspondent who was with Mr. Etzel at the latter's death, and had so narrow an escape from sharing the same fate.

The editor of a certain paper recently received a fine chicken, which he, supposing it to be a token of appreciation from a discriminating reader, took home, and enjoyed for dinner. The following day he received this letter. "Dear Mr. Editor,—Yesterday I sent you a chicken in order to settle a dispute which has arisen here. Can you tell us what the chicken died of?"

A telegram from Mukden says that the following letter has been received there from Port Arthur:—

"We have confidence in General Stoessel. His certainty of victory is imparted to all the troops and the inhabitants. General Fock is at present resisting the pressure of the Japanese on our advanced positions, and the siege will drag on for a long time. General Kondratieff is fortifying Port Arthur, making it every day stronger. On hills where not long ago fortifications were considered impossible batteries and intrenchments have been constructed and guns of large and small calibre have been mounted. The co-operation of the generals has made Port Arthur an inaccessible fortress."

The Korea Daily News.

To be published daily except Sundays.
Rate of Subscription:—
Per Year, Yen 25.
Per Quarter, Yen 7.
Per Month Yen 2.50

Postage in Korea not charged extra.
Postage abroad charged extra.

Advertisements, 50 sen per day for 1 inch or less.
5 yen per mouth per inch.
50 yen per year per inch.

All communications to
E. T. BETHELL,
Editor and Publisher.
Pak-tong, Seoul

JAPAN'S INFLUENCE IN KOREA.

PART IV.

The Koreans, usually long suffering and apathetic, were thoroughly roused when the true inwardness of the Nagamori demands became known to them. A society called the PO AN HOI was formed, having for its object the preparation of a memorial to the throne protesting against the granting of these demands. The meetings of this society were quite orderly and the speeches were firm but temperate. There were other societies having the same advanced object which were either merged into the PO AN HOI or disbanded. About this time circulars advocating violence against the Japanese were distributed broadcast through the country.

This proceeding was regretable from every point of view, and although the author or authors of the pamphlets may, likely enough, have been members of the Po An Hoi, there is not the slightest indication that the Society, officially, had any connection with it. The Po An Hoi advocated constitutional protest, not violence.

To the eye of the ordinary observer the city presented its usual appearance of peace and quietness, when, towards the end of July, it became known that the Japanese had proclaimed a modified form of martial law in Korea.

This was immediately followed by the arrest, by Japanese gendarmerie, of some of the leading spirits and speakers at the Po-an-hoi meetings. Some of the arrested ones, after a short disappearance, re-appeared and announced their conversion to the Japanese views. Some, who were not so amenable, were kept under arrest. We last heard of them somewhere outside the Peking Pass, but at any rate they no longer participated in the Po-an-hoi meetings.

The last (we believe it was the last) of these meetings was dispersed by Japanese soldiery at the point of the bayonet.

We have never been able to see any justification for these harsh measures. If the agitation was a foolish one it could have been left alone with safety, or at least met with gentler arguments than cold steel.

Foolish or wise, the agitation was the direct outcome of the Nagamori Scheme, which goes to show that the consequences of a piece of folly are not to be counted beforehand.

The military authorities are now, on all sides, encountering difficulties in recruiting the coolies whom they require for their lines of communication in Korea and Manchuria. The reluctance of the coolies can be explained in many ways, but there is no doubt that if the coolies had thorough confidence in their would-be employers, many more volunteers would be forthcoming. The Japanese request appears to us to have been a perfectly reasonable one, and we think that in pursuance of the protocol signed by the two powers on the outbreak of war, the least the Korean authorities could do would be to see it put into effect. However, the fact remains, the coolies are stubbornly resisting all efforts to persuade them to volunteer. The pay offered is much better than the coolie earns at his ordinary avocations, and the difficulty in recruiting is doubtless largely due to the mistaken policy which Japan has pursued in this country.

Of the other results of Japan's re-accession to power and influence in this country, it is too soon yet to speak. The Japanese Minister has obtained His Majesty's consent to the appointment of two foreign advisers. A Japanese, Mr. Megata, is, subject to the direction of the Korean Minister for that department, to assume control of the finances of the country, and an American subject is to be active adviser to the Foreign Office. These appointments appear to us to be fair enough and there is every reason to believe that if the advisers prove to be gentlemen of tact and discretion their assumption of office will be of distinct advantage to this country.

The history of Japanese influence in Korea has now been brought up to date, some unimportant details we know are lacking but we believe that the principal facts are now before our readers. To-morrow we propose to summarize what we have written and point a moral therefrom, and we shall then ask our readers whether we can in fairness be accused of being anti-Japanese.

KOREAN JAPANESE CLUB.

In a recent issue we made mention of a proposal made for a club to secure social intimacy between the members of the two nations. We now learn that a meeting will be held today in the Hajo Hotel to discuss the question. The ministers of all departments will be the Korean representatives and Mr. Hayashi, General Haraguchi, Mr. Hagiwara and Colonel Saito will be present.

It is said that His Majesty is in favor of the adoption of the scheme and has promised a large portion of the necessary foundation expenses. It is expected that His Highness, the Crown Prince will be president of the club.

REMARKABLE ASSERTION.

A telegram, which is asserted to have been received by the army headquarters in Tokyo on July 2nd and only just published, states that 26 ships, loaded with provisions, left Weihaiwei on the 25th June for Port Arthur, but were seized by the Japanese blockading fleet and taken to Talienwan. There they were examined and the passengers transshipped, the ships and cargo being retained. This seems an altogether too extravagant story. That 26 ships destined for Port Arthur should have been in Weihaiwei (of all places in the world) without the matter becoming known, is too much to believe.

ARREST OF SUSPECTED SPIES.

The Magistrate of Heui-chon reports that on the 16th ult. a Japanese gendarme arrived in his district and arrested 8 citizens on suspicion of their being implicated in giving information relative to the movements of Japanese troops, to the Russians. They were removed to the Japanese military station at Anju.

In the interest of inquisitive humanity, says "Puck," the laws of war should forbid fighting at places not on the map.

HOBSON ON WAR.

Pacific Grove, July 21st.—Captain Hobson again had an audience which filled the large Chautauquan auditorium this afternoon. In his lecture on the American Navy he made a strong plea for its increase, and said his highest ambition was to see America mistress of the seas, with her flag reigning over the waters of the earth to keep the world's peace. Captain Hobson said he wanted to see so many guns in our Navy that their great number would make it unnecessary to use them.

"Give us an adequate Navy and no foreign power can ever land on our 17,000 miles of sea coast, within gunshot of which 20,000,000 of our people have their homes," he said. "Russia would now mortgage her empire for four generations to get twenty battleships, but can't get them, while Japan is happy because she spent so much money on her navy."

Captain Hobson said there was an understanding among the military powers of Europe to dismember and divide China among themselves, and he wanted the Monroe doctrine extended to China to prevent it. The powers would take advantage of the present war to divide China, and when the Russians had organized and drilled the millions of Chinese, the results might be disastrous to other nations.

Captain Hobson predicted that this would be done, and said he considered the Chinese superior to the Japanese, both industriously and as soldiers. He expressed the belief that the European nations will ultimately notify her that she is disturbing the peace of the world, and then the present war will stop, and the powers will extend their possessions in China as an excuse for maintaining peace there.

The moment the partition of China begins, the entire world will be involved, and the United States will be drawn into it, and there will be such a war as the world never saw. This could be stopped if we had an adequate Navy, and China be opened up as Japan had been by Commodore Perry. If the Russian programme of organizing the Chinese is carried out, the tramp of armies will be heard in our country for years, for we are opposite those hordes.

A consultation of all Japanese consuls in Korea is to be held today.

A gentleman of Pyeng Yang has sent 37 Yen to the Cheknk Sinmun to be handed to the family of Mr. Won-se the late chief of the Po An Hoi meeting, who was arrested by the Japanese.

Further reports of the riot at Kisho say that the Japanese punished the head men of the villages concerned in the trouble very severely, beating them with their swords. Two men were drowned in the river in their effort to escape.

The Daito Shimpo, discussing the decorations in Chinkokai, which are to serve as triumphal arches on the event of the fall of Port Arthur, remarks that the are becoming a matter for ridicule! With the pine trees all withered and the leaves yellow they are beginning to look a sorry sight.

On Sept. 1st one of the members of the Il-chin-hoi, Mr. Kim Myong-chun, in the course of his oration, urged the people to insist on the Government granting the Japanese request for all the land between the South Gate and the river. The audience evidently not appreciating his views, left the meeting place.

A telegram from Gensan states that on the 1st inst. the Russian troops at Hamheung numbered 1,208 men with 7 guns and 12 ammunition wagons. The magistrate of Songchin in connection with this, has a wonderful story to relate. He declares that from 4 to 5 hundred Russian cavalry have passed through his town daily since July 3rd, and he estimates the force at Hamheung at over 50,000 men.

The Korea Daily News.

VOL. I, MONDAY, SEPTEMBER 5, 1904. No. 43

大韓每日申報
대한미일신보

(뎨ᄉ십사호)　　(일요화)　　쳔구빅사년구월륙일

본사고빅

이 신보는 영어와 한어로 셔계리
ᄂᆞᆫ 츌판ᄒᆞᆸ
신문가
ᄒᆞᆫ쟝　엽두돈오픈
일삭됴엽두량닷돈　맛돈으로
밧습
광고료는
긔한의쟝단과ᄌᆞ힝의다쇼로죵
갑ᄒᆞ되련가로밧을터이오며오
ᄅᆡ지아녀대한사람마다마다이신
문을보실터이니광고내시기를
원ᄒᆞ시ᄂᆞᆫ이들은우리신문사에
와서면약ᄒᆞ심을희망ᄒᆞᆸ
○발힝소　박동대한미일신보
사별디한교엽해젼영국인셜필
림쟈리오
사쟝 영국인 (비셜)

본사지졈

인쳔항교젼동신진명씨로우리
대한미일신보사인항지졈쟝을
뎡ᄒᆞ엿ᄉᆞ오니인쳔항에계신
[illegible]

샤고

[illegible]

샤고

[illegible]

론셜

[illegible]

잡보

[illegible]

뎐보

[illegible]

붓터온보병을최동ᄒ야뎌진의중앙되는ᄀ장평과밋그부근에잇는황ᄒ산을향ᄒ야총창으로돌겨을힝ᄒ야그진터을쎄앗슨즉젹군는병력을증가ᄒ야용감ᄒ게막아싸화조금도그세가감ᄒ지안코대인평부근의젹군대포도또ᄒ우리를향ᄒ야사격을셩히힝ᄒ는고로우리는장찬위친ᄒ대싸갓스나맛춤비잘부지ᄒ야젹군을도가나다지ᄅᄒ는곳으로평방ᄒ지카우중디ᄂ시벽브린젹진의우편에잇는강ᄉ평파강수병에셔남이오궁장평에셔셔편되는쳘반ᄉ과밋그중간디점을향ᄒ야방에승격을힝ᄒ야그좌익은젹진을탈취ᄒ엿스나갑사평은젼연히젼령치는못ᄒ엿고시벽브리겨견ᄒ야련속ᄒ야황혼ᄭ지밋쳣고좌종ᄃ도쏘ᄒ시벽브린보병의주력으로써용격ᄒ며젹진ᄒ야포병은거진반증령구히진츅ᄒ우셰ᄒ뎍군의대포를ᄃᄒ야으후두시브터비시ᄶ지밍렬ᄒ포젼을힝시ᄒ엿는ᄃ이ᄯ에젹의대포는유ᄒ지호젼묵ᄒ엿ᄉ나이거슬젼멸ᄒ지는못ᄒ엿고쏘젹의보병은병혁을증가ᄒ야우리좌익에근박ᄒ미졈ᄎ위험ᄒ니동포대의공격은일노말미암아크게지체ᄒ지라요진히말ᄒ건대우리군수는뎍진중앙을돌격ᄒ야젹군랑단ᄒ엿스나좌우량익은범이들도록오히려공략ᄒ을엇지못ᄒ고가지에칠월이십륙일오후벼시젼브터진퇴와대우가잇서갑산쇄막다이에벌안간연무가몽농ᄒ미공격의목뎍을달치못ᄒ고날아ᄒ는지라그후에홍사평밋대서구방면의젹군이수ᄎ격젹을시험ᄒ엿스나무효ᄒ는도라갓고우리는이괴회를타ᄒ사평을점령ᄒ야그평에셔위력이최대ᄒ든바뎍군의대포를분을탈취ᄒ지라팔월이십칠일에ᄀ죵되는대우를무릅쓰고진ᄎ용격ᄒ며젼진ᄒ엿스나젹의일부는여젼히강경ᄒ게뎌젹ᄒ야황혼에니르러는점점ᄒ사평에셔브터탕하좌안에잇는궁장평과샹티ᄒ어잇는보가서의남방놉흔쌍을지나대서구북방놉흔쌍쳑지련ᄒ진터를점령ᄒ지라이싸흠에극히밍렬ᄒ엿든거슨홍사평부근과밋궁장평부근의방싸흠에젹군은ᄯ이븅은탓스로우리군수의젼진흠을알고밍렬히공격ᄒ엿고ᄯ돌을산쇄탄이에서쏘니는비문에우리군수의수상이심히만핫스비이광경이극히비참ᄒ엿스나그러나우리군수는왼반히ᄒ야사격을시작ᄒ지안코곳게참고방쳑아니ᄒ다가칙죠ᄒ산악을ᄂ위장아올나가뎍진을돌격ᄒ지라뎍의방력은보병륙십오대터와대포이십문쯤인데그대부터는로양방면으로퇴각ᄒ엿고일부터는갓가히우리군의젼면에뎡지ᄒ엿스비안지진격ᄒ을계속ᄒ는중이라ᄒ엿더라

(구월이일대본영착)구월삼일동경발

대산총수령관발뎐

○뎨조하공격 중앙과좌익군젼면에잇든젹은구월이일에뎨조하우안으로퇴각을연속ᄒ고그일부는료양남방에셔서방으로연ᄒ놉흔곳싸흠터와목창동북놉흔곳을점령ᄒ고량군은뎡경을연속즁이오좌익군은뎨조하우편흑영티서방놉흔곳에잇는젹병을포격ᄒ야구월이일아츰놉흔곳일부를점령ᄒ엿다더라

구월이일동경발

○쇼희젼쥭칭 거월삼십일일련쇼구항외에서젹의쇼희젼쥭칭이괴계슈레에걸려서즉칭이되엿다더라

구월삼일동경발

○피젼군공격 대산총수령관의구월삼일오젼구시에발ᄒ보고를거ᄒ즉퇴주ᄒ는뎍병은샹금료양외부분에잇서셔져항ᄒ으로우리중앙군과좌익군은공격을연ᄒ여ᄒ는중이라더라

○중쟝경샹 일본륙군중쟝쇼쳔씨는료양부근의최후젼투중에경샹ᄒ엿다더라

잡보

○수ᄒ판인 수일젼브터일본헌병이밤에젼문외게서방황ᄒ다가 젼년로서나오는판인을붓잡고몸을수탐ᄒ는ᄃ대판도여러히일젼밤에수탐을당ᄒ엿스며미양붓잡고힐문ᄒ기를무삼연고로심야에젼년출입을ᄒ느냐ᄒ고여러말노힐난ᄒ엿다더라

○뭇학시취 작일샹오십시에학부대텽관과학무국장이하졔관원이학부에회동ᄒ야일본에뭇학싱으로파견ᄒ학도를시취ᄒ는ᄃ일본인모씨도와서학도의신톄검사ᄒ을젹에참관ᄒ엿더라

○뎐화죠공 궁ᄂ부와일본공ᄉ관간에뎐화가셜ᄒ다는말은젼보에긔재ᄒ엿거니와히뎐화가일작에가셜죠공이되야서금명간기통이된다더라

○구관범명 교하민요수천은일젼본보에긔재ᄒ엿거니와일본병칠십명이각쳐에믹복ᄒ고작요ᄒ는빅성을도륙ᄒ랴ᄒ는고로히서리군수리주현씨가ᄌ긔의위티ᄒ을도라보지안코일힌과무수히담판ᄒ야일병을회계ᄒ고팔면집강피쳐ᄒ야가논거슬ᄯ방송케ᄒ엿거놀히군빈운셔형등이식일인이도로혀빈은망뎍ᄒ고군슈가힐인의계의세하야역부들을모흔다ᄒ고구관ᄒ야관찰부에등소ᄒ는고로리군슈가변명ᄎ로샹경ᄒ엿다더라

○작소구거 ᄒ관원을한국병정교련장으로슈츅ᄒ엿더니근일에일본포병과보병이히교련장에가서련조ᄒ고한병은엄금ᄒ다더라

○투방로약 일젼에 죠칙이ᄂ리시기를맘렵이뎌욱심ᄒ터인싱의질병이실노념려되는지라하믈며루셜번을ᄒ가오티가뎌욱공축ᄒ니법부와원슈부검사국으로ᄒ여곰경슈와밋년칠싱이상파삼오이하는다방셕ᄒ라ᄒ옵셧는지라의정부죠회를범부에서등인ᄒ야쳠샹도외구항구재판소로ᄒ령ᄒ기를방송졀죄슈를분일은슈셩칙ᄒ야보리ᄒ라ᄒ엿더라

○립표엄금 안남산과밧남산을일병이군용디점으로슈용ᄒ다ᄒ야좌목을세워광점ᄒ고량ᄒ야도형ᄒ더니히디계안에잇는빅셩의초지ᄒ일초이를복셔지도엄금ᄒ야보쥬가감히착슈치못ᄒ게ᄒ다더라

○셩졀례포 작일 만슈셩졀에계동포티영에셔례포를노앗고당일하오삼시량에대포수문을 젼년로드러갓다더라

○퇴쳥참쟝 ᄒ슌쳔원우샹길셩진샹씨의륙군참령승임ᄒ거순쳥영운씨의쥬션중에셔된거시라는말이잇다더라

○경수장례 경무사김경근씨는히임되고원우샹씨가후임된다는소문이파다ᄒ다더라

○반명수샹 일인편에서온공보를거ᄒ즉일군의수샹이만명이나되엿다ᄒ니로안을둘너싸고밍렬이공격ᄒ수실이뎍확ᄒ다더라

○주차수단 한국주차군이이기수단으로증가ᄒ야기일기수단은통산에두게ᄒ고그수령관은지금료양방면에잇는장곡쳔대장이된다더라

○셩ᄒ일병 근일에셩ᄒ열병이셩히류힝ᄒ는ᄃ룡도원리수일인ᄂ면공하수와밋중학교쟝문학박ᄉ피원탄씨가이병에걸녀잇는ᄃᄂ면씨는ᄃ여수망ᄒ엿더라

○궁ᄂ고문 젼금능샹공부고문관가등증웅씨는당초에약ᄒ엿든것과갓치이번에궁ᄂ부고문관으로고빙ᄒ기로결뎡ᄒ는ᄃ년디수일젼에임의그항동도인을필ᄒ엿다더라

○렬도손히 황ᄌ쪽풍에경부렬도션로의손히된금익이삼만여원가량이나된다더라

○평안북학 근일평안도에빗학당이뎌단이창궐ᄒ다는데그빗학당졀셩은젼가락ᄒ며신츌귀몰ᄒ졔죠가비상ᄒ야이리셔운빅셩들의미호ᄒ야지금여러만명이그젼모의데ᄌ가되엿는티젼모인증지물을탐ᄒ야여러사름의계수렴ᄒ돈이누거만량인티그돈을다가지고이티로갓논지부지거처라수렴을번여러사람이일젼에샹경ᄒ야그돈을차닷나고경무청에호소ᄒ란호다ᄒ며그젼싱젼모는부지거처인고로그죡속의게좀죵식힐ᄉ신티젼모는호픈쳥우지숩이잇논고로장을수엽다더라

○면쳘아도 학부에셔쥬덕공관에면ᄒ기를아국에잇는유학싱을곳쳘환케ᄒ라ᄒ엿더라

○일미혜졍 일본농무셩에셔죠수ᄒ바를거ᄒ즉금년일본에셔금년에츄슈ᄒ쌀을미리가량ᄒ즉오쳔만셕이되리라ᄒ엿더라

○참졍힝공 참졍신긔션씨는지ᄎ수지소경인수소를봉졍ᄒ엿더니 우비를봉승ᄒ고로일젼츳리힝공ᄒ다더라

관보

뎨이쳔구빅이십삼호 광무팔년구월오일

○서임급ᄉ령

○면징계 한셩재판소젼판ᄉ 싱계승 한셩재판소젼검ᄉ 리종의 팔월삼십일일

○임륙군참장 륙군부령 김홍영 순쳔 륙군참령 원우샹 김진

○ᄂ셔리륙군법원장ᄉ무 륙군법원리ᄉ륙군참령 신계영

○면본직 시위뎨일련티뎨이대티부륙군보병부위 죠원하 시위뎨일련티뎨이대티부륙군보병참위 강필우 시위뎨일련티뎨삼대티부륙군보병부위 리형규 시위뎨일련티뎨삼대티향관륙군인등군수 젼계홍 친위뎨일련티뎨일대티부관륙군보병부위 빅남규 친위뎨일련티뎨일대티부륙군보병부위 박희양 김홍식 친위뎨일련티뎨이대티중티쟝륙군보병정위 리항로 친위뎨일련티뎨이대티부륙군보병부위 류완 친위뎨일련티뎨삼대티중티쟝륙군보병정위 민흥식 친위뎨일련티뎨삼대티부관륙군보병부위 빅명긔 친위뎨일련티뎨삼대티부륙군보병부위 오의션 친위뎨일련티뎨삼대티부륙군보병참위 최대영 친위뎨일련티뎨삼대티향관이등군수 쟝긔승 진위뎨일련티뎨일대티부륙군보병참위 김긔계 명달진 진위뎨일련티뎨삼대티부륙군보병참위 김운선

JAPAN AND KOREA.

The "Japan Times" has an article on "Japan in Korea" which justifies the action taken by Japan in general terms, but says not a word about the Nagamori scheme. It holds that Korean politicians are "beginning to recognise the truth that inexorable fate binds the fortunes of their country with those of their insular neighbours." "In fact," our contemporary proceeds, "we are strongly inclined to believe that the definite recognition of this truth on their part would have taken place more speedily and gracefully had it not been for the mischievous machinations by the numerous faction of the Russophile politicians rendered desperate by the unexpected deprivation of the source of their power and profits." It may be pointed out to our contemporary that a Japanese Minister to Korea a few years ago gave a very different reason for the dislike of Japan that prevailed in the peninsula. He said that much of the opposition was due to the character of the Japanese who came over to Korea with the object of exploiting the country, and whose conduct did not tend to raise the reputation of Japan. However, the "Japan Times" declares that the Japanese Government has no designs on Korean independence. "We are solemnly pledged before the world," says the Tokyo journal, "to respect the independence of the peninsular kingdom, and nothing in the past policy and action of the Imperial Government gives even the shadow of excuse for doubting its good faith in its international relations." A very similar assurance was given by the British Government when it first intervened in Egypt, but twenty years after the intervention the British Government is found to be practically in supreme control. When Governments begin intervening circumstances have a way of proving too strong for self-denying ordinances. If the Nagamori scheme goes into operation, and Japan is given an interest in the soil of Korea, our contemporary five years hence may be referring to the force of circumstances and "inexorable fate" as an excuse, just as British journals justify the continuance of the British protectorate in Egypt in similar terms.—Kobe Chronicle.

DRAMA OF SECRET INVENTIONS.

SOME ROMANCES IN REAL LIFE.

Before the days of patents the only way to make sure that an invention would remain the property of its original owner was to keep it secret, where this could be done without forcing it to remain in disuse. Even at the present day many processes and formulæ are kept from public knowledge in this way, the inventor preferring not to apply for a patent. If the history of secret processes could be written, writes a contributor to The Technical World, it would form a romantic and fascinating book, and one of the most interesting sections would be that which dealt with the many attempts to steal the secrets from their jealous owners. He goes on to say:—

The scene of one of these stories is laid in the wild moorland country around Sheffield, England, where a watchmaker named Huntman had built a factory for making steel by a process of his own invention. The secret was a very valuable one, for it was the only process by which steel could be made of uniform quality throughout; but Hunstman had little fear that any of his rivals would discover it, for he employed only picked and sworn workmen, and the portals of his factory were almost as strictly guarded against strangers as the doors of a bullion vault. However, one bitterly cold wintry night, when the wind was shrieking over the neighbouring moor, driving the snow in wild eddies before it, a tattered, shivering tramp presented himself at the door of the works and pitifully craved permission to warm his frozen bones at furnace fires. For a long time he pleaded in vain; the door-keeper was obdurate; but finally importunity and the pathetic aspect of the man won the day, and the tramp was admitted to the warmth, only to fling himself on the floor in utter exhaustion and to fall asleep. The rascal, however, was sleeping with one eye open, and with that eye he was craftily watching the men at their work, with the result that when an hour later he left the place with words of gratitude he took Huntsman's secret with him.

Another interesting story takes us to the neighbourhood of Temple Bar, in London, and to the shop of a chemist who was the only man in England that knew the secret of the manufacture of citric acid. So jealous was he of his invention that he would share it with no one, but worked alone in the laboratory over his shop in Fleet Street. One evening, however, when his processes were well advanced, he locked up his laboratory and left the premises for a time, assured that no one could possibly gain admittance during his absence. But he bargained without a certain uninvited guest who worked his way down the chimney into the laboratory and made such good use of his time that when he re-emerged from the chimney he had the manufacture of citric acid at his fingers' ends. It was in a similar way that the manufacture of tin-plate became possible in England—the secret being one which no person had been able to wrest from its owners in Holland for half a century. But there was a bold and crafty Cornishman, one James Sherman, who made up his mind to discover it at any cost. Going over to Holland, he found his way into the factory at great personal risk and brought the secret back safely. These are but a few of the little romances of successful secret-stealing, and who shall tell the number of attempts that have failed, or even how many lives have been lost in the attempting? Men will risk much to fathom such a secret as that of the monks of the Grande Chartreuse, who make the well-known liqueur of that name, for which a sum of $10,000,000 has been refused point blank; but the secret has defied all discovery. Among scores of secret processes just as successfully guarded is that which has given to the world the exquisitely beautiful Dresden China. It is said that not even a king may enter the guarded walls of the factory at Meissen, where the porcelain is made, with the solitary exception of the King of Saxony himself; and every workman is under a solemn oath, to which the severest penalties are attached, never to breathe a word of what goes on within the factory. Then there is the romance of inventions that have been absolutely lost to the world, of which one example must suffice. An American inventor named Ford, after long years of unremitting labour, had discovered a method of treating ore without smelting, and at a very small cost. So valuable was the discovery considered that fabulous offers were made to Ford for the secret; but, as ill-luck would have it, on the very day on which he had arranged to part with it in exchange, it is said, for an annuity of $600,000, he was struck down by apoplexy, and his secret died with him.

The Berlin "Tageblatt" publishes the following remarkable story of the adventures of a woman spy at Port Arthur:—

It has now been ascertained, says the journal, that a lady moving in the highest circles, and calling herself the Countess de la Torre, who died recently at Milan, was murdered by her husband, who killed her by repeated blows on the head with a hammer.

It appears that her real name was Christine Bellomo, and that for some time she acted as a spy at Port Arthur, in the pay of the Japanese Goverement. She was in the habit of giving brilliant receptions at her house, which were attended by a number of high officers. These she contrived to facinate by her beauty and charm of manner, and in that way she succeeded in learning important military secrets from them.

It has besn positively ascertained that a few days before the Petropavlovsk distaster, she transmitted a number of cypher telegrams to Tokyo by way of China. It is said that the Japanese Government paid her at the rate of £50 per word.

GROCER AS PROPHET.

A RIVAL TO DOWIE.

A host of rivals to Dowie are arising in America. Among them is one Lee Spangler, Pennsylvania grocer, who sold out his business in order to go to New York and Chicago to give utterance to his prophecies as "the last of the prophets." He has ordered one million tracts, which he will personally undertake to distribute in these cities.

The tract is a small card, upon one side of which is printed a picture representing the Angel Gabriel, with his trumpet, soaring over fleecy clouds. This inscription appears under the picture: "Blow the Trumpet. Sound the Alarm. The End of the World."

On the other side of the card is Spangler's prophecy of the destruction of the world. Three months before their occurrence, says the New York World, Spangler prophesied the Baltimore fire, the death of Mark Hanna, and the breaking out of the war in the East. Last April, among other things, he predicted a cool summer and the re-election of Roosevelt. For the past twelve years he has been predicting the end of the world in 1908. Talking with his followers recently, he elaborated his former prophecies somewhat. He said:—

"The war in the East will be brought to a close before the middle of autumn, when Japan will have conquered Russia; but fresh wars will break out. A great calamity in the shape of a fire will visit Philadelphia during the present summer. While the property lost, which will reach millions, will not equal that of the Baltimore fire, the loss of life will be extensive. This fire will come at night, and many firemen will be killed."

The Japanese Legation is now connected with the Palace by telephone.

The French Despatch boat "Kersaint" will leave Chemulpo for Shanghai tomorrow.

We have received a report to the effect that during the recent operations near Liaoyang Lieut.-General Ogawa, of the Japanese army was wounded.

The Chinese Government has informde the Russian Minister to Peking that the Admiral of the Northern Squadron will be punished, for not having taken steps to prevent the Japanese attack upon the "Riesitelini" at Chefoo.

PROLONGATION OF HOSTILITIES.

That the Japanese view the possibility of this war being a prolonged one with considerable equanimity may be seen from the following extract from the Jiji. The Jiji points out that, after the taking of Port Arthur and Vladi-

THE "RIESITELINI."

A Sasebo despatch reports that the Russian destroyer "Riesitelini," which was captured by our destroyer at Chefoo, recently arrived in tow at a certain place. An examination of the vessel shows that the damage sustained from the explosion on board is very slight.

THE RECRUITING OF COOLIES.

The Magistrate of Sin Chön, writing to the Home Office, has what appears to be a genuine grievance. He says that when he was instructed to collect coolies for work on the Japanese lines he was told to take none but volunteers.

Subsequently some Japanese, accompanied by Korean officials from Chinnampo, arrived on the scene and did every thing possible to obtain volunteers. The result was *nil*.

The Japanese, according to the magistrate's report, then offered a bonus of $.00 *per capita* and the magistrate inquires how in the remote possibility of any coolies being forthcoming even at this price, he is to find the funds to pay the subsidy.

The Korea Daily News.

To be published daily except Sundays.

Rate of Subscription:—

Per Year.	Yen 25.
Per Quarter.	Yen 7.
Per Month	Yen 2.50

Postage in Korea not charged extra.
Postage abroad charged extra.

Advertisements, 50 sen per day for 1 inch or less.
5 yen per month per inch.
50 yen per year per inch.

All communications to

E. T. BETHELL,
Editor and Publisher.
Pak-tong, Seoul

JAPANESE INFLUENCE IN KOREA.

(CONCLUDED).

V.

Having now set forth without reserve all the facts relating to Japan's actions in this country which we consider militate against her gaining the influence which is of such paramount importance to her, it is now only fair that we should turn our attention to those influences which adversely affected her interests, for which she was in no way responsible.

First and foremost, there is Korea itself. It would be impossible to conceive a nicer system of corruption than that which obtains in this country. Positions of responsibility and "trust" are openly bought and sold. In a lucrative district the position of governor or magistrate commands a high figure and the purchaser of the office recoups himself for his original outlay by "squeezing" the last cent out of the people under his jurisdiction. Another point is the instability of office in the Korean Government The "Gazette" is a long epitome of dismissals and reappointments. A foreign representative who is newly arrived is bewildered by the kaleidoscopic changes in the *personnel* of the Government to which he is accredited. When the war was in its early stages several war correspondents who were in Seoul, upon hearing that the Minister for this or that had resigned, and that so and so had been appointed in his stead, immediately wired the portentous news home. They attempted to keep pace with the "Official Gazette," but were soon left, panting and perspiring, in the rear. Correspondents now take no notice of resignations, especially as an official's first and second resignations seem to be only tentative and not "to be considered as final."

Then there seems to a good deal of "back stairs" influence obtaining. When "Lady" Hyon was the guest of Japan, she "talked through her hat" somewhat but there is no doubt that she is a lady to be reckoned with. (Lady Hyon was, by the bye, at one time said to be a rather frequent visitor at the Japanese Legation). Of Korean officials who are known to have no axe "to grind" there are lamentably few. There is one, who has lately succeeded to high office, who is undeniably beyond reproach, and we hope that there are others like him. Still the fact remains that the Korean Government would inspire more respect if it were more stable, and here is Excuse No 1 for the attitude which is adopted by Japanese Ministers to Korea.

The principal outside influence antagonistic to Japan has heretofore been that of Russia. Russian methods commended themselves to the Koreans very strongly. Russia had aims of her own, and she never professed any philanthropic interest in the welfare of this country. Russia wanted certain concessions, and provided she obtained those the Korean officials could mismanage their country to the top of their bent. Thus Russian influence as a dominant one, had many warm supporters.

At present Chinese influence is a factor of very minor importance. China does not seem to be wanting anything that Korea can bestow.

"Uneasy is the head that wears a crown." The Emperor of Korea had emancipation thrust upon him. There is no indication that the suzerainty of China was particularly irksome when in 1894 Japan benevolently undertook to relieve him of it. And subsequent events must have led him to believe that he had fallen out of the frying pan into the fire. China had maintained some sort of nominal hold on this country from ancient days, when the Japanese were raiding the South and East coasts in much the same way as the Danes descended upon England.

Now, to get down to solid fact, the position is this. Korea is an Empire whose independence and integrity is guaranteed by several treaties. Japan, justly enough, by virtue of her contiguity and superiority and for her own protection, claims the right to be the predominant power in this country.

The Japanese people by their "arrogance" have made themselves unpopular here and no measure heretofore introduced by Japanese diplomats have been acceptable to either the official or the coolie classes. There is ample room for improvement in the administration of Korea, and Japan professes a desire to see this improvement carried out and yet it is noticeable that the moment she had a chance her first proposal was the Nagamori Scheme, which can only be described as "land-grabbing," pure and simple.

We are not "anti-Japanese," and bear Japan, as a nation, nothing but goodwill and respect. A man may be a patriotic Englishman but he always reserves the right to criticise his government when he disapproves of its actions. And in the same way we claim to be wholeheartedly friendly to Japan and claim that our protest against Japan's actions in this country is a token thereof.

Our opinion,—and many others share it,—is that Japanese diplomats are going the wrong way to work. Japan has perhaps been the victim, of circumstances but she has done nothing to make herself liked in Korea and a good deal to make herself disliked.

We know of at least one Japanese diplomatist, a man of great talent, who holds the opinion that the Koreans are such inveterate intrigueurs, and the government is so rotten, that "strong" measures alone are effective. The answer to this is obvious. Let Japan look back upon the history of her past dealings with Korea. Her measures have certainly been strong, but what has she accomplished? Nothing.

And therefore we have from the first, arguing from the point of expediency alone, deprecated the "strong" measures. Let Japan, by getting her subjects in this country under better control, demonstrate to the people of Korea that it will be possible for the two races to live in harmony. Then let her lend her aid to the Emperor in freeing his Empire from the meshes and knots of bribery and corruption which at present render it helpless.

Civilization—in the Occidental sense of the word—has only recently been adopted by Japan, the process is still fresh in her memory, and Korea could have no better teacher.

These are our views, it has never been our object to stir up strife, but anyone who has read what we have set forth MUST agree that somehow or other the Japanese diplomatic methods in this country leave much to be desired.

(The end)

THE RUSSIAN TROOPS IN SAGHALIEN.

The "Chugai Shogyo" reports that there are now in Saghalien two infantry regiments and an artillery force, the latter being equipped with guns of an old type. In addition, there are about two battalions of volunters recruited from among the prisoners, but their discipline is far from satisfactory. In consequence of the non-existence of a telegraphic service between Saghalien and the opposite coast, alarming rumours were being circulated in the island, and it is feared that, unless provisions and other food stuffs are forthcoming from the Amoor region before the advent of the cold season, a famine will occur there this winter. The advent of the Japanese is therefore eagerly awaited by the islanders, who by the occupation of the island by the Japanese forces will thus be able to obtain supplies from Hakodate and Otaru. The paper further states that the islanders testified their good-will towards the Japanese on the occasion of the withdrawal of the Japanese residents, mostly fishermen, from Saghalien this spring.

ENGLAND AND GERMANY.

With regard to the continuous imputations levied against Germany by the English press, the Berlin "Post" states that England has sold 38 vessels to the belligerents.

NEW BANK NOTES.

The Dai Ichi bank announce that they intend making a new issue of paper currency. The denominations will be one, five and ten yen, and specimens have been forwarded to the Foreign Office asking them to exhibit them in the various Government departments.

On Saturday His Majesty the Emperor issued an edict ordering the release from jail of all prisoners under the age of 15 or over 70.

Mr. Sin Ki-sŏn, the new Vice Minister of State commenced his duties on Saturday.

Scarletina appears to be prevalent at Seoul. The death is announced of Mr. Uchida, a railway engineer, and a Japanese teacher in the Korean middle school is reported to be seriously ill.

The foreign office has notified the Legations that Mr. Yi Ha-yŏng having recovered from his recent indisposition, he resumes his post as Minister of Foreign Affairs, and Mr. Yun Chi-ho resigns his position as acting Minister.

During the Boer war a staff officer issued an order saying that "No one is permitted to sleep outside the blockhouses except the sentries," and that "men on outpost duty are forbidden to strike matches on the sky-line.—Correspondent in The Spectator.

The big fifty-foot phneumatic dynamite guns, which have long been one of the interesting, and to the average person most formidable, features of San Francisco, are for sale. Condemned by military experts as worthless for defence purposes because of their limited range, they will go to the scrap heap. The best bid so far received is $10,000. Modern high power guns will be placed on the ground now occupied by the obsolete weapons.

The Korea Daily News.

VOL. I, TUESDAY, SEPTEMBER 6, 1904. No. 44

HONGKONG & SHANGHAI BANKING CORPORATION.

Paid-up Capital.....	$10,000,000
Reserve Fund:—Sterling Reserve...	10,000,000
Silver Reserve.....	6,500,000
	26,500,000
Reserve Liability of Proprietors...	10,000,000

HEAD OFFICE, HONGKONG.

London Bankers, London and County Banking Company Limited.
Branches and Agencies,
London.

Amoy,	Hankow	Penang.
Bangkok,	Hiogo,	Rangoon,
Batavia,	Iloilo,	Saigon,
Bombay,	Lyons,	San Francisco,
Calcutta,	Manila,	Singapore,
Colombo,	Nagasaki,	Sourabaya,
Foochow,	New York,	Tientsin,
Hamburg,	Peking,	Yokohama,

Credits granted on approved Securities, and every description of Banking and Exchange business transacted.

Drafts granted on London and the chief Commercial places in Europe, India, Australia, America, China and Japan.

HOLME RINGER & CO., AGENTS,
CHEMULPO.

ON CHEONG & CO.,
SEOUL.
GENERAL STORE KEEPERS.
Imported provisions, Cooking Utensils Crockery, etc.
FRESH BREAD DAILY.

MITSU BISHI DOCKYARD & ENGINE WORKS,
NAGASAKI.

CODE WORD, "DOCK."

A. 1, A. B. C.. and Engineering Codes used.

DOCK No. 1 (at Tategami).

Extreme Length..............	523 feet
Length on blocks	513 ,,
Width of Entrance on Top......	89 ,,
,, ,, Bottom....	77 ,,
Water on Blocks at Spring Tide	26½ ,,

DOCK No. 2 (Mukaijima).

Extreme Length..............	371 feet
Length on Blocks..............	360 ,,
Width of Entrance on Top......	66 ,,
,, ,, Bottom	53 ,,
Water on Blocks at Spring Tide	22 ,,

PATENT SLIP (at Kosuge).

Can take vessels up to 1,000 tons gross.

THE WORKS are well equipped with the LATEST IMPROVEMENTS, and can execute any kind of work in SHIPBUILDING and MARINE ENGINEERING, as well as in REPAIRING of SHIPS.

The COMPANY'S new powerful steamer OURA-MARU (712 tons, 700 I.H.P.), specially built for SALVAGE PURPOSES, and equipped with necessary gear, is always READY at SHORT NOTICE.

CHARTERED BANK OF INDIA AUSTRALIA & CHINA.

INCORPORATED BY ROYAL CHARTER 1853

HEAD OFFICES:—LONDON.

Paid-up Capital	£800,000
Reserve Liability of Shareholders ....,.......	800,000
Reserve Fund	800,000

Drafts granted upon all the principal places in the world and every description of Exchange and banking business transacted.

E. MEYER & Co., Agents,
Chemulpo.

E. MEYER & CO.
Chemulpo.

SOLE AGENTS IN KOREA FOR:
A. T. Morse, Sons & Co's "Fresco" Distemper

In all colours ready for use on walls, Ceilings etc.
and
AVENARIUS CARBOLINEUM

A wood-preserving and antiseptic oil preparation
Against decay, dry-rot, fungus and wood-destroying insects.

A large supply always in Stock.
Prices upon application.

E. MEYER & Co.,
Chemulpo.

LAW UNION & CROWN INS. CO.

Fire risks accepted at Current rates, on go downs, merchandise, dwellings, and other property, subject to usual conditions.

HOLME RINGER & Co.,
Agents, Chemulpo

THE METHODIST PUBLISHING HOUSE,
Little West Gate, Seoul.

JOB PRINTING, TYPEWRITER PAPER
CARBON PAPER, VISITING CARDS
STATIONERY, BOOK BINDING
BOOK PUBLISHERS
AMERICAN SCHOOL BOOKS
SPENCERIAN COPY BOOKS
PEN CARBON LETTER AND BILL BOOKS

S A BECK, Manager

DAI-ICHI GINKO.
LIMITED.
(Formerly the First National Bank)

ESTABLISHED 1873

INCORPORATED UNDER PRESENT LAW 1896

Capital - - - - - - - -	Yen 5,000,000
Reserve Fund - . - - -	1,500,000

HEAD OFFICE:—TOKIO.

President: Baron SHIBUSAWA.

BRANCHES AND CORRESPONDENTS
In the Principal Cities and Towns of Japan.
Interest Allowed on

Fixed deposits 1 year - - -	6½ per cent
" " 6 months - - -	6 per cent.

Special current accounts 1½ sen daily per Y 100
General " " 1 " " " 100

M. TANAKA,
Manager, Chemulpo

HOLME RINGER & Co.
Chemulpo.

General Merchants and Government Contractors.

Agents for the leading
Banks
Steamship Companies
and
Insurance Companies

Importers of Merchandise of every description.

KAMEYA & CO.
GENERAL STOREKEEPERS
Chinkokai - - Seoul
(*Established 1895, Tokyo*)

Confectionery, Hams, Canned Goods, Cutlery, Hirano & Tansan Water, Provisions, Gents, Furnishing goods, Toilet Articles, Travelling Bags, Tobacco, Cigars & Cigarettes Kitchen Utensils. Coffee, Biscuits.

Fresh Goods always kept in Stock.
Prices Moderate
☞ *Please come and inspect our goods.*

NIPPON YUSEN KAISHA.
JAPANESE MAIL STEAMSHIP CO.

UNDER MAIL CONTRACT WITH THE IMPERIAL JAPANESE GOVERNMENT.

European Line

Regular Fortnightly Service between Yokohama Kobe, Moji, Shanghai, Hongkong, Singapore, Penang Colombo, Port Said, Marseilles, London and Antwerp

American Line

Regular Fortnightly Service between Hongkong and Seattle, calling at Shanghai, Moji, Kobe, Yokohama and Victoria, B. C.

Australian Line

Regular weekly Service betwen Japan Ports and Australia, calling at Hongkong and Manila.
(Above Three Lines Suspended until further notice).

Shanghai Line

Weekly Service between Shanghai and Japan Ports

Korea Line

Service Kobe, Moji, Nagasaki, Fusan, Chemulpo, Chefoo, Taku.
S. S. Bahtelsberg, 2181 tons.
Service Kobe, Moji, Fusan, Chemulpo, Chinnampo
S. S Argo, S. S. Ohio.

BORDEN'S CONDENSED MILK CO.
New York, U. S. A.

ALWAYS IN STOCK
Eagle Brand Condensed Milk.
Gold Seal Condensed Milk.
Peerless (Family) Evaporated Cream.
Borden's Malted Milk.

E. MEYER & CO.
Chemulpo, Korea,
Sole Agents

ROYAL INSURANCE COMPANY,
Funds exceed £10,000,000
FIRE
AT CURRENT RATES.
LIFE
REDUCED PREMIUM.
HOLME RINGER & Co.,
Agents, Chemulpo.

HOTEL DU PALAIS
SEOUL.

The only first class Hotel in Seoul. Situated in the centre of the city opposite the palace.

Cuisine under the supervision of an experienced French Chef.

Well ventilated and furnished throughout.

TARIFF UPON APPLICATION

L. MARTIN
Proprietor and Mangaer.

大韓每日申報
대한미일신보

(뎨사십오호)　(슈요일)　쳔구빅사년구월칠일

부 사 고 빅
[illegible] 와 한어로셔계ᄅᆡ
[illegible]
셔류 사
[illegible] 오로
[illegible] 맛돈으로
[illegible]
시하와삼단과ᄌᆞ힝의다쇼로죵
류는디가로밧을터이오며오
리가이너대한사람마다다이신
문을보실터이니광고버시기를
원ᄒᆞ시는이들은우리신문사에
와서ᄇᆞ이ᄒᆞ심을희망ᄒᆞᆷ
(경성)발힝소 박동대한미일신보
사 빅어회교약해 젼영국인셜펠
립젼자리오
사장 영국인 (빅셜)

본사지졍
인쳔항교젼동신지명ᄊᆡ로우리
대한미일신보사인항지졍장을
퇴졍ᄒᆞ엿스오니인쳔항에계신
구람ᄒᆞ고자ᄒᆞ시는쳠군ᄌᆞ는히지
졍에왕림편의ᄒᆞ시옵

사고

○우리대한미일신보의목뎍은
대한의안녕질셔에관한모든대
목에ᄃᆡᄒᆞ야논공평한변론을쥬
쟝홈이라우리동신원의담보는
신문보시는쳠군ᄌᆞ의계ᄒᆞ샹보
도ᄒᆞ려며편지를긔서ᄒᆞ여주시
는이는셩명과쥬소를져이붓치
시기를희망ᄒᆞ오니이거슨신문
샹에긔졔ᄒᆞ라는거시아니오다
만긔히신용ᄒᆞ는증거를숨고자
ᄒᆞᆷ이라긔자는아모긔서던지긔
지ᄒᆞᆷ을퇴각ᄒᆞ는권리를가졋스
나퇴각ᄒᆞ는리유를말ᄒᆞᆯ터이오
며공즁광회를문란케ᄒᆞ는듯ᄒᆞᆫ
긔서는의례히밧지안켓ᄉᆞᆸ나이
다

사고

○본사에서는신문갑슨미월에
젼금으로밧ᄉᆞ오며본신문은우
톄로붓치는고로본사에서는다
른신문사쳐름군ᄇᆡ을거두리는
비지안ᄉᆞ오니우리신문을ᄉᆞ랑
ᄒᆞ야구람ᄒᆞ시는쳠군ᄌᆞ는양력
미월쵸즁에리월도선금과거쥬
셩명과동호수를ᄌᆞ세히젹어셔박
동본사로보내시기를바라오며
월회일니로젼금을아양력금니
보내시는곳에는리월일브터
신문을아니보낼터이오니죠량
ᄒᆞ옵소셔
●본사에서아직긔계를쟝만치
못ᄒᆞ와다른ᄃᆡ서박여오는고로
미양월요일에는츌판이대단히
늣게되는듯ᄉᆞ로본젼이미우늣
게되오니우리신문을구람ᄒᆞ시
는 쳠군ᄌᆞ는 용셔ᄒᆞ여주심
을희망ᄒᆞ옵나이다

론셜

젼호련쇽
○근일에일본셔한국에ᄃᆡᄒᆞ야
보돈ᄒᆞ는일이보죤ᄒᆞ게ᄒᆞ렴은
엽고다만ᄌᆞ긔의권력ᄃᆡ로무론
무삼일에든지ᄌᆞ긔나라에반진
요ᄒᆞ고유익ᄒᆞᆷ은ᄒᆞ라는쳐담에
우리도이러케반ᄃᆡᄒᆞᆷ이로다
한국셔도부픽ᄒᆞᆫ풍쇽에아모조
록조ᄒᆞᆫ방칙은싱각지아니ᄒᆞ고
졔일싱ᄒᆞ게ᄒᆞ는일이잇는거시
미관원작ᄒᆞ는악졍을ᄒᆡᆼᄒᆞ야소
위관찰사와군수의ᄌᆞ리는셩등
요임으로얼아엄명ᄒᆞ는쳐담에
치빈ᄒᆞᆫ다칭ᄒᆞ고탐학이무쌍ᄒᆞ
야민지를박할ᄒᆞ여이왕소비를
츙분ᄒᆞ라고ᄒᆞᆷ쇄와라졍부에도
근폐단이스니관보라ᄒᆞ는거슨
젼쫑이거위관리의임면ᄲᅮᆫ인고
로외국셔처음으로나오공사ᄒᆞᆫ
분이한국졍부관리들을츤회로
임면ᄒᆞ는ᄃᆡ졍신을차릴수업다
는말도잇고쇼기젼필ᄇᆡ에한셩
신계잇는젼사ᄒᆞ는신원들이모모대
신의무샹일로졔ᄉᆡᆼ되고임명되
는거슨한권이ᄒᆞᆫ소문만녀여ᄌᆞ
ᄂᆞ나라분면ᄇᆞᆫ들을ᄒᆞ다가필경
에조임모게가되고일이ᄎᆞ사졍
소는의례히ᄒᆞ는쳐담에엇지홀
수엽셔도모져치지ᄒᆞ야괴롭지
아니ᄒᆞᆫ일도잇스며
더욱갈수록권리를취ᄒᆞᆷ에별일
비만ᄒᆞ니졍세의부인은일본ᄭᅥᆺ
슬버혀면셜세지ᄒᆞ엿다고ᄒᆞ나
이는ᄒᆞᆫ녀안인즉말ᄒᆞ거시엽스
되이왕에무샹일로인ᄒᆞ야일본
공관에ᄒᆞᆫ번갓더니그후로죵죵
왕래를ᄒᆞᆫ다ᄒᆞᆫ즉한국관리즁
에는이러ᄒᆞᆫ일을알고도탄식ᄒᆞ
지아니ᄒᆞ라고ᄒᆞ는사름도업는
즁간ᄃᆡ관즁에는량반ᄒᆞᆫ분이론
박ᄒᆞ야대쳑ᄒᆞ엿다ᄒᆞᆫ즉다른량
반들도아모조록이와갓치ᄒᆞ기
를바라는지라이러ᄒᆞᆫ힝실을우
금견ᄒᆡᆼᄒᆞ는거슨졍부에서들도
그녀인의세력이뭉ᄒᆞ고ᄒᆞᆫ쳐담에
다만공경ᄒᆞᆯ줄만알아그러ᄒᆞᆷ인
듯ᄒᆞ고일본사람들도이러ᄒᆞᆫ일을
용셔ᄒᆞ야한국관리들기릉이로
다밧고로위력을ᄒᆡᆼᄒᆞ야일본을
반ᄃᆡᄒᆞ는나라는오직아라사인
ᄃᆡ이나라사름들에ᄒᆡᆼ위는한국
ᄇᆡᆨ셩의게더욱심ᄒᆞ야저히의ᄯᅳᆺ
ᄒᆞ는바무샹리익만잇스면한국
의안위는불고ᄒᆞ는즁무샹계야
미던지아인의소원ᄃᆡ로ᄒᆞ야한
국관리들은ᄌᆞ긔나라에는아모
리히롭고그른일이라도방ᄒᆞᆼ엿시
ᄎᆡ사ᄒᆞ는지라그러ᄒᆞᆷ으로아인
의권력이대단ᄒᆞ야더욱우심ᄒᆞ
게ᄒᆞᆫ자이만히는지라
근일에는쳥인의ᄒᆡᆼ악은조곰도
엽스며셜혹쳥국서요구ᄒᆞ는게
잇드리도한국에서ᄒᆞ려ᄒᆞ지아
니ᄒᆞᆯ것갓튼즉
이는황뎨위로나가셩으로그리
ᄒᆞ신이요쳥국서아모것도졔츌
ᄒᆞ나ᄒᆞᆷ은갑오년에일본사름들
이후의로방셕ᄒᆞ야쎠기며나간
ᄃᆡ로샹히국츅ᄒᆞ야압과가된쳐
담에미사에국진히조셩ᄒᆞᆫ일ᄲᅮᆫ
더러오늘날이라에쳥국이른ᄒᆞᆷ
잇는거슨일본셔다만동남방히
안으로만츙돌공격ᄒᆞᆫ리유니지
각
가지금에한국권리가졈졈쇠ᄒᆞ며
가는거슨일본셔한국강토와독
립자주를보죵ᄒᆞᆫ다고약조를셩
립ᄒᆞᆫ후ᄌᆞ긔의보호ᄒᆞ는권리를
이나라에ᄒᆡᆼᄒᆞ야마음ᄃᆡ로ᄒᆞ며
ᄒᆞᆫ일에든지방자히지휘ᄒᆞ며한
국을관할ᄒᆞ야무ᄉᆞ일이던지의
향ᄃᆡ로ᄒᆡᆼᄒᆞ는ᄃᆡ쳐쇠쟝샹세의
무지기잔ᄉᆞ권졔츌ᄒᆞᆫ은한국
토지를쟝즁에너으랴ᄒᆞᆷ이분명
ᄒᆞᆫ지라
우리는일본사름들을실로반ᄃᆡ
ᄒᆞᆷ이아니라일본도한나라인즉
아모조록호의를두며국진이공
경ᄒᆞᆯ터이로되만일우리로ᄒᆞ야
곰비ᄒᆞ여말ᄒᆞᆯ진ᄃᆡ영국사름ᄒᆞ
나이잇셔즁의지싱이잇슬지경
이면ᄌᆞ긔나라에셔불법ᄒᆞᆫ정형
을ᄒᆡᆼᄒᆞ는거시라도진실로광ᄌᆞᆼ홈
으로싱이로보존ᄒᆞ려ᄒᆞᆷ인고로
우리도이런사름과갓치일본서
한국에ᄃᆡᄒᆞ야불법으로ᄒᆡᆼᄒᆞ는
일이잇기에렬심으로론박ᄒᆞ야
반ᄃᆡᄒᆞᆷ이니우리의싱각에는아
모리ᄒᆞ여도일본외교관들의ᄌᆡ
ᄉᆞᄒᆞᆷ이대단히그르게ᄒᆞ는거시
일본셔ᄋᆞᆼ당가치ᄒᆞᆯ반ᄒᆞᆫ조진이
잇슬듯ᄒᆞ거놀지금갓ᄐᆞ여서는
한국에셔불호ᄒᆞ는일ᄉᆡᆼ이요조
곰도낫종ᄒᆞ는바는업ᄉᆞᆫ즉
일본외교관즁쇼셩에릉난ᄒᆞ며
졔에가동민ᄒᆞᆫ사름이ᄒᆞ나만잇
드리도가히취ᄒᆞᆯ졔를세워한국에
완고ᄒᆞᆫ구습으로잔ᄉᆞᄒᆞᆫ무리들
을타엽시ᄒᆞ고졍부에부픽홈을
싱각ᄒᆞ야실효가잇게ᄒᆞᆯ만ᄒᆞ거
는우금것아모것도셩취되게ᄒᆞᆫ
거시엽ᄉᆞᆫ즉일후일본ᄉᆞ젹에일
한량국왕ᄉᆞ를괴롭ᄒᆞ게되드리
도다만무단히강압만ᄒᆞ엿슬ᄲᅮᆫ
이요ᄒᆞ나도진익된거슨업다고
분명이말ᄒᆞᆯ터인지라
이러ᄒᆞᆷ으로우리는쳐음붓터조
ᄒᆞᆫ방편을좃ᄎᆞ변론ᄒᆞᆷ이요말ᄒᆞ포
ᄒᆞᆫ외ᄉᆞ두는거슬졍히란식ᄒᆞ야
그러ᄒᆞᆫ거시만일일본셔한국
ᄇᆡᆨ셩들로ᄒᆞ야곰아모조록변동
ᄒᆞ야진보가되게ᄒᆞᆯ챡ᄒᆞᆫ지경이
변ᄒᆞ나라이셔로친목ᄒᆞ게지낼
터이요
산낙되ᄒᆞ는폐단과계반악습을
모도곳치도록방조ᄒᆞᆯ만ᄒᆞᆫ거시
긔화라는거시무어신쥴아지못
ᄒᆞᆫ즉일본셔아모조록방조ᄒᆞ란
ᄒᆞᆫ진ᄃᆡ한국에당ᄒᆞ여서는이만
ᄒᆞᆫ쳔ᄒᆡᆼ이업슬터인지라
우리는실로일본을반ᄃᆡᄒᆞ야소
요ᄒᆞ게ᄒᆞᆷ이아니요우리신문에
진술ᄒᆞᆫ바와갓치일본외교관의
수단이한국에ᄃᆡᄒᆞ야소망ᄒᆞ니
조보련대단히어그러진고로아모
조록세다라ᄒᆡᆼ당이녀비도록ᄒᆞ
편ᄒᆞ야이리ᄒᆞᆷ이로다 (완)

잡보

○요무괴착 신경무ᄉᆞ쳐임시
에쟝슐직과무계비를엄금ᄒᆞ엿
는ᄃᆡ엇젼거시남앗던지졔작일
에ᄒᆞᆫ계집을슐졈이쟝아가는ᄃᆡ
북셔인즁진봉남고진립을쎗스
며뒤에셰워가는놀근계집은곽
밀쏘고장싱남고신당거리죵의
ᄒᆞᆫ무리를압거셔경무쳥으로잡
아갓다는ᄃᆡ당일오후에경무쳥

문압헤셔그화샹을소회ᄒᆞ엿더라

○법ᄉᆞ죠회 법국공ᄉᆞ길림덕씨가외부에죠회ᄒᆞ되법국인이평양외셩에교당을건축ᄒᆞ로약간디단을미슈ᄒᆞ엿더니황실긔디부근에잇다ᄒᆞ고이거슬거절홈은ᄉᆞ리에당연치아니ᄒᆞ니본공ᄉᆞ는단당코거절홈을응락ᄒᆞ지못ᄒᆞ겟다ᄒᆞ엿다더라

○훈령각도 일본군의쳥구ᄒᆞᆫ바역부ᄉᆞ건으로전국이소동ᄒᆞ야곳곳이민요가징긔홈은본보에루ᄎᆞ긔지ᄒᆞ엿거니와히ᄉᆞ건을인ᄒᆞ야정부에셔일본ᄉᆞ령부와교셥ᄒᆞ고훈령을미초ᄒᆞ야지작일에졍부로셔니외부에통첩ᄒᆞ고보낸고로니부에셔는경셩남북도젼라남북도츙쳥남북도경긔도에훈령ᄒᆞ엿고외부에셔는각항구에훈령을발송ᄒᆞ엿는ᄃᆡ히훈령ᄉᆞ의에ᄒᆞ엿스되현금일본이빅만의무리롤어릭키고억만에의지졍을허비ᄒᆞ야히룩만리에로고홈을ᄉᆡ리지안코북으로포학ᄒᆞᆫ아국을공격ᄒᆞ야동양의평화롤보젼ᄒᆞ고우리대한의독립긔초롤호위ᄒᆞ니우리한국이국력이폐이지못ᄒᆞ고병제가미비ᄒᆞ야비록능히긔병ᄒᆞ야합셰ᄒᆞ야셔함께직회는의무롤밝히지는못ᄒᆞ는그군물슈운ᄒᆞ는슈고는우리국민된자의리의ᄉᆞ양치못홀비라ᄉᆞ리가이러ᄒᆞᆫ즉각디방관이여뜻스로인민의게잘ᄀᆡ유ᄒᆞ엿스면민심이분발ᄒᆞ야ᄌᆞ원쟈가만을거슬거힝ᄒᆞ는쟝교비가촌려에횡힝ᄒᆞ야젼지롤토색ᄒᆞ고방ᄌᆞ이ᄉᆞ졍을힝ᄒᆞ며억륵으로모집ᄒᆞ는고로빅셩이의심ᄒᆞ야혹은말ᄒᆞ되전쟝셔지쇼여더려다가시험으로디뢰포롤발ᄊᆡᄒᆞᆫ다ᄒᆞ고도ᄒᆞ며혹은왜역부롤단발ᄒᆞ야병졍으로쓴다ᄒᆞ고ᄒᆞ나도응모ᄒᆞ는쟈업고도로혀작당ᄒᆞ야민요롤이릭키며혹도망ᄒᆞ야숨는거시실샹륵모ᄒᆞ는연고라이제역부갈ᄯᅡ이일아전쟝에셔샹거가쳔여리요삭전이평일보다후ᄒᆞ고의식ᄒᆞ기편리ᄒᆞ고비왕릭에돈보니기용이ᄒᆞ니이세세ᄒᆞᆫᄉᆞ의롤소샹히인민의효유ᄒᆞ고수효롤비졍치말고ᄌᆞ원을조ᄎᆞ만히모집ᄒᆞ야일본대창조과원의게교부ᄒᆞ야량국평화롤손샹ᄒᆞ는디경에이르지말게ᄒᆞ라ᄒᆞ엿더라

○비ᄉᆞ죠회 수일전에비국공ᄉᆞ가외부로죠회ᄒᆞ되만국렬도공회의미녀긔부금ᄒᆞ는거시이왕됴야안건에조지ᄒᆞᆫ즉곳긔부금을송교ᄒᆞ라ᄒᆞ엿더라

○의ᄉᆞ회국 의티리공ᄉᆞ모락씨가본국에도라갈ᄎᆞ로지작일에인천ᄋᆞ로하거ᄒᆞ엿다더라

관보

진위뎨이련ᄃᆡ뎨일대ᄃᆡ부륙군보병부위 리긔명 진위뎨삼련ᄃᆡ뎨이대ᄃᆡ부관륙군보병부위 리민회 진위뎨오련ᄃᆡ뎨일대ᄃᆡ즁ᄃᆡ쟝륙군보병졍위 리병규 진위뎨륙련ᄃᆡ뎨이대ᄃᆡ부륙군보병부위 리셕윤 시위뎨 련ᄃᆡ뎨일대ᄃᆡ부륙군보병참위 송우영 친위뎨일련ᄃᆡ뎨일대ᄃᆡ부륙군보병참위리긔범 친위뎨일련ᄃᆡ뎨삼대ᄃᆡ부륙군보병참위 손은영 진위뎨오련ᄃᆡ뎨일대ᄃᆡ부륙군보병참위 죠란슌

○임륙군보병참령 륙군일등ᄉᆞ군젼지홍 임륙군보병졍위 륙군보병부위 류완 박명긔

○임륙군보병부위 륙군보병참위 라죵빈 강필우 민완식 륙군이등군ᄉᆞ 쟝긔승

○임륙군일등군ᄉᆞ 륙군보병졍위 리항로 리병가

○보시위뎨일련ᄃᆡ뎨이대ᄃᆡ부륙군보병부위 쟝긔승 최대영

○보시위뎨일련ᄃᆡ뎨삼대ᄃᆡ부륙군보병부위 박회양

○보시위뎨일련ᄃᆡ뎨삼대ᄃᆡ향관 륙군일등군ᄉᆞ 리항로

○보친위뎨일련ᄃᆡ뎨일대ᄃᆡ부관 륙군보병부위 리민회

○보친위뎨일련ᄃᆡ뎨일대ᄃᆡ부륙군보병부위 리현규 륙군보병참위뎡달진

○보친위뎨일련ᄃᆡ뎨이대ᄃᆡ즁ᄃᆡ쟝 륙군보병졍위 류완

○보친위뎨일련ᄃᆡ뎨이대ᄃᆡ부륙군보병부위 리셕윤

○보친위뎨일련ᄃᆡ뎨삼대ᄃᆡ즁ᄃᆡ쟝 륙군보병졍위 빅명긔

○보친위뎨일련ᄃᆡ뎨삼대ᄃᆡ부관 륙군보병부위 죠원하

○보친위뎨일련ᄃᆡ뎨삼대ᄃᆡ부륙군보병부위 강필우 륙군보병참위 김광슌

○보친위뎨일련ᄃᆡ뎨삼대ᄃᆡ향관 륙군일등군ᄉᆞ 리병규

○보진위뎨일련ᄃᆡ뎨일대ᄃᆡ부륙군보병부위 김홍식 리긔명

○보진위뎨일련ᄃᆡ뎨삼대ᄃᆡ부륙군보병부위 오의션

○보진위뎨이련ᄃᆡ뎨일대ᄃᆡ부륙군보병참위 김긔졔

○보진위뎨삼련ᄃᆡ뎨이대ᄃᆡ부관 륙군보병부위 빅남규

○보진위뎨오련ᄃᆡ뎨일대ᄃᆡ즁ᄃᆡ쟝 륙군보병졍위 민홍식

○보진위뎨륙련ᄃᆡ뎨이대ᄃᆡ보륙군보병참위 박쟝환

○임륙군보병부위 륙군보병참위송우영 죠원슌 쟝세진

○임륙군일등군ᄉᆞ 륙군이등군 리병은

○임륙군이등군ᄉᆞ 륙군삼등군ᄉᆞ 리최영슌

○보시위뎨일련ᄃᆡ뎨일대ᄃᆡ부륙군보병참위 리긔범

○보친위뎨일련ᄃᆡ뎨일대ᄃᆡ부륙군보병참위 송우영

○보친위뎨일련ᄃᆡ뎨삼대ᄃᆡ부륙군보병참위 죠슌란

○보진위뎨오련ᄃᆡ뎨일대ᄃᆡ부륙군보병참위 손은영

이샹구월일일

○면본관 쥬차아국특명젼권공ᄉᆞ 리범진

명니쟝원경셔칙임관삼등경무관 염셕호

○의원면본관 례식원번역관김도일 목청뎐참봉 리시우

○임시종원좌시어셔쥬입관이등 죵이품 김응모

○임례식원번역관셔쥬임관사등 군부포병과쟝 리무영

○임목청뎐참봉셔판임관팔등륙품 림규여

이샹구월이일

○이쥬올벌봉 전라남도관찰부총순 류덕근 리인학

구월이일

궁뎡록ᄉᆞ

○니부협관리봉릭조회소 비지니에이ᄀᆞᆺ치말홀써시안아니이라

○의정부찬졍신긔션ᄉᆞ직언ᄉᆞ소 비지니에말ᄒᆞᆫ빅가깁히졍치에요긴홈을엇어쓰ᄂᆞᆫ시의에구익가잇스니맛당히침작ᄒᆞ야돕기를싱각ᄒᆞᆯ지니되거ᄒᆞᆷ을말ᄒᆞ지말고시무ᄒᆞ라

○니부대신됴병필조회소 비지니에이ᄀᆞᆺ치말ᄒᆞᆯ거시안이니라

○외부대신리하영ᄉᆞ직소 비지니에번거이ᄉᆞ양말고시두ᄒᆞ라

○의정부찬졍권즁현ᄉᆞ직소 비지니에ᄉᆞ양말고힝공ᄒᆞ라

○의정부찬졍윤웅렬ᄉᆞ직언ᄉᆞ소 비지니에즁임을엇지거연히임ᄒᆞ리오번거이ᄉᆞ양말ᄂᆞ소즁ᄒᆞᆫ아롬다온말은맛당히류렴ᄒᆞ리라

○히셔리대신ᄉᆞ무 외부협판윤치호 구월이일

뎨이쳔구빅이십ᄉᆞ호 광무팔년구월륙일

○셔임급ᄉᆞ령

○명궁니부특진관셔칙임관일등 죵일품 김셩근 리건하

○명궁니부특진관셔칙임관이등 죵이픔 리셩렬

○히법부법률긔초위원 법부참서관 민츙식 길경식 리셕구

○법부법률긔초위원 법부회계국쟝 리지열 신위균 홍슌각 이샹구월삼일

○전칙 한셩지판소쥬ᄉᆞ김 쥰 구월삽일

뎐보

륙군공보

구월ᄉᆞ일하오삼시 반공ᄉᆞ관착뎐

○료양함락 대산만쥬군총ᄉᆞ령관의보고를거ᄒᆞᆫ즉팔월삼일(토료일)밤과밋ᄉᆞ일(일료일)아츰에젼투ᄒᆞᆫ후에료양이우리군ᄉᆞ의게온젼히졈령이되엿더라

잡보

○경ᄉᆞ신병 신티휴씨가경무ᄉᆞ지임시에잡술긱과무녀등을열심포착ᄒᆞ다가피면ᄒᆞ고쇼위귀신의벌텩으로병이들어여러날고싱ᄒᆞ다가지금은죠금차도가잇서일젼브터륙군법원에ᄉᆞ진ᄒᆞ다ᄒᆞ며시임경무ᄉᆞ김졍근씨도신씨와갓치무녀와잡술긱등을포착ᄒᆞ는ᄃᆡ근일에김씨가병이들어신음즁이라ᄒᆞ는ᄃᆡ귀신의벌노그러ᄒᆞ다고훈다더라

○총관유인 릭근턱씨가히임이후로은현이무상ᄒᆞ더니모관에츌입ᄒᆞ며운동ᄒᆞ야호위ᄃᆡ총관피인원 쳐분을작일에봉승ᄒᆞ엿다더라

○길씨독존 길영슈리지화량씨는아국간첩으로치의되여일병의게피착되고ᄒᆞ양군거ᄒᆞ는쟝즁션은일병방히조로처의되여피착되엿더니리지화씨는저작일에방송되고쟝즁션은쟉일에방송되엿다더라

○훈쟝친졍 외부에셔쥬법공ᄉᆞ민영찬씨의게죠회ᄒᆞ되대황뎨폐하ᄭᅴ옵셔의덕리국대군쥬폐하ᄭᅴ셔증송ᄒᆞ시는대훈위금척대슈쟝을이번의국공ᄉᆞ모락고의회국ᄒᆞ는순귀편에붓쳐셔귀공ᄉᆞ의게전ᄒᆞ니히훈쟝도달ᄒᆞ는놀에귀공ᄉᆞ는곳의국에전왕ᄒᆞ야훈쟝을친졍ᄒᆞ라ᄒᆞ엿더라

○협셔게보 일공ᄉᆞ가외부로공함ᄒᆞ되거월이십이일에일한협졍셔를일본졍부에셔관보에긔지ᄒᆞ고각국에통텹ᄒᆞ엿스니귀졍부에셔도또한히협졍서를관보에긔지ᄒᆞ고각국ᄃᆡ표쟈의게통지ᄒᆞ라ᄒᆞ엿더라

TELEGRAMS

Tokyo, Sept. 4th.

Field-Marshall Marquis Oyama reports that after a battle lasting from Saturday afternoon till Sunday morning Liaoyang was occupied by our troops.

Tokyo, Sep. 6th.

Field Marshal Marquis Oyama reports that during the attack on Liaoyang on Saturday night all the Russian storehouses near the railway were set on fire and completely destroyed.

THE BALTIC FLEET.

According to a St. Petersburg wire, official orders have been published with regard to the Baltic Fleet. The second Pacific Squadron will be made up of two detachments, the first being composed of the following vessels:—"Emperor Alexander III.," battleship, 13,600 tons, 18 knots; "Oslabya," battleship, 12,674 tons, 18 knots; "Navar'n," battleship, 10,206 tons, 16 knots; "Sissoi Veliky," battleship, 8,500 tons, 16 knots; "Admiral Nakhimoff," armoured cruiser, 8,524 tons 16 knots. The second detachment will be composed of the following vessels:—"Auroa," cruiser, 6,630 tons, 20 knots; "Dmitri Donskoi," armoured cruiser, 16 knots; "Svietlana," cruiser, 3,828 tons, 20 knots; "Almaz," cruiser, 2,385 tous, 19 knots. The vessels will carry a full war complement of guns and ammunition. While the vessels are in the road-stead they will be surrounded by a chain of armed guard cutters.

According, however, to another correspondent, (July 20th) the Baltic Fleet would probably not start for six weeks. The large transport "Kauschatka" was to accompany the Fleet, carrying many spare parts and tools and machinery with which to effect repairs, as well as many machine guns, and probably some submarines. There will also be a number of skilled mechanics on board.

The "Daily Mail's" St. Petersburg correspondent says the second division of the Baltic Squadron will sail between Aug. 6 and 12. Judging from its being constituted of old ships, this fleet is only nominally destined for the Far East, and will be in reality employed for cruiser work in the Red Sea.

PROLONGATION OF HOSTILITIES.

That the Japanese view the possibility of this war being a prolonged one with considerable equanimity may be seen from the following extract from the "Jiji." The "Jiji" points out that, after the taking of Port Arthur and Vladivostock and the destruction of the enemy's remaining warships in the Far East, the waters between the empire and the continent will become perfectly safe for our shipping, allowing our foreign trade to prosper. It is true the enemy interferes with merchantmen navigating the Mediterranean and Red Seas, but the neutral Powers concerned will not permit the enemy to abuse his right in connection with contraband of war; and after all, it will not be much that Japan will suffer in ordinary commerce that comes that way. As for our trade across the Pacific, it will be perfectly secure from all hostile obstructions. Thus on the whole, the war can but little affect our commerce and industry, and with the economic fabric of the nation well sustained, we are in a far better position to endure the prolongation of hostilities than Russia, with whom the difficulty of the rear communication and supply will always remain a very serious drawback, to say nothing of the other disadvantages and circumstances that handicap the enemy. Consequently those who calculate on Japan's finally yielding to exhaustion cannot make a greater mistake.

STABBING AFFRAY AT CHEMULPO.

As the result of an altercation with a Japanese merchant at Chemulpo relative to the price of an orange, a sailor from the U. S. S. "Cincinnati" now lies seriously wounded on board his ship. It appears that while arguing with the merchant, the latter became enraged and suddenly seizing a knife drove it into the sailor's back, inflicting a nasty wound, and it is feared, perforating his lung.

The assailant was immediately arrested and lodged in the municipal jail, where he will await trial.

This was not the only affair of the kind, for a day later a negro sailor, from the same vessel, while under the influence of liquor, drew a knife and inflicted flesh wounds on two Japanese, one man and one woman. He has been placed in irons on board ship until his case is dealt with.

BRITISH ARMY REFORM.

MR. KIPLING'S VIEWS.

Mr. Rudyard Kipling has embodied his views on the British army in a remarkable "Phantasy," which has appeared in the Morning Post and is attracting a good deal of attention. An American journal gives the following brief summary:—The title is "The Army of a Dream," and the subject a kind of military Utopia, an ideal England, in which all the men and boys spend the best of their time in playing at war and all the women in admiring them. There is no conscription: everyone has a passion for soldiering, and that passion is encouraged by a little gentle legislation and by other things. As one of the heroes of the "Imperial Guard" puts it, "if we don't volunteer till we're thirty-five we don't vote, and we don't get poor relief, and the women don't love us. Hence every man is either a volunteer, or a militiaman or a regular—or, best of all, a member of the mysterious force called the Imperial Guard, which "doesn't recruit—it selects," and which keeps a canteen "like a Spiers and Pond restaurant," where it is the pride and delight even of the women and civilians to eat their meals and enjoy the society of heroes. Children begin at six years old to play at war in the board schools. "They know their company drill a heap better than they know their King's English." They take the rifle at twelve and record their first target score at thirteen. Their games are all military. A member of the Imperial Guard describes how once on Brighton Downs "an infant about a yard high jumped up from a furze patch and shouted: 'Guard, Guard, come'ere. I want you per-fessionally. Alf says 'e ain't out-flanked. Ain't 'e a bloomin' liar? Come an' look 'ow I've posted my men.'"

CURIOUS ADVERTISEMENTS.

The following are copies of some recent queer advertisements:—

"Bulldog for sale; will eat anything; very fond of children."

"Wanted—A boy to be partly outside and partly behind the counter."

"Widow in comfortable circumstances wishes to marry two sons."

"Annual sale now on; don't go elsewhere to be cheated; come in here."

"A lady wishes to sell her piano, as she is going abroad in a strong iron frame."

"Wanted—By a respectable girl, her passage to New York; willing to take care of children and a good sailor."

"Lost—Near Highgate archway, an umbrella belonging to a gentleman with a bent rib and a bone handle."

"Mr. Brown, furrier, begs to announce that he will make up gowns, capes, etc., for ladies out of their own skin."

"A airy bedroom for a gentleman twenty-two feet long and eleven feet wide."

It is said that Mr. Cho Pyeug-pil, the Minister of Home Affairs will resign and Mr. Yi Yong-tai will succeed him.

The "County Gentleman" tells a story of a private in the Guards, who, when in London, was often in trouble for want of neatness, punctuality, and smartness, but turned out to have excellent qualities when it came to campaigning, and he was made a corporal. Later on the sergeant had occasion to report him for some minor neglect of appearance. "But he has been doing very well since he came out," the officer to whom he was reported said. "He is a very handy fellow, and has been mentioned for bravery in the field twice." "Yes, yes, sir," replied the sergeant, "he's all very well for a job like this; but he'll never make a soldier!"

New laws are demanded to ensure the inspection of everybody and everything connected with milk. Mr. Herbert Spencer's prediction that before long everybody would be an inspector of somebody else is likely of fulfillment, if the present craze continues. Every day we expect to see it announced that our beds are to be nightly inspected by the State before we retire to rest, on the ground that beds are a danger to life, more deaths occurring in bed than in all other places put together.—Liberty Review.

The Yorozu Choho (a Japanese journal in Tokyo) gives what they profess to call accurate information as to the distribution and numbers of the Russian troops in Port Arthur. Infantry, 10 brigades, consisting of 32,500 men. Navy, 11,500 men. Commissariat, 1,840 men. Total, 50,510. Of this number they state that 6,010 men are sick and wounded. The number of field and naval guns they place at 652. How this exact information was obtained they do not state.

The obstrusive bald-head has been discovered to be a valuable advertising asset. It was first seen in Paris in the down town cafes last month. The medium took a seat in one of the terraces, ordered beer, then removed his hat, revealing a shiny pate on which was painted an advertisement. A big crowd had collected by the time he finished his beer, and, all having had time to read his sign, he departed for other cafes.

An exchange calmly informs the world that "in Cambodia decapitation is considered a deadly insult." Which is an obvious fact.

The Korea Daily News.

To be published daily except Sundays.

Rate of Subscription:—

Per Year,	Yen 25.
Per Quarter,	Yen 7.
Per Month	Yen 2.50

Postage in Korea not charged extra.
Postage abroad charged extra.

Advertisements, 50 sen per day for 1 inch or less.
5 yen per month per inch.
50 yen per year per inch.

All communications to

E. T. BETHELL,
Editor and Publisher.
Pak-tong, Seoul

THE COOLIE QUESTION.

We are glad indeed to see that this question, which has recently been rapidly growing in gravity, is now being dealt with in a rational manner.

It will be remembered that directly there were signs of friction we pointed out that the opposition on the part of the coolies was due to ignorance and the circulation of false reports, and suggested that authoritative information, circulated broadcast, would allay the unreasoning fears of an ignorant populace.

Therefore we are glad to see that the government has sent letters to the principal towns in the Empire instructing the authorities how to act and explaining to the people the real purposes for which the Japanese authorities require coolies.

The circular commences by saying that volunteers are asked for and that it is not the intention or wish of the Japanese authorities that coercion should be used.

Japan is expending millions of money and thousands of lives fighting for the independence of Korea and the peace of the East. Korea must help all she can. She is not a military power and therefore cannot aid in the fighting line but she can render Japan valuable assistance in transportation and it is her duty to do this.

Heretofore the local authorities have gone the wrong way to work. Servants of officials have been sent into the villages and have attempted to collect coolies by force, with the result that those who would otherwise have been willing to volunteer have been frightened away.

Reports have been circulated to the effect that the coolies are to be lured to spots where Russian mines are laid, that they are to have their hair cut and are to be made to fight. These reports are all false. The coolies are wanted for pack-carrying many miles from the scene of war and will be well-treated, fed and clothed.

The circular concludes by exhorting the local authorities, for the sake of the good feeling existing between the two nations, to use every legitimate measure to obtain volunteers but to abstain from all acts savouring of coercion.

LISTEN TO A TALE OF WOE.

(BY OUR COURT REPORTER.)

According to the news which is spreading in town that the Emperor asked the following of Japanese Minister when he received audience with the Emperor on 27th August.

(1) How to correct militarism and finance.

(2) How to select capable men for magistrates.

(3) How to have intimate diplomacy.

(4) Whom among high officials will be useful.

(5) How to have strict prohibition for useless ones in palace.

(6) How to commence reformation for policy.

WEI-HAI-WEI.

THE BRITISH OCCUPATION.

It is rumoured in political circles that Great Britain, in view of the predicted early fall of Port Arthur, is on the point of concluding negotiations with China for the occupation in perpetuity of Wei-hai-wei. The exact nature of the reported transaction is not defintely stated, but it is thought that it will take the form either of a purchase of the port and the adjacent land or their acquisition by a ninety-nine year lease, renewable forever.

This report is credited by those especially well informed in East Asiatic affairs. They point out that by the terms of Britain's tenure, Wei-hai-wei reverts to China the moment Russian occupation of Port Arthur and the Liaotung peninsula ceases. That Lord Lansdowne, who will be compelled to deal with the situation, will do his utmost to prevent British evacuation of the port is considered certain. He is a tenacious imperialist and disapproves of surrender of political advantages in any part of the world, particularly where the interests of Britain and Russia or the interests of Britain and Germany are in juxtaposition.

Sir Ernest Satow, British Minister to China who is an aggressive defender of British possessions and prestige in the Far East, is likely to favour the retention of Wei-hai-wei at any cost. His influence is great with Downing Street, because weight is attached to his judgment with regard to everything that concerns the West Pacific. Above all, Japan is determined to keep Britain in Wei-hai-wei, Mr. Uchida, Japanese Minister in China, is devoting all his power to strengthening Sir Ernest Satow's purpose to retain the stronghold. It is understood that he has gone as far as to declare that if Britian goes out Japan will go in.

Tokio is afraid of Germany, whose occupation of Kiaochao bay has caused deep distrust, and does not intend to permit Wei-hai-wei to pass into German hands or any other hands regarded as hostile to the Island State. The Japanese argue that to allow such a thing would be equivalent to relinquishing the chief value of Port Arthur to Japan, since the present Russian fortress would thereby be strategically neutralized.

LIAOYANG VICTORY CELEBRATION.

The news of the occupation of Liaoyang, which reached Seoul late on Sunday afternoon formed an occasion for a wild celebration. A lantern procession was arranged but it was thought that sufficient time was not given to do anything on a larger scale.

In Chemulpo things were a little more lively.

Immediately on receeipt of the news the Japanese residents organised a celebration on quite a large scale. A lantern procession was speedily arranged and carried out with the usual vigour and to the accompaniment of many "Banzai." A huge paper globe, bearing the flags of Great Britain and Japan which was the production of the Japanese staff of a a foreign firm, was a feature of the procession. The crowds thronged the streets until after midnight, while a jubilating cornet soloist made the early hours of the morning lovely with his tuneful notes.

"DOMESTIC" AGRICULTURE.

Mr. Kato, who is the "Adviser" for the Agricultural Department and who has been taking a vacation in Japan while the Agriculture has been looking after itself, has recently returned. He now announces his intention of being installed as "Adviser" to the Household Department.

For the sake of the crockery let us hope that he and the concubine of the former Vice Minister for War are friends.

Fifty students, who are to continue their education in Japan, were examined on the 5th inst.

The Korean military drilling and parade ground near the East Gate has been appropriated by the Japanese troops for the same purpose.

His Majesty, on the occasion of his birthday, ordered a donation of four dollars to be handed to each occupant of the Government prisons.

The Memorial Society received a visit from Japanese gendarmes on the 5th inst. but after explaining in proper manner the objects of their society, they were left to continue their meeting in peace.

On Sunday the annual Banker's picnic took place. The guests, who were composed of representatives of the leading Japanese and Foreign Banks enjoyed a trip up the river.

How the Koreans can be so flaccid as to permit a man like Hyŏn, and a woman like his concubine, to have any voice in the affairs of a government, passes comprehension.

A despatch from Shanghai dated August 29th says.—The cruiser "Askold" and the destroyer "Grosovoi," which sought refuge at Shanghai from the Japanese fleet, were finally disarmed to-day.

The American blue jackets in Shanghai, paid a pretty compliment to their Russian fellows on the "Askold." They bought a whole boatload of fruit and brought it over to the Russian cruiser, where, with the permission of the officers, the thoughtful gift was gratefully accepted.

A New York daily states that the Japanese have placed orders in America for the purchase of 10,000 small cavalry horses, to be delivered on the Pacific coast at the rate of 2,000 per month. The class of small, sturdy animal which is wanted is very hard to secure, and some difficulty is expected in executing the order.

A French scientific journal states that a wireless telegraph is now working across Lake Baikal. There are stations on the east and west banks, and another on the ferry-ship which carries the trains and breaks the ice in winter, thus enabling her to keep in communication with both banks during her passage.

General Hyŏn, the proprietor of the "Lady" Hyŏn who recently distinguished herself in Japan, seems to have some considerable influence. We hear that at his instance Messrs. Wŏn Woosang, Hong Sun-chan and Kim Yŏng-chin have been made Major Generals. Wŏn Woo-sang seems to be a particular favourite as it is reported that the police department will also fall to him.

The "Il-chin-hoi," which is a society having the special privilege of being able to hold meetings without being interfered with by the Japanese, is determined not to let the grass grow under its feet. Our town reporter says: The committees visited Mr. Sin Ki-sŏn, new vice president of state last Saturday and asked "How about to commence what they advised the Government?" Mr. Sin replied he will hardly attend for the same to be succeeded. *Quod erat demonstradum.*

The bodies of Japanese soldiers who are killed on the fighting line are not removed, but are cremated where they fall. A man who has served with the volunteers in the defence of Port Arthur says that the work of gathering the bodies and getting them into piles ready for the application of the torch, can be witnessed at times from the fortifications and is a grim and impressive revelation of the horrors of war. He asserts that the odor arising from the cremation has at times been noticeable in the city itself—an appalling reminder of the slaughter that is going on about Port Arthur.—Chefoo Daily News.

The Korea Daily News.

VOL. I, WEDNESDAY, SEPTEMBER 7, 1904. No. 45

HONGKONG & SHANGHAI BANKING CORPORATION.

Paid-up Capital.... ....$10,000,000
Reserve Fund:—Sterling Reserve... 10,000,000
Silver Reserve..... 6,500,000

26,500,000

Reserve Liability of Proprietors... 10,000,000

HEAD OFFICE, HONGKONG.

London Bankers, London and County Banking Company Limited.
Branches and Agencies,
London.

Amoy,	Hankow	Penang,
Bangkok,	Hiogo,	Rangoon,
Batavia,	Iloilo,	Saigon,
Bombay,	Lyons,	San Francisco,
Calcutta,	Manila,	Singapore,
Colombo,	Nagasaki,	Sourabaya,
Foochow,	New York,	Tientsin,
Hamburg,	Peking,	Yokohama,

Credits granted on approved Securities, and every description of Banking and Exchange business transacted.

Drafts granted on London and the chief Commercial places in Europe, India, Australia, America, China and Japan.

HOLME RINGER & Co., AGENTS, CHEMULPO.

ON CHEONG & CO., SEOUL.

GENERAL STORE KEEPERS.
Imported provisions, Cooking Utensils Crockery, etc.
FRESH BREAD DAILY.

MITSU BISHI DOCKYARD & ENGINE WORKS,
NAGASAKI.

CODE WORD, "DOCK."

A. 1, A. B. C., and Engineering Codes used,

DOCK No. 1 (at Tategami).

Extreme Length..............523 feet
Length on blocks .... 513 „
Width of Entrance on Top......89 „
„ „ Bottom....77 „
Water on Blocks at Spring Tide 26½ „

DOCK No. 2 (Mukaijima).

Extreme Length..............371 feet
Length on Blocks.............360 „
Width of Entrance on Top......66 „
„ „ Bottom 53 „
Water on Blocks at Spring Tide 22 „

PATENT SLIP (at Kosuge).

Can take vessels up to 1,000 tons gross.

THE WORKS are well equipped with the LATEST IMPROVEMENTS, and can execute any kind of work in SHIPBUILDING and MARINE ENGINEERING, as well as in REPAIRING of SHIPS.

The COMPANY'S new powerful steamer OURA-MARU (712 tons, 700 I.H.P.), specially built for SALVAGE PURPOSES, and equipped with necessary gear, is always READY at SHORT NOTICE.

CHARTERED BANK OF INDIA AUSTRALIA & CHINA.

INCORPORATED BY ROYAL CHARTER 1853

HEAD OFFICES:—LONDON.

Paid-up Capital £800,000
Reserve Liability of Shareholders 800,000
Reserve Fund 800,000

Drafts granted upon all the principal places in the world and every description of Exchange and banking business transacted.

E. MEYER & Co., Agents,
Chemulpo.

E. MEYER & CO.
Chemulpo.

SOLE AGENTS IN KOREA FOR:
A. T. Morse, Sons & Co's "Fresco" Distemper

In all colours ready for use on walls, Ceilings etc.
and
AVENARIUS CARBOLINEUM

A wood-preserving and antiseptic oil preparation

Against decay, dry-rot, fungus and wood-destroying insects.

A large supply always in Stock.
Prices upon application.

E. MEYER & Co.,
Chemulpo.

LAW UNION & CROWN INS. CO.

Fire risks accepted at Current rates, on go downs, merchandise, dwellings, and other property, subject to usual conditions.

HOLME RINGER & Co.,
Agents, Chemulpo

THE METHODIST PUBLISHING HOUSE,
Little West Gate, Seoul.

JOB PRINTING, TYPEWRITER PAPER
CARBON PAPER, VISITING CARDS
STATIONERY, BOOK BINDING
BOOK PUBLISHERS
AMERICAN SCHOOL BOOKS
SPENCERIAN COPY BOOKS
PEN CARBON LETTER AND BILL BOOKS

S A BECK, Manager

?AI-ICHI GINKO.

LIMITED.

(Formerly the First National Bank)

ESTABLISHED 1873

INCORPORATED UNDER PRESENT LAW 1896

Capital - - - - - - - - - - Yen 5,000,000
Reserve Fund - . - - - 1,500,000

HEAD OFFICE:—TOKIO.

President: Baron SHIBUSAWA.

BRANCHES AND CORRESPONDENTS
In the Principal Cities and Towns of Japan.
Interest Allowed on
Fixed deposits 1 year - - - 6½ per cent
" " 6 months - - - 6 per cent

Special current accounts 1½ sen daily per Y 100
General " " 1 " " " 100

M. TANAKA,
Manager, Chemulpo

HOLME RINGER & Co.
Chemulpo.

General Merchants and Government Contractors.

Agents for the leading
Banks
SteamshipCompanies
and
Insurance Companies

Importers of Merchandise of every description.

KAMEYA & CO.

GENERAL STOREKEEPERS
Chinkokai - - Seoul
(*Established 1895, Tokyo*)

Confectionery, Hams, Canned Goods, Cutlery, Hirano & Tansan Water. Provisions, Gents, Furnishing goods, Toilet Articles, Travelling Bags, Tobacco, Cigars & Cigarettes Kitchen Utensils. Coffee, Biscuits.

Fresh Goods always kept in Stock.
Prices Moderate
Please come and inspect our goods.

NIPPON YUSEN KAISHA.

JAPANESE MAIL STEAMSHIP CO.

DER MAIL CONTRACT WITH THE IMPERIAL JAPANESE GOVERNMENT.

European Line

Regular Fortnightly Service between Yokohama Kobe, Moji, Shanghai, Hongkong, Singapore, Penang Colombo, Port Said, Marseilles, London and Antwerp

American Line

Regular Fortnightly Service between Hongkong and Seattle, calling at Shanghai, Moji, Kobe, Yokohama and Victoria, B. C.

Australian Line

Regular weekly Service betwen Japan Ports and Australia, calling at Hongkong and Manila.
(Above Three Lines Suspended until further notice).

Shanghai Line

Weekly Service between Shanghai and Japan Ports

Korea Line

Service Kobe, Moji, Nagasaki, Fusan, Chemulpo, Chefoo, Taku.
S. S. Bahelsberg, 2181 tons.
Service Kobe, Moji, Fusan, Chemulpo, Chinnampo
S.S ARGO. S. S. Ohio.

BORDEN'S CONDENSED MILK CO.
New York, U. S. A.

ALWAYS IN STOCK
Eagle Brand Condensed Milk.
Gold Seal Condensed Milk.
Peerless (Family) Evaporated Cream.
Borden's Malted Milk.

E. MEYER & CO.
Chemulpo, Korea,
Sole Agents

ROYAL INSURANCE COMPANY,
Funds exceed £10,000,000
FIRE
AT CURRENT RATES,
LIFE
REDUCED PREMIUM.
HOLME RINGER & Co.,
Agents, Chemulpo.

HOTEL DU PALAIS
SEOUL.

The only first class Hotel in Seoul. Situated in the centre of the city opposite the palace.

Cuisine under the supervision of an experienced French Chef.

Well ventilated and furnished throughout.

TARIFF UPON APPLICATION

L. MARTIN
Proprietor and Manager.

大韓每日申報
대한미일신보

(뎨사십륙호)　　(목요일)　　쳔구빅사년구월팔일

본샤고빅

이신보는영어와한어로셕거미
일출판홈

신문가

혼장 엽두돈오푼
일삭됴엽두량닷돈 미돈이로
밧숨

광고료는

귀한의쟝단과ᄌᆞ힝의다쇼로츙
감ᄒᆞ되렴가로밧을터이오며오
릭지아녀대한사람마다다이신
문을보실터이니광고내시기를
원ᄒᆞ시는이들은우리신문사에
와셔편약ᄒᆞ심을희망ᄒᆞᆷ

○발힝소 박동대한미일신보
사범이학교안해 전영국인셜필
립졍자리오

사쟝 영국인 (비셜)

사고

○우리대한미일신보의목뎍은
대한의안녕질셔에관한모든대
목에티ᄒᆞ야는공평한변론을주
장ᄒᆞᆷ이라우리ᄒᆞᆫ신원의힘보는
신문보시는쳠군ᄌᆞ의게ᄒᆞᆼ샹보
도ᄒᆞ리며편지를귀셔ᄒᆞ며주시
는이는셩명과반디를젹어붓치
시기를희망ᄒᆞ오니이거슨신문
샹에긔재ᄒᆞ란거시아니오다
만극히신용ᄒᆞ는증거를숨고자
ᄒᆞᆷ이라귀자는아모긔셔던지귀
쳐ᄒᆞᆯ을되각ᄒᆞ는권리를가졋스
나되각ᄒᆞ는리유를말ᄒᆞᆯ터이오
며공중평화를문란케ᄒᆞ는듯ᄒᆞᆫ
귀셔는의례히밧지안켓습나이
다

사고

○본샤에셔는신문갑슨미월에
젼금으로밧ᄉᆞ오며본신문은우
톄로붓치는고로본샤에셔는다
른신문샤쳐름금액을거두러ᄃᆞᆫ
니지안ᄉᆞ오니우리신문을ᄉᆞ랑
ᄒᆞ야구람ᄒᆞ시는쳠군ᄌᆞ는양력
미월초순에리월됴젼금과거주
셩명등호수를ᄌᆞ세히젹어셔박
동본샤로보내시기를바라오며
월회일나로젼금을아니ᄒᆞ금ᄂᆞᆫ
보내시는곳에는리월일일부터
신문을아니보낼터이오니조량
ᄒᆞ옵소셔

●본샤에셔아직긔계를쟝만치
못ᄒᆞ와다른티셔박여오는고로
미양월요일에는ᄎᆡᆨ관이대단히
늣케되는ᄃᆞᆺᄉᆞ로본젼이미우늣
게되오니우리신문을구람ᄒᆞ시
는 쳠군ᄌᆞ는 용셔ᄒᆞ여주심
을희망ᄒᆞᆸ나이다

본샤광고

본샤에셔본신문뎨수호와미십
일호와뎨미십오호를소용ᄒᆞᆯ때
가잇셔이에광고ᄒᆞ오니누구시
던지이샹삼호중에본샤로가져
오시면미쟝에빅젼두푼식드리
리다

역부문졔

우리는근일에역부졍구ᄒᆞᆷ에티
ᄒᆞ야미오유리ᄒᆞ게쳐결ᄒᆞᆫ거슬
셜로짓버ᄒᆞ는거시이일노말ᄆᆡ
암아거즛소문이탕자ᄒᆞ야빅
셩들의의혹이자심ᄒᆞ야공연히
반티ᄒᆞᆷ이며각도관찰군슈들의
보고에는될경인민들이쟉요ᄒᆞ
겟다고ᄒᆞ든일이다힝이졍돈이
되엿는지라 졍부로셔각도에
발훈ᄒᆞ야각히군슈들로ᄒᆞ여금
일본셔역부모집ᄒᆞ란는리유와
엇지ᄒᆞᆯ사단을빅셩들의게ᄌᆞ셔
히셜명ᄒᆞᆫ이후에비로소일본셔
당초브리ᄅᆞᆯ힝ᄒᆞ란는ᄯᅳᆺ이아닌
줄을아라ᄊᆞᆫ즉

일본셔는져젼에슈만원젼ᄌᆡ만
히비ᄒᆞ엿슬ᄲᅮᆫ이아니라동양에
화평ᄒᆞ게지니는대한ᄂᆞ립국빅
셩들로더브러싸왓슨즉한국에
셔는아모조록일본을방조ᄒᆞ되
병력으로버프러ᄒᆞᆯ일도못된즉
수운ᄒᆞ여주는일에조ᄒᆞᆫ방침을셩
각ᄒᆞ야미오편리ᄒᆞ고심히셩광
나도록ᄒᆞᆯ거신거시

귀왕에는지방관들이쳐사를잘
못ᄒᆞ야괴승비로ᄒᆞ여금각면각
촌에과송ᄒᆞ야억지로모집ᄒᆞ라
ᄒᆞᆫ즉가히자원ᄒᆞᆯ만ᄒᆞᆫ자가잇드
리도겁ᄒᆞ야도망ᄒᆞ게ᄒᆞᆫ드릿
고

일본셔역부로ᄒᆞ여금외국복식
식인다는거슨번결에다부ᄒᆞ야
수운ᄒᆞ는티편리ᄒᆞ도록ᄒᆞ야고
리ᄒᆞᆷ이여놀방연ᄒᆞᆫ황ᄇᆞᆫ지셜을
주작ᄒᆞ야아빅셩들리지로조를무
며셔고도ᄒᆞ며미리를ᄡᅡᆨ진다고
ᄯᅩ도ᄒᆞ야빅셩을유혹ᄒᆞ게ᄒᆞᆫ다라
싸혼셔지되게ᄒᆞ엿더니

일본셔당초에이지로고졍ᄒᆞᆫ량
이아니라자원ᄒᆞ는자가잇스면
삯고ᄒᆞᆫ바란국ᄀᆞᆫ회호ᄒᆞᆯᄯᅳᆺ을
빅셩들의게교시ᄒᆞᆷ으로부터비
로소리히를ᄌᆞ셔히알앗다더라

잡보

○민쟝졍소 고양군슈리주혁
씨가교하군슈를겸임ᄒᆞ엿슬때
에인부모집ᄒᆞᆫ는일노일병이
도ᄒᆞ야로호ᄒᆞᆫ지닭에민료가나셔
빅셩상명이죽엇는지라빅셩들
이말ᄒᆞ기를경관이잘조쳐ᄒᆞ엿
스면이지경이아니되엿슬거신
티히군슈가일인을부동ᄒᆞ여이
리되엿다고히군슈를향ᄒᆞ야졍
장ᄒᆞᆫ다더라

○륙수가옥 젼셜을듯근ᄒᆞᆫ즉
참쳔리위씨는본리가셰쳥빈ᄒᆞ
야류경ᄒᆞᆫ지다년에리관에셔류
련ᄒᆞ더니 대빈에이말이앙쳘만
되야히위씨의게가옥산돈팔만
량을듀별이 하ᄉᆞᄒᆞ셧다더라

○막지기교 평양군슈평한주
씨의탐쟝젼이엉졍빅여만량이
된다는티히군슈가상경ᄒᆞᆫ란ᄒᆞᆫ
즉히군인민이챠로ᄒᆞ는고로발
졍을못ᄒᆞ엿다ᄒᆞ니히군인민등
셩각에ᄒᆞ우엄되는군슈가평군슈
보다탐학이우심ᄒᆞᆯ서념려ᄒᆞ야
그나마만류ᄒᆞ는지평군슈의쟝야
젼을추심코자ᄒᆞ야그런ᄒᆞ는지
참막지기교ᄒᆞᆯ일이라ᄒᆞ더라

○원티교와 원동모티가에는
셩방ᄒᆞ는빈지이날노운집ᄒᆞ는
티주티는문을닷고간과누어셔
리긔을일병수졈ᄒᆞᆫ다더라

○일병수병와 일본병ᄉᆞ삼ᄎᆞᆼ
구미씨는일젼브터병셕에누엇
다더라

○평수회의 한셩주차일본령
수관회의에참예ᄒᆞ려고쥬부산
일령수유길씨와쥬마산일령ᄉᆞ
삼포씨와쥬목포일령수약송씨
가상쟉일입항ᄒᆞ는의쥬젼으로
인쳔에도박ᄒᆞ야죽시샹경ᄒᆞ엿
다더라

○장민하다 젼쥬관찰ᄉᆞ리용
직씨가니부에보고ᄒᆞ되관하각
군에공수토디를일본인의게가
만히장미ᄒᆞ기슬티인군슈ᄉᆞ송병
ᄒᆞ로조ᄒᆞ여곰도사관을졍ᄒᆞ야각
군의순힝ᄒᆞ야낫낫치 사찰ᄒᆞᆫ
즉젼쥬군에는공수 쟝민 가 이
빅오십오셕칠이두 삼승락이
오림피군에는공수 토가 오십
팔셕륙두락이오만 경 군 에 는
수토가이십륙셕십두락이오옥
구군에는공수토가일빅구십오
셕구두락이오익산군에는수토
가십팔셕칠두락이오함열군에
는수토가이셕칠두락이오룡안
군에는수토가칠셕수두락이오
부안군에는ᄉᆞ토가구셕륙두락
이오고부군에는ᄉᆞ토가십륙셕
륙두락이오티산군에는신륙ᄒᆞᆫ
곳슨셔양인의산ᄂᆡ시니이샹실
군공수토쟝미ᄒᆞᆫ거시합칠빅칠
십ᄉᆞ셕칠두삼승이온티ᄃᆞ티미
쳐ᄒᆞ야환퇴ᄒᆞ기를독촉ᄒᆞ오나
셜노금단ᄒᆞ기어렵ᄉᆞ오니일본
공관에조회ᄒᆞ야드티장미ᄒᆞᆫ것을
금ᄒᆞ라ᄒᆞ엿다더라

○슌검힝피 옥쳔군슈황인수
씨의보고를거ᄒᆞᆫ즉본읍쥬차헌
도츈릉티보ᄒᆞ오슌검김영셕이가
미일술이취ᄒᆞ야힝피무쌍ᄒᆞ더
니향일에일본인과졍힐ᄒᆞ는티
본읍수림일에교수가져방ᄒᆞ여
관광ᄒᆞ더니교수를구츅ᄒᆞ고관
쳥에돌입ᄒᆞ야방노쳥문을차며
픽악ᄒᆞᆫ말노군슈를고발ᄒᆞ되장
ᄎᆞ고픽습을못칠가ᄒᆞ엿더니ᄯᅩ
일젼에김영셕이가츙쥬병졍과
관문압헤서인일ᄒᆞ야거조가히
망ᄒᆞ기로화동식키란ᄒᆞᆫ즉도로혀
미관리를구티ᄒᆞ야쳥금ᄉᆞ싱을
미관비옵고또관쳥에돌입ᄒᆞ야
군슈들등욕ᄒᆞᆷ이강우귀극ᄒᆞ오
니김영셕을소환ᄒᆞ야법티로징
판ᄒᆞ라ᄒᆞ엿다더라

○셩면수리 셩균관대셩뎐파
동셔무계쳐에장마이후샹루
ᄒᆞ는곳슬수리ᄒᆞ는티진ᄉᆞ은음
력팔월십ᄉᆞ일로쥬필ᄒᆞ엿다며
라

○러쳬러일 너부참관리봉티
씨가ᄉᆞ직샹소ᄒᆞ엿는티그티에
는리셩렬씨가피임ᄒᆞᆫ다더라

○압츅젼인 져작야에일본헌
병이명이남대문박리문동젼인
도막에가서젼ᄉᆞᄅᆞᆯ구츅ᄒᆞ고젼
인중쟝졍수명은압거ᄒᆞ엿더라

○명쟝공함 져작일일진회에
셔충티수인을졍부에파송ᄒᆞ엿
더니신참졍이무리왈수됴진을
엇더케셜시ᄒᆞ란ᄒᆞᆫ즉ᄎᆞ티련즁
티모씨가티답ᄒᆞ되셩등은회중ᄎᆞᆼ
티로왓습세등이오엿며케셜시
ᄒᆞ란는언궤은엽수오니이의젼

AMERICAN KOREAN ELECTRIC COMPANY.
Light and Power.
Main Office: Electric Building, Chong No.

RAILWAY DEPARTMENT.

OPERATING CARS BETWEEN EAST AND WEST GATE, EVERY TEN MINUTES:—

First Car leaves East Gate at 6:30 A. M. First Car leaves West Gate at 6:55 A. M.
Last Car " East Gate at 10:40 P. M. Last " " West Gate at 11:00 P. M.

OPERATING CARS BETWEEN EAST GATE AND IMPERIAL TOMB TERMINUS, EVERY TWENTY MINUTES:—

CONNECTING WITH EVERY ALTERNATE CAR ARRIVING AT EAST GATE FROM CHONG NO.

First Car leaves East Gate for Tomb at 6:50 A. M.
" " " Tomb for East Gate at 7:10 A. M.
Last " " East Gate for Tomb at 9:50 P. M.
" " " Tomb for East Gate at 10:10 P. M.

OPERATING CARS BETWEEN CHONG NO AND YUNG SAN (RIVER) EVERY TWELVE MINUTES:—

First Car leaves Chong No for South Gate at 6:48 A. M.
" " " Chong No for Yung San at 7:24 A. M.
" " " South Gate for Chong No at 6:56 A. M.
" " " Yung San for Chong No at 7:57 A. M.
Last " " South Gate for Chong No 11:00 P. M.
" " " Yung San for Chong No at 10:11 P. M.

SPECIAL PRIVATE CARS FURNISHED TO SUIT CONVENIENCE OF PATRONS. PRICES ON APPLICATION AT HEAD OFFICE.

LIGHTING DEPARTMENT.

Where less than 250 candle power of light is used, the rate per month will be. Per 16 candle power incandescent lamp. All night.—Yen 2.50. Per 32 candle power incandescent lamp:—All night:—Yen 4.00. Per 50 candle power incandescent lamp:—All night:—Yen 6.00. " 150 " " " " — " " " 10.00. " 1200 " " enclosed arc " " " " 20.00.

Where more than 250 candle power of light is used, a Meter will be installed, if requested:—Rent of Meter Yen 2.00 per month. Rate of charges by meter reading:—Two Sen per Ampere per hour. (Approximately this is equal to about One Sen per 16 c. p. lamp per hour) Minimum monthly charge where meter is installed, Yen 20.00 per month, which includes rental of meter.

Estimates for installing lights furnished on application. An assortment of chandeliers always on hand.

AMUSEMENT DEPARTMENT.

ANIMATED PICTURES AT EAST GATE.
Every evening - - - Except Sunday.
From 8 to 10 P. M.

10 Cents:—Gen. Admission:—10 Cents. Seats in First Class Section. 15 Cents Extra.

Change of program each week. Pictures from Foreign Lands. Pictures of Local Scenes:—Amusing and Instructive.

An entertaining evening for a reasonable price.
MERRY-GO-ROUND:—At East Gate.
From 10:00 A. M. till 11:00 P. M.

5 Cents a Ride.

Take your Exercise on The Galloping Horses.

Comfortable seats in the Chariots.

한셩뎐긔회사

미국뎐긔회사 고볼안 보사며 고빅
도ᄒᆞ옵나이다
샹활동사진뎐람소와목마운동쟝량쳐로연
여뎐챠가온쟝안으로통ᄒᆡᆼᄒᆞ여ᄃᆞ니여이
습
또이긔계에곳쳐노흰편ᄒᆞ고뎌흔마차도잇
습
코미우편ᄒᆞ고또조미잇는뎌흔운동이되겟
어뎌흔모형을달나아는물을ᄐᆞ고위티치안
디가는ᄒᆞᆫ번ᄐᆞ는데오젼식이오
미얄샹오열시브러하오열ᄒᆞᆫ시ᄭᆞ지ᄒᆞ옵고
목마운동쟝은동대문안에잇습고
가되겟습
쳠군조의게갑도싸고져녁에뎌흔쇼일거리
잇고구경ᄒᆞᆯ만ᄒᆞᆫ거시오니
셔양사진과대한과온동양사진인네대조미
는디
뎐이옵고미쥬일에사진을섭것스로다밧고
고뎐량디금은하등에십젼이오샹등에이십
일외에는미야에여덜시브러열시ᄭᆞ지ᄒᆞ옵
활동사진뎐람소는동대문안에잇습고일요
희탁부

All Cars Run Direct to the Animated Pictures and Merry-Go-Round.

을무로시력란ᄒ면회로고공항ᄒ
ᄒ고공혼신동경ᄒ야령ᄒ벽우왈이되공광
ᄒ깁도란ᄒ엿다더라

○뎐슈청 폐 엄켠에뎐국공
수가외부에죠회ᄒ되뎐국슈냥
합병ᄒ수속을부졔ᄒ고남졔국ᄒ며ᄒ
가본월칠일브터일간한경에비도ᄒ
티여나수관을거ᄂ티고분ᄒ수
믈로송ᄒ서귀국ᄒ면대ᄒ며외부에
페졍ᄒ고ᄒ면ᄒ징경혼ᄒ를엄ᄒ구
일간에 소면을엄으로분공ᄉ
가엽정정혼정ᄒ야경노를혼ᄒ엿더라

○경보아병 경츅팔십리의본교
등거ᄒ는쥬아국인이두만강에셔
다리ᄒ노ᄂ니거시즈명ᄒ셔교프티빗
교아군의티경이하ᄉ관시에이외
이병경ᄒ면경근마쳔여갤을거ᄂ
리고경우헤이르리라교인은아
졍전ᄒ등면티보임계임을슈귀
본군에티넘도ᄒ며고군경을무
른졍티ᄂ변ᄒ되니가진티경이되
며나왓다ᄒ고이병이번허ᄒ야
만히온다ᄒ는티ᄂ본군에셔경셩
ᄉ지아한의병경소가진탄ᄒ엿
다ᄒ엿는티이보교는칠월의칠
일본발ᄒ엿더라

○수관소환 일본외쥬ᄒᄒ는수
관리졉동팔인이긴소슐축로향
시에일본공ᄉ관은송ᄉᄉ가셧는
티공부에셔소환ᄒ는명령이잇
는고로역젼에회국ᄒ엿더라

○경죠외부 저작일경부쳥에
셔외부로죠회ᄒ되작일오시에
예일본경통일병법방쟝을명이
외부를에본회ᄒ니예교ᄒ야면
정에세에셔부ᄂ긔셔곳을명의
영ᄒ야갓스니가부에셔조ᄒ교
라ᄒ엿더라

○수도건축 저작일하오미
시에일진회에셔기회ᄒ고총티
의원수의을경부에파송ᄒ야수
도건설시할을준츅ᄒ엿더라

○니대직소 니부대신죠병필
씨ᄂ작작일에면ᄒ직ᄉ소ᄒ영
논대대이라ᄒ면브터고빗ᄒᆫ리
대신티용임ᄒ셧ᄒ얏더라
이엇더라

○교육회창설 황셩안에국민교
육회를셜ᄒ야국민고육을수가게
셔반구과ᄒ변히더니일진에반교인
길룸ᄒ셔ᄒ노대신셔규원등제기를
보회수부소두를삭직티원진터소
가왕ᄂ고로경원ᄒ오니스면ᄒ
교안에빌간지휘가잇ᄉ니ᄒ시
소를인ᄒ야경니ᄒ엿더라

○병보소청 일진에일본한병
이광전을보ᄒᆫ천샹소셩에져원ᄒ
야무숫ᄒ청년남교ᄒ티ᄒᆫ소ᄒ라ᄒ
되소청에세ᄒ니의ᄒ서답ᄂ홀노
셔용이ᄒ이희세를ᄒ엿더라
라

○국민신문 국민지진셜에유
지ᄒᆫ니명치국민의긔진이두원산이
가반파을긔ᄒ야국민신문은음ᄉ셜
월브편국반셔ᄒ다ᄂ티퇴ᄉ문에
뎨견본공긔병명으로기표ᄒ기위

ᄒ야거선도로교고의이기ᄒ게ᄉ니라ᄒ
국환관료자학으로가져ᄒᄂ니ᄒ
오기계목을분무ᄒ야위경국교
육부ᄂ아부샹교엽부게ᄒ바가
잇고기외에로ᄉ계문ᄒ는만가
기ᄉ샹관리재죠ᄒ등죠지는다
허시문ᄒ셔분본글으샹연유시
경현셥ᄂ티인고ᄒ이오심원시
인터받ᄒ사원을보교ᄒ아다면
라

○주회변빗 변천군ᄉ체취우
계가로포죠ᄉ를경ᄒ엿는ᄃ야시
거ᄒ는주가리빈이도져구죠의
빈교로셔군스가ᄃ상군에죠회
ᄒ는주가를영ᄒ야보내ᄒ엿ᄃ
나본동에셔시형ᄒ지이죠ᄒ리군
수가경칙를보니셔려쥬가ᄂ를
청치ᄒ야문죠ᄒᆯ이ᄉ에주가스인
의계시변ᄒ엿는티우사르빈이나
리가샹ᄒ지라팽티원의로엿앗고
피여인일천에샹샤ᄒ죽주가가무
죄ᄒ즁노신빗되엿더더라

○면거회장 한성미전구ᄉ샹에
셔군자가에면과를로진승셥쟝ᄒ
야서문밧신면디면ᄒ셔셔소두문밧
과차경거장으로가는길운호죡ᄒ
인로ᄒ야승쳐합이서소거지ᄉ곳
가회부셩ᄒ고ᄒ곳에면거표과
ᄂ경걸소승ᄒ고시소를진츅ᄒ던
인면그디ᄂ면차에셔나면대거
를일이비ᄒ니니가ᄂ되과경면
일을경ᄒ니되과가는면ᄒ니
렁ᄒ빈티도면과를ᄒ니죠이나ᄌ이
다ᄒ면쳐의금면쳔역ᄉ지경조ᄂ
ᄂ즁에셔면아국으ᄒ시문ᄉ동면
가ᄉ경인은진회체로의분동안되
니계셔장ᄒ여오어ᄉ무에비
ᄒ야고료ᄒ고피ᄂ터졈셜게료쓰
본셔인본에디도ᄒ영는디두과
일안에세과을ᄋ졉ᄒ티이외셩님
에지곰면차가다둥와이업는본분
여ᄇ곳시로면차를를륭니죠ᄒ며도
혼면과의슈용경을증가ᄒ는티
과계경부ᄒ기로주무ᄒ는ᄂ이가
일의지경ᄒ엿는티경구ᄒ지로
가위국셔오는티로츅시 작ᄒ
엿는셩되리라더라

○쇼션경페 한성소운ᄒ큐일
셔가셔며남본부에소선지하나
ᄒᆫ는티경ᄒ폐읍된다더라

○경소견경 경무수긴경곤셰
논빌토원랑긍ᄋ로진일음ᄒ교그
티에논경경ᄂ우샹셔가되팀ᄒ
엿ᄐ라

○한저견병 한셩져관소에셔
게변교시ᄒ엿는티그소이를등
ᄒᆯ도무분이로ᄒ스ᄂ지원모가
친졍ᄒ게ᄒ교주작에계읍을ᄒ
야쥬기로경시ᄒ되리안알분가를
지계밀경우에는계ᄋ을맛리가원
조와지간을미리경지ᄒ며죠유
직교기필일동안에금세ᄒ면니라
ᄒ면진인의회동ᄒ야경셜ᄒ리그
ᄒ게셔오ᄂ야경ᄒ이잇스면교
쳥ᄒ게ᄒ교오송는편의계안동

ᄒ야미도로샹에셔공포ᄒ게ᄉ오
셩등동의셔로도경셩에는밍송
을아니ᄒ기로ᄒ이라더라

○일진회명 잘셰셔 지각일경부
에셔 일진회로공합ᄋ엿ᄂ티참
경ᄉ과전의회의셩경경을아니ᄉ세
엿다ᄒ야경부로각송ᄒ엿더니
가부ᄒ에회도경을히이분회
에러도ᄒ엿는티경공회나ᄀ계
수도건셜셰서룰진송ᄒ
ᄒ라ᄒ엿ᄂ넌회즁에셔동의ᄒ
되 회신를존즁케ᄒ교국가ᄀ
소를공교계흥을연ᄒ며케설시보
명세ᄒᆫ는과진인민이ᄉ면경게하
호ᄒᆫ는과계ᄀ진정을엇ᄒ과계실시ᄒ는명해ᄒ일
명ᄒᆫ는과진인미ᄉ엿경지경이각
흥을엇더케ᄒ엿ᄂ니ᄒ케롤일흘
일부에서경문ᄒ아면셰셔를경
호ᄂᆫ소 회셔의권문을일아가저교
죵경도저ᄒᄂ회이 되던네셔이되
샤엽와견각권이엽이셔의되어ᄉ
거ᄉ시니어 희방여원이자가ᄀ거의
셰이를리여서이외소로부니에졔
의소에셔경인의미셔를경경
ᄒ야파로는후에면세서류샹ᄉ며
셔경부에계경ᄒ오교ᄒ엿더라

○경로감뎡 주면묘판점셔브
유리원의가졍빌미으례슈유흥
교리가국ᄒ가곰로게셔병이나
셔계교비와무셜 셰도보ᄂ녀세
나교외부로면분ᄒ엿더라

○경여경면 이분분감면에셔쇼
금셔보영게영ᄒ는소를금부두교
이셔기경보로한국셔를명죄조
흉과면ᄂ지ᄒ는등권을휘득ᄒ지로
면판간이고오은동ᄒ교보ᄒ와분의
무셔ᄒ에경구ᄒᄂ티헤이무원
셔도고게ᄒᄂ도아주기를ᄂ시오
ᄒ엿ᄂ더라

○일슈츅교 일진회에일본손수
가변에헙교엣등일어와셔헝교원
학을거ᄒ셔학교학도의수표를경
이갓더라

○연초견팀 일본인성상을견
탕세가답면케조와경미를팀전
을흔국경부에게증ᄒ고일분수
의도와죠을엇어지금비밀이교
셔ᄒ야가지게약을계졀ᄒ게되
엿다더라

외보

○렴경료청 빌링뎐보를거혼즉
법경에셔쳐에셔ᄒ는ᄂ괴외시
일진교본은그사셔에는ᄒ야문경리
미병민수국ᄂ두료견국의평화
를헙ᄒ기에심ᄒ라ᄒ엿
더라

○러쇼도병 즁원로셔샹셔
전과ᄒ는바러쇼구에잇는로국
병함은수리ᄒ거ᄒ칙경치못ᄒ티
기모사케무분는를기ᄒ즉로
기ᄒ계셔불ᄒ엿다더라

보병실 샴만이쳔오
빅인
슈병 일만이쳔오빅인

요셕포병 수쳔륙빅칠십인
보즁병이긔대티 일쳔팔빅
수셥인
합계 오만오빅십인
빅에병병 칠쳔구빅인
륭군샹병 수쳔칠빅오십
인
희군샹병 일쳔이빅륙십
인
실수젼투원 삼만륙쳔륙빅
인
야젼즁경포
요셕포
시로노흔희군포
합계 륙빅오십이문

○로례인졍 로국통신사면의
보에왈로국황뎨는황ᄌ를탄싱
ᄒ던티관ᄒ야조칙을반포ᄒ엿는
티그요령은좌와곳ᄒ니
뎨일 일반인민과륙히군인에
티ᄒ야형벌을폐ᄒ는ᄉ
뎨이 디방에와긔타죠세의체
납ᄒ것ᄉ뎡혼ᄒ는ᄉ와금은일
병됴금됴ᄉ
뎨삼 국수범죄인에게티ᄒ야
는일면금번엉ᄒ며ᄋ
뎨수 분관ᄒ디에티ᄒ야ᄂᆫ엇
던죠세는물론ᄒ며ᄌ티로도터
슈룰특사ᄒ며이외께통별ᄒ허
면을영ᄒ야명국ᄒ흔구효ᄒ는긔
금을증야샹빗오십만마국(일
화이십오계)을원ᄒ수ᄒ
뎨오 유티이외께티ᄒ야는병
력에디ᄒ야비샹금에드ᄂ거술팅
감ᄒ수
뎨륙 일본과젼쟁ᄒ는티셔에서ᄉ
망ᄒ장교와및하ᄉ병졸의유족
의게티ᄒ야그보호ᄒ며로효ᄒ
ᄂ방법을경구ᄒᄂᆫ수
이외에또로뎐좌수를마샤밧ᄉᆯ
ᄒ며빅벌의게ᄀ닐티를무일을구
교샤범엿분분(일화칠십오젼)
을하ᄉᄒ엿더라

○화티즈병변셔 거월이십륙
일샹히발젼보를거혼즉로국정티
즈변명셔순ᄒ변빈혼의시으로형
ᄒ엿는티샹셔를보ᄒ엿ᄂ츙ᄒ로노
할교경희ᄒ보를화뎐봉ᄒ는ᄅ게ᄉ사ᄒ
엿다ᄒ엿더라

관보

관보뎨이쳔구빅이십오호
광무팔년구월칠일

○서임급ᄉ령
○승셔원필관오등 진위대참
렵디메일ᄃ대부구군의보 지
도일
구월삼일

○음지경면보수즈수 셔면임관
오등 팡양면보수즈수 리봉
종

○금삼셥봉 긔셩면보수즈수
리봉죵
이상구월오일

○시심칠광봉 증뇌부쥬ᄉ 김
샹슌

A FOREIGN OPINION OF THE JAPANESE ARMY.

The "London Standard's" special correspondent with the First Army, in the course of an interesting letter dated Feng-huang-cheng, May 25, says:—

To form any estimate of the character of men without a knowledge of their language and thoughts is a rash enterprise. It is like a deaf man trying to converse with a mute. But observation and experience may make good some of the defects of silence. During two months we have seen the Japanese soldier under nearly all the conditions of war save that of defeat or repulse. We have watched him in barracks and on the march; in battle and in camp; we have beheld him in torrid heat, in rain and cold; we have seen him hauling heavy burdens over difficult roads, and on guard at the outposts; we have observed him under the surgeon's knife and in that long, deadly zone of rifle fire, which is the most powerful factor in battle. Under all these conditions, he has displayed the qualities of a race of fighting men—perfect discipline, inexhaustible energy and endurance, and patience, reckless courage, and absolute disregard for danger. It is our custom to speak of "the little Jap," but in the Army—and especially in the Artillery—are many men of more than average height, and regiment after regiment might be inspected without discovering any of those weaklings whom we describe by the euphemism "specials." They are all men of the age of full physical development, whose uniform size and strength have impressed even the Chinese—themselves a tall and vigorous race. "The Japanese," said an intelligent Manchurian, "are sure to win, for they are not like the Russian soldiers—tall and short, young and old." On the march each man carries his fifty-six pounds and thirteen ounces, and lives on a few handfuls of rice and vegetables. From this, too, the Chinese have drawn a moral, after the manner peculiar to the East. For them the white rice, or "chin-mei," is a lordly dish, compared with which the dark, hard bread and brown biscuit of the Russian is poor and tasteless, and therefore denotes inferiority. It is curious to find that on this question of diet our own Sikhs are of the same opinion as the Chinese. In the march to the relief of the Legations at Peking, the Sikhs observed the Russian soldiers with curiosity and closeness of a potential enemy, and expressed the confident opinion that there is "nothing to fear from men who eat black bread."

According to regulations, the daily ration of the Japanese soldier is one quart of rice, one third of a pound of beef, one-third of a pound of vegetables, and one-sixth of an ounce of saké, or rice spirit. But beef is scarce in Manchuria, and pork is too dear to feed an Army, so that the private has to be content with rice and vegetables and an occasional ounce or two of tinned meat. Luxuries such as tea, milk, and jam he never dreams of, and his whole ration would serve only to whet the appetite of Tommy Atkins. Yet the Japanese soldier is always in good condition, and seems capable of any fatigue. He will draw a cart or a gun with a cheerfulness that is amazing to anyone familiar with European soldiers. The care that he takes of his rifle shows his determination to use it with effect. On the march he puts a cork in the barrel and a cloth round the breech, so that dust and rain cannot touch it. In camp, as on the march, he is quiet and orderly and self-possessed, displaying none of that superabundance of animal spirits and "deviltry" which is characteristic of the British soldier in the field. This solemn demeanour is peculiar to the race, and cannot be mistaken for feeble vitality. When Japanese soldiers amuse themselves they do so thoroughly. Their songs and choruses have the lilt of battle, and their wrestling and sports attest their vigour and keenness. But it is in fight that they manifest their highest and most attractive qualities. The officer who leads in a charge need never look over his shoulder; they will follow him to the last man, even through that long horizontal zone of rifle fire which, according to some tacticians and theorists, is as impassable as the entrance to the Garden of Eden, over which was placed a flaming sword that turned every way.

This estimate of the Japanese soldier may be open to the criticism that justly applies to the unqualified eulogies of travellers and excursionists who must be held responsible in some measure for the impetuous Chauvinism of Japan. Events may demonstrate its error. We have, I admit, yet to see the Japanese in conflict with equal or superior numbers; we have yet to witness their demeanour in adversity; to regard them under conditions that test the real fibre and temper of a race. Personally, I feel confident that they will endure the ordeal like men, and that, whatever may be the issue of this great struggle, the rank and file of the Japanese Army will establish a lasting fame for personal valour and patriotic devotion. Of the officers I am not qualified to speak with any degree of certainty. Our opportunities of observation have been very limited, for reasons that no doubt seem adequate to the members of the Headquarter Staff in Tokyo, though they appear to us childish. That the officer is brave may be taken for granted; he comes of the Samurai class, and to the instincts of the soldier has added a training not inferior to that of the European officer. He may seem a trifle academic, and his constant reference to the drill book may sound a little pedantic. A Staff Officer, describing the capture of the Russian batteries at Hamatan, was impressed not so much by the gallantry of the resistance as by the fact that the gunners, before surrendering, disabled their artillery and "did everything in accordance with the rules laid down in the drill book." Because of this habit of deferring to authority, some people are prone to conclude that the Japanese are mere copyists and are wanting in the power of initiative. But no mere copyist could ever be so self-confident, if we accept as self-confidence what some may call conceit—qualities hard to distinguish between in strong men....

Of the Japanese Cavalry I cannot speak. We have seen them only in small bodies on the march and in camp. They certainly impress one as being bad horsemen and bad horse-masters, and their horses are poor. Nevertheless, we hear remarkable tales of their prowess against the Cossacks. We are told of two squadrons putting to flight a regiment or polk of Cossacks, and of a handful of troopers routing squadrons of this famous irregular cavalry. It may be that the Cossack is played out, but it would be well to wait a little before despising him. There are other Cossacks beside those who are settled in Manchuria and Siberia, and it may be that when he retires instead of fighting, he is only acting "in accordance with the rules laid down in the Drillbook," which says that it is the duty of patrols and outposts to observe and not to fight. The Artillery is in every respect admirable, and the new Arisaka quick-firing steel gun, with a range of five thousand yards, has proved a most serviceable weapon. It is to be regretted that the re-armament is not complete. In the howitzer the field gun has a powerful ally upon which the Japanese place great reliance. The value of indirect fire has long been recognised, and howitzers were used for field work in South Africa. Their efficiency not only against trenches and gun emplacements, but in open country, was demonstrated on the Yalu, where howitzer and shrapnel worked in unison and practically as one weapon, a howitzer shell being followed immediately by a hail of shrapnel. It will be instructive to note how this combination works out in practice, and to discover some evidence that may enable experts to determine the relative efficiency of shrapnel and common shell.

The measles, now epidemic in Kansas, has given the doctors a chance to circulate an ancient joke. They say that the German measles come from a germ; French from a Parisite, and the Irish from a Mikerobe.

Concerning the question of whether the Baltic fleet will or will not go out to the Far East, a correspondent of the Westminster Gazette says:—"They cannot now avoid sending it, even if they wished it to remain in the Baltic. Before Kuropatkin left for the East he is credited with having stated that none of the Japanese who had landed in Korea would go back to Japan alive and that peace would be signed in Tokio. The Russian Press has since then done its best to work up popular feeling and enthusiasm, and have been more successful than they hoped for. The working-classes in the great centres of population are at last fully awake, and now want to have Kuropatkin's promise made good. Murmurings have already been audible in the public streets, and more would be likely to happen did it not become evident that the Government were not 'putting their backs into it.'' So it comes about that the Baltic fleet, cost what it will, is going to the East. The Government is fully aware of the state of affairs, and see clearly that the only way of avoiding a revolution is to see the thing through.

ROYAL NEWSPAPER.

The Emperor of Austria was the first royal personage to have a newspaper published for his own private perusal. About thirty years ago he thought it would be a nice idea to have each important article condensed by a competent writer, and the results written out on small square sheets, which are then slipped into a binding cover and laid on His Majesty's breakfast table.

Nothing that concerns him, agreeable or disagreeable, is ever omitted, and to make certain nobody is fooling him he occasionally orders a fresh bundle of papers to see if his orders are obeyed. True, the Emperor loses a lot of amusing things, as every one does who cannot read a newspaper for himself; but he is now an old man and doesn't like to try his eyes too long at a time. His royal newspaper was likewise adopted by other European monarchs, until the more modern kingships found they were not getting all the news, and they took to doing their own "condensing" and skimming. King Edward is an indefatigable newspaper reader, despite his "busy day" programme.

It is reported that the Amir of Afghanistan is showing a great interest in the war. Special mounted messengers carry him the latest cablegrams daily. He constantly expounds these messages in durbar, and quotes the Japanese successes as showing what a nation can do when thoroughly united. It is believed that the Russian reverses have made a great impression in Afghanistan.

The heart of Jumbo, the famous elephant, which died six years ago, is now in the possession of a doctor in America, and will shortly be dissected by the students of an American university. It is the largest heart in the world, weighing 35½lbs., and measuring 28in. by 24in.

The Korea Daily News.

To be published daily except Sundays.

Rate of Subscription:—

Per Year,	Yen 25.
Per Quarter,	Yen 7.
Per Month	Yen 2.50

Postage in Korea not charged extra.
Postage abroad charged extra.

Advertisements, 50 sen per day for 1 inch or less.
5 yen per month per inch.
50 yen per year per inch.

All communications to

E. T. BETHELL,
Editor and Publisher.
Pak-tong, Seoul

THE WAR.

We have received from the front, reports of the fighting from the 25th to the 29th, culminating in the occupation of Anping and Anshantien.

The fighting appears to have been of the most desperate character, and the conditions terrible enough to have debarred any army but the Japanese from taking the offensive. The Japanese appear to argue that however bad the weather and roads are, they are equally bad for the enemy, and in fact, the Japanese seem to have a talent for turning adverse conditions to good account.

The fight appears to have been a fairly even one, for although General Kuroki succeeded in his object of driving the Russians out of Anping, and across the Tango river, the Russians do not appear to have retreated in the disorder which one would have expected of an army when a river crosses its line of retreat.

On the 25th the Japanese forces moved forward to attack the Russians, and before dawn on the 26th, a battle was raging the whole length of a front of over twelve miles. The Russian position was an excellent one. They were drawn up on the outermost of a succession of mountain ridges. These ridges were intersected by fields of grain, and as fast as the Russians were driven from one range, they retired to the next and so on. The Russian troops are said to have fought with great courage and even recklessness, but little by little Kuroki drove them back, and before noon had succeeded in turning their left flank after very heavy fighting and a spirited counter attack. In this action the Russians lost eight guns which were in position on the summit of a cliff. These the Japanese captured, by scaling the cliff in the face of an avalanche of rocks hurled on them from above. This dashing assault cost many of the Japanese soldiers their lives.

At noon the Russian centre began to fall back. The Japanese took the ridge at the point of the bayonet, and finally, finding themselves enfiladed by a mountain battery which the Japanese had brought to bear, the Russians evacuated the position altogether.

In the meantime the attack on the Russian right was meeting with no success. The Russian artillery was superior to the Japanese in quality and numbers, and their lines were strongly entrenched. By nightfall no impression had been made on the Russian position and both armies bivouaced in the open. The night was a terrible one, the rain falling in torrents, and the next morning it was found that many of the wounded had died from exposure.

On the 27th, with undiminished energy, General Kuroki's troops continued their attack on the Russian centre and left. The conditions were terrible, the heavy rain had turned the roads into quagmires, and many of the artillery horses died from fatigue and exposure. Soldiers immediately took their places and the army steadily advanced, shelling the Russians out of position after position and by five o'clock in the evening the Russian rearguard retreated from Anping, and fording the Tougho, took shelter in the hills on the other side. During this retreat the Russians lost very heavily from the Japanese artillery fire, but, owing to the difficult nature of the country, the Japanese infantry made no attempt to pursue them.

In the meantime the endeavours of the Japanese centre and left to dislodge the Russian right were futile. The Russian guns were well placed and well served and commanded the whole field. Japanese infantry advancing to the attack were repeatedly repulsed, whole battalions being decimated. It was at this point that the Japanese sustained the greater part of their casualties.

However, the approach of the two other Japanese armies from the south finally caused the Russian right to fall back towards Liaoyang, and bringing artillery to bear, the Japanese shelled the Russians from all their positions to the north and west of Anping.

Detaching his main column from the main army, Kuroki then made a sweeping movement with the object of menacing the Russian communications north of Liaoyang. The details of this movement are not to hand, but the news of the Japanese occupation of Liaoyang indicates that it was entirely successful.

Eight Korean officers, who were attached to the 1st Japanese army, returned to Seoul on the 5th inst.

The Japanese news offices in Seoul and Chemulpo are closed for two days in celebration of the Liaoyang victory.

His Excellency the German Minister has applied to His Majesty for an audience on the 9th instant as he desires to present the German vice Admiral and his staff.

Further reports relative to a tobacco monopoly in this country, are continually circulating. It appears that Mr. Nagamori is again the moving spirit in the new enterprise

Mr. Yu Ki-won, the secretary of the legation in Berlin, started out on a visit to Korea, but only reached half way when serious illness laid him by the heels. He telegraphs for money to meet his expenses.

His Majesty hearing that Mr. Ho We, Assistant Councillor of State recently arrived from a country magistracy, is a poor man and cannot afford the expenses of town life, has ordered the payment of $2,800 to enable him to buy a house.

An extremely belated despatch, dated July 18th, comes from the Kamni of Kyeng-hung and states that the bridge built by the Russians across the Tumen was nearly completed, also he had an interview with Major Kim In-su, who told him he was in command of a Russian regiment. A brigadier-general with a force of 600 officers and men and 1,000 horses had passed through on their way south, early in July. Military stations had been established south to Kyeng-syong.

ELECTRIC CAR SERVICE TO BE ENLARGED.

The American Korean Electric Company is about to extend its electric railway tracks from the foot of the hill outside of West Gate along the street leading to the West Gate Railway Station, to a point immediately adjacent to the Passenger Depot, where a ticket office and waiting room will be erected. This will obviate the long walk from the train to the electric cars, and will be appreciated particularly in inclement weather. Work will be commenced on this improvement today or tomorrow.

The Company will shortly commence operating cars every five minutes between West Gate and East Gate, a doubling of the present service, which is at ten minutes intervals. The materials necessary for putting in the extra passing tracks required for this service have arrived in Japan and are expected here within a fortnight.

Several new car lines, to portions of the city and suburbs now without car service, also the addition of engines and dynamos giving an increased capacity for electric lighting, have been decided on by the Directorate, the installation of which will be completed as soon as the required materials can be procured from abroad.

PRISONERS OF WAR.

The Japan Times remarking on prisoners in the hands of the Russians says "Owing to the absence of detailed information, the exact number of Japanese prisoners in the hands of the enemy is not known, but it is believed in official quarters that they exceed three hundred and of them the prisoners from the Izumi Maru and the Kinshu Maru alone number 287.

We remember that 12 men including Major Togo were taken prisoners near Wiju at the outset of the war, but there is no indication as to when and where the other man, who brings the total up to 300, was captured,

THE IL CHIN HOI.

It appears to us that the Japanese authorities would do well to withdraw their support from this society. The Koreans freely allege that its objects are not of the harmlessly Utopian character they profess to be and that on the contrary it is a distinct menace to the welfare of the Empire. If the origiual programme of the society is to be adhered to, it is much too vague and nebulous for anything to be accomplished, and if, on the other hand, it is being departed from, some investigation should be made into the real aims of the society.

As an indication of the lines along which an investigation might proceed we may say that it is alleged of the Il Chin Hoi, that the society is not a representative one but is "packed." That many of its meetings are secret. That its real objects are diametrically opposed to those of the Po An Hoi, which was a society formed to protest against the granting of the Nagamori demands.

TENNIS.

At 4 P.M. today on the Seoul Union court, tennis matches will be played between H. M. S. "Phoenix" and Seoul. Seoul will be represented by Messrs. Hulbert, Turner, Davidson and Porter.

On the 5th inst. some Japanese gendarmes went to a hillside cave inhabited by beggars and picking out four of the strongest carried them off. As this indicates work for the beggars, it seems a very good plan and further steps taken in the same direction should be much appreciated. Firstly, it rids the city of a lot of useless loafers and secondly it will help to fill the demand for coolies.

The Korea Daily News.

VOL. I, THURSDAY, SEPTEMBER 8, 1904. No. 46

HONGKONG & SHANGHAI BANKING CORPORATION.

Paid-up Capital..... ....$10,000,000
Reserve Fund:—Sterling Reserve... 10,000,000
Silver Reserve..... 6,500,000

26,500,000
Reserve Liability of Proprietors... 10,000,000

HEAD OFFICE, HONGKONG.

London Bankers, London and County Banking Company Limited.

Branches and Agencies, London.

Amoy,	Hankow	Penang,
Bangkok,	Hiogo,	Rangoon,
Batavia,	Iloilo,	Saigon,
Bombay,	Lyons,	San Francisco,
Calcutta,	Manila,	Singapore,
Colombo,	Nagasaki,	Sourabaya,
Foochow,	New York,	Tientsin,
Hamburg,	Peking,	Yokohama,

Credits granted on approved Securities, and every description of Banking and Exchange business transacted.

Drafts granted on London and the chief Commercial places in Europe, India, Australia, America, China and Japan.

HOLME RINGER & Co., AGENTS, CHEMULPO.

ON CHEONG & CO., SEOUL.

GENERAL STORE KEEPERS.
Imported provisions, Cooking Utensils Crockery, etc.
FRESH BREAD DAILY.

MITSU BISHI DOCKYARD & ENGINE WORKS,

NAGASAKI.

CODE WORD, "DOCK."

A. 1, A. B. C., and Engineering Codes used.

DOCK No. 1 (at Tategami).

Extreme Length..............523 feet
Length on blocks .... 513 ,,
Width of Entrance on Top......89 ,,
,, ,, Bottom....77 ,,
Water on Blocks at Spring Tide 26½ ,,

DOCK No. 2 (Mukaijima).

Extreme Length..............371 feet
Length on Blocks............360 ,,
Width of Entrance on Top......66 ,,
,, ,, Bottom 53 ,,
Water on Blocks at Spring Tide 22 ,,

PATENT SLIP (at Kosuge).

Can take vessels up to 1,000 tons gross.

THE WORKS are well equipped with the LATEST IMPROVEMENTS, and can execute any kind of work in SHIPBUILDING and MARINE ENGINEERING, as well as in REPAIRING of SHIPS.

The COMPANY'S new powerful steamer OURA MARU (712 tons, 700 I.H.P.), specially built for SALVAGE PURPOSES, and equipped with necessary gear, is always READY at SHORT NOTICE.

CHARTERED BANK OF INDIA AUSTRALIA & CHINA.

INCORPORATED BY ROYAL CHARTER 1853

HEAD OFFICES:—LONDON.

Paid-up Capital £800,000
Reserve Liability of Shareholders 800,000
Reserve Fund 800,000

Drafts granted upon all the principal places in the world and every description of Exchange and banking business transacted.

E. MEYER & Co., Agents, Chemulpo.

E. MEYER & CO.
Chemulpo.

SOLE AGENTS IN KOREA FOR
A. T. Morse, Sons & Co's "Fresco" Distemper

In all colours ready for use on walls, Ceilings etc.
and
AVENARIUS CARBOLINEUM

A wood-preserving and antiseptic oil preparation

Against decay, dry-rot, fungus and wood-destroying insects.

A large supply always in Stock.
Prices upon application.

E. MEYER & Co., Chemulpo.

LAW UNION & CROWN INS. CO.

Fire risks accepted at Current rates, on go downs, merchandise, dwellings, and other property, subject to usual conditions.

HOLME RINGER & Co., Agents, Chemulpo

THE METHODIST PUBLISHING HOUSE,
Little West Gate, Seoul.

JOB PRINTING, TYPEWRITER PAPER
CARBON PAPER, VISITING CARDS
STATIONERY, BOOK BINDING
BOOK PUBLISHERS
AMERICAN SCHOOL BOOKS
SPENCERIAN COPY BOOKS
PEN CARBON LETTER AND BILL BOOKS

S. A. BECK, Manager.

DAI-ICHI GINKO.

LIMITED.

(Formerly the First National Bank)

ESTABLISHED 1873

INCORPORATED UNDER PRESENT LAW 1896

Capital - - - - - - - - - Yen 5,000,000
Reserve Fund - - - - - 1,500,000

HEAD OFFICE:—TOKIO.

President: Baron SHIBUSAWA.

BRANCHES AND CORRESPONDENTS
In the Principal Cities and Towns of Japan.

Interest Allowed on

Fixed deposits 1 year - - - 6½ per cent
" " 6 months - - - 6 per cent

Special current accounts 1½ sen daily per Y 100
General " " 1 " " " 100

M. TANAKA, Manager, Chemulpo

HOLME RINGER & Co.
Chemulpo.

General Merchants and Government Contractors.

Agents for the leading
Banks
Steamship Companies
and
Insurance Companies

Importers of Merchandise of every description.

KAMEYA & CO.
GENERAL STOREKEEPERS
Chinkokai - - Seoul
(*Established 1895, Tokyo*)

Confectionery, Hams, Canned Goods, Cutlery, Hirano & Tansan Water. Provisions, Gents, Furnishing goods, Toilet Articles, Travelling Bags, Tobacco, Cigars & Cigarettes Kitchen Utensils. Coffee, Biscuits.

Fresh Goods always kept in Stock.
Prices Moderate
Please come and inspect our goods.

NIPPON YUSEN KAISHA.

JAPANESE MAIL STEAMSHIP CO.

DER MAIL CONTRACT WITH THE IMPERIAL JAPANESE GOVERNMENT.

European Line

Regular Fortrightly Service between Yokohama Kobe, Moji, Shanghai, Hongkong, Singapore, Penang Colombo, Port Said, Marseilles, London and Antwerp

American Line

Regular Fortnightly Service between Hongkong and Seattle, calling at Shanghai, Moji, Kobe, Yokohama and Victoria, B. C.

Australian Line

Regular weekly Service betwen Japan Ports and Australia, calling at Hongkong and Manila.

(Above Three Lines Suspended until further notice).

Shanghai Line

Weekly Service between Shanghai and Japan Ports

Korea Line

Service Kobe, Moji, Nagasaki, Fusan, Chemulpo, Chinnampo, Taiku.
S. S. Bahelsberg, 2181 tons.
Service Kobe, Moji, Fusan, Chemulpo, Chinnampo
S. S ARGO, S. S. Ohio.

BORDEN'S CONDENSED MILK CO.

New York, U. S. A.

ALWAYS IN STOCK
Eagle Brand Condensed Milk.
Gold Seal Condensed Milk.
Peerless (Family) Evaporated Cream.
Borden's Malted Milk.

E. MEYER & CO.
Chemulpo, Korea,
Sole Agents

ROYAL INSURANCE COMPANY,
Funds exceed £10,000,000
FIRE
AT CURRENT RATES.
LIFE
REDUCED PREMIUM.
HOLME RINGER & Co., Agents, Chemulpo.

HOTEL DU PALAIS
SEOUL.

The only first class Hotel in Seoul. Situated in the centre of the city opposite the palace.

Cuisine under the supervision of an experienced French Chef.

Well ventilated and furnished throughout.

TARIFF UPON APPLICATION

L. MARTIN
Proprietor and Mangaer.

大韓每日申報

대한ᄆᆡ일신보

(뎨사십칠호) (금요일) 쳔구ᄇᆡᆨ사년구월구일

본사고

이신보는영어와한어로셔게ᄆᆡ일출판ᄒᆞᆸ

신문가

ᄒᆞᆫ장 엽두돈오푼

ᄒᆞᆫ삭 됴엽두량닷돈 빅돈으로 반삭

광고료는

귀한의쟝단과ᄌᆞ항의다쇼로좃감ᄒᆞ되별가로받을터이오매오퇴지아니ᄒᆞ대한사람마다이신문을보실터이니광고내시기를원ᄒᆞ시ᄂᆞᆫ이들은우리신문사에와셔면약ᄒᆞ심을희망ᄒᆞᆸ

○발행소 박동대한ᄆᆡ일신보사벽어학교엽해젼영국인셜필립졍자리오

사쟝 영국인 (비셜)

사고

○우리대한ᄆᆡ일신보의목뎍은대한의안녕질셔에관한모든뎨목에ᄃᆡᄒᆞ야ᄂᆞᆫ공평한변론을쥬쟝ᄒᆞ올이라우리동신원의담보ᄂᆞᆫ신문보시ᄂᆞᆫ쳠군ᄌᆞ의게ᄒᆞᆼ샹보도ᄒᆞ리며편지를긔셔ᄒᆞ여주시ᄂᆞᆫ이ᄂᆞᆫ셩명과반ᄃᆡ를젹어붓치시기를희망ᄒᆞ오나비긔ᄒᆞᆯ신문샹에긔ᄌᆡᄒᆞᆯ거시아니오ᄃᆞᆫ만국ᄒᆞᆯ신용ᄒᆞᄂᆞᆫ증거를삼고자ᄒᆞᆷ이라긔자ᄂᆞᆫ아모긔셔던지긔ᄌᆡᄒᆞᆷ을되ᄀᆞᆺᄒᆞᄂᆞᆫ권리를가졋스니취ᄒᆞᆯ만ᄒᆞᆫ리유를말ᄒᆞᆯ터이오며공즁평화를문란케ᄒᆞᄂᆞᆫ듯ᄒᆞᆫ귀셔ᄂᆞᆫ의례히밧지안켓ᄉᆞᆸ니다

사고

○본사에셔ᄂᆞᆫ신문갑ᄉᆞᆫᄆᆡ월에션급으로밧ᄉᆞ오며본신문은우체로붓치ᄂᆞᆫ고로본사에셔ᄂᆞᆫ다른신문사처럼금행을거두러도니지안ᄉᆞ오니우리신문을ᄉᆞ랑ᄒᆞ야구람ᄒᆞ시ᄂᆞᆫ쳠군ᄌᆞᄂᆞᆫ향ᄒᆡ비셩명ᄒᆞᆫ호수와쥬소를ᄌᆞ세히젹어셔박쥬동본샤로보내시기를바라오며금월회일노브터션금을아니보내시ᄂᆞᆫ곳에ᄂᆞᆫ리월일일브터ᄒᆞᆫ신문을아니보낼터이오니조량ᄒᆞ옵소셔

●본사에셔아직귀게들쟝만치못ᄒᆞ와다론데셔박여오ᄂᆞᆫ고로ᄆᆡ양월요일에ᄂᆞᆫ출판이대단히늣게되ᄂᆞᆫ듯ᄉᆞ오니본젼이ᄆᆡ우늣게되오니우리신문을구람ᄒᆞ시ᄂᆞᆫ쳠군ᄌᆞᄂᆞᆫ 용셔ᄒᆞ여쥬심을희망ᄒᆞᆸ니이다

본샤광고

본사에셔본신문뎨ᄉᆞ호와뎨싱일호와뎨기셩오호를소용ᄒᆞᆯᄯᆡ가잇셔이에광고ᄒᆞ오니누구시던지이샹삼호중에본사로가져오시면ᄆᆡ쟝에빅젼두푼식드리리다

론셜

뎐쟁소식

○거월이십오일로붓터ᄆᆡ셩구일셔지셔로싸와안평과밋안산쳔두곳졈령ᄒᆞ엿다ᄂᆞᆫ보고를게ᄒᆞᆫ즉그싸홈에아라사에셔뒤젹ᄒᆞ야방어ᄒᆞᆷ이심히굿세되일본셔도승습ᄒᆞ야용ᄆᆡᆼᄒᆞᆷ이강경ᄒᆞᆫ엿시되엿다ᄂᆞᆫᄃᆡ그ᄯᆡ에맛참ᄃᆡ우가쪽주ᄒᆞ야광국비셔로동병ᄒᆞᆷ에ᄃᆡ단비불리ᄒᆞᆷ은피ᄎᆞ일반이나그러ᄒᆞ나일본셔ᄂᆞᆫ거묘ᄒᆞᆫ계교를써단항이괴ᄒᆞ취ᄒᆞᆯ이되엿다ᄂᆞᆫ티

다만교젼일향에흑목대쟝의망뎨로안평싸를니모라단ᄒᆞ고갑소셕지진ᄂᆞᆫ계ᄒᆞ엿스나그러ᄒᆞ나아국핀졸들리갈ᄯᆡᄂᆞᆫ알시조ᄒᆞ되여모도뵈아지아니ᄒᆞᄂᆞᆫ지라그런고로일본군ᄃᆡ에셔이십오일에군ᄉᆞ를졔츅ᄒᆞ야식이영리를젼진ᄒᆞ야그이튼날두에아병으로ᄒᆞ여곰셔로맛나싸왓ᄂᆞᆫ뒤아병들은산샹에결진ᄒᆞ여ᄒᆞᆫ요히계에ᄋᆞ거ᄒᆞ엿슴을ᄡᅡᆷ도가히ᄎᆡ티ᄒᆞ엿ᄂᆞᆫ고로모도리진세ᄒᆞ야주의건이귀ᄒᆞ되면만엿진예셔군ᄉᆞ를뎌칠ᄒᆡ보ᄒᆞ면그귀산샹으로츅츅퇴귀ᄒᆞᄂᆞᆫ지라이ᄇᆡᆨ조ᄒᆞ라에좌익디병으로ᄒᆞ여곰아병을흑목대쟝은승승쟝구ᄒᆞ야습ᄒᆞ야승쳡ᄒᆞ엿다ᄂᆞᆫ뒤일본군ᄉᆞ들은바위졀벽에다사다리를놋코긔여올나가아병의가진총을써던병이나세샷스되산샹으로셔일병의올나옴을향ᄒᆞ야방ᄒᆞ엿ᄉᆞᆫ닭에일병의샹ᄒᆞᆫ쟈ᄂᆞᆫ만히이되엿고그날오젼에아병의본진이졈졈퇴츅ᄒᆞᄂᆞᆫ지라일병들이귀히희들엇더니산마루로좃ᄎᆞ총을노와아병을쳘귀ᄒᆞ도록ᄒᆞ엿고

ᄯᅩ우익뒤병은맛나지못ᄒᆞ야셩공치못ᄒᆞ엿다ᄂᆞᆫ뒤더ᄇᆡ에아국포병의수효가일본과비교ᄒᆞ면싱히만홀ᄲᅮᆫ더러ᄯᅩᄒᆞᆫ진세가견엉ᄒᆞᆫ중맛츰일모ᄒᆞᆫ석담에련ᄒᆞ야싸호지못ᄒᆞ고야영을ᄇᆡ푸러밤을지ᄂᆡᆯ새ᄃᆡ우가쪽주ᄒᆞ야샹과갓치나리ᄂᆞᆫ지라그의일아츰에비로소군ᄉᆞ의사샹을헤아렷다ᄒᆞ며

이십칠일에흑목ᄃᆡ쟝의군ᄉᆞ가아병을공격ᄒᆞᄂᆞᆫ뒤미싸홈이가히ᄉᆞ롬으로ᄒᆞ여곰ᄃᆡ경실ᄉᆡᆨᄒᆞ게ᄒᆞᆯ만ᄒᆞᆫ즁ᄃᆡ우로인ᄒᆞ야모든길이긔쳔과ᄎᆞᆺᄂᆞᆫ고로포병의마필은긔관포를ᄭᅳᆯ티지못ᄒᆞ야수운젼치못ᄒᆞ며군ᄉᆞ들은일향오후다섯시조음되여아병의후뒤가면져안평싸에셔퇴ᄒᆞ야당호셔으로다라낫ᄂᆞᆫ뒤이곳에죡장산이수방으로들너가젓ᄂᆞᆫ지란이아벼에일병의포격ᄒᆞᆷ을인ᄒᆞ야아병의손히가블소ᄒᆞ나지향을ᄌᆞ세히알수업ᄂᆞᆫ고로련ᄒᆞ야쌧지못ᄒᆞ엿다ᄒᆞ며

보병들은여러번공격ᄒᆞ야물리쳣스되사샹이반치아니ᄒᆞᆷ은대뒤병즐이수방으로덤뷔여피진ᄒᆞᆫ닭이라ᄒᆞ며

궬경에남방으로보낸군ᄉᆞ―아병을에워싸고진터를포격ᄒᆞ야취ᄒᆞ려ᄒᆞᆯ시맛츰흑목대쟝이ᄌᆞ귀의군ᄉᆞ로ᄒᆞ여곰수방으로분파ᄒᆞ야요양을협낙ᄒᆞ엿다ᄒᆞᆫ즉아샹보ᄂᆞᆫ아즉보지못ᄒᆞ엿스되일병의요양졈령ᄒᆞᆷ은분명ᄒᆞᆫ듯ᄒᆞ도다

잡보

○구락부회동 지작일하오륙시에한일구락부에셔일본인모모졔씨가과셩관에셔회동ᄒᆞ엿ᄂᆞᆫ뒤일공ᄉᆞ림권조씨ᄀᆞᆺ쳥에되엿스며대한칙임관을일졔히쳥요ᄒᆞ야구락부원가옥과소용즙물픔장만홀수를샹의ᄒᆞ엿다ᄒᆞ더라

○니ᄃᆡ샹소 니부ᄃᆡ신조병필씨가지쟉샹소에즉지시무ᄒᆞ라ᄒᆞ옵신 우비를승ᄒᆞ엿스ᄂᆞᆫ귀어히도레ᄒᆞ라ᄒᆞ고지작일에샹ᄎᆞ샹소를ᄒᆞ엿더라

○경찰발명 일작에니현쟝샹덕ᄎᆞ씨집에셔엇더ᄒᆞᆫ신병을사회되은ᄒᆡᆼ가양우산일병을잡어가ᄂᆞᆫ거슬헌병이장아일본경찰셔로보내엿더니일본경관이대한경찰이졈졈발명된다고대단칭ᄎᆞᄒᆞ엿다더라

○비밀신문 지작일경무청에셔경무ᄉᆞ이하각경관이신문계에회동ᄒᆞ야차오팔시붓터신시되지비밀히죄인을신문ᄒᆞ엿ᄂᆞᆫᄃᆡ그죄인은동학과빌학의유라ᄒᆞ더라

○부등진복 지작일진신소청에셔대첩ᄎᆞ샹소를진정ᄒᆞ란ᄒᆞ고ᄃᆡ안분젼에진복ᄒᆞ란ᄒᆞᄂᆞᆫ티일본헌병수령부에셔헌병을파송ᄒᆞ야헝문ᄒᆞ되소청에셔ᄒᆞᄂᆞᆫ일이다일본을빙쳑ᄒᆞᄂᆞᆫ운동이니샹소를못ᄒᆞ리라ᄒᆞᄂᆞᆫ고로진복지못ᄒᆞ엿다더라

○ᄌᆞ차문슈 지작일에일본수령부참모부관증위후등진ᄊᆡ가니부ᄃᆡ신을방문ᄒᆞ고말ᄒᆞ되롱쳔군슈를리경직으로환임하송ᄒᆞ던지그럿치아니ᄒᆞ면곳슈포ᄒᆞ던지신임ᄒᆞ야즉히송ᄒᆞ라ᄒᆞ엿더라

○광쥴면보 평남관찰ᄉᆞ리즁하씨의면보를거ᄒᆞᆫ즉강쳐에장복ᄒᆞ엿든동학당이셔울셔둥문이왓다ᄒᆞ고삼등군에도회ᄒᆞ야국ᄉᆞ를위ᄒᆞ야장ᄎᆞᆺ경셩으로향ᄒᆞᆫ다ᄒᆞ기로슌검을파송ᄒᆞ야졍탐ᄒᆞᄂᆞᆫ중이오니샹탐ᄒᆞᄂᆞᆫ되로졍보ᄒᆞ겟다ᄒᆞ엿다더라

○광쥴우보 ᄯᅩ보고ᄒᆞ기를평양쥬차일본수령관이공함ᄒᆞ되군ᄉᆞ샹쇼용ᄎᆞ로평양셔문에ᄃᆡ동강ᄂᆞᆫ티셔지표목을세우고가그린표한안에ᄂᆞᆫ수령관의인가엽시ᄂᆞᆫᄉᆞ수로히향ᄆᆡᄒᆞ던지되ᄆᆡᄒᆞ던지가옥을걸구ᄒᆞ던지디향을금츅ᄒᆞ지못ᄒᆞ되만일위형ᄒᆞᄂᆞᆫ자ᄂᆞᆫ군률로시ᄒᆡᆼᄒᆞ겟다ᄒᆞ고디방도본을보ᄂᆡᆫ고로본관찰ᄉᆞ가히용ᄒᆞᆷ수의문시ᄒᆡᆼ치못ᄒᆞ켓다고루ᄎᆞ교셥ᄒᆞ되듯지안ᄊᆞ오며ᄯᅩ본군수의보고를거ᄒᆞ온즉일병이보통문안으로셩으로

봇더들너셔분외진두쳐지표롱운셰운고토쟉간ᄒᆞᆫ즉외셩젼국쥬희가셩오픽에 황궁 궤궁졍양문함구ᄒᆞᆫ이표목ᄌᆞ희안에싸비여드럿다ᄒᆞ엿스오니그외향을알수업셔경부지령을기다련오매분파찬이고림표ᄒᆞᆫ스진예티ᄒᆞ야시방치못ᄒᆞᆫ즉노히병쳠에용함ᄒᆞ엿더니뢰칵ᄒᆞ고밧져안엇다ᄒᆞ엿더라

○병련쳥거 일젼에일본헌병비경무남서에뒤도ᄒᆞ야하기를쳥ᄒᆞᆫ즉수무불즉금와시ᄒᆞ야랑군이방ᄒᆞᆨᄒᆞ야쳐취ᄒᆞ기로쳥약ᄒᆞᆫ다ᄒᆞ엿ᄂᆞᆫ디일인거루더에ᄂᆞᆫ뢰국인아참결붕용조칭ᄒᆞᆫ기로ᄒᆞᆫ다더라

○참졍용함 일젼에참졍신긔션씨가일진회에용함ᄒᆞᆫ젼문은췌엽긔취ᄒᆞ노니공헥소뢰 졍복자ᄅᆞ헌금ᄒᆞᆫ세가위미부젼ᄒᆞᆫ거손표야가디우탄ᄒᆞᄂᆞᆫ바열녀니귀회중에셔수묘긴을도리본쟉경부에티결ᄒᆞᆫ셥허ᄒᆞ기를권면ᄒᆞ니국민의충이지싱을알지랑고희ᄒᆞᆫ남수됴진비대경령샏이오명세ᄒᆞᆫ됴목이엉스니디시쥬명을디ᄒᆞ야방편을상시ᄒᆞ라

의정부참졍신긔션 랄쟝
일진회쟝 윤시병 좌하

○류학싱소환 경부에서상쥬ᄒᆞ되헌금일아기젼지시를방ᄒᆞ야모묘가죠결ᄒᆞ엿셔니야국에파견ᄒᆞᆫ공햑싱리게하비보닉기반편ᄒᆞ오니헌햑도등을소환ᄒᆞ을이하여ᄒᆞ을지근 ᄒᆞ와봉지외쥬되엿더라

○포살요인 평벽관찰수리옹필씨보고에ᄒᆞ엿스되쥬차일주일본소령관산연쟝지의조회를졉준ᄒᆞᆫ은즉ᄒᆞ기를회친거민우궤슈우비숀킹을ᄒᆞ리응몽긴회틔오헌이랑자아병이안쥬등은승ᄒᆞᆫ뵈에아병으로뎌브리동싱함긔ᄒᆞ야이를본군소상혜방취동ᄒᆞᆫ고로군등포서행ᄒᆞ야왕렬히싱오여ᄒᆞ히오안을포살ᄒᆞ엿노라ᄒᆞ엿다고ᄒᆞ엿더라

○도망츄거 평리원수가의부에조회ᄒᆞ되일본병참부인거리즈길의관할ᄒᆞᆫ일본공관에잇ᄂᆞᆫ티병기쟝에범인ᄒᆞᆫ고로치티단챵승본쥬의게츌감ᄒᆞᆯ수로자너괴월네티부로조회ᄒᆞ엿더니샹금회부미보수뢰싱ᄒᆞ야츄호지라또회조회ᄒᆞ니허티단가에편화동쳔원ᄂᆞᆫ죵시본ᄂᆞᆫ흔으로송교ᄒᆞ라ᄒᆞ엿더라

○쳔쳔군보 쳔쳔군슈가외부에보고ᄒᆞ되일본군용뎐도를헌금시셕ᄒᆞᄂᆞᆫ티원ᄀᆞᆯ드의에본군남면도사포에셔원뎐도에이르기서지별도치셥ᄒᆞ부셜고자ᄒᆞ야들내가득ᄒᆞᆯ거슨셜못된곡식을원병배하라고인민의게독촉ᄒᆞᄂᆞᆫ고로셩진항ᄒᆞ며샤탈하다호곽ᄒᆞᄂᆞᆫ경상은과연참불인견미오니이수상으로일공관에조회ᄒᆞ야헌뎐도티에신쳐ᄒᆞ야츄수ᄒᆞᆫ후에헌뎐도를시부ᄒᆞ야이창양ᄒᆞᆫ빗셩을안도케ᄒᆞ라ᄒᆞ엿더라

○옥뎨미령 두수운쥬 뎨황에뎨폐하게오셔일젼붓터 옥뎨미령ᄒᆞ신하게시다더라

○뎍함도인 뎍국군함닙게이졔작일에인항에졍박ᄒᆞ엿더라

○창거죵방 일젼에진신소쳥에서상소ᄒᆞ고진복ᄒᆞ란듸일노분보에긔지ᄒᆞ엿거니와계문ᄒᆞᆫ졍싱소수외ᄂᆞᆫ이왕루츠상소와동일ᄒᆞ다ᄒᆞ고홍졍엑박계빈셰아하뵈며명이ᄒᆞᆫ명ᄒᆞ엿ᄂᆞᆫ티쳐힘ᄒᆞᆫ티ᄒᆞᆫ졍쥬잡ᄒᆞᆫ티닐병챵관암ᄒᆞᆫ티로붕슈샹셰와따유칭셜인이대한문젼에진복ᄒᆞ엿더니 뎨나뢰셔비셔승을 명송ᄒᆞ샤샹소ᄂᆞᆫ곳봉입ᄒᆞ고즉시하비됨딤이니리거ᄒᆞ란ᄒᆞ노조응예회헌병이뤼도ᄒᆞ야금ᄒᆞᄂᆞᆫ고로진복은못되엿고리범챵셰돌을마샹구츅ᄒᆞ다디착거ᄒᆞᄂᆞᆫ티풍우굿치모라가더니일보ᄒᆞᆫ후에노혀왓다더라

○싱셰츌셩 싱상ᄒᆞᆫ셰ᄂᆞᆫ조궤원칭비시국에맛지아니ᄒᆞᆫ고로향데로ᄂᆞᆫ리갈츠로등문외로츌거ᄒᆞ엿더라

○함쟝영셩 죄쟉일덕국함쟝이하계쟝관이영셩ᄒᆞ야쟈쟉일에덕어학교를관광ᄒᆞ엿더라

○이수졍셩 이티리공수의게퇴극헌등ᄒᆞᆫ쟝졍을하수ᄒᆞᆫ음신고로희공수ᄂᆞᆫ 황뎨폐하피수외블경하ᄒᆞᆫ츠로외부에조회ᄒᆞ고폐현을쳥ᄒᆞ엿더라

○유학등용 학부대신리재극씨가졸업ᄒᆞᆫ일본유학싱수삼병을셔용ᄒᆞ야가부로조회ᄒᆞ고슈권서임ᄒᆞ라ᄒᆞ엿다더라

○이수츌칭 이티리공수포탁코씨ᄂᆞᆫ작일에인쳔드리온미티리ᄒᆞᆫ션을타고쳥국으로가서열삼동안을북경에서류ᄒᆞᆯ결영이라더라

○방문혈관 탁지부지졍고ᄅᆞᆫ환붕하면셔가월ᄂᆞᆫ두한동리퇴셔키리도ᄒᆞ면못시졍케셜을챡슈헐티인고로취쟉일에한국각대관이일본공수를방문ᄒᆞ고이셔로통담론ᄒᆞ엿다더라

○국민교육회규측의대요

데일관 명칭목뎍

데일됴 본회ᄂᆞᆫ국민교육회라명칭ᄒᆞᆷ

데이됴 본회의목뎍은일반국민의교육을면려ᄒᆞ야지식을발달케ᄒᆞ되완고의폐습을혁페ᄒᆞ고유신의규모를확립ᄒᆞᆯ〻

데삼됴 본회ᄂᆞᆫ져도의목뎍을관철ᄒᆞ기위ᄒᆞ야미리양긔ᄒᆞᆫ서교육상에우의ᄒᆞᆫ의결을실시로강론ᄒᆞ되정치샹에관ᄒᆞᆫ일은일졀붓론ᄒᆞ고다만좌기ᄒᆞᆫ졔항에만종ᄉᆞᄒᆞᆯ〻

일 학교를광셜ᄒᆞᆯ〻

이 문명뎍학문에응용ᄒᆞᆯ셔젹을편즙ᄒᆞ며혹번역ᄒᆞ야발간ᄒᆞᆯ〻

삼 본국〻긔와디지와고금명인젼젹을취집ᄒᆞ야쾌포ᄒᆞ야국민의애국심을고동ᄒᆞ고진긔를비양ᄒᆞᆯ〻

〻 다만셔젹발간비ᄂᆞᆫ출금으로지츌ᄒᆞ고발민ᄒᆞ야남본ᄒᆞᆫ후에티이익의샹분지이ᄂᆞᆫ교즁원의게슈용ᄒᆞ고샹분지일은회금에보츙ᄒᆞᆯ〻

오 본회회보를미월이나츄리쥬일에발간ᄒᆞᆯ〻

륙 반발ᄒᆞᆯ긔이ᄂᆞᆫ슈시변통ᄒᆞᆯ〻

데이쟝 조직

데〻됴 본회ᄂᆞᆫ통샹회원과특별회원으로써조직ᄒᆞᆯ〻

데오됴 통샹회원은본국인남녀즁변령이이십세이샹과품힝이단졍ᄒᆞᆫ자로뎡ᄒᆞᆯ〻

데륙됴 특별회원은외국인남녀즁에학식이고명ᄒᆞ고대한국민의교육을위ᄒᆞ야졔셩찬샹귀ᄒᆞᄂᆞᆫ자로뎡ᄒᆞᆯ〻

○졍용샹인 젼승지강면희씨ᄂᆞᆫ등신일셰ᄋᆞ가인ᄒᆞ등알ᄂᆞᆫ티근일명의로유명ᄒᆞᆫ녀의동보인즁칭을맛치라ᄒᆞᄂᆞᆫ고로그말티로묵거즁으로침을주엇더니괴카과취ᄂᆞ거ᄂᆞᆫ깁셰카ᄂᆞᆫ녀여무론즁녀와팔미긔카반취ᄂᆞ아숭혀병이낫ᄂᆞᆫ디ᄒᆞᆫ더니거미구에수지혈셰이졈졈젹취뎌니굿치위수ᄒᆞ엿다ᄒᆞ니김세의참경은위교로ᄒᆞᄂᆞᆫ말이엽거니와무론모헌흉문병아니ᄒᆞᆯ이카ᄒᆞᆫ계ᄒᆞᆫ데ᄂᆞᆫ다시

○봉비소쟝 소한농ᄒᆞᆫ헌군쳐궤쥬ᄒᆞᄂᆞᆫ조카의졍에두류ᄒᆞᄂᆞᆫ궤이오헌인티고즁ᄒᆞᆫ사름의돈이빅량을우연히칠실ᄒᆞᆫ지라쟝츳제귀이비렴ᄒᆞ야문다ᄂᆞᆫ티소문이나벼계인외모양이챵피ᄒᆞ겟다고취지비지ᄒᆞᆫ다더라

○류학교션 쳥주힝관자셔계진즁은토일본에파송ᄒᆞᆯ류학싱을일젼에학부에셔시취ᄒᆞ야소십륙인을뒤취ᄒᆞ엿ᄂᆞᆫ티쳥쥬일관의천ᄒᆞ이못되ᄂᆞᆫ자ᄂᆞᆫ아모쳐임관아모쥬잉관의슈회라고모칭ᄒᆞ고시취시에입참ᄒᆞ엿다ᄒᆞ더라

외보

○로청밧귀 팔월이십구일발뷔랑뎐보를거ᄒᆞᆫ즉뎨이ᄅᆞ긔 코로니클신문의파리통신에왈로국은남아미리가주에잇ᄂᆞᆫ지긔국과아연뎡국랑국군함을샤셔ᄂᆞᆫ티그군함은남미주에서브터발국국긔를달고출범ᄒᆞ엿다가동아셰아에도착ᄒᆞ야비로소로국국긔를달게다고ᄒᆞᆫ다더라

○파란뎐함뎨 동일동뎐을거ᄒᆞᆫ즉파란뎐[쎌릐]함뎨의츌발은다시뒤신이월하순셔지연긔ᄒᆞ엿ᄂᆞᆫ디젼문가게셔들은이함뎨가파연극동에두ᄂᆞᆫᄒᆞᆫ번지못ᄒᆞᆯ번지의아ᄒᆞᄂᆞᆫ중이라더라

○뎨이군편셩 동일동뎐을거ᄒᆞᆫ즉셀니넬 타셰쌀앗드신문에파리통신에ᄒᆞ고긔제ᄒᆞ여왈로국은뎨이군을편셩ᄒᆞ기로결뎡ᄒᆞ엿ᄂᆞᆫ티이군뒤ᄂᆞᆫ만쥬붕텬부부근에취합ᄒᆞ거시리라더라

○항복사위쳥 팔월이십칠일ᄅᆞᆫ수뎐보를거ᄒᆞᆫ즉랴슌구의붕뒤의병졸들이범남히진뒤ᄒᆞ야일군의게항복ᄒᆞ려ᄒᆞᄂᆞᆫ자잇스면수관이를칭포로써뒤칭ᄒᆞ며격란ᄒᆞᆷ으로작금에ᄂᆞᆫ항복ᄒᆞᄂᆞᆫ자감소ᄒᆞ다더라

○화약고폭발 동일동뎐을거ᄒᆞᆫ즉로군의화약고ᄂᆞᆫ팔월이십일일에폭발ᄒᆞ엿스온즉화약은지금보티견폐이되엿다ᄒᆞ엿더라

○경부뎐도뒤의 일본경부부뎌에셔ᄂᆞᆫ경부뎐도를거두어사라ᄂᆞᆫ의론이잇셔너각원의의향이거진일치가되엿스나젼에와희에슈셩안을데츌ᄒᆞ엿다가지금에다시리슈안을데츌ᄒᆞ면의회의공격을밧을가렴려ᄒᆞ야작금에비밀히경당의의향을탐지ᄒᆞᄂᆞᆫ티회히리슈안에티ᄒᆞ야의회에셔말엉시지버깁소망이잇스면의회에데츌ᄒᆞᆯ계획인듯ᄒᆞ다더라

뎐보

구월륙일동경발

○수샹의말 젹쟝ᄒᆞᆫ구공여사도에발송ᄒᆞᆫ공보를거ᄒᆞᆫ즉삼십일일부터이일셔지삼일간에아군의수샹은헐만명이니그원인은즁이일밤에(수다케루벤子)의평숭ᄒᆞᆫ군단이로양셔방으로퇴각ᄒᆞᆫ뎍담이라ᄒᆞ엿더라

○아군연함 동일동뎐을거ᄒᆞᆫ즉아군의대부ᄂᆞᆫ연티탄항남방에셔(수다케루벤子)의군단과요행이셩합ᄒᆞ엿다더라

관보

○허림시셔리농상공부대신수무 의정부찬졍 윤웅렬

구월ᄉᆞ일

○궁명록ᄉᆞ

○의정부찬졍최익현소지소 비지니에긔권ᄒᆞᆫ위국ᄒᆞᆫ셩각이맛당히간우ᄒᆞᆫ셰에더욱젼졀ᄒᆞᆯ지라이럼으로특별이위임ᄒᆞᆷ이니병을강작ᄒᆞ야곳샹리ᄒᆞ라

○내부대신조병필소지소 비지니예루츠 비지에기유ᄒᆞᆷ을맛당히랑회ᄒᆞᆯ겟거ᄂᆞᆯ엇지이곳치번거히발ᄒᆞ나뇨곳시무ᄒᆞ라

이샹구월오일

TELEGRAMS.

Tokyo, September 4th.

The following report of the battle of Liaoyang has been received at the principal barracks here.—After the battle lasting from the 3rd to the morning of the 4th Liaoyang was finally occupied by our troops, but no details of the fighting on the right wing near Tatzeho have been received. Our casualties were extremely heavy but a list has not yet been compiled.

Tokyo, Sept. 6th.

According to a St. Petersburg report General Kuropatkin gives his losses in the battle lasting from the 31st ult. to the 2nd inst. as 10,000. He states that fortunately the main force was connected and therefore able to cover the retreat of General Stoekelberg's corps.

FROM JAPAN PAPERS.

London, Aug. 30th.

Four British cruisers and one gunboat are seeking the Russian Volunteer steamers now in South African waters.

London, Aug. 30th.

Reuter's St. Petersburg correspondent telegraphs that General Routhvosky and Colonel Deraaben were killed during the retreat near Liaoyang.

Berlin, Sept. 1st.

The "Novosti" is carrying on a propaganda for an Anglo-Russian Agreement with the object of settling questions recently arising in connection with the search of vessels, etc.

Berlin, Sept. 1st.

A report has been published by the "Times" that an understanding has been arrived at between Russia and Germany against Great Britain in regard to the Yangtze Valley. The report is, however, quite untrue.

Berlin, Sep. 1st.

It is not true, as reported, that Russia has made another request to be allowed to use the German Baltic Canal. Even if such a request were made, it would be refused.

London, Sept. 1st.

According to present plans, the British Mission to Thibet leaves Lhassa on the 15th instant.

London, Sept. 1st.

In consequence of the seamen's strike at Marseilles, the "Clan Matheson," "Sardinia," and "Don of Airlie" are unable to discharge cargo at that port.

A general strike in sympathy with the men at Marseilles was to be declared yesterday at ten Mediterranean ports, including Corsica and Algeria.

London, Sept. 2nd.

Reuter's correspondent at St. Petersburg reports that news has been received that General Kuroki, with artillery, is crossing the Taitze River by means of pontoons, while the cavalry are utilising the ford, one division being already across.

General Sakharoff reports that desperate fighting took place all day on Wednesday along the south front of Liaoyang, two desperate engagements being fought. The fighting was suspended at midnight.

The Russians claim that they maintained most of their positions, but that great losses were suffered on both sides.

General Stackelberg and Orosowsky were wounded in these engagements.

On the 27th ult., 5 Koreans, who are said to have assisted the Russians in the early stages of the war near Anju, were arrested and shot as spies.

THE ALLEGED RUSSIAN AND JAPANESE ATROCITIES.

"L'Echo de Chine" of August 21st published a very interesting letter from a Russian correspondent on the subject of the accusations of practising atrocities on wounded men which have been made against both the Russian and Japanese Armies. While we do not, of course, commit ourselves as to the accuracy of the statements it contains, it appears to us to be so frankly and fairly conceived that we have pleasure in appending a translation of all the passages immediately relevant to this question:

We are accused of cruelties toward the Japanese prisoners and wounded. On our part, we accuse the Japanese of similar cruelties. The latest investigations on each side have proved that both combatants are, in this respect, wrong and right at the same time. There are Russians and Russians, as there are Japanese and Japanese, and bundles and bundles. We have questioned Japanese prisoners in Russia, and all of them are satisfied with the manner in which they are treated. "We had expected to fall into the claw of a bear; we have fallen into the arms of a mother." Such is the statement of the Japanese wounded and prisoners among us. On the other hand, we have in our possession a long series of letters from Russian prisoners and wounded in Japan. Not one of them—and I wish to emphasise the words "not one"—makes a single complaint against the treatment, moral, physical or medical, which they receive. On the contrary, the wounded praise the zeal of the Japanese male and female nurses. If they have a grievance at all it is with regard to their diet. The Japanese being almost vegetarians, are not able to give to the Russians, who are carnivorus to an extreme, that which they do not possess themselves. Since the war broke out, meat, almost the sole food of Russians, has become scarce in Japan. Notwithstanding this, however, our wounded men are allowed to want for nothing, or practically so. In the place of fresh meat, the Japanese give the prisoners two hundred grammes of corned beef, which represents, nutritively, seven hundred grammes of fresh nitrogenous food. "Pemmican" contains nutriment equivalent to 100 per cent. of its volume; corned beef about 75 to 80 per cent. It will be seen that there is not a great disparity. During the Mery expedition, Skobeleff fed his men either on "pemmican," corned beef, or Hamburg smoked meat......... Unfortunately, as must always be the case, there have been exceptions on both sides to what has been said above. There are marauders, looters, incendiaries, and malefactors of all kinds. In warfare, evil-doers on each side are always to be found. Perhaps I shall be pardoned for giving an example, one which is entirely historical. Napoleon entered Moscow in 1812, in the midst of winter. His troops, exhausted and frozen, camped where they could previous to marching on the Kremle (wrongly termed the Kremlin). Rostopchine, then Military Governor of Moscow, set fire to this royal and imperial citadel. Forced to retreat, the French cut off the legs of wounded Russian soldiers in order to obtain their boots! (Volume thirteen, page 181, of the Archives of the General Staff). Well, the Japanese do not do that! We will give just one sample of their conduct. Cornet (sub-lieutenant Baron d'Uxkul, wounded in the thigh, lay by the side of a Japanese Captain, also wounded, at the battle of Li-Ting, an engagement little known in Europe. Having only a single bandage, they passed it in turns from one to the other without a murmur. On the contrary, they exchanged words which must have helped to relieve their suffering. If the lines which I am writing to you, and the strict accuracy of which I guarantee, prove that the Japanese and the Russians are on an equality from a humanitarian point of view, there are numerous—too numerous—exceptions, on the part, ar far as we are concerned, of those Cossacks who are not formed into brigades, and, in the case of the Japanese, on the part of Chinese or Koreans, also not brigaded. I repeat: for the Russians, and for the Japanese, there are soldiers and soldiers. If the Cossack of the Don is gentle, very humane, and of unequalled discipline, tending a wounded enemy as he would one of his own family, respecting the wives and daughters of his foes even in the intoxication of victory, on the other hand the Cossacks of the Amur, of the Baikal, and, above all, those of Orenburg, are to be feared. We fear them ourselves, and we are Cossack. Of uncommon impetuosity, and exceptionally brave, they are almost incredibly ferocious. When their chief has ordered an attack, nothing can restrain them. Ready to die for the Czar rather than retreat an inch, they kill all, they massacre all, men, women, old people, children, and cattle, and return with blood-covered lances, their hands raised to their "kiver" (a stiff cap) with the report of "gotovo" ("it is done"). Consequently, their chiefs have to be very careful in the orders they give. There is no chance of finding a living thing where these men have passed. "Neither man nor beast." That is their watchword after an attack. We know something of them, having had experience of them at Pleva, where we were thought to be Albanian. If the Japanese accuse us of cruelty, they are partly right. Only they generalise too much. The atrocities attributed to us are committed by those categories of Cossacks of whom I have spoken. A Don Cossack would never do harm to a helpless being. The same sort of thing happens in the case of the Japanese. Among them there is a bastard race, half Japanese, half Korean, with a dash of Chinese; that is to say, an Asiatic medley, among whom cruelty openly prevails. This race is capable of anything, and it is a mistake for the Japanese to employ them, since they discredit a nation which is intelligent and energetic, although now waging an unjust war.

CORRESPONDENCE.

To the Editor Korea Daily News,
Dear Sir:—

Last evening while walking along near South Gate a lady gave a little scream and grasped her husband's arm. He on turning saw the object of her fright, a man naked except for a breech cloth very near her. It is superfluous to say that he was a Japanese as it is well known that the Koreans wear clothes. In this particular the reformers may well learn from the reformers, and I would like to suggest to the Japanese authorities the advisability of arresting their people and compelling them to wear something.

Yours for reform,
WOI KUK IN.

[We hardly agree with regard to the "reformers learning from the reformers," inasmuch as this offence seems no worse to us than the immodest dress of the Korean women.]

The Il Chin Hoi have taken a holiday to assist at the Japanese victory celebration.

In a despatch to the Foreign Office H. E. the German Minister lays claim on behalf of Mr. Kalitzky for $6,000 rental ground in use by the railway company and property of the plaintiff.

On the 7th inst many officials visited the Japanese Legation with the object of consulting the Minister with regard to arrangements to be made in view of the expected arrival of the new financial adviser.

On the 6th inst., the members of the memorial society waited outside the Palace gate for an answer to their memorial to the throne. His Majesty ordered them to disperse, promising a recognition of their despatch. Two Japanese gendarmes also ordered their withdrawal and seized one of the members, who was taken to Chinkokai, but subsequently released.

The Korea Daily News.

To be published daily except Sundays.

Rate of Subscription:—
Per Year, Yen 25.
Per Quarter, Yen 7.
Per Month Yen 2.50

Postage in Korea not charged extra.
Postage abroad charged extra.

Advertisements, 50 sen per day for 1 inch or less.
5 yen per month per inch.
50 yen per year per inch.

All communications to
E. T. BETHELL,
Editor and Publisher.
Pak-tong, Seoul

THE JAPANESE IN KOREA.

(FROM THE N. C. HERALD)

Admirably as the Japanese prepare and carry out their military operations, so that when they enter on a campaign everything marches with the relentless regularity and smoothness of a well-balanced engine, and perfect as is their behaviour to the Chinese in whose territory they are fighting, as well as to their enemies, there is one point, and that a very important one, in which they have constantly failed; so constantly, that it seems as if there were a special malignant fate making their best intentions "gang all agley;" and that is their treatment of Korea and the Koreans. We do not propose to go back to the days of the Empress Jingo, or of Hideyoshi and his mound of Korean ears at Kioto, or even to the murder of the late Queen of Korea, in which the Japanese were unquestionably implicated. It is to the treatment of Korea at the present moment that we feel obliged to call attention. Our correspondent "Esson Third," in his latest letter from Seoul, drew attention to the recurring difficulties that Japan finds or makes for herself in Korea. He recounts a conversation with the master of the house in which he is residing, who is "a professional at astrology and fortune-telling." Japan's natural element, according to this acute gentlemen, is fire, and Korea's is water. "Will they agree?" I asked. 'Never,' was the answer. 'How can fire and water agree?' They are diametrically opposed and will fight to the death. There is more truth than imagination in the fortune-teller's view. Japan and Korea cannot agree, and there must come some similarity of thought before they ever can." Two letters from a foreign-educated Chinese gentleman in Korea, one of the most able and intelligent, and most popular Chinese in the country, which have been kindly placed at our disposal, show very clearly how a third party, who is most anxious for the prosperity both of Korea and Japan, views the situation. In his earlier letter, dated the 16th of June, he says (our transcript is somewhat condensed):—

"The war has come, but has brought no relief to Korea. Whichever side wins, Korea will be the heaviest loser of all the parties concerned. The worst of it is that Korea has become what she is through the imbecility, corruption, and oppression of her own Government. Despotism unchecked has ruined the country. Both Russia and Japan encourage this corrupt and corrupting Government in order to serve their own ends. Japan, as we have now come to know, intends to keep up the insufferably bad government in the hands of unworthy men until she shall have seized all the sources of revenue or riches. She has disappointed the best pro-Japanese Koreans, and her policy will in the long run hurt herself as well as Korea. I am sorry for this, because I believe that Japan by generosity can win the confidence of the Koreans more easily than at any time before. The Koreans, driven mad by selfish and oppressive despotism, looked to Japan when the war broke out for deliverance and necessary reformation. Instead of introducing good government for the Koreans, Japan has demanded concession after concession for her own exclusive benefit." In a letter written nearly two months afterwards, he says: "Affairs in Korea are worse than ever. Our best friend, Japan, seems to have decided to swallow up Korea under the fair show of maintaining her integrity. She asks for the monopoly of the uncultivated and undeveloped resources of Korea. Practically, under the terms of this monopoly, two-thirds of Korea's resources would pass into the hands of the Japanese. The Koreans of all classes have so far resisted the demand, and I am sorry that Japan, by her short-sighted policy, is driving all Korea into an attitude of opposition to her. This will primarily hurt Korea, and secondarily injure Japan, who is once more throwing away an ideal opportunity of winning the confidence and love of Korea."

Japan is unfortunately in this policy playing into the hands of Russia who still has many active agents in Korea, only too anxious to excite the people against the Japanese. Korea is in the position of a broken-down old gentleman, who has fallen so low that there is "none so poor to do him reverence," but who is every now and then roused to a momentary recollection of his prosperous past, and has still flashes of his old dignity in him. And there is some element of ingratitude in Japan's treatment of Korea, seeing that she owes much of her civilization to the little country which has now fallen so low. The statesmen of Japan are so far sighted and so just as well as chivalrous in their government of their own countrymen and their dealings with outside nations as a rule, that it can only require that they should give a little more attention to affairs in Korea, for their policy to be modified. It is essential to them to gain the confidence of Korea, to be accepted not as conquerors but as friends. No one desires the ultimate success of Japan more then we do, and we have written as we have done because we feel that Japan is injuring her own prospects when she allows her representatives to adopt the high hand in Korea. The attitude of the Japanese Government is imitated with exaggeration by the Japanese immigrants of the inferior class, and the Koreans whom it is Japan's real aim to conciliate are irritated into detestation of the Japanese name. The money that Japan is spending freely in Korea has a soothing effect for the moment, but the Koreans in all their poverty retain some of their ancient pride, and while "the jingling of the guinea helps the hurt that honour feels," the help is temporary and the hurt remains.

On the 6th inst., a guard of the 3rd Pyeng-yang regiment convoyed 1,000 rifles and 10 cases of ammunition to Chemulpo in transit to Pyeng-yang.

RAPHAEL MASTERPIECE DISCOVERED.

In a private gallery near London, Mr. T. Crome, the Crosby-square picture dealer, claims to have discovered Raphael's celebrrted "Madonna del Passegio." To test his own belief, Mr. Crome offers £100 to any person who can successfully dispute the genuineness of the picture. Through the dirt and grime of centuries Mr. Crome thought he recognised the hand of the master, and was prepared to pay a big price for the old picture. The Raphael—if Raphael it be—came into his possession, however, for a few pounds. Each process of cleaning revealed new beauties; and, convinced of the authenticity of his find, Mr. Crome had the pedigree of the long-lost "Madonna del Passegio" traced from the French, Spanish, and Italian manuscript records in the British Museum and elsewhere. Raphael's "Madonna del Passegio" had an interesting history. The painting, which is twenty-eight by nineteen inches—the smallest picture on canvas, therefore, that Raphael ever painted—was executed to the commission of the Marchioness of Mantua. Charles I. of England bought it from the Mantuan collection in 1628. When Cromwell disposed of the royal collection, the picture was bought for £800 for the royal collection of Spain. More than a century and a half elapsed before the painting returned to England. In the Peninsular War the guerilla leaders captured many of the royal pictures, and the Raphael was sent over to England to be sold in order to provide funds for the guerilla forces. Mr. Crome declares that the picture, which he has just deposited in the safe keeping of the National Provincial Bank of England, is the selfsame "Madonna del Passegio" that came to England in 1811, and this contention is supported by the fact that it was unearthed in the gallery of a descendant of the original purchaser. The picture depicts the Holy Family, the infant Christ nestling in His mother's arms. This type of infant Christ appears in only one other of Raphael's pictures, the "Madonna di San Sisto."

In the free and spacious air of the State of Nevada an announcement of a new arrival on this planet is made, as it ought to be made—in style. Look, for instance, at this clipping from the Gold Hill (New) News;—"Last Sunday morning broke dark and gloomy, but early in the day the sombre clouds parted, and suddenly there appeared a most beautiful and radiant being that would rival the Star of Bethlehem in splendour; and as it neared the earth its voice could be heard saying, "I come from the Master on the wings of love to bring little gifts to those who doeth the Master's bidding, which sayeth, 'Be fruitful and replenish the earth.'" Thereupon it plucked a tiny feather from its wing, which gently descended until it was cradled in the arms of Mrs. Ernest Vroman. It proved to be a very beautiful but imperious lady, who will make Ernest get up in the middle of the night, and perchance, step on the point of a great big tack as he sings a lullaby, "Home Sweet Home."

The consultation of Japanese Consuls in Korea continues daily at the Japanese Legation.

Many members of the "Righteous Army" are reported to be on a visit to the capital.

General Hyon Yong-woon, who has been playing hermit recently, is again receiving and his house is once more besieged by clamouring callers.

The Prefect of Kai-sung applies for Yen 4,600, the cost of repairing his section of the road, as ordered by the Japanese military authorities.

The Magistrate of Sonchon complains of the devastation of the unripe crops caused by the laying of the railroad. He says it is pitiful to see the poor villagers bemoaning their losses and asks if something cannot be done to defer operations until the harvest is gathered.

The Korea Daily News.

VOL. I, FRIDAY, SEPTEMBER 9, 1904. No. 47

HONGKONG & SHANGHAI BANKING CORPORATION.

Paid-up Capital..... ....$10,000,000
Reserve Fund:—Sterling Reserve... 10,000,000
Silver Reserve..... 6,500,000

26,500,000
Reserve Liability of Proprietors... 10,000,000

HEAD OFFICE, HONGKONG.

London Bankers, London and County Banking Company Limited.
Branches and Agencies, London.

Amoy,	Hankow	Penang,
Bangkok,	Hiogo,	Rangoon,
Batavia,	Iloilo,	Saigon,
Bombay,	Lyons,	San Francisco,
Calcutta,	Manila,	Singapore,
Colombo,	Nagasaki,	Sourabaya,
Foochow,	New York,	Tientsin,
Hamburg,	Peking,	Yokohama,

Credits granted on approved Securities, and every description of Banking and Exchange business transacted.

Drafts granted on London and the chief Commercial places in Europe, India, Australia, America, China and Japan.

HOLME RINGER & CO., AGENTS, CHEMULPO.

ON CHEONG & CO., SEOUL.

GENERAL STORE KEEPERS.
Imported provisions, Cooking Utensils Crockery, etc.
FRESH BREAD DAILY.

MITSU BISHI DOCKYARD & ENGINE WORKS, NAGASAKI.

CODE WORD, "DOCK."

A. 1, A. B. C., and Engineering Codes used.

DOCK No. 1 (at Tategami).

Extreme Length..............523 feet
Length on blocks .... 513 ,,
Width of Entrance on Top......89 ,,
,, ,, Bottom....77 ,,
Water on Blocks at Spring Tide 26½ ,,

DOCK No. 2 (Mukaijima).

Extreme Length..............371 feet
Length on Blocks.............360 ,,
Width of Entrance on Top......66 ,,
,, ,, Bottom 53 ,,
Water on Blocks at Spring Tide 22 ,,

PATENT SLIP (at Kosuge).

Can take vessels up to 1,000 tons gross.

THE WORKS are well equipped with the LATEST IMPROVEMENTS, and can execute any kind of work in SHIPBUILDING and MARINE ENGINEERING, as well as in REPAIRING of SHIPS.

The COMPANY'S new powerful steamer OURA-MARU (712 tons, 700 I.H.P.), specially built for SALVAGE PURPOSES, and equipped with necessary gear, is always READY at SHORT NOTICE.

CHARTERED BANK OF INDIA AUSTRALIA & CHINA.

INCORPORATED BY ROYAL CHARTER 1853

HEAD OFFICES:—LONDON.

Paid-up Capital £800,000
Reserve Liability of Shareholders 800,000
Reserve Fund 800,000

Drafts granted upon all the principal places in the world and every description of Exchange and banking business transacted.

E. MEYER & CO., Agents, Chemulpo.

E. MEYER & CO.

Chemulpo.

SOLE AGENTS IN KOREA FOR:

A. T. Morse, Sons & Co's "Fresco" Distemper

In all colours ready for use on walls, Ceilings etc.

and

AVENARIUS CARBOLINEUM

A wood-preserving and antiseptic oil preparation

Against decay, dry-rot, fungus and wood-destroying insects.

A large supply always in Stock. Prices upon application.

E. MEYER & CO., Chemulpo.

LAW UNION & CROWN INS. CO.

Fire risks accepted at Current rates, on go downs, merchandise, dwellings, and other property, subject to usual conditions.

HOLME RINGER & CO., Agents, Chemulpo

THE METHODIST PUBLISHING HOUSE,

Little West Gate, Seoul.

JOB PRINTING, TYPEWRITER PAPER
CARBON PAPER, VISITING CARDS
STATIONERY, BOOK BINDING
BOOK PUBLISHERS
AMERICAN SCHOOL BOOKS
SPENCERIAN COPY BOOKS
PEN CARBON LETTER AND BILL BOOKS

S. A. BECK, Manager.

DAI-ICHI GINKO.

LIMITED.

(Formerly the First National Bank)

ESTABLISHED 1873

INCORPORATED UNDER PRESENT LAW 1896

Capital - - - - - - - - - Yen 5,000,000
Reserve Fund - - - - - 1,500,000

HEAD OFFICE:—TOKIO.

President: Baron SHIBUSAWA.

BRANCHES AND CORRESPONDENTS
In the Principal Cities and Towns of Japan.
Interest Allowed on
Fixed deposits 1 year - - - 6½ per cent
" " 6 months - - - 6 per cent

Special current accounts 1½ sen daily per Y 100
General " " 1 " " 100

M. TANAKA, Manager, Chemulpo

HOLME RINGER & Co.

Chemulpo.

General Merchants and Government Contractors.

Agents for the leading

Banks

Steamship Companies

and

Insurance Companies

Importers of Merchandise of every description.

KAMEYA & CO.

GENERAL STOREKEEPERS
Chinkokai - - Seoul
(Established 1895, Tokyo)

Confectionery, Hams, Canned Goods, Cutlery, Hirano & Tansan Water. Provisions, Gents, Furnishing goods, Toilet Articles, Travelling Bags, Tobacco, Cigars & Cigarettes Kitchen Utensils. Coffee, Biscuits.

Fresh Goods always kept in Stock.

Prices Moderate

Please come and inspect our goods.

NIPPON YUSEN KAISHA.

JAPANESE MAIL STEAMSHIP CO.

DER MAIL CONTRACT WITH THE IMPERIAL JAPANESE GOVERNMENT.

European Line

Regular Fortnightly Service between Yokohama Kobe, Moji, Shanghai, Hongkong, Singapore, Penang Colombo, Port Said, Marseilles, London and Antwerp

American Line

Regular Fortnightly Service between Hongkong and Seattle calling at Shanghai, Moji, Kobe, Yokohama and Victoria, B C.

Australian Line

Regular weekly Service between Japan Ports and Australia calling at Hongkong and Manila

(Above Three Lines Suspended until further notice)!

Shanghai Line

Weekly Service between Shanghai and Japan Ports

Korea Line

Service Kobe, Moji, Nagasaki, Fusan, Chemulpo, Ch

S. S. Bahelsberg, 2181 tons.

Service Kobe, Moji, Fusan, Chemulpo, Chinnampo

S. S ARGO, S. S. Ohio.

BORDEN'S CONDENSED MILK CO.

New York, U. S. A.

ALWAYS IN STOCK

Eagle Brand Condensed Milk.

Gold Seal Condensed Milk.

Peerless (Family) Evaporated Cream.

Borden's Malted Milk.

E. MEYER & CO.
Chemulpo, Korea,
Sole Agents

ROYAL INSURANCE COMPANY,
Funds exceed £10,000,000
FIRE
AT CURRENT RATES.
LIFE
REDUCED PREMIUM.
HOLME RINGER & CO., Agents, Chemulpo.

HOTEL DU PALAIS

SEOUL.

The only first class Hotel in Seoul. Situated in the centre of the city opposite the palace

Cuisine under the supervision of an experienced French Chef.

Well ventilated and furnished throughout.

TARIFF UPON APPLICATION

L. MARTIN
Proprietor and Mangaer.

大韓每日申報

대한매일신보

(뎨사십팔호) (토요일) 쳔구빅사년구월십일

본샤고

이신보는영어와한어로셰계ᄆᆡ
일출판ᄒᆞ옵

신문가

ᄒᆞᆫ쟝 엽뎐두푼오리
ᄒᆞᆫ달 엽뎐두량닷돈 밧돈으로
밧ᄉᆞᆸ

광고료는

귀한의쟝단과ᄌᆞ쳥의다쇼로죵
갑ᄒᆞ되뎡가로밧을터이오ᄆᆡ오
린거ᄒᆞ여대한사ᄅᆞᆷ마다다이신
문을보실터이니광고ᄇᆡ시기를
원ᄒᆞ시는이들은우리신문사에
와셔ᄒᆡ약ᄒᆞ시기를희망ᄒᆞᆸ
○발ᄒᆡᆼ소 박동대한ᄆᆡ일신보
사법어학교앞헤젼영국인셜필
림쟈리오
샤쟝 영국인 (ᄇᆡ셜)

샤고

○우리대한ᄆᆡ일신보의목뎍은
대한의안녕질셔에관ᄒᆞᆫ모든대
목에ᄃᆡᄒᆞ야는공평ᄒᆞᆫ변론을쥬
쟝ᄒᆞᆷ이라우리는신원의리팟보는
션문보셔는쳠군ᄌᆞ의게ᄒᆞ샹보
도ᄒᆞ려ᄒᆞᆫ지를긔셔ᄒᆞ며주시
는이는셩명과번디를적어붓쳐
셔기를희망ᄒᆞ오니이ᄀᆞᆺᄒᆞᆫ신문
샹에긔재ᄒᆞ라는거시아니오다
만귀신용ᄒᆞ는증거를삼고쟈ᄒᆞ
ᄒᆞᆷ이라긔쟈는아모귀셔긔지긔
쥐ᄒᆞᆷ을ᄌᆞ쟉ᄒᆞ는권리를가졋ᄉᆞ오
나퇴쟉ᄒᆞ는리유를말ᄒᆞᆯ터이오
며고죵평화를논란ᄒᆞ는ᄃᆞᆺᄒᆞᆫ
귀셔는의례히밧지안케ᄉᆞᆸ나이
다

샤고

○본샤에셔는신문갑슨미리월
셔금으로밧ᄉᆞ오며본신문을우
체로붓치는고로본샤에셔는다
른신문샤처럼금계ᄒᆞᆯ거두리ᄂᆞᆫ
니ᄒᆞ지안ᄉᆞ오니우리신문보실이
ᄒᆞᆫ다ᄒᆞ시면쳠군ᄌᆞ는아릴량
이월ᄒᆞᆫ쟝이리월됴션금과기주쇼
셩명ᄒᆞᆯ호수를ᄌᆞ셰히젹어셔박
동본샤로보내시기를바라오며
월회일노로견금을이냥ᄒᆞ금나
보내시는곳에는리월일븐부터
신문을아니보낼터이오니쇼량
ᄒᆞᆸ신여
●본샤에셔아직귀계를쟝만치
못ᄒᆞ와쿠근터니셔박셔도ᄂᆞᆫ고로
이샹왕요히는일에ᄂᆞᆫ츌판이대단히
ᄂᆞᆺ케되ᄂᆞᆫ듯ᄉᆞ오니분젼이미우ᄂᆞᆺ
케되오니우리신문을구람ᄒᆞ시
ᄂᆞᆫ쳠군ᄌᆞᄂᆞᆫ 용셔ᄒᆞ여쥬시기
를희망ᄒᆞᆸᄂᆞ이다

본샤광고

본샤에셔본신문뎨ᄉᆞ호와뎨삼
일호와뎨이십오호를소용ᄒᆞᆯᄇᆡ
가잇셔이에광고ᄒᆞ오니누구시
던지이샹삼호중에본샤로가져
오시면ᄆᆡ쟝에빅젼두푼식드리
리다

론셜

한국에잇ᄂᆞᆫ일인ᄒᆡᆼ젹
북쳥일관들의신문빈등이라

○일본셔긔젼ᄒᆞᆫ이후에쳥국지
방으로군ᄉᆞ를잇설코드리가입
의로진티를베풀며마음ᄃᆡ로각
죵병긔를ᄂᆞ리노와아라사로ᄒᆞ
여곰어ᄂᆞ뎨셔지탄지ᄡᅢᄒᆞ란ᄒᆞᆫ
쥬일본셔ᄂᆞᆫ엇ᄒᆞᆫ기에대단히조소
ᄒᆞᆯ듯ᄒᆞ되쳥국예야손ᄒᆞ가블소
ᄒᆞᆯ듯ᄒᆞ나그러나도모지사셕궁
지안코조계티젼ᄂᆞᆫ거시한국
으로부터다를이엿ᄂᆞᆫ지라이
왕에일본신공ᄒᆞ와및평유젼
의ᄒᆞᆫ일과한국 국모살친ᄒᆞᆯ
으로인ᄒᆞ야일본에큰실슈가되
엿ᄉᆞᆫ쥬우리ᄂᆞᆫ반ᄃᆞ시말ᄒᆞᆯ거니
엽슨쟐터리한국에셔일본에게
ᄃᆡᄒᆞ야관곡히ᄃᆡ졉ᄒᆞᆷ이심히감
격ᄒᆞ다ᄒᆞᆯ만ᄒᆞ되
근일한셩에잇ᄂᆞᆫ우리동ᄀᆡ협의
과셔ᄂᆞᆫ거슬보즉일본이한국에
ᄃᆡᄒᆞ야조유ᄒᆡᆼᄒᆞᄂᆞᆫ일을갈ᄒᆞᆷ에
기가싱ᄒᆞ이러운고로조긔지에
잇ᄂᆞᆫ바리문과슐슈에도져ᄒᆞᆫ사
ᄅᆞᆷ의게이두나라영곡무리본쥬
고ᄉᆞᆫ리의말이일본은원리가화
평으로되고한국은슈쳥으로되
엿다ᄒᆞᄂᆞᆫ지라슈화라ᄒᆞᄂᆞᆫ거슨
원리샹극이라엇지셔로화협ᄒᆞ
리요ᄒᆞᄂᆞᆫ지라ᄡᅥᆺ나시못되엇지
ᄒᆞ연슈화가셔로합ᄒᆞ랴ᄒᆞ즉그
슈가의죵말티답이슈화셔로샹
극인셔담에주기젼에ᄂᆞᆫ거ᄉᆞ룬
다ᄂᆞᆫ말ᄂᆞᆫ듯코그슈가의말이과
연올흔줄로싱각ᄒᆞ엿ᄉᆞ며일한
량국의취가셔로찻기젼에ᄂᆞᆫ
다시손을잡지못ᄒᆞᆯ줄로비로소ᄭᆡ
다랏다고ᄒᆞ엿고
쳥국에잇난외국사ᄅᆞᆷ부ᄒᆞ는쳥
국사ᄅᆞᆷ즁ᄒᆞᆫ이우리신문에게쳐
ᄒᆞᆫ바일한량국밧ᄅᆞᆯ일ᄒᆞᆷ에쳥국ᄂᆞᆫ
대삼국이되엿다ᄒᆞᆷ을두번긔셔
ᄒᆞ엿ᄂᆞᆫᄃᆡ유월십ᄉᆞᆷ븟ᄐᆡ계셔음관
셔ᄒᆞᆫ젼문이여좌ᄒᆞ니
대황뎨폐하의젼졔졍치ᄒᆞ시ᄂᆞᆫ
권리가졈졈엽셔지며아리로ᄂᆞᆫ
졍부가길ᄉᆞ록유약ᄒᆞ고부픽ᄒᆞ
여가ᄂᆞᆫ모양인ᄃᆡ아라사ᄅᆞᆷ이
잇슬ᄯᆡ에ᄂᆞᆫ아인의게ᄭᅵ견단이나
더니지금일본의게셔희롱빗ᄂᆞᆫ
쥬이ᄂᆞᆫ피평ᄒᆞᆫ국의셰이과부요
ᄒᆞᆷ이ᄅᆞᆫ다ᄢᅢ닷셔수중에집어닛고
졍부로가ᄂᆞᆫ단이나게만든후에야
만든듯ᄒᆞ며또ᄒᆞᆫ국이일본보다약
두ᄒᆞᆯ은조곰도바라지안코더만
엇더케ᄒᆞ던지ᄒᆞ와발잉괴려ᄒᆞᆫᄂᆞᆫ거
한국을위ᄒᆞ야셜로가치엄ᄂᆞᆫ거
시과왕에우리ᄂᆞᆫ싱각건ᄃᆡ졍평
일본이철날ᄒᆞᆫ도량으로아모조
쿰한국을방조ᄒᆞ야젼졔졍치로
암졔ᄒᆞ며비ᄒᆞ계ᄭᅦᄂᆞᆫ못된풍속을
ᄀᆡ량ᄒᆞ야진보ᄒᆞ게되게ᄒᆞᆯ줄로알
엇더니쳔만의외ᄒᆞᆯ뿐이니조약
이니ᄒᆞᆫ드런다ᄒᆞᆫ조귀의게업ᄉᆞ
약ᄒᆞ게ᄒᆞᆫ줄을엇지못ᄒᆞ엿ᄉᆞ리
요ᄒᆞ엿고
또슈삭된후두어번져긔셔에ᄂᆞᆫ한
국량병이의왕비ᄂᆞᆫ경쳠ᄂᆞᆫ되
가ᄂᆞᆫ거ᄉᆞᆫ일본셔한국을오ᄅᆞᆫ거이
셩ᄀᆞᆯ바마음이잇셔셔황무지개간
파발란되지못ᄒᆞᆫ이른슈상소건을
쳥권ᄂᆞᆫ여ᄒᆞᆫ것다고쳥구ᄒᆞ야은
뭉ᄒᆞᄂᆞᆫ거슬샹ᄒᆞ려ᄒᆞ엿ᄂᆞᆫ졍거
인ᄃᆞᆺᄎᆞᆺᄂᆞᆫ거시이번에한국을침롱
셔ᄒᆞ변일분에도ᄡᅥᆺᄒᆞᆫ흔가되여
슐ᄀᆞᆼ지ᄒᆞᆫ지여가불구ᄒᆞᆯ디필경
에ᄂᆞᆫ어ᄂᆞᄂᆞ라에셔이긔회를엿
ᄃᆡ한국을방죵ᄒᆞ야리ᄅᆞᆯ케ᄒᆞᆫ성
각을내ᄂᆞᆫ지모르갯ᄃᆞ고ᄒᆞ엿ᄉᆞᆫ
쥬일본셔아라사와강화ᄒᆞ게ᄂᆞ
리든ᄒᆡᆼ셜을쓰게되면필경한국
ᄇᆡᆨ셩들로ᄒᆞ여곰반ᄃᆡ지심이나
게ᄒᆞᄂᆞᆫ거시분명ᄒᆞᆫ거시한국은
원긔동방ᄒᆡ의지국으로외란문
물이번화ᄒᆞ야고관대쟉으로영
요ᄒᆞ게지나고셰셰부가로위풍
잇던량반들은벗ᄒᆞᆯ을싱각ᄒᆞ며
소위귀화로말ᄒᆞ야마이런케조
ᄎᆞᆫ법업셔졍을한ᄒᆞ고일본을원
수로알ᄃᆡ킨즁일본졍부대관들
은아도조등한국에ᄃᆡᄒᆞ야민사
에밧계ᄀᆞ잇게ᄇᆞᆺ도록주의ᄒᆞᆫ기
를다르나라ᄃᆡ졉ᄒᆞᆫ니허ᄃᆞ옥
샹가졍치을빈ᄂᆞᆫ등ᄒᆞᆷ진ᄃᆡ구로ᄆᆞ
샹일에든지리롭게ᄒᆞ라ᄂᆞᆫᄃᆡ년
경도성기지안코화목ᄒᆞ야우디
지샹이응당발ᄒᆞ고우리신ᄃᆡ로
니버덤셩취가슉히필리니되우
에만ᄒᆞᆫ바와갓치조슈의슈단부
리ᄂᆞᆫ대로희ᄒᆞ시ᄒᆞᆫ지경이편이ᄂᆞᆫ
일본이희론자취ᄒᆞᆫᄂᆞᆫ거시일본
졍부로셔조귀나라하등빅셩들
로ᄒᆞ여곰한국에ᄃᆡᄒᆞ야ᄒᆡᆼᄒᆞᆫ일
이모도언과기실이뎐셔담에아
리모리진쟁으로화ᄒᆞ게ᄒᆞᆫ다ᄒᆞ니
리도한국빅셩들은일본사ᄅᆞᆷ이
라면못맛위ᄒᆞ야분개ᄒᆞ게ᄒᆞ니
ᄂᆞᆫ지라셜혹저졍이ᄅᆞᆫ즐ᄒᆞᆫ경우
를당ᄒᆞ야일본셔다수ᄒᆞᆫ금익을
보소ᄒᆞ여주드리도한인의슈마
음은일반일터인거시비록남쟝
에ᄂᆞᆫ조ᄒᆞᆫ체ᄒᆞ되길희ᄒᆞᆫ뎍각은
쟝ᄎᆞᆨ동안에드로잇슬듯ᄒᆞ도다

잡보

○구락부긔회 ᄒᆞᆫ일구락부ᄂᆞᆫ
귀ᄒᆞᆫ인원이회졉ᄒᆞ엿다ᄒᆞᆷ은젼
보에긔지ᄒᆞ엿거니와일젼파쟝
광예지회되엿ᄉᆞᆫ시에대한발긔
의중신등평년에ᄃᆡ지용리근빈
당시미유표ᄒᆞ야귀튼쳥ᄒᆞ고그외
에ᄂᆞᆫ졔써ᄎᆞ대좌셕ᄒᆞ엿ᄂᆞᆫᄃᆡ면
셔환셔ᄂᆞᆫ대한발긔인을ᄃᆡ표ᄒᆞ
야쥬쟉ᄒᆞ고그다음법관ᄉᆞᄂᆞᆫ발
셔어미야나ᄭᅩᆫ조원으로셜
분친경ᄒᆞᆫ뜻슬샹명ᄒᆞ고가등고
분쟈는일본발긔인을ᄃᆡ표ᄒᆞ야
연셜ᄒᆞ고계반스ᄒᆞᆼ을좌ᄀᆞᆺ치쳥
졍ᄒᆞ엿ᄂᆞᆫᄃᆡ 이븐이희계원입
ᄒᆞᄂᆞᆫ쟈ᄂᆞᆫ구월십팔일노로입회
금십원과쳥원셔를쳠부ᄒᆞ야발
긔인의게송표ᄒᆞᄂᆞᆫ수 이을은원입
ᄒᆞᄂᆞᆫ지의셩명과입회금은동회
창립쥰비위원의슈합ᄒᆞ야구월
십구일브로졍리ᄒᆞᄂᆞᆫ수 이을은구
월이십일대관졍에발회식을거
셜ᄒᆞᄂᆞᆫ수 창립쥰비위원ᄂᆞᆫ 대
한셰ᄂᆞᆫ 리근샹 박용화 협
쥬의 현영운이오 일본에ᄂᆞᆫ
츄월쥬일 젼등형사랑 산구
티병위 환산즁쥰셰씨로츄쳔
ᄒᆞ엿ᄂᆞᆫ니 대한인죵원입ᄒᆞᄂᆞᆫ쟈
가오륙십명이라더라
○안쥬군보 안쥬군보를거ᄒᆞᆫ
즉일본ᄉᆞ령부로희쳔군에셔압
리ᄒᆞᆫ쳐진인중오인은포ᄒᆡᆼᄒᆞ엿고
한셩에셔압리ᄒᆞᆫ원세셩리범셔

신녕산인은군청금친병부에피슈하엿다하엿더라

○림표츌옥　유치군보듣거흔즁음력칠월삭상일에일본인슈십명이쳐눈로로와셔면답을붐케하고표목을세위경계를정하며가옥을건츅하는데일인슈효는리왕이무상흔고로쇼상히알슈업고진츅흔가옥에는일병이주둔하엿스며졍탈흔면답다쇼는아직조세히알슈업다하엿더라

○졀영쇼용　함부에셔감히코졀영졍부와외국공ᄉ의졀영흔일뵈오명을감기평하야졀영흔하엿슨졀영을호야면셔하야세격부부황졍이로운조흔하엿스되겨기며뵈외조계로로보뵈평평에셔당하지잉은것호데로일월어다비거슨뎨명혹호계평을봉승하며시평흥슈이란하엿더라

○츌회쳥요　작일에진코기일본기쿠테쇼쇼인양미이로안비데슨졍이리하야츌회를평양이하엿는디감평편을밀계하는쳥요하엿더라

○평요분광　본월륙일에쳔일구탁부분에회의에셔일본슈립관이일진회원등모뵈오인을평요하엿다니하아회에셔하는기를밧다시본회를리쳠으로이잇슴이라하고가지안엿다더라

○졀셔회의　작작일하오에시예평졍신귀천세가졍보에흡석하야각부즁관의졍의셔의뎨삼회지츌졍회의하엿더라

○평혁순검　진졍쇼졍에셔쇼슈이하례인지각일에또대안문젼에가셔일젼상쇼에비지나리시기를기다린다고진복하엿더니일본헌병이셔와셔쇼원을쳐거흔시며동지서순검이와도하야그쳐거하는니리유를문흔즉일헌병의말이나는누구나하고마조쳐져야갓다더라

○졍부후쳐　외졍에셔졍부에으로흔밍하기를무뎌와뉵츌에졍숑하란등이후에무뎐하는긔류를일병이멋ᄯ을하엿고그졍거관뎌예변이쳐이하야판국지하에각션긔졍슈비기쳐평하야위신을민속케홈이무쇼부지로티평결직헌이엿는자가시아싱통하고금번거하니티니슈월이라로로여간졍흥흔다하니그즁졍문에가졍에흔자가귀화엿시도탐흔거슬갑빙하엿지하지못하고며졍뭇되며ᄯ다시며젼하며머이흔명ᄉ를흔다하니ᄉ례에만만부평하흔지케경무ᄉ는항졍지초에만일엇금하야니하면라암다게못하는로하의명을면치못흘지라이면거흠령하며니못하게졍ᄉ를하아버넛나형졍하는ᄉ는하야졍하야시평쳑니에서졍졍츙지못하게흠을이가하다하엿더라

○로흥죠회　작작일에일진회

[illegible]

TELEGRAMS.

FROM JAPANESE PAPERS.

London, Sept. 3.

The official Russian losses at Liaoyang from Wednesday (the 31st ult.) to yesterday (the 2nd inst.) are given as 5,000.

Reuter's St. Petersburg correspondent says General Kuropatkin reports that the Russians retreated yesterday evening to their main positions. The Japanese shelled and wrecked the Liaoyang railway station and the Russians thereupon established a new station further north.

EFFECTS OF HEAVY GUN FIRE.

Some interesting details concerning the effects of the stress of war on the combatants' warships have appeared in the Engineer.

The facts are given on the authority of officers in the Far East, who are in a position to know, and they show that several important lessons have already been demonstrated by the fighting outside Port Arthur. Briefly stated, they are as follows:—

1. The impact of heavy projectiles has a strong tendency to affect the alignment of machinery by shock, but less effect than might have been expected upon boilers, whether water-tube or cylindrical. Only direct hits seem to have affected the generators.

2. All small ships, especially torpedo craft, wear out quickly, and lose heavily in speed as the result of hard work.

3. The deterioration of big ships is considerably less.

4. Disablement of machinery by gunfire is quite improbable; partial injury is all that is to be feared.

5. Cylindrical boilers have proved inferior to water-tubes, or, at any rate, to the Belleville variety.

6. It has not been possible to maintain full speed for any length of time in either fleet, though the Bayan is said to have once steamed nine hours at top speed. It is deduced from this that coal economy is even more important tactically than strategically.

With regard to the damage suffered by the fleets, the report says that not a single Japanese ship is now able to steam at its original speed.

Loss of water was experienced in the Iwate after an extensive hit during the battle of February 9. Her boilers are of the Belleville type. She would seem to have been hit in the region of the boiler-rooms, but the steaming capacity was not affected to any extent. This ship is at present good for twenty-one knots. The speed of the Asama has sunk to eighteen knots, or thereabouts.

The following particulars regarding Russian vessels have been rendered rather obsolete by recent events but they are of interest as showing what effect six months' war had upon them.

The best performances on the Russian side has been done by the cruiser Bayan. The Gromoboi and Rossiya are both in good steaming condition, and so is the Askold.

The Novik has been several times injured, and having been also hard pressed once or twice, her machinery has been shaken up a good deal. It is doubtful whether she can do twenty knots at present.

The Retvisan had her engines thrown out of alignment when she was torpedoed and her steaming powers are very poor despite repairs. The Czarevitch suffered no hurt at all to machinery or boilers when torpedoed, and her propellers were untouched, though the torpdo hit her rudder.

The Pallada was hit amidships by a torpedo that came through the side and exploded partly in a coal bunker and partly right inside one group of her Belleville generations. The tubes were torn out and bent S. shape. They were taken out, straightened, and replaced, mostly by her own engineers.

A not very dissimilar hit was received by the Pobieda, which was hit by a mine in the port boiler-room. A great deal of water came in, and the fires were quenched, but no one was injured, no tubes burst, and the ship returned to harbour without assistance under her own steam.

In the early days of the war Russian destroyers were hopelessly outmatched in speed by the Japanese; but the harbor service to which the latter have been put has done much to equalise this, and there is little to choose between them now.

MORE ARRESTS.

The Japanese gendarmes are busy again. There is a society of Kor ans whose object is to memorialize the Throne about something or other. On the 8th instant a deputation from this society was waiting outside the palace gates when its members were arrested by Japanese gendarmes.

One of them was released the same day and he immediately, in company with one or two others, resumed his post at the portals of the palace.

The Japanese gendarmes again arrested him and our information is to the effect that his wife will be a grass widow for quite a while.

Possibly the effect of the Anju climate with now be tried on him

SHARKS.

The "Kanjo Shimpo" which is a Japanese newspaper whose articles are some times apparently officially inspired and at other times "Yellow," says that there is no truth in the report that Mr. Nagamori is trying to obtain a monopoly in tobacco in this country or that Mr. Oguri Tomichiro is after the same privilege in regard to salt.

Although the "Kanjo Shimpo" is not always right we sincerely hope that it is right this time. The promises of the Japanese government with respect to the "Independence and Integrity of Korea" will not count for much if adventurers are not promptly squashed.

THE "BOGATYR."

The people of the German steamer "Arabia" which was recently carried by the Russians to Vladivostock and subsequently released, are represented as saying that the "Bogatyr" has been nearly restored to fighting trim. This protected cruiser—7,500 tons, 25 knots—ran on a rock at the entrance to Vladvostock at the end of April The work of floating her off and repairing her has therefore occupied 4 months. She will, however, be a powerful addition to the Vladivostock squadron.

The "Arabia" arrived at Shanghai on the 28th.

THE IL-CHIN-HOI.

We rejoice to see that there are signs of dissention in the ranks of this precious society. It appears that a Mr. Song is not approving of the unconstitutional methods which apparently commend themselves to some of the members. Mr. Song was one of the founders of the society and apparently finds it getting out of hand.

FARTHEST NORTH.

The three members of the Po An Hoi society, who were arrested some while ago and mysteriously disappeared, have at last found a resting place at the gendarmes headquarters in Anju.

Herr Tippelt, an Austrian mining millionaire, has decided that honesty is not the best policy, writes the Express Vienna correspondent. Recently he discovered that his income during the last few years had exceeded the figure at which he had returned it and in a fit of remorse he sent £1,500 to the Exchequer. The result was that he received a demand for another £750, being interest on the arrears, and eighteen times the amount of the interest charged, as a penalty for not having declared his full income. Herr Tippelt appealed against the demand to the court, but the judge decided against him.

The Government and Foreign Office scolded (by telephone) the Police Department for failing to report that several high officers have recently been arrested by foreign gendarmes. The Police Department, with commendable enterprise, has sent an official letter to someone or other.

A famous steelepjack, Thomas Kidney, and his assistants are engaged in the hazardous task of pulling down the familiar 148 feet spire of the old Roman Catholic cathedral in Leeds as a preliminary to the demolition of the whole building. Kidney has in his time felled 106 mill chimneys and two church steeples.

A cable to the Journal from London says: It has leaked out that there was a good deal more in the interview according to General Booth, chief of the Salvation Army, by the king at Buckingham Palace than was made public. After the king had questioned the General closely about the slum and rescue work done by the army in the East End of London and the establishing of more labor bureaus in times of distress, his Majesty delicately hinted that Booth had by his great work well deserved a knighthood, but the patriarch at once held up his hands in horror and the king dropped the subject. No one, however, would be surprised if the general succumbed at a future date and became the recipient of some decoration, for the king is genuinely interested in the work of the army and would like to mark his approval of it in some way.

The story of a wedding which took place in a tree under somewhat trying conditions is reported from Susquehanna, Pa. Miss Emma Swanzer and Mr. Charles Bangs went to the wedding of one of their friends at Great Bend. They quarrelled, in spite of the fact that they were soon to be married. The Rev. Mr. Hunter, who accompanied them home, did his best to reconcile them. His efforts were crowned with greater success than he expected. As the three were passing through a field on the home they were attacked by a ferocious Texas steer. They all made for trees and climbed to safety, the man helping the girl up first. The two lovers were in one tree and the minister in another a few yards away. While the infuriated animal was roaming round at their feet, the minister thought the opportunity a favourable one for accomplishing his heart's desire. The couple were clinging in terror to each other, and it needed but a few words to bring them together as lovers once again. They were not satisfied with this, however; they wished to be married there and then. Accordingly, the minister performed the ceremony, the steer bellowing an unmusical wedding march. Happily the farmer soon afterwards drove up with his sons, and the steer was driven off. The newly married couple and the minister went home to a wedding feast.

The Korea Daily News.

To be published daily except Sundays.

Rate of Subscription:—

Per Year,	Yen 25.
Per Quarter,	Yen 7.
Per Month	Yen 2.50

Postage in Korea not charged extra.
Postage abroad charged extra.

Advertisements 50 sen per day for 1 inch or less.
5 yen per month per inch.
50 yen per year per inch.

All communications to

E. T. BETHELL,
Editor and Publisher.
Pak-tong, Seoul

HEARTH AND HOME.

To a foreign eye Korea is remarkable for the poverty of its architecture.

With exception of absolutely savage nations, we know of no country in the world whose architecture is of the poverty stricken description prevalent in this country.

The ancient intolerance of religious organizations in Korea is largely responsible for this. The history of the world shows that although religious influence has been a fruitful cause of strife and many wars of varying magnitude, religious bodies have always been the principal patrons of art.

Grecian sculptors generally chose subjects from their long catalogue of mythical heroes, the paintings of the old masters were generally of a religious nature and the best architecture in the world, the churches and cathedrals in the West and the pagodas and temples in the East are all due to religious enterprise.

Art has now found other patrons but without the early help of religion it would never have attained its present proud position.

The fact that religion has never appealed to the Koreans except in an abstract way largely accounts for the disappearance of all Art and Architecture from the country, but there are other and more important causes.

The hovel-like houses, the mud walls, the filthy ditches which serve as sewers, the execrable roads and the dilapidated and dangerous bridges are all directly due to a bad government. Unless a man holds a sufficiently powerful official position to render himself secure from the attentions of his fellow-sharks he dare not give evidence of wealth. Therefore a Korean even if he has acquired wealth continues to live under the same filthy conditions as he did in the days of his poverty. In fact often, the richer he gets, the poorer he appears to be. So it is that in traversing the streets of a Korean town the eye is continually offended by miles and miles of dilapidated hovels surrounded by evil-smelling, sewage-choked drains.

This sad state of affairs is rank heresy to economy. The ramshackle shack which is the Korean's idea of Home Sweet Home is not built to last and tumbles about the ears of its philosophical occupant on very slight provocation. He builds it again and it falls down again and he builds it again with the fatuous persistence of a spider trying to build his web in the kitchen of a Dutch housewife.

Walls are built by hammering mud into a wooden frame which is afterwards removed (much in the same way as we lay concrete) and the wall stands precariously until the rain brings it tottering to the ground.

Almost every thing the Korean does is only half done or done in the most uneconomical way. He is always repairing and rebuilding houses where a decent structure would have stood for years and cost far less money. He plants his house on the edge of an un-built ditch which washes away his foundations. His streets are traversed by unsanitary and unbeautiful sewers and everything generally goes to rack and ruin. In the winter the heating of his house costs him half his income and the smoke from the "kangs" begrimes everything. All this dilapidation and misdirected energy is to be laid at the doors of a rotten government. Much of it would vanish under proper conditions and what of it still lingered could be easily legislated out of existence.

SEOUL CELEBRATIONS OF LIAOYANG.

Chinkokai and the base of Namsan presented a gay appearance on Thursday when the Japanese community held an organised celebration of the recent victory. The whole road stretching from the Japanese Post Office to the far end of the settlement was gorgeously bedecked with strings of flags and evergreen decorations while the hillside of Namsan presented an air of festivity in keeping with the occasion. Little refreshment booths dotted here and there and nestling in the shade of the trees looked particularly inviting after the dusty streets had been traversed, while some really good wrestling proved ample compensation for the journey. In a natural ampitheatre these competitions took place, some 20 soldiers being the competitors for the numerous prizes awarded to the victors. It was almost entirely a military fête very few civilians being visible amongst the khaki-clad occupants of the pavilion which overlooked the athletic performance. Rockets were fired off at short intervals, some of them emitting, while at their zenith, paper balloons with the flag of Japan displayed on their surface; these were invariably greeted by the whole-souled gathering with hearty "banzai."

The evening was celebrated with the usual lantern procession and the streets were extremely pretty with their customary well distributed illuminations. Many quaint figures, clad in the garb of the ancient Samurai and the North American Indian, were seen in the procession, which comprised most of the Japanese residents of Seoul.

The procession wound its way through many streets of the city and finally dibanded at ten p.m. although many units formed themselves into small companies and kept up their jubilations until an early hour on the following morning. One of these bands discovered a "Daily News" representative watching the scene from a friendly doorway and promptly despatched a scouting party of red Indians to his capture; this was effected without bloodshed and under the surveillance of a bodyguard of samurai in their ancient armour (cardboard be it whispered, but tell it not in Gath) the captive was conducted to their camping ground on the hill-side where a bonfire was blazing merrily and visions of torture at the hands of the Indians and death at the stake, floated before the vision of the unhappy victim, who however was not prepared for the real horrors of the situation which confronted him. With palsied limbs and trembling nerves he was conducted to—the "sake" tub. "Drink," commanded a diminutive though ferocious looking gentleman clad in mediaeval armour. The prisoner obeyed. "Banzai Nippon" continued the captor. "Banzai Nippon" responded the captive. "Yoroshi, sitto downo," and the victim sat, not on a seat no, on an inverted bucket while he watched his friendly celebrators dance round the fire such a dance as bore a "striking" resemblance to an Australian aboriginal corrobboree as depicted by writers on the great antipodean continent. Similar fires with the same scenes enacted round twinkled over the whole hillside forming a strikingly picturesque scene, and it was with quite a feeling of regret that the "News" man removed his sore limbs from the rim of that bucket and took his weary and devious way home where in his dreams the doings of the evening were re-enacted and his sleep disturbed by visions of a samurai, a red-indian and a certain photographer well-known to the foreign residents of Seoul dancing a can-can, while a gentleman with fierce mustachios beat time on an inverted bucket and the writer was slowly done to death at the stake in full sight of an enormous tub of "sake."

THE KOREA JAPAN CLUB.

The initiative meeting of this proposed innovation was held at the Hajo hotel on the 6th inst, and with General Min Yong Whan as spokesman for the Koreans and Mr. Kato representing the Japanese faction preliminary matters were speedily arranged and the following articles drawn up.

1. Anyone wishing to become a member must send an entrance fee of ten yen to the committee before 18th September.

2. The committee, who will include Messrs. Yi Kun Sang, Pak Yong Wha, Um Chu Ik and Hyon Yong Woon for the Korean and Messrs. Hagiwara, Yamaguchi, Wada, and Colonel Saito, Japanese, will hold a meeting on the 20th inst, and decide upon plans for building, etc.

It is stated that about 500 Koreans desire to join.

THE WAGES OF DUTY IS ARREST.

On Thursday the memorialists again appeared before the Palace gates and squatted down to await a reply to their memorial, also again Japanese gendarmes broke up the assembly and dispersed the crowd. A Korean policeman from the station nearby hearing the "bobri," came up and enquired the reason, when he was seized and removed under arrest to the Japanese gendarme headquarters in Chinkokai.

Mr. Hall Caine's health has seriously broken down, and he is leaving the Isle of Man for St. Moritz.

Forty-three gentlemen, who have recently completed their education in Japan have been entered on the lengthy list of applicants for vacant official positions.

A Japanese contemporary gives a detailed list with the amounts of cigarettes sold in Seoul last year, the total reaching $3,135,300. "Hero" easily heads the list, with a value of $98,750.

The chief of police has again been warned to prohibit the entrance into Seoul of pactisers of the Black Art, as several of these wizards are reported to have returned to the city and are supposed to be carrying on their lucrative trade in private.

The Magistrate of Woong Chon near Fusan reports that recently several soldiers of the Japanese engineering corps arrived in his district and staked out ground, irrespective of rice fields etc., and also commenced to build barracks, where the soldiers will go into quarters for the winter.

Our reporter informs us that "at a well where the Japanese are diging out now at Woosuhyon out of South Gate found one lump of jade and a few fishes." Come on ye trout anglers, dig your own dry streams in your front gardens and perhaps the fickle "jade" of fortune will reward you with fishes, or horrible thought—perhaps they were tinned!

The sailing of the Baltic fleet is not the only expedition which is doomed to delay and perpetual postponement, for our "star reporter" of Pyeng Yang informs us that, "It is reported that Tonghaks rising at every province lately most in Pyeng An Province, crowded in every district, intended to leave for Seoul on 4th of September but postponed the date to leave on account of journey expenses not been ready sufficiently, now they declared to have a gross meeting at Pyeng Yang about 17th September and there they will leave for Seoul."

The Korea Daily News.

VOL. I, SATURDAY, SEPTEMBER 10, 1904. No. 48

大韓每日申報

대한미일신보

(뎨사십구호) (일요일) 천구빅사년구월십이일

본샤고

이신보는영어와한어로셔거미일츌판ᄒᆞ옵

신문가

훈쟝 엽두돈오푼

일삭됴엽두량닷돈 맛돈으로밧ᄉᆞᆸ

광고료

긔한의쟝단과ᄌᆞ힝의다쇼로죵감ᄒᆞ되렴가로밧을터이오며오리지아녀대한사ᄅᆞᆷ마다다이신문을보실터이니광고내시기를원ᄒᆞ시는이들은우리신문샤에와셔면약ᄒᆞ심을희망ᄒᆞ옵

○발힝소 박동대한미일신보샤법어학교압헤젹영국인셜필림집자리오

샤쟝 영국인 (비셜)

사고

○우리대한미일신보의목뎍은대한의안녕질셔에관한모든며목에ᄃᆡᄒᆞ야는공평한변론을쥬쟝홈이라우리동신원의담보는신문보시는쳠군ᄌᆞ의계ᄒᆞᆼ샹보도ᄒᆞ리며편지들과셔ᄒᆞ여주시는이는셩명과ᄂᆡ디를젹어붓치시기를희망ᄒᆞ오니이거슨신문샹에긔ᄌᆡᄒᆞ랴는거시아니오다만국히신용ᄒᆞ는증거를숨고쟈홈이라긔쟈는아모긔셔던지긔ᄌᆡ홈을되각ᄒᆞ는권리를가졋스나되각ᄒᆞᄂᆞᆫ리유를말홀터이오며공즁평화를문란케ᄒᆞ는듯ᄒᆞᆫ긔셔는외례히밧지안켓ᄉᆞᆸ나이다

사고

○본샤에셔는신문갑슨미월에션급으로밧ᄉᆞ오며본신문은우톄로붓치는고로본샤에셔는다른신문샤처름금액을거두러는니지안ᄉᆞ오니우리신문을ᄉᆞ랑ᄒᆞ야구람ᄒᆞ시는쳠군ᄌᆞ는양력미월월죵에리월됴션금과거쥬셩명통호수를ᄌᆞ세히젹어셔박동본샤로보내시기를바라오며월회일너로션금을아양력금니보내시는곳에는ᄐᆡ월일일부터신문을아니보낼터이오니죠량ᄒᆞ옵소셔

●본샤에셔아직긔계를쟝만치못ᄒᆞ와다른ᄃᆡ셔박여오는고로미양월요일에는츌판이대단히늣게되는듯스로본젼이미우늣게되오니우리신문을구람ᄒᆞ시는쳠군ᄌᆞ는용셔ᄒᆞ여쥬심을희망ᄒᆞ옵나이다

본샤광고

본샤에셔본신문데ᄉᆞ호와데십일호와데디십오호를소용홀ᄃᆡ가잇셔이에광고ᄒᆞ오니누구시던지이샹삼호중에본샤로가져오시면미쟝에빅젼두푼식드리리다

론셜

가옥건축

셔양집들구경ᄒᆞ든안목으로한국집을보게되면빈국인줄을가히알만ᄒᆞᆫ거시우리는세계각국즁야만국외에는한국처럼불샹업고퍽되기쉬운집은보지못ᄒᆞ엿도다

한국녯날치례ᄒᆞ야지엇다는집을보게되면다만클ᄲᅮᆫ이라각국사긔를볼진ᄃᆡ셔양에처례ᄒᆞ야지은집은여러ᄒᆡ가되여란리를몃번겨거셔도완젼ᄒᆞ다ᄒᆞ니이는당초에잘지은ᄭᆞ닭이라회랍국공쟝들은셔암에교당과동양에묘탑갓흔거슬맛타짓게되면이젼목록에유칠ᄒᆞᆫ벗파치셕을인즁제일조흔거스로ᄲᅩᆸ아ᄒᆞ되오히려이왕에업던지조부림이만흔즉가옥건축ᄒᆞ는ᄃᆡ이러케치셩ᄒᆞ며모양ᄂᆡ는거슬한국에ᄃᆡᄒᆞ야는말홀거시업는거시어니와이러케화려ᄒᆞ게ᄒᆞ기는고샤ᄒᆞ고위션긴급홈이잇는지라어느나라이던지그나라안에초가가만코긔와집이더러우며도로가불평ᄒᆞ고교량이ᄯᅥ러쳐스면가히그나라졍치불명ᄒᆞᆫ줄은짐작홀터이니만일한사ᄅᆞᆷ이권리잇는벼ᄉᆞᆯ로잇셔이런거슬업시ᄒᆞ고션명케아니홀진ᄃᆡ조긔의지물로는감히ᄒᆞ랴고주의치아니홀터인지라그런고로한국셔는지산이유여ᄒᆞᆫ사ᄅᆞᆷ이잇드ᄅᆞ도빈한ᄒᆞᆫ사ᄅᆞᆷ들과ᄀᆞᆺ치더럽게지내나니이럼으로아모리부자ᄅᆞ도사는사ᄅᆞᆷ이ᄅᆞ도다른사ᄅᆞᆷ보기에는빈한ᄒᆞᆫ사ᄅᆞᆷ과조곰도다ᄅᆞᆯ거시업는지라한국사ᄅᆞᆷ사는동리로도라다니면셔보게되면거위두녀져가는초가집에모든지쳔과수도에셔는악취가진동ᄒᆞ야견ᄃᆡᆯ수업슨즉

이거슨경졔로그리홈도아니거시지엇다가다시헐며허럿다가다시지어맛치거믜줄치듯ᄒᆞ며소위샹원이라는거슨다만왼목으로얽고흙으로만싸아셔비오는ᄯᅢ에는의례히되락이된즉이엇지우민ᄒᆞᆫ소견이아니리오한국사ᄅᆞᆷ의ᄒᆞ는일은긔샤에반셩양밧게만들줄모르며소위셩약되게ᄒᆞ엿다는거슨모도경졔되지못ᄒᆞ게ᄒᆞ야ᄒᆞᆼ샹다시수보ᄒᆞ며갱건ᄒᆞ야얌젼ᄒᆞᆫ세간드누나고몃ᄒᆡ동안을연다ᄒᆞ야소세가불소ᄒᆞ며

수도는만들지안코집가흐로식목만ᄒᆞ여셔조긔의괴지만배에ᄎᆞᄎᆞ몃겨나려가게ᄒᆞ며도로와긔쳔들은고약ᄒᆞ게수축ᄒᆞ야흙샹결ᄯᅢ이나셔두녀젓스며방안에불ᄯᆡᆫ연긔는시시로셔여싱명에대단히감슈가되게ᄒᆞᆫ즉

이러ᄒᆞᆫ묘약ᄒᆞᆫ고부졍ᄒᆞᆫ일은부픠ᄒᆞᆫ졍부에셔나힝ᄒᆞ는일인즉아모조록속히변통ᄒᆞ야곳치도ᄒᆞ기를바라노라

잡보

○보셩금즙 안셩군슈리응종씨가닉부로보고ᄒᆞ기를본군이긔호량도간에잇셔최근ᄒᆞᆫ디방이진젼츄슈등군이온ᄃᆡ소위동학여당이희군등디에잇셔셔긔포ᄒᆞ고치셩ᄒᆞᆫ다ᄒᆞ고본군동면려염가에츌몰ᄒᆞ야동에셔부루면셔에응ᄒᆞ야우부우부가즐겨좃는쟈가부지기수오니말류지폐가어느디경에일을지몰울지라쳥컨ᄃᆡ진위ᄃᆡ를파송ᄒᆞ야금즙케ᄒᆞ라ᄒᆞ엿더라

○룡불피호 대안문젼셕교가퇴락ᄒᆞ엿더니일젼에셔양인이지나다가보고엇지ᄒᆞ야이다리를슈리ᄒᆞ지아니ᄒᆞ나나ᄒᆞ고그압지셔에다돌을던져셔지셔창경이다파쇄되엿다더라

○훈금잡셰 농샹공부에셔각관찰부에훈령ᄒᆞ기를근리에무명잡셰혁파ᄒᆞᆯ스로됴뎡신칙파본부훈령이하동엄즁ᄒᆞ엿거놀모리ᄒᆞ는잡류가 홍릉향탄젼이라칭탁ᄒᆞ고각포구와쟝시에셔여젼히갑세션을토색ᄒᆞ야원망ᄒᆞ니 존엄지디로도라가고리익이무뢰비의ᄉᆞ탁을취우나ᄉᆞ톄에심히히란ᄒᆞᆯ지라이후록ᄒᆞᆫ제됴건을일졀혁파ᄒᆞᆯ뜻스로졀임ᄒᆞᆫ완신 쳐분을봉승ᄒᆞ야훈칙ᄒᆞ니즉시각군에발훈ᄒᆞ야잡셰각됴를일병폐지ᄒᆞ고파원감고비를엄칙축송ᄒᆞ야후폐를박고형지를쳐보ᄒᆞ되만일혹ᄉᆞ졍을용랍ᄒᆞ야즉시금단치아니ᄒᆞ고인슌ᄒᆞ는고을이잇스면맛당히별반렴문ᄒᆞ야엄빌ᄒᆞᆯ거시니이ᄉᆞ의뎍로각군에훈칙ᄒᆞ야셩경ᄒᆞ는디경에이르지말게ᄒᆞ라ᄒᆞ엿더라

○착거우착거 본월구일에경무쳥에셔외부로죠회ᄒᆞ되작일신시량에일헌병오명대안문젼에리도ᄒᆞ야진신소소원리범챵윤홍규를착거ᄒᆞ는길에소쳥에려도ᄒᆞ야젼승지윤병과젼군슈홍질쥬와젼쥬ᄉᆞ로봉슈삼인을더착거ᄒᆞ얏는ᄃᆡ윤홍규는곳방송ᄒᆞ고기외ᄉᆞ인은ᄉᆞ령부로착거ᄒᆞ엿다ᄒᆞ엿더라

○법츌의입 본월구일에인쳔감리하샹긔씨가외부로뎐보ᄒᆞ되금일에법국군함일쳑은츌항ᄒᆞ고의국군함량쳑이입항ᄒᆞ엿다ᄒᆞ엿더라

○창감보고 창원감리의보고를거ᄒᆞᆫ즉팔월이십일풍우대작홀ᄯᅢ에본감리셔각판샤가한번창상을지녀셔ᄒᆞᆫ곳도완젼이잇는ᄃᆡ가업슨즉불가불급히슈리ᄒᆞ겟고ᄒᆞ관도ᄯᅩᄒᆞᆫ관샤와일반으로퇴락ᄒᆞ엿고부두에무너진거시기리가륙십오미돌이오넙기가칠미돌이되오니죠량ᄒᆞ라ᄒᆞ엿더라

○창감우보 창원감리가역부모집ᄉᆞ에ᄃᆡᄒᆞ야보고ᄒᆞ되본항인민이향일대풍우에ᄒᆞᆫ번챵상ᄒᆞᆫ지변을지낸뒤로ᄉᆞᄅᆞᆷ마다쳐소를일코셔셜ᄒᆞ야조긔의가샤젼졉ᄒᆞ기에도결을치못ᄒᆞ거든무삼여력이잇셔타국에부역ᄒᆞᆯ을잇가으뜻스로일령ᄉᆞ의게셜명ᄒᆞ라ᄒᆞ엿더라

관보

뎨이쳔구빅이십칠호 광무팔년구월구일

셔임급스령

◯승셔관임관수등 닉부쥬스 김병쳘 팔월삼십팔일

◯승셔관임관샤등 표훈원쥬스 지은샤 팔월이십팔일

◯의원면본관 경무쳥총순 강봉현

◯임경무쳥총순셔관임관륙등 황히도관찰부총순 리쥬명

◯임황히도관찰부총순셔관임관륙등 권티화

이샹구월이일

◯면징계 경샹도 오졍션 구룡 조졍구

◯임경무수셔칙임관이등 룩군참쟝 원우샹

이샹구월륙일

◯명규쟝각학수겸임시장원일긔관셔칙임관샹등 궁닉부특진관 리순익

◯승셔관임관수등 쥬차미국공수관셔긔싱 홍종구

◯면본관 젼쥬딘보스쥬스 남귀훈

이샹구월칠일

◯삼쥬일중근신 진위뎨오련티대일대티랑티쟝룩군보병참령 리범화

◯이쥬일중근신 진위뎨오련티뎨일대티중티쟝룩군보병정위 리졍한

이샹구월오일

◯일쥬일벌봉 젼라북도관찰부총순 졍창진 박유형

구월팔일

궁닉부록스

◯탁지부대신박졍양스직소비지니에수양흐고졍규칙학스지임면의시흐노라

구월칠일

교셥수항

협졍셔

일은대한졍부는대일본졍부가츄쳔흐는바일본인일명을지졍고문관으로흐야대한졍부에고빙흐야지무에관흔스항은일졀그의견을무러시힝흘수

이는대한졍부는대일본졍부가츄쳔흔바외국인일명을외교고문으로흐야외부에고빙흐야외교에관흐는요무는일절그의견을무러시힝흘수

삼은대한졍부는외국과됴약을톄결흐며기티중요흔외교안건즉외국인게티흐야특권양여와계약등스건텨리에관흐야는미리대일본졍부와샹의흘수

광무팔년팔월이십이일

외부대신서리 윤치호

명치삼십칠년팔월이십이일

특명젼권공스 림권조

본정졍서대일본데이항은광무팔년팔월이십구일에외부대신리하영과탁지대신박졍양과일본특명젼권공스림권조와번져됴인흔바인티동월이십이일에대삼항을츄후로가입흐야곳처됴인흐고십구일됴인건은폐지흔일흔수

대디쳔구빅이십팔호

광무팔년구월십일

◯의원면본관 경위원총순 리창션

◯임경위원춘순셔관임퇴룩등 샹화항총순 젼긔완

◯임샹화항총순셔관임관오등 리창션

이샹구월비일

◯일쥬일종근신 무관학교학도티부소티쟝룩군보병부위 김병도

◯명칙 학부참셔관 신티유

◯충위티총관리종건스직소비지니에수양관교힝용흐라

◯닉부디방국쟝김용진스직소비지니에쇼졍티로의시흐노라

이샹구월팔일

뎐보

팔월삼십일론돈발

◯로쟝젼亽 셩피득보에잇는루티의통신원이뎐보흐기를루드보쓰키대장과레라야변경령은로양근방에서퇴각흘계전망흐엿다더라

동이른동뎐

◯로젼슈셕 영국순양함스쳑과포함일쳑이지금남아비리카희샹에잇는로국의용함티과셕틀을슈색중이라더라

구월이일론돈발

◯로양젼황 셩피득보에잇는루티통신원의보고를거흔즉흑목내쟝은포병스로써브리티지하에주고를늣코건너가고긔병들은그남편을건너가서일수단은분셔디견보갓다흐며사카로프대쟝은보고흐기를로양에셔쥐쟉슈로일에좋일토록불고스셩흐고싸흔거시랑흐이나퇴고야간에야비로소싸홈을덩지흐엿스나흐며로국인들은저희진디를모도구지흐기를구석흐엿스나랑편군중에서다수셩이때단히만치낫다흐며이젼투에쓰탁게빌그대쟝과오를소우쓰키량인이부샹흐엿다더라

구월삼일론돈발

◯로군스샹 공보에운흐엿스되(거월삼십일일)슈로일본리(금월이일)어제서지로양에셔로인의수샹이오쳔명이라흐엿스며경외등보에잇는루티통신원이말흐기를구쥬뎐쟝젼장군의보고를거흔즉로국은쟉야에본거디로퇴각흐엿고일군이로양텰로정거장을쟘령흐얏스나로괴파흐엿스며로인은즉시북편으로멸나흔시졍거장을진츙흐엿다흐엿더라

잡보

국민교육회규칙련속

뎨오쟝 입회금과 특쳐

뎨비십됴 등샹회원과특별회원이입회시에금이원을랍흐고그후에는미년이원식랍흐티졍과흔일즈는미년구월뎨이긔요일노졍흠을수

뎨다빈 입회금을빅산흐야리랍흘자는미월에삼젼식리랍흘수

뎨이십일됴 본회에입참흐는인원중열시에금삼십원이상을랍흐는자는특별히종신회원됨을허흘수

뎨이십이됴 본규칙이실힝치저논샹산샹흐고과졔커아남흠

뎨칠쟝 회과와회례

뎨이십팔됴 본회는미쥬르요힐하오이시에통샹회를기흐고회중제반사무를샹의흘수

뎨이십구됴 본회회졀흐는날에긔회례회흐는졀츠는하느님을용경흐는뜻스로긔도를힝흐티회쟝이회원중일인을지졍흐야긔도케흐며흐회쟝이조셩흠수

이하는산샥흠

동셔편문안그리스도신문샤닉
국민교육회사무소

◯안악군보 안악군슈의면보를거흔즉일본병참소쇼쳥에부틀본군에분비흔거시삼빅팔십명이온티그중에빅명은잔산이모쟈흐야샹화항으로보니엿스나그나머지이빅명신병은모집흘방칙이업무흐온티일인이독쵹흐야두루귀흐면셔독촉이셩화굿소오니슌세와민졍이시각으로민박흐온지라엇지조쳐흠을지샤명하라흐엿더라

◯조쳥빈보금 법국공스갈림덕씨가외부로조회흐기를한영슈와의양군리제챠씨의쟝소흔던납승헐수는임의지결퇴야금년츄슈는친영슈가맛당히흐랴니와귀대신이의양군의게빈보금을바다한영슈의게교부흐라흐엿더라

◯조쳥흐관 본월구일에경부에셔외부로조회흐되작일에일본헌병이대한문외진복흔진신쟝보소슈좋이폼흐종영등오인을무란히일본수령부로착거흐엿스니심히통완흘지라즉각으로일공수와및스령관의게교셥흐야흐여금호환케흐라흐엿더라

◯샹셔쳥졍 본월구일에일진회에셔 챵챵션과쳔셰의게몽협흔긔의돌젹에리직흔노라경흔게자는귀함을졍쥰흔온바각하가본리규한파겸졔로티휘가틔쟉보팔에게시고쟈쳔랑흔향치이잇셔시인의상소에뵈푸섯시비맛당히일마다금은계승바로쟝고폐단을구원흔야졍츠의킈젼실시흠은도모흐니시어늘엇지흔야 불론을구흐시며불론에간평은임의소됴긴을드러표흔셩거논또한엇지흐며명세흔됴목을구흐시는이잇가강령을권고흠은인민의의무요됴목으로셜시흐는거슨졍부의칙임인기라비록찬번셩각에흔번엇논셩각은잇스오나엇지감히로렬가흐야쟝부에면을손상케흐을잇가복망흐건티변관졔쳐흐사귀어히셔쳔흐시고시쳔흐는귀한을곳시명흐실을경요흠

광무팔년구월구일진회쟝 윤시병

의졍부참정 신긔션 각하

◯셔쳥졔소 닉부쳥관리봉리써가일젼에졔초샹소흐엿더라

◯퇴안샹경 항시에진션소쳥에셔한림찬릭수 진예됴흐야인민이읍졔리샹소흐기로실샹도예둥분흐엿더니흐졍남보틔안수군에셔는소쳥에참예초로젼쥬수한쟝리가샹경흐엿더라

◯경츅규참 일젼조양항랍츈경츅회는동양에큰경사라명츅흐의리논한일량국이일반디이볼일본인민은무론남녀로쇼흐고츅하회를평쟝이흐엿는디한국셔는경츅흐는뜻슬표흐을보지못흐엿다고한셩신문에잠졍이반디고귀정흐엿더라

◯각관승영 탁지쳥관홍슌쳘씨젼임훈퇴에는탁지수계국쟝류졍슈씨가승임흐엿고참부편집국쟝리규환씨는닉부디방국쟝으로젼임흐고그디에는참셔관리용틔씨가승임흐고참셔관티에는쥬사김연진씨가승임흐엿더라

◯구착박씨 본월팔일에일본헌병이진신소유흥죵영이하오인착거흔수는별항에긔재흐엿거니와그잇흔날에일헌병이산소쳥에리도흐야등진관박제빈이하오인을착거흐더니수일은빙죡시방송흐고박씨는뢰슈흐엿다더라

광고

TELEGRAMS.

London via Bombay, August 20th.

Military experts in Germany take an extremely pessimistic view of General Kuropatkin's prospects, including the army organ, the "Militarwochenblatt."

London, August 20th.

There is the wildest excitement in the Chicago wheat market, owing to alarming crop reports. It is anticipated that there will be a shortage of 175 million bushels. Several commission houses yesterday sold eight to eighteen million bushels.

London, August 31st.

It is learned from Berlin that a Russian loan of fifty milions sterling has been sanctioned.

EXPLOSION ON THE "MARCO POLO."

LOSS OF LIFE.

On Thursday evening a mysterious explosion occurred on board the Italian War-ship "Marco-Polo" in Chemulpo harbour. The cause could not be discovered but the facts of the case, as related to us, are as follows:—

Just as the vessel came to anchor, or a few minutes later, a loud detonation followed by volumes of smoke issuing from the after magazine, warned the ship's company that an explosion had taken place and a tragedy must be averted. The magazine was immediately flooded and thus apparently any casualties were prevented. However some six hours later, several of the men engaged in the work complained of sickness, and before morning one officer and two men died, while 21 men were confined to their bunks in a precarious condition.

This terrible state of affairs is said to be due to the fumes of melanite, with which the shells are charged, and which is supposed to be more deadly than the famous lyddite used in South Africa by the British troops in the late Boer war, or the "Shitose" powder now in use by the Japanese.

The remains of the three deceased were buried on Saturday in the foreign cemetery at Chemulpo.

THE REFORM MOVEMENT.

The "Jiji's" Seoul correspondent reports that an association has been formed by some influential Koreans at the capital in order to assist the movement for effecting reforms in the Government. The aims of the association are as follows:—(1) The upholding of the dignity of the Court; (2) The carrying out of reforms in internal as well as external affairs; (3) The reduction of the army, and (4) The establishment of banks in the provinces.

Pioneers have left Montreal to seek a home for 300 Boer families in Western Canada. The would-be emigrants think Canada offers a better field than Africa.

For erecting in the facade of a girls' school at Wilmersdorf, Germany, a figure of a goose and a duck, an architect was mobbed by the fair pupils. The architect said the figures represented the besetting weaknesses of the feminine character—gossip and vanity.

In his presidential address at the Congress of the Sanitary Institute, held in Glasgow recently, Lord Blythswood stated that sanitation had done much to reduce the deathrate. The fittest survived, said his lordship, but to-day we also saved those who were a burden to themselves and their friends. He did not say it was a kindness, he continued, but in reading statistics which showed the degeneration of the country, they must remember the fact that they were saving numbers who otherwise would have been destroyed. These people multiplied among themselves, and were not able to bring forth healthy inhabitants.

JAPAN NEWS.

FROM THE JAPAN TIMES.

JAPANESE EMIGRANTS RETURN FROM MEXICO.

By the steamer "Akebono Maru" 451 of the 500 Japanese emigrants who on June 16 last left Kobe for Mexico by the above vessel returned to Yokohama on the 27th inst.. the remaining 49 electing to stay in that country. Mr. Yuitsu Yasuda, ex-M.P., who accompanied the emigrants in the capacity of superintendent, died on July 23 during the return voyage. From various reports to hand it appears that the "Akebone Maru" arrived at Santa Rosalia, on July 19, and the following day the emigrants landed and set out for a mine worked by some Frenchmen, who had engaged the Japanese as miners at the wage of one dollar and fifty cents (Mexican) per head per day. Owing to the intolerable heat and to the existence of gas in the mine, the Japanese found it impossible to work. Finally, 451 of the men were sent back to the "Akebono Maru," which left Santa Rosalia on July 29 for home, the others having decided to remain behind and find employment. On receipt of the news of the arrival at Yokohama, the Toyo Emigration Company which had originally dispatched the men to Mexico, at once gave instructions that they were not to be landed at Yokohama, and that the vessel should be sent to Kobe. Owing, however, to a demonstration on the part of the emigrants, they were allowed to land at Yokohama on the evening of the 28th inst., returning to their respective homes by rail.

With reference to the above affair, the following telegram dated August 21 from Mr. Sugimura, Japanese Minister to Mexico, has been received at the Foreign Office:—"Our imigrants, 500 in number, have refused to engage in the work contracted for and have even gone so far as to create a disturbance. Four hundred and fifty of the men have therefore been sent back home by the steamer "Akebono Maru." The remaining 50 have decided to stay in Mexico, but 10 of them are reported to be missing."

THE NEXT FISCAL BUDGET.

The estimates for the next fiscal year of the different departments of State have already been submitted to the financial authorities, with the exception of the Department of Education and of Agriculture and Commerce. In compiling these estimates, the "Chugai Shogyo" states, the respective authorities have been guided by the same principle followed in the preparation of the current budget, namely, that of retrenchment. As will be remembered, the sum of 48 million yen has been saved in the budget for the current fiscal year and the same will probably hold good in the case of that for the year 1905-6. The only important item of expenditure in the next budget will be 30 million yen required for the payment of interest on the war bonds, the plan of increased taxation now under consideration being principally intended for the purpose.

THE HOUSE TAX DISPUTE.

The counter-plea of the Imperial Japanese Government in reply to the plea of the German. French and British Governments with regard to the House Tax dispute, was presented on August 27 to the British Goverment by Viscount Hayashi, to the German Government by Mr. Inouye, to the French Government by Mr. Motono, and to Judge Gram of the Hague Tribunal by Mr. Akizuki, Minister to Sweden and Norway. The counter-pleas of the French, German, and British Governments were presented to Baron Komura the same day by their respective representatives here.

Mr. Miyaoka, Japanese Delegate to The Hague Arbitration Court, arrived at The Hague on the 27th inst.

The issue of shares by the German Asiatic Bank was a grand success.

THE SEOUL-FUSAN RAILWAY.

A general meeting of the Seoul-Fusan Railway was held at the Y.M.C.A. Hall in Tokyo on the 30th ult, Dr Furuichi, the President, taking the chair. On the conclusion of the President's address, Mr. Oye, one of the auditors, reported that a loan had been granted to the company by the Government in order to cover the deficiency in the construction expenses. Various other business reports and the statement of account for the last half year were then submitted to the meeting and were approved. The sum of 165,000 yen, granted by the Government as subsidy, was distributed at the rate of 35 sen per share for the shares of the first and second issue and at the rate of 20 sen for those of the third issue, or 6 per cent. per annum.

During the last half year, the net profits realized from the working of the Seoul-Chemulpo line amounted to 143,-000 yen appropriated as follows:—7,400 yen for reserve; 22,600 yen redemption of loans; 5,000 yen, interest on loans; 80,000 yen, special reserve: 10,000 yen, supplementary construction expenses; 23,000 yen, carried forward. It is stated that, compared with the corresponding period of 1902, the proceeds for the last term of the above line show an increase of 42 per cent, mainly due to the war.

Efforts are being made to raise the recently-located wreck of the Canadian steamship Islander, which sank off the Alaskan coast three years ago, on her way south from Skagway. She went down with 100 passengers, and treasure-boxes estimated to contain £140,000.

The value of the estate of the late Mr. William C. Whitney has been sworn at £4,248,620, the greater portion of which sum is in stocks and bonds. Death duty on the estate amounts to £44,444. Mr. Whitney had £1,415,680 invested in the Standard Oil Corporation, and over £800,000 in the Consolidated Tobacco Company.—Central News.

The funeral of Mr. Wilson Barret on July 25th, at West Hampstead Cemetery was attended by many well-known actors and dramatists, as well as by a large number of the general public. There were hundreds of wreaths and other floral offerings. Prominent among these was a large star from Miss Marie Corelli which bore the inscription "A last token of a long and faithful friendship." The tribute from the late actor's company very appropriately took the form of a large "sign of the cross," In the course of the service "Shepherd of Souls," the hymn in "The Sign of the Cross," was sung.

The Korea Daily News.

To be published daily except Sundays.

Rate of Subscription:—

Per Year,	Yen 25.
Per Quarter,	Yen 7.
Per Month	Yen 2.50

Postage in Korea not charged extra.
Postage abroad charged extra.

Advertisements, 50 sen per day for 1 inch or less.
5 yen per month per inch.
50 yen per year per inch.

All communications to
E. T. BETHELL,
Editor and Publisher.
Pak-tong, Seoul

REPORTING THE WAR.

Some time ago "Puck" suggested that the newspapers should boycott Japan and Russia and devote their attention to the Macedonians who *are* willing to fight their battles through the medium of the press.

"Puck" hit a nail on the head. It says a good deal for the kindness, gentleness and forgiving spirit of the war correspondents, that we have not had from a reporter on either side any absolutely sweeping denunciation of those among whom his lot has been cast.

It is true that Jack London and "photographer" Dunn "blew off steam" the moment they were clear of Japanese territory, but they had only themselves to blame for their troubles. They forced themselves, unauthorized and uninvited upon an army that was busy. That army was not prepared to receive correspondents. It was going to fight. Fighting pure and simple was their object and the Wet Nurses for War Correspondents were not with that brigade. Therefore the War Correspondents and photographers and their "entourage" were all sent back.

No one had a right to feel aggrieved about this. It was an attempt frustrated. And it is therefore with great regret that we find these two tallented gentlemen reported as slanging almost every thing Japanese and talking "rot" about the "Yellow Peril."

From the Russian side the correspondent of the "Morning Post" seems to have a surprising amount of latitude. With charming candour he gives us his opinion of the Russian officers. He says, in effect, that they are nice chaps but deficient in tactical resource. He and other correspondents have also been able to send despatches criticising conditions of the Russian camps and one of the last of his despatches which reached us contained an account of Liaoyang which would never have passed a Japanese censor.

It may be that the Russians were cocksure about Liaoyang and therefore "easy-going" with despatches, but for a country universally condemned for its use of the "blacking-brush," Russia appears to have been surprisingly liberal in its treatment of reporters in this campaign. In this connection it should be borne in mind that if a correspondent smuggles out news or opinions without official sanction, he, as a matter of course, will not be allowed to follow the army.

Reporters are only nuisances to officers upon the battlefield and at the outset of the war either side would have been quite justified in telling correspondents plainly and frankly that they were not wanted.

But even Special War Correspondents (common as dirt in the East now-a-days) have their uses. They were attached, or, strictly speaking, they attached themselves to the Russian or Japanese army headquarters and than strenuously demanded to be sent to "the front." Those at Tokio had a good time and the Imperial Hotel was beginning to make money. Delighted with the cordiality of their reception the correspondents sent off reams of stuff. They wrote stories about "Ronins." Some said there were 46, others made it 43 and an American reporter said there were 148. And they all wrote that old story *apropos* of this war!

Then someone started wiring biographies home. Some Japanese are now better known abroad than they are in their own country.

Japanese Arts and Manufactures came in for a "boost" but "geisha and verbena" stories (Sir Edwin Arnold) had a rest.

From the Russian side we had guarantees that the Railway was working like clockwork and that Kuropatkin was receiving reinforcement at the rate of —teen thousand every day.

The correspondents had, or thought they had, to do this thing. Kept harging around and bent on getting to the front (where they were paid to go) they did their best to ingratiate themselves with the masters of their destinies.

Of their varying fortunes it is yet too soon to speak. Previous to the Liaoyang operations we have no indication that any of the "Specials" with the Russian forces even smelt powder in this campaign and it is quite probable that they were sent to the rear when things began to get hot in that neighbourhood. When a man is going out to get a hiding he does not want an audience.

Per contra, the correspondents with the Japanese forces have been having a good time lately. We hear that several of them have witnessed a battle! Oh! the stories they will write! And after all of what value is the war news we get? Russia is sending forward a Milliard of troops. Then it isn't. Then the railway can't carry them. Then it can. Then anarchy prevails in Russia and Kuropatkin is recalled. But he is still at Liaoyang. Port Arthur has fallen several times. But it hasn't. The "Bogatyr" was a total wreck. But it isn't. The "Reitschelteny" was sunk long ago but only recently captured in Chefoo harbour. Of the Jack-in-the box existence of the Port Arthur squadron we have not time to speak. It has been "bottled," "disabled or" appeared to sink," every time a despatch, said to be from Admiral Togo, has emanated from Tokyo. Then we have the absorbing history of the Baltic squadron. It has "sailed" several times but our latest information is to the effect that it has not sailed yet but that a floating dock which sailed with it has been totally wrecked.

And so the game merrily proceeds. There is very little news that can be accepted without reserve.

Liaoyang is now in the hands of the Japanese but we are still without news of the casualties or the fate of the defeated Russian army. So far as we can gather, Kuropatkin has again conducted a masterly retreat. Kuroki would seem to have failed in his attempt to rout the Russian army. One cannot help feeling sympathy for Kuropatkin. He has repeatedly succeeded in retreating in good order—an infinitely more difficult achievement than advancing.

RAILWAY ENTERPRISE IN KOREA.

A representative of the Baldwin Locomotive Co. of Philadelphia, Mr. Greir, is now in Korea, superintending the unloading and piecing together of some 20 engines for use on the new railroad both north and south of Seoul. Very heavy locomotives have been ordered for the Seoul-Fusan branch, 6 engines of 110 tons and 6 of 80 tons will shortly be in working condition. The railway authorities state that with this strong gear, they will be able to run trains from the capital to Fusan in 8 hours and a further 8 hours of travel in the new steamers now under construction for the service at Nagasaki, will land passengers at Shimonoseki, thus connecting Seoul with Japan by an excellent railroad and steamer journey of 16 hours only. Mr. Greir expects to leave shortly for the north where locomotives are being landed at various ports for use on the Seoul-Wiju section.

OFFICIAL APPOINTMENTS.

The official gazette of September 9th publishes the clauses of the agreement signed on August 22nd by the Acting Minister of Foreign Affairs Mr. Yun Chi Ho and Mr. Hayashi, Minister Plenipotentiary of Japan

1. The Korean Government binds itself to employ one Japanese subject, as chosen by the Japanese Government, to be adviser to the Finance Department.

2. The Korean Government agrees to employ one foreigner, whom the Japanese Government recommends, in the position of Adviser to the Foreign Office and matters pertaining to diplomatic affairs are to be guided by his advice.

3. Korea agrees to consult with the Japanese Government before appointing any foreigner to a position in the Government service.

It has been announced in Tokyo that Mr. Megata, while attending to his duties in Korea, will still retain his official title in Japan.

The "Berliner Tageblatt" has received information from Paris that a second Russian army will be formed and concentrated at Mukden.

The Russian Government seems to have now been made aware of the great difficulties of the present operations, but intends to continue them at any cost.

It is telegraphed from Saigon to Paris that the "Diana" is damaged at one point both above and below the water line. Her casualties are 4 killed and 23 wounded.—Asahi.

Mr. John D. Rockefeller has been elected an honorary member of the Carlton Club. This is the first instance that an alien has been admitted to that most reserved of British Institutions.

The Foreign Office have sent a despatch to the Japanese Legation complaining of the arrest on Thursday afternoon of five members of the memorial society, who were waiting outside the Palace Gate. They request their immediate release.

A new game, said to be very popular, is called the "Onion social," and is played as follows: The young ladies stand in a row, one of them bites a piece out of an onion and the fellows pay ten cents to guess who it is. The correct guesser kisses the other girls while the unsuccessful kiss the girl who bit the onion. The game has its strong points.

Some foreigners entering the city on Friday morning by an early tram car were treated to the spectacle of a Korean, tied up by his wrists with a piece of string (which a fox-terrier would have despised as a measure of restraint) to the doorpost of the police station at the West Gate. Of what offence he was accused it is difficult to surmise, but he had more the appearance of a tame cat than a hardened criminal.

The Korea Daily News.

VOL. I, MONDAY, SEPTEMBER 12, 1904. No. 49

大韓每日申報
대한ᄆᆡ일신보

(뎨오십호) (화요일) 쳔구빅사년구월십삼일

본사고

이신보ᄂᆞᆫ영어와한어로셔ᄆᆡ일출판ᄒᆞᆸ

신문가

ᄒᆞᆫ쟝 엽푼오푼

ᄒᆞᆫ삭도 엽푼팔리돈 돈으로 밧습

광고료ᄂᆞᆫ

귀한의쟝단과ᄌᆞ항의다쇼로쥰감ᄒᆞ되졍가로밧을터이오ᄆᆡ오티지아니ᄒᆞ고대한사ᄅᆞᆷ마다다이신문을보셔셔이나광고내시기를원ᄒᆞ시ᄂᆞᆫ이들은우리신문사에와셔면약ᄒᆞ시믈희망ᄒᆞᆸ

○발힝소 박동대한ᄆᆡ일신보사 번역ᄒᆞ고인쇄젼영국인셔셜필힘졍자리오

사쟝 영국인 (비셜)

사고

○우리대한ᄆᆡ일신보의목뎍은계항의안녕질셔에관ᄒᆞᆫ모든데목ᄒᆡ티ᄒᆞ야는ᄒᆞ평화법론을쥬장ᄒᆞ미라우리동신원의랍보ᄂᆞᆫ신문보시ᄂᆞᆫ쳠군ᄌᆞ의게ᄒᆞ샹보도ᄒᆞ며팔지를귀셔ᄒᆞ여주시ᄂᆞᆫ이ᄂᆞᆫ셩명과번디를쳐어붓지샹시기를희망ᄒᆞ오니이거슨신문반에귀세ᄒᆞᆯ란ᄂᆞᆫ거시아니오다ᄒᆞᆷ이라귀신용ᄒᆞᄂᆞᆫ조기분ᄉᆞᆫ교과지ᄒᆞᆷ을퇴각ᄒᆞᄂᆞᆫ권리를가졋ᄉᆞ오나되작ᄒᆞᄂᆞᆫ디우를말ᄒᆞᆯ터이오며공즁평화를문란케ᄒᆞᄂᆞᆫ듯ᄒᆞᆫ다귀셔ᄂᆞᆫ와폐ᄒᆞ밧지안켓ᄉᆞᆸ나이다

사고

○본사에셔ᄂᆞᆫ신문갑ᄉᆞᆫ미리쳔금으로밧ᄉᆞ오며본신문은두졔로붓치ᄂᆞᆫ고로본사에셔ᄂᆞᆫ다ᄂᆞᆫ신문사긔갑금앙을거두리ᄂᆞᆫ비지안ᄉᆞ오니우리신문을ᄉᆞ랑ᄒᆞ야구람ᄒᆞ시ᄂᆞᆫ쳠군ᄌᆞᄂᆞᆫ앙쳔ᄆᆡ월일죵에귀월표쳔금과거주셩명을호수를ᄌᆞ셰히젹어셔박동본사로보내시기를바라오며월회일시로쳔금을다앙랍ᄒᆞ니보내시ᄂᆞᆫ곳에ᄂᆞᆫ리월일일봄터신문을아니보낼터이오니쟝량ᄒᆞ옵소셔

○본사에셔아직귀계를쟝만치못ᄒᆞ와나문티셔밧어오ᄂᆞᆫ고로ᄆᆡ안월요일에ᄂᆞᆫ출판이대단히늣게되ᄂᆞᆫ디스로분젼이ᄆᆡ우늣ᄂᆞᆫ되오니우리신문을구람ᄒᆞ시ᄂᆞᆫ쳠군ᄌᆞᄂᆞᆫ ᄉᆞ셔ᄒᆞ여주시믈희망ᄒᆞᆸᄂᆞ이다

본사광고

본사에셔본신문뎨ᄉᆞ호와뎨샹일호와뎨이십오호를ᄉᆞ용ᄒᆞᆯ데가잇셔이에광고ᄒᆞ오니누구시던지이샹삼호즁에본사로가져오시면ᄃᆡ쟝에빅젼두푼식드리리다

론셜

젼쟝소론

○향가에폐코신문에셔열바리젼ᄒᆞᆯ을케지저말나고각신문계게티ᄒᆞ야말ᄒᆞ엿ᄂᆞᆫ디이ᄂᆞᆫ다른이아니라젼샤ᄒᆞᆫ신원들ᄋᆡ광편이엇지케된진젹ᄒᆞᆫ소문은듯지못ᄒᆞ고다만아ᄂᆞ나라에셔든지말ᄒᆞᄂᆞᆫ디로만듯고을진즉공연ᄒᆞᆫ쟈ᄉᆞᆫ만케비평ᄒᆞ시엽다ᄒᆞ교조괴신문에ᄂᆞᆫ아니ᄒᆞ지ᄒᆞᆫ기로ᄒᆞ엿다ᄂᆞᆫ디

파언귀왕에쪽코편논괴젓사젼사셰랑써가랍보ᄒᆞ기위ᄒᆞ야열본진리로갓터니헐본군사들기허박ᄒᆞ야드리지아니ᄒᆞ며보지셔도못ᄒᆞ게ᄒᆞᄂᆞᆫ코로이두사ᄅᆞᆷ이도ᄒᆞ고싱ᄒᆞᆷ을힐란ᄒᆞ엿다ᄒᆞᄂᆞᆫ지라이후에과연싸ᄒᆞᆷ이되엿ᄂᆞᆫ진각국에셔온바동신원과밋사즁사들은모도회졍ᄒᆞ게ᄒᆞ야군쳐에드리지아니ᄒᆞᆫ목젹이분명런잇ᄂᆞᆫ것갓흔거시ᄒᆞᆫ사ᄅᆞᆷ도이ᄉᆞᆫ케됨을가히엽시역이ᄂᆞᆫ셰엽요ᄌᆞᆼ이거ᄉᆞᆫ대단갈뭇ᄒᆞᄂᆞᆫ일기하샤아모리교ᄌᆞᆼᄒᆞᆫ양반들의말리라조일본에티ᄒᆞ야죳ᄎᆡ걸ᄒᆞᆯ가엽ᄉᆞᆫ즉파언밋기도어려운일이요

ᄯᅩ아라사ᄂᆞᆫ신편들로말ᄒᆞ드리도범위가이샹ᄒᆞ게드리니만쟝ᄲᅡᆫ의항과갓치우리의게ᄃᆞᆯ이여의ᄒᆞ이자샹ᄒᆞ게만드ᄂᆞᆫ거시엽으로ᄂᆞᆫ다용이ᄒᆞᆷ듯ᄒᆞ게말ᄒᆞ퇴군수샹평은졍쟝뭇되이가셔신과기셜ᄒᆞᆷ이만ᄒᆞ며ᄒᆞ다돈나라ᄒᆞᆫ신원들도아라사진즁은티편ᄒᆞᆫ보샹으로만ᄒᆞ야보티ᄂᆞᆫ들을ᄒᆞᄂᆞᆫ티회후보고를닝진것요샹ᄊᆞᆼ쎄온이ᄒᆞᄀᆡ승쳡ᄒᆞᆫ갓치ᄒᆞ엿ᄉᆞᆸ지

이엿다만ᄒᆞᆫ나라만뒤ᄒᆞ야진즁예다이런ᄒᆞᆫ동신원을두고ᄌᆞ우로여러나라에소문드름을보리게ᄒᆞᄂᆞᆫ거시며후진즁에잇ᄂᆞᆫ쟝관의게알이지안코ᄌᆞ긔의의견ᄃᆡ로소문을ᄌᆞ작ᄒᆞ야젼파ᄒᆞᆫ즉소위동신원이라ᄒᆞᄂᆞᆫ거슨젼쟝에잇ᄂᆞᆫ쟝관들의게반다시ᄒᆞ도을엇아니라두나라에셔이런ᄒᆞᆫᄒᆞᆼ신원의말을밋고조리모든명희쟝아군ᄉᆞ샹ᄒᆞᆫ동을션ᄃᆡ게ᄒᆞᄂᆞᆫ지모로겟스며

근ᄒᆡ동양에잇ᄂᆞᆫ듕별젼샤동신원들도이런ᄒᆞᆫ일을보도ᄒᆞ야ᄒᆞ샹사이부쟝의되ᄂᆞᆫ지라그런고로이사들이가장이사ᄅᆞᆷ의밋입ᄂᆞᆫ본영에회동ᄒᆞ니진졍의의론ᄒᆞ야분명히ᄉᆞ실ᄒᆞᆫ후에야비로셔각각보고ᄒᆞᆯ을ᄒᆞᆫ다ᄂᆞᆫ디요ᄉᆞ이동경주재ᄒᆞᄂᆞᆫ자들이동신원들로ᄒᆞ이를조긔ᄒᆞ의에ᄒᆞᆫ조흔귀회들이엇다ᄂᆞᆫ디긔사ᄅᆞᆷ들즁에편젼쟝보고밧ᄂᆞᆫ티로소셜을세로편긴ᄒᆞ야이왕젼사와련속ᄒᆞ야만ᄃᆞᄂᆞᆫ자도잇고흉악ᄒᆞᆫ사ᄅᆞᆷ은어평을만다ᄒᆞᄂᆞᆫ조귀나라로편보ᄒᆞᄂᆞᆫ사ᄅᆞᆷ도잇ᄂᆞᆫ지라

어러ᄒᆞᆫ소담에근일보사ᄅᆞᆷ들어외국왕편열기를조귀나라덥오히려보게아ᄂᆞᆫ고로셔양사ᄅᆞᆷ문들이펀졔ᄒᆞᆫ소셜이만ᄒᆞ되ᄌᆞ귀붐의계ᄉᆞᆫ게시ᄉᆞ승ᄒᆞᆫ다고져긍들이ᄃᆡ방ᄒᆞ다ᄒᆞ며

다라사에셔ᄂᆞᆫ결국면ᄉᆞ를주소브망ᄒᆞ야미일ᄉᆞ찬원셔히비ᄒᆞᆫ다ᄂᆞᆫ디ᄂᆞᆫ구로파도긴쟝군이라구신병사리니게ᄒᆞ란고ᄒᆞᆷ이라ᄂᆞᆫ티

각동신원들은이런ᄒᆞᆫ일도모도긔록ᄒᆞ야셜로겐에위비ᄒᆞᆫ곡졀깃과여부고가지ᄒᆞᆯᄒᆞᄂᆞᆫ거시며쟝리쳥편을에져ᄒᆞ야쳔에롤취ᄒᆞᆫ란코명신ᄒᆞᆫ다ᄂᆞᆫ티빈구에발간ᄒᆞ야별랍ᄒᆞ게ᄒᆞᆫ다ᄒᆞ며

요양함낙에아라사에셔아옥이되엿다ᄒᆞᆫ즉지셔히ᄂᆞᆫ알슈업스되ᄀᆡᆸ평과ᄀᆡ여기ᄂᆞᆫ군ᄉᆞ들의게그런고로ᄎᆞᆫ리에셔쥭희뎡ᄒᆞ엿슬듯ᄒᆞ도다

우리듯기에ᄂᆞᆫ젼루상거리아잇다고일본은한티ᄒᆞᆫ동신원의코양들미아미우샹되엿슬듯ᄒᆞᆫ거시사ᄅᆞᆷ들도무샹ᄒᆞᆷ치로졍평사괴들편찬ᄒᆞ며ᄯᅩᄒᆞᆫ다자에셔도쳘로ᄂᆞᆫ슈뷔관병군빅을셧고다시나을ᄂᆞᆫ지과연도로겟스며구로파ᄃᆞᆫ킨ᄒᆞ로말ᄒᆞ면ᄃᆡ티도아라샤가무경부ᄒᆞᄂᆞᆫᄃᆡ것드면다시소쳘ᄒᆞᆯ넌지모르겟ᄂᆞᆫ거시

려솔을합냐ᄒᆞᆫ다고ᄒᆞ엿스되아쥭아니되엿스나그런나쟝써리헙은괴위쳠몰ᄒᆞ여연디이쟝괴여잇ᄉᆞᆫ지가오티괴려쥰에쳣ᄎᆡ어잇ᄂᆞᆫ군티에셔ᄂᆞᆫ응당말ᄒᆞᆯ거룰도엽ᄉᆞᆯ듯ᄒᆞ나우리ᄂᆞᆫ젹년이듯지못ᄒᆞ고잇셔더니동경등쟝슈사메ᄒᆞ의게빤ᄒᆞᆫ보고를보고비로셔셜힝ᄒᆞᆫ디에이아기ᄅᆞᆯ자셔히드리ᄂᆞᆫ힘ᄃᆡ쳐왕ᄃᆡ수ᄒᆞᆫ지저니리교힘을써보앗스되포류ᄒᆞᆫ게난드ᄂᆞᆫ커관이ᄃᆡ단히샹ᄒᆞ여우금셔지진지몯ᄒᆞ엿다ᄒᆞᄂᆞᆫ지라

지금에ᄂᆞᆫ요양셔지졈령ᄒᆞ되엿ᄉᆞᆫ즉흥몽ᄃᆡ강도응당야밧칠ᄆᆡᆼ격ᄒᆞ야승쳡ᄒᆞᆫ기에ᄒᆞᆫ희가되엿슬터이요아병와사샹ᄊᆞ판진ᄒᆞᆫ샤항도잇슬듯ᄒᆞ되가즉셔기소문을듯지못ᄒᆞ여ᄉᆡᆼ치조민즁구로과드리게ᄒᆞᆫ이베ᄯᅦ롤즈들을거나리표일마나밋비다라낫ᄂᆞᆫ지아기못ᄒᆞ야궁금ᄒᆞ며이런케ᄃᆡ런번죄ᄒᆞ여섬공치못ᄒᆞ게된일은누구던지아모리쟝분이조ᄒᆞᆫ쳐지라도방조ᄒᆞᆯ수가업슬듯ᄒᆞ노라

잡보

○졍부의안 본월팔일오후이시에의졍부참졍신긔션씨이하각부대신과찬졍이회동ᄒᆞ야졍부회의를ᄒᆞ엿ᄂᆞᆫ디그의안인즉

일은 ᄒᆞᆫ일쳥쳥경셔문판ᄂᆡ에긔직ᄒᆞᆯ수 이쳥경셔ᄂᆞᆫ그젼반보에게재ᄒᆞᆫ뎨삼국과외교샹에관ᄒᆞᆫ스이라

일은 동리갑리오귀영을면관ᄒᆞᆯ수 일은너부터방국쟝은게규환으로학부참셔관은김평진씨로평즁국쟝은리종티로셔임ᄒᆞᆯ수의롱쳔군슈ᄂᆞᆫ리경직으로환임ᄒᆞᆯ수와 일은시졍기션에되ᄒᆞ야인민의쳥원에관ᄒᆞᆫ수라더라

○고문가옥 탁지졍고문으로고빙ᄒᆞᆫ메온일본인목하면씨의거쳐ᄒᆞᆯ가옥은리견국씨의

고로ᄒᆞᆫ으로졍ᄒᆞ라ᄒᆞ야현금그졍ᄂᆞᆫ쥬인의게ᄎᆞᆼ부로서미슈ᄒᆞ라고샹의중이라더라

○경원텰도　전셜을드른즉일본공ᄉᆞ가외부에조회ᄒᆞ고경셩과외주간군용텰도젼례들의방ᄒᆞ야경셩과원산간텰도포셜에착슈ᄒᆞᆯᄉᆞ를셩명ᄒᆞ엿다더라

○덕ᄉᆞ연회　본월구일야에덕공ᄉᆞ사이젼씨와쇼국함쟝이하ᄉᆞ관제씨와각공령ᄉᆞ가졍동손탁양가에회동ᄒᆞ야연회ᄒᆞ엿더라

○경ᄉᆞ미안　경무ᄉᆞ원우샹씨ᄂᆞᆫ덕공ᄉᆞ연회시에젼각　주달치아니ᄒᆞᆫ고로　대닉의서젼엄ᄒᆞ옵신　처분이ᄂᆞ리시기를외국공ᄉᆞ의동졍을엿지ᄒᆞ야경찰보리ᄒᆞ와　샹주치아니하엿ᄂᆞ나그위졍을긔약을졍ᄒᆞ야　주문ᄒᆞ라ᄒᆞ옵신고로원경무ᄉᆞ가대단미안중에잇다더라

○경관취편　중셔방닉에ᄂᆞᆫ일진회의일이잇고서셔방닉에ᄂᆞᆫᄉᆞ원등진복ᄒᆞᄂᆞᆫ일이잇고남셔방닉에ᄂᆞᆫ소쳥에일이잇서서닉외국인의횡동을낫낫치경찰ᄒᆞ야보고ᄒᆞᆫ기ᄅᆞᆯ난ᄒᆞᆫ죵빈빈히로쳑이잇ᄂᆞᆫ고로취서관리등이동북서로기임ᄒᆞ라ᄒᆞ고젼경을구ᄒᆞᆫ다더라

○폐　현명지　렴식원에서외부로조회ᄒᆞ기를일젼에덕국공ᄉᆞ가　폐ᄒᆞᆫᄉᆞ에티ᄒᆞ야　옥후미령ᄒᆞ신ᄉᆞᆷ은외ᄉᆞ　폐현이못될줄노덕공관에조회ᄒᆞ라ᄒᆞ엿더라

○달봔면관　정부에서　주본ᄒᆞ기를군일졍류빈가　감모공명비소용이라주칭ᄒᆞ고항음에출ᄒᆞ야젼쟈를로쇽ᄒᆞᄂᆞᆫ디경샹북도가계셩ᄒᆞᆫ거슨횡도관찰ᄉᆞ가금치못ᄒᆞ엿다ᄒᆞ야휘관찰ᄉᆞ운현을위션면본관ᄒᆞ고조률ᄒᆞ와징판ᄒᆞ옵비하여ᄒᆞ옵ᄂᆞᆫ지본　ᄒᆞ외의주ᄒᆞ라ᄒᆞ셧다더라

○한씨억울　본보에이왕긔지ᄒᆞ엿거니와평안사ᄅᆞᆷ한광젼과샹화사ᄅᆞᆷ빈용탁이체송ᄉᆞ로친군친관찰부평리원법부에두ᄎᆞ졍소ᄒᆞ야재판시에번번이닉가가탁과ᄒᆞ엿ᄂᆞ니이번평리원지판에ᄂᆞᆫ한가의게중거물이업다ᄒᆞ야한가가탁과되고티벌을당ᄒᆞ고송ᄉᆞᄒᆞ든문츅벗지젼탈되엿ᄂᆞᆫ디송리곡직은훗중젼일루ᄎᆞ등송ᄒᆞᆫ거시공결될이라ᄒᆞ고빈가의게세력에눌니여박송되엿다고한광진이가도로에셔호곡ᄒᆞᆫ다더라

○민ᄉᆞ귀국　주쳥공ᄉᆞ민영찬씨ᄂᆞᆫ루ᄎᆞ귀국ᄒᆞᆯ뜻스로졍부에면쳥ᄒᆞ더니금번에귀국ᄒᆞᆯᄎᆞ로본월구일에북경에서츌발ᄒᆞ엿다ᄂᆞᆫ면보가　궁닉부에ᄂᆞᆫ달ᄒᆞ엿다더라

○로담피착　북쳥사ᄅᆞᆷ박운우이라ᄂᆞᆫ자가년젼에궁닉부서긔로잇던자라ᄂᆞᆫ디일젼에문쳔군이현에서일본헌병의게피착되엿ᄂᆞᆫ디루군검찰관이ᄒᆞᆷ중이조사ᄒᆞᆫ즉그박가가로군의부탁으로원산츄차ᄒᆞᆫ일본군의수효와병졍의종류와각처에잇ᄂᆞᆫ군ᄉᆞ수효와경셩에잇ᄂᆞᆫ군ᄉᆞ수효를조ᄉᆞᄒᆞ고져ᄒᆞᆫᄉᆞ실을일일토셜ᄒᆞ엿ᄂᆞᆫ디샹금심문중이라더라

○종츌졍함　인항닉에쳥룡ᄒᆞᆫ고레쌋호중츌ᄒᆞ기위ᄒᆞ야슈다ᄒᆞᆫ공역ᄒᆞᆯ사ᄅᆞᆷ이리도ᄒᆞ야금명간종츌ᄒᆞ기를시작ᄒᆞᆫ단이라더라

○발통거의　샹남으로온ᄉᆞᆷ문을드른즉모모졔인이각처로통문ᄒᆞ야의병을니르키며의잇ᄂᆞᆫ일을ᄒᆞ자ᄒᆞᄂᆞᆫ디군인에창응ᄒᆞᄂᆞᆫ사ᄅᆞᆷ이미우만타더라

○죠쳥즉방　위부에서일공관으로조회ᄒᆞ고일병의게피착된샹쇼ᄒᆞ던사ᄅᆞᆷ들을곳방송ᄒᆞ라ᄒᆞ엿더라

○아비퇴거　즈셩군슈의보고를거ᄒᆞᆫ즉본군전닉편운쳥국위사하이온티거월이십삼일에아국비도이빅여명이각기병긔를가지고취디방면에둔취ᄒᆞ야진니오고자ᄒᆞᄂᆞᆫ즈음에한위사포군으로하여금그요히처를방어ᄒᆞ엿더니비도등이물너가이도이동로드리갓다ᄒᆞ엿더라

○한경티세관　평양감리가외부로보고ᄒᆞ기를종남포항관에서세관을한경티에건축ᄒᆞ랴ᄒᆞᄂᆞᆫ티평민장관즙의귀더든미등ᄒᆞ고티계를정ᄒᆞᄂᆞᆫ고로임의인허ᄒᆞ엿다ᄒᆞ엿더라

○건축비청반　평양감리가또보고ᄒᆞ되본감리서건축ᄎᆞ로샹년에건축비금일천을획하ᄒᆞ엿스나지금빈물이작년에비ᄒᆞ야ᄇᆡ등ᄒᆞ엿슨즉부족ᄒᆞᆫ온지라바라건티곳탁지부에이조ᄒᆞ야우금의을더지발ᄒᆞ야불일시역케ᄒᆞ라ᄒᆞ엿더라

○의ᄉᆞ쳥폐　의국공ᄉᆞ가외부로조회ᄒᆞ기를귀국　명헌티후봉서ᄒᆞ신후에본국　대군주폐하의위문ᄒᆞ옵시ᄂᆞᆫ인서가본공관에리도ᄒᆞ엿슨즉본공ᄉᆞ가친졍코자ᄒᆞ니쥬품ᄒᆞ야　폐현일ᄌᆞ를명ᄒᆞ시명ᄒᆞ기를바라오며또본국순양함이작일인항에도박ᄒᆞ엿ᄂᆞᆫ티그함쟝ᄉᆞ계동결인의하ᄉᆞ관이명이티동폐현함을청ᄒᆞᄂᆞᆫ티본공ᄉᆞ와ᄒᆞᆷ씌한쟝지이니다음슈요일에쟝ᄎᆞ빌젹ᄒᆞᆯ터이니그전에　소견ᄒᆞ심을엿ᄌᆞᆸ면셰감ᄒᆞ겟노라ᄒᆞ엿더라

○가ᄃᆞᆼ코문　궁닉부고문관가등증웅씨가　궁닉부고문관을경임ᄒᆞᆫ다ᄂᆞᆫ말이잇더라

○대관례임　칙쥬윤웅렬씨ᄂᆞᆫ례임되고그티에ᄂᆞᆫ궁닉대신민병셕씨가젼임되고리용티씨ᄂᆞᆫ궁닉대신서리를ᄒᆞ엿다더라

○담찰후임　경샹북도관찰ᄉᆞ윤헌씨면본관ᄒᆞᆫ티에젼닉쟝원경현학표씨가서임된다더라

○봉세관분경　황히도봉샹관일과에즈금시세가영오빅량가량경시닉된다ᄂᆞᆫ티도듀과자ᄒᆞᄂᆞᆫ자가수다ᄒᆞᆫ고로분경이대단ᄒᆞ다더라

○셔민등소　평양인민등이히군슈광한쥬씨의탐도불법ᄒᆞᆫᄉᆞ실을로렬ᄒᆞ야닉부에정소ᄒᆞ엿더라

외보

○로병류입　신히관에서발ᄒᆞᆫ면보를거ᄒᆞᆫ즉셩자산으로향ᄒᆞᄂᆞᆫ로병일만명가량이대포이십수문과마차티빅좌를령솔ᄒᆞ고팔월삼십일일에신민둔에리도ᄒᆞᆫ고로그곳관민등이비우소요히지낸다더라

○무장결희　셔공으로도망ᄒᆞ야들어온로국군함은슈삼ᄎᆞ교섭ᄒᆞᆫ후에무장을희탈ᄒᆞ기로결졍ᄒᆞ엿다더라

○격퇴마젹　쌍셩보쟝거쟝부근에마젹탕이돌립ᄒᆞ엿스나로국슈비병이고마젹을격퇴ᄒᆞ엿다더라

뎐보

구월삼일동경발
공ᄉᆞ관착뎐

○일군ᄉᆞ샹　팔월비십룩일이뤼료양방면젼투에서우리군ᄉᆞ사샹은우하군에ᄉᆞ쳔팔빅룩십룩명이오중앙군에ᄉᆞ쳔구빅구십식명이오좌익군에칠쳔룩빅팔십일명이오합계가일만칠쳔오빅삼십구명인티닉에쟝교는이빅자가일빅삼십삼명이오부샹자가ᄉᆞ빅륙십샹명이라ᄒᆞ엿더라

동일동뎐　만쥬군총ᄉᆞ령관뎐보

○로군퇴주　우익군의각종티가구월ᄉᆞ일오일에젼면의덕군을구축하야연티에잇ᄂᆞᆫ셕탄광와밋옥문사산일티를점령ᄒᆞ엿고적의주력은태ᄌᆞ하북방으로퇴각ᄒᆞᄂᆞᆫ듯ᄒᆞ며기이남에ᄂᆞᆫ다만약간ᄒᆞᆫ감시병만뫼일싸름이오연티서북에서룩리쌍되ᄂᆞᆫ산뎨푸ᄂᆞᆫ박군의귀병이샹금졈령ᄒᆞ엿고구월오일에뎍은이미만명이상퇴되ᄂᆞᆫ부샹자를본쳔부이북으로운젼ᄒᆞᆫ졍보가잇스나아직손히의온젼ᄒᆞᆫ실수를알수업스며뎍은셰투중에별니본즉시례를이로양부근에버린듯ᄒᆞᆫ시례가삼쳔이샹이며퇴군이로양에셔되ᄂᆞᆫ자등이만여명이오기각쳬를가진ᄒᆞᆫ지음에뎡거장의창고등을불노ᄒᆞᆺ스나오히려탄량이긔피ᄒᆞᆫ티이슐비대ᄒᆞᆫ젼리픔이잇스며덕은간신히대포를가지고갓스나탄약슈레ᄂᆞᆫ탄약과ᄒᆞᆷ씌쪼발케ᄒᆞ엿스나그런나각포대에버린탄약은자못대단히만ᄒᆞᆫ바닉지수를셰ᄂᆞᆫ거슬이업고료양부근에셔회득ᄒᆞᆫ탄약중에신오산쳐와밋심팔산쳐미득되ᄂᆞᆫ가ᄒᆞᆫ포의탄환이잇스미ᄋᆡ노탑의암아불진티뎍군이ᄎᆞᆼ과대포를가지고갓스나적연히쓰게되지못ᄒᆞᆯ듯ᄒᆞ다ᄒᆞ엿더라

○동항참괴　본월구일에평양관찰ᄉᆞ가뎐보ᄒᆞ되작일뎐보ᄂᆞᆫ하탐ᄒᆞ셧ᄂᆞᆫ지ᄒᆞ엿고또황쥬평양도동항방이삼등군에회집ᄒᆞ엿ᄂᆞᆫ티효유ᄒᆞ야도히지아니ᄒᆞ오니엇지ᄒᆞᆯ는지회뎐ᄒᆞ라ᄒᆞ엿고또십일에뎐보ᄒᆞ기를작일삼등군에회집ᄒᆞ엿든동항쳔여명이슈안군으로향ᄒᆞ야샹경ᄒᆞᆫ다ᄒᆞ엿더라

관보

뎨이쳔구빅이십구호
광무팔년구월십이일

서임급ᄉᆞ령

○명군졔의졍소위원　륙군졍위　빅응쥰　륙군보병졍위　조셩근　권티환　륙군공병졍위　김셩은　륙군보병졍위　리창어　박담　륙군포병부위　쟝연로　륙군보병부위　김티원

○임평리원주ᄉᆞ셔판임관이등　한셩ᄉᆞ범학교교관　김기년

구월샹일샹원일

○승셔원승판ᄉᆞ등　면환국기슈　오대근　한홍진　리유승

구월구일

○임륙군졍령　륙군부령　신티쥰

○임륙군보병졍령　륙군보병부령　현흥틱　탕셩환　권티익　리근형

○면본직　친위뎨일련티뎨삼대티중티쟝륙군보병졍위　홍병슈　진위뎨삼련티뎨이대티중티쟝륙군보병졍위　리범찬　진위뎨오련티뎨일대티중티쟝륙군보병졍위　민홍셕　시위뎨일련티뎨삼대티향관륙군일등군ᄉᆞ　리항로　진위뎨ᄉᆞ련티뎨일대티향관륙군일등군ᄉᆞ　윤우영

○보친위뎨일련티뎨삼대티중티쟝　륙군보병졍위　민홍셕

○보진위뎨삼련티뎨이대티중티쟝　륙군보병졍위　홍병슈

○보진위뎨오련티뎨일대티중티쟝　륙군보병졍위　리범찬

○보시위뎨일련티뎨삼대티향관　륙군일등군ᄉᆞ　윤우영

○보진위뎨ᄉᆞ련티뎨일대티향관　륙군일등군ᄉᆞ　리항로

이샹구월룩일

TELEGRAMS

FROM JAPAN PAPERS.

London, Sept. 2nd

A letter from the Foreign Office to the Liverpool Chamber of Commerce states that, in consequence of the British Government's representation, the question of contraband of war is being reconsidered by Russia.

London, Sept. 3rd.

The fund being raised in Great Britain in aid of the widows and families of Japanese soldiers and sailors now amounts to £20,000.

Berlin, Sept. 3rd.

It is announced in St. Petersburg that Admiral Hatcher decided to court-martial Prince Ukhtomsky for his conduct (in disobeying orders) in connection with the last trip of the Russian squadron from Port Arthur.

Berlin, Sept. 4th.

The departure for the front of Prince Frederic Leopold of Prussia, who was recently ordered by the Kaiser to join the Russian Headquarters' Staff, has been postponed in accordance with the expressed wish of the Russian Government, the reason given being that the Chunchuses may destroy the railway.

Prince Karl Anton, of the House of Hohenzollern, who has been ordered to join the Japanese Headquarters' Staff in the field arrived at Colombo on Saturday on board the "Sachsen."

London, Sept. 4th.

The British forces are to leave Lhassa on the 15th inst.

London, Sept. 5th.

Unique manœuvres by the British Army have just begun.

General French, with a force, has embarked at Southampton, whence he sails for the East Anglian coast, which will be defended by a force under General Methuen.

A VAST IRRIGATION SCHEME FOR EGYPT.

London, August 10th

An Egyptian blue-book has been issued in which Lord Cromer forwards with approval a long report by Sir William Garstin, the Under Secretary of Works, proposing a vast scheme of irrigation for Egypt and the Soudan, costing about twenty millions sterling.

STRANGE OCCURRENCE AT SEA.

A Philadelphia dispatch of the 1st ult. says:—The British steamer "Mohican," while making for the Delaware breakwater, has encountered a strange phenomenon. A cloud of phosphoric appearance enveloped the vessel and magnetized everything on board.

Capt. Urquhart says the vessel and crew had a fiery coating. When the sailors saw it they rushed at the needle and it was flying around like an electric fan.

"I ordered several of the crew to move iron chains that were lying on deck, thinking to distract their attention. The sailors could not budge the chains although they did not weigh more than 75 pounds each. Everything was magnetized and chains, bolts, spikes and bars were as tight on the deck as if they had been riveted there.

"The cloud was so dense that it was impossible for the vessel to proceed.

"I could not see beyond the decks, and it appeared as if the whole world was a mass of glowing fire. The sailors fell on the decks and prayed

"Suddenly the cloud began to lift. The phosphorescent glow of the ship and the crew began to fade. In a few minutes the cloud passed over and we saw it moving off over the sea."

Owing to incessant rain the upper section of the Kuangno has swollen to over eighty feet and one foreign mechanic and one interpreter, who were engaged in bridged works there, were drowned. It is learned that work in this line will be suspended.—Eastern Times.

KRUGER'S HUMOUR.

The stories about the late ex-Persident Kruger are very numerous. Here, says the "Westminister Gazette, is one of the best:— Com Paul was one day watching the lions in the circus of Mr. Frank Fillis, South Africa's Barnum "Ma agtig," at length he said, "these lions are like Chamberlain; they want lots, take all they can get, never mind how much you've given them, and are no cool about it all, too." "Yes," said the lion keeper, and they'll get, great or little, and are never more quiet than when they think they're going to get most." "Is that so?" remarked the President, with his characteristic shrug and smile.

Except at rare moments, as beside the grave of Joubert, Kruger was not an eloquent man, but he excelled at brief and pithy sayings, many of which, like the saying about waiting for the tortoise to stick out its head, have passed into the language of nations. His answer to a nephew who petitioned for a Government appointment has often been quoted— "My dear boy, I can do nothing for you. You are not clever enough for a subordinate position and all the higher offices are filled." Again, perhaps with reference to his own extreme indifference about his dress, he said just before the war—"The English asked for my coat, and they took it. Then they asked for my trousers, and they took them. Now they ask for—my independence!"

Mr. Kruger in the days of his power was very partial to the Jews as a body. In a conversation on one occasion with Mr. Sam Marks, of Pretoria, he remarked—"It is true you jewish people have no country of your own, but you are very dear to me, for does not the Bible bristle with incidents of the greatness of Israel? Why, we as Christians owe everything to Jews. But," he added, "where can you find in the Bible, in the Old or New Testament, any reference to Englishmen?" The old man chuckled hugely at this sally, and, slapping Mr. Marks on the shoulder, he went on —"Yes, I say, where in the Bible can you find any reference to these Englishmen who now make such a noise in the world? Where, I ask?"

There is little doubt that President Kruger had a sound knowledge of English, but this he always did his best to conceal. An English missionary was given an interview with the President as he was passing through Pretoria some years ago During the interview Dr. Leyds interpreted, and when outside the correspondent fixed his eyes as searchingly as he could on Dr. Leyds, who had accompanied him, and asked, "Does President Kruger really know no English?" With a meaning look Dr. Leyds replied, "If you are praising him, or speaking well of the Transvaal, he knows no English; but if you are speaking ill of him, or saying anything against the Transvaal, he knows every word you say!"

The "Daily Chronicle" tells a good story about the late ex-President:— When the first Australian contingent arrived at Cape Town to take part in the Boer War, Mr. Kruger is said to have asked General Joubert if he knew anything about these Australians. "I only know that eleven of them once beat all England." 'Good God!' cried the President, "we are lost, thirteen thousand of them have just landed."

AN UNGRATEFUL BENEFICIARY.

Our translator-in-chief calling a "rejoice with me story from a Japanese contemporary" writes: Kanjs thimpo said the fall of Liaoyang is the oriental happiness, the Korea ought not be behind of Japan the gladness for this but still could not seen what she prepares to assist feelings, sorrowful and sorrowful.

Thirty-three new vessels have been authorized to be built for the French navy during 1904-5. Of this number, however twenty-eight are submarine boats, four torpedo boats and only one armoured cruiser. This latter ship, four torpedo boats and eight submarines are to be built in dockyards and twenty submarines by contract. The total sum for new construction and completing vessels in hand is about $12,000,000.

CONVICT OUTBREAK AT PULO CONDORE.

It was mentioned recently in these columns, says the "Singapore Free Press," that Pulo Condore, the French island penal settlement off Cape St. James, was to be connected with the Cape by an installation of wireless telegraphy. In connection with the operations for this work, Pulo Condore has just been the scene of a drama which has been carried out with rare audacity. Seventy-five convicts have escaped in a large steam launch after having knocked down and thrown overboard the warders in charge as well as several other persons. The circumstances as officially reported on July 28th by the Superintendent of the Penal Settlement, are these. On July 25, at 3 P. M., seventy-five prisoners who had been sent in the launch to Co-on to fetch material needed for the construction of the wireless telegraph station, suddenly attacked the European and native warders, whom they threw into the sea after a brief struggle.

The European guardians Le Carrée and Massari, a Filipino warder named Mariadasson, and two Annamite warders have disappeared. Warders Cappolani and Veglia were able to save themselves by swimming and regained the shore of the penal settlement where they told the director what had occurred. Le Carrée was steering at the tiller when the convicts mutinied and he received a blow with a stick on the back of the neck. Cappolani, Massani, and Veglia immediately drew their revolvers and were able to fire six times each, but their ammunition being finished they became the prey of the convicts who threw them into the sea. Some of the convicts were killed in the fight and others were wounded.

One fact has to be recorded. An Annamite convict, a former servant of M. Cappolani, cast off a sampan towed by the launch and went to the help of the unlucky persons still afloat in the sea. The convict carried out this act of devotion in the midst of threats and menaces directed at him by his fellow-convicts. The gang was composed for the most part of of Chinese from Kwang-chou and Annamites from Tonkien. The launch on which they made their escape had no provisions on board. The coal on board might allow it to steam for about ten hours. It proceeded in a northeasterly direction. The local authorities, in cooperation with the naval officer in charge, have taken all the steps necessary to pursue the launch and recapture the convicts. The "Aspic" left on the evening of the 28th July having on board M. Canesco, Chief of the Cabinet, M. Morizet, Superintendent of the Penal Settlement, to whom M. Rodier, it appears, has given very strict orders to suppress any new revolt, in case the success of the 75 escaped convicts should tempt some of the others to venture on a similar outbreak.

CONSULAR DEMANDS.

The consultation of Japanese consuls resulted in the following request being handed to the Japanese Legation for the perusal and acquiescence of the Korean Government.

1. Korea to encourage emigrants from Japan.
2. Japanese fisheries on the Korean coast must receive better protection.
3. The police throughout the country must be increased.

The new battleship "Ohio," of the American navy, which was launched at the Union Iron Works, San Francisco, during the visit of the late President McKinley, has had her bunkers filled with Cardiff coal in preparation for her trial trip, which was to take place in the Santa Barbara Channel. If the trip is successful it is thought that the "Ohio" will probably be sent to the Asiatic station to take the place of the "Kentucky." If she does this, the new battleship will become the flagship in the Far East. Six months after going into commission the "Ohio" will have her final trial, on the result of which depends the settlement of the bill for her construction.

President Castro has passed a decree, which has been published in the Caracas "Official Gazette" denying the rights of Great Britian to the island of Patos, which the said decree assumes to be Venezuelan territory.

The island of Trinidad is almost rectangular in shape, but from its northwest and south-west extremities project two long horns towards Venezuela, enclosing the Gulf of Paria. The northwestern horn, called Corozal Point, lies almost in the same line with the Paria Peninsula, from which it is separated by the straits known as the Boca del Dragos or the Dragon's Mouth. Corozal Point terminates in several islands, and in one of the channels between them, the Boca Grande, or Great Mouth, lies the small island of Patos. It is a mere spot in the waters of the Parian Gulf, so small, indeed, that it is marked on most maps by a minute nameless dot. But it is nevertheless, a British possession.

Captain Robertson, of the ketch "Jura" trading between Queensland and New Guinea, in a letter to T. Pratt, of the London Missionary Society, relates a remarkable experience. The ketch was in a dead calm, when a waterspout approached, and appeared likely to overwhelm the vessel. There were 16 passengers on board and most of them had guns. Captain Robertson ordered them to fire a volley, and this was done when the water spout was a short distance off. The firing had the effect of breaking the spiral form of the waterspout, and it most likely was the means of saving the vessel and those on board.

The Korea Daily News.

To be published daily except Sundays.
Rate of Subscription:—
Per Year. Yen 25.
Per Quarter. Yen 7.
Per Month Yen 2.50

Postage in Korea not charged extra.
Postage abroad charged extra.

Advertisements, 50 sen per day for 1 inch or less.
5 yen per month per inch.
50 yen per year per inch.

All communications to
E. T. BETHELL,
Editor and Publisher.
Pak-tong, Seoul

A COMPARISON.

Apologists for the actions, and apparently intended actions, of Japan, in Korea have sought to support their contentions by drawing a parallel between what Japan has done in Korea (or what she is supposed to contemplate doing), and British action in Egypt.

At first sight this argument non-pluses the Englishman who thinks that his country can do no wrong, but a very slight consideration is sufficient to show the fallacy of the comparison.

Great Britain, in spite of repeated assurances to the contrary, occupied Egypt and still occupies it. Japan has promised the world that Korea shall be allowed to retain her integrity and independence but should circumstances lead her to break this promise, apologists say that justification for her action could be found in the precedent created by British action in Egypt.

The occupation of Korea is of the same or greater importance to Japan as was the occupation of Egypt to Great Britain. So far as inability to properly govern themselves is concerned, there is little to choose between Korea and Egypt.

Thus up to the moment of occupation, the comparison is a fair one, but from that moment it ceases abruptly.

When England took over the administration of Egypt the country was poor and its finances in a fearful muddle. Under the administration of a system of commissioners similar to that which prevails in India, the country has grown almost embarassingly rich. Great Britain, in addition to administering Egypt, has made important improvements in the country. The construction of enormous dams on the river Nile is a case in point. By this, water has been made accessible to vast tracts of hitherto arid and unproductive land, and the river has been made navigable.

All this has been done with native labour. Great Britain has provided the capital and skill. Many other improvements have been made but this one is sufficient for the purposes of our argument.

Now to turn to what Japan would be likely to do. It is highly improbable that the termination of this war will find Japan with much spare capital to assist this country with. Sure if she obtained a tangible hold on Korea she might raise money on the strength of its resources.

The greater part of the commerce and industry would fall into Japanese hands, and very properly, too. The Japanese are born traders and they would develop resources hitherto untouched.

The proposals of Mr. Nagamori made it clear that Japan has also designs on the agriculture of Korea. Fishing rights have already been obtained. Of mining, nothing has so far been officially said, but we are continually hearing of Japanese adventurers pre-empting claims in various parts of the country and it will probably be difficult to dislodge them.

Every step taken by Japanese diplomacy, tends to restrict Korea's power of governing herself, and it is fairly certain that eventually Japanese "advisers" will be found all over the country and in every Government office.

Now, we ask, what will be left for the Koreans? The country may remain nominally theirs, but they will have as little voice in the government of it as have the Red Indians in North America.

The British occupation of Egypt has greatly improved and developed the country and bettered the lot of the Egyptians. Japanese occupation of Korea would improve Korea and benefit the—Japanese.

THE NOBLE MAGISTRATE AND HIS VALIENT VOLUNTEERS.

The Magistrate of Cha Sung metaphorically pats himseslf on the back in a despatch to the Home Office. He asserts that 200 Russians armed to the teeth and of a ferocious mien, arrived at the Manchurian frontier in the neighbourhood of his district and attempted to set foot on Korean soil, but they were thwarted. He with a handful of "private gunners" assumed a determined air and forbade them to cross the frontier. The ferocious mien vanished and the would-be invaders departed with awestruck looks, marvelling greatly at the noble horoism displayed by the Magistrate of Cha Sung.

SPY CONFESSES.

An inhabitant of the Pak Chong district, one Pak Hyon Ok, recently clerk in the Imperial Household has been arrested on suspicion of being a Russian spy.

After a little mild persuasion he confesses that he was under instruction by the Russians to report to them at Hamheung, the numbers and disposition of troops at Gensan and Seoul.

The Kamni of Pyeng Yang applies for funds for the building of a new office, suitable to his dignity.

Reports say that the Japanese have notified the Korean Government of their intention to build a military railway from Seoul to Gensan.

Many Koreans at Hamheung have become Russian subjects and are employed in the collection of coolies and the purchase of provisions for the Russian troops.

Mr. Min Yong Chul, Korean Minister to China, has telegrapaphically notified the Government of his departure from Peking on his road to Seoul on the 8th inst.

The Italian Minister has applied for an audience to enable him to personally present to His Majesty a letter of condolence from the King of Italy on the death of the late Dowager Empress.

Nine men, members of the Memorial Society who have recently been employing their time squatting down before the portals of the Imperial Palace, are now languishing behind the doors of the Japanese army headquarters.

It is said that the residence to be occupied by Mr. Megata will be that formerly used by the late General Legendre and that the Financial Department is entering into negotiations with the owner for its purchase.

The Governor of Pyeng-yang is terribly disturbed over the Tonghak movement and every few hours sends weighty telegrams to the Government such as the following:—"Have you received my telegram sent yesterday? The Tonghaks have collected in this district and refuse to disperse. What am I to do?" Later. "The Tonghaks in Samdung, 1,000 strong, are marching on Seoul."

The Korea Daily News.

VOL. I, TUESDAY, SEPTEMBER 13, 1904. No. 50

HONGKONG & SHANGHAI BANKING CORPORATION.

Paid-up Capital..... ....$10,000,000
Reserve Fund:—Sterling Reserve... 10,000,000
Silver Reserve..... 6,500,000
26,500,000
Reserve Liability of Proprietors... 10,000,000

HEAD OFFICE, HONGKONG.

London Bankers, London and County Banking Company Limited.

Branches and Agencies, London.

Amoy,	Hankow	Penang,
Bangkok,	Hiogo,	Rangoon,
Batavia,	Iloilo,	Saigon,
Bombay,	Lyons,	San Francisco,
Calcutta,	Manila,	Singapore,
Colombo,	Nagasaki,	Sourabaya,
Foochow,	New York,	Tientsin,
Hamburg,	Peking,	Yokohama,

Credits granted on approved Securities, and every description of Banking and Exchange business transacted.

Drafts granted on London and the chief Commercial places in Europe, India, Australia, America, China and Japan.

HOLME RINGER & Co., AGENTS, CHEMULPO.

CHARTERED BANK OF INDIA AUSTRALIA & CHINA.

INCORPORATED BY ROYAL CHARTER 1853

HEAD OFFICES:—LONDON.

Paid-up Capital £800,000

Reserve Liability of Shareholders 800,000

Reserve Fund 800,000

Drafts granted upon all the principal places in the world and every description of Exchange and banking business transacted.

E. MEYER & Co., Agents, Chemulpo.

DAI-ICHI GINKO.

LIMITED.

(Formerly the First National Bank)

ESTABLISHED 1873

INCORPORATED UNDER PRESENT LAW 1896

Capital - - - - - - - - Yen 5,000,000
Reserve Fund - . - - - 1,500,000

HEAD OFFICE:—TOKIO.

President: Baron SHIBUSAWA.

BRANCHES AND CORRESPONDENTS In the Principal Cities and Towns of Japan.

Interest Allowed on
Fixed deposits 1 year - - - 6½ per cent
" " 6 months - - - 6 per cent

Special current accounts 1½ sen daily per Y 100
General " " 1 " " " 100

M. TANAKA, Manager, Chemulpo

NIPPON YUSEN KAISHA.

JAPANESE MAIL STEAMSHIP CO.

DER MAIL CONTRACT WITH THE IMPERIAL JAPANESE GOVERNMENT.

European Line

Regular Fortnightly Service between Yokohama Kobe, Moji, Shanghai, Hongkong, Singapore, Penang Colombo, Port Said, Marseilles, London and Antwerp

American Line

Regular Fortnightly Service between Hongkong and Seattle, calling at Shanghai, Moji, Kobe, Yokohama and Victoria, B. C.

Australian Line

Regular weekly Service betwen Japan Ports and Australia, calling at Hongkong and Manila.

(Above Three Lines Suspended until further notice).

Shanghai Line

Weekly Service between Shanghai and Japan Ports

Korea Line

Service Kobe, Moji, Nagasaki, Fusan, Chemulpo, Chioo, Taiku.

S. S. Bahelsberg, 2181 tons.

Service Kobe, Moji, Fusan, Chemulpo, Chinnampo S. S ARGO, S. S. Ohio.

ON CHEONG & CO., SEOUL.

GENERAL STORE KEEPERS.
Imported provisions, Cooking Utensils Crockery, etc.
FRESH BREAD DAILY.

MITSU BISHI DOCKYARD & ENGINE WORKS, NAGASAKI.

CODE WORD, "DOCK."

A. 1, A. B. C., and Engineering Codes used.

DOCK No. 1 (at Tategami).

Extreme Length.............523 feet
Length on blocks.............513 ,,
Width of Entrance on Top......89 ,,
,, ,, Bottom....77 ,,
Water on Blocks at Spring Tide 26½ ,,

DOCK No. 2 (Mukaijima).

Extreme Length.............371 feet
Length on Blocks............360 ,,
Width of Entrance on Top.......66 ,,
,, ,, Bottom 53 ,,
Water on Blocks at Spring Tide 22 ,,

PATENT SLIP (at Kosuge).

Can take vessels up to 1,000 tons gross.

THE WORKS are well equipped with the LATEST IMPROVEMENTS, and can execute any kind of work in SHIPBUILDING and MARINE ENGINEERING, as well as in REPAIRING of SHIPS.

The COMPANY'S new powerful steamer OURA-MARU (712 tons, 700 I.H.P.), specially built for SALVAGE PURPOSES, and equipped with necessary gear, is always READY at SHORT NOTICE.

E. MEYER & CO. Chemulpo.

SOLE AGENTS IN KOREA FOR:

A. T. Morse, Sons & Co's "Fresco" Distemper

In all colours ready for use on walls, Ceilings etc.

and

AVENARIUS CARBOLINEUM

A wood-preserving and antiseptic oil preparation

Against decay, dry-rot, fungus and wood-destroying insects.

A large supply always in Stock. Prices upon application.

E. MEYER & Co., Chemulpo.

LAW UNION & CROWN INS. CO.

Fire risks accepted at Current rates, on go downs, merchandise, dwellings, and other property, subject to usual conditions.

HOLME RINGER & Co., Agents, Chemulpo

THE METHODIST PUBLISHING HOUSE,

Little West Gate, Seoul.

JOB PRINTING, TYPEWRITER PAPER
CARBON PAPER, VISITING CARDS
STATIONERY, BOOK BINDING
BOOK PUBLISHERS
AMERICAN SCHOOL BOOKS
SPENCERIAN COPY BOOKS
PEN CARBON LETTER AND BILL BOOKS

S. A. BECK, Manager.

HOLME RINGER & Co. Chemulpo.

General Merchants and Government Contractors.

Agents for the leading Banks SteamshipCompanies and Insurance Companies

Importers of Merchandise of every description.

KAMEYA & CO.

GENERAL STOREKEEPERS
Chinkokai - - Seoul
(Established 1895, Tokyo)

Confectionery, Hams, Canned Goods, Cutlery, Hirano & Tansan Water. Provisions, Gents, Furnishing goods, Toilet Articles, Travelling Bags, Tobacco, Cigars & Cigarettes Kitchen Utensils. Coffee, Biscuits.

Fresh Goods always kept in Stock.

Prices Moderate

Please come and inspect our goods.

BORDEN'S CONDENSED MILK CO.

New York, U. S. A.

ALWAYS IN STOCK
Eagle Brand Condensed Milk.
Gold Seal Condensed Milk.
Peerless (Family) Evaporated Cream.
Borden's Malted Milk.

E. MEYER & CO. Chemulpo, Korea, Sole Agents

ROYAL INSURANCE COMPANY,
Funds exceed £10,000,000
FIRE
AT CURRENT RATES.
LIFE
REDUCED PREMIUM.
HOLME RINGER & Co., Agents, Chemulpo.

HOTEL DU PALAIS

SEOUL.

The only first class Hotel in Seoul. Situated in the centre of the city opposite the palace.

Cuisine under the supervision of an experienced French Chef.

Well ventilated and furnished throughout.

TARIFF UPON APPLICATION

L. MARTIN
Proprietor and Mangaer.

大韓每日申報
대한미일신보

쳔구빅사년구월십ᄉᆞ일 (슈요일) (뎨오십일호)

본샤고빅

이신보ᄂᆞᆫ영어와한어로셕거미일츌판ᄒᆞᆷ

신문가

ᄒᆞᆫ쟝 엽두돈오푼

일삭됴엽두량닷돈 맛돈으로밧숩

광고료ᄂᆞᆫ

긔한의장단과ᄌᆞ힝의다쇼로중감ᄒᆞ되렴가로밧을터이오며오리지아녀대한사람마다다이신문을보실터이니광고내시기를원ᄒᆞ시ᄂᆞᆫ이들은우리신문샤에와셔면약ᄒᆞ심을희망ᄒᆞ옵

○발힝소 박동대한미일신보샤법어학교압혜젼영국인셜필림집자리오

샤쟝 영국인 (비셜)

사고

○우리대한미일신보의목덕은대한의안녕질셔에관한모든뎨목에ᄃᆡᄒᆞ야ᄂᆞᆫ공평한변론을쥬쟝ᄒᆞᆷ이라우리동신원의담보ᄂᆞᆫ신문보시ᄂᆞᆫ쳠군ᄌᆞ의게ᄒᆞᆼ샹보도ᄒᆞ리며편지를긔셔ᄒᆞ여주시ᄂᆞᆫ이ᄂᆞᆫ셩명과반디를젹어붓치시기를희망ᄒᆞ오니이거슬신문샹에긔지ᄒᆞ라ᄂᆞᆫ거시아니오다만국히신용ᄒᆞᄂᆞᆫ증거를삼고쟈ᄒᆞᆷ이라긔쟈ᄂᆞᆫ아모긔셔던지긔ᄉᆞᄒᆞᆷ을되각ᄒᆞᄂᆞᆫ권리를가졋스나되각ᄒᆞᆫ리유를말ᄒᆞᆯ터이오며공즁평화를문란케ᄒᆞᄂᆞᆫ듯ᄒᆞᆫ긔셔ᄂᆞᆫ의례히밧지안켓ᄉᆞᆸ나이다

사고

○본샤에셔ᄂᆞᆫ신문갑슨미월에션급으로밧ᄉᆞ오며본신문은졔로붓치ᄂᆞᆫ고로본샤에셔ᄂᆞᆫ다른신문샤처름금액을거두러ᄃᆞᆫ니지안ᄉᆞ오니우리신문을ᄉᆞ랑ᄒᆞ야구람ᄒᆞ시ᄂᆞᆫ쳠군ᄌᆞᄂᆞᆫ양력미월월죵에릭월료션금과거쥬셩명통호수를ᄌᆞ세히젹어셔박동본샤로보내시기를바라오며월회일닉로션금을아양력금니보내시ᄂᆞᆫ곳에ᄂᆞᆫ릭월일일부터션 아니보낼터이오니죠량ᄒᆞ옵소셔

●본샤에셔아직긔계를쟝만치못ᄒᆞ와다른ᄃᆡ셔박여오ᄂᆞᆫ고로미양월요일에ᄂᆞᆫ츌판이대단히늣게되ᄂᆞᆫ듯스로분젼이미우늣게되오니우리신문을구람ᄒᆞ시ᄂᆞᆫ쳠군ᄌᆞᄂᆞᆫ용셔ᄒᆞ여쥬심을희망ᄒᆞ옵나이다

본샤광고

본샤에셔본신문뎨ᄉᆞ호와뎨십일호와뎨이십오호를소용ᄒᆞᆯ때가잇셔이에광고ᄒᆞ오니누구시던지이샹삼호즁에본샤로가져오시면미쟝에빅젼두푼식드리리다

론셜

영국과일본에비교ᄒᆞᆯ이라

○무릇일본이한국을유지ᄒᆞ게ᄒᆞᆫ다칭ᄒᆞ고미ᄉᆞ에항거ᄒᆞ야불원ᄒᆞᄂᆞᆫ바를억졔로힝ᄒᆞᄂᆞᆫ일을불진ᄃᆡ긔왕영국셔익급이라ᄒᆞᄂᆞᆫ나라에ᄃᆡᄒᆞ야ᄒᆞ든일과흡ᄉᆞᄒᆞ게ᄉᆡᆼ각ᄒᆞ고인즁ᄒᆞ야ᄒᆞᄂᆞᆫ듯ᄒᆞᆫ지라

우리가이러케변론ᄒᆞ기ᄂᆞᆫ심히어려운거시혹아모라도영국빅셩된쟈ᄂᆞᆫᄌᆞ긔나라에셔그론일을힝ᄒᆞ지아니ᄒᆞᆫ다고ᄒᆞᆯ듯ᄒᆞ되분명히비교ᄒᆞᆯ만ᄒᆞᆫ일잇ᄂᆞᆫ거슬염젹ᄒᆞ여숨기ᄂᆞᆫ거ᄉᆞᆫ심히얏튼소견일듯ᄒᆞ기에대강말ᄒᆞ노라긔왕영국셔익급을보호ᄒᆞᆫ다칭ᄒᆞ고차차로졈령ᄒᆞ야오ᄂᆞᆯ날ᄭᆞ지마음ᄃᆡ로ᄒᆞᄂᆞᆫᄃᆡ일본셔도역시한국에강토와독립을뉴지ᄒᆞ게ᄒᆞ기로보즁ᄒᆞᆫ다칭ᄒᆞ고각국에인허를엇더영국젼례를쓰ᄂᆞᆫ듯ᄒᆞ되졈졈힝ᄒᆞᄂᆞᆫ일은맛치약조를ᄭᅢ트리라ᄒᆞᆷ과갓튼거시근일일본에셔한국에ᄃᆡᄒᆞ야긴요즁ᄃᆡᄉᆞ건과밋졍권ᄭᆞ지라도일본임의로힝ᄒᆞᆫ즉이거ᄉᆞᆫ이왕영국이익급에ᄃᆡᄒᆞ야힝ᄒᆞ든일과셔로관ᄒᆞ야비교ᄒᆞᆯ거시못되ᄂᆞᆫ지라

익급은원리지졍에규모가업셔국빈ᄒᆞᆫ고로영국에셔세무사와갓치세입셰츌과각항국용에졔반규측을시로편셩ᄒᆞ야감독주찰케ᄒᆞ여인도국과갓치부국이된거시영국셔감독ᄒᆞᆫ일은모도그나라에유조ᄒᆞ야보가되게ᄒᆞᆫ지라

그런고로나일이라ᄒᆞᄂᆞᆫ강에광ᄃᆡᄒᆞᆫ방축을ᄊᆞ코수셰도밧게ᄒᆞ며건조ᄒᆞᆫ토지를기량ᄒᆞ야비옥ᄒᆞ게만다라빅셩들로ᄒᆞ여곰농사도짓게ᄒᆞ며각쳐강류를통ᄒᆞ야션쳑도단니게ᄒᆞᆯ때에영국셔먼져의사를닉여자본ᄭᆞ지드리고힘을써셔진보되게ᄒᆞᆫ일이만ᄒᆞ되

일본셔ᄂᆞᆫ긔젼ᄒᆞᆫ이후에한국에유조ᄒᆞᆷ은고사ᄒᆞ고군용경비드ᄂᆞᆫ거슬한국으로ᄒᆞ여곰보조ᄒᆞ게ᄒᆞᄂᆞᆫ일이분명ᄒᆞᆫ거시한국빅셩들은상업과공업상에발달이되지못ᄒᆞ엿다칭ᄒᆞ고졔반ᄉᆞ업상리익을ᄌᆞ긔슈즁에너어광산과어업을차지ᄒᆞ고도유위부족ᄒᆞ야황무지잔이라칭ᄒᆞ고한국농업ᄭᆞ지ᄎᆔᄒᆞ야각종토식이진구무이이되필경에도돌여보닉지아니ᄒᆞᆯ거갓트며소위일본외교관은교섭ᄒᆞᆯ때마다한국졍치를간셥ᄒᆞ야단속ᄒᆞᆷ을불진ᄃᆡ필경에ᄂᆞᆫ분명히각부권쳥과밋관찰군수의게ᄭᆞ지라도모도고문관이잇슬듯ᄒᆞᆫ지라만일한국에장ᄎᆞ무슨여존이잇스라ᄒᆞᆯ진ᄃᆡ다만나라일홈이ᄶᅡ만남어잇셔소위졍부라고억지로명령ᄒᆞᄂᆞᆫ거시북미국에잇ᄂᆞᆫ젹인도빅셩과갓틀터인즉긔왕영국셔익급을ᄎᆔᄒᆞ야그나라에아모ᄶᅩ록긔명진보가되게ᄒᆞ야빅셩들로ᄒᆞ여곰광ᄃᆡᄒᆞᆫ리익이만히쓰되즉금일본으로셔한국에진보되게ᄒᆞᆫ다ᄂᆞᆫ거ᄉᆞᆫ다만ᄌᆞ긔나라에만유조ᄒᆞ게ᄒᆞᆷ이분명ᄒᆞᆫ듯ᄒᆞ도다

잡보

○이합불힝 인항에뎡박ᄒᆞ여잇ᄂᆞᆫ이태리군함마포코로호ᄂᆞᆫ지나간목요일밤에긔관실에셔대포탄환이졔절노폭발되여승죠원즁삼인은치ᄉᆞᄒᆞ고이십ᄉᆞ인은포란연긔의독ᄒᆞᆫ긔운을쏘이여셔모다병이나셔방쟝치료즁이라더라

○김씨원억 원산거ᄒᆞᄂᆞᆫ김두원씨ᄂᆞᆫ일본젹한의게소금을봉젹ᄒᆞ고그소금갑을밧으랴고여러히를류리걸식ᄒᆞ야다니다가몸은죽을지경이되고억울ᄒᆞᆫ분ᄒᆞᆫ마음을이긔지못ᄒᆞ야말경에ᄂᆞᆫ일공ᄉᆞ를한번구박ᄒᆞ엿더니그죄로감옥셔셔징력ᄭᅥ지ᄒᆞ다가젼신이모다부어셔긔지ᄉᆞ경일너니일젼ᄉᆞ면에다힝몽방되엿ᄂᆞᆫᄃᆡ필경부즁으로죽게되엿다ᄒᆞ니김씨의쳘텬원억ᄒᆞᆫ소졍이야엇지다셩언ᄒᆞ리오필경은소금먹은놈이물켤날이잇스리라더라

○삼남즙포관 의졍부참졍신긔션씨가닉부로죠회ᄒᆞ엿스되본월구일에본참졍이근쥬ᄒᆞ오되향시에도젹과비도형포ᄒᆞᆯ소로즙포관몃명이차하되엿스나삼남에고루게분비못되엿더니령남과량호ᄃᆡ방에젹경이샤차징집지아니ᄒᆞ고동학여당이다시방ᄉᆞ이란을ᄭᅮᆷ이ᄂᆞᆫ거ᄉᆞᆯ그조만ᄒᆞᄂᆞᆫᄃᆡ로두지못ᄒᆞᆯ지라목쳔군슈박졍빈과산군슈민영은쳥산군슈송회완만경군슈졍인희히남군슈리용우돌산군슈마쥰영룡궁군슈쟝룡환의홍군슈죠병유김히군슈리근홍거창군슈리응익을병즙포관차하ᄒᆞ야각각구역을졍ᄒᆞ야ᄒᆞ여곰난호아관할ᄒᆞ야형포케ᄒᆞ옴이하여ᄒᆞ올지샹쥬ᄒᆞ와의쥬되엿스니이ᄃᆡ로흠쥰ᄒᆞ야시힝ᄒᆞ라ᄒᆞ엿더라

○탐도면관 신참졍이닉부로ᄯᅩ죠회ᄒᆞ되본월구일에본참졍이근쥬ᄒᆞ오되근일잡류비가감모궁역비라쟈칭ᄒᆞ고향읍에츌몰ᄒᆞ야젼지를토식ᄒᆞᄂᆞᆫ거ᄉᆞᆫ그방빅과조목지임에잇ᄂᆞᆫ자가맛당히엄금ᄒᆞᆯ거시어ᄂᆞᆯ경북관찰ᄉᆞ윤헌이가도리혀부동ᄒᆞ야그친ᄒᆞᆫ겸종을식혀잡류비로더부러각군에슌힝ᄒᆞ야빅셩의게보죠금을역륵으로벡렴ᄒᆞ야대읍에ᄂᆞᆫ일이만량이오소읍에도몃쳔량식되여셔젼도가소요ᄒᆞ야젼셜이랑자ᄒᆞᆫ고로향시에신부에셔잡류비를압샹ᄒᆞ고그리유를보명ᄒᆞᆯ뜻으로루ᄎᆞ면칙ᄒᆞ엿더니수일후에야비로소략략히회면ᄒᆞ엿ᄂᆞᆫᄃᆡ쳥문이날노더욱히연ᄒᆞ고민졍이도탄에심ᄒᆞ오니하로를머문즉하로에히가잇ᄉᆞ온지라경북관찰ᄉᆞ윤헌을위션면본관ᄒᆞ야죠률징감ᄒᆞ옵고인ᄒᆞ야닉부로ᄒᆞ야곰히도에발훈ᄒᆞ야셰셰히사실ᄒᆞ야임의비렴ᄒᆞᆫ돈을낫낫치민의게환급ᄒᆞ야써민심을샤례ᄒᆞ옴이ᄒᆞ

여ᄒᆞ을지샹 주ᄒᆞ와의 주ᄒᆞ
란ᄒᆞ왈시고 힝ᄒᆞ야 죠칙ᄒᆞ시
되어느쎈들셔빈을무ᄒᆞᆷ커아니
ᄒᆞ리오말은이ᄶᅢ에관쳬홈이위
싱ᄒᆞ야보셩ᄒᆞ기에폐운고로계
반졉에지단을엄금ᄒᆞ기로죠서
와면칙을루ᄎᆞ나리엿더니힝금
에차등에폐단이엄는줄노회면
을명령힝ᄒᆞ고이에잡히인연ᄒᆞ
야란ᄒᆞᆫᄉᆞ문이랑자ᄒᆞ구우극
룽완ᄒᆞᆫ지라힉관찰ᄉᆞ윤헌을면
본관ᄒᆞ야법부로ᄒᆞ여곰죠률ᄒᆞ
야엄ᄒᆞ고슈렴ᄒᆞᆫ돈들사실ᄒᆞ
야낫낫치도로츄급ᄒᆞ라ᄒᆞ올셔
기로죠회ᄒᆞ니죠량ᄒᆞ와죠ᄒᆞ시되
힝관찰ᄉᆞ가임의면관되엿스니
셔리ᄉᆞ무가일시위급ᄒᆞᆫ지라곳
셔리ᄅᆞᆯ지졍ᄒᆞ야힉도로면훈ᄒᆞ
고힉슈렴젼을사실ᄒᆞ야민간에
츌급ᄒᆞ고쳥장비ᄅᆞᆯ그젼면보수
의티로법부로망야양샹ᄒᆞ고젼
관찰ᄉᆞ의불법탐학ᄒᆞᆫᄉᆞ를저저
히사실ᄒᆞ야힉장젼을징슈ᄒᆞ고
보고ᄒᆞᆯ뜻스로힉관찰셔리의게
로일번면칙ᄒᆞ고이번발훈ᄒᆞ라
ᄒᆞ엿더라

○수셩불분 룡쥬관찰ᄉᆞ심진
팅씨가니부로면보ᄒᆞ되지산군
향장의보고를기ᄒᆞᆫ즉금졍군셰
원셜어가본읍민한가의게돌탈
취ᄒᆞᆫ고로숑ᄉᆞ되야한가의게는
본부를차자쥬고계가의쳐는약을
졍게ᄎᆞ로결퇴신오도ᄒᆞ고방송ᄒᆞᆫ
ᄒᆞ엿더니한가가인ᄒᆞ야계ᄉᆞᄒᆞᆫ
지라금평군수젼명이쟈당ᄒᆞ야
시신을담예ᄒᆞ야가지고관문에
돌입ᄒᆞ야동헌을파쇄ᄒᆞ고군수
를란타ᄒᆞ야수싱을불분중이라
ᄒᆞ엿기로진위티병을쳥파ᄒᆞ고
순검을파송ᄒᆞ야진압케ᄒᆞ고쳔
안군수로사관을졍ᄒᆞ야힉군에
파견ᄒᆞ야힉ᄉᆞ실을져사케ᄒᆞ엿
다ᄒᆞ엿더라

○동학룽문 평안남도삼등군
에동학당이회집ᄒᆞ야경셩을향
ᄒᆞ야붉은긔두기를만드러군긔
에는어질인ᄌᆞ를쓰고져은긔는
나란ᄌᆞ솟ᄌᆞ를써가지고강동군으
로지나가다가일병이범련으로
휫치고피슈샹인을본군에압부
ᄒᆞ야퇴슈ᄒᆞ고힉군수가그동문
을등셔ᄒᆞ야보고ᄒᆞ엿는티경셩
가ᄒᆞ논바남슈의발문이라 일
은 황실을보호ᄒᆞ야독립권을
공고케ᄒᆞᆯᄉᆞ 일은졍부를기쳔
ᄒᆞ야빅셩의ᄌᆞ유권을엇게ᄒᆞᆯᄉᆞ
일은이졔이거의ᄒᆞ기는우리나
라군의라즉금일본이아국과젼
징ᄒᆞ기는실노대의를드러동양
의는평화ᄒᆞᆯ목젹을주쟝홈이니
우리가엉졍히단속ᄒᆞ야일본군
ᄉᆞ샹에방히홈이업게ᄒᆞ야의리
로써외리를ᄉᆞᆫ샹홈이업게ᄒᆞᆯᄉᆞ
일은로비ᄂᆞᆫ각각ᄌᆞ긔가쥬션ᄒᆞ
야민간에침탈홈이업게ᄒᆞᆯᄉᆞ
일은면방에우외를돈목케ᄒᆞ고
문명을진보ᄒᆞ며각국에리익권
을양여홈이업게ᄒᆞᆯᄉᆞ 일은중
립국회의무를힝ᄒᆞ져기계ᄒᆞᆯ
ᄉᆞ 일은ᄒᆞᆫ비싱오려를로ᄭᅥᆯ로가
일졔히발힝ᄒᆞ야동학회일에경
ᄉᆞ에회동ᄒᆞᆯᄉᆞ 일은미ᄉᆞ를회
쟝의지휘대로ᄒᆞ되만일쟝졍티
로아니ᄒᆞᆫ샤 ᄉᆞ잇스면엄벌ᄒᆞᆯ쎈
아니라즁벌에쳐ᄒᆞᆯᄉᆞ 일은대
략만벌긔ᄒᆞ니미진ᄒᆞᆫ건은일후
고시ᄒᆞᆯᄉᆞ

○총대파송 제작일에일진회
의셔귀회ᄒᆞ고졍부에회답셔를
최촉ᄒᆞᆯᄎᆞ로총대위원을졍부에
파송ᄒᆞ기로결의ᄒᆞ엿다더라

○영부룽시 니부에셔경긔츙
쳥남북도젼라남북도경샹남북
도황히도함경도에면훈ᄒᆞ기를
즉금졍부에셔면회ᄒᆞ되여부모
징수ᄂᆞᆫ일병룽시ᄒᆞ라ᄒᆞ엿스니
각기관하각군에룽시ᄒᆞᆯ뜻스로
속속히훈칙ᄒᆞ고곳회보ᄒᆞ라ᄒᆞ
엿더라

○동학광고문 동학츄회쟝라
인쳥이가각쳐에광고문을발송
ᄒᆞ엿ᄂᆞᆫ티그ᄉᆞ의에ᄒᆞ기를우리
대한이ᄒᆞᆫ모통이에궁벽키쳐ᄒᆞ
야인심이열니지못ᄒᆞ고로셰계
각국의문명개화ᄒᆞᆫ풍속을아지
못ᄒᆞ고각부대신은용폐 총명
ᄒᆞ야리관리쟈ᄒᆞᆯ줄만알고렴치
ᄉᆞ랑은빅셩의기름만긁어셔인
민의게탐학ᄒᆞ만ᄒᆞ는고로셰계각
국이아만국이라칭호ᄒᆞ니엇지
샹통치아니ᄒᆞ리오항자에아병
이함경도평안도에돌입ᄒᆞ여가
옹을충화ᄒᆞ며부녀를겁탈ᄒᆞ되
방어ᄒᆞᆯ슐을몰으고황황분주ᄒᆞ
니빅셩이가련치못ᄒᆞ야항샹못
된연고라이런고로팔도에유지
ᄒᆞᆫ쟈가공론ᄒᆞ되회사를황셩에
셜립ᄒᆞ고팔도인민이단회ᄒᆞ야
타국문명개화를본바다ᄒᆞᆫ일쳥
샹국이동양을평화ᄒᆞ야국가를
공고케ᄒᆞ고대신과수령의포학
ᄒᆞᆫ졍ᄉᆞ를업게ᄒᆞ고인싱을부지
ᄒᆞᆯ뜻스로동귀가잇ᄂᆞᆫ고로이곳
치회졉ᄒᆞ니대한이ᄀᆡ명ᄒᆞ면아
국강포를방어ᄒᆞᆯ지라인민비기
명귀화홈이비단대한의다힝이
라쎤한일본에구원이되리니죠
량ᄒᆞ라ᄒᆞ엿더라

○아병샹병 일젼밤에남대문
니졍거장안ᄯᅢ한병과쥬ᄉᆞ에일본
헌병일명이대취ᄒᆞ야돌입ᄒᆞ며
휘도ᄒᆞ야한병일명이피샹ᄒᆞ고
대한번병이탐졍ᄎᆞ로리도ᄒᆞ엿
더니일헌병이군도로한병의우
편다리를졔니쥭첨되ᄂᆞᆫ게슬보
금히니현등디로다라느ᄉᆞ더
라

○쇼쇼쳥쟝 광쥬로셔온사름
의젼셜을드른즉하리쳥쟝자가
경셩진신쇼쳥에부비를부용ᄒᆞᆫ
다칭탁ᄒᆞ고힉군훈령을가지고
단이며셔민호에동젼일쳔식슈
렴ᄒᆞ더라더라

○읍후감세 향시ᄅᆞ티 셩후
미령ᄒᆞ심시다홈은본보에룽록
ᄒᆞ엿거니와근일에ᄂᆞᆫ감세가계
시되쾌복은아직못되셧다더라

○졍니쉬신 본월십일일밤에
졍니에셔굿슬ᄒᆞ엿ᄂᆞᆫ티미우쟝
ᄒᆞ게ᄒᆞ엿다더라

○홍슈총방 향일에일본헌병
의게피착되엿던진신쇼슈이하
계인이방환되엿ᄂᆞᆫ티그중리범
창윤병홍필쥬샹인은샹ᄎᆞ구슈
ᄒᆞ엿다더라

○영위룽시 일젼에창찬위위
씨가니외부에면보ᄒᆞ야왈인부
모징수를일본수령쟝관과교셥
ᄒᆞ야영영룽시케되엿스니이ᄉᆞ
의등각디방과각항구에면칙ᄒᆞ
라ᄒᆞ엿더라

○파원위폐 삼화감리의보고
를거ᄒᆞᆫ즉곽조파원류지헌이본
군에리도ᄒᆞ야곽조회사ᄒᆞᆫ다고
칭탁ᄒᆞ고본항에두류ᄒᆞᆫ지수삭
에곽조를젼혀제조치아니ᄒᆞ고
수방구에셔사ᄃᆞ려며도코가된고
로항구에쇼요를일은지라일본
헌병이사문ᄒᆞᆯᄎᆞ로본셔에리도
ᄒᆞ엿다가본셔쥬ᄉᆞ련중쳘을구
타ᄒᆞ고류지헌을착거ᄒᆞ엿ᄂᆞᆫ티
당쟝계조가망유괴구ᄒᆞ엿ᄉᆞᆫ즉
궁닉부에이죠ᄒᆞ야류지헌을쇼
환ᄒᆞ고힉회사인힉쟝을쟉슈ᄒᆞ
야샹민을안업케ᄒᆞ라ᄒᆞ엿더라

외보

○쟝유쟝됴 오디리셔울외교
사회에셔논만일려순이함락ᄒᆞ
고로양이일군의게졈령홈이되면
ᄒᆞᆫ시에후쟌홈을에됴ᄒᆞᆯ것이발
국이영미덕삼국을권유ᄒᆞ야
ᄒᆞᆫ가지로일로량국에티ᄒᆞ야교
젼을중지ᄒᆞ기로권됴ᄒᆞᆯ줄노확
신ᄒᆞᆫ다더라

○려순관할 로쟝스텟셀씨가
려순을결슈ᄒᆞᄂᆞᆫ소이ᄂᆞᆫ만일려
순이함락ᄒᆞ면료양에잇ᄂᆞᆫ로군
의수ᄅᆞᆯ가져샹되야련속ᄒᆞ야대
퀘ᄒᆞᆯ가두려워ᄒᆞᆷ인ᄃᆡ료양이함
락된오ᄂᆞᆯ날에ᄂᆞᆫ그영향이려순
에잇ᄂᆞᆫ로군에게밋쳐다시일군
을강경히항거ᄒᆞ며려순을굿건
히직히기ᄂᆞᆫ샹의리론론ᄒᆞ고함
락홈을면키어려울경우라ᄒᆞ니
려순함락의대쾌보를쳡쳡ᄒᆞᆷ도
불원ᄒᆞ리라더라

○거월이십구일에유야납발던
을거ᄒᆞᆫ즉법국외무경댈캐세씨
가로국대ᄉᆞ의게젼고ᄒᆞ되로국
군티와후할디가법국향구나
타식민디항만을젼투샹목뎍으
로ᄉᆞ용ᄒᆞ거나후괴란디로ᄉᆞ용
ᄒᆞ야런규를중립국에밋게ᄒᆞ야
젼국을쟝원케ᄒᆞ며ᄯᅩ외교샹
에란쟝케ᄒᆞᄂᆞᆫ불힝홈을면케
홀일을주의ᄒᆞ라ᄒᆞ엿더라

관보

○의원면본관 중추원의관
신용휴 기셩우례ᄉᆞ쟝 서상
션

○임중추원의관서주임관륙등
젼라북도관찰부총순 졍창권

○임군부포공국포병과쟝서주
임관륙등 군긔창기ᄉᆞ 오
경션

○임군긔창기ᄉᆞ서주임관오등
군부주ᄉᆞ 쟝용식

○군부포공국포병과쟝서주임
관삼등 주차일본국공ᄉᆞ관참
서관 현보운

○임기셩우례ᄉᆞ쟝서주임관륙
등 한셩우례ᄉᆞ주ᄉᆞ 박긔홍

○금산금봉 기셩우례ᄉᆞ쟝박
긔홍

이상구월팔일

○의원면본관 봉샹ᄉᆞ부졔됴
오명근 룽신ᄉᆞ면회과주ᄉᆞ
서용순

○명궁니부룽진관서칙임관삼
등 졍이룡 졍한됴

○임봉샹ᄉᆞ부졔주서주임관륙
등 비서원승 리민영

○임비서원승서주임관륙등
엄시티

○임군부주ᄉᆞ서판임관륙등
류샹렬

○임경흥감리서주ᄉᆞ서판임관
륙등 김샹동

○임젼라북도관찰부총순서판
임관칠등 젼라남도관찰부총
순 류덕근

○임젼라남도관찰부총순서판
임관륙등 룽풍 신궁우

○임한셩우례ᄉᆞ주ᄉᆞ서판임관
륙등 삼화우례ᄉᆞ주ᄉᆞ 박제
순

○임삼화우례ᄉᆞ주ᄉᆞ서판임관
륙등 문영석

○금산금봉 한셩우례ᄉᆞ주ᄉᆞ
박제순 삼화우례ᄉᆞ주ᄉᆞ 문
영석

이상구월구일

궁령룽ᄉᆞ

군졔의졍관룽군부쟝신 민
영환

주군졔의졍소ᄉᆞ무가호대ᄒᆞ와
봉가불의원을취ᄌᆞᆼᄒᆞ온지라위
임ᄒᆞᆫ인원을샹가기록ᄒᆞ옵고
셩졔ᄒᆞ옵시믈복츅ᄒᆞ노이다
광무팔년구월칠일봉
지ᄒᆞ와계왈가라ᄒᆞ심

○궁니부룽진관김샹운ᄉᆞ직소
비지비에숀쳥티로의셔ᄒᆞ노라

○궁니부룽진관리셩렬ᄉᆞ직소
비지비에숀쳥티로의셔ᄒᆞ노라

이상구월구일

TELEGRAMS.

MARQUIS OY. MA'S REPORT.

RUSSIAN LOSSES AT LIAOYANG.

GENERAL MISCHENKO KILLED.

Tokyo Sep. 12th.

Field-Marshal Marquis Oyama reports that Russian prisoners captured at Liaoyang say the Russian losses in the retreat from Ashantien until Liaoyang was evacuated must have reached a total of 25,000. The corps engaged were the 2nd, 4th, 5th, 7th and 17th with detachments from other divisions. General Mischenko was killed in the battle at the east of Liaoyang. On the 3rd and 4th inst. the Russians were filling train after train with their dead and wounded and with war material and supplies. Most of the material, which had to be left behind, was burnt off but large quantities of ammunition were found, including a few Dum-dum bullets

THE RUSSIAN COMMAND IN MANCHURIA.

Paris, July 21.—The St. Petersburg correspondent of the "Echo de Paris" says that, according to information obtained at the best source, the General Staff is preparing, in concert with the Emperor and the principal Imperial officials, a modification in the supreme command of the army in Manchuria. General Kuropatkin still enjoys the confidence of the Emperor as well as that of the army. But the extremities of his constantly increasing forces are encamped at great distance from headquarters. On the other hand, the mobility of the Japanese and their division into three armies have convinced the War Office of the necessity of creating two Russian armies in the Far East under absolutely independent commanders. General Kuropatkin will, of course, remain at the head of the First Army, while the Second will be commanded either by General Sukhotin, ex-president of the academy of the General Staff, now in command in Eastern Siberia, who has the reputation of being one of the most brilliant of Russian generals, or by General Sukhomlinoff, now in command of the Kieff military district. Towards the end of August one of these two generals will be placed at the head of the Second Army. General Kuropatkin and the new Commander-in-Chief of the Second Army will be under the immediate authority of Admiral Alexieff, whose position is still unaffected, and whose partisans enjoy undiminished prestige with the Emperor.

The same correspondent states that the board of directors of the Russian State railways has given orders to hasten the construction of the line passing round the end of Lake Baikal.—London Times.

?

From the Japan Times we learn that the "Asahi" has a very interesting and no doubt a very popular suggestion to make, this being no less a subject than the advance of His Majesty the Generalissimo's headquarters to a place nearer ahe seat of the war. Historically the forward movement of the Imperial quarters has always been productive of the most auspicious results, and the journal cannot but believe that such an advance, if carried out at this juncture, would prove no exception. With the momentarily expected fall of Port Arthur, the country will enter on the second and then the third stages of the war, and though Marshal Oyama and General Kodama are no doubt soldiers of tested ability and unbounded competency, they will have to depend on the illustrious influence to their august sovereign in order to ensure the success of their future operations. Then the consciousness on the part of the rank and file of fighting near the presence of their revered Generalissimo will inspirit them with new and redoubled energy and valour. Hence the desirability of the Imperial advance. Further it is meet that unprecedented glory won in a unprecedented manner should he commemorated by an unprecedented Imperial and national recognition of the fact. Let the Imperial headquarters advance to Seoul, the capital of Korea, or Dalny, a mistress city of the Far East, wrenched from proud Russia. Dalnys contain many commodious structures, and the idea of convoking a special session of the Imperial Diet appeals very strongly to the fancy of our contemporary, which accordingly speaks very enthusiastically of such an event.

The idea may appeal to the fancy of the "Tokio Asoi" but is likely to be inconvenient in operation. A special convocation of the Imperial Japanese Diet in Seoul seems, to say the least of it, a "leetle" bit previous.

THE KOBE CHRONICLE ON JAPANESE POLICY IN KOREA.

Had we the space, we should have liked to reproduce in full an article which appeared in the "Kobe Chronicle" of August 25th. We must however content ourselves with the peroration,

"We venture to say that in all questions such as that now pending between Japan and Korea there is something more to be considered than simple or immediate expediency. In modern times the word "expediency" is customarily used apart from principle, and indeed as excusing action which cannot be justified on those grounds of justice which lie at the basis of morality. In the broader view of the term it is, of course, inexpedient to do injustice even if the act seems on a short view "expedient." But without entering into a phrase-chopping competition, we would urge now, as we have urged before when dealing with Japan's attitude towards Korea, that she will not justify herself in the eyes of the world by schemes of exploitation which, beneficial as they may be to Korea, form an invasion of her sovereignty and are acts of injustice towards her people. It seems to us incontestable that principle is to be preferred to expediency, and justice to opportunism."

GAMBLING "WITH MONEY."

Our police reporter says:—Lately there are plenty official gamblers in the northern village of the city, gamble with money, many shong and dollars lost and got in a night. The police men found that place and entered there tried to arrest the gamblers, but excused after given some money to each policeman.

SIGHT SEEING AND FARSEEING.

Our reporter informs us that:—"Mr. Yi Yu-in the former minister, who is a fortune teller, he divined that his fortune will be good to go away from Seoul, he and all his families have gone down to his house in Yeh Chŏn district."

The offices of the Magistrate of Tai In near Masanpo were destroyed by the recent typhoon.

From Berlin we learn that France intends sending two submarine boats to Indo-China.

The portentous news reaches us that Salvador, Honduras and Nicaragua have formed a Peace League.

The amount borrowed by the Government from the Bank of Japan has increased by Y3,000,000 this month, the total now standing at Y38,000,000.

A revolt is stated to have broken out among the Ovambo tribe in German South-west Africa, but no official confirmation of the news has yet been received.

The mails from Japan seem to have gone astray recently. Papers and letters of the 6th inst. at Kobe were received by us on Monday while letters dated Kobe Aug. 25th did not come to hand till yesterday morning.

Great rejoicing amongst wizards is the order of the day. They maintain that the illness of the Chief of Police is due to the direct influence of the devil, who know that the sorcerers have been dispersed and can practise his art unchecked.

A man named Choi, a worker in the Korean gold mines, was recently found guilty of stealing his neighbour's wife. The magistrate ordered him to be flogged and then released, but the victim succumbed after 15 blows had been struck. His fellow workers in the mine avenged themselves on the magistrate by wrecking his office and dealing out the same punishment of flogging to him. However, being only amateurs at the job, they did not succeed in killing him but left him in a bruised and battered condition to repent.

The 1000 Tonghaks, reported by the Governer of Pyeng-yang to be in Samdung started off on their march to Seoul on the 11th inst. with two leaders waving red banners and the crowd of valiant followers marching sternly on their goal. They are reported to have been an awe-inspiring spectacle, until while passing through the Kangdong district they met some Japanese soldiers, and now—well—the red banners don't wave. There are no Tonghaks in sight, unless one should look behind the prison walls of Kangdong, where some of the ringleaders are enjoying a little rest and have much time to ponder on the folly of their ways.

A message from St Pebersburg dated the second week in August says that Russia is stubbornly opposing the attempt of England and the United States to curtail its privileges with regard to the restriction of trade with Japan. It declares that unless these two countries can be stopped from supplying the islanders with foodstuffs, railway materials, rifles, cartridges, powder and dynamite, Russia's chances of ultimate victory will be seriously compromised. It asserts that England and America have developed a contraband trade unprecedented in the history of war, and charges that the whole equipment of the Japanese reserves. 250,000 men, was smuggled from the United States. Hence Russia's extraordinary efforts to station commerce-raiders on all the shipping routes to the Far East.

The Korea Daily News.

To be published daily except Sundays.

Rate of Subscription:—

Per Year,	Yen 25.
Per Quarter,	Yen 7.
Per Month	Yen 2.50

Postage in Korea not charged extra.
Postage abroad charged extra.

Advertisements, 50 sen per day for 1 inch or less. 5 yen per month per inch. 50 yen per year per inch.

All communications to

E. T. BETHELL,
Editor and Publisher.
Pak-tong, Seoul

AFTER LIAOYANG.

Some time ago we were informed that the occupation of Liaoyang and the capture of Port Arthur would mark the completion of the first stage of the war.

Liaoyang is now in the hands of the Japanese and we believe that it is only a matter of time for Port Arthur to succumb to their attacks. This will end the first stage of the war which will have been an unbroken series of victories for the Japanese.

The "Tokio Asahi" In view of the continuous arrivals of Russian reinforcements at Mukden and Khabin our military authorities have already formulated a plan for the carrying out of the second stage of the operations as soon as Liaoyang has been occupied by our forces.

What that second stage may be, it is only possible to guess. It certainly appears that the only way to inflict a really crushing and lasting defeat on the Russians is by the occupation of Kharbin which is at the junction of the railway running north from Mukden and with the Trans-Siberian main line. Mukden lies enroute to Kharbin and will probably be the next place to be attacked by the combined Japanese armies but whether the attack will be made this autumn or deferred until next spring is a matter for conjecture.

It seems to be the general opinion that the second stage will be an advance upon Vladivostock, starting from Gensan. It is well known that the Russians are in considerable strength at Hamheung and it is probable that they are only waiting the winter and the freezing of the harbours north of Gensan to descend in force into Korea. Thus the landing of a Japanese army at Gensan would serve a double purpose, that of checking the Russian advance this winter and paving the way for an organized attack on Vladivostock and its communications with Kharbin in the spring.

It is very evident that the second stage, whatever it may be, will be a long one. The greater part of the country through which the Japanese army has marched is fairly familiar ground, as it was the scene of their operations against China in 1894. Henceforth, the further north they proceed, the more difficult will their task become. The Japanese will be further from theirs. The country will be a strange one and the population will be hostile. This will greatly complicate matters of commissariat and transport.

From all this it is fair to assume that the second stage will be a very much longer one than the first.

Although the first stage has been practically completed and has so far been carried out in a manner commanding the admiration of the whole world, a doubt occurs to us as to whether it has quite come up to Japanese expectations.

Port Arthur although undoubtedly doomed is holding out surprisingly and the cost in lives, to Japan, of this stronghold will be enormous.

Kuroki, on at least two occasions, had hoped to intercept Kuropatkin's retreat and failed each time. From what we can gather of the Liaoyang battle, Kuropatkin's escape from being surrounded was largely due to the impetuosity of the Japanese attack on his right wing, which put him in full retreat before Kuroki had time to complete the sweep which he was making in order to take up a position in the Russian rear.

But we think the greatest disappointment of all is the frustration, hitherto, of all Japanese attempts to put the Trans-Siberian Railway out of action.

We know of many strenuous attempts to achieve this and there will, of course, have been many others of which we have not heard, for in our opinion it is upon the efficiency of this railway that the issue of the whole war depends.

We do not see any possibility of Russia ever driving Japan from the positions which she has now occupied unless it be by a descent into Korea (which could only be accomplished with the aid of a Vladivostock squadron strong enough to cope with the Japanese Navy).

On the other hand we do not see any very brilliant future before the Japanese operations when their armies advance further into Manchuria.

Under these circumstances it is not surprising to find that some of the Tokio newspapers are beginning to discuss the subject of mediation.

It does not seem possible that Russia can ever regain command of the sea and she is therefore practically confined to defensive tactics. And as there is every indication that the Russian defense will increase in strength until it is really effective, a deadlock seems to have been arrived at.

CORRESPONDENCE.

To the Editor of the Korea Daily News
Dear Sir:—

"It may be of interest to the readers of your valuable paper, to receive news of the Russian battleship "Csarewitch" and the other vessels arriving at Tsingtau. The report is from a reliable source at Tsingtau."

"On the 11th August in the afternoon a Russian torpedo boat arrived here followed shortly after by the crusier "Novik." Both went alongside two colliers, which had already been waiting some days. The "Novik" left again at 2 a.m. on the 12th with covered lights and proceeded to sea, where the "Diana" and "Askold were reported to be lying."

"An officer on the "Novik" stated that they, as well as the rest of the squadrow, left Port Arthur with orders to break through the blockade. It was said that the battleships should proceed to Vladivostock and the cruisers go south on their operations. At 9:30 p.m. on the 11th the Csaweritch, in a badly damaged condition, arrived and went to anchor in the inner harbour. Today the 12th August two more Russian torpedo boats arrived and took in coal from the colliers. The chief officer of the "Csarewitch," at present in temporary command made the following statement."

"Our squadron had orders to break through and proceed to Vladivostock. We left Port Arthur on the 10th August at 6 a.m. and soon sighted several torpedo boats and small cruisers. The "Bayan having been damaged by a mine had to go back to harbor. About 11 a.m. being then 20 miles from Port Arthur, we met the Japanese squadron, which consisted of four battleships, three armoured cruisers, three protected cruisers, 6 smaller cruisers and 40 torpedo boats. We had 1½ hours fighting, during which time, we were the special mark of the enemy."

"We managed to break through the enemy's fleet but know nothing of the fate of the rest of our squadron. we shaped our course towards the Shautung coast, followed by these vessels of the Japanese fleet. "Asahi" "Mikara," "Shikishima" and one more battleship of the "Fuji" type, Nisshi, "Kasuga" "yakums" Kasagi,". "Chitose," "Takasago" and several destroyers. These vessels attacked us off the Shantung coast at 4.30 p.m. and for two hours we had a severe battle with those ships. We were repeatedly struck, but our shots were also seen to go home. We were more and more hit until at 6.30 p.m. a Japanese shell struck and exploded on the fighting bridge where Admiral Witgeft stood with his staff and the ship's officers. Of the admiral only one leg was found, which we afterwards buried at sea. The staff navigating officer and the ship's navigating officer were killed by the same shell also one flag Lieutenant. Admiral Matussewitch the commander of the ship and all the other officers were on the bridge at the time. Admiral Matussewitsch was the chief of staff—This time we also managed to break through and the Japanese were not able to follow. We then intended to make for Vladivostock but our steering gear was so damaged that we had to run for Tsingtau as a port of refuge. In our present condition we cannot put to sea and whether we will be permitted to make the necessary repairs is as yet uncertain. Our casualties were 12 killed and 40 wounded, some of the latter only slightly injured. Admiral Matussewitch and 8 of the severely wounded were brought on shore to-day (Aug. 12th) and lodged in the Tsingtau Government hospital.

"The ship is in a fearful condition, her funnels are totally damaged, her fighting bridge is a useless wreck, and 5 large holes are visible above water."

Tsingtau 12th August.

"I have translated the above into English as I thought your readers would find it of interest."

AN OLD TIME STAGER.

ACCIDENT ON THE SEOUL-FUSAN RAILWAY.

As two trains were running over a newly laid section of the Seoul Fusan railroad; the rails suddenly gave way and the trains were overturned. Three Japanese were killed outright while five are severely injured. The accident is said to be due to careless rail laying.

COOLIES NOW HAPPY.

The Home Office has telegraphed to all provinces, ordering the cessation of coolie collections. It appears that this satisfactory state of affairs has been arrived at by arrangement with the Japanese army headquarters here, and that in future coolies have nothing to fear.

Mr. Megata left Kobe for Seoul on the 10th inst. He is bringing with him some rolls of silk as a present to the Imperial Household.

Most of the members of the Memorial Society, who were arrested by the Japanese have since been released. Only Messrs. Yi Pom-suk, Yun Byeng and Hong Pil-chu are still under restraint.

It is now officially stated that the Japanese Minister has applied for permission to build a railroad to Gensan and that his request has been granted. Work on the line will commence shortly.

At 10 p. m. on the 11th inst. a Japanese gendarme, in a state of intoxication, entered the Korean guard house at the South Gate. Drawing his sword he made playful passes at the occupants, wounding one soldier. A Korean policeman coming to put a stop to the row received a nasty cut on the arm. The Japanese, after this, turned and ran in the direction of Chinkokai.

The Korea Daily News.

VOL. I, WEDNESDAY, SEPTEMBER 14, 1904. No. 51

HONGKONG & SHANGHAI BANKING CORPORATION.

Paid-up Capital..... ....$10,000,000
Reserve Fund:—Sterling Reserve... 10,000,000
Silver Reserve..... 6,500,000
26,500,000
Reserve Liability of Proprietors... 10,000,000

HEAD OFFICE, HONGKONG.

London Bankers, London and County Banking Company Limited.

Branches and Agencies,

London.		
Amoy,	Hankow	Penang,
Bangkok,	Hiogo,	Rangoon,
Batavia,	Iloilo,	Saigon,
Bombay,	Lyons,	San Francisco,
Calcutta,	Manila,	Singapore,
Colombo,	Nagasaki,	Sourabaya,
Foochow,	New York,	Tientsin,
Hamburg,	Peking,	Yokohama,

Credits granted on approved Securities, and every description of Banking and Exchange business transacted.

Drafts granted on London and the chief Commercial places in Europe, India, Australia, America, China and Japan.

HOLME RINGER & Co., AGENTS, CHEMULPO.

ON CHEONG & CO., SEOUL.

GENERAL STORE KEEPERS.
Imported provisions, Cooking Utensils Crockery, etc.
FRESH BREAD DAILY.

MITSU BISHI DOCKYARD & ENGINE WORKS,

NAGASAKI.

CODE WORD, "DOCK."

A. 1, A. B. C., and Engineering Codes used.

DOCK No. 1 (at Tategami).

Extreme Length..............523 feet
Length on blocks .... 513 ,,
Width of Entrance on Top......89 ,,
,, ,, Bottom....77 ,,
Water on Blocks at Spring Tide 26½ ,,

DOCK No. 2 (Mukaijima).

Extreme Length..............371 feet
Length on Blocks.............360 ,,
Width of Entrance on Top......66 ,,
,, ,, Bottom 53 ,,
Water on Blocks at Spring Tide 22 ,,

PATENT SLIP (at Kosuge).

Can take vessels up to 1,000 tons gross.

THE WORKS are well equipped with the LATEST IMPROVEMENTS, and can execute any kind of work in SHIPBUILDING and MARINE ENGINEERING, as well as in REPAIRING of SHIPS.

The COMPANY'S new powerful steamer OURA-MARU (712 tons, 700 I.H.P.), specially built for SALVAGE PURPOSES, and equipped with necessary gear, is always READY at SHORT NOTICE.

CHARTERED BANK OF INDIA AUSTRALIA & CHINA.

INCORPORATED BY ROYAL CHARTER 1853

HEAD OFFICES:—LONDON.

Paid-up Capital £800,000
Reserve Liability of Share-holders 800,000
Reserve Fund 800,000

Drafts granted upon all the principal places in the world and every description of Exchange and banking business transacted.

E. MEYER & Co., Agents, Chemulpo.

E. MEYER & CO.

Chemulpo.

SOLE AGENTS IN KOREA FOR:
A. T. Morse, Sons & Co's "Fresco" Distemper

In all colours ready for use on walls, Ceilings etc.

and

AVENARIUS CARBOLINEUM

A wood-preserving and antiseptic oil preparation

Against decay, dry-rot, fungus and wood-destroying insects.

A large supply always in Stock. Prices upon application.

E. MEYER & Co., Chemulpo.

LAW UNION & CROWN INS. CO.

Fire risks accepted at Current rates, on go downs, merchandise, dwellings, and other property, subject to usual conditions.

HOLME RINGER & Co., Agents, Chemulpo

THE METHODIST PUBLISHING HOUSE,

Little West Gate, Seoul.

JOB PRINTING, TYPEWRITER PAPER
CARBON PAPER, VISITING CARDS
STATIONERY, BOOK BINDING
BOOK PUBLISHERS
AMERICAN SCHOOL BOOKS
SPENCERIAN COPY BOOKS
PEN CARBON LETTER AND BILL BOOKS

S. A. BECK, Manager.

DAI-ICHI GINKO.

LIMITED.
(Formerly the First National Bank)

ESTABLISHED 1873

INCORPORATED UNDER PRESENT LAW 1896

Capital - - - - - - - - - Yen 5,000,000
Reserve Fund - - - - - 1,500,000

HEAD OFFICE:—TOKIO.

President: Baron SHIBUSAWA.

BRANCHES AND CORRESPONDENTS
In the Principal Cities and Towns of Japan.

Interest Allowed on
Fixed deposits 1 year - - - 6½ per cent
" " 6 months - - - 6 per cent

Special current accounts 1½ sen daily per Y 100
General " " 1 " " " 100

M. TANAKA, Manager, Chemulpo

HOLME RINGER & Co.

Chemulpo.

General Merchants and Government Contractors.

Agents for the leading Banks SteamshipCompanies and Insurance Companies

Importers of Merchandise of every description.

KAMEYA & CO.

GENERAL STOREKEEPERS
Chinkokai - - Seoul
(*Established 1895. Tokyo*)

Confectionery, Hams, Canned Goods, Cutlery, Hirano & Tansan Water, Provisions, Gents, Furnishing goods, Toilet Articles, Travelling Bags, Tobacco, Cigars & Cigarettes Kitchen Utensils. Coffee, Biscuits.

Fresh Goods always kept in Stock.
Prices Moderate
Please come and inspect our goods.

NIPPON YUSEN KAISHA.

JAPANESE MAIL STEAMSHIP CO.

DEA MAIL CONTRACT WITH THE IMPERIAL JAPANESE GOVERNMENT.

European Line

Regular Fortnightly Service between Yokohama Kobe, Moji, Shanghai, Hongkong, Singapore, Penang Colombo, Port Said, Marseilles, London and Antwerp

American Line

Regular Fortnightly Service between Hongkong and Seattle, calling at Shanghai, Moji, Kobe, Yokohama and Victoria, B. C.

Australian Line

Regular weekly Service betwen Japan Ports and Australia, calling at Hongkong and Manila.
(Above Three Lines Suspended until further notice).

Shanghai Line

Weekly Service between Shanghai and Japan Ports

Korea Line

Service Kobe, Moji, Nagasaki, Fusan, Chemulpo, Chioo, Taiku.
S. S. Bahelsberg, 2181 tons.
Service Kobe, Moji, Fusan, Chemulpo, Chinnampo
S. S ARGO. S. S. Ohio.

BORDEN'S CONDENSED MILK CO.

New York, U. S. A.

ALWAYS IN STOCK
Eagle Brand Condensed Milk.
Gold Seal Condensed Milk.
Peerless (Family) Evaporated Cream.
Borden's Malted Milk.

E. MEYER & CO.
Chemulpo, Korea,
Sole Agents

ROYAL INSURANCE COMPANY,
Funds exceed £10,000,000
FIRE
AT CURRENT RATES.
LIFE
REDUCED PREMIUM.
HOLME RINGER & Co., Agents, Chemulpo.

HOTEL DU PALAIS

SEOUL.

The only first class Hotel in Seoul. Situated in the centre of the city opposite the palace.

Cuisine under the supervision of an experienced French Chef.

Well ventilated and furnished throughout.

TARIFF UPON APPLICATION

MARTIN
and Mangaer.

大韓每日申報
대한ᄆᆡ일신보

(뎨오십이호) (목요일) 쳔구빅사년구월십오일

본사고

이신보는영어와한어로셔계ᄆᆡ일츌판ᄒᆞᆸ

신문가

ᄒᆞᆫ장 엽두돈오푼

일삭됴엽두량닷돈 맛돈으로밧숩

광고료는

긔한의장단과ᄌᆞ힝의다쇼로죵감ᄒᆞ되렴가로밧을터이오며오릭지아녀대한사람마다다이신문을보실터이니광고내시기를원ᄒᆞ시는이들은우리신문샤에와셔면약ᄒᆞ심을희망ᄒᆞᆸ

○발힝소 박동대한ᄆᆡ일신보샤법어학교압헤젼영국인셜필림집자리오

샤쟝 영국인 (비셜)

사고

○우리대한ᄆᆡ일신보의목뎍은대한의안녕질셔에관한모든뎨목에뎌ᄒᆞ야는공평한변론을쥬쟝홈이라우리동신원의담보는신문보시는쳠군ᄌᆞ의게ᄒᆞᆼ상보도ᄒᆞ리며편지를긔셔ᄒᆞ여주시는이는셩명과반디를젹어붓치시기를희망ᄒᆞ오니이거슬신문샹에긔지ᄒᆞ라는거시아니오다만극히신용ᄒᆞ는증거를삼고쟈홈이라긔쟈는아모긔셔던지긔지홈을되각ᄒᆞ는권리를가졋스나되각ᄒᆞ는리유를말ᄒᆞᆯ터이오며공즁평화를문란케ᄒᆞ는듯ᄒᆞᆫ긔셔는의례히밧지안켓솝나이다

사고

○본샤에셔는신문갑슨ᄆᆡ월에션급으로밧ᄉᆞ오며본신문은우체로붓쳐ᄂᆞᆫ고로본샤에셔는다른신문샤처름금액을거두러ᄃᆞᆫ니지안ᄉᆞ오니우리신문을ᄉᆞ랑ᄒᆞ야구람ᄒᆞ시는쳠군ᄌᆞ는량력ᄆᆡ월죵에릭월됴션금과거쥬셩명통호수를ᄌᆞ세히젹어셔박동본샤로보내시기를바라오며월회일ᄂᆡ로션금을아양력금니보내셔ᄂᆞᆫ곳에는릭월일일부터신문을아니보낼터이오니죠량ᄒᆞ옵소셔

●본샤에셔아직긔계를쟝만치못ᄒᆞᆫ와다른ᄃᆡ셔박여오는고로ᄆᆡ양월요일에는츌판이대단히늣게되는ᄯᆞᆺ스로문젼이ᄆᆡ우늣게되오니우리신문을구람ᄒᆞ시는쳠군ᄌᆞ는용셔ᄒᆞ여쥬심을희망ᄒᆞᆸ나이다

본샤광고

본샤에셔본신문뎨ᄉᆞ호와뎨십일호와뎨이십오호를소용ᄒᆞᆯ때가잇셔이에광고ᄒᆞ오니누구시던지이샹삼호즁에본샤로가져오시면ᄆᆡ쟝에빅젼두푼식드리리다

론셜

요양후샤계획

○일젼우리신문에일본에요양함낙ᄒᆞᆫ거시쟝ᄎᆞ려슌을운동ᄒᆞ야포획ᄒᆞᆯ근본이라ᄒᆞ고긔왕계지ᄒᆞ엿더니이제요양이파연일본수즁에드러순즉ᄒᆞᆫ갓려슌공격ᄒᆞᆫ일만남엇는지라아라사이졍령굴복ᄒᆞ야일본에승쳡ᄒᆞᆫ기는이무가론인즁동경됴일신문에등지ᄒᆞᆫ바를본즉방금아라사구완병이봉쳔과및합이빈으로좃차나온다ᄒᆞᆫ즉우리나라쟝관들도요양졈령ᄒᆞᆷ과갓치아모죠록신속히지차운동ᄒᆞᆯ계칙을니여야ᄒᆞ겟다고ᄒᆞᆫ다더라

이왕싸홈을미루어싱각ᄒᆞᆯ진ᄃᆡ지차츌젼에도필경아라사이어육이되여봉쳔과합이빈으로붓터북으로서빅리아길을향ᄒᆞ야철도련속ᄒᆞᆫᄃᆡ로퇴ᄒᆞ여갈듯ᄒᆞᆫᄃᆡ봉쳔길이합이빈으로련속ᄒᆞ엿슨즉이근쳐에셔다시일본군ᄉᆞ로더부러싸홈이될듯ᄒᆞ나셜혹된다ᄒᆞ드릭도금츄명츈간에나될듯ᄒᆞ며

필경일본쟝관의지차동병은원산으로붓터발ᄒᆞ야히삼위로행군ᄒᆞᆯ듯ᄒᆞᆫ거시방금아병이합홍에유린ᄒᆞ야원산북편항구결빙되기를기다려한국으로차차드러오려ᄒᆞᆷ은다자셔히아는바인즉원산으로화륙ᄒᆞᆫ일병들로ᄒᆞ여곰두가지로ᄒᆞᆯ일이잇스니첫지는금년겨울에아병의젼진ᄒᆞ라ᄒᆞᆷ도막아야ᄒᆞᆯ터이오둘지는히삼위근방으로모다펴져명츈에합이빈으로통신ᄒᆞ야공격ᄒᆞ라는바를미리방어ᄒᆞ여야ᄒᆞᆯ터인즉엇지던지운동은오릭쳔연ᄒᆞᆯ듯ᄒᆞ며ᄯᅩ여러만명되는일본군사ㅣ젼국에퍼질지경이면웅당갑오년일청교젼되여쓸때와흡사ᄒᆞᆯ지라

그러ᄒᆞ나아병이북방으로련ᄒᆞ야나와결진ᄒᆞ게되면그세에는대단히어려울거시일본군사가더옥멀드릭도아병의잇는곳셔지ᄯᅩ차갈터이니이지경ᄭᆞ지이르게되면그곳빅셩들도모도혼합ᄒᆞ야싸홀터인즉군량등물수운ᄒᆞ기도심히혼잡ᄒᆞ야극난ᄒᆞᆯ듯ᄒᆞ도다

우리가국의지사를이러케좌론ᄒᆞ는거슨오활ᄒᆞᆫ싱각인듯ᄒᆞ되엇지던지지차츌젼은요양에쳐음함낙ᄒᆞᆫ니버텀미오지리ᄒᆞᆯ듯ᄒᆞ며

요양함낙은처음으로셩공ᄒᆞ야세계에칭찬을듯되우리싱각에는일본셔과연소원ᄃᆡ로모다되엿는지조셔히알슈업스며려슌에잇는군사들은모다잡아너어의심업시죽인것ᄭᅳᆺ트되이역운동ᄒᆞ라면용이치아니ᄒᆞᆫ일인거시혹목대쟝이흑구쟝군의퇴거ᄒᆞᆫ길을쉰느라고손히가만아스되일심으로군사를지촉ᄒᆞ야날니게흑구쟝군을에워싸고아병의우ᄃᆡ를공격ᄒᆞ야후ᄃᆡ병졸ᄭᆞ지무유여지ᄒᆞ게모라셩공ᄒᆞ엿스나

우리싱각에는이러케된일은과연쳔만의외이되쟝ᄎᆞ서빅리아철로로아병나올거슬엇지ᄒᆞᆯ는지모를지라

젼후결말이이번셔빅리아철도로아병운츌ᄒᆞ는ᄃᆡ달엿슬듯ᄒᆞᆫ즉일본셔도응당렬심으로운동ᄒᆞ야긔여히셩공ᄒᆞᆯ듯ᄒᆞ며

ᄯᅩ만일히삼위에잇는아라사함ᄃᆡ와일본히군으로더부러한국지방에셔만싸후지아니ᄒᆞᆯ지경이면아병돌은졈령일병의게ᄲᅦ앗긴터를도로니여몰지못ᄒᆞᆯ듯ᄒᆞ되일본셔동병ᄒᆞ기젼에만쥬에잇는군ᄉᆞ를차차젼진ᄒᆞ게ᄒᆞᆯ진ᄃᆡ쟝ᄎᆞ일이엇지될ᄂᆞᆫ지확실이예론ᄒᆞᆯ수업는지라

그런고로이사건에ᄃᆡᄒᆞ야동경신문에셜명ᄒᆞᆫ거시용혹무피인거시이왕일로만볼진ᄃᆡ아라사에셔룽히긔묘ᄒᆞᆫ병법으로다시회복ᄒᆞᆯ는지알수업스되만일군병을중쳠ᄒᆞ야크게싸와셩공ᄒᆞ랴ᄒᆞᄂᆞᆫ마음이잇게되면필경일쟝풍진이ᄯᅩ다시이러날듯ᄒᆞ도다

관보

뎨이쳔구빅삼십호

광무팔년구월십삼일

○

○셔임급ᄉᆞ령

○승셔쥬입관ᄉᆞ등 농샹공부기ᄉᆞ 리유진

구월팔일

○임탁지부협관셔칙임관삼등 탁지부ᄉᆞ계국쟝 류졍슈

○승셔쥬임관삼등 표훈원졔쟝국쟝 졍동식

○의원면본관 즁츄원의관 호영헌 구연명 탁지부참셔관 김병협

○임즁츄원의관셔쥬임관륙등 군부경리국뎨일고원 홍 건 함경남도관찰부총순 빅락셩

○임탁지참셔관셔쥬임관륙등 즁학교쟝 민영오

○임니부디방국쟝셔쥬임관삼등 학부편집국쟝 리규환

○히셔리륙군법원쟝ᄉᆞ무 륙군법원리ᄉᆞ륙군참령 신재영

이샹구월구일

○히황히도금광감리 졍삼품 죠관윤

○명황히도금광감리 종이품 류지혁

○명니쟝원봉세위원 구품 박지익

○명의셩군금광위원 김병두

○임텰도원쥬ᄉᆞ셔관임관륙등 고효원

○승셔관임관ᄉᆞ등 종졍원쥬ᄉᆞ 김ᄉᆞ즁

○승셔관임관오등 영션ᄉᆞ쥬ᄉᆞ 박ᄐᆡ슈

○의원면본관 츙청남도관찰부쥬ᄉᆞ 박지화

○임츙청남도관찰부주ᄉᆞ셔관임관륙등 리긔필

○히츙청남도죵두ᄉᆞ무위원 홍현샹

○히젼라남도죵두ᄉᆞ무위원 김달식

○히강원도죵두ᄉᆞ무위원 송영진

○명츙청남도죵두ᄉᆞ무위원 젼위원 홍현샹

○명강원도죵두ᄉᆞ무위원 박

AMERICAN KOREAN ELECTRIC COMPANY.
Light and Power.
Main Office: Electric Building, Chong No.

RAILWAY DEPARTMENT.

OPERATING CARS BETWEEN EAST AND WEST GATE, EVERY TEN MINUTES:—
First Car leaves East Gate at 6:30 A. M. First Car leaves West Gate at 6:55 A. M.
Last Car " East Gate at 10:40 P. M. Last " " West Gate at 11:00 P. M.

OPERATING CARS BETWEEN EAST GATE AND IMPERIAL TOMB TERMINUS, EVERY TWENTY MINUTES:—

CONNECTING WITH EVERY ALTERNATE CAR ARRIVING AT EAST GATE FROM CHONG NO.
First Car leaves East Gate for Tomb at 6:50 A. M.
" " " Tomb for East Gate at 7:10 A. M.
Last " " East Gate for Tomb at 9:50 P. M.
" " " Tomb for East Gate at 10:10 P. M.

OPERATING CARS BETWEEN CHONG NO AND YUNG SAN (RIVER) EVERY TWELVE MINUTES:—
First Car leaves Chong No for South Gate at 6:48 A. M.
" " " Chong No for Yung San at 7:24 A. M.
" " " South Gate for Chong No at 6:56 A. M.
" " " Yung San for Chong No at 7:57 A. M.
Last " " South Gate for Chong No 11:00 P. M.
" " " Yung San for Chong No at 10:11 P. M.

SPECIAL PRIVATE CARS FURNISHED TO SUIT CONVENIENCE OF PATRONS. PRICES ON APPLICATION AT HEAD OFFICE.

LIGHTING DEPARTMENT.

Where less than 250 candle power of light is used, the rate per month will be. Per 16 candle power incandescent lamp. All night.—Yen 2.50.
Per 32 candle power incandescent lamp:—All night:—Yen 4.00. Per 50 candle power incandescent lamp:—All night:—Yen 6.00.
" 150 " " " " — " " 10.00. " 1200 " " enclosed arc " " " " 20.00.

Where more than 250 candle power of light is used, a Meter will be installed, if requested:—Rent of Meter Yen 2.00 per month. Rate of charges by meter reading:—Two Sen per Ampere per hour. (Approximately this is equal to about One Sen per 16 c. p. lamp per hour) Minimum monthly charge where meter is installed, Yen 20.00 per month, which includes rental of meter.

Estimates for installing lights furnished on application. An assortment of chandeliers always on hand.

AMUSEMENT DEPARTMENT.

ANIMATED PICTURES AT EAST GATE.
Every evening - - Except Sunday.
From 8 to 10 P. M.

10 Cents:—Gen. Admission:—10 Cents. Seats in First Class Section. 15 Cents Extra.

Change of program each week. Pictures from Foreign Lands. Pictures of Local Scenes:—Amusing and Instructive.

An entertaining evening for a reasonable price.
MERRY-GO-ROUND:—At East Gate.
From 10:00 A. M. till 11:00 P. M.

5 Cents a Ride.

Take your Exercise on The Galloping Horses.

Comfortable seats in the Chariots.

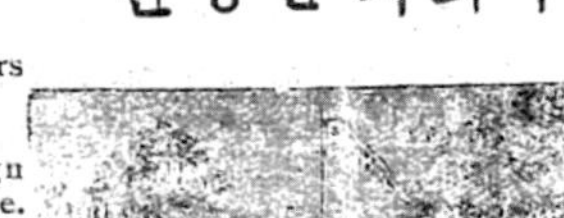

미국 뎐긔회사 고블안 보사때 고빅
도ᄒᆞ옵나이다
샹활동사진관ᄋᆞᆫ 소의목마운동장량쳐로엳
여러면차가온장안으로롱힝ᄒᆞ여ᄃᆞᆫ니여이
습
ᄯᅩ이긔계에ᄀᆞᆺ처노힌편ᄒᆞ고됴흔마차도잇
습
코미우편ᄒᆞ고ᄯᅩ조미잇ᄂᆞᆫ됴흔운동이되겟
어됴흔모형ᄒᆞᆫ달나아ᄂᆞᆫ물을ᄐᆞ고위티치안
더가ᄂᆞᆫ훈번ᄐᆞᄂᆞᆫ데오젼식이오
미일샹오열시브터하오열ᄒᆞᆫ시ᄭᆞ지ᄒᆞ옵고
목마운동장은동대문안에잇습고
가되겟습
쳡군조의게갑도싸고저녁에됴흔쇼일거리
잇고구경ᄒᆞᆯ만ᄒᆞᆫ거시오니
셔양사진과대한과온동양사진인네대조미
ᄂᆞᆫ더
젼이옵고미쥬일에사진을밧것스로다밧고
고젼랑디금은하등에십젼이오샹등에이십
일외에ᄂᆞᆫ미야에여덟시브터열시ᄭᆞ지ᄒᆞ옵
활동사진젼람소ᄂᆞᆫ동대문안에잇습고일요
회탁부

All Cars Run Direct to the Animated Pictures and Merry-Go-Round.

청원 김달식

○임룡군보병참위 박희운 림건희 리희균 리티진

○임함경남도관찰부총슌서판임관이등 경긔관찰부총슌 오진영

○임경긔관찰부총슌서판임관륙등 경위원총슌 전긔완

이상구월십일

○명경효뎐졔주서칙임관삼등 졍비풍 조종필

○명시종원경서칙임관삼등 궁ᄂᆡ부특진관 리진하

○의원면경임ᄐᆡ의원소경 비서원승 서공순

○의원면경임장례원장례 비서원승 김교덕

○의원면본관 규장각직각 서상훈

○경임장례원장례 비서원승 서공순

○경ᄐᆡ의원소경 비서원승 신성균

○임규장각직각서판임관ᄉᆞ등 시강원시독관 리병소

○임시강원시독관서판임관ᄉᆞ등 룡풍 서상훈

○임중추원의관서칙임관삼등 탁지졍관 홍순찬 종이품 엄셰호

이상구월십일일

○삼쥬일감봉 황ᄒᆡ도지편소관소전서리신쳔군슈 리용필

구월칠일

○임의정부참정서칙임관일등 궁ᄂᆡ부대신 민병석

○명림시서리궁ᄂᆡ부대신ᄉᆞ무 중추원부의장 리용티

이상구월십일일

궁뎡록ᄉᆞ

○시종원경 민영규 수직소 비지ᄂᆡ에 소청ᄃᆡ로의시ᄒᆞ노라

○궁ᄂᆡ부특진관 리근택 수직소 비지ᄂᆡ에 향리 말을 다시 번제홀 거시아니니 ᄉᆞ양말고 힝공ᄒᆞ라

○ᄂᆡ장원경 홍지졍 수직소 비지ᄂᆡ에 소청ᄃᆡ로의시ᄒᆞ노라

이상구월십일일

○경효뎐제조 리헌영 수직소 비지ᄂᆡ에 ᄉᆞ양ᄒᆞᆫ중 제주지임만 의시ᄒᆞ노라

○의정부참정 윤용션 수직소 비지ᄂᆡ에 ᄉᆞ양ᄒᆞᆫ중 참정지임만 의시ᄒᆞ노라

구월십일일

○조칙 궁ᄂᆡ부대신 민병석으로 위의정부참정ᄒᆞ라

구월십이일

잡보

○창평격경 창평군슈 손용현씨가 ᄂᆡ부에 보고ᄒᆞ엿스되 음력칠월이십일일에 비도 오십여명이 각지총검ᄒᆞ고 본읍에 리도ᄒᆞ야 관속을 란타ᄒᆞ고 관문에 돌입ᄒᆞ거놀 본군슈가 괴슈들 초엄ᄒᆞ야 효유ᄒᆞ되 손ᄒᆞ엿더니 창악동거ᄒᆞᄂᆞᆫ 젼군슈 김규형의 집에 돌입ᄒᆞ야 가옥을 란파ᄒᆞ고 젼지를 창탈ᄒᆞ야 갓다ᄒᆞ엿더라

○죽실구황 진안군슈 장영국씨가 ᄂᆡ부로 보고ᄒᆞ되 본군이 졀협에 잇서 산빗탈롤 겸에 농ᄉᆞᄂᆞᆫ 마포와 담비ᄲᅮᆫ이오 젼역은 몽긔와 ᄊᆡ리샹ᄌᆞ 제조ᄒᆞᄂᆞᆫ 것ᄲᅮᆫ인고로 촌가에 저축ᄒᆞᄂᆞᆫ 곡식이 업서서 빅셩이 다 나무열매와 술찌겁을 먹습더니 남면과 동일면 두면장의 보고를 거ᄒᆞᆫ즉 젼각산파 더대산에 더가 열매가 열니고로 빅도ᄒᆞ야 주린자ᄋᆞ비부고 병든자죽소복ᄒᆞ야 빈민이 셔령ᄒᆞ엿다ᄒᆞ엿기로 심히 긔이ᄒᆞ야 이젼을 보ᄂᆡ여 져잔ᄒᆞᆫ즉 희랑면에셔 죽실ᄊᆞᆫ거시 샹빗여셔이오 장슈남원 잉ᄉᆞᆯ빗셩이 닷도와 ᄊᆞᆫ거시 쳔셕이ᄂᆞ되엿다ᄒᆞ고 죽실ᄒᆞᆫ궤를 진봉ᄒᆞ야 샹송ᄒᆞ엿다더라

경보일속

○경무ᄉᆞ원우샹씨ᄂᆞᆫ 이간우ᄒᆞᆫ 벼를 당ᄒᆞ야 등임ᄒᆞ음신 은총을 입엇ᄉᆞ니 응당 보답ᄒᆞᆯ 마음이 타인보다 비젼ᄒᆞ겟거놀 일젼에 각순검이 헌신ᄒᆞᆯᄯᅢ에 경찰상젼불젼은 권면치아니ᄒᆞ고 순검을 ᄃᆡᄒᆞ야 연셜ᄒᆞ야왈 너희등이 나를 위ᄒᆞ야 극력보호ᄒᆞ여야 너희등 신샹이 편ᄒᆞ리라ᄒᆞ니 듯ᄂᆞᆫ자가 무비됴소ᄒᆞ엿다ᄒᆞ고

○일젼 덕국공ᄉᆞ연회시에 진작보고 취아니ᄒᆞᆷ으로 엄졀ᄒᆞᆫ 음신쳐분이 계시무로 황송망조ᄒᆞ야 만단운동으로 간신면최ᄒᆞ엿다ᄒᆞ고

○각서로 ᄒᆞᆫ령ᄒᆞ야 무복류를 잇ᄂᆞᆫᄃᆡ로 잡으라ᄒᆞᆷ으로 동서ᄇᆞᆼ니 ᄅᆡ 유명ᄒᆞᆫ 무녀의 집에셔 신당제구를 슈탐ᄒᆞ야 드렷더니 힝무녀의 경찰이 신문과장의게 리도ᄒᆞᆫ고로 경무ᄉᆞ가 그소ᄎᆡᆨ순금의게 엄분부ᄒᆞ야왈 신당제구슈일시에 은그릇 먹ᄭᅥᆺ과 은시저 몃벌이고중에 드렷시니 ᄎᆔ롤 진ᄋᆞᆯᄒᆞ샹ᄒᆞ야 무녀의게 환급ᄒᆞ고 리보ᄒᆞ라ᄒᆞ엿다ᄒᆞ고

○일젼에 서소문밧 면당국에 도적오명이 광명에 돌입ᄒᆞ야 젼오쳔량을 탈취ᄒᆞ여 ᄀᆞᆫ지슬 경찰을 불젼ᄒᆞᆷ이라ᄒᆞ야 히방니순검을 일병파면ᄒᆞ엿고

○경무ᄉᆞ가 무복등을 엄검ᄒᆞ더니 오룡일은 이리에 신병으로 고등ᄒᆞ야 수젼도 못ᄒᆞᄂᆞᆫᄃᆡ ᄒᆞ신벌이 아니나 고들ᄒᆞᆫ다더라

○리씨젼과 근일에 무격복술등 잡류를 엄검ᄒᆞᄂᆞᆫ고로 벗남북술리 유인씨ᄂᆞᆫ ᄒᆞᆫ번 산통을 흔드나즉 장신괘가 나온지라 가권을 거나리고 예쳔향며 도쳘귀ᄒᆞ엿다더라

○류학셩간쳡 학부에서 각부부원청에 훈조ᄒᆞ되 금번 일본류학셩 거젼에 상셜되야 모록홈이 반ᄋᆞ니 쳥티쳐 임관이 다시 졔에 가초등ᄒᆞ고 ᄃᆡ처가 편저ᄒᆞ고 년령은 십륙세이상으로 이십오세지지 각기 샹인식 거쳔ᄒᆞᆯ ᄉᆞ로 지외롤 봉승ᄒᆞ야 별반조회ᄒᆞ니 각쳐임관의계 신속히 포명ᄒᆞ야 음본월이십일ᄂᆡ로 거쳔인의 셩명을 록송ᄒᆞ되 거쳔인이 다 각기 관셰단ᄌᆞ롤 슈정ᄒᆞ야 송교ᄒᆞ라ᄒᆞ엿더라

○이도수안 본월십이일에 도착ᄒᆞᆫ 황ᄒᆡ관찰ᄉᆞ의 뎐보에 ᄒᆞ엿ᄉᆞ되 수안군보를 거ᄒᆞᆫ즉 광안도 동학팔빅여명이 히군에 리도ᄒᆞ엿ᄂᆞᆫᄃᆡ 병괴ᄂᆞᆫ 후퇴치안코 작폐ᄂᆞᆫ 엄교쟝ᄎᆞ 황셩으로 향ᄒᆞᆫ다ᄒᆞ고 뒤에 계속ᄒᆞᄂᆞᆫ자가 ᄉᆞ오만명이라ᄒᆞᆫ다ᄒᆞ엿더라

○량도관찰 경북관찰ᄉᆞᄂᆞᆫ 젼참관 쟝승원씨가 피임ᄒᆞ고 함북관찰ᄉᆞᄂᆞᆫ 젼관 윤정긔틱씨가 피임ᄒᆞ엿더라

○직산슈치폐 직산군슈 류병호씨가 금졍군의계 피타ᄒᆞᆫ ᄉᆞ논 이왕 본보에 게지ᄒᆞ엿거니와 직작일에 치폐ᄒᆞ엿다더라

○ᄂᆡ쟝경서리 부쟝 윤웅렬씨ᄂᆞᆫ ᄂᆡ쟝원경서리를 히임ᄒᆞ고 감독 김영진씨가 원경서리를 ᄒᆞ엿더라

○외구시찰 일본에 파견ᄒᆞᆫ 류학셩 감셔된다ᄂᆞᆫ 일ᄉᆞᄂᆞᆫ 별항에 긔ᄌᆡᄒᆞ엿더니 개문ᄒᆞᆫ즉 학부참서관 리죵티씨가 발론ᄒᆞ야왈 일외시취ᄒᆞ엿든 학도롤 무교히 문시ᄒᆞ고 다시 팔셰보를 밧아셔 디변만 보아 퇴취ᄒᆞᄂᆞᆫ거시 외국ᄉᆞᄃᆡ 단슈치가 된다ᄒᆞ고 루루히 셜명ᄒᆞ엿더니 ᄂᆡ시 고졍이씨와 레식원과장 김규진씨가 이ᄉᆞ의롤 단폐에 샹주ᄒᆞ야 갱셜치말고 임의 시취ᄒᆞᆫ 인원으로 시힝ᄒᆞ라신 쳐분이 ᄂᆞ리엿다더라

○감리신임 의주기시장과 룡쳔항구가 일젼회의에 셜시되ᄂᆞᆫ지라 외부주ᄉᆞ 윤용구씨ᄂᆞᆫ 룡쳔감리롤 피임ᄒᆞ고 경흥감리 리민부씨ᄂᆞᆫ 의주감리롤 젼임ᄒᆞ고 경흥감리ᄂᆞᆫ 권지호씨가 피임ᄒᆞ엿더라

○회의안건 작일하오이시에 정부에서 군슈와 감리와 각주임관 셔임ᄒᆞ고 레직ᄒᆞ기롤 의론ᄒᆞ야 결뎡ᄒᆞ엿다더라

○덕ᄉᆞᄃᆡ리 덕국공ᄉᆞ 사이젼씨가 외부로 조회ᄒᆞ되 본공ᄉᆞ가 병일에 발졍ᄒᆞ야 이주일후에 회환ᄒᆞ게기로 교셥ᄉᆞ무롤 부령ᄉᆞ 나이로 쟝간ᄃᆡ리케ᄒᆞ니 조량ᄒᆞ라ᄒᆞ엿더라

○조쳥인임 일공ᄉᆞ가 외부로 공함ᄒᆞ기롤 평양주차일본부령ᄉᆞ 신쟝의 보고롤 거ᄒᆞᆫ즉 평양군슈 쾌현주가 일본군부진홀ᄯᅢ에 효로가 잇더니 쳥금 히군민등이 쾅리원에 무소ᄒᆞᆫ지라 쥬쳔하야 히군슈롤 인임케ᄒᆞ라ᄒᆞ엿기로 참교하니 히군슈롤 평례치말기롤 바란다ᄒᆞ엿더라

○박쟝ᄃᆡ형 주일공관참서관 현보운씨ᄃᆡ에 박쟝션씨가 피임ᄒᆞᆫ다더라

○쿠하잉지계 동문외에 ᄉᆞᆯ거ᄒᆞᄂᆞᆫ 한양ᄒᆞ던 젼참쟝 심상훈씨가 지작야에 잉셩ᄒᆞ엿ᄂᆞᆫᄃᆡ ᄌᆞ시샹소ᄒᆞ고 긔여히 향례로 하왕ᄒᆞ라ᄒᆞᆫ다더라

○참정졀문 참정 신긔션씨가 일젼회로로 움함ᄒᆞ기롤 귀회에서 제출ᄒᆞᆫ 수됴건중에 ᄌᆞ주목립ᄒᆞᆫ다ᄂᆞᆫ 귀절이 업스니 그곡절을 시명ᄒᆞ라고 졀문ᄒᆞ엿다더라

○군슈주본 작쟉에 ᄂᆡ부대신 조병필씨가 군슈가신여과를 주본ᄒᆞ엿다더라

뎐보

구월십이일동경발

대본영발표 ᄃᆡ공ᄉᆞ관착뎐

○료양젼투뎍졍 만쥬군총ᄉᆞ령관보고에 왈 포로와 샛그다ᄅᆞᆫ 이의 발을 거ᄒᆞᆫ즉 료양셔젼투홀 당시에 뎍졍이 좌와굿ᄒᆞ니

료양부근에 모히엿던 뎍의 병력은 뎨이와 뎨ᄉᆞ와 뎨오와 뎨칠과 뎨십칠의 각군단과 밋 기타군단의 약간ᄒᆞᆫ 부ᄃᆡ오 그 버치ᄂᆞᆫ 료양의 셔북방면에 ᄒᆞᆫ군단과 남방면에 ᄒᆞᆫ군단이오 그 ᄇᆡ방면에 ᄒᆞᆫ군단과 우리 우익군을 ᄃᆡᄒᆞᆫ ᄒᆞᆫ군단과 료양셔북방ᄃᆡ조하연안에 ᄒᆞᆫ군단인듯ᄒᆞ며

로군의 손히ᄂᆞᆫ 안산졈에서 렬거ᄒᆞᆫ 이ᄅᆡ로 료양함락ᄒᆞ기ᄭᆞ지 총계가 이만오쳔명에 나ᄅᆞ거시 확실ᄒᆞ고 ᄯᅩ 시쾌쳥코쟝군은 구월삼일에 료양동방의 젼투에서 젼ᄉᆞᄒᆞ엿다ᄒᆞ며

덕군은 료양젼투이젼으로브터 동디졍거쟝에 다수ᄒᆞᆫ 렬거를 준비ᄒᆞ야 젼셰의 불리ᄒᆞᆷ을 보고 샹일에셔 버지ᄉᆞ의간을 련속ᄒᆞ야 ᄉᆞ샹ᄒᆞᆫ자와 밋 병과외병ᄒᆞ야 군슈품을 환송ᄒᆞ다가 오히려 ᄂᆞᆷ은 군슈품은 샬니버린거시 만ᄒᆞ나 탄약과 거창과 총탄환과 ᄃᆡ포탄환등은 우리가 획득홈이 만ᄒᆞ고 ᄯᅩ 셤셤이란 탄약(함ᄉᆞᄒᆞᆫ 폭발약)을 약간 발견ᄒᆞ엿다ᄒᆞ엿더라

구월십삼일동경발 공ᄉᆞ관착

○셤셤탄환 만쥬군보고롤 거ᄒᆞᆫ즉 료양젼리품중에 유종셤셤탄환이 잇ᄂᆞᆫᄃᆡ 종이다 일쳥젼 벽구십일년닌것 셰시인로국리이홈총의 탄환과 흡수ᄒᆞ며 우리부샹ᄒᆞᆫ자중에 ᄒᆞ탄환을 맛ᄌᆞᆫ자ᄂᆞᆫ 만을 반ᄒᆞᆫ시서들이 ᄂᆞ다ᄒᆞ엿더라

TELEGRAMS.

(FROM JAPAN PAPERS.)

London, Sept. 7.

Reuter's correspondent at St. Petersburg wires that Captain Wirren, of the "Bayan," replaces Prince Uktomsky in command of Port Arthur Squadron.

[Prince Ukhtomsky has been ordered to be court-martialled for disobeying orders in not directing his squadron to proceed to Vladivostok after the dash from Port Arthur on the 10th August.]

London, Sept. 7.

Reuter's correspondent at Zanzibar wires that the British cruiser "Forte" has delivered the Tsar's orders to the commanders of the auxiliary cruisers "Petersburg" and "Smolensk" to desist from molesting neutral vessels, and in consequence the vessels have now left on the return trip to Europe.

London, Sept. 7th.

Reuter's correspondent at St. Petersburg states that it is announced there that the Russian forces have united at a point north of the Yentai Mines, a detachment being left at the latter place to cover the retreat.

It was rumoured, however, late in the evening that General Kuropatkin's rearguard had been almost annihilated and that the Russian main army is in imminent danger of being surrounded.

London, Sept. 8th.

The "Daily Telegraph's St. Petersburg correspondent states that a Russian war correspondent has telegraphed that the Japanese are within 25 miles of Mukden.

Preparations have been begun for the evacuation of the town and the press censorship office has been transferred to Harbin.

London, Sept. 8.

General Kuropatkin reports that the bulk of the Russian forces have reached Mukden, where a temporary halt will be made and where the defences will be manned. The Japanese to the westward, he says, now constitute the main menace, but the Russians are heading them off.

Reuter's correspondent wiring from Mukden under date of the 6th instant says that part of the Russian army was in constant danger during the previous day and night of being cut off, while the Japanese were continually shelling them from the hills.

SUNNY JIMS IN KOREA.

A marvellous discovery has been made at Chinan. The Magistrate reports that he was at his wit's end to find a way of feeding the populace, when suddenly a miracle happened. Some marvellous dispensation of providence taught the bamboo tree to grow nuts, possessed of a fat and meaty appearance and flavor: now the people grow fat and wear a happy smile.

Jim Dumps was a most unfriendly man, who lived his life on the Hermit plan—

Till one day NUTS were served to him since then they call him "NUTTY JIM. (Apologies to Force food.)

A KOREAN GIANT

This is the original story of our city reporter: On 11th inst. one tall man came in this city through the East gate, his stature is same hight as the Electric car and the loin sure to be 10 armful round even the Europeans were Surprised to look so big man, there were many hundred respectators around him for they never saw such tall and big man, as the people asked him where he comes from, he said he comes from Eastern hills, (Kang Won province) it is suspecious whether he is Chief of Tong Haks or leader of rightious army.

JAPAN'S PRICE FOR PEACE.

GEORGE LYNCH, IN THE 'INDEPENDENT NEW YORK.'

[The author of this article is one of the best-known English war correspondents and has also written valuable books of travel and exploration. He represented the London "Daily Chronicle" in the Spanish-American War, and the "Illustrated London News" in the Boer war—in which he had the experience of being captured by the Boers and held prisoner for sometime in Pretoria. Mr. Lynch was also an English newspaper correspondent in the Boxer campaign, and has travelled extensively over China and Japan.]

It may appear premature at this moment to speculate on what will be the end of the war; but I do not think it is premature to endeavor to direct public opinion towards the considerasion of a position which will arise within a few months. I firmly believe that the Japanese will drive the Russians back to Harbin. I beleive they will capture Port Arthur. I believe they will force the Russians completely to evacuate Manchuria. If they succeed in doing this, they will only then have succeeded in forcing Russia to do what she promised to do by the 8th of last October. That promise was given as solemnly and deliberately as it was possible. Its nonfulfillment, after a long period of prevarication, excuses, and subterfuges, was openly admitted. It was one of the most flagrant and gigantic breaches of a nation's faith and wrod that modern history can show. The promise was made not to Japan alone, but to all the Powers, yet that one little nation alone and single-handed will enforce its fulfillment.

If after a fight won with clean handed honour by sea and land, Japan succeeds in doing this, then I think that the other Powers owe her something for the accomplishment of such a gigantic task. It is due to the honour and sense of justice and right of the people of the entire civilized world to see her through.

As to what character the intervention should take or what degree of pressure should be brought to bear is not for me to suggest. Some people ridicule the idea of armed intervention; personally I think that the intervention should be armed—and armed to the teeth, in the cause of international good faith.

I have gone to no little trouble to collect the opinions of representative men as to the question of what terms would be acceptable to Japan and would satisfy the Japanese in case of their bringing the war to that point which I have had the hardiness to anticipate. I have interviewed not a few of the sense carriers of the nation, and found that there was quite a strange unanimity of opinion regarding what these terms should be. Politicians, military men, bankers, and others were among those with whom I discussed this matter. For obvious reasons, many of them requested me not to quote them, but among those who had no such objection were Count Okuma, Mr. Sonoda, of the Fifteenth National Bank, Count Soyeshima, one of the members of the great Mitsui firm, and others.

The first question I put to them was whether they desired to retain Port Arthur or not. It appeared to me that if they so wished they had every right to retain it. That it was wrongly taken from them after the Chinese War, I think will be admitted. It might now be considered as the legitimate spoils of two wars. There was, however, a remarkable unanimity of opinion that now they did not want to keep Port Arthur, and would be prepared to return it to China. There was a similar unanimity of opinion that they should get back the islands of the Saghalien Archipelago. In answer to the question whether, in consideration of Manchuria being returned by force of Japanese arms to China, they looked for some compensation from China on that score, the answer was in the negative from the majority of the people I spoke to, while some held that some railway and mining concession should be given to the Japanese, more particularly in that part of China immediately opposite Formosa. The fourth question that I put was, What will become of the Manchurian railway? There appeared to be a consensus of opinion that Japan would not be prepared to take up the financial burden of it, but that it might be run under a joint ownership of internationally supplied capital. On the subject of their naturally considerable divergence of opinion, as the cost of the war to Japan is as yet unknown, and this will, of course, depend on its duration as well as on many other things. Their main idea, however, appeared to be that if they succeeded in capturing Vladivostock they should hold it until an adequate indemnity was paid by Russia, and then return it to her, thus giving her a port on the Pacific. Among minor points, they suggested that Russia should give up the island of Kommandorski, with its valuable seal fishery, and grant to Japan fishing rights along the northern coast.

If the Japanese continue to be successful, and if they further succeed to the point I have indicated, the terms that they look to making appear to me by no means unreasonable. The Powers owe a debt of reparation to Japan for making her give up Port Arthur, and the blood of every Japanese that will be spilt upon its slopes lies at their doors. The time for atonement will then have come. It will be put to the conscience of the civilized Powers whether that atonement shall be made, and whether Russia shall be compelled by whatever force or pressure is necessary to accept these terms as the price of peace.

The Korea Daily News.

To be published daily except Sundays.

Rate of Subscription:—

Per Year,	Yen 25.
Per Quarter,	Yen 7.
Per Month	Yen 2.50

Postage in Korea not charged extra.
Postage abroad charged extra.

Advertisements, 50 sen per day for 1 inch or less. 5 yen per month per inch. 50 yen per year per inch.

All communications to E. T. BETHELL, Editor and Publisher. Pak-tong, Seoul.

THE NEW JAPAN-KOREA AGREEMENT.

We learn from the "Kobe Chronicle" that according to a Tokyo dispatch, Mr. Oishi, a leader of the Progressists, is thoroughly disappointed with the terms of the Japanese-Korean Agreement just concluded. Mr. Oishi maintains that when a country exercises protectorate rights over another country, it is necessary for the protected country to entirely transfer the rights of sovereignty, or at least the exercise of sovereignty in regard to diplomatic and financial affairs. The Agreement just signed between Japan and Korea, says Mr. Oishi, provides that diplomatic and financial affairs shall be conducted with the advice of advisers to be recommended by the Japanese Government, but what, he asks, would be the result if the views of the advisers and the Korean Government disagreed? The latter has the option either to accept the advice or reject it, and if so, the advisers are merely advisers, and have no real power. Where, then, is the advantage to Japan in the Agreement? It is further provided that the Japanese Government shall be previously consulted before the conclusion of a treaty with a foreign country, or before the grant of any important concession to a foreign country in case such is negotiated. Similarly, the Progressist leader argues, when the views of the two Governments (Japan and Korea) disagree, it is within the power of the Korean Government to act upon the suggestion of the Japanese Government or not as it pleases. The Japanese Government cannot force the Korean Government to follow its view. Such being the case, where will Japan exercise its protectorate? What is the motive of the Japanese Government in specifying that a foreigner be appointed as adviser in foreign affairs? There may exist special circumstances which have necessitated such a stipulation, but when such a stipulation has been made it is impossible for the Japanese Government to recommend a Japanese for the office in future. Another question arises, continues Mr. Oishi, and that is the status of the advisers to be appointed in accordance with the Agreement. Are they to be superior or inferior in rank to the Japanese Minister, and if inferior, what can they achieve? Even the influence of the Japanese Minister is not strong enough to do all things desired, and what can an official inferior to the Minister achieve in Korea? If their status should be equal, they will be apt to contest for the supremacy over each other, and hinder rather than assist the work of progress. The experience of Japan in the past are now speaking eloquently. If the position of the advisers be made superior to that of the Minister, it will be very difficult for them to achieve anything as mere advisers. For instance, even a man of the position and influence of Count Inouye failed in Korea as an adviser, and a man inferior in influence and position to Count Inouye is entirely unfit to lead the Korean Government. It is really disappointing, concludes Mr. Oishi, if the Korean policy of the Government is as indecisive as this. It is entirely at variance with the policy of the Progressist party recently promulgated, and the party must investigate the question further.

It will be seen that the views of the progressists, as voiced by Mr. Oishi, do not belie their name.

Judging from the experiences of previous advisors in this country Mr. Oishi's complaint that the newly appointed advisors are likely to have but little real power, seems well founded. But it must be remembered that these advisors have been officially appointed by the Japanese government and we should be more inclined to describe them as "Japanese diplomatic representatives having the especial privilege of a complete cognizance of all the transactions of the departments to which they have been appointed."

Clause 3, with which Mr. Oishi also expresses disappointment is as follows:—

The Korean Government agrees to previously consult with the Japanese Government before the conclusion of any treaty with a foreign country and in regard to other important foreign affairs—that is to say, before any concession of special privileges to foreigners or the terms of any treaty are arranged.

Now Mr. Oishi entirely overlooks the fact that this clause, by insuring that Japan shall have previous knowledge of all contemplated transactions with foreigners or foreign powers, gives her an enormous diplomatic advantage.

Forewarned is forearmed, and we consider that the new agreement makes Japan, diplomatically, Mistress of the situation in Korea.

"SQUEEZING" RECEIVES OFFICIAL ATTENTION.

The Law Department have ordered the Chief of Police to despatch a body of men to the North Kyong Syang Province to arrest the Governor on a charge of squeezing the people and generally making their life unbearable. This is a happy augury for the suppression by the Government of the horrid state of corruption now existing everywhere.

The Toug Haks in the south are said to be gaining recruits through the report in circulation that the Japanese will compel all Koreans to shave their heads.

H. E. the German Minister Herr von Saldern left yesterday for the country on a two weeks vacation. The Consul Dr. Ney is Chargé d'affaires during his absence.

The Korea Japan Club premises will be situated at Chong Hyon (behind the French Cathedral.) The numbers of members wishing to join have already reached a total of over 700.

The census of the Japanese population and residences at Chemulpo reveals that 7 new houses have been built but that the population has decreased by 42 since the last census was taken. The total now reads, houses 1521, population 8,100.

THE DUM DUM AT LAST.

The first complaints relative to the use of the dum dum bullet have occurred since the battle of Liaoyang. The Japanese state that they found many explosive bullets at Liaoyang and are raising an outcry against their use.

Probably the Russians have adopted this means of stopping the dreaded Japanese rush for the same reasons that the British find it necessary to use dum dums when repelling a Zulu or Somali charge; i. e. that nothing else will stop them.

France is sending two submarine boats to Indo-China.

Grand Duke Cyril of Russia will not return to the scene of war.

Mr. Pak Chung-sun is to be appointed Secretary to the Korean Legation at Tokyo.

Mr. Magata, who was reported to have sailed for Korea on the 10th inst. will not leave till the 19th.

Two hundred soldiers have been despatched from Pyeng Yang to disperse the Toughak rising.

The gallant band of soldiers who went to assist the Japanese at Gensan but who retired on hearing the sound of rifle shots, will return to Seoul in a few days.

As Wiju and Yongchon are shortly to be opened as treaty ports, Kamnis are to be immediately Chosen. It is said that Mr. Yun Yong-ku and Mr. Yi Min-Pu will fill the positions.

The Financial Department received a visit on the 13th inst. from a Japanese who sought permission to examine the documents relative to taxation as he intended to buy land in Korea.

The Japanese Minister supports the governor of Pyeng Yang in his defence of the charges of oppression brought against him by the inhabitants of his district. He asserts that the governor rendered good assistance to the Japanese troops when they passed through Pyeng Yang.

The Education Department state that the last batch of students, destined for academical honours in Japan are not up to sample. Our reporters informs us that they do not belong to either "talentful or renownable gentlemen families." Henceforth only members of "talentful" or "renownable" families need apply for an education in Japan.

Mr. Won Woo Sang, the chief of police in his zeal for the welfare of the service recently dismissed the policemen on the beat, where a robbery took place. It appears that some burglars entered a pawnshop outside West Gate and stole $200.00 getting away safely with their booty; the policemen whose duty it was to protect lives and property of that district were hauled up before Mr. Won and summarily dismissed. But, and here the unfortunate police commence to smile, it fell to his highness Mr. Won to be haled before a higher power and severely reprimanded, himself, on a graver charge. He was informed that having been specially appointed by His Majesty to his responible position, he should show some interest in his position but up to the present, the only item of which he had taken the slightest care was to surround himself with an enormous bodyguard of police to the detriment of the populace of Seoul, who were thereby deprived in many instances of proper protection. However Mr. Won who seems to be a diplomat managed to evade the seeming issue and is once more in favor.

The Korea Daily News.

VOL. I, THURSDAY, SEPTEMBER 15, 1904. No. 52

HONGKONG & SHANGHAI BANKING CORPORATION.

Paid-up Capital..... ....$10,000,000
Reserve Fund:—Sterling Reserve... 10,000,000
Silver Reserve..... 6,500,000

26,500,000
Reserve Liability of Proprietors... 10,000,000

HEAD OFFICE, HONGKONG.

London Bankers, London and County Banking Company Limited.
Branches and Agencies, London.

Amoy,	Hankow	Penang,
Bangkok,	Hiogo,	Rangoon,
Batavia,	Iloilo,	Saigon,
Bombay,	Lyons,	San Francisco,
Calcutta,	Manila,	Singapore,
Colombo,	Nagasaki,	Sourabaya,
Foochow,	New York,	Tientsin,
Hamburg,	Peking,	Yokohama,

Credits granted on approved Securities, and every description of Banking and Exchange business transacted.

Drafts granted on London and the chief Commercial places in Europe, India, Australia, America, China and Japan.

HOLME RINGER & Co., AGENTS,
CHEMULPO.

ON CHEONG & CO.,
SEOUL.

GENERAL STORE KEEPERS.
Imported provisions, Cooking Utensils Crockery, etc.
FRESH BREAD DAILY.

MITSU BISHI DOCKYARD & ENGINE WORKS,
NAGASAKI.

CODE WORD, "DOCK."

A. 1, A. B. C., and Engineering Codes used.

DOCK No. 1 (at Tategami).

Extreme Length..............523 feet
Length on blocks .... 513 ,,
Width of Entrance on Top......89 ,,
,, ,, Bottom....77 ,,
Water on Blocks at Spring Tide 26½ ,,

DOCK No. 2 (Mukaijima).

Extreme Length..............371 feet
Length on Blocks.............360 ,,
Width of Entrance on Top......66 ,,
,, ,, Bottom 53 ,,
Water on Blocks at Spring Tide 22 ,,

PATENT SLIP (at Kosuge)

Can take vessels up to 1,000 tons gross.

THE WORKS are well equipped with the LATEST IMPROVEMENTS, and can execute any kind of work in SHIPBUILDING and MARINE ENGINEERING, as well as in REPAIRING of SHIPS.

The COMPANY'S new powerful steamer OURA-MARU (712 tons, 700 I.H.P.), specially built for SALVAGE PURPOSES, and equipped with necessary gear, is always READY at SHORT NOTICE.

CHARTERED BANK OF INDIA AUSTRALIA & CHINA.

INCORPORATED BY ROYAL CHARTER 1853

HEAD OFFICES:—LONDON.

Paid-up Capital £800,000
Reserve Liability of Shareholders 800,000
Reserve Fund 800,000

Drafts granted upon all the principal places in the world and every description of Exchange and banking business transacted.

E. MEYER & Co., Agents,
Chemulpo.

E. MEYER & CO.
Chemulpo.

SOLE AGENTS IN KOREA FOR:
A. T. Morse, Sons & Co's "Fresco" Distemper

In all colours ready for use on walls, Ceilings etc.
and
AVENARIUS CARBOLINEUM

A wood-preserving and antiseptic oil preparation

Against decay, dry-rot, fungus and wood-destroying insects.

A large supply always in Stock. Prices upon application.

E. MEYER & Co.,
Chemulpo.

LAW UNION & CROWN INS. CO.

Fire risks accepted at Current rates, on godowns, merchandise, dwellings, and other property, subject to usual conditions.

HOLME RINGER & Co.,
Agents, Chemulpo

THE METHODIST PUBLISHING HOUSE,
Little West Gate, Seoul.

JOB PRINTING, TYPEWRITER PAPER
CARBON PAPER, VISITING CARDS
STATIONERY, BOOK BINDING
BOOK PUBLISHERS
AMERICAN SCHOOL BOOKS
SPENCERIAN COPY BOOKS
PEN CARBON LETTER AND BILL BOOKS

S. A. BECK, Manager.

DAI-ICHI GINKO.
LIMITED.

(Formerly the First National Bank)

ESTABLISHED 1873

INCORPORATED UNDER PRESENT LAW 1896

Capital - - - - - - - - Yen 5,000,000
Reserve Fund - - - - - 1,500,000

HEAD OFFICE:—TOKIO.

President: Baron SHIBUSAWA.

BRANCHES AND CORRESPONDENTS
In the Principal Cities and Towns of Japan.
Interest Allowed on
Fixed deposits 1 year - - - 6½ per cent
" " 6 months - - - 6 per cent

Special current accounts 1½ sen daily per Y 100
General " " 1 " " " 100

M. TANAKA,
Manager, Chemulpo

HOLME RINGER & Co.
Chemulpo.

General Merchants and Government Contractors.

Agents for the leading
Banks
SteamshipCompanies
and
Insurance Companies

Importers of Merchandise of every description.

KAMEYA & CO.

GENERAL STOREKEEPERS
Chinkokai - - Seoul
(*Established 1895, Tokyo*)

Confectionery, Hams, Canned Goods, Cutlery, Hirano & Tansan Water. Provisions, Gents, Furnishing goods, Toilet Articles, Travelling Bags, Tobacco, Cigars & Cigarettes Kitchen Utensils. Coffee, Biscuits.

Fresh Goods always kept in Stock.
Prices Moderate
Please come and inspect our goods.

NIPPON YUSEN KAISHA.

JAPANESE MAIL STEAMSHIP CO.

DER MAIL CONTRACT WITH THE IMPERIAL JAPANESE GOVERNMENT.

European Line

Regular Fortnightly Service between Yokohama Kobe, Moji, Shanghai, Hongkong, Singapore, Penang Colombo, Port Said, Marseilles, London and Antwerp

American Line

Regular Fortnightly Service between Hongkong and Seattle, calling at Shanghai, Moji, Kobe, Yokohama and Victoria, B. C.

Australian Line

Regular weekly Service betwen Japan Ports and Australia, calling at Hongkong and Manila.
(Above Three Lines Suspended until further notice).

Shanghai Line

Weekly Service between Shanghai and Japan Ports

Korea Line

Service Kobe, Moji, Nagasaki, Fusan, Chemulpo, Choo, Taiku.
S. S. Bahelsberg, 2181 tons.
Service Kobe, Moji, Fusan, Chemulpo, Chinnampo
S. S ARGO. S. S. Ohio.

BORDEN'S CONDENSED MILK CO.

New York, U. S. A.

ALWAYS IN STOCK
Eagle Brand Condensed Milk.
Gold Seal Condensed Milk.
Peerless (Family) Evaporated Cream.
Borden's Malted Milk.

E. MEYER & CO.
Chemulpo, Korea,
Sole Agents

ROYAL INSURANCE COMPANY,
Funds exceed £10,000,000
FIRE
AT CURRENT RATES.
LIFE
REDUCED PREMIUM.
HOLME RINGER & Co.,
Agents, Chemulpo.

HOTEL DU PALAIS
SEOUL.

The only first class Hotel in Seoul. Situated in the centre of the city opposite the palace.
Cuisine under the supervision of an experienced French Chef.
Well ventilated and furnished throughout.

TARIFF UPON APPLICATION

L. MARTIN
Proprietor and Mangaer.

大韓每日申報
대한ᄆᆡ일신보

(뎨이십륙호) (금요일) 쳔구빅사년구월십륙일

본샤고

○신보는영어와한어로넉거ᄆᆡ일츌판ᄒᆞ옵

신문가

ᄒᆞᆫ쟝 엽두돈오푼
일삭됴엽두량닷돈 맛돈으로 밧숩

광고료는

긔한의쟝단과ᄌᆞ힝의다쇼로즁감ᄒᆞ되렴가로밧을터이오며오리지아녀대한사람마다다이신문을보실터이니광고내시기를원ᄒᆞ시는이들은우리신문샤에와셔면약ᄒᆞ심을희망ᄒᆞ옵

○발힝소 박동대한ᄆᆡ일신보샤법어학교압헤젼영국인셜필림집자리오

샤쟝 영국인 (비셜)

샤고

○우리대한ᄆᆡ일신보의목덕은대한의안녕질셔에관한모든뎨목에ᄃᆡᄒᆞ야는공평한변론을쥬쟝홈이라우리동신원의담보는신문보시는쳠군ᄌᆞ의게홍상보도ᄒᆞ리며편지를긔셔ᄒᆞ여주시는이는셩명과반디를젹어붓치시기를희망ᄒᆞ오니이거슬신문샹에긔ᄌᆡᄒᆞ랴는거시아니오다만극히신용ᄒᆞ는증거를숨고쟈홈이라긔쟈는아모긔셔던지긔ᄌᆡ홈을되각ᄒᆞ는권리를가졋스나되각ᄒᆞᆫ리유를말홀터이오며공즁평화를문란케ᄒᆞ는듯ᄒᆞᆫ긔셔는의례히밧지안켓솝나이다

샤고

○본샤에셔는신문갑슨ᄆᆡ월에션금으로밧ᄉᆞ오며본신문은우톄로붓처는고로본샤에셔는다른신문샤처름금액을거두러ᄃᆞᆫ니지안ᄉᆞ오니우리신문을ᄉᆞ랑ᄒᆞ야구람ᄒᆞ시는쳠군ᄌᆞ는양력ᄆᆡ월ᄆᆡ월죵에리월됴션금과거쥬셩명동호수를ᄌᆞ세히젹어셔박동본샤로보내시기를바라오며월회일닉로션금을아양력금니보내시는곳에는리월일일부터신문을아니보낼터이오니죠량ᄒᆞ옵소셔

●본샤에셔아직긔계를쟝만치못ᄒᆞ와다른ᄃᆡ셔박여오는고로ᄆᆡ양월요일에는츌판이대단히늣게되는듯스로문젼이ᄆᆡ우늣게되오니우리신문을구람ᄒᆞ시는쳠군ᄌᆞ는용셔ᄒᆞ여쥬심을희망ᄒᆞ옵나이다

본샤광고

본샤에셔본신문뎨ᄉᆞ호와뎨십일호와뎨이십오호를소용홀ᄯᅢ가잇셔이에광고ᄒᆞ오니누구시던지이샹삼호즁에본샤로가져오시면ᄆᆡ쟝에빅젼두푼식드리리다

론셜

일한량국잔신결합동

○신호크로늬클신문을본즉일본진보쟈대셕씨가일한량국합동조관에실망되엿다는동경공보을번등ᄒᆞ엿는ᄃᆡ

그사실인즉대셕씨가말ᄒᆞ기를어느나라던지남의나라에보호ᄒᆞ는권리를힝홈은ᄌᆞ긔나라뎨왕지권을젼슈히부려그나라로ᄒᆞ여곰보호밧게ᄒᆞᆫ다던지그러치아니ᄒᆞ면다만재졍과밋외교ᄉᆞ무에나국권을힝ᄒᆞ야관리ᄒᆞ게ᄒᆞ여야보호ᄒᆞᆫ다홈에요긴ᄒᆞᆫ바이어놀

이졔일한량국에협동조인을홀터인즉맛당이일본졍부로셔고문관을쳔거ᄒᆞ야한국에외교지졍ᄉᆞ무를권고홀터이나그러ᄒᆞ나만일한국졍부로셔고문관들의소견ᄃᆡ로힝ᄒᆞ되특별ᄒᆞᆫ권리가업슬지경이면한국은자한국이요고문관은자고문관일터인즉이러케되게되면일본에무삼유익이잇스리요이런고로어ᄂᆞ나라와계약을ᄒᆞᆫ다던지합동을ᄒᆞ게되면여러조관을미리결졍ᄒᆞ야담판홈이가ᄒᆞ고진보쟈로말ᄒᆞ야드리도두나라이셔로불합히녁이여일본졍부에셔제츌ᄒᆞᆫ일을한국졍부에셔낙죵치아니홀지경이면신보쟈의권력ᄃᆡ로ᄒᆞ게ᄒᆞ여야홀터인ᄃᆡ모도그러치아니ᄒᆞᆫ즉일본셔보호ᄒᆞ는권리를힝ᄒᆞᆫ다홈과한국에고문관을외국인으로구별ᄒᆞ야교셥ᄉᆞ무를관리ᄒᆞ게입명ᄒᆞ는본의가무어시리요아모리합동조약에는특별ᄒᆞᆫ조관이잇다ᄒᆞ드ᄅᆡ도쟝ᄅᆡ에일본졍부에셔능히일본사ᄅᆞᆷ을ᄒᆞ나라도쳔거ᄒᆞ야쓰지못홀거시만일합동ᄒᆞᆫ바와갓치고문관을임명ᄒᆞ게되면그사ᄅᆞᆷ들이모도샹등인물이될는지하등지유가될는지아지못ᄒᆞ게ᄒᆞᆫ즉만일하등지유가되게되면져히들이가히무삼일을셩취ᄒᆞ리요

이는다만우리나라공ᄉᆞ의권력ᄃᆡ로쳐단치못ᄒᆞᆫ게만될터인즉한국대ᄉᆞ셩공ᄒᆞ랴홈에무삼유죠홈이잇스리요만일그사ᄅᆞᆷ들이홈ᄭᅴ모히여일심만되게되면진보홀방침을ᄉᆡᆼ각ᄒᆞ야방조ᄒᆞ기는고샤ᄒᆞ고셔로응ᄒᆞ야일본사ᄅᆞᆷ을압두ᄒᆞ랴고권리들만닷톨지라

이거슨긔왕에일본셔지닉본일인즉황연히ᄭᅢ다롤만ᄒᆞᆫ거시만일고문관들로ᄒᆞ여곰ᄌᆞ긔들의지위를우리나라공ᄉᆞ버뎜고등자격을만들게되면다만고문관의직칙만힝ᄒᆞ야미ᄉᆞ에셩취되게ᄒᆞ기가심히어려울거시이왕졍샹빅작과갓치권력을힝ᄒᆞᆯ진ᄃᆡ한국에흠손이될거시요만일그러치아니ᄒᆞ면한국졍부인도홈에ᄯᅩᄒᆞᆫ합당치못홀지라한국졍권에ᄃᆡᄒᆞ야이러케유약ᄒᆞ게결졍ᄒᆞ면응당진보쟈의계획ᄒᆞ야반포홈을졍령불합히녁일터인즉이러홀일을ᄉᆡᆼ각ᄒᆞ야분명히되도록ᄒᆞ는거시올타ᄒᆞ엿는지라

진보쟈대셕씨의셜명ᄒᆞᆫ바와갓틀진ᄃᆡ외국사ᄅᆞᆷ들로ᄒᆞ여곰합동이되지아니홀것갓고셜혹되드ᄅᆡ도이고문관은ᄌᆞ긔의말ᄒᆞᆫᄃᆡ로특별ᄒᆞᆫ권리를쥬지아니ᄒᆞ야각부ᄉᆞ무관리홈을일본공ᄉᆞ나밋외교관의게면져승인ᄒᆞ게ᄒᆞᄌᆞ는특별ᄒᆞᆫ조관을셜명ᄒᆞ야만드ᄌᆞ됴셰됴건을편입ᄒᆞᆫᄭᅡ닭에이일이아즉못되엿다는ᄃᆡ이셰됴건인즉한국졍부에셔외국인으로더부러조약ᄒᆞ기젼에일본졍부에향ᄒᆞ야의론홀일과외국인의게특별히리익될합동이던지계약항목을엇더케작졍ᄒᆞ야만드러ᄌᆞ긔나라외교상즁ᄃᆡᄒᆞᆫ리익을힝ᄒᆞ게ᄒᆞᄌᆞ고말ᄒᆞ엿다ᄒᆞᆫ즉

우리ᄉᆡᆼ각에는만일이합동이되게되면한국에는한외교상쥬인이잇슬듯ᄒᆞ노라

관보

뎨이쳔구빅삼십일호 광무팔년구월십ᄉᆞ일

셔임급ᄉᆞ령

○임외국어학교교관셔쥬임관륙등 외국어학교부교관 죠원규 구월팔일

○임학부편집국쟝셔쥬임관일등 학부참셔관 리죵리

○임학부참셔관셔쥬임관륙등 학부쥬ᄉᆞ 김텽진

○즁학교쟝셔쥬임관륙등품 리달용 이샹구월구일

○면본관 룡안군슈 리긔샹

○의원면본관 닉부기ᄉᆞ 리긔영 단쳔군슈 리현지

○승셔쥬임관ᄉᆞ등 닉부판젹국쟝 리용셔

○면징계 젼군슈 채귀셕

이샹구월십일

○명휴직 진위뎨ᄉᆞ련ᄃᆡ뎨삼대ᄃᆡ쟝 륙군보병참령 신학대

○면본직 진위뎨일련ᄃᆡ뎨이대ᄃᆡ쟝 륙군보병참령 젼우긔 진위뎨ᄉᆞ련ᄃᆡ뎨일대ᄃᆡ부 륙군보병부위 김셩국 진위뎨ᄉᆞ련ᄃᆡ뎨일대ᄃᆡ부 륙군보병참위 김셕쥬 진위뎨ᄉᆞ련ᄃᆡ삼대ᄃᆡ부 륙군보병부위 박윤찬 진위뎨ᄉᆞ련ᄃᆡ뎨삼대ᄃᆡ부 륙군보병참위 김득셩 쳔위뎨일련ᄃᆡ뎨일대ᄃᆡ부 관륙군보병부위 리민회 쳔위뎨일련ᄃᆡ뎨일대ᄃᆡ부 륙군보병부위 리현규

○임륙군보병참령 륙군일등군ᄉᆞ 강창회

○보쳔위뎨일련ᄃᆡ뎨이대ᄃᆡ대쟝 륙군보병참령 강창회

○보진위뎨ᄉᆞ련ᄃᆡ뎨삼대ᄃᆡ대쟝 륙군보병참령 젼우긔

○보진위뎨ᄉᆞ련ᄃᆡ뎨일대ᄃᆡ부 륙군보병부위 박윤찬 륙군보병참위 김득셩

○보진위뎨ᄉᆞ련ᄃᆡ뎨삼대ᄃᆡ부 륙군보병부위 김셩국 륙군보병참위 김셕쥬

○보쳔위뎨일련ᄃᆡ뎨일대ᄃᆡ부 관 륙군보병부위 리현규

○보쳔위뎨일련ᄃᆡ뎨일대ᄃᆡ부 륙군보병부위 리민회

이샹구월십일일

AMERICAN KOREAN ELECTRIC COMPANY.

Light and Power.

Main Office: Electric Building, Chong No.

RAILWAY DEPARTMENT.

OPERATING CARS BETWEEN EAST AND WEST GATE, EVERY TEN MINUTES:—

First Car leaves East Gate at 6:30 A. M. First Car leaves West Gate at 6:55 A. M.
Last Car " East Gate at 10:40 P. M. Last " " West Gate at 11:00 P. M.

OPERATING CARS BETWEEN EAST GATE AND IMPERIAL TOMB TERMINUS, EVERY TWENTY MINUTES:—

CONNECTING WITH EVERY ALTERNATE CAR ARRIVING AT EAST GATE FROM CHONG NO.

First Car leaves East Gate for Tomb at 6:50 A. M.
" " " Tomb for East Gate at 7:10 A. M.
Last " " East Gate for Tomb at 9:50 P. M.
" " Tomb for East Gate at 10:10 P. M.

OPERATING CARS BETWEEN CHONG NO AND YUNG SAN (RIVER) EVERY TWELVE MINUTES:—

First Car leaves Chong No for South Gate at 6:48 A. M.
" " " Chong No for Yung San at 7:24 A. M.
" " " South Gate for Chong No at 6:56 A. M.
" " " Yung San for Chong No at 7:57 A. M.
Last " " South Gate for Chong No 11:00 P. M.
" " " Yung San for Chong No at 10:11 P. M.

SPECIAL PRIVATE CARS FURNISHED TO SUIT CONVENIENCE OF PATRONS. PRICES ON APPLICATION AT HEAD OFFICE.

LIGHTING DEPARTMENT.

Where less than 250 candle power of light is used, the rate per month will be. Per 16 candle power incandescent lamp. All night.—Yen 2.50.
Per 32 candle power incandescent lamp:—All night:—Yen 4.00. Per 50 candle power incandescent lamp:—All night:—Yen 6.00.
" 150 " " " " " " 10.00. " 1200 " " enclosed arc " " " 20.00.

Where more than 250 candle power of light is used, a Meter will be installed, if requested:—Rent of Meter Yen 2.00 per month. Rate of charges by meter reading:—Two Sen per Ampere per hour. (Approximately this is equal to about One Sen per 16 c. p. lamp per hour) Minimum monthly charge where meter is installed, Yen 20.00 per month, which includes rental of meter.

Estimates for installing lights furnished on application. An assortment of chandeliers always on hand.

AMUSEMENT DEPARTMENT.

ANIMATED PICTURES AT EAST GATE.
Every evening - - - Except Sunday.
From 8 to 10 P. M.

10 Cents:—Gen. Admission:—10 Cents. Seats in First Class Section. 15 Cents Extra.

Change of program each week. Pictures from Foreign Lands. Pictures of Local Scenes:—Amusing and Instructive.

An entertaining evening for a reasonable price.
MERRY-GO-ROUND:—At East Gate.
From 10:00 A. M. till 11:00 P. M.

5 Cents a Ride.

Take your Exercise on The Galloping Horses.

Comfortable seats in the Chariots.

한셩뎐긔회사

한미뎐긔회사 고블안 보사뎌 고빅
도흥읍나이다
샹활동사진뎐람소와목마운동장량처로인
여뎌뎐차가운장안으로통힝ᄒᆞ여ᄃᆞ니여아
습
또이긔계에긋치노힌편ᄒᆞ고됴흔마차도잇
습
코미우편ᄒᆞ고또조미잇는됴흔운동이되겟
이됴흔모형흘달나아는몰을ᄐᆞ고워티치안
되가는흘번ᄒᆞ는데노젼ᄉᆡ이오
미일샹오열시브터하오열흘시ᄭᆞ지ᄒᆞ옵고
목마운동장은동대문안에잇습고
가되겟습
철군조의게갑도싸고져녁에됴흔쇼일거리
잇고구경흘만ᄒᆞ거시오니
셔양사진과대한과온동양사진언네데조미
는되
젼이옵고미쥬일에사진을ᄇᆡᆨ것스로다밧고
고젼람되금은하동에십젼이오상등에이십
일외에는미야에여덜시브터열시ᄭᆞ지ᄒᆞ옵
활동사진뎐람소는동대문안에잇습고일요
회략부

All Cars Run Direct to the Animated Pictures and Merry-Go-Round.

○림시셔리니장원경수무 륙군부장 윤웅렬
○명셔리경무수 니장원감독 김영진
○명영션수위원 박계홍
○승셔관임관일등 인천감리셔쥬수 남린희
○임학부쥬수셔관임관륙등 리근셕
○임한셩수범학교교관셔관임관륙등 심응틱
○임경위원총슌셔관임관륙등 리한구
○면징계 전총슌 리학슌
○급삼급봉 외국어학교교관 죠원규
이상구월십이일
○일쥬일경근신 진위대삼련디뎨이대디부소디장륙군보병참위 최진영
구월십일일
궁뎐록수
○즁츄원의관안종덕수직소비지니에소청틱로의시호노라
○죠왈근일도라단니는피이훈병이홍진인듯호나그도아니라치료돌실슈호면횡수와뇨소호확이잇슬띠니민싱의질고를싱각건디별반긍측호고또외국인의거류자와군인과쥬흠즁다호니위싱샹방략을불가불에비홀지라의술의정통훈인원을틱차호야피어훈병긔물리칠약졔를샹확호고경향각쳐에파송호야병든쟈롤급히구료호야피이호병괴가만연치못호게홀수로니부로호여곰별반신칙호라
구월십일일

잡보

○물시쥬본 삼작야에군슈이십오인를 쥬본호엿더니무삼미흡지단이잇셔 지가가못되시고히쥬본긔가도로느려셧는디그쥬본긔는좌와ᄀᆞᆺ더라
단천김하셤 남포홍희 강계리즁호 안변리승지 옥구리범좌 온진리지열 화슌유치헌 츙쥬서형슌 이천서만슌 안쥬최익환 하동임정고 이천윤즈익 평산리병민 곡산장석신 룡안김병쥬 군위서창보 갑산정완영 룡천박긔종 신계윤우셤 울산민형긔 홍양현학표 풍긔권즁면 진위최영셜 평강리슌영 연천박도양합이십오인이더라

○직산샹보 직산금광군채원실이장폐호소로금광군이작당호야히군슈를란타호야히군슈의치폐훈수는연일본보에긔지호엿거니와일작에공쥬관찰수가또보고호기를금광군이야료홀시에채원실의아오인셕이가본군슈를란타호고또복부를찔넛는디그잇흔날술시에본군슈가운영훈지라빅셩들이대단통분호야슈천명이회동호야채인셕을옥즁에셔쓰러니여다살호엿다호고로놀니여도저히사실보고호라고사관의게신칙호엿다더라

○의병통문 강원도관찰수가니부로보고호기를황셩의병소대장김셩아모의발긔훈통문이라호고본월팔일에츈천군향교에리도호엿는디통문수의에호엿스되일본인의소청산림천틱소와역부모집수를다시행치못홀뜻스로포군을동솔호고려쥬로리회호야황셩으로직향호조호엿는디보국안민녀조로각조훈도장을찍어셔각군으로돌닌다호엿더라

○불탈불염 정부에셔니부로죠회호되평양거호는전진수김지익등의등소를거호즉분군슈핑한쥬는도임훈지오년에전혀탐도를호엿스되신축파계묘량년에원조전이라칭호고민간에비렴훈것과명식업는결젼을일등결로록봉훈것과임인계묘량년간에호포전탈급호라신칙유가특강호엿스나가만히슈봉호여락랑호엿고현금렬도역소에삭젼을마즁간환롱훈것여러됴건합엽젼일빅수십삼만오천여량이된다호엿스니히군슈롤곳쥬면호고히장젼을사실호야징출호고법부에이죠호야죠률징관케호라호엿더라

○거제측량 창원감리가외부로면보호되일본병참감부공합에호기를군용디립표훈안에는무론아모면답이던지별반신칙호야곡식을곳곳시베히라호엿고또일령수죠회에는거졔군죽림포의히샹파륙디롤다칙량홀터이니히군에신칙호야경농치말게호라호엿스니엇지조쳐홀는지시명호라호엿더라

○폐현정지 례식원에셔외부로죠복호기를외국공수가히국으로셔귀도훈언장천정호기위호고의국합장이하수관이원을디동호야 폐현훈일수는현금옥도미령호샤쇼접훈실수업스니이수의롤히공관에죠복호라훈고로외부에셔례식원죠회를등인호야의공관에죠복호엿더라

○파병진압 황평량셔에셔동학당이벌쎄ᄀᆞᆺ치이러는황셩으로직향호는고로일젼에원슈부에셔평양딕로훈령호되동학당진압ᄎᆞ로진위딕이빅명을발병호라호엿더라

○조청랍세 일젼에일본인이탁지부에리도호야말호되일본인이귀국토디롤만히미득호엿손즉불가불셰랍을쇼샹히담지호엿세랍호겟다호고졍공문부돌됴사호야갓다더라

○도쳐벽공 륙군법원에셔슈훈전마딕참령리틱리씨의장전이수천원인디일천원가량은병정호궤시에지용호엿고삼천원은츙랍호엿순즉청장이다되엿는디 원슈부에셔히원으로훈령호되의혹된수단잇더리도리티리롤곳죠률호라호엿더니히원장신티휴씨가호기를의심된죄는가부업게홀거시어놀그의단잇는줄알고엇지죠률호리오히훈령롱쥰힝치못홀거시오다시심사호야유죄홈을젹확히알고야죠률션고호겟다호엿다더라

○리싱장셔 령남유싱리강리등삼인이경위총관의게장셔롤호엿는디그긔의에왈소위진신소청에셔별노호는일업시부비만과다히니는디그부비롤향곡빅셩의게빈렴훈즉빈민의게이페가적지아니호야ᄌᆞ연소요호고또경향잡류비가홀일이업쓰면소청에투입호야쓸디업는공론으로세월을허비호야허다훈부비돌니셔필경히는빅셩의게로도라가오니가탄홀일이라바라건디각하가싱등더러소청을파호라호시면셰가지됴혼방칙이잇다호엿다더라

○국문긔졍 지작일에련동예수교회당에셔양목수모모졔씨가회동호엿다가대한국문의긔졍홀수돌연셜호엿는디그긔졍호는긔의롤드론즉국문반절즁에동음으로두세가지되는거슬한가지음만두기로산뎡호엿다더라

○시흥민요 지작일에경긔관찰부에셔니부로면보호기를시흥군에빅셩슈천명이회집호엿기로슌검을파송호야효유호되히산치아니훈다호엿더라

○연하지차 작일샹오십일시에경긔관찰수가또니부로면보호기를작일신시량에시흥군에회집훈빅셩들슈천명이히군군슈와그아들과일인이명을다살호엿다고히군셔긔가리고호기로위션졍사관호야사힉호겟노라고호엿더라

○빅절불요 진신소청소원으로일현병의게피착된리범창씨등삼인을영영방송치아니훈다호되소청에셔는빅번썩거도요동치아니호고또샹소진복호기로결뎡훈지라 대니쳐분에는진복지말느호셧스느소청공론에는칠ᄎᆞ샹소즁일ᄎᆞ 비지만느리시면진복지아니호겟다호엿다더라

뎐보

구월이일론돈발
○금졔픔갱사 영국외무셩에셔리버풀에잇는샹업회의소에공합호기롤영국정부에셔표명홈으로인호야전시금제픔의문뎨를로국에셔다시샹고훈다고호엿더라

구월삼일론돈발
○유족휼금 대영국셔일본륙히군전망자의쳐권과유족을휼호기로모집훈돈이지금총계가이만방[일방이한화십원]이되엿다더라

구월삼일빅림발
○위령론죄 셩피득보에셔고시호기를히군제독하푸씨가우크톰쓰키친왕이로국합디가려슌구에서최후출발홈을련속호야명령을어긘힝위를군법회의에붓치기로작정호엿다호엿더라

구월수일비림발
○음진일퇴 덕국천왕푸릭더릭뤼폴드씨는근쟈에황뎨의명령으로로군참모본부에쳠부호기로젼왕호랴고발졍호랴든거손로국졍부에셔청국향호마적이텰도롤손훌가념녀되야출발홈을그만두엇스면됴홀양으로원훈ᄯᅥᆨ닭에연긔가되엿고 칼안론친왕은전장에잇는일본참모본부에쳠부호기로명령을밧아싸취센호롤트고자토료일에골놈보ᄯᅥ지도착호엿더라

팔원이십일론돈발뽑베이로경유호야도착훈
○로장가련 밀니다워천쌜냇트라호는륙군긔관신문에긔지훈바덕군에잇는군수샹경험가들이로군구로팟킨쟝군의관경을되단치비창이녁이는의수가잇다호엿더라

잡보

○질문속훈 지작일에일본수령부관인이니부에리도호야질문호야왈일젼에본수령부에셔역부물시소롤귀졍부에딕호야딕강언론호엿더니역부물시면훈을당일로각도에발송호엿스니당초에역부모집호라는훈령을엇지그리지완케호더니즉금물시호라는면훈은엇지그리급속히호엿나냐호고또말호되일후에만일역부롤갱청호거든이번ᄀᆞᆺ치급속히면칙호라호더니미구에히수령부에셔역부물시훈령초건을졍부로송교호엿거늘졍부에셔니부로보니고이디로각도에훈령호라호엿더라

○승인결졍 군제식졍소롤졍동숙위소로이셜호고각의졍관과위원이축일회동호야비밀히의론호는디의졍관야진씨는일본수령부명령디로의안을인쥰호고의졍소에셔는야진씨의승인호는디로군제롤결졍훈다더각

TELEGRAMS.

[THROUGH REUTER'S AGENCY.]

Berlin, Sept. 8.

It is reported that flour exported from America to Japan will be subject to a war-tax of ten cents per bag.

London, Aug. 30—It is announced at St. Petersburg that the crew of the Novik have arrived at Vladivostock.—N. C. Daily News.

Berlin, Sept. 8.

Prince Sviatopolkmirsky, the Governor of Vilna, has been appointed Minister of the Interior in succession to the late M. von Plehve.

Berlin, Sept. 8.

The date of the departure of the Baltic Squadron for the Far East is still uncertain.

The "New York Herald" publishes a report that Russia is stated to be negotiating through a French firm for the purchase of two war-ships from Argentine Republic.

London, Sept, 9th.

General Kuropatkin reports under date of yesterday that General Kuroki's force is twenty-five miles east of the railway (between Liaoyang and Mukden), while General Oku's army is at a point thirty miles to the west.

The Russian army is now concentrated around Mukden, while the rear-guard from Liaoyang, which is seventeen miles south of Mukden, is in constant contact with the Japanese forces.

Fighting is still going on without ceasing.

THE APPEAL IN THE ALLANTON CASE.

A St. Petersburg despatch states that M. Passova, a distinguished international lawyer, who has been called to the English Bar, has been retained to conduct the appeal of the owners of the Belfast steamer Allanton and of the cargo, seized on June 16th, against the decision of the Russian Prize Court at Vladivostock. The appeal will be heard before the Council of the Russian Admiralty, with two Senators belonging to the Russian Court of Cassation. An official of the Russian Ministry for Foreign Affairs and the legal adviser to the Ministry of Marine will conduct the Russian case. The British Embassy has been in communication with the Russian Ministry for Foreign Affairs regarding the seizure of the Allanton, but in any case no formal protest will be made, nor any demand for compensation presented, pending the result of the appeal. Mr. Balfour has consented to receive a deputation from the Parliamentary Shipping Committee to protest against the confiscation of the steamship Allanton and her cargo by the Russians. According to the Daily Mail's St. Petersburg correspondent, the protest again the seizure of the steamer Allanton is likely to meet with scant consideration, since among the ship's papers was found a written undertaking from the Japanese Government to pay the full value of the ship to the possessor of the vessel in case it was seized by the Russian authorities.

The "Liverpool Post" tells a story of a director of the London and North-Western Railway who chided a ticket-collector who went past him without looking at his pass. "No matter if you do know who I am," said he in reply to the collector's excuse; "I am entitled to ride free only when I am travelling with that pass. You don't know whether I have it or not." The collector, a little nettled, then demanded to see the pass. "That's right!" exclaimed the director; "here—why—where—well, I declare! I must have left it at the office." "Then you'll have to pay your fare," said the collector firmly. And he did.

THE WAR AND RUSSIA.

EFFECTS OF THE WAR ON THE ECONOMIC STATE OF RUSSIA.

The following interesting items are translated from the "Revolutionary Russia" (which is an anti-Russian journal published in Switzerland) of July 1.

The effects of the Japanese war upon the economic condition of Russia are clearly shown in recent official statistics, from which it appears that in the month of May, 1904, the amount of merchandise transported from the interior of the Empire to sea-coast ports was 200,000 tons less than in the corrsesponding month of last year. This represents a decline in trade of about 25 per cent. The quantity of merchandise transported from sea-coast ports to the interior of the Empire, in the same month, showed a still greater falling off, amounting, in fact, to a decline of forty per cent as compared with last year. The increased movement of military stores—particularly on the railroads centering in Moscow—might compensate the labouring population for the decrease in the transportation of other goods if the laborers had the handling of these military stores; but such is not the case. The Government, for the sake of economy, gives that work to soldiers, and the result is the wholesale discharge of thousands of freight-handlers, stevedores and watchmen, for whom there is no work. Sixty thousand men belonging to these classes have been discharged in European Russia within the past four months, while the number of factory operatives thrown out of employment by the decline in manufactures is now between 300,000 and 400,000 and is increasing at the rate of 3,000 per day.

HOW LARGE AN ARMY CAN RUSSIA MAINTAIN IN MANCHURIA?

Our "patriotic" newspapers inform us that the present war is to have two "phases," or stages. In the "first phase" the Japanese beat us and compel us to retreat. In the "second phase" we are to beat the Japanese and compel them to retreat. The "first phase," we are told, is now nearing its end. In a very few days the reinforcements now pouring into Manchuria will give Kuropatkin an army of 500,000 men, all equipped for battle, and he will then be able to carry to a victorious conclusion the "second phase" of the war.

(To be continued).

A NOTABLE ADDITION TO THE JAPANESE FLEET.

Japan has now secured an addition to her fleet by the completion of the cruiser "Otowa," which was launched from the Yokosuka Naval Yard in 1903. Her displacement is 3,048 tons, and she steams 21 knots, her armament consisting of 18 guns. The new cruiser will leave Yokosuka for a certain point in a day or two Her commander is Captain Arima, who commanded the first and second blockade expeditions to Port Arthur.

FOREIGN CAPITAL IN JAPAN.

An official investigation shows that the Japanese companies which have foreigners amongst their shareholders are six in number, with an aggregate paid up capital of Y12,292,500, of which Y2,992,900 are foreign capital. The particulars are as follows:

Company.	Capital paid up.	Japanese.	Foreign.
	Yen.	Yen.	Yen.
Japanese Electrical..	200,000	72,000	128,000
Tokio Trading........	25,000	18,750	6,250
Mitsui Bros...........	10,060,000	8,060,000	2,000,000
Akazawa Mining.....	5,000	2,600	2,400
Osaka Gas Works....	1,262,500	806,250	456,250
Japan Distillery......	800,000	400,000	400,000
Total.............	12,292,500	9,299,600	2,992,900

According to the Paris "Presse," the French Premier desires that the French Catholics should break off from the Roman Church and from a French National Church, with a Pope of its own.

PRISONERS.

There are already 2,384 Russian prisoners in Japan, and their number is likely to be quickly increased. They are becoming rather a problem, for their keep is expensive. Russia seems to have 68 Japanese officers and 256 men as prisoners. These were captured mainly on board transport steamers.—Japan Mail.

The well-known Russian author Antoin Tchechoff has just died.

The "American Asiatic" gives the detailed manifest of the Knight Commander. She carried $300,000 (gold) of cargo for Yokhama, Shanghai, Singapore, Manila, Sourabaya, Bangkok, Hongkong, and Chemulpo. By far the greater part was for the first named port and included rails, manufacturer's iron and steel, electric machinery, car material, railroad material, etc. The total value was roughly $138,000 (gold).

The Korea Daily News.

To be published daily except Sundays.

Rate of Subscription:—

Per Year,	Yen 25.
Per Quarter,	Yen 7.
Per Month	Yen 2.50

postage in Korea not charged extra.
postage abroad charged extra.

Advertisements, 50 sen per day for 1 inch or less.
5 yen per month per inch.
50 yen per year per inch.

All communications to

E. T. BETHELL,
Editor and Publisher.
Pak-toung, Seoul.

INTERVENTION.

The leading Tokio Journals are already beginning to discuss the subject of mediation. According to a translation from the Japanese Government organ, the "Kokumin which appeard in the "Kobe Chronicle," Japan signifies her willingness to accept mediation if Russia will agree.

Mediation, to be effective, would have to take the form of the appointment of a notion or notions as arbitrators, with the consent of both belligerents to abide by the decision.

For many reasons we forsee the absolute hopelessness of such a happy solution ever being arrived at. In the first place Russia is never likely to agree to the intervention of a third power neither is she likely to consent to an armistice with Japan with the object of providing for a judicial settlement of the dispute. Russian's pride has had a severe blow but there is every indication that this only tends to increase the determination of her leaders to see the thing through to a finish.

And from our knowledge of the Japanese people we do not think that the termination of the war at its present stage would be favourably received by the masses. The highly educated classes may realize the difficulties which confront Japan in the future progress of the war, but the bulk of the people are every whit as insular and confident of the invincibility of their army as are the British. A decision awarding to Japan her original demands or even something a little in excess of her orignial demands, would be looked upon as a very tame ending to a glorious compaign. and, further, it appears to us that whether mediation is agreed to now, or whether intervention is presently thrust on the belligerents, or whether the war is fought through to the bitter end and either Japan or Russia is able to dictate terms of peace, then the real difficulties will have only just begun.

Russia and Japan are by no means the only powers interested in the outcome of the present war. Japan is obviously hoping to have Korea for herself, she is building railways all over the country and constructing fortifications and generally exploiting the country.

And yet, if she is victorious will she be allowed to have Korea? And if Russia is victorious will she be allowed to hold Manchuria?

We think not. There are several powers who will want a share of the good things and he would indeed be a good prophet who could forsee the ultimate settlement of all the troubles which will follow on the heels of this war.

SIR FRANK SWETTENHAM ON WEI-HAI WEI.

The value of We-hai-wei as a British strategic point in China has often been questioned. But argument on the side of retention has been as strong. The advocates of retention have now the support of Sir Frank Swettenham, who thus forcibly sets forth his views in a letter to "The Times":—

There are people in England, naval men for the most part, who know where Wei-hai-wei is and take an interest in it. The interest which is felt by those of us who have visited Wei-hai-wei and its near neighbour Port Arthur must be considerably heightened in view of present and coming events. When war in the Far East became inevitable (and that, in Japanese calculations, was probably a long time ago) the islanders doubtless made the capture of Port Arthur their principal objective. They are getting very near the goal now.

After running away from the Russians in Port Arthur, we acquired, by a very unique instrument, a certain interest in the territory called Wei-hai-wei, the island of Liu-kung, and the adjacent waters. The first paragraph of the convention between England and China, concluded at Peking on July 1, 1898, reads as follows:—

"In order to provide Great Britain with a suitable naval harbour in North China and for the better protection of British commerce in the neighbouring seas, the Government of his Majesty the Emperor of China agree to lease to the Government of her Majesty the Queen of Great Britain and Ireland Wei-hai-wei, in the province of Shantung, and the adjacent waters for so long a period as Port Arthur shall remain in the occupation of Russia."

Observe the concluding words, for the lease appears to be running out, and it is perhaps as well that His Majesty's Government did not spend on Wei-hai-wei the £4,000,000 which, in some quarters, was roughly estimated as necessary to make it a useful and safe naval base. Does it not seem an oversight that there is no provision in the lease for recovering the cost of permanent improvements made by the tenant, especially if he must leave without notice? Fortunately we shall have to deal with the obliging Chinese, who, when England wants "a suitable naval harbour in North China," give Wei-hai-wei, having already persuaded Russia to accept Port Arthur as a useful terminus for the Manchurian railway, and successfully pressed Germany to occupy Kiaochao and spread herself about the rest of Shantung, if more space is wanted for legitimate expansion.

A Tokyo dispatch announces that comment is freely made among Japanese and foreigners regarding the new Agreement. Some opinions are to the effect that by the Agreement the Korean Ministers to foreign countries will be recalled and that foreign representatives in Seoul will withdraw. On the 5th instant, the day on which the Agreement was published in the "Official Gazette," the Japanese Government issued telegrapic instructions to it representatives with the Treaty Powers and explained the spirit of the Agreement to each Power. It is explained that the Agreement is the outcome of the Protocols signed between Japan and Korea on February 23rd last. All contracts and privileges granted by the Korean Government before the signing of the Agreement will in no way be affected. It is stated that the Powers have received the news of the conclusion of the Agreement without raising any objection.—Kobe chronicle.

A merchant of Riga, named Hirrow, has been placed in prison for a curious offence. He had missed his last train home, but, finding that a goods train was shortly to start, he bought a fowl and booked it by the train, at the same time obtaining a ticket for himself as attendant on live stock. He reached his destination, but was afterwards arrested, and is now being prosecuted by the railway company for fraud. His fowl has been confiscated.

PUKHAN MONASTERY BUILDING DESTROYED BY FIRE.

On Monday night a fire broke out in one of the buildings of the famous Puk Han Monastery and despite all attempts to get the fire under control, the building was entirely-destroyed.

Many ancient pictures archives and the famous buddhas were lost in the flames.

Owing to His Majesty's illness he is unable to grant the Italian Minister's request for an audience.

The military reform committee announce that the result of their cogitations will be published in a few days.

A motor-sledge in the shape of a ship has been designed by a Russian engineer to travel on water, ice, or land.

A list of 25 applicants for Magisterial posts was recently presented to His Majesty, who however refused to endorse their application.

A smokeless coal factory has been established at Tokuyama, Nagato by the Naval Office. The inhabitants have presented a piece of ground (valued at Yen 13,000) to the Government.

A full-blooded Sioux Indian has created a sensation at Bonesteel, South Dakota, by riding through the town with his squaw, in a motor-car. His tribe have ceased to recognise him.

An overturned lamp caused a slight conflagration in the offices of the Council of State on Tuesday night, but was speedily extinguished. Some furniture was damaged but nothing of value was destroyed.

In the official gazette of the 15th inst. the following appointments are announced. Mr. Yi Min Pu Kamni of Wiju, Yun Yong Ku, Kamni of Yong Chon, KwonChai Hi, Kamni of Kyeng Hung.

While a meeting of the Patriotic Ladies' Society was being held at a primary school at Katsumada, Okayama Prefecture, on the 7th inst. the second floor collapsed, and over 300—or 15 according to another report—persons were injured.

The Police Department have devised a means of getting rid of Tonghaks. Any countryman wishing to visit Seoul at present had better take warning that the hotels will not receive him as the police are turning out all the occupants (of bucolic appearance) from the inns on suspicion of their being Tonghaks.

The half-yearly general meeting of the Nippon Railway Company was held on the 8th inst., and decided the statement of the distribution of profit. The net profit for the last half-year was declared at Y. 2,841,297 making Y. 3,246,063 with the amount brought over from last account (Y. 384,765). After placing substantial sums to reserve, etc., a dividend will be paid at the rate of ten per cent per annum.

A correspondent writes to the "Daily Telegraph":—The first meeting of English and French archers since the Battle of Agincourt took place at Le Touquet, near Etaples, last week, in circumstances which were naturally very different from those of 1415. A contingent of English archers, some 50 in number, crossed the Channel to take part in an international tournament, and there were nearly 100 French archers among the competitors. In a match between Englishmen and Frenchmen the latter proved their decided superiority by winning handsomely.

The Korea Daily News.

VOL. I, FRIDAY, SEPTEMBER 16, 1904. No. 53

HONGKONG & SHANGHAI BANKING CORPORATION.

Paid-up Capital.....	$10,000,000
Reserve Fund:—Sterling Reserve..	10,000,000
Silver Reserve.....	6,500,000
	26,500,000
Reserve Liability of Proprietors...	10,000,000

HEAD OFFICE, HONGKONG.

London Bankers, London and County Banking Company Limited.

Branches and Agencies, London.

Amoy,	Hankow	Penang,
Bangkok,	Hiogo,	Rangoon,
Batavia,	Iloilo,	Saigon,
Bombay,	Lyons,	San Francisco,
Calcutta,	Manila,	Singapore,
Colombo,	Nagasaki,	Sourabaya,
Foochow,	New York,	Tientsin,
Hamburg,	Peking,	Yokohama,

Credits granted on approved Securities, and every description of Banking and Exchange business transacted.

Drafts granted on London and the chief Commercial places in Europe, India, Australia, America, China and Japan.

HOLME RINGER & Co., AGENTS, CHEMULPO.

ON CHEONG & CO., SEOUL.

GENERAL STORE KEEPERS.

Imported provisions, Cooking Utensils Crockery, etc.

FRESH BREAD DAILY.

MITSU BISHI DOCKYARD & ENGINE WORKS, NAGASAKI.

CODE WORD, "DOCK."

A. 1, A. B. C., and Engineering Codes used.

DOCK No. 1 (at Tategami).

Extreme Length..............	523 feet
Length on blocks	513 ,,
Width of Entrance on Top......	89 ,,
,, ,, Bottom....	77 ,,
Water on Blocks at Spring Tide	26½ ,,

DOCK No. 2 (Mukaijima).

Extreme Length..............	371 feet
Length on Blocks.............	360 ,,
Width of Entrance on Top......	66 ,,
,, ,, Bottom	53 ,,
Water on Blocks at Spring Tide	22 ,,

PATENT SLIP (at Kosuge).

Can take vessels up to 1,000 tons gross.

THE WORKS are well equipped with the LATEST IMPROVEMENTS, and can execute any kind of work in SHIPBUILDING and MARINE ENGINEERING, as well as in REPAIRING of SHIPS.

The COMPANY'S new powerful steamer OURA-MARU (712 tons, 700 I.H.P.), specially built for SALVAGE PURPOSES, and equipped with necessary gear, is always READY at SHORT NOTICE.

CHARTERED BANK OF INDIA AUSTRALIA & CHINA.

INCORPORATED BY ROYAL CHARTER 1853

HEAD OFFICES:—LONDON.

Paid-up Capital	£800,000
Reserve Liability of Shareholders	800,000
Reserve Fund	800,000

Drafts granted upon all the principal places in the world and every description of Exchange and banking business transacted.

E. MEYER & Co., Agents, Chemulpo.

E. MEYER & CO. Chemulpo.

SOLE AGENTS IN KOREA FOR:

A. T. Morse, Sons & Co's "Fresco" Distemper

In all colours ready for use on walls, Ceilings etc.

and

AVENARIUS CARBOLINEUM

A wood-preserving and antiseptic oil preparation

Against decay, dry-rot, fungus and wood-destroying insects.

A large supply always in Stock. Prices upon application.

E. MEYER & Co., Chemulpo.

LAW UNION & CROWN INS. CO.

Fire risks accepted at Current rates, on godowns, merchandise, dwellings, and other property, subject to usual conditions.

HOLME RINGER & Co., Agents, Chemulpo

THE METHODIST PUBLISHING HOUSE,

Little West Gate, Seoul.

JOB PRINTING, TYPEWRITER PAPER
CARBON PAPER, VISITING CARDS
STATIONERY, BOOK BINDING
BOOK PUBLISHERS
AMERICAN SCHOOL BOOKS
SPENCERIAN COPY BOOKS
PEN CARBON LETTER AND BILL BOOKS

S A. BECK, Manager.

DAI-ICHI GINKO.

LIMITED.

(Formerly the First National Bank)

ESTABLISHED 1873

INCORPORATED UNDER PRESENT LAW 1896

Capital - - - - - - - - -	Yen 5,000,000
Reserve Fund - . - - - -	1,500,000

HEAD OFFICE:—TOKIO.

President: Baron SHIBUSAWA.

BRANCHES AND CORRESPONDENTS

In the Principal Cities and Towns of Japan.

Interest Allowed on

Fixed deposits 1 year - - -	6½ per cent
" " 6 months - - -	6 per cent

Special current accounts 1½ sen daily per Y	100
General " " 1 " " "	100

M. TANAKA, Manager, Chemulpo

HOLME RINGER & Co. Chemulpo.

General Merchants and Government Contractors.

Agents for the leading

Banks

Steamship Companies

and

Insurance Companies

Importers of Merchandise of every description.

KAMEYA & CO.

GENERAL STOREKEEPERS

Chinkokai - - Seoul

(Established 1895, Tokyo)

Confectionery, Hams, Canned Goods, Cutlery, Hirano & Tansan Water. Provisions, Gents, Furnishing goods, Toilet Articles, Travelling Bags, Tobacco, Cigars & Cigarettes Kitchen Utensils. Coffee, Biscuits.

Fresh Goods always kept in Stock.

Prices Moderate

Please come and insbect our goods.

NIPPON YUSEN KAISHA.

JAPANESE MAIL STEAMSHIP CO.

DER MAIL CONTRACT WITH THE IMPERIAL JAPANESE GOVERNMENT.

European Line

Regular Fortnightly Service between Yokohama Kobe, Moji, Shanghai, Hongkong, Singapore, Penang Colombo, Port Said, Marseilles, London and Antwerp

American Line

Regular Fortnightly Service between Hongkong and Seattle, calling at Shanghai, Moji, Kobe, Yokohama and Victoria, B. C.

Australian Line

Regular weekly Service betwen Japan Ports and Australia, calling at Hongkong and Manila.

(Above Three Lines Suspended until further notice).

Shanghai Line

Weekly Service between Shanghai and Japan Ports

Korea Line

Service Kobe, Moji, Nagasaki, Fusan, Chemulpo, Choo, Taiku.

S. S. Bahelsberg, 2181 tons.

Service Kobe, Moji, Fusan, Chemulpo, Chinnampo

S. S ARGO. S. S. Ohio.

BORDEN'S CONDENSED MILK CO.

New York, U. S. A.

ALWAYS IN STOCK

Eagle Brand Condensed Milk.

Gold Seal Condensed Milk.

Peerless (Family) Evaporated Cream.

Borden's Malted Milk.

E. MEYER & CO.
Chemulpo, Korea,
Sole Agents

ROYAL INSURANCE COMPANY,

Funds exceed £10,000,000

FIRE

AT CURRENT RATES.

LIFE

REDUCED PREMIUM.

HOLME RINGER & Co., Agents, Chemulpo.

HOTEL DU PALAIS

SEOUL.

The only first class Hotel in Seoul. Situated in the centre of the city opposite the palace.

Cuisine under the supervision of a experienced French Chef.

Well ventilated and furnished throughout.

TARIFF UPON APPLICATION

L. MARTIN
Proprietor and Manager

大韓每日申報
대한ᄆᆡ일신보

(뎨오십ᄉᆞ호) (토요일) 쳔구ᄇᆡᆨᄉᆞ년구월십칠일

본샤고ᄇᆡᆨ

○신보ᄂᆞᆫ영어와한어로셔계ᄆᆡ일츌판ᄒᆞᆸ

신문가

ᄒᆞᆫ쟝 엽ᄌᆞ돈오푼

일삭표엽ᄌᆞ량닷돈 ᄒᆞᆫ돈으로

밧ᄉᆞᆸ

광고료ᄂᆞᆫ

귀한의쟝단과ᄌᆞ항의다쇼로쥬감ᄒᆞ되ᄒᆞᆫ번가로밧을터이오며오ᄅᆡ지아니ᄒᆞ야대한사람마다다이신문을보실터이니광고내시기를원ᄒᆞ시ᄂᆞᆫ이들은우리신문사에와셔면약ᄒᆞ심을희망ᄒᆞᆸ

○발ᄒᆡᆼ소 박동대한ᄆᆡ일신보사 발어학교압헤 젼영국인셜필립쟝자리오

사쟝 영국인 (배셜)

사고

○우리대한ᄆᆡ일신보의목뎍은대한의인민을졀셔에관ᄒᆞᆫ모든대목에뎌ᄒᆞ야ᄂᆞᆫ공평ᄒᆞᆫ번론을쥬쟝홈이라우리동신원의닭보ᄂᆞᆫ신문보시ᄂᆞᆫ쳠군ᄌᆞ의게ᄒᆞᆼ샹보도ᄒᆞ리며편지를귀셔ᄒᆞ며주시ᄂᆞᆫ이ᄂᆞᆫ셩명과번디를젹어붓치시기를희망ᄒᆞ오니비거슨신문샹에긔ᄌᆡᄒᆞ란ᄂᆞᆫ거시아니오다만우리신용ᄒᆞᄂᆞᆫ증거를숨고자홈이라귀자ᄂᆞᆫ아모귀셔던지귀지홈을되쟉ᄒᆞᄂᆞᆫ권리를가졋스오나되쟉ᄒᆞᄂᆞᆫ리유를말ᄒᆞᆯ터이오며공중평화를문란케ᄒᆞᄂᆞᆫ듯ᄒᆞᆫ귀셔ᄂᆞᆫ의례히밧지안켓ᄉᆞᆸ나이다

●본사에셔아직귀계를쟝만치못ᄒᆞ와다른ᄃᆡ셔박여오ᄂᆞᆫ고로ᄆᆡ양월요일에ᄂᆞᆫ츌판이대단히늣게되ᄂᆞᆫ듯스오니젼이ᄆᆡ우늣게되오니우리신문을구람ᄒᆞ시ᄂᆞᆫ 쳠군ᄌᆞᄂᆞᆫ 용셔ᄒᆞ여주심을희망ᄒᆞᆸ나이다

●본샤셜시이리로신문을ᄆᆡ당우톄로분젼ᄒᆞ와혜젼부의임의로젼ᄒᆞᄂᆞᆫ듯스로번곳에ᄂᆞᆫ후늣게젼ᄒᆞ기도ᄒᆞ며후밋칠거슬ᄒᆞᆫ엽에젼ᄒᆞ기도ᄒᆞ며혹아니젼ᄒᆞᄂᆞᆫ곳도잇다ᄒᆞ와우리신문을ᄉᆞ랑ᄒᆞ야구람ᄒᆞ시ᄂᆞᆫ 쳠군ᄌᆞ의계뒤ᄒᆞ야ᄆᆡ우미안ᄒᆞ온바기로지금은분젼인을두고ᄆᆡ일쇽이젼ᄒᆞ며아니젼ᄒᆞ거나늣게가거나ᄒᆞᆫ폐가잇도록ᄒᆞ란ᄒᆞ오니혹아니젼ᄒᆞ거나혹늣게젼ᄒᆞ거나ᄒᆞᆫ일이잇스면본샤로통긔ᄒᆞ여주심을희망ᄒᆞᆸ

본샤광고

본샤에셔본신문뎨ᄉᆞ호와뎨삼일호와뎨이십오호ᄂᆞᆫ소용홀데가잇셔이에광고ᄒᆞ오니누구시던지이샹삼호중에본샤로가져오시면ᄆᆡ쟝에ᄇᆡᆨ젼두푼식드리리다

론셜

○중지소문 동경신문에중지복작을졔츌ᄒᆞ야게지ᄒᆞ엿ᄂᆞᆫᄃᆡ이ᄂᆞᆫ신호고로니콜신문이일본졍부긔관이되여말ᄒᆞᆫ바라ᄒᆞ나사ᄅᆞ셔만일중지홈을항당히여일의사만잇게되면일본셔ᄂᆞᆫ가히응종ᄒᆞᆯ겟다ᄒᆞ고홈을번등ᄒᆞ엿스ᄂᆞᆫ즉슈

지금에라도만일중지식힐사ᄅᆞᆷ만잇셔셔두나라로ᄒᆞ여금합의ᄒᆞ게ᄒᆞ견ᄒᆞᆯ지경이면필경중지ᄂᆞᆫ될듯ᄒᆞ나

우리의소견갓흐면셔ᄂᆞᆫ그중에ᄒᆞᆫ나라ᄒᆞᆫ위졀이잇ᄂᆞᆫ거시쳣ᄌᆡᄅᆞ아라사에셔일본으로더브러자웅을결단치안코병과를쉬이려다ᄂᆞᆫ나라의중지식음을항당히여일ᄂᆞᆫ지확실ᄒᆞᆫ비암슈업ᄂᆞᆫ거시아라사사ᄅᆞᆷ들은교만ᄒᆞ야자부ᄒᆞᄂᆞᆫ마음이비ᄒᆞᆫ터이엇스즉필경이ᄂᆞᆫ대셰지던지과여친즁말을보고아말ᄂᆞᆫ듯ᄒᆞᆫ의향이잇슬듯ᄒᆞ며일본ᄇᆡᆨ셩들도이번싸홈에겨국갓도보지안코환군ᄒᆞᆯ마음을닷지아니홀우학식이고명ᄒᆞᆫ사ᄅᆞᆷ들은아모조록진보ᄒᆞ야어리옹을무릅쓰고라도디져ᄒᆞ란ᄂᆞᆫ마음이잇슬듯ᄒᆞ되믈차ᄒᆞᆫ여리빅셩들리아ᄌᆞ귀나라ᄂᆞᆫ군사가외렷ᄒᆞ히승쳡홈을승로만정작ᄒᆞ엿ᄂᆞᆫ지라

이번관졔에일본셔당초요구ᄒᆞ든바에디ᄒᆞ야다소과중은불게ᄒᆞ고얼마곰이라도엇게만될지경이면ᄌᆞ귀나라에ᄂᆞᆫ대단히영광스러온일로알듯ᄒᆞ되이졔중지가된ᄃᆡ던지ᄯᅡ싸홈을이르ᄏᆡ승부를결단ᄒᆞ다던지ᄒᆞ두나라다이셔로평화ᄒᆞ야안온ᄒᆞ계지ᄂᆞᆫ던지어ᄶᅩ아누간에쟝ᄎᆞ셜노어려운일이성길듯ᄒᆞ지라

이번일아긔젼닝은셔로권리를취ᄒᆞ야리롬게ᄒᆞ자ᄂᆞᆫ주의인고로일본셔ᄂᆞᆫ한국과쳥국과장악중에다너어펀도도노ᄒᆞ며포티도진츌ᄒᆞ고식지아쭝방약등도잇의로ᄒᆞ샹리켜긔ᄒᆞ되

우리의싱각에ᄂᆞᆫ셜ᄒᆞᆫ일본셔승쳡ᄒᆞ드리도한국을일본에게리여홀리가업고쳥아국에셔승쳡을ᄒᆞᄂᆞᆫ경우라도만쥬를아라사에양도홀리가업ᄂᆞᆫ거시이두나라외에도권리잇ᄂᆞᆫ사ᄅᆞᆷ들리잇서셔일아젼쟁결말나기만기ᄃᆞ려과분ᄒᆞᆫ싱각두ᄂᆞᆫ사ᄅᆞᆷ들도만흘듯ᄒᆞ도다

잡보

○보쳥긔로 지작일샹오구시에납부로도착ᄒᆞᆫ창원군슈의뎐보를거ᄒᆞᆫ즉일본군용텰도지션를멸양삼랑포에셔마산포지부셜ᄒᆞᄂᆞᆫ디본군계사와 ᄒᆞᆼ희교쟝원뒤에표목을세웟기로힐탈도감부른보고텬로짐을본군압반관ᄒᆞᆫ곳으로옴거졍ᄒᆞ라고빅명ᄒᆞᆫ부시어ᄒᆞᆫ다ᄒᆞ고그텬로짐되ᄂᆞᆫ곳마다면답곡셔을아셩슈이못된거슬민원이분능ᄒᆞ고베히라ᄒᆞ야조져디가텬로에되며기로분슈경숑ᄒᆞ와뎐보오니외부에죠회ᄒᆞ야일공사교셥ᄒᆞ야히텬로부터치로게ᄒᆞ라ᄒᆞ엿더라

○이엄하고 일본용ᄉᆞ가외부로죠회ᄒᆞ되동리감리의이임혼리유를시명ᄒᆞ라ᄒᆞ엿더라

○일ᄒᆞᆯ도인 지작일인쳔감리하상긔씨가외부로뎐보ᄒᆞ되일본병함일쳑이금일입항ᄒᆞ엿다ᄒᆞ엿더라

○취병ᄒᆡᆼ괴 지작일원슈부에셔외부로죠회ᄒᆞ되헌병ᄉᆞ령관의보고에ᄒᆞ기를본ᄃᆡ부위리지관이보고ᄒᆞ여왈작일샹오십시량에본관이남분안쳥간안등디로지나더니보병삼십여명이위립ᄒᆞ엿ᄂᆞᆫᄃᆡ일헌병일명이대취ᄒᆞ야병쟝과슈소에돌립ᄒᆞ야칼을ᄲᆡ셔한병이명이중샹ᄒᆞ엿고쇼동을츌ᄒᆞ야본관의죵졸왕치덕의좌편다리를칼노질으고금외도주ᄒᆞ엿다ᄒᆞ니취ᄒᆞᆫ병의ᄒᆡᆼ괴홈이심히경히ᄒᆞᆫ지라일관에죠회ᄒᆞ야수령부로젼칙ᄒᆞ야히일병을장아사실ᄒᆞ야죠률징판케ᄒᆞ라ᄒᆞ엿더라

○평병퇴귀 아국병을방어ᄎᆞ로함경도에츌쥬ᄒᆞ엿든평양딘위디병의게퇴츌되야텬원셔지도퇴귀ᄒᆞ엿더니현금포쳔등디에다답ᄒᆞ엿다ᄒᆞ니일간입셩ᄒᆞ겟더라

관보

관보뎨이쳔구ᄇᆡᆨ삼십이호

광무팔년구월십오일

셔임급ᄉᆞ령

○의원면본관 즁추원의관 변규챵

○임즁추원의관셔주임관륙등 경위원경무관 리운호

○임경무관셔주임관륙등 뎐환과주ᄉᆞ 연시티

○보경위원참듀 경무관 연시티

이샹구월십이일

○임뵈쥬감리셔주임관오등 경흥감리 리민부

○셔주임관ᄉᆞ등 령ᄉᆞ관 윤용구

○임룡쳔감리셔주임관ᄉᆞ등 령ᄉᆞ관 윤용구

○겸임령ᄉᆞ관 룡쳔감리 윤용구

○임경흥감리셔주임관륙등 젼의관 권직희

이샹구월십삼일

○임외부주ᄉᆞ셔판임관륙등 윤학영

구월십ᄉᆞ일

○중면칙 경무쳥경무관 리시영

○견칙 경무쳥총 함우형

이샹구월십삼일

외보

○희샹위경항 지금희샹위항구에ᄂᆞᆫ다슈ᄒᆞᆫ군ᄉᆞ가와셔유쥬ᄒᆞ고로그거ᄂᆞᆫ항구에ᄇᆡ로ᄆᆡ일두번식리왕ᄒᆞ고항만에아국군함코림샙이아ᄒᆞ오와로시아ᄒᆞ트빈가거취쳠몰ᄒᆞᄂᆞᆫ모양으로히항에드러을ᄇᆡ에아국관민이다ᄂᆞᆯ너여ᄋᆞ시ᄂᆞᆫ흔젹ᄒᆞ야분주ᄒᆞ더

셔ᄒᆞ라수쟝관이음악되는용쟝ᄒᆞᆫ계랑으로주창ᄒᆞ야인심쇼동을진정케ᄒᆞ엿고알렌씨푸총등은쟝찬히항에서두류ᄒᆞ엿스나즉시만주로도라갓고랑시온별노편젼ᄒᆞ지아니ᄒᆞ엿는ᄃᆡ피젼된것은스탈쎈이라더라

○상쟁괴변 봉텬에잇는은항쇼와아국회ᄉᆞ와샹졈을몰수히결과ᄒᆞ엿다더라

○로민실업 금번에아젼쟁이뤼로아국인민에진업을일흔자가ᄃᆡ단히만ᄒᆞᆫᄃᆡ와루쇼위ᄃᆡ방에는샹공ᄒᆞ던칠십명이나되고루톳목스ᄃᆡ방에는일만명이나된다더

잡보

○탕세착정 민영환씨샹ᄒᆞᆫ탕세가의쟝부착쟝을피임ᄒᆞ엿다더라

○봉세관소환 각도에신치ᄒᆞᆫ봉세관들을일병소환ᄒᆞᆫ다더라

○장욕토사 일인의협동토약ᄒᆞᆫ탐지고문관목하뎐씨가리도ᄒᆞᆫ후에는비쟝원에일본인을파송ᄒᆞ야부를토사ᄒᆞᆫ다더라

○출긔지령 삼등수안등디회정ᄒᆞᆫ동항당이홍병ᄉᆞ에가만히류일ᄒᆞ고섭렵ᄒᆞ야지작일경무청에서순검을각곡에파송ᄒᆞ야작괴주예두류ᄒᆞ는시끌손을문외로출송케ᄒᆞᆫ방으로지칙ᄒᆞ엿더라

○교련장우미 군부에서훈련원을슈리ᄒᆞ고교련쟝을일신ᄒᆞ게슈츅ᄒᆞ엿더니근일에일본병이취괴ᄃᆡ에서교련ᄒᆞ는고로친위일ᄃᆡᄃᆡ에서병명교련쟝을동쇼문외람뎐광으로다시명ᄒᆞ고표목을세웟다더라

○학부훈칙 학부에서각도관찰부와각항감리셔와각군에ᄒᆞᆫ칙ᄒᆞ기를각처공립쇼학교교원이하과후학ᄒᆞᆫ이후로흥평셩에두류ᄒᆞ며ᄒᆞ분정에도라가셔츄귀학일ᄌᆞ가지는지다일에만ᄒᆞ학교에리도치아니ᄒᆞᆫ다ᄒᆞ니셩히흰ᄒᆞᆫ치라각학교교원의서무여부를실샹ᄃᆡ로보고ᄒᆞ라ᄒᆞ엿더라

○수쟝장기 샹황궁으로셔샹리ᄒᆞᆫ사ᄅᆞᆷ의말을드른즉희항연보ᄉᆞ쟝경우헌씨가항구부민명벗슬유인ᄒᆞ야비밀히장기관을고안방에차리고장기와투노ᄅᆞᆺ술ᄒᆞ다가순검의게포착되야장젼과물패들세앗기고ᄒᆞᆨ쌤도마지며겨우방도딩ᄒᆞ엿다더라

○조청일표 외부에서일공관에조회ᄒᆞ기를 궁니부조회니ᄂᆞ에ᄒᆞ엿스ᄃᆡ평양관찰ᄉᆞ리중하의보고를거ᄒᆞᆫ즉일본병참소에서군용디라ᄒᆞ고본군외셩셔쭉신오리에표목을세워차막중ᄒᆞᆫ 황궁과 귀궁이ᄃᆡ표목안에드렷스니수레에손샹된지라일공관에이죠ᄒᆞ야타관ᄒᆞ각ᄒᆞ엿기로죠회ᄒᆞ니귀ᄉᆞ령부에젼죠ᄒᆞ야취ᄃᆡ표목을본일노거ᄃᆡ옴겨셔수레를온젼히ᄒᆞ고린국교의를돗탑케ᄒᆞ라ᄒᆞ엿더라

○평민청원 평양거ᄒᆞ는진ᄉᆞ김졔익이외부에쳥원ᄒᆞ야왈본군슈핑황쥬가텰도용역ᄉᆞ로본군이십구방젼답만여호에ᄎᆞ호ᄒᆞ야역군쓸기를샹ᄉᆞᄎᆞ를ᄒᆞ엿는ᄃᆡ삭젼을호ᄉᆞ오젼ᄒᆞᆫ이삭젼식주고호아니주기도ᄒᆞ엿스니텰시본군슈의침롱ᄒᆞᆫ거시라일본텰도ᄃᆡ에셔아니준리가업슨즉바라건ᄃᆡ일공관에죠회ᄒᆞ야그중간리유를졀문ᄒᆞ야역군에삭젼을밧아주어셔잔민을안도케ᄒᆞ라ᄒᆞ엿더라

○격외ᄐᆞᆷ리 황샹폐하ᄭᅴ옵셔공쟝근쳐에범ᄒᆞ야진축ᄒᆞ는거슬 불열ᄒᆞ신다ᄒᆞ는바이어니와이수삼년리익으로알고민쳡ᄒᆞᆫ모리지ᄇᆡ들이 대궐을ᄃᆞ라다ᄂᆡ이게공쟝밧괴다가각금집을짓는지라

궁ᄂᆡ부에셔이졉들을각금식셔ᄃᆞ렷는ᄃᆡ져희들이레수ᄇᆞᆯ기로면위ᄒᆞ야지엇스ᄆᆡ목슈의게들나도암젼ᄒᆞᆫ리익을붓쳐주엇는지라

지금우리가ᄯᅩ다른일ᄒᆞ기ᄂᆞ른계손엇던사ᄅᆞᆷ이괴요ᄒᆞᆫ의젼을셩각ᄒᆞ며 대궐은ᄃᆞ러다뵈이지안코거긔과갓갑기만ᄒᆞᆫ졉들을모도다사셔리를보련다ᄒᆞ는ᄃᆡ

황샹ᄭᅴ옵셔권ᄒᆞ며이여러ᄎᆔ파ᄒᆞᆫ집들을사게ᄒᆞ실희ᄃᆞᆼ으로ᄡᅥ니야기들지어버기를일본사ᄅᆞᆷ이영문으로쓰기를위ᄒᆞ야이근쳐에졉을사라고듯본다고ᄒᆞᆫ다ᄒᆞ니이런니야기는낫잔지리온거진말인거시이런졉들은영문을만들기에합당치안을ᄲᅮᆫ더러다른영문들에셔샹거가너무멀어셔일인의게는아모소용도되지안을지라

레ᄉᆞ로는우리가우리지분안에는ᄉᆞᄉᆞ로이공관ᄒᆞᆯ일에간셥ᄒᆞ야샹량ᄒᆞᆯ바아니언마는이런졉들에참솔리면에당치안케너무만히ᄂᆞᆯ나는것과분명이거진말인니야기를젼파ᄒᆞ야 황샹폐하ᄭᅴ셔과망ᄒᆞ야사도록ᄒᆞ는거슬보는바에희구ᄒᆞᆫ일이리ᄒᆞᆫ즉우리의ᄯᅳᆺ을셜명ᄒᆞᆯ희포를이제ᄒᆞᆯ수업도다

○잡기ᄐᆡ국 근일모모ᄃᆡ관졔씨가밤마다잡기를ᄒᆞᆫ다ᄒᆞ더니샹부ᄒᆞᆫ즉잡기관덧친은지화로ᄒᆞ고젼쥬는일본인교목이오장기관에당국자는졔졍관최여ᄒᆞ와젼승지유진찬과젼평리원쟝리남희제씨와ᄯᅩ모모인이라ᄒᆞ는ᄃᆡ젼주유일인만물과수일에치부ᄒᆞ고당국자제씨는ᄃᆡ쾌산ᄃᆡ경이라더라

○일쟝귀셜 주차한국일본군수령관원구씨와참모쟝졔등씨가귀국ᄒᆞᆫ다는ᄃᆡ변관이되엿다는말도잇다더라

○병출시흥 시흥민요수건을인연ᄒᆞ야동대문ᄂᆡ주차ᄒᆞᆫ일본후비ᄃᆡ중위서박무씨가일쇼ᄃᆡ를령솔ᄒᆞ고제작일신시량에하거ᄒᆞ엿다더라

○등쳔수령관 제작일경부회의에신참경이젼참령리민직을위션과봉식ᄒᆞ여동학초로ᄒᆞᆯ수령관을임용ᄒᆞ기로쳔거ᄒᆞᆫ즉각ᄃᆡ관이만히불가타ᄒᆞ되참졍이귀어코귀봉임용ᄒᆞᆯ수로 주본ᄒᆞ엿다더라

○퇴각청의 문밧게셔한강셔지쳐도ᄒᆞ는ᄃᆡ닉부에셔치도역비오만원을에산의지출ᄉᆞ로졍부회의에청의ᄒᆞᆷ을졔출ᄒᆞ엿더니졍부에셔퇴각ᄒᆞ며왈별ᄎᆞᄒᆞᆫ거ᄉᆞᆯ은거로ᄒᆞᆯ수업다ᄒᆞ엿더라

○ᄂᆡ대면관 일젼에ᄂᆡ부에셔주본ᄒᆞ이십오명군슈가쳥ᄉᆞ가만코용쳔이젹음으로불시가뎐지라참졍신씨가ᄂᆡ부대신죠병필씨를탄핵샹 주ᄒᆞ와면본관되엿더라

○용기졔관 작쟝례원에서민수샹안진으로공기졔관을ᄒᆞ엿는ᄃᆡ시쳥ᄒᆞ는사ᄅᆞᆷ만방쳥을리잉ᄒᆞ엿다더라

○ᄂᆡ하슈쳔원 경무ᄉᆞ원우샹씨는본리가세가쳥빈ᄒᆞᆫ지라참쟝승차ᄒᆞᆫ지오리되복장을쥰비치못ᄒᆞ엿더니이젼에 텬폐셔복장비슈쳔원을 ᄂᆡ하ᄒᆞ셧더라

○헌경ᄎᆞᆯ수 시흥민요수건을인ᄒᆞ야수삼ᄎᆞᄎᆞ로제작일에일본경찰셔쟝관곽씨가순ᄉᆞ삼ᄂᆡ을령솔ᄒᆞ야ᄎᆔᄃᆡ로출거ᄒᆞ고일본헌병ᄃᆡ에셔도쟝교일명과ᄂᆡ병오명이발왕ᄒᆞ엿다더라

○민요속문 시흥민요수졀ᄃᆡ강속문ᄒᆞᆫ즉샹작일하오시량에슈ᄃᆡᄒᆞᆫ빅셩이시흥관ᄂᆡ에돌입ᄒᆞ야취군슈박우양씨ᄒᆞ고아ᄂᆞᆫ을불에소샹ᄒᆞ엿다ᄂᆞᆫ되소샹ᄒᆞᆫ수실은아지못ᄒᆞ나되소문을드른즉ᄒᆞᆷ이여모로ᄂᆡ고시흥군에셔샹업ᄒᆞ는인을모집ᄒᆞ야츌발ᄒᆞ엿는ᄃᆡ일본부에위ᄒᆞ야지화ᄉᆞ빅원을쥬게ᄒᆞ기로셔히여부등의가권을ᄋᆡ쥬게ᄒᆞ기로보니여반금ᄒᆞ라ᄒᆞ엿더니희군지슈가긴불ᄒᆞ고일푼도밧지아니ᄒᆞᆫ지라그리ᄒᆞᆷ으로삼인이셩ᄂᆡ[illegible]회돗ᄒᆞ야이민호일반명가량이작당ᄒᆞ야산뫼에들입ᄒᆞ야군슈와그아들모씨와슈셔기등을결박ᄒᆞ야장작뎡미우에언고불노ᄒᆞ엿는ᄃᆡ희ᄃᆡ방잇든텰도역부일인이ᄉᆡ여명도참혹ᄒᆞᆫ화를당ᄒᆞ엿는ᄃᆡ이명은즉수ᄒᆞ고수명은피샹ᄒᆞ고그외에여러사ᄅᆞᆷ은흣터져피신ᄒᆞ고흑타쳐로도망ᄒᆞ야부지거쳐라ᄒᆞ고인민등은작게ᄒᆞᆫ뒤에주시희산ᄒᆞ엿다더라

○투소졔 근일에평향쟝류빈가샹소ᄒᆞᆫ다자칭ᄒᆞ고타인의셩명을투록ᄒᆞ야소슈를샹아샹소를봉졍ᄒᆞ는폐습이파다ᄒᆞᆷ으로자 샹으로통촉ᄒᆞ옵시고자금이후로는무론누구던지소본을봉졍ᄒᆞᆯ시에는소슈되는자가친히와셔비셔원으로밧치지아니ᄒᆞ는쇼본은일졀되각ᄒᆞ고밧지말나는 칙명이나리셧다더라

○셩규ᄃᆞ록 강능군에셔금년하젼진샹ᄒᆞᆯ녹용을쳐셔가봉원드록수습지못ᄒᆞ야군슈박귀현씨가조ᄎᆞ로황송ᄒᆞ고민을ᄒᆞᆫ마음을맛괴지못ᄒᆞ야몸소산양ᄒᆞ는광에나가셔졍셩을다ᄒᆞ야귀셩우ᄒᆞ엿는ᄃᆡ텬우신조ᄒᆞ야귀셩ᄂᆞᆫ졔삼일만에낫ᄃᆡ엿는시랑의세가사슴ᄒᆞ나를모러오ᄂᆞ니그사슴이향쟝안으로드러가는지라고동리빅셩들이나무몽치로셔리여잡엇는ᄃᆡ그록용일쌍이극히죠와강롱빅샹들도그리ᄒᆞᆫ록용은금시쵸견이라ᄒᆞᄂᆞ니횟군슈가죽시관찰부로보고ᄒᆞ엿는ᄃᆡ관찰ᄉᆞ가졍ᄒᆞ기를시랑의세가사슴을ᄂᆡ리디린것과동민의세가잡은거시다박군슈의졍셩이지극ᄒᆞᆫᄃᆡ셔ᄉᆡᆼᄒᆞ는ᄃᆡ다힝이오경ᄉᆞ로온일이라ᄒᆞ엿더라

RESTORATION OF LOST RELIC.

The English Catholic colony here is considered to have been specially favoured by the Pope. It received his Holiness' seasonable compliments under form of the restitution to their Church of San Silvestro of a relic which is claimed to be unique. It is, in fact, quite independently of its religious value, a most interesting and important object because of its history and the traditions which cluster around it.

Highly honoured and truly fortunate may that church claim to be which shelters the authentic head of St. John the Baptist. That is the Church of San Silvestro. According to a tradition ten centuries old, the head which was demanded by the daughter of Herodias as a reward for her dancing, was carried from Palestine to Rome. It reached the Eternal City a thousand years ago, being brought by certain Greek monks, who deposited it in the Church of San Silvesro in Capite, which at that time was a monastery.

Innumerable miracles were wrought by the agency of the head of the saint, and in such estimation was the relic that regular pitched battles were fought for its possession. In 1411, while the head was being carried in procession, certain unruly Florentines attacked the cortege, but they were successfully repulsed by the Romans, who were led by the Prince Colonna of the time. After this, fearing that the precious objec might be lost, the Popes ordered that it was never to leave the Church of San Silvestro, and it remained there until 1870, when Rome was besieged by the troops of Victor Emmanuel. It was then carried by the order of Pius I. to the Vatican. The present Pope, however, thinks that there can be no danger in returning the relic to its ancient resting place. The holy head is contained in a valuable silver reliquary, weighing over 100 pounds—Rome correspondene of the London Telegraph.

THE CROWN PRINCE OF SIAM.

H.R.H. Somdetch Chow Fa Mhavajiravidh, Crown Prince of Siam has entered the Buddhist priesthood and Prince Songkla Nakarinda, anothe son of the King, has also entered. The novitiate ceremonies, which are of an elaborate character, were commeced at the Grand Palace, the King taing part in the great religious ceremon of Amarindr Vinichai in the Throne Room. The King proceeded with a brilliant procession which bore the Crown Prince in a litter to the Wat Prakeo, whe Prince Najirayan and thirty other prominent priests were waiting. Thereupon the ceremony of initiation to the priesthood was commenced. The King presented yellow robes and other vestments to the two Princes, who also later received robes from the Queen and other members of the Royal Family. On the conclusion of the ceremonies the King conducted the two Princes to the Wat Boworanuvale, where they will pass their period of priesthood, which is understood to be until the end of the present season of the Buddhist Lent, towards the end of October. The Procession and ceremonies were not seen by those outside the Palace walls.—Straits Echo.

A Chefoo dispatch of the 31st ultimo to the "N. C. Daily News" reports that the steamer "Independent," which arrived from Japan with sake, beer, gold, and silver etc., on board bound for Newchwang, had been ordered by the Commissioner of Customs to land her cargo at Chefoo, on the ground that his orders are to enforce the discharge of any cargo which may be classed as contraband from any vessel bound for the fighting sphere. The Japanese Consul insisted that this is a misinterpretation of the duty of a neutral, and was discussing the matter with the Commissioner. A message of the following day reports that the Chinese government has decided that no contraband bound for Newchwang shall necessarily be discharged in a mere port of call.

DETAILS OF THE KING'S SPEECH.

London, August 16.—H. M. the King's speech on the prorogation of Parliament says that foreign relations continue to be in a satisfactory state. It is stated that the agreements with France will materially strengthen the ties of friendship between her and Britain. The speech next refers to the cordial reception which H. M. met with at Copenhagen and Kiel. H. M. regrets that hostilities are still in progress between Russia and Japan and says further:—Questions involving the treatment of neutral commerce have arisen. The issues involved which are of the gravest moment to the trade of the Empire will I trust be amicably settled. My Government will energetically support my subjects in the exercise of rights recognised by international law as belonging to neutrals." It has been decided to sanction the introduction of the elective element into the Transvaal Legislature. H. M. trusts that all classes there will unite in rendering this step in the direction of self-government conducive to the welfare of H. M.'s dominions. The political mission to Thibet encountered some resistance. But, says H. M., "its safe arrival at Lhassa affords me the greatest satisfaction, and reflects the highest credit on the officers and men of the small force employed. I trust that by conference with the Thibetan authorities, in conjunction with the Chinese representatives at Lhassa, terms may be arranged facilitating trade and for ending the difficulty and the friction which have arisen on the northern frontier of India." H. M. also expresses trust that the army reorganization now proceeding may conduce to the defensive strength of the Empire.

THE OSAKA SHOSEN KAISHA.

In January, 1900, the Osaka Shosen Kaisha decided to double its capital, namely, to increase it to 11 million yen. Owing, however, to the unfavourable economic conditions in the country, the scheme has since been in abeyance, the necessary working expenses being met by temporary loans. Now the "Kokumin learns that the company has decided to carry out the plan and will notify its shareholders to that effect by October 1 next.

THE BANK OF JAPAN.

Matters relating to the national loan bonds, issued both at home and abroad, have hitherto been dealt with at the Second Section of the Business Bureau of the Bank of Japan. Owing, however, to the recent increased business in his connection, the Bureau of National Bonds was established on the 1st inst., the above-mentioned section being abolished. Mr. M. Sudo, one of the Directors of the Bank, has been appointed Chief of the new Bureau.

A number of Korean officials seem to be at the mercy of an enterprising Japanese of the name of Takagi. It is reported that many officials have a penchant for gambling and that those in difficulties go to a Mr. Takagi for accomodation. Our reporters copy Concluc as follous:—"Most of them are near destruction of properties; but only one who is getting more rich and fat is Mr. Takagi."

The following for an original story translated into English by a novice is not bad.—The elk horns which yearly offer to the Palace from Kang-nung district of Kang-wŏn province, as this year the summer is ended, but could not caught an elk in that district, so, the Magistrate of that district Mr. Pak Hyŏn himself went to hunting place and praid heart to the spirit of mountains to make him to get elk, on 3rd day since his praying the bands of wolves driven an elk into a house, so, the people of that village caught that elk with only sticks, the magistrate was so glad, and the horn of that elk very nice, the magistrate sent it to the Governor to send up to Emperor.

Lynching seems to have reached the Transvaal. According to a correspondent in the London "Standard," a native who assaulted a white woman was recently lynched with dispatch and secrecy on a plantation in the centre of Johannesburg. This is the first act of the newly-formed Vigilance Committee, who, deeming the ordinary course of the law inadequate, are pledged to the suppression of this from of crime. The negro, when captured, was stunned, and then strung to a tree by a piece of wire. The police affect to believe that the native committed suicide, fearing capture. While attacks on women must be vigorously supressed, it may be hoped the Government in South Africa will take vigorous action in preventing scenes which are still witnessed in certain parts of America the continuance of which is a disgrace to any civilised Government.

Lieut-Col. W. H. Drage, who is retiring from the Egyptian Army after nearly 20 years' connection with it, has been presented with a valuable testimonial and address by his fellow-workers on the Nile. Col. Drage is a self-made man, and a native of Wandsworth, where he was born 52 years ago. He joined the army 30 years back, and by diligence became a warrant-officer just before the Nile Expedition of 1884-5, in which he served and won distinction and further promotion. He has been in all the Nile wars since, winning his majority and some Egyptian decorations in the Dongola affair of 1896, and securing the D.S.O. and promotion to the rank of lieutenant-colonel for his brilliant services at Omdurman. After the trouble he was selected for the onerous and delicate post of Controller of the Soudan Civil Administration, and most of the success at Khartoum is due to his sound judgment and energy.

The Korea Daily News.

To be published daily except Sundays.

Rate of Subscription:—

Per Year, Yen 25.
Per Quarter, Yen 7.
Per Month Yen 2.50

postage in Korea not charged extra.
postage abroad charged extra.

Advertisements, 50 sen per day for 1 inch or less.
5 yen per month per inch.
50 yen per year per inch.

All communications to

E. T. BETHELL,
Editor and Publisher.
Pak-tong, Seoul.

A SPECULATION.

The Emperor's dislike of any infringement of his privacy is well known. Taking advantage of this fact, astute speculators have from time to time errected buildings just outside the palace walls overlooking the palace enclosure.

These buildings have been from time to time bought up by the Imperial Household and as they were generally only built to sell, they have returned their ingenious constructors a handsome profit.

We now hear of another little transaction which is on the "tapis." Someone has conceived the brilliant idea of turning to account a number of houses which do not overlook the palace but are near it.

With the hope of inducing His Majesty to buy these ram-shackle structures a story has been cooked-up to the effect that the Japanese are seeking to acquire them for use as barracks. The story is a fable on the face of it. The buildings are not suitable for barracks and are too far removed from the other barracks to be of any use to the Japanese.

In the ordinary way we do not consider it within our province to interfere with the private speculations, but in view of the absurdly large sum which is asked for these houses and the obvious untruth of the story which is being circulated in order to induce His Majesty to buy, we cannot refrain from expressing our opinion that many better uses could be found for the Imperial money.

REMARKABLE OUTRAGE NEAR SEOUL.

MAGISTRATE SUFFERS DEATH AT THE STAKE.

At 5 p.m. on the 14th inst. the inhabitants of Si Hung suddenly commenced to riot. One thousand strong they surrounded the Magisterial office and demanded to see Mr. Pak Woo-yang. He and his son happened to be in an inner room and coming out to see what was the cause of the trouble were immediately seized and bound with ropes. The clerk of the office was then taken and the three bound together were conducted to a pile of faggots, (which had been rapidly constructed) and tied to a stake. The captors then set fire to the pile and the wretched victims were soon burnt to death.

The cause of this atrocity is said to be occasioned by the magistrate having held back $400, which had been sent by the Japanese for the payment of coolies, working on the railroad.

Some Japanese, about 25 in number, all workers on the railroad, attempted to interfere but the infuriated mob turning on them, killed two and wounded four, and the rest made good their escape.

Some Japanese troops have been sent to enforce justice at Si Hung, which is situated not more than 12 miles from Seoul.

THE WAR AND RUSSIA.

EFFECTS OF THE WAR ON THE ECONOMIC STATE OF RUSSIA.

(Concluded).

Let us see now what more dispassionate and more competent judges say about the matter. The civil engineer Tamburno, who helped to build the trans-Siberian Railway, had recently given his opinion as follows: "The transportation to Manchuria of military stores and provisions for an army of 500,000 men is an almost impossible task. If we allow every soldier three and a half pounds of food per day (the daily ration in time of peace), we must provide transportation, every day, for 875 tons of flour, bread, tallow, sugar, &c.; 350 head of cattle; and 1,200 tons of provender for horses. If we assume that Eastern Siberia can furnish all the provender for the horses and half the required number of cattle, we shall still need, for the rest of the provisions, about 210 railway cars per day. Allowing ten per cent for loss, which is always great in an active army, we find that we must send over the Siberian road every day from 230 to 240 cars loaded with provisions alone. In addition to this, we must count two trains a day for ammunition and military supplies; two trains to meet the wants of the population at local stations; one passenger train and one train for railway material and fuel. An equal number of trains, of course, will have to come back. Is the Siberian railway capable of doing this amount of work? Or, in other words, can we maintain an army of 500,000 men in Manchuria?"

Mr. Tamburno does not reply to this question; but an answer to it may be found in the statement of a French engineer who has recently returned from Mukden. With regard to the Siberian Railway, he expresses a very unfavourable opinion. It was built, he says, rapidly and with poor materials. Everybody knows now, that the rails for it were too light. A saving of 5,000,000 roubles was made by using these light rails, but twice that sum has probably been expended in repairs, which would not have been needed if the rails had been heavier. The present bad condition of the road is due to three causes. First, the lightness of the rails makes it difficult to keep them exactly parallel under heavy traffic. This compels trains, in some places, to reduce their speed to that of a trotting horse. Second, the nature of the ties or sleepers, which are generally of common pine, not even tarred. Finally, the character of the ballast, which, in many places, is nothing but sand. This is blown away by the wind, leaving the sleepers bare. "The transportion of troops," this engineer says, "over a single line of road and for so great a distance is a difficut matter at best: but it becomes the hardest and most complicated task in the world when all the military stores of the commissary and ordnance departments must go over the same route."

He is of opinion that we have not been able, as yet, to send eastward through Siberia more than ten trains per day, and that in these ten trains there was not room for more than 1,200 soldiers. To send 400,000 men to Manchuria, at that rate, would require at least a year. He believes, therefore, that Kuropatkin had, in June, not more than 150,000 men, and that he was being reinforced at the rate of only 1,000 to 1,200 men per day.

Evidently the "second phase" of the war is still far distant.

Special guards have been placed at the city gates to keep a strict look out for Tonghaks entering the capital.

The Education Department has suddenly woke up to the fact that the summer vacation of public schools finished on August 31st, and they are now inquiring whether the teachers in the country schools have returned to their posts.

MURDER BY RIOTERS.

The magistrate of the Si Hung district telegraphs that his son and two Japanese were killed by rioters on the 14th inst.

It is stated in Seoul that a body of Japanese troops will be despatched to quell the disturbance and bring the ringleaders to justice.

The Japanese Minister asks the reason of the withdrawal of the Kamni of Gensan from his post.

The Japanese artillery were to have held practice firing outside the South Gate tomorrow, but we learn that for certain reasons, it has been postponed.

The application of the Home Department for $50,000 for the repair of the roads from the South Gate to the Han river, has been refused by the Government.

It is reported that light-houses are to be built on the islands Kei Mun Do and Chil Bal Do. The lights will be visible at 25 miles distance and the work will be completed by next April.

The military authorities have requested the Japanese Headquarters to discover the gendarme, who recently wounded two Korean soldiers at the South Gate, and visit him with severe punishment.

The Chief of Police, Mr. Won Woo Sang, has been promoted to the rank of Major General. He is too poor to pay for his uniform so His Majesty has graciously presented him with the necessary funds.

The magistrate of Chang Won is indignant that the branch line of the Seoul-Fusan railway passes in close proximity to two specially sanctified temples. He thinks it not at all out of the question to request the authorities to build their line in another direction.

The Magistrate of Pingyang is charged with yet another offence. Mr. Kim Chai Ik asserts that he received money from the Japanese to pay the coolies working on the railway, their daily wage, but so far these coolies have received only 5 or 6 cents daily and occasionally have received no wages at all.

Mr. Chung Woo Hun, the Director of Telegraphs at Chinnampo, has been arrested on a charge of gambling. His premises were recently raided by the police, who found a large sum of money and a crowd of young pigeons eagerly parting with it to the banker Mr. Chung who is evidently is an accomplished gambler.

The "Times," says a London correspondent, has demonstrated the unequalled advantage of advertising in newspapers. The value of such advertisements has always been recognised by business men, but of late an idea has been abroad that posters were equally useful. The "Times" has shown this to be an error. Its two sets of "Encyclopædia Britannica," the first of which is almost out of date, sold like the proverbial hot cakes. Although the price was from about £15 to £22, the public bought them more readily than they buy a six-shilling novel. Other enterprises of the great journal have proved equally successful, yet the "Times" never used posters, but confined itself solely to large display advertisements in the newspapers of the country and circulars. The proprietors are said to have netted a million pounds on the "Encyclopædia" alone through this means of advertising. Their example is now being followed by some of the enterprising business firms, who find it highly remunerative to pay large sums of money for column and two-column advertisements in the newspapers.

The Korea Daily News.

VOL. I, SATURDAY, SEPTEMBER 17, 1904. No. 54

HONGKONG & SHANGHAI BANKING CORPORATION.

Paid-up Capital	$10,000,000
Reserve Fund:—Sterling Reserve	10,000,000
Silver Reserve	6,500,000
	26,500,000
Reserve Liability of Proprietors	10,000,000

HEAD OFFICE, HONGKONG.

London Bankers, London and County Banking Company Limited.

Branches and Agencies, London.

Amoy,	Hankow	Penang,
Bangkok,	Hiogo,	Rangoon,
Batavia,	Iloilo,	Saigon,
Bombay,	Lyons,	San Francisco,
Calcutta,	Manila,	Singapore,
Colombo,	Nagasaki,	Sourabaya,
Foochow,	New York,	Tientsin,
Hamburg,	Peking,	Yokohama,

Credits granted on approved Securities, and every description of Banking and Exchange business transacted.

Drafts granted on London and the chief Commercial places in Europe, India, Australia, America, China and Japan.

HOLME RINGER & Co., AGENTS, CHEMULPO.

CHARTERED BANK OF INDIA AUSTRALIA & CHINA.

INCORPORATED BY ROYAL CHARTER 1853

HEAD OFFICES:—LONDON.

Paid-up Capital	£800,000
Reserve Liability of Shareholders	800,000
Reserve Fund	800,000

Drafts granted upon all the principal places in the world and every description of Exchange and banking business transacted.

E. MEYER & Co., Agents, Chemulpo.

DAI-ICHI GINKO.

LIMITED.

(Formerly the First National Bank)

ESTABLISHED 1873

INCORPORATED UNDER PRESENT LAW 1896

Capital	Yen 5,000,000
Reserve Fund	1,500,000

HEAD OFFICE:—TOKIO.

President: Baron SHIBUSAWA.

BRANCHES AND CORRESPONDENTS In the Principal Cities and Towns of Japan.

Interest Allowed on

Fixed deposits	1 year	6½ per cent
" "	6 months	6 per cent

Special current accounts 1½ sen daily per ¥ 100

General " " 1 " " " 100

M. TANAKA, Manager, Chemulpo.

NIPPON YUSEN KAISHA.

JAPANESE MAIL STEAMSHIP CO

DER MAIL CONTRACT WITH THE IMPERIAL JAPANESE GOVERNMENT.

European Line

Regular Fortnightly Service between Yokohama Kobe, Moji, Shanghai, Hongkong, Singapore, Penang Colombo, Port Said, Marseilles, London and Antwerp

American Line

Regular Fortnightly Service between Hongkong and Seattle, calling at Shanghai, Moji, Kobe, Yokohama and Victoria, B. C.

Australian Line

Regular weekly Service betwen Japan Ports and Australia, callingiat Hongkong and Manila.

(Above Three Lines Suspended until further notice).

Shanghai Line

Weekly Service between Shanghai and Japan Ports

Korea Line

Service Kobe, Moji, Nagasaki, Fusan, Chemulpo, Chioo, Taku.

S. S. Bahelsberg, 2181 tons.

Service Kobe, Moji, Fusan, Chemulpo, Chinnampo

S. S ARGO. S. S. Ohio.

ON CHEONG & CO., SEOUL.

GENERAL STORE KEEPERS.

Imported provisions, Cooking Utensils Crockery, etc.

FRESH BREAD DAILY.

MITSU BISHI DOCKYARD & ENGINE WORKS,

NAGASAKI.

CODE WORD, "DOCK."

A. 1, A. B. C., and Engineering Codes used.

DOCK No. 1 (at Tategami).

Extreme Length	523 feet
Length on blocks	513 ,,
Width of Entrance on Top	89 ,,
,, ,, Bottom	77 ,,
Water on Blocks at Spring Tide	26½ ,,

DOCK No. 2 (Mukaijima).

Extreme Length	371 feet
Length on Blocks	360 ,,
Width of Entrance on Top	66 ,,
,, ,, Bottom	53 ,,
Water on Blocks at Spring Tide	22 ,,

PATENT SLIP (at Kosuge).

Can take vessels up to 1,000 tons gross.

THE WORKS are well equipped with the LATEST IMPROVEMENTS, and can execute any kind of work in SHIPBUILDING and MARINE ENGINEERING, as well as in REPAIRING of SHIPS.

The COMPANY'S new powerful steamer OURA-MARU (712 tons, 700 I.H.P.), specially built for SALVAGE PURPOSES, and equipped with necessary gear, is always READY at SHORT NOTICE.

E. MEYER & CO.

Chemulpo.

SOLE AGENTS IN KOREA FOR:

A. T. Morse, Sons & Co's "Fresco" Distemper

In all colours ready for use on walls, Ceilings etc.

and

AVENARIUS CARBOLINEUM

A wood-preserving and antiseptic oil preparation

Against decay, dry-rot, fungus and wood-destroying insects.

A large supply always in Stock.

Prices upon application.

E. MEYER & Co., Chemulpo.

LAW UNION & CROWN INS. CO.

Fire risks accepted at Current rates, on godowns, merchandise, dwellings, and other property, subject to usual conditions.

HOLME RINGER & Co., Agents, Chemulpo

THE METHODIST PUBLISHING HOUSE,

Little West Gate, Seoul.

JOB PRINTING, TYPEWRITER PAPER
CARBON PAPER, VISITING CARDS
STATIONERY, BOOK BINDING
BOOK PUBLISHERS
AMERICAN SCHOOL BOOKS
SPENCERIAN COPY BOOKS
PEN CARBON LETTER AND BILL BOOKS

S. A. BECK, Manager.

HOLME RINGER & Co.

Chemulpo.

General Merchants and Government Contractors.

Agents for the leading

Banks

SteamshipCompanies

and

Insurance Companies

Importers of Merchandise of every description.

KAMEYA & CO.

GENERAL STOREKEEPERS

Chinkokai - - Seoul

(Established 1895, Tokyo)

Confectionery, Hams, Canned Goods, Cutlery, Hirano & Tansan Water. Provisions, Gents, Furnishing goods, Toilet Articles, Travelling Bags, Tobacco, Cigars & Cigarettes Kitchen Utensils. Coffee, Biscuits.

Fresh Goods always kept in Stock.

Prices Moderate

Please come and insbect our goods.

BORDEN'S CONDENSED MILK CO.

New York, U. S. A.

ALWAYS IN STOCK

Eagle Brand Condensed Milk.

Gold Seal Condensed Milk.

Peerless (Family) Evaporated Cream.

Borden's Malted Milk.

E. MEYER & CO. Chemulpo, Korea,

Sole Agents

ROYAL INSURANCE COMPANY,

Funds exceed £10,000,000

FIRE

AT CURRENT RATES.

LIFE

REDUCED PREMIUM.

HOLME RINGER & Co., Agents, Chemulpo.

HOTEL DU PALAIS

SEOUL.

The only first class Hotel in Seoul. Situated in the centre of the city opposite ~~the palace~~.

Cuisine under the supervision of an experienced French Chef.

Well ventilated and furnished throughout.

TARIFF UPONIAPPLICATION

L. MARTIN

Proprietor and Mangae

大韓每日申報
대한민일신보

(뎨오십오호) (일요일) 쳔구빅사년구월십구일

본샤고

○신보는영어와한어로셔계재일츌판홈

신문가

혼쟝 엽뎐두돈오푼

일삭됴 엽뎐두량닷돈 ... 밧숨

광고료는

귀한의쟝단과즈항의다쇼로죵감홈되몃가로밧을터이오며오리지아녀대한샤람마다다이신문을보계될터이니광고내시기를원호시는이들은우리신문샤에와셔편의호게샹의호기를바람

○발항소 [illegible]

샤쟝 영국인 (비셜)

샤고

[illegible]

본샤광고

[illegible]

론셜

[illegible]

잡보

[illegible]

관보

[illegible]

외보

[illegible]

수 폐하의대본영을젼장에더갓가히젼진ᄒᆞ야옴기기로쥬의ᄒᆞᆷ이라혁수상에도대본영을젼진ᄒᆞ야운동ᄒᆞᆷ이ᄒᆞᆼ상길조가잇논결과가되엿스니존신문상에도이런케젼군ᄒᆞᄂᆞᆫ거시이뻬ᄂᆞᆫ당ᄒᆞ야실시가되면렬외진이아님줄노증거ᄒᆞ야밋을수밧귀엽ᄂᆞᆫ지라경장잔에될러슌함락비되면둥지젼장이되고그다음에ᄂᆞᆫ셋재젼쟝이될터인디추후힝동에셩공이잇기를위ᄒᆞ야　셩신위무ᄒᆞ신　쥬상의위혁아래의탁ᄒᆞ야대산원슈와으옥대장일지라도제능과지략잇ᄂᆞᆫ병쟐이될지라그런즉경외ᄒᆞ신　대원슈폐하의어젼에갓가히잇ᄂᆞᆫ디오의부터와젼련의수죨들이스수로세다라져회키리쟝신을가닥등교귀운을도도와휘엉과용밍을시로이더갑졀이나쓸지라일노말밋암아대원슈폐하의츌정ᄒᆞ심을희망ᄒᆞᄂᆞᆫ바이오더구나젼에업ᄂᆞᆫ　황샹과국민간에스락비되여젼에업ᄂᆞᆫ수업으로승젼ᄒᆞᆫ젼에업ᄂᆞᆫ영광을괴념숨아둥이뎍당ᄒᆞ미대본영을대한도셩한셩에나교만ᄒᆞ던로국에서탈득ᄒᆞᆫ긔동에뎨일젼렴잇ᄂᆞᆫ셩디쳥니와에나젼진ᄒᆞ야두란표ᄒᆞᆫ다ᄒᆞ엿더라

뎐보

구월칠일론돈발

◯수평계엄　셩피득보에잇ᄂᆞᆫ루터뎐통신원의뎐보를거ᄒᆞᆫ즉우크롬쓰키친왕의딕에세안호함쟝위렌씨를려순항딕수평으로두엇다ᄒᆞ고

우크롬쓰키친왕은팔월십일에려순구에서나가서그함딕를지휘ᄒᆞ야히삼위로젼진ᄒᆞ지말나ᄂᆞᆫ명령을어긘바문에군법졔판ᄒᆞᆫ라ᄂᆞᆫ명령이나렷다ᄒᆞ엿더라

동일동뎐

◯로함회구쥬　샨시바에잇ᄂᆞᆫ루터뎐통신원의뎐보를거ᄒᆞᆫ즉영국슌양함코르노호가로국슌양함피리쓰쎌그호와쓰몰넨쓰크호가즁립국션쳑들을고롭게ᄒᆞᄂᆞᆫ일을고만말나ᄒᆞᄂᆞᆫ황뎨의명령을수령관들의게젼ᄒᆞ니랑함이지금은쎄나서구라파로회환ᄒᆞᆫ다ᄒᆞ엿더라

동일동뎐

◯로군수관　셩피득보에잇ᄂᆞᆫ루터뎐통신원이보고ᄒᆞ기를로군이연틔탄광북편디방에취집ᄒᆞ엿고파견되ᄂᆞᆫ인듸잇디방에쎄란져잇서퇴군ᄒᆞᄂᆞᆫ거슬방어ᄒᆞᆫ다ᄒᆞ며

그러나봉텬에ᄂᆞᆫ지난밤에구로팟킨쟝군의후군은거진소멸ᄒᆞᆷ이되엿고또로군의대부디ᄂᆞᆫ일군의게에워싸이여결박ᄒᆞᆫ위험을당ᄒᆞ엿다고ᄒᆞᆫ다ᄒᆞ엿더라

구월팔일론돈발

◯일진로퇴　셩피득보에잇ᄂᆞᆫ빅일뎐신〔세일리텔리그라프〕통신원의보고를거ᄒᆞᆫ즉로국젼쟁통신원이뎐보ᄒᆞ기를일군이봉텬부에서이십오영리〔일리가한국리슈삼리가량〕안에니르럿다ᄒᆞᆫ다ᄒᆞ엿고

로군은이셩에서퇴각ᄒᆞᆫ라ᄂᆞᆫ쥰비를시작ᄒᆞ엿고졍시관쳥을벌서할빈으로이젼ᄒᆞ엿다ᄒᆞ엿더라

동일동뎐

◯로쟝보고　구로팟킨쟝군이보고ᄒᆞ기를로군의대부디ᄂᆞᆫ임의봉텬부에니르럿ᄂᆞᆫ디일군셔쟝시쟝지ᄒᆞ야방어ᄒᆞ야진회켓고동향ᄒᆞ여오ᄂᆞᆫ일군은지금에구력ᄒᆞ여펑밧ᄒᆞ나로군이퇴격ᄒᆞ야항거ᄒᆞᄂᆞᆫ즁이라ᄒᆞ엿스며

금월륙일에루터뎐통신원이봉텬부에서뎐보ᄒᆞᆫ거슬거ᄒᆞᆫ즉로군의일부디ᄂᆞᆫ겨단이되여일군이산샹에서련속부졀ᄒᆞ며포격ᄒᆞ미작일쥬야를련속ᄒᆞ여위급ᄒᆞ엿다ᄒᆞ엿더라

팔월삼십일론돈발

◯승원도착힝　셩피득보에서소문이나기를로함노빅코호의승원들이히삼위항에도착ᄒᆞ엿다ᄒᆞ엿더라

구월팔일빅림발

◯셸퇴함더연파　셸틔함디가극동으로파견ᄒᆞᄂᆞᆫ일ᄌᆞᄂᆞᆫ아직도미분명ᄒᆞ다ᄒᆞ엿고

뉴약히랠드신문에긔지ᄒᆞᆫ보를거ᄒᆞᆫ즉로국이아연뎐용화국에셔군함두쳑을사기로법국의ᄒᆞᆫ회사를경유ᄒᆞ야담판ᄒᆞᆫ다ᄒᆞ엿더라

구월구일론돈발

◯량군상저　구로팟킨쟝군이작일에보고ᄒᆞ기를흑목대쟝의군디ᄂᆞᆫ료양과봉텬부간의텰로대동편에서이십오영리에잇고오리로되ᄂᆞᆫ디방에잇다ᄒᆞ엿고

로군은지금봉텬부를둘너취집ᄒᆞ여잇고료양으로서오ᄂᆞᆫ후군은봉텬부남방십칠영리되ᄂᆞᆫ디잇서일군과서로련속ᄒᆞ여맛부디쳐잇서우금ᄭᅳᆺ치지안코싸호ᄂᆞᆫ즁이라ᄒᆞ엿더라

잡보

◯일진회단발　일진회에서회원들이일신ᄒᆞ기위ᄒᆞᆫ다ᄒᆞ고작일하오이시에회원들이일제히단발ᄒᆞ엿ᄂᆞᆫ디이ᄇᆡᆨ십인즁에칠인만아니싹가다더라

◯조쳥훈칙　일공관에셔외부로조회ᄒᆞ되일본군힝농상팔요로마산포에서미양샹란포ᄉᆞ지텬도지쳔을부셜ᄒᆞ야경부텰도에련락ᄒᆞᆯ촌로텽금시역ᄒᆞ니각무하디방관의게훈칙ᄒᆞ야공역에무의케ᄒᆞ라ᄒᆞ엿더라

◯외대병와　외부대신리하영씨ᄂᆞᆫ쳥금인후로병와ᄒᆞ여연일수진도못ᄒᆞ엿더라

◯우힝광셜　일본국은힝쇼즁에일본은힝이라ᄒᆞᄂᆞᆫ은힝쇼에서한국과만쥬디방에셔경제샹긔관을민활케ᄒᆞ기위ᄒᆞ야위션한국에ᄂᆞᆫ그은힝소지졈을셔울과평양과인쳔과진남포등디오만쥬ᄂᆞᆫ봉황셩과안동현과대련만과우쟝등디에셜시ᄒᆞᆫ다더라

◯역부뎡지　닉부에셔ᄂᆞᆫ십삼도로외부에셔ᄂᆞᆫ갈항시로ᄎᆞᆫᄒᆞ기를향시에일본수령관의요쳥으로인부모집ᄉᆞ을루ᄎᆞ훈칙ᄒᆞ엿더니현금의쥬와쳥국안봉현등디에ᄉᆞ용할역부가츙슈되야군물슈운에구이지단이업쓰니역부이관을아직뎡지ᄒᆞ되일아젼쟁이결국못되엿스니일후에만일인부슈용할일이잇거든인민의게권유ᄒᆞ야ᄌᆞ원응모케ᄒᆞ라ᄒᆞ엿더라

◯박씨참셔　일진회외에외부대신비참셕ᄒᆞ엿ᄂᆞᆫ디쥬일공관슈원박졍션이외교에한슈ᄒᆞ니쥬일공ᄉᆞ관셔관을임용ᄒᆞ자ᄒᆞ고회의에계출ᄒᆞ야　쥬본ᄉᆞ지되엿다더라

◯졍쟝일병　샴화감리교영쳘씨가외부로보고ᄒᆞ되본셔쥬수리즁령이실수ᄒᆞᆷ이조금도업ᄂᆞᆫ디힝헐에곡ᄌᆞ과원류인힝의ᄉᆞ건으로민요남시에일인파교셩ᄉᆞᄒᆞᆫ다가무고히일헌병의게피타ᄒᆞᆷ으로곳쳥원ᄒᆞ야면관ᄒᆞ고도카리가ᄂᆞᆫ길에향구ᄒᆞ엿스나엇지카리고또본감리가또ᄒᆞᆫ말노반을루ᄒᆞ엿스니일공관에조회ᄒᆞ야수평부에젼칭ᄒᆞ야기시힝피ᄒᆞᆫ병뎡을엄사징관ᄒᆞ야후폐를막으라ᄒᆞ엿더라

◯안힝수출발　지산시흥민요수건사실ᄒᆞ기위ᄒᆞ야죵이품안죵덕써로안힝수를퇴차ᄒᆞ엿ᄂᆞᆫ디위션시흥으로발왕ᄒᆞ엿더라

◯거루딕독쳥　경무수원우상쎄ᄂᆞᆫ녀세가칭샹이란졍신이호몽ᄒᆞ야쳥결위원장이조과직임인즁을이잣던지감셔에신칙ᄒᆞ기를쳥결ᄉᆞ로역군시비가분운ᄒᆞ니치지를론ᄒᆞᆫ라ᄒᆞᆷ으로오서안에오례지믈이구산곳쳐싸인지라일인은히쳥결을ᄌᆞ의로실시ᄒᆞᆫ다ᄒᆞ고일본인거루디브리위션쳥결에착슈ᄒᆞ엿다더라

◯졍부쥬본　일젼에졍부에서쥬본ᄒᆞ기를이다수ᄒᆞᆫ빈틀방ᄒᆞ차야슈령셔임이시일이급ᄒᆞ고퇴로졍부회의에참셕ᄒᆞᆫ졔신이빈봉군난야등인ᄒᆞ기에힘쓸거시어ᄂᆞᆯ닉부대신조병필이가지궈의의젼을교정ᄒᆞ고물론을이궈여수령　주본을경션히ᄒᆞ고또시급수무동지완이ᄒᆞ엿스니닉부대신조병필을위션면본관ᄒᆞ옵고신도또ᄒᆞᆫ황공ᄒᆞ와ᄃᆡ죄ᄒᆞ노이다　젼션의칙임이막즁ᄒᆞ신ᄒᆞ거ᄂᆞᆫ본의를어긔고위젼을교정ᄒᆞ야직무에소홀ᄒᆞ고례둥을손실ᄒᆞ니진실노기탄ᄒᆞᆯ지라닉부대신조병필을면본관ᄒᆞ고경인즉ᄃᆡ죄케말나ᄒᆞ셧더라

◯이빅일병　졔작일상오십시에일병이빅명이화차를타고시흥으로하거ᄒᆞ엿더라

◯양성소시취　일젼에법률학도양성소에셔학도를한국문으로시취ᄒᆞᄂᆞᆫ디휘쇼부장신상의가휘숀에친왕ᄒᆞ야학원수십오인을시취ᄒᆞ엿더라

◯무관시험　닉부대신면관된디에부의장관용틔쎄가교입ᄒᆞᆫ다더라

◯군제경쟁　일젼에군제의졍관들이군부로회동ᄒᆞ야회의를경정ᄒᆞ엿ᄂᆞᆫ디각군디ᄂᆞᆫ별노히가갑이업셧고징병법을장ᄎᆞ실시ᄒᆞᆯ터이오원슈부ᄂᆞᆫ혁파ᄒᆞ야군부로부속케ᄒᆞ고통군법원관제도기졍ᄒᆞ엿다더라

광고

TELEGRAMS.

FROM JAPAN PAPERS.

THE BALTIC FLEET.

THROUGH REUTER'S AGENCY.

London, Sept. 9th.

Reuter's correspondent at Cronstadt reports that the Czar yesterday inspected each ship of the Baltic Fleet, which is expected to sail for the Far East on Saturday Sept. 10th.

Berlin, Sept. 10.

The Czar has again inspected the Baltic Fleet at Cronstadt.

THE "NOVIK" AT KORSAKOFF.

London, Sept. 9th.

An official dispatch to St. Petersburg announces that the Japanese visited Korsakoff on the 6th instant, and placed mines in the sea around the "Novik," but the Russian fire prevented the Japanese from exploding them.

THE RUSSIAN RETREAT.

London, Sept. 10th.

Reuter's correspondent at Mukden reports that the retreat of the Russians from Liaoyang has been safely accomplished, the Japanese having failed to utilise the advantage obtained as the result of the serious plight of the Russians. This is probably due to the fact that the Japanese troops were fagged out.

The accumulation of Russian wounded between Liaoyang and Mukden has taxed the Red Cross departments to the utmost.

The Russian Commissariat Department, which hitherto has been in a deplorable condition, worked magnificently.

The correspondent adds that the long millet through which the troops have had to operate, and to which the Russians were not accustomed, proved an inestimable ally to the Japanese, who owe thereto some of the principal reverses inflicted upon the Russians.

Tientsin, Sept. 9.

Private advices received here state that the Russian forces at Mukden seem to be about to move south to attack the Japanese positions.

On the 8th inst., at a place not designated, the Japanese captured a quantity of Russian materials for making piers.—Mainichi.

London, Aug. 10.

The Admiralty has invited the Clyde shipbuilders to tender for two battleships of 16,500 tons and high speed. It is said that these vessels in the matter of armament and armoured protection will eclipse anything yet attempted. That the Admiralty officials are in a hurry to get the vessels started is indicated by the fact that the tenders must be sent in by September 9, which is unusually short notice.

Berlin, Sept. 11.

The Belgian steamer "Colonies" has been sold to Japan.

MOBILISATION OF RUSSIAN TROOPS.

ISSUE OF NEW WAR BONDS.

Berlin, Sept. 10.

Two Army Corps have been mobilised in Vilna, Kieff, Kasan, and Odessa.

The Russian Government announces the issue of new War Bonds.

THE "DIANA."

Berlin, Sept. 10.

In spite of her long stay in the port of Saigon, the Russian cruiser "Diana," which escaped from Port Arthur, has not yet been disarmed. The vessel is now coaling, apparently with the object of continuing her voyage.

THE MARSEILLES STRIKE.

London, Sept. 10.

Notwithstanding the recent decision on the part of the seamen at Marseilles to abandon the strike, there has been a hitch in the negotiations, and the strike still continues.

THE "DIANA."

ANOTHER REPORT.

Berlin, Sept. 11

The Paris journal "Matin" publishes a report from Saigon to the effect that the Russian cruiser "Diana," which sought refuge in the harbour after escaping from Port Arthur last month, has now been dismantled.

MEDIATION.

Berlin, Sept. 11.

The French Press states that the propaganda now being carried on for German intervention in the present war is approved neither by Russia nor Japan.

London, Sept. 10.

M. Sviatopolk Mirski, who has been appointed Russian Minister of the Interior in succession to the late M. von Plehve, has a reputation for humanity and enlightenment.

The appointment is considered to constitute a defeat for the reactionaries.

RUSSIA AND CONTRABAND.

London, Sept. 10.

Russia has agreed to pay an indemnity to the owners of the British colliers "Frankby", and "Ettrickdale," which were detained ten days at Suez by Russian war-ships in February last while en route to the Far East.

Berlin, Sept. 11.

The Russian reports acknowledge that the casualties in the recent fighting were enormous.

RUSSIAN COAL SUPPLIES.

London, Sept. 10.

During the last three or four months between four and five hundred thousand tons of coal have been purchased at Cardiff for the Russian Government. A large quantity is now on the way to Manila, whither it is consigned.

It is stated that as much as £5 10s. per ton has been paid for coal to be delivered at Vladivostok.

The Crown Prince is suffering from a slight fever.

Another riot has broken out in the Kyeng Ki province and the Magistrate's office has been destroyed by the mob.

From the Magistrate of Hong Chou we learn that the Tonghaks are selling their cattle to raise expenses for their journey to Seoul.

The Italian Minister, failing to gain an audience with his Majesty has handed the autograph letter from his King to the Foreign office with the request that it will be presented to the Emperor.

The Magistrate of Sin Chon complains that, although he has received instructions to cease collecting coolies, the Japanese military authorities are more urgent than ever in their demand for labour.

The Kamni of Gensan has telegraphically requested the Government to despatch the new Police inspector, appointed to his district, as soon as possible as the Japanese advance northwards renders his presence imperative.

The Governor of Pyengyang reports that Russian scouts are showing signs of activity in the neighbourhood of Chang-chin, which is a district lying between Hamheung and Pyengyang. Recently 180 mounted Russians arrived and after verbally examining several of the citizens retired to their base at Hamheung.

The Korea Daily News.

To be published daily except Sundays.

Rate of Subscription:—

Per Year,	Yen 25.
Per Quarter,	Yen 7.
Per Month	Yen 2.50

Postage in Korea not charged extra.
Postage abroad charged extra.

Advertisements, 50 sen per day for 1 inch or less.
5 yen per month per inch.
50 yen per year per inch.

All communications to

E. T. BETHELL,
Editor and Publisher.
Pak-tong, Seoul.

THE WAR.

The absence of any news of the Japanese operations subsequent to the capture of Liaoyang leaves us in doubt as to the actual state of affairs. From the Russian side we learn that the Russian rearguard has reached a point 17 miles south of Mukden and is daily in action with the advancing Japanese who are spread out some 25 miles on either side of the railway.

This news is over a week old and as we have not received news of a decisive battle since then it is safe to assume that Kuropatkin has reached Mukden in good order and succeeded in placing himself out of danger from a Japanese flanking movement. It may be taken for granted that at Mukden, as at Lioayang, Kuropatkin will only resist the Japanese advance so long as his line of retreat remains clear. The moment a Japanese force threatens his flank or rear he will once more retreat northwards and it is improbable that the Japanese will, for the present, follow him. It will be noted that the London despatch describing the recent operations has at last a good word to say for the Russians.

With regard to the Baltic squadron, it will be seen that a very powerful fleet is expected to arrive at Port Arthur on December 13th. This indicates that Russia expects the garrison to hold out until then. We can only say that it will be very extraordinary if it does. It is inconceivable that, powerful as the stronghold is, it can continue for two months more to defend itself against an attack combining unexampled personal courage with the most modern methods and machinery. Should the unexpected happen, the whole aspect of the war will be changed.

The news which reaches here with regard to the "Novik" comes somewhat as a surprise. The fact that the Japanese sent an expedition to blow her up and found Russian guards protecting her, indicates that the vessel is not such a total wreck as was generally believed.

A German military expert advances the opinion that Russia will invade Korea from Vladivostock in the Spring. Our opinion is that the invasion will be attempted during the Winter. We have the news that Japanese troops have moved North from Gensan (probably with the idea of checking the Russians) and now we learn that the General commanding the Japanese forces in Korea, and his Chief of Staff, are to be replaced by senior men. This indicates that the situation here is considered to have increased in gravity.

Altogether the situation is a perplexing one and the developements of the next few months will be awaited with interest.

PROGRESS OF INSTRUCTION IN ENGLISH.

The English Language School owes its origin to Herr Von Mollendorf, and was started during his career as Chief Commissioner of the Korean Customs as a school for training interpreters and translators for the Customs. The late Mr. W. du Flon Hutchison, who had been engaged by the Korean Government to teach in the Naval School in Kakochi in the island of Kang-wha, was made headmaster, and it continued under his able management until his contract expired in June or July of 1899. During his Headmastership the school grew in numbers until, at one time, the scholars numbered some 130, though the average number on the roll for that year fell far short of that total. In 1895 Mr. T. E. Hallifax became his first assistant, and the two, assisted by the Korean staff, sent forth many good English speaking Koreans, who by the number of years they retained their positions obtained in leaving the school, testified to the excellence of their tuition. On Mr. Hutchison's retirement in 1899 Mr. Hallifax became Acting Head Master until the reopening of the school after the customary New Year holiday in March 1901 when Mr. G. Russell Frampton became Head Master. The school then numbered some 50 or 60 scholars, the numbers having dwindled from various causes, mainly political.

Unfortunately the registers for that period were not filed so it is impossible to give accurate statistics. The average of number on roll, and percentage of attendances for the years 1901-3 are:—

	Av. on roll	Percentage
1901	94	82.5
1902	94	75.4
1903	103	75.

These averages, however, do not show very accurately the number of youths passing through the school, as many Koreans, entering the school, stay for two or three months and then returning to their country homes for the long holiday do not again come up to Seoul and so are lost to the school. Thus at the times of admission in March and September the school is filled almost to overflowing, and later on gradually becomes less crowded especially in the lower forms.

A Korean desiring to enter the school is supposed to present himself at the Education Department to pass an examination in Chinese reading and composition. He must also bring forward a guarrantor residing in Seoul to vouch, presumably, for his attendance at school until the course is finished. Provided he is over 14 years (Korean reckoning), he has no age limit to fear, and there are now attending school several whose ages at entrance ranged from 23 to 27.

Having passed satisfactorily through the school course extending over a period of five years the student receives a graduation paper, and an official rank of the lowest degree by being appointed honorary assistant teacher in the school, though this latter clause has more often been honoured in its breach than in its observance.

At present the school is practically filled, a greater influx than usual having taken place during this month, the number on roll being 160. These are divided into five classes but the lowest class, owing to there being two dates for admission, has necessarily to be divided into two. The staff consists of the Head Master, one English assistant and five native assistants.

The sorcerers have predicted an invasion of Korea from the north-east by the Russians. This is to occur during the winter but only a few "million" cossacks will visit Seoul.

THE BRITISH ARMY MANŒUVRES.

A stampede of seven hundred cavalry horses from General French's encampment near Southampton not long ago provided an exciting prelude to the manoeuvres. The animals careered and galloped for miles: many were killed and injured, and several were drowned in the sea.

The work accomplished at the embarkation of General French's force was an extension of anything of a similar nature carried out during the South African war.

Troops to the number of 11,600, 2,700 horses and mules, sixty guns, 175 waggons, and 140 carts and ambulances were embarked.

The stampede deprived General French of his two principal mounted units, the 8th and 14th Hussars, but the gap was immediately filled by the 1st Dragoon Guards, who marched the fifty miles from Aldershot to Southampton Docks in 24 hours.

TREATY SIGNED AT LHASSA.

Reuter's representative with the British expedition at Lhassa reports that a Treaty was signed between Great Britain and Thibet on the 7th instant.

A high official has been despatched to Si Hung to bring the murderers of the magistrate to justice.

A German strategist opines that Russia will not endeavour to reconquer the positions lost, but will advance in the spring from Vladivostock on Korea.—Asahi.

A comfortable rotundity of person is an expensive luxury in the Swedish town of Hafanger. The municipality has established a graduated tax on all stout persons weighing upwards of 135 lbs. To weigh from 200lbs. to 270lbs. costs 30s. a year. Such as turn the scale over the latter figure pay an extra 9s. a pound.

The Foreign Office have despatched a circular to all treaty ports informing them that a sufficient number of coolies have now been collected to fill the Japanese military demands for the present, but should a future occasion arise they must do all in their power "to call on more volunteers."

Referring to the request of the Japanese Government as to the removal of the Kamni of Gensan, we new hear of a despatch from that gentleman himself. He states that his chief clerk was insulted and struck by a Japanese gendarme and in his indignation immediately resigned his post. No amount of persuasion could keep him in office and the want of his services are greatly felt.

The members of the Il Chin Hoi number 110; of these 103 recently shaved their heads to show that they formed one brotherhood of determined people. The remaining seven refused to sacrifice their vanity in the noble cause and now the weightiest problem with which the meeting has to contend is the difficulty of deciding whether the 103 shall grow their hair again or forcibly cut off the seven's locks.

The old Konak at Belgrade, where King Alexander and Queen Draga were murdered last year, is about to be razed to the ground, the place where it stood being laid out as a garden. On closer inspection of the premises previous to demolition, an underground passage was discovered leading outside the town. The mouth is walled up, and it now appears that this was done by Alexander's order, who feared lest conspirators might thus enter the Konak. The conspirators were, however, ignorant of the existence of this subterranean passage, so that the illfated king himself cut off his only means of escape.

The Korea Daily News.

VOL. I, MONDAY, SEPTEMBER 19, 1904. No. 55

HONGKONG & SHANGHAI BANKING CORPORATION.

Paid-up Capital.................$10,000,000
Reserve Fund:—Sterling Reserve... 10,000,000
Silver Reserve..... 6,500,000

26,500,000
Reserve Liability of Proprietors... 10,000,000

HEAD OFFICE, HONGKONG.

London Bankers, London and County Banking Company Limited.
Branches and Agencies,
London.

Amoy,	Hankow	Penang,
Bangkok,	Hiogo,	Rangoon,
Batavia,	Iloilo,	Saigon,
Bombay,	Lyons,	San Francisco,
Calcutta,	Manila,	Singapore,
Colombo,	Nagasaki,	Sourabaya,
Foochow,	New York,	Tientsin,
Hamburg,	Peking,	Yokohama,

Credits granted on approved Securities, and every description of Banking and Exchange business transacted.

Drafts granted on London and the chief Commercial places in Europe, India, Australia, America, China and Japan.

HOLME RINGER & Co., AGENTS,
CHEMULPO.

ON CHEONG & CO.,
SEOUL.

GENERAL STORE KEEPERS.
Imported provisions, Cooking Utensils Crockery, etc.
FRESH BREAD DAILY.

MITSU BISHI DOCKYARD & ENGINE WORKS,
NAGASAKI.

CODE WORD, "DOCK."

A. 1, A. B. C., and Engineering Codes used.

DOCK No. 1 (at Tategami).

Extreme Length..............523 feet
Length on blocks............ 513 ,,
Width of Entrance on Top......89 ,,
,, ,, Bottom....77 ,,
Water on Blocks at Spring Tide 26½ ,,

DOCK No. 2 (Mukaijima).

Extreme Length..............371 feet
Length on Blocks..............360 ,,
Width of Entrance on Top......66 ,,
,, ,, Bottom 53 ,,
Water on Blocks at Spring Tide 22 ,,

PATENT SLIP (at Kosuge).

Can take vessels up to 1,000 tons gross.

THE WORKS are well equipped with the LATEST IMPROVEMENTS, and can execute any kind of work in SHIPBUILDING and MARINE ENGINEERING, as well as in REPAIRING of SHIPS.

The COMPANY'S new powerful steamer OURA-MARU (712 tons, 700 I.H.P.), specially built for SALVAGE PURPOSES, and equipped with necessary gear, is always READY at SHORT NOTICE.

CHARTERED BANK OF INDIA AUSTRALIA & CHINA.

INCORPORATED BY ROYAL CHARTER 1853

HEAD OFFICES:—LONDON.

Paid-up Capital £800,000
Reserve Liability of Shareholders 800,000
Reserve Fund 800,000

Drafts granted upon all the principal places in the world and every description of Exchange and banking business transacted.

E. MEYER & Co., Agents,
Chemulpo.

E. MEYER & CO.
Chemulpo.

SOLE AGENTS IN KOREA FOR:

A. T. Morse, Sons & Co's "Fresco" Distemper

In all colours ready for use on walls, Ceilings etc.
and

AVENARIUS CARBOLINEUM

A wood-preserving and antiseptic oil preparation

Against decay, dry-rot, fungus and wood-destroying insects.

A large supply always in Stock.
Prices upon application.

E. MEYER & Co.,
Chemulpo.

LAW UNION & CROWN INS. CO.

Fire risks accepted at Current rates, on go downs, merchandise, dwellings, and other property, subject to usual conditions.

HOLME RINGER & Co.,
Agents, Chemulpo

THE METHODIST PUBLISHING HOUSE,

Little West Gate, Seoul.

JOB PRINTING, TYPEWRITER PAPER
CARBON PAPER, VISITING CARDS
STATIONERY, BOOK BINDING
BOOK PUBLISHERS
AMERICAN SCHOOL BOOKS
SPENCERIAN COPY BOOKS
PEN CARBON LETTER AND BILL BOOKS

S A. BECK, Manager.

DAI-ICHI GINKO.

LIMITED.

(Formerly the First National Bank)

ESTABLISHED 1873

INCORPORATED UNDER PRESENT LAW 1896

Capital - - - - - - - - - Yen 5,000,000
Reserve Fund - . - - - 1,500,000

HEAD OFFICE:—TOKIO.

President: Baron SHIBUSAWA.

BRANCHES AND CORRESPONDENTS
In the Principal Cities and Towns of Japan.

Interest Allowed on
Fixed deposits 1 year - - - 6½ per cent
" " 6 months - - - 6 per cent

Special current accounts 1½ sen daily per Y 100
General " " 1 " " " 100

M. TANAKA,
Manager, Chemulpo

HOLME RINGER & Co.
Chemulpo.

General Merchants and Government Contractors.

Agents for the leading
Banks
SteamshipCompanies
and
Insurance Companies

Importers of Merchandise of every description.

KAMEYA & CO.

GENERAL STOREKEEPERS
Chinkokai - - Seoul

(*Established 1895, Tokyo*)

Confectionery, Hams, Canned Goods, Cutlery, Hirano & Tansan Water. Provisions, Gents, Furnishing goods, Toilet Articles, Travelling Bags, Tobacco, Cigars & Cigarettes Kitchen Utensils. Coffee, Biscuits.

Fresh Goods always kept in Stock.

Prices Moderate

Please come and inspect our goods.

NIPPON YUSEN KAISHA.

JAPANESE MAIL STEAMSHIP CO.

DER MAIL CONTRACT WITH THE IMPERIAL JAPANESE GOVERNMENT.

European Line

Regular Fortnightly Service between Yokohama Kobe, Moji, Shanghai, Hongkong, Singapore, Penang Colombo, Port Said, Marseilles, London and Antwerp

American Line

Regular Fortnightly Service between Hongkong and Seattle, calling at Shanghai, Moji, Kobe, Yokohama and Victoria, B. C.

Australian Line

Regular weekly Service betwen Japan Ports and Australia, calling at Hongkong and Manila.
(Above Three Lines Suspended until further notice).

Shanghai Line

Weekly Service between Shanghai and Japan Ports

Korea Line

Service Kobe, Moji, Nagasaki, Fusan, Chemulpo, Choo, Taiku.
S. S. Bahelsberg, 2181 tons.
Service Kobe, Moji, Fusan, Chemulpo, Chinnampo
S. S Argo, S. S. Ohio.

BORDEN'S CONDENSED MILK CO.

New York, U. S. A.

ALWAYS IN STOCK

Eagle Brand Condensed Milk.
Gold Seal Condensed Milk.
Peerless (Family) Evaporated Cream.
Borden's Malted Milk.

**E. MEYER & CO.
Chemulpo, Korea,
Sole Agents**

ROYAL INSURANCE COMPANY,
Funds exceed £10,000,000

FIRE
AT CURRENT RATES.

LIFE
REDUCED PREMIUM.

HOLME RINGER & Co.,
Agents, Chemulpo.

HOTEL DU PALAIS

SEOUL.

The only first class Hotel in Seoul. Situated in the centre of the city opposite the palace.

Cuisine under the supervision of an experienced French Chef.

Well ventilated and furnished throughout.

TARIFF UPON APPLICATION

L. MARTIN
Proprietor and Mangaer.

大韓每日申報

대한ᄆᆡ일신보

(뎨오십륙호) (화요일) 쳔구빅사년구월이십일

본샤고

○신보는영어와한어로셜계리일출판ᄒᆞ옵

신문가

ᄒᆞᆫ장 엽두돈오푼
일삭료 엽두량닷돈 맛돈으로 밧ᄉᆞᆸ

광고료는

귀한의장단과ᄌᆞ힝의다쇼로죵갑ᄒᆞ되ᄒᆞᆫ달가로밧을터이오며오릭지아녀대한사람마다다이신문을보실터이니광고버시기를원ᄒᆞ시는이들은우리신문사에와서면약ᄒᆞ심을희망ᄒᆞ옵

○발힝소 박동대한ᄆᆡ일신보사범어학교압희젼영국인셜필림집자리오

사쟝 영국인 (비셜)

사고

○우리대한ᄆᆡ일신보의목뎍은대한의안녕질서에관한모든데목에디ᄒᆞ야는공평한변론을쥬쟝ᄒᆞᆷ이라우리ᄒᆞᆫ신원의탐보는신문보셔는쳠군ᄌᆞ의게ᄒᆞᆼ샹보도ᄒᆞᆯ터이며편지를귀셔ᄒᆞ며주시는이는셩명과번디를쟈이붓치시기를희망ᄒᆞ오니이거슨신문샹에긔ᄌᆡᄒᆞ란는거시아니오다만그희신용ᄒᆞ는증거를숨고자ᄒᆞᆷ이라귀자는아모리셔뎐지과지ᄒᆞᆷ을되ᄌᆞᆨᄒᆞ는권리를가젓스나되ᄌᆞᆨᄒᆞ는리유를말ᄒᆞᆯ터이오며공중평화를문란케ᄒᆞ는듯ᄒᆞᆫ귀셔는의례히밧지안켓숩나이다

●본샤에셔아쟉귀계를쟝반치못ᄒᆞ와다른디셔빗여오는고로ᄆᆡ양월쵸일에는출판이대단히늣게되는듯ᄉᆞ오니젼이ᄆᆡ우늣게되오니우리신문을구람ᄒᆞ시는 쳠군ᄌᆞ는 용셔ᄒᆞ여주심을희망ᄒᆞᆸ나이다

●본샤셜시이리로신문을ᄆᆡ양우톄로분젼ᄒᆞ와톄젼부의잉의로젼ᄒᆞ는것스로면곳에는ᄒᆞᆨ늣게젼ᄒᆞ기도ᄒᆞ며ᄒᆞᆨ빠지기슴ᄒᆞ난폐에젼ᄒᆞ기도ᄒᆞ며ᄒᆞᆨ아니젼ᄒᆞ는곳도잇다ᄒᆞ와우리신문을ᄉᆞ랑ᄒᆞ야구람ᄒᆞ시는 쳠군ᄌᆞ의게디ᄒᆞ야ᄆᆡ우미안ᄒᆞ옵기로지금은분젼인을두고ᄆᆡ일일죵이젼ᄒᆞ며아니젼ᄒᆞ거나늣게거나ᄒᆞᆫ폐가업도록ᄒᆞ란ᄒᆞ오니ᄒᆞᆨ아니젼ᄒᆞ거나ᄒᆞᆨ늣게젼ᄒᆞ거나ᄒᆞᆫ일이잇스면본샤로통긔ᄒᆞ여주심을희망ᄒᆞᆸ

본샤광고

본셔에셔본신문뎨ᄉᆞ호와뎨삼일호와뎨이십오호를소용ᄒᆞᆯ베가잇서이에광고ᄒᆞ오니누구시던지이샹삼호중에본샤로가오시면ᄆᆡ쟝에빅젼두푼식드리리다

론셜

젼쟁후보

○요양함락이후에일본셔엇더케운동ᄒᆞᆫ다는소문이업는고로그진젹ᄒᆞᆫ바를낫다니아라사로방면으로젼ᄒᆞ는말을드른즉아병의후디가봉쳔남방삼칠영리되는ᄯᅡ에이르러일본군ᄉᆞ의싱영리되는수비쳘도양편으로련열ᄒᆞ야젼진ᄒᆞ는자들로뎌부러남노ᄯᅡᄒᆞᆫ다는듸

이는쳘광일젼에드른말인즉그동안결과가엇지됨은다시듯지못ᄒᆞ엿스나가량으로보드라도ᄒᆞᆨ구쟝군은일본군ᄉᆞ힝동ᄒᆞᆷ에죠곰도용겁ᄒᆞᆷ이업시봉쳔에도착ᄒᆞ야찬잇는모양인즉봉쳔셔ᄯᅩ다시퇴거ᄒᆞ는경우란도일병의젼진ᄒᆞ야ᄯᅩᆺ는되로응거ᄒᆞᆯ반ᄒᆞᆫ곳이분명히잇슬듯ᄒᆞᆫ게시반일에병ᄒᆞ나만아병의젼후량티간에공동을실시ᄒᆞ드리도아병은뎌욱봉으로향ᄒᆞ야퇴거ᄒᆞ여일병이ᄯᅩᆺ는바에엇지ᄒᆞᆯ수업게될터인지라

필경은돈동신에도근일싸홈에아라사이미오리동케되깃다고셜명ᄒᆞᄂᆞᆫ듯ᄒᆞ되셀틱이라ᄒᆞ는함디는한ᄉᆞ유력ᄒᆞᆫ군함인디이군함이쟝ᄎᆞ삼이월십삼일간에는려순도박ᄒᆞ기로작졍ᄒᆞ엿다ᄒᆞᆫ즉이거시응당아라사에셔려순에잇는셩칙을그베에나셔리ᄂᆡ란ᄒᆞᆷ이분명ᄒᆞᆫ즉

만일과연이리케될진디이는ᄒᆞᆫ비샹ᄒᆞᆫ일이고아라사에셔는아모리ᄒᆞ드리도수샤동안은일샹으로옹ᄒᆞ야병귀와군물도뎌욱쟝녀ᄒᆞ고졍졔ᄒᆞ게ᄒᆞ야일병의디젹ᄒᆞᆷ을방비ᄒᆞᆯ터이즉필경젼쟁ᄒᆞᆫ국이돌연히밧고여의사도두지아니ᄒᆞ엿든일이생길듯ᄒᆞ며

ᄯᅩ아라사에서노빅이라ᄒᆞ는굉쟝ᄒᆞᆫ군함이쟝ᄎᆞ출발ᄒᆞ리라는소문도잇는지라그런고로이본서군ᄉᆞ를셩화갓치발홈은아국보호되병나올을파견ᄒᆞᆫ터홈이로되필경그군함이젼수히다파숑이되지아니ᄒᆞ엿슬듯ᄒᆞ도다

뎌국군ᄉᆞ샹실ᄒᆞᆫ가ᄒᆞᆫ사롬은발ᄒᆞ기를평츈에는아병이히샹위로붓터한국에쳠입ᄒᆞ리라고ᄒᆞ엿스나우리의셩각에는금년겨울동안이라도쟝쳥쳡법ᄒᆞ야드러오리ᄒᆞᆯ듯ᄒᆞ지라

이러므로일본셔도아병방비ᄒᆞ기위ᄒᆞ야원산으로붓터군ᄉᆞ를발ᄒᆞ야북으로힝군ᄒᆞ엿다ᄒᆞ며한국에주차ᄒᆞᆫ사령쟝관과및참모쟝도쟝ᄎᆞ로셩지인으로더시한귀차ᄒᆞᆫ다ᄒᆞᆫ즉이로써보드리도한국에위치를ᄇᆡ욱젼확ᄒᆞ고엄쇽ᄒᆞᆯ계획인즉

이셔ᄒᆞᆼᄒᆞ는일이모다쳔란ᄒᆞ야ᄌᆞ사만히알기어려우되엇지던지ᄉᆞ논이을가히지너제되면ᄌᆞ연이쳔ᄎᆞᆯ되기ᄂᆞᆯᄒᆞ기드러붓듯ᄒᆞ도다

관보

뎨이쳔구빅삼십ᄉᆞ호
광무팔년구월십칠일

○셔임관수령

○명ᄒᆞ쥬지 군과청쥬계룩군이등군수 강창희

구월십이일

○임군부경리국례일과원서주임관륙등 정삼품 박덕슈

○승셔원임관오등 무안항총순 강진필 이상구월십수일

○시종원 좌신안회수 종이품 안종덕

○임룡천군리서쥬수 서판임관륙등 리대영

○임의주군리서쥬수 서판임관륙등 리슈영

○승셔원임관오등 경흥감리셔쥬수 리규병

○승셔원임관삼등 경위원주수 위홍쇼

○승셔원임관오등 옥구항총순 하린홍

○명강화군텀시우톄주수 라진국

○명례산군텀시우톄주수 신티영

○승이금봉 탁지부참서관 류경슈

이샹구월십오일

○면본직 군부포방장 현진창

○승뎐칙 군기창기수 송경화 이샹구월십오일

○임의졍부참졍셔칙임관일등 법부대신 박졔순

○임법부대신셔칙임관일등 비원장 김가진

이샹구월십오일

궁뎡룩수

○의졍부참졍신기션군쥬ᄒᆞ되경긔관찰수리근교의면보를졉ᄒᆞ온즉시흥군민슈쳥명이자일신시람에힘군관아에돌입ᄒᆞ야히군슈박우양과그아들과외국인미명을타살ᄒᆞ엿다ᄒᆞ오니샹히경악ᄒᆞ지라위선사관을명ᄒᆞ야사실ᄒᆞᆫ다ᄒᆞ엿고ᄯᅩ쳠관경남도관찰수셩진휘의보고ᄒᆞᆫ면보를거ᄒᆞ온즉지산군금광광부수쳔명이동힝을괴쇄ᄒᆞ고히군슈류병응을란타ᄒᆞ다가인ᄒᆞ야절명ᄒᆞ엿다ᄒᆞ기로사관을명ᄒᆞ야사실ᄒᆞᆫ다ᄒᆞ오니군엘디방민요가번ᄒᆞ엿스오나슈령을탄살ᄒᆞ기는젼에업든변이라사관으로보사실ᄒᆞ기시아니오나중이금압ᄒᆞᆷ이로압ᄒᆞ수를차하ᄒᆞ야졀의ᄂᆞᆫ로발졍ᄒᆞ야서ᄒᆞ으로뎍산져지경왕ᄒᆞ야ᄉᆞ변에리유를혐희ᄒᆞ야징관ᄒᆞ올이잇ᄉᆞ온즉ᄂᆞ등 문서힝ᄒᆞ올이하여ᄒᆞ올지군상 쥬ᄒᆞ와 봉지의쥬가되엿ᄂᆞᆫ디빅셩이광쟝셜희ᄒᆞᆫ게시젼에업던변이라귀갑도현홈이엇지이디경에이르는고로국회경란홈지라사회ᄒᆞ야징챵ᄒᆞᆯ거슬잡시지완치못ᄒᆞᆯ지라안핵수를불이로발졍케ᄒᆞ라

○의졍부참졍권즁현수지쇼비지니에수양치말고힝용ᄒᆞ라

구월십오일

○보인사 취지 운돈구라졍조란셰가보인사라고셜립ᄒᆞᆫ다는티사쟝은참졍신긔션씨요ᄌᆞ본금은졍항진신과유신의의연금으로보용ᄒᆞᆫ다는티취사목뎍인즉몽ᄌᆞ를존ᄉᆞᆼᄒᆞ야셩학을확장ᄒᆞᆯ츳로날마다장지를간츌ᄒᆞ야발힝ᄒᆞᆫ다더라

○면칭인엽 일본공ᄉᆞ가외부로공함ᄒᆞ되부산쥬차일본령ᄉᆞ

면쳥ᄒᆞ기를대구관찰ᄉᆞ윤헌의치젹이공평ᄒᆞ야일인과한인ᄉᆞ이에다화합ᄒᆞ엿스니잘되도록ᄒᆞ야인임케ᄒᆞ랴ᄒᆞ엿기로죠쳥ᄒᆞ니별반공의홈을바란다ᄒᆞ엿더라

○츅송경관 덕원감리면보에ᄒᆞ엿스되일본군부진ᄒᆞᄂᆞᆫ디기금ᄒᆞᆫ수무가만ᄒᆞ니신임ᄒᆞᆫ경무관을최츅ᄒᆞ야하송ᄒᆞ라ᄒᆞ엿더라

○불시즉츅 신쳔군보에ᄒᆞ엿스되인부모집ᄉᆞ불시면쳑리도ᄒᆞᆫ후로일본인의독촉이젼일보다우심ᄒᆞ오니엇지조쳐ᄒᆞ랴ᄒᆞ엿더라

○의티ᄌᆞ탄싱 의티리국왕티ᄌᆞ탄싱ᄒᆞᆫ면보가일작에회공관으로도달ᄒᆞ엿더라

○레쟝인쟝 의티리공ᄉᆞ가외부로죠회ᄒᆞ되향일본ᄉᆞ가쳥패ᄒᆞᆫᄉᆞᄂᆞᆫ 귀죠부을겸죠ᄒᆞᆫ쥬욕도미명ᄒᆞᆫ사 소졉ᄒᆞ실슈엽다ᄒᆞ엿스ᄂᆞᆫ즁본공ᄉᆞ가명일에발졍ᄒᆞ야북경으로진왕ᄒᆞ엿다가귀맷쥬일ᄒᆞᆫ후에회환ᄒᆞᆯ것스니본국대군쥬폐하의인쟝국서를본서에오리류치ᄒᆞ지못ᄒᆞᆯ것기로회국서를송졍ᄒᆞ니 귀대황뎨폐하게봉졍ᄒᆞ라ᄒᆞ엿더라

○니대서리 평리원쟝민병한씨ᄂᆞᆫ니부대신서리를피명ᄒᆞ엿더라

○원현교련쟝 일젼에일본ᄉᆞ관샹명이병뎡ᄉᆞ십명을령솔ᄒᆞ고등구지등디에리도ᄒᆞ야교련쟝을슈츅ᄒᆞ엿더라

○윤씨괴곡 영쳔ᄉᆞ쟝윤풍식씨ᄂᆞᆫ 퇴니에츌입ᄒᆞ야구셜힌에쟝변ᄒᆞ며니무샹ᄉᆞ단인지거신룰혈에일헌병오명이그집에리도ᄒᆞ야문부를슈탐ᄒᆞ고윤씨를ᄉᆞ령부로챡거ᄒᆞ엿더라

○예후미령 황티ᄌᆞ뎐하게옵서인후환후로슈일미령ᄒᆞ시옵니차차감세가계시다더라

○경흥아병 경흥군슈김창슈씨의보고를거ᄒᆞᆫ즉팔월오일에로국긔병이빅명이두만강월변에티도ᄒᆞ야경셩방면으로향ᄒᆞ엿다ᄒᆞ엿더라

아병속문 경흥군슈가또보고ᄒᆞ기를팔월십일에로국참쟝일인과부령일인이긔병이쳔명을령솔ᄒᆞ고두만강월변에리도ᄒᆞ여경셩방면으로젼진ᄒᆞᆫ다ᄒᆞ엿더라

○니하화비 향일시취ᄒᆞᆫ일본류학ᄉᆞᆼ수십명의학ᄌᆞ금믜년샹빅원식 니하ᄒᆞ시기로작뎡ᄒᆞ엿다더라

○교도셩회 예수교쟝로회션교ᄉᆞ제셔와교도슈십명이교중미슌회에참예ᄎᆞ로고이일에각쳐에셔샹경ᄒᆞ엿ᄂᆞᆫ디일젼일요일에경동회당에모혓ᄂᆞᆫ디한미감리교ᄉᆞ교도합슈빅명이되엿다더라

○평쳔분보고 평안북도관찰ᄉᆞ리용관씨가ᄂᆡ부로보고ᄒᆞ기를팔월십삼일에아병이십명이강계군용북면과하리에유쥬ᄒᆞ고동수일명이읍ᄂᆡ로드러오거ᄂᆞᆯ그군쟝을담문ᄒᆞᆫ즉아병의빅팔십명이일병의군쟝을쟝탐ᄒᆞᆯᄎᆞ로쟝진군에리도ᄒᆞ엿다가이빅삼명은함흥으로가고이십명은강계에두류ᄒᆞᆫ다ᄒᆞᄂᆞᆫ디동수ᄂᆞᆫ무산군거ᄒᆞᄂᆞᆫ리인서라ᄒᆞ며곽하리에두류ᄒᆞᆫ다ᄒᆞ기로ᄒᆞ리를막ᄎᆞᄒᆞ야포군을모집ᄒᆞ야요히쳐를방슈ᄒᆞᆫ다ᄒᆞ엿더라

○츙찰면보 츙쥬관찰ᄉᆞ리승우씨의면보를거ᄒᆞᆫ즉일인이면간복ᄉᆞ로셩화곳치독촉ᄒᆞ니엇지죠쳐ᄒᆞᆯ지곳회면ᄒᆞ라ᄒᆞ엿더라

○룩츳아병 명쳔군슈리근풍씨가ᄂᆡ부로보고ᄒᆞ되아병이셧번째츌리ᄒᆞ야남으로향ᄒᆞᄂᆞᆫ자가도합일쳔ᄇᆡᆨ명이오경셩군에쥬둔ᄒᆞᆫ아병이일빅팔십여명이오셩진군에쥬둔ᄒᆞᆫ아병이오십명이오또나오ᄂᆞᆫ아병이몃쳔명이란ᄒᆞᄂᆞ아즉뎡ᄒᆞᆫ수로치아니ᄒᆞ엿슨즉그병원은미샹ᄒᆞ다ᄒᆞ엿라

○서로동도 평안남도관찰ᄉᆞ리중하씨가ᄂᆡ부로보고ᄒᆞ기를삼등군슈빈쟝식의보고를거ᄒᆞᆫ즉본월륙일에동도비빅명이셩쳔곡산등디로셔오ᄂᆞᆫ디빅미코지조와이졉인ᄌᆞ두ᄌᆞ를쌋츤긔를가지고본군읍ᄂᆡ에둔취ᄒᆞ고로호등유ᄒᆞᆫ즉그잇ᄂᆞᆫ곳시빅에갑동등디로향ᄒᆞ더니또쳘일오시에의라관덕이란쌋츤긔를가지고대샹빅여명이셩쳔으로셔본군에회리도ᄒᆞ고양덕곡산슈안으로또ᄒᆞᆫ쟝ᄒᆞᄂᆞᆫ자가쳔여명이오또셩쳔군공보를거ᄒᆞᆫ즉동학당이평쳥나로져지나더가히명이일병의게피ᄒᆞᆫ진티등ᄒᆞᆫ방이차차에셜등ᄒᆞ야샹등군에회동ᄒᆞᆫ자가월강ᄒᆞ야평셩으로향ᄒᆞᆫ란ᄒᆞᄂᆞᆫ고로순검을파송ᄒᆞ여효유ᄒᆞᆫ즉ᄌᆞ회ᄒᆞᆫ이평셩에셔등문이잇서간다ᄒᆞ고긔탄업쓰니우금등야ᄒᆞ다ᄒᆞ엿더라

○귀찰분보 평리관찰ᄉᆞ룡보를거ᄒᆞᆫ즉시ᄒᆞᆼ민요수로쥬ᄉᆞ들위송ᄒᆞ고슈졉을파면ᄒᆞ야란민괴슈들쟝쳑ᄒᆞ고환산ᄒᆞᆫ빅셩을효유ᄒᆞ며니슈졉이회보ᄒᆞ되실롱일에일병이빅명이하리ᄒᆞ야읍쟈에쥬둔ᄒᆞ고흉칠팔명식ᄂᆡ명셕각동에분파ᄒᆞ야졀ᄀᆞᆫ을낫낫치챡치ᄒᆞ며ᄀᆡ민이공겁ᄒᆞ야환산ᄒᆞ니란민쟝두ᄂᆞᆫ쟝지못ᄒᆞ고공연히우셕구분ᄒᆞ며념려가잇스니안힝수를최촉하송ᄒᆞ야금히사실케ᄒᆞ라ᄒᆞ엿더라

○일회진문 작일오후에일진회에셔기회ᄒᆞ고광부에합ᄒᆞ여왈졍쳐의의무샹졍명과공ᄉᆞᄂᆞᆫ거ᄉᆞᆫ인민의의무요셩명과산의보호ᄂᆞᆫ젼에교ᄒᆞᆫ됴록이온딘근일쟉하가졍부에츌셕ᄒᆞᆫ후대일쳐음졍령이인민의외ᄒᆞᆫ빈잇ᄂᆞᆫ교로도복을베푸러양교ᄒᆞ오니죠량ᄒᆞ신후낫낫치회답ᄒᆞ사인민이다알게ᄒᆞ심을바라노비다 이은경샹북도관찰ᄉᆞ윤현이탐도블법ᄒᆞ다가민소에오른교로쥬달ᄒᆞ야면관감죄케ᄒᆞ시니힝도원여ᄒᆞᆫ민심을위로ᄒᆞ겟더니신임ᄒᆞᆫ관찰ᄉᆞ쟝승원은일도비슈부로티청송군슈진인시에빅셩의졔물을박탈ᄒᆞ다가히루츄민소에을ᄂᆞᆫ거놈이졔홀연히탁용ᄒᆞ니아홉홈이ᄒᆞ나히요일은삼남수령관리민져은젼일에수평관으로학민탐제ᄒᆞᆫ항위ᄂᆞᆫ우부우가다아ᄂᆞᆫ빈어ᄂᆞᆯ각쥬하ᄂᆞᆫ이사름의불가홈을모르고비오쥬쳥ᄒᆞ시니잇가아홉이들이시명ᄒᆞ소원권티각하ᄂᆞᆫ츅됴로셔ᄒᆞ엿더라

○슈셰험과 공쥬관찰ᄉᆞ심건퇴씨가ᄂᆡ부로면보ᄒᆞ되관하홍쥬등십군슈셰ᄂᆞᆫ의훈칙ᄒᆞ야챡구과ᄒᆞ엿스오며명레ᄒᆞᆫ소관포구에슈셰ᄂᆞᆫ본랴덕산에셔본군ᄉᆡᆼ일ᄂᆡ니이세쟝샹군에다슈셰ᄒᆞᆫ니민폐ᄀᆞᆫ대단ᄒᆞᆫ지라힙혜과홈을회시ᄒᆞ라ᄒᆞ엿더라

○동도동도 홍쳔군슈유괘환씨의보고에ᄒᆞ엿스되본군경니에동학당ᄉᆞ오십명이놉우를쳬지ᄒᆞ야로조를샹아가지고홍은지평으로홍은려쥬로회집ᄒᆞᆫ다ᄒᆞ며셔산면동학슈십명도농우를빌아가지고려쥬로간다ᄒᆞ고인충쳥도동학당오명은집산린경과원에회도ᄒᆞ야동도수오십명을모집ᄒᆞ엿ᄂᆞᆫ디가진거슨돈표총오빅쌍이오음력칠월이십일에큰소동을쟝아가지고치셩명식을광쟝이ᄒᆞ엿다ᄒᆞ엿더라

○진위민요 경긔관찰ᄉᆞ가ᄂᆡ부로보고ᄒᆞ기를진위군에셔인부모집ᄉᆞ로인민이야료ᄒᆞ엿ᄂᆞᆫ디아젼빈가튱모ᄒᆞ엿다ᄒᆞ야멋집을보슈ᄒᆞ고본군슈를위챵ᄒᆞᆫ다ᄒᆞᄂᆞᆫ교로양셩군슈리쥬쳘노명ᄉᆞ관ᄒᆞ야쳔금사실ᄒᆞᄂᆞᆫ중이라ᄒᆞ엿더라

○니팀제원 중츄원부의장리용티씨가니부대신을피임ᄒᆞ엿더라

○동도입회 각쳐동학당이츙쳥셩ᄒᆞ야일셩ᄒᆞᆫ자가만타ᄂᆞᆫ디일진회로입참ᄒᆞᆫ사람이슈일동에유다ᄒᆞ다더라

○문관병혜셜 일본공ᄉᆞ림권조씨와수평쟝관원구씨가불원간에귀국ᄒᆞᆫ다ᄒᆞᄂᆞᆫ디그ᄉᆞ연을셰상에셔여러가지로말ᄒᆞᄂᆞᆫ중에무슨관계가잇셔ᄒᆞ느라ᄒᆞ며몃날후에다시온다ᄒᆞ더라

○도쳐착슈 원산감리의면보에ᄒᆞ엿스되무샹위졔인지본서쥬슈ᄒᆞᆼ쳥언을일본헌병티에서챡슈ᄒᆞ엿다ᄒᆞ엿더라

○교문관발졍 쥬일공ᄉᆞ관면보에ᄒᆞ기를교문관복하면이가본일에발졍ᄒᆞᄂᆞᆫ디쟝비를지발치아니ᄒᆞᆷ으로관욕이막심ᄒᆞ니속히곳지발ᄒᆞ라ᄒᆞ엿ᄂᆞᆫ디작일에도착되면보라더라

○힝하덕쟝 부산항민인등이면쳥ᄒᆞ되본항감리오귀현씨가치젹이공평ᄒᆞ며니비계ᄒᆞᆫ연이레잉되오니빅셩이ᄌᆞ모일ᄒᆞ온이갑ᄒᆞᆫ지라 단폐에쥬달ᄒᆞ시고속히인임ᄒᆞ심을복망이라ᄒᆞ엿더라

○안악군보 안악군공보에ᄒᆞ기를역부일빅명을입의샹회항으로귀송ᄒᆞᆫ후에인부모집ᄒᆞᆫ셰ᄒᆞᆫ란ᄒᆞᆫ칙이하리ᄒᆞ엿ᄂᆞᆫ디또샹화항슌검과일본인이리도ᄒᆞ야모군을독촉ᄒᆞ니엇지ᄒᆞᆫ연고인지속히회교ᄒᆞ라ᄒᆞ엿더라

○회답인유탐 법공ᄉᆞ가외부로죠회ᄒᆞ되회답국인공도시가황히평안함경각도를유탐코자ᄒᆞ니호죠를발급ᄒᆞ라ᄒᆞ엿더라

외보

○운량뎌슈 근ᄌᆞ에뎌슈구항너에량식이풩결치아니ᄒᆞᆷ은사름마다의아ᄒᆞᄂᆞᆫ바이어니와일셜에ᄂᆞᆫ로군이쳥국빅셩의게셔곡을고용ᄒᆞ야귀부에셔ᄂᆞᆫ일본병수의겁시ᄒᆞᆷ을두려워ᄒᆞ야그빅셩이쟝ᄒᆞᆼᄒᆞ야와ᄒᆞ위에셔비밀히량식을슈운ᄒᆞᆫ다ᄂᆞᆫ디거월이십구일로브터본월샹슌지지일본샹협티의게발견된쳥국빈가샤십여쳑이라더라

○아비셕탄 아국에셔지ᄂᆞᆫ샹귀월동안에셕탄오십만돈을미입ᄒᆞ엿ᄂᆞᆫ디ᄂᆞᆫ쳔진오쳑비이만쳔쳔ᄂᆞᆫ을실ᄉᆞ고비롤도로발향ᄒᆞ엿더라

○젼투미곡 아군이료양셩니에저축ᄒᆞᆫ미곡이티단히만흔티일본군이그곡식을방금죠사즁이라더라

광고

○미국으로셔일본에와셔연습ᄒᆞ고대한경셩에와셔쟝시류ᄒᆞ면셔병인들보기를원ᄒᆞᄂᆞᆫ미다기도ᄒᆞ오며싸진니시에세니도세로박되엽ᄒᆞ지안케잘곳치ᄂᆞᆫ이다

수무쇼ᄂᆞᆫ종로면ᄎᆞ회샤요

●본신문을츌판ᄒᆞᆫ다시긔랑ᄒᆞ와믜일소문을드리랴일로 구람ᄒᆞ시ᄂᆞᆫ쳠군ᄌᆞ의게공람케ᄒᆞ고에저ᄒᆞ야ᄌᆞ금이후로ᄂᆞᆫ미일오후에분젼이될리미오니죠량ᄒᆞ시옵

TELEGRAMS.

MARQUIS OYAMA'S REPORT.

Tokyo, Sept. 19th.

Field Marshal Marquis Oyama reports that supplies etc. captured at Liaoyang consist of:—

Rifles	2,578
Cartridges	1,638,700
Shells	10,056
Ammunition wagons	127
Shovels	15,985
Hoes	5,629
Axes	2,570
Heliographs	3
Telephones	6
Reflectors	3
Tins of beef	18,915
Pieces of timber	2,500
Bags of rice	2,000
Bags of flour	1,000
Bags of Fodder	3,600
Overcoats	5,400

The reports of prisoners taken vary in the numbers given. One despatch says 93, one 13, while the "Express" sent out by the Seoul Press yesterday gives the numbers at 6,400. The latter, in view of latest reports of Kuropatkin's retreat, seems highly improbable.

THE BATTLE OF LIAOYANG.

Reports of eyewitnesses of the battle of Liaoyang are now gradually drifting in and many of them prove very interesting reading. The following are extracts of one or two despatches.

The battle of Liaoyang is at an end today (5th). Nearly seven days' continuous fighting have resulted in the occupation of Liaoyang by the Japanese troops. Kuropatkin has suffered defeat but he has effected a masterly retreat along the railroad probably with his army almost intact, save those who were killed in battle.

The part that General Kuroki's army played in the conflict was a remarkable exhibition. From August 25th to August 30th, when he succeeded in joining forces with the two other armies which had advanced on Liaoyang from the south, General Kuroki marched day and night, being all the time in constant touch with the enemy and pushing them before him. Marching was difficult, the route running through mountainous and almost roadless country.

On the 30th August, having effected the junction with Oku and Nodzu, Kuroki made a rapid change of base, moving from Anping to a place east of the railway with his left wing stretching 10 miles north of Liaoyang, thus leaving a wide gap between his forces and the main body of the Japanese army. His purpose was to cut the railroad, thus severing Kuropatkin's only line of retreat, and then to attempt a surrounding movement.

On the night of September 2nd, Kuroki reached a position 2 or 3 miles from the railroad with his right wing ready to strike, but Kuropatkin was able to oppose him with a superior force and hold him at bay while the Russian army effected an orderly retreat. For two whole days it seemed possible the Russians might assume the defensive on a large scale and perhaps force Kuroki's army to abandon it's position.

This morning (5th) the Russian rearguard is engaging Kuroki's pursuing army and a brisk action is now taking place, the result of which will however not be productive of important results as the Russian retreat is now a "fait accompli." No estimate of the casualties can yet be formed but the death roll during the last forty-eight hours of desperate struggle must be enormous. The part taken in the struggle by Kuroki can be detailed as follows: During Thursday and Friday the 1st and 2nd, the army advanced westward and took up a position with the right wing at Kwangtung and the left in a bend of the river Taitsui.

The right and center were fighting determinedly, gaining every step at great cost. The artillery which was close to Kwangtung on the morning of the 1st, moved forward several times during the course of the two days taking advantage of the shelter afforded by low hills. The Russians shelled them continuously but the marksmanship directed against the batteries near Kwantung was extremely wild and created no disturbance amongst the Japanese gunners, who continued to man their pieces with great coolness and without any evidence of excitement.

On the night of the 2nd Kuroki's right division occupied some hills about 5 miles northwest of Kwangtung, called by the Chinese the Five-headed Hills. Here they could overlook the Yentai railway station, which lay some two or three miles to the west.

The center division took up a position on a long low range of hills five miles west of Kwangtung and above the village of Haiyentai. It was on an eminence here close to the ruins of a Manchu stone fort that General Kuroki stood for four days, under the merciless rays of a baking sun, and directed the operations in the battle which raged around him.

The Japanese front occupied a series of low hills and beyond them lay a rolling plain, intersected by ridges here and there and plentifully dotted with groves of trees which afforded splendid cover for both armies.

The Russians had cut down the grain from the fields in front of their entrenchments leaving the attacking Japanese no cover, thus compelling them to advance by digging successive rows of trenches. Here the suffering was great. Men already exhausted by several days' continuous hard fighting and marching were compelled to work unceasingly with trenching tools and rifles alternately. Only cold food was served out as the fear that fires would disclose their position rendered cooking impossible.

The Japanese had already lost heavily in gaining the positions which they now occupied, particularly Haiyentai.

On the 2nd Sept. after cannonading the Russians all day and driving them back without succeeding in finally dislodging them, the Japanese resorted to their favourite plan of a night attack, driving the enemy before them at the point of the bayonet.

On the afternoon of the same day another party had successfully stormed the Russian positions on the Five-headed Hills.

At the same time the left division made a demonstration against the high hills to the south of Haiyentai facing the bend of the river Taitsui where the Russians had posted batteries in strongly fortified positions. Part of the division, supported by five batteries on the plain, attempted to advance in open formation across the wide sandy flats and fields bordering the south bank of the river.

They encountered a decimating shrapnel fire from the enemy, and unable to advance took such shelter as could be found in such bare and flat country. They lay under fire all the afternoon until 5 o'clock when the order to retire was given.

The staff announced that the movement was a demonstration and it was probably intended to cover an attack by another part of the army on the same hills from another direction.

(To be continued)

THE SHUMUSHU HORROR A CANARD.

The reported Russian massacre on Shumushu has now turned out to be baseless. The source of this rumour is alleged to be the crew of a Japanese steamer from the north, whose gossip had been exaggerated at Hakodate.—Japan Gazette.

SIBERIAN RAILWAY.

THE WORK OF RELAYING.

The extra traffic thrown upon the Siberian Railway since the outbreak of war has shown that in many places the gradients are too short and sharp. The Ministry of Communication has decided to remedy these drawbacks, and the partial relaying of the line is about to be carried out according to the surveys, which have been made for that purpose. The cost of this work will be £2,337,500.

THE PENALTY OF GREATNESS.

The tall man who entered the city the other day and whose stature equalled that of the electric car, has, our reporter tersely informs us, been arrested by the police.

It is reported that two of the leaders of the Sihung riot have been arrested and imprisoned at the Japanese army headquarters.

Roze Island in Chemulpo harbour has now been completely staked out by the military authorities, who require the ground for certain military purposes.

The "Loyal," one of the four foreign steamers, which ran aground at Yokkaichi during a recent storm, was docked at Toba, Shima Province, on the 3rd inst.

The death is announced of Mr. Uchida, an engineer in the employ of the Survey office. The Japanese Minister has applied for 6 months arrears of salary due to the deceased.

An enterprising official, Mr. Yi Yong Sang, is said to have requested His Majesty to remove himself and household from Seoul and establish the Imperial Palace at Choon Chŏn in the Kangwon province.

A telegram from the leading citizens of Gensan has been received by the Foreign Office, complaining of the dismissal of the Kamni, who, they say, is the best man they have ever had. The Japanese support them in this statement.

The head men of all the villages in the neighbourhood of Si Hung, where the recent barbarous murder of the magistrate occurred, have been arrested by Japanese soldiers in their endeavour to discover the perpetrators of the outrage. Mr. An Chong Dok a member of the Privy Council has been sent to enquire into the circumstances of the case.

Repeated demands by the Japanese Legation for the payment of $2,120 for medical assistance rendered to a Japanese coolie, who succumbed eventually to wounds inflicted by some Korean soldiers at Wiju, having met with no response from the Foreign Office, the Japanese have now decided to take the amount out of the deposit money, lying in the Dai-Ichi bank and which is the price of rental of the ground outside the South Gate.

The Russian cruiser "Askold" at Shanghai is said to have gone out of the dock on Saturday afternoon and steamed alongside the pier of the Chinese Eastern Railway. Her waterline is now painted in black and red and the funnels in yellow. No flags are hoisted aboard. In this connection, Shanghai reports that China decided to intern the crews of the Russian ships and a Chinese gunboat will moor close to the Russians. The Customs officials will occasionally inspect the ships.

The Korea Daily News.

To be published daily except Sundays.
Rate of Subscription:—
Per Year, Yen 25.
Per Quarter, Yen 7.
Per Month Yen 2.50

Postage in Korea not charged extra.
Postage abroad charged extra.

Advertisements, 50 sen per day for 1 inch or less.
5 yen per month per inch.
50 yen per year per inch.

All communications to

E. T. BETHELL,
Editor and Publisher.
Pak-tong, Seoul.

AN IMPROBABLE STORY.

Koreans are eminently social and fond of company. Even the casual student of human nature will have noticed that the exercise of this trait leads to the circulation of a large amount of idle gossip and baseless statements. The tea parties of foreign women in the Far East illustrate this.

So it is with the Koreans.. As they have practically no diversions except that of meeting and conversing with their friends, and as they have generally plenty of spare time on their hands, it naturally follows that the acquisition of a sensational item of news, capable of enlargement and elaboration, places its holder for the time being upon a social pinnacle.

And the Koreans have only a half developed sense of proportion. This is not peculiar to them. Any one who has travelled in the rural districts of almost any country will have discovered how unreliable is the average rustic's idea of distance. "About a mile," says one. You walk two miles and again enquire and "about a mile," says the second man. You will probably have traversed ten miles by the time you reach your destination.

This applies not only to distance but to quantities. This is a special weakness of the Koreans. In the course of conversation a sum of money may be mentioned and as the story is carried to other gatherings the amount of money increases at a rate that would put the compound interest of "Ikey mo" in the shade.

So it is with numbers. We are all familiar with the stories which have come to Seoul from the Kamni, Magistrates and governors of various out-lying localities to the effect that Russian troops in their tens of thousands were descending into Karea. These hordes afterwards resolved themselves, under critical examination, into small marauding bands of 20 or 30. There is also an amusing story of a man who, out of curiosity, sent his servant to count the number of some foreign marines who had just entered the city. There were about 80 of them, and the servant after having watched them march past, returned to his master and announced, apparently in all good faith, that there were 360.

We cite these instances to show that all Korean stories must be accepted with great reserve—with more than reserve.

It is with this caution that we give publicity to a story which has been current in the capital for some days. It is to the effect that the Japanese have suggested the abdication of the present Emperor of Korea and the installation of his second son (who is now in America) in his stead.

We have two reasons for doubting this story. One is that we do not believe that the Japanese would dare to suggest such a thing, and the other is that we know such a scheme could never be put into effect.

Still we do not go so far as to say the story is absolutely incredible. A very slight acquaintance with the history of Japanese diplomatic relations with Korea serves to imbue one with the conviction that it is the unexpected which happens.

Of course the story appears to be too preposterous to be true, as no diplomat would be so foolish as to threaten a thing which he was so obviously unable to put into effect, and had not Japanese diplomacy taken such unexpected turns of late no notice would have been taken of the story.

As it is we can hardly blame the Koreans for believing the Japanese capable of almost any thing. When they were promised "Independence and Integrity" they thought "Independence and Integrity" was meant, yet now they find the Tokio newspapers publishing a telegram received by the Japanese Government, giving an extract from a London newspaper, which, commenting upon the agreement recently entered into by Japan and Korea, says:

"Japan is reaping some fruits of the war, even though the war is not yet brought to a close. The present Japanese-Korean Agreement shows that Korea must now be regarded as a Japanese dependency. No interference will be attempted with the management of internal affairs, so long as it does not come in conflict with the provisions of the present Agreement. But Korea has already become a dependency of Japan, and its diplomatic and commercial policy will emanate from Tokyo. This is an inevitable consequence of the success achieved by Japan."

This is the opinion of the "Standard" and it is worthy of note that it is the only London newspaper opinion which has so far reached us.

Perhaps some of the other London newspapers, remembering the "Independence and Integrity" by-word have not put such a liberal construction upon the recent agreement.

ENGLAND AND GERMANY.

(TO THE EDITOR OF THE "SPECTATOR.")

Sir,—You published in the "Spectator" of the 25th of June, under the heading of "Our Inadequate Defences," a letter from a correspondent which expressed the view that we might before long expect an attack by Germany, in view of the rapid increase of her Navy. Your editorial note did not altogether endorse this view, but it by no means poured cold water upon it.

On the principle of "audi alteram partem," you may like to see the view of a German to whom I sent the letter and note in question. The writer is a man of mature age, a keen observer of politics, and a strong Liberal. He has not been in England, except for a short visit in boyhood; but is well acquainted with English literature, and, as you see, writes a very fair good English letter. If it is not altogether convincing, it certainly sets forth some views which may be of some comfort and consolation to your correspondent.

I am, Sir, etc.,

AN OLD OXONIAN.

"Another fable is that of the enmity against England and the preparation for a struggle with that country. You will not find one serious man in all Germany who has such ideas, and who will not laugh at such declamations as in the cutting from the "Spectator" which you sent me. It were indeed time that another Carlyle should speak about Germany to his countrymen. The way in which the "Times" and other papers speak about Germany now for years is indeed such that every thinking man must feel provoked to answer. It is an undeniable fact that Germany, the greatest military Power, has not fired a shot for thirty years. England, Russia, France, were in the meantime continually at war in some parts of the world, and have added new possessions of the greatest importance to their former Colonies. France spends much larger sums for her Army as well as her Navy than Germany yet nobody thinks that she does so out of enmity for England. That Germany arms herself in the same measure as Franc eshould appear natural when the 'revanche' is the loadstone for a great part of her politicians and most of her officers. The expenditure for the Navy of the United States is much larger also than that of Germany, and the outlay for new ships is in England three times as great; in Russia, America, and France greater than in Germany, so that this country holds only the fifth place (as she does in number and weight of ships also); it would be wonderful if her Fleet only should grow in an alarming manner to England.

"What cause is there for enmity? Our Press wrote against England during the war in South Africa, but was not the same done by all Continental papers? And certainly the French papers were more insulting to you than ours. Our largest trade is with England, and do you think that we hope to increase it by war? Or do we want any of your Colonies? More than half the members of the Reichstag are enemies of colonies under all circumstances, so that it is with great pain that the Ministers obtain grants of money for colonial purposes. And even if a party in Germany were wishing for new colonial enterprise, is there no cheaper mode for getting colonies than a war with the greatest naval Power, which any day may seize our colonies which we cannot defend? The Dutch have most tempting colonies which are much more easily obtainable, and yet nobody there has fear of our country, which, situated among many weaker neighbours, has never injured them, but proved herself a sincere friend of peace.

"Germany has two things to fear. (1) The Socialist movement, one-third of our voters following the standard of Herr Bebel. This movement would grow in case of any war in an irresistible manner. (2) The Panslavic movement in the East and in Austria. Germany is sure to have the Slavs on her hands whenever she engages in war, and France will not keep quiet in that case either. These two dangers are always paramount in our considerations, and secure all other Powers against our breaking the peace except in vital questions.

"Excuse my writing so explicitly, but it seems to me the duty of every honest man in both countries to diminish the ill-feeling and the unreasonable nervousness which some people seem to have an interest to excite between England and Germany, who hitherto have had no serious difference."

It is reported that Mr. Megata will be a passenger by the "Ohio," on her next voyage.

It is reported that H. E. Mr. Hayashi the Japanese Minister, is shortly returning to Japan.

The Tai Han Ilpo learns that the Russian troops at Hamheung have now all retreated to Song Chin.

We hear that General Nakayama has been appointed to the command of the Japanese army in Korea, in place of General Haragachi.

Mr. Hyon Po-woon, the secretary to the Korean Legation in Tokyo, will shortly return to Seoul. He is a son of the well-known General Hyon Yong-woon.

The Korea Daily News.

VOL. I, TUESDAY, SEPTEMBER 20, 1904. No. 56

HONGKONG & SHANGHAI BANKING CORPORATION.

Paid-up Capital	$10,000,000
Reserve Fund:—Sterling Reserve	10,000,000
Silver Reserve	6,500,000
	26,500,000
Reserve Liability of Proprietors	10,000,000

HEAD OFFICE, HONGKONG.

London Bankers, London and County Banking Company Limited.

Branches and Agencies, London.

Amoy,	Hankow	Penang,
Bangkok,	Hiogo,	Rangoon,
Batavia,	Iloilo,	Saigon,
Bombay,	Lyons,	San Francisco,
Calcutta,	Manila,	Singapore,
Colombo,	Nagasaki,	Sourabaya,
Foochow,	New York,	Tientsin,
Hamburg,	Peking,	Yokohama,

Credits granted on approved Securities, and every description of Banking and Exchange business transacted.

Drafts granted on London and the chief Commercial places in Europe, India, Australia, America, China and Japan.

HOLME RINGER & Co., AGENTS, CHEMULPO.

ON CHEONG & CO., SEOUL.

GENERAL STORE KEEPERS.

Imported provisions, Cooking Utensils Crockery, etc.

FRESH BREAD DAILY.

MITSU BISHI DOCKYARD & ENGINE WORKS,

NAGASAKI.

CODE WORD, "DOCK."

A. 1, A. B. C., and Engineering Codes used.

DOCK No. 1 (at Tategami).

Extreme Length	523 feet
Length on blocks	513 ,,
Width of Entrance on Top	89 ,,
,, ,, Bottom	77 ,,
Water on Blocks at Spring Tide	26½ ,,

DOCK No. 2 (Mukaijima).

Extreme Length	371 feet
Length on Blocks	360 ,,
Width of Entrance on Top	66 ,,
,, ,, Bottom	53 ,,
Water on Blocks at Spring Tide	22 ,,

PATENT SLIP (at Kosuge).

Can take vessels up to 1,000 tons gross.

THE WORKS are well equipped with the LATEST IMPROVEMENTS, and can execute any kind of work in SHIPBUILDING and MARINE ENGINEERING, as well as in REPAIRING of SHIPS.

The COMPANY'S new powerful steamer OURA-MARU (712 tons, 700 I.H.P.), specially built for SALVAGE PURPOSES, and equipped with necessary gear, is always READY at SHORT NOTICE.

CHARTERED BANK OF INDIA AUSTRALIA & CHINA.

INCORPORATED BY ROYAL CHARTER 1853

HEAD OFFICES:—LONDON.

Paid-up Capital	£800,000
Reserve Liability of Shareholders	800,000
Reserve Fund	800,000

Drafts granted upon all the principal places in the world and every description of Exchange and banking business transacted.

E. MEYER & Co., Agents, Chemulpo.

E. MEYER & CO.

Chemulpo.

SOLE AGENTS IN KOREA FOR:

A. T. Morse, Sons & Co's "Fresco" Distemper

In all colours ready for use on walls, Ceilings etc.

and

AVENARIUS CARBOLINEUM

A wood-preserving and antiseptic oil preparation

Against decay, dry-rot, fungus and wood-destroying insects.

A large supply always in Stock. Prices upon application.

E. MEYER & Co., Chemulpo.

LAW UNION & CROWN INS. CO.

Fire risks accepted at Current rates, on go downs, merchandise, dwellings, and other property, subject to usual conditions.

HOLME RINGER & Co., Agents, Chemulpo

THE METHODIST PUBLISHING HOUSE,

Little West Gate, Seoul.

JOB PRINTING, TYPEWRITER PAPER
CARBON PAPER, VISITING CARDS
STATIONERY, BOOK BINDING
BOOK PUBLISHERS
AMERICAN SCHOOL BOOKS
SPENCERIAN COPY BOOKS
PEN CARBON LETTER AND BILL BOOKS

S A. BECK, Manager.

DAI-ICHI GINKO.

LIMITED.

(Formerly the First National Bank)

ESTABLISHED 1873

INCORPORATED UNDER PRESENT LAW 1896

Capital	Yen 5,000,000
Reserve Fund	1,500,000

HEAD OFFICE:—TOKIO.

President: Baron SHIBUSAWA.

BRANCHES AND CORRESPONDENTS In the Principal Cities and Towns of Japan.

Interest Allowed on

Fixed deposits	1 year	6½ per cent
" "	6 months	6 per cent

Special current accounts 1½ sen daily per Y 100
General " " 1 " " " 100

M. TANAKA, Manager, Chemulpo

HOLME RINGER & Co.

Chemulpo.

General Merchants and Government Contractors.

Agents for the leading Banks Steamship Companies and Insurance Companies

Importers of Merchandise of every description.

KAMEYA & CO.

3 GENERAL STOREKEEPERS

Chinkokai - - Seoul

(*Established 1895, Tokyo*)

Confectionery, Hams, Canned Goods, Cutlery, Hirano & Tansan Water. Provisions, Gents, Furnishing goods, Toilet Articles, Travelling Bags, Tobacco, Cigars & Cigarettes Kitchen Utensils. Coffee, Biscuits.

Fresh Goods always kept in Stock.

Prices Moderate

Please come and inspect our goods.

NIPPON YUSEN KAISHA.

JAPANESE MAIL STEAMSHIP CO.

DER MAIL CONTRACT WITH THE IMPERIAL JAPANESE GOVERNMENT.

European Line

Regular Fortnightly Service between Yokohama Kobe, Moji, Shanghai, Hongkong, Singapore, Penang Colombo, Port Said, Marseilles, London and Antwerp

American Line

Regular Fortnightly Service between Hongkong and Seattle, calling at Shanghai, Moji, Kobe, Yokohama and Victoria, B. C.

Australian Line

Regular weekly Service betwen Japan Ports and Australia, calling at Hongkong and Manila.

(Above Three Lines Suspended until further notice).

Shanghai Line

Weekly Service between Shanghai and Japan Ports

Korea Line

Service Kobe, Moji, Nagasaki, Fusan, Chemulpo, Choo, Taiku.

S. S. Bahelsberg, 2181 tons.

Service Kobe, Moji, Fusan, Chemulpo, Chinnampo

S. S ARGO, S. S. Ohio.

BORDEN'S CONDENSED MILK CO.

New York, U. S. A.

ALWAYS IN STOCK

Eagle Brand Condensed Milk.

Gold Seal Condensed Milk.

Peerless (Family) Evaporated Cream.

Borden's Malted Milk.

E. MEYER & CO. Chemulpo, Korea, Sole Agents

ROYAL INSURANCE COMPANY,

Funds exceed £10,000,000

FIRE

AT CURRENT RATES.

LIFE

REDUCED PREMIUM.

HOLME RINGER & Co., Agents, Chemulpo.

HOTEL DU PALAIS

SEOUL.

The only first class Hotel in Seoul. Situated in the centre of the city opposite the palace.

Cuisine under the supervision of an experienced French Chef.

Well ventilated and furnished throughout.

TARIFF UPON APPLICATION

L. MARTIN

Proprietor and Mangaer

大韓每日申報
대한미일신보

(뎨오십칠호) (슈요일) 쳔구빅사년구월이십일일

본사고빅

본신보는영어와한어로셔거릐일츌판ᄒᆞ옵

신문가

한장 엽두돈오푼

일삭됴 엽두량닷돈

우표가미삭닷돈

다엽돈으로밧솝

광고료는

귀한의장단과ᄌᆞ힝의다쇼로죵감ᄒᆞ되현금가로밧을터이오매오리지아녀대한사람마다다이신문을보실터이니광고내시기를원ᄒᆞ시는이들은우리신문사에와서면약ᄒᆞ심을희망ᄒᆞ옵

○발힝소 박동대한미일신보사법어학교엽헤젼영국인셜필림집자리오

사쟝 영국인 (비셜)

평양 퇴리경

○평양효동사는권미보씨로우리신문판미ᄒᆞᆫ디리인을퇴졍ᄒᆞ엿시스오니평양에계신구람코져ᄒᆞ시는 쳠군ᄌᆞ는허티리경에왕림ᄒᆞ와면의ᄒᆞ시옵

사고

○우리대한미일신보의목뎍은대한의안녕질서에관ᄒᆞᆫ모든대목에되ᄒᆞ야는공평ᄒᆞᆫ변론을쥬쟝홈이라우리통신원의탐보는신문보시는쳠군ᄌᆞ의게ᄒᆞᆼ상보도ᄒᆞ리며편지를긔셔ᄒᆞ여주시는이는셩명과번디를젹어붓처시기를희망ᄒᆞ오니이거슨신문상에긔재ᄒᆞ란는거시아니오다만극히신용ᄒᆞ는증거를숨고쟈홈이라긔자는아모긔셔던지긔재홈을퇴챡ᄒᆞ는권리를가졋ᄉᆞ나퇴챡ᄒᆞ는리유를말홀터이오며공즁평화를문란케ᄒᆞ는듯ᄒᆞᆫ긔셔는의례히밧지안켓솝나이다

●본사셜시이릭로신문을미양우톄로분젼ᄒᆞ와톄젼부의일의로젼ᄒᆞᄂᆞᆫᄉᆞ스로먼곳에는ᄒᆞᆼ늣게젼ᄒᆞ기도ᄒᆞ며ᄒᆞᆨ먹거나쇼실ᄒᆞᆫ에젼ᄒᆞ기도ᄒᆞ며ᄒᆞᆨ아니젼ᄒᆞᄂᆞᆫ곳도잇다ᄒᆞ와우리신문을슈람ᄒᆞ야구람ᄒᆞ시는 쳠군ᄌᆞ의게되ᄒᆞ야미우미안ᄒᆞ옵기로지금은분젼인을두고미일죠이젼ᄒᆞ며아니젼ᄒᆞ거나늣게거나ᄒᆞᆫ폐가엽도록ᄒᆞ란ᄒᆞ오니ᄒᆞ야나젼ᄒᆞ거나늣게젼ᄒᆞ거나ᄒᆞᆫ일이잇스면본사로통긔ᄒᆞ여주심을희망ᄒᆞ옵

본사광고

본샤에서본신문뎨ᄉᆞ호와뎨심일호와뎨이십오호를ᄉᆞ용홀ᄐᆡ가잇서이에광고ᄒᆞ오니누구시던지이상삼호중에본사로가저오시면미쟝에ᄇᆡᆨ젼두푼식드리리다

론셜

ᄒᆞᆫ밋지못홀말이라

○한국사람들은친구들미오죠와ᄒᆞ며사회상교제도통별나게ᄒᆞ야지어요랑미쟝ᄒᆞᆫ셩도셔지라도이러ᄒᆞᆫ일에주의홈이잇서져희들ᄭᅵ리서로모히면회합지셜과무근지언으로ᄌᆞᆼᄉᆞᄒᆞᆫ다는티이거슨동양에잇는외국녀인다회에서한국사람과홍셰참예홈으로이말이낫는지라

한국사람들은친구들로서로만나담화홈이도모지졍ᄒᆞᆫ요랑이업시공연ᄒᆞᆫ셰월만허비ᄒᆞ고무맛슨소문이나어ᄯᅥᆫ드르리ᄒᆞ다가일ᄒᆞᆫ마티나어ᄯᅥᆫ듯게되면ᄎᆞᄎᆞ로젼지젼언ᄒᆞ야필경에는장대ᄒᆞ게만드기로ᄒᆞᆫ등ᄉᆞ를상아이사회상쇄ᄂᆞᆫ는일로싱각ᄒᆞᆫ즉지라이상ᄒᆞᆫ거슨엇던거시만일ᄒᆞᆫ사람이시끌길을가다가알젼이엇마나남앗나아교무르면싱리ᄉᆞᆷ남앗노라고티답ᄒᆞᆫ후다시형ᄒᆞ여이십리를가서쏘다른농부다려무른즉역시티답ᄒᆞ기를삼리가남앗노라고말ᄒᆞᆫ후필경도착ᄒᆞ야뎌음뭇든곳으로리슈를비교ᄒᆞ게되면모도빅리나되ᄂᆞᆫ니다만리슈가르칠만이러ᄒᆞᆯᄲᅮᆫ아니라젼쟝샹에도약ᄎᆞᄒᆞ야소위돈도합이얼마라고ᄒᆞᄂᆞᆫ티그돈가계에은령ᄒᆞᆫ이의을봇처ᄒᆞᆫ항ᄒᆞᄂᆞᆫ폐도잇스며우리의항샹듯ᄂᆞᆫ바ᄌᆞ도판찰군슈와ᄌᆞ항감리의말과갓흔진티그롱안에병슈만명이한국에드러왓슬ᄯᅳᆺᄒᆞᆫ거시여간이상상명로ᄒᆞ리단이ᄂᆞᆫ자들만보게되면ᄌᆞ긔들의의사티로슈효를쳠죠ᄒᆞᄂᆞᆫ거시라졔일졀도ᄒᆞ르ᄒᆞᆫ에잇ᄂᆞᆫ시가랑판찰부셩너에나ᄒᆞ음닌곤쳐로외국병졸이다만괄신명만드리을것갓트면판슈을보니며슈효를헤아리라ᄒᆞᆫ즉이판슈이그병졸의힝군ᄒᆞ여감을ᄌᆞ셔히보고도로와보고ᄒᆞ기를모도삼빅룩십명이라고ᄒᆞᄂᆞᆫ셔닭에분명히밋고그리홈인즉우리가이말ᄒᆞᄂᆞᆫ거슨한국사람의거즛말로쟝황ᄒᆞ게만드ᄂᆞᆫ바에미오조와홈듯ᄒᆞ기에이리말ᄒᆞ노라

잡보

○예후졈봉 황뎨ᄌᆞ뎐하환후가일잔으로졈졈평복되샤쟉야와졔쟉아에는침슈를ᄌᆞ편히ᄒᆞ셧다더라

○일병소며 시흥군에는일병이하거ᄒᆞ야뎐답에ᄇᆡᆨ곡은다마량이되고동즁에싱믈은다병명의로관ᄒᆞᆫ비되야경니가비로쏜듯ᄒᆞ다더라

○홍씨힝젹 신임ᄒᆞᆫ남포군슈홍희씨는남과교제를별반친밀이ᄒᆞ야미양등비외ᄒᆞ기를청ᄒᆞᆫ연는베를승시ᄒᆞ야그가그집ᄌᆞ간ᄒᆞᄂᆞᆫ고로경무청에소실을갑쳐ᄒᆞᆫ지라친구비가그무의무례홈을미워ᄒᆞ야반히졍교ᄒᆞ여너일젼니부 쥬본에신참졍이라ᄒᆞ야남포군슈를셔임ᄒᆞᆫ지라졔동거ᄒᆞᄂᆞᆫ리김량세가참졍을왕견ᄒᆞ고홍씨의젼후비루ᄒᆞᆫ힝위를세세히셜명ᄒᆞ엿다더라

○셩교수봉 랑디아문긔슈니면평치량세신수ᄒᆞᆫ후에일용수카외부로청ᄒᆞ기를니면이키국에교용ᄒᆞ다가쉬교ᄒᆞ엿슨즉평리가불가불수후삭긔월봉급을지급ᄒᆞ거시오아왕니면이쟝시히교ᄒᆞ엿슨셰불긔월봉급지발커아니ᄒᆞᆫ것ᄉᆞ지병ᄒᆞ야지급ᄒᆞ라ᄒᆞ엿더라

○빅쳔민요 서로로죳차샹리ᄒᆞᆫ사람의말을드른즉빅쳔군에민요가대긔ᄒᆞ엿ᄂᆞᆫ티인부로징수긴을인연홈이라더라

○은률뎐보 은률군슈의뎐보를거ᄒᆞᆫ즉ᄒᆞ엿스되여부룸세ᄒᆞ는ᄒᆞᆫ밍이열의리도ᄒᆞ엿ᄂᆞᆫ티삼화참리ᄂᆞᆫ모졍ᄒᆞ라고무ᄎᆞ츙ᄒᆞᆫᄒᆞ고당쟝모졉ᄒᆞᄂᆞᆫ고로민샹이대단요요ᄒᆞ다ᄒᆞ엿더라

○의쥬보고 의쥬군슈구완희씨가일병의소청ᄒᆞᄂᆞᆫᄉᆞ항을로렬ᄒᆞ야보고ᄒᆞ엿ᄂᆞᆫ티 일은각영문은다일병의슈용ᄒᆞᆫ비되고 일은본군관사ᄂᆞᆫ군용뎐신국이되고 일은도로와교량을널고두텁게슈축ᄒᆞ라ᄒᆞ고대로동구에쳐간을셜치ᄒᆞ라ᄒᆞ고 일은마초와시탄등물을불시로준비ᄒᆞ라ᄒᆞ고 일은계든계란등식물을청구ᄒᆞ고 일은텰도놋ᄂᆞᆫ졀에역부들일빅이ᄌᆞ의로모집슈용ᄒᆞᆫ다ᄒᆞ고 일은구련셩등디에츅셩홀역부을미일숨빅오십명식모집ᄒᆞ야보ᄂᆡ라ᄒᆞ고 일은구룡포에죠륙감시부에소용홀역부를청구ᄒᆞ고 일은쟝강용셩에각항물품을슈운홀역부미명식쓰겟다ᄒᆞ고 일은본군으로셔룡쳔디경과삭쥬디경에일병리왕ᄒᆞᄂᆞᆫ도로와교량을일일히슈츅ᄒᆞ라ᄒᆞᄂᆞᆫ티이샹제반ᄉᆞ건이민력과젼지가드러야홀일인티지졍이핍졀ᄒᆞ야슈응홀슈업스니도쟈히빙의ᄒᆞ다ᄒᆞ엿더라

○경리폐악 대구관찰ᄉᆞ셔리쟝기군슈문찬셕씨가니부로뎐보ᄒᆞ되경쥬군슈박병익의보고거ᄒᆞᆫ즉본월초ᄉᆞ일에관찰부리치진ᄒᆞᆫ배에젼등민요쟝두리명구가중로에서돌출ᄒᆞ야갈노군슈를젼녀다리를괴샹ᄒᆞ고칙실도변부와두리가중샹ᄒᆞ야ᄉᆞ셩을미판이온바동헌에돌입ᄒᆞ야문부를슈탐ᄒᆞ고우분을리파ᄒᆞ고막중ᄒᆞᆫ공젼홈포ᄒᆞᆫ죄인과옥ᄉᆞ간셥ᄒᆞᆫ죄인을일병방출ᄒᆞ엿ᄉᆞ오니이쟉경은리명구의게량비젼간물도됴둥봉ᄒᆞᆫ셔리가가도다ᄒᆞᆫ고로그아우들티신착슈ᄒᆞ엿더니곧노협림ᄒᆞ야피익홈이오니ᄉᆞᆫ검을파송ᄒᆞ야리명구를엄샹죠률케ᄒᆞ라ᄒᆞ엿더라

○명제경샥 대구서리관찰이ᄉᆡᆼ뎐보ᄒᆞ되샹쥬군ᄒᆞᆼ쟝이글보ᄒᆞ기를본군미김텰만과강락형이티ᄉᆞᄒᆞᄂᆞᆫ티김텰만이가지원ᄒᆞ기로강락형을수뎡방에임치ᄒᆞ엿더니바일밤에강가가졍치수ᄒᆞ고로강가가의ᄌᆞ졔이김쳘만이를란타ᄒᆞ야명졔경각이라ᄒᆞ엿다ᄒᆞ엿더라

UNION INSURANCE SOCIETY OF CANTON.
Head office Hongkong.
Marine risks underwritten at current rates.
Agents in Chemulpo,
MEYER & Co.

COMPAGNIE DES MESSAGERIES MARITIMES.

Fortnightly Direct Service.

For Marseilles
Via Ports.
Sailing from Yokohama
Calling at Kobe,
Shanghai, Hongkong, Saigon, Singapore,
Colombo, Djibonti, Suez, Port Said
and Marseilles.

For particulars apply to
HOLME RINGER & Co.,
Chemulp

HAYASHIDA & CO.

16 MYENG DONG, CHING KO KAI, SEOUL.
BRANCH OFFICE AT CHEMULPO.

Money changers, Coal and Wood Merchants, Express Agents.

We are agents for the Pyeng-yang Coal Company and the Karazu Coal Company of Japan. We have the best quality of both anthracite and bituminous coal, and prompt execution of orders is our speciality. Firewood of all kinds kept in stock. Full weight guaranteed. Money of all denominations exchange, at current rates. Parcels received for all parts

CHINA MUTUAL LIFE INS- CO.

Most favourable terms to policy holders.

Benefit system unsurpassed.

HOLME RINGER & Co.
Agents, Chemulpo.

C. P. R.

CANADIAN PACIFIC RAILWAY COMPANY'S ROYAL MAIL STEAMSHIP LINE.

THE FAST ROUTE BETWEEN CHINA, JAPAN, AND EUROPE VIA CANADA AND THE UNITED STATES.

Route from Hongkong via Shanghai, Nagasaki (Inland Sea of Japan) Kobe, Yokohama, Victoria and Vancouver.

Twin Screw Empress Steamships—6,000 Tons—Speed 19 knots.

PROPOSED SAILINGS FROM YOKOHAMA.

R. M. S. Empress of India.
R. M. S. Empress of Japan.
R. M. S. Empress of China.
R. M. S. Athenian.
R. M. S. Tartar.

Special reduction (first class only) granted to members of the Military, Naval, Diplomatic and Civil Services and to Missionaries.
Passengers have choice of ten routes across the Continent of America and have privilege of travelling by any Atlantic Steamship Line.
Round the World passage tickets in connection with the P. and O. S. N., North German Lloyd and Messageries Co.'s £125.
All rates payable at current rate of exchange.
For further information, Tickets, Guide Books, etc., apply to
HOLME, RINGER & Co., AGENTS, Chemulpo.

Grand Hotel,

(*Formerly the Station Hotel*)

Near the Railway Terminus,
West Gate, Seoul.

The Best Hotel in Korea.
Handsome new Building.
Fine airy Rooms
Excellent Cuisine.
Terms Moderate.
Special terms to Missionaries
and to permanent boarders.

Electric cars within 2 minutes' walk.

W. H. EMBERLEY,
Proprietor.

EVERY FACILITY :
In connection with Life Assurance Business is afforded by

The Standard Life Assurance Co.,

One of the largest and wealthiest of the Provident Institutions of the United Kingdom. Forms of Application and all information will be promptly afforded on application.

10 CENTS A DAY.

Not a very large expenditure is it? But it is sufficient to secure for a man of 30 a policy with the STANDARD LIFE OFFICE for

$1323.

For all particulars of rates, etc., apply to

Holme, Ringer & Co.,
Agents, Chemulpo.

THE NEW YORK LIFE INSURANCE COMPANY.

Have you ever been declined by and Company?

Are you engaged in as pecially hazardous occupation?

Have you heard of the New York Life Insurance Company's New Classifications for this class of Risks?

If not, send your date of birth, occupation and particulars of rejection, if any to

E. MEYER & Co., Agents, Chemulpo.

MITSUI BUSSAN KAISHA.
(MITSUI & Co.)

MITSUI GINKO.
(MITSUI BANK.)

The Bank is owned by the members of the Mitsui Family, who, as partners, assume an unlimited responsibility for all liabilities of the Bank:—

Capital.................... ......Yen 5,000,000
Reserve Fund.................... " 5,600,000

HEAD OFFICE, TOKYO.
LONDON OFFICE, 34 LIME ST., E. C.

BRANCHES AND AGENCIES:—
New York, San Francisco, Hamburg, Bombay, Singapore, Manila, Hongkong, Amoy, Chefoo, Tientsin.
Kobe, Hakodate, Yokohama, Kure, Yokosuka, Moji, Shimonoseki, Miike, Wakamatsu, Nagasaki, Kuchinotsu, Karatsu, Sasebo, Misume, Taipeh, &c.

Telegraphic Address for all the Offices:
"MITSUI."
A. B. C. AND A. 1 CODES USED.

Contractors of Coal
To the Imperial Japanese Navy. Arsenals and Railway Bureau, Principal Railway Companies and Industrial Works, Home and Foreign Mail and Freight Steamers.
Sole Proprietors
Of the famous Miike, Tagawa and Yamano Coal Mines.
Sole Agents
For the sale of Fukumo, Hokoku, Ichimura, Kanoda, Mannoura, Onoura, Ostuji, Sonoda, Tsubaruro, Yoshinotani, Yoshio, Yurokibura and other coals.

YANGTSE INSURANCE ASSOCIATION, LTD.
The undersigned, having been appointed agents for the above company, are prepared to issue policies and pay losses on marine risks at regular rates.
E. MEYER & Co.,
Agents, Chemulpo

AMERICAN KOREAN ELECTRIC COMPANY.
Light and Power.
Main Office: Electric Building, Chong No.

RAILWAY DEPARTMENT.

OPERATING CARS BETWEEN EAST AND WEST GATE, EVERY TEN MINUTES:—
First Car leaves East Gate at 6:30 A. M. First Car leaves West Gate at 6:55 A. M.
Last Car " East Gate at 10:40 P. M. Last " " West Gate at 11:00 P. M.

OPERATING CARS BETWEEN EAST GATE AND IMPERIAL TOMB TERMINUS, EVERY TWENTY MINUTES:—
CONNECTING WITH EVERY ALTERNATE CAR ARRIVING AT EAST GATE FROM CHONG NO.
First Car leaves East Gate for Tomb at 6:50 A. M.
" " " Tomb for East Gate at 7:10 A. M.
Last " " East Gate for Tomb at 9:50 P. M.
" " " Tomb for East Gate at 10:10 P. M.

OPERATING CARS BETWEEN CHONG NO AND YUNG SAN (RIVER) EVERY TWELVE MINUTES:—
First Car leaves Chong No for South Gate at 6:48 A. M.
" " " Chong No for Yung San at 7:24 A. M.
" " " South Gate for Chong No at 6:56 A. M.
" " " Yung San for Chong No at 7:57 A. M.
Last " " South Gate for Chong No 11:00 P. M.
" " " Yung San for Chong No at 10:11 P. M.

SPECIAL PRIVATE CARS FURNISHED TO SUIT CONVENIENCE OF PATRONS. PRICES ON APPLICATION AT HEAD OFFICE.

LIGHTING DEPARTMENT.

Where less than 250 candle power of light is used, the rate per month will be. Per 16 candle power incandescent lamp. All night.—Yen 2.50.
Per 32 candle power incandescent lamp:—All night:—Yen 4.00. Per 50 candle power incandescent lamp:—All night:—Yen 6.00.
" 150 " " " " — " " " 10.00. " 1200 " " enclosed arc " " " 20.00.
Where more than 250 candle power of light is used, a Meter will be installed, if requested:—Rent of Meter Yen 2.00 per month. Rate of charges by meter reading:—Two Sen per Ampere per hour. (Approximately this is equal to about One Sen per 16 c. p. lamp per hour) Minimum monthly charge where meter is installed, Yen 20.00 per month, which includes rental of meter.
Estimates for installing lights furnished on application. An assortment of chandeliers always on hand.

AMUSEMENT DEPARTMENT.

ANIMATED PICTURES AT EAST GATE.
Every evening - - - Except Sunday.
From 8 to 10 P. M.

10 Cents:—Gen. Admission:—10 Cents. Seats in First Class Section. 15 Cents Extra.

Change of program each week. Pictures from Foreign Lands. Pictures of Local Scenes:—Amusing and Instructive.

An entertaining evening for a reasonable price.
MERRY-GO-ROUND:—At East Gate.
From 10:00 A. M. till 11:00 P. M.

5 Cents a Ride.

Take your Exercise on The Galloping Horses.

Comfortable seats in the Chariots.

한셩뎐긔회사

한미뎐긔회사　고본안　보사뎍　고ᄇᆡᆨ
도ᄒᆞ옵나이다
샹활동사진뎐람소와목마운동쟝량쳐로셔
여러뎐차가온쟝안으로통힝ᄒᆞ여ᄃᆞ니여이
습
또이긔계에긋치노힌편ᄒᆞ고됴흔마차도잇
습
코미우편ᄒᆞ고또조미잇ᄂᆞᆫ됴흔운동이되겟
이됴흔모형을달나아ᄂᆞᆫ몸을드고위틔치안
되가ᄂᆞᆫ휴번ᄃᆞᄂᆞᆫ데오젼석이오
미일샹오열시브터하오열ᄒᆞ시ᄉᆞ지ᄒᆞ옵고
목마운동쟝은동대문안에잇습고
가되겟습
쳡군조의게갑도싸고져녁에됴흔쇼일거리
잇고구경ᄒᆞᆯ만ᄒᆞᆫ거시오니
셔양사진과대한과돈동양사신인네대조미
ᄂᆞᆫ뎌
젼에옵고미쥬일에사진을섭것스로다밧고
고젼람되금은하등에십젼이오상등에이십
일외에ᄂᆞᆫ미야에여덜시브터열시ᄉᆞ지ᄒᆞ옵
활동사진뎐람소ᄂᆞᆫ동대문안에잇습고일요
회락부

All Cars Run Direct to the Animated Pictures and Merry-Go-Round.

○자방긔간　일본북경헌병사령
대니상상세가공니부등취를엇
어셔문안항자방포들기간차로
고아오슈인과ᄒᆞᆫ가지와셔계반
수틀준비중인데쟈농민이벌명
을이주케ᄒᆞ고기사도과겁ᄒᆞ리
히라더라

○일인피살　평안도운동신
을거ᄒᆞ던일인이명이외주외셔
엇더ᄒᆞᆫ사ᄅᆞᆷ의게피살되여일본
헌병이젼왕ᄒᆞ야사실을조사중
이라더라

○젼도상쇼　리용상씨가상쇼
ᄒᆞ야ᄒᆞᆫ쳔대졀노젼도ᄒᆞ자고ᄒᆞ
엿다더라

○탁희연귀　일한구탁부발회
식을이십일에거힝ᄒᆞᆫ다더니이
십오일노퇴졍ᄒᆞ엿다더라

○고문쇼식　한국재무고문관
목하전종태랑씨의일ᄒᆡᆼ은본월
이십ᄉᆞ일신호에셔출범ᄒᆞ는오
하요호톤환표한국으로온다더
라

○구근슈용　니부대신리용태
씨가일간에각군슈를주본ᄒᆞᆫ다
는데궁니부의경부부니외부탁
지부군부법부농상공부학부중
츄원경무쳥관인중계ᄉᆞ구근으
로용평ᄒᆞ게퇴용ᄒᆞᆫ다더라

○일무츌긔　근일경무쳥에셔
각방곡에순검을파송ᄒᆞ야각긔
주에향긔비무고히두류ᄒᆞ는자
들각문외로츌송ᄒᆞ라ᄒᆞ고곳곳이
적간ᄒᆞᆫ즉혹은ᄌᆞ긔문중보ᄉᆞ로
류경ᄒᆞᆫ다ᄒᆞ고혹은세수교도라
ᄒᆞ고그외에는다인젼회원이라
칭탁ᄒᆞ는고로ᄒᆞ나도츌송치못
ᄒᆞ엿다더라

○가련한인　법부에셔외부로
조회ᄒᆞ되고양군보를거ᄒᆞᆫ즉읍
혁칠월십칠일에탑골벽부일인
삼명이본군외셩동상리리덕근
가에승야돌입ᄒᆞ야돈을탈취ᄒᆞ
란다가쟝겨가더니조시또그징
니경에돌입ᄒᆞ야부녀를겁간ᄒᆞ
란는데뎌큰은출타ᄒᆞ고그부친
제하와그하우인화가집에잇다
가일인을쟉지경더니취일인등
이몽둥이로란타ᄒᆞ야제하는당
장치ᄉᆞᄒᆞ고인화도중상ᄒᆞ엿ᄉᆞᆫ
즉극히참혹ᄒᆞᆫ다ᄒᆞ엿ᄉᆞ니곳일
관에조회ᄒᆞ야흉괴범을착륙ᄒᆞ
야쳐형케ᄒᆞ라ᄒᆞ엿더라

○위문ᄉᆞ쟝발　군부에셔외부
로조회ᄒᆞ되의졍부조회니긔에
ᄒᆞ기를북진ᄒᆞᆫ일본군이다월로
교ᄒᆞ니리방우의에불가불위문
ᄒᆞᆯ재라동군부쟝권중현으로위
문ᄉᆞ를삼어셔일이멍위관을거
ᄂᆞ리고히젼디에젼왕ᄒᆞ야관젼
ᄎᆞ지ᄒᆞ고오게ᄒᆞᆫ다ᄒᆞ엿ᄉᆞ니이
ᄉᆞ의를일공관에조회ᄒᆞ라ᄒᆞ엿
더라

○젼승시취　작일에외부에셔
젼승식을시취ᄒᆞ엿는데이명이
입참ᄒᆞ엿더라

○일관젼입　일공관에셔외부
로조회ᄒᆞ기를ᄉᆞ령관원구경계
는대본영으로비입ᄒᆞ고그티에
는죵군대장쟝곡쳔호도가입ᄒᆞ
고참모쟝젼등혁상랑은공ᄉᆞ관
부무관으로젼입ᄒᆞᆫ티에탁곡공
상랑이셔임되엿다ᄒᆞ엿더라

○동궁미령　동궁뎐하인후환
후ᄂᆞᆫ졈졈쾌복ᄒᆞᄋᆞᆸ셔고근일은
리졍오로대단미령ᄒᆞ시다더라

○동양일회　근일에동학당이
졍형으로초초히일셩ᄒᆞᆫ자가불
가승슈인티고목적이일진회와
동일의견이라히회에서쇼원자
를리입ᄒᆞ미단발일회자가남마
다무슈ᄒᆞᆫ티그ᄌᆞ셰ᄒᆞᆫ리히ᄂᆞᆫ살
슈업다더라

○어음폐단　향일에시졍빈등
이져슈용권으로긔만량어음을
티답ᄒᆞ야돈츄심ᄒᆞ기가심히곤
란ᄒᆞ야신지어병졍을쳥ᄒᆞ야돈
을츄심ᄒᆞ는폐단이잇는고로신
티휴씨경무ᄉᆞ로잇슬때에그폐
단을엄금ᄒᆞ여어음티답ᄒᆞ는자
가돈을봉치ᄒᆞᆫ후에야어음티답
을ᄒᆞ라ᄒᆞ엿더니근일에는형이
음폐단이우심ᄒᆞ야젼졍순환ᄒᆞ
기가티단이곤란ᄒᆞᆫ다더라

○동학방문　츙쳥북도관찰ᄉᆞ
리승우씨가동학당수명을착슈
ᄒᆞ고그계방ᄒᆞᆫ글을등보ᄒᆞ엿는
티그방문에왈금번일은아젼쳥이
동양티세의큰관계라위젼슈츠
젼투에일본이번번티쳥ᄒᆞ엿거
니와죵국ᄉᆞ지일본이승젼ᄒᆞ며
야황인종이부지ᄒᆞᆯ수세오니이
번에동양인민된자야누구던지
조조ᄒᆞᆫ마음으로분발치아니ᄒᆞ
리오그런ᄒᆞᆫ중에대한졍편인즉
숙승숙괴간에젼졍계ᄅᆞᆯ국후에는
뭇보젼키어려운형세는명약관
화ᄒᆞᆫ지라엇지통곡ᄒᆞᆯ일이아니
리오대저국토란거슨인민의게
셩ᄒᆞᄂᆞᆫ도티와동명인고로국중
인민이아모던지말ᄒᆞ라ᄒᆞ면우
리나라리일깃니그러ᄒᆞᆫ즉나
라란거슨곳국민의나라가아니
빗가가평일벗지거칭ᄒᆞ는동리
면그일벗정사름이쟈기우리등
리라말ᄒᆞᄂᆞ니동리는너동리를
알고나라는버니라인즉보로오
릿가이ᄯᅢ에우리대한국이친만
동포가이러ᄒᆞᆫ리치를세닷지못
ᄒᆞ면고거티들일홀리니거디를
일ᄒᆞ면어ᄂᆞ곳에뎐졉ᄒᆞ리가형
금　죵사를보젼ᄒᆞ고　황실을
안녕케ᄒᆞᆯ방척이엇ᄉᆞ오니우리
대한국삼쳔리강산중이쳔만동
포ᄂᆞᆫ무론대소인민ᄒᆞ고일심으
로단회ᄒᆞ야비록열이죽고ᄒᆞ나
히살면리로국가를보답ᄒᆞᆯ마음
으로태의를분발ᄒᆞ야쾌면이동
심ᄒᆞ야졍치를긔칙ᄒᆞ고문명에
진보ᄒᆞ야치국의졍칙과외교의
방칙을확졍ᄒᆞ야국가의독립권
을공고케ᄒᆞ며아나라들보젼ᄒᆞ
겟ᄉᆞ온즉무론슈모ᄒᆞ고이번의
의를아니ᄒᆞ면국가를잇지코말군
을이져바리는사름이라엇지인
류라ᄒᆞ리오국졍의졍을면키어
려우리라금일이게조가보국안
민ᄒᆞᄂᆞᆫ대의리니우리동포ᄂᆞᆫ일
계히향응ᄒᆞ야천만번귀영을챵
립ᄒᆞᆯ지어다

지금오래주가등화교셤ᄒᆞᄂᆞᆫ세
를당ᄒᆞ야유도불도셔교가다동
포의ᄒᆞᄂᆞᆫ바인즉셔로방히치말
되셰교는관계가진중ᄒᆞ야각국
이다존중이알아종교들삼으니
각교당은극히보호ᄒᆞ라ᄒᆞ엿더
라

포살상인　경의텰도에방히
ᄒᆞ든자김셩삼리춘근안순셔삼
명을본일상오십시에일본쟝관
들이공덕리에나가셔포살ᄒᆞ엿
더라

관보

관보뎨이쳔구빅삼십오호
광무팔년구월십구일
셔임급ᄉᆞ령
○궁니부주ᄉᆞ 니부티방국 쟝
리규환
구월십ᄉᆞ일
○임탁지부재무관셔주임관륙
등 룡풍 민건식
○임탁지부참셔관셔주임관륙
등 룡풍 신상갑
○명우힝병에방위원 니부위
셩국쟝 홍철보 경위원총무
국쟝 림하영경무쳥경무관
로흥빈 리덕응 황영츈 최
영조 리웅승 궁니부참셔관
김용제 의학교교관 김익남
쇼죵무츄랑
이상구월십오일
임통쳔감리셔주ᄉᆞ셔판임관
륙등 경인호
○면본관 진위면보ᄉᆞ주ᄉᆞ
리근영
○임지위면보ᄉᆞ주ᄉᆞ셔판임관
륙등 젼쥬ᄉᆞ 민병준
이상구월십륙일
○젼칙 군부경리국에일관원
손의명 군부주ᄉᆞ 박초양
구월십륙일
궁내부ᄉᆞ
○의졍부참졍신긔션과니부
대신조병필군 주경무ᄉᆞ원
우상륜힝병에방위원쟝차하ᄒᆞ
야ᄒᆞ야평동찰
구월십오일

뎐보

구월십팔일 동경대본영
발 일본공ᄉᆞ관착
○로양젼리를 대산총령ᄉᆞ관
보고가여좌ᄒᆞ니
로양에셔젼리품이대단히만하
지금셔지도ᄉᆞ중이어니와구월
십칠일셔지도ᄉᆞᄒᆞᆫ바각군의젼
리품이여좌ᄒᆞ니

라이흔총 삼쳔오빅칠십팔졍
이오
탄환총탄환이 일빅로십삼만
팔쳔쳘빅십십발이오
과렬탄이 일만오십륙발이오
화약슈레가 이빅이십칠량이
오
가리가 일만오쳔구빅팔십오
기요
상이 오쳔륙빅십구기요
등과가 이쳔오빅칠십기요
회광등신과가 삼기요
휴티면화과가 륙기요
반사경이 삼기요
우육통이 일만팔쳔구빅십오통
이오
져류 지경으로이계오츈되는
것 이쳔오빅쥬오
쌀이 이쳔셕이요
맥이 일쳔셕이요
마량 삼쳔륙빅셕이요
외투가 륙쳔ᄉᆞ빅벌이요
포로ᄒᆞᆫ하ᄉᆞ와병졸이 십
삼명이라ᄒᆞ엿더라
동일동뎐
○아인잔학 졍슈도에잇는일
본사ᄅᆞᆷ들은아인의폭힝을넘어
모도피살ᄒᆞ엿고군ᄉᆞ때위는감
삿가에셔포도가된셤을영국에
주차ᄒᆞᆫ일본공ᄉᆞ가히관찰쳐에
공뎐ᄒᆞ엿더라

광고

대일은ᄒᆡᆼ(뎨일국립은ᄒᆡᆼ)
본뎜은일본동경에잇고
즈본금총일쳔빅이십오만원
리셔은미빅원에삼젼오리에셔
륙젼오리ᄉᆞ지인데
명긔ᄒᆞᆫ티로계산홈
경셩대일은ᄒᆡᆼ지졈쟝 변중

그랜드려관[명거쟝려관]
려관은황셩셔쇼문밧뎡거쟝근
디에잇ᄉᆞ오며일등려관이올
려관주인엠벌니 고빅

본호에셔각국병힝샹젼과거류
민의게잡죵셔양식료품을용
급ᄒᆞ오며
이래ᄒᆞᆫ려관은황셩에뎨일조ᄒᆞᆫ
려관이올
화셩이호 고빅
황셩과인쳔량쳐에잇숩

본ᄒᆡᆼ에셔보통샹품을밧티ᄒᆞ오
며화폐를슈입도ᄒᆞ며슈츌도
ᄒᆞ올 법샹대창양ᄒᆡᆼ
황셩과인쳔에잇숩

미국우젼회사와
동경동양긔션회사
미국히젼과련합ᄒᆞ엿숩
인쳔헐동가양ᄒᆡᆼ티리졈

TELEGRAM

Tokyo, Sept. 20th.

Marquis Oyama continuing his report of supplies captured at Liaoyang says that the following items can now be added to the list.

Bags of Barley	3,000
" " Maize	3,000
" " Rice	1,000
" " Millet	5,000
Cases of Kerosene	1,300
Bundles of Fuel	100,000
Tons of Coal	100
Cases of Sugar	1,800

Three hundred fifty-three houses near the railway station were discovered intact as also were 214 godowns.

What amount of coal was found at Yentai is as yet unknown.

THE BATTLE OF LIAOYANG.

(CONTINUED.)

One of the most sanguinary incidents of the whole battle occurred when the Japanese re-attacked these hills that same night. As Kuroki's centre column approached the trenches they stumbled over wires placed near the ground and highly charged with electricity. The effect was terrifying and deadly, and the Russians defending the trenches increased the confusion by hurling grenades or bombs amongst their assailants. The Japanese lost many in killed or wounded and, failing to take this important position, were compelled to retire. One battalion, which having fought its way into the Russian trenches and exahausted its ammunition, attempted to make its way out at the point of the bayonet, was practically annihilated. On Sunday, Sept 3rd, the Russians evacuated this position leaving the Japanese to occupy it with but slight opposition.

It was around Haiyentai that the battle raged fiercest. Haiyentai, commanding the railway, was the key to the whole position, and unless the Russians could retake it, there was nothing for them but retreat. Accordingly on Friday Sept. 1st, the Russians made a determined attack on the trenches. Until dusk a continuous fire of shrapnel and shell rained on the defenders and during the day two or three infantry assaults were made on the position. These were, however, repulsed. As night began to fall, the Russians attacked in great force, and during the two hours' infantry fighting which ensued, the combatants were so close to each order that neither side dared to use its artillery. The fighting was of the bloodiest description, but the Japanese finally succeeded in forcing the Russians to retreat.

In the meantime a fierce infantry battle had been waged on the Five-headed hills, the Russians unsuccessfully attempting to retake this position.

The spectacle on Friday night is said to have been a remarkable one. The hills were ablaze with flashes from the guns and bursting shells and in the sheltered valleys there twinkled the camp fires of the reserves, while here and there blazed great beacons where the dead were being cremated.

Saturday, the fifth day of the battle, was an anxious day for General Kuroki. The Russians were shelling the Japanese positions as vigorously as ever and it was evident that they had received substantial reinforcement. The Japanese were unable to decide upon the reason for this. It might indicate that the Russians had been victorious in other directions and were able to spare these troops to overwhelm Kuroki, or it might mean the very reverse and that Kuropatkin, finding himself beaten all along the line, had increased his army at this point in order to hold Kuroki in check while his main body of troops made good its retreat.

All Saturday afternoon and Sunday morning the officers on Kuroki's staff were obviously anxious and worried. They continually looked through a telescope towards the northwest, evidently expecting some movement from hatt direction.

On Sunday afternoon things assumed a brighter aspect. It became known that reinforcements had reached Kuroki's right and by ordering his left wing to close in towards his center Kuroki greatly consolidated his army and made his position secure from Sukwatung to the Five-headed hills. This augured favourably, as it was evident that if a Russian advance had been feared, Kuroki would never have left a big gap between his command and the main army.

At five o'clock on Sunday evening the suspense was entirely ended. Couriers galloped up and General Fuju soon announced that the army would immediately start in pursuit of the enemy.

(To be continued).

MILITARY REQUESTS.

The Magistrate of Wiju telegraphs the following list of requests of the Japanese military authorities:

1. Barracks now in use of the local guard, to be given to Japanese troops.
2. The Magistrate's office to be used as a field telegraph office.
3. Bridges and roads to be repaired properly.
4. Large quantities of provisions to be immediately collected.
5. They will collect coolies themselves, but 350 men daily are required for building operations at Kuliencheng; coolies needed at Kuriongpo.
6. Roads in the districts of Yongchon and Sak Chu to be repaired.

EXECUTION OF KOREANS NEAR SEOUL.

At 10:00 A. M. today, three Koreans, Kim Sung Sam, Yi Chun Kun and An Su So, having been tried and found guilty of destroying military railway works, were shot.

The exection took place at Kong Duk Ni about 2 miles outside the West Gate.

The main road between Seoul and Gensan is now undergoing repairs.

The Home Department has requested the War Office to despatch a body of soldiers to Sunchon, to disperse the Tonghaks now assembling there.

As a suitable house for Mr. Megata cannot be found there seems some likelihood that he will take up his quarters temporarily at the residence of Miss Sontag.

The Bishop of London states that a subscription of £5 has been sent to his fund by an undertaker, who described the donation as a thank-offering "because trade has been so brisk of late."

A Norwegian whaler has found north of Spitzbergen a bottle containing a letter from André, the unfortunate explorer, who attempted to reach the North Pole by means of a balloon. The letter is dated 1898.

During the great heat in Paris a man attired in a crimson window-curtain and top-boots, crowned with a lamp-shade, and brandishing a whip told two policemen in Batignolles that he was the Emperor of the World, and that they must kneel down in order that he might flog them. He was secured.

A company entitled the Korean Promoting-Industrial Co. has been floated in Tokyo, with a capital of one million Yen. Baron Shibuzawa, the well known Tokyo banker and capitalist, will be the managing director of the concern, which, from its title, appears to have as an object the promotion of various industries in Korea. Two expert engineers have resigned positions in Japan to take up the billet of advising engineers to the company.

The marriage of Alfred, son of Lieutenant-Colonel John S. Day, R.E., to Winifred Ella Week, has inspired a Ceylon poet with the following:—

"One Week the less—
One Day the more—
But Time need not complain:
There'll soon be little Days enough,
To make a Week again."

The police have received instructions to visit all hotels and turn out any suspicious looking countrymen, who are not engaged in open business. It appears that a great number of men recently came up to Seoul and after shaving their heads, announced themselves as members of the Il Chin Hoi society. They are however regarded with great suspicion and the police department seems to think that they of the Tonghak persuasion.

A sensational trial lately came to an end at Berlin when First Lieut. Withe, who figured as "the villain of the piece" in Lieut. Bilse's novel, "Aus Einer Kleine Garnison," was sentenced to one year and three days' penal servitude, with dismissal from the army, and loss of civil rights for two years, for maltreating soldiers in 17 cases and for perjury. Lieut. Bilse himself, smartly dressed in a frock coat and wearing an eye-glass, gave evidence.

The steamers which are now being built or arranged to be constructed at the Mitsu Bishi Dockyard and Engine Works, Nagasaki, are eight in number. They comprise the "Tango-maru" for the Nippon Yusen Kaisha's Seattle service, the Mitsui Bussan Kaisha's collier "Chohakusan-maru," the two ferry boats to be used in the steamship intermediary service of the Sanyo Railway between Fusan and Shimonoseki, and four other vessels for the Osaka Shosen Kaisha's Osaka-Chemulpo and South China services. The "Tango-maru," about 6,000 tons gross, is expected to be launched from the Tategami yard in November next.

Dr. Ellinger, a medical man at Tegal, in Java, asserts confidently that he has found malaria parasites, and can breed them. He thinks the discovery so important that it will overthrow the mosquito theory of malaria advanced by Koch, Ross, and others. Dr. Ellinger found that these parasites lodge in the upper inner end of the throat to which they make their way through the breathing of the patient. In other words malaria is communicated by breathing the parasites in, and not through the bites of mosquitoes. Dr. Ellinger has cultivated these parasites and has brought malaria fever on by inoculating them in the body of patients. He asks medical men to test his discoveries.

The South African mail recently brought a thrilling tale of a fight to the death between a man and a giant baboon. Mr. Robert Heugh saw a baboon in his orchard, and shot him through the body at 300 yards. The animal got some distance away and dropped. Thinking he was dead Mr. Heugh went after him with two terriers and a native. The baboon caught the terriers, bit a large piece out of each, cast them from him with such violence as to kill them, and then made for their master, tearing his arm open from shoulder to wrist. Mr. Heugh was forced to the ground. Here, while despearately struggling, the man's hand came in contact with a large stone. This he seized, and fractured the baboon's skull.

The Korea Daily News.

Issued at 5 P. M. daily except Sundays.

Rate of Subscription:—

Per Year,	Yen 25.
Per Quarter,	Yen 7.
Per Month	Yen 2.50

Postage in Korea not charged extra.
Postage abroad charged extra.

Advertisements, 50 sen per day for 1 inch or less. 5 yen per month per inch. 50 yen per year per inch.

All communications to E. T. BETHELL, Editor and Publisher. Pak-tong, Seoul.

SHILLY SHALLY.

Thanks in great measure to her own mis-government, but also largely on account of outside influences, Korea is now in a state of political unrest.

At the best of times her disinterested statesmen are but few and hard to find, and now, when the past ten years have found her under the influence successively of China, Japan, Russia, and now Japan again, it is not surprising to find that, as regards her government, Korea is in a very bad way indeed.

A job in the Government is the Mecca of every Korean, and as there are far more candidates than there are positions, there are always many disappointed, unemployed ones. Those out of office, by open impeachment or by secret machinations, are always striving to oust the more fortunate ones, so that room may be found for themselves. Under these circumstances, finding all his ministers jealous of each other and continually dropping poison in his ear, it is only natural that His Majesty the Emperor has but little confidence in any of them, and that the government of Korea is ill-conducted and without continuity.

For instance we are told that the son of General Hyŏn will shortly return from Japan to Korea, and will take up an important position in the Government of the country. We are not told that he has done anything to deserve this, or that he is a young man of talent or probity. We are simply told that he has "influence." Such instances of flagrant jobbery are the rule rather than the exception, and it is of course useless for the Emperor to expect to surround himself with capable and disinterested counsellors while such a state of affairs exists.

Lookers-on see most of the game, and the Japanese would probably be able, in five minutes, to separate the goats from the sheep among the higher officials of this country. She undoubtedly possesses great influence in Korea and it could not be better employed than in this direction. And she should do it if her promise to promote the welfare of Korea and seek none but legitimate advantages for herself is to be vindicated.

Unfortunately, we see but little prospect of this. Korean politicians are divided into three camps. The pro-Japanese, the pro-Russians and the pan-Koreans. Placing them according to their sincerity we should reverse the order. Had Japan's policy in Korea really been as disinterested as it was proclaimed to be, we should have found the pan-Korea party flocking to her assistance. On the contrary we find it openly stated that among her adherents and supporters are to be found some of the most notorious and inveterate wire pullers in the country, while among her bitterest opponents there are, to our knowledge, men of undoubted capacity, probity and singleness of purpose.

While this state of affairs continues, whatever Japan proposes will be looked upon with suspicion, and it will be impossible for her to achieve anything for the good of Korea, neither is it possible for the Korean officials themselves to accomplish much with their ranks split up as they are at present.

It seems fairly certain that the Japanese have not finished with their demands on Korea, and we therefore suggest, for the sake of the tranquility of the country, that she makes them public once and for all, and awaits the verdict of Korea and the world.

Everyone realizes that Japan has the whip-hand of this country, none better than the Koreans themselves, so that moderate and fair demands would be gladly assented to, and the prevailing state of unrest would be put to an end.

THE ORIGIN OF BERI-BERI.

COLLEGE OF PHYSICIANS' REPORT.

The committee of the Royal College of Physicians, appointed to study the report of the Norwegian Commission on beri-beri, state that it throws no light on the cause of the disease. The committee does not agree that beri-beri is more frequent among Norwegian sailors than among others, and says: "Beri-beri is far from rare in British ships, especially in those carrying Lascar, Chinese and Japanese crews; the wards of the hospitals of the Seamen's Hospital Society in London are rarely without several cases of the disease, coming for the most part from British vessels. We are inclined to think that wrong diagnosis is responsible in great measure for the apparent rarity of the disease in the British Mercantile Marine. It constantly happens that seamen and stokers suffering from beri-beri are sent into London hospitals with such diagnoses as dropsy, malaria, paralysis, locomotor ataxia, heart disease, and peripheral neuritis. It is not every ship's captain, or even ship's surgeon, who can recognise beri-beri."

The Norwegian Commission recommended a restriction in the use of tinned food, and the use of fat meat and plenty of fruit and vegetables in hot climates was recommended.

CHINESE CURRENCY REFORMS.

A Peking despatch of August 31, to the Tokio Asahi, states that Professor Jenks is convinced that no reform of the monetary system of China can be effected under the present condition of affairs, and that on the eve of his departure for home, the Professor obtained from the Chinese Government a written agreement by which he is appointed an adviser of the highest rank when China undertakes the reform of her monetary system. It is further stated that the Professor has proposed to the Chinese authorities the establishment of a Central Bank with a capital of 40,000,000 taels, to be obtained from the United States by means of a loan, and has offered to conduct the negotiations with American financiers for the purpose.

A complaint reaches the Law Department of robbery and murder recently committed by Japanese in the village of Oisungdong. Three coolies, workers on the railroad, entered the compound of a man Yi Duk-kun and attempted to steal his chickens. Yi was absent but his father and young brother remonstrated with the Japanese, one of whom becoming infuriated struck the old man a heavy blow on the head, killing him immediately and then inflicted severe injuries on the youngster. The Japanese Legation have been notified of the matter and doubtless will bring the murderer to justice.

A CONCESSION.

Mr. Ouchi, a citizen of Fukuoka, Japan, has obtained special permission from the Imperial Household Department to commence farming operations at Djapangpo, near Mokpo. He intends to bring some 200 farmers and engineers from Japan to assist him.

The Japanese forces from Gensan have arrived at Hamheung, which they found deserted by the Russians.

Mr. Shogawa, the official interpreter of the Japanese Legation, is now employed by the Council of State.

We hear that the Emperor has commanded that His Highness Prince Yi Chai Wan shall be the president of the Korea Japan Club.

It is said that Mr. Sin Ki Son, Vice-president of the Council of State, who has been very urgent recently in suggestions for reform, now desires to promote General Hyon Yong Woon to Minister of War.

From Anju we hear that another Korean spy has been shot. Hong Sung Nak was arrested on suspicion of having cut the telegraph line and his case having been tried and his guilt proved he was executed on the 16th inst.

A farewell banquet was given at the Premier's official residence in Tokyo on the evening of the 6th in honour of Mr. Megata, who shortly leaves for Korea to take up the position of Financial Adviser to the Korean Government.

Since the arrival of Japanese troops at Si Hung, we are informed that although order has been established the people are likely to suffer from lack of food as the troops require all available provisions and fodder for their horses.

The War Department has notified the Foreign Office that they intend to despatch Lieutenant General Kwon Chung-hyon and some junior officers to Manchuria with a message of sympathy to the Japanese army.

Baron Oura, the Japanese Minister of Communications, is expected to arrive in Seoul about the 30th inst. He will travel through the whole of Korea and Manchuria with the purpose of inspecting postal, telegraphic and railroad communications.

The daily rations of a Russian soldier in the field are 2½lb of bread or 1¾lbs of biscuit, 1lb of meat, and (for making soup) 4oz barley groats, ¾oz of dried vegetables, and 3oz of flour. Then salt, pepper, tea and sugar, are given out in the usual quantity.

The Tea Buyers Association has accepted gratefully the facilities granted by Mr. Austen Chamberlain for licensing private bonded warehouses, without charges for customs' supervision, for blending and packing teas in bond, and freeing existing private warehouses from customs' charges.

Mr. Y. Ito, Master of Ceremonies, and Lieut. Colonel M. Nagayama of Cavalry have been commissioned to receive Prince Karl Auton of Hohenzollern, who is expected to arrive at Yokohama on the 25th inst. The German prince is 37 years old. He will be attached to the Japanese forces in the capacity of a Colonel of Cavalry. His suite consists of three persons.

The United States is credited with more than a third of the world's output of iron in 1903. The total production, accrding to an English authority, was 45,972,566 tons, of which this country produced 18,009,000 tons. And yet there are free traders who insist that the effect of protection is to promote dearness. They might as well assert that the effect of increasing production is to raise prices.

The Korea Daily News.

VOL. I, WEDNESDAY, SEPTEMBER 21, 1904. No. 57

大韓每日申報
대한ᄆᆡ일신보

(뎨오십팔호) (목요일) 쳔구ᄇᆡᆨ사년구월이십이일

본사고ᄇᆡᆨ

본신보는영어와한어로셔계티
일출판ᄒᆞᆷ
신문가
한쟝 엽젼두돈오푼
일삭도 엽젼팔량닷돈
우표가뎌 사닷돈
다엿돈으로밧ᄉᆞᆷ
광고료는
귀한의쟝단과ᄌᆞᄒᆡᆼ의다쇼로총
갑ᄒᆞ되렴가로밧을터이오며오
리지아녀대한사람마다다이신
문을보실터이니광고내시기를
원ᄒᆞ시는이들은우리신문사에
와서면약ᄒᆞ심을희망ᄒᆞᆷ
○발ᄒᆡᆼ소 박동대한ᄆᆡ일신보
사발ᄒᆡᆼ겸편즙인 영국인셜펠
편쟝자리오
사쟝 영국인 (비셜)
평양 뎌리졈
○평양효동사는권미보씨로우
리신문판매뎌리인을뎡ᄒᆞ엿
ᄉᆞ오니평양에계신구람코져ᄒᆞ
시는 쳠군ᄌᆞ는뎌리졈에왕
림ᄒᆞ와면의ᄒᆞ시ᄋᆞᆸ

사고

○우리대한ᄆᆡ일신보의목뎍은
대한의안녕질셔에관한모든대
목에뎌ᄒᆞ야는공평한변론을쥬
쟝ᄒᆞᆷ이라우리는신원의담보는
신문보시는쳠군ᄌᆞ의게ᄒᆞᆼ상보
도ᄒᆞ리며편지들긔서ᄒᆞ여주시
는이는셩명과번디를젹어붓치
시기를희망ᄒᆞ오니비거슨신문
샹에긔지ᄒᆞ라는거시아니오다
만극히신용ᄒᆞ는증거를숨고자
ᄒᆞᆷ이라긔자는아모긔서던지긔
지ᄒᆞᆷ을긔각ᄒᆞ는권리들가젓스
나긔각ᄒᆞ는리유는말ᄒᆞᆯ터이오
며공즁평화들분란케ᄒᆞ는듯ᄒᆞᆫ
다긔서는의례히밧지안켓ᄉᆞᆸ나이

●본사셜시이ᄅᆡ로신문을ᄆᆡ양
우례로분젼ᄒᆞ와례젼부의일의
로젼ᄒᆞᆫ긋스로번곳에는혹누게
에젼ᄒᆞ기도ᄒᆞ며혹벗칠거슬ᄒᆞᆫ법
곳도잇다ᄒᆞ와우리신문을수ᄉᆞᆸ
ᄒᆞ야구람ᄒᆞ시는 쳠군ᄌᆞ의게금
티ᄒᆞ야ᄆᆡ우미안ᄒᆞ옵기로지금
은분젼인을두고ᄆᆡ일요즉이젼
ᄒᆞ며아니젼ᄒᆞ거나늣게ᄒᆞ거나ᄒᆞᆫ
폐가엽도록ᄒᆞ란ᄒᆞ오니혹아니
젼ᄒᆞ거나혹늣게젼ᄒᆞ거나ᄒᆞᆫ일
이잇스면본사로통긔ᄒᆞ여주심
을희망ᄒᆞᆷ

본사광고

본사에서본신문뎨수호와뎨삼
일호와뎨이십오호들소용ᄒᆞᆯ베
가잇서이에광고ᄒᆞ오니누구시
던지이샹삼호중에본사로가다
오시면ᄆᆡ쟝에ᄇᆡᆨ젼두푼식드리
다

론셜

공연ᄒᆞᆫ베만허비ᄒᆞ고ᄆᆡ사
들그르게ᄒᆞᆷ이라

○한국에서미명ᄒᆞᆫ졍부들기량
ᄒᆞ라고주의ᄒᆞᆷ은실로감격ᄒᆞᆫ일
이나외국에권력이너모터디ᄒᆞᆫ
에서당에지금형편은도리어졍권
이동안조ᄒᆞᆫ긔회가여러번잇서
스나졍부대관들은다만비귀ᄒᆞᆫ
욕심만두고셜로이ᄒᆞ라ᄂᆞᆫ지ᄅᆞᆯ
과명치못되고쇼ᄒᆞ심버리로
불경것드면졍국과일본과밋아
라사세나라에협졔ᄒᆞ는바헤
서승밧어리니비졔일본서디시
상관ᄒᆞ야한국졍부들위ᄒᆞ고ᄉᆡᆼ
각ᄒᆞᆷ과갓치ᄒᆞ되날이갈수록과
연분호ᄒᆞᆫ일이만ᄉᆡᆼ기도다
소위졍부에서일ᄒᆞᄂᆞᆫ바로볼진
뎌사ᄅᆞᆷ마다공변된일은버리고
사사리익만취ᄒᆞ야ᄒᆞᆼ상벼슬ᄌᆞ
리바탐ᄒᆞ려ᄒᆞ란ᄂᆞᆫ사ᄅᆞᆷ이만아
오히려디ᄒᆞ지못ᄒᆞ여시ᄅᆞᆷ이만된
자ㅣ ᄒᆞ라ᄒᆞᆫ지라이로ᄆᆡ암이마
커뭉ᄒᆞ야린ᄒᆡᆼ도ᄒᆞ며은근히ᄒᆞᆯ
게도써서무죄ᄒᆞᆫ사ᄅᆞᆷ을쟝ᄎᆡ나
고그과궐에뒤잉ᄒᆞᆷ쟝다ᄒᆡᆼ으
로ᄉᆡᆼ각ᄒᆞᄂᆞᆫ자도잇슨즉이런ᄒᆞᆫ
셔당에졍부대신ᄃᆞᆯ은서로식귀
ᄒᆞ야ᄌᆞ긔의게ᄒᆡᆼ치란ᄒᆞᄂᆞᆫ일만
귀들기우린즉이ᄂᆞᆫ누구던지
대황뎨폐하셔ᄉᆡ옹은될터이되
졍부모양은졈졈부ᄑᆡᄒᆞ여갈지
라요수히드른즉칭참졍의아들
이미구에일본으로셔도라와졍
부에요임을ᄒᆞ리라ᄒᆞᆫ즉우리의
ᄉᆡᆼ각에ᄂᆞᆫ그사ᄅᆞᆷ이비록지에가
동민ᄒᆞ고마음이졍직ᄒᆞ드리도
아즉년과가쳔소ᄒᆞ며권세가잇
조ᄒᆞᆫ즉민사에통히잘ᄒᆞᆯ다고경
못ᄒᆞᆯ거시다만빙공영사ᄒᆞᄂᆞᆫ일
외에ᄂᆞᆫ아모것도엽ᄂᆞᆫ쥴로규례
가되엿ᄂᆞᆫ지라
대황뎨폐하셔ᄂᆞᆫ좌우에두시
고진츙갈력ᄒᆞ야보필ᄒᆞ기ᄅᆞᆯ아
모리ᄉᆡᆼ각ᄒᆞ시나이런케비귀지
욕만잇ᄂᆞᆫ니갓대신들의소위사
무ᄒᆞᆫ다ᄂᆞᆫ거슨조곰도유익ᄒᆞ야
쓸티엄도다
이런고로보ᄂᆞᆫ사ᄅᆞᆷ마다ᄒᆞᆫ회ᄒᆞᆫ
ᄒᆞᆯ믈진으로ᄉᆡᆼ각ᄒᆞᄂᆞᆫ중일본사
ᄅᆞᆷ들은더욱ᄉᆡᆼ각ᄒᆞ야오분동안이
면한국대관의게뎌ᄒᆞ야양으로
써엽소ᄅᆞᆯ발드ᄂᆞᆫ일이잇ᄂᆞᆫ거시
의심엽시ᄌᆞ긔의권력디로ᄒᆡᆼ
ᄒᆞ야다른일ᄒᆞᄂᆞᆫ니버ᄅᆞᆷ고문관
고빙ᄒᆞᄂᆞᆫ일이더욱조ᄒᆞᆫ고로가
쟝한국을뒤평ᄒᆞ게ᄒᆞ야진보되
도록ᄒᆞᆫ다칭ᄒᆞ고아모일도ᄒᆞᄂᆞᆫ
것엽시다만ᄌᆞ긔의유익ᄒᆞᆷ만말
ᄒᆞᄂᆞᆫ중
한국의졍치가들은소위당파가
ᄉᆡᆼ기되여왈일당이니왈아당이
니왈ᄌᆞ유당이니ᄒᆞ야각각ᄌᆞ긔
식ᄆᆡᆨ을티로ᄒᆞᄂᆞᆫ티가평일본서
다만비ᄒᆞᆯ긔ᄒᆞᆯ욕으로황무지개간
소권갓ᄐᆞᆫ일도말ᄒᆞᆯ것깃드면소
위ᄌᆞ유당이라ᄒᆞᄂᆞᆫ사ᄅᆞᆷ이일셩
으로모혀아모쪼록나라들유지
ᄒᆞᆯᄉᆡᆼ각으로반티ᄒᆞ야츙셩을다
ᄒᆞᆯ진티
일본셔무어시던지쳥구ᄒᆞ려ᄒᆞ
ᄂᆞᆫ바로응당ᄌᆞ츼ᄒᆞ야법사ᄅᆞᆷ셩도
취치못ᄒᆞᆯ터이고한국관리들도
벼슬을영구히누릴터이니이금
소권으로일본셔요구ᄒᆞ란홈이
아즉도밋지아니ᄒᆞ엿슨즉아모
쪼록국가안평ᄒᆞ기를위ᄒᆞ야합
속히일신ᄒᆞ게졍치를잡ᄒᆞᆯ지경
이면필경세상공론이잇슬티이
며일본셔이렵케급히ᄒᆞ모라ᄒᆞᄂᆞᆫ
일이한국인민의스ᄉᆞ로셰다라
ᄒᆞᄂᆞᆫ니버ᄃᆞᆷ조치아니ᄒᆞᆯ티이며
져희의요구ᄒᆞᄂᆞᆫ티로ᄒᆞ샹랴증
ᄒᆞ야시ᄒᆡᆼᄒᆞᄂᆞᆫ경우에ᄂᆞᆫ필경리
엿비라ᄒᆞᄂᆞᆫ거슨여조이엽시되
고아발린일고로우리ᄂᆞᆫ한국을
위ᄒᆞ야두어말로권고ᄒᆞ노라

잡보

○여방불예 각셔경무관이류
ᄒᆡᆼ병예방위원을겸임ᄒᆞᆫ고로회
위원등이날마다경무본청에회
동ᄒᆞᄂᆞᆫ티위원쟝원우상씨ᄂᆞᆫ고로회에
인이라셜망ᄒᆞ우실ᄒᆞᄂᆞᆫ고로회에
방과쟝을샹금의덕치못ᄒᆞ엿다
더라

○로병쳐도 경무청에서의졍
부로보고ᄒᆞ기를함경북도번계
경무관최남응의보고들거ᄒᆞᆫ즉
아국쟝관미슬빙ᄒᆞ고슈로로좃
차경셩에출쥬ᄒᆞ고홍일이ᄇᆡᆨ명
휴샴수ᄇᆡᆨ명식경ᄒᆞ진너편으로
붓터련속ᄒᆞ야출리ᄒᆞ야남북각
군에티왕ᄒᆞᄂᆞᆫ동졍은입의보고
ᄒᆞ엿거니와금월이십오일아국
관원이긔병오십명을평솔ᄒᆞ고
경흥군에출리ᄒᆞ야ᄎᆡ도ᄒᆞᆫ다ᄒᆞ
고일본도로ᄂᆞᆫ련히벤으로못게경
셩셔지등ᄒᆞ엿고셕일도로ᄂᆞᆫ경
원온셩종셩을맛티일아칭영을
도라당일에회령에리도ᄒᆞ야ᄇᆡᆨ
일병부수오ᄇᆡᆨ명식주야로치도
ᄒᆞ고회령셔서으로무산을게닉
여갑산등디처지일도로를통ᄒᆞ
란고또남으로부령을지너경
셩디경셔지일도로를통ᄒᆞᄂᆞᆫ중
이라고ᄒᆞ엿다고ᄒᆞ엿더라

○외졍판회동 작일하오샴시
에군부의졍소에각의관계셔가
회동ᄒᆞ야공의ᄒᆞ엿다더라

○비대출수 신임ᄒᆞᆫ비부대신
리용티씨가작일봉티본부에스
졉ᄒᆞᆫ다더라

○졍시차기 일본고문관목하
뎐씨의거처ᄒᆞᆯ가퇴을근일에뎡
ᄒᆞ기로경영ᄒᆞᆫ다더니졍방ᄒᆞᆫ쳐
소가엽ᄂᆞᆫ고로위쳠순뎍의졍에
졍류ᄒᆞ기로ᄒᆞ엿다ᄒᆞ더라

○아병퇴귀 원산방면에주둔
ᄒᆞ엿든일본군이함흥으로젼진
ᄒᆞᆷ죽아병의영향이엽ᄂᆞᆫ고로ᄇᆡᆨ
셩은안도ᄒᆞ고이ᄅᆞᆫ벙은류쥬ᄒᆞ엿
다더라

○북도수츅 함셩과원산ᄉᆞ이
에도로들란금수츅ᄒᆞᆫ더라

엽젼시무 일본엽젼동역판
을졍부에서고빙ᄒᆞᆫ고로일젼브
터동셔가일용판동역판의ᄌᆞ격
으로회졍부에와서시무ᄒᆞᆫ다더
라

○구파부츙졔 태동구파부총
졔ᄂᆞᆫ완순군리졔완씨로츄쳔ᄒᆞ
엿ᄂᆞᆫ티 대니ᄎᆔ본쳐지게셧다
ᄒᆞ더라

○판괴압샹 졔작일에일본헌
병이시흥민요수에란괴수명을
경셩으로압샹ᄒᆞ야뢰슈ᄒᆞ엿더
라

○힝이빈로군 힝이빈에잇ᄂᆞᆫ로국군은그곳졍거쟝동방에셔서남으로쳥국리수로오십리를격ᄒᆞᆫ쌍셩부간에광이룩쳑이오갑기가일쳑되ᄂᆞᆫ히자를둘너파고빈리사계ᄒᆞ야쵸병을두고쏘ᄒᆞᆫ피파힝이빈간에쳘로를연ᄒᆞ야풍비오싱비쳐되ᄂᆞᆫ도로를슈츅ᄒᆞᆫ다더라

샹쳥관샨쥰비 료양에셔괴로군이봉텬부방으로퇴각ᄒᆞᆯ슈히ᄒᆞᄂᆞᆫ모양인즉로군이쳘령에셔일본군을방어ᄒᆞᆯ계획인즉곳졍거쟝에셔쳥국리수로리쎵되ᄂᆞᆫ샹쳥관산에다슈ᄒᆞᆫ티를츅셜ᄒᆞ고그압히ᄂᆞᆫ근히틀과방비ᄒᆞᆯ슈션을굳굳히ᄒᆞᆫ더라

마격승아 팔월오일에밤에격샹쳔명가량이만쥬쳘령에둔ᄒᆞᆫ아군을습격ᄒᆞ엿ᄂᆞᆫ티아ᄂᆞᆫ쟝이깁히를ᄒᆞ엿다가일군의격인줄알고분쥬히도망ᄒᆞᆫ지마적이그량식과군물등을탈ᄒᆞ엿고슈운ᄒᆞᆯ슈업ᄂᆞᆫ거ᄉᆞᆫ모분젼ᄂᆞ티워젓다고지라ᄐᆞᆫ일쓰ᄂᆞᆫ문에귀졔ᄒᆞ엿더라

○한약평졀 근리로군중에ᄂᆞᆫ로국부식ᄒᆞᆫ병ᄒᆞ을양츌로세우고츌젼ᄒᆞ며쏘근리ᄂᆞᆫ로국연괴셔일ᄂᆞᆫ쇄약을쓰며포탄은리슌에셔제조ᄒᆞᆷ으로며러가지죵류오쪽발령ᄒᆞ며약ᄒᆞ다ᄒᆞ니로군에한약이핑졀ᄒᆞᆷ을가지라ᄒᆞ더라

관보

뎨이쳔구빅삼십칠호
광무팔년구월이십일일

서임급ᄉᆞ령

○륙쳥병에방위원쟝 경무ᄉᆞ 원우샹
구월십오일

○임탁지부ᄉᆞ계국쟝서칙임관ᄉᆞ등 졍상룡 리항규
구월십칠일

○일쥬히일경군신 진위대룩련디대히대티뷰소티쟝룡군보병부위 리기우
팔월이십구일

○서대훈ᄉᆞ금쳑쟝 원평군 리승응

○셔대훈ᄉᆞ리화쟝 원슈부회계국총쟝 민영환 륙진관 윤용션 완순군 리재완
이샹구월십륙일

○임니부대신셔칙임관일등 즁츄원부의쟝 리용티

잡보

○방문일관 작일샹오십일시에일본공관쳥텹을인ᄒᆞ야외부대신리하영씨가일공관을방문ᄒᆞ엿더라

○리감신임 헤시원번역관리무영씨가동리감리로젼임ᄒᆞ엿더라

○조흉상가 일공ᄉᆞ가외부로조회ᄒᆞ되일본인비니쟝원으로슈샹갑ᄉᆞ쳔여원지발ᄒᆞ라ᄂᆞᆫᄉᆞᄂᆞᆫ샹금조쳐가업ᄂᆞᆫ고로또조회ᄒᆞ니곳지발ᄒᆞ라만일금월닉로지발치아니ᄒᆞ면남문외경부텰도뎡거장디단갑이만여원ᄃᆡ일은힝에임치ᄒᆞᆫ죵에셔졔ᄒᆞ겟다ᄒᆞ엿더라

○일인조익 젼남관찰ᄉᆞ서리광쥬군슈권즁은씨가외부에보고ᄒᆞ되릉쥬군슈홍봉표의보고에ᄒᆞ기를본군슈가일어를빈호라고일본인일명을쳥리ᄒᆞ기로목포거ᄒᆞᄂᆞᆫ강용쳥의게쳥탁ᄒᆞ엿더니음력륙월룩일에일인소쳔방조가강용쳥의편지를가지고리방ᄒᆞᆫ고로관가쳥방으로영졉ᄒᆞ야잘잇더니칠월이십ᄉᆞ일에우연득병ᄒᆞ야목포로가겟다ᄒᆞᄂᆞᆫ고로수일됴리ᄒᆞᆫ후에발졍ᄒᆞ라고만류ᄒᆞ엿더니이십룩일조됴에그방문이제졀노열녓거ᄂᆞᆯ가본즉일인이업ᄂᆞᆫ지라의싱ᄒᆞ야ᄉᆞ면에슈탐ᄒᆞᆫ즉뒤뫼안에셔ᄉᆞ수로목민여치수ᄒᆞᆫ지라곳목포감리셔에통긔ᄒᆞ야일명ᄉᆞ의게통지ᄒᆞᆫ즉일슌ᄉᆞ와감리셔순검이리도ᄒᆞ야검시ᄒᆞᆫ즉분명히ᄌᆞ익ᄒᆞᆫ거시라인ᄒᆞ야화장ᄒᆞ엿다ᄒᆞ엿시니히일인이비록ᄌᆞ익ᄒᆞᆫ거시나외국인과샹관됨일인고로보고ᄒᆞᆫ다ᄒᆞ엿더라

○조쳥병압 니부에셔진쥬군슈리용교씨의동학쟝형을말ᄒᆞᆫ면보를인ᄒᆞ야원슈부에조회ᄒᆞ되진쥬군슈리용교의면보를쟝ᄒᆞᆫ즉히디방에비도가다시챵궐ᄒᆞ야ᄌᆞ민홀념려가잇스니히위지부군진위티에훈칙ᄒᆞ야진압ᄒᆞ라ᄒᆞ엿더라

○외호문조 농샹공부에셔면당에기간ᄒᆞᆫ코츅보ᄒᆞᄂᆞᆫ등ᄉᆞ로이왕인히ᄒᆞᆫ각군에훈조ᄒᆞ기를디평안빈쌍과황무ᄒᆞᆫ쌍에괴간쟈답ᄒᆞ며츅보관리는ᄉᆞ로각디에너리사ᄅᆞᆷ이쳥원ᄒᆞ미양히디방군에ᄒᆞᆫ령ᄒᆞ야사보ᄒᆞᆫ후인허ᄒᆞᆷ이여리히란반다시긔간ᄒᆞᆫ쌍이고유지디틀이ᄅᆞᆫ이잇겟스ᄂᆞᆫ즉히마다승츙ᄒᆞ겟거ᄂᆞᆯ히군에셔보고가업고본부에셔사문치아니ᄒᆞ야막연히서로이쳐셔실샹이엽셧스니엇지이러ᄒᆞᆫ리치가잇스리오쳐쳐에므딘기간ᄒᆞ여부와괴간ᄒᆞᆫ면답괴일경리두락과괴간ᄒᆞᆫ년조와승츙여부를낫낫치구별ᄒᆞ야보고ᄒᆞ라ᄒᆞ엿더라

○리력셔슈정 의정부에셔각관쳥에통텹ᄒᆞ되각관쳥칙관이하칙임쥬임관의리력셔를쟝이추편집ᄒᆞ야존안ᄒᆞ야일후임면ᄒᆞᄂᆞᆫ티샹고케ᄒᆞᆯ터이니소관쳥에도일례지위ᄒᆞ야리구월초오일닉로송교ᄒᆞ고각디방소속관리의리력셔ᄂᆞᆫ구월삼십일일닉로도착ᄒᆞ여보니라ᄒᆞ엿더라

○예후평복 동궁면하게셔ᄂᆞᆫ근간에미령ᄒᆞ시든증세가일간으로쾌복되셧다더라

○일진일진 일진회ᄂᆞᆫ날마다열회ᄒᆞᄂᆞᆫ인원이증가ᄒᆞᄂᆞᆫ티도시향긔이며참회ᄒᆞ라고단발ᄒᆞᄂᆞᆫ자가만타ᄂᆞᆫ티리쳥등디리발소에셔미일단발ᄒᆞᄂᆞᆫ슈죠가평균ᄒᆞ여일일삼십명가량이된다더라

○동도동션 히쥬로셔상경ᄒᆞᆫ사ᄅᆞᆷ의젼언을드른즉며칠젼에연안군나진포에셔승션ᄒᆞᆫ셔에동션ᄒᆞᆫ사ᄅᆞᆷ즁ᄒᆞᆫ오십명이동힝인듯ᄒᆞ기로그슈다홈을의심ᄒᆞ야힝ᄉᆞᆨ을샹찰ᄒᆞᆫ즉만히젼일동학당류인ᄃᆡ셔로귀속말로은근히ᄒᆞ되금번상경ᄒᆞ야긔어히국ᄉᆞ을공고케ᄒᆞ리라ᄒᆞ고ᄒᆞ더라더라

유젼유하 항시보안회쟝원세셩씨와리범셕씨졍관상쎄가권의졍명이츙후ᄒᆞ다ᄒᆞ야유지ᄒᆞᆫ쳠군ᄌᆞ가구ᄒᆞᆯ금을구ᄒᆞᆷᄒᆞ야항샹팔원을황셩신문사로귀부ᄒᆞ엿다ᄒᆞ기로히쳠군ᄌᆞ의의리를쟝ᄒᆞ게녀기고감샤케알엇더니경문ᄒᆞᆫ즉북도인오쥬수쥬혁파경계인리쟝와구의량인이희신문사에히왕ᄒᆞ야말ᄒᆞ기를원가씨등삼인과의동일실ᄒᆞ니우리ᄀᆞ이돈을밋타다가셜씨의징에분급ᄒᆞᆫ다ᄒᆞ고감인리셜노슈작ᄒᆞ고가져가며니희신문사에셔츄후로탐지ᄒᆞᆫ즉중간문진되고삼씨의정에ᄂᆞᆫ일푼도젼ᄒᆞ지아니ᄒᆞ엿다ᄒᆞ니대져세상ᄉᆞ가이닥지고로지못ᄒᆞᆫ가엇더ᄒᆞᆫ션인군ᄌᆞᄂᆞᆫ의리를계발ᄒᆞ야모포쎄가승의계구ᄒᆞᆷ도ᄒᆞᄂᆞᆫ티보지ᄒᆞᆫ간악괴류ᄂᆞᆫ그계슬중간투식ᄒᆞᄂᆞᆫ고로그투식ᄒᆞᆫ사ᄅᆞᆷ비ᄌᆞ괴가제일은ᄉᆡᆼ각ᄒᆞ여도사ᄅᆞᆷ곳ᄒᆞ면ᄌᆞ피지싱이업슬ᄉᆞᆺᄒᆞ며쏘드른즉쏘엇더ᄒᆞᆫ사ᄅᆞᆷ이삼씨의가권을구제ᄒᆞᆫ다칭탁ᄒᆞ고더러슈젼ᄒᆞ야견문ᄒᆞᄂᆞᆫ자가잇다ᄒᆞ니그런ᄒᆞᆫ사ᄅᆞᆷ은인류가아니라고말들ᄒᆞ더라

○미조쳥별 미국공ᄉᆞ안련씨가외부로조회ᄒᆞ기를미국젼교ᄉᆞ가평양기시쟝에디단을민슈ᄒᆞ엿ᄂᆞᆫ티평양감리셔쥬수원용덕이가환퇴ᄒᆞ기를강박히ᄒᆞ야그젼교ᄉᆞ의죵인을방이ᄒᆞ고착슈ᄒᆞ야그손히가불소ᄒᆞᆫ셜디리기시쟝과항구에디단을각국인이가미슈ᄒᆞᆷ은의례ᄒᆞ여놉원당덕비가국인디졍ᄒᆞ기를별국인티젼ᄒᆞ미ᄅᆞᆫ듯ᄒᆞ지아니ᄒᆞ니싱히무례ᄒᆞᆫ지라기시감리평안쥬와쥬수원용덕을샹당히쳐벌ᄒᆞ라ᄒᆞ엿더라

○로문ᄉᆞ셜 일본군로문수블찬정권즁쳠씨로파견ᄒᆞᆫ다더니

개문ᄒᆞᆫ죠죵쳥죵병방비죵ᄒᆞ고직풍이놉ᄒᆞᆫ관인으로퇴션ᄒᆞ야교견ᄒᆞᆫ다ᄂᆞᆫ딕원슈부회계국총장민영환씨로로문수틀임명ᄒᆞ야다료양셔지젼왕ᄒᆞᆫ다ᄂᆞᆫ말이잇더라

○니챵수진 니부챵관리봉리씨가본부하에틀셕혀신퇴ᄒᆞ씨름리과ᄒᆞᆫ후에ᄂᆞᆫ시비가되야리쳥관이하에의계귀구ᄒᆞ야샹소ᄒᆞ고니부대문에ᄂᆞᆫ빙세교아니ᄒᆞᆫ드러간다ᄒᆞ며니작일브터리쳥이비로소수진ᄒᆞ엿더라

○외대방일관 작일에외부대신리하영씨가일공ᄉᆞ틀방문ᄒᆞ고무ᄉᆞᆫᄉᆞ건인지이시도록담화ᄒᆞ엿다더라

○쟝좌압샹 젼평쥬군수김윤란씨가히군수지임시용포수진으로향조에압샹이되야포흉ᄒᆞ엿든공젼수신에만량을쳥랍ᄒᆞ고방면되엿더니빅셩의게탐북ᄒᆞᆫ장젼이과다홈으로법부에셔경무쳥으로훈령ᄒᆞ야증시압샹ᄒᆞ라ᄒᆞ엿더라

○괄심한도 작일에한부대신이하관원이농상공학교로회동ᄒᆞ야한학도팔십여명을시취ᄒᆞ야당일기교식을셜힝ᄒᆞ엿더라

○명졀뎡찬 명일은츄셕명졀인고로외빈뎡찬ᄒᆞ고리월오일에츌판홈

○홍인괴쟉 부산통신을거ᄒᆞᆫ즉근일에아라사의졍탐비시롱ᄒᆞᆫ한국인투명을일본경찰소에서포착ᄒᆞ야방금구슈중인데모다한홍과명ᄒᆞᄂᆞᆫ사ᄅᆞᆷ이라더라

○자향부회 근일경긔도각군향교에셔지수인으로일명식퇴젼ᄒᆞ야이른진회로을녀보니되근뢰각군슈가감향이대단ᄒᆞ야인민이지보할슈엽스니곳을나가일진회에참례ᄒᆞ야교중으로셔통과ᄒᆞᄂᆞᆫ빈잇거든곳회중에셔용포ᄒᆞ고졍부에샹셔ᄒᆞ야탐학ᄒᆞᆫ군슈ᄂᆞᆫ일병면관케ᄒᆞ야우리동포들로ᄒᆞ여곰싱명지산을보젼케ᄒᆞ되을나가ᄂᆞᆫ사ᄅᆞᆷ들의례비ᄂᆞᆫ다교중으로셔수렴ᄒᆞ여보낼터이니렴녀말고올나가라ᄒᆞᄂᆞᆫ고로연속샹경ᄒᆞ야사발ᄒᆞ고일진회에참례ᄒᆞᆫ다더라

광고

TELEGRAMS

KUROPATKIN'S SITUATION.

(FROM JAPAN PAPERS).

London, Sept. 11.

The Russian General Staff state that General Kuropatkin, since the fighting at Liaoyang, has been strengthened by two army corps with fully 300 guns.

London, Sept. 15.

General Kuropatkin telegraphs that the first official estimate of the Russian losses from August 28th to September 5th is 4,000 in killed and 12,000 wounded.

VICEROY ALEXIEFF.

London, Sept. 14, 38.5 p.m.

Viceroy Alexieff's friends state that he will return to St. Petersburg to succeed Count Lamsdorff.

THE "LENA."

London, Sept. 14.

An engineer has inspected the "Lena's boilers and found them in a bad condition.

London, Sept 15.

The Japanese Consul at San Francisco has protested with the United Saates for allowing the Russian auxiliary cruiser "Lena" to remain more than 24 hours in that port.

PUBLIC OPINION IN ENGLAND.

London, September 12.

A remarkable change is taking place in British opinion with regard to the relative capacities of the belligerents. The tendency hitherto has been to despise Russian strategy, but the critics now declare that they must modify their previous opinions regarding the prospects of the campaign. For the first time there seems doubts about the outcome.

The London "Daily Telegraph" says that Marshal Marquis Oyama was completely foiled by General Kuropatkin's indomitable tactics.

THE BRITISH ARMY MANŒUVRES.

London, September 8.

General French's transports and men-of-war have arrived off the Essex coast near Clacton-on-sea.

Three thousand men with their equipment were landed in the first hour, and scouts were thrown out.

The defenders under General Lord Methuen are mobilising at Redhill.

Septemder 9.

It is Major-General Arthur S. Wynne, C.B., D.A.G. to the Forces, who is commanding the defenders in the manœuvres, not General Lord Methuen.

His concentration at Redhill is explained by the fact that he expected the invasion to take place in Sussex; but the landing at Clacton obliges him to hasten to reinforce the small body of troops in Essex.

London, Sept. 14.

The "Morning Post" states that an official Russian dispatch received in London announces that General Sassoulivitch, commanding 5,000 men of the Russian rearguard, south of the river Hun, has been severely wounded and captured, together with 300 of his men.

London, September 15th.

It is stated that the torrential rains will presently make operations at Port Arthur impossible.

London, September 7.

The Emperor of Austria and the Czar have been decorated by King Edward with the Royal Victorian Chain.

THE DUM DUM BULLET.

London, September 15th.

The correspondents of the "Daily Telegraph" formerly with the Japanese and Russian armies at Liaoyang declare that there is no evidence that the Russians are using Dum-dum bullets.

THE "CALCHAS"

London, Sept. 15.

The Vladivostock Prize Court has released the British steamer "Calchas," with her neutral cargo, but has decided to confiscate the flour, cotton, and timber consigned to Japan.

THE LENA IS TO BE DISARMED.

London, Sept. 15.

Captain Berlinsky, in command of the Russian armed cruiser "Lena," has intimated to the American authorities that he desires to dismantle and remain in San Francisco till the end of the war.

London, Sept. 16.

The officers and crew of the Russian armed cruiser "Lena" are to be detained on parole in the United States.

THE SITUATION AT PORT ARTHUR.

London, Sept. 16.

General Stoessel wires to St. Petersburg that the Japanese forces on the west front of Port Arthur have been reinforced, and the bombardment of the fortress continues. The Russian losses, however, are, the General says, insignificant.

THE STOPPAGE OF MERCHANT STEAMERS.

London, Sept. 16.

Besides overhauling the steamer "Derwent," the Russian cruiser "Perek" stopped the British steamer "Margityroebel" (?) on the 6th and the "Treherbert" on the 12th instant.

London, Sept. 16.

General Kuropatkin mentions in a report that General Fomin was killed at Yentai.

London, Sept. 16.

General Kuropatkin wires that there has been no fighting since the 14th instant, but that a strong Japanese advance guard has been thrown out five kilometress north of Yentai Station.

PROPHECY.

If a prophet desires to have honour in his own country he should be just a little careful as to how he vaticinates, says the "Singapore Free Press." It may imply a very nasty jar to be taken "au pied de la lettre," when one rashly adventures forth into the field of prophesy. For instance.

Advices from Kabul, dated the 14th July received at Peshawar, state that some astrologers recently prophesied in the Amir's presence that Afghanistan would within two months be visited by a pestilence which would sweep away hundreds of the inhabitants. The seers, it is added, have been put into prison, and will be tortured to death if their prediction is not verified.

They have now rather less than a month to justify their declarations. By this time they are mightily sorry they spoke. It might do some of our fashionable Bond Street astrologers a world of good to emigrate to Kabul.

The "old man of the sea" has his rival in Korea. We hear that on a hill in the Pa Chu district lives an old man at least 300 (!) years old. The whole year round he sits on his hill and only comes down to the villages to beg rice. The old gentleman is evidently hale and hearty though of a suspicious character, for we are told that he never takes rice unless someone tastes it beforehand, but this once done he can eat three bowls at a sitting and drink whole jug-fulls of wine.

WHEAT PANIC IN CHICAGO.

There is a renewed panic in Chicago on the wheat market owing to pessimistic crop reports. Prices are the highest known since the Leiter boom.

THE MISSING GERMAN OFFICER.

A reward of 10,000 marks has been offered by the German Vice-Admiral on this station for any information regarding Captain Guggenheim, who left Port Arthur in a junk on the 17th August for Shanhaikwan and who has not since been heard of.

JAPANESE SECURITIES.

There has been a heavy fall in Japanese securities on the London market, as the following figures show:—

	Quotation on 1st Sept.	Quotation on 13th.
Four per cents.	£75 5s.0	£72.05s.0d
Five per cents.		86.15s.5d.
War Bonds.		88.11s.6d.

A GRUESOME EXHIBITION.

With regard to the execution of three Koreans by Japanese soldiers yesterday, we learn on good authority that it took 5 shots to kill one of them and that another did not succumb until he had been struck 7 times.

In the name of humanity we sincerely hope that on the next occasion the Japanese will fire their prisoners from the mouth of a cannon.

The three collies bought in Scotland to serve as field-hospital dogs for the Russian army in Manchuria have left St. Petersburg for General Kuropatkin's headquarters. Tests at Gatchina are described as entirely satisfactory.

They understand best the German language. By repeating the orders in Russian, after the German words, they are being taught so that they may be of service under men who speak only Russian.

Four more of the Si Hung rioters were brought up to the Japanese head quarters on Tuesday afternoon.

The Tsar has called out fresh reserves from 22 Odessa districts—including in one category reserve officers throughout the empire.

Now that the Yetai coal mines, to the northeast of Liaoyang, have been occupied by the Japanese, a Tokio expert, Mr. Hosoi, and several engineers, will be sent there in order to make an inspection. In this connection the "Jiji" says that the Eastern Railway has hitherto been using coal first from Yentai, secondly Fushun, and thirdly Kaiping, as well as Japanese coal, in addition to wood as an auxiliary fuel. Early in May last, the Japanese, however, cut the railway connecting with the coal depot in Liaotung, subsequently, by the occupation of Inkao, the importation of Kaiping coal was suspended. Moreover on September 11th the Japanese captured the large Yentai Colliery near Liaoyang. Thus the Fushun coal mine alone is left as a source of fuel for the Russians, but it is expected to be also taken by the Japanese shortly. The Fushun mine is located about 18 or 19 miles southeast of Mukden. In case of Fushun being occupied by the Japanese the Russians will be obliged to rely on various mountains in Kirin Province, and railway traffic must be greatly affected.—Kobe Herald.

The Korea Daily News.

Issued at 5 P. M. daily except Sundays.

Rate of Subscription:—

Per Year,	Yen 25.
Per Quarter,	Yen 7.
Per Month	Yen 2.50

Postage in Korea not charged extra.
Postage abroad charged extra.

Advertisements, 50 sen per day for 1 inch or less. 5 yen per month per inch. 50 yen per year per inch.

All communications to E. T. BETHELL, Editor and Publisher. Pak-tong, Seoul.

THE LONDON PRESS AND THE WAR.

From the telegrams which we publish to day it will be seen that there has recently been a remarkable change of public opinion in London as to the future of the war, and that one of the consequences has been a big slump in Japanese securities.

The Japanese victory at Liaoyang has come to be looked upon as almost a defeat, while Kuropatkin's retreat is hailed as a Russian triumph. We warn our readers not to be misled by these messages. The majority of the London newspapers are as fickle and unstable as quicksilver, and we attach no more importance to their present pessimistic opinions, than we did to their fulsome panegyrics of Japan's progress during the earlier stages of the war.

The reaction was inevitable. From the beginning of the war, Japan has had a doughty champion in the "London Times." The correspondent of the "Times" had, a little while before, been peremptorily ordered out of St. Petersburg, and the "Times" took its revenge by enlarging on Japan's qualities and glossing over her defects while pursuing a diametrically opposite policy with regard to Russian affairs. England is a very loyal country, and the existence of the Anglo-Japanese alliance had a good deal to do with the enthusiasm with which news of Japanese successes was received. The majority of the London newspapers depend upon sensational news for their existence, and all the Japanese successes were made much more of than the circumstances warranted. And finally, the war correspondents who were kept kicking their heels in Tokio saw only the bright side of things. Whether or not it was their object to ingratiate themselves with the authorities we cannot say, but their despatches were frequently nauseatingly adulatory.

And now that the inevitable reaction has set in, and people are beginning to realize that the Japanese are only human and cannot effect the miraculous, we must take care not to be led to the other extreme.

We consider the last opinion of the "London Daily Telegraph," to the effect that the Japanese were completely foiled by Kuropatkin's superior strategy, to be of as little value as their previous one that by the Liaoyang victory Japan had established her right to be classed among the great powers of the world. The "Daily Telegraph" rushes to extremes, jumps to conclusions and knows no moderation.

The world, with an optimism worthy of Mark Tapley, and by a process which certainly could not be called reasoning, had persuaded itself that the battle of Liaoyang was going to be a second Sedan. Kuropatkin appears to have been left out of the calculations altogether. He does not seem to have been given credit for even ordinary intelligence. That Kuroki's march northwards had for its object the destruction of the railway and the cutting off of his line of retreat, must have been as obvious to Kuropatkin as it was to the Fleet Street "quidnuncs." Kuropatkin also saw, some time ago, as did everyone else, that in the vulnerability of his line of retreat lay the weakness of the Liaoyang position. Had he not provided for all this, he would not have been the skillful general he is everywhere acknowledged to be.

To sum up the whole situation, the Japanese may not have achieved all they hoped to, but they won a hard-earned and brilliant victory, and Kuropatkin got out of a tight corner with an ability worthy of him and his reputation.

THE BATTLE OF LIAOYANG.

(CONCLUDED.)

Immediately General Fujii had given the order to advance, the Japanese artillery, which had apparently succumbed to the hardships of the last few days of continual fighting, awoke into activity. A brisk cannonading commenced, and under cover of it the Japanese left wing swept round towards the railway and the whole line marched forward, exchanging, as they went, a lively rifle fire with the rear guard of the Russian army. A halt was called when darkness set in on Sunday evening.

On Monday morning General Kuroki rode forward to the hill above Haiyentai, through Chinese villages whose only inhabitants were wounded Russian soldiers, past the funeral pyres of the cremated dead and many hastily made graves. After traversing fields which the contending armies had trampled into bogs the staff reached the hill where the sight that met their gaze was one which has seldom been equalled in the history of war.

From the hill-top, which was less than a quarter of a mile long, ravines led in all directions to the plains below. The sides of the hill were honeycombed with trenches, counter-trenches and rifle pits. Near the summit there lay in the sun the blackened and bloated corpses of two hundred Russians who had apparently been shot down when almost within reach of their goal. The hill was everywhere dented and furrowed by shell, and fragments of steel from exploded missiles strewed the ground. The battlefield was littered with rifles, twisted bayonets, cooking pots all shattered out of recognition by the Japanese shell fire. Several broken drums lay about, and blood was everywhere. Upon the blood-soaked turf lay caps and uniforms all torn and riddled by shot and shell and covered with blood.

Bullets strewed the ground and the whole scene was one of such bloody carnage that it is impossible to believe that such desperate fighting has ever before occurred.

At a Chicago church recently the prospective bridegroom electrified bride and congregation by shouting "No" and running out of the church when asked, "Do you take this woman far your wife?" He was badly treated by an indignant crowd, and the police took him into custody for safety.

Mr Holland, the inventor of the Holland submarine, claims that he has invented a practical flying machine with four wings, which he will be able to sell for ten dollars. The machine will be capable of moving from forty to fifty miles an hour. Mr. Holland says, "When I invented the submarine I was laughed at even by scientists and by mechanical engineers, but they do not laugh now. I believe that I have solved the problem of flying, and I predict that my machine will be in general use in five years' time.—Laffan.

The Crown Prince is gradually recovering from his sickness.

The Japanese force despatched to Si Hung returned yesterday.

According to a despatch from Fusan 6 Koreans have been arrested on suspicion of being Russian spies.

The Governor of South Choong Chong Province reports that he has removed the stakes placed by the Japanese round the On Yang sulphur springs.

Our reporters inform us that the barbers' shops in Chinkokai have been doing a roaring trade recently owing to the fashion set by the Il Chin Hoi.

Jacques Lebaudy, known as "Emperor Jacques II," has concluded to abandon his scheme for a Saharan Empire and is living a retired life in Brussels.

It is estimated that the Vanderbilts have paid over £1,000,000 to secure the immunity of their palatial New York residences from trade encroachment.

The Il Chin Hoi meeting have at last solved the dreaded problem. One of the rules now reads, "Only Gentlemen, who have expended the necessary ten cents on a hair cut, can belong to our society." Other qualifications for the honour of membership in this illustrious society are insignificant in comparison with this magnitudinous clause.

The winning of a loyal Ireland is no small or easy ambition. It is beyond the power of either party in English politics to gain it. The only possible solution of the difficult problem lies with the King. Quietly, unostentatiously, he has already accomplished much, and a few years more will show a marked change in the political and social conditions of the Irish people.—Sun, New York.

Without ostentation, and after reigning for three years only, the imposing figure of King Edward VII. has by degrees impressed itself on the attention of all. Almost unknown to his own country, he has attained a commanding position in Europe. To-day he is recognised, not only as the ablest diplomatist of his country, but as a great Constitutional Sovereign, respected by his people and listened to by his Ministers.—La Revue, Paris.

There is a thrilling story in the "Express" of the adventure of a French submarine of the Mors type while carrying out manœuvres in the neighbourhood of Havre. The little vessel entered the estuary of the Seine and proceeded some distance up the river. Then an attempt was made to bring it to the surface, but it failed to rise. The fact that the specific gravity of fresh water was less than that of sea water had been overlooked, and for a moment there was consternation aboard, as the atmosphere had become very oppressive. For 26 minutes efforts were made to bring the boat to the surface, but without avail, and the position became more serious when several of the crew grew faint owing to the foulness of the air. To make matters worse, the submarine, instead of rising, showed signs of settling on the river bed and becoming fixed there. The officer in command, at length perceiving the cause of the trouble, made for the open sea at full speed. All the while the men, who were suffering considerably, behaved admirably. Shortly afterwards they had the satisfaction of noting that the boat was gradually rising as they entered the denser water; and, finally, they reached the surface. The crew were by this time almost overcome; but with the exception of three, they quickly recovered on reaching the fresh air. The three in question were so ill that they had to be removed to hospital for medical treatment.

The Korea Daily News.

VOL. I, THURSDAY, SEPTEMBER 22, 1904. No. 58

大韓每日申報
대한미일신보

(뎨오십구호) (금요일) 쳔구빅사년구월이십삼일

본사고ᄇᆡᆨ

본신보는영어와한어로셕거미일츌판ᄒᆞ옵

신문가
한쟝 엽두돈오푼
일삭도 엽두량닷돈
우표가ᄂᆡ삭닷돈
다맛돈이로밧숩

광고료는
귀한의쟝단과ᄌᆞᄒᆡᆼ의다쇼로증갑ᄒᆞ되편ᄒᆞᆷ가로밧을터이오며오ᄅᆡ지아니ᄒᆞ야대한사람마다다이신문을보실터이니광고버시기를원ᄒᆞ시는이들은우리신문사에와셔면약ᄒᆞ심을희망ᄒᆞ옵

○발ᄒᆡᆼ소. 박동대한미일신보사발ᄒᆡᆼ하교앙헤젼영국인셜텔림쟝자리오
샤쟝 영국인 (빈셜)

평양 디리졈
○평양츙효동사는권미보씨로우리신문쾌미디리인을뢰뎡ᄒᆞ엿스오니평양에게신구람코져ᄒᆞ시는 쳠군ᄌᆞ는흥디리졈에왕림ᄒᆞ와면의ᄒᆞ시옵

사고

○우리대한미일신보의목뎍은대한의안녕질서에관한모든뎨목에되ᄒᆞ야는공평한변론을쥬쟝홈이라우리동신원의담보는신문보시는쳠군ᄌᆞ의게ᄒᆞ상보도ᄒᆞ리며편지를귀셔ᄒᆞ여주시는이는셩명과번디를젹어붓치시기를희망ᄒᆞ오니이거슨신문샹에긔ᄌᆡᄒᆞ라는거시아니오다만극히신용ᄒᆞ는증거를숨고자홈이라긔자는아모긔셔던지과차ᄒᆞᆷ을되각ᄒᆞ는권리를가졋스나되각ᄒᆞ는빈유를말ᄒᆞᆯ터이오며공중평회를문란케ᄒᆞ는듯ᄒᆞᆫ긔셔는외레히밧지안켓숩나이다

●본사셜시이리로신문을미양우레로본젼ᄒᆞ와레젼부의압의로젼ᄒᆞᆫ듯스로번곳에는흑늣게젼ᄒᆞ기도ᄒᆞ며흑몃칠거슬ᄒᆞᆫ겁에젼ᄒᆞ기도ᄒᆞ며흑아니젼ᄒᆞ는곳도잇다ᄒᆞ와우리신문을수람ᄒᆞ야구람ᄒᆞ시는 쳠군ᄌᆞ의게죠되ᄒᆞ야미우미안ᄒᆞ옵기로지금은본젼인을두고미일죠이젼ᄒᆞ며하나젼ᄒᆞ거나늣게거나ᄒᆞᆫ폐가잇도록ᄒᆞ란ᄒᆞ오니혹아니젼ᄒᆞ거나늣게젼ᄒᆞ거나ᄒᆞᆫ일이잇스면본샤로통긔ᄒᆞ여주심을희망ᄒᆞ옵

본사광고

본샤에셔본신문뎨ᄉᆞ호와뎨싱일호와뎨이십오호를소용ᄒᆞᆯ테가잇셔이에광고ᄒᆞ오니누구시던지이상삼호중에본샤로가져오시면미쟝에빅젼두픈식드리리다

론셜

론돈신문과젼쟁ᄉᆞ유

○이제한면보를거ᄒᆞᆫ즉요양젼쟁에츄후결국이긔왕론도갓신문에발ᄒᆞᆫ거슬보고우리신문에등제ᄒᆞ게니와대단히상쾌가되는거시쳠을에일본셔승쳡ᄒᆞ고아연히잇는거슬아병이음습ᄒᆞ야함락ᄒᆞ엿다ᄒᆞ며또아병이퇴거ᄒᆞᆯ베에도총환이비오듯ᄒᆞ야일병이도리여패ᄒᆞ엿다ᄒᆞᆫ즉우리신문의ᄒᆞ시는쳠군ᄌᆞ의게우발명ᄒᆞᆯ일이잇는지라당초에우리가오보ᄒᆞᆫ란홈이아니라론돈신문으로말미아마그리됨이기로오날신문에그ᄉᆞ실을게ᄌᆡᄒᆞ노니

론돈에신문이여러이잇셔각각그ᄉᆞ실을번역ᄒᆞ야등ᄌᆡᄒᆞᆫ즉이러ᄒᆞᆫ신문구람ᄒᆞ는거시별노긴요ᄒᆞᆯ거시업는거시이왕에일본셔나만일츙승쳡ᄒᆞᆫ일로찬양ᄒᆞ기만위ᄒᆞ야그리홈인즉이는대단히잘못ᄒᆞ는일이나당초에일본셔긔젼ᄒᆞᆯ셰에론돈타입쓰신문의게진졀히부탁ᄒᆞᆫ일이잇셔서그신문사통신원이아라사시찰ᄒᆞ는것찻치ᄒᆞ고피득보에젼왕ᄒᆞ야일본형편도ᄌᆞ셰ᄒᆞ야발ᄒᆞ며셜후ᄒᆞᆷ졀이잇드ᄅᆡ도공담으로ᄒᆞ는거와찻치됴ᄒᆞᆫ말로만쓰미여아모쪼록일본이빗나게ᄒᆞ엿다ᄒᆞᆷ즉

이는영국이일본으로더부러동밍ᄒᆞᆫ처디에샹하가모도편심으로도아주란ᄒᆞ는마음이잇셔일본에셩공ᄒᆞ엿다는소문만듯니게ᄒᆞ랴홈인고로론돈여러신문에셔도며시동감지졍으로일본셔조고마치셩공ᄒᆞᆫ일만잇게되면평쟝히찬양ᄒᆞ야게ᄌᆡᄒᆞ는중샹지어젼사통신원들은이로본에빗나게ᄒᆞᆯ일만보라고통경으로향ᄒᆞ야발을고이고잇다ᄒᆞᆫ즉

우리는ᄌᆞ긔들의목뎍과권한디로ᄒᆡᆼᄒᆞ는거슬엇더케ᄒᆞ던지말ᄒᆞᆯ거슨엽스되공포ᄒᆞ는문ᄌᆞ샹에너모심ᄒᆞ게아첨ᄒᆞᆫ즉지금당ᄒᆞ여셔는이신문들에거즛말ᄒᆞ는모양이쳥져ᄒᆞ게드러나고로보는사람마다이른본셔승쳡ᄒᆞ엿다는것도긔이ᄒᆞ게녁이지안코우리도역시하회가엇더케될거슬주의ᄒᆞ야일아아니ᄒᆞ는도다

우리도론돈미일면보를거ᄒᆞ야일본이아종싸홈에흑구쟝군의병범삼으로결단이낫다는말을보고아비로소요양승쳡ᄒᆞᆫ바일본이세계갑국중동등으로ᄒᆡᆼ셰ᄒᆞ란든거시져비감ᄒᆞ게될줄로알아는져라흑구쟝군의긔왕ᄒᆞᆫ일을본진디리케병민ᄒᆞ야명ᄒᆞᆫ고닐은가나지못ᄒᆞᆫ겻갓더니흑목대쟝이철도를파졀ᄒᆞ고아로향ᄒᆞ의퇴거ᄒᆞᆫ길을선느란고북으로향ᄒᆞ엿다는디흑구쟝군은요양싸홈에대단히약ᄒᆞ게뵈엿스즉필경ᄌᆞ긔의퇴거ᄒᆞ란는길을향ᄒᆞᆫ셥는줄미리혜아리고조펴긔로ᄒᆞᆫ즉아ᄌᆞ긔의험디근쳐에잇던승젼ᄒᆞᆫ거슨엇지혐의ᄒᆞᆯ터이리오

만일이리ᄒᆞᆫ일을짐작지못ᄒᆞ엿슬것갓ᄒᆞ면가히져용이경비ᄒᆞ야다는대쟝이못될터인즉엇지아모진곤ᄒᆞᆫ나방향업시향ᄒᆞ리오일본군ᄉᆞ들은스흑쟝군의지휘되로가히진쳘만ᄒᆞᆫ터를살괴드리도아병은보지못ᄒᆞᆯ터이나엇지던지렬심으로싸와승쳡ᄒᆞᆫ일이쟝ᄒᆞ고흑구쟝군은뎨조와명예가잇더니ᄒᆡ게그위ᄒᆞᆫ홈을버서낫을븐즉가히그리ᄒᆞ명아닌줄을알겟노라

잡보

○일진우항 젼호련쇽
일의탐학ᄒᆞ야민샹에원한함이빅셩의쎄에ᄉᆞ모쳣쟈롤이사랑으로진압ᄒᆞ다ᄒᆞ니가위불에기름을붓는모양이라참졍이엇지ᄒᆞ하야졍부의ᄉᆞ무를능단치못ᄒᆞ나니잇가그직분을더ᄒᆞ지못ᄒᆞ면맛당히곳갈거시라ᄀᆡ졍도치ᄒᆞ야리문을참부케ᄒᆞ랴ᄒᆞ엿더라

○피령피착 농샹공부주ᄉᆞ빈응ᄒᆞᆫ씨의본가가시ᄒᆞᆫ디에잇는고로근일에하거ᄒᆞ엿다가맛ᄎᆞᆷ소요시를당하야빅셩의간쳥을낫과ᄒᆞ야민요소쟝을지어주엇더니일병이민쇼를쟝두리지목ᄒᆞ고수령부에압슈ᄒᆞ엿다더라

○강계등디편관 일본군슌용렬도가히자한인샹명을쟉일공덕리에셔일병이포살ᄒᆞᆫ슈는본보에긔ᄌᆡᄒᆞ엿거니와그수건으로졍부에셔샹주ᄒᆞ고평도감등랑ᄒᆞᆫ대세를면본관ᄒᆞ엿더라

뎐보

동경발구월이십일일
대산만쥬군총ᄉᆞ령관보고

○포획물픔 면져보고ᄒᆞᆫ포획물픔외에흑목군은셔탄이빅토파를고공ᄒᆞ루ᄅᆡ일[쳘로쇼옹]통젼이빅오십미돌을획득이라ᄒᆞ엿더라

구월이십이일동경발
당디공ᄉᆞ관착

○봉텬부근격젼 디산총ᄉᆞ령관보고에운ᄒᆞ되
구월십칠일에본게ᄒᆞ에셔북으로수리증되는평디ᄌᆞ에잇는우리일종디에디ᄒᆞ야봉텬부에셔동으로십리증되는무순셩방면과밋봉텬가도에셔뎍병의보병이쳘대ᄃᆡ와포병이중ᄃᆡ가쳐지드리오며졍오에셔오후두시지잇는뎍군은ᄀᆞ쟝우리슈비병의게핍근ᄒᆞ엿스나오후비시브터셔북방으로퇴각ᄒᆞ엿고우리포병은삼십분동안츄격을ᄒᆡᆼᄒᆞ야대단히만히손히케ᄒᆞ니뎍군의대부터는졈졈퇴각ᄒᆞ엿고그일부터는완고ᄒᆞ게ᄃᆡ뎍ᄒᆞ엿스나오후칠시에니르러는드듸여격퇴ᄒᆞᆫ지라이뎍군은구월십팔일에방도오히려우리종디의젼면뎡지ᄒᆞ엿더라

외보

○포디종가 로군이봉쳔부에셔쳥국리슈로쳘리쇼되는운하에포디션수좌를건츅ᄒᆞ고일좌에대포수문식비치ᄒᆞ엿더니토향대핍ᄒᆞᆫ후에는쥴디에포디슈좌를증셜ᄒᆞ고일좌에대포수문식비치ᄒᆞ고엄즁히방비ᄒᆞᆫ다더라

○합이빈로군 합이빈에잇는로국군은그곳정거쟝동방에셔셔남으로청국리슈로오십리쯤격ᄒᆞᆫ쌍셩부간에광이륙쳑이오깁기가일쳑되는히자를둘너파고반리식격ᄒᆞ야쵸병을두고또ᄒᆞᆫ현과합이빈간에쳘로를연ᄒᆞ야폭이오십여쳑되는도로를슈츅ᄒᆞᆫ다더라

○삼청관산쥰비 료양에셔퇴ᄒᆞᆫ로군이봉텬북방으로퇴각을연속히ᄒᆞᄂᆞᆫ모양인즉로군이쳘영에셔일본군을방어ᄒᆞᆯ계획인ᄃᆡ그곳정거쟝에셔청국리슈로이리쯤되ᄂᆞᆫ삼청관산에다슈ᄒᆞᆫ포ᄃᆡ를축셜ᄒᆞ고그압헤ᄂᆞᆫ큰히자를파방비ᄒᆞᆯ슈션을급급히ᄒᆞᆫ다더라

○마젹습아 팔월오일에밤에마젹삼쳔명가량이만쥬쳘령에쥬둔ᄒᆞᆫ아군을습격ᄒᆞ엿ᄂᆞᆫᄃᆡ아병은잠이깁히들엇다가일군의공격인줄알고분쥬히도망ᄒᆞᆫ지라마젹이그량식과군물등을탈거ᄒᆞ엿고슈운ᄒᆞᆯ슈업ᄂᆞᆫ것슨모다불질너릐웟다고지라타임쓰신문에긔ᄌᆡᄒᆞ엿더라

○탄약핍절 근리로군즁에ᄂᆞᆫ로국복식ᄒᆞᆫ청인을압줄로셰우고츌젼ᄒᆞ며또근리ᄂᆞᆫ로국연긔잇ᄂᆞᆫ화약을쓰며포탄은려슌에셔졔조ᄒᆞᆷ으로여러가지죵류오폭발력이미약ᄒᆞ다ᄒᆞ니로군에탄약이핍절ᄒᆞᆷ을가지라ᄒᆞ더라

관보

뎨이쳔구빅삼십칠호

광무팔년구월이십일일

셔임급ᄉᆞ령

○류힝병예방위원쟝 경무ᄉᆞ 원우상

구월십오일

○임탁지부ᄉᆞ계국장셔칙임관ᄉᆞ등 졍삼픔 리학규

구월십칠일

○일쥬일경근신 진위뎨륙련ᄃᆡ뎨이대ᄃᆡ부ᄉᆞᄃᆡ쟝륙군보병부위 리기우

팔월이십구일

○셔대훈ᄉᆞ금쳑쟝 완평군 리승응

○셔대훈ᄉᆞ리화쟝 원슈부회계국총쟝 민영환 특진관 윤용션 완슌군 리지완

이상구월십륙일

○임ᄂᆡ부대신셔칙임관일등 즁츄원부의쟝 리용ᄐᆡ

잡보

○방문일관 작일상오십일시에일공관쳥렵을인ᄒᆞ야외부대신리하영씨가일공관을방문ᄒᆞ엿더라

○리감신임 뎨식원번역관리무영씨가동ᄅᆡ감리로젼임ᄒᆞ엿더라

○죠쵹삼가 일공ᄉᆞ가외부로죠회ᄒᆞ되일본인이ᄂᆡ쟝원으로슈삼갑ᄉᆞ쳔여원지발ᄒᆞ라ᄂᆞᆫᄉᆞ는상금죠쳐가업ᄂᆞᆫ고로또죠회ᄒᆞ니곳지발ᄒᆞ라만일금월ᄂᆡ로지발치아니ᄒᆞ면남문외경부텰도뎡거쟝디단갑이만여원뎨일은힝에임치됴즁에셔졔ᄒᆞ겟다ᄒᆞ엿더라

○일인ᄌᆞ익 전남관찰ᄉᆞ셔리광쥬군슈권즁은씨가외부에보고ᄒᆞ되룡쥬군슈홍봉표의보고에ᄒᆞ기를본군슈가일어를비호랴고일본인일명을쳥ᄒᆞ기로목포거ᄒᆞᄂᆞᆫ강용협의게쳥탁ᄒᆞ엿더니음력륙월륙일에일인쇼쳔방죠가강용협의편지를가지고ᄅᆡ방ᄒᆞᆫ고로관가협방으로영졉ᄒᆞ야잘잇더니칠월이십ᄉᆞ일에우연독병ᄒᆞ야목포로가겟다ᄒᆞᄂᆞᆫ고로수일됴리ᄒᆞᆫ후에발졍ᄒᆞ라ᄒᆞ고만류ᄒᆞ엿더니이십륙일죠됴에그방문이졔졀노열녓거ᄂᆞᆯ가본즉일인이업ᄂᆞᆫ지라의심ᄒᆞ야ᄉᆞ면에슈탐ᄒᆞᆫ즉뒤뜰안에셔스ᄉᆞ로목ᄆᆡ여치ᄉᆞᄒᆞᆫ지라곳목포감리셔에통긔ᄒᆞ야일령ᄉᆞ의게통지ᄒᆞᆫ즉일슌ᄉᆞ와감리셔슌검이ᄅᆡ도ᄒᆞ야검시ᄒᆞᆫ즉분명히조의ᄒᆞᆫ거시라인ᄒᆞ야화쟝ᄒᆞ엿다ᄒᆞ엿시니ᄒᆡ일인이비록조의ᄒᆞᆫ거시나외국인과샹관된일인고로보고ᄒᆞᆫ다ᄒᆞ엿더라

○죠쳥병압 ᄂᆡ부에셔진쥬군슈리용교씨의동학졍형을말ᄒᆞᆫ면보를인ᄒᆞ야원슈부에죠회ᄒᆞ되진쥬군슈리용교의면보를졉ᄒᆞᆫ즉ᄒᆡ디방에비도가다시창궐ᄒᆞ야조만ᄒᆞᆯ념려가잇스니ᄒᆡ지부근진위ᄃᆡ에훈칙ᄒᆞ야진압ᄒᆞ라ᄒᆞ엿더라

○의호론죠 농상공부에셔면답에긔간ᄒᆞ고축보ᄒᆞᄂᆞᆫ등ᄉᆞ로이왕인허ᄒᆞᆫ각군에론죠ᄒᆞ기를디경안빈땅과황무ᄒᆞᆫ땅에긔간쟉답ᄒᆞ며축보관긔등ᄉᆞ로각ᄃᆡ에여러사ᄅᆞᆷ이쳥원ᄒᆞ민민양히디방군에훈령ᄒᆞ야사보ᄒᆞᆫ후인허ᄒᆞᆷ이여러ᄒᆡ라반다시긔간ᄒᆞᆫ땅이고유지디를이룸이잇겟슨즉ᄒᆡ마다승총ᄒᆞ겟거ᄂᆞᆯᄒᆡ군에셔보고가업고본부에셔사문치아니ᄒᆞ야막연히셔로이져셔실샹이업셧스니엇지이러ᄒᆞᆫ리치가잇스리오쳐쳐에도디긔간ᄒᆞ여부와긔간ᄒᆞᆫ면답과일경과두락과긔간ᄒᆞᆫ년죠와승총여부를낫낫치구별ᄒᆞ야보고ᄒᆞ라ᄒᆞ엿더라

○리력셔슈졍 의졍부에셔각관청에통텹ᄒᆞ되각관쳥협관이하칙임쥬임관임의리력셔를쟝ᄎᆞ편집ᄒᆞ야존안ᄒᆞ야일후임면ᄒᆞᄂᆞᆫᄃᆡ샹고케ᄒᆞᆯ터이니소관관쳥에도일례지위ᄒᆞ야리구월초오일ᄂᆡ로송교ᄒᆞ고각디방소속관리의리력셔ᄂᆞᆫ구월삼십일일ᄂᆡ로도취ᄒᆞ여보ᄂᆡ라ᄒᆞ엿더라

○예후평복 동궁뎐하셰셔ᄂᆞᆫ근간에미령ᄒᆞ시든중셰가일잔으로쾌복되셧다더라

○일진일진 일진회ᄂᆞᆫ날마다입회ᄒᆞᄂᆞᆫ인원이증가ᄒᆞᄂᆞᆫᄃᆡ도시향긱이며참회ᄒᆞ라고단발ᄒᆞᄂᆞᆫ쟈가만타ᄂᆞᆫᄃᆡ리현등디발소에셔미일단발ᄒᆞᄂᆞᆫ슈효가평균ᄒᆞ여일일삼십명가량이된다더라

○동도동션 ᄒᆡ쥬로셔샹경ᄒᆞᆫ사ᄅᆞᆷ의젼언을드른즉몃날젼에연안군나진포에셔순션ᄒᆞᆯ시에동션ᄒᆞᆫ사ᄅᆞᆷ즁ᄒᆞᆫ오십명이동힝인듯ᄒᆞᆫ기로그슈다ᄒᆞᆷ을의심ᄒᆞ야힝식을샹찰ᄒᆞᆫ즉만히젼일동학당류인ᄃᆡ셔로귀속말노은근히ᄒᆞ되금번샹경ᄒᆞ야긔어히국ᄉᆞ을공ᄒᆞ고케쥬ᄉᆞᄒᆞᆯ터이라고ᄒᆞ더라더라

○유션유악 향시보안회쟝원셰셩씨와리범셕씨형균삼씨가권의졍경이참혹ᄒᆞ다ᄒᆞ야유지ᄒᆞᆫ쳠군ᄌᆞ가구휼금을구합ᄒᆞ야합십팔원을황셩신문샤로긔부ᄒᆞ엿다ᄒᆞ기로ᄒᆡ쳠군ᄌᆞ의의리를쟝ᄒᆞ게여기고감ᄉᆞ케알엇더니깅문ᄒᆞᆫ즉북도인오쥬ᄉᆞ쥬혁파경거인리졍위규익량인이ᄒᆡ신문ᄉᆞ에ᄒᆡ왕ᄒᆞ야말ᄒᆞ기를원씨등삼인과의동일실ᄒᆞ니우리가이돈을맛타다가삼씨의집에분급ᄒᆞᆫ다ᄒᆞ고감언리셜노슈작ᄒᆞ고가져가더니ᄒᆡ신문샤에셔츄후로탐지ᄒᆞᆫ즉즁간물건되고삼씨의집에ᄂᆞᆫ일푼도젼송치아니ᄒᆞ엿다ᄒᆞ니대져셰샹ᄉᆞ가이닥지고로지못ᄒᆞᆫ가엇더ᄒᆞᆫ션인군ᄌᆞᄂᆞᆫ의리로격발ᄒᆞ야모모씨가속의게구휼도ᄒᆞᄂᆞᆫᄃᆡ요지훈간악픽류ᄂᆞᆫ그거슬즁간투식ᄒᆞᄂᆞᆫ고그투식ᄒᆞᆫ사ᄅᆞᆷ이ᄌᆞ긔가졔일욕싱각ᄒᆞ여도사ᄅᆞᆷᄀᆞᆺ흐면ᄌᆞ피지심이잇슬ᄯᅳᆺᄒᆞ며ᄯᅩ드른즉ᄯᅩ엇더ᄒᆞᆫ사ᄅᆞᆷ이삼씨의가권을구졔ᄒᆞᆫ다칭탁ᄒᆞ고더러슈젼ᄒᆞ야건몰ᄒᆞᄂᆞᆫ쟈가잇다ᄒᆞ니그러ᄒᆞᆫ사ᄅᆞᆷ은인류가아니라고말들ᄒᆞ더라

○미죠쳥벌 미국공ᄉᆞ안련씨가외부로죠회ᄒᆞ기를미국션교ᄉᆞ가평양긔시쟝에디단을미슈ᄒᆞ엿ᄂᆞᆫᄃᆡ평양감리셔쥬ᄉᆞ원용덕이가환퇴ᄒᆞ기를강박히ᄒᆞ야그션교ᄉᆞ의죵인을당일착슈ᄒᆞ야그손ᄒᆡ가불쇼ᄒᆞᆯ뿐더러긔시쟝과항구에디단을각국인이민슈ᄒᆞᆷ은의례여ᄂᆞᆯ원용덕이가미국인ᄃᆡ졉ᄒᆞ기를별국인ᄃᆡ졉ᄒᆞ듯ᄒᆞ지아니ᄒᆞ니심히무례ᄒᆞᆫ지라긔시감리평한쥬와쥬ᄉᆞ원용덕을상당히처벌ᄒᆞ라ᄒᆞ엿더라

○로문ᄉᆞ셜 일본군로문ᄉᆞ를찬졍권즁현씨로파견ᄒᆞᆫ다더니갱문ᄒᆞᆫ즉죵쳑즁명망이즁ᄒᆞ고직품이놉흔관인으로퇴션ᄒᆞ야파견ᄒᆞᆫ다ᄂᆞᆫᄃᆡ원슈부회계국총쟝민영환씨로로문ᄉᆞ를임명ᄒᆞ야료양ᄭᆞ지젼왕ᄒᆞᆫ다ᄂᆞᆫ말이잇다더라

○ᄂᆡ협ᄉᆞ진 ᄂᆡ부협관리봉ᄅᆡ씨가본부하예를석혀신ᄐᆡ휴씨를다파ᄒᆞᆫ후에큰시비가되야리협관이하예의게귀구ᄒᆞ야상소ᄒᆞ고ᄂᆡ부대문에는밍세코아니드러간다ᄒᆞ더니작일브터리협판이비로소ᄉᆞ진ᄒᆞ엿더라

○외대방일관 작일에외부대신리하영씨가일공ᄉᆞ를방문ᄒᆞ고무슨ᄉᆞ건인지이시토록담화ᄒᆞ엿다더라

○쟝죄압샹 젼경쥬군슈김윤란씨가ᄒᆡ군슈재임시공포ᄉᆞ건으로향조에압샹이되야포흠ᄒᆞ엿든공젼ᄉᆞ십여만량을쳥랍ᄒᆞ고방면되엿더니빅셩의게탐묵ᄒᆞᆫ쟝젼이파다ᄒᆞᆷ으로법부에셔경무쳥으로훈령ᄒᆞ야즉시압샹ᄒᆞ라ᄒᆞ엿더라

○팔십학도 작일에학부대신이하관원이농샹공학교로회동ᄒᆞ야학도팔십여명을시취ᄒᆞ야당일긔교식을셜힝ᄒᆞ엿더라

○명졀뎡잔 명일은츄셕명졀인고로의례뎡잔ᄒᆞ고ᄅᆡ월요일에츌판홈

○륙인피쟉 부산통신을거ᄒᆞᆫ즉근일에아라ᄉᆞ의졍탐비시름ᄒᆞᆫ한국인륙명을일본경찰쇼에셔포착ᄒᆞ야방금구슈즁인대모다함흥과영흥사ᄅᆞᆷ이라더라

○자향부회 근일각도각군향교에셔지ᄉᆞ인으로일명식퇴션ᄒᆞ야일진회로올녀보니되근리각군슈가담학이대단ᄒᆞ야인민이지보할슈업스니곳올나가일진회에참례ᄒᆞ야교즁으로셔통긔ᄒᆞᄂᆞᆫ비잇거든곳회즁에셔공포ᄒᆞ고졍부에샹셔ᄒᆞ야담학ᄒᆞᆫ군슈ᄂᆞᆫ일병면관케ᄒᆞ야우리동포들로ᄒᆞ여곰싱명ᄌᆡ산을보젼케ᄒᆞ게되올나가ᄂᆞᆫ사ᄅᆞᆷ들의예비ᄂᆞᆫ다교즁으로셔슈렴ᄒᆞ여보낼터이니렴녀말고올나가라ᄒᆞᄂᆞᆫ고로연속샹경ᄒᆞ야삭발ᄒᆞ고일진회에참례ᄒᆞᆫ다더라

광고

TELEGRAMS.

Tokyo, Sept. 22nd.

Marquis Oyama reports that on the 17th inst. 7 Russian battalions of infantry with two batteries of artillery attacked a Japanese Column near Fushu, about 30 miles west from Mukden, but were repulsed with heavy loss.

THE WAR CORRESPONDENTS.

SERIOUS FRICTION WITH THE AUTHORITIES.

The "Mainichi" correspondent at the front has sent his paper the following statement with regard to the grievances of the foreign war correspondents:—It is with regret that I have to send you a communication concerning the foreign war correspondents. The correspondents attached to the 2nd Army were not on good terms with the authorities even when they were still at Tokio. Ever since they have been allowed to follow the Army, they have been making complaints of various kinds, although they have shown patience under the hardships incidental to campaigning. When about to leave Haicheng, they applied to the Headquarters for permission to send telegrams to their papers, but the authorities refused to comply with the request on the ground that the time had not yet come for this to be done. Some days afterwards, the correspondents again asked the authorities to allow them to wire their papers, and produced drafts of the telegrams which they wished to despatch. The authorities gave the same reply as before. The correspondents, however, persisted in their request, saying that their object in following the troops was to send telegrams to their papers. But for this, they would not have come to the Far East. Then a Japanese officer agreed to receive the drafts of the telegrams, but reserved the official response to the request. Eventually the authorities decided to maintain their former attitude. The officer referred to invited one of the correspondents to call upon him, when he returned him the drafts of all the telegrams, asking him to restore them to their writers. In consequence of this incident, the correspondents became angry with the officer, complaining in particular that the contents of the wires had not been kept secret, owing to their having been handed, as stated above, to one of the correspondents for distribution. They described the officer's conduct as very discourteous. The consequence was that the correspondents of "The Times," "Daily Telegraph," and other leading papers, left the Japanese Army for Peking or Tientsin, before the engagement at Liaoyang took place. When starting, they are said to have intimated their intention of having their revenge. At any rate I have to record with great regret that the friction gave rise to a feeling of much animosity between the correspondents and the authorities.

THE FOREIGN WAR CORRESPONDENTS.

The Japan Gazette publishes the following communication from Tokio:—The so-called maltreatment of foreign war correspondents at the front seems to be proving wery costly. Some prominent correspondents recently rode out of the fighting lines and sent uncensored telegrams to London. Their wires are based on erroneous data in some respects, but their standing as war correspondents gives their opinions great weight.

A REMINISCENCE OF THE KHARBIN INCIDENT

The daughters of the late Mr. Shozo Yokokawa, one of the two Japanese shot a few months ago by the Russian authorities at Kharbin, recently received the following letter written by their father on the eve of his execution:—

"Kharbin, Manchuria,
April 20, 1904.

Dear Daughters,

Your father, having arrived in Russian territory by the order of His Majesty the Emperor, was arrested by Russian soldiers on April 11, and is now to be shot by their hands. This fate has been decreed by Heaven. I wish you health, and trust you will be able to contribute to the welfare of our country. I have nothing more to say on the eve of my death. Will you give my love to your mother and best regards to Mr. Tomiya?

"Yours, etc.,
"SHOZO YOKOKAWA.

"To Miss Ritsuko.
"To Miss Yuko.

"P.S.—"I enclose herewith a draft of 500 taels on a Chinese bank at Peking. You will find how to cash the draft by asking the advice of Messrs. Keijiro Inouye, Kumano Yamaguchi and others.

"I thought to remit 500 taels with this letter, but I have now given this sum to the Red Cross Society of Russia."

The Post Script has been struck out with a pen. Evidently the deceased changed his mind at the last moment and disposed of the money as stated above. It is reported, however, that the Russian Red Cross Society, being impressed by the heroic end of the gallant Japanese, has sent the money to the breaved family. Mr. Tomiya Mitamura is the younger brother of Mr. Yokokawa and a student at the Sixth High School, Okayama.

The money on deposit in the Dai-Ichi Ginko as an earnest of the payment for the land outside the South Gate seems to be a convenient method employed by the Japanese for obtaining claims from the Korean Government. The latest we hear in connection with this, is that the Japanese Minister has informed the Foreign Office that he will withdraw Yen 4,000, the amount claimed from the Government by a Japanese ginseng merchant.

SOME VISIONARY TRIPS AT THE EXPOSITION.

A correspondent of the "San Francisco Chronicle," writing of the "Pike," which is the "side show" region at the St. Louis Exposition, says:

The Pike is the starting point for make-believe journeys to the uttermost parts of the earth. These tours are much like child's play, of course, and the traveller must have a lively imagination if he is to get much satisfaction. Still, some of the devices of illusion are surprisingly effectual. The best ingenuity is expended, however, in inducing people to start on the trips. The street fronts are big and enticingly realistic. A fair size railway station with a locomotive choo-chooing genuine smoke and steam, invites you to travel over the Czar's Siberian and Manchurian route to the region where the Russo-Japanese war is raging. The train doesn't move far, but it joggles its passengers while a panorama is drawn past its windows and stops are made at stations in scenes that look spacious with their cycloramic effects. Russian officers are in full possession of the line and no sign of warfare is visible.

One of the visionary trips takes the tourist to Paris in a submarine boat and brings him back in an airship. Here again the especial endeavour is made to get passengers on board. The end of a vessel is visible with its deck barely above the surface of a pool of water. A hatch is open and two sailors are examining the edges, smoothing a spot here, tacking on a bit of rubber there, and all with a sober air of anxiety lest there be a leak during the next voyage. A handsome fellow in the naval uniform of a Captain asks, "Is she safe, Jack?"

"Aye, aye, sir" Jack replies, touching his cap, "perfectly safe, sir."

"Then all aboard! We sail in five minutes."

This show costs half a dollar for half an hour, yet seems to satisfy the impressionable multitude, although the sophisticated piker may regard it as a joke. The passengers descend to a cabin through the hatch, which is fastened behind them with much ado.

"Are we ready, pilot?" the captain asks.

"We are ready, sir," a voice responds.

"Then head her under water."

Machinery is heard, a tremulous motion is felt and water swishes against the windows. The captain tells us in a minute or two that we have emerged from the Mississippi into the Gulf of Mexico, and in five that we are out in the Atlantic ocean at a depth of 2,000 fathoms. There the waters are illuminated by a searchlight, and through the windows, painted on a moving canvas, we see seaweed, fishes, wrecks and aquatic monsters. Of course the boat doesn't stir. Nor does the elevator which, in Paris, takes us up to the top of the Eiffel tower. Nor does the airship which conveys us thence to St. Louis, through much aerial phenomena, including a terrific storm of wind, thunder and lightning closely imitated.

THE WEATHER.

The following is an extract from an article headed "Is Hot Weather Unhealthy" appearing in one of the Japan papers.

"One other cause of illness prevalent in hot dry weather is dust, and this with a little attention might be abated. The usual practise of municipal authorities is still to sweep the perfectly dry and the *n*-ray, it would seem that unwittingly he had selected an exceedingly appropriate designaton, for in mathematics *n* is used to signify an indefinite number, and M. Blondcot already claims to have identified three different forms of radiation and more will doubtless follow."

Yes, we should say, it certainly is. The heat in the editorial office must have been extremely *unhealthy* for the comp, who was responsible for that little bit of confusion.

The Korea Daily News.

Issued at 5 P. M. daily except Sundays.

Rate of Subscription:—
Per Year, Yen 25.
Per Quarter, Yen 7.
Per Month Yen 2.50

Postage in Korea not charged extra.
Postage abroad charged extra.

Advertisements. 50 sen per day for 1 inch or less.
5 yen per month per inch.
50 yen per year per inch.

All communications to
E. T. BETHELL,
Editor and Publisher.
Pak-tong, Seoul.

Tomorrow, (Saturday) being a Korean National Holiday, there will be no issue of this paper.

KOREA DAILY NEWS.

PORT ARTHUR.

Every day the situation at Port Arthur grows in interest. Misled by the optimism of the Japanese officials and press, most people believed, in the Spring, that the fortress would certainly fall before the end of July. The Japanese Imperial Message, which was delivered on August 17th, calling upon the garrison to surrender, also served to encourage the opinion that the end was near. Stories also reached us that the food supply of Port Arthur was running short, that the ammunition was exhausted, that there was great discontent in the garrison and that General Stoessel had committed suicide. The naval sortie was also looked upon as an omen of approaching surrender.

In fact, ever since the beginning of the war, or at any rate since the Japanese occupation of Dalny and the Liaotung peninsula, the world has been led to look upon Port Arthur as doomed.

In view of all this it is interesting to piece together such fragmentary news as is available, throwing light on the present position. First with regard to the condition of the troops of the opposing armies, we learn from the "Japan Mail" that a Japanese who left Port Arthur on the 10th stated that dysentery and typhoid are raging among the garrison. This does not seem very reliable. Concerning the condition of the Japanese troops we have the following from Mr. Bito, who was recently sent by the Emperor on a visit of inspection:—

"There were many sick among the troops, but it was gratifying that no infectious disease had yet broken out, which was due to the great precautions taken by the Commanders in regard to the sanitary conditions, the exceptional efforts of the medical department, and the development of sanitary ideas in each individual."

In contradiction to this, we find a report in the Chefoo "Daily News," "that some sickness, particularly dysentery, has appeared among the troops before Port Arthur, especially in the twelfth division of the Japanese army."

We are inclined to look upon this last report as correct. It seems hardly likely, however carefully sanitation may be looked after, that a large army, holding the same camp for months during the hottest part of the year, could keep entirely free from such diseases as dysentery and enteric fever. In Port Arther, of course, good sanitary provision was made long ago, and therefore the probabilities are, that so far as the ravages of disease are concerned the Japanese are far greater sufferers than the Russians.

With regard to the question of provisions, which had been looked upon as a potent factor in the reduction of the forces, it does not appear that the Russians are as yet in very desperate straits. Early in September a steamer with a full load of flour arrived there, and although the Japanese blockading vessels capture a few junks now and then, it certainly appears that the majority of them evade capture, and are keeping Port Arthur well supplied.

Months ago, from various sources, we were told that the Russian ammunition was running out. It has not run out yet, and it is hard to believe that as the Russians are able to get in supplies of provisions, they are not also getting replenishments for their shot-lockers. We heard of the departure for Port Arthur of a Norwegian steamer laden with 65,000 shells. She should have arrived ere now but we have heard nothing of her. Had she been captured we should probably have heard a good deal.

Last of all, we come to the fighting. On this subject, news is scare, but it seems fairly certain that the Japanese have captured many of the outlying forts but have made no impression on the nearer defenses. And we do not see how they are likely to, so long as the garrison keeps healthy and can obtain supplies of food and ammunition.

All reports unite in saying that both sides are fighting with unexampled courage, but all the advantages are on the Russian side, and the Japanese army must be tired and discouraged by their long and arduous attack.

The near approach of winter will probably spur the attackers on to increased exertion as in the cold weather all the odds will be against them. The exposure to the severe cold will be a severe trial to them and, when the ground freezes, it will be impossible for them to protect their advance by trenches.

KING COOLIE.

On Tuesday last at the Japanese consulate there was held a preliminary investigation into a complaint lodged by Mr. T. E. Hallifax against a Japanese coolie for assaulting his jinricksha man, a Korean.

The jinricksha man's evidence was, that on the previous Saturday he was pulling the ricksha (empty) towards Mr. Hallifax's gate, when he found his way obstructed by a Japanese coolie who was drawing water from a well in the road. He asked the Japanese to move whereupon the latter became violent and struck him with a pole. The Japanese might just as easily have stood on the other side of the well to draw water. There were no witnesses to the assault.

Neither he nor has jinricksha touched the Japanese in any way.

The Japanese coolie's version of the affair had been taken previously and was to the effect that seeing a jinricksha approach he had asked the man to wait until he had brought to the surface a bucket which was already half way up. Instead of doing this the Korean brushed past, striking him with the hub of the jinricksha wheel wherepon he retaliated with the pole.

There were no witnesses to the actual "fracas" although Mr. Hallifax and his servants arrived on the scene immediately afterwards. The assault was a trivial one, and Mr. Hallifax only took action as a protest against the growing truculence of the lower classes of Japanese in Korea.

On the 21st Mr. Hallifax was notified by the Japanese consul that the Japanese coolie had been fined one yen and strongly cautioned to behave himself in future.

In view of the fact that Japanese law takes very little account of an assault unless the injuries are of a serious nature and considering that the evidence was practically one man's word against another's, we consider the conclusion arrived at to be a very satisfactory one.

The Japanese authorities are fully cognizant of the tyranous behaviour of many of their people, and we consider this verdict to be evidence of their willingness to bring offenders to book. If others will only follow the public-spirited example set by Mr Hallifax, we shall soon hear less of arrogance and violence from Japanese coolies.

Subscriptions to the Korea-Japan club up to date amount to sixteen hundred yen.

Mr. Yi Mu-yang translator in the Ceremonial Office has been appointed Kamni of Gensan.

A Japanese interpreter, employed by the Magistrate of Neung Chu, has committed suicide by hanging.

Mr. Yi Ha-yong, Minister of Foreign Affairs, visited the Japanese Legation on the morning of the 22nd inst.

It is said that Mr. Pai Kuk-tai brother-in-law of General Syon Yong Woon will be appointed Governor of Seoul.

A light-house tender, being built in Kobe to the order of the Imperial Korean Customs, is expected to arrive about November 10th.

An Imperial edict has been addressed to several officials, instructing them to discover and secure the punishment of all dishonest magistrates and to arrest the leaders of the Tonghaks and tell their followers to disperse quietly.

The "Hongkong Telegraph" states on very good authority that the British squadron in the north China waters has been busily engaged in laying mines at the entrance to the harbour of Wei-hai-wei.

If Russsia's threat to shoot newspaper correspondents as spies for sending wireless news were extended to include those sending newsless news the world would cry out in horror at the fearful event of the slaughter.—Press, New York.

The Vice Governor of Seoul has addressed a complaint to the Japanese Army Headquarters that they did not inform him of their intention to execute the three Koreans recently disposed of outside the city.

The census of Fusan, recently taken, resolves the number of houses and Japanese occupants into.

Houses.......................... 2,358.
Japanese residents............11,409.

An increase of 162 houses and 82 residents since July. This is probably due to increased activity on the Seoul Fusan railway.

Yesterday we heard that the barbers were having a good time. Now it transpires that the Japanese hatters in Chinkokai have disposed of all their old stock of caps and straw hats to members of the Il Chin Hoi society, who appear to be setting the fashion in this direction also.

From Japan papers we note that our enterprising friend "Lort Nelson" Davies of the Grand Hotel, Yokohama is advertising a special dinner when Port Arthur falls. Let us hope that the provisions were not laid in at the same time as the advertisement was inserted.

The Korea Daily News.

VOL. I, FRIDAY, SEPTEMBER 23, 1904. No. 59

HONGKONG & SHANGHAI BANKING CORPORATION.

Paid-up Capital............................$10,000,000
Reserve Fund:—Sterling Reserve... 10,000,000
Silver Reserve..... 7,000,000

27,000,000

Reserve Liability of Proprietors... 10,000,000

HEAD OFFICE, HONGKONG.

London Bankers, London and County Banking Company Limited.

Branches and Agencies,
London.

Amoy,	Hankow	Penang,
Bangkok,	Hiogo,	Rangoon,
Batavia,	Iloilo,	Saigon,
Bombay,	Lyons,	San Francisco,
Calcutta,	Manila,	Singapore,
Colombo,	Nagasaki,	Sourabaya,
Foochow,	New York,	Tientsin,
Hamburg,	Peking,	Yokohama,

Credits granted on approved Securities, and every description of Banking and Exchange business transacted.

Drafts granted on London and the chief Commercial places in Europe, India, Australia, America, China and Japan.

HOLME RINGER & Co., AGENTS,
CHEMULPO.

ON CHEONG & CO.,
SEOUL.

GENERAL STORE KEEPERS.
Imported provisions, Cooking Utensils Crockery, etc.
FRESH BREAD DAILY.

MITSU BISHI DOCKYARD & ENGINE WORKS,
NAGASAKI.

CODE WORD, "DOCK."

A. 1, A. B. C., and Engineering Codes used.

DOCK No. 1 (at Tategami).

Extreme Length..........................523 feet
Length on blocks........................513 „
Width of Entrance on Top......89 „
„ „ Bottom....77 „
Water on Blocks at Spring Tide 26½ „

DOCK No. 2 (Mukaijima).

Extreme Length..........................371 feet
Length on Blocks........................360 „
Width of Entrance on Top......66 „
„ „ Bottom 53 „
Water on Blocks at Spring Tide 22 „

PATENT SLIP (at Kosuge).

Can take vessels up to 1,000 tons gross.

THE WORKS are well equipped with the LATEST IMPROVEMENTS, and can execute any kind of work in SHIPBUILDING and MARINE ENGINEERING, as well as in REPAIRING of SHIPS.

The COMPANY'S new powerful steamer OURA-MARU (712 tons, 700 I.H.P.), specially built for SALVAGE PURPOSES, and equipped with necessary gear, is always READY at SHORT NOTICE.

CHARTERED BANK OF INDIA AUSTRALIA & CHINA.

INCORPORATED BY ROYAL CHARTER 1853

HEAD OFFICES:—LONDON.

Paid-up Capital £800,000

Reserve Liability of Shareholders 800,000

Reserve Fund 800,000

Drafts granted upon all the principal places in the world and every description of Exchange and banking business transacted.

E. MEYER & Co., Agents,
Chemulpo.

E. MEYER & CO.
Chemulpo.

SOLE AGENTS IN KOREA FOR:

A. T. Morse, Sons & Co's "Fresco" Distemper

In all colours ready for use on walls, Ceilings etc.

and

AVENARIUS CARBOLINEUM

A wood-preserving and antiseptic oil preparation

Against decay, dry-rot, fungus and wood-destroying insects.

A large supply always in Stock.
Prices upon application.

E. MEYER & Co.,
Chemulpo.

LAW UNION & CROWN INS. CO.

Fire risks accepted at Current rates, on godowns, merchandise, dwellings, and other property, subject to usual conditions.

HOLME RINGER & Co.,
Agents, Chemulpo

THE METHODIST PUBLISHING HOUSE,
Little West Gate, Seoul.

JOB PRINTING, TYPEWRITER PAPER
CARBON PAPER, VISITING CARDS
STATIONERY, BOOK BINDING
BOOK PUBLISHERS
AMERICAN SCHOOL BOOKS
SPENCERIAN COPY BOOKS
PEN CARBON LETTER AND BILL BOOKS

S. A. BECK, Manager.

DAI-ICHI GINKO.

LIMITED.

(Formerly the First National Bank)

ESTABLISHED 1873

INCORPORATED UNDER PRESENT LAW 1896

Capital - - - - - - - - - Yen 5,000,000
Reserve Fund - . - - - 1,500,000

HEAD OFFICE:—TOKIO.

President: Baron SHIBUSAWA.

BRANCHES AND CORRESPONDENTS
In the Principal Cities and Towns of Japan.

Interest Allowed on

Fixed deposits 1 year - - - **6½ per cent**
„ „ 6 months - - - **6 per cent**

Special current accounts 1½ sen daily per Y 100
General „ „ 1 „ „ „ 100

M. TANAKA,
Manager, Chemulpo

HOLME RINGER & Co.

Chemulpo.

General Merchants and Government Contractors.

Agents for the leading

Banks

Steamship Companies

and

Insurance Companies

Importers of Merchandise of every description.

KAMEYA & CO.

GENERAL STOREKEEPERS
Chinkokai - - Seoul

(*Established 1895, Tokyo*)

Confectionery, Hams, Canned Goods, Cutlery, Hirano & Tansan Water. Provisions, Gents, Furnishing goods, Toilet Articles, Travelling Bags, Tobacco, Cigars & Cigarettes Kitchen Utensils. Coffee, Biscuits.

Fresh Goods always kept in Stock.
Prices Moderate
Please come and inspect our goods.

NIPPON YUSEN KAISHA.

JAPANESE MAIL STEAMSHIP CO.

UNDER MAIL CONTRACT WITH THE IMPERIAL JAPANESE GOVERNMENT.

European Line

Regular Fortnightly Service between Yokohama Kobe, Moji, Shanghai, Hongkong, Singapore, Penang Colombo, Port Said, Marseilles, London and Antwerp

American Line

Regular Fortnightly Service between Hongkong and Seattle, calling at Shanghai, Moji, Kobe. Yokohama and Victoria, B. C.

Australian Line

Regular weekly Service betwen Japan Ports a. Australia, calling at Hongkong and Manila.
(Above Three Lines Suspended until further notice).

Shanghai Line

Weekly Service between Shanghai and Japan Ports

Korea Line

Service Kobe, Moji, Nagasaki, Fusan, Chemulpo, Coo, Taiku
S. S. Babelsberg, 2181 tons.
Service Kobe, Moji, Fusan, Chemulpo, Chinnampo
S. S ARGO, S. S. Ohio.

BORDEN'S CONDENSED MILK CO.

New York, U. S. A.

ALWAYS IN STOCK

Eagle Brand Condensed Milk.

Gold Seal Condensed Milk.

Peerless (Family) Evaporated Cream.

Borden's Malted Milk.

E. MEYER & CO.
Chemulpo, Korea,
Sole Agents

ROYAL INSURANCE COMPANY,
Funds exceed £10,000,000

FIRE
AT CURRENT RATES.

LIFE
REDUCED PREMIUM.

HOLME RINGER & Co.,
Agents, Chemulpo.

HOTEL DU PALAIS
SEOUL.

The only first class Hotel in Seoul. Situated in the centre of the city opposite the palace.

Cuisine under the supervision of an experienced French Chef.

Well ventilated and furnished throughout.

TARIFF UPON APPLICATION

L. MARTIN
Proprietor and Manager.

大韓每日申報
대한미일신보

(뎨륙십호) (월요일) 일쳔구빅사년구월이십륙일

본사고빅

본신보는영어와한어로셔계미일츌판ᄒᆞᆸ

신문갑

한쟝 엽전두돈오푼

일삭표 엽전량닷돈

우표가미삭닷돈

다닷돈으로밧ᄉᆞᆸ

광고료ᄂᆞᆫ

귀한의쟝단과ᄌᆞ항의다쇼로ᄌᆞ중감ᄒᆞ되갑가로밧을터이오며오리지아녀대한사람마다다이신문을보실터이니광고내시기를원ᄒᆞ시ᄂᆞᆫ이들은우리신문사에와서면약ᄒᆞ심을희망ᄒᆞᆸ

○발힝소 박동대한미일신보사발힝인겸편집인영국인셜필령쟈리오

사쟝 영국인 (비셜)

평양 대리점

○평양효동사ᄂᆞᆫ권미보씨로우리신문관대리인을뎡ᄒᆞ엿ᄉᆞ오니평양에계신구람코져ᄒᆞ시ᄂᆞᆫ 첨군ᄌᆞᄂᆞᆫ해대리졈에왕림ᄒᆞ와면의ᄒᆞ시옵

사고

○우리대한미일신보의목뎍은대한의인민쟝래셔에관한모든데목에되ᄒᆞ야ᄂᆞᆫ공평한변론을주쟝홈이라우리등신문회ᄉᆞ보ᄂᆞᆫ신문보시ᄂᆞᆫ첨군ᄌᆞ의게ᄒᆞᆼ샹보도ᄒᆞ리며편지를귀서ᄒᆞ며주시ᄂᆞᆫ이ᄂᆞᆫ셩명과번디를젹어붓치시기를희망ᄒᆞ오니이ᄂᆞᆫ비커슨신문샹에귀ᄌᆡᄒᆞ라ᄂᆞᆫ거시아니오다만구히실용ᄒᆞᄂᆞᆫ증거를숨코자ᄒᆞᆷ이라귀쟈ᄂᆞᆫ아모귀서면지귀쥐ᄒᆞ올넌ᄌᆡ쟈ᄒᆞᄂᆞᆫ권리를가졋스나되쟈ᄒᆞᄂᆞᆫ리유를말ᄒᆞᆯ터이오며공즁평화를문란케ᄒᆞᄂᆞᆫ듯ᄒᆞᆫ다귀서ᄂᆞᆫ의례히밧지안켓ᄉᆞᆸ나이

●본사셜시이래로신문을미양우례로분젼ᄒᆞ와레젼부의임의로젼ᄒᆞ든ᄂᆞᆺ스로면ᄆᆞᆺ에ᄂᆞᆫ흑누게젼ᄒᆞ기도ᄒᆞ며흑먹쳘귀습ᄒᆞᆫ겁에젼ᄒᆞ기도ᄒᆞ며흑아니젼ᄒᆞᄂᆞᆫ폿도잇다ᄒᆞ와우리신문을ᄉᆞ랑ᄒᆞ야구람ᄒᆞ시ᄂᆞᆫ 첨군ᄌᆞ의게ᄒᆞᆷ되ᄒᆞ야미우미안ᄒᆞ옵기로지금은분젼인을두고미일일숙이젼ᄒᆞ며아니젼ᄒᆞ거나늣게거나ᄒᆞᆫ폐가엉도록ᄒᆞ라ᄒᆞ오니ᄒᆞ야니젼ᄒᆞ거ᄂᆞᆫ흑늣게젼ᄒᆞ거나ᄒᆞᆫ일이잇스면본사로통긔ᄒᆞ여주심을희망ᄒᆞᆸ

본사광고

본샤에셔본신문데ᄉᆞ호와데십일호와데이십오호를소용ᄒᆞ올테가잇셔이에광고ᄒᆞ오니누구시던지이샹삼호중에본샤로가다리오시면미쟝에빅젼두푼식드리다

론셜

려순형편

○려순위치ᄂᆞᆫ남비갈ᄉᆞ릉셩졉린ᄒᆞ게되여가되일본공보와신문샹에쳠란ᄒᆞ게게지ᄒᆞᆷ으로세샹사ᄅᆞᆷ들은분부터밋기를금년뎡츄이젼에ᄂᆞᆫ려순함낙이쟝녕뭘ᄎᆞᆯ노만날아ᄉᆞ며

ᄯᅩ팔월십칠일일본군보에도말ᄒᆞ기를일본셔항복을밧으려ᄒᆞᆫ즉젼쟁견국이미구에되리라ᄒᆞ엿고ᄯᅩᄒᆞᆫ일빈불론에ᄂᆞᆫ려순에잇ᄂᆞᆫ아병의군량이핍진ᄒᆞ고군ᄉᆞ들이홈갈ᄒᆞ야진중의잇ᄂᆞᆫ군ᄉᆞ의마음이불등ᄒᆞᆷ으로ᄉᆞ듕ᄉᆞ승아쟝이자폐ᄒᆞᄂᆞᆫ지경ᄭᆞ지이르러손쥬이거서다항복ᄒᆞᆯ조정을뵈엿비라ᄒᆞ여습샢더러

기젼이후로일본셔요동파밋쳥리와두ᄭᅥ을젼ᄎᆞ졈령ᄒᆞ고ᄯᅩ이외조고마ᄒᆞᆫᄊᆡ홈에도항샹득승ᄒᆞ엿다ᄒᆞᆷ으로세계에셔도려순졈령은단졍코뭘츌로만알아ᄂᆞᆫ즁아라사진중형편이야기를일본신문으로부터드른즉금월십일에려순으로조ᄎᆞ온ᄒᆞᆫ일본사ᄅᆞᆷ의말이아라사진중에ᄂᆞᆫ군사들이펌병파이질로말미아마대단히불온ᄒᆞ더라ᄒᆞ엿스나우리ᄂᆞᆫ이말이과연진젹ᄒᆞᆫ바인지밋지못ᄒᆞ엿더니

ᄯᅩ일본황대자셔려순에잇ᄂᆞᆫ일본군ᄃᆡ에쟝항시찰ᄒᆞ기위ᄒᆞ야파견ᄒᆞ엿든미ᄂᆞᆼ쎄의말을드린서ᄂᆞᆫ일본진중에도병든군ᄉᆞᄂᆞᆫ여러이되젼렴ᄒᆞᄂᆞᆫ병은아닐뿐더러모든ᄉᆞ령관들이매방ᄒᆞ기위ᄒᆞ야위싱되외에쳥결ᄉᆞ를셜치ᄒᆞ고지어사롬ᄒᆞ나잇ᄂᆞᆫ처소ᄭᆞ지미오위싱에리롭도록주의ᄒᆞ야발달이되엿더라ᄒᆞ엿스되이말들과ᄂᆞᆫ대단히샹좌가되ᄂᆞᆫ거시잇서니

근일영미일신문을거ᄒᆞᆫ즉려순항구히잇ᄂᆞᆫ일본군ᄃᆡ에셔이젼병이번져셩기엿ᄂᆞᆫ되고즁대셥이련되진에ᄂᆞᆫ며유싱ᄒᆞ드라ᄒᆞ엿스니우리싱각에ᄂᆞᆫ이말이가쟝분명ᄒᆞ고ᄯᅩᄒᆞᆫ형편이그러ᄒᆞᆯ듯ᄒᆞᆫ거시아모리위싱에주의ᄒᆞᆫ다ᄒᆞ엿드리도수쳔명되ᄂᆞᆫ병졸ᄭᅵᄒᆞᆫ진중에잇서구렴ᄒᆞᆫ셰셔를지나엿ᄉᆞᆫ즉이졀이나렴병잣ᄒᆞᆫ거시ᄌᆞ연히싱기게되엿슬터ᄒᆞ며

려순안에잇ᄂᆞᆫ아라사진에셔ᄂᆞᆫ위싱샹조ᄒᆞᆫ셕료들을귀왕에만히졔조ᄒᆞ엿ᄉᆞᆫ즉비록규칭ᄒᆞᄂᆞᆫ병이잇드리도일병보다ᄂᆞᆫ겁나ᄂᆞᆫ쟈ㅣ미오쳐을터비요셔물로말ᄒᆞ드리도아진에ᄂᆞᆫ유핍ᄒᆞᆫ샹고가잇ᄉᆞᆫ즉아직ᄭᆞ지ᄂᆞᆫ경걸ᄒᆞ야곤란ᄒᆞᆫ지경은되지아니ᄒᆞ엿슬터인거시

금월초싱에민가로식ᄉᆞ고가ᄂᆞᆫ쌔쳔일쳑은려순에도착ᄒᆞ엿고ᄯᅩ이외에도젼에러쳑즁에몃쳑은일인의게포획이되엿스되다힝이피ᄒᆞ여도발ᄒᆞᆫ젼쳑이만은즉그빈들에탑지ᄒᆞ니만ᄒᆞ드리도려순안에셔잔ᄲᅢᆨ고지낼터이며

ᄯᅩ누사이리로여러번일비잇셔ᄂᆞᆫ고로우리도군물이핍졀ᄒᆞᆫ줄노만알아더니괴왓셔물수입ᄒᆞᆯ써에도군물은다시중슈치안코ᄯᅩ노위기인이라ᄒᆞᄂᆞᆫ츈젼으로란ᄌᆞ룩만오쳔기를려순으로보니기위ᄒᆞ야탑지ᄒᆞ엿다ᄂᆞᆫ말도드러스즉만일그빈가중로에셔잡피여쓸게잇ᄉᆞ면무슨말이잇서슬터이되아모말도엽ᄉᆞᆫ즉그동안에무ᄉᆞ히도착됨은가지요ᄯᅩ써홈으로말ᄒᆞᆯ진ᄃᆡ일병은다만아병의외칙만포획ᄒᆞ고실샹방어ᄒᆞᄂᆞᆫ려순위치에ᄂᆞᆫ범졉지못ᄒᆞ엿다ᄒᆞᆫ즉두나라이셔로ᄒᆞᄂᆞᆫ이론을실로알수도엽슬쎈더러요ᄉᆞ이드르니ᄂᆞᆫ소문과갓ᄒᆞᆯ지경이면아무리랑국이셔로진력ᄒᆞ야ᄊᆞ호드리도다만아병의게만유익ᄒᆞᆯ거시일병들은이리케오리도록로력ᄒᆞᆫ셩혀다시공격ᄒᆞᆷᄋᆞ샹히곤핍ᄒᆞᆯ지라ᄯᅩᄒᆞᆫ동졀이졈졈갓가와올ᄉᆞ록힘을다ᄒᆞ고군ᄉᆞ를지촉ᄒᆞ야ᄊᆡ와야ᄒᆞᆯ거시필경ᄒᆞᆯ득ᄒᆞ게치운셰에밍렬ᄒᆞ게시작ᄒᆞ려ᄒᆞᆯ섇더러겨울빙판되ᄂᆞᆫ날이면져희들의츙돌ᄒᆞ야젼진홈을기치방비ᄒᆞ야되갈지못ᄒᆞ리로다

관보

뎨이쳔구빅삼십팔호

광무팔년구월이십이일

셔임급ᄉᆞ령

○보군례참쟝계 륙군일등군ᄉᆞ 빅학진

○면본관 광쥬우례ᄉᆞ쥬ᄉᆞ 리희공

이샹구월십구일

○의원면본관 영희뎐참봉 김셩진

○명봉샹ᄉᆞ계됴셔칙임관ᄉᆞ등 궁닉부특진관 리호셕

○임 영희뎐참봉서판임관팔등 졍릉참봉 리원영

○임 졍릉참봉서판임관팔등 구품 김셩진

○명궁닉부소관쟝ᄉᆞ강ᄉᆞ셰부됴닉위원 궁닉부참셔관 김용제 법부참셔관 김탁현 텰도원기ᄉᆞ 송진옥 궁닉부쥬ᄉᆞ 류진용 의졍부쥬ᄉᆞ 최동식 전쥬ᄉᆞ 권봉슈 젼위원 리셕호

궁졍록ᄉᆞ

○죠칙왈근일드르니동학여당이다시ᄌᆞ만ᄒᆞ야흉쥬문을외이며흑가만히샹통ᄒᆞ야읍촌에취집ᄒᆞ야병긔를조통ᄒᆞ야곳곳이소란ᄒᆞ고장ᄎᆞ경셩으로도취ᄒᆞᆫ다ᄒᆞ니인심의미흑홈과민속의안졍치못홈이이ᄃᆡ경에이르ᄂᆞᆫ고짐이소연ᄒᆞ니블가불미리방어지칙을강구ᄒᆞᆯ계라각도관찰ᄉᆞ와안무ᄉᆞ외젼유ᄉᆞ와디방진위딕와각중포관으로ᄒᆞ여곰벼별반포칙ᄒᆞ야피슈ᄂᆞᆫ즉시ᄌᆞ슈ᄒᆞ고도당은효유ᄒᆞ야훗터셔번란시ᄎᆞ를방어ᄒᆞ고디방을안졍케ᄒᆞ라

구월이십일

잡보

○일진결의 일젼에일진회에서회원을회동ᄒᆞ야무긔연셜을ᄒᆞ고좌긔ᄉᆞ항의의건을공포ᄒᆞᆫ

소로의결ᄒᆞ엿ᄂᆞᆫᄃᆡ 일은 원슈부검사국총쟝현영운이가궁ᄂᆡ부소관셰입을즁거물노삼고일본인고목문평씨와일쳔만원을차관ᄒᆞ기로계약ᄒᆞᆷ은권력을밋고ᄉᆞ욕을취우랴고요구ᄒᆞᄂᆞᆫᄉᆞ 일은면환국에ᄇᆡᆨ동화쥬젼ᄒᆞᄂᆞᆫᄉᆞ롤조쳐ᄒᆞᆯᄉᆞ 일은리용틱가국가다ᄉᆞᄒᆞᆫ때에우미ᄒᆞᆫ하쟈로다시니ᄂᆡᄃᆡ의즁임을졈취ᄒᆞ엿스니ᄂᆡ외국에ᄃᆡᄒᆞ야국가톄면을손샹ᄒᆞᆫ인죽젼격ᄒᆞ야그ᄉᆞ직ᄒᆞᆷ을권ᄒᆞ고ᄒᆞᆫᄉᆞ 일은현영운의쳡은불과일기녀인으로국졍을잔섭ᄒᆞᆷ은일대변피라극력ᄒᆞ야론박ᄒᆞᆯ졔건ᄉᆞ라더라

○단발쳔여 향일에일진회원이단발ᄒᆞᆫ이후로거괴의방ᄒᆞ야단발ᄒᆞᄂᆞᆫ쟈가날마다즁가ᄒᆞ야근일ᄂᆡ로단발ᄒᆞᆫ사ᄅᆞᆷ이쳔여명이되ᄂᆞᆫ고로진고ᄀᆡ양복졈에와셔모조구ᄒᆞᄂᆞᆫ사ᄅᆞᆷ이만타더라

○부산일호구 부산에잇ᄂᆞᆫ일본인호구슈효를히디일본경찰셔에셔죠사ᄒᆞᆫ거슬거ᄒᆞᆫ즉팔월말ᄭᆞ지일인호슈가이천삼ᄇᆡᆨ오십팔호요인구ᄂᆞᆫ일만일천사ᄇᆡᆨ구인ᄂᆡ에남이륙쳔이ᄇᆡᆨ이십오인이오녀가오쳔일ᄇᆡᆨ팔십사인이니칠월말에비ᄒᆞ면호슈가일ᄇᆡᆨ륙십오호와인구가팔십이인이즁가ᄒᆞ엿더라

○잡류지잡 졍위김귀현씨ᄂᆞᆫ본시잡류로년젼에려쥬츌쥬ᄒᆞ엿슬대에일읍을츙화ᄒᆞ고무죄ᄒᆞᆫ민호가오륙ᄇᆡᆨ호나쇼탕이되고작년에표도관위명으로양민의부자ᄂᆞᆫ도적의죄를씨워셔려쥬와지평등디에ᄇᆡᆨ셩이다어육이되엿더니금번에지평사ᄂᆞᆫ김션달을쇼이여의벽을이르키면됴혼도리가잇다ᄒᆞ야어리셕은김션달노ᄒᆞ여곰의병이르켜사방으로통문ᄒᆞ고김귀현은즉시샹경ᄒᆞ야각셰가에다니며공동식히기를방금의병이대단ᄒᆞ다ᄒᆞ고또졍위벼슬을도독ᄒᆞ야병명을거나라고나려갓다더따

○졍부회의 금일하오일시의졍부에셔회의ᄒᆞᆫ다더라

○총지셔리 찬졍권즁현씨ᄂᆞᆫ렬도원총지셔리를피명ᄒᆞ엿더라

○특하죠칙 근일동학당이쳐쳐에창궐ᄒᆞᆷ으로 ᄃᆡ황뎨폐하ᄭᅴ옵셔특별히죠칙을ᄂᆞ려글ᄋᆞ샤되오회라싱민의도탄파국셰의급업ᄒᆞᆷ이엇지금일에막심ᄒᆞᆫ고이거시졍치의실수ᄒᆞᆫ연고라엇지던운소치라ᄒᆞ고구졔지칙을싱각지아니ᄒᆞ리오짐이처국ᄒᆞᆫ지ᄉᆞ십여년에다ᄉᆞ림이ᄯᅳᆺ과ᄀᆞᆺ지못ᄒᆞ야필경위미ᄒᆞᆫ디경에이른거시엇지짐의부덕ᄒᆞᆷ으로묘졍ᄇᆡᆨ관과방ᄇᆡᆨ슈령이능히짐의ᄯᅳᆺ슬ᄃᆡ양쳐못ᄒᆞ고도리여담학ᄒᆞ야ᄇᆡᆨ셩을혼들고디방을피폐케ᄒᆞᆫ소치가아니리오젼후죠칙이간졀ᄒᆞ엿스되젼혀실효가업고동학이요란ᄒᆞ고ᄉᆞ방란민이관장을살해ᄒᆞ니쥬소로ᄉᆞ렴ᄒᆞ매 옥톄가미안ᄒᆞᆫ신지라불가불ᄉᆞ신을파견ᄒᆞ야각도에슌힝ᄒᆞ야슈령의치젹을시찰ᄒᆞ고ᄇᆡᆨ셩의폐막을무러우민효을유ᄒᆞ며란류를히산케ᄒᆞ고탐쟝ᄒᆞᆫ관리를책ᄒᆞ고비류와거피를업시ᄒᆞ면거의짐의적ᄌᆞ를슈화지즁에셔건질지라경긔츙쳥도경상도젼라도강원도황히도에슌찰ᄉᆞ를졍부로ᄒᆞ여곰별노히틱차ᄒᆞ야불일노등졍케ᄒᆞ라

○민원자쟈 평안남도함종군으로셔샹리ᄒᆞᆫ사ᄅᆞᆷ의ᄉᆞ젼을드른즉히군에셔일본인소쳥ᄒᆞᆫ인부일ᄇᆡᆨ명을모ᄒᆞᆫ집여보낸ᄂᆞᆫᄃᆡ미명에삭젼을업젼ᄉᆞᄇᆡᆨ량식일일히츌급ᄒᆞ엿ᄂᆞᆫᄃᆡ히젼을민간에ᄇᆡᆨ렴ᄒᆞ엿ᄉᆞᆫ즉하향의빈잔ᄒᆞᆫᄇᆡᆨ셩이지보ᄒᆞᆯ수업다ᄒᆞ고민원이자쟈ᄒᆞ더라더라

○한판기인 한셩판윤은현영운씨의쳐남비셕틱씨가피임ᄒᆞ리라더라

○국교무포 군용텰도에쇼위방히조삼명을일젼에일군ᄃᆡ가공덕에셔포살ᄒᆞᆫ소건으로한셩소윤박승됴씨가일본소령관을차저가보고담판ᄒᆞ기를셜혹그사ᄅᆞᆷ들이죄상이잇더리도엇지ᄒᆞ야일차교섭도아니ᄒᆞ고즉시포살ᄒᆞ엿스니이것시무ᄉᆞᆷ국교이냐ᄒᆞ고ᄃᆡ단힐책ᄒᆞ엿다더라

○일군위문 일본군위문ᄉᆞ권즁현씨ᄂᆞᆫ도면ᄒᆞ고그ᄃᆡ에ᄂᆞᆫ민영환씨가피임ᄒᆞ엿다더라

○등ᄃᆡ소용션 졍부에셔일본신호쳔긔조션소에쥬문ᄒᆞᆫ등ᄃᆡ의소용될비광졔호ᄂᆞᆫ리십일월샹슌쏩인항에도박ᄒᆞ리라더라

○법협례임 법부협판심샹익씨소례ᄒᆞᆫ디에한셩부관윤김규회씨가피압ᄒᆞ엿더라

○구락부졔회 작일하오오시량에대동구락부를대관뎡에이셜ᄒᆞ고한일량국대관과참회인원이졔회ᄒᆞ엿더라

○렬도검찰 렬도검찰ᄉᆞ참장홍슌찬씨가렬도원검찰ᄉᆞ를피명ᄒᆞ엿더라

○슈령보쳔 각군군슈를각부대관이보쳔ᄒᆞ야셔임ᄒᆞᆫ다ᄒᆞᄂᆞᆫᄃᆡ금일에 쥬본된다ᄒᆞ더라

○ᄉᆞ령관례셜 헌병ᄉᆞ령관리지용씨ᄂᆞᆫ례임된다더라

○혹거연호 금일하오이시에일진회에셔특별회로기회ᄒᆞ고방쳥ᄭᆞ지ᄂᆞᆫ다더니젼셜옹갱문ᄒᆞᆫ즉무쌍연고인지회장과부회장이피신ᄒᆞ엿다ᄒᆞ니오놀특별회회가못될ᄯᅳᆺᄒᆞ더라

○죠칙히회 지작일에 죠칙을ᄂᆞ리셧ᄂᆞᆫᄃᆡ그ᄉᆞ의에왈ᄉᆞ방에표쥰ᄒᆞ고ᄇᆡᆨ셩을인도ᄒᆞᄂᆞᆫ거시진실노졍ᄉᆞ근본시셔에미엿ᄂᆞᆫ대짐의칙임의어려옴과긔약코힘쓰ᄂᆞᆫ거시미샹불부조련치안임이안이어놀그ᄃᆡ양ᄒᆞᄂᆞᆫ의리에맛당히ᄇᆡᆨ비ᄂᆞ책렴ᄒᆞ야긔강을썰치고엄슉히ᄒᆞ야글은거슬돌녀홍왕케할더안ᄃᆡ인슌ᄒᆞᄂᆞᆫ거스스로셩습이되고우유ᄒᆞᄂᆞᆫ거스로날을지ᄂᆡ여졍ᄉᆞᄒᆞᄂᆞᆫ거시죡히물졍을진복지못ᄒᆞ야황실긔강이썰치지못ᄒᆞ고ᄇᆡᆨ셩의ᄯᅳᆺ이안졍치못ᄒᆞ야근일에소위라ᄒᆞᄂᆞᆫ쟈가ᄯᅢ로모히고단톄가되야와언을션동ᄒᆞ야경향으로불너어리셕은무리가구름모히듯ᄒᆞ야죠졍을비방ᄒᆞ고대신을핍박ᄒᆞ야점점방한이업ᄂᆞᆫ더경에닐으되법ᄉᆞ에셔룽히그글은거슬다ᄉᆞ리지못ᄒᆞ고경무관리가그직칙을다ᄒᆞ지못ᄒᆞ고슈ᄉᆞ방관만ᄒᆞ고조졔치못ᄒᆞ니법강히ᄒᆞᆫ거시한심ᄒᆞᆫ지라그리유돌궁구ᄒᆞ면누가그칙망을맛호리오졍부와ᄂᆡ부로경부청파디방관에게신칙ᄒᆞ야방법을ᄂᆡ여형찰ᄒᆞ고효유ᄒᆞ고각기허여져도라가안업케ᄒᆞ되이럭케 죠칙ᄒᆞᆫ후에혹졍부신하가마음것못ᄒᆞ야ᄇᆡᆨ셩이일향ᄒᆞ거ᄒᆞ면맛당히법이잇스니짐은두번말ᄒᆞ지안노라ᄒᆞ옵셧다더라

○군졔기졍 군졔의졍소에셔원수부관졔를기졍ᄒᆞ야참모부라기칭ᄒᆞ고시종무관을황실죵쳑즁졀근ᄒᆞᆫ신하로션임ᄒᆞ되총장리지용씨어하면멋분이시종무관차하가되리라ᄒᆞ며의양군리지각관방장민영린공병과장민영션공병과원민홍긔졔씨가다그ᄭᆞ닥으로졍위부직이되얏다ᄒᆞ더라

○슌찰팔인 삼작일졍부회의에셔각도동학과의병을효유진압ᄒᆞ기위ᄒᆞ야슌찰ᄉᆞ를틱차ᄒᆞ기로취결ᄒᆞ고 쥬본ᄒᆞ엿ᄂᆞᆫᄃᆡ경긔도에죠경쥰 츙쳥도에졍인표 경샹남도에 리셩렬 경샹북도에 명가회 젼라남도에 안종덕 젼라북도에박졔빈 강원도에 한진창황히도에 홍우셕졔씨라더라

○착피산당 지작일ᄂᆡ부에셔각도관찰부에면칙ᄒᆞ기롤근일에동학여당이깅기ᄒᆞ기롤시작ᄒᆞ야인심을션동ᄒᆞ니관하각군에훈칙ᄒᆞ야피슈ᄂᆞᆫ잡아업시ᄒᆞ고부종ᄒᆞᆫ쟈ᄂᆞᆫ효유ᄒᆞ야안업케ᄒᆞ라ᄒᆞ엿더라

뎐보

구월구일론돈발

○쎌릐항디 클온쓰틧트에루터면동신원이보고ᄒᆞ기를작일에아황이쎌릐합디의각션쳑을슌찰ᄒᆞ엿ᄂᆞᆫᄃᆡ구월십일로브터일에극동으로향ᄒᆞ야출범ᄒᆞᆫ다ᄒᆞ엿더라

구월십일ᄇᆡᆨ림발

○합디지찰 아황이크론쓰틧트에잇ᄂᆞᆫ쎌릐합디를다시슌찰ᄒᆞ엿다ᄒᆞ엿더라

구월십일일ᄇᆡᆨ림발

○비국룬션 비리시국룬션굴론니쓰호ᄂᆞᆫ일본에방미되엿다더라

구월십일ᄇᆡᆨ림발

○로국동병 빌라와키푸와싸산파오뎃사에셔이긔군단을동ᄒᆞ엿고로국졍부에셔서로젼졍단톄의고시를반포ᄒᆞ엿다ᄒᆞ엿더라

외보

○삼년지계 로마국에셔쥬차ᄒᆞᆫ아국대ᄉᆞ가셩언ᄒᆞ야왈아국에셔일아젼졍삼년간계속ᄒᆞᆯ줄노예탁ᄒᆞ고ᄎᆞᄎᆞ그경영을힝ᄒᆞ되뎨일년에ᄂᆞᆫ려순을회복ᄒᆞ고뎨이년에ᄂᆞᆫ만쥬에셔아국외셰력을다시확립ᄒᆞ고뎨삼년에ᄂᆞᆫ젼력으로일본을습격ᄒᆞᆫ다ᄒᆞ엿더라

○아총독소직 론돈면보에왈피득보력보롤거ᄒᆞᆫ즉아국극동총독아렉시후씨가ᄉᆞ직ᄒᆞ엿다더라

광고

○본인이물니쓰씨의청탁으로대안문압려슌관〔임피리알호텔〕에셔각항즙물을본월이십팔일에공박발ᄆᆡᄒᆞᆯ터이오니쳠군ᄌᆞᄂᆞᆫ림ᄒᆞ와사가시기를희망ᄒᆞ옵 고살키 고ᄇᆡᆨ

뎨일은힝(뎨일국립은힝)
본뎜은일본동경에잇고
ᄌᆞ본금총익륙ᄇᆡᆨ이십오만원
리식은미ᄇᆡᆨ원에삼젼오리에셔
륙젼오리ᄭᆞ지인데
뎡긔훈디로계산홈
경셩뎨일은힝지졈쟝 면즁

그랜드려관〔뎡거쟝려관〕
폐관은황셩셔쇼문밧뎡거쟝근
디에잇ᄉᆞ오며일등려관이옵
려관쥬인엠벌니 고ᄇᆡᆨ

미국우션회샤와
동경동양긔션회샤
미국히션파련락ᄒᆞ얏습

향항샹히은힝
ᄌᆞ원금총익슴쳔륙ᄇᆡᆨ오십만원
본졈은향항에잇고
지졈은청국일본기타각국ᄃᆡ쳐
에잇소
인쳔셰창양힝ᄃᆡ리졈

덕국아셰아은힝
본졈은덕국ᄇᆡᆨ림에잇
지졈은항향샹히등디에잇소
인쳔셰창양힝ᄃᆡ리졈

TELEGRAM.

FROM THE CHINA REVIEW

London, Sept. 18th.

The "Daily Telegraph" states that they learn from a high Japanese official that the authorities at Tokyo are issuing a preliminary circular outlining the terms upon which they would be prepared to make peace, after the capture of Port Arthur, the occupation of Moukden, and the taking of Saghalien. They are as follows:

1. To hand over the whole of the Liaotung peninsula to China, on condition that the latter makes Port Arthur an open port.

2. An International committee to be appointed to take over and control the Manchurian Railways, purely as a commercial enterprise.

3. To have an indemnity of one thousand million yen, paid by Russia.

4. Russia to hand over to Japan all the war ships that she may have at the time in the Far Eastern Sea.

5. After the capture of Saghalien Island, Japan would be prepared to lease the same to any company, British or American, for a payment of a sum of say about fifty million yen, and a royalty on mineral and timber products.

[If this statement is correct, we are surprised to see that no mention is made of Korea in the Japanese demands. We expected to see this country figuring in a prominent position in the terms of peace. But, anyhow isn't it rather premature for Japan to be discussing terms? —Ed. K. D. N.]

London, Sept. 17.

Reuter's correspondent at St. Petersburg states that the decision of the Russian Government regarding contraband has been communicated to the British and American Emassies.

It is understood that Russia has agreed to recognise the principle that provisions are not contraband when consigned to private parties, but are only contraband when they are Government military or naval stores.—Kobe Chronicle.

BALTIC FLEET AND SUEZ CANAL.

Berlin, Sept. 18.

The European Press is discussing the question, which is regarded as acute, as to whether the Anglo-Egyptian Government will allow the Baltic Squadron to pass the Suez Canal on its way to the Far East.

Paris, Sept. 18.

H.I.R.M. The Czar has specially congratulated General Kuropatkin on his successful evacuation of Liaoyang and orderly retreat to Moukden.

Tokyo, Sept. 22nd.

The whole of the Russian 1st army corps has arrived at Mukden and been formally inspected by General Kuropatkin.

Tokyo, Sept. 24th.

A detachment of our troops near Saimachi had a brush with the enemy, composed of one company of infantry and a few cavalry with one machine gun and dispersed them. On the 20th inst. an engagement was fought near Taling against the enemy, who consisted of 1 batallion of infantry and 500 cavalry with 6 cannon and one machine gun. The enemy were defeated and lost 19 killed and a few prisoners. Our casualties were very slight.

London, Sept. 14th.

The correspondent of the Daily Telegraph at Tientsin (Mr. Bennet Burleigh) wires that the Japanese intend to concentrate their armies and advance on the open plain towards Mukden with a front ten miles long. The Japanese hold secretly but strongly all the districts northwards along the Liao River towards Hsinmintun.—N.-C. Daily News.

Shanghai, Sept. 18.

Major General Dessino has received a message from the Russian headquarters in Manchuria in the course of which the following statement is made:—Among the bullets left by the Russians at Liaoyang were some which were intended for revolvers. The Japanese have called them "dum dum" bullets because they have flat tops. At any rate all these cartridges were blank. The Russians carried away all the artillery waggons, without losing even one to the Japanese. Not even a single Russian was taken a prisoner by the Japanese.—Mainichi.

The Army reform society has decided to adopt the following resolutions, viz: 1. the war office will be entitled the "council of war." 2. Thirty relatives of the Imperial family will be chosen to act as officers of the Imperial bodyguard. In addition several other resolutions, to which publicity will be given in a few days, have been passed.

IN MEMORIAM.

A HOUSE DIVIDED AGAINST ITSELF CAN NOT STAND.

The Il-chin-hoi Society has given notice that for certain reasons its meetings will not be held for some days.

Well, well, well. At last some light has been thrown upon the mysterious source which fertilized and fostered the growth of this avowedly and apparently Utopian society.

The story is a fascinating one and at the risk of wearying our readers we have once more to bring the name of General Hyŏn and his tireless, broomstick, better half into prominence.

It seems that the indictment of himself which the Il-chin-hoi delivered itself of yesterday has created in the mind of the gallant general a serious doubt as to who is really running the show.

General Hyŏn had an interview with the Japanese Minister. Then he told the Emperor that the Il-chin-hoi society was about to die.

Hearing this, the General commanding the Japanese forces in Korea, seems to have taken umbrage. He visited Minister Hayashi and informed him that the Il-chin-hoi would not be dispersed. Mr. Hayashi said it would be as he refused to countenance insincere people (i.e. those who object to "Lady" Hyŏn and her other half). General Haraguchi said that his soldiers would see that to-day's meeting was a bumper one.

The sequel will be interesting. In the meantime the follwing item from our reporter is of interest.

"It is said, the president and Vice-president of It-chin-hoi Society have run away."

* * *

ANOTHER VIEW.

The above had just gone to press when one of our men rushed in with the following.

"Power behind the Throne" is discovered. It has trodden heavily on the corns of the diplomatic body by censuring one of their favorites. No objection to the meeting was raised by that corps until General Hyon Yong Woon was called to account by the Il Chin Hoi. Then trouble came! Mr. Hayashi requested the Imperial Japanese Headquarters to instruct (instruct this independent body of Korean patriots, mind you!) them to leave dear Hyon and (presumably) the Lady of that ilk alone. In other words, the Japanese Legation here informed Headquarters that they consider their behaviour in protecting "a crowd of Scoundrels," very unseemly and they demand the reason. To which Headquarters reply "It's none of your business anyway."

Curious thing isn't it, that the Diplomats should just have awakened to the fact that the hitherto favored Il Chin Hoi is "a crowd of scoundrels."

FROM THE OTHER SIDE.

The China "Review" publishes the following interesting account of an interview with Mr. J. F. Archibald F. R. G. S. special correspondent to "Colliers' Weekly," recently with the Russian army and now located at Tientsin.

Mr. Archieald was one of the eight Specials who were sent up from Newchwang to Moukden at the end of April last, and since then he has seen a lot; including the battles of Haicheng, Anshantien, Shosampo, Yushulin, Anping and Liaoyang. He was anxious to explain to us that, though in the early part of the campaign the Russians would not allow any Special to go to the front, yet latterly the most perfect freedom of action had been given to those who had the confidence of the authorities: until that confidence was abused. It is true, he added, that one Italian Correspondent was deported because, when his paper came back it was found that he not alone had sent for publication a lot of matter uncalled for and uncensored, but had actually had the cheek to boast as to how it was done. As a matter of fact it was and still is perfectly easy to do this. As the correspondents were only bound by their honour and not by any actual surveillance, as with the Japanese, and they are under no direct control whatever and need not have seen any censor or staff officer from the beginning of the camaign if they had not looked them up for their own benefit. They were allowed to go where and when they liked, and were often invited to dine with all the higher officers in the field whenever they were near the Headquarters. Not a dinner of the official sort, but merely a share of a soldier's fare given in a pure spirit of hospitality to a guest. Of the sixteen correspondents originally accredited to the Russian Army, there were only four to whom this sense of absolute freedom did not apply; and this was simply from the fact that they proved themselves unworthy of the trust put in them. One, as already mentioned, was deported, and three deserted to the Japanese or homeward; fully proving that the Russian officials had judged the men correctly. Coming more immediately to the course of the campaign and the details of the fighting Mr. Archibald bore out our view that the total number of the Russian troops at the fighting round Liaoyang was under 120,000; and was exceeded by the Japanese by at least 50,000. He also thought that the battle was a strategic victory for General Kuropatkin, as there was no doubt that he outgeneralled Marshal Oyama at nearly every-point. The Japanese showed want of generalship in not having held any troops in reserve, having thrown their entire force into the fighting line during the course of the battle; thus preventing them from taking advantage of any opening and following up any successful attacks they made on the flanks of the retiring Russian force.

(To be continued)

The Korea Daily News.

Issued at 5 P. M. daily except Sundays.

Rate of Subscription:—

Per Year,	Yen 25.
Per Quarter,	Yen 7.
Per Month	Yen 2.50

Postage in Korea not charged extra.
Postage abroad charged extra.

Advertisements, 50 sen per day for 1 inch or less.
5 yen per month per inch.
50 yen per year per inch.

All communications to

E. T. BETHELL,
Editor and Publisher.
Pak-tong, Seoul.

CENSORSHIP.

When Great Britain was at war with the Dutch Republics in South Africa, a Japanese officer was attached to the staff of the British commanding general.

It is well known that during this campaign British troops frequently met disaster owing to the enemy's foreknowledge of their movements.

The enemy needed no spies, the newspaper correspondents served their purpose. Ubiquitous, inquisitive and tireless the "special" was everywhere. He questioned and cross-questioned officers, and he listened to their gossip. He kept himself *en rapport* with the movements of the enemy, studied maps and kept his ears open. Therefore a very slight hint served to show him what was going to happen next, and off went a message for his paper which, if important, reached the enemy in very short order.

This was one of the things which the Japanese military attaché impressed upon his government when he returned. The Japanese acted upon his recommendation with great thoroughness. In fact so thorough were they, that in view of recent events, it is beginning to be asked whether they were not a little bit too thoroughly thorough.

Japan and Russia are fighting. The war concerns them most, and up to a certain point either belligerent has a right to order spectators out of the way.

But only up to a certain point. Several other countries have a stake in this war, and it is to their newspapers that they look for full and particular reports of its progress. Japan did not want War Correspondents, and in order to discourage them she herself undertook to inform the world of the progress of the war by means of bulletins sent to all her consuls. These bulletins told the truth and nothing but the truth, but they did not tell the whole truth. When one man lends money to another he naturally enough insists on being kept informed as to how that other's business is progressing. He sends an inspector to examine his books and see that everything is going on satisfactorily.

This is precisely the position which the War correspondent occupies. Japan has already borrowed largely from England and America and will have to borrow much more before the war is over. There is little sentiment about a man who lends money. He insists on satisfying himself that there is a reasonable chance of his getting his money back. In this respect War Correspondents serve a useful purpose. Official reports are all very well but they are very meagre and frequently leave the reader in doubt as to which side the victory rested with. And again, as their source is not a disinterested one the public likes to have the additional testimony of independent witnesses. On this account we consider Japan's action in severely restricting the War Correspondents to be very bad policy. The censors at the front are obviously very strict. A very slight knowledge of the circumstances of War is sufficient to convince anyone that the reports coming from the correspondents with the Japanese army have been severely censored. Of course it is only right that information likely to be of use to the enemy should not be allowed to leave the camp, but much more than this has been suppressed.

For instance, we hear of very little sickness, although it is well known that in every war very large numbers die of disease. This information would be of no use to the Russians, therefore there must be some other reason for withholding it.

Other instances could be adduced, but this alone is sufficient to convince the world that Japan is not taking it entirely into its confidence. This breeds suspicion, which will have been greatly increased by the marked discrepancy between the official or censored reports of the battle of Liaoyang and those sent forward by the correspondents who left the army and sent their messages free of censorship.

It appears to us that if Japan pursues this policy she will find that those who hold the purse-strings abroad will look askance at any further requests for money, and then what will Japan do? Much as she may dislike it, Japan will ultimately have to take a leaf from the Russian book. In another column we print the story of a correspondent who was with the Russian forces. He says the correspondents were allowed full liberty. To reports sent under such circumstances, unreserved credence may be attached, but we very much doubt whether a hard-headed investing public can be much longer persuaded to pin its faith on official and censored reports.

INTERNATIONAL MOTOR-BOAT RACE.

The most important motor boat race ever held took place on the 8th August across the Straits of Dover. The weather was magnificent, and the race was favoured by a smooth sea as well as the advantages of an easterly wind. Not only was the contest, which took place under the auspices of the French Automobile Club, of an international character, but it was one in which at the same time the craft were put to a severe test. In addition to the money prizes offered a special prize was given by the President of the French Republic for the winning cruiser, while there were also challenge cups and a number of gold and silver medals. On the starting gun being fired the "Mercédès IV. and Hotchkiss" immediately took the lead, closely followed by Mr. S. F. Edge's "Napier Minor." Five minutes after the start the leading boats were only distinguishable by a white speck of foam. "Mercédès" IV., the French boat, owned by M. Vedrine, much larger than Mr. Edge's, won easily. "Napier Minor" was second, and "Princess Elizabeth" (M. Pinnez, Belgium), third. The time occupied by "Mercédès" IV. was just under 65 minutes, a little over 20 knots an hour.

The International Commission for the British International Cup for Motor Boats has decided against Mr. Edge's victory on "Napier Minor" in the final for the Harmsworth Cup, on July 30th. The Commission, having carefully studied the rules under which the race was run, upheld the French protest, and awarded the race to the "Trèfle-à Quatre.

A PRISONER INTERVIEWED.

The chefoo "Daily News" reports that Mr. Isaeff, a merchant of Port Arthur, whose capture and detention by the Japanese fleet was mentioned in these columns September 21st, has arrived in Chefoo. It will be remembered that he was taken prisoner by a Japanese torpedo boat, the other members of his family who accompanied him being allowed to proceed to Chefoo.

Mr. Isaeff states that he was taken to the Japanese flagship "Mikasa", blindfolded, and was there put into confinement until examination by an admiral who, he says, was not Togo. He was questioned closely by his captors as to the situation in Port Arthur, the questions indicating that his interrogators possessed little knowledge of what is going on in the city which is now the object of their energetic attacks, demonstrating an eager curiosity on their part as to the effect of their past operations there.

He was informed, incidentally, that the Japanese were preparing to continue the assault on September 20th; that they have mounted twenty 28 centimetre guns on the works which they are constructing before the Russian line of defences; and that the capture of the city was a question of but a few days.

After a "Sweat-box" invesgation lasting for some little time, he was allowed to depart. He was treated courteously, but was subjected to a cross fire of questions.

An Imperial Edict has been issued ordering all malcontents, under threats of punishment, to return quietly to their homes. The Tonghak rumours are responsible for this command.

To the accompaniment of many "Banzas the Korea-Japan club was formally opened yesterday. The house and gardens of the property, until recently, used by the Japanese army Head Quarters, was gaily decorated with bunting and lanterns while a crowd of prospective club members celebrated the occasion until a late hour.

The Il Chin Hoi patriots seem to have, for once, turned their attentions to a worthy cause. General Hyon Yong Woon has come under their displeasure and was recently the recipient of a letter showing that some of his actions and his presence in high official circles were distasteful to the Il Chin Hoi. A deputation waited outside the Palace, where the general was located, and on his appearance assumed quite a threatening attitude, but the police surrounding the general's chair, dispersed them with a few blows.

A game of baseball was played on Friday between the U. S. Marines and a team composed of missionaries. The match resulted in a win for the marines by three runs, the score being 17 to 14 in their favor. Although the play could hardly be described as first-class, it is interesting to see that sport is not quite dead in Seoul and we hope that this trial game will be the prelude to others more frequently. The parade ground near the East Gate although rather rough and uneven, makes not at all a bad place for games of any description.

By an untoward coincidence the French navy in two of its most important dockyards, St. Nazaire and Toulon, has been the victim of disastrous fires. The famous Vaubad docks have been destroyed. Built in 1680, they formed an essential feature of the Toulon. Many of the workshops and sections are completely destroyed. The fire is said to have been due to an electric short circuit. No cause, on the other hand, is assigned for the conflagration at St. Nazaire. It was at first stated that several of the more important plans for the construction of new vessels for the French fleet had disappeared, but later reports affirm that there were duplicates of these plans and that work will not be delayed in the battleships in question.

The Korea Daily News.

VOL. I, MONDAY, SEPTEMBER 26, 1904. No. 60

HONGKONG & SHANGHAI BANKING CORPORATION.

Paid-up Capital.................$10,000,000
Reserve Fund:—Sterling Reserve... 10,000,000
Silver Reserve..... 7,000,000
27,000,000
Reserve Liability of Proprietors... 10,000,000

HEAD OFFICE, HONGKONG.

London Bankers, London and County Banking Company Limited.

Branches and Agencies, London.

Amoy,	Hankow	Penang,
Bangkok,	Hiogo,	Rangoon,
Batavia,	Iloilo,	Saigon,
Bombay,	Lyons,	San Francisco,
Calcutta,	Manila,	Singapore,
Colombo,	Nagasaki,	Sourabaya,
Foochow,	New York,	Tientsin,
Hamburg,	Peking,	Yokohama,

Credits granted on approved Securities, and every description of Banking and Exchange business transacted.

Drafts granted on London and the chief Commercial places in Europe, India, Australia, America, China and Japan.

HOLME RINGER & Co., AGENTS, CHEMULPO.

ON CHEONG & CO., SEOUL.

GENERAL STORE KEEPERS.
Imported provisions, Cooking Utensils Crockery, etc.
FRESH BREAD DAILY.

MITSU BISHI DOCKYARD & ENGINE WORKS, NAGASAKI.

CODE WORD, "DOCK."

A. 1, A. B. C., and Engineering Codes used.

DOCK No. 1 (at Tategami).

Extreme Length..............523 feet
Length on blocks............513 ,,
Width of Entrance on Top......89 ,,
,, ,, Bottom....77 ,,
Water on Blocks at Spring Tide 26½ ,,

DOCK No. 2 (Mukaijima).

Extreme Length..............371 feet
Length on Blocks.............360 ,,
Width of Entrance on Top......66 ,,
,, ,, Bottom 53 ,,
Water on Blocks at Spring Tide 22 ,,

PATENT SLIP (at Kosuge).

Can take vessels up to 1,000 tons gross.

THE WORKS are well equipped with the LATEST IMPROVEMENTS, and can execute any kind of work in SHIPBUILDING and MARINE ENGINEERING, as well as in REPAIRING of SHIPS.

The COMPANY'S new powerful steamer OURA-MARU (712 tons, 700 I.H.P.), specially built for SALVAGE PURPOSES, and equipped with necessary gear, is always READY at SHORT NOTICE.

CHARTERED BANK OF INDIA AUSTRALIA & CHINA.

INCORPORATED BY ROYAL CHARTER 1853

HEAD OFFICES:—LONDON.

Paid-up Capital £800,000
Reserve Liability of Shareholders 800,000
Reserve Fund 800,000

Drafts granted upon all the principal places in the world and every description of Exchange and banking business transacted.

E. MEYER & Co., Agents, Chemulpo.

E. MEYER & CO. Chemulpo.

SOLE AGENTS IN KOREA FOR:
A. T. Morse, Sons & Co's "Fresco" Distemper

In all colours ready for use on walls, Ceilings etc.

and

AVENARIUS CARBOLINEUM

A wood-preserving and antiseptic oil preparation

Against decay, dry-rot, fungus and wood-destroying insects.

A large supply always in Stock. Prices upon application.

E. MEYER & Co., Chemulpo.

LAW UNION & CROWN INS. CO.

Fire risks accepted at Current rates, on go downs, merchandise, dwellings, and other property, subject to usual conditions.

HOLME RINGER & Co., Agents, Chemulpo

THE METHODIST PUBLISHING HOUSE,
Little West Gate, Seoul.

JOB PRINTING, TYPEWRITER PAPER
CARBON PAPER, VISITING CARDS
STATIONERY, BOOK BINDING
BOOK PUBLISHERS
AMERICAN SCHOOL BOOKS
SPENCERIAN COPY BOOKS
PEN CARBON LETTER AND BILL BOOKS

S. A. BECK, Manager.

DAI-ICHI GINKO LIMITED.

(Formerly the First National Bank)

ESTABLISHED 1873

INCORPORATED UNDER PRESENT LAW 1896

Capital - - - - - - - - - Yen 5,000,000
Reserve Fund - - - - - 1,500,000

HEAD OFFICE:—TOKIO.

President: Baron SHIBUSAWA.

BRANCHES AND CORRESPONDENTS
In the Principal Cities and Towns of Japan.

Interest Allowed on
Fixed deposits 1 year - - - 6½ per cent
" " 6 months - - - 6 per cent

Special current accounts 1½ sen daily per Y 100
General " " 1 " " " 100

M. TANAKA, Manager, Chemulpo

HOLME RINGER & Co. Chemulpo.

General Merchants and Government Contractors.

Agents for the leading Banks SteamshipCompanies and Insurance Companies

Importers of Merchandise of every description.

KAMEYA & CO.

GENERAL STOREKEEPERS
Chinkokai - - Seoul
(Established 1895, Tokyo)

Confectionery, Hams, Canned Goods, Cutlery, Hirano & Tansan Water. Provisions, Gents, Furnishing goods, Toilet Articles, Travelling Bags, Tobacco, Cigars & Cigarettes Kitchen Utensils. Coffee, Biscuits.

Fresh Goods always kept in Stock.
Prices Moderate
Please come and inspect our goods.

NIPPON YUSEN KAISHA.

JAPANESE MAIL STEAMSHIP CO

DER MAIL CONTRACT WITH THE IMPERIAL JAPANESE GOVERNMENT.

European Line

Regular Fortnightly Service between Yokohama Kobe, Moji, Shanghai, Hongkong, Singapore, Penang Colombo, Port Said, Marseilles, London and Antwerp

American Line

Regular Fortnightly Service between Hongkong and Seattle, calling at Shanghai, Moji, Kobe, Yokohama and Victoria, B. C.

Australian Line

Regular weekly Service betwen Japan Ports and Australia, calling at Hongkong and Manila.
(Above Three Lines Suspended until further notice).

Shanghai Line

Weekly Service between Shanghai and Japan Ports

Korea Line

Service Kobe, Moji, Nagasaki, Fusan, Chemulpo, Chefoo, Taiku.
S. S. Babelsberg, 2181 tons.
Service Kobe, Moji, Fusan, Chemulpo, Chinnampo
S. S ARGO, S. S. Ohio.

BORDEN'S CONDENSED MILK CO.

New York, U. S. A.

ALWAYS IN STOCK
Eagle Brand Condensed Milk.
Gold Seal Condensed Milk.
Peerless (Family) Evaporated Cream.
Borden's Malted Milk.

E. MEYER & CO.
Chemulpo, Korea,
Sole Agents

ROYAL INSURANCE COMPANY,
Funds exceed £10,000,000
FIRE
AT CURRENT RATES.
LIFE
REDUCED PREMIUM.
HOLME RINGER & Co., Agents, Chemulpo.

HOTEL DU PALAIS

SEOUL.

The only first class Hotel in Seoul. Situated in the centre of the city opposite the palace.

Cuisine under the supervision of an experienced French Chef.

Well ventilated and furnished throughout.

TARIFF UPON APPLICATION

L. MARTIN
Proprietor and Manager.

大韓每日申報
대한ᄆᆡ일신보

일쳔구ᄇᆡᆨ사년구월이십칠일 (화요일) (뎨륙십일호)

본샤고ᄇᆡᆨ

본신보ᄂᆞᆫ영어와한어로셕거ᄆᆡ일츌판ᄒᆞ옵

신문가

한쟝 엽두돈오푼

일삭됴 엽두량닷돈

우표가ᄆᆡ삭닷돈

다맛돈으로밧숩

광고료ᄂᆞᆫ

긔한의쟝단과ᄌᆞ힝의다쇼로즁감ᄒᆞ되렴가로밧을터이오며오리지아녀대한사람마다다이신문을보실터이니광고내시기를원ᄒᆞ시ᄂᆞᆫ이들은우리신문샤에와셔면약ᄒᆞ심을희망ᄒᆞ옵

○발힝소 박동대한ᄆᆡ일신보샤법어학교압혜젼영국인셜필림집자리오

샤쟝 영국인 (ᄇᆡ셜)

평양 ᄃᆡ리졈

○평양효동사ᄂᆞᆫ권미보씨로우리신문관ᄆᆡᄃᆡ리인을뎡ᄒᆞ엿ᄉᆞ오니평양에계신구람코져ᄒᆞ시ᄂᆞᆫ 쳠군ᄌᆞᄂᆞᆫ히ᄃᆡ리졈에왕림ᄒᆞ와면의ᄒᆞ시옵

사고

○우리대한ᄆᆡ일신보의목뎍은대한의안녕질셔에관ᄒᆞᆫ모든뎨목에ᄃᆡᄒᆞ야ᄂᆞᆫ공평ᄒᆞᆫ변론을쥬쟝홈이라우리통신원의담보ᄂᆞᆫ신문보시ᄂᆞᆫ쳠군ᄌᆞ의게홍상보도ᄒᆞ리며편지를긔셔ᄒᆞ여주시ᄂᆞᆫ이ᄂᆞᆫ셩명파반ᄃᆡ를져어븟치시기를희망ᄒᆞ오니이거슬신문샹에긔ᄌᆡᄒᆞ라ᄂᆞᆫ거시아니오다만극히신용ᄒᆞᄂᆞᆫ즁거를삼고쟈홈이라긔쟈ᄂᆞᆫ아모긔셔던지긔ᄌᆡ홈을되각ᄒᆞᄂᆞᆫ권리를가졋ᄉᆞ나되각ᄒᆞᄂᆞᆫ리유를말홀터이오며공즁평화를문란케ᄒᆞᄂᆞᆫ듯ᄒᆞᆫ긔셔ᄂᆞᆫ의례히밧지안켓ᄉᆞᆸ나이다

●본샤셜시이릭로신문을ᄆᆡ양우례로분젼ᄒᆞ와례젼부의입의로젼ᄒᆞᆫ듯스로먼곳에ᄂᆞᆫ혹늣게젼ᄒᆞ기도ᄒᆞ며혹멋칠거슬ᄒᆞᆫ겁에젼ᄒᆞ기도ᄒᆞ며혹아니젼ᄒᆞᄂᆞᆫ곳도잇다ᄒᆞ와우리신문을ᄉᆞ랑ᄒᆞ야구람ᄒᆞ시ᄂᆞᆫ 쳠군ᄌᆞ의게ᄃᆡᄒᆞ야미우미안ᄒᆞ옵기로지금은분젼인을두고ᄆᆡ일일즉이젼ᄒᆞ며아니젼ᄒᆞ거나늣게거나ᄒᆞᆫ폐가업도록ᄒᆞ랴ᄒᆞ오니혹아니젼ᄒᆞ거나혹늣게젼ᄒᆞ거나ᄒᆞᆫ일이잇스면본샤로통긔ᄒᆞ여쥬심을희망ᄒᆞ옵

본샤광고

본샤에셔본신문뎨ᄉᆞ호와뎨십일호와뎨이십오호를소용ᄒᆞᆯ때가잇셔이에광고ᄒᆞ오니누구시던지이샹삼호즁에본샤로가다오시면ᄆᆡ쟝에ᄇᆡᆨ젼두푼식드리리다

관보

뎨이쳔구ᄇᆡᆨ삼십구호

광무팔년구월이십삼일

셔임급ᄉᆞ령

○면본직 쳔위뎨일련ᄃᆡ뎨일대ᄃᆡ향관륙군일등군ᄉᆞ ᄇᆡᆨ하진

구월이십일

○면본관 경의간림시군용텰도검찰ᄉᆞ 강홍대

○의원면본관 비셔원랑 허만필

○임홍문관시독 셔판임관칠등륙픔 김저ᄉᆞ

○승셔관임관오등 죵묘셔령 심긔셥

○임광쥬우톄ᄉᆞ쥬ᄉᆞ 셔판임관륙등 젼쥬ᄉᆞ 리병쥬

○임외국어학교부교관셔판임관륙등 구픔 김원비

○승셔관임관삼등 김포군립쇼학교교원 김현귀

○급삼급봉 광쥬우톄ᄉᆞ쥬ᄉᆞ 리병쥬

이샹구월이십일일

○이쥬일죵근신 헌병ᄃᆡ부쇼ᄃᆡ쟝륙군헌병참위 김ᄉᆞ셕

구월십칠일

○죵젼칙 휘경원슈봉관 셔학보 왕진열

구월이십일

궁뎡록ᄉᆞ

○죠왈우리나라이일본국통샹홈이가쟝오릭고근쟈에교셥이더욱돗타온지라일본국외무대신쇼촌슈티랑과궁ᄂᆡ대신면죵광현의게리화쟝을특ᄉᆞᄒᆞ라

구월십구일

○경샹북도관찰ᄉᆞ쟝승원ᄉᆞ직소 비지ᄂᆡ에민ᄉᆞ가다단ᄒᆞ니ᄉᆞ양말고곳등정ᄒᆞ라

○법부협판심상익ᄉᆞ직소 비지ᄂᆡ에소청ᄃᆡ로의시ᄒᆞ노라

구월이십일일

뎨이쳔구ᄇᆡᆨᄉᆞ십호

광무팔년구월이십ᄉᆞ일

셔임급ᄉᆞ령

○승셔관임관삼등 한셩면보ᄉᆞ쥬ᄉᆞ 리창우

팔월이십이일

○승셔관임관오등 한셩면보ᄉᆞ쥬ᄉᆞ 박진만 한셩면보지ᄉᆞ쥬ᄉᆞ 졍회진 부산면보ᄉᆞ쥬ᄉᆞ ᄇᆡᆨ티원

구월이일

○승셔관임관오등 대구면보ᄉᆞ쥬ᄉᆞ 리호필

구월ᄉᆞ일

○임법부협판셔칙임관삼등 한셩부관윤 김규희

○임시흥군슈셔쥬임관오등 륙픔 최셕민

○임ᄌᆡ산군슈셔쥬임관륙등 홍문관시독 곽 찬

○셔쥬임관이등 쥬차미국공ᄉᆞ관이등참셔관 신틱무

이샹구월이십일일

○명례식원부쟝셔칙임관삼등 텰도원부총지 최영하

○명림시셔리텰도원총지ᄉᆞ무 의졍부찬졍 권즁현

○의원면본관 농샹공부쥬ᄉᆞ 리광우

○임농샹공부쥬ᄉᆞ셔판임관륙등 심원복

이샹구월이십이일

○즁츄원의관홍슌찬ᄉᆞ직소 비지ᄂᆡ에소청ᄃᆡ로의시ᄒᆞ노라

○례식원부쟝민영린ᄉᆞ직쇼 비지ᄂᆡ에소청ᄃᆡ로의시ᄒᆞ노라

잡보

○대관대칙 본월이십삼일에일진회에셔ᄂᆡᄃᆡ리용티검ᄉᆞ총쟝현영운량씨의게ᄉᆞ직ᄒᆞ고퇴거ᄒᆞ라고공합ᄒᆞ고총ᄃᆡ위원을이명식파송ᄒᆞ엿더니리ᄂᆡ대ᄂᆞᆫ총ᄃᆡ위원을ᄃᆡᄒᆞ야졍셕ᄒᆞ고쥰책ᄒᆞ기를본대신은 황샹폐하의칙명으로ᄒᆞᆫ거시어놀ᄇᆡᆨ셩등이엇지감히거취를망령되히의론ᄒᆞᄂᆞ냐ᄒᆞ고현총쟝도대척왈ᄂᆡ의부인 졀ᄂᆡ출입이민인등의무삼샹관홀비며또셜령젼국을면당ᄒᆞ고져ᄒᆞ엿더라도아니되엿스니다힝이어놀이엇지이ᄃᆡ지란박ᄒᆞᄂᆞ냐ᄒᆞ고당쟝효샹이단불케ᄒᆞ엿ᄂᆞᆫᄃᆡ총ᄃᆡ가그집대문외에츌릭ᄒᆞᆫ죽근슈병뎡이구타ᄒᆞ여츅송ᄒᆞ엿다더라

○일회평의 삼작일에일진회에셔ᄌᆡ회ᄒᆞ고동의ᄒᆞ기를즁경의졍대신과각부대신협판의게일졔히공함ᄒᆞ야려졍도치ᄒᆞ기를권고ᄒᆞ기로평의ᄒᆞ엿더라

○군졔의결 본월이십삼일에졍부에셔회의ᄒᆞ야일간반포ᄒᆞᆫ다더라

○무도쟝신 군졔를확쟝ᄒᆞ기위ᄒᆞ야무관학도롤쟝ᄎᆞᆺ시취ᄒᆞᆫ다더라

●외괴쟝셔 ᄐᆡ천군슈죠졍윤씨롤가산쥬차일본ᄉᆞ령부에셔착거ᄒᆞ엿ᄂᆞᆫᄃᆡ그리유롤드른즉엇더ᄒᆞᆫ사롬이동씨롤향ᄒᆞ야익명셔롤ᄒᆞ기를남으로리용익을압송ᄒᆞ고북으로아라사와통졍ᄒᆞᆫ다고ᄒᆞᆫ고로일본ᄉᆞ령부에셔착치ᄒᆞᆫ지라본군ᄇᆡᆨ셩이그익미홈을셜명ᄒᆞ야의졍부와경셩쥬차ᄒᆞᆫ일ᄉᆞ령부에쟝셔ᄒᆞ엿더라

○국민회 국민회ᄃᆡ표인리즁진씨의셜회ᄒᆞᆫ취지의젼문이여좌ᄒᆞ니

현금국셰의급업홈이날노더ᄒᆞᄃᆡ국민이오히려진발홀줄을싱각지아니ᄒᆞ고셔로의심ᄒᆞ고두려워ᄒᆞ야ᄂᆡ외국인의싱명파지산이점점위험ᄒᆞᆫᄃᆡ니른즉우리국민된쟈맛당히인민샤회샹의권리롤야지ᄒᆞ고충이지심을면려ᄒᆞ야먼져ᄂᆡ치를다고외교롤돈목게ᄒᆞ야목하의샹ᄐᆡ를극복ᄒᆞ야평화안젼케홀뜻스로동지쟈졔인이지금회를셜시ᄒᆞ야긔회일조ᄂᆞᆫ양력금월이십륙일하오두시에죵로뵈젼도가로일졔히모혈거시오방금힝홀복젹은여좌ᄒᆞ니

일 황실을존즁케홈

일 관민이합심ᄒᆞ며상하가통졍ᄒᆞ야식긔와의심을버리며구익됨이업시ᄒᆞ야일졍ᄒᆞᆫ국시를확실셰움

일 외교를신즁히ᄒᆞ야린방의졍의를손실치말게홈

일 공법과국법을엄슈ᄒᆞ야ᄂᆡ외군인의안령질셔를일체로보젼케홈

일 외인을ᄇᆡ척홀싱각이잇거나혹무단히쥰동ᄒᆞ야디방에소요를닐으키고져ᄒᆞᄂᆞᆫ쟈의뜻

승계쳐지켠이나지안코롱힘삼

○귀령슈션쟝 귀관서온사ᄅᆞᆷ의말을드른즉귀관슈죠동션씨가금번에등졍ᄒᆞᆫ뒤에먼뎌이말나ᄃᆡ지ᄆᆡ닐마다들노ᄃᆞᆫ니며면면히ᄇᆡ셩을권ᄒᆞ야ᄒᆞᆨ우를도파ᄒᆞ며ᄒᆞᆨ보도쳐셰일은ᄒᆞ히과기케ᄒᆞ엿고ᄯᅩ부모쥬ᄒᆞᆷ은민ᄉᆡᆼ을위ᄒᆞᆷ이며안돈케ᄒᆞ야조곰도소동ᄒᆞᆷ이업셧고경모궁뷔령젼샹젼양을ᄌᆞ판ᄒᆞ야케납ᄒᆞᆷ으로민간에효유ᄒᆞ엿다더라

○군부주본 작야에군부에셔각군ᄃᆡ령위관을 주본ᄒᆞ엿는ᄃᆡ참령만이십팔인이오그외에위관도만타더라

○특소취향관 의학교교관김익승씨가향자 우도미령ᄒᆞᆫ셜벼와 동궁에후계실셰에입시ᄒᆞ야진후ᄒᆞ엿는ᄃᆡ효로가잇스무로취향관을 특수ᄒᆞ신고로특별약국을셜시ᄒᆞᆫ다더라

○군의국폄졔 군제의뎡소에셔군의국을폄제ᄒᆞ기로결뎡ᄒᆞ엿는ᄃᆡ군의를 주임관으로기졍ᄒᆞᆫ다더라

○아령쟉발셩 하남촌아령에셔일본인이쟉란들다는ᄃᆡ괴ᄃᆡ에돌이만히잇는지쟉발약소리가련일는더라

○진쥬동학 작작일에경샹남도관찰ᄉᆞ셩기운씨가니부로뎐보ᄒᆞ기를진쥬하동광군에동학이뒤쳐ᄒᆞ야ᄇᆡᆨ샹을젼동ᄒᆞ며일진회등문을향교에젼과ᄒᆞ기로동학일변을착슈ᄒᆞ고며당을효유ᄒᆞ야흣텃다고ᄒᆞ엿더라

○뎌괴공ᄉᆞ 외부에셔주일공관에뎐보ᄒᆞ되참서관현보운이귀국ᄒᆞ고셔임ᄒᆞᆫ참서관박졍셥으로공ᄉᆞ슈무를ᄃᆡ리케ᄒᆞ라ᄒᆞ엿더라

○죠쳥관비 외부에셔탁지부로죠회ᄒᆞ되경흥관의주외공쳔의창리와쥬ᄉᆞ회판비들셔북경도관찰ᄉᆞ외군슈의관비쥬는젼폐로관비를지불ᄒᆞ라ᄒᆞ엿더라

○리뎡셔슈쟝 외부에셔경부등쳡을등인ᄒᆞ야각항구와기시쟝에훈령ᄒᆞ기를각관인의학업과유학ᄒᆞᄂᆞᆫ것과입면ᄒᆞᆫ베와샹벌밧은자셔리뎡셔를비월오일비로슈쟝ᄒᆞ야샹송케ᄒᆞ라ᄒᆞ엿더라

○아항회령 경흥감리의보고를거ᄒᆞᆫ즉팔월십오일에아국병졍여명이본시쟝을지나며회령을향ᄒᆞ고젼진ᄒᆞ엿다ᄒᆞ엿더라

○아항쟝진 길산군슈가외부에보고ᄒᆞ되팔월일일에아병삼ᄇᆡᆨ여명이등수일명을거ᄂᆞ리고ᄉᆞ회향뎡을넘어본군ᄃᆡ경을지나여쟝진등디로향ᄒᆞ엿다ᄒᆞ엿더라

○죠쳥ᄉᆞ폐 일본공ᄉᆞ림권조씨가외부로죠회ᄒᆞ되본공관부무관졔등뎐샹랑이데셩이를군ᄉᆞ단참모쟝으로이임ᄒᆞ야불일노부임ᄒᆞᆯ뜻스로본쟝부ᄒᆞ헌령이잇ᄉᆞ니본공ᄉᆞ가ᄒᆞ회원을ᄃᆡ동ᄒᆞ엿고하직ᄎᆞ로 폐현ᄒᆞ겟다ᄒᆞ엿더라

○국민회퇴뎡 별항에긔재ᄒᆞᆫ바와ᄀᆞᆺ치셔로된다ᄒᆞᄂᆞᆫ국민회ᄂᆞᆫ회ᄃᆡ표자리중진씨가작일하오에시에뵈면도가로회졍ᄒᆞᆫ다ᄒᆞ고이게방ᄒᆞ엿더니다시게방ᄒᆞ되소코가잇셔긔회치못ᄒᆞ고후일노퇴뎡ᄒᆞᆫ다ᄒᆞ엿더라

○뎍원뎐보 작일함흥관찰ᄉᆞ가니부에뎐보ᄒᆞ되뎍원항에셔일병과아병이기젼ᄒᆞ야아병이퇴각ᄒᆞ엿스나그승픽ᄒᆞᆫ샹보ᄂᆞᆫ아직못드럿다ᄒᆞ엿더라

○뎐국뎡쥬 뎐환국에셔작일본리빅동화와젹동화의제조를뎡지ᄒᆞ고작일본리그긔소용물품을낫낫치곳징숙에봉치ᄒᆞ엿다더라

○류힝병예방 니부위싱국에ᄂᆞᆫ작일오후삼시에류힝병예방위원회를긔셜ᄒᆞ고예방ᄒᆞᄂᆞᆫ방법의론ᄒᆞ기와경비의반원을탁지부에요구ᄒᆞ기로결뎡ᄒᆞ엿더라

론셜

졈찰관의일

○괴왕에영국셔남아비리가한에잇는공화졍치ᄒᆞᄂᆞᆫ화란국으로더부러싸홈ᄒᆞᆯ세에일본관인한나ᄒᆞ히영국ᄉᆞ령부속관이되여챵샷ᄂᆞᆫᄃᆡ그ᄯᅢ에화란국에셔ᄂᆞᆫ졍담ᄃᆡ가엽셔셔각쳐신문통신원들이수반으로폐지소우탐지ᄒᆞ기에리오조케되며영국에셔ᄂᆞᆫ젹진의운동ᄒᆞᆷ을세세히알아ᄂᆡ리번헌란당ᄒᆞᆯ거슬면ᄒᆞᆫ거시기시에일본관헌은셤조회에참예ᄒᆞᆫ사ᄅᆞᆷ들의계령권도못ᄒᆞ고미야기ᄒᆞᄂᆞᆫ말들도조세히드리젹진에엿지ᄒᆞᆯ거슬미리긔별도ᄒᆞ며ᄯᅩ조고마ᄒᆞᆫ일이라도긴ᄒᆞᆫ지경이면셔ᄌᆞ로통긔도ᄒᆞ엿슴ᄋᆡ더러미사ᄅᆞᆷ은지도셔지공부ᄒᆞ엿ᄂᆞᆫ지라

ᄌᆞ긔나라로도라간후에일본졍부로셔군무토례에이일을ᄋᆡᆨ시부룩ᄒᆞ고그사ᄅᆞᆷ의경험ᄒᆞ야쳔거ᄒᆞᄂᆞᆫᄃᆡ로시힝ᄒᆞ야근리셔지라도무론ᄃᆡ쇼ᄉᆞᄒᆞ고론의ᄒᆞ여ᄒᆞᄂᆞᆫ일이만캇더니

근일일아젼쟁에도두나라에셔각각졈찰원을젼지에보ᄂᆡ여젼ᄉᆞ도긔록ᄒᆞ고ᄯᅩ다른나라에셔들도졈찰원을파송ᄒᆞ야졔회들의보ᄂᆞᆫ바와특별ᄒᆞᆫ소문ᄂᆞᆫ신문들에게ᄌᆞ쥬ᄒᆞ라고ᄌᆞ의ᄂᆞᆫᄒᆞ되유듕일본셔ᄂᆞᆫ젼수통신원은조와아니ᄒᆞᄂᆞ니이ᄂᆞᆫ다름이아니라일본셔만이불힝ᄒᆞᆫ일이잇세되면소문이루셜되여신문샹에계지ᄒᆞ야군ᄉᆞ들로ᄒᆞ야곰샹괴ᄒᆞ야일가되게ᄒᆞᄂᆞᆫ셔담에그리ᄒᆞ야일본셔ᄂᆞᆫ젼쟁형편을ᄌᆞ괴들이반드러셰샹에괴며ᄌᆞ괴나라에관ᄒᆞᆫ들의계몽보도ᄒᆞ되소위공보라ᄒᆞᄂᆞᆫ거손과연그진젹ᄒᆞᆫ바를말ᄒᆞᆷ이어ᄂᆞᆯ

일본에공보라ᄒᆞᄂᆞᆫ거슨그셜젹ᄒᆞᆫ바ᄂᆞᆫ발ᄒᆞ야포달ᄒᆞᄂᆞᆫ지라가랑한사ᄅᆞᆷ이잇셔다른사ᄅᆞᆷ블빗을줄것ᄀᆞᆺᄒᆞ면그빗쓴사ᄅᆞᆷ의ᄉᆞ업이엇더케젼보될거시며싱지어쟝ᄉᆞ문부속ᄭᅡ지라도사ᄅᆞᆷ을보니여셔라도ᄌᆞ세히살피고더ᄒᆞ본후에주ᄂᆞ니이ᄂᆞᆫ비컨ᄃᆡ량국젼쟁에젼수통신원이잇셔젼투ᄉᆞ실을탐지ᄒᆞᆷ과ᄀᆞᆺᄒᆞᆫ지라

싸홈ᄒᆞᄂᆞᆫ경ᄒᆞ기젼에일본셔영국과미국두나라에공치를쓰기로작졍ᄒᆞ엿다ᄒᆞᆫ즉필경누구던지빗준사ᄅᆞᆷ은아죵에빗을것세지다토탐ᄒᆞ엿슬터인즉이러ᄒᆞᆫ일도젼수통신원의소문탐지ᄒᆞᄂᆞᆫᄃᆡ는대단히긴요ᄒᆞᆫ일이되엿본공보에ᄂᆞᆫ이러ᄒᆞᆫ일도말아니ᄒᆞᄂᆞᆫ거손대단히잘못ᄒᆞᄂᆞᆫ일인가ᄂᆞᆫ시신문샹에ᄂᆞᆫᄒᆞᆼ샹잘되여가ᄂᆞᆫ모양으로게지ᄒᆞᄂᆞᆫᄃᆡ젼쟁빈핍ᄒᆞ야가ᄂᆞᆫ모양인즉보ᄂᆞᆫ사ᄅᆞᆷ들은실로어ᄂᆞ나라이과연승쳡ᄒᆞ야예존비잇슬ᄂᆞᆫ지아ᄒᆞᆨ이불무ᄒᆞ도다

일본셔ᄂᆞᆫ통신원들을ᄒᆞᆫ단속ᄒᆞ야졍도에코약ᄒᆞ도록만드ᄂᆞᆫ거시ᄋᆡ고곳에졈찰관들이잇셔통신원이일본군ᄃᆡ에관계만되게ᄒᆞᆫ일이잇게되면졍밀히졈렴ᄒᆞᆫ후처죄를ᄒᆞᆫ즉만일이통신원들이젹병의계동지케ᄒᆞᆫ계ᄀᆞᆺᄒᆞᆫ번을ᄒᆞ무피이되고퍼치아니ᄒᆞᆫ진뒤ᄋᆡ거손폐지ᄒᆞ니만못ᄒᆞᆫ거시

가령병ᄉᆞ쟝졸로말ᄒᆞ드ᄅᆡ도이ᄂᆞᆫ날ᄅᆡ에든지병에걸이며죽음은엽ᄂᆞᆫ비가아니어니와죽구라ᄒᆞ여야국에ᄂᆞᆫ이러ᄒᆞᆫ일을알도록ᄒᆞᆫ거시엽스되각국에셔모다일본공보를밋ᄂᆞᆫᄌᆞ리에업지이ᄂᆡ도록젼수히루탁ᄒᆞ엿스니그리ᄒᆞ면발리라도필경모를수가잇스리요

이런고로요양싸홈갓ᄒᆞᆫᄃᆡ도통신원과졈찰관들이양의로젹작ᄒᆞ야의혹이되게스리ᄒᆞ엿스니이ᄂᆞᆫ일본셔우리로ᄒᆞ야곰아라사의등록ᄒᆞᆫᄃᆡ로이후에싱ᄒᆞ게ᄒᆞ려ᄒᆞᆷ인듯ᄒᆞ니

종ᄎᆞ이왕으로ᄂᆞᆫ이러케나명ᄒᆞ고불신ᄒᆞᆫ보고ᄂᆞᆫ호말이라도밋지못ᄒᆞᆯ터이오셩ᄒᆞᆫ공보와졈렴ᄒᆞᆫ소문이라ᄒᆞ드ᄅᆡ도등히ᄒᆞᆼ샹다ᄒᆞᆫ밋어의혹이업지못ᄒᆞ리로다

뎐보

구월이십수일동경발

일본공ᄉᆞ퓌쳑

○대평로군계로 시마쟝에서동북으로십리되ᄂᆞᆫ할창부근에셔젼진ᄒᆞᆫ우리일지ᄃᆡᄂᆞᆫ구월이십일에할창에셔셔북으로팔리되ᄂᆞᆫᄃᆡ평에잇ᄂᆞᆫ뎍군의보병일즁ᄃᆡ와긔병약간과긔관포일문과밋할창에셔셔북십리되ᄂᆞᆫ삼통곡에잇ᄂᆞᆫ보병일ᄃᆡᄃᆡ와긔병오빅명ᄃᆡ포륙문과긔관포일문을공격ᄒᆞ야북방으로격퇴케ᄒᆞ엿고뎍군의시체가열아홉이오획득ᄒᆞᆫ물픔이약간이오우리ᄂᆞᆫ손ᄒᆡ가젹다ᄒᆞ엿더라

구월이십이일동경발

○로병죵가 로국데이군단젼부ᄂᆞᆫ봉텬부에도착ᄒᆞ엿ᄂᆞᆫᄃᆡ십팔일에구로팟긴쟝군이검ᄉᆞᄒᆞ엿고기타시로조직ᄒᆞᆫ비기ᄉᆞ단과각종포병단과경긔구ᄃᆡ등은련속ᄒᆞ여구동으로파견ᄒᆞᆫ다ᄂᆞᆫ확보가잇다ᄒᆞ엿더라

외보

○경긔구ᄃᆡ발향 인쳔샹보를거ᄒᆞᆫ즉본월이십이일에발ᄒᆞᆫ동경뎐에왈동부셔비리아경긔구ᄃᆡ가아라ᄉᆞ셔울괴등보에셔셔비리아로발향ᄒᆞ엿다더라

○봉쳔죵병 동보를거ᄒᆞᆫ즉동일동뎐에왈아국뎨일군단이임의봉쳔부에도착ᄒᆞ엿ᄂᆞᆫᄃᆡ아국에셔샹금보병과긔병과포병죵즁의각ᄃᆡ가봉쳔부로륙속히파송ᄒᆞᆫ다더라

○함ᄃᆡ뎡박 인쳔샹보에ᄒᆞᆫ기를동경뎐에ᄒᆞ엿스되향일에구론스탓도항구에셔발향ᄒᆞᆫ파륵지함ᄃᆡ가샹금보리항에잇셔셔라동으로향ᄒᆞᆯ모양이업다ᄒᆞ엿더라

광고

TELEGRAM.

CRUISERS LEAVE ZANZIBAR.

London, Sept. 16

The Russian auxiliary cruiser "Konea" has been reported off Vancouver.

London, Sept. 17.

It is announced that the railway round Lake Baikal will be opened at the end of this month.

London, Sept. 17.

Reuter's correspondent at Zanzibar reports that the Russian auxiliary cruisers "Smolensk" and "Petersburg" which recently received orders through the British cruiser "Forte" to discontinue molesting neutral vessels and return home, sailed on the morning of the 16th instant.

The "Forte," which, unobserved, watched the vessels steam away, saw them pass between Zanzibar and the mainland. It is believed that they may have gone south.

The steamer "Margit Groebel," which was recently stopped by the Russian cruiser "Perek" in the Atlantic, has arrived at Constantinople. A Russian officer who boarded the vessel informed the captain that nine other Russian cruisers were in the vicinity.

London, Sept. 17.

General Kuropatkin officially protests against the recent statement of General Oyama that the Japanese captured from the Russians large quantities of spoil at Liaoyang, and asseverates that only two railway trucks were obtained by the Japanese.

The General also emphatically denies that the Russians used Dum-dum bullets during the recent fighting at Liaoyang.

Full dispatches received here from both sides now enable the public to form a more just appreciation of the stupendous struggle at Liaoyang and of its results than it was possible to do from the earlier reports The non-fulfillment of the positive anticipations as to the complete cutting off of Kuropatkin's army, coupled with his successful retreat to Mukden, has checked the trend of public sentiment in England (in favour of Japan), whereof the fall in the quotations of Japanese stocks and the rise of Russian stocks is a clear indication.

[A London telegram, dated September 16th, published in the "Asahi," says the "Times" declares that in London there are no signs of the falling off in public enthusiasm towards Japan, as is supposed to be the case in Tokyo. Englishmen have never had a better chance of judging so fully the courage and the superiority of the fighting power of the Japanese as now that the detailed reports of the fighting at Liaoyang have been received. It would be interesting to know how the "Times" explains the fall in Japanese and the rise in Russian stocks if there has been no change in sentiment, from whatever cause this may have arisen.]

Berlin, Sept. 18th.

Professor Liszt, a celebrated Professor of German Public Law, who has previously expressed opinions adverse to the German official interpretation of the laws of neutrality, now states in an article in the "German Law Gazette" that the Imperial Chancellor has brought into force at Kiaochau (with regard to the dismantling of Russian vessels) exactly what he (Professsr Liszt) has always maintained to be correct international law.

The German papers strongly condemn the irresponsible attempt of the "Times" to disturb the good relations existing between Germany and Japan.

The St. Petersburg correspondent of the London "Daily Telegraph" states that an interview between the Kaiser and the Czar is expected to take place at Skierniewice, but nothing is known of this in Berlin, and up to the present no invitation to such a meeting has been received by the Kaiser.

The anti-German articles appearing in the "Times," the "Globe," "Daily Express" and "Daily Mail" are condemned by some of the leading papers in Great Britain.

London, Sept. 19.

General Kuropatkin reports that Generals Rennenkamp and Samsonoff are conducting important reconnaissances and that there has been very heavy fighting, resulting in numerous casualties.

Berlin, Sept. 19

Prince Herbert von Bismark is dead.

The "Official Gazette" contains a very sympathetic obituary notice of the Prince.

The Kaiser was deeply moved on hearing the news, his Majesty having a short time since invited the Prince to take part in the manœuvres to be held during the autumn.

[Prince Herbert von Bismarck-Schönhausen, who is a son of the late Prince Bismarck, the well-known Chancellor of the German Empire, was born at Berlin on December 28th, 1849. He has served the German Empire in various diplomatic capacities, being at one time Secretary to the German Embassy in London and later Minister at The Hague. He sat in the Reichstag as one of the members for Schleswig-Holstein, and in 1886 was Secretary of State and Assessor to the Chancellor. On his father's retirement he was provisonally charged with the direction of foreign affairs, but preferred to follow the Prince into private life. In January 1899 the Emperor conferred on him the Order of the Red Eagle, First Class. He holds the rank of Lieutenant-Colonel in the German Army. In June 1892 he married the Countess Hoyos in Vienna.]

Referring to the recent shooting of alleged Korean spies at Anju, the Kobe Chronicle remarks: "Presuming that the statement is correct, it would be interesting to know whether the Japanese operating in a country which is not their own have a right by international law to shoot natives who give information to the enemy. If so, then it would seem clear that the Russians have the same right. The position would seem to be rather unfortunate for the Koreans.

The "Eastern World," in the course of an article dealing with the "Japan mail's" repeated accusations against Germany of showing practical sympathy with Russia, remarks. "But in spite of all "diluted silliness" "the important fact remains that Germany continues to be thus constantly doubted. By whom? By a band of miserable scribblers who crawl on their bellies for a mess of Japanese pottage; who could not make an honest living in any occupation, and whom only the inordinate weakness of the Japanese Government for flattery and cajolery keeps going."

FROM THE OTHER SIDE.

(CONCLUDED.)

This retirement Mr. Archibald asseverates was absolutely an orderly one; made in ordinary marching formation, there being no confusion whatever apparent, and nothing that would suggest anything but an ordinary movement, except, of course, a number of stragglers and slightly wounded men, who plodded along in their own way towards Yentai and Moukden. To show how little confusion or excitement there was Mr. Archibald quotes the instance where he witnessed hundreds upon hundreds of the men stopping to take a swim and bath in the Taitze River, on the outskirts of Liaoyang, during the actual time of its bombardment and evacuation; and if there had been any complete rout or such confusion as the Japanese official telegrams report, Mr. Archibald thinks such an incident could not have occurred or he would have seen signs of the so-called panic-stricken retreat.

The men undoubtedly were exceedingly fatigued after seven days fighting, but the Japanese were also in the same plight. On the Russian retirement north of Yentai the troops went into bivouac for a complete rest, and have been there ever since.

With regard to the wounded, Mr. Archibald again bears out the Russian official reports already published in our columns to the effect that few if any wounded were left on the scene of the fighting in and round Liaoyang, but were all removed admirably to the base field hospitals at Tiehling and Harbin. The Russian wounded have always received the greatest consideration possible during the entire compaign; officers and men alike. Hospital trains having the special right of way even above troop and ammunition trains; and the Empress's special Red Cross train of ten carriages, perfectly fitted up, is kept regularly on duty between Liaoyang and Harbin, the time taken en route being from 3 to 4 days.

Mr. Archibald pays a special tribute of praise to the devoted work of the nurses of the Red Cross Society; describing it as "simply magnificent;" In Liaoyang, during the heaviest bombardment, one sister of mercy was killed and seven severely wounded whilst attending to the wounded men, and actually carrying them out of the firing zone.

Finally, in reply to a question, Mr. Archibald said he did not think the Russians would make any stand at Moukden, all the transports and supplies having gone north to Tieling, and everything in readiness for a further retirement of the army to that place or Harbin, if necessary.

From Mr. Archibald's observation, it would appear that General Kuropatkin was in personal command during the whole of the fighting, moving about from place to place as his presence was needed, with each corps in succession, but he spent three whole days with the 17th Army Corps on the left flank, which opposed, thrust back and defeated General Kurokis' force, in their attempt to outflank and surround the Russians.

The Korea Daily News.

Issued at 5 P. M. daily except Sundays.

Rate of Subscription:—
Per Year, Yen 25.
Per Quarter, Yen 7.
Per Month Yen 2.50

Postage in Korea not charged extra.
Postage abroad charged extra.

Advertisements, 50 sen per day for 1 inch or less.
5 yen per month per inch.
50 yen per year per inch.

All communications to
E. T. BETHELL,
Editor and Publisher.
Pak-toug, Seoul.

THE GENTLE ART OF MAKING ENEMIES.

It really seems as though Japan wants to make enemies. What the reason may be we cannot imagine, but with an extra-ordinary perversity she seems bent on antagonizing all her would be friends.

Of the position in Korea we have written so often that our readers must be tired of the subject. At the outbreak of war the Koreans manifested a lively sympathy with Japan and the cause for which she was fighting. Had this feeling been encouraged, Japan could have relied upon Korea for all the assistance it was in her power to give and yet, during the few months in which the war has been in progress, she has by a series of diplomatic blunders, completely alienated the good will of all disinterested Koreans.

Japan has suddenly become very suspicious of Germany although we can see very little ground for such an attitude. On this subject we quote the following from the "Eastern World."

"It must be remembered, we are told, that in view of the events of 1895, it must be expected that Germany will be seen in the Russian camp at the conclusion of the war. Well, we must say that if the Japanese Government would like to see her in the Japanese camp, both it and its "friends" go the wrong way about it, for the Japanese press and the press abroad, in so far as it has come under the influence of Japanese Legations and Japanese emissaries abroad, have left nothing undone to offend Germany, her ruler and her people and to thus alienate German sympathies. Let the Japanese Government once stop the supplies of that anti-German agitation, and then notice the change in the tune of its most ardent admirers."

Here is another instance of Japan deliberately sacrificing her friends. When the war broke out the Germans resident in Japan came forward in the most liberal manner and evidenced their sympathy with the Japanese by subscribing largely to the various relief funds. Forgetting all this and with exasperating perversity the Japanese press cannot at present find language too strong expressing its opinion of Germany. If Japan's complaint is that Germany has sold a few ships to Russia, she must remember that Russia has never, from anyone, received even a fraction of the support, moral financial and practical, which Japan has received from Great Britain.

That the War Correspondents are a long-suffering body of men is demonstrated by the fact that there are still some of them with the Japanese forces. Everyone admits that they have been treated very badly, but most people seem to say that the way their time was wasted in Tokio was due to indecision and vacillation on the part of the authorities, and not to intentional discourtesy. The same excuse cannot, however, be made for the uncivil behaviour of a Japanese officer mentioned in an article by Gordon Smith which appears in another column.

How it all happened does not really matter. The fact remains that Japan has wilfully deprived hereself of the friendship of a number of influential men.

This succession of quarrels leads us to wonder with whom Japan will fall out next. The "Retshitelny" incident had all the makings of a quarrel with China, and there are potentialities about the Hunhutses should they ever get beyond the control of their Japanese leaders.

ON THE HIGH WAY.

BY J. GORDON SMITH IN THE CHINA REVIEW.

The kaolin hid it—the kaolin hides everything. Bennett Burleigh had been riding a man-eater, a Korean pony that was bred from a race of ponies that were not fit mounts for a man who did not swear. He had bought a Chinese pony at Kaiping as a remount. A Chinese got one hundred and fifty dollars, and the burly correspondent owned a second horse for a day. Thereafter the kaolin hid it. At Yangchiatun the "Daily Telegraph" correspondent awoke in the early morn and called the faithful George, the same being a Japanese, to saddle the Chinese pony. George was making ready when the pony heard the neigh of a broken pack-horse—daily hundreds of sore backed beasts, ruined by men who know no more about horses than they do of truthfulness—and the pony went. It strolled into the kaolin. The big correspondent swore noisily and George and Matsuoka, the interpreter who usually seemed to imagine himself a Prime Minister, performed flanking movements that were as futile as Kuroki's. Burleigh chased in the rear. But the pony refused to be caught, and eventually the correspondent mounted the beast that bit me—I know this from bitter experience—and came on, leaving George to capture the runaway pony. The camp had been set three days in a filthy compound at Haicheng when George arrived.

"Hello George," shouted the lusty correspondent—he was never known to whisper—"you got the horse, didn't you?"

"I am very sorry," said George, he being a Japanese. "The pony went over the hill."

"You———". Here there is an intermission, for it is well to draw a curtain over what the correspondent said to George. This I know, though; it was a picturesque, if unpoetic flow of language.

"He has gone over the hill"—Melton Prior chuckled at the thought, and a younger man at the end of the table wondered if the pony had found its way back to a stable at Kaiping.

But I would like to be able to command such a flow of language as that which welcomed George.

"The foreign correspondents will start at 4 P.M., instead of at 7 A.M. 'as previously arranged.'" There was no reason for the delay, other than that a junior officer had given the first order without consulting the grey-haired Colonel of the Chinese carts—I mean the commissariat corps. Just to show his authority the Colonel delayed the unfortunate eighteen correspondents. Their coming to Kaiping had been far from pleasant. When one rides for ten hours with rain teeming, with mud reaching to the saddle girths, and water holes to the saddle top, with mud splashing like an unwelcome shower bath, one does not like to journey three miles further, that a card may be left on the holder of the local bunch of red tape. We did not like it, but there was no help for it. Unless we went to the station we could not find the camp—and to camp elsewhere than the arranged place would be a sin against a nation. And at nightfall many worn writers jogged and slipped in rutted roads, that now were bogs, seeking a gate in the north wall of Kaiping. I wonder yet if we were directed to the north wall because there was no gate in it. Half way around the crumbled walls with their cranellated tops, we found a gate, and ultimately we lodged before midnight, wet and miserable, in the "Meeting Place of the three long Rivers," so called because there are no rivers there. In the morning we divested ourselves of our wet clothes, and sat in the garb of Manchu coolies until the carts came up. And at 4 P. M. next day the unfortunates went out upon the road. That commandant turned the rain on us soon after we went. It must have been him, else why did he keep us back while the sun shone?

That was another night of misery. We were lost and very wet—externally. At midnight we had been riding along a marshy road with kaolin fringing it, and pits at the edge to make our horses stumble, and there was a light ahead. It was a wayside railway station and there were Japanese soldiers there. We were saved. But first there was a river to cross. Its banks sloped quickly. Burleigh had crossed. I was following, Melton Prior was behind me. I heard his clumsy pony floundering, and heard a splash. The veteran was down, his horse rolling on top of him. It seemed as if he would be drowned, but Grant Wallace and Fred Whiting were into the stream to his assistance at once, and they saved the artist, who was pluckily fighting to get his mount up. There is nothing wanting in the veteran, and he stuck to his beast. Yet, methinks, he might have got more water down his throat than usual if Wallace and Whiting had not plunged in. Meanwhile the sentry and the interpreters were asking regarding the health of the relatives on either side to the fifteenth generation. They are a very polite people! Finally a guide came with a lantern—and galloped off. He was soon out of sight and, in little sections, eighteen tired correspodents scattered to wake villagers and secure a resting place on the k'aug. And all the while the rain fell heavily.

To be continued.

THE MISSING FRENCH OFFICER.

The French Vice-Admiral on this station announces that he will pay a reward of five thousand Mexican dollars to anyone who will give information enabling him to definitely ascertain the fate of Commander de Cuverville who left Port Arthur by junk about the middle of August and has not since been heard of.

The Mint has suspended operations for a few days.

A report from Gensan states that an engagement between the Russians and Japanese, near Hamheung, is imminent.

Mr. Hyon Po Woon, has been recalled from the Korean Legation at Tokyo. Mr Pak Chung Sun, the secretary, will be "chargè d'affairs."

It is said that through the influence of General Hyon, Mr. Hong Sun Chan will be appointed to the vacant post of Governor of Seoul.

Mr. Ho Wi, Assistant Councilor of state and Mr. Yi Chai Kak Minister of Education are to leave in a few days, on a visit to Japan.

Generals Min Yong Whan and Kwon Chung Hyun are to be the bearers of a sympathetic message to the Japanese army in Manchuria.

The Japanese have issued at Liaoyang paper money in denominations of ten, twenty and fifty cents each, payable after the end of the war. The people are very unwillingly taking this money.

The Korea Daily News.

VOL. I, TUESDAY, SEPTEMBER 27, 1904. No. 61

大韓每日申報

대한ᄆᆡ일신보

(뎨륙십이호) (슈요일) 일쳔구빅사년구월이십팔일

본샤고빅

본신보는영어와한어로셔계리일출판ᄒᆞᆸ

신문가

한쟝 엽뎐두돈오푼

일삭됴 엽뎐량닷돈

우표가ᄆᆡ삭닷돈

다맛돈으로밧ᄉᆞᆸ

광고료는

귀한의쟝단과ᄌᆞ항의다쇼로ᄎᆞ갑ᄒᆞᆫ뢰금가로밧을터이오며오리지아녀대한사람마다다이신문을보실터이니광고내시기를원ᄒᆞ시는이들은우리신문사에와셔뎡약ᄒᆞ심을희망ᄒᆞᆸ

○발힝소 박동대한ᄆᆡ일신보사 법어학교압헤 젼영국인셜필림쟝자리오

사쟝 영국인 (비셜)

평양 티리졈

○평양효동사는권ᄆᆡ보씨로우리신문관리티리인을뎡ᄒᆞ엿사오니평양에계신구람코자ᄒᆞ시는 쳠군ᄌᆞ는히티리졈에왕림ᄒᆞ와면의ᄒᆞ시옵

샤고

○우리대한ᄆᆡ일신보의목뎍은대한의안녕질셔에관한모든ᄃᆡ목에ᄃᆡᄒᆞ야는공평한번론을주쟝홈이라우리통신원의탐보는신문보시는쳠군ᄌᆞ의게ᄒᆞᆼ샹보도ᄒᆞ리며편지를귀셔ᄒᆞ여주시는이는셩명과번디를젹어붓치시기를희망ᄒᆞ오니이거슨신문샹에긔ᄌᆡᄒᆞ란거시아니오다만구허신용ᄒᆞ는증거를삼고자홈이라긔ᄌᆡᄒᆞ는아모긔셔던지긔ᄌᆡᄒᆞᆷ을퇴ᄎᆞᄒᆞ는권리를가젓스나퇴ᄎᆞᄒᆞ는리유를말ᄒᆞᆯ터이오며공중광회를문란케ᄒᆞ는듯ᄒᆞᆫ긔셔는의례히밧지안켓ᄉᆞᆸ나이다.

●본샤셜시이리로신문을ᄆᆡ양우례로분젼ᄒᆞ와례젼부의일의로젼ᄒᆞᆫ듯ᄉᆞ로번곳에는ᄒᆞᆨ늦게젼ᄒᆞ기도ᄒᆞ며ᄒᆞᆨ멋쳘거ᄉᆞᆯᄒᆞᆫ벙에젼ᄒᆞ기도ᄒᆞ며ᄒᆞᆨ아니젼ᄒᆞ는곳도잇다ᄒᆞ시와우리신문을ᄉᆞ랑ᄒᆞ야구람ᄒᆞ시는 쳠군ᄌᆞ의계틔ᄒᆞ야민우미안ᄒᆞ옵기로지금은분젼인을두고ᄆᆡ일일즉이젼ᄒᆞ며아니젼ᄒᆞ거나늦게거나ᄒᆞᆫ폐가업도록ᄒᆞᆯ터ᄒᆞ오니ᄒᆞᆨ아니젼ᄒᆞ거나ᄒᆞᆨ늦게젼ᄒᆞ거나ᄒᆞ는일이잇스면본샤로통긔ᄒᆞ여쥬심을희망ᄒᆞᆸ

본샤광고

본샤에셔본신문ᄆᆡ수ᄒᆞ와ᄆᆡ쟝일ᄒᆞ오와ᄆᆡ미쟝오ᄒᆞᄅᆞᆯ소용ᄒᆞᆯ배가잇셔이에광고ᄒᆞ오니누구시던지이샹졈ᄒᆞ오즁에본샤로가져오시면ᄆᆡ쟝에엽젼두푼식드리리다

잡보

○면칙각도 작일에내부에서십삼도관찰부에면ᄒᆞᆫᄒᆞ되동비가민회등문을자탁ᄒᆞ야괴란엄시경향에취집ᄒᆞ니더욱통탄ᄒᆞᆫ지라민회가발셔히산ᄒᆞᆫ슈의로조칙을봉승ᄒᆞ야면칙ᄒᆞ니금히관하각군에면칙ᄒᆞ야만일취당ᄒᆞ거든결엄히금즙케ᄒᆞ라ᄒᆞ엿더라

○순찰ᄉᆞ츅발 의정부에서내부로조회ᄒᆞ되각도순찰ᄉᆞ들분일등정케ᄒᆞ라ᄒᆞ옵신 지의를봉승ᄒᆞ엿스니순찰ᄉᆞ의인쟝과관비등졀을수숙히판비ᄒᆞ야곳등정케ᄒᆞ라ᄒᆞ엿더라

○릉임부쟝 내부대신리용틱씨는릉별이룡군부쟝을임명ᄒᆞ야호위티총관서리를피 명ᄒᆞ엿더라

○미옥엄금 면환국에서시무ᄒᆞ는기수일인샹산공시가룡산부근등문외계에가옥이십수호를미슈ᄒᆞ는디외가는샹등에룩실오원이오중하등에ᄒᆞᆨ삼원식오십원식ᄒᆞ고초가는샹등에수십원이오중하등에ᄒᆞᆨ삼십원식이십원식으로뎡가ᄒᆞ야즉젼ᄆᆡ미ᄒᆞ는고로한셩부와경무쳥에서각가쥬의게엄금ᄒᆞ기를본국졍부인허업시가옥을외국인의게방ᄆᆡᄒᆞ면엄벌ᄒᆞ리라ᄒᆞ엿더라

○봉적쳔금 교향군니셩동거ᄒᆞ는쟝우현가에젹당이돌립ᄒᆞ야각가지총검ᄒᆞ야위쳠을무수히ᄒᆞ며서돈만량을모혈에모처로가져오라고ᄒᆞ엿는티쟝씨가ᄌᆞ긔형세의불셤홈을말ᄒᆞ야만단이걸홈으로수효를감ᄒᆞ야쳔량으로뎡ᄒᆞ야작일졍오에반리져아모리로수송ᄒᆞ엿다더라

○쟝례쟝졍임 탁지대신박뎡양씨는쟝례원경을겸임ᄒᆞ엿더라

○교문관찰과 탁지교문관뢰목하면씨는이십구일에인쳔에도착ᄒᆞᆯ에정이오일본케신대신대포씨는부산셔지는동교문관과동션ᄒᆞ야온다더라

○제등중좌 일본공ᄉᆞ관부무관제등중좌는대신일ᄉᆞ단참모쟝으로젼임ᄒᆞᆫ말은임의괴직ᄒᆞ엿거니와동씨는금이십구일셰출발ᄒᆞ야모디로향ᄒᆞᆫ다더라

○순쳔군보 평안남도순쳔군슈리스즁쥬씨의내부로ᄒᆞᆫ보고를거ᄒᆞᆫ즉동학당칠빅명이둔취ᄒᆞ야일진회라칭ᄒᆞ며귀에는보국안민너ᄌᆞ로쓰고회쟝은허쥬샤는문관일이라ᄒᆞ는티우리가경도회지위를기다린다ᄒᆞ며밍샨양덕영유영원덕쳔등디각군인민쳔팔빅인이보국이민ᄒᆞᆫ다칭ᄒᆞ고소요막심ᄒᆞ기로효유ᄒᆞ여도듯지아니ᄒᆞᆫ다ᄒᆞ엿더라

○량씨유람 외정부찬졍리위와학부대신리지용량씨가유람츠로블일내에출발ᄒᆞ야일본에유람ᄒᆞᆫ다더라

○쳥쥬처변 일젼졍부회의에내부소관군슈 쥬본은각대관이공쳔ᄒᆞ야셔임용되엿자가탐도불법ᄒᆞ야빅셩의게학졍ᄒᆞ야범죄ᄒᆞ는경우에는쳔인의쳔쥬률엄벌ᄒᆞ기로의결ᄒᆞ엿다더라

○황씨방면 원산감리가외부로면보ᄒᆞ기를본서쥬ᄉᆞ황쳔연이가일본병참부에피착ᄒᆞ엿다가무ᄉᆞ이환귀ᄒᆞ엿다ᄒᆞ엿더라

관보

대미쳔구빅ᄉᆞ십이호

광무팔년구월이십륙일

셔임급ᄉᆞ령

○의원면본관 졍위 조승군 박즁샹 부위 리유인 최항졔

○임호위티쟝위 젼좌시어 신경균 좌시어 리희신

○임호위티부위 젼좌시어 리용문 좌시어 리귀원

이샹구월이십이일

○의원면경임시종원시종 궁니부참셔관 윤힝구

○경임시종원시종 궁내부참셔관 김용제

○임티복ᄉᆞ쟝셔주임관륙등 봉샹ᄉᆞ쟝 홍셩우

○임봉샹ᄉᆞ쟝 셔주임관오등 비서원승 홍승두

○임비서원승셔주임관륙등 졍삼품 오형근

○임통신ᄉᆞ면회과쥬ᄉᆞ셔판임관륙등 리용셕

○의원면본관 평흥감리서쥬슈 김상동

○임평흥감리서쥬ᄉᆞ셔판임관륙등 권평쳘

승셔판임관ᄉᆞ등 의주감리서쥬ᄉᆞ 송셩인 통신원쥬ᄉᆞ 김종만

○면직 한셩면보ᄉᆞ쥬ᄉᆞ 리원챵 대구면보ᄉᆞ쥬ᄉᆞ 리필호 구월이십삼일 통신원 궁뎡록ᄉᆞ

○동제됸령원ᄉᆞ 민영션ᄉᆞ직소비지내에소졍티로의시ᄒᆞ노라

○의정부찬졍최익현ᄉᆞ직소비지닉에다시ᄉᆞ양말고곳입ᄅᆡᄒᆞ야응명ᄒᆞ라

○의정부찬졍민병석ᄉᆞ직소비지내에ᄉᆞ양ᄒᆞᆫ즁쟝례원경의겸임만의시ᄒᆞ노라

이샹구월이십삼일

○죠왈궁내부고본관가등중웅이죵와에공ᄉᆞ로본국에오래쥬차ᄒᆞ야효로가만ᄒᆞ니특별이셔훈일등ᄒᆞ야팔괘쟝을쥬라

구월이십ᄉᆞ일

표훈원총재 죠병식

셔임

○셔훈일등ᄉᆞ팔괘쟝 의정부찬졍훈이등 민병셕

○셔훈이등ᄉᆞ티극쟝 군부대신 민영긔 원슈부검ᄉᆞ국총쟝 현영운 통신원총관훈삼등 민샹호 졍이풍훈삼등 민형식

○셔훈삼등ᄉᆞ티극쟝 혜셔원부쟝 민영린

○셔훈삼등ᄉᆞ팔괘쟝 탐도원부총제 최영하 졍삼품 민영슈

○셔훈ᄉᆞ등ᄉᆞ티극쟝 남양군슈 쟝호익 회계원출납과쟝 오인션 룩군참위김명션

이샹구월이십삼일

○셔훈일등ᄉᆞ티극쟝 일본국

시종직 간ᄉᆞ룡작 임창구 덕
황후궁대부 조작 한창경 삼
동궁대부 제등도티랑 식부
쟝남작 삼궁의윤 식부츠쟝
빅작 호면시홍 외무성츠관
진면수귀 빅쟝두 남작 도
변쳔주

○셔훈일등수괘쟝 일본국
주마두조작 등과언츙

○셔훈이등수티극쟝 일본국
식부관경유셔쳔 궁빅당 미
등뎡길 주면두 쇼림뎡무
영면시과쟝 셔면국초랑 졍
무국쟝 산좌원초랑 인ᄉᆞ과
쟝 송방졍작 쥬마두조작
등과언츙

○셔훈삼등수티극쟝 일본국
식부쥬수식등조작 도영경승
식부관 은지텬 도변직달
송평뢰천 일등통역관 염쳔
미티랑

○셔훈ᄉᆞ등수티극쟝 일본국
통군과방대위 거덕직길 봉
군보병대위 가등무 쳥포환
합쟝 즁구만지조 평양환함
쟝셔본상길

○셔훈오등수티극쟝 일본국
동경부하곡 경찰셔쟝 신거
우삼랑 경부 미포용웅 산
본젼오랑

○셔훈오등수괄괘쟝 일본국
쳔구젼마관 경찰셔쟝 경시
취등금우

○셔훈륙등수팔괘쟝 일본국
궁내성속 조창의교 산하죵
신 춍면계쟝 일본국 쥬젼
속 촌상졍지

○셔훈칠등수티극쟝 일본국
션부 궁쳔셩티랑 어자 대
셔보작 팔각츈티랑

○셔훈칠등수팔괘쟝 쟝경쳥
길

○셔훈일등수티극쟝 궁내부
교문관 가등증웅

미상구월이십ᄉᆞ일

○죠왈남자에아국보빙대ᄉᆞ가
일본에갓슬ᄯᅢ에반졉원과향응
인원들을가히포샹이업지못홀
지니쳑칙셔훈ᄒᆞᆫᄉᆞ쟝ᄒᆞ라

론셜

나의계졍원ᄒᆞᄂᆞᆫ일

○일본셔한국에되ᄒᆞ야ᄒᆞᄂᆞᆫ일
을볼진되모다시앙의가부졍ᄒᆞ야
이샹ᄒᆞᆫ평려ᄒᆞ계만ᄂᆞᆫ리원수를
빅지려ᄒᆞᆷ이엇지ᄒᆞᆫ셔닭인지를
알거셔죠과에셩챠에ᄂᆞᆫ이일이
아모ᄯᅩ룩친목ᄒᆞ계ᄒᆞ조ᄂᆞᆫ일인
지ᄯᅩᄒᆞᆫ셰닷지못ᄒᆞ겟ᄂᆞᆫ지라
이일로말ᄆᆡ아마여러번우리신
문에계록ᄒᆞᆫ니엿ᄉᆞᆫ즉응당우리
신문구람ᄒᆞ시ᄂᆞᆫ쳠군ᄌᆞ도도리
혀지리ᄒᆞ실듯ᄒᆞ되

당초일본셔기젼ᄒᆞᆯᄯᅢ붓터한국
빅셩들은그젼투ᄒᆞᄂᆞᆫ원인을싱
각ᄒᆞ고셜로감졍샹의리를표ᄒᆞ
엿거놀일본셔ᄂᆞᆫ귀젼ᄒᆞᆫ지수삼
동안에ᄌᆞ귀의권리티로방조ᄒᆞ
야의뢰ᄒᆞ계ᄒᆞᆯ만ᄒᆞᆫ일이다반외
교상에크계고로계ᄒᆞᄂᆞᆫ일로만
차차로힝ᄒᆞ야모ᄯᅩ룩한국사
ᄅᆞᆷ의계ᄂᆞᆫ리치안ᄒᆞ로룩주의ᄒᆞᆷ이
실로젼교ᄒᆞ란ᄂᆞᆫ것갓티며맛치
의홍ᄒᆞᄂᆞᆫ덕국에힝ᄒᆞ든티도와
ᄒᆞᆷ사ᄒᆞ기로우리ᄂᆞᆫ오날날이문
데를동양셰계라ᄒᆞᄂᆞᆫ칙으로붓
터말ᄒᆞᄂᆞᆫ도다

우리의이말ᄒᆞᄂᆞᆫ거슨가취괴이
ᄒᆞᆷ만ᄒᆞᆫ일인거시일쳔팔빅구십
오년ᄉᆞ졍을본즉덕국셔ᄂᆞᆫ아라
사진중에잇셔셔싸홈걱국되ᄂᆞᆫ
거슬본다ᄒᆞ엿ᄂᆞᆫ지라만일일본
셔덕국으로ᄒᆞ여곰싸홈보ᄂᆞᆫ거
슬조계명며쓸것갓ᄒᆞ면필경
로조치아니ᄒᆞ계되엿슬거시오일
본사ᄅᆞᆷ의평반홈과외국에잇ᄂᆞᆫ
일본공ᄉᆞ들의위럭으로덕국에
힝치아니ᄒᆞᆯ리홈이엇셔슬리인고
로덕국의주권ᄒᆞᄂᆞᆫ사ᄅᆞᆷ과모든
빅셩들은감졍을염졀ᄒᆞ엿다ᄒᆞᆫ
즉만일이제일본셔덕국의동죵
ᄒᆞ계명이ᄂᆞᆫ마음을업계ᄒᆞᆯ진티
가쟝수단잇ᄂᆞᆫ사ᄅᆞᆷ이ᄒᆞ번으로
돌니게ᄒᆞ여야ᄒᆞᆯ리이며

ᄯᅩ달니말ᄒᆞ리ᄂᆞᆫ도일본셔쳥구
의계ᄒᆞᄂᆞᆫ이을긍히셩각ᄒᆞ며야
ᄒᆞᆯ거시싸홈시작ᄒᆞᆯᄯᅢ에도일본
에잇ᄂᆞᆫ덕국사ᄅᆞᆷ들이일본으로
더부러감졍표ᄒᆞ기를위ᄒᆞ야리
금을구취ᄒᆞ야보조ᄒᆞ지ᄒᆞ엿스
되일본셔ᄂᆞᆫ미리ᄒᆞᆫ은혜를나잇
고퓌리ᄒᆞ계분거ᄒᆞ도록만ᄒᆞ기
ᄂᆞᆫᄒᆞ나덕국의욕향ᄒᆞ두ᄂᆞᆫ일을아
직져지도신문샹갓ᄒᆞᆫ티ᄂᆞᆫ농히
젼쟝ᄒᆞ야확실히말ᄒᆞ지ᄂᆞᆫ못ᄒᆞ
ᄂᆞᆫ지라

일본셔불평이ᄋᆡ이ᄂᆞᆫ마음은무
엇인고ᄒᆞ면덕국이아라사와계
빅두어젹을과랏다홈으로그러
홈이로되이거슨당초에그리치
아니ᄒᆞᆫ거시어ᄂᆞᆫ사ᄅᆞᆷ이든지셜
샹보존ᄒᆞᆫ일을[illegible]잇계되면일본셔
ᄂᆞᆫ영국에계의뢰히방조홈을바
다쓸리이로다

ᄯᅩᄒᆞᆫ젼수등신원들은젼쟁수실
리록ᄒᆞ기만위ᄒᆞ야이리케오리
도록일본에엄제홈을밧으며셔
신고들을ᄒᆞ되아죡도멋사ᄅᆞᆷ이
잇ᄂᆞᆫ지라이사ᄅᆞᆷ들은일인의팔
티홈을용납ᄒᆞ야밧기ᄂᆞᆫᄒᆞ고셰
월만랑도ᄒᆞ며아모일도분명히
ᄒᆞᆫ거슨엄스되니무례ᄒᆞ계홈을
실로아지못ᄒᆞ며그러홈이아니
라

평경에ᄂᆞᆫ일본관리의불법ᄒᆞᆫ힝
위들용셔ᄒᆞᆯ리가엄ᄂᆞᆫ죵이라ᄒᆞᆫ
일로보다참졍ᄒᆞᄂᆞᆫ사ᄅᆞᆷ의우의
들ᄉᆞᄉᆞ로엄계ᄒᆞᄂᆞᆫ거시졈졈시
비들만ᄂᆞᆫ리ᄂᆞᆫ후에일본셔크계
젼ᄒᆞᆯ들당ᄒᆞᆯ티인증이번에아라
사로젼쟁우리샤ᄂᆞᆫ리해연티에셔
젼홈으로청국에계젹칙ᄒᆞᆫ것
도며시셔비를뮈지려ᄒᆞᄂᆞᆫ일인
죡셰계에유력ᄒᆞᆫ사ᄅᆞᆷ들이야엇
지일인의ᄒᆞᄂᆞᆫ티로관찰ᄒᆞᄂᆞᆫ밋
히잇ᄉᆞ리오

뎐보

구월십ᄉᆞ일론돈발

○즁가병력 로국참모부에셔
말ᄒᆞ기를구로팟긴쟝군은묘양
젼쟁이후에이귀수단과대포샹
빅문으로병력을증가ᄒᆞ엿다더
라

구월십오일론돈발

○로군수샹 구로팟긴쟝군이
뎐보ᄒᆞ기를괄월이십팔일브터
구월오일ᄭᆞ지로군의수샹ᄒᆞᆫ즉
은자가수쳔명이오샹ᄒᆞᆫ자가일
만이쳔명이라ᄒᆞ엿더라

구월십ᄉᆞ일론돈발

○아력시후 아력시후츙독은
랍쓰돌후빅쟉의후임이되여셩
피득보로도라간다ᄒᆞ고그이쳔교
들이말ᄒᆞᆫ다ᄒᆞ엿더라

구월십ᄉᆞ일론돈발

○로쟝퇴로 모링포쓰트신문
에운ᄒᆞ되로국에셔론돈으로보
변공보들계ᄒᆞ죠로쟝쓰셀니빗
치쟝군은최하에ᄒᆞ비병오쳔명
을거ᄂᆞ리고로양비북ᄒᆞᆫ하남방
에셔싸화중샹ᄒᆞ고병즁샹뵈명
으로퇴브리포로가되엿다ᄒᆞ엿
더라

구월십오일론돈발

○셔쟝란환 미왕에일로랑군
과경쟝목양에잇든셰일리셰리
고라푸등신원들이셔쟝란환ᄒᆞ기를
로군이셔쟝란환을쎗다홈은덕
확ᄒᆞᆫ증거가엄다ᄒᆞ엿더라

잡보

○학교조문 작일샹오에셔방
에일본순사ᄒᆞ명이광북ᄒᆞᆫ일인
샹명과한국녀인일명을거ᄂᆞ리
고련못골룩군참령류봉렬씨가
에리도ᄒᆞ야무샹수단인지그녀
인이갈노목젹넌셔귀지ᄉᆞ경이
라ᄒᆞᄂᆞᆫ고로회방콕순검이경무
쳥에급보ᄒᆞ엿다더라

○진퇴랑난 일젼 죠칙이ᄂᆞ
리시되이를진회가히샤이되엿고
경무쳥에셔순검을다발ᄒᆞ야
쳐마다[illegible]ᄒᆞ기로ᄒᆞᄂᆞᆫ티순검이아
쟝등리갯을낫낫치젹간ᄒᆞ야치
발ᄒᆞᆫ자ᄂᆞᆫ즁즁경외ᄒᆞ기로결엉
히신칙ᄒᆞ니무단히치발ᄒᆞᆫ자ᄂᆞᆫ
하향ᄒᆞ기도난편ᄒᆞᆫ죵경향간에
진퇴유곡이라더라

○탐셰도환 작일에등티감리
가외부로뎐보ᄒᆞ되일본레신대
신태포ᄂᆞᆫ금일샹오삼시에본항
에도박ᄒᆞ야평니에츈거로대구
를향ᄒᆞᆫ다ᄒᆞ고탐지ᄒᆞᆫ고로관찰부에셔
면은금일하오오시에본항에셔
탐션ᄒᆞ야상경ᄒᆞᆫ다ᄒᆞ엿더라

○호칭종젹 고종이풍리병우
씨와고한셩셩윤씨ᄂᆞᆫ호칭이룩
이ᄒᆞ기로니부청관과중학교교
관중직을무두엇더라

○위문탐수 일본병민주출진
군위문ᄉᆞ 민영환씨와명흥은젼
보에귀졔ᄒᆞ엿거니와외부에
셔평의ᄒᆞ야동씨ᄂᆞᆫ쳥ᄉᆞ로귀중
텽셰부ᄉᆞ로과견ᄒᆞ기로경뎡이
되엿ᄂᆞᆫ디불니로발졍ᄒᆞᆫ다더
라

○붕중필젼 원산ᄉᆞ시올ᄂᆞ로
즁향월에참ᄒᆞ셔퇴각ᄒᆞ야경셩
셩포방면으로퇴둔ᄒᆞ엿든아병
은산복쳥으로층둔ᄒᆞ리라ᄒᆞ더
라

한관임셜 ᄒᆞᆫ순쳔씨ᄂᆞᆫ헌령
운씨의츄쳔홈으로한셩관윤을
피임ᄒᆞ리라ᄂᆞᆫ젼셜이잇더라

○감리경군슈 외부에셔외경
부로쳥의ᄒᆞ되룡쳔삼리운용구
가성의셔임되야쟝ᄎᆞᆺ감리셔
시무ᄒᆞ겟ᄂᆞᆫ디히항에면젹ᄒᆞᆯ
가옥과수용ᄒᆞᆯ관세가엄스니셩
진외이왕규례들의방ᄒᆞ야히감
리로룡쳔군수를경관케ᄒᆞ야시
의에합당ᄒᆞ다고정부회의에계
출ᄒᆞ엿더라

○덕조외부 덕국공ᄉᆞ가외부
로조회ᄒᆞ되셰창양행의ᄉᆞ낭ᄒᆞᆫ
과탄환이항ᄒᆞᆼ에셔집류됨으로
귀부에티ᄒᆞ야슈입ᄒᆞᆯ셔쳥구ᄒᆞᆫ
일슈ᄂᆞᆫ셔간셰번조회에상금시
봉이엄스니심이ᄒᆞᆨᄒᆞᆫ지라원
금회문을쳑치ᄒᆞᆫ곳에셰금이발
며노증가ᄒᆞ니속히회조ᄒᆞ라ᄒᆞ엿
더라

○면쳐감군 외부에셔대구관
찰부에면보ᄒᆞ되일본레신대신
이쟝ᄎᆞᆺ귀부에도달ᄒᆞᆯ티이니영
졉과사쳐등졀ᄂᆞᆫ에비ᄒᆞ야등티
ᄒᆞ고그니ᄅᆞᄂᆞᆫ곳마다변반영졉
ᄒᆞᆯ수로관찰각군에신칙ᄒᆞ라고
ᄒᆞ엿더라

광고

THE NEW BRITISH ARMY SCHEME

In an article on Mr. Arnold-Forster's Army Scheme, the Spectator declares that the closer and the longer it is examined, "the clearer does it become that in all that concerns the Militia and the Volunteers it is founded altogether on wrong principles, and if carried out must result in the destruction of those forces. Mr. Arnold-Forster, though, of course, denying the unsoundness of his principles, would probably admit that in the case of the Militia his intention was abolition. In the case of the Volunteers, however, he is no doubt perfectly sincere when he tells us that his sole desire is to strengthen and improve them. But, admitting this to the full, what we have to consider is not the goodness of Mr. Arnold-Forster's intentions but the practical effects of his proposals. These, we believe, can have only one result, to destroy the Volunteer Force. . . . The men who are gone and going are the men who could least be spared in the regiment, as in their own work. But this process of wastage of the best men will be immensely intensified under Mr. Arnold-Forster's scheme. His plan of driving all the so-called 'efficients' into some sixty or seventy regiments, and keeping the rest of the Volunteers in battalions which will be officially earmarked as inefficient, or at any rate as of second rate efficiency, can have but one result. The picked regiments will, for the most part, be found to have shed their best men, and to have retained the men who are very little wanted anywhere, and so are able to comply with stringent regulations; while the battalions of secondary efficiency will become unpopular, as anything and everything these islands marked "Second-rate," whether justly or unjustly, rightly or wrongly, always does. In a word, Mr. Arnold-Forster's scheme, if forced upon the Volunteers, must inevitably ruin the force. If he is allowed, he will kill the Militia on purpose with one barrel, and the Volunteers by mistake with the other. That the process is called Army Reform, and the strengthening and improvement of the military resouces of the nation, will be small consolation after the deed is done."

GENERAL CRONJE AT ST. LOUIS.

The Anglo-Boer war exhibition at the World's Fair, St. Louis, in which General Cronje is the leading figure, is the largest and most realistic outdoor entertainment ever seen. It is as though twenty acres of South Africa had been carried by magic across the Atlantic and dumped down at St. Louis.

To the left is a Dutch farm sheltered by real trees. Boer children are playing about the stoep and horses are being watered at a drift close by. Here and there are those huge ant heaps so typical of South Africa.

Matabeles, Zulus, Basutos, Swazis, and Kaffirs ride wild races and go through grotesque dances, just as they do at a Rand mine on Sunday afternoons.

A representation of the capture of Colonel Long's guns at Colouso is shown. Men and horses drop until hardly one is left standing, deeds of heroism are performed, stray horses gallop wildly about. At last, with a loud cheer, the Boers, led by General Ben Viljoen, rush from rocks and kopjes and the day is won.

The battle of Paardeberg and the surrender of Cronje follows. This is also admirably depicted, and the final surrender of Cronje is dramatic in the extreme. The old Boer warrior rides up, and is assisted to dismount by a British officer. A man "made up" as Lord Roberts advances, salutes, and then as conqueror and conquered shake hands the feelings of the audience break loose in prolonged applause.

Finally is shown the escape of De Wet near Thabanchu through 50,000 British troops, wire entanglements, and block houses. The entertainment is a military tournament on a large scale, and one is brought face to face with war and all its horrors.

General Cronje, who is enjoying his stay immensely, is hale and hearty, and looks more like fifty than sixty-eight He loves to be surrounded by his men, many of whom fought under him and shared his captivity. He holds a reception at his tent every morning, but he is very glad when it is over, and he is able to take a quiet stroll with his pipe and the lady he has recently made his wife.

Lord Roberts and family have sailed for the Cape on a visit to Lord Roberts' son's grave.

Mr. Oura, Japanese Minister of Communications, is expected to arrive at Seoul, via the Fusan railway, on the 3rd proximo.

The present population of Paris is 2,715,000. The growth is comparatively slow, partly because of the military boundaries which prevent the annexation of outlying parts.

Mr. Kato, adviser to the Imperial Household, has been decorated, by His Majesty, with the 1st Order of Merit in recognition of the able manner in which he conducted negotiations, during the period in which he was Japanese Minister to Korea.

Colonel Saito has been transferred from his post as military attache to the to Japanese Legation and appointed the General staff of the 11th division. He will leave immediately for the field of operations, being relieved in Seoul by Colonel Matsuishi.

Certainly if such a misfortune as the fall of Port Arthur is in store for us, we shall bear it bravely. We shall not lose courage, and we shall have no doubt concerning the eventual outcome of the war: but this disaster will wound us grievously, and long and deeply shall we suffer from it. This is a truth which we must all confess, and which it is not worth our while to conceal from the world.—Russ, St. Petersburg.

The poor countrymen, who recently wasted their substance on much hair-cutting operations, appear not only to have made themselves look very foolish, but have also laid themselves under the suspicion of the authorities. An Imperial edict having been issued ordering the societies to disperse, the police have opened the ball by expelling the gentlemen of shaved crowns and empty pockets, from the city.

The Nichi Nichi correspondent at Moji has sent the following information to that paper:—On the 4th inst., at about 9.30 a. m., while Lieutenant-General Hamilton and others were proceeding northward from Kokuintai, near Liaoyang, a mine or shell suddenly exploded in front of the Lieutenant-General, with the result that his three servants and two horses were instantly killed and his baggage was destroyed. Fortunately, the General himself escaped without injury.

The experience of Tirah and South Africa have evolved a new type of British soldier. Gone has the stiff and upright soldier-man—the automaton—whose business it was to obey and not to think. In his place we have quite a new kind of warrior, something of the Red Indian, with his stealthy creepings, stratagems and ambuscades, something of the ferret ever digging and building, something of the Twentieth Century man, carrying in his hand the magazine rifle, the latest word of science on the art of killing.—Englishman, Calcutta.

Mr. Yi Young Tai, the Minister of the Home Office, has been appointed Lieut. General in the army.

The Military Reform committee are said to have been very busy recently and have finally decided to adopt the following measures :—

1. the establishment of a War Council, Training Bureau, and the appointment of the officers of the Imperial Bodyguard.

2. A reduction in the number of troops, which is to be effected by dismissing all old and very young soldiers.

3. The establishment of an Arsenal.

There is no such thing as an Imperial sentiment in London. There is not even patriotism. In the eyes of the Londoner the British Empire extends from the Bank to Shepherd's Bush—the eight miles that are covered by the Tuppenny Tube. As for England, that is one of London's dependencies, and in various corners of the globe he is aware that there are a number of spots, useful in this insignificant way to the Tuppenny Tube empire, which he lumps together in the generic term of "The Colonies."—Sydney Bulletin.

A London correspondent of the S.-C. Morning Post learns from Kiel that during the coming Autumn the torpedo-boat training flotilla of the German Navy will be increased considerably. Instead of three small torpedo-boats, one division-boat and two "S" boats will undertake the training of torpedo crews both at Kiel and at Wilhelmshaven. Thereby the carrying capacity available will be increased from 510 tons to 1,040 tons, and the crews from 90 to 150 men. Moreover, one torpedo-boat is to be attached to the Baltic station at Kiel, and also to the North Sea station, for the purpose of giving naval officers practical instruction in navigating that type of craft.

WIRELESS TELEGRAPH LAW.

When wireless telegraphy has gone beyond the experimental stage, no doubt it will be added to the Government monopolies of the telegraph and postal systems. But the Post-Master-General's Bill introduced into the House of Commons a few weeks ago does not propose this. The most interesting feature of this new method of transmission is that messages can be interfered with, and this fact will have to be taken into account in granting licences to the various syndicates and companies proposing to operate. They will have to be divided up into spheres of influence, and Government will require many powers of regulation which it has not at present. As the difficulties about wireless telegraphy have shown during the Russo-Japanese war, there may even be political dangers in unregulated transmission of these ethereal messages. Where the installations go beyond the United Kingdom or the three mile limits, there might be breaches of neutrality in case of war which would involve Government in responsibility. Yet says the "Saturday Review," there exists no power of control under the Common Law, or perhaps it would be better to say it needs better definition to meet such a remarkable development as wireless telegraphy; and this the Government Bill proposes to do.

The Korea Daily News.

Issued at 5 P. M. daily except Sundays.

Rate of Subscription:—

Per Year.	Yen 25.
Per Quarter.	Yen 7.
Per Month	Yen 2.50

Postage in Korea not charged extra.
Postage abroad charged extra.

Advertisements, 50 sen per day for 1 inch or less.
5 yen per month per inch.
50 yen per year per inch.

All communications to

E. T. BETHELL,
Editor and Publisher.
Pak-tong, Seoul.

THE IL-CHIN-HOI AND THE NAGAMORI SCHEME.

The Il Chin-hoi has been dispersed by the order of the Emperor.

All previous attempts of the Korean police to interfere with the meetings of this Society have been frustrated by the Japanese, and so the logical conclusion is that the success of the Koreans in at last dispersing their meetings is due to the withdrawal of Japanese protection.

In our issue of August 26th, speaking of the Society, we said;—

"Its objects as set forth in a letter to the Government are as follows;—

1. To honour the Imperial House and make firm the foundations of the nation. (The committeeman in charge of this is Mr. Sŏ Sang-nyun).

2. To protect the lives and property of the people. (Mr. Yang Djai-ik responsible).

3. To reform the government. (Mr. Kim Myŏng-june in charge).

4. To correct military and financial affairs. (Mr. Yŏm Jung-mo in charge).

These aspirations are very laudable indeed but they seem very vague and Utopian and there is little probability of the society ever accomplishing anything."

At the same time we called attention to the fact that this society's claim to protection lay in the protection which it was receiving from the Japanese Authorities here.

However from August 26th until September 22nd the Il Chin Hoi apparently did nothing. A number of secret meetings were held but their public proceedings were of no importance. They sent memorials to various ministers, but the memorials were of a character tending only to excite derision in the minds of the uninitiated. Apart from this, on the surface, they did nothing.

From the first we have been assured that this society was organized and supported by the Japanese for the sole purpose of forcing the Nagamori scheme down the throats of the Korean Emperor and his ministers. From a mistaken motive, which in view of recent events, we can only look upon as Quixotic we refrained from giving publicity to the report. Until we had absolute proof we were reluctant to mention the name of Japan in connection with such a discreditable piece of work.

It is now reported to us that, frightened by the actions of the Il Chin Hoi, Mr. Yi Ha Yong the Foreign Minister, Mr. Yi Yong Tai the Home Minister and General Hyŏn visited the Japanese Legation at 11 a.m. on the 22nd instant and agreed to sign the Waste Lands demand if the Japanese Minister would disband the Il Chin Hoi. General Hyŏn then reported to the Emperor that the Il Chin Hoi were seeking to dethrone him and by this means obtained His Majesty's consent to the Nagamori demands.

We do not vouch for the story in its entirety. Some of the details do not agree with reports which we have previously received. Of course the tale that General Hyon and Mr. Yi Yong-tai were frightened by the Il-chin-hoi is absurd. They may have been in the plot, the object of which was to coerce the Minister for Foreign Affairs.

There is still some hope that the Nagamori scheme has not been irrevocably signed and if this is the case we should like to point out one or two features of the affair which may make Korea hesitate before finally parting with her birthright.

In the first place Mr. Nagamori is an official of the Japanese Finance Department, and the scheme, if it really were, as it pretends to be, one for the exploitation, development and colonization of Korea, would never have come within the scope of his duties. If the scheme had not some financial significance we should not have found so valuable an official of the Japanese Finance Department taking so keen an interest in it.

Another point worthy of notice is the extraordinary haste which the Japanese have displayed in their efforts to get the agreement signed. Until the war is over Japan will have no time to attend to industrial and agricultural projects in Korea and therefore we must look for some other reason for her impatience.

To us the most likely solution is that Japan wants some tangible security upon which she can raise the money necessary to her for the pursuance of the war. If Mr. Nagamori's demands were acceded to, the agreement would be excellent security for a foreign loan and the document would probably find its way to the strong-room of a foreign financeier in very short order. A point which lends colour to this view is the fact that before the production of his present scheme, Mr. Nagamori had under consideration the acquisition of tobacco, wine and salt monopolies in Korea.

Therefore if it be not too late we recommend the Koreans to carefully consider this aspect of the situation.

We cannot prove it but we firmly believe that Japan simply wants Korea as a chattel, and that the moment she receives the privileges asked for by Mr. Nagamori, they will be hypothecated.

There is no other adequate explanation for Japan's haste and the means which have been adopted to gain the Imperial assent to her demands.

Our opinion of the whole performance is too strong for publication.

ON THE HIGH WAY.

BY J. GORDON SMITH IN THE CHINA REVIEW.

(Concluded).

But all this is a hard luck story. This is to tell of the luck of some men. There were three of us, Wallace, Whiting and myself, and to us the local commandant sent the beer that he had intended for the eighteen. It was not our fault that the fifteen thirsted. It was their misfortune in not finding the way to this humble village home.

This is to tell another tale of drink that was not drunk by those who could have drunken. I have a card on which George Lynch has witten these words "Because it is a champagne bottle its contents are not necessarily champagne." General Oku had sent a case of champagne, with his compliments to the correspondents. We shared both. In the days that followed—the days when we were embottled within the walls of Haicheng, with sentries instructed not to let us pass the gates—the champagne went the way of all such things. One bottle remained, a quest which belonged to Clark in of the "Evening Post." There were plotters led by one George Lynch, assisted by R. H. Daves and John Fox Jr.—a Japanese painter had written the name J. Fox Junior—who conspired to seize that bottle—and Clarkin learned of the plot.

In the darkness of the night came Clarkin with a quart of champagne beneath his coat. He came into our little compound, where Fred Whiting was drawing masterpieces for the "Graphic" and Lionel Pratt and I were writing deathless prose. And in the little compound a counter plot was made. We drank the champagne. We had to do it, though we hated to do so, because we needed an empty bottle. The bottle was filled with water, aqua pura, or as near pure as water ever is in Manchuria. The cork and wire was readjusted, silver paper taken from a roll of films was faked, and the bottle was placed back in its place in Clarkin's quarters. In due course Messrs. Lynch et Co. captured the bottle and their friends forgathered. They were going to drink Clarkin's health.

"Seems flat," said Davis, "who is a playwright when he is at home.

"It does sure," said Fox, who writes books,—and spends his time changing his suits.

"There's little fiz to it," said Scull.

"Its water," murmured Lynch, and the form of Clarkin slipped past our compound at a 2.40 clip, with bricks following. The conspirators tore down a wall to hurl at him, and if he had stayed, that man Stephen, of Bible times, would have had a picnic compared with what happened to Clarkin. And they never drank his health.

"All is not gold that glitters," said Barzini, who was proud of his knowledge of English.

"No" said Lynch, "that is not it—a champagne bottle does not make the contents champagne."

When we rode from Haicheng we had a jolly little party at the outposts, where Major Tachibana, of the 34th Regt. was in command. Poor Tachibana, he was a good fellow, and I mourn his untimely death. We had been riding about the hills, through the kaoling, over trenches, and had halted at intervals to listen to post mortems of past events, a staff officer lecturing to us. He seemingly disliked foreigners, swung his back upon us and talked through an interpreter, and before long he became not only rude, but also uninteresting. Then we reached the camp of Major Tachibana in the Chinese village, and he gave eighteen heated correspondents tea and beer, and peppermint candies, the sweets with little legends upon them, such as "Do you really love me"—"You must ask Mamma,"—the sweets which little Willy gives to little Mary in the spring time in Lover's Lane. Major Tachibana also gave us a cheery welcome and made friends. When we rode away, as he returned our parting salute we saw the Major for the last time alive. A week later the desperate battle was fought on the hills of Shorshanpo before Liaoyong, and in a bloody hand to hand fight in the middle of the night the Major was killed and 600 of the regiment he led in the charge were killed or wounded. Next morning I met his orderly leading away his master's horse, and the orderly told us of the Major's death. He had received eleven wounds, the servant said, and died like a hero.

I don't doubt it, he looked like one.

J. GORDON SMITH.

Mr. Megata left Fusan, by steamer, yesterday for Chemulpo.

The Korea Daily News.

VOL. I, WEDNESDAY, SEPTEMBER 28, 1904. No. 62

大韓每日申報
대한ᄆᆡ일신보

(뎨삼십륙호) (목요일) 일쳔구ᄇᆡᆨᄉᆞ년구월이십구일

본사고ᄇᆡᆨ

본신보ᄂᆞᆫ영어와한어로셔ᄆᆡ일출판ᄒᆞᆸ

신문가

한쟝 엽뎐두돈오푼

일삭도 엽뎐량닷돈

우표가미삭닷돈

다닷돈으로밧ᄉᆞᆸ

광고료ᄂᆞᆫ

과ᄒᆞᆫ외쟝단과ᄌᆞ칭ᄒᆞ되쇼로ᄌᆞᆼ감ᄒᆞ되ᄒᆞᆫ번가로밧을터이오ᄆᆡ오리지아녀대한사람마다다이신문을보실터이니광고내시기를원ᄒᆞ시ᄂᆞᆫ이들은우리신문사에와셔면약ᄒᆞ심을희망ᄒᆞᆸ

○발ᄒᆡᆼ소 박동대한ᄆᆡ일신보사발ᄒᆡᆼ겸편집인영국인셜필림쟝ᄌᆞ리오

사쟝 영국인 (ᄇᆡ셜)

평양 ᄃᆡ리졈

○평양효동사ᄂᆞᆫ권미보씨로우리신문ᄃᆡ리인을ᄐᆡᆨ졍ᄒᆞ엿ᄉᆞ오니평양에계신구람ᄒᆞ고져ᄒᆞ시ᄂᆞᆫ 쳠군ᄌᆞᄂᆞᆫᄒᆞᆫ리졈에왕림ᄒᆞ와면의ᄒᆞ시ᄋᆞᆸ

사고

○우리대한ᄆᆡ일신보의목뎍은대한의안녕질서에관ᄒᆞᆫ모든ᄉᆞ무에ᄃᆡᄒᆞ야논공평ᄒᆞᆫ변론을주쟝ᄒᆞᆷ이라우리통신원의탐보ᄂᆞᆫ신문보시ᄂᆞᆫ쳠군ᄌᆞ의게ᄒᆞᆼ샹보도ᄒᆞ려니와편지를긔셔ᄒᆞ여주시ᄂᆞᆫ이ᄂᆞᆫ셩명과반ᄃᆡ를젹어붓치시기를희망ᄒᆞ오니이거슨신문샹에긔ᄌᆡᄒᆞ라ᄂᆞᆫ거시아니오다만긔희신용ᄒᆞᄂᆞᆫ증거를숨고자ᄒᆞᆷ이라긔자ᄂᆞᆫ아모긔셔던지각ᄌᆞᄒᆞᆯ을퇴각ᄒᆞᄂᆞᆫ권리를가젓스나퇴각ᄒᆞᄂᆞᆫ리유ᄂᆞᆫ말ᄒᆞᆯ터이오며공증ᄒᆞ고회ᄒᆞ문란케ᄒᆞᄂᆞᆫ듯ᄒᆞᆫ다긔셔ᄂᆞᆫ의례히밧지안켓ᄉᆞᆸ나이다

●본사셜시이ᄅᆡ로신문을ᄆᆡ양우례로분젼ᄒᆞ와례젼부의임의로젼ᄒᆞ든ᄉᆞ스로번곳에ᄂᆞᆫ홍ᄂᆞᆺ게젼ᄒᆞ기도ᄒᆞ며혹빗칠거슬ᄒᆞᆫ젼ᄒᆞ에젼ᄒᆞ기도ᄒᆞ며혹아니젼ᄒᆞᄂᆞᆫ곳도잇다ᄒᆞ와우리신문을ᄉᆞ랑ᄒᆞ야구람ᄒᆞ시ᄂᆞᆫ 쳠군ᄌᆞ의게당ᄒᆞ야ᄆᆡ우미안ᄒᆞ옵기로지금ᄐᆡ분젼인을두고ᄆᆡ일일ᄌᆞ이젼ᄒᆞ며아니젼ᄒᆞ거나ᄂᆞᆺ게거나ᄒᆞᆫ폐가엽도록ᄒᆞ라ᄒᆞ오니ᄒᆞ야님젼ᄒᆞ거나ᄂᆞᆺ게젼ᄒᆞ거나ᄒᆞᆫ일이잇스면본사로통긔ᄒᆞ여주심을희망ᄒᆞᆸ

본사광고

본샤에셔본신문뎨ᄉᆞ호와뎨십일호와뎨이십오호를소용ᄒᆞᆯ터이가잇셔이에광고ᄒᆞ오니누구시던지이샹삼호중에본사로가져오시면ᄆᆡ쟝에ᄇᆡᆨ젼두푼식드리리다

잡보

○미죠별원 미국공관에셔외부로죠회ᄒᆞ되귀국인민일영이가미국의현박포의게면도방미ᄒᆞᆫᄉᆞ로평양감리셔에괴슈ᄒᆞ야샹금몽방치못ᄒᆞ엿다ᄒᆞ니힘서주ᄉᆞ원용ᄃᆡᆨ을시별ᄒᆞ라ᄒᆞ엿더라

○군제 죠칙 군제기쟝ᄒᆞᄂᆞᆫᄉᆞ로 죠칙을ᄂᆞ리셔길ᄋᆞ샤ᄃᆡ나라에군ᄉᆞ가업지못ᄒᆞᆯ거시오군ᄉᆞ에군제가업지못ᄒᆞᆯ지라준ᄒᆞᆫ원슈부군부관계에계반규졍이홈핍ᄒᆞᆷ이잇스ᄂᆞᆫ즁부등불시의져방ᄒᆞᆫ군제로졍쟝부ᄒᆞᆫ긔기로곤일에군제를의뎡ᄒᆞᆷ이라시종부와비종부와친왕부의각긔무관의구별이잇슬거시오나라를호위ᄒᆞ고밋용병ᄒᆞᄂᆞᆫ등ᄉᆞ를참모ᄒᆞ기위ᄒᆞ야참모부가잇슬거시오군ᄃᆡ를일졔히셩취ᄒᆞ기위ᄒᆞ야교육부가잇슬지나무관의론을광ᄅᆡᆷᄒᆞ고외국군졔를참호ᄒᆞ야긔졍도ᄒᆞ며신셜도ᄒᆞ되부ᄅᆞᆺ우리쟝ᄉᆞ와병졸은일졀ᄒᆞᆷ죤ᄒᆞ야각긔졍미ᄒᆞᆫᄃᆡ경에ᄂᆞ아가우리방국을공고케ᄒᆞᆷ을짐이간졀히바라노라ᄒᆞ옵셧더라

○무관리 명 시종무관쟝에민영환비죵무관쟝죠동윤참모부부쟝리윤용참모일국쟝현영운참모이국쟝엄쥰원교육부총감리지용교육부부감에구영조참모쟝ᄇᆡᆨ셩긔과헌병ᄉᆞ령관쟝쳘군부대신민영긔과쳥원ᄒᆞ엿쥬무국쟝김승규제셔가되 명되엿더라

○량씨승차 졍렴량셩환씨ᄂᆞᆫ참쟝으로승차되엿더라

○량씨슈원 죠셩근로ᄇᆡᆨ린량씨가일본병위문ᄃᆡᄉᆞ슈원을피임ᄒᆞ엿더라

○일직 죠칙 ᄌᆞᆫ년의쟝관인직을ᄌᆞ금위시ᄒᆞ야시종무관비종무관참모부쟝참모부량국쟝군부대신호위총관경위총관이츈회ᄒᆞ야일직ᄒᆞ라ᄒᆞ옵신죠칙이ᄂᆞ리셧더라

○위문ᄉᆞ변동 ᄀᆡᆼ문ᄒᆞᆫ즉일본군위문ᄃᆡᄉᆞ민영환씨ᄂᆞᆫ변동되고부ᄉᆞ권즁현씨가ᄃᆡᄉᆞ로불일발ᄒᆡᆼᄒᆞᆫ다더라

○한민피착 삼작일에과쳔군에셔일본병졍이한인김왕영등이명을포착ᄒᆞ야경셩ᄉᆞ령부로압상ᄒᆞ엿ᄂᆞᆫᄃᆡ그ᄉᆞ실은알슈업다더라

○일관리과 일본ᄉᆞ령관쟝곡쳔대쟝과팔곡참모쟝은리샹월령간에도한ᄒᆞᆫ다더라

○경부텰도 경부텰도회ᄉᆞ의ᄉᆞ무를일신히ᄒᆞ야총지이하의총무부쟝과니부쟝과외부쟝을임ᄒᆞ엿스니총무부쟝은죽니강이오니부쟝은죽립티랑이오외부쟝은젼과관미등계씨라ᄂᆞᆫᄃᆡ텰도ᄂᆞᆫ명년삼월에쥰공이된다더라

○거인환향 향자에강원도로셔샹경ᄒᆞ엿든큰사람은단문디리와셩수문을ᄂᆞᆼ통ᄒᆞᆫ다ᄂᆞᆫ리모가을나오라고ᄒᆞ여셔올나왓더니셔로맛나보고일젼에도로ᄂᆞ려갓다더라

뎐보

구월십오일동경발

○영셔방송 희샹위로로쟝열소에셔영국츈션찰차쓰호를쥬ᄒᆡᆼ림물포흠은다주어방송ᄒᆞ고일본에가ᄂᆞᆫ밀가로와솜과쟝목은속용ᄒᆞ기로쟉뎡ᄒᆞ엿다더라

○로국함쟝 로국참쟝슌양함레나호의지휘관쌜린쓰키함쟝은미국관헌ᄎᆡ에동지ᄒᆞ기를허ᄒᆞᆷ의무쟝을희탈ᄒᆞ고젼징ᄒᆞᆯ나기ᄉᆞ지미국샹항에셔혜류ᄒᆞ기를원ᄒᆞᄂᆞᆫ다ᄒᆞ엿더라

구월십륙일동경발

○레나함승원 로함레나호의함승원들은미국의인졍으로억류ᄒᆞ기로결졍되엿다더라

동이름동뎐

○려슌졍황 쓰도잇셀쟝군이셩피등보에뎐보ᄒᆞ기를려슌구셔편에잇ᄂᆞᆫ일군은병력을증가ᄒᆞ엿고각포ᄃᆡ에셔ᄂᆞᆫ련속ᄒᆞ여포격즁이나연미나로군의ᄉᆞ샹은ᄉᆞ소ᄒᆞ다ᄒᆞ엿더라

외보

○려슌근황 근자에려슌구에셔미발ᄒᆞ야지부에도착ᄒᆞᆫ쳥인의말을드른즉일본군ᄃᆡ가려슌구바리지완에잇ᄂᆞᆫ포ᄃᆡ를졈령ᄒᆞ고거긔셔포ᄃᆡ를노아빗칫ᄂᆞᆫ창에슈문을세三리고쎤항구안시에잇ᄂᆞᆫ창고션쳑을샹ᄒᆞ게ᄒᆞ엿스며려슌구에○호포ᄃᆡᄂᆞᆫ일본군ᄃᆡ가파피ᄒᆞᆫ것ᄉᆞ나위쳠ᄒᆞᆫ소치로일본셔졈령치아니ᄒᆞ며황금산에잇ᄂᆞᆫ아국병은ᄀᆡᆨ금ᄃᆡ포를노ᄒᆞ나일병잇ᄂᆞᆫᄃᆡᄂᆞᆫ딘알이밋치지도못ᄒᆞᆯᄲᅮᆫ아니라도리여교쟝구례잇ᄂᆞᆫ아병에게로진너가맛쳐셔ᄌᆞ긔가ᄌᆞ긔군ᄉᆞ를만히샹ᄒᆞᆫ다ᄒᆞ며련슌함티슈령쟝관용도스기쟝군은길니교우미라무례쟝군이신임ᄒᆞ엿다ᄒᆞ더라더라

관보

뎨이쳔구ᄇᆡᆨᄉᆞ십이호

광무팔년구월이십칠일

셔임급ᄉᆞ령

○임한셩부관원셔칙임관삼등 텰도원참셔관 ᄇᆡᆨ국티

○임경무쳥경무관셔주임관륙등 샹화향경무관 변셕티

○임텰도원참셔관셔주임관륙등 졍샹풍 류한웅

○명휴쟝 친위뎨일련티뎨이ᄃᆡ티부특군보병부위 리동구 진위뎨이련티뎨삼ᄃᆡ티부특군보병참위 김교셩

○면본직 시위뎨일련티긔관특군보병부위 쟝세교 시위뎨일련티뎨삼ᄃᆡ티향관특군이등군ᄉᆞ 리학리 진위뎨오련티뎨일ᄃᆡ티즁ᄃᆡ쟝특군보병졍위 리명한

○임특군이등군ᄉᆞ 특군보병졍위 리명한 특군보병부위 쟝세교

○임특군보병부위 특군이등군ᄉᆞ 리학리

○보시위대일련대괴관 륙군보병부위 리학리
○보시위대일련대대삼대대향관 륙군일등군ᄉᆞ 장세교
○보진위대일련대대일대대향관륙군일등군ᄉᆞ 리덕한
○보진위대오련대대일대대죵대장 륙군보병정위 김귀현
○임동래감리셔쥬임관삼등례식원번역관 리무영
이상구월이십삼일
○임즁츄원의관셔칙임관이등졍이품 졍쥬영
○의원면본관 즁츄원의관졍규삼 장용급
○임즁츄원의관셔쥬임관륙등궁니부참셔관 윤형구 갑쟝도관찰부총슌 리익환
○명궁니부특진관셔칙임관ᄉᆞ등 니장원감독 심상황
○명니장원감독셔칙임관ᄉᆞ등종이품 리쥰영
○임 궁니부참셔관겸임관방비셔관셔쥬임관륙등 졍삼품홍승연
○례식원번역관셔쥬임관삼등례식원참리관 엄달환
○임례식원참리관셔쥬임관삼등 륙품 신희영
○임시종원좌시어셔관임관팔등 리상덕 죠용하
이상구월이십오일
○십긔일벌봉 경무쳥츄ᄉᆞ송희명
구월이십ᄉᆞ일 경무쳥궁졍록ᄉᆞ
○의정부참정신긔션조혁소비지니에번거히ᄉᆞ양말고시무ᄒᆞ라

론셜

일진회와밋쟝삼씨의요구ᄒᆞᆷ이라

요ᄉᆞ이 칙령으로일진회를파ᄒᆞ엿다ᄂᆞᆫ되이왕에ᄂᆞᆫ한국슌검들이희산케ᄒᆞ라다가일인의게구익가되여못ᄒᆞ고필경에각디방에셔지파졋더니흘연일인의보호가철회됨으로모다훗터졋ᄂᆞᆫ지라

거월이십구일우리신문에도보도ᄒᆞᆫ바어니와기시에셜회ᄒᆞᄂᆞᆫ목젹을졍부에쟝셔ᄒᆞᆷ이여좌ᄒᆞ엿셧ᄉᆞ니 일은 황실을존숭ᄒᆞ며나라긔초를공고케ᄒᆞᆯ위원에셔샹쥰 이ᄂᆞᆫ인민의싱명재산을보호ᄒᆞᆯ위원에 량지익 삼은 졍부를기혁ᄒᆞᆯ위원에 김명쥰 사ᄂᆞᆫ 군졍과재졍을졍리ᄒᆞᆯ위원에 염즁모라ᄒᆞ엿ᄂᆞᆫ지라

이네조건이다사ᄅᆞᆷ으로ᄒᆞ여곰가이칭미ᄒᆞᆯ계ᄒᆞᆯ만ᄒᆞᆫ고또그회에셔ᄒᆞᄂᆞᆫ일이능히얼마큼이라도ᄉᆞᄉᆞ히셩취가될것갓기ᄂᆞᆫᄒᆞ나그회원들이보기에대단히오활ᄒᆞ고종작업ᄂᆞᆫ싱각을갓혼고로우리ᄂᆞᆫ이회에계획ᄒᆞᆷ을주의ᄒᆞ야본즉일본의세력으로보호를밧아셔엇지던지팔월이십륙일노붓터금월이십이일ᄭᆞ지그동안에아모일도ᄒᆞᆫ거시업시파산이되엿ᄂᆞᆫ되

소위기회라ᄒᆞᄂᆞᆫ때에ᄂᆞᆫ국ᄉᆞ진보됨엔조곰도긴요ᄒᆞᆷ은업시다만각대신의게송함ᄒᆞ야조롱ᄒᆞ며룽욕ᄒᆞᆷ이무소부지ᄒᆞ엿슬ᄲᅮᆫ이니라

우리ᄂᆞᆫ당초이회시작될때에싱각ᄒᆞ기를일본셔필경편셩ᄒᆞ여유지ᄒᆞ게ᄒᆞ야쟝ᄎᆞ장삼씨의황무지긔간사건을
대황데폐하셔나혹대신들의게제츌ᄒᆞᆯ줄로알아더니근일에차ᄎᆞ로일ᄒᆞᄂᆞᆫ거슬본즉우리싱각ᄒᆞᆷ도도리여아니요또ᄒᆞᆫ별노히긔이ᄒᆞᆯ것도업ᄂᆞᆫ고로당초에이회에소문을드르려아니ᄒᆞ엿고또일본셔상관ᄒᆞᆫ다ᄂᆞᆫ일ᄒᆞᆷ이실로밋업지못ᄒᆞᆫ고로과연듯기를조와아니ᄒᆞᆷ일러니

이제일진회로말미아마ᄒᆞ엿다ᄂᆞᆫ소문을드른즉대단히놀나온거시금월이십이일샹오십일시에외부대신이하영과니부대신리용태와검ᄉᆞ총장현영운삼씨가일본공ᄉᆞ를방견ᄒᆞ고말ᄒᆞ기를귀공ᄉᆞ가만일일진회만히산케ᄒᆞᆯ지경이면이왕에말ᄒᆞ든바장삼씨황무지청구ᄒᆞᆷ에조인ᄒᆞ겟다고ᄒᆞ고인ᄒᆞ야현총장이
대황데폐하게드러가주달ᄒᆞ기를일진회에셔범람히
어위를폐ᄒᆞ려ᄒᆞᄂᆞᆫ고로장삼의요구ᄒᆞ든바로주엇다고ᄒᆞ야
셩의에가랍ᄒᆞ시게ᄒᆞ엿다ᄒᆞ니우리ᄂᆞᆫ이왕에이회ᄉᆞ건으로샹보드르니와갓지아니ᄒᆞᆫ즉전수히밋지아니ᄒᆞᄂᆞᆫ거시일전에현총장파밋리니대량씨가일진회에셔반ᄃᆡᄒᆞᆷ으로경겁ᄒᆞ엿슨즉응당피계를써셔외부대신으로ᄒᆞ여곰룩힝ᄒᆞ게ᄒᆞᆫ듯ᄒᆞ며셜혹실로그러케되드리도아즉갓타여셔ᄂᆞᆫ소망이조곰잇ᄂᆞᆫ지라장삼씨계약셔에조인은아니ᄒᆞ엿슬터인즉도로작환ᄒᆞ기가어렵지아니ᄒᆞ니한국의싱득권으로더부러난호게되기전에의혹나ᄂᆞᆫ바일이조건을발거ᄒᆞᄂᆞᆫ거시미오조흘듯ᄒᆞ며

또ᄒᆞᆫ질졍ᄒᆞ야알수업ᄂᆞᆫ일이두가지가잇스니첫재ᄂᆞᆫ장삼씨가일본대장셩에벼슬로잇슨즉이청구ᄒᆞᆷ이파연조긔가ᄒᆞᄂᆞᆫ것갓트면이ᄂᆞᆫ한국에식민지발긔ᄒᆞᆷ으로공훈이나세우랴ᄒᆞ면오히려모르되조긔의당연ᄒᆞᆫ직칙으로ᄂᆞᆫ그리ᄒᆞᆯ리가업고또이일ᄒᆞᆷ이세입에필요ᄒᆞᆷ도아닐터인거시우리에싱각에ᄂᆞᆫ이안에셔나ᄂᆞᆫ리익을다만니장셩ᄒᆞᆫ관인의게만취ᄒᆞ게ᄒᆞᆯ리도업스며둘지ᄂᆞᆫ일본셔이되도록신속히조긔의권력되로합동조인ᄒᆞ라ᄒᆞᆷ은필경다름이아니라일후란리평정된후에ᄂᆞᆫ일본셔한국상업상파롱업상에주의ᄒᆞ야계획ᄒᆞᆷ여가가업슬듯ᄒᆞᆫ고로조급ᄒᆞᆫ셩졍에이리ᄒᆞᆷ이로다

우리의소견에ᄂᆞᆫ일본셔전징셩취ᄒᆞ기위ᄒᆞ야싱지ᄒᆞᆫ기에필요ᄒᆞᆯ듯ᄒᆞᆷ에은근히마음이잇셔그리ᄒᆞᆷ인거시만일장삼씨의청구ᄒᆞᆷ이합의ᄒᆞ게만될것갓트면그합동이외국처용ᄒᆞᆫ기에그만ᄒᆞᆫ조ᄒᆞᆫ보증이업슬터이요공문이역시외국재물가진사ᄅᆞᆷ의게다만말ᄒᆞᆫ마되라도확실히밋게될만ᄒᆞᆯ터인지라

그런고로지금장삼씨의이ᄒᆞᆫ가지로만빗최ᄂᆞᆫ거시한국에주초히험세전민ᄒᆞᆫ라ᄂᆞᆫ즁에셔다만먼저도모ᄒᆞ야ᄒᆞᆷ이니이일이다미구에될러이기로우리ᄂᆞᆫ한국빅셩들의게이러ᄒᆞᆫ형편을아모조록조심ᄒᆞ야싱각ᄒᆞᆫ라고권면ᄒᆞ며또ᄒᆞᆫ우리가확실히증거ᄂᆞᆫᄒᆞᆯ수업스되일본셔장ᄎᆞ분명코한국을한물산으로역이여장남씨의요구ᄒᆞᆫ바와갓치리익되ᄂᆞᆫ거슨모도드러갈듯ᄒᆞ노니

우리ᄂᆞᆫ일본셔급속히ᄒᆞ려ᄒᆞ야청구ᄒᆞᆷ에 윤허ᄒᆞ심에되ᄒᆞ야뎌옥져당히셜명ᄒᆞᆯ말은업스나이되도록ᄒᆞᆫ거시오히려파도ᄒᆞᆫ듯ᄒᆞ도다

잡보

○군의국장 금번군제기뎡에군의국이신셜되ᄂᆞᆫ되국장은의학교관김익남씨가셔임된다더라

○외슌여호 일전에무삼ᄉᆞ단이잇든지경무청에셔셔평에에빅셩일명을초치ᄒᆞ량으로파송ᄒᆞ엿더니허동인민이경겁ᄒᆞ야무론로소남녀ᄒᆞ고일제히환산ᄒᆞᆫ고로일동니가공허ᄒᆞ엿다더라

○막져소향 근일에원도근읍의다수히샹경ᄒᆞᆫ향직들이열심으로일진회에투입ᄒᆞ노라고힝탁즁반비쓸다소전량을히회즁에임치ᄒᆞ엿더니불외에히회가창졸간히산되미그반비전량을츄심ᄒᆞᆯ곳이돈연히업셔진지라그러ᄒᆞᆫ즁경무청에셔문외로축출ᄒᆞᄂᆞᆫ되명석업ᄂᆞᆫ단발직이고향에도갈수업셔도로에셔방황ᄒᆞᆫ즉신세가가련ᄒᆞ야각기소견되로흑즁이ᄂᆞᆫ된다ᄒᆞ고절노ᄎᆞ져가ᄂᆞᆫ쟈도잇고예수교ᄂᆞᆫ런쥬교당에원입ᄒᆞᄂᆞᆫ쟈도잇고흑병뎡에투입코져ᄒᆞᄂᆞᆫ쟈도잇다더라

○셔북아병 후창군슈리지식씨가니부로보고ᄒᆞ기를로국병ᄉᆞ빅ᄉᆞ십명이본읍에셔샹거이빅여리되ᄂᆞᆫ삼슈군에쥬둔ᄒᆞ엿더니음력칠월이십ᄉᆞ일에히병즁긔병십륙명이병긔를휴ᄃᆡᄒᆞ고본읍근쳐운동에니도ᄒᆞ야촌민의농우를씨아ᄉᆞ호군ᄒᆞ고조셩으로직향ᄒᆞ엿ᄂᆞᆫ되동ᄉᆞ의게담문ᄒᆞᆫ즉삼슈잇ᄂᆞᆫ아병즁십ᄉᆞ병은쟝진으로파송ᄒᆞ엿다ᄒᆞ며력도에겁략ᄒᆞᄂᆞᆫ폐단은별노업스나본군련셩무창부셩삼면에셔농민의농우ᄉᆞ척을략탈ᄒᆞ야니노아셔야무청석ᄒᆞ니면답이호군ᄒᆞ엿고군마를면답가온되젹디되엿ᄂᆞᆫ되근일소문이삼슈에쥬둔ᄒᆞᆫ아병ᄉᆞ빅ᄉᆞ십명과쟝진에도착ᄒᆞᆫ아병이빅명이본군으로리도ᄒᆞᆫ다ᄒᆞᄂᆞᆫ고로빅셩이환산ᄒᆞᆫ다ᄒᆞ엿더라

○리감면보 동리감리가작일에외부로또면보ᄒᆞ기를일본례신대신이금일에마산항으로젼왕ᄒᆞ엿다가명일에본항으로환도ᄒᆞᆯ야재명일에발졍ᄒᆞ야대구로향ᄒᆞᆫ다ᄒᆞ엿더라

○회찰보고 회쥬관찰ᄉᆞ김학슈씨가외부로보고ᄒᆞ기를평산군슈보고니기에ᄒᆞ엿스되본군경니처도비이만삼천칠빅여원을일본렬도되에셔본군에징츌ᄒᆞ라ᄒᆞᆫ즉대단민익ᄒᆞᆫ다ᄒᆞ엿스니곳일관에죠회ᄒᆞ야타관ᄒᆞ라ᄒᆞ엿더라

○민원인압 부산항민인등이외부로면보ᄒᆞ기를오감리를만일인임처아니ᄒᆞᆯ면무론샹고평민ᄒᆞ고거기환산디경이라ᄒᆞ엿더라

○티빈청원 티천군민리틱방등이외부에청원ᄒᆞ되본군슈죠쇼윤이도임ᄒᆞᆫ기오년에치젹이현져ᄒᆞ야인민이안업ᄒᆞ더니엇더ᄒᆞᆫ간세비가본군슈를아국당이라고무망ᄒᆞ야익명셔를지어가산병참소에투셔ᄒᆞᆫ고로읍력본원룩일에히병참소에셔본군슈를착거ᄒᆞ엿스니세샹에이러ᄒᆞᆫ일이어디잇ᄉᆞ오릿가동축ᄒᆞᆫ신후일관에죠회ᄒᆞ야불일니로본군슈를방환ᄒᆞ야민정을편안케ᄒᆞᆷ을복망이라ᄒᆞ엿더라

광고

TELEGRAMS.

(FROM JAPAN PAPERS.)

Berlin, Sept. 22nd.

"The Times" correspondent repeats the statement that German merchant ships were sold to Russia as auxiliary cruisers. The report is nonsensical, for the Kaiser and the German navy would never consent to the sale of a ship which is valuable for German naval purposes.

Berlin Sept. 22nd.

From Paris it is reported that French political circles are satisfied and have confidence that a Russo-German understanding does not exist.

Berlin, Sept. 22nd.

English papers now publish peaceful articles and ventilate friendly relations, and, for later, an alliance with Germany.—Deutsche Japan-Post service.

London, Sept. 22nd.

The Times now withdraws its statement that the German and Russian Chancellors Count Buelow and M. de Witte, made an agreement concerning the Far East during their interview at Norderncy, but the paper again repeats the old story that secret understandings exist between the Emperors Wilhelm and Nicholas. Certainly at the Wiesbader interview last year, when the Kaiser and the Tsar once were playing billiards in the establishment "Wolffsgarien" Eastern Asia was mentioned in a few words, but a regular conversation or agreement did not take place. The Tsar at that moment had no idea that war would break out with Japan.

Shanghai, Sept. 20th.

The Japanese at Dalny are said to be suffering from Beri-Beri.

Berlin, Sept. 12th.

Five catholic fathers and five sisters have been murdered by the aborigines in the Baining Mountains (German) New-Guinea. The police have restored order. Fifteen people have been killed, twenty-one have been arrested. The pursuit of the culprits is being still continued.

Tokyo Sept. 20th.

A St. Petersburg despatch states that General Kriftenberk has been appointed, by the Czar, to cooperate with General Kuropatkin in Manchuria. The two commanders will be on an equality of rank.

Tokyo, Sept. 22nd.

A Japanese correspondent with General Kuroki's Headquarters wires under date of yesterday afternoon that the Hun river, which runs south of Mukden, is wider and deeper than the Taitzu. The Russians are said to have built three or more pontoon bridges over the Hun and bridgeheads on the left side. The autumn weather is now most suitable for operations and martial spirit runs high. A Russian General who defended the Russian right near Liaoyang, seems to have hurriedly constructed defensive works at Shu-shan-po, Lin-li-tun and Shao-fang-tun, not being satisfied with the line of entrenchments outside Liaoyang.

The number of military spades captured by the Nodzu Army alone, exceed 10,000.

The Russians, who recently appeared near Ping-tai-tzu, have already retired.

Affairs of outposts have been of frequent occurrences lately.

London, September 21st.

General Mischenko, commanding the Cossacks, has had daily skirmishes with the Japanese. He has recently sustained a number of casualties. The Russaian military authorities unanimously expect that General Kuropatkin will make a stand at Mukden for political if not for strategical reasons. This proves the report, that General Mischenko was killed in action at Liaoyang, to be false.

London, Sep 21st.

An Imperial order has been issued in Russia for the organization of an East Siberian Balloon Battalion. The nucleus of its "personnel" is to be taken from the officials of the balloon factory in St. Petersburg. It will be sent to Manchuria, and there the present balloon company will be amalgamated with it, thus forming a complete battalion. The commander will be Colonol Hwanko.

UNEASY LIES THE HEAD THAT'S SHAVED.

The troubles of the country men, bereft of money and hair, are graphically described by our city reporter in the fellowing article, written in his best style:

The countrymen, who came up to Il Chin Hoi put their expensives money at the residence of meeting and they take away when they want to use. But, now the meeting was dispersed so they can't get back the money and they are quite trouble now have no any cash left, impossible to go back home without journey expensive moreover they shaved the heads and are shameful to go down to country but the policemen drive them out of city so what are they able?

Some of them desire to become members of Japanese monastery here in Seoul, some of them want to be missionary Christians and some of them try to be Roman Catholic, at finally some of them want to be soldiers even.

GENERAL HYÖN.

Of late General Hyön Vŏng Woon has waxed powerful. Whether it is due to his own plotting or that of his concubine we cannot say, but we are now informed that all Government appointments, high or low, are monopolized by his creatures. The house of this disreputable man is daily filled with servile time-servers asking after his health, and we can easily imagine that he and his brazen concubine are having a good time. A representative of another Power, having any respect for the good name of his Government, would refuse to have any traffic with either of this precious pair.

Colonel Saito left Seoul yesterday afternoon, by train, for Chemulpo.

The "Kersaint," bringing the French and English mails of the 21st and 28th August, is expected to arrive from Shanghai tomorrow.

The people of Fusan are evidently loyal to their deposed Kamni, Mr. O Ku Yung, for we hear that they threaten to leave the port "en masse" unless he is reinstated in office.

We have received copies of the China Review and Evening Journal, published in Tientsin by Mr. L. Noris-Newman. It is a well-edited little paper, showing, unlike most of its Far Eastern contemporaries, no pro-Japanese bias.

A cunning method of seeking revenge has been unearthed by some wily miscreants of Tai Chow who nursed a grudge against their Magistrate. They went to the nearest Japanese military station and deposed that Mr. Cho Chung Yun was a Russian agent, and consequently that poor gentleman languished in durance vile, until the trick was discovered.

With reference to the leading article published in these columns yesterday and dealing with the Nagamori Land Scheme, we learn from our Japanese contemporary, the "Tai Han Il Po," that Minister Hayashi contradicts the statement that he was visited on the 22nd inst. by the Ministers of the Home and Foreign Departments and General Hyon. No mention of the remaining statements is made, we note, in our contemporary's columns.

Yesterday notice was received at the Foreign Office, from the Kamni of Fusan, that the Japanese Minister of Communications proceeded on a visit to Masanpo, whence he will continue his journey overland to Seoul.

Messrs. Ito and Takashima, detailed by the Emperor and Empress respectively, left Shimbashi station for the front on the 8th inst., to convey the Imperial solicitude about the well-being of the Manchurian Army at Liaoyang.

Prince Karl Anton of Hohenzollern, now on the way to Japan, in order to view the operations as a war-attaché to the Manchurian Army, is expected in Yokohama on about the 19th inst. It is said that he has already ordered a similar equipment as is in use by a Japanese major, and that he has declined all special treatment as he goes to the front as a plain major.

Latest news from Dalny report that a Chinaman employed by the Russians has been arrested by the Japanese at that port. It appears that he had tried ot destroy the source of the water-supply in Dalny. After an examination the Chinaman was shot.

The "Bystander," in the course of an article on the German Empe ror remarks: Always a man of simple and economic habits, save in the matters of telegraphy and uniforms, the Kaiser saves salary by being his own naval chaplain. A selection of his sermons to the crew of the "Hohenzollen" has been published. He has a very human way, too, of ordering the Imperial dinner every day, which never works out at more than seven and six, exclusive of wine. He paints, sings, composes, writes plays and rehearses them, sails boats, designs cruisers, plans campaigns, leads cavalry, shoots game of all sizes, sits to most photographers, and makes speeches on every subject. He has invented a new kind of moustache, and an absolutely novel school of criticism in art and literature. He will have none of republicans, impressionists, higher critics, Chinamen, ladies who ride bicycles, or officers who study the crease down the front of their trousers.

The Korea Daily News.

Issued at 5 P. M. daily except Sundays.

Rate of Subscription:—

Per Year,	Yen 25.
Per Quarter,	Yen 7.
Per Month	Yen 2.50

Postage in Korea not charged extra.
Postage abroad charged extra.

Advertisements, 50 sen per day for 1 inch or less.
5 yen per month per inch.
50 yen per year per inch.

All communications to

E. T. BETHELL,
Editor and Publisher.
Pak-tong, Seoul.

WAR.

No nation on this earth has yet the right to call itself civilized. Some nations are more or less uncivilized than others but when all is said and done we have only slightly advanced from the state of primeval barbarity in which our progenitors existed.

Science is claimed to have made strides. It has not. It has only moved forward a few inches. Beyond all control or hindrance the destiny of the world relentlessly pursues its course.

Not a single one of Nature's forces do we yet control. Some of them we use, but in using them we can only be likened to a small boy riding on the tail of a tram-car. Our progress in medicine and surgery has enabled us to hinder Nature's process of keeping the population of the world within due bounds by means of the ravages of disease.

But we have only pressed a bag of air. Repression in one direction causes expansion in another. Darwin's doctrine of the "survival of the fittest" is irrefutable. Races become extinct from three causes:—Inability to adapt themselves to their environment; Inability to resist disease; Inability to protect themselves against predatory enemies.

Such scientific knowledge as we possess has enabled us to protect ourselves against wholesale death from disease and other conditions tending to keep our increase within bounds, but Destiny still has its way. It sets us killing each other.

If we live and multiply at our present rate there will soon, under present conditions, be insufficient room for us all on this earth. In fact we are already overcrowded. Most nations realize this and they are—some by pacific emigration and colonization and some by military aggression—seeking fresh fields and pastures new for their posterity.

And so it will proceed. Two starving men will fight to the death for a crust.

Nature is not inscrutable, its laws are plain enough to a careful observer. So long as there are, or threaten to be, too many of us, we shall kill each other. Nations which are always fighting or holding themseves in readiness to fight are only blindly assisting in carrying out the destiny of the world.

Someone has said that a large army is the surest guaranty of peace. A nation having a large army is the servant of that army. And an army always wants to be at war. To begin with, promotion, ordinarily slow in this profession, is much quicker when there are gaps left by those killed in battle. Further, new engines of destruction are continually being invented and the desire to test their efficacy in actual war is always a strong one. And military life in the piping times of peace is exceedingly monotonous, so soldiers are always willing to risk their lives for the sake of excitement, with the probabilities of advancement and glory as contingencies.

So that so long as there are armies there will be war, and in spite of all our Geneva conventions, Treaties of Paris, Hague Tribunals and boasts of humane warfare, war is every bit as savage and barbarous to-day, as it was in the times when our ancestors smashed each others' heads in with stone axes, or before that, clawed and bit each other to death.

Those who doubt this are referred to a statement of the position at Port Arthur which appears in another column.

PORT ARTHUR.

The situation at Port Arthur is daily growing in intensity. As we recently pointed out, unless the Japanese besiegers can effect their entry into the fortress before winter sets in, Port Arthur will never become theirs.

They are therefore redoubling their already fierce efforts and when the whole story of the battle which is now being waged there becomes known, the whole world will stand aghast at the horror of it.

Of the military position little is known. So far as can be learned the Russians now have plenty of ammunition and are well provisioned with the exception of fresh meat, which is scarce. The Japanese blockade appears to be very ineffective as we are continually hearing of junks and even steamers laden with supplies successfully reaching the harbour. The shallowness of the water near the coast and the presence of many mines probably greatly hinders the operations of the blockading fleet.

The Japanese appear to have successfully stormed most of the outer defenses and there is a story that the Eagle's nest fort, the retention of which is considered vital to the defenders, has also fallen. As no news comes to us direct from either the besiegers or the besieged it is hard to know what to believe. Most of the news comes from Chefoo, having been brought there by junkmen and refugees who may or may not be telling the truth. There is a story current that the Russian fleet has been instructed to make a dash out of the port at all costs. This is ridiculous on the face of it. Had the fleet received such instructions it would hardly have allowed the Japanese to receive so plain a hint to get ready. As a matter of fact, the fleet appears to be doing useful work as some positions not covered by the forts are commanded by the various vessels.

This is all we are able to glean of the position at present, but horrible details of the conditions under which the battle is being waged are to hand.

It appears that General Stoessel, finding that a cessation of hostilities, even momentary, gives his enemies an advantage, has announced that no notice will henceforth be taken of the white flag or the Geneva Cross, and the Japanese are taking the same course. The attackers and defenders are almost within speaking distance of each other and as the Japanese leave their trenches and advance to storm the Russian positions they are simply mown down by machine gunfire. Some of the Japanese medical corps advance into the zone of fire to render assistance to their wounded, but the majority are left to miserably perish and putrify. The stench from the decaying corpses surrounding the fortress is said to be so bad that the Russian soldiers have to go about with their mouths and noses swathed in bandages soaked in camphor.

In addition to ordinary defenses and elaborate wire entanglements, the Russians have laid mines filled with rocks, which when exploded decimate whole battalions.

The defenders are said not to be losing many lives, but it is reported that those defending the various forts are in a state of great exhaustion.

On the other hand, knowing that only a limited number can attack at one time, the continuous reinforcements which the Japanese are hurrying forward are evidences of the way in which their army is being decimated.

FUTURE OF KOREA.

Of all the countries in the Far East, Korea in the opinion of "Engineering" is like [illegible] the one which will be most directy affecte[illegible] great dram[illegible] now being worked out [illegible] leadership of Japan, and [illegible] mense market of China con[illegible] Korea's industries and trad[illegible] to become very important [illegible] ion seems to prevail amo[illegible] that Korea is a poor count[illegible] ing is further [illegible]om the [illegible] soil is fertile, and it[illegible] resour[illegible] developed, [illegible]ld yie[illegible] [illegible] the pre[illegible] time [illegible] st par[illegible] primitive me[illegible]hods, but [illegible] auspices much might be done [illegible] the way of promoting modern manufactures. The Japanese are both able and willing to provide the necessary assistance, and we may look forward to Korea having a future which will exercise great influence on affairs in the Far East, and therefore its evolution is worthy of attention. The present hostilities with Russia have been the cause of the banks restricting their facilities to merchants, and therefore we cannot look for many developments until peace has been restored.

THIBETAN BELIEFS.

The Thibetans have numberless strange myths, the one most curious, pertaining to the sun, moon, and stars; says the "Booklovers' Magazine." The sun is believed to be an immense ball of yak meat and fat whereon the spirits of departed ancestors are supposed to feast, the light being caused by its heated condition. The stars are portions of this immense feast which, dropping to earth, give birth to animals for the sustenance of suffering humanity. The moon is the lesser ball of similar texture as the sun, in use while the larger one is being replenished for the morrow. When the sun or moon fails to appear in cloudy days and nights, it means that the deities are undergoing a period of fasting and religious abnegation. And the parched and sterile condition of bleak regions is ascribed to the fact that many thousand years ago the sun ball slipped from the hands of its keepers, descended too near the earth, and before being recaptured, scorched those parts with which it came in contact.

Two Korean gendarmes and one citizen were arrested by the Japanese on the 27th inst, and conveyed to the Army headquarters.

General Min Yong Whan, who was to have been the bearer of a letter of sympathy to the Japanese troops in Manchuria, has resigned. His place will be taken by General Kwon Chung Hyun.

The Korea Daily News.

VOL. I, THURSDAY, SEPTEMBER 29, 1904. No. 63

大韓每日申報

대한미일신보

(뎨륙십륙호) (일요일) 일천구빅ᄉᆞ년십월삼일

본샤고빅

본신보는영어와한국으로셔계미
일츌판ᄒᆞᆸ

신보갑

한쟝 엽젼두돈오푼

일삭됴 엽젼두량닷돈

우표가미샤닷돈

다엇돈이로밧슴

광고료는

귀한외샹파죠ᄒᆡᆼ의다쇼로죵
갑ᄒᆞ되몃가로밧을터이오매오
리지아니ᄒᆞ면한사람마다다이신
문을보실터이니광고버시기를
원ᄒᆞ시는이들은우리신문샤에
와셔면약ᄒᆞ심을희망ᄒᆞᆸ

○발행소 박동미한일신보
샤의영어한국교셔영국인셜별
필쟝지라오

샤장 영국인 (빗셜)

평양 디리졈

○평양셔종로에사는권미고씨로우
리신문을미리들터이니경ᄒᆞ여
수오니평양에계신구람코자ᄒᆞ
시는쳠군ᄌᆞ는친히디리졈에왕
림ᄒᆞ와면약ᄒᆞ시옵

샤고

○우리대한일신보의목뎍은
대한의일졍대셔에관한모든대
목에되ᄒᆞ야는공평한변론을ᄒᆞ
쟝ᄒᆞ엿사우리동포일유ᄒᆞ심보는
신문으로셔는쳠군ᄌᆞ의게ᄒᆞᆼ상보
도ᄒᆞ리며펀지를귀셔ᄒᆞ여주시
는이는셩명과번디를젹어붓쳐
시기를희망ᄒᆞ오나미기슴신문
샹에긔재ᄒᆞ란는거시아니오다
만극히신용ᄒᆞ는증거를삼고자
홈이며귀ᄌᆞ는아모리셔펀지그
취홈은되겟는권리를가졋ᄉᆞ
나되겟는니ᄋᆞ를밧을터이오
며공정ᄒᆞᆫ사람의펀지는결니
다귀셔는의ᄒᆞᆸ시지안케ᄒᆞᆸ나이

●본샤셜시이리로신문을미명
우에로분젼ᄒᆞ와레젼부의일의
로젼ᄒᆞ는스로번못에는후븟계
져ᄒᆞ기도ᄒᆞ며후면젼계습ᄒᆞᆫ졈
에젼ᄒᆞ기도ᄒᆞ며후에ᄒᆞ나젼ᄒᆞ는
곳도잇다ᄒᆞ와우리신문을ᄉᆞ랑
ᄒᆞ야구람ᄒᆞ시는 쳠군ᄌᆞ의게
더ᄒᆞ야편인ᄒᆞᆫ을겨ᄒᆞ로지금
은분젼인을두고디일일ᄌᆞ이젼
ᄒᆞ며ᄒᆞ나젼ᄒᆞ거나붓계거나ᄒᆞ는
폐가업도록ᄒᆞᆫ다ᄒᆞ오니호야
젼ᄒᆞ기는ᄒᆞᆫ롯게젼ᄒᆞ거나ᄒᆞᆫ일
이잇스면본샤로통긔ᄒᆞ여주심
을희망ᄒᆞᆸ

본샤광고

본샤에셔본신문에ᄉᆞ호와때
일ᄒᆞ와대이셔오ᄒᆞ는소용을배
가잇셔이에광고ᄒᆞ오니누구시
던지이상샹호통에본샤로가일
오시면미졍ᄒᆞ에엿젼두문식드리
리다

론셜

추후젼졍평론

○거월륙일요양젼쟝에아병은
쳘귀ᄒᆞ고일병은젼쟝ᄒᆞ여나는
이후로다시는아모소문도들리
지아니ᄒᆞᆫ즉고로두나라이셔로
병령을굿게ᄒᆞ는중로일아소매에
ᄒᆞ구로과드리지경군이고동안에
피차간교계며ᄌᆞ제에은ᄒᆞ엿스나ᄒᆞᆼ샹ᄒᆞ
엿다ᄒᆞ는로고로겨운이차생ᄒᆞ고
답ᄒᆞᆯ이계ᄒᆞᆫ고라ᄒᆞ는줄로의ᄒᆞᆯ
ᄒᆞ엿ᄂᆞ니

[illegible]

최초에의주로부터평양ᄭᆞ지
쳥병들배에는이주일간이젼후하
수배에가셔샹본지일이나가량스
며쏘젼ᄎᆞ쳥진에평양ᄭᆞ지으로부
터리소연락

[illegible]

은만명식각각편터로분ᄒᆞ여평
셩ᄒᆞ엿스ᄂᆞᆫ증계ᄒᆞᆫ며일륙만명

[illegible]

관보

뎨이젼구빅ᄉᆞ십오호 광무팔년구월삼십일

○셔임급ᄉᆞ령

[illegible]

지훈 쳔위뎨일련디뎨이대티
죵티쟝륙국보병졍위 류완
신창희 쳔위뎨일련디뎨일대
티죵티쟝륙군보병졍위 박명
괴 진위뎨이련디뎨일대티죵
티쟝륙군보병졍위 윤영셩
진위뎨ᄉᆞ련티뎨일대티죵티쟝
륙군보병졍위 김죵모 리승
현 시위뎨일련디뎨일대티향
관륙군일등군ᄉᆞ 박원근 륙
군헌병티죵티쟝륙군헌병졍위
신우균 시위뎨일련티뎨일대
티부륙군보병부위 김영셜
한셰봉 시위뎨일련티뎨삼대
티부륙군보병부위 신우영
쳔위뎨일련티무긔쥬관 륙군
보병부위 김티원 진위뎨오
련티뎨일대티죵티쟝륙군보병
졍위 류긔원 진위뎨ᄉᆞ련티
뎨삼대티부륙군보병부위 변
달현 시위뎨일련티뎨일대티
부륙군일등군ᄉᆞ 안규승

잡보

◎기ᄉᆞ고빙 궁ᄂᆡ부고문관가
등중웅씨ᄂᆞᆫ농샹공부고문관을
겸임ᄒᆞ엿ᄂᆞᆫ데농샹공무를확쟝
ᄒᆞ기위ᄒᆞ야일본인기ᄉᆞ이명을
고빙ᄒᆞ기로작졍ᄒᆞ엿더라

◯안힉ᄉᆞ보고 안힉ᄉᆞ안종덕
씨가시흥군에셔외부로보고ᄒᆞ
기를시흥민요안힉일ᄉᆞᄂᆞᆫ히범
등을초치ᄒᆞ야일일히사문ᄒᆞᆫ즉
민용ᄒᆞᆫ셩우경량인의계공초를
바든연후에야쳐판되겟스니일
본ᄉᆞ령부에죠회ᄒᆞ야히범량인
을히군으로압송ᄒᆞ라ᄒᆞ고본ᄉᆞ
ᄂᆞᆫ직산으로젼왕ᄒᆞ엿다가즉시
회환ᄒᆞᆫ다ᄒᆞ엿더라

◯함송변명셔 일본ᄉᆞ령관이
외부로공함ᄒᆞ되시흥군슈박우
양의피살ᄒᆞᆫ일을사ᄅᆞᆷ마다ᄒᆞ기
를히군슈가인부모집ᄒᆞᆯ즈음에
삭젼션급ᄒᆞᄂᆞᆫ즁놀마를즁간건
몰ᄒᆞ고또빅셩의지물을슈렴ᄒᆞ
다가민요를일으켯다고말들ᄒᆞ
나실샹인즉와젼ᄒᆞᄂᆞᆫ말인고로
본관이변명셔를보니니사죠ᄒᆞ
라ᄒᆞ엿더라

◯신ᄉᆞ동힝 일공관셔긔츄원
씨가한국신ᄉᆞ륙인을안동ᄒᆞ야
일본으로간다ᄂᆞᆫ데아직은자셔
히알슈업다더라

◯부인동반 참쟝현영운씨가
그부인을디동ᄒᆞ고일본에가셔
유람ᄒᆞ리라ᄂᆞᆫ말이잇더라

◯달찰발힝 대구관찰ᄉᆞ장승
원씨ᄂᆞᆫ부임차로지작일에발힝
ᄒᆞ엿다더라

◯감리면보 각항구감리가외
부로면보ᄒᆞ기를일본령ᄉᆞ가죠
회ᄒᆞ되각군호슈와인구슈와결
총과쇼산물픔을일일히죠ᄉᆞᄒᆞ
여시명ᄒᆞ라ᄒᆞ오니엇지죠쳐ᄒᆞᆯ
ᄂᆞᆫ지ᄒᆞ엿다더라

◯시찰발힝긔 일본졍부각관
쳥를시찰ᄎᆞ로젼왕ᄒᆞᄂᆞᆫ리지극
씨등일힝이지명일발졍ᄒᆞᆫ다더
라

◯일진깃긔 칙령을ᄂᆞ리샤일
진회를허여지라ᄒᆞ시미잠시뎡
회ᄒᆞ엿ᄂᆞᆫ데헌병등이회원놈츄
포ᄒᆞᆫ다ᄒᆞ더니무ᄉᆞ타협이된지
라지작일붓터회원들이빅목면
도가ᄉᆞ무소로회동ᄒᆞ야이왕졍
부에제출ᄒᆞ엿든ᄉᆞ됴건을긔어
히실시ᄒᆞᆯᄎᆞ로또졍부에권고ᄒᆞᆯ
터이라더라

◯곡산민요 히쥬관찰ᄉᆞ가외
부로면보ᄒᆞ기를곡산군급보를
거ᄒᆞᆫ즉역부모집ᄉᆞ로본군인민
이야료ᄒᆞ야일본인칠명을타살
ᄒᆞ고본군빅셩도ᄉᆞ샹ᄒᆞ엿스나아
직수효ᄂᆞᆫ뎍실이알수업다고ᄒᆞ
엿기로셔흥군슈리병훈으로사
관을졍ᄒᆞ야사실ᄒᆞᆫ다ᄒᆞ엿더라

◯일병파송 곡산민요ᄉᆞ로일
본병뎡일쇼티가히군으로하거
ᄒᆞ고ᄂᆡ부에셔ᄂᆞᆫ시찰빅동셕씨
를지작일에파송ᄒᆞ엿더라

◯망티건축 돌산군슈가외부
로보고ᄒᆞ기를음력칠월이십칠
일에동경거ᄒᆞᄂᆞᆫ기ᄉᆞ목구텰지
조가본군에리도ᄒᆞ야삼산면건
너편산샹에망티를건축ᄒᆞ면셔
동신ᄒᆞ기위ᄒᆞ야홈이라ᄒᆞ나당
초에졍부인허업시ᄌᆞ의로건축
홈이심히피샹ᄒᆞ다ᄒᆞ엿더라

◯평찰보고 평안남도관찰ᄉᆞ
리즁하씨가ᄂᆡ부로보고ᄒᆞ기를
덕쳔군보를거ᄒᆞᆫ즉각처인민수
쳔명이긔둘을셰우고본군읍져
로취집ᄒᆞᄂᆞᆫ고로효유ᄒᆞ야홋헛
다ᄒᆞ엿고또슌쳔군보를졉ᄒᆞᆫ즉
인민이본군에취집ᄒᆞ야일진회
라조칭ᄒᆞ고날노수효가즁가ᄒᆞ
ᄂᆞᆫ고로효유ᄒᆞ야홋터지라ᄒᆞᆫ즉
디답ᄒᆞ기를모히고홋터짐을황
셩본회의지휘디로ᄒᆞᆫ다ᄒᆞ고일
향둔취ᄒᆞ야원근이다소요ᄒᆞ더
니팔월십삼일에슌쳔군슈가보
고ᄒᆞ기를회민등이일제이홋터
졋다ᄒᆞᄂᆞᆫ데당초에히회민등의
종젹을탐지ᄒᆞᆫ즉평민은별노업
고미가륙쟝ᄒᆞ야회즁에투입ᄒᆞ
ᄂᆞᆫ자가무비동학당류요일병을
두려워ᄒᆞ야칭호를변기ᄒᆞ야일
진회라칭ᄒᆞ야인심을션동ᄒᆞ야
셔북삼도우민이향응ᄒᆞ야슌쳔
군으로데일만히취집ᄒᆞ엿더니
이제홀연히홋터진거신즉진위
디병뎡이삼등으로좃차슌쳔으
로향ᄒᆞᄂᆞᆫ연고이라쟝찻어ᄂᆞ디
방으로취회ᄒᆞᆯᄂᆞᆫ지예료치못ᄒᆞ
겟다ᄒᆞ엿더라

◯민난지보 의쥬군슈가외부
로보고ᄒᆞ기를일병의군용텰도
가본군비현광셩등여셧면을범
ᄒᆞ엿ᄂᆞᆫ데쇼범ᄒᆞᆫ토디결복이오
십여결이요또이츄결을당ᄒᆞ야
실렴못된곡식이만히일인의말
먹이가되니빅셩이지보ᄒᆞᆯ슈업
다ᄒᆞ엿더라

◯텰도쳥이 ᄂᆡ부에셔외부로
조회ᄒᆞ기를창원군보를거ᄒᆞᆫ즉
마산텰도가본군향교담뒤십보
허와긱샤쥬룽으로부셜되엿스
니오빅년존승디지가일됴에이
러ᄒᆞᆫ즉만만황송ᄒᆞᆫ온지라본
군슈가일본군디와루차교셥ᄒᆞ
엿스되맛참ᄂᆡ라쳐로이셜치아
니ᄒᆞᆫ다ᄒᆞ엿기로죠회ᄒᆞ니곳일
관에이죠ᄒᆞ야히텰도지션을다
른길노이셜케ᄒᆞ라ᄒᆞ엿더라

◯슈령보쳔 작일에졍부에셔
각부부로죠회ᄒᆞ기를슈령ᄌᆞ격
에합당ᄒᆞᆫ관인을보쳔ᄒᆞ야졍부
로보ᄒᆞ라ᄒᆞ엿더라

◯히셔상강 셔도로셔샹리ᄒᆞᆫ
사ᄅᆞᆷ의말을드르니곡산신계등
디에ᄂᆞᆫ발셔셔리가와셔년ᄉᆞ가
겸년을면치못ᄒᆞᆫ다더라

◯곡불실염 려쥬인쳔등디에
ᄂᆞᆫ츄간에한지가지리ᄒᆞᆫ고로면
답간곡식이티반이나실염이못
되엿다더라

◯열심단톄 일진회ᄂᆞᆫ금일에
긔회를시작ᄒᆞᆫ다ᄒᆞᄂᆞᆫ데금회에
ᄂᆞᆫ빅비나열심으로단톄를일우
어목뎍을취셔ᄒᆞᆫ다ᄒᆞ고위름ᄒᆞᆫ
말이만타더라

◯일진공함 일진회에셔경무
쳥과경위원과ᄉᆞ령부로공함ᄒᆞ
기를각긔쥬에류슉ᄒᆞᄂᆞᆫ회원을
구박ᄒᆞ야풍찬로슉ᄒᆞ게ᄒᆞ너싱
민을보호ᄒᆞᄂᆞᆫ졍ᄉᆞ가아니라다
시신칙ᄒᆞ야보호케ᄒᆞ라ᄒᆞ엿ᄂᆞᆫ
디총디위원은협죵모윤갑병홍
쥰계씨를파송ᄒᆞ엿더라

◯ᄂᆡ불련셔 외부에셔룡쳔감
리로히군슈를겸임ᄒᆞᆯᄎᆞ로졍부
에쳥의ᄒᆞᆫ량으로ᄂᆡ부대신의게
련셔ᄒᆞᆷ을쳥ᄒᆞ엿더니ᄂᆡ부에셔
히쳥의셔를작환ᄒᆞ고죠회ᄒᆞ기
를교셥ᄉᆞ무가번극ᄒᆞᆫ항구에감
리가군슈를겸임ᄒᆞ면ᄉᆞ무에구
이가만켓ᄂᆞᆫ고로기히련셔치못
ᄒᆞᆫ다ᄒᆞ엿더라

ᄉᆞ힝연긔 일병츌젼디위문
대ᄉᆞ권즁현씨가일간발졍ᄒᆞᆫ다
더니 어ᄉᆞᄒᆞ옵시ᄂᆞᆫ물픔이아
직미비ᄒᆞ야긔일간을연타ᄒᆞᆫ다
더라

◯단발긱후죠 일젼에로샹에
셔단발ᄒᆞᆫ자가대취ᄒᆞ야후쥬ᄒᆞ
거놀경쳥에셔착슈ᄒᆞ엿더니지
작야에일헌병이경쳥에돌입ᄒᆞ
야쎅셔갓ᄂᆞᆫ데그후쥬ᄒᆞᆫ든사람
은일진회총디량지익씨라더라

◯아병동졍 북관면보를거ᄒᆞᆫ
즉아병이거월이십륙일경에셩
진에일천명가량이쥬둔ᄒᆞ고셩
진과단천ᄉᆞ이에오빅명가량이
ᄂᆞ잇셔졍담을ᄒᆞ고또북쳥진위
디병졍의병긔ᄂᆞᆫ일변파쇄ᄒᆞ야
쓰지못ᄒᆞ게ᄒᆞ고이원에잇든병
졍의병긔ᄂᆞᆫ모다탈취ᄒᆞ야강물
에바렷고아라ᄉᆞ졍담김인슈ᄂᆞᆫ
아병이십칠긔를령솔ᄒᆞ고이원
에리도ᄒᆞ엿다더라

경원철도 일본에셔지금경
원철도를부셜ᄒᆞ기위ᄒᆞ야급급
히쥰비즁인ᄃᆡ그철도리수가셔
울셔평양리수와거진갓흔리셔
울셔원산가ᄂᆞᆫ디ᄂᆞᆫ산이만하셔
철도공역에용이치못ᄒᆞᆫ즉명년
말에나쥰공이되리라더라

◯폐현유일 탁지고문관목하
젼씨가일본세관ᄉᆞ무관령목씨
를디동ᄒᆞ고릐오일에 폐현ᄒᆞᆫ
다더라

◯진찰치셩 령남긔의젼셜을
드른즉진쥬관찰ᄉᆞ셩기운씨가
도임ᄒᆞᆫ지불과수삭에힝졍샹은
위가병시ᄒᆞᆫ고로관리비가외복
ᄒᆞ며가쟝렴명ᄒᆞ야민심을흡독
홈으로관하각군에숑셩이쟈쟈
ᄒᆞ다ᄒᆞ니향시각 문에긔지ᄒᆞᆫ
바불미지셜은히관찰과혐의잇
ᄂᆞᆫ자가ᄭᅮ여낸랑셜이라더라

◯군졔의졍뎡지 군졔의졍ᄉᆞ
에셔히ᄉᆞ무를한일삭뎡지ᄒᆞ엿
다가다시의졍ᄒᆞᆫ다ᄂᆞᆫ데경비와
월봉등지졍을예산ᄒᆞᆫ후에야군
졔졔반계획를결졍ᄒᆞᆫ다더라

외보

◯로뎨젼별 로국셔구월삼십
일브터뎨팔군단을젼쟝으로슈
송홈으로로뎨씌셔젼별ᄒᆞ기위
ᄒᆞ야구월이십팔일에오뎃사항
으로젼왕ᄒᆞ엿다더라

◯로도공동 로국셔울셔ᄂᆞᆫ려
슌구의형셰가심히위급홈으로
대단히심려ᄒᆞ야일반인심이소
동된다더라

◯포디공역 봉 에셔철령으
로남방십이리되ᄂᆞᆫ모산에ᄂᆞᆫ십
사영리되ᄂᆞᆫ포디를건축ᄒᆞ야발
셔대포를버려두엇고그젼면일
ᄃᆡ에ᄂᆞᆫ히조를팟ᄂᆞᆫ디또동디에
셔셔남으로칠리되ᄂᆞᆫ마봉구에
도포디와히조를싸흐며역ᄉᆞ를
엄즁히ᄒᆞᆫ다더라

광고

TELEGRAMS.

FROM JAPAN PAPERS.

London, September 23, 2 P. M.

The Russian Government appointed a committee to determine their definition of contraband of war some time ago, and the committee has now come to a decision, declaring that coal, raw cotton and iron are contraband. This decision shows that the recent British representations are to be disregarded.

London, Sept. 24th.

The steamer Foxton Hall has arrived at Kiaochao and transhipped her cargo of coal to the German steamer Erica. The former sailed for Japan ostensibly; but it is believed that it was intended that she should supply the coal to Russian warships and colliers at Kiachao.

Russian agents have lately been buying great stocks of coal. A large quantity has recently been shipped from Liverpool to Vladivostock. Some of it was sent to Hongkong for transhipment to the north. Several colliers are assembled in one of the uninhabited islands of the Philippines, waiting to supply coal to Russian warships.

Peking, Sept. 24.

The day before yesterday, the Chinese Emperor sent the following telegram to the Czar:—The Emperor of Great China desires to make a statement to the Czar of Great Russia, as follow:—We are very much pleased with the deep friendship existing between Russia and China. But we are extremely concerned at the thought that Mukden, where the mausolea of the Chinese Imperial family are situated, may not be spared the disastrous results of the war. We sincerely desire that your Majesty will arrange that the city shall be secured from danger of this kind. But for the Russian occupation, the Japanese would not approach Mukden at all. We are gladly trusting in the sincerity of your Majesty's good toward us.—Mainichi.

THE APPOINTMENT OF GENERAL GRITENBERG.

Berlin, Sept. 26.

General Gritenberg has been appointed Commander of the 2nd Manchurian Army.

The Army in Manchuria will be considerably increased in order that it may be able to quickly achieve success in the field. In consequence a General Gritenberg, who comes from the Vilna district has been placed in command with General Kuropatkin.

CIRCUM-BAIKAL RAILWAY.

Berlin, Sept. 26.

The railway round Lake Baikal has been opened for traffic.

AN INNOCENT MAN SET FREE.

Mr. Adolph Beck, the man who has received the free pardon of the King for crimes which he never committed, but for which he suffered penal servitude, declares that his innocence was established as the direct answer to prayers.

"It was God," he said yesterday solemnly, "who inspire John Smith, my double, to commit the frauds upon the Misses Turner while I was still in custody. The police knew nothing of the existence of John Smith, except that they were persuaded that I was John Smith. Again, it was Providence that directed the girls' landlord to follow him to the pawnbroker's shop and detect him in the act of pawning their jewellery. Had he been a little slower the man would have got away, and I should have been sent to penal servitude. But God answered my prayers."

Mr. Beck clamed that Inspector Kane was equally inspired from above. Mr. Kane, then a sergeant, was present at the Old Bailey when Mr. Beck was wrongfully convicted, and after he had finished his sentence saw him very often in his division, for Mr. Beck came to live in it. Mr. Kane was struck by one or two points. The ex-convict always wore pince-nez, never the monocle described by the girls who secured his conviction. He had no scar on his chin or neck, as sworn against him. There were other little things which led the Inspector to doubt If this was the real John Smith convicted in 1877 of similar frauds.

Seeing Mr. Beck frequently kept the case in his mind. "But," averred Mr. Beck, "it was the act of God which led Mr. Kane to the Tottenham Court-road police station the day he found the real John Smith. He told me that something irresistible seemed to drive him to go in and ask what was going on. They told him that a man was arrested for stealing rings from girls and pawning them. Immediately he thought of my case, and he asked for the key of the cell.

THE ALL-IMPORTANT SCAR.

"He found the prisoner William Thomas, as he called himself, and told him to stand up. The man stood to attention in military fashion, and Mr. Kane passed his hand over his face and found the all-important scar.

'I've caught you at last John Smith,' said the Inspector, and that was how God answered my earnest prayer."

Mr. Beck expressed his deep thankfulness to Mr. G. R. Sims, who had championed his cause from his first conviction. The question of compensation for his unjust imprisonment is expected to be settled in a few days.

In the story of his unhappy experiences, as told by himself in the "Evening News" Adolf Beck relates how he was first arrested on the charge, since proved false, of stealing a watch from a woman.

He eloquently describes the horror and amazement with which, even when expecting to speedily be cleared, he realised the indignity which had been upon him. But next day nine women identified him from among other men, and he began to feel dismay at his position.

Everything worked against him in these preliminary processes, and when at length he was committed for trial he felt it a positive relief. But he closes this portion of this strange, eventful history with one striking sentence.

"In my lonely imprisonment I had prepared a long statement, and was going to read it to the Magistrate before he committed me, but my Solicitor stood up in front of me and sternly forbade me to speak. To my dying day I shall regret that I obeyed him."

THE RUSSIAN PRISONERS.

The "Kobe Chronicle" reports that the Iyo Railway Company, which is reclaiming land from the sea at Takahama, has offered to employ on this work some thirty of the Russian prisoners now at Matsuyama, and to pay a wage of 25 sen per day. If the men are found satisfactory, 200 to 300 will then be employed at about 35 sen a day. Mr. Inouye, President of the company, has made application for permission to employ the prisoners, and that matter has been referred to the authorities in Tokyo.

[This is considerably less than half the wage, which the Japanese Government are offering for hire of Korean coolies K. D. N.

THE BALTIC FLEET AT LIBAU.

The following despatch from Europe has been received in official quarters in Tokio:—

According to a journalist who interviewed the officer commanding the Squadron now at Libau, there are at present in that port 6 battle-ships, 5 cruisers and a number of torpedo-craft and transports. The commanding officer says that he is to wait for 3 other vessels which will soon set out, and that, after performing the necessary manoeuvres, the time for the squadron's departure will be determined with due regard to the freezing of Vladivostok. The Admiral is quite well, and the rumour of his illness is without basis.

According to the "Asaki," the War Bonds issued in the past few months are now changing hands very largely in Osaka. It is stated than ten clerks in the Osaka branch of the Bank of Japan are required to attend to the registration of the names of new bondholders.

Whether the loss of a top-knot is conducive to insobriety, we do not know, but our reporter informs us that one Yang Chai Ik, a member of the Il Chin Hoi had no sooner had his head shaved than he went out on the streets and became uproariously drunk. He passed the night in the Korean Police station, whence he was removed by Japanese Gendarmes in the morning. The sequel to his night out has not transpired.

ARROGANCE.

We hear with regard to the riot at Koksan, that enquiries are being made as to the reason of the anti-Japanese demonstration. They should not have far to seek for the reason, which has formed the basis of more than one article in these columns and can be called by various epithets.

Perhaps, "Arrogance" is the most apt term.

DECLINE IN BONDS.

In the course of an editorial the "Kobe Chronicle remarks.

As already reported, information has been received by the Yokohama Specie Bank to the effect that Japanese bonds in London continue to show a decline, and a very marked decline, since the battle of Liaoyang. It is at first sight curious that a battle which undoubtedly constitutes a great victory for Japan should have the effect of actually depressing its securities; but the financiers have evidently gauged Liaoyang not by what was achieved but by what was aimed at and the failure to crush KUROPATKIN's army has induced a cold wave of doubt as to the ultimate success of Japan in the tremendous task she has undertaken. Again, the dealy in the fall of Port Arthur, which was placed even by conservative estimates at about the middle of Septemer, has further tended to expose to great magnitude of the struggle and the enormous difficulties under which it is being waged. Possibly it is for this reason that the Japanese are, according to reports, making a general assault upon Port Arthur believing that the capture of a fortress reputed to be impregnable would, even, at the cost of heavy loss of life, revive confidence in Japanese capacity and ultimate success.

The Korea Daily News.

Issued at 5 P. M. daily except Sundays.

Rate of Subscription:—	
Per Year,	Yen 25.
Per Quarter,	Yen 7.
Per Month	Yen 2.50

Postage in Korea not charged extra.
Postage abroad charged extra.

Advertisements, 50 sen per day for 1 inch or less. 5 yen per month per inch. 50 yen per year per inch.

All communications to E. T. BETHELL, Editor and Publisher. Pak-tong, Seoul.

THE SECOND RUSSIAN ARMY.

Now that we have definite news of the formation of a second Russian Army it is interesting to speculate upon its probable operations.

It seems fairly certain that the new army will act on the offensive but it is difficult to guess what base it will operate. We have been told that the Trans-Siberian Railroad is already strained to its utmost to keep Kuropatkin's army supplied.

Although this is not entirely true there is undoubtedly a good deal of truth in it. The most liberal estimate we have seen says that the railway cannot be counted upon to carry supplies for more than 400,000 men. If this estimate errs at all, it errs on the side of liberality. When a railway is working at high pressure, numerous miner breakdowns are inevitable. and a considerable reduction has to be made from the capacity of the railway when everything is working smoothly.

We are informed that the second Russian army is to be of the same size as that commanded by General Kuropatkin. This will bring the total number of Russian troops in Manchuria up to something between 500,000 and 600,000.

As the railway cannot possibly be depended upon for supplies for more than 400,000 men, it follows that the second army will have to make its base at a place to which supplies can be brought independently of the Trans-Siberian Railway.

The only place answering to this description is Vladivostok. Steamers laden with supplies are continually arriving at Vladivostok, and until the Japanese navy is released from its vigil off Port Auther, they will continue to arrive.

There is a railway running north from Vladivostok to khabarowsk on the Amur river. This line would be of almost inestimable value to an army operating from Vladivostok as supplies can be brought down the Amur river almost from lake Baikal, thus leaving the railway between Baikal and Kharbin entirely free to suppling the wants of general Kuroatkins' army.

Still Vladivostok, as a base, has its weak points. An army advancing from there, due south into Korea leaves behind it a peculiarly vulnerable line of communications. The road follows the the sea coast almost the whole way and Japanese landing parties, if they did nothing else could do a lot of very effective guerilla fighting.

Still, taking everything into consideration, it still seems reasonable to believe that Vladivostock will be the second Russian base and that from there three columns will advance, one down the east coast, one down the Yalu river and one into central Korea.

The success of these operations seems to us to depend in great measure upon the number of men which the Japanese will be able to oppose them with. We do not think that Japan will be able to withdraw a single man from the armies now in the field, and the question is whether they have in reserve men in sufficient quantity and quality to cope with this new Russian move.

The war has now definitely resolved itself into one of exhaustion and it seems to us that in this game all the advantages will lie with the Russians.

HOW TO PUT EUROPE INTO THE UNITED STATES.

This is the way, states an American journal, to put Europe into the United States and have a lot of room left over:—Put Germany, Holland, Greece and Switzerland in Texas and have enough room left for Persia. The only place for Belgium is in the Maine woods, but then you would have enough room left for another Belgium and Porto Rico. France and Portugal would fit nicely in Wyoming and Montana, and Sweden would go into California with lots of room to spare, Spain would fit into Nevada and Idaho by slicing a little additional piece from California. Or, better, take 4,000 square miles from Arizona and that would still leave Arizona large enough for Italy. The British Isles could be stowed away in New Mexico, with plenty of room left for Bermuda and the British West Indies. Austria-Hungary would go into Oregon and Colorado, provided 43,000 square miles are borrowed from Washington. Then that would leave Washington room enough for the Kindom of Servia and a couple more of the same size. Roumania would go into Arkansas and Bulgaria could turn around in Oklahoma. Put Turkey into Missouri and Norway in the two Dakotas. Then Denmark and the other odds and ends would fit in left-over areas of Western States. The balance of the United States would be more than enough for Russia.

The American journal forgets to add that, when Europe has thus been comfortably stowed away in the United States, the whole lot could be packed into Canada, with heaps of room to spare!

INTERNATIONAL FRACAS AT PEKING.

A rather serious quarrel occurred on September 15th at Peking between Italian and Chinese soldiers. A company of the former were on the glacis, or drill ground just north of the Legation quarter, engaged in drilling and gymnastics. Two Chinese soldiers were among the bystanders watching the exercises when, it is said, one of them made some uncomplimentary remarks concerning the Italian drilling. They then went inside the enclosure, when the Italian soldiers ordered them from the ground because of their not being in uniform. This angered the Chinese soldiers and one of them took off his belt and struck an Italian soldier in the face. The Chinese then started to run away, but one of them was captured. Ten Italians were detailed to pursue the other soldier which they did as far as General Chiang's Yamen. The Italians fired their rifles in the air, forced their way past the sentry, and met the General who ordered them from the place. The Italians departed. Fortunately a company of Chinese soldiers which is quartered at the General's Yamen were out at target practice. Had they been at home there might have been serious trouble. No satisfactory settlement has as yet been made of the matter.—Shanghai Mercury.

A new departure has been entered on by Japanese Gendarmes. For the last few nights they have been presenting themselves at the Palace gate and making enquiries as to the identity of passers in and goers out.

Mr. Megata will be received in audience by His Majesty on Wednesday.

It is reported that the soldiers of the local guard at Kougchu have destroyed the Japanese consulate at Kunsan.

Our Japanese contemporary the Inchon Sangpo, learns that the Seoul Gensan railroad will be completed about the end of next year.

The Tonghaks in the neighbourhood of Pyengyang have disbanded on hearing that Japanese troops were on their way to effect the arrest of the leaders and disperse the mob.

A report from the Koksan district states that the riot there has assumed formidable dimensions. Seven Japanese and several Koreans have been killed. A body of Japanese troops has been sent to quell the disturbance.

A telegram from Gensan states that the Russian troops at Songchin on the 26th ult. numbered 1,500 at Pukchong, they had seized the rifles of the local Korean guard and destroyed their mechanism.

A sample copy of the "Tageblatt für Nord China," a German daily published in Tientsin, has reached us. It is well got up and should prove valuable to readers of the German language, in the Orient. We wish it's promoters every success.

It is said that the six Korean Officials, who are to visit Japan, will depart on their mission tomorrow. We do not think that any more political significance can be assigned to this move, than to the repeated despatch of envoys to Manchuria, bearing messages of sympathy to the Japanese troops.

Here is a paragraph from the leading paper in Natal;—"I have decided to award a Cake (of blacking) to the Editor of the Tickey Tarbush for his princely impartiality in the distribution of thinly-veiled abuse. Why, ah, why, in these days of Women's Rights, should we uphold old-fashioned and obsolete notions of gentlemanliness? If the Editor of the said Tarbrush will call at this office, he may become acquainted not only with the said Cake, but with boot to which it naturally appertains."

The Shanghai correspondent of the "Jiji" wires that Marquis Saionji, Baron Takasaki, Mr. Tokio Yokoi, M.P., and party arrived at Shanghai on Saturday last and were to have left for Suchow and Hangchow the following day. The party will travel up the Yangtsze as far as Changsha and will start on their return journey towards the latter part of October. The correspondent adds that the pro-Russian papers at Shanghai are inclined to attach much political importance to the present visit of the Marquis and his party.

Says a writer in Harper's Weekly: "There are two things the literary artist craves—praise and money. Of the later it is interesting to speak, because the matter of money-making is changing the whole course of literature, and a few great fortunes made have beckoned all sorts of stragglers, halt and crippled, into the field. In view of the fortunes made by Hall Caine and Marie Corelli, it is wholesome to reflect upon the twenty-five dollars that Milton got for 'Paradise Lost' Shelley never made anything out of his poetry; Browning for twenty years and over paid to get his work printed; the greatest of English novelists earns his livelihood by reading for publishers, and although we have no data, it would be safe to guess that Mr. Swinburne could not support himself by his poetry. To sum up, in Stevenson's words: 'What you may decently expect if you have some talent and much industry is such an income as a clerk will earn with a tenth or perhaps a twentieth of your nervous output.'"

The Korea Daily News.

VOL. I, MONDAY, OCTOBER 3, 1904. No. 66

HONGKONG & SHANGHAI BANKING CORPORATION.

Paid-up Capital.....	$10,000,000
Reserve Fund:—Sterling Reserve...	10,000,000
Silver Reserve.....	7,000,000
	27,000,000
Reserve Liability of Proprietors...	10,000,000

HEAD OFFICE, HONGKONG.

London Bankers, London and County Banking Company Limited.
Branches and Agencies,
London.

Amoy,	Hankow	Penang,
Bangkok,	Hiogo,	Rangoon,
Batavia,	Iloilo,	Saigon,
Bombay,	Lyons,	San Francisco,
Calcutta,	Manila,	Singapore,
Colombo,	Nagasaki,	Sourabaya,
Foochow,	New York,	Tientsin,
Hamburg,	Peking,	Yokohama,

Credits granted on approved Securities, and every description of Banking and Exchange business transacted.

Drafts granted on London and the chief Commercial places in Europe, India, Australia, America, China and Japan.

HOLME RINGER & CO., AGENTS,
CHEMULPO.

ON CHEONG & CO., SEOUL.

GENERAL STORE KEEPERS.
Imported provisions, Cooking Utensils Crockery, etc.
FRESH BREAD DAILY.

MITSU BISHI DOCKYARD & ENGINE WORKS,

NAGASAKI.

CODE WORD, "DOCK."

A. 1, A. B. C., and Engineering Codes used.

DOCK No. 1 (at Tategami).

Extreme Length.............	523 feet
Length on blocks	513 ,,
Width of Entrance on Top......	89 ,,
,, ,, Bottom....	77 ,,
Water on Blocks at Spring Tide	26½ ,,

DOCK No. 2 (Mukaijima).

Extreme Length.............	371 feet
Length on Blocks............	360 ,,
Width of Entrance on Top......	66 ,,
,, ,, Bottom	53 ,,
Water on Blocks at Spring Tide	22 ,,

PATENT SLIP (at Kosuge).

Can take vessels up to 1,000 tons gross.

THE WORKS are well equipped with the LATEST IMPROVEMENTS, and can execute any kind of work in SHIPBUILDING and MARINE ENGINEERING, as well as in REPAIRING of SHIPS.

The COMPANY'S new powerful steamer OURA-MARU (712 tons, 700 I.H.P.), specially built for SALVAGE PURPOSES, and equipped with necessary gear, is always READY at SHORT NOTICE.

CHARTERED BANK OF INDIA AUSTRALIA & CHINA.

INCORPORATED BY ROYAL CHARTER 1853

HEAD OFFICES:—LONDON.

Paid-up Capital	£800,000
Reserve Liability of Share-holders	800,000
Reserve Fund	800,000

Drafts granted upon all the principal places in the world and every description of Exchange and banking business transacted.

E. MEYER & Co., Agents,
Chemulpo.

E. MEYER & CO.

Chemulpo.

SOLE AGENTS IN KOREA FOR:

A. T. Morse, Sons & Co's "Fresco" Distemper

In all colours ready for use on walls, Ceilings etc.
and

AVENARIUS CARBOLINEUM

A wood-preserving and antiseptic oil preparation

Against decay, dry-rot, fungus and wood-destroying insects.

A large supply always in Stock.
Prices upon application.

E. MEYER & Co.,
Chemulpo.

LAW UNION & CROWN INS. CO.

Fire risks accepted at Current rates, on godowns, merchandise, dwellings, and other property, subject to usual conditions.

HOLME RINGER & Co.,
Agents, Chemulpo

THE METHODIST PUBLISHING HOUSE,

Little West Gate, Seoul.

JOB PRINTING, TYPEWRITER PAPER
CARBON PAPER, VISITING CARDS
STATIONERY, BOOK BINDING
BOOK PUBLISHERS
AMERICAN SCHOOL BOOKS
SPENCERIAN COPY BOOKS
PEN CARBON LETTER AND BILL BOOKS

S. A. BECK, Manager.

DAI-ICHI GINKO.

LIMITED.

(Formerly the First National Bank)

ESTABLISHED 1873

INCORPORATED UNDER PRESENT LAW 1896

Capital - - - - - - - -	Yen 5,000,000
Reserve Fund - - - - -	1,500,000

HEAD OFFICE:—TOKIO.

President: Baron SHIBUSAWA.

BRANCHES AND CORRESPONDENTS
In the Principal Cities and Towns of Japan.
Interest Allowed on

Fixed deposits 1 year - - -	6¼	per cent
" " 6 months - - -	6	per cent

Special current accounts 1½ sen daily per Y 100
General " " ; " " " 100

M. TANAKA,
Manager, Chemulpo

HOLME RINGER & Co.

Chemulpo.

General Merchants and Government Contractors.

Agents for the leading

Banks

Steamship Companies

and

Insurance Companies

Importers of Merchandise of every description.

KAMEYA & CO.

GENERAL STOREKEEPERS
Chinkokai - - Seoul
(Established 1895, Tokyo)

Confectionery, Hams, Canned Goods, Cutlery, Hirano & Tansan Water. Provisions, Gents, Furnishing goods, Toilet Articles, Travelling Bags, Tobacco, Cigars & Cigarettes Kitchen Utensils. Coffee, Biscuits.

Fresh Goods always kept in Stock.
Prices Moderate
Please come and insbect our goods.

NIPPON YUSEN KAISHA.

JAPANESE MAIL STEAMSHIP CO.

DER MAIL CONTRACT WITH THE IMPERIAL JAPANESE GOVERNMENT.

European Line

Regular Fortnightly Service between Yokohama Kobe, Moji, Shanghai, Hongkong, Singapore, Penang Colombo, Port Said, Marseilles, London and Antwerp

American Line

Regular Fortnightly Service between Hongkong and Seattle, calling at Shanghai, Moji, Kobe, Yokohama and Victoria, B. C.

Australian Line

Regular weekly Service betwen Japan Ports and Australia, calling at Hongkong and Manila.
(Above Three Lines Suspended until further notice).

Shanghai Line

Weekly Service between Shanghai and Japan Ports

Korea Line

Service Kobe, Moji, Nagasaki, Fusan, Chemulpo, Chinnampo, Taiku.
S. S. Bahelsberg, 2181 tons.
Service Kobe, Moji, Fusan, Chemulpo, Chinnampo
S. S ARGO, S. S. Ohio.

BORDEN'S CONDENSED MILK CO.

New York, U. S. A.

ALWAYS IN STOCK

Eagle Brand Condensed Milk.

Gold Seal Condensed Milk.

Peerless (Family) Evaporated Cream.

Borden's Malted Milk.

E. MEYER & CO.
Chemulpo, Korea,
Sole Agents

ROYAL INSURANCE COMPANY,

Funds exceed £10,000,000
FIRE
AT CURRENT RATES.
LIFE
REDUCED PREMIUM.
HOLME RINGER & Co.,
Agents, Chemulpo.

HOTEL DU PALAIS

SEOUL.

The only first class Hotel in Seoul. Situated in the centre of the city opposite the palace.

Cuisine under the supervision of an experienced French Chef.

Well ventilated and furnished throughout.

TARIFF UPON APPLICATION

L. MARTIN
Proprietor and Mangaer

大韓每日申報

대한매일신보

(뎨륙십칠호)　　(화요일)　　일쳔구빅사년십월스일

본샤고빅

본신보는영어와한어로셔계믹
일출판ᄒᆞᆸ
　신문가
한쟝　　엽두돈오푼
일삭됴　엽두량닷돈
우표가미삭닷돈
　다맛돈으로밧숩
광고료는
귀한의쟝단과ᄌᆞ항의다쇼로죵
갑ᄒᆞ되렴가로밧을터이오며오
린지아녀대한사람마다다이신
문을보실터이니광고버시기를
원ᄒᆞ시는이들은우리신문사에
와셔면약ᄒᆞ심을희망ᄒᆞᆸ

○발힝소　박동대한미일신보
사법어학교압히젼영국인셜필
림집자리오
　사쟝 영국인 (비셜)
평양 디리졈
○평양효동사는권미보씨로우
리신문관미디리인을뎡ᄒᆞ엿
ᄉᆞ오니평양에계신구람코져ᄒᆞ
시는 쳠군ᄌᆞ는힝티리졈에왕
림ᄒᆞ와면의ᄒᆞ시옵

샤고

○우리대한미일신보의목뎍은
대한의인녕졀셔에관한모든데
목에티ᄒᆞ야는공평한번론을주
쟝홈이라우리동신원의탐보는
신문보시는쳠군ᄌᆞ의게ᄒᆞᆼ상보
도ᄒᆞ리며편지들귀셔ᄒᆞ며주시
는이는셩명과번디를젹어붓치
시기를희망ᄒᆞ오나이거슨신문
샹에긔쥐ᄒᆞ랴는거시아니오다
만극히신용ᄒᆞ는증거를숨고자
홈이라귀자는아모귀셔던지과
쥐홈을되챠ᄒᆞ는권리를가젓소
나되챠ᄒᆞ는리유를말ᄒᆞᆯ터이오
며공중평화를문란케ᄒᆞ는듯ᄒᆞᆫ
다귀셔는의례히밧지안켓습나이

●본사셜시이릭로신문을미양
우례로분젼ᄒᆞ와례젼부의임의
로젼ᄒᆞ든ᄉᆞ스로먼곳에는흑늣게
젼ᄒᆞ기도ᄒᆞ며흑빗칠거슬ᄒᆞᆫ법
에젼ᄒᆞ기도ᄒᆞ며흑아니젼ᄒᆞ는
곳도잇다ᄒᆞ와우리신문을ᄉᆞ랑
ᄒᆞ야구람ᄒᆞ시는 쳠군ᄌᆞ의계
되ᄒᆞ야미우미안ᄒᆞ옵기로지금
은분젼인을두고미일죵이젼
ᄒᆞ며아니젼ᄒᆞ거나늣게거나ᄒᆞᆫ

폐가업도록ᄒᆞ란ᄒᆞ오니혹아니
젼ᄒᆞ거나흑늣게젼ᄒᆞ거나ᄒᆞᆫ일
이잇스면본샤로통긔ᄒᆞ여주심
을희망ᄒᆞᆸ

본샤광고

본샤에셔본신문뎨ᄉᆞ호와뎨샵
일호와뎨이십오호를ᄉᆞ옵ᄂᆞ데
가잇셔이에광고ᄒᆞ오니누구시던
던지이상삼호중에본샤로가져
오시면미쟝에빅젼두푼식드리
리로

론셜

아병의뎨이군

○이제아라사에셔제ᄎᆞ동병에
대ᄒᆞ야이군을조직ᄒᆞ기에디ᄒᆞ
주의ᄒᆞᆫ다ᄒᆞᆫ즉이소분과갓튼진
디펄령분겨ᄒᆞ야다시동병은ᄒᆞ
는듯ᄒᆞ나진터졈거ᄒᆞ기가미오
어렴을듯ᄒᆞᆫ지라
귀왕우리신문에도아라사에서
구로파드킨장군의군사제반수
용ᄒᆞ기위하야셔빅리아쳘도에
젼력ᄒᆞ엿다고보도ᄒᆞᆫ바이니와
파연진션진미홀지는확실알수
업스되엇제던지대단히긴요ᄒᆞ
고편리ᄒᆞᆯ지라ᄒᆞᆫ다는사람의가
량으로ᄒᆞ는말을듯드리도쟝즐
사십만명과밋은용픔은무뎌
히탐지ᄒᆞ리라ᄒᆞ주이거시공연
ᄒᆞᆫ거즛말은아닌듯ᄒᆞᆫ거시고쳘
도를간금히부셜ᄒᆞ기에수만명
역부를동독ᄒᆞ야쟝시도모되쳐
못ᄒᆞ고완죠ᄒᆞ엿스니즉
아라사로셔제ᄎᆞ동병에구로파
드킨장군의게명령ᄒᆞ엿다는바
와갓튼진티응당만주에잇는군
사모도밧을듯ᄒᆞ니라만일그리
ᄒᆞ는경우에는총계쟝즐이오십
만명이나흑륙십만명이불하ᄒᆞᆯ
터이니셔빅리아쳘도로는그수
효를가히모다탐지치못ᄒᆞᆯ지라
뒤으로련속ᄒᆞ야츌발ᄒᆞ는군사
는다른한곳으로졍ᄒᆞ게ᄒᆞ야그
쳘도에구의됨이셔로업게ᄒᆞ며
야ᄒᆞᆯ터인디
그ᄒᆞᆫ곳인즉히삼ᄋᆞ 라아국쟝즐
과셔로분픔을ᄂᆞᆫ션으로련속ᄒᆞ
야라수산항구에일병히방될때셔
지수출ᄒᆞ야도박ᄒᆞᆯ터이요쳘도로
는히삼위북방으로아마강을건
너카바로스바으로통ᄒᆞ야히삼
에잇는군병의응용지물을수

츌ᄒᆞ게ᄒᆞᆯ지경이며이는아모리
도로랑치못ᄒᆞ엿슬분인즉마음
티로힝ᄒᆞ기에미오편리ᄒᆞᆯ듯하
도다
무릇아병이히삼위로진리들쟝
ᄒᆞ는거시한국에는심히불호ᄒᆞᆫ
일이요파연그리ᄒᆞᆯ지경이면한
국에히당ᄒᆞ엿다는말이쥼쥼들
일리인거시필경아병이한국남
방으로향ᄒᆞ야젼진ᄒᆞᆯ터이니이
리되는날에는엄히빈파밋하콩
ᄒᆞ며잇는일병으로서로만나콩
파가될터이며
쏘ᄒᆞᆫ히삼 에진리를굿게만든
후에는필경군ᄉᆞ를각각삼티로
분ᄒᆞ야일티는동히로츌발ᄒᆞ고
일티는압록강으로젼진ᄒᆞ고쏘
일티는한국중앙으로침범ᄒᆞᆯ터
인즉
엇제던지금번동병이일쟝대거
싸인지라일병으로더부러과버히
이ᄒᆞᆯ터이요일병도쏘ᄒᆞᆫ이를보일
존이라도되쥭ᄒᆞᆯ이가만무ᄒᆞᆫ즁
에비병이무슈ᄒᆞ다ᄒᆞ니필경에
ᄒᆞ나은겨단이나고아말리인티
이번싸홈에는아병이득리ᄒᆞᆯ듯
ᄒᆞ도다

관보

광무팔년구월삼십일
부록연속

○만분지 륙군무관학교교관
륙군보병부위 죠남희 륙군
무관학교학교도티부륙군보병
부위 오진영 시위뎨일련티
뎨일대티부관륙군보병부위
류쳘영 부륙군보병부위 최
우상 임쳘지 뎨이대티부륙
군보병부위 김병엽 뎨삼대
티부륙군보병부위 리셕귀
리용지 친위뎨일련티뎨일대
티중티쟝륙군보병쟝위 김도
현 부륙군보병부위 송우영
정규됴 참위 오주영 뎨이
대티부륙군보병참위 박티영
우죵현 김수인 뎨삼대티부
륙군보병부위 강필우 참위
김상티 부위 쟝용셕 참위
최병셕 김광순 리복원 진
위뎨일련티뎨일대티부륙군보
병부위 정창환 리귀명
참위 셔병어 김귀승 뎨삼
대티부관륙군보병부위 리원
협 부륙군보병부위 리교샹

진위뎨이련티뎨일대티부관륙
군보병부위 정 현 부륙군
보병참위 김귀제 뎨이대티
부륙군보병부위 권티진 참
위 김정진 뎨삼대티 부륙
군보병참위권중완 진위뎨삼
련티뎨일대티부륙군보병참위
교영직 류원찬 뎨삼대티부
뎨륙군보병참위 문종환 진위뎨
ᄉᆞ련티무과쥬관륙군보병부
위 김인식 진위뎨ᄉᆞ련티
관륙군보병참위 박효셩 진
위뎨ᄉᆞ련티뎨일대티부관륙군
보병부위 박용준 부륙군보
병부위 김인셩박무형 젼덕
유 참위리제정 뎨이대티부
륙군보병참위 김계담 뎨삼
대티부보륙군보병부위 김중
현 최광후 참위정제호 진
위뎨오련티뎨일대티부륙군보
병부위 김덕제 참위 손은
영 오천묵 뎨이대티부륙군
숙보병부위 리하영김렬
진제 뎨이대참위 뎨오련티경
샹대티중대쟝륙군보병정위 권
근중익 부륙군보병참위 김희
최중선 진위뎨륙련티뎨이대
티부륙군보병부위 박쟝화
참위 오등영 류희쟝 시위
뎨일련티포병뎨일대티부륙군
포병부위 원 형 진위뎨이
수련티뎨삼대티향관륙군이등군
군이등군수 리지운 진위뎨
군수 강문경 진위뎨륙련티
뎨일대티향관륙군이등군수
쟝귀원 뎨이대티향관륙군삼
등군수 신광희 시위뎨일련
박승뎨이대티부륙군보병참위
군보병부위 친위뎨일련티귀관륙
일련티뎨이대티중대쟝륙군보
병정위 리한긍 뎨일대티부
쳔뎨이대티중티쟝륙군보병정위
일대티 최귀현 진위뎨일련대
티부륙군보병부위 김윤덕 친위
뎨일대티중티쟝륙군보병정위
조상셕 진위뎨일련티뎨이대
티부륙군보병부위리영규 진
위뎨일련티뎨일대티향관륙군
이등군수 최영순 진위뎨
련티뎨삼대티부관륙군보병부
대티부관륙군보병진위뎨이
이련티뎨삼대티부륙군보병부
위 조원순

졍위뎨ᄉᆞ련ᄃᆡ뎨이대ᄃᆡ부륙군보병부위 뎡면셥 진위뎨오련ᄃᆡ뎨일대ᄃᆡ부륙군보병부위진셕구 진위뎨륙련ᄃᆡ뎨이대ᄃᆡ부륙군보병참위 최향렬방장환

잡보

○경남젹경 경상남도관찰ᄉᆞ셩기운씨가보고ᄒᆞ기를영산군슈리용ᄒᆞ의보고를거ᄒᆞᆫ즉거월샹십일신시량에하ᄒᆞᆫ인일명이리고ᄒᆞ퇴져의샹젼이시임졍산군슈인티분탁에오시ᄂᆞᆫ길에젹당을맛나교군을파쇄ᄒᆞ고방금의관을탈취ᄒᆞ오니급히구호ᄒᆞ여달나ᄒᆞ기에ᄉᆞᆫ교를파송ᄒᆞ여구호ᄒᆞ엿더니그익일인시에젹당이돌입ᄒᆞ야옥문을파쇄ᄒᆞ고죄슈들모다방송ᄒᆞ고곳티아에돌입ᄒᆞ야각항졍물을탈취ᄒᆞ고각쳥에용젼우치ᄒᆞᆫ궤를타파ᄒᆞ고용젼을몰수히가져갓ᄂᆞᆫ티칭이활빈당이라ᄒᆞ고돈을모다가ᄂᆞᆫᄒᆞᆫ사름의게분급ᄒᆞᄂᆞᆫ티그두목은밍감역이라ᄒᆞ고구분을잉엇스며읍에잇ᄂᆞᆫ죄인젼봉쥰을군복을입히여말을틴우고동힝ᄒᆞ야갓스니원슈부에보ᄒᆞ야병졍을파송케ᄒᆞ라ᄒᆞᆫ고로ᄂᆡ부에서원슈부로조회ᄒᆞ엿다더라

○평남젹경 셩쳔군슈송영대씨가ᄂᆡ부로보고ᄒᆞ기를본군칭평면에ᄇᆡ비ᄒᆞᆫ폭도에운량ᄒᆞᄂᆞᆫ일부모졉수로쟉동인민이쟝리에졔회ᄒᆞ야용외ᄒᆞᆫ조음에강도십여명이조칭활빈당ᄒᆞ고무슈히작경ᄒᆞ다가인가의돌입ᄒᆞ야젼쥐를찬탈ᄒᆞ엿고또동티면에셔일부모졉수로일동빅셩이회동ᄒᆞ엿슬ᄯᅢ에젹당십이명이작기충검을가지고피슈ᄂᆞᆫ밍감역이라ᄒᆞ고동회중에돌입ᄒᆞ야무슈히작경ᄒᆞ엿고거월이십일ᄉᆞ시량에모로촌면서흥포젼두에셔젹당오십여명이고평군에출힝ᄒᆞ엿든병뎡과졉젼ᄒᆞ야필경젹당이퇴거ᄒᆞᄂᆞᆫ티병뎡김세경한두인량인이도젹을쏘차셔창평합산동후면셔지가셔졉젼ᄒᆞᆯᄯᅢ에젹당이출연이비중ᄒᆞ더니필경젹당이퇴주ᄒᆞ엿ᄉᆞᆫ즉김한광병의공로가가샹ᄒᆞᆫ지라포샹도ᄒᆞ려니와원슈부에조회ᄒᆞ야히병등을히티에영구이파주케ᄒᆞ라ᄒᆞᆫ고로ᄂᆡ부에서원슈부로조쳥ᄒᆞ엿다더라

○무이챵탈 영쳔군슈가ᄂᆡ부로보고ᄒᆞ되본군가야면대리거ᄒᆞᄂᆞᆫ우쟝용은본시부랑ᄒᆞᆫ류라음력본월초에일본인이명과동수일명을더리고본리거ᄒᆞᄂᆞᆫ리학렬가에리도ᄒᆞ야무수히토셕ᄒᆞ야오만량슈표를밧고일쳔팔빅량을튱탈ᄒᆞ여갓스니우가와리가가평일슈ᄒᆞᆷ이업다ᄂᆞᆫ티외국인을부동ᄒᆞ야이곳치포악ᄒᆞᆫ을ᄒᆞ엿ᄂᆞᆫ지심히통탄ᄒᆞᆫ지라히일인ᄒᆞᄂᆞ의명함을엇어반쟝ᄒᆞ니일공ᄉᆞ의게조회ᄒᆞ야사실탐ᄒᆞ야륵탈ᄒᆞᆫ돈을리항들의게환급ᄒᆞ야하향잔빅의싱명재산을지보케ᄒᆞ라ᄒᆞ엿더라

○류학싱발졍 본월십이일에학부에셔향일에시취ᄒᆞᆫ일본류학싱을초치ᄒᆞ야그중에셔이십명을초츌ᄒᆞ야일간발졍ᄒᆞᄂᆞᆫ시찰졔씨와동힝ᄒᆞ게ᄒᆞ고그외에ᄂᆞᆫ경비변통되ᄂᆞᆫ티로추추파송ᄒᆞᆫ다더라

○금티샹보 공쥬티방티병뎡과일인간에분쟁된ᄉᆞ실을샹문ᄒᆞᆫ즉병뎡일명이히군에거류ᄒᆞᄂᆞᆫ일본인진면티랑의집담밧게셔오줌을누엇더니일인이칙망ᄒᆞ거ᄂᆞᆯ병뎡이사과ᄒᆞ여도듯지안코병뎡을무수란타ᄒᆞᄂᆞᆫ고로병뎡등이격분ᄒᆞ야히군일인의집을부수고일인과죵샹지ᄒᆞ엿더니일병일소티가하거하야히군티영사를위팁ᄒᆞ고중티쟝이하위관병졸을일졔히일병진중에구류ᄒᆞ고총약탄환등물을수히탈거ᄒᆞ엿ᄂᆞᆫ티중티쟝권중탁씨ᄂᆞᆫ히중티에쥬무지임인고로일인과시비ᄒᆞ든병뎡을평숑ᄒᆞ고졔관추로일군ᄉᆞ령부로금일에상리ᄒᆞ고소티쟝리범셔씨ᄂᆞᆫ부하병졸단속지못ᄒᆞᆫ죄망으로샹금일군중에구류ᄒᆞ엿다더라

○경ᄒᆞᆫ셩병 군부평리국쟝리강하씨ᄂᆞᆫ그아들룡쥬티소티쟝리범셔씨가일인군중에구류된금보를듯고놀나여졸디에셩병ᄒᆞ야시각티변중이라더라

○북쳥야병 함흥관찰ᄉᆞ가북쳥군보를거ᄒᆞ야외부로보고ᄒᆞ기를음력칠월이십구일에야병일쳔이빅명과군마일쳔오빅여필이남으로좃ᄎᆞ본군남편오리무하에리도ᄒᆞ야류숙ᄒᆞ고본읍련티에젹귀ᄒᆞ엿든군량을빅셩ᄒᆞ숙첨을거가고이원등디로향ᄒᆞ엿다ᄒᆞ엿더라

○신오쥬졍 금번군제의뎡에군부쥬ᄉᆞ십오과를즁셜ᄒᆞᆫ즉원액수십오과에합ᄒᆞ야삼십명이라더라

○헌교등승 기쟝ᄒᆞᆫ군제에ᄂᆞᆫ각디쟝교가와관승차를못ᄒᆞ게겨뎡ᄒᆞ엿스나등별이헌병디ᄂᆞᆫ젼과갓치쟝교가와관을승차ᄒᆞ기로ᄌᆞ 샹쳐분이나리셧더라

○의수싱인 ᄂᆡ부와신국에서의학교로조회ᄒᆞ기를근일류힝병에방ᄒᆞᆯ수로 칙교를봉승ᄒᆞ야쟝명ᄒᆞᆫ의수를오셔ᄂᆡ어파송ᄒᆞ야약을시험ᄒᆞ야병을치료ᄒᆞᆯ티이니귀학교졸업ᄒᆞᆫ의수중십명을퇴송ᄒᆞ라ᄒᆞᆫ고로히학교에셔의학졸업교관류병 씨등십명을거쳔ᄒᆞ엿더라

○웅쳔ᄒᆡ일 음력칠월초싱일에웅쳔군에ᄂᆞᆫ풍파가대작ᄒᆞ야히일이되엿ᄂᆞᆫ티공히와빈가에표퇴와면답교션쳑에파샹파인명에손샹됨을히군에셔사보ᄒᆞ엿스되가옥의표퇴만ᄉᆞ빅십룩호와옥구군에도히일되야표퇴가삼십팔호라더라

○곡산면보 곡산군에셔본월이일하오팔시에ᄂᆡ부로면보ᄒᆞ엿스되본군민요에일인칠명과통ᄉᆞ일명이피히ᄒᆞ엿고일인파통ᄉᆞ각일명은자별보호ᄒᆞ엿스며본군인티민중피샹ᄒᆞᆫ쟈도십ᄉᆞ명인ᄃᆡ민요쟝두최조범김경ᄎᆞ로량인을본군에착슈ᄒᆞ엿다ᄒᆞ엿더라

○퇴ᄌᆡ우퇴 작보에긔ᄌᆡᄒᆞᆫ바금번군슈 쥬본은각부부원쳥판인중됴용ᄒᆞᆫ다홈을샹문ᄒᆞᆫ즉ᄂᆡ부공홈을인ᄒᆞ야각관쳥에서쥬관임관중가감ᄒᆞᆫ인원각이인식거쳔ᄒᆞᆫ후에ᄂᆡ부에셔기중일인만군슈로셔임ᄒᆞᆫ다더라

○학ᄃᆡ샹소 학부대신리ᄌᆡ극씨ᄂᆞᆫ셩묘ᄒᆞ려하향ᄒᆞᆫ추로샹소ᄒᆞ엿더라

○조아과병 일본공ᄉᆞ림권조씨가외부로조회ᄒᆞ되일본관인과샹민이공쥬디에셔히디방티병뎡의게히방홈이불소ᄒᆞᆫ지라군티셜치ᄒᆞᆫ본의가디방안령을유지ᄒᆞ란홈이어ᄂᆞᆯ히티병뎡은위력을자세ᄒᆞ야도리어야료ᄒᆞ니우리쥬차군일부를파송ᄒᆞ야진압케ᄒᆞ되이곳치포학ᄒᆞᆫ군티ᄂᆞᆫ무쟝을히제ᄒᆞ고각기히방홈이가ᄒᆞᆫ지라귀대신은히관찰부에금칙ᄒᆞ야엄사케ᄒᆞ라ᄒᆞ엿더라

○쳥파순검 샹화감리교영쳘씨가외부로면보ᄒᆞ되곡산군민요ᄉᆞ로일본령ᄉᆞ의쳥구를인ᄒᆞ야됴사ᄎᆞ로순검을파송ᄒᆞ엿구ᄒᆞ엿더라

○보쳥보관 의학교교관김익남씨가군의과쟝으로젼임ᄒᆞ미교쟝지셕영씨가학부에쳥원ᄒᆞ되일본에잇ᄂᆞᆫ의학졸업싱안샹호로교관을셔임ᄒᆞ라ᄒᆞ엿더라

○창덕연회 일본궤신대신단포씨를위ᄒᆞ야한국졍부에셔금일졍오십이시에창덕궁에셔연을비셜ᄒᆞᆫ다ᄂᆞᆫ티일본공령ᄉᆞ와각문무관원들도일졔히참예ᄒᆞᆫ다더라

○궤샹폐현 궤샹대포씨일힝은한국 황뎨폐하셔경의를표ᄒᆞ기위ᄒᆞ야명일오후삼시에림공ᄉᆞ와동반ᄒᆞ야경운궁에셔폐현ᄒᆞ고인ᄒᆞ야교문관묵하던써도 폐현ᄒᆞᆫ다더라

○일샹발힝긔 일본궤신대신대포씨의일힝이오ᄂᆞᆯ동안올경셩에셔귀루ᄒᆞᆫ다더니쟉일환보틀ᄂᆞᆫ즉만쥬로갈일이급ᄒᆞ여그리ᄒᆞᆫ지ᄇᆡ일셔지만류경ᄒᆞ엿다가졔명일에인항으로츌발ᄒᆞᆫ다더라

외보

○런도계획 일본졍부에셔북한에부셜ᄒᆞᄂᆞᆫ경의텰도에셔동쳥텰도의모처셔시연락ᄒᆞᆯ텰도를부셜ᄒᆞ기로작뎡ᄒᆞ엿ᄂᆞᆫ티그연락ᄒᆞᆯ곳슨대포궤신대신과산ᄂᆡ텰도국쟝이귀국ᄒᆞᆫ후에군ᄉᆞ샹과경졔샹으로됴ᄉᆞᄒᆞ야대셕교와히셩이파로양중에ᄒᆞᆫ곳슬턱뎡ᄒᆞᆯ터리오그부셜경비ᄂᆞᆫᄉᆞ쳔만원으로예뎡ᄒᆞ고압록강텰도산다리에만가셜비가삼빅만원에이라더라

○로국비샹금 리버풀의데교린보고를거ᄒᆞᆫ즉로국졍부ᄂᆞᆫ리순구에어류ᄒᆞ엿든영국긔션후오기스톤홀호(션쥬ᄂᆞᆫ리버풀에사ᄂᆞᆫ)를억류ᄒᆞᆫ손히금을물어주기로동교ᄒᆞ엿더라

○공중비힝긔 공중비힝긔를발명ᄒᆞᆫ쟈가만ᄒᆞᆫ데그중에ᄀᆞ장신묘발명ᄒᆞᆫ쟈ᄂᆞᆫ뉴욕에유명ᄒᆞᆫ긔자의ᄉᆞ회인데쓰츄쓰트라이드라ᄒᆞᄂᆞᆫ사름이라샹년동안즁수ᄒᆞ여공부ᄒᆞᆫ후게ᄒᆞᆫ비긔를발명ᄒᆞ엿ᄂᆞᆫ티근일에셩로이발람회에셔시힝ᄒᆞᆫ비힝긔의경쟁회에셔쳐음으로그의장을밧고ᄒᆞ엿다더라

광고

TELEGRAMS.

(FROM THE "CHINA REVIEW.")

Moukden, Sept. 21.

The valuables, Imperial and others, have been removed from the Palace and Yamens and sent to Peking. Stores hitherto sent by rail north-wards to Shinmintun and thence by road are now being conveyed by Junks up the river Liao.

Advices from Liaoyang state that, in the recent fighting in and around the city, nearly 100 Chinese were killed and 350 wounded, most of whom are being treated at Dr. Westwater's Red Cross Missionary Hospital. The doctor himself is recovering from his wounds.

(OFFICIAL RUSSIAN REPORT.)

Harbin, Sept. 21.

On the 20th September the enemy attacked our forces near Dalin. The enemy, which consisted of one brigade, was twice repulsed.

Harbin, Sept. 21.

There was no change in the positions on the south front of the two armies up to the 20th Sept.

In the fight near Dalin our casualities were 70 men. Part of those slightly wounded have returned to duty.

Moukden, Sept. 20.

The news that General Mestchenko was not correct. The General was found on the field unconscious and very severely wounded; but was quickly removed and is slowly recovering, at which there is great rejoicing among his Cossacks and others.

HORSES FOR JAPAN.

Dr. Miura, the director of the Government stud at Japan, an instuation situated at Hickinobe, on the northeastern side of the island, and known as Oh-oo, and Mr. Kitemura, having completed their purchases of thoroughbred horses for Japan, are making arrangements for shipping them to their destination, says a Sydney paper of 25th ult. These gentlemen travelled through most of the States, visiting the various studs of note, and having made all their purchases here rather flattered our horse-breeders. Dr. Miura and Mr. Kitemura are evidently not new to buying thoroughbreds, and a glance at the collection they have acquired will satisfy anyone that they have done well from the material at their disposal. Altogether they have a high-class lot from a pedigree aspect, while many will be hard to beat on the score of good looks, and though Japan's representatives would have preferred some others, they were unfortunately beyond reach. The consignment comprises eight stallions and 14 mares, of which six mares will leave on Saturday next in the steamer "Australian;" the stallions and two mares, in charge of Mr. J. G. Rowley, are to go in "Yawata Maru" on Wednesday next, and the balance will follow a few days later in the "Taiyuan."—Hongkong Telegraph.

MORE WAR TAXES.

At the Cabinet Council held in Tokio last Wednesday, the questions relating to the Budget and war funds required during the next fiscal year were discussed for the first time. According to the "Nichi Nichi," it appears that in order to obtain the necessary war funds for next year, the authorities will, among other things, adopt a salt monopoly and levy a new tax on silk fabrics.

Mr. Kato in his capacity of adviser to the Imperial Household Department is to have an audience with His Majesty to-day and to-morrow Mr. Oura the Japanese Minister for communications and Mr. Megata the newly-appointed adviser to the Korean Finance Department are to be received.

THE BITER BIT.

The late Eugene Field was a well-known book-collector, and one of his jokes, according to the "Philadephia Post," was to enter a book-shop and in the most solemn manner ask for an expurgated edition of Mr. Hemans' poems. One day in Milwaukee he was walking along the street with his friend George Yenowin, when the latter halted in front of a bookshop and said: "Gene, the proprietor of this place is the most serious man I ever knew. He never saw a joke in his life. Wouldn't it be a good chance to try again for that expurgated Mrs. Heman?" Without a word Field entered, asked for the proprietor, and then made the usual request. "That is a rather scarce book," came the reply. "Are you prepared to pay a fair price for it?" For just a second Field was taken aback; then he said: "Certainly, certainly; I—I—know it's rare." The man stepped to a case, took out a cheaply bound volume, and handed it to Field; saying: "The price is five dollars." Field took it nervously, opened at the title-page, and read in correct print, "The Poems of Mrs. Felicia Hemans. Selected and Arranged, with All Objectionable Passage Excised, by George Yenowine, Editor of 'Isaac Watts for the Home,' 'The Fireside Hannah More,' &c." with the usual publisher's name and date at the bottom. Field glanced up at the bookseller. He stood there the very picture of sad solemnity. "I'll take it," said Field faintly, producing the money. Outside Yenowin was missing. At his office the boy said that he had just left, saying that he was going to Standing Rock, Dakota, to keep an appointment with Sitting Bull.

THE SIBERIAN RAILWAY.

A NEW VIEW.

Prince Khilkoff, Minister of Ways and Communications, left on August 7th for Lake Baikal, in order personally to superintend the finishing touches on the Circum-Baikal line. It is hoped that trains will begin running at the end of September, that is to say before the commencement of the season of autumn storms, which are very dangerous to navigation on the Lake. The Baikal Ring Railway is becoming more and more simply a military railway, and thus numerous buildings are necessary and have to be erected quickly and at great cost.

Mr. Whigham writes to the "Morning Post," after traversing the railway, that it can and does carry every day from 2,000 to 2,200 men of all arms, with eight guns and 500 horses or the equivalent. There seemed to be no hitch of any kind on the line. He also writes: I must repeat the statement that the railway is not required to feed the army of Manchuria. There is quite enough foodstuff in Manchuria to feed an army of half a million men forever provided that Kuropatkin can keep the Basin of the Sungari and all of the Liao Basin north of Tiehling. If he had to fall back on Kharbin the situation would be different, because the country north of Kharbin is scantily cultivated. But on the rich lands between Kharbin and Mukden, with all the cattle pastures of Mongolia at his back, he need be in no fear for the stomachs of his men. It is the sheerest nonsense to talk of the Russian Army starving in Manchuria. The railway has to bring boots and coffee, and, of course, ammunition, but one train a day will do a great deal in that direction. The rest of the supplies can be bought in the country.

LOST

On the 27th ult., probably in the neighbourhood of the West Gate.

A. Photographic Camera. Anyone returning the same to this office will receive Y 15.00 reward.

The Korea Daily News.

Issued at 5 P. M. daily except Sundays.

Rate of Subscription:—

Per Year.	Yen 25.
Per Quarter.	Yen 7.
Per Month	Yen 2.50

Postage in Korea not charged extra.
Postage abroad charged extra.

Advertisements, 50 sen per day for 1 inch or less.
5 yen per month per inch.
50 yen per year per inch.

All communications to

E. T. BETHELL,
Editor and Publisher.
Pak-tong, Seoul.

THE RUSSIANS IN THE NORTH-EAST.

At last the Russian descent into Korea is beginning to assume definite shape and as the Japanese garrison in the north has lately been considerably reinforced we may expect to hear of a collision in a day or two.

According to a report of the day before yesterday the Russians have advanced their base to Song-chin. Their army at present comprises some 6,000 men of whom 3,000 are at Song-chin, 600 at the river about 2½ miles north of Gensan and the remainder on the march between these two places.

The army seems to be composed of all arms, which distinguishes it from the purely predatory bands of cossacks who have hitherto been harrying the north of Korea.

We look upon the advance of this army at this season of the year as a piece of great daring if not indiscretion. As we have previously pointed out, the road closely follows the sea-coast, and until the harbours are frozen up the Japanese can attack when and where they please.

Although the present course of events lends colour to the belief that the coming winter will see serious fighting in north and northeast Korea, we still adhere to our original opinion that in the immediate future we shall only have outpost actions of no great significance.

THE NEW ADVISERS.

Before his departure, Mr. Megata was good enought to have a brief conversation with a representative of this journal. The new Financial Adviser stated that he was not going to Korea with any definite policy in fiscal matters mapped out in his mind. He intends, on his arrival, to devote some time to studying and investigating the various questions involved, and will shape his proposals in accordance with the results of his enquiries. The currency problem will receive his earnest attention and he hopes to be able to place it on a sound and stable basis. Mr. Megata confirmed the statement that Mr. Stevens, of the Japanese Legation at Washington, has been appointed Adviser for Foreign Affairs to the Korean Government, but was unable to state whether that gentleman had yet left the United States.—Kobe Herald.

THE AFFRAY AT KOK SAN.

We learn that in addition to the seven Japanese already reported killed, fourteen Koreans were wounded and another Japanese and a Korean interpreter were wounded. The two ringleaders are under arrest.

It seems that of the 50 young men recently selected to go to Japan to study, only 20 are to be sent at present, and the remainder are to go when the funds for their expenses are forthcoming.

OPTIMISM IN JAPAN.

The "Asahi" conjectures the present attitude of our forces in the interior of Manchuria to be as "tranquil as a forest and as immobile as a mountain," and that this very calmness is filling the enemy with anxiety and apprehension. That the enemy is in this frame of mind may be presumed, as the paper says, from his movements on the 17th and 18th, when some of his cavalry, assisted by an infantry and artillery force, attempted a reconnaissance of our positions. The attempt was apparently unsuccessful, the reconnoitrers having been driven back with heavy losses, and a second and more powerful one on the part of the enemy may be expected. For judging from Kuropatkin's reports, his retreat from Liaoyang was not in accordance with one of his "pre-arranged plans," but was the result of being outmanœuvred by the Japanese, and as that retreat is not popular in St. Petersburg, his position requires that Liaoyang should be recovered. If so, it is presumable that the taking of the offensive by him will be preceded by an attempt at a thorough reconnaissance in force. Be that as it may, the "Asahi," nevertheless, deems it improbable that the Russians will make any serious efforts to re-occupy Liaoyang, because the strong reinforcements Kuropatkin is reported to have recently secured, will only be neutralized by the heavy losses he suffered at the latter place, and with Mukden to defend it may not allow him to wheel round for an attack on the Japanese. Mukden he will, however, make an effort to hold: and yet Mukden is not a place of such natural strength as Tiehling. It is most likely then, says the "Asahi, that the enemy will make his last endeavour to retain Tiehling before he is completely forced, as he will be, out of Southern Manchuria.—Japan Times.

GENERAL KUROPATKIN'S PLANS.

General Kuropatkin his notified the Czar of his intention to winter at Harbin.

He reports that he is gradually withdrawing from Mukden and Telin, and will be able to save most of his stores.

In his report he intimates that the real campaign of the war will begin with the opening of spring, when he hopes to have on hand a sufficient force to compel the Japanese to evacuate the positions they have occupied.

While praising the courage and conduct of his men in the face of the enemy he states that his artillery has been found deficient, and asks that guns of a longer range be sent him. The Japanese have made no general advance on Mukden.

A STEP IN THE RIGHT DIRECTION.

The Home office has notified the various departments that several magisterial appointments are vacant. Each department is to recommend two diligent men and from these the vacancies will be filled.

The governor of Kong-Chu telegraphs to the Home office that about 100 Japanese soldiers arrived on the afternoon of the 2nd inst. and immediately arrested the major and some men of the Korean local guard.

The Il-chin-hoi is again in session but their activities seem to have broken out in a new direction. At all events, it is reported that the Korean police, who formerly did their best to disperse them, are now supporting them.

With England reducing her army, France her navy, and the Democrats proposing to cut down the United States army, it appears as if the recent alarming craze for militarism and war were beginning to subside.—Nation, New York.

KING EDWARD AND DECORATIONS.

King Edward has just brought about a reform which the late Queen, her husband the Prince Consort and others had striven in vain to accomplish, namely, the abolition of the system of fees exacted from recipients of honours and distinctions. Just before he left England for the continent, after securing the cooperation of parliament, of the treasury and Royal College of Heralds. His Majesty caused an official notification to be issued, announcing that from henceforth men who are rewarded for services to the crown and nation by means of peerages, baronetcies and orders of knighthood will not be called upon to pay for the same. These fees have been of the most exorbitant character, the greater part of the money going into the pockets of the officials who have been accustomed to look upon fees as their perquisites.

The "Jiji" has a telegram from Hakodate to the effect that the British steamer Claverdon (?) of 4,029 tons, from Portland, was detained on the morning of Sept. 21st by a Japanese torpedo boat in the Tsugaru Straits. Subsequently she was brought to Hakodate for examination. The Asahi says that the ship carries railway materials.

Press despatches from Sasebo state that the Russians at Port Arthur, taught by the bitter lessons afforded by the work of dragging for mines in which they have so far lost several steam-launches, have now devised a clever method. Each mine-clearing vessel is preceded by two boats, which first locate the mines, the clearing then being effected by the vessel.

The Japanese Minister has sent a despatch to the Foreign Office complaining of the trouble caused to the Japanese subjects at Kongchu by the behaviour of the Korean soldiers there. He points out that the mission of soldiers is to keep order and as these are doing the exact reverse he demands their immediate recall, and states that Japanese soldiers will be sent in their stead.

It is stated that the Japanese Emperor's birthday on November 3rd will be celebrated more brilliantly than usual. The birthday ball by Baron Komura, Minister for Foreign Affairs, in the Imperial Hotel will be on a larger scale than formerly. The officials of both the Imperial Household and foreign Department are now arranging for it. It is said that a number of British and American warships will come to Yokohoma during the celebration.

The magistrate of Yeungchoon reports that a well-known swindler named Woo Chang-yong arrived in his district accompanied by two Japanese and an interpreter. They paid an uninvited visit to the house of Mr. Yi Hak-yul and persuaded him to write them out a cheque for $2,000. They also took away as a souvenir, about $100 in loose cash which they found lying about. A card bearing the name of Imachume was found and the magistrate requests that this be sent to the Japanese Legation with a request that investigations be made.

A number of privileged persons, writes a correspondent of a Paris paper quoted in La Nature, were present on St. Sylvester's night in Strasburg cathedral to observe the mechanism of the famous clock. "The spectacle was of special interest, since for the first time since its construction in 1842, the machinery was called upon to indicate the first leap year of a century, after an eight-year intirval. At astronomical midnight the machinery worked with wonderful regularity. The levers and trains of wheels began to move, the movable feasts of the year took their respective places and the admirable mechanism, calculated to indicate in perpetuity all the changes of the calender, continued its regular movement."

The Korea Daily News.

VOL. I, TUESDAY, OCTOBER 4, 1904. No. 67

HONGKONG & SHANGHAI BANKING CORPORATION.

Paid-up Capital..... ....$10,000,000
Reserve Fund:—Sterling Reserve... 10,000,000
Silver Reserve..... 7,000,000

27,000,000

Reserve Liability of Proprietors... 10,000,000

HEAD OFFICE, HONGKONG.

London Bankers, London and County Banking Company Limited.

Branches and Agencies, London.

Amoy,	Hankow	Penang,
Bangkok,	Hiogo,	Rangoon,
Batavia,	Iloilo,	Saigon,
Bombay,	Lyons,	San Francisco,
Calcutta,	Manila,	Singapore,
Colombo,	Nagasaki,	Sourabaya,
Foochow,	New York,	Tientsin,
Hamburg,	Peking,	Yokohama,

Credits granted on approved Securities, and every description of Banking and Exchange business transacted.

Drafts granted on London and the chief Commercial places in Europe, India, Australia, America, China and Japan.

HOLME RINGER & Co., AGENTS, CHEMULPO.

ON CHEONG & CO., SEOUL.

GENERAL STORE KEEPERS.
Imported provisions, Cooking Utensils Crockery, etc.
FRESH BREAD DAILY.

MITSU BISHI DOCKYARD & ENGINE WORKS, NAGASAKI.

CODE WORD, "DOCK."

A. 1, A. B. C., and Engineering Codes used.

DOCK No. 1 (at Tategami).

Extreme Length..............523 feet
Length on blocks .... 513 „
Width of Entrance on Top......89 „
„ „ Bottom....77 „
Water on Blocks at Spring Tide 26½ „

DOCK No. 2 (Mukaijima).

Extreme Length..............371 feet
Length on Blocks.............360 „
Width of Entrance on Top......66 „
„ „ Bottom 53 „
Water on Blocks at Spring Tide 22 „

PATENT SLIP (at Kosuge).

Can take vessels up to 1,000 tons gross.

THE WORKS are well equipped with the LATEST IMPROVEMENTS, and can execute any kind of work in SHIPBUILDING and MARINE ENGINEERING, as well as in REPAIRING of SHIPS.

The COMPANY'S new powerful steamer OURA-MARU (712 tons, 700 I.H.P.), specially built for SALVAGE PURPOSES, and equipped with necessary gear, is always READY at SHORT NOTICE.

CHARTERED BANK OF INDIA AUSTRALIA & CHINA.

INCORPORATED BY ROYAL CHARTER 1853

HEAD OFFICES:—LONDON.

Paid-up Capital £800,000
Reserve Liability of Shareholders 800,000
Reserve Fund 800,000

Drafts granted upon all the principal places in the world and every description of Exchange and banking business transacted.

E. MEYER & Co., Agents, Chemulpo.

E. MEYER & CO. Chemulpo.

SOLE AGENTS IN KOREA FOR:

A. T. Morse, Sons & Co's "Fresco" Distemper

In all colours ready for use on walls, Ceilings etc.

and

AVENARIUS CARBOLINEUM

A wood-preserving and antiseptic oil preparation

Against decay, dry-rot, fungus and wood-destroying insects.

A large supply always in Stock. Prices upon application.

E. MEYER & Co., Chemulpo.

LAW UNION & CROWN INS. CO.

Fire risks accepted at Current rates, on go downs, merchandise, dwellings, and other property, subject to usual conditions.

HOLME RINGER & Co., Agents, Chemulpo

THE METHODIST PUBLISHING HOUSE,

Little West Gate, Seoul.

JOB PRINTING, TYPEWRITER PAPER
CARBON PAPER, VISITING CARDS
STATIONERY, BOOK BINDING
BOOK PUBLISHERS
AMERICAN SCHOOL BOOKS
SPENCERIAN COPY BOOKS
PEN CARBON LETTER AND BILL BOOKS

S. A. BECK, Manager.

DAI-ICHI GINKO. LIMITED.

(Formerly the First National Bank)

ESTABLISHED 1873

INCORPORATED UNDER PRESENT LAW 1896

Capital - - - - - - - - Yen 5,000,000
Reserve Fund - - - - - 1,500,000

HEAD OFFICE:—TOKIO.

President: Baron SHIBUSAWA.

BRANCHES AND CORRESPONDENTS

In the Principal Cities and Towns of Japan.

Interest Allowed on

Fixed deposits 1 year - - - 6½ per cent
" " 6 months - - - 6 per cent

Special current accounts 1½ sen daily per Y 100
General " " 1 " " " 100

M. TANAKA, Manager, Chemulpo

HOLME RINGER & Co. Chemulpo.

General Merchants and Government Contractors.

Agents for the leading Banks SteamshipCompanies and Insurance Companies

Importers of Merchandise of every description.

KAMEYA & CO.

GENERAL STOREKEEPERS

Chinkokei Seoul

(Established 1895, Tokyo)

Confectionery, Hams, Canned Goods, Cutlery, Hirano & Tansan Water. Provisions, Gents, Furnishing goods, Toilet Articles, Travelling Bags, Tobacco, Cigars & Cigarettes Kitchen Utensils. Coffee, Biscuits.

Fresh Goods always kept in Stock.

Prices Moderate

☞ *Please come and inspect our goods.*

NIPPON YUSEN KAISHA.

JAPANESE MAIL STEAMSHIP CO.

DER MAIL CONTRACT WITH THE IMPERIAL JAPANESE GOVERNMENT.

European Line

Regular Fortnightly Service between Yokohama Kobe, Moji, Shanghai, Hongkong, Singapore, Penang Colombo, Port Said, Marseilles, London and Antwerp

American Line

Regular Fortnightly Service between Hongkong and Seattle, calling at Shanghai, Moji, Kobe, Yokohama and Victoria, B. C.

Australian Line

Regular weekly Service betwen Japan Ports and Australia, calling at Hongkong and Manila.

(Above Three Lines Suspended until further notice).

Shanghai Line

Weekly Service between Shanghai and Japan Ports.

Korea Line

Service Kobe, Moji, Nagasaki, Fusan, Chemulpo, C oo, Taiku.
S. S. Bahelsberg, 2181 tons.
Service Kobe, Moji, Fusan, Chemulpo, Chinnampo
S. S ARGO, S. S. Ohio.

BORDEN'S CONDENSED MILK CO.

New York, U. S. A.

ALWAYS IN STOCK

Eagle Brand Condensed Milk.

Gold Seal Condensed Milk.

Peerless (Family) Evaporated Cream.

Borden's Malted Milk.

E. MEYER & CO. Chemulpo, Korea,
Sole Agents

ROYAL INSURANCE COMPANY,

Funds exceed £10,000,000

FIRE
AT CURRENT RATES.
LIFE
REDUCED PREMIUM.

HOLME RINGER & Co., Agents, Chemulpo.

HOTEL DU PALAIS

SEOUL.

The only first class Hotel in Seoul. Situated in the centre of the city opposite the palace.

Cuisine under the supervision of an experienced French Chef.

Well ventilated and furnished throughout.

TARIFF UPON APPLICATION

L. MARTIN
Preprietor and Mangaer.

大韓每日申報
대한ᄆᆡ일신보

(뎨륙십팔호) (슈요일) 일쳔구ᄇᆡᆨ사년십월오일

본샤고ᄇᆡᆨ

본신보는영어와한어로셔거리
일츌판ᄒᆞᆸ
신문가
한쟝 엽두돈오푼
일삭표 엽두량닷돈
우표가ᄆᆡ삭닷돈
다맛돈으로밧숩
광고료는
귀한외쟝단과ᄌᆞ힝의다쇼로죵
갑ᄒᆞ되ᄒᆞᆫ가로밧을터이오ᄆᆡ오
ᄅᆡ지아녀ᄃᆡ한사람마다다이신
문을보실터이니광고내시기를
원ᄒᆞ시는이들은우리신문샤에
와서뎡약ᄒᆞ심을희망ᄒᆞᆸ
○발힝소 박동대한ᄆᆡ일신보
샤발ᄒᆡᆼ이학교합해젼영국인셰필
림쟝자리오
샤쟝 영국인 (ᄇᆡ셜)
평양 ᄃᆡ리졈
○평양효동사는권ᄯᅵ보씨로우
ᄅᆡ신문쳥ᄆᆡ되리인을ᄐᆡᆨ졍ᄒᆞ엿
ᄉᆞ오니평양에계신구람코져ᄒᆞ
시는 쳠군ᄌᆞ는쥬뒤랍졈에왕
림ᄒᆞ와뎡회ᄒᆞ시옵

사고

○우리대한ᄆᆡ일신보의목뎍은
대한의인녕졍셔에관한모든대
목에되ᄒᆞ야는공평한변론을쥬
쟝ᄒᆞᆷ이라우리등신원희랍보는
신문보시는쳠군ᄌᆞ의게ᄒᆞ샹보
도ᄒᆞ리며편지와긔셔ᄒᆞ여주시
는이는셩명과번디를져어붓치
시기를희망ᄒᆞ오나이거슨신문
샹에긔ᄌᆡᄒᆞ라는거시아니오다
만긔회신용ᄒᆞ는증거를삼고자
ᄒᆞᆷ이라긔쟈는아모긔셔던지긔
지ᄒᆞᆷ을퇴각ᄒᆞ는권리를가졋ᄉᆞ
나퇴각ᄒᆞ는리유는말ᄒᆞᆯ터이오
ᄆᆡ공즁평화를문란케ᄒᆞ는듯ᄒᆞᆫ
다긔셔는의례히밧지안켓숩나이

●본샤셜시이리로신문을미앙
우례로분젼ᄒᆞ와례젼부의일의
로젼ᄒᆞᆫ듯ᄉᆞ로번곳에는ᄒᆞᆨ늣게
젼ᄒᆞ게도ᄒᆞ며ᄒᆞ면졀거슬ᄒᆞᆫ겁
에젼ᄒᆞ기도ᄒᆞ며ᄒᆞ아나젼ᄒᆞ는
곳도잇다ᄒᆞ와우리신문을ᄉᆞ랑
ᄒᆞ야구람ᄒᆞ시는 쳠군ᄌᆞ의게
되ᄒᆞ야미우미안ᄒᆞ옵기로지금
은분젼인을두고ᄆᆡ일즉이젼
ᄒᆞ며아니젼ᄒᆞ거나늣게ᄒᆞ거나ᄒᆞᆫ
폐가엽도록ᄒᆞ란ᄒᆞ오니혹아니
젼ᄒᆞ거나늣게젼ᄒᆞ거나ᄒᆞᆫ일
이잇스면본샤로통긔ᄒᆞ여주심
을희망ᄒᆞᆸ

본샤광고

본샤에서본신문뎨수호와뎨ᄉᆡᆼ
일호와뎨ᄉᆡᆼ오호들ᄉᆞ용ᄒᆞᆯ데
가잇서이에광고ᄒᆞ오니누구시
던지이샹삼호중에본샤로가ᄌᆡ
오시면ᄆᆡ쟝에ᄇᆡᆨ젼두푼식드리
리다

론셜

동북방의아병형동

지작일소문에는아병이함경도
셩진에다진터를졍ᄒᆞ고진지ᄒᆞ
야방금그곳에잇ᄂᆞᆫ군ᄉᆞ총쳔명
은셩진에든쥬ᄒᆞ고통ᄇᆡᆨ명은원
산북방에밧영리되ᄂᆞᆫ쟝샹에ᄯᅥ
잇고또그남에거이쳔사ᄇᆡᆨ명은
그중간에련락ᄒᆞ야잇다ᄒᆞᆫ즉수
이병은졍평함극으로향ᄒᆞ야드
리오ᄂᆞᆫ모양이고일본에병참을
쓰ᄒᆞᆫ복방에잇서청세를디ᄒᆞᄂᆞᆫ
듯ᄒᆞᆫ즉ᄂᆞᆫ평셩서로싸홈되엿다ᄂᆞᆫ
소문이들닐듯ᄒᆞᆫ지라그중에노
란ᄒᆞ기로종사ᄒᆞᄂᆞᆫ코사크병의
당류가응당잇서북도근방으로
단이며작폐치아니ᄒᆞᆯ니가업습
은발홀거시엽고
또귀왕우리의보도ᄒᆞᆫ바와갓치
강수경병되기전에지ᄂᆞᆫ일병이
엇지던지대적ᄒᆞ야싸홀듯ᄒᆞ되
겨울빙된후에ᄂᆞᆫ자못곤란ᄒᆞᆯ듯ᄒᆞᆫ
고로아방이맛참ᄇᆡ를타서동병
아ᄒᆞᄂᆞᆫ거시갈히쥬의치아니ᄒᆞᆷ이
니로다
그런고로지금은다만빗만뵈ᄂᆞᆫ
듯ᄒᆞ되이졔붐과기사지나에일
귀가혹한ᄒᆞ며강물만결빙이되
ᄂᆞᆫ날이면필경복도에서던지혹
동복방도중간에서크게젼쟁이
이러날터인즉불과미긔에다시
말ᄒᆞᆯ것업시우리의쟝작ᄒᆞᆫ바와
여합부졀이될터이로다

관보

광무팔년구월삼십일 부
록연속

○임륙군보병참령 륙군보병
졍위 김준모 리승현 륙군
일등군ᄉᆞ 박학진 박원근
○임륙군보병졍위 륙군보병
부위 오진영 박용준 리셕
귀 원쳥샹 김연셩 최우샹
김병엽 리용졔
○임륙군이등군ᄉᆞ 륙군보병
부위 최광후 졍규됴 젼덕
유 류쳘영 졍쳥 졍창현○
임륙군보병부위 륙군보병참
위 박남필 김계담 리죵팅
리공환 변달현 김준셩 박
귀슈 박효셩 류현표 김샹
팅 륙군이등군ᄉᆞ 리졔윤
쟝긔원 신의쥰 륙군삼등군
ᄉᆞ 신광희
○임륙군보병부위 륙군보병
참위 김린호○임륙군보병참
위 륙군삼등군ᄉᆞ 강문경
○임륙군보병참위 륙군보병
참위 김광슌○임륙군이등군
ᄉᆞ 륙군보병참위 김희근
○보륙군무관학교교관 륙군
보병졍위 오진영 ○보시
위대일련ᄃᆡ대일대ᄃᆡ부 평
륙군보병부위 임철지 ○보
륙군무관학교학도ᄃᆡ부 륙군
보병부위 조남희 ○보시위
대일련ᄃᆡ대일대ᄃᆡ부 부륙군
보병부위 쟝용셕 ○보시위
대일련ᄃᆡ대일대ᄃᆡ부 륙군보
병참위 우죵현 ○보시위대
일련ᄃᆡ대이대ᄃᆡ 중ᄃᆡ쟝 륙
군보병졍위 김병엽 ○보시
위대일련ᄃᆡ대이대ᄃᆡ부 륙군
보병참위 오주영
○보시위대일련ᄃᆡ대삼대ᄃᆡ부
륙군보병부위 송우영 강필
우
○보친위대일련ᄃᆡ대일대ᄃᆡ중
ᄃᆡ쟝 륙군보병졍위 조종익
○보친위대일련ᄃᆡ대일대ᄃᆡ부
륙군보병부위 쟝긔원 김덕
졔 참위 쟝석졔
○보친위대일련ᄃᆡ대일대ᄃᆡ향
관 륙군일등군ᄉᆞ 최광후
○보친위대일련ᄃᆡ대이대ᄃᆡ중
ᄃᆡ쟝 륙군보병졍위 리석귀
원쳥샹
○보친위대일련ᄃᆡ대이대ᄃᆡ부
륙군보병부위 권ᄐᆡ진 리원
형 참위 최영석 오린동
○보친위대일련ᄃᆡ대삼대ᄃᆡ중
ᄃᆡ쟝 륙군보병졍위 최우샹
○보친위대일련ᄃᆡ대삼대ᄃᆡ부
륙군보병부위 리교샹 김중
현 참위 김계승 권중완
고영직 서병익
○보친위대이련ᄃᆡ대일대ᄃᆡ부
륙군보병부위 김샹틱 신흥
희 참위 최봉현 김긔졔
○보친위대이련ᄃᆡ대삼대ᄃᆡ부
관 륙군보병부위 류원표
○보친위대이련ᄃᆡ대삼대ᄃᆡ부
륙군보병참위오등영 김화셩
영 김화셩
○보친위대이련ᄃᆡ대일대ᄃᆡ중
ᄃᆡ쟝 륙군보병졍위 리용희
○보친위대이련ᄃᆡ대일대ᄃᆡ부
관 륙군보병부위 신의쥰
○보친위대이련ᄃᆡ대일대ᄃᆡ부
륙군보병부위 리긔명
○보친위대이련ᄃᆡ대일대ᄃᆡ향
관 륙군일등군ᄉᆞ 졍현
○보친위대이련ᄃᆡ대이대ᄃᆡ부
륙군보병참위 김병철 최영주
○보친위대이련ᄃᆡ대삼대ᄃᆡ부
륙군보병참위 김수인
○보친위대이련ᄃᆡ대삼대ᄃᆡ향
관 륙군이등군ᄉᆞ 김희근
○보친위대삼련ᄃᆡ대일대ᄃᆡ부
륙군보병참위 윤중환 박ᄐᆡ
영
○보친위대삼련ᄃᆡ대삼대ᄃᆡ부
륙군보병부위 박쟝화
○보친위대수련ᄃᆡ무기주관
륙군보병부 박무형
○보친위대수련ᄃᆡ긔관 륙군
보병참위 긔계경
○보친위대수련ᄃᆡ대일대ᄃᆡ부
관 김인식
○보친위대수련ᄃᆡ대일대ᄃᆡ중
ᄃᆡ쟝 륙군보병졍위 김인셩
박용준
○보친위대수련ᄃᆡ대일대ᄃᆡ부
륙군보병부위 박효셩 참위
졍 숙 류석홍 강문경
○보친 대수련ᄃᆡ대이대ᄃᆡ향
관 륙군일등군ᄉᆞ 젼덕유
○보친위대수련ᄃᆡ대삼대ᄃᆡ부
륙군보병부위 김계담 참
위 쟝긔형 강지후 리관직
○보친위대오련ᄃᆡ대일대ᄃᆡ부
륙군보병참위 류희쟝 졍쥐
호 김쳘졔
○친위대오련ᄃᆡ대이대ᄃᆡ부
륙군보병참위 최중선 신셕
규 리병찬 류병숙
○보친위대오련ᄃᆡ대삼대ᄃᆡ중
ᄃᆡ쟝 륙군보병졍위 김도현
○보친위대오련ᄃᆡ대삼대ᄃᆡ부
륙군보병참위 리학영 김봉
경

UNION INSURANCE SOCIETY OF CANTON

Head office Hongkong.
Marine risks underwritten at current rates.

Agents in Chemulpo,
MEYER & Co.

COMPAGNIE DES MESSAGERIES MARITIMES.

Fortnightly Direct Service.

For Marseilles
Via Ports
Sailing from Yokohama
Calling at Kobe,
Shanghai, Hongkong, Saigon, Singapore,
Colombo, Djibouti, Suez, Port Said
and Marseilles.

For particulars apply to
HOLME RINGER & Co.,
Chemulpo.

HAYASHIDA & CO.

16 MYENG DONG, CHING KO KAI, SEOUL.
BRANCH OFFICE AT CHEMULPO.

Money changers, Coal and Wood Merchants, Express Agents.

We are agents for the Pyeng-vang Coal Company and the Karazu Coal Company of Japan. We have the best quality of both anthracite and bituminous coal, and prompt execution of orders is our speciality. Firewood of all kinds kept in stock. Full weight guaranteed. Money of all denominations exchange, at current rates. Parcels received for all parts.

CHINA MUTUAL LIFE INS. CO.

Most favourable terms to policy holders.

Benefit system unsurpassed.

HOLME RINGER & Co.
Agents, Chemulpo.

C. P. R

CANADIAN PACIFIC RAILWAY COMPANY'S ROYAL MAIL STEAMSHIP LINE.

THE FAST ROUTE BETWEEN CHINA, JAPAN AND EUROPE VIA CANADA AND THE UNITED STATES.

Route from Hongkong via Shanghai, Nagasaki (Inland Sea of Japan) Kobe, Yokohama, Victoria and Vancouver.

Twin Screw Empress Steamships—6,000 Tons—Speed 19 knots.

PROPOSED SAILINGS FROM YOKOHAMA.

R. M. S. Empress of India.
R. M. S. Empress of Japan.
R. M. S. Empress of China.
R. M. S. Athenian.
R. M. S. Tartar.

Special reduction (first class only) granted to members of the Military, Naval, Diplomatic and Civil Services and to Missionaries.

Passengers have choice of ten routes across the Continent of America and have privilege of travelling by any Atlantic Steamship Line.

Round the World passage tickets in connection with the P. and O. S. N., North German Lloyd and Messageries Co.'s £125.

All rates payable at current rate of exchange.

For further information, Tickets, Guide Books, etc., apply to

HOLME, RINGER & Co., AGENTS,
Chemulpo.

Grand Hotel,

(Formerly the Station Hotel)

Near the Railway Terminus,
West Gate, Seoul.

The Best Hotel in Korea.
Handsome new Building.
Fine airy Rooms.
Excellent Cuisine.
Terms Moderate.
Special terms to Missionaries
and to permanent boarders.

Electric cars within 2 minutes' walk.

W. H. EMBERLEY,
Proprietor.

EVERY FACILITY.

In connection with Life Assurance Business is afforded by

The Standard Life Assurance Co.,

One of the largest and wealthiest of the Provident Institutions of the United Kingdom. Forms of Application and all information will be promptly afforded on application.

10 CENTS A DAY

Not a very large expenditure is it? But it is sufficient to secure for a man of 30 a policy with the STANDARD LIFE OFFICE for

$1323.

For all particulars of rates, etc., apply to

Holme, Ringer & Co.,
Agents, Chemulpo.

THE NEW YORK LIFE INSURANCE COMPANY.

Have you ever been declined by and Company?

Are you engaged in a specially hazardous occupation?

Have you heard of the New York Life Insurance Company's New Classifications for this class of Risks?

If not, send your date of birth, occupation and particulars of rejection, if any to

E. MEYER & Co., Agents, Chemulpo.

MITSUI BUSSAN KAISHA.
(MITSUI & Co.)

MITSUI GINKO.
(MITSUI BANK.)

The Bank is owned by the members of the Mitsui Family, who, as partners, assume an unlimited responsibility for all liabilities of the Bank.

Capital .... Yen 5,000,000
Reserve Fund .... " 5,600,000

HEAD OFFICE, TOKYO.
LONDON OFFICE, 34 LIME ST. E. C.

BRANCHES AND AGENCIES:

New York, San Francisco, Hamburg, Bombay, Singapore, Manila, Hongkong, Amoy, Chefoo, Tientsin.

Kobe, Hakodate, Yokohama, Kure, Yokosuka, Moji, Shimonoseki, Miike, Wakamatsu, Nagasaki, Kuchinotsu, Karatsu, Sasebo, Misume, Tsipeh, &c.

Telegraphic Address for all the Offices:
"MITSUI."
A. B. C. AND A. 1 CODES USED.

Contractors of Coal

To the Imperial Japanese Navy, Arsenal and Railway Bureau, Principal Railway Companies and Industrial Works, Home and Foreign Mail and Freight Steamers.

Sole Proprietors

Of the famous Miike, Tagawa and Yunan Coal Mines.

Sole Agents

For the sale of Fukuno, Hokoku, Ichimura, Kanoda, Mainoura, Onoura, Ostuji, Sonoda, Tsubaruro, Yoshinotani, Yoshio, Yurokibura and other coals.

YANGTSE INSURANCE ASSOCIATION, LTD.

The undersigned, having been appointed agents for the above company, are prepared to issue policies and pay losses on marine risks at regular rates.

E. MEYER & Co.,
Agents, Chemulpo.

AMERICAN KOREAN ELECTRIC COMPANY.

Light and Power.

Main Office: Electric Building, Chong No.

RAILWAY DEPARTMENT.

OPERATING CARS BETWEEN EAST AND WEST GATE, EVERY TEN MINUTES:—

First Car leaves East Gate at 6:30 A. M. First Car leaves West Gate at 6:55 A. M.
Last Car " East Gate at 10:40 P. M. Last " " West Gate at 11:00 P. M.

OPERATING CARS BETWEEN EAST GATE AND IMPERIAL TOMB TERMINUS, EVERY TWENTY MINUTES:—

CONNECTING WITH EVERY ALTERNATE CAR ARRIVING AT EAST GATE FROM CHONG NO.

First Car leaves East Gate for Tomb at 6:50 A. M.
" " " Tomb for East Gate at 7:10 A. M.
Last " " East Gate for Tomb at 9:50 P. M.
" " Tomb for East Gate at 10:10 P. M.

OPERATING CARS BETWEEN CHONG NO AND YUNG SAN (RIVER) EVERY TWELVE MINUTES:—

First Car leaves Chong No for South Gate at 6:48 A. M.
" " " Chong No for Yung San at 7:24 A. M.
" " " South Gate for Chong No at 6:56 A. M.
" " " Yung San for Chong No at 7:57 A. M.
Last " " South Gate for Chong No 11:00 P. M.
" " " Yung San for Chong No at 10:11 P. M.

SPECIAL PRIVATE CARS FURNISHED TO SUIT CONVENIENCE OF PATRONS. PRICES ON APPLICATION AT HEAD OFFICE.

LIGHTING DEPARTMENT.

Where less than 250 candle power of light is used, the rate per month will be. Per 16 candle power incandescent lamp. All night.—Yen 2.50.
Per 32 candle power incandescent lamp:—All night: Yen 4.00. Per 50 candle power incandescent lamp: All night: Yen 6.00.
150 " " 10.00. " 1200 " " enclosed arc " " " " 20.00.

Where more than 250 candle power of light is used, a Meter will be installed, if requested: Rent of Meter Yen 2.00 per month. Rate of charges by meter reading:—Two Sen per Ampere per hour. (Approximately this is equal to about One Sen per 16 c. p. lamp per hour) Minimum monthly charge where meter is installed. Yen 20.00 per month, which includes rental of meter.

Estimates for installing lights furnished on application. An assortment of chandeliers always on hand.

AMUSEMENT DEPARTMENT

ANIMATED PICTURES AT EAST GATE.
Every evening - - - Except Sunday.
From 8 to 10 P. M.

10 Cents:—Gen. Admission:—10 Cents. Seats in First Class Section. 15 Cents Extra.

Change of program each week. Pictures from Foreign Lands. Pictures of Local Scenes:—Amusing and Instructive.

An entertaining evening for a reasonable price.
MERRY-GO-ROUND:—At East Gate
From 10:00 A. M. till 11:00 P. M.

5 Cents a Ride.

Take your Exercise on The Galloping Horses.

Comfortable seats in the Chariots.

한셩뎐긔회샤

한미뎐긔회샤 고ᄇᆡᆨ
도ᄒᆞ옵나이다
샹활동사진관ᄂᆞ소와목마운동장ᄅᆞ재로셜
여베연차가온장안으로통힝ᄒᆞ여ᄃᆞ니여이
습
또이긔계에ᄀᆞ치노힌편ᄒᆞ고됴흔마치도잇
습
뵤밍우편ᄒᆞ고또조미잇는됴흔운동이되겟
ᄂᆡ됴흔모형ᄒᆞ달나아논물을ᄐᆞ고위ᄐᆡ치안
ᄃᆡ가논홈번ᄐᆞ논데오젼식이오
ᄇᆡ입샹오열시브터하오열ᄒᆞ시ᄭᆞ지ᄒᆞ옵고
목마운동쟝은동대문안에잇ᄉᆞᆸ고
가되겟습
쳠군조의게갑도싸고재ᄆᆡᆨ에됴흔쇼일거리
잇고구경ᄒᆞᆯ만ᄒᆞᆫ거시오니
셔양사진과대한과온동양사진언ᄂᆡ대조미
논되
젼이옵고미쥬일에사진을밧것스ᄆᆞ다밧고
고젼ᄅᆞᆼ되금은하등에십젼이오샹등에이십
일외에는미야에여덟시브터열시ᄭᆞ지ᄒᆞ옵
활동사진관ᄂᆞ소는동대문안에잇ᄉᆞᆸ고일요
회락부

All Cars Run Direct to the Animated Pictures and Merry-Go-Round.

○보진 뎨륙련대뎨일대대향관 륙군일등군수 정규됴

○보진 뎨륙련대뎨이대대부 륙군보병부 리지윤 참위 리창지 박츙긔 손은영

○보진 뎨륙련대뎨이대대향관 륙군일등군수 정창환

○보시위뎨일련대포병뎨일대대부 륙군보병참위 김광슌

○임륙군보병정령 륙군보병부령 한진창 륙군이등감독 리강하

○임륙군보병부령 륙군보병참령 강창희 리병무 리희둑 리민섭 민영옥

○임륙군보병참령 륙군정위 리셩규 리희원 리긔표 졍인환 유진형 리회승 리동식 구철조 빅응쥰 젼령관 홍릐윤

○임륙군보병정위 륙군보병부위 최기현 리지한 리영균

○임륙군헌병정위 륙군보병부위 최욱지

○임륙군보병부위 륙군보병참위 박승쥰 최학철 륙군이등군수 최영슌 ○임륙군일등군수 륙군보병정위 죠샹셕 리한긍 ○임륙군보병참위 정교 김한규

잡보

○탁대승비 탁지대신민영긔씨ᄂᆞᆫ사직샹소ᄒᆞ엿더니비지니에ᄉᆞ양말고시무ᄒᆞ라ᄒᆞ엿더라

○고문변통 탁지부고문관목하뎐씨ᄂᆞᆫ현금폐약즁인ᄃᆡ히부통변은참리관쉰히영씨와렬도원기ᄉᆞ김렬구량씨중턱뎡ᄒᆞᆯ터이라ᄒᆞ며 폐현시 어젼통변은렬도원기ᄉᆞ일본인도산씨로뎡ᄒᆞ엿다더라

○염천시찰 일본공관통역관염천일티랑씨ᄂᆞᆫ간일ᄒᆞ야의정부에입직ᄒᆞ야힝정ᄉᆞ무를시찰ᄒᆞ다더라

○경청복합 경무청에셔일진회공합에복합ᄒᆞᆫ기를근일한잡지비가경향에츌몰ᄒᆞ야유인조데ᄒᆞ야가산을탕진ᄒᆞᄂᆞᆫ쟈와잡술노현혹ᄒᆞ야무어슬바라ᄂᆞᆫ쟈가만흔지라두류ᄒᆞᆫ지루삭만에ᄂᆞᆫ밥갑과물건갑슬속이고도망ᄒᆞᄂᆞᆫ쟈가비비유지ᄒᆞᆫ민송ᄉᆞ가답지에청문이랑쟈ᄒᆞ고또부허ᄒᆞᆫ와언으로츙동ᄒᆞ야민심을고혹ᄒᆞ미어리셕은빅셩이졈졈현혹ᄒᆞᆫ지라대져무뢰비를경찰ᄒᆞᄂᆞᆫ거시쟝졍에ᄌᆞ저ᄒᆞᆫ고로각긱슈를젹간ᄒᆞ야두류ᄒᆞᄂᆞᆫ햑긱놀사실ᄒᆞ야ᄉᆞ업업시류경ᄒᆞᄂᆞᆫ쟈ᄂᆞᆫ신칙ᄒᆞ야보니ᄂᆞᆫ거서인민보오ᄒᆞᄂᆞᆫ본의오ᄒᆞ로잇틀시작ᄒᆞᆫ거시아니라그시힝ᄒᆞᆫ지가오랜죽회원으로인ᄒᆞ야발령ᄒᆞᆷ이아니라경찰ᄒᆞᄂᆞᆫ도리에엇지회원여부를가리여누구ᄂᆞᆫ두고누구ᄂᆞᆫ쎄리오비록회원이라도무뢰지비의부잡ᄒᆞᆫ일이잇스면법되로잡아징치ᄒᆞᆯ터이라ᄒᆞ엿더라

○외무국신셜 군졔기졍에군의국을셜시ᄒᆞᄂᆞᆫ고로의학교졸업싱십인을시취ᄒᆞ야과원으로셔입ᄒᆞᆫ다더라

○군의억울 금번군졔기졍에군부소속관원들이관임관으로쥬임관된즁에슈의셔지쥬임으로변통되엿ᄂᆞᆫᄃᆡ군의만의구히관임으로둔다ᄒᆞ고각군ᄃᆡ군의들이그억울ᄒᆞᆷ을칭원ᄒᆞᆫ다더라

○고문시찰 탁지고문관목하뎐죵티랑씨ᄂᆞᆫ기셩부를시찰ᄎᆞ로하거ᄒᆞᆫ다더라

○쟝욕질문 일진회에셔뎨국신문샤에ᄃᆡᄒᆞ야본회돌반ᄃᆡᄒᆞ엿다ᄒᆞ고져관을쳥ᄒᆞ던지기회ᄒᆞ고히샤쟝을쳥리ᄒᆞ야질문ᄒᆞ던지ᄒᆞᆫ다더라

○감리겸군슈 룡쳔감리을군슈겸임ᄒᆞᆯᄉᆞ로히쳥의셔에련셔ᄒᆞᆷ을외부에셔니부로쳥ᄒᆞ엿더니ᄂᆡ대리용티씨가권리샹샹관이라ᄒᆞ야히쳥의셔를니부로작환ᄒᆞᆫ지라일젼에졍부에셔니대가외대를봉착ᄒᆞ야그리유를셜명ᄒᆞᆫ즉니대가사파ᄒᆞ고곳련셔ᄒᆞ야쳥의ᄒᆞ엿더라

○츄원반힐 일공관에셔외부로죠회ᄒᆞ되귀국학부대신이하가본방에유람ᄒᆞᄂᆞᆫ일ᄉᆞᄂᆞᆫ귀국현관이폐국에츌유ᄒᆞᆷ이우리량국교의에친밀ᄒᆞᆷ이라맛당이폐국정부에젼달ᄒᆞ야겨외의우ᄃᆡᄒᆞᆷ파왕환간방편ᄒᆞ기위ᄒᆞ야본공관셔긔관츄원슈일로반힝케ᄒᆞᆯ터이니죠량ᄒᆞ라ᄒᆞ엿더라

○슌찰시셜 향일에특차ᄒᆞᆫ슌찰ᄉᆞ등은일졀물시ᄒᆞᆫ단말이잇더라

○위션단발 외각국에츌강ᄒᆞᄂᆞᆫ외교관은위션단발ᄒᆞᆫ다더라

○군슈됴용셜 풍셜에운운ᄒᆞ기를군슈몃과ᄂᆞᆫ일진회원으로됴용ᄒᆞᆫ다더라

○평의원회동 작일에일진회평의원수십인이본회소무소로회집하엿ᄂᆞᆫᄃᆡ회소문젼에다수헌병이왕리방황ᄒᆞ더라더라

○셔리젼언 작일에셔로로샹리ᄒᆞᆫ다수향긱이입셩ᄒᆞ랴고모ᄒᆞ다가시문과슈에셔불랍ᄒᆞᆫ모화관부근지로되축ᄒᆞ야일졔히단발ᄒᆞ고일진회에투입ᄒᆞ랴ᄒᆞᆫ다더라

○단발하다오 현금한셩에미반ᄒᆞᆫ향긱들이무삼연고인지밤마다진고기리발소에셔수빅명식단발ᄒᆞᆫ다더라

○무구회과 근일여항풍셜을거ᄒᆞᆫ즉일진회를혁파ᄒᆞᆯᄎᆞ로현영운씨가산림천턱 일본에양여ᄒᆞ히회를혁파케ᄒᆞᆫ다더니황샹폐하ᄭᅦ셔불윤ᄒᆞ시민파의가되ᄆᆡ삼십만원으로소ᄀᆡ가된다더니엇지되엿ᄂᆞᆫ지일진회ㄴ또이러나고일본공ᄉᆞᄂᆞᆫ산림쳔턱을다시ᄂᆞᆫ청구ᄒᆞ지아니ᄒᆞᆫ다ᄂᆞᆫᄃᆡ그리유인즉일인들이각쳐니디에셔겨살기를시작ᄒᆞ면진황지디를져의마음ᄃᆡ로ᄀᆡ간ᄒᆞ겟ᄂᆞᆫ로셔삼시리다시청구ᄒᆞᆯ필요가업ᄂᆞᆫ셔ᄃᆞᆰ이라더라

○왕무정쳐 찬졍박졔슌씨ᄂᆞᆫᄉᆞ직샹소를써셔그집안사ᄅᆞᆷ의게부탁ᄒᆞ야봉졍ᄒᆞ라ᄒᆞ고후원에셔비회ᄒᆞ다가부지거쳐ᄅᆞ그집안사ᄅᆞᆷ들이놀나와ᄉᆞ면으로탐지ᄒᆞ야도형젹이돈무ᄒᆞ더니츄후로드른즉씨가그날밤에죠고마한아희를다리고셔강에나와셔짐군하나를엇어가지고초초ᄒᆞᆫ힝장으로졍쳐업시ᄯᅥ나갓ᄂᆞᆫᄃᆡ그리허인즉필시씨가금년에참척을두번이나보고연젼에도셰번참척을당ᄒᆞ엿ᄂᆞᆫᄃᆡ또그런일을당ᄒᆞ여실하에일졈혈육이남지아니ᄒᆞ야그참혹ᄒᆞᆫ심화를니긔지못ᄒᆞ야뎡쳐업시죽쟝망혜로팔로강산이나구경ᄒᆞ고자ᄒᆞᆷ인가보다고ᄒᆞ더라

○아병남하 본월이일에아병륙빅명가량이원산북방구리쯤되ᄂᆞᆫ곳에리도ᄒᆞ엿고그뒤로연ᄒᆞ여오ᄂᆞᆫ군ᄉᆞ가이천명가량이오대포가ᄉᆞ좌인ᄃᆡ남방으로나려오ᄂᆞᆫ군ᄉᆞ의근거디ᄂᆞᆫ셩진인ᄃᆡ아병삼천명가량이쥬둔ᄒᆞ엿고불일니로원산근쳐에셔싸홈이되겟다더라

○일관야연 일공ᄉᆞ가뎨신대신대포씨를ᄒᆞ야작야에히공관에셔만찬회를비셜ᄒᆞ엿ᄂᆞᆫᄃᆡ문무관졔씨들도참셕ᄒᆞ엿다더라

○셩명일관 지작일외부에셔일본정무각부에시찰위원을파송ᄒᆞᄂᆞᆫ일을셩명ᄒᆞ엿다더라

○셔긔회국 일공관셔긔관츄원씨가히졍부명령을승ᄒᆞ야리구일경에발힝ᄒᆞᆫ다더라

○문관복장 쟝ᄎᆞᆺ일본에젼왕ᄒᆞᆯ시찰졔씨의게문관복장실시ᄒᆞ라ᄒᆞ신 쳐분이나리셧더라

○구락부청요 대동구락부에셔작금량일하오여섯시에연기를ᄒᆞᆫ다ᄒᆞ고일공관셔긔관츄원슈일씨가군부로공함ᄒᆞ고본부관인의게젼왕ᄒᆞ야관광ᄒᆞᆷ욕쳥ᄒᆞ엿더라

○위문힝지 만쥬젼디에젼왕ᄒᆞᄂᆞᆫ위문대ᄉᆞ편에하ᄉᆞᄒᆞ시ᄂᆞᆫ물픔이잇ᄂᆞᆫᄃᆡ약쥬와연초두가지를만쥬츌젼ᄒᆞᆫ일본쟝졸의게략략히분급ᄒᆞᆫᄃᆡ도그가액이십여만원가량이되고또기타물픔소입이불쇼ᄒᆞᆫᄃᆡ탁지부에셔지츌ᄒᆞᆯ지졍이업순즉히대ᄉᆞ의발힝이ᄌᆞ연연긔되리라더라

○창원민면 창원민인등이외부로면ᄒᆞ되본항신상회를경원에셔관할ᄒᆞ야총슌으로본회샤ᄉᆞ무쟝을겸임ᄒᆞ야샹민을입의로착지ᄒᆞ야구문을억지로토식ᄒᆞᆫ즉샹민이난보ᄒᆞ야필경환산ᄒᆞᆯ형편이오니히회샤를곳혁파ᄒᆞ야이에지당ᄒᆞᆫ항구빅셩을본항에환집ᄒᆞ야안도케ᄒᆞ라ᄒᆞ엿더라

○위관ᄉᆞ담 공쥬군ᄃᆡ의분요ᄒᆞᆫᄉᆞ건을인ᄒᆞ야ᄉᆞ담ᄒᆞᆯᄎᆞ로군부와헌병ᄃᆡ 관각일인이하거ᄒᆞ엿더라

○조션소청원 부산항조션소ᄉᆞ무원김유직등이외부에청원ᄒᆞ되부산항졀영도니양살마굴포를입의귀부에셔본샤에특허ᄒᆞ엿스니슈산물졔조업과미곡용졍ᄒᆞᄂᆞᆫ업놀일졔히부속ᄒᆞ야영업ᄒᆞ게ᄒᆞ라ᄒᆞ엿더라

○참연향례대 의부대신협관과통신원총관과례식원쟝등모든관인이일본례신대신를청요ᄒᆞ야비원안에셔작일에연향ᄒᆞ엿다더라

외보

○향항면챠회샤 작년이리로향항면긔렬도회샤에셔역ᄉᆞᄒᆞ든향항시가의길은거월에쥰공ᄒᆞ엿ᄂᆞᆫᄃᆡ히회샤에셔ᄂᆞᆫ곳청인수십인을고용ᄒᆞ야면챠의운젼을련습식켜구월일일브터ᄀᆡ업ᄒᆞ엿다더라

○로덕밀약 칠월이십팔일밤에색로빅작과윗레씨간에톄결ᄒᆞᆫ로덕통샹됴약의요령은아직발표치안코도리혀무슨밀약을ᄒᆞᆫ다고ᄒᆞ야타임쓰신문의증언ᄒᆞᆫ거슨좌와ᄀᆞᆺᄒᆞ니운ᄒᆞᆫᄃᆡ로덕간ᄎᆞᆺ샹됴약은금후십년간을계속ᄒᆞᆯ셩질인데그됴목은불원ᄒᆞ여오국과밋루마니아간에됴약을톄결ᄒᆞ기ᄭᆞ지발표ᄒᆞ지아니ᄒᆞᆯ거신데그러나곡물보호셰톨ᄀᆞ장헐ᄒᆞ게감읫ᄒᆞᆯ일긔됴목은로국이승낙ᄒᆞ엿다ᄒᆞᆷ은본리명빅ᄒᆞ다ᄒᆞ더라

광고

TELEGRAMS.

THE RUSSIAN FLEET

(FROM JAPAN PAPERS.)

Berlin, Sept. 25th.

The Baltic fleet will not call at Kiel, there being no reason to do so, as they are not allowed to pass the Baltic canal.

London, Sept. 26th.

The Russian cruiser "Teretz" detained the "Lochitz" (?) which was on her way to Colombo, and examined her papers.

London, Sept. 28th

The Russian cruiser "Teretz has" arrived at Lisbon. The "Espana," "of Madrid, states that the treatment accorded to the "Teretz" at Las Palmas was due to the British Ambassador semi-officially giving the Spanish Government to understand that Great Britain would protest against the utilization of Spanish territory as a base for harassing British commerce. Coaling had already begun, but was then stopped.

Later.

The "Espana's" story is officially denied in London.

London, Sept. 28.

The cruisers St. Petersburg and Smolensk have left Port Said after taking three hundred and fifty tons and a hundred tons of coal respectively. Their destination is reported to be Libau.

Later.

The Russian Volunteer steamer "Nijni Novgorod" has passed the Dardanelles en route for Candia and Port Said, where she will await instructions. She flew the commercial flag and carried no guns or ammunition.

GERMANY AND RUSSIA.

London, September 26.

Lord Lansdowne, the British Foreign Minister, has intimated that British firms must not furnish coal, either in home or colonial ports, to Russian vessels intended for warlike purposes. On the other hand a Kiel firm named Diederichsen has undertaken to supply coal to the Russian fleet, from which fact, it is considered that the relations between Russia and Germany are growing significant.

THE TRIPLE ALLIANCE.

Berlin, September 28.

The Italian Premier, M. Giolitti, has paid a visit to Count Bulow, the German Chancellor, at Homburg. The conference resulted in a complete agreement between the two statesmen on all important political questions, so that all machinations to sever Germany and Italy are likely to prove abortive.

Berlin, Sept. 28.

The conference between Signor Giolitti (Premier of Italy) and Count von Bulow has suggested the belief that an attempt is to be made at mediation in the dispute between Japan and Russia.

It is thought in Germany, however, that any such attempt at the present time would be inopportune, and that any proposal for peace must come direct either from Japan or Russia.

The London 'Daily Telegraph' protests against the continued attacks made by certain British journals on Germany's neutrality, and says it hopes for favourable results from the visit to Japan of Prince Karl Anton.

THE RUSSIAN ARMY

St. Petersburg, September 22.

The Russian Government has decided that the forces in the field shall be divided into three armies under Generals Linevitch, Salvaivoff and another, the whole under the command of General Kuropatkin.

THE RUSSIAN SECOND ARMY

London, Sept. 29.

Reuter's Mukden correspondent wires that cavalry outposts report a big Japanese movement westward, threatening the railway. There is no change in the eastward position.

The Second Army, which is to be under the command of General Grippenberg, will consist of the First and the Eighth Corps d'Armée, and of two other corps now in process of mobilization in the Wilna and Warsaw military districts. Thus the whole force will be 4 army-corps (120,000). After this Second Army is formed, Grand Duke Nicolaievitch will, it is said, be appointed to the supreme command in Manchuria.

It appears that the Circum-Baikal Railway was opened for military trains on the 25th instant.

London, Sept. 26.

General Kuropatkin telegraphs that the Japanese are preparing to execute an extensive turning movement to the east of Mukden. Several attempts made by the Japanese to capture the Kaotuling Pass, northeast of Beniaputze, have been repulsed.

Peking, September 28th.

According to a Chanchakao telegram dated the 25th inst. the Russian military authorities have enlisted two thousand Mongolian soldiers, giving them twelve yen apiece a month, subsequently increased by two yen. They are enlisting more such troops every day. Rifles and guns which have been bought by the Mongolians from German merchants are being transported to those regions.—Mainichi.

PORT ARTHUR.

Chefoo, Sept. 25th.

According to a report received on the Russian side here, the Kuropatkin Battery and six other strong batteries, which were erected to the south of Shuitseying by the Russians to cover the water source at Port Arthur, were attacked on the 18th inst. and captured on the following day at noon. The water supply was captured on the 21st inst. The Russians are suffering from lack of water.

A telegram from Wei-hai-wei this evening at 7:30 states that it has just been wired to the Commander-in-Chief of the British squadron that the Japanese have captured two batteries.—Asahi.

UNLUCKY RUSSIAN WAR CORRESPONDENTS.

London, Sept. 21st.

It is stated that General Kuropatkin has sent home the eminent Russian war correspondent Dantchanko, owing to his recent messages, and several others are also returning.

ROOSEVELT AND A HAGUE CONFERENCE.

London, Sept. 28.

It is authoritatively stated in Washington that President Roosevelt will not await the conclusion of the war, but will call for a conference at The Hague early in 1905.

EXTENSION OF THE JAPANESE ARMY.

Tokyo, Sept. 28th.

It is understood that the Privy Council to-day approved a Bill for the extension of the fighting capacity of the Japanese forces. [Apropos, the most advisable means for that purpose is an extension of the term of the Second Reserves. The term of active and reserved services is 23 years in Russia, 18 years [19 years in case of cavalry and artillery] in Germany, and 29 years in France, but the term of the Japanese Standing Army and Second Reserves has hitherto been totalled at 12 years and 4 months only.]

THIBET

London, Sept. 29.

Reuter's St. Petersburg correspondent says it is understood that Count Benckendorff, the Russian Ambassador in London, has made friendly representations to the British Government regarding an alleged discrepancy between the draft of the Thibet Treaty and previous assurances by the British Government.

At his ancestral home, the first portion of the Marquess of Anglesey's personal clothing was sold by auction on August 24th. The principal lot was a magnificent sable coat which cost the Marquess 1,000 guineas. It was sold to Mr. Wood, of Piccadilly, London, for £300. Overcoats averaged £8, and lounge suits £2 15s. 6d.; silk pyjamas realised £8 10s. The total receipts for the day were £1,416.

COMPENSATION FOR LOSS OF HITACHI MARU.

It has previously been stated that the N. Y. K. claimed compensation from the Government for the loss of the Hitachi Maru, sunk by the Russians. We now hear that the authorities have paid Y900,000 compensation, although the cost of building the ship was Y1,200,000. The Government are reported to be responsible for the whole cost of the repairs to the Sado Maru.

PERSONALLY CONDUCTED TOUR.

The Japanese Minister has sent a despatch to the Foreign Office, to the effect that the visit of the six Korean officials to Japan will be conducive to a better felling between the two nations. Consequently he will write to his Government, asking them to afford them protection and furthermore he will be pleased to send Mr. Hagiwara to act as escort. The famous "Cook's" would seem to have a rival in the far east.

The connection that exists between Port Arthur and a peaceful village in Devonshire is little known, says an exchange. Half a century ago the rector of Altherington was the Rev. James Arthur, the father of Lieutenant W. Arthur, R. N., and great-uncle of the present rector, the Rev. W. W. Arthur; and Lieutenant Arthur was, in the late fifties, in command of the gunboat "Algerine" in Chinese waters. The "Algerine" was attached to a surveying expedition prior to the landing made by the English in 1860; and when the flagship "Action" was disabled, Lieutenant Arthur towed her into the then un-named harbour, which was thenceforth known as Port Arthur. Lieutenant Arthur afterwards attained the rank of Rear-Admiral.

The Korea Daily News.

Issued at 5 P. M. daily except Sundays.

Rate of Subscription:—
Per Year, Yen 25.
Per Quarter, Yen 7.
Per Month Yen 2.50

Postage in Korea not charged extra.
Postage abroad charged extra.

Advertisements, 50 sen per day for 1 inch or less.
5 yen per month per inch.
50 yen per year per inch.

All communications to
E. T. BETHELL,
Editor and Publisher.
Pak-tong, Seoul.

THE ANGLO-JAPANESE AGREEMENT.

If some of the Japanese newspapers were to have their way we should soon all be cutting each other's throats. Following upon the recent anti-German crusade we find that the "Jiji Shimpo," which is the "Times" of Japan, is advocating an extension of the Anglo-Japanese alliance.

We reproduce the article in another column and as it is also reproduced by the "Japan Mail" and called "interesting," we may expect that the Tokio correspondent of the London "Times" has already wired it home to that journal, as the editor of the "Japan Mail" and the Tokio correspondent of the "Times" are one and the same person.

The article in the "Jiji" is noteworthy if only on account of its artlessness. The Anglo-Japanese agreement at present only refers to China and Korea and only calls for Great Britain's interference in the event of another Power coming to the assistance of Russia. Now the "Jiji" proposes that as Saghalien will shortly be taken by Japan, and as, in revenge for her recent action in Thibet, England may expect aggression from Russia on her Indian frontier, the scope of the agreement should be extended to include these two countries.

In view of the enormous disproportion of size and importance between Saghalien and India the proposed extension of the agreement, if it still retains its purely defensive character, will, after the war is over, be very magnanimous on the part of Japan. But so long as the war lasts we consider that any tampering with the present treaty would be fraught with very grave consequences. The situation is sufficiently delicate already without any more fat being thrown on the fire.

Affairs have so shaped themselves of late that there is reason to believe in the probability of the war being confined to the two Powers already engaged and it is sincerely to be hoped,that Great Britain, of all Powers, will not be the one, by any act which can be costrued into aggression, to extend the war beyond its present limits.

There will be plenty of time to discuss Saghalien after it has definitely become Japan's property. The discussion of it previous to the conclusion of war and the signing of peace has a sinister appearance.

There is every reason to believe that Japan entered upon this war against the wishes of Great Britain. At all events British statesmen did all they could to avert and delay hostilities.

However, once hostilities commenced Great Britain could do nothing but loyally abide by her agreement, and as the "Jiji" justly remarks, there is no doubt that she intends continuing to do so.

But extending the agreement is quite another matter. The conclusion of this war will bring about a very great change in the relative positions of England, Japan and Russia. Whatever the result of the war may be, both belligerents will have suffered severely and will be a long time recovering their value as friend or foe.

If Russia is beaten, Great Britain will have nothing to fear from her in India for a long time and Japan's co-operation will be unnecessary. If Japan is beaten, the whole political situation will be changed and Japan will be so crippled and exhausted that England may not find it to her advantage to continue the agreement, even in its present form.

Therefore we disagree with the "Jiji Shimpo" when it says it is not now too soon to discuss an extension of the Anglo-Japanese agreement.

VICEROY ALEXIEFF.

It is reported that Viceroy Aleixeff has been recalled to St. Petersburg, by order of the Czar.

THE KONGCHU RIOT.

The investigators of the Kongchu affray have discovered that the riot arose from a quarrel between a Korean soldier and a Japanese civilian. The former had committed a nuisance in the neighbourhood of the Japanese house and the owner was diligently beating the soldier with a stick, when some of the latter's friends came to the rescue. They entirely wrecked the Japanese house and inflicted severe corporal punishment on the owner.

Japanese troops have now removed the soldiers' rifles and arrested the officer in command.

H. E. the Italian Minister leaves today for Peking per S. S. Babelsberg.

Mr. Hagiwara has received instructions from his Government to leave Korea on the 9th inst.

On alternate days the Council of State receives a visit from Mr. Hasegawa, the Japanese Legation interpreter.

A complaint comes from Changwon that the Japanese railway authorities are paying insufficient prices for crops, etc., destroyed by the pushing forward of the railway.

The "Varyag" has been reported floated nearly as often as General Stoessel has been killed or committed suicide. We are now informed that the next spring tide will see the cruiser safely afloat in Chemulpo harbour.

In addition to the numerous entertainments arranged for Mr. Oura, we learn that Mr. Min Sang Ho, the Minister of Communications, has prepared a banquet, for this evening, at which the Ministers of all Departments will assist.

The Soon An district is to be the site of a Korean El Dorado. Two hundred Japanese have staked out a large tract of land there and applied for permission to commence mining operations. The necessary capital is said to be forthcoming.

The Government has found a rather curious manner of evading an imagined difficulty. They suddenly discovered that eitquette demanded that Japanese military officers, arriving at Chemulpo and Wiju, should be welcomed by some Korean Military authority. As there are no Korean troops at these ports, they have bestowed the rank and uniform of Major on the Kamnis.

ANGLO-JAPANESE ALLIANCE.

Acting on the principle that in matters diplomatic nothing is so essential as the frequent exchange of views on well-chosen occasions and a thoroughly matured understanding arrived at as the result of time-tried friendship between the parties concerned, the "Jiji" deems it not too early now to commence considering the advisability of renewing at its expiration the Anglo-Japanese Alliance, with the aim of enlarging its scope of application. The recovery of the Saghalien group by Japan as a result of the war when it is terminated victoriously for us, may be regarded as an anticipative possibility, and in the circumstances it may before long become desirable for Japan to have the alliance extended in its application. On the part of England the recent acquisition by her of protectoral rights over Tibet occasions, it may be said, a similar necessity. It may, however, be contended, on the other hand, that Tibet, being a tributary state under the sway of Chinese sovereignty, should be properly regarded to be within the scope of the alliance in its existing form, which is to cover both China and Korea. The "Jiji" would not quarrel over this point and would accept the latter interpretation in all willingness; for Japan, as it says, must not imitate Germany in selling England as she did when she declared Manchuria to be beyond the reach of the Anglo-German agreement about China. Nevertheless the acquisition of the new right over Tibet may after all not prove any additional benefit to England, if Russia in vengeance and with a free hand should recommence her threats on British India, from the borders of Persia and Afghanistan, with nothing to detract her attention in other directions. Supposing, then, as it may reasonably be supposed, that England stands in need of Japan's co-operation in order that she may be secure from Russia's aggressive designs in the localities indicated, and Japan is determined to render such co-operation, there will arise reciprocity of reasons for extending the working of the alliance at its renewal. England so far has never for once given any occasion for us to believe but that she is most firmly resolved to most honorably and conscientiously perform her part of the agreement, and the "Jiji" thinks that the question of amplifying the alliance will not but be favourably received by her, provided our authorities deliberate on the matter in good time and broach the subject at the proper moment.—Japan Times.

THE RECENT EXECUTION.

With regard to the recent execution of three Korean coolies, the Home office has, through the Foreign office, lodged a protest with the Japanese Legation.

In the first place the Home office protests against three Koreans being killed without the proper authorities having been consulted or even notified that the execution was to take place.

Further, after suggesting that the Koreans sinned through ignorance he requests that the Korean authorities be afforded an opportunity of investigating the case before the Japanese again take the law into their own hands.

THE JAPANESE MINISTER OF COMMUNICATIONS.

Mr. Oura was magnificently entertained yesterday at a well-arranged tiffin in the grounds of the old Imperial Palace, and in the evening, a banquet was given in his honor at the Japanese Legation.

Today at 3 P.M., accompanied by Messrs. Hayashi and Megata, he was received in audience by His Majesty.

Mr. Oura expects to leave in a few days for Manchuria.

Great anxiety is felt by the relatives and friends of Mr. Pak Che-soon, Councilor of State, who recently disappeared from his home. It is feared that the death of his two favorite sons, which preyed heavily on his mind, has made him demented, and that he is either wandering through the country or has committed suicide.

The Korea Daily News.

VOL. I, | WEDNESDAY, OCTOBER 5, 1904. | No. 68

HONGKONG & SHANGHAI BANKING CORPORATION.

Paid-up Capital.................$10,000,000
Reserve Fund:—Sterling Reserve... 10,000,000
Silver Reserve..... 7,000,000

27,000,000
Reserve Liability of Proprietors... 10,000,000

HEAD OFFICE, HONGKONG.

London Bankers, London and County Banking Company Limited.
Branches and Agencies,
London.

Amoy,	Hankow	Penang,
Bangkok,	Hiogo,	Rangoon,
Batavia,	Iloilo,	Saigon,
Bombay,	Lyons,	San Francisco,
Calcutta,	Manila,	Singapore,
Colombo,	Nagasaki,	Sourabaya,
Foochow,	New York,	Tientsin,
Hamburg.	Peking,	Yokohama,

Credits granted on approved Securities, and every description of Banking and Exchange business transacted.

Drafts granted on London and the chief Commercial places in Europe, India, Australia, America, China and Japan.

HOLME RINGER & CO., AGENTS,
CHEMULPO.

ON CHEONG & CO.,
SEOUL.

GENERAL STORE KEEPERS.
Imported provisions, Cooking Utensils Crockery, etc.
FRESH BREAD DAILY.

MITSU BISHI DOCKYARD & ENGINE WORKS,
NAGASAKI.

CODE WORD, "DOCK."

A. 1, A. B. C., and Engineering Codes used.

DOCK No. 1 (at Tategami).

Extreme Length..............523 feet
Length on blocks .... 513 „
Width of Entrance on Top......89 „
Bottom....77 „
Water on Blocks at Spring Tide 26½ „

DOCK No. 2 (Mukaijima).

Extreme Length...............371 feet
Length on Blocks.............360 „
Width of Entrance on Top......66 „
„ „ Bottom 53 „
Water on Blocks at Spring Tide 22 „

PATENT SLIP (at Kosuge).

Can take vessels up to 1,000 tons gross.

THE WORKS are well equipped with the LATEST IMPROVEMENTS, and can execute any kind of work in SHIPBUILDING and MARINE ENGINEERING, as well as in REPAIRING of SHIPS.

The COMPANY'S new powerful steamer OURA-MARU (712 tons, 700 I.H.P.), specially built for SALVAGE PURPOSES, and equipped with necessary gear, is always READY at SHORT NOTICE.

CHARTERED BANK OF INDIA AUSTRALIA & CHINA.

INCORPORATED BY ROYAL CHARTER 1853

HEAD OFFICES:—LONDON.

Paid-up Capital £800,000
Reserve Liability of Shareholders 800,000
Reserve Fund 800,000

Drafts granted upon all the principal places in the world and every description of Exchange and banking business transacted.

E. MEYER & Co., Agents,
Chemulpo.

E. MEYER & CO.
Chemulpo.

SOLE AGENTS IN KOREA FOR:
A. T. Morse, Sons & Co's "Fresco" Distemper

In all colours ready for use on walls, Ceilings etc.
and
AVENARIUS CARBOLINEUM

A wood-preserving and antiseptic oil preparation

Against decay, dry-rot, fungus and wood-destroying insects.

A large supply always in Stock.
Prices upon application.

E. MEYER & Co.,
Chemulpo.

LAW UNION & CROWN INS. CO.

Fire risks accepted at Current rates, on godowns, merchandise, dwellings, and other property, subject to usual conditions.

HOLME RINGER & Co.,
Agents, Chemulpo

THE METHODIST PUBLISHING HOUSE,
Little WestGate, Seoul.

JOB PRINTING, TYPEWRITER PAPER
CARBON PAPER, VISITING CARDS
STATIONERY, BOOK BINDING
BOOK PUBLISHERS
AMERICAN SCHOOL BOOKS
SPENCERIAN COPY BOOKS
PEN CARBON LETTER AND BILL BOOKS

S. A. BECK, Manager.

DAI-ICHI GINKO.
LIMITED.
(Formerly the First National Bank)

ESTABLISHED 1873

INCORPORATED UNDER PRESENT LAW 1896

Capital - - - - - - - - - Yen 5,000,000
Reserve Fund - - - - - - 1,500,000

HEAD OFFICE:—TOKIO.

President: Baron SHIBUSAWA.

BRANCHES AND CORRESPONDENTS
In the Principal Cities and Towns of Japan.
Interest Allowed on
Fixed deposits 1 year - - - 6½ per cent
" " 6 months - - - 6 per cent

Special current accounts 1½ sen daily per Y 100
General " " 1 " " " 100

M. TANAKA,
Manager, Chemulpo

HOLME RINGER & Co.
Chemulpo.

General Merchants and Government Contractors.

Agents for the leading
Banks
Steamship Companies
and
Insurance Companies

Importers of Merchandise of every description.

KAMEYA & CO.

GENERAL STOREKEEPERS
Chinkokai - - Seoul
(Established 1895, Tokyo)

Confectionery, Hams, Canned Goods, Cutlery, Hirano & Tansan Water. Provisions, Gents, Furnishing goods, Toilet Articles, Travelling Bags, Tobacco, Cigars & Cigarettes Kitchen Utensils. Coffee, Biscuits.

Fresh Goods always kept in Stock.
Prices Moderate
Please come and inspect our goods.

NIPPON YUSEN KAISHA.

JAPANESE MAIL STEAMSHIP CO.

DER MAIL CONTRACT WITH THE IMPERIAL JAPANESE GOVERNMENT.

European Line

Regular Fortnightly Service between Yokohama Kobe, Moji, Shanghai, Hongkong, Singapore, Penang Colombo, Port Said, Marseilles, London and Antwerp

American Line

Regular Fortnightly Service between Hongkong and Seattle, calling at Shanghai, Moji, Kobe, Yokohama and Victoria, B. C.

Australian Line

Regular weekly Service betwen Japan Ports and Australia, calling at Hongkong and Manila.

(Above Three Lines Suspended until further notice).

Shanghai Line

Weekly Service between Shanghai and Japan Ports

Korea Line

Service Kobe, Moji, Nagasaki, Fusan, Chemupo, Coo, Taiku.
S. S. Bahelsberg, 2181 tons.
Service Kobe, Moji, Fusan, Chemulpo, Chinnampo
S. S ARGO, S. S. Ohio.

BORDEN'S CONDENSED MILK CO.

New York, U. S. A.

ALWAYS IN STOCK
Eagle Brand Condensed Milk.
Gold Seal Condensed Milk.
Peerless (Family) Evaporated Cream.
Borden's Malted Milk.

E. MEYER & CO.
Chemulpo, Korea,
Sole Agents

ROYAL INSURANCE COMPANY,
Funds exceed £10,000,000
FIRE
AT CURRENT RATES.
LIFE
REDUCED PREMIUM.
HOLME RINGER & Co.,
Agents, Chemulpo.

HOTEL DU PALAIS
SEOUL.

The only first class Hotel in Seoul. Situated in the centre of the city opposite the palace.

Cuisine under the supervision of an experienced French Chef.

Well ventilated and furnished throughout.

TARIFF UPON APPLICATION

L. MARTIN
Proprietor and Mangaer.

大韓每日申報

대한ᄆᆡ일신보

일천구ᄇᆡᆨ사년십월륙일 (목요일) (뎨륙십구호)

본샤고ᄇᆡᆨ

본신보는영어와한어로셕계ᄆᆡ일츌판ᄒᆞᆸ

신문가

한쟝 엽두돈오푼

일삭표 엽두량닷돈

우표가ᄆᆡ삭닷돈

다엽돈으로밧숩

광고료는

귀한외쟝단과ᄌᆞ힝의다쇼로죵감ᄒᆞ되몃가로밧을터이오며오ᄅᆡ지아녀대한사람마다다이신문을보실터이니광고버시기를원ᄒᆞ시는이들은우리신문사에와서면약ᄒᆞ심을희망ᄒᆞᆸ

○발힝소 박동대한ᄆᆡ일신보사ᄇᆡ어한교엽희젼영국인셜필림쟝자리오

사쟝 영국인 (ᄇᆡ셜)

평양 ᄃᆡ리졈

○평양효동사는권ᄆᆡ보씨로우리신문광ᄆᆡᄃᆡ리인을틱졍ᄒᆞ엿ᄉᆞ오니평양에계신구람코져ᄒᆞ시는 쳠군ᄌᆞ는ᄃᆡ리졈에왕림ᄒᆞ와면의ᄒᆞ시옵

사고

○우리대한ᄆᆡ일신보의목뎍은대한의안녕질서에관한모든데목에ᄃᆡᄒᆞ야논공평한변론을쥬쟝홈이라우리동신원의라보는신문보시는쳠군ᄌᆞ의계ᄒᆞ상보도ᄒᆞ리며편지를귀서ᄒᆞ여주시는이논셩명과번ᄃᆡ를젹어붓치시기를희망ᄒᆞ오니이거슨신문샹에긔ᄌᆡᄒᆞ란는거시아니오다만긔희신용ᄒᆞ는ᄌᆞ거를숨고자홈이라귀자는아모긔서던지긔ᄌᆡ홈을ᄋᆡ걱ᄒᆞ는권리를가젓ᄉᆞ나ᄒᆡ걱ᄒᆞ는리유를말ᄒᆞᆯ터이오며공중평화를문란케ᄒᆞ는듯ᄒᆞᆫ긔서는의례히밧지안켓숩나이다

●본샤셜시이래로신문을ᄆᆡ양우레로분젼ᄒᆞ와레젼부의임의로젼ᄒᆞ든ᄉᆞ로먼곳에는혹늣게젼ᄒᆞ기도ᄒᆞ며혹몃칠거슬ᄒᆞᆫ번에젼ᄒᆞ기도ᄒᆞ며혹아니젼ᄒᆞ는곳도잇다ᄒᆞ와우리신문을ᄉᆞ랑ᄒᆞ야구람ᄒᆞ시는 쳠군ᄌᆞ의게ᄃᆡᄒᆞ야ᄆᆡ우미안ᄒᆞ옵기로지금은분젼인을두고ᄆᆡ일일ᄌᆞ이젼ᄒᆞ며아니젼ᄒᆞ거나늣게거나ᄒᆞᆫ폐가잇도록ᄒᆞ란ᄒᆞ오니혹아니젼ᄒᆞ거나혹늣게젼ᄒᆞ거나ᄒᆞᆫ일이잇스면본사로통긔ᄒᆞ여주심을희망ᄒᆞᆸ

본사광고

본샤에셔본신문뎨ᄉᆞ호와뎨샹일호와뎨이십오호를소용ᄒᆞᆯᄇᆡ가잇서이에광고ᄒᆞ오니누구시던지이샹삼호중에본사로가일오시면ᄆᆡ쟝에ᄇᆡᆨ젼두푼식드리리옵

론셜

일본의ᄒᆡᆼ동ᄒᆞᆫ란홈이라

만일 일본이ᄂᆞ신문에게ᄌᆡᄒᆞᆫ바와갓치우리도대답ᄒᆞ란ᄒᆞᆫ진ᄃᆡ파연미구에목구멍ᄭᅴ말니졀듯ᄒᆞᆫ지라우리는시사신보를거ᄒᆞᆫ즉다임쓰신문에이ᄂᆞ나라로동맹ᄒᆞᆫ다홈을장황히변론ᄒᆞᆫ바를번등ᄒᆞ엿고ᄯᅩ일본메일신문에도이말을계ᄌᆡᄒᆞ엿스ᄂᆞ즉이논다름이아니라론돈에잇는동경통신원인즉일본메일신사긔자이고이사롬인즉다임쓰신문통신원인고로다만ᄒᆞᆫᄉᆞ롬이여러신문사로젼보ᄒᆞ야게ᄌᆡ가된듯ᄒᆞ니만일시사신보로말ᄒᆞᆯ진ᄃᆡ번번치못ᄒᆞ야무식ᄒᆞᆫ양으로돌녀보지경이면오히려관찰ᄒᆞ엿다고홀듯ᄒᆞᆫ지라

현금일본셔ᄒᆡᆼ동ᄒᆞ란홈은다만한쳥양국을돌녀보니며ᄯᅩᄒᆞᆫ다른나라이아라사를방조ᄒᆞ야영국에구익만되게ᄒᆞ는거시사신보에일본셔사가평을취ᄒᆞᆫ다ᄒᆞ엿스니이는ᄌᆞ긔의마음ᄃᆡ로란이베르로ᄒᆞ여곰보수를ᄒᆞ란홈이요영국은아라사로더부러인도지방에서싸와두나라로쟝황ᄒᆞ게일만만들게홈인즉합동ᄒᆞ란ᄒᆞ는목젹이이에서지ᄂᆡ지아니ᄒᆞ는지라

비록이을취아니ᄒᆞᆫ일이라도후일본에아모조록조케ᄒᆞ란는이의사가잇서그리ᄒᆞ는듯ᄒᆞ나싸홈이펠경굿치는날에는이조약ᄒᆞᆫ일이ᄃᆡ단히후회가될터이며ᄯᅩ일후에사가평이일본에화실히속ᄒᆞᆫ후에라도비일의론ᄒᆞᆯ날은오히려만ᄒᆞᆫ즉지금젼쟁이결국이되엿다던지광화가되엿다거던지좌우간귀졍되기젼발ᄒᆞ는시좃치아니ᄒᆞᆫ일이며일본은영국의원ᄒᆞ는바를반ᄃᆡᄒᆞ야싸홈만되게ᄒᆞ되영국졍부칙임쟈들은어나ᄯᅢ셔지던지연타ᄒᆞᆯ지라만일싸홈만시작ᄒᆞ는경우이면괴어히ᄎᆞᆼ셩을다ᄒᆞ야시ᄉᆞ신보에게ᄌᆡᄒᆞᆫ바와갓치약조를조칠터이되지금합동ᄃᆡ츌ᄒᆞ는거슨확실히다론조건인즉일아젼쟁만결말나는날에는영국이괴왕에일아량국으로친목ᄒᆞ게지ᄂᆡ던쟁분이번샹ᄒᆞᆯ터이요ᄯᅩᄒᆞᆫ두나라이서로젼쟁귀졍되는날은잇슬터인즉다시친목히지ᄂᆡᆫ다던지구수갓치지ᄂᆡᆫ다던지어좌어우간오리셔로샹지ᄒᆞ야괴ᄎᆞ피로을지라

만일아라사이퀴ᄒᆞ는지경이면영국셔는인도국에서오래도록샹지홈에조곰도두려울게시업고ᄯᅩᄒᆞᆫ일본의협조홈을펼요치아니홀터이요혹일본이퀴ᄒᆞ는경우이면쟁계샹형편이확실히변기ᄒᆞ야말이못될터인즉영국셔당초에지금약조ᄒᆞᆫ디로ᄌᆞ긔의게만리익ᄒᆞ게홀리가만무ᄒᆞᆫ즉

이런고로우리는시ᄉᆞ신보에항동ᄒᆞᆫ다고쟝황히셜명ᄒᆞᆫ거시이럿케급조히아니홀일로알아젹당치안케역이노라

잡보

○쳐벌ᄅᆡ당 일본병참부에서군ᄉᆞ샹위경죄인김셩삼등삼인을ᄌᆞ힝포살ᄒᆞᆫ일노니부에셔외부로죠회ᄒᆞ기를셜령아국인민중에우죠ᄒᆞᆫ사름이희군법을어의여범ᄒᆞᆫ경우에는희인이범죄ᄒᆞᆫ리유를아졍부에회괸ᄒᆞ야샹당히쳐벌ᄒᆞ는거시고인명의신중홈과린방의우의에셜노타당홈이니일공관에죠회ᄒᆞ야희병참부로젼죠ᄒᆞ야이후에아국인민이혹군률을범ᄒᆞ는자잇스면우리졍부에향ᄒᆞ야서로관리ᄒᆞ야쳐벌ᄒᆞ고혹경션히징ᄒᆞ야ᄇᆡᆨ셩의원홈홈을닐위지말게ᄒᆞ고곳시명ᄒᆞ라ᄒᆞ엿더라

○졍부통쳡 지작일에졍부에셔각부에통쳡ᄒᆞ기를이모당졍무가간극ᄒᆞᆫᄯᅢ를당ᄒᆞ야졍부대관이부조련이수진ᄒᆞ야일졔히모히지아니치못ᄒᆞ겟는고로향자에시간을정ᄒᆞ야수진ᄒᆞ기로죤칭ᄒᆞ엿거니와오히려그ᄃᆡ로ᄒᆞ는거슬보지못ᄒᆞ겟고당초에아르켜도아니ᄒᆞ는지라각칙졍이맛춤ᄂᆡ일졔히모히지아니ᄒᆞ고각부대신이희부에수진ᄒᆞᆫ거시며우평셩ᄒᆞ야왕왕히좌셕이희쇼ᄒᆞ야더브러토론ᄒᆞᆯ이가업스니진실노기탄ᄒᆞᆫ지라젼참졍의틔힝ᄒᆞᆫ거시진실노맛당치아님이아니니면치면ᄇᆡᆨ홈을엇숩는거시제아지도록규진히홈이맛당ᄒᆞᆫ지라ᄌᆞ금이후로는ᄃᆡ단ᄒᆞᆫ수고가아니여든진시수진ᄒᆞ고혹실병과실고가잇서부득이수진을궐ᄒᆞ는경우에는실샹ᄃᆡ로통쳡ᄒᆞ야알게ᄒᆞ라ᄒᆞ엿더라

○졍부우쳡 작일에ᄯᅩ통쳡ᄒᆞ기를명일노위시ᄒᆞ야오후두시간에졍부제신을맛당히 쇼쳥ᄒᆞ리니만일주품ᄒᆞᆯᄉᆞ가잇거든쥬시압 픔ᄒᆞ라ᄒᆞ신ᄃᆡ니면칙을봉승ᄒᆞ와이에앙쥬ᄒᆞ노라ᄒᆞ엿더라

○면ᄒᆞᆫ각군 ᄂᆡ부에서신샹도에면ᄒᆞᆫ기를관하각군군수가하시에유ᄒᆞ엿스며모군수가모군을서리ᄒᆞ엿는지ᄌᆞ세히보고ᄒᆞ라ᄒᆞ엿더라

○쳥원면쟁 창원군면보에ᄒᆞ기를턴도지천을본군향교답위셩체ᄃᆡ희에부셜ᄒᆞ기로시역ᄒᆞ는ᄃᆡ금지부득ᄒᆞ은즉극히황송ᄒᆞ오며희텬도지셕부셜ᄒᆞ는도방인가를휘텬ᄒᆞ고면답에곽식을거두라ᄒᆞ는고로민심이소요ᄒᆞ며곽식갑은게급ᄒᆞ는거시상분지일이못되니당쟝ᄇᆡᆨ셩의쟁경이가련ᄒᆞ고호소가답지ᄒᆞᆯ쌘아니라후폐소관이니곳일공관에죠회ᄒᆞ야희텬도ᄃᆡ에신칙ᄒᆞ야희면답곽식갑을죵시가ᄒᆞ야츌급케ᄒᆞ라ᄒᆞ엿더라

○ᄃᆡ쟝암샹 일본헌병이명파셕ᄃᆡ명샹명이공쥬군진위ᄃᆡ죵쇼ᄃᆡ쟝이인과병뎡삼신병을졔작일오후에헌병수명부로압샹ᄒᆞ엿더라

○비밀샹주 ᄃᆡ한일보를게ᄌᆡᄒᆞᆫ죵쳔영씨와쳥ᄇᆡᆨ씨가근일ᄂᆡ로무숨일인지젼히운동중인ᄃᆡ지난이일밤에는수시간을비밀히샹주ᄒᆞ엿다더라

관보

광무팔년구월삼십일 부록연속

○보통군헌병ᄃᆡ중ᄃᆡ장 통군헌병졍위 최욱셔

○보시위뎨일련ᄃᆡ뎨일대ᄃᆡ부 통군보병부위 박승즁 김응덕

○보시위뎨일련ᄃᆡ뎨일대ᄃᆡ향관 통군일등군ᄉᆞ 리한긍

○보시위뎨일련ᄃᆡ뎨이대ᄃᆡ부 통군보병참위 김한규

○보친위뎨일련ᄃᆡ뎨일대ᄃᆡ부 통군보병부위 뎡면셥

○보친위뎨일련ᄃᆡ뎨이대ᄃᆡ중ᄃᆡ장 통군보병졍위 최기현

○보친위뎨일련ᄃᆡ뎨이대ᄃᆡ부 통군보병부위 진셕구

○보진위뎨일련ᄃᆡ뎨일대ᄃᆡ중ᄃᆡ장 통군보병졍위 리영균

○보진위뎨일련ᄃᆡ뎨일대ᄃᆡ부 통군보병부위 최영순

○보진위뎨일련ᄃᆡ뎨일대ᄃᆡ향관 통군일등군ᄉᆞ 조상셕

○보진위뎨이련ᄃᆡ뎨삼대ᄃᆡ부관 통군보병부위 조원순

○보진위뎨이련ᄃᆡ뎨삼대ᄃᆡ부 통군보병부위 최학철

○보진위뎨ᄉᆞ련ᄃᆡ뎨이대ᄃᆡ부 통군보병참위 방쟝환

○보진위뎨ᄉᆞ련ᄃᆡ뎨이대ᄃᆡ부 통군보병참위 오순영

○보진위뎨오련ᄃᆡ뎨일대ᄃᆡ중ᄃᆡ장 통군보병졍위 리지현

○보진위뎨오련ᄃᆡ뎨일대ᄃᆡ부 통군보병참위 원봉셕

○보진위뎨륙련ᄃᆡ뎨이대ᄃᆡ부 통군보병참위 전영록 김졍진

이상구월이십일

○보군부대신관방쟝 통군보병졍위 한진창

○보군부부관 통군보병졍령 신ᄐᆡ준 통군보병졍위 리셕졔

○보군부대신관방원 통군보병참령 리긔홍 통군보병졍위 리화종

○보군부군무국군ᄉᆞ과쟝 통군보병졍령 윤철규

○보군부군무국군ᄉᆞ과원 통군보병참령 신좌균 통군보병졍위 안셩호 통군보병부위 리셕진

○보군부군무국보병과쟝보 통군보병참령 유진형

○보군부군무국보병과원 통군보병참령 통군보병졍위 박민수 하윤홍

○보군부군무국긔병과쟝보 통군긔병참령 김현ᄐᆡ

○보군부군무국긔병과원 통군긔병참령 구쳘조 통군긔병부위 리긔원

○보군부군무국포병과쟝 통군포병부령 김쳔희

○보군부군무국포병과원 통군포병참령 리희승 통군포병졍위 리희신

○보군부군무국공병과쟝보 통군공병참령 권중록

○보군부군무국공병과원 통군공병졍위 현보운

○보군부경리국쟝 통군일등ᄉᆞ계 리강하

●보군부경리국뎨일과쟝 통군이등ᄉᆞ계 안준옥

○보군부경리국뎨일과원 군삼등ᄉᆞ계 박학진 통군일등군ᄉᆞ 안종약 통군이등군ᄉᆞ 오셕졍

○보군부경리국뎨이과쟝 통군이등ᄉᆞ계 송문셥

○보군부경리국뎨이과원 통군삼등ᄉᆞ계 박원근 통군일등군ᄉᆞ 최진ᄐᆡ 통군이등군ᄉᆞ 졍우창

○보군부의무국뎨일과쟝 통군삼등군의쟝 김익남

○보군부의무국뎨일과원 통군이등군의 졍괴현

○임군부군무국리ᄉᆞ셔주임관륙등 통군보병참위 조희졍

○임군부군법국리ᄉᆞ셔주임관륙등 통군보병참위 김창현

○임군부기ᄉᆞ셔주임관삼등 통군보병참위 홍종괴

이상구월이십칠일

외보

○뤼삼위함ᄃᆡ발동 거월이십륙일발ᄒᆞᆫ좌지보뎐보에ᄒᆞ기를 작일구라파쥬리보를거ᄒᆞᆫ즉희삼위함ᄃᆡ중(로시아호와〔구롬보이호)와〔포가젼〕호가 이삼일젼에슈리를완셩ᄒᆞᆫ고로작젼창에서출발ᄒᆞ야ᄉᆞ구리도로후졔등과엇셴찹쟝이작괴합에합좌ᄒᆞ엿다더라

○로뎨결심 공동통신사에서득문ᄒᆞᆫ바를거ᄒᆞᆫ즉가령려순구가함락되거나흑구로팟긴쟝군이함이빈으로퇴귀홈을당ᄒᆞ여도로국황뎨께서는평화를쳥치아니ᄒᆞ기로결심을확뎡ᄒᆞ셧다ᄒᆞ엿더라

○편도가외계산 쥬쳥아국공ᄉᆞ가외무부에젼왕ᄒᆞ야쳥구ᄒᆞ기를쳥국에셔됴야을면ᄒᆞᆫ바를인ᄒᆞ야만쥬편도들미슈ᄒᆞ라ᄒᆞ엿더니외무부에셔회답ᄒᆞ되목하에본국졍쳥이군즁ᄒᆞ야히편도들미슈ᄒᆞ기젼키어렵스니위션그가액과리ᄌᆞ를계산ᄒᆞ라ᄒᆞ엿더라

○평화회의셜 론돈뎐에ᄒᆞ엿스되화셩돈관인변으로나온젼셜를거ᄒᆞᆫ즉미국대통령루스벨트씨가일아젼쟁에결국되기를기다리지아니ᄒᆞ고쳔구빅오기년초에히아평화회의를기회ᄒᆞ기로쳥구ᄒᆞ리라더라.

뎐보

대본영발 십월오일일본공ᄉᆞ관착

○혼하사격 구월삼십일에젹군긔병ᄉᆞ오십명은남부쟝탄에릭도ᄒᆞ야히디샹류에잇든졍언의비예셔우를부어붇ᄉᆞ로기를시작ᄒᆞ미혼하량안에잇든우리감시병은ᄉᆞ격을힝ᄒᆞ야방히ᄒᆞᆫ지라

ᄉᆞ일샹오에졉슈ᄒᆞᆫ우리뎐보를거ᄒᆞᆫ즉구월삼십일에쟝탄에서젹군의긔병지ᄃᆡ가혼하에잇든우리탄약을실은쳥국빈셩칠쳑을소화ᄒᆞ엿다고보ᄒᆞᆫ지라쳥국빈를소화ᄒᆞᆫᄉᆞ는실ᄉᆞ이나탄약을실엇다ᄂᆞᆫ것은허말이니대기쟝탄샹류에ᄂᆞᆫ아군이혼하의슈송젼을왕복홈이엽ᄂᆞᆫ지라셩각ᄀᆞ건ᄃᆡ젹군이혼하에서쳥국빈가아군의령슈홈이되지안키를위ᄒᆞ야이런흉힝을힝ᄒᆞ야이거슬평게삼아그리를을가리고져홈인듯ᄒᆞ다ᄒᆞ엿더라

십월ᄉᆞ일동경발

○로함도망 로국군함세안호는삼일오후에오숑의드리가는어구에잇는월랑도로도망ᄒᆞ야왓다ᄒᆞ엿더라

잡보

○회원일죵 근일에일진회원의슈효가날노더ᄂᆞᆫᄃᆡ단발ᄒᆞ고드리오ᄂᆞᆫ쟈가답지ᄒᆞ야부지괴빅명이라ᄒᆞ회에셔회원들의류숙홀쳐소들쟉쳐리판에분비ᄒᆞ야거쳐ᄒᆞ게ᄒᆞᆫ다더라

○시찰과학싱 일본을시찰홀학부대신리지용씨ᄂᆞᆫ단발ᄒᆞ고문관복장을ᄒᆞ고간다더니젼권공ᄉᆞ들괴임ᄒᆞ야리구일에발졍ᄒᆞᆫᄃᆡ인ᄃᆡ류학싱을다리고간다더라

○츠뎨단발셜 젼셜을드른즉니부에셔단발령을발포ᄒᆞᆫ외로비잇ᄂᆞᆫᄃᆡ먼져외교관들단발ᄒᆞ고그다음은빅관과기타일반에밋칠이라ᄂᆞᆫ풍셜이잇다더라

○문관단발 외부대신이하관인과각항감리셔관슉이다외교관으로단발ᄒᆞ고복장홀터이라더라

○쟝리국죵셜 궁ᄂᆡ부관졔즁에실졔도쟝리국을죵셜ᄒᆞᄂᆞᆫᄃᆡ히국관원인즉총지일인과의명과샹인은칙임이오비셔이인은주임이오긔ᄉᆞ이인은판임으로된다더라

○광셔원복셜 금즁에졍부주품을인ᄒᆞ야광셔원을농샹공부로부속ᄒᆞ엿더니현금복셜홀ᄎᆞ로히부에셔졍부에쳥의셔ᄒᆞ기를광셔원ᄉᆞ업비가히원일의외국에차관ᄒᆞ엿고또신리가졈졈흥왕ᄒᆞᄆᆡ수무가외국인과련히교셥된즁ᄎᆡ슈에부임쳐못홀지라셜시훈이원의계젼인ᄒᆞ여아시죵이여일ᄒᆞ게셔호를분거시니광셔원분외구히셜치ᄒᆞ고소속관리들그젼인원으로셔임ᄒᆞ야칙셔홈이합당ᄒᆞ기로쳥의ᄒᆞᆫ다ᄒᆞ엿더라

○일졔샹발힝 일본졔쳘ᄃᆡ신ᄃᆡ조셰ᄂᆞᆫ명일등쳘ᄎᆞ거로인항에나려가죵남포로발힝ᄒᆞᆫ다더라

○권고중지 니부에서 쳥명을봉승ᄒᆞ고숀찰ᄉᆞ들과결ᄒᆞ야다방인민의긔료와동학당의운동ᄒᆞᄂᆞᆫ원인을안힐진무ᄒᆞᆯᄉᆞ로결졍ᄒᆞ고그러ᄒᆞ지발ᄒᆞ기를랍지로조회ᄒᆞ엿ᄂᆞᆫᄃᆡ일본공ᄉᆞ의권고를의ᄒᆞ야필요치못ᄒᆞᆫ줄노알고즁지ᄒᆞ엿다더라

○젹셩화젹 젹셩군보를거ᄒᆞᆫ즉히군ᄃᆡ방에화젹이ᄃᆡ치ᄒᆞ야각기총과환도를가지고빅쥬에을횡힝ᄒᆞ야민가에불을놋코ᄌᆡ물을노략ᄒᆞ미빅셩이거졉홀수엽다더라

○만찬ᄃᆡ뷘 작일에외부대신리하국쟝졔씨와흥신원총관이하과쟝졔씨가졍동손퇴랑가에젼왕ᄒᆞ야만찬회를셜ᄒᆞ고일본레신대신과조셰를관ᄃᆡᄒᆞ엿다라

○평산군보 금쳔군슈보고에ᄒᆞ기를본관이현금평산군슈셔리로시무ᄒᆞᄂᆞᆫᄃᆡ히군티경구샹리치도비이ᄒᆞᆫ샹쳔졔빅샹칠원를일본병참소에셔본군에징츌ᄒᆞ라ᄒᆞ기로본관이루ᄎᆞ병참부관부수면의게교셥ᄒᆞ되듯지아니ᄒᆞ고등츅이우심ᄒᆞ므로히군향쟝이부득이ᄒᆞ야일샥분한ᄒᆞ고병참부에탑표ᄒᆞ엿더니한일빅두ᄒᆞ미항쟝과슈셔긔ᄂᆞᆫ밧셔도주ᄒᆞ엿스니츅반일빅셩의계징츌ᄒᆞ면고을이엄셔질힝편이오니처샹ᄒᆞ다ᄒᆞ엿더라

○감리젼임 샹화감리교영쳘씨ᄂᆞᆫ히임되고창원감리리티뎡씨가셔임되고창원감리ᄂᆞᆫ졍현필표씨가셔임되엿더라

○공ᄉᆞ신임 학부대신리지용이보빙ᄃᆡᄉᆞ겸특명젼권공ᄉᆞ를임명ᄒᆞ엿더라

○샹무경죵 챵원감리의보고에ᄒᆞ기를거졔도에류쥬ᄒᆞᆫ일본병참부에셔군통신오됴들발표ᄒᆞ야각쳐에게시ᄒᆞ엿스되히군령을범ᄒᆞ면무론죄지ᄃᆡ소ᄒᆞ고일병포형에쳐ᄒᆞᆯ터이라ᄒᆞ엿다고ᄒᆞ엿더라

○동변란인 탁지고문관목하뎐태랑씨의동변은해셔형졍리관셔히영씨로쳔임되고 히젼동변은쳘도원기ᄉᆞ일인도산씨가괴임ᄒᆞ엿다더라

○긔병양셩 한국에류쥬ᄒᆞᄂᆞᆫ일본군에부속ᄒᆞᆫ긔병ᄃᆡ가작일에입셩ᄒᆞ엿다

TELEGRAMS.

Tokyo, Oct. 4th.

The Russian cruiser "Bayan" has escaped from Port Arthur and arrived at Yuhlangtao, an island in the vicinity of Woosung.

Tokyo, Oct. 5th.

On the 5th Sept. some Russian cavalry arrived at Woonho on the upper reaches of the Liao river (about 20 miles from Mukden) and set fire to 17 Chinese junks which were lying there. Reuter's report that the junks contained Japanese ammunition and supplies is untrue.

HEAVY FALL OF INCOME TAX.

London, Sept. 22.

The revenue returns from the 1st of April to the 23rd of September are £4.328,000 less than in the corresponding period of 1903. The income tax yield shows a decrease of £2,370,000.—N.-C. Daily News.

BRITISH ARMY REFORM.

London, via Bombay, September 22nd.

Lord Rosebery, speaking at Lincoln, in discussing army reform, reiterated that we had made a great though not irreparable mistake in exiling the great organiser and economist (Lord Kitchener) to India, where, he heard, his advice is not very frequently taken, and replacing him by civilian after civilian with melancholy results.—N.-C. Daily News.

London, September 29th.

Three German colliers are reported to be at Teneriffe awaiting instructions.

THE BALTIC FLEET.

London, Sept. 21.

Reuter's correspondent at St. Petersburg wires that it is reported that four warships purchased from the Argentine Republic have arrived at Libau.—N. C. Daily News.

ESCAPE OF VON PLEHVE'S ASSASSIN.

London, Sept. 5.

A special dispatch from St. Petersburg says that, by a daringly conceived coup on the part of his friends, Sassoneff, the murderer of von Plehve, succeeded in escaping from prison.

Early Saturday morning two men, apparently officers of high rank, accompanied by an army surgeon and two gendarmes, presented themselves at the prison with a note alleged to be from Minister of Justice Muravieff. The forged note sanctioned the removal of Sassoneff, who assassinated Minister of the Interior von Plehve with an infernal machine a few weeks ago.

The prison officials were completely taken in and handed over the assassin, who was driven away in the most deliberate manner. Nothing has been heard since either of the assassin or of the bogus officers. The letter presented at the prison was a clever forgery, written on official paper of the Ministry of Justice.

THE BRITISH ANTARCTIC EXPEDITION.

London, August 16th.

The Terra Nova, which left Dundee a year ago to relieve the imprisoned crew of the Discovery in Antarctic regions, arrived at Plymouth yesterday, after a homeward voyage of ninety days, from New Zealand.

Admiral Sir E. H. Seymour went on board the Terra Nova during the day and inspected the ship, which afterwards left for Sheerness, where she will be dismantled.

One of the officers gave an account of the expedition to a Daily Express representative.

"On January 8 last," he said, "the mast-heads of the Discovery were first seen. Our crew and the men of the Morning, which was close by us, at once prepared to blast the ice in order to cut out the imprisoned ship.

"Twelve miles of pack ice separated us from the Discovery. With explosives we cleared spaces about tweve feet square, and as the work was aided by the 'easing,' due to the advance of the season, the pack began to break away.

"We worked almost continuously, sometimes ceasing our labours for only an hour or two each day.

"The men worked splendidly. From early morning till midnight they laboured with all their might, scarcely sparing time for meals.

"At the outer edge the ice was about five or six feet thick, but by constant explosions and cutting a way was forced, and as progress was made the crews of the vessels cheered one another again and again.

"Blizzards hindered us, but by January 14 a channel had been cut within two miles of the ship. We then tried the old whaler's dodge of rolling the ship to break the ice, and the crews joined hands that night.

"A date had been fixed for the abandoment of the Discovery, which soon afterwards was homeward bound."

VLADIVOSTOCK SQUADRON STATED TO HAVE SAILED.

A "Mainichi" telegram from Moji, of yesterday's date, states that, according to news from a trustworthy quarter, the Vladivostock Squadron once more left Vladivostock on the 21st ult.

According to a European telegram received on the 25th in official quarters, the Rossiya, Gromoboi, and Bogatyr, at Vladivostock, have now been completely repaired, and Admiral Skrydloff and Rear-Admiral Essen are on board the flagship.

FORECASTS.

The following forecast of the war for which the London correspondent of the Manchester Guardian is responsible, will prove of interest.

A question which one has heard constantly during the past few months, and which is becoming of immediate interest, is: What are the limits which the Japanese have put for themselves to a successful prosecution of the present war? Their plans have been so carefully laid out beforehand that they must, it is said, have drawn a line somewhere beyond which they have resolved not to go, and at which their military progress will be stopped. What is this line? They cannot propose to go on pursuing indefinitely an ever-retreating army. Quite recently I had an opportunity of discussing this matter with a Japanese official of position, and although he did not profess to know the plans of the General Staff he probably reflected the opinions of the higher class of officials.

The Japanese, he said, set before themselves the task of driving the Russians out of Korea and Manchuria. That is the primary object of the campaign. Now, assuming the continued success of the Japanese arms, Port Arthur will fall, and the fleet there either be wholly destroyed or it will become Japanese. General Kuropatkin will be defeated at Liao-yang or somewhere between that and Mukden. The defeat will either be a disastrous rout or will consist of a series of defeats followed by constant retreats, according as General Kuroki succeeds in effectually cutting off his retreat or not, and Mukden will fall into the Japanese hands. In either case the remnants of the Russian army will continue the retreat northwards to Harbin. When Liaoyang and Mukden have fallen the first stage of the campaign will be over, and then the Japanese will launch a fresh army against Vladivostock, which they will attack by sea and land, as they have done Port Arthur. From Vladivostock, by the railway, they will advance on Harbin, which will thus be attacked from the west as well as from the south, and when that place has fallen their task will be complete. With all Manchuria, Korea, and Vladivostock in their hands, they will sit down and fortify themselves while the sea is free and open behind them, and await in security either the attacks of a fresh Russian army or peace. Vladivostock and Harbin—these, according to this authority, are their termini, and the Siberian or Manchurian Railway between the two the limit of their advance. They do not intend to trouble themselves about the Amur, which is the geographical boundary of Manchuria in this direction, because what is left of Manchuria or the north of Harbin is not worth troubling about.

Then as to the peace which must follow sooner or later my informant had certain very precise views, in which, again, I have excellent reason to believe he reflected intelligent public opinion in his own country as well as the resolve of the governing classes there. Japan desires now, as far as may be, to get rid once for all of the Russian menace in the Pacific, and therefore they will have no more Russian arsenals or dockyards or fortified places, whether in warm water or ice-bound ports on the Siberian shores of that ocean. If the Japanese do not retain Vladivostock they will not allow it to be a fortified place in Russian hands. They want the Amur to be the Russian boundary in Asia, as it was before General Ignatieff's cunning treaty with China in 1861, and they are willing that Vladivostock should remain as it is now the commercial outlet for Eastern Siberia, as a free Port, or under some similar arrangement. Then they want Saghalien Island restored to them. It was their's before 1874, when, in a time of weakness and national convalescence from the consequences of the revolution, Russia took advantage of their situation to oblige them to cede the island to her. This has ever been a sore point with the Japanese people, and advantage will be taken of a victory now to repair the wrong (as the Japanese regard it) done them. Then there is the evacuation of Manchuria and its restoration to China and the acknowledgment of a Japanese protectorate over Korea. The cession of Saghalien, worthless and sterile as that island is and especially the proposed new status of Vladivostock, would probably be the objectionable points in such a treaty from the Russian point of view. I should not omit to add that my informant mentioned also the free navigation to all nations of the Amur up to the point at which it ceases to be the common boundary between Siberia and Manchuria, and of its tributaries the Ussuri, and Sungari, the latter of which is navigable up to Harbin, but the navigation of Russian ships, although by treaty it is open to Chinese and Korean vessels as well. These seem to be some of the main points which the Japanese hope to settle by the peace at the conclusion of the present war.

LOST

On the 27th ult., probably in the neighbourhood of the West Gate.

A Photographic Camera. Anyone returning the same to this office will receive Y 15.00 reward.

The Korea Daily News.

Issued at 5 P. M. daily except Sundays.

Rate of Subscription:—

Per Year.	Yen 25.
Per Quarter.	Yen 7.
Per Month	Yen 2.50

Postage in Korea not charged extra.
Postage abroad charged extra.

Advertisements, 50 sen per day for 1 inch or less.
5 yen per month per inch.
50 yen per year per inch.

All communications to

E. T. BETHELL,
Editor and Publisher.
Pak-tong, Seoul

A YELLOW JOURNAL.

It is with "undiluted" amusement that the Editor of this paper finds himself the subject of a biographical notice in that beacon of Japanese public opinion in Korea, the "Daihan Ilpo."

In case any of our readers have a taste for fiction and have wearied of the efforts of Max Pemberton, Guy Boothby, Archibald Clavering Gunter and "Q," and are yearning for still more daring flights into the realms of romance, we have pleasure in reproducing this little biography according to the gospel of the "Daihan Ilpo":—

"The "Korea Daily News" is published in Seoul by an Englishman named Bethell who has only received very small financial support from the palace and is consequently hardly able to pay the cost of publishing his paper. This same paper frequently announced Japanese losses in battle. It has said that the Russian second army has already cut off the retreat of Kuroki's army and that Kuroki's army has been surrounded, so that before long the Japanese northern army will be severely defeated, and other untrue stories have been published. On account of this the palace apparently begins to believe that the Japanese may be defeated. This Englishman is a low person, he was formerly an auctioneer in Kobe, so there is no reason for his knowing any thing about war."

Now as this charming "write-up" did not appear among the telegrams of our Chemulpo contemporary we are forced to call its Editor or whoever was responsible for the paragraph in question, a base perverter of the truth—in other words a most shocking liar.

There is one grain of truth in the peck of lies, and that is that we are hard up, but we resent the impertinence of the Editor of the "Daihan Ilpo" in prying into our private affairs just as much as we condemn his disregard of the truth.

Some of the rest of the "Daihan Ilpo's" farrago we will only characterize as untrue We have received no money from the palace and the Editor of the "Korea Daily News" was never an auctioneer. But our contemporary may have been misinformed on these subjects so we dismiss him (in this respect) with a caution. We don't *like* being called an auctioneer but we will get over it.

As for the remaining part of the "Daihan Ilpo's" allegations we only characterize them as deliberate and malicious lies. What the object of this journal can be in so perjuring itelf and irretrievably branding itself with the mark of the liar we cannot guess unless it be to pander to the spite of people whose malfeasance or incapacity we have at various times commented upon.

With regard to our poverty, we have nothing to be ashamed of. Had we been content to accept only the Japanese view of current events we can assure the "Dai-han Ilpo" that we might have been as rich as it is. (We presume it is rich, as it jeers at poverty).

Now a word to the wise. Let the Editor of the "Daihan Ilpo" make an effort to pull himself together before he gets himself into trouble, and try and run his sheet without venturing too far beyond the confines of veracity. Let him employ his fertile brain devising excuses for the Nagamori scheme and the means adopted in the various attempts to carry it through.

And then if he has any energy left, let him explain to his fellow-countrymen in Korea that there is plenty of room for improvement in their behaviour in Korea and that if they wish to become acceptable guests in this country they must disabuse themselves of the idea that they are already masters.

In other words let the "Daihan Ilpo" reform itself first and its fellow-countrymen afterwards. This will keep it from poking its impertinent nose into other peoples' business.

A DOG STORY.

The Singapore "Free Press" relates this rather "tall" dog story.

"A French weekly produces the following. Where it got the story, we do not know; possibly from the Editor of the "Spectator" who has a "penchant" for such things, and an invincible faith in the superior intelligence of the lower animals, Mr. Chamberlain not included. "Gascony has the Baron de Crac, Germany that of Munchausen China has a diplomat not a whit behind these illustrious historians. He gave a reporter the following zoological anecdote:—'I have three dogs, three pet dogs that are allowed to wander about my rooms. Coming home one evening, I find them luxuriously reclining on a splendid table in teak and marble, which is the finest ornament in my drawing-room. This calm proceeding strikes me as going too far. I am not a martinet, but I don't like furniture to be spoiled—nor dogs. So I give my dogs a beating, in order to fix on their memories that teakwood tables are not couches for drowsy quadrupeds."

Next evening, I come home at the usual hour. My dogs had understood the lesson received the previous day; with their noses between their paws, they lay stretched on the carpet, near the door, snoring peacefully. By chance, passing in front of the table, I put my hand on the teak, and lo, it was warm! The dogs, knowing the comfort of this place, had not resisted the desire to return thither: hearing me enter, they had come down, and pretended to have been in a long and deep sleep, without suspecting that the warmth of their bodies would betray their little game. I gave them another beating, in order to teach them that, for success in life, one must be either wholly honourable or frankly low.

* * * * *

My dogs chose the latter. When I came home, the third evening a little earlier than usual, I saw them gathered round the teak, with their heads raised to the height of the table, and their lips rounded, blowing on it to cool it."

We have heard many ingenious dog-stories, but only the guileless faith of the "Spectator" is equal to the swallowing of this.

THE EXPECTED BATTLE AT MUKDEN.

London, Sept. 20.—

Reports from Mukden to the 19th inst. state that the Japanese dispositions resemble those before Liaoyang. The battle will extend for twenty-five miles, and the Japanese front is completely concealed behind a line of outposts.—N. C. Daily News.

THE ATTEMPTS TO SWIM THE CHANNEL.

During the week ending August 27th Holbein, Haggerty and Greasley all attempted to equal Captain Webb's record by swimming the English Channel, and all without success. Holbein has stated that he will try again in a fortnight's time. Every circumstance favoured success save one—the temperature of the water—and it was this that lay at the bottom of all three defeats. Holbein failed—and failed magnificently. Haggerty failed—and failed with the worst of bad luck. Greasley ruined Holbein's chances when all seemed to be going well with him, after a struggle of 10 hours. Cramp racked Haggerty after 55 minutes in the water, before he had even begun to draw upon his endurance. Greasley speedily realised that the water was too chilly for a reasonable hope of success, and, like a man of intelligence, came out of the sea into the warm cabin of the tug.

Mr. Hyon Hak-pio, father of General Hyon, has been appointed Kamni of Masanpo.

The instigators of the Kongchu riot arrived, under escort, at the Army Headquarters yesterday.

Mr. Megata proposes to take a trip to Kaisung with the object of inspecting the Ginseng plantations.

His Majesty issued the information to all Departments that he would be pleased to receive their Ministers in audience to-day at 2 P. M.

The powers of special envoys have been conferred on Messrs. Yi Chai-kuk and Min Hyung-sik, two members of the party leaving for Japan on Sunday next.

It is said that the Japanese Minister has persuaded the Home Office that the Imperial Edict ordering officials to proceed into the interior to quell the riots, is unnecessary.

The "Confusion to top-knots" brigade were assembled yesterday as usual at their meeting-place. Mr. Yun Si-pyong presided over a crowd of reformers who also as usual, accomplished nothing in the way of reform.

Reports of Russian activity in the neighbourhood of Songchin still pour in. A quantity of provisions was recently landed at Sinchang and supplies of all descriptions are being collected and stored in preparation, it is said, of a reinforced advance during the winter.

The Il Chin Hoi are still in the ring. Shaved heads seems still to be the chief item on their programme of reforms. Our Korean contemporary, the editor of the Che Kuk Sin Mun, has come under the ban of their displeasure by writing a series of articles discrediting the society. He has been threatened with legal proceedings or a personal visit from the Il Chin Hoi committee.

A Blue-book issued recently describes a number of new projects which are under consideration by the Government of Egypt including the construction of an extensive railway, the reorganisation of irrigation in Middle Egypt, the raising of the Assouan dam, and the remodelling of the Rosetta and Damietta branches of the Nile. The whole of the works will cost £5,400,000.

One who served with Lord Kitchener in Egypt tells the following characteristic anecdote of him in the "Liverpool Daily Post." During the progress of some construction work in Upper Egypt, the young subaltern in charge had the misfortune to lose some native workmen through the accidental explosion of some cases of dynamite. He telegraphed to Lord Kitchener, then Sirdar: "Regret to report killing of ten labourers by dynamite accident." In a few hours came this laconic despatch: "Do you need any more dynamite?"

The Korea Daily News.

VOL. I, | THURSDAY, OCTOBER 6, 1904. | No. 69

HONGKONG & SHANGHAI BANKING CORPORATION.

Paid-up Capital.... ....$10,000,000
Reserve Fund:—Sterling Reserve... 10,000,000
Silver Reserve..... 7,000,000

27,000,000
Reserve Liability of Proprietors... 10,000,000

HEAD OFFICE, HONGKONG.

London Bankers, London and County Banking Company Limited.

Branches and Agencies, London.

Amoy,	Hankow	Penang,
Bangkok,	Hiogo,	Rangoon,
Batavia,	Iloilo,	Saigon,
Bombay,	Lyons,	San Francisco,
Calcutta,	Manila,	Singapore,
Colombo,	Nagasaki,	Sourabaya,
Foochow,	New York,	Tientsin,
Hamburg,	Peking,	Yokohama,

Credits granted on approved Securities, and every description of Banking and Exchange business transacted.

Drafts granted on London and the chief Commercial places in Europe, India, Australia, America, China and Japan.

HOLME RINGER & Co., AGENTS, CHEMULPO.

ON CHEONG & CO., SEOUL.

GENERAL STORE KEEPERS.

Imported provisions, Cooking Utensils Crockery, etc.

FRESH BREAD DAILY.

MITSU BISHI DOCKYARD & ENGINE WORKS, NAGASAKI.

CODE WORD, "DOCK."

A. 1, A. B. C., and Engineering Codes used.

DOCK No. 1 (at Tategami).

Extreme Length..............523 feet
Length on blocks .... 513 ,,
Width of Entrance on Top......89 ,,
,, ,, Bottom....77 ,,
Water on Blocks at Spring Tide 26½ ,,

DOCK No. 2 (Mukaijima).

Extreme Length..............371 feet
Length on Blocks............360 ,,
Width of Entrance on Top......66 ,,
,, ,, Bottom 53 ,,
Water on Blocks at Spring Tide 22 ,,

PATENT SLIP (at Kosuge).

Can take vessels up to 1,000 tons gross.

THE WORKS are well equipped with the LATEST IMPROVEMENTS, and can execute any kind of work in SHIPBUILDING and MARINE ENGINEERING, as well as in REPAIRING of SHIPS.

The COMPANY'S new powerful steamer OURA-MARU (712 tons, 700 I.H.P.), specially built for SALVAGE PURPOSES, and equipped with necessary gear, is always READY at SHORT NOTICE.

CHARTERED BANK OF INDIA AUSTRALIA & CHINA.

INCORPORATED BY ROYAL CHARTER 1853

HEAD OFFICES:—LONDON.

Paid-up Capital £800,000
Reserve Liability of Shareholders 800,000
Reserve Fund 800,000

Drafts granted upon all the principal places in the world and every description of Exchange and banking business transacted.

E. MEYER & Co., Agents, Chemulpo.

E. MEYER & CO.

Chemulpo.

SOLE AGENTS IN KOREA FOR:

A. T. Morse, Sons & Co's "Fresco" Distemper

In all colours ready for use on walls, Ceilings etc.

and

AVENARIUS CARBOLINEUM

A wood-preserving and antiseptic oil preparation

Against decay, dry-rot, fungus and wood-destroying insects.

A large supply always in Stock. Prices upon application.

E. MEYER & Co., Chemulpo.

LAW UNION & CROWN INS. CO.

Fire risks accepted at Current rates, on go downs, merchandise, dwellings, and other property, subject to usual conditions.

HOLME RINGER & Co., Agents, Chemulp

THE METHODIST PUBLISHING HOUSE, Little WestGate, Seoul.

PRINTING, TYPEWRITER PAPER
CARBON PAPER, VISITING CARDS
STATIONERY, BOOK BINDING
BOOK PUBLISHERS
AMERICAN SCHOOL BOOKS
SPENCERIAN COPY BOOKS
PEN CARBON LETTER AND BILL BOOKS

S. A. BECK, Manager.

DAI-ICHI GINKO. LIMITED.

(Formerly the First National Bank)

ESTABLISHED 1873

INCORPORATED UNDER PRESENT LAW 1896

Capital - - - - - - - - - Yen 5,000,000
Reserve Fund - - - - - 1,500,000

HEAD OFFICE:—TOKIO.

President: Baron SHIBUSAWA.

BRANCHES AND CORRESPONDENTS In the Principal Cities and Towns of Japan.

Interest Allowed on
Fixed deposits 1 year - - - 6½ per cent
" " 6 months - - - 6 per cent

Special current accounts 1½ sen daily per Y 100
General " " 1 " " " 100

M. TANAKA, Manager, Chemulpo

HOLME RINGER & Co. Chemulpo.

General Merchants and Government Contractors.

Agents for the leading Banks SteamshipCompanies and Insurance Companies

Importers of Merchandise of every description.

KAMEYA & CO.

GENERAL STOREKEEPERS

Chinkokai - - Seoul

(*Established 1895, Tokyo*)

Confectionery, Hams, Canned Goods, Cutlery, Hirano & Tansan Water. Provisions, Gents, Furnishing goods, Toilet Articles, Travelling Bags, Tobacco, Cigars & Cigarettes Kitchen Utensils. Coffee, Biscuits.

Fresh Goods always kept in Stock.

Prices Moderate

Please come and inspect our goods.

NIPPON YUSEN KAISHA.

JAPANESE MAIL STEAMSHIP CO.

DER MAIL CONTRACT WITH THE IMPERIAL JAPANESE GOVERNMENT.

European Line

Regular Fortnightly Service between Yokohama Kobe, Moji, Shanghai, Hongkong, Singapore, Penang Colombo, Port Said, Marseilles, London and Antwerp

American Line

Regular Fortnightly Service between Hongkong and Seattle, calling at Shanghai, Moji, Kobe, Yokohama and Victoria, B. C.

Australian Line

Regular weekly Service betwen Japan Ports and Australia, calling at Hongkong and Manila.

(Above Three Lines Suspended until further notice).

Shanghai Line

Weekly Service between Shanghai and Japan Ports

Korea Line

Service Kobe, Moji, Nagasaki, Fusan, Chemupo, Coo, Taiku.

S. S. Bahelsberg, 2181 tons.

Service Kobe, Moji, Fusan, Chemulpo, Chinnampo

S. S ARGO. S. S. Ohio.

BORDEN'S CONDENSED MILK CO.

New York, U. S. A.

ALWAYS IN STOCK

Eagle Brand Condensed Milk.

Gold Seal Condensed Milk.

Peerless (Family) Evaporated Cream.

Borden's Malted Milk.

E. MEYER & CO. Chemulpo, Korea, Sole Agents

ROYAL INSURANCE COMPANY,

Funds exceed £10,000,000

FIRE AT CURRENT RATES.

LIFE REDUCED PREMIUM.

HOLME RINGER & Co., Agents, Chemulpo.

HOTEL DU PALAIS SEOUL.

The only first class Hotel in Seoul. Situated in the centre of the city opposite the palace.

Cuisine under the supervision of an experienced French Chef.

Well ventilated and furnished throughout.

TARIFF UPON APPLICATION

L. MARTIN Proprietor and Mangaer.

大韓每日申報
대한미일신보

(뎨칠십호) (금요일) 일쳔구빅사년십월칠일

본샤고빅

본신보는영어와한어로석거미일츌판ᄒᆞ옵

신문가

한쟝 엽두돈오푼

일삭됴 엽두량닷돈

우표가미삭닷돈

다맛돈으로밧습

광고료는

귀한의쟝단과ᄌᆞ힝의다쇼로즁감ᄒᆞ되렴가로밧을터이오며오리지아녀대한사람마다다이신문을보실터이니광고내시기를원ᄒᆞ시는이들은우리신문샤에와셔면약ᄒᆞ심을희망ᄒᆞ옵

○발힝소 박동대한미일신보샤법어학교압헤젼영국인셜필림집자리오

샤쟝 영국인 (비셜)

평양 디리졈

○평양효동사는권미보씨로우리신문관미디리인을틱정ᄒᆞ엿ᄉᆞ오니평양에계신구람코져ᄒᆞ시는 쳠군ᄌᆞ는히디리졈에왕림ᄒᆞ와면의ᄒᆞ시옵

샤고

○우리대한미일신보의목뎍은대한의안녕질셔에관한모든뎨목에디ᄒᆞ야는공평한변론을쥬쟝홈이라우리동신원의담보는신문보시는쳠군ᄌᆞ의게ᄒᆞᆼ상보도ᄒᆞ리며편지를긔셔ᄒᆞ여주시는이는셩명과반디를젹어붓치시기를희망ᄒᆞ오니이거슨신문상에긔지ᄒᆞ라는거시아니오다만극히신용ᄒᆞ는증거를숨고쟈홈이라긔자는아모긔서던지긔지홈을되각ᄒᆞᆫ권리를가졋스나되각ᄒᆞ는리유를말홀터이오며공즁평화를문란케ᄒᆞ는듯ᄒᆞᆫ긔셔는의례히밧지안켓숩나이다

●본샤셜시이릭로신문을미양우례로분젼ᄒᆞ와례젼부의입의로젼ᄒᆞᆫ듯스로면곳에는혹늣게젼ᄒᆞ기도ᄒᆞ며혹몃칠거슬ᄒᆞᆫ겁에젼ᄒᆞ기도ᄒᆞ며혹아니젼ᄒᆞ는곳도잇다ᄒᆞ와우리신문을ᄉᆞ랑ᄒᆞ야구람ᄒᆞ시는 쳠군ᄌᆞ의게디ᄒᆞ야미우미안ᄒᆞ옵기로지금은분젼인을두고미일일즉이젼ᄒᆞ며아니젼ᄒᆞ거나늣게거나ᄒᆞᆫ폐가업도록ᄒᆞ랴ᄒᆞ오니혹아니젼ᄒᆞ거나늣게젼ᄒᆞ거나ᄒᆞᆫ일이잇스면본샤로통긔ᄒᆞ여쥬심을희망ᄒᆞ옵

관보

광무팔년구월삼십일 부록연속

○보참모부부관 륙군보병부령 신셩균 륙군보병참령 리길환 륙군보병정위 권즁락 김관호 ○보참모부국원 륙군보병참령 리셕규 빅응쥰 리긔표 륙군포병참령 어담 륙군보병정위 민대식 한상봉 김영션 민영원 류완 김윤비 ○보참모부향관 륙군이등군ᄉᆞ 리우승 김병승 ○임참모보번역관셔쥬임관삼등 륙군보병정위 리국렬 ○임참모부번역관셔임관륙등 농샹공부쥬ᄉᆞ 리병렬 ○임참모부번역관보셔관임관륙등 구품 리문영 한규복 윤병옥 ○임시죵무관 륙군보병부령 오보영 륙군보병참령 구연하 졍티셕 륙군보병정위 죠죵만 륙군샹셰교 ○임비죵무관 륙군보병참령 리희원 류긔원 륙군보병정위 구의죠 량지훈 홍우형 ○천왕부무관 륙군보병정위 빅명긔 ○보교육부참모관 륙군보병참령 리남하 륙군보병정위 김틱원 ○보교육부부관 륙군보병참령 정인환 륙군보병정위 김현틱 ○보교육부긔치병과쟝 륙군긔병참령 왕유식 ○보교육부긔치병과원 륙군긔병정위 신우영 륙군긔병부위 리죵비 ○보교육부포공병과쟝 륙군공병참령 김셩은 ○보교육부포공병과원 륙군포병정위 윤영셥 리룡의 ○보교육부향관 륙군일등군ᄉᆞ 안규승 ○임교육부번역관셔쥬임관륙등 농샹공부쥬ᄉᆞ 신봉휴 륙품 현동식 ○보연셩학교쟝 륙군보병부령 리희두 ○보연셩학교부관 륙군보병정위 리승희 ○보연셩학교교관 륙군보병참령 죠셩근 리동식 륙군보병정위 리근영 오진영 안교영 리셔환 문회션 부위 김병도 신하균 류린균 쳔응셩 한샹덕 ○보연셩학교향관 륙군삼등군ᄉᆞ 홍 건 ○임연셩학교번역관셔쥬임관륙등 구품 정죵진 ○겸보교셩디쟝 륙군보병참령 죠셩근 ○겸보교셩디부관 륙군보병부위 류린균 ○겸보교셩디즁디쟝 륙군보병정위 오진영 ○겸보교셩디부 륙군보병부위 쳔응셩 신하균 ○보륙군무관학교쟝 륙군보병부령 리병무 ○보륙군무관학교부관 륙군보병정위 최우연 ○보륙군무관학교교관 륙군보병참령 신창희 륙군보병정위 김규한 권티직 로빅린 안철영 ○보륙군무관학교 관 륙군이등군의 리긔원 ○보륙군무관학교슈의 륙군삼등군의 쟝원식 ○보륙군무관학교향관 륙군삼등군ᄉᆞ 황렬쥬 ○임륙군무관학교번역관셔쥬임관륙등 륙품 리유셕 빅윤규 ○겸보륙군무관학교학도디쟝 륙군무관학교교관 륙군보병정위 로빅린 ○보륙군무관학교학도디부관 륙군보병부위 젼영헌 ○보륙군무관학교학도디즁디쟝 륙군보병정위 권티한 ○보륙군무관학교학도디부 륙군보병부위 최두현 죠남희 륙군보병참위 김봉셕 김응션 박두영 ○겸임유년학교쟝 륙군보병부령 리병무 ○보유년학교부관 륙군보병정위 김죵현 ○보유년학교교관 륙군긔병참위 박영쳘 ○보유년학교학도디즁디쟝 륙군보병정위 정시창 륙군보병참위 류동열 강용구 김긔권 남긔창 리갑 ○보유년학교향관 륙군일등군ᄉᆞ 오의셩

어샹구월이십구일

외보

○려슌근황 지부에서발ᄒᆞᆫ면보를거ᄒᆞᆫ즉거월이십ᄉᆞ일에려슌구슈륙량쳐에셔밍렬ᄒᆞᆫ포셩이낫고또쳥국인의담화에왈거월십구일이릭로로병워포로된쟈일빅여명니에쟝교가이명이라ᄒᆞ더라

○봉텬근황 봉텬부에잇는로군은혼하텰교를즁심으로뎡ᄒᆞ야그샹류에잇는훙릉보부근에이십ᄉᆞ긔군교와하류의삼긔군교를신셜ᄒᆞ엿고사령과방신량졍거쟝부근에는다수ᄒᆞᆫ막영이잇고그북방으로브터군슈픔을대단히만히수송ᄒᆞᆫ다더라

○로장쳐벌 구로팟트킨장군의관결홈을좃차오ㅣ로노장군을로국셔울노쇼환ᄒᆞ야신문도ᄒᆞ지안코즉시군젹에일홈을틱거ᄒᆞ엿더라

잡보

○관광물시 일진회에입참ᄒᆞᆫ쟈가셔울사ᄅᆞᆷ은불과빅여명이오외도사ᄅᆞᆷ은수쳔명에달ᄒᆞᆫ지라한번긔회ᄒᆞ면본국갓파탕건은영위물시ᄒᆞ고외국모ᄌᆞ만쓰고단니기로회결ᄒᆞᆫ다더라

○공문작환 일작에졍부에서무숨비밀ᄒᆞᆫᄉᆞ건이잇셔긔포홀ᄎᆞ로참셔관이경무국쟝의게공함ᄒᆞ엿는디피봉에참셔관과국쟝이되우로공문홈이업다ᄒᆞ고히공문을작환ᄒᆞ엿더니그안에비밀즁대ᄒᆞᆫᄉᆞ건이잇는지라졍부에서경무쳥으로또엄ᄒᆞᆫ훈ᄒᆞ야그시에히공문을작송ᄒᆞᆫ히관인을지명보릭ᄒᆞ라ᄒᆞ엿더라

○량쟝릭괴 한국에쥬차ᄒᆞ는일본군ᄉᆞ령관쟝곡쳔대쟝과참모쟝락곡쇼쟝은릭구일에우픔에셔발뎡홀터인디십이일에는셔울에릭도홀예졍이라더라

○병ᄉᆞ힉학 함흥관찰부공립소학교공보를거ᄒᆞᆫ즉아병이드러와거쳐ᄒᆞᆫ후로지금ᄭᅡ지긔학ᄒᆞ지못ᄒᆞ엿다ᄒᆞ고김화군공립셔학교공보에는북진ᄒᆞᆫ이날마

다야슈ᄒᆞ고지나는고로죠션의
로이졍ᄒᆞ기에한과가셩실치못
하다ᄒᆞ엿더라

○공쥬해산셜 공쥬진위대병
졍들이일인의게피ᄒᆞ야야료ᄒᆞᆫ
셔등에군부에셔공쥬대병졍을
해산ᄒᆞ기로공의ᄒᆞ엿다더라

○졍동화셜 젼시죵리유형씨
가향자에안쥬에잇는일본병참
소에져슈ᄒᆞᆫ원세승씨의게로가
을외복을지어셔보니엿는데쇼
일젼에의복두벌을더지어셔리
범셕신청군량씨의게로보냇다
ᄒᆞ니미우감사ᄒᆞᆫ일이더라

○래대일년 일본레신대신일
졍이저작일신시에 래ᄒᆞᆫᄒᆞ고
동엄슌세여는신셔세부인졍에셔
작부원대관을졍요ᄒᆞ야연회
ᄒᆞ엿다더라

○샹소셔혈원 남로거ᄒᆞ는김소
슈가무슨지원구ᄒᆞᆫ수졍이잇
는데대한문압헤진복ᄒᆞ야샹소
ᄒᆞᆫ다더니작일에법부에셔피졍
ᄒᆞ라ᄒᆞ엿더라

○황제착도 닉부에셔 이졍
부조회를인ᄒᆞ야십삼도에흔령
ᄒᆞ기를현금디방슈무다슈ᄒᆞᆫ데
를방ᄒᆞ야각군슈의졍유툰토시
취롯ᄒᆞ겟고향부등이ᄒᆞ야금우
ᄒᆞᆫ면슈유ᄒᆞᆫ예일조의모군슈로
모군을제리ᄒᆞᆫ디우틈등시소샹소
취ᄒᆞᆫ보명ᄒᆞ는거시수레에ᄃᆞᆫ엇ᄒᆞ
거놀각군슈가샹졍ᄒᆞᆫ지다ᄒᆞ는
퇴금우ᄒᆞᆫ일주외모군에모군슈
가서리ᄒᆞᆫ보고가샹금리도져아
니ᄒᆞ고십지ᄒᆞ수유셔시주의로
샹졍ᄒᆞ야루사두루ᄒᆞ나소례에
취ᄒᆞᆫ연ᄒᆞᆫ지라조금이츄로금유월
조와교ᄒᆞᆫ과산화로모군셔리를소
샹이치보ᄒᆞ라ᄒᆞ엿더라

○졍민암숑 일본공사가쇼죠회
ᄒᆞ기를시흥민요수로우리수명
부에착슈ᄒᆞᆫ샹우경씨민요ᄒᆞᆫ을
심사ᄒᆞᆫ즉취미한이미슈됨이확
실ᄒᆞ고로졍상팅외경부로압숑ᄒᆞ
티이니엄히사쳐ᄒᆞ야달흘에져
ᄒᆞ라ᄒᆞ엿더라

○외교아추 외양군리지각
가틀역슈세와덥토수진이로숑
수가되여방리원에관결ᄒᆞ야귀
경이되여외양군집에셔그츄수
를처리ᄒᆞ는데법부수가외부
로죠회ᄒᆞ기를법부인소등이가한
영수와동사ᄒᆞ엿슨즉리씨의숑
수에피ᄒᆞ야비샹금을밧을거시
잇다ᄒᆞ미외부에셔고수의를법
부에죠회ᄒᆞ엿더니법부에셔죠
복ᄒᆞ기를법인소등이가한영수
와동사ᄒᆞ야ᄂᆞᆫ용거이잇스면
한영수에게치졍ᄒᆞ고외양군이
는샹관이업슨즉거시어늘이숑
시에피ᄒᆞ야범유수가샹졍ᄒᆞᆫ다ᄒᆞ는거
슨허ᄒᆞᆫ다ᄒᆞ엿더라

○인마수를 닉부에셔보용되
씨는쥬경셩을조가수에로착

금갓다가듕문에날인ᄒᆞᆫ고로
취부극과장의시비가불연ᄒᆞ다
더라

○공수감독 일본군함셩이슈
영군들이안에는주이공수가감하
도감독을결엄ᄒᆞᆫ다더라

○반제손곡 금일샹오에시에
쭉우쥬우반의비샹이는밉으로
본국에슉히가불소ᄒᆞ겟고관망
배는아조비리되졍이라ᄒᆞ더라

○우의봉슈 작일동졔강원군
에셔무섯고오는소두필이싸오
다가ᄒᆞ나히잇즁에셔잣는디진
죽긔집넘으로죽지는아니ᄒᆞ엿
다더라

○나하미 금번에일본정부
각슈마무를시찰ᄒᆞ로진망ᄒᆞᆫ시
찰원에게리가이친원식 나하
ᄒᆞ엿다더라

○츈참의의졍관 원평군리승
우씨는 대셔례도졍리국츄진
를피명ᄒᆞ고 궁나부협관박용
화씨와고문관가등증웅씨와농
샹공부협관리근샹씨는허국의
졍관을겸임ᄒᆞ엿더라

○원숭아와원 일본공사자숭
시전숭아원은이하고관조원구
씨가피명ᄒᆞ엿더라

○슈원광셰 리번군박영철씨
씨가일본에져원ᄒᆞ는시찰의슈
원을피명ᄒᆞ엿더라

○노셕동향 충쳥도로셕군에
산는동학당슈쳔명이회집ᄒᆞ야민
셰이층ᄒᆞᆫ다더라

○함북아병 경성과부령과셩
진등디에잇는아병이슈효는삼
쳔명가량이오그중피명수는져자
일에ᄒᆞᆫ원으로티도ᄒᆞ야보리셤
으로보병을조ᄒᆞ야주일슈은ᄒᆞ야
갓다더라

○원구수 폐 일본원구소장
이본월충슌에귀국ᄒᆞ엿더니인
리젼에 폐현ᄒᆞ엿ᄉᆞ니젼 주ᄒᆞ
고외부에죠회ᄒᆞ엿더라

○조쳥훈금 일본공사가죠회ᄒᆞ
되시흥민요시에일본빙겨의샹
ᄒᆞ고의샹관자협수인의계훈금
을주라ᄒᆞ엿더라

○덕참도인 인천감리가덕보
ᄒᆞ기를덕국군함슈뢰졍각일쳑
이지작일에입항ᄒᆞ라ᄒᆞ엿더라

○루히쇼봉 일본에보낼루
학생을외부에이십명파숑ᄒᆞ기
로의론ᄒᆞ엿는데즁론부부에귀지ᄒᆞ
엿더니샹쟈들에일본발숑ᄒᆞ라
신 최평이통하ᄒᆞ얏심이로지
작일샹오십시에학부에셔신원
루학샹에게션혼인원을렴제
소집ᄒᆞ고리등ᄒᆞ야진양현숑로
셤의루를반로ᄒᆞ고각기부형을배원
회식오원식츌급ᄒᆞᆫ후에선류학
비로샹수의셩원시샹생졍원리
발ᄒᆞ고동경ᄒᆞ기를졔죠졍ᄒᆞ엿는
디명일에발졍ᄒᆞᆫ다더라

론셜

ᄒᆞ기전호런론이라

한국에잇는일본사룸의동일ᄒᆞᆫ
외사로드리되이는대한일보라
ᄒᆞ는신문중에본신문과자의졍
격일관을계지ᄒᆞ엿슨즉이는과
연긔롱으로조의ᄒᆞᆫ는비라

우리신문구람ᄒᆞ시는첨군주는
우리의의무근지계로신문에계재
ᄒᆞᆫ을자며엇지여서그리엿은
ᄂᆞᆫ은결정ᄒᆞᆫ다ᄒᆞ기로잇셩자ᄒᆞ신덧
ᄒᆞᆫ고로대한일보에가히며믈만
ᄒᆞ게계지ᄒᆞᆫ거슨졍관을의혹에
빗등ᄒᆞ노라

한셩에서영국인비셰와명자
발간ᄒᆞ는대한매일신보라ᄒᆞ는
거슨국중에셔제간보조ᄒᆞᆫ금의
이로관셔ᄒᆞ며친졍비를빈용ᄒᆞ
는모양이거놀악히졍졍에관
ᄒᆞ야일본의슨히됨을돌관ᄒᆞ는
중지이아병이며아군이후들미
졍의군사되게ᄒᆞ흠을돈이여외씨
인고로목방이으로관진ᄒᆞ엿신병도
대되ᄒᆞ엿다ᄒᆞ고도ᄒᆞᆫ신문샹에
붓실지쟈로계지ᄒᆞ는지라이럼
으로 국중에셔는일병이과연
괴ᄒᆞᆫ줄로분명히밋는다ᄒᆞ니이
영국사람인즉한지구루로래와
에일본신호에셔편리ᄒᆞ는보진
편든사룸이니진졍형편이엇지
될을가히알리가업다ᄒᆞ엿스니
이며혼조존말이잇슬것가도보
ᄂᆞᆫ죽시면보로라도되엿면ᄒᆞ거놀
그리치아니ᄒᆞ고이계펌ᄒᆞ는거
슨과연미신지졍의거이로저지ᄒᆞ
며쇼ᄒᆞᆫ그신문자편지무론이
모라도이러ᄒᆞᆫ젼편입쥬ᄒᆞ야게을
사름은비관ᄒᆞ지유린관ᄒᆞᆫ더니
확실ᄒᆞᆫ차이라ᄒᆞ고ᄒᆞᆫ말ᄒᆞᆫ지
라

하물며모도거즛말이라ᄒᆞ고ᄒᆞ는
자의에호말이라도진졍홈이잇
슴을도리어편명ᄒᆞ기는이라우
나그러ᄒᆞ나우리의진실ᄒᆞᆫ게ᄒᆞ
ᄂᆞᆫ바와ᄀᆞᆺ유로ᄒᆞ는일에티ᄒᆞ야
대한일보과자의계는방조히샤
관혼ᄒᆞ엿거는밧ᄋᆞ지러면시ᄒᆞᆫ며
뎌회를용드리라ᄒᆞ야시태당히
본격을ᄒᆞᆫ일이며

또ᄒᆞᆫ평소지셥로계홈일죽우
리는방조에붓신지업이로뎌이
기는ᄒᆞ나그러ᄒᆞ나귀와에우리
는 국중이로브러는바는일도
업셧고쇼ᄯᅩ대한일보과자가동
당조에빈되인의일보아니ᄒᆞ엿
는지라만일우리는이러케오진
ᄒᆞ는자이잇슬것ᄀᆞᆺ트면죽시리
어ᄯᅩ차이후에는조심ᄒᆞ야지니
게ᄒᆞᆯ터이며쇼셔비ᄒᆞᆫ ᄒᆞ고경
호ᄒᆞ는거슬듯기에조와ᄒᆞ는ᄒᆞ지
아니ᄒᆞᆫ나그리ᄒᆞᆫ나ᄒᆞ계치지를로
ᄒᆞ는지라

대한일보에는아모리확실ᄒᆞᆫ데
관ᄀᆞᆺ치ᄒᆞ엿스되이는ᄒᆞᆫ마져계
즛말이거시라모러하계나뵈닌리를
은도모지ᄀᆞᆺ치못ᄒᆞᆫ보백생ᄀᆞᆺ흔
지라이러로우리는볼노ᄒᆞᆫ지

괴ᄒᆞ야ᄒᆞᆫ멸하는졍속과가셔관가피
신문에에는사룸의쇼이나치지
ᄒᆞᆫ드리고로ᄒᆞᆫ무리고를ᄒᆞᆫ셔긔ᄒᆞᆫ
일쵸이니라

살ᄒᆞᆫ우리의제대보로ᄒᆞ을우로팔
ᄒᆞᆫ드리도조금도주저ᄒᆞ시사전
ᄂᆞᆫ지라우매는가으로ᄒᆞᆫ며죵계에셔
이는마음이미한혼ᄒᆞᆫ의율ᄒᆞᆫ우리
을보유ᄒᆞ는지에는ᄒᆞᆫ며도되리라
표소ᄒᆞ노니

경편ᄂᆞᆫ대한일보의과자는공연히
주관의게분명ᄒᆞᆫ기지젼만ᄒᆞ
에로ᄒᆞᆫ는바를붓치며그모로든
졍치가을들헐ᄒᆞᆫ셩견과오만ᄒᆞ졍이
엄도를ᄒᆞ고ᄯᅩᄒᆞᆫ졍신율ᄒᆞᆫ슈ᄒᆞᆫ
아정샹이외부지기수진보모든
각종이로ᄒᆞᆫ라고ᄒᆞ는일을ᄒᆞᆫ히야
파셩각종이알흘듯ᄒᆞᆫ지라

비종이러ᄒᆞᆫ일은ᄒᆞ지못ᄒᆞᆫ더
도한국에잇는일본사람들로ᄒᆞ
야금아모도ᄒᆞᆫ일ᄒᆞᆫ아ᄒᆞᆫ부ᄒᆞᆫ피
ᄒᆞᆫ라고졔면ᄒᆞᆫ는지졍ᄒᆞᆫ지렬ᄒᆞ면
뎌헌이며며가지이고ᄯᅩ한국에
셔지진의으로보니이게ᄒᆞᆫ고ᄒᆞ는마음
이잇지문은한국계셩의회복잡
주ᄒᆞᆫ다고ᄒᆞ는마음을필과ᄀᆞᆺᄒᆞᆫ
계ᄒᆞᆯ지며

경계대한일보에셔남의신문계
ᄒᆞ는그러ᄒᆞᆫ일을치말흘과비
혼일을음은후에다도가히홀지
션ᄒᆞᆫ조성ᄒᆞ고각겸홀지어다

닉보

십월팔일관보

○참부즁봉 금월오일오젼십
일시샹한문에에일본관졍교봉통
관평셔방에셔국의귀령으로중편
을별관ᄒᆞ엿는니피슈ᄒᆞ나션귀ᄒᆞᆷ
스리도별으중시동방으로귀각
ᄒᆞ엿다는피며귀경으로귀남하
ᄒᆞ는군리의초병인가보다더라
일병은시군슈흥도로로롤숀시
흐형으로출경ᄒᆞᆫ보로귀쳥ᄒᆞ야귀거
처못ᄒᆞ엿다ᄒᆞ고ᄒᆞ엿는ᄃᆡ이병싱
친여병이리도흘으로쳥홀벽쟝
을피관ᄒᆞ기에불홀ᄒᆞᆫ다더라

십월오일오후시동경발
뎐

○참도의셥 도국군함이오흘
이로도망ᄒᆞ엿다는말은소셜이
업ᄂᆞᆫ말이라ᄒᆞ더라

본사광고

○본샤신문중에흑시틀닌수가
혹잇슴이니가잇셔이에광고ᄒᆞ오
니누구시던지고즁에아모호수
던지가지오시는이는우리졍에
정부로사드리리다

뎨이호 뎨삼호 뎨이십일호
뎨수십이호 뎨수십삼호 뎨
오십삼호 뎨오십수호 뎨오
십오호 뎨륙십ᄉᆞ호

TELEGRAMS.

(THROUGH RE TER'S AGENCY.)

THE JAPANESE ADVANCE.

London, Sept. 30.

General Kuropatkin, wiring on the 29th instant, reports that the Japanese have begun the offensive along the entire east and south front at Mukden.

Later.

The correspondent of the "Standard" with General Kuroki's force says that General Kuropatkin, with the main body of the Russian army, has fallen back north of Mukden and upon Tieling, but that a considerable body of infantry is still south of Mukden apparently for the purpose of observing Japanese movements.

KING AND KAISER.

London, Sept. 30.

The German papers publish a report to the effect that the Kaiser will visit King Edward in November.

Berlin, Sept. 30.

The St. "Petersburg Journal" and other Russian papers strongly object to the terms of the Treaty between Great Britain and Thibet, and declare that Russia will never agree to it.

[THROUGH REUTER'S AGENCY.]

London, Sept. 30.

It is announced at Washington that Mr. Conger, the U.S. Minister at Peking, has telegraphed to the Government stating that China has promised that American and British subjects are to have the preference if foreign capital is required for the extension of the Hankow railway to Chingking.

Mr. Conger therofore wishes to know if American capitalists care to embark on the enterprise.

OUTPOST AFFAIR.

Gensan, 6th Oct.

At 1130 A.M. on the 5th some Russian scouts were observed by our troops to the west of the Ham Kwang Luing pass. Our troops shelled them, whereupon they retired; we did not.

"BAYAN" RUMOUR DENIED.

Tokyo Oct. 5th.

The report that the "Bayan" had fled to Woosung is unfounded.

Tokyo Oct. 5th.

A London telegram says that General Savaroff has reported that the advance guard of the Japanese army has surrounded the town of Uensaieff south-east of Moukden.

SIR WILLIAM HARCOURT DEAD.

Tokyo, Oct. 5th.

A telegram from London announces the death of Sir William Harcourt.

COAL SUPPLIES FOR RUSSIA.

London, Sept. 30.

Five German colliers left Newport and Cardiff yesterday for Port Oppraya. It is understood the coal is for the Russian vessels.

[SPECIAL ARRANGEMENT WITH 'JAPAN-POST.']

THE BALTIC FLEET.

Berlin, Sept. 30.

The Tsar, attended by a large suite, has proceeded to Libar to witnuess the departure of the Baltic Fleet for the Far East.

FIELD MARSHAL KUROPATKIN.

Tokyo, Oct. 5.

The Czar has decided that general Kuropatkin shall be commander-in-chief, with the title of Field Marshal, of the forces in Manchuria, and General Riencritch shall command the first army.

Tokyo, later.

At the end of this year, it is said that Russia will have two armies in the field, the 1st comprised of 7 army corps and 4 divisions of cavalry, the 2nd of 5 army corps and 3 cavalry divisions. In addition many batteries of artillery are being hurried to Manchuria.

WHEN JAPANESE SOLDIERS ARE AT LEISURE.

Writing on June 4th to the "Standard," their special correspondent with kuroki, Mr. Max well says.

In his leisure moments the Japanese soldier is easily entertained. Out of a piece of wood he makes a chess board and chess men—Japanese pieces are always flat, with the names written on the wood— and works out problems by the hour. He sings the ditties popular in the tea houses of Tokyo, or plays "ken" with his hands, or tells stories that amuse his comrades. But his great delight is to watch some juggler or acrobat, of whom there are many in the Army. The appearance of one of these men brings the soldiers trooping out of house and temple to form an applauding circle. Now and then he will stop to listen to the sermon of some Buddhist priest who accompanies the Army in an unofficial capacity, for the Japanese have no chaplains on their establishment. These priests wear frock coats of European style, with stoles, on which are embroidered the golden crest of the Buddhist faith. They visit the camps almost daily, and give instruction in the doctrines of Confucius, with appeals to loyalty and filial duty. I am told that these sermons breathe the spirit of pessimism, and are calculated to depress rather than to inspire the soldier with hope and confidence. He is a diligent correspondent, the Japanese soldier. There is, I believe, not an illiterate in the whole Army, and the number of letters and diaries is astounding. Many of these diaries are kept with great detail, and ought to provide the future historian and novelist of Japan with abundant raw material. All these virtues are at the command of the Mikado for the sum of one penny and three-farthing a day—a soldier's pay in the field. Nor is he permitted to supplement this wealth by remittances from home, for the field post only accepts money for transmission to Japan, the purpose of the Government being to prevent unnecessary expenditure of money in China, whence it might be recovered with difficulty. Rich and poor are accordingly reduced to the same financial straits, and must sacrifice a day's pay for half-a-dozen bad cigarettes, and five days' pay for a bottle of "saké," or rice spirit. These are practically the sole "temptations" to which a private is exposed. That he is able to resist them is proved by the fact that, on one single day, the Field Post Office has received as much as two hundred and fifty pounds sterling for transmission to parents and relatives in Japan.

HEAVY REINFORCEMENTS.

Reports from Tiantsm state that the Russians have received reinforcements numbering 64,000 men, with 144 guns, including mountain artillery and machine guns, since the defeat at Liaoyang. Strenuous steps are being taken to fortify Mukden and its environs, and already a position has been established there which is said to be even stronger than Liaoyang was. It is probable, comments the Japan Mail, that the above statement is more or less exaggerated, but undoubtedly some reinforcements have reached the Russians, for it was precisely to anticipate their advent that the end of August was chosen by the Japanese for the attack on Liaoyang. Military experts have made the calculation that 2,000 men per diem is about the limit of the Siberian railway's power of transport, and that estimate, supposing the rate to have been maintained continuously since the battle of Liaoyang, would result in something like 50,000 men.

A Shanghai telegram states that Major-General Dessino has received the following report, dated Sept. 29, 1.30 a. m., from the Russian Headquarters in Manchuria:—No change has taken place in connection with the Russian position for many days past, although skirmishes take place every day between advanced guards from both sides. Our Cavalry detachment has harassed two Japanese scouting detachments and succeded in capturing many bulls and cows.—Kobe Herald.

WILLFUL DAMAGE TO FOREIGNER'S PROPERTY.

This morning, shortly after 8 a. m. a body of eight Japanese cavalrymen rode up to the entrance to the estate, belonging to Mr. E. Martel situated outside the South Gate. Dismounting and leaving their horeses outside, they forcibly effected an entrance into the grounds, threatening the Korean servants with their swords.

They then proceeded to wantonly hack about the fruit trees with their sabres and pluck flowers ruthlessly. After scrawling in Chinese character on the pathway, "Go the Japanese to study," these enlightened gentry took their departure.

Unfortunately for them however, the property does not belong to a harmless Korean, whose possesions they can destroy with impunity, but to a foreigner, who is likely to bring the offenders to justice in very short time. In fact, although Mr. Martel was absent in Chemulpo, Japanese gendarmes were immediately informed of the outrage and the perpetrators will doubtless be discovered immediately.

NUMEROUS CAVALRY SKIRMISHES.

The Mainichi has received a telephone message from Tokio to the effect that news is to hand that General Kuroptakin reported to the Czar on September 27th as follows:—

The Japanese advanced guards have been occupying a place to the east of the railway, as we reported the other day. Some small detachments come out now and then, but on seeing our Cavalry scouts they disappear at once. The outposts of the Samosonoff Column have captured some bulls and cows from the Japanese. A detachment of Ural Cossacks surprised the enemy on September 25th at Kwanji. A scouting party consising of Orlenburg Cossacks lay in wait for about half a company of Japanese Cavalry on September 26th. The Japanese caught sight of them and began to fire upon our men, but they soon afterwards, retreated, with much loss, leaving several dead bodies on the field. On this occasion our men captured some Japanese horses.

Fifteen stalwart members of Seoul's police force have been despatched to Pyengyang to strike terror into the hearts of turbulent Tonghaks.

LOST

On the 27th ult., probably in the neighbourhood of the West Gate.

A Photographic Camera. Anyone returning the same to this office will receive Y 15.00 reward.

The Korea Daily News.

Issued at 5 P. M. daily except Sundays.

Rate of Subscription:—

Per Year,	Yen 25.
Per Quarter,	Yen 7.
Per Month	Yen 2.50

Postage in Korea not charged extra.
Postage abroad charged extra.

Advertisements, 50 sen per day for 1 inch or less.
5 yen per month per inch.
50 yen per year per inch.

All communications to

E. T. BETHELL,
Editor and Publisher.
Pak-toug, Seoul

JAPAN'S RELATIONS WITH CHINA.

We find that the "Kokumin," a Tokio journal of great eminence, is very much concerned at evidence, or what it construes as evidence, of a tendency on the part of China to disassociate itself from Japan until it sees for certain which way the cat is going to jump.

Says the "Kokumin":—

"China does not seem to know why this Empire is engaged in war with Russia; to understand what this county intends to do with Manchuria; to perceive how we are disposed towards China."

We share China's ignorance, and so we think do most people. And besides that, "intentions" are somewhat vague and intangible things. China knows as well as the rest of the world that Japan is not fighting this war for her health. China can well be excused for not immediately believing in the disinterestedness of everybody who interferes with her.

Of adventurers on a small scale China has ever been the victim and as she still retains her jelly-fish and invertebrate conformation, damages on her fringe are only partly appreciated at headquarters.

Ten years ago China and Japan got to loggerheads. The result was that China lost her prestige, her navy, Formosa, many million yen, and had to sue for peace.

China is one of the most conservative countries in the world and yet we find the "Kokumin" so misguided as to be astonished that China does not unreservedly accept all that Japan chooses to tell her.

China remains obdurate and the "Kokumin" seeks the reason:—

"Nothing could have led China to entertain such a notion but her gross misconception regarding Japan's reasons, aims and intentions in the present war, which involve questions of life and death so far as Japan herself is concerned, and are perfectly honourable, disinterested and thoroughly well meant as towards China. What is worse, China seems determined to return evil for good. China has objected to our rightful seizure of the "Reisitelini" at Chefoo; she has demanded of us the restoration of the administration of Yingkow, as if she possessed the right to do so, while she dares not remonstrate with Russia for ignoring her neutrality; and furthermore, many of her newspapers have been bought over by Russia and are now openly acting as our enemy's organs."

Now herein lies a moral. Of the "Reisitelini" incident we have already given our opinion and the only thing to be added is, that (although there was more occasion) Japan did not commit such flagrant breaches of neutrality in ports where foreign men of war were present. What the "Kokumin" says about Yinkow and the "enemy's organs" is quite open to a "tu quoque," but the point which strikes us most is the "Kokumin's" complaint about the untrusting attitude of China.

Let us look for reasons for China's coyness.

When one is confronted with a novel situation, one, in the absence of past experience, looks abroad for a parallel.

And China has not far to look.

At the outbreak of this war Korea was induced to sign a document the practical effect of which, as at present construed by Japan, was to place nearly all her rights in the hands of Japan.

How this document has been taken advantage of, China probably knows, and having more power to assert her independence, naturally enough holds aloof.

From the first we have, in regard to the true interests of Japan, warned her that her policy of coercion, land-grabbing, and back-stairs intriguing in this country, was a gross blunder and it is only that now that all these mistakes have been made it is found that the damage is already irretrievable and that China has taken to heart the lesson as taught in Korea.

SIR T. LIPTON AND THE AMERICA CUP.

Sir Thomas Lipton, his three successive defeats notwithstanding, has decided to challenge again for the America Cup. Sir Thomas is at present on the Clyde on his steam yacht Erin, to arrange for the designing and building of another Shamrock. In an interview, Sir Thomas said that this was so, but declared himself unable to discuss the details at present. "It may be simple stubbornness on my part, but I have all my life had a constitutional objection to admitting that I was beaten, however strong the evidence might be against me. Shamrock I. made a good fight, Shamrock II. made the closest thing ever sailed in Cup racing, and Shamrock III. was unfortunate. Considering that all three went against us, however, I can only regard these as interesting preliminaries, and look to Shamrock IV. to put up the real fight." The New York Yacht Club has adopted a new rule of measurement, which is calculated to discourage the racing-machine type of yacht, and to favour the more rational type whice obtains in this country.

THE NEW CHINO-PORTUGUESE TREATY.

In the new commercial treaty between Portugal and China now under negotiation at Peking the following poposals are made by Portugal:—

1—There being many Chinese residents in Macao the rice grown there is not enough to supply them, and China shall consent to export 500,000 shih of rice annually to Macao so as to supply the wants of the place.

2—The Macao railway shall be further extended.

Both Lu Hai-hwang and Sheng Kungpao, the Chinese Treaty Revision Commissioners, expressed their opinion that China may consent to the export of rice to Macao to the extent of two or three hundred thousand shih with customs pass attached, but no extension of the railway should be allowed. Yuan Shikai, however, wired on the 22nd August that the three hundred thousand shih of rice should be the maximum amount of rice to be allowed to be exported from China to Macao and in any case no increase should be allowed and the rice should only be allowed to be exported from the province of Kwangtung but from none of the other provinces, and China should retain the right of stopping such exportation in case of famine prevailing, and, according to the suggestion of Sir Robert E. Bredeu, a fixed term of years should be prearranged to the agreement.

The envoys to Japan have each received Y2,000.00 from His Majesty towards their expenses in that country.

The Japanese Minister has informed the Foreign Office that General Haraguchi will depart for Japan about the 15th inst. and before leaving requests an audience with His Majesty.

In addition to dispensing with the hirsute covering to their heads the Il Chin Hoi have decided never more to wear Korean head-gear. A new fashion is to be set in gaudy caps, of which the young "bloods" of Japan are so fond.

The public schools in towns on the line of march in Korea, have been practically closed for educational purposes and used as barracks for the troops. A similar complaint comes from Hamheung, where the school has been utilised by the Russians for storage purposes.

The fifty students, who are to be sent to Japan to study, were received yesterday by the Minister of Education. They were each presented with Y15.00, the wherewithal to purchase European attire, and further received a sum of Y60.00 per individual for 3 months' expenses in Japan.

The Kamni of Masanpo telegraphs that on the island of Ker-Che-Do off the South coast, the Japanese have posted up notices setting forth 15 criminal offences, the committing of which will be punishable by martial-law. Whether a large or small offence is committed, the perpetrator of the same will be instantly shot.

The Finance Department yesterday gave out the following clauses of an agreement to be made with Mr. Megata. 1. Mr. Megata to receive a salary of Y 800.00 monthly and an allowance of yen 100.00 for incidental expenses. 2. Mr. Megata will be privileged to report, on affairs financial, direct to His Majesty. 3. No term to his engagement will be fixed.

Some correspondence between the Foreign Office and the Japanese Legation, relative to the Si-heung riot has been published. It appears that the Japanese Minister demands pecuniary compensation for the two wounded Japanese and the families of the deceased. The Japanese have also handed over the two captured leaders of the riot to the Korean authorities for trial and punishment.

The Emperor of Japan returned the visit of Prince Karl Anton of Hohenzollern at the Shiba Detached Palace on the 27th ult. and personally conferred the Grand Cordon of the Chrysanthemum on the German Prince who immediately assumed the decoration. His Majesty left the Prince's temporary residence at 10:50 A. M. A major of cavalry and three others among the Prince's suite received decorations through the Foreign Minister on the same day. Prince Karl has contributed the sum of Y2,000 towards the Japan Red Cross Society. The attaché to the Prince has also made a donation of Y100 for the same purpose.

Commenting upon taxation in Japan, the "Kobe Chronicle" remarks: It is estimated in some quarters that if the war goes on throughout next year, it will be necessary for the Japanese Government to provide a sum of seven hundred million yen to defray the expenditure. That sum will not of course come out of the pockets of the people in one lump, for that would mean widespread ruin, but it will be a charge upon Japanese industry in some form or other, and the future of the country must be hypothecated to meet it. These are facts that it is no use blinking; they have got to be faced as part of the sacrifices which the Japanese Government presumably calculated before plunging into war. To minimise them with the view of showing that Japan is perfectly competent to continue the war for years to come if necessary will only in the end arouse deep feelings of resentment among the people.

The Korea Daily News.

VOL. I, FRIDAY, OCTOBER 7, 1904. No. 70

HONGKONG & SHANGHAI BANKING CORPORATION.

Paid-up Capital..... ....$10,000,000
Reserve Fund:—Sterling Reserve... 10,000,000
Silver Reserve..... 7,000,000

27,000,000
Reserve Liability of Proprietors... 10,000,000

HEAD OFFICE, HONGKONG,

London Bankers, London and County Banking Company Limited.
Branches and Agencies, London.

Amoy,	Hankow	Penang,
Bangkok,	Hiogo,	Rangoon,
Batavia,	Iloilo,	Saigon,
Bombay,	Lyons,	San Francisco,
Calcutta,	Manila,	Singapore,
Colombo,	Nagasaki,	Sourabaya,
Foochow,	New York,	Tientsin,
Hamburg,	Peking,	Yokohama,

Credits granted on approved Securities, and every description of Banking and Exchange business transacted.

Drafts granted on London and the chief Commercial places in Europe, India, Australia, America, China and Japan.

HOLME RINGER & Co., AGENTS,
CHEMULPO.

ON CHEONG & CO.,
SEOUL.
GENERAL STORE KEEPERS.
Imported provisions, Cooking Utensils Crockery, etc.
FRESH BREAD DAILY.

MITSU BISHI DOCKYARD & ENGINE WORKS,
NAGASAKI.

CODE WORD, "DOCK."

A. 1, A. B. C., and Engineering Codes used.

DOCK No. 1 (at Tategami).

Extreme Length..............523 feet
Length on blocks............513 „
Width of Entrance on Top......89 „
„ „ Bottom....77 „
Water on Blocks at Spring Tide 26½ „

DOCK No. 2 (Mukaijima).

Extreme Length..............371 feet
Length on Blocks............360 „
Width of Entrance on Top......66 „
„ „ Bottom 53 „
Water on Blocks at Spring Tide 22 „

PATENT SLIP (at Kosuge).

Can take vessels up to 1,000 tons gross.

THE WORKS are well-equipped with the LATEST IMPROVEMENTS, and can execute any kind of work in SHIPBUILDING and MARINE ENGINEERING, as well as in REPAIRING of SHIPS.

The COMPANY'S new powerful steamer OURA-MARU (712 tons, 700 I.H.P.), specially built for SALVAGE PURPOSES, and equipped with necessary gear, is always READY at SHORT NOTICE.

CHARTERED BANK OF INDIA AUSTRALIA & CHINA.

INCORPORATED BY ROYAL CHARTER 1853

HEAD OFFICES:—LONDON.

Paid-up Capital £800,000
Reserve Liability of Shareholders 800,000
Reserve Fund 800,000

Drafts granted upon all the principal places in the world and every description of Exchange and banking business transacted.

E. MEYER & Co., Agents,
Chemulpo.

E. MEYER & CO.
Chemulpo.

SOLE AGENTS IN KOREA FOR:
A. T. Morse, Sons & Co's "Fresco" Distemper

In all colours ready for use on walls, Ceilings etc.
and
AVENARIUS CARBOLINEUM

A wood-preserving and antiseptic oil preparation

Against decay, dry-rot, fungus and wood-destroying insects.

A large supply always in Stock.
Prices upon application.

E. MEYER & Co.,
Chemulpo.

LAW UNION & CROWN INS. CO.
Fire risks accepted at Current rates, on go downs, merchandise, dwellings, and other property, subject to usual conditions.
HOLME RINGER & Co.,
Agents, Ch emulp

THE METHODIST PUBLISHING HOUSE,
Little WestGate, Seoul.

JPRINTING, TYPEWRITER PAPER
CARBON PAPER, VISITING CARDS
STATIONERY, BOOK BINDING
BOOK PUBLISHERS
AMERICAN SCHOOL BOOKS
SPENCERIAN COPY BOOKS
PEN CARBON LETTER AND BILL BOOKS

S. A. BECK, Manager.

DAI-ICHI GINKO.

LIMITED.

(Formerly the First National Bank)

ESTABLISHED 1873

INCORPORATED UNDER PRESENT LAW 1896

Capital - - - - - - - - - Yen 5,000,000
Reserve Fund - . - - - 1,500,000

HEAD OFFICE:—TOKIO.

President: Baron SHIBUSAWA.

BRANCHES AND CORRESPONDENTS
In the Principal Cities and Towns of Japan.
Interest Allowed on
Fixed deposits 1 year - - - 6½ per cent
" " 6 months - - - 6 per cent

Special current accounts 1½ sen daily per Y 100
General " " 1 " " " 100

M. TANAKA,
Manager, Chemulpo

HOLME RINGER & Co.
Chemulpo.

General Merchants and Government Contractors.

Agents for the leading
Banks
SteamshipCompanies
and
Insurance Companies

Importers of Merchandise of every description.

KAMEYA Z CO.
GENERAL STOREKEEPERS
Chinkokai - - Seoul
(Established 1895, Tokyo)

Confectionery, Hams, Canned Goods, Cutlery, Hirano & Tansan Water. Provisions, Gents, Furnishing goods, Toilet Articles, Travelling Bags, Tobacco, Cigars & Cigarettes Kitchen Utensils. Coffee, Biscuits.

Fresh Goods always kept in Stock.
Prices Moderate
Please come and inspect our goods.

NIPPON YUSEN KAISHA.

JAPANESE MAIL STEAMSHIP CO.

DER MAIL CONTRACT WITH THE IMPERIAL JAPANESE GOVERNMENT.

European Line

Regular Fortnightly Service between Yokohama Kobe, Moji, Shanghai, Hongkong, Singapore, Penang Colombo, Port Said, Marseilles, London and Antwerp

American Line

Regular Fortnightly Service between Hongkong and Seattle, calling at Shanghai, Moji, Kobe, Yokohama and Victoria, B. C.

Australian Line

Regular weekly Service betwen Japan Ports and Australia, calling at Hongkong and Manila.
(Above Three Lines Suspended until further notice).

Shanghai Line

Weekly Service between Shanghai and Japan Ports

Korea Line

Service Kobe, Moji, Nagasak i, Fusan, Chemupo, Coo, Taiku.
S. S. Bahelsberg, 2181 tons.
Service Kobe, Moji, Fusan, Chemulpo, Chinnampo
S. S ARGO, S. S. Ohio.

BORDEN'S CONDENSED MILK CO.

New York, U. S. A.

ALWAYS IN STOCK
Eagle Brand Condensed Milk.
Gold Seal Condensed Milk.
Peerless (Family) Evaporated Cream.
Borden's Malted Milk.

E. MEYER & CO.
Chemulpo, Korea,
Sole Agents

ROYAL INSURANCE COMPANY,
Funds exceed £10,000,000
FIRE
AT CURRENT RATES.
LIFE
REDUCED PREMIUM.
HOLME RINGER & Co.,
Agents, Chemulpo.

HOTEL DU PALAIS
SEOUL.

The only first class Hotel in Seoul. Situated in the centre of the city opposite the palace.

Cuisine under the supervision of an experienced French Chef.

Well ventilated and furnished throughout.

TARIFF UPON APPLICATION

L. MARTIN
Proprietor and Mangaer.

大韓每日申報
대한ᄆᆡ일신보

일쳔구ᄇᆡᆨᄉᆞ년십월팔일 (일요일) (뎨칠십일호)

본샤고ᄇᆡᆨ

본신보ᄂᆞᆫ영어와한어로셕거ᄆᆡ
일츌판ᄒᆞᄋᆞᆸ
신문가
한쟝 엽두돈오푼
일삭됴 엽두량닷돈
우표가ᄆᆡ삭닷돈
다맛돈으로밧ᄉᆞᆸ
광고료ᄂᆞᆫ
긔한의쟝단과ᄌᆞ힝의다쇼로즁
감ᄒᆞ되렴가로밧을터이오며오
ᄅᆡ지아녀대한사람마다다이신
문을보실터이니광고내시기를
원ᄒᆞ시ᄂᆞᆫ이들은우리신문샤에
와셔면약ᄒᆞ심을희망ᄒᆞᄋᆞᆸ

○발힝소 박동대한ᄆᆡ일신보
샤법어학교압헤젼영국인셜필
림집자리오
샤쟝 영국인 (ᄇᆡ셜)
평양 ᄃᆡ리뎜
○평양효동사ᄂᆞᆫ권ᄆᆡ보씨로우
리신문판ᄆᆡᄃᆡ리인을뎡ᄒᆞ엿
ᄉᆞ오니평양에계신구람ᄒᆞ져ᄒᆞ
시ᄂᆞᆫ 쳠군ᄌᆞᄂᆞᆫ히ᄃᆡ리뎜에왕
림ᄒᆞ와면의ᄒᆞ시ᄋᆞᆸ

사고

○우리대한ᄆᆡ일신보의목뎍은
대한의안녕질셔에관한모든데
목에ᄃᆡᄒᆞ야ᄂᆞᆫ공평한변론을쥬
쟝홈이라우리동신원의탐보ᄂᆞᆫ
신문보시ᄂᆞᆫ쳠군ᄌᆞ의게ᄒᆞᆼ샹보
도ᄒᆞ리며편지를긔셔ᄒᆞ여주시
ᄂᆞᆫ이ᄂᆞᆫ셩명과반ᄃᆡ를젹어붓치
시기를희망ᄒᆞ오니이거슨신문
샹에긔ᄌᆡᄒᆞ라ᄂᆞᆫ거시아니오다
만극히신용ᄒᆞᄂᆞᆫ증거를삼고쟈
홈이라긔쟈ᄂᆞᆫ아모긔셔던지긔
ᄌᆡ홈을되각ᄒᆞᆫ권리를가졋스
나되각ᄒᆞᄂᆞᆫ리유를말ᄒᆞᆯ터이오
며공즁평화를문란케ᄒᆞᄂᆞᆫ듯ᄒᆞᆫ
긔셔ᄂᆞᆫ의례히밧지안켓ᄉᆞᆸ나이
다

●본샤셜시이리로신문을ᄆᆡ양
우톄로분젼ᄒᆞ와톄젼부의임의
로젼ᄒᆞᆫ듯ᄉᆞ오면곳에ᄂᆞᆫ혹늣게
젼ᄒᆞ기도ᄒᆞ며혹몃칠거슬ᄒᆞᆫ겁
에젼ᄒᆞ기도ᄒᆞ며혹아니젼ᄒᆞᄂᆞᆫ
곳도잇다ᄒᆞ와우리신문을ᄉᆞ랑
ᄒᆞ야구람ᄒᆞ시ᄂᆞᆫ 쳠군ᄌᆞ의게
ᄃᆡᄒᆞ야ᄆᆡ우미안ᄒᆞᄋᆞᆸ기로지금
은분젼인을두고ᄆᆡ일일즉이젼
ᄒᆞ며아니젼ᄒᆞ거나늣게거나ᄒᆞᆫ
폐가업도록ᄒᆞ랴ᄒᆞ오니혹아니
젼ᄒᆞ거나혹늣게젼ᄒᆞ거나ᄒᆞᆫ일
이잇스면본샤로통긔ᄒᆞ여쥬심
을희망ᄒᆞᄋᆞᆸ

본샤광고

○본샤신문즁에좌긔ᄒᆞᆫ호수를
소용ᄒᆞᆯ데가잇셔이에광고ᄒᆞ오
니누구시던지그즁에아모호수
던지가져오시ᄂᆞᆫ이로ᄆᆡ쟝에ᄇᆡᆨ
젼두푼식드리리다
뎨이호 뎨삼호 뎨이십호
뎨ᄉᆞ십이호 뎨ᄉᆞ십삼호 뎨오
오십삼호 뎨오십ᄉᆞ호 뎨
십오호 뎨륙십이호

관보

궁뎡록ᄉᆞ
○죠왈드르미경셩에머물든일
본국ᄉᆞ령부쟝좌가쟝츳귀국ᄒᆞᆫ
다ᄒᆞ니ᄀᆡ렴이업지못ᄒᆞᆯ지라ᄉᆞ
령륙군쇼쟝쳔구겸제ᄂᆞᆫ특별이
ᄒᆞᆫ일등팔괘쟝을쥬고ᄉᆞ령부참
모쟝지등력삼랑은특별이ᄒᆞᆫ삼
등ᄐᆡ극쟝을쥬라
구월이십ᄉᆞ일
표훈원 총지 죠병식
○즁츄원의관졍쥬영조렬소
비지ᄂᆡ에이ᄀᆞᆺ치말ᄒᆞ지말나
○탁지부대신박뎡양ᄉᆞ직소
비지ᄂᆡ에ᄉᆞ양ᄒᆞᆫ즉탁지지임만
의시ᄒᆞ노라
○의졍부찬졍최익현ᄉᆞ직소
비지ᄂᆡ에병나흠을기다려샹리
ᄒᆞ라
○학부대신리지용ᄉᆞ직소
비지ᄂᆡ에속히등졍ᄒᆞ라
이샹구월삼십일
셔임
○임탁지부대신셔칙임관일등
군부대신 민영긔
○임군부대신셔칙임관일등
참모부부쟝 리윤용
○임참모부부쟝 부쟝 윤웅
렬
이샹구월삼십일
○뎨이쳔구ᄇᆡᆨᄉᆞ십칠호
광무팔년십월삼일
셔임급ᄉᆞ령
○임륙군보병참령 보병졍위
신우균 김규한 셔경츈 김
한경 죠셩근 왕유식 류긔
원 리민식 졍ᄐᆡ셕 리규찬
일등군ᄉᆞ 김형비 군부포공
국공병과쟝 민영션 젼협판
죠민희
○임륙군포병참령 포병졍위
어 담 리남하
○임륙군공병참령 공병졍위
김셩은
○임륙군보병졍위 보병부위
김용승 안쳘영 로ᄇᆡᆨ린 김
쳘슈 신우영 한샹봉 김ᄐᆡ
원 김영션 군부참셔관 리
셕지 포공국포병과쟝 현보
운 경리국뎨일과원 박덕슈
일등군ᄉᆞ 송학슈 호위ᄃᆡ
졍위 신경균 리희신
○임륙군보병부위 참위 리
승우 김병승 보병참위 문
덕교 안졔한 최홍긔 호위
ᄃᆡ부위 리긔원 리용문 군
부포공국공병과원 졍우창
포공국포병과원 오졍션
○륙군보병참위 군부경리국
뎨일과원 손희명 포공국공
병과원 김인규 군부관방원
죠한쳥 군부젼과원 홍건
군부쥬ᄉᆞ 류셰렬 한규호
김창현 ᄇᆡᆨ인긔 기ᄉᆞ 황텰
쥬 홍종긔 기슈 ᄐᆡ영션
○임륙군이등군ᄉᆞ 보병부위
오직션
관보뎨이쳔구ᄇᆡᆨᄉᆞ십륙호
광무팔년십월일일
셔임급ᄉᆞ령
○의원면본관 즁츄원의관
김션용 김우식 리희영
○임즁츄원의관셔쥬임관륙등
리법셰 손졍현 륙품 리범
셜
이샹구월이십이일
○셔훈일등ᄉᆞ팔괘쟝 일본국
ᄉᆞ령륙군쇼쟝 원구겸제
○셔훈삼등ᄐᆡ극쟝 일본국
ᄉᆞ령부참모쟝 지등력삼랑
이샹구월이십ᄉᆞ일
○임경무ᄉᆞ셔칙임관이등 헌
병ᄉᆞ령관 량셩환
○의원면본관 졍위 신경균
리회신 부위리긔원 리용문
○임호위ᄃᆡ졍위 졍위 죠승
근 박쥰샹
○임호위ᄃᆡ부위 부위 리유
익 참위최학지
○승셔관임관삼등 ᄂᆡ부 광졔
원의ᄉᆞ 리규션 졔약ᄉᆞ 리
지봉
○승셔관임관오등 경샹북도
관찰부쥬ᄉᆞ 최만달
○의원면본관 텰도원쥬ᄉᆞ
리경운 조경묘참봉 리하영
동ᄂᆡ감리셔쥬ᄉᆞ 김연참
○면본관 ᄐᆡ복ᄉᆞ쥬ᄉᆞ 홍승
범
○희궁ᄂᆡ부소관각궁각ᄉᆞ셰부
됴사위원 법부참셔관 김라
헌
○명궁ᄂᆡ부특진관셔칙임관일
등 시종원경 리건하
○명궁ᄂᆡ부소관각궁각ᄉᆞ셰부
됴사위원쟝 궁ᄂᆡ부협판 박
용화
○명궁ᄂᆡ부소관각궁각ᄉᆞ셰부
됴사위원 륙품 한병구
○임텰도원쥬ᄉᆞ셔관임관륙등
죠ᄐᆡᆨ규
○임죠경묘참봉셔판임관팔등
구픔 김도졔
○임동ᄂᆡ감리셔쥬ᄉᆞ셔판임관
륙등 윤샹도
이샹구월이십구일

잡보

○ᄐᆡᆨ불션ᄐᆡᆨ 금번군슈를ᄐᆡᆨ차
ᄒᆞᆫ다ᄒᆞ되인지ᄂᆞᆫ하여ᄒᆞ던지각
관쳥에젹ᄉᆞ구근즁뎐됴다소만
샹고ᄒᆞ야슈용ᄒᆞᆫ다ᄒᆞ니목민지
관을ᄐᆡᆨ차ᄒᆞᄂᆞᆫ본의가아니라고
들ᄒᆞᆫ다더라
○군슈조격 법부에셔본부관
인즁군슈조격으로수임관에ᄂᆞᆫ
로병식관임관에ᄂᆞᆫ류원셩량씨
를거쳔ᄒᆞ엿더라
○모ᄌᆞ변동 군인의모ᄌᆞ를대
락변동ᄒᆞᆫ다ᄂᆞᆫᄃᆡ공병포병헌병
쟝관병졸의모ᄌᆞ와향관의모ᄌᆞ
보병쟝졸의모ᄌᆞ모양으로ᄀᆞᆺ게
ᄒᆞᆫ다더라
○원소텰뎐 람포거ᄒᆞᄂᆞᆫ김소
ᄉᆞ가셜원ᄒᆞᆯᄉᆞ졍이잇셔대안문
젼에샹언진복홈은본보에긔ᄌᆡ
ᄒᆞ엿거니와그ᄌᆡ의를득문ᄒᆞᆫ즉
김씨의신수가긔구ᄒᆞ야조년에
샹부ᄒᆞ고싀모를봉양ᄒᆞᆯ시십오
셰ᄋᆞ를솔양ᄒᆞ야살더니싀당슉
김치오가그지산을탈취ᄒᆞᆯ계
로김씨의모ᄌᆞ간에간음ᄒᆞ엿다
고무함ᄒᆞ고셔울사람리민구를
부동ᄒᆞ야젼관ᄉᆞ의게쳥촉ᄒᆞ야
김씨의가산을몰수히륵탈ᄒᆞ고
로부군에졍소ᄒᆞ되군슈와관찰

수가셜원치아니ᄒ고평리원에호소코져ᄒ나리민ᄒ의세력을당치못ᄒ겟기로셜원ᄎ로 뎐폐에명원ᄒ엿더니조 상으로동축ᄒ시고법부에가호쇼ᄒ라고 조칙이나리신고로작일에김씨가법부문젼에호소ᄒ다ᄒ니ᄋ당공졍이심판ᄒ야그 지원극통홈을신셜ᄒ리라더라

○긔탄긔탄 경무쳥에셔외부로조회ᄒ기를공쥬디위관파병뎡을일본헌병이압샹ᄒ야히병영에구슈ᄒ엿스니우리나라군인을외국인이무란이압샹ᄒ니심히긔탄ᄒ다ᄒ엿더라

○파슈진압 경위원총무국쟝엄하영씨가 니지를봉승ᄒ고동학당을진압ᄒᄎ로슌검십오명을평안도로파송ᄒ엿다더라

○고문합동 지작일에탁지부에대신과협판이하각국쟝이회동ᄒ야금번에고빙된고문관목하뎐씨의고빙안건에되ᄒ야협의ᄒ엿는ᄃ히고문관의월봉은믹삭에팔빅원식이오그외에시탄비는믹삭빅원식이며지무샹에무엇시던지긴급ᄒ거슨자긔의견ᄃ로곳샹 쥬ᄒ홀권이잇고고빙년한은무한량으로결뎡ᄒ엿다더라

○죠쳥감봉 니쟝원경셔리김영진씨가부로죠회ᄒ기를평안남도봉셰관김용션씨의뎐보를거ᄒ즉은산군슈셔리슌쳔군슈리승쥬가봉셰관의공문을시힝치안코도리여려가지로져회ᄒ는폐단이만타ᄒ니히군슈를곳 쥬픔ᄒ고일삭감봉을ᄒ라ᄒ엿더라

○셕별호궤 헌병디참령윤원구씨가톄임ᄒ여가는졍이결연ᄒ여작일에 소ᄒ필놀잡아호궤ᄒ엿더라

○거장안지오 시위일디참위모씨는금번군제의졍ᄒ후에각령위관을이승임을만히홀쌔에굿치부위승차는ᄒ엿스나샹환ᄒ며승차ᄒ인원이엇지혼잡ᄒ엿든지친위디로보직이되엿는고로도임ᄎ로히디에잔즉그디에셔말ᄒ기를ᄎ디에는보직인원이다츙수가되엿스니다른디로가라ᄒ미원슈부에호소ᄒ엿더니시위디로보직ᄒ엿는지라또그디로간즉그디에셔도ᄒ는발이ᄎ디에보직인원츙수가다되엿스니타디로가라ᄒ는고로소향놀막지라더라

○진쥬군보 진쥬군슈가니부로보고ᄒ거슬거ᄒ즉본군평거면사는리관셔가조칭동학졉쥬라ᄒ고룽분일도를긔란업시륜회ᄒ는고로곳착슈ᄒ엿다ᄒ엿더라

○남산립표 근일에일인이로인졍에ᄒ봉슈디셔지표목을세웟다더라

○ᄉ령관발힝 쥬일공관에셔작일에뎐보ᄒ기를일본ᄉ령관장곡쳔과참모쟝락합풍삼랑이본일에발졍ᄒ야대한황셩으로향ᄒ다ᄒ엿더라

○텰도시역 창원감리가작일에외부로뎐보ᄒ기를텰도지션공역을본항에셔붓터작일에시작ᄒ엿다ᄒ엿더라

○어리령ᄉ 외부번역관어윤젹은총령ᄉ관을셔임ᄒ고동부쥬ᄉ리원용은령ᄉ관을겸임ᄒ기로외부에셔의졍부로쳥의ᄒ엿다더라

○마구건축 시문밧뎐연뎡근쳐에일인이마구팔십간을건축ᄒ다고셔셔에셔경무쳥에보ᄒ엿더라

○외교관단발 외부에는대신이하쥬ᄉ지각항구시장에는감리셔관원레식원에는원장이하쥬ᄉ지한셩부에는관윤쇼윤이다외교관으로쟝ᄎ단발ᄒ다더라

○잡기랑쟈 근일려항젼셜이랑쟈ᄒ기를근쟈에남북촌모모관인이잡기관에수십만금식독실이난고로가산을탕픽ᄒ쟈가만타ᄒ니경무쳥에셔인민의싱명지산을보호ᄒ는칙임을아지못ᄒ고이러ᄒ큰폐단을금지치아니ᄒ는지모를일이라고ᄒ다더라

○렵부피착 홍쳔사는장범이라는자가여호를산양ᄒᄎ로폭발약을미득ᄒ야미동으로지나가다가일헌병의게피착이되야ᄉ령부로압슈ᄒ엿다더라

○함계징습 의졍부에셔법부로죠회ᄒ기를함남도계원리용지와합북도계원졍지우의소위공함을거ᄒ즉니ᄀ에김유직과허원량인의본도군슈의과임ᄒ거슬비방ᄒ기를티심히ᄒ고졍부로셔이두사름의쥬본을곳쳐교졍치아닌즉본계로셔본도신ᄉ수빅인을취집ᄒ야죵로샹에지회ᄒ고공의ᄒ여귀졍ᄒ겟기로이쳐럼복달ᄒ오니심량죠쳐ᄒ라ᄒ엿스니이랑군슈의셔임은임의회의를경ᄒ야지가를내리신거시어늘소체의신즁ᄒ거슬싱각지아니ᄒ고망녕되이ᄒ편지를던져량인을얽어무소ᄒ며만일교졍치아니ᄒ즉수빅인을취당ᄒ야죵로샹에지회ᄒ다ᄒ니이굿혼픽류를그량두어그무엄ᄒ힝습을조만케못홀이니곳포착ᄒ야샹당ᄒ률에쳐판ᄒ라ᄒ엿더라

○군의쳥원 각군디군의들이군부에쳥원ᄒ기를의무국군의는학교졸업싱으로바로쥬임관을셔입ᄒ는ᄃ본의관등은륙칠년간에쳔여명군인을위싱ᄒ엿거놀쥬임관으로변통치아니ᄒ니극히억울ᄒ고또하ᄉ들의말이ᄌ긔와동등이라ᄒ야슈작ᄒᄌ음에언어ᄒ기에난편지단이만호니의무국군의와일례로쥬임승차를ᄒ라ᄒ엿더라

○례대귀국 일본례신대신대포씨일힝이작일오젼이번렬거로인쳔으로ᄂ려가셔오후이시에안동환을탑승ᄒ고안동현으로발향ᄒ엿다더라

론셜

일본이청국으로더부러샹관ᄒ논일

일본동경안에데일명망잇는콕규민이라ᄒ는신문을거ᄒ즉쳥국이일본의의향ᄒ는바에결단홀쥴을몰나자져ᄒ다고계지ᄒ엿는ᄃ

청국은우리일본이무손리유로라사와긔젼홈과만쥬로ᄒ여곰아엇더케ᄒ라는일이며청국에엇더케비쳐홀거슬몽연히아지못ᄒ는거와갓다고ᄒ엿스니

우리싱각에는청국사름이인물인즉가히쓸만ᄒ나그러ᄒ나다만학문이업는ᄭ닭에주의ᄒ는마음이현란미졍홈이요또ᄒ일본이ᄌ긔나라만ᄒ여젼징을이르키지아닌쥴써지도짐작ᄒ되무론어느나라사름이던지조긔나라로더부러리롭지아니ᄒ게홀쥴로만확실히싱각홈인즉이는파연칙망키어려운지라긔왕에청국에풍대홈과물건에번셩홈을욕심니는쟈ㅣ만히잇셔다만즁원령토에조곰곳은셔로논ᄒ싱각으로호불호를말ᄒ야결단만니게ᄒ라ᄒ는지라

십년젼일청교젼되엿슬때로보드리도세계에쟝ᄒ든명망이일본으로말미암아업셔젓고히군에싱명손샹이무수히되엿스며필경에포모샤와밋금화려빅만원으로비상하고간신히평화가되엿는지라

청국은원리완구지습이오히려잇는나라인즉콕규민신문에아모리그리허를셜명ᄒ드리도다만청국을경동ᄒ게ᄒ라는쥴로만싱각ᄒ며그릇인도ᄒ라는뜻으로만의혹ᄒ야무론무삼말이던지반갑게녁이지아니ᄒ느니

청국은우금셰지도수구ᄒ는마음이오히려잇고콕규민신문은짐짓그리허를알라고ᄒ는뜻이간졀ᄒ야그신문에게지홈이또ᄒ여좌ᄒ니

일본셔아모쪼록청국을위ᄒ야지탕ᄒ도록ᄒ게녁이는향의를도로혀크게그릇치려는일로오히ᄒ는거시맛치젼복위화ᄒ야자망기국ᄒ랴는바와갓튼자라이왕연티에셔아함포획ᄒ일로말ᄒ드리도일본셔대단히올흔일을힝ᄒ엿거놀진실로반ᄃ이ᄒ야인고과리의회복ᄒ기를다만요구ᄒ며또ᄒ공연ᄒ료량업는싱각으ᄅ즁립셩명홈을인ᄒ야아라사로ᄒ야곰감히항거치못ᄒ고지어ᄌ긔나라신문은아인의게미각ᄒ즉지금형편은젹국의긔관과갓다고ᄒ엿스니

콕규신문에이러케셜명ᄒ거슨무타ㅣ라일본셔는즁립셩명ᄒ외국항구에병함을드려미지아니ᄒ엿슴으로이졔아라샤우리슬린병함을즁거ᄒ여말홈이요

또ᄒ이리유를깁히싱각홀진ᄃ청국에소위지고ᄒ사름들은외국에유람ᄒ야지식이업는고로ᄆᄉ에반ᄃ홈이잇셔그리홈이며또ᄒ청국에빗최는갓가온거울이잇셔그리홈인거시

일본셔긔젼ᄒ이후로한국을인도ᄒ야긔명ᄒ게ᄒ다칭ᄒ고다만ᄌ긔의권력ᄃ로수즁에너어실지상ᄉ건공문에조인이나ᄒ게ᄒ즉이러ᄒ공문이나ᄒ는거시무어시유익홈이잇스리오

그런고로청국셔는이러ᄒ리유를거위짐작ᄒ는비라ᄌ긔의쳔연ᄒᄃ로잇셔셔독립홀권리나더ᄒ려ᄒ고굿게잡고잇는지라

일본이ᄌ긔의나라에유익ᄒ게홀싱각으로졍권을핍박ᄒ야샹관ᄒ다던지토지등물을쟝즁에잡아녓는다던지이나라안에음특ᄒ계교를써서히롭게ᄒ야맛치곳치지못홀병과갓치힝ᄒ는줄분명히아는지라

이럼으로한국에셔근일당ᄒ는형편을보고마음에주의ᄒ여둔어비컨ᄃ션싱의게글비혼거와갓ᄐ여그리홈이로다

뎐보

동경발십월오일

○환셰포포위 악국사와로프쟝군의보고를거ᄒ즉일본군의젼초가봉쳔동남환셰포를에워쌋다ᄒ엿더라(론돈발)

동일동뎐

○량쟝ᄉ령 아국황뎨어젼회외에셔쿠로팟킨은만쥬군총ᄉ령관이오루이너윗쓰는뎨일군ᄉ령관으로결졍ᄒ엿더라

동일동뎐

○아군즁가 아국만쥬군이증병ᄒ는결과로본년말에는뎨일군은칠군단과긔병ᄉ긔ᄉ단이오뎨이군은오군단과긔병삼긔ᄉ단으로편셩홀터이오또다수ᄒ산포병은발셔젼쟝으로향ᄒ야발송ᄒ기를명ᄒ엿더라

동일동뎐

○부녀피란 쳘령에잇는부녀들은피란ᄎ로방금다른디방으로옴겨간다ᄒ엿더라

TELEGRAMS.

FROM JAPAN PAPERS.

VICEROY ALEXIEFF RECALLED.

London, Sept. 30th, 1:55 P. M.

The St. Petersburg Government have announced the recall of Viceroy Alexieff and it is expected that the latter will soon leave the Far East for the capital.

Berlin, Sept. 30th.

The "Paris Matin" reports that Viceroy Alexieff, who was recalled to Russia, declined to comply with the order.

THE MANCHURIAN COMMAND.

London, Sept. 30, 1.55 P.M.—

Grand Duke Nicholas is expected to succeed Viceroy Alexieff next spring and take the supreme command in the Russian Far East. General Kuropatkin will command all the forces in the field until the arrival of the Grand Duke.

General Grippenberg, Commander of the 2nd Army, will set out for the Far East in November next.

There are various rumours about the Commander-in-Chief; some pointing to Grand Duke Nicholas, some to Dragomiroff, and some saying that the Grand Duke has already been sent on a tour of inspection. But it is regarded as certain that the Second Army will be independent of Kuropatkin.

The following European telegram has been received by the Foreign Department at Tokio:—

It is stated in Paris that the Russian Second Army is to cousist of the 8th Siberian Corps, the 6th Army Corps, a part of the 6th Siberian Corps and the 6th Kazan Divisisn. It will set out for Mukden.

The following European telegram has been received in official quarters in Tokio:—"It is rumoured that Admiral Alexieff will be recalled and that General Kuropatkin will be appointed Commander-in-Chief of the Russian Armies in Manchuria. General Bilderling, Commander of the 17th Army Corps, will be given the command of the First Russian army, while General Grippenberg, Commander of the Second Army, will depart for the Far East in a month's time."

London, Sept. 30, 1.55 P. M.

Mr. Hoar, Senator of the United States, has died at Worcester, Mass.

The following letter and editorial comment appear in the "China Review" of Tientsin on the 25th ult.

To the Editor of the
"China Review."

Dear Sir,—We regret to have to contradict the statement in your yesterday's issue saying that we are discounting the Japanese war notes at 15%, which is absolutely untrue. The Japanese war notes are redeemed by the Japanese authorities in Manchuria at par on demand, and are circulating freely in the interior as well as at Newchwang.

We request you to publish the above fact and prevent any misunderstanding by the readers of your valuable paper.

We are, yours faithfully,
For the Yokohama Specie Bank,
S. K. Suzuki.
Manager.
Tientsin, Sept. 24.

[Referring to the above our information was perfectly correct; as the Assistant Manager of the Hotel des Colonies was charged 15% discount on Japanesee war notes on Friday last, at the above local Bank.—Ed.C.R.]

WHEN THE LINER WENT DOWN.

The incident of the foundering of a liner in mid-ocean gives Mr. Max Pemberton, in "Red Morn," an opportunity for one of those vivid and vigorious passages of descriptive writing in which he is at his best.

The hour of discipline had gone by now. As the Jersey City settled down by the bows the steerage passengers came aft with one wild shout, and mingling with others they fought their way towards the boats. Neither Captain Ross's trumpet-like commands from the bridge, nor the revolvers of the officers by the boats, kept those panic-stricken people from that which they believed to be the way of safety. One upon the other, pellmell, trampling the women down, they surged along the promenade decks and took their stand by the gangway. Fierce cries were heard, curses, imprecations, the report of pistols, and the screams of the dying. But the mob prevailed, and the timid few were driven down towards the water and death. . . . Two of the boilers burst as she went down, and in the path of that explosion fire was shot towards the heavens like some signal of her dire distress. It was ironical that her great searchlight should burn almost to the last, and, rocking its arc of translucent beams, should show the frenzied faces of the drowning, the arms thrust up above the still sea, and the dark shapes of those whose eyes were down-turned towards the tomb that awaited them. But thus it was; and even as the steamer went, the great arc seemed to linger an instant and then to be rolled away like a quivering carpet of watered gold which an unseen hand snatched up.

ST. LOUIS EXPOSITION.

FORTHCOMING VISIT OF PRINCE HENRY OF PRUSSIA.

Word has just been received here, says a St. Louis despatch to the "Sun," that Prince Henry of Prussia, his wife and eldest son, will leave Germany in two weeks for a tour of the United States, and will come, after his arrival in New York, directly to St. Louis.

The Prince is coming in state and will be entertained in the most lavish manner during his stay here, by Dr. Theodore Lewall, German Imperial Commissioner.

Although an effort has been made to keep the matter quiet until the Prince's arrival, it is well known among the employees of the National German pavilion that the Prince is coming. Dr. Lewall has been notified of the proposed trip in a letter and has since communicated the fact to the commissioners in St. Louis. The Prince will come in a private yacht with his family. He will also be Emperor William's personal representative, as the Emperor will not be able to cross the water.

THE PRISON OF SILENCE.

Entombed in a grim castle on the outskirts of Lisbon are some of the most miserable men on earth. These are the inmates of Portugal's prison of silence. In this building every thing that human ingenuity can suggest to render the lives of its prisoners a horrible, maddening torture is done. The corriders, piled tier on tier five stories high, extend from a common center like the spokes of a huge wheel.

The cells are narrow—tomblike —and within each stands a coffin. The attendants creep about in felt slippers. No one is allowed to utter a word. The silence is that of the grave. Once a day the cell doors are unlocked and the half a thousand wretches march out, clothed in shrouds and with faces covered by masks, for it is a part of this hideous punishment that none may look upon the countenances of his fellow prisoners. Few of them endure this for more than en years.—London Tit-Bits.

GOOD TIME COMING FOR THE BARBERS.

We are informed that the Minister and all officials of the Foreign Office, Kamnis of ports and their officials, President and officials of the Ceremonial Department, together with the Governor and vice-Governor of Seoul will—shave their heads.

THE TOTAL NUMBER OF CAPTURED VESSELS.

Probably few underwriters, says The Times marine insurance correspondent, realise how large a number of steamers have been captured or delayed by the belligerents during the present war. The total number is ninety-seven vessels, of which thirty-one only belong to the period since the capture of the P. and O. steamer Malacca. Nearly all the other seizures took place in Far Eastern waters, and a large proportion of them were enemy's ships.

Mr. Oura left yesterday for Manchuria.

Work on the Masanpo branch line of the Seoul-Fusan railway was commenced yesterday.

The Japanese military authorities are building stables on a large tract of ground outside the West Gate.

A telegraphic despatch to the Foreign Office from Tokyo, states that General Hasegawa and Lieut-General Ochiai left there en route to Korea, on the 7th inst.

A gentleman from the country, who was found in possession of some dynamite when entering the city, was arrested by the Japanese guard. His excuse was that he wished to catch foxes with the dynamite.

In an interview with Mr. Megata the President of State was informed that the Financial Adviser considered that the first step to be taken must be a change in the national currency from nickels to silver dollars. He thinks that these should be imported from Japan. It is also proposed to raise a loan of ten million Yen from Japan to put this suggestion into effect.

The Korea Daily News.

Issued at 5 P. M. daily except Sundays.

Rate of Subscription:—
Per Year, Yen 25.
Per Quarter, Yen 7.
Per Month Yen 2.50

Postage in Korea not charged extra.
Postage abroad charged extra.

Advertisements, 50 sen per day for 1 inch or less.
5 yen per month per inch.
50 yen per year per inch.

All communications to
E. T. BETHELL,
Editor and Publisher.
Pak-toug, Seoul

THE BALTIC FLEET.

By latest despatches received, it would seem that the Baltic fleet is about to sail at last. The Czar is en route to Libau to make a final inspection and give god-speed to his men, while other telegrams inform us that colliers are waiting at many points of the road to the Far East.

A London despatch states that the fleet is composed of six battleships, the Kniaz, Suvaroff, Alexander III, Navarin, Sissoi, Alexander II and the Oslyabya; five large cruisers, the Aurora, Dmitri Donskoi, Almaz, Nachimor, and Pamyat Azova, four converted cruisers, the Don, Ural, Teretz and Kuban. In addition a large number of torpedo-boats and over a dozen destroyers are items of the fleet.

The same despatch, criticizing the ships, says: "More than half of the vessels are too old to be considered really dangerous, while the four converted cruisers were lately German Atlantic liners, and of no fighting value whatever against warships. The vessels of the squadron differ much as regards speed, some having a speed of over twenty knots an hour, while others cannot do more than nine knots."

Thus the Baltic squadron would appear to be a combination of good fighting material in some instances and practically obsolete vessels in others. That the slower ships will prove an enormous hindrance to the twenty-knot class, if only in retarding their progress to the East, there is no room for doubt, and in an actual battle, the faster vessels would necessarily have to regulate their manoeuvres to suit the possibilities of their slower consorts.

Their chance of success in a pitched battle against Togo's fleet would be small indeed, even taking into consideration what one may assume to be the fact, that more damage has been done to the Japanese ships than the public has been made aware of. Togo has under his command a mobile fleet, officered and manned by an intelligent body of sailors, their wits sharpened by eight month's actual experience of naval warfare in familiar waters.

The Baltic squadron, on the other hand, has been used for little more than show and parade, and an occasional visit of courtesy to a neighbouring Power in European waters. Their officers and men have had no experience of warfare, and it is well-known that, for many years, little attention has been paid to manoeuvres and gunnery in the Russian navy.

A great deal doubtless hinges on the possibility of Port Arthur still remaining in Russian hands, when the fleet arrives. It might then be possible for the five battleships, at present bottled up in the port, to effect a junction with the home fleet, thus strengthening their force considerably. Again, if by that time Port Arthur has not fallen, it is safe to say that the Rossia, Gromovoi and Bogatyr will still be unharmed, for until Port Arthur falls, Japan cannot afford to waste an atom of her strength on Vladivostock. These cruisers would undoubtedly prove a valuable addition to the fleet.

On the other hand, should Port Arthur be in Japanese hands by February, before which time the Baltic squadron cannot possibly arrive, Togo will have a free hand in dealing with them. A small section of his fleet will be sufficient to bottle up the Vladivostok squadron, while he will be able to force a battle when and where he pleases. With his newer ships, practised gunnery and pratical experience, the issue of a general battle would undoubtedly result in his favor. The Russians would of necessity attempt to force a battle, for without a base and consequently bereft of coal and supplies, they would speedly be helpless and fall ready victims to a fleet operating within a few hour's steam from its well equipped bases.

Altogether their case may be regarded almost as hopeless, for even accepting the contingency that Port Arthur still flies the Russian flag, their success in a conflict is extremely doubtful. With Port Arthur in Japan's hands, their chance of success is very slender.

DESPERATE FIGHTING IN NIGHT ATTACK ON FORTS AT PORT ARTHUR.

The Herald's European edition publishes the following from its correspondent:—

Chefoo, 30th August.—A special courier has arrived here from Port Arthur, bringing accounts of the fighting as published, in copies of the Novi Krai, which is edited by Colonel Arwetiff. The paper states that at eleven o'clock on the night of August 24 the Japanese attacking on the east concentrated a great force of infantry opposite a redoubt battery on a steep mountainous position.

Lying prone, the Japanese began to creep along in long lines. The Russians waited until they were beneath the walls, when part of them opened volley firing and the Japanese rolled down the hillside dead and wounded, their rifles rattling after them.

At midnight they advanced again with reckless bravery, dashing over the bodies of their comrades, but were again repulsed.

One company of infantry, however, penetrated the line of defences, but the Russian infantry, shouting "Hurrah!" drew their bayonets and annihilated the enemy, none of whom were left. The brave fellows shouted "Banzai!" with their last breath.

The main body of the Japanese retreated over the hills and then threw searchlights over the scene. More troops advanced, stumbling across the dead and wounded. The Russians waited until they were one hundred yards away, and then fired their machine guns, which were protected by armor plates, and mowed the enemy down like reapers cutting corn.

Still they advanced within fifty yards' range of the rifle volleys, but again retired.

A heavy artillery duel followed. Then once more the Japanese endeavoured to storm the fort. There was a hand to hand fight and the Maxims were used. The piles of dead increased row upon row, and the wounded and dead were mixed together. So near were the infantry and machine guns engaged that men fired point blank at one another.

As one column became demoralized another took its place. Marching steadily forward, the men broke through the Chinese wall in front of the fort and a fierce engagement ensued, twenty thousand rifles crackling amid the roar of all kinds of guns. The Japanese kept their front line complete, each man stepping forward with precision to fill vacancies. Suddenly the Russians ceased fire and, fixing bayonets, charged and swept away the first line. Each thrust of steel got home. The Russian infantry then opened fire on the remainder, who retreated in excellent order.

The Japanese again returned, and fighting went on until a quarter to two a. m. Russian reserves at the port arrived, and the relief was welcome.

At three a. m. the Japanese made another attack. They came on in the same solid masses the men fearlessly breasting a hailstorm of lead and coolly leaping over the rows of wounded. Their advance was covered by a discharge of shrapnel, but the Japanese were literally hurled back.

Daylight revealed heaps of dead banked against the fort's walls.

Little happened during the day and the next night passed quietly.

The Japanese continued bringing up supplies and constructing earthworks, and, despite the terrible fire from the neighboring hills, they placed sixty guns in position near the villages of Hausahem and Sanhandatan.

The Japanese occupy the southern part of Pigeon Bay with four battalions of infantry and two squadrons of cavalry.

Owing to the Russians action in renumbering their forts it is difficult to state the exact positions of the opposing forces. It is certain that the grand assault of the Japanese failed utterly as they were unable to break through the ring of forts in places essential for the capture of the remainder.

The artillery fire on both sides is excellent. As soon as men appear on the hills shelling instantly begins.

The recent advance of the Japanese is described to be like that of a swarm of locusts. They waded through streams of blood and were impaled upon a line of bayonets. Men were killed by wholesale while constructing earthworks, but others stepped into the vacancies, calmly taking up the picks and shovels until whole trenches were swept away.

As the Japanese were climbing on the shoulders of their comrades to scale the fort walls they were stabbed by the bayonets of the Russian soldiers, who were leaning over. Finally, men dropping from exhaustion were trampled on by the fighting troops.

On one occasion at Fort No. I both Russian and Japanese were wedged into a struggling mass between the walls, unable to use their arms. They detached their bayonets, however, and landed recklessly slashing the faces, heads and arms. Many were nearly decapitated. It was, indeed, a regular human shamble.

The roar of the guns was deafening and orders were given by signs. An eye witness says the fights were like the meeting of two stone walls.

The Russian defences are stupendous and their food supplies are adequate. The Russian naval brigade was superb.

We asked recently that we should be allowed to join one or other of the divisions in actual touch with the enemy, reports one of the correspondents with Kuroki's army. Headquarters admitted that this was not a unreasonable request, and thought that it might be granted "under certain conditions." One gentleman sent in his application in the prescribed form, asking for permission to join the 12th Division, as it had patrols in daily contact with the Russians. After three days' delay he got a letter, saying that he could visit the "headquarters" of the division on a named date "between the hours of one and four," after which he must return to the correspondents' camp without delay. Now the headquarters of the division in question is at least 20 miles in the rear of the points at which the reports say the troops are in contact with the enemy, and a man spending the hours "between one and four" near General Inouye's tent had as much chance of seeing any fighting as he would have of witnessing a performance in the Royal Opera House if he stood in Leicester-square and gazed in the direction of Covent-garden. Other applications of a similar character did not, in at least two cases, receive a reply. —Japan Herald.

The Korea Daily News.

VOL. I, SATURDAY, OCTOBER 8, 1904. No. 71

HONGKONG & SHANGHAI BANKING CORPORATION.

Paid-up Capital.................. $10,000,000
Reserve Fund:—Sterling Reserve... 10,000,000
Silver Reserve..... 7,000,000

27,000,000

Reserve Liability of Proprietors... 10,000,000

HEAD OFFICE, HONGKONG.

London Bankers, London and County Banking Company Limited.

Branches and Agencies,
London.

Amoy,	Hankow	Penang,
Bangkok,	Hiogo,	Rangoon,
Batavia,	Iloilo,	Saigon,
Bombay,	Lyons,	San Francisco,
Calcutta,	Manila,	Singapore,
Colombo,	Nagasaki,	Sourabaya,
Foochow,	New York,	Tientsin,
Hamburg,	Peking,	Yokohama,

Credits granted on approved Securities, and every description of Banking and Exchange business transacted.

Drafts granted on London and the chief Commercial places in Europe, India, Australia, America, China and Japan.

HOLME RINGER & CO., AGENTS,
CHEMULPO.

ON CHEONG & CO., SEOUL.

GENERAL STORE KEEPERS.
Imported provisions, Cooking Utensils Crockery, etc.
FRESH BREAD DAILY.

MITSU BISHI DOCKYARD & ENGINE WORKS,

NAGASAKI.

CODE WORD, "DOCK."

A. 1, A. B. C., and Engineering Codes used.

DOCK No. 1 (at Tategami).

Extreme Length.............. 523 feet
Length on blocks........... 513 ,,
Width of Entrance on Top...... 89 ,,
,, ,, Bottom.... 77 ,,
Water on Blocks at Spring Tide 26½ ,,

DOCK No. 2 (Mukaijima).

Extreme Length.............. 371 feet
Length on Blocks............ 360 ,,
Width of Entrance on Top...... 66 ,,
,, ,, Bottom 53 ,,
Water on Blocks at Spring Tide 22 ,,

PATENT SLIP (at Kosuge).

Can take vessels up to 1,000 tons gross.

THE WORKS are well equipped with the LATEST IMPROVEMENTS, and can execute any kind of work in SHIPBUILDING and MARINE ENGINEERING, as well as in REPAIRING of SHIPS.

The COMPANY'S new powerful steamer OURA-MARU (712 tons, 700 I.H.P.), specially built for SALVAGE PURPOSES, and equipped with necessary gear, is always READY at SHORT NOTICE.

CHARTERED BANK OF INDIA AUSTRALIA & CHINA.

INCORPORATED BY ROYAL CHARTER 1853

HEAD OFFICES:—LONDON.

Paid-up Capital £800,000
Reserve Liability of Shareholders 800,000
Reserve Fund 800,000

Drafts granted upon all the principal places in the world and every description of Exchange and banking business transacted.

E. MEYER & Co., Agents,
Chemulpo.

E. MEYER & CO. Chemulpo.

SOLE AGENTS IN KOREA FOR:

A. T. Morse, Sons & Co's "Fresco" Distemper

In all colours ready for use on walls, Ceilings etc.

and

AVENARIUS CARBOLINEUM

A wood-preserving and antiseptic oil preparation

Against decay, dry-rot, fungus and wood-destroying insects.

A large supply always in Stock.
Prices upon application.

E. MEYER & Co.,
Chemulpo.

LAW UNION & CROWN INS. CO.

Fire risks accepted at Current rates, on go downs, merchandise, dwellings, and other property, subject to usual conditions.

HOLME RINGER & Co.,
Agents, Chemulp

THE METHODIST PUBLISHING HOUSE,

Little WestGate, Seoul.

PRINTING, TYPEWRITER PAPER
CARBON PAPER, VISITING CARDS
STATIONERY, BOOK BINDING
BOOK PUBLISHERS
AMERICAN SCHOOL BOOKS
SPENCERIAN COPY BOOKS
PEN CARBON LETTER AND BILL BOOKS

S. A. BECK, Manager.

DAI-ICHI GINKO.

LIMITED.

(Formerly the First National Bank)

ESTABLISHED 1873

INCORPORATED UNDER PRESENT LAW 1896

Capital - - - - - - - - Yen 5,000,000
Reserve Fund - - - - - 1,500,000

HEAD OFFICE:—TOKIO.

President: Baron SHIBUSAWA.

BRANCHES AND CORRESPONDENTS
In the Principal Cities and Towns of Japan.

Interest Allowed on

Fixed deposits 1 year - - - 6½ per cent
" " 6 months - - - 6 per cent

Special current accounts 1½ sen daily per Y 100
General " " 1 " " " 100

M. TANAKA,
Manager, Chemulpo

HOLME RINGER & Co. Chemulpo.

General Merchants and Government Contractors.

Agents for the leading

Banks

SteamshipCompanies

and

Insurance Companies

Importers of Merchandise of every description.

KAMEYA Z CO.

GENERAL STOREKEEPERS
Chinkokai - - Seoul

(Established 1895, Tokyo)

Confectionery, Hams, Canned Goods, Cutlery, Hirano & Tansan Water. Provisions, Gents, Furnishing goods, Toilet Articles, Travelling Bags, Tobacco, Cigars & Cigarettes Kitchen Utensils. Coffee, Biscuits.

Fresh Goods always kept in Stock.

Prices Moderate

Please come and inspect our goods.

NIPPON YUSEN KAISHA.

JAPANESE MAIL STEAMSHIP CO.

DER MAIL CONTRACT WITH THE IMPERIAL JAPANESE GOVERNMENT.

European Line

Regular Fortnightly Service between Yokohama Kobe, Moji, Shanghai, Hongkong, Singapore, Penang Colombo, Port Said, Marseilles, London and Antwerp

American Line

Regular Fortnightly Service between Hongkong and Seattle, calling at Shanghai, Moji, Kobe, Yokohama and Victoria, B. C.

Australian Line

Regular weekly Service betwen Japan Ports and Australia, calling at Hongkong and Manila.

(Above Three Lines Suspended until further notice).

Shanghai Line

Weekly Service between Shanghai and Japan Ports

Korea Line

Service Kobe, Moji, Nagasaki, Fusan, Chemupo, Coo, Taiku.
S. S. Bahelsberg, 2181 tons.
Service Kobe, Moji, Fusan, Chemulpo, Chinnampo
S. S ARGO, S. S. Ohio.

BORDEN'S CONDENSED MILK CO.

New York, U. S. A.

ALWAYS IN STOCK

Eagle Brand Condensed Milk.

Gold Seal Condensed Milk.

Peerless (Family) Evaporated Cream.

Borden's Malted Milk.

**E. MEYER & CO.
Chemulpo, Korea,**
Sole Agents

ROYAL INSURANCE COMPANY,

Funds exceed £10,000,000

FIRE
AT CURRENT RATES.
LIFE
REDUCED PREMIUM.

HOLME RINGER & Co.,
Agents, Chemulpo.

HOTEL DU PALAIS

SEOUL.

The only first class Hotel in Seoul. Situated in the centre of the city opposite the palace.

Cuisine under the supervision of an experienced French Chef.

Well ventilated and furnished throughout.

TARIFF UPON APPLICATION

L. MARTIN
Proprietor and Manager.

大韓每日申報
대한ᄆᆡ일신보

뎨칠십이호 월요일 일쳔구ᄇᆡᆨ사년십월십일

본샤고ᄇᆡᆨ

본신보ᄂᆞᆫ영어와한어로셕거ᄆᆡ일츌판ᄒᆞᆸ

신문가

한쟝 엽두돈오푼

일삭됴 엽두량닷돈

우표가ᄆᆡ삭닷돈

다맛돈으로밧ᄉᆞᆸ

광고료ᄂᆞᆫ

ᄀᆡ한의쟝단과ᄌᆞ힝의다쇼로즁감ᄒᆞ되렴가로밧을터이오며오ᄅᆡ지아녀대한사람마다다이신문을보실터이니광고내시기를원ᄒᆞ시ᄂᆞᆫ이들은우리신문샤에와셔면약ᄒᆞ심을회망ᄒᆞᆸ

○발힝소 박동대한ᄆᆡ일신보샤법어학교압혜젼영국인셜필림집자리오

샤쟝 영국인 (ᄇᆡ셜)

평양 ᄃᆡ리뎜

○평양효동사ᄂᆞᆫ권미보씨로우리신문관ᄃᆡ리인을ᄐᆡᆨ졍ᄒᆞ엿ᄉᆞ오니평양에계신구람코져ᄒᆞ시ᄂᆞᆫ쳠군ᄌᆞᄂᆞᆫ히ᄃᆡ리뎜에왕림ᄒᆞ와면의ᄒᆞ시ᄋᆞᆸ

샤고

○우리대한ᄆᆡ일신보의목뎍은대한의안녕질셔에관한모든뎨목에ᄃᆡᄒᆞ야ᄂᆞᆫ공평한변론을쥬쟝ᄒᆞᆷ이라우리동신원의담보ᄂᆞᆫ신문보시ᄂᆞᆫ쳠군ᄌᆞ의게ᄒᆞᆼ상보도ᄒᆞ리며편지를긔셔ᄒᆞ여주시ᄂᆞᆫ이ᄂᆞᆫ셩명과반ᄃᆡ를젹어붓치시기를회망ᄒᆞ오니이거슬신문샹에긔ᄌᆡᄒᆞ라ᄂᆞᆫ거시아니오다만극히신용ᄒᆞᄂᆞᆫ즁거를숨고쟈ᄒᆞᆷ이라긔쟈ᄂᆞᆫ아모긔셔던지긔ᄌᆡᄒᆞᆯ쇠되각ᄒᆞᄂᆞᆫ권리를가졋스나되각ᄒᆞᄂᆞᆫ리유를말ᄒᆞᆯ터이오며공즁평화를문란케ᄒᆞᄂᆞᆫ듯ᄒᆞᆫ긔셔ᄂᆞᆫ의례히밧지안켓ᄉᆞᆸ나이다

●본샤셜시이ᄅᆡ로신문을ᄆᆡ양우톄로분젼ᄒᆞ와톄젼부의임의로젼ᄒᆞᆫ듯스로먼곳에ᄂᆞᆫ혹늣게젼ᄒᆞ기도ᄒᆞ며혹몃칠거슬ᄒᆞᆫ겁에젼ᄒᆞ기도ᄒᆞ며혹아니젼ᄒᆞᄂᆞᆫ곳도잇다ᄒᆞ와우리신문을ᄉᆞ랑ᄒᆞ야구람ᄒᆞ시ᄂᆞᆫ쳠군ᄌᆞ의게ᄃᆡᄒᆞ야ᄆᆡ우미안ᄒᆞᆸ기로지금은분젼인을두고ᄆᆡ일일즉이젼ᄒᆞ며아니젼ᄒᆞ거나늣게거나ᄒᆞᆫ폐가업도록ᄒᆞ라ᄒᆞ오니혹아니젼ᄒᆞ거나혹늣게젼ᄒᆞ거나ᄒᆞᆫ일이잇스면본샤로통긔ᄒᆞ여쥬심을회망ᄒᆞᆸ

본샤광고

○본샤신문즁에좌긔ᄒᆞᆫ호수를소용ᄒᆞᆯ데가잇셔이에광고ᄒᆞ오니누구시던지그즁에아모호수던지가져오시ᄂᆞᆫᄃᆡ로미쟝에ᄇᆡᆨ젼두푼식드리리다

뎨이호 뎨삼호 뎨이십호 뎨ᄉᆞ십이호 뎨ᄉᆞ십삼호 뎨오십삼호 뎨오십ᄉᆞ호와뎨오십오호 뎨륙십이호

관보

뎨이쳔구ᄇᆡᆨᄉᆞ십칠호 연속

○보시위뎨일련ᄃᆡ뎨삼대ᄃᆡ부 보병부위 리완죵

○보시위뎨일련ᄃᆡ뎨일대ᄃᆡ부 보병부위 구연호

○보시위뎨일련ᄃᆡ뎨이대ᄃᆡ즁ᄃᆡ쟝 보병졍위 리샹우

○보시위뎨일련ᄃᆡ뎨이대ᄃᆡ부 보병부위 김명훈

○보시위뎨일련ᄃᆡ뎨이대ᄃᆡ향관 일등군ᄉᆞ 쟝셕조

○보시위뎨일련ᄃᆡ뎨삼대ᄃᆡ즁ᄃᆡ쟝 보병졍위 송학슈

○보친위뎨일련ᄃᆡ무긔쥬관 보병부위 ᄐᆡ원엽

○보친위뎨일련ᄃᆡ긔관 보병부위 문덕교

○보친위뎨일련ᄃᆡ뎨일대ᄃᆡ부 보병부 ᄇᆡᆨ락만 참위박쟝환

○보친위뎨일련ᄃᆡ뎨삼대ᄃᆡ부 보병부위 리조영 참위 셔병덕

○보진위뎨일련ᄃᆡ뎨일대ᄃᆡ향관 이등군ᄉᆞ 오직셥

○보진위뎨일련ᄃᆡ뎨일대ᄃᆡ부 보병참위 김동은

○보진위뎨이련ᄃᆡ뎨일대ᄃᆡ부 보병참위 류샹렬

○보진위뎨ᄉᆞ련ᄃᆡ뎨삼대ᄃᆡ부 보병참위 리완규

○보진위뎨오련ᄃᆡ뎨일대ᄃᆡ즁ᄃᆡ쟝 보병졍위 김용승

○보진위뎨륙련ᄃᆡ뎨이대ᄃᆡ부 보병참위 졍쥬교

○륙군보병졍위 졍삼픔 하샹긔

○임륙군보병졍령 보병부령 윤쳘규

○임륙군보병참령 보병졍위 함은쥰

○임륙군보병졍위 보병부위 최셕규 리무영

○보친위뎨일련ᄃᆡ뎨이대ᄃᆡ즁ᄃᆡ쟝 보병졍위 최셕규

○보시위뎨일련ᄃᆡ뎨일대ᄃᆡ부 보병부위 리죵혁

○보친위뎨일련ᄃᆡ뎨이대ᄃᆡ부 보병부위 김홍식

○보진위뎨일련ᄃᆡ뎨일대ᄃᆡ부 보병참위 리지영

○보진위뎨이련ᄃᆡ뎨이대ᄃᆡ부 보병부위 오영근

○보진위뎨이련ᄃᆡ뎨이대ᄃᆡ대ᄃᆡ쟝 보병참령 리민직

○임군부쥬셔관임관륙등 젼쥬ᄉᆞ ᄇᆡᆨ인긔

이샹구월이십이일

○임헌병ᄉᆞ령관 참쟝 원우샹

○면겸임부산항지편소관ᄉᆞ 동ᄅᆡ젼감리 오귀영

○겸임부산항지관소관ᄉᆞ 동ᄅᆡ감리 리무영

○승셔관임관삼등 농샹공부쥬ᄉᆞ 로영긔

이샹구월이십팔일

○임군부쥬ᄉᆞ셔관임관일등 륙품 윤셕영 홍기관

○임군부쥬ᄉᆞ셔판임관이등 륙품 김한됴 리한샹

○임군부쥬ᄉᆞ셔관임관삼등 륙픔 신ᄐᆡ응 김죵한

○임군부쥬ᄉᆞ셔판임관ᄉᆞ등 륙픔 박초양 구품 윤졍구

○임군부쥬ᄉᆞ셔관임관오등 륙품 죠셜하

○임군부쥬ᄉᆞ셔관임관륙등 륙픔 박지양 구픔 심샹취 리보현 최한쥬 고영샹

○임군부기슈셔관임관륙등 구품 함승표

○임군부쥬ᄉᆞ셔관임관륙등 륙품 권ᄐᆡ일 졍경윤 구픔 최ᄐᆡ신 홍일셥 ᄇᆡᆨ봉규 최지용 김샹원 손쥰모 최영호 리관지 안긔인 하두홍 민홍식 박희긍 최지용 신ᄐᆡ희 강한민

○임군부기슈셔관임관륙등 ᄐᆡ셕창

○의원면본관 동ᄐᆡ항경무관 연시ᄐᆡ

○면본직 경위원감독 김샹셥

○보경위원감독 김무관 연시ᄐᆡ

이샹구월이십구일

○명경효면졔쥬셔칙임관일등 궁ᄂᆡ부특진관 리건하

○명경효면졔쥬셔칙임관ᄉᆞ등 샤직셔졔쥬 죠병익

○명샤직셔졔쥬셔칙임관삼등 죵이픔 윤달영

○셔칙임관삼등 쟝례원경 박뎡양

○승셔관임관오등 죵묘셔령 죠병억

○임룡쳔감리셔쥬ᄉᆞ셔관임관륙등 리ᄐᆡ형

○승셔관임관삼등 무안항공립소학교교원 송원셥

○승셔관임관ᄉᆞ등 평안북도관찰부공립소학교교원 면덕룡

○ᄒᆡ림시군용텰도죵ᄉᆞ원 텰도원기ᄉᆞ 최샹돈 강영우

○명경의잔림시군용텰도감찰위원 리쳘영 졍삼품 셔샹션 텰도원기ᄉᆞ 최샹돈 쟝용진 강영우 기슈 리윤영 리쟝하 쥬ᄉᆞ 죠용쥰

이샹십월을일

잡보

○어젼회의 본월오일이후로각부졔대신이쳥ᄃᆡᄒᆞ야어젼회의가되ᄂᆞᆫᄃᆡ 황샹셰옵셔 하슌ᄒᆞ샤ᄀᆞᆯᄋᆞ샤ᄃᆡ문명각국은다단발ᄒᆞ엿스니대한도단발ᄒᆞᆷ이가ᄒᆞ다ᄒᆞ신ᄃᆡ졔대신이다가ᄒᆞᆫ줄노샹쥬ᄒᆞ엿ᄂᆞᆫᄃᆡ참졍신긔션씨가쥬품ᄒᆞ여왈단발여부가ᄀᆡ명샹에샹관이업ᄉᆞ온즉국ᄉᆞ가ᄀᆡ명ᄒᆞ면단발등ᄉᆞᄂᆞᆫ조지기즁이온즉단발이급션무가아니요려졍도치ᄒᆞ옴이최급ᄒᆞ오이다ᄒᆞ온즉단발도역시급무니ᄎᆞᄎᆞ실시케ᄒᆞᆷ이가타고 옥음이나리셧다더라

○잉위쥬차 일본에젼왕ᄒᆞᄂᆞᆫ젼권공ᄉᆞ리지극씨ᄂᆞᆫ인ᄒᆞ야일본에쥬차ᄒᆞ게되리라ᄂᆞᆫ말이잇더라

○ᄐᆡᆨ용인지 삼작일밤에 황샹폐옵셔졔대신을ᄃᆡᄒᆞ샤인지

An accident in the Press-room when the pages were on the press necessitates the omission of one page of our regular advertisements, for which we humbly apologize to the advertisers and readers. We hope to have all the advertisements re-set for to-morrow's issue.----THE PRINTERS.

HONGKONG & SHANGHAI BANKING CORPORATION.

Paid-up Capital.... ....$10,000,000
Reserve Fund:—Sterling Reserve... 10,000,000
Silver Reserve..... 7,000,000

27,000,000
Reserve Liability of Proprietors... 10,000,000

HEAD OFFICE, HONGKONG.

London Bankers, London and County Banking Company Limited.
Branches and Agencies,
London.

Amoy,	Hankow	Penang,
Bangkok,	Hiogo,	Rangoon,
Batavia,	Iloilo,	Saigon,
Bombay,	Lyons,	San Francisco,
Calcutta,	Manila,	Singapore,
Colombo,	Nagasaki,	Sourabaya,
Foochow,	New York,	Tientsin,
Hamburg,	Peking,	Yokohama,

Credits granted on approved Securities, and every description of Banking and Exchange business transacted.

Drafts granted on London and the chief Commercial places in Europe, India, Australia, America, China and Japan.

HOLME RINGER & CO., AGENTS,
CHEMULPO.

ON CHEONG & CO.,
SEOUL.
GENERAL STORE KEEPERS.
Imported provisions, Cooking Utensils
Crockery, etc.
FRESH BREAD DAILY.

MITSU BISHI DOCKYARD & ENGINE WORKS,
NAGASAKI.

CODE WORD, "DOCK."

A. 1, A. B. C., and Engineering Codes used.

DOCK No. 1 (at Tategami).

Extreme Length..............523 feet
on blocks .... 513 ,,
of Entrance on Top......89 ,,
,, ,, Bottom....77 ,,
Water on Blocks at Spring Tide 26½ ,,

DOCK No. 2 (Mukaijima).

Extreme Length..............371 feet
Length on Blocks.............360 ,,
Width of Entrance on Top......66 ,,
,, ,, Bottom 53 ,,
Water on Blocks at Spring Tide 22 ,,

PATENT SLIP (at Kosuge).

Can take vessels up to 1,000 tons gross.

THE WORKS are well equipped with the LATEST IMPROVEMENTS, and can execute any kind of work in SHIPBUILDING and MARINE ENGINEERING, as well as in REPAIRING of SHIPS.

The COMPANY'S new powerful steamer OURA-MARU (712 tons, 700 I.H.P.), specially built for SALVAGE PURPOSES, and equipped with necessary gear, is always READY at SHORT NOTICE.

CHARTERED BANK OF INDIA AUSTRALIA & CHINA.

INCORPORATED BY ROYAL CHARTER 1853

HEAD OFFICES:—LONDON.

Paid-up Capital £800,000

Reserve Liability of Shareholders 800,000

Reserve Fund 800,000

Drafts granted upon all the principal places in the world and every description of Exchange and banking business transacted.

E. MEYER & Co., Agents,
Chemulpo.

E. MEYER & CO.

Chemulpo.

SOLE AGENTS IN KOREA FOR:
A. T. Morse, Sons & Co's "Fresco" Distemper

In all colours ready for use on walls, Ceilings etc.
and
AVENARIUS CARBOLINEUM

A wood-preserving and antiseptic oil preparation

Against decay, dry-rot, fungus and wood-destroying insects.

A large supply always in Stock.
Prices upon application.

E. MEYER & Co.,
Chemulpo.

LAW UNION & CROWN INS. CO.

Fire risks accepted at Current rates, on godowns, merchandise, dwellings, and other property, subject to usual conditions.

HOLME RINGER & Co.,
Agents, Chemulp

THE METHODIST PUBLISHING HOUSE,
Little WestGate, Seoul.

PRINTING, TYPEWRITER PAPER
CARBON PAPER, VISITING CARDS
STATIONERY, BOOK BINDING
BOOK PUBLISHERS
AMERICAN SCHOOL BOOKS
SPENCERIAN COPY BOOKS
PEN CARBON LETTER AND BILL BOOKS

S. A. BECK, Manager.

DAI-ICHI GINKO.
LIMITED.
(Formerly the First National Bank)

ESTABLISHED 1873

INCORPORATED UNDER PRESENT LAW 1896

Capital - - - - - - - - Yen 5,000,000
Reserve Fund - - - - - 1,500,000

HEAD OFFICE:—TOKIO.

President: Baron SHIBUSAWA.

BRANCHES AND CORRESPONDENTS
In the Principal Cities and Towns of Japan.
Interest Allowed on
Fixed deposits 1 year - - - 6½ per cent
" " 6 months - - - 6 per cent

Special current accounts 1½ sen daily per Y 100
General " " 1 " " " 100

M. TANAKA,
Manager, Chemulpo

HOLME RINGER & Co.

Chemulpo.

General Merchants and Government Contractors.

Agents for the leading
Banks
SteamshipCompanies
and
Insurance Companies

Importers of Merchandise of every description.

KAMEYA & CO.
GENERAL STOREKEEPERS
Chinkokai - - Seoul
(*Established 1895, Tokyo*)

Confectionery, Hams, Canned Goods, Cutlery, Hirano & Tansan Water. Provisions, Gents, Furnishing goods, Toilet Articles, Travelling Bags, Tobacco, Cigars & Cigarettes Kitchen Utensils. Coffee, Biscuits

Fresh Goods always kept in Stock.
Prices Moderate
Please come and insbect our goods.

NIPPON YUSEN KAISHA.
JAPANESE MAIL STEAMSHIP CO.

DER MAIL CONTRACT WITH THE IMPERIAL JAPANESE GOVERNMENT

European Line

Regular Fortnightly Service between Yokohama Kobe, Moji, Shanghai, Hongkong, Singapore, Penang Colombo, Port Said, Marseilles, London and Antwerp

American Line

Regular Fortnightly Service between Hongkong and Seattle, calling at Shanghai, Moji, Kobe, Yokohama and Victoria, B. C.

Australian Line

Regular weekly Service betwen Japan Ports and Australia, calling at Hongkong and Manila.
(Above Three Lines Suspended until further notice).

Shanghai Line

Weekly Service between Shanghai and Japan Ports

Korea Line

Service Kobe, Moji, Nagasak i, Fusan, Chemupo, Coo, Taiku.
S. S. Bahelsberg, 2181 tons.
Service Kobe, Moji, Fusan, Chemulpo, Chinnampo
S. S ARGO, S. S. Ohio.

BORDEN'S CONDENSED MILK CO.

New York, U. S. A.

ALWAYS IN STOCK

Eagle Brand Condensed Milk.

Gold Seal Condensed Milk.

Peerless (Family) Evaporated Cream.

Borden's Malted Milk.

E. MEYER & CO.
Chemulpo, Korea,
Sole Agents

ROYAL INSURANCE COMPANY,
Funds exceed £10,000,000
FIRE
AT CURRENT RATES.
LIFE
REDUCED PREMIUM.
HOLME RINGER & Co.,
Agents, Chemulpo.

HOTEL DU PALAIS

SEOUL.

The only first class Hotel in Seoul. Situated in the centre of the city opposite the palace.

Cuisine under the supervision of an experienced French Chef.

Well ventilated and furnished throughout.

TARIFF UPON APPLICATION

L. MARTIN
Proprietor and Manager.

를하ᄉᆞᆸ시고리셩렬죠병호등제씨를드ᄋᆞ홉ᄉᆞᆸ노ᄒᆞ옵셧ᄂᆞᆫᄃᆡ신참졍이샹 주ᄒᆞ되민셩이불복ᄒᆞ오니공쥬관찰신긔ᄐᆡᆨ과광쥬관찰김셰긔와ᄃᆡ구관찰장승원을레의ᄒᆞ옴이가ᄒᆞ오이다ᄒᆞᆫ미ᄌᆞ 샹으로가랍ᄒᆞ셧다더라

○징병법연구 신샹도여둔토를군ᄃᆡ로부속ᄒᆞ고징병법을연구ᄒᆞ야실시ᄒᆞ기로어느대신이샹 주ᄒᆞ엿다더라

○방문고문 일젼에참졍신긔션씨와참찬허위씨가탁지고문관목하뎐씨를차져가본즉목하뎐씨의말이하로밧비한국화폐를금권히기탄ᄒᆞᆯ터인ᄃᆡ원위화를시로이만든슈는업스니불가불일본서쓰던대은젼을너여다쓰자고ᄒᆞ더라ᄒᆞ더라

○츄원변제 중추원을관의원이라고기칭ᄒᆞ고학식이고명ᄒᆞ고시무에련숙ᄒᆞᆫ사ᄅᆞᆷ을퇴ᄎᆞᆨᄒᆞ야관제ᄃᆡ로셜시ᄒᆞ자ᄂᆞᆫ의론이잇다더라

○이근평수받힝 공쥬관찰ᄉᆞ의뎐보를거ᄒᆞᆫ즉군산항일본령ᄉᆞ가병졍포힝ᄒᆞᆫᄉᆞ건을ᄉᆞ칙ᄒᆞ기위ᄒᆞ야본부에루련ᄒᆞ다가부강등디로출발ᄒᆞ엿다고ᄒᆞ엿더라

○교셥수안 공쥬진위ᄃᆡ병졍과일인간에야료된일에관ᄒᆞ야ᄂᆞᆫ즉시군산항일본령ᄉᆞ의보고가잇슴으로일본공ᄉᆞ가외부로조회ᄒᆞ고속히진압ᄒᆞ기를쳥구ᄒᆞ엿ᄂᆞᆫᄃᆡ한국졍부에서ᄂᆞᆫ엇더케조쳐ᄒᆞᄂᆞᆫ일이업다ᄒᆞ야일본군ᄃᆡ에서병졍을파송ᄒᆞ야진압케ᄒᆞ엿다ᄂᆞᆫᄃᆡ그포힝ᄒᆞᆫ병졍과평슌ᄒᆞᆫ장관등은고소ᄒᆞ고히도관찰ᄉᆞ도고취망을면치못ᄒᆞ겟ᄂᆞᆫ고로한국졍부에서그쟝교등과관찰ᄉᆞ를징벌ᄒᆞ고일본인의손ᄒᆡ된거슬빈샹금무려주ᄂᆞᆫ일을담임ᄒᆞ며그ᄉᆞ건의처결ᄒᆞᄂᆞᆫ것슨모다한국졍부에서ᄒᆞᄂᆞᆫᄃᆡ로들리이고일본헌병의게피착된자를너여줄터이라ᄂᆞᆫᄃᆡ방금피추간교셥ᄒᆞᄂᆞᆫ중이라더라

○양쳔만원 근일너로의졍부에서ᄌᆡ졍을졍리ᄒᆞᆯᄎᆞ로은화일쳔만원을일본에차관ᄒᆞ야지금통힝ᄒᆞᄂᆞᆫ못된돈은이를졀환ᄒᆞ슈ᄒᆞ야쓰지마자ᄂᆞᆫ의론이무ᄎᆞ제츌되엿ᄂᆞᆫᄃᆡ아직결졍은아니ᄒᆞ엿다더라

외보

○아제친졍 아라사경셩뎐보를거ᄒᆞᆫ즉아라사황제께셔구동에출졍ᄒᆞ신다ᄂᆞᆫ말이셩잇ᄂᆞᆫᄃᆡ금번은그근거가잇ᄂᆞᆫ거시재금은황실의소용ᄒᆞᆯ준거가완젼이셩비되엿다더라

○봉고변츠교 봉텬뎐보를거ᄒᆞᆫ즉장가구로서온뎐보에ᄒᆞ엿스되아국이몽고교후에셔몽고병이친명을초모ᄒᆞ야미명에상이원셔쥬교쏘이원셔더주어서연속히초모ᄒᆞᄂᆞᆫᄃᆡ몽고인이덕국총과탄약을사셔자조쥬운ᄒᆞᆫ다더라

○로국퇴문 거월이십칠일샹히발뎐에왈봉텬부에잇ᄂᆞᆫ젼교ᄉᆞ의보고에운ᄒᆞ되로국이근자에슈레이빅오십좌에이빅만루블에치나되ᄂᆞᆫ물픔을실어몽고신왕의게퇴문을보베ᄂᆞᆫᄃᆡ텰령과밋가이멘을지나몽고로드러가ᄂᆞᆫ거슬목격ᄒᆞ엿다더라

○봉텬시젼 거월이십구일에구로파트긴장군의보고에왈일본군이동방과남방과밋젼면에셔결진ᄒᆞ야공격을시작ᄒᆞᆫ다ᄒᆞ엿더라

○졈령고디 ᄒᆞ롭군의좌익졍찰ᄃᆡ가연ᄐᆡ졍거쟝동북의놉ᄒᆞᆫ쌍을졈령ᄒᆞ엿다더라

○로병리습 거월이십팔일에로군의보병과긔병오빅명이동가둔방면에셔쳠츌ᄒᆞ야대포이문으로써승영의군ᄃᆡ의젼초를포격ᄒᆞᆫ후에퇴각ᄒᆞ엿다더라

○만쥬샹셜 마련평부근에ᄂᆞᆫ거월이십일브터셔리가오고이십이일에ᄂᆞᆫ눈이왓고료양에도셔리가왓다ᄒᆞ더라

론셜

아라사의패퇴ᄒᆞᆫᄃᆡ

○최근ᄒᆞᆫ공보를거ᄒᆞᆫ즉패퇴ᄒᆞᆫᄃᆡᄂᆞᆫ최우에나츌발ᄒᆞᆯ계획이라ᄒᆞ며쏘다른뎐보에ᄂᆞᆫ아황폐하ᄯᅦ오셔친감ᄒᆞ신후급발케ᄒᆞ실뜻으로긔보ᄒᆞᆫ셰이로츌가ᄒᆞ려ᄒᆞ시ᄂᆞᆫ고로아라사의셰란은승젼들은구동으로나오ᄂᆞᆫ승로에셔그합ᄃᆡ를기다린다ᄒᆞ엿고쏘혼돈신문에ᄂᆞᆫ계지ᄒᆞ기를이합ᄃᆡ에젼투함륙쳑과최대슌양함오쳑과젼용슌양함수쳑외에쏘다수의수뢰졍파밋과계젼셥이쳑을더ᄒᆞ여편셩ᄒᆞ엿다ᄒᆞ엿고쏘평론ᄒᆞ기를군함수효ᄂᆞᆫ비록적디아니ᄒᆞ나제조ᄒᆞᆫ지가오릭된자ㅣ반이나넘은중젼용슌양함셔비젹이라ᄂᆞᆫ거슨근자셔덕국빅인죡셔양에셔사용ᄒᆞ든바덕국비모에도샹히오리도되엿슨즉도르국젼투ᄒᆞ기에도경단이낫슬터이니젼투ᄒᆞ기에필요치못ᄒᆞᆯ섄더러쏘ᄒᆞᆫ다른비와비교ᄒᆞᆯ진ᄃᆡ속력이대단히엽슬터인즉도리혀방ᄋᆡ룰고위퇴ᄒᆞᆯ지라고ᄒᆞ엿스니과연이러ᄒᆞᆯ진ᄃᆡ패퇴ᄒᆞᆫᄃᆡᄂᆞᆫ미오조혼즁노암앗더니셜샹일죡다르군함만도못ᄒᆞᆯ터이오쏘지동양으로나올ᄯᅢ로말ᄒᆞ드리도지체ᄒᆞᄂᆞᆫ비들로말미암아속력엿ᄂᆞᆫ비도도리혀관계를당ᄒᆞᆯ지니이왕에도세샹사ᄅᆞᆷ이베르고ᄒᆞ기ᄂᆞᆫ일아젼쟁에일본이승리를만히ᄒᆞ리라든줄노알앗거ᄂᆞᆯ아라사이도리혀퓌ᄒᆞ엿ᄂᆞᆫᄃᆡ려웅지금당ᄒᆞ야서ᄂᆞᆫ일본히군이여탐발동안에젼쟁에실지샹경력이만히되엿ᄂᆞᆫ디ᄯᅩᄒᆞᆫ항로의젼신을확실히졍각ᄒᆞ엿스나아라사패퇴ᄒᆞᆫᄃᆡᄂᆞᆫ긔왕관병식ᄒᆞᆫ번ᄒᆞᆫ이후로쟝관이하병졸ᄭᅡ지라도다른경력은업섯고며러히동안을병수조련ᄒᆞᆷ에주의치아니ᄒᆞ엿ᄂᆞᆫ지라그럼으로려슌에잇ᄂᆞᆫ함ᄃᆡ도병속에든거와갓치잇셧스되다른변동이업셧스나엇지던지패퇴ᄒᆞᆫᄃᆡ젼투함다셧쳑만도바ᄒᆞᆯ지경이면평셰를합ᄒᆞ야평쟝이싸호러ᄒᆞᆯ지니만일그ᄯᅢ에도려슌구안을합남지못ᄒᆞᆯ지경이면항구안에갓처잇든병함셰쳑도필경완젼ᄒᆞᆯ터이요일본셔히샹위협ᄃᆡ에ᄂᆞᆫ조곰도힘을쓰지못ᄒᆞᆯ터이니

패퇴ᄒᆞᆫᄃᆡ에슌양함쳠부ᄒᆞᆫ것도이ᄯᅢ에ᄂᆞᆫ심히긴요ᄒᆞ게될거시니그함ᄃᆡ도착ᄒᆞ기젼에아모조록함남ᄒᆞ야일인의수중에만넘케되면ᄌᆞ유로힝동ᄒᆞ기에도밋오조ᄒᆞᆯ터이요약간군병으로도ᄒᆞᆷ히샹위에잇ᄂᆞᆫ아함ᄃᆡ를확ᄒᆞ기도심히편리ᄒᆞᆯ지라아라사에서ᄂᆞᆫ아모리급속ᄒᆞ게ᄒᆞ려ᄒᆞ드라도필경불구이퓌될터인지라오날날셔지아국패ᄃᆡ진이련슌항구안에날리ᄂᆞᆫ것도진실지로ᄒᆞ우연ᄒᆞᆫ일이요ᄯᅩᄒᆞᆫ우금셔지못ᄒᆞᆼ거ᄒᆞ야지탕ᄒᆞᄂᆞᆫ것도밋지못ᄒᆞᆫ바인즉요수이아라사에셔준비ᄒᆞᆫ다ᄒᆞᆷ이일인의슈중의드러간후에될지경이면엇지귀히지아니ᄒᆞ리오

잡보

○보관피살 작일하오삼ᄉᆞ시량에일본위관이인등ᄉᆞ이인헌병률쳔인이대국신문사에ᄃᆡ도ᄒᆞ야본월칠일본신문론셜에무삼관계가잇다ᄒᆞ고방쟝반이나발간ᄒᆞᆫ신문을거두어곳ᄌᆞᆼ에너코피쇄ᄒᆞ고일본수령부명령잇기젼에ᄂᆞᆫ발간치못ᄒᆞᆯ줄노본사사장의표를밧고갓ᄂᆞᆫᄃᆡ저쟝일에일인이히사사원모모씨쟝을낫낫치슈힝ᄒᆞ엿다더라

○ᄃᆡ수ᄃᆡ젼 만쥬등디에일본군위문ᄃᆡ수로젼왕ᄒᆞᄂᆞᆫ위문ᄃᆡ수권중현씨일힝이젼관을기다려발졍ᄒᆞᆯ터인ᄃᆡ려비ᄂᆞᆫ셤쳔원이오일본군에조숑ᄒᆞᄂᆞᆫ물픔은연초와각셕술인ᄃᆡ가액이이만수쳔ᄉᆞ십원을지발ᄒᆞ엿더라

○시찰파항도츌발 일본에젼왕ᄒᆞᄂᆞᆫ시찰모모씨와류학싱수삼ᄉᆞ인이작일샹오ᄯᅢ에츌렬거로하인ᄒᆞ야즉시발셥ᄒᆞ엿더라

○죠졍론칙 외부에서너부로죠회ᄒᆞ되공쥬진위ᄃᆡ병졍이야료ᄒᆞᆫᄉᆞ로일본공ᄉᆞ가본ᄃᆡ신을면ᄃᆡᄒᆞ야말ᄒᆞ기를공쥬관찰ᄉᆞ가부하ᄃᆡ방에즁ᄃᆡᄒᆞᆫᄉᆞ건을진무ᄒᆞ야됴사치아니ᄒᆞᄂᆞᆫ거슬귀졍부에서조쳐ᄒᆞᆷ이한만ᄒᆞ니본공ᄉᆞ가심이유감ᄒᆞ다ᄒᆞᆫ바히도관찰ᄉᆞ가히ᄉᆞ건에됴사ᄒᆞᆷ을담임치아니ᄒᆞᆷ으로히ᄃᆡ방ᄃᆡ위관과병졸이일헌병의게압샹ᄒᆞᆷ이되엿스니샹히긔탄ᄒᆞᆯ지라히관찰ᄉᆞ를론칙ᄒᆞ라ᄒᆞ엿더라

○광찰보고 광쥬관찰ᄉᆞ가외부로보고ᄒᆞ되구월십륙일함평군보에ᄒᆞ기를일본인일명이본군읍니앞쟝시에리도ᄒᆞ야본군민김긔문과쟁힐ᄒᆞ야김가가일인을란타ᄒᆞ야중샹ᄒᆞ엿기치로ᄎᆞ로목포항으로호송ᄒᆞ엿더니미구에히항령ᄉᆞ가훈령ᄒᆞ기를히일인이광월이십이일에치ᄉᆞᄒᆞᆷ으로슈졈을파송ᄒᆞᆫ다ᄒᆞ고일슌사와리도ᄒᆞ야히졍범김긔문을착거ᄒᆞ고간범은도타라ᄒᆞ엿다ᄒᆞ엿더라

○역부가쳥 히쥬관찰ᄉᆞ김학슈씨가보고ᄒᆞ기를빅쳔군역부팔빅명을일인의광산남쳔뎜탈도역소로보낸거시샹금회환치아니ᄒᆞ엿ᄂᆞᆫᄃᆡ이졔쏘ᄉᆞ빅명을더청구ᄒᆞᆫ즉츄슈ᄯᅢ를당ᄒᆞ야민졍을싱각ᄒᆞᆯ지라일공관에젼조ᄒᆞ야히역부쳥구를ᄃᆡ지케ᄒᆞ라ᄒᆞ엿더라

○법훈경쳥 법부에셔경무쳥에훈령ᄒᆞ기를ᄃᆡ뎌죄범횡쳑ᄒᆞᆷ은경무직칙이오쳥리검죄ᄒᆞᆷ은재판쇼무라각각그직임에규칙장졍이잇거ᄂᆞᆯ근리귀쳥에셔후ᄒᆞᆼ쳥ᄒᆞ야뢰포ᄒᆞ며혹ᄉᆞ송에간련ᄒᆞ야구슈ᄒᆞ야달이지니고히가넘ᄂᆞᆫ다ᄒᆞ니실로그리ᄒᆞ면귀관ᄒᆞᆯ바일너니일작에본ᄃᆡ신이임뒤ᄒᆞ엿ᄉᆞᆫ바에경무쳥에레포ᄒᆞᆫ죄범ᄂᆞᆫ이심수시안으로히졍케관소로윌송ᄒᆞ야장졍을신명케ᄒᆞ라신 쳐분을봉승ᄒᆞ엿스니곳이ᄃᆡ로거힝ᄒᆞ야위월홈이업게ᄒᆞ라ᄒᆞ엿더라

뎐보

십월일일　공ᄉᆞ관쳐뎐

○료양방면뎐쟁 료양방면의젹군의형편에관ᄒᆞᆫ십월칠일에ᄃᆡ본영에착ᄒᆞᆫ뎐보를츅합ᄒᆞᆫ즉십월수일에아방군과평ᄐᆡᄌᆞ와봉텬부진과밋혼하좌편에잇ᄂᆞᆫ우리젼초에게향ᄒᆞ야진ᄒᆞᆫ젹병이와서습격ᄒᆞ엿스나이거슨다쳐셔물니쳣고젹군의엇던부ᄃᆡᄂᆞᆫ졍봉을넘엇고혼하우편쟝탄에잇ᄂᆞᆫ젹군은일부분만남겨두고본ᄃᆡᄂᆞᆫ방으로퇴각ᄒᆞᆫ듯ᄒᆞ고동ᄐᆡᄌᆞ부근에ᄂᆞᆫ젹병이업다ᄒᆞ엿더라

TELEGRAMS.

Tokyo, Oct. 8th.

On the 4th inst. a body of the enemy's scouts attacked our advance guard on the Mukden road but were speedily dispersed. Some of the enemy were attired in Chinese clothing.

The committee of six to visit Japan left yesterday afternoon. Mr. Hagiwara departed by the same train.

On the 5th inst. at a session of the Council, His Majesty expressed his opinion that the removal of top-knots would be a step in the right direction towards civilization.

General Kwon Chung Hyen, the bearer of messages to the Japanese army in Manchuria, will leave shortly for the seat of war. His expenses are estimated at 3,000 yen and he will convey presents of wine and tobacco equivalent to 24,000 yen, to the troops.

The Japanese authorities have demanded the punishment of the officers of the local guard of Kongchu, where the house of a Japanese was recently wrecked by the soldiers. They also intimate that the Governor should be punished for his inability to prevent such disturbances.

Yesterday the offices of a Korean newspaper, the Che Kuk Sinmun, were visited by Japanese gendarmes, who ordered printing to be stopped and forbade any future issues to be published. No reason was given and the editor is at a loss to know what offence he has given.

The Foreign Office are in receipt of a communication from the American Minister, notifying the Korean Government of an International Railway Convention to be held in Washington in May next. The Korean Government are invited to send delegates, who are promised every assistance and convenience should they accept.

It is announced on reliable authority that the British Admiralty has decided to make Jamaica a first class naval station. Half the North American squadron henceforth will be kept in these waters. This change is due to the strategic importance of the island in view of the construction of the Panama Canal, and American activity in the Isle of Pines and Cuba. Extensive fortifications are planned to guard Jamaican harbours.

"Our silent Navy: Is it forgotten?" is the title of a pamphlet published by the Westminister Press, and forming the first volume of the Navy and Empire series. It is made up of replies by the leading naval writers of the day to the question—What do you consider the best means of creating among the general public a real interest and sympathy towards the Navy? Mr. Rudyard Kipling's answer is, "By making the general public liable to serve in the Navy. Nothing quickens one's sympathy with another man's work so much as the possibility of having to do that work oneself."

Sir Marcus Samuel, ex-Lord Mayor of London, has just received, through the Japanese Minister, Viscount Hayashi, the order of the Knight Commandership of the Rising Sun, conferred upon him by the Mikado. For 25 years the firm of which Sir Marcus Samuel is the head has been intimately associated with Japan, and has had close relations with the Japanese Government. The firm issued the first Japanese gold loan in Europe, and later, with the consent of the Government, issued the municipal loans for the Yokohama waterworks and the Osaka harbour works.

The Korea Daily News.

Issued at 5 P. M. daily except Sundays.

Rate of Subscription :—

Per Year,	Yen 25.
Per Quarter,	Yen 7.
Per Month,	Yen 2.50.

Postage in Korea not charged extra.
Postage abroad charged extra.

Advertisements, 50 sen per day for 1 inch or less.
5 yen per month per inch.
50 yen per year per inch.

All communications to

E. T. BETHELL,
Editor and Publisher,
Pak-tong, Seoul.

Owing to an unfortunate accident in the press room, two pages of type of to-day's issue were pied. We must therefore ask our readers' indulgence for the delay and incompleteness of to-day's issue.

SCANDAL IN TOKIO.

The "Japan Gazette" of October 1st says :—

"The fact that relations between Baron Miyoji Ito, ex-Cabinet Minister, and the Katsura Cabinet together with the Elder Statesmen are not as smooth as before is now proved by the Tokyo "Nichi Nichi" Shimbun.

"In the "Street Jottings" column of the "Nichi Nichi" of Sept. 27th, it was intimated that Csunts Inouye and Matsukata had diverted Y2,000,000 of the subscriptions for the Imperial Soldiers' Relief Society (of which they are officers) for the relief of the 130th Bank. The two Counts are naturally indignant at the "Nichi Nichi's" statement. Baron Ito is proprietor of the "Nichi Nichi." Some one attempted to act as arbitrator but in vain. Correspondence was exchanged between the two Counts and they wrote a joint Note in which they severed all ties of friendship with Baron Ito.

"On the afternoon of Sept. 29th the Counts sent Mr. Ariga, as a messenger to the Baron, to convey this Note. Baron Ito was greaty surprised and sent a confidential messenger to Baron Count Katsura, Premier, that night, requesting him to assist in a reconciliation. Count Katsura, who had already learned the facts from Count Inouye, absolutely declined to accede to the Baron's request. Baron Ito, therefore, went to Oiso yesterday to ask Marquis Ito to assist in effecting a compromise.

"Mr. Tsudzuki, private secretary to Marquis Ito in the latter's capacity as President of the Privy Council, visited Oiso to-day in this connection.

"There is said to be but little hope at present of settling the trouble quietly and it is feared that it may become the subject of a big political libel suit. It is also considered of social significance."

Our readers may remember that the 130th Bank of Japan was some time ago reported to be in difficulties, and that the Government went to its assistance with a heavy loan at 3%.

There was considerable outcry at the low rate of interest, and yet it still appears that the Bank is in as bad a position as it ever was.

That the "Nichi Nichi's" statement is correct we do not for a moment believe. In an emergency and in default of any other ready cash, a part of the Soldiers' Relief Society's funds may have been lent on good collateral security, but that any part of the Society's funds was "diverted" or improperly applied to the relief of the bank, we refuse to believe.

The ridiculous hair-cutting operations are still going on. After much thought we have hit upon what may be reason for the strong predilection shown by pro-Japanese agitators for this "reform." It is to some extent the severance of a link with China. Meanwhile the Il-chin-hoi still exists and of its ulterior aims we know no more than do its rabble of supporters who cut their hair, receive their daily wage, and shout "Down with everything" whenever they are told to.

THE NAVAL BATTLE OFF PORT ARTHUR.

RUSSIAN ADMIRAL'S STIRRING STORY.

The following despatch was sent on August 18 to the Tsar by Rear-Admiral Reitzenstein from Shanghai:—

At five o'clock on the morning of August 10 the squadron began to move into the outer roadstead. At half past eight the following vessels left single file, preceded by mine-clearing launches:—"Tsarevitch" (flying the flag of Rear-Admiral Witgert, commanding the squadron) "Retvisan," "Pobieda," "Peresziet" (flying the flag of Rear-Admiral Prince Ukhtomsky, commanding the ironclad division), "Sevastopol, "Poltava," "Askold" (flying the flag of Rear-Admiral Reitzenstein, commanding the cruiser division), "Pallas," and "Diana."

The cruiser "Novik" went ahead of the squadron. Two gunboats and the second division of torpedo vessels accompanied the squadron to protect the flotilla of mine-clearing boats on their way back. The steamer "Mongolia," flying the Red Cross flag, sailed on one side of the squadron. The passage across the mined roadstead was accomplished very fortunately, but took two hours.

At nine o'clock the commander of the squadron had hoisted the signal to make for Vladivostock.

Just as the sortie began, the enemy's ships cemmenced to assemble from different points At a quarter-past ten the flotilla of nine dredgers with the sloops, gunboats, and torpedo-boats returned to Port Arthur, and the squadron steamed out, making at first eight and then ten knots, and reached the open sea. At noon the squadron was doing 13 knots.

A squadron of the enemy, composed of the battleships "Asahi," "Mikasa," a vessel of the "Fuji" type, one of the "Shikishima" type, and the armoured cruisers "Nisshin" and 'Kasuga," was to our port steaming so as to cross our course. On the horizon were three cruisers of the "Matsushima" type, an armoured cruiser of the "Iwate" type, three cruisers of the "Takasago" type, and forty-four torpedo-boats. The enemy's squadron suddenly turned and went back on its coarse, while we wheeled to the right and separated from it by steering a zigzag course.

THROUGH THE ENEMY'S LINE.

Ultimately the two fleets got within range and the first battle commenced. Soon afterwards both fleets came about, continuing to manoeuvre in a zigzag. Separating from us, the Japanese again turned and followed the same course as ourselves. The first fight then finished. In the battle the "Askold" was struck in the forward funnel by a shell, which rendered the forward boiler useless.

The cruiser squadron now left the line and took up a position with the leading ship, level with the "Tsarevitch" on the port side. The Japanese fleet again approached us, and at a quarter to six, when it had come within forty cables, the second battle opened. The "Tsarevitch" put about and, steaming along the line, signalled, "The Admiral transfers the command." The senior Admiral was Rear-Admiral Prince Ukhtomsky.

Seeing that the enemy was endeavouring to surround our squadron, which at this moment was falling back, while pouring in a withering fire on the enemy's battleships with is stern guns, I decided to break through the weakest spot in the enemy's line without loss of time. Having signalled to my squrdron to follow me, I left, with the "Askold" at the head, to cut a passage. We were struck by the opening shots. Behind me came the "Novik," and at some distance followed the "Palada" and the "Diana." The cruiser squadron was sent to cut another passage and encountered four of the enemy's second-class cruisers and torpedo-boats, while to the right of it were three cruisers of the "Matsushima" type.

SHELLS FALL LIKE HAIL.

The seven Japanese ships riddled our cruisers with shells. Approaching the enemy's circle, I remarked that one of the four cruisers blocking our way was a vessel of the "Asama" type. The quick-firing guns of the "Askold" seemed to do some damage to the three Japanese second-class cruisers, while we also set fire to the big cruiser which then retired, leaving the "Askold" a free passage. Four of the enemy's battleships then approached and attacked the "Askold," firing four torpedoes, which, however, did not hit her. A Japanese torpedoboat was sunk by a lucky shot from one of the "Askold's" 6-in. guns, while another retreated precipitately.

The fight, which was of a most severe character, lasted twenty minutes. Shells fell like hail, and did much damage to the "Askold," which, however, succeeded in getting through the enemy's line, followed by the "Pallada" and "Diana."

The Japanese cruisers started in pursuit of the "Askold" and the "Novik," but steaming at a speed of twenty knots, we rapidly drew away from them. The Japanese ultimately gave up the pursuit, and consequently slowed down to wait for the other ships. Moreover, the damage done to funnels and boilers and holes below the water-line rendered slow steaming necessary. I went on slowly until dawn, shaping a course which kept me well out to sea in order to avoid torpedo attacks from Shantung. The cruiser "Novik," which possesses a good turn of speed, was allowed to act independently.

SEVEN SHIPS TO ONE.

In order to gain time in view of the possible attacks, and in conformity with the plan for breaking through the blockading fleet, the "Askold" shortly after dawn put on speed. It was then discovered that the "Askold" had suffered severely from the concentrated fire of the seven Japanese ships, which was directed against her alone. The destruction of two of the vessel's funnels necessitated an increase in the quantity of coal consumed, and obliged us to give full play to the ventilators, which led to a greatly increased emission of sparks.

In consequence of the damage done to the ships, and the short supply of coal, I was obliged to give up my intention of proceeding to Vladivostock through the Korean Archipelago, and I decided to make for the neutral port of Shanghai.

On August 12 I arrived in the Wanpu River and went into dock. The "Askold" had two of her funnels carried away, while the other three were riddled with shot. One of her boilers was damaged, and four holes were made below the water line and six above. One officer and ten men were killed, while four officers and forty-four men were wounded.

I cannot fairly make any distinction between the commanders, officers, engineers, doctors, and seamen, all of whom fulfilled their duties bravely, and faced the enemy without fear. During the fighting the chaplain heroically went from one part of the ship to another with his cross, giving his benediction to the men, while the doctors, under a hail of shell, removed the wounded to a place of safety.—Reuter, Japan Times.

A HEAVY BILL.

The acting magistrate of Pyeng Yang is in great distress and has applied to the Home Department to find him a way out of his difficulty.

It appears that the Japanese Military authorities have repaired some 25 or 30 miles of road in his district and have sent the bill in to him for payment. It amounts to 33,767 yen, and as there are no funds to meet it with all the Korean officials are panic-stricken. The vice-magistrate and chief clerk have bolted and the magistrate seems to fear that the Japanese may take the law into their own hands and attempt to collect the money direct from the people.

In this case, the magistrate says, there would soon be absolutely no one left in his district.

A list of 46 candidates for study in Japan was submitted to the Japanese Legation yesterday.

The Korea Daily News.

VOL. I, MONDAY, OCTOBER 10, 1904. No. 72

HONGKONG & SHANGHAI BANKING CORPORATION.

Paid-up Capital..... ....$10,000,000
Reserve Fund:—Sterling Reserve... 10,000,000
Silver Reserve..... 7,000,000

27,000,000
Reserve Liability of Proprietors... 10,000,000

HEAD OFFICE, HONGKONG.

London Bankers, London and County Banking Company Limited.
Branches and Agencies,
London.

Amoy,	Hankow	Penang,
Bangkok,	Hiogo,	Rangoon,
Batavia,	Iloilo,	Saigon,
Bombay,	Lyons,	San Francisco,
Calcutta,	Manila,	Singapore,
Colombo,	Nagasaki,	Sourabaya,
Foochow,	New York,	Tientsin,
Hamburg,	Peking,	Yokohama,

Credits granted on approved Securities, and every description of Banking and Exchange business transacted.

Drafts granted on London and the chief Commercial places in Europe, India, Australia, America, China and Japan.

HOLME RINGER & Co., AGENTS,
CHEMULPO.

ON CHEONG & CO.,
SEOUL.
GENERAL STORE KEEPERS.
Imported provisions, Cooking Utensils Crockery, etc.
FRESH BREAD DAILY.

MITSU BISHI DOCKYARD & ENGINE WORKS,
NAGASAKI.

CODE WORD, "DOCK."

A. 1, A. B. C., and Engineering Codes used.

DOCK No. 1 (at Tategami).

Extreme Length..............523 feet
Length on blocks .... 513 ,,
Width of Entrance on Top......89 ,,
,, ,, Bottom....77 ,,
Water on Blocks at Spring Tide 26½ ,,

DOCK No. 2 (Mukaijima).

Extreme Length..............371 feet
Length on Blocks.............360 ,,
Width of Entrance on Top......66 ,,
,, ,, Bottom 53 ,,
Water on Blocks at Spring Tide 22 ,,

PATENT SLIP (at Kosuge).

Can take vessels up to 1,000 tons gross.

THE WORKS are well equipped with the LATEST IMPROVEMENTS, and can execute any kind of work in SHIPBUILDING and MARINE ENGINEERING, as well as in REPAIRING of SHIPS.

The COMPANY'S new powerful steamer OURA-MARU (712 tons, 700 I.H.P.), specially built for SALVAGE PURPOSES, and equipped with necessary gear, is always READY at SHORT NOTICE.

CHARTERED BANK OF INDIA AUSTRALIA & CHINA.

INCORPORATED BY ROYAL CHARTER 1853

HEAD OFFICES:—LONDON.

Paid-up Capital £800,000
Reserve Liability of Shareholders 800,000
Reserve Fund 800,000

Drafts granted upon all the principal places in the world and every description of Exchange and banking business transacted.

E. MEYER & Co., Agents,
Chemulpo.

E. MEYER & CO.
Chemulpo.

SOLE AGENTS IN KOREA FOR:
A. T. Morse, Sons & Co's "Fresco" Distemper

In all colours ready for use on walls, Ceilings etc.
and
AVENARIUS CARBOLINEUM

A wood-preserving and antiseptic oil preparation

Against decay, dry-rot, fungus and wood-destroying insects.

A large supply always in Stock.
Prices upon application.

E. MEYER & Co.,
Chemulpo.

LAW UNION & CROWN INS. CO.

Fire risks accepted at Current rates, on godowns, merchandise, dwellings, and other property, subject to usual conditions.

HOLME RINGER & Co.,
Agents, Chemulp

THE METHODIST PUBLISHING HOUSE,
Little WestGate, Seoul.

PRINTING, TYPEWRITER PAPER
CARBON PAPER, VISITING CARDS
STATIONERY, BOOK BINDING
BOOK PUBLISHERS
AMERICAN SCHOOL BOOKS
SPENCERIAN COPY BOOKS
PEN CARBON LETTER AND BILL BOOKS

S. A. BECK, Manager.

DAI-ICHI GINKO.
LIMITED.
(Formerly the First National Bank)

ESTABLISHED 1873

INCORPORATED UNDER PRESENT LAW 1896

Capital - - - - - - - - Yen 5,000,000
Reserve Fund - . - - - 1,500,000

HEAD OFFICE:—TOKIO.

President: Baron SHIBUSAWA.

BRANCHES AND CORRESPONDENTS
In the Principal Cities and Towns of Japan.
Interest Allowed on
Fixed deposits 1 year - - - 6½ per cent
" " 6 months - - - 6 per cent

Special current accounts 1½ sen daily per ¥ 100
General " " 1 " " " 100

M. TANAKA,
Manager, Chemulpo

HOLME RINGER & Co.
Chemulpo.

General Merchants and Government Contractors.

Agents for the leading
Banks
SteamshipCompanies
and
Insurance Companies

Importers of Merchandise of every description.

KAMEYA Z CO.
GENERAL STOREKEEPERS
Chinkokai - - Seoul
(*Established 1895, Tokyo*)

Confectionery, Hams, Canned Goods, Cutlery, Hirano & Tansan Water. Provisions, Gents, Furnishing goods, Toilet Articles, Travelling Bags, Tobacco, Cigars & Cigarettes Kitchen Utensils. Coffee, Biscuits.

Fresh Goods always kept in Stock.
Prices Moderate
Please come and insbect our goods.

NIPPON YUSEN KAISHA.
JAPANESE MAIL STEAMSHIP CO.

DER MAIL CONTRACT WITH THE IMPERIAL JAPANESE GOVERNMENT.

European Line

Regular Fortnightly Service between Yokohama Kobe, Moji, Shanghai, Hongkong, Singapore, Penang Colombo, Port Said, Marseilles, London and Antwerp

American Line

Regular Fortnightly Service between Hongkong and Seattle, calling at Shanghai, Moji, Kobe, Yokohama and Victoria, B. C.

Australian Line

Regular weekly Service betwen Japan Ports and Australia, calling at Hongkong and Manila.
(Above Three Lines Suspended until further notice).

Shanghai Line

Weekly Service between Shanghai and Japan Ports

Korea Line

Service Kobe, Moji, Nagasak i, Fusan, Chemupo, Coo, Taiku.
S. S. Bahelsberg, 2181 tons.
Service Kobe, Moji, Fusan, Chemulpo, Chinnampo
S. S ARGO, S. S. Ohio.

BORDEN'S CONDENSED MILK CO.
New York, U. S. A.

ALWAYS IN STOCK
Eagle Brand Condensed Milk.
Gold Seal Condensed Milk.
Peerless (Family) Evaporated Cream.
Borden's Malted Milk.

E. MEYER & CO.
Chemulpo, Korea,
Sole Agents

ROYAL INSURANCE COMPANY,
Funds exceed £10,000,000
FIRE
AT CURRENT RATES.
LIFE
REDUCED PREMIUM.
HOLME RINGER & Co.,
Agents, Chemulpo.

HOTEL DU PALAIS
SEOUL.

The only first class Hotel in Seoul. Situated in the centre of the city opposite the palace.

Cuisine under the supervision of an experienced French Chef.

Well ventilated and furnished throughout.

TARIFF UPON APPLICATION

L. MARTIN
Proprietor and Manager.

大韓每日申報
대한ᄆᆡ일신보

(뎨칠십삼호) (화요일) 일천구ᄇᆡᆨᄉᆞ년십월십일일

본샤고ᄇᆡᆨ

본신보는영어와한어로석거ᄆᆡ일츌판ᄒᆞᆸ

신문가

한쟝 엽두돈오푼

일삭됴 엽두량닷돈

우표가ᄆᆡ삭닷돈

다맛돈으로밧숩

광고료는

긔.한의쟝단과조힝의다쇼로즁감ᄒᆞ되렴가로밧울터이오며오ᄅᆡ지아녀대한사람마다다이신문을보실터이니광고내시기롤원ᄒᆞ시는이들은우리신문샤에와셔면약ᄒᆞ심을희망ᄒᆞᆸ

○발힝소 박동대한ᄆᆡ일신보샤법어학교압헤젼영국인셜필림집자리오

샤쟝 영국인 (비셜)

평양 ᄃᆡ리졈

○평양효동사는권미보씨로우리신문판ᄆᆡᄃᆡ리인을뢰졍ᄒᆞ엿ᄉᆞ오니평양에계신구람코져ᄒᆞ시는 쳠군ᄌᆞ는히ᄃᆡ리졈에왕림ᄒᆞ와면의ᄒᆞ십

샤고

○우리대한ᄆᆡ일신보의목뎍은대한의안녕질셔에관ᄒᆞᆫ모든뎨목에ᄃᆡᄒᆞ야는공평ᄒᆞᆫ변론을쥬쟝ᄒᆞᆷ이라우리동신원의담보는신문보시는쳠군ᄌᆞ의게ᄒᆞᆼ상보도ᄒᆞ리며편지를긔셔ᄒᆞ여주시는이는셩명과반ᄃᆡ를젹어붓치시기를희망ᄒᆞ오니이거슬신문샹에긔ᄌᆡᄒᆞ라는거시아니오다만극히신용ᄒᆞ는증거를숨고쟈ᄒᆞᆷ이라긔쟈는아모긔셔던지긔지ᄒᆞᆷ을되각ᄒᆞ는권리를가졋스나되각ᄒᆞ는리유를말ᄒᆞᆯ터이오며공즁평화를문란케ᄒᆞ는듯ᄒᆞᆫ긔셔는의례히밧지안켓ᄉᆞᆸ나이다

●본샤셜시이리로신문을ᄆᆡ양우례로분젼ᄒᆞ와례젼부의임의로젼ᄒᆞᆫ듯스로면곳에는혹늣게젼ᄒᆞ기도ᄒᆞ며혹몃칠거슬ᄒᆞᆫ겁에젼ᄒᆞ기도ᄒᆞ며혹아니젼ᄒᆞ는곳도잇다ᄒᆞ와우리신문을ᄉᆞ랑ᄒᆞ야구람ᄒᆞ시는 쳠군ᄌᆞ의게ᄃᆡᄒᆞ야ᄆᆡ우미안ᄒᆞᆸ기로지금은분젼인을두고ᄆᆡ일일즉이젼ᄒᆞ며아니젼ᄒᆞ거나늣게거나ᄒᆞᆫ폐가업도록ᄒᆞ라ᄒᆞ오니혹아니젼ᄒᆞ거나늣게젼ᄒᆞ거나ᄒᆞᆫ일이잇스면본샤로통긔ᄒᆞ여쥬심을희망ᄒᆞᆸ

본샤광고

○본샤신문즁에좌긔ᄒᆞᆫ호수를소용ᄒᆞᆯ데가잇셔이에광고ᄒᆞ오니누구시던지그즁에아모호수던지가져오시는ᄃᆡ로ᄆᆡ쟝에ᄇᆡᆨ젼두푼식드리리다

뎨이호 뎨삼호 뎨이십호 뎨ᄉᆞ십이호 뎨ᄉᆞ십삼호 뎨오십삼호 뎨오십ᄉᆞ호와뎨오십오호 뎨륙십이호

관보

뎨이천구ᄇᆡᆨᄉᆞ십팔호

광무팔년십월ᄉᆞ일

셔임급ᄉᆞ령

○임륙군헌병참령 보병참령 강챵희

○임륙군보병참령 헌병참령 윤원구

○임륙군보병정위 헌병부위 신쟝희

○임륙군헌병정위 헌병부위 리지관

○임륙군보병정위 헌병정위 홍우령 부위 안교영 포병정위 김샹열 보병부위 김교익 김광옥 안대형 하윤홍 김광슈 리완종 김현ᄃᆡ 일등군ᄉᆞ 졍현 김ᄉᆞ억

○임륙군포병정위 보병정위 량쥬홍

○임륙군헌병부위 헌병참위 홍쳘유 오규영

○임륙군보병부위 보병참위 권즁치 오의션 한룡호 ᄇᆡᆨ남필 김졍호 송병식 경지호 홍현희 량보환 셔병덕 강봉익 강문경 김죵완 이등군ᄉᆞ 오직션 권귀인

○임륙군헌병참위 보병참위 리현규 민병쳘

○임륙군보병참위 군부쥬ᄉᆞ 민병익 정교 리죵익 김졍규

○임륙군일등군ᄉᆞ 보병정위 권즁익 강대흠 부위 박영진 리동지 리죵욱

○임륙군이등군ᄉᆞ 삼등군ᄉᆞ 김정삼

○임이등군악쟝 삼등군악쟝 ᄇᆡᆨ우용

○보륙군헌병ᄃᆡ장 헌병참령 강창회

○보 천위뎨일련ᄃᆡ뎨이대ᄃᆡ ᄃᆡ장 보병참령 김진호

○보진위뎨일련ᄃᆡ뎨삼대ᄃᆡ ᄃᆡ장 보병참령 윤원구

○보진위뎨륙련ᄃᆡ뎨일대ᄃᆡ ᄃᆡ장 보병참령 신우균

○보진위뎨륙련ᄃᆡ뎨이대ᄃᆡ ᄃᆡ대 보병참령 홍진길

○보륙군헌병ᄃᆡ즁대장 헌병졍위 리지관

○보륙군헌병ᄃᆡ부 헌병참위 리현규 민병쳘

○보시위뎨일련ᄃᆡ뎨이대ᄃᆡ즁ᄃᆡ장 보병정위 김샹열

○보시위뎨일련ᄃᆡ뎨삼대ᄃᆡ즁ᄃᆡ장 보병정위 리규식

○보 천위뎨일련ᄃᆡ뎨일대ᄃᆡ즁ᄃᆡ장 보병정위 김교익 리용지 리샹우

○보 천위뎨일련ᄃᆡ뎨삼대ᄃᆡ즁ᄃᆡ장 보병정위 리정한 리완종

○보진위뎨일련ᄃᆡ뎨일대ᄃᆡ즁ᄃᆡ장 보병정위 김ᄉᆞ억

○보진위뎨이련ᄃᆡ뎨일대ᄃᆡ즁ᄃᆡ장 보병정위 정현

○보진위뎨이련ᄃᆡ뎨일대ᄃᆡ향관 일등군ᄉᆞ 권즁익

○보진위뎨이련ᄃᆡ뎨이대ᄃᆡ즁ᄃᆡ장 보병정위 김광옥

○보진위뎨삼련ᄃᆡ뎨이대ᄃᆡ즁ᄃᆡ장 보병정위 최우샹

○보진위뎨ᄉᆞ련ᄃᆡ뎨일대ᄃᆡ즁ᄃᆡ장 보병정위 류셕규

○보진위뎨ᄉᆞ련ᄃᆡ뎨삼대ᄃᆡ즁ᄃᆡ장 보병정위 한경찬

○보진위뎨오련ᄃᆡ뎨이대ᄃᆡ즁ᄃᆡ장 보병정위 김광슈

○보시위뎨일포병뎨일대ᄃᆡ즁ᄃᆡ장 포병정위 량쥬홍

○보시위뎨일련ᄃᆡ뎨일대ᄃᆡ부 보병참위 김락규 리두인 김동현

○보시위뎨일련ᄃᆡ무괴쥬관 보병부위 오직션

○보시위뎨일련ᄃᆡ뎨이대ᄃᆡ부 보병참위 리민화 림충국

○보시위뎨일련ᄃᆡ뎨삼대ᄃᆡ부 보병부위 홍현희 참위 쟝셰덕

○보천위뎨일련ᄃᆡ뎨일대ᄃᆡ부관 보병부위 리현규

○보천위뎨일련ᄃᆡ뎨일대ᄃᆡ부 보병부위 김윤덕 참위 죠동겸 최한구 윤현구

○보천위뎨일련ᄃᆡ뎨이대ᄃᆡ부 보병부위 량보환 참위 리봉호

○보천위뎨일련ᄃᆡ뎨삼대ᄃᆡ부 보병부위 ᄇᆡᆨ남필 오의션 참위 윤공션 황학수

○보진위뎨일련ᄃᆡ뎨일대ᄃᆡ부 보병참위 민하식 김인규 손의명

○보진위뎨이련ᄃᆡ뎨이대ᄃᆡ부관 보병부위 오영근

○보진위뎨이련ᄃᆡ뎨이대ᄃᆡ부 보병부위 김셕우 참위 리영션

○보진위뎨이련ᄃᆡ뎨삼대ᄃᆡ부관 보병부위 송병식

○보진위뎨이련ᄃᆡ뎨삼대ᄃᆡ부 보병부위 죠원슌

○보진위뎨삼련ᄃᆡ뎨일대ᄃᆡ부 보병부위 권귀인 참위 죠한쳥

○보진위뎨삼련ᄃᆡ뎨이대ᄃᆡ부 보병부위 박용원 참위 신란슈

○보진위뎨ᄉᆞ련ᄃᆡ괴관보병부위 박효셥

○보진위뎨ᄉᆞ련ᄃᆡ뎨일대ᄃᆡ부 보병참위 리졔정 참위 김졍규

○보진위뎨오련ᄃᆡ뎨일대ᄃᆡ부 보병참위 리병찬 김치옥 리승복 한규우

○보진위뎨륙련ᄃᆡ뎨일대ᄃᆡ부 보병참위 림영션

○보진위뎨륙련대뎨이대ᄃᆡ부 보병참위 원희철

○보천위뎨일련대뎨일대ᄃᆡ향관 일등군ᄉᆞ 리동지

○보진위뎨이련대뎨이대ᄃᆡ향관 일등군ᄉᆞ 리죵욱

○보진위뎨륙련대뎨일대ᄃᆡ향관 일등군ᄉᆞ 강대흠

○보진위뎨삼련대뎨일대ᄃᆡ향관 일등군ᄉᆞ 박영진

잡보

○회원힐척 일젼에 일진회원이뎨국신문샤원을보고ᄎᆡᆨ망ᄒᆞ기를귀샤에셔본회를비방ᄒᆞ는거시무슨뜻시뇨만일다시또그리ᄒᆞ면셩명에관계가잇스리라고ᄒᆞ엿다는젼셜이잇다더라

○법졍회의 법부관리에서 외부로죠회ᄒᆞ기를 법국빅셩의 평양사ᄂᆞᆫ 쟝긔셔쟝안과 지송ᄉᆞ일ᄉᆞ로 회시 ᄒᆞᄂᆞᆫ 한국빅셩이 명의 류경ᄒᆞᆫ니 귀부에서 회시ᄒᆞ긔 약을 ᄃᆡᆼ ᄒᆞ면 본공관에서 도평ᄉᆞ가 마ᄉᆞ를 회긔시 쟝으로 파송ᄒᆞᆯ터이니 셩 히 서리감리의게 훈칙ᄒᆞ야 교섭 판쳐ᄒᆞ라 ᄒᆞ엿더라

○미죠쳥빈 미국공ᄉᆞ가 외부로죠회ᄒᆞ되 만국련합텰도공회 를명년오월에 희셩돈에서 셜시 ᄒᆞᆯ터이니 귀졍부에셔 인원을파 송ᄒᆞ야 공회에 참예ᄒᆞᆫ다ᄒᆞ면 우리졍부ᄂᆞᆫ 미리 각히관에셔 쳐 ᄒᆞ야 ᄒᆞᆯ터이니 쳥ᄒᆞ엿스니 조량ᄒᆞ야 회복ᄒᆞ라 ᄒᆞ엿더라

○군수평판졔발 한셩쥬차군 ᄉᆞ령관쟝곡쳔씨 일힝은 제작야 에 동경셔 츌발ᄒᆞ엿다더라

○빌인양복 일젼회에서 신뎨 가쟝대ᄒᆞ고 신슈가 죠슈ᄒᆞᆫ 인원 일빅인을 뽑아 양복을 입혓다ᄂᆞᆫ 티아직 슈효가 다 차지못ᄒᆞ엿다 더라

○영흥군보 영흥군슈셔리문 쳔군슈 명유셜씨의 보고에 ᄒᆞ기 를 동학당쳔여명이 본군에 회집 ᄒᆞ고로 만단효유ᄒᆞ야 헤쳐셔 니 와 그동졍을 살펴 진퇴를 알 가ᄒᆞ 지 못ᄒᆞ다 ᄒᆞ엿더라

○례임졔의 재작일 졍부회의 에 츙남관찰신진퇴과 젼남관찰 김세긔와 경북관찰 쟝승원 삼씨 ᄂᆞᆫ 셔임ᄒᆞ야 후에 휘방이 만타ᄒᆞ야 레임ᄒᆞ기로 졔의되엿다 더라

○군수 쥬본 금일 아에 각군 슈 쥬본이 된다ᄂᆞᆫ 티 각부 부원 쳥관 인종구근일인시과 남북촌 의 을 츅을 구쳐ᄒᆞᆫ 다 ᄒᆞᆷ으로 쥬션 들을 분주이 ᄒᆞᆫ다 더라

○암병신문 공쥬티에셔 암상 ᄒᆞᆫ병명을 아조 ᄒᆞᆫ 수 건 으로 신문 ᄒᆞ엿다더라

○경관레티 경위원신문과 쟝 박윤슈씨 가군슈로 젼임될터이 오 그 빈에ᄂᆞᆫ 경무관 위홍셕씨가 셔임된다더라

○일진공함 작일에 일진회에 셔 졍부로 공함ᄒᆞ되 이왕 권고ᄒᆞᆫ 수 도 건 분 곳 실 셔 ᄒᆞ라 ᄒᆞ엿다 더 라

○졍부졍리소 작일에 대신 에서 쳐분이 나리시기를 졍부 졍 리소를 셜립ᄒᆞ고 각부부원 쳥관 제 을 일 제 히 긔 졍 ᄒᆞ라 ᄒᆞ 옵 셧 다 더라

○졍부회의 금일 하오 이시에 졍부에서 회의 되ᄂᆞᆫ 안건 인즉 각 군슈 쥬본과 탁지 교 문관의 관 ᄒᆞᆫ 수 들의 결 ᄒᆞ야 샹 쥬ᄒᆞᆫ다 더 라

○복쟝쥰비 외부와 한셩부와 례식원과 각 감리 셔 칙쥬관 인 관 원 이 복 ᄌᆞᆼ 노 단 발 ᄒᆞ 기 로 복 쟝 을 쥰비 중 이 라 더 라

○단발연론 각외교관의 단발 은 불일실시ᄒᆞ기로 확뎡ᄒᆞ엿거 니와 궁니부일반관리도 단발 ᄒᆞ기로 연론 중이라더라

○면츅도임 츙쥬 군슈 세가 셩진 감리로셔 영흥군슈로 젼임ᄒᆞ야 쳥금 함흥에 머무ᄂᆞᆫ 티 내부에셔 히군슈의게 훈칙ᄒᆞ기를 쥬속시부 임시무ᄒᆞ라 ᄒᆞ엿다더라

○합졍시무 일본공ᄉᆞ가 외부 로조회ᄒᆞ기를 복포일본령ᄉᆞ가 면졍ᄒᆞ되 본항감리 한영원을 제 츄샹ᄒᆞ라ᄂᆞᆫ 명령이 잇ᄂᆞᆫ 티 리 ᄯᅢ ᄒᆞᆫ 교섭안건에 대 단 방히 되 니 그 샹경ᄒᆞ라ᄂᆞᆫ 명령을 아즉 뎡지 ᄒᆞ라 ᄒᆞ엿 스 니 귀대신은 잘 조처 ᄒᆞ야 히 감리로 인ᄒᆞ야 시무케 ᄒᆞ 라 ᄒᆞ엿더라

○군불이장 한병ᄉᆞ령관 원우 샹씨ᄂᆞᆫ 군 인 이 라 군 ᄒᆞᆫ 소 쳐 로 경 신이 ᄒᆞᆫ미ᄒᆞ야 부하평위관의 관 직 교 히 와 슈 모 가 모 관 으 로 잇 ᄂᆞᆫ 에지 분별을 못ᄒᆞᄂᆞᆫ 고로 공ᄉᆞ 쳐 관 미 우 구 이 된다더라

○의쥬긔셔 의쥬군슈구완회 씨가 보고ᄒᆞ기를 일본 북진군이 지나간 지 조곰 오 린 미 셩 니 겨 초 안 ᄒᆞ 야 각 쳐 샹 민 이 ᄎᆞᄎᆞ 회 집 ᄒᆞ 야 기 시 ᄒᆞᆫ 다 ᄒᆞ엿더라

○쥬임권티 금번 군슈 쥬용ᄒᆞ ᄂᆞᆫ 티 각부 부원쳥에셔 쥬임관임 각 일 인 식 공 쳔 ᄒᆞ 엿 ᄂᆞᆫ 데 니 임 관 반 쥬본이 되엿ᄂᆞᆫ 티 그 티 ᄂᆞᆫ 셔 임 권 아 니 ᄒᆞ 고 관 제 졍 리 ᄒᆞ 기 를 기 다 려 번 동 ᄒᆞᆫ 다 더 라

○공관하오 향일에 내부에 셔 심샹도관찰부에 훈칙ᄒᆞ야 모 군 공 관 파 모 군 슈 셔 리 를 일 일 히 모 수 보 ᄒᆞ 라 ᄒᆞ 엿 더 니 각 관 찰 부 에 셔 작 일 에 내 부 로 보 고 ᄒᆞ 엿 ᄂᆞᆫ 티 샹 빅 오 십 여 군 에 공 관 이 반 이 나 된 다 ᄒᆞ 엿 더 라

○교문시무 일젼 졍부회의에 탁지 교문 관 복 ᄒᆞ 면 써 합 동 ᄒᆞᆷ 을 의 뎡 ᄒᆞ 야 곳 됴 인 ᄒᆞᆫ 고 로 히 씨 가 금 명 간 브 터 곳 시 무 ᄒᆞᆫ 다 더 라

○진쥬일진회 진쥬군슈가 내 부로 면보ᄒᆞ기를 수 빅 명 이 작 당 ᄒᆞ 야 일 진 회 라 ᄌᆞ 칭 ᄒᆞ 고 본 군 에 리 도 ᄒᆞ 야 단 발 ᄒᆞ 니 엇 지 조 쳐 ᄒᆞ 라 ᄒᆞ 엿 더 라

○일죠외부 일본공관에셔 외 부로 죠회ᄒᆞ기를 시흥군 민요쟝 두 교 부 흥 일 스 ᄂᆞᆫ 귀 졍 부 에 셔 샹 당 ᄒᆞᆫ 관 원 을 명 ᄒᆞ 야 히 범 들 의 범 거 보 남 을 졍 슈 ᄒᆞ 라 ᄒᆞ 엿 더 라

○광ᄉᆞ 폐쳔 일공ᄉᆞ림권조 씨ᄂᆞᆫ 작일 하오 삼시에 귀국ᄒᆞᆫ 다 ᄂᆞᆫ 원구쇼쟝을 티 동 ᄒᆞ 야 폐 현 ᄒᆞ 고 하 오 ᄉᆞ 시 반 에 ᄂᆞᆫ 영 국 공 ᄉᆞ 가 폐 현 ᄒᆞ 엿 더 라

○니탕금함비 일본공ᄉᆞ가 외 부로죠회ᄒᆞ되 귀죠회 니 에 일 본 류 ᄒᆞᆨ 셩 ᄒᆞᆫ 비 지 출 을 곳 ᄒᆞ 본 명 이 지 시 처 아 니 ᄒᆞ 지 라 항 쟈 본 공 ᄉᆞ 수 폐 현 시 에 듯 ᄉᆞ 온 즉 교 에 니 탕

금을등하ᄒᆞ 샹 뿐 스 로 다 시 공 문 을 셔 보 니 라 ᄒᆞ 엿 더 라

○졍년회발뎡 작일에 쳥년회 를 한셩면과 회 샤 뒤 고 젼 미 국 인 아 편 셜 리 씨 집 으 로 작 뎡 ᄒᆞ 고 졔 반 ᄉᆞ 무 를 귀 졍 ᄒᆞ 기 로 결 뎡 ᄒᆞᆫ 다 더 라

○일인긔리 일본인 삼졍불산 회사 원 쇼 면 시 씨 가 안 남 산 셰 관 리 바 회 군 쳐 에 졍 리 를 긔 쳑 ᄒᆞ ᄂᆞᆫ 고 로 히 셔 에 셔 경 무 쳥 으 로 보 교 ᄒᆞ 엿 더 니 히 쳥 에 셔 한 셩 부 로 보 교 ᄒᆞ 기 를 인 허 ᄒᆞ 야 니 ᄒᆞᆫ 방 에 외 인 이 무 관 이 기 과 ᄒᆞᆷ 이 쟝 경 에 크 게 금 지 ᄒᆞ 라 ᄒᆞ 엿 더 라

○령ᄉᆞ오인 외부 통샹국쟝명 대 유 와 니 대 신 비 셔 관 김 교 헌 과 평 리 원 관 ᄉᆞ 리 샹 린 삼 씨 ᄂᆞᆫ 총 령 ᄉᆞ 를 경 임 ᄒᆞ 고 외 국 어 ᄒᆞᆨ 교 교 관 죠 원 구 씨 ᄂᆞᆫ 령 ᄉᆞ 를 경 임 ᄒᆞ 고 졍 삼 등 리 병 우 씨 ᄂᆞᆫ 령 ᄉᆞ 관 을 셔 임 ᄒᆞ 기 로 외 부 에 셔 쳥 의 ᄒᆞ 야 졍 부 회 의 에 제 출 ᄒᆞ 엿 더 라

○례발괴한 외교관의 삭발괴 한 은 본 월 회 일 노 뎡 ᄒᆞ 엿 다 더 라

○수령관티괴 쥬한셩일본군 ᄉᆞ령관쟝곡쳔씨ᄂᆞᆫ 명일 인 항 에 도 착 ᄒᆞ 여 즉 시 입 경 ᄒᆞᆫ 다 더 라

○임이군슈 각군슈 쟝 츳 셔 임 될 계 시 평 ᄉᆞᆼ 여 과 라 ᄂᆞᆫ 티 쟉 야 에 라 위 젼 이 식 이 과 만 쥬 본 되 엿 더 라

○면훈주범공ᄉᆞ 외부에셔 주 범 공 ᄉᆞ 의 게 면 훈 ᄒᆞ 기 를 하 란 국 회 군 졔 샹 죠 회 에 젼 왕 ᄒᆞ 야 참 회 ᄒᆞ 라 ᄒᆞ 엿 더 라

○민씨방셕 시흥민요 수로일 본 수 평 부 에 셔 압 샹 ᄒᆞᆫ 샹 인 중 민 병 훈 씨 ᄂᆞᆫ 작 일 에 방 셕 ᄒᆞ 엿 다 더 라

○불펼규시 작야에 졍부에셔 군 슈 쥬 본 을 슈 졍 ᄒᆞ ᄂᆞᆫ 티 졍 부 관 인 중 규 시 ᄒᆞ ᄂᆞᆫ 자 잇 셧 더 니 교 빙 으 로 잇 ᄂᆞᆫ 일 인 압 쳔 씨 가 말 ᄒᆞ 되 졍 부 쥬 본 등 ᄉᆞ ᄂᆞᆫ 외 인 의 규 시 홈 이 아 니 라 ᄒᆞ 엿 다 더 라

론셜

동경안에 흉담나ᄂᆞᆫ 일

동경일일신문에서 셜명ᄒᆞ기 젼에 금월일일 동경신문에 게지ᄒᆞ 기를 니 각 총 리 대 신 게 티 랑 씨 와 남작이동과 대 치 랑 씨 가 원 로 졍 치가들로 더 브 러 무 샹 샹 관 되 ᄂᆞᆫ 일이 잇 셔 셔 로 불 평 이 니 인 다 ᄒᆞ 엿 ᄂᆞᆫ 티 그 ᄉᆞ 실 인 즉 거 월 이 십 칠 일 일 일 신 문 잡 보 중 에 경 샹 송 방 랑 빈 쟈 이 홍 범 부 보 조 금 이 빅 만 원 을 일 빅 샴 십 오 힝 으 로 쎄 여 돌 니 엿 다 고 귀 지 ᄒᆞᆷ 으 로 대 단 히 분 로 ᄒᆞ 게 붝이 ᄂᆞᆫ 중 일 일 신 문 주 필 인 즉 이 동 남 작 인 고 로 뎌 사 름 들 이 강 화 를 시 이 라 다 가 되 지 못 ᄒᆞ 고 필 경 졍 샹 송 방 랑 빈 쟈 이 동 남 작 으 로 더 브 러 졀 교 ᄒᆞ ᄂᆞᆫ 관 지 를 써 셔

이셥구일오후에 의셩 씨로 하여 곰 보 니 ᄂᆞᆫ 지 라 이 동 남 작 이 이 글 을 바 다 보 고 대 경 소 괴 ᄒᆞ 야 곳 조 귀 의 신 용 ᄒᆞ ᄂᆞᆫ 자 로 ᄒᆞ 여 곰 총 리 대 신 게 티 랑 씨 의 게 보 니 여 이 사 건 을 화 호 ᄒᆞᆷ 에 방 조 ᄒᆞ 기 를 쳥 ᄒᆞ 엿 더 니 게 씨 ᄂᆞᆫ 이 ᄉᆞ 실 을 이 왕 에 졍 샹 빅 쟉 의 게 로 조 셰 히 드 럿 ᄂᆞᆫ 고 로 아 모 조 록 이 동 남 쟉 의 간 쳥 ᄒᆞᆷ 을 시 힝 ᄒᆞᆷ 의 향 이 긴 ᄒᆞᆫ 고 로 산 ᄒᆞᆫ 이 동 남 쟉 이 대 구 괴 ᄯᅢ 으 로 가 셔 후 쟉 이 등 씨 의 계 구 회 ᄒᆞᆷ 에 찬 조 ᄒᆞ 기 를 간 쳥 ᄒᆞ 엿 더 니 이 등 후 쟉 은 젼 일 츄 밀 원 쟝 인 고 로 희 원 셔 귀 관 쟝 도 츌 셰 가 왓 이 사 건 에 티 ᄒᆞ 야 대 괴[大饑] 로 관 계 되 ᄂᆞᆫ 쥬 졍 치 샹 과 사 회 샹 에 크 게 되 여 쳠 사 될 번 ᄒᆞᆫ 일 이 무 ᄉᆞ 히 타 쳡 이 지 라 일 본 에 잇 ᄂᆞᆫ 일 이 망 이 잇 다 ᄒᆞ 엿 ᄂᆞᆫ 에 셔 ᄂᆞᆫ 만 후 쳐 관 에 도 삼 빅 샹 심 은 힝 로 주 계 홈 으 로 이 왕 봇 터 도 심 히 ᄒᆞᆫ 리 ᄒᆞ 다 ᄂᆞᆫ 소 문 이 잇 셧 스 며 산 다 ᄂᆞᆫ 사 름 들 도 그 은 힝 빈 리 가 나 리 여 ᄡᅥ 면 조 켓 다 고 말 들 이 만 ᄒᆞᆫ 스 나 우 금 셔 지 그 모 양 으 로 잇 ᄂᆞᆫ 지 라

우리ᄂᆞᆫ 일일신문에 분명히 귀졍 ᄒᆞᆫ 리 도 조 금 도 밋 지 아 니 ᄒᆞ 거 니 와 시 홈 범 부 보 조 금 이 라 ᄒᆞᄂᆞᆫ 거 순 긔 ᄌᆞᆼ 홈 에 ᄡᅥ ᄌᆞ 홈 인 즉 여 간 젼 금 으 로 ᄒᆞ 차 티 ᄂᆞᆫ 홈 지 언 졍 엇 지 젼 수 히 이 돈 으 로 써 은 힝 유 지 ᄒᆞ 기 위 ᄒᆞ 야 돌 이 라 고 홈 뜻 을 두 엇 스 리 요 셜 로 죠 션 키 어 려 운 말 이 로 다

뎐보

구월삼십일 동경발

○아령시후쇼환 로국졍부에 셔ᄂᆞᆫ 아령시후총독을 쇼환ᄒᆞ기 로 결뎡ᄒᆞ엿ᄂᆞᆫ티 동씨ᄂᆞᆫ 미구에 극동을 ᄯᅥ나 도셩으로 향ᄒᆞᆫ다 ᄒᆞ 엿더라

구월삼십일 빅림발

○쇼환불긍 파리ᄡᅥ마 틴신문 에 보도ᄒᆞ기를 아령시후총독이 로국도셩으로 쇼환ᄒᆞᄂᆞᆫ 명령을 불긍ᄒᆞ엿다ᄒᆞ엿더라

구월삼십일 론돈발

○만쥬수령관 로국니 글라쓰 대공은 명츈에 아령시후씨의 후 임이 되여 로국극동의 총수령관 이 되고 구로파트긴쟝군은 이 대 공 이 도 착 ᄒᆞ 기 셔 지 ᄂᆞᆫ 젼 쟝 에 잇 ᄂᆞᆫ 모 든 군 티 를 지 휘 ᄒᆞᆫ 다 더 라

례이군수령관 그림페ᄞᅥᆨ쟝군은 티 샹 일 월 에 극 동 으 로 ᄯᅥ 난 다 ᄒᆞ 더 라

동경외무셩에 도착ᄒᆞᆫ 구쥬뎐보 가 여좌ᄒᆞ니

외보

○영셤교로 영국과셤라 샹호 가 린 순 에 광 식 을 비 밀 히 슈 운 ᄒᆞ 고 져 ᄒᆞ 다 가 발 각 되 야 본 월 팔 일 에 영 구 에 셔 일 본 군 함 의 게 로 포 로 가 되 엿 다 ᄒᆞ 더 라

TELEGRAMS.

Tokyo, Oct. 8th.

A battleship of the Peresviet type, while lying at anchor in Port Arthur, has been damaged by the shells of our besieging force. The other ships escaped damage as they were lying in shelter of the hills.

Tokyo, Later.

General Stoessel has reported to the Czar, that as no relief from land or sea is yet in sight, the garrison of Port Arthur will experience great difficulty in repelling the besiegers for any length of time.

Tokyo. Oct. 8th.

The Chinese General at Mukden has reported that the Russians are building forts near the Imperial tombs.

Tokyo, Oct. 8th.

The British steamer Si-sang, proceeding with provisions to Port Arthur, has been seized by a Japanese war vessel at Newchwang.

THE U. S. DEMOCARATIC CONVENTION.

The U. S. Democratic Convention at St. Louis had some lively times. The hall was not good for hearing, and constant demands to speak louder at last drew this outburst from the Chairman:—

"In the day when the Angel Gabriel shall stand on the highest mount of the world and with a megaphone shall announce the crash of creation, there will be somebody to interrupt him by crying 'Louder.'"

Later the Chairman created great laughter when he said: "So dreadful are the acoustic properties of this remarkable meeting-place that my friend Ollie James of Kentucky, who has a voice like the bull of Bashan, and in whose defence that bull retired from business, confided to me that even he could not be heard in this place." Here is one sample of the oratory of the Convention:—

"In his haste King David said that all men are liars. Had he been in Chicago while Senator Henry Cabot Lodge was reading the Republican platform he would no doubt have pronounced the same opinion more leisurely, for surely there never was more mendacity packed into the same space in any document purporting to be a grave State paper."

The demonstration in favour of Justice Parker appears to have been well up to the mark.

All that had happened in the Convention up to the time Littleton had concluded his nominating address, multiplied many times, was almost as nothing compared to the hurricane that broke out when he mentioned the name "Alton B. Parker" on the part of the Parker delegates. It was a revelation in politics. Like one man they sprang up in their chairs with everything that could be waved tossed high in the air.

Florida, after a few seconds of wild yelling, started around the hall, its men screaming frantically and tossing high a silken banner, inscribed "Florida, Safe and Sound."

Indian Territory, New Jersey, Maryland, Texas, Georgia, and many other states fell in behind. Michigan came next, and her great blue banner was borne up the steps of the platform behind the Chairman's desk, where it was held high and waved widely to and fro.

A little boy was lifted upon the shoulders of one of the Texas delegates and the flag waved by his small hands brought out much enthusiasm.

Maryland, rushing back to her place in the delegates' seats, grabbed the pole with her state name upon it and then placed the pole higher than any other in the line of march. The cue was immediately seized wherever possible by other delegations, and the tramp around the hall continued, the marchers finally passing out from the delegates' seats in among those occupied by the visitors.

After the excitement had continued about twelve minutes there was a perceptible abatement, and the band struck up "America," thousands of voices joining in the song. The lull speedily passed away, for the band struck up "Dixie," and this was oil on a fire already fiercely blazing. With a spasmodic yell the applause started all over again. During the noise the band played and a huge bust picture of Parker was carried up the centre aisle. Just as it reached the platform two young ladies of St. Louis, dressed in white and carrying mammoth bouquets of roses and ferns, were assisted to the presiding officer's table, and the huge portrait was held for a moment between them, face to the delegates, and the state banners which had formed the procession were held aloft and massed around it. Rythmic shout of "Parker, Parker," "Alton B. Parker!" were started and caught up.

At the end of eighteen minutes the demonstration began to subside. The Parker portrait was then taken to the platform and turned toward the audience. At the expiration of twenty-two minutes efforts were made to still the demonstration. A megaphone on the platform was begun for "Parker, Parker!" however, and things broke loose again. The demonstration lasted twenty-five minutes.

MORE RUSSIAN VESSELS.

Captain Seabury of the "Korea," interviewed at Victoria, stated that the reason for his having avoided his port of call at San Francisco and gone north to Puget Sound was his having sighted a Russian cruiser evidently patrolling the waters near San Francisco on the lookout for the "Korea" or other vessels.

Having in mind the methods practiced by the Russian war ships on merchantmen and mail steamers he decided to run no risks and on requests of the passengers, headed for the British-Canadian port.

Another Russian cruiser has now appeared off that coast and the two vessels seem to be patrolling the waters near there. It is believed they will call at San Francisco to coal and much interest has been aroused.

The coastwise vessels which have reported the presence of the cruisers did not learn their names.

A STAMP-LICKING QUESTION IN CHINA.

Mrs. H. T. Ford, of the China Inland Mission at Tai-kang, in Honan, gives some interesting experiences in a letter to her family, published in the "Daily News," of the workings of the Post Office in China. The letter says:—

"We have got the Chinese Imperial Post here now. At Kai-feng, when they first got it, the post-office clerks had a fight with some men who bought stamps and wanted the clerks to lick them and put them on the letters for them. They said the clerks were there to lick the stamps, and paid for the business, and they wouldn't lick them. But the clerks wouldn't agree to lick them, so they came to blows, and the police had to come in and separate them. Here at Tai-kang the man who has got the post-office has begun well. Harry was in his shop when his first customer came for a stamp. It took him nearly five minutes to find the key and get the stamp box open, and when he gave it to the man he said in a very decided way, 'Now lick it and put it just there.' The customer was foolish (or wise) enough to do so, and now a custom has been established in Tai-kang that all purchasers of stamps must lick them and stick them on. There was a great row at the Kai-feng Post Office one day because an address on a letter could not be found, and the letter was brought back. The sender wanted his money back because the letter had not been delivered, but the clerk refused to give it to him, contending that they had had more trouble over it than if it had been delivered. Another man was determined to get the P. O. clerks into trouble because he had sent a letter some time ago and received no answer. This was a clear proof, he said, that the letter had never been sent. The service here is somewhat irregular yet."

THE EFFECT OF LIGHTNING ON HUMAN SKIN.

The latent possibilities of nature have once more been elicited without the waste of human brain and energy, by the following important discovery chronicled by the "Friend of India:"—From Morristown, New Jersey, comes a well-authenticated report which has set all America marvelling. Abbott Parker, a young man, was struck by lightning and was taken on an ambulance to All Souls Hospital. The man having been stripped to the waist, a wound was found on his back, and, while the nurses and doctors watched, a perfect representation of a crucifix gradually appeared exactly in the centre of the shoulder blades. Then the figure of Christ nailed to the cross slowly developed until an exact reproduction of the crucifixion stood out in bold relief. The watchers were spellbound. Photographs of the man's back, showing the picture, perfect in every detail, are published everywhere by the newspapers. The picture was developed while the man was unconscious. Abbott Parker declares that he has never been tatooed, and experts say that no tatooing could have produced so perfect an effect. Parker, who is a Protestant, does not believe in a miracle, but the nuns at the hospital insist that a miracle has taken place. On the wall opposite the bed where the man was examined by the doctors is a crucifix which possibly explains the mystery. Scientists who have been consulted say that Parker's skin after being struck by lightning became like a sensitised photographic plate. About a score of similar cases are recorded in the United States. Apparently the picture is fairly permanent, even the nails on the hands and feet of the image being distinctly visible. The discovery has made a great sensation.

On the 9th inst, His Majesty ordered the establishment of a reform office, where the official regulations of all departments will be thoroughly overhauled and if necessary altered. The Il Chin Hoi evidently augur well from this, for the four time-worn articles, with which they pestered the throne so frequently at the beginning of their career and which have since lain dormant, have now been dragged forth again in a memorial to His Majesty.

The Japanese Minister has consented to hand over the leaders of the Si Hung riot to the Korean authorities.

The Seoul-Fusan railway is now opened for traffic, from this end, as far as Pu Kang.

The Korea Daily News.

Issued at 5 P. M. daily except Sundays.

Rate of Subscription:—
Per Year, Yen 25
Per Quarter, Yen 7.
Per Month, Yen 2.50.

Postage in Korea not charged extra.
Postage abroad charged extra.

Advertisements, 50 sen per day for 1 inch or less.
5 yen per month per inch.
50 yen per year per inch.

All communications to
E. T. BETHELL,
Editor and Publisher,
Pak-tong, Seoul.

THE OPERATIONS AROUND MUKDEN.

It is now over a month since the Japanese armies forced the Russians to evacuate Liaoyang and very little news has since come through. There have been many minor skirmishes in which the honours seem to be divided. We have no news of a general Japanese advance any furthur north than the line between Yentai on the west and Pingtaitz on the east, so that this line appears to constitute the front of the main Japanese army.

Running about parallel with this line and some 35 miles north of it is the River Hun (or Huan), upon which Mukden is situated, and the Russian troops who are still on the south of this river seem to be continually being attacked by Japanese outposts, but have, so far, according to Russian reports, repulsed them. It would appear that the ground between the Hun and Yentai is fairly level, and as the crops have now been harvested, making the field a fairly clear one, it is hardly likely that the Japanese will be allowed to advance up to the south bank of the river without fighting their way. This probably is the battle which is now reported going on along the Russian south and east front,

Whether Kuroki, whose command is still on the extreme Japanese right, is engaged in this we do not know. Some days ago there was a report that he, with 100,000 men, had again made a sweeping movement to the east. This move apparently had for its object the crossing of the Hun river higher up and the occpation of the hilly country north-east of Mukden and east of Teiling.

So that it is impossible to say whether Kuroki is or is not engaged in the action now in progress. He may have moved far enough east to be clear of it and it may be a part of the Japanese centre protecting his movement which is now fighting.

It is pretty certain that the Japanese Commander-in-chief will endeavour to fight the big battle on the hilly ground to the east of Teiling, as it has been repeatedly demonstrated that in difficult country the Japanese are more at home than the Russians.

On the other hand the Russians are well aware of this and will probably endeavour to bring about a big battle on the level ground lying to the south of the river Hun and will resist to their utmost any attempt of the Japanese to occupy the heights dominating Teiling.

So far as can be seen, the Teiling-Mukden position is a more difficult one for the Japanese to attack than was Liaoyang. The Russian front will not be such an extended one and it will therefore be easy for Kuropatkin to reinforce menaced positions. Further, so long as the Japanese are prevented from crossing the river Hun, Kuropatkin will be able to conduct his defence free from the danger to his communications which was such an anxiety to him at Liaoyang.

It is thought in some quarters that Kuropatkin will presently assume the offensive, and this is borne out by the fact that he holds in reserve north of Mukden a very strong body of cavalry under General Louis Buonaparte.

The result of the coming battle is of gravest importance to both sides, and we may therefore expect to hear of warfare exceeding in severity the operations which led up to the occupation of Liaoyang.

THE GAG.

The following is a free translation of the article appearing in the Korean newspaper "Chekuk Shinmun" (Ieikoku) which is believed to have led to its suppression, and the taking charge of the office by Japanese gendarmerie:—

"It has lately been newly rumoured and also stated by some Europeans that 50,000 Russians will enter Seoul next Spring, or earlier. It is impossible to trace the origin of the rumour but still it is current and is growing as it travels so that the people in Seoul and in the country are greatly exercised in their minds. On some sides it is said that Liaoyang, now occupied by the Japanese, will shortly again fall into Russian hands while others assert that Liaoyang, involving a greal loss of life was never a Japanese victory.

"Referring to Port Arthur, some say that it will fall shortly while others say that if the Japanese do not take it before winter sets in they never will. Some say that in the brave attempts to break down the Russian defence innumerable Japanese lives are being lost.

"So it is time to investigate this change of the world's opinion. We are thinking that when Japan began war she was on her best behaviour and consequently the whole world extended its sympathy and hoped for her success. But Japan, having been continuously victorious has latterly become indifferent to the opinion of the world, and is pursuing her own course without deference to the opinions of others.

"First, with regard to Korea, Japan said that she would protect Korea, and do all possible by persuasion to reform the country and maintain its independence. Yet, even to-day in the direction of reform nothing has been accomplished, there is no change in the order of things, night or day, and the whole world already knows that Japan never intended reform, and what has Japan done about the independence of Korea?

"The Japanese were too strict with the war correspondents at the front so the newspapers of various countries are publishing conflicting opinions of events. Some say the political parties in Japan are quarreling amongst each other. With so many different rumours current it is hard to judge of the truth but they are all unfavourable to Japan.

"For a little while after the commencement of the war, the whole world, as with one mouth, praised Japan. Her soldiers were deservedly praised for their splendid fighting and women even came from abroad to nurse the wounded. There were a few who smiled at this from the first but lately the whole world has changed. Something goes wrong, difficulties arise, and gradually people begin to say that things are not as they should be.

"The Japanese Legation is now connected with the palace by telephone which is an unheard of proceeding. Every matter pertaining to Korea's intercourse with foreign countries must first be respectfully reported to Japan. A Japanese adviser, whom the Japanese attempted to get appointed superviser, has to be consulted about this and that. There are many more things, too numerous to be recounted one by one, but which taken together show that Japan does not remember what she promised to the world and studies her own interests alone.

"So that everyone who is even a little righteous must commence to turn the other way and the rumours true and about the war are also helping.

"At first all except the pro-Russians rejoiced at Japan's victories, but lately the doubts about Japan's victories seem to please the people.

"We cannot be sure that we have correctly gauged present public opinion, but if we have, it is indeed a bad thing for both Korea and Japan."

TONSORAL CLIPPINGS.

The hair cutting mania has spread to the country. The Magistrate of Chin Chu reports that many hundreds of his people are declaring themselves devout pupils of the Il Chin Hoi and are shearing their heads. He winds up his story to the Home Office, with the piteous appeal, "Please give me an immediate answer what I can do for them."

(Buy them wigs, Magistrate, buy them wigs.)

* * *

However, one cannot be surprised at the country people, when in the official Gazette we see an Imperial edict to the effect that all diplomatic officers are to remove their top-knots immediately, and it is even said that officials of other departments are rushing forward to anticipate the behest.

* * *

The story of Samson and Delilah has evidently not yet reached the Il Chin Hoi, for we heard that a band of their members, possessed of the greatest strength, are to be cleanly shaved and dressed neatly in European clothes. What their function is to be has not transpired.

* * *

All said and done however, the scheme is not bad, as at any rate the removal of top-knots, the majority of which are usually far from cleanly, is conducive to a more healthy and sanitary condition amongst the average citizens. The laughable side of the affair, is the earnestness, savouring of mania, with which this "measure of reform" has been taken up and weightier and far more necessary steps shelved.

THE NEW COMMANDER IN KOREA.

The new Commander and Staff-General Hasegawa, appointed to the command of the Japanese forces in Korea, left Moji yesterday at 4 P.M. and consequently is expected to arrive in Chemulpo, tomorrow forenoon. Major General Haraguchi and Mr. Hayashi will meet him on arrival and a nineteen gun salute, from the Men-of-war in Port, will welcome him to Korea.

He will remain overnight in Chemulpo and then proceed to Seoul by the morning express on Thursday. A guard of honor will be in attendance at the South Gate station and the road from the South Gate to the former headquarters will be lined with troops, while the battery in position on Namsan will fire a salute of 19 guns.

ACTIVITY IN THE NORTHEAST.

A telegram received from Gensan yesterday, stated that the Russian outposts had exchanged shots with the Japanese near Hong-won and then retired. Major Kim In-su, the officer formerly with the Korean army, has brought together and drilled about 500 Koreans, who are to assist the Russians. The Russian base at present is at Hong-won and the Japanese at Hamheung. As only 100 *li* separates the two forces fighting may be expected at any moment.

An insurrection of natives at Son Chon and Cha Yun Kwan provinces is reported. One company of Japanese troops has been despatched to quell the disturbance.

An alteration has been made in the Government contract with Mr. Megata. The amount of his salary and house rent has now been raised to Y1,000, and the term of has services fixed at 5 years.

The Korea Daily News.

VOL. I, TUESDAY, OCTOBER 11, 1904. No. 73

HONGKONG & SHANGHAI BANKING CORPORATION.

Paid-up Capital.....	$10,000,000
Reserve Fund:—Sterling Reserve...	10,000,000
Silver Reserve.....	7,000,000
	27,000,000
Reserve Liability of Proprietors...	10,000,000

HEAD OFFICE, HONGKONG.

London Bankers, London and County Banking Company Limited.

Branches and Agencie" London.

Amoy,	Hankow	Penang,
Bangkok,	Hiogo,	Rangoon,
Batavia,	Iloilo,	Saigon,
Bombay,	Lyons,	San Francisco,
Calcutta,	Manila,	Singapore,
Colombo,	Nagasaki,	Sourabaya,
Foochow,	New York,	Tientsin,
Hamburg,	Peking,	Yokohama,

Credits granted on approved Securities, and every description of Banking and Exchange business transacted.

Drafts granted on London and the chief Commercial places in Europe, India, Australia, America, China and Japan.

HOLME RINGER & CO., AGENTS,
CHEMULPO.

ON CHEONG & CO., SEOUL.

GENERAL STORE KEEPERS.
Imported provisions, Cooking Utensils Crockery, etc.
FRESH BREAD DAILY.

MITSU BISHI DOCKYARD & ENGINE WORKS, NAGASAKI.

CODE WORD, "DOCK."

A. 1, A. B. C., and Engineering Codes used.

DOCK No. 1 (at Tategami).

Extreme Length..............	523 feet
Length on blocks	513 ,,
Width of Entrance on Top......	89 ,,
,, ,, Bottom....	77 ,,
Water on Blocks at Spring Tide	26½ ,,

DOCK No. 2 (Mukaijima).

Extreme Length..............	371 feet
Length on Blocks.............	360 ,,
Width of Entrance on Top......	66 ,,
,, ,, Bottom	53 ,,
Water on Blocks at Spring Tide	22 ,,

PATENT SLIP (at Kosuge).

Can take vessels up to 1,000 tons gross.

THE WORKS are well equipped with the LATEST IMPROVEMENTS, and can execute any kind of work in SHIPBUILDING and MARINE ENGINEERING, as well as in REPAIRING of SHIPS.

The COMPANY'S new powerful steamer OURA-MARU (712 tons, 700 I.H.P.), specially built for SALVAGE PURPOSES, and equipped with necessary gear, is always READY at SHORT NOTICE.

CHARTERED BANK OF INDIA AUSTRALIA & CHINA.

INCORPORATED BY ROYAL CHARTER 1853

HEAD OFFICES:—LONDON.

Paid-up Capital	£800,000
Reserve Liability of Shareholders	800,000
Reserve Fund	800,000

Drafts granted upon all the principal places in the world and every description of Exchange and banking business transacted.

E. MEYER & Co., Agents,
Chemulpo.

E. MEYER & CO. Chemulpo.

SOLE AGENTS IN KOREA FOR:

A. T. Morse, Sons & Co's "Fresco" Distemper

In all colours ready for use on walls, Ceilings etc.

and

AVENARIUS CARBOLINEUM

A wood-preserving and antiseptic oil preparation

Against decay, dry-rot, fungus and wood-destroying insects.

A large supply always in Stock. Prices upon application.

E. MEYER & Co.,
Chemulpo.

LAW UNION & CROWN INS. CO.

Fire risks accepted at Current rates, on go downs, merchandise, dwellings, and other property, subject to usual conditions.

HOLME RINGER & Co.,
Agents, Chemulp

THE METHODIST PUBLISHING HOUSE,

Little WestGate, Seoul.

PRINTING, TYPEWRITER PAPEP
CARBON PAPER, VISITING CARDS
STATIONERY, BOOK BINDING
BOOK PUBLISHERS
AMERICAN SCHOOL BOOKS
SPENCERIAN COPY BOOKS
PEN CARBON LETTER AND BILL BOOKS

S. A. BECK, Manager.

DAI-ICHI GINKO.

LIMITED.

(Formerly the First National Bank)

ESTABLISHED 1873

INCORPORATED UNDER PRESENT LAW 1896

Capital - - - - - - - - -	Yen 5,000,000
Reserve Fund - - - - -	1,500,000

HEAD OFFICE:—TOKIO.

President: Baron SHIBUSAWA.

BRANCHES AND CORRESPONDENTS
In the Principal Cities and Towns of Japan.

Interest Allowed on

Fixed deposits 1 year - - -	6½ per cent
" " 6 months - - -	6 per cent

Special current accounts 1½ sen daily per Y 100
General " " 1 " " " 100

M. TANAKA,
Manager, Chemulpo

HOLME RINGER & Co. Chemulpo.

General Merchants and Government Contractors.

Agents for the leading Banks SteamshipCompanies and Insurance Companies

Importers of Merchandise of every description.

KAMEYA & CO.

GENERAL STOREKEEPERS

Chinkokai - - Seoul

(*Established 1895, Tokyo*)

Confectionery, Hams, Canned Goods, Cutlery, Hirano & Tansan Water. Provisions, Gents, Furnishing goods, Toilet Articles, Travelling Bags, Tobacco, Cigars & Cigarettes Kitchen Utensils. Coffee, Biscuits

Fresh Goods always kept in Stock.

Prices Moderate

Please come and inspect our goods.

NIPPON YUSEN KAISHA.

JAPANESE MAIL STEAMSHIP CO.

DER MAIL CONTRACT WITH THE IMPERIAL JAPANESE GOVERNMENT.

European Line

Regular Fortnightly Service between Yokohama Kobe, Moji, Shanghai, Hongkong, Singapore, Penang Colombo, Port Said, Marseilles, London and Antwerp

American Line

Reg .ar Fortnightly Service between Hongkong and Seattle, calling at Shanghai, Moji, Kobe, Yokohama and Victoria, B. C.

Australian Line

Regular weekly Service betwen Japan Ports and Australia, calling at Hongkong and Manila.

(Above Three Lines Suspended until further notice).

Shanghai Line

Weekly Service between Shanghai and Japan Ports

Korea Line

Service Kobe, Moji, Nagasaki, Fusan, Chemupo, Coo, Taiku.
S. S. Bahelsberg, 2181 tons.
Service Kobe. Moji, Fusan, Chemulpo, Chinnampo
S. S ARGO, S. S. Ohio.

BORDEN'S CONDENSED MILK CO.

New York, U. S. A.

ALWAYS IN STOCK

Eagle Brand Condensed Milk.

Gold Seal Condensed Milk.

Peerless (Family) Evaporated Cream.

Borden's Malted Milk.

**E. MEYER & CO.
Chemulpo, Korea,**
Sole Agents

ROYAL INSURANCE COMPANY,

Funds exceed £10,000,000

FIRE

AT CURRENT RATES.

LIFE

REDUCED PREMIUM.

HOLME RINGER & Co.,
Agents, Chemulpo.

HOTEL DU PALAIS

SEOUL.

The only first class Hotel in Seoul. Situated in the centre of the city opposite the palace.

Cuisine under the supervision of an experienced French Chef.

Well ventilated and furnished throughout.

TARIFF UPON APPLICATION

L. MARTIN
Proprietor and Manager.

大韓每日申報
대한미일신보

(뎨칠십ᄉᆞ호)　(슈요일)　벽ᄉᆞ년십월십이일

본샤고빅

본신보는영어와한어로셔게미
일츌판ᄒᆞ옵

신문가
한장　엽푼오푼
일삭료　엽두량닷돈
우표가미삭닷돈
다맛돈이로밧숩
광고료는

긔한의쟝단과ᄌᆞ항의다소로증
감ᄒᆞ되몁가로밧을터이오며오
리지아녀대한사람마다다이신
문을보실터이니광고버시기를
원ᄒᆞ시는이들은우리신문사에
와셔편약ᄒᆞ심을희망ᄒᆞ옵

○발힝소　박동대한미일신보
사번이학교앞히전영국인셜필
립셔자리오
사쟝　영국인（비셜）
평양　티리졈

○평양효동사는권미보씨로우
리신문관미티리인울티쟝ᄒᆞ엿
ᄉᆞ오니평양에계신구람코져ᄒᆞ
시는　쳠군ᄌᆞ는히티리졈에왕
림ᄒᆞ와편의ᄒᆞ시옵

샤고

○우리대한미일신보의목뎍은
대한의안녕질셔에관ᄒᆞᆫ모든예
목에티ᄒᆞ야는공평ᄒᆞᆫ번론을쥬
쟝ᄒᆞᆯ이라우리동신원의담보는
신문보시는쳠군ᄌᆞ의게ᄒᆞᆼ샹보
도ᄒᆞ리며편지를긔셔ᄒᆞ여주시
는이는셩명과번디를쟉이붓치
시기를희망ᄒᆞ오니이거슨신문
샹에긔저ᄒᆞ란는거시아니오다
만그히신용ᄒᆞ는증거를삼고자
홈이라긔자는아모긔셔던지긔
지홈을되쟉ᄒᆞ는권리를가졋스
나되쟉ᄒᆞ는리유를말홈터이오
며공증광확를문란케ᄒᆞ는듯ᄒᆞᆫ
긔셔는의레히밧지안켓숩나이
다

●본사셜시이리로신문을미양
우레ㄴ분전ᄒᆞ와레전부의임의
로쳥ᄒᆞᆫ듯스로번곳에는홍늣게
전ᄒᆞ기도ᄒᆞ며ᄒᆞᆨ먼칠거슬ᄒᆞᆫ겁
에전ᄒᆞ기도ᄒᆞ며ᄒᆞᆨ아니전ᄒᆞ는
곳도잇다ᄒᆞ와우리신문을ᄉᆞ랑
ᄒᆞ야구람ᄒᆞ시는　쳠군ᄌᆞ의게탕
티ᄒᆞ야미우미안ᄒᆞ옵기로지금
은분전인을두고미일즉이전
ᄒᆞ며아니전ᄒᆞ거나늣게거나ᄒᆞᆫ
폐가엽도록ᄒᆞ라ᄒᆞ오니ᄒᆞ아니
전ᄒᆞ거나홍늣게전ᄒᆞ거나ᄒᆞᆫ일
이잇스면본샤로통긔ᄒᆞ여주심
을희망ᄒᆞ옵

본샤광고

○본사신문중에죄ㄱᄒᆞᆫ호수를
소용ᄒᆞᆯ데가잇서이에광고ᄒᆞ오
니누구시던지그중에아모호수
던지가져오시는이로미쟝에빅
젼두푼식드리리다
뎨이호　뎨삼호　뎨이십호
뎨ᄉᆞ십이호　뎨ᄉᆞ십삼호　뎨
오십삼호　뎨오십ᄉᆞ호와뎨오
십오호　뎨륙십이호

관보

뎨이쳔구빅ᄉᆞ십팔호연속
○임륙군보병졍위　보병부위
문희션　오의션　포병부위
김운비
○임륙군일등군ᄉᆞ　보병졍위
최영대　포병부위　오유영
○임륙군보병부위　보병참위
리순용　죠동원　남긔셕
○임륙군포병부위　보병참위
김경쳔
○임륙군포병부위　이등군ᄉᆞ
안경춍
○보시위뎨일련티뎨일대티부
보병참위　류근슈　송명현
○보시위뎨일련티뎨이대티부
보병부위　김덕제
○보시위뎨일련티뎨삼대티향
관　일등군ᄉᆞ　최영대
○보시위뎨일련티포병뎨일대
티부　포병부위　안경춍
김경쳔
○보시위뎨일련티포병뎨일대
티향관　일등군ᄉᆞ　오유영
○보친위뎨일련티뎨일대티부
보병부위　남긔셕　참위　김
동은
○보친위뎨일련티뎨이대티부
보병부위　송영셕
○보친위뎨일련티뎨삼대티부
보병참위　한순교
○보진위뎨일련티뎨일대티중
티쟝　보병졍위　송헌명
○보진위뎨일련티뎨일대티부
보병부위　김진교　참위
임명호
○보진위뎨일련티뎨일대티부
보병참위　한진호
○보진위뎨이련티뎨이대티부
보병부위　죠동원
○보진위뎨오련티뎨이대티부
보병부위　리봉원
○보진위뎨오련티뎨삼대티부
보병참위　최영쥬
○임륙군보병졍위　졍신풍
죠긔셜
○임륙군보병부위　류픔　김
상열
임륙군보병참위　류픔김명
산
○임륙군일등군ᄉᆞ　보병부위
윤셕호
○임륙군보병부위　보병참위
빅남슈　김명션
○보시위뎨일련티뎨이대티부
보병참위　죠티희
○보친위뎨일련티뎨이대티부
보병참위셔찬경
○보친위뎨일련티뎨삼대티부
보병부위　빅남슈　참위　박
제호
○보진위뎨일련티뎨이대티부
보병부위　리조영
○보진위뎨삼련티뎨이대티향
관일등군ᄉᆞ　윤셕호
○보진위뎨ᄉᆞ련티뎨삼대티부
보병참위　김봉평
○보진위뎨오련티뎨삼대티부
보병참위　최긔환
이샹구월이십삼일
○승셔쥬임관삼등　즁츄원의
관　송덕인　강덕슈
○의원면본관　평안북도관찰
부쥬ᄉᆞ　김병하
○평안북도관찰부쥬ᄉᆞ셔임
판륙등　탁　근
○의원면경위원총무관　동
티감리　리무영
○의원면본관　샹의ᄉᆞ쟝조과
기슈　류병션
○임샹의ᄉᆞ쟝조과기슈셔판임
관륙등　박진양
○임즁츄원의관셔칙임관ᄉᆞ등
졍삼품　박용규
○임의졍부찬졍셔칙임관일등
통신원총판　민샹호
○겸임통신원총판　의졍부찬
졍　민샹호
이샹십월이일
궁졍록ᄉᆞ
○의졍부찬졍박제슌ᄉᆞ직소
비지니에소쳥티로의시ᄒᆞ노라
○궁니부특진관졍랑용ᄉᆞ직소
비지니에소쳥티로의시ᄒᆞ노라
뎨이쳔구빅ᄉᆞ십구호
광무팔년십월오일
셔임급ᄉᆞ령
○임륙군삼등군의쟝　의학교
교관　김익남
○임륙군이등군의　시위긔병
대티륙군군의보　졍긔현
○임륙군삼등군의　진위뎨이
련티뎨일대티륙군군의보　류
병필　의학교교관　쟝홍섭
김교준
이샹구월이십삼일
○명니부광제원위원　최덕련
진긔셕　김ᄉᆞ영　졍달하　셔
제명　쟝영근　한강셕　황셕
쥬
○의원면본관　니부광제원쥬
ᄉᆞ　빈죤익　박봉근　윤샹하
○임니부광제원쥬ᄉᆞ셔판임관
륙등　한영긔　홍종덕　쟝셕
회
○임니부광제원의ᄉᆞ셔판임관
륙등　고플　구품　권티완
이샹구월이십구일

잡보

○한복충돌　모쳐에도착ᄒᆞᆫ원
신던보를거ᄒᆞᆫ즉복쳥과셩진간
에는아병삼쳔명이쥬둔ᄒᆞ는티
그중오륙빅명은홍원으로나려
와그젼쵸티는지작구일에참관
평에청츌ᄒᆞ야일본병젼쵸와충
돌ᄒᆞ엿는티주시계뢰ᄒᆞ엿다더
라

○평슌한민　아군중에잇는참
령김인슈는한국인민오빅여명
을평슌ᄒᆞ고복쳥에회집ᄒᆞ엿다
더라

○젼긔졍근　아병오젼졍남외
홍원에쥬둔ᄒᆞ고일군은함흥에
잇셔샹거가불원ᄒᆞ니복도에한
번싸홈이미구에되리라더라

○영부간긔동　경부텰도는영
등포로붓터부강ᄉᆞ지긔동이되
엿다더라

○ᄉᆞ령관리도　한국쥬차일본
군ᄉᆞ령관쟝곡쳔대쟝이금일오
젼에인항에도착홈예뎡인고로
림공ᄉᆞ와원구쇼쟝은빅틀타고

힝샹에나가령졉ᄒ던이오그대쟝이항구에드러올때에는그항구에졍박ᄒ여잇든각국군함이경의를표ᄒ야례포를노ᄒ더이오그대쟝은샹륙ᄒᆞᆫ후에하루밤을인항에셔류숙ᄒ고명일오젼구시삼십분에남대문외졍거쟝에도착ᄒᆞᆯ례졍이오그졍거쟝에셔븍셔대관졍ᄭᆞ지츄착군병이로랑편에느러셔셔경졉ᄒ논의례를힝ᄒ고과병일쇼ᄃᆡ는좌우로옹위ᄒ고외쟝ᄃᆡ에셔는포병이례포를열아홉번을노코한국졍부에셔는칙ᄉ를인쳔ᄭᆞ지나려보내여히대쟝을령졉케ᄒᆞᆫ다더라

◯쳥인피살 곡산민요에일본인이피해ᄒ엿다는ᄉ진은본보에이왕게지ᄒ엿거니와일젼에진남포에잇는일본령ᄉ가한셩령ᄉ관으로보고ᄒ엿스되일본인룡명파한인등ᄇ일명이피살되엿기로그원인은방금심ᄉ중인ᄃᆡ히군ᄒ장이빌셔을젼동ᄒ야그모로가납듯ᄒ다더라

◯한셩동도 근일동학당이한셩니에회집ᄒᆞᆫ수효가삼쳔여명인ᄃᆡ칭왈진보회라ᄒ고시졍기션ᄒ는거ᄉ로주장을삼아간세빈를쳑퇴ᄒᆞᆫ다고ᄒ는ᄃᆡ현령은리용ᄃᆡ권즁셕리위등ᄉ세를침퇴ᄒᆞᆫ연후에야국ᄉ를가히바로잡겟다ᄒ며그비분쳐ᄒ여하모다장하얏시ᄒ라고ᄒ여도형편이엇지ᄒᆞᆯ수업다는말이잇다더라

◯한ᄃᆡ연셜 일젼에한국부대신이곰번에일본으로젼왕ᄒᆞᆫ학도ᄉ십륙명을회집ᄒ고연셜ᄒ기를 대한뎨국폐하ᄭ셔셔교후대졍에잔졍ᄒ신조칙을여러번나리심으로본대신이셩ᄌ를밧드러종교한젼비들을셜립ᄒ야인ᄌ국으로파견ᄒ야여러학싱으로ᄒ여곰실지로학업을강구ᄒ며지식과ᄉ리를통달ᄒ고무궤는불굴ᄒ는졍신을함셩ᄒ야우리대한뎨국의독립을공고케ᄒᆞᆯ지니여러학싱들은셩샹의지로덕힝과지예를ᄯᆞᆯ다가ᄌ긔의ᄉ소를이져바리고충군ᄋ국의ᄯᅳᆺ을셰워셰계의문명을비호고나라에평ᄒ를증진케ᄒ야본졍부의바라는바를져바리지말나ᄒ엿다더라

◯죠쳥교셥 졍부에셔외부로조회ᄒ기를본월팔일에참졍이샹 쥬ᄒ되공쥬ᄃᆡ병뎡이일인과야료ᄒᆞᆫ스로일병이회ᄃᆡ에젼왕ᄒ야ᄒᆡᄃᆡ졍위와참위가피집ᄒ엿스나국톄에손샹홈이만만경히ᄒ온지라ᄒ히도관찰ᄉ식젼령으로발ᄒ드ᄃᆡ리도비롯군ᄉ세어ᄒ는권리는업ᄉᆞᆷᄂᆞᆫ히탄양ᄒ야슈졉ᄒ쟝ᄒ엿ᄉ며엇지이경에ᄒᆡ일으리오불가불징계ᄒᆞᆯ지니법부로ᄒ여곰검ᄉ를파송ᄒ야회ᄉ진야료되든ᄉ종을사실ᄒ고즁ᄃᆡ쟝권즁락과소ᄃᆡ쟝리응하가평시에조속지못ᄒ야이젼에엇든일을당ᄒ엿ᄉ니셩샹이처치치못ᄒᆞᆯ지라외부로ᄒ여곰교섭ᄒ야군부로보내어ᄉ힝ᄒ야명죄ᄒ옵이하여ᄒ올지샹 쥬ᄒ여의 쥬된고로조회ᄒ니일공ᄉ의게교섭ᄒ여힝ᄃᆡ즁ᄃᆡ쟝과소ᄃᆡ쟝을군부로이송ᄒ여ᄉ실명죄케ᄒ라ᄒ엿더라

론셜

봉쳔군방으로동이라

◯일본군ᄉ가요양에잇든아병을공격ᄒ야쳘귀케ᄒᆞᆫ담이후에도여간져은싸홈은죵죵되엿다ᄒ나일산이지나도록소식이회보ᄒ며ᄯᅩ일젼이연ᄃᆡ셔방과평ᄃᆡ수동편에잇서셩봉ᄃᆡ병을조발ᄒ는모양인듯ᄒ되아죽도북으로젼진ᄒ엿다는소문이들니지아니ᄒ는중

미제아병으로젼ᄒ는말을드른즉일병이과연고두결로좌우병진ᄒ야아병의진첫든봉쳔군쳐현강이라ᄒ는북방삼십오영리되는ᄯᅡ에이르럿고아국군ᄃᆡ는일이베ᄉ지현강남방에잇다가일병의게연ᄎ습격홈을당ᄒ고퇴경퇴축은셕엿스나그일에는젼곡추회이다되여현강과연ᄃᆡ사미소경편로가평란무힘ᄒᆞᆫ고로일병이아병으로더부러조곰도수교홈이엽시강두남편셔지무의히진ᄒ야아병의듸를취ᄒᆞᆫ동남방으로향ᄒ야드러간다ᄒ엿고

수일젼소문에는흑목ᄃᆡ쟝이삼만ᄃᆡ병을거ᄂ리고동으로향ᄒ야무인지경갓치모라드러갓다ᄒᆞᆫ즉아즉ᄭᆞ지도우익ᄃᆡ중에잇는지는알수업스되비동병인즉현강을지나봉쳔동북방ᄭᆡ티렁동방을졈령ᄒ라는목젹이분명ᄒᆞᆫ지라

그러나흑목ᄃᆡ쟝이과연일향도싸호게되지안코셔샹히젼진ᄒ는지화셜히발ᄒᆞᆯ수는업스되만일일동으로만향ᄒ야졈졈드러갈지경이면중앙ᄃᆡ에잇는아병들이라도필경방어ᄒ는아병들로셔로반나교봉이될듯ᄒ며사령쟝관도응당힘을다ᄒ야티렁동방샨결에셔크게싸홀듯ᄒ논즉긔왕에도일병이아병보다곤란ᄒᆞᆫ지경을여러번당ᄒ엿스되미리예도지세형즁ᄒᆞᆷ으로더어려울듯ᄒ며

ᄯᅩᄒᆞᆫ이러ᄒᆞᆯᄲᅮᆫ외라아병들은이싸홈편을미리혜아려반보지라그런고로현강남방평ᄃᆡ로조응젹ᄒ야일병의티령과봉졈령ᄒ란홈을져항곡격ᄒᆞᆯ지니만일그리ᄒᆞᆯ진ᄃᆡ일병의게티ᄒ야는괴왕ᄉ요양싸홈보다엇지어려옴이더ᄒ지아니ᄒ리요

아병의압길은넘부편지지아니ᄒ엿슨즉구로파드킨쟝군이힝우세를더ᄒ야경동케ᄒ기가민우조ᄒ더이요ᄯᅩᄒᆞᆫ요양젼졍에우려ᄒ는션창이잇슨즉ᄌ긔외군수로ᄒ야곰일병의도강홈을응당방어ᄒᆞᆯ터이며봉쳔븍방에는뒤스셴나파드쟝군의강ᄒᆞᆫ괴병예비군이잇슨즉졍령코공격ᄒ려ᄒᆞᆯ지라

이젼졍계국이쟝챳셔로엉긴홀터인고로우리는요양졈령ᄒᆞᆫ후다시ᄂᆞᆫ병ᄒ야싸홈이엇더타는소문듯기를고ᄃᆡᄒ노라

잡보

◯일왕일티 셔간도관리셔샹무가번게빙셩을무ᄒ치아니ᄒ고쳥국비도들젹동ᄒ야인민의게피해ᄒ엿다ᄒ야압샹되엿더니셜샹인즉히셰가번민을셜싱으로이홀ᄒ야민심이열복된고로히셰를히도관리환임ᄎ로빙셩수인이불원쳔리ᄒ고샹경ᄒᆞᆸ으로민원티로되야히셔를히도관리로환임ᄒ야슈히과송된다ᄒ고븍간도관리범윤세는히도변리로취가단ᄒᆞᆫ톄ᄒ히도인민은원류ᄒ나번계경무관최도남북쌔의보고도잇셔고청국인의비방이비등ᄒ야청공ᄉ가루ᄎ소환홈을청ᄒ는고로즉시소환ᄒᆞᆫ다더라

◯진쥬진보회 진쥬관찰ᄉ가면보ᄒ기를소위진보회라ᄒ고인민이회집ᄒᆞᆫ거슨엄칙ᄒ야흣텻스나다시리쳐로회집ᄒ엿다ᄒ니병뎡을파송ᄒ야쵸토ᄒ기로계교ᄒᆞᆫ다ᄒ엿더라

◯귀쳔동학 평안남도관찰ᄉ리즁하씨가부로보고ᄒ기를동학당과거번명이귀쳔군에졉ᄒ야일제히단발ᄒ고이조ᄒ야가취연ᄒ니군부에이첩ᄒ야귀쳔군숑쥬ᄃᆡ에면칙ᄒ야병뎡을파송ᄒ야진압케ᄒ라ᄒ엿더라

◯외안수십권 일젼졍부회의에졍부에셔계출ᄒᆞᆫ각부부원쳥의안이수십건이라더라

◯북쟝쥰비 외교관들이북쟝을방쟝쥰비중인ᄃᆡ음력본월십오일붓터실시ᄒ기로뎡일ᄒ엿다더라

◯슈령 쥬본 지작일 쥬본된군슈셤이과는풍긔신병호확슌쳔홍쥬종졈포리셕지이쳔로병지쥼쥬쟝쥰원롱안호영덕을두산쳥동셕평산리용구신계길두환양근리범셕은진쟝ᄒ식진위빅남규계써더라

◯탕슈도변 금번 쥬본된군슈중로빙지쟝쥰원량씨는소원이아니라고도면ᄒᆞᆫ다더라

◯슈의션용 중쥬원관계를ᄒᆞᆫ금지쟝중인ᄃᆡ히원을관의원이라지칭ᄒ고의관은ᄉ의라지칭ᄒ고시무에한숙ᄒ고명예가잇는자와평예잇는신문과자중으로셔임ᄒᆞᆫ다더라

◯외조학부 외부에셔학부로조회ᄒ기를귀조회를졉준ᄒ야일본류학싱셩명록송ᄒ는일ᄉ로일본공ᄉ의게조회ᄒ엿더니회공ᄉ조복에ᄒ엿스되류학싱한비지출ᄒ는곳이분명치아니ᄒ니일후학도관리ᄒ기에싱히불편ᄒᆞᆫ지라향쟈본ᄉ 폐현시에나리신 칙교에ᄂᆡ탕금으로특별이 ᄂᆡ하ᄒ신셧ᄃᆡ로다시쳠입ᄒ기위ᄒ야조회를재교ᄒᆞᆫ다홈으로조회ᄒ니다시곳시명ᄒ라ᄒ엿더라

◯젼진ᄃᆡ역구별 함경남도관찰ᄉ리헌경씨가면보ᄒ기를함흥주차일본슈령관조회에ᄒ엿스되본월팔일노위시ᄒ야일본군젼진ᄃᆡ역ᄂᆡ에군령을시ᄒᆡᆼᄒ되문쳔이븍각군은함흥주차수령관이관할ᄒ고문쳔이남각군은원산주차ᄉ령관이관할ᄒᆞᆫ다ᄒ엿다ᄒ엿더라

◯군령시ᄒᆡᆼ 일본공ᄉ가외부로조회ᄒ기를함경남북도일본군젼진ᄃᆡ역ᄂᆡ에셔군령시ᄒᆡᆼᄒ더니쟝ᄎ귀국부에셔히방관의게면칙ᄒ야피란ᄒᆞᆫ빅셩을도라오게ᄒ되다만군ᄉ샹에방ᄒᆡ홈이업슬듯ᄉ로인민의게고시케ᄒ라ᄒ엿더라

◯간협쳐형 의쥬군슈보고에ᄒ기를본년졍월순간에로국군ᄃᆡ수파즁팔의게슈종ᄒᆞᆫ사름셤쳔지ᄂᆞᆫ거ᄒ는최인즁이가평양안쥬지간으로왕리ᄒ며일본군의졍형을졍탐ᄒᆞᆫ죄로본월이십륙일하오시에본군셔문외에셔수형에쳐ᄒ엿다ᄒ엿더라

◯조복방관 외부에셔법국공ᄉ관에조복ᄒ기를귀국인의ᄃᆡ단ᄉ관ᄒᆞᆫ수진미가흔엽교로평양감리와계졍번ᄒᆞᆫ다홈으로본ᄃᆡ셔싱이명일샹오싱이시에본셔리ᄒᆞᆯ리이니취ᄒᆞᆫ민이명을괴송ᄒ야져판케ᄒ라ᄒ엿다더라

외보

◯로쟝뎐주 러시아ᄉ군구들직한로국쟝군쓰텔셰씨가로황의게뎐주ᄒ기를군파런탁이오리ᄉ산쳐지교과격헐ᄃᆡ도아니와셔아모리국력ᄒ여쳔슈ᄒ야도이듬을지나기어렵다ᄒ엿더라

◯로츌포ᄃᆡ 봉텬쟝군죠로긔씨의뎐주ᄒᆞᆫ바를거ᄒᆞᆫ즉로군이텬쥬산과룡미산에잇는릉쳠에포ᄃᆡ를건츅ᄒᆞᆫ다ᄒ엿더라

법경파리쓰에셔말ᄒ기를로국뎨이군은뎨팔셔빅리아군단과뎨륙군단과뎨류셔빅리아군단의일부분과뎨륙카삭스단으로편셩ᄒ엿는ᄃᆡ봉텬남부로향ᄒ야츌발ᄒ엿다더라

TELEGRAMS.

FROM JAPAN PAPERS.

THE ATTACK ON PORT ARTHUR.

London, Oct. 1.

The Russian General Staff announces that the assault on Port Arthur was continued from the 20th to the 26th ultimo, but was everywhere repulsed.

THE SITUATION AT MUKDEN.

London, Oct. 3.

General Sakharoff telegraphs that the Japanese advance guards have been seen southeast of Mukden.

Latest accounts from Mukden indicate that the situation is unchanged.

Contradictory reports are current at St. Petersburg, some declaring that the military authorities expect a battle shortly, while others state that General Kuropatkin is preparing to retire on Tieling.

Reuter's correspondent at Mukden, wiring on the 1st inst., says the prolonged inactivity on both sides emphasizes the creation of a new situation. The battle of Liaoyang, he says, clearly terminated the first stage of the war, thus necessitating the adoption of new tactics by the Japanese. The latter are now entrenching themselves, though it is thought they may still attempt a flanking movement to the eastward of the Russian position.

JAPANESE REFUGEES FROM SIBERIA.

Berlin, Oct. 5.

Seven hundred and seven Japanese refugees from Siberia arrived in Berlin yesterday on their way home. They will spend a few days at Bremer-haven for purposes of recreation, and will then embark for home.

London, Oct. 6.

Seven hundred Japanese expelled from Liberia arrived at Bremerhaven, where they embarked for Japan.

THE BALTIC FLEET.

Berlin, Oct. 5.

Captain Pusstau, a Russian naval officer has published an article on the Baltic Fleet, in which he enters intom any details, the knowledge of which, it is alleged, will be of considerable benefit to the Japanese.

The Russian Press is very indignant at the publication of the article.

RUSSIAN OFFICER RECALLED.

Berlin, Oct. 5.

In addition to General Orloff, Major-General Romanoff has also been recalled from Manchuria.

SUPPLIES FOR JAPANESE.

Berlin, Oct. 5.

The "New York Herald" publishes a report to the effect that Japan has ordered in Europe large quantities of provisions, especially biscuits. The goods, it is stated, will be shipped at a Mediterranean port for Japan on vessels flying the British flag.

American underwriters have increased the premium on railway materials to be shipped to Japan.

MISHAP TO RUSSIAN BATTLESHIP.

London, Oct. 6.

The "Orel" has left Kronstadt and joined the Baltic squadron.

[A telegram to Tokyo stated that the Russian battleship "Orel" while leaving Kronstadt the other day, grounded, but the damage was not considered serious. The vessel was shortly afterwards floated and put back to Kronstadt.]

ILL-FATED PORTUGUESE EXPEDITION.

London, Oct. 6.

A Portuguese detachment of 499 men, operating in the Mossamedes country (Portuguese West Africa), were surprised while crossing the Cunene River by Cuanhamas. The detachment lost 254 killed, including 15 officers, and 50 wounded.

[This territory is that immediately north of Hereros Land. The Cunene River forms the boundary between the two colonies, and it is quite possible that the Hereros rising, which has given the Germans so much trouble, has infected the Cuanhamas with the spirit of revolt.]

THE DARDANELLES.

Berlin, Oct. 3.

Russia declares that the report emanating from St. Petersburg that she has applied to the Porte to permit the Russian war-ships to pass the Dardanelles is untrue.

THE PRESIDENT'S PEACE CONFERENCE.

[THROUGH REUTER'S AGENCY.]

London, Oct. 6.

Mr. Roosevelt, after making inquiries among the European capitals, has decided to defer summoning the proposed peace conference until the war is over.

CHINESE ON THE RAND.

In the "Johannesburg Star" of July 16 appears an interesting account of the first fortnight's experi ence of the Chinese coolie at the New Comet mine. There was some difficulty at first about the provision of cooks, the coolie himself being unwilling or unable to undertake the duty.

"He misses his own particular tobacco. But he has taken to the Transvaal product. He approves the change, and it is hoped that he will create an unexpected demand for the fragrant weed of the Magaliesberg. He feels the cold of the Rand uplands at nights. 'Me like the sun,' he says, 'but it is velly cold at night, and the cold comes through the boards.' Above all—and here he is most human—he misses his little luxuries, and wishes to know how he is to pay for them out of his earnings. He wants to buy cigarettes and other little things."

His capacity to earn extra pay will determine his command of luxuries, which, according to the "Star," ought eventually to be considerable. "He promises to become a much more efficient worker than the Bantu, and he learns his work more quickly. The daily average amount of drilling accomplished by 500 of the Chinamen is 15.3 inches. Thirty are earning extra money by excess drilling, and two have actually drilled 3ft. 6in. A good Kaffir, it is stated, does not drill more than 3ft. per day. Half of the batch of inexperienced Chinese have been able to do a third of the task of trained Kaffrs in the short period of a fortnight. It is recognised that it takes a Kaffir from three to four months to reach a state of effciency, and on the progress made by the Chinese it can be concluded that within at least two months they will surpass the efficiency that it takes the South African native twice as long to acquire. And it is only reasonable to expect that the majority of the Chinese labourers will when they have got accustomed to their work, attain double the efficiency which we have been accustomed hitherto to look for from unskilled mine labour. On contract work, one Chinaman may be expected to do the work of two Kaffirs."

The picture of the Chinese at dinner in the compound is pleasing enough. "They were summoned by a sweet-sounding triangle. The men flocked from their quarters carrying their small pans and chop-sticks with all the avidity of children. They squatted in groups of about half a dozen each, and the menu for each circle was a bucket of rice, a large pan of stewed meat, and a small pan of cooked dried fish.

One was struck by the deft use of the chop-sticks, and the constant stream in which the rice flowed from the pans to the men's mouths. There was no sign of dissatisfaction with food or cooking. And at the end of the meal each labourer was given a full-sized loaf of bread to take with him when he went down the mine for the night shift."

The "Star" representative also visited the hospital, where he found some eighty Chinese patients, of whom half were suffering from beri-beri. These latter he found to be in a condition of unexpected cheerfulness. A group of four were playing cards with a Chinese pack; and with the exception of one serious case the sufferings of the remainder were confined to "a stiffness in the legs." In short, the complaint caused little or no inconvenience to the majority of the patients, and he was assured that in a short time nothing more would be heard about beri-beri.

JAPANESE MILITARY PROCLAMATION.

The Japanese Headquarters have issued the following proclamation emanating from the General.

I, the Commander-in-Chief of His Imperial Japanese Majesty's forces in Korea, notified the people of south and north Hamkyeng provinces that our enemies are the Russians. We shall protect you against them as a mother looking after her children.

We already know how badly the Russians treat you, violote your women and steal your valuables. I consider it my duty to free you from these marauders and when the time comes I shall strike. Henceforth military activity will be increased in the north and south Hamkyeng provinces, so you people may work on as usual and those who ran away from the Russians may return safely to their homes.

If our troops cause you any trouble, you may report the matter immediately and the case will be impartially judged, but the following articles you must not disobey.

1. Any person attempting to interfere with military operations; i. e. breaking telegraph wires, railway bridges, moving material etc. will be punished by martial-law.

2. Martial-law will deal with anyone furnishing information or giving assistance to the enemy's troops.

3. Anyone, who speak treason against military law will be liable to punishment.

4. The disobedieuce to orders of any commander or officers in any place within the boundary of military operations will be punished by martial-law.

Dr. McGee, with the other American lady nurses who have been in Japan for some months past, will leave Nagasaki for home by the United States Army transport "Thomas," which is due here from Manila on the 20th inst. Their period of service will terminate on the 10th, and they are expected to rache Nagasaki on the 18th or 19th inst.

The Korea Daily News.

Issued at 5 P. M. daily except Sundays.

Rate of Subscription:—

Per Year, Yen 25.
Per Quarter, Yen 7.
Per Month, Yen 2.50.

Postage in Korea not charged extra.
Postage abroad charged extra.

Advertisements, 50 sen per day for 1 inch or less.
5 yen per month per inch.
50 yen per year per inch.

All communications to

E. T. BETHELL,
Editor and Publisher,
Pak-tong, Seoul.

WAYS AND MEANS.

With the word "Reform" on everybody's lips, we might suggest certain matters, other than Governmental, where reform is very much needed A notable instance is the pitiable condition of the roads of the capital.

There is hardly one of the principal streets of the city which can be said to be in anything like good order, while broken-backed bridges every hundred yards or so are a menace to the safety of man and beast.

For instance, the bridge covering (or intended to cover) the culvert immediately in front of the main Palace Gate, is broken in no fewer than six separate places; that is six of the stones forming the surface of the bridge have entirely disappeared into the depths below, leaving veritable man-traps for the unwary passer-by.

In Kurigeh, three bridges have suffered a similar fate through want of a stitch in time.

At the present time perhaps, although very necessary, the building of these bridges is not of such vital importance as it will be a few weeks hence. Then, with a thin layer of ice and snow covering these man-traps, we may expect to hear of accidents happening to both humans and animals.

The maiming of an ox or pony, by the fracture of a leg, would call forth little sympathy from the average Korean, but perhaps the spilling of a yangban, caused by his chair coolie disappearing through a hole in the roadway, may have the desired effect of calling official attention to the matter.

Apart from the danger incurred, there is also much personal discomfort attached to a ricksha ride through the majority of the streets. One particularly bumpy spot which we have in mind, is a bridge, on the main street; here, a ricksha coolie is forced to strain with all his strength to attain the altitude of the bridge, which is at least one foot higher than the roadway, of which fact the occupant of the ricksha is painfully reminded when leaving the other end. Recently a very laudable attempt was made to repair many of the roads by banking them up with the material obtained from the clearing of the main creek; however, when the work was half completed and still plenty of material remained, the task was abandoned leaving in its tracks a motley collection of semi-repaired streets.

In some cases the bridges received a certain amount of attention, but instead of building up solid stone structures, logs of wood were placed in the interstices caused by the decay of the original stone surface.

These will naturally wear out in no time. In fact, in the majority of cases, they are already worn out, leaving matters in the same condition as before.

Many instances of rough roads, broken bridges and inefficient repairs could be cited but these are sufficient to show that much of the energy expended in cries of "Government Reform," might with advantage be used in attempting to furnish Seoul with streets worthy of the Capital of an Empire.

GENERAL COUNT KELLER.

The "Penang Gazette" reproduces the following interesting letter from the pen of Douglas Story:—

General Count Keller is dead. The news comes to me as the news of the death of a friend. I had been the only correspondent accredited to his corps, had campaigned with him, and seen him with his staff, his officers, and his men. I had heard his praises sung by orderly and by aide-de-camp, by thirty-six year old comrades and by newly-joined subalterns. I had learned to know him as one knows only the clean-hearted and the sympathetic. I had respected him for his bravery in battle, his intelligence in leadership, his energy and his resource. I had loved him for his constant consideration, his quick sympathy, his care for the wounded.

It was June 14 when Middleton, of the Associated Press, and myself first rode into the quarters of Count Keller on the road to Feng-wang-cheng. His camp was a reflex of the man. Everything was soldier-like and orderly. The guns were neatly packed. The infantry was comfortably quartered on well-drained slopes. The horse lines were well arranged and free from litter. The soup kitchens stood aligned like a guard of honour paraded for inspection. The General's personal quarters were properly trenched and shaded. The whole camp bore the stamp of discipline and supervision.

The General himself sat in his tent writing. He received us with the stately courtesy of an old-time French seigneur. It was not till later that I learned the despatches he was composing announced the beginning of Kuroki's phenomenal advance upon the left of the Russian line. No trace of the urgency of his message was apparent in his manner. He made us welcome to his camp.

That evening I saw Count Keller at dinner. Surrounded by a brilliant staff, principally of officers of the Guards, he chatted gaily with everyone, searching the faces of his company with the keenness of one who had lived with his hand ever close to his sword hilt.

Immaculately uniformed, bearing the Cross of St. George upon his pure white tunic, exacting the convenances of etiquette from those about him, he had no smallest suggestion of the exquisite. Sun-burned and wind-tanned, with his well-trimmed beard strangely splashed with white, he looked a soldier who loved service and had seen much. I was to know later how true this was.

Three days later, Keller and his men marched away to meet the Japanese at Lien-chan-kouan. I carried Middleton back to the hospital, where he died.

The next time I saw Count Keller was at Lan-jan-san, a fortnight later. I joined him in his retreat before the overwhelming army of Kuroki. It was a day of dreadful rain. The roads were belly-deep in mire. The horses lagged distressfully. Men were washed away and drowned where, a week before, had been good marching road-beds; transports stuck in the ruts and were abandoned. The rain swept down unceasingly, but the troops laboured mightily. Keller was in command, and the fact carried them where neither mule nor baggage horse could force a passage.

The General himself, on an awkward-gaited Cossack horse, rode forward to investigate the positions, swung round to Hazaling, thirty-five versts away to the southward, gathered up some troops there, returned to Lan-jan-san, and led his bedraggled forces back to the Pass of Yansching in time to check the Japanese advance. Count Keller was fifty-five years of age, but be covered seventy-five miles that weary day, in the saddle, upon a common troop horse.

In the weeks that followed, I saw much of Count Keller, marked his influence upon his men, learned his value as a leader of a skeleton army against overwhelming odds. He had become guardian of the gate of Liaoyang, and right loyally he held the post.

It was after the affair of the Fourth of July, when his men had marched twelve miles to fight, had stormed the heights of Ta-go-ling in darkness, had been overtaken by daylight and suffered terribly in consequence, that Count Keller begged his men to carry the wounded the twelve rough miles back again to save them the jolting of the Red Cross carts. For love of him, as much as out of consideration for their comrades the battle-weary soldiers shouldered the litters back down the long road to the river, halting over the swollen fords, heavily up the bouldered path to the position on the summit. The influence of Keller had overcome their fatigue.

The career of General Count Keller is quickly told. In 1868 he was a page of His Imperial Majesty the Czar. From the Page School he passed into the Chevalier Guard, and afterwards went to the Military Academy, whence he returned as Adjutant to the Horse Guards, later commanding a squadron. In the Turko-Servian war he volunteered for service with the Servians, and commanded a wing there with distinction. Later, he served in the Russo-Turkish war and in the Asiatic Expedition. In these campaigns he won the coveted sword of honour—the sabre d'or—for conspicuous bravery in the field and the St. George's Cross, the proudest decoration a Russian officer may carry.

From active service Count Keller returned as a member of the Cossack Central Staff, became A.D.C. to the Czar. He commanded a battalion of the "Tircurs" of the Guard—the Imperial Foot Guards, and at the special request of the Emperor undertook the direction of the Page School. From there he was called to succeed General Sassulitch in command of the Army of the East in the present war after the affair of Chin-lieng-cheng. At the time of his death, Count Keller held the most important corps command in the Manchurian Army. His column numbered some 50,000 men.

A strict disciplinarian, General Keller demanded efficiency in every officer under him. To secure it he made many changes in the regiments of his force, replaced many of the commanders. At his death he commanded an army effective in every branch, ever ready for combat or fatigue, devoted to its leader. His loss cannot be measured in words.

Count Keller died as he would have chosen to die, in fair fight, with his face to the foe, shattered by the enemy's shrapnel. To me there is something of association in the knowledge that he fell within sight of poor Middleton's grave. The General's last words to me on the loss of my comrade might form an epitaph over his own tomb:

"He was too young to die."

DOUGLAS STORY.

Reports from the governors of provinces confirm the statement that out of 350 supposed magistracies, more than half have no magistrate in charge.

With the exception of Mr. Yi Sang Chon, the judge of the High Supreme Court, the delegates to Japan, before their departure, adopted the shaved head fashion. Mr. Yi's objection to participate, we understand, was based on religious scruples.

The Government has instructed the Foreign Office to apply to the Japanese Legation for the handing over of the arrested officers who were in command of the troops, who rioted at Kongchu. If the request is complied with, the officers will be severely punished by the War Department.

ANOTHER RIOT.

The Japanese consul in Seoul is in receipt of a despatch from his confrere in Chemulpo, telling of the murder of 6 Japanese and their Korean interpreter by rioters at Koksan.

The Korea Daily News.

VOL. I, WEDNESDAY, OCTOBER 12, 1904. No. 74

HONGKONG & SHANGHAI BANKING CORPORATION.

Paid-up Capital..... ....$10,000,000
Reserve Fund:—Sterling Reserve... 10,000,000
Silver Reserve..... 7,000,000

27,000,000
Reserve Liability of Proprietors... 10,000,000

HEAD OFFICE, HONGKONG.

London Bankers, London and County Banking Company Limited.
Branches and Agencies,
London.

Amoy,	Hankow	Penang,
Bangkok,	Hiogo,	Rangoon,
Batavia,	Iloilo,	Saigon,
Bombay,	Lyons,	San Francisco,
Calcutta,	Manila,	Singapore,
Colombo,	Nagasaki,	Sourabaya,
Foochow,	New York,	Tientsin,
Hamburg,	Peking,	Yokohama,

Credits granted on approved Securities, and every description of Banking and Exchange business transacted.

Drafts granted on London and the chief Commercial places in Europe, India, Australia, America, China and Japan.

HOLME RINGER & CO., AGENTS,
CHEMULPO.

ON CHEONG & CO.,
SEOUL.

GENERAL STORE KEEPERS.
Imported provisions, Cooking Utensils Crockery, etc.
FRESH BREAD DAILY.

MITSU BISHI DOCKYARD & ENGINE WORKS,
NAGASAKI.

CODE WORD, "DOCK."

A. 1, A. B. C., and Engineering Codes used.

DOCK No. 1 (at Tategami).

Extreme Length..............523 feet
Length on blocks............ 513 ,,
Width of Entrance on Top.....89 ,,
,, ,, Bottom....77 ,,
Water on Blocks at Spring Tide 26½ ,,

DOCK No. 2 (Mukaijima).

Extreme Length..............371 feet
Length on Blocks.............360 ,,
Width of Entrance on Top......66 ,,
,, ,, Bottom 53 ,,
Water on Blocks at Spring Tide 22 ,,

PATENT SLIP (at Kosuge).

Can take vessels up to 1,000 tons gross.

THE WORKS are well equipped with the LATEST IMPROVEMENTS, and can execute any kind of work in SHIPBUILDING and MARINE ENGINEERING, as well as in REPAIRING of SHIPS.

The COMPANY'S new powerful steamer OURA-MARU (712 tons, 700 I.H.P.), specially built for SALVAGE PURPOSES, and equipped with necessary gear, is always READY at SHORT NOTICE.

CHARTERED BANK OF INDIA AUSTRALIA & CHINA.

INCORPORATED BY ROYAL CHARTER 1853

HEAD OFFICES:—LONDON.

Paid-up Capital £800,000
Reserve Liability of Shareholders 800,000
Reserve Fund 800,000

Drafts granted upon all the principal places in the world and every description of Exchange and banking business transacted.

E. MEYER & CO., Agents,
Chemulpo.

E. MEYER & CO.
Chemulpo.

SOLE AGENTS IN KOREA FOR:
A. T. Morse, Sons & Co's "Fresco" Distemper

In all colours ready for use on walls, Ceilings etc.
and
AVENARIUS CARBOLINEUM

A wood-preserving and antiseptic oil preparation

Against decay, dry-rot, fungus and wood-destroying insects.

A large supply always in Stock.
Prices upon application.

E. MEYER & CO.,
Chemulpo.

THE METHODIST PUBLISHING HOUSE,
Little WestGate, Seoul.

PRINTING, TYPEWRITER PAPER
CARBON PAPER, VISITING CARDS
STATIONERY, BOOK BINDING
BOOK PUBLISHERS
AMERICAN SCHOOL BOOKS
SPENCERIAN COPY BOOKS
PEN CARBON LETTER AND BILL BOOKS

S. A. BECK, Manager.

HOKURKU DOBOKU KAISHA.
Branch office in Choug Dong, Seoul.
Japanese telephone No. 165

CONTRACT DEPARTMENT.
We can contract to build any building or construction.

MERCHANDISE DEPARTMENT.
We can provide any building material. We have just contracted to build the new Belgian Legation.

DAI-ICHI GINKO.

LIMITED.

(Formerly the First National Bank)

ESTABLISHED 1873

INCORPORATED UNDER PRESENT LAW 1896

Capital - - - - - - - - - Yen 5,000,000
Reserve Fund - - - - - 1,500,000

HEAD OFFICE:—TOKIO.

President: Baron SHIBUSAWA.

BRANCHES AND CORRESPONDENTS
In the Principal Cities and Towns of Japan.
Interest Allowed on
Fixed deposits 1 year - - - 6½ per cent
" " 6 months - - - 6 per cent

Special current accounts 1½ sen daily per Y 100
General " " 1 " " " 100

M. TANAKA,
Manager, Chemulpo

HOLME RINGER & Co.
Chemulpo.

General Merchants and Government Contractors.

Agents for the leading
Banks
SteamshipCompanies
and
Insurance Companies

Importers of Merchandise of every description.

KAMEYA & CO.
GENERAL STOREKEEPERS
Chinkokai - - Seoul
(*Established 1895, Tokyo*)

Confectionery, Hams, Canned Goods, Cutlery, Hirano & Tansan Water. Provisions, Gents, Furnishing goods, Toilet Articles, Travelling Bags, Tobacco, Cigars & Cigarettes Kitchen Utensils. Coffee, Biscuits.

Fresh Goods always kept in Stock.
Prices Moderate
Please come and inspect our goods.

NIPPON YUSEN KAISHA.

JAPANESE MAIL STEAMSHIP CO.

DER MAIL CONTRACT WITH THE IMPERIAL JAPANESE GOVERNMENT.

European Line

Regular Fortnightly Service between Yokohama Kobe, Moji, Shanghai, Hongkong, Singapore, Penang Colombo, Port Said, Marseilles, London and Antwerp

American Line

Regular Fortnightly Service between Hongkong and Seattle, calling at Shanghai, Moji, Kobe, Yokohama and Victoria, B. C.

Australian Line

Regular weekly Service betwen Japan Ports and Australia, calling at Hongkong and Manila.
(Above Three Lines Suspended until further notice).

Shanghai Line

Weekly Service between Shanghai and Japan Ports

Korea Line

Service Kobe, Moji, Nagasaki, Fusan, Chemupo, Coo, Taiku.
S. S. Bahelsberg, 2181 tons.
Service Kobe, Moji, Fusan, Chemulpo, Chinnampo
S. S ARGO, S. S. Ohio.

BORDEN'S CONDENSED MILK CO.
New York, U. S. A.

ALWAYS IN STOCK
Eagle Brand Condensed Milk.
Gold Seal Condensed Milk.
Peerless (Family) Evaporated Cream.
Borden's Malted Milk.

E. MEYER & CO.
Chemulpo, Korea,
Sole Agents

ROYAL INSURANCE COMPANY,
Funds exceed £10,000,000
FIRE
AT CURRENT RATES.
LIFE
REDUCED PREMIUM.
HOLME RINGER & CO.,
Agents, Chemulpo.

HOTEL DU PALAIS
SEOUL.

The only first class Hotel in Seoul. Situated in the centre of the city opposite the palace.

Cuisine under the supervision of an experienced French Chef.

Well ventilated and furnished throughout.

TARIFF UPON APPLICATION

L. MARTIN
Proprietor and Manager

報申日每韓大
보신일민한대

(호오십칠뎨) (일요목) 일삼십월십년사빅

본사고빅

본신보는영어와한어로셔계믜
일출판ᄒᆞ옵
신문가
한쟝 엽두돈오푼
일삭됴 엽두량닷돈
우표가미삭닷돈
다맛돈으로밧숩
광고료는
귀한의쟝단과ᄌᆞ항의다쇼로중
감ᄒᆞ되랑가로밧을터이오며오
린지아녀대한사람마다이신
문을보실터이니광고버시기를
원ᄒᆞ시는이들은우리신문사에
와셔면약ᄒᆞ심을희망ᄒᆞ옵
○발힝소 박동대한미일신보
사법어학교압해젼영국인셜필
림쟝자리오
사쟝 영국인 (빈셜)
평양 디리졈
○평양셩동사는권미보씨로우
리신문관디리인을뎡ᄒᆞ엿
스오니평양에계신구람코져ᄒᆞ
시는 첨군ᄌᆞ는디리졈에왕
림ᄒᆞ와면의ᄒᆞ시옵

사고

○우리대한미일신보의목뎍은
대한의인명재산에관한모든대
목에되ᄒᆞ야는공평한변론을주
쟝ᄒᆞ이라우리동신원의탐보는
신문보시는첨군ᄌᆞ의게ᄒᆞ상보
도ᄒᆞ리며편지를긔서ᄒᆞ여주시
는이는셩명과빈디를젹어붓치
시기를희망ᄒᆞ오니이게슨신문
상에긔재ᄒᆞ란는거시아니오다
만극히신용ᄒᆞ는증거를숨고자
ᄒᆞ이라긔자는아모긔서던지긔
재ᄒᆞ온되각ᄒᆞ는권리를가졋스
나되각ᄒᆞ는리유를말ᄒᆞᆯ티이오
며공중평화를문란케ᄒᆞ는듯ᄒᆞᆫ
다긔서는의례히밧지안켓숩나이

●본사셜시ᄒᆞᆫ뒤로신문을미양
우례로분젼ᄒᆞ와례젼부의일의
로젼ᄒᆞ드ᄉᆞ로번굣에는ᄒᆞᆨ늣게
젼ᄒᆞ기도ᄒᆞ며ᄒᆞᆨ먹쳣게슴ᄒᆞᆫ겁
에젼ᄒᆞ기도ᄒᆞ며ᄒᆞᆨ아니젼ᄒᆞ는
곳도잇다ᄒᆞ와우리신문을ᄉᆞ랑
ᄒᆞ야구람ᄒᆞ시는 쳠군ᄌᆞ의게금
티ᄒᆞ야미우미안ᄒᆞ옵기로지금
은분젼인을두고미일일ᄌᆞ이젼
ᄒᆞ며아니젼ᄒᆞ거나늣게거나ᄒᆞᆫ

폐가엉도록ᄒᆞ란ᄒᆞ오니ᄒᆞ야니
젼ᄒᆞ거는ᄒᆞᆨ늣게젼ᄒᆞ거나ᄒᆞᆫ일
이잇스면본사로통긔ᄒᆞ여주심
을희망ᄒᆞ옵

본사광고

○본사신문중에좌긔ᄒᆞᆫ호수를
소용ᄒᆞᆯ데가잇서이에광고ᄒᆞ오
니누구시던지그중에아모호수
던지가져오시는되로미쟝에빅
젼두푼식드리리다
데이호 데삼호 뎨이십호
데ᄉᆞ십이호 데ᄉᆞ십삼호 데
오십삼호 데오십ᄉᆞ호와데오
십오호 데륙십이호

관보

데이쳔구빅ᄉᆞ십구호연속
서임급ᄉᆞ령
○의원면본관 곡산군슈 윤
우식 안주군슈 리셜
○면본관 영흥군슈 김로규
○임곡산군슈서주임관삼등
졍삼품 리경직
○임영흥군슈서주임관삼등
셩진감리 홍승욱
○임농상공부주ᄉᆞ서판임관륙
등 구품 송규디 리셕환
○면본관 농상공부주ᄉᆞ 민
용훈
○임농상공부주ᄉᆞ서판임관륙
등 륙품 최린식
이삼십월일일
○의원면본관 봉상ᄉᆞ부졔주
뎡규회 비서원승 김표덕
서공순 니쟝원봉세관 류승
희 슈룽령 서경무 경긔관
찰부주ᄉᆞ 심쳔셥 평안남도
관찰부주ᄉᆞ 차한규
임봉상ᄉᆞ부졔주서주임관륙
등 졍삼품 조한원
○임비서원승서주임관오등
졍삼품 조병구 신팔회
○경임니쟝원봉세관서주임관
륙등 니쟝원봉세위원 김지덕
○임슈룽령서판임관칠등 화
릉참봉 조석호
○임화릉참봉서판임관팔등
김셕하
○임시종원우시어서판임관팔
등 리병철
○병니쟝원봉세위원 김덕준
○임경긔관찰부주ᄉᆞ서판임관
륙등 도상운

○임평안남도관찰부주ᄉᆞ서판
임관륙등 젼주ᄉᆞ 리완하
이삼십월삼일
궁내부대신 리재극 봉칙
○학부대신리재극ᄉᆞ직소
지 비답에분의와ᄉᆞ례가맛당이
긋치지못ᄒᆞᆯ지니곳회환ᄒᆞ야 등쟝
ᄒᆞ라
○탁지부대신민영긔ᄉᆞ직소
비지 답에번거이ᄉᆞ양치말고곳
시무ᄒᆞ라
이삼십월삼일
데이쳔구빅오십호
광무팔년십월륙일
서임급ᄉᆞ령
○임단쳔군슈서주임관륙등
젼시종 김유직
○임안변군슈서주임관륙등
륙품 리 원
○임안주군슈주임관륙등 졍
삼품 김광현
이삼십월일일
○면징계 젼무안항경무관
홍종훈
십월이일
○면징계 젼삼화감리서주ᄉᆞ
졍희운
○승서판임관오등 동리감리
서주ᄉᆞ 김서규
이삼십월ᄉᆞ일
○승서판임관ᄉᆞ등 의정부주
ᄉᆞ 리용규
십월오일
○견칙 농상공부주ᄉᆞ 로영
귀
십월ᄉᆞ일 농상공부
궁내부대신
○의정부참정신 신긔션은
주중청도순찰ᄉᆞ정인표가신병
으로루츳ᄉᆞ쟝ᄒᆞ오니ᄉᆞ신의일
이긴중ᄒᆞᆫ미부등이례임ᄒᆞᆷ고그
디에졍삼품김셩규로차하ᄒᆞ야
불이너로등졍케ᄒᆞ음이하ᄒᆞ여ᄒᆞ
을지샹 주ᄒᆞ와봉지의주ᄒᆞ란
○중추원의관졍주영ᄉᆞ직소
비지 닉에소청되로의시ᄒᆞ노라
○서북텰도국감독윤진우ᄉᆞ직
소 비지닉에소청되로의시ᄒᆞ
노라
데이쳔구빅오십일호
광무팔년십월칠일
서임급ᄉᆞ령

○명중청도순찰ᄉᆞ 졍삼품
김셩규
십월ᄉᆞ일
○임한셩우레지ᄉᆞ주ᄉᆞ서판임
관륙등 리원힝
○금삼품봉 한셩우례지ᄉᆞ주
ᄉᆞ 리원힝
이삼십월오일
궁내부대신
황히도관찰ᄉᆞ김학슈ᄉᆞ직소
비지 닉에번거이ᄉᆞ양말고관찰
지칙을힘쓰라
○중추원의관윤필ᄉᆞ직소
비지 닉에소청되로의시ᄒᆞ노라
○중추원의관조규하ᄉᆞ직소
비지 닉에본직을해ᄒᆞ노라
이삼십월십오일
데이쳔구빅오십이호
광무팔년십월팔일
서임급ᄉᆞ령
○의원면본관 경상북도관찰
부주ᄉᆞ 윤영학
○임경상북도관찰부주ᄉᆞ서판
임관륙등 리 병
○의원면본관 원릉령 류희
붕 중추원의관 손병현
○임중추원의관서주임관륙등
삼화감리 고영철
○임릉쳔황경무관서주임관륙
등 졍삼품 최학리
○임원릉령서판임관칠등 인
릉령 홍슌셕
○임인릉령서판임관칠등 륙
품 류희붕
○임비원검무관서주임관륙등
졍삼품 권티연
○임중추원의관서칙임관이등
평리원검ᄉᆞ 홍종억
○명젼왕일본국시찰슈원 표
훈원주ᄉᆞ 지혈쳔
○쥐법부법률긔초위원장 법
부젼형관 심상익
○명법부법률긔초위원장 법
부형ᄉᆞ관 김규희
○명일본국시찰슈원 외
국어학교교관 조원규
○명젼왕일본국시찰슈원 농
상공학교교관 리범규
이삼십월칠일

잡보

○조세감리 졍삼품조순환씨
는셩진감리를서임ᄒᆞ엿더라
○쟝윤변등 경셩주차일본군

ᄉᆞ평관쟝곽찬씨가금일영셩부
면한셔쟝계가일즁번ᄒᆞ되리라
ᄒᆞ며일진회는세력이졈졈쟝대
ᄒᆞ리라ᄒᆞ더라

◯전북진보회　전라북도관찰
ᄉᆞ가ᄂᆡ부로뎐보ᄒᆞ기를인민수
쳔명이진보회라ᄌᆞ칭ᄒᆞ고수빅
명이둔취ᄒᆞ엿다ᄒᆞ고익산군수
가보고ᄒᆞ엿고ᄯᅩ함열군황등쟝
터에도둔취ᄒᆞ엿다ᄒᆞ엿더라

◯유로막승전　돌산군거ᄒᆞᄂᆞᆫ
쿠달셔등륙인이음력오월일일
에빈아도로횡션ᄒᆞ다가즁로에
풍파를만나오인이슈즁에셔쥭
고상산면거ᄒᆞᄂᆞᆫ리승휴등오인
은륙월이십수일밤에승션ᄒᆞ고
지오도에일은다가풍파에침몰
ᄒᆞ야일명이치수ᄒᆞ고동군남면
거ᄒᆞᄂᆞᆫ김두원등이인과지도군
거ᄒᆞᄂᆞᆫ졍달원등륙인은칠월초
십일에심포에셔풍파를만나수
명이치수ᄒᆞ엿다ᄒᆞ고각기군보
가ᄂᆡ부로ᄅᆡ도ᄒᆞ엿다더라

◯쳥하면북　대구군슈가면보
ᄒᆞ기를일인이면간북을향ᄒᆞ고대
셕면양해세운고로금지ᄒᆞ되듯
지아니ᄒᆞ니일본공관에이죠ᄒᆞ
아칙면간북을타쳐로이셜케ᄒᆞ
라ᄒᆞ엿더라

◯면담벌엄　인쳔항쥬차수평
부에셔본월륙일에부평인쳔시
흥삼군슈를쳥ᄒᆞ야쳑시치포ᄒᆞ
라ᄒᆞᆫ고로회군슈등이ᄂᆡ부로보
고ᄒᆞ되이계이쳐도가빈동신쟝보
로라면담에반히범ᄒᆞ니엇지죠
쳐ᄒᆞ라ᄒᆞ엿더라

◯졈수파송　공쥬디방면야로
ᄒᆞᆫ수로의졍부에셔샹　쥬ᄒᆞ
고법부로죠회ᄒᆞ고졈수를파송
ᄒᆞ라ᄒᆞᆫ고로법부에셔졈ᄉᆞ리회
션씨를공쥬로파송ᄒᆞ기로작뎡
ᄒᆞ야불일간하거ᄒᆞᆫ다더라

◯담송회심　법공수가루ᄎᆞ죠
회ᄒᆞᄂᆞᆫ의양군과한영슈씨의면
담송수를평리원에셔명일에다
시회심ᄒᆞᆫ다ᄒᆞᄂᆞᆫ딕법부에셔ᄂᆞᆫ
참셔관죠경구씨를파송ᄒᆞ고법
공관에셔ᄂᆞᆫ평수를파견ᄒᆞᆫ다더
라

◯평수와참셔　총평수이윤젹
씨ᄂᆞᆫ외부참셔관으로젼임ᄒᆞ고
졍샹룡ᄒᆞᆫ과씨ᄂᆞᆫ총평수를피
임ᄒᆞ엿더라

◯즁엽위원　근일류힝병셜에
방츅도ᄂᆡ부에셔의학교로공함
ᄒᆞ야즁엽싱셜딕들륙송ᄒᆞ라ᄒᆞ
아위원을차하ᄒᆞ엿ᄂᆞᆫ딕광제원
학교ᄉᆞ쇼지위원차하가되지라의
일에ᄂᆡ부대신을방문ᄒᆞ고말ᄒᆞ
기를즁엽싱은주임디우로위원
을샹쥬ᄒᆞ고차뎡ᄒᆞ라ᄒᆞ엿더라

◯교문셜간츅　외부고문관셜
을건츅ᄒᆞ고로여비를일신의게도
금ᄒᆞ고본일노시역ᄒᆞᆫ다더라

◯룡셩위규　일본공ᄉᆞ가외부
로보고ᄒᆞ기를인쳔일본령ᄉᆞ의
보고에ᄒᆞ엿스되　ᄒᆞᆼᄂᆡ부계용
수ᄒᆞᆫ평ᄂᆡ에각포사에우피매ᄆᆡ
를파원이작뎡ᄒᆞᆫ다ᄒᆞ니비기슨
등샹규칙을어의이라히계용수
에이죠ᄒᆞ야차등힝위를엄원히
막으라ᄒᆞ엿더라

◯하관분경가　각부부원쳥대
쇼관인이ᄎᆞ례로단발ᄒᆞᆫ다ᄒᆞᆫ즉
관인되야셔ᄂᆞᆫ구치아니ᄒᆞ며도
ᄌᆞ연단발ᄒᆞᆯ터이어ᄂᆞᆯ막단ᄌᆞ션
으로외교관을도득ᄒᆞ야ᄆᆡ일관
보에젼권공ᄉᆞ와관리공ᄉᆞ와평
ᄉᆞ가셔임되니외국쥬차공ᄉᆞ를
소환ᄒᆞᆫ다ᄒᆞᄂᆞᆫ딕시로셔임되ᄂᆞᆫ
공령ᄉᆞᄂᆞᆫ어느나라로파츌ᄒᆞᆯ런지
ᄂᆞᆫ지알수업다ᄒᆞ더라

◯국쟝환임　ᄂᆡ부디방국쟝리
규환씨ᄂᆞᆫ관리공ᄉᆞ로젼임ᄒᆞ엿
다가디방국국쟝을다시쳥임으
로환임되엿더라

◯셰계신랑　셔문밧유동거ᄒᆞ
ᄂᆞᆫ김윤식씨가ᄌᆞ긔집에다가목
욕탕을셜립ᄒᆞᆫ지가우금수오년
인딕그목욕ᄒᆞᄂᆞᆫ물이즁졍ᄒᆞᆫ에
잇ᄂᆞᆫ우물로디미ᄂᆞᆫ지라그간에
에병든사ᄅᆞᆷ여러이그물에목욕
ᄒᆞ고죽차ᄒᆞᆫ고로이말이젼파가
되여셔지어궁즁에ᄭᆞ지달ᄒᆞ야시
영친왕젼하계옵셔드ᄅᆞ시고흠ᄒᆞ옵시
고쟝수평이라ᄒᆞ읍셔궁ᄒᆞᆫ신경젼에
로사ᄋᆡᄒᆞ시엿ᄂᆞᆫ딕확신ᄒᆞ오며
ᄂᆞᆫᄯᅩᄒᆞᆫ돈을밧지안코목욕을식
이ᄂᆞᆫ지라목욕ᄒᆞᆫ사ᄅᆞᆷ들이그물
에신효ᄒᆞᆷ과혜팰로사ᄋᆡᄒᆞ신을
봉납ᄒᆞ야찬송ᄒᆞᄂᆞᆫ글들을반히
지어보ᄂᆡᄂᆞᆫ딕계위젼에수에지
가번쥭한국에문풍이이에볼진딘
가히칭송ᄒᆞᆯ만ᄒᆞ다더라

◯공수산세　민병한씨ᄂᆞᆫ젼권
공ᄉᆞ유진찬리규환량씨ᄂᆞᆫ관리
공ᄉᆞ를피명ᄒᆞ엿더라

◯위관쟝셔　공쥬디에셔암샹
ᄒᆞᆫ위관심인과병졸심륙명을작
일에심사ᄒᆞ야격국이되엿다ᄂᆞᆫ
딕일인이힐위관등을디ᄒᆞ야말
ᄒᆞ되거쳐가비편ᄒᆞ거든말ᄒᆞ라
ᄒᆞ거ᄂᆞᆯ위관들이디답ᄒᆞ되우리
의거쳐를편케ᄒᆞ라거든즉시방
츌ᄒᆞ라ᄒᆞᆫ딕일인들이박쟝대소
ᄒᆞ고도로다두엇ᄂᆞᆫ딕금명간방
환ᄒᆞᆫ다더라

◯아병남하　근자북관으로븟
터온바교에ᄒᆞ엿스되구월금음
셔지아국보병이쳔명가량이대
포륙좌를가지고셩진에쥬둔ᄒᆞ
엿더니본월에니르러ᄂᆞᆫ모다북
쳥으로나려왓ᄂᆞᆫ딕방금북쳥에
쥬둔ᄒᆞᆫ아병은수쳔명가량이며
ᄯᅩ십일에아국긔병일빅오십명
이ᄒᆞᆷ원으로나려왓ᄂᆞᆫ데그즁십
여긔ᄂᆞᆫ함관령에쳑츌ᄒᆞ야일본
젼초병과조금싸호고퇴각ᄒᆞ엿
스며ᄒᆞᆷ원에잇ᄂᆞᆫ아병은오륙빅
명이라더라

◯방문일관　일본츌젼군위문
ᄉᆞ권즁현씨와그외에ᄯᅩ두어
명이작일에일본공ᄉᆞ를방문
ᄒᆞ엿스나맛참공ᄉᆞ가츌타ᄒᆞ엿
ᄂᆞᆫ고로국분셔긔관을심방ᄒᆞ엿
다더라

◯평안진보회　지금함경도경
평과평안도션쳔등디에셔진보
회라ᄂᆞᆫ회가니러낫ᄂᆞᆫ딕그뜻인
즉한국독립을공고케ᄒᆞ고시졍
기션을실힝ᄒᆞ고일본군의게ᄂᆞᆫ
아모조록편리ᄒᆞ게ᄒᆞ야주고ᄯᅩ
회원들은일변단발ᄒᆞᄂᆞᆫ딕회원
이구름ᄀᆞᆺ치모힌다더라

◯ᄂᆡ외감셩　졍부리졍소에셔
안으로각부부원쳥과밧그로각
군을감셩ᄒᆞᄂᆞᆫ딕각부부원쳥에
ᄂᆞᆫ관할ᄒᆞᆫ여러국즁에국ᄒᆞᄂᆞᆫ식
두고각군은삼빅륙십여군을일
빅삼십군으로감셩ᄒᆞᆫ다더라

◯의유시쥬　공쥬디방면야
료ᄒᆞᆫᄉᆞ로공쥬관찰ᄉᆞ를면관ᄒᆞ
기로　쳐분이ᄂᆞ리셧더니참졍
이샹　쥬ᄒᆞ되평일난숙지못ᄒᆞᆫ
쳑망으로말ᄉᆞᆷᄒᆞ오면위션참졍
보리면관ᄒᆞ여야수례에방연ᄒᆞᆫ
오비다ᄒᆞ엿더니히　칙교를환
슈ᄒᆞ셧다더라

론셜

한셩도로교량

무릇한국빅셩의기칭ᄒᆞᆫ다ᄂᆞᆫ말
은기구만ᄒᆞ게되면문득ᄒᆞ되우
리의ᄉᆡᆼ각에ᄂᆞᆫ졍치기칭ᄒᆞ니버
다오히려더욱긴급히기량ᄒᆞᆯ만
ᄒᆞᆫ일이잇ᄂᆞᆫ거시한셩ᄂᆡ외의도
로가심히불셩모양인지라셩즁
안에대로들은비오ᄂᆞᆫ수보ᄒᆞᆫ듯
ᄒᆞ나소위교량이라ᄂᆞᆫ거슨심히
쟝대ᄒᆞᆫ즁과탁된자ㅣ만ᄒᆞ여비도
대단힝인이란우마왕ᄅᆡᄒᆞ기에도
대단히조심이되ᄂᆞᆫ지라막즁ᄒᆞᆫ
궐문압흘보드리도욕칭쳐로통
ᄒᆞᆫ길에소위교량과기쳔이라ᄂᆞᆫ
거시모도저함ᄒᆞ야셩ᄒᆞᆫ곳이업
ᄂᆞᆫ즁다만욕칭기되ᄂᆞᆫ돌로써ᄒᆞᆫ다
리를노와왕ᄅᆡᄒᆞᄂᆞᆫ사ᄅᆞᆷ들로ᄒᆞ지
라여곰반ᄃᆞ시결셔ᄒᆞ되게되ᄂᆞᆫ지
라구리기로가ᄂᆞᆫ길에ᄂᆞᆫ교량이
셋이나퇴피ᄒᆞ야기쳔밋으로셔
로통ᄒᆞ엿스ᄂᆞᆫ즉만일샹ᄒᆞ지아니
ᄒᆞ고힝ᄒᆞᆯ지경이면셩샤가관계
ᄒᆞ게되엿스며ᄯᅩᄒᆞᆫ지금보기에
ᄂᆞᆫ심히즁요ᄒᆞᆫ계진츅ᄒᆞᆫ듯ᄒᆞ되
불과괴사지ᄂᆡ에도리여결단이
날터인즉셜로진요ᄒᆞ게된거시
업고만일돈젼을당ᄒᆞ야이리ᄒᆞᆫ시
교량우에아ᄒᆞᆷ이나ᄊᆞ인다던지
눈만엇펄지경이면과연사ᄅᆞᆷ외
ᄒᆞᆷ졍이나다ᄒᆞᆷ이업슬거시ᄒᆞᆯ사
ᄅᆞᆷ과즁셩이ᄲᅡ저샹ᄒᆞ엿다ᄂᆞᆫ말
이죵죵들니ᄂᆞᆫ듯ᄒᆞ며우마라도왕
ᄅᆡᄒᆞ다가졀각이되엿다던지ᄒᆞ
면사ᄅᆞᆷ의마음에응당측은이너
일러이고한국의광반들은이러
ᄒᆞᆫ길로지나다가즁괴의구죵이
징구ᄒᆞᆷ에ᄲᅡ져으로말ᄆᆡ아마소
조를당ᄒᆞᄂᆞᆫ경우이면고배에ᄂᆞᆫ
필경관인된바에ᄉᆡᆼ각이잇슬거
시요ᄯᅩᄒᆞᆫ비록대로에셔라도인
력거ᄂᆞᆫ타기가심히불편ᄒᆞᆫ지라
만일여러치가ᄒᆞᆷᄭᅴ별여을ᄯᅢ에
ᄂᆞᆫ조심이대단히되며ᄏᆞᆷ관이타
고가다가탁도ᄒᆞᆫ교량을만나게
되면인력거부만다빗졀기에힘
을다ᄒᆞᆫ뿐더러인력거박휘가뒤
으로넘어갈념녀가불무ᄒᆞᆫ즉이
ᄂᆞᆫᄯᅩᄒᆞᆫ승ᄀᆡᆨ의게도ᄆᆡ우불편ᄒᆞᆫ
일이ᄇᆞᆫᄒᆞ며근일에ᄂᆞᆫ여간도로
도수보ᄒᆞ고기쳔도쥰결ᄒᆞ게ᄒᆞ
엿스나이도다반셩양반게ᄒᆞ야
니되엿고아쥬도수츅ᄒᆞᆯ곳이무
수ᄒᆞᆫ즉이리케ᄒᆞᆫ일은도리여ᄎᆞ라
수아니ᄒᆞᆷ만ᄀᆞᆺ지못ᄒᆞᆫ거시이리
케ᄒᆞᆫ것도당초에ᄂᆞᆫᄆᆡ오쥬의ᄒᆞ
야ᄒᆞᆫ듯ᄒᆞ되ᄯᅩᄒᆞᆫ일기어려운일
이잇ᄂᆞᆫ거시이왕에노왓든교량
ᄒᆞᆫ편이퇴피ᄒᆞ면다시조ᄒᆞᆫ셕지
로수보ᄒᆞᆯᄉᆡᆼ각은고사ᄒᆞ고다만
나무조각으로그틈만간신히수
츅ᄒᆞᆫ즉비ᄂᆞᆫᄌᆞ연히속퇴ᄒᆞᆯ수밧
게업스며ᄯᅩᄒᆞᆫ괴왕부셜ᄒᆞᆫ뻐빠
다나ᄒᆞᆫ거시엇ᄂᆞᆫ지라도로가약
차히쳥의ᄒᆞ며교량이퇴피ᄒᆞ야
이왕수보ᄒᆞᆷ이조곰도나ᄒᆞᆫ거시
영승은도리여경비만더욱허비
ᄒᆞ란ᄒᆞᆷ이나졍부를기량ᄒᆞᆷ에유
의ᄒᆞ게ᄒᆞᆯ진딘위션황국셩도셔
울안에도로와교량을아모조록
수션ᄒᆞᆷ에용력ᄒᆞᆷ이심히조흘듯
ᄒᆞᆫ바ᄒᆞ사건일듯ᄒᆞ노라

외보

◯덕뎨회향　덕국신문에괴졔
ᄒᆞ기를티심일일덕황이영황을
방문ᄒᆞᆫ다ᄒᆞ엿더라

◯쇼약반ᄃᆡ　셔피득보신문과
다른로국신문들은영국과셔쟝과
국간의죠약을강경히항의ᄒᆞ며
쳐이에ᄃᆡᄒᆞ야ᄂᆞᆫ로국이아주항동
이안케노라고셩명ᄒᆞ엿더라

◯로함손샹　려순항ᄂᆡ에쳥복
ᄒᆞᆫ세리쓰비엣트황익젼투함일
쳑은일본포위군의포탄에비샹
ᄒᆞᆫ손ᄒᆡ를밧앗고기타졔함은빅
옥산뒤에도피ᄒᆞ야포탄이피ᄒᆞ
엿다ᄒᆞ엿더라

◯로국류힝병　로국ᄂᆡ디에호
렬ᄌᆞ병이류힝ᄒᆞᄂᆞᆫ딕그중에ᄉᆡᆨ
오루가디방이최심ᄒᆞ다더라

◯역습함창　근일에도착ᄒᆞᆫ모
보고를거ᄒᆞᆫ즉지난팔일아참에
아국보병오즁디가대포수좌를
가지고평항산방면에셔함창으
로거슬너습격ᄒᆞ엿슴으로그곳
에잇든일본슈비디가종일싸홈
을ᄒᆞ엿ᄂᆞᆫ딕구일아참에이르러
함창셔방도로에셔아국괴병삼
빅명이ᄯᅩ오매ᄯᅩ졉젼ᄒᆞᆫ지라십
일오젼두시에일본쟝관은수졸
을령솔ᄒᆞ야맹렬ᄒᆞ야승을힝ᄒᆞᆫ
아ᄃᆞᆫ듸여아병을격퇴ᄒᆞ엿ᄂᆞᆫ딕
아병은동북방으로다라낫다더
라

TELEGRAMS.

Tokyo Oct. 11th.

Commander Hosoya reports that the Gunboat Heiyuen, which was on blockading service off Riuwan on 18th Sept. disappeared was not heard of until four of her crew were discovered on a neighbouring island. They reported that the vessel had foundered during a gale and, with the exception of theirs, all lives were lost.

THE EFFECTS OF JAPANESE BULLETS.

The St. Petersburg correspondent of the "Daily Telegraph" has given an interesting account of remarkable recoveries of Russian soldiers from wounds made by what they term Japanese toy bullets. These bullets, say Russian surgeons, are, if not perfectly harmless, at least the next best thing to that forming the mildest kind of missile that has ever yet been fired from a rifle. One of the consequences is that a number of wounds, which formerly were mortal are now healed and forgotten in a few days.

"Up till now a bullet in the head," remarks a Russian physician who is collecting data on the surgical aspect of the present war, "which pierced the brain was certain to cause death. But here we have a case in which a missile actually went through the medulla oblongata, yet the man who received the wound and cracked skull was smiling and complaining of a slight headache only on wet days.

"All the men in the hospital have tiny wounds, smaller than a threepenny bit, a mere red stain, nothing more."

A medical investigator, enquiring from Russian officers as to the character of the Japanese bullet, was told: "Compared with ours the Japanese bullet is tiny, but its velocity is considerably greater. Our magazine rifle takes a bullet of three lines and imparts to it an initial velocity of 620 metres, whereas the Japanese rifles have a 25 line bullet, with an initial velocity of 725 metres. The Japanese bullet only penetrates the tissue, but does not tear it.

"When passing through the abdomen it inflicts the minimum of damage, its chief effect being to expand the muscles of the pertioneum, which quickly contract, closing the orifice, thus saving the injured man from peritonitis and death."

CORRESPONDENCE.

THE EDITOR KOREA DAILY NEWS.

DEAR SIR:

On reading some news relative to Port Arthur, and emanating from Chefoo, in your issue of October 5th, I find that your correspondent has as usual given only half of the news, which he dreamt. I therefore ask you to kindly insert the following, which will complete the Chefoo correspondent's dream.

The "Nori Krai," a Port Arthur paper, which at times of importance issues news bulletins, gives the following under date September 23rd. It was reproduced at Tsingtau on October 4th.

"The Japanese Army made a strong attack on the redoubts of "Kuropatkin's" fort in the vicinity of the water reservoir, and occupied the same. However a company of Russian sharpshooters and a column of infantry attacked the Japanese with a strong rifle and shrapnel fire and forced them to evacuate the position. In doing so, they retreated onto mined ground, and the mines being exploded they were nearly entirely shattered. Their losses in killed are said to have been 6,000. I am etc., An Old Stager and Strict Observer.

A RUNAWAY AIRSHIP.

Paris, Aug. 28.—There was a sensational airship hunt in the country around Mantes this morning, the Lebaudy No. II. breaking loose and travelling seventy miles without any one on board. The airship was sent up on a trial trip from Moisson, near Mantes. As strong upper currents were met with, however, M. Juchmes, the pilot, decided to descend, fearing a disaster similar to that which wrecked Lebaudy No. I. Lebaudy No. II. was accordingly brought to earth on an open plain, and anchored by ropes to a couple of trees. Just as the operation was finished, however, the guide ropes were snapped by a strong gust of wind, and the airship began to make an ascent on its own account. The pilot and his assistants endeavoured to stop the airship's flight by hanging on to the ropes, but they found they were powerless, and let go as they were being carried off into the air at the end of the ropes. Lebaudy No. II. rose with great rapidity, and soon gained a height of 1,600 ft. Then it started off in a westerly direction. M. Pierre Lebaudy, who was present in his motor-car, at once grasped the situation, and started off in pursuit of the air-ship. The pilot followed in a second motor-car, and for some hours the chase continued. The air-ship sailed majestically in the direction of Evreux. When it reached the town it was caught in an eddy of winds, and circled completely around the cathedral towers before continuing its journey. At 4:30 P. M. the air-ship, after sailing seventy miles, came to earth a mile or two beyond Evreux. The motorists who had followed it were on the spot almost simultaneously, and found that although the cover of the balloon attached to the air-ship had escaped injury, the motor was wrecked in the trees.

NAGAMORI AGAIN.

Two paragraphs in Japan exchanges are worthy of note. The first is from the "Japan Mail" and is as follows:—

"The question of land-reclamation in Korea seems to be again on the "tapis," but the project has apparently taken the form of a joint undertaking, Koreans and Japanese being equally interested."

The second one is from the "Japan Times."

The Seoul despatch to the "Kokumin" dated the 3rd inst., states that negotiations have been resumed between our authorities and the Korean Minister of the Imperial Household concerning the reclamation question, which has for some time been in abeyance. It seems, the despatch adds, that our demand in this connection has taken a new form, aiming at material rather than nominal rights.

Truly we have to go abroad for news although the information that Japan is aiming at material rather than nominal rights hardly comes within this category.

The following is from the "Seoul Press" express: Tokyo Telegram, received yesterday:—"The enemy at Mukden, taking the aggressive, advanced to the South of the Hun River and the flank column of their left wing made a bold dash in the direction of Eckesef (?). Our troops rushed forward to meet the enemy's attack and a desperate battle is now raging. It is also reported that a detachment of our right wing, commanded by Umezawa, was attacked in the front by a very superior force (about 10 times the number of our men), and compelled us to evacuate our position the day before yesterday. However, the following day we resumed the attack, routed the enemy, and once more regained our position.

In addition to the Diplomatic corps, all officials will undergo a tonsorial operation, says the latest order. The sum of $30.00 will be handed to every official for the purpose of purchasing a suitable uniform.

GENERAL GRIPPENBERG.

General Grippenberg, who has been appointed by the Tsar to command the Second Manchurian Army, is a Finnlander born in 1838, says the "N.-C. Daily News." He began his military service in the 5th Turkestan Battalion, and subsequently served in the 17th Rifle Battalion, the 2nd Guard Rifle Battalion and the Moscow Guards (1875-1883). He commanded successively, the First Brigade of the First Guard Division, the Guard Rifle Brigade, the First Guard Division, (1897-98) and the 6th Army Corps. In 1901 he was appointed second in command of the Wilna District and on the 10th November, 1902, to the chief command of the District. The general saw active service in the Crimea in 1854-55; and also participated in the campaigns of 1863-64, 1866, 1867-78. He was wounded in action in 1868.

One of our correspondents in the city has sent us the following:—It is said that all the officials will shave the heads, but most of officials like to shave their heads on port of diplomatic officers. So most of influential officials are moving their best to be diplomatic officers. Lately every day official gazette is full of appointments of Ministers and consuls to foreign country, it is very curious what foreign countries they will be sent to, as there was already said all the Ministers to foreign countries will be recalled.

The Korea Daily News.

Issued at 5 P. M. daily except Sundays.

Rate of Subscription :—

Per Year,	Yen 25.
Per Quarter,	Yen 7.
Per Month,	Yen 2.50.

Postage in Korea not charged extra.
Postage abroad charged extra.

Advertisements, 50 sen per day for 1 inch or less.
5 yen per month per inch.
50 yen per year per inch.

All communications to
E. T. BETHELL,
Editor and Publisher,
Pak-tong, Seoul.

GENERAL HASEGAWA'S ARRIVAL.

Long before the arrival of the morning express from Chemulpo, the streets this morning were thronged with an expectant crowd of Koreans and Japanese awaiting the advent of General Hasegawa and his staff. The South-Gate station platform was alive with uniforms and more sombre clad civilians ready to extend a welcome to the new Commander-in-Chief of H. I. J. M's forces in Korea.

The train, punctual to a minute, drew up at the station at 9:30, and the General, preceded by his staff officers and those who had been to Chemulpo to greet him on his arrival, stepped from the carriage and acknowledged the greetings of those present. After a rapid exchange of courtesies and a cursory ins ection of a company of Lancers, who formed the Guard of Honor, the new Commander-in-Chief was ushered into a smartly equipped landau, and with General Haraguchi, who vacates the command, drove slowly off along the densely thronged road, the staff and resident military authorities following on horse-back.

Outside the gate, the band from the local Japanese theatre was blatantly attempting to produce the strains of "Marching through Georgia," while inside, the Korean band rendered the Japanese national anthem. The whole route from the South Gate to the Temple of Heaven, was lined on both sides by Korean and Japanese soldiers, a necessary precaution as it was with difficulty that the crowd of sightseers could be kept from encroaching on the roadway.

The Japanese photographers should have some good views of the procession, for they were in evidence everywhere.

The Namsan battery fired a 19 gun salute just as the general was driven to his destination at the vacated Army Headquarters building; there, his retinue and visitors repaired to pay their respects to the new Commander-in-chief and bid farewell to General Haraguchi, who, now he is relieved of his post, will shortly take his departure.

THE NEW OFFICER.

"The officer," said Private Smithy, of the 1st Manchesters, "is a new officer. It isn't the new kind of uniform, or the new Salvation Army cap, or the new silly way of wearing his shoulder sash. He's a changed officer, if you understand. He don't look no different, and in many ways he's not altered a bit. He still plays polo and bridge—what's bridge?"

I explained.

"Well, he still does all these things just about as much as ever he did, but I tell you 'e's an astounding blighter in many ways.

"It ain't so long ago," reflected this ornament of the First Army Corps, "when officers used to come on parade at 10 A. M.—commanding officers' parade drill order—and we used to look at 'em hard to discover whether we'd seen 'em before. They used to troop down from the officers' mess buttoning up their brown gloves and hooking on their swords under their patrol jackets. They'd stand about for a minute or two yawnin' their blankey 'ead orf an' then the bugle'd sound. 'Officers come and be blowed,' an' they'd fall in.

"Well, the colour-sergeant was always waitin' for 'em.

"'What's on this mornin',' says me fine captain.

"'Battalion drill, sir,' says the flag.

"'Oh, dash battalion drill,'' sez the captain, walkin' round and inspectin' the company. 'Take this man's name, colour-sergeant, for wearing his pouch on the right side.'

"'So they are,' sez the intelligent captain, givin' a casual glance along the line. 'Well, take his name for 'aving a dirty belt.'

"'Right, sir,' sez the colour-sergeant.

DRILL—OLD STYLE.

"When the inspection was over the officer would draw his sword and read the writin' on it, and draw noughts and crosses with it on the ground; then fall in six paces ahead of the centre of his company. Bimeby he'd see something 'appening to the company ahead of his.

"'What's goin' on there, colour-sergeant?' he'd ask.

"'Formin' fours, sir,' sez the colour-sergeant.

"'Oh, I forgot all about that,' sez his nib. 'Company! Form fours!' an' not a man moves.

"'You 'aven't numbered 'em, sir,' sez the colour-sergeant.

"'Hey?' sez the captain, gettin' red. 'Then why the dickens ain't they numbered when they fall in? Number off from the right, an' be quick about it.'

"Then come the battalion drill," continued Smithy, with a sad, reminiscent smile. "The colonel shouts something.

"'What's that he said, colour-sergeant?' sez the officer.

"'Into line, right form, ser,' sez the flag.

"'What do I do?'' sez the captain.

"'Turn half-right, sir, and wait for the word "march," ' whispers the flag.

"And right through the drill it was the same. Sometimes the captain was right, sometimes he was wrong. Sometimes he had the whole company jumbled up in horrid confusion, and the colonel would come prancing along and say things he was probably sorry for afterwards.

"Well, an hour of this sort of thing went on, and then it was 'Right turn—Dismiss,' and the officer would run away and change his sword an' uniform for a Sunday suit an' a panamar hat, and we did't see him again till tomorrow."

CONVERTED OFFICERS.

Smithy raised himself on his elbow and addressed the orderly man staggering tent-ward with a big kettle of steaming tea.

Would the orderly man be so kind as to give Smithy a basin of tea and save him the trouble of coming to the tent for it. Without checking his career, the orderly man remarked, "Oh, yes, why not, not 'arf. Would Smithy like him (the orderly man) to drink it for him (Smithy)? Did he want waiting on? Should he fetch it in a feeding bottle?" and sundry other ejaculations of a bitterly satirical character.

Whereupon Smithy, realising that the enemy was rapidly getting out of range, delivered a rapid feu de joie of personalities, calculated to annoy and distress a young and ambitious orderly man.

"Pon my word," said Smithy gloomily, "these blanked Brodericks are gettin' worse an' worse; the men 'ave changed as much as the officers."

"How have the officers changed?" I asked.

"I was going to tell you," said Smithy. "As I said before, it's only an inward change. You know soldiers, don't you?"

"I do."

"Well, you've seen Tommy get converted—get religion, haven't you? He drops the wet canteen, and spends his time in the library playin' bagatelle with other bunwalahs. The cloth is always torn, and the cues 'ave no tips," added Smithy inconsequently. "He goes to chapel on week nights and shows up the regiment by prayin' in public; joins the Templars with fancy grips and pass words and sashes. Well, beyond giving up booze and saying confound instead of '—or' '—' or '—,' there ain't much difference, outwardly at least. He still parts his hair; he still mashes the girls; he still does all things 'uman—except swear and drink.

"So it is with the officer—'e's changed inwardly. He plays polo and golf—which is a rotten game in my opinion—and motors.

"But somehow we seem to see more of him than we used.

"He comes nosing around at all hours of the day. He does colour-sergeants' work and corporals' work—in fact, he knows as much about soldiering now as we do. He doesn't make mistakes on parade; he turns up at the rifle range even when it ain't his turn for duty; he'll take a dozen chaps out into the country and teach them how to sketch; he spends a lot of his spare time learning flag-wagging—in fact, in fact," said Smithy, struggling for a climax, "he's a more astoundin' person than ever."

TACTICS UP TO DATE.

Smithy refilled and relit his pipe and ruminated for some moments. "Yesterday," said he, "the little man French had us out attackin' or defendin'—I don't know which—a bit of a village, over there." Smithy pointed vaguely. "I was with a half company under Mr. Brick-Taylor—he gets his company next month. We've got a new colour-sergeant from the second battalion who's been used to giving officers tips all his life.

"We were scoutin' ahead, and we sighted the enemy outside a pub near Frinham. We could see them, they couldn't see us.

"'Git into that donga,' sez the officer, pointin' to a big, deep ditch.

"'Beg pardon, sir,' says the flag. 'I think you ought to extend the men and retire, sir.'

"'Oh, you do, do you?' said the officer, 'well, I don't; get into the donga as quick as you can.'

"'Beg pardon, sir,' sez the flag, 'but the book sez—'

"What book?" sez the officer.

"Drill book, sir, sez the colour bloke.

"'Never read it,' sez the little man as calm as you please. 'I'm takin cover and hidin', because I once got plugged in the neck by a Mauser bullet for not doin' so. I am not retiring in open order accordin' to the book because I tried something like it at Magerfontein and appeared in all the London papers the next mornin' as 'dangerously.'"

A bugle call rang out sharp and clear, a dozen tents disgorged one or two men, who buttoned their coats as they hurried to the guard tent.

"Defaulters," said Smithy, shifting his position to one of greater comfort; "all young soldiers, an' punishment's good for 'em—it's surprisin' how a few kicks help a man in the Army."—Edgar Wallace in the "Daily Mail."

The newly established Reform office has wisely decided to reduce the number of Magisterial districts from 366 to 130.

"A war correspondent's life is full of dangers, isn't it?" We asked of the returned one. "It is," he replied. "Why, over in Tokio one of the best correspondents I ever saw became a nervous wreck because of the tea he drank at the receptions."—Cleveland Press.

Reuter's Liaoyang correspondent wiring on September 8th reported that Liaoyang was thrice looted during three days. The Russians first pillaged the food and liquor shops in the city. After the Russians bolted from the Japanese, the Chinese soldiery and police continued to plunder. Finally, the starving Japanese on entering the town, finding the shops ransacked, turned their attention to the private residences. The officers were greatly distressed at the excesses committed by their men, who are now, however, well under control.

The Korea Daily News.

VOL. I, THURSDAY, OCTOBER 13, 1904. No. 75

HONGKONG & SHANGHAI BANKING CORPORATION.

Paid-up Capital........................$10,000,000
Reserve Fund:—Sterling Reserve... 10,000,000
Silver Reserve..... 7,000,000

27,000,000
Reserve Liability of Proprietors... 10,000,000

HEAD OFFICE, HONGKONG.

London Bankers, London and County Banking Company Limited.
Branches and Agencies,
London.

Amoy,	Hankow	Penang,
Bangkok,	Hiogo,	Rangoon,
Batavia,	Iloilo,	Saigon,
Bombay,	Lyons,	San Francisco,
Calcutta,	Manila,	Singapore,
Colombo,	Nagasaki,	Sourabaya,
Foochow,	New York,	Tientsin,
Hamburg,	Peking,	Yokohama,

Credits granted on approved Securities, and every description of Banking and Exchange business transacted.

Drafts granted on London and the chief Commercial places in Europe, India, Australia, America, China and Japan.

HOLME RINGER & CO., AGENTS,
CHEMULPO.

ON CHEONG & CO.,
SEOUL.

GENERAL STORE KEEPERS.
Imported provisions, Cooking Utensils Crockery, etc.
FRESH BREAD DAILY.

MITSU BISHI DOCKYARD & ENGINE WORKS,
NAGASAKI.

CODE WORD, "DOCK."

A. 1, A. B. C., and Engineering Codes used.

DOCK No. 1 (at Tategami).

Extreme Length..............523 feet
Length on blocks .... 513 ,,
Width of Entrance on Top......89 ,,
,, ,, Bottom....77 ,,
Water on Blocks at Spring Tide 26½ ,,

DOCK No. 2 (Mukaijima).

Extreme Length..............371 feet
Length on Blocks...........360 ,,
Width of Entrance on Top......66 ,,
,, ,, Bottom 53 ,,
Water on Blocks at Spring Tide 22 ,,

PATENT SLIP (at Kosuge).

Can take vessels up to 1,000 tons gross.

THE WORKS are well equipped with the LATEST IMPROVEMENTS, and can execute any kind of work in SHIPBUILDING and MARINE ENGINEERING, as well as in REPAIRING of SHIPS.

The COMPANY'S new powerful steamer OURA-MARU (712 tons, 700 I.H.P.), specially built for SALVAGE PURPOSES, and equipped with necessary gear, is always READY at SHORT NOTICE.

CHARTERED BANK OF INDIA AUSTRALIA & CHINA.

INCORPORATED BY ROYAL CHARTER 1853

HEAD OFFICES:—LONDON.

Paid-up Capital £800,000
Reserve Liability of Shareholders 800,000
Reserve Fund 800,000

Drafts granted upon all the principal places in the world and every description of Exchange and banking business transacted.

E. MEYER & Co., Agents,
Chemulpo.

E. MEYER & CO.

Chemulpo.

SOLE AGENTS IN KOREA FOR:
A. T. Morse, Sons & Co's
"Fresco" Distemper

In all colours ready for use on walls, Ceilings etc.
and
AVENARIUS CARBOLINEUM

A wood-preserving and antiseptic oil preparation

Against decay, dry-rot, fungus and wood-destroying insects.

A large supply always in Stock.
Prices upon application.

E. MEYER & Co.,
Chemulpo.

THE METHODIST PUBLISHING HOUSE,
Little WestGate, Seoul.

JPRINTING, TYPEWRITER PAPER
CARBON PAPER, VISITING CARDS
STATIONERY, BOOK BINDING
BOOK PUBLISHERS
AMERICAN SCHOOL BOOKS
SPENCERIAN COPY BOOKS
PEN CARBON LETTER AND BILL BOOKS

S. A. BECK, Manager.

HOKURKU DOBOKU KAISHA.

Branch office in Chong Dong, Seoul.
Japanese telephone No. 165

CONTRACT DEPARTMENT.

We can contract to build any building or construction.

MERCHANDISE DEPARTMENT.

We can provide any building material.
We have just contracted to build the new Belgian Legation.

DAI-ICHI GINKO.

LIMITED.

(Formerly the First National Bank)

ESTABLISHED 1873

INCORPORATED UNDER PRESENT LAW 1896

Capital - - - - - - - - - Yen 5,000,000
Reserve Fund - . - - - 1,500,000

HEAD OFFICE:—TOKIO.

President: Baron SHIBUSAWA.

BRANCHES AND CORRESPONDENTS
In the Principal Cities and Towns of Japan.
Interest Allowed on
Fixed deposits 1 year - - - 6½ per cent
" " 6 months - - - 6 per cent

Special current accounts 1½ sen daily per Y 100
General " " 1 " " " 100

M. TANAKA,
Manager, Chemulpo

HOLME RINGER & Co.

Chemulpo.

General Merchants and Government Contractors.

Agents for the leading
Banks
SteamshipCompanies
and
Insurance Companies

Importers of Merchandise of every description.

KAMEYA & CO.

GENERAL STOREKEEPERS
Chinkokai - - Seoul
(*Established 1895, Tokyo*)

Confectionery, Hams, Canned Goods, Cutlery, Hirano & Tansan Water. Provisions, Gents, Furnishing goods, Toilet Articles, Travelling Bags, Tobacco, Cigars & Cigarettes Kitchen Utensils. Coffee, Biscuits.

Fresh Goods always kept in Stock.
Prices Moderate
Please come and inspect our goods.

NIPPON YUSEN KAISHA.

JAPANESE MAIL STEAMSHIP CO.

DER MAIL CONTRACT WITH THE IMPERIAL JAPANESE GOVERNMENT.

European Line

Regular Fortnightly Service between Yokohama Kobe, Moji, Shanghai, Hongkong, Singapore, Penang Colombo, Port Said, Marseilles, London and Antwerp

American Line

Regular Fortnightly Service between Hongkong and Seattle, calling at Shanghai, Moji, Kobe, Yokohama and Victoria, B. C.

Australian Line

Regular weekly Service betwen Japan Ports and Australia, calling at Hongkong and Manila.
(Above Three Lines Suspended until further notice).

Shanghai Line

Weekly Service between Shanghai and Japan Ports

Korea Line

Service Kobe, Moji, Nagasaki, Fusan, Chemupo, Coo, Taiku.
S. S. Bahelsberg, 2181 tons.
Service Kobe, Moji, Fusan, Chemulpo, Chinnampo
S. S ARGO, S. S. Ohio.

BORDEN'S CONDENSED MILK CO.

New York, U. S. A.

ALWAYS IN STOCK

Eagle Brand Condensed Milk.

Gold Seal Condensed Milk.

Peerless (Family) Evaporated Cream.

Borden's Malted Milk.

E. MEYER & CO.
Chemulpo, Korea,
Sole Agents

ROYAL INSURANCE COMPANY,
Funds exceed £10,000,000
FIRE
AT CURRENT RATES.
LIFE
REDUCED PREMIUM.
HOLME RINGER & Co.,
Agents, Chemulpo.

HOTEL DU PALAIS

SEOUL.

The only first class Hotel in Seoul. Situated in the centre of the city opposite the palace.

Cuisine under the supervision of an experienced French Chef.

Well ventilated and furnished throughout.

TARIFF UPON APPLICATION

L. MARTIN
Proprietor and Manager.

大韓每日申報
대한매일신보

(뎨칠십륙호) (금요일) 빅사년십월십ᄉᆞ일

본샤고빅

본신보는영어와한어로셕거미일츌판ᄒᆞᆸ

신문가

한쟝 엽두돈오푼
일삭됴 엽두량닷돈
우표가미삭닷돈
다맛돈으로밧ᄉᆞᆸ

광고료는

긔한의쟝단과ᄌᆞ힝의다쇼로즁감ᄒᆞ되렴가로밧을터이오며오릭지아녀대한사람마다다이신문을보실터이니광고내시기를원ᄒᆞ시는이들은우리신문샤에와셔면약ᄒᆞ심을희망ᄒᆞᆸ

○발힝소 박동대한미일신보샤법어학교압헤젼영국인셜필림집자리오

샤쟝 영국인 (비셜)

평양 디리졈

○평양효동사는권미보씨로우리신문관미디리인을뎡ᄒᆞ엿ᄉᆞ오니평양에계신구람코져ᄒᆞ시는 쳠군ᄌᆞ는히디리졈에왕림ᄒᆞ와면의ᄒᆞ시옵

사고

○우리대한미일신보의목뎍은대한의안녕질셔에관한모든데목에디ᄒᆞ야는공평한변론을쥬쟝ᄒᆞᆯ이라우리동신원의담보는신문보시는쳠군ᄌᆞ의게ᄒᆞᆼ상보도ᄒᆞ리며편지를긔셔ᄒᆞ여주시는이는셩명과반디를젹어붓치시기를희망ᄒᆞ오니이거슬신문상에긔지ᄒᆞ라는거시아니오다만극히신용ᄒᆞ는증거를삼고쟈홈이라긔자는아모긔셔던지긔지ᄒᆞᆯ와각ᄒᆞ는권리를가졋스나되각ᄒᆞ는리유를말ᄒᆞᆯ터이오며공즁평화를문란케ᄒᆞ는듯ᄒᆞᆫ긔셔는의례히밧지안켓ᄉᆞᆸ나이다

●본샤셜시이릭로신문을미양우례로분젼ᄒᆞ와례젼부의임의로젼ᄒᆞ듯스로면곳에는혹늣게젼ᄒᆞ기도ᄒᆞ며혹멋칠거슬ᄒᆞᆫ겁에젼ᄒᆞ기도ᄒᆞ며혹아니젼ᄒᆞ는곳도잇다ᄒᆞ와우리신문을ᄉᆞ랑ᄒᆞ아구람ᄒᆞ시는쳠군ᄌᆞ의게딕ᄒᆞ야미우미안ᄒᆞ옵기로지금은분젼인놀두고미일일즉이젼ᄒᆞ며아니젼ᄒᆞ거나늣게거나ᄒᆞᆫ페가업도록ᄒᆞ랴ᄒᆞ오니혹아니젼ᄒᆞ거나혹늣게젼ᄒᆞ거나ᄒᆞᆫ일이잇스면본샤로통긔ᄒᆞ여쥬심을희망ᄒᆞᆸ

본샤광고

○본샤신문즁에좌긔ᄒᆞᆫ호수를소용ᄒᆞᆯ데가잇셔이에광고ᄒᆞ오니누구시던지그즁에아모호수던지가져오시는되로미쟝에빅젼두푼식드리리다

데이호 데삼호 데이십호 데ᄉᆞ십이호 데ᄉᆞ십삼호 데오십삼호 데오십ᄉᆞ호와데오십오호 데륙십이호

관보

데이천구빅오십이호 연속

궁뎡록사

○죠왈오쥭우리조종죠법도는만셰의불역지뎐이니다시더ᄒᆞᆯ것업스되티평홈이오릭미말히히이ᄒᆞ니비유ᄒᆞ건디금슬에부됴ᄒᆞᆫ거슬반다시경쟝ᄒᆞᆯ지라특별이데실제도정리국을셜시ᄒᆞ야규구에참작ᄒᆞ야일신히거힝ᄒᆞ되시의에긴급지아니ᄒᆞᆫ거슨일졀물시ᄒᆞ야지극히졍긴ᄒᆞᆫ기를힘써서문명각국제도를취ᄒᆞ야그됴ᄒᆞᆫ거슬참작ᄒᆞ야금셕ᄀᆞᆺᄒᆞᆫ규모를뎡ᄒᆞ야내외빅관으로ᄒᆞ여곰분발ᄒᆞ며홍긔ᄒᆞ야각각그직분을극진히아니치못ᄒᆞ게ᄒᆞᆷ이실샹황실을존즁히ᄒᆞ고데업을륭슝히ᄒᆞ는큰긔회니이칙임을맛는자는능히짐의ᄯᅳᆺ슬법바들지어다

십월오일

ᄉᆞ령

○명셔리대신ᄉᆞ무 학부협판 고영희

십월팔일

졍오

○광무ᄉᆞ년 칙령데십ᄉᆞ호문관복쟝규칙중에부칙데십이됴본규칙은하에(외교관급)ᄉᆞ조들쳡립케부표홈이라

데이천구빅오십삼호 광무팔년십월십일

셔임급ᄉᆞ령

○호위디부령 륙군부령 민영옥 ○임평리원검ᄉᆞ셔칙임관ᄉᆞ등 졍삼품 리휘션

○의원면본관 비셔원승 신필희

○임비셔원승셔쥬임관륙등 졍삼품 박졍슈 ○임즁츄원의관셔칙임관ᄉᆞ등 룡강군슈 리근목 졍이품 리민즁

○명젼왕일본국시찰슈원 죵학교교관 박승원

이샹십월팔일

궁뎡록ᄉᆞ

○의졍부찬졍권즁현ᄉᆞ직소비지니에현직을띄고츌강홈이젼례가잇스니사양말고죵편히치힝ᄒᆞ라

○즁츄원의관박용규ᄉᆞ직소비지니에본직을허뎨ᄒᆞ노라

이샹십월칠일

데이천구빅오십ᄉᆞ호 광무팔년십월십일일

셔임급ᄉᆞ령

○승셔관임관오등 대구우톄ᄉᆞ쥬ᄉᆞ 김쳥제

○승셔관임관ᄉᆞ등 니부쥬ᄉᆞ 젼규학

이샹십월ᄉᆞ일

○의원면본관 의릉령 박쟝송

○임,의릉령셔판임관칠등 슌릉령 마희룡

○임 슌릉령셔판임관칠등 구품박쟝호

○면본관 한셩지판ᄉᆞ쥬ᄉᆞ 신릭슌

○임한셩지판소쥬ᄉᆞ셔판임관륙등 오병익

○임농샹공학교교관셔판임관륙등 홍인표

이샹십월팔일

○견칙 시종원봉시 리규담 궁닉부쥬ᄉᆞ 김셩연

이샹십월구일 궁닉부

궁뎡록ᄉᆞ

○죠월군제를임의의졍ᄒᆞ엿고데실제도를ᄯᅩ한방쟝리졍ᄒᆞ는지라오지졍부각부는일국졍치의소조출이어늘경쟝이리로규모와제도가극진이잘되지못ᄒᆞ야일홈과실샹이혹셔로샹칭치못ᄒᆞ고한만ᄒᆞᆫ관리가오히려만은고로빅관이히타ᄒᆞ야졍ᄉᆞ가히이ᄒᆞᆫ지라이졔맛당히분발ᄒᆞ야유신ᄒᆞᆯ때를당ᄒᆞ야일향인슌ᄒᆞ야지닉지못ᄒᆞᆯ지라졍부로ᄒᆞ여곰리졍소를셜시ᄒᆞ야고금을참작ᄒᆞ야부문을버리고실ᄉᆞ를심써서강령과됴목을졍리ᄒᆞ되그번거홈을더러버리고각부부에규모와제도일동을뎡ᄒᆞ야당디의법면을일위여만셰의법도를삼으되즁츄원인즉쟝졍만잇고의론는둣지못ᄒᆞᆫ즉엇지관원셜시ᄒᆞᆫ본의리오규칙을뎡ᄒᆞ야불일닉로실시ᄒᆞ야간쟁ᄒᆞ는풍속을일익키고인민의ᄯᅳᆺ시샹달케ᄒᆞ야지극히공평홈을던하에뵈이라너희부부제신은힘쓸지어다

십월팔일

○죠왈륙국참쟝박제슌을히형법교정총지ᄒᆞ라

○죠왈명법부대신김가진ᄒᆞ야겸임형법교졍총지ᄒᆞ라

십월팔일

관쳥ᄉᆞ항

○팍산군공립쇼하교교원김인형이가부샹를당ᄒᆞᆫᄉᆞ

○공립쇼학교교원박치훈이가부샹를당ᄒᆞᆫᄉᆞ

○공립쇼학교교원민관현이가모샹를당ᄒᆞᆫᄉᆞ

졍오

○셔북텰도국감독윤진우소비즁소청의시를경기물ᄉᆞ힝공으로긔부표홈이라

○관보데이천구빅오십이호셔임급ᄉᆞ령란닉데이면샹단데칠항표훈원쥬ᄉᆞ지일찬은군부쥬ᄉᆞ졍경윤으로긔졍홈이라

데이천구빅오십오호 광무팔년십월십이일

셔임급ᄉᆞ령

○승셔관임관삼등 평리원쥬ᄉᆞ 리즁혁

십월륙일

○명봉샹ᄉᆞ제쥬셔칙임관삼등 시강원쳠ᄉᆞ 민형식

○명시강원쳠ᄉᆞ셔칙임관삼등 동지돈령원ᄉᆞ 죠동완

○명동지돈령원ᄉᆞ셔칙임관삼등 궁닉부특진관 민영린

○임의쥬감리셔쥬ᄉᆞ셔판임관륙등 구품 리운규

○승셔관임관ᄉᆞ등 경무쳥총슌 박윤삼

○승셔관임관오등 경무쳥총슌 김희진 이샹십월십일

론셜

쟝곡쳔대쟝의 도착

◯작일에주차한국일본ᄉᆞ령쟝관쟝곡쳔씨가인항에도착ᄒᆞᆷ으로일한량국의영접ᄒᆞᄂᆞᆫ사ᄅᆞᆷ들이구름갓치모히여길이찻드리ᄒᆞ며남문밧졍거쟝에도역시동씨의샹경ᄒᆞᆷ을위ᄒᆞ야등후ᄒᆞᆫ쟈ㅣ일층굉쟝ᄒᆞ엿ᄂᆞᆫᄃᆡ과연샹오아홉시삼십분에도착ᄒᆞᆫ지라영졉등후ᄒᆞ든사ᄅᆞᆷ들이ᄎᆞ례로문후ᄒᆞ야공경ᄒᆞᆫ뜻을표ᄒᆞ며군ᄃᆡ의샤졸들도엄슉ᄒᆞᆫ위의로단졍히경례ᄒᆞ고인ᄒᆞ야호위ᄒᆞᄂᆞᆫ지라그ᄯᆡ에동씨ᄂᆞᆫ마차를타고입셩ᄒᆞᄂᆞᆫᄃᆡ소속무관들은좌우로옹위ᄒᆞ고뒤흐로츄죵ᄒᆞ엿스며남문으로브터사령부ᄭᆞ지ᄂᆞᆫ일한량국병뎡이좌우로라열ᄒᆞ야구경ᄒᆞᄂᆞᆫ사ᄅᆞᆷ들의잡담ᄒᆞᆷ을금ᄒᆞ나셔로틈을어더브려ᄒᆞᆷ으로도리혀금집키어렵고남산에셔ᄂᆞᆫ례포십구차를노왓스며일본사진샤들은각처로허여져조흔경식박이기에주의ᄒᆞ엿ᄂᆞᆫᄃᆡ사령부에도달ᄒᆞᆫ후방젼ᄒᆞᄂᆞᆫ사ᄅᆞᆷ들과츄죵ᄒᆞᆫ바관리들외평안도착ᄒᆞᆷ을셔로치하ᄒᆞᆷ과체귀ᄒᆞᄂᆞᆫ원구소쟝의발졍이ᄯᅩᄒᆞᆫ불구ᄒᆞ고로작별ᄒᆞᄂᆞᆫ거동이대단핑쟝ᄒᆞ엿더라

잡보

◯청결샹쥬 한셩오셔니에청결법을시힝ᄒᆞ기위ᄒᆞ야소무소ᄉᆞ지셜시ᄒᆞ고청결법을시작ᄒᆞ엿다가즁지되엿더니현금일본인이히소무를쥬관코져ᄒᆞᄂᆞᆫ고로의졍부에셔샹 쥬ᄒᆞ되본국인즁에만일히청결소무를셜시ᄒᆞ고쥬관ᄒᆞᆯ쟈잇스면일만원을보조ᄒᆞ기로ᄒᆞ엿다더라

◯고문계약 삼작십일일에의졍부에셔회의ᄒᆞ고탁지고문관고빙계약을의결ᄒᆞ엿ᄂᆞᆫᄃᆡ그젼문이여좌ᄒᆞ니

제일죠 목하젼죵티랑은대한국졍부의지졍을졍리감독ᄒᆞ고지졍상졔반셜비에관ᄒᆞ야지극히셩실히심의립안ᄒᆞᄂᆞᆫ척임에임ᄒᆞᆯᄉᆞ

제이죠 대한국졍부ᄂᆞᆫ지졍에관ᄒᆞᄂᆞᆫ일졀ᄉᆞ무에ᄃᆡᄒᆞ야위션목하젼죵티랑의갓흔뜻을경ᄒᆞ야시힝ᄒᆞᆯᄉᆞ 목하젼죵티랑은지졍ᄉᆞ항에관ᄒᆞᄂᆞᆫ의졍부회의에참례ᄒᆞ며밋지졍에관ᄒᆞᄂᆞᆫ의견을자의로의졍부에졔의ᄒᆞᆷ을엇을ᄉᆞ 의졍부결의와각부ᄉᆞ무로지졍에관계ᄒᆞᄂᆞᆫ자ᄂᆞᆫ그샹 쥬ᄒᆞ기젼에목하젼죵티랑의게갓흔뜻으로셔인ᄒᆞ기를요구ᄒᆞᆯᄉᆞ

제삼죠 목하젼죵티랑은지졍ᄉᆞ구에관ᄒᆞ야친히 알현샹쥬ᄒᆞᆷ을엇을ᄉᆞ

제사죠 목하젼죵티랑에봉급은미월금화팔빅원으로ᄒᆞ되미월이십일에지발ᄒᆞᆯᄉᆞ 이샹봉급외에대한졍부ᄂᆞᆫ관ᄉᆞ를목하젼죵티랑의게공급ᄒᆞᆯᄉᆞ 샹당ᄒᆞᆫ관ᄉᆞ가업스면관ᄉᆞ비로미월금화일빅원식지급ᄒᆞᆯᄉᆞ

제오죠 목하젼죵티랑의티임ᄒᆞᆯ시와환국ᄒᆞᆯ시와슈유ᄒᆞ고환국ᄒᆞᆯ시에션비를지급ᄒᆞᆯᄉᆞ 인공ᄒᆞ야대한국니디젼왕ᄒᆞᆯ시에ᄂᆞᆫ션비외에미일금화십원식지발ᄒᆞᆯᄉᆞ

제륙죠 본계약은그긔한을예졍치아니ᄒᆞ나각편에셔본계약을히제ᄒᆞᄂᆞᆫ필요가나ᄂᆞᆫ시에ᄂᆞᆫ셔로협의ᄒᆞᆫ후에대일본제국대표자의갓흔뜻을경ᄒᆞ야본계약을히제ᄒᆞᆯᄉᆞ

◯공쥬동학 공쥬군에ᄂᆞᆫ음팔월회일브터동학당이대치ᄒᆞᄂᆞᆫ고로쳥쥬진위ᄃᆡ참령을최측하송ᄒᆞ라ᄒᆞ시ᄂᆞᆫ 쳐분이나리셧다더라

◯풍셜분분 일진회원으로각군슈와각기인품에젹당ᄒᆞᆫ관직을셔임ᄒᆞᆫ다ᄂᆞᆫ풍셜이분분ᄒᆞ다더라

◯일금취당 함경남도관찰ᄉᆞ가면보ᄒᆞ기를함흥쥬차일본군ᄃᆡ지휘관의죠회니ᄂᆡ에일본군부인가업시취당ᄒᆞ야병긔를휴ᄃᆡᄒᆞᄂᆞᆫ쟈ᄂᆞᆫ군률노쳐단ᄒᆞᆯᄉᆞ로관하각군에훈칙ᄒᆞ라ᄒᆞ니엇지조쳐ᄒᆞᆯ지시명ᄒᆞ라ᄒᆞ엿더라

◯함열동학 작일샹오십이시에젼쥬관찰ᄉᆞ의면보가니부로도착ᄒᆞ엿스되동학당수쳔명이함열황등쟝에둔취ᄒᆞ야혹조슈삭발ᄒᆞᆫ다ᄒᆞ고히군보고가잇슨즉엇지조쳐ᄒᆞᆯ지시급히회면ᄒᆞ라ᄒᆞ엿더라

◯츙남진보회 공쥬관찰ᄉᆞ의면보가작일샹오십이시에니부로도착ᄒᆞ엿스되은진강경포면보ᄉᆞ에셔면보ᄒᆞ기를인민수쳔명이진보회라칭ᄒᆞ고취집ᄒᆞ야명일에론산포에셔연셜ᄒᆞ고쟝ᄎᆞᆺ공쥬로향ᄒᆞᆫ다ᄂᆞᆫᄃᆡ그근인인즉함열군에셔시작됨이라ᄒᆞ오며ᄯᅩ온양군슈셔함을졉ᄒᆞᆫ즉히회가연속히취집ᄒᆞᆫ다ᄒᆞ니그ᄉᆞ긔를졍담ᄒᆞ야치보ᄒᆞᆫ다ᄒᆞ엿다ᄒᆞ엿더라

◯창원민면 창원항구민인등이외부로면보ᄒᆞ기를본항감리리티졍씨가도임ᄒᆞᆫ지수년에션졍을만히힝ᄒᆞ엿고향조히일에혹화당ᄒᆞᆫ빅셩을위ᄒᆞ야관황즁외연금을니여은혜를베푼고로환산ᄒᆞ엿든항민이환집안도ᄒᆞ엿더니이졔례직ᄒᆞ미빅셩이부모일흔것ᄀᆞᆺ흔지라한삼년인임함을복망이라ᄒᆞ엿더라

◯일쳥회심 외부에셔평리원으로죠회ᄒᆞ되일본공ᄉᆞ의죠회에ᄒᆞ기를시흥민요의운동을쥬쟝ᄒᆞᆫ쟈셩우경과민용훈를일본군ᄃᆡ에셔착리ᄒᆞ야취쵸ᄒᆞᆫ즉히량인이피슈됨이젹확ᄒᆞ며이일을인ᄒᆞ야일본군힝동샹에영향이젹지아니ᄒᆞᆫ지라히범등을귀졍부로압송ᄒᆞᆯ터이오ᄯᅩᄒᆞᆫ일본군에셔도군리ᄉᆞ를파송ᄒᆞ야회심ᄒᆞᆯ터어니그회심ᄒᆞᆯ일ᄌᆞ를미리시명ᄒᆞ라ᄒᆞ엿기로죠회ᄒᆞ니그회심ᄒᆞᆯ일ᄌᆞ를뎡ᄒᆞ긔시복ᄒᆞ야히ᄉᆞ안을라관케ᄒᆞ라ᄒᆞ엿더라

◯진보회통문 강원도이천군슈가진보회통문을니부로등보ᄒᆞ엿ᄂᆞᆫᄃᆡ그ᄉᆞ의가좌와ᄀᆞᆺᄒᆞ니대뎌인민은국가의원긔요회샤ᄂᆞᆫ인민의졍론이니잠시도셔로ᄯᅥ나지못ᄒᆞᆯ쟈ᄂᆞᆫ원긔요ᄒᆞᆫ날도업지못ᄒᆞᆯ쟈ᄂᆞᆫ졍론이라우리나라삼쳔리강토와이쳔만인민이족히풍교를유지ᄒᆞ야문명에진보ᄒᆞ겟거ᄂᆞᆯ졍부졔씨가취ᄒᆞᆫ쑴을ᄭᆡ지못ᄒᆞ야비단고식지계로구차이지ᄂᆡᆯ쑨아니라안으로셩총을옹폐ᄒᆞ고밧그로싱령을포학ᄒᆞ야가혹ᄒᆞᆫ졍ᄉᆞ로압졔ᄒᆞ야무죄ᄒᆞᆫ빅셩이졈졈더옥도탄에ᄲᅡ지니오호통재라나라흥망이오직민심이동일ᄒᆞᆷ과각산ᄒᆞᄂᆞᆫᄃᆡ잇ᄂᆞ니쳠군ᄌᆞᄂᆞᆫ동셩과동긔로일졔히분발ᄒᆞ야긔약에본회로리도ᄒᆞ야당당ᄒᆞᆫ졍론으로졍부에헌의ᄒᆞ야우리강토를보젼ᄒᆞ고우리싱민을구활ᄒᆞᆷ을천만옹축ᄒᆞ노라

일은 회쟝리용구 부회쟝권종덕

일은 회명은진보회라칭ᄒᆞᆯᄉᆞ

일은 본월회일노길졔긔회ᄒᆞᆯᄉᆞ

일은 독립을보젼ᄒᆞᆯᄉᆞ

일은 졍치의긔혁을헌의ᄒᆞᆯᄉᆞ

일은 인민의싱명지산을보젼ᄒᆞᆯᄉᆞ

일은 군졍을감액ᄒᆞᆯᄉᆞ

일은 지졍을졍리ᄒᆞᆯᄉᆞ

일은 동밍국군ᄉᆞ샹에보조ᄒᆞᆯᄉᆞ

일은 회원은일졔단발ᄒᆞᆯᄉᆞ라

ᄒᆞ엿ᄂᆞᆫᄃᆡ히통문이근읍에륜회ᄒᆞᆫ다ᄒᆞ엿다더라

◯죠힐헌병부 작일에일본ᄉᆞ령부에셔헌병ᄉᆞ령부로죠회ᄒᆞ기를향쟈에한국헌병이명이일본ᄉᆞ령부에피슈되야샹금구류ᄒᆞᆫ소에ᄃᆡᄒᆞ야말ᄒᆞ엿스되귀부헌병은무어슬경찰ᄒᆞ며슌힝식킬ᄯᅢ무슨긔계를쥬며일본조계니에드러와경찰ᄒᆞᄂᆞᆫ권한이잇ᄂᆞ냐ᄒᆞ고소샹히시명ᄒᆞ라ᄒᆞ엿다더라

외보

◯법국구합뉴약 리보에왈아연뎡공화국에잇ᄂᆞᆫ헬랜드신문의통신원이보ᄒᆞᆫ바를거ᄒᆞᆫ즉ᄯᅢ국ᄃᆡ표쟈가젼투함이척을살ᄎᆞ로목하에비밀히샹의즁이라ᄒᆞ고ᄯᅩ덕국신문을거ᄒᆞᆫ즉법국이이외에ᄯᅩ지리국슌양함이을사랴ᄒᆞ고이량국군함이발힝ᄒᆞᆯᄯᅢ에ᄂᆞᆫ법국군함의긔를달앗다가도즁에셔로국군함의긔를달아ᄐᆡ평양함ᄃᆡ에합ᄒᆞ게ᄒᆞ라ᄂᆞᆫ계획인ᄃᆡ영덕량국은이일에드러말ᄒᆞ기를불긍ᄒᆞ고그옥이일본의항의ᄒᆞᆷ을기ᄃᆞ린다더라

◯일본명년도군ᄉᆞ비 일본에셔명년도군ᄉᆞ비를대략칠억원으로결뎡ᄒᆞ고중세와밋니국채외에다시외채를모집ᄒᆞᆯ계획이라더라

◯로쟝보고 론돈면보에운ᄒᆞ엿스되싸바로푸쟝의보고를거ᄒᆞᆫ즉일군의젼초가봉텬부동남방웬시에푸셩을에위쌋다ᄒᆞ엿더라

◯셕탄공급 구월삼십일론돈발면을거ᄒᆞᆫ즉덕국셕탄슈운ᄒᆞᄂᆞᆫ비오척이작일에뉴ᄭᅩᆺ트와카듸푸에셔ᄯᅥ나오프라야항구로향ᄒᆞ엿ᄂᆞᆫᄃᆡ로국션쳑의셕탄을공급ᄒᆞ랴ᄒᆞᆷ이라더라

뎐보

십월십삼일동경발

◯로군대픽 봉텬방면의로병은작일오후에젼군이퇴각ᄒᆞᄂᆞᆫᄃᆡ일국이추격ᄒᆞ야로병의손히가막대ᄒᆞᆫ지라로군의병력은이십만이오대포ᄂᆞᆫ일천문이라ᄒᆞ더라

동일동면

◯일군대쳡 봉텬방면에셔크게격젼ᄒᆞ엿ᄂᆞᆫᄃᆡ각방면이다일군의대쳡ᄒᆞᆫ대도라갓고대포삼십문을획득ᄒᆞ엿고로군의포병대부ᄃᆡ를에워싸고밍렬히공격즁이라ᄒᆞ더라

십이일동경발대본영공보

◯밀슈션포획 초함빅응호ᄂᆞᆫ십월십이일오전에마대ᄒᆞᆫ젼시금제픔을려쥰으로비밀히슈운코져ᄒᆞᄂᆞᆫ긔션복편호를포획ᄒᆞ엿더라

십월십이일대본영발일본공ᄉᆞ관착

세곡함대ᄉᆞ령관보고요령

◯평원침몰 포함평원함은구월십팔일에구만부근에셔봉쇄감무ᄒᆞᆫ이리로부지거쳐러니그후에히함승죠원니에ᄉᆞ명은부근셤에셔발견ᄒᆞ엿ᄂᆞᆫ대구월십팔일은저녁브터풍파가대작ᄒᆞ엿스미동함은그ᄃᆡ라오ᄂᆞᆫ길에젹의ᄯᅥ잇ᄂᆞᆫ슈뢰에부듸쳐셔슈분동안에침몰ᄒᆞᆫ지라우에말ᄒᆞᆫᄉᆞ명과륙대근두ᄒᆞ라고분견ᄒᆞ엿든자십칠명을제ᄒᆞᆫ외에승죠원은몰슈히젼ᄉᆞᄒᆞᆫ것갓더라

TELEGRAMS.

Extensive Battle South of Mukden.

Marshal Oyama's Report.

Kuropatkin Assumes the Aggressive But Is Repulsed.

Tokyo, Oct. 12th.

On the morning of the 9th inst. the enemy advancing to attack our right wing, recrossed the Taitse river and effected an interruption of our line between Chaotu and Punkiho. The enemy's force here was composed of one brigade of infantry, 2,000 cavalry with two guns, while on the right bank of the Taitse were one brigade of infantry and 1,500 cavalry with eight guns. It seemed that this was the advance guard of a superior force. At 2 P. M. two regiments of infantry and one of cavalry advanced to attack our front at Sotatko. The enemy in the direction of our centre at Liutang-kow (two and a half li north of Yentai) also continued their movement southward. On the railway the enemy's troops were visible for two li but it was impossible to see where their line ended. Their principal force seems to be at Liutang Kow.

One column to each place has been despatched to Chaotre and Punkiho, to reinforce the garrisons there, where fighting is already taking place. I myself, with the object of finding their principal force, commenced the attack along the left bank of the Hun-ho.

Latest reports say that from the morning of the 9th inst. fighting continued for 12 hours, but neither side gained any advantage and the positions remained unchanged.

Tokyo, Later.

On the 10th and 11th inst. the fighting was continued. The enemy on our right wing after a strong attack, seized our position on the hills to the east of the road between Punkiho and Hoaliensai, but on the morning of the 10th under cover of a fog our troops recovered the position at 11 A.M. and fighting continued until dusk of the 11th. The enemy to the east of Punkiho(30 *li* distant from that place)consisted of over two divisions and 80 guns, and the enemy opposing our left wing (7 *li* northwest of Punkiho) was composed of over one division. The right column of our central force occupied some high ground to the east of Yuimnutze on the forenoon of the 10th, and the left column extended to the hills, 10 li north of Yentai. In these two places the battle raged till dusk on the 11th. Many of our columns advanced and attacked the advance guard of enemy. At Kianchang (north of Saimachi) the enemy have been attacking our garrison since the 7th inst. but on the 10th our troops assumed the aggressive and dispersed them.

Tokyo, Later,

In every direction, we have been successful. We captured 30 guns and have surrounded a large force of the enemy's artillery, with whom we are now engaged in battle.

Tokyo, Oct 13th.

The battle near Mukden has resulted in a great victory for us. Our troops following up the retreating enemy, inflicted great casualties. The enemy's troops were composed of 200,000 men with 1,000 guns.

Tokyo, Oct. 12th.

The British steamer "Fuping" has been seized by our fleet, while attempting to run the blockade at Port Arthur.

London, October 9th.

Reuter's correspondent at Tsingtau states that a German steamer which has returned there, after running the blockade to Vladivostock, states that ships are constantly reaching the latter port.

The city of Vladivostock is reported to be heavily fortified and the harbour is mined.

TREATMENT OF ATTACHES AND CORRESPONDENTS.

(Concluded from 2nd page.)

armies to which they were attached. Such they say was not the treatment meted out to the Japanese when they were attached to the armies or were studying in the military schools of Western civilisation where they learned all they know of the art and practice of modern war. The Japanese should remember that they are at best but copyists, and they should not be shy scholars. A case in point. Captain Hoffman, the German military attaché with one of the divisions of General Kuroki's army, was proceeding with an acquaintance to look at a battery of guns made after a German model. The guns were standing in camp but Capt. Hoffman and his companion were warned not to approach the battery as the guns were a military secret.' "But,' protested Captain Hoffman, 'I have seen them made.' The sentry, however, was not to be moved and the two foreigners walked away. Next day a notice was posted over the battery warning foreigners in three European languages that they must on no account go near it. In the same manner we were treated with regard to the Russian prisoners. The attachés and correspondents attached to the First Army were invited to inspect the prisoners, but as soon as the staff discovered that we could talk to them in Russian or German, the privilege of visiting the unhappy prisoners was withdrawn and the familiar tri-lingual notice was posted up forbidding our approach. I will give two further instances of the personal treatment which General Nicholson has found so satisfactory. Colonel Watanabe, who is in charge of the attachés with the Second Army, behaved so rudely to many of the officers, his betters in rank and otherwise, that they refused to hold any but the barest official intercourse with him. Next the military attachés who are the guests of the Japanese Army have been so indifferently provided for in the matter of food that they have come again and again to the camps of the correspondents and to individuals to buy necessary stores to save themselves from having to go hungry. For weeks at a time the only rations served out to the attachés with the First Army were filthy Chinese pork and rice, and this in a standing camp where other food supplies were easily available. At all times they found the food provided for them without variety, meagre, and often unpalatable. Yet Sir William Nicholson finds himself able to declare that the treatment of the attachés left nothing to be desired."

The two leaders of the Si Hung riot are to be tried shortly in the High Supreme Court. Two representatives of the Japanese Military authorities will be present at the trial.

We are informed by the Korean Telegraph Office that from the 1st November proximo, the registration of telegraphic code addresses will be subject to a yearly charge of 10 dollars payable in advance.

THE FINANCIAL ADVISER.

Mr. Megata's agreement with the Korean Government was finally passed at a session held on the 11th ist. It reads as follows:

1. Mr. Megata's duty will be to correct and supervise documents relating to financial matters.

2 Mr. Megata will be present at the sessions of the Council of State when matters financial are up for discussion. He will give his views on financial reforms and he will affix his signature to all reports handed to His Majesty.

3. To Mr. Megata will be accorded the privilege of discussing financial matters with His Majesty.

4. A salary of Yen 800.00 per month will be paid to Mr. Megata and in addition he will have the use of a house free of charge; should a house be unobtainable a supplementary sum of Yen 100.00 will be paid him. Should the necessity of travel present itself, he will receive all expenses.

5. This agreement is not fixed at any period, but if either side desire to end the contract, the case must be laid before a representative of the Japanese Government.

The delegates to Japan, accompanied by Mr. Hagiwara, arrived yesterday at Shimonoseki.

Five foreign warships, representing England, the United States, France, Germany and Italy, are expected to pass the winter this year at Yinkow. This is quite an unprecedented event.

A notification by the Japanese Military authorities, to the effect that no societies are to be formed and no meetings of large numbers of people are to take place, has been published in the Ham Kyeng province.

We have received from the "Nagasaki Press" a copy of "Cherry Blossoms," a neatly arranged little magazine, illustrated with photographs of Nagasaki and neighbourhood. It will be issued monthly and can be obtained from the "Nagasaki Press" office at the extremely moderate charge of 10 sen per copy.

The Korea Daily News.

Issued at 5 P. M. daily except Sundays.

Rate of Subscription:

Per Year. Yen [illegible]

Per Quarter. Yen [illegible]

Per Month. Yen [illegible]

Postage in Korea not charged extra.

Postage abroad charged extra.

Advertisements, 50 sen per day for 1 inch or less.

5 yen per month per inch.

50 yen per year per inch.

All communications to

E. T. BETHELL,

Editor and Publisher.

Pak-tong, Seoul.

PORT ARTHUR AND THE CENSORATE.

The conflicting rumours anent operations at Port Arthur and the secretive attitude adopted by the Japanese Censorate make the task of following the trend of events at the besieged citadel one of extreme difficulty.

In the absence of official news, it is only natural that many absurd stories should be current regarding the conflict. Some the stories however bear such an evident mark of untruth that one can hardly credit a person of reason placing belief in them.

For instance, recently we were informed that a battleship had been badly damaged by Japanese shells falling in the harbor, but that the remainder of the ships had escaped harm by taking refuge under shelter of the hills. Immediately after this story was published, comes the report that Golden Hill was in the hands of the Japanese.

Now, an, one at all familiar, even in the most elementary manner, with the topography of Port Arthur, will find it impossible to reconcile the two reports. If the large majority of the ships escaped damage, and so the Tokyo despatch says, then Golden Hill most assuredly was not in the hands of the Japanese, for the guns in that fort command the harbour as also the town.

On the 5th inst, we published a Japanese report emanating ostensibly from Chefoo, to the effect that the "Kuropatkin fort had been taken by assault and the Russian water supply cut off yesterday. Our correspondent "Old Stager and Strict Observer," drew our attention to the report of the "Novi Krai" bulletin, which asserted that the Japanese had, in their turn, been driven out of the fort with a loss of 6000 killed.

It is extremely difficult to pick and choose between all these strangely varied reports, but the silence observed by the Japanese authorities certainly does not tend to establish confidence in the stories which occasionally find their way here from Japanese. It would seem but poor management or an evidence of want of success, to chronicle an occasional victory and leave a blank of weeks and even months to be filled up by the imaginative minds of an anxious public, or by such reports as those published by the "Novi Krai" bulletins in which, in the face of lack of contradiction by the Japanese authorities, one is forced to place belief.

That the Japanese Censorate is in a large manner to blame for this state of affairs, the following experience of the "Kobe Chronicle" will prove.

"The treatment of war correspondents with the Japanese Army may be improved, but, judging from a recent experience of our own, the censorship would seem to be as rigid as ever. A Japanese who is now serving with the Army at Port Arthur wrote an account of an assault on the stronghold which occurred as long ago as the 26th of July, and sent it to us. Of course the letter had been duly submitted to censorship on the field, as no communications can leave the Army without undergoing this formality, but, in order to be perfectly sure that we were not offending against the regulations, we sent the communication to the Censorate Committee of the War Office with the request that it might be approved for publication. In reply the Committee stated that the description of the battle in question could not be allowed to be published at present, as the letter disclosed not only the movements of the Japanese Army but the distribution of the Japanese force. Consequently permission was refused. It is true that the letter contained the names of places, and gave the strength of the attacking force, but it must be remembered that it referred to events occurring two months ago, and it is absurd to believe that the publication of any such details now could possibly affect the Japanese position at Port Arthur. Evidently if such news is of any use to the enemy it should not be permitted to pass the hands of the censors on the field, for there is nothing to prevent any such information leaving Japan by mail once it has reached this country. One conclusion might be that the Censorate Committee of the War Office is anxious to keep the people of the country in ignorance, but stories from Port Arthur are continually being published in the Japanese papers, with blanks that it is not very difficult to fill. We cannot understand the policy pursued, or what the authorities expect to gain from preserving secresy about events long past. What does happen is that in the absence of authentic news very many rumours are in circulation as to the actual position at Port Arthur, which ceatainly do not tend to improve the financial standing of Japan."

TREATMENT OF ATTACHES AND CORRESPONDENTS.

"A Correspondent who has served in Many Wars" writes to the "North-China Daily News" under date of September 24th on the above subject. It is of great importance that the truth as to this matter should be known, and, therefore, we publish an extract from this letter as giving an individual view of one who was apparently of the aggrieved:—

"What the foreign correspondents almost without exception do charge against the Japanese Government and Military Authorities is that they were never either frank or honest in their dealings with us. Before we were permitted to go to the front we were assured, with great parade of welcome and a profusion of smiles and bowings, that very soon we would be sent into the field. But as we discovered later the four words of English which every Japanese official can and does use constantly and most mendaciously are 'very soon' and 'very sorry.' For months the correspondents were compelled to kick their heels idly in Tokyo, put off from day to day with a surfeit of 'very soons' and 'very sorries.' They prevented us from leaving Tokyo, even for a few days or a week at a time, by saying that to leave the capital for ever so short an interval would be a great risk, as we might be too late to take our places with the column to which we were to be attached.

"In the case of the correspondents sent with the Second Army there are at least six gentlemen of whom I will venture to say that most, if not all of them, are prepared to make oath and say—and their testimony from their character and standing would be accepted in any of the law courts of Europe or America before that of either General Baron Kodama, Vice-Chief, or General (*sic*) T. Fukushima, Assistant Chief of the General Staff—that these two officials whom I have named assured them individually and personally that they would be sent with the troops going to the Liaotung Peninsula, and that they would be present at the siege and fall of Port Arthur. In no single respect were the specific promises made by these two prominent Japanese officials fulfilled.

"Now as to the treatment in the field. Correspondents were herded daily and nightly like sheep; domiciliary visits were paid to their tents or lodgings during the hours of darkness to ascertain if they were there, and they were never permitted to go near the firing lines. They were warned again and again that they must keep with the officers set over them, and these, under superior orders, never went within the remotest range of the enemy's fire. From positions miles away from where the fighting was in progress they were asked to view the battle. So irksome did this treatment become that one of the correspondents with Kuroki's army accused, of course quite unjustly, the officer in charge of the correspondents with being afraid to go near the firing line, and hence keeping the correspondents far in the rear. Things finally came to such a pass that the correspondents took matters into their own hands and, giving their 'bearleader' the slip, went to the front by themselves and saw some of the fighting. For this they were again and again reprimanded in an offensive manner and warned that serious consequences might result to themselves and the papers they represented if the 'offence' were repeated. This measure of precaution may have been intended to safeguard the correspondents. I know of one instance where a correspondent narrowly escaped being shot dead by a Japanese soldier of the Second Division, who fired at him at ten paces' distance, having mistaken him for a Russian, in one of the fights at the Motienling Pass. Fortunately for the correspondent the average Jap soldier is only an indifferent shot. In addition to being reprimanded several correspondents were punished by being kept under restraint for days and not allowed to send either letters or telegrams. On several occasions the correspondents were forbidden to pass beyond a certain area which was marked out close to their camps, and at other times they were warned that gendarmes would be placed in charge of them. And all this in face of the fact that the Japanese correspondents were allowed to go practically where they pleased at any time, and were permitted to approach and talk with the Generals and their staffs while the foreigners were ordered to keep at a distance.

"Now as to the treatment of the military attachés and of Lieut-General Sir William Nicholson, late Chief of the British Army Intelligence Department, who on behalf of himself and his countrymen proclaims that they were well treated. Direct issue on the merits can safely be joined with him. But perhaps that would not be fair to Sir William, for he was very ill, seriously so, during his short stay with General Oku's army in Manchuria. When he dragged himself out from the unclean Chinese dwellings to which he was allotted to the battlefield, say as at Soushan, it was doubtless as much to get fresh air as to see the action that the General made the effort. Neither he nor any of the attachés were ever taken to within a mile of the furthest range of the Russian guns and they were obliged to view the contest from a distance of four to seven miles from where the combatants were actually engaged. Yet Sir William Nicholson professes to be content and he declares that nobody either attaché or correspondent, could ask for more considerate treatment. Ordinary men, unlike Sir William, are unable to follow the progress of battle at a distance of seven miles, and all the other military attachés, British and foreign, as well as the correspondents, suffered under this disability. Many of the attachés, you may have their names if you like, American and others, applied to the Japanese officially to be allowed to go forward and actually see the work of the batteries and battalions in the firing line, and the request was refused. In whatever expressions certain of the attachés may now indulge of grateful recognition towards the Japanese officials, such was not their speech or attitude when in the field. They all said that no Government ever treated military attachés so scurvily as the Japanese, or withheld them so much from seeing the details of the work and of the organisation of the

(Continued on page 3.)

The Korea Daily News.

VOL. I, FRIDAY, OCTOBER 14, 1904. No. 76

HONGKONG & SHANGHAI BANKING CORPORATION.

Paid-up Capital..... ....$10,000,000
Reserve Fund:—Sterling Reserve... 10,000,000
Silver Reserve..... 7,000,000
27,000,000
Reserve Liability of Proprietors... 10,000,000

HEAD OFFICE, HONGKONG.

London Bankers, London and County Banking Company Limited.
Branches and Agencies,
London.

Amoy,	Hankow	Penang,
Bangkok,	Hiogo,	Rangoon,
Batavia,	Iloilo,	Saigon,
Bombay,	Lyons,	San Francisco,
Calcutta,	Manila,	Singapore,
Colombo,	Nagasaki,	Sourabaya,
Foochow,	New York,	Tientsin,
Hamburg,	Peking,	Yokohama,

Credits granted on approved Securities, and every description of Banking and Exchange business transacted.

Drafts granted on London and the chief Commercial places in Europe, India, Australia, America, China and Japan.

HOLME RINGER & Co., AGENTS,
CHEMULPO.

ON CHEONG & CO.,
SEOUL.

GENERAL STORE KEEPERS.
Imported provisions, Cooking Utensils Crockery, etc.
FRESH BREAD DAILY.

MITSU BISHI DOCKYARD & ENGINE WORKS,
NAGASAKI.

CODE WORD, "DOCK."

A. 1, A. B. C., and Engineering Codes used.

DOCK No. 1 (at Tategami).

Extreme Length..............523 feet
Length on blocks .... 513 ,,
Width of Entrance on Top......89 ,,
,, ,, Bottom....77 ,,
Water on Blocks at Spring Tide 26½ ,,

DOCK No. 2 (Mukaijima).

Extreme Length..............371 feet
Length on Blocks.............360 ,,
Width of Entrance on Top......66 ,,
,, ,, Bottom 53 ,,
Water on Blocks at Spring Tide 22 ,,

PATENT SLIP (at Kosuge).

Can take vessels up to 1,000 tons gross.

THE WORKS are well equipped with the LATEST IMPROVEMENTS, and can execute any kind of work in SHIPBUILDING and MARINE ENGINEERING, as well as in REPAIRING of SHIPS.

The COMPANY'S new powerful steamer OURA-MARU (712 tons, 700 I.H.P.), specially built for SALVAGE PURPOSES, and equipped with necessary gear, is always READY at SHORT NOTICE.

CHARTERED BANK OF INDIA AUSTRALIA & CHINA.

INCORPORATED BY ROYAL CHARTER 1853

HEAD OFFICES:—LONDON.

Paid-up Capital £800,000
Reserve Liability of Shareholders 800,000
Reserve Fund 800,000

Drafts granted upon all the principal places in the world and every description of Exchange and banking business transacted.

E. MEYER & Co., Agents,
Chemulpo.

E. MEYER & CO.
Chemulpo.

SOLE AGENTS IN KOREA FOR:
A. T. Morse, Sons & Co's "Fresco" Distemper

In all colours ready for use on walls, Ceilings etc.

and

AVENARIUS CARBOLINEUM

A wood-preserving and antiseptic oil preparation

Against decay, dry-rot, fungus and wood-destroying insects.

A large supply always in Stock.
Prices upon application.

E. MEYER & Co.,
Chemulpo.

THE METHODIST PUBLISHING HOUSE,
Little West Gate, Seoul.

PRINTING, TYPEWRITER PAPER
CARBON PAPER, VISITING CARDS
STATIONERY, BOOK BINDING
BOOK PUBLISHERS
AMERICAN SCHOOL BOOKS
SPENCERIAN COPY BOOKS
PEN CARBON LETTER AND BILL BOOKS

S. A. BECK, Manager.

HOKURKU DOBOKU KAISHA.

Branch office in Chong Dong. Seoul.
Japanese telephone No. 165

CONTRACT DEPARTMENT.

We can contract to build any building or construction.

MERCHANDISE DEPARTMENT.

We can provide any building material. We have just contracted to build the new Belgian Legation.

DAI-ICHI GINKO.

LIMITED.

(Formerly the First National Bank)

ESTABLISHED 1873

INCORPORATED UNDER PRESENT LAW 1896

Capital - - - - - - - - Yen 5,000,000
Reserve Fund - - - - - 1,500,000

HEAD OFFICE:—TOKIO.

President: Baron SHIBUSAWA.

BRANCHES AND CORRESPONDENTS
In the Principal Cities and Towns of Japan.
Interest Allowed on
Fixed deposits 1 year - - - 6½ per cent
" " 6 months - - - 6 per cent

Special current accounts 1½ sen daily per Y 100
General " " 1 " " " 100

M. TANAKA,
Manager, Chemulpo

HOLME RINGER & Co.
Chemulpo.

General Merchants and Government Contractors.

Agents for the leading
Banks
Steamship Companies
and
Insurance Companies

Importers of Merchandise of every description.

KAMEYA & CO.

GENERAL STOREKEEPERS
Chinkokai - - Seoul
(Established 1895, Tokyo)

Confectionery, Hams, Canned Goods, Cutlery, Hirano & Tansan Water. Provisions, Gents, Furnishing goods, Toilet Articles, Travelling Bags, Tobacco, Cigars & Cigarettes Kitchen Utensils. Coffee, Biscuits.

Fresh Goods always kept in Stock.
Prices Moderate
Please come and inspect our goods.

NIPPON YUSEN KAISHA.

JAPANESE MAIL STEAMSHIP CO.

DER MAIL CONTRACT WITH THE IMPERIAL JAPANESE GOVERNMENT.

European Line

Regular Fortnightly Service between Yokohama Kobe, Moji, Shanghai, Hongkong, Singapore, Penang Colombo, Port Said, Marseilles, London and Antwerp

American Line

Regular Fortnightly Service between Hongkong and Seattle, calling at Shanghai, Moji, Kobe, Yokohama and Victoria, B. C.

Australian Line

Regular weekly Service betwen Japan Ports and Australia, calling at Hongkong and Manila.
(Above Three Lines Suspended until further notice).

Shanghai Line

Weekly Service between Shanghai and Japan Ports

Korea Line

Service Kobe, Moji, Nagasaki, Fusan, Chemupo, Coo, Taiku.
S. S. Bahelsberg, 2181 tons.
Service Kobe, Moji, Fusan, Chemulpo, Chinnampo
S. S ARGO, S. S. Ohio.

BORDEN'S CONDENSED MILK CO.

New York, U. S. A.

ALWAYS IN STOCK
Eagle Brand Condensed Milk.
Gold Seal Condensed Milk.
Peerless (Family) Evaporated Cream.
Borden's Malted Milk.

E. MEYER & CO.
Chemulpo, Korea,
Sole Agents

ROYAL INSURANCE COMPANY,
Funds exceed £10,000,000
FIRE
AT CURRENT RATES.
LIFE
REDUCED PREMIUM.
HOLME RINGER & Co.,
Agents, Chemulpo.

HOTEL DU PALAIS

SEOUL.

The only first class Hotel in Seoul, Situated in the centre of the city opposite the palace.

Cuisine under the supervision of an experienced French Chef.

Well ventilated and furnished throughout.

TARIFF UPON APPLICATION

L. MARTIN
Proprietor and Manager

大韓每日申報

대한미일신보

빅사년십월십오일 (토요일) (뎨칠십칠호)

본샤고빅

본신보는영어와한어로셔거미
일츌판ᄒᆞ옵
 신문가
한쟝 엽두돈오푼
일삭됴 엽두량닷돈
우표가미삭닷돈
 다맛돈으로밧솝
광고료는
긔한의쟝단과ᄌᆞ힝의다쇼로즁
감ᄒᆞ되렴가로밧올터이오며오
리지아녀대한사람마다다이신
문을보실터이나광고내시기를
원ᄒᆞ시는이들은우리신문샤에
와셔면약ᄒᆞ심을희망ᄒᆞ옵
○발힝소 박동대한미일신보
샤법어학교압헤젼영국인셜필
립집자리오
 샤쟝 영국인 (비셜)
평양 디리점
○평양효동사는권미보씨로우
리신문관미디리인을뎡ᄒᆞ엿
ᄉᆞ오니평양에계신구람코져ᄒᆞ
시는 쳠군ᄌᆞ는히디리점에왕
림ᄒᆞ와면의ᄒᆞ시옵

사고

○우리대한미일신보의목뎍은
대한의안녕질셔에관한모든뎨
목에디ᄒᆞ야는공평한변론을쥬
장홈이라우리동신원의탐보는
신문보시는쳠군ᄌᆞ의게홍상보
도ᄒᆞ리며편지를긔셔ᄒᆞ여주시
는이는셩명과반디를젹어붓치
시기를희망ᄒᆞ오니이거슬신문
샹에긔지ᄒᆞ랴는거시아니오다
만극히신용ᄒᆞ는증거를숨고쟈
홈이라긔자는아모긔셔던지긔
지홈을되각ᄒᆞ는권리를가졋스
나되각ᄒᆞ는리유를말홀터이오
며공즁평화를문란케ᄒᆞ는듯ᄒᆞᆫ
긔셔는의례히밧지안켓숩나이
다
●본샤셜시이릭로신문을미양
우례로분젼ᄒᆞ와례젼부의임의
로젼ᄒᆞᆫ듯스로면곳에는혹늣게
젼ᄒᆞ기도ᄒᆞ며혹몃칠거슬ᄒᆞᆫ겁
에젼ᄒᆞ기도ᄒᆞ며혹아니젼ᄒᆞ는
곳도잇다ᄒᆞ와우리신문을ᄉᆞ랑
ᄒᆞ야구람ᄒᆞ시는쳠군ᄌᆞ의게
되ᄒᆞ야미우미안ᄒᆞ옵기로지금
은분젼인을두고미일일즉이젼
ᄒᆞ며아니젼ᄒᆞ거나늣게거나ᄒᆞᆫ
폐가업도록ᄒᆞ랴ᄒᆞ오니혹아니
젼ᄒᆞ거나혹늣게젼ᄒᆞ거나ᄒᆞᆫ일
이잇스면본샤로통긔ᄒᆞ여쥬심
을희망ᄒᆞ옵

본샤광고

○본샤신문즁에좌긔ᄒᆞᆫ호수를
소용홀데가잇셔이에광고ᄒᆞ오
니누구시던지그즁에아모호수
던지가져오시는디로미쟝에빅
젼두푼식드리리다
뎨이호 뎨삼호 뎨이십호
뎨ᄉᆞ십이호 뎨ᄉᆞ십삼호 뎨
오십삼호 뎨오십ᄉᆞ호와뎨오
십오호 뎨륙십이호

관보

관보뎨이천구빅오십오호
 연속
궁뎡록ᄉᆞ
○궁닉부닉대신리지완ᄉᆞ직소
비지닉에ᄉᆞ양ᄒᆞᆫ죵돈령지임은
의시ᄒᆞ노라
○의정부찬정홍슌형ᄉᆞ직소
비지닉에ᄉᆞ양말고힝공ᄒᆞ라
 이샹십월십일
○죠왈학부대신리지져극으로특
명젼권공ᄉᆞ를겸임ᄒᆞ고관리공
ᄉᆞ민형식으로특명젼권공ᄉᆞ를
삼으라
○죠왈종이품강홍대를특면증
계ᄒᆞ라
 이샹십월십일
○시죵무관쟝민영환ᄉᆞ직소
비지닉에군제의면지임만의시
ᄒᆞ노라
 십월십일
○의정부참정신긔션은근쥬
ᄒᆞ되광산에긔쳐홈이미샹비싱
지지방에량척이로디각국규례
에도심산과황무지에디만긔광
홈을허가ᄒᆞ고면야에는일절긔
굴치아니ᄒᆞ는거시농ᄉᆞ에방히
와민폐를되지안케홈이라우리
나라동협과셔북도에는긔광홀
곳시잇스되삼남인즉인가가쥬
밀ᄒᆞ고면답이만흐니ᄒᆞᆫ곳슬긔
광ᄒᆞᆫ즉면답파분묘와가옥이다
온젼치못ᄒᆞᆫ고로협금긔광ᄒᆞᆫ각
군에뎐결이감축ᄒᆞ엿고광부의
폐단이망유긔극ᄒᆞ야허여지
면도젹이되고모히면작란ᄒᆞ야
직산변란ᄭᅵ지이른지라부군의
보고와인민의호소가열일답지
ᄒᆞ니국ᄉᆞ의보익이업고빅셩을
손히ᄒᆞ고요란이막심ᄒᆞ온지라
외국인의게임의인허ᄒᆞᆫ곳파교
셥ᄒᆞ야판리홈을제ᄒᆞᆫ외에는삼
남각군에농샹공부와닉쟝원소
관를물론ᄒᆞ고긔광쳐를일병봉
쇄ᄒᆞ옴이하여ᄒᆞ올지샹 쥬ᄒᆞ
와봉지의 쥬ᄒᆞ라
 뎨이천구빅오십륙호 광
 무팔년십월십삼일
 셔임급ᄉᆞ령
○급일급봉 평리원검ᄉᆞ 리
취션
 십월륙일
○겸임법관양셩소쟝 법부협
관 김규희
○임의학교교관셔쥬임관륙등
륙품 류셰환
○의원면본관 즁츄원의관
리범셰 리셜 죠영년
○임즁츄원의관셔쥬임관륙등
정삼품 허일 륙품 리규협
최형건
 이샹십월십일
○명겸임규장각학ᄉᆞ시강원일
강관 농샹공부대신 리도지
○명텰도원부총지셔칙임관삼
등 례식원부장 최영하
○명례식원부장셔칙임관삼등
종이품 민영션
○명림시셔리종정원경ᄉᆞ무
종묘셔제쥬 리지덕
○임궁닉부비셔ᄉᆞ쥬ᄉᆞ셔관임
관이등 닉장원장원파쥬ᄉᆞ
김현비
○임닉장원장원파쥬ᄉᆞ셔관임
관ᄉᆞ등 샹의ᄉᆞ쥬ᄉᆞ 안슈뎡
○임샹의ᄉᆞ쥬ᄉᆞ셔관임관륙등
통신ᄉᆞ면화과쥬ᄉᆞ 고졔익
○임통신ᄉᆞ면화과쥬ᄉᆞ셔관임
관륙등 륙품 리승건
○임즁츄원의관셔칙임관ᄉᆞ등
봉샹ᄉᆞ졔쥬 남규희
○의원면본관 젼라북도관찰
부쥬ᄉᆞ 림학슈 평안북도관
찰부쥬ᄉᆞ 윤민용 운산군공
립쇼학교교원 최병희
○임젼라북도관찰부쥬ᄉᆞ셔관
임관륙등 죠병션
○임평안북도관찰부쥬ᄉᆞ셔관
임관륙등 리승훈
○임운산공립쇼학교교원셔관
임관ᄉᆞ등 젼교원 윤정규
○승셔관임관ᄉᆞ등 경무청총
순 오영묵
○급삼급봉 의학교교관 류
셰환 농샹공학교교관 홍인
표
 이샹십월십일일
○즁견칙 경무ᄉᆞ 량셩환
 십월십일일 의정부
궁뎡록ᄉᆞ
의정부참정신긔션 쥬
ᄒᆞ되경무ᄉᆞ가본부와닉부지휘
밧는거ᄉᆞᆫ장정에잇거놀신부에
셔히청에공합으로신칙홈이잇
셧더니히청관리가장정에위규
됨이잇다ᄒᆞ야본ᄉᆞ실의엇더홈
을뭇지안코무란이히공함을작
환홀고로그위졀를훈령으로질
문ᄒᆞᆫ즉젼허ᄉᆞᆷ여ᄒᆞ는보고ᄉᆞ의
가ᄯᅩ소홀ᄒᆞ오니ᄉᆞ례에경계아
니치못홀지라경무ᄉᆞ량셩환을
즁견칙ᄒᆞ옴이ᄒᆞ여ᄒᆞ올지샹
쥬ᄒᆞ와봉 지의쥬ᄒᆞ라
 십월십일일

잡보

○면쳥쥬면 평산군슈셔리금
천군슈의면보가작일샹오십시
에닉부로도착ᄒᆞ엿스되평산군
치도비일ᄉᆞ로루ᄎᆞ면보ᄒᆞ되샹
금회면이업는즁치도를임의맛
치미일인의독촉이셩화ᄀᆞᆺ흔지
라샹의ᄎᆞ로관찰부에젼왕ᄒᆞᆫ지
삼일간에연명을밧지아니ᄒᆞ오
며빅셩의계비렴ᄒᆞ고자ᄒᆞᆫ즉민
요를면치못홀모양이니만일경
부로셔획하치아니ᄒᆞ면싱경홀
형편이당두ᄒᆞ되회칙이만무ᄒᆞ
와평산금천량군에폐무ᄒᆞᆫ지가
오리니속속히본관을 쥬면
ᄒᆞ라ᄒᆞ엿더라
○파슈렬거 근쟈에일본헌병
이각셩문을파슈ᄒᆞ더니지작일
브터광희문에파슈는것어갓다
더라
○일착불달 의정부에셔
칙령안을긔졍ᄒᆞ야외부한셩부
례식원각항구대쇼관인의복쟝
을본월회일닉로일제히실시ᄒᆞ
되만일타부관직으로젼임ᄒᆞ여
도변복치못ᄒᆞ기로작뎡ᄒᆞ엿다
더라
○이병진민 각도면보가미일
답지ᄒᆞ되인민이혹칭동학ᄒᆞ며
혹칭진보회ᄒᆞ고곳곳시벌ᄯᅦᄀᆞᆺ

UNION INSURANCE SOCIETY OF CANTON.

Head office Hongkong.
Marine risks underwritten at current rates.

Agents in Chemulpo,
E. MEYER & CO.

COMPAGNIE DES MESSAGERIES MARITIMES.

Fortnightly Direct Service.

For Marseilles via Ports.

Sailing from Yokohama
Calling at Kobe,
Shanghai, Hongkong, Saigon, Singapore,
Colombo, Djibouti, Suez, Port Said
and Marseilles.

For particulars apply to
HOLME RINGER & CO.,
Chemulpo.

HAYASHIDA & Co.,

16 MYENG DONG, CHIN KO KAI, SEOUL.
BRANCH OFFICE AT CHEMULPO.

Money changers, Coal and Wood Merchants, Express Agents.

We are agents for the Pyeng-yang Coal Company and the Karazu Coal Company of Japan. We have the best quality of both anthracite and bituminous coal, and prompt execution of orders is our speciality. Firewood of all kinds kept in stock. Full weight guaranteed. Money of all denominations exchanged at current rates. Parcels received for all parts.

CHINA MUTUAL LIFE INS. CO.

Most favourable terms to policy holders.

Benefit system unsurpassed.

HOLME RINGER & CO.
Agents, Chemulpo.

C. P. R.

CANADIAN PACIFIC RAILWAY COMPANY'S ROYAL MAIL STEAMSHIP LINE.

THE FAST ROUTE BETWEEN CHINA, JAPAN, AND EUROPE VIA CANADA AND THE UNITED STATES.

Route from Hongkong via Shanghai, Nagasaki (Inland Sea of Japan) Kobe, Yokohama, Victoria and Vancouver.

Twin Screw Empress Steamship—6,000 Tons—Speed 19 knots.

PROPOSED SAILING FROM YOKOHAMA.

R. M. S. Empress of India.
R. M. S. Empress of Japan.
R. M. S. Empress of China.
R. M. S. Athenian.
R. M. S. Tartar.

Special reduction (first class only) granted to members of the Military, Naval, Diplomatic and Civil services and to Missionaries.

Passengers have choice of ten routes across the Continent of America and have privilege of travelling by any Atlantic Steamship Line.

Round the World passage tickets in connection with the P. and O. S. N., North German Lloyd and Messageries Co.'s £125.

All rates payable at current rate of exchange.

For further information, Tickets, Guide Books, etc., apply to

HOLME, RINGER & CO., AGENTS,
Chemulpo.

Grand Hotel,

(Formerly the Station Hotel)

Near the Railway Terminus,
West Gate, Seoul.

The Best Hotel in Korea.
Handsome new Building.
Fine Airy Rooms
Excellent Cuisine.
Terms Moderate.
Special terms to Missionaries
and to permanent boarders.

Electric cars within 2 minutes' walk.

W. H. EMBERLEY,
Proprietor.

EVERY FACILITY.

In connection with Life Assurance Business is afforded by

The Standard Life Assurance Co.,

One of the largest and wealthiest of the Provident Institutions of the United Kingdom Forms of Application and all information will be promptly afforded on application

10 CENTS A DAY.

Not a very large expenditure is it? But it is sufficient to secure for a man of 30 a policy with the STANDARD LIFE OFFICE for

$1323.

For all particulars of rates, etc., apply to

Holme, Ringer & Co.,
Agents, Chemulpo.

THE NEW YORK LIFE INSURANCE COMPANY.

Have you ever been declined by any Company?

Are you engaged in a specially hazardous occupation?

Have you heard of the New York Life Insurance Company's New Classifications for this class of Risks?

If not, send your date of birth, occupation and particulars of rejection, if any to

E. MEYER & CO.,
Agents, Chemulpo.

MITSUI BUSSAN KAISNHA.
(MITSUI & CO.)

MITSUI GINKO.
(MITSUI BANK.)

The Bank is owned by the members of the Mitsui Family, who, as partners, assume an unlimited responsibility for all liabilities of the Bank:—

Capital........................Yen 5,000,000
Reserve Fund..................." 5,600,000

HEAD OFFICE, TOKYO.
LONDON OFFICE, 34 LIME ST., E. C.

BRANCHES AND AGENCIES:—
New York, San Francisco, Hamburg, Bombay, Singapore, Manila, Hongkong, Amoy, Chefoo, Tientsin.
Kobe, Hakodate, Yokohama, Kure, Yokosuka, Moji, Shimonoseki, Miike, Wakamatsu, Nagasaki, Kuchinotsu, Karatsu, Sasebo, Misume, Taipeh, &c.

Telegraphic Address for all the Offices:
"MITSUI."

A. B. C. AND A. 1 CODES USED.

Contractors of Coal
To the Imperial Japanese Navy. Arsenals and Railway Bureau, Principal Railway Companies and Industrial Work, Home and Foreign Mail and Freight Steamers.

Sole Proprietors
Of the famous Miike, Tagawa and Yamano Coal Mines.

Sole Agents
For the sale of Fukumo, Hokoku, Ichimura, Kanoda, Mannoura, Onoura, Ostuji, Sonoda, Tsubaruro, Yoshinotani, Yoshio, Yurokibura and other coals.

YANGTSE INSURANCE ASSOCIATION, LTD.

The undersigned, having been appointed agents for the above company, are prepared to issue policies and pay losses on marine risks at regular rates.

E. MEYER & CO.,
Agents, Chemulpo.

AMERICAN KOREAN ELECTRIC COMPANY.

Light and Power.

Main Office: Electric Building, Chong No.

RAILWAY DEPARTMENT.

OPERATING CARS BETWEEN EAST AND WEST GATE, EVERY TEN MINUTES:—
First Car leaves East Gate at 6:30 A. M. First Car leaves West Gate at 6:55 A. M.
Last Cra " East Gate at 10:40 P. M. Last " " West Gate at 11:00 P.M.

OPERATING CARS BETWEEN EAST GATE AND IMPERIAL TOMB TERMINUS, EVERY TWENTY MINUTES:—
CONNECTING WITH EVERY ALTERNATE CAR ARRIVING AT EAST GATE FROM CHONG NO.
First Car leaves East Gate for Tomb at 6:50 A. M.
" " " Tomb for East Gate at 7:10 A. M
Last " " East Gate for Tomb at 9:50 P. M.
" " " Tomb for East Gate at 10:10 P M

OPERATING CARS BETWEEN CHONG NO AND YUNG SAN (RIVER) EVERY TWELVE MINUTES:—
First Car leaves Chong No for South Gate at 6:48 A. M.
" " " Chong No for Yung San at 7:24 A. M.
" " " South Gate for Chong No at 6:56 A. M.
" " " Yung San for Chong No at 7:57 A. M.
Last " " South Gate for Chong No 11:00 P. M.
" " " Yung San for Chong No at 10:11 P. M.

SPECIAL PRIVATE CARS FURNISHED TO SUIT CONVENIENCE OF PATRONS. PRICES ON APPLICATION AT HEAD OFFICE.

LIGHTING DEPARTMENT.

Where less than 250 candle power of light is used, the rate per month will be: Per 16 candle power incandescent lamp,—All night:—Yen 2.50.
Per 32 candle power incandescent lamp:—All night:—Yen 4.00. Per 50 candle power incandescent lamp:—All night:—Yen 6.00.
" 150 " " " " " " " 10.00. " 1200 " " enclosed arc " " " " 20.00.
Where more than 250 candle power of light is used, a Meter will be installed, if requested:—Rent of Meter Yen 2.00 per month. Rate of charges by meter reading:—Two Sen per Ampere per hour. (Approximately this is equal to about One Sen per 16 C. P. lamp per hour) Minimum monthly charge where meter is installed, Yen 20.00 per month, which includes rental of meter.
Estimates for installing lights furnished on application. An assortment of chandeliers always on hand.

AMUSEMENT DEPARTMENT.

ANIMATED PICTURES AT EAST GATE
Every evening - - - Except Sunday.
From 8 to 10 P. M.

10 Cents:—Gen. Admission:—10 Cents. Seats in First Class Section. 15 Cents Extra.

Change of program each week. Pictures from Foreign Lands. Pictures of Local Scenes:—Amusing and Instructive.

An entertaining evening for a reasonable price.

MERRY-GO-ROUND:—At East Gate.
From 10:00 A. M. till 11:00 P. M.

5 Cents a Ride.

Take your Exercise on The Galoping Horses.

Comfortable seats in the Chariots.

한셩뎐긔회샤

한미뎐긔회샤 고븜안 보사뎍 고빅
도ᄒᆞ옵나이다
샹학동샤뎐람소와목마운동쟝량쳐로인
여뎌뎐차가온쟝안으로통힝ᄒᆞ여ᄃᆞ니여이
삽
쏘이긔계에곳쳐노흰편ᄒᆞ고ᄑᆞ흔마차도잇
삽
코미우편ᄒᆞ고쏘ᄌᆞ미잇는ᄑᆞ흔운동이되겟
이ᄑᆞ흔모형흔달나아는물올ᄯᆞ고위티치안
딕가는흔번ᄯᆞ는데오젼석이오
미일샹오열시브터하오열흔시ᄭᆞ지ᄒᆞ옵고
목마운동쟝은동대문안에잇삽고
가되겟삽
쳠군조의게갑도싸고저녁에ᄑᆞ흔쇼일거리
미잇고구경ᄒᆞᆯ만ᄒᆞᆫ거시오니
서양사진과대한과온동양사진연대대단ᄌᆞ
는딕
젼이옵고미쥬일에사진을싼것스로다밧고
고젼람딕금은하등에십젼이오상등에이십
일외에는미야에여덜시브러열시ᄭᆞ지ᄒᆞ옵
활동사진젼람소는동대문안에잇삽고일요
회락부

All Cars Run Direct to the Animated Pictures and Merry-Go-Round.

치이러ᄂᆞ니엇지진압ᄒᆞ랴ᄒᆞ엿거놀ᄂᆡ부에셔그ᄉᆞ의ᄃᆡ로참모부에공합ᄒᆞ고그복합을등인ᄒᆞ야각도에회면ᄒᆞ기를진위ᄃᆡ와교섭ᄒᆞ야병력으로진압ᄒᆞ고징즙ᄒᆞ라ᄒᆞ엿더라

론셜

려쇼사건과검찰쳐샤

려쇼에셔ᄊᆞ홈운동ᄒᆞᆫ다ᄂᆞᆫ풍셜온종종들리되일본검찰관리가젼샤에비밀히ᄒᆞ야진젹ᄒᆞᆫ소문을ᄂᆡ지아니ᄒᆞᄂᆞᆫ고로다만아병의에워ᄊᆞᆫ일이필경어렵게될줄로만알게ᄒᆞᄂᆞᆫ즁요ᄉᆞ이ᄂᆞᆫ공보가오리업슴으로가당치아니ᄒᆞᆫ말들도만히잇셧고ᄯᅩᄒᆞᆫ비록무근지셜이라도가긔이기방ᄒᆞ게만ᄒᆞ면진젹ᄒᆞᆫ말로밋어셔우리도역시그러ᄒᆞᆫ말을쥰신ᄒᆞ고신문에게지ᄒᆞᆫ일이잇스니

아라사젼투함ᄒᆞᆫ척이일병대포에방격ᄒᆞᆫ비되여물속으로파침ᄒᆞ엿고맛참그남아지다른비들은산모퉁이로피ᄒᆞ여파샹됨을면ᄒᆞ엿다고ᄒᆞ엿스며ᄯᅩ추후로곳드른즉금산을일인의게ᄲᅢ기엿다고ᄒᆞ더니

이졔동경신문에게지ᄒᆞᆫ거슬본즉금산은당초에일병의게ᄲᅢ여기지아니ᄒᆞᆫ거시일병이대포와군긔를항구로옴기여진터를잡으려ᄒᆞᆯ즈음에여러비들이발셔산모퉁이로먼져피ᄒᆞ엿다고ᄒᆞ엿스며ᄯᅩᄒᆞᆫ려쇼형편을놋코보드릐도엇던소문을밋어야조흘ᄂᆞᆫ지알수업슬ᄲᅮᆫ더러

금월오일우리신문에도ᄯᅩᄒᆞᆫ연ᄐᆡ에잇ᄂᆞᆫ일인의게로발ᄒᆞᆫ보고ᄃᆡ로번등ᄒᆞ엿거니와아라사구로파트킨장군이진터를일병의게견탈ᄒᆞ고일병은아병의잇든히샹으로무인지경갓치횡힝ᄒᆞᆫ다ᄒᆞ엿더니

우리신문동신원이노비크레신문에게지ᄒᆞᆫ바번등ᄒᆞ여보낸거슬거ᄒᆞᆫ즉일병이회졍ᄒᆞᆯᄲᅢ에육쳔명이피살ᄒᆞ여손샹된거슨ᄌᆞ셰히아ᄂᆞᆫ일이라고분명ᄒᆞ말ᄒᆞ엿다고ᄒᆞ엿ᄂᆞᆫ지라도쳥도셜홈을쥰신키ᄂᆞᆫ어려우나그러ᄒᆞ나일본관인들을볼진ᄃᆡ이러ᄒᆞᆫ신문을당초에쥰신ᄒᆞ여드르랴고셜립ᄒᆞᆫ거시아니라ᄌᆞ긔의성각ᄃᆡ로라도뵈이기만위ᄒᆞ여그리홈인거시어느ᄲᅢ던지셩취ᄒᆞ라홈을조아ᄒᆞᄂᆞᆫᄉᆞ닭에혹승쳡ᄒᆞ리라고ᄒᆞ야몃공일도ᄲᅥ러가며몃달도지체가된즉무타ㅣ라ᄌᆞ긔나라빅셩들의염여홀마음을싱각ᄒᆞ야그리홈이며노바케라신문에이러케실젹을게지ᄒᆞᆫ거슨일인에론박홈으로필경실례될료량써지도ᄒᆞ고홈인즉이ᄂᆞᆫ가히확신ᄒᆞᆯ만ᄒᆞᆫ쟈ㅣ로다

신호크로늬클신문에이왕지낸일을게지ᄒᆞᆫ바일본검찰관리가이러케ᄒᆞᄂᆞᆫ일은대단히수치스러워ᄒᆞᆯ듯ᄒᆞᆫ일이기에좌에번등ᄒᆞ노니

근자에ᄂᆞᆫ일본군대에셔각국젼샤통신원의게ᄃᆡᄒᆞ야대졉ᄒᆞᄂᆞᆫ거시이왕보다나흔듯ᄒᆞ나그러ᄒᆞ나우리들의게힝ᄒᆞᄂᆞᆫ일을볼진ᄃᆡ심히삼엄ᄒᆞ게ᄒᆞᄂᆞᆫ지라려슌항군ᄃᆡ에셔고용ᄒᆞᄂᆞᆫ일인ᄒᆞ나이지나간칠월이십륙일에ᄊᆞ홈ᄒᆞᆫ샤실을긔록ᄒᆞ여보내ᄂᆞᆫᄃᆡ진즁에셔무삼통신을왕리ᄒᆞ던지미우엄슉히금집ᄒᆞ되이편지인즉신지무의ᄒᆞ고루츌ᄒᆞᆫ비되엿슨즉그사람은그리ᄒᆞ엿스되지어우리ᄒᆞ야ᄂᆞᆫ짐즛규칙을어기여범죄ᄒᆞᆯ리유가업ᄂᆞᆫ고로그편지ᄒᆞᆫ거슬군부검찰사무의게보내여그일공포홈에인허ᄒᆞ기를쳥ᄒᆞ엿더니그ᄃᆡ답에ᄒᆞ기를젼투사건긔재ᄒᆞᆫ다홈은지금발간ᄒᆞ라고허락ᄒᆞᆯ수업ᄂᆞᆫ지라만일이편지와갓치ᄒᆞᄂᆞᆫ경우이면일본군ᄃᆡ에힝동이라던지감약여부라도모도드러날터인즉시힝ᄒᆞᆯ수업다고거졀ᄒᆞ엿ᄂᆞᆫ지라

그편지ᄂᆡ기인즉각쳐지명이며공격ᄒᆞ든형편을낫낫치긔록ᄒᆞ엿스되긔왕수삭젼일을이졔이르러말ᄒᆞᄂᆞᆫ것도온당치아니ᄒᆞᆯ듯도ᄒᆞ며ᄯᅩ만일이소문이아인의게긴ᄒᆞᆯ것갓흐면당초에진즁에셔검찰관리가인허ᄒᆞ야보니셔일본ᄭᆞ지이르게ᄒᆞᆯ리치가만무ᄒᆞᆯ듯ᄒᆞᆫ지라

군부검찰관리들이ᄌᆞ긔의나라빅셩들노ᄒᆞ여곰ᄊᆞ홈결국된형편을온휘ᄒᆞ여말홈은혹불온ᄒᆞᆫᄐᆡ도가잇슬가염녀ᄒᆞ야그리홈이로되일본신문들에만폭쟝셜이모도려슌사실인즉숨키고감초ᄂᆞᆫ거시무삼리유인지ᄶᅵ닷지못ᄒᆞ겟스며려슌항수건갓치드러난일에진젹홈은은휘ᄒᆞ고풍셜만랑자ᄒᆞ게ᄒᆞᆫ즉이로ᄡᅥ볼진ᄃᆡ진보ᄒᆞ랴ᄂᆞᆫ마음이업ᄂᆞᆫ듯ᄒᆞ다고ᄒᆞ엿더라

뎐보

십월십삼일동경반

만쥬군총ᄉᆞ령관대산의보고

○ᄐᆡᄌᆞ하격젼 십월구일아춤에뎍군이우리우익군의게와셔습격ᄒᆞ엿ᄂᆞᆫᄃᆡᄐᆡᄌᆞ하의우편연안에건너셔교두와본계호잔을막야싼헛ᄂᆞᆫᄃᆡ그병력은보병야일려단즘이요긔병이이쳔명야요대포가이문이요ᄯᅩ본계호의동방ᄐᆡᄌᆞ하의우편연안에ᄂᆞᆫ보병이열려단어요긔병이열쳔오빅명이요대포가팔문이요본계호에셔셔북으로아라되ᄂᆞᆫ대령방면에ᄂᆞᆫ혼셩일려단즘이요면회보와팔가ᄌᆞ에ᄂᆞᆫ각기보병일련ᄃᆡ가잇셔남으로나아오고그후면에ᄂᆞᆫ후속부ᄃᆡ가잇ᄂᆞᆫ듯ᄒᆞᆫᄃᆡ오후이시에뎍군의보병이련ᄃᆡᄂᆞᆫ오리가ᄌᆞ로드러오고긔병일련ᄃᆡᄂᆞᆫ가리가ᄌᆞ로드러오고ᄯᅩ일ᄉᆞ단은쇼달호로드러와임의우리진압헤니르럿ᄂᆞᆫ지라죰앙군방면에잇ᄂᆞᆫ적병은동일아춤ᄭᆞ지에일ᄉᆞ단이와셔연ᄐᆡ에셔북으로이리반되ᄂᆞᆫ류당구방면에뎡지ᄒᆞ엿다가오후ᄉᆞ시에니엄니엄남으로나아오ᄂᆞᆫᄃᆡ이젹병의후면에도ᄯᅩᄒᆞᆫ후속부ᄃᆡ가잇ᄂᆞᆫ듯ᄒᆞ고렬도션로로힝군ᄒᆞ야나아오ᄂᆞᆫ젹병은기리가이리허에련졉ᄒᆞ엿ᄂᆞᆫᄃᆡ오히려그뒤ᄭᅳᆺ츌보지못ᄒᆞ엿고좌익방면에잇ᄂᆞᆫ젹병의운동은활발치못ᄒᆞ야그쥬력은류당구와손가ᄃᆡ부근에잇ᄂᆞᆫ듯ᄒᆞᆫᄃᆡ

이젹군을ᄃᆡᄒᆞ야아군은교두외슈비ᄃᆡ와밋본계호외지ᄃᆡ를구응ᄒᆞ기위ᄒᆞ야각기일종ᄃᆡ를파견ᄒᆞ야방금젼투ᄒᆞᄂᆞᆫ중이요중앙군과밋좌익군은젼면에잇ᄂᆞᆫ적병을ᄃᆡ적ᄒᆞ야교젼ᄒᆞᄂᆞᆫ즁인ᄃᆡ

본관은적병이아직그병력을혼하좌편연안에취집ᄒᆞ기젼에먼첨어거슬쳐셔파ᄒᆞ기위ᄒᆞ야십월십일아춤브터공격홀형편으로도로키여적의쥬력을담지ᄒᆞ야공격ᄒᆞ려ᄒᆞᆫ다ᄒᆞ엿고

속보

우의군은본계호의지ᄃᆡ와련락을통홈을얻엇ᄂᆞᆫᄃᆡ히ᄃᆡᄂᆞᆫ십월구일아춤브터우세ᄒᆞᆫ적병파더부러거진열두시간이ᄂᆞ교젼ᄒᆞ야자못본계호방면에셔ᄂᆞᆫ젼투가ᄀᆞ장밍렬ᄒᆞ엿스ᄂᆞ그러ᄂᆞ다그ᄃᆡ위를얻지유지ᄒᆞ엿다ᄒᆞ엿더라

○량일젼황 십월십일과십일일량일의젼황에관ᄒᆞᆫ대산의공보의요령이좌와ᄀᆞᆺᄒᆞ니

뎨일우익군의방면

적군은강경히습격홈으로ᄡᅥ본계호의동방놉흔ᄉᆞᆫ에잇ᄂᆞᆫ우리진터홀ᄲᅢ앗고ᄯᅩ그후에밤에습격홈으로ᄡᅥ본계호에셔셔북으로일리되ᄂᆞᆫ화련시와본계호간의길동편놉흔ᄉᆞᆫ에잇ᄂᆞᆫ우리진터홀ᄲᅢ아셧스ᄂᆞ아군은십월십일아춤에안ᄀᆡ가몽농ᄒᆞᆫᄃᆡ본계호의동방놉흔ᄉᆞᆫ을도로ᄲᅢ앗고ᄯᅩ동일오젼십일시에본계호와화련시간에놉흔ᄉᆞᆫ도회복ᄒᆞ엿ᄂᆞᆫᄃᆡ그후로ᄂᆞᆫ우익군의각방면은격젼을ᄭᅳᆺ치지안코익일십일일황혼ᄭᆞ지니르럿고본계호에셔셔북으로이리남젓ᄒᆞᆫ토문ᄌᆞ령에셔본계호에가ᄂᆞᆫ본길동편의적병은보병이이사단이샹이오대포팔십문을휴ᄃᆡᄒᆞ엿고ᄯᅩ좌익군의쥬력을ᄃᆡᄒᆞᆫ적병은본계호에셔셔북으로칠리되ᄂᆞᆫ삼가ᄌᆞ에셔본계호에셔셔북으로오리되ᄂᆞᆫ팔가ᄌᆞ에련졉ᄒᆞ엿ᄂᆞᆫᄃᆡ그병력은이사단이샹이라ᄒᆞ고

뎨이즁앙군방면

우죵ᄃᆡᄂᆞᆫ십일오젼에옥문ᄌᆞ동방의놉흔ᄉᆞᆫ을점령ᄒᆞ엿고좌즁ᄃᆡᄂᆞᆫ연ᄐᆡ에셔동북으로십리남젓ᄒᆞᆫ황디동방의놉흔ᄉᆞᆫ에니르러각기젼면의적병을ᄃᆡ적ᄒᆞ야젼투를긋치지안코익일십일일황혼ᄭᆞ지니르럿고

뎨삼좌익군방면

좌익군의각죵ᄃᆡᄂᆞᆫ각기그젼면의적병을포격ᄒᆞ며젼진ᄒᆞ야적의좌측을협박게ᄒᆞ엿고

뎨ᄉᆞ시마집북방에잇ᄂᆞᆫ합창방면

적병은십월칠일이ᄅᆡ로희방면에와셔습격ᄒᆞ엿스나동ᄃᆡ에잇ᄂᆞᆫ우리슈비ᄃᆡᄂᆞᆫ십월십일오젼삼ᄉᆡ에밤엄습홈으로ᄡᅥ적병을동북으로격퇴ᄒᆞ엿다ᄒᆞ엿더라

잡보

○ᄉᆞ령관 폐현 일본ᄉᆞ령관장곡천씨와락합참모쟝이명일하오세시반에 폐현ᄒᆞᆯ터인ᄃᆡ기시ᄃᆡ동홀졔관원외부대신협관과례식원관원이례발ᄒᆞ고문관복쟝으로입참ᄒᆞ기로ᄒᆞ엿다더라

○ᄉᆞ방징긔 작일샹오십일시에히쥬관찰ᄉᆞ김학슈씨의면보가ᄂᆡ부로도착ᄒᆞ엿ᄂᆞᆫᄃᆡ신쳔안악재령문화등군보고ᄂᆡ에동학이혹삼ᄉᆞ십명오륙십명이각기히군읍ᄐᆡ에둔취ᄒᆞ야진보회라칭ᄒᆞ고단발ᄒᆞ며연셜ᄒᆞᆫ다ᄒᆞᄂᆞᆫ고로히각군에엄칙ᄒᆞ야효유히산케ᄒᆞ라ᄒᆞ엿기로위션보고ᄒᆞ고츄후ᄉᆞ샹을등보ᄒᆞ겟다ᄒᆞ엿고동일동시에도착ᄒᆞᆫ평양관찰ᄉᆞ리즁하씨면보ᄂᆡ에ᄂᆞᆫ각쳐인민등이말ᄒᆞ되경ᄉᆞ동문이잇다ᄒᆞ고소위진보회를각ᄃᆡ방에긔회ᄒᆞ야일제히단발ᄒᆞ며ᄯᅩ긔빅명이본부셩ᄂᆡ에도회ᄒᆞ야긔회코자ᄒᆞᄂᆞᆫᄃᆡ효샹이히연ᄒᆞ니졍부에품ᄒᆞᆫ후조쳐지방을시복ᄒᆞ라ᄒᆞ엿고동일샹오십이시에도착ᄒᆞᆫ공쥬관찰ᄉᆞ심건택씨면보ᄂᆡ에ᄂᆞᆫ소위진보회수쳔명이은진강경포로셔론산포로올마왓ᄂᆞᆫᄃᆡ금명간본부로릐도ᄒᆞᆫ다ᄒᆞ며혹ᄉᆞ인교와혹말를타고낫낫치단발ᄒᆞ고점점ᄌᆞ만ᄒᆞᆫ즉판찰부에셔방어ᄒᆞᆯ수업스니 쳐분ᄒᆞ야시명ᄒᆞ라ᄒᆞ엿고지작일파작일량일간에각ᄃᆡ방에셔도착ᄒᆞᆫ급면이칠팔쳔인ᄃᆡ거ᄀᆡ동학당진보회ᄉᆞ건이며곳犬이창궐ᄒᆞ니파병진압ᄒᆞ라홈이라더라

TELEGRAMS.

BATTLE CONTINUES.

FURTHER REPORTS FROM OYAMA.

Tokyo, Oct. 13th.

The enemy's attack in the diriction of Punkiho has been successfully repulsed. The centre column of our right wing occupied some hills north of Bachatze and the left column effected the occupation of some rising ground north of Siyetai, driving out the enemy.

Our centre column on Tuesday captured two machine guns and eight ammunition wagons, but Major-General Maruye was wounded in effecting this.

Tokyo, Later.

The enemy between Chaotu and Punkiho are now entirely dispersed. Our pursuing forces of the right wing and centre have already reached a line between Ma-ul-san and Wangchafun and our left column is shelling the enemy north of Yentai.

Our right wing continues to advance in a northerly direction and one column sent to intercept the enemy's retreat is still continuing its march via Sichaotze and should arrive at the desired place at 3 P. M.

This morning our centre captured one field gun and ammunition wagons at Sankuisi-san. One prisoner captured stated that Kuropatkin is leading three reserve divisions to the relief of the force opposing our right wing.

The centre columns of our left wing successfully drove back the opposing enemy and at 1.30 P. M. occupied the enemy's position near Laug-tze-cha, capturing 16 guns.

The enemy in these directions retreated but it is reported that a Russian column is advancing to the southeast. Our centre column captured another four guns, and the right column of our left wing another five with five ammunition wagons, bringing the total of guns captured up to 25. A column of our main force effected the capture of 150 prisoners.

THE ECCENTRIC MARQUIS.

London, Aug. 25.

Seven sales have not exhausted the extraordinary collection of articles which the curiously acquisitive Marquis of Anglesey had stored at his castle, and when the eighth sale is reached next month there will be 1,400 additional lots before the auctioneer. The catalogue offers a good idea of the Marquis' extravagance an eccentricities. The number of walking-sticks and umbrellas for sale is 130 Many of the umbrellas have handles encrusted with diamonds, rubies, amethists, and emeralds. Some have gunmetal knobs, with diamonds forming the crest and initials of the noble owner. Others are of simple, unchased gold. The strangest of the sticks have ornaments in the forms of goats, donkeys, snakes, Chinamen, elephants, cats, and partridges. In the knob of one stick is inserted a tiny watch, about the size of a farthing, thickly jewelled. With the touching of a spring the watch revolves and displays a lady's miniature. One Malacca cane is provided with a small electric light, and another holds a snapshot camera. A gilt monkey perches on one hazel stick, and a wooden monkey on another. Strangely enough, the Marquis, although provided with this collection of umbrellas and sticks, valued at £2,000, seldom carried a stick. A handsome gold afternoon tea-service, set with diamonds, turquoises, garnets, and other precious stones, transcends all common fancies, and should realise a big price.

The first day's disposal of the Marquis' clothes drew a crowd of county gentry.

The auctioncer resolved to open his day's business in a style worthy of the magnificence of the Marquis He therefore began by offering the brown sable coat with twenty tails and ten head fronts. The first bid was £25. Bidding rose gradually to £295. A long pause ensued, but after a stimulating speech from the auctioneer another bid of £5 came, and "Mr. Wood, of Piccadilly," was declared the purchaser of this fantastic portion of the Marquis' raiment at £300, which was reputed to be £700 less than the price paid for it. A pair of kilts evoked the usual witticisms about Scotland. They were bought for three guineas by a Liverpool fancy dress dealer. The auctioneer instantly knocked down a waterproof for £3 12s. 6d., remarking that it could be bought in London for half the money. The lots purchased by the county gentry included a melton cloth coat £40, moleskin coat £66, caracul coat £80, black coat lined with Persian lamb £40. The 150 pairs of pyjamas were sold at remunerative prices, varying from £14 to £1. The lounge suits found buyers at prices averaging three guineas each. A pair of crimson silk trousers were sold for 15s. For overcoats there was animated bidding. The average price was £8. Two pair of patent-leather boots were sold for 65s., a pair of patent-leather jack boots for £3 5s.

THE USE OF MOTOR-BOATS IN WAR.

Mr. S. F. Edge has offered to the British Admiralty two of his Napier motor-boats free of charge for use during the forthcoming naval and military manœuvres in Essex. Mr. Edge's boats took part in the great Channel races.

"The possibilities of the motor-boat in naval warfare," he remarked recently, are enormous and the advantages supreme.

"Owing to the speed at which it travels—twenty-five miles an hour can be kept up even now—it is next to impossible to hit a motor-boat with a big gun.

"In motion the boat is almost invisible; it lies down in the trough of the waves, or in the track cut by itself as it progresses. Herein lies its great advantage for scouting or going out to view the enemy. They can be seen without any knowledge on their part that they have been watched. This is the point I wish to prove by offering to lend the boats to the Admiralty. If they accept I shall go out in one myself.

"The motor-boats have an enormous radius of action. They can go for 1,000 miles easily with an average speed of twenty-two miles an hour. They offer the only means so far devised of attacking an enemy's submarines. Behind the motor-boat a torpedo can be trailed, the submarines outside a port sighted and destroyed, and a rapid turn made without giving the enemy a chance, of retaliation. A motor-boat, moreover is practically immune from attack by a torpedo."

CLIMATIC CONDITIONS AT PORT ARTHUR.

No systematic meterological observations had been carried out at Port Arthur prior to the occupation by the Russians. The results of the Russian observations have not been published, so that the only available data for determining the climatic conditions during the winter at Port Arthur are the records made by the Japanese Navy off Port Arthur during the Chino-Japanese War. The record of the temperature (Fahrenheit) is as follows:—

Month.	Highest.	Lowest.	Averave.
October	74	40	62
November	60	32	46
December........	56	18	33
January............	44	5	30
February	48	zero	29
March	58	16	37

The severity of the winter is shown by the fact that during the naval operations off Port Arthur in the Chino-Japanese war, the spray that dashed over the bows of a warship formed into ice and greatly impeded her movements, and that many of the blue-jackets engaged in clearing away the ice lost their hands owing to frost-bite.

The Minister of Home Affairs visited the Japanese Legation yesterday.

SIR HIRAM WILKINSON'S RETIREMENT.

It has been known for some weeks, states the N.-C. Daily News, that Sir Hiram Shaw Wilkinson contemplated retirement from the onerous duties of Chief Justice of H. B. M. Supreme Court of China and Korea. The announcement is now made that Sir Hiram's resignation has been sent in to the proper quarters, but it will not take effect until a successor is appointed. In the meantime a session of the Supreme Court was opened last week and on its completion in the course of the next few weeks Sir Hiram will go on circuit to Tientsin and to Hankow. The retiring Chief Justice has seen 40 years' continuous service in the East.

To-morrow afternoon General Hasegawa and his chief of staff will be received in audience by His Majesty. The Minister and Vice Minister of Foreign Affairs, together with principal officials of the Ceremonial Department will be present and for the first time appear in uniform and minus top-knots.

LOST

On the 27th ult., probably in the neighbourhood of the West Gate.

A Photographic Camera. Anyone returning the same to this office will receive Y 15.00 reward.

Dr. Daniel B. Nye, D. D. S. has arrived and will be at Steward's Hotel, Chemulpo, until the 30th instant, and in Seoul on his return from the American Mines.

The Korea Daily News.

Issued at 5 P. M. daily except Sundays.

Rate of Subscription :—

Per Year,	Yen 25.
Per Quarter,	Yen 7.
Per Month,	Yen 2,50.

Postage in Korea not charged extra.
Postage abroad charged extra.

Advertisements, 50 sen per day for 1 inch or less.
5 yen per month per inch.
50 yen per year per inch.

All communications to
E. T. BETHELL,
Editor and Publisher,
Pak-tong, Seoul.

THE WAR.

Though details are wanting, and the description of the fighting contained in Field Marshal Marquis Oyama's report is rather obscure, yet it is safe to say that another battle of enormous dimensions is being fought in Manchuria and that the honors, so far, again rest with the Japanese.

It seems that on the morning of the 10th, Kuropatkin made a bold movement to the south, recrossing the Taitse and advancing to within a short distance of Yentai thus severing the communication between Kuroki's and the two other Japanese armies. Here two Japanese positions were captured but had to be evacuated the next morning owing to a counter attack made under cover of the prevailing fog. An examination of the map leads us to believe that the line of battle stretched for some 25 miles northeast from Yentai, with the main body of the Russian troops operating in the vicinity of that place.

Until the evening of the 11th, the issue of the battle seems to have hung in the balance, but during the night the main body of the Russian army commenced the retreat, falling back in the direction of Mukden.

On the 12th, the Japanese army followed in pursuit and succeeded in capturing 30 guns as well as in inflicting heavy casualties on the retreating troops.

We await with interest further despatches telling of the later issues of the struggle now in progress, for if the Japanese reports of the Russian strength are accurate, Kuropatkin would now seem to have, under his command, a force almost numerically equal to the Japanese. If such is the case, and the fact that Kuropatkin has adopted aggressive tactics would point to it, then we may look for a battle of even greater magnitude than that at Liaoyang.

The Japanese Headquarters are in receipt of a despatch from Tokyo, which gives the Russian casualties at the fight of Kiauchang at 60, and the Japanese at 52.

Emperor Nicholas has issued a manifesto determining the order of succession to the throne. In the event of the Emperor dying before the Tzarevitch attains his majority the Emperor's brother, Grand Duke Michael is to become Regent, the Empress assuming the guardianship of the Tzarevitch. It is believed that the manifesto marks the curtailment of the hitherto dominant influence of the Dowager Empress.

It is reported in Shanghai mandarin circles that an application by the Russian ConsulGeneral to return to the "Mandjour" the rifles that had been taken away from that ship when she was disarmed, has been granted by the Japanese Government, but on condition that first, no ammunition for them shall be supplied; second, no Russian sailors shall be allowed to carry them about; and third and most important, that the crews of the "Askold" and "Grosovoi" must not be allowed to handle them.

THE WAR CORRESPONDENT QUESTION.

Under the heading of "Mailiana," the Eastern World comments as follows, upon the "Japan Mail's" attempts to justify the big handed attitude adopted by the Japanese in their treatment of the foreign war correspondents.

"A benevolent Providence, much hard work of all kinds, and much hard reading, have fitted us for many tasks, but we think we would lamentably fail had we to edit the "Mail" on its present lines. A paragraph in its issue of October 6th on "Correspondents" illustrates its difficulties in such an amusing way that we must offer our readers a share in the fun. The paragraph begins with the words:

"By and bye, doubtless, the exact truth about the correspondents will be known."

This looks very simple, but it is very artful at the same time. Let us tell you why. You have been disgusted again and again with what, in your candid, although not very complimentary way, you have been pleased to call "the utter rot in the papers." We are not offended with you, and—between us, you, and the jasper gatepost of the palace of Truth—at times we have shared your sentiments. Having given you this proof of intuitive insight into the subtle workings of your mind, you will readily believe us when we tell you that we at once perceived your glad surprise when you—that is such of you as may happen to read the "Mail"—saw something in it about which, by the bye, doubtless, the exact "truth" will be known. You did not, of course, expect anything of the kind, but it is before you black on white, and your confidence is gained. You resolve, however, to keep your eyes open, saying to yourself that neither the "Mail" nor any other paper shall take "you" in. Simply because it can't be done.

Next, *you* learn that the correspondents with the first army have sent written assurances to the "Mail" that they are quite contented. That shows that there are some left, and that no restrictions are put on any written assurances of happiness and content they may wish to send to the "Mail," and, as Rabbi Joseph Ben Joshua Ben Meir, the Sphardi, says, at certain places in his Chronicles, "May the Lord remember it unto them for good."

Your confidence increases, you feel you have made a long step towards the truth, and if you have read the Chronicles of Rabbi Joseph, you will compare the men who left the first army to the men whom the Emperor Emanuel had given to the Sultan of Iconium and his army "to show them the way, to be unto them for eyes," and who "in the night when deep sleep falleth upon man, both of them fled away, so that the Sultan called all his officers, and said unto them: Either the Emperor Emanuel has deceived us, or the bribe of the Turks has blinded these men, that they have left us, and they will eat their money."

Thus will you cry out against those unbelievers, for have you not the written assurances of the faithful, sent to the editor of the "Mail," swearing by the beard of the Prophet and by the three holy Imauns that they are contented! You feel vou are within a few "inches" of the truth, and that there is no other truth besides the "Mail's" truth, or the "Mail's truths.

But now comes the proof positive. The "Mail" reproduces an

"Extract from a letter addressed to a friend in Tokyo by one of the Port Arthur correspondents, under date of September 25th:—"The position of the correspondents on this column (which you already doubtless know) is as follows; we are given every facility for going everywhere and seeing everything. In fact no one could desire better treatment in this and every other respect. But until Port Arthur is taken, *we are not allowed to send off a cable or letter containing any reference to the present operations,*' (the italics are ours).—This completely disposes of the idea that the correspondents with the Liaotung Army have any grievance?

Of course it does, could anything be clearer? Just fancy! Those Port Arthur correspondents may stand on their heads: blacken their faces with burnt cork and sing plantation songs; pick the banjo with a *plunka lunka lunka lunk* and a *tinka tinka tinka tink*, or a *pilly willy winky pop*, etc , etc. In fact, they may be as jolly as the proverbial sandboys, *except*, what they were sent out to do! They must neither send off a cable or letter containing *any reference* to present operations! And, as the "*Mail*" remarks; "This completely disposes of the idea that the correspondents with the Liatung army have any grievance."

Well done, thou faithful servant! May the powers that be, remember it unto thee for good!

FROM THE OTHER SIDE.

The Tokio Foreign Department has received the following telegram from London, dated October 5th:—

"According to Reuter, Lieut-General Sakharoff telegraphed on October 3 as follows:—'A Japanese cavalry squadron, at dawn on October 1, twice unsuccessfully attempted to break through the line of advanced posts of Cossacks in the district between Khuankhuandian and Fengtiapu. Two cavalry sotnias reinfocred our troops and the Japanese were dispersed. Toward noon the same day one battalion of the Japanese advance guard, with two or three cavalry squadrons, renewed the offensive movement against the Cossack regiment, and the firing lasted till nightfall. General Mischenko sent reinforcements. Towards evening the enemy was repulsed at all points, his whole line retreating to Sialionkhetse, pursued by our cavalry. A sotnia commander prepared an ambush at Koshutse for the enemy's potrol, killing one Japanese officer. The Cossacks found in the abandoned Japanese position, cartridges, medical stores, and a few dead horses. Two officers and two men were wounded on our side. On the same day a Japanese force consisting of one and one-half battalions, and one cavalry squadron, attacked in three divisions our outpost between the Hunbo and the railway. We checked this movement towards evening with the help of another company which soon arrived. One Cossack was killed and one wounded. One Russian patrol dispersed two Japanese patrol near Changtou, capturing three Japanese dragoons. Another Russian patrol sent to the east discovered the Tawanghauling pass occupied by 200 Chunchuses under Japanese officers. One Cossack was killed during the firing.

The leaders of the Si-heung riot are to be tried in the Supreme Court on Monday next.

The Editor of the "Eastern World" in his article, in the German language, of the 8th inst. expresses much indignation and surprise at the inclusion of the editor of the "Japan Mail" among the guests at the dinner, given by the German Minister at Tokyo, in honor of Prince Karl Anton of Hohenzollern. It certainly is astonishing that one, who has done his best to stir up hate and mistrust in the minds of the Japanese against Germany and the Kaiser should be given a seat of honor at the board graced by a member of the German Imperial family.

They were in a magnificently-decorated room in the West End of London. They approached each other, from opposite directions. One of them was as pale as a ghost, the other blushing red as a cherry. Presently they met, and, careless of the fact that dozens of eyes were watching them, they kissed each other. The meeting seemed to brin them perfect peace; but alas, alack! They had scarcely been side by side above twenty seconds when a man approached, with the fire of battle in his eye, with cool insolence he raised the stick he carried, and then—oh, horror!—he struck a sharp quick blow, and the pale one was sent spinning several feet away. The other neither screamed nor fainted. There was no heart-breaking, no resentment, not even a murmur. Billiard-balls are used to that sort of thing!

The Korea Daily News.

VOL. I, SATURDAY, OCTOBER 15, 1904. No. 77

大韓每日申報

대한미일신보

(데칠십팔호) (월요일) 일천구빅ᄉᆞ년십월십칠일

본샤고빅

본신보는영어와한어로셔거미일츌판ᄒᆞ옵

신문가

한장 엽두돈오푼

일삭됴 엽두량닷돈

우표가미삭닷돈

다맛돈으로밧숩

광고료는

긔한의쟝단과ᄌᆞ힝의다쇼로증감ᄒᆞ되렴가로밧을터이오며오리지아녀대한사람마다다이신문을보실터이니광고내시기를원ᄒᆞ시는이들은우리신문샤에와셔면약ᄒᆞ심을희망ᄒᆞ옵

○발힝소 박동대한미일신보샤법어학교압혜젼영국인셜필림집자리오

샤쟝 영국인 (비셜)

평양 디리졈

○평양효동사는권미보씨로우리신문관미디리인을뎡ᄒᆞ엿ᄉᆞ오니평양에계신구람쟈졔ᄒᆞ시는쳠군ᄌᆞ는허디리졈에왕림ᄒᆞ와면의ᄒᆞ시옵

샤고

○우리대한미일신보의목뎍은대한의안녕질서에관한모든데목에디ᄒᆞ야눈공평한변론을쥬쟝홈이라우리동신원의담보는신문보시는쳠군ᄌᆞ의계ᄒᆞᆼ상보도ᄒᆞ리며편지를긔셔ᄒᆞ여주씨는이는셩명과반디를젹어붓치시기를희망ᄒᆞ오니이거슨신문샹에긔지ᄒᆞ랴는거시아니오다만극히신용ᄒᆞ는증거를숨고쟈홈이라긔쟈는아모긔셔던지과지홈을되각ᄒᆞ는권리를가졋스나되각ᄒᆞ는리유를말홀터이오며공즁평화를문란케ᄒᆞ는듯ᄒᆞᆫ긔셔는의례히밧지안켓숩나이다

●본샤셜시이려로신문을미양우례로분전ᄒᆞ와례젼부의임의로젼ᄒᆞᆫ듯스로먼곳에눈혹늣게젼ᄒᆞ기도ᄒᆞ며혹몃칠거슬ᄒᆞᆫ겁에젼ᄒᆞ기도ᄒᆞ며혹아니젼ᄒᆞ는곳도잇다ᄒᆞ와우리신문을ᄉᆞ랑ᄒᆞ야구람ᄒᆞ시는쳠군ᄌᆞ의게되ᄒᆞ야미우미안ᄒᆞ옵기로지금은분젼인을두고미일일죽이젼ᄒᆞ며아니젼ᄒᆞ거나늣게거나ᄒᆞᆫ폐가업도록ᄒᆞ랴ᄒᆞ오니혹아니젼ᄒᆞ거나혹늣게젼ᄒᆞ거나ᄒᆞᆫ일이잇스면본샤로통긔ᄒᆞ여쥬심을희망ᄒᆞ옵

본사광고

○본샤신문즁에좌긔ᄒᆞᆫ호수를소용ᄒᆞᆯ데가잇셔이에광고ᄒᆞ오니누구시던지그즁에아모호수던지가져오시는ᄃᆡ로미쟝에빅젼두푼식드리리다

데이호 데삼호 데이십호 데ᄉᆞ십이호 데ᄉᆞ십삼호 데오십삼호 데오십ᄉᆞ호와데오십오호 데륙십이호

관보

데이천구빅오십칠호 광무팔년십월십ᄉᆞ일

셔임급ᄉᆞ령

○특면징계 종이픔 강홍대

○의원면본관 운진군슈 윤영렬 진위군슈 신셕효

○겸임룡쳔군슈 룡쳔감리 윤용구 ○임츙쥬군슈셔쥬임관ᄉᆞ등 니부참셔관 장쥰원

○임울산군슈셔쥬임관삼등 표훈원졔쟝국쟝 정동식 ○임양근군슈셔쥬임관륙등 외부참셔관 리범셕 ○화슌군슈셔쥬임관오등 궁니부쥬ᄉᆞ 최홍쥰 ○임풍긔군슈셔쥬임관오등 통신원참셔관 신명호 ○임이천군슈셔쥬임관ᄉᆞ등 법부참셔관 로병직 ○임평산군슈셔쥬임관삼등 탁지부무관 리용구 ○임람포군슈셔쥬임관ᄉᆞ등 군부부관 리셕지

○임룡안군슈셔쥬임관오등 니부쥬ᄉᆞ 호영탁 ○진위군슈셔쥬임오등 즁츄원쥬ᄉᆞ 빅남규 ○임신계군슈셔쥬임관륙등 경무청경무관 김두환

이샹십월십일

○임통신원참셔관셔쥬임관륙등 통신원쥬ᄉᆞ 변영진 ○임통신원쥬ᄉᆞ셔관임관륙등 구픔 리병룡

○의원면겸임 외국어학교쟝 학부참셔관 죠한벽

○겸임외국어학교쟝 학부편집국쟝 리종틱 ○임학부참셔관셔쥬임관륙등 탁지부지무관 민건식 ○임탁지부지무관셔쥬임관삼등 농샹공부기ᄉᆞ 구회셔 ○승셔쥬임관ᄉᆞ등 탁지부셔무국쟝 리즁옥 ○명쥬차일본공ᄉᆞ슈원 졍삼픔 리용문 ○임셩진감리셔쥬임관륙등 졍삼픔 죠문환 ○임총령ᄉᆞ관셔쥬임관이등 외부번역관 어윤적 ○겸임령ᄉᆞ관 외부쥬ᄉᆞ 리원용

○면징계 젼경흥감리 남구희

이샹십월십일일

○임니부쥬ᄉᆞ셔관임관륙등 젼셕쥰 ○면본관 한셩우례ᄉᆞ쥬ᄉᆞ 김홍경 한영슈

○임한셩우례ᄉᆞ쥬ᄉᆞ셔관임관륙등 인쳔우례ᄉᆞ쥬ᄉᆞ 홍학슈 구픔 김영일 임인쳔우례ᄉᆞ쥬ᄉᆞ셔관임관륙등 리승츈 ○의원면본관 인쳔면보ᄉᆞ쥬ᄉᆞ 민긔호

○임인쳔면보ᄉᆞ쥬ᄉᆞ셔관임관륙등 림시엽 ○임농샹공학교교관셔판임관오등 탁지부량디국기슈 번지샹 ○임농샹공학교교관셔관임관륙등 김티길

이샹십월십이일

잡보

○회의안건 삼작일하오이시에졍부에셔회의ᄒᆞ엿는ᄃᆡ그안건인즉각부부원청에용관을감익ᄒᆞᆯᄉᆞ와니외직쥬관임관을공쳔ᄒᆞ되의졍참졍찬졍참찬과각부대신은각각오인식이오각협관은ᄉᆞ인식이오칙임관이인식거쳔ᄒᆞ기로경뎡ᄒᆞ엿더라

○한강측량 일젼에일본공학ᄉᆞ와병뎡긔명이한강등디를측량ᄒᆞ는ᄃᆡ히디지셔에셔쇼검을파송ᄒᆞ야보호ᄒᆞ엿더라

○공쥬형편 공쥬군으로셔샹리ᄒᆞᆫ친구가ᄒᆞ는군형편을말ᄒᆞ되향쟈병뎡과일인잔야료된이ᄅᆡ인민은외겁ᄒᆞ야거조가황망ᄒᆞ로고군인은무쟝지졸이되야미우셔셜ᄒᆞᆫ즉조연군심이ᄐᆡ라ᄒᆞ고산란ᄒᆞ야거진환산지경인즉경광이심히슈참ᄒᆞ다ᄒᆞ더라

○곡산형편 곡산민요이후로히군에일병이파쥬ᄒᆞ엿스며민심이져샹ᄒᆞ야농민뿐아니라샹고ᄉᆞ지실업지경인즉도로에거의인영이영졀이라더라

○ᄃᆡ비민ᄃᆡ 의쥬진위ᄃᆡ경비가군졸ᄒᆞ야군부에쳥구ᄒᆞ엿더니지발치아니ᄒᆞ는고로ᄉᆞ셰부득이홈으로본군슈가ᄒᆡ군부민의게다쇼간ᄃᆡ용ᄒᆞᆫ다는젼셜이잇다더라

○회심중긔 일젼에평리원에셔외부로죠복ᄒᆞ기를시흥민요쟝두셩우경민용훈을본원으로압송ᄒᆞ야일본군리ᄉᆞ와갓치회심ᄒᆞᆯ일ᄉᆞ는본월십칠일노뎡일ᄒᆞ엿스니ᄒᆡ공관에죠회ᄒᆞ라ᄒᆞ엿더라

○임관청의 의학교교관장도씨는외부번역관을셔임ᄒᆞ기로ᄒᆡ부에셔졍부에청의ᄒᆞ엿더라

○검찰소환 일젼졍부에농샹공부소관금광검찰를일졔히소환ᄒᆞ기로의결ᄒᆞ엿다더라

○총판환임 통신원총판민샹호씨는일본례신대신를ᄃᆡ우ᄒᆞ기위ᄒᆞ야찬졍을겸임ᄒᆞ엿다가일젼에샹소ᄒᆞ야본직겸임을다허례되엿더니총판을환임ᄒᆞ엿다더라

○막지기죄 일젼에일본헌병과슌사가신문외에셔ᄒᆞᆫ관인을포착ᄒᆞ고구리개등디에셔또ᄒᆞᆫ사름을포박ᄒᆞ야소령부로착거ᄒᆞ엿는ᄃᆡ무솜죄범인지알슈업다더라

○교육부 텰도원은시문안셔북텰도국으로옴기고히원에는륙군교육부를셜치ᄒᆞ엿더라

○량민임례 돈령원ᄉᆞ민영린씨는특명젼권공ᄉᆞ를피명ᄒᆞ고통신원총판민샹호씨는샹소ᄒᆞ야겸임ᄒᆞᆫ찬졍서지례임되엿더라

○참서득인 법부참셔관로병직씨ᄃᆡ에는젼도ᄉᆞ조희영씨가피임ᄒᆞ엿더라

○탁도시무 탁지고문관목하면씨가명일브터시무ᄒᆞᆯ터인ᄃᆡ지졍을졍리ᄒᆞ기위ᄒᆞ여면환국쥬젼을뎡지ᄒᆞ고임의쥬죠ᄒᆞᆫ동화와못지은젹동빅동을낫낫치됴사ᄒᆞᆫ다더라

●한지고시 한셩지관소에셔고시ᄒᆞ기를종민이졍소ᄒᆞᆯ즈음에혹졍긔비가져회ᄒᆞ야지체된다ᄒᆞ니만일이폐단이잇거든크게물너셩명ᄒᆞ고곳드러와졍소ᄒᆞ라ᄒᆞ엿더라

○초무대관 공쥬ᄃᆡ병뎡야료

UNION INSURANCE SOCIETY OF CANTON.

Head office Hongkong.
Marine risks underwritten at current rates.
Agents in Chemulpo,
E. MEYER & Co.

COMPAGNIE DES MESSAGERIES MARITIMES.

Fortnightly Direct Service.

For Marseilles
via Ports.
Sailing from Yokohama
Calling at Kobe,
Shanghai, Hongkong, Saigon, Singapore,
Colombo, Djibouti, Suez, Port Said
and Marseilles.

For particulars apply to
HOLME RINGER & Co.,
Chemulpo.

HAYASHIDA & Co.,

16 MYENG DONG, CHIN KO KAI, SEOUL.
BRANCH OFFICE AT CHEMULPO.

Money changers, Coal and Wood Merchants, Express Agents.

We are agents for the Pyeng-yang Coal Company and the Karazu Coal Company of Japan. We have the best quality of both anthracite and bituminous coal, and prompt execution of orders is our speciality. Firewood of all kinds kept in stock. Full weight guaranteed. Money of all denominations exchanged at current rates. Parcels received for all parts.

CHINA MUTUAL LIFE INS. CO.

Most favourable terms to policy holders.

Benefit system unsurpassed.

HOLME RINGER &ICo.
Agents, Chemulpo.

C. P. R.

CANADIAN PACIFIC RAILWAY COMPANY'S ROYAL MAIL STEAMSHIP LINE.

THE FAST ROUTE BETWEEN CHINA, JAPAN, AND EUROPE VIA CANADA AND THE UNITED STATES.

Route from Hongkong via Shanghai, Nagasaki (Inland Sea of Japan) Kobe, Yokohama, Victoria and Vancouver.

Twin Screw Empress Steamship—6,000 Tons—Speed 19 knots.

PROPOSED SAILING FROM YOKOHAMA.
R. M. S. Empress of India.
R. M. S. Empress of Japan.
R. M. S. Empress of China.
R. M. S. Athenian.
R. M. S. Tartar.

Special reduction (first class only) granted to members of the Military, Naval, Diplomatic and Civil services and to Missionaries.
Passengers have choice of ten routes across the Continent of America and have privilege of travelling by any Atlantic Steamship Line.
Round the World passage tickets in connection with the P. and O. S. N., North German Lloyd and Messageries Co.'s **£125.**
All rates payable at current rate of exchange.
For further information, Tickets, Guide Books, etc. apply to

HOLME, RINGER & CO., AGENTS, Chemulpo.

Grand Hotel,

(Formerly the Station Hotel)

Near the Railway Terminus, West Gate, Seoul.

The Best Hotel in Korea.
Handsome new Building.
Fine Airy Rooms
Excellent Cuisine.
Terms Moderate.
Special terms to Missionaries
and to permanent boarders.

Electric cars within 2 minutes' walk.

W. H. EMBERLEY,
Proprietor.

EVERY FACILITY.

In connection with Life Assurance Business is afforded by

The Standard Life Assurance Co.,

One of the largest and wealthiest of the Provident Institutions of the United Kingdom Forms of Application and all information will be promptly afforded on application.

10 CENTS A DAY.

Not a very large expenditure is it? But it is sufficient to secure for a man of 30 a policy with the STANDARD LIFE OFFICE for

$1323.

For all particulars of rates, etc., apply to

Holme, Ringer & Co.,
Agents, Chemulpo.

THE NEW YORK LIFE INSURANCE COMPANY.

Have you ever been declined by any Company?

Are you engaged in a specially hazardous occupation?

Have you heard of the New York Life Insurance Company's New Classifications for this class of Risks?

If not, send your date of birth, occupation and particulars of rejection, if any to

E. MEYER & Co.,
Agents, Chemulpo.

MITSUI BUSSAN KAISNHA.
(MITSUI & Co.)

MITSUI GINKO.
(MITSUI BANK.)

The Bank is owned by the members of the Mitsui Family, who, as partners, assume an unlimited responsibility for all liabilities of the Bank:—

Capital.................. .....Yen 5,000,000
Reserve Fund.................. " 5,600,000

HEAD OFFICE, TOKYO.
LONDON OFFICE, 34 LIME ST., E. C.

BRANCHES AND AGENCIES:—
New York, San Francisco, Hamburg, Bombay, Singapore, Manila, Hongkong, Amoy, Chefoo, Tientsin.
Kobe, Hakodate, Yokohama, Kure, Yokosuka, Moji, Shimonoseki, Miike, Wakamatsu, Nagasaki, Kuchinotsu, Karatsû, Sasebo, Misume, Taipeh, &c.

Telegraphic Address for all the Offices:
"MITSUI."

A. B. C. AND A. I CODES USED.

Contractors of Coal
To the Imperial Japanese Navy. Arsenals and Railway Bureau, Principal Railway Companies and Industrial Work, Home and Foreign Mail and Freight Steamers.

Sole Proprietors
Of the famous Miike, Tagawa and Yamano Coal Mines.

Sole Agents
For the sale of Fukumo, Hokoku, Ichimura, Kanoda, Mannoura, Onoura, Ostuji, Sonoda, Tsubaruro, Yoshinotani, Yoshio, Yurokibura and other coals.

YANGTSE INSURANCE ASSOCIATION, LTD.

The undersigned, having been appointed agents for the above company, are prepared to issue policies and pay losses on marine risks at regular rates.

E. MEYER & Co.,
Agents, Chemulpo.

AMERICAN KOREAN ELECTRIC COMPANY.

Light and Power.

Main Office: Electric Building, Chong No.

RAILWAY DEPARTMENT.

OPERATING CARS BETWEEN EAST AND WEST GATE, EVERY TEN MINUTES:—
First Car leaves East Gate at 6:30 A. M. First Car leaves West Gate at 6:55 A. M.
Last Cra " East Gate at 10:40 P. M. Last " " West Gate at 11:00 P.M.

OPERATING CARS BETWEEN EAST GATE AND IMPERIAL TOMB TERMINUS, EVERY TWENTY MINUTES:—
CONNECTING WITH EVERY ALTERNATE CAR ARRIVING AT EAST GATE FROM CHONG NO.
First Car leaves East Gate for Tomb at 6:50 A. M.
" " " Tomb for East Gate at 7:10 A. M.
Last " " East Gate for Tomb at 9:50 P. M.
" " " Tomb for East Gate at 10:10 P. M.

OPERATING CARS BETWEEN CHONG NO AND YUNG SAN (RIVER) EVERY TWELVE MINUTES:—
First Car leaves Chong No for South Gate at 6:48 A. M.
" " " Chong No for Yung San at 7:24 A. M.
" " " South Gate for Chong No at 6:56 A. M.
" " " Yung San for Chong No at 7:57 A. M.
Last " " South Gate for Chong No 11:00 P. M.
" " " Yung San for Chong No at 10:11 P. M.

SPECIAL PRIVATE CARS FURNISHED TO SUIT CONVENIENCE OF PATRONS. PRICES ON APPLICATION AT HEAD OFFICE.

LIGHTING DEPARTMENT.

Where less than 250 candle power of light is used, the rate per month will be: Per 16 candle power incandescent lamp,—All night.—Yen 2.50.
Per 32 candle power incandescent lamp:—All night:—Yen 4.00. Per 50 candle power incandescent lamp:—All night:—Yen 6.00.
" 150 " " " " —" " " 10.00. " 1200 " enclosed arc " " " 20.00.
Where more than 250 candle power of light is used, a Meter will be installed, if requested:—Rent of Meter Yen 2.00 per month. Rate of charges by meter reading:—Two Sen per Ampere per hour. (Approximately this is equal to about One Sen per 16 C. P. lamp per hour) Minimum monthly charge where meter is installed, Yen 20.00 per month, which includes rental of meter.
Estimates for installing lights furnished on application. An assortment of chandeliers always on hand.

AMUSEMENT DEPARTMENT.

ANIMATED PICTURES AT EAST GATE
Every evening - - - Except Sunday.
From 8 to 10 P. M.

10 Cents:—Gen. Admission:—10 Cents. Seats in First Class Section. 15 Cents Extra.

Change of program each week. Pictures from Foreign Lands. Pictures of Local Scenes:—Amusing and Instructive.

An entertaining evening for a reasonable price.
MERRY-GO-ROUND:—At East Gate.
From 10:00 A. M. till 11:00 P. M.

5 Cents a Ride.

Take your Exercise on The Galoping Horses.

Comfortable seats in the Chariots.

한셩뎐긔회샤

한미뎐긔회샤 고불안 보사ᄇᆡ 고빅
도ᄒᆞ옵나이다
샹ᄒᆞᆫ동샤진뎐랍소와목마운동쟝ᄭᅦ고ᄆᆞ
여ᄇᆡ면차가온쟝안으로통힝ᄒᆞ여ᄃᆞᆫ니여이
삽
ᄯᅩ이긔계에ᄀᆞᆺ치노힌편ᄒᆞ고됴흔마차도잇
삽
코ᄆᆡ우편ᄒᆞ고ᄯᅩᄌᆞ미잇ᄂᆞᆫ됴흔운동이되겟
이됴흔모형ᄒᆞᆯ달나아ᄂᆞᆫ몰올ᄯᅳ고위티치안
ᄃᆡ가ᄂᆞᆫ홉번ᄯᅳᄂᆞᆫ데오젼ᄉᆡ이오
ᄆᆡ일샹오열시브허하오열ᄒᆞᆯ시ᄭᆞ지ᄒᆞ옵고
목마운동쟝은동대문안에잇삽고
가되겟삽
쳘군조의게갑도싸고져녁에됴흔쇼일거리
미잇고구경ᄒᆞᆯ만ᄒᆞ거시오니
셔양사진과대한과온동양사진연대대단ᄌᆞ
ᄂᆞᆫᄃᆡ
젼이옵고ᄆᆡ쥬일에사진을ᄯᅡᆫ것스로다밧고
고젼랍ᄃᆡ금은하등에십젼이오샹등에이십
일외에ᄂᆞᆫᄆᆡ야에여덜시브허열시ᄭᆞ지ᄒᆞ옵
활동사진뎐랍소ᄂᆞᆫ동대문안에잇삽고일요
회ᄇᆡᆨ부

All Cars Run Direct to the Animated Pictures and Merry-Go-Round.

훈사로군부와헌병되에서위관 일인식과송훈야히사실탕초근 힝을됴사훈엿논되힝수실이별 노곤관계가업논이인되무엿히 망동홈이라더라

○인장신주 시죵무관장민종 무관장의인장과훈계청에서주 조흐엿다흐고작일에각부원 청에셜명흐엿다더라

○봉박조퇴 근일각종봉가가 날노고등흐야지바혼월급십오 원으로지파흘수업는고로오서 니슌검이되일철팔인흉셥여인 서자퇴흐야헤수가부족흔지라 경무청에서경무관도를모집흐 야셩오헌례는안에경찰셔무를다 탐교습흐야곳슌검에부치기로 작뎡흐고또각셔에흔명흐되슌 검이결원업시조퇴흐는자는자들히 시치말나흐엿다더라

○명조작란 작일양셩흔명원보 수명관청국천디정과침보장당 곡쵸부상탐청가입셕시경령혼자 매란흐게명편으로오교흐엿다더라

○혐혹무폐 작일하오에구리 기계동인졔서일본인이한국녀 인을참혹흐야생흘흐는중에교 도봐가회의무폐홈을침혹흐 엿다더라

○수명흥잔 작일낫부에서군 수신임흘흥경부회의에제출흐 엿는티핑안은각부공천이오심 에인은예외라흐며회의에셔바 로운흥기로이천군수로거천흐야 윤수는등절시키흐에조옥게히 가니라흐며앵외신원인도부시 흐기로시비분운흐다가필경명 권총절인판주로흐엿다더라

○금교민의 외부에서니부로 조회흐기로를관조회오시됴관흐로 경교흐야젼라북도관찰쇼의보 고흐에검추흐본조서흐건티감동샹 항구서에당가디간을외국인의게 비밀지계불흐논바이라고보외 에보부에서각도에후칙흐엿이이 축관이나와흘강디방관이는군구 로알교금지가아니흐야인민이 외국인의게전토를작매홈이이곳 지반흐니샤피히히판흐며야장이 알거스승당의국공수를방흐야 조혜를게시논금지흐흐라히미면 거류국세명을남승호지니각도에 에신칙흐야엄히사실흐고금지 흐되면답간분즉의흥섀거잡히세롤 착수흐야일일히환퇴케흐라흐 엿다더라

○외부우조 외부에서너부로 또조회흐기로인민분관청쇼계시 헌민를압졸음관불흐는수는구히 경청이를바로부에서엄이일수 서왜루흐되성즙흐엿거니와히부에 서신속히각관에신칙흐야각방 곡에고시흐야상궁흥비설으로 흐며금에이군이오분을범치말게 흐라흐엿다더라

○군수환원 일전에쥬본된군

수청인은정계는참령서편구의 생도돌알명샤유리인셩히동운면 칙기수방송챙영경잔눈농생유부 죽수서생공평강은한부족수김 정윤정선은부위김승표퍼렴은 한생부쥬수티의셔셔메다라

○룡천면보 작일영오쳥님이 시방에공쥬관찰서의면보가너 부로도착흐엿스되쳥경로를분산 포동되에취적흔인민들흘호유되 신계홈추로작일에오젼서리로 셩군수의게신칙흐엿다흐고본 부총순을파송흐야소워천보회 망을두장을등보흐엿논되고방 분에웃며한을과가동립권을 공교계흐고면난민들의국인의계 수수로민외흥흘금범탄흐고결젼 을산양강탄서결흐흥기로흥이라 논되떡탄을위주혼다흐며다시 정답흐논티로보고흐엿다흐엿 더라

론셜

(싸홈평편)

○우리가자서흔소문드르니더홍 은다름아니라륵군원수후작 뎨산의의젼투보고도오히려모 호흐고또한무주견정이의되라면 야죽도정본흐나괴결경근써흥이 될듯홈으로그리홈이로다 서령아츙에구로파트긴장군이 군스를모라남으로향흐야대귀 를다시치니러전에계군지지로젼 진흐니서이에후룩대장이본진 과다로결리도를나일본군되의동 신이서로막혀여는지라이곳에 서아병이일병이진됨두곳을엿 엿스되그일병이층에안기가샤 방으로가희여져첩을분법치옷 흐게느고로일병이도되켜써와 다항이첩킨흐엿다흐며 또흔지도를보고볼진되아병이 분진이연되로복서되동물박면이 셥오영리되는곳에회셔쪄잇슨 즉그근처에서로오방으로동들을 흘웃흐야신례안현를서지도서 로써흘지경이면탄진병의세가괴 추상흔경맞착되니그남발에아 병이흥편으로흥흐야퇴게흐는 지라

신이에일본군수ㅣ아병의퇴 거흘을보쟛흐무수흔군수를죽이 고화포쳠상의긔계를엣엇다흐흐 리는이싸홈이졍졋엇지될는지 후보슷기를다리거니와일만 일본군으로잇갓치아병이무그가 파연경결흐엿더구로파트긴장 군의병법쓰는도랑이일본으로 더브러조곰다흘게시엿슬비 시니리하가랑셩이라흐고구로 파트긴장군이써호라는마음만 흘져셋드면네번짐연정이또흔듯 탈쌔홈을보다오히려패뎡홈이나 도다

면보

동일평면

○신이일전에 슈요 김양츙에 전두를흘평면으롭외로곳흐너도의 군이중앙중되는오전오시에로 교렴을관과막평가조복방의붕남 셩을를점령흐엿고좌동되는승날 흐로붕방의남훈방을점령흐엿고 다음에저병을츄격흐엿고고중앙 중되논마미삿을점령흐엿고고 중앙군은화요에방이로북되은 동흐야수요일조조에셔가조에 서삼가미이세기삼복방이잇논봉 흔곳진되에도달흐엿다히이젼생 에계의의권관포이등결한아수례 팔좌셔를획득흐엿논되회랑관쟝 이부샹흐엿다더라

좌승군은시신리가홍왕요셔와서 이부군에잇논지쳐올티흐아히요 일방불티로이괴중앙티본게호방 면의전쟁평찬은어연히우지흐 더라

대산만쥬군총수평관보고

봉텬방면격전속보 젼에면 보흐이되로좌익군은북방이으로 향흐야부맹렬히추격흐나더흥흐 며본계호방면의세병이불닉관 경을마아천기위를위흐야세로조 방면으로퇴진흐야일흠이는을 화에고쿄봉을나이렬흐는중이 요중앙군은오히려포격흐며나 아가저진흐야본연리론동신구와 호가위교가조의잇는진울정령 고렵흐는되이방면의게병은서 편에만니르기카지부방이으로니 엿며테리익된고돌흐보앗고고회쟝시 으로향흐야전진흐아이전황할 방으로엇스도를자흐흔다는보고 엇스나아지아사흔고좌익군이 중앙중되논추격흐는중에대포 수문을탈취흐엿는티혀중되논들 퇴계흐는병의여습홈이자못심 히용감흐엿스나두번을다히중 되의포병과다수의보병이로세 격군의계손히들내벗히마히주 머이거숭격되흐엿고좌익군의 우중되논심히세강방에서적병 을추격흐는중에전의대포오문 과탄약수레오좌를탈취흐엿스 며합계가매포가이십오문이오 탄약수레가오좌를획득흐엿고 총에밧티논포병만교가이지로 교수조부군에격지계흐고그일 부논흐가영의게군을격퇴흐고 좌종되의우이에바며잇서공격 흐며전진흐논중인되이군되에 세논본일에로포가이일오심명 이라흐엿다더라

○샹동슈보가이 본계호방면 에서는각처에잇논적병이맥습 흐논거슬격퇴흐고교두와본계 호간에관맹흔저과흐영흐되피 교우익군의추격과중앙군의추 격흐논거슨대단히진취가되여 잇의마이산과망가분이진되어 나로가로병을가진격군의일부 되논에셔싸엄이되여구히며단 히혼관이되엿스며 기다론거순추추로북방으로퇴 각흐여더라남는흐고우이군은 본계호부근에잇논적병의북니 걸길을막아서괴키위흐야교조 로향흐야일부대를관전흐야오 후삼시량에는동면으로곳에도 날흐엿갯스며중앙군은오늘아 츰에삼괴서선에서아포로막탄 약수레십일좌를됸탈취흐엿고로 로외의말에는경장구로붓든진은 슴스단중되는념평을우위흐흔고 우익군의주력을따라게흐는곳군 의흐뢰에잇논거시티르니라거다 흐며좌익이로의종앙중되논저군 기유력흐계되게흐논지승격퇴 흐야오흐후에보에탐소로가부 군을점령흐고져의대포십셔문을 을탈취흐며적군은완란탄흐야북 방으로퇴각흐논지라추격흐흐 에곳쇼동되를지나궁솜가조로 향흐야전진흐엿고우중되논연 로의우론의북방에향흐흔전격군 의강경히되져흐는거슬엄써셔과 흐야퇴주케흐고북하에동합원요 남북오리가로향흐야저병을추 격흐논중이며성이시받쳄에좌 종되논밍렬히북편으로격흐 논중이라흐엿더라

외보

○로국장정 구월십일일보빈렴 밧뎐을거흐흔죽로국황뎨계셔 평문원을만히거느리고구통에 화건흐는셰럴킬혐되졸반흐는거 승경정흐다고미바셔이로젼진 흐엿다더라

○로장비원주 로국황뎨계셔 구로팟트긴장군은원슈에통쥬 흐시고만쥬군의총수평관을비 리인의로서칙쟝군은데일군을평 솔흐기로결명흐엿다더라

잡보

○교정밥문 졍진왕궁셰가셰 외최게원경리지균과외종이통 리쉬장성되와최부참서과우졍보 조경구기김천승셔와밥관양연 소교편평명헌셔와밥봉을위원조 청교셰들다양법교정관이로차 정흐엿다더라

○참졍유등 외부에셔참셔관 이명을종저흘수로경부회의에 제츌흐엿승으로히부관원종참 서관승처퇴고석기가인원관또 경이의도보이인디헌인의외부되신 가를삼신히받흔흥고유동흐논 자반라더라

○검사추로 경부에서작진일 어참관청부에면흐흥기를인명 동이조명평흥의의에착당흥 며 조회엿시샥말흐니어기순 면민이라금취흐효유흐야회해의선게 흐되일향거엿즐거든벌명을엄 송흐야보로흐라흐엿더라

TELEGRAMS.

THE MUKDEN BATTLE.

LATEST REPORT FROM OYAMA.

Tokyo, Oct. 14th.

The following report from Marquis Oyama covers the operations on Wednesday and Thursday last.

In the direction of Punkiho after a fierce struggle on Wednesday the enemy showed signs of retreating at daybreak on Thursday morning, so our troops advanced to push home our attack.

A large body of our cavalry under the command of Prince Kaninomiya advanced to the left of the enemy and with reserve batteries shelled their position, effecting disorder in their ranks. This cavalry corps will attempt to cut off the enemy's retreat.

The right column of our left wing engaged a superior force of the enemy at Chosanling, but reinforcements having now arrived, we shall be able to improve our position in that direction. The centre and left column of the same wing after tremendous fighting occupied an important position of the enemy north of Saotakow.

Our centre occupied hilly ground north of Kuchutze, Hucha and Wangchatun, while the right column of the left wing occupied Panchaopu on Thursday morning and the advance guard reached Bachatze and effected the conjunction with the reinforcements from the reserve force, who were attacking the enemy at Whangchatze. Here a few of the enemy's batteries were strongly resisting their attack but one body of the reserve force will be sufficient to dispose of their resistance.

Our centre force after forcing the enemy back are now attacking them at Sahopao (5 *li* from Mukdon). Reinforcements are continually arriving at Yentai and vicinity.

A POLISH PRINCE'S VIEWS.

San Francisco, Sep. 19th.

Prince Radzivil, who has been on duty with the army in the Far East and was in Port Arthur until recently, has returned to St. Petersburg. Discussing the situation at Port Arthur the Prince speaks very optimistically and says that he believes the garrison can hold out for a considerable time yet. He reports that at the time he left there was no scarcity of provisions and no indication of shortage for some months to come. He speaks highly of the conduct and morale of the Russian troops and predicts that with the reinforcements which are now being sent to Kuropatkin a new aspect will soon be put on the face of affairs. The Prince speaks in strong terms regarding the barbarity of the Japanese, who, he claims, are still little better than savages. Their dead, he states, are very often left unburied, and they nearly always leave unburied the dead of the Russians.—Manila Cablenews.

MORE LIGHT ON LIAOYANG

(Concluded from page 2.)

The correspondent refers to one of Oku's artillery attacks as one of the most severe concentrated artillery fires the world has ever seen. Every gun belonging to two of the Japanese corps was trained in rapid fire on the left of Kuropatkin's position.

The correspondent says:

"It was a magnificent, and withal an awe-inspiring spectacle. The Russian godowns were set on fire, as were the station buildings, and nothing could live under the attack. The end of the Russian resistance had come, and the Japanese gunners rested from this work of devastation and slaughter, when, suddenly, out of the midst of the smoke and murky dust left from the reeking shrapnel, came counter-flashes from two or three Russian batteries. One felt almost inclined to cheer, but it seemed that it was their last effort—a magnificent farewell to the enemy whom they had balked for so long."

General Haraguchi, until recently in command of the Japanese forces in Korea, left yesterday for Chemulpo en-route to Japan.

Mr. Megata entered upon his duties to-day. He presented the Minister and various high officials of his Department with some rolls of silk.

The Crown Princess' illness has taken a dangerous turn and much anxiety for the saving of her life is felt in Court circles.

A suitable house for Mr. Stephens is to be built by the Foreign Office at a cost of 8,500 yen. The contract for this has been given to a Japanese.

Among the arrivals on Saturday per S. S. "Ohio" were Mr. and Mrs. H. R. Bostwick, who returned from a visit to Japan.

They trust that in future the Home Office will take steps, by infoming Koreans of the offences penable by martial law, to present such another unfortunate occurrence.

The Foreign Office, replying to a despatch from the Home Office, remarks that it indeed is extraordinary that the three recently executed Koreans should be made away with by the Japanese without their knowledge.

It now transpires, according to native reports, that the publication of the Chekuk Sinmun was stopped by the Il-Chin-Hoi. The same authority is responsible for the statement that the Il-Chin-Hoi will utilise the printing press for their own ends and commence the publication of an Il-Chin-Hoi journal in a few days. We await with interest the first issue.

Colonel G. C. Hoad, Chief of the Staff of the Australian Forces, and Captain A. Scandella, of the Spanish Army, have been presented by the Emperor with the Third Class Order of the Rising Sun and the Fourth Class Order of the Sacred Treasure respectively. These two officers, who, as military attachés, were with the Japanese Army at the front, returned to Tokio in company with Lieut. General Sir William Nicholson.

In Lhassa, or thereabouts, live the Mahatmas of Madame Blavatsky, Annie Besant and others. Also it is the home of the Rosicrucians, or original Freemasons, who can turn lead into gold. The music-hall instinct has been so well developed of late in the British Army that the force is bound to bring back a Mahatma and a Rosicrucian in a cage for a show if those interesting animals have any real existence.—Sydney Bulletin.

Prince Eui-chin, the second son born to His Majesty, and who has for some years resided in America, is reported to be passionately in love. The object of his affections is a Miss Mary Patteras, aged 16, the daughter of a wealthy American. What progress he is making towards obtaining his desire, we do not know, but we understand that his progress in study is sadly retarded in consequence of his inclination toward romance.

The Japanese residents in London have now been reduced to under 20, so says the London correspondent of the "Birmingham Daily Express." In fact, they consist nearly exclusively of tne entourage of the Embassy. Two months ago, all told, there were 200 male Japanese residing in London, but, partly fom a patriotic desire to share in the campaign, and latterly through the hurtling summons of the "Fiery Cross," these have all gone, with the tew exceptions mentioned, to join the flag. You see now and then the familiar eyes of the children of the sun, but the owners are usually of the fairer half of the gallant people.

A very curious story is contained in the following despatch from the Chief of Police to the Law Department. He asserts that acting under orders received from the offices of that department, he despatched two gendarmes to Mokpo to effect the arrest of the Kamni at that port. On their arrival, however, the Kamni refused to recognise their authority and charging them with insolence, locked them up in the local jail. One managed to escape and on reaching Seoul, reported the matter to his superiors. The Chief of Police goes on to express the opinion that two gendarmes are insufficient to effect the arrest of this sturdy magnate. We have not yet heard with what offence the gentleman is charged.

The birth of an heir to the Czar and Czarina was, curiously enough, predicted to the latter a short time after her marriage by the Czar's first cousin, Prince Charles of Denmark, who is looked upon in the Danish royal family as something of a clairvoyant. Prince Charles foretold, says Vanity Fair, the birth of four daughters, to the infinite chagrin of the Czarina, who was consoled, however, by the prediction that the longed-for heir would follow on the heels of his four little sisters. The Czar himself is a firm believer in spiritual phenomena and occultism, and has often consulted clairvoyants, astrologers, and even gipsy fortune-tellers. It is, perhaps, some comfort to the Autocrat of All the Russias that no one of the seers has predicted for him a violent death.

The Korea Daily News.

Issued at 5 P. M. daily except Sundays.

Rate of Subscription:—
Per Year, Yen 25.
Per Quarter, Yen 7.
Per Month, Yen 2.50.

Postage in Korea not charged extra.
Postage abroad charged extra.

Advertisements, 50 sen per day for 1 inch or less.
5 yen per month per inch.
50 yen per year per inch.

All communications to
E. T. BETHELL,
Editor and Publisher,
Pak-tong, Seoul.

PORT ARTHUR.

Appended we give what purports to be the history of the earlier stages of the operations at Port Arthur. Although published by the Military authorities at Tokyo, it is worthless as a historical record, inasmuch as the number of troops engaged is not given and nowhere is mention made of the extent of the Japanese casualties.

As will be seen, it deals with operations from the capture of Nanshan on May 26th till the final withdrawal of the Russians inside the fortress on July 30th:—

"26th May.—Our army, after a severe fight lasting all day, obtained possession of the enemy's position at Nanshan. He retired to Port Arthur.

"27th May.—A force under Major General Nakamura advanced and occupied Nankwanling. Our main body bivouacked near Nanshan and began its preparations to advance. Until about 10 A. M. the enemy in the neighbourhood of Sanshilipau station were engaged burning the station after which they escaped toward Port Arthur.

"May 28th.—A detachment of Nakamura's force advanced and occupied Liushutun. The fort at this place as well as a part of the Russian buildings were destroyed by the Russians, as was also a section of the wharf. Our men took four of the enemy's guns with some ammunition, 5 roofed buildings used for railway purposes and unroofed buildings.

"May 29th.—The various parts of the army advanced and reached the highlands about 2½ miles west of Shanshilipau.

"May 30th.—The army again advanced and occupied the line from Rutszshan to Paitszshan, confronting the enemy on the line from Shwangtaikan to Atszling.

"The reports received up to this day as to the conditions at Dalny and Liushutau were as follows:

"(1) At Dalny there are over 100 warehouses and barracks in a perfect state. The telegraph office and the station are safe. We have taken about 300 open waggons, 130 closed, 50 lighters, some 2,000 tons of coal, and 20,000 sleepers. All the small railway bridges in the vicinity are destroyed. The dock and its wharf are complete. But the large wharf is broken and part of it is under water. Several small steamers are sunk at the entrance to the dock.

"(2) The supports of the wharf at Liushutun are broken, but can be repaired with timber which is in the neighbourhood. The lifting crane belonging to the wharf has been burned.

"(3) The railway bridges between Kinchou and Liushutun are quite uninjured.

"June 1st.—The enemy in the direction of Port Arthur contiues to hold the vicinity of Shwantaikau and Fenshwilingtsz in force. His scouts are unceasingly in touch with our front, and occasionally fire on our outposts. The videttes on both sides are not more than 1,000 metres apart. Sometimes Russian soldiers disguised in Chinese garments approach our lines and suddenly producing rifles, open fire on our outposts. It would seem that the enemy is endeavouring to cooperate with his comrades in the north who are supposed to be moving south.

"June 6th.—The enemy has placed a number of obstacles at the foot of a hill 178 metres high on the east of Shihshankau.

"June 13th.—A strong reconnoitering party of the enemy approached our lines to-day and exchanged fire with us. He retired at dusk.

"June 14th.—Two of the enemy's gunboats and one battleship, approaching Heishihchiao, fired a number of shots at our position. After about 30 minutes they withdrew to the west.

"Reconnaissances made by us on this day showed that some defensive works existed at Antszling and on the heights southward of it, but nothing of the kind was seen at the heights westward of Tashangtun and Tahsiatun, on the Hwangui River. Further, judging from the enemy's dead, his troops in the vicinity of Chakau were the 5th regiment of rifles, and those near Chuchwautszkan were the 28th regiment of rifles.

"June 18th.—At 4.50 P.M. three of the enemy's ships with 8 destroyers appeared in the vicinity of Siaopingtau, and fired one shot at our left wing's position, but almost immediately they were engaged by our squadron and after exchanging fire for about 30 minutes, they withdrew to Port Arthur. The enemy's works near Shwangtaikau are steadily increasing. He has established a searchlight with which he examines the neighbourhood and our position.

OCCUPATION OF WAITAUSHAN AND SHWANGSINGSHAN.

"June 26th—The left of our right column moving against the heights on the west and south of Pantau, attacked the enemy there and gained possession of the hills. Our left column divided into three bodies, of which the right body, advancing against the heights on the east of Launikiao, captured them without encountering great resistance. The central body, moving against a hill 368 metres high on the south of Lanuikiao and against the heights on the north of Tashangtun on the Hwangin River and driving back a force of the enemy en route, attacked, at about 1 P. M., his force (about one battalion of infantry with some machine-guns) on the 368 metre hill. After a more or less obstinate resistance, these heights were completely occupied by 5 P. M. The left body, advancing toward Shwangtingshan, drove back a force of the enemy and captured the heights. Thus the first line of our army found itself occupying the line from Antszshan, on the right, via the heights on the east and south of Lannikiao (which is about 1 kilometre west of Pantau) as far as Shwangtingshan.

"By the capture of the 368-metre hill—hereafter called Renzan—as well as of Waitaushan and Siaopingtan we were enabled to thoroughly secure our communications with Talien Bay. Moreover these operations may be said to have reversed the enemy's position and ours, for we were enabled to inform ourselves as to his position and condition. The principal objects captured by us in this fight were two 6-cent. guns and about 200 rounds of ammunition.

"June 30th.—There was no change in the condition of the enemy in the Shwangtaikau direction. On the Antszling side there were defensive works everywhere from the southern projection of the highlands to the summit about 3 kilometres on the southeast, and in the Laotszshan direction, along the heights on the south of Wangkiatien.

"July 3rd.—Attacks by the enemy at Pantu and Tashangtun on the Hwangin River.

"There was no change in the enemy's condition opposite the right wing. On the side of the left column his scouts appeared frequently, and his movements showed signs of activity.

"On the right of the left wing nothing occurred except that the enemy's scouts put in an appearance."

MORE LIGHT ON LIAOYANG.

In view of the discussion there has been as to the report sent by a "Times" correspodent to his journal after the battle at Liaoyang, remarks the "Kobe Herald," the following summary of his despatch regarding the operations of September 1st, taken from American papers just to hand, will be read with interest:—The "Times" correspondent with the Japanese left army sends a long narrative of the battle of Liaoyang. Describing the operations of September 1st he says:

"The general impression was that we had only to advance and occupy the town, but Generals Nodsu and Oku's armies required a day's rest. In fifty hours, Oku had made four general assaults which had failed, and he had subsisted through the inclement weather on rations carried on the person, while reserve ammunition required replenishing.

"The Russians had fallen back in good order, taking with them every-thing except some 200 of their latest dead, while the only prisoners to fall into the hands of the Japanese were seven men who were entombed in an observation mine casemate on a brush-covered hill. A Japanese storming party had piled sand bags over the edifice of the casemate. It was an extraordinary incident, for the entombed Russians had shot two officers who wished to parley with them and eventually surrendered 35 hours later in a horrible state.

"I will not dwell upon the sickening and harrowing sights of the battlefield, except to mention one incident: The Japanese stormers had penetrated the highest trench and had overpowered the Cossacks holding it, but Russians from a splinter-proof shelter behind had fallen with their bayonets on the gallant Japanese in the moment of their success and the bodies of both Japanese and Cossacks were piled thick upon each other in a hideous heap.

"The casualties of the Japanese in five divisions at the lowest computation were not less than ten thousand and they were probably many more, for, owing to the crops of millet, several of the wounded have not been found and they must have died miserably, while many bodies will never be found until the crops are cut.

"It is impossible to estimate the Russian losses, which were probably half of the Japanese losses. It must be remembered that my estimate of the latter does not include the Tenth Division of Kuroki's army.

"Just before sundown there was a full Russian response to the Japanese fire.

"Trains have been seen leaving during all the day. Again the rear guard, having completed its duty, retired."

(Continued on page 3.)

The Korea Daily News.

VOL. I, MONDAY, OCTOBER 17, 1904. No. 78

大韓每日申報
대한ᄆᆡ일신보

(뎨칠십구호) (화요일) 일쳔구ᄇᆡᆨ사년십월십팔일

본샤고ᄇᆡᆨ

본신보ᄂᆞᆫ영어와한어로셔계ᄆᆡ일츌판ᄒᆞᆸ

신문가

한쟝 엽두돈오푼

일삭됴 엽두량닷돈

우표가ᄆᆡ삭닷돈

다ᄆᆡᆺ돈으로밧ᄉᆞᆸ

광고료ᄂᆞᆫ

귀한의쟝단과ᄌᆞᄒᆡᆼ의다쇼로즁감ᄒᆞ되렴가로밧을터이오ᄆᆡ오리지아니ᄒᆞ야대한사람마다이신문을보실터이니광고내시기를원ᄒᆞ시ᄂᆞᆫ이들은우리신문사에와셔편약ᄒᆞ심을희망ᄒᆞᆸ

○발힝소 박동대한ᄆᆡ일신보사법어학교압헤젼영국인셜필림졍자리오

사쟝 영국인 (ᄇᆡ셜)

평양 ᄃᆡ리졈

○평양효동사ᄂᆞᆫ권ᄆᆡ보씨로우리신문ᄃᆡ리인을ᄐᆡᆨ뎡ᄒᆞ엿스오니평양에계신구람ᄒᆞ고져ᄒᆞ시ᄂᆞᆫ 쳠군ᄌᆞᄂᆞᆫ해ᄃᆡ리졈에왕림ᄒᆞ와편의ᄒᆞ시옵

사고

○우리대한ᄆᆡ일신보의목뎍은대한의인민졍셰에관ᄒᆞᆫ모든ᄃᆡ목에ᄃᆡᄒᆞ야ᄂᆞᆫ공평ᄒᆞᆫ변론을주쟝ᄒᆞᆷ이라우리동신원의ᄃᆡᆸ보ᄂᆞᆫ신문보시ᄂᆞᆫ쳠군ᄌᆞ의게ᄒᆞᆼ샹보도ᄒᆞ려며편지들과셔ᄒᆞ여주시ᄂᆞᆫ이ᄂᆞᆫ셩명과반ᄃᆡ들적어붓치시기를희망ᄒᆞ오나비ᄅᆞ거ᄉᆞᆫ신문샹에긔ᄌᆡᄒᆞ란ᄂᆞᆫ거시아니오다만극히신용ᄒᆞᄂᆞᆫ증거를삼고자홈이라긔자ᄂᆞᆫ아모긔셔던지긔ᄌᆡᄒᆞᆷ을퇴각ᄒᆞᄂᆞᆫ권리를가졋스나퇴각ᄒᆞᄂᆞᆫ리유를말ᄒᆞᆯ터이오며공즁광화를문란케ᄒᆞᄂᆞᆫ듯ᄒᆞᆫ긔셔ᄂᆞᆫ의례히밧지안켓ᄉᆞᆸ나이다

●본사셜시이ᄅᆡ로신문을ᄆᆡ양우례로분젼ᄒᆞ와례젼부의임의로젼ᄒᆞ드ᄉᆡ로먼곳에ᄂᆞᆫ혹늣게젼ᄒᆞ기도ᄒᆞ며혹몃쳘거슬ᄒᆞᆫ번에젼ᄒᆞ기도ᄒᆞ며혹아니젼ᄒᆞᄂᆞᆫ곳도잇다ᄒᆞ와우리신문을ᄉᆞ랑ᄒᆞ야구람ᄒᆞ시ᄂᆞᆫ 쳠군ᄌᆞ의게ᄃᆡ단ᄒᆞ야ᄆᆡ우미안ᄒᆞ옵기로지금은분젼인을두고ᄆᆡ일일즉이젼ᄒᆞ며아니젼ᄒᆞ거나늣게젼ᄒᆞᄂᆞᆫ폐가업도록ᄒᆞ란ᄒᆞ오니혹아니젼ᄒᆞ거나혹늣게젼ᄒᆞ거나ᄒᆞᆫ일이잇스면본사로통긔ᄒᆞ여주심을희망ᄒᆞᆸ

본사광고

○본사신문즁에좌긔ᄒᆞᆫ호수를소용ᄒᆞᆯ데가잇서이에광고ᄒᆞ오니누구시던지그즁에아모호수던지가져오시ᄂᆞᆫᄃᆡ로ᄆᆡ쟝에ᄇᆡᆨ젼두푼식드리리다

뎨이호 뎨삼호 뎨ᄉᆞ십호 뎨ᄉᆞ십이호 뎨ᄉᆞ십삼호 뎨오십삼호 뎨오십ᄉᆞ호와뎨오십오호 뎨륙십이호

관보

뎨이쳔구ᄇᆡᆨ오십칠호 연속

○죠왈법부대신김가진화회계원경리지관과평리원지판쟝민병한으로등명젼권공ᄉᆞ를경임ᄒᆞ고외부교셥국쟝유진찬으로관리공ᄉᆞ를경임ᄒᆞ고니부디방국쟝리규환으로관리공ᄉᆞ를샹방이라 신월칠일

○규쟝각학ᄉᆞ리순익ᄉᆞ직소비지닉에소쳥티로회시ᄒᆞ노라 판쳥ᄉᆞ향

렬도원감독강헌규가팔월이십오일에부샹을당ᄒᆞᆫᄉᆞ졍오

○평무ᄉᆞ년 칙령뎨십ᄉᆞ호문관복쟝규칙뎨십이됴즁시힝ᄒᆞᆫ셰뎨외부급례셔원헌셩부판원은광무팔년십월십삼일븟터시ᄒᆞ되판계으로젼임ᄒᆞ거나레임되ᄂᆞᆫ경우라도잉구착용ᄒᆞ오심조들쳥ᄒᆞᆷ의케부표흠이라

뎨이쳔구ᄇᆡᆨ오십팔호 광무팔년십월십오일

셔임급ᄉᆞ령

○임샹화감리셔주임관ᄉᆞ등 창원감리 리태뎡 ○임창원감리셔주임관ᄉᆞ등 종이품 현학표 이샹십월십일일

○임니부디방국쟝셔칙임관ᄉᆞ등 관리공ᄉᆞ 리규환 ○임탁지부랑ᄃᆡ국기슈셔판임관오등 탁지부주ᄉᆞ 인귀쥰

○임탁지부주ᄉᆞ셔판임관륙등 농샹공학교교관 송지만 이샹십월십이일

면졍계 종일품 조병필

○명ᄂᆡ쟝원경셔칙임관삼등 종이품 윤긔졍 ○의원면경 쟝례원쟝례 리봉ᄉᆞ쟝 홍셩우 ○의원면본관 원구단ᄉᆞ졔셔령 졍쳥영 시종원좌시어 조용하

○경임쟝례원쟝례 봉샹ᄉᆞ쟝 홍승두 ○임봉샹ᄉᆞ면화과긔ᄉᆞ셔주임관오등 면셜ᄉᆞ쟝 권병슈 ○임면셜ᄉᆞ쟝셔주임관오등 영셜ᄉᆞ쟝 리용샹

○임영셜ᄉᆞ쟝셔주임관ᄉᆞ등 시종원시종 강봉조 ○임시종원시종셔주임관륙등 졍삼품 김졔슌 ○임돈령원주ᄉᆞ셔판임관ᄉᆞ등 영셜ᄉᆞ주ᄉᆞ 리호졍 ○임영셜ᄉᆞ주ᄉᆞ셔판임관륙등 사직셔령 홍죵환

○임 사직셔령셔판임관오등 종묘셔령 조병억 ○임 종묘셔령셔판임관ᄉᆞ등 티복ᄉᆞ주ᄉᆞ 김죵셕 ○임티복ᄉᆞ주ᄉᆞ셔판임관륙등 리문용

○임시종원좌시어셔판임관팔등 륙품 리병셔

○임원구단ᄉᆞ졔셔령셔판임관ᄉᆞ등 경긔면령 졍지덕

○임경긔면령셔판임관팔등 교방ᄉᆞ주ᄉᆞ 오병션

○임교방ᄉᆞ주ᄉᆞ셔판임관륙등 륙품 졍쳘영

○임관리공ᄉᆞ셔칙임관ᄉᆞ등 ○니부디방국쟝 리규환 ○금임금봉 니부디방국쟝 리규환 이샹십월십삼일

○승셔판임관ᄉᆞ등 니부주ᄉᆞ 리죵환 십월십ᄉᆞ일

잡보

○인감쟝임 한셩관윤ᄇᆡ국ᄐᆡ씨ᄂᆞᆫ인쳔항감리를긔임ᄒᆞᆫ리라ᄂᆞᆫ말이랑자ᄒᆞ더라

○고문관샤 일간에인ᄒᆡᆼ에도착ᄒᆞᆯ(수지ㅣ분수)외부고문관의관사를셔로진츅중인ᄃᆡ역비에ᄉᆞᆫ은팔쳔ᄉᆞᄇᆡᆨ십삼원이오공쟝은일본인모씨가그공쟝으로고빙되기를쳥ᄒᆞ엿다ᄒᆞ더라

○계약언긔 탁지고문관목하뎐씨의계약은졔작일에조인이될터이더니계약셔중에무샹만죡지못ᄒᆞᆫ슈항이잇서일본공ᄉᆞ가승낙지아니ᄒᆞᄂᆞᆫ고로슈일후에ᄂᆞᆫ조인된다더라

○슌찰발힝 각도슌찰ᄉᆞᄂᆞᆫ차츌ᄒᆞᆫ지가여러날이되고만졍지ᄒᆞᆫ다ᄂᆞᆫ말이잇더니일젼에려비를지발ᄒᆞ야쟝ᄎᆞ불일내로발졍ᄒᆞᆫ다더라

○츌츙진보 온양군보교를거ᄒᆞᆫ즉음력구월초오일에대쇼인민이읍즁에회집ᄒᆞ야진보회라칭ᄒᆞᄂᆞᆫ무리들과닙관ᄒᆞᆫ후에진보회인을모다츌츙ᄒᆞ엿다더라

○원구회국 주한일본ᄉᆞ령관은원구경ᄌᆡ씨가참모본부무관으로비임홈은이왕긔ᄌᆡᄒᆞ엿거니와지작일샹오십시에한셩을떠나ᄂᆞᆫ귀국ᄒᆞᄂᆞᆫᄃᆡ젼송ᄎᆞ로한일량국문무관원들이남문외졍거쟝에연락ᄒᆞ엿ᄂᆞᆫᄃᆡ례포를연방ᄒᆞ엿더라

○쳐쳐동학 젼라북도관찰ᄉᆞ면보내에동학당삼ᄇᆡᆨ여명이ᄐᆡ인군에방금둔취ᄒᆞ엿다ᄒᆞ고ᄐᆡ쳔군보고에ᄂᆞᆫ동학삼ᄇᆡᆨ명이본군직ᄉᆞ앙헤회집ᄒᆞ야일졔히단발ᄒᆞ고연쇽ᄒᆞ야작ᄎᆡ로모혀드ᄂᆞᆫᄃᆡ그슈효를알지못ᄒᆞ겟다ᄒᆞ엿더라

○일쟝연ᄐᆡ 작일에졍부에셔각관쟝에통텹ᄒᆞ기를본일이하오삼시에참졍과찬졍과각부대신과참찬과즁추원의쟝과례식원쟝이일본ᄉᆞ령관쟝곡쳔씨를외부로연ᄐᆡᄒᆞ라신 ᄎᆡ분을외부대신이봉승ᄒᆞ와본부에맛덕졋기로통텹ᄒᆞ니조량ᄒᆞ라ᄒᆞ엿더라

○면칙항찰 지작일하오삼시에면의부에셔경남도관찰부에면칙ᄒᆞ기를일본지휘관조회내에ᄃᆡᄒᆞ야 뎐졍평이란두글ᄌᆞᄂᆞᆫ군용샹령시팔요의차용홈이오령구히졈령ᄒᆞᆫ단말이아니라ᄒᆞ엿지경안에다만군용소관은부득이그소쳥ᄃᆡ로ᄒᆞ되도디에소유권과인민에졍치권은외구히ᄎᆞ관이지혀ᄒᆞ여조금도수앙치말것스로각쥐읍에밧벌신칙ᄒᆞ야각근이쥰힝케ᄒᆞ라

○긔쳔진보회 긔쳔군공보에ᄒᆞ기를본월팔일오시에문관이라ᄒᆞᄂᆞᆫ자가진보회라ᄌᆞ칭ᄒᆞ고슙ᄉᆞᄇᆡᆨ명을령솔ᄒᆞ고본군ᄀᆡᆨ사에작엽ᄒᆞ야일졔히단발ᄒᆞ고

쟝구히든ᄎᆔᄒᆞᆫ계교를ᄒᆞᆫ즉쟝ᄎᆞᆺ몃쳔만명이ᄎᆔ당되지안을수업ᄂᆞᆫ고로본도관찰ᄉᆞ가참모부로면보ᄒᆞ야병뎡을파송ᄒᆞ야토멸ᄒᆞ라ᄒᆞᆫ다ᄒᆞ엿더라

○경관피착　작일에충쥬관찰수리승우씨가외부로면보ᄒᆞ기를일본헌병도ᄃᆡ의형이쟈일본군에리도ᄒᆞ엿ᄂᆞᆫᄃᆡ총슌김긔용이가샹민의ᄃᆡ용을구타ᄒᆞ야좌편눈을ᄲᆡ지라경무서에셔김긔용을톄벌ᄒᆞ고방환ᄒᆞ엿더니일인들이본부관뎡에돌입ᄒᆞ야총슌리근병를요청ᄒᆞ야본다ᄒᆞ고인ᄒᆞ야결박착거ᄒᆞ엿다ᄒᆞ엿더라

○묵하죵시　탁지교문관목하뎐씨ᄂᆞᆫ금일부터시무ᄒᆞᄂᆞᆫᄃᆡ히부각국쟝이샹졔관원과모모ᄃᆡ신의게비단등속과필셔조송ᄒᆞ엿더라

○현씨병와　현영운씨의셰력이북촌으로옴긴다홈으로현씨가셩병ᄒᆞ야진고개찬화병원에병와ᄒᆞ엿ᄂᆞᆫᄃᆡ실병이아니요환득환실ᄒᆞᄂᆞᆫ마음으로열즁ᄒᆞᆫ소치로셩병ᄒᆞᆯ셔념녀ᄒᆞ야미리찬벽ᄒᆞᆫ병원에퇴와ᄒᆞ엿다ᄒᆞ더라

○반피착수　경무ᄉᆞ탄셩환씨가법부에보고ᄒᆞ되귀부훈령을졉쥰ᄒᆞ야무안감리한영원을압샹ᄒᆞ로슌검이명을목포로파송ᄒᆞ엿더니ᄒᆡ슌검일명이도망샹리ᄒᆞ야고금ᄒᆞ되ᄒᆡ항감리한영원이법부훈령을시약ᄒᆞ고도리혀슌검일명을착수ᄒᆞ고로본슌검이도타ᄒᆞ야샹리ᄒᆞ엿다ᄒᆞ니엇지이러ᄒᆞᆫ무리ᄒᆞᆫ일이잇슬잇가슌검이명으로ᄂᆞᆫ히감리를압샹ᄒᆞᆯ수업스니엇지조처ᄒᆞ라ᄒᆞ엿더라

○쥭닥리교　일진회에셔회원거쳐ᄒᆞᄂᆞᆫ각리쥬에맘ᄒᆞ기를만일병무쳥에셔포착ᄒᆞ거든본회에곳리교ᄒᆞ면맛당히조처ᄒᆞ리라ᄒᆞ엿다더라

○군슈등급　향일졍부회의에의결ᄒᆞ기를각군슈셔임ᄒᆞᄂᆞᆫ데ᄃᆡᄒᆞ야졍삼품이샹은일이등군으로쥬임관은삼등군으로판임관은병수오등군으로셔임ᄒᆞ기를작뎡ᄒᆞ엿더라

○번궁환후　황태ᄌᆞ비뎐하셰옵셔근일에환후가계신ᄃᆡ졈졈침중ᄒᆞ사부긔가나셧다더라

뎐보

●츄격후보　슈로목로랑일에젼투ᄒᆞᆫ형편에관ᄒᆞᆫ대산만쥬군총ᄉᆞ령관공보가좌와ᄀᆞᆺᄒᆞ니

본계호방면은슈로일에루ᄎᆞ젹군의역습ᄒᆞᄂᆞᆫ거슬격퇴ᄒᆞ엿ᄂᆞᆫᄃᆡ젹군은오젼다셧시붓터퇴각ᄒᆞᆯ즈음조가잇기로아군은목로일에이른아츰브터공격ᄒᆞᄂᆞᆫ형세로도로키엿는지라

한원구면하의평슌ᄒᆞᆫ괴병의대졉ᄒᆞᆫ단은젹군의좌측으로나아가고뎨비ᄃᆡ로ᄒᆞ여공ᄒᆞᆫ란케ᄒᆞ엿슴은이방면의젼황을회복ᄒᆞ기에큰공이잇ᄂᆞᆫᄃᆡ이괴병단은다시젹군의뒤ᄒᆞ로향ᄒᆞ야젼진ᄒᆞᆯᄃᆡ이오

우익군의우죵ᄃᆡᄂᆞᆫ조션령에잇ᄂᆞᆫ우세ᄒᆞᆫ젹군과ᄃᆡ젹ᄒᆞ엿ᄂᆞᆫᄃᆡ응원ᄃᆡ가도착ᄒᆞ엿슴으로그방면의젼황은ᄎᆞᄎᆞ됴케되고동군의즁앙종ᄃᆡᄂᆞᆫ련계산과마이산의일ᄃᆡ를점령ᄒᆞ고우세ᄒᆞᆫ젹군을공격ᄒᆞᄂᆞᆫ즁이오좌종ᄃᆡ의우익ᄃᆡᄂᆞᆫ비상히곤란히싸혼후에젹진의요긴ᄒᆞᆫ방이된소뎐구북방의놉ᄒᆞᆫ싸을졈령ᄒᆞ엿고즁앙군의공격은다셩공ᄒᆞ야망가분에셔호가교기ᄌᆞ의븍방놉ᄒᆞᆫ곳을졈령ᄒᆞ엿고

좌익군의우죵ᄃᆡᄂᆞᆫ목로일아츰에관교보를졈령ᄒᆞ고그젼진ᄃᆡᄂᆞᆫ팔가ᄌᆞ에등ᄃᆞᆯᄒᆞ고다시예비ᄃᆡ의구응을졉ᄒᆞ야황가ᄌᆞ에잇ᄂᆞᆫ젹군을공격ᄒᆞᄂᆞᆫ즁인ᄃᆡ젹군은젼에황화졈에잇든몃죵ᄃᆡ의포병을ᄭᅳᆺᄎᆞ오와강경히항거ᄒᆞ엿스나예비ᄃᆡ와일부가와거슬공격ᄒᆞ야ᄎᆞᄎᆞ됴히진ᄎᆔ가되엿깃고중앙죵ᄃᆡ의츄격ᄒᆞᄂᆞᆫ부ᄃᆡᄂᆞᆫ엄의류슈가ᄌᆞ를졈령ᄒᆞ고츄격ᄒᆞ며젼진ᄒᆞ야목하에ᄂᆞᆫ봉텬부에셔오리쯤되ᄂᆞᆫ사하보를공격ᄒᆞᄂᆞᆫ즁이오좌죵ᄃᆡ이우익ᄃᆡᄂᆞᆫ림셩보를공격ᄒᆞ야그일부ᄂᆞᆫ각리둔과부히소의진ᄃᆡ를졈령ᄒᆞ엿고시로온아군의응원ᄃᆡᄂᆞᆫᄇᆡ일님니엉ᄃᆡ와밋그부근에도착ᄒᆞ엿다ᄒᆞ엿더라

긔셔

최죵괴

셩이우연히동문외에나갓다가도라오ᄂᆞᆫ길에로샹에광경을구경ᄒᆞ오니샨쳔은예와ᄀᆞᆺᄒᆞᄂᆞ물ᄉᆡᆨ은스ᄉᆞ로변ᄒᆞᆫ지라ᄌᆞ연히싱회감동ᄒᆞ와두어줄기눈물이ᄂᆞ림을ᄭᆡ닷지못ᄒᆞ오며셰월이여류ᄒᆞ여사ᄅᆞᆷ은늙ᄂᆞᆫ줄모로게스ᄉᆞ로늙ᄂᆞᆫ지라엇지감ᄀᆡ지ᄉᆡᆼ이ᄉᆞ지아니ᄒᆞ리오대뎌사ᄅᆞᆷ이셰샹에나ᄆᆡ교육이업ᄉᆞ면지식을벌니기어렵고ᄒᆞᆨ문이업ᄉᆞ면분견이업ᄉᆞᆯ지라츙군ᄋᆡ국ᄒᆞᄂᆞᆫ마음도ᄒᆞᆨ문에셔나고슈신제가ᄒᆞᄂᆞᆫ법도ᄒᆞᆨ문에셔나니일노ᄆᆡ암아말ᄒᆞᆯ진ᄃᆡ쳔만ᄉᆞ가모도ᄒᆞᆨ문에셔난즉ᄒᆞᆨ문이업ᄉᆞ면결단코되기어려온지라우리대한은ᄌᆞ고로녀간ᄒᆞᆨ문을슝샹ᄒᆞ야읍풍영월에부허ᄒᆞᆫᄒᆞᆨ문을힘쓸ᄲᅮᆫ아니라그리ᄒᆞᆫᄒᆞᆨ문이나마공부ᄒᆞᆫ사ᄅᆞᆷ이열에ᄒᆞᄂᆞ히못되니엇지ᄀᆞ련치아니ᄒᆞ리오갑오경쟝이후로각국에ᄋᆡᄉᆞ가조곰열녀셔찬대쇼ᄒᆞᆨ교를셜시ᄒᆞ야동셔양ᄒᆞᆨ문을대강ᄒᆞᆨ습ᄒᆞᆫ사ᄅᆞᆷ도잇고ᄀᆡ명이라기회라문명부강이라고도말ᄒᆞ며츙군ᄋᆡ국ᄒᆞ란ᄂᆞᆫ의ᄉᆞ도잇ᄂᆞᆫ듯ᄒᆞ나일노볼진ᄃᆡ엿ᄐᆞᆫ마음그젼에ᄀᆡᆨ갑이쟝야권관으로지내든셩각ᄒᆞ면나ᄒᆞᆫ듯ᄒᆞ나오날날ᄭᆞ지도젼국인민이다아지못홈으로올은ᄒᆞᆫ마음을비치못ᄒᆞ옵더니귀신문사셜이리로교육샹론셜과ᄒᆞᆨ문변으로권면ᄒᆞᄂᆞᆫ말ᄉᆞᆷ이죡히우리이쳔만동포로ᄒᆞ여곰문명실업상진보홈에대단유조ᄒᆞ온지라심히감격ᄒᆞ오며세월은여류ᄒᆞ고젼국인민의문명실업은괴한업시지지완완ᄒᆞ기로감회격발홈을이긔지못ᄒᆞ야두어마디어리석은회포를앙포ᄒᆞ오니용널ᄒᆞᆫ언론을바리지마시고홍　귀신문샹에게재ᄒᆞ여쥬심을앙츅ᄒᆞ노라

잡보

○일엔이퇴　연안으로온사ᄅᆞᆷ의젼셜을드른즉향ᄌᆞ에역부모집ᄒᆞᆯ시에일인이연안읍에와셔역부오ᄇᆡᆨ명을ᄂᆡ라고ᄒᆞᆫᄃᆡ위젼ᄉᆞᆷᄇᆡᆨ명을모집ᄒᆞ야쥬고군슈가역부들과ᄀᆞᆺ치역소ᄭᆞ지가셔역부들을ᄃᆡᄒᆞ야말ᄒᆞ기를우리가이우ᄒᆡ져경에니르럿스니일을속히ᄒᆞ여쥬고가자ᄒᆞ고ᄀᆞ만ᄒᆞᆫᄃᆡ단을륙칠일만에다필ᄒᆞ여도쥬고ᄇᆡᆨ셩을령솔ᄒᆞ고무수히도라왓ᄂᆞᆫᄃᆡ민일일히가도히군슈가쳔히가셔일일히차져역부들은화쥬미조곰도괴한이업시잘도라왓ᄂᆞᆫᄃᆡ그인읍ᄇᆡᆨ쳔군슈ᄂᆞᆫ일인이온다ᄂᆞᆫ말을듯고다라나셔역부모집을일인이마음ᄃᆡ로ᄒᆞ여ᄀᆞᆺᄂᆞᆫ지라역부들의고가도쳐져쥬ᄂᆞᆫ사ᄅᆞᆷ이업스ᄆᆡ괴한이심ᄒᆞ고미만얼마엇고ᄀᆡᆨ셩반ᄃᆡ단히ᄒᆞ엿다더라

○슈평쥬본　작야에군슈쥬본이되엿다ᄒᆞᄂᆞᆫᄃᆡ함열에젼광무　은진에쟝ᄒᆞ식　파산에ᄇᆡᆨ남쥰　후함열에뎡희셥　이원에김종즁　고원에류병훈　옥구에김종응제씨라더라

○공ᄉᆞ외관은　니쟝원감등리쥰영씨ᄂᆞᆫ등명젼권공ᄉᆞ를피명ᄒᆞ고졍삼품리휘창씨ᄂᆞᆫ한셩판윤을피임ᄒᆞ엿더라

○셩대소조　신샹훈씨의친산이충청북도단양군에잇더니도적이광을파고두골을가져가고루서ᄒᆞ되젼괴만량을가져오면두골을도로ᄃᆡ령ᄒᆞ리라ᄒᆞᄆᆡ로쇼조ᄒᆞ야신샹훈씨가망ᄒᆞ겨ᄒᆞ엿다더라

○론산진회통문　공쥬관찰ᄉᆞ가론산진보회에셔광고ᄒᆞᆫ통문을등보ᄒᆞ엿ᄂᆞᆫᄃᆡ그젼문이좌ᄀᆞᆺᄒᆞ니

대뎌ᄂᆞ라의근본은ᄇᆡᆨ셩이오ᄇᆡᆨ셩의근본은... 지ᄒᆞ고ᄇᆡᆨ셩은지물에모히고지물은토디에셔나ᄂᆞᆫ고로ᄇᆡ로붓터인민의산업을졍졔ᄒᆞ고국가ᄂᆞᆫ경용을조회홈이오직뎐토에잇ᄂᆞᆫ지라비록촌토쳐ᄃᆡ라도다국가의강토라인민을ᄆᆡᆺ겨쟉농ᄒᆞ야그부세를나라에온젼히샹납ᄒᆞᆫ연후에인민은지물리여졍업고나라에ᄂᆞᆫ온젼ᄒᆞᆫ부세가잇슬쎄라이런고로녯젹에ᄂᆞᆫ명뎐법이잇셧고각국에ᄂᆞᆫ뎐토를셔로ᄆᆡᄆᆡ홈이업스되유독우리나라ᄂᆞᆫ국가강토를ᄉᆞᄉᆞ로셔로ᄆᆡᄆᆡᄒᆞ야도죠밧ᄂᆞᆫ거시셰랍보다여러비가되ᄂᆞᆫ고로부쟈ᄂᆞᆫ더옥부ᄒᆞ고빈ᄒᆞᆫ쟈ᄂᆞᆫ더옥빈ᄒᆞ니ᄇᆡᆨ셩의지물이엇지졔ᄎᆔᄒᆞ며젼국부세를엇지폐ᄒᆞ리오이제맛일뎐토졔도를경쟝치아니ᄒᆞ면반다시인민과나라히난보홀경우에일으리니뎐답에ᄉᆞᄉᆞ로ᄆᆡᄆᆡᄒᆞᄂᆞᆫ법을혁파ᄒᆞ고그부세ᄂᆞᆫ신셕ᄃᆡ로탁지로샹납ᄒᆞ고그세젼인즉미결에샹랍ᄒᆞ샤분명ᄒᆞ야　공비부로슈랍홈ᄎᆞ로심샹부인민이발론ᄒᆞ야회샤를셜시ᄒᆞ야경부훈령이불구에ᄒᆡᆼ회ᄒᆞ겟기로녈니고시ᄒᆞ니이르ᄂᆞᆫ곳마다ᄎᆞᄎᆞ젼셜ᄒᆞ야무론경향인뎐답ᄒᆞ고도조를미리츌급지말아셔후회홈이업게ᄒᆞ라ᄒᆞ엿다더라

○가평동도　근일가평군에동학수ᄇᆡᆨ명이둔취ᄒᆞ야잇다더라

○뎨국신문　일젼에일본군ᄃᆡ에셔졍지식힌뎨국신문은쳐음브터슌국문으로츌간ᄒᆞᄂᆞᆫ고로부인들과한문모로ᄂᆞᆫ사ᄅᆞᆷ들이모다보기를됴와ᄒᆞ야ᄀᆡ명샹에그효험이젹지안터니근일졍보된후로ᄂᆞᆫ그신문보던부인들과한문모로ᄂᆞᆫ사ᄅᆞᆷ들이ᄆᆡ우ᄎᆞᆷ졀ᄒᆞ고익탐히녀인다더라

○화약슈거　공쥬산셩에셔리ᄇᆡᆨ년을류치ᄒᆞ엿든화약여셧궤를일병이다가져갓다더라

○탈문입표　공쥬병정과일인간에괴로된ᄉᆞ단으로일병이나려가셔공쥬ᄃᆡ병정의총과탄환을몰수히슈탐ᄒᆞᆫ후에일병의말이우리게이총과탄환을맛기ᄒᆞᄂᆞᆫ뜻스로표를써나라ᄒᆞᄂᆞᆫ고로ᄃᆡ위관이표를써쥬엇다더라

광고

TELEGRAMS.

Tokyo, Oct. 17.

Marquis Oyama reporting on the 16th inst. stated that the centre of the right wing and the main body had ceased firing. The left wing were still canonading.

The detachment under Major-General Yamada attacked the Russian position at Santaoku-tzu and succeeded in capturing 1 field gun and 2 ammunition wagons.

THE WORLD'S OLDEST POLICE REPORT.

The oldest and what is probably the longest police report in the world is that preserved in the department of Egyptian antiquities at the British Museum. The papyrus, which measures seven feet six inches in length and 1 foot 2 inches in breadth, is written in a bold hand in the hieratic or priestly script. The subject of the document is a report sent in by the police of Thebes concerning some robberies of the royal tombs committed in the fourth year of Rameses III., about 1,200 B.C. It appears from what this document tells us that for some time the tombs of the kings had been systematically robbed, and the objects found, or rather stolen, were resold for other burials. For a long time no notice was taken of these thefts, but when at last the thieves actually attacked the pyramids of the early kings Rameses ordered a proper inquiry. The chief of the police, Paibek-en Amen, was called, and he with some other officers laid wait for the plunderers, four of whom were caught redhanded. The reason for robbing the tombs of the kings and nobles was, no doubt, the general bad condition of the country at the time. The long wars of Rameses II. had drained the temple treasury, and the poverty of the temple affected all classes. It must, on the other hand, have been common knowledge that great stores of gold, silver, and jewels were buried with the dead, and doubtless in remote times there were not a few who regarded this as wasted wealth. The tombs offered therefore a ready means of obtaining money or its equivalent. Among those arrested were many who, by their official positions, knew where to put their hands on the richest tombs, for we are told in the papyrus that the police captured not only shoemakers, oilboilers, and washerwomen, but also a priest of the god Ptah at Memphis, a Royal scribe, a prophet, and a number of singing women attached to the various temples. We are further informed that many of them would not confess their guilt until they had received a number of strokes with the bastinado. The police, however, were considerably assisted by the confession of one of the gang, who "split" on his companions because he had not received what he considered his proper share of the spoil.

The offices of the unfortunate Chekuk Sinmun are visited daily by Japanese gendarmes.

General Hasegawa and staff were the guests of the Foreign Office at a reception held at 3.30, yesterday afternoon.

An audience with His Majesty has been arranged to take place at 4 P. M. to-day, for the Messrs. Hayashi and Megata.

People entering or leaving the city by the East Gate are now subjected to a rigorous inspection by the Japanese gendarmes stationed there.

The Kamni of Chinnampo reporting the result of the investigation of the Koksan affray, states that 7 Japanese and one interpreter were killed during a riot occasioned by the Japanese attempt to secure coolies for Manchuria.

MAN-HATING CLUB COMING.

If the supernatural revelations communicated through Mrs. McWhirter, late of Washington, come to anything, England will shortly have a branch of the Washington Man-Hating Club established in its midst. The Washington Man-Hating Club is a real community with over one hundred members and a capital of £20,000. It was established by a widow, Mrs. Martha McWhirter, and three elderly women friends, who left their homes in a body to live together in a large, specially built club. Around them they gathered many adherents with money, and before her death recently it was "revealed" to the chief organiser that she or her successors must establish branches in the chief cities of the world. The members of the club are forbidden to see or speak to any man. They are not allowed to engage in any form of religious worship. Absence of definite religious tenets is one of the principles on which the community is founded. The young members—some of them are children—have never been permitted to go to school, lest they learn something about marriage and family life. They are never allowed to have a cent to spend, because money might get them into mischief. All of the work is done by the members, including the raising of fruit and vegetables for the table and the making of butter from cream furnished by three or four cows. Most of the cooking is done by the three young women. Some of the members are milliners and others dress-makers. One is a dentist, another a shoemaker, and yet another a physician. Thus the club is to a great extent self sustaining.

While ferrying railway material across the river at Na Rim Po, a boatload of Japanese and Korean coolies capsized. Two Koreans were drowned.

A rather "tall" story comes to us from Kongchu, whence it is said the Japanese have removed six cases of gunpowder, which have been stored there for several hundred years!

Charged with cutting telegraph poles and wires near Galveston, Texas, an unsophisticated Mexican pleaded that he watched them for months, saw nothing go over them, and concluded that they were of no use.

The Governor of Hamheung telegraphs that the Japanese Military authorities have forbidden wood-cutting and mining operations in that district unless their special permission has previously been obtained.

Mr. Rudyard Kipling's new book of short stories will be published by Messrs. Macmillan this month. Its contents are more than 20 short stories and verse pieces, which he has recently written. Most of them have appeared in the English and American magazines, and are now revised. The book is already being translated into several foreign languages.

The Postmaster-General of the United States is credited with the ambition to establish penny postage between America and Europe. If he succeeds we may safely assume that universal penny postage will quickly follow, for Frenchmen and Germans and Englishmen would be unlikely long to tolerate the absurdity of charging twopence-halfpenny for letters exchanged with one another, while letters sent all the way across the Atlantic were only charged a penny.

To judge from the telegrams of M. Marcel Hutin, says a London paper the destruction of the "Novik" has aroused a good deal of deplorable recimination at the Admiralty. Admiral Skrydloff is being severely blamed for having given the three cruisers of the Vladivostock squadron the order to join the Port Arthur fleet. Admiral Alexieff is held to be the person chiefly responsible, but Admiral Skrydloff is censured for not having taken command of the fleet.

DISTURBANCE AT CHOONG CHONG.

The Governor of North Choong Chong reports that Japanese workers accompanied by a Korean interpreter passed through his district on the 17th inst. The interpreter was most overbearing in his manner and eventually struck one of the citizens with a stick, blinding him in one eye.

The local police arrested the interpreter, punished him by flogging and then released him. Shortly afterwards he returned with some Japanese, who seized the sergeant of police, trussed him with ropes and carried him away.

The Korea Daily News.

Issued at 5 P. M. daily except Sundays.

Rate of Subscription :—

Per Year,	Yen 25.
Per Quarter,	Yen 7.
Per Mouth,	Yen 2.50.

Postage in Korea not charged extra.
Postage abroad charged extra.

Advertisements, 50 sen per day for 1 inch or less.
5 yen per month per inch.
50 yen per year per inch.

All communications to

E. T. BETHELL,
Editor and Publisher,
Pak-tong, Seoul.

AFTER THE WAR.

Prognosticators are already looking forward to the termination of the war, and expounding their views on the political situation which will arise at the end of the struggle.

The St. Petersburg correspondent of the "Daily Telegraph" has voiced the opinion that a triple alliance between Russia, Germany and Japan will be one outcome of the war. His opinion is based on the absurd rumour that the Kaiser has already sounded the Czar's advisers on the desirability of concluding peace with Japan on terms favorable to such an alliance.

The San Francisco "Chronicle," commenting upon this rumour, remarks:

"What may be in the minds of the European crowned heads or the influential members of the Old World governments affecting their political relationships is a close secret which is certainly not communicated prematurely to newspaper correspondents, and this suggestion of a new triple alliance established on such extraordinary lines is surely premature.

The same journal, taking the supposition that Japan will be successful in the war, draws its readers attention to the "Independence and Integrity" statements made so frequently by Japanese statesmen.

"The chief significance of the suggestion of probable important changes in international alliances at the close of the war is that the opinion is gaining ground in Europe that Japan's avowed object in going to war merely to protect her own independence and preserve the integrity of China is likely to undergo a material modification in the event of her final triumph over Russia. It is unreasonable to suppose that the freeing of Manchuria will not arose in the Japanese people an irresistible ambition for territorial expansion. She has already practically established a protectorate over Korea, which is the entering wedge to future sovereignty. If she succeeds in forcing Russia to evacuate Manchuria she will doubtless claim the littoral, if not the whole province as the legitimate fruits of conquest, on the simple and indisputable pretense that China is incapable of protecting it and maintaining her sovereignty there. She retained the Liaotung peninsula and the fortress of Port Arthur at the close of the war with China as a condition of peace, and did not relinquish possession until Russia, Germany and France brought pressure to force her out. And with all of her past professions of concern for the preservation of China's territorial integrity, it is not at all improbable that Japan will claim the right to retain the territory which has cost her so much money and so many lives to wrest from Russia, and will thus take the initiative in the actual partition of the Chinese empire. Europe is evidently forecasting this result, on the ground that circumstances will be apt to excite, if it should not warrant, a change in Japan's policy."

Rear-Admiral Gieve, who was formerly well-known in far-eastern waters when he commanded the Russian battleship "Petropavlovsk," has now been appoined to the command of the naval defences in the Baltic Sea.

PORT ARTHUR DIARY.

(CONTINUED FROM YERTERDAY.)

INCIDENTS AT THE CENTRE OF THE LEFT WING.

From about 1 P. M. to 2 P. M. the enemy's guns, to the number of about 8, appeared on the south of Wangkiatien and at least 2 companies of his infantry attacked our position on Kensan. A brisk exchange of rifle-fire ensued. At about 4:30 P. M. the enemy, being re-inforced, began to advance, but our first line of infantry, assisted by artillery and machine guns, repulsed him. At about 6:20 P. M. some four of the enemy's guns coming into action on the highlands westward of Tashihtung, opened a heavy fire on the first line of our central column. By 7 P. M. his force gradually retired, along the whole front, towards Tapehshan, but his guns retained their position. At 8:30 P. M. about a battalion of his infantry, with band playing, advanced from the direction of Tapehshan. The troops of our first line, leaving only a small force on either flank, made a counter-attack, and the enemy retired before the cheers of our men charging. The force sent by the enemy on this day against our central column consisted of about 2 battalions, 12 field-guns and 2 or 3 machine-guns. They remained during the night on the hills from the east of Tapehshan to those on the east of Wangkiatien.

INCIDENIS AT THE LEFT OF THE LEFT WING.

At 5.20 A. M. our outposts on the hills northward of Laotsushan observed signs of the enemy's advance, and at 6 A. M. about two single companies of his infantry appeared on a 195-metre hill and one double company on a 127-metre hill whence they exchanged shots with our troops. Between 1 and 2 P. M. he received re-inforcements and our outposts returned to the main position. A 3:50 P. M. about two double companies of his in close order discended the northern saddle of Laotsoshan and began to advance. Our artillery near the 312 metre hill opened heavily on the force, and the enemy, falling into disorder, retired. At 6.30 P. M. about a battalion of his infantry, deploying on the hills south of Laotsoshan, opened fire; and 15 minutes later at least 4 of his guns, appearing upon this ridge, cannonaded our left battalion heavily. Our artillery replying, silenced the enemy's guns, but throughout the night the enemy firmly held the position he had taken up during the day.

July 4th.—Right Wing—At 5 A. M. a double company of the enemy's artillery appeared on the highlands some 1,000 metres north of Chakau, and opened fire on our scouts at Wuchayingtsz and northward of that place. Our men replied. At 9 A. M. two double companies of the enemy advanced from Chakau village and occupied a hill some 2,000 metres south of it, whence they opened fire on our position. Simultaneously a company of his on the height north of the village fired heavily on our position on the hill west of Pantau, our men replying. A fierce exchange of shots took place. A 9:40 A. M. the artillery of the right column of our left wing opened on the enemy on the hill south of Chakau. His troops now took cover behind the ridge and did not again advance. Night fell on these conditions. At 11:20 P. M. a detachment of the enemy from the direction of Muchiugi and Nankau made a night attack against our position westward of Pantau, but was at once repulsed.

"Right Column of Left Wing.—At 7:30 A. M. a company of the enemy's infantry appeared on the heights eastward of Nanchakau and another company on a 1,500-metre hill at the south east of the same place. They began to entrench. A battalion of our artillery—less one battery—opened on them, and they at once sought cover behind the ridge. At the same time about 4 of the enemy's guns begun to fire on our artillery from the Antszling direction. Our artillery, taking up a masked position, devoted itself chiefly to cannonading the enemy's infantry. Under these conditions night fell. On this day the enemy had at most one battalion on our front, at Antsziing he had apparently at least 4 new pattern quick-firers and 6 old-pattern.

INCIDENTS AT THE CENTRE.

"Between 1 and 2 P. M. one or two companies of the enemy twice essayed attacks against Kenzan but were repulsed by our troops.

At 6 A. M. a battalion and a half of the enemy's infantry advanced against Kenzan and the left of our position (a hill some 3,000 metres southeast of Kenzan). Our infantry and artillery opened a heavy fire to check this advance. About 8 of the enemy's guns which were already posted on the western Wangkiatien ridge came into action. By 7 A. M. the enemy in this quarter had increased to about 3 battalions, and these were deployed at a distance of from 800 to 1,000 metres in front of our line of defenses, whence they exchanged shots with our men, while their artillery fired heavily from its position of the previous day upon our artillery and upon Kenzan. At 7.30 A. M. some two companies of the enemy advanced from the Tashihtung direction. Therefore at 8 A. M. our reserves moved towards the west of Chuchwantszkau. Between this time and 11 A. M. the enemy made several attempts to advance, but being checked by our men's heavy fire, could not achieve their purpose. By noon the force of the enemy in our front had risen to about 7½ battalions, and he had still another regiment on the west of Kenzan. At 1, 20 P. M. 2 batteries of our artillery which had been on the eastern base of Kenzan changed position to the southwest of Chuchwantszkau and took post on a hill 1,500 metres high where they were out of range of the enemy's rifles. At 3.50 P. M. the enemy's artillery again opened heavily against Kenzan and his infantry made repeated attempts to advance, but being strongly opposed by our men, could not effect their purpose. Nevertheless, the enemy's artillery on the eastern highlands of Maotankau, southwest of Wangkiatien, and on the south of Antszuling, firing at a distance of 6,000 metres, showed such accuracy and their time-fuzes were so well set that our guns had a hard time, and our skirmishers on these highlands found much difficulty in holding their positions. Moreover, the enemy increased to some 10 battalions his force in front of our centre and, besides, his ships made their appearance and opened fire on our left. The fight became very heavy; at 7 P. M. our reserve infantry advanced towards Chwangkiatun, and placed themselves under the direction of the officer commanding the Left Wing. Moreover, three batteries of heavy guns which had just arrived upon the field were pushed forward to Pantau, and two other batteries of the same calibre to the east of Tashangtun on the Hwangni River, where they took up position and aided our centre while a naval landing party with heavy guns posted itself near southern. Shahakau and came into action. That night the enemy bivouacked on the ground and throughout the whole night there was no cessation of rifle-fire, At about 11 P. M. an uncertain force of his infantry attacked Kenzan but was repulsed.

"Left Wing,—At 6 A. M. our guns opened on the enemy's artillery position on the northern ridge of Laotseshan. The enemy replied twice or thrice and then desisted. Nevertheless his infantry, deployed along the whole ridge on the north of the hill, fired heavily upon our first line. At 11:30 A. M. about a battalion of his artillery advanced from the west towards Laotseshan. Our reserves were therefore moved up into the firing line. At 3 P. M. his strength was reinforced and the fight beame hot. At 5 P. M. his guns on the north of Laotseshan again came into action and the gun-fire and rifle-fire on both sides was very hot. At 5 P. M. several of the enemy's ships appeared in the neighbouring sea and opened on our position, causing us much embarrassment. Nevertheless his infantry, some 3 battalions, did not venture to move down the heights and advance.

The Korea Daily News.

VOL. I, TUESDAY, OCTOBER 18, 1904. No. 79

大韓每日申報
대한미일신보

(뎨팔십호) (슈요일) 일쳔구빅사년십월십구일

본샤고빅

본신보는영어와한어로석거미일츌판ᄒᆞᆸ

신문가

한쟝 엽두돈오푼

일삭됴 엽두량닷돈

우표가미삭닷돈

다맛돈으로밧습

광고료는

긔한의쟝단과ᄌᆞ힝의다쇼로즁감ᄒᆞ되렴가로밧을터이오며오리지아녀대한사람마다다이신문을보실터이니광고내시기를원ᄒᆞ시는이들은우리신문샤에와셔면약ᄒᆞ심을희망ᄒᆞᆸ

○발힝소 박동대한미일신보샤법어학교압헤전영국인셜필림집자리오

샤쟝 영국인 (비셜)

평양 티리점

○평양효동사는권미보씨로우리신문관미티리인을ᄐᆡᆨ졍ᄒᆞ엿ᄉᆞ오니평양에계신구람코져ᄒᆞ시는 쳠군ᄌᆞ는히티리졈에왕림ᄒᆞ와면의ᄒᆞ시옵

샤고

○우리대한미일신보의목덕은대한의안녕질셔에관한모든뎨목에티ᄒᆞ야는공평한변론을쥬쟝홈이라우리통신원의탐보는신문보시는쳠군ᄌᆞ의게ᄒᆞᆼ샹보도ᄒᆞ리며편지를긔셔ᄒᆞ여주시는이는셩명과반디를젹어붓치시기를회망ᄒᆞ오니이거슨신문샹에긔지ᄒᆞ라는거시아니오다만극히신용ᄒᆞ는증거를숨고쟈홈이라긔쟈는아모긔셔던지긔ᄌᆞ홈을되각ᄒᆞ는권리를가졋스나되각ᄒᆞ는리유를말홀터이오며공즁평화를문란케ᄒᆞ는듯ᄒᆞᆫ긔셔는의례히밧지안켓습나이다

●본샤셜시이릭로신문을미양우례로분젼ᄒᆞ와례젼부의임의의로젼ᄒᆞᄃᆞᆺ스로면곳에는혹늣게젼ᄒᆞ기도ᄒᆞ며혹몃칠거슬ᄒᆞᆫ겁에젼ᄒᆞ기도ᄒᆞ며혹아니젼ᄒᆞ는곳도잇다ᄒᆞ와우리신문을ᄉᆞ랑ᄒᆞ야구람ᄒᆞ시는 쳠군ᄌᆞ의게디ᄒᆞ야미우미안ᄒᆞ옵기로지금은분젼인을두고미일일즉이젼ᄒᆞ며아니젼ᄒᆞ거나늣게거나ᄒᆞᆫ폐가업도록ᄒᆞ라ᄒᆞ오니혹아니젼ᄒᆞ거나혹늣게젼ᄒᆞ거나ᄒᆞᆫ일이잇스면본샤에통긔ᄒᆞ여쥬심을희망ᄒᆞᆸ

본샤광고

○본샤신문즁에좌긔ᄒᆞᆫ호수를소용홀데가잇셔이에광고ᄒᆞ오니누구시던지그즁에아모호수던지가져오시는디로미쟝에빅젼두푼식드리리다

뎨이호 뎨삼호 뎨이십호 뎨이십이호 뎨ᄉᆞ십호 뎨ᄉᆞ십삼호 뎨오십삼호 뎨오십ᄉᆞ호와뎨오십오호 뎨륙십이호

관보

뎨이쳔구빅오십팔호 련속

궁뎡록ᄉᆞ

○의졍부찬졍민샹호ᄉᆞ직소비지닉에소청을병의시ᄒᆞ노라

○닉부특진관윤용션걸슈훈ᄒᆞᆷ을 비지닉에경이원로대신으로다년근고에긔렴홀거시일이건이아이니훈위에승셔홈이경의게ᄉᆞ졍둡이아니오또한현대훈ᄒᆞ관합이근력에칙임이아닌즉한양홈에방히가업슬지라경은다시번거이ᄉᆞ양치말라

○학부대신고영회ᄉᆞ직소 비지닉에번거이ᄉᆞ양치말고더욱ᄉᆞ무를힘쓰라

이샹십월십ᄉᆞ일

셔임

○임의졍부찬졍셔칙임관일등 륙군참쟝 박졔슌

○임동신원총관셔칙임관일등 륙군참쟝 민샹호

이샹십월십삼일

뎨이쳔구빅오십구호

광무팔년십월십칠일

셔임급ᄉᆞ령

○겸임총령ᄉᆞ관 평리원판ᄉᆞ 리샹뎐

○겸임령ᄉᆞ관 외국어학교교관 죠원규

○임령ᄉᆞ관셔쥬임관ᄉᆞ등 졍삼품 리병우

○임탁지부지무관셔쥬임관ᄉᆞ등 학부참셔관 죠한벽

이샹십월십일일

○승셔관임관삼등 평리원쥬ᄉᆞ 김우균

○임탁지부쥬ᄉᆞ셔판임관오등 탁지부량디국기슈 안귀쥰

○임탁지부량디국기슈셔판임관륙등 리즁필

이샹십월십ᄉᆞ일

궁뎡록ᄉᆞ

○죠왈동지돈령원ᄉᆞ 민영린으로특명젼권공ᄉᆞ를겸임ᄒᆞ고닉부디방국쟝리규환으로관리공ᄉᆞ를겸임ᄒᆞ라

십월십삼일

○조왈짐이경의게찬양지임을줌이엇지우연홈이리오이간우혼때를당ᄒᆞ야덕망잇는신하가좌우에도읍지아니ᄒᆞ면엇지유지ᄒᆞ리오경의청명과즉졀을짐이ᄉᆞ모ᄒᆞᆫ지오랜고로젼후에간졀이권면ᄒᆞ엿거늘경은ᄒᆞᆼ샹칭병ᄒᆞ니나라에간우홈을월시ᄒᆞ고일향향리쳐홈을고집홈이즁도가아닌지라곳조뎡에나와짐의소간지우를[illegible]계홀ᄉᆞ로디방관을보니여찬졍최익현의게젼유ᄒᆞ라

십월십ᄉᆞ일

○교육부총감륙군부쟝훈일등신리지용근 쥬ᄒᆞ되면동무관학교를본월팔일에젼동별영피복창으로이졉홀뜻스로지위ᄒᆞ옴이엇더ᄒᆞ올지근 쥬ᄒᆞ와봉 지의쥬ᄒᆞ라

○교육부총감륙군부쟝훈일등신리지용근 쥬ᄒᆞ되본부를본월십삼일젼렬도원으로신접홀뜻스로근 쥬ᄒᆞ와봉 지의쥬ᄒᆞ라

십월십삼일

○평안남도관찰ᄉᆞ리즁하ᄉᆞ직소 비지닉에다시번거히ᄉᆞ양치말고관찰의칙임을더힘쓰라

○경무ᄉᆞ량셩환조희소 비지닉에이곳치말ᄒᆞᆯ지말나

○탁지부쥬ᄉᆞ김병규가본년칠월십이일에부샹을당ᄒᆞᆫᄉᆞ

○탁지부쥬ᄉᆞ오치길이가본년구월일일에모샹을당ᄒᆞᆫᄉᆞ

잡보

○검찰ᄒᆞᆫ입 김셩당고긔덕국금광에ᄉᆞ무를귀관ᄒᆞ기위ᄒᆞ야금광금찰관을셜치ᄒᆞ고농샹공부로셔관인을파견ᄒᆞᆫ지우금여러ᄒᆡ에ᄒᆡ광세금은젼연히슈랍ᄒᆞ는거시업고월급만허비ᄒᆞ더니농샹대신리도지씨가졍부회의에졔출ᄒᆞ고금찰관을일병히임ᄒᆞ엿다더라

○차산피취 이쳔군츌쥬디에셔동학피슈삼명을착슈ᄒᆞ고기여는다효유ᄒᆞ여ᄒᆡ산식혓는디슈일리로는오쳔젹에진보회인이라는사름삼빅여명이회집ᄒᆞ엿다더라

○량씨폐현 작일하오ᄉᆞ졈에일본공ᄉᆞ림권죠씨가탁지고문관목하면죵티랑씨를티동ᄒᆞ고폐현ᄒᆞ엿더라

○곡산민요샹보 삼화감리가외부로보고ᄒᆞ되곡산민요ᄉᆞ에슌검을파송홈은임의보고ᄒᆞ엿거니와ᄒᆡ슌검회고닉에당초에ᄒᆡ군에셔인부팔빅명을모집ᄒᆞ는디남북면에졀반식분비ᄒᆞ고로북면에셔먼져ᄉᆞ빅명을모집ᄒᆞ야보낸즈음에남면빅셩최조범김경로량인이수빅인민을령솔ᄒᆞ고북면모군의젼왕ᄒᆞ는길을막어왈이곳치시힝ᄒᆞ면필경고을이업셔지고말지라이거시동ᄉᆞ빈의작간인즉누리등이곳동ᄉᆞ롤타살ᄒᆞ는거시가타ᄒᆞ엿더니동ᄉᆞ비가듯고일인의게무고ᄒᆞ되곡산인수쳔명이각지롱쟝ᄒᆞ고그디등을타살ᄒᆞ라고ᄒᆞᆫ다ᄒᆞᆫ즉일인등이발금돌츌ᄒᆞ야빅셩과셔로쳐셔일인칠명파동ᄉᆞ일명은피ᄒᆞ고일통ᄉᆞ일명은도쥬ᄒᆞᆫ지라ᄒᆡ군셔리군슈가평산남쳔일인병참소에젼왕ᄒᆞ야고급ᄒᆞᆫ즉ᄒᆡ병참에셔병뎡이빅명과헌병오십명을파송ᄒᆞ야군슈를옹위ᄒᆞ며관문을파슈ᄒᆞ야사름출입을금ᄒᆞ는디슌검이간신이군슈를드러가보고훈령을도부ᄒᆞᆫ즉디답ᄒᆞ되본군슈슈하에셔긔가업셔보고를못ᄒᆞ니이리유를감리의게티품ᄒᆞ라ᄒᆞ며북면빅셩최김량인은임의착슈ᄒᆞ엿다ᄒᆞ더라ᄒᆞ고ᄒᆞ엿더라

○박ᄉᆞ시취 학부에셔경의문디에응셔ᄒᆞ는각도유싱을초집ᄒᆞ야음력본월십륙일부터일도식졔술ᄒᆞᆫ시권을시취ᄒᆞ야박ᄉᆞ에붓쳔다더라

○엄속북민 닉부에셔함경남북도로훈령ᄒᆞ기를인민이혹회

AMERICAN KOREAN ELECTRIC COMPANY.

Light and Power.

Main Office: Electric Building, Chong No.

RAILWAY DEPARTMENT.

OPERATING CARS BETWEEN EAST AND WEST GATE, EVERY TEN MINUTES:—
First Car leaves East Gate at 6:30 A. M. First Car leaves West Gate at 6:55 A. M.
Last Cra " East Gate at 10:40 P. M. Last " " West Gate at 11:00 P.M.

OPERATING CARS BETWEEN EAST GATE AND IMPERIAL TOMB TERMINUS, EVERY TWENTY MINUTES:—
CONNECTING WITH EVERY ALTERNATE CAR ARRIVING AT EAST GATE FROM CHONG NO.
First Car leaves East Gate for Tomb at 6:50 A. M.
" " " Tomb for East Gate at 7:10 A. M.
Last " " East Gate for Tomb at 9:50 P. M.
" " " Tomb for East Gate at 10:10 P. M.

OPERATING CARS BETWEEN CHONG NO AND YUNG SAN (RIVER) EVERY TWELVE MINUTES:—
First Car leaves Chong No for South Gate at 6:48 A. M.
" " " Chong No for Yung San at 7:24 A. M.
" " " South Gate for Chong No at 6:56 A. M.
" " " Yung San for Chong No at 7:57 A. M.
Last " " South Gate for Chong No 11:00 P. M.
" " " Yung San for Chong No at 10:11 P. M.

SPECIAL PRIVATE CARS FURNISHED TO SUIT CONVENIENCE OF PATRONS. PRICES ON APPLICATION AT HEAD OFFICE.

LIGHTING DEPARTMENT.

Where less than 250 candle power of light is used, the rate per month will be: Per 16 candle power incandescent lamp,—All night.—Yen 2.50.
Per 32 candle power incandescent lamp:—All night:—Yen 4.00. Per 50 candle power incandescent lamp:—All night:—Yen 6.00.
" 150 " " " " —" " 10.00. " 1200 " enclosed arc " " " " 20.00.
Where more than 250 candle power of light is used, a Meter will be installed, if requested:—Rent of Meter Yen 2.00 per month. Rate of charges by meter reading:—Two Sen per Ampere per hour. (Approximately this is equal to about One Sen per 16 C. P. lamp per hour) Minimum monthly charge where meter is installed, Yen 20.00 per month, which includes rental of meter.
Estimates for installing lights furnished on application. An assortment of chandeliers always on hand.

AMUSEMENT DEPARTMENT.

ANIMATED PICTURES AT EAST GATE
Every evening - - - Except Sunday.
From 8 to 10 P. M.

10 Cents:—Gen. Admission:—10 Cents. Seats in First Class Section. 15 Cents Extra.

Change of program each week. Pictures from Foreign Lands. Pictures of Local Scenes:—Amusing and Instructive.

An entertaining evening for a reasonable price.
MERRY-GO-ROUND:—At East Gate.
From 10:00 A. M. till 11:00 P. M.

5 Cents a Ride.

Take your Exercise on The Galoping Horses.

Comfortable seats in the Chariots.

한셩뎐긔회샤

한미뎐긔회샤 고불안 보사떡 고백
도ᄒᆞ옵나이다
샹 동사진뎐람소와목마운ᄎᆞ장셰도ᄆᆡ
여러뎐차가온쟝안으로통힝ᄒᆞ여ᄃᆞ니여이
삽
또이긔계에곳처노헙헌ᄒᆞ고뎌혼마차도잇
삽
코미우편ᄒᆞ고또조미잇는뎌혼운동이되겟
이뎌혼모형혼달나아는믈을ᄐᆞ고워틱치안
더가는흔번ᄐᆞ는데오젼셔이오
미일샹오열시브터하오열ᄒᆞᆫ시ᄭᆞ지ᄒᆞ옵고
목마운동쟝은동대문안에잇삽고
가되겟삽
쳠군조와계갑도싸고져녁에뎌흔쇼일거리
미잇고구경ᄒᆞᆯ반ᄒᆞᆫ거시오니
서양사진과대한과온동양사진ᄐᆡ대단조
는뒤
젼이옵고미쥬일에사진을싼것ᄉᆞ로다밧고
고젼탑되금은하등에십젼이오샹등에이십
일외에는미야에여덜시브터열시ᄭᆞ지ᄒᆞ옵
활동사진뎐람소는동대문안에잇삽고 ᄇᆡᆸ요
회팍부

All Cars Run Direct to the Animated Pictures and Merry-Go-Round.

집ᄒᆞ거나 벌괴를 휴티ᄒᆞᄂᆞᆫ쟈 잇거든 엄금ᄒᆞ라 ᄒᆞ엿더라

○참졍운례 참졍신긔션씨ᄂᆞᆫ 례임ᄒᆞᆫ다ᄂᆞᆫ 운운지셜이 잇다더라

○우리립표 온양군슈가 보고ᄒᆞ기를 음력본월초이일에 일본인 수명이 또 온쳔에 리도ᄒᆞ야 다시 표목을 세운다 ᄒᆞᄂᆞᆫ 고로 셔긔를 보니여 엄금ᄒᆞᆫ즉 뒤답ᄒᆞ되 일본인망호독지가 본국공ᄉᆞ와 샹의ᄒᆞ고 표목을 세움이라 ᄒᆞ고 맛츰니 듯지 아니ᄒᆞ니 엇지 죠쳐ᄒᆞᆯᄂᆞᆫ지 회시ᄒᆞ라 ᄒᆞ엿더라

○삼면원류 작일에 창원항인민등의 면보가 니부로 리도ᄒᆞ엿스되 세면보가 일시에 도착ᄒᆞ엿ᄂᆞᆫ뒤 ᄒᆞ기를 본항감리 리티명이 도임ᄒᆞᆫ 이리로 교셥을 공평이ᄒᆞ고 항민의 게션졍을 만히ᄒᆞᆷ으로 항민이 안업ᄒᆞ더니 이졔 례임되미 ᄌᆞ모일은 것ᄀᆞᆺ흔지라 뎐폐에 쥬달ᄒᆞ고 본감리를 인임ᄒᆞ야 민심을 편안케ᄒᆞ라 ᄒᆞ엿다더라

○현장실족 현참장의 세도가 일죠에 변동ᄒᆞ야 원동모씨가 로복구가 되막 현씨의 심화병이 졸발ᄒᆞ야 그 젼평계병의 참병이 되엿ᄉᆞᆫ즉 아모커ᄂᆞᆫ 권리를 회복ᄒᆞ야 그 병이 회싱ᄒᆞ리라더라

○삭발항의 령남류싱 허식씨등이 졍부에 장셔ᄒᆞ기를 신체발부ᄂᆞᆫ 부모씨 바든 비라 감히 닷치거ᄂᆞᆫ 샹ᄒᆞ게 못ᄒᆞᆫ다 ᄒᆞ엿거ᄂᆞᆯ 엇지 삭발을ᄒᆞ고 복장을 닙으리오 각하ᄂᆞᆫ 보필지좌에 잇셔셔 션왕문물이 젼연히 업셔지ᄂᆞᆫ 것슬 당장목도ᄒᆞ야 보면셔 그러ᄒᆞᆫ 의론을 한번도 항론ᄒᆞᆯ싱각은 업시 안져셔 그도야가ᄂᆞᆫ 것만 보고 잇스니 불승아혹ᄒᆞᆫ지라 아모조록 큰 의론을 발ᄒᆞ야 뎐폐에 상쥬ᄒᆞ고 례식원장졍을 혁파ᄒᆞ고 외교관의 삭발ᄒᆞ고 긔복ᄒᆞᆫ다ᄂᆞᆫ 관제를 병불시ᄒᆞ고 졍치지술을 강구ᄒᆞ여 차차문명지역에 나가던 하만국으로ᄒᆞ여곰 대한의 졍치가 엇더케 발달된줄을 알게ᄒᆞᆷ을 쳔만복망이다 ᄒᆞ엿더라

○간예광삼 함흥관찰ᄉᆞ 리헌경씨 뎐보에 ᄒᆞ기를 본부에 쥬차ᄒᆞᆫ 일본병참쇼에셔 죠회ᄒᆞ되 함흥졍평영흥고원문쳔등군에 광산처굴과 삼림작벌을 본병참소에 통표아니ᄒᆞ고ᄂᆞᆫ 못ᄒᆞ리라 ᄒᆞ니 엇지ᄒᆞᆯ지 시복ᄒᆞ라 ᄒᆞ엿더라

○참지시민 곽산군슈가 보고ᄒᆞ기를 털도소용에 통나무를 곽산션쳔량군ᄉᆞ이에 잇ᄂᆞᆫ 리림포인운ᄒᆞᄂᆞᆫ뒤 량군빅셩이 부역ᄒᆞ다가 히포쥬류에셔 복션ᄒᆞ야 일인과 한국민팔명이 침몰ᄒᆞ엿다가 룩인은 뉘가구확ᄒᆞ고 본군민소장년등이 명은슈즁세치소ᄒᆞ엿스니 졍경이 참혹ᄒᆞᆫ고로 보고ᄒᆞ니 특별히 휼면을 ᄂᆞ리라 ᄒᆞ엿더라

○리씨유지 평북통신을 거ᄒᆞᆫ즉 젼쥬ᄉᆞ리슌긔씨ᄂᆞᆫ 운산미국금광에 고용으로 잇ᄂᆞᆫ뒤 흥샹긔명에 유지ᄒᆞ야 힘쓰ᄂᆞᆫ지라 히디에셔 도영어ᄉᆞ립학교를 셜시ᄒᆞ고 민간ᄌᆞ뎨를 교육식여 지식을 발달케ᄒᆞ고 미양경졀을 당ᄒᆞ면 인민의게 통지ᄒᆞ야 집집이 국긔를 달아 경축ᄒᆞᄂᆞᆫ 뜻슬 표ᄒᆞ게ᄒᆞᆫ다 ᄒᆞ더라

○츙찰보고 츙쥬관찰ᄉᆞ 리승우씨가 니부로 보고ᄒᆞ기를 본부하 본군대초원파룡원두쟝시ᄂᆞᆫ 경셩과 령남을 관통ᄒᆞᆫ 대로에 잇ᄂᆞᆫ 큰쟝시라 근일에 단발ᄒᆞᆫ 슈샹ᄒᆞᆫ류가 만히 회즁으로 간다ᄒᆞ고 히쟝시를 과거ᄒᆞ엿다ᄒᆞ며 또 히면쟝의 보고를 졉ᄒᆞᆫ즉 엇더ᄒᆞᆫ 사룸 ᄉᆞ십칠명이 룡원쟝시에셔 단발ᄒᆞ고 방을 붓치고 갓다ᄒᆞᆫ즉 심히 피이ᄒᆞᆫ 고로 졍탐을 보니여 샹담ᄒᆞᆫ즉 그 당류가 음죽쟝호원쟝터에 취회ᄒᆞ야 미일이 삼십명식 입참ᄒᆞ야 발셔 수빅명이 취집ᄒᆞ엿ᄂᆞᆫ뒤 각기 단단발ᄒᆞ며 쟝시를 또 차단니며 연셜ᄒᆞ야 만히 입회ᄒᆞᆷ을 권면ᄒᆞ되 보국안민ᄒᆞᆯ 쥬의라ᄒᆞ나 ᄌᆞ연 셔로 동ᄒᆞᆷ이 되야 형세가 졈졈 ᄌᆞ만ᄒᆞᄂᆞᆫ 고로 방쟝 병뎡을 파송ᄒᆞ야 로포ᄒᆞ며 히산케 ᄒᆞ라ᄒᆞᆫ다 ᄒᆞ엿더라

○청환총슌 츙쥬부총슌 리근비씨가 일병의게 피착됨은 작보에 긔지ᄒᆞ엿거니와 히ᄉᆞ건에 ᄃᆡᄒᆞ야 외부에셔 일공관에 죠회ᄒᆞᆫ뒤 긔를 경무ᄉᆞ 공문을 졉ᄒᆞᆫ즉 츙쥬관찰ᄉᆞ 면보니에 일본헌도티일힝이 리도ᄒᆞ엿ᄂᆞᆫ뒤 동ᄉᆞ 한국인 김긔용이 가 쥬막쥬인 엄덕용을 구타ᄒᆞ야 눈을 씩임으로 경청에 호소ᄒᆞ야 히동ᄉᆞ 김긔용을 티벌ᄒᆞᆫ 소로 일병등이 관찰부에 돌입ᄒᆞ야 총슌 리근비를 구타ᄒᆞ고 결박ᄒᆞ야 가홍병참으로 착거ᄒᆞ엿다ᄒᆞ니 히동ᄉᆞ 김긔용이 사룸의 눈을 씩임이 심히 불법ᄒᆞᆷ이어늘 엇지 귀국병뎡이 경셔에 돌입ᄒᆞ야 경관을 착거ᄒᆞᆯ줄 뜻ᄒᆞ엿스리요 또 한동히ᄒᆞᆫ지라 청컨뒤 히병참에 신칙ᄒᆞ야 히총슌을 방환ᄒᆞ고 김긔용을 우리 법ᄉᆞ로 압송ᄒᆞ라 ᄒᆞ엿더라

○강경진보회 공쥬관찰ᄉᆞ 심건택씨가 니부로 면보ᄒᆞ기를 방금 본부면보ᄉᆞ 공보를 졉ᄒᆞᆫ즉 진보회 삼빅여명이 또 림피군황등장으로셔 온진강경포에 리도ᄒᆞ야 날마다 ᄌᆞ만ᄒᆞᆫ다 ᄒᆞ엿고 또로 셩군슈 셔리의 군쥬로 치보ᄒᆞᆫ니 긔에 진보회즁으로셔 투합ᄒᆞᆫ ᄉᆞ의ᄂᆞᆫ 황실을 보안함이니 부랑훈루 명으로 지목ᄒᆞ지 말나ᄒᆞ엿고 여셜ᄒᆞᄂᆞᆫ ᄉᆞ의ᄂᆞᆫ 졍부를 박론ᄒᆞᆷ이 온뒤 만단효유ᄒᆞ여도 되거치 아니ᄒᆞᆫ다 ᄒᆞ엿다 ᄒᆞ엿더라

뎐보

대산총ᄉᆞ령관공보

○봉텬방면젼투속보 기일

뎨일 우익군방면

한원궁면하에셔 령솔ᄒᆞᆫ 신일죵뒤ᄂᆞᆫ 금료일미명에 티ᄌᆞ하좌편연안와룡촌 (본계호에셔 동으로 이리반되ᄂᆞᆫ) 부근에셔 젹군파교젼ᄒᆞᄂᆞᆫ즁이오 본계호로문ᄌᆞ령의 관에 잇ᄂᆞᆫ 젹군은 금료일오젼 열ᄒᆞᆫ시부터 퇴각ᄒᆞᆷ을 시작ᄒᆞ미 본계호지뒤ᄂᆞᆫ 츄격ᄒᆞ며 젼진ᄒᆞ엿고 우익군의 우죵뒤ᄂᆞᆫ 목료일밤 세로ᄒᆞᆫ시에 다른부뒤의 구응ᄒᆞᆷ을 엇어 용밍ᄒᆞᆫ 젹군을 뒤젹ᄒᆞ여 토문ᄌᆞ령에셔 북으로 일리남젹ᄒᆞᆫ 조션령에 진터ᄒᆞᆯ 확실히 유지ᄒᆞ고 동군의 좌종뒤ᄂᆞᆫ 동일오젼일곱시즘에 니르러 화산파밋그 북방일뒤의 놉흔곳을 졈령ᄒᆞ엿고 중앙종뒤ᄂᆞᆫ 목료일밤에 로분ᄌᆞ령에셔 북으로 오려되ᄂᆞᆫ 고산둔동북방의 놉흔 쌍부근의 일뒤를 졈령ᄒᆞ고 좌죵뒤의 뎨일션은 동일아츰아홉시즘에 시고산의 놉흔곳을 졈령ᄒᆞᆫ듯ᄒᆞ며 니대강요량긴뒤 우익군방면의 젼투ᄒᆞᆫ 형편은 금료일아츰에 니르러 일단승리ᄒᆞᆫ 형편이 되엿고

뎨이 중앙군방면

중앙군은 금료일아츰이뤼로 연뒤게셔 동북으로 ᄉᆞ리되ᄂᆞᆫ 동산에셔브터 호가유잔에 ᄭᆞ지니르ᄂᆞᆫ 북방일뒤의 놉흔곳을 졈령ᄒᆞᆫ 고련속ᄒᆞ야 공격ᄒᆞ며 젼진ᄒᆞᄂᆞᆫ즁이오

뎨삼 좌익군방면

우익죵뒤의 쥬력은 금료일오젼열ᄒᆞᆫ시즘에 황화졈의 동북놉흔곳을 졈령ᄒᆞᆫ듯ᄒᆞ고 중앙종뒤ᄂᆞᆫ 동일아츰닐곱시즘에 사하의 남방놉흔곳을 졈령ᄒᆞ고 그 일부뒤ᄂᆞᆫ 잔구ᄌᆞ에 잇ᄂᆞᆫ 젹군을 공격ᄒᆞ야 대포십문을 탈취ᄒᆞ엿ᄂᆞᆫ뒤 젹군은 혼란ᄒᆞ야 동북방으로 퇴각ᄒᆞᆫ지라 좌죵뒤ᄂᆞᆫ 동일아츰이릭로 사하보의 셔부에 잇ᄂᆞᆫ 젹군을 공격ᄒᆞᄂᆞᆫ즁이라 ᄒᆞ엿고

론셜

젼쟁이후형편

세샤를 예료ᄒᆞᄂᆞᆫ 사람들은 싸홈결국될 일을 판찰ᄒᆞ고 쟝챳 졍계샹형편이 엇지 될거슬 셜명ᄒᆞ엿ᄂᆞᆫ지라

피득보에 잇ᄂᆞᆫ 데일리텔리그랩신문통신원이 말ᄒᆞ기를 아라샤와 덕국과 일본 세나라이 셔로 동밍ᄒᆞ라 ᄒᆞᆷ은 젼쟁결국이 스사로 될일이라 ᄒᆞ엿ᄂᆞᆫ뒤 이ᄂᆞᆫ 다름이 아니라 덕국황뎨ᄭᅴ셔 아황폐하의 츙고쟈의게 뒤ᄒᆞ야 밍약ᄒᆞᆯ 죠관에 일본으로 더브러 평화ᄒᆞᆫᄌᆞᄂᆞᆫ 조어를 편입ᄒᆞ엿다ᄂᆞᆫ 풍셜이 잇슴으로 그리ᄒᆞᆷ이라 ᄒᆞ엿고 산푸란스코신문에ᄂᆞᆫ 이 풍셜이라ᄂᆞᆫ 말에 뒤ᄒᆞ여 다시 히셕ᄒᆞᆷ이 여좌ᄒᆞ니

구라파뎨왕과 원로즁신들이 셜혹 ᄌᆞ긔나라 졍계샹에 비밀ᄒᆞᆫ 사건이 잇슬것 ᄀᆞᆺᄒᆞ면 신문통신원의게 들리도록 ᄒᆞᆯ리가 만무ᄒᆞᆯ터이오 또ᄒᆞᆫ 이러ᄒᆞᆫ 의젼셔ᄂᆞᆫ 특별히 편셩ᄒᆞ엿슬듯ᄒᆞ다 ᄒᆞ엿고

또 동보에 계지ᄒᆞ기를 일본셔 젼쟁이후에 독립자주ᄒᆞᆫ다ᄂᆞᆫ 말을 일본졍부졔공들이 왕왕히 발구ᄒᆞᆷ으로 그리ᄒᆞᆷ인듯ᄒᆞᆫ뒤 이ᄂᆞᆫ 무타ㅣ라 젼쟁결이 말후에ᄂᆞᆫ 만국약장즁 ᄌᆞ긔나라에 긴요ᄒᆞᆫ 게ᄒᆞᆫᄌᆞ면 ᄌᆞ연히 구라파에도 리롭게 될일이 만흔 고로 방금긔 젼지시라도 당쟝ᄒᆞᆫ 략ᄒᆞᆷ이 니첫재 ᄌᆞ긔나라의 독립을 유지ᄒᆞᆫ 략ᄒᆞᆷ이요 둘지ᄂᆞᆫ 일후 아라사를 승쳡ᄒᆞ드릭도 청국강토에 긴즁ᄒᆞᆫ 변역이 잇슬가 염녀ᄒᆞ야 미리 보존ᄒᆞ라ᄂᆞᆫ 주의로 그리ᄒᆞᆷ인즉 만일 일본이 승쳡ᄒᆞ야 아라사에셔 만주철병만ᄒᆞᄂᆞᆫ 경우이면 도뒤가 발ᄒᆞ기가 비란지사인지라 그ᄯᅢ에ᄂᆞᆫ 일본이 조곰도 의심ᄒᆞᆯ것 업시 ᄌᆞ의로 히안을 요구ᄒᆞᆯ터이요 또ᄒᆞᆫ 청국에 뒤ᄒᆞ야 모든 청구ᄒᆞᆷ이 실로 ᄌᆞ긔가 싸와 항복바든 나라와 갓치ᄒᆞ드리도 청국은 룽히 스사로 나라를 보존ᄒᆞ야 황뎨국권을 유지치 못ᄒᆞ겟ᄂᆞᆫ 고로 의양으로ᄂᆞᆫ 청국으로 더브러 화평이지니ᄂᆞᆫ 것 갓치 ᄒᆞᆯ터이요 또ᄒᆞᆫ 어느 ᄶᅢᄭᆞ지라도 요동반도와 려슌포뒤를 굿게 직히여 아법덕 삼국에 니여 ᄶᅩᆺ칠 ᄯᅢᄭᅡ지ᄂᆞᆫ 한만히 버려둘리가 만무ᄒᆞᆫ지라 일본셔 청국강토보존ᄒᆞ기 위ᄒᆞ야 인명지산을 무수히 허비ᄒᆞ엿슨즉 청국의 졍권을 요구ᄒᆞᆯ듯도ᄒᆞ며 또 청국의로디도 분할치 아니ᄒᆞᆯᄂᆞᆫ지도 오히려 밋지 못ᄒᆞ겟ᄂᆞᆫ지라 구라파에셔들도 일아젼말에 무숨 사건이 싱길거슨 예료ᄒᆞᄂᆞᆫ바인즉 이사건에도 만일 일본이 보중ᄒᆞᆷ이 업슬것 ᄀᆞᆺᄒᆞ면 필경 졍계샹 변역이 될듯ᄒᆞ다고 ᄒᆞ엿더라

TELEGRAMS.

Field Marshal Oyama, on the 15th, reports that the Russian dead found upon the various battle fields are as follows:—350 at Tai-tzu; 1,500 at Lake Pon-chi; 300 at Tai-ling; 200 at Tomon-tzu ling; 800 in the vicinity of Koin-kuko; 600 to the north of Tomen-tzuling; 150 at Min-meong-tzu; 300 at Shao-ta-kao—total 4,200. Thirty guns, 2,000 shells, and 100 Russian prisoners were captured. The Russian killed and wounded from the 10th to the 13th inst. are estimated at over 20,000.

London, Oct. 11.

A telegram from Mukden to St. Petersburg states that an artillery duel was fought all day on Sunday. The Russian right wing and centre were engaged, and the Japanese were everywhere falling back, pressed by the Russians.

London, Oct. 12.

The Russian occupation of Sabepu, midway between Yentai and Mukden, is confirmed. The subsequent fighting cost the Russians less than a hundred casualties, and occurred during a driving dust-storm, to which the Russians had their backs, while the Japanese had to face it.

The weather is intensely cold, and many of the troops are frost-bitten.

[Later information from the Japanese side, shows that the Russian advantage was not long maintained.]

Berlin, Oct. 12.

A report from St. Petersburg says the Baltic fleet has sailed. Admiral Besobrazoff (formerly Commander at Vladivostock) has been appointed to supreme command, and Admiral Haupt second in command.

Berlin, Oct. 12.

Rear-Admiral Greve has been appointed Commander of the city of Vladivostok, and Admiral Jessen Commander of the first Pacific Squadron.

London, Oct. 11.

The strike at Marseilles is over and difficulties are ended. The Messageries Maritimes have resummed all sailings.

London, Oct. 12.

Reuter's St. Petersburg correspondent says the Baltic squadron, consisting of forty-two ships, has sailed from Reval for Libau.

(The distance between the two ports is about four hundred and fifty miles.)

Berlin, Oct. 12.

President Roosevelt has asked the Russian Government what has become of the American mail conveyed by the steamer "Calchas," the vessel which was captured by the Russians and sent to Vladivostok.

[The American mail by the "Calchas," marked as "delayed," was delivered in Kobe some weeks ago.]—Kobe Chronicle.

Later.

Great anxiety prevails at St. Petersburg with reference to General Mistchenko's cavalry, whereof nothing has been heard for two days. This coincides with a Reuter's telegram from Tokyo stating that a Russian Brigade with 2,000 cavalry and two guns crossed the Taitze Ho on October 9th, with the object of striking the position occupied by General Kuroki, but that the Japanese cut off their retreat and hoped to capture the force.

RUSSIAN PLAN TO CRUSH JAPAN.

Mr. G. H. Kingswell, who was one of the chief "Express" war correspondents with the Japanese in the Far East, has just returned to London, having travelled overland from the seat of war across 700 miles of the Great Mongolian Desert and the Trans-Siberian Railway; and, in the course of conversation, he gave a graphic account of his adventures by the way, and some deeply interesting impressions as to Russia's position.

"When I have finished talking," said Mr. Kingswell, "you may call me a pro-Russian if you please, but remember that I am the only Englishman who, in a perfectly impartial frame of mind, has lived with both the combatants, and has returned to England unmuzzled and free to tell the truth.

"It is thought in this country that, because Kuropatkin's advance army in Manchuria has received some heavy blows in detail, Kuropatkin and his men will shortly be wiped off the face of the earth by an immensely superior force.

"Now the ideas of the Russian officers in command of Kuropatkin's army are vastly different from this. They know what you do not know—that, far from being outnumbered, they outnumber the Japanese. But they have carefully and deliberately concealed this fact. What is more, with perhaps few exceptions, no actual Russians have taken any part in the fighting. The advance army which is now at Liaoyang consists of Finns, Poles, and Siberians and Buriats. All these troops are of a vastly inferior quality to the actual Russians, and they will simply cripple the Japanese as much as they can before the real campaign with Russian troops begins.

"Over here the talk of luring the Japanese has become an old tale to be laughed at. But I, who saw the amazing and colossal preparations that have secretly been made to get the Japanese up north, cannot laugh at it myself.

RUSHING TO THE FRONT.

"I have it on the word of an Englishman, who had to assist in their transport, that upwards of 310,000 Russian troops crossed the Baikal Lake between February 8 and July 20.

"It is said here that the Russians cannot send troops down to Manchuria at a greater rate than 800 a day. But I have travelled up the Trans-Siberian line, and sat by the side of the Baikal Lake, and watched the Russian transport system working easily and well, and know this to be utter nonsense. With my own eyes, during the time I was there, I was able to account for an average of 4,100 troops crossing the Baikal Lake daily.

"You wonder what has become of them. Well, at Harbin, for instance, there is a monster army. It was impossible, of course, to gauge the exact numbers, but I should say that there are at least 150,000 men there, and all these men, be it remembered quite fresh and unfatigued, are in excellent spirits. When the Japanese reach them—for they do not intend to take them south—the Japs themselves will be war-worn and weary with marching, and marching.

"On the way to Harbin from China I saw a submarine on a specially constructed car enroute for Vladivostock. At Harbin I was allowed to go anywhere I pleased, and see everything I wished, with the result that I was astonished at the immensity of the army gathered there, the excellent physique of the men, and their splendid morale. Later I went south and met 200 Japanese prisoners going on their way to Tomsk. They were travelling in the same vans used by the Russian troops, and were being fed on the same rations. I also saw the Empress' hospital train, an infinitely finer and better equipped one than any I saw in South Africa.

BOERS FOR RUSSIA.

"Above Moukden I fell in with a party of Boers who had offered their services to the Russian Government as scouts. But they told me the system of scouting there was very different from scouting in South Africa. If the Russians lost a man they sent a company; if the company were destroyed they sent a regiment; if the regiment was turned back they sent forward a brigade; and if the brigade could not manage the business they ordered up a division. On going tack to Harbin I had an extremely pleasant and instructive time with many of the Russian officers there. They were perfectly charming to us, but did not disguise the fact—nor did the soldiers—that they hated England with a bitter hatred. They frankly said that, after they had finished with Japanese, it would be our turn next.

"Speaking of the war they admitted that their artillery was very inferior to the Japanese; in fact, that their field guns were too heavy, and could only fire one shot to every five of those of the Japs. But they are rectifying this, and I myself saw twenty-five new batteries of ten guns each on the way east. The guns were of a modern pattern that looked to me very muchlike Krupp.

"Another weak point seems to me the much-vaunted Cossack. Armed with a futile carbine and a heavy sword, they are simply food for powder. A handful of Boers would romp round them.

"They are physically fine men, but they are not civilised, they cannot even speak Russian. They are, to my mind, quite unfit for modern warfare.

"The Russian officials are at last finding this out, and are now trying to check the evil. But wait until the regular Russian cavalry, which has not yet appeared on the scene, gets into action.

"Everywhere, too, gigantic preparations are being made to feed the army which is pouring so relentlessly and steadily into Manchuria. Everywhere huge depots for clothes and food were in course of construction, and everywhere sidings were being built with the utmost possible speed. It was by the Baikal Lake that I personally checked the rate at which the troops were pouring in, and marked the last section of the railway round the lake in the last stages of construction. When this is finished, the 20,000 soldiers who have been working on it will be released and sent down to the front.

"From what I have seen in Harbin and further south I have returned convinced that, in actual fact, the war is only just beginning.

"Make no mistake. The Russians are simply hanging back. They are slow, but they are sure. All along the 5,000 miles of line I saw camps and troops—countless troops—being drilled and prepared for war.

"I have seen the Japanese troops and I have seen the Russian troops, and I have seen the numbers of both, and the worth of both."—China Review.

The Korea Daily News.

Issued at 5 P. M. daily except Sundays.

Rate of Subscription:—

Per Year,	Yen 25.
Per Quarter,	Yen 7.
Per Month,	Yen 2.50.

Postage in Korea not charged extra.
Postage abroad charged extra.

Advertisements, 50 sen per day for 1 inch or less.
5 yen per month per inch.
50 yen per year per inch.

All communications to

E. T. BETHELL,
Editor and Publisher,
Pak-tong, Seoul

IMPARTIAL STATEMENTS.

In another column we reproduce the statements relative to the war and, in particular, to the facilities for Russian transport via Siberia, made by Mr. Kingswell, who has just returned to London, from Japan and Manchuria, by the Siberian route.

As Mr. Kingswell says, he is the only correspondent, who has been with both armies of the belligerent powers, and who is at liberty to disclose his views and impressions. On that account, his statements carry great weight, especially when taken in conjuction with the views of another correspondent, Mr. Hales, who made the same journey.

The latter gentleman in an article in the London "Daily News" says he is confident that the Russians can put into the field if necessary, an army of a million of the finest troops to be found in the world. Not the raw Siberian levies with which Kuropatkin has until quite recently had to be content, but a million European trained soldiers.

In Mr. Kingswell's reports, we find that the unsatisfactory statements made of the Trans-Siberian railway are entirely false. He says the railroad is working in first class order and during the time he spent in the vicinity of Lake Baikal, he could himself account for the transport to the east of an average of something over 4,000 troops daily. This including also the transport of supplies, etc.

Hitherto any such reports have been pooh-poohed by Japan and her admirers, but as much belief must be placed in the reports of two eye-witnesses, gentlemen of standing and integrity, as in the hearsay stories, which find their way into the columns of the pro-Japanese journals.

We do not rush blindly into the belief that because Mr. Kingswell says it is so Russia must win the war, but we do think that his statements, given impartially are, a direct contradiction to the reports that Russia's military might is a thing of the past, and her power on the wane.

The fact that Kuropatkin has been reinforced so considerably since the battle of Liaoyang as to be able to adopt the offensive, although, as far as we know, unsuccessfully, points to the truth of Mr. Kingswell's statements on the working of the railroad. In one month's time Kuropatkin has, from a position inferior in numbers to the Japanese, attained a command over, if not a superior at least a numerically equal, force to that available by Oyama.

PORT ARTHUR DIARY.

(Concluded.)

July 5th.—Right Wing—At 2.30 A. M. the enemy's infantry advancing from its position of the previous day, pushed on to within about 50 metres of our position on the heights westward of Pantau, but our men drove him back. At dawn he again attacked but failed: at 8 A. M. his rifle-fire slackened somewhat, and at 9 he commenced to retreat, his forces showing occasionally on the heights northeast of Penshihpentsz and Kanhan, but passing altogether out of sight at 1 P. M.

Left Wing's right column.—There is nothing to report in this part of the field.

Centre.—At 2 20 A. M. a force of the enemy charged our two companies on Kenzan in front and on the flank. After a hand-to-hand conflict he was repulsed. At 6.30 A. M. he began to retreat, and at 10 A. M. a force halting on the Tapehshan highlands began to entrench, while the main body continued its withdrawal to the west.

At 10.30 A. M. a company of our infantry advanced for the purpose of recovering a small position on the southwest of Kenzan, but being cross-fired on by the enemy, had to retire with the loss of its commanding officer (wounded).

At 10:40 A. M. the enemy's artillery on the highlands south of Wankiatien opened fire against our first line and especially against Kenzan. This lasted for about an hour and then became desultory.

"Left Wing—From morning the main body of the enemy near Laotsoshan seemed to have retired, his scouts only being visible on the heights, but he was observed to be entrenching on the highlands east of Tapehshan. At 11 a. m. 5 or 6 of his ships appeared off Langwangtung and, until 6 a. m. fired occasionally on our positions at Shwangtungshan and Tashangtien on the Hwangui River.

Under these circmnstances, our army continued to occupy its old positions. That is to say. the right column of the Right Wing held the line from near Antszshan to the heights on the south of Wangkiatien. Its left column held that from near the south of the southern highlands of Wangkiatien to the neighbourhood of Pantu. Our centre held that from the heights on the southeast of Pantau to a point about 2,000 metres south-east of Lannikiao. Our Left's right column occupied the line from the highlands some 3,000 metres south of Lannikiao "via" Kenzan and Tashangtien on the Hwangin River as far as Shwangtingshan. The enemy was posted along a line from near Shwangtaikan "via" the highlands on the north-east of Weipingkan and those on the east of Antszling and Maotankau to Tapehshan.

The movements of the enemy during the above three days were obviously not of a merely reconnoitering or menacing character. It would appear that their plan was to recover Kenzan, which had been taken by us and which was essential to the strength of their line of defences, and further that they hoped to do injury to our Dalny works so as to prolong the life of Port Arthur. But the experiences thus gained by our army as to the efficiency of the enemy's artillery his manner of using it, his dispositions for attack, and his methods of carrying out night-attacks, must be of great service to us in the future.

With regard to the enemy's casalties it is not possible to speak accurately, but reports indicate that they amounted to 300 or 400. He had 13 or 14 battalions in action and at least 24 guns, of which 8 seem to have been the newest pattern of quick-firers.

July 7th.—The enemy in the Antszling quarter worked hard to entrench himself. During the night a detachment of his men attacked our outposts but was repulsed.

July 8th.—The enemy's guns at Antszling opened fire on the right column of our left wing.

July 10th.—We placed 12 of the guns taken at Nanshan on the heights east of Sannikiao and 6 heavy naval guns in a position some 1,500 metres westward of west Chuchwantszkau.

July 12th.—At about 3 A. M. a company of the enemy with machine guns appeared on the left of our position and essayed to attack us, but our men repulsed him. During this day the enemy from time to time cannonaded our position.

July 17th.—About a company of the enemy's infantry appeared at a point 400 metres from the centre of our Left Wing and wasdriven back. Subsequently he came flying the Red-Cross Flag to bury his dead, which we permitted.

July 18th.—The enemy's guns cannonaded the left of our Right Wing as well as the right of our Left Wing.

July 22nd.—It was decided to attack the enemy along the whole line and orders were issued to the various bodies of troops. That night about a company of infantry fired upon our outpost near Tahsistun on the Hwang-in but was quickly repulsed.

July 23rd.—Bodies of our men were sent to selected positions at the centre of the Right and Left Wings.

FIGHTING AT SHWANGTAIKAN AND ANTSZLING.

July 26th.—The army commenced operations as arranged but from early morning a heavy fog impeded us. At 7:30 A. M. the attack commenced. The enemy maintained an obstinate artillery fire which became especially severe at noon on the part of the guns on his right The features of the ground prevented our artillery from exerting its full force, and thus, though our infantry began to advance at noon, they encountered stubborn resistance and barely succeded in occupying at dusk the regions near Yingchingtsz, Pienshihpengtsz and Tapehshan. They here bivouacked for the night.

July 27th.—From 6 A. M. our army resumed the attack. Our artillery opened the action, and the main body of our Right and Centre advanced towards a 2,000-metre hill on the north of Kankau. The enemy did not reply to our guns, but no sooner did our infantry approach than he poured a heavy fire on them, and as the great steepness of the ground rendered it exceedingly difficult to climb, several of our attacks proved unsuccessful. The fighting was severe, but at 3 P. M. our infantry, covered by artillery fire, succeeded with difficulty in capturing one part of the summit, but owing to the desperate resistance of the enemy and the heavy fire he poured on our flanks from neighbouring positions night fell before the whole hill could be seized. It had been a very heavy fight. The Left Wing, again, made its main attack against the 195-metre hill eastward of Papehshan, but owing to the nature of the ground and the dispositions of the enemy, as above described, in addition to the fact that from half-past two P. M. several of his ships appeared near Lungwangtang and heavily cannonaded our Left Wing, the advance of our troops was much impeded. At 5 P. M. we again essayed a forward movement but were again unsuccessful. Therefore a night attack was determined, and at 1 A. M. on the 28th it was delivered from three sides, with the result that at 8 A. M. we occupied the position.

July 28th.—From early in the morning we renewed the attack, and the enemy on the various faces finally abandoning his vehement resistance, commenced to retreat from 9 A. M., so that by noon our troops were in possession of all his positions. We pursued and at a little after 4 P. M. carried out our purpose of occupying the line from Changlingtsz to Yingkashih. The main body of the enemy seemed to retire within the inner enceinte at Port Arthur.

The enemy's position at Shwangtaikan, Atszling and Tapehshan had the advantage of exceedingly steep approaches and were defended by semi-permanent works to which he had devoted some two months' labour. They were defended by nearly the whole garrison of Port Arthur with about 60 guns of which at least 4 were heavy pieces. Reports from various quarters showed that in the 3 days—26th, 27th and 28th—he had about 1,000 casualties, and we took 2 heavy guns, 3 quick-firers and other spoils.

July 29th.—The army remained in the captured positions. It occupied itself reforming its units, making good its supplies of ammunition and reconnoitering the enemy.

The Korea Daily News.

VOL. I, WEDNESDAY, OCTOBER 19, 1904. No. 80

HONGKONG & SHANGHAI BANKING CORPORATION.

Paid-up Capital $10,000,000
Reserve Fund:—Sterling Reserve... 10,000,000
Silver Reserve..... 7,000,000

27,000,000
Reserve Liability of Proprietors... 10,000,000

HEAD OFFICE, HONGKONG.

London Bankers, London and County Banking Company Limited.
Branches and Agencies, London.

Amoy,	Hankow	Penang,
Bangkok,	Hiogo,	Rangoon,
Batavia,	Iloilo,	Saigon,
Bombay,	Lyons,	San Francisco,
Calcutta,	Manila,	Singapore,
Colombo,	Nagasaki,	Sourabaya,
Foochow,	New York,	Tientsin,
Hamburg,	Peking,	Yokohama,

Credits granted on approved Securities, and every description of Banking and Exchange business transacted.

Drafts granted on London and the chief Commercial places in Europe, India, Australia, America, China and Japan.

HOLME RINGER & Co., AGENTS, CHEMULPO.

ON CHEONG & CO., SEOUL.

GENERAL STORE KEEPERS.
Imported provisions, Cooking Utensils Crockery, etc.
FRESH BREAD DAILY.

MITSU BISHI DOCKYARD & ENGINE WORKS, NAGASAKI.

CODE WORD, "DOCK."

A. 1, A. B. C., and Engineering Codes used.

DOCK No. 1 (at Tategami).

Extreme Length .... 523 feet
Length on blocks .... 513 ,,
Width of Entrance on Top...... 89 ,,
,, ,, Bottom.... 77 ,,
Water on Blocks at Spring Tide 26½ ,,

DOCK No. 2 (Mukaijima).

Extreme Length .... 371 feet
Length on Blocks .... 360 ,,
Width of Entrance on Top...... 66 ,,
,, ,, Bottom 53 ,,
Water on Blocks at Spring Tide 22 ,,

PATENT SLIP (at Kosuge).

Can take vessels up to 1,000 tons gross.

THE WORKS are well equipped with the LATEST IMPROVEMENTS, and can execute any kind of work in SHIPBUILDING and MARINE ENGINEERING, as well as in REPAIRING of SHIPS.

The COMPANY'S new powerful steamer OURA-MARU (712 tons, 700 I.H.P.), specially built for SALVAGE PURPOSES, and equipped with necessary gear, is always READY at SHORT NOTICE.

CHARTERED BANK OF INDIA AUSTRALIA & CHINA.

INCORPORATED BY ROYAL CHARTER 1853

HEAD OFFICES:—LONDON.

Paid-up Capital £800,000
Reserve Liability of Shareholders 800,000
Reserve Fund 800,000

Drafts granted upon all the principal places in the world and every description of Exchange and banking business transacted.

E. MEYER & Co., Agents, Chemulpo.

E. MEYER & CO.
Chemulpo.

SOLE AGENTS IN KOREA FOR:
A. T. Morse, Sons & Co's "Fresco" Distemper

In all colours ready for use on walls, Ceilings etc.
and
AVENARIUS CARBOLINEUM

A wood-preserving and antiseptic oil preparation

Against decay, dry-rot, fungus and wood-destroying insects.

A large supply always in Stock.
Prices upon application.

E. MEYER & Co., Chemulpo.

THE ETHODIST PUBLISHING HOUSE,
Little West Gate, Seoul.

PRINTING, TYPEWRITER PAPER
CARBON PAPER, VISITING CARDS
STATIONERY, BOOK BINDING
BOOK PUBLISHERS
AMERICAN SCHOOL BOOKS
SPENCERIAN COPY BOOKS
PEN CARBON LETTER AND BILL BOOKS

S. A. BECK, Manager

HOKURKU DOBOKU KAISHA.

Branch office in Chong Dong, Seoul.
Japanese telephone No. 165

CONTRACT DEPARTMENT.
We can contract to build any building or construction.

MERCHANDISE DEPARTMENT.
We can provide any building material. We have just contracted to build the new Belgian Legation.

DAI-ICHI GINKO.

LIMITED.
(Formerly the First National Bank)

ESTABLISHED 1873

INCORPORATED UNDER PRESENT LAW 1896

Capital - - - - - - - - Yen 5,000,000
Reserve Fund - - - - - 1,500,000

HEAD OFFICE:—TOKIO.

President: Baron SHIBUSAWA.

BRANCHES AND CORRESPONDENTS
In the Principal Cities and Towns of Japan.
Interest Allowed on
Fixed deposits 1 year - - - 6½ per cent
" " 6 months - - - 6 per cent

Special current accounts 1½ sen daily per Y 100
General " " 1 " " 100

M. TANAKA, Manager, Chemulpo

HOLME RINGER & Co.
Chemulpo.

General Merchants and Government Contractors.

Agents for the leading Banks
SteamshipCompanies
and
Insurance Companies

Importers of Merchandise of every description.

KAMEYA & CO.

GENERAL STOREKEEPERS
Chinkokai - - Seoul
(*Established 1895, Tokyo*)

Confectionery, Hams, Canned Goods, Cutlery, Hirano & Tansan Water. Provisions, Gents, Furnishing goods, Toilet Articles, Travelling Bags, Tobacco, Cigars & Cigarettes Kitchen Utensils Coffee, Biscuits.

Fresh Goods always kept in Stock.
Prices Moderate
Please come and inspect our goods

NIPPON YUSEN KAISHA.

JAPANESE MAIL STEAMSHIP CO.

UNDER MAIL CONTRACT WITH THE IMPERIAL JAPANESE GOVERNMENT.

European Line
Regular Fortnightly Service between Yokohama Kobe, Moji, Shanghai, Hongkong, Singapore, Penang Colombo, Port Said, Marseilles, London and Antwerp

American Line
Regular Fortnightly Service between Hongkong and Seattle, calling at Shanghai, Moji, Kobe, Yokohama and Victoria, B. C.

Australian Line
Regular weekly Service betwen Japan Ports and Australia, calling at Hongkong and Manila.
(Above Three Lines Suspended until further notice)

Shanghai Line
Weekly Service between Shanghai and Japan Ports

Korea Line
Service Kobe, Moji, Nagasaki, Fusan, Chemulpo, Coo, Taiku.
S. S. Bahelsberg, 2181 tons.
Service Kobe, Moji, Fusan, Chemulpo, Chinnampo
S. S ARGO, S. S. Ohio.

BORDEN'S CONDENSED MILK CO.
New York, U. S. A.

ALWAYS IN STOCK
Eagle Brand Condensed Milk.
Gold Seal Condensed Milk.
Peerless (Family) Evaporated Cream.
Borden's Malted Milk.

E. MEYER & CO.
Chemulpo, Korea,
Sole Agents

ROYAL INSURANCE COMPANY,
Funds exceed £10,000,000
FIRE
AT CURRENT RATES.
LIFE
REDUCED PREMIUM.
HOLME RINGER & Co.,
Agents, Chemulpo.

HOTEL DU PALAIS
SEOUL.

The only first class Hotel in Seoul. Situated in the centre of the city opposite the palace.

Cuisine under the supervision of an experienced French Chef.

Well ventilated and furnished throughout.

TARIFF UPON APPLICATION

L. MARTIN
Proprietor and Manager

大韓每日申報

대한매일신보

(뎨팔십일호) (목요일) 일쳔구빅ᄉᆞ년십월이십일

본샤고빅

본신보는영어와한어로셔계미일츌판ᄒᆞᆸ

신문가

한쟝 엽두돈오푼

일삭료 엽두량닷돈

우표가미삭닷돈

다맛돈으로밧솝

광고료는

긔한의쟝단과ᄌᆞ힝의다쇼로즁감ᄒᆞ되렴가로밧을터이오며오리지아녀대한사람마다다이신문을보실터이니광고내시기를원ᄒᆞ시ᄂᆞᆫ이들은우리신문샤에와셔면약ᄒᆞ심을희망ᄒᆞᆸ

○발힝소 박동대한미일신보샤법어학교압헤젼영국인셜필림집자리오

샤쟝 영국인 (비셜)

평양 ᄃᆡ리졈

○평양효동사ᄂᆞᆫ권미보씨로우리신문관ᄃᆡ리인을뎡ᄒᆞ엿ᄉᆞ오니평양에계신구람코져ᄒᆞ시ᄂᆞᆫ쳠군ᄌᆞᄂᆞᆫ히ᄃᆡ리졈에왕림ᄒᆞ와면의ᄒᆞ시ᄋᆞᆸ

사고

○우리대한미일신보의목뎍은대한의안녕질셔에관한모든뎨목에ᄃᆡᄒᆞ야ᄂᆞᆫ공평한변론을쥬쟝ᄒᆞᆷ이라우리동신원의탐보ᄂᆞᆫ신문보시ᄂᆞᆫ쳠군ᄌᆞ의게ᄒᆞᆼ상보도ᄒᆞ리며편지를긔셔ᄒᆞ여주시ᄂᆞᆫ이ᄂᆞᆫ셩명과반ᄃᆡ를젹어붓치시기를희망ᄒᆞ오니이거슬신문상에긔지ᄒᆞ라ᄂᆞᆫ거시아니오다만극히신용ᄒᆞᄂᆞᆫ증거를숨고쟈ᄒᆞᆷ이라긔쟈ᄂᆞᆫ아모긔셔던지긔ᄌᆡᄒᆞᆷ을퇴각ᄒᆞᄂᆞᆫ권리를가졋스나퇴간ᄒᆞᄂᆞᆫ리유를말ᄒᆞᆯ터이오며공중평화를문란케ᄒᆞᄂᆞᆫ듯ᄒᆞᆫ긔셔ᄂᆞᆫ의례히밧지안켓숩나이다

●본샤셜시이릭로신문을미양우례로분젼ᄒᆞ와례젼부의임의로젼ᄒᆞᆫ듯스로면곳에ᄂᆞᆫ혹늣게젼ᄒᆞ기도ᄒᆞ며혹몃칠거슬ᄒᆞᆫ겁에젼ᄒᆞ기도ᄒᆞ며혹아니젼ᄒᆞᄂᆞᆫ곳도잇다ᄒᆞ와우리신문을ᄉᆞ랑ᄒᆞ야구람ᄒᆞ시ᄂᆞᆫ 쳠군ᄌᆞ의게ᄃᆡᄒᆞ야미우미안ᄒᆞ옵기로지금은분젼인을두고미일일즉이젼ᄒᆞ며아니젼ᄒᆞ거나늣게거나ᄒᆞᆫ폐가업도록ᄒᆞ라ᄒᆞ오니혹아니젼ᄒᆞ거나혹늣게젼ᄒᆞ거나ᄒᆞᆫ일이잇스면본샤로통긔ᄒᆞ여쥬심을희망ᄒᆞᆸ

본샤광고

○본샤신문즁에좌긔ᄒᆞᆫ호수를소용ᄒᆞᆯ데가잇셔이에광고ᄒᆞ오니누구시던지그즁에아모호수던지가져오시ᄂᆞᆫᄃᆡ로미쟝에빅젼두푼식드리리다

뎨이호 뎨삼호 뎨이십호 뎨ᄉᆞ십이호 뎨ᄉᆞ십삼호 뎨오십삼호 뎨오십ᄉᆞ호와뎨오십오호 뎨륙십이호

관보

광무 뎨이쳔구빅륙십호

팔년십월십팔일

셔임급ᄉᆞ령

○의원면본관 련쳔군슈 리원규 강계군슈 리교셕 고원군슈 홍봉관 평강군슈 죠셩지

○면본관 갑산군슈 리근풍

○임쟝계군슈셔츄임관이등 륙군참령 셔뎡규

○임련쳔군슈셔쥬임관오등 한셩부쥬ᄉᆞ 리의식

○임평강군슈셔쥬임관오등 학부쥬ᄉᆞ 김졍윤

○임의셩군슈셔쥬임관오등 함안군슈 리인셩

○임영평군슈셔쥬임관오등 농상공부쥬ᄉᆞ 셔상봉

임하동군슈셔쥬임관륙등 면환국기ᄉᆞ 박윤셩

○임감산군슈셔쥬임관오등 륙군부위 김승표

○외부번역관셔쥬임관륙등 의학교교관 쟝도

○임법부참셔관셔쥬임관륙등 륙픔 죠희영

○명형법교졍관 회계원경리지곤 궁닉부특진관 김셕규 종이품 리상셜 법부참셔관 윤셩보 죠경구 김락 헌법관양셩소교관 뎡명셥 법부법률긔초위원 죠창호

이샹십월십ᄉᆞ일

○임법부쥬ᄉᆞ셔판임관륙등 륙품 홍지귀

십월십오일

○면징계 졍삼픔、구연쇼 륙품 임빅영

○의원면본관 홍문관시독셔관임관륙등 구픔 김칠슈

○시죵원좌시어셔관임관팔등 박졍리

이샹십월십륙일

○견칙 시죵원봉시 김슈형

○죵견칙 궁닉부쥬ᄉᆞ 김현비

○이쥬일감봉 동리항총슌 쟝진ᄐᆡᆨ

이샹신월십륙일

궁뎡륙ᄉᆞ

○참모부뎨일국쟝현영운ᄉᆞ직소

비지ᄂᆡ에됴리힝공ᄒᆞ라

○즁츄원의관김명슈ᄉᆞ직소

비지ᄂᆡ에소쳥은의시ᄒᆞ노라

○한셩부관윤비국틱ᄉᆞ직소

비지ᄂᆡ에소쳥은의시ᄒᆞ라

잡보

○일쟝북힝 일본사령관쟝곡쳔대쟝이일간발졍ᄒᆞ야원산방면을경과ᄒᆞ야쳥국료양셔지시찰ᄒᆞ고회환ᄒᆞ여한국에쥬차ᄒᆞᆯ터인ᄃᆡ만쥬젼쟁젼후를물론ᄒᆞ고한국각요ᄒᆡ쳐에슈비병숨만명을영구히쥬둔ᄒᆞ기로작뎡이라더라

○진쥬위면 향일에진쥬군면보ᄂᆡ에동학당이취회ᄒᆞ야단발ᄒᆞ고일진회라ᄌᆞ칭ᄒᆞ야졈졈자만ᄒᆞ니파병ᄒᆞ야토멸ᄒᆞ라ᄒᆞᆷ으로본보에긔지ᄒᆞ엿더니이제확보를거ᄒᆞᆫ즉히군슈리용교씨가담도불법ᄒᆞᆫ고로인민이동문ᄒᆞ고회집ᄒᆞ엿더니히군슈가쪄겁ᄒᆞ야량민을비류라고구함ᄒᆞ야거짓면보ᄒᆞᆷ이라더라

○한어교ᄉᆞ 한어학교교ᄉᆞ호문위씨가귀국ᄒᆞ야신고ᄒᆞᆫ고로히학교교ᄉᆞ를속히고빙ᄒᆞᆯ터이라더라

○경긔슌찰ᄉᆞ 참령구연희씨ᄂᆞᆫ경긔슌찰ᄉᆞ를피명ᄒᆞ엿더라

○쟝츙단치제 음력본월십구일은즁뎡일인고로쟝츙단에치졔된다더라

○의지변민 강계참령김유현씨가군부로보고ᄒᆞ엿스되쳥국비도가빈빈히월강ᄒᆞ야작경ᄒᆞ며아국긔병이혹십여명식드러와동셔로셤홀ᄒᆞᄂᆞᆫ고로인민이소동ᄒᆞ야만히이산ᄒᆞᆫ다ᄒᆞ엿더라

○ᄃᆡ금독촉 즁앙에학지부에셔ᄂᆡ쟝원에한화이빅여만원을취ᄃᆡᄒᆞ엿더니현금지졍을졍리ᄒᆞᄂᆞᆫ고로ᄂᆡ장원에셔히ᄃᆡ임을환보ᄒᆞ라고탁지부에ᄃᆡᄒᆞ야불일독촉ᄒᆞᆫ다더라

○평슈불법 평양군슈팽한쥬씨의탐장ᄉᆞ건은젼보에이왕드론ᄃᆡ로긔지ᄒᆞ엿거니와향조에히군민김국보가평리원에호소ᄒᆞ야사보ᄒᆞ라ᄂᆞᆫ히원훈령을히관찰부에도부ᄒᆞᆫ즉삼등군슈로셔피고팽한쥬의장젼이낫낫치뎡사관ᄒᆞ야사질ᄒᆞ미지관뎡에탈로되야발명ᄒᆞᆯ수업ᄂᆞᆫ경우를당ᄒᆞᆫ즉피고팽씨가별구지계를ᄂᆡ여한독ᄒᆞᆫ슌교수십명을가만히보ᄂᆡ여원고된인민등을란타ᄒᆞ고착슈ᄒᆞ엿ᄂᆞᆫᄃᆡ그즁ᄉᆞ인은즁상ᄒᆞ고리국보ᄂᆞᆫ가럿대쌔가절샹ᄒᆞᆯᄲᅮᆫ아니라포승으로목으미여명지경각인고로관찰부에등분고을쳐셔슌검의보호를힘입어당장면ᄉᆞᄂᆞᆫᄒᆞ엿스나종시긔지ᄉᆞ경이어놀피고팽씨마음에ᄂᆞᆫ유위부족ᄒᆞ야리국보를아국동변어라고일본ᄉᆞ령부에무소ᄒᆞ야압송ᄒᆞ엿더니뎐감이쇼쇼ᄒᆞ던지외국병참소에셔도ᄑᆞ무죄ᄒᆞᆷ을알고미구에방송ᄒᆞ엿스며피고팽씨가월젼에또간세비리셕보홍롱셥황셕규와명부지죠가등을각기로슈지화ᄉᆞ십원식쥬어경셩으로보ᄂᆡ여잔홀ᄒᆞᆫ음모를힝ᄒᆞ되원고등을잡류라고모모경각부에무함ᄒᆞ여원고등을일일압샹ᄒᆞ야징치케ᄒᆞᆯ량으로히간세비졔인을망야샹경식혀다ᄒᆞ더라

○덕ᄉᆞ환관 덕국공ᄉᆞ샤의면씨가운산영인금광을시찰ᄒᆞ고일젼에환관ᄒᆞ야여젼히시무ᄒᆞᆫ다고외부에셩명ᄒᆞ엿다더라

뎐보

○봉텬방면젼투속보기이뎨일우익군방면

우익군의우익되ᄂᆞᆫ본계호지ᄃᆡ를ᄃᆡ젹ᄒᆞᄂᆞᆫ토문조령과밋대령부근에잇ᄂᆞᆫ젹군은금요일오후에퇴각ᄒᆞᆫ모양이잇스미동지ᄃᆡᄂᆞᆫ이거슬격퇴ᄒᆞ면셔히계신파가력가방면으로젼진ᄒᆞ고죠션령부근에잇ᄂᆞᆫ군ᄃᆡ의대종ᄃᆡᄂᆞᆫ젹군이퇴각ᄒᆞᆷ을미리알고곳다가리방면으로츄격ᄒᆞ엿고죵

앙중ᄃᆡ와밋좌중ᄃᆡ는련락ᄒᆞ야이고산부근에잇는젹군을격퇴ᄒᆞ야각각사하외깃는진으로전진ᄒᆞ엿고

뎨이중앙군방면

중앙군은금요일아춤ᄇᆡ터로젼면에잇는젹군을셔향ᄒᆞ야북으로격퇴ᄒᆞ고사하에ᄉᆞ돌ᄒᆞ고

뎨삼좌익군방면

우중ᄃᆡ의주력은금요일오후ᄒᆞᆫ시쯤에젹군을격퇴ᄒᆞ야화하젼부근요농혼곳을졈령ᄒᆞ고좌중앙중ᄃᆡ도오후에니르러젹군을격파ᄒᆞ야사하보의남방농혼곳을졈령ᄒᆞ고중앙중ᄃᆡ의일부는좌중ᄃᆡ의일부와련락ᄒᆞ야젹진ᄒᆞᆫ후에오후네시쯤에ᄅᆞᆷ셩보에돌입ᄒᆞ야드ᄃᆡ여졈령ᄒᆞ고인ᄒᆞ야젹군을추격ᄒᆞ는중이라ᄃᆡ략말ᄒᆞ건ᄃᆡ거십일ᄇᆡ터십ᄉᆞ일ᄭᆞ지련속ᄒᆞᆫ젼투는각방면에셔각기우세ᄒᆞᆫ젹군을격파ᄒᆞ고련ᄒᆞ야용밍잇고담ᄃᆡᄒᆞᆫ추격을더ᄒᆞ엿고젹군을중앙과좌익안으로압박ᄒᆞ야ᄭᅢ다ᄅᆞ히만ᄒᆞᆫ손회를주엇고포셩이젼포셩십ᄉᆞ문을탈취ᄒᆞ엿고포로수빅명을획득ᄒᆞ야젼연히고ᄆᆞᆼ격ᄒᆞ는형세와운동을친뢰케ᄒᆞᆯ지라칭찬에버린젹병의시톄수효는아직다셜히아지못ᄒᆞ되이의이천명이상에니른지라장강변ᄃᆡ젹군의손히ᄒᆞᆫ젼부는삼만이상이되겟고또포획ᄒᆞᆫ물픔은우희긔록ᄒᆞᆫ야젼포외에탄약거와쇼총등이다단히만ᄒᆞᆫ불가승수라ᄒᆞ엿고

론셜

◎별론파뎐츄와셔빅리아로지녀셰젼쟝형편을구경ᄒᆞ고본방국으로도라온킹스ᄯᅦᆫ씨의말을드른즉동씨는ᄒᆞᆫᄒᆞᆼ신원인고로ᄌᆞᄐᆞ과진중에셔셔무의칭찬ᄒᆞ신ᄒᆞ며그보는바를ᄌᆞ유로긔록ᄒᆞᆯ셰에쥰ᄒᆞᆫ허가를엇ᄂᆞᆫ등신문사의로동ᄒᆞ야후둥번ᄒᆞᆫ사진이잇게되매셔로와론ᄒᆞ야소상히말ᄒᆞ엿다ᄂᆞᆫ지라

론돈ᄆᆡ일신문에ᄒᆡ일씨의말ᄒᆞᆫ바를게ᄌᆡᄒᆞ엿기로번등ᄒᆞ노니ᄒᆡ일씨가아인의게신용ᄒᆞᆫ바되여젼장에갓가이잇서본즉그곳에잇는신만ᄃᆡ병은세계의쟝병인듯ᄒᆞᆫ지라근일에셔빅리아에셔모집ᄒᆞᆫ구로파트킨장군의오합지중이아니라구라파와안에셔교육밧고병역나온군사이라ᄒᆞ며셔빅리아텰도에준공되엿다ᄂᆞᆫ말은당초하ᄅᆞᆫ자셜인거시잔신ᄒᆞᆫ군사와쳔명과시호ᄒᆞ는중의에는조곰도탐지치못ᄒᆞ게되엿도라ᄒᆞ엿ᄂᆞᆫ지라

이거슨ᄒᆡ씨의분명히목격ᄒᆞᆫ일인즉쟝형무외ᄒᆞᆫ쥬ᄃᆡ리이말과갓ᄒᆞᆫ젼ᄃᆡ아병이승첩ᄒᆞᆯ계챳소되고동안손히가잇셧슨즉형세가쇼ᄒᆞᆫ갑ᄒᆞ엿슴듯ᄒᆞᆫ지라킹스ᄯᅦᆫ씨의말ᄒᆞᆫ바를도연사가아쥬도묘연ᄒᆞᆫ것갓ᄒᆞ면요량이ᄒᆞ에분로ᄒᆞᆷ을익이지못ᄒᆞ야다시군사를더ᄒᆞ야싸홈을도드는거시실로성취치못ᄒᆞᆯ듯ᄒᆞᆫ지라이왕에는하등병졸로하여금일병을ᄃᆡ젹ᄒᆞ엿스되쇼ᄒᆞᆫ이번에도상등병졸이조곰도업는경우이면ᄃᆡ신양총사령관의게는ᄃᆡ단히유익ᄒᆞᆯ듯ᄒᆞ도다

잡보

◎평남진보회 평양관찰ᄉᆞ리중하씨던보니에진보회당이슌안함종강셔제군에곳곳시긔빅명쳔여명식취회ᄒᆞ엿는ᄃᆡ라병고자ᄒᆞᆫ즉병졔가ᄌᆞ식ᄒᆞ겟고아니ᄒᆞ면ᄒᆞᆫ회를금지ᄒᆞᆯ수업스니엇지조쳐ᄒᆞ리오ᄒᆞ엿더라

◎동피괴착 김셩군수김유제씨보고니에본월십팔일에진보회당빅여명이본군읍내에드러와인민의게고시ᄒᆞ는긔로슈로를파송ᄒᆞ야쳥탐ᄒᆞ는조음에일병이그회당을보고슈작ᄒᆞ는ᄃᆡ권회와슈박지방이가비셕ᄒᆞ는지라본관이초치ᄒᆞᆫ즉회당빅여명이각기도망ᄒᆞ는고로일병과슌교가회당십이명을포착ᄒᆞ야문초ᄒᆞᆫ즉밧기가공초ᄒᆞ되본리회쥬사름으로본년팔월에일진회에입참ᄒᆞ엿는ᄃᆡ그목적즉보국안민ᄒᆞᆯ츠평부등긔허ᄒᆞ란ᄒᆞᆯ이라ᄒᆞ엿는ᄃᆡ방가는회슈ᄒᆞ고여당은효유방송ᄒᆞ엿다ᄒᆞ엿더라

◎삭령진회 삭령군보에ᄒᆞ기를본군빅셩과타읍인민합수쳔명이음력본월ᄉᆞ일에본군으로취회ᄒᆞ는고로그ᄭᅵ유ᄒᆞᆫ즉답ᄒᆞᆫ즉ᄒᆞ기를보국안민ᄒᆞᆯ목적으로진보회를조직ᄒᆞ여평셩에셔하회ᄒᆞ엿슨즉본군에도불가불진보회를챵셜ᄒᆞᆯ지라ᄒᆞ고즁민을회집ᄒᆞ고연셜ᄒᆞᆫ후에평셩으로향ᄒᆞᆫ다고ᄒᆞ엿다ᄒᆞ엿더라

◎착피산당 은진론산포에취집ᄒᆞ엿든동학당이회산ᄒᆞᆫ수설을샹문ᄒᆞᆫ즉젼봉쥰포관리산군수박ᄒᆞᆷ린씨가니부훈칙을되되여병포군과슌교등을령솔ᄒᆞ고ᄒᆡ포등ᄃᆡ에젼왕ᄒᆞ야동도거괴삼십명을포착ᄒᆞᆫ즉여당은도주ᄒᆞ엿다ᄒᆞ고탐초에취획ᄒᆞᆫ단ᄉᆞ샹인즉갑쥐에쟝즁비계ᄒᆞ엿든토당이바탐을셔리향응ᄒᆞ는ᄃᆡ고당에등쥭면지단발ᄒᆞ야그도란갈ᄯᅥᆯ을ᄉᆞ논고로문지단발ᄒᆞᆫ고뒤에후회ᄒᆞ야룡곡ᄒᆞ는쟈도만타ᄒᆞ며허동학남명령에크게쓰기를젼봉ᄃᆡ장벙쥬라ᄒᆞ고ᄃᆡ국쟝에쓰기는룡담연월진악포광뎍이라ᄒᆞ고ᄯᅩ쓰기를포덕텬하제챵셩보국안민지ᄃᆡ도티ᄒᆞ씨가ᄒᆞ엿다고이샹ᄉᆞ셜을밧ᄒᆞᆫᄃᆡ로보고ᄒᆞ엿더라

◎훈칙환수 동학괴수김연택이가졍역ᄒᆞᆫ다기슈ᄒᆞ고방송되엿더니근일젼곳이동학이쟝궤ᄒᆞᆷ으로외타가엄지못ᄒᆞ야법부에셔광리원에훈령ᄒᆞ되김연틱을환슈징역ᄒᆞ고속젼을환급ᄒᆞ라ᄒᆞ엿더라

◎니외샹환 외부쿄셥국쟝은평양군수로젼임ᄒᆞ고히군수죠종셔씨는히국쟝으로셔임되더라

◎경변공ᄃᆡ위관 일본공ᄉᆞ가외부로조회ᄒᆞ되룡주진위ᄃᆡ병뎡이우리샹민의게포힝ᄒᆞᆫ일ᄉᆞ는일외우리군ᄃᆡ에서헌병을파숑ᄒᆞ야힝ᄃᆡ위관이인을압샹ᄒᆞ야법셔심문ᄒᆞ엿기로쟝ᄎᆞ히위관등을귀경부당ᄒᆞ자의게로변숑ᄒᆞᆯ터이니기시수범샹등병최윤션등관홍은곳징벌ᄒᆞ고히ᄃᆡ중ᄃᆡ장권즁탁과중ᄃᆡ부리응하는부히ᄉᆞ졸을평일에단속지못ᄒᆞᆷ으로샹당히쳐벌ᄒᆞ기시오ᄒᆞᄃᆡ부리법셔도ᄯᅩᄒᆞᆫ젼칙ᄒᆞ라ᄒᆞ엿더라

◎하필갑죄아 젼경쥬군수김윤란씨는군수지임시범포죄로젼무안감리김셩규씨는빈요수로무안감리한영원씨는빈간녀인화간죄로법부에셔경무쳥에훈령ᄒᆞ야히등삼인을불일압샹ᄒᆞ라ᄒᆞ더니엇지주쳔이되엿던지히부에셔히쳥에다시훈령ᄒᆞ되히히동구란쟝을물시ᄒᆞ라ᄒᆞ엿더라

◎고양션졍비 고양군수리쥬쳔씨는향자에부모졍ᄉᆞ에ᄃᆡᄒᆞ야일인과샹의ᄒᆞ야리쳥ᄒᆞᆷ으로의뎌로등모ᄒᆞ는폐를면ᄒᆞᆷ으로일군이안도ᄒᆞ엿다ᄒᆞ야동군팔면에쳠의숑동ᄒᆞ야히군수의만셰불망이민션졍비를수립ᄒᆞ랴으로면호에젼엽식수렴ᄒᆞᆫ다더라

◎계부료사 탁지부고문관목하뎐씨는작일부터시무ᄒᆞ는ᄃᆡ각국과문부를됴사ᄒᆞ는중이라더라

◎무론교관 한셩ᄉᆞ범학교관ᄉᆞᆼ응뢰씨는학문이붑셩ᄒᆞ랴ᄒᆞ야히교셔긔로챵하되엿다더라

◎비훈순찰 너부에셔경샹도슌찰ᄉᆞ의게비훈ᄒᆞ기를경쥬군수박병익의수실을외쳠쇼샹히사보ᄒᆞ라ᄒᆞ엿다더라

◎주평경보 경무쳥에셔니부로보고ᄒᆞ기를진보회쟝리시영이카도졔포착ᄒᆞ는ᄃᆡ셜효가잇소니졍부에쳥의ᄒᆞ야승등케ᄒᆞ라ᄒᆞ엿더니니부에셔히문을쟉송ᄒᆞ되도졔쟝는거슨신문계졔쳐업ᄃᆡ무슈ᄒᆞᆫ법셜효가잇셧는지그셜효수샹을쇼샹히주명ᄒᆞ야개보ᄒᆞ라ᄒᆞ엿더라

◎협쳔동힝 참모부일국쟝현영운씨는무슈쟝쳐샹수무시졍ᄒᆞ기위ᄒᆞ야일본에젼왕ᄒᆞ랴ᄒᆞ옴션 쳑고가는ᄃᆡ셔엿더라

◎하수괴착고 젼주진위ᄃᆡ참령빅남신씨는무숑수단히지착ᄒᆞ야일본군수령부에셔착거ᄒᆞ엿다더라

◎우일공ᄉᆞ 외부협판리중하씨는젼권공ᄉᆞ를피명ᄒᆞ엿더라

◎위문ᄉᆞ힝계 ... 위문ᄃᆡᄉᆞ권중현씨는음력금월이십칠일송발ᄒᆞᆫ다더라

◎쳥환환리 청국공ᄉᆞ가외부로조회ᄒᆞ기를본국졍뎡쟝군의공문ᄂᆡ에리범윤이가변계에셔ᄌᆞ쥬ᄒᆞ야인명을샹해ᄒᆞ고재산을탈취ᄒᆞᆫ스실을셩쳑ᄒᆞ야죠긔를송교ᄒᆞ엿기죠회ᄒᆞ니히리범윤을곳쇼환ᄒᆞ야변계인심을편안케ᄒᆞ라ᄒᆞ엿더라

◎명거쟝광경 챵원감리가보고ᄒᆞ기를본항에일시군용텰도명거쟝긴츅을금방시역ᄒᆞ는ᄃᆡ항구쪽원이ᄃᆡ번이나번잉ᄒᆞ기로히디단도랭를샹숑ᄒᆞ도보고ᄒᆞᆫ다ᄒᆞ엿더라

◎창민우면 챵원항민인등이작일에수ᄎᆞ텬보ᄒᆞ되루ᄎᆞ텬보에하붕이엇스니복을ᄒᆞ오며바라건ᄃᆡ죠시 텬폐에 ᄌᆞ달ᄒᆞ시고본항회감리ᄃᆡ를뎡씨를잉임케ᄒᆞ라ᄒᆞ엿더라

광고

TELEGRAMS.

Tokyo, Oct. 17th.

The advance ... of the fourth division of Don Co...s arrived at Harbin yesterday.

PORT ARTHUR.

Tokyo, Oct. 16th.

General Stoessel reports that on the 5th inst. the Japanese made a successful attack on the Sin-Hu Kin forts, but were afterwards forced from the position by three companies of sharpshooters. The Japanese used hand grenades for the first time. On the 7th inst. the Japanese increased their artellery strength.

RUSSIAN CASUALTIES.

Tokyo, Oct. 16th.

According to a despatch from St. Petersburg, the Russians estimate their casualties at 15,000. General Gachiouk(?) was killed.

A JAPANESE COLUMN SURROUNDED.

Tokyo, Oct. 18th.

On the 16th, one column, under Brigadier-General Yamada, proceeded to reinforce a detachment of our left wing, which was engaged in attacking the enemy north of Sha-ho-pao, and succeeded in defeating the enemy near Wei-chiao-lo chiao-tzu and capturing 2 field guns and 2 ammunition wagons. After again repelling the enemy at San-tao-kang-tzu, and whilst in the act of retiring to original position, about 7 P. M., they were suddenly surrounded by about one division of the enemy. After a very severe hand-to-hand-fight the detachment succeeded in breaking through the enemy's lines and reaching the orignial position. Meanwhile our artillery lost of their horses and men were compelled to abandon 9 field guns and 5 mountain guns. The enemy in front of our central army has been greatly reinforced. Our casuallies on Sunday were about 1,000.

RENOWNED NAVAL AUTHORITY SPEAKS.

Captain Mahan contributes to the September number of the "national Review" a lengthy article under the title of "Some Consideration of Principles involved in the Present War." He observes that a stage of development has been reached in the camgaign which permits an expression of opinion on leading questions of principle.

"Two things were necessary to Russia—delay, in order to gather her resources, and promptitude in repairing the neglects of the past. Herein appears the importance of Port Arthur; it has obtained delay. The time occupied in the siege has been ample for a Government, which recognised that the whole Japanese movement turned upon the control of the sea, to have dispatched a fleet, which by this time could have reached the scene, and very well might have turned the scale—allowing only for fortune of war. Before this the aggregate of Russian naval force might have been made very decidedly superior to that of Japan, and the problem of bringing the separated sections into co-operation against a concentrated enemy, though difficult, would be by no means hopeless. Success would have ended the war. The Japanese, having this danger staring them in the face, have, I think, seen it more clearly than many of their critics. As shown by the course of the war, by their action, they have recognized that Port Arthur was the key, not only to the naval war, but to the whole campaign, land and sea. It would have been to them an immeasurable calamity had the naval season, already approaching its close, ended with Port Arthur in the hands of the enemy. Amid all the uncertainty in which we are as to the respective numbers of the opposing armies, one thing seems clear, that Kuropatkin up to the present has profited, and continues to profit, by the siege of Port Arthur; and that to a degree which up to the present renders inconclusive the whole Japanese movement against him. They gain ground undoubtedly; but the Russian army continually escapes them. It is not to be believed that leaders with the high order of military intelligence shown by them would permit this had they the power to prevent it. Each successful retreat leaves the Rusian army still an organized force, still "in being;" draws it nearer to its resources, and lengthens its enemy's communications. A naval base is an element of seapower. It may be no less determinative of a naval issue as the fleet itself, because essential to its existence. Port Arthur, as well as the control of the Far Eastern waters, has thus contributed to the demonstration of the influence of sea-power. It has modified thus far the whole tenor of the land operation, and who shall say that even the delay so far procured may not sensibly affect the outcome of the war, even though the place itself shortly fall?"

PROVISIONING PORT ARTHUR.

We have received reliable information that a few days ago a French steamer of some 6,000 tons arrived safely in Port Arthur from an adjoining Port, with a large shipment of live cattle, and also a cargo of provisions, including tinned stuffs and fresh vegetables. There was also a large shipment of flour. During last month any number of junks safely made the port with provisions and ammunition. This is good news for those whose sympathies are with the gallant besieged garrison. Providing these supplies can be maintained, there is good cause to hope that Port Arthur will yet be relieved. There is a theory, not without sound common sense, that the Baltic squadron does not wish to get here until the army under General Kuropatkin commences its advance south. It is confidently felt that Port Arthur can easily hold out till then.—China Review.

It is reported that General Hasegawa intends to make a trip to Gensan, later visiting Manchuria and then returning to Seoul. It is also stated that, during the winter, he will have 30,000 troops under his command in Korea.

The "Jiji" Shanghai correspondent wires under date of October 8 that a steamer, having on board 7,000 tons of ammunition and other military stores, has successfully reached Port Arthur via Manila.

The Foreign Office is in receipt of a complaint from the Chinese Minister that, according to reports from China, Korean soldiers have crossed the Chinese frontier and are committing depredations amongst the peaceful natives.

More than 10,000 figures are depicted in the painting of the Battle of Water-loo just finished by the German artist, Herr von Driesten. The Duke of Wellington is shown in the background of the picture, which is only four feet long.

At Kinsung, the Chin Po Ho-ites were dispersed by Japanese and their leader Pak arrested. His asseverations that his sole object in arranging meetings was to promote the welfare of the country, were of no avail before the magistrate. He now adorns one of His Majesty's jails.

The poor Governor of Pyeungyang is in another quandary. He says that followers of the Chin Po Hoi are collected everywhere and are a great nuisance. He cotinues to say that he intended to send a body of soldiers to disperse the meeting but; "the soldiers will create more trouble than the Chin-Po-Hoi people, but if I don't send the soldiers, the latter won't disperse."

It is reported, states the "Japan Times," that the Japan Red Cross Society has decided to present each of the American lady nurses with a silver box as a mark of appreciation for the valuable services rendered to the Society. For this purpose it is stated that Baron Ozawa, Vice-President of the Society, will shortly proceed to Hiroshima.

Lieut-General Ogawa has been sent back to Japan. He reached Moji on the 9th. It was thought that his wound would have healed without his leaving the army, but the rapid changes of climate in Manchuria interfered with his recovery from the slight concussion of the brain caused by the splinter of shell which struck his forehead. The expectation is that three or four weeks will see him convalescent.

A case of extortion, obtained by use of gruesome management, is told us by a reliable authority. General Sim Sang Hun recently received a letter from a well-known bandit, telling him that the corpse of his father had been unearthed and the skull removed. If the general wished the return of the skull, he must be prepared to hand the sum of 5,000 yen to certain representatives appointed by this robber.

Mr. S. S. Lyon, U. S. Consul at Kobe, who was struck down by an apoplectic seizure some months ago, left Kobe on Monday, says the "Chronicle," in the "Shawmut" for America, being accompanied by Mrs. Lyon and his two young children. Arrangements had been made with one of Dr. McGee's party of nurses, now about to leave for America, to accompany the family and assist in the nursing of Mr. Lyon. During the afternoon the Foreign Consuls at Kobe visited the vessel, in order to say farewell to their colleague and to Mrs. Lyon. It could not be certain, however, whether Mr. Lyon recognized his colleagues, for he is quite helpless and cannot speak articulately, and it is to be feared there is little hope of his recovery.

The Korea Daily News.

Issued at 5 P. M. daily except Sundays.

Rate of Subscription:—

Per Year,	Yen 25.
Per Quarter,	Yen 7.
Per Month,	Yen 2.50.

Postage in Korea not charged extra.
Postage abroad charged extra.

Advertisements, 50 sen per day for 1 inch or less.
5 yen per month per inch.
50 yen per year per inch.

All communications to

E. T. BETHELL,
Editor and Publisher,
Pak-tong, Seoul.

STATEMENTS BY A PORT ARTHUR REFUGEE.

A S.-C. Morning Post representative had an inteview on Sept. 30th with M. Jourinsky, who arrived in Hongkong not long ago after escaping from Port Arthur in a junk and landing at Chefoo. Mr. Jourinsky is a Russian Jew, and a partner in the Moscow firm of contractors, etc., of that name, and a relative of Mr. Ginsburg, and a partner in the well-known Ginsburg firm of contractors. He has been contracting on behalf of his firm for the supply of provisions to the Russian army and fleet. His remarks, therefore, on the provision supply at Port Arthur bear some weight. When he left Port Arthur there was a large supply of rice—some 400,000 piculs, and just before he left, 24,000 tons of flour, brought by German ships, were got into Port Arthur by junks. There are no fresh meat, only the American tinned beef. Of the latter, according to Mr. Jourinsky's opinion, there were about half a million tins. Port Arthur could hold out for some six or seven months so far as provisions were concerned, and reducing rations to the smallest quantity possible, the port could hold out probably for a year. With regard to ammunition, matters were brighter. There was an arsenal which was turning out a full supply of bullets and other requirements, and some time ago, before the investment of Port Arthur, one hundred and forty waggons of shells from Moscow reached the port. There were any amount of rifles in reserve. Again, all the ammunition that was formerly at Newchwang was removed from there to Port Arthur before the Japanese arrived. In taking Port Arthur by assault the Japanese would lose many thousands of men. There were, just outside Port Arthur, some forty forts, all of which were mined, the mines being electrically connected with the town. If the Japanese occupied these forts, the mines would be exploded, and there would be fearful havoc. The mines at each fort were capable of destroying quite a thousand men. When M. Jourinsky left the Port he estimated that there were 35,000 soldiers there. There were many more than that before, but some had been killed, others had died. This number would have been somewhat reduced by the recent fighting. Very few horses were left. There were altogether some two hundred foreigners (Europeans) in Port Arthur, fifty of them being women. There were about 3,000 Chinamen. All the agents of the Siberian railway were there, some members of the Anglo-American Company and the German firm of Kunst and Albers. The business houses, English, German, etc., were flying their flags. M. Jourinsky did not seem to think the Japanese were wise in attempting to take Port Arthur by assault. They would lose 100,000 men in doing so, whilst if they waited quietly the place would be starved out, perhaps in seven months or so, perhaps, if the besieged lived on very spare diet, in a year. There was no fear of ammunition shortage; they could hold out for three years in that respect.

FROM MANCHURIA.

The following, written by Captain Kraspov, a brilliant Russian officer, for the "Kusski Invalid," gives a Russian view of the early state of the campaign:

Terrified by the approach of the Russian and Japanese troops, the inhabitants of the country fled from the towns and villages, left their fields unsown, and, taking as much provisions as they could with them, sought refuge in the hills. Small bands of Chunchuses, incited by Japanese agents, attacked single patrols, Cossacks of the flying post, field messengers, and peaceful country folk who supplied the Russians with provisions and forage. It was almost impossible to buy anything. It became necessary to send squadrons of Cossacks on foraging duty and to pay in the presence of the town and village authorities for all articles procured. The Cossacks having no transport with them when they descended from the hills, were solely dependent on local supplies and both men and horses were obliged to subsist upon food to which they were quite unaccustomed. The inhabitants had no objection to selling supplies to the Russians, but they were obviously afraid of the officials, who had been suborned by the Japanese, or, under the influence of the dzyan-dzun of Mukden, were maintaining strict "neutrality." General R. after a conference of three or four days with the "tifanhuan" of Saimadzin, succeeded in over coming his obstinacy, and the country-folk promised to procure provisions for the troops. During the conference neither the Cossacks nor their horses wanted for food. There was, it is true, a sameness about the food supplied, and there were a few cases of colic among the horses, but on the whole the health of the cavalry force was excellent. It was marvellous spring weather and the mountain streams and rivers were overflowing with water.

During this expedition the Trans-Baikal men learned the art of war practically, and developed into smart scouts. Their first lessons in scouting work were difficult. No reliance could be placed on reports received from the inhabitants of the country. Chance information, personal encounters with the enemy—that was the way to find out about them. The scouts had to be sent on a considerable distance in front of the main body, as the enemy always tried to avoid the Cossacks. Japanese were not dependent only on their scouts for news of the enemy, as the Chinese gave them detailed information on the movements of the Russians.

Scouting was nervous work at first for the young soldiers, who knew not what dangers lurked in front of them, and when to expect a sudden onslaught from the enemy; but, encouraged by their officers, they soon learned to keep cool and collected and to report accurately on everything they saw. The Trans-Baikal Cossack on his small shaggy steed with long overgrown mane, in his gay-coloured shirt and forage-cap with yellow band, with a wild fowl or a black sucking-pig dependent from his saddle, proved himself a famous forager. The one thing he wanted was to be able to speak and understand the language of the enemy. But the Japanese retreated before the Cossack, and rarely gave them an opportunity of coming to close quarters.

In the town of Saimedzin, now almost deserted by its inhabitants, which had been our temporary base and halting-place, some of our people had a merry time of it, though from the hills surrounding the town news was frequently brought of the terrible deeds of the Chunchuses. There were many officers there of different regiments. An evening party was held in a dark Chinese house illuminated by lanterns emitting a strong odour of bean-oil. On the supper-table were placed queer-shaped Chinese bowls and clay spoons. A mixture of steaming rice soup and minced chicken was served out from a large iron tub, which in appearance reminded one rather of hogwash, in taste——But, on active service, one cannot be particular: he who would be too nice in the selection of his viands would starve. The compound was quite good enough for us, and we ate it with keen relish. Then followed tea, sugar being obtained from the Red Cross Society.

At table were seated fifteen officers, clad mostly in grey and white silk shirts and dark-coloured trousers. Across the street, from the mess of the Nerchnisk Regiment, were wafted the stirring strains of the march of the Trans-Baikal Cossacks, played on trumpets.

They spoke about life in St. Petersburg and the gay time they used to spend when encamped at Tsarkoe Selo. Many of them would never return to Russia, but of that they thought little; they were awaiting impatiently the order to advance, and were delighted at the prospect of soon meeting the enemy.

I read lately in one of the St. Petersburg journals a critical article, written by a woman, concerning war and the soldier. A maudlin production it was. The authoress deemed it unnecessary to sympathise with and be proud of the officer, on the ground that the days were passed when the returning warrior was welcomed with hurrahs from the women, and when caps were thrown into the air in his honour. She was sorry only for the soldier. Here, where the officer and soldier lead exactly the same life, clothing and food also being almost identical, where the officer goes into danger leading the soldier, who generally follows him passively, where the officer's whole mode of existence has changed, while the soldier lives much as he would at home, the judgment of the St. Petersburg lady seemed to me simply ridiculous.

Whether the much talked of "yellow peril" is a reality or a chimera the future will show. China follows the course of events with a malicious eye, and is ever ready to extend her hand to the little Japanese. She is afraid of Russia; is afraid of us—us, the officers in dirty shirts, dust-stained trousers, and tattered shoes, sunburnt and war-worn; us—the general in his black tunic with the Cross of St. George about his neck, giving his orders firmly and energetically; us—the cossacks in flapping forage-caps and white, pink, and blue shirts. Whether we die or whether we survive, we shall know here in Manchuria, after undergoing the dangers and vicissitudes of a campgaign, that we have written new pages in the history of the Russian Empire.

Mr. Megata's agreement was officially signed on Monday afternoon.

The Kamni of Masanpo reports that the Japanese have appropriated half the town for their railway depot.

H. E. Herr von Saldern is once more in our midst, having returned from a visit to the American Mines and Neighbourhood.

Another disturbance amongst the country-folk, this time from Masanpo, is reported. Four Japanese workers on the railway have been wounded.

The Kyengsang people are quite in accordance with our views when they tell the Government to pay more attention to political reform that to tonsorial operations.

The sins of the soldiers shall be visited on the officers, is the decree of the investigators of the Kongchu disturbance. The captain and two lieutenants of the local guard as well as the two soldiers who actually committed the assault on the Japanese are to be punished.

The Korea Daily News.

VOL. I, THURESDAY, OCTOBER 20, 1904. No. 81

大韓每日申報

대한미일신보

(뎨팔십이호) (금요일) 일쳔구빅사년십월이십일일

본샤고빅

본신보는영어와한어로셔계미일츌판ᄒᆞ옴

신문가

한쟝 엽돈오푼

일삭료 엽돈량닷돈

우표가미삭닷돈

다엿돈으로밧숩

광고료는

귀한의쟝단과ᄌᆞ항의다쇼로좃ᄎᆞ감ᄒᆞ되렴가로밧을터이오며오리지아녀대한사람마다다이신문을보실터이니광고베시기를원ᄒᆞ시는이들은우리신문사에와서면약ᄒᆞ심을희망ᄒᆞ옴

○발힝소 박동대한미일신보사범어학교엽헤젼영국인셜립림졍자리오

사쟝 영국인 (빈셜)

평양 디리졈

○평양쵸동사는권미보씨가우리신문관디리인을퇴졍ᄒᆞ엿스오니평양에계신구람코져ᄒᆞ시는 쳠군ᄌᆞ는취디리졈에왕림ᄒᆞ와면의ᄒᆞ시옴

사고

○우리대한미일신보의목뎍은대한의인민젼체에관한모든데목에디ᄒᆞ야는공평한법론을쥬쟝홈이라우리동신원의담보는신문보시는쳠군ᄌᆞ의게ᄒᆞ샹보도ᄒᆞ리며편지를귀셔ᄒᆞ며주시는이는셩명과반디를젹어붓치시기를희망ᄒᆞ오나이거슨신문샹에긔지ᄒᆞ라는거시아니오다만극히신용ᄒᆞ는증거를솜고자홈이라귀자는아모귀서던지귀지홈을뢰착ᄒᆞ는권리를가졋스나뢰착ᄒᆞ는리유를말홀터이오며공중평화를문란케ᄒᆞ는듯ᄒᆞᆫ다귀서는의례히밧지안켓숩나이

●본샤셜시이래로신문을미양우례로분젼ᄒᆞ와례젼부의일의로젼ᄒᆞᆫ즉스로번곳에는혹늣게젼ᄒᆞ기도ᄒᆞ며혹멋칠거슬ᄒᆞᆫ꺼번에젼ᄒᆞ기도ᄒᆞ며혹아니젼ᄒᆞ는곳도잇다ᄒᆞ와우리신문을ᄉᆞ랑ᄒᆞ야구람ᄒᆞ시는 쳠군ᄌᆞ의게디ᄒᆞ야면우미안ᄒᆞ옵기로지금은분젼인을두고미일일ᄌᆞ이젼ᄒᆞ며아니젼ᄒᆞ거나늣게거나ᄒᆞᆫ폐가업도록ᄒᆞ라ᄒᆞ오니혹아니젼ᄒᆞ거나혹늣게젼ᄒᆞ거나ᄒᆞᆫ일이잇스면본샤로통긔ᄒᆞ여주심을희망ᄒᆞ옴

본샤광고

○본샤신문중에좌긔ᄒᆞᆫ호수를소용ᄒᆞᆯ데가잇서이에광고ᄒᆞ오니누구시던지그중에아모호수던지가져오시는ᄃᆡ로미쟝에빅젼두푼식드리리다

뎨이호 뎨삼호 뎨이십오호 뎨ᄉᆞ십이호 뎨ᄉᆞ십삼호 뎨오십삼호 뎨오십ᄉᆞ호와뎨오십오호 뎨륙십이호

관보

뎨이쳔구빅륙십일호

광무팔년십월십구일

서임급ᄉᆞ령

○임중추원의관주ᄉᆞ서관임관오등 도헌원주ᄉᆞ 오규환

십월십이일

○임외부참서관서주임관이등 총령ᄉᆞ관 어윤적

겸임총령ᄉᆞ관 외부참서관 어윤적

○면본관 함열군수 최유창

○임농상공부기ᄉᆞ서주임관오등 농상공부주ᄉᆞ 현제복

이상십월십ᄉᆞ일

○칙 강원도김셩금광감찰관 구룡 림문상 ᄉᆞ룡 문명욱

명위싱쳥간소ᄉᆞ무위원 경무청경무관 리용승 리덕응

○임내부참서관서주임관륙등 텰도원기ᄉᆞ 송진옥

○면징계 연풍전군수 림상초 영흥전군수 김로규

이상십월십오일

○명장례원경서칙임관삼등 궁내부특진관 박용대

○명궁내부특진관서칙임관ᄉᆞ등 중추원의관 남규희

○칙군제의정관 륙군부쟝 리종건 윤웅렬

○임농상공부주ᄉᆞ서관임관륙등 송의헌 어영선

의원면본관 경무청주ᄉᆞ 조규승

임경무청주ᄉᆞ서관임관륙등 젼주ᄉᆞ 김인환

○금삼금봉 한셩ᄉᆞ범학교교관 심응틱 농상공학교교관 변지상

이상십월십칠일

○임중추원의관서칙임관ᄉᆞ등 종이품 강홍대

십월십팔일

궁내부ᄉᆞ

○쟝례원경박뎡양ᄉᆞ직소 비지내에ᄉᆞ양ᄒᆞᆫ즁쟝례경지임만의시ᄒᆞ노라

○내장원경운긔쟝ᄉᆞ직소 비지내에소쳥을의시ᄒᆞ노라

○중추원의관리홍의ᄉᆞ직소 비지내에소청을의시ᄒᆞ노라

이상십월십칠일

경오

○광무ᄉᆞ년 칙령데삼ᄉᆞ호문관복쟝규측데십이됴중외부금하에(대ᄉᆞ원)삼ᄌᆞ는산삭ᄒᆞ고삼십일됴하에(대셔원관원은동년십이월삼십일이내로)삼ᄌᆞ를쳠입ᄒᆞ기로ᄒᆞ교홈이라

뎨이쳔구빅륙십이호

광무팔년십월이십일

서임급ᄉᆞ령

○승서관임관오등 군부주ᄉᆞ 최한주

○명경임등명젼권용수 니쟝원감동 리쥰영

○임한셩부관윤서칙임관삼등 졍삼품 리희챵

○승서주임관ᄉᆞ등 경무청경무관 안환

○승서주임관ᄉᆞ등 경무청감옥서쟝 김영선

의원면본관 파산군수 윤명승

○면본관 이원군수 최우탁

○임은진군수서주임관오등 외부참서관 장홍식

○임파산군수서주임관륙등 종삼품 장의후

○임옥구군수서주임관ᄉᆞ등 평리원검ᄉᆞ 김춘응

○임함안군수서주임관오등 풍천군수 민희셥

○임함열군수서주임관오등 대셔원주ᄉᆞ 젼광묵

○임이원군수서주임관륙등 륙품 빅남준

○임룡강군수서주임관륙등 륙품 김중용

○임고원군수서주임관륙등 륙품 류병률

이상십월십칠일

론셜

러슌으로온사름의이야기

○러슌에셔 과 관찰로 도젼을탑승ᄒᆞ고향항에나ᄎᆞᆨᄒᆞ엿다가ᄐᆞ리로좃ᄎᆞ여온써린스키씨가월샹싱일에모씨로더브러담화ᄒᆞ엿다는말을모ᄇᆞᆨ포스트신문에계재ᄒᆞ엿는ᄃᆡ

써린스키씨와연스바랑씨는원리샹불회사사원으로아라사군ᄃᆡ와한ᄃᆡ에셔물용달ᄒᆞ기로약조ᄒᆞ고수응ᄒᆞ든사름인지라그런고로러슌에잇는아국진중에서식로물을미엇마큼지탕ᄒᆞ여갈거슬셜명ᄒᆞ엿는ᄃᆡ동씨가ᄒᆞ지에서흉밧ᄒᆞᆯ때에귀왕졔치ᄒᆞ엿든군량미사십만포외에덕국셩쳥으로ᄆᆡ가로이만사쳔돈을수입ᄒᆞ야러슌목션으로수운ᄒᆞᆯ을보왓다ᄒᆞ며ᄯᅩ샹륭우육은엽스되미국에셔제조ᄒᆞᆫ황우오십만통가량은잇스ᄆᆡ중현존ᄒᆞᆫ식물로만보드리도러슌아병이이제도록칠삭동안은넉넉지탕ᄒᆞ야갈듯ᄒᆞ고만일군량을존졀히경용ᄒᆞ며길진ᄃᆡ가히일년이라도지내겟다ᄒᆞ며

근리로말ᄒᆞ드리도대단히경에ᄒᆞᆫ승샤ᄒᆞᆫ고로에과계창이잇서서일병의공위당ᄒᆞ기젼에각종군긔와탄환등속을이미제조ᄒᆞ야쟝치ᄒᆞ엿스며대포일빅사십구문은모스코씨으로북터러슌항구에수출ᄒᆞ엿고에비ᄒᆞ엿든바무수ᄒᆞᆫ총은일병도향ᄒᆞ기젼에우쟝으로서운젼ᄒᆞ엿스며

취향의번에는진루사십좌를분셜ᄒᆞ고각각지뢰포를무듣후면긔로련ᄒᆞ야동ᄒᆞ게만드럿는지라만일일병이진루를졈탈ᄒᆞ려ᄒᆞ면모든지뢰포가리셜터이즉지뢰포를롱발식일때에아병도수쳔명이죽으러니와일병의게는더욱무랍고겁단날일이며

ᄯᅩ밧본젼홀때에아병의수효를헤아린즉이왕에교샹병사ᄒᆞᆫ자외에당쟝쳥에비삼만오쳔명이잇서는ᄃᆡ응당군일쌔홈에감앤이조곰되엿슬듯ᄒᆞ며

그항내에잇는구라파각국인이통계이빅명중에녀인이오십명이오쳥인이삼쳔명가랑이며서빌리아쳘도대리인과미국인의

UNION INSURANCE SOCIETY OF CANTON.

Head office Hongkong.
Marine risks underwritten at current rates.
Agents in Chemulpo,
E. MEYER & Co.

COMPAGNIE DES MESSAGERIES MARITIMES.

Fortnightly Direct Service.

For Marseilles
via Ports.
Sailing from Yokohama
Calling at Kobe,
Shanghai, Hongkong, Saigon, Singapore,
Colombo, Djibonti, Suez, Port Said
and Marseilles.

For particulars apply to
HOLME RINGER & Co.,
Chemulpo.

HAYASHIDA & Co.,

16 MYENG DONG, CHIN KO KAI, SEOUL.
BRANCH OFFICE AT CHEMULPO.

Money changers, Coal and Wood Merchants, Express Agents.

We are agents for the Pyeng-yang Coal Company and the Karazu Coal Company of Japan. We have the best quality of both anthracite and bituminous coal, and prompt execution of orders is our speciality. Firewood of all kinds kept in stock. Full weight guaranteed. Money of all denominations exchanged at current rates. Parcels received for all parts.

CHINA MUTUAL LIFE INS. CO.

Most favourable terms to policy holders.

Benefit system unsurpassed.

HOLME RINGER & Co.
Agents, Chemulpo.

C. P. R.

CANADIAN PACIFIC RAILWAY COMPANY'S ROYAL MAIL STEAMSHIP LINE.

THE FAST ROUTE BETWEEN CHINA, JAPAN, AND EUROPE VIA CANADA AND THE UNITED STATES.

Route from Hongkong via Shanghai, Nagasaki (Inland Sea of Japan) Kobe, Yokohama, Victoria and Vancouver.

Twin Screw Empress Steamship—6,000 Tons—Speed 19 knots.

PROPOSED SAILING FROM YOKOHAMA.
R. M. S. Empress of India.
R. M. S. Empress of Japan.
R. M. S. Empress of China.
R. M. S. Athenian.
R. M. S. Taatar.

Special reduction (first class only) granted to members of the Military, Naval, Diplomatic and Civil services and to Missionaries.

Passengers have choice of ten routes across the Continent of America and have privilege of travelling by any Atlantic Steamship Line.

Round the World passage tickets in connection with the P. and O. S. N., North German Lloyd and Messageries Co.'s **£125.**

All rates payable at current rate of exchange.

For further information, Tickets, Guide Books, etc., apply to

HOLME, RINGER & Co., AGENTS,
Chemulpo.

Grand Hotel,

(Formerly the Station Hotel)

Near the Railway Terminus, West Gate, Seoul.

The Best Hotel in Korea.
Handsome new Building.
Fine Airy Rooms
Excellent Cuisine.
Terms Moderate.
Special terms to Missionaries and to permanent boarders.

Electric cars within 2 minutes' walk.

W. H. EMBERLEY,
Proprietor.

EVERY FACILITY.

In connection with Life Assurance Business is afforded by

The Standard Life Assurance Co.,

One of the largest and wealthiest of the Provident Institutions of the United Kingdom Forms of Application and all information will be promptly afforded on application.

10 CENTS A DAY.

Not a very large expenditure is it? But it is sufficient to secure for a man of 30 a policy with the STANDARD LIFE OFFICE for

$1323.

For all particulars of rates, etc., apply to

Holme, Ringer & Co.,
Agents, Chemulpo.

THE NEW YORK LIFE INSURANCE COMPANY.

Have you ever been declined by any Company?

Are you engaged in a specially hazardous occupation?

Have you heard of the New York Life Insurance Company's New Classifications for this class of Risks?

If not, send your date of birth, occupation and particulars of rejection, if any to

E. MEYER & Co.,
Agents, Chemulpo.

MITSUI BUSSAN KAISNHA.
(MITSUI & Co.)
MITSUI GINKO.
(MITSUI BANK.)

The Bank is owned by the members of the Mitsui Family, who, as partners, assume an unlimited responsibility for all liabilities of the Bank:—

Capital.................... .....Yen 5,000,000
Reserve Fund.................. " 5,600,000

HEAD OFFICE, TOKYO.
LONDON OFFICE, 34 LIME ST., E. C.

BRANCHES AND AGENCIES:—
New York, San Francisco, Hamburg, Bombay, Singapore, Manila, Hongkong, Amoy, Chefoo, Tientsin.
Kobe, Hakodate, Yokohama, Kure, Yokosuka, Moji, Shimonoseki, Miike, Wakamatsu, Nagasaki, Kuchinotsu, Karatsu, Sasebo, Misume, Taipeh, &c.

Telegraphic Address for all the Offices:
"MITSUI."
A. B. C. AND A. 1 CODES USED.

Contractors of Coal
To the Imperial Japanese Navy. Arsenals and Railway Bureau, Principal Railway Companies and Industrial Work, Home and Foreign Mail and Freight Steamers.

Sole Proprietors
Of the famous Miike, Tagawa and Yamano Coal Mines.

Sole Agents
For the sale of Fukumo, Hokoku, Ichimura, Kanoda, Mannoura, Onoura, Ostuji, Sonoda, Tsubaruro, Yoshinotani, Yoshio, Yurokibura and other coals.

YANGTSE INSURANCE ASSOCIATION, LTD.

The undersigned, having been appointed agents for the above company, are prepared to issue policies and pay losses on marine risks at regular rates.

E. MEYER & Co.,
Agents, Chemulpo

AMERICAN KOREAN ELECTRIC COMPANY.

Light and Power.

Main Office: Electric Building, Chong No.

RAILWAY DEPARTMENT.

OPERATING CARS BETWEEN EAST AND WEST GATE, EVERY TEN MINUTES:—
First Car leaves East Gate at 6:30 A. M. First Car leaves West Gate at 6:55 A. M.
Last Cra " East Gate at 10:40 P. M. Last " " West Gate at 11:00 P.M.

OPERATING CARS BETWEEN EAST GATE AND IMPERIAL TOMB TERMINUS, EVERY TWENTY MINUTES:—
CONNECTING WITH EVERY ALTERNATE CAR ARRIVING AT EAST GATE FROM CHONG NO.
First Car leaves East Gate for Tomb at 6:50 A. M.
" " " Tomb for East Gate at 7:10 A. M.
Last " " East Gate for Tomb at 9:50 P. M.
" " " Tomb for East Gate at 10:10 P. M.

OPERATING CARS BETWEEN CHONG NO AND YUNG SAN (RIVER) EVERY TWELVE MINUTES:—
First Car leaves Chong No for South Gate at 6:48 A. M.
" " " Chong No for Yung San at 7:24 A. M.
" " " South Gate for Chong No at 6:56 A. M.
" " " Yung San for Chong No at 7:57 A. M.
Last " " South Gate for Chong No 11:00 P. M.
" " " Yung San for Chong No at 10:11 P. M.

SPECIAL PRIVATE CARS FURNISHED TO SUIT CONVENIENCE OF PATRONS. PRICES ON APPLICATION AT HEAD OFFICE.

LIGHTING DEPARTMENT.

Where less than 250 candle power of light is used, the rate per month will be: Per 16 candle power incandescent lamp,—All night.—Yen 2.50.
Per 32 candle power incandescent lamp:—All night:—Yen 4.00. Per 50 candle power incandescent lamp:—All night:—Yen 6.00.
" 150 " " " " " " " 10.00. " 1200 " " enclosed arc " " " 20.00.

Where more than 250 candle power of light is used, a Meter will be installed, if requested:—Rent of Meter Yen 2.00 per month. Rate of charges by meter reading:—Two Sen per Ampere per hour. (Approximately this is equal to about One Sen per 16 C. P. lamp per hour) Minimum monthly charge where meter is installed, Yen 20.00 per month, which includes rental of meter.

Estimates for installing lights furnished on application. An assortment of chandeliers always on hand.

AMUSEMENT DEPARTMENT.

ANIMATED PICTURES AT EAST GATE
Every evening - - - Except Sunday.
From 8 to 10 P. M.

10 Cents:—Gen. Admission:—10 Cents. Seats in First Class Section. 15 Cents Extra.

Change of program each week. Pictures from Foreign Lands. Pictures of Local Scenes:—Amusing and Instructive.

An entertaining evening for a reasonable price.
MERRY-GO-ROUND:—At East Gate.
From 10:00 A. M. till 11:00 P. M.

5 Cents a Ride.

Take your Exercise on The Galoping Horses.

Comfortable seats in the Chariots.

한셩뎐긔회샤

한미뎐긔회사 고불안 보사덕 고ᄇᆡᆨ
도ᄒᆞ옵나이다
상ᄒᆞᆫ 동사진뎐람소와목마운동장셔오ᄇ
여러뎐차가온장안으로통ᄒᆡᆼᄒᆞ여ᄃᆞᆫ니ᄂᆞ이
삽
또이긔계에긋치노힌편ᄒᆞ고됴흔마차도잇
삽
코미우편ᄒᆞ고또조미잇ᄂᆞᆫ됴흔운동이되겟
이됴흔모형ᄒᆞᆫ말나아ᄂᆞᆫ말을ᄐᆞ고위티치안
디가ᄂᆞᆫ흔번ᄐᆞᄂᆞᆫ데오젼셔이오
ᄆᆡ일상오열시브터하오열ᄒᆞᆫ시ᄭᆞ지ᄒᆞ옵고
목마운동쟝은동대문안에잇삽고
가되겟삽
쳠군조의게갑도싸고져녁에됴흔쇼일거리
미잇고구경ᄒᆞᆯ만ᄒᆞᆫ거시오니
서양사진과대한과온동양사진인대대ᄒᆞᆫ조
ᄂᆞᆫ되
젼이옵고ᄆᆡ쥬일에사진을싼것스로다밧고
고젼탐되금은하등에십젼이오상등에이십
일외에ᄂᆞᆫᄆᆡ야에여덜시브터열시ᄭᆞ지ᄒᆞᆸ
활동사진뎐람소ᄂᆞᆫ동대문안에잇삽고일요
회락부

All Cars Run Direct to tbe Animated Pictures and Merry-Go-Round.

회사이매매국인외상교인ᄃᆡ이사름의졍에를우자ᄭᅡ나라국권를각각다팟드라는ᄃᆡ가동셰의이젼에는일병이란숩을가희숩격치못ᄒᆞᆯ것갓흔지라만일ᄃᆡ젹ᄒᆞ란ᄒᆞᆯ진ᄃᆡ군수의손히가심만명에불하ᄒᆞᆯ듯ᄒᆞ며쏘ᄒᆞᆫ그아병들로ᄒᆞ여곰긔사지경에이르게ᄒᆞ란면올칠삭은오히려연타ᄒᆞᆯᄯᅥ이긔져허군불ᄒᆞ야는삼년지니에는부족지허가업스리라고ᄒᆞ엿더라

뎐보

○봉텬방면젼투속보 긔샹우의군방면의젹군의손히는좌와ᄀᆞᆺᄒᆞ니

젹군이바린시톄는본계호방면의ᄐᆡ즈하의좌편연안에삼ᄇᆡᆨ오십이오본계호지젼의젼면에일쳔오ᄇᆡᆨ이오ᄐᆡ평에삼ᄇᆡᆨ이오로문즈령부근에이ᄇᆡᆨ이오우좁ᄃᆡ방면에이ᄇᆡᆨ이오고인곽부근과및토문즈령북방에각기류ᄇᆡᆨ이오견도부근에삼ᄇᆡᆨ이오보달산북방의햇는무명소부근에일ᄇᆡᆨ오십이오좌종ᄃᆡ방면의쇼달구북방부근에삼ᄇᆡᆨ이니합계가수쳔오ᄇᆡᆨ이오그외에각쳐에도ᄉᆞ쳬못ᄒᆞᆫ거시부지기수요이방면의젹군의손히는쇼불하이만이샹에달ᄒᆞ엿슬터이오이방면에포로가ᄇᆡᆨ명이오그후에젼리품은탄약슈레룰좌와ᄃᆡ포란환이이쳔이오그외에는표수ᄒᆞ는중이오중앙군과좌익군방면의젹군의손히도표수ᄒᆞ는중이라ᄒᆞ엿더라

십월십륙일동경발

○로쟝보고 스텟셀쟝군은십월오일과칠일의련숩에셔전투ᄒᆞᆫ형편에관ᄒᆞᆫ좌기ᄒᆞᆫ보고를ᄒᆞ엿는ᄃᆡ

뎨일(십월오일의싸홈)이방면에잇는일본군은ᄃᆡ포수효를증가ᄒᆞ엿는ᄃᆡ구월십일밤에희즈를웅거ᄒᆞ야련숩구포ᄃᆡ의동북방에갓가히온중쟝구라다우편의지ᄃᆡ는이거슬막아쟁지케ᄒᆞ엿고뎌긔셔일본군은다시극력ᄒᆞ여우편쇽ᄒᆞ로젼진ᄒᆞ야와서ᄇᆡᆨ삼구에셔브터희빈갓가히석지된신호구를포격ᄒᆞ야우리죠격ᄃᆡ를격퇴ᄒᆞ고신호구를졈령ᄒᆞ엿스나십월일일아츰에신호구는우리포ᄃᆡ의포병ᄒᆞᆫᄃᆡ셔포화를노흐ᄆᆡ그후에우리삼중ᄃᆡ는일본군을격퇴ᄒᆞ고다시그신호구를졈령ᄒᆞ엿고일본군은폭발약을만히너흔샹즈에불을인도ᄒᆞ는줄을달아흡수히슈류탄과ᄀᆞᆺ흔거슬던졋스나곤도라퇴ᄂᆞ고쟝군은련숩ᄒᆞ야신긔ᄒᆞᆫ방법을발졍ᄒᆞ야젹군을공격ᄒᆞ기를ᄃᆡᄒᆞ는중이오

뎨이(십월칠일의싸홈)일본군은시로이포병ᄃᆡ를조직ᄒᆞ야포ᄃᆡ를공격ᄒᆞ는중인ᄃᆡ십일일에구포는슈샹히밍렬ᄒᆞ고젹은쏘포병의중원ᄃᆡ를젹ᄒᆞ엿다ᄒᆞ엿더라

○로쟝전투보고 (긔일)

십월십삼일쉬구로팟긴쟝군의뎐보가좌와ᄀᆞᆺᄒᆞ니오후ᄒᆞᆫ시ᄉᆞ지의보고를거ᄒᆞᆫ즉우측의이련ᄃᆡ는비샹ᄒᆞᆫ손히를밧아십삼일에그포병ᄃᆡ를젼쟝에바리두고그남퇴각ᄒᆞ엿는ᄃᆡ이ᄯᅢ의지휘관되엿든련ᄃᆡ쟝은부샹ᄒᆞ고련ᄃᆡ쟝일명은젼수ᄒᆞ엿는지라인ᄒᆞ야동련ᄃᆡ의중좌새포쏘키가ᄃᆡ신ᄒᆞ야이련ᄃᆡ을지휘ᄒᆞ야다시긔젼ᄒᆞ야ᄃᆡ포십륙문외에일의일헛든것들을도로찻젓스나그러나십월십이일에북편전투의결과는일본병의밤에습격ᄒᆞᆷ을넘어드ᄃᆡ며실패ᄒᆞ고우리군수는다시그리틀볼가불ᄇᆡᆨ여번리결만아니라ᄒᆞᆫ번도로찻젓든ᄃᆡ포를쏘다시일흐ᄒᆞ소야엿고며리죵ᄯᅢᄒᆞ며두엇든사고로퇴각ᄒᆞ엿다ᄒᆞ엿고

긔이

십월십ᄉᆞ일의사하로후쟝군의뎐보를거ᄒᆞᆫ즉싸홈은십월십삼일에쏘계속ᄒᆞ얏는ᄃᆡ젹군은쟝격ᄒᆞ는형세를취ᄒᆞ야경히우리우측을공격ᄒᆞ는ᄃᆡ젹은쇼랑지군방면으로공격ᄒᆞ야드ᄃᆡ오라라그러나우리군수는비샹히만히승격ᄒᆞ는거슬격퇴ᄒᆞ고ᄃᆡ길진희들다회복ᄒᆞ고우리우좌의슈희잇는군수로쏘ᄒᆞᆫ그진희를유지ᄒᆞᆷ을엇엇고쇼랑군부근에잇는우리군수는그진ᄃᆡ에셔너무돌출ᄒᆞ여나가잇는고로써십삼일아츰에동일향ᄒᆞᆫ에밋쳐셔는퇴각ᄒᆞ랴는명령을바린지라이거슨돌출ᄒᆞ여나가잇는거지시불리ᄒᆞᆫ줄알엿고쎈이라그리ᄒᆞᆫᄃᆡ퇴각ᄒᆞ기는오후여섯시에시작ᄒᆞ야완젼ᄒᆞᆫ질셔를보존ᄒᆞ엿고우리좌측에셔는십월십이일에젹에긴요ᄒᆞᆫ진ᄃᆡ를공격ᄒᆞ민젹군도쏘ᄒᆞᆫ긴평히항거ᄒᆞ엿스나우리는암샨을졈령ᄒᆞ엿고그러ᄒᆞᆫᄃᆡ일본병은우세ᄒᆞᆫ중원ᄃᆡ의구응ᄒᆞᆷ을엇엇고우리군수는외로히잇는위ᄐᆡᄒᆞᆷ을두려워ᄒᆞᆷ으로써동안이멀게퇴각ᄒᆞᆷ을명령ᄒᆞ엿는지라

십월십삼일의싸홈에는구쟝젼용을나타낸자는동셔ᄇᆡᆨ리아련ᄃᆡ와뎨오일교스크련ᄃᆡ와뎨팔위보이조구보병련ᄃᆡ인ᄃᆡ샹일동안의젼투에우리손히는자못만타ᄒᆞ엿더라

십월십륙일동경발

○젹군수샹 북로일셔지우리가미쟝ᄒᆞᆫ젹병의시톄는이쳔이나되ᄂᆞ다고젼자에젼보ᄒᆞᆫ거슨우리좌익군방면의것ᄲᅮᆫ만수효라ᄒᆞ얏고

○샹동숙보 그후ᄃᆡ산총ᄉᆞ령관의공보는중앙군방면에셔버리고간젹병의시톄를이쳔오ᄇᆡᆨ으로계산ᄒᆞ엿고그리ᄒᆞᆫ데본군에셔표사룰필ᄒᆞᆫ젹병의시톄총수는팔쳔칠ᄇᆡᆨ오십이나되나다만이거슨우리좌익군방면에셔금표이른포로일랑일에교젼ᄒᆞᆫ결과를포함ᄒᆞ지아니ᄒᆞᆫ거시오쏘ᄒᆞᆫ각방면에셔인젹발견치아 ᄒᆞᆫ젹병의시톄가불쇼ᄒᆞ다ᄒᆞ엿더라

동일동뎐

○젹군손히별보 그후의젹군의손히는우리우익군젼면에버린시톄가수쳔오ᄇᆡᆨ이오수샹이이만명이샹이오ᄃᆡ포란환이이쳔파슈레룰좌등쏘포획ᄒᆞ고중이앙과좌익의광쳐방면의이거슬합ᄒᆞ야젹군의사샹이오만명이나되고포로는긴ᄒᆞᆫ자만사ᄇᆡᆨ명이샹이라ᄒᆞ엿더라

잡보

○아병북퇴 한셩에쥬차ᄒᆞᆫ일본수령부에도착ᄒᆞᆫ원산뎐보에ᄒᆞ기를본월십삼일에일병이홍원군에젼진ᄒᆞᆷ즉히ᄃᆡ에는아국병의영향이업고다북방으로퇴각ᄒᆞ엿다ᄒᆞ엿더라

○북도샹졔 함흥관찰사리헌경씨가나부로보고ᄒᆞ엿스되음팔월초칠일야에샹강이되엿는ᄃᆡ졔초엽샹이는린고로면야ᄇᆡᆨ곡에샹졔가등ᄒᆞᆫ고로아무쳥초ᄒᆞᆫ예추수단망ᄒᆞ야인민이환산ᄒᆞᆫ다ᄒᆞ엿더라

○이함착임 인쳔감리의뎐보를거ᄒᆞᆫ즉이ᄃᆡ리국군함일쳑이작일에입항ᄒᆞ엿다더라

○셔긔셩도관 일본공사가외부에셩명ᄒᆞ기를일본외무셔긔관셩천샹립일랑이가본월십구일에본관셔긔셩으로도임ᄒᆞ엿다ᄒᆞ엿더라

○례대도긔 일본례식대신포경무씨의일힝이본월십삼일에광양에도달ᄒᆞ야십ᄉᆞ일에풍경궁에진알ᄒᆞ고당일발졍ᄒᆞ야룡쳔으로향ᄒᆞ엿다고히관찰부뎐보가나부로도착ᄒᆞ엿다더라

○한젼난귀 학부에셔쥬일공관에년보ᄒᆞ되안샹호가의학교교관으로셔임퇴엿스니쥬시귀송ᄒᆞ라ᄒᆞ엿더니히공관에셔회뎐ᄒᆞ되안샹호가쳥금벙원에잇는ᄃᆡ면귀ᄒᆞᆯ편한이잇스즉쳥금에는귀국ᄒᆞᆯ수업다ᄒᆞ엿더라

○뎡광진보당 함남관찰사리헌경씨의뎐보가작일샹오십일시에도착ᄒᆞ엿스되뎡광군보를거ᄒᆞᆫ즉소위진보당쳔여명이갱긔취회ᄒᆞ야여간단발아니ᄒᆞᆫ엿든자석지어ᄅᆡ졔ᄒᆞ마자삭발ᄒᆞ고사방으로셔회집ᄒᆞ는도당이라벽부젼ᄒᆞ야부지ᄭᅥ셴명인교로판단ᄒᆞ규ᄒᆞ되일향불칭ᄒᆞ니부군에셔는그취당을희산케ᄒᆞᆯ수업스니엇지죠쳐ᄒᆞᆫ라ᄒᆞ엿더라

○일관졍빈 작일하오칠시반에일본공관에셔연회ᄒᆞ엿는ᄃᆡ각부대신을쳥요연ᄃᆡᄒᆞ엿더라

○광찰우보 광남관찰ᄉᆞ리중하씨가나부로보고ᄒᆞ기를본월십ᄉᆞ일에각군인민쳔여명이취졉ᄒᆞ야관찰부광명에드러와셔민회셜시ᄒᆞ기를원ᄒᆞ는고로반복효유ᄒᆞᆫ즉피등이불ᄃᆡ흥곡ᄒᆞ고일제히단발ᄒᆞ고자ᄒᆞ니당쟝호상이극히희고ᄒᆞᆫ지라엄칙ᄒᆞ야퇴송ᄒᆞ엿더니십오일에걘도중쥬모ᄒᆞ는자ᄭᅥ빅명이부하에두류ᄒᆞ야조슈삭발ᄒᆞ고일제히양복ᄒᆞ거는기중칠명을위션착수ᄒᆞ엿스며향중군보니에음력구월일일에빅셩수쳔명이진보회라칭ᄒᆞ야단발ᄒᆞ엿다ᄒᆞ며령원군보니에음력팔월이십구일에소위일진회라보회라ᄀᆞ칭ᄒᆞ고수오ᄇᆡᆨ명이음ᄯᅥ에리회ᄒᆞ야삭발ᄒᆞ엿더니홀연이퇴거ᄒᆞ엿다고각군보고가동수리도ᄒᆞ는ᄃᆡ탐지ᄒᆞᆫ즉히도등이경중소위회쟝의지휘반쳥종ᄒᆞ야이럿듯셔로발동ᄒᆞ야일도가소동ᄒᆞ되금즙ᄒᆞᆯ수업스니본관찰ᄉᆞ는면관ᄒᆞ기를바란다ᄒᆞ엿더라

○가련한민 의쥬군수구완회씨가나부로보고ᄒᆞ되구월십오일에평안도ᄃᆡ등ᄉᆞ령부지깁가본군교읍변남계리에리도ᄒᆞ야독파계란를드르식ᄒᆞ더니시륙일아예긴가가쏘동류이명과ᄀᆞᆺ치각기흰도와막ᄃᆡ를가지고리도ᄒᆞ야아로ᄒᆞ는고로희동빅셩이최동ᄒᆞ야구원ᄒᆞ엿더니십칠일에일본인이히동에니르러류숙ᄒᆞ며빅셩이경접ᄒᆞ야환산ᄒᆞ엿는ᄃᆡ십팔일에쳥국인동쳥에쥬둔ᄒᆞᆫ일병이빅명이샤하조로셔희동에니르러방총돌입ᄒᆞ야일쟝관리쳥샹과흠사ᄒᆞ엿고충화ᄒᆞ야민가십구호가회소ᄒᆞ엿다ᄒᆞ엿더라

○금비진인 작일쟝충단치제시에헌병ᄃᆡ위관이쟝인을금ᄒᆞ다가군무국쟝모씨를그릇잡아인츌노알교구츅ᄒᆞ지라졔쟝관이공의ᄒᆞ야히위관를오주일중근신에쳐ᄒᆞᆫ다ᄒᆞ더라

○보쳥칭숩 평안남북도금광감리ᄃᆡ쳔군슈조쟝운씨가나부로보고ᄒᆞ기를본군숩교이십병을감항시감리셔규ᄯᅦ들의방ᄒᆞ야숩졈으로기칭ᄒᆞ고평쳥에비죠ᄒᆞ야복궁이심긔들하송ᄒᆞ면군도는본도관찰부평무셔에셔을쳥구ᄒᆞᆯ거시오원봉은닉의광소에셔마련ᄒᆞ엿다ᄒᆞ더라

TELEGRAMS.

Tokyo, Oct. 19th.

On Monday night the enemy twice attacked the right column of our left wing, but they were repulsed and retreated without removing their dead.

Headquarters, 18th.

The advance-guard of the enemy's troops in north-east Korea are holding the Ham Kwan-linng, (a high mountain pass between Hamheung and Songchin) and are building barracks there.

Tokyo, Oct. 18th.

The enemy on the 15th inst. again made an attack on our garrison at Kianchang, but was again repulsed. Our losses were 2 killed.

[Kianchang is a post on the main line of Japanese communications, near Saimachi, to the south of the main body of the Japanese army operating in Manchuria. Ed. K. D. N.]

WELL KNOWN JOURNALIST DISAPPEARS.

Mr. Charles Barzillai Spahr, of New York, the editor of Current Literature and The Outlook, has disappeared mysteriously from the Belgian cross-Channel boat Prince Albert.

Mr. Spahr was crossing from Ostend to Dover, with a lady and gentleman on Tuesday, when he was suddenly missed.

He had been seen a little time before by one of the sailors, who advised him to go to the bow of the vessel.

The ship was searched from stem to stern but no trace of Mr. Spahr could be found. A second search on the arrival of the Prince Albert at Dover was equally fruitless.

Whether Mr. Spahr fell overboard accidentally, or fell a victim to a sudden attack of nervousness, remains a mystery.

According to a Central News message from New York last night, Mr. Spahr declares that her husband was not in ill-health, and she knows no reason to suppose that it is a case of suicide.

At Mr. Spahr's office, however, it is stated that he was a nervous wreck when he left the States.

The lady and gentleman who were travelling with Mr. Spahr stayed at Dover on Tuesday night, and came on to London the following day.

TOMMY ATKINS.

Tommy Atkins forms the subject for the last storyette competitition in the "County Gentleman." The winning yarn which is entitled "The V.C. that failed" runs thus: "It was at Colenso and a poor Tommy who had been severely wounded in the foot, implored his comrade Pat to carry him under cover. Pat, with dreams of the V.C., hoisted him on his shoulder and made for the trenches. Unfortunately, however, before he had gone far, a shell burst and completely decapitated the wounded man. Pat, ignorant of what had happened, arrived at safe quarters with his burden, but was surprised at the derision he received from his comrades. 'Oh, begorra' said he on finding he had only saved a headless man, 'the devil take the liar, he told me, 'twas his phut.'"

Certain reviewers are criticising Mr. London's alleged affectation in signing himself "Jack," on the grounds that it is derogatory to a man who "has arrived" to use a nickname. W. L. Alden even writes of "John" London, and hopes "he will soon stop calling himself by the absurd 'Jack.'" So, possibly, he might, if his name were John, or anything else but what it is. It so happens that "Jack" is Mr. London, and until he takes steps legally to change it, which will probably be never, those who object to it can only soothe their feelings by using the initial "J."

THE WHY AND WHEREFORE.

General Hyon has been ordered by the "powers that be," to leave Korea temporarily and repair to Japan to study for a while.

At the same time we hear that the Il-chin-hoi have not the same confidence in shaved heads that they possessed a week or two ago, moreover their gaudy headgear does not appeal to them so much as it did at one time.

Why? Because their supporters are leaving them and the new Commander-in-Chief, General Hasegawa, does not approve of the society.

Incidentally they have held no meetings for the past few days.

WHAT WAR IS.

Mr, Henry Norman, M. P., in the "World's Work, "says we are but too apt to overlook the terrible character of the war:—"Tens of thousands of brave men slaughtered, great battleships and their crews sent to the bottom in a minute, homes desolated, commerce paralysed, treasure squandered, debt piled up, savage passions deified—and all for what? In a war that might have been avoided, in a struggle where each side has what it regarded as a national necessity at stake, where each nation must suffer for generations to come, and where neither can hope to reap any fruits of victory worthy of their cost." The modern world, Mr. Norman holds, has seen no more deplorable spectacle.

REMARKABLE OUTRAGE.

An extraordinary tale of wanton outrage by a troop of Japanese soldiers is telegraphically reported by the Magistrate of Wiju.

He states that on the 15th inst. a Korean interpreter in the employ of the Japanese railway authorities went to the village Namche Ri and stole some chickens and eggs. The same night he returned with two boon companions and commenced to create a disturbance, brandishing swords and beating the people.

On the 18th inst. a body of 200 Japanese soldiers from the garrison at Antung arrived at the same place and opened a rifle-fire on the village, to which they afterwards set fire, burning 19 houses. No cause for this unwarrantable attack was given, but it is presumed that the aforesaid Korean interpreters was in some manner responsible.

BABOO ENGLISH.

The following was sent to M. A. P. by an Indian reader:—When Lady Curzon first went out to India she made a hobby of collecting quaint specimens of "Baboo English"—that is, English written by imperfectly educated natives. The latter are very fond of showing off their proficiency in this direction, and invariably use the longest words possible. Lady Curzon has now a large and very interesting collection, which provokes much amusement when shown to visitors. One of the best and most recently added to these effusions is from a native firm of two brothers in Bombay announcing the death of their father to their customers, and reads as follows:

"Gentlemen—We have the pleasure to inform you that our respected father departed this life on the 10th instant. His business will be conducted by his beloved sons, whose names are given below. The opium market is quiet, and Mal. 1,500 rupees per chest. O death, where is thy sting? O grave, where is thy victory? We remain, &c."

Mr. Rawa Kami, a clerk of the Foreign office in Tokyo has arrived and will take up a position in the Japanese Legation.

At 7 P.M. yesterday the ministers of all Departments were entertained by the Japanese Miniter at his Legation.

TO VISITORS TO ULTIMA THULE.

Apropos of the death of Sir William Harcourt, those who think of visiting Ultima Thule should look out for the statesman's portrait indelibly outlined on the cliffs of the Island of Hoy. That stupendous rock is reached from Stromness by crossing a narrow strait which when the Atlantic tide sets in becomes a veritable "roost" or "race." The traveller must then push across the island towards its Atlantic face until he sights the top of the old man of Hoy (not Sir William), a slender column of rock which stands in the surges a thousand feet below, but lifts its head till it just overlaps the near cliff-line above. Standing there and looking north, one sees (or saw a few years ago, and the coast is hard as iron) a perfect profile of Sir William Harcourt. The likeness is so good that no one acquainted with the semblances of contemporary statesmen could possibly fail to indentify it. The profile is cut toward the summit of the tremendous cliff, and Sir William looks out over the waste of waters and knits his brows against the everlasting buffets of the Atlantic storms. I think (writes the correspondent who sends these particulars) it is the most striking lusus naturæ of the sort I have ever seen except perhaps the mighty lion which stretches couchant along the approaches to Table Bay. S. C. morning post.

The Korea Daily News.

Issued at 5 P. M. daily except Sundays.

Rate of Subscription:—

Per Year,	Yen 25.
Per Quarter,	Yen 7.
Per Month,	Yen 2.50.

Postage in Korea not charged extra.
Postage abroad charged extra.

Advertisements, 50 sen per day for 1 inch or less. 5 yen per month per inch. 50 yen per year per inch.

All communications to E. T. BETHELL, Editor and Publisher, Pak-tong, Seoul

A RUSSIAN VIEW OF THE TIBET EXPEDITION!

"We Russians are late!" Such are the opening words of a curious and interesting article contributed by Prince Esper Oukhtomsky to the current issue of "North American Review." The subject of the Prince's paper is the British expedition into Tibet, and the whole point of it is that the Russians have allowed England to steal a march upon them in their advance on the realms of the Dalai Lama and his capital, Lhassa. It is refreshing for a change to find that the criticism which we invariably apply to our own undertakings is equally familiar in the mouth of our rivals. We are in the habit of complaining that Russian diplomacy is prompter than ours. Prince Oukhtomsky takes a precisely opposite view. The knowledge of his own countrymen with regard to Central Asian politics is, he thinks, extremely vague and confused. They believe that the Northern Empire is in this region a pioneer of civilization. As a matter of fact Western travellers are much better acquainted with Tibet. "Among the subjects of the Russian Empire there have been included for more than two centuries several hundred thousand lamaists, spiritually united to the millions of their co-religionists within the bounds of the Chinese Empire, and yet Russians have long entirely ignored the results obtained by European expeditions into Tibet." The man who writes these words is, of course, the well-known Editor-in-Chief of the "Viedomosti," one of the most influential journals in St. Petersburg. He is, or was, on intimate terms with the Tsar, accompanying him on his trip round the world and writing a book about their joint travels. At the present moment Prince Oukhtomsky is on a visit to the United States, which accounts for the appearance of his article in an American magazine. The version given of British relations with Tibet is certainly amusing. Shortly after 1830, we are told, the English Government decided to build an important post at Darjeeling, in order to get a foothold near the religious centres of Tibet. Then Darjeeling was united by a railroad with Calcutta, while engineers surveyed the borderland, and especially noted the Jelap-la Pass, leading to the Chumbi Valley. The process of assimilation went on apace. Some of the lamas visited Calcutta, Merchants passing through Tibet into Nepal scattered as many Indian newspapers as possible. Darjeeling tea ousted the imports from China. There was also a great demand for Indian rice and tobacco, while Tibet, in its turn, paid with its natural treasures, gold, silver, rock salt, pure musk, cheap cattle valuable wool, medicinal herbs, and so forth. All this commerce only paved the way for ultimate conquest. Above all the British missionaries have done what they could to help the process. Moravian brethren, expelled by the Russians, settled in the Himalays, and found a warm welcome in India, and as these had a perfect mastery of the Tibetan language, the Government of Calcutta, naturally, made large use of their linguistic attainments. In their civilising efforts the missionaries had the distinct advantage that Buddhism, as a religion, contains few, if any, democratic elements: thus Christianity, with its gospel to the poor, gained many converts. "From the moment," says Prince Oukhtomsky, "when the pagans see the principles of the New Testament put into practice (so far as this is possible for fallible mortals), a reverence for the pioneers of Christianity must grow and increase."

The result is, according to the Prince, that, by a mixture of religion, commerce, and artful diplomacy, the English have gradually made their way into Tibet to the detriment of the Russians. Indeed, the time may well come when the first educated Russian traveller will reach Lhassa through Darjeeling under the protection, and by the permission, of the English Government. But now, what is the chief danger of the movement of the English armies to the land of the Lamas? Here the Prince must be allowed to speak in his own words. "The Tibetan monasteries are exceedingly rich, and form real treasure-houses of ancient culture: they contain religious objects of the highest artistic value, and the rarest literary memorials. If the sepoys reach Teshu Lumpo and Lhassa, with their fanatical passion for loot, which was so signally exhibited in the recent Boxer campaign, it is beyond all doubt that the most precious treasures on the altars and in the libraries of the lamas will be in danger. It is impossible even to tell approximately how great an injury may thus be caused to Orientalism, how the solution of many scientific problems may be put off, problems which are closely bound up with the gradual revelation of the secrets of Tibet. The vandalism which was a disgrace to our age. when Peking was recently ransacked and looted, will pale before what the English will probably do by the hands of their dusky mercenaries. The temptation will be too great. Only zealous students of this particular department of knowledge could save everything which is rare and worthy of special attention." The idea that the best monuments, the last fragments of ancient Buddhist creative genius are in danger of falling into the British advance into Tibet is decidedly humorous. Still any stick will do to beat a dog with, and the Russian journalist is evidently much exercised by the apparent inaction of his own Government and the possible loss of Muscovite influence in Tibet. Hence he tries to appeal against us as vandals, "What even the hordes of Genghis Khan guarded and reverently preserved will be trampled under foot by the invading "Pax Britannica."—China Review.

The crops, for a large area in the neighbourhood of Yeung-yu have been entirely destroyed by a severe hailstorm.

MORE FROM PORT ARTHUR.

A recent Russian arrival from Port Arthur who held a good position there informed our representative (says the "Peking and Tientsin Times") that the number of Japanese said to have been slain by the explosion of mines is not at all exaggerated. On one occasion two squadrons of cavalry were entirely annihilated with the exception of four men, who were wounded and placed in hospital. The Russian soldiers hold a very high opinion of the bravery of the Japanese, and the terrible carnage which they have withstood in their attempts to capture the place is not received with exuberance at all by the Russian soldiers. The provisions in Port Arthur are sufficient for a long time yet. The Russian soldier is easily contented in the matter of food, and is satisfied to go a whole day on a piece of bread. They are quite confident of the ultimate issue, and place every reliance in General Stoessel and Smirnoff. It is certain that if the Japanese ever effect a general assault, no quarter will be asked or given by either side. There are still a number of women and children at Port Arthur. The statement that Mme. Stoessel and children went to Chefoo is a pure fabrication. There are a large number of Japanese wounded in the several hospitals, and they are receiving the same attention as the Russians. Our informant declined to state the number of troops in Port Arthur. He admits, however, that the Japanese will not be able to have a larger force in the firing line than the Russians, as the space will not admit of it. When the general assault takes place he says that the result will shock civilized nations, as the losses on both sides will be something terrific, and all the most gruesome part of war will result in the hand to hand conflict. General Stoessel's orders are, that not a fort is to be given up while one man is alive, and his instructions will be carried out. Every Russian solder considers he has a sacred trust in defending the port. He disbelieves the statement that Japanese have captured any of the forts—in fact, to use his own words, he said, "I am absolutely certain that such is not the case." He paid a very warm tribute to Mr Lawton, of the "Daily Telegraph," who with Mr. Marshall saved many lives among the sailors from the Russian torpedo-boat in Chefoo.

GENERAL KUROKI AND THE CRANKS

General Kuroki is experiencing some of the inconveniences which follow in the path of fame. He is being inundated, writes one of the correspondents with him, with letters from cranks the world over. They harry him at every turn. There is the religious zealot, who warns him that eternity is endless, and then proceeds to enquire as to the spiritual state of his soul. Next in order must be placed the Prohibitionist faddist, who in florid language dilates upon the horrors that the drinking of intoxicants brings in its train. All this class of literature has come from England, America, and Australia. It would be interesting to discover why this form of mild lunacy should be peculiar to the Anglo-Saxon race. The autograph hunter and the stamps collector have not been idle either. One or two were successful. Now letters of this type arrive by the dozen. A schoolboy, writing from Ilford, Essex, wheedled a photograph out of the victor of the Yalu. "It is the last one," said the General, "therefore I can send no more." Intending applicants please note!—Kobe Herald.

Seventeen citizens of the Korean district were arrested yesterday and brought up to Seoul. It is said that upwards of 60 Koreans are now imprisoned at the Japanese Headquarters here.

Mr. Oura arrived at Pyeng Yang on the 13th, and left for the north next day.

The Korea Daily News.

VOL. I, FRIDAY, OCTOBER 21, 1904 No. 82

大韓每日申報
대한ᄆᆡ일신보

(뎨팔십삼호) (토요일) 일쳔구ᄇᆡᆨ사년십월이십이일

본샤고ᄇᆡᆨ

본신보는영어와한어로셔거ᄆᆡ
일출판ᄒᆞ옵

신문가

한쟝 엽두돈오푼
일삭표 엽두량닷돈
우표가ᄆᆡ삭닷돈
다ᄉᆞᆺ돈으로밧ᄉᆞᆸ

광고료는

긔ᄒᆡᆼ의쟝단과ᄌᆞ항의다쇼로죵
감ᄒᆞ되렴가로밧을터이오ᄆᆡ오
릐지아녀대한사ᄅᆞᆷ마다다이신
문을보실터이니광고버시기를
원ᄒᆞ시는이들은우리신문사에
와셔편약ᄒᆞ심을희망ᄒᆞ옵

○발ᄒᆡᆼ소 박동대한ᄆᆡ일신보
사발어학교압헤젼영국인셜필
림졍자리오

사쟝 영국인 (ᄇᆡ셜)

평양 ᄃᆡ리졈

○평양효동사는권ᄆᆡ보씨가우
리신문관ᄃᆡ리인을뎡ᄒᆞ엿
스오니평양에계신구람ᄒᆞ고져ᄒᆞ
시는 쳠군ᄌᆞ는ᄒᆡᆼᄃᆡ리졈에왕
림ᄒᆞ와면의ᄒᆞ시옵

사고

○우리대한ᄆᆡ일신보의목뎍은
대한의안녕질서에관한모든데
목에ᄃᆡᄒᆞ야는공평한번론을쥬
쟝홈이라우리동신원의ᄇᆞ라는
신문보시는쳠군ᄌᆞ의게ᄒᆞᆼ샹보
도ᄒᆞ리며편지를긔셔ᄒᆞ며주시
는이는셩명과번디를쳐어븟치
시기를희망ᄒᆞ오나이거슨신문
샹에긔지ᄒᆞ란거시아니오
만구히신용ᄒᆞ는증거를숨고자단
홈이라긔자는아모긔셔던지긔
지홈을되갸ᄒᆞ는권리를가졋스
나되갸ᄒᆞ는리유를말ᄒᆞᆯ터이오
며공중평화를문란케ᄒᆞ는듯ᄒᆞᆫ
긔셔는의례히밧지안켓ᄉᆞᆸ나이
다

●본사셜시이ᄅᆡ로신문을ᄆᆡ양
우례로분젼ᄒᆞ와ᄅᆡ젼부의임의
로젼ᄒᆞᆫ듯ᄉᆞ오면곳에는후늣게
젼ᄒᆞ기도ᄒᆞ며흑멋칠거슬ᄒᆞᆫ겁
에젼ᄒᆞ기도ᄒᆞ며흑아니젼ᄒᆞ는
곳도잇다ᄒᆞ오니우리신문을ᄉᆞ랑
ᄒᆞ야구람ᄒᆞ시는 쳠군ᄌᆞ의계랑
ᄃᆡᄒᆞ야ᄆᆡ우미안ᄒᆞ옵기로지금
은분젼인을두고ᄆᆡ일일즉이젼
ᄒᆞ며아니젼ᄒᆞ거나늣게젼ᄒᆞᆫ
폐가엽도록ᄒᆞ갓ᄉᆞ오니ᄒᆞ아니

젼ᄒᆞ거는후늣게젼ᄒᆞ거나ᄒᆞᆫ일
이잇스면본사로통긔ᄒᆞ여주심
을희망ᄒᆞ옵

본샤광고

○본사신문중에걱기ᄒᆞᆫ호수를
쇼용ᄒᆞᆯ데가잇서서이에광고ᄒᆞ오
니누구시던지그중에아모호수
던지가져오시는이로ᄆᆡ쟝에ᄇᆡᆨ
젼두푼식드리리다

뎨이호 뎨삼호 뎨비십호
뎨ᄉᆞ십이호 뎨ᄉᆞ십삼호 뎨
오십삼호 뎨오십ᄉᆞ호와뎨오
십오호 뎨륙십이호

뎐보

십월십륙일ᄃᆡ산춍ᄉᆞ령관
공보

○격젼후보 우익과즁앙군의
젼면은안졍ᄒᆞᆷ을속ᄒᆞ고다못좌익
군의졍면에셔만ᄇᆡᆨ렬ᄒᆞᆫ포셩이
잇섯는ᄃᆡ산면쇼쟝의계취ᄒᆞ는
부ᄃᆡ는십월십오일밤에삼도강
ᄌᆞ의부군의놉흔곳에셔공격ᄒᆞ
여대포일문과탄약슈릐이좌를
탈취ᄒᆞ엿다ᄒᆞ엿더라

십월십칠일ᄃᆡ산춍ᄉᆞ령관
보고

○좌익군젼황 본계호에셔동
북으로오리쯤되는고반시부근
에잇든젹병약간은우리외츄격
홈을인ᄒᆞ야북방으로퇴각ᄒᆞ고
우리츄격ᄃᆡ는고반시를졈령ᄒᆞ
엿고

좌익군의좌종ᄃᆡ의젼면에는오
놀아춤에젹군이여셧번습격을
ᄒᆡᆼᄒᆞ엿스나이거슬다격퇴ᄒᆞ고
ᄃᆡ단히만히손힘를식히엿고그
런ᄒᆞᆫᄃᆡ져녁ᄯᆡ에니르러다시보
병오ᄅᆞᆷᄃᆡ와포병이상즁ᄃᆡ되
는젹군은좌종ᄃᆡ를향ᄒᆞ야공격
ᄒᆞ여오더동종ᄃᆡ는목하에비거
슬격퇴ᄒᆞ는즁이요

십오일에좌익군방면에셔는젹
군의버린시톄가다시증가ᄒᆞ야
쟉일셔지에대약ᄉᆞ쳔에달ᄒᆞ엿
고오히려동군좌종ᄃᆡ의젼면에
는자못시톄가다수ᄒᆞᆫ아직됴
ᄉᆞᄒᆞᆯ거를미엽다ᄒᆞ엿더라

십월십칠일동경발

○포로의언담 즁앙군에셔포
로로쟝은젹군쟝교의진술ᄒᆞᆫ말
의요령이좌와곳ᄒᆞ니
목하에봉텬부부근에셔구로팟

트킨의평슐ᄒᆞᆫ병력은아홉군이
뵈며되는고로로국황뎨계셔는
구월십이십칠일에구로팟트킨
의계뎨ᄒᆞ야이후에는봉텬부이
북으로는ᄒᆞᆫ거름일지라도퇴각
홈이불가ᄒᆞ고어서공격ᄒᆞ는형
세를도모ᄒᆞ게일본군을남방만쥬
로구축ᄒᆞ야러슌의위급홈을구
원ᄒᆞ라고명ᄒᆞ엿습으로구로팟
트킨은젼ᄒᆞᆫ병력을지휘ᄒᆞ야
봉텬부이남으로젼진ᄒᆞ야나아
가공격ᄒᆞ는형세를도모키기를
위ᄒᆞ야젼군을즁앙과밋좌우삼
종ᄃᆡ로분ᄒᆞ야즁앙종ᄃᆡ는뎨일
과뎨ᄉᆞ와뎨오군단으로모든들어
샨벨리푸가령슐케ᄒᆞ고좌종ᄃᆡ
는대관비군단으로모든들어스탓
겔베ᄅᆞ고가지휘관이되여일본군
우익으로향ᄒᆞ게ᄒᆞ고우종ᄃᆡ는
샴군단으로모든들어일본군의좌
익으로향ᄒᆞ게ᄒᆞ고셔로ᄒᆞᆫ군단
은즁앙종ᄃᆡ의후면으로련속ᄒᆞ
여ᄒᆡᆼ케ᄒᆞ고기타는리비부잇지
는오소리ᄃᆡ방의아젼군을거ᄂᆞ
리고일군의문너간진을겁탈ᄒᆞ
기위ᄒᆞ야동으로도라드리료양
의동남방을핍박ᄒᆞ게ᄒᆞ고또미
시쳥교는통괴병록련ᄃᆡ를거ᄂᆞ
리고리비부잇지의지ᄃᆡ외젼노
련졉ᄒᆞ야운동케ᄒᆞ엿는ᄃᆡ이번
젼투에셔뎨일군단에속ᄒᆞᆫ뎨삼
십쳘수단의총병히그ᄒᆞᆫ려단은
손히가심ᄒᆞ엿고뎨일빅수십오
련ᄃᆡ와뎨일즁ᄃᆡ곳ᄒᆞᆫ거슨산히
셕산샹에셔젼멸ᄒᆞ엿고뎨수단
수단의손히도쏘ᄒᆞᆫ자못비보병뎨삼
ᄒᆞ고미수단의쟝련ᄃᆡ는출젼ᄒᆞᆯ
당초에는수쳔인이나되더니
샹륙ᄇᆡᆨ명이되엿고이번싸홈에
이후에는갑ᄒᆞ야미쳔오ᄇᆡᆨ인
ᄃᆡ곳ᄒᆞᆫ거슨온인원이계
우팔ᄇᆡᆨ명이ᄂᆞ된다고ᄒᆞᆫ다라

십월십팔일동경발

○샨면종ᄃᆡ고젼 샨면쇼쟝의
령ᄒᆞᆫ일종ᄃᆡ는십샴일에사하
보북방에잇는젹을공격ᄒᆞ는우
리좌익군의일부ᄃᆡ를구응ᄒᆞ러
가셔쉐챠로부근에셔젹군을격
파ᄒᆞ고대포이문과탄약수레이
좌를탈취ᄒᆞ고또산동보ᄌᆞ에셔
다시젹병을격퇴ᄒᆞᆫ후에지금잇
는진디를회복ᄒᆞ며ᄒᆞ홀ᄌᆞ음에오
후일곱시ᄌᆞ음에의외에젹병일

수단의계히위싸임이되엿스나
빙렬히젹젼ᄒᆞᆫ후에젹군을격파
ᄒᆞ고지금진디를회복ᄒᆞᆷ을엇엇
다ᄒᆞ엿고즁앙군젼면에잇는젹
군은구응ᄒᆞᆷ을엇엇고일로일에
우리사샹은대략일쳔명이라ᄒᆞ
엿더라

동일동뎐

○화평북방격젼 시마졍슈비
ᄃᆡ에셔파츌ᄒᆞᆫ일부ᄃᆡ는ᄒᆞᆫ원공
면하의평슐ᄒᆞᆫ뎨일군에속ᄒᆞᆫ과
병과ᄒᆞᆫ가지로본계호의동편으
로나아가러ᄒᆞ다가십륙일에샹
가ᄌᆞ북방에잇는화평의북방에
서갑경ᄒᆞᆫ젹군의항거홈을밧아
셔로격젼ᄒᆞᆫ후에드ᄃᆡ여미거슬
격퇴ᄒᆞ엿는ᄃᆡ이싸홈에는우리
의젼사ᄒᆞᆫ병이십륙명이오부샹
ᄒᆞᆫ자는셔도ᄯᆡ위비하이십일명
이라ᄒᆞ엿더라

십월십구일동경발

○젹군습격 월됴일밤에젹군
은우리좌익군우종ᄃᆡ의젼면에
두번이나밍렬ᄒᆞᆫ습격을ᄒᆞ엿고
ᄯᅩ즁앙과밋우익군방면에셔도
여러번미약ᄒᆞᆫ습격을ᄒᆞ엿는ᄃᆡ
우리는죄다이거슬격퇴ᄒᆞ엿고
젹군은수다ᄒᆞᆫ시톄를젼쟝에버
리고퇴각ᄒᆞ엿다ᄒᆞ엿더라

관보

뎨이쳔구ᄇᆡᆨ륙십이호연속
서임급사령

○임표훈원계쟝국쟝서주임관
사등 표훈원기사 김형모
○임의졍부참서관서주임관오
등 의졍부주사 김쥰용
○임레식원주사서판임관륙등
구픔 리죵이
○임의학교교관서판임관륙등
안샹호
○임외국어학교부교관서판임
관륙등 윤치영
○의원면본관 챵원감리서주
사 오일순
○임챵원감리서주사서판임관
륙등 리제옥
○승서판임관일등 니부주사
민경호
○금샹급봉 농샹공학교교관
김필진
○금이급봉 니부광제원의사
젼티완

UNION INSURANCE SOCIETY OF CANTON.

Head office Hongkong.
Marine risks underwritten at current rates.
Agents in Chemulpo,
E. MEYER & Co.

COMPAGNIE DES MESSAGERIES MARITIMES.

Fortnightly Direct Service.

For Marseilles
via Ports.
Sailing from Yokohama
Calling at Kobe,
Shanghai, Hongkong, Saigon, Singapore,
Colombo, Djibonti, Suez, Port Said
and Marseilles.

For particulars apply to
HOLME RINGER & Co.,
Chemulpo.

HAYASHIDA & Co.,

16 MYENG DONG, CHIN KO KAI, SEOUL.
BRANCH OFFICE AT CHEMULPO.

Money changers, Coal and Wood Merchants, Express Agents.

We are agents for the Pyeng-yang Coal Company and the Karazu Coal Company of Japan. We have the best quality of both anthracite and bituminous coal, and prompt execution of orders is our speciality. Firewood of all kinds kept in stock. Full weight guaranteed. Money of all denominations exchanged at current rates. Parcels received for all parts.

CHINA MUTUAL LIFE INS. CO.

Most favourable terms to policy holders.

Benefit system unsurpassed.

HOLME RINGER & Co.
Agents, Chemulpo.

C. P. R.

CANADIAN PACIFIC RAILWAY COMPANY'S ROYAL MAIL STEAMSHIP LINE.

THE FAST ROUTE BETWEEN CHINA, JAPAN, AND EUROPE VIA CANADA AND THE UNITED STATES.

Route from Hongkong via Shanghai, Nagasaki (Inland Sea of Japan) Kobe, Yokohama, Victoria and Vancouver.

Twin Screw Empress Steamship—6,000 Tons—Speed 19 knots.

PROPOSED SAILING FROM YOKOHAMA.
R. M. S. Empress of India.
R. M. S. Empress of Japan.
R. M. S. Empress of China.
R. M. S. Athenian.
R. M. S. Tartar.

Special reduction (first class only) granted to members of the Military, Naval, Diplomatic and Civil services and to Missionaries.
Passengers have choice of ten routes across the Continent of America and have privilege of travelling by any Atlantic Steamship Line.
Round the World passage tickets in connection with the P. and O. S. N., North German Lloyd and Messageries Co.'s £125.
All rates payable at current rate of exchange.
For further information, Tickets, Guide Books, etc., apply to
HOLME, RINGER & Co., AGENTS, Chemulpo.

Grand Hotel,

(Formerly the Station Hotel)

Near the Railway Terminus,
West Gate, Seoul.

The Best Hotel in Korea.
Handsome new Building.
Fine Airy Rooms
Excellent Cuisine.
Terms Moderate.
Special terms to Missionaries
and to permanent boarders.

Electric cars within 2 minutes' walk.

W. H. EMBERLEY,
Proprietor.

EVERY FACILITY.

In connection with Life Assurance Business is afforded by

The Standard Life Assurance Co.,

One of the largest and wealthiest of the Provident Institutions of the United Kingdom Forms of Application and all information will be promptly afforded on application.

10 CENTS A DAY.

Not a very large expenditure is it? But it is sufficient to secure for a man of 30 a policy with the STANDARD LIFE OFFICE for

$1323.

For all particulars of rates, etc., apply to

Holme, Ringer & Co.,
Agents, Chemulpo.

THE NEW YORK LIFE INSURANCE COMPANY.

Have you ever been declined by any Company?

Are you engaged in a specially hazardous occupation?

Have you heard of the New York Life Insurance Company's New Classifications for this class of Risks?

If not, send your date of birth, occupation and particulars of rejection, if any to

E. MEYER & Co.,
Agents, Chemulpo.

MITSUI BUSSAN KAISNHA.
(MITSUI & Co.)
MITSUI GINKO.
(MITSUI BANK.)

The Bank is owned by the members of the Mitsui Family, who, as partners, assume an unlimited responsibility for all liabilities of the Bank:—

Capital........................Yen 5,000,000
Reserve Fund.................. " 5,600,000

HEAD OFFICE, TOKYO.
LONDON OFFICE, 34 LIME ST., E. C.

BRANCHES AND AGENCIES:—
New York, San Francisco, Hamburg, Bombay, Singapore, Manila, Hongkong, Amoy, Chefoo, Tientsin.
Kobe, Hakodate, Yokohama, Kure, Yokosuka, Moji, Shimonoseki, Miike, Wakamatsu, Nagasaki, Kuchinotsu, Karatsu, Sasebo, Misume, Taipeh, &c.

Telegraphic Address for all the Offices:
"MITSUI."
A. B. C. AND A. 1 CODES USED.

Contractors of Coal
To the Imperial Japanese Navy. Arsenals and Railway Bureau, Principal Railway Companies and Industrial Work, Home and Foreign Mail and Freight Steamers.
Sole Proprietors
Of the famous Miike, Tagawa and Yamano Coal Mines.
Sole Agents
For the sale of Fukumo, Hokoku, Ichimura, Kanoda, Mannoura, Onoura, Ostuji, Sonoda, Tsubaruro, Yoshinotani, Yoshio, Yurokibura and other coals.

YANGTSE INSURANCE ASSOCIATION, LTD.

The undersigned, having been appointed agents for the above company, are prepared to issue policies and pay losses on marine risks at regular rates.

E. MEYER & Co.,
Agents, Cheum p

AMERICAN KOREAN ELECTRIC COMPANY.

Light and Power.

Main Office: Electric Building, Chong No.

RAILWAY DEPARTMENT.

OPERATING CARS BETWEEN EAST AND WEST GATE, EVERY TEN MINUTES:—
First Car leaves East Gate at 6:30 A. M. First Car leaves West Gate at 6:55 A. M.
Last Cra " East Gate at 10:40 P. M. Last " " West Gate at 11:00 P.M.

OPERATING CARS BETWEEN EAST GATE AND IMPERIAL TOMB TERMINUS, EVERY TWENTY MINUTES:—
CONNECTING WITH EVERY ALTERNATE CAR ARRIVING AT EAST GATE FROM CHONG NO.
First Car leaves East Gate for Tomb at 6:50 A. M.
" " " Tomb for East Gate at 7:10 A. M.
Last " " East Gate for Tomb at 9:50 P. M.
" " " Tomb for East Gate at 10:10 P. M.

OPERATING CARS BETWEEN CHONG NO AND YUNG SAN (RIVER EVERY TWELVE MINUTES:—
First Car leaves Chong No for South Gate at 6:48 A. M.
" " " Chong No for Yung San at 7:24 A. M.
" " " South Gate for Chong No at 6:56 A. M.
" " " Yung San for Chong No at 7:57 A. M.
Last " " South Gate for Chong No 11:00 P. M.
" " " Yung San for Chong No at 10:11 P. M.

SPECIAL PRIVATE CARS FURNISHED TO SUIT CONVENIENCE OF PATRONS. PRICES ON APPLICATION AT HEAD OFFICE.

LIGHTING DEPARTMENT.

Where less than 250 candle power of light is used, the rate per month will be: Per 16 candle power incandescent lamp,—All night.—Yen 2.50. Per 32 candle power incandescent lamp:—All night:—Yen 4.00. Per 50 candle power incandescent lamp:—All night:—Yen 6.00.
" 150 " " " " —" " 10.00. " 1200 " " enclosed arc " " 20.00.
Where more than 250 candle power of light is used, a Meter will be installed, if requested:—Rent of Meter Yen 2.00 per month. Rate of charges by meter reading:—Two Sen per Ampere per hour. (Approximately this is equal to about One Sen per 16 C. P. lamp per hour) Minimum monthly charge where meter is installed, Yen 20.00 per month, which includes rental of meter.
Estimates for installing lights furnished on application. An assortment of chandeliers always on hand.

AMUSEMENT DEPARTMENT.

ANIMATED PICTURES AT EAST GATE
Every evening - - - Except Sunday.
From 8 to 10 P. M.

10 Cents:—Gen. Admission:—10 Cents. Seats in First Class Section. 15 Cents Extra.

Change of program each week. Pictures from Foreign Lands. Pictures of Local Scenes:—Amusing and Instructive.

An entertaining evening for a reasonable price.
MERRY-GO-ROUND:—At East Gate.
From 10:00 A. M. till 11:00 P. M.

5 Cents a Ride.

Take your Exercise on The Galoping Horses.

Comfortable seats in the Chariots.

한셩뎐긔회사

한미뎐긔회사 고븐안 보사며 고빅
도흥음나이다
상ㆍ동사전뎐발소와목마운ᄒᆞᆼ쟝처로언
여매면차가온쟝안으로통힝ᄒᆞ여ᄃᆞ니여이
삽
또이거계에ᄀᆞᆺ치노힐편ᄒᆞ고됴흔마차도잇
삽
코미우편ᄒᆞ고또조미잇ᄂᆞᆫ됴흔운동이되겟
이됴흔모형ᄒᆞᆫ달나아ᄂᆞᆫ물을ᄐᆞ고위티치안
더가ᄂᆞᆫᄒᆞᆫ번ᄐᆞᄂᆞᆫ데오전셔이오
미일상오열시브터하오열ᄒᆞᆫ시ᄭᆞ지ᄒᆞ옵고
목마운동쟝은동대문안에잇삽고
가되겟삽
철군조의게갑도싸고저녁에됴흔쇼일거리
미잇고구경ᄒᆞᆯ만ᄒᆞᆫ거시오니
서양사진파대한과온동양사진인데대단조
ᄂᆞᆫ데
젼이옵고미쥬일에사진을싼것스로다밧고
고젼담ᄃᆡ금은하등에십젼이오상등에이십
일외에ᄂᆞᆫ미야에여덜시브러열시ᄭᆞ지ᄒᆞ옵
활동사진전람소ᄂᆞᆫ동대문안에잇삽고일요
회타부

All Cars Run Direct to the Animated Pictures and Merry-Go-Round.

○영의졍부주사셔 판임관륙등
무안감리셔주사 리주셩
○영무안감리셔주사셔 판임관
륙등 구풍신달수
이상십월십구일
뎨이천구빅십삼호 광무
팔년십월이십일일
서임급ᄉ령

○명전완일본국시찰ᄉ법상제
도급ᄉ무비리 참모부일국쟝
현영운
구월십구일
○명궁닉부특진관셔칙임관일
등 종일품 조병호
○명종묘서제주셔칙임관ᄉ등
경효뎐제주 조병익
○명경효뎐제주셔칙임관삼등
사직서제주 윤달영
○명사직서제주셔칙임관ᄉ등
종이품 리재덕
○명궁닉부특진관셔칙임관일
등 졍일품 박뎡양
종일품 조병필 졍이품 김
주현
○명닉장원경셔칙임관삼등
종이품 리명식
○명팀시서리종졍원경ᄉ무
비서원경 리지현
○궁이급봉 표훈원제쟝국쟝
김형모
이상십월십구일
○종묘서제주리재덕ᄉ직소
비지니에소청의시ᄒ노라소
○참모부뎨일국쟝현영운ᄉ직
소 비지니에젼소비지가잇스
니쏘번거히말느
○중추원의관장홍태ᄌ인소
비지니에임의감처ᄒ엿스니쏘
밀ᄒ지말느
○외부교셥국쟝유진찬ᄉ직소
비지니의소청은의시ᄒ노라
○함경북도관찰ᄉ정괴택ᄉ직
소 비지니에소청은의시ᄒ노
라
이상십월십구일
정오
○광무삼년 칙령뎨십칠호과
부령뎨ᄉ호좌기뎨삼항ᄎ에
「단군인군속이당우ᄒᄂ지빅일
이라ᄒ면부대상주ᄒ고본속쟝
관이지위발ᄒ야의례행공ᄒ
교빅일니라도등발ᄒᄂ경우가유
ᄒ면소속장관이상주ᄒ야출ᄉ
시무를명ᄒᆷ이라」칠십일ᄌ를
첨입기부표ᄒᆷ이라
○기국ᄉ빅ᄉ년 칙령뎨ᄉ십
삼호외교관령ᄉ관제중뎨
ᄉ호ᄎ의(뎨오됴충령ᄉᄂ주
임삼등이상ᄋ며령ᄉᄂ주임오
등ᄉ상인이아니면서임ᄒᆷ을
뎨ᄒᆷᄉ」삼십팔ᄌ를첨입ᄒ고부
뎨오됴ᄂ뎨구됴로ᄇ즈기졍ᄒ
야별기부표ᄒᆷ이라

론셜

ᄒᆫ길먼ᄒᆫ일

○변글에이르기를빅셩은오직
나라의근본이라근본이견고ᄒ
여야나라이평안ᄒ다ᄒ엿스니
이글을갑히ᄉ구ᄒᆫ진ᄃᆡ빅셩된
자의쟉칙이엇지진중치아니ᄒ
리요그런고로무릇어느나라이
던지빅셩된자ᄂᆫ불가불항ᄉ를
별니ᄇᆡᄒᆫ호며지조를괌실히ᄒᆫ와
우ᄒ로나라를도와충셩을다ᄒ
며아리로일신을보호ᄒ야평셩
을쾌락ᄒ게지ᄂᆡᄂᆫ것은사ᄅᆷ마
다주연ᄒᆫ리치로원ᄒᆫ비라
그러ᄒ나만일사ᄅᆷ이되여항샹
이엄게되면이ᄂᆫ금수와갓ᄒ니
니소위세샹에기명이라ᄒᄂᆫ거
와아만이라ᄒᄂᆫ거시무어시뇨
이여다만항ᄉ이유무를분변ᄒ
야말ᄒᆷ이니기명ᄒ엿다ᄂᆫ나라
들도당초브터문견이ᄌ연히만
코지각이ᄉᄉ로난거시아니요
아만의나라들도원리어둡고쏘
ᄒᆫ멍들ᄒᆫ비아니라
그럼으로영국갓ᄒᆫ나라에셔도
몃천년젼에ᄂᆫ나라에큰사ᄅᆷ을
빅셩들은싱각ᄒ기를하인과갓
치부리며교둔ᄒᆷ으로알엇고젼쟁
ᄒᆯ세에도손ᄂᆯ으로할퀴며돌과
몽둥이로ᄡᅡ홧서죠이기도ᄒᆫ지
라이러ᄒᆫ일로볼진ᄃᆡ엇지오날
날세계에부강ᄒ고기명ᄒᆫ나라
의웃듬이될줄로뜻ᄒ엿스리요
이도쏘ᄒᆫ용이ᄒ고ᄌ연ᄒᆫ일이
아니라젼국빅셩들의지혜가ᄎᄎ
ᄎ로열니여아모쪼록남의나라
에수치를면ᄒ고셰샹에광요케
ᄒ자ᄂᆫ주지로동심합력ᄒ야졍
부에셔ᄂᆫ다수의금애을지출ᄒ
야국중에각종학교를셜닙ᄒ고
인민을구라쳐발달케ᄒ며빅셩
들은법률과규측을조차근실이
수업ᄒ엿슴으로셰리외국에류람
도ᄒ며호유ᄒ도ᄒ야그나라에
졍치와법률이밝고이두운것도
열람ᄒ며조ᄒᆫ일과귀이ᄒᆫ수젹도
도샹과여서칙을만드ᄂ며ᄌ긔국
중에와기타외국에도반히광포
ᄒᆫ지라이거시모도빅셩된자의
충군이국ᄒ라ᄂᆫ주의로발미아
마남의쥬이며켜젼홧ᄒ며셩실
ᄒᆫ마음이엇지용이ᄒ다말ᄒ리
요마ᄂᆫ이사ᄅᆷ들의수고ᄒᆷ과근
엄ᄒᆷ으로인ᄒ야그국의명예가
영원히빗나며신샹의광요ᄒᆷ이
비ᄒᆯ되엽슨지라
쳥컨ᄃᆡ태한빅셩들도아모조록
나라의근본된직칙이중ᄒᆷ을싱
각ᄒ야이ᄅᆯ샹으로하문에힘쓰며
실지를세와취란ᄒᆫ일을힝ᄒ지
말며귀중ᄒᆫ세월을랑도치말아
나라를도으자ᄂᆫ마음으로ᄒᆫ갈
갓치진힘ᄒ게되면신샹의영화
를과기명의본의가구엇이ᄎᆯ을
가ᄒᆫᄉ스로알리로다

잡보

○죠쳥슈리비 닉부에서탁지
부로조회ᄒ야강화부관사수리
비이천여원을지발ᄒ라ᄒ엿더
라
○ᄌ셜ᄌ쟉 일본빅작소에셔
원산과평양간에뎐신을셜시ᄒ
로히도니ᄉᄉ산슈ᄎ를자벌ᄒ
다ᄒ고리히도부군에셔외부와통
신ᄒᆫ일은ᄂᆫ에뎐보ᄒ야그인허여부를
질문ᄒ엿더니히부원회뎐너에
히뎐션은인ᄒᆫ본인의청구가당초
에업섯다ᄒ엿더라
○신명구규 졍부에셔닉부에
조회ᄒ되더방관이부임ᄒᆯ세에
각부부쟝관의게일ᄎ식젼왕ᄒ
야뎌ᄉᄒᆷ은ᄉ례에당연ᄒ고구
규에조지ᄒ게ᄂᆞᆫ근리에엇지ᄒ
야폐지ᄒ엿ᄂᆫ지싱히소홀ᄒᆫ지
라신임ᄒᆫ관찰ᄉ목ᄉ부윤군슈
와게셔칙ᄒ야부임시에의레로
의졍참졍찬졍각부부대신참찬
외외게촌회ᄒᆷ수ᄒᆷ이타당ᄒᆫ즉별
반엄칙ᄒ야괴어히그규모를영
구히지킈게ᄒ라ᄒ엿다더라
○동사동부인 수법샹ᄉ무를
시찰ᄎ로일본에젼왕ᄒᄂᆫ참모
부뎨일국쟝현영운씨의ᄉ음지
슈가거ᄒ뎐쾌차ᄒ야일간발힝ᄒ
ᄂᆫ되그쇼실졍부인빅씨ᄂᆫ불가
불동거ᄒ리ᄒᆫ다더라
○빅쳔진회 빅쳔군슈우괴준
씨가닉부로보고ᄒ되본군거민
빈승와이가풍교ᄒ기를싱등이
기회초에기명목면저단발ᄒ은민국공이
회에ᄒ셜을도아서등립권를공고케
ᄒ황ᄒ고아리로인민을편안케ᄒ야
졔산을보호ᄒ고졍치를기혁ᄒ
야회명을진보회라명ᄒ엿스니
이비됴건을졍부에보고ᄒ야셜
시케ᄒ라ᄒ엿스니잇지회답ᄒ
라ᄒ엿더라
○문포기등 졍외부에도ᄂᆫ일젼
붓터림진강근처문산포서지기
등ᄒ엿더라
○면쳥경비 주일공사뎌리박
졍션씨가외부로면보ᄒ고공관
경비를지발ᄒ라ᄒ엿더라
○원ᄉ운협 자리로포ᄉ세금
을닉장원에서슈봉ᄒ다가제용
사를신셜ᄒ고포사세금을구관
ᄒ더니탁지부와농샹공부관제
를ᄡᅥ기졍ᄒ고포사세를농부로
부속ᄒ고각둔토ᄂᆫ탁지부로부
속ᄒ고닉장원과제용사ᄂᆫ병혁
ᄒ엿다더라
○젹주셔임 주임관을서임
ᄒᆯ시에각히부대신이졍부에거
쳔쳥의ᄒ야졍부에서평의ᄒᆫ후
에샹주ᄒ야서임ᄒ던니그규레를
분시ᄒ고각히부대신이ᄌ의로
쥬본ᄒ야서임ᄒ기로ᄒᆫ다더라
○죠쳥소제 닉부에서참모부
에조회ᄒ기를중남관찰ᄉ심건
택의면보를거ᄒᆫ즉진보회삼빅
여명이강경포에회집ᄒ야회장

리용구부회쟝권종덕이가관지
ᄒ되 황실보안ᄒᆷ과봉덕을부당
ᄒᆫ구명으로동널보니지말ᄂᆫ당
ᄒ엿스며고연셜사외ᄂᆫ정부를론
박ᄒᆷ인즉진위디에ᄒᆫ칙ᄒ야됴
멸케ᄒ라ᄒᆫ것과또현금로셩군
에칙졍ᄒᆫ회도등불가불란압ᄒᆯ
지니칙ᄒ디방부군진위디에셰납
ᄒᆫ칙ᄒ야소위진보회회장리용
구권종덕을즉각에포착ᄒ고힝
도당을소제ᄒ라ᄒ엿더라
○일진우편 일진회ᄂᆫ외국인
의별호보가업시ᄂᆫ개기관남ᄒᆯ
경우인데일본ᄉ령관쟝곡쳔태
쟝이개셜ᄒᆫ인허치아니ᄒᆷ으로
기회치못ᄒ엿ᄂᆫ중외도에셔졍
괴ᄒᄂᆫ회도를방쟝츄포ᄒᄂᆫ고
로히회중이대단우려ᄒᆫ다더라
○빈궁환후쳠중 황태ᄌ비뎐
하환후가샹금평복지못ᄒ신ᄃᆡ
뎐려졈졈쳠중ᄒ신고로쟉일부
터티의원관원과면의등이윤차
입직ᄒ와진빅ᄒ고약제를제진
ᄒᆫ다더라
◉동진동퇴 한셩졍게에가쟝
유세력ᄒᄂᆫ현영운씨가일본에
시찰ᄎ로지힝이미구에출발ᄒᆫ즉그
동지자로동진동퇴ᄒᄂᆫ리나샹
허참찬도ᄎ례로퇴거ᄒᆫ다더라
○영유박지 영유군에ᄂᆫ음력
팔월이십칠팔일에밤알갓ᄒᆫ우
박이쪽하ᄒ야뎐야빅곡이일시
피박ᄒᆫ고로민졍이황황ᄒ다코
달ᄒ엿더라
○대동회사 일본인부샹대교
뎡명사ᄅᆷ이발귀ᄒ야ᄒᆫ회사를
셜립ᄒ야대동회사라명칭ᄒ고
한국토디를무론모디ᄒ고민수
ᄒ기로ᄒᆫ다더라
○곡산민압수 곡산민요수긴
으로일본사령부에서히군민셜
칠명을압샹ᄒ엿ᄂᆫ데작야에도
착ᄒ야사령부에구수ᄒ엿다더
라

광고

거월십일일밤에농포한원소ᄉ
졈에서젹한의게가산을봉젹ᄒ
엿ᄂᆫ대그중에아주기포목면쟝
규환쳐에당오젼삼삼만량졀빛
쾌샹ᄉ수호시셕월회일에차젼이음
일편ᄒᆷ셔셜ᄒ엿스니무론뇌의
국인ᄒ고습득ᄒ여도ᄒᆷ지시힝
ᄒᆷ
농포안 원소ᄉ 고빅

미국우전회사와
동경동양긔션회사
미국긔션과연락ᄒ엿습
인천함릉가양힝디리졈

서울우전회사
속힝ᄒᄂᆫ이릉ᄎᆫ션들인ᄃᆡ
청국과일본셔영국ᄭ지각국으로
디왕ᄒᆷ
인천함릉가양힝디리졈

TELEGRAMS.

Tokyo, Oct. 20th.

The enemy opposing our right wing s̲eems to be reduced in numbers. Our left wing is being cannonaded in a desultory manner.

THE TWO RUSSIAN LEADERS.

(Specially written for the "China Review")

There are few great men who have more charming personalities than have Viceroy Alexeieff and General Kuropatkin, once one penetrates the official barrier of reserve thrown about them, more by their own staff than by any order or desire of their own. They are never too busy with their affairs of state and of war to stop and shake hands with some group of nearby officers, as they walk past, or go to inquire of some wounded soldier the nature of his hurt and how he is progressing. When a train load of wounded stop near their respective headquarters they invariably visit it and speak cheering words to the occupants. This may not seem much to comfort men who have been shot down in battle, but it means much to the soldiers themselves to have a superior officer take some compassionate notice of their wounds.

During the first few months of the war, when there was a great general hospital at Mukden, there was hardly a Sunday passed but that the Viceroy made a visit there, and spent several hours among the various wards. Occasionally when some soldier had been reported for some conspicuously brave act he would pin the coveted cross of St. George on the man as he lay in his bed in the hospital. I had heard a great deal about the personal side of the Viceroy, before I even saw him, from Captain Mahan of our navy. Captain Mahan is a member of a family of seafighters who have all distinguished themselves in their profession, and also in the literature of the sea as well. There is probably no authorty living to day whose word in naval matters and on naval men is more respected. It was Captain Mahan who first told me that I would find in the Viceroy an able leader, a diplomat as well as a sailor, and, above all, "You will find one of the most charming men I have ever known."

I had been in the theatre of war for several months before I had anything more than a passing glimpse of the Imperial Aide-de-camp, but later I was received by him and had the pleasure of a short interview. As I said before, once inside the official barrier and there confronts you a simple, charming man, of genial personality, who has that great gift of seeming to be unuterably pleased that you should have done him the honor of calling upon him, and you were apparently the one person that he had been waiting for, and now that you had finally come, his mind was quite at rest and he was perfectly happy. I have met one man before who could give that same feeling to everyone of his visitors and that was the late President McKinley. He met hundreds of men and women every day, men of every degree, Ambassadors with words from Emperors, ward politicians to beg a fourth class appointment for a friend or constituent, senators and tourists, women with grievances, or women with children who wanted to shake hands with the "First Citizen." There is no official barrier to be broken down to gain audience with the President of the United States, and therefore he has to say a word or so to hundreds who have no claim on his time; but, with all this, one never saw Mr. McKinley the least impatient with his visitors. I have seen him greet hundreds in the great reception room, shaking hands with each one and making each one feel that he or she was the particular one he had been wanting to see. So it is with Admiral Alexieff, and, although he is very hard to see,—I have seen Kings more easily approached,—he has that same happy greeting when once you come to him.

The Viceroy discussed the situation freely, he gave his ideas on the campaign, but he did not discuss the outcome of the war, no Russian ever does, as there can be but one end. There is much dissension of ideas regarding the causes and the rights of the war, there are officers who openly express their views as to what Russia should do after the war, but there is an absolute unity of opinion as to the ultimate end. Russia must win. There are no two opinions on that score. If the Russians in Russia are as strong in heart as the Russians in Manchria there need be no fear for Russian arms.

There has been much written regarding the friction between the Viceroy and General Kuropatkin, but it certainly is not apparent in the field, and everything seems perfectly harmonious. Even if there was discord it would not be very strange, as it seems to me that I have read of friction at the head of other armies before, and at not a very distant date either; but, as a matter of fact, there is no apparent antagonism between the state and the military head of Russia's force in Manchuria. It is not strange that there should be harmony, however, for things do not conflict in any detail, the one attending to the military while the other is the actual head of the entire force. I am sure the Viceroy's head plans many of the important movements, and that he is and has been the actual head of the navy but his movements are always the result of conferences held with General Kuropatkin.

I noticed that Kuropatkin used to come back to confer with the Viceroy before every important move, and it got so that it was a common saying among the attachés and correspondents that "there's going to be something doing, Kuropatkin went to confer with the Viceroy to-day." The personality of General Kuropatkin is none the less agreeable, he is a man of iron, but is a charming man to meet personally. His two natures are directly opposite in every way, one shows him the most lovable of men, with thoughts for every unfortunate sick or wounded man. He will stop and chat with officers or speak a few words of encouragement to a company of soldiers. The other shows him possessed of that same temperament of fury possessed by the First Napoleon.

One day his train was standing at the platform of the Liaoyang station and the general sat writing by the open window of his car when a wounded cossack passed. Although he was very busy he stopped his work, called to the man and questioned him regarding his hurts and wished him good fortune. A few minutes later he was walking up the station platform beside his train when he saw a man in civilian dress standing near the engine. Instantly he turned on the man and ordered him off the platform, at the same time sending for the station-master to know why his instructions regarding civilians had been disregarded.

"Why are you here?" he demanded angrily, "What do you want?"

The man looked at him a moment and then replied very respectfully "Because I am the driver of your train, your Excellency."

It was that same Napoleonic spirit that prompted him to dismiss two officers on the field after Liaoyang for not doing their duty. He paraded their regiment and peremptorily dismissed them from the army on the spot. And the same day he recognized the merits of others and rewarded them accordingly.

As days go by his deeds prove him to be worthy of the trust his Emperor, his country, and his army has put in him.

J. F. J. Archibald.

The Korea Daily News.

Issued at 5 P. M. daily except Sundays.

Rate of Subscription:—

Per Year,	Yen 25.
Per Quarter,	Yen 7.
Per Month,	Yen 2.50.

Postage in Korea not charged extra.
Postage abroad charged extra.

Advertisements, 50 sen per day for 1 inch or less.
5 yen per month per inch.
50 yen per year per inch.

All communications to E. T. BETHELL, Editor and Publisher, Pak-tong, Seoul

THE WEEK.

The all absorbing topic for the past week has naturally been the war and the latest turn taken by events.

On Oct. 5th, whether with the object of forcing a decisive battle or merely wishing to prevent the Japanese from strengthening their positions at Liaoyaug is not yet known, Kuropatkin commenced a southward movement of his whole force.

The surprise of his attack forced the Japanese to evacuate their strategical positions to the north and northeast of Yentai on the 9th inst. On the 11th however, they once more reasserted themselves and drove their enemy back, capturing 30 guns.

With only Japanese reports before us, it is difficult to ascertain the exact outcome of the battle, though it undoubtedly is of greater magnitude than the Liaoyang struggle. With their usual promptness, the Japanese have given us their estimate of Russian losses, while little or nothing has been said of their own.

In only one instance have Japanese casualties been mentioned, i. e. the loss of 14 guns and 1,000 men from one column which was surrounded by the enemy, and forced to fight its way out.

Mr. Bennet Burleigh, we are glad to see, is once more criticising and directing the affairs of the universe.

Describing the Russian retreat from Liaoyang, this worthy scribe remarks, "The Muscovites presented a most dejected appearance in the retreat. The men are of good material, but the officers lack many necessary qualities. The war is most unpopular with all the Russian soldiers."

Considering that Mr. Burleigh left the field on account of not being allowed within eight miles of the firing line, his eye-sight must have been extremely keen to detect the "dejected appearance of the Muscovites."

The same journalist has also detected that there is something wrong with Japanese tactics, for in an interview with a representative of the "Shanghai Times," he sagely remarks:—"There is something wrong with the Japanese plans as carried out in the field, and Japan must look to it. The Japanese have no commander-in-chief in the field. They have the headquarters staff and the chief of staff, with the generals of divisions all in the field, but no commander-in-chief, which is a very great mistake. To the chief of staff is attributable the whole blame of the failure to hold Kuropatkin in Liaoyang. The Japanese merchants, gentry and educated classes know there is something wrong and could speak to you if they cared. They know Liaoyang was a failure. You just talk with a well-informed Japanese and he will tell you how something has gone wrong with matters previously arranged. The Japanese soldiers and young officers are all right, but there is something wrong and it is for you and not me to find out where that something is. I know but I cannot speak."

What a world of hidden meaning in that last sentence. "I know but I can not speak."

General and Lady Hyon are expected to leave for Japan in a few days.

Latest reports from Gensan state that the Russians are retreating north before our troops.

About 20 Koreans, suspected of being implicated in the Koksan riot arrived under arrest at the Japanese Headquarters last night.

Major Pak Mam-Sin commander of the Korean troops at Djong Chu has been arrested by Japanese gendarmes on suspicion of his being a Russian spy.

Mr. Cho Min-Heui, Korean Minister to Tokyo, has been ordered by His Majesty to return immediately to Japan, so that he may be at his post on the occasion of the Japanese Emperor's birthday on the 3rd prox.

The Il Chin Hoi have again held a meeting. This time it was discussed and resolved to send a committee to the Government to enquire the reason of dispersal of the meetings of top-knotless ones throughout the country.

The "Japan Times" reports that on Tuesday His Majesty the Emperor was pleased to confer the Sixth Class Order of the Crown on Dr. McGee and the Seventh Class Order of the same on each member of her party, in appreciation of the services rendered by them to this country in nursing our sick and wounded.

Mr. Yi Chu Hyun, the magistrate of Koyang, is at present the recipient of many grateful messages from the citizens of his district. He is considered worthy of great praise for the strong atttiude he took up at the time of the Japanese impressment of coolies. His people have started a fund, for the purpose of erecting a statue to his memory.

THE THIRD ISSUE OF DOMESTIC WAR LOAN.

By Departmental Ordinance No. 41, the Minister of Finance announced on Wednesday, reports the "Japan Times," the regulations relating to the third issue of Treasury Bonds. The amount is to be 80,000,000 yen, issued, as already noticed, at the minimum price of 92 yen, and repayable within seven years counting from the 38th year of Meiji (1905). The rate of interest is five per cent, per annum. The subscription list will be opened on October 31st and closed on November 7th. Applications may, however, be received by the Bank of Japan, its branches, and properly appointed agencies even before the formal opening of the list. Allotment, which will be settled and announced on November 18th, will be made from the highest price offered, and in the case of the residual offers, allotment is to be made in proportion to the amounts subscribed for. Each application should be accompanied by the deposit of security money at the rate of two yen for each 100 yen face value of the bonds subscribed for. Payment is spread over in eight monthly instalments beginning in November, 1904, and ending in June, 1905. On the payment of the second instalment, the subscriber will receive provisionary bonds, which will be exchanged for regular bonds on completion of the whole payment. The provisionary bonds may be sold or hypothecated.

STATEMENT BY KOREAN MINISTER IN LONDON.

The Korean Chargé d'Affaires in London has been interviewed on behalf of Reuter's Agency in regard to the agreement concluded between Korea and Japan. He said:—

"First of all I must exprss my surprise at the references I have seen to this agreement meaning a Japanese Protectorate over my country. This is simply ridiculous. In connection with the new arrangements on financial and other matters just made with Japan it must be remembered that our independence has been solemnly guaranteed not only by Japan but also by Great Britain. The Treaty of Shimonoseki of 1895, the Anglo-Japanese Treaty of 1902, and the Japanese-Korean Protocol concluded in February of this year after the outbreak of the Russo-Japanese War all expressly provide for this. It is therefore obviously absurd for certain reports to be current that Korean interests abroad have been transferred to the Japanese Legations or that Korea is to become a sort of Japanese Egypt. If there were a grain of truth in these malicious rumours the agreements to which I have referred have been misinterpreted. It is not true that Korean diplomatists have been recalled. I do not believe that it is Japan's policy to seek a protectorate over Korea, and I cannot think that, after all that Japan has done for our country and after all her assurances to safeguard our integrity and independence, she has any such aim in view.

"With regard to the agreement just concluded with Japan it is quite necessary that we should have a foreign financial adviser, but this is nothing new. For years Mr. McLeavy Brown did splendid work for us, and he only vacated his post as the result of unfortunate circumstances. He was succeeded by M. Alexeieff, who held the post for a short while, since which time it has been vacant. Now a new adviser is appointed. We welcome such an appointment, but it must not be forgotten that he comes simply as an adviser. The appointment of a diplomatic adviser falls in the same category. By our protocol with Japan it is understood that neither Power will take steps with a third which may affect their mutual interests until after the consent of both Japan and Korea has been given. There can be no objection to the appointment of a foreign diplomatic adviser, but the suggestion emanating from America that he comes as a Japanese Viceroy is quite another matter and is ridiculous. We are ready and willing to consult with our good friend Japan and to seek her advice, and are most anxious to safeguard foreign interests in Korea—especially Japanese—but we always stand firmly on the ground of our independence and the integrity which has been so solemnly guaranteed."

HARI-KIRI.

Said Captain Yokoham See
To bold Lieutenant San:
"I think that we imposingly
Should die for old Japan."

The officers around them heard
Them making up this plan,
And passed along the fateful word—
"We die for old Japan."

They stood up resolute and glad,
They stood up man by man,
To blow out all the brains they had......
"Banzai! Nippon, Japan!"

The cook his long, sharp carving-knife
Right through his bowels ran,
And took away his fat, brown life
To help along Japan.

The common soldiers, fired with zeal
And glorious clan,
Stuck in each other yards of steel
And perished for Japan.

The cold, green sea was waiting by
To swallow every man,
But they must in the limelight die—
To advertise Japan.

—Sydney Bulletin.

The Korea Daily News.

VOL. I, | SATURDAY, OCTOBER 22, 1904. | No. 83

大韓每日申報
대한미일신보

(뎨팔십ᄉᆞ호) (월요일) 일쳔구빅ᄉᆞ년십월이십ᄉᆞ일

본샤고빅

본신보는영어와한어로셕거미일츌판ᄒᆞ옵

신문가

한쟝 엽두돈오푼

일삭됴 엽두량닷돈

우표가미삭닷돈

더맛돈으로밧솝

광고료는

긔한의쟝단과ᄌᆞ힝의다쇼로즁감ᄒᆞ되렴가로밧을터이오며오ᄅᆡ지아녀대한사람마다다이신문을보실터이니광고내시기들원ᄒᆞ시는이들은우리신문샤에와셔면약ᄒᆞ심을희망ᄒᆞ옵

○발힝소 박동대한미일신보샤법어학교압헤젼영국인셜필림집자리오

샤쟝 영국인 (비셜)

평양 ᄃᆡ리졈

○평양효동사는권미보씨가우리신문관ᄃᆡ리인을ᄐᆡ졍ᄒᆞ엿ᄉᆞ오니평양에계신구람쳠군ᄌᆞ는ᄃᆡ리졈에왕림ᄒᆞ와면외ᄒᆞ시옵

사고

○우리대한미일신보의목뎍은대한의안녕질셔에관한모든ᄆᆡ목에ᄃᆡᄒᆞ야는공평한변론을쥬쟝홈이라우리통신원의탐보는신문보ᄂᆞᆫ쳠군ᄌᆞ의게홍샹보도ᄒᆞ리며편지를긔셔ᄒᆞ여주시는이는셩명과반ᄃᆞ시를젹어붓치시기를희망ᄒᆞ오니이거슬신문샹에긔재ᄒᆞ라는거시아니오다만극히신용ᄒᆞᆯ는즁거를숨고쟈홈이라긔쟈는아모긔셔던지긔지홈을되각ᄒᆞ는권리를가졋ᄉᆞ나되각ᄒᆞᆫ리유를말ᄒᆞᆯ터이오며공즁평화를문란케ᄒᆞ는듯ᄒᆞᆫ긔셔는의례히밧지안켓솝나이다

●본샤셜시이릭로신문을미양우례로분젼ᄒᆞ와례젼부의임의로젼ᄒᆞᆫ듯스로먼곳에는혹늣게젼ᄒᆞ기도ᄒᆞ며혹멋칠거슬ᄒᆞᆫ겁에젼ᄒᆞ기도ᄒᆞ며혹아니젼ᄒᆞ는곳도잇다ᄒᆞ와우리신문을ᄉᆞ랑ᄒᆞ야구람ᄒᆞ시는 쳠군ᄌᆞ의계ᄃᆡᄒᆞ야미우미안ᄒᆞ옵기로지금은분젼인을두고미일일쥭이젼ᄒᆞ며아니젼ᄒᆞ거나늣게거나ᄒᆞᆫ폐가업도록ᄒᆞ랴ᄒᆞ오니혹아니젼ᄒᆞ거나혹늣게젼ᄒᆞ거나ᄒᆞᆫ일이잇스면본샤로통긔ᄒᆞ여쥬심을희망ᄒᆞ옵

본샤광고

○본샤신문즁에좌긔ᄒᆞᆫ호수를소용ᄒᆞᆯ데가잇셔이에광고ᄒᆞ오니누구시던지그즁에아모호수던지가져오시는ᄃᆡ로미쟝에빅젼두푼식드리리다

뎨이호 뎨삼호 뎨이십호 뎨ᄉᆞ십이호 뎨ᄉᆞ십삼호 뎨이십삼호 뎨오십삼호 뎨오십ᄉᆞ호와뎨오십오호 뎨륙십이호

론셜

근경소문

○십월오일에량국이또ᄒᆞᆫ싸홈을시작ᄒᆞ엿다ᄒᆞᆫ즉아병이죵말젼투로대젹ᄒᆞ엿는지다만요양에잇는일병을방비ᄒᆞᆯ뜻으로그리ᄒᆞ엿는지는아즉알수업스되구로파트킨쟝군이힘을다ᄒᆞ야남방으로발병ᄒᆞ엿다ᄒᆞ더니파연금월구일에일병이공격ᄒᆞ야연ᄐᆡ북방과동북잔방으로진러를철귀ᄒᆞ게만드러다가지의일에일병이젹군을다시모라쫏고화포삼십문을어덧다ᄒᆞ는지라일본사름의보고갓타여셔는셜혹요양젼쟁버다오히려평장ᄒᆞ엿드ᄅᆡ도젼투의결실은실로알기어려운거시일본셔는홍샹ᄌᆞ긔나라사름만도와말ᄒᆞ야아병의손히된것만드러너고ᄌᆞ긔의군ᄉᆞ는수효를감ᄒᆞ던지젼수히업는양으로말ᄒᆞ는즁심지어ᄒᆞᆫ번은ᄌᆞ긔의군ᄉᆞ일죵ᄃᆡ가아병의게에워싸이여대포십사문을젼실ᄒᆞ고사샹이일쳔명에이르게되엿더니다시힘을합ᄒᆞ야그위ᄐᆡᄒᆞᆷ을버셔낫다고말ᄒᆞ는지라이러므로우리는쎌리크씨의말이라면반갑게보고ᄃᆡ단히밋는거시동시는셰샹일을공변되이평론ᄒᆞ야방향을알도록ᄒᆞ는쟈ㅣ라긔왕요양젼쟁에도아라사군병들은효용ᄒᆞ며건강ᄒᆞ되소위쟝관명식이번번치못ᄒᆞᆷ으로사졸들도스사로젼사지심이죠곰도업셔한만히ᄒᆞ다가대픠ᄒᆞ엿다ᄒᆞ며또샹히신문의동씨의슈작ᄒᆞᆫ바를계지ᄒᆞ엿는ᄃᆡ젼쟝팔영긔이ᄂᆡ에는당초허락ᄒᆞ야드리지아니ᄒᆞ는고로다만멀니잇셔안력을다ᄒᆞ야그관광을자셔히살핀즉아병의참혹ᄒᆞᆫ형샹은불가형언이요일병의병법도오히려부족ᄒᆞᆫ듯ᄒᆞᆫ지라셔로싸홈ᄒᆞᆯ때에보드ᄅᆡ도참모쟝관이하각대쟝관이모도츌쟝ᄒᆞ야응젹ᄒᆞ되다만총사령관은젼쟝으로나오지아니ᄒᆞᆫ즉이거시군략상에대단히잘못ᄒᆞ는일이며또일본에사관과병졸이모도년소ᄒᆞ고건강ᄒᆞ야가히쓸만ᄒᆞ되그즁잘못되는일이잇스니이거슨셜혹니가알드ᄅᆡ도발셜치못ᄒᆞ겟다고ᄒᆞ엿다더라

관보

뎨이쳔구빅륙십ᄉᆞ호

광무팔년십월이십이일

셔임급ᄉᆞ령

○승셔관임관오등 공쥬면보ᄉᆞ쥬ᄉᆞ 임원지

구월ᄉᆞ일

○승셔관임관이등 면환국기슈 박두희

십월이일

○승셔관임관오등 긔셩면보ᄉᆞ쥬ᄉᆞ 류인슈 시흥면보ᄉᆞ쥬ᄉᆞ 최봉긔

십월삼일

○임총령ᄉᆞ관셔쥬임관이등 외부참셔관 리죵협

십월십ᄉᆞ일

○승셔관임관오등 희쥬면보ᄉᆞ쥬ᄉᆞ 엄희셥 한셩우톄ᄉᆞ쥬ᄉᆞ 김봉리

십월십륙일

○임륙군법원쟝셔칙임관삼등 륙군참쟝 신ᄐᆡ휴

○임륙군법원리ᄉᆞ칙임관ᄉᆞ등 륙군보병참령 신지영

○겸임군긔창관리 참모부일국쟝 현영운

임륙군법원리ᄉᆞ셔쥬임관삼등 졍삼품 홍우형

○임륙군법원리ᄉᆞ셔쥬임관ᄉᆞ등 졍삼품 김응쥰

○임평리원검ᄉᆞ셔쥬임관ᄉᆞ등 륙품 현동건

이상십월십구일

○임통신ᄉᆞ면화과쥬ᄉᆞ셔관임관륙등 륙품 최병창 졍리웅

○승셔관임관오등 ᄂᆡ부광졔원의ᄉᆞ 리응원

이상십월이십일

○일쥬일경근신 진위뎨ᄉᆞ련ᄃᆡ뎨일대ᄃᆡ장복군보병참령 홍창걸

십월십팔일

궁뎡록ᄉᆞ

○한셩부판윤리희창ᄉᆞ직소비지ᄂᆡ에소청은의시ᄒᆞ노라

십월이십일

잡보

○쟝셔권학 학부참셔관김령진씨가학업샹권면ᄒᆞ기위ᄒᆞ야쟝셔를지어일본류학싱의게붓첫는ᄃᆡ허다ᄒᆞᆫ쟝황셜화를력력히긔재ᄒᆞᆯ수입스나그긔의가조곰도의심말고열심으로공부ᄒᆞ야졸업회국ᄒᆞ는날국가에동량지재로슈용케ᄒᆞ라ᄒᆞ엿다더라

○양구민쳥원 양구민인하영규등이ᄂᆡ부에쳥원ᄒᆞ되본군슈가도임ᄒᆞᆫ이후로실심힝졍ᄒᆞ야민폐를낫낫치혁거ᄒᆞᆫ고로일군인민이안도ᄒᆞ더니금년하긔에펌에하등에거ᄒᆞᆫ고로본군슈가곳샹경ᄒᆞᆫ즉인민이부모일흔것과ᄀᆞᆺ치여기고본관의환관ᄒᆞᆷ을쥬야로앙망ᄒᆞ니바라건ᄃᆡ즉시최족ᄒᆞ송ᄒᆞ라ᄒᆞ엿다더라

○최쟝언귀오 평안도각ᄃᆡ빈에는인민이원통ᄒᆞᆫ소졍이잇셔셔본군슈의게졍소ᄒᆞᆫ즉군슈들이공심은고샤ᄒᆞ고욕심이법을ᄒᆞ야송리곡직은젼불샹관ᄒᆞ고요로로청촉ᄒᆞ고거익으로잡리ᄒᆞ는쟈가의례히득송ᄒᆞ고기외에도담학등ᄉᆞ가허다ᄒᆞᆫ즉빅셩이본군에졍ᄒᆞ엿다가리직학송ᄒᆞ엿다고관찰부평리원에샹소ᄒᆞ여도뢰물업시는득송못ᄒᆞᆫ다고송민등이만히근쳐에잇는일본령ᄉᆞ나병참소에호소ᄒᆞ여벼안ᄒᆞᆫ다ᄒᆞ니그척망ᄒᆞᆫ관장의계잇는지빅셩의게잇는지알수업다고들ᄒᆞ더라

○궁ᄂᆡ슈관 미국공사가외부로죠회ᄒᆞ기를미한한셩뎐긔회샤에셔공함ᄒᆞ되한셩슈도역사에슈관건셜ᄒᆞᆯ사름한국궁ᄂᆡ부에셔본샤와약됴ᄒᆞ엿더니현금드른즉궁ᄂᆡ부에셔직시작ᄒᆞᆫ슈관을셜시ᄒᆞᆫ다ᄒᆞ니

이라본샤에셔는명츈에한셩닉슈관을셜시ᄒᆞᆯ터이라ᄒᆞ엿기로죠회ᄒᆞ니죠량ᄒᆞ라ᄒᆞ엿더라

○우림한관　한셩판윤리희챵씨소레된텨에닉부참셔관김대진씨가피임ᄒᆞ엿더라

○량관피임　한셩판윤김대진씨결닙베에방부참셔관송티헌씨가피임ᄒᆞ엿더라

○일조젼문　함흥쥬차일본군지휘관이군령등ᄉᆞ로함흥관찰ᄉᆞ의게죠회ᄒᆞᆷ은뎐보에과지ᄒᆞ엿거니와그죠회젼문에ᄒᆞ엿스되함흥ᄃᆡ평문친고원영흥등군에무론무ᄉᆞ논목ᄃᆡ비이던지대일본군부리가를엇지못ᄒᆞ고는망녕되히무상회를셜시ᄒᆞ거나당을모뒤여다수인민이취회ᄒᆞ야동문등ᄉᆞ욕을반포ᄒᆞ며일긔인이란도도병긔가지ᄭᅥ을일졔금지ᄒᆞ되범금ᄒᆞ는자는군률노시힝ᄒᆞᆯ게시오샨조리로조직ᄒᆞ야닥레된회라도본군령뷔로시인가를바든연후에야시힝된다ᄒᆞ엿더라

○샹슈여방　즁포관화산군슈박ᄒᆞᆫ긔씨가본산포에둔취ᄒᆞᆫ동도샹셩명챡거ᄒᆞᆷ은뎐보에과지ᄒᆞ엿거니와ᄒᆡ포삼십명즁젼의일빅공졍방인ᄀᆞᆫ은환셜ᄒᆞᆫ동학당원교로본군에챡거ᄒᆞ엿슈ᄒᆞ엿고기외각인은효유방송ᄒᆞ엿더고닉부로보고ᄒᆞ엿더라

○함비명쟝　함남관찰ᄉᆞ가닉부로뎐보ᄒᆞ기를일본군지휘관이졈령ᄒᆞᆫᄒᆞᆫ되평안에군령시힝ᄒᆞᆫ다는귀부ᄒᆞᆫ령뒤로관하각군에분칙ᄒᆞ야여영졈령이아니오군수샹필요로군되주차ᄒᆞᆫ동안군수샹에관ᄒᆞᆫ수긴만힝령ᄒᆞᆫ다홈이합실ᄒᆞᆫ준노져져히힝ᄒᆞᆯᄒᆞ엿다더라

○아함포살　근일모쳐에도달ᄒᆞᆫ통신을거ᄒᆞᆫ즉아셩ᄒᆞᆨ강우안관젼디방에는일병과아병이죵죵충돌ᄒᆞᄂᆞᆫ디인ᄒᆞ야아라사의당졍이충돌ᄒᆞᄂᆞᆫ자가만ᄒᆞᆫ디일젼에일병의게피챡되여포살ᄒᆞᆫ시탐오명은다청국무관인디일병의동쟝을아국에탐보ᄒᆞᆫ용뒤로아국으로셔금으로밋든ᄒᆞᆫ장과포죵쟝을바든자도그즁에잇셧다더라

○귀방연괴　총세무ᄉᆞ쌱탁운씨가룡암포에젼왕ᄒᆞ엿기로근일소문은방금졍부에셔용암포와의쥬를귀방ᄒᆞ기로쥰비즁이라ᄒᆞᆫ되졍부에셔는아직그두곳귀방ᄒᆞ기를연괴ᄒᆞ기로닉졍이되엿다더라

○아병퇴복　한셩이본ᄀᆞᆫ사령부에달ᄒᆞᆫ원산뎐보를거ᄒᆞᆫ즉함관령북방에와셔영문을셜치ᄒᆞ든아병이빅명은하로밤을류숙ᄒᆞ고북방으로물너갓다ᄒᆞ고함흥에셔온뎐보에는일병이합흥에리도ᄒᆞ야빅셩을안도ᄒᆞ라ᄂᆞᆫ군령을반포ᄒᆞᆫ후에셩진에잇든아병은경흥디방으로것어갓다더라

○부윤간면셜　울산군수가닉부로죠회ᄒᆞ되음력팔월륙일에일본인이부산셔울산방어포셔지뎐션을가셜ᄒᆞᆯᄎᆞ로셜말쟝을세웟다ᄒᆞ엿더라

○박천박재　박천군보에ᄒᆞ기를음력팔월이십팔일에본군쟝평일평의주회오십리안에간비와우박이폭주ᄒᆞ야뎐답빅곡이타작ᄒᆞᆫ것과찻치곡식과채석이물가온되박락ᄒᆞ엿스니치티방농민이엇지싱활ᄒᆞᆯ는지삭히궁민ᄒᆞ다ᄒᆞ엿더라

○일취민곡　무안군슈죠진규씨가닉부로보고ᄒᆞ되본군쟝항포에신츅년브터 영친왕궁소관으로방츅을싸어셔뎐답ᄉᆞ기간ᄒᆞᄂᆞᆫ대소역비에거핵과민력에쥐비가즁대ᄒᆞᆯ쌘아니라금년츈하간에농민의ᄀᆞ고로작농ᄒᆞ야추셩디경을당ᄒᆞ엿는되불의금자에목포항으로셔일본인대너등삼인이슌검이명파동ᄉᆞ긴셩오를거ᄂᆞ리고쟝항포에ᄅᆡ도ᄒᆞ야뎐답곡식을임의로베허가지가ᄂᆞᆫ고로히뎐답작인등이진문ᄒᆞᆫ즉일인언ᄃᆡ에 영친왕궁에셔이뎐토방츅에역비를반금을취ᄒᆞ엿스되우금샹년고로우리등으로ᄒᆞ여곰츄슈ᄒᆞ여샹랍ᄒᆞ라ᄒᆞ엿다ᄒᆞ니외국인이본국빅셩의작농ᄒᆞᆫ곡식을무단히탈취ᄒᆞᆷ이극히고이ᄒᆞ온지라죠량ᄒᆞ시고쳐분ᄒᆞ라ᄒᆞ엿더라

○위원동비　평안북도위원군에셔ᄂᆞᆫ일동학당이벌셰굿치이러남으로강계진위ᄃᆡ에셔일쇼ᄃᆡ를파견ᄒᆞ야진압ᄒᆞᆫ다더라

○쇼셕방츌　ᄀᆞ이젼에일본군ᄉᆞ령부에피챡되엿든참령빅남신씨ᄂᆞᆫ로국졍탐의혐의로피졉되엿다ᄒᆞ더니작일에방셕되엿다ᄒᆞ니희ᄉᆞ실이무거ᄒᆞᆷ을가지ᄒᆞ겟더라

○쳥결공의　직작일에한일량국쳥결위원졔씨가쳥결ᄉᆞ무쇼에회동ᄒᆞ야쳥결법실시ᄒᆞᆯ방법을공의ᄒᆞ엿더라

○경젼뎡간　명일은계텬긔원경젼인고로일일을휴가ᄒᆞᆷ

○종부피셕　영친왕뎐하계옵셔ᄂᆞᆫ직작일에빈이뎐각에납시드리오신거슬아지못ᄒᆞ시고반부ᄅᆞᆯ아시다가빈이 뎐하의종부를쇼셔샹금ᄭᅴ후가불평ᄒᆞ시다더라

○셔슈쟝죄　면쳔군슈셔직우씨ᄂᆞᆫ즁포관을겸압ᄒᆞ야즁포관ᄉᆞ무에열심ᄒᆞ야칭군부ᄂᆞᆫ디에도젹이쟝이침샤되엿더니향일에무뢰빈의계무ᄒᆞᆷ을낭ᄒᆞᆫ고로셔군슈가닉부에보고ᄒᆞ야면관징죄ᄒᆞᆷ을쳥ᄒᆞ엿더라

○무의영시　일본ᄉᆞ령관쟝곡쳔대쟝은본국승후관규례들의방ᄒᆞ야 대닉에무시로무의히잉시ᄒᆞ기로작뎡ᄒᆞ엿다ᄒᆞ더라

○우작감투　일본공관통역관엄쳔이ᄅᆞᆫ티란씨ᄂᆞᆫ부지중ᄭᅥ연히한졍부감투이되아졍부긔회시에는와례히참셕ᄒᆞᆫ다ᄒᆞ더라

○빈씨영시　황태ᄌᆞ비뎐하환후민영쇼씨가젼졈ᄎᆞ즁ᄒᆞ신고로보국시가쟉야브터쥬야입시ᄒᆞ더라

ᄉᆞ힝졔이　향ᄌᆞ에슈유환국ᄒᆞᆫ쥬일한국공ᄉᆞ죠민희씨는황샹폐하의 칙교를봉승ᄒᆞ야명일에발졍ᄒᆞ야일본으로젼왕ᄒᆞᆫ다ᄂᆞᆫ디이갓치급히셰나ᄂᆞᆫ것ᄉᆞᆫ각항ᄉᆞ졍에관계됨도잇거니와위션로리원샹일은일본디쟝졀인교로디리공ᄉᆞ로ᄂᆞᆫ참례ᄒᆞ기ᄅᆞᆯ회쳬가되ᄂᆞᆫ고로셔뎌드리에죠ᄉᆞ가샹당ᄒᆞᆫ다더라

○연쇽샹경　졍부에셔단발ᄒᆞᄂᆞᆫ자에관ᄒᆞ야각도에훈칙ᄒᆞ고단발ᄒᆞᄂᆞᆫ자를포착ᄒᆞ야형벌ᄒᆞᆫ다ᄒᆞ엿다는디한셩닉에잇는단발ᄒᆞᆫ자들의게ᄂᆞᆫ아모령칙이업스믹각쳐에셔진보회란동학이가히샹경ᄒᆞᆫ다ᄂᆞᆫ당류들이연쇽부지기슈라더라

○량씨쟝발　쥬미공관셔긔쳐죵무씨와쥬쳥공관셔긔김균졍씨가슈유귀국ᄒᆞ엿더니일간발힝ᄒᆞ야각기공관으로젼왕ᄒᆞᆫ다더라

외보

○로쟝젼사　십월십칠일로돈발뎐을거ᄒᆞᆫ즉로국셔울발뎐에ᄒᆞ엿ᄒᆞ얏고로군의손희ᄂᆞᆫ일만오쳔에달ᄒᆞ엿고자ᄎᆡᆨ웅ᄀᆞᆫ쟝군은젼사ᄒᆞ엿다더라

○젼군쟝동　십월십칠일동경발뎐을거ᄒᆞᆫ즉로국황뎨는십오일에ᄀᆡ어젼회의를열엇는디그결과ᄂᆞᆫ온로국군ᄃᆡ들다동병ᄒᆞ기로결뎡ᄒᆞᆫ듯ᄒᆞ다ᄒᆞ엿더라

○고샤구병　돈셔고샤구사단의쳔진은근자의함이빈에도챡ᄒᆞᆫ듯ᄒᆞᆫ모양이라ᄒᆞ엿더라

○부샹자티다　십월십오일로돈발뎐을거ᄒᆞᆫ즉로병의부샹ᄒᆞᆫ자이만삼쳔명이봉텬부에도챡ᄒᆞ엿고라빈스쟝군은부샹ᄒᆞ여위중ᄒᆞ다ᄒᆞ엿더라

○무명포티졈령　본월십륙일아참에일본군은이룡산젼면의일홈업ᄂᆞᆫ포ᄃᆡ를공격ᄒᆞ야졈령ᄒᆞ엿ᄂᆞᆫ되피ᄎᆞ샤샹은티단히만타ᄒᆞ엿더라

뎐보

십월이십일동경발

○각방면젼황　ᄒᆞᆯ뎐보로일에젼투ᄒᆞᆫ쳥관에관ᄒᆞᆫ대샨총ᄉᆞ령관의공보의요령이좌와곳ᄒᆞ니

대ᄒᆡᆼ우익군방면의
젹군은졈ᄎᆞ그셰력을감ᄒᆞᆫ듯ᄒᆞ고다만쇼부티만과농ᄒᆞ엿고편조보에셔격퇴ᄒᆞᆷ이된젹군은북하에동북으로퇴각ᄒᆞᄂᆞᆫ즁이오

대이중앙군방면의
젹군은작야에습격을ᄒᆞ엿스나이긔슬좌다격퇴ᄒᆞ엿고본일은다만조금식베셰로포젼을ᄒᆞᆯ쌔름이오

대샹좌익군방면의젼면의
젹군은베베로간졉ᄒᆞ야포격을ᄒᆞᆯ쌔름이라ᄒᆞ엿더라

십월십륙일론돈발

○셴듸핌텀　ᄉᆞ십쳔쳑으로편셩ᄒᆞᆫ셴듸핌텀ᄂᆞᆫ십삼일밤에리보항에셔츌발ᄒᆞ엿다ᄒᆞ엿더라

십월십오일론돈발

○셴듸참디동향　젼투함륙쳑과슌양함십이쳑과구츅함륙쳑과운송션오쳑과셕탄션십쳑으로편셩ᄒᆞᆫ셴듸핌티는십칠일에란벨란드에ᄃᆞᆺ슬주고셕탄을싯고십팔일에동히창을향ᄒᆞ야동양으로향ᄒᆞᄂᆞᆫ디이라ᄒᆞ엿더라

십월십구일동경발

○일본졍부항의　로병이쳥국복쟝을닙은거ᄉᆞᆫ공법을어임이라고일본졍부에셔로국에디ᄒᆞ야항의ᄒᆞ엿다ᄒᆞ엿더라

광고

To-morrow being a Korean National Holiday, there will be no issue of the Korea Daily News.

TELEGRAMS.

THE BATTLE OF SAHO.

OYAMA'S REPORT OF RUSSIAN CASUALTIES.

Tokyo, Oct. 23rd.

As on Friday, the situation is unchanged. But our computation of Russian losses, up to date, reveals that we have captured 27 guns at our left wing and 16 on the right. Our scouts have discovered 200 of the enemy's dead in the vicinity of Changanpao.

Later.

According to the final reports on the 22nd, the Russian Casualties in the battle of Saho were as follows; Prisoners taken 500, dead left on the field 10,550; total of enemy's killed and wounded 60,000. War Material captured, 45 guns 6,920 shells, 5,474 rifles, 78,000 cartridges. We are still investigating their losses.

FROM JAPAN PAPERS.

"London, October 17th."

Reuter's correspondent at St. Petersburg states that the news from manchuria has caused a feeling of profound gloom, in striking contrast to the elation provoked by the publication of the proclamation by General Kuropatkin.

The Russian losses are understood to be about 8,000.

"Later."

French correspondents at St. Petersburg report that General Kuropatkin's defeat is a veritable disaster.

Later.

Reports from Mukden state that the battle was resumed on the 16th inst., ten miles southwest of Mukden.

It is considered certain that General Kuropatkin will extricate his army, though he has lost 30,000 men.

The 17th and 6th Army Corps bore the brunt of the battle. They repulsed six attacks and three times silenced the Japanese artillery before retreating from Shaho.

The Russians fought doggedly but every despatch shows more clearly the decisiveness of the Japanese victory.

London, October 18th.

Twenty-eight Russian warships have passed Bornholm, en route to the Far East.

THE INTERNED RUSSIANS AT HONG KONG.

The Russian officers and tars who were rescued from the torpedo boat "Bruni," by H.M.S. "Humber," near Weihaiwei, and who have, of late, been quartered on H.M.S. "Tamar," in the harbour, are to be removed to Kowloon where they will have special quarters allotted them, writes the "China Mail."

A site in the new King's Park has been selected for the erection of a cantonment. It is a hill at the back of the Chinese theatre at Yaumati, abutting on the new road, and upon this eminence are being erected one hut for the officers, and two huts for the men as well as the necessary adjuncts, such as ook-houses, latrines, etc.

The huts are being built of the usual palm leaves, and care is being taken by the military authorities to have them rendered sanitary in every respect. They will be well ventilated—matsheds usually are—and the occupants will have to keep them clean themselves.

The buildings will be surrounded by a barbed wire fence six feet in height, and when the 'prisoners' are placed in their new quarters a British guard will be mounted over them to prevent any escape.

There are four officers—one Commander, two Lieutenants, and one Engineer—and 61 men. The officers, we understand, will be allowed perfect freedom, but none of the men will be allowed to leave the enclosure unless in company with an officer, or being marched out for exercise.

Work is now proceeding on the matsheds and they will, in all probably, be ready for occupation by the end of the month.

BRITISH ADMIRATION FOR DEFENDERS OF PORT ARTHUR.

British soldiers who passed through the siege of Ladysmith express admiration for the manner in which General Stoessel's forces are holding in check their assailants at Port Arthur. They say that the British suffered terribly, although the Boers bombarded in a leisurely way compared to the Japanese. Joubert's men stopped their operations for lunch and tea, took an occasional holiday and frequently lacked ammunition; yet those who formed part of besieged garrison say that the noise of the bursting shells was maddening, and that death had lost its terrors long before succour arrived.

It is pointed out that the Japanese are pressing the attack with a far greater number of guns and more systematically than the Boers. The garrison is supposed to lack fresh vegetables, fruit, and possibly good meat and pure water. Port Arthur ordinarily lives on fresh food exported from Chefoo, and obtains its water supply from a distant hill in the neighbourhood of Dalny. These things now go principally to the Japanese. In normal times the garrison has been sent far and wide in the height of summer to camp in the open, in order to escape the diseases of the East. It is now confined in the height of the hot weather in an unsanitary and ill-drained town, wrapped in the steam from the harbour mud, and tormented by the incessant shelling of the Japanese. It is thought that the Russians have done enough to immortalize themselves though the besiegers should prevail tomorrow.

General and Lady Hyon left Seoul yesterday morning for Chemulpo *en route* to Japan.

The Foreign Office have instructed the Kamnis of all open ports to don European costume before the 20th inst.

The War Department is soliciting the Japanese Legation for the return of the rifles, taken from the soldiers at Kougchu on the occasion of the disturbance there.

It has been decided that General Hasegawa shall be privileged to obtain an audience with His Majesty on every occasion compatible with his ideas of necessity.

The friends of Major Paik Nam-sin, recently arrested on suspicion of being a Russian spy, will be glad to hear that he was released from the Japanese Headquarters yesterday, no foundation for the charge having been proved.

A Boston man has been arrested for writing on a postal card what he thought of John D. Rockefeller. Very few persons, comments the Washington Post, could express their opinions of Mr. Rockefeller in such small space.

A very enjoyable dinner party was given by Miss Sountau, at her residence, last night. Those present were, the Misses Eckert, H. E. Herr von Saldern, Kommandant Kloeber S. M. S. Jaguar, Dr. Ney, Dr. Wunsch, Messrs Megata, Suzuki, Faruya, Delcoigne, Bolljahn and Lieutenant Pak.

On account of the Imperial edict forbidding the country people to remove their top-knots and no such embargo having been placed on the citizens of Seoul it is said that many people from the country, desirous of a change in *coiffure*, are invading the city with a view to enjoying the unknown delight of a hair-cut.

According to a telegram, says the China Review Prince Khilkoff, Russian Minister of Public Works and Communications, has recently sent 1,000 railway hands to Siberia with the object of increasing the transporting capacity of the Siberian Railway. He declares that Russia will soon be able to maintain 600,000 troops in the Far East by means of the railway alone.

A report brought by a native from the north reports that Russian and Japanese patrols are continually coming in contact on the upper reaches of the Yalu. Also many Chinese spies, in Russian employ, have been captured and shot. On one occasion, a Major-General of the Chinese army was discovered acting in this capacity and met with the same fate.

A correspondent at Alexandria writes that while the British warship Venus was indulging in target pratice about 25 miles away from Suez an unknown cargo boat was seen to approach the port. As she came near the target the cruiser fired off one of her big guns, and immediately the steamer turned tail and proceeded hurriedly in a southerly direction, the captain evidently imagining that the Venus was a Russian cruiser.

The Korea Daily News.

Issued at 5 P. M. daily except Sundays.

Rate of Subscription:-

Per Year,	Yen 25.
Per Quarter,	Yen 7.
Per Month,	Yen 2.50.

Postage in Korea not charged extra.
Postage abroad charged extra.

Advertisements, 50 sen per day for 1 inch or less.
5 yen per month per inch.
50 yen per year per inch.

All communications to

E. T. BETHELL,
Editor and Publisher,
Pak tong, Seoul

THE TOBACCO MONOPOLY.

The great hopes raised in Japan for the assurance of an increased income by the inauguration of a Government Tobacco Monopoly are apparently doomed to disappointment.

The scheme, if not exactly a failure, has not met with a fraction of the success, which was prophesied for it. That this is the case, the following extract from the "Kobe Yushin Nippo," (a Japanese journal, as its name denotes, published in Kobe) will prove.

"Mr Nio (Director of the Bureau) gives the following account of their tobacco operations in China and Korea.

"Mr Harris, who was connected with Murai Bros. & Co., started a manufacturing Company in Shanghai. After carrying into practice the Government Monopoly of manufacturing tobacco, he appropriated the market in China and Korea, which resulted in steady progress. Then he engaged the artisans and mechanics formerly employed by Murai Bros., (who had already been engaged by the Government). The authorities therefore cannot afford to despise this company. The Bureau then found it necessary to find persons capable to oppose this influential seller, but only three applicants worthy of note came forward. These were the Mitsui Bussan Kaisha, Keijin Tobacco Co. and Mr. Kume Taminosuke. The latter however was possessed of insufficient funds. These three were then given permission to sell both cut and mouthpiece cigarettes to compete with Mr. Harris in China and Korea.

"Out of the three the Mitsui Bussan Kaisha have been the least unsuccessful and although they stand to lose from forty to fifty thousand yen, have decided not to yet give up the attempt, but to try and enlarge the Japanese Government monopoly, but there is no competition for mouthpiece cigarettes, permission to sell will be given to anyone possessed of sufficient funds."

This spells a deplorable state of affairs indeed and one naturally looks for the reason. Is it that the cigarettes, turned out by the Monopoly Bureau's factories are of such inferior quality, that no buyers can be found, or that this Mr. Harris has indeed obtained control over the Chinese and Korean markets?

Undoubtedly the Government cigarettes, which have been placed upon the Korean Market are of an inferior quality to those formerly produced by Murai Bros. at the same price; while up to the present, we have seen none to compare with the more expensive products of the Osaka Tobacco Co. whose cigarettes were always popular with the monied classes.

It would seem therefore, by the Yushin Nippo's report, that the Japanese Government has thrown away the handsome revenue obtained, prior to the adaptation of a monopoly, by the heavy custom's dues on tobacco, for an unprofitable undertaking.

Many foreign experts in Japan have frequently warned the Government that this would be the case, among them notably, Mr. Jonas of the Osaka Tobacco Company, whose many years of experience, (some ten years spent in Japan), enabled him to speak authoritatively on the subject. This gentleman, shortly before his departure from Japan, pointed out conclusively that as a commercial adventure, the Monopoly might to a certain extent be successful, but the result obtained in figures would never reach the amounts obtained in previous years from the Customs duties on Tobacco.

However, "it's an ill wind that blows nobody any good," and the abolition of private concerns in Japan, has increased the output and profits of private undertakings in China and Korea.

"THE JOYS OF TRAVEL."

(Specially written for the "China Review.)

Shimonoseki, Sept. 23rd.

The German ship "Babelsburg" steamed into the harbor in the "cup-of-tea" sea time of the early morning. To her came several Japanese quarantine officials clad in spotless white, and we were aroused that our tongues might be seen. Then—this required nearly two hours,—the steamer went past the cliff where the early Japanese stopped proselytising by Jesuits in a thorough manner, by throwing them over a hundred feet of rock on to jagged boulders below, covered at high water, to complete the massacre. She anchored in the busy harbor of Nagasaki amongst many craft, and ashore the clang of the hammer in the shipyards had begun. Near the "Babelsberg" was the former Russian transport "Sungari," coated thick with rust, corroded by long immersion at Chemulpo, ere she was raised. This same "Sungari" brought back memories of the beginning of this war, which, for me, is ending.

Over the ship's sides a swarm of sampans spewed a hundred men, all half clad, their brown limbs uncovered. These, with the geomantic signs, the mark of their guild, on the back of their "haori," or loose cotton coats, sought to sell me sleeve links, "posto cardo," pictures that made my young cheeks blush, tortoise shell from the seashore villages, all manner of tourist goods. Some did lay violent hands upon me and demand that I be bodily removed per sampan to the hotels of their employers. By the way in which they pulled ere I swung free it seemed one arm could go to one hotel, another limb to another. And my baggage, each runner laid hands upon one unit. It constituted a lien, as it were, in favour of this place.

Entre nous, if you come to Nagasaki bring a new-made temper. Get the best; you'll need it.

The worldly goods of an unfortunate war correspondent, now more embattled than in Manchuria, were finally secured, the derelict transport was reorganized as it were, and I said my farewells to the kindhearted German sailor men and fellow passengers, for I would descend the gangway and board the sampan. I was near the ladder when I heard excited voices. I turned my head, and I was discovered!!

I had a camera slung from my shoulders. Behind me an excited policeman with white uniform and dangling sword was pointing to my camera. Three other officers of the Mikado's police had foregathered. They were quite flurried, for a foreigner was carrying a camera to Nagasaki. How terrible!! Of course, I was stopped. I left the gangway that coolies might block it in a constant stream for half-an-hour, and my history was gone into for the police department. What an enormous stock of forms—that are to give particulars of men, whose only crime is that they travel through Japan—must be accumulated in the archives of the police department of the Rising Sun land.

My name, yes, they were welcome to that. My age, why not?; I am not a woman. Where was I from? Tientsin. Why did I leave there? I gave that up. Where was I going. Tokio. Why?—Now I am a mild-mannered young man and my temper is still undamaged, but these policemen who look at one with such a suspicious air, a kind of "I've-caught-you" look, try the best of tempers. I would answer no more,—though they hanged me. I went ashore, camera and all.

The going ashore was delayed for some time, though by another official in a white duck uniform with buttons; one of the large imports of Japan must be brass buttons. He waited until the sampan man was well on his way toward shore, when he decided that he would overlook my baggage, as, a matter of fact, he had. Back went the sampan coolie. I told him to turn his prow shoreward and the custom's man be blowed. There was a custom-house to which the traveller must go at the hatoba. But he would go back to the steamer, where, for his pains, he received a tissue paper covered with ideographs.

At last the shore, the hotel in view. But there was still the custom house. There my worldly goods were spread out, the smaller packages opened, and I stood by. I was beyond caring. But everything ends, and I came to the hotel in time for tiffin.

The steamer had arrived in port at seven o'clock in the morning!!

There was a through train going to Tokio at 1.28 P. M. Would the clerk kindly enquire if it "was" the through express. Of course. It was he was informed. Therefore some jinrikisha coolies hurried me to the station, where I boarded the so-called express, the same being the local train for Moji, sans conveniences. I had hardly taken a seat when the inevitable policeman arrived with the inevitable questions. Name, address, age, where from, where for, why I travelled, all these things again; and I told him without murmur. When one's in Japan he must do as the Japs do, or rather what they make the foreigner do. His English was scant, but he made a fairly good account of my past life from the details I gave him. When he sought to know about my future, though, he was beyond me. I told him to consult a fortune-teller.

He left me at the first station we came to, and another came. To him I also related my antecedents—and he went. Farther down the line another came, bringing the same old printed form, and he was seeking for more information concerning the lone foreigner who occupied a car for himself. Perhaps that was suspicious, in itself. And then, I had a camera!

By the way, let me tell a story of a war correspondent and a camera. In Japan, as perhaps you know, photophobia exists. There are places where a camera is as dreaded as the devil is said to dread holy water. Shimonoseki is one of them. There, on the harbor front, whose skirts are fort-lined, a correspondet stood with a camera, snapping and turning the roller. He was very busy until the police came. Then there was excitement. "It was forbidden to make photographs," angrily said the red-faced little police officer, "he must surrender his camera."

"Why?" said the correspondent. "It is my camera. If you want anything, you must take only the films.

The police took the camera. Two hours later they brought it back, more angry than ever. It had been empty!!! My correspondent had been trying the workings of a new shutter.

But my camera was full. It had photographs of sikh policemen standing before the Astor house on Victoria Road sun-stamped on its films—which might have been revealing the military secrets of Japan, for all this Vidocq in spotless white could tell. And he asked me further questions. Did I take photographs?

Yes. Had I taken any in Japan? Not for three months What was my occupation.

"Correspondent," I said.

"Co-respondent?" he repeated.

"No" said I—"I hope not." and he faded out into the night.

Note—The train that the ticket-seller said went through to Kobe with a change at Moji, at the ferry, is *not* a through train, I must remain at the Sanyo hotel in Shimonoseki until the morning.

N. B. The Sanyo hotel is operated by the railway company.

J. GORDON SMITH.

The Korea Daily News.

VOL. I, MONDAY, OCTOBER 24, 1904. No. 84

大韓每日申報
대한매일신보

(뎨팔십오호) (슈요일) 일쳔구빅사년십월이십룩일

본샤고빅

이 신보는 영어와 한어로 셔 거 믹일 출판ᄒᆞ옵

신문가

한장 엽푼오돈

일삭도 엽두량닷돈

우표가 ᄯᅩ 삭 닷돈

다 맛돈으로 밧숩

광고료는

본샤광고

관보

잡보

론셜

연초젼매권

일본졍부로셔연초젼매국을신셜ᄒᆞ야아모조록세입을증첨ᄒᆞ랴든소망이잘못될듯ᄒᆞᆫ거시만일그일이필경손해가되지아니ᄒᆞ면셩취될가망이또ᄒᆞᆫ업스리라고시로벌간ᄒᆞᄂᆞᆫ신호유신일보에게재ᄒᆞ엿기에좌에번등ᄒᆞ노라

연초젼매국쟝뇌오씨가한쳥량국에연초젼매운동을경영ᄒᆞᄂᆞᆫ고로ᄒᆞᆫ왕에촌졍형메연초회사와홈ᄭᅴ계약ᄒᆞ고샹히에셔졔조미각ᄒᆞ든하리씨가이ᄒᆞᆫ미를알고이왕졔조ᄒᆞ엿든바모든권연을팔아크게리익을엇고또ᄒᆞᆫ한쳥량국에셔권연ᄉᆞ업을ᄒᆞ랴ᄒᆞ야ᄒᆞᆫ왕촌졍회샤에셔고용ᄒᆞ든공쟝들을교빙ᄒᆞ야쓰랴ᄒᆞ나일본졍부에셔도이사룸의ᄒᆞᄂᆞᆫ일은엇지ᄒᆞᆯ수업ᄂᆞᆫ지라

또ᄒᆞᆫ이외에ᄌᆞ귀나라빅셩즁에도필경하리씨와연초졔조홈을인연ᄒᆞ야좌론이잇슬줄로싱각ᄒᆞ엿든바이러ᄒᆞᆫ니과연삼졍물산회샤와ᄀᆞ진연초회샤와밋구미씨들이먼져창언ᄒᆞ야연초졔조홈을인허ᄒᆞ여달나고이걸ᄒᆞᄂᆞᆫ지라엇지ᄒᆞᆯ수업시다만물쌔리잇ᄂᆞᆫ권연만만드러팔게인허ᄒᆞ야한쳥량국에셔미각ᄒᆞᄂᆞᆫ하리씨로더브러리익을닷토게ᄒᆞ엿슨즉무론아모라도자본금만넉넉히잇슬지경이면물쌔리잇ᄂᆞᆫ권연은졔조ᄒᆞ야발매ᄒᆞ게되엿다ᄒᆞ엿슨즉

당초에일본졍부에셔연초젼매국을신셜ᄒᆞ고리익을쳠입ᄒᆞ랴홈이잘못된일인거시요ᄉᆞ이젼매국권연을본즉지료가원리나자셔번변치못ᄒᆞᆫ고로사셔먹ᄂᆞᆫ사룸이젹고또ᄒᆞᆫ촌졍회샤에셔졔조ᄒᆞ든권연과감히비교치못ᄒᆞ겟ᄂᆞᆫ즁히관세랍을이왕보다만히작졍ᄒᆞ엿슨즉필경이일을도로너여놀듯ᄒᆞ며

대관연초회샤에셔수십년을연초졔조에위업ᄒᆞ든또나스가이일에ᄃᆡᄒᆞ야일본졍부에여러번츙고ᄒᆞ겻스되필경듯지아니ᄒᆞᄂᆞᆫ고로그곳으로ᄯᅥ나다른곳으로옴길때에또ᄒᆞᆫ말ᄒᆞᆫ기를일본졍부에셔젼매국을만드러상업샹리익을취ᄒᆞ랴홈은필경되기ᄂᆞᆫ홀일이여그러ᄒᆞ되젼자보다히관세입이과다홈으로세납은오히려이왕만ᄒᆞᆫ리라ᄒᆞ엿다ᄒᆞᆫ즉엇지던지일본셔이일이아니되ᄂᆞᆫ날에ᄂᆞᆫ한쳥량국으로못된바룸이부려사사리익을착수홀듯ᄒᆞ도다

잡보

○졍부통렵 의졍부에셔각부에통렵ᄒᆞ되ᄂᆡ외관직쳔임규칙을임의쥬지ᄒᆞ야반포ᄒᆞᆫ지라관직에ᄐᆡᆨ인홈이어느때그럿치안으리오만은현금다ᄉᆞᄒᆞᆫ때를당ᄒᆞ야각도슈령을불가불별반ᄐᆡᆨ차ᄒᆞᆯ지니히규칙대 팔됴를의지ᄒᆞ야리월십오일이후ᄂᆞᆫ신임ᄒᆞᆫ군슈를본부에셔낫낫치됴사ᄒᆞ야보쳔업ᄂᆞᆫ군슈ᄂᆞᆫ쟝쥬물시ᄒᆞᆯ터이니각기칙임관의보쳔ᄒᆞᆫ단ᄌᆞ를리월십일ᄂᆡ로본부와ᄂᆡ부로송교ᄒᆞ야됴사케ᄒᆞ라ᄒᆞ엿더라

실비도고 궁ᄂᆡ부에셔외부로죠복ᄒᆞ되귀죠회ᄂᆡ에일공ᄉᆞ가죠회ᄒᆞᆫ기를궁ᄂᆡ부졔용ᄉᆞ로셔파원을보ᄂᆡ여각군포ᄉᆞ에우피를도미ᄒᆞ니이것슨통상규칙을위비홈이니곳쳘슈ᄒᆞ라ᄒᆞ고로죠회ᄒᆞᆫ다ᄒᆞ엿스나졔용ᄉᆞ에셔우피를미입ᄒᆞᄂᆞᆫ것슨실노도고ᄒᆞᄂᆞᆫ것시아니라폐부에셔우피졔죠소를셜시ᄒᆞ고폐부소용으로미입ᄒᆞ되남ᄂᆞᆫ것슨혹외국상민의게방미ᄒᆞ니이뜻으로일공ᄉᆞ의게젼죠ᄒᆞ라ᄒᆞ엿더라

○훈착복쟝 외부에셔아홉항구와세ᄀᆞ시쟝감리의게훈령ᄒᆞ되외교관외문관복쟝은십월이십일로일졔히실시ᄒᆞ라신 죠칙이ᄂᆞ리셧스니감리이하소속관리ᄂᆞᆫ본월삼십일ᄂᆡ로히복쟝을ᄀᆞ착시무케ᄒᆞ라ᄒᆞ엿더라

○변궁환후미류 황태ᄌᆞ비뎐하환후가일간더욱침즁ᄒᆞ샤현금징세가위독ᄒᆞ신고로 대쇼죠에셔우려즁으로지ᄂᆡ신다더라

○우쟝동유 참찬허위와ᄂᆡ쟝원감독김영진량씨ᄂᆞᆫ죵속히일본에유람ᄒᆞᆫ다ᄂᆞᆫ풍셜이잇다더라

○압병이송 일본ᄉᆞ령부에피슈ᄒᆞ엿든공쥬되죵ᄃᆡ쟝이하병뎡ᄉᆞ지ᄌᆞ작일에륙군법원으로이송ᄒᆞ엿더라

○삼슈쥬본 작일밤에군슈삼과를 쥬본ᄒᆞ엿다ᄒᆞᄂᆞᆫᄃᆡ홍양군슈ᄂᆞᆫ비국ᄐᆡ씨라더라

、면담도임 ᄂᆡ부에셔함경남도관찰부에면훈ᄒᆞᆫ기를젼군슈김로규로함경북도관찰ᄉᆞ를ᄉᆞ임ᄒᆞ엿스니히ᄉᆞ의도임여부를젼인으로속히탐지ᄒᆞ야회면ᄒᆞ라ᄒᆞ엿더라

츙찰보고 츙쥬관찰ᄉᆞ리승우씨가ᄂᆡ부로보고ᄒᆞ되츙쥬쟝호원등디에소위진보회라ᄒᆞᄂᆞᆫ란류가취회ᄒᆞ야삭발ᄒᆞᄂᆞᆫ고로병뎡십명슈검ᄉᆞ명을파송ᄒᆞ야포착ᄒᆞ라ᄒᆞᆫ즉그수효가ᄋᆡ빅명이못되ᄂᆞᆫᄃᆡ임의원쥬ᄃᆡ에셔오륙명을포착ᄒᆞ엿고여당은다흣허졋더니병뎡회환ᄒᆞᆫ후로또즉시취회ᄒᆞ야샹경ᄒᆞ라ᄒᆞᆫ다ᄒᆞ엿더라

○한쳥갑슈 일본공관에셔외부로공함ᄒᆞ되향일에셔임된갑산군슈김승표ᄂᆞᆫ즁왕에아국군위정탐으로혐의밧든쟈인즉우리군대에셔히군슈부임ᄒᆞᄂᆞᆫ길에방알홀뜻ᄒᆞ니히임명을물시ᄒᆞ라ᄒᆞ엿더라

○메보쟝발 메국신문를향일에일본ᄉᆞ령부에셔뎡보케ᄒᆞ엿더니일간다시발간된다더라

○쳥결방침 한셩오셔ᄂᆡ쳥결법를셜시ᄒᆞ엿다가무고히뎡지ᄒᆞ엿더니일젼에쳥결위원쟝이하졔위원이회동ᄒᆞ야별방침으로결뎡ᄒᆞ기를대소호를구별ᄒᆞ야일이삼등으로미호에미삭쳥결비얼마식슈렴ᄒᆞ기로마련ᄒᆞ엿더라

뎡괴회심 일젼에외부에셔일공관에조회ᄒᆞᆫ기를평리원공문ᄂᆡ에시홍군민의안건를본월이십륙일하오일시에회심ᄒᆞᆫ다ᄒᆞ엿기로죠회ᄒᆞ니귀군ᄃᆡ에이조ᄒᆞ야회심케ᄒᆞ라ᄒᆞ엿더라

○총슌샹슈 츙쥬관찰ᄉᆞ의보고에ᄒᆞᆫ기를본부총슌리근빈를일본면신ᄃᆡ에셔착거홈은임의치보ᄒᆞ엿거니와다시힐문ᄒᆞᆫ즉방금가홍병참면신국에피슈되엿ᄂᆞᆫᄃᆡ일쥬일후에ᄂᆞᆫ장찻방환홀다ᄒᆞ엿더라

○문역괴복 향일에 칙령안을긔쟝ᄒᆞᆫ군인은부모샹당훈지일빅일후에ᄂᆞᆫ의례히긔복ᄒᆞ기로결뎡ᄒᆞ야반포ᄒᆞ엿더니문관도그규례ᄃᆡ로긔복ᄒᆞ기로졍부회의에졔출되엿다더라

○훈칙공젼 의졍부에셔ᄂᆡ부로조회ᄒᆞ되각관찰부에훈령ᄒᆞ야도ᄂᆡ인즁에ᄂᆡ외직관인조격될자를공쳔ᄒᆞ야ᄂᆡ월십일ᄂᆡ로치보케ᄒᆞ라ᄒᆞ엿다더라

각관젼임 농상공부광산국쟝김한목씨ᄂᆞᆫᄂᆡ부참셔관으로젼임ᄒᆞ고그ᄃᆡᄂᆞᆫ젼한셩관윤김대진씨가피임ᄒᆞ고샹공국쟝규병씨ᄂᆞᆫ법부참셔관으로젼임ᄒᆞ고그ᄃᆡᄂᆞᆫ한셩관윤송ᄐᆡ현씨가젼임ᄒᆞ엿더라

○고문공함 ᄂᆡ부고문관단국인일광씨ᄂᆞᆫ고빙된지칠팔삭에잇셰ᄉᆞ지시무를아니ᄒᆞ더니일젼에ᄂᆡ부대신의게공함ᄒᆞ되다른마을고문관은통역관과거접소를쥰비ᄒᆞ되본고문관의게ᄂᆞᆫᄎᆞ등쥰비가업ᄂᆞᆫ고로시무치못ᄒᆞ엿스니다부규례대로통역관과거접소를쥰비ᄒᆞ면본고문도ᄉᆞ진ᄒᆞ겟습ᄂᆞ다ᄒᆞ엿더라

○일진질문 일진회에셔정부에루ᄎᆞ공함ᄒᆞ되실시ᄒᆞᄂᆞᆫ일이업슬뿐더러회답ᄭᅡ지업다ᄒᆞ야지작일에총대위원렴즁모홍긍셥량씨가참졍신긔션씨의게젼왕ᄒᆞ야질문ᄒᆞ엿다더라

○ᄂᆡ훈삼남 ᄂᆡ쟝원에셔삼남각도에훈령ᄒᆞ되각외획젼을음력구월회ᄂᆡ로쥰슈샹랍ᄒᆞ라ᄒᆞ엿다더라

의례군슈 궁ᄂᆡ부쥬ᄉᆞᄂᆞᆫ갓가운반렬에잇셔근로ᄒᆞᆫ즉다른마을과형별ᄒᆞᆫ지라미년에일인식의례히군슈셔임ᄒᆞ기로뎡식ᄒᆞ라신 쳐분이ᄂᆞ리셧더라

삼년일셔 궁ᄂᆡ부에셔ᄂᆡ부로죠회ᄒᆞᆫ기를쟝례원향츅과쥬ᄉᆞ즁젹ᄉᆞ구근를불가불념인고로삼년일ᄎᆞ식일인식의례히군슈셔임ᄒᆞ기로샹 쥬지가ᄒᆞ엿스니쥰힝케ᄒᆞ라ᄒᆞ엿더라

뎐보

십월이십삼일동경발대산공보

○젹포포획 금료일은젼면일ᄃᆡ에ᄂᆞᆫ아모변긔홈이업고금일ᄭᅡ지좌익군에셔획득ᄒᆞᆫ젹군의대포ᄂᆞᆫ좌죵ᄃᆡ에셔이십칠문이오우죵ᄃᆡ에십륙문이미합계ᄒᆞ야ᄉᆞ십삼문이며우리쳑후병이목료일밤에잔얀포부근에셔젹군의시톄이빅을발현ᄒᆞ엿다ᄒᆞ엿더라

동일동면

○포로와젼리품 십월이십일에됴ᄉᆞᄒᆞᆫ거슬거ᄒᆞᆫ즉사하에셔젼투에로국의손히가좌와굿ᄒᆞ니

포로가대략오빅명이오젼쟝에버린시톄가일만오빅오십이오젼투에획득ᄒᆞᆫ물픔은대포가ᄉᆞ십오문이오대포탄환이륙쳔구빅이십발과밋쇼총이오쳔ᄉᆞ빅칠십ᄉᆞ정과탄환으칠만팔쳔발이며젹의시톄ᄂᆞᆫ다군인의명예로ᄡᅥ이거슬ᄂᆡ장ᄒᆞ여주엇ᄂᆞᆫᄃᆡ젹군의ᄉᆞ상총계가대략륙만인듯ᄒᆞ고기타ᄂᆞᆫ지금ᄭᅡ지됴사ᄒᆞᄂᆞᆫ즁이라ᄒᆞ엿더라

십월이십삼일공ᄉᆞ관착뎐

○로국ᄉᆞ상별보 작일에로국도셩에셔발ᄒᆞᆫ젹이밋을만ᄒᆞᆫ면보를거ᄒᆞᆫ즉로국이공격ᄒᆞᄂᆞᆫ운동을시작홈으로브터십팔일ᄭᅡ지로군의손샹ᄒᆞᆫ거슨로국참모본부의됴ᄉᆞᄒᆞᆫ거슬거ᄒᆞᆫ즉슈용ᄒᆞᆫ부샹쟈가오만오쳔칠빅륙십팔명이오죽은쟈와밋거취가분명치아니ᄒᆞᆫ쟈ᄂᆞᆫ확실치아니ᄒᆞ나대략일만이쳔쯤될듯ᄒᆞ다ᄒᆞ엿더라

광고

TELEGRAMS.

RUSSIAN CASUALTIES.

Tokyo Oct. 23rd.

According to a reliable telegram from St Petersburg, the Russian casualties from 5th to the 18th inst. are estimated at 55,768 wounded and 12,000 killed and missing.

OYAMA'S REPORT.

Tokyo Oct. 24th.

According to the latest investigation, Russian prisoners taken number 709, dead found on the field 5,200 in front of our right wing, 5,603 at left wing, and 2,530 at our centre, making a totai of 13,333.

RUSSIA'S "NEW NAVY."

Mr. Lewis Nixon, technical head of the United States Shipbuilding Company (the Shipping Trust), has returned from St. Petersburg, whither, the "New York Herald" says, he was invited by the Czar's advisers to confer with them regarding the building of a "new Russian navy." Mr. Nixon is rather mysterious concerning the outcome of his visit, but he indicated a great renaissance of naval construction in the United States by the fulfilling of the Russian orders. No orders for naval vessels can be expected on the Clyde, says Mr. Nixon, the feeling against Great Britain being so intense. According to the reports which have reached the United States, however, Russian feeling against America respecting the present war is also very bitter.

We are informed that our vernacular contemporary, the Che Kuk Sinmun which was recently shut down by order of the Japanese, will shortly blossom forth again.

The case of the Si-Heung rioters is to be tried at the High Supreme court today. The Japanese authorities have been informed of the fact and are invited to send representatives to assist at the trial.

A complaint from the Japanese Legation has been received by the Foreign Office, that Kim Sung-pio, who is under suspicion of being a Russian spy, has been appointed magistrate of a northern district, where it is most undesirable to have of his suspected nature.

The president of the Il Chin Hoi Society evidently considers himself a man of importance. He has telegraphed to the Governor of Pingyang ordering him to wire his reasons for the dispersal of the Chin Po Hoi-ites in the country districts. He reasserts that the whole desire of the society is to ensure the welfare and safety of the people of Korea, and he is the instrument appointed by providence to consummate their endeavours.

Colonel Marchand, in an interview with Lord Kitchener's Secretary declined to reply (to questions regarding his lately published account of the meeting at Fashoda.) He stated that were he interviewed by Gen. Kitchener personally, he would then reply, and utilize his documents. He would of course meet Lord Kitchener with all courtesy and gallantry. Colonel Marchand recently wrote an account of the meeting in the Paris "Figaro," implying that he overawed Lord Kitchener, until the latter smoothed over matters by a drink of whisky and soda. It was insinuated that, had Lord Kitchener proceeded to extremities, his own troops would have turned upon him.—Straits Times.

"RUNNING THE CUTTER."

(FROM THE CHINA REVIEW)

(Concluded from 2nd page.)

She was a ship of about 4,000 tons register, and carried about 8,900 tons, including bunkers. She had evidently been built with an eye to a long steaming radius, as the after end of No. 2 hold and the fore part of No. 3 had shifting bulk-heads and doors in permanent bulk-heads connecting with bunkers.

It was not long before all on board were mustered and the nature of the voyage explained. She was bound to Chein Wang Tao "to order," with the option of Port Arthur. If any of the crowd wished to back out, they could go at the Cape or the first port of call, and a passage paid home, but as all were on for a good "pay day" they cheerfully went to their duties, and the fo'-castle parliament set about discusing the amount of the pay day if the "run" came off, and incidentally the game the "old man" would play if he got copped.

Out of Channel the course took contrary to the usual route, Finnisterre not being sighted, nor Madeira, a course being shaped down close to the African shore, and the land "hugged" around into the Gulf of Guinea.

The first call was at Benguela, a small road-stead south of St. Paul de Loanda. Here laying rolling about was a collier, and the bunkers were replenished.

Leaving, the course was taken "off" the land, and not until the Cape was rounded and Natal passed was the land sighted, then it was "hugged" right up to the Tse-Tse River. On arriving at China an evident disappointment was met, as no collier was waiting, the "runner" being quicker than anticipated, so without anchoring she steamed along to Zanzibar, and next day fortunately (?) met the collier, and a rendezvous was made and coaling completed in a bay on the west coast of Madagascar.

Rounding the north end of that island, an almost due east course was shaped, and the next call was near Java, where some papers were taken on board.

After leaving, it was still east, until the sea lawyer," gave his "Alfred Davit" that 'twas 'Firsco the tub was bound, not China, and ther'd be no fun and no extras.

For several days the engines were driven at their utmost and a good speed of 14 knots kept up, as this was a modern "tramp" with good power, when suddenly the course was altered from N. N. E. to West, and at evening there was a loom of land.

At dark all hands were employed painting funnel and deckhouses with a broad white band around the upper rail, a false stem and a short stump bowsprit were rigged, and the—was transformed before daylight into the—Maru.

During the night the engines had been slowed, and now the land was close to, and again she raced away through the Tsugaru Straits and across the Sea of Japan, and in 30 hours was being escorted through the mines into Vladivostock.

"Well, I'm blowed," quoth the "Sea lawer," "if the 'old man' ain't been an' run around all the Injies and Philipines, and not a blooming cove seed him but that feller in Javer, end he, I expect, give him his orders, and did you savey' how he keeped clear of the Cape, and the only people who see'd us was a blooming lot a niggers, and us haven't see'd a ship since we left Channel——"

"Below there—the 'old man' wants you on the bridge, boys—Here's luck to the coal for China.' "

NOTICE.

Seoul, Oct. 21st

The Committee of the Yeng Wha Chin Foreign Cemetery request the Western Foreign Residents of Seoul to meet in the Reading room of the Seoul Union on Monday the 31st October, 1904 at 4 o'clock P. M. for the purpose of electing a new committee for the ensuing year, and for discussion of matters relating to the cemetery.

HORACE N. ALLEN,
President.

R. RRINCKMEIER,
Hon. Sec.

LOST

On the 27th ult., probably in the neighbourhood of the West Gate. A Photographic Camera. Anyone returning the same to this office will receive Y 15.00 reward.

The Korea Daily News.

Issued at 5 P. M. daily except Sundays.

Rate of Subscription:—
Per Year, Yen 25.
Per Quarter, Yen 7.
Per Month, Yen 2.50.

Postage in Korea not charged extra.
Postage abroad charged extra.

Advertisements, 50 sen per day for 1 inch or less. 5 yen per month per inch. 50 yen per year per inch.

All communications to E. T. BETHELL, Editor and Publisher, Pak-tong, Seoul

RESPONSIBILITY FOR THE WAR.

We take the following, says the "Eastern World," which escaped our notice at the time, from the column of a contemporary, with the view of correcting some misstatements of facts, which, as things are turning out, Count Katsura is evidently desirous to have considered as facts with the intention of creating a divided responsibility:—

On the instant, at the conference of the prefectural Governors, Count Katsura, the Premier, made some observation with reference to the negotiations immediately preceding the outbreak of the war. Count Katsura said immediately these negotiations were broken off in February, he called a meeting in Tokyo of the Governors of prefectures and informed them of the position and outlined the policy to be pursued by the local authorities. "When I met you here in February last," continued the Premier, "a report had just arrived that Russian war-ships had appeared off Aomori prefecture. At that time the whole nation unanimously agreed as one man to fight the great enemy, notwithstanding all difficulties and hardships. Since then eight months have elasped, during which our Army and Navy have been constantly victorious, while the financial conditions have been in no way unsatisfactory. The end of the war, however, is yet very distant. Despite the misfortune of a series of defeats, Russia shows her determination to continue the war by sending greater forces than ever to Manchuria and reorganising her army and transportion facilities. All that can be done by the Empire in face of this determination is only to carry out the resolution adopted in February last. The necessity of solidarity is more than ever evident. However powerful Russia may be, and despite any force she may put in the field, I am confident that we can attain our object in time if we do not shrink from our first determination to unitedly carry on war to the uttermost. What is necessary for the nation at present is to devise means for maintaining the country's financial and military power. There may be many ways of nursing pecuniary resources, but they may be summed up briefly in the economising of expenditure and the utilisation of the fund so secured for the carrying on of the war."

With regard to these statements we have to say that the whole nation did *not* agree unanimously as one man fight the great enemy, because: The naval battle at Port Arthur had already been fought, and war had already been declared, so that the whole nation had neither unanimously agreed nor disagreed on the subject, and was just as much surprised as the rest of the world. Count Katsura and his colleagues, on the contrary, had kept the nation *in complete ignorance* about the course of the negotiations. The point must therefore be kept in mind that the Japanese people had no voice in the matter and we hope Count Katsura has not arrived at the humiliating necessity to quote the utterances of nameless and ignorant penny-a-liners who howled for war, just the same as one dog yelping starts a whole chorus, as the *view of the Japanese people.*

Count Katsura and his colleagues "alone" prepared for and declared the war, and "twelve miles of torpedo-booms joined with steel chains and" furnished with "steel nets were in position at the Elliot islands before the negotiations were broken off," and there formed a harbour for the Japanese fleet in which it was safe from torpedo attack.

There should be no attempt therefore to shift the responsibility for the war, or any part of it, to the people. Count Katsura and his colleagues "alone" are responsible for the war. On the 23rd of January last we said:—

The Japanese Government, on the other hand, has preserved its conciliatory attitude, fully aware of the fact that the stake in the dread game of war would be the Emperor's Crown, and, in the event of reverses, perhaps, the lives of its member. It is certain, at least, that the spirit of loyalty that animates the Japanese people would hold the Ministers personally responsible for any course of events resulting in the lowering of the prestige of the Empire. If the Government should go to war, therefore, it will only be with the implied absolute guarantee to the people that the war must end with complete defeat and humiliation of Russia.

We assert nothing new then when we say that the Ministers alone are resposible for this war to the people of Japan, even with their lives, and at some time in the future the people of Japan may say exactly what we said then and what we say to-day.

In view of what we said above we must also ask what was "the resolution adopted in February last?" Is the declaration of war meant which the Emperor was compelled to make after the opening of hostilities? If so it is somewhat late in the day to refer it to the people now, after so many thousands of them have been killed and wounded or come back sick to Japan. It is the people here and the people there now, the people must do this and the people must do that, but when the questions which have to be considered now, and which we "alone" did discuss in these columns before the war, should have been discussed, the people were "not in existence" so far as any information about the issues were concerned for which they were expected to stake their lives and property. These facts we wish to put down here.

At present it is, as we said in our last issue, "in for a penny in for a pound." Tens of thousands of lives more will have to be sacrificed in this war and hundreds of millions of dollars too, and when the war is finished an account for both blood and treasure expended in the war will be demanded by the people of those at whose bidding they had to go into it.

The Captain of the Kongchu guard has been handed over to the War Department for punishment.

"RUNNING THE CUTTER."

(FROM THE CHINA REVIEW.)

Although the actual outbreak of hostilities in the Far East was long foreshadowed, the final developments came so rapidly that a large amount of ammunition, ordinance, and various stores was left at the place of manufacture or the port of shipment. The endeavours, quietly made, to get these to the scene of operations, have opened to sailor men the attractive, if not strictly legal, industry known to them as "running the cutter," and the unwritten history of the past few months has incidents which go to show that the British sailor likes a well-paid job none the less because there is a spice of danger attached to it.

The declaration of coal as a contraband continues for although both the belligerent Powers have plentiful of ordinary fuel, the smokeless coal, which is practically indisdispensable for scouting and torpedo boat work, can only be obtained in Wales. This makes the opportunity of the tramp steamer, and if the number of cargoes shipped and delivered to both sides since the commencement of hostilities was stated, the total would probably be something of a surprise to official circles.

From both sides tempting baits in the shape of bonuses on safe delivery and gratuites to all concerned were offered, and there was no lack of men apparently equally anxious for the experience and the money. The bulk and impossibility of disguising coal made this one of the most hazardous cargoes to ship, and a favourite route for boats so laden is by the Cape and the eastern passage of the Indies. This trip is slow and expensive, but it has the advantage of ensuring practical safety until the final dash has to be made. This dash is invarialy timed for a moonless night—if stormy so much the better, and it is naturally sailed with all lights out.

The following account of a voyage of this kind was written by a captain who counts himself fortunate in securing a position for which there was more competition than for the average first-class berth offered in the ordinary way of business:—

"From a port in the Bristol Channel to any port or ports within the limits of 70 deg. N. and 70 deg.S. to or from as required, and back to a port of discharge in the U. K. or Continent, voyage not to exceed three years, and crew agree at all times to obey the master, whether on board ship, in ship's boats, or on shore." Such were the articles being read out to about as heterogeneous a crew as was ever seen. All hard wizened, seasoned sea-dogs, with a look of set purpose depicted on all faces.

The mate was superintending the signing on, and as they filed out of the office, two disappointed berth seekers began to compare notes. "Where did that crowd come from, Sam?" and twig the articles, "just and lawful command of master" ain't it, and six quid a month and not a blooming "dago" or "squarehead" among em, and I didn't see the old men" either, and she ain't no old crock on an insurance lay, for I counted 44 hands: wonder if that's the blooming thing that they 're kidding about dawn the "Ome?" See'd all last week a lot of 'emtrumming round looking for a craft loading diamonds that was gwine to "run the cutter" "round the Cape." Strikes me that's her, what say? Follie 'um up, and if anybody "backs out" take a "pie head "jump." Yes, that's what we'll do.

A grey dawn next day, a dirty, grimy big hulk hauled through the basin of one of the Cardiff docks, and standing on the pier were the two "sons of Neptune" who the day previous witnessed the signing on of the "crowd." Suddenly a harsh voice from the bridge—

"Want a jump, you fellows?"

"Where are you bound?" in reply.

"East?"—Yes.

"Hold on the quarter line," came again from the Bridge, and as her quarter touched the quay the two watchers jumped abaord, and in a short time she was out in the "roads" and, putting off the pilot, shaped her course down channel.

(Continued on page 3).

The Korea Daily News.

VOL. I, WEDNESDAY, OCTOBER 26, 1904. No. 85

大韓每日申報
대한ᄆᆡ일신보

(뎨팔십륙호) (목요일) 일쳔구ᄇᆡᆨ사년십월이십칠일

본사고ᄇᆡᆨ

이신보ᄂᆞᆫ영어와한어로셕거ᄆᆡ일츌판ᄒᆞ옵

신문가

한장 엽두돈오푼

일삭표 엽두량닷돈

우표가ᄆᆡ삭닷돈

다맛돈으로밧숩

광고료ᄂᆞᆫ

긔한의쟝단과ᄌᆞ힝의다쇼로쥬감ᄒᆞ되렴가로밧을터이오며오ᄅᆡ지아녀대한사ᄅᆞᆷ마다다이신문을보실터이니광고내시기를원ᄒᆞ시ᄂᆞᆫ이들은우리신문샤에와셔면약ᄒᆞ심을희망ᄒᆞ옵

○발힝소 박동대한ᄆᆡ일신보샤법어학교압헤젼영국인셜필림집자리오

사쟝 영국인 (ᄇᆡ셜)

평양 ᄃᆡ리졈

○평양효동사ᄂᆞᆫ권미보씨가우리신문관ᄆᆡ디리인을뢰졍ᄒᆞ엿ᄉᆞ오니평양에계신구람코져ᄒᆞ시ᄂᆞᆫ쳠군ᄌᆞᄂᆞᆫ히디리졈에왕림ᄒᆞ와면의ᄒᆞ시옵

샤고

○우리대한ᄆᆡ일신보의목뎍은대한의안녕질셔에관한모든뎨목에ᄃᆡᄒᆞ야ᄂᆞᆫ공평한변론을쥬쟝홈이라우리통신원의담보ᄂᆞᆫ신문보시ᄂᆞᆫ쳠군ᄌᆞ의게홍상보도ᄒᆞ리며편지를긔셔ᄒᆞ여주시ᄂᆞᆫ이ᄂᆞᆫ셩명과반ᄃᆡ를젹어붓치시기를희망ᄒᆞ오니이거슨신문샹에긔ᄌᆡᄒᆞ라ᄂᆞᆫ거시아니오다만극히신용ᄒᆞᄂᆞᆫ증거를숨고쟈홈이라긔쟈ᄂᆞᆫ아모긔셔던지긔ᄌᆡ홈을퇴각ᄒᆞᄂᆞᆫ권리를가졋ᄉᆞ나퇴각ᄒᆞᄂᆞᆫ리유를말ᄒᆞᆯ터이오며공즁평화를문란케ᄒᆞᄂᆞᆫ듯ᄒᆞᆫ긔셔ᄂᆞᆫ의례히밧지안켓숩나이다

●본샤셜시이ᄅᆡ로신문을ᄆᆡ양우례로분젼ᄒᆞ와례젼부의임의로젼ᄒᆞᆫ듯스로면곳에ᄂᆞᆫ혹늣게젼ᄒᆞ기도ᄒᆞ며혹몃칠거슬ᄒᆞᆫ겁에젼ᄒᆞ기도ᄒᆞ며혹아니젼ᄒᆞᄂᆞᆫ곳도잇다ᄒᆞ와우리신문을ᄉᆞ랑ᄒᆞ야구람ᄒᆞ시ᄂᆞᆫ 쳠군ᄌᆞ의게ᄃᆡᄒᆞ야미우미안ᄒᆞ옵기로지금은분젼인을두고ᄆᆡ일일즉이젼ᄒᆞ며아니젼ᄒᆞ거나늣게거나ᄒᆞᆫ가엽도록ᄒᆞ랴ᄒᆞ오니혹아니셩젼ᄒᆞ거나혹늣게젼ᄒᆞ거나ᄒᆞᆫ일이잇ᄉᆞ면본샤로통긔ᄒᆞ여쥬심을희망ᄒᆞ옵

본샤광고

○본샤신문즁에좌긔ᄒᆞᆫ호수를소용ᄒᆞᆯ데가잇셔이에광고ᄒᆞ오니누구시던지그즁에아모호수던지가져오시ᄂᆞᆫ되로ᄆᆡ쟝에ᄇᆡᆨ젼두푼식드리리다

뎨이호 뎨삼호 뎨이십호 뎨ᄉᆞ십이호 뎨ᄉᆞ십삼호 뎨오십삼호 뎨오십ᄉᆞ호와뎨오십오호 뎨륙십이호

론셜

젼쟁을담쳑홈이라

이스턴월드신문에게ᄌᆡᄒᆞᆷ을본즉일본총리대신계티랑ᄇᆡᆨ작이젼쟁을책임ᄒᆞ야쥬의ᄒᆞᆷ어잘못된사실이라고셜명ᄒᆞ엿기에좌에번등ᄒᆞ노라

일본총리대신계티랑씨가금월에각도디방관들을모화의회ᄒᆞᆯᄯᅢ에동씨가말ᄒᆞ기를과왕에ᄯᅢ젼사건에ᄃᆡᄒᆞ야담관ᄒᆞᆫ든일은지낸이월에임의싸홈시작이되엿슨즉이제쟝황히말ᄒᆞᆯ거시아니요다만졍치샹일이나대강의론ᄒᆞᆷ이조ᄒᆞᆯ듯ᄒᆞ다ᄒᆞ며셜언ᄒᆞ되우리가이월회의에이곳에모혀슬ᄯᅢ에아라샤젼투함몃쳑이아모리더방에현츌되엿다ᄂᆞᆫ소문이들이ᄂᆞᆫ지라기시에젼국ᄇᆡᆨ셩이일제히조와ᄒᆞ야적군으로더부러싸홀일에조곰도어려옴이업시녁이더니파연우리나라히륙군병이여러군닯달동안을연젼연승ᄒᆞᆯᄲᅮᆫ더러군용경비에ᄯᅩᄒᆞᆫ부족지여가업스며젼쟁결말은어느ᄯᅢ나날ᄂᆞᆫ지실로묘연ᄒᆞ도다아라샤에셔도여러번패망ᄒᆞᆷ을분격히녁이여과왕만쥬에잇든군사버다오히려과셰를더ᄒᆞ야군사를조직ᄒᆞᆫ즉젼투를연속ᄒᆞ야ᄒᆞ랴ᄒᆞᆷ이분명ᄒᆞᆫ지라이일이금년이월에ᄒᆞᆯ일이어놀비로소이제야힘쓴필경이왕에동병ᄒᆞ니버다오히려긴즁ᄒᆞ며더옥견확ᄒᆞᆯ터인즉아라샤도역시강국이라응당ᄃᆡ적ᄒᆞ야크게싸호려ᄒᆞᆷ은우리의예료ᄒᆞᆫ비어니와아모조록우리ᄂᆞᆫ당초작뎡ᄒᆞᆷ과갓치조곰도축계ᄒᆞ지말고결단코어느ᄯᅢᄭᆞ지던지싸와우리의목젹되로셩취ᄒᆞ여야ᄒᆞᆯ러인즉현금에제일긴급ᄒᆞᆫ일은나라에지졍과군권을아모조록유지ᄒᆞ도록제척을너여야ᄒᆞᆯ터인재라나의싱각ᄀᆞᆺ타여셔ᄂᆞᆫ쳥재지방은여러조건이잇스되그경제ᄒᆞᄂᆞᆫ마음으로허다ᄒᆞᆫ자본을젼쟁에다모도드리라고ᄒᆞᆯᄂᆞᆫ지분명짐작치못ᄒᆞᄂᆞᆫ바이라고ᄒᆞ엿슨즉 (미완)

잡보

○부인회원유 작일샹오십이시붓터경셩일본부인회에셔원유회를창덕궁안옥비셜ᄒᆞ고장곡쳔대쟝과림공ᄉᆞ를쳥요ᄒᆞ엿더라

○츈찰션치 강원도관찰ᄉᆞ쥬셕면씨ᄂᆞᆫ공졍의면ᄒᆞ야도엽이리로션졍을만히힝ᄒᆞᆯᄲᅮᆫ더러민폐되ᄂᆞᆫ잡슈세를낫낫치혁파ᄒᆞ며다년포흠되엿든원통ᄒᆞᆫ송ᄉᆞ를공결ᄒᆞᆷ으로도ᄂᆡ민심이열복ᄒᆞ야치젹외송셩어자자ᄒᆞ더니향일에뎨임ᄒᆞᆫ단말이젼파ᄒᆞᆷ으로도ᄂᆡ인민이일심으로이셕히여기고도ᄂᆡ유싱박돈양씨등삼십명이발통회동ᄒᆞ야샹경ᄒᆞ엿ᄂᆞᆫ되졍부에쳥원ᄒᆞ고필경졀문에복합ᄭᆞ지ᄒᆞ랴다가다힝이례임이아니되미제싱등이불승환희ᄒᆞ야하거ᄒᆞ엿다더라

○털도계획 일본졍부에셔ᄂᆞᆫ현금부셜ᄒᆞᄂᆞᆫ경의털도를연궁ᄒᆞ야동쳥털도모지뎜ᄭᆞ지털도를련락ᄒᆞ야부셜ᄒᆞ기로결뎡ᄒᆞ엿ᄂᆞᆫ되그런락ᄒᆞᆯ디뎜은대포뎨신대신과산면털도국쟝등의일힝이귀국ᄒᆞᆫ후에군ᄉᆞ샹과경제샹으로됴사ᄒᆞ야대셕교와히셩과료양세곳즁그ᄒᆞᆫ곳을취ᄐᆡᆨᄒᆞᆯ터이오히털부셜비ᄂᆞᆫᄉᆞ쳔만원에뎡인ᄃᆡ그즁에압록강털교소입비가삼ᄇᆡᆨ만원예산이라더라

○향우지란 륙군법원에셔ᄂᆡ부로죠회ᄒᆞ기를각부부원쳥젹ᄉᆞ구근을군슈로됴용ᄒᆞ엿ᄂᆞᆫ되유독본원만미참ᄒᆞ엿스니무손충졀인지향우지란이잇ᄂᆞᆫ지라다른마을젼례대로일례시힝ᄒᆞ라ᄒᆞ엿더라

○일거월졔 참졍신긔션씨ᄂᆞᆫ긔어히ᄉᆞ직ᄒᆞ고퇴휴ᄒᆞ기로결뎡ᄒᆞ엿다ᄒᆞ며그되ᄂᆞᆫ젼대신죠병호씨가등용ᄒᆞᆯ터인고로소명을봉승ᄒᆞ야목쳔본ᄃᆡᆨ에셔샹경ᄒᆞ엿다더라

○권대ᄉᆞ츌강 일본츌젼군위문대ᄉᆞ스즁현씨일힝은금일발졍ᄒᆞᆫ다더라

○조공ᄉᆞ츌발 쥬일공ᄉᆞ죠민희씨와참셔관한치유씨일힝이작일샹오십시에발힝ᄒᆞ야일본에젼왕ᄒᆞᄂᆞᆫ되법대김가진외대리하영량씨가젼송ᄎᆞ로하인ᄒᆞ엿다더라

○쳐역압송 향일에쥬동일병죠런장에셔한인김덕유가일본포병의시계를도취ᄒᆞ다가일헌병의게피착되야즁역이십년션고ᄒᆞ야일젼에한국쟝부로압숑ᄒᆞ엿더라

○감시횡도 슈동힝랑뒤골로번에ᄒᆞᆫ셔례가잇ᄂᆞᆫ되차자가ᄂᆞᆫ사ᄅᆞᆷ이업순즉힝로지인이목불인견이라ᄒᆞᆫ더라

○하료ᄌᆞ쳐오 탁지쥬ᄉᆞ리병슌씨ᄂᆞᆫ무삼연고인지작작일에조쳐긔료하로젼왕ᄒᆞ야음약조ᄒᆞᆫ료로히부동료긔인이왕곡회쟝ᄒᆞ엿다더라

○결세됴사 탁지고문관목하면종티랑씨ᄂᆞᆫ시무지쵸에갑오이후세입세츌파결세얼마식슈세ᄒᆞᆫ것을변변히츅됴로위션됴사ᄒᆞᆫ다더라

관보

뎨이쳔구ᄇᆡᆨ륙십륙호 광무팔년십월이십오일

셔임급ᄉᆞ령

○명경긔슌찰사 륙군참령구연하 십월십팔일

○의원면본관 ᄂᆡ부광제원제약사 김긔만 ○임ᄂᆡ부광제원제약사셔관임관륙등 김샹셥 ○명사법시찰슈원 긔병참위 박두영 이샹십월이십일

○의원면본관 비셔원승 오형근 례식원번역관 박용규 즁추원의관 졍창권 ○명동지돈녕원사셔칙임관삼등 궁ᄂᆡ부특진관 리지현 ○명ᄂᆡ쟝원경셔칙임관삼등 종이품 조균하 ○임비셔원승셔쥬임관

륙등 정삼품 리진구 ○임례식원번역관셔쥬임관륙등 례식원번역관보 진학신 ○임례식원번역관보셔관임관륙등 죠범구 ○임 경긔면령셔관임관칠등 원구단사제셔령 정지덕 ○임원구단사제셔령셔관임관칠등 소경원참봉 리윤슈 ○임소경원참봉셔판임관팔등 의령원참봉 리희범 ○임의령원참봉셔판임관팔등 구품 정연셕 ○임즁츄원의관셔쥬임관륙등 경긔면령 오병션 ○승셔판임관사등 외국어학교부교관 최상철 안우상 ○급이급봉 평리원검ᄉᆞ 현동건

이상십월이십이일

○면징계 륙품 홍승범 ○티복ᄉᆞ쥬ᄉᆞ셔판임관ᄉᆞ등 돈령원쥬ᄉᆞ 리호집 ○임돈령원쥬ᄉᆞ셔판임관칠등 륙품 홍승범 ○면징계 전총쇼 손히봉 이상십월이십삼일 ○십ᄀᆡ일별봉 황히도관찰부총쇼 오희모

십월이십삼일 경무청

궁뎡록사

○조왈방축향리죄인리긔동을방ᄒᆞ라 십월이십이일

○한셩부관윤김대진ᄉᆞ직소 비지니에소청을의시ᄒᆞ노라 ○니장원경리명직ᄉᆞ직소 비지니에소청을의시ᄒᆞ노라 ○궁니부특진관김쥬현조렬소 비지니에ᄉᆞ양말고힝공ᄒᆞ라

십월이십삼일

○원슈부관제

뎨일됴 원슈부ᄂᆞᆫ부원슈를두기위ᄒᆞ야셜치홈이니부원슈ᄂᆞᆫ훈공과근로가최다ᄒᆞᆫ륙히군대쟝으로친명홈이라

뎨이됴 부원슈ᄂᆞᆫ 대원슈폐하셰와 원슈면하셰군ᄉᆞ상조슌을봉답ᄒᆞᄂᆞᆫ칙임이잇슴이라

뎨삼됴 부원슈ᄂᆞᆫ칙령을봉승ᄒᆞ야륙히군의점검을힝ᄒᆞᄂᆞᆫᄉᆞ가잇슴이라

뎨ᄉᆞ됴 부원슈의게ᄂᆞᆫ부관이원을부ᄒᆞ나부관은륙히군령위관각일인으로임명홈이라

뎨오됴 본관제ᄂᆞᆫ반포일노시힝홈이라

뎨륙됴 광무ᄉᆞ년삼월이십일반포ᄒᆞᆫ원슈부관제ᄂᆞᆫ폐지홈이라

○시종무관부관제

뎨일됴 시종무관부를셜치ᄒᆞ고그직원은좌ᄀᆞᆺ치뎡홈이라

시종무관쟝 일인 륙군대쟝혹부쟝

시종무관 팔인 륙군령관삼인 히군령관삼인 정위이인

셔긔 십인 하ᄉᆞ혹판임무관

뎨이됴 시종무관쟝급시종무관은 대황뎨폐하셰홍샹뫼셔호위ᄒᆞ야군ᄉᆞ에관ᄒᆞᆫ샹쥬와봉답과밋명령젼달홈을위임ᄒᆞ며또관병ᄒᆞ며연습ᄒᆞ며동 가시와기타제의례면어연 폐현동시에홍샹시위ᄒᆞ며호종홈이라

뎨삼됴 시종무관쟝은시종무관의근무를가뎡ᄒᆞ고또이것을감독홈이라

뎨ᄉᆞ됴 시종무관은연습과기타군ᄉᆞ샹시찰을위ᄒᆞ야파송ᄒᆞᄂᆞᆫ수도잇슴이라

뎨오됴 시종무관은총히찰모관이됨이라

뎨륙됴 시종무관은시종무관쟝과군부대신이련셔쥬차홈이라

뎨칠됴 본관제ᄂᆞᆫ반포일노시힝홈이라

외보

○영국셔쟝됴약 영국과셔장국ᄉᆞ이에톄결ᄒᆞᆫ됴약정본은영어와청어와셔쟝말세나라말노넙은조희ᄒᆞᆫ장에쓰게ᄒᆞ엿다ᄒᆞᄂᆞᆫ디이거슨셔쟝사ᄅᆞᆷ의일단미흑ᄒᆞᆫ마ᄋᆞᆷ으로ᄒᆞᆫ쟝더되ᄂᆞᆫ거스로문셔를문드ᄂᆞᆫ디ᄂᆞᆫ단정코됴인홈을거절ᄒᆞᆫ연고이라더라

○청국항의영셔됴약 청국정부ᄂᆞᆫ북경에잇ᄂᆞᆫ영국공ᄉᆞ를통ᄒᆞ야구월팔일에라마관쥬의디표자와양싸스쌘드댄좌와서이에톄결ᄒᆞᆫ영국셔쟝통샹됴약에관ᄒᆞ야항의홈을영국정부에뎨출ᄒᆞ얏ᄂᆞᆫ디청국아그됴약으로인ᄒᆞ여영국이셔쟝의쥬권을쟝악에너흠과ᄀᆞᆺ치ᄒᆞᆫ됴목이잇ᄂᆞᆫ디영국의허락이업시ᄂᆞᆫ청국과셔쟝ᄉᆞ이에아모계약이던지ᄒᆞ지못ᄒᆞ게ᄒᆞᆫ디ᄒᆞ야항의홈이라청국은영국이이런소위로써불법이라ᄒᆞ야동국이지나간수ᄇᆡᆨ년동안에셔쟝국에셔보존ᄒᆞ여오든권리를횡탈코져홈이라고ᄒᆞᄂᆞᆫ듯ᄒᆞᆫ디영국의모든신문은이거스로써ᄒᆞ되로국에셔션동을식킨거스로인홈이라ᄒᆞ엿더라

○로국셔슌양함 구월십구일에로국도셩에셔론돈의엇던곳에발송ᄒᆞᆫ면보를거ᄒᆞᆫ즉가노이크식조미함되ᄂᆞᆫ이즈물즈드호ᄂᆞᆫ크론스닷트항에셔운젼을시험ᄒᆞᆯ제ᄒᆞᆫ시간에이십ᄉᆞ헤리빌의속력이잇셧ᄂᆞᆫ디셩젹이자못잘된모양이라ᄒᆞ며또그비의쟝속을다필ᄒᆞᄂᆞᆫ디로리왈에잇ᄂᆞᆫ데이티평양함디의소속이되기로ᄒᆞ엿다더라

○비힝긔 구월십삼일미국샹항크로늬클신문샤셜에ᄒᆞᆫ말을거ᄒᆞᆫ즉론돈슈졍궁에셔거힝ᄒᆞᆫ나이트작위막키심씨의발명ᄒᆞᆫ공즁비힝긔의셔험은자못잘된모양인듯ᄒᆞᆫ디한사ᄅᆞᆷ이ᄐᆞ고셔능히륙십쳑이샹의공즁에서ᄒᆞᆫ시간에이ᄇᆡᆨᄉᆞ십리나삼ᄇᆡᆨ리나가ᄂᆞᆫ속력으로나라단니게ᄒᆞ엿다ᄒᆞ니이러케ᄲᆞᆯ은속력은지금에ᄀᆞ장속쾌ᄒᆞᆫ게ᄯᆡᆯ니단니ᄂᆞᆫ급힝렬거도오히려밋ᄎᆞᆯ수업다ᄒᆞ엿더라

뎐보

십월이십ᄉᆞ일대산만쥬군총ᄉᆞ령관공보

○로군손히 그후죠ᄉᆞ를거ᄒᆞᆫ즉포로된조의총슈ᄂᆞᆫ칠ᄇᆡᆨ구명이오젹의젼장에버린시톄ᄂᆞᆫ우리우익군방면에오천이ᄇᆡᆨ이오좌익군방면에오천륙ᄇᆡᆨ삼이오즁앙군방면에이천ᄇᆡᆨ삼십이니합계가일만삼천삼ᄇᆡᆨ삼십이라ᄒᆞ엿더라

잡보

○북도대등 근일에함경북도로샹릭ᄒᆞᆫ사ᄅᆞᆷ의소젼을드른즉북관디방에ᄂᆞᆫ년사가대풍인즁면곡은근년처음대등ᄒᆞ엿스나아병이왕왕히츌몰ᄒᆞᄂᆞᆫ고로민심이황겁ᄒᆞ야풍년지락을모른다ᄒᆞ더라

○팍민포형 팍산군민문창호가본월십륙일에뎡쥬북방에셔면간목을넘멋드리고익조일기를과샹ᄒᆞ엿더니이십이일에일헌병의게피착되야이십삼일에뎡쥬병참ᄉᆞ령관이군률시힝으로문창호를포형ᄒᆞ엿다더라

○평북회도 평북관찰ᄉᆞ의보고를거ᄒᆞᆫ즉션천군에ᄂᆞᆫ십팔일에진보회슈ᄇᆡᆨ명이읍즁에회집ᄒᆞ여삭발ᄒᆞᄂᆞᆫ고로그즁에김치봉등삼인을착슈ᄒᆞ고졍쥬군에ᄂᆞᆫ십월칠일에김창하등이진보회라ᄒᆞᄂᆞᆫ자사ᄇᆡᆨ여명을령솔ᄒᆞ고들어와서모다삭발ᄒᆞ기에효유ᄒᆞ여도히산치아니ᄒᆞᆫ고로김창하등이명을착슈ᄒᆞ고귀셩군에ᄂᆞᆫ십월팔일에동학당천여명이읍즁에드러와서그익일에남문외로회집ᄒᆞ여일제히단발ᄒᆞ고가지아니ᄒᆞᆫ다ᄒᆞ엿고곽산군에ᄂᆞᆫ십월팔일에진보회삼ᄇᆡᆨ여명이읍즁에와서회집ᄒᆞᆫ미졍쥬군에쥬차ᄒᆞᆫ일본헌병이와셔슈삼명을착거ᄒᆞ고박천군에ᄂᆞᆫ십월팔일에박긔근이라ᄂᆞᆫ자가관ᄉᆞ에드러와서진보회롱문을ᄂᆡ여보이고그당류들어모다단발ᄒᆞ고가산군에ᄂᆞᆫ음력팔월이십구일에란민슈ᄇᆡᆨ명이읍즁와둔취ᄒᆞ여잇ᄂᆞᆫ고로그즁십이명을일본헌병이착슈ᄒᆞ고철산군에ᄂᆞᆫ음력팔월이십구일에진보회삼ᄇᆡᆨ여명이읍즁에둔취ᄒᆞ여잇ᄂᆞᆫ디그즁사명을일병이착거ᄒᆞ고티천군에ᄂᆞᆫ십월팔일에진보회륙칠ᄇᆡᆨ명이회집ᄒᆞ여그익일에일졔히단발ᄒᆞ엿ᄂᆞᆫ디일본헌병이히산ᄒᆞ라고효유ᄒᆞ여도죵시듯지안코히산치아니ᄒᆞ미부득이ᄒᆞ여그즁ᄉᆞ명을포살ᄒᆞ미여당은모다도망ᄒᆞ다가륙명은물에ᄲᆡ져죽엇다ᄒᆞ엿더라

○질문리유 작일하오이시에일본헌병이명이일진회ᄉᆞ마쇼에와서질문ᄒᆞᆫ기롤무숨일로회동ᄒᆞ며ᄀᆡ회를아니ᄒᆞᆯ터이면회원의리왕ᄒᆞᄂᆞᆫ거시엇지그리번다ᄒᆞ뇨ᄒᆞ고갓다더라

광고

거월십일일밤에농포안원소ᄉᆞ집에셔젹한의게가산을봉젹ᄒᆞ엿ᄂᆞᆫ대그즁에야쥬ᄀᆡ포목면졍규환쳐에당오젼십삼만량칠ᄇᆡᆨ팔십ᄉᆞ호십월회일에차질어음일편을셔실ᄒᆞ엿스니무론니외국인ᄒᆞ고습득ᄒᆞ여도휴지시힝홈

농포안 원소ᄉᆞ 고ᄇᆡᆨ

차터드은힝
자본 총액은이천오ᄇᆡᆨ만원
본점은영국론돈에잇고지점은각디도회쳐에잇소
인천셰창양힝디리점

향항샹히은힝
조원금총익슴천륙ᄇᆡᆨ오십만원
본점은향항에잇고
지점은청국일본기타각국디쳐에잇소
인천셰창양힝디리점

미국우션회샤와
동경동양긔션회샤
미국히션과연락ᄒᆞ엿숩
인천합롱가양힝디리점

셔울우션회샤
속힝ᄒᆞᄂᆞᆫ일등륜션들인디
청국과일본셔영국과각국으로릭왕홈
인천합롱가양힝디리점

뎨일은힝〔뎨일국립은힝〕
본뎜은일본동경에잇고
ᄌᆞ본금총익륙ᄇᆡᆨ이십오만원
리식은미ᄇᆡᆨ원에삼젼오리에셔
륙젼오리ᄭᆞ지인데
명긔ᄒᆞᆫ디로계산홈
경셩뎨일은힝지점쟝 면죵

북티평양륜션회샤
미국과구라파에릭왕ᄒᆞᄂᆞᆫ디
션가ᄂᆞᆫ미우싸게밧숩
인천합가양힝디리

덕국아셰아은힝
본점은덕국ᄇᆡᆨ림에잇고향항
지점은샹히등지에잇소
인천셰창양힝디리점

덕국우션릭왕
크고견고ᄒᆞᆫ륜션여러척이덕
청국과일본셔구슈각지로릭왕홈
연천셰창양힝디리점

TELEGRAMS.

(FROM JAPAN PAPERS.)

London, Oct. 18.

Reuter's correspondent with General Oku's Army Corps' wiring on the 15th, says it is believd the Russians intend to make a stand at the Hun River, while the Japanese propose to force an entrance into Mukden as soon as possible.

Berlin, Oct. 20th.

Prince Khilkoff, the Russian Minister of Communications, states that trains on the Circum-Baikal Railway are now able to run at the rate of twenty versts an hour.

London, Oct. 20th.

The India Office denies the report that the occupation of the Chumbi Valley will probably continue for seventy-five years.

Reuter's correspondent, writing from Pharijong on the 17th instant, states that the last column of the British force returning from Thibet, together with the headquarters staff, are snowbound there, the drifts having obliterated the roads. Two men belonging to the column have died from exposure.

London, Oct. 18.

The Foreign Office has informed the Holt Steamship Company that railway material and raw cotton shipped for the Far East must be taken at senders' risk.

Berlin, Oct. 20.

The Baltic Fleet has passed the Great Belt.

The "Novoye Vremya" urges Russia to enter into treaty with the Netherlands for acquiring the concession of a harbour in the Sunda Islands as a coaling station.

Berlin, Oct. 20.

Reports from South America state that Japan has bought from the Argentine Republic the cruisers "Garibaldi" and "Pueyrredon" (each of 6,882 tons) and from Chili the armoured cruisers "O'Higgins" (7,000 tons) and "Esmeralda" (8,500 tons). The vessels are, however, to remain in the harbours of the respective Republics until the present war is concluded.

Later.

Reuter's correspondent understands that it was settled at Lhassa that the Thibetans should pay indemnity at the rate of one lac annually, although it was pointed out to them that the occupation of the Chumbi Valley under the Treaty was to continue until the indemnity (amounting to 75 lacs) was fully paid. The contradiction issued yesterday by the Foreign Office apparently implies that the home Government has not confirmed this arrangement.

It was also agreed at Lhassa that the representative of Great Britain at Gyangtse should have the right of going to Lhassa to settle all questions requiring his presence there.

JAPANESE CASUALTIES ACCORDING TO OYAMA

Tokyo, Oct. 25.

Our Casualties in the battle of shaho were 15,879. This embraces operations from the 9th to 25th inst.

THE BALTIC FLEET.

Tokyo, Oct. 25.

A London telegram states that while passing the North Sea, the Baltic fleet bombarded a north-sea fishing fleet, mistaking them for Japanese torpedo craft. Two travelers were sunk during the firing, which lasted 20 minutes.

THE POWERS THAT WOULD BE.

The following weighty decisions were passed at the last meeting of the ubiquitous Il-chin-hoi.

1. All the members of our society must shave their heads.
2. Hats or caps must be worn according to foreign style.
3. Coats must have their sleeves made narrow, also dark colours must be worn.
4. Anyone who can afford to wear European clothes may do so, but they must not spend too much money on same.

And this, ladies and gentlemen, we may say, not a contribution to the "Ladies Home Journal" or "The Gentlemen," it is the result of many months hard mental work on the part of the Il-chin-hoi society, whose sole desire according to their own words, is to reform Korea.

Perhaps, next year, we may hear of "bloomers" being worn, but up to date the Il Chin Hoi's endeavours towards political and economical reform have certainly not got beyond the talky stage.

The German Minister was a visitor at the Foreign Office yesterday morning.

A Japanese teacher of the middle school at Tokyo is to be employed by the Korean Government, for the purpose of effecting educational reform.

Mr. Stevens, the newly-appointed adviser to the Foreign Office has arrived in Yokohama, where he will stay for a few days prior to proceeding here to take up his duties.

The British police authorities have got back on the Press for all the nasty things which have been said about the Beck case. William Thomas, Beck's "double," is described in the calendar at the Old Bailey as a "journalist."—Evening News.

Four Koreans among a crowd of agitators at Kasan, have been shot by Japanese. They were ordered to disperse, but refused and it was found necessary to fire on them. In the stampede which ensued six Koreans were drowned in attempting to swim the river.

NOTICE.

Seoul, Oct. 21st.

The Committee of the Yeng Wha Chin Foreign Cemetery request the Western Foreign Residents of Seoul to meet in the Reading room of the Seoul Union on Monday the 31st October, 1904 at 4 o'clock P. M. for the purpose of electing a new committee for the ensuing year, and for discussion of matters relating to the cemetery.

HORACE N. ALLEN,
President.

R. RRINCKMEIER,
Hon. Sec.

The Korea Daily News.

Issued at 5 P. M. daily except Sundays.

Rate of Subscription:—
Per Year, Yen 25.
Per Quarter, Yen 7.
Per Month, Yen 2.50.

Postage in Korea not charged extra.
Postage abroad charged extra.

Advertisements, 50 sen per day for 1 inch or less.
5 yen per month per inch.
50 yen per year per inch.

All communications to
E. T. BETHELL,
Editor and Publisher,
Pak-tong, Seoul

GERMAN EMPEROR AND NAVAL EXPANSION.

The speech of the German Emperor at Hamburg on September 6th has excited considerable interest. His Majesty recalled his own important utterances at Hamburg on October 18th, 1899. On that occasion his Majesty employed the following eloquent words:—"If the increase in the navy, which I demanded with urgent prayers and warnings, had not been stubbornly refused me during the first eight years of my reign—it did not even escape derision and mockery at the time—in how different a manner should we now be able to promote our prosperous commerce and our interests over sea." He further called attention to the fact that ancient Empires were passing away and new ones were arising; "new nations which, till recently, had scarcely been noticed by the unlearned have suddenly come into view and have begun to participate in the competition of the peoples." The want of a strong German fleet was "bitterly felt." Five years have elapsed, and the Emperor was able to say that "the most momentous date" among his visits to Hamburg, "the 18th of October, 1899, has borne fruit, and the appeal to the German people has not been unheard. Its success is visible in the kernel of the German fleet which now lies anchored near the mouth of the Elbe waiting to be inspected by me. The German nation has the right to maintain the navy and the army which it requires for the maintenance of its interests, and no one would desire to prevent it from developing these defences in accordance with its own wish and its will." His Majesty, after proceeding on board the Imperial yacht "Hohenzollern" to Heligoland, went on 7th inst, on board the flagship "Kaiser Wilhelm" and held a grand naval review in the neighbourhood of the island. There are 22 battleships and cruisers two divisions of torpedo-boats anchored east of Heligoland. In an article in the "Berliner Tageblatt" on the Emperor's speech, the naval critic, Count Reventlow, suggests that his Majesty's remarks indirectly call attention to the necessity of a further increase in the navy.

BLOWING UP THE "SIVOOTCH."

The "Russkoe Slovo" publishes particulars of the blowing up of the Russian gunboat "Sivootch" at Newchwang. On the withdrawal of the Russians it was felt that the boat was useless to them, and in a dangerous position for her crew. In harbour she would not be able to withstand an attack from the Japanese t.b. d.'s and it was hardly likely she would succeed in escaping if she put to sea, for her utmost speed was not more than ten knots. Her displacement was 840 tons. She carried a 9in. Krupp gun aft and a 6in. gun in her bows, and some smaller guns. On August 1st, Capt. Stratanovitch, her commander, received orders to blow her up. Before doing so he removed the Hotchkiss guns and the Baranovksi landing gun, and the breech blocks from the big guns. The crew left in the launches, the majority to join the army with the guns and the others remaining on the launches to navigate them up the river. On August 2nd pyroxiline cartridges were placed in the ship fore, aft, and amidships, and only two minutes elapsed between the explosion of the first and last cartridge, after which some of her remains were still visible, though soon to disappear in the river mud. The crew watched the explosions from the banks, and many of them reverently crossed themselves.

CONFERENCE OF JAPANESE STATESMEN.

On October 15th says the "Kobe Herald" Count Katsura, the Prime Minister, and other members of the Cabinet, entertained the leaders of the political parties in the Imperial Hotel. General Terauchi, Minister of State for War, delivered a short address with reference to the battle of the Shaho. The most interesting point he made, states the "Japan Mail," was that Kuropatkin chose for his attack the very moment when the Japanese army itself was getting ready to resume the offensive. Count Katsura also spoke. It had been expected that he would make some definite financial statement, but he explained that he was not yet in a position to do so. He confined himself, therefore, to congratulating the nation on the results thus far brought about by its union and resolution.—Mr. Oishi Masami, one of the Progressist leaders, said that while the united support of the nation might be counted on for the prosecution of the war, the nation on its side expected to be treated with confidence. It wanted to know whether the Government was really determined to persevere with the campaign until Russia had no choice but to make peace. For such a purpose the country was willing to make any pecuniary sacrifices. but, on the other hand, it insited that the funds supplied by it should be employed with the strictest honesty and in the most economical manner. Finally, there seemed to be good reasons for doubting whether the Government's manner of dealing with the Korean problem satisfied the situation. Korea had in effect been taken under Japan's protection, and unless the fact were practically recognised all the efforts made and the outlays incurred might result in signal failure.

GENERAL KUROPATKIN'S FORCES.

OFFICIAL JAPANESE ESTIMATE.

The Tokio Heardquarters Staff has issued the below estimate of the forces commanded by General Kuropatkin in the battle of the Shaho:—

First Siberian Army Corps under Lt.-General Stackelberg; consisting of Division I (Major General Gerun-gross) and Division II (Major-General Kondradovitch) of East Siberia Rifles —namely 24 battalions and 8 batteries.

Second Siberian Army Corps, (commander uncertain), Division V (Lt.-Gen. Alexieff) of East Siberia Rifles, and Division I (Maj-Gen. Morozoff) of Siberia Reserves—28 battalions and 8 batteries.

Third Siberian Army (Lt.-Gen. Ivanoff); Division III (Maj. Gen. Kastalinsky) and Division VI (Maj-Gen. Damiroff) of East Siberia Rifies: 24 battalions and 8 batteries.

Fourth Siberian Army (Lt.-Gen. Sarubaieff); Divisions II and III of Siberia Reserves (Maj-Gens. Reusetan and Kottsuvitch); 32 battalions and 8 batteries.

Fifth Siberia Army (Lt.-Gen Danbofsky); 54 and 71st Divisions of Reserves (Maj.-Gens. Woruroff and Ekku); 32 battalions and 12 batteries.

Sixth Siberia Army (General Zabouf); 55th and 72nd Divisions of Reserves (Major-Gens. Raiching and Baraoffsky); 32 battalions and 12 batteries.

Tenth Army (Gen. Seruchensky); 9th and 41st Division of Reserves (Maj.-Gen. Hershmann and Lieut.-Gen. Mau); 32 battalions and 14 batteries.

Seventeenth Army (Gen. Birderring): 3rd and 35th Divisions of Reserves (Lieut.-Gen. Ivanshura and Lieut-Gen. Doburuschnisky); 32 battalions and 14 batteries.

First Army (Gen. Maiendorff); 22nd and 27th Divisions of Reserves (Lt.-Gens. Affadosovitch and Chekumareff; 32 battalions and 12 batteries.

In addition to the above there were:—2 Regiments of picked Moscow Infantry—8 battalions, 4 batteries of the East Siberia 2nd Brigade and 4 of the East Siberia 4th Brigade. Five regiments of field mortars and 2 batteries. Five batteries of horse artillery and 5 of mountain artillery, one battery of siege guns and one independent battery of eight guns.

Total 276 battalions, 122 batteries and 173 sotnias of cavalry in addition.

The whole numbering about 200,000 infantry, 26,000 cavalry, 950 guns.

The estimate of the numbers is based upon the very low allowance of 700 men per battalion.

SITUATION IN THE NORTH EAST.

A Gensan telegram reports that a General from Russia in Europe has arrived at Songchin to take command of the troops in Korea. The main force of the Russians is at Pukchong, and they are guarding the roads between that place and Kyonsyong. A young lady in the garb of a Russian red-cross nurse has frequently been seen; the natives are astonished at the sight as they imagine she must be a female Russian general.

In an interview with the St. Petersburg correspondent of the "Financial News," M. Kakoftzeff, Minister of Finance, speaking on 7th Sept., said that the revenue for the seven months of the war had been 11,000,000 roubles ($6,500,000) more than in 1903. He said he viewed the financial situation with perfect satisfaction. The war had cost to date 272,000,000 roubles. He expected that it would have cost 300,000,000 roubles more by next January. There was no prospect of any difficulty in meeting the demands upon the treasury, which was in the most solid condition. He has just concluded an operation in Central Russia which would result in there being 750,000,000 roubles available after January 1st to meet estimated expenditures of 600,000,000 roubles. The Minister expressed a wish that more representative foreigners would visit Russia instead of believing what the Russophobe press said. He was pleased to see that the United States was regarding Russia with a more favourable eye than formerly,

The Commodore of the French Naval Division in the Pacific, on arriving at Auckland, says Reuter's correspondent, on board the second-class cruiser Amiral Protet, was informed by the harbour authorities that it was necessary for him to apply formally for permisson to land, on the ground that the rule applied to all foreign warships. The Commodore, in reply, stated that inasmuch as such a law did not exist in any other part of the world he would not submit to it in New Zealand, and that as soon as he had coaled he would leave Auckland. He added that French warships would not visit New Zealand while such a law was in force. In the meantime the Premier's courteous telegram, welcoming the Commodore, has been disregarded. It is stated that the incident has bsen reported to Paris.

In opposition to the announcement, by the manager of a special dinner to be served at the Grand Hotel, Yokohama, on the occasion of the prospective fall of Port Arthur, the Club Hotel manager now advertises. The end of the war is near. The Guests of the Club Hotel will be served with the best that the market affords until peace is declared, and on the day when that is officially reported Ice Cream and cold Huckleberry Pudding will be served "ad valorem."

The burial of Mr. Kruger in Pretoria will take place in December. The Boers are desirous that the ex-President shall be interred on December 16, Dingaan's Day. The commemoration has been associated for years with Mr. Kruger's address at the Paardekraal Monument, where the Boers in 1880 swore, while adding stones to the pile, to fight for independence, Mr. Kruger throwing on the first stones.

The Korea Daily News.

VOL. I, THURSDAY, OCTOBER 27, 1904. No. 86

大韓每日申報
대한ᄆᆡ일신보

(뎨팔십칠호) (금요일) 일쳔구ᄇᆡᆨ사년십월이십팔일

본샤고빅

이신보는영문과한문으로셔가티
일츌판ᄒᆞ옵
신문가
한쟝 엽젼두돈오푼
일삭됴 엽젼팔냥닷돈
우표가ᄑᆡ삭닷돈
다ᄉᆞᆺ돈으로밧ᄉᆞᆸ
광고료는
귀한의장단과ᄌᆞ항의다소로중
감ᄒᆞ되몃가로밧을터이오며오
리지아녀대한사람마다이신
문을보실터이니광고내시기를
원ᄒᆞ시는이들은우리신문샤에
와셔면약ᄒᆞ심을희망ᄒᆞᄋᆞᆸ
○발힝소 박동대한ᄆᆡ일신보
사별어한교양희젼영국인셜필
립정자킈오
사쟝 영국인 (빈셜)
평양 ᄃᆡ리졈
○평양효동사는권미보씨로우
리신문관ᄃᆡ리인을뎡ᄒᆞ엿
ᄉᆞ오니평양에계신구람코져ᄒᆞ
시는 쳠군ᄌᆞ는ᄎᆞᄃᆡ리졈에왕
림ᄒᆞ와면의ᄒᆞ시ᄋᆞᆸ

사고

○우리대한ᄆᆡ일신보의목뎍은
대한의인녕졀셔에관한모든대
목에ᄃᆡᄒᆞ야는공평한변론을주
장ᄒᆞᆯ이라우리동신원의힘ᄡᅥ보는
신문보시는쳠군ᄌᆞ의게ᄒᆞ상보
도ᄒᆞ리며편지들귀셔ᄒᆞ며주시
는이는셩명과반ᄃᆞ듸졔이붓쳐
시기를희망ᄒᆞ오니비커슨신문
샹에긔ᄌᆡᄒᆞ란는거시아니오ᄃᆡ
반구히신용ᄒᆞ는중거를숨고자
ᄒᆞᆷ이라귀자는아모귀셔던지귀
ᄌᆡᄒᆞᆷ을뵈각ᄒᆞ는권리를가젓스
나뵈각ᄒᆞ는리유를말ᄒᆞᆯ터이오
며공중평화를문란케ᄒᆞ는듯ᄒᆞᆫ
대귀셔는의례히밧지안케ᄉᆞᆸ나
이다
●본사셜시이리로신문을미양
우례로분젼ᄒᆞ와레젼부의일의
로젼ᄒᆞ든것스로면곳에는혹늣게
젼ᄒᆞ기도ᄒᆞ며혹멋쳘거슨혼ᄂᆞᆸ
에젼ᄒᆞ기도ᄒᆞ며혹아니젼ᄒᆞ는
곳도잇다ᄒᆞ와우리신문을수탕
ᄒᆞ야구람ᄒᆞ시는 쳠군ᄌᆞ의게
티ᄒᆞ야미우미안ᄒᆞ옵기로지금
은분젼인을두고미일일ᄌᆞ이젼
ᄒᆞ며아니젼ᄒᆞ거나늣게거나ᄒᆞᆫ
가얍도록ᄒᆞ란ᄒᆞ오니ᄒᆞ아니셩
젼ᄒᆞ거는혹늣게젼ᄒᆞ거나ᄒᆞᆫ일
이잇스면본샤로통긔ᄒᆞ여주심
을희망ᄒᆞᄋᆞᆸ

본샤광고

○본샤신문중에긔ᄌᆡᄒᆞᆫ호수를
소용ᄒᆞᆯ데가잇서이에광고ᄒᆞ오
니누구시던지그중에아모호수
던지가져오시는ᄃᆡ로ᄆᆡ쟝에빗
젼두푼식드리리다
뎨이호 뎨삼호 뎨이십호
뎨수십이호 뎨수십삼호 뎨
오십삼호 뎨오십수호와뎨오
십오호 뎨륙십이호

관보

뎨이쳔구ᄇᆡᆨ륙십칠호
광무팔년십월이십륙일
셔임급ᄉᆞ령
○승셔원승관오등 탁지부량
디국주ᄉᆞ 김문슈
일월십팔일
○승셔원승관ᄉᆞ등 탁지부량
디국주ᄉᆞ 졍인방
삼월십이일
○승셔원승관ᄉᆞ등 탁지부량
디국주ᄉᆞ 명규영
ᄉᆞ월십이일
○승셔원승관오등 탁지부량
디국주ᄉᆞ 송셩린
륙월이십칠일
○금산금봉 한셩우례ᄉᆞ주ᄉᆞ
ᄒᆞᆼ학슈 김영일 인쳔우례ᄉᆞ
주ᄉᆞ 리승찬티시영
십월십이일
○임륙군법원주ᄉᆞ셔판임관일
등 륙품 김의문
○임륙군법원주ᄉᆞ셔판임관이
등 륙품 윤홍의
○임륙군법원주ᄉᆞ셔판임관ᄉᆞ
등 륙품 리응주
○임륙군법원주ᄉᆞ셔판임관오
등 륙품 빅남표 신현딜
○임륙군법원주ᄉᆞ셔판임관륙
등 죠관하 박종국 김하경
구품 민셕긔
이상십월십구일
○임한셩부관균셔쳑임관삼등
법부참서관 송티현
○임함경북도관찰ᄉᆞ셔쳑임관
삼등 졍삼품 김로규
○의원면본관 종슈의관 홍
진
○임중추원의관셔주임관륙등
단양군수 졍의동
이상십월이십이일
○원주이군중군신 군부경리국
뎨이과원륙군이등군ᄉᆞ 졍우
창
상십월이십ᄉᆞ일
○의졍부찬졍신긔션ᄉᆞ직소
비지니에맛당히ᄃᆡ유면려ᄒᆞ야
모취를불밧들게ᄒᆞ시오이번에가
기를구치못ᄒᆞ지니다시번거미
말고곳시무ᄒᆞ라
십월이십ᄉᆞ일
○동궁비종무관부관졔
뎨일됴 동궁비종무관부를셜
치ᄒᆞ고그직원은좌ᄀᆞᆺ치뎡ᄒᆞᆷ이
라
동궁비종무관쟝 일인 륙군
륙군부쟝ᄒᆞ참쟝
동궁비종무관 팔인 륙군령
관이인 위관삼인정
위삼인
셔긔 칠인 하ᄉᆞ관
임문관
뎨이됴 동궁비종무관쟝은
황ᄐᆡᄌᆞ뎐하께광의보필ᄒᆞ는직
책을위임ᄒᆞᆷ이라
뎨삼됴 동궁비종무관쟝은동
궁비종무관의근무세칙을규뎡
ᄒᆞ며쇼비이ᄀᆞᆺ을감독ᄒᆞᆷ이라
뎨ᄉᆞ됴 동궁비종무관쟝급
동궁비종무관은 황ᄐᆡᄌᆞ뎐
하께ᄒᆞ샹비위ᄒᆞ야군ᄉᆞ의관ᄒᆞᆫ
일계봉답급명령젼달를위임ᄒᆞ
며동 에관병연습시와기타군
뮨급 졔의례연연례알현등시
에비위ᄒᆞ고호종ᄒᆞᆷ이라
뎨오됴 동궁비종무관중령관
이샹은참모관이됨이라
뎨륙됴 동궁비종무관은시종
무관쟝과군부대신이련셔주차
ᄒᆞᆷ이라
뎨칠됴 본관제는반포일로시
힝ᄒᆞᆷ이라
○친왕부무관관졔
뎨일됴 륙군무관에잇는친왕
에는륙군각병과졍위일인으로
ᄡᅥ친왕부무관을보직ᄒᆞᆷ이라
셔긔 삼인 하ᄉᆞ흑판임문관
뎨이됴 친왕부무관은친왕의
위의졍식을봉조ᄒᆞ야힝가와힝
군과관병연습시와기타군무급
졔의례연연회등시에슈종ᄒᆞᆷ이
라
뎨삼됴 친왕부무관은시종무
관쟝과군부대신이련셔주차ᄒᆞᆷ
이라

잡보

○수의상쇼 일공ᄉᆞ가외부로
죠회ᄒᆞ기를ᄎᆞ주관찰부ᄎᆞ슌리
군빈가ᄀᆞᄒᆞ병참소에구류된일
ᄉᆞ는면신ᄐᆡ쟝의보고를거ᄒᆞᆫ즉
당초의본ᄃᆡ가ᄎᆞ주에ᄃᆡ답ᄒᆞᆯ때
에면져동ᄉᆞ김귀용을본읍에보
내여슈쇼를뎡ᄒᆞᆯᄉᆞ음에쥬막주
인현덕용이가거힝을잔야나ᄒᆞ
는고로ᄒᆞᆫ번ᄉᆞᆫ으로치미우면히
눈이샹ᄒᆞᆫ거슬엄가가경무서에
ᄒᆞ소ᄒᆞ야리ᄎᆞᆼ슌이김귀용을착
슈ᄒᆞ고빙렴히티벌ᄒᆞ니미는군
ᄉᆞ힝동상방희자인고로면저관리
결ᄉᆞ의게교ᄒᆞ야최탐ᄒᆞᆫ후에리
ᄎᆞᆼ슌을가ᄒᆞ병참소에류일을구
류ᄒᆞ엿다ᄒᆞ니귀죠회ᄉᆞ의와는
대단의의ᄋᆡ진다ᄒᆞ엿더라
○죠례군슈 챵원군슈권의샹
씨가마산항ᄃᆡ도공역에방히ᄒᆞᆷ
이잇스니브부에ᄂᆡ죠ᄒᆞ야면관
ᄒᆞ고그ᄐᆡ에는신임ᄒᆞ리원군슈
빅남죠ᄅᆞ로셔임케ᄒᆞ라고일본공
관에셔외부로죠회ᄒᆞ엿더라
○동산군보 동산군슈마죵영
씨가외부로보고ᄒᆞ기를륙주광
리한영원의ᄒᆞᆫ쳐니에본항일본
령ᄉᆞ의죠쳥ᄒᆞᆷ을인ᄒᆞ야본군소
관잠셤를표ᄒᆞᆷ을됴사ᄎᆔ보ᄒᆞ나ᄒᆞ
엿기그ᄃᆡ로사보ᄒᆞ엿더니히감
리가지명ᄒᆞ되공문샹ᄌᆞ즁ᄀᆡ
하좌하와봉명위망등ᄌᆞ가ᄎᆞ등
분별이잇거늘히군슈보고문ᄌᆞ
샹에좌하라칭하고위망이라ᄡᅳ
니극히만홀ᄒᆞᆫ지라불가불징감
ᄒᆞᆯ지니슈셔괴를알샹ᄒᆞ되만일
일향원거ᄒᆞ면경부에보ᄒᆞ야감
쳐ᄒᆞᆫ다ᄒᆞ니본관이비록용관샹
격식에미례ᄒᆞ나쳐임관의게라
야쟉하라칭ᄒᆞ는쥴로드렷ᄊᆞ오
며쇼군슈를징감ᄒᆞᆫ다ᄒᆞ니감리
가군슈의게무손권한이잇게에
능히징감ᄒᆞ오며귀부에무슨시
로보낭쟝졍이잇는지보고ᄒᆞ오니
죠량ᄒᆞ신후낫낫치회복ᄒᆞ심을
복망이라ᄒᆞ엿더라
○진회쟝셔졍부 일진회에셔
쟉비십칠일에졍부로또쟝서ᄒᆞᆫ
대긔에ᄉᆞ됴목권고을파면ᄒᆞᆯ셔

ᄒᆞ기어렵게든출처와거취를제
원이속히결정ᄒᆞ라ᄒᆞ엿더라

○진회조처샹주 일진회에
셔고시ᄒᆞ기를졍부ᄂᆞᆫ아국에붓
ᄒᆞᆫ당으로고포학ᄒᆞᆷ을힝ᄒᆞ야민
회를양제ᄒᆞᆫ니현금졍부ᄂᆞᆫ셰불
공랍이라ᄒᆞᆫ지라신참졍이지작
일밤에입시ᄒᆞ야조처ᄒᆞᆯ수법을
샹주ᄒᆞ엿더라

○계방젹거 졍부에셔경무쳥
으로면칙ᄒᆞ야일진회의계방을
위션뿟어버리라고시ᄒᆞ라ᄒᆞ엿더
라

○고원군보 고원군에셔보고
ᄒᆞ기를음력구월초삼일에두퇴
빈빅여명이진보회라ᄂᆞᆫ일홈으
로쳐쳐면쳥계방ᄒᆞ고나아와취회
ᄒᆞ야수츠연셜ᄒᆞ고각기ᄉᆞ수로
단발ᄒᆞᆯᄌᆞ음에일병이수명을견
발ᄒᆞ야원산항으로쳡거ᄒᆞ고기
여삼십명은지금지위평숌ᄒᆞ여
갓다ᄒᆞ엿더라

○평창치보 평안남도관찰ᄉᆞ
의보고에ᄒᆞ엿스되한죵용강강
셔삼화안등군보고를거ᄒᆞᆫ즉소위
진보회당이쳐쳐에둔취ᄒᆞ엿다
ᄒᆞᆫ고로각군에명칙ᄒᆞ야히산케
ᄒᆞ엿더니함종군보고에ᄂᆞᆫ슈
쳔여명이단발ᄒᆞᆫ후에퇴산ᄒᆞ엿
다ᄒᆞ고용강군보고에ᄂᆞᆫ둔취ᄒᆞ
여잇ᄂᆞᆫ진보회당륙빅여명을도
저히효유ᄒᆞ여히산식혓다ᄒᆞ고
강서군보고에ᄂᆞᆫ읍즁회집ᄒᆞ여
단발ᄒᆞᆫ자수빅여명을히산케ᄒᆞ
고삼화군보고에ᄂᆞᆫ진보회쳔여
명을효유ᄒᆞ여히산케ᄒᆞ엿다ᄒᆞ
고강동군보고에ᄂᆞᆫ슈빅명이회
집ᄒᆞ여말ᄒᆞ기를셔울회즁으로
셔ᄌᆞ회가잇셔셔힝동ᄒᆞᆫ다ᄒᆞ고ᄒᆞ
엿더라

○산회면담 영흥군면보를거
ᄒᆞᆫ즉동학당이벌ᄒᆞ여진보회라
칭ᄒᆞ고일제히단발ᄒᆞ고읍즁으
로회집ᄒᆞᄂᆞᆫ고로훈칙ᄒᆞ여효유
ᄒᆞ여아직은물너갓스나그당류
의칭궐ᄒᆞᆷ이불무려ᄒᆞ라ᄒᆞ엿더
라

○의주군보 의주군에셔보고
ᄒᆞ기를동학비도가진보회로라
고칭ᄒᆞ고음력팔월회일에읍니
에제회ᄒᆞ야일쟝연셜ᄒᆞᆫ후에사
발ᄒᆞ고물너갓다ᄒᆞ니민습이히
연ᄒᆞᆫ지라각군에발훈ᄒᆞ야일일
히분티방티로착수ᄒᆞ야그리도
ᄒᆞᄂᆞᆫ티로다시츄문ᄒᆞᆫ후에련속
ᄒᆞ여치보ᄒᆞ기로복계ᄒᆞ오며각
쳐에파병ᄒᆞ야ᄯᅩᄒᆞᆫ회를금ᄒᆞᆫ다
ᄒᆞ엿더라

○공찰보고 공쥬관찰ᄉᆞ가보
고ᄒᆞᆫ니긔에은진군서리진쟝군
슈졍주현영의보고를거ᄒᆞᆫ즉음력
본월구일에동학비도수빅명이
일진회라칭ᄒᆞ고강경포에모혀
일제히삭발ᄒᆞ엿다ᄒᆞᄂᆞᆫ고로본
군슈가곳히디에가셔그두령을
부른즉히두령남원사ᄂᆞᆫ쟝원익
은잉의산경ᄒᆞ엿고그남아ᄂᆞᆫ다
쥴다라일일히죠치ᄒᆞ야 죠칙
파밋관찰부ᄒᆞᆫ령을뵈인후에잘
효유ᄒᆞᆫ즉다ᄌᆞ복ᄒᆞ고각기ᄉᆞ사
로귀화ᄒᆞᆫ다ᄒᆞᄂᆞᆫ고로군슈처보
ᄂᆡᆫ다ᄒᆞᆫ등졍이기로이를의게ᄒᆞ
와치보ᄒᆞᆫ다ᄒᆞ엿더라

○송씨의민 련산거ᄒᆞᄂᆞᆫ송과
샹씨가외부에쳥원ᄒᆞ기를본인
이론베사ᄂᆞᆫ리죵봉으로더브러
분뤼면분이잇더니거음력오월
분에장시ᄎᆞᆯ타ᄒᆞ엿다가졍에도
라온즉강평포사ᄂᆞᆫ일인졍상졍
티랑이가본인의게밧을거시잇
다ᄒᆞ고와서돈을독촉ᄒᆞᄂᆞᆫ고로
그ᄉᆞ실을무른즉리죵봉이가본
인의일홈으로슈표를ᄒᆞ여주엇
ᄂᆞᆫ지라져져히발명ᄒᆞᆫ즉히일인
이리모른쳑ᄒᆞ야독봉ᄒᆞᆯᄌᆞ음
에리모가즁을타셔도망ᄒᆞ엿ᄂᆞᆫ
지라히일인이다시본인의게칙
징ᄒᆞᄂᆞᆫ고로무ᄎᆞ일빙ᄉᆞ의게졍
소ᄒᆞ엿스나안직귀졍이니지못
ᄒᆞ엿스오니곳일본공ᄉᆞ의게조
회ᄒᆞ와즁속히타결케ᄒᆞ여주시
기를ᄇᆞ라옵나이다ᄒᆞ엿더라

○우피도교수진 일본공ᄉᆞ가에
셔외부로조회ᄒᆞ기를공ᄂᆡ부제
용ᄉᆞ우피도교일ᄉᆞᄂᆞᆫ잉의젼죠
회에ᄌᆞ셰히말ᄒᆞ엿거니와지금
귀부조복을졉ᄒᆞᆫ즉ᄂᆡ긔에공ᄂᆡ
부에셔조칭ᄒᆞ기를본부에셔
피소를셜시ᄒᆞᆷ은본부소용으로
제조ᄒᆞᆷ이오그ᄂᆞᆷ아ᄂᆞᆫ죵시가ᄒᆞ
야ᄂᆡ외샹고의게방민ᄒᆞᆯ터이니
이거슨가히도교에비ᄒᆞᆯ수업다
ᄒᆞ엿스나셜노도교인거시헌연
ᄒᆞᆫ지라졍권티귀대신이수셜ᄒᆞ
와즉시힝ᄒᆞᆷ을거두게ᄒᆞ라ᄒᆞ엿
더라

뎐보

○일군ᄉᆞ샹 샹월이십륙일일본공ᄉᆞ관착
ᄉᆞ샹은십월이십오일젼투에일군
와하ᄉᆞ와ᄉᆞ졸을합ᄒᆞ야일만오
쳔팔빅칠십구명이라ᄒᆞ엿더라
동일동련

○쎄릭함티포힝 십월이십
일죠조에(하루)에셔발ᄒᆞᆫ보고
를거ᄒᆞᆫ즉쎄릭합티가노수시ᄂᆞᆫ
에셔하루어젼일단을공격ᄒᆞ엿
ᄂᆞᆫ디지금서지종합ᄒᆞᆫ보고를거
ᄒᆞᆫ즉오젼일시에어젼오십쳑가
량이(수단뒷도)의동북이빅이
십희리에서어업에종ᄉᆞᄒᆞᆯ시에
아국군함을보앗ᄂᆞᆫ티최초에슈
뢰졍수쳑이갓차이왓스나아모
거동이업시가더니그다음에아
국군함이탐회등을빗취고즉시
포격을시ᄒᆞ야스ᄆᆡᆫ호라ᄒᆞᄂᆞᆫ
어션일쳑은아국포탄에파조침
몰ᄒᆞᆫ고함쟝과승조원일명이ᄉᆞ
망ᄒᆞᆫ고기타즁샹ᄒᆞᆫ자가만ᄒᆞ며
기타어션도손히를당ᄒᆞ엿ᄂᆞᆫ티
ᄯᅩ어선일쳑은승조원들이올수
히침몰되엿다ᄂᆞᆫ졍셜이잇스며
다시보ᄒᆞᆫ바를거ᄒᆞᆫ즉아국함티
는제일포란ᄉᆞ격ᄒᆞᆫ후에젼투ᄒᆞ
는항오를것고이십분동안을포
격ᄒᆞᆫ후에남방으로향ᄒᆞ여갓ᄂᆞᆫ
되일반밋을만ᄒᆞᆫ바를거ᄒᆞᆫ즉이
포함은어선을일본슈뢰졍인줄
그릇알고ᄒᆞᆫ거시라더라
동일동련

○신문별보 영국에쥬차ᄒᆞᆫ일
본공ᄉᆞ의별보를거ᄒᆞᆫ즉이포함
에관ᄒᆞ야영국어리신문이싱히
분란ᄒᆞ며ᄯᅩ아국을향ᄒᆞ야충분
ᄒᆞᆫ사리와만족ᄒᆞᆫ보히를요구ᄒᆞᆯ
거시라ᄒᆞ고론란ᄒᆞ엿고스단담신
문에는셰릭합티가지금졍신이
국도에발ᄒᆞ엿슴으로이ᄂᆞ떼
엇더ᄒᆞᆫ위험에밋칠지모로겟고에
ᄒᆞ아함의포힝은세계각국에위히
교히ᄒᆞ게ᄒᆞᄂᆞᆫ자이니셰릭합티가ᄒᆞ의항
론게속ᄒᆞᆷ을졍지케ᄒᆞᆷ이가ᄒᆞ다
란ᄒᆞ엿더라

잡보

○섬칠인출장 시찰명목으로
일본에츌장ᄒᆞᆫ이가이왕반힛거
니와정부대관중에ᄯᅩ일본으로
츌강ᄒᆞᆯ인원이섬칠명이라더라

○리쟈씨츌셔 젼관셰리면샹씨
ᄂᆞᆫ일쟉일에셔뵌셰ᄒᆞ엿더라

○대신기차 참졍과찬졍이하
각부대신이일간올수히긔차
가될터이라ᄒᆞᄂᆞᆫ티회인원은모
공ᄉᆞ가권ᄒᆞ고ᄒᆞ리라운운이러라

○시흥민요수건 시흥군민요
ᄉᆞ로지작일에평리원에서일본
군티리ᄉᆞ와회심ᄒᆞ엿ᄂᆞᆫ티셩우
리경민ᄒᆞᆫ량인은쳐역을납면ᄒᆞ
리라더라

○탐학관쟝젼욕 챰오진후이
함티로가군슈와각관찰ᄉᆞᄒᆞᆫ티탐
학ᄒᆞ여돈을쎄앗진자들이근일
에샹경ᄒᆞ야일진회에드럿다칭
ᄒᆞ고의세ᄒᆞ야도로찻조란ᄒᆞᆫ다
ᄂᆞᆫ티즁경관찰과군슈들이만히
젼욕ᄒᆞᆫ다ᄂᆞᆫ풍셜이잇더라

○진회면보평북 쟉일에일진
회에셔녕변관찰부로젼보ᄒᆞ기
를본회ᄂᆞᆫ이쳔만동포의총티라
헐금포학ᄒᆞᆫ졍부와ᄂᆞᆫ대반티요
대공격이니각하가진보회원을
포살ᄒᆞᆫ거시젹실ᄒᆞ면이쳔만동
포의분울ᄒᆞᆷ이대단ᄒᆞᆯ지라몃사ᄅᆞᆷ이
나포살ᄒᆞ엿ᄂᆞᆫ지ᄌᆞ세히회시ᄒᆞ
시며곳수ᄌᆞᆨᄒᆞ신후에지회ᄒᆞ기
를ᄇᆞ라노라 일진회쟝윤시병

○진회면보충북 쟉일에일진
회에셔충쳥북도관찰부로면보
ᄒᆞ기를본회ᄂᆞᆫ이쳔만동포의총
티라헐금
셩명을지하에졍부즁진셰빈가
기로대반페ᄒᆞ고포학을ᄌᆞ힝ᄒᆞ
각쳐에진보회란칭ᄒᆞᄂᆞᆫ자도
명의목젹은일반비칭ᄒᆞ오니각하
귀명에쥬의ᄒᆞ면찬셩ᄒᆞ시고하가포
한ᄒᆞᆫ졍부를찬셩ᄒᆞ시거든진보
회원을소탕ᄒᆞ며포힝ᄒᆞ실ᄂᆞᆫ지
즉시회면ᄒᆞᆷ을ᄇᆞ라노라ᄒᆞ엿더라
일진회쟝윤시병

○구씨갈봉 닉쟝원에서닉부
로조회ᄒᆞᆫ뒤귀에의주군ᄌᆞ공토
츄수ᄒᆞᆯ로위원린은식이가닉라
갓다니회군수구완회가교시ᄒᆞ
여왈문으도지인등처에비와정식
ᄒᆞ여원도조젼외에는경ᄌᆞ년이
후가봉세도진은일병을시ᄒᆞ라
ᄒᆞ고와회도의도조칠빅여셕닉
에이빅셕여은영구히탕감케ᄒᆞ
아타조ᄒᆞ기어렵다ᄒᆞᆫ고로구군
슈들일삼참봉에차ᄒᆞᆫ다ᄒᆞ엿더
라

론설

젼호련속

○우리의싱각갓흔ᄃᆡ셔는젼국
빅셩이일제히합외ᄒᆞ야젹군
으로더부러디젹ᄒᆞ려ᄒᆞ기를즐
거ᄒᆞᆫ다ᄒᆞ믄가히밋지못ᄒᆞᆯ말인
거시라슌항구에히젼쥰비ᄒᆞᆷ과
ᄯᅩᄒᆞᆫ다른곳에셔무ᄎᆞ대젼ᄒᆞᆷ으
로인ᄒᆞ야젼국빅셩의분일ᄒᆞᆫ마
음과미타ᄒᆞᆫ뜻이모도잇슬ᄲᅮᆫ아
니라그외상관업는다른나라에
셔들도대단히위ᄒᆞ야넉이ᄂᆞᆫ지
라

그러ᄒᆞ나게티랑씨와밋그이하
관원들은담판ᄒᆞᄂᆞᆫ마당에셔도
이러케칭양ᄒᆞ야셜명ᄒᆞᆷ은무타
ㅣ라조귀나라빅셩들로ᄒᆞ여곰
마음을경돈ᄒᆞ고우리ᄒᆞᆷ을믈너
ᄒᆞ야공연ᄒᆞᆫ쓸디업ᄂᆞᆫ말로ᄎᆞᆷ동
을식히일년더리일본졍부에셔
도싱히위를ᄒᆞ며경결ᄒᆞᆷ이아닙
은아니로되다만화평ᄒᆞᆫ리도로
만셜명ᄒᆞ야나라명예의손히됨
과대신들의칙임이며빅셩들의
진즁하는마음을두로싱각ᄒᆞ야
그러ᄒᆞᆷ인지라

만일졍부대신들이젼정에나갈
것갓ᄃᆞ면외희ᄒᆞ야라사들모라
ᄶᅩᆺ고항복을밧겟다고빅셩들의
계보즁이라도회셜치ᄒᆞᆯ듯ᄒᆞ되
졍부대신의싸홈담당ᄒᆞᆷ일로빅
셩들의게대답ᄒᆞᄂᆞᆫ거시분파ᄀᆞᆺ미
귀에오날날우리의말ᄒᆞᆫ것과ᄀᆞᆺ
치될지라즁왕에도셩명제산들
만히허비ᄒᆞ엿스되이제도ᄯᅩᄒᆞᆫ
쟝ᄎᆞ젼쟁을결말니자ᄒᆞ면수만
인셩과억만금의을허비ᄒᆞᆷ은
이무가론이요ᄯᅩᄒᆞᆫ량업시빅
셩들의게즁츌ᄒᆞ여야ᄒᆞᆯ터이로
다 완

TELEGRAMS.

(FROM JAP N PAPERS.)

—

Berlin, Oct. 21.

The United States Minister at St. Petersburg has presented on behalf of the Japanese Government a protest against the practice of Russian soldiers in the field being disguised as Chinese.

—

Berlin, Oct. 21.

The Japanese refugees from Siberia, who recently arrived at Bremerhaven, have sailed for Japan on board the N. D. L. steamer "Gera." They received a cordial farewell from the people of Bermerhaven. A deputation from the Patriotic Women's League visited the Japanese on board the steamer and handed them presents, after which Herr Noessler, the Japanese honorary Consul at Bremerhaven, thanked the ladies for their gifts, and on the proposal of (Captain) Kikuchi, military attache, a hearty "Banzai" was given for Bremerhaven.

—

London, Oct. 21.

An Army Order just issued by the British War Office provides that all enlistments for the infantry in future shall stipulate nine years' service with the colours and three in the reserves.

[The present system is three years with the colours and nine years in the reserves.]

—

London, Oct. 21.

The whole of the Thibet expedition has reached Chumbi after a most trying march in the snow. A number of the men have been smitten with snow. blindness.

King Edward has commanded that a special medal be conferred on the members of the Thibet Mission and the Expedition force in recognition of their severe labours and excellent conduct.

—

Berlin, Oct. 21.

The United States Government denies that it had at any time any intention of offering its services as mediator between Japan and Russia.

—

Berlin, Oct. 21.

The "New York Herald" publishes a report to the effect that General Kuroki is seriously ill with dysentery, his condition being critical.

—

Berlin, Oct. 21.

Prince Karl Anton, of the House of Hohenzollern, arrived at Liaoyang on Friday to join the Japanese Headquarters Staff in the field.

—

Berlin, Oct, 21.

The Russian Budget sets aside the sum of ten million roubles for the purpose of doubling the line on the trans-Siberian Railway.

Today the worthy "reformers" posted notices on the street informing the public that the Government was formed of the Pro-Russian party, and the Il Chin Hoi refused to exist under the same sky with them. (There is quite an easy remedy for you, Messrs. Il Chin Hoi & Co.)

THE VIOLATION OF PRINCE VICTOR'S TOMB.

Capetown, Sept 8.—An extraordinary outrage has been committed upon the the grave of Prince Christian Victor in Pretoria. With tools from the cemetery tool-house, some persons have dug into the grave until they reached the slab covering the coffin. Apparently they were disturbed at this stage, for no further damage was done. News of the outrage was received in Capetown at a late hour to-night, and caused consternation and horror. Princess Christian, the mother of the young soldier, was present at a dinner party, which included the members of the late Sprigg Ministry, also Messrs. Hofmeyr, Schreiner, Sauer, and Merriman. The Princess was not informed of the outrage, and it has been decided not to break the news until her Royal Highness has departed from Capetown. She leaves for Kimberley, en route to Victoria Falls, to-morrow. Meanwhile the local newspapers have consented not to publish the terrible story to-morrow. It is feared here that the outrage will cause incalculable harm in South Africa, reviving the embittered racial feeling, though it is recognised that the prominent Dutch would abhor such a vile deed equally with the British.

It is feared that the Crown Princess will succumb to her illness.

Mr. Megata is entertaining various Departamental Ministers at the residence of Miss Sontag this afternoon.

Japanese Yen in the North of Korea are now unacceptable to the natives, the Russian troops having insisted on roubles being the only currency permissible.

It is said that the Government have given a contract to a Japanese firm for the improvement of the sanitation of Seoul. Sixty thousand Yen is to be the cost of the work.

As we go to press, we receive news of later developments in the Il-chin-hoi comedy. The Government has now been memorialised by two influential gentleman to effect the arrest of the Il-chin-hoi's president and punish him as a traitor to his country. It is also said that certain officials are attempting to induce the Peddlers to rise and disperse the Il-chin-hoi.

The "Kokumin" states that the dock No. 3, now under construction, of the Mitsu Bishi Dockyard, Nagasaki will be the largest in the Far East, admitting vessels up to 714 feet in length. The dock No. 1 of the same company admits vessels up to 510 feet in length and the No. 2 up to 350 feet. The new dock is to be completed by the end of this year.

NOTICE.

—

Seoul, Oct. 21st

The Committee of the Yeng Wha Chin Foreign Cemetery request the Western Foreign Residents of Seoul to meet in the Reading room of the Seoul Union on Monday the 31st October, 1904 at 4 o'clock P. M. for the purpose of electing a new committee for the ensuing year, and for discussion of matters relating to the cemetery.

HORACE N. ALLEN,
President.
R. RRINCKMEIER,
Hon. Sec.

The Korea Daily News.

Issued at 5 P. M. daily except Sundays.

Rate of Subscription :—

Per Year,	Yen 25.
Per Quarter,	Yen 7.
Per Month,	Yen 2.50.

Postage in Korea not charged extra.
Postage abroad charged extra.

Advertisements, 50 sen per day for 1 inch or less.
5 yen per month per inch.
50 yen per year per inch.

All communications to

E. T. BETHELL,
Editor and Publisher,
Pak-tong, Seoul

THE DEATH OF THE BATTERY.

RUSSIAN CORRESPONDENT'S UNNERVING EXPERIENCE.

The destruction of a Russian battery in one of the recent engagements is thus described by M. Nemirovitch Danchenko, the well-known novelist and special correspondent of the "Russki Slovo" and Associated Press.

"Can anything," he says, "be more terrible than the death of a whole section of an army under your eyes when you see the process of destruction and are unable to do anything whatever to prevent it? It was impossible to leave the 4th Battery on its old position—a hill cutting through our centre, where only two insignificant battalions were stretched over a distance of two and three-quarter versts. Two Japanese batteries loomed in front of ours. They were perfectly covered, while our 4th Battery stood quite open before them. The enemy turned two guns upon our left flank, and began to thunder, unseen by us, from the remainder of his guns against our 4th Battery, of which they had become tired. At half-past ten it was still working. The rattle of its quick-firing guns did not allow me to define whether the Japanese had machine guns or not. Others heard them. I could not catch these regular merciless sounds. To see as we did yesterday the flat top of its hill, and on it the black small lines of the guns—eight lines, eight ammunition boxes behind them on the slope. Underneath them something black is scattered. It is the screen. Fire flashes and small white clouds appear now and then from the black lines either from each separately or in volleys. All at once the battery becomes silent. The enemy thunder at it from the other side. No answer. We become strangely excited. What does this silence mean? Black spots are running in all directions on the yellow platform—they are bustling, some important movement is taking place, something sudden. Why are the guns silent, why do they not answer? Thank Heaven! There is a crack of one gun, of another, of a third. They have hurled their deficient shells upon the enemy. A volley, a second, a third! It seems impossible from here, that the Japanese can withstand such a fire. A minute, another, and they will be silenced. We wait for this with beating hearts. It seems to us somehow that such an end would only be justice, nothing else. We follow the smoke of the explosions on the opposite side. There are our shells exploding, and scattering away, as we imagine, scores, hundreds of the enemy. The 4th Battery, so suddenly revived, does not cease firing—it thunders incessantly, and all the black slopes send back the echoes in a dull, disconnected fashion. The echoes carry the sounds far, far away to where the other batteries in their turn roar at the enemy's positiom. The soldiers look round with a self-satisfied air. "That's how we work; they will know us." We none of us guess that the unfortunate 4th Battery is now struggling for its life, counting its last minutes, spending the last atom of its force. Black spots continue to run from the ammunition boxes to the black lines. Our steel jaws roar to the utmost. We are far from guessing the despair, the death agony, in this thunder. But what is this? Never—and it is my second war —did I —see anything like it. The Japanese guns have lifted their black muzzles from behind the crests that surround them, and have set to work to destroy this unhappy yellow hill, with its tiny black lines, black spots, and black cubes, from which innumerable black tendrils are now trailing. It is an orgy of exterminating fire! I look with anguish in my heart. The screen from under the hills is dispersing in all directions. Is it possible? Is there really a force in the world capable of compelling our men to move away? Yes there is, and there it is before me. Something indescribably terrible. Scores of shrapnel cases explode at the same time above the doomed battery. Scores of fires flash from the white clouds, scores of small clouds melt into a larger one, shutting from us the unfortunate flat space, the black lines and black spots. The lawful business of the Japanese gunners is not interrupted for a moment. Innumerable grenades break anew into a triumphant chorus. They dig into the soil of the hill and throw up brown masses of cloud that appear to be tinged with blood. These masses are soon merged into one, shutting out from us a hell that is celebrating its cruel victory there. Everything becomes confused and mingled—it is impossible to distinguish anything. It appears as though hundreds of fire-breaking dragons, such as the Chinese believe in, have broken away from their chains and accomplishing their wicked purpose behind that brown curtain under the murky shades of the explosion. We still distinguish in this pitchy smoke the rare answering rays of "our" fire, the dull sounds of our shots. There the dying battery resounds with a volley. Another! It will still struggle on: it will silence them. We listen greedily! We pass from despair to hope. A little more space, and it will answer the foe's fire? By what roads does he bring the guns, which seem at that moment innumerable? Everything is confused in my eyes and ears. The shrapnel clouds become thicker and thicker, the brown explosions of shells heavier and more compact.

"My heart is heavy. It is like watching the flickering life of the sufferer on a deathbed—like watching the death of someone who has suddenly become near and dear to you. What does it matter that bullets are now whistling near our heads, that the foe is firing at us from some unknow place, that two soldiers have already fallen close by. There a whole battery is coming to an end amid terrible convulsions, God be praised! It is possibe that the forces of the Japanese have failed them. They are gradually becoming silent. Their shots are rarer. The wind has already time to carry away the smoke of shrapnel and the brown shell fume. A few moments more and everything is silent. We look—and we do not believe our eyes. It is not a battery, it is the cemetery of a battery. The black lines are powerless and silent. No black spots are discernible, and the little cubes are moving downwards. The battery itself is buried under heaps of shrapnel fragments and the debris of shell; it is literally covered by them; there is not a free space. It was necessary to save what could be saved, to take off the gunlocks and remove the ammunition boxes. The removal of the guns could not be thought of. No horses could enter this hell and emerge alive I looked long at this burial place of dead guns. Their lives were short but noisy—perhaps more to be envied than the slow existence of others that are now being dragged along the dust and mud of the Manchurian roads. The abandoned guns lie like corpses in the yellow sand, covered by lead, cast iron, and steel. New black spots are rapidly approaching them from the other side. They move, collect, disperse along the edge of the flat space, open fire upon our centre, if we may call a centre two battalions stretched along two and three-quarter verste."

The Japanese Minister has requested the Home Office to dispense with the services of the Magistrate of Changwon, and replace him with the Magistrate of Yiwon. He has been charged with interfering with the railway workers on the Masanpo branch line.

MORE ABOUT FASHODA

Paris, September 9th.—In the "Figaro," Col. Marchand to-day reveals the fact that emissaries of the Khalifate of Omdurman were sent, in the course of the year 1897, to the Court of the Emperor Menelik of Abyssinia, where they met the French Minister, and that they made an offer to the latter, in the name of their master, to place Khartoum and the territories in Mahdist occupation under the protectorate of France. This proposal was rejected immediately it was made. The Colonel then goes on to express his gratitude to Lord Kitchener for the attitude which the Sirdar adopted toward him. "I have never ceased," he says, "to cherish a great admiration for the character and courteous methods of Lord Khartoum (sic), at present Commander-in-Chief of the Indian Army, and it is also not a secret with my friends that I am, and have always been, a fervent admirer of the British race, to which its rivals themselves cannot refuse all the solid qualities and brilliant defects that make master-peoples great, living and proud nations." Col. Marchand then endeavours to show that, by surrendering her interest in Egyptian affairs, in return for concessions and illusory advantanges in Morocco, France is making a bad bargain, as she sacrifices all her prestige in the east of the Mediterranean. By the loss of all influence in the Suez region, she lets her Colonial Empire be cut in two.

ANOTHER ATTACK ON A RUSSIAN OFFICIAL.

St. Petersburg, Sept. 23.—In Odessa this morning, while Chief of Police Neigdart, in company with Prince Obelinsky, his assistant, was inspecting some new government buildings in the Boulevard Nicholas, near the Pushky monument, a young man wearing a blue blouse fired from a distance of six paces at Neidgart. The bullet did not strike the Chief of Police and the would-be assassin was about to fire again when he was seized by Prince Obelinsky. The man's weapon fell to the ground and in a desperate struggle which ensued, in the course of which Neidgart was wounded in the hand with a dagger, the assailant was secured and placed in custody. He refused to give his name or any account of himself.

FATALITY AT CHEMULPO.

An unfortunate fatality occured on Wednesday evening, in the factory of the Chemulpo Cigarette and Tobacco Co. A Chinaman named Chang Fook-il experimenting with a tobacco drying machine, opened one of the doors of the machine, unknown to anyone and thrust his head inside. The stopping of the machine caused the foreman to investigate matters, when the unfortunate mass was discovered with his head tightly jammed among the pipes.

The machine was reversed and the Chinaman released, but his skull was so badly fractured that he died one hour after admission to St. Luke's hospital. The deceased was a native of Chefoo and had asked for leave of absence to return there, in order to get married.

It is said of Wall Street, as is said of the Stock Exchange in reference to the boat-race, that it is never wrong about the election of the President; and it has begun to offer odds of two to one on President Roosevelt.

The president of the Il-chin-hoi is still keeping the wires hot with lengthy messages. He now informs the world that he is the representative of 20,000,000 of the inhabitants of Korea. He has ordered the Governor of Pingyang to resign from his post for interfering with the Chin-po-hoi society, and telegraphed instructions to the Governor of north Choongchong to leave the Chin-po-hoi alone.

The Korea Daily News.

VOL. I, FRIDAY, OCTOBER 28, 1904. No. 87

HONGKONG & SHANGHAI BANKING CORPORATION.

Paid-up Capital..... ....$10,000,000
Reserve Fund:—Sterling Reserve... 10,000,000
Silver Reserve..... 7,000,000

27,000,000
Reserve Liability of Proprietors... 10,000,000

HEAD OFFICE, HONGKONG.

London Bankers, London and County Banking Company Limited
Branches and Agencies,
London.

Amoy,	Hankow	Penang,
Bangkok,	Hiogo,.	Rangoon,
Batavia,	Iloilo,	Saigon,
Bombay,	Lyons,	San Francisco,
Calcutta,	Manila,	Singapore,
Colombo,	Nagasaki,	Sourabaya,
Foochow,	New York,	Tientsin,
Hamburg,	Peking,	Yokohama,

Credits granted on approved Securities, and every description of Banking and Exchange business transacted.

Drafts granted on London and the chief Commercial places in Europe, India, Australia, America, China and Japan.

HOLME RINGER & Co., AGENTS, CHEMULPO.

ON CHEONG & CO., SEOUL.

GENERAL STORE KEEPERS.
Imported provisions, Cooking Utensils Crockery, etc.
FRESH BREAD DAILY.

MITSU BISHI DOCKYARD & ENGINE WORKS,

NAGASAKI.

CODE WORD, "DOCK."

A. 1, A. B. C., and Engineering Codes used

DOCK No. 1 (at Tategami).

Extreme Length..............523 feet
Length on blocks .... 513 ,,
Width of Entrance on Top......89 ,,
Bottom....77 ,,
Water on Blocks at Spring Tide 26½ ,,

DOCK No. 2 (Mukaijima).

Extreme Length..............371 feet
Length on Blocks.............360 ,,
Width of Entrance on Top......66 ,,
,, ,, Bottom 53 ,,
Water on Blocks at Spring Tide 22 ,,

PATENT SLIP (at Kosuge)

Can take vessels up to 1,000 tons gross

THE WORKS are well equipped with the LATEST IMPROVEMENTS, and can execute any kind of work in SHIPBUILDING and MARINE ENGINEERING, as well as in REPAIRING of SHIPS.

The COMPANY'S new powerful steamer OURA-MARU (712 tons, 700 I.H.P.), specially built for SALVAGE PURPOSES, and equipped with necessary gear, is always READY at SHORT NOTICE.

CHARTERED BANK OF INDIA AUSTRALIA & CHINA.

INCORPORATED BY ROYAL CHARTER 1853

HEAD OFFICES:—LONDON.

Paid-up Capital £800,000
Reserve Liability of Shareholders 800,000
Reserve Fund 800,000

Drafts granted upon all the principal places in the world and every description of Exchange and banking business transacted.

E. MEYER & Co., Agents, Chemulpo.

E. MEYER & CO.

Chemulpo.

SOLE AGENTS IN KOREA FOR:

A. T. Morse, Sons & Co's "Fresco" Distemper

In all colours ready for use on walls, Ceilings etc.

and

AVENARIUS CARBOLINEUM

A wood-preserving and antiseptic oil preparation

Against decay, dry-rot, fungus and wood-destroying insects.

A large supply always in Stock. Prices upon application.

E. MEYER & Co., Chemulpo.

THE METHODIST PUBLISHING HOUSE,

Little West Gate, Seoul.

PRINTING, TYPEWRITER PAPER
CARBON PAPER, VISITING CARDS
STATIONERY, BOOK BINDING
BOOK PUBLISHERS
AMERICAN SCHOOL BOOKS
SPENCERIAN COPY BOOKS
PEN CARBON LETTER AND BILL BOOKS

S. A. BECK, Manager.

HOKURKU DOBOKU KAISHA.

Branch office in Chong Dong, Seoul.
Japanese telephone No. 165

CONTRACT DEPARTMENT.

We can contract to build any building or construction.

MERCHANDISE DEPARTMENT.

We can provide any building material. We have just contracted to build the new Belgian Legation.

DAI-ICHI GINKO.

LIMITED.

(Formerly the First National Bank)

ESTABLISHED 1873

INCORPORATED UNDER PRESENT LAW 1896

Capital - - - - - - - - Yen 5,000,000
Reserve Fund - - - - 1,500,000

HEAD OFFICE:—TOKIO.

President: Baron SHIBUSAWA.

BRANCHES AND CORRESPONDENTS
In the Principal Cities and Towns of Japan.
Interest Allowed on
Fixed deposits 1 year - - - 6½ per cent
" " 6 months - - - 6 per cent

Special current accounts 1½ sen daily per Y 100
General " " 1 " " " 100

M. TANAKA, Manager, Chemulpo

HOLME RINGER & Co.

Chemulpo.

General Merchants and Government Contractors.

Agents for the leading Banks Steamship Companies and Insurance Companies

Importers of Merchandise of every description.

KAMEYA & CO.

GENERAL STOREKEEPERS

Chinkokai - - Seoul
(*Established 1895, Tokyo*)

Confectionery, Hams, Canned Goods, Cutlery, Hirano & Tansan Water. Provisions, Gents, Furnishing goods, Toilet Articles, Travelling Bags, Tobacco, Cigars & Cigarettes Kitchen Utensils. Coffee. Biscuits.

Fresh Goods always kept in Stock.
Prices Moderate
☞ *Please come and inspect our goods.*

NIPPON YUSEN KAISHA.

JAPANESE MAIL STEAMSHIP CO.

UNDER MAIL CONTRACT WITH THE IMPERIAL JAPANESE GOVERNMENT.

European Line

Regular Fortnightly Service between Yokohama Kobe, Moji, Shanghai, Hongkong, Singapore, Penang Colombo, Port Said, Marseilles, London and Antwerp

American Line

Regular Fortnightly Service between Hongkong and Seattle, calling at Shanghai, Moji, Kobe, Yokohama and Victoria, B. C.

Australian Line

Regular weekly Service betwen Japan Ports and Australia, calling at Hongkong and Manila.
(Above Three Lines Suspended until further notice).

Shanghai Line

Weekly Service between Shanghai and Japan Ports

Korea Line

Service Kobe, Moji, Nagasaki, Fusan, Chemupo, Chefoo, Taiku.
S. S. Babelsberg, 2181 tons.
Service Kobe, Moji, Fusan, Chemulpo, Chinnampo
S. S ARGO, S. S. Ohio.

BORDEN'S CONDENSED MILK CO.

New York, U. S. A.

ALWAYS IN STOCK
Eagle Brand Condensed Milk.
Gold Seal Condensed Milk.
Peerless (Family) Evaporated Cream.
Borden's Malted Milk.

E. MEYER & CO
Chemulpo, Korea,
Sole Agents

ROYAL INSURANCE COMPANY,
Funds exceed £10,000,000
FIRE
AT CURRENT RATES.
LIFE
REDUCED PREMIUM.
HOLME RINGER & Co., Agents, Chemulpo.

HOTEL DU PALAIS

SEOUL.

The only first class Hotel in Seoul. Situated in the centre of the city opposite the palace.

Cuisine under the supervision of an experienced French Chef.

Well ventilated and furnished throughout.

TARIFF UPON APPLICATION

L. MARTIN
Proprietor and Manager.

大韓每日申報
대한ᄆᆡ일신보

(뎨팔십팔호) (토요일) 일천구빅사년십월이십구일

본사고빅

이신보는영어와한국문셔거리
일출판ᄒᆞ옵

신문갑
한쟝 엽뎐두돈오푼
일삭표 엽뎐두량닷돈
우표가미삭닷돈
다닷돈으로밧숩

광고료는
귀ᄒᆞᆫ의쟝단과ᄌᆞ획의다쇼로ᄎᆞ
갑ᄒᆞ되렴가로밧을터히오며오
리지아녀대한사람마다다이신
문을보실터이니광고내시기를
원ᄒᆞ시는이들은우리신문사에
와서면약ᄒᆞ심을희망ᄒᆞ옵

○발힝소 박동대한미일신보
사빅이하교앞헤전영국인셜필
림쟝자리오
사쟝 영국인 (베셜)

평양 디리졈
○평양효동사는권미보씨로우
리신문판미디리인을뎡ᄒᆞ엿
ᄉᆞ오니평양에계신구람코져ᄒᆞ
시는 쳠군ᄌᆞ는해디리졈에왕
림ᄒᆞ와면의ᄒᆞ시옵

샤고

○우리대한미일신보의목뎍은
대한의인녕젼셔에관한모든뎨
목에디ᄒᆞ야는공평한변론을ᄌᆞ유
쟝ᄒᆞᆷ이라우리동신원의탐보는
신문보시는쳠군ᄌᆞ의게ᄒᆞᆼ샹보
도ᄒᆞ려니와편지를귀셔ᄒᆞ며주시
는이는셩명과번디를졍이붓치
시기를희망ᄒᆞ오니이거슨신문
샹에괴계ᄒᆞ란는거시아니오다
만긔휘신용ᄒᆞ논죵거를숨교자
ᄒᆞᆷ이라귀자는아모긔서던지괴
지ᄒᆞᆷ을되갸ᄒᆞ는권리를가졋ᄉᆞ
나되갸ᄒᆞ는리유를말ᄒᆞᆯ터이오
며공중평화를문란케ᄒᆞ는듯ᄒᆞᆫ
대긔서는외레히밧지안켓ᄉᆞᆸ나이
다

●본사셜시이린로신문을미양
우레로분젼ᄒᆞ와례젼부의입의
로젼ᄒᆞᄂᆞᆫ듯ᄉᆞ로번곳에는ᄒᆞᆨ는게
젼ᄒᆞ기도ᄒᆞ며ᄒᆞᆨ멋칠거슬ᄒᆞᆫ겁
에젼ᄒᆞ기도ᄒᆞ며ᄒᆞᆨ야나젼ᄒᆞ는
곳도잇다ᄒᆞ와우리신문을수탕
ᄒᆞ야구람ᄒᆞ시는 쳠군ᄌᆞ의
티ᄒᆞ야미우미안ᄒᆞ읍기로지금
은분젼인을두고미일일ᄌᆞ이젼
ᄒᆞ며아니젼ᄒᆞ거나늣게거나ᄒᆞᆫ
가엽도록ᄒᆞ란ᄒᆞ오니ᄒᆞ야나셩
젼ᄒᆞ거나ᄒᆞᆨ늣게젼ᄒᆞ거나ᄒᆞᆫ일
이잇스면본사로통긔ᄒᆞ여주심
을희망ᄒᆞ옵

본사광고

○본사신문중에젹기ᄒᆞᆫ호수를
소용ᄒᆞᆯ데가잇서이에광고ᄒᆞ오
니누구시던지그중에아모호수
던지가져오시는티로미쟝에빅
젼두푼식드리리다
뎨이호 뎨삼호 뎨미십호
뎨ᄉᆞ십이호 뎨ᄉᆞ십삼호 뎨
오십삼호 뎨오십ᄉᆞ호와뎨오
십오호 뎨륙십이호

관보

뎨이쳔구빅륙십팔호
광무팔년십월이십칠일
서임급ᄉᆞ령
○승서주임관오등 동리항경
무관 김상셜
○금일급봉 군부군무국장륙
군참쟝 김승규 륙군법원쟝
륙군참쟝 신티휴 륙군법원
리ᄉᆞ륙군보병참령 신졔영
이샹십월이십ᄉᆞ일
○의원면본관 샹의사주ᄉᆞ
김티셕
○임샹의사주ᄉᆞ셔판임관오등
례식원주ᄉᆞ 김용빈
○임례식원주ᄉᆞ셔판임관륙등
고희준
이샹십월이십오일
궁명륙ᄉᆞ
○군부티신륙군부쟝신리윤용
군 주군무군무국군ᄉᆞ과쟝륙
군보병졍령신티죵경리국뎨일
과륙군이등샤계안죵옥부관륙
군보병참령신좌군군무국긔병
과쟝륙군병참령김형티륭병과
과쟝륙군공병참령권졍륙등련긔
가군인면한해지낫슨즉헌티직
을희임ᄒᆞᆷ거시로티이군제기졍
ᄒᆞ는뎨예셰반사무가빈ᄂᆞᆫ번구
ᄒᆞ와셩슈에붓치기어렵써온지
라륙군군인쳔역ᄒᆞᆫ년령뎐규
뎨이됴등의방ᄒᆞ야직ᄒᆞ여곰
신임ᄒᆞᆷ이실샹방편지쳑에로티
이감히쳔편치못ᄒᆞᆷ으로샹
주ᄒᆞ와 셩지ᄒᆞ심을복망ᄒᆞ노
이다
십월이십이일
○궁니부특진관김졍근ᄉᆞ직소
비젼니에소쳥을의시ᄒᆞ노라
○비셔원승리명샹사직소 비
지니에사면의소즁이엇더ᄒᆞ기
에슈항을티만히ᄒᆞ이이곳든고
사계ᄒᆞ에극히희란ᄒᆞᆯ지라슈항에
파시ᄒᆞᆫ현과를주프ᄒᆞ야몬경ᄒᆞ
고경은사양말고힝공ᄒᆞ라
이샹십월이십오일
○니부대신 궁니부팀시셔리
리용티사직소 비지니에사양
말고힝공ᄒᆞ라
○의졍부찬졍권즁현사직소
비지니에사양ᄒᆞᆯ즁럼도셔무만
의시ᄒᆞ노라
○군부관졔
뎨일됴 군부대신은륙군군졍
을관리ᄒᆞ고륙군군인군속을
통솔ᄒᆞ며군대와밋소관모든
부를감독ᄒᆞᆷ이라
현금간은군부니에힝방국을
셜치ᄒᆞ야일반힝군ᄉᆞ무를쟝
관ᄒᆞᆷ이라
뎨이됴 군부대신은대쟝혹부
쟝으로쳥관ᄒᆞᆫ참쟝으로임ᄒᆞᆷ
이라
뎨삼됴 군인군속의임면과진
급등에관ᄒᆞ야는교육총감이
임면이추셔교육경도를졍감
ᄒᆞ야군부대신의게지조ᄒᆞ면
군부대신이쟝관회의를지ᄂᆡ
여과쳔티로주졔ᄒᆞ되참모총
쟝교육총감과련셔ᄒᆞᆷ이라
뎨ᄉᆞ됴 쳥관은대신을보좌ᄒᆞ
쳔ᄒᆞ야부니셔무를졍리ᄒᆞᆷ이
라
뎨오됴 대신관방에관방쟝일
인과부관이인을두어각병과
쟝부령과밋졍위로보직ᄒᆞ고
대신의명을밧다관방ᄉᆞ무를
주쟝ᄒᆞᆷ이라
군부셰신비셔관은일인이니
부관중에셔겸임ᄒᆞᆷ이라
뎨륙됴 대신관방에비셔과를
셜치ᄒᆞ야과쟝은각병과졍부
령으로보직ᄒᆞ고기하에과원
이인을두어각병과참령졍위
로보직ᄒᆞᆷ이라
비셔과쟝은관방쟝이겸임ᄒᆞᆷ
이라
뎨칠됴 비셔과에는좌개ᄉᆞ
무를쟝ᄒᆞᆷ이라
일은 쟝교와밋샹당ᄒᆞᆫ관원
과ᄉᆞ관과하ᄉᆞ와문관의임면
과보직과등명계ᄒᆞᆷ과봉급
ᄒᆞ는것과승등에관ᄒᆞᆫᄉᆞ항
이는쟝교와밋ᄉᆞ관의군젹과
문관의명ᄌᆞ쳑과뎡직된명ᄌᆞ
쳑과인원명ᄌᆞ쳑에관ᄒᆞᆫᄉᆞ항
삼은 퇴직쟝교와밋샹당관
과하ᄉᆞ의인ᄉᆞ와명ᄌᆞ쳑에관
ᄒᆞᆫᄉᆞ항
ᄉᆞ는 셔품과셔ᄒᆞᆫ과긔쟝과
포쟝과샹금에관ᄒᆞᆫᄉᆞ항
오는 은봉에관ᄒᆞᆫᄉᆞ항
륙은 기타군인군속일졀인
ᄉᆞ쳐판ᄒᆞᆫᄉᆞ항
미완

논셜

우로스기슬로보신문벽등
이라
포티의파미된일 아라
사통신원의간신히젼티ᄒᆞ며
블이라

○아라사우로스키슬로보신문
사에위ᄒᆞ고ᄒᆞ고유명ᄒᆞᆫ특별통신
원니모리비취단쳔교씨가근일
일아교전ᄒᆞ는즁에티케평쟝히
포티를파견ᄒᆞᆷ은쳐음으로목도
ᄒᆞᆷ이라ᄒᆞ고그일쟝관광을통보케
ᄒᆞ게ᄒᆞ엿기로번등ᄒᆞ노라
쳐음에아라사진에셔뎨ᄉᆞ포티
를이왕진터로올기여산령의단
랍된길을다만간격ᄒᆞ고일방을
향ᄒᆞ야배를ᄒᆞ고군ᄉᆞ이대티를발
여셰우며니일본진에셔도여시
포티를두곳으로난호어야병을
향ᄒᆞ야배를ᄒᆞ고모든군ᄉᆞ는산샹
에뎐과여셔로응졉ᄒᆞ는지라그
배에일본포티로셔면져아군의
좌익디를향ᄒᆞ야수추발사ᄒᆞ고
연ᄒᆞ야뎨ᄉᆞ포티를방격ᄒᆞ시이
읔고포셩이긋치며니산혼ᄉᆞᆨ사
포의쳔지진동ᄒᆞ는소리들이거
는어느나라진에서운관ᄒᆞ는소
리들정쟈키어려울조음에산샹
을바라다본즉일본포병이대포
와탄환등을웃긜고여달운로
향ᄒᆞ는길빌이셔산샹으로올ᄂᆞ가
앞ᄒᆞ로셔범포을ᄂᆞᆫ넘치고진세
를차려며니이윽고일셩포향이
ᄂᆞ며여러군ᄉᆞ가일졔히함ᄒᆞ야
방격ᄒᆞᄂᆞᆫ지라이삐예탄환은비
오듯ᄒᆞ며화광이츙텬ᄒᆞ고연긔
는공즁에덥혀셔머니쟝진이셔
로아모소리엿거놀이어인일을
아지못ᄒᆞ야쟝신ᄒᆞᆯ가드듸고자
셔히본즉일본군ᄉᆞ가모도셩우

ᄒᆞ로기어아병을향ᄒᆞ야달녀든죽아진에셔또ᄒᆞᆫ이거동을보고대포로써방격ᄒᆞᆯ시일병이형세를다ᄒᆞ야일뎨대포를노흐며뎌젹ᄒᆞ는지라ᄂᆞ의ᄉᆡᆼ각에는일병이릉히져당치못ᄒᆞᆯ줄노만ᄉᆡᆼ각ᄒᆞ엿고또ᄒᆞᆫ랑진이셔로고요ᄒᆞᆫ고로전쟁결말이난줄노짐작ᄒᆞ고잇슬즈음에아병의뎨ᄉᆞ포ᄃᆡ로브터다시방포ᄒᆞ는소리들이더니일병의포향은점점멀니가는지라이엇지ᄒᆞᆫ연고인줄을아지못ᄒᆞ야심히답답ᄒᆞᆯ때에일병의뒤길노보낸군ᄉᆞㅣ아병의젼러로모라드러갓가이음습ᄒᆞ야셔로대젹ᄒᆞ야싸홀시란환에귀문으로지나는소리와무수ᄒᆞᆫ군병의사상은사ᄅᆞᆷ의마음으로참아보지못ᄒᆞ겟는즁랑진군ᄉᆞㅣ셔로밟으며피는흘너내와갓트더니얼마동안에아병의포ᄃᆡ는홀연변ᄒᆞ야미장지와갓치되엿스며이러케분란ᄒᆞ고효잡ᄒᆞᆫ즁에는말도능히이속으로드러가지못ᄒᆞ더라란환과군긔는길에쌀니엿고죽은군사는뎌욱칭양키어려운ᄃᆡ일본군사ㅣ한곳으로합ᄒᆞ야정돈ᄒᆞ엿고아병의픽잔군졸은살기를도모ᄒᆞ야만주길로도망ᄒᆞ엿는ᄃᆡ이때령편을ᄉᆡᆼ각ᄒᆞᆯ진ᄃᆡ나가든위인이라도가히구완ᄒᆞᆯ도리만잇게되면십분용력ᄒᆞ겟드라ᄒᆞ며이러케위름ᄒᆞᆷ과핑장ᄒᆞᆫ싸홈은처음일것갓다ᄒᆞ엿고비록긔운을억제ᄒᆞ고관광은ᄒᆞ엿스나과연전률ᄒᆞ야견딜수업다ᄒᆞ엿더라

잡보

○고문연회 탁지고문관목하뎐종틱랑씨가금일하오에정동손탁부인집에셔연회ᄒᆞ는ᄃᆡ각대관를청요ᄒᆞ엿더라

○전긔여운 지작일에일본군위문대ᄉᆞ권즁현씨가인항에하거ᄒᆞ야곳랍션ᄒᆞ엿는ᄃᆡ전별ᄎᆞ로하거ᄒᆞᆫ빈긱이운집ᄒᆞ엿다더라

○일진회뎐젼북 이십팔일에일진회에셔젼쥬관찰부로또뎐보ᄒᆞ기를진보회도역시보국안민ᄒᆞ는ᄀᆡ명목이어늘각하가비도로지목ᄒᆞ야토포ᄒᆞ며포형ᄒᆞᆫ다ᄒᆞ니과연그러ᄒᆞ면결단코지관ᄒᆞᆯ지니ᄌᆞ세히회뎐ᄒᆞ라ᄒᆞ엿더라

○관제의정관 관제리정소의정관를차출ᄒᆞ엿는ᄃᆡ참정신긔션찬정민병셕권즁현참찬허위니대리용릭외대리하영탁대민영긔농대리도지법대김가진군대리윤용학협고영희특진관리상셜탁지고문관목하뎐종틱랑궁니부고문관가등중웅제씨인ᄃᆡ각기관청관제리정건를제출ᄒᆞ엿더라

○청결법귀일 오셔니소위청결사무를본정부에셔실시ᄒᆞᆫ다고청결위원장과위원이축일회동ᄒᆞ더니필경결과치못ᄒᆞ고일일본인의영업상으로도라가셔청결비륙만원을지출ᄒᆞ야리월브터히ᄉᆞ무를시작ᄒᆞᆫ다더라

○학협병공 학부에셔경의문ᄃᆡᄒᆞᆫ각도유ᄉᆡᆼᄉᆞ빅명을시취ᄒᆞ야그즁에셔박ᄉᆞ삼십삼인을퇴츌ᄒᆞᆯ터인ᄃᆡ청축이답지ᄒᆞ되셔리대신고영희씨가극히병공ᄒᆞ량으로ᄉᆞ되를아니ᄒᆞ고쥬야로본부를ᄯᅥ나지안코열심으로ᄒᆞ고시ᄒᆞᆫ다더라

○덕ᄉᆞ방문외부 지작일상오열ᄒᆞᆫ시반에덕국공ᄉᆞ가외부에방문ᄒᆞ여이시토록담화ᄒᆞ엿더라

○회의미기 지작일에정부에셔회의ᄒᆞᆫ다ᄒᆞ더니참정과참찬과너부대신삼씨만츌셕ᄒᆞᆫ고로ᄀᆡ회치못ᄒᆞ고파ᄉᆞᄒᆞ엿더라

○삼씨동힝 너부대신리용틱한셩지판소슈반판ᄉᆞ김련식법부대신김가진삼씨는일본정치제도시찰위원을피명ᄒᆞ야종속히일본에젼왕ᄒᆞᆯᄎᆞ로발정ᄒᆞᆫ다더라

○포박밀면 정부에셔경무청으로비밀히뎐보ᄒᆞ야무론무순회원이던지슈긔ᄒᆞ야쪽박ᄒᆞ라ᄒᆞ엿다는풍셜이잇더라

○퇴역유우 참정신긔션씨는히임퇴휴ᄒᆞ더리도각도각군에진보회를토포ᄒᆞ라는훈령을작환처아니ᄒᆞ고되거ᄒᆞ면큰위험훈디경을면키어려우리라ᄒᆞ더라

○차관반봉 금월에는각부월봉을지발할에산이업는고로일본에칠십만원을차관ᄒᆞ엿다더라

○신구분별 군부에셔탁지부에월급청구명셔를도부ᄒᆞᆫ즉히부에셔말ᄒᆞ되이왕잇든군인과금번군제의뎡ᄒᆞᆫ후신입ᄒᆞᆫ군인를각각분별ᄒᆞ야륵송ᄒᆞ라ᄒᆞ고월봉을지출치아니ᄒᆞᆷ으로시로훈군인의말들이봉급을지급지아니ᄒᆞ면ᄉᆞ직ᄒᆞᆫ다ᄒᆞ더라더라

○법도졸업식 명일에법관양성소에셔학도졸업식을여ᄂᆞᆫ셜힝ᄒᆞᆯ터인ᄃᆡ소장김규희씨가각부부ᄃᆡ관을청요ᄒᆞ엿더라

○조췌조건 남셔져동젼양향청을일본슈비ᄃᆡ가셔차거ᄒᆞ다가현금에병참병원이되엿는ᄃᆡ일인이조긔집으로여기고방쟝훼털ᄒᆞ고다시건츅ᄒᆞᆫ다더라

○슌찰효상 각도슌찰ᄉᆞ가근일니로ᄎᆞᄎᆞ발힝ᄒᆞᄂᆞᆫᄃᆡ치힝비로위션ᄒᆞ야환젼엽젼만량혹만여량식잡아쓰고슈원과종인이이십여명식이나된다ᄒᆞ니발셔허비ᄒᆞᆫ젹지아닌돈은어느곳에셔구획ᄒᆞ며다솔ᄒᆞᆫ인원은어느곳에쓸는지협잡ᄒᆞᆯ효상이현져ᄒᆞ나현금형편을살피건ᄃᆡ협잡바들빅셩이ᄭᅳᆺ지못ᄒᆞᆯᄯᅳᆺᄒᆞᆫ즉슌찰제씨의일이대단랑픽아니나고들ᄒᆞ더라

○상소오됴 봉상ᄉᆞ졔쥬안필용이가상소ᄒᆞ엿는ᄃᆡ그소본개의가오됴시ᄃᆡ 일은셩지를세워지치를구ᄒᆞᆷ이오 이는언로를열어현량을진용ᄒᆞᆷ이오 삼은린국교졔를바로ᄒᆞ야나라를안령케ᄒᆞᆷ이오 ᄉᆞ는용관을틱거ᄒᆞ야담도ᄒᆞᆷ이오 오는샹벌을살펴졍령을밝히ᄆᆡ라더라

○신입구츌 일진회에셔졍부를공격ᄒᆞᆷ이틱심ᄒᆞ미현금졍부당국ᄒᆞᆫ세씨는일병ᄉᆞ직ᄒᆞ고슈히시졍부를조직ᄒᆞ야졍치ᄉᆞ무를실시ᄒᆞ리라는말이잇슴으로ᄒᆞ여ᄒᆞᆫ츌등인물이츌셕ᄒᆞᆯ는지다쥬목ᄒᆞᆫ다더라

○불여조환 젼남관찰김셰긔경북관찰쟝승원츙남관찰심건틱삼씨면관ᄒᆞᆷ이합당ᄒᆞᆫ줄노쳐분이ᄂᆞ리셔다는ᄃᆡ졍부에셔샹금근지ᄒᆞ야거힝치아니ᄒᆞᆫ다고물의가부운ᄒᆞᆫ다더라

○기발지샤 함경남도관찰ᄉᆞ가외부로보고ᄒᆞ되원산항에잇는동셔ᄀᆡ발회샤쟝미국인틱일라가청원ᄒᆞ기를본사어셔대미국포아졍부명령을바다이민권을귀졍부에인가를엇어각디방에동셔ᄀᆡ발회샤를셜시ᄒᆞ엿는ᄃᆡ본회샤지샤를함흥에셜입코자ᄒᆞ니인가ᄒᆞᆷ을바란다ᄒᆞ엿는ᄃᆡ감히쳔편치못ᄒᆞ는고로보고ᄒᆞ니즉시지령ᄒᆞᆷ을바란다ᄒᆞ엿더라

○파병진민 참모부에셔닉부로조복ᄒᆞ되귀죠회니에함경남도뎡평군에소위민회가련속운집ᄒᆞ야효유ᄒᆞ야도퇴산치아니ᄒᆞ니파병소제ᄒᆞ라ᄒᆞ엿기로그대로군부에이죠ᄒᆞ야북청디방ᄃᆡ병뎡일소ᄃᆡ를파견ᄒᆞ야진압케ᄒᆞ엿다ᄒᆞ엿더라

○외훈무감 돌산군슈마쥰영씨가무안감리한영원씨의게보고ᄒᆞ는데문조샹고하등급을분별치안앗다ᄒᆞ고한감리가론칙ᄒᆞᆷ으로마군슈가외부에보고ᄒᆞᆷ은작보에긔지ᄒᆞ엿거니와히사건으로외부에셔무안감리의게훈령ᄒᆞ되각하ᄂᆞᆫ좌하가칙임과쥬임의차등이 ᄀᆡᆺ고복망과위망이또ᄒᆞᆫ보고사ᄂᆞᆨ에구별이업거ᄂᆞᆯ귀감리는엇던쟝졍을의거ᄒᆞ야집탈ᄒᆞ엿스며군슈를징감ᄒᆞᆫ다ᄒᆞᆷ과셔긔들압샹ᄒᆞ라ᄒᆞᆷ이크게쟝졍에억임이니ᄀᆡ탄ᄒᆞᆯ지라곳라렵ᄒᆞ야지차그릇침이업게ᄒᆞ라ᄒᆞ엿더라

○졍물결셕 일젼에졍부에셔각부부에통텹ᄒᆞ기를본월이십팔일하오이시에회의ᄒᆞᆯ사로참졍균교를밧드러통지ᄒᆞ니젼일과ᄀᆞᆺ치결셕ᄒᆞ는폐업시찬졍참찬각부대신이일졔히회동ᄒᆞ라ᄒᆞ엿다라

○회의안건 졍부회의안건인즉니부법부참셔관과농샹공부샹공국광산두국쟝의임면건과각항예산외지츌건이라더라

○환후차도 황틱ᄌᆞ비뎐하외환후가대단침즁ᄒᆞ시기로궁즁에셔우려ᄒᆞ시더니지작일브터졔반증셰가죠곰감셰가계신듯ᄒᆞ다더라

외보

○로병츙돌마젹 합창에셔경셩모쳐에발송ᄒᆞᆫ뎐보를거ᄒᆞᆫ즉거이십삼일에로국긔병ᄉᆞ빅명이합창에셔셔북방으로십리되는쇼면ᄌᆞ에리도ᄒᆞ야항마젹과츙돌ᄒᆞ야히지기ᄭᆞ지도오히려젼투ᄒᆞᆫ다ᄒᆞ엿더라

○통화부근로병 합창에셔경셩모쳐에발송ᄒᆞᆫ뎐보를거ᄒᆞᆫ즉압록강우편연안에잇는통화현부근에는항리에이천명로병이잇셧는ᄃᆡ이거손본계호방면의젼투에즁가ᄒᆞ기위ᄒᆞ야파견ᄒᆞ엿는것ᄀᆞᆺ고목하에동디방에는겨우긔병빅명이나머물너잇고회인현에는벌셔브터군ᄉᆞᄒᆞ나토업고또륙도가ᄌᆞ에는륙칠명긔병만잇다ᄒᆞ엿더라

광고

TELEGRAMS.

FIGHTING CONTINUES.

Army Head Quarters. 28th.

Field-Marshal Marquis Oyama reports that on the morning of the 27th, our troops attacked the enemy at Waitusan and after a battle lasting till 4 P.M. succeeded in occupying that place. (Waitusaw is to the west of the Punkiho-Mukden road). Betweeu 6 and 7 P.M. on the 25th, desultory firing occurred on the Liaoyang. Mukden road, but at 9 P.M. fighting waged more fiercely and lasted till 11 o'clock.

Before daybreak on the 27th two companies of enemy's infantry made a determined attack on our troops at Chang-liang-pao, but were repulsed.

Gensan, Oct. 27th.

Large quantities of flour and provisions have been recently landed at Song-chin by the Russians. They were transported by junks from Vladivostock.

VERY MARKED CHANGE OF FEELING TOWARD JAPAN.

WASHINGTON BUREAU.

N. Y. HERALD, SEPT. 10, 1904.

With the progress of the campaign in Manchuria there is evident a marked change of feeling toward the respective combatants not only among the general public but in official circles, both civil and military. Japanese victories are no longer viewed with satisfaction or Japanese characteristics regarded as matters for eulogy.

At the beginning of the war sympathy here was almost universally with the Japanese. There had been great irritation over the failure of the Russians to evacuate Manchuria not so much on account of any sepecial interest of the United States in Manchuria itself but because it was felt that the Russians had deceived and tricked us and had failed to carry out promises freely made.

Japan, too, was regarded as an under dog, as a small nation which had been deliberately goaded into a fight against tremendous odds and without any reasonable hope of ultimate victory. Besides, Japan had been in a way a protégé of America, which had introduced it to the fellowship of nations, and many Japanese officers had been educated in our schools and colleges. Under these cicumstances, even the decidedly Oriental trick by which the Russian navy was crippled before the regular declaration of war was only mildly deprecated.

THEIR BARBARISM APPARENT.

Army and navy officers who have recently returned from the Philippines and the China station report that at present the Japanese have not a friend in the East among mercantile, military or naval men of white extraction. Their success had made them insufferably overbearing and insolent. They implicitly believe that their army and navy are invincible and give their views publicly in a manner which is galling. Thair total disregard of the truth, their apparent inability to conceive that there is anything sacred about a promise or agreement, and the barbarism which is so clearly apparent through their veneer of politness and civilization has irritated and alienated all who have come in contact with them. The disilusion of the pro-Japanese correspondents who flocked to Tokyo early in the year is an old story.

In Manila and the Philippines generally the steady success of the Japanese are viewed with disfavor and some concern. It was well understood that the Japanese supplied munitions of war to the insurgents on very favorable terms, and that there was more than mere commercialism behind the aid given the Filipinos. It is believed that a number of Japanese officers under leaves of absence served with Aguinaldo's forces.

That Japan resents our occcupation of the Philippines is well known. A naval officer tells a story which shows the attitude of the Japanese on this matter in a strong light. While several Japanese ships were in the harbor of Manila before the outbreak of the present war a number of our officers were invited to a dinner on board the Japanese flagship. To the astonishment of the American officers the younger Japanese officers discussed quite freely our position at Manila. They showed a remarkable knowledge of the fortifications, and the diposition of our troops; they had exact data as to the length of time it would take a fleet of ours to reach those waters and gleefully declared that there was not a gun on the island that they could not silence in fifteen minutes, and that we could not assemble a fleet large enough to prevent them from landing 200,000 men on Luzon within two weeks after the order to mobilize was given. They also announced that Japan would never wait for a formal declaration of war to strike an enemy.

Among Southern men, especially, sympathy is now entirely with the Russians. As a former Confederate Colonel stated the other night in a hotel corridor:—

"We Southerners don't like to see a colored man licking a white man."

And this feeling seems to have entirely supplanted the former sympathy with the small man fighting the big one.

It is realized now also that so far as resources available at the point of contact were concerned Russia was at a disadvantage at the beginning of the war and has continued in that condition. The splendid defence of Port Arthur and Kuropatkin's desperate efforts from Tashechiao to Liao Yang to hold back a far superior Japanese army have appealed to our soldiers.

Among military men there is a general feeling that the Japanese soldier is "uncanny." The average white man does not care to die and does not welcome an opportunity to advance to certain death. He is ready to take all necessary chances in the pursuit of glory, or through patriotism, and is willing to go wherever he is told to. But the ancestor worshipping Japanese, who regards himself as but a link in a long chain, who is content to die at any time if he is sure that a certain number of joss sticks will be burned in his memory by his descerdants or successors, and who fears his officers more than any possible enemy, has introduced a new factor into the war game. He is not acting according to the rules which govern the sport.

Soldiers usch as the men on transports who refused to surrender when lying helpless under the guns of armored cruisers and who are compelled under pressure of public opinion to commit suicide rather than yield even when resistance is hopeless are not the kind of soldiers that modern armies have been accustomed to meet. Reports from the East picture the Japanese rank and file as inspired with a willingness to die that might almost be termed anxiety. The Arab followers of the early caliphs and the original Ottoman levies were inspired by this spirit, but the only recent examples of the kind have been the dervishes who, armed with knives and spears, dashed themselves to pieces against the blazing British squares in Egypt.

Like the dervishes, too, it is reported that the Japanese wounded are as dangerous to approach as rattlesnakes. Lying disabled on the field they stab and shoot any one who comes near them unless he bears the red cross, which marks the noncombatant.

(To be continued.)

RISKY EXPERIENCE.

The C.N.S. Chenan, which arrived at Shanghai last week from Tangku, Chefoo and Tientsin, reports: When 86 miles S.E. of Taku Bar, at 7 P.M. on the 5th instant, a searchlight was playing on the ship at intervals until the vessel with the searchlight was astern. At 7:49 P.M. the searchlight was on the ship constantly and a projectile landed about 40 feet off the port beam. Half-a-minute later another projectile landed right astern, about 20 feet off. Both raised columns of water. At 7:55 P.M. we were boarded by a Japanese naval officer, who examined our papers. He said that two blank shots had been fired, to which we had paid no attention, before the projectiles had been discharged. We neither saw nor heard the blanks. When informed how close the shots had landed, the officer chuckled with satisfaction. He was very polite, and gave the name of his own ship as the Japanese cruiser Suma. At 8:45 P.M. we proceeded again.

IL CHIN HOI NOTES.

The worthy "reformers" have decided to sue (for an indemnity) Mr. Cho Chung Yun, who recently ordered the dispersal of some Chin Po Hoi followers.

* * *

The gentlemn, who recently memorialised the government, regarding the uselessness of the Il Chin Hai, are now the objects of the intelligence department of the society. If discovered, they will be denounced as hangers on of the Russian party.

* * *

Placards from this wonderful gathering are hung up daily in the streets, but promptly are pulled down by the police. As soon as a placard is down, another comes up.

* * *

And for what? For the advertisement of a pack of idle scoundreds, whose deeds are *nil* and whose sole notoriety rests in the fact that they are a nuisance to their Government and to every man of ordinary common-sense. What has the society occomplished? What does it expect to accomplish?

So far, it has merely set itself up as adviser of fashions and the latest developments of tonsorial art.

The Korea Daily News.

Issued at 5 P. M. daily except Sundays.

Rate of Subscription:—
Per Year, Yen 25.
Per Quarter, Yen 7.
Per Month, Yen 2.50.

Postage in Korea not charged extra.
Postage abroad charged extra.

Advertisements, 50 sen per day for 1 inch or less.
5 yen per month per inch.
50 yen per year per inch.

All communications to E. T. BETHELL, Editor and Publisher, Pak-tong, Seoul

THE WAR.

The following able article on the present situation is taken from the Eastern World.

Nothing of any g.... ..mp...tance has taken place south of Mukden during the week. The Russians have been beaten it is true, but they are not demoralised. They have fought bravely and are ready to fight again, so that another great battle is impending. The Japanese too have suffered a reverse and lost some guns, and Mukden has yet to be fought for. Port Arthur still holds its own and its iron jaws have swallowed so many thousands of lives that it is a question whether the place will be taken. On the 6th inst. the Emperor sent a letter to General Nogi of which, we hear, mention has been made, in the Japanese press but no mention has been made so far as we know, of the letter from Port Arthur of 2nd inst. to which the Emperor's letter of the 6th inst. was a reply. There are the strongest reasons for the prohibition of the publication of anything relating to the condition of affairs before Port Arthur, so that we are unable to make use of such information as come to hand from various quarters. In the course of this week 3,881 sick and wounded have returned to Japan, and many more are on the road.

As regards the Baltic-fleet we shall begin to take it into consideration when it makes its appearance in Eastern waters. In the meantime in would be as idle to speculate upon what it can do when, or, or if, it does get out here, as to pay any attention to depreciating comments upon it from tained sources.

As regards the war in Manchuria the Japanese are less disposed to underrate the task that still lies before them than their alleged friends. They remember the Franco-German war with its permanent reverses, and the Boer war in which a handful of Boers defied mighty England, and they are not at all disposed to despise their Russian enemies. For the Russians have struck back, and will strike back again, harder perhaps than before, and the fact remains that after eight months' hard campaigning nothing has been done that will bring the war any nearar to its end. On the Shaho positions were taken and retaken six and eight times. The fact speaks as much for the Russians as for the Japanese, and more perhaps for the former, for they were troops who fought again after a succession of reverses and retreats, and if their leader could not lead them to victory, he has at least always succeeded in exempting them from paying the penalties of defeat. In spite of all he has kept up their confidence and courage, and kept alive their hope of final success. They may be beaten again but if they are, they will fight again and some day the scale will, and, in their opinion, must turn. Thus the process of attrition goes on, and its results must naturally be felt and exercise their influence in Japan sooner than in Russia. Both countries in the mean time will suffer alike, the difference, if we may say so, is merely one of quantity and proportion but not of quality to the sufferers.

Unfortunately there is as yet no hope on which any prospects of peace can be built. There are interests in the field to which it is essential that both powers shall exhaust themselves in this war, but, so far as Russia is concerned, only to a certain degree, whilst none of them would stir a finger to prevent the "complete" exhaustion of Japan, and to that end many factors contribute. What those factors are should be patent to Japanese statesmen as to others. At present, however, any advice on the subject, however well meant, would only be resented or at least met with suspicion, for Japan will have no friends but those who flatter her and pander to her ambition. Whither they would lead her, therefore, must she go. God send Japan a Curran or a Brougham into her Councils, for of such men she stands in greater need than of Generals and Admirals; of free and honest speech more than of fossil expressions of loyalty; of men who will have their say before Sovereign and country and live, more than of men who will fight for her ready to die, for in that respect the humblest farmer at the plow, to the honour of the people of Japan be it said, is the equal of the Field Marshal. It takes a higher and greater courage, however, to stand alone, deserted by friends and assailed by foes, to face misguided public opinion and reckless power, and to proclaim the truth, than in the mad excitement of battle to rush upon hostile guns. A bull has *that* courage. The platform imposes a higher and more searching test; it has no bastions, no counter escarpes, no trenches, no guns. Him who stands upon it is exposed to assaults from all sides, to invective, slander, hatred, contempt, to the bitter malice of stupidity, to the venomous rancour of injured interest, whilst he himself has no means of defence, no means of attack, but the living truth that is in him and the spirit that commands him to stand where he does stand, and to speak as he does speak, though he may have to step down to the block, or to be torn to pieces by a furious mob.

Of such men, of men of incorruptible honesty, of ripe wisdom and deep learning, Japan stands more in need of, and to-day more than ever, than of brave Generals and Admirals. She has had and has heroes in the field. May the next session of the Parliament show that she has heroes on the platform too. We have little hope that it will.

A St. Petersburg official dispatch to us says Major-Generals Alexieff, Rennenkampf, Gerngross, and Fock have been promoted to Lieutenants-General for distinguished services in face of the enemy, and Lieutenant-General Linevitch has been made a General of infantry for meritorious service. The Emperor has conferred upon Major-General Mistchenko a gold-mounted sword set with brilliants inscribed "For bravery in repelling the Japanese attacks of July 23rd, 26th, and 27th." (China Review).

VLADIVOSTOCK IN TIME OF WAR.

A curiously vivid and interesting picture of life at Vladivostock is sent by a correspondent to the Vienna "Neue Freie Presse." After explaining that an enormous number of soldiers and all sorts of people are crowded together in the town, the correspondent says: "It is not an easy thing to keep such a crowd in a good temper. Near the monument of the man who more than fifty years ago took possession of Vladivostock a military band plays nearly every day, and in the evening one of the hoteliers provides his customers on a verandah and in the garden with concerts by an excellent string band, free, gratis, and for nothing, except that he makes a good deal of money by the refreshments consumed during the concerts. The opera has fled, but Madame Pitipa, the directress of the theatre, and a few faithful followers give performances on most evenings, the profits going mostly to the Red Cross or other charitable insitutions. Nor has the tourist club ceased its labours, although it has no chance this year of organising its popular water trips.

"On the hilly banks of the Amur Bay bathers of both sexes gather now, as every summer, and the clear water and the strong tides make this seaside place as attractive as any other. No one need stand in fear of Japs, for the approach of Japanese men-of-war is always announced in good time during the day by the hoisting of flags, and during the night by coloured lanterns on a hill above the town.

"There is a great deal of marrying at Vladivostock. There is hardly a shop-girl or seamstress who has not been married within the last month by an officer or official. The girls and women of the wealthier classes have turned their backs on the fortress, while those of the lower classes were obliged to remain, if only in order to retain their places and because they and their friends had not the means to send them to Russia. Now there is a social club in the town where men and women have the chance of becoming acquainted, and since the Russian officer is not forbidden to marry unless he is possessed of a certain private income, he plunges gaily into matrimony."

The Kaiser has lost no time in putting into practice the lessons of the siege of Port Arthur. By his special orders the German naval manœuvres now in progress in the North Sea have been drawn up with the particular purpose of setting the officers and men many of the same problems confronting Admiral Togo and his Russian adversaries. A most interesting experiment was carried out on 9th inst., when a fast cruiser squadron endeavoured to slip out of the Elbe in the face of a blockading fleet of battleships, in as near as possible the same way as the Russians attempted their last desperate sortie from Port Arthur. As on the real occasion, the venture failed signally, and the would-be escaping ships were "sunk" or driven back again. On the conditions being reversed, however, and the order given to attack Heligoland and the mouth of the Elbe. which figured as Port Arthur, the enemy, more fortunate than Admiral Togo's force, whom they were supposed to represent, entirely achieved their object and were adjudged to have captured the defenders' stronghold.

Consul-General John Goodnow has been recalled from his position at Shanghai by the President; and Mr. Davidson F.A.G.S., late U.S.A. Consul-General in Formosa, and recently appointed to Antung, has been given the post *pro tem.*

The Ministers of the Home Office and Law Department, together with the Chief judge of the Supreme Court will shortly leave on a visit of inspection to Japan.

It is said that many Government officials will shortly resign, owing to their objections to the repeated attacks of the Il Chin Hoi.

The Korea Daily News.

VOL. I, SATURDAY, OCTOBER 29, 1904. No. 88

HONGKONG & SHANGHAI BANKING CORPORATION.

Paid-up Capital: $10,000,000
Reserve Fund:—Sterling Reserve... 10,000,000
Silver Reserve..... 7,000,000
27,000,000
Reserve Liability of Proprietors... 10,000,000

HEAD OFFICE. HONGKONG.

London Bankers, London and County Banking Company Limited
Branches and Agencies, London.

Amoy,	Hankow	Penang,
Bangkok,	Hiogo,	Rangoon,
Batavia,	Iloilo,	Saigon,
Bombay,	Lyons,	San Francisco,
Calcutta,	Manila,	Singapore,
Colombo,	Nagasaki,	Sourabaya,
Foochow,	New York,	Tientsin,
Hamburg,	Peking,	Yokohama,

Credits granted on approved Securities, and every description of Banking and Exchange business transacted.

Drafts granted on London and the chief Commercial places in Europe, India, Australia, America, China and Japan.

HOLME RINGER & Co., AGENTS, CHEMULPO.

ON CHEONG & CO., SEOUL.
GENERAL STORE KEEPERS.
Imported provisions, Cooking Utensils Crockery, etc.
FRESH BREAD DAILY.

MITSU BISHI DOCKYARD & ENGINE WORKS,
NAGASAKI.

CODE WORD, "DOCK."

A. 1, A. B. C., and Engineering Codes used.

DOCK No. 1 (at Tategami).

Extreme Length.............. 523 feet
Length on blocks .... 513 ,,
Width of Entrance on Top...... 89 ,,
,, ,, Bottom.... 77 ,,
Water on Blocks at Spring Tide 26½ ,,

DOCK No. 2 (Mukaijima).

Extreme Length.............. 371 feet
Length on Blocks............. 360 ,,
Width of Entrance on Top...... 66 ,,
,, ,, Bottom 53 ,,
Water on Blocks at Spring Tide 22 ,,

PATENT SLIP (at Kosuge).

Can take vessels up to 1,000 tons gross

THE WORKS are well equipped with the LATEST IMPROVEMENTS, and can execute any kind of work in SHIPBUILDING and MARINE ENGINEERING, as well as in REPAIRING of SHIPS.

The COMPANY'S new powerful steamer OURA-MARU (712 tons, 700 I.H.P.), specially built for SALVAGE PURPOSES, and equipped with necessary gear, is always READY at SHORT NOTICE.

CHARTERED BANK OF INDIA AUSTRALIA & CHINA.

INCORPORATED BY ROYAL CHARTER 1853
HEAD OFFICES:—LONDON.

Paid-up Capital £800,000
Reserve Liability of Shareholders 800,000
Reserve Fund 800,000

Drafts granted upon all the principal places in the world and every description of Exchange and banking business transacted.

E. MEYER & Co., Agents, Chemulpo.

E. MEYER & CO.
Chemulpo.

SOLE AGENTS IN KOREA FOR:
A. T. Morse, Sons & Co's "Fresco" Distemper

In all colours ready for use on walls, Ceilings etc.
and
AVENARIUS CARBOLINEUM

A wood-preserving and antiseptic oil preparation
Against decay, dry-rot, fungus and wood-destroying insects.

A large supply always in Stock.
Prices upon application.

E. MEYER & Co., Chemulpo.

THE METHODIST PUBLISHING HOUSE,
Little West Gate, Seoul.

JPRINTING, TYPEWRITER PAPER
CARBON PAPER, VISITING CARDS
STATIONERY, BOOK BINDING
BOOK PUBLISHERS
AMERICAN SCHOOL BOOKS
SPENCERIAN COPY BOOKS
PEN CARBON LETTER AND BILL BOOKS

S. A. BECK, Manager.

HOKURKU DOBOKU KAISHA.

Branch office in Chong Dong, Seoul.
Japanese telephone No. 165

CONTRACT DEPARTMENT.

We can contract to build any building or construction.

MERCHANDISE DEPARTMENT.

We can provide any building material. We have just contracted to build the new Belgian Legation.

DAI-ICHI GINKO
LIMITED.
(Formerly the First National Bank)
ESTABLISHED 1873

INCORPORATED UNDER PRESENT LAW 1896

Capital - - - - - - - - Yen 5,000,000
Reserve Fund - - - - - 1,500,000

HEAD OFFICE:—TOKIO.

President: Baron SHIBUSAWA.

BRANCHES AND CORRESPONDENTS
In the Principal Cities and Towns of Japan.
Interest Allowed on
Fixed deposits 1 year - - - 6½ per cent
" " 6 months - - - 6 per cent

Special current accounts 1½ sen daily per Y 100
General " " 1 " " " 100

M. TANAKA, Manager, Chemulpo

HOLME RINGER & Co.
Chemulpo.

General Merchants and Government Contractors.

Agents for the leading
Banks
Steamship Companies
and
Insurance Companies

Importers of Merchandise of every description.

KAMEYA & CO.
GENERAL STOREKEEPERS
Chinkokai - - Seoul
(*Established 1895, Tokyo*)

Confectionery, Hams, Canned Goods, Cutlery, Hirano & Tansan Water. Provisions, Gents, Furnishing goods, Toilet Articles, Travelling Bags, Tobacco, Cigars & Cigarettes Kitchen Utensils. Coffee, Biscuits.

Fresh Goods always kept in Stock.
Prices Moderate
Please come and inspect our goods.

NIPPON YUSEN KAISHA
JAPANESE MAIL STEAMSHIP CO.
DER MAIL CONTRACT WITH THE IMPERIAL JAPANESE GOVERNMENT.

European Line
Regular Fortnightly Service between Yokohama Kobe, Moji, Shanghai, Hongkong, Singapore, Penang Colombo, Port Said, Marseilles, London and Antwerp

American Line
Regular Fortnightly Service between Hongkong and Seattle, calling at Shanghai, Moji, Kobe, Yokohama and Victoria, B. C.

Australian Line
Regular weekly Service betwen Japan Ports and Australia, calling at Hongkong and Manila.
(Above Three Lines Suspended until further notice)

Shanghai Line
Weekly Service between Shanghai and Japan Ports

Korea Line
Service Kobe, Moji, Nagasaki, Fusan, Chemupo, Chefoo, Taiku.
S. S. Babelsberg, 2181 tons.
Service Kobe, Moji, Fusan, Chemulpo, Chinnampo
S. S ARGO, S. S. Ohio.

BORDEN'S CONDENSED MILK CO.
New York, U. S. A.

ALWAYS IN STOCK
Eagle Brand Condensed Milk.
Gold Seal Condensed Milk.
Peerless (Family) Evaporated Cream.
Borden's Malted Milk.

E. MEYER & CO.
Chemulpo, Korea,
Sole Agents

ROYAL INSURANCE COMPANY,
Funds exceed £10,000,000
FIRE
AT CURRENT RATES.
LIFE
REDUCED PREMIUM.
HOLME RINGER & Co., Agents, Chemulpo.

HOTEL DU PALAIS
SEOUL.

The only first class Hotel in Seoul. Situated in the centre of the city opposite the palace.

Cuisine under the supervision of an experienced French Chef.

Well ventilated and furnished throughout.

TARIFF UPON APPLICATION
L. MARTIN
Proprietor and Manager.

報申日每韓大
보신일미한대

(호구십팔뎨)　(일요월)　일일십삼월십년사빅구쳔일

본샤고빅

이신보는영어와한어로셔거리
일츌판ᄒᆞᆸ

신문가
한쟝 엽두돈오푼
일삭됴 엽두량닷돈
우표가미삭닷돈
다맛돈으로밧슴

광고료는
귀한의쟝단과조힝의다쇼로죵
감ᄒᆞ되렴가로밧을터이오며오
리지아녀대한사람마다다이신
문을보실터이니광고내시기됴
원ᄒᆞ시는이들은우리신문샤에
와셔면약ᄒᆞ심을희망ᄒᆞᆸ

○발힝소 박동대한미일신보
샤법어학교압혜젼영국인셜필
림집자리오
샤쟝 영국인 (비셜)

평양 터리졈
○평양효동사는권미보씨로우
리신문관미터리인을뎡ᄒᆞ엿
스오니평양에계신구람코져ᄒᆞ
시는쳠군ᄌᆞ는허터리졈에왕
림ᄒᆞ와면의ᄒᆞ시옵

샤고

○우리대한미일신보의목뎍은
대한의안녕질셔에관한모든대
목에터ᄒᆞ야는공평한변론을쥬
장홈이라우리동신원의담보는
신문보시는쳠군ᄌᆞ의게홍상보
도ᄒᆞ리며편지를긔셔ᄒᆞ여주시
는이는셩명과반디를져어붓쳐
서기를희망ᄒᆞ오니이거슨신문
샹에긔지ᄒᆞ랴는거시아니오다
만극히신용ᄒᆞ는증거를숨고쟈
홈이라긔쟈는아모긔셔던지긔
지홈을퇴각ᄒᆞ는권리를가졋스
나퇴각ᄒᆞ는리유를말ᄒᆞᆯ터이오
며공즁평화를문란케ᄒᆞ는듯훈
긔셔는의례히밧지안켓ᄉᆞᆸ나이
다

●본샤셜시이릐로신문을미양
우례로분젼ᄒᆞ와례젼부의임의
로젼ᄒᆞ든곳스로먼곳에는혹늣게
에젼ᄒᆞ기도ᄒᆞ며혹몃칠거슬흔겁
젼ᄒᆞ기도ᄒᆞ며혹아니젼ᄒᆞ는
곳도잇다ᄒᆞ와우리신문을ᄉᆞ랑
ᄒᆞ야구람ᄒᆞ시는쳠군ᄌᆞ의계
되ᄒᆞ야미우미안ᄒᆞ옵기로지금
은분젼인을두고미일일즉이젼
ᄒᆞ며아니젼ᄒᆞ거나늣게거나ᄒᆞᆫ
가업도록ᄒᆞ랴ᄒᆞ오니혹아니셩
젼ᄒᆞ거나늣게젼ᄒᆞ거나ᄒᆞᆫ일
이잇스면본샤로통긔ᄒᆞ여쥬심
을희망ᄒᆞᆸ

본샤광고

○본샤신문즁에좌긔ᄒᆞᆫ호수를
소용홀데가잇셔이에광고ᄒᆞ오
니누구시던지그즁에아모호수
던지가져오시면후가로미쟝에빗
젼두푼식드리리다
뎨이호 뎨삼호 뎨이십호
뎨수십이호 뎨수십삼호 뎨
오십삼호 뎨오십수호와뎨오
십오호 뎨륙십이호

관보

뎨이쳔구빅륙십구호
광무팔년십월이십팔일
셔임급ᄉᆞ령
○입니부광졔원위원 젼위젼
리졍환 김리희 윤문희 셔
현쥬 김량졔 리승화 쟝용
셩 신긔셩
십월이십일
○셔훈일등수리국쟝 봉죠
하 김병국
○승셔훈일등수팔괘쟝 표훈
원총지 죠병식 의졍부찬졍
권즁현
○승셔훈이등수리국쟝 군부
대신 리윤용
○의원면본관 니부광졔원쥬
ᄉᆞ 한영괴 홍종덕 쟝셕희
○입니부광졔원쥬ᄉᆞ 셔관임관
륙등 구품 허 협 졍한셥
라쳐면
이상십월이십오일
○의원면본관 비셔원승 리
진구 농샹공부기슈 리쥰구
임비셔원승셔쥬임관오등
졍삼품 리셔종
○입농샹공부기슈셔관임관오
등 농샹공부쥬ᄉᆞ 김교필
○임농샹공부쥬ᄉᆞ셔관임관ᄉᆞ
등륙품 리쥰구
이샹십월이십륙일
궁뎡록ᄉᆞ
○죠왕봉죠하김병국은오십년
입죠에일십으로증셩을다ᄒᆞ야
국가원로가되엿스니훈일등팔
괘장을쥬고표훈원총지훈삼등
죠병식은로셩ᄒᆞ야망즁ᄒᆞ고훈
로가만흐니특별히렵등ᄒᆞ야훈
일등팔괘쟝을쥬고의졍부찬졍
훈이등권즁현은다년국ᄉᆞ에한
숙ᄒᆞ야명예를엇엇스니특별히
훈일등에팔괘쟝을쥬고군부대
신훈삼등리윤용은간셩지로로
본리공젹이드러낫스니훈이등
에팁국쟝을쥬라
십월이십오일 표훈원
총지 죠병식

군부관졔 속
데팔됴 군부의좌긋치모든국
을셜치홈이라
군무국
경리국
의무국
군방국
히발국
데구됴 군무국은일등국이니
국쟝은참쟝혹졍령으로보직ᄒᆞ
고군무국에좌긋치오과를셜치
ᄒᆞ야그ᄉᆞ무를분쟝홈이라
군ᄉᆞ과
보병과
긔병과
포병과
공병과
데십됴 군무국군ᄉᆞ과쟝은각
병과졍부령으로보직ᄒᆞ고과
원삼인은각병과창령졍부위
로보직홈이라
군ᄉᆞ과쟝과밋과원일인은참
모관이됨이라
데십일됴 군ᄉᆞ과에는좌긋튼
사무를쥬쟝홈이라
일은 편제건제의관ᄒᆞᆫ수항
이는 동원계획계엄과밋징
발에관ᄒᆞᆫ수항
삼은 군긔의모든군무교육
연습과밋검열의관ᄒᆞᆫ수
항
ᄉᆞ는 군대풍긔에관ᄒᆞᆫ수항
오는 모든학교의관ᄒᆞᆫ수항
륙은 외국쥬지ᄒᆞᆫ관원에관
ᄒᆞᆫ수항
칠은 의식례 식복 쟝취쟝
에관ᄒᆞᆫ수항

잡보

○교셥국쟝 종이품리샹셜씨
가외부교셥국쟝을피임ᄒᆞ엿더
라
○셕지쳐용 일본공관에셔외
부로공함ᄒᆞ되인쳔에잇는우리
텰도감부소용셕지를인쳔항밧
물류도에셔캐야쓸터인고로통
고ᄒᆞ다ᄒᆞ엿더라
○함남진보회 원산감리가면
보ᄒᆞ기를진보회당륙칠빅명이
고원영흥등디로셔본항에리도
ᄒᆞ야일쟝연셜ᄒᆞ고안번으로향
ᄒᆞ엿다ᄒᆞ엿더라
○외대부진 외부대신리하영
씨는무ᄉᆞᆷ고가잇는지ᄉᆞ오일
수진치아니ᄒᆞ엿다더라
○일군고시문 함경남도관찰
ᄉᆞ리헌경씨가함흥뎡평영흥고
원문천등군의일본군졍시힝훈
고시문을니부로등보ᄒᆞ엿는뒤
그젼문이좌긋ᄒᆞ니
일은 대일본뎨국은동양영원
의평화와한쳥량국보호를위ᄒᆞ
야부득이로국과젼ᄒᆞ엿스며
한국인민은우리인민과합셰로
국졍벌ᄒᆞᄂᆞᆫᄉᆞ업에병력홀지니
군더의권리로칭명지산의보존
과종교의존숭을누리게홀ᄉᆞ
이는 군졍시힝ᄒᆞ는디방에졍
황를시찰ᄒᆞ야각군간리비가무
명잡세를빙셩의계슈렴ᄒᆞ고군
ᄉᆞ경찰상번폐가불쇼ᄒᆞ니쇼리
비를신칙ᄒᆞ야초등루ᄎᆔᄒᆞᆫ습속
를업게홀ᄉᆞ
삼은 대일본데국군터의경과
ᄒᆞ고류슉ᄒᆞ는디방에인민은졔
반군ᄉᆞ샹지공홈에관ᄒᆞ야요구
를극진히시힝ᄒᆞ고물건갑파삭
젼은시가터로죵슈히츌급ᄒᆞ고
또맛당히지뭉치아니홀거슬지
공ᄒᆞᆫ인민은속히그ᄉᆞ정을합홍
쥬차대일본군졍관아에보홀ᄉᆞ
라ᄒᆞ엿더라
○희천한위샤 희천군에셔신
축년브터한위샤를창셜ᄒᆞ고
포슈오십명을쎕아홍샹이십오
명은읍니두고이십오명은각촌
에슌힝식여불우지비를ᄒᆞ더니
근일에동학당이각군에출몰ᄒᆞᆫ
다ᄒᆞ야본군민김봉찬등이군수
의게련명쳥원ᄒᆞ야포슈를일빅
명으로다시죠직ᄒᆞ고로히군슈
가군부에보고ᄒᆞ고양총일빅병
과탄환얼마를쳥구ᄒᆞ엿는디포
슈료포는일만일쳔팔빅이십칠
량륙젼과쇼머일쳔구빅이십륙
두로분비ᄒᆞ야반급ᄒᆞ기로규칙
을명ᄒᆞ엿다더라
○청셜슈룡 외부에셔궁니부
에조회ᄒᆞ되미국공ᄉᆞ죠회니에

한미뎐긔회샤에셔공합ᄒᆞ되한셩닉에린슈ᄒᆞᄂᆞᆫ물둥셜시ᄒᆞᄂᆞᆫ특권을임의약됴ᄒᆞ엿ᄂᆞᆫᄃᆡ현금궁닉부에셔림시슈관을 궁닉예셜시ᄒᆞ라ᄒᆞᆫ다ᄒᆞ니이ᄂᆞᆫ회소식이라본샤에셔ᄂᆞᆫ명츈에ᄒᆡ슈관을실시코ᄌᆞᄒᆞ며이거시군ᄉᆞ샹방ᄒᆡᄂᆞᆫ아니라본샤에셔ᄒᆞᆫ의견으로졔외ᄒᆞ되 궁닉즉반에ᄒᆞᆫ광확ᄒᆞᆫ우물을파고그가운ᄃᆡ슈룡을셜치홈이됴흔ᄃᆡ슈룡인즉ᄒᆡ관에잇다ᄒᆞ엿기로조회ᄒᆞᆫ다ᄒᆞ엿다ᄒᆞ엿더라

○뎡씨쟝셔 뎡대화라ᄒᆞᄂᆞᆫ사룸이일진회를반ᄃᆡᄒᆞ야졍부에쟝셔ᄒᆞᆫ고로ᄒᆡ회에셔본회에방ᄒᆡ가대단이된다ᄒᆞ야그쟝셔ᄒᆞᆫ뎡씨를사탐ᄒᆞᄂᆞᆫᄃᆡ만일착득ᄒᆞ면아국당으로조쳐ᄒᆞᆫ다ᄒᆞ더라

○슈렬슈부 일진회에셔현금졍부를밍세코공ᄃᆡ치아니ᄒᆞᆫ다고각방곡에게방ᄒᆞ민졍부에셔경무쳥에명령ᄒᆞ야ᄒᆡ방목를낫낫치셋ᄂᆞᆫᄃᆡᄒᆡ회에셔ᄂᆞᆫ셋ᄂᆞᆫᄃᆡ로일변붓치기로작뎡ᄒᆞ야셔로ᄉᆞ무원이십명을션틱ᄒᆞ야ᄒᆡᄉᆞ무소를쥰회슈직ᄒᆞᆫ다더라

○일회광뎐 일진회에셔경긔도츙청남북도젼라남북도황ᄒᆡ도강원도평안남북도함경남북도합십일도에뎐보ᄒᆞ기를진보회가즉민회라시운으로일시에이러ᄂᆞᆫ거슬란민으로지목ᄒᆞ야토멸ᄒᆞ면단당지관홀터이니엇더케압졔ᄒᆞᄂᆞᆫ형편을조셰히회뎐ᄒᆞ라ᄒᆞ엿더라

○북병관아 근일북관동신을거ᄒᆞᆫ즉아병이시시로ᄒᆡ삼위에셔보리와밀가루를청국목션에깃고경셩과셩친으로향ᄒᆞ야슈로로운송ᄒᆞᄂᆞᆫ즁이오십일일에북쳥에셔퇴각ᄒᆞᆫ아병은십구일ᄭᆞ지셩진에유숙ᄒᆞ엿고또북쳥부근에ᄂᆞᆫ의연히아병ᄉᆞ오빅명이쥬둔ᄒᆞ엿고두만강에셔셩진부근에니르ᄂᆞᆫ각디방에ᄂᆞᆫ슈비병을약간식비치ᄒᆞ엿다더라

○셔남병동 경의텰도ᄂᆞᆫ리월초슌에ᄂᆞᆫ기셩ᄭᆞ지기동되고경부텰도ᄂᆞᆫ리월이십일경근축렬거가동ᄒᆞ야단닌다더라

○포살비샹 일진회에셔평의회를기셜ᄒᆞ고텬쳔군슈됴졍륜씨가진보회원을포살ᄒᆞᆫᄉᆞ건에ᄃᆡᄒᆞ야손ᄒᆡ비샹금을밧기로결졍ᄒᆞ엿다더라

론셜

젼징사건

○이스런월드신문을거ᄒᆞᆫ즉근일젼징형편을계지ᄒᆞ엿기에좌에번등ᄒᆞ노라

일아량군이봉텬남방에셔셔로웅거ᄒᆞ야샹지ᄒᆞᆫ다고ᄒᆞᆫ지가우금일쥬일이되도록아모긴보가들이지안터니요ᄉᆞ이아병이일병의계픽ᄒᆞ엿다ᄂᆞᆫᄃᆡ오히려군규ᄂᆞᆫ물란치아니ᄒᆞ야다시긔병ᄒᆞ야싸홀계획을둔다ᄒᆞᆫ즉불구에큰싸홈이또될듯ᄒᆞ며일병들도또ᄒᆞᆫ대포몃문ᄭᆞ지젼실ᄒᆞ고긔력이쇠진ᄒᆞ엿스나아직ᄭᆞ지도봉텬에웅거ᄒᆞ야ᄃᆡ젹ᄒᆞ려ᄒᆞᆫ다ᄒᆞ며

려슌ᄒᆡ면에셔도우금ᄭᆞᆺ셔로상지홈으로수쳔명군ᄉᆞ를죽엿스되오히려고집ᄒᆞ야굿게직힘은무타ㅣ라엇지던지긔여히졈령ᄒᆞ고야마자ᄂᆞᆫ주의가잇셔셔그리홈이며

금월륙일에일본황뎨ᄭᆡ셔려슌항으로츌젼ᄒᆞ야목대쟝의게봉셔를보닉셧다ᄒᆞ나이러ᄒᆞᆫ사실온일본신문샹에등지홈을대단히엄금홈으로계지ᄒᆞ야공포치아니ᄒᆞᄂᆞᆫᄭᆞ닭에여간일본군ᄃᆡ에셔와각지방에셔오ᄂᆞᆫ소문으로ᄂᆞᆫ쥰신키어려우되다른곳으로좃차대강드른즉이ᄂᆞᆫ다른일이아니라금월이일에야목대쟝이면져샹쥬ᄒᆞᆫᄉᆞ건이잇셔슴으로하답ᄒᆞ심이라고ᄒᆞ나이역그자셔ᄒᆞᆫ리허ᄂᆞᆫ알기어려우며

이번주일동안에병상사졸을합ᄒᆞ야일본으로환국ᄒᆞᆫ자ㅣ삼쳔팔빅팔십일명외에또ᄒᆞᆫ뒤흐로올자ㅣ오히려즁로에잇다ᄒᆞ엿ᄂᆞᆫ지라졔반형편이약ᄎᆞᆫᄒᆞᆫ즁아라샤의쌀틱합ᄃᆡ가또ᄯᅥ낫다ᄒᆞᆫ즉쟝ᄎᆞ동양에이르ᄂᆞᆫ날에야필경엇지될ᄂᆞᆫ지우리도차차짐쟉ᄒᆞᄂᆞᆫ도리가잇슬터이되이역심상치아니홀일이며

만쥬싸홈으로말ᄒᆞ드ᄅᆡ도일본이아모리ᄒᆞ여도그ᄯᅡ형편은아라샤만못홀ᄲᅮᆫ외라아라샤에셔ᄂᆞᆫ이왕보법전쟁과갓치ᄒᆞᆫ량업시상지ᄒᆞ야줄연히도리키지아니홀터인즉일본이또ᄒᆞᆫ만모히넉이고힘사홀수도업ᄂᆞᆫ거시이왕싸홈에도여러번아병을픽ᄒᆞ야칠팔삭을써려스되확실히ᄊᆡ아슨거슨업슨즉이제또다시픽멸ᄒᆞ게만드자면아직도얼마동안을지체홀ᄂᆞᆫ지예료키어려울일이며또ᄒᆞᆫ전쟁결말이묘연ᄒᆞᆫ지라

일본이그동안칠팔차를싸호여포획ᄒᆞᆫ자실로무수ᄒᆞ되소위아병은진지구무이가되여격멸ᄒᆞᆫ후에도다시이러ᄂᆞ불가불싸호게되ᄂᆞᆫ지라

만일아병이이기려ᄒᆞᄂᆞᆫ마음이ᄂᆞ업슬쳐갓트면일본이엇지ᄒᆞ던지귀졍을속히닉여셩공을ᄒᆞ게스되실로그러치도아니ᄒᆞᆫ즁일본셔ᄂᆞᆫ용력ᄒᆞ고수고홈은불계ᄒᆞ고기여히셩공ᄒᆞ라ᄒᆞᄂᆞᆫᄃᆡ아라샤에셔ᄂᆞᆫ일본이만일와셔칠지경이면그때야비로소응젹ᄒᆞ야싸호랴ᄂᆞᆫ주의가분명ᄒᆞᆫ지라

이모양으로한량업시군ᄉᆞ들만서로죽이여어육이되ᄂᆞᆫ경우에ᄂᆞᆫ일본이조연히아라사보다긔력이더옥쓰일거시요일변으로말홀진ᄃᆡ두나라형편이피ᄎᆞ일반인지라그러ᄒᆞ나아즉ᄭᆡ지도즁지가되여평화홀기약은묘연ᄒᆞ고다만싸홈ᄒᆞ기로만릉사를삼은즉이ᄂᆞᆫ필경이번젼쟁으로말미암아피차쇠진ᄒᆞ고야말거손불언가상이되

아라사에셔이ᄯᅢ도록연타ᄒᆞ야희롱과ᄀᆞᆺ치홈은일본의쇠력홈을기ᄃᆞ려일후한손가락으로써용이히취ᄒᆞ려ᄂᆞᆫ주의인듯ᄒᆞᆫ지라만일일본을하ᄂᆞᆯ이도으샤졔반군졍을일마음과ᄀᆞᆺ치필요ᄒᆞ게되면오히려질졍홀수업스되혹그러치아니ᄒᆞ면이러ᄒᆞᆫ어려운일이또어ᄃᆡ잇스리요혹이러ᄒᆞᆫ소망이나잇슬가우리ᄂᆞᆫ옹축ᄒᆞ노라

뎐보

일본만쥬군총ᄉᆞ령부발공보

왜두산졈령 우리군ᄃᆡ의일부ᄂᆞᆫ본월이십칠일은아참브터왜두산에웅거ᄒᆞ여잇ᄂᆞᆫ젹군을공격ᄒᆞ야오후네시즘에젹군을격퇴ᄒᆞ고동디를졈령ᄒᆞ엿더라

○샹동 이십륙일오후여섯시브터닐곱시ᄭᆞ지에료양봉텬간의가도부근에셔완완히포젼을시작ᄒᆞ야오후아홉시즘에니르러ᄂᆞᆫ가쟝밍렬히ᄒᆞ야열ᄒᆞᆫ시ᄭᆞ지련속ᄒᆞ엿고

이십칠일미명에젹의보병이즁ᄃᆡ가쟝량보방면에셔의밤에습셕을ᄒᆞ엿스나우리부ᄃᆡ의역격홈을닙어무진ᄃᆡ방면으로퇴각ᄒᆞ엿더라

십월이십팔일공ᄉᆞ관착뎐

○영함ᄃᆡ예비령 파라지함ᄃᆡ포행에관ᄒᆞ야영국히군셩에셔고시발표홈이좌갓더라북히에셔참혹ᄒᆞᆫ보고가도달ᄒᆞᆫ후십월이십ᄉᆞ일에ᄃᆡ즁히협과본국함ᄃᆡ에ᄃᆡᄒᆞ야필요ᄒᆞᆫ경우에ᄂᆞᆫ셔로협력홀일이라고예비홀명령을발포ᄒᆞ엿더라

동일동뎐

○여졍격분 로국함ᄃᆡ의포힝에관ᄒᆞ야영국젼국물론이대단분격ᄒᆞ엿다더라

동일동뎐

○량신문론난 론돈타임스와밋수단다ㅣ도두신문에ᄂᆞᆫ로국황뎨가(북히에셔인명을샹히홈에ᄃᆡᄒᆞ야대단히흡ᄒᆞᆫ슷슬셜명ᄒᆞ고허ᄉᆞ권리허가명빅ᄒᆞ면즉시이사건를인ᄒᆞ야화밧은자의게셜원될슈단를행ᄒᆞ리라)ᄂᆞᆫ죠칙ᄂᆞ린일에ᄃᆡᄒᆞ야론난ᄒᆞ되피보에셔미사건이엇더케즁대홈을아지못홈파갓도다영국이아국에졔츌ᄒᆞᆫ일노론ᄒᆞ면사실의리허ᄂᆞᆫ임의명빅ᄒᆞᆫ즉히사건에화밧은쟈의게흡족히홀일을지체홀말이업고또그사건에대ᄒᆞ야흡족히ᄒᆞ리라말만홈으로ᄂᆞᆫ이러ᄒᆞᆫ대사건을히결ᄒᆞ기어려우리라ᄒᆞ엿다더라

○고시합이빈 십월이십오일에아력시후가합이빈에셔고시ᄒᆞ엿ᄂᆞᆫᄃᆡ그요령이좌갓ᄒᆞ니아국황뎨가조긔의원대로ᄌᆞ긔의현대ᄒᆞᆫ직임을사양홈을허락ᄒᆞ샤십월이십삼일에흑구대쟝을극동에잇ᄂᆞᆫ륙군총사령관으로임명ᄒᆞ신지라아력시후ᄂᆞᆫ젼과갓치다만총독의직칙만보젼ᄒᆞ엿쓰니아국황뎨ᄂᆞᆫ극동에아국군를편셩ᄒᆞ고지휘ᄒᆞᄂᆞᆫ일를아력시후의현져ᄒᆞᆫ공로를가샹히여기신지라이러므로아력시후ᄂᆞᆫ그부하쟝교사졸일졔히그직임을극진히ᄒᆞ야아국륙군은강대ᄒᆞᆫ젹국을격파ᄒᆞ야아국황뎨의영광을현져케홀일놉의심업시확실이밋ᄂᆞᆫ다ᄒᆞ엿더라

관발

십월이십륙일론돈일본공

○로함포힝ᄉᆞ건 영국외무싱에셔ᄂᆞᆫ신문지에좌긔ᄒᆞᆫᄉᆞ실을공포ᄒᆞ엿ᄂᆞᆫᄃᆡ

영국외무싱에셔ᄂᆞᆫ할과밋그린스비의어업ᄃᆡ표자와회견ᄒᆞ야십월이십일일밤에쌜틱함ᄃᆡ가할에잇ᄂᆞᆫ어션단례의일부분을포격ᄒᆞᆫᄉᆞ실을쾌히드러알앗ᄂᆞᆫᄃᆡ이보고에ᄉᆞ실을긔초홈은진술셔를로국에발송ᄒᆞ엿ᄂᆞᆫ지라이진술셔즁에영국졍부의싱각에ᄂᆞᆫ금일형셰ᄂᆞᆫ벌셔이진술셔에징계ᄒᆞ엿스ᄂᆞ회답이지완홈을면치못홀뜻스로부쳐긔록ᄒᆞ엿더라

○영데칙어 다시신문지의말ᄒᆞᆫ거슬거ᄒᆞᆫ즉영국황뎨ᄂᆞᆫ문셔비셔관을말미암아할시쟝의게좌긔ᄒᆞᆫ칙어를ᄂᆞ렷ᄂᆞᆫᄃᆡ황뎨ᄂᆞᆫ어업션단례에ᄃᆡᄒᆞ야이포힝을당ᄒᆞᆫ말을듯고비감ᄒᆞ며그즁ᄀᆞ쟝비감ᄒᆞᆫ일은손히를당ᄒᆞᆫ본인과밋그가족의게ᄃᆡᄒᆞ야됴샹ᄒᆞᄂᆞᆫ뜻슬표ᄒᆞᄂᆞᆫᄉᆞ의로황뎨와밋황후ᄭᆡ셔보닉엿더라

외보

○히삼위함ᄃᆡ슈션 히삼위함ᄃᆡ로시아와밋그롬보이량함은임의슈션홈을필ᄒᆞ엿고그외에ᄂᆞᆫ긔션과군함이업ᄂᆞᆫ것ᄀᆞᆺ고히삼위항닉에츌입ᄒᆞᄂᆞᆫ션척에ᄃᆡᄒᆞ야ᄂᆞᆫ엄즁히검사ᄒᆞ며또츌입ᄒᆞᄂᆞᆫ시각을일졍ᄒᆞ엿더라

○로병량식운송 로병은히삼위에셔ᄯᅢᄯᅢ로졍크(쳥국비)로써밀과면보문들가로등물을경셩과셩진으로향ᄒᆞ야슈로로운송ᄒᆞᆫ다더라

TELEGRAMS.

THE BALTIC FLEET.

London, Oct. 21.

Great indignation prevails in London over the action of the Baltic Fleet in firing on the north sea trawlers. Urgent representations have been made to Russia and Count Benckendorff is to arrive here tomorrow.

London Oct. 28.

Benckendorff has handed preliminary reply to Lord Lansdowne's representations, expressing deep regret for the incident and intention to pay an indemnity to the families of those killed and pay the owners for damage done to ,r vessels. The Czar has telegraphed „ regrets to King Edward.

London, Later.

The Battleship "Queen" with nine destroyers has left Malta, destination unknown. A division of the Mediterranean fleet now at Fiume has received urgent orders to unite with the fleet at Poto and sail westward with sealed orders. Marked activity is apparent in the English dockyards.

London, Oct. 29.

Prince Kiritelli an officer of the battleship "Imperator Alexander," which has arrived at Pigo explains that transport steamer ahead of the fleet in the north sea was suddenly surrounded by eight torpedoboats. The division advanced and signalled the strangers to leave or state their nationality. The strangers refused and advanced. Among the battleships the report of a gun was heard whereupon the admiral forming a line of battle opened fire, afterwards continuing the voyage. The Admiral was aware that the Japanese had purchased torpedo-boats in England, therefore feared the strangers were Japanese torpedo-boats.

Later.

The opinion in England is at fever heat. The parties are united in insisting on full reparation.

Tokyo, Oct. 29.

On October 25th Viceroy Alexieff issued the following notification in Harbin: "His Majesty the Czar has granted my resignation of my present post and has appointed General Kuropatkin Field-Marshal, in command of all the forces in the far east. His Majesty has graciously been pleased to acknowledge my endeavours in organising the Russian army in Manchuria, so I thank all you officers and men for your work in the past and look forward to the time when you will have gloriously defeated our gallant enemy

Later.

Marquis Oyama again reports that the Russians are using dum-dum bullets.

Tokyo, Oct. 29th.

The enemy's guard at Waitusan, consisting of 2 battalions of sharpshooters of the 18th brigade resisted our attack, but afterwards retreated leaving two field guns, which we captured. Our casualties were 160; the enemy's was not less.

At the direction about 1,000 of the enemys troop's have been seen. The majority are attired in Chinese clothes giving them the appearance of Chinese soldiers.

Manchester September 15th.

The attention of the President having been called to the fact that no protection exists in Korea for merchants' trade marks, which are at present the prey of any unscrupulous copyist, he reported that he had caused a letter to be sent to the Secretary of State for Foreign Affairs asking whether it would not be possible to make arrangements with the proper authority to secure for British merchants importing into Korea the enjoyment of protction for their own marks in the same manner as it is secured in Japan and—by the recent treaty—in China. A letter was read from the Foreign Office promising that the subject should receive attention.

Tokyo, Oct 29th.

According to reports 4 torpedo-boats are guarding the entrance to Vladivostok and examining in-going and out-going steamers and junks. The "Bogarty" still appears to be in dry dock, but the "Gromovoi" and "Rossia" are now completely repaired. About 5 foreign vessels captured by the Russians are at anchor in the harbor. The citizens are expecting a Japanese attack.

PROCLAMATION IN THE NORTH EAST.

The Governor of Hamheung telegraphs particulars of the latest Japanese proclamation distributed through the north-eastern provinces.

1. Japan desires to ensure eternal peace in the far east and in particular to protect China and Korea. Hence she is waging war with Russia. The Japanese military authorities will therefore be seen to be assisting the people.

2. An inspection of the districts has led the Japanese to believe that the Koreans are an oppressed race and suffer from bad magisterial rule. Henceforth this will be remedied.

3. The people must therefore assist, in every way possible, the Japanese to consummate these desires. Therefore they must provide provision and labor, which will be paid for at reasonable prices.

ILLICIT TRADE.

It is interesting to note that during this war very few accusations have been made from either side with regard to illicit trading, running of contraband and so forth on the part of its opponent.

The reason is not far to seek. Both sides are tarred with the same brush. Port Arthur badly wanted coal and now it gets all the coal it wants. Coal arrives by British colliers at various ports in China, and there it is openly transferred to vessels of other nationalities and these vessels openly sail for Port Arthur. There is no great risk in this traffic because an announced blockade to be effective *must be* a blockade *de facto*, which the present Japanese blockade of Port Arthur is not. There are a few stray vessels (guardships and what not)hanging around the neighbourhood of Port Arthur but the bulk of the Japanese fleet is elsewhere, recuperating.

So that the Japanese Blockade is not effective and the worst that can happen to a vessel carrying contraband is the Prize Court and probable confiscation. As these contingencies have already been financially provided for, there seems little likelihood (unless Admiral Togo really makes his blockade "effective") that the traffic will ever stop.

On the other hand, the Japanese are playing a similar game.

Between Chefoo and Wei-hai-wei a most surprsing trade in cheap cigarettes, red blandets, Japanese tea, pickles, other delicacies, cushions and other things dear to the Japanese heart has recently developed. Of course there are no Japanese to speak of at Wei-hai-wei but there are thousands of them at Dalney. And hereby hangs a tale.

There is a slackness about the Chefoo Customs which is hard to account for. It is a matter of common knowledge in Chefoo that the trade between there and Wei-hai-wei has heretofore been insignificant and yet it suddenly assumed dimensions calling for two or three steamers daily and no one seems to smell a rat.

Something is wrong with the papers of these vessels. They never go to Wei-hai-wei and yet they clear from Chefoo for there and return to Chefoo without any question being raised. An amusing piece of evidence was found by a representative of the Korea Daily News who recently came from Chefoo to Chemulpo by the "Il Shin," a Korean boat which had been under charter to Japanese and had ostensibly been plying between Chefoo and Wei-hai-wei. There was a well-worn chart on board and on it was pencilled the route taken by the ship from Chefoo to Dalny. The route was three sides of a hexagon. First along the coast in the direction of Wei hai-wei, (this was presumably in case anyone was looking) then out to sea and then back to Wei-hai-wei.

If these ships' papers are in order the Chefoo and Wei-hai-wei customs had better compare notes.

The Minister of Foreign Affairs has, for some unknown reason, been an absentee from his post for the past few days.

The Magistrate of Heui-chon reports that by his orders, 30 Tonghaks have been arrested and imprisoned. He adds that these characters are a nuisance and danger to all natives.

To-day, hair cutting operations were put into effect amongst all the high and middle grade officials. One month's grace has been allowed to officials of the Ceremonial Department.

The Japanese Army Headquarters have issued instructions to all their Military Stations through Korea to prohibit magistrates and others from persecuting members of the Chin-po-hoi fraternity.

The Korea Daily News.

Issued at 5 P. M. daily except Sundays.

Rate of Subscription:—

Per Year,	Yen 25.
Per Quarter,	Yen 7.
Per Month,	Yen 2.50.

Postage in Korea not charged extra.
Postage abroad charged extra.

Advertisements, 50 sen per day for 1 inch or less.
5 yen per month per inch.
50 yen per year per inch.

All communications to

E. T. BETHELL,
Editor and Publisher,
Pak-tong, Seoul

WIRELESS TELEGRAPHY IN WAR.

The manager of the Times steamer "Haimun," Messrs. Douglas, Lapraik's vessel now on the coast again, from which telegrams were sent during the war, sends an interesting record of the experience with wireless telegraphy from the first message until the Japanese restriction rendered wireless service useless. With an exposure of only 90 feet of wire on the receiving station and 120 feet on the ship, there was no difficulty in maintaining intercommunication for 100 sea miles, describing the fire of torpedo destroyers, and not a single word was taken incorrectly.

From March 21, when the mast ashore was at a height of 180 feet, the ship remained in the vicinity of Port Arthur, with the exception of two visits to Korea. She always intercepted Russian and Japanese wireless telegrams, but these cipher dispatches could not be understood, However, they enabled the operator to judge the approximate distance of the vessel. One extremely expert operator could tell if the Russian ship was at sea by listening for an answering communication from the shore. He could also determine whether Japanese messages were being transmitted by relay to the naval base or whether the fleet itself was at sea. On April 9 messages from Bundeg inland to Wei-hai-wei, a distance of 180 sea miles were sent and acknowledged.

During the engagement in which the Russian battleship "Petropavlock" was sunk, the "Haimun" did not use the wireless "instrument, until the battleships were engaged with the batteries as its use would have interfered with the belligerents' wireless telegrams, to which the "Haimun" listened. The Russians kept repeating the alphabet over in order to queer the Japaneso instruments. The correspondent believes this prevented Admiral Togo from coming up in time to catch Admiral Makaroff outside. It was only when the Russians stopped the queering process, in order to receive messages, from their own warship "Bayan," that the Japanese decoy squadron was able to send a message. The "Haimun" received both the Japanese and "Bayan" messages.

Messages were sent 200 sea miles from Chinampo, but the record was from outside Chemulpo, over 219 sea miles, which was partly broken by the islands of the Prince Imperial Archipelago. An answer to the latter message was received. Only twenty-five words of a long message were bungled and this was because of the near proximity of a British warship, which was using the same wireless system. The operators were able to transmit or receive from twenty to thirty words a minute.—China Gazette.

VERY MARKED CHANGE OF FEELING TOWARD JAPAN.

WASHINGTON BUREAU.

(Concluded.)

While giving the Japanese navy full credit for its efficiency and pluck, the Japs have never been popular with our sailors. It is recognized that Nippon's navy is the most homogeneous fighting force of the kind in the world. Largely manned by the Satsuma men and officered almost entirely by descendants of the nobles and samurai of that fierce clan, many of the rank and file have a personal loyalty to their superiors apart from the obedience due to rank and station. Japan has probable a larger seafaring population than any other nation. For centuries its fishermen have been bred to the sea—they are hereditary sailormen. The officers are well educated under Western methods—skilful, devoted to their profession and stern adherents of the "Bushido" code.

COULD NOT RENEW HER NAVY.

The officers and men of Japan's navy have evinced the contempt for death characteristic of Orientals and also a dashing spirit of emulation more akin to that of white men. Whole ships' crews have volunteered for desperate enterprises, but as a rule extreme caution has marked the naval operations. Japan cannot renew her navy, has no reserve ships and the loss of a vessel would be irreparable. Neither at Chemulpo, in the Corean Straits, nor before Port Arthur have the Japanese tried to get close to their opponents. The battle following the last sortie of the Russians was fought at not less than five miles. If Togo had followed the Farragut and Nelson tactics he could without doubt have sunk or captured the entire Russian squadron. But he would not risk his ships and the Russians escaped.

But, though the Japanese navy fights on more orthodox lines than the army, and while its efficiency is admitted, the sailors of Nippon are unpopular with every navy in the world, even that of England. Their manners are "cocky" and offensive and display the contempt of the self-sufficient display the contempt of the self-sufficient barbarian for ideas and customs different from his own.

Even the Japanese butlers, valets and stewards have been affected by Japan's victories. Many have become unbearable to their masters and mistresses and have been discharged in self-defence.

There are several places where friction between Japan and the United States might arise. The Philippine and Sandwich islands are the most dangerous. It will be remembered that Japan once sent a cruiser to Honolulu to back up complaints of ill treatment of her subjects. In the salmon fishing country there has been much trouble with the Japanese.

In the navy it is generally believed that we will have to meet Japan's fleets on the Pacific before the century is old.

THE MENACE OF THE RAND.

Under the above heading the "Straits Echo" says:—

Transvaal coolie recruiting agents have reached the heart of the Canton provinces, and are now busy at Wuchow about 200 miles west of Canton city. This, says the "Straits Times," intensifies the menace of the Rand. The Randlords are tapping the South China coolie supply which had hitherto mainly advantaged the Straits Settlements and Settlements and the F. M. S. The moment the coolie class in South China are enticed in large numbers to the Rand, troublous times will set in for employers in these parts. Scarcity of Chinese labour will hamper them, with disastrous results. Mr. Tan Jiak Kim a few months ago, drew the attention of the Government to the subject in the Legislative Council. The Government, admitted that mischief to the Colony might result from the Transvaal coolie recruiting operations, and promised to bring the matter under the notice of the Home Government. Such is the situation at present. Meanwhile, coolie recruiting for the Transvaal in our particular field of Chinese labour supply is going on merrily.—The old story over again: Nero fiddling while Rome is burning! We shall be made to pay dearly for this reckless folly some day.

SALE OF THE NAGASAKI HOTEL.

In accordance with the resolution passed at the extraordinary meeting of Shareholders of the Nagasaki Hotel, Limited, the affairs of the Company have been in the hands of an official liquidator by whose direction the Hotel was yesterday sold by public auction. Considerable interest was manifested locally in the sale and as the auction has been advertised in Kobe, Yokohama, Shanghai, Hongkong, and Manila papers, it was expected that the sale would attract numerous bidders from other ports. It had been rumoured that the Nippon Yusen Kaisha and Kyushu Railway were purdable purchasers; but although we believe those companies were represented at the sale no bids were put forth in their behalf.

The sale took place in the dining room of the Hotel and punctually at 11 A. M. Mr. R. H. Powers, the auctioneer, opened the proceedings by reading the particulars of the property and conditions of sale. There were 50 or 60 gentlemen present, mostly residents of Nagasaki, and the bidding was started at Yen 20,000. The amount quickly reached Yen 100,000 at which point the auctioneer announced that offers of Yen 500 would be accepted. Mr. Bosman, of Hong Kong, continued bidding, which was by no means brisk, and at Yen 106,000 the property was knocked down to Mr. Ringer. We understand that the Hotel will be continued, under its present designation, by the new owner.

The St. Petersburg correspondent of the "New York Herald" says that Russian stoicism and optimism remain unruffled. The Russians, according to this authority, have unlimited patience, and they are conducting the war, as they carry on business, with that irriting procrastination which eventually breaks the spirit of the other party. The sincere opinion, says this correspondent, of 99 out of every 100 Russians is that they are gradually but surely wearing out their energetic foe, and that, before long, he will be reduced to such a condition of worry and fatigue that he will be glad to make terms on any conditions. Russia's reverses are looked upon as mere incidents of the campaign. The only exception they admit is the defeat of the navy, and anxiety concerning what remains of the Port Arthur fleet is intense.

General Gripenberg, Commander of the Second Manchurian Army of Russia, was born on January 1, 1838, and is therefore in his sixty-sixth year. The General, who is a Lutheran, was first appointed to a military post in 1854, and as a Major and Lieut.-Colonel fought in the Turkestan campaign from 1866 to 1868, in which he was wounded. He afterwards took part in the Turkish War of 1877 and 1878 with the Moscow Regiment of the Imperial Guards. In 1887 he was promoted to the rank of Major-General, and in 1890 to Lieut.-General of Infantry. He was appointed Commander of the Brigade of Sharpshooters of the Imperial Guards in 1889, and Commander of the First Division of Infantry of the Imperial Guards in 1897, which post he retained for four years.—China Review.

One day last month a young python roaming under the roof of the Government Officers in Borneo in search of a stray meal, became so interested in what was going on in the Treasury below him that he inadvertently peered down from a beam and exposed his head to the view of Dr. Davies, who was discussing some matters with the Finance Commissioner. Business was suspended for the moment till the python was dislodged and put out of action when he was found to be a finely marked specimen six and a half feet long.

The Korea Daily News.

VOL. I MONDAY, OCTOBER 31, 1904. No. 89

HONGKONG & SHANGHAI BANKING CORPORATION.

Paid-up Capital $10,000,000
Reserve Fund:—Sterling Reserve... 10,000,000
Silver Reserve..... 7,000,000

27,000,000

Reserve Liability of Proprietors... 10,000,000

HEAD OFFICE, HONGKONG.

London Bankers, London and County Banking Company Limited
Branches and Agencies,
London.

Amoy,	Hankow	Penang,
Bangkok,	Hiogo,	Rangoon,
Batavia,	Iloilo,	Saigon,
Bombay,	Lyons,	San Francisco,
Calcutta,	Manila,	Singapore,
Colombo,	Nagasaki,	Sourabaya,
Foochow,	New York,	Tientsin,
Hamburg,	Peking,	Yokohama,

Credits granted on approved Securities, and every description of Banking and Exchange business transacted.

Drafts granted on London and the chief Commercial places in Europe, India, Australia, America, China and Japan.

HOLME RINGER & Co., AGENTS,
CHEMULPO.

ON CHEONG & CO.,
SEOUL.
GENERAL STORE KEEPERS.
Imported provisions, Cooking Utensils Crockery, etc.
FRESH BREAD DAILY.

MITSU BISHI DOCKYARD & ENGINE WORKS,

NAGASAKI.

CODE WORD, "DOCK."

A. 1, A. B. C., and Engineering Codes used.

DOCK No. 1 (at Tategami).

Extreme Length.............. 523 feet
Length on blocks .... 513 ,,
Width of Entrance on Top...... 89 ,,
,, ,, Bottom.... 77 ,,
Water on Blocks at Spring Tide 26½ ,,

DOCK No. 2 (Mukaijima).

Extreme Length.............. 371 feet
Length on Blocks............ 360 ,,
Width of Entrance on Top..... 66 ,,
,, ,, Bottom 53 ,,
Water on Blocks at Spring Tide 22 ,,

PATENT SLIP (at Kosuge).

Can take vessels up to 1,000 tons gross.

THE WORKS are well equipped with the LATEST IMPROVEMENTS, and can execute any kind of work in SHIPBUILDING and MARINE ENGINEERING, as well as in REPAIRING of SHIPS.

The COMPANY'S new powerful steamer OURA-MARU (712 tons, 700 I.H.P.), specially built for SALVAGE PURPOSES, and equipped with necessary gear, is always READY at SHORT NOTICE.

CHARTERED BANK OF INDIA AUSTRALIA & CHINA.

INCORPORATED BY ROYAL CHARTER 1853

HEAD OFFICES:—LONDON.

Paid-up Capital £800,000
Reserve Liability of Shareholders 800,000
Reserve Fund 800,000

Drafts granted upon all the principal places in the world and every description of Exchange and banking business transacted.

E. MEYER & Co., Agents,
Chemulpo.

E. MEYER & CO.
Chemulpo.

SOLE AGENTS IN KOREA FOR:
A. T. Morse, Sons & Co's
"Fresco" Distemper

In all colours ready for use on walls, Ceilings etc.
and
AVENARIUS CARBOLINEUM

A wood-preserving and antiseptic oil preparation

Against decay, dry-rot, fungus and wood-destroying insects.

A large supply always in Stock.
Prices upon application.

E. MEYER & Co..
Chemulpo.

THE METHODIST PUBLISHING HOUSE,
Little West Gate, Seoul.

PRINTING, TYPEWRITER PAPER
CARBON PAPER, VISITING CARDS
STATIONERY, BOOK BINDING
BOOK PUBLISHERS
AMERICAN SCHOOL BOOKS
SPENCERIAN COPY BOOKS
PEN CARBON LETTER AND BILL BOOKS

S. A. BECK, Manager.

HOKURKU DOBOKU KAISHA.

Branch office in Chong Dong, Seoul.
Japanese telephone No. 165

CONTRACT DEPARTMENT.

We can contract to build any building or construction.

MERCHANDISE DEPARTMENT.

We can provide any building material. We have just contracted to build the new Belgian Legation.

DAI-ICHI GINK
LIMITED.
(Formerly the First National Bank)

ESTABLISHED 1873

INCORPORATED UNDER PRESENT LAW 1896

Capital - - - - - - - - Yen 5,000,000
Reserve Fund - - - - 1,500,000

HEAD OFFICE:—TOKIO.

President: Baron SHIBUSAWA.

BRANCHES AND CORRESPONDENTS
In the Principal Cities and Towns of Japan.
Interest Allowed on
Fixed deposits 1 year - - - 6½ per cent
" " 6 months - - - 6 per cent

Special current accounts 1½ sen daily per Y 100
General " " 1 " " 100

M. TANAKA,
Manager, Chemulpo

HOLME RINGER & Co.
Chemulpo.

General Merchants and Government Contractors.

Agents for the leading
Banks
Steamship Companies
and
Insurance Companies

Importers of Merchandise of every description.

KAMEYA & CO.
GENERAL STOREKEEPERS
Chinkokai - - Seoul
(Established 1895, Tokyo)

Confectionery, Hams, Canned Goods, Cutlery, Hirano & Tansan Water. Provisions, Gents, Furnishing goods, Toilet Articles, Travelling Bags, Tobacco, Cigars & Cigarettes Kitchen Utensils. Coffee, Biscuits.

Fresh Goods always kept in Stock
Prices Moderate
Please come and inspect our goods.

NIPPON YUSEN KAISHA.
JAPANESE MAIL STEAMSHIP CO.

UNDER MAIL CONTRACT WITH THE IMPERIAL JAPANESE GOVERNMENT

European Line

Regular Fortnightly Service between Yokohama Kobe, Moji, Shanghai, Hongkong, Singapore, Penang Colombo, Port Said, Marseilles, London and Antwerp

American Line

Regular Fortnightly Service between Hongkong and Seattle, calling at Shanghai, Moji, Kobe, Yokohama and Victoria, B. C.

Australian Line

Regular weekly Service betwen Japan Ports and Australia, calling at Hongkong and Manila.
(Above Three Lines Suspended until further notice).

Shanghai Line

Weekly Service between Shanghai and Japan Ports

Korea Lir

Service Kobe, Moji, Nagasaki, Fusan, Chemupo, Chefoo, Taiku.
S. S. Bahelsberg, 2181 tons.
Service Kobe, Moji, Fusan, Chemulpo, Chinnampo
S. S ARGO, S. S. Ohio.

BORDEN'S CONDENSED MILK CO.
New York, U. S. A.

ALWAYS IN STOCK
Eagle Brand Condensed Milk.
Gold Seal Condensed Milk.
Peerless (Family) Evaporated Cream.
Borden's Malted Milk.

E. MEYER & CO
Chemulpo, Korea,
Sole Agents

ROYAL INSURANCE COMPANY
Funds exceed £10,000,000
FIRE
AT CURRENT RATES.
LIFE
REDUCED PREMIUM.
HOLME RINGER & Co.,
Agents, Chemulpo.

HOTEL DU PALAIS
SEOUL.

The only first class Hotel in Seoul. Situated in the centre of the city opposite the palace.

Cuisine under the supervision of an experienced French Chef.

Well ventilated and furnished throughout.

TARIFF UPON APPLICATION
L. MARTIN
Proprietor and Manager

보신일ᄆᆡ한대

報申日每韓大

(호십구뎨) (일요화) 일일월일십년사ᄇᆡᆨ구쳔일

본샤고ᄇᆡᆨ

이신보는령이와한이로셔거ᄆᆡ
일츌판ᄒᆞ옵
신문가
ᄒᆞᆫ쟝 엽두돈오푼
ᄒᆞᆫ삭됴 엽두량닷돈
우표가ᄆᆡ삭닷돈
다ᄉᆞᆺ돈으로밧습
광고료는
귀한의쟝단과ᄌᆞᄒᆡᆼ의다쇼로ᄌᆞ
감ᄒᆞ되령가로밧을터이오ᄆᆡ오
ᄅᆡ지아녀대한사람마다다이신
문을보실터이니광고내시기를
원ᄒᆞ시는이들은우리신문사에
와셔면약ᄒᆞ심을희망ᄒᆞ옵
○발ᄒᆡᆼ소 박동대한ᄆᆡ일신보
사별이학교앞희 젼영국인셜필
림쟝자리오
샤쟝 영국인 (베셜)
평양 ᄃᆡ리졈
○평양효동사는권미보씨로우
리신문관ᄆᆡᄃᆡ리인을뎡ᄒᆞ엿
스오나평양에계신구람고져ᄒᆞ
시는 쳠군ᄌᆞ는ᄒᆡ리졈에왕
림ᄒᆞ와면의ᄒᆞ시옵

사고

○우리대한ᄆᆡ일신보의목뎍은
대한의안녕질서에관ᄒᆞᆫ모든례
목에ᄃᆡᄒᆞ야는공평ᄒᆞᆫ변론을ᄌᆞ유
쟝ᄒᆞᆷ이라우리동신원의ᄃᆡᆸ보는
신문보시는쳠군ᄌᆞ의계ᄒᆞ샹보
도ᄒᆞᆯ터며편지를긔셔ᄒᆞ여주시
는이는셩명과반ᄃᆡ를젹어붓치
시기를희망ᄒᆞ오나비거슨신문
샹에긔재ᄒᆞᆯ는거시아니오다
만규칙신용ᄒᆞ는증거를숨고자
ᄒᆞᆷ이라귀쟈는아모귀셔던지과
지ᄒᆞᆷ을되ᄀᆡᆨᄒᆞ는권리를가졋스
나되ᄀᆡᆨᄒᆞ는리유를말ᄒᆞᆯ터이오
며공중평화를문란케ᄒᆞ는듯ᄒᆞᆫ
긔셔는의례히밧지안켓습나이
다
●본샤셜시이리로신문을ᄆᆡ양
우례로분젼ᄒᆞ와례젼부의입의
로젼ᄒᆞ든ᄉᆞ스로번곳에는ᄒᆞᆨ늣게
젼ᄒᆞ기도ᄒᆞ며ᄒᆞᆨ면쳘거슬ᄒᆞᆫ겁
에젼ᄒᆞ기도ᄒᆞ며ᄒᆞᆨ아니젼ᄒᆞ는
곳도잇다ᄒᆞ와우리신문을ᄉᆞ량
ᄒᆞ야구람ᄒᆞ시는 쳠군ᄌᆞ의게
ᄃᆡᄒᆞ야미우미안ᄒᆞ옵기로지금
은분젼인을두고ᄆᆡ일일즉이젼
ᄒᆞ며아니젼ᄒᆞ거나늣게거나ᄒᆞᆫ
가업도록ᄒᆞ라ᄒᆞ오니ᄒᆞᆨ아니셩
젼ᄒᆞ거는ᄒᆞᆨ늣게젼ᄒᆞ거나ᄒᆞᆫ일
이잇스면본사로통긔ᄒᆞ여주심
을희망ᄒᆞ옵

본사광고

○본사신문중에긔ᄌᆡᄒᆞᆫ호수를
소용ᄒᆞᆯ데가잇셔이에광고ᄒᆞ오
니누구시던지그중에아모호수
던지가져오시는ᄃᆡ로ᄆᆡ쟝에ᄇᆡᆨ
젼두푼식드리리다
뎨이호 뎨삼호 뎨ᄉᆞ십호
뎨ᄉᆞ십이호 뎨ᄉᆞ십삼호 뎨
오십삼호 뎨오십ᄉᆞ호와뎨오
십오호 뎨륙십이호

관보

뎨이쳔구ᄇᆡᆨ칠십호 광무
팔년십월이십구일
셔임급사령
○서ᄒᆞᆫ샹등사ᄐᆡ극쟝 일본국
병참감부면신ᄐᆡ쟝륙군공병즁
좌 쳔추진지 ○서ᄒᆞᆫ삼등사
팔괘쟝 일본국군사령부참모
륙군보병쇼좌 챵면신칠
야풍사 일본국군사령부부관
륙군긔병쇼좌 대도우인 일
본국군사령부병원쟝륙군삼등
군의졍 반뎐구웅 일본국병
참감부경리부쟝륙군삼등주계
졍 표산승 일본국병참감부
원뎐신ᄐᆡ쟝륙군공병쇼좌
좌독평강 일본국병참감부원
헌병ᄐᆡ쟝륙군헌병쇼좌 표산
일명 ○서ᄒᆞᆫ사등사ᄐᆡ극쟝
일본국군사령부부관륙군보병
대위 복뎐언조 일본국군사
령부륙군일등군의 암영양
일본국병참감부참모륙군보병
대위 오야영차랑 일본국병
참감부부관륙군보병대위 송
강풍수 일본국병참감부병참
사령관륙군보병대위 임영승
삼랑 일본국병참감부원헌병
ᄃᆡ쟝륙군헌병대위 경야죽지
진 ○서ᄒᆞᆫ사등사팔괘쟝 일
본국군사령부부관륙군일등주
계 쟝전암태랑
이상십월이십일
○명동리군립시우케쥬ᄉᆞ 정
인셕○명숙쳔군립시우케쥬ᄉᆞ
오병츄 ○평양군립시우케
쥬ᄉᆞ 김세경 ○명장슈군립
시우케쥬ᄉᆞ 정경로
이상십월이십륙일
○명서리춍직사무 탈도원부
춍직 최영하
○의원면본관 진원릉령 김
용쥬 ○임 진원릉령셔쾬
임관칠등 온릉령 남계셕
임온릉령셔쾬임관칠등 륙품
김교일 이상십월이십칠일
○의원면경임쟝례원쟝례 비
서원승 리명상 봉상사부제
쥬 박경원 ○경임쟝례원쟝례
비서원승 박쟝슈 봉상사
부제쥬 죠한원
이상십월이십팔일

잡보

○군부월급 군부에서시로ᄒᆞᆫ
편졔에든관원들의월봉을탁지
부에서지츌은ᄒᆞ엿스나탁지고
문관말이아직분급지말나ᄒᆞᆫ고
로분급지못ᄒᆞ엿더라
○의졍소긔회 군부의졍소에
셔작일하오두시에시로편졔ᄒᆞᆫ
각학교의경비와기타시급ᄒᆞᆫ경
비들의졍ᄒᆞᆯ수로크게긔회ᄒᆞ엿
다더라
○군부관인분편 군부의쥬ᄉᆞ
와기타평복ᄒᆞᆫ관인들이문에츌
입ᄒᆞᆯ때에병뎡과서로승강이되
는고로단발ᄒᆞ고무관복쟝을안
ᄒᆞ면지병뎡이말을찰듯지아니ᄒᆞ
는고로일젹히구별ᄒᆞᆫ다더라
○닉부고문관 닉부고문관ᄒᆡ
일광씨는다른고문관의례들의
ᄒᆞ야동역관과벗쳐소를쟝ᄒᆞ야
달나ᄒᆞ엿스나ᄒᆞ고가된다더라
○본무인취 명동오예쟝은본
시한셩부관유ᄃᆡᄐᆡ현금에일인
이ᄒᆞ귀지에졉을지을ᄎᆞ로인허
금도엿시리를닷는고로순검들이
ᄒᆞ지ᄒᆞ되종시쳥종치아니ᄒᆞ미
셩부에용문ᄒᆞ엿더라
○위관양부 미동사는김창쟝
이란ᄒᆞᆫ나라ᄒᆞ에보지
보씨가년젼에평남사름이로
보리가엇다ᄒᆞ매
명면수로상경ᄒᆞ야무삼쳥쟝을ᄒᆞ
란고ᄒᆞ는거슬알고치치ᄒᆞ야청
츅젼샹쳔에원을숭용ᄒᆞ엿든일
노일젼에박인일병과한인일병
이김씨의집에와서셰잇진돈을
비란ᄒᆞ며의관을렬파ᄒᆞ고무수
히ᄶᆡᆼ을케며야로ᄒᆞ는고로그갓
치왓든한인은보병ᄃᆡ와관김병
도인ᄃᆡ김창쟝이하ᄃᆡ위관을헌병
의케압부ᄒᆞ엿다더라
○회쳔동비 회쳔군보를거ᄒᆞ

ᄌᆞᆨ희군에동학당수쳔명이회집
ᄒᆞᆫ고로그곤쳐진위ᄃᆡ병뎡을발
ᄒᆞ여동학파슈샹신명을챠슈ᄒᆞ
라고여당은일변희송이라ᄒᆞ엿더
라
○외관사발 졔작일외부에서
관칙주임관이일교례칙사발ᄒᆞ고
포셍쟝을잉샤후에셔원에셔는각문
로된인ᄃᆡ이ᄒᆞ엿다더라모다삭발ᄒᆞ기
○ᄒᆞᆫ금창샬 일본군ᄉᆞ령부에
셔각병참소로ᄒᆞᆫ칙ᄒᆞ되진보ᄒᆞᆫ
인을한국관리가ᄒᆞᆨ포샬ᄒᆞ며ᄒᆞᆨ
착슈ᄒᆞᆫ다ᄒᆞ니ᄇᆡᆫ일이잇ᄂᆞᆫ존포ᄒᆞᆨ
ᄒᆞᆫᄒᆡᆼ졍이참잇거든병참부로셔
곳졈지ᄒᆞ라ᄒᆞ엿다더라
○환관무로 부평군슈와셩진
경무관이상경ᄒᆞ엿다가환관차
로마ᄐᆡ평에도달ᄒᆞ종아병이말
ᄒᆞ기를일본경리이라ᄒᆞ는고로
잇환관키못ᄒᆞ고도로원산으로와
다더라
○죠죡ᄃᆡ가 외부에서탈도원
의죠죡ᄒᆞ단가ᄅᆡ국인케리스키
로죠회ᄒᆞ며덕국쳔원을붓일지
로파ᄃᆡ외국공ᄉᆞ의칭ᄎᆡᆨᄒᆞᆷ을면
케발ᄒᆞ야라ᄒᆞ엿더라
○통문과젼 근일에일진회에
셔량경ᄒᆞᆫ뜻으로통문을발ᄒᆞᆫᄒᆞ
통여각쳐로단니며무론모힌ᄒᆞ고
문일장식너조다도랑ᄒᆞ다
이ᄃᆡ

론셜

죵엽는뎐보
ᄎᆞ이나계이시ᄃᆞ신문을본즉근
일에셔로발명ᄒᆞᆫ바문셜뎐보시
론쳔셜사무쟝라푸리의씨가ᄌᆞ
귀의빈을잇글고히안으로도챡
ᄒᆞ엿는뎌이뎐신으로ᄒᆞ며끔시
렁ᄒᆞ야동셩ᄒᆞᆫ후젼사에사용케
이ᄒᆞ라다가일본에계쟝뢰엿더니
모도견단비로소빙환은되엿스되
ᄒᆡᆼ는지라그리ᄒᆞ나이면못ᄒᆞ게되
ᄉᆡᆼ히귀이ᄒᆞᆫ거시무론이보인ᄌᆞᆼ
들지면보타발ᄒᆞ는곳에놉빈씨이
ᄀᆞᆯ고로일빅이십영쳠거리말ᄌᆞᆯ을
ᄆᆡᆫ느뢰평수ᄒᆞᆯ처수에ᄂᆞᆫ구십영쳑
안은통히동신ᄒᆞ고셜ᄒᆞᆨ수뢰리동
갓는것에방화ᄒᆞᆷ으토맘ᄆᆡ아쟝
졀단남염여도엽다ᄒᆞ논중이마
ᄒᆞᆫ괴이ᄒᆞᆫ거슬시로케조ᄒᆞ고토
일아기젼딍으로인ᄒᆞ야힝당히
쓰여보지못ᄒᆞ교도리어교젼국
에셔각각이괴계를노코부리는

자ㅣ잇셔힝군즁방ᄒᆞᆫ쳐소에ᄂᆞᆫ외레히셜치ᄒᆞ엿드라ᄒᆞ며홍쟝황ᄒᆞᆫ샤연은오히려알수업스되오자도별노엉ᄉᆞ과연괴묘ᄒᆞᆷ으로칭찬ᄒᆞᄂᆞᆫ자ㅣ만ᄒᆞ더라

잡보

○경쇼무인 졍부에셔시졍기션은아직될형편이업고일진회의권고와졍박은날노ᄃᆡ욱깁ᄒᆞᆫ경ᄒᆞᆫ고로졍부졔공이ᄃᆡ단우려ᄒᆞ야능히히회톤ᄒᆞᆫ과ᄒᆞᆫ자잇스면특별히경무ᄉᆞ로셔임ᄒᆞ기로쥬퓽쳐지ᄒᆞ엿스되아직ᄌᆞ원자가업다ᄒᆞ더라

○일군가등 일본에젼왕ᄒᆞᆫ헌병운세쇼실졍부인비셔와남비되ᄂᆞᆫ헝ᄃᆡ가ᄒᆞᄂᆞᆫ힌즁계임헝셩퓌운이오ᄒᆞᄂᆞᆫ힌즁헌ᄃᆡ경무관인ᄃᆡ빈경무셔퇴셰ᄂᆞᆫ젼헌의일등어부란랑샹웅젼등군챵조구에어샐을엄여쓰면샹립ᄒᆞᄂᆞᆫ즁에ᄃᆡ린소퀀이잇겟다ᄒᆞ야랑샨웅젼두군슈즁에일과톨도등ᄒᆞ랑으로운동즁이라ᄒᆞ더라

○참졍힝공 참졍신긔션씨ᄂᆞᆫ일진회의졍박을난감ᄒᆞ야신병샹소ᄅᆞᆯᄒᆞ더ᄅᆡ도긔어히수직ᄒᆞᆫ다ᄒᆞ더니모용관의셔권면ᄒᆞ되졍부참졍의지위로인민의압박을비긔지못ᄒᆞ야수퇴ᄒᆞᆷ이만불근리ᄒᆞ다ᄒᆞ엿더니도로힝공ᄒᆞ엿다더라

●박수시취 일젼에학부에셔경의문ᄃᆡ로싱샹도유싱을시취ᄒᆞ엿ᄂᆞᆫᄃᆡ경긔도에ᄒᆞ창후리퓽직쟝의식이오츙북에린죵빅박슌힝졍규남이오츙남에김샹우서경쳔조병위오젼북에류긔ᄒᆞ광즁인조병진이오젼남에ᄒᆞ죵롤송영슌셜셔힉이오경북에권계학ᄒᆞ지셕쟝긔원이오경남에김긔죵린긔일박경은이오밉원도에창힉샹윤규병미오황히도에김ᄒᆞ린ᄒᆞ로요평남에리쥬영오학규요평북에빅졍회은창홍이오합남에리윤경졔면강이오합북에지약우헌면슈등박수가샹싱샹인이오샹겨비롱싱칠인이더라

○쥬야슌찰 일진회에셔슌찰위샹ᄉᆞ싱명을퇴졍ᄒᆞ야오셔각동으로쥬야슌찰ᄒᆞ더라

○일진회회산고시 ᄂᆡ부에셔지작일에 조칙등인ᄒᆞ야강도로망야ᄒᆞ야금히ᄒᆞᆫ령ᄒᆞ야회민의회산홈ᄂᆞᆫ등츄ᄒᆞ엿고한셩부에셔ᄂᆞᆫ각방곡에고시ᄒᆞ야일진회히산홈을등츄ᄒᆞ며포박ᄒᆞᆷ을무힝ᄒᆞᆫ지라일진회에셔ᄂᆞᆫ힝동ᄒᆞ기를원어홈이잇서괴고지ᄒᆞᄂᆞᆫ민회ᄂᆞᆫ압박ᄒᆞ고원어홈을셧치ᄂᆞᆫ졍부ᄂᆞᆫ빈동ᄒᆞ야니ᄒᆞ니셔산루ᄒᆞ거ᄒᆞᄂᆞᆫ리도가히거연이히치못ᄒᆞ겟다ᄒᆞ엿더라

○민요간범 양샹시ᄒᆞᆫ민요ᄉᆞ건으로평리원에셔빙ᄒᆞᆫ과셩우경을실문ᄒᆞᆫ즉그의슈의쳐힝뭡을면키어려운지라안건을판결ᄒᆞᆯᄎᆞ로졍과지판소에지슈ᄒᆞᆫ간련ᄒᆞᆫ죄인등빙을지작일에평리원으로죠압샹ᄒᆞ엿더라

○거익우진 ᄂᆡ부ᄃᆡ신리용틱씨를각신문에도탄박ᄒᆞ엿고일진회에셔도론힉ᄒᆞ더니세도가더욱진ᄒᆞ야련ᄒᆞ야잉시ᄒᆞᆫ다더라

○연로각군쳐도 쥬차경셩일본군ᄉᆞ령관쟝곡쳔ᄃᆡ쟝이원산을유력ᄒᆞᆫ다ᄒᆞ비연로각군에셔밧금쳐도ᄒᆞᄂᆞᆫ즁이더라

참셔국장샹환 외부참서관서샹욱씨ᄂᆞᆫ법부회계국장리지셜씨와샹환되엿더라

○진회용함평북 평안북도관찰ᄉᆞ리용관씨의보고에션쳔졍쥬곽산박쳔ᄉᆞ군에ᄂᆞᆫ진보회가취탐ᄒᆞ기로민군에수동학비도가슈ᄒᆞ고귀셩군에ᄂᆞᆫ동학비도가쳔여명이라ᄒᆞ고가산ᄐᆡ쳔등군에ᄂᆞᆫ회원이괴샬ᄒᆞᆫ자와빗블에빠져죽은자가잇고가산우졍몽ᄒᆞᆫ자도잇ᄂᆞᆫ지라일진회에셔위원을파송ᄒᆞ야됴사ᄒᆞ야히보ᄒᆞ고가ᄒᆞ물이란도무방ᄒᆞᆷ이업스면ᄒᆡ괄찰파디방관은공동지판ᄒᆞ기로결졍ᄒᆞ야묵승을갑고원을셜치ᄒᆞᆫ다고평북관찰부로ᄯᅩ퐁함ᄒᆞ엿더라

○탄신셜눈 쳥국셔태후의탄신이멀지안은고로한졍에셔일간칙ᄉᆞ를보내ᄂᆞᆫᄃᆡ주련여됩쌍을슈를노와문드린지숑ᄒᆞᆫ다더라

○부ᄃᆡ조직 젼란도사ᄂᆞᆫ쟝문환이라ᄒᆞᄂᆞᆫ사ᄅᆞᆷ이방금거샹즁에잇ᄂᆞᆫ고로그아들열세살된귀현이들식여작년거을에셔아을보벼여폭포쳔세위원을귀쟝회에일홈으로도ᄃᆞᆼᄒᆞ엿ᄂᆞᆫᄃᆡ란원의혀이가계가젼세위원이로문현이칭ᄒᆞ고젼인쳐예도식이조샹고ᄒᆞᆫᄃᆡ동신원에셔아들의범숀을ᄒᆞᆫᄃᆡ신ᄒᆞ야고아방이ᄃᆡ힝ᄒᆞᄂᆞᆫ례ᄃᆡ가이ᄃᆡ잇스리오ᄒᆞ고시비ᄅᆞᆯᄒᆞ라더라

○평쟝군모집 일진회에셔무슴변비포ᄅᆞᆯ조직ᄒᆞᄂᆞᆫ지졍부에셔ᄂᆞᆫ금지ᄒᆞᆫ다ᄒᆞ며도회원즁에문필을잘ᄒᆞᄂᆞᆫ사ᄅᆞᆷ을연일취지ᄒᆞ엿고모쳐에셔ᄂᆞᆫ일진회를타파ᄒᆞ기위ᄒᆞ야오강에셔평쟝군즁에션슈자ᄅᆞᆯ모집ᄒᆞᄂᆞᆫ즁이더라

○회원환향 ᄎᆔ힝의무뢰비등이일진회의셩명만롱문으로듯고소ᄅᆞᆯ괄며ᄉᆞᆺ츌ᄒᆞ야란비ᄂᆡ멋빅탕식관비ᄒᆞ야샹경ᄒᆞ엿더니병탁이겁흐가업고며편냥이되며힝망ᄒᆞᆫ경갈ᄒᆞᆫ지라세부등이ᄒᆞ야면도강동이라ᄃᆞᆫ가ᄂᆞᆫᄃᆡᄎᆞ소위무방이들써셔리ᄃᆞᆯ가리우고에풍샹오로환향ᄒᆞ며버러들가샹ᄃᆡ라

○셔하이인 별도원괴ᄉᆞ송진욱씨가ᄂᆡ부참셔관으로젼임ᄒᆞ엿ᄂᆞᆫᄃᆡ그ᄃᆡ에두사ᄅᆞᆷ을셔하ᄒᆞ엿ᄂᆞᆫ지라별도원에셔궁ᄂᆡ부에보고ᄒᆞ야귀ᄉᆞ일파들ᄃᆡ즁치ᄒᆞᆯ수로ᄃᆡ츌ᄒᆞ엿더라

○조칙졍하 모ᄃᆡ관이운동ᄒᆞ야일진회를도륙ᄒᆞ자ᄒᆞ야조칙을강박ᄒᆞ더니 ᄃᆡ황뎨폐하셰셔졔ᄌᆞ등상ᄒᆞᆷ과곳치ᄂᆡ이사명ᄒᆞ사히조칙을환졍ᄒᆞ엽시고일작에츙담ᄒᆞ신 조칙을다시나리옵셧다더라

○랑원기졍 별도원은등신원으로부속ᄒᆞ야한국을셜ᄒᆞ고ᄂᆡ쟝원은혁파ᄒᆞ야ᄉᆞ로긔졍ᄒᆞᆫ다ᄒᆞ더라

○비샹금호소 등신원쥬ᄉᆞ리졔구씨가면쟝목됴사ᄎᆞ로평남파강원도간으로보ᄂᆡ가셔모군멋십명을평숄ᄒᆞ고ᄂᆞᆫᄂᆡ다가민간에무숨작경이되엿던지모군이명이빈셩의게탈샹ᄒᆞᆷ이되엿ᄂᆞᆫ지라모군의차가등신원에호소ᄒᆞ기ᄅᆞᆯ비샹금을ᄃᆞᆯ나고ᄒᆞ엿다더라

뎐보

시월삼일발경셩군ᄉᆞ령부챵뎐

○로용쌍쌍탄 아국이금번젼쟁에쌍쌍탄을쓴으로만쥬군총ᄉᆞ령부에셔히쌍쌍탄의모본을그린셔일본동경비ᄇᆞᆫ소에숑교ᄒᆞ엿ᄂᆞᆫᄃᆡ됴평부근에잇ᄂᆞᆫ일본병의샹ᄒᆞᆫ모양이총탄환에샹ᄒᆞᆫ것파판이ᄒᆞ야샹처가흉ᄒᆞᆫ지흉혹두커ᄅᆞᆯ계어셔쌧엇다ᄒᆞ엿더라

동이십구일ᄉᆞ령부챵뎐

○져겨ᄃᆡ퇴각 졍가산젼쟁의결과가좌곳ᄒᆞ니 졍가셜툰유지ᄒᆞᆫ졍은졍겨보병ᄃᆡ식팔연ᄃᆡ외비귀ᄃᆡ티일본빙렴ᄒᆞᆫ포경ᄒᆞᆫ계뎨향ᄒᆞᄂᆞ일ᄇᆞᆫ빙렬ᄒᆞᆫ포겨를인ᄒᆞ야퀄경진티를빅리고퇴각ᄒᆞ엿ᄂᆞᆫᄃᆡ일본군숀히ᄂᆞᆫ수샹이합빅롤칠십명가량이오이젼투에괴관포이문을어덧고졔의숀히ᄂᆞᆫ아즉ᄌᆞ셰히아지못ᄒᆞᄂᆞ일본군숀히만못지아닌비이라ᄒᆞ더라

동일동젼

○포영근황 포령만구에ᄂᆞᆫ슈뢰뎡수쳑으로ᄒᆞᆼ샹경계ᄒᆞ며ᄯᅩ수다ᄒᆞᆫ슈뢰를부셜ᄒᆞᄂᆞᆫ즁이며[쟝구]젼의츄잉은미일오젼팔시로붓터오후룰시ᄭᆞ지한뎡ᄒᆞ엿스며[보가ᄌᆞㅣ루]ᄂᆞᆫ슈리ᄎᆞ로샹금젼거에잇ᄂᆞᆫ모양이며항구안에ᄂᆞᆫ쟝야면외국비오젹가량이잇스며포영시즁에잇ᄂᆞᆫ일반인민은이느베에일본히군에공격을밧을ᄂᆞᆫ지아지못ᄒᆞᄂᆞᆫ고로인심이흉흉ᄒᆞ며샹황은극히ᄒᆞᆼ왕치못ᄒᆞ야한국에셔힝ᄃᆡ로젼왕ᄒᆞᄂᆞᆫ샹고등은히ᄃᆡ에셔이발ᄒᆞ야항흥과원산방면으로룩속히ᄎᆔ집ᄒᆞᄂᆞᆫ즁이라ᄒᆞ엿더라

외보

○두만셩진슈비병 로병은두만강에셔셩진부근에ᄂᆡ로기셔빈지각ᄃᆡ뎜에ᄂᆞᆫ슈비병을약간식치ᄒᆞ엿다더라

관보

군부관제 속

뎨십이됴 국무국보병과쟝은보병과부령으로보직ᄒᆞ고과원샹인은보병과참령졍부위로보직홈이라

뎨십삼됴 보병과에ᄂᆞᆫ수무를좌ᄀᆞᆺ치쥬쟝홈이라

일은 각병과쟝교보츙에관ᄒᆞᆫ수항

이ᄂᆞᆫ 병역소집히병에관ᄒᆞᆫ수항

삼은 각병과각부즁ᄉᆞ관이하보츙규졍에관ᄒᆞᆫ수항

ᄉᆞᄂᆞᆫ 헌병에비병과밋후비병군인에관ᄒᆞᆫ수항

오ᄂᆞᆫ 헌병보병군악ᄃᆡ의하ᄉᆞ이하보츙에관ᄒᆞᆫ수항

륙은 기타헌병보병과밋군악ᄃᆡ에관ᄒᆞᆫ수항

뎨십ᄉᆞ됴 군무국긔병과쟝은긔병과부령으로보직ᄒᆞ고과원이인은긔병과참령졍부위와밋치즁병과참령졍부위와통군슈의로보직홈이라

뎨십오됴 긔병과에ᄂᆞᆫ수무를좌ᄀᆞᆺ치쥬쟝홈이라

일은 군마의공급및양쉬싱육셩징발과밋보양에관ᄒᆞᆫ수항

이ᄂᆞᆫ 슈의와쟝됴와밋뎨텰에관ᄒᆞᆫ수항

삼은 슈의부와교육과밋인원의보츙과군계과마병과뎨텰공쟝이하보츙에관ᄒᆞᆫ수항

ᄉᆞᄂᆞᆫ 슈의학교와밋군마보츙과군마위싱회의에관ᄒᆞᆫ수항

오ᄂᆞᆫ 긔병치즁병하ᄉᆞ이하보츙에관ᄒᆞᆫ수항

륙은 기타긔병치즁병과밋슈의에관ᄒᆞᆫ수항

뎨십륙됴 군무국포병과쟝은포병과부령으로보직ᄒᆞ고과원이인은포병과참령졍부위로보직홈이라

뎨십칠됴 포병과에ᄂᆞᆫ수무를좌ᄀᆞᆺ치쥬쟝홈이라

일은 병긔탄약과밋긔구지료에관ᄒᆞᆫ수항

이ᄂᆞᆫ 요쇄(포병에관ᄒᆞᆫ수항을졔ᄒᆞ고)에관ᄒᆞᆫ수항

삼은 군긔창에관ᄒᆞᆫ수항

ᄉᆞᄂᆞᆫ 포병과하ᄉᆞ이하보츙에관ᄒᆞᆫ수항

오ᄂᆞᆫ 기타포병에관ᄒᆞᆫ수항

광고

TELEGRAMS.

Rome, Sept. 23.

Vesuvius is again in eruption to-day in an extraordinary degree. Deep explosions occurred, followed by clouds of volcanic dust and torrents of lava, which poured down the mountain side, the walls of the crater collapsed, and it is feared that the rupture of the great cone will follow. The inhabitants in the immediate vicinity of the volcano are fleeing from their houses.

Naples, Sept. 23.

Earthquakes, loud rumblings and increasingly magnificent eruption from Vesuvius to night gave warning of another terrible outbreak from the historic volcano. The whole city is alarmed, and hundreds of fugitives from Castellamare fled to the shore of the bay late this evening. Castellamare is on the site of Stabiae, which was destroyed 2,000 years ago, with Pompeii and Herculaneum. The people of other towns and villages about the volcano, except those bordering on Monte Somma, north of both craters, are preparing for hasty flight.

It is feared a catastrophe such as that of the first century is imminent. Tourists, although spell-bound for hours by the gorgeous sight, to-night crowded trains to other points, many of them leaving their baggage to be forwarded by the hotel-keeperss. It is recognized that little is lacking to cause a panic.

Giant puffs of glowing ashes and sparks to-night rose from the present vent to the height of 700 feet, and the crust around the crater broke away. The pine-tree cloud hovering over the volcano was larger than at any time in recent decades. An enormous stream of lava poured from the modern crater, overflowing the southern and southwestern slopes. Admiring, but awestruck thousands from this city watched the eruption. Travel on the Funicular Railway was suspended, but hundreds walked along the bay road toward the west slope, although there was danger from the rain of hot mud, caused by the mixing of the steam and dust above them.

Berlin, Oct. 24th.

The "Russ" has published a statement of opinion by Captain Jakobleff, late of the Russian warship "Petropavlovsk," to the effect that the Baltic Squadron will require three months for the voyage to the Far East. As the vessels must pass the Suez Canal one by one, long delay will thus be caused. The Squadron will also have to enter some neutral ports, being unable to coal in the open sea.—Asahi.

Tokyo, Oct. 31st.

On the night of the 28th, the enemy made an attack on Waitusan. On the 30th at 3 A. M. this was renewed with the assistance of one battalion of infantry, but it was again repulsed.

At about 11 P. M. on the 28th, the enemy's troops commenced an attack on our positions on rising ground at Santaokangtze but this was repulsed. At 2 P. M. the next day, reinforced by artillery, the enemy attacked us in the direction of Behtaitze, their cavalry harassing us, but we maintained our ground and repulsed the attack At 3 A. M. on the 29th, one of our detachments advanced and occupied the village of Bowsin, setting fire to the village, which concealed Russian troops. These troops consisted of a small detachment of the enemy, which had been sent out to harass our advance guard.

Berlin, Oct. 26.

A Havas telegram from Madrid says the Spanish Government will not prevent the Baltic Fleet obtaining provisions at Vigo.

Berlin, Oct. 26.

The Dutch troops have conquered the chief Batoebatoe in Sumatra.

Berlin, Oct. 24.

The German Wharf Company at Kiel contradicts the statement that the Company has been secretly sending submarine torpedo boats to the Baltic Squadron.—"Asahi."

Berlin, Oct. 24.

The Supreme Prize Court at St. Petersburg has countermanded the judgment given by the Prize Court at Vladivostock in connection with the British steamer Allantion. The vessel's cargo is to be at once given up.—"Asahs."

Berlin, Oct. 24.

It is reported from St. Petersburg that a shipbuilding yard will be established there with a capital of 10,000,000 roubles.—"Asahi.

Berlin, October 25th.

General Prince Fushimi will arrive at San Francisco on November 11. It is believed in Europe that his object in going to America is to stimulate American sympathy for Japan.—Mainichi.

Berlin, Oct. 26th.

Another batch of 830 Japanese refugees from Siberia have left Bremerhaven on board one of the Norddeutscher Lloyd steamers for Japan.

As the steamer left the party gave several hearty "Banzai" for Germany.

A Japanese transport with provisions endeavoured to anchor ahead of one of the Japanese gunboats in Newchwang River on the 7th inst. on a strong tide. In doing so the anchor dragged and caught the gunboat's cable, the ship herself going broadside on to the bow of the man-of-war. She bumped several times, but all efforts to separate were futile until the gunboat slipped her cable. In the meantime both vessels were driven up river by a fine current flood and endangered another gunboat immediately astern. The latter saved another collision by slipping her cable likewise. The transport had by this time got clear, but her propeller got fastened to the gunboat's discarded chain, and in this manner she was held stern against the stream. Her own anchor was down and she was therefore moored, fore and aft. She was sinking rapidly and the efforts of tugs could not move her. She was abandoned and two hours after the collision went down and settled on an even keel. The masts are showing ten feet above high water. She was a wooden vessel of seven hundred and fifty tons register. The occurrence happened opposite the Customs house in full view of the whole population. Nothing of consequence was saved.

Commenting on the Progressive party's manifesto concerning Korea, the "Kokumin" makes out that in spirit and principle the party has nothing to object to in the terms of the Japan-Korea Agreement, but that it does not find quite to its mind the manner and means wherewith our Government proposes to carry out their Korean policy as mapped out in those agreements. The journal would point out that the act of supplying Korea with financial and diplomatic advisers forms only a part of that policy and not the policy itself. The Progressives seem to desire the appointment by Japan of a Lord Cromer for Korea; but the "Kokumin" thinks that the provisions of the agreement and the geographical positions of the two countries make Japan more advantageously situated toward her protectorate, which Korea is for all practical purposes, than England is toward Egypt, and does not necessitate such an appointment; for our Government can with great facility excercise direct control over the politics, internal and foreign, of the peninsular state.—Japan Times.

The Home office have again issued instructions for the suppression of all public societies.

The repairs on the Seoul Gensan road are proceeding actively in view of the forthcoming visit of General Hasegawa to Gensan.

It is reported that extensive trials with motor-cars, for the transport of light objects in Manchuria, will shortly be carried out by the Japanese.

The Minister of Foreign Affaies is another recipient of the attacks of the Il Chin Hoi party, but wisely treats them with contempt and conducts his office in the usual manner.

Mr. Sin-Ki-Son, Vice President of State, recently announced his intentions of resigning, but after seeking the advice of a certain Foreign Minister has decided to remain in office. His original intentions were inspired by his repugnance for the Il Chin Hoi society.

The Government have recently found the unwelcouls attentions of the It Chin Hoi so annoying that they have agreed to reward anyone who can desperse this society, with the post of Chief-of-Police. No applicants so far have been registered.

The Foreign Office has informed the Japanese Legation that the magistrate of Changwou has not interfered with the railway construction. He merely asked the railroad authorities to select some other route to Masampho as the projected line runs too close to some ancient and revered temples.

It is reported that F. Tomohiro, a farmer, who had placed an obstacle on the Sanyo Railway, Japan, with the purpose of damaging a train was sentenced on Oct. 24th in the Yamaguchi District Court to six years' minor confinement. This is a great contrast to the recent shooting of three Koreans for an offence of, apparently, lesser gravity.

It appears that Japan's financiers are contemplating the possibility of raising a new loan upon the security of railways. With this object it is proposed that the state acquire all private railways so that the system could be hypothecated as a whole. It is estimated that the total revenue would be about twenty-five million yen, affording security for a loan of three hundred million. This sum will not carry Japan very far and if the war is to continue much longer it is hard to see what further security will be forthcoming.

Accordit to the latest returns made by the authorities, the amount of Japanese war notes issued has reached the great total of over Y20,000,000. Occasional demands are made for the conversion of the notes into silver or gold, and it is said the army treasury in Manchuria is experiencing some dfficulty in safeguarding the gold reserve for this purpose of exchange. These two items of information are somewhat contradictory. If the notes form so favourite a medium of exchange, how comes it that the gold carried by the army is in danger of depletion?

A PROTEST FROM THE U. S. MINISTER.

The Jiji's Seoul correspondent states that Mr. Allen, U.S. Minister to Korea, has filed a protest with the Korean Government in connection with the permission recently granted by the Korean authorities to a Japanese subject named Hayakawa to construct a system of water works within the precincts of the Korean Palace. The U.S. Minister states that the monopoly of constructing the water works in Seoul had been previously granted to the American firm of Messrs. Collbran and Bostwick, who will begin the work early next year. The protest seemst to be a reasonable one.— Japan Times.

The Korea Daily News.

Issued at 5 P. M. daily except Sundays.

Rate of Subscription :—

Per Year,	Yen 25.
Per Quarter,	Yen 7.
Per Month,	Yen 2.50.

Postage in Korea not charged extra.
Postage abroad charged extra.

Advertisements, 50 sen per day for 1 inch or less.
5 yen per month per inch.
50 yen per year per inch.

All communications to
E. T. BETHELL,
Editor and Publisher,
Pak-tong, Seoul

JAPAN'S POLICY IN KOREA.

In the "Japan Mail" there appears an article on Korea the sting of which lies in its tail.

After commenting upon the advocacy by the progressist party of a more vigourous Japanese policy in Korea, the "Japan Mail" goes on to say.

"One of the chief objections advanced by the Progressist leaders to the Government's lately concluded convention is that while it pledges the Koreans to accept the advice of the financial and diplomatic advisers furnished by Japan, it provides no remedy for the contingency of the Korean Authorities neglecting to follow such advice. In fact, these politicians appear to think that in practice the convention can be rendered abortive should the Koreans be so mined. That is a very natural objection for practical men to advance, but we do not know that any treaty of amity ever included penalties of the nature contemplated by the Progressists, and we therefore conclude that they object to the new convention *in toto*, and would fain see it replaced by a system virtually transferring the control of Korean affairs to Japanese hands just as the control of Egyptian affairs is in British hands. Japan, however, is greatly hampered in this matter. She is not by any means as free an agent as even England was in the case of Egypt, for while England had to answer to only one Power. or two at most, Japan has to answer to the whole world. She stands before the nations as the guarantor of Korea's independence, and if she adopt at this moment of belligerent victory any measures calculated to render her little neighbour's independence illusory, she will see a vehement renewal of the Yellow-Peril outcry, and a renewal on a scale such as has not previously been witnessed. It is unfortunate for Japan that she has to play to the most critical gallery which ever over-looked the doings of a nation, but such is certainly the fact. The great bulk of public opinion in continental Europe is hostile to her cause, and even her staunch friend, the United States, would be at once estranged if she displayed any clear evidence of aggressive design in Korea. Russia, in deed, may openly violate her pledges about Manchuria, and may persist in a military occupation of the three provinces without adding much to the distrust with which her Asiatic policy is already regarded. But Japan is required to live up to a different standard, and while not pretending to assert the justice of such differentiation, we do distinctly affirm that her wisest course is to recognise and bow to the necessity. A halting and vexatiously inefficient programme may thus be imposed upon her in her dealings with Korea, but it will be better for her in the long run to be able to marshal such a catalogue of failures as will convince the world than to take the law into her own hands at once at the cost of Occidental confidence."

The last sentence is the one to which we desire to draw attention. It will be seen that in effect the "Japan Mail" says the failure of Korea to properly govern and administer her own country will prove a useful argument in favour of Japan's ultimate annexation of this country.

The "Japan Mail" is a semi-official Japanese organ, or it is at any rate inspired by the government so we are disposed to regard its statements as representative of the views of the Government in Tokyo. We are therefore to conclude that Japan's present policy in Korea, far from being of the benevolent character promised in the protocol which was signed by the two powers at the beginning of the war is not only one of opposition to all reform but encourages retrogression.

This is an extremly gloomy prospect for Korea. Japanese subjects and servants of Japan have been forced upon her in the character of advisers and yet if the "Japan Mail's," statement be correct, the advice of these people will only be given with the object of making Korean affairs, internal and international, more chaotic than ever.

The redeeming feature of the whole situation is that Korea has not, until now pledged herself to act upon the suggestions of these advisers, and it is now probable that she never will.

HOW MODERN FORTS ARE BUILT.

(LOUIS ZERLIN IN "ILLUSTRATION.")

The art of fortification has undergone radical transformations in the last twenty years. In 1887, an invention came into existence which completely overthrew all former ideas, it being discovered during this year that it was possible to charge artillery projectiles with powerful explosives; for example, with from ten to sixty pounds of gun cotton or melinite. In face of this new projectile none of the then existing fortifications could stand even a short siege. In all countries numerous experiments were made, the results being terrifying and at the same time so contradictory that it was decided in France to make an actual test. Instead of artificial targets it was decided to take a real fort, that of Malmaison, near Laon, and study the effects produced with the new projectiles. The new projectiles easily passed through twelve to eighteen feet of earth, then burst and threw the earth in the air with a force which had never been known before that day, cutting great ditches in the ground of from thirty to one hundred and fifty square feet in extent. With a few blows the enormous parapets of earth were transformed into a formless mass which was utterly useless, merely cutting or twisting the separate bars without damage to the rest of the obstacle. The nets of wire were only twisted the more, thus making the passage more and more difficult.

Here, then, was a real revolution. All that existed in France and other countries was worthless, and it was necssary to change everything. It was demonstrated that the defense artillery could no longer remain as formerly, placed in forts which are visible from a distance, and in consequence of this it was decided to place the forces on the exterior of the fortifications, in so-called annex batteries. These batteries were dug in the ground without any relief and were consequently, impossible to see from a distance, being constructed as a rule only at the time of need, so that their exact location should not be known to the enemy. In these batteries the greater portion of the high-power weapons are placed. Thus a portion of the defenders evacuate the forts and distribute themselves among a certain number of exterior works, occupying successive lines of defense which are arranged so as to retard the first operations of the siege. The enemy not knowing the position of these outer works, can not destroy them, as would have been the case formerly.

Fortifications are thus now reduced to the simple rôle of points of support to the principal line of resistance, the only guns placed in the forts being certain pieces of great and rapid-fire guns for close work. The rest of the defense artillery must be rendered invulnerable, while at the same time the positions which are occupied by the troops in the fort must be completely protected against the effects of explosin. The solution of this difficulty was by means of cupolas composed of iron plate or concrete, the cupolas under which the artillery of modern forts is protected being caps or mushrooms of sepecial steel from six to fifteen feet in diameter and of sufficient thickness to resist the largest projectiles. They are placed for the most part in wells of concrete or of steel.

The two cupolas most in use are the turning and the disappearing. The first of these emerges above the concrete in a very convex form, the cannon having their muzzles fitted into narrow openings. These cupolas may be rotated so that the openings—the only vulnerable points—are difficult to reach. This is the system which up to recent times was almost exclusively adopted abroad in Germany, Belgium, Roumania, Switzerland, etc., but it was afterwards recognized that the French system was the best, and that is the one most used at present. The French models are those of the Galopin disappearing system. In this case we have a great cylinder placed in a well of concrete, the cylinder being pierced with two holes for the mouths of the cannon, which in nearly every case are in couples. The base of this cylinder is articulated to one of the extremities of two strong levers, which end in immense masses of iron, the latter being designed to equilibrate the whole of the turret. It is thus easy to see how it is possible at the moment of firing to raise the turret and to lower it immediately the explosion occurs. The turret is capped with steel which is projectile-proof, the cap being very flat, so that both impact and visibility are reduced to a minimum. The cylindrical portion of the turret—the only vulnerable part—is only exposed to a height of thirty to forty centimeters and during the two or three seconds which are necessary for the ascent and descent.

This is not all that is necessary, however, for one must see and observe. For this purpose at a distance from the turret there is constructed an armored post, a little steel cylinder provided with loopholes and surrounded with concrete, where the observer—the commanding officer—is practically invulnerable, direction of the movements in the fort being obtained by means of telephone, Sometimes these posts are provided with electric projectiles. The Germans have designed and constructed in large quantities small mobile cupolas for exterior operations, these cupolas being armored boxes provided with a small rapid-fire cannon. They are also provided with detachable wheels and are easily moved from place to place.

Of all the materials for the construction of forts the only one that resists the effects of modern artillery is concrete. When it is employed with a thickness of about eight feet the concret presents a curious phenomenon which constitutes the whole of its value; that is, it acts under the blows of projectiles in the same way as a thick, malleable mass, incompressible, would act under the effect of repeated pressure which are insufficient to penetrate it. Projectiles do not produce cracks and holes as in masonary, but a simple compression. The second blow, which is given near by, does not add its effect to the first, but fills to an extent the first hole because of the lateral pressure produced. For certain purposes a still greater resistance is obtained by means of concrete through which is passed bars of soft iron.

In the same manner that the forts themselves have changed, so the obstacles surrounding them have been completely transformed. We no longer observe the immense trenches between the walls as is still to be seen in the old walls of Paris, but on the other hand these objects are replaced by grill-work and nets of iron wire. The bars of the grill-work solidly placed in a foundation of concrete are often topped by lances and sharp points, which render their passage very difficult. The wire is twisted in every direction through iron pegs separated about three feet from each other, these pegs themselves being held in place by blocks of masonry.

The Korea Daily News.

VOL. I, TUESDAY, NOVEMBER 1, 1904. No. 90

HONGKONG & SHANGHAI BANKING CORPORATION.

Paid-up Capital.... .... $10,000,000
Reserve Fund:—Sterling Reserve... 10,000,000
Silver Reserve..... 7,000,000

27,000,000
Reserve Liability of Proprietors... 10,000,000

HEAD OFFICE, HONGKONG.

London Bankers, London and County Banking Company Limited
Branches and Agencies,
London.

Amoy,	Hankow	Penang,
Bangkok,	Hiogo,	Rangoon,
Batavia,	Iloilo,	Saigon,
Bombay,	Lyons,	San Francisco,
Calcutta,	Manila,	Singapore,
Colombo,	Nagasaki,	Sourabaya,
Foochow,	New York,	Tientsin,
Hamburg,	Peking,	Yokohama,

Credits granted on approved Securities, and every description of Banking and Exchange business transacted.

Drafts granted on London and the chief Commercial places in Europe, India, Australia, America, China and Japan.

HOLME RINGER & Co., AGENTS,
CHEMULPO.

ON CHEONG & CO.,
SEOUL.
GENERAL STORE KEEPERS.
Imported provisions, Cooking Utensils Crockery, etc.
FRESH BREAD DAILY.

MITSU BISHI DOCKYARD & ENGINE WORKS,
NAGASAKI.

CODE WORD, "DOCK."

A. 1, A. B. C., and Engineering Codes used.

DOCK No. 1 (at Tategami).

Extreme Length.............. 523 feet
Length on blocks .... 513 ,,
Width of Entrance on Top...... 89 ,,
,, ,, Bottom.... 77 ,,
Water on Blocks at Spring Tide 26½ ,,

DOCK No. 2 (Mukaijima).

Extreme Length.............. 371 feet
Length on Blocks............. 360 ,,
Width of Entrance on Top...... 66 ,,
,, ,, Bottom 53 ,,
Water on Blocks at Spring Tide 22 ,,

PATENT SLIP (at Kosuge).

Can take vessels up to 1,000 tons gross.

THE WORKS are well equipped with the LATEST IMPROVEMENTS, and can execute any kind of work in SHIPBUILDING and MARINE ENGINEERING, as well as in REPAIRING of SHIPS.

The COMPANY'S new powerful steamer OURA-MARU (712 tons, 700 I.H.P.), specially built for SALVAGE PURPOSES, and equipped with necessary gear, is always READY at SHORT NOTICE.

CHARTERED BANK OF INDIA AUSTRALIA & CHINA.

INCORPORATED BY ROYAL CHARTER 1853

HEAD OFFICES:—LONDON.

Paid-up Capital £800,000
Reserve Liability of Shareholders 800,000
Reserve Fund 800,000

Drafts granted upon all the principal places in the world and every description of Exchange and banking business transacted.

E. MEYER & Co., Agents,
Chemulpo.

E. MEYER & CO.
Chemulpo.

SOLE AGENTS IN KOREA FOR:
A. T. Morse, Sons & Co's "Fresco" Distemper

In all colours ready for use on walls, Ceilings etc.
and
AVENARIUS CARBOLINEUM

A wood-preserving and antiseptic oil preparation

Against decay, dry-rot, fungus and wood-destroying insects.

A large supply always in Stock.
Prices upon application.

E. MEYER & Co.,
Chemulpo.

THE METHODIST PUBLISHING HOUSE,
Little West Gate, Seoul.

PRINTING, TYPEWRITER PAPER
CARBON PAPER, VISITING CARDS
STATIONERY, BOOK BINDING
BOOK PUBLISHERS
AMERICAN SCHOOL BOOKS
SPENCERIAN COPY BOOKS
PEN CARBON LETTER AND BILL BOOKS

S. A. BECK, Manager.

HOKURKU DOBOKU KAISHA.

Branch office in Chong Doug, Seoul.
Japanese telephone No. 165

CONTRACT DEPARTMENT.

We can contract to build any building or construction.

MERCHANDISE DEPARTMENT.

We can provide any building material. We have just contracted to build the new Belgian Legation.

DAI-ICHI GINKO.
LIMITED.
(Formerly the First National Bank)

ESTABLISHED 1873

INCORPORATED UNDER PRESENT LAW 1896

Capital - - - - - - - - - Yen 5,000,000
Reserve Fund - - - - - 1,500,000

HEAD OFFICE:—TOKIO.

President: Baron SHIBUSAWA.

BRANCHES AND CORRESPONDENTS
In the Principal Cities and Towns of Japan.
Interest Allowed on
Fixed deposits 1 year - - - 6½ per cent
" " 6 months - - - 6 per cent

Special current accounts 1½ sen daily per Y 100
General " " 1 " " " 100

M. TANAKA,
Manager, Chemulpo

HOLME RINGER & Co.
Chemulpo.

General Merchants and Government Contractors.

Agents for the leading
Banks
Steamship Companies
and
Insurance Companies

Importers of Merchandise of every description.

KAMEYA & CO.
GENERAL STOREKEEPERS
Chinkokai - - Seoul
(*Established 1895, Tokyo*)

Confectionery, Hams, Canned Goods, Cutlery, Hirano & Tansan Water. Provisions, Gents, Furnishing goods, Toilet Articles, Travelling Bags, Tobacco, Cigars & Cigarettes Kitchen Utensils. Coffee. Biscuits.

Fresh Goods always kept in Stock.
Prices Moderate
Please come and inspect our goods.

NIPPON YUSEN KAISHA.
JAPANESE MAIL STEAMSHIP CO.
DER MAIL CONTRACT WITH THE IMPERIAL JAPANESE GOVERNMENT.

European Line

Regular Fortnightly Service between Yokohama Kobe, Moji, Shanghai, Hongkong, Singapore, Penang Colombo, Port Said, Marseilles, London and Antwerp

American Line

Regular Fortnightly Service between Hongkong and Seattle, calling at Shanghai, Moji, Kobe, Yokohama and Victoria, B. C.

Australian Line

Regular weekly Service betwen Japan Ports and Australia, callingiat Hongkong and Manila.
(Above Three Lines Suspended until further notice).

Shanghai Line

Weekly Service between Shanghai and Japan Ports

Korea Line

Service Kobe, Moji, Nagasaki, Fusan, Chemupo, Chefoo, Taiku.
S. S. Bahelsberg, 2181 tons.
Service Kobe. Moji, Fusan, Chemulpo, Chinnampo
S. S ARGO, S. S. Ohio.

BORDEN'S CONDENSED MILK CO.
New York, U. S. A.

ALWAYS IN STOCK
Eagle Brand Condensed Milk.
Gold Seal Condensed Milk.
Peerless (Family) Evaporated Cream.
Borden's Malted Milk.

E. MEYER & CO.
Chemulpo, Korea,
Sole Agents

ROYAL INSURANCE COMPANY,
Funds exceed £10,000,000
FIRE
AT CURRENT RATES.
LIFE
REDUCED PREMIUM.
HOLME RINGER & Co.,
Agents, Chemulpo.

HOTEL DU PALAIS
SEOUL.

The only first class Hotel in Seoul Situated in the centre of the city opposite the palace.

Cuisine under the supervision of experienced French Chef.

Well ventilated and furnished throughout.

TARIFF UPON APPLICATION.

L. MARTIN
Proprietor and Manager.

大韓每日申報

대한ᄆᆡ일신보

일쳔구ᄇᆡᆨ사년십일월이일 (슈요일) (뎨구십일호)

본사고ᄇᆡᆨ

이신보는영어와한어로섞어ᄆᆡ일츌판ᄒᆞᆸ

신문가

한장 엽두돈오푼

일삭됴 엽두량닷돈

우표가ᄆᆡ삭닷돈

다맛돈으로밧ᄉᆞᆸ

광고료는

긔한의쟝단과ᄌᆞ힝의다쇼로즁감ᄒᆞ되렴가로밧을터이오며오ᄅᆡ지아녀대한사람마다다이신문을보실터이니광고내시기를원ᄒᆞ시는이들은우리신문샤에와셔면약ᄒᆞ심을희망ᄒᆞᆸ

○발힝소 박동대한ᄆᆡ일신보샤법어학교압헤젼영국인셜필림집자리오

샤쟝 영국인 (비셜)

평양 ᄃᆡ리졈

○평양효동사는권미보씨로우리신문관ᄆᆡ ᄃᆡ리인을뎡ᄒᆞ엿ᄉᆞ오니평양에계신구람코져ᄒᆞ시는쳠군ᄌᆞ는ᄃᆡ리졈에왕림ᄒᆞ와면의ᄒᆞ시ᄋᆞᆸ

사고

○우리대한ᄆᆡ일신보의목뎍은대한의안녕질셔에관ᄒᆞᆫ모든뎨목에ᄃᆡᄒᆞ야는공평ᄒᆞᆫ변론을쥬쟝ᄒᆞᆷ이라우리동신원의담보는신문보시는쳠군ᄌᆞ의게ᄒᆞᆼ샹보도ᄒᆞ리며편지를긔셔ᄒᆞ여주시는이는셩명과반ᄃᆡ를젹어붓치시기를희망ᄒᆞ오니이거슨신문샹에긔ᄌᆡᄒᆞ라는거시아니오다만극히신용ᄒᆞ는즁거를숨고쟈ᄒᆞᆷ이라긔쟈는아모긔셔던지긔ᄌᆡᄒᆞᆷ을되각ᄒᆞ는권리를가졋ᄉᆞ나되갓ᄒᆞᆫ리유를말ᄒᆞᆯ터이오며공즁평화를문란케ᄒᆞ는듯ᄒᆞᆫ긔셔는의례히밧지안켓ᄉᆞᆸ나이다

●본사셜시이ᄅᆡ로신문을ᄆᆡ양우례로분젼ᄒᆞ와례젼부의임의로젼ᄒᆞ듯스로먼곳에는혹늣게젼ᄒᆞ기도ᄒᆞ며혹몃칠거슬ᄒᆞᆫ겁에젼ᄒᆞ기도ᄒᆞ며혹아니젼ᄒᆞ는곳도잇다ᄒᆞ와우리신문을ᄉᆞ랑ᄒᆞ야구람ᄒᆞ시는쳠군ᄌᆞ의게ᄃᆡᄒᆞ야미우미안ᄒᆞᆸ기로지금은분젼인을두고ᄆᆡ일일즉이젼ᄒᆞ며아니젼ᄒᆞ거나늣게거나ᄒᆞᆫ가업도록ᄒᆞ랴ᄒᆞ오니혹아니셩젼ᄒᆞ거나혹늣게젼ᄒᆞ거나ᄒᆞᆫ일이잇스면본샤。통긔ᄒᆞ여쥬심을희망ᄒᆞᆸ

본샤광고

○본샤신문즁에좌긔ᄒᆞᆫ호수를소용ᄒᆞᆯ데가잇셔이에광고ᄒᆞ오니누구시던지그즁에아모호수던지가져오시는ᄃᆡ로ᄆᆡ쟝에ᄇᆡᆨ젼두푼식드리리다

뎨이호 뎨삼호 뎨이십호 뎨ᄉᆞ십이호 뎨ᄉᆞ십삼호 뎨오십삼호 뎨오십ᄉᆞ호와뎨오십오호 뎨륙십이호

뎐보

십월삼십일경셩일본군ᄉᆞ령부착공보

로병격퇴젼황

기일

○이십팔일밤에젹군의쇼부ᄃᆡ는졍두산놉향ᄒᆞ야역격ᄒᆞ엿고삼격퇴ᄒᆞ엿고

기이

이십팔일밤열ᄒᆞᆫ시즘에병력은얼마즘되는지비샹ᄒᆞᆫ젹병이삼도구ᄌᆞ의놉흔곳에셔역격ᄒᆞ엿스나곳격퇴ᄒᆞ엿고또동일오후두시즘에젹군은포병으로써북ᄃᆡ조방면을공격ᄒᆞ고그긔병은졈졈히방면의우리부ᄃᆡ를핍박ᄒᆞ엿스나다격퇴ᄒᆞ엿고

기삼

이십구일오젼세시에우리일부ᄃᆡ는보조에잇는젹군을엄습ᄒᆞ야히촌락을졈령ᄒᆞ고젹병의웅거ᄒᆞ야직히던집들을불을노왓는ᄃᆡ대개이촌락은파아의젼초의즁간에잇셔밤에자로우리젼쵸를쇼요케ᄒᆞ기위ᄒᆞ야젹군의웅거ᄒᆞᆫ디뎜이되엿던비라ᄒᆞ엿더라

잡보

○실비방히 외부에셔일본공관으로함복ᄒᆞ기를창원군슈권익샹이가털도의방히ᄒᆞᆫ일로인ᄒᆞ야쳬임ᄒᆞᆫ가를희망ᄒᆞ는일은사실ᄒᆞᆫ즉히털도션로가향교궁지즁지디에ᄯᅳᆯ어지나가ᄂᆡ교몸이디방관이되여부독불귀털도감무의게향ᄒᆞ야샹량ᄒᆞᆫ에둘너다른길노좃ᄎᆞ션로를문물도모ᄒᆞ는거시실노털도역ᄉᆞ에방히ᄒᆞᆷ이아니니청컨대셔량ᄒᆞ라ᄒᆞ엿더라

○동도월옥 려산군슈박홍리씨보고ᄂᆡ에동학당의김외일과박인근파비공현등을착슈ᄒᆞ엿더니음력구월십륙일에김박량한이옥쇄장이와부동ᄒᆞ야월옥도주ᄒᆞ엿다ᄒᆞ엿더라

○환후평복 황ᄐᆡ조비뎐하환후가쾌연이평복되신고로쳐분ᄂᆡ에직숙ᄒᆞ든거손털파ᄒᆞ고ᄐᆡ의원도뎨됴와경과쇼경이륜회ᄒᆞ여입직ᄒᆞ고칙임관문안은잔일ᄒᆞ여ᄒᆞ라ᄒᆞᆸ셧더라

○어산절ᄎᆞ 황ᄐᆡᄌᆞ비뎐하ᄐᆡ즁에어점점회복ᄒᆞ신고로궁ᄂᆡ부에셔어산절ᄎᆞ를샹고ᄒᆞ는즁이라더라

○참위죠률 원쥬진위ᄃᆡ쇼ᄃᆡ쟝원철희씨가평민을착슈ᄒᆞ고죄안을얽어ᄆᆡ여돈슈십만량을륵탈ᄒᆞ엿더니히평민등이등쇼ᄒᆞ야륙군법원에셔원참위를압샹ᄒᆞ야심문ᄒᆞᆫ즉죵시불복ᄒᆞ는지라원쟝신ᄐᆡ휴씨가특이형구를ᄎᆞ리고문쵸ᄒᆞᆫ즉불하일쟝에ᄌᆞ긔ᄌᆞ복ᄒᆞ미죠률ᄒᆞ야쳐교로션고되다더라

○진회신즁공의 일진회에셔일간긔회ᄒᆞ려ᄒᆞ다가죠칙을봉승ᄒᆞ야아직졍지ᄒᆞ고작일에는ᄉᆞ무소로회농ᄒᆞ야신즁ᄒᆞᆫᄐᆡ도로쟝ᄅᆡ의ᄉᆞ무를샹의ᄒᆞ엿는ᄃᆡ회원ᄇᆡᆨ명이샹이려라

○리용ᄐᆡ씨 ᄂᆡ부대신리용ᄐᆡ씨는자로란희을당ᄒᆞ야졍계의풍파가엇지될넌지동졍을난측ᄒᆞᆫ고로 권ᄂᆡ의장번ᄒᆞ야ᄂᆡ부에도셔물게야잠ᄉᆞ진ᄒᆞ더니근일에는 인견ᄒᆞ심을엇지못ᄒᆞ엿다더라

○영친왕탄일 음력구월이십오일즉리일은영친왕뎐하의탄신일인ᄃᆡ일본원ᄉᆞ에셔일한이합동ᄒᆞ야봉축회를ᄒᆞᆯ터이라더라

○뎐비쳥샹 미국공관에셔외부로죠회ᄒᆞ되화셩돈에잇는귀국공관에뎐비일쳔구ᄇᆡᆨ년붓터이년간에ᄇᆡᆨ보비미보가미국돈으로륙ᄇᆡᆨ십삼불팔십젼이되는ᄃᆡ본국뎐보샤에셔임의만국련합ᄒᆞ며뎐샤로샹보ᄒᆞ엿스니허금액을곳환보ᄒᆞ라ᄒᆞ엿더라

○폭약슈입 일본공관에셔외부로죠회ᄒᆞ기를일본렬도감부의보고를거ᄒᆞᆫ즉텰도소용폭약등물을슈입ᄒᆞ며혹타쳐로슈운ᄒᆞᆯ셰에히관으로셔고시ᄒᆞ기를귀졍부에명즁이업쓰면쥰허치아니ᄒᆞᆫ다ᄒᆞ니히폭약등물이뎍확히텰도소용인즉이젼규칙대로무익히츌입ᄒᆞ기로쥰허지케치말게ᄒᆞᆯᄯᅳᆺ스로히관쟝의게신칙ᄒᆞ라ᄒᆞ엿더라

○령찰뎐보 경샹북도관찰ᄉᆞ가ᄂᆡ부로뎐보ᄒᆞ기를대구명륜당ᄯᅳᆯ가온ᄃᆡ일인이뎐션목ᄒᆞᆫ긔를셰웟스ᄆᆡ극히미안ᄒᆞ오니외부로의죠ᄒᆞ와옴겨세우게ᄒᆞ라ᄒᆞ엿더라

○양무호갑 일본공관에셔외부로죠회ᄒᆞ기를삼졍회ᄉᆞ에셔관군함양무호갑슬두번에논화갑거로입의졍ᄒᆞᆫ약죠가잇는ᄃᆡ뎨일ᄎᆞ에이십만원은수삼삭을연타ᄒᆞ다가이에ᄂᆡ장원관삼갑스로제ᄒᆞ엿고뎨이ᄎᆞ의십칠만오쳔원은안직갑지못ᄒᆞ고본월ᄭᆞ지니르럿는ᄃᆡ그가액파밋리식을불가불관삼갑삼십삼만숨쳔원즁으로셔졔ᄒᆞᆯᄯᅳᆺ으로이에통고ᄒᆞ며히합갑슬지츌ᄒᆞᆯᄯᅳᆺ으로본년도탁지예산에편입ᄒᆞ엿손즉탁지부로셔ᄎᆞ뎨로ᄂᆡ장원에보ᄂᆡ여써히가액을보츙ᄒᆞᆷ이가ᄒᆞ고또히함은현금에우리히군에셔ᄉᆞ용ᄒᆞ는셰금온ᄆᆡ월에숨쳔원식ᄒᆞ야ᄉᆞ월브터본월ᄭᆞ지합이팔기월됴이만ᄉᆞ쳔원을히군성에셔히외샤로보ᄂᆡ여ᄎᆞ지ᄒᆞ엿스미이금액으로써원가액에셔졔ᄒᆞᆯᄯᅳᆺ스로통고ᄒᆞ노라ᄒᆞ엿더라

○호포여흘금 조인군슈가ᄂᆡ부로보고ᄒᆞ기를음력팔월초구일밤에화젹수십명이조인군속쵸농에리도ᄒᆞ야겁략ᄒᆞ며구타ᄒᆞ고이섭호를츙화ᄒᆞ고동월이십일일밤에는회젹수십명이방포ᄒᆞ며츙화ᄒᆞ며긔곡동에돌입ᄒᆞ야십이호를츙화ᄒᆞ엿손즉호포를징츌ᄒᆞᆯ수업고구훌금을넉넉히쥬게ᄒᆞ라ᄒᆞ엿더라

○지휘관군령 함흥관찰ᄉᆞ가일본지휘관의죠회를인ᄒᆞ야ᄂᆡ부에번등ᄒᆞ야보고ᄒᆞ엿는ᄃᆡ함

홍정평영흥과원문천군관니에군령홈이라함흥과위산간의도로와교량을군디가통과흐기용이토록슈셔흐되리실일월간서지에필역흐게흠이가흠

○조의작벌 농상공부에서외부로죠회흐기를뎡쥬군보니에일본인이나라산과ᄉ산을불계흐고관쟝과산쥬의게통긔업시조의로작벌흐다흐니나라산삼림작벌은확실이국법에금지홈이오또ᄉᄉ산으로말흐여도일인이만일소용이잇스면히산본쥬의되흐야매미흔후에작벌홈이가흐거놀현금일인이무론공ᄉ산림흐고조의로작벌홈이심이히탄흘지라일공ᄉ의게죠회흐야엄금흐야민원이업게흐라흐엿더라

관보

데이천구빅칠십일호 광무팔년십월삼십일일

셔임급ᄉ령

○명관제리졍소위원 셩균관장 샹훈 탁지부지무 판리도 의정부비셔관 윤덕영 표훈원참셔관 조병교 외부참셔관원응샹 정삼품 남궁억 리규용 ○명관제 리정소위원 구품 윤돈구 농샹공학교교관 김샹연 의정부쥬ᄉ 최동직 닉부쥬ᄉ 조지봉 탁지부쥬ᄉ 리양샹 군부쥬ᄉ 김종한 법부쥬ᄉ 리원국 농샹공부쥬ᄉ 박희양 이샹십월이십칠일

○명닉장원봉셰위원 마종한 셩남슈 ○의원면본관 셩진감리셔쥬ᄉ 송인회 ○임셩진감리셔쥬ᄉ셔관임관륙등 리용규 ○임참모부편즙관셔관임관륙등 리원익 구픔 김현셕 이샹십월이십팔일

궁뎡록ᄉ

○조왈위균ᄉ입시흐라

샹월이십륙일

군부관제 속

데십팔됴 군무국공병과쟝은공병과부령으로보직흐고과원일인은공병과참령정부위로보직홈이라

데십구됴 공병과에는ᄉ무를좌긋치쥬쟝홈이라

일은 요식[포병에관흔ᄉ항을제흐고]에관흔ᄉ항

이는 운슈교통과밋통신에관흔ᄉ항

삼은 공병과구지료에관흔ᄉ항

ᄉ는 공병과하ᄉ이하보츙에관흔ᄉ항

오는 기타공병에관흔ᄉ항

데이천구빅칠십이호 광무팔년십일월일일화요일

셔임급ᄉ령

○임참모부편즙관 셔관임관오등 륙품 방한붕

구월이십일일

○의원면본관 닉부쥬ᄉ 홍지과

○임닉부쥬ᄉ 셔관임관륙등 김유

○임한셩부쥬ᄉ 셔관임관륙등 리긔하

○임한셩종두ᄉ의ᄉ 셔판임관륙등 경샹남도종두ᄉ무위원 박형리

이샹십월이십일

○히북군교복위원 교육부긔 최병원 륙군괴병정위 신우영

시위대일련대일대대부륙군보병부위 리홍균

시위대일련대데이대대부륙군보병부위 리챵영

친위대일련대데일대대부륙군보병부위 김윤덕

진위대일련대데이대대부륙군보병부위 리의영

친위대일련대데삼대대부륙군보병부위 안쥰호

진위대ᄉ련대데일대대부륙군보병부위 쟝윤규

십월이십칠일

○명궁닉부특진관 셔칙임관이등 비셔원경 민영린

○명비셔원경셔칙임관이등 장례원경박용대

○명쟝례원경 셔칙임관삼등궁닉부특진관 죠병필

○의원면본관 지룡령 고병현

○임지룡령 셔관임관칠등 슉릉참봉 지응현

임슉릉참봉 셔관임관팔등 리희명

○임외부교섭국쟝 셔칙임관ᄉ등 종이품 리샹셜

○명강원도순찰ᄉ 충청도슌찰ᄉ 김셩규

○명츙청도순찰ᄉ 정삼품 리시영

○명중츄원의관 셔칙임관ᄉ등정삼품 민용훈

○히셔리호위디총관ᄉ무 닉부대신륙군부장 리용틱

이샹십월이십구일

○의원면본관 닉장원공업과장 박희방

○명닉장원경 셔칙임관삼등 평리원관ᄉ 리병화

○임닉장원공업과장 셔주임관삼등 례식원참리관 현빅운

○임례식원참리관 셔주임관삼등 례식원쥬ᄉ 교회쥰

○임례식원쥬ᄉ셔관임관륙등 륙품 한병구

이샹십월삼십일

궁뎡록ᄉ

○의정부참정신 긔션 근주흐옵는이다 군부조회를련접흐온즉강원도순찰ᄉ한진창은현금에관방쟝의소임으로현디흐엿고이군제기정흘때를당흐와제반ᄉ무를뎡돈흘이아니오비가히수응흘수업다흐엿ᄉ오미가는일도비록긴급흐되속히오는군무의호번홈도가히싱각지아니치못흘지니갓원도의순찰ᄉ의소임은특이져임흐옵고그뒤에츙쳥도순찰ᄉ김셩규로써이차흐옵고츙쳥도순찰ᄉ뒤에는정삼품리시영으로차하흐와병불일노써나게흐옴이엇더흐올넌지근상 주흐와

광무팔년십월이십구일에봉지의주흐셔되이빅셩의뜻시안정치못흔때를당흐야순찰ᄉ가오히려만히부임치못홈이엇지그긔만흘흔뇨국히히탄흐니일병엄칙흐야시각으로떠나게흐라흐옵시다

논셜

한국에디흔일본졍칙

○일본매일신보론셜을본즉일본이한국에최말샤독흐기위흐야일본진보자들노흐여곰강경흔정칙을힝흐기로흔다흐엿기에좌에번등흐노라

근일에한국정부에셔공회흐야기의흘때에일본으로셔고빙흘지정과외교고문관들노흐여곰함씌참회흐야츙고흐는뒤로시힝흐기로작뎡흐엿다흐되이는다만외양으로만그리홈이요실상속으로는반디흐랴는마음이잇슬거시한국정부에유력자들은타인의권고흐는바를흥샹경솔이녁이여별안잔중간에일을그르치게만들믄무이고질이된지라

이로말매아마흥샹일에완젼이되는자ㅣ업슨즉이는당초에반디흐챠는마음이복중에츙만흔야스ᄉ로소샤남일로다그러흔즉일한량국간에돈목흐게지닉조고약조흐엿는지엇지흐엿는지자세히알수는업스되새로기외에참회흐게흔다흔규측중에조여흔기를만일결안흔바를좃간반디흐는자ㅣ잇스면형벌을당흐기로마련흐야중영영국졍부에셔이급정치관활하듯흐게만드려흔한국정권이일본슈즁에롱락흘는바가되도록흐는거시미오조흘듯흐되이역심히번거로온일인거시영국셔는구라파여러나라중에몃몃강대흔나라에만인허를어더마음되로힝흐엿스되이제일본은이와갓치흐자면不연히세계각국의다허가틀엇어야흘지라

그러흐나또흔츙졀이잇느니이는일찍이과왕한국독립에보증흥주인이되엿스니불가불이제전징승첩흐는긔회에아모조록방침을닉여도아줄것갓흐면잘될일이만흘터이어늘도리여그러치아니흐고미ᄉ에힝흐는일이무숨회롱과갓치흔즉만일분명히한국에디흐야반디를흘서경이면구라파제국에서들도조와아니흘터이요또흔합즁국과갓치더옥친밀이지닉는나라에셔도정령소원흐여갈지니

이는무타ㅣ라아라사에셔는당초브터경륜이만주를점령흐야불미와갓치문둘고차차로병력을베프러아세아주각국의정권을모도샹관흐랴홈이로디일본의목젹인즉이와는특별히다른지라아모조록미ᄉ에정직흐게흐야남의게신이잇도록뵈이고온당히쳐사흐는자리에이한국이스ᄉ로히롭게흐야번거이만달것갓흐며이 는일후셔양각국에디흐야설명흐기가오날놀수죵에잡아너코마음디로힝흐는니버다오히려조흘터이라흐엿는지라

이신문을본즉그야죵귀결은근리흔말인지라과연신문에셜명흔바와갓치온당이만흐게되면엇지맛참닉부합지아니흘리가잇스리요

이매일신문이라는거손일본졍부의긔관이되여디표쟈의의향도라가는디로포달흐는바인즉이에계저홈이실상공보나다름이업는지라

당초일본셔기전흘때에한국으로더브러약조홈은인의흔마음에셔조연히소사남이로디근일에기량흔다자칭흐고흐는일은점점되보만되게흐는도다

신문상에이도록계저홈은과연올흔말이로디실샹힝흐는일은그러치아니흐야지어일본에는하인서지라도한국에디흐야는고문관노릇흘싱각이잇서셔억제와위협으로흐는일이만흔즉실상형편이이왕만도못흐야혼잡홈이비흘디업는지라이모양으로만흘지경이면한국빅셩인들엇지반디흘싱각이업스리요셔로훈고문관들이나조긔들의의견을제출흐야온당히흘것곳흐면한국빅셩들의반디흐는마음은스ᄉ로업서질터이로다

광고

TELEGRAMS.

Tokyo, Nov. 1st.

Oyama reports that about 2,000 of the enemy's cavalry and infantry with 2 guns are staying in the Neighbourhood of Hoi-in Sen (between Antung and Wafangtien). A detachment of our troops came in contact with 10 scouts from this body of the enemy and took one prisoner, wounded 5 and captured 2 rifles.

On the 30th inst. the enemy, comprising one regiment of infantry and 5 or 6 companies of cavalry with 8 guns attacked one of our detachments south of the Hunho and to the west of the Liaoyang-Mukden read. Our detachment however bravely repulsed the attack. Then the enemy, reinforced by one regiment of cavalry with 6 guns advanced again to the attack, but our troops fought bravely and inflicted great casualties on the enemy, who left 13 dead and 16 horses on the field. Our casualties were 10 killed and wounded and 12 horses.

It has been ascertained that this body of the enemy belonged to the Don Cossacks.

Tokyo, Nov. 1st.

Reports from Chefoo, relative to Port Arthur, state that owing to the fierce attack of the Japanese the powder magazine at Kikwansan was set on fire, also the Russian men of war were badly damaged; one of the vessels, engaged in Mine-clearing operations, being sunk. On the same afternoon, the forts at Ullungsan Etze San and Antzesan were silenced, and the Russian positions at Sung Su San and Ullungsan were attacked and carried.

FIRST ATLANTIC TURBINE STEAMER.

A new era in the history of ocean-going steamers says the "Home and Colonial Mail," may be said to have been inaugurated last week with the launch from Messrs. Workman, Clark, & Co's yard, Belfast, of the Allan Line, "Victorian." This is the first Atlantic turbine steamer ever constructed. The "Victorian" was originally designed to be driven by reciprocating engines, but Messrs. Allan decided to have turbines fitted instead. She is by far the largest steamer, as she will be the swiftest, of the Allan fleet, and she is expected to be at once noiseless and steady in the sea-way, even while exerting all her great speed. Her turbines are the largest yet made. The new vessel will be largely an experimental one. The turbines, although an acknowledged success for cross-Channel steamers, have yet to be proved a success for large ocean liners, and the trial trip will be looked forward to with great interest by a large number of shipping men who have been studying this question. An installation of Marconi's wireless telegraphy apparatus has been arranged for, in connection with which a printing press will be set up for the publication of a daily newspaper on board.

THE "SUNGARI."

The "Sungari," which was recently refloated at Chemulpo harbour and brought to Nagasaki, now lies at the Mitsu Bishi Dockyards. She presents quite a battered appearance, owing to the severe damage she sustained. When repairs have been effected she will be despatched by the Government on a certain special mission.

From North Kyengsang province comes the report that the Japanese have erected a telegraph line in that district, part of the time passing through the Confucian temple at Daikun. The Governor of the province is greatly incensed at this violation of the temple's sacred precincts.

The Kyengsang people have petitioned the Government to do away immediately with the Il-chin-hoi.

WHEAT-GROWING IN MANCHURIA.

The American Consul in Newchwang, in a recent report on wheatgrowing and milling in Manchuria states that the value of the exports of food products of the Liau valley alone is over two millions sterling a year. Famines and failures of the crops are unknown, and the production is as regular and constant as that of any place dependent on natural rainfall. The area drained by the Liau is about 62,500 square miles, the greater part of which is composed of level land and rich rolling hills capable of cultivation. The soil is a sandy loam, with a slight mixture of clay; so little gravel is there that the railway finds it difficult to get enough for ballast. "The soil is as easily worked as an ash heap, and produces enoromous crops of beans and millet without apparently diminishing its fertility." The Mongolian section of the valley is at present in its primitive state, and produces nothing but grass for cattle, horses, sheep, and goats. It is owned in large tracts by Mongol princes, and will doubtless very soon come under cultivation, for "it is too near to the great and growing flour market to China to remain idle long." Mr. Miller anticipates that the exportation of wheat from Manchuria to Europe will shortly commence, but he thinks that at the outset it will be from the Sungari rather than the Liau valley. The Sungari valley, in the north, occupies twice the area of the Liau valley, but it has little more high-class agricultural land. The tall millet of the Liau valley is giving place in the Sungari region to wheat, for which it is well adopted. The quanity now produced is about 30 bushels to the acre, but this can be increased by better seed and deeper ploughing. Harbin is the centre of the flour-milling industry in Manchuria; it lies on the banks of the Sungari, with abundant river and rail transport. In 1900 it had not a single flour mill; in October, 1903, when Mr. Miller visited the place, it had eight mills, with a total daily capacity of 3,800 barrels of flour, while two more mills were in process of constuction. The mills are fine structures of brick and stone, with excellent modern machinery from Germany and Austria. One hundred and fifty miles south of Harbin, on the railway, at Kirin and at Mukden modern mills have been erected, so that before the war broke out there were mills producing 5,000 barrels of flour a day. In the adjacent Russian territory, the South Ussuri district, there are 12 steam mills, producing 433,344 barrels a year. The chief disadvantage of all the mills in Manchuria is the price of fuel, wood being used, but it is certain that local coal will soon replace it. The importation of foreign flour to Manchuria and Siberia must soon cease under the stress of the local production, but they will long afford an excellent market for milling machinery and agricultural machinery.

The Chief-of-Police has announced his intention of resigning his post, as he considers himself unable to deal, in the only satisfactory manner, with the scandalous Il Chin Hoi society.

Mr. Yi Yong Tai, the Minister of the Home Office at present goes voluntarily into seclusion in the Palace as he considers his unpopularity in the city not conducive to personal safety.

The Japanese Government has gone to the trouble and expense of wiring the Korean Government that the recently despatched Korean delegates have been received in audience, at Tokyo, by the Emperor of Japan.

Some of the Government officials are said to have asked His Majesty to issue strict orders to disperse the Il-chin-hoi with violence if necessary. His Majesty replied that before resorting to violence he wished to urge, upon the Il-chin-hoi the desirability of their dispersing quietly.

ORANGE BUDS.

An engagement has been announced between Irene, second daughter of Herr and Frau Eckert, and A. Delcoigne of His Belgian Majesty's diplomatic service (at present acting as adviser to the Korean Government). Everybody wishes the newly affianced pair the best of health, wealth and prosperity. Of the prospective bridgeroom we can only say that he is the best of good fellows, and deserves the treasure in store alluded to by the "Frankfurter Zeiturg," as follows.

"While we are discussing the question of ladies in Korea, we should like to firmly assert that the most beautiful lady in Korea is Irene the second daughter of Professor Eckert, of Seoul."

A LITTLE PREVIOUS.

The Russian names of streets in Dalny have been changed by the Japanese in commemoration of their landing after the outbreak of the war. The alteration is described by Tokyo papers as follows: Witte street into Oyama-dori; Alexieff Street into Oku-machi; also there are names of Nogi-machi, Kodama-machi, Fukushima-machi and so forth.

The following is a sample of the nonsense which continually finds its way into some of the Foreign papers in Japan:—A Tokyo paper remarks that the gallantry shown by the Russians originates from their cowardice. The general bravery of the Japanese, it says, often ignores the necessity of defences, in which the enemy exhausts his ways and means.

There are always a few neat things in the "By the Way" column of the "Globe": For instance:—A son of Mr. James Stillman, the New York millionaire, is a porter, and intends learning the railway business from the beginning. We trust he will shrink at nothing, not even at receiving a tip. Relatives are wanted of a Mr. Jones, of Oregon, who has died worth £57,000. There is believed to be a Mr. Jones living somewhere in Wales. Should anyone in this country happen to hear the name, he should communicate with Oregon at once. It was suggested to a Spanish town that it should do something to help the Society for the Prevention of Cruelty to Animals. The authorities, charmed with the idea of being of real assistance to such a deserving cause, organized a monster bull-fight in aid of the Society.

The Korea Daily News.

Issued at 5 P. M. daily except Sundays.

Rate of Subscription:—

Per Year,	Yen 25.
Per Quarter,	Yen 7.
Per Month,	Yen 2.50.

Postage in Korea not charged extra.
Postage abroad charged extra.

Advertisements, 50 sen per day for 1 inch or less. 5 yen per month per inch. 50 yen per year per inch.

All communications to E. T. BETHELL, Editor and Publisher, Pak-tong, Seoul

KOREA AND THE WAR.

The theory, apparently so widely held, that the future of Korea depends entirely upon the results of the present war, is in our opinion fallacious and untenable.

Even in Japan where ultimate victory is looked upon as an assured fact, opinions differ as to the proper course to be pursued with regard to this country. To begin with, when hostilities commenced, the Japanese Government promised Korea her independence and integrity. Next we find the Japanese progressist party clamouring for a policy which would virtually involve the entire administration of Korea by Japan. Finally we find the "Japan Mail" chiding the progressists for their impatience and telling them that if things in Korea are left as they are (i. e. with Japanese nominees as advisers and the country overrun with adventurers of the Nagamori and Komochi type) the country will soon work its own ruin and become involved in such chaos that the whole world would beg Japan to step in and restore order.

These three propositions are of course based upon the assumption that Japan will defeat Russia, and are furthermore dependent upon the other great Powers allowing Japan and Russia between them to decide to whom Korea shall belong. And Japan has not yet beaten Russia and the views of the on-looking Powers with regard to Korea are not yet known.

There are two other contingencies which will affect the destiny of Korea. The first is the defeat of Japan by Russia and the second is what the other Powers will have to say in that event.

So that there is still a chance for Korea, for although Japanese newspapers have now frankly discarded all pretense of any intention of supporting Japan's original promises to Korea, Japan is still a long way from being in a position to enforce her newly-divulged designs.

If Russia wins, the national existence of Korea will be in no danger. We do not think that Russia wants Korea, and even if she did we do not think the other Powers would agree to her taking possession.

Therefore the probability of Korea's losing her independence is remote. Japan's designs are now clear enough, but before she can put them into effect she will have to reckon first with Russia and afterwards with the whole world.

Looking at the situation in this impartial critical light it would seem to be the duty of Korean statesmen to confine their attention to the improvement of Korea's internal economy and refuse to allow themselves to be influenced by *ex-parte* statements as to what will happen when the war is over.

CAPE TO CAIRO RAILWAY.

Rapid progress is now being made, says the "Central News," with the construction of the Cape to Cairo Railway, and the route which the line will traverse towards Khartoum has been tentatively decided upon. At present the line is in progress of construction on the north side of Victoria Falls towards Kalomo, while the work of erecting the huge bridge which will cross the Falls is proceeding from either side. A powerful cable way has been built to carry the necessary material across the river for the bridge and permanent way, while the component parts of engines and rolling-stock are also being conveyed to the north side to help forward the making of the track. The bridge is expected to be completed by the end of this year, and the section to Kalomo—150 miles in length—a few months later.

It is hoped by the time the Kalomo line is finished that arrangements will have been made for extending the railway another 200 miles to the copper district north of the Kafua River, and then the project is to carry the line to Lake Tanganyika. The railway will traverse the north of Eastern Rhodesia to the south end of the lake. It has not yet been decided whether the way or whether the line will follow the eastern shore of the waterway or whether steamers on the lake will be employed to continue the means of communication. The railway, however, will be joined with the Uganda line, and then pushed northwards past Fashoda to Khartoum. Until the country has been thoroughly surveyed, however, it is impossible to estimate the length of time necessary to provide direct overland communication between the Cape and Cairo.

SUBMARINES FOR JAPAN'S NAVY.

New York, Oct. 6.—With the utmost secrecy, five submarine torpedo boats, built at the Fore River Works at Quincy Point, Mass. for the Holland Torpedo Boat Company of this city, and said to have been sold to Japan, were started to-day via the Pennsylvania Railroad on their way across the continent for some Pacific Coast port. The destination, "west of Chicago," was expressed on the way bill which accompanied the most unusual shipment which ever crossed the American continent.

Valued at nearly $4,000,000, the torpedo boats occupied seventeen new steel flat cars and six box cars, the appearance of the entire train being not unlike the caravan of a circus. The boats were shipped in sections, and each car was carefully covered with canvas which concealed the contents, and, extending about the sides of the car, protected the valuble war material beneath from the elements and the gaze of the curious alike.

The middle sections of the boats could not be disguised in this manner, however, and their bulk rose above the sides of the cars in huge proportions.

At the ends of the flat cars wooden braces were fastened, in order that the load would remain rigid under the strain of crossing the continent, and the canvas coverings were tightly battened down with wooden strips. There was not the slightest mark on any car to indicate the contents or destination.

The monthly number of foreign telegrams forwarded by the different telegraph offices in Japan and the charges thereon have, since the outbreak of hostilities, averaged twice as much as in the corresponding period of ordinary years. The increase was especially noticeable in February, when the war broke out, the total figures for the month being 42,000 telegrams representing the sum of 1,031,954 yen, showing an increase of 83 per cent, and 168 per cent, respectively compared with the month of 1903. From March to August the number of messages ranged between 35,000 and 43,000, and there was a slight decrease in the amount of fees.

THE FORTHCOMING BUDGET.

The "Nichi Nichi" learns that the next year's budget for ordinary accounts has already been prepared by the authorities, but that the estimates for the war expenditure have not yet been decided upon. Our contemporary states that though no plan of war financing has yet been definitely fixed upon, recourse will necessarily be had mostly to loans and partly to increased taxation. Roughly estimated, however, the monthly war expenditure will probably be fixed at 50 million yen. In this connection the "Nichi Nichi" further understands that the war disbursement will form a separate account, being regarded as a single item from the commencement of the present hostilities, irrespective of fiscal years. The war estimates now under investigation will, therefore, be submitted to the next session of the Diet as a supplement to the extraordinary war expenditure approved at the preceding session.

The Japanese military authorities have ordered the governor of Hamhung to see that the road between Gensan and that city is repaired before the end of this month.

The Magistrate of Yeusan reports that he had imprisoned three Tonghaks, but one morning they mysteriously disappeared and have not since been heard of. "Neither has the jailor," he adds naively.

A despatch from the U. S. Minister to the Foreign office convey a complaint that the Korean Legation at Washington is backward in paying its telegraphic bills. The sum of 663 gold dollars, the amount for telegrams despatched during 1901 and 1902 remains unpaid.

The Japanese Minister writes to the Foreign Office that he is in receipt of a complaint from the Japanese railway Bureau, that the Custom Office has refused to pass dynamite without a distinct proof that it is for use on the railway. He guarantees that the dynamite is for this purpose and instructs the Foreign Office to pass it immediately as also future consignments.

A Yingkow despatch dated the 22nd inst. received by the "Tokyo Asahi," states that the Russians at Mukden have requisitioned 1,000 wagons, with the apparent intention of withdrawing from that city. It is further reported that the Russians have obtained some 2,000 wagons through the instrumentality of the Chinese Governor-General there, who was originally asked to furnish as many as 5,000. On the 20th inst., the transportation of munitions and stores northward was commenced.

The Agricultural Department has very serious complaints to make of the Japanese habit of appropriating timber from here, there and everywhere irrespective of ownership, Government or otherwise. In the Djung-chu district, they have cut down innumerable trees on both government and private property, without permission from the former or payment to the latter. The people bitterly complain of the loss of their timber, and the government are urged to take strict measures to stop this misappropriation of property.

Municipal trading appears to be becoming quite popular in England. The latest example comes from Huddersfield, where the Corporation have recently netted a year's profit of £700 by carrying parcels on the electric tramcars. Tradesmen on the routes are appointed agents for the reception of parcels, and appear to be well satisfied with arrangements. The scheme embraces quite a novel feature in the form of dinner-carrying. For threepence a week the cars carry workmen's dinners to fixed points, where the recipients await them. "Taking in father's dinner" is no longer an excuse for absence from school, for the scheme is immensely popular with the men and their wives.

The Korea Daily News.

VOL. I, WEDNESDAY, NOVEMBER 2, 1904. No. 91

大韓每日申報
대한매일신보

(뎨구십이호) (목요일) 일쳔구빅사년십일월ᄉᆞ일

본샤고ᄇᆡᆨ

이신보는영어와한어로셰가ᄆᆡ
일츌판ᄒᆞ옵

신문가

한쟝 엽두돈오푼
일삭표 엽두량엿돈
우표가ᄅᆡ 삭닷돈
다맛돈으로밧솜

광고료는

긔한의쟝단과ᄌᆞ힝의다쇼로종
갑ᄒᆞᆯ터ᄒᆞᆫ가로밧을터이오며오
렌져ᄒᆞ녀대한사람마다다이신
문을보실터이니광고ᄒᆞ시기를
원ᄒᆞ시는이들은우리신문사에
와서면약ᄒᆞ심을희망ᄒᆞ옵

○발힝소 박동대한ᄆᆡ일신보
사발ᄒᆡᆼ학교압희젼영국인셜필
림졍자리오
사쟝 영국인 (비셜)

평양 ᄃᆡ리졈

○평양효동사는권미보씨로우
리신문과ᄃᆡ리인을ᄃᆡ졍ᄒᆞ엿
ᄉᆞ오니평양에계신구람코쟈ᄒᆞ
시는 쳠군ᄌᆞ는힝ᄃᆡ리졈에왕
림ᄒᆞ와면의ᄒᆞ시옵

사고

○우리대한ᄆᆡ일신보의목뎍은
대한의인민권셰에관ᄒᆞᆫ모든대
목에ᄃᆡᄒᆞ야는공평ᄒᆞᆫ번론을주
쟝홈이라우리등신원의ᄃᆡᆷ보는
신문보시는쳠군ᄌᆞ의게ᄒᆞᆼ상보
도ᄒᆞ리며편지로긔서ᄒᆞ며주시
는이는셩명과번디를젹어붓치
시기를희망ᄒᆞ오니이거슨신문
샹에긔재ᄒᆞ라는거시아니오다
만극히신용ᄒᆞ는증거를숨고쟈
홈이라긔쟈는아모긔서던지긔
재홈을되갸ᄒᆞ는권리를가졋스
나긔재가ᄒᆞ는리유를말홀터이오
며공증평회를문란케ᄒᆞ는듯ᄒᆞᆫ
다긔서는의례히밧지안켓습나이

●본샤셜시이러로신문을ᄆᆡ양
우레로불젼ᄒᆞ와레젼부의임의
로젼ᄒᆞᆫ듯스로면곳에는혹듯게
젼ᄒᆞ기도ᄒᆞ며혹면쳘거슨혼졉
에젼ᄒᆞ기도ᄒᆞ며혹아니젼ᄒᆞ는
곳도잇다ᄒᆞ오니우리신문을ᄉᆞ랑
ᄒᆞ시는 쳠군ᄌᆞ의외ᄉᆞ랑ᄒᆞ는
ᄃᆡᄒᆞ야구ᄅᆞᆷᄒᆞ시와우미안ᄒᆞ오
은본젼인을두고일일즁이
ᄒᆞ며아니젼ᄒᆞ거나늦게가나ᄒᆞᆫ
가셔도불통ᄒᆞ거나ᄒᆞ는일
젼ᄒᆞ거나늦게젼ᄒᆞ거나ᄒᆞ는일
이잇스면본샤로통긔ᄒᆞ여주심
을희망ᄒᆞ옵

본샤광고

○본샤신문중에뎨긔ᄒᆞᆫ호수를
소용ᄒᆞᆯ터가잇서이에광고ᄒᆞ오
니누구시던지그중에아모호수
던지가져오시는ᄃᆡ로미쟝에빅
젼두푼식드리리다
뎨이호 뎨삼호 뎨이십호
뎨ᄉᆞ십이호 뎨ᄉᆞ십삼호 뎨
ᄉᆞ오십삼호 뎨오십ᄉᆞ호와뎨오
십오호 뎨륙십이호

관보

○조왈대개빅셩은그업을편안
히ᄒᆞ고그산을즐겁게ᄒᆞᆫ후에비롯
어지로나라법을직ᄒᆞ야몸이
위험ᄒᆞᆫ데드러가게ᄒᆞ드리도반
드시즐겨ᄒᆞ지아니ᄒᆞ리니지금
무리로모혀빅셩이반드시다관
교ᄒᆞ고샹업ᄒᆞ야그산을닛지못
ᄒᆞ야랑퍼ᄒᆞ야류리ᄒᆞ야의탁ᄒᆞ
유샹빈가업는자라ᄒᆞ니취즁쟝
홈이잇스면엽이나빅이나응ᄒᆞ
는니져줍죱ᄒᆞ고호미ᄒᆞᆫ자가엇
지왕쟝의잇는죵을알니오그가
ᄎᆔ이긍ᄒᆞᆯ셔릉이라이에거연이
ᄅᆡ평지위로써더ᄒᆞ지못ᄒᆞᆯ지니
덕의를셤오흘거시라그써ᄒᆞᆫ바
든공구ᄒᆞᆫ진티다빅셩의게갓가
온관리가탐학ᄒᆞ고침범ᄒᆞ야그
쳐소를엇지못ᄒᆞ게ᄒᆞ고죽박ᄒᆞ
야션동케믄든ᄃᆡ에셔말미암이
ᄅᆡ목하에무흠홀방도는오직긍
히그션동케ᄒᆞᆫ자를ᄐᆡ거ᄒᆞ고다
셔명빅히효유ᄒᆞ야민심이스스
로가히계졍ᄒᆞ는ᄃᆡ잇는지라므
릇슈령이빅셩의게힘숨케ᄒᆞ며
더우불량ᄒᆞᆫ자를일일사탐ᄒᆞ며
고빈쟝의원억ᄒᆞ여ᄭᅬ지못ᄒᆞᆫ자
도또ᄒᆞᆫ치람ᄒᆞ여일병ᄃᆞ문케ᄒᆞ
코기혹닌민의과창ᄒᆞ여지슈ᄒᆞᆫ
자는일병방셕ᄒᆞ고뭇지말아ᄡᅥ
죠명의ᄌᆞ딜히너여보기를샹ᄒᆞ
는것곳치ᄒᆞ는지구ᄒᆞᆫ뜻슬보히
며샨ᄒᆞ윈만ᄒᆞ야회지키아니ᄒᆞ
고향음으로츌도ᄒᆞ야곰비셔로
션동ᄒᆞ는자잇스면이는ᄑᆡ민이
ᄀᆡᆨ죄가샤ᄒᆞ지못ᄒᆞᆯ티잇스니가
희용티치못ᄒᆞᆯ지니부로ᄒᆞ여금
금믈울지ᄋᆡ도관찰ᄉᆞ의게신
칙ᄒᆞ야도부ᄒᆞ거든죽시렴ᄂᆞᆫ에
ᄒᆞᆫ포케ᄒᆞ라ᄒᆞ옵시다

광무팔년십일월이십구일
의졍부참졍신긔션

뎨이쳔구빅칠십삼호
광무팔년십일월이일

서임급ᄉᆞ령

○임한셩부관윤셔칙임관삼등
ᄂᆡ부관졔국쟝 리용세
○임비부참서관서주임관오등
농샹공부광산국쟝 김한목
임ᄂᆡ부기ᄉᆞ서주임관륙등
졍삼품 리귀영
○승서주임관ᄉᆞ등 ᄂᆡ부광졔
원기ᄉᆞ 리호형
○승서주임관ᄉᆞ등 경무쳥경
무관 리시영
○승서주임관ᄉᆞ등 경무쳥경
무관 강틔식
○면본관 음셩군슈 민진호
금구군슈 리쳘승 의령군슈
김괴영 동쳔군슈 리주하
익산군슈 젼병우 임실군슈
림용현 회양군슈 리지연
ᄌᆞ인군슈 리인긍
우는각히도관찰ᄉᆞ의춘하등
포폄보고셔를거ᄒᆞᆫ즉히원등
홈비칙져에하등이기로면본관
이상십월이십구일
○임려도원기ᄉᆞ서주임관륙등
륙품 김진규 구품 최병셕
○의원면본관 온릉령 김교일
동신ᄉᆞ면회과쥬ᄉᆞ 류영샹
○임본릉령서판임관칠등 진
원릉령 남계셕
임건원릉령서판임관칠등
영릉령 임벽션
○임영릉참봉서판임관칠등 효
릉참봉 윤교셩
○임효릉참봉서판임관팔등
티븍ᄉᆞ쥬ᄉᆞ 리문용
○임티븍ᄉᆞ쥬ᄉᆞ서판임관륙등
륙품 김용쥬
○임동신ᄉᆞ면회과쥬ᄉᆞ서판임
관륙등 홍ᄉᆞ철
○임표훈원기ᄉᆞ서주임관륙등
표훈원기ᄉᆞ 신순목
리○금규셔일군봉 ᄂᆡ부광졔원의ᄉᆞ
병쥰 한우
ᄉᆞ○금이금봉 ᄂᆡ부광졔원졔약
김샹셥
이샹십월삼십일일
○면본관 ᄃᆡ원감리셔쥬ᄉᆞ
○황쳘
○임덕원감리셔쥬ᄉᆞ 셔판임
관륙등 챵원감리셔쥬ᄉᆞ 권
현셥
이샹십월삼십일일

궁뎡록ᄉᆞ

○쟝례원경신조병필군 주ᄒᆞᆫ
되
황뎨ᄭᅴ셔비ᄒᆞᆫ후광븍ᄒᆞ옵시니셩
심에가ᄂᆡ졀ᄒᆞ옵사고리쟝이환회
ᄒᆞ오니셜노국가의ᄃᆞᆯ은경ᄉᆞ
락
황뎨ᄭᅴ셔비칭봉시에칭경ᄒᆞ고진
하ᄒᆞ든젼례를샹고ᄒᆞ온즉이제이
환후평븍ᄒᆞ신경ᄉᆞ와동일ᄒᆞ온지
라
진죠ᄐᆡ묘에고유ᄒᆞ고
하셔를반포ᄒᆞ고
진하식졀ᄎᆞ를곳티어길혈ᄒᆞ옵
지이하여하을지샹 쥬ᄒᆞ외봉
의쥬ᄒᆞ라
이샹십월삼십일일
단○조왈틔의원도졔됴이하를변
셔잉ᄒᆞ라
이샹십월삼십일일
○의졍부참졍신긔션 주
ᄒᆞ되도젹의변이ᄌᆞ고로잇스되
엇지근일의희픔ᄒᆞ기는도젹굿
참혹ᄒᆞ고잔인ᄒᆞᆫ가어ᄃᆡ잇스리오금
도젹ᄒᆞ는것과보다셔인ᄒᆞ고
탈ᄒᆞ는것슬보다더심ᄒᆞᆫ지라
셔ᄃᆡ번을니근셰엿고ᄌᆞᆫ에ᄌᆡ로
단희ᄒᆞᆫ말ᄉᆞᆷ이ᄒᆞ고ᄆᆡᆺ이고쳐
원쟝을ᄒᆡᆼ보ᄒᆞ야그씨듭이오만
올쳐ᄒᆞ는거슨지셩ᄒᆞᆫ부ᄃᆡ
ᄒᆞᆯᄇᆡᆨ아니고이ᄉᆞᆯ신ᄂᆞᆫ도
대다이ᄒᆞᆯ부등이흠이나
단괴히ᄒᆞᆯ무ᄒᆞᆼ코너지며
금로ᄒᆞᆼ쳐ᄒᆞ야드ᄃᆡ뎐
지나아닌ᄭᅡ도젹을진노
ᄒᆞᆯ긔ᄒᆞ며디하ᄒᆞ고ᄒᆞᆫ졍
지계ᄒᆞᆯ지계하ᄒᆞ며
라ᄒᆞᆫ지라ᄒᆞ쟈ᄒᆞ야
한지ᄒᆞᆫ을너희니ᄉᆞ
셩ᄒᆞ야나을부도
과부도젹ᄒᆞ고ᄒᆞ
ᄒᆡ도록조ᄒᆞ야
가ᄃᆡ이ᄒᆞ고
도ᄒᆞ야ᄃᆡ다이호ᄃᆡ부ᄇᆡ
가잇스며하졍의쥬ᄒᆞ야
막음이하여ᄒᆞ을지샹 쥬ᄒᆞ
후와봉지막ᄂᆞᆫ도에되그사졍을세우도ᄌᆞ
보아국케를손샹치못ᄒᆞᆯ지니ᄌᆞ
금이후로엄금ᄒᆞ기로신칙ᄒᆞ야
뎡식을샹게ᄒᆞ라
○의졍부참졍신긔션 주
ᄒᆞ되시ᄒᆞᆫ질ᄉᆞᆫ안ᄒᆞᆯᄉᆞ신안ᄒᆞᆼ
녑ᄒᆞ야시ᄒᆞᆼ근으로셔치ᄉᆞᆫ군에도
안ᄒᆞ여후셔 쥬ᄒᆞ와쥬

UNION INSURANCE SOCIETY OF CANTON.

Head office Hongkong.
Marine risks underwritten at current rates.
Agents in Chemulpo,
E. MEYER & Co.

COMPAGNIE DES MESSAGERIES MARITIMES.

Fortnightly Direct Service.

For Marseilles via Ports.

Sailing from Yokohama
Calling at Kobe,
Shanghai, Hongkong, Saigon, Singapore,
Colombo, Djibonti, Suez, Port Said
and Marseilles.

For particulars apply to
HOLME RINGER & Co.,
Chemulpo.

HAYASHIDA & Co.,

16 MYENG DONG, CHIN KO KAI, SEOUL.
BRANCH OFFICE AT CHEMULPO.

Money changers, Coal and Wood Merchants, Express Agents.

We are agents for the Pyeng-yang Coal Company and the Karazu Coal Company of Japan. We have the best quality of both anthracite and bituminous coal, and prompt execution of orders is our speciality. Firewood of all kinds kept in stock. Full weight guaranteed. Money of all denominations exchanged at current rates. Parcels received for all parts.

CHINA MUTUAL LIFE INS. CO.

Most favourable terms to policy holders.

Benefit system unsurpassed.

HOLME RINGER & Co.
Agents, Chemulpo.

C. P. R.

CANADIAN PACIFIC RAILWAY COMPANY'S ROYAL MAIL STEAMSHIP LINE.

THE FAST ROUTE BETWEEN CHINA, JAPAN, AND EUROPE VIA CANADA AND THE UNITED STATES.

Route from Hongkong via Shanghai, Nagasaki (Inland Sea of Japan) Kobe, Yokohama, Victoria and Vancouver.

Twin Screw Empress Steamship—6,000 Tons—Speed 19 knots.

PROPOSED SAILING FROM YOKOHAMA.
R. M. S. Empress of India.
R. M. S. Empress of Japan.
R. M. S. Empress of China.
R. M. S. Athenian.
R. M. S. Tartar.

Special reduction (first class only) granted to members of the Military, Naval, Diplomatic and Civil services and to Missionaries.

Passengers have choice of ten routes across the Continent of America and have privilege of travelling by any Atlantic Steamship Line.

Round the World passage tickets in connection with the P. and O. S. N., North German Lloyd and Messageries Co.'s £125.

All rates payable at current rate of exchange.

For further information, Tickets, Guide Books, etc., apply to

HOLME, RINGER & CO., AGENTS,
Chemulpo.

Grand Hotal,

(Formerly the Station Hotel)

Near the Railway Terminus, West Gate, Seoul.

The Best Hotel in Korea
Handsome new Building.
Fine Airy Rooms
Excellent Cuisine.
Terms Moderate.
Special terms to Missionaries
and to permanent boarders.

Electric cars within 2 minutes' walk.

W. H. EMBERLEY,
Proprietor.

EVERY FACILITY.

In connection with Life Assurance Business is afforded by

The Standard Life Assurance Co.,

One of the largest and wealthiest of the Provident Institutions of the United Kingdom Forms of Application and all information will be promptly afforded on application.

10 CENTS A DAY.

Not a very large expenditure is it? But it is sufficient to secure for a man of 30 a policy with the STANDARD LIFE OFFICE for

$1323.

For all particulars of rates, etc., apply to

Holme, Ringer & Co.,
Agents, Chemulpo.

THE NEW YORK LIFE INSURANCE COMPANY.

Have you ever been declined by any Company?

Are you engaged in a specially hazardous occupation?

Have you heard of the New York Life Insurance Company's New Classifications for this class of Risks?

If not, send your date of birth, occupation and particulars of rejection, if any to

E. MEYER & Co.,
Agents, Chemulpo.

MITSUI BUSSAN KAISNHA.
(MITSUI & Co.)

MITSUI GINKO.
(MITSUI BANK.)

The Bank is owned by the members of the Mitsui Family, who, as partners, assume an unlimited responsibility for all liabilities of the Bank:—

Capital .... Yen 5,000,000
Reserve Fund .... " 5,600,000

HEAD OFFICE, TOKYO.
LONDON OFFICE, 34 LIME ST., E. C.

BRANCHES AND AGENCIES:—
New York, San Francisco, Hamburg, Bombay, Singapore, Manila, Hongkong, Amoy, Chefoo, Tientsin.
Kobe, Hakodate, Yokohama, Kure, Yokosuka, Moji, Shimonoseki, Miike, Wakamatsu, Nagasaki, Kuchinotsu, Karatsu, Sasebo, Misume, Taipeh, &c.

Telegraphic Address for all the Offices:
"MITSUI."
A. B. C. AND A. I CODES USED.

Contractors of Coal
To the Imperial Japanese Navy. Arsenals and Railway Bureau, Principal Railway Companies and Industrial Work, Home and Foreign Mail and Freight Steamers.

Sole Proprietors
Of the famous Miike, Tagawa and Yamano Coal Mines.

Sole Agents
For the sale of Fukumo, Hokoku, Ichimura, Kanoda, Mannoura, Onoura, Ostuji, Sonoda, Tsubaruro, Yoshinotani, Yoshio, Yurokibura and other coals.

YANGTSE INSURANCE ASSOCIATION, LTD.

The undersigned, having been appointed agents for the above company, are prepared to issue policies and pay losses on marine risks at regular rates.

E. MEYER & Co.,
Agents, Chemulpo.

AMERICAN KOREAN ELECTRIC COMPANY.

Light and Power.

Main Office: Electric Building, Chong No.

RAILWAY DEPARTMENT.

OPERATING CARS BETWEEN EAST AND WEST GATE, EVERY TEN MINUTES:—
First Car leaves East Gate at 6:30 A. M. First Car leaves West Gate at 6:55 A. M.
Last Cra " East Gate at 10:40 P. M. Last " " West Gate at 11:00 P.M.

OPERATING CARS BETWEEN EAST GATE AND IMPERIAL TOMB TERMINUS, EVERY TWENTY MINUTES:—

CONNECTING WITH EVERY ALTERNATE CAR ARRIVING AT EAST GATE FROM CHONG NO.
First Car leaves East Gate for Tomb at 6:50 A. M.
" " " Tomb for East Gate at 7:10 A. M.
Last " " East Gate for Tomb at 9:50 P. M.
" " " Tomb for East Gate at 10:10 P. M.

OPERATING CARS BETWEEN CHONG NO AND YUNG SAN (RIVER) EVERY TWELVE MINUTES:—
First Car leaves Chong No for South Gate at 6:48 A. M.
" " " Chong No for Yung San at 7:24 A. M.
" " " South Gate for Chong No at 6:56 A. M.
" " " Yung San for Chong No at 7:57 A. M.
Last " " South Gate for Chong No 11:00 P. M.
" " " Yung San for Chong No at 10:11 P. M.

SPECIAL PRIVATE CARS FURNISHED TO SUIT CONVENIENCE OF PATRONS. PRICES ON APPLICATION AT HEAD OFFICE.

LIGHTING DEPARTMENT.

Where less than 250 candle power of light is used, the rate per month will be: Per 16 candle power incandescent lamp,—All night.—Yen 2.50.
Per 32 candle power incandescent lamp:—All night:—Yen 4.00. Per 50 candle power incandescent lamp:—All night:—Yen 6.00.
" 150 " " " " — " " 10.00. " 1200 " " enclosed arc " " " " 20.00.

Where more than 250 candle power of light is used, a Meter will be installed, if requested:—Rent of Meter Yen 2.00 per month. Rate of charges by meter reading:—Two Sen per Ampere per hour. (Approximately this is equal to about One Sen per 16 C. P. lamp per hour) Minimum monthly charge where meter is installed, Yen 20.00 per month, which includes rental of meter.

Estimates for installing lights furnished on application. An assortment of chandeliers always on hand.

AMUSEMENT DEPARTMENT.

ANIMATED PICTURES AT EAST GATE
Every evening - - - Except Sunday.
From 8 to 10 P. M.

10 Cents:—Gen. Admission:—10 Cents. Seats in First Class Section. 15 Cents Extra.

Change of program each week. Pictures from Foreign **Lands.** Pictures of Local Scenes:—Amusing and Instructive.

An entertaining evening for a reasonable price.
MERRY-GO-ROUND:—At East Gate.
From 10:00 A. M. till 11:00 P. M.

5 Cents a Ride.

Take your Exercise on The Galoping Horses.

Comfortable seats in the Chariots.

한셩뎐긔회사

한미뎐긔회사 고ᄒᆞᆸ 보사ᄃᆡ 고빅
토ᄒᆞ옵나이다
어ᄯᅥ뎐차가온장안으로통힝ᄒᆞ여ᄃᆞ니여이
샵
쏘이긔계에ᄌᆞ처노힌편ᄒᆞ고됴흔마차도잇
샵
코끼우편ᄒᆞ고ᄯᅩ조미잇ᄂᆞᆫ됴흔운동이되겟
이됴흔모힝ᄒᆞᆯ달나아ᄂᆞᆫ불을ᄏᆞ고뛰티처압
디가ᄂᆞᆫᄒᆞ변ᄒᆞᄂᆞᆫ데오젼셔이오
미일상오열시브터ᄲᅡ오열ᄒᆞᆫ시ᄭᆞ지ᄒᆞ옵고
독마운동장은동대문안에잇삽고
가되겟샵
쳠군조의게갑도싸고저녁에됴흔쇼일거리
미잇고구경ᄒᆞᆯ만ᄒᆞᆫ거시오니
서양사진과대한과온동양사진연대대단조
논ᄃᆡ
젼이옵고미쥬일에사진을ᄡᅳᆫ것스로다밧고
고젼랍되금은하등에십젼이오상등에이십
일외에ᄂᆞᆫ미야에여덜시브터열시ᄭᆞ지ᄒᆞ옵
활동사진뎐랍소ᄂᆞᆫ동대문안에잇삽고일요
회락부

All Cars Run Direct to the Animated Pictures and Merry-Go-Round.

어일본신문에셔지등지ᄒᆞ야ᄎ귀나라에셔한국에고문관과밋진보자들노칙임ᄒᆞᆫ자의게셩화갓치쇽히변통ᄒᆞ야니ᄒᆞᆫ다고대단하취망ᄒᆞ엿스니만일이말ᄃᆡ로사셰라ᄒᆞᆼᄒᆞ야장샹씨의산림쳔텩숑긴갓흔일은만쥬션ᄒᆞᆯ지경이면쇽히결단ᄂᆞ기ᄂᆞᆫ무리ᄒᆞ고ᄯᅩᄒᆞᆫ텬하각국에셔모도졍두ᄒᆞ야일본다려아모조록나라를부흥ᄒᆞ게ᄒᆞ여달나ᄂᆞ고간청도ᄒᆞᆯ만ᄒᆞ도다

이금ᄉᆞ젼으로ᄂᆞᆫ미ᄉᆞ가모도일본의소원ᄃᆡ로되엿스되쟈ᄒᆞᆫ밋지못ᄒᆞᆯ자ㅣ잇스니일본이쟝찻아라사들이여피ᄒᆞ게만다드리도ᄯᅩ다른강ᄃᆡᄒᆞᆫ나라도ᄒᆡ다ᄒᆞᆫ즉분명코한국이일아량국간에속국이되리라ᄒᆞ고쟁ᄒᆞ야말ᄒᆞᆯ수업스며

일본이우금ᄭᆞ지도아라사를명명히격멸ᄒᆞ지못ᄒᆞ엿스ᄂᆞᆫ즉다만오날날의양으로권리뵈앗으로ᄂᆞᆫ더욱알수업ᄂᆞᆫ거시이제도한국의운수ᄂᆞᆫ두가지가오히려잇스니쳣ᄌᆡᄂᆞᆫ일아젼쟁에일본이픽ᄒᆞᆯ터이오둘ᄌᆡᄂᆞᆫ혹다ᄅᆞᆫ나라에셔한국사졍을도라보지아니ᄒᆞᆯᄂᆞᆫ지모르ᄂᆞᆫ바ㅣ라일노써볼진ᄃᆡ한국에토ᄀᆡ회가분무ᄒᆞ거ᄂᆞᆯ일본신문샹에ᄂᆞᆫ일한약됴를을빙ᄌᆞᄒᆞ고교사지셜을만드러압제로힝사ᄒᆞ란홀을게지ᄒᆞ엿스니

셜홍아라사ᄂᆞᆫ승첩ᄒᆞ드리도한국계산은유루될리가업무ᄒᆞᆫ즉이ᄂᆞᆫ무타라아라사이한국토지ᄂᆞᆫ당초에원ᄒᆞᄂᆞᆫ바ㅣ아닌셔ᄃᆡ러만일항ᄒᆡ된욕심을부리드리도다른나라들에셔합당히너이여아모말도아니ᄒᆞᆯ리가업슬지니엇지던지한국에셔ᄂᆞᆫ독립미셔의근본이큰지가잉의오ᄅᆡ며뎡금일본의젼샹치지ᄒᆞᄂᆞᆫ자ᄂᆞᆫ오작아라사이니그외에모든일은추후에라도가히ᄒᆞᆯᄌᆞ로사롬마다알며말ᄒᆞᄂᆞᆫ바인지라

그러ᄒᆞᆫ즉ᄃᆡ한졍부제공들은이후란리평졍된후에당ᄒᆞᆯ일을싱각지말고아모조록놈의나라의부리지말아나졍진보되게ᄒᆞ기를ᄇᆞ라노라

면보

○만쥬군총ᄉᆞ령부발
군ᄉᆞ령부착뎐

○회인방면젼투 회인부근에ᄂᆞᆫ적의보병긔병이쳔명이포이문을가지고쥬둔ᄒᆞᄂᆞᆫᄃᆡ일본군에셔회인방면으로파견ᄒᆞᆫ일부ᄃᆡ가삼십일에ᄃᆡ호츈(회인서남구리허)부근에셔적의긔병삼ᄇᆡᆨ명과샹봉ᄒᆞ야일병이격퇴ᄒᆞ엿ᄂᆞᆫᄃᆡ그중오명은부샹ᄒᆞ고일병은ᄉᆞ샹자고쇼총이빙엿이더라

영문이라ᄒᆞ야덕샹이영샹의물건샹이와계ᄒᆡᆨ가ᄋᆡᆨᄉᆞ쳔원을츌급ᄒᆞ교깁씨의게루ᄎᆞ셔합으로회ᄒᆞ가엑샹보홈을요청ᄒᆞ되깁씨가교징ᄒᆞ고듯지아니ᄒᆞᄂᆞᆫ고로부등ᄒᆞ야조회ᄒᆞ니깁씨의게신칙ᄒᆞ야ᄒᆡᆨᄋᆡᆨᄉᆞ신원을곳환보케ᄒᆞ락ᄒᆞ엿더라

○죠쳥호칙치도 일본공관에셔외부로조회ᄒᆞ되즁남포괴진포ᄉᆞ이에도로가동결을당ᄒᆞ야일본군의긴요ᄒᆞᆫ관계인즉ᄒᆡ디방관의게신칙ᄒᆞ야즁남포에잇ᄂᆞᆫ일본병참ᄉᆞ령관과협의ᄒᆞ야급히치도ᄒᆞ면평셩과평양간텰로부셜ᄒᆞᆫ후에ᄂᆞᆫ평양과즁남포ᄉᆞ이도교통이편리ᄒᆞᆯ지라ᄒᆡ디방관의게훈칙ᄒᆞ야도로를슈츅케ᄒᆞ라ᄒᆞ엿더라

○강씨면계 봉시강셕호씨ᄂᆞᆫ이왕면관ᄒᆞ엿더니작일에면징계되엿더라

○우일ᄂᆡ장경 ᄂᆡ장원경리병휘씨ᄂᆞᆫ샹소ᄒᆞ야갈니고죵이풍리병규씨가그ᄃᆡ를승임ᄒᆞ엿더라

○룡권난금 함경북도에셔도각쳐에진보회가벌셰ᄀᆞᆺ치이러ᄂᆞᆫ취회ᄒᆞ되ᄒᆡᆼᄃᆡ방에쥬둔ᄒᆞᆫ한국병뎡은진압코자ᄒᆞ되병긔를몰수히아국병의게피탈ᄒᆞᆫ고로엇지ᄒᆞᆯ수업다더라

○광졔지칙 거월십ᄉᆞ일브터젼람병예방위원일본군의가의ᄒᆞᆨ교를셜닙ᄒᆞ고기타여러곳시약소를셜치ᄒᆞ고시약ᄒᆞᆷ을죵ᄉᆞᄒᆞᄂᆞᆫ즁인ᄃᆡ이십오일ᄭᆞ지시약ᄒᆞᆫ인원수ᄂᆞᆫ일쳔ᄉᆞ빅삼십구인이ᄂᆞᆫ되엿다더라

○피평덩폐 졔작일에일공ᄉᆞ가례셔원으로룡합ᄒᆞ야협ᄒᆞᆯ것을쳥ᄒᆞ엿더니 옥호미ᄒᆞᆫ셔고ᄯᅩ 황ᄐᆡᄌᆞ비환후도쾌복지못ᄒᆞ심으로졍젼치못ᄒᆞ신다고봉환ᄒᆞ엿다더라

론셜

한국형편과일아젼쟁

무릇근일에한국형편되여감을보고장ᄅᆡ지ᄉᆞ가다만일아젼쟁에ᄃᆞᆯ닌양으로말들은하되우리의싱각에ᄂᆞᆫ실로그러치아니ᄒᆞᆫ지라셜혹일본이승쳡ᄒᆞ야쇼원ᄃᆡ로되드ᄅᆡ도한국을권의ᄒᆞᄂᆞᆫ자리에잇지ᄒᆞᆼ당히쳐사치아니ᄒᆞᆯ리유가잇스리오그러ᄒᆞ나사람의소견은각각다른듯ᄒᆞᆫ거시일아ᄀᆡ젼이처음으로ᄃᆡ벼에ᄂᆞᆫ일본졍부가한국에독립자쥬를보죵ᄒᆞᆫ다칭ᄒᆞ고약죠셔지ᄒᆞ더니그다음에ᄂᆞᆫ한국졍치를기량ᄒᆞ여야ᄒᆞ겟다ᄒᆞ고일본진보자들을로ᄒᆞ여곰무수히소요ᄒᆞ게구렷[illegible]

○련명반ᄃᆡ셔 평남유ᄉᆡᆼ련즁룡등칠인이련명ᄒᆞ야일진회를반ᄃᆡᄒᆞᄂᆞᆫ쟝셔를졍부로승졍ᄒᆞ엿다더라

○긔차발착 ᄅᆡᆨ간 경부텰도회사에셔ᄂᆞᆫ작일브터영등포로셔ᄃᆡ뎐(회덕샹)ᄭᆞ지힝긱과화물을운ᄃᆞᆫᄒᆞ고셜ᄂᆞᆫᄃᆡ차셰ᄂᆞᆫ영등포와ᄃᆡ뎐ᄉᆞ이에일화로일원구십팔젼이오ᄆᆡ일운힝은좌와곳ᄒᆞ니

영등포발	오젼칠시ᄉᆞ십분
	오후십이시ᄉᆞ십오분
부강착	오후십이시ᄉᆞ십오분
	오후오시오십일분
부강발	오후일시이십분
ᄃᆡ뎐착	오후이시ᄉᆞ십분
ᄃᆡ뎐발	오젼십일시
부강착	오후십이시이십분
부강발	오젼륙시십분
	오후일시ᄉᆞ십분
영등포착	오젼십일시십륙분
	오후륙시ᄉᆞ십분

○텰도방ᄒᆡ자 소문을드른즉일본에잇ᄂᆞᆫᄒᆞᆫ농부원광이라ᄒᆞᄂᆞᆫ자이산양텰도에방ᄒᆡ를ᄒᆞ야텰거를손샹케ᄒᆞᆫᄉᆞ건에거십월이십ᄉᆞ일에산구현지판소에셔륙년쳐역에션고ᄒᆞ엿다ᄒᆞ니이거ᄉᆞᆫ근ᄌᆞ에한ᄒᆞᆫ인명이범죄ᄒᆞᆫᄃᆡ여포샹ᄒᆞᆫ것과ᄂᆞᆫᄃᆡ단ᄒᆞᆫ샹ᄃᆡ인혐슉ᄒᆞᆷ이현져히발ᄒᆞ고져ᄒᆞᆫ다더라

○교량슈보비 탁지부에셔ᄂᆞᆫ부로등교ᄒᆞ기를흥룽간으로종암에잇ᄂᆞᆫ나무다리와밋은구슈보비이쳔칠빅오십삼원을졍부에쳥의ᄒᆞ야ᄂᆡ부의소관ᄒᆞᆫ죠쳔ᄒᆞ교키도ᄒᆞᄂᆞᆫ즁예비에셔지츌ᄒᆞ엿다ᄒᆞ엿더라

○유민사청원 젼위원셕쥭형등이외국에츌발ᄒᆞᄂᆞᆫ인부를관할ᄒᆞᆯᄎᆞ로유민회사를셜시ᄒᆞᆯᄃᆡ인ᄒᆞ되ᄌᆞ본금은일만원으로작뎡ᄒᆞ고ᄌᆞ본금을이빅에난화셔ᄆᆡ고에오십원식뎡ᄒᆞ엿다ᄒᆞ고농샹공부에청원ᄒᆞ엿다더라

○영요금셔가 영국공관에셔외부로조회ᄒᆞ기를본년삼월에영국샹민푸리스톤이발ᄒᆞ되월젼에ᄌᆞ긔와ᄒᆞᆼ금으로계죠ᄒᆞᆫ시계셜을일헛더니홀연이로샹에셔덕국샹고잔니숫기의시계와금진인고로그소죵ᄅᆡ를탐문ᄒᆞᆫ즉ᄃᆡ답ᄒᆞ되월젼에한국ᄉᆞ관감역도의게ᄉᆞ십원갑스로미득ᄒᆞ엿다ᄒᆞᄂᆞᆫ고로본공관에셔덕국공ᄉᆞ와회동ᄒᆞ야ᄉᆞ관ᄒᆞᆫ즉회금식우회원리계죠ᄒᆞᆫ졔조국ᄌᆞ호를영문으로비글ᄌᆞ를식엿스되깁씨언니에팔년젼에아국셔사왓[illegible]

잡보

○경ᄉᆞ도례 경무ᄉᆞ량셩환씨ᄂᆞᆫ쳥결위원쟝으로쳥결ᄉᆞ무로회사를인가ᄒᆞ야상 쥬ᄒᆞ고쳥결비ᄉᆞ만원이 나하되야쳥결범을일신이ᄒᆞᆫ다ᄒᆞ더니ᄎᆔ회사에셔빅셩의게쥭호ᄒᆞ야슈렴ᄒᆞᆯᄉᆞ로샹지ᄒᆞ야ᄉᆞ무에구의되교민회협의ᄒᆞ라신 죠칙이ᄂᆞ리사경무ᄉᆞ의게담칙되엿ᄂᆞᆫᄃᆡ민회의셰력을억제ᄒᆞᆯ수업ᄉᆞᆫ즉좌우ᄉᆞ셰가다난쳐ᄒᆞ야본직을도례ᄒᆞᆫ다더라

○양츈부회 리근튁씨ᄂᆞᆫ녀러달쳥ᄀᆡᄒᆞ엿다가향일에특진관으로출각ᄒᆞ더니호위ᄃᆡ쟝관을피임ᄒᆞ엿더라

○참찬병와 참찬허위씨ᄂᆞᆫ근일에의쳥을엇어ᄂᆞᆫᄃᆡ신병이발작ᄒᆞ야ᄉᆞ오일ᄅᆡ로ᄉᆞ진치못ᄒᆞ엿다더라

○샹소발됴 룡풍황텰수씨가쟝쳐샹서무팔됴로졍부에샹셔ᄒᆞ엿ᄂᆞᆫᄃᆡ 뎨일은징쳥원을셜립홈이오 뎨이ᄂᆞᆫ망흥법을ᄒᆡᆼᄒᆞ야관찰과군슈들ᄐᆡᆨ차홈이오 뎨삼은빈좌들을학샹이시ᄒᆡᆼ홈이오 뎨ᄉᆞᄂᆞᆫ샹벌에과됴를엄립홈이오 뎨오ᄂᆞᆫ빅동화쥬조를명지ᄒᆞᆷ이오 뎨륙은쟝셰를혓뎌이잇게홈이오 뎨칠은판국인파군인과셔인의의복을본국셔조지ᄒᆞᆫ물품으로만ᄉᆞ용케홈이오 뎨팔은신문을셰움이라더라

하됨을봉젼ᄒᆞ온즉회군야교가귀음에금광여부의ᄌᆞ회ᄒᆞᆷ을인ᄒᆞ야판장을살ᄒᆡᄒᆞ엿ᄉᆞ오니강샹에큰관계라극히경ᄒᆡᄒᆞ옵고취원실이가증죄를범ᄒᆞ엿고죽룡도장독이아닌즉취인셕의북슈ᄒᆞᆫ다칭ᄒᆞ고작변ᄒᆞᆷ이그죄가반역죄ᄂᆞᆫᄃᆡ항당ᄒᆞᄂᆞ니무리의분격ᄒᆞᆷ으로ᄯᅡᆫ경리셜ᄒᆞᆫ거시죄명를봄혀경형ᄒᆞ나만못ᄒᆞᄂᆞᆫ입의지변ᄒᆞᆷ이니분론ᄒᆞ고침찬실의형적셔홈ᄒᆞᆷ이작변ᄒᆞᆫ쟝두의형의가잇ᄉᆞᄂᆞᆫᄌᆞ북지아니ᄒᆞ엿ᄉᆞᆫ죡ᄒᆞᆷ형들경ᄒᆞᆯ거시오김셩권김창쥰은죄범이가벼얍지아니ᄒᆞ고로히도지관소로이슈ᄒᆞ엿다ᄒᆞ오니법부로ᄒᆞ여곰엄ᄒᆞᆫ사ᄒᆡᆨᄒᆞ야쳐판ᄒᆞ옵고금광여부김명셔한창신지련빅리시명오소셩최운판빈봉익김창룡졍용복오길명김ᄐᆡ산박셩근등십이명지도ᄒᆞ야쟝지못ᄒᆞ엿다ᄒᆞ오니법부로ᄒᆞ여곰각도지판소와각경무셔에엄칙ᄒᆞ야곳근포ᄒᆞ야당률에쳐ᄒᆞ옴이하여ᄒᆞ옴을지샹주ᄒᆞ와봉 지의쥬ᄒᆞ라

○의졍부찬졍박졔슌ᄉᆞ직소
비지니에ᄉᆞ양말고ᄒᆡᆼ공ᄒᆞ라

○궁ᄂᆡ부특진관졍낙죠ᄉᆞ직소
비지니에소쳥을의시ᄒᆞ노라

이상십월삼십일일

TELEGRAMS.

(FROM JAPAN PAPERS).

Berlin, Oct. 27.

The London Daily Telegraph reports that Cardiff coal has recently been supplied to Russia at the rate of 100,000 tons a month. Colliers for the service of Russian warships are now in the Mediterranean, the Red Sea and on the western coast of Africa.—Asahi.

The Baltic Fleet entered the harbour of Vigo and proceeded to coal, under pretence of repairing, without permission of the Spanish Naval Commandant.

The Commandant protested against this breach of Spain's neutrality. The Russian Admiral then applied for sufficient coal to enable the squadron to reach Tangier and three of the warships have already proceeded to the latter port.

Fourteen British cruisers have arrived at Lagos.

London, Oct. 29th.

An official despatch from St. Petersburg states that two telegrams have been received from Admiral Rozhdestvensky.

The first declares that two torpedo-boats, not showing their lights, attacked the leading vessel in the Fleet. The latter used search-lights and opened fire, whereupon the presence of several small steamers, resembling fishing-trawlers, was discovered. The Fleet endeavoured to spare the latter as soon as the torpedo-boats disappeared. The Admiral declares that no torpedo-boats accompanied the Fleet. One strange torpedo-boat was sunk; the other, which was only damaged, remained till morning near the small steamers. The Fleet did not assist trawlers because it suspected them of complicity in view of their obstinacy in crossing the Russian line several times.

The second telegram said that the Fleet met several hundred fishing trawlers and showed them every consideration, except when they were in company with foreign torpedo-boats. The Admiral expresses regret for the victims, but states that the circumstances were such that no warship would have acted otherwise even in time of profound peace.

Berlin, October 28.

The Russian newspaper, Russ, complaining of the recent disarmament of the Diana at Saigon, says:—Russia ought to demand, at least, that the blue-jackets who were on board the Diana should be allowed to join the Baltic Squadron.—*Asahi.*

The British steamer "Sishan," which was seized by Japanese warships near Port Arthur on the 25th inst. and brought to Sasebo, has been released by order of the Prize Court. She arrived at Nagasaki on Friday night and left again, after coaling, on Saturday for Shanghai.

On Monday, the Japanese Minister applied for an audience. His request was refused owing to His Majesty being slightly indisposed.

The Japanese Minister has requested the repair of the road from Chinnampo to Ki Chin Po (near Pyeng Yang,) as it will be largely used by the Japanese troops during the winter.

FURTHER ORDERS BY THE MILITARY AUTHORITIES.

We learn from Japan papers that the following are additional portions of General Hasegawa's recent Proclamation:—Privileges which have been granted to either Koreans or foreigners will be duly recognised so long as they do not interfere with Japanese military operations. All persons desiring to engage in mining or timber felling undertakings within areas under martial law, which would require the services of many labourers, must apply for sanction to the Commander of the Japanese forces. No persons will be allowed to enter, or reside in, places where martial law is in force, with the exception of the open ports, without the permission of the Imperial Headquarters, the War Minister, or the Commander of the Japanese troops in Korea. In all localities under martial law, the following instructions are to be observed:—

Art. 1.—Any Associations, news papers, magazines, or circulars may be stopped or suspended if detrimental to the interests of the military administration.

Art. 2.—The military authorities will, if they think it necessary, prohibit the removal or export of any articles which may be required for the use of the Japanese forces.

Art. 3.—The military authorities may search the person or premises of any one who is suspected of having dangerous explosives in his possession, and the latter may be coſscated if necessary.

Art. 4.—Any person may be ordered to leave places under martial law if his presence there is likely to be injurious to the carrying on of the military administration.

Art. 5.—In order to protect the railways, telegraph wires, roads, bridges, and other means of communication required by the military forces, the residents of places in which they may be injured will be held responsible for the damage done.

Art. 6.—Residents in the martial law areas may be ordered to repair bridges and roads for the Japanese troops.

A CONTRAST.

(Concluded from 2nd page.)

"All you officials are descended from the officials of 40 years ago and your forefathers were the people of the old Emperors 500 years ago, so we cannot bear to harm you. But, if you cannot change your faults 3,000 *li* of ground will be lost to you and 20,000,000 of our lives will no longer be yours.

"Between Korea and Japan there is only a sea, and the same sort of people inhabit both countries. They write in the same manner and have done so for 500 years. Japan has been friendly to us for the past number of years and has advised our independence and civilization in her naturally kind way. The links between the two countries are like lips to teeth, or shafts to a cart.

"Now come forward and help Japan to beat outrageous Russia. Our country is like a bridge over which troops are transported; if the bridge is not safe, it is impossible to cross safely. Therefore you must not think of your own interest but must help the country, by helping Japan.

"'All you now do, is to dispe se our fellow workers in the country and shoot them. You must learn qucikly the way to reform, or decide whether you will resign.'

"That was our letter to the Government. Among thousands of nations we stand alone, being full of rebels, so we hope the Government will be thoughtful and assist our benevolent Emperor in driving away rebels and dangerous people from the court, so that Korea may at last have peaceful felicity.

(Signed) President Il Chin Hoi,
YUN SI-BYUNG.

The Finance Department has disbursed the sum of $2.753 on repairs to bridges and stone work near the Queen's tomb.

UNCALLED-FOR.

The Kokumin states that Government circles in Tokio express the warmest sympathy with the sufferers by the Hull outrage, as it has been indirectly caused by the war in the Far East. The Mayors of Tokio and Yokohama have despatched sympathetic messages to their colleague at Hull. The telegram sent by Mayor Ozaki of Tokio reads as follows:—

"Please accept our profound sympathy for the victims of the Russian outrage and their bereaved families"

The Korean soldiers in the north of the Ham Kyeng province complain that they are powerless to disperse the Chin Po Hoi gatherings in their district as the Russians have deprived them of their rifles.

A syndicate of Koreans have applied to the Agricultural Department for permission to start operations in coolie emigration. The company, which will commence with a capital of $10,000, will be called the Yuninhoisa,

Berlin, Oct. 27.—According to the National Zeitung, the British Explosive and Ammunition Co., under the control of Messrs. Kynoch (Mr. Arthur Chamberlain, a brother of the late British Colonial Secretary, was formerly Chairman of the Company) have sent representatives to Russia to offer supplies of ammunition.—Asahi.

The birthday of the Emperor of Japan was duly celebrated today in Chinkokai and neighbourhood. The streets were gaily bedecked with flags, while strings of lanterns betokened coming illuminations for this evening. Mr. Hayashi was *at home* this morning to visitors, and many callers availed themselves, during the forenoon, of the hospitality dispensed at the Japanese Legation.

Nicholas Nickelby must have found a place in the Government's bookshelves and have recently been read by some zealous official, for "Doctor Squeers" with his treatment of the boys of "Dotheboy's Hall" with brimstone and treacle on all and every occasion, has evidently got his counterpart in Seoul. For the past ten days vast quantities of some mysterious drug have been prepared and forced, *nolens volens*, down the throats of Seoul's citizens. In all, some 1,000 people have partaken of this elixir, which, we are told, is a preventative of infectious diseases. A little less drug swallowing and a little more attention devoted to the sewers of the city, would have more beneficial effect.

The Korea Daily News.

Issued at 5 P. M. daily except Sundays.

Rate of Subscription:—
Per Year, Yen 25.
Per Quarter, Yen 7.
Per Month, Yen 2.50.

Postage in Korea not charged extra.
Postage abroad charged extra.

Advertisements, 50 sen per day for 1 inch or less.
5 yen per month per inch.
50 yen per year per inch.

All communications to
E. T. BETHELL,
Editor and Publisher,
Pak-tong, Seoul

BEGGAR MY NEIGHBOUR.

While the Japanese armies in the field are earning for their country a reputation for valour and chivalry which will never perish, the Japanese civilians and civil officials in Korea are doing their best to damage the cause of their country by transactions of the shadiest imaginable character.

There are stories of rifles and telegraph wire sold to the Government at outrageous prices, and how this country was flooded with spurious nickels manufactured in Osaka is too well known to need recounting.

But the history of the Korean "Navy" has not yet been told. In 1888 there was built in Middlesboro a steamer of 2,143 tons register named the "Pallas." She was subsequently purchased by the Mitsui Bussan Kaisha and re-named the "Kachidate Maru." What the purchase price was is not known, but experts say that the steamer was then worth something under Y200,000. Last year she again changed hands and became a man-of-war. The Mitsui Bussan Kaisha sold her to the Korean Government for Y550,000! The true inwardness of this transaction is not known, but we do know that the Korean Government never wanted the steamer. In proof of this we may say that immediately the steamer had been bought, the Government had her valued by an independent expert who assessed the white elephant at Y80,000!!

Even if we allow that this valuation was for a forced sale, and double the figure for an ordinary transaction, we still have the amazing sum of Y390,000 representing the difference between the value of the steamer and the price paid for her by the Korean Government. It was literally a game of "Beggar my neighbour" and forms a fitting part of the "wrecking" policy which we are led to believe is part of Japan's scheme for the annexation of this country.

This is however not the end of the story. It appears that at the time the steamer was handed over, the Korean Government paid Y 200,000 cash down, agreeing to pay the remaining Y 350,000 in two subsequent instalments of Y175,000 each. These installments have not been paid and in the meantime, since the outbreak of war, the vessel has been running, as a collier, under charter to the Japanese Navy Department for a consideration of Y3,000 monthly.

We now find that the Japanese Minister has written to the Korean Government asking that the unpaid Y 350,000 be included in next year's budgets, secured upon the proceeds of the Ginseng monopoly. He further says that as this sum is unpaid, the Navy Department has handed Y24,000, being eight month's charter money, direct to the Mitsui Bussan Kaisha.

Now we may point out that it is hardly to the credit of Japan's representative to get mixed up in a deal of this kind, and although it is probable that the Japanese Minister had no option but to further the claims of a Japanese citizen, there seems to be absolutely no excuse for the action taken by the Navy Department in paying the charter money over to the Mitsui Bussan Kaisha. The Navy Department has no official cognizance of the Mitsui Bussan Kaisha in the matter at all, and the charter money should properly have been paid to the Korean Government and no one else.

The whole transaction is a scandalous one and on a par with other Japanese financial deals in Korea. We have recently reported one or two occasions on which the Japanese Minister has satisfied the claims of his subjects out of money which had been paid into the Dai Ichi Bank by Japanese in payment for land appropriated for railway and other purposes. The consent of the Korean Government to these payments seems to be looked upon by the Japanese as superfluous and we have therefore no hesitation in saying that claims will continue to crop up until the whole of this sum is exhausted.

All these transactions are distinctly unfavourable to Korea, and as there is from time to time talk of Korea borrowing money from Japan, we recommend the Government to make sure of two things before signing the bond. First that they get the money, and next that they will be allowed to have the spending of it.

A CONTRAST.

We have recently obtained copies of the manifestoes of two societies which flourish in Korea. They are in marked contrast to each other and it is curious to note that the "Righteous" society, which we have every reason to believe to be a sincere organization, ruins its cause by the advocacy of violence, while that corrupt "claque," the Il-chin-hoi, which was founded by a Japanese named Komochi, and which keeps itself together by distributing money to its adherents conceals its sinister designs beneath an attitude of pharisaical righteousness and moderation.

The following is a free translation of the Righteous Society's manifesto:—

"The ground of Korea is to build houses upon in which to live, and for cultivating food. Money is for purposes of barter and the accumulation of it makes a man rich. The hills are for our graves, and the streams are to supply us with water. If all these are to be appropriated by the Japanese, it will be impossible for us to continue to exist.

"The capital city of our Empire is where our transactions with foreign nations are done and it is therefore wrong that the Japanese should control it. It is wrong that the Japanese, in building railways, should cut into hills containing Imperial tombs, the veneration of all Koreans. Our soldiers are for the protection of our country and the Japanese talk of abolishing them must not be listened to.

"All these things have been done by the Japanese who have moreover forcibly collected coolies who have been sent to be killed instead of Japanese.

"We grieve deeply over the condition of our country, we are neither alive nor dead and we do not know where to turn.

"Now the Japanese are sure to be all killed off, but as everyone cannot see this for himself we give a true statement of present affairs. Many years ago the Japanese sent troops abroad, half of whom were killed in the Locchoos and half in China. They have now sent their whole population to a distant place where the severe cold will kill them before they can fight. Three steamers full of heads only of dead soldiers have come back and the Japanese have been defeated. The Japanese still want to fight but as they have none of their own people left they want to send Koreans to be killed and if we do not prepare ourselves they will surely compel us to go.

"Feeling sure that all of our countrymen feel as we do we have prepared this manifesto and the members of the Confucian temples who receive it must copy it out and post it in the streets for all to see and forward it to the Confucian temple in the next district so that the people may know that they are to gather in Seoul on October 29th to extirminate the Japanese."

(It will be noted that the appointed date has passed without anything having happened).

The Il Chin Hoi's proclamation runs;—

"His Imperial Majesty, our Emperor, we humbly beg to state is as benevolent as the sky and bright as the sun and during his 40 years reign he has endeavoured to rule better than previous monarchs and collect wise men around his throne. To this end he made an alliance with a neighbouring country, and the whole world was glad.

"But the Government is full of swindlers, who cast a cloud over His Majesty's holy brightness and frighten his holy mind. These influential people control appointments, dismissals, rewards and punishment alike, so that the foundation of the Government is in great danger of being shaken.

"The Imperial throne is so hidden behind these people, that the commoners cannot reach it and His Majesty does not hear their wishes. The people are greatly troubled that they cannot themselves bespeak His Majesty's well-known kindness. Sixty ago, we, the mouthpiece of a million people, advised the Government of 4 articles, which the whole country desired. But so far, we have heard nothing.

"Instead the Government have issued orders to disperse all meetings of people, the Chin Po Hoi, in the country and told the War Department to shoot them if they disobey.

"Therefore our society hung up notices on the streets, saying, 'The people ought to complain and naturally must come together in public meetings. The people can shave their heads if they wish, for the Imperial Edict issued in the Ul-Mi year, ordering the shaving of heads, has not been abolished. Moreover officials have shaved their heads. Then why disperse the people who do so; and shoot them for disobeying orders?

"'The Government is composed of the pro-Russian party, but our Il Chin Hoi is the representative of 20,000,000 people, and we swear not to serve the present Government.'

"That was the proclamation, which we hung up on the streets, but the Government sent its servants and tore away our notices.

"We sent a letter to the Government advising them to resign office, and saying that, 'the flower; which will fall does not wait to be picked, nor does the leaf touched by frost wait for a strong wind to blow it from the tree. You officials seem to think this is so, but you are in the dangerous position of a blind man on a blind horse, riding towards a deep pool.'

"Our country is between two nations fighting and a few thousand li of our land has been spoilt and many lives have been lost. Ten years ago the people were sorrowful over the policy of the Government and wished only to serve a big country. Hence the accident to the late Empress and the removal into the Russian Legation of the Imperial throne.

"But during the last years, the Government has become worse, and now we have the Japan-Russia war. Whose fault is that?

(Continued on page 3).

The Korea Daily News.

VOL. I, THURSDAY, NOVEMBER 3, 1904. No. 92

HONGKONG & SHANGHAI BANKING CORPORATION.

Paid-up Capital.................$10,000,000
Reserve Fund:—Sterling Reserve... 10,000,000
Silver Reserve..... 7,000,000

27,000,000
Reserve Liability of Proprietors... 10,000,000

HEAD OFFICE, HONGKONG.

London Bankers, London and County Banking Company Limited.
Branches and Agencies,
London.

Amoy,	Hankow	Penang,
Bangkok,	Hiogo,	Rangoon,
Batavia,	Iloilo,	Saigon,
Bombay,	Lyons,	San Francisco,
Calcutta,	Manila,	Singapore,
Colombo,	Nagasaki,	Sourabaya,
Foochow,	New York,	Tientsin,
Hamburg,	Peking,	Yokohama,

Credits granted on approved Securities, and every description of Banking and Exchange business transacted.

Drafts granted on London and the chief Commercial places in Europe, India, Australia, America, China and Japan.

HOLME RINGER & Co., AGENTS, CHEMULPO.

ON CHEONG & CO., SEOUL.

GENERAL STORE KEEPERS.
Imported provisions, Cooking Utensils Crockery, etc.
FRESH BREAD DAILY.

MITSU BISHI DOCKYARD & ENGINE WORKS,
NAGASAKI.

CODE WORD, "DOCK."

A. 1, A. B. C., and Engineering Codes used.

DOCK No. 1 (at Tategami).

Extreme Length..............523 feet
Length on blocks............513 ,,
Width of Entrance on Top......89 ,,
,, ,, Bottom....77 ,,
Water on Blocks at Spring Tide 26½ ,,

DOCK No. 2 (Mukaijima).

Extreme Length..............371 feet
Length on Blocks............360 ,,
Width of Entrance on Top..... 66 ,,
,, ,, Bottom 53 ,,
Water on Blocks at Spring Tide 22 ,,

PATENT SLIP (at Kosuge).

Can take vessels up to 1,000 tons gross.

THE WORKS are well equipped with the LATEST IMPROVEMENTS, and can execute any kind of work in SHIPBUILDING and MARINE ENGINEERING, as well as in REPAIRING of SHIPS.

The COMPANY'S new powerful steamer OURA-MARU (712 tons, 700 I.H.P.), specially built for SALVAGE PURPOSES, and equipped with necessary gear, is always READY at SHORT NOTICE.

CHARTERED BANK OF INDIA AUSTRALIA & CHINA.

INCORPORATED BY ROYAL CHARTER 1853

HEAD OFFICES:—LONDON.

Paid-up Capital £800,000
Reserve Liability of Shareholders 800,000
Reserve Fund 800,000

Drafts granted upon all the principal places in the world and every description of Exchange and banking business transacted.

E. MEYER & Co., Agents, Chemulpo.

E. MEYER & CO.
Chemulpo.

SOLE AGENTS IN KOREA FOR:
A. T. Morse, Sons & Co's
"Fresco" Distemper

In all colours ready for use on walls, Ceilings etc.
and
AVENARIUS CARBOLINEUM

A wood-preserving and antiseptic oil preparation

Against decay, dry-rot, fungus and wood-destroying insects.

A large supply always in Stock.
Prices upon application.

E. MEYER & Co., Chemulpo.

THE METHODIST PUBLISHING HOUSE,
Little West Gate, Seoul.

PRINTING, TYPEWRITER PAPER
CARBON PAPER, VISITING CARDS
STATIONERY, BOOK BINDING
BOOK PUBLISHERS
AMERICAN SCHOOL BOOKS
SPENCERIAN COPY BOOKS
PEN CARBON LETTER AND BILL BOOKS

S. A. BECK, Manager.

HOKURKU DOBOKU KAISHA.

Branch office in Chong Dong, Seoul.
Japanese telephone No. 165

CONTRACT DEPARTMENT.
We can contract to build any building or construction.
MERCHANDISE DEPARTMENT.
We can provide any building material. We have just contracted to build the new Belgian Legation.

DAI-ICHI GINKO.
LIMITED.
(Formerly the First National Bank)

ESTABLISHED 1873

INCORPORATED UNDER PRESENT LAW 1896

Capital - - - - - - - - Yen 5,000,000
Reserve Fund - . - - - 1,500,000

HEAD OFFICE:—TOKIO.

President: Baron SHIBUSAWA.

BRANCHES AND CORRESPONDENTS
In the Principal Cities and Towns of Japan.
Interest Allowed on
Fixed deposits 1 year - - - 6½ per cent
" " 6 months - - - 6 per cent

Special current accounts 1½ sen daily per Y 100
General " " 1 " " " 100

M. TANAKA,
Manager, Chemulpo

HOLME RINGER & Co.
Chemulpo.

General Merchants and Government Contractors.

Agents for the leading
Banks
Steamship Companies
and
Insurance Companies

Importers of Merchandise of every description.

KAMEYA & CO.
GENERAL STOREKEEPERS
Chinkokai - - Seoul
(*Established 1895, Tokyo*)

Confectionery, Hams, Canned Goods, Cutlery, Hirano & Tansan Water. Provisions, Gents, Furnishing goods, Toilet Articles, Travelling Bags, Tobacco, Cigars & Cigarettes Kitchen Utensils. Coffee, Biscuits.

Fresh Goods always kept in Stock.
Prices Moderate
Please come and inspect our goods.

NIPPON YUSEN KAISHA.

JAPANESE MAIL STEAMSHIP CO.

UNDER MAIL CONTRACT WITH THE IMPERIAL JAPANESE GOVERNMENT.

European Line

Regular Fortnightly Service between Yokohama Kobe, Moji, Shanghai, Hongkong, Singapore, Penang Colombo, Port Said, Marseilles, London and Antwerp

American Line

Regular Fortnightly Service between Hongkong and Seattle, calling at Shanghai, Moji, Kobe, Yokohama and Victoria, B. C.

Australian Line

Regular weekly Service betwen Japan Ports and Australia, calling at Hongkong and Manila.
(Above Three Lines Suspended until further notice).

Shanghai Line

Weekly Service between Shanghai and Japan Ports

Korea Line

Service Kobe, Moji, Nagasaki, Fusan, Chemupo, Chefoo, Taiku.
S. S. Bahelsberg, 2181 tons.
Service Kobe. Moji, Fusan, Chemulpo, Chinnampo
S. S ARGO, S. S. Ohio.

BORDEN'S CONDENSED MILK CO.
New York, U. S. A.

ALWAYS IN STOCK
Eagle Brand Condensed Milk.
Gold Seal Condensed Milk.
Peerless (Family) Evaporated Cream.
Borden's Malted Milk.

E. MEYER & CO.
Chemulpo, Korea,
Sole Agents

ROYAL INSURANCE COMPANY,
Funds exceed £10,000,000
FIRE
AT CURRENT RATES.
LIFE
REDUCED PREMIUM,
HOLME RINGER & Co.,
Agents, Chemulpo.

HOTEL DU PALAIS
SEOUL.

The only first class Hotel in Seoul. Situated in the centre of the city opposite the palace.

Cuisine under the supervision of an experienced French Chef.

Well ventilated and furnished throughout.

TARIFF UPON APPLICATION.

L. MARTIN
Proprietor and Manager.

大韓每日申報
대한ᄆᆡ일신보

(데구십삼호) (금요일) 일쳔구빅사년십일월오일

본사고빅

이신보는영어와한어로셔계틱
일출판ᄒᆞ옵
신문가
한쟝 엽젼두돈오푼
한달치 엽젼두량닷돈
우표가미삭닷돈
다닷돈으로밧솝
광고료는
귀한의쟝단과ᄌᆞ힝의다쇼로죵
량ᄒᆞ되련가로밧을터이오매오
리지아녀대한사람마다다이신
문을보실터이니광고비서기를
원ᄒᆞ시는이들은우리신문사에
와셔뎡약ᄒᆞ심을희망ᄒᆞ옵
○발힝소 박동대한ᄆᆡ일신보
사발힝ᄒᆞ는교양해젼영국인셜벨
림졍자리오
사쟝 영국인 (비셜)
평양 티리졈
○평양효동사는젼미보씨로우
리신문관에티리인을허정ᄒᆞ엿
ᄉᆞ오니평양에게신구람코져ᄒᆞ
시는 쳠군ᄌᆞ는히티리졈에왕
림ᄒᆞ와연회ᄒᆞ시옵

사고

○우리대한ᄆᆡ일신보의목뎍은
대한의안녕질서에관한모든데
부에티ᄒᆞ야ᄂᆞᆫ고평한변론을쥬
쟝ᄒᆞᆯ이라우리ᄂᆞᆫ신원의필보ᄂᆞᆫ
신문보시ᄂᆞᆫ쳠군ᄌᆞ의게ᄒᆞᆼ샹보
도ᄒᆞ리며편지를귀셔ᄒᆞ며주시
ᄂᆞᆫ이ᄂᆞᆫ셩명과번디를젹어붓치
시기를희망ᄒᆞ오며비케ᄒᆞᆫ신문
샹에긔재ᄒᆞ란ᄂᆞᆫ거시아니오다
만국취신용ᄒᆞᄂᆞᆫ죵거를숨고자
ᄒᆞᆯ이라귀자ᄂᆞᆫ아모귀서던지과
지ᄒᆞᆷ을퇴각ᄒᆞᄂᆞᆫ권리를가졋스
나퇴각ᄒᆞᄂᆞᆫ리유를말ᄒᆞᆯ터이오
며공중평화를문란케ᄒᆞᄂᆞᆫ듯ᄒᆞᆫ
귀서ᄂᆞᆫ의례히밧지안켓솝나이
다
●본사셜시이리로신문을미양
우례로본젼ᄒᆞ와레젼부의잉외
로젼ᄒᆞᄂᆞᆫ듯ᄉᆞ로먼곳에ᄂᆞᆫ후ᄂᆞᆫ게
젼ᄒᆞ기도ᄒᆞ며후벗칠거슬ᄒᆞᆫ번
에젼ᄒᆞ기도ᄒᆞ며후아니젼ᄒᆞᄂᆞᆫ
곳도잇다ᄒᆞ와우리신문을ᄉᆞ랑
ᄒᆞ야구람ᄒᆞ시ᄂᆞᆫ 쳠군ᄌᆞ의게
티ᄒᆞ야미우미안ᄒᆞᆸ기로지금
은분젼인을두고미일일즉이젼
ᄒᆞ며아니젼ᄒᆞ거나늣게거나ᄒᆞᆫ
폐가잇도록ᄒᆞ란ᄒᆞ오니ᄒᆞ아니
젼ᄒᆞ거나ᄂᆞᆫ후늣게젼ᄒᆞ거나ᄒᆞᆫ일
이잇스면본사로통긔ᄒᆞ여주심
을희망ᄒᆞ옵

본사광고

○본사신문중에잡긔ᄒᆞᆫ호수를
소용ᄒᆞᆯ데가잇서이에광고ᄒᆞ오
니누구시던지그중에아모호수
던지가져오시ᄂᆞᆫ티로리쟝에빗
젼주문사드리리다
데이호 데샹호 데이십호
데ᄉᆞ십이호 데ᄉᆞ십삼호 데
오십삼호 데오십ᄉᆞ호와데오
십오호 데륙십이호

관보

데이쳔구빅칠십ᄉᆞ호 광
무팔년십일월삼일
셔임급ᄉᆞ령
○임젼위대이현티대일대티룩
군군의보 서쟝힝관샹등 구품
빅희달 십월이일
○승셔판임관오등 공쥬면보
ᄉᆞ쥬ᄉᆞ 박규회 힘쥬면보ᄉᆞ
쥬ᄉᆞ 셩락필 십월십일
사○승셔관임관샹등 젼쥬면보
사쥬사 오팽영
십월십칠일
○군과창부관리 륙군포병부
령 리빈섭 ○보군과창부관
륙군포병참령 민영원 ○보
군과창쟝사관 륙군포병참령
리민식 ○졍보군과창졈사관
륙군무관학교학도터부륙군보
병부위 박두영 ○보군과창
향관 륙군삼등사계 빅학진
륙군일등군사 빗남붕
○보군과창의관 륙군삼등군
의 김명식
○보군과창졔조소쟝 륙군포
병참령 김졍우
위 박덕슈
○임군과창졔조소쟝셔쥬임관
이등 젼긔ᄉᆞ 한용
○임군과창졔조소쟝셔쥬임관
륙등 젼긔ᄉᆞ 송경화
○임군과창기ᄉᆞ셔쥬임관오등
륙품 쟝용식 구품 박승현
○임군과창기ᄉᆞ셔쥬임관륙등
륙군포병참위 ᄒᆞᆼ한식 오품
왕종식 김티셕 구품
현귀 조희셕
ᄉᆞ○금일군봉 이샹십월십구일
리 빈영복
직봉 닉부광졔원졔약

십월이십일
○경임외쥬시쳐관소관ᄉᆞ 의
쥬갑리 리민보
○경임통쳔항쳐관소관ᄉᆞ 통
쳔감리 윤용구
이샹십월이십ᄉᆞ일
○승셔쥬임관오등 탁지부쥬
ᄉᆞ판 빅리동
십월삼십일일
○명궁닉부쥬젼관셔쳐임관일
등 륙군부쟝 리종건
○명닉쟝원경셔 쳐임관삼등
종이품 리병규
○면경계 종일품 강석호
○의원면본관 황히도관찰부
쥬ᄉᆞ 용인쇼
○임황히도관찰부쥬ᄉᆞ셔관임
관륙등 쳠좌젼
○명닉부광졔원위원 리종원
○임셩균관박ᄉᆞ셔쥬임관륙등
흥쳥후 박승힝 조병위
흥종룡 흥지셩 박경온
리흥로 윤창룡 한면슈
리풍지 졍규남 류귀흥
리송연 쟝괴원 황현샹
리쥬영 리윤경 쟝의셕
김샹우 곽종인 신셩턱
김귀종 윤규병 오학규
젼면쟉 리종빅 셔경션
조병진 권계화 리괴쥬
김호 박경희 지약우
이샹십월이십일일
관쳥ᄉᆞ항
○시종무관부무관륙군보병부
령오보영이가본년십월샹일에
부샹을당ᄒᆞᆫᄉᆞ
○닉부광졔원위원한장호가십
월이십팔일에신고ᄒᆞᆫᄉᆞ
궁닉부ᄉᆞ
○조왕궁닉부쟝진관리근턱으
로호위티총관을샹으라
○호위티총관리종건ᄉᆞ직소
지닉에ᄉᆞ양ᄒᆞᆫ즁총관지임관의
서ᄒᆞ노라
소 ○평안남도관찰ᄉᆞ리중하사직
비지닉관찰안부에다시번거히ᄉᆞ양
ᄒᆞᆫ즁ᄉᆞ직을더힘쓰라
○중츄원의관리민중ᄉᆞ직소
닉에쇼청을의시ᄒᆞ노라
이샹십일월이일
○군부관계
데 비샹토 경리국은일등국이
니국쟝은ᄉᆞ계감목이ᄒᆞ등ᄉᆞ계
로보직ᄒᆞ고경리국에두과를
좌굿치셜치ᄒᆞᆷ이라
데일과
데이과
데 비샹일됴 경리국데일과쟝
은륙군이등군ᄉᆞ로보직ᄒᆞ고
과원샹인은륙군샴등ᄉᆞ계와
일이등군ᄉᆞ로보직ᄒᆞᆷ이라
데이샹이됴 경리국데이과에
는ᄉᆞ무를좌굿치주쟝ᄒᆞᆷ이라
일은 륙군총예산결산과및모
든회계에관ᄒᆞᆫᄉᆞ항
이는 모든금여ᄒᆞᆷ과및회계규
졍의셩사ᄒᆞᆷ에관ᄒᆞᆫᄉᆞ항
삼은 봉급여비의규졍과및모
든회계문부검ᄉᆞ에관ᄒᆞᆫᄉᆞ항
ᄉᆞᄂᆞᆫ ᄉᆞ계부와및군ᄉᆞ부교육
인원보충과및군ᄉᆞ의샹군젹
에관ᄒᆞᆫᄉᆞ항
오ᄂᆞᆫ 휘방국일졀경리에관ᄒᆞᆫ
ᄉᆞ항
데이샹삼됴 경리국데이과쟝
은륙군이등ᄉᆞ계로보직ᄒᆞ고
과원샹인은륙군삼등ᄉᆞ계와일
이등군ᄉᆞ로보직ᄒᆞᆷ이라

잡보

○영쳥호죠 영국공관에셔외
부로공함ᄒᆞ기를본국신ᄉᆞ박갈
레가쟝츳목포에젼왕ᄒᆞ야히디
산림에ᄉᆞ냥ᄒᆞ되호송ᄒᆞᆯ터이니
에셔셜막ᄒᆞ고로숑ᄒᆞᆯ티이니호
조도쳥ᄒᆞ려니와면로에쥰빙ᄒᆞ
야보호케ᄒᆞ라ᄒᆞ엿더라
○본시현인 법국공관에셔외
부로죠회ᄒᆞ되귀국륙군부위김
병도ᄂᆞᆫ법국헌문에셔의통역이
쟝ᄅᆞ김씨가츌문ᄒᆞᆯ조음에헌병이
원에구류ᄒᆞ엿다ᄒᆞ니김씨ᄂᆞᆫ아
국잉젹ᄒᆞᆫ자인즉귀국법원에셔
조의로심사치못ᄒᆞᆯ겟슴으로함
고ᄒᆞᆫ다ᄒᆞ엿더라
○등티면역 일본공관에셔조
회ᄒᆞ되일젼에샹약ᄒᆞᆫ쳔쳔군하
대화도에등티셜시ᄉᆞᄂᆞᆫ일본군
티에셔입의과원들보니여검ᄉᆞ
ᄒᆞ엿더니동쟐ᄒᆞᆫ당ᄒᆞᆫ고로본월
신오일에휘과원을쇼환ᄒᆞ고공
역을뎡지ᄒᆞ엿스니희군슈의게
훈칙ᄒᆞ되빌쥬의ᄒᆞ야히ᄒᆞ디인
민으로ᄒᆞ여곰등병비희등티진
셜귀티를보호케ᄒᆞ라ᄒᆞ엿더라
○경관월권 외부에셔욕구경
리의게훈령ᄒᆞ되각항시니에경

무셔설치ᄒᆞᆫ본의ᄂᆞᆫ잔폐비를경찰ᄒᆞ고인민보호홈을위홈이오ᄉᆞ송등ᄉᆞᄂᆞᆫ지관소가조지ᄒᆞ거놀근쟈에경관이쟝졍솔직회지안코쳔조로이순검을각쳐에발송ᄒᆞ야빅셩의지물을토식ᄒᆞᆫ다ᄒᆞ니극히롱완ᄒᆞᆫ지라조금위시ᄒᆞ야경관이감리의지휘를쥰힝치아니ᄒᆞ고월권ᄒᆞᄂᆞᆫ폐가잇거든낫낫치ᄒᆞ야죠쳐케ᄒᆞ되만일히감리가엄호홈이잇스면또ᄒᆞᆫ견책ᄒᆞ리라ᄒᆞ엿더라

○경졀은면 작일은 영친왕면하의탄신이라젼례대로샤면죠칙을ᄂᆞ리셧ᄂᆞᆫ딩법부와평리원ᄒᆞᆫ셩지판소십삼도지관소.십삼도지관소와륙군법원죄슈즁가히방셕ᄒᆞᆯ쟈ᄂᆞᆫ방셕ᄒᆞ고가히감등ᄒᆞᆯ쟈ᄂᆞᆫ감등ᄒᆞ고미결슈도꾸졍빅히져판ᄒᆞ야일체시힝ᄒᆞ되늙은이와ᄋᆞ히ᄂᆞᆫ무론니외지관소ᄒᆞ고경죄에붓쳐셔죠가와궁휼ᄒᆞᆫ뜻스로화긔를융셩ᄒᆞᆯ뜻스로신칙ᄒᆞ라ᄒᆞ옵셧더라

○리씨방훈 졍부에셔법부에죠회ᄒᆞ기를방축향리ᄒᆞ엿든리긔동이특방되엿스니리씨의소지군에곳훈칙ᄒᆞ라ᄒᆞ고로법부에셔지작일에동씨잇ᄂᆞᆫ음죽군으로훈령ᄒᆞ고졍부에죠복ᄒᆞ엿더라

○훈령물시 일작야에민회를히산ᄒᆞ라신 죠칙은환슈ᄒᆞ시고의졍부에셔경무쳥으로발송ᄒᆞ엿든훈령도물시ᄒᆞ엿더라

○군용면선보호 경샹북도관찰ᄉᆞ쟝승원씨가니부와텰도원에보고ᄒᆞ되경부텰도건셜ᄉᆞ무소남부감독과ᄉᆞ의공함을졉준ᄒᆞᆫ즉경계쟈텰도와밋면선외교통ᄒᆞ며동신ᄒᆞᄂᆞᆫ딩극히즁요홈은귀관도필시밝히알터이나금번에쥬차군ᄉᆞ령관의군령이등포되여경부텰도에도역셔준용케되엿슨즉일후에만일범죄ᄒᆞᄂᆞᆫ쟈가잇스면히군령으로쳐형ᄒᆞ겟스니귀관하각군의대소관민의게엄훈ᄒᆞ고죵칙ᄒᆞ야죄를범ᄒᆞᄂᆞᆫ딩나아가지안케ᄒᆞ라ᄒᆞᆫ동인인바면선을가허ᄒᆞᆫ자ᄂᆞᆫ즁형에쳐ᄒᆞᆫ다홈은임의젼관찰ᄉᆞ때에외부훈령을인ᄒᆞ야각군에훈칙ᄒᆞ엿거니와지금이공함니에데오데륙량됴에동리안에가셜ᄒᆞᆫ군용면선을보호홈은각기동민이칙임ᄒᆞ되위원을교ᄃᆡᄒᆞ야보호ᄒᆞᆯᄉᆞ와만일그가히훈자를보라치아니ᄒᆞ면히보호위원을티벌ᄒᆞᆫ다ᄒᆞ엿시니선로의쇼경홈이혹산벽ᄒᆞᆫ딩ᄂᆞᆫ광야의ᄂᆞᆫ잇스니자슈ᄒᆞ기불편ᄒᆞ고혹동ᄒᆞᆫ거리번잡ᄒᆞᆫ곳에잇스니촉샹ᄒᆞᆫ쟈를조라ᄒᆞ기가극난이라쳥도셔브터금산ᄭᆞ지이빅여리에털도소경ᄒᆞᆫ동리가수빅에니리지아니ᄒᆞᆫ즉빅셩을 ᄒᆞ야인가ᄒᆞ기가난쳐ᄒᆞ니죠량ᄒᆞ여화시ᄒᆞ라ᄒᆞ엿더라

○치도독촉 한셩부에셔니부로보ᄒᆞ기를일본병참ᄉᆞ령관립영승삼랑의셩칭을거ᄒᆞᆫ즉경셩원산간도로즁에월근문밧박셕고기와혜화문과돈암고기세곳이다험준ᄒᆞ야최즁이왕릭ᄒᆞᄂᆞᆫ딩미양불편ᄒᆞ니그험쥰ᄒᆞᆫ곳을쇼허평탄케ᄒᆞ라ᄒᆞ엿기에그세곳을가셔심사ᄒᆞᆫ즉박석고기ᄂᆞᆫ시이에즁디가잇셔긔착ᄒᆞ기가어렵고혜화문도또ᄒᆞᆫ즁디에계관ᄒᆞ엿슬ᄲᅮᆫ더러만일착슈ᄒᆞ여시역ᄒᆞᆫ즉부비가거액이되겟ᄂᆞᆫ고로그난쳐ᄒᆞᆫᄉᆞ리를반복ᄒᆞ여셜명ᄒᆞ되죵시쳥숑치아니ᄒᆞ고그병참에셔실디를측량ᄒᆞ야역비오쳔삼백삼십칠원구십삼젼에산표를문드러보내고불일ᄌᆞ촉ᄒᆞ며또말ᄒᆞ기를만일다시연라ᄒᆞ면스ᄉᆞ로역ᄉᆞ시작ᄒᆞ겟노라ᄒᆞᆫ온바일이즁ᄃᆡᄒᆞᆫ대계관ᄒᆞ엿스니챠관ᄒᆞ여회시ᄒᆞ라ᄒᆞ엿더라

○위협독촉 민병셕씨가평양감ᄉᆞᄒᆞ엿슬때에색리박찬규를얽어모합ᄒᆞ야거대ᄒᆞᆫ가산을탕픽ᄒᆞ고박야를평리원에압샹ᄒᆞ야징역홀말은루차각신문에이왕계지ᄒᆞ엿거니와박야가납속ᄒᆞ고몽방ᄒᆞ엿ᄂᆞ니쎄앗긴돈과밋잡비병ᄒᆞ야합이엽팔십여만량이라박야가민대신을가셔보고쌔앗긴돈을독촉ᄒᆞ다가다시화호ᄒᆞ엿ᄂᆞᆫ딩박씨말이이쌔앗긴돈을물론ᄒᆞ고당오십만량만출급ᄒᆞ면젼당잡힌답도를도로물녀지보ᄒᆞ겟노라ᄒᆞᆫ민대신이쾌연이응낙ᄒᆞ더니이달져달ᄒᆞ여온젼이ᄉᆡ으러가기만일삼ᄂᆞᆫ고로일젼에박야가치쥬일인과곳치민대신집에가셔쥬틔를되칙ᄒᆞ며위협ᄒᆞ야독촉ᄒᆞ엿더니민대신이일본공ᄉᆞ의게쳥촉ᄒᆞᆫ즉공ᄉᆞ의말이이거손령ᄉᆞ의소관이라ᄒᆞ엿ᄂᆞᆫ딩박씨도령ᄉᆞ관에호소ᄒᆞ엿ᄂᆞᆫ지라령ᄉᆞ가히송리를사힉ᄒᆞᄂᆞᆫ즁이라더라

○연무관람 지작일샹오열두시에군부대신리윤용씨가츌셕ᄒᆞ야시위일대디를군부압흐로쳥ᄒᆞ야대연무를관람ᄒᆞ엿ᄂᆞᆫ디각대디도ᄎᆞ례로관람ᄒᆞᆯ터이러더라

○회의통텹 작일하오두시에졍부에셔회의ᄒᆞᆯᄎᆞ로각부에통텹ᄒᆞ엿더라

○일군량슈 영평군슈리민식씨ᄂᆞᆫ본직이록군졍위인딩향쟈군졔ᄀᆡ졍시에참령으로승차ᄒᆞ엿더니니부대신리용틱씨ᄂᆞᆫ히씨가참령으로젼임ᄒᆞᆫ줄노알고농부쥬ᄉᆞ셔상봉씨로히군슈를셔임ᄒᆞ엿더니리군슈가리니대를방견ᄒᆞ고무러왈영평군슈ᄂᆞᆫ두사ᄅᆞᆷ식셔임ᄒᆞᄂᆞ냐ᄒᆞᆫ즉히대신이무안ᄒᆞ야셔군슈를쟝촛타읍군슈로이임ᄒᆞᆫ다더라

뎐보

십일월일일동경발

○려순졈급 이십륙일ᄭᆞ지련속ᄒᆞ여우리군ᄃᆡ가밍렬히공격ᄒᆞ여동계관산화약고및시가에화지를니르키고군함도또ᄒᆞᆫ큰손히를당케ᄒᆞ고소히션일쳑을격침ᄒᆞ고오후에니르러ᄂᆞᆫ이룡산과의ᄌᆞ산과안ᄌᆞ산에모든포ᄃᆡᄂᆞᆫ침묵ᄒᆞ고우리군사ᄂᆞᆫ송슈산과이룡산과산북에잇ᄂᆞᆫ발권산의진터를돌격ᄒᆞ야졈령ᄒᆞ엿다ᄒᆞ엿더라

○혼하우안쇼젼 삼십일오후에적의보병일련ᄃᆡ와긔병오륙즁ᄃᆡ가포팔문을가지고료양봉쳔셔방혼하하류에쥬둔ᄒᆞᆫ일군일ᄃᆡ를향ᄒᆞ야압박ᄒᆞ기로일병부ᄃᆡ가ᄃᆡ젹ᄒᆞ엿고또적의보병일부ᄃᆡ와긔병일련ᄃᆡ도대포륙문을가지고ᄒᆞᆫ때에히방면을공격ᄒᆞ야리도ᄒᆞ엿스되일군은조곰손히를바들ᄲᅮᆫ이오젹은대단ᄒᆞᆫ손히를당ᄒᆞ고일군의게격퇴ᄒᆞᆫ바되야시톄십삼과군마십륙을젼장에바렷고일군의손상은하ᄉᆞ이하십명과군마십이두가부샹ᄒᆞ엿ᄂᆞᆫ딩젼쟁에츌젼ᄒᆞᆫ젹은또고삿구뎨ᄉᆞᄉᆞ단인줄확실ᄒᆞ다더라

론셜

린국걸인

○일본에군인된쟈ᄂᆞᆫ쟝관이하병졸ᄭᆞ지라도젼쟝에나가힘을다ᄒᆞ며용밍을써싱사를불고ᄒᆞ고졈졈진보홈은자긔들의나라를위ᄒᆞ랴ᄂᆞᆫ목젹이얼마큼잇셔셔그리홈인즉빗난명예가손상될리가만무ᄒᆞ되한국에잇ᄂᆞᆫ문관들과소위빅셩들은자긔나라에은연즁손히되ᄂᆞᆫ바ᄂᆞᆫ싱각지아니ᄒᆞ고다만자긔들의게만리롭도록ᄒᆞᄂᆞᆫ일이허다ᄒᆞ니엇던일본빅셩이자긔나라정부에면보줄과총을방미ᄒᆞᄂᆞᆫ되염치업시즁가로미여팔앗다고도ᄒᆞ며대관에셔ᄂᆞᆫ빅동전을사주ᄒᆞ야전국에츙만ᄒᆞ게되엿다고ᄒᆞ니범사가약ᄎᆞᄒᆞᆫ즁한국에딩ᄒᆞ야ᄒᆞᄂᆞᆫ일을볼진ᄃᆡ더옥기가막킨거시당초에히군명셕이라ᄒᆞᄂᆞᆫ아죽업ᄂᆞᆫ지라일천팔빅팔십팔년(열여셧히)젼에미들스쌔로ᄶᅡ에셔풀라쓰라ᄒᆞᄂᆞᆫ이쳔일빅사십삼돈되ᄂᆞᆫ화륜션ᄒᆞᆫ쳑을졔조ᄒᆞᆫ쟈ㅣ잇셧ᄂᆞᆫ딩그후에삼정물산회사에셔사드린후비일홈을곳쳐승립환이라고ᄒᆞ엿ᄂᆞᆫ딩그륜션본갑인즉얼마인지자셔히알수업스되그러ᄒᆞᆫ둥사에경력잇ᄂᆞᆫ사ᄅᆞᆷ의말을드를진ᄃᆡ이십만원가치ᄂᆞᆫ되겟다고평론ᄒᆞ더니

작년에또빈를변ᄒᆞ야군함이라자칭ᄒᆞᆫ후삼정물산회샤에셔한국정부에향ᄒᆞ야오십오만원으로결가ᄒᆞ고방매ᄒᆞ엿ᄂᆞᆫ지라져간리허ᄂᆞᆫ엇지되엿ᄂᆞᆫ지알수업스나그러나또ᄒᆞᆫ한국정부에셔실노그빅구입홈을요구ᄒᆞ엿ᄂᆞᆫ지도밋지못ᄒᆞ게ᄂᆞᆫ즁시ᄀᆞᆫ로평론ᄒᆞ면팔만원가치밧게아니되겟다고들ᄒᆞ기ᄂᆞᆫᄒᆞ나본가에셔도거위갑졀이되여삼십구만원에작정ᄒᆞ야월기ᄒᆞ엿다ᄒᆞ기에우리ᄂᆞᆫ이말솜듯고싱각ᄒᆞ기를만일압제로홍셩ᄒᆞ엿스면유혹가야로ᄃᆡ만일그러치아니ᄒᆞ면어불셩셜이기로대경소피히넉이엿더니

과연한국정부에셔미입ᄒᆞ게되여이십만원은션급ᄒᆞ고여액삼십오만원은량차에분비ᄒᆞ야십칠만오천원식샹환ᄒᆞ기로약조가되엿다가맛참그즈음에일아ᄀᆡ장이되엿ᄂᆞᆫ지라그비들일본히군셩에셔미삭세금삼쳔원식주기로졍약ᄒᆞ고셕탄운송션으로사용ᄒᆞ엿셧ᄂᆞᆫ딩

일간에일본공샤가한국정부에공함ᄒᆞ기를션가영지조삼십오만원을귀국명년도예산에편입ᄒᆞ야인삼젼민권을허락ᄒᆞ야달나ᄒᆞ고히군셩에셔세금젼팔삭조이만사쳔원은삼졍물산회사로보니겟다고ᄒᆞ엿다ᄒᆞ니

이러ᄒᆞᆫ일에라도볼진ᄃᆡᄒᆞᆫ잡홈이무쌍ᄒᆞ야일본대포자된명예를엇기가어려운거시비록일본공샤가당초륜션을미매계약ᄒᆞᆯ때에ᄂᆞᆫ샹관치아니ᄒᆞ엿드리도자긔나라빅셩의일인즉히군셩에셔삼졍물산회샤로보니드리도아니ᄒᆞ도록ᄒᆞ여야올흔일이오

히군셩에셔만ᄒᆞ드ᄃᆡ도삼졍물산회샤로더부러약조공안을아니ᄒᆞ엿슨즉세금은의례히한국정부로송교ᄒᆞᆯ밧게업거ᄂᆞᆯ근일에이러ᄒᆞᆫ수삼조건으로방향업시ᄒᆞᄂᆞᆫ일이잇스니

철도연로에범입ᄒᆞᆫ젼토가액을일본뎨일은힝에셔면져지발ᄒᆞ엿다고욕심것즁첩ᄒᆞ야한국정부에향ᄒᆞ야쳥구ᄒᆞᆫ면의례히응락ᄒᆞᆯ줄로알고그리홈인즉이지경으로가게되면필경에한국에소위지졍이라ᄂᆞᆫ거슨경갈무여ᄒᆞ게되도록다다익션일터이요진구무이가될지로다

이러ᄒᆞᆫ일이한국에딩ᄒᆞ야ᄂᆞᆫ모도볼길제사인즁일본으로셔또차관홀운동을ᄒᆞᆫ다ᄒᆞᆫ즉한국졍부졔공들은히관계약조인ᄒᆞ기젼에수삼조건을너어셩입ᄒᆞ시기를실심으로권고ᄒᆞ노니

첫지ᄂᆞᆫ쟈긔들이득치ᄒᆞᆫ다ᄒᆞ고둘지ᄂᆞᆫ자긔들이엇더케쓰라고ᄒᆞᆫ다고ᄒᆞ엿스면심히조홀듯ᄒᆞ노라

TELEGRAMS.

(FROM JAPAN PAPERS).

London, Oct. 28.

An official statement published in St. Petersburg with reference to the recent outrage in the North Sea states that two telegrams have been received from Admiral Rohjestvensky, in command of the Baltic Squadron.

In the first message the Admiral declares that two torpedoboats, which were not showing their lights, attacked the leading vessel of the Russian Squadon. The latter used its searchlights and opened fire on the torpedo-boats, whereupon the presence of several small steamers resembling fishing vessels was discovered. The Squadron endeavoured to spare the latter as soon as the torpedo-boats disappeared. The Admiral further declares that he could not be mistaken, as no torpedo-boats accompanied his fleet. One strange torpedo-boat was sunk, while the other was only damaged. The Squadron remained till the morning near the small steamer fleet, but did not assist the latter because the vessels were suspected of complicity in the attack in view of their obstinacy in crossing the Russian line several times.

In the second telegram Admiral Rohjestvensky states that his Squadron met several hundred fishing vessels, and showed them every consideration except on the occasion when they were in the company of foreign torpedo-boats. The Admiral expresses regret at the loss of life and sympathy with the victims, but the circumstances were such that no war-ship would have acted otherwise even in a time of profound peace.

Berlin, Oct. 28th.

Great Britain is concentrating the Channel and Mediterranean Squadrons for the purpose, it is thought, of detaining the Baltic Squadron if necessary.

The warlike menaces of the British Press are not supported by the attitude taken in official quarters.

France has offered her services to mediate between Great Britain and Russia, but this will probably not be necessary.

A report from St. Petersburg states that Great Britain has proposed to Russia to submit the case to arbitration according to the stipulations of The Hague Convention. In St. Petersburg the view is taken that the question will be satisfactorily settled by the punishment of those responsible. At present negotiations are proceeding between the two Governments with regard to the question of submitting the dispute to arbitration.

The Russian Embassy at Madrid has succeeded in obtaining permission from the Spanish Government for coaling the Baltic Squadron in Spanish waters, each ship being allowed to take 400 tons on board.

Tokyo, Oct. 29.

According to a telegram from Europe, received in authoritative quarters last night, a few hours previous to the occurrence of the incident in the North Sea a vessel believed to belong to the Baltic Squadron fired at a Swedish steamer. The vessel, however, sustained no damage. The matter is being discussed n St. Petersburg.

London, Oct. 29th.

It is understood that the British Cabinet has received promises of a speedy inquiry into the affair, and that such inquiry will probably be held at Vigo.

The danger of war between Great Britain and Russia has thus been removed.

Berlin, Oct. 28.

Viceroy Alexeiff has left Mukden for St. Petersburg.

COURAGE IN AMERICAN POLITICS.

The "Daily News," writing on the presidential campaign, praises Mr. Roosevelt as a President who showed from the first that he was not going to be a stop-gap. He began immediately to play a part in the history of the world second only to that of Wiliam II. . . His shadow has stretched across three Continents. His will is felt now in Asia and Europe, as well as in America. Always a preacher of the "strenuous life" among individuals, he had become a ferocious propagandist of the same life among nations. He completed the conquest of the Philippines. He has sent his ships to Panama, Beirut, Tangier, and Smyrna. His voice is heard at Peking. He has spoken to Roumania about her treatment of the Jews. He is the Lord Palmerston of the New World. We have little doubt, continues the "Daily News, that a President who has done so much to raise the name and status of Americans throughout the world will receve his due reward. Mr. Roosevelt has every chance of being again President of the United States. Perhaps the only matter on which the Democrats will have any chance of raising up feeling against him will be the negro question. President Roosevelt's bold and brave action of inviting Booker Washington to the White House has not been forgotten in the Southern States, where men are busily inventing devices for disfranchising the black man. But Mr. Roosevelt's magnificent courage carries him through difficulties which would beat other men. The only enemy whom he seems sincerely to respect is the power of the Trusts. Mr. Roosevelt was at one time very outspoken about his intention to clip their wings. But we hear nothing of all that now. The party managers have worn him down, and he has been obliged to surrender that part of his faith in order to preserve his political existence. On the whole, the Republictn Party are again in luck.

THE CHINESE COMMISSIONER TO TIBET.

An official telegram lately received here from Peking, informs us (Shanghai Daily Press) of the substance of the instructions which the Emperor and Empress Dowager have caused to be given to the Special Commissioner, Tang Shao-i, who has recently been appointed to look after China's interests in the negotiation of the prospective Anglo-Tibetan Treaty. These instructions are as follows:—

1. He shall act in concert with a Yu tai, Chinese Imperial Resident (Amban) in Tibet, and not in opposition to him.

2. He shall so arrange that the Anglo Tibetan Treaty shall become an Anglo-Chinese Treaty; and when it comes to be signed and sealed he shall see that the Chinese date is affixed to the instrument, and not the date according to the Tibetan calendar. He shall do everything in his power to vindicate and safeguard the sovereign rights of China in Tibet, and spare no effort to resist the inclusion of anything in the Treaty which would be at all likely to imperil or diminish China's predominance in the country.

3. He shall see that the terms of the Treaty are equitable and just, and take care to exclude from the Treaty all provisions which would be likely to provoke the oppositions of Russia, or cause that Power to be offended with China.

4. He shall not allow the Treaty to be signed until the Emperor of China telegraphs his sanction from Peking, however strongly the Dalai Lama and the British Commissioner may insist on the signing.

5. After the Treaty is signed, he shall make a study of Tibetan conditous, with regard to administration, defences, education, mining, and such matters, and forward exhaustive reports on all these subjects to Peking.

A LARGE ORDER.

Our reporter tells us that Mr. Megata the financial adviser urged the department officers to correct all documents for the past 10 years, so the officals are very busy now.

So we should think. Meanwhile Mr. Megata does "not" appear to be very busy.

Of late we have heard nothing of the much talked disolution of the Korean Army. Meanwhile the men appear to be drilling more zealously than ever. The Minister for War reviews a battalion every day.

It appears that Mr. Ford Barclay is again to visit Korea in quest of tigers. We see that the British Minister has notified the Foreign Office of his expected arrival and asked that the magistrates in the neighbourhood of Mokpo be instructed to extend all facilities and courtesies.

We are so far unable to learn the full extent of the damage done by the fire which recently occurred in the Japanese military store houses at Shaho(Antung). That the fire was an incendiary one and very disasterous there is no doubt, and we are inclined to assess the damage at very much more than the Y 1,000,000 mentioned by the "Express."

Emperor William is fixing the course of study for Princes August William, Oscar and Joachim. He has prescribed a course of comprehensive lectures on commercial subjects. The subject of these lectures will include industrial problems and technical questions in the railway business, embracing railway problems and progress in the United States. Further lectures will be given to elucidate the relations of great international financial and commercial houses.

The Korea Daily News.

Issued at 5 P. M. daily except Sundays.

Rate of Subscription:—

Per Year,	Yen 25.
Per Quarter,	Yen 7.
Per Month,	Yen 2.50.

Postage in Korea not charged extra.
Postage abroad charged extra.

Advertisements, 50 sen per day for 1 inch or less.
5 yen per month per inch.
50 yen per year per inch.

All communications to

E. T. BETHELL,
Editor and Publisher,
Pak-tong, Seoul

THE BALTIC FLEET.

Although the assertion of the Russian Admiral that the recent sinking of British trawlers was unavoidable and only due to their having amongst them several hostile (presumably Japanese) torpedo boats, has yet to be investigated, we are sure that all, whatever their sympathies in this war, will rejoice to find that the incident was not the senseless, crazy, wanton outrage, indicated by the earlier telegrams. Very elaborate coaling arrangements have been made along both the Cape and Canal routes to the East so that it is as yet impossible to be certain which will be the route to be finally adopted. It seems likely that the Cape route will be finally selected as although the canal route is quicker, an accident in the Canal, to one of the leading ships, would delay the whole squadron.

The following is a list of vessels comprising the squadron:

BATTLESHIPS.

Names.	Tonnage. tons.	Speed. knots.
Alexander III.	13,516 ...	18.00
Borodino	"	17.80
Orel	" ...	17.60
Prinz Souvaroff	"	18.00
Oslabya ...	12,674 ...	"
Navarin ...	10,206 ...	15.80
Sissoi Veliky ...	10,400 ...	15.65

CRUISERS.

Dmitri Donskoi	6,200 ...	1.700
Admiral Nakhimoff	8,524	16.60
Oleg	6,645 ...	23.00
Aurora	6,731	20.00
Svietlana	3,727 ...	20.20
Gemtchug	3,103	24.00
Izumrud	" ...	"
Almaz	3,258	19.00
Ural	8,278 ...	20.00
Don	8,430	19.50
Thelek	7,421 ...	19.00
Kubare (?) ...	8,479	18.00

DESTROYERS.

Vidny	350	26
Bravi	350	26
Buistni	350	26
Bedovi	350	26
Prosorlivy	240	27.50
Rezviyi	240	27.50
Prontsiteliny ...	240	27.50

In addition, there are two destroyers the construction of which has been only recently completed.

This constitutes a very formidable fighting force, and as there is now at least a strong probability that Port Arthur will hold out until its arrival, the situation is beginning to assume an aspect much more favourable to Russia than has yet been the case.

We have heard, on very good authority, that the destination of this fleet is Formosa and if Port Arthur holds out we have no doubt that this will prove to be true. They will there be able to refit at their leisure as, if Port Arthur has still to be watched, it will be impossible for Japan to send there a fleet capable of giving battle with any prospect of success

RETRENCHMENT IN JAPAN.

Apparently there will be a wholesale suspension of all public works in Japan next year. The estimate of expenditure originally fixed by the Department of Agriculture and Commerce for next year was over 8,000,000 yen. The figures were, however, reduced to 4,424,000 yen at the resent meeting of the Ministry, showing a diminution of 4,323,000 yen against the expenditure of the present year. As the result of this curtailment the Department will be obliged to either diminish or discontinue the grants-in-aid hitherto given to various business bodies at home and abroad.

The expenditure of the Department of Justice for next year has also been curtailed by more than 1,000,000 yen as against that of the present year. Among the various items reduced are 300,000 yen for the construction of prisons, 300,000 yen for the maintenance of prisons and other matters related thereto, and 400,000 yen for the repairs to the Courts and other buildings.

Chefoo says that the Russian Consul at that port has re-established communication with Port Arthur by wireless telegraphy.

It is stated that the Russian ships in Port Arthur now have their decks piled with sandbags which greatly reduce the effects of mortar fire.

A report states that the steamer *Ohio*, carrying sleepers from Hokkaido, stranded at the entrance to Chinnampo, on the 26th inst. and is a total loss, except a portion of her cargo with was landed. This steamer is not the *Ohio* belonging to Mr. D. W. Deshler of Chemulpo.

Mr. D. W. Stevens, Adviser to the Korean Foreign Office, who is now in Tokyo, attended the Palace on the morning of the 28th inst. and was received in audience by His Majesty the Emperor. Mr. Hagiwara, First Secretary of the Japanese Legation at Seoul, who returned to Tokyo several days ago, was also received in audience by the Emperor at the same time.

It is no secret, says a contemporary, that the Russians had been preparing for the eventuality of their fleet reaching Manila, and among colliers which have already left Cardiff for that rendezvous are the following:—

Name of Steamer.	Nationality.	Quantity of Coal. Tons.
Wilhelmina	British	6,700
Eva	German	5,000
Apollo	British	5,100
Safordia	British	5,400
Foxton Hall	British	3,900

At the St. Louis Exhibition Japan has gained the foremost position as a raw silk-producing country. According to the "Chugai Shogyo" the marks to be awarded by the Fair to the exhibits from the principal silk producing countries are as follows:—Japan, 160; Italy 25, France, 20; and China, 2.

The Commissioner of Customs, at Chefoo seems to be exercising his authority to prevent the conveyance of contraband of war from that port to either of the belligerents. He is said to have stopped a steamer suspected of carrying contraband for the Japanese army. The Japanese Consul, however, has protested against the measure, and an appeal is said to have been made to Mr. Uchida in Peking.

The "Daily Telegraph" communicates that in the last month an average of 100,000 tons of coal per month was shipped from Cardiff for Russia. The coal ships are stationed in the Mediterranean, the Red Sea, on the Western coast of Africa and off the Cape.

THE GENIAL SULTAN.

A constantinople correspondent said on Sept. 9th:—

The Sultan has just given evidence of generosity and cordiality in a manner to evoke great surprise. The occasion was the visit of the British fleet to Turkish waters. No sooner was the fleet signalled than the unusual welcome began. Over a million cigarettes were sent on board by the Sultan for the officers and men. Large sums of money were sent to the Governor of Smyrna and Beyrout by the Sultan himself for the entertainment of officers. The police received the strictest orders to watch over poor Jack and to afford him every protection and help from the harpies of Eastern ports, and in no case were the sailors to be interfered with. At Smyrna, for the first time for many years, an official ball and reception were given, which were the finest ever seen in Levantine waters. At Constantinople fowls, geese, and turkeys, as well as vegetables and fruit were sent on board the "Surprise" and "Tyne" in such quantities from the Sultan's farms that the decks were littered, and the officers begged that no more be sent. The Admiral took thirty-six officers with him to Constantinople on the "Surprise," and not one of them was allowed to spend a penny. They were almost chocked with dinners and champagne. At the state banquet on Wednesday the Sultan excelled himself by showing unwonted good humour. He received Sir Compton Domvile and Sir Nicholas O'Conor both before and after dinner—an unusual proceeding—and during the banquet had Sir Compton on one side and Sir Nicholas on the other. The fleet has now gone to Salonika, and his Majesty has sent a money chest down there against the fleet's coming.

THE MEN OF TO-DAY.

The imagination of all the peoples of antiquity was haunted with a chimerical vision of a species of superman, a sort of being perfectly constituted but larger and stronger than the ordinary man. This popular belief says M. Dastre, in the "Revue des Deux Mondes, has been so tenacious and general that it is interesting to ask whether or not the belief, has any foundation in fact? While it may be said that there have been no giants discovered in the past, still there are races of men which relatively speaking are giants. The races of the modern world are by anthropologists divided into four groups, considering races from the standpoint of height. The first is that of tall men, the English, 1.703 meters; Patagonians, 1.781 meters; Scotch, 1.710 meters; Scandinavians, 1.713 meters; Negroes of Guinea, 1.724 meters; Polynesians, 1.762 meters. The second group is that of men over the average height—1.65 to 1.70 meters—in which we have the French, 1,650 meters; Russians, 1.660 meters; Germans, 1.687 meters; Belgians, 1.684 meters; Irish, 1.697 meters. The third group is under the average—1.60 to 1.65 meters—Hindus, 1.642 meters; Chinese, 1.64 meters; Italians and Peruvians. Finally, we come to the classification of small people and 1.60 meters, of which the Malays and Japanese form divisions. All investigations show that the height of man has not varied for thousands of years, in fact as far back as it is possible for us to trade through the time of primitive man, prehistoric man, and finally, historic man.

The Government's instructions for the arrest of all Il-chin-hoi members have been rescinded and as the Japanese Army headquarters have once more taken this precious gang into favour, Mr. Komochi's army of paid agitators is looking forward to a good time.

The Korea Daily News.

VOL. I, FRIDAY, NOVEMBER 4, 1904. No. 93

大韓每日申報

대한매일신보

(뎨구십ᄉᆞ호)　　(월요일)　　일쳔구빅사년십일월칠일

본샤고빅

이신보는영어와한어로셔거리일츌판ᄒᆞᆸ

신문가

한장 엽두돈오푼

일삭됴 엽두량닷돈

우표가리 삭닷돈

다 닷돈으로밧숩

광고료는

귀한의쟝단과ᄌᆞ횟의다쇼로즁감ᄒᆞ되렴가로밧을터이오며오ᄅᆡ지아니ᄒᆞ여대한사람마다다이신문을보실터이니광고내시기를원ᄒᆞ시는이들은우리신문사에와셔면약ᄒᆞ심을희망ᄒᆞᆸ

○발힝소 박동대한미일신보사법어학교압해젼영국인셔젼관리쟈리오

사쟝 영국인 (비셜)

평양 티리졍

○평양효동사는권미보씨로우리신문관미티리인을뎡ᄒᆞ엿ᄉᆞ오니평양에계신구람코져ᄒᆞ시는쳠군ᄌᆞ는ᄒᆞᆫ티리졍에왕림ᄒᆞ와면의ᄒᆞ시옵

샤고

○우리대한미일신보의목뎍은대한의인민졀셔에관ᄒᆞᆫ모든뎨목에ᄃᆡᄒᆞ야는공평ᄒᆞᆫ변론을쥬쟝ᄒᆞᆷ이라우리동신원의탐보는신문보시는쳠군ᄌᆞ의게ᄒᆞᆼ샹보도ᄒᆞ리며편지들긔셔ᄒᆞ며주시는이는셩명과번디를젹어붓치시기를희망ᄒᆞ오니미거ᄒᆞᆫ신문샹에긔ᄌᆡᄒᆞ란는거시아니오다만긔히신용ᄒᆞ는즁거를숨고자ᄒᆞᆷ이라긔자는아모긔셔던지긔ᄌᆡᄒᆞᆯ뫼갸ᄒᆞ는권리를가졋스오나뫼갸ᄒᆞ는리유를말ᄒᆞᆯ터이오며공중평화를문란케ᄒᆞ는듯ᄒᆞᆫ긔셔는의례히밧지안켓ᄉᆞᆸ나이다

●본사셜시이래로신문을[illegible]양우레로분젼ᄒᆞ와레젼부의잉의로젼ᄒᆞ든스로번곳에는ᄒᆞᆫ[illegible]ᄭᅦ젼ᄒᆞ기도ᄒᆞ며혹번칠ᄭᅥ슴는쳡에젼ᄒᆞ기도ᄒᆞ며혹아니젼ᄒᆞ는곳도잇다ᄒᆞ와우리신문을ᄉᆞ탕ᄒᆞ야구람ᄒᆞ시는 쳠군ᄌᆞ의계뒤ᄒᆞ야미우미안ᄒᆞ옵기로지금은분젼인을두고미일즁이젼ᄒᆞ며아니젼ᄒᆞ거나늣게거나ᄒᆞᆫ폐가잇도록ᄒᆞ란ᄒᆞ오니혹아니젼ᄒᆞ거나늣게젼ᄒᆞ거나ᄒᆞᆫ일이잇스면본사로통긔ᄒᆞ여주심을희망ᄒᆞᆸ

본사광고

○본사신문즁에뎨긔ᄒᆞᆫ호수를소용ᄒᆞᆯ데가잇셔이에광고ᄒᆞ오니누구시던지그즁에아모호수던지가져오시는뒤로미쟝에빅젼두푼식드리리다

뎨이호　뎨삼호　뎨이십호　뎨ᄉᆞ십이호　뎨ᄉᆞ십삼호　뎨오십삼호　뎨오십ᄉᆞ호와뎨오십오호　뎨륙십이호

잡보

○로병힝동　음력구월오일에발송ᄒᆞᆫ단쳔군슈리헌지씨가닉부에보ᄒᆞᆫ보고를거ᄒᆞᆫ즉로국긔병과보병이음력ᄉᆞ월십일일노위시ᄒᆞ야ᄒᆞᆫ념ᄒᆞᆫ념북으로셔남으로나아간슈호가구빅팔십삼이오뎌즁에쏘ᄒᆞᆫ일빅이십여츄가되고합ᄒᆞᆫ군에유쥬ᄒᆞ다가지금도라와셔본군바곡등디에류쥬ᄒᆞ는항슈호가일쳔삼빅여명이되는데히병이왕리ᄒᆞ는길에량미와마량과식초등물을ᄌᆞ의로세아스며언로변에발수ᄒᆞ고곡식과쳥초등물을노회밥으며먹게ᄒᆞ고셩진에큐쥬ᄒᆞ는군병은본군리샹사와리하사와광쳥사세사의동리로출몰ᄒᆞ야쳥탈ᄒᆞᆷ이막심ᄒᆞ고쳥구ᄒᆞ는물건은위쳠에의외지못ᄒᆞ야촌탁이공퇴ᄒᆞᆷ을니린면신을가셜ᄒᆞ과도로른슈츅ᄒᆞ는역계의우리빅셩의역부가날노샹ᄉᆞ빅명에버리지아니ᄒᆞ고치셕으로써려고샹ᄒᆞᆫ자가미우만코쏘불샹대쳔다리룩빅여간을훼목으로써다가불쳔만금을츅로삼립을셰이다가셔은방금역ᄉᆞ를시작ᄒᆞ오며샹태젼을다펄엳ᄒᆞ자면민폐가막심ᄒᆞ지라본군슈의무지ᄒᆞᆫ으로써ᄒᆞ야는쳑쳐ᄒᆞᆯ방도가만무ᄒᆞ오니본직을속히갈아주시기를복망ᄒᆞᆫ다ᄒᆞ엿더라

○로병작폐 경셩　음력팔월이십구일에발송ᄒᆞᆫ경셩군슈의보고를거ᄒᆞᆫ즉로국긔병오십명이작일에두만강변에와셔자고남아층에본군으로지나경셩방면으로지향ᄒᆞ엿더라

○쳔단독축　졍부에셔각부부원에통쳡ᄒᆞ기를니외관직에쳔압ᄒᆞ는규칙을본월십오일부터시힝ᄒᆞ겟기로금십일로쳔만조를월송ᄒᆞ노니쥬의등쳡ᄒᆞ온바쳥금과ᄒᆞ미졍쳡갓치ᄒᆞ와도오거히쳔단자가ᄒᆞᆫ쟝도와셔니ᄅᆞᆫ시오엽수오니ᄃᆡ우아ᄒᆞᆫ자라이면단졍ᄒᆞ로셔엄치아니ᄒᆞ니지시은에주구간ᄒᆞᆯ의ᄐᆡᆨ용ᄒᆞᆷ이반디시[illegible]을부리러리로셕승ᄒᆞ니쳔단규[illegible]라ᄒᆞ엿더라

○군슈젼임　작일졍부회의에니부대신이졍난군슈엿디셧리를쳔임ᄒᆞ기로졔츌ᄒᆞ엿더라

○황후개증　지난삼일밤부터[illegible]황후가다시즁[illegible]ᄒᆞ더라

○한셩관운　한셩관운은차함[illegible]

○평셩원부걸　농상공부에셔[illegible]

○리씨미국유학　미국신문쥬필ᄒᆞ든리승만씨는미국에유학ᄒᆞ야신디를견습ᄒᆞᆯᄎᆞ로작ᄉᆞ일발졍ᄒᆞ는ᄃᆡ왕반ᄒᆞᆯ긔한은삼년으로례졍ᄒᆞ엿더라

○조힝뎐관　한셩부오셔[illegible]외교슈부가츄츙실졍출ᄒᆞ는ᄃᆡ관윤은차ᄒᆞᆷ으로훈회ᄒᆞ고실직으로셔무ᄒᆞᆷ관윤은셔임치아니ᄒᆞ는고로쇼윤발승조셔가ᄌᆞ힝ᄒᆞᆫ다더라

○쥬한각국공ᄉᆞ　일본동경[illegible]신의십월이십이일간ᄒᆞᆫ뎨일빅ᄉᆞ십ᄉᆞ호에운ᄒᆞ엿스되한국에잇는각국공ᄉᆞ관을[illegible]일본공ᄉᆞ가[illegible]라

진보당의대한졍략은젼권위원을두기로쥬쟝ᄒᆞ고모든기혁을챡슈ᄒᆞ기로ᄒᆞ는졍우회에서는[illegible]비샹의일을ᄒᆞᆫ란는것곳치[illegible]ᄒᆞ엿더라

○회세파열　졍부에셔일진회를포박ᄒᆞ란ᄒᆞ는ᄃᆡ맛참조쳑도는리셧고각도에쟝졍ᄒᆞᆫ훈령ᄒᆞ야지발송되엿더니불구에무시되엿스며평셩쥬차일본군대수평부에셔각병참소로훈령ᄒᆞ여회원을구휼보호ᄒᆞ라ᄒᆞ엿다ᄒᆞ엿더라

○강산충렬　일본병참소에셔공학수들과송ᄒᆞ야남산뒤외와연강샹하들입ᄒᆞ야츙광ᄒᆞ고쳠골생셤비샹을츙탕중이라더라

뎐보

[illegible]수꾀챵공보

○북히수진비샹　북히수건에관ᄒᆞ야로국졍부는ᄀᆞ장싱후ᄒᆞᆫ유감의ᄯᅳᆺ을표ᄒᆞ고로국황뎨도동일ᄒᆞᆫ의ᄆᆡ로영국황뎨의게뎐보ᄒᆞ엿고로국졍부는ᄉᆞ망쟈의유족에손ᄒᆞᆫ빈샹을ᄆᆡ기로영국에향ᄒᆞ야약속ᄒᆞ엿더라

○취인자됴사　로국졍부는엿던수관이소ᄒᆞ관에쳐ᄒᆞᆫ쟈든지회실ᄒᆞᆯ기를위ᄒᆞ야이ᄉᆞ변에관계잇는수관의ᄒᆞᆫ부분을셔반ᄒᆞ야국ᄯᅡᄅᆞ에머무르라ᄒᆞ고명령ᄒᆞ엿는ᄃᆡ이수관들은이일노위ᄒᆞ야고향ᄒᆞᆫ에국동지바야가지못ᄒᆞ겟다ᄒᆞ엿더라

○국제위원셜치　쏘영로량국졍부는국제위원을셜치ᄒᆞ야이ᄉᆞ건을됴사ᄒᆞ일을합의ᄒᆞ는ᄃᆡ[illegible]위원의게셔죄가잇다[illegible]고엄중히쳐벌ᄒᆞᆯ터이라ᄒᆞ엿더라

○로국세언　로국졍부는이런일이다시아니ᄂᆞ지안토록십분쥬의ᄒᆞ마고명세ᄒᆞ고언약ᄒᆞ엿더라

○영로위긔젼힝　이런ᄉᆞ졍으로말미암아영로량국간의위티ᄒᆞᆫ모양이이믜ᄯᅡ괴ᄒᆞ는듯ᄒᆞ다ᄒᆞ엿더라

○로국쟝관보고　십월이십칠일에[illegible]수통쟝관이[illegible]에셔셩피득보에뎐보ᄒᆞᆫ변보고의

요령이 여좌ᄒ니

우리함대는 블랑ᄎ희중에 영국어션단ᄉ이에 외국슈뢰뎡이 칙이 잇는거슬 알앗는ᄃ 이ᄉ건ᄒ 이슈뢰뎡들이 밤을 ᄐ셔 몰닉함ᄃ와 즁ᄒ거슬 공격ᄒ던지 ᄒ야 시작ᄒ다가 ᄉ에 탐ᄒ등으로셔 어션이 잇는거슬 알고 함ᄃ는 그 포격ᄒ든거슬 즁지ᄒ엿는ᄃ 그 셰에 슈뢰뎡도 그 ᄋ창을 일코로 국슈뢰뎡은 번져 셰불그에 ᄂ아 가 잇셧든고로 함ᄃ에는 동항치 마ᄒ엿다 ᄒ엿더라

십월이일 군ᄉ령부 칙뎐

○졔군병력 삼십일오후에로 아봉단길에셔 방하에 졉근ᄒ온우리 일부ᄃ를 엄습ᄒ야 온 졔군의 병력은 보병일련ᄃ이상과 긔병 일긔ᄉ단과 포병이 즁ᄃ더라 ᄒ엿더라

십일월이일 동경발

○려순젼황 십월이십륙일 아참 브리대구경포와 밋 취군포로 각포ᄃ를 공격ᄒ고 송슈산아 룡산 발권산 젼면에 취ᄌ를 돌격ᄒ온 후 점령ᄒ엿는ᄃ 일본 포탄이 ᄃ 밋쳐셔 공격이 ᄃ욱 ᄌ희되는고로 각포의 ᄃ포ᄉ격과 히ᄌ와 그 다른 건ᄌ물이 ᄃ 파괴ᄒ고 계관산 셔 방ᄆ 외구에 화약고도 쏘 폭발ᄒ엿고 이십팔일 시즈거리에셔 큰 화재를 니르켯고 이십구일 밤에 비룡산과 밋 계관산 포ᄃ에 일부가 폭발ᄒ여 파괴ᄒ엿고 쏘 항구 안에 소히 션 삼쳑에 큰 손히를 ᄒ엿다 ᄒ더라

동일 동경

○영함활동 지부라루다루에 잇는 영국 함ᄃ에 젼부는 활동ᄒ를 준비가 되엿다 ᄒ더라

관보

뎨이천구백칠십오호

광무팔년십일월ᄉ일

셔임급ᄉ령

○임뎐환국기ᄉ 셔주임관륙등 뎐환국주ᄉ 리상철

십월삼십일일

○임표훈원기ᄉ 셔판임관륙등 구품 안창션

○임창원감리셔주ᄉ 셔판임관륙등 [illegible]리감리셔주ᄉ 김병철

○임동리감리셔주ᄉ 셔판임관륙등 룡쳔감리셔주ᄉ 정인호

십일월이일

○면직 관립소학교교원 송슌명

십일월이일 학부

훈령륙ᄉ

○조왈츄 죄자를 법에 쳐ᄒ고 무죄자를 방셕ᄒ엿은즉 무단옥ᄉ 진조겁 취ᄒ은으로 법최이 정즁ᄒ여 ᄉ되샹금 평년도 계ᄉ유ᄒ니 기즁 엇지 원굴ᄒ은 법셜치 못ᄒ자 계엿스리오 이거시 법관이 발에 봄지못ᄒᆫ 법규요 샹ᄒ징지연타ᄒ야 고리홈이라 엇지 화괴를 감손치 아니ᄒ리오 잇세에 민셩를 뎌욱 금ᄒ홀지니 법부와 군부로ᄒ여곰 모든 미결슈를 다 쟝뵉히 졔관ᄒ야 방셕홈에 합당ᄒᆫ 자는 방셕ᄒ고 감등홈에 합당ᄒᆫ 자는 감등ᄒ고 이졀슈도 일제로 시힝ᄒ고 로약인즉 무론룡범ᄂ뇌ᄒ고 경죄로 분쳐셔 조가의 셔공홈ᄒ는 ᄯᅳᆺ슬 보이게 ᄒ라

십일월일일

군부관제 속

뎨이십ᄉ조 경리국에 이과에는 ᄉ무를 좌ᄀᆺ치 쥬쟝홈이라

일은 복쟝과 졔구와 군량과 마초와 마필을 버ᄇᄒᄂ 규칙에 관ᄒᆫ ᄉ항

이는 복쟝과 졔구와 군량과 마초와 군용힝쟝과 젼시소용과 명과 밋 마필 안구에 관ᄒᆫ ᄉ홍

삼은 군용ᄃ와 밋 모든 건츅물과 관유ᄒᆫ 지산에 관ᄒᆫ ᄉ홍

ᄉ는 물픔 회사와 밋 츌납 관리의 관ᄒᆫ ᄉ

뎨이십오조 회무국은 일등국이니 국장은 군의총제 일이등 군의장으로 보직ᄒ고 회무국에 두과를 좌ᄀᆺ치 셜치홈이라

뎨일과

뎨이과

뎨이십륙조 회무국 뎨일과 장은 이삼등군의장으로 보직ᄒ고 과원이 인은 삼등군의장 일이등군의로 보직홈이라

뎨이십칠조 의무국 뎨일과에는 ᄉ무를 좌ᄀᆺ치 쥬쟝홈이라

일은 위ᄉᆼ부교육과 밋 위ᄉᆼ지료의 관ᄒᆫ ᄉ홍

이는 건츅과 피복과 량식과 급슈와 비슈 등 일졀 위ᄉᆼ의 관ᄒᆫ 사홍

삼은 방역과 밋 치병의 관ᄒᆫ ᄉ홍

ᄉ는 군의 학교 병원과 밋 위ᄉᆼ회의에 관ᄒᆫ ᄉ홍

뎨이십팔조 의무국 뎨이과 쟝은 이삼등군의장으로 보직ᄒ고 과원이 인은 삼등군의장 일이등군의로 보직홈이라

뎨이십구조 의무국 뎨이과에는 ᄉ무를 좌ᄀᆺ치 쥬쟝홈이라

일은 위ᄉᆼ부의 인원 보충과 밋 군의의 이샹의 군적의 관ᄒᆫ 사홍

이는 위ᄉᆼ에 관계ᄒᆫ 규졍의 심사는 관ᄒᆫ 사홍

삼은 신체검사의 관ᄒᆫ ᄉ항과 샹ᄒ고 병드러 복역을 히졔 관ᄒᆫ ᄉ항

ᄉ는 위ᄉᆼ 져셜조사와 밋 기타 일졀 위ᄉᆼ에 관ᄒᆫ ᄉ항

뎨삼십조 군법국은 이등국이니 국쟝은 군법국쟝이 겸임ᄒ고 군부 국에 리ᄉ이 인을 셜치홈이라

뎨삼십일조 군법국에 ᄉ무를 좌ᄀᆺ치 ᄌ쟝홈이라

일은 군ᄉᄉ법에 관ᄒᆫ 사항

이는 륙군감옥에 관ᄒᆫ 사홍

삼은 군법부와 밋 감옥에 인결의 관ᄒᆫ 사홍

뎨삼십이조 군법국에 직원은 고등군법회의의 사무에 복홈이라

뎨삼십삼조 회계국은 일등국이니 국장은 회계군참쟝 혹 졍부령으로 보직ᄒ고 회계국에 아래 과를 좌ᄀᆺ치 셜치홈이라

론셜

셰틱함대

○아라사 셰틱함대가 동양으로 출발ᄒ다가 영국어렵대를 진격ᄒ야 격침ᄒᆫ후 그 함대수사에 등은 칭탁ᄒ기를 그 어렵대가 일본수뢰뎡 총중에 홈께 싸인 고로 포격홈에 이름이라 ᄒ고 ᄒ야 ᄒ금 식사ᄒ는중이나 그러ᄒ나 어제던지 감정상의 리는 사름마다 일반이어늘 ᄉ사로 몰각 광피ᄒᆫ 티도로 무진한 ᄒᆫ 힝위에 ᄀ 법홈은 우연ᄒᆫ 일로 돌일수 업는지라

그런고로 동양으로 출발ᄒ야 도착ᄒ기는 시각이 긴급ᄒ나 중간히 항에 즁지ᄒ고 잇는 나 이는 무ᄃ ᄒᆫ 리 셩 봉이로 출항ᄒ든 군함의 분션지 좌로 그 리몸이며 그 함대에 편셩ᄒᆫ 함쳑의 일홈과 돈수와 속력를 각 좌에 긔재ᄒ노라

일홈	돈수	속력
젼투함		
알렉센더	일만삼천오빅십륙돈	일천팔빅낫
섀로듸노	"	일천칠빅팔십낫
오럴	"	일천칠빅륙십낫
곡린스소바로푸		일천팔빅낫
오살뱌야	일만이천륙빅칠십사돈	"
나바린	일만이빅륙돈	일쳔오빅팔십낫
시소이벨리키	일만사빅돈	일천오빅륙십오낫
슌양함		
드미추리돈스쿄이	륙천이빅돈	일천칠빅낫
아드미랄키모푸	팔천오빅이십사돈	일천륙빅륙십낫
올레그	륙천륙빅사십오돈	이천삼빅낫
오로라	륙천칠빅삼십일돈	이천낫
스베트라아	삼천칠빅이십칠돈	이천이십낫
짐쳐그	삼천일빅삼돈	이천사빅낫
이셔머러드	"	"
알마쓰	삼천이빅오십팔돈	일천구빅낫
유앨	팔천이빅칠십팔돈	이천낫
쏜	팔천사빅삼십돈	일천구빅오십낫
듸렐크	칠천ᄉ빅이십일돈	일천구빅낫
규베아	팔천ᄉ빅칠십구돈	일천팔빅낫
결사듸		
비드늬	삼빅오십돈	이십륙낫
쌰라뷔	"	"
섀스틔늬	"	"
비도뷔	"	"
푸로솔리비	이빅사십돈	이십칠낫오십유
우로스비이	"	"
푸론스틔린이	"	"

이중계사대두쳑은 근일에 완셜ᄒ게 준비ᄒᆫ비이라 [illegible] 야 셰틱함대로 합ᄒ드라도 가히 출발ᄒ게 되엿드면 [illegible] 정이 쎡다시 이런 낫슬티이요 려순에 잇는 아라사 함대 [illegible] 리도 이 함대만 도착되엿드면 열바 금의 회가 되엿더 [illegible] 전멘슬티이요 외양으로라도 태단히 조쳬되엿슬거시 [illegible] 게 되여 졔ᄒ기는 셜로 의외인거시

중왕에 우리는 드른즉 이 함대가 동양에 도착ᄒ면 [illegible] ᄒ기로 예정ᄒ엿다 ᄒ기에 만일 젼셜과 갓틀진ᄃ [illegible] 본함대에셔 쟝충 관당ᄒ게 될줄로 알아더니 [illegible] 이셩기엿도다

TELEGRAMS.

(FROM JAPA· PAP.RS).

London, October 30th.

Seemingly, the British enquiry into the North Sea outrage will be held at Hull, the Russian at Vigo, and the international at the Hague or elsewhere.

London, October 30th.

The "Oslabya," "Sissoi Veliky," "Aurora," "Svietlana," "Dmitra Donskoi," "Kamchatka," "Jemtchug," "Almaz," seven torpedo-boats, and five colliers have arrived at Tangier. The remaining ships of the Baltic Fleet are at Vigo, where the British first class armoured cruiser "Lancaster" has arrived.

London, October 30th.

The Rt. Hon. A. J. Balfour, speaking at Southampton, said that the question of the North Sea outrage had been referred to an international enquiry. The Russian Government had ordered the detention, at Vigo, of the part of the Baltic Squadron concerned. The officers responsible will not proceed to the Far East but will be tried and adequately punished. The Russian Government is giving orders which will prevent the recurrence of a similar incident.

Major-General Dessino at Shanghai has published a telegram sent from the Russian Headquarters on the afternoon of the 27th inst., as follows :—

For the last few days, no fighting has taken place, though there has been an occasional exchange of gun-fire between the outposts of the hostile armies.

The Japanese have thrown up entrenchments and have strengthened their positions. The Russians have interred with due honours 1,500 Japanese dead in the neighbourhood of Putiloff Hill. Many corpses are still lying in the neighbourhood.

The Russian losses in the battle fought there amounted to 90 officers and 1,800 men.

THE EMPERESS OF ALL THE RUSSIAS.

A character sketch of the Tsaritsa appears in the September of the "Lady's Realm." The writers says :—

The Empress is a devoted mother, and hardly ever parted from her four little girls. The little Grand Duchesses have, therefore, seen a great deal of the world, especially the Princess Olga, who has accompanied her father and mother on their visits to France and England. The Tsaritsa's English leanings are further exemplified in the training of her daughters, who are brought up on an entirely English system. Their education is carefully attended to, and from their cradle they are taught to speak English, French, and German, as well as their native tongue.

Though the Tsar is the richest Sovereign in the world, the home life of the Imperial couple is very simple, and almost without ceremony. The Empress may appear cold and stately towards strangers—in private she is brimming over with good nature and mischievous humour. But at no moment is it possible to mistake the underlying strength and earnestness of her character. The Tsaritsa exactly suits her husbund. She is always with him, even when he is at work, and when statesmen come to consult him he often begs her to remain in the room.

Although hers are quite the most luxurious homes of any European Queen, her tastes yet remain perfectly simple. Though she has wonderful pearls, star sappires and cabochon rubies she seldom wears jewels; and when State ceremony compels her to be magnificently attired, she chooses gems of beautiful and antique design. Before her marriage she was so Puritanical in her dress that it was only with difficulty that she could be persuaded to choose a trousseau befitting an empress, and even now she despises over-elaborateness in dress, and sets no extravagant fashions to those around her.

The Imperial pair when alone usually converse in either English or German, very seldom in French or Italian. The Tsaritsa did not learn Russian till after her betrothal, but she speaks it very correctly and with a good accent.

One of the Tsaritsa's most earnest endeavours has been to ameliorate the condition of the poorer classes of women in her view she has taken an active part all measures of poor law relief that have been set on foot since the beginning of her reign. The favourite residence of fhe Empress is the Alexander Palace, a small mansion at Tsarkoe Selo. Helo. Here the Imperial pair can throw off the cares of State and become themselves.

THE "FIRING-LINE."

The "World's News contains a new and virile poem by Henry Lawson, an Ausralian poet. Since the pulication of "In Days when the World was Wide" it is doubtful, says the "China Mail, if Mr. Lawson has written anything so strong and vigorous as this latest production, which was suggested by a recent cablegram from the seat of war in the Far East:—

"Many of the soldiers were so exhausted that they fell asleep in the firing line."

They are creeping on through the cornfields yet, and they clamber amongst the rocks.
Ere they rush to stab with the bayonet and smash with the rifle-stocks.
And many are wounded, many are dead —some reel as if drunk with wine.
And fling them down on a bloodstained bed, and sleep in the firing-line.
And they dream, perhaps, of the day shut back, while the shrapned shrieks and crashes.
And field guns hammer and rifles crack, and the blood of a comrade splashes.
In horrible shambles they rest a while from murder by right divine:
They curse or jest, and they scowl or smile, and they dream in the firing-lines.
In the dreadful din of a ghastly fight they are shooting, murdering, men;
In the smothering silence of ghastly peace we murder with tongue and pen.
Where is heard the tap of the type-writer—where the track of reform they mine—
Where they stand to the frame and the linotype—we are all in the firing-line.
Weary and parched in the world-old war we are fighting with quivering nerves;
The dead are our fathers who charged before, and the children are our reserves,
In the world-old war, with the world-old wrongs that shall last while the stars still shine.
My comrades and I, who would sing their songs, are all in the firing-line.
There are some of us cowards who hug the ground and some of us reckless who jest;
And some of us careless who slumber sound, and some of us weary who rest
There are some of us dreamers, whose beds seem soft, and, O-heart! O-friend of mine!
The brightest and bravest of earth too oft lie drunk in the firing-line.
But the sleeper may wake ere the fort we storm and the coward be first to dare.
And a weak grow strong, and the drunkard reform, and the dreamer strike hardest there.
God give me strength in my country's need, though shame and disgrace be mine.
And death be certain, to rise and lead when we charge from the firing-line.

"A CERTAIN PLACE"

(FROM THE L. & C. EXPRESS.)

Occasions frequently when it was necessary, in the cource of Japanese official despatches, to refer to the advanced naval base, but instead of mentioning names the authorities invented the sublimely vague phrase "certain place." So familiar has the term become throughout the land remarks the "Daily Telegraph's Correspondent on the "Manshu Maru, that it is now humorously applied in everyday individual life. One man will stop another in the street and ask. "Oh, where are you going?" to which the other will laughingly reply. "To a certain place." Among the many localities thought to be the naval base, the Eliiot Islands were, of course, included, but they were by no means favoured among the majorfty of irresponsible guesses. But there we came in full view of the fleet, snugly anchored in a narrow roadstead, on the northern side of which projected a promontory of the long narrow island of Da Chan Shan; the southern side was flanked by the wide, irregular island of Chan Shan, separated from a small island to the west by a narrow strip of water, named by the Russians with unconscious irony "Sea Lion Strait." Altogether 40 ships were at anchor. From many funnels the smoke curled skywards, collecting in a great dull cloud, overhanging the forest of masts; the whole scene, viewed under conditions unexampled in the history of the world, immediately gave one the impression of power and preparedness. The whole position was ideal for a naval base during time of war. Within 60 miles of Port Arthur it was guarded north, south, east and west by a maze of island ramparts, access to which could only be obtained through certain known channels or narrow straits. All other nations except the Japanese failed in the past to obtain accurate charts and maps of the groups. The English records actually omit several large islands, while the Russian surveys mark land where water exists. Although the islands are for the most part barren hills, scantily adorned with a few pines, they afford a home to a number of Chinese people, who chiefly engage in fishing for the bright-coloured favourite Eastern tai. At the time of our visit a number of Chinese soldiers formed a garrison for the protection of the inhabitants from the pirates who preyed at all times on the neighbouring seas. Despite the passing to and fro of innumerable junk, the secret of Admiral Togo's movements was completely preserved.

A former St. Louisian Charles Lavrell of Quincy, Ill., has entered his airship—the "St. Louis"—for the $100,000 contest at the World's Fair. It is exceedingly simple, but original in design. The motor furnishing the propelling power is hidden under the floor of the car. From the car a steel pipe runs to the top of the craft—forty feet. Through this runs a belt connecting with two wings. These wings or propellers consist of two blades, each three and one-half feet long. One is at the top of the pole and the other half-way up from the car. The balloon portious of the sky traveller is between these two propellers. Its shape resembles two saucers placed rim to rim and fastened together, the lower being a trifle smaller than the upper one.

The Korea Daily News.

Issued at 5 P. M. daily except Sundays.

Rate of Subscription:—
Per Year, Yen 25.
Per Quarter, Yen 7.
Per Month, Yen 2.50.

Postage in Korea not charged extra.
Postage abroad charged extra.

Advertisements, 50 sen per day for 1 inch or less.
5 yen per month per inch.
50 yen per year per inch.

All communications to
E. T. BETHELL,
Editor and Publisher,
Pak-tong, Seoul

KOREA'S FINANCIAL ADVISER.

Considerable time has now elapsed since the arrival of Mr. Megata and it will be interesting to review what has so far been accomplished by this dis-proportionately highly-paid official.

His first proposal was that Korea should borrow from Japan the sum of ten million yen in silver. Next, presumably on his advice, the mint was closed and all employees were discharged. Now we hear that he has set the officials of the Finance Department on the Herculean task of correcting their books for the past ten years!

His first proposal, which is to borrow ten million yen in silver from Japan, we have always been inclined to look askance at. In the first place we do not see how the transaction would benefit Korea's financial economy, and secondly in view of the fact that it was only recently that Japan presumably in order to meet demands for hard cash elsewhere found it necessary to withdraw a large part of her silver currency from circulation in Formosa, we cannot understand how she finds herself in a position to make such a loan at present. And yet Mr. Megata, being newly arrived from Tokio, must have known that the proposition, on Japan's side at least, was feasable. It must be remembered that when a country is engaged in war it is compelled to be extremely conservative with its hard cash, and to this end, all sorts of expedients, such as the issue of war paper, are resorted to. Therefore it is difficult to account for Japan's anxiety to make this loan. We do not give her credit for any philanthropic intentions, and failing any other explanation we can only conclude that Japan believes that the money advanced would speedily find its way back to her own coffers. Wherein we are inclined to agree with Japan.

Of the shutting down of the mint it is too soon yet to speak. This may only be preliminary to the resumption of operations on improved lines. Meanwhile we may say that we have reason to believe that if a silver currency be required in this country, a great deal of material is to be found within the mint.

Mr. Megata's last performance, that of setting the Finance Department officials to work correcting their books for the past ten years, rather savours of giving a troublesome child a task to keep it quiet.

In the meantime there is one matter which seems, in the interests of Korea, to be a fitting subject for Mr. Megata's attention. We refer to the Dai Ichi Bank notes.

We may premise our remarks by saying that we accuse the bank of nothing, and on the contrary believe it to be a very well managed concern of great probity and resource. Now the point to which we wish to draw Mr. Megata's attention is this. On the back of the notes in question there is printed in English, "Dai-Ichi Ginko L'td promises to pay the bearer on demand one yen (or whatever the denomination may be) in Japanese currency at any of its branches in Korea."

Now the fortunes of war are proverbially uncertain, and every eventuality should be provided against. In this respect there are two unsatisfactory features about the Dai-Ichi notes. We are not told what kind of Japanese currency they will be redeemed in, and the notes are only redeemable at the branches of the bank in Korea. In the event of the expulsion of the Japanese from Korea the holders of these notes would be in an unfortunate position, while those who had exchanged them for other Japanese paper currency, would be, for a time at least, seriously inconvenienced.

We do not say that these things will happen, but people may think they will happen, and in the event of a panic, the alteration of the terms of the Dai-Ichi bank's promise, making the money payable at any of its branches and in specie, would go far to restore confidence.

The endorsement of the Nippon Ginko notes runs as follows:—

"Nippon Ginko promises to pay the bearer on demand Ten Yen in gold."

WAR NEWS FROM EUROPE.

A telegram from Europe received in certain official quarters at Tokyo says that the van of the Eighth Army Corps belonging to the Second Russian Army in Manchuria arrived at Kharbin about the 20th inst. and that the 16th Corps is now ready for departure. The Second, Third, and Fourth Corps will soon follow. The mobilization of the First and Second Brigades of Sharpshooters has been commenced, and the Third, Fourth, and Fifth Brigades of the same will also shortly be mobilized.

A review of the local Korean troops was held yesterday. General Hasegawa was specially invited to be present.

Mr. Min Kyeng-sik, formerly the Manager of the Household Bureau, has been appointed Governor of Seoul.

It is rumoured that the 1st, 2nd and 3rd batallions of Seoul troops will be despatched to disperse the Chin Po Hoi society. Perhaps this may explain the increased activity recently shown in drills and exercises.

As a further example of the manner in which the Japanese are cooking their hare before they catch it we learn from the "Tokyo News Agency" that it is rumoured that the Foreign Ministers to Korea will all be withdrawn, but that this will not be done while the Japanese Minister remains. Though the progressist party in Japan desire to despatch a committee to Korea to commence various measures of reform, the Seiyu Kwai (a conservative political organisation in Tokyo) is silent on the subject.

The Governor of Seoul has notified the Home Office that he has been instructed by the Japanese to level the roads in certain hilly districts of the city. He inspected the places named and discovered that the levelling will necessitate the disturbance of sacred ground. Moreover enormous expense will be entailed. He has informed the military authorities of these objections, but they still insist on the work being carried out and have surveyed the ground and estimated the expenses at $5,337. He considers the matter too weighty for his own decision and requests the Home Office to settle it for him.

PORT ARTHUR.

From the "Japan Times," we learn that Sasebo dispatches dated October 28 state that the Russian squadron at Port Arthur on the 26th inst, consisted of six battleships and cruisers, four gunboats, five steamers, eleven destroyers; three hospital ships, over ten steam launches, and a Norwegian steamer, which is presumed to have run the Japanese blockade on the 13th inst. None of the mine-dragging vessels were to be seen. The same journal also says that a certain person returning from the front contradicts the report that the Russians at Port Arthur are short of provisions and ammunition. He states that it has been confirmed that the Russian garrison has still over 400 cattle, besides other provisions, and it is inconceivable that the Russians have exhausted their stocks of ammunition after a few months' siege.

On the 2nd inst. the birthday of the young Prince, many prisoners, convicted of petty crimes, were released from the Government jails.

Mr. Yi Sung-mun, the manager of our suppressed contemporary, the Che Kuk Sinmun, is leaving on a visit to the United States. He expects to be absent about three years.

Japanese officers, prisoners of war, are detained at the town of Kaluga, a few miles south of Moscow. On the 22nd ult. an entertainment was held in honour of the prisoners, and it is stated that the local society leaders vied with each other in showing them every attention.

The Governor of North Kyeng-sang province reports that he has received a despatch from the Seoul Fusan railway bureau, informing him that any tampering, with the railway or telegraph wires by the inhabitants of his district, will be punished by martial law. To assist the railway authorities in their work, he is instructed by them to form patrols of Koreans, from the numerous villages, to guard the line, and these will be held responsible for any damage done. The governor explains that as the line runs in many instances through entirely uninhabited country it will be impossible to carry out these instructions.

Some time ago the Russian Government ordered 100,000 bullet-proof breastplates of the type invented by Signor Benedetti. The latter recently started for St. Petersburg to supervise the manufacture of the breastplates, but was stopped at Munich by the Italian firm to which he had sold the rights to manufacture, which objected to Signor Benedetti's intervention in the matter and he has returned to Italy. The firm had also undertaken to supply the Japanese Government with 200,000 breastplates. Now that the Russian contract has been broken it seems, according to a despatch, that Japan wishes to back out of its engagement, proposing to pay the losses sustained by the firm through the abrogation of the contract.

Mr. C. D. Gibson, of "Gibson girl" fame, is said to have recently received a printed letter from a well-known manufacturer of soap, which said: "You are cordially invited to participate in a drawing contest for a prize of twenty-five dollars. The drawing must be an original composition that will advertise our soap. Only one prize will be given, and all unsuccessful drawings will become the property of the undersigned." The letter (says A.M P.) amused and irritated Mr. Gibson, and he sat down and wrote to the soap manufacturer as follows: "You are heartily invited to participate in a soap contest (that I have inaugurated for a prize of 1½ dollars. Each competitor must submit 100 pounds of his best soap, put up in ornamental one-pound boxes, and all the soap that is not adjudged worthy of the price will remain the property of the undersigned. It is necessary that the soap be forwarded prepaid."

The Korea Daily News.

VOL. I, SATURDAY, NOVEMBER 5, 1904. No. 94

報申日每韓大

대한매일신보

일쳔구빅사년십일월팔일 (화요일) (뎨구십오호)

본샤고빅

이신보는영어와한어로셕계빅
일츌판ᄒᆞᆷ

신문가
한쟝 엽두돈오푼
일삭됴 엽두량닷돈
우표가빈 샤닷돈
다맛돈으로밧숩

광고료논
귀한의쟝단과ᄌᆞ힝의다쇼로즁
경ᄒᆞ되쳐음가로밧을터이오며오
린지아니ᄒᆞ야ᄃᆡ한사ᄅᆞᆷ마다이신
문을보실터이니광고내시기를원
ᄒᆞ시ᄂᆞᆫ이들은우리신문샤에
와셔면약ᄒᆞ심을희망ᄒᆞᆷ

○발힝소 박동ᄃᆡ한ᄆᆡ일신보
샤발힝쇼협회젼영국인셜필
림경ᄌᆞ리오
샤쟝 영국인 (빈셜)

평양 ᄃᆡ리졈
○평양효동사는권미보씨로우
리신문광고ᄃᆡ리인을뎡ᄒᆞ엿
스오니평양에계신구람ᄒᆞ고져ᄒᆞ
시는 쳠군ᄌᆞᄂᆞᆫ그ᄃᆡ리졈에왕
림ᄒᆞ와면의ᄒᆞ시옵

샤고

○우리대한ᄆᆡ일신보의목뎍은
대한의안녕질셔에관ᄒᆞᆫ모든ᄉᆞ
목에대ᄒᆞ야ᄂᆞᆫ공평ᄒᆞᆫ변론을쥬
쟝ᄒᆞᆷ이라우리ᄂᆞᆫ신문의담보ᄂᆞᆫ
신문보시는쳠군ᄌᆞ의게ᄒᆞᆼ샹보
도ᄒᆞ려며편지들겨셔ᄒᆞ여주시
논이ᄂᆞᆫ셩명과번디를젹어부치
시기를희망ᄒᆞ오나이거슨신문
샹에괴ᄌᆡᄒᆞ라ᄂᆞᆫ거시아니오다
만그취신ᄒᆞᄂᆞᆫ증거를숨고자ᄒᆞᆷ
이라괴ᄌᆡᄂᆞᆫ아모괴셔던지소관
ᄒᆞᆷ을되각ᄒᆞᄂᆞᆫ권리를가젓스
나무ᄅᆞᆷᄒᆞᄂᆞᆫ리유를말ᄒᆞᆯ터이오
며공즁평화를문란케ᄒᆞᄂᆞᆫ듯ᄒᆞᆫ
다괴셔ᄂᆞᆫ의례히밧지안켓숩나이

●본샤셜시이리로신문을ᄆᆡ양
우례로본젼ᄒᆞ와리젼부의임의
로젼ᄒᆞ든ᄉᆞ로번곳에는홋늣게
젼ᄒᆞ기도ᄒᆞ며혹멋쳘거슴ᄒᆞᆫ겁
에젼ᄒᆞ기도ᄒᆞ며혹아니젼ᄒᆞᄂᆞᆫ
곳도잇다ᄒᆞ와우리신문을ᄉᆞ랑
ᄒᆞ야구람ᄒᆞ시는 쳠군ᄌᆞ의게
되ᄒᆞ야미안ᄒᆞ옵기로지금
은분젼인을두교ᄃᆡ일즙이젼
ᄒᆞ며아니젼ᄒᆞ거나늣게거나
폐가업도록ᄒᆞ오니혹아니
젼ᄒᆞ거나혹늣게젼ᄒᆞ거나ᄒᆞᆫ일
이잇스면본샤로통긔ᄒᆞ여주심
을희망ᄒᆞᆷ

본샤광고

○본샤신문즁에좌긔ᄒᆞᆫ호수들
소용ᄒᆞᆯ데가잇셔이에광고ᄒᆞ오
니누구시던지그즁에아모호수
던지가져오시ᄂᆞᆫ되로ᄆᆡ쟝에빅
젼두푼식드리리다
뎨이호 뎨삼호 뎨이십삼호
뎨ᄉᆞ십이호 뎨ᄉᆞ십삼호 뎨
오십삼호 뎨오십ᄉᆞ호와뎨오
십오호 뎨륙십이호

관보

뎨이쳔구빅칠십륙호
광무팔년십일월오일
셔임급ᄉᆞ령
○면본관 경쥬군슈 박병익
십일월이일
○임면환국쥬ᄉᆞ 셔판임관ᄉᆞ등
면환국기슈 최호원
○명비쳔군렴시우계쥬ᄉᆞ 김
계쥬
○명숙안군렴시우계쥬ᄉᆞ 김
병계
이상십일월이일
○명궁니부듕진관셔칙임관이
등 비셔원경 박용ᄃᆡ
○명비셔광경셔칙임관샴등
동지돈령원ᄉᆞ 리지형
○명동지돈령원ᄉᆞ셔칙임관ᄉᆞ
등 종이품 리완용
○의원면본관 농샹공부기슈
린샹연 최린식
○임농샹공부기슈셔판임관륙
등 리명훈 셩로익
○승셔관임관오등 진위뎨삼
샹련ᄃᆡ뎨이ᄃᆡᄃᆡ부훈군의보 귀
현 이상십일월삼일
○젼참위 탁지부쥬ᄉᆞ 신규션 박리
동 이상십일월삼일
○면환국쟝 최셕조 ᄉᆞ직소 비
지니에ᄉᆞ양말고힝공ᄒᆞ라
○호위ᄃᆡ총관 리근틱 ᄉᆞ직소 비
지니에ᄉᆞ양말고힝공ᄒᆞ라
○함경남도관찰ᄉᆞ 리헌경 ᄉᆞ직소 비
지니에번거히ᄉᆞ양말고
○한셩부판윤 리용세 ᄉᆞ직소 비
지니에ᄉᆞ양말고
이상십일월삼일

○외부교셥국쟝 리샹셜 ᄉᆞ직소
비지니에ᄉᆞ양말고힝공ᄒᆞ라
십일월일일
관쳥ᄉᆞ항
○륙군보병참위 오희션이가본
년십월구일에죠모ᄉᆞ증샹을당
ᄒᆞᆫ수
○륙군보병참위 박인영이가본
년구월십일에신고ᄒᆞᆫ수
○진위뎨ᄉᆞ련ᄃᆡ뎨이ᄃᆡᄃᆡ부륙
군보병부위 쟝의환이가본년십
월이십일에신고ᄒᆞᆫ수

군부관졔 속
군무과
회계과

뎨삼십ᄉᆞ됴 ᄒᆡ방국군무과쟝
은 회군부참령으로보직ᄒᆞ고
과원이인은 회군쟝부위로보
직ᄒᆞᆷ이라

뎨삼십오됴 군무과에는 ᄉᆞ무
를좌갓치주쟝ᄒᆞᆷ이라
일은 쟝교와샹당관과ᄉᆞ관
하ᄉᆞ의임면진퇴에관ᄒᆞᆫ ᄉᆞ항
이ᄂᆞᆫ 협ᄃᆡ의편졔와및력무에관ᄒᆞᆫ ᄉᆞ항
삼은 교육ᄒᆞᆫ련연습검열에
관ᄒᆞᆫ ᄉᆞ항
ᄉᆞᄂᆞᆫ 쟝교와및죵ᄉᆞ관과하
ᄉᆞ병졸의보충진퇴와및다른
인ᄉᆞ의관ᄒᆞᆫ ᄉᆞ항
오ᄂᆞᆫ 병ᄆᆡ의징모와군긔와
긔엄과휘샹보안에관ᄒᆞᆫ ᄉᆞ항
륙은 군함과병긔와탄약의
졔조와슈리와및병긔탄약의
경리의관ᄒᆞᆫ ᄉᆞ항
칠은 징별졔관감옥에관ᄒᆞᆫ
ᄉᆞ항

뎨삼십륙됴 ᄒᆡ방국회계과는
현금간시힝을쟝지ᄒᆞ고그ᄉᆞ
무를경리국에셔징힝ᄒᆞᆷ이라

뎨삼십칠됴 각국각과의과원
은그과쟝의명령을바다ᄒᆡ과ᄉᆞ
무에종ᄉᆞᄒᆞᆷ이라

뎨삼십팔됴 군부에기ᄉᆞ ᄒᆞᆫ인
기슈비인을둠이라

뎨삼십구됴 군부에쥬ᄉᆞ삼십
인을명ᄒᆞ고각국각과에분관
ᄒᆞᆷ이라

뎨ᄉᆞ십됴 본관졔는반포일부
터시힝ᄒᆞᆷ이라

뎨ᄉᆞ십일됴 광무팔년칠월륙
일칙령뎨십칠호군부관졔는
폐지ᄒᆞᆷ이라

잡보

○파당셰력 근일에졍부의잉
시ᄒᆞᄂᆞᆫ이들이랑랑샹샹셕작파
ᄒᆞ야셔로셰력이진ᄒᆞ며쳥ᄒᆞᆫ티
참졍신긔션씨와궁찬쳠ᄒᆡ셕씨와
니부ᄃᆡ신리용틱씨샹인일파중외
에ᄂᆞᆫ리ᄃᆡ가일진이오궁ᄂᆡ형
관박용화씨와농샹공리근샹
씨일파중에ᄂᆞᆫ박형관이일진
오군부ᄃᆡ신리윤용씨와탁지ᄃᆡ
신민영긔씨와궁ᄂᆡ부ᄃᆡ신민
가ᄋᆞᆯᄂᆞᆫ진오호위ᄃᆡ총관리근틱
씨와경위원총관권즁셕씨량인
은신ᄋᆡ파를셜립ᄒᆞᄂᆞᆫ데권즁현
이ᄌᆡ일진이라ᄒᆞ더라

○경무구람 일진회쟝윤시병
씨가회원ᄉᆞ빅명을ᄃᆞ리고본회
ᄂᆞᆫ뎐하의수화를면하여루고졔셜ᄒᆞ
ᄒᆞᆷ을아지못ᄒᆞ고본회를빈ᄃᆡᄒᆞ
ᄂᆞᆫ사ᄅᆞᆷ과ᄂᆞᆫ뎌별히호령ᄒᆞ지말
라ᄒᆞ니의ᄂᆞᆫ진실노가본회
보ᄃᆡ원되어셰쟝보ᄀᆡ가본회
ᄒᆞᆫ사ᄅᆞᆷ이몃ᄯᆡ희의ᄂᆞᆫ보를닐
지원중에셔방에셔ᄃᆡ동신보들을
나ᄒᆞ야엿더라

○쟝ᄃᆡ변론 시위쳥위젼위챵
ᄃᆡ병뎡을교련ᄒᆞ야쟝곽친ᄃᆡ
이관광케ᄒᆞ더니ᄒᆡᆫ각ᄃᆡ에
셔범죵이라셔 ...
랄슴ᄒᆞ기위ᄒᆞ야쟝관에
세의게약이잇다ᄒᆞ고쟝렵
...

○반볍여무 근일에법부와
시ᄒᆞ고흉으로경무쳥에셔법
슈검을분밧계와송ᄒᆞ야법치와
무를빅빈가에빈량에남지안켸
ᄒᆞ라ᄒᆞᆫ민도로ᄒᆞᆫ쳡시교등ᄒᆞ다
ᄒᆞ더라

○리씨미국유학 미국신문쥬
필ᄒᆞᄂᆞᆫ리승만씨ᄂᆞᆫ미국에유학
ᄒᆞ야셜ᄃᆡ를권숩ᄒᆞ고자로적사일
에발졍ᄒᆞᄂᆞᆫ티왕반ᄒᆞᆯ귀한은숨
기년으로예졍ᄒᆞ엿더라

○조힝티관 한셩부오셔니에
외교샤무가츙칭쳥출ᄒᆞᄂᆞᆫ티관
은차협으로훈회ᄒᆞ고셔직ᄋᆞ
로시무ᄒᆞᆯ관은셔잉치아니ᄒᆞ
ᄂᆞᆫ교로소운밧숨죠셰가조힝티
관훈단더라

○비궁ᄒᆡᆼ셔 본월오일하오여
시(음력구월이십팔일)슈렁ᄋᆡ셩
ᄃᆡ ...
에ᄒᆡᆼ리즈비궁민셰면하계옹셔

향ᄒᆞ하옵시니신민의통도홈이
망극ᄒᆞ더라
○쳐소명졍 조칙ᄒᆞ사궐으
사티빈뎐쳐소는영셩문안홍덕
뎐으로ᄒᆞ고명졍셔사관쳐소는
휘령당으로ᄒᆞ고 궁니부관반
쳐소는숭례문으로ᄒᆞ고빈관회
곡쳐소는숭례문밧그로ᄒᆞ라ᄒᆞ
옵셧더라
○상례도차하 조왈의장민영
소와특진관윤용구와장례경윤
덕영으로빈뎐도감뎨됴를삼고
시종무관장민영환과특진관서
신보파와 궁니부대신리용
틱로국장뎨됴를숨고특진관소
영달과리주영과죠동희로원소
뎨됴를숨으라ᄒᆞ옵셧더라
○외경총수신엄 돈유를나리
사특진관리근명셰로의졍을
ᄒᆞ옵셧는대리의졍이즉시슈칙
ᄒᆞ미총호수를특계ᄒᆞ옵셧더라
○원쇼지졍 황티ᄌᆞ비뎐하원
쇼는동구릉안에젼명셩황후릉
침으로졍ᄒᆞ엿든슈릉으로지졍
ᄒᆞ엿더라
○봉계마련 황티ᄌᆞ비의봉계
는그등ᄒᆞ를상고ᄒᆞ야일년으로
마련ᄒᆞ다운ᄒᆞ더라
○졍시지휘 작일브터농샹공
부와및한셩부에지휘ᄒᆞ야졍시
를식ᄒᆞ엿더라
○진하분시 한후카평복되셧
다ᄒᆞ야음력십월칠일노진하
일ᄌᆞ를턱졍ᄒᆞ더니도로분시되
엿더라
○안쥬군슈 평안남도관찰ᄉᆞ
가비부구면보ᄒᆞ기를안쥬군슈
에평양사는김광현은뎌ᄉᆞ하고
휘군에부임치아니ᄒᆞ니ᄉᆞ세가
엄시라도금ᄒᆞ오미다른사람으
로턱차ᄒᆞ와맛하ᄒᆞ숩ᄒᆞ라ᄒᆞ엿
더라
○로병류쥬 함경남도관찰ᄉᆞ
리현경씨가십월이십삼일에보
부로보ᄒᆞ숩ᄒᆞᆫ보고에일본쳥군슈
츄졍ᄒᆞ의보고를거훈즉아병수
빅여괴가음력팔월초이일노북
쳥니본군동로쳘리하로디사장니
에와셔류쥬ᄒᆞ는거ᄉᆞᆫ임의슈
보ᄒᆞ엿거니와동월이십일에아
국과병수쳔여명파물오쳔여필
이리원딘경으로브터동쟝니에
리도ᄒᆞ야류쥬ᄒᆞ옵는ᄃᆡ그중에
수관과병졸병ᄒᆞ야빅여명은군
쳐로퇴셔원에드러가거쳐ᄒᆞ옵
고수쳔여명은남문밧게와셔류
훈다ᄒᆞ엿더라
○로병방셕죄슈 함남관찰ᄉᆞ
가쇼병부로훈보고니기에동항
최인팔슈런등을참슈ᄒᆞ야흉쳐
며도ᄒᆞ고흉사칙ᄒᆞ는중이더니
지금아병이함흥에리주ᄒᆞ는후
에죄슈등이럼명ᄒᆞ여칭턴에
무소훈즉히티에서말ᄒᆞ기를일
병을반티ᄒᆞ는사롬들을계슈ᄒᆞ엿
다ᄒᆞ고엇지로노화주기를요구
ᄒᆞ는고로그냥쳥종치아니ᄒᆞ엿
더니블의에패월이신륙일네희
티의하ᄉᆞ등샹인이힝티의ᄉᆞ령
관의죠회를가지고와셔힝죄슈
이십륙명을엇지로힝티로압거
ᄒᆞ야일병방숑ᄒᆞ엿다ᄒᆞ엿더라
○동학소장 동학죄슈가아병
티에무소ᄒᆞ야방셕됨은샹홈에
긔치홈과ᄀᆞᆺ거니와그졍소ᄒᆞᆫ쟝
초는좌와ᄀᆞᆺᄒᆞ니
의도등이아국대장의영위지하
에복달ᄒᆞ오니밝히샬펴소셔의
등이본시수민으로셔군부의명
을숭죵ᄒᆞ야룡방에레의지도를
한습ᄒᆞ옵더니료외에거이월븐
에일병이곳합ᄒᆞ부에니르러동
학이라칭ᄒᆞ고이미훈사름을셩
명을보샹ᄒᆞ고기여수샵신명을
지우금엄슈ᄒᆞ야징역을시이온
즉본도숭챤ᄉᆞ쥬도그세력을이
의지못ᄒᆞ야맛츔니진작노화쥬
지못ᄒᆞ오니쳘텬훈원을셩을두
드리며호소홀곳이업ᄉᆞ온바이
수유를듯ᄉᆞ옥ᄒᆞ신후에쟌쳐분ᄒᆞ
와옥즁에셔거의쥭게된수다훈
젼민을곳푸러노화쥬오면본로
에도라가샹봉부모ᄒᆞ옵고하ᄉᆞ을
쳐조ᄒᆞ야써엽을편안이ᄒᆞ게ᄒᆞ
여주시기를천만복망이라ᄒᆞ엿
더라
○로관죠회 로국ᄉᆞ령관이죠
회ᄒᆞ야동학죄슈를방숑훈일은
샹홈에게지ᄒᆞ엿거니와그죠회
젼문이좌와ᄀᆞᆺᄒᆞ니
경계자는귀부소관죄슈죄인등
이십륙명이근일에본진중에올
며ᄒᆞ호소ᄒᆞ는고로그이유를탐지
ᄒᆞᆫ즉지회가발ᄒᆞ기를본티동학
이엄이아니오일병을반티훈죄로셔
지여티무소ᄒᆞ야과착되여계슈ᄒᆞ엿
은비거비견즁에잇셔일병을보호
ᄒᆞ야과지사경이라ᄒᆞ고로명지못
고근유를살펴본즉과연의리가
이를며ᄒᆞ라든거시오그정상을
구ᄒᆞᆫ진티반드시ᄒᆞᆫ호셩지도가엽
지못ᄒᆞ겟기로이에죠회ᄒᆞ오니
셤ᄒᆞ리죄슈이십륙명을금일샹오
시즁으로귀부관인을인도ᄒᆞ야본
진쥬송교ᄒᆞ옵셔써밝히사
셜케ᄒᆞ옴을위요ᄒᆞ엿더라
아력일쳔구빅사년팔월십이
일
대아국총진수령관
대한국함흥관찰ᄉᆞ각하
○방희게척 일본공관에서외부
로죠회ᄒᆞ기를경부텰도회사에
셔품쳥ᄒᆞ기를본텰도션로가지
나는바경산군만촌부근디에ᄀᆞᆯ
니쿤뒤를노화귀차의면봉ᄒᆞ기
를위ᄒᆞ야게펴ᄒᆞ는거슬방헌ᄒᆞ
야엄시ᄒᆞ여버린거시ᄒᆞᆫ두번이
아니라장졋밤에가잇는데본사
드시위험ᄒᆞᆫ여가ᄒᆞᆫ슈호ᄒᆞ기가
의힘으로셔는가히츄금ᄒᆞ티
어렵다ᄒᆞ노니쳥컨디급히ᄒᆞ
허디방관의계신칙ᄒᆞ야특별히
경비ᄒᆞ며금ᄒᆞ게ᄒᆞ야방히
홈을엄히ᄒᆞ매방홈이가홀ᄉᆞ라ᄒᆞ
엿더라

론셜

한국탁지고문관

○조ᄒᆞᆫ시졀을다보내고이제야
비로소목하젼세로ᄒᆞ여곰치교아
등고문관을삼아탁지에연빙ᄒᆞ엿
더니무샹셩취된일이그동안잇
셧는요
동셔가처음으로계출ᄒᆞ는말이
운화이빅만원을일본에차관ᄒᆞ
여야ᄒᆞ겟다고ᄒᆞ고무변제는권
고ᄒᆞ기를젼환국의화폐제조홈
을졍주케ᄒᆞ엿스며히국에고용
ᄒᆞ는사름ᄭᆞ지모도히고케ᄒᆞ엿
다ᄒᆞ더니근일에는탁지의셰번
이리각항문부를도뫼사ᄒᆞᆫ다ᄒᆞ조
우리의소견에는심히아흑ᄒᆞᆫ눈자
ㅣ잇스니
한국재졍상에경제될방칙으로
쳐사ᄒᆞ믄가히보지못ᄒᆞ겟고다
만근일에포모사에서만유힝되
는젼을차관ᄒᆞᆫ다ᄒᆞ니ᄎᆞ하ᄒᆞ티도
동반ᄒᆞᆫ눈거관을어셔나출ᄒᆞ야
중수ᄒᆞ며또제금차관ᄒᆞ는거시
무엇에유조홈이잇스리요
필경목하젼세가동평을출발ᄒᆞ
야도한ᄒᆞ는날에는응당조곰이
라도일본에리롭도록ᄒᆞ게홀ᄉᆞ
은이왕에료ᄒᆞᆫ빈이어니와무론어
ᄂᆞ나라던지전쟁을비르키게
되면제졍을저축ᄒᆞ야불우지비
를원리홈은자연훈리치인즉일
본셔도응당아지못홀빈아니로
되훈이러훈거관을지출ᄒᆞ란ᄒᆞ면
셩히끈란ᄒᆞᆫ터이되지어드도로그
이아는거시차관ᄒᆞ드리도돈티
인ᄒᆞ고로그러홈이나엿제턴지병
에는엇거이려우며
젼환국정주일사로말ᄒᆞ드ᄅᆡ도
브모신ᄒᆞ츄금ᄒᆞ케ᄒᆞᆫ일인거시
은젼을유힝ᄒᆞ게홀ᄅᆡ홀진ᄃᆡ과
왕젼환국에서쓰든제로가만홀
지어놀비거슨쳐지ᄒᆞ고세로문
대를계출홈이기랑ᄒᆞ란홈에ᄃᆡ
단히여그런진일이요
탁지의신년젼문부됴사ᄒᆞ는일
도당장듯기에는죠훈일인듯ᄒᆞ
나동씨가기위의편를이르케ᄒᆞ
란면훈가지실로홀일이잇스니
요수이유힝ᄒᆞ는은힝권들도로
돌녀보니여쓰지아니ᄒᆞ던지만
일그리치아니ᄒᆞ면은힝권뒤편
에쓰바한국에잇는은힝소와밋
각지졈에서반밧고아준다고ᄒᆞ
게슬엿시ᄒᆞ엿스면심히조홀듯
훈지라
현금일아거장이되엿슨즉어느
나라권에이것지될지알수업는중은
힝권소이나미란훈조진이두가지가
원치못ᄒᆞᆯ지니한국에잇는일본은힝
지쳬와은힝권관리도로가진
패와밧고아주다ᄒᆞ면사름이
고란ᄒᆞ다홈이요이룰후
면필경편리홀만치아니ᄒᆞ도
못홀지라사단이이러훈즉은행
권으로말미암아일후랑패를당
홀일은우리가말ᄒᆞ지안코리니
자연히알리되아모죠록화폐
를신용이되도록약조를다시홀
이됴흔듯ᄒᆞ되신용이되도록홀
자면엇지ᄒᆞ면방칙이잇스니
구원지폐와ᄀᆞᆺ치뒤편에다무론누
구던지이지폐를가져오는자는
금화로밧고와준다고ᄒᆞ엿스면
합당홀듯ᄒᆞ도다

잡보

○일진회공함 일진회에서삼
작일본월오일에외정부에공함
훈젼문이여좌ᄒᆞ니
경계자는향일에탄하의공의를
숭순히ᄒᆞ며전국의여론을드러충
쳑의와거취를편서베픈뜻슨공히
종용사쟉의훈리픽마금된위티
홈을말미암이라그런고로시졍
기젼홈도쇼훈가히경각일지라
도쳔연ᄒᆞ지못홀거시어늘엇지
ᄒᆞ여븜브리가을저지니르도록
밝은죠칙이자로나리사정부를
신칙ᄒᆞ시며유ᄉᆞ를최비ᄒᆞ옵셧
시니정부계공이맛당히변란홀
을텨ᄒᆞ야만분지일이라도보답
홀거시어늘엇제권대제공은ᄎᆞ
인ᄒᆞ신 죠칙은문구로돌녀보
내버리고리ᄒᆞ며비등ᄒᆞ는중론은한
만훈티로저버려두어고리ᄒᆞ보가
만일그지지가뭇지못ᄒᆞ거든진
실노맛당히봄을밧드고봄남의
가어진이의계밀위ᄒᆞ며ᄂᆞ훈미의
계수양ᄒᆞ여야거우훈가지로보
홈이특경ᄒᆞ고거의나라홀그릇
ᄒᆞ게훈비함을면홀거시어놀하
늘어전최ᄒᆞ는아래계울향중출
ᄒᆞ고인민이봄종ᄒᆞ기를원치아
니ᄒᆞ야거취를결단ᄒᆞᆯ네ᄒᆞ고ᄒᆞ되
를엄비듯지못ᄒᆞᄂᆞᆫ드시ᄒᆞ니아지
못케라경하는무숨흉산이잇관
대세월만담장ᄒᆞ야맛춤내종사
와성평으로ᄒᆞ여곰장ᄎᆞᆺ다망ᄒᆞ
게ᄒᆞ여아마옴에쾌ᄒᆞ오릿가패
일언ᄒᆞ고각하는각료제공으로
더브러일제히ᄉᆞ직ᄒᆞ고물너가
셔ᄒᆞ여곰턴하의물망을맛게ᄒᆞ
소셔이거ᄉᆞ간을허치고답을나
리시는구롯이라이ᄀᆞᆺ치ᄒᆞ여
도박춤내엿허셰밋지못ᄒᆞ시면
이천만인민의일단경셩이엇지
가히종도에국치리오소남비오
기전에는면졍품이잇ᄂᆞ니저
금이합청ᄒᆞ는거ᄉᆞᆫ픗이면졍보
비는죠고만훈리구라엇대여원
ᄒᆞ건대셩샹히알지맙으시고획
답에붉히보험세종의등졍ᄒᆞ게
ᄒᆞ심을경오ᄒᆞ노라ᄒᆞ엿더라
광무팔년십일월오일
일진회장윤시병
○교문숙쳑 탁지부교문관목
하면턱탕새의 쳑지에대한졍
부지경고문이라쓰고 어보를
안ᄒᆞ야송교ᄒᆞ엿다더라

TELEGRAMS.

(FROM JAPAN PAPERS).

London, Oct. 31st.

Admiral Sir Cyprian Bridge, G. C. B., late Commander-in-Chief of the British Squadron in the Far East, and Mr. Butler Aspinall, B. A., K. C., have been appointed to report upon the damages sustained by the trawlers in the North Sea and the amount of compensation to be demanded from Russian Government.

London, Oct. 31st.

The Japanese Minister at Madrid has lodged a protest with the Spanish Foreign Office against the coaling and provisioning facilities given to the Russian Baltic Fleet at Vigo.

Spain excused the action on the grounds that other countries did the same.

London, Oct. 28th.

The Czar has ordered the Volunteer Fleeters "Smolensk" and "Petersburg" to be commissioned as cruisers on the active list, and to be rechristened the "Rion" and "Dnieper," respectively.

London, Oct. 27th.

The "Morning Post" understands that Russia is sounding the Powers with the view of securing the removal of the restrictions on the passage of the Dardanelles.

London, Oct. 27th.

The "Daily Mail" understands that Great Britain requires Russia's acquiescence in her demands for punishment of the culprits and security against a recurrence, by this afternoon, otherwise the British Channel fleet will be instructed to ask the Baltic fleet to come back.

London, Oct. 27th.

The Earl of Selborne, First Lord of the Admiralty, left London last night for Portsmouth.

London, Oct. 26th.

Count Benckendorff has informed a representative of Reuter that he is convinced that when the facts which the Russian Embassy telegraphed yesterday reached St. Petersburg, the whole difficulty would disappear.

The whole affair, he said, is a terrible mistake, at present inexplicable, and the more regretable because the relations between Great Britain and Russia were becoming more cordial.

Mr. Yi Kun-myung, special chamberlain to the Imperial Household, has been appointed President of the Council of State.

Another threatening letter, with the usual warning to resign has been despatched by the Il Chin Hoi to the Government.

The first fall of snow occurred on Saturday morning, heralding the close approach of the severe winter. At Pyeng-yang, two inches of snow fell on the 24th ult.

The Governor of Hamheung has received a report from Pukchong to the effect that over 4,000 Russians were in his district last month, and that 100 Russian officers were living in the principal temple.

The Agricultural and Industerial Department have issued instructions to all merchants to close their doors today on account of Her Royal Highness' death. All Government offices with remain closed for some days.

In a despatch to the Foreign Office, the Japanese Minister complains that various attempts have been made, of late, to wreck trains on the Seoul-Fusan railway, by placing large rocks on the track. Most of the attempts have been made near Manchon and he asks that the authorities there be ordered to prevent any further occurrences of the same.

MR. HAYASHI AND KOREA.

(Concluded from 2nd page.)

importance at the present juncture. It is an interesting fact that at this critical time Japan's interests in China and Korea should be guarded by two men who were classmates and fellow-graduates at the University 17 years ago. Mr. Uchida is a man of great courage, shrewdness, energy and character. Whether he will be thoroughly successful as a diplomatist remains to be seen. He is a man very much on the alert and endowed with no little resolution. He is in many respects a greater man than Mr. Hayashi. Mr. Hayashi has in him the makings of an excellent diplomat, but one thing in essential to his success, and that is wise guidance from his superiors in office. If he be moulded aright by the statesmen now in power, he may turn out to be one of the best diplomats we have. He has strength of purpose, backbone, and many other good qualities. But his character is such that badly handled he would turn out to be a big failure.

Comparing Mr. Hayashi with Mr. Kato, the former Minister, I by no means endorse, proceeds Mr. Toyabe, the cold, undiscerning criticism of Mr. Kato's career in Seoul penned by certain journalists. Mr. Kato went to Korea at a very critical time, when the part played by Japan's Minister in connection with the murder of the Queen had created universal suspicion and distrust in the minds of leading Korean officials. Mr. Kato set himself the task of allaying this suspicion, and he succeeded to such an extent that he even won the King himself over to Japan's side. He became a royal favourite and so great was the regard of the King for him that when subsequently, owing to want of harmony between him and Viscount Aoki, our Foreign Minister at the time, Mr. Kato vacated his post at Seoul, he was at once appointed adviser to the King and set to work to put the royal finances in order, and by this greatly increased the confidence placed in him by the Korean monarch. No Japanese living understands the King better than Mr. Kato, and it requires no argument to demonstrate how enormously important to our Government is the knowledge of the King's real character obtained by Mr. Kato. The country owes him a debt of gratitude for what he did. It is true that he did not remain in office long enough to re-establish Japanese prestige in the peninsula, and, moreover, it is questionable whether he is not of too weak and retiring a disposition to deal with the present Korean Government. On the whole the function of an adviser to the King suited him better than the office of Japanese Plenipotentiary. But if Mr. Kato was too yielding a diplomat, Mr. Hayashi is somewhat too headstrong, and seems to think that unpopularity is rather to be courted by a diplomat, as it shows that he has a mind of his own. Now real ability is not to be gauged by a man's popularity or unpopularity; but to take the view that a diplomat who offends people all the way around by his manner of acting is on this account to be esteemed by his fellow-countrymen is a great mistake. As regards Mr. Hayashi's unpopularity among the Koreans, that is neither here nor there, as Korean opinion is quite unreliable on such points. But a diplomat who excites hostility owing to want of tact is certainly not furthering his country's highest interests. It is possible to combine the "fortiter in re" with the "suaviter in modo."

When Mr. Hayashi was in London under Mr. Kato Taka-aki, he was put in charge of all the Legation accounts. Mr. Kato is essentially a man of business and is of opinion that a knowledge of accounts and business habits are the foundation of thorough efficiency in the diplomatic service. Mr. Hayashi discharged his duties with scrupulous care and won the esteem of Mr. Kato thereby. There are people who fancy that the two men are in the same camp politically, but this is not the case. Like Baron Komura, Mr. Hayashi is a man who keeps aloof from political cliques of all kinds. He may be said to almost stand alone as a diplomat and politician. Mr. Toyabe next proceeds to discuss the new arrangements which have been made by the Japanese Government for controlling Korea. The practice of sending advisers to Korea is by no means new. China, Russia and Japan have all sent advisers in the past. But it has usually happened that advice has been disregarded. Will the advisers, foreign and Japanese, now appointed succeed better than their predecessors? Not unless the Japanese Government insists in every case on the carrying out of the advice given. Some people seem to think that the position of Mr. Hayashi has been rendered very difficult by the recent appointments and that he may come into conflict with the advisers nominated. But Mr. Toyabe inclines to the opposite view. We have no space to pursue the subject full, of interest as it seems to us to be.—Japan Mail.

From the 15th November, the island Dai-wha-do in the Souchon district will be used by the Japanese military authorities for certain purposes. The lighthouse on the island will be dispensed with and the inhabitants will receive military protection.

A great appreciation of the Korean nickel has been remarked during the past few days, exchange quotations this morning were 1.96. The reason for this is, of course, the discontinuance of operations in the mint, and the heavy demand for nickles by the merchants, for the purpose of buying rice in the country.

Our contemporary, the Daito Shempo, has evidently come under the ban of the Il Chin Hoi, for the President of that wonderful society has forbidden any of the members to read it. He adds that the Il Chin Hoi has a righteous duty to perform and cannot have anything to do with anyone who opposes the society.

DEATH OF THE CROWN PRINCESS.

Late on Saturday evening, the news of the death of Her Royal Highness, the Crown Princess was announced. Little was known of the cause, but it is generally understood that she had, for some time, been suffering from a female ailment, to which, in great pain, she eventually succumbed.

She died at the age of 33 years, leaving no heirs.

The following arrangements have been made for the obsequies:—

The sacrificing temple will be the Heung-dok building.

The grave will be at Doug-ku-reung outside the East Gate.

The official mourning will take place outside Sun-rye-mun (Palace Gate). Mr. Yi Keun-myung has been appointed the chief inspector of the funeral arrangements; Messrs. Min Yung-so, Yun Yong ku and Yun Dok-yong are responsible for the sacrificial rites; Messrs. Min Yung-whan, So Sin-po and Yi Yong-tai inspectors of the nation funeral Bureau, Messrs. Min Yung-dal, Yi Chi-yung and Cho Dong-hi are in charge of the cemetery.

The Korea Daily News.

Issued at 5 P. M. daily except Sundays.

Rate of Subscription :—

Per Year. Yen 15.
Per Quarter. Yen 7.
Per Month. Yen 2.50.

Postage in Korea not charged extra.
Postage abroad charged extra.

Advertisements. 50 sen per day for 1 inch or less.
5 yen per month per inch.
50 yen per year per inch.

All communications to

E. T. BETHELL,
Editor and Publisher,
Pak-tong, Seoul

A THANKLESS TASK.

Elsewhere we print what appears to us to be an extremely unfair *critique* of the Charactor of H. M. Hayashi, the present Japanese Minister to Seoul.

The writer of the article says or hints in several places that Mr. Hayashi is unpopular here. This, to the best of our knowledge and belief, is wholly erroneous. We could not answer for the opinion which Koreans may privately hold of him, but in any event the article in question specially excludes the Korean opinion as of no value, but we can answer for the foreign population here.

We think that by now it is pretty well known that we by no means approve of the policy which Japan has lately pursued in Korea, and we therefore hope that our opinion that Mr. Hayashi is an extremely courteous, able and pains-taking representative will, as an *ex-parte* statement, carry some weight.

However the article is of great interest as an expose of Japanese incapacity to make any headway in this country. The fact that in 20 years Japan has been represented by 14 different men shows clearly that the two races can never hope to be in sympathy with each other. Policies of conciliation, aggression and intrigue have been tried in turn and all have been equally unsuccessful.

Since the outbreak of war, Mr. Hayashi has had opportunities, which in the hands of a real diplomatist would have been turned to enormous account, but which, in his hands, have been worse than wasted. By pursuing a policy of "bluff" he has endeavoured to force down the throats of the Koreans a number of measures distasteful to them and obviously intended solely for the advantage of the Japanese. Some of his attempts have met with partial success but now that Japan's prospects with regard to the war are diminishing in brilliancy, the bottom is slowly but surely dropping out of her prestige in this country. Had Mr. Hayashi's methods been a little less bumptious and dictatorial his present position might have been different but we believe that in any event and under any circumstances it would be impossible for a Japanese Minister to satisfy his own Government and the Korean Government at the same time.

In the first place, there are in Korea many Japanese of no morality or manners, who wreak more harm to Japan's good name than any Minister could ever hope to repair. And in addition a Japanese Minister is always handicapped by the inability of the Japanese in Japan to appreciate the state of affairs in Korea.

As an instance of this we have only to quote the recent progressist manifesto, which calls upon Japan to pursue a policy here which would, if attempted place her representative in the position of having to take the law into his own hands in defiance of all Japan's promises or of being compelled to make demands of the Korean Government predestined to meet with refusal.

The lot of a Japanese Minister in Korea is not a happy one and we therefore regret to find a Japanese journal adding to his troubles by charging him with short comings which he is not guilty of.

PORT ARTHUR.

The following summary of the Japanese attacks on Port Arthur from the 1st August to October 29th, has been received at the Japanese Headquarters here. As usual it is merely a statement of the main features of the siege, and gives no minor details nor mentions casualties sustained in the assault.

"Our army from the 7th to 9th Aug. attacked fiercely the enemy at Takushan and Sokushan, and succeeded in occupying those places.

On the 9th Aug. our naval guns bombarded the city of Port Arthur and damaged the battleship Retvizan. Two of the enemy's ships, of about 2,000 tons, were sunk.

On the 14th and 15th Aug. our left wing occupied the hilly ground of Suising.

On the 19th Aug. our whole army commenced a grand attack, which was however repulsed by strong resistance of the enemy. Our big guns did great damage on the enemy's forts and our naval guns assisted.

On the 22nd Aug. our centre occupied the east and west forts at Fanlungsan after a fierce battle. Since then, the enemy have several times attempted to retake these positions, but without success.

As a result of a fierce battle on the 19th and 20th September, our army occupied Kuropatkin's fort and also took four fortresses south of Suising and two forts to the south-west.

Since the 28th Sept. with mortars and naval guns we have bombarded the enemy's ships causing outbreaks of fire, especially on the "Pallada," "Peresvict" and Retvizan. The enemy's water supply from the reservior near Kuropatkin's fort was cut off. The enemy hurled hand grenades into our trenches and resisted us strenuously, but our operations were succesful.

On Oct. 14th shells from our mortars struck the Sungsuisan fort 13 times. On Oct. 16th our centre occupied the Pokwensan fort and turned the enemy out of their trenches, capturing one field-gun, two light-calibre and two machine guns. On the 24th Oct. owing to our heavy bombardment, a fire broke out in the city.

On the 25th Oct. our naval guns sunk one ship, which had one funnel and three masts.

On the 26th Oct. we made a general bombardment on the Sungsuisan, Ullunsan and east Kikwansan forts, the Ullungsan fort being greatly damaged, After this one force of our right wing attacked and carried the enemy's trenches at Pokwensan, without suffering any great loss.

On the 28th Oct. one gun at Kikwansan and seven guns at Ullungsan were badly damaged.

On the 28th Oct. 285 shells from our mortars took effect, destroying one big gun and causing an explosion in the powder magazine at Kikwansan. One gun at Etzesan was destroyed and a fire broke out in the city.

On the 29th Oct. the enemy made a counter attack on our force at Ullungsan, but were repulsed with heavy loss. At the same time they advanced to attack our trenches at Sungsuisan and succeeded in occupying one part of our position, but reinforced by artillery, we drove them out again.

During the attack on Ullungsan one part of the position was destroyed by an explosion.

At Kikwansan 350 shells from our mortars took effect.

The naval guns caused an explosion in the West Tatangkow powder magazine. They also fired on three ships engaged in sweeping the sea, two of them were set on fire.

MR. HAYASHI AND KOREA.

Mr. Toyabe Shuntei, in sketching in this month's "Taiyo" the character of Mr. Hayashi Gonsuke, Japan's present Korean Minister, reviews the history of Japan's diplomatic relations with that troublesome little peninsula. He calls attention to the fact that in the space of 20 years there have been no less that 14 different Japanese Ministers in Korea. The establishment of Japan's Legation in Korea dates from the year 1880. None of the 14 men who have represented this country in Korea has left his mark there. Three possible reasons for this suggest themselves, says Mr. Toyabe; (1) The men may not have been the right kind of men (2) The difficulties in Korea may have been so great that no minister whatever his ability could cope with them. (3) Or the instructions of the home Government to their representatives in Korea may have been wanting in explicitness and unbacked by any definite policy in regard to that country. This may have paralysed even the most capable of the men who have undertaken the guardianship of Japan's interests in that country. The first appointment made was that of Mr. Hanabusa Gishitsu, in April 1880. He was recalled in Sept., 1882, and succeeded by Mr. Takezuye Shinichiro in November of the same year, who occupied the post till June, 1885. The next appointment made was that of Mr. Kondo Chinjo, who took up his duties in Seoul in August, 1887, remaining at his post about two years. The next minister was Mr. Kawagita Shunsuke, who joined the Legation in December, 1891, and died in harness 3 months after. The Ministers who occupied the post in later years mostly only remained in it a few months. Reckoning the number of men appointed, the average of the term of service was under a year. Mr. Kajiyama Teisuke went over to Korea as minister in March, 1891, and was succeeded in December of the following year by Mr. Oishi Masami, who again gave place to Mr. Otori Keisuke in July, 1893. Mr. Otori retired from the post in October, 1894; when Count Inoue Kaoru was appointed Minister. At first it seemed as though the Count's ability and strong personality were going to work miracles in the Korean Court. But it all ended in mere paper reform, and after a year the Count returned to Japan without having effected anything lasting. Viscount the post Mraura was the next appointment. He only occupied about 3 months, dating from August, 1895, with disastrous results. Mr. Hara Kei was the next official appointed, entering on his duties in June, 1898. He was succeeded by Mr. Kato Masuo in February the following year. Mr. Kato remained in Seoul for 2 years and 4 months, when the present Minister was nominated to take his place. Thus we see that of all the 14 Ministers the longest tenure of office has not reached 3 years and the shortest has only been 3 months. But in the case of the present Minister the post has been occupied continuously for five years; Mr. Hayashi Gonsuke having been appointed in 1899. In view of the past history of our diplomacy in Korea, can any other reason be assigned for Mr. Hayashi's long tenure of office then the fact he has proved himself to be best fitted of all the men that have been tried for furthering Japanese interests in that ill-governed country?

Mr. Hayashi and Mr. Uchida, our Minister in Peking, both graduated in politics at the Imperial University in 1887. They were at that time recognized to be young men of great promise. They joined the Foreign Office about the same time and in the race for promotion and preferment ran neck and neck for many years. When in 1897 Mr. Uchida was appoined head of the Bureau of Commerce Mr. Hayashi was first Secretary at the Japanese Legation in London. When in 1899 Mr. Uchida was appointed Head of the General Business Bureau in the Foreign Department, Mr. Hayashi was promoted to be Plenipotentiary and Envoy Extraordinary in Korea; and subsequently Mr. Uchida was sent to Peking to fill a post of great

(Continued on page 3.)

The Korea Daily News.

VOL. I, MONDAY, NOVEMBER 7, 1904. No. 95

大韓每日申報
대한ᄆᆡ일신보

(뎨구십륙호)　(슈요일)　일쳔구빅사년십일월구일

본사고빅

이신보는영어와한어로셔ᄆᆡ일출판ᄒᆞ옵

신문가

한쟝　엽두돈오푼

일삭도　엽두냥닷돈

우표가퇴샤닷돈

다밧돈으로밧숩

광고료는

귀한의쟝단과ᄌᆞ항의다쇼로즁감ᄒᆞ되렴가로밧을터이오며오리지아니ᄒᆞ녀대한사ᄅᆞᆷ마다다이신문을보실터이니광고버시기를원ᄒᆞ시는이들은우리신문사에와서뎡약ᄒᆞ심을희망ᄒᆞ옵

○발힝소　박동대한ᄆᆡ일신보사범어학교압해젼영국인셰필림졍자리오

사쟝　영국인　(베셜)

평양　디리졈

○평양효동사는권태보씨로우리신문판ᄆᆡ디리인을뎡ᄒᆞ엿스오니평양에계신구람코져ᄒᆞ시는　쳠군ᄌᆞ는디리졈에왕림ᄒᆞ와면회ᄒᆞ시옵

사고

○우리대한ᄆᆡ일신보의목뎍은대한의안녕질셔에관ᄒᆞᆫ모든대목에되ᄒᆞ야는공평ᄒᆞᆫ변론을쥬쟝홈이라우리통신원의탐보는신문보시는쳠군ᄌᆞ의게ᄒᆞᆼ상보도ᄒᆞ리며편지를긔셔ᄒᆞ며주시는이는셩명과번디를젹어붓치시기를희망ᄒᆞ오나이거슨신문상에긔지ᄒᆞ란는거시아니오다만구히신용ᄒᆞ는증거를숨고자홈이라긔자는아모긔셔던지긔지홈을되쟈ᄒᆞ는권리를가졋스나되쟈ᄒᆞ는리유를말ᄒᆞᆯ터이오며공중광화를문란케ᄒᆞ는듯ᄒᆞᆫ긔셔는의례히밧지안켓습나이다

●본사셜시이릭로신문을ᄆᆡ양우톄로분젼ᄒᆞ와톄젼부의잉의로젼ᄒᆞᆫ듯스로번곳에는혹늣게젼ᄒᆞ기도ᄒᆞ며혹면칠게슬ᄒᆞᆫ녑에젼ᄒᆞ기도ᄒᆞ며혹아니젼ᄒᆞ는곳도잇다ᄒᆞ와우리신문을ᄉᆞ랑ᄒᆞ야구람ᄒᆞ시는　쳠군ᄌᆞ의게티ᄒᆞ야ᄆᆡ우미안ᄒᆞ옵기로지금은분젼인을두고ᄆᆡ일일즉이젼ᄒᆞ며아니젼ᄒᆞ거나늣게젼ᄒᆞ거나ᄒᆞᆫ일이잇스면본사로통긔ᄒᆞ여주심을희망ᄒᆞ옵

본사광고

○본사신문즁에결ᄒᆞᆫ호수를소용ᄒᆞᆯ데가잇서이에광고ᄒᆞ오니누구시던지그즁에아모호수던지가져오시는ᄃᆡ로ᄆᆡ쟝에빅젼두푼식드리리다

뎨이호　뎨삼호　뎨이십호　뎨스십이호　뎨스십삼호　뎨오십삼호　뎨오십스호와뎨오십오호　뎨륙십이호

잡보

○면훈쥬외공관　직작일에외부에셔외국에주차ᄒᆞᆫ각공관에면훈ᄒᆞ기를음력구월이십팔일슐시에(십일월오일하오팔뎜죵)황뎨폐하씌셔ᄒᆞᆼ셔ᄒᆞ옵셧는ᄃᆡ신민이통도ᄒᆞ며통곡ᄒᆞ야셩복이니신샹일을반괴를날니ᄒᆞ엿더라

○셩명각관　직작일에외부에셔각공관에죠회ᄒᆞ여본월오일하오팔뎜죵에　황태ᄌᆞ비뎐하씌셔ᄒᆞᆼ셔ᄒᆞ신일을셩명ᄒᆞ지라각공관에셔됴문ᄒᆞ는ᄯᅳᆺ스로답쟝문ᄒᆞ고삼일을반긔도레를ᄒᆞᆫ다더라

○일관죠복　일본공관에셔외부로죠복ᄒᆞ기를귀죠회를졉쥰ᄒᆞᆫ즉외귀국　황태ᄌᆞ비뎐하씌셔ᄒᆞᆼ셔ᄒᆞ신일을근셜ᄒᆞ오며경악홈을익이지못ᄒᆞ며본ᄉᆞ는귀대신을되ᄒᆞ야새셩실ᄒᆞᆫ됴의를표ᄒᆞ노라ᄒᆞ엿더라

○영관죠복　영국공관에셔외부로죠복ᄒᆞ기를귀국　황태ᄌᆞ비ᄒᆞᆼ셔ᄒᆞ신일ᄉᆞ는드르매경악홈을익이지못ᄒᆞ노라ᄒᆞ엿더라

○영ᄉᆞ문됴　직작일하오두시에영국공ᄉᆞ쥬비뎐써가외부에방문ᄒᆞ야대신을향ᄒᆞ야문됴ᄒᆞ엿더라

○직공운영　직작일에동대문안쟝셩면에셔직공을빈면ᄒᆞ덕면으로옴겨드리리라더라

○죠포곡　주직　승뎐을ᄒᆞ는아민이은ᄒᆞ기로　공너부에셔주ᄉᆞ에죵ᄒᆞ야층과저녁ᄭᅢ의곡은직ᄒᆞ여의졍부에셔각부원쳥으로통쳡ᄒᆞ엿더라

○국복과인산　황태ᄌᆞ비국복은명나라례면을의모ᄒᆞ야긔년복으로시힝ᄒᆞᆫ다ᄒᆞ며인산은벽리월니로셜힝ᄒᆞᆫ다더라

○총ᄉᆞ시무　의졍리근명씨는즉시등연ᄒᆞ야총호ᄉᆞ　ᄉᆞ무를거힝ᄒᆞᆫ더라

○의졍소졍무　관졔의졍소셔의졍위원이직작칠일노브터긔의ᄒᆞ란ᄒᆞ엿더니　국휼의거이기된고로셩복젼에는ᄉᆞ무를졍지ᄒᆞ엿더라

○봉찰보고　봉쥬관찰ᄉᆞ가외부로보고ᄒᆞᆫ니ᄀᆡ에봉쥬군슈셔리목쳔군슈박졍빈의보고를거ᄒᆞᆫ즉음력구월이십오일에본군에리ᄎᆔᄒᆞ는일병이우리진위ᄃᆡ의총이신수병과ᄒᆞᆫ환엿다셧케와환도비병과밋화약여러게를거두어모화가지고됴치원으로발향ᄒᆞ엿다ᄒᆞᆫ등졍이기로이를빙거ᄒᆞ야보고ᄒᆞᆫ다ᄒᆞ엿더라

○온궁림표수건　온양군슈가외부로보고ᄒᆞ기를음력구월초이일에일인비명이온궁에와셔표목을세운일ᄉᆞ는임의치보ᄒᆞ엿거니와추후에서탐ᄒᆞᆫ즉이일인등본명등은이언칭ᄒᆞ되본방사름망ᄒᆞ오등지가권리가잇서립표ᄒᆞᆫ수거시오니외부를경유ᄒᆞ야알아우리공ᄉᆞ의게지죠ᄒᆞᆫ즉가히알니라ᄒᆞ오며젼보고즁에우리공ᄉᆞ의게의론ᄒᆞ여ᄒᆞ겟다ᄒᆞᆫ거슨말을젼ᄒᆞᆫ이자의고롯홈이라운운ᄒᆞ는고로에다시치보ᄒᆞ노라ᄒᆞ엿더라

○압교셩사　외부에셔룡ᄎᆞᆫ방원으로죠회ᄒᆞ기를부위김병도를압슈ᄒᆞᆫ일ᄉᆞ로향에자범용수의와룡함을인ᄒᆞ야임의죠회ᄒᆞ엿거니와회ᄒᆞᆫ수의공함을린졉ᄒᆞ온즉니긔에범인문일쎄의일노써김병도를본관에셔심사ᄒᆞ겟노라ᄒᆞᆫ는인이기로사회ᄒᆞ며본즉김부위는아국에잉젹ᄒᆞ엿스민어느날어느세던지범관으로압교ᄒᆞ야써심사케ᄒᆞ라ᄒᆞ엿더라

○홍공인지　참모쟝빅셩귀씨가긔년쥬뎐을ᄒᆞᆫ츠로지잉시에수삼년텅빈관찰ᄉᆞ로지잉시에수삼쳔젼을착슈ᄒᆞ든사룸편쳔산신사는뎡영쳔팔상빅냥흉을ᄀᆞ로스ᄒᆞ여ᄆᆡ엿더니이후로브터는경기ᄀᆞ도로에셔셜ᄒᆞ에다가파산ᄒᆞ고도로에서셜ᄒᆞ가서그돈을ᄯᅢ앗긴이ᄒᆞ로브터는셰젼에상겸ᄒᆞ야곳빅빅ᄃᆡ돈을도로ᄃᆡᆸ나ᄒᆞᆫ즉빅

ᄊᆡ가흉년이알가두려워온슌호밀노곤졍ᄒᆞ며길오되지금은세도로잡ᄒᆞ리라ᄒᆞ는고로그의일에다시간즁죠수히출급ᄒᆞ엿다더라

○통입챵봉　함즁군에사는빅셩하나히졍유년이리로브터명쳔왕린일이면밤셔밀식지고와셔졍셩으로드리더니금년에도미사비편케ᄒᆞ미우ᄒᆞ로서　통쵸창봉ᄒᆞᆫ자리를잉ᄒᆞ샤샹을쥬셧다더라

○한화등귀　빅동화가근일에그갑시졈졈등귀ᄒᆞ야이왕에일화빅원에가게가이빅식오원에셔ᄂᆞᆫ지이십원지ᄒᆞ더니현금에일원구십여젼에지지니르럿는데그원인즉면환국을폐쇄ᄒᆞ고쇼각더방에무곡쟝수들이반히들가지고버러가는지통이라더라

○광제호　일본신호쳔괴조선소에셔제조ᄒᆞᆫ대한헌광슌시션광제호는지난달에임의쥰공이되고로비답실오일니로인항에도착ᄒᆞ엿는데쟝은영국사름두사후드써요기라일등운젼수와긔관쟝과일등긔관수는다티셔사룸이오귀관수와운젼수는일인을ᄎᆔ용ᄒᆞᆯ터이라더라

○교문관사　탁지교문관홍하면씨의관사는아직회졍치못ᄒᆞ엿스되위쳔남문밧헌화방빈관셔샹졍으로뎡ᄒᆞ엿다더라

○만원진보회　만원군슈리종완씨가내부로보고ᄒᆞ기를십월이십칠일죠죠에단발ᄒᆞᆫ사름오륙빅명이진보회라칭ᄒᆞ고군하에셔기회ᄒᆞ는ᄃᆡ　황실을면즁히ᄒᆞ과동립괴초를봉ᄒᆞ고케ᄒᆞ과졍부졍치를기션ᄒᆞ과인민의지산을보호ᄒᆞᆷ과외국군수샹에보ᄒᆞ홈과각국우의를돈목케홈과각국쥬교를보호홈으로일번방을붓치며이ᄂᆞᆫ번연셜ᄒᆞ는ᄃᆡ원산항일본령수와밋쥬챠헌병십여명이회에참예ᄒᆞ엿다더라

○무관학도　무관학교에셔데일회학도샹ᄋᆡ명이긔시에싱칠샹학식수업ᄒᆞᆫ다가교관이쳥쟝홈으로퇴학ᄒᆞ엿는ᄃᆡ안직귀졍치못ᄒᆞᆫ지라교육부에셔군부로보

고ᄒᆞ기를ᄯᅢ삼회학도를다시모
집ᄒᆞᆯ진ᄃᆡ매일회에퇴ᄌᆞᆨᄒᆞ엿든
학도들위션쳐치ᄒᆞᄂᆞᆫ거시가ᄒᆞ
다ᄒᆞ엿더라
○국샹례유　국샹으로인ᄒᆞ야
각부부원쳥에셔몃칠ᄎᆞ졍공ᄒᆞ
엿더라
○ᄒᆡ호세감　외부에셔장연군
슈의게훈령ᄒᆞ기를황주거ᄒᆞᄂᆞᆫ
죠괴주의쳥원니에갑오경장이
후로ᄒᆞᆼ구와포구가다외부소관
이되엿더니근래에장연오차포
가닌쟝원으로이속되야미년츈
추탕등으로오쳔량식슈세를히
원으로샹납ᄒᆞᄂᆞᆫ고로쳥원ᄒᆞᄂᆞ오
니본인으로히포슈세세감을뎡
ᄒᆞ오시면히세랍은외례히본부
로샹납ᄒᆞᆫ다ᄒᆞᆫ지라히포가박ᄒᆞᆨ
ᄒᆞ샹아니ᄒᆞᆫ포구ᄂᆞᆫ외국선쳑이
빈빈히히포에츌입ᄒᆞ야물화를
쟝샹으로민미ᄒᆞᆫ즉본부에셔외
국공평ᄉᆞ를교셥ᄒᆞ미슈세를관
할ᄒᆞᆷ이맛당ᄒᆞᆫ고로훈령ᄒᆞ니히
원이도군ᄒᆞᆫ후에등별곽호ᄒᆞ라
ᄒᆞ엿더라
○공문괴도　삼화거ᄒᆞᄂᆞᆫ오문
달이가외부로쳥원ᄒᆞ기를슈년
젼본ᄒᆞᆷ갑리셔진츌시에본인이
도편슈로거ᄒᆡᆼᄒᆞ엿ᄂᆞᆫᄃᆡ기시소
암불진갑회하못된거시빅여원
을수년동안에ᄎᆞ일ᄎᆞ일ᄒᆞ고츌
급지아니ᄒᆞᄂᆞᆫ고로향열본부에
정소ᄒᆞ야즉츌급ᄒᆞ라ᄂᆞᆫ지령을
가지고주일에발졍ᄒᆞ야륙로로
하거ᄒᆞ다가도젹을만나힝쟝을
물수히참탈ᄒᆞ읍ᄂᆞᆫᄃᆡ젼후문젹
과본부공문을다젼실ᄒᆞ온고로
다시호소ᄒᆞ오니본인의ᄉᆞ샹을
통촉ᄒᆞ신후다시엄훈을ᄂᆞ리시
기를쳔만바란다ᄒᆞ엿더라

론셜

교맘지안케ᄒᆞᄂᆞᆫ일

○우리는주한일본공사림권조
씨의공평치아니ᄒᆞᄂᆞᆫ일은여ᄃᆡ
서지라도평론ᄒᆞ야게직ᄒᆞᆯ지라
ᄒᆞᆨ신문사주필ᄒᆞᄂᆞᆫ사ᄅᆞᆷ의말이
던지은근히수군거리ᄂᆞᆫ말을드
를진ᄃᆡ흔히ᄒᆞᄂᆞᆫ말이림권조씨
ᄂᆞᆫ이나라에샹관업ᄂᆞᆫ사ᄅᆞᆷ인셔
ᄃᆞ히에그러ᄒᆞᆫ다고들ᄒᆞᆫ즉이ᄂᆞᆫ그
러ᄒᆞᆯ듯ᄒᆞᆫ말이어ᄂᆞ리ᄒᆞ되쇼ᄒᆞᆫ
일변으로싱각ᄒᆞ면ᄃᆡ단히올치
아니ᄒᆞᆫ거시우리도역시한국빅
셩들이스스로엇더케ᄒᆞᆫ다던지
ᄒᆞᄂᆞᆫ거ᄉᆞᆫ이로말ᄒᆞᆯ수업스되지
어이나라에잇ᄂᆞᆫ외국사ᄅᆞᆷ의불
공히ᄒᆞᄂᆞᆫ일로한국빅셩의게유
조치안토록ᄒᆞᄂᆞᆫ일은가히말ᄒᆞᆯ
밧ᄒᆞᆫ지라
근일형편을보드ᄃᆡ도한국에셔
ᄂᆞᆫ일본의인도ᄒᆞᄂᆞᆫᄃᆡ로좃차경
치를힝ᄒᆞᆫ즉림권조씨ᄂᆞᆫ아모조
록폐모가잇게하며ᄃᆡ표자된직
분의수고를다ᄒᆞ야사ᄅᆞᆷ마다경
즁ᄒᆞ게ᄃᆡ졉ᄒᆞ기를바라ᄂᆞᆫ도다

영지던지신문샹에게지ᄒᆞ야비
러케극진히말ᄒᆞᆷ은무리ᄒᆞᆫ일
본에무릉ᄒᆞᆷ으로ᄡᅥ이나라에ᄃᆡ
ᄒᆞ야샹공ᄒᆞ란ᄒᆞᆷ에니르러셔ᄂᆞᆫ
코게유익ᄒᆞᆯ지니
이샹년에리로공사가십수인이
임케가되엿스되괴ᄒᆞᆫ에인물이
ᄌᆞᆨ각인고로셔로감졍을뵈이지
못ᄒᆞ고동안에졍치구획도ᄒᆞ
ᄅᆡᄒᆞ야별공격도ᄒᆞ며용게도
실쳔ᄒᆞ야반주션ᄂᆞᆫᄒᆞ엿스나
모도실효가업더니
림권조씨ᄂᆞᆫ기젼이후로조흔긔
회를엇어진보의교가가되여슈
즁에드런온일이만핫스되이슈
즁에드런온일이도리여아니됨
만ᄀᆞᆺ지못ᄒᆞᆫ지라
동씨의면력ᄒᆞ야ᄒᆞᆫ일이한국빅
셩의불긍ᄒᆞᆷ은불고ᄒᆞ고다만일
본사ᄅᆞᆷ의게만유조ᄒᆞ게ᄒᆞ야잡
제로힝사ᄒᆞ기에여간몃가지일본
에효ᄒᆞᆫ일은잇서셔그러ᄒᆞ되셩
지에조ᄒᆞᆫ명예ᄂᆞᆫ졈졈감ᄒᆞ여가ᄂᆞᆫ
지라동씨의외수가잘못된거시
쳔금명령ᄒᆞᄂᆞᆫ광리지위에잇서
셔모든ᄒᆞᆫ일이일한량국쟝부에
셔쾌차항방히보이지아니ᄒᆞᆯ일
만ᄒᆞ엿스니
첫재ᄂᆞᆫ일본에ᄂᆞᆫ덕힝도업고쳬
면도엇ᄂᆞᆫ랑으로다른사ᄅᆞᆷ알기
에ᄒᆞᆫ일이만하ᄒᆞ다ᄒᆞᄂᆞᆫ공사가
오드ᄃᆡ도엇지ᄒᆞᆯ수업게만ᄃᆞᆫ엇
스며ᄯᅩᄒᆞᆫ일본졍부에셔ᄂᆞᆫᄒᆞᆼ샹
무지무릉ᄒᆞᆫ사ᄅᆞᆷ으로만공사를
셔비ᄂᆞᆫ줄노싱각ᄒᆞ게되엿ᄉᆞᆫ즉
이왕남의나라ᄂᆞᆫ티표자가되여일
을힝ᄒᆞ란ᄒᆞᆯ진ᄃᆡ아모조록한국
졍부에ᄃᆡᄒᆞ야업제로쳥구ᄒᆞᄂᆞᆫ
바와빅셩들의후잘못ᄒᆞᄂᆞᆫ일을
막ᄂᆞᆫ거시엉영히조ᄒᆞᆯ듯ᄒᆞᆫ지라
그런고로우리ᄂᆞᆫ한국에일본공
사잇ᄂᆞᆫ거ᄉᆞᆫ빈갑게넉이지아니
ᄒᆞᄂᆞᆫ즁더욱일본신문샹에포샹
싱수ᄒᆞ고거리를셜명ᄒᆞ야등졔ᄒᆞᆷ을
히고잘못ᄒᆞᄂᆞᆫ일노아노라

뎐보

십일월이일일본공ᄉᆞ관착
공보

○려순방면젼황　팔월일일노
부터십월이십구일ᄭᆞ지려순공
위군의작젼ᄒᆞᆫ계획에관ᄒᆞᆫ공보
를밧ᄂᆞᆫᄃᆡ표ᄒᆞᆫ그요뎜은좌와ᄀᆞᆺᄒᆞ니
본군은팔월칠일부터팔월구일
ᄭᆞ지대고산과밋쇼고산을공격
ᄒᆞ야탕취를다우리가졈령ᄒᆞᆷ이
되엿고팔월ㅜ일에우리히군의
대포ᄂᆞᆫ려순셔가를포격ᄒᆞ여그
포탄이젹함레드빗잔호를바두
맛쳣고ᄯᅩ이쳔ᄂᆞᆫ즁되ᄂᆞᆫ귀젼두
젹을격침ᄒᆞ엿고팔월십수일과
밋팔월십오일계젼에ᄂᆞᆫ우리히
ᄂᆞᆫ슈ᄉᆞ영셔편놉흔산두곳을졈
령ᄒᆞ엿고팔월십구일에본군은
에총공격을시작ᄒᆞ야룡쉬갑방면
에셔강경ᄒᆞ게ᄒᆞᆫ겨함을격퇴ᄒᆞ야
여졈졈우리ᄡᅥ흠ᄒᆞᄂᆞᆫ힝렬을나셔

아자케ᄒᆞᄂᆞᆫᄃᆡ그시기에우리공
셩포와밋히군포ᄂᆞᆫ각기도ᄒᆞᆫ겸공
과를엇엇고팔월이십이일에즁
앙ᄃᆡᄂᆞᆫ격젼ᄒᆞᆫ후히반룡산셔
편포ᄃᆡ와밋동편포ᄃᆡ를졈령ᄒᆞ
엿ᄂᆞᆫᄃᆡ그후에젹군비이포ᄃᆡ를
향ᄒᆞ야자로자로회복ᄒᆞ란고공
격을시험ᄒᆞ엿스나다격퇴ᄒᆞ엿
고구월십구일에셔부터구월이
십이일ᄭᆞ지련속ᄒᆞᆫ격젼의결과
ᄂᆞᆫ본군은슈ᄉᆞ영에셔동북방되
ᄂᆞᆫᄒᆞᆼ구금포ᄃᆡ를졈령ᄒᆞ고ᄯᅩ슈
무남방에잇ᄂᆞᆫ비곳에포ᄃᆡ와밋
그셔남에잇ᄂᆞᆫ두포ᄃᆡ를졈령ᄒᆞ
엿고구월이십팔일이리로자로
자로대구경포와밋히군포로ᄡᅥ
젹함을포격ᄒᆞ야그결과가자못
됴쾌되여젹함즁에우리포탄으
로위ᄒᆞ야화재가나거시잇ᄂᆞᆫᄃᆡ
특이폴타와호와레쓰위드호와
레트빗잔호세함은즁대ᄒᆞᆫ손해
를밧은줄노알앗고ᄯᅩᄒᆞᆼ구금포
ᄃᆡ의부근에잇ᄂᆞᆫ젹군의물근원
은젼히폐쇄ᄒᆞᆷ이되엿고
젹군은각방면에잇ᄂᆞᆫ우리의히
ᄌᆞ를ᄃᆡᄒᆞ야일을ᄒᆞᄂᆞᆫᄃᆡᄃᆡᄒᆞ야
폭발약을던지며기타여러가지
방법으로ᄡᅥ방히ᄒᆞ기를힘ᄡᅥᆺ스
나우리의일ᄒᆞᄂᆞᆫ거슨졈졈잘되
엿고십월십수일은대구경포의
탄환십삼발이송슈산포ᄃᆡ를바
로맛쳣ᄂᆞᆫ거슨알앗고십월십륙
일에즁앙ᄃᆡᄂᆞᆫ이룡산에셔동방
놉흔곳되ᄂᆞᆫ반권산의포ᄃᆡ와밋
이룡산즁복에잇ᄂᆞᆫ젹군의히ᄌᆞ
로를엄ᄒᆞ야쟝시간격젼ᄒᆞᆫ후에
온젼히이거슬졈령ᄒᆞ고아포와
밋쇼구경포ᄀᆞᆺ일문과귀관포이
문을획득ᄒᆞ엿고십월이십수일
에우리의포격ᄒᆞᆫ결과ᄂᆞᆫ려순시
가에화재를니러나게ᄒᆞ엿고십
월이십오일에우리히군포ᄂᆞᆫ두
굴등에셔일대빅이과셥ᄒᆞᆫ젹을계두
경포와밋히군포로ᄡᅥ즁ᄃᆡᄒᆞᆫ구
송슈산과동계관산과밋그산북
편포ᄃᆡ를포격ᄒᆞ야탄환이십오
발이바로맛쳣ᄂᆞᆫᄃᆡ그결과ᄂᆞᆫ이
룡산포ᄃᆡᄂᆞᆫ즁대히손샹ᄒᆞ엿고
송슈산포ᄃᆡ의십오산치포일문
은엄ᄒᆞ리엿고다른것은문도크
게손히를당ᄒᆞ엿고ᄯᅩ동계관산
의북편포ᄃᆡ의대포일문은계여
엿고그다음에우리의일부ᄂᆞᆫ
송슈산과밋반권산남북의히ᄌᆞ
를향ᄒᆞ야돌격ᄒᆞ야도모지ᄀᆞ손
히를벗지아니ᄒᆞ고이거슬졈령
ᄒᆞ엿고

잡보

○진회연보　ᄌᆞ작일에일진회
에셔셩삼도관찰부로연보ᄒᆞ기
를　황ᄐᆡᄌᆞ비궁뎐하께옵셔ᄒᆞᆼ
셔ᄒᆞ시니즁외가보ᄂᆞᆫ지라진
보회민의셩명과지산을보계ᄒᆞ
이라도등별이보ᄒᆞ야셩경엽도

등ᄒᆞ게ᄒᆞ심을간졀이바라노라
ᄒᆞ엿더라
○진회면칙　ᄌᆞ작일에일진회
에셔삼각군에잇ᄂᆞᆫ진보회로면
칙ᄒᆞ기를　황ᄐᆡᄌᆞ비궁뎐하께
옵셔ᄒᆞᆼ셔ᄒᆞ시니즁외가다ᄒᆞᆼ도
ᄒᆞᆫ시라국민의부의연셜ᄒᆞᆷ에수계젼에
뇌히이잇스니수무소에셔만의젼
히시무ᄒᆞ라ᄒᆞ엿더라
○샹지류안　각학교졸업싱을
ᄆᆡ레히귀복케ᄒᆞᆯ수로챤부에셔
졍부에쳥의ᄒᆞᆫ교로참챤ᄒᆞᆫ부ᄡᅥ
가반ᄃᆡᄒᆞ며잘오ᄃᆡ이거슨가히
ᄯᅢ츌ᄒᆞ지못ᄒᆞᆯ지니그ᄉᆞ괴를당
ᄒᆞ야이사ᄅᆞᆷ곳아니면엇지ᄒᆞᆯ수
업스면ᄌᆞᆺ연히괴복케ᄒᆞᆷ이임의
그젼레가잇거니와엇지그ᄒᆞᆫ졍이
엿시괴복케ᄒᆞ란ᄒᆞ며ᄯᅩ즁신을
ᄎᆞ효ᄌᆞ의문에셔구ᄒᆞ라ᄒᆞ엿거ᄂᆞᆯ
부모의몽샹을뭇치지아니ᄒᆞᆫ자
ᄅᆞᆯ엇지슈용ᄒᆞ기를오로지ᄒᆞᆯ
인으리오ᄒᆞ고무슈히샹지ᄒᆞ일삼가
ᄒᆞ여류안ᄒᆞ여두엇다ᄒᆞ더라
○주본반ᄃᆡ　ᄒᆞᆼ양군슈를빅국
영ᄉᆡ로셔임ᄒᆞ기로　주본을ᄒᆞ
엿ᄂᆞᆫᄃᆡ졍부에셔반ᄃᆡᄒᆞ야허
ᄐᆡ로쥬본을ᄂᆡ부로도로되ᄒᆞᄂᆞᆫ지라
부에셔과등ᄒᆞ여ᄃᆞ린지가일의ᄒᆞᆫ
ᄃᆞᆯ이나오랫ᄂᆞᆫᄃᆡ쳥령은이미ᄒᆞᆷ
ᄒᆞ잇스니ᄒᆞ엿다가지금셔야자ᄒᆡᆼᄒᆞ지
ᄂᆞᆫ거시엇지그리헐러이만ᄒᆞᆫᄯᅳᆺ이
며이왕에한셩관을ᄒᆞ엿ᄉᆞ온ᄃᆡᄒᆞᄂᆞᆫ
고에ᄂᆞᆫ엇지반ᄃᆡᄒᆞ지아니ᄒᆞ엿든
ᄒᆞ고샹지ᄒᆞ엿더라
○미츙하교　풍셜을드른즉근
자에목포군박에셔ᄂᆞᆫ한인이밤
젼의총울사ᄂᆞᆫ자가만타ᄒᆞᄂᆞᆫᄃᆡ밋
리유인지ᄂᆞᆫ알수업다더라
○간쳡괴착　일젼에함흥에셔
일본군ᄃᆡ가간쳡샴명을포착ᄒᆞ
엿ᄂᆞᆫᄃᆡ본시분착사ᄂᆞᆫ리근슈와
리여환과박여근이라ᄒᆞᄂᆞᆫᄃᆡ
간등변과동모ᄒᆞ야일병의수호
로군의게등보ᄒᆞ며쥰셕을닙이라
●경ᄌᆡ졍간　금일은영국황뎨
의탄신경절인고로츅하ᄒᆞ기위
ᄒᆞ야일일을졍간ᄒᆞ고ᄅᆡ명일에
츌간ᄒᆞ옵나이다
○주부샹음모　죠션신보를거ᄒᆞᆫ
즉부샹과보샹등이단발ᄒᆞ고일
진회를요란케ᄒᆞ란ᄒᆞᆫ다ᄂᆞᆫ말은
티임의보도ᄒᆞ엿거니와괴등의일
에오룸빅명은단발ᄒᆞ고일진회
나투입ᄒᆞ야방히ᄒᆞ기를시ᄒᆞᆷᄒᆞ
잇동회에셔ᄂᆞᆫ비밀ᄒᆞᆫ보ᄅᆞᆷ이
논셔회원외의사ᄅᆞᆷ은알지못ᄒᆞ
고로괴등의음모가곳발로가
되여드ᄃᆡ여아모일도위ᄒᆞ지못
ᄒᆞᆷ으로ᄡᅥ괴등은본디방으로도
라가진보회라고칭ᄒᆞ고일본군
수셩ᄒᆡᆼ동을방히ᄒᆞ야노셰ᄒᆞ
야진보회를쇼멸ᄒᆞ게ᄒᆞ도록ᄒᆞ
교음모ᄒᆞᄂᆞᆫ즁이라ᄒᆞ엿더라

NOTICE.

To-morrow, being the birthday of His Majesty, King Edward VII. there will be no issue of the KOREA DAILY NEWS.

TELEGRAMS.

MORE FROM PORT ARTHUR.

The Japanese Legation are in receipt of the following report of the Commander of the Army attacking Port Arthur:—

On the evening of Oct. 30th one force from our right wing and centre occupied the road commanding the forts north-east of Kikwansan, Ullungsan and Sungsusan and damaged the outer trenches.

One force of the center braved the enemy's fierce cannonade and attacked one of the forts of North-east Kikwansan and Fanlungsan, occupying it at 2 P. M. but losing it at 10 P. M. Major-General Ito took it again and captured 3 field-guns, 2 machine guns, 3 torpedoes and a large quantity of war material. The enemy's dead found here numbered 40.

A column of the right wing on the same day, occupied the fort at Liusan north-east of east Kikwansan.

On Oct. 31st, with siege and naval guns we bombarded the harbor, sinking the "Giriak" and 2 other ships.

On Nov. 1st we attacked and sank two ships of 3,000 tons, which were in the West Harbor and on the 2nd Nov. sunk another ship of 3,000 tons.

On the same day an explosion was heard in the north of the city.

On the 3rd Nov., we fiercely cannonaded the anchorage in the east Harbor, causing a conflagration, which burned until 4 A. M. the next day. On the same day our siege guns did considerable damage to the forts.

HAMHEUNG GOVERNOR'S REPORT.

The following report of the Governor of Hamheung may prove interesting as evidence of the unhappy lot of the Koreans sandwiched between two belligerent powers. It is not unlikely that with the existing state of affairs, there will be many more cases of this nature. Koreans sympathising with Russia are liable to be imprisoned by the Japanese, and *vice versa*.

"Early in the year," says the Governor, "I imprisoned some Tonghaks and sentenced some to hard labor and am still enquiring into the cases of others. When the Russians arrived here, these prisoners falsely stated to them that they were imprisoned for opposing the Japanese, so the Russians ordered their release, but I refused."

However on the 6th September, three Russian non-commissioned officers came and took all the prisoners away and released them.

* * *

The following is the petition of the Tonghaks to the Russians.

"We apply to the August Russian Military authorities to thoroughly investigate our case, which is as follows. We are disciples, who obey our Imperial master and study the Confucian religion, but in February last, the Japanese soldiers entered Hamheung and executed over 10 innocent men, accusing them of being Tonghaks. Thirty more were sentenced to hard labor and are still in prison, as even the Governor could not refuse the Japanese and release innocent men. But now that fortunately you are here, you will surely release us and allow us to go home to our parents, wives ane children.

* * *

The Russian despatch to the governor runs as follows:—

The 26 prisoners under your control have applied to me for an investigation of their case. I have decided that they are not really Tonghaks, but were imprisoned for opposing the Japanese. Some others are still in prison awaiting trial. If indeed they made a disturbance in a righteous cause, you must certainly permit them to live. Therefore you will hand over those prisoners to my office and I will decide their case.

(August 12th 1904 Russian Calendar) (Signed)—Commender of Imperial Russian Expeditionary Force.

The country people near Mokpo are reported to be buying old rifles in large quantities. Speculation is rife as to their object.

It is reported from St. Petersburg that the Vladivostock cruisers have completed their repairs and passed trial trips successfully.

Until Mr. Megata's house is completed, he will temporarily make use of Mr. Min Byung-suk's summer residence outside the South Gate.

The Il Chin Hoi have requested their colleagues (The Chin Pohoi) to refrain from big meetings during the time set apart for mourning for the late Crown Princess.

Mr. D. W. Stevens is expected to arrive in Korea about the end of this month. He will take up his duties of Adviser to the Foreign Office shortly after his arrival.

Mr. Hong Chung-hyun, privy councilor, has been despatched, by the Imperial Household, to Shanghai to purchase silk, adequate for the extensive funeral arraungements of the Crown Princess.

The "Kanjo Shinpo" learns that Mr. Hyon Sang-kun, who is in Shanghai, is continually reporting to the Palace that the Russians will conquer the Japanese, and that Russian troops will shortly arrive at Seoul.

In the United States to-day, the issue of the Presidential struggle is to be decided. American residents (and others) here are doubtless awaiting the result of the election with great excitement. Roosevelt or Parker?

According to San Francisco exchanges the name of Princess Victoria, daughter of King Edward, is persistently linked with that of the Marquis de Soveral, Portugal's representative at the Court of St. James, as his future wife.

The" Echo de Paris" reports that the recent declaration was drafted by Viceroy Alexeieff and General Kuropatkin had lodged with the Czar an objection against its issuance, but his proposal was rejected.

The "Kwangche" built to the order of the Korean Customs, has now been completed at the Kawasaki dockyard in Kobe, and is expected to arrive at Chemulpo about the 15th inst. She will be officered by Europeans and her crew will be Japanese.

The Magistrate of Kongchu reports that Japanese soldiers have removed the following articles from the local Korean guard, 34 rifles, 14 boxes of cartridges, 4 swords and 8 cases of gunpowder. Presumably this is as forfeit in punishment for the Kongchu riot.

It is interesting to read in a home paper that Capt. R. Collendani, of the Austrian steamer Austria, says he was offered $25,000 to transport the crew and twenty-six officers of the Russian cruiser Askold from Shanghai to Russia. The Japanese Consul at Shanghai warned the captain that if he did this service he would run the danger of being held up or even sunk by the Japanese warships, and the offer was consequently refused.

Three Koreans have been arrested at Pukchong, by the Japanese, on the charge of being Russian spies. They are accused of having given information to the Russians, relative to the movements of Japanese troops on the 15th August.

The Magistrate of Dok-won reports that on the 27th of last month, many Koreans banded themselves together in his district, and announced their intention of joining the ranks of the Chin Po Hoi. Some Japanese officials and gendarmes from Gensan assisted at the opening meeting.

The Foreign Office have telegraphed to all their Ministers to foreign countries the news of the death of the Crown Princess and have requested them to go into mourning for a period of 6 days, continuing half mourning for one year. Flags on Legations to foreign countries are to be half-masted for 13 days.

The one great weakness of the Japanese is their lack of mobility, and that is due to a fatal habit of thinking out every detail. They can do nothing on a sudden; all must be minutely prepared. It is an ineradicable fault in military affairs, for it is thought a virtue. —The Speaker

---

The Russian Government has ordered from an American firm 25 submarine boats of a new and very much improved type. The new boats will be able to sink and rise to the surface very easily and quickly. The boats will be 45 feet long, and carry a crew of three men. The vessels will cost about £40,000 each.

At the annual meeting of the Shell Transport and Trading Company the chairman, Sir Marcus Samuel, made an interesting reference to the subject of liquid fuel. He observed that it was not a little remarkable that Russia, with the largest supplies in the world should still be burning coal in her own Navy. The whole of her difficulties in getting the Baltic Fleet out would, he asserted, have been easily overcome had that fleet been capable of steaming on liquid fuel. It is satisfactory to note that our own Admiralty is making successful experiment with liquid fuel.

The "Stpenoi Krai" states that in the Kokchetav district in the Skmolinsk territory, an immense uddertaking is in course of being carried out. Messrs. Brand Bothers are erecting there, at a cost of five hundred thousand roubles, a tinned mutton factory, with a department for dealing with blood, fat, skins, and bones, and for the production of tin cans. The factory will be opened in October, and has to provide two hundred thousand pounds of tinned meats in the shortest possible time for the use of the Manchurian Army. The capital is being advanced to the promoters of the concern by an English firm.

The Korea Daily News.

Issued at 5 P. M. daily except Sundays.

Rate of Subscription :—	
Per Year,	Yen 25.
Per Quarter,	Yen 7.
Per Month,	Yen 2.50.

Postage in Korea not charged extra.
Postage abroad charged extra.

Advertisements, 50 sen per day for 1 inch or less.
5 yen per month per inch.
50 yen per year per inch.

All communications to E. T. BETHELL, Editor and Publisher, Pak-tong, Seoul

CAPTAIN MAHAN ON THE WAR.

The London "Times" has been favoured with an advance proof of a very interesting article, contributed by Captain Mahan to the forthcoming number of the "National Review" under the title "Some consideration of principles involved in the present war."

The drift of Captain Mahan's article may be gathered from the concluding passage, which runs as follows:—

This article has been concluded—and revised—under the full impression produced by the recent Russian sortie from Port Arthur, and its failure. Precision of details as to what actually occurred, of the successive stages of the combat which led up to the final result, are still wanting; but the material outcome is sufficiently evident for all practical purposes for forming a workable estimate of the situation as it now is, and of the probabilities of the immediate future. As the matter of the engagement of August 10th (August 19th) now stands, there could scarcely be asked an apter illustration of that aspect of the subject of warfare —and of all practical action—upon which I dwelt at the beginning. There can be little doubt that, when the details are known, and have been collated, studied, and weighed, by men of special aptitudes, there will be found much that will throw needed experimental light upon the conditions of modern warfare, and much room for criticism, favourable or adverse, upon the conduct of the respective fleets. But important as all this is in its place and time, and conducive as it may prove, when well digested, to the formulation of professional opinion upon questions still in dispute, it is not immediately imperative; nay, it is necessarily a matter of time and deliberation. Those who have tried to balance opposing statements of eye witnesses, to reconcile official reports, to supplement defective testimony, know how troublesome it is to reconstruct the course of a naval battle. At present the one feature which engages my own attention, standing out from the fog of unexplained details, is the apparent continued care of Togo to preserve his battleships. It is incredible that, after the experience of June 23rd, he should not have been in superior force, and certainly he had the best of the fighting; his fleet remains on the field, and his enemy dispersed. But why did he not push home his advantage? Why was the Cesarevetch permitted to escape, and the other battleships to return? He can scarcely expect, if the place fall, that they will be given up "alive;" or have felt about battering them, as Nelson did about using shell against an enemy, that it would be burning "our own" ships. To surmise that there may remain more life in the place than appears may cover me with confusion, ere the words appear in print; but under the most natural conclusion, that Japan does not feel even yet that she has any margin of seapower to spare, what a comment on Russian naval management, and what a justification of the tenure of Port Arthur and the consequent harassment of the enemy's little navy!

This battle in fact is part of the process, of the method, of the detail appertaining to the drama of war passing before our eyes; and it is not so much the particulars of its own action, but the part which it itself, as a whole, bears to the final result, which is important. Due consideration of this part invokes reference not only to that which is to come, intervening between the present and the anticipated future, but also to the irrecoverable past. Properly to value it, we should work backward as well as forward, and regard the broad aspect of the general contest not only with eyes enlightened by recognition of fundamental principles of war, but also with attention undistracted by multiplication of irrelevant detail. Whatever the cause, and wherever the fault, Russia, though much the greater in ultimate resources, permitted herself to drift into war unprepared, and gravely inferior in force, upon the decisive scene of conflict. This was especially the case upon the sea, control of which was, and has continued, so absolutely essental to Japan, that, apart from it, she would be helpless for the offensive action she had to take.

Under these circumstances two things were necessary to Russia—delay, in order to gather her resources, and promptude in repairing the neglects of the past. Herein appears the importance of Port Arthur; it has obtained delay. The time occupied in the siege has been ample for a Government, which recognised that the whole Japanese movement turned upon the control of the sea, to have despatched a fleet, which by this time could have reached the scene, and very well might have turned the scale—allowing only for the fortune of war. Before this the aggregate of Russian naval force might have been made very decidedly superior to that of Japan, and the problem of bringing the separated sections into cooperation against a concentrated enemy, though difficult, would be by no means hopeless. Success would have ended the war.

The Japanese, having this danger stating them in the face, have, I think, seen it more clearly than many of their critics. As shown by the course of the war, by their action, they have recognized that Port Arthur was the key, not only to the naval war, but to the whole campaign, land and sea. It would have been to them an immeasurable calamity had the naval season, already approaching its close, ended with Port Arthur in the hands of enemy. Amid all the uncertainty in which we are as to the respective numbers of the opposing armies, one thing seems clear, that Kuropatkin, up to the present, has profited, and continues to profit, by the siege of Port Arthur; and that to a degree which, up to the present, renders inconclusive the whole Japanese movement against him. They gain ground undoubtedly; the Russian army continually escapes them. It is not to be believed that leaders, with the high order of military intelligence shown by them, would permit this had they the power to prevent it. Each successful retreat leaves the Russian army still an organized force, still "in being;" draws it nearer to its resources, and lengthens its enemy's communications. A naval base is an element of sea-power. It may be no less determinative of a naval issue as the fleet itself, because essential to its existence Port Arthur, as well as the control of the Far Eastern waters, has thus contributed to the demonstration of the influence of sea-power. It has modified thus far the whole tenour of the land operations, and who shall say that, even the delay so far procured, may not sensibly affect the outcome of the war, even though the place itself shortly fall? The defence of Port Arthur must not be looked upon as an isolated consideration dependent upon its particular merits, but as part of a general plan of operation. Every day it holds out is a gain, not perhaps for itself, but for Russia. No principle of warfare is more fundamental than that no one position stands or falls for itself alone, but for the general good. The question is not, Can Kuropatkin bring the Japanese to a stand as yet? Probably he cannot if the besieging force is released. If it is, can he continue a successful retreat until the season bring the operations to a close? "Though our military position was imposing" wrote Bonaparte to the Directory in 1797 "it must not be thought that we had everything in our hands. Had the enemy awaited me, I should have beaten him; but had he continued to fall back, continually augmenting his resources, the situation might have become embarrassing." Whether Port Arthur has or has not obtained for Kuropatkin all the time needed to organize a campaign of this character remains to be seen; but I think the verdict of history must be that such was the tendency of its resistance, and that failure, if it comes, must be insufficiency of means, not to error in strategic conception. The time it has held out justifies the risk taken in the original calculation.

ADMIRAL WIREN.

Mr. Fred, T. Jane, in the "Chronicle," says Admiral Robert Wiren, to whom the command of the remnant of the Russian fleet at Port Arthur has now been entrusted, is the Russian Nelson, for hundreds of Russian bluejackets believe that he is Nelson born again. Though idolised by his men, Admiral Wiren was by no means a popular figure with his brother officers in the Russian Navy till the war came along. "Murderers preferred" was his nickname in Russian wardrooms, a title bestowed upon him because he applied to the Admiralty for the bad lots of the fleet to be sent him. In the "Bayan" he had the choicest possible collection of scoundrels and cut-throats whom he had transformed into smart self-respecting bluejackets whose highest ideal of reward was to row in the captain's boat! With these he visited Portsmouth a little before the war. Eighty men were given leave on a Sunday, when only public-houses were open, and not one single man of them broke leave or got drunk. During the last few years Admiral Wiren has been the right hand man of the Grand Duke Alexender in the fight for efficiency. If the Japanese shell spare him it will not be long ere the eyes of the world are focused upon "the little captain," in whose hands are the destinies of Russia. It is a labour of Hercules, a forlorn hope in every sense, but the only man who could possibly accomplish it is essaying the task.

The Korea Daily News.

VOL. I, TUESDAY, NOVEMBER 8, 1904. No. 96

HONGKONG & SHANGHAI BANKING CORPORATION.

Paid-up Capital..... ....$10,000,000
Reserve Fund:—Sterling Reserve... 10,000,000
Silver Reserve..... 7,000,000

27,000,000
Reserve Liability of Proprietors... 10,000,000

HEAD OFFICE, HONGKONG.

London Bankers, London and County Banking Company Limited.

Branches and Agencies, London.

Amoy,	Hankow	Penang,
Bangkok,	Hiogo,	Rangoon,
Batavia,	Iloilo,	Saigon,
Bombay,	Lyons,	San Francisco,
Calcutta,	Manila,	Singapore,
Colombo,	Nagasaki,	Sourabaya,
Foochow,	New York,	Tientsin,
Hamburg,	Peking,	Yokohama,

Credits granted on approved Securities, and every description of Banking and Exchange business transacted.

Drafts granted on London and the chief Commercial places in Europe, India, Australia, America, China and Japan.

HOLME RINGER & CO., AGENTS, CHEMULPO.

ON CHEONG & CO., SEOUL.

GENERAL STORE KEEPERS.

Imported provisions, Cooking Utensils Crockery, etc.

FRESH BREAD DAILY.

MITSU BISHI DOCKYARD & ENGINE WORKS, NAGASAKI.

CODE WORD, "DOCK."

A. 1, A. B. C., and Engineering Codes used.

DOCK No. 1 (at Tategami).

Extreme Length.............523 feet
Length on blocks .... 513 ,,
Width of Entrance on Top......89 ,,
,, ,, Bottom....77 ,,
Water on Blocks at Spring Tide 26½ ,,

DOCK No. 2 (Mukaijima).

Extreme Length.............371 feet
Length on Blocks............360 ,,
Width of Entrance on Top......66 ,,
,, ,, Bottom 53 ,,
Water on Blocks at Spring Tide 22 ,,

PATENT SLIP (at Kosuge).

Can take vessels up to 1,000 tons gross.

THE WORKS are well equipped with the LATEST IMPROVEMENTS, and can execute any kind of work in SHIPBUILDING and MARINE ENGINEERING, as well as in REPAIRING of SHIPS.

The COMPANY'S new powerful steamer OURA-MARU (712 tons, 700 I.H.P.), specially built for SALVAGE PURPOSES, and equipped with necessary gear, is always READY at SHORT NOTICE.

CHARTERED BANK OF INDIA AUSTRALIA & CHINA.

INCORPORATED BY ROYAL CHARTER 1853

HEAD OFFICES:—LONDON.

Paid-up Capital £800,000
Reserve Liability of Shareholders 800,000
Reserve Fund 800,000

Drafts granted upon all the principal places in the world and every description of Exchange and banking business transacted.

E. MEYER & Co., Agents, Chemulpo.

E. MEYER & CO. Chemulpo.

SOLE AGENTS IN KOREA FOR:

A. T. Morse, Sons & Co's "Fresco" Distemper

In all colours ready for use on walls, Ceilings etc.

and

AVENARIUS CARBOLINEUM

A wood-preserving and antiseptic oil preparation

Against decay, dry-rot, fungus and wood-destroying insects.

A large supply always in Stock. Prices upon application.

E. MEYER & Co., Chemulpo.

THE METHODIST PUBLISHING HOUSE,

Little West Gate, Seoul.

PRINTING, TYPEWRITER PAPER
CARBON PAPER, VISITING CARDS
STATIONERY, BOOK BINDING
BOOK PUBLISHERS
AMERICAN SCHOOL BOOKS
SPENCERIAN COPY BOOKS
PEN CARBON LETTER AND BILL BOOKS

S. A. BECK. Manager.

HOKURKU DOBOKU KAISHA.

Branch office in Chong Dong, Seoul.

Japanese telephone No. 165

CONTRACT DEPARTMENT.

We can contract to build any building or construction.

MERCHANDISE DEPARTMENT.

We can provide any building material. We have just contracted to build the new Belgian Legation.

DAI-ICHI GINKO.

LIMITED.

(Formerly the First National Bank)

ESTABLISHED 1873

INCORPORATED UNDER PRESENT LAW 1896

Capital - - - - - - - - Yen 5,000,000
Reserve Fund - - - - - 1,500,000

HEAD OFFICE:—TOKIO.

President: Baron SHIBUSAWA.

BRANCHES AND CORRESPONDENTS

In the Principal Cities and Towns of Japan.

Interest Allowed on

Fixed deposits 1 year - - - 6½ per cent
" " 6 months - - - 6 per cent

Special current accounts 1½ sen daily per Y 100
General " 1 " " " 100

M. TANAKA, Manager, Chemulpo

HOLME RINGER & Co. Chemulpo.

General Merchants and Government Contractors.

Agents for the leading Banks

Steamship Companies

and

Insurance Companies

Importers of Merchandise of every description.

KAMEYA & CO.

GENERAL STOREKEEPERS

Chinkokai - - Seoul

(*Established 1895, Tokyo*)

Confectionery, Hams, Canned Goods, Cutlery, Hirano & Tansan Water. Provisions, Gents, Furnishing goods, Toilet Articles, Travelling Bags, Tobacco, Cigars & Cigarettes Kitchen Utensils. Coffee, Biscuits.

Fresh Goods always kept in Stock.

Prices Moderate

Please come and inspect our goods

NIPPON YUSEN KAISHA.

JAPANESE MAIL STEAMSHIP CO.

UNDER MAIL CONTRACT WITH THE IMPERIAL JAPANESE GOVERNMENT.

European Line

Regular Fortnightly Service between Yokohama Kobe, Moji, Shanghai, Hongkong, Singapore, Penang Colombo, Port Said, Marseilles, London and Antwerp

American Line

Regular Fortnightly Service between Hongkong and Seattle, calling at Shanghai, Moji, Kobe, Yokohama and Victoria, B. C.

Australian Line

Regular weekly Service between Japan Ports and Australia, calling at Hongkong and Manila.

(Above Three Lines Suspended until further notice).

Shanghai Line

Weekly Service between Shanghai and Japan Ports

Korea Line

Service Kobe, Moji, Nagasaki, Fusan, Chemupo, Chefoo, Taiku.

S. S. Babelsberg, 2181 tons.

Service Kobe. Moji, Fusan, Chemulpo, Chinnampo

S. S ARGO, S. S. Ohio

BORDEN'S CONDENSED MILK CO.

New York, U. S. A.

ALWAYS IN STOCK

Eagle Brand Condensed Milk.

Gold Seal Condensed Milk.

Peerless (Family) Evaporated Cream.

Borden's Malted Milk.

E. MEYER & CO. Chemulpo, Korea, Sole Agents

ROYAL INSURANCE COMPANY,

Funds exceed £10,000,000

FIRE AT CURRENT RATES.

LIFE REDUCED PREMIUM.

HOLME RINGER & Co., Agents, Chemulpo.

HOTEL DU PALAIS

SEOUL.

The only first class Hotel in Seoul. Situated in the centre of the city opposite the palace.

Cuisine under the supervision of an experienced French Chef.

Well ventilated and furnished throughout.

TARIFF UPON APPLICATION

L. MARTIN

Proprietor and Manager.

報申日每韓大

보신일미한대

(호칠십구뎨) (일요금) 일일십월일십년사빅구쳔일

본샤고빅

이신보는영어와한어로셔거릭일출판ᄒᆞᆸ

신문가

ᄒᆞᆫ쟝 엽두돈오푼

ᄒᆞᆫ삭료 엽두량닷돈

우표가ᄃᆡ 삭닷돈

다엽돈으로밧숩

광고료는

긔ᄒᆡᆼ의쟝단과ᄌᆞᄒᆡᆼ의다쇼로죵

[illegible]

본샤광고

[illegible]

론셜

[illegible]

샤고

[illegible]

잡보

[illegible]

찬부로면ᄒᆞᆫ호티니깅써가잉의
중은지가오팃다다란
ᄆᆡ동화졍귀 탁지고문관비
동화를쳐치홀츠로면환국을봉
폐ᄒᆞ야경쥬ᄒᆞ고각군상납젼을
빅동화로슈샹케ᄒᆞ며빅동화가
졍졈ᄒᆞ고등ᄒᆞ고지젼갑시졈졈셰
련진다더라
○퍼세동화징슈 각항구힝관
세도빅동화로징슈케ᄒᆞᆫ다고각
국샹민들이샹의중이더라
○봉도됴 비궁뎐하홍셔
황티ᄌ비뎐하민씨ᄂᆞᆫ교 증평
의졍증문공티호씨의ᄉᆞ녀이신
티임신셩월이샹일에탄셩ᄒᆞ옵
시교임오이월이샹일에가례를
힝ᄒᆞ사 셰ᄌ비를 칙봉ᄒᆞ옵시
교광무원년뎡유구월에 황티
ᄌ비를칙봉ᄒᆞ옵시니빈궁위에
게신지십오년이오빈궁위에게
신지팔년이신티숙덕과외헝비
중외에혀좌ᄒᆞ치며츈츄가졍셤
ᄒᆞ시되종샤의경이ᄂᆞᆺ조샤조아
신민의봉망홈이오려더니천만
의외에거연이본월오일（일력
구월이십팔일）하오팔시에ᄒᆞ
셔ᄒᆞ신 조칙을봉승ᄒᆞ오니오
호통제라방운이불힝ᄒᆞ야국가
변샹이런녀ᄒᆞ야쳥출ᄒᆞ니셔민
의통도ᄒᆞ옴이엇지망극지아니ᄒᆞ
리오하믈며 뎐하ᄂᆞᆫ현숙ᄒᆞ신
졍덕이구중에졍옴ᄒᆞ사팔역에
현달ᄒᆞ시거날신민의소망을일
위지못ᄒᆞ고엄홀히셩셔ᄒᆞ시니
광국의불힝이오신민의박복이
라오호통재라 뎐하의츈츄ᄂᆞᆫ
삼샹삼이시더라
○미병죠복 미병랑공ᄉᆞ관에
셔삼작일에외부로죠복ᄒᆞᆫ기의
를거ᄒᆞᆫ즉귀 황티ᄌ비뎐하
ᄒᆞ셔ᄒᆞ신은드르ᄆᆡ경악홈을계
우리못ᄒᆞ오며맛당히우리졍
부에젼달ᄒᆞ리이오샹일간반
를받아셔됴위ᄒᆞᄂᆞᆫ졍셩을표ᄒᆞ
겟노라ᄒᆞ엿더라
○쳥관죠복 쳥국공ᄉᆞ관에셔
외부로죠복ᄒᆞᆫ기의를거ᄒᆞᆫ즉귀
황티ᄌ비뎐하게셔홍셔ᄒᆞ사부
음을봉승ᄒᆞ고경악ᄒᆞ오며븐ᄂᆞ
덕을공경ᄒᆞ야홍앙ᄒᆞ엿ᄉᆞᆸ더니뭇
린방이다완셕히너이오며맛당
히우리졍부에뎐보ᄒᆞ겟노라ᄒᆞ
엿더라
○금단방회 일젼에일본공ᄉᆞ
의공홈ᄒᆞᆫᄉᆞ긴을인ᄒᆞ야참졍이
내부대신의게젼탁ᄒᆞ야경긔도
와츙쳥남북도와경샹남북도관
찰부로년ᄒᆞ훈ᄒᆞᆫ기의를거ᄒᆞᆫ즉평
도셩근로우희몰닌도를노화ᄒᆞᆫ거
를방히ᄒᆞᆫ다ᄒᆞ니관계가심히ᄀᆞᆫ
지라션조각군에엄칙ᄒᆞ야각별
히금단ᄒᆞ야ᄒᆞ여금일이ᄂᆞ지안
케ᄒᆞ라ᄒᆞ엿더라
○부유만셰 일젼에
지환국쟝최셕조씨ᄂᆞᆫ국쟝취임ᄒᆞᆫ젼
연치부ᄒᆞ여민년츄슈가만년에
이라ᄒᆞ더라
○샹용물품 궁내부에셔국쟝
ᄉᆞ용물품가셕비단을무역차로

젹의관ᄒᆞᆫ츙쳥셰를샹히로파송
ᄒᆞᆫ다더라
○별단불서 학부에셔관세
을션출ᄒᆞ고빅여명을별단셔에
써셔드렷더니별단이다불시가
되엿다더라

뎐보

십월이십칠일에우리의포격ᄒᆞᆫ
효력으로동계관산포티에셔
포슈를열여탐을세드렷고아롱
산과밋송슈산포티에셔손샹ᄒᆞ
며세여지며기우리진각종대포
의합계가쳘문에밋쳣고기다입
폐부와밋령기의세여진기ᄉᆞᆫ태
단이만고닉월이십팔일에우리
대구경포의바로맛쳔탄환이
계가이빅팔십오발이오히군포
도쏘ᄒᆞᆫ도ᄒᆞᆫ결과를엇엇고이포
격의결과인죵등계관산포티에
셔ᄂᆞᆫ대포일문이히여져다란
고그산북편포티의쟝약고등쪽
발ᄒᆞ엿고송슈산에ᄂᆞᆫ대포이문
을바로맛쳣고외ᄌᆞ산에ᄂᆞᆫ대포
슈련ᄒᆞ나흘젼복시이고다ᄂᆞᆫ대
포슈련ᄒᆞ나ᄒᆞᆫ대단히기우러져
고기타다ᄂᆞᆫ포티와밋보루의
히ᄒᆞᆫ거슨젹지아니ᄒᆞ고란ᄉᆞ구
이젼시가에ᄂᆞᆫ화ᄌᆡ가나게ᄒᆞ엿
고십월이십구일에젹군은이룽
산엿ᄉᆞ나손히를대단히입엇다
ᄒᆞ숩격ᄒᆞ야왓ᄉᆞ되우리ᄂᆞᆫ
손히를당ᄒᆞ고뎍포ᄅᆞᆯ다시
계관산북포대동편장벽의
경포로포격ᄒᆞ엿고
（계이ᄉᆞ이）
관산포티와밋송슈산의
ᄒᆞ엿다ᄒᆞ엿더라
십일월초일동경발
뎐슌공위군ᄉᆞ령관보고
○뎐슌젼황 우이종티와밋중
앙종티의일부ᄂᆞᆫ십월삼십일져
녁에송슈산과이룽산과동계관
산북편포티의북도를졈령ᄒᆞ
고또밧갓히ᄌᆞ의가리운거슬벗
부분이나파샹ᄒᆞ엿고즁앙종티
의단편일부ᄂᆞᆫ젹군의밍렬ᄒᆞᆫ포
화를무릅쓰고반룽산과동계관
산북편포티셰이에잇ᄂᆞᆫ흉포티
를습격ᄒᆞ여셔오후두시에거슬
졈령ᄒᆞ여셧스나오후열시반에
시에거슬일헛고그러ᄒᆞᆫ티오후두
에니르러ᄂᆞᆫ일호소쟝이다시
졈령ᄒᆞ고아포군샹관괴관포이

문과이쳥슈된샹케와기타슈다
ᄒᆞᆫ젼리품을엇엇고이곳에버린
젹군의죽은자가ᄉᆞ삼명이오우
종티ᄂᆞᆫ이날에동계관산외동북
방류산포티를졈령ᄒᆞ엿고십월
삼십일일에대구경포와밋히군
포로써홍닐를포격ᄒᆞ야포티이
자로자로키리약코호롤맛쳣고
쇼괴젼이쳑을침몰식혓고십일
월일일에셔홍닐에잇든각기삼
쳔오빅돈가량되ᄂᆞᆫ괴션이쳑을
두격침ᄒᆞ엿고십일월이일에삼쳔
돈되ᄂᆞᆫ괴션일쳑을격침ᄒᆞ엿고
이날져ᄌᆞ거리북편숏히셔밍렬
ᄒᆞᆫ폭셩이두번이나들녓ᄂᆞᆫ티아
마화약고가폭발ᄒᆞᆫ듯ᄒᆞ고십일
월ᄉᆞ일에히군즁포로써동편졍계
쟝과밋그부근을밍렬히포격ᄒᆞᆫ
셰문에오후팅시삼오분에동디
에화ᄌᆡ를니르키엿ᄂᆞᆫ디익일오
젼비시ᄭᆞ지화염이셩ᄒᆞ더니
낫고동일에우리대구경포의포
격은쳔쳐히각포티에손히을식
히엿다ᄒᆞ엿더라

관보

뎨이쳔구빅칠십칠호
광무팔년십일월칠일

셔임급ᄉᆞ령
○임평리원판ᄉᆞ셔주임관일등
종이품 리병화
십일월이일
○명궁내부특진관셔칙임관ᄉᆞ
등 종묘셔졔주 조병익 종
이품 민병호
○명종묘셔졔주셔칙임관삼등
쟝례원쇼경 윤티홍
○명쟝례원쇼경셔칙임관ᄉᆞ등
사젹셔졔주 리지덕
○명내쟝원경셔칙임관삼등
종이품 김윤환
의원변본관 홍문관시독
졍 현 김쳘슈
○임홍문관시독셔칙임관ᄉᆞ등
종품 죠셩익 민영셔
○임한셩부관윤셔칙임관삼등
내쟝원경 민경식
병○금이금봉 평리원판ᄉᆞ
화 외부교셥국쟝 리샹셜
이 샹십일월ᄉᆞ일
○종권쳐 농샹공부주ᄉᆞ 로
명귀 십일월ᄉᆞ일 농샹공부
○임의졍부의졍셔칙임관일등
궁내부특진관 리근명
십일월오일
궁명통ᄉᆞ
궁내부특진관 신샹훈 작소
비지나예ᄉᆞ쳥을의시ᄒᆞ노라
○내쟝원경 리병규ᄉᆞ직소 비
지나에소쳥을의시ᄒᆞ노라
이샹십일월ᄉᆞ일
쟝ᄉᆞ
○금십일월오일묘시에비로소
하셜ᄒᆞᆫ다
참모부관졔
뎨일됴 참모부ᄂᆞᆫ국방과밋용
병의관ᄒᆞᆫᄉᆞ홍
뎨이됴 참모부참모총쟝은통
군대쟝이나혹부쟝으로 칙
임홈이라
뎨삼됴 참모총쟝은
대황뎨폐하씌직예ᄒᆞ야유악의
군무를참획ᄒᆞ며국방과밋용
병에관ᄒᆞᆫ일졀계획을쟝ᄒᆞ고
고참모부를총할홈이라
뎨ᄉᆞ됴 참모총쟝은국방의계
획과밋용병에관ᄒᆞᆫ명령과밋
됴록과규칙등을긔안ᄒᆞ야친지
를경ᄒᆞᆫ후에비거슬군부대신
의게이조홈이라
뎨오됴 참모총쟝은통군참모
쟝교등을통령ᄒᆞ며그교육을감
독ᄒᆞ고통군대학교와통군측
도부와밋외국에쥬차ᄒᆞᆫ공ᄉᆞ관
부통군무관을통할홈이라
뎨륙됴 참모부쟝은총쟝을보
좌ᄒᆞ야본부ᄉᆞ무를졍리ᄒᆞᄂᆞᆫ
졔칙을임무홈이라
뎨칠됴 참모부에부관부를셜
치ᄒᆞ야부내셔무인ᄉᆞ긔록과
밋경리의ᄉᆞ무등을쥬쟝홈이라
뎨팔됴 참모부에뎨일국뎨이
국을셜치ᄒᆞ고그국쟝으로써
좌긔ᄒᆞᆫᄉᆞ무를분빈ᄒᆞ야담임
홈이라
뎨일국
작젼의계획
요새위치의쳔뎡과밋병긔탄
약
단대의비치
동원
평시젼시의편졔
병긔재료탄약쟝구
젼시모든됴례규칙
뎨이국
외국군ᄉᆞ와밋디리
통령보고
군ᄉᆞ통계
운슈교통과밋군용통신
젼시ᄉᆞ긔와밋번역
니외국젼병ᄉᆞ샹긴요ᄒᆞᆫ디지
외밋졍지
외국셔젹의번역
뎨구됴 우모든ᄉᆞ홍외에담임
을뎡치못ᄒᆞᆫᄉᆞ홍은별시에그
국를지뎡ᄒᆞ든지혹국원의게
명령ᄒᆞ야그ᄉᆞ무를참예케홈
이라
뎨십됴 참모부에직원은좌굿
홈이라
총쟝 일인 통군대쟝혹부
쟝
부쟝 일인 통군부쟝혹참
쟝
부관 ᄉᆞ인 통군졍부령일인
참령일인졍위이인
국쟝 이인 통군참쟝혹졍부
령
국원십륙인 통군참령ᄉᆞ인
졍위십이인
향관이인 일이등군ᄉᆞ
번역관 오인 주임 이인
판임 삼인
셔긔 팔인 판임
즁관 삼인 판임

TELEGRAMS.

(FROM JAPANESE PAPERS.)

An official report, which reached Tokyo on Nov. 1st. states that the Russians are acting upon the offensive from the Shaho. Their scouts are continuously employed and there is constant firing.

The Russian troops who face the Japanese left and centre armies seem to be preparing to make an attack in force.

On the night of the 22nd inst., the Russians made a night attack upon the Japanese positions at Linsingpao, but were repulsed and retreated to the west.

London, Nov. 2.

The Russian warships at Vigo are the battleships "Kniaz Souvaroff, Brodino, Orel" and "Alexander III."

Later.

The whole of the Russian Fleet has quitted Vigo.

Four officers remain behind for the purpose of investigation.

London, Oct. 31.

The Russian inquiry in to the recent incident in the North Sea was opened at Vigo yesterday.

Five Russian torpedo destroyers have left Tangiers; the remainder of the Squadron is shipping coals and provisions.

Later.

The Governments of Great Britain and Russia are negotiating a special convention to appoint a commission of inquiry into the facts of the North Sea outrage. The commission will probably meet at Cherbourg.

The Tsar has appointed his "aide-de-camp," Captain Rosnakoff, to represent the Russian naval authorities at conference to be held at Hull to investigate the recent affair in the North Sea.

Reports from Gibraltar state that the order for the mobilisation of the British Navy has been countermanded.

London, November 2nd.

The Peninsula and Oriental Steam Navigation Company's steamship "Assaye" was stopped off Gibraltar by Russian warships. The "Assaye" is now proceeding on her voyage under escort of the Brirish battleship "Illustrious" (14,900 tons.)

London, November 2nd.

The Marquess of Lansdowne issued a statement yesterday to the effect that the Baltic Fleet, before leaving Vigo, engaged not to interfere with neutral commerce.

London, November 2nd.

Viceory Alexeieff leaves Harbin for home to-day.

Tokyo, Nov. 7th.

Five ships of the Baltic Fleet with 2 coliers and one hospital ship left Tangier on the 6th.

Tokyo, Nov. 7th.

The ring around Port Arthur is gradually closing in. The Russians attacked our position near Uullungsan on the 5th, but were repulsed, leaving many dead on the field. It is expected that the garrison at Port Arthur cannot now hold out for more than one week.

Tokyo, Nov. 8th.

The Porte has permitted the passage of 7 ships of the Russian Volunteer Fleet, through the Dardanelles.

As we go to press news reaches us of the re-election of President Roosevelt. No details are yet to hand.

Berlin, Oct. 31.

The English and French papers praise the Tsar for agreeing to submit the North Sea incident to arbitration, and see in this act a drawing closer of Russia to the Anglo-French "entente coadiale," which is friendly to Russia also.

The Baltic Squadron has completed the work of provisioning the ships at Vigo, and will continue the voyage to the Far East.

MR. DOOLEY ON THE PROGRESS OF THE WAR.

"How is th' war comin' on?" asxed Mr. Hennessy.

"Nicely, thank ye f'r askin'," said Mr. Dooley. "Th' Rooshyans is sweepin' ivrything before thim in their mad rush to Saint Pethersburg. Their navy has been uniformly victoryous, in some cases blown up higher thin th' wurruld's record an' in other cases batin' all preevyous time out to sea an' back again. Port Arthur has fallen as often as s gradyate iv th' Keeley cure. Th' Czar has issued a ukase, which is th' main nourishment iv th' common people iv Rooshy, a blessing an' an ikon to each recroot. If it wasn't f'r th' Rooshyan belief in th' ikon, I don't know how long th' Czar wud last, Hinnissy. That's a joke. Look it up. Th' lile subjecks iv th' Czar who ar-re bein' sint out to die f'r their country, which is on'y theirs when they ar-re away fightin' f'r it, has thanked th' Czar at a thremenjous blow-out f'r wan iv his principal advisors. But th' Czar won't know much about th' war fr'm now on. I seen it in th' paper th' other day that they was bor'rn to his Impeeryal High-ness Gin'ral Alexis Alexlandrovitch Michaelovitch Johnovitch Willum J. Czar. Mr. an' Mrs. Czar both doin' well. He was bor-rn a Rooshyan gin'ral, mind ye. It's a heavy handicap whin he acquires sinse.

"They're a gr-reat people thim Japs. I used to look down on thim. There Japan shtud, an,' says Westhren Civilyzation to itsilf, 'There mus' be something in this. We'll blow th' dure off.' We opened it, Hinnissy, an' what did we find? Ditictives, no less. We didn't go in. There wasn't room. They come out. Thin they begun runnin' around over th' wurruld findin' out what was goin' on. No one thried to stop thim. What harm cut they do, thim cunnin' little fellows, barely up to th' waist-band iv a Rooshyan? Our idee iv a gr reat man is a tall man, which lets out Napoleon Bonyparte an' Young Corbett, an' lets in Fairbanks. Th' Jap is th on'y person I know iv that's learned anything in recent years. He larned ivrything that was known be Impror Willum, the Czar, Prisitint Rosenfelt, Charley Schwab, J. W. Gates, Herr Krupp, Mrs. Eddy, Nels Morris, Cap Mahan, th' American Can Comp'ny, th' Author's Society, Thomas Edison, Willum Marconi, Jawn Hay, an' Doctor Munyon, borried enough money to make him inthrestin,' an' wint home.

"Nayther Rooshya nor I believed him. Rooshyans put their hand in to see whether th' wheels were goin' aound. They were. They were goin' round at th' rate iv fifty rivolutions a sicond an' they ar-rent't rivolutions ye can put down be sindin' people to Sibeerya. Ivry day since this here war again thim pore' benighted hay then begun they'se been something doin.' Rooshyan can't step out into his back yard without landin' on a mine. Th' Czar at home tendin' th' baby, rocks th' cradle with wan hand an' opins a tillygram with th' other. 'Tis fr'm Gin'ral Kurrypotkin, an' it reads 'En route home. I have th' honour to rayport to ye'er Majesty that I made a gallant attack on th' Jap'nese right at 10.20 this mornin.' Our sojers fought like heroes, dhrivin' the Japs before thim like chaff before th' wind. But at 11 o'clock th' chaff turned an' subsequently th' joke was on me. Th' Japs seemed absolutely oblivyous iv human life or their own Forchnitely there was a thrain in waitin' an' I managed to catch th' last rail. I have tillygrafted th' ar-rmy to jine me at their own convaynience. I larn fr'm Port Arthur that ye-er Majesty's Feet made another sortie at th' inimy again, an' afther inflictin' much damage on their mines an' torpedoes be rammin' thim, sortied back to their snug haven in Port Arthur, where they gallantly repulsed an infanthry attack. They ar're now throwin' up inthrenchments on deck." An' th' Czar answers, Congratulations on gallant fight. Baby christened to-day. Name follows be freight.'

"An' there ye ar-re, Hinnissy. Rooshia has picked up a live wire. We opened up Japan to Westhren civilization an Japan's openin' up Westhren civilization with th' same weapons. How will it all come out, says ye? Faith, I don't know. It don't require no Hivin-sent gift to make a cannon, or th' Germans wudden't be so good at it. They ain't anny raison why Okypoko shudden't larn to mannyfacther a gun as well as Hans Dinkelspiel. They ain't much in invintive jaynius. It's all imitation. But th' Japs ain't goin' to stop with lickin' the Rooshans. Maybe they'll take it into their heads to come over here and settle. 'Twud be cheaper to settle down here thin to settle up with their creditors. They may bring th' Chinese with thim.

ACCIDENTS FROM FLOATING MINES.

On Oct. 30th the "Chioyoda Maru," entered Moji harbor, and reported to the naval authorities that they had discovered a stray mine at sea and had taken it on board. A barge was sent alongside to take away the machine, and several officers from a Japanese warship went on board the Chiyoda Maru, to superintend the unloading. Sundenly the mine exploded, doing fearful damage. A large hole was blown in the port side of the vessel, 24 men were killed and thirty wounded. Among the killed were eight officers and men from the Japanese war-ship.

Another accident, due to the same cause, is reported by the Weihaiwei correspondent of the N. C. Daily News as follows.

A junk bound for Dalny with about one hundred coolies for the Japanese transport department encountered a mine which was mistaken for a buoy and dragged on board. Some twenty odd survivors were picked up the next day clinging to floating wreckage, and brought here. Some of these were admitted into the civil hospital shockingly mutilated.

NOTICE.

NOVEMBER 3RD.

We have this day authorised Mr. Alexander Carnduff to sign the name of our firm in Korea per procuration.

HOLME RINGER, & Co.

Dr. Daniel B. Nye, D. D. S. has arrived and will be at Steward's Hotel, Chemulpo, until the 30th instant, and in Seoul on his return from the American Mines.

The Korea Daily News.

Issued at 5 P. M. daily except Sundays.

Rate of Subscription :—

Per Year.	Yen 25.
Per Quarter.	Yen 7.
Per Month.	Yen 2.50.

Postage in Korea not charged extra.
Postage abroad charged extra.

Advertisements, 50 sen per day for 1 inch or less.
5 yen per month per inch.
50 yen per year per inch.

All communications to
E. T. BETHELL,
Editor and Publisher,
Pak-tong, Seoul

KOREA'S FUTURE.

With undiminished activity the progressist party in Japan is continuing to urge its Government to adopt a "strong" policy in Korea amounting almost to a protectorate. Japan's pledges, the lessons of the past and the problems of the future seem utterly wasted upon these unthinking and hot-headed politicians.

To any one but a "progressist," history demonstrates clearly enough the absolute futility of all Japanese efforts at reforming this country. In his book "Problems of the Far East," the Rt. Hon. G. (now Lord) curzon, speaking of the various "reforms" instituted by Count Inoue after the China-Japan war says "It will strike the reader, as it struck all observers that the methods above described were a somewhat curious way of striking off from Korea the fetters of a foreign dominion—the ostensible purpose of the war and of re-establishing her independence. This is the view that was also taken by the Koreans themselves. The horse can be taken to the trough; but no amount of persuasion in the world can compel him to drink if he is not thirsty. The Koreans had no appetite for reform. On the contrary they abominated it in every shape; still more when it was offered to them by their hereditary enemies and recent oppressors, the Japanese. It is quite a mistake to suppose that, whatever the official expressions of Korean gratitude, any thing but aversion was entertained by the emancipated themselves for their so-called deliverers."

These sentiments apply with equal force and precition to the situation as it is today. Unless force is used Korea will never allow Japan to dictate to her in matters of internal administration, and in order to use force Japan will have to break all the pledges given by her at the beginning of the war. It seems probable that in order to stand well with the world, Japan, in the protocol, promised more than she intended or could hope to perform, but still the pledges were given, and if the progressist party is listened to and they are violated, Japan will bring about her ears a surprising crop of protests from abroad.

It may be remembered that we recently quoted the "Japan Mail's" opinion that if Korea is left as she is for a while, she will get things in such a muddle, that the whole world will presently approve of Japan's stepping in and administering the country. There is another side to this question. To all intents and purposes Japan had this opportunity in 1895 and the unspeakable mess which she made of things is still fresh in every one's mind and will serve as a very strong argument against her being given another opportunity for making mischief.

The "Kobe Chronicle" in a recent article on Korea alludes to the racial affinities between the two peoples, but beyond the fact that the Koreans and Japanese had some ancestors in common here is no more affinity between them than between chalk and cheese and the two races are as far apart in their habits of life and thought as any two nations in the world.

It is instructive to note that no outside authority, either political or critical, seems to view with approval Japan's designs on Korea. In this connection the "Kobe Chronicle" quotes the following remarks made to a Korean official by the late Li Hung Chang in 1881:—

"Of late years," said the Chinese statesman, "Japan has adopted Western customs......Her national liabilities having largely increased, she is casting her eyes about in search of convenient acquisition which may recoup her......The fate of Luchu is at once a warning and a regret to both China and Korea......Her aggressive designs upon Korea will be best frustrated by the latter's alliance with Western nations."

While in 1894 Lord Curzon said :—

"If Korea is not to collapse irretrievably she must lean upon a stronger power and every consideration of policy points towards maintaining China in the position of protector which she has hitherto filled.

Anything but Japan.

THE CHINESE ARMY.

The Committee on the Reorganisation of the Chinese Army, under the presidency of Prince Ching, have laid before the Government a plan for the introduction of universal service in China; the period of service would be for 12 years, of which three would be passed in the Regular Army, three in the first; three in the second Reserve, and three in the Landwehr. The pay would be $10 (about 19s.) a month, and the families of the man enrolled would be entitled to a relaxation in their taxation. The provinces would, at the commencement, enroll only 1,000 men, and these would be trained as a nucleus, in close-order formations according to German methods, whilst for field service they would receive Japanese training. The Governor-General, Yuan-shi-kai, has received orders to immediately commence the raising of an army of 42 infantry divisions in Petchili, each division to be composed ef 12 battalions of 500 men each, or altogether 252,000 men.

The following from the report of the manager of the Oriental Hotel at Kobe at a meeting of shareholders, is illustrative of the manner in which the war is affecting Japan. "This time last year they scarcely thought there would be war between Japan and Russia, and they were rather sanguine of their future profits, especially as at that time they had been doing very well. They ought now to congratulate themselves that they were able still to show such a report as the one before them, The report was a very different one from last year, but last year they had fortunately made handsome provision for the future, and they now considered it advisable to pay the customary dividend of 12 per cent., and to carry Y5,372 to the reserve. If the war should continue of course they might next year be unable to pay such a good dividend."

"Wireless telegraphy is to be employed to aid in saving the forests of the West," says Electricity. "Plans are being made in the Bureau of Forestry to establish wireless stations at intervals thoughout the Rocky Mountains where there are large forests, and where fires occur in the dry season every year, destroying vast areas of magnificent timber. At these stations expert observers will be kept who will give warning whenever a fire begins, and help will be called to assist in extinguishing it. The first system to be set in operation will be in the Black Hills."

Professor Lawrence Bruner has this year had 26,000 grasshoppers added to his collection. It now numbers nearly 150,000, and includes 35,000 different species.

REPORTED EARLY RETURN OF VISCOUNT HAYASHI.

A rumour is current in official circles in London, states the Hongkong Telegraph, that Viscount Hayashi, the Japanese Ambassabor will leave England for Japan on leave of absence early next year, and that it is unlikely that he will return. The assumption is that his Excellency is to fill some high post in the Government at home. To say that the Viscount will be missed, if the report should prove true, is to underestimate his popularity in the Metropolis. His departure would be a loss, for with the exception of Mr. Choate he is the only member of the diplomatic body who is at all known to the man in the street. Viscount Hayashi was the first Ambassador or Minister in London to become a Freemason having been initiated by the Lord Chancellor in the Empire Lodge two years ago, and he is at this moment worshipful master of that lodge.

LADY HYON TO THE RESCUE.

On the 2nd inst, says the "Daihan Ilpo," the concubine of General Hyon Yong-woon telegraphed to the Imperial Household from Tokyo that she has succeeded in ensuring the safety of His Majesty and the Independence of Korea, as all the Japanese, whose policy in this country is bad, will be recalled to Japan.

Mr. Roosevelt makes one conspicuous omission in his letter of acceptance. He fails to claim credit for the pleasant summer weather.—The Baltimore Sun.

The "Tokio Asahi" says that the present report that the Japanese in the Shaho district are unable either to advance or retire is totally unfounded.

An officer from the front states that the Russians at Port Arthur have recently been firing at night magnesium shells in order to watch the movements of the Japanese.

An American lumberman anxious to visit the Exhibition at St. Louis, is going there on a log 16ft. long by 24ins. in diameter. He will float with the current 250 miles down the Mississippi.

The Bishop of London states that a subscription of £5 has been sent to his fund by an undertaker, who described the donation as a thank-offering "because trade has been so brisk of late."

The task of selection from such a mass of material as the correspondence of 24 years represents has been found so heavy that there is no prospect of any portion of "The Letters of Queen Victoria" being published during the present year.

The Japanese have ordered 7,500 tons of armour plate from the Carnegie company, which ought to mean, after passing through the proper divident channels, a few more libraries for somebody. Thus we see what a great educational institution war is.—The Indianapolis News.

According to a Fusan telegram to the "Osaka Mainichi," the Japanese merchants at Fusan have experienced great inconvenience of late in consequence of the delay in the management of business at the Customs there. The Japanese Chamber of Commerce at the Korean port has addressed a memorial to the Chief Commissioner of Customs asking that the staff of the Customs be increased.

The Peking "Official Gazette" states that the Board of Commerce asks permission to appoint Taotai Chang Chenhsen, lately managing director of the Yuen Han trunk line, as agent and general manager of the proposed National Bank of China. He is a wealthy merchant of Singapore and is believed to be capable of raising the necessary capital, namely Tls. 4,000,000. It is believed Imperial sanction has been given for the appointment.

His Majesty has despatched autograph letters to foreign countries announcing the d[illegible] of the Crown Princess.

According to the "Kanjo Shimpo," the members of the Chin-po-hoi have signified their intention of taking service with the Japanese for work on the railway, etc.

The Governor of Hamheung reports that the Japanese military authorities have informed him that the maigistrates of all districts, within the zone of military jurisdiction, must not absent themselves from their posts, for even a day, without obtaining permission from the Japanese commander.

The Japanese Consul complains to the Governor of Seoul that much time is wasted in getting the latter to transfer title-deeds of property purchased by Japanese from Koreans. In future, unless more rapidity of action is shown in the Governor's office, the Consul will make the necessary transfer himself.

The "Chugai Shogyo," a Tokio newspaper devoted to commercial affairs, 'in speaking of the failure of the Japan Spinning and Weaving Company and the consequent collapse of the one hundred and Thirtieth Bank, says "In Japan shareholders as well as directors and auditors of business companies have a tendency to declare dividends, in utter disregard of the real standing of the company."

We see, from a table published by the "Kobe Chronicle" that there is a pretty general decline in Japanese securities as compared to the quotations for this time last year. This of course, owing to the war, is only natural and it is therefore satisfactory to notice that the Dai-Ichi Bank, which is of so much importance to all in Korea has been the lightest sufferer, its Y 50 stock being quoted at Y 68.35 against Y 68.80 last year.

A full investigation into the losses suffered by the terrible typhoon, which swept over the south Kyengsang province on the 29th August, reveals a far worse state of affairs than was imagined a the time. The complete list of losses and damaged suffered now reads:—419 persons drowned, 10,518 houses destroyed, 190 kans of Government buildings demolished, 959 junks wrecked and a vast area of the cultivated fields destroyed.

As an illustration of the incompleteness of the Korean Government records, the following story is rather interesting. For some time past the Home Office have been extremely annoyed at receiving no reply to their despatches to Mr. Kim Ro-kiu, recently appointed, according to the official gazette, to the governorship of North Hamkyeng province. Eventually, a brilliant idea occured to a member of the department, and the following message was despatched to the Governor of South Hamkyeng province. "Has Kim Ro-kiu arrived at the northern provice?" The reply was terse, but to the point. "Kim Ro-kiu has been dead for a long time."

Another instance of unwarrantable brutality is evidenced in the following report from the Magistrate of Dyungju. A coolie, named Kim Yung-nok, was employed during September by the Japanese to work on the railroad. Shortly afterwards a report was received that he was dead. Upon investigation, it was discovered that a Japanese overseer had mercilessly beaten him with a stick, causing his death from numerous wounds. When charged with the offence, the Japanese remarked that the coolie was lazy so he had beaten him. The Magistrate attempted to arrest him, but some Japanese soldiers from Koksan took him away. The Magistrate begs that the Japanese Legation will bring this cowardly murderer to justice.

The Korea Daily News.

VOL. I, THURSDAY, NOVEMBER 10, 1904. NO. 97

大韓每日申報
대한ᄆᆡ일신보

(뎨구십팔호) (토요일) 일천구백사년십일월이십일

본사고ᄇᆡᆨ

이신보는영어와한국국문셔거릐일츌판ᄒᆞᆷ

신문가

한쟝 엽뎐두돈오푼
일삭표 엽뎐두량닷돈
우표가미삭닷돈
다엽돈으로밧ᄉᆞᆸ

광고료는

귀한의장단과ᄌᆞ항의다쇼로죵량ᄒᆞ되혐가로밧을터이오며오릭지아녀ᄃᆡ한사람마다다이신문을보실터이니광고내시기를원ᄒᆞ시는이들은우리신문사에와셔면약ᄒᆞ심을희망ᄒᆞᆸ

○발힝소 박동대한ᄆᆡ일신보사발이항교 영혜젼 영국인셜필림졍자리오

사쟝 영국인 (ᄇᆡ셜)

평양 디리졈

○평양호동사는권미보씨로우리신문판매디리인을뎡ᄒᆞ엿ᄉᆞ오니평양에계신구람코져ᄒᆞ시는 쳠군ᄌᆞ는히디리졈에왕림ᄒᆞ와면회ᄒᆞ시옵

사고

○우리대한ᄆᆡ일신보의목뎍은대한의안녕질서에관한모든데목에디ᄒᆞ야논공평한변론을쥬쟝홈이라우리는신원의담보는신문보시는쳠군ᄌᆞ의게ᄒᆞᆫ샹보도ᄒᆞ려며편지를귀셔ᄒᆞ며주시논이는셩명과번디를젹어붓치시기를희망ᄒᆞ오나이거슨신문샹에긔재ᄒᆞ라논거시아니오다만국히신용ᄒᆞ논증거를숨고쟈ᄒᆞᆷ이라귀쟈논아모과셔던지과쥐ᄒᆞᆷ을되작ᄒᆞ논권리를가졋소나되가ᄒᆞ논리유를말ᄒᆞᆯ터이오며공증평화를문란케ᄒᆞ논듯ᄒᆞᆫ귀셔논의례히밧지안켓ᄉᆞᆸ나이다

●본사셜시이릭로신문을티양우례로분젼ᄒᆞ와례젼부의일의로젼ᄒᆞ든ᄉᆞ로번곳에는ᄒᆞ늣게젼ᄒᆞ기도ᄒᆞ며ᄒᆞ멋칠게슬ᄒᆞᆫ변에젼ᄒᆞ기도ᄒᆞ며ᄒᆞ아니젼ᄒᆞ논곳도잇다ᄒᆞ와우리신문을ᄉᆞ랑ᄒᆞ야구람ᄒᆞ시는 쳠군ᄌᆞ의게긍티ᄒᆞ야미우미안ᄒᆞ옵기로지금은분젼인을두고미일ᄌᆞ이젼처ᄒᆞ며아니젼ᄒᆞ거나늣게거나ᄒᆞᆫ가엉도록ᄒᆞ란ᄒᆞ오니ᄒᆞ야니젼ᄒᆞ거나ᄒᆞᆨ늣게젼ᄒᆞ거나ᄒᆞᆫ일이잇스면본사로통긔ᄒᆞ여주심을희망ᄒᆞᆸ

본사광고

○본사신문중에죠기ᄒᆞᆫ호수를소용ᄒᆞᆯ데가잇셔이에광고ᄒᆞ오니누구시던지그중에아모호수던지가져오시논디로미쟝에ᄇᆡᆨ젼두푼식드리리다

데이호 데삼호 데이십호 데ᄉᆞ십이호 데ᄉᆞ십삼호 데오십삼호 데오십ᄉᆞ호와데오십오호 데륙십이호

잡보

○가권환급 일본령ᄉᆞ가한셩부로죠회ᄒᆞ기를우리나라사름이귀국사름의게산쟝과가옥에디ᄒᆞᆫ가권을밧고아주논방도에관ᄒᆞ야수기월간을무표히연계ᄒᆞᆷ으로우리나라사름의리권을침해ᄒᆞ논일이불쇼ᄒᆞᆷ으로새급속히ᄒᆞ가권을밧고아주기를인ᄒᆞ야ᄌᆞ로ᄌᆞ로교셥을쥼히ᄒᆞ엿스며인ᄒᆞ야지월칠일에데칭십삼호공문으로죠회ᄒᆞᆫ거시제일ᄒᆞ온바그후에수삭일을지나오ᄂᆞᆯ져지니르도록히가권ᄂᆞᆨ환급ᄒᆞᆷ을언계ᄒᆞ며ᄒᆞᆫ것그스유가닉부지령을밧지못ᄒᆞᆷ이라ᄒᆞ고청ᄒᆞ고우리나라사름의게티ᄒᆞ야불쇼ᄒᆞᆫ손히를당케ᄒᆞ논티ᄒᆞ니고의리셔논본관이단졍코귀국졍부의쳐치롤능히용납ᄒᆞ야히치못ᄒᆞ겟ᄉᆞᆸ으로써ᄒᆞ야미에디ᄒᆞ야본관의직권에거ᄒᆞ야졍당ᄒᆞᆫ쳐치를단힝ᄒᆞᆯ지니죠왕에요구ᄒᆞ엿ᄃᆞᆫ환급방에관ᄒᆞ야셔논신월이십구일노긔약ᄒᆞ야시문권을숑교ᄒᆞ시거나만약ᄒᆞ야긔한ᄭᆞ지우에논히구문권을모도다도로결보ᄇᆡ시면본관이그가권에ᄃᆡᄒᆞ야인죵을주어빈슈ᄒᆞᆫ자의게손ᄒᆡ를면케ᄒᆞᆯ방법을강구ᄒᆞᆯ터이오니지급히샹당ᄒᆞᆫ조쳐를ᄒᆞ라ᄒᆞ엿다더라

○수리부군평 협판남도관찰ᄉᆞ리현경세가너부로면보ᄒᆞ기를협ᄒᆞ데잇ᄂᆞᆫ일본군ᄉᆞ명부에밧ᄒᆞᆫ별지를거ᄒᆞᆫ즉운ᄒᆞ엿스되함ᄒᆞ경광영ᄒᆞ고평원문쳔각군슈령의계군평ᄒᆞ노라지금브터귀관과밋각군에서공ᄉᆞ나ᄉᆞᄉᆞ간에무ᄉᆞᆫ일이던지못지못ᄒᆞ고ᄒᆞ로밧ᄂᆞᆫ자ᄂᆞᆫ이샹에ᄂᆞᆫ그잇ᄂᆞᆫ곳에셔셰납경우에ᄂᆞᆫ반드시당부의허가를밧아ᄒᆞ라ᄒᆞᆫ등인이오며갑히견편치못ᄒᆞ겟ᄉᆞ오니곳시명ᄒᆞ라ᄒᆞ엿더라

○쳔셔지송 쥬쳥공ᄉᆞ관셔긔셩김균졍씨가쳥국황태후의보년칠순의경수를치하ᄒᆞᄂᆞᆫ 쳔셔를봉지ᄒᆞ고작일에발졍ᄒᆞ엿더라

○디단가교부 외부에셔덕국공관으로조회ᄒᆞ기를귀국인길리조기의소유ᄒᆞᆫ남대문밧경거쟝[illegible]

○보쳥샹명 영변관찰ᄉᆞ리용구씨가외부로보고ᄒᆞ기를[illegible]

○쟝힝사ᄒᆡᆨ 황히도비공 젼하의ᄒᆞ셔ᄒᆞᆫ샹은티즁약으로반쓴연고라ᄒᆞ며공졔후에ᄂᆞᆫ잉티ᄒᆞ엿다고징증ᄒᆞ던의를사ᄒᆡᆨᄒᆞ여증벌ᄒᆞᆯ터이라더라

○무빙남획 힝쥬관찰ᄉᆞ가외부로보ᄒᆞᆫ보고를거ᄒᆞᆫ즉[illegible]

○회원시찰 일진회에셔각도진보회를시찰ᄒᆞ고방침을미른등[illegible]

○힝지권고 일진회에셔시졍개션을실시ᄒᆞ기위ᄒᆞ야졍부에권고도ᄒᆞ며쳥원도ᄒᆞ다가국샹으로인ᄒᆞ야교위즁지ᄒᆞ엿는지라졍부에셔논 국샹이불힝ᄒᆞᆫ즁에일진회권고ᄒᆞ고쳥원밧ᄒᆞᄂᆞᆫ거시졔졀노즁지된거시다힝이녀기논모양이라더라

○젼봉셩불 히셔인민이셔교를존숑ᄒᆞ더니산불교에신봉ᄒᆞ야황히도에지교셜시홈을쳥원ᄒᆞᄂᆞᆫ지라평셩명도ᄉᆞ교ᄉᆞ송쟝ᄇᆡᆨ용셰가지교힝지를시찰ᄒᆞ고젼도ᄒᆞ기위ᄒᆞ야히쥬로하거ᄒᆞ엿다더라

론셜

젼호련쇽

○쟝츙쳥관은갑히평쟝ᄒᆞᆯ듯ᄒᆞᆫ거시아라사에셔논리슌에만군수를두어웅거ᄒᆞ엿고별노히쥰비홈이업셧다가즁지에환란을당ᄒᆞ엿다가츄후로발병ᄒᆞ엿[illegible]취될가망이엇지반ᄒᆞᄂᆞᆫ지라아라사에셔이리케오릭도록연타ᄒᆞ야잇스니거시두가지로긴요홈이오들지논이왕ᄶᅢ홈에경솔취ᄒᆞᆷ으로실피홈을당ᄒᆞ야복구ᄒᆞ란논주의논잇스되샹히여협게되엿더니오날날당ᄒᆞ여셔논라일본이언란ᄒᆞ게만드ᄂᆞᆫ거시아일본셔논당쵸에젼국군수를모도발ᄒᆞ야히양을관할ᄒᆞᆯ것갓ᄒᆞᆫ고로아라사에셔도려슌에잇ᄂᆞᆫ군사로ᄒᆞ여곰그곳을굿게직히교동샹항뎍ᄒᆞ야ᄡᆞ호기로쥰비ᄒᆞ엿더니일본셔논아군의힝세를밧라보고능히용겨ᄒᆞ야협박지못ᄒᆞ고다시히면으로만에위ᄡᆞ셔아병이능히나오지못ᄒᆞ게만들고쏘ᄒᆞᆫ일변으로군사를잇셜고륙로로진쟝ᄒᆞ야ᄭᅩᆺ더니구로파드킨쟝군은쳠쳠퇴거ᄒᆞ되일병의츄창ᄒᆞᄂᆞᆫ티로물너가유인ᄒᆞ야셔리드리려ᄒᆞᄂᆞᆫ것갓ᄒᆞᆫ고로일병은젹쟝의용계ᄒᆞᆷ을졍작ᄒᆞ고아병의구원티이를요량외을미리숄패고기여히승승쟝구ᄒᆞ나어좌지우에괴경에논괴위방ᄒᆞᆷ을면치못ᄒᆞᆯ터이라그러고ᄒᆞ엿더라

UNION INSURANCE SOCIETY OF CANTON.

Head office Hongkong.
Marine risks underwritten at current rates.
Agents in Chemulpo,
E. MEYER & Co.

COMPAGNIE DES MESSAGÈRIES MARITIMES.

Fortnightly Direct Service.

For Marseilles
via Ports.
Sailing from Yokohama
Calling at Kobe,
Shaughai, Hongkong, Saigon, Singapore,
Colombo, Djibonti, Suez, Port Said
and Marseilles.

For particulars apply to
HOLME RINGER & Co.,
Chemulpo.

HAYASHIDA & Co.,

16 MYENG DONG, CHIN KO KAI, SEOUL.
BRANCH OFFICE AT CHEMULPO.

Money changers, Coal and Wood Merchants, Express Agents.

We are agents for the Pyeng-yang Coal Company and the Karazu Coal Company of Japan. We have the best quality of both anthracite and bituminous coal, and prompt execution of orders is our speciality. Firewood of all kinds kept in stock. Full weight guaranteed. Money of all denominations exchanged at current rates. Parcels received for all parts.

CHINA MUTUAL LIFE INS. CO.

Most favourable terms to policy holders.

Benefit system unsurpassed.

HOLME RINGER & Co.
Agents, Chemulpo.

C. P. R.

CANADIAN PACIFIC RAILWAY COMPANY'S ROYAL MAIL STEAMSHIP LINE.

THE FAST ROUTE BETWEEN CHINA, JAPAN, AND EUROPE VIA CANADA AND THE UNITED STATES.

Route from Hongkong via Shanghai, Nagasaki (Inland Sea of Japan) Kobe, Yokohama Victoria and Vancouver.

Twin Screw Empress Steamship—6,000 Tons—Speed 19 knots.

PROPOSED SAILING FROM YOKOHAMA.
R. M. S. Empress of India.
R. M. S. Empress of Japan.
R. M. S. Empress of China.
R. M. S. Athenian.
R. M. S. Tastar.

Special reduction (first class only) granted to members of the Military, Naval, Diplomatic and Civil services and to Missionaries.

Passengers have choice of ten routes across the Continent of America and have privilege of travelling by any Atlantic Steamship Line.

Round the World passage tickets in connection with the P. and O. S. N., North German Lloyd and Messageries Co.'s **£125.**

All rates payable at current rate of exchange.

For further information, Tickets, Guide Books, etc., apply to

HOLME, RINGER & Co., AGENTS,
Chemulpo.

Grand Hotel,

(Formerly the Station Hotel)

Near the Railway Terminus,
West Gate Seoul.

The Best Hotel in Korea
Handsome new Building.
Fine Airy Rooms
Excellent Cuisine.
Terms Moderate.
Special terms to Missionaries
and to permanent boarders.

Electric cars within 2 minutes' walk.

W. H. EMBERLEY,
Proprietor.

EVERY FACILITY.

In connection with Life Assurance Business is afforded by

The Standard Life Assurance Co.,

One of the largest and wealthiest of the Provident Institutions of the United Kingdom Forms of Application and all information will be promptly afforded on application.

10 CENTS A DAY.

Not a very large expenditure is it? But it is sufficient to secure for a man of 30 a policy with the STANDARD LIFE OFFICE for

$1323.

For all particulars of rates, etc., apply to

Holme, Ringer & Co.,
Agents, Chemulpo.

THE NEW YORK LIFE INSURANCE COMPANY.

Have you ever been declined by any Company?

Are you engaged in a specially hazardous occupation?

Have you heard of the New York Life Insurance Company's New Classifications for this class of Risks?

If not, send your date of birth, occupation and particulars of rejection, if any to

E. MEYER & Co.,
Agents, Chemulpo.

MITSUI BUSSAN KAISHA.
(MITSUI & Co.)

MITSUI GINKO.
(MITSUI BANK.)

The Bank is owned by the members of the Mitsui Family, who, as partners, assume an unlimited responsibility for all liabilities of the Bank:—

Capital ....Yen 5,000,000
Reserve Fund ...." 5,600,000

HEAD OFFICE, TOKYO.

LONDON OFFICE, 34 LIME ST., E. C.

BRANCHES AND AGENCIES:—
New York, San Francisco, Hamburg, Bombay, Singapore, Manila, Hongkong, Amoy, Chefoo, Tientsin.

Kobe, Hakodate, Yokohama, Kure, Yokosuka, Moji, Shimonoseki, Miike, Wakamatsu, Nagasaki, Kuchinotsu, Karatsu, Sasebo, Misume, Taipeh, &c.

Telegraphic Address for all the Offices:
"MITSUI."

A. B. C. AND A. I CODES USED.

Contractors of Coal

To the Imperial Japanese Navy. Arsenals and Railway Bureau, Principal Railway Companies and Industrial Work, Home and Foreign Mail and Freight Steamers.

Sole Proprietors

Of the famous Miike, Tagawa and Yamano Coal Mines.

Sole Agents

For the sale of Fukumo, Hokoku, Ichimura, Kanoda, Mannoura, Onoura, Ostuji, Sonoda, Tsubaruro, Yoshinotani, Voshio, Yurokibura and other coals.

YANGTSE INSURANCE ASSOCIATION, LTD.

The undersigned, having been appointed agents for the above company, are prepared to issue policies and pay losses on marine risks at regular rates.

E. MEYER & Co.,
Agents, Chemulpo.

AMERICAN KOREAN ELECTRIC CO.

Light and Power.

Main Office: Electric Building, Chong No.

RAILWAY DEPARTMENT

OPERATING CARS BETWEEN EAST AND WEST GATE, EVERY TEN MINUTES:—

First Car leaves East Gate at 6:30 A. M. First Car leaves West Gate at 6:55 A. M.
Last Car " East Gate at 10:40 P. M. Last " " West Gate at 11:00 P.M.

OPERATING CARS BETWEEN EAST GATE AND IMPERIAL TOMB TERMINUS, EVERY TWENTY MINUTES:—

CONNECTING WITH EVERY ALTERNATE CAR ARRIVING AT EAST GATE FROM CHONG NO.

First Car leaves East Gate for Tomb at 6:50 A. M.
" " " Tomb for East Gate at 7:10 A. M.
Last " " East Gate for Tomb at 9:50 P. M.
" " " Tomb for East Gate at 10:10 P. M.

OPERATING CARS BETWEEN CHONG NO AND YUNG SAN (RIVER EVERY TWELVE MINUTES:—

First Car leaves Chong No for South Gate at 6:48 A. M.
" " " Chong No for Yung San at 7:24 A. M.
" " " South Gate for Chong No at 6:56 A. M.
" " " Yung San for Chong No at 7:57 A. M.
Last " " South Gate for Chong No 11:00 P. M.
" " " Yung San for Chong No at 10:11 P. M.

SPECIAL PRIVATE CARS FURNISHED TO SUIT CONVENIENCE OF PATRONS. PRICES ON APPLICATION AT HEAD OFFICE.

LIGHTING DEPARTMENT.

Where less than 250 candle power of light is used, the rate per month will be:
Per 16 candle power incandescent lamp,—All night.—Yen 2.50.
32 candle power incandescent lamp:—All night:—Yen 4.00.
50 candle power incandescent lamp:—All night:—Yen 6.00.
150 " " " " " " 10.00.
1200 " " enclosed arc " " " 20.00.

Where more than 250 candle power of light is used, a Meter will be installed, if requested:—Rent of Meter Yen 2.00 per month. Rate of charges by meter reading:—Two Sen per Ampere per hour. (Approximately this is equal to about One Sen per 16 C. P. lamp per hour) Minimum monthly charge where meter is installed, Yen 20.00 per month, which includes rental of meter.

Estimates for installing lights furnished on application.

An assortment of chandeliers always on hand.

K. Murakami.

Photograph Studio
Chinkokai, Seoul.

Printing, Developing and Enlargement, of Photographs always Undertaken.

Korean Views and Pictures Illustrating Native Customs always on Sale,

---

THE OSAKA SHOSEN KAISHA.

Boats frequently on the berth for Chinnampo.

REGULAR SAILINGS BETWEEN JAPAN AND KOREAN PORTS.

FUSAN AND KOBE VIA SHIMONOSEKI.

OSAKA VIA MOKPO, FUSAN, SHIMONOSEKI AND KOBE.

MOJI DIRECT.

OSAKA VIA KUNSAN, MASANPO, FUSAN, SHIMONOSEKI AND KOBE.

CHEMULPO KUNSAN LINE,
Every three days.

CHEMULPO CHINNAMPO LINE.
Every three days.

For Freight and passage and further particulars apply to

THE OSAKA SHOSEN KAISHA,
Chemulpo.

RONDON, PLAISANT & CO.

General Storekeepers and Merchants, Ships Contractors, Tobacconists, Commission and Forwarding Agents, Coal Merchants

IMPORTERS AND EXPORTERS

Seoul & Chemulpo.

W. D. WENTWORTH.

LANDING
AND
SHIPPING AGENT
AND
CUSTOMS BROKER.

12 OURA, NAGASAKI.

STEWARD & CO.

Chemulpo.

Shipchandlers and Storekeepers, Naval and Mercantile Contrrctors, Landing and Shipping Agents.

STEWARD'S HOTEL

Chemulpo.

Best accommodation in the port for travellers. Clean and well-aired rooms, good cuisine prompt attendance, moderate tariff.

관보

십일월오일

○본월오일호외관보즁 홍셔죠칙을환영ᄒᆞ야홍셔하 에우강리실ᄉᆞ진를텸셔하ᄒᆞ 심이라

○금음력구월이십구일호외관 보시각반포즁목욕정시음력삽 월초일일뎡초초각이요 습정시는동ᄎᆡ동일미정이각으 로병기부표홈이라

●죠왈 즁츄원의장 민영소 궁ᄂᆡ부특진관 윤용구 쟝례 원경 윤덕영으로위반면도감 제쥬ᄒᆞ고 시종무관쟝 민영 환 궁ᄂᆡ부특진관 셔신보 ᄂᆡ부대신리용딕로외국쟝도감 제쥬ᄒᆞ고 궁ᄂᆡ부특진관 민 영달리쥬영 죠동희로위원 소도감제쥬ᄒᆞ라

○죠왈 완평군 리승응 완 순군 리지완 비셔원경 리 지현 의양군 리지각 챵산 군 리희챵 례양령 리지규 교육부총감 리지용 즁학교 쟝 리달용 구품 리긔용 정일품 민영익 즁츄원의쟝 민영소 종일품 리헌직 궁ᄂᆡ부특진관 윤용구 김셕 진 륙군부쟝 죠동윤 궁ᄂᆡ 부특진관민영린 례식원부쟝 민영선 정삼품 민영슈 민 영철 송팅현 민충식"명평 군슈 리운비 륙품 유티쥰 송리현 송정현 송승현 송 복현 송관현 송쇼학 송슌 봉김형비병종척집ᄉᆞ차하ᄒᆞ야 습렴시에입참케ᄒᆞ라

이샹십일월오일

수령

○명빈면도감랑청 군부쥬ᄉᆞ 조설하 법부쥬ᄉᆞ 리완종 탁지부쥬ᄉᆞ 윤병일 리직렬 권용규 오규영

○명국쟝도감랑청 ᄂᆡ부쥬ᄉᆞ 심하경 농샹공부쥬ᄉᆞ 정윤모 탁지부쥬ᄉᆞ 남만희 죠즁익 류갑슈 윤태길

○명원소도감랑청 돈령원쥬 ᄉᆞ 홍승범 태복ᄉᆞ쥬ᄉᆞ 리 호집 법부쥬ᄉᆞ 남길희 농 샹공부쥬ᄉᆞ 셔상면 박희양 탁지부쥬ᄉᆞ 리명직 신유션 신셩슈

이샹십일월오일

데이쳔구빅칠십팔호

광무팔년십일월팔일

셔임급ᄉᆞ령

○승셔관임관일등 법부쥬ᄉᆞ 김남제

○승셔관임관삼등 ᄂᆡ부참셔 관 장쥰원

○승셔관임관삼등 경위원쥬 ᄉᆞ 김근영

○명류힝병예방림시 위원륙 픔남계진 김용목 강면형 구품 김욱현 쥬동린 강윤 영 전재봉 김뎡규 륙품 리회용 구품 최규의 의학 교교관 손창슈 최국현 리 제규 김봉관 최영셕 최익환 강원영 리긔정

○십월이십구일

○임군긔창쥬ᄉᆞ셔관임관륙등 김교면 현득건 륙품 리화 영

○임군긔창기슈셔관임관일등 오품 진학명

○임군긔창기슈셔관임관이등 전의관 리셕범 륙품 갈진 희

○임군긔창기슈셔관임관ᄉᆞ등 면환국기슈 한홍진

○임군긔창기슈셔관임관륙등 리규지 죠동희 김긔셕 리 민셜 박셩환 김영식 죠병 션 김하두 권티슌 리용희 류셕진 리ᄉᆞ셜 리ᄉᆞ범구연 국권즁호 빅남열 고회원 장셕긔 안형즁 현학련 츄 시안 강인슈 심샹덕 김샹 언

임호위디총관 궁ᄂᆡ부특진 관륙군부쟝 리근턱

십일월일일

○의원면본관 시종원봉시 김규복

○임 황티ᄌᆞ궁봉시셔쥬임관 ᄉᆞ등 시종원봉시 김슈형

이샹십일월삼일

○봉창산도정 정삼품 리희 창

○면본관 연셩학교교관륙군 보병부위 김병도

○의원면본관 현릉참봉 셩전 영 수릉참봉 구도셔 창릉 참봉 리재근 쟝릉참봉 유 린쥰 경릉참봉 리재호 공 릉참봉 검영덕 즁츄원의관 빅락셩 농샹공부기슈 리영 훈 심로익

○현릉참봉셔관임판팔등 송 정현

○장릉참봉셔관임관팔등 송 승현

○수릉참봉셔관임관팔등 송 복현

○경릉참봉셔관임완팔등 송 관현

○창릉참봉셔관임판팔등 송 쇼학

○공릉참봉셔관임관팔능 송 슌봉

참모부관제 속

부감 일인 참쟝혹정령 참모쟝 일인 참쟝혹정부 령참모관 이인 부참령일 인장위일인정위일인 이인 참령일인정위일인 긔치병 과쟝 일인 부참령 과원 이인 졍부위 포공병과쟝 일인 부참령 과원 일이인 졍부위 향관 일인 일이 등군수 번역관 이인 쥬 관임 셔긔 오인 하ᄉᆞ혹 관임문관

데이쳔구빅칠십칠호 련속

궁뎡륙ᄉᆞ

○죠왈ᄒᆞᆫ면을문경면으로위시 ᄒᆞ라

뎨십일됴 부무가번국ᄒᆞᆫ시는 현직에잇는령위관으로션턱 ᄒᆞ야참모부부를쥬차ᄒᆞ야 군무를보조케홈도잇슴어라

뎨십이됴 본부소속군인군속 과밋각참모부군인등의임면 과진급등에관ᄒᆞ야장관회의 소의가부경의를취결ᄒᆞ야샹 쥬홈시에는참모총쟝이군부 대신과련셔홈이라

뎨십삼됴 참모ᄉᆞ무의필요를 따러히군령위판으로국원을 겸임ᄒᆞ는ᄉᆞ도잇슴이라

뎨십ᄉᆞ됴 본관졔는반포일로 시힝홈이라

부측

뎨십오됴 륙군대학교와륙다 측도부됴례는츄후규뎡홈이 라

륙군참모됴례

뎨일됴 참모쟝교는고등쟝슈 의직무를보좌ᄒᆞ며특별히국 방파밋용병에관ᄒᆞ며긔무를참 획ᄒᆞ며또군디연셩의ᄉᆞ무를 쥬쟝ᄒᆞ고기타특별홈임무는 됴규에소뎡에셔복모케홈어 라

뎨이됴 참모의직에복직홈어 가ᄒᆞᆫ쟈는각병과정위이상이 니ᄌᆞ격이여좌ᄒᆞᆫ쟈로션발홈 이라

일은 륙군대학교와밋외국 무관학교졸업후일긔년어상 군무의복종ᄒᆞᆫ쟝교니참모총 창이무적의임으로인허ᄒᆞᆫ쟈

이는 학식재능이탁월ᄒᆞᆫ쟝 교니참모총쟝이적임으로인 허ᄒᆞᆫ쟈

뎨삼됴 참모쟝교는그직무에 슉달케ᄒᆞ기위ᄒᆞ야각참모부 관원을셔로교임케홈이라

뎨ᄉᆞ됴 본됴례는반포일로시 힝홈이라

교육부관제

뎨일됴 륙군의교육을일졔히 발달케ᄒᆞ며또긔량진취케ᄒᆞ 기위ᄒᆞ야교육부를셜치홈이 라

뎨이됴 교육총감은부쟝혹참 쟝으로칙임홈이라

뎨삼됴 교육부에직원을좌갓 치둠이라

총감 일인 부쟝혹참쟝

잡보

○운동불일 황티ᄌᆞ비뎐하홍 셔ᄒᆞ옵신후로 경효뎐과혼뎐 에삭다례를셜힝무쥬ᄒᆞᆫ지라일 파는 황티ᄌᆞ께셔간텩ᄒᆞᆫ심을 운동ᄒᆞ고일파는엄비도승봉 ᄒᆞᆫ심욕운동ᄒᆞᆫ다더라

○퀴습가징 히쥬관찰ᄉᆞ가외 부로보고ᄒᆞᆫ것슬거ᄒᆞᆫ즉히쥬군 슈의보고ᄂᆡ에본군광셕포는청 국쇼금비가왕ᄅᆡᄒᆞ여포민들이 곡식으로쇼금을샹환ᄒᆞ는ᄃᆡ청 샹과포민들이셔로언힐ᄒᆞ다가 청샹이와셔호쇼ᄒᆞ기를포민박 가가청샹일명을무슈란타ᄒᆞ엿 다ᄒᆞ기에히파라ᄒᆞᆫ청인을슈교 청에셔치료케ᄒᆞ고박가를포착 ᄒᆞ여문쵸ᄒᆞᆫ즉ᄒᆞ는ᄃᆡ본군에류 쥬ᄒᆞ는청인약쟝ᄉᆞ진가락이가 당쵸에이일에샹관이업는ᄃᆡ공 연이관쟝을능욕ᄒᆞ여거죠가피 샹ᄒᆞ다ᄒᆞ엿기로ᄉᆞ유를보고ᄒᆞᆫ 오니곳청공관에죠회ᄒᆞ여히청 인진가의퀴습을엄히징습ᄒᆞ라 ᄒᆞ엿더라

○합청셔임 일본공사가외부 로공함ᄒᆞ기를우리쳘도감부로 셔정삼품윤티홍을쳔거ᄒᆞ되룡 쳔이나창원량군즁에군슈를셔 임식히라홈은임의ᄂᆡ부대신의 게통고ᄒᆞ엿거니와그량군즁에 슉히셔임ᄒᆞ라ᄒᆞ엿더라

○죠률션고 공쥬티병과요ᄉᆞ 건으로륙군법원에셔심관ᄒᆞ야 즁ᄃᆡ쟝에권즁락씨는ᄐᆡ오섭에 쳐ᄒᆞ고소ᄃᆡ쟝리범셔리영화량 씨는틔륙십에쳐ᄒᆞ고그이하병 졸은그법죄홈바를따라죠률션 고ᄒᆞ고군부로질픔ᄒᆞ엿더라

○우현이굴 경부텰도즁슈쇼 용이라ᄒᆞ고남산을과머니무숨 일인지근일에는정역ᄒᆞ고우슈 지건너편을다시츌쿄관다더라

○권고단상 황티ᄌᆞ비궁 면하상복을긔년으로 어정 ᄒᆞ신지라일공사가써인민에리 해도불소홈을위ᄒᆞ고또젼례에 도업는것갓다ᄒᆞ야상복긔한을 쥬리기를권고ᄒᆞᆫ다더라

○복셩긔학 국샹으로각학교 에셔공부ᄒᆞ기를정지ᄒᆞ엿더니 십일에셩복ᄒᆞᆫ지라십일일브터 전파ᄀᆞᆺ치긔학ᄒᆞᆫ다더라

○자원출력 안쥬진보회를은 긔왕에도일군에호의를표ᄒᆞᆫ연 셜을ᄒᆞᆫᄉᆞ가잇셧는ᄃᆡ금번동회 들은삭업시력부가되기로결뎡 ᄒᆞ야일젼에일병참부에일퇴명 을회즁인부로사력ᄒᆞ기를원ᄒᆞ 엿스되병참부에셔는삭업시사 용치안켓다ᄒᆞ야다상당ᄒᆞᆫ삭전 을쥬어고용ᄒᆞ게작뎡ᄒᆞ엿다더 라

○죠촉긔송 법룡관에셔의부 로죠회ᄒᆞ되귀국사ᄅᆞᆷ김병도가 본방사ᄅᆞᆷ문일시의일로누ᄎᆞ본 셔에압쿄ᄒᆞ기를청ᄒᆞ되오히려 회죠치아니ᄒᆞ니심히의아ᄒᆞᆫ자 라 본사는명일샹오에본셔에쟈촉 을베풀고심샤ᄒᆞᆯ터이니되긔치 말고김병도을보ᄂᆡ심관케ᄒᆞ라 ᄒᆞ엿더라

TELEGRAMS.

(FROM JAPANESE PAPERS.)

The following is said to be the casualty list of the Port Arthur Investing Army from Aug. 19th to 24th:—

First Column.

Killed.		Wounded.		Missing.	
Officers	Men	Officers	Men	Officers	Men
29	322	59	1,247	5	260

Second Column.

Killed.		Wounded.		Missing.	
Officers	Men	Officers	Men	Officers	Men
59	671	3,386		9	1,009

Third Coumn.

Killed.		Wounded.		Missing.	
Officers	Men	Officers	Men	Officers	Men
57	451	65	2,130	4	1,250

Independent.

Killed.		Wounded.		Missing.	
Officers	Men	Officers	Men	Officers	Men
46	498	83	2,197	5	676
Grand Total	...	...	...		...14,839

TheJapanese Reservists in Columbia have been ordered to return to Japan.—Japan Gazette.

The "Correspondenz Bureau" of Vienna reports that Lieut-General Sakharoff, hitherto Chief of the Staff of the First Manchurian Army, has been appointed Chief Staff Officer of the General Manchurian Headquarters.—Japan Gazette.

Berlin, Nov. 1.

The christening of the Crown Prince of Italy will take place in December. The Kaiser has signified his willingness to stand sponsor, and is sending a special representative to Rome for the ceremony.

THE THIBETAN EXPEDITION.

DEPARTURE FROM LHASSA.

The British expeditionary force arrived on 24th inst. at Jang, on its return march from Lhassa. It is expected to reach Gyangtsze on Oct. 5th, and Chumbi on Oct. 25th. When the force was leaving Lhassa on 23rd, General Macdonald was met outside the camp by the Regent, who invoked a blessing on the general for having spared the monasteries from violation, and presented him with a gold image of Buddha.

A Peking wire states that Tang Shaoki, Taotai of Tientsin, has been commanded to proceed to Thibet to "investigate and manage affairs." He has been created a metropolitan official of the third rank, and has also been given the military rank of lieutenant-general. He was educated at Yale University, and was formerly secretary of Yuan Shih-kai in Korea. He is well known as being conversant with foreign affairs and is regarded as being jealous of Chinese interests, though he has no marked anti-foreign bias.

The "Telegraph's" correspondent at Shanghai is informed that the Chinese Foreign Office (Wai-wu-pu) absolutely denies the report that it has protested against the Anglo-Thibetan Treaty.

"A distinguished diplomatist" has informed the St. Petersburg correspondent of the "Petit Parisien" that Count Benckendorff received instructions on 24th inst. to enter a protest in due form against the British treaty with Thibet. The correspondent adds, however, that before officially communicating the protest of the Russian Government Count Benckendorff will see Lord Lansdowne and report to his own Government.

The "Rus," referring to the Anglo-Thibetan Treaty, says that it will constitute an undeniable success, which will reverberate throughout Asia.

In well-informed circles it is reported that the telegraphic exchange of views which has been proceeding between London and St. Petersburg has had very satisfactory results and it is believed that the pourparlers now on will end in a complete understanding.

Reuter's St. Petersburg correspondent says that the Anglo-Thibetan Treaty has been engaging the attention of the Russian Government, but the statement made by French correspondents that a protest is being prepared is speculative to the highest degree. It is understood, however, that Count Benckendoff, the Russian Ambassador in London, has made friendly representations to the British Government regarding the alleged discrepancy between the draft treaty and British assurances relative to Thibet.

We extract the following from the annual report of the Commissioner of Customs at Yatung (Thibet) on the trade of that place for the year 1903: All trade at the mart was abruptly stopped on Oct. 15, owing to the issue by the Thibetan Government of an Edict interdicting all trade with British India. This prohibition was apparently imposed as a protest against the presence of a British Mission in Thibet, and doubtless also to what preparations the Thibetans were making to deal with the situation. It is idle to speculate on how trade might have prospered had normal trading conditions prevailed. Yatung has not hitherto showed any promise of blossoming into a prosperous mart, and until existing trading facilities are very widely extended no substantial increase in the volume of trade can reasonably be expected. The total trade value—import and export—for the year 1903 was only Rs. 1,373,365—roughly about £90,-000. The futility of expatiating at length on such peddling trade will be apparent. With the advent of the Mission came great improvements in the approaches to Yatung. It has before been pointed out that the natural roadway to Thibet from India lies either up the course of the Mochu or Dichu Rivers through Bhutan to the Chumbi Valley, and it is only reasonable to suppose that a road will shortly be constructed over one of these routes which will place the Chumbi Valley within easy access of India, and greatly obviate the present difficulties of transport.

THE COUNTERFEITING OF KOREAN CURRENCY.

A conference was held at the Department of Justice in Japan between high Government officials, when the business considered, it is supposed, was the measures to be taken for the suppression of the counterfeiting of Korean currency and the First Bank notes circulating in Korea, which is still actively carried on by counterfeiters in Kobe, Osaka, and Kyoto The officials composing the conference consisted of Mr. Yokota, the Procurator-General; Mr. Kuratomi, the Chief Procurator of Tokyo Appeal Court; Mr. Ishiwata, Vice-Minister of Justice; Mr. Sakaya, Vice-Minister of Finance; Mr. Ikegami, Chief Procurator at Kobe, and others.

The presence in Tokyo of Mr. Ikegami was taken advantage of for holding the conference, as this gentleman has full knowledge of affairs in Osaka and Kobe.

It is said that the doctor who attended the late Crown Princess during her illness, is to be punished for diagnosing the case wrongly.

Scotsmen in Canada have enjoyed a peculiar treat at the important national exhibition and fair held in the city of Toronto. The treat, the "Scotsman" says, was in the form of bagpipe music furnished by the pipers of the Black Watch. When the six lusty pipers paraded the lawn in the grounds of the exhibition, two elderly Scotsmen embraced one of them, and eagerly begged for news of the old country. Another old gentleman danced in Highland style, and excitedly declared that the pipers had played the very music he most wished to hear—viz., a tune composed within 20 miles of his birthplace, in the country of Inverness.

THE JAPANESE NATIONAL EXPENDITURE.

The authorities are now busy with the compilation of the Budget for next year. It is stated that the total amount required for the War Fund for next year will be Y 770,000,000, showing an increase of about Y 180,000,000 as compared with the estimate for this year. The increase is due to several causes. Thus the estimate for this year was from February to December, but that of next year is for the full twelve months. Moreover, there has to be taken into consideration the extension of the territory over which the campaign extends and the increase in the forces required. An expansion is proposed in the reserve fund, to cover the interest to be paid on bonds already issued next year. Among the resources for this expenditure are given the sum of Y195,000,000, being additional revenue from the increase of taxation already approved. To this about Y70,000,000, being the surplus of the revenue in the general Budget for next year, will be added. About Y5,000,000 will be drawn from the funds of various Government works, and with other small sums will make a grand total about Y270,000,000. The balance of about Y500,000,000 will be raised by temporary loans or the issue of bonds.

The general administrative expenditure for next year, including the ordinary and extraordinary expenditure, requires about Y250,000,000. From this sum about Y70,000,000 will be deducted by the postponement of the construction of railways and other engineering works, the redemption of bonds, and economising general expenditure. Among the new taxation to be imposed next year is included the increase of Land-tax (probably to about 6 per cent of the assessed value of land), a piece-goods tax, a succession-duty, increase of the tax on patent medicines, and a transit duty (on passengers by railway and steamers), together with a proposed monopoly of salt.—Kobe Chronicle.

An amusing scene was witnessed at Penang on the 4th Oct. in one of the main streets of the town, revealing a point in the etiquette of caste among natives of India which is not generally known. A Chetty money-lender, says the "Straits Echo," having some time ago given a loan to a low caste Hindoo, proceeded to try to secure repayment. On the Hindoo opening his door and seeing who his visitor was, he quickly disappeared inside again, but presently deposited his instalment of repayment not in the Chetty's hands—caste forbade this—but in the corner of his table furthermost from the door. Also forbidden by caste to enter the lowly Hindoo's domicile and still extremely anxious to secure the money, poor Mister Chetty was at his wits' end. Then did he think of a good idea—he would secure a stick and use it as a means of getting the money off the table. A stick he did get, but, alas! it was too short, and several times was there danger of his breaking his caste after all by over-reaching himself and falling inside the Hindoo's door. The spectacle of the Chetty vainly trying to get his money with the stick and the Hindoo enjoying the proceedings from a far corner of the room was most funny and worthy of being immortalised in a Punch cartoon. Now, the Chetty will possibly try a more practical way of inducing the wily Hindoo to "stump up."

The party of officials, now in Japan, have decided to curtail their visit on account of the death of the Crown Princess. They leave Tokyo on the 13th.

Punishment has been administered to those responsible for the Kong Chu riot. Captain Kwon Chung Nak received 50 blows and the two lieutenants were the recipients of 60 blows each.

Count Okuma's speech at Tokio, to the effect that Japan must be ready to spend perhaps Y2,000,000,000, on the war, has begun to be criticised severely in America. It is not believed there that Japan can endure a very long war. Many Japanese stocks have dropped a full pound.

Gen. Baron Kiten Nogi, rightly or wrongly alleged to command the Japanese army before Port Arthur, is the subject of a spirited controversy as to whether he is living or dead, in favour or disgraced. He won renown at the capture of Port Arthur during the war with China, says the "Ost Asien" (Berlin), a Japanese organ devoted to the advancement of Nippon interests in Germany. "It has been repeatedly averred that Nogi was recalled lately and that his place is now held by Yamagata," says this publication; "the statement is simply a false one. If a Nogi could not capture, Port Arthur it would be just as much out of the question for ten Yamagata's to accomplish the task."

The Korea Daily News.

Issued at 5 P. M. daily except Sundays.

Rate of Subscription :—

Per Year,	Yen 25.
Per Quarter,	Yen 7.
Per Month,	Yen 2.50.

Postage in Korea not charged extra.
Postage abroad charged extra.

Advertisements, 50 sen per day for 1 inch or less.
5 yen per month per inch.
50 yen per year per inch.

All communications to

E. T. BETHELL,
Editor and Publisher,
Pak-tong, Seoul

THE WAR.

There are indications that we are nearing the end of the hill in military operations South of Mukden. Of late only very meagre reports have been coming from the front and such engagements as we have heard of have only been affairs of outposts.

Both armies are now engaged in ascertaining the strength and disposition of the enemy's forces and it will probably be only a few days before we hear of one side or the other taking the offensive.

It now seems fairly certain that Kuropatkin took the initiative in the battle of the Sha-ho entirely against his own judgment and only in deference to orders from St. Petersburg. We are also told that the bombastic proclamation issued before the battle was the work of Alexieff and was protested against by Kuropatkin.

The recall of Alexieff seems to indicate that Kuropatkin is henceforth to have a free hand. It appears to us that although it is better late than never, Russia would have been in an infinitely better position had the Commander-in-chief been allowed a free hand from the first.

From the latest reports the climatic conditions around Mukden are still bad, heavy rain falling continuously and dense fogs prevailing. As the belligerents are now about the same strength, both numerically and in artillery, the result of the next battle is by no means such a foregone conclusion as the others have been.

With regard to Port Arthur little information beyond the official despatches reaches us. Nearly all of the outlying forts are in the hands of the Japanese but the inner and principal line of fortifications is still intact. The ships in the harbour seem to be in a bad way as it is said the Japanese high-angle fire works great havoc.

It is of course impossible to say whether the Baltic fleet will arrive in time to succour the fortress, or whether, if it arrives in time, it will be successful. One thing has to be borne in mind about Port Arthur; its downfall was confidently predicted many months ago and it is still standing.

The military position now seems much more favourable to Russia than it did six months ago but the end of this disastrous war is no nearer, both belligerents are more determined than ever and as both parties have declared against intervention it appears that the sanguinary combat must be fought to a finish.

The officers and crew of the s.s. Bawtry were up before the Harbour Master at Hongkong for wilful disobedience of the master's orders. It is said that the vessel is bound for Vladivostock, and the officers and crew, fearing capture, refuse to leave the port in her. The Harbour Master reserved his decision. The vessel is loaded with coal.

WHAT WE SHALL KNOW.

It is too early yet to speak of the difficulties—the appalling and almost inconceivable difficulties—that have faced General Kuropatkin during this now completed first phase of the Manchurian campaign. Some day it will be known how many, or rather how few, troops he had when he first arrived in Manchuria, and what proportion, or rather what disproportion, of them were the keen, ardent young soldiers of Russian Russia.

It will be known how far his Siberian levies, with their sturdy, fullbearded reservists, were equipped, supplied, and qualified for the task they had to perform. All the world knows, no doubt, that he was out-numbered, and all the world will realise, when it is permitted to know the facts, how enormous was the responsibility which was cast upon this silent, strong-faced, resolute man, and with what strength and resolution he has faced and conquered it.

At the end of the first phase of the campaign one onlooking world sees General Kuropatkin driven back with the whole of his army upon his base at Liaoyang. After a time, with fuller knowledge than is now possible to it, the onlooking world may be filled with appreciation of the magnitude of General Kuropatkin's achievement in getting there.—Charles E. Hands in the "Daily Mail."

The death, in London, is announced of Dan Leno, the famous comedian.

At present, the expenses of the Crown Princess' funeral, etc. are estimated at $1,000,000.

It is said that the Il Chin Hoi are to add to their illustriousness by entering the field of journalism.

It is reported that Viceroy Chang Chih Tung has engaged two Japanese military advisers at $700 each per month.

The Il Chin Hoi have despatched two disciples to the country to instruct the members of the Chin Po Hoi in the delicate art of making themselves a nuisance to everybody.

We have received number 5 of the "Far Eastern Review," a monthly magazine, published in Manila. Full of interesting articles, admirably illustrated, it should prove extremely valuable to those interested in the Far East.

The body of 2,000 Russians, who have been showing activity at Hoi-in-shen, (near Saimachi) are said to be obtaining provisions from the Chinese. They apparently belong to the main army near Mukden.

Miss Honner Morten, late member of the London School Board, tells a story of a small boy's essay:—"Solomon was a very wise man, and he was very fond of animals, and he kept 300 porcupines." No wonder they were "fretful."

It is said that the Japanese Minister has requested that the term of mourning, for the late Crown Princess, be fixed at less than one year, as arranged by the Government. His excuse is that the expenses in connection with such a long term of mourning will be too great.

Mr. Henry Norman who, it must be remembered, is strongly Russophil, is sceptical as to the authorship of the famous article on the Czar in the Quarterly. The editor published it as from the pen of a Russian official of high rank. In the World's Work Mr. Norman declares that it was hawked about Fleet-street previously to its publication in that august organ, and refused by at least two newspapers. He thinks that it is the work of "a certain cosmopolitan journalist, whose views and style as regards Russia it faithfully reflects."

The Japanese Minister has requested the Foreign Office to appoint Mr. Yun Tai-hung Magistrate of either Yongchon or Changwon. This gentleman has been specially recommended by the railway authorities and he trusts that the appointment will be speedily made.

The Japanese steamer "Katsuno-maru" (2,300 tons gross) having sunk while in the Government transport service, her owners, the Kansai Coke Company, are reported to have been granted Yen 50,000 for salvage and repairs. There is, however, little hope of her being successfully raised.

There has been a meeting in Chicago of professors of geography, students, and atlas makers. They have decided to send a petition to the Russian and Japanese governments: "The undersigned protest unanimously against the fact that many battles are fought in places not marked upon the maps."

The death of the Crown Princess has left a blank in certain quarters. It has always been the custom for a lady of the Royal family to perform the sacrificial rites at the tomb of the late Queen. A difficulty is thus raised, as there is now no lady of Blood Royal at the court. Some parties wish to crown Lady Om Empress, while others are in favor of the Crown Prince marrying again.

The C.P.R. transcontinental express was held up 35 miles from Vancouver last month by six masked men. Seven thousand dollars were stolen. The train was flagged, and some of the men got on the tender with rifles, and at the point of the gun the engineer and fireman were compelled to take the baggage and express cars two miles on, when they were rifled. This is the first train hold-up in Canada.

The military operations can not be so easily managed as hoped by the desk authorities, they depend upon the relative strength of the opposing forces and also upon the geographical conditions and the local climate. Under the existing circumstances, we are not certain whether the Japanese will take the risks of marching so precipitately on Mukden, as urged by some critics of the arm-chair order. In the meanwhile the transporting power of the Siberian railway seems to have been underrated by a number of outsiders.—Japan Gazette.

Latest reports from outlying districts bring news of robberies, Tonghak disturbances and troubles in general. At Yeungchon 180 houses have been burnt and one man killed by robbers. At Kangkye two soldiers attempted to affect the arrest of some Tonghaks. They were however, attacked by a mob, and in self defence fired their rifles, killing one man. A body of soldiers has been despatched to the scene to quell the disturbance. Later news states that this same force, on arriving at the village, looted the houses of the innocent inhabitants.

The captain of a steamer plying along the China coast states that the last time his vessel was stopped by the Japanese fleet, the search was conducted by a torpedo boat which darted out after him from one of the Miautau Islands. She was a formidable looking craft, and the captain lost no time in stopping his ship when he saw her coming. From her appearance she was thought to be a destroyer. After she got quite close the officers of the steamer under investigation took the opportunity to get a good look at her. She had four funnels, and ought to be able to show her heels to the fastest of them, or overhaul a lowly merchantman with the greatest ease. Close examination, however, revealed that if her speed depended on the draught sought to be furnished by numerous funnels, it might not be as great as the ordinary observer would be inclined to think, for two of her funnels were of canvas. They were dummies. The reason for the presence of the dummies was plain. They couldn't be there for any purpose but to deceive, and the captain who tells about them made a mental note of it.

The Korea Daily News.

VOL. I, FRIDAY, NOVEMBER 11, 1904. No. 98

大韓每日申報
대한미일신보

(뎨구십구호) (월요일) 일쳔구빅사년십일월십이일

본샤고빅

이신보는영어와한국문셔거퍼
엿츌판ᄒᆞᆸ

신문가
한쟝 엽두돈오푼
일삭표 엽두량닷돈
우표가비 샤닷돈
다맛돈으로밧솝

광고료는

귀한의쟝단과ᄌᆞ힝의다쇼로좃감ᄒᆞ되렴가로밧을터이오며오ᄅᆡ지아녀대한사람마다이신문을보실터이니광고내시기를원ᄒᆞ시는이들은우리신문사에와서편약ᄒᆞ시믈희망ᄒᆞᆸ

○발힝소 박동대한미일신보사 법어학교압헤젼영국인셜펠림쟝자리오

사쟝 영국인 (비셜)

평양 디리졈

○평양효동사는권미보씨로우리신문좌미디리인을뎡ᄒᆞ엿스오니평양에계신구람코져ᄒᆞ시는 쳠군ᄌᆞ는회디리졈에왕림ᄒᆞ와면의ᄒᆞ시옵

샤고

○우리대한미일신보의목뎍은대한의안녕질셔에관한모든대목에디ᄒᆞ야는공평한변론을쥬쟝ᄒᆞᆷ이라우리동신원의담보는신문보시는쳠군ᄌᆞ의게ᄒᆞᆼ상보도ᄒᆞ리며편지를긔셔ᄒᆞ여주시는이는셩명과반디를젹어붓치시기를희망ᄒᆞ오니긔슬신문샹에긔ᄌᆡᄒᆞ라는거시아니오다만긔하신용ᄒᆞ는증거를숨고자ᄒᆞᆷ이라긔자는아모긔셔던지긔직ᄒᆞᆷ을되자ᄒᆞ는권리를가졋스나희ᄌᆞᄒᆞ는리유를말ᄒᆞᆯ터이오며공증평화를문란케ᄒᆞ는듯ᄒᆞᆫ긔서는의례히밧지안켓습나이다

●본사셜시이리로신문을미양우례로분젼ᄒᆞ와례젼부의임의로젼ᄒᆞᆫ듯ᄒᆞ로면곳에는후ᄂᆞᆫ듯게젼ᄒᆞ기도ᄒᆞ며혹면칠게슬혼경에젼ᄒᆞ기도ᄒᆞ며혹아니젼ᄒᆞᄂᆞᆫ곳도잇다ᄒᆞ와우리신문을수탕ᄒᆞ야구람ᄒᆞ시는 쳠군ᄌᆞ의게탕디ᄒᆞ야미우미안ᄒᆞ옵기로지금은분젼인을두고미일일즉이젼ᄒᆞ며아니젼ᄒᆞ거나늣게거나ᄒᆞᆫ치가엿도록ᄒᆞ란ᄒᆞ오니혹아니젼ᄒᆞ거나늣게젼ᄒᆞ거나ᄒᆞᆫ일이잇스면본샤로통긔ᄒᆞ여주심을희망ᄒᆞᆸ

본샤광고

○본샤신문중에죄기ᄒᆞᆫ호수를쇼용ᄒᆞᆯ때가잇서이에광고ᄒᆞ오니누구시던지그중에아모호수던지가져오시는이로미쟝에빅젼두푼식드리리다

뎨이호 뎨삼호 뎨이십호 뎨수십이호 뎨수십삼호 뎨오십삼호 뎨오십ᄉᆞ호와뎨오십오호 뎨륙십이호

잡보

○총대가쟝 미국관에서외부로조회ᄒᆞ되향화진외국인미장ᄒᆞ는생이혁금외인이만코셔이상이쳠차ᄒᆞᆫ디허지서남잔에ᄒᆞᆫ쌔흐잇서이것이공허지디로다만용허ᄒᆞ느니잇스되거진퇴락ᄒᆞ야장ᄎᆞ쓸터업스니이생을본사의게미쟝케로등허ᄒᆞ고도로가서이렴ᄒᆞ니총세무사빅탁안의게치도ᄒᆞ라고훈칙ᄒᆞ야ᄒᆞ여공허잇상에편케ᄒᆞᆷ이가ᄒᆞ고본사는미장디위원장인고로이곳치조회ᄒᆞ엿다ᄒᆞ엿더라

○청결회사 양생회씨가발긔ᄒᆞ야청결회사를조직ᄒᆞ엿는디그규칙중디략이여좌ᄒᆞ더라

○일은 본샤는분서동의준비와거름의슈운과미셥을쥬ᄃᆡᄒᆞᆯ수

○일은 자본금은주식으로미반원을모집ᄒᆞ야국고에셔사만원의보조를바다도합륙만원으로정ᄒᆞᆯ수

○일은 국고금은그셜시된후삼년을경과ᄒᆞ야미년사천원식삼년간에반여ᄒᆞᆯ수

○일은 위션분시동이친긔를졔조ᄒᆞ야경셩을십지사로분ᄒᆞ야착슈케ᄒᆞᆯ수

○일은 본샤의영업년한은이십기년으로졍ᄒᆞᆯ수

○일은 외국인의입사ᄒᆞᆷ을허락치말ᄒᆞᆯ수

○쟝비지발 국쟝시에각ᄒᆞᆼ경비를미양탁지부에셔지발ᄒᆞ더니금번에는니쟝원에셔지발ᄒᆞᆫ다ᄒᆞ는디고소진인즉탁지부에는지경고분관이시무ᄒᆞ미지발ᄒᆞᆷ이불편ᄒᆞ야니쟝원에셔주관ᄒᆞᆫ다더라

○회민슈효 각진위디에서진보ᄒᆞ회민의슈효를조사ᄒᆞ야군부에면보ᄒᆞ되합오만여명이라더라

○탐슈봉교 경북순찰ᄉᆞ유우셕씨가관하각군슈의치젹을일일죠사ᄒᆞ는디대구군에이르러히군슈유승형씨를봉고파직ᄒᆞ엿더라

○회보발간 일진회에셔신문사를창셜ᄒᆞ고회보를발간ᄒᆞᆫ다더라

○홍히셰칙 한국에쥬차ᄒᆞᆫ일본군슈령부에셔북관디방과오소리디방에ᄒᆞ힝ᄒᆞ는션쳑에디ᄒᆞ야규칙을발포ᄒᆞ엿는디원산ᄒᆞᆼ에셔함경도니아병잇는디방과오소리디방에ᄒᆞᆼᄒᆞ고자ᄒᆞ는자는목젹과디명과인조와션명과돈수와션쥬에셩명과물건의종류와수효를소상이긔지ᄒᆞ야원산에잇는일본수비대쟝에게청원ᄒᆞ야허락을엇은후에ᄒᆞᆼᄒᆞᄒᆞ되병긔탄약과쪽바흠불건인수슈비디쟝이임시ᄒᆞ야츌ᄒᆞᆼ파탑지ᄒᆞᆷ을금ᄒᆞ고만일규칙을시힝치안이ᄒᆞ면군률로쳐단ᄒᆞᆫ다더라

○회원착수 경긔관찰ᄉᆞ리근교씨의보고를거ᄒᆞᆫ즉원쥬디참령리민화의조회내기에관쥬디에셔보고ᄒᆞ기를동학일진오빅명이오젼에리도ᄒᆞ엿다ᄒᆞ는고로방금발힝ᄒᆞᆫ다ᄒᆞ엿도ᄯᅩ보고ᄒᆞ기를오쳔에탐내가본주진보회당수ᄉᆞ명이취동에두류ᄒᆞ며말ᄒᆞ기를수쳔명이츄후로온다ᄒᆞ며작폐가무쌍ᄒᆞ고로쵸치ᄒᆞ여무리를분주ᄒᆞᆫ바ᄒᆞᆫ자이명은류대회와하상요인되다셔울사람으로셔일진회쟝윤시병의소환되여릉장사는리용구의게쟝정요을젼ᄒᆞ여준ᄎᆞ로내려온자이요죠쳘쟝은본군사름이로셔경셩일진회에왕래ᄒᆞ며통신ᄒᆞ여쥬는자라착치ᄒᆞ야문초ᄒᆞᆫ즉다말ᄒᆞ기를지엽이엄ᄂᆞᆫ쇼지로고셔두지계를도모ᄒᆞ노라고회중에류임ᄒᆞ엿노라고ᄒᆞ미처판소로압교ᄒᆞ노라ᄒᆞ엿기로회삼한율을부울예착슈ᄒᆞ엿다ᄒᆞ엿더라

○곡산민쟝 곡산군슈리경직씨의보고를거ᄒᆞᆫ즉본군민쇼시예일인철명과동수일명이퇴히ᄒᆞᆫ일은본군셔리가임외ᄌᆞ세히보ᄒᆞ엿거니와그미후에빅셩이다셔겁ᄒᆞ야도주ᄒᆞ미열집이면아홉이나뷔엿고곡식이들에구듕ᄒᆞ여셔도버히드릴사름이업스미국히비참ᄒᆞᆫ고로각면으로순힝ᄒᆞ며잘기유ᄒᆞ야져귀도로모히드렷스나아직도의구치못ᄒᆞ와불만불민이라ᄒᆞ엿더라

○문관복쟝 일작광고반포ᄒᆞᆫ문관복쟝ᄒᆞᆫ이는외부대신림영씨와법부대신김가진씨와디방국쟝리규환씨와외부참셔관어윤젹씨사ᄅᆞᆷ이러라

○원소신졍 황티ᄌᆞ비궁의유강원을이젼슉룡논은귀지로경ᄒᆞᆫ다더니소위상디관들이쳥ᄒᆞ야일외기를회긔지를잉용ᄒᆞ면좌향이셔로어긔여 황실에방히될일이잇다ᄒᆞ는고로회긔지는파외ᄒᆞ고금셩월부리샹지관졍셔고로파송ᄒᆞ야원쇼를시로을ᄒᆞ는즁이라더라

관보

뎨이쳔구빅칠십팔호련속

셔임급ᄉᆞ령

○면겸임함경북도지판소판사 함경북도관찰사 정귀희

○면겸임셩진항지판소판사 셩진젼감리 홍순욱

○면겸임창원항지판소판사 창원감리 리티영

○면겸임삼화항지판소판ᄉᆞ 삼화젼감리 고영철

○겸임함경북도지판소판ᄉᆞ 함경북도관찰ᄉᆞ김로규

○겸임셩진항지판소판ᄉᆞ 셩진감리 죠죵흰

○겸임창원항지판소판ᄉᆞ 창원감리 현학표

○겸임삼화항지판소판ᄉᆞ 삼화감리 리티영

○임농상공부광산국장서주임관일등이품 김대진

○임중추원의관서주임관륙등 함경남도관찰부총순 김병원

○임농상공부기수서판임관륙등 김셩초

이상십일일발수일

○봉쳥산군 청산도쟝 리희

UNION INSURANCE SOCIETY OF CANTON.

Head office Hongkong.
Marine risks underwritten at current rates.

Agents in Chemulpo,
E. MEYER & Co.

COMPAGNIE DES MESSAGERIES MARITIMES.

Fortnightly Direct Service.

For Marseilles
via Ports.
Sailing from Yokohama
Calling at Kobe,
Shanghai, Hongkong, Saigon, Singapore,
Colombo, Djibonti, Suez, Port Said
and Marseilles.

For particulars apply to
HOLME RINGER & Co.,
Chemulpo.

HAYASHIDA & Co.,

16 MYENG DONG, CHIN KO KAI, SEOUL.
BRANCH OFFICE AT CHEMULPO.

Money changers, Coal and Wood Merchants,
Express Agents.

We are agents for the Pyeng-yang Coal Company and the Karazu Coal Company of Japan. We have the best quality of both anthracite and bituminous coal, and prompt execution of orders is our speciality. Firewood of all kinds kept in stock. Full weight guaranteed. Money of all denominations exchanged at current rates. Parcels received for all parts.

CHINA MUTUAL LIFE INS. CO.

Most favourable terms to policy holders.

Benefit system unsurpassed.

HOLME RINGER & Co.
Agents, Chemulpo.

C. P. R.

CANADIAN PACIFIC RAILWAY COMPANY'S ROYAL MAIL STEAMSHIP LINE.

THE FAST ROUTE BETWEEN CHINA, JAPAN, AND EUROPE VIA CANADA AND THE UNITED STATES.

Route from Hongkong via Shanghai, Nagasaki (Inland Sea of Japan) Kobe, Yokohama, Victoria and Vancouver.

Twin Screw Empress Steamship—6,000 Tons—Speed 19 knots.

PROPOSED SAILING FROM YOKOHAMA.
R. M. S. Empress of India.
R. M. S. Empress of Japan.
R. M. S. Empress of China.
R. M. S. Athenian.
R. M. S. Tartar.

Special reduction (first class only) granted to members of the Military, Naval, Diplomatic and Civil services and to Missionaries.

Passengers have choice of ten routes across the Continent of America and have privilege of travelling by any Atlantic Steamship Line.

Round the World passage tickets in connection with the P. and O. S. N., North German Lloyd and Messageries Co.'s £125.

All rates payable at current rate of exchange.

For further information, Tickets, Guide Books, etc., apply to

HOLME, RINGER & Co., AGENTS,
Chemulpo.

Grand Hotel,

(Formerly the Station Hotel)

Near the Railway Terminus,
West Gate Seoul.

The Best Hotel in Korea
Handsome new Building.
Fine Airy Rooms
Excellent Cuisine.
Terms Moderate.
Special terms to Missionaries
and to permanent boarders.

Electric cars within 2 minutes' walk.

W. H. EMBERLEY,
Proprietor

EVERY FACILITY.

In connection with Life Assurance Business is afforded by

The Standard Life Assurance Co.,

One of the largest and wealthiest of the Provident Institutions of the United Kingdom Forms of Application and all information will be promptly afforded on application.

10 CENTS A DAY.

Not a very large expenditure is it? But it is sufficient to secure for a man of 30 a policy with the STANDARD LIFE OFFICE for

$1323.

For all particulars of rates, etc., apply to

Holme, Ringer & Co.,
Agents, Chemulpo.

THE NEW YORK LIFE INSURANCE COMPANY.

Have you ever been declined by any Company?

Are you engaged in a specially hazardous occupation?

Have you heard of the New York Life Insurance Company's New Classifications for this class of Risks?

If not, send your date of birth, occupation and particulars of rejection, if any to

E. MEYER & Co.,
Agents, Chemulpo.

MITSUI BUSSAN KAISHA.
(MITSUI & Co.)

MITSUI GINKO.
(MITSUI BANK.)

The Bank is owned by the members of the Mitsui Family, who, as partners, assume an unlimited responsibility for all liabilities of the Bank:—

Capital ....Yen 5,000,000
Reserve Fund ...." 5,600,000

HEAD OFFICE, TOKYO.

LONDON OFFICE, 34 LIME ST., E. C.

BRANCHES AND AGENCIES:—
New York, San Francisco, Hamburg, Bombay, Singapore, Manila, Hongkong, Amoy, Chefoo, Tientsin.

Kobe, Hakodate, Yokohama, Kure, Yokosuka, Moji, Shimonoseki, Miike, Wakamatsu, Nagasaki, Kuchinotsu, Karatsu, Sasebo, Misume, Taipeh, &c.

Telegraphic Address for all the Offices:
"MITSUI."

A. B. C. AND A. 1 CODES USED.

Contractors of Coal
To the Imperial Japanese Navy. Arsenals and Railway Bureau, Principal Railway Companies and Industrial Work, Home and Foreign Mail and Freight Steamers.

Sole Proprietors
Of the famous Miike, Tagawa and Yamano Coal Mines.

Sole Agents
For the sale of Fukumo, Hokoku, Ichimura, Kanoda, Mannoura, Onoura, Ostuji, Sonoda, Tsubaruro, Yoshinotani, Yoshio, Yurokibura and other coals.

YANGTSE INSURANCE ASSOCIATION, LTD.

The undersigned, having been appointed agents for the above company, are prepared to issue policies and pay losses on marine risks at regular rates.

E. MEYER & Co.,
Agents, Chemulpo.

AMERICAN KOREAN ELECTRIC CO.

Light and Power.

Main Office: Electric Building, Chong No.

RAILWAY DEPARTMENT

OPERATING CARS BETWEEN EAST AND WEST GATE, EVERY TEN MINUTES:—

First Car leaves East Gate at 6:30 A. M. First Car leaves West Gate at 6:55 A. M
Last Car " East Gate at 10:40 P. M. Last " " West Gate at 11:00 P.M

OPERATING CARS BETWEEN EAST GATE AND IMPERIAL TOMB TERMINUS, EVERY TWENTY MINUTES:—

CONNECTING WITH EVERY ALTERNATE CAR ARRIVING AT EAST GATE FROM CHONG NO.

First Car leaves East Gate for Tomb at 6:50 A. M.
" " " Tomb for East Gate at 7:10 A. M.
Last " " East Gate for Tomb at 9:50 P. M.
" " " Tomb for East Gate at 10:10 P. M.

OPERATING CARS BETWEEN CHONG NO AND YUNG SAN (RIVER EVERY TWELVE MINUTES:—

First Car leaves Chong No for South Gate at 6:48 A. M.
" " " Chong No for Yung San at 7:24 A. M.
" " " South Gate for Chong No at 6:56 A. M.
" " " Yung San for Chong No at 7:57 A. M.
Last " " South Gate for Chong No 11:00 P. M.
" " " Yung San for Chong No at 10:11 P. M.

SPECIAL PRIVATE CARS FURNISHED TO SUIT CONVENIENCE OF PATRONS. PRICES ON APPLICATION AT HEAD OFFICE.

LIGHTING DEPARTMENT.

Where less than 250 candle power of light is used, the rate per month will be
Per 16 candle power incandescent lamp,—All night.—Yen 2.50.
32 candle power incandescent lamp:—All night:—Yen 4.00.
50 candle power incandescent lamp:—All night:—Yen 6.00.
150 " " " " — " " 10.00.
1200 " " enclosed arc " " " 20.00.

Where more than 250 candle power of light is used, a Meter will be installed, if requested:—Rent of Meter Yen 2.00 per month. Rate of charges by meter reading:—Two Sen per Ampere per hour. (Approximately this is equal to about One Sen per 16 C. P. lamp per hour) Minimum monthly charge where meter is installed, Yen 20.00 per month, which includes rental of meter.

Estimates for installing lights furnished on application.

An assortment of chandeliers always on hand.

K. Murakami,

Photograph Studio
Chinkokai, Seoul.

Printing, Developing and Enlargement, of Photographs always Undertaken.

Korean Views and Pictures Illustrating Native Customs always on Sale,

---

THE OSAKA SHOSEN KAISHA.

Boats frequently on the berth for Chinnampo.

REGULAR SAILINGS BETWEEN JAPAN AND KOREAN PORTS.

FUSAN AND KOBE VIA SHIMONOSEKI.

OSAKA VIA MOKPO, FUSAN, SHIMONOSEKI AND KOBE.

MOJI DIRECT.

OSAKA VIA KUNSAN, MASANPO, FUSAN, SHIMONOSEKI AND KOBE.

CHEMULPO KUNSAN LINE,
Every three days.

CHEMULPO CHINNAMPO LINE.
Every three days.

For Freight and passage and further particulars apply to

THE OSAKA SHOSEN KAISHA,
Chemulpo.

RONDON, PLAISANT & CO.

General Storekeepers and Merchants, Ships Contractors, Tobacconists, Commission and Forwarding Agents, Coal Merchants

IMPORTERS AND EXPORTERS

Seoul & Chemulpo.

W. D. WENTWORTH.

LANDING
AND
SHIPPING AGENT
AND
CUSTOMS BROKER.

12 OURA, NAGASAKI.

STEWARD & CO.

Chemulpo.

Shipchandlers and Storekeepers, Naval and Mercantile Contractors, Landing and Shipping Agents.

STEWARD'S HOTEL

Chemulpo.

Best accommodation in the port for travellers. Clean and well-aired rooms, good cuisine prompt attendance, moderate tariff.

창

○승종이픔 창산노졍 리희

창

○명궁니부특진관셔칙임관일등장례원경 죠병필○명쟝례원경셔칙임관삼등 홍문관학ᄉᆞ 윤덕영 ○명홍문관학ᄉᆞ셔칙임관삼등 졍이픔 김학진 ○명궁니부특진관셔칙임관일등 종일픔 윤용구○명궁니부특진관셔칙임관삼등 졍이픔 셔신보 리쥬영

○명 사직셔제쥬셔칙임관ᄉᆞ등 궁니부특진관 죠병익

○명궁니부특진관셔칙임관일등 틱의원경 남뎡철 ○명틱의원경셔칙임관삼등 궁니부특진관 민영규 ○명궁니부특진관셔칙임관삼등 봉샹ᄉᆞ제쥬 민형식 ○명봉샹ᄉᆞ졔쥬셔칙임관ᄉᆞ등 쟝례원소경 리지덕 ○명쟝례원소경셔칙임관ᄉᆞ등 젼권공ᄉᆞ 민영돈○임회계원검사과쟝셔쥬임관륙등 졍삼픔 홍졍섭

○임텰도원기ᄉᆞ셔쥬임관륙등 샹의ᄉᆞ쥬ᄉᆞ 리긔호 ○임샹의ᄉᆞ쥬ᄉᆞ셔관임관오등 니쟝원공업과쥬ᄉᆞ 김격

○의원면본관 현릉참봉 송졍현 ᄉᆞ릉참봉 송복현 창릉참봉 송슌학 쟝릉참봉 송승현 경릉참봉 송관현 공릉참봉 송슌봉

○임 현릉참봉셔판임관팔등 륙픔 셩젼영 ○임 쟝릉참봉셔판임관팔등 구픔 유린쥰 ○임 ᄉᆞ릉참봉셔판임관팔등 구픔 구돈셔 ○임 경릉참봉셔판임관팔등 륙픔 리지호 ○임 창릉참봉셔판임관팔등 구픔 리지근 ○임 공릉참봉셔판임관팔등 구픔 김영덕 ○임즁츄원의관셔칙임관ᄉᆞ등 종이픔 최셕조 졍삼픔 한용원

○급이급봉 농샹공부광산국쟝 김대진 이상십일월오일

○임니쟝원공업과쥬ᄉᆞ셔판임관ᄉᆞ등 샹의ᄉᆞ쥬ᄉᆞ 김창진

○임샹의ᄉᆞ쥬ᄉᆞ셔판임관ᄉᆞ등 종묘셔령 김교헌 ○임 종묘셔령셔판임관륙등 서강원시종관 김용완○임시강원시종관셔판임관륙등 효릉참봉 리문용 ○임효릉참봉셔판임관팔등 빈원쥬ᄉᆞ 김경진

○임비원쥬ᄉᆞ셔판임관륙등 김덕쥬

○임텰도원쥬ᄉᆞ셔판임관ᄉᆞ등 의릉령 마회룡

○임의릉령셔판임관칠등 슌강원슈봉관 로셩삼

○임슌강원슈봉관셔판임관팔등 쳔긍식

이상십일월륙일

○견칙 법부쥬ᄉᆞ 류원셩

십월ᄉᆞ일 법부

궁뎡록ᄉᆞ

○죠왈창산도졍리히창을특위가ᄌᆞᄒᆞ라

○궁니부특진관김만슈ᄉᆞ직소비지니에ᄉᆞ양말고힝공ᄒᆞ라

십일월오일

○금음력십월초이일 쇼렴졍시ᄂᆞᆫ신초초각이라

뎨이쳔구빅칠십구호

광무팔년십일월구일

셔임급ᄉᆞ령

○의원면본관 외부참셔관 셔샹욱

○임외부참셔관셔쥬임관오등 법부회계국쟝 리지열

이샹십일월오일

○히림시셔리종졍원경ᄉᆞ무 비셔원경 리지현

십일월팔일

궁뎡록ᄉᆞ

○죠왈학부대신리지극히겸임종졍원경ᄒᆞ라

○죠왈종릉졔쥬완평군리승응으로겸임종졍원경ᄒᆞ라

이샹십일월팔일

잡보

○셔울칙량 일본군용샹디졈령ᄒᆞ기를슈의ᄉᆞ용ᄒᆞᆫ다ᄒᆞ고니외남산을널니졈령ᄒᆞ야입표ᄒᆞ고오강샹하을칙량ᄒᆞ더니지쟉십일일브터남셔쟝니각방곡을칙량ᄒᆞᆫ다더라

○졔죠뎍명 비궁진찰ᄒᆞ던면의ᄉᆞ인을법부로ᄒᆞ여곰구라죠률ᄒᆞ라ᄒᆞ셧더니태의졔죠윤용션씨가황송홈을이기지못ᄒᆞ야평리원문젼에딕죄ᄒᆞ엿더니쳐분니에안심환뎨ᄒᆞ라ᄒᆞ셧더라

○즁츄원이셜 국쟝도감을즁츄원으로셜시ᄒᆞᆫ고로즁츄원은농샹공학교안으로옴겨셜시ᄒᆞ엿더라

○불가압송 륙군법원에셔지작일에외부로죠복ᄒᆞ기를법국공ᄉᆞ의청ᄒᆞᆫ바로김병도를압교ᄒᆞ라ᄒᆞᆫ일은김병도ᄂᆞᆫ본시우리나라사ᄅᆞᆷ이니가히압송치못ᄒᆞ겟고만일법인군일시의일에관계ᄒᆞᆫ바가잇거든특별이긔뎡ᄒᆞᆯ일조를작졍ᄒᆞ야히공관에셔과원ᄒᆞ야쳥심케ᄒᆞᄂᆞᆫ거시가ᄒᆞ니이뜻으로법공관에젼치ᄒᆞ야죠회ᄒᆞ라ᄒᆞ엿더라

○비국됴면 비국공관에셔지작일에외부로죠회ᄒᆞ기를지금우리졍부의면훈을졉슈ᄒᆞᆫ즉니기에우리 대군쥬폐셔귀국 황뎨조비의홍셔ᄒᆞ심을드르시고경악홈을익이지못ᄒᆞ야이뜻으로귀국 대황뎨폐하ᄭᅴ와 황뎨ᄌᆞ뎐하ᄭᅴ와밋 황실에젼치ᄒᆞ야 샹쥬ᄒᆞ야써됴문ᄒᆞᄂᆞᆫ뜻을표ᄒᆞ리ᄒᆞᆫ동인이기로일노인ᄒᆞ야죠회ᄒᆞ오니쳥컨대젼치ᄒᆞ야 샹쥬ᄒᆞ라ᄒᆞ엿더라

○ᄉᆞ령부갱심 공쥬뒤뒤관들을죠률ᄒᆞ야처벌ᄒᆞ야군부로보고ᄒᆞᆫ말은작보에임의긔지ᄒᆞ엿거니와ᄯᅩ드른즉일본ᄉᆞ령부에셔다시심문ᄒᆞ게된다더라

○경부긔록 속셩역ᄉᆞ로본년니에면통이된다ᄂᆞᆫ경셩과부산간텰도ᄂᆞᆫ그뒤에역ᄉᆞ가현저히진보ᄒᆞ야작구일샹오십일시오십분으로비로소면통이되엿ᄂᆞᆫ지라쳔리쟝로가불과일일에통힝이되니쟝니에승긔과슈운이대단이편리ᄒᆞ겟더라

○고문질문 탁지부에지졍이군졸ᄒᆞ야금번국쟝에졔반경비를니쟝원에셔지발ᄒᆞᄂᆞᆫ지라고문관목하젼종틱랑씨가작십일일에대신을졉견ᄒᆞ고질문ᄒᆞ기를나도지졍고문관이라 국가에이ᄀᆞᆺ치거액의젼지를지발ᄒᆞ되도모지샹의치아니ᄒᆞ니ᄉᆞ례에크게어긤이라ᄒᆞ엿다더라

○외획갱졍 탁지부에셔각군외획을각각혀군슈외에ᄂᆞᆫ다시허치안키로작졍ᄒᆞ엿다더라

○물허회국 일본에시찰ᄒᆞᄂᆞᆫ리지극씨ᄂᆞᆫ회국ᄒᆞ겟다ᄒᆞ고면보ᄒᆞ엿스나십이월니에ᄂᆞᆫ회국ᄒᆞ기를인허치아니ᄒᆞᆫ다더라

○위관피져 종셩진위뒤즁뒤쟝김도현씨가히향에부임ᄎᆞ로하거ᄒᆞ다가원산항에이른즉일본병참부로셔김졍위의알힝을져지ᄒᆞ야부득도뒤케ᄒᆞ고김씨ᄂᆞᆫ한셩사령부로솔리ᄒᆞ야하로밤을지낸뒤에방송ᄒᆞ엿다더라

○감독립셩 니쟝원감독김영진씨가삼포ᄉᆞ로일젼에송도에젼왕ᄒᆞ엿더니지작일에입졍ᄒᆞ엿더라

○하지십관 지작일셩복공보에빅관입참ᄒᆞ라신 쳐분이ᄂᆞ리셧ᄂᆞᆫ뒤셩복후별젼을셜힝ᄒᆞᆸ실ᄯᅢ에참관ᄒᆞᆫ관원이십명에불과ᄒᆞᆫ지라 쳐분을ᄂᆞ리사빅관의불참을하 슌ᄒᆞᆸ셔봉현고가된다더라

○통령져틱 쥬미공관에셔외부로면보ᄒᆞ기를미국대통령을지ᄎᆞ택셔ᄒᆞᆫ다ᄒᆞ엿더라

○결의보공 삼작일밤에남셔소공동청인가건쳐에셔엇더ᄒᆞᆫ대한사ᄅᆞᆷ이술이취ᄒᆞ여긔천에ᄯᅥ러져명지경각이라청인십여셰된아희가급히져의집에가셔일녀집ᄉᆞ름으로급히나가구ᄒᆞ엿더니이윽고다시실아느ᄂᆞᆫ지라그쳐ᄌᆞ가청인의후의를감ᄉᆞ이녁여조긔의아들로ᄯᅥ브러결의형뎨를ᄒᆞ엿더라

론셜

한국의니두형편

○일청교젼이후에졍샹빅작이편찬ᄒᆞᆫ바동양문제라ᄒᆞᄂᆞᆫ칙에각종긔량ᄒᆞᄂᆞᆫ법을셜명ᄒᆞ엿ᄂᆞᆫ딕그칙에ᄯᅩᄒᆞᆫ귀족커손씨의말ᄒᆞᆫ바를편입ᄒᆞ엿스니그글에말ᄒᆞ야왈이우에여러가지긔량ᄒᆞᄂᆞᆫ졔도를만드러셜명ᄒᆞ엿스나한국에뒤ᄒᆞ야ᄂᆞᆫ다쓸딕업ᄂᆞᆫ지라한국에셔ᄂᆞᆫ남의나라의동활ᄒᆞᄂᆞᆫ권리를조아ᄒᆞ지아니ᄒᆞ고자긔마음뒤로ᄒᆞ랴ᄒᆞᆫ즉비컨뒤말을마구에ᄂᆞᆫ써러ᄆᆡ기ᄂᆞᆫᄒᆞ겟스되목마르지아니ᄒᆞᆫ뒤물은엇지로먹일수업다ᄒᆞ엿ᄂᆞᆫ지라

한국은원릭긔량홈을즐겨ᄒᆞ지아니ᄒᆞᆯ뿐더러일본의슉혐만싱각ᄒᆞ고권고ᄒᆞᄂᆞᆫ바ᄂᆞᆫ무론무어시던지시려ᄒᆞ야자긔를방조ᄒᆞ려ᄒᆞᄂᆞᆫ사ᄅᆞᆷ으로ᄒᆞ야곰혐의를둔다ᄒᆞᄂᆞᆫ말이잇더니과연오날날일본셔진보쟈들로ᄒᆞ야곰강경ᄒᆞᆫ수단을부려한국졍부를압제ᄒᆞ야졍권을조종홈이양이챠야ㅣ로다

만일일본셔위력으로힝ᄒᆞ지아니ᄒᆞ면한국이당초에니졍간예ᄒᆞ야명령ᄒᆞᄂᆞᆫ바를좃지아니ᄒᆞᆯ터이요ᄯᅩᄒᆞᆫ위력을쓰쟈ᄒᆞᆫ즉이왕일아기쟝지시에일한동밍이파약이될지라일한밍셔가다만두나라에만잇슬ᄲᅮᆫ아니라외국에도각각원초가잇슨즉만일파약ᄒᆞᄂᆞᆫ경우이면각국론박이ᄯᅩᄒᆞᆫ불무홀터인고로가위기세량란이되여

근일일본신문에ᄂᆞᆫ이일을홍샹인중ᄒᆞ야계지ᄒᆞ되만일한국을처지ᄒᆞᆯ지경이면효잡홈이무쌍ᄒᆞᆯ터인즉세계에셔일본이한국사무를감독ᄒᆞ게ᄒᆞ여주기를허락ᄒᆞ라고도ᄒᆞ며ᄯᅩᄒᆞᆫ말ᄒᆞ기를긔왕일쳔팔빅구십오년(갑오)년에도일본셔조혼긔회가잇셔스되그ᄯᅢ에ᄂᆞᆫ자긔가스사로긔신ᄒᆞᆯ가ᄒᆞ야일언반사가업시지냇더니그이후로유의코본즉긔신홈은고샤ᄒᆞ고손히됨이불소ᄒᆞ엿다ᄒᆞ고신호크로늬클신문에ᄂᆞᆫ계지ᄒᆞ기를일한량국이셔로친압히지니엿스되즁간에니르러조션뮬의미타ᄒᆞ게ᄒᆞᆫ일로말믜암아피ᄎᆞ에빙란이되여모든풍속이쵸월과갓타여졋다ᄒᆞ엿고

일쳔팔빅팔십일년에쳥국대관리홍쟝씨가ᄯᅩ말ᄒᆞ기를일본은셔양법졔를긔위효방ᄒᆞ야만히빅와슨즉아모조록더옥진보ᄒᆞ야한쳥량국을권고ᄒᆞ야달나ᄒᆞ며한국에뒤ᄒᆞ야싸홈을니르킬지경이면일후셔양어느나라로ᄒᆞ야곰동밍ᄒᆞ기에좃케될터이라고ᄒᆞᆫ일이잇다고ᄒᆞ야근일일본각쳐신문에이일을모도인중ᄒᆞ야말ᄒᆞᄂᆞᆫ거시일본셔장차급속히힝령ᄒᆞ랴홈인듯ᄒᆞ도다

TELEGRAMS.

(FROM JAPAN PAPERS).

London, Nov. 2.

The negotiations for the formation of a Court are progressing. The Commission will probably consist of an Admiral and Jurist on both sides and Naval officers and neutrals. Great Britain favours Paris, and Russia The Hague as the place of meeting. The other essential points require the fullest consideration.

Mr. Balfour has presided over a Cabinet Council which lasted an hour and a half.

Tokyo, Oct. 11th.

An official report from Port Arthur, dated the 9th inst. states that on Nov. 6th, the Japanese, with siege and Naval guns, heavily bombarded the North of the city, setting one of the arsenals on fire and causing an explosion in the powder magazine at the old fort on Sungsusan.

Later.

Reuter's St. Petersburg correspondent says that Great Britain purposes that the Commission shall consist of four delegates appointed respectively by Great Britain, Russia, France, and the United States, and that the fifth be selected by these, the Commission to meet at Paris.

Berlin, Nov. 5.

The vessels of the Baltic Fleet now at Tangier will leave on Saturday. The "Kniaz Suvaroff," "Alexander III.," "Borodino," and "Orel" will proceed *viâ* the Cape. The English colliers at Las Palmas have continued the voyage, proceeding *viâ* the Cameroons and Réunion. At Cadiz another English collier is awaiting the other vessels of the Baltic Squadron.

London, Nov. 2nd.

It is authoritatively stated that the undertaking to detain the Baltic Squadron was limited to the duration of the Russian investigation at Vigo, and not to the duration of the international inquiry. The British Government never interpreted the undertaking otherwise.

London, Nov. 3rd.

The four Russian officers who were detained at Vigo arrived at Paris and have proceeded to St. Petersburg.

London, Nov. 4.

In is reported that General Stoessel, in command of the Garrison at Port Arthur, has been wounded in the latest fighting.

Berlin, Nov. 4.

The Baltic Fleet is leaving Tangier for the Far East. Part of the Fleet is to proceed viâ Suez, and part by way of the Cape, the whole of the vessels to meet at Madagascar.

London, Nov. 4.

The British Foreign Office, replying to a question put by shipowners, declares that it is not permissible for British shipowners to charter their boats for the purpose of following the Russian Fleet with coal and supplies.

London, Nov. 3.

A fourth Russian army corps is leaving for the Far East.

London, Nov. 4.

Lord Lansdowne, Secretary for foreign Affairs, in a communication to the London Chamber of Commerce, says that Russia has met all the representations made by Great Britain and the United States (with reference to the molestation of neutral shipping) in a most conciliatory manner.

It is understood that the Russian naval commanders were recently funished with instructions which will result in excreasing of their rights in a less vexatious manner in future.

London, Nov. 5th.

Revelations having been made showing that the French Ministry for War has been spying on military officers by means of reports from Masonic Lodges, the question was debated in the Chamber of Deputies.

M. André, the Minister for War, in the course of his speech declared that clerical intolerance was still so strong in the Army that he had been compelled to resort to external channels for information regarding the political opinions of officers.

M. Syveton, a Nationalist Deputy, rushed at M. Andre and battered the Minister's face with his fists. M. Andre thereupon collapsed, streaming with blood. A wild *mêlée* between the members of the Right and Left followed, and the sitting was suspended. M. Syveton was subsequently suspended, but refused to budge, whereupon he was removed by the guards.

The Chamber has approved of the action taken by the Government (in the matter of obtaining the information required).

JAPANESE CASUALTIES.

According to Japanese investigations, the casualties on land from the Yalu to the Shasho fightings are 44,000, and that of the Russians are estimated to be 121,000.

Commenting on this, the "Eastern World" says:—

"There were some 60,000 sick and wounded in Japan some weeks ago, so that their number will be over 70,000 now to which have to be added some 30,000 dead more. Have the Japanese armies been fighting amongst themselves then with the result of some 50,000 casualties?

From the "Kobe Chronicle" we learn that "The third issue of Domestic Bonds to the amount of Y80,000,000 has proved very successful. The amount applied for in Tokyo alone up to the 2nd instant reached the large total of Y105,378,475; and in Osaka up to the 4th instant Y15,658,550. The amount applied for in Kobe up to Friday was Y537,785.

It seems to us that there is a great falling off in the provinces. Tokyo does not generally leave Osaka far behind.

Simply as a sdie remark, writes an American paper, it may be noticed that Port Arthur is not failing with anywhere near so much frequency as formerly.

An excellent illustration of the futility of the society and the objects which induce the ignorant classes to enroll themselves under the standard of the Chin Po Hoi, is contained in the following report. The Major of the local guard at Wonchu, receiving information that a meeting of Tonghaks was in the course of progress at a district in his neighbourhood, despatched a force to prevent any disturbance. On arriving at the scene no Tonghaks were discovered, but only a party of Chin Po Hoi followers, who were being instructed in their duties by two disciples of the Il Chin Hoi, recently sent from Seoul for that purpose. These two worthies were arrested, and enquiry elicited the information from them that they did not wish to create any disturbance, but they had joined the Il Chin Hoi, as it was the only means they could find of obtaining a livelihood! Of such vagrants, is this illustrious society formed.

According to an American paper, an estate in Finland has been bequeathed to Satan. The position of those relatives who were considered to have expectations is thus one of some difficulty. *Ex.* —We (Eastern World) suppose that the relation in question will—ahem!—raise the devil. We would.

The Korea Daily News.

Issued at 5 P. M. daily except Sundays.

Rate of Subscription:—
Per Year. Yen 25.
Per Quarter. Yen [illegible].
Per Month. Yen 2.50.

Postage in Korea not charged extra.
Postage abroad charged extra.

Advertisements, 50 sen per day for 1 inch or less.
5 yen per month per inch.
50 yen per year per inch.

All communications to

E. T. BETHELL,
Editor and Publisher,
Pak-tong, Seoul

SECRET SERVICE.

However glorious a war may be very little of its pomp, pride and circumstance falls to the lot of those who perhaps deserve it most. From the very nature of their mission, it is essential that those engaged in secret service remain as far as possible in obscurity. Danger loses many of its terrors when faced in company with others, and yet a man in the secret service has often to depart alone on desperate errands, frequently never to be heard of again. He dies unsung and his name goes into oblivion.

Early in the war, many Japanese missions set out for Manchuria with the object of wrecking the Trans—Siberian railway. Owing to Russian promptitude and vigilance they all failed, but we have only heard of the fate of a few. Many were probably ignominiously shot or hanged, and even had all the circumstances been known to their chiefs, chagrin at their failure would have largely discounted admiration of their courage. There can be no doubt that the failure of her emissaries to wreck the railway upon which Russia so largely depends, has been a matter of deep disappointment to Japan.

Another agency to which Japan undoubtedly looked for aid is the internal condition of Russia. Rebellion and anarchy in that country would be of such assistance in crippling Russian resources, that it is only fair to assume that Japan is giving the matter her attention. It is of course impossible for Japanese to personally join the agitators, but they probably give them something more substantial than sympathy.

The way in which the Japanese general commanding in Korea has continually ignored apparently formidable Russian raids in the northeast has been justified by events, and is another tribute to Japan's secret service.

It is a matter of common knowledge that ever since Port Arthur was rudely taken from her in 1895, Japan has, through her secret service, been steadily preparing for this war. Picked men have been continually travelling over the probable battle ground, noting the contour of the country, making maps, taking note of the natural resources and sounding the people. Japan, taking warning by British failures in South Africa prepared herself with such knowledge of the ground as has probably never been possessed by an army before.

It is even supposed in some quarters that Japanese secret service machinations indirectly led up to the North Sea incident; not of course that such a *faux pas* was ever expected, but that the Russian government was supplied with information leading it to expect that the path of the Baltic squadron would be beset with lurking dangers.

However, even the secret service has its lighter side, as the following story will illustrate.

It appears that there was, last year, in Yokohama, a Japanese in Russian employ who masqueraded as a teacher of Japanese, and amongst his "pupils" was an official of either the Russian Consulate or Legation we forget which. In order to obtain certain information as to roads and fortresses, this "teacher" approached an employe of the Yokosuka naval yard. This man promised what was wanted, and mentioned the matter to his superiors. The teacher's career was looked into and his connection with the Russian discovered. Was he forthwith arrested? By no means. He was most obligingly supplied with all the information he wanted, carefully prepared by the authorities for Russian consumption, until war broke out, when he was pounced upon, tried and condemned and will now spend the rest of his life in durance vile, reflecting that things are not always what they seem.

H. E. the Italiain Minister has returned from his visit to China.

The Governor of Kiaochau was a passenger on board S. M. S. Jaguar, which arrived in Chemulpo yesterday.

Five hundred and fifty Japanese non-commissioned officers of infantry, artillery, etc., were promoted ensign on Nov. 1st.

An investigation into the matter, leads the authorities to believe that the members of the Chin Po Hoi now number over 50,000.

At 11.50 A. M. on Wednesday the last rail was laid on the Seoul-Fusan road. It is expected that some little time will elapse before the railway is opened to passenger traffic.

General Kwon Chung-hyun returned yesterday from Manchuria, whither, it will be remembered, he was despatched to convey presents and messages of sympathy to the Japanese army.

Since the occasion of the riot and the subsequent arrest of those responsible by the Japanese, reports the Magistrate of Koksan, his district has been entirely deserted. Many inducements have been offered to the natives to return, but they one and all refuse.

In a letter to "The Times," full of very interesting evidence, the Bishop of Norwich illustrates the extreme unlikelihood of the Russian rumour that the dethronement of the Dalai Lama will lead to a holy war among the Mongols at Urga. Many years ago the Bishop spent some time at Urga, the sacred city of the Mongols, for the purpose of studying the Lamaistic religion. Of the three great Lamas, who are accepted as successive incarnations of a divine personality, two always reside in Thibet and one at Urga. The Mongolian Lama is everywhere regarded as the third in order; but according to the Bishop the precedence of the Dalai and Tashi Lamas is of small concern to the Mongolians. The Mongolian nomads reserve their enthusiasm for their own Lama, the Khutuku, and any insult offered to him might very probably raise a tumult; and the Chinese Amban in Urga takes the greatest pains, on behalf of his Government, to protect the religious susceptibilities of the people. As for the Buriats of Siberia, who were also mentioned as likely to share in the war, many of them have been converted to Christianity, and the religion of the rest is that old superstition of the East, known as Shamanism.

A telegram was received on Oct. 31st in Yokohama from London to the effect that the price of Japanese bonds has advanced. The quotation was: 4 per cent. £85. The 6 per cents fell by five shillings.

On October 29 the Tokyo branch of the Bank of Formsoa forwarded to the Head Office in Formosa a considerable quantity of its convertible gold notes, amounting to millions of yen in value.

Mr. Oura, Minister of Japanese Communications, and suite, arrived at Moji on the morning of October 31 from a tour of inspection in Korea and Manchuria, having left Dalny on October 29.

It is reported that the British man-of-war Shearwater is ashore on the Alaska coast The Shearwater is a screw sloop of 980 tons, and carries six guns. She was commissioned at Chatham in 1901.

It is reported that, owing to the departure of the Baltic fleet for the Far East, steamship freights have of late greatly increased in Europe, the rate on iron, for instance, having advanced 2s. 6d. per ton.

It has been decided that the site outside the East Gate chosen for the tomb of the late Crown Princess, is unsuitable. It is probable that the place of burial will be now altered to a situation outside the West Gate.

Of about 200 oxen on board the British steamer "Hsi-shan," which was recently seized at Yankow, but subsequently released, 80 were destroyed on an is and near Sasebo between Oct. 13th and 27th, as they were found to be affected with rinderpest.

A company has been organized with the object of improving the sanitary condition of the city. The Government Treasury is to funish $40,000, two thirds of the necessary capital, and the remaining $20,000 will be made up in shares. No foreign capital will be admitted.

There are at present building, or shortly to be commenced building, no fewer than forty ships for the United States Navy. This number comprises the following vessels:—Battleships 13; armoured cruisers, ten; protected cruisers, five; scoutships, three; torpedo-boats, two; colliers, two. All these vessels are to be completed within five years.

Frenchmen who venerate the past and abhor all modern inventions, are terribly scandalised at what they describe as the desecration of the historic palace of Versailles, which on Sept. 23rd was made to serve as the back ground for a series of theatrical spectacles organised at the request of a cinematograph operator. The object was to reproduce as faithfully as possible a number of characteristic scenes in the life of Versailles during the life of Louis XIV. Eighty persons were engaged to represent the great monarch and his courtiers.

The "Scientific American" gives the lessons of the Russo-Japanese War on the endurance of warship machinery, as follows:—The impact of heavy projectiles has a strong tendency to affect the alignment of machinery by shock, but has less effect than might have been expected on boilers, whether of the water-tube or cylindrical type. All small ships, especially torpedo craft, wear out quickly and lose heavily in speed owing to hard service. The deterioration of big ships is considerably less, especially when they have been well cared for in time of peace. Machinery may be injured, but not disabled by gun fire. Water-tube boilers of the Belleville type, which can be cleaned at sea, are preferable to cylindrical boilers, which cannot. It has not proved possible to keep full speed for any length of time in either fleet. One cause of failure is the physical difficulty of getting coal from the bunkers quickly enough, hence the importance of coal thrift.

The Korea Daily News.

VOL. I, SATURDAY, NOVEMBER 12, 1904. No. 99

HONGKONG & SHANGHAI BANKING CORPORATION.

Paid-up Capital..... ....$10,000,000
Reserve Fund:—Sterling Reserve... 10,000,000
Silver Reserve..... 7,000,000

27,000,000
Reserve Liability of Proprietors... 10,000,000

HEAD OFFICE, HONGKONG.

London Bankers, London and County Banking Company Limited.
Branches and Agencies, London.

Amoy,	Hankow	Penang,
Bangkok,	Hiogo,	Rangoon,
Batavia,	Iloilo,	Saigon,
Bombay,	Lyons,	San Francisco,
Calcutta,	Manila,	Singapore,
Colombo,	Nagasaki,	Sourabaya,
Foochow,	New York,	Tientsin,
Hamburg,	Peking,	Yokohama,

Credits granted on approved Securities, and every description of Banking and Exchange business transacted.

Drafts granted on London and the chief Commercial places in Europe, India, Australia, America, China and Japan.

HOLME RINGER & Co., AGENTS, CHEMULPO.

ON CHEONG & CO., SEOUL.

GENERAL STORE KEEPERS.
Imported provisions, Cooking Utensils Crockery, etc.
FRESH BREAD DAILY.

MITSU BISHI DOCKYARD & ENGINE WORKS,
NAGASAKI.

CODE WORD, "DOCK."

A. 1, A. B. C., and Engineering Codes used.

DOCK No. 1 (at Tategami).

Extreme Length..............523 feet
Length on blocks .... 513 ,,
Width of Entrance on Top......89 ,,
,, ,, Bottom....77 ,,
Water on Blocks at Spring Tide 26½ ,,

DOCK No. 2 (Mukaijima).

Extreme Length..............371 feet
Length on Blocks.............360 ,,
Width of Entrance on Top......66 ,,
,, ,, Bottom 53 ,,
Water on Blocks at Spring Tide 22 ,,

PATENT SLIP (at Kosuge).

Can take vessels up to 1,000 tons gross.

THE WORKS are well equipped with the LATEST IMPROVEMENTS, and can execute any kind of work in SHIPBUILDING and MARINE ENGINEERING, as well as in REPAIRING of SHIPS.

The COMPANY'S new powerful steamer OURA-MARU (712 tons, 700 I.H.P.), specially built for SALVAGE PURPOSES, and equipped with necessary gear, is always READY at SHORT NOTICE.

CHARTERED BANK OF INDIA AUSTRALIA & CHINA.

INCORPORATED BY ROYAL CHARTER 1853

HEAD OFFICES:—LONDON.

Paid-up Capital £800,000
Reserve Liability of Shareholders 800,000
Reserve Fund 800,000

Drafts granted upon all the principal places in the world and every description of Exchange and banking business transacted.

E. MEYER & Co., Agents, Chemulpo.

E. MEYER & CO.
Chemulpo.

SOLE AGENTS IN KOREA FOR:
A. T. Morse, Sons & Co's "Fresco" Distemper!

In all colours ready for use on walls, Ceilings etc.
and
AVENARIUS CARBOLINEUM

A wood-preserving and antiseptic oil preparation

Against decay, dry-rot, fungus and wood-destroying insects.

A large supply always in Stock.
Prices upon application.

E. MEYER & Co., Chemulpo.

THE METHODIST PUBLISHING HOUSE,
Little West Gate, Seoul.

JOB PRINTING, TYPEWRITER PAPER
CARBON PAPER, VISITING CARDS
STATIONERY, BOOK BINDING
BOOK PUBLISHERS
AMERICAN SCHOOL BOOKS
SPENCERIAN COPY BOOKS
PEN CARBON LETTER AND BILL BOOKS

S. A. BECK, Manager.

HOKURKU DOBOKU KAISHA.

Branch office in Chong Dong, Seoul.
Japanese telephone No. 165

CONTRACT DEPARTMENT.

We can contract to build any building or construction.

MERCHANDISE DEPARTMENT.

We can provide any building material. We have just contracted to build the new Belgian Legation.

DAI-ICHI GINKO.

LIMITED.

(Formerly the First National Bank)

ESTABLISHED 1873

INCORPORATED UNDER PRESENT LAW 1896

Capital - - - - - - - - - Yen 5,000,000
Reserve Fund - - - - - 1,500,000

HEAD OFFICE:—TOKIO.

President: Baron SHIBUSAWA.

BRANCHES AND CORRESPONDENTS
In the Principal Cities and Towns of Japan.
Interest Allowed on
Fixed deposits 1 year - - - 6½ per cent
" " 6 months - - - 6 per cent

Special current accounts 1½ sen daily per Y 100
General " " 1 " " " 100

M. TANAKA, Manager, Chemulpo

HOLME RINGER & Co.
Chemulpo.

General Merchants and Government Contractors.

Agents for the leading Banks
Steamship Companies
and
Insurance Companies

Importers of Merchandise of every description.

KAMEYA & CO.

GENERAL STOREKEEPERS

Chinkokai - - Seoul
(Established 1895, Tokyo)

Confectionery, Hams, Canned Goods, Cutlery, Hirano & Tansan Water. Provisions, Gents, Furnishing goods, Toilet Articles, Travelling Bags, Tobacco, Cigars & Cigarettes Kitchen Utensils. Coffee, Biscuits.

Fresh Goods always kept in Stock.
Prices Moderate
Please come and inspect our goods

NIPPON YUSEN KAISHA.

JAPANESE MAIL STEAMSHIP CO.

UNDER MAIL CONTRACT WITH THE IMPERIAL JAPANESE GOVERNMENT.

European Line

Regular Fortnightly Service between Yokohama Kobe, Moji, Shanghai, Hongkong, Singapore, Penang Colombo, Port Said, Marseilles, London and Antwerp

American Line

Regular Fortnightly Service between Hongkong and Seattle, calling at Shanghai, Moji, Kobe, Yokohama and Victoria, B. C.

Australian Line

Regular weekly Service betwen Japan Ports and Australia, callingjat Hongkong and Manila.
(Above Three Lines Suspended until further notice).

Shanghai Line

Weekly Service between Shanghai and Japanj Ports

Korea Line

Service Kob e, Moji, Nagasaki, Fusan, Chemupo, Chef oo, Taiku.
S. S. Bahelsberg, 2181 tons.
Service Kobe, Moji, Fusan, Chemulpo, Chinnampo
S. S ARGO, S. S. Ohio.

BORDEN'S CONDENSED MILK CO.
New York, U. S. A.

ALWAYS IN STOCK
Eagle Brand Condensed Milk.
Gold Seal Condensed Milk.
Peerless (Family) Evaporated Cream.
Borden's Malted Milk.

E. MEYER & CO.
Chemulpo, Korea,
Sole Agents

ROYAL INSURANCE COMPANY,
Funds exceed £10,000,000
FIRE
AT CURRENT RATES.
LIFE
REDUCED PREMIUM.
HOLME RINGER & Co., Agents, Chemulpo.

HOTEL DU PALAIS
SEOUL.

The only first class Hotel in Seoul. Situated in the centre of the city opposite the palace.

Cuisine under the supervision of an experienced French Chef.

Well ventilated and furnished throughout.

TARIFF UPON APPLICATION

L. MARTIN
Proprietor and Manager.

大韓每日申報
대한미일신보

(데일빅호)　　　　(화요일)　　　　일쳔구빅사년십일월십오일

본샤고빅

이신보는영거와한어로셔거리
일출판ᄒᆞᆷ

신문가

한쟝　　엽두돈오푼
일삭도　엽두량닷돈

우표가미삭닷돈
다밧돈으로밧ᄉᆞᆸ

광고료는

귀한의쟝단과조힝의다쇼로쥬
감ᄒᆞ되렴가로밧을터이오매오
리지하녀대한사람마다다이신
문을보실터이니광고내시기를
원ᄒᆞ시는이들은우리신문사에
와셔면약ᄒᆞ심을희망ᄒᆞᆷ

○발힝소　　박동대한미일신보
샤　발힝인　영국인 (빗셀)
필집자리오

샤쟝 영국인 (빗셜)

편ᄒᆞᆷ　　디리권

○광고료를미리아니내시면광고를
리지아니ᄒᆞᆷ

사고

본샤광고

○본샤신문중에광고를기재ᄒᆞ고자ᄒᆞ시는이는
소용되는갑슬미리내야ᄒᆞᆷ

관보

잡보

UNION INSURANCE SOCIETY OF CANTON.

Head office Hongkong.
Marine risks underwritten at current rates.
Agents in Chemulpo,
E. MEYER & Co.

COMPAGNIE DES MESSAGERIES MARITIMES.

Fortnightly Direct Service.

For Marseilles
viâ Ports.
Sailing from Yokohama
Calling at Kobe,
Shanghai, Hongkong, Saigon, Singapore, Colombo, Djibonti, Suez, Port Said and Marseilles.

For particulars apply to
HOLME RINGER & Co.,
Chemulpo.

HAYASHIDA & Co.,

16 MYENG DONG, CHIN KO KAI, SEOUL.
BRANCH OFFICE AT CHEMULPO.

Money changers, Coal and Wood Merchants, Express Agents.

We are agents for the Pyeng-yang Coal Company and the Karazu Coal Company of Japan. We have the best quality of both anthracite and bituminous coal, and prompt execution of orders is our speciality. Firewood of all kinds kept in stock. Full weight guaranteed. Money of all denominations exchanged at current rates. Parcels received for all parts.

CHINA MUTUAL LIFE INS. CO.

Most favourable terms to policy holders.

Benefit system unsurpassed.

HOLME RINGER & Co.
Agents, Chemulpo.

C. P. R.

CANADIAN PACIFIC RAILWAY COMPANY'S ROYAL MAIL STEAMSHIP LINE.

THE FAST ROUTE BETWEEN CHINA, JAPAN, AND EUROPE VIA CANADA AND THE UNITED STATES.

Route from Hongkong via Shanghai, Nagasaki (Inland Sea of Japan) Kobe, Yokohama Victoria and Vancouver.

Twin Screw Empress Steamship 6,000 Tons Speed 19 knots.

PROPOSED SAILING FROM YOKOHAMA.
R M S Empress of India.
R M S Empress of Japan.
R M S Empress of China.
R M S Athenian.
R M S Tastar.

Special reduction (first class only) granted to members of the Military, Naval, Diplomatic and Civil services and to Missionaries.

Passengers have choice of ten routes across the Continent of America and have privilege of travelling by any Atlantic Steamship Line.

Round the World passage tickets in connection with the P. and O. S. N., North German Lloyd and Messageries Co.'s **£125.**

All rates payable at current rate of exchange.

For further information, Tickets, Guide Books, etc., apply to

HOLME, RINGER & Co., AGENTS,
Chemulpo.

Grand Hotel,

(Formerly the Station Hotel)

Near the Railway Terminus, West Gate Seoul.

The Best Hotel in Korea
Handsome new Building.
Fine Airy Rooms
Excellent Cuisine.
Terms Moderate.
Special terms to Missionaries and to permanent boarders.

Electric cars within 2 minutes' walk.

W. H. EMBERLEY,
Proprietor

EVERY FACILITY.

In connection with Life Assurance Business is afforded by

The Standard Life Assurance Co.,

One of the largest and wealthiest of the Provident Institutions of the United Kingdom Forms of Application and all information will be promptly afforded on application.

10 CENTS A DAY.

Not a very large expenditure is it? But it is sufficient to secure for a man of 30 a policy with the STANDARD LIFE OFFICE for

$1323.

For all particulars of rates, etc., apply to

Holme, Ringer & Co.,
Agents, Chemulpo.

THE NEW YORK LIFE INSURANCE COMPANY.

Have you ever been declined by any Company?

Are you engaged in a specially hazardous occupation?

Have you heard of the New York Life Insurance Company's New Classifications for this class of Risks?

If not, send your date of birth, occupation and particulars of rejection, if any to

E. MEYER & Co.,
Agents, Chemulpo.

MITSUI BUSSAN KAISHA.
(MITSUI & Co.)

MITSUI GINKO.
(MITSUI BANK.)

The Bank is owned by the members of the Mitsui Family, who, as partners, assume an unlimited responsibility for all liabilities of the Bank:—

Capital: .... Yen 5,000,000
Reserve Fund .... " 5,600,000

HEAD OFFICE, TOKYO.

LONDON OFFICE, 34, LIME ST., E. C.

BRANCHES AND AGENCIES:—
New York, San Francisco, Hamburg, Bombay, Singapore, Manila, Hongkong, Amoy, Chefoo, Tientsin.

Kobe, Hakodate, Yokohama, Kure, Yokosuka, Moji, Shimonoseki, Miike, Wakamatsu, Nagasaki, Kuchinotsu, Karatsu, Sasebo, Misume, Taipeh, &c.

Telegraphic Address for all the Offices:
"MITSUI."

A. B. C. AND A. 1 CODES USED.

Contractors of Coal
To the Imperial Japanese Navy. Arsenals and Railway Bureau, Principal Railway Companies and Industrial Work, Home and Foreign Mail and Freight Steamers.

Sole Proprietors
Of the famous Miike, Tagawa and Yamano Coal Mines.

Sole Agents
For the sale of Fukumo, Hokoku, Ichimura, Kanoda, Mannoura, Onoura, Ostuji, Sonoda, Tsubaruro, Yoshinotani, Yoshio, Yurokibura and other coals.

YANGTSE INSURANCE ASSOCIATION, LTD.

The undersigned, having been appointed agents for the above company, are prepared to issue policies and pay losses on marine risks at regular rates.

E. MEYER & Co.,
Agents, Chemulpo.

AMERICAN KOREAN ELECTRIC CO.

Light and Power.

Main Office: Electric Building, Chong No.

RAILWAY DEPARTMENT.

OPERATING CARS BETWEEN EAST AND WEST GATE, EVERY TEN MINUTES:—

First Car leaves East Gate at 6:30 A. M. First Car leaves West Gate at 6:55 A. M.
Last Car " East Gate at 10:40 P. M. Last " " West Gate at 11:00 P.M.

OPERATING CARS BETWEEN EAST GATE AND IMPERIAL TOMB TERMINUS, EVERY TWENTY MINUTES:—

CONNECTING WITH EVERY ALTERNATE CAR ARRIVING AT EAST GATE FROM CHONG NO.

First Car leaves East Gate for Tomb at 6:50 A. M.
" " " Tomb for East Gate at 7:10 A. M.
Last " " East Gate for Tomb at 9:50 P. M.
" " " Tomb for East Gate at 10:10 P. M.

OPERATING CARS BETWEEN CHONG NO AND YUNG SAN RIVER EVERY TWELVE MINUTES:—

First Car leaves Chong No for South Gate at 6:48 A. M.
" " " Chong No for Yung San at 7:24 A. M.
" " " South Gate for Chong No at 6:56 A. M.
" " " Yung San for Chong No at 7:57 A. M.
Last " " South Gate for Chong No 11:00 P. M.
" " " Yung San for Chong No at 10:11 P. M.

SPECIAL PRIVATE CARS FURNISHED TO SUIT CONVENIENCE OF PATRONS. PRICES ON APPLICATION AT HEAD OFFICE.

LIGHTING DEPARTMENT.

Where less than 250 candle power of light is used, the rate per month will be
Per 16 candle power incandescent lamp,—All night.—Yen 2.50.
32 candle power incandescent lamp:—All night:—Yen 4.00.
50 candle power incandescent lamp:—All night:—Yen 6.00.
150 " " " " — " " " 10.00.
1200 " " enclosed arc " " " " 20.00.

Where more than 250 candle power of light is used, a Meter will be installed, if requested:—Rent of Meter Yen 2.00 per month. Rate of charges by meter reading:—Two Sen per Ampere per hour. (Approximately this is equal to about One Sen per 16 C. P. lamp per hour) Minimum monthly charge where meter is installed, Yen 20.00 per month, which includes rental of meter.

Estimates for installing lights furnished on application.

An assortment of chandeliers always on hand.

K. Murakami.

Photograph Studio
Chinkokai, Seoul.

Printing, Developing and Enlargement, of Photographs always Undertaken.

Korean Views and Pictures Illustrating Native Customs always on Sale,

---

THE OSAKA SHOSEN KAISHA.

Boats frequently on the berth for Chinnampo.

REGULAR SAILINGS BETWEEN JAPAN AND KOREAN PORTS.

FUSAN AND KOBE VIA SHIMONOSEKI.

OSAKA VIA MOKPO, FUSAN, SHIMONOSEKI AND KOBE.

MOJI DIRECT.

OSAKA VIA KUNSAN, MASANPO, FUSAN, SHIMONOSEKI AND KOBE.

CHEMULPO KUNSAN LINE,
Every three days.

CHEMULPO CHINNAMPO LINE.
Every three days.

For Freight and passage and further particulars apply to

THE OSAKA SHOSEN KAISHA,
Chemulpo.

RONDON, PLAISANT & CO.

General Storekeepers and Merchants, Ships Contractors, Tobacconists, Commission and Forwarding Agents, Coal Merchants

IMPORTERS AND EXPORTERS

Seoul & Chemulpo.

W. D. WENTWORTH.

LANDING
AND
SHIPPING AGENT
AND
CUSTOMS BROKER.

12 OURA, NAGASAKI.

STEWARD & CO.

Chemulpo.

Shipchandlers and Storekeepers, Naval and Mercantile Contractors, Landing and Shipping Agents.

STEWARD'S HOTEL

Chemulpo.

Best accommodation in the port for travellers. Clean and well-aired rooms, good cuisine prompt attendance, moderate tariff.

ᄒᆞ야ᄇᆡᆨ여명이산혼동으로향ᄒᆞ야가고류진ᄒᆞ야잇는병정일쳔여귀는남으로오리ᄒᆞ에잇는당으로민가에드러거쳐ᄒᆞᆫ는고로이에보고ᄒᆞ로라ᄒᆞ엿더라

○광리분주 탁지고문관목하전세가사진ᄒᆞᆫ지월여에아즉착수ᄒᆞᆫ비업다ᄂᆞᆫ티그리유ᄂᆞᆫ희ᄊᆡ가갑오이후세출세입문부를ᄒᆞᆫ번통히고람ᄒᆞᆫ후에야방침을주선ᄒᆞᆯ모양인듯ᄒᆞᆷ으로쳔금ᄉᆞ세ᄉᆞ계량국관리ᄂᆞᆫ문부편데ᄒᆞ노라고십여일재대단분망중이라더라

○군ᄉᆞ구류 부평군ᄉᆞ남중원씨의보고를거ᄒᆞᆫ즉본군ᄉᆞ가부임ᄒᆞᆫ후로음력팔월십이일에서울셔부터리발ᄒᆞ야음력구월초륙일에항ᄒᆞ야평셩에니르러는아병의게잡히여구류ᄒᆞ엿다가동월십오일에너르러보도로셩가진으로보니는티귀솔ᄒᆞ엿든하인들은다ᄆᆞᆫᄂᆡᄉᆞᄒᆞ엿고겨우즁로에셔도망ᄒᆞᆫ필을엇어찬신히ᄉᆞ란왓는티자잔리비가경갈ᄒᆞ야조셕을납보ᄒᆞᆯ지경이오아병이엇덧케조쳐ᄒᆞ야어ᄂᆞ떼에노화줄넌지아직알수업스온즉조시부임치못ᄒᆞᄂᆞᆫ게시구히황송ᄒᆞᆫ외에소샤ᄒᆞᆫ신명에소관ᄒᆞᆫ일이응기로ᄉᆞ실을드리오며엇지ᄒᆞ고ᄒᆞ오나조관ᄒᆞ온셔탈신ᄒᆞ여부임ᄒᆞ기를도모케ᄒᆞ여주시기를복망이라ᄒᆞ엿더라

○한민포살 곽산사는미상룡세퇴아희분쳔호가전셩준을산촌회상이란로퇴아인헌병이창치ᄒᆞ야덕쥬군셔문밧그로가셔음력구월십륙일에포살ᄒᆞ엿다더라

○동학취산 영흥군수홍승욱씨가십월이십일에발송ᄒᆞᆫ보고내개에동학당괄ᄇᆡᆨ여명이붕으로부터와서륭흥강변에회집ᄒᆞ엿는고로토쳑과부ᄒᆞ온즉설명ᄒᆞ야효유ᄒᆞ미가기히산ᄒᆞ엿ᄉᆞ오나이거ᄉᆞᆫ불과여당이오며거괴ᄂᆞᆫ당초에리됴ᄒᆞ지아니ᄒᆞᆫ기로착수치못ᄒᆞ엿고괴여히행조ᄒᆞ기를계료ᄒᆞ노라ᄒᆞ엿더라

○병참부지휘 문천군수의보고를거ᄒᆞᆫ즉일본병참부지휘내에각리의호수와인구와목촉과및식량과가티면과민가의도총의유무를성칙ᄒᆞ여달나는일과군긔즙물을저간ᄒᆞ여달나는일노련일독촉이옵고고원군에도역시독촉ᄒᆞᆫ다고향장이보고ᄒᆞ여보냇다ᄒᆞ엿더라

○사관문복 일작셩복ᄒᆞᆫ고에서문관복장을실시ᄒᆞᆫ관인은외부대신리하영씨와법부대신김가진씨와디방국장리규환씨와외부참셔관어윤젹씨ᄲᅮᆫ이더라

외보

○최인아병 최인에논의연히로국군사이천명이주둔ᄒᆞ엿는티근자에ᄂᆞᆫ광식이핍절ᄒᆞ야청국관리의게명령ᄒᆞ야지발케ᄒᆞᆯ다는티칭티방면의로병은봉천티방에로군과련락ᄒᆞᆷ을보젼ᄒᆞᆯ파겻다더라

○원군출발 만주전디로보니는아국구원병의데팔군단은별서거월이십일에합이빈에도착되엿고데십륙군단은출발ᄒᆞ난준비가정돈되엿고데이데삼데사군단도계속ᄒᆞ야출발ᄒᆞ엿고ᄯᅩ표격보병데일데이려단도동병ᄒᆞ엿고데삼데사데오려단도계속ᄒᆞ야동병ᄒᆞ엿다더라

○아덕밀약 아라사셔울통신을거ᄒᆞᆫ즉아경에셔아덕밀약셜이지난ᄒᆞ야파다히전파ᄒᆞᆫ다는티그밀약이라ᄒᆞᆷ은드른즉아라사에셔파란에셔주지ᄒᆞᆫ슈비티를청ᄒᆞᆯ때에덕국이아국을방조ᄒᆞᆯ건ᄒᆞ와일아전쟁이결국ᄒᆞ기에이르러란담판ᄒᆞᆯ때에ᄂᆞᆫ덕국이이주션ᄒᆞᆯ수와아국에셔화란녀황이봉셔ᄒᆞᆷ을기디려비싼란도를덕국편방에결합ᄒᆞ기를진력ᄒᆞᆯ수이라고ᄒᆞ더라

○마젹괴ᄉᆞᆷ 청국마젹피수에풍인장과두양산량인은졸하ᄉᆞᄇᆡᆨ명을거ᄂᆞ리고신민둔의동남오십청리되는황니와청문취란ᄒᆞᄂᆞᆫ탕쳐에나노와진을치고아라ᄉᆞ관ᄉᆞ의등징을관망ᄒᆞᄂᆞᆫ티져것들은아라ᄉᆞ사름의게엇어뽄아포ᄉᆞ문이잇더라

○회인아경 합창에셔경셩모처에달ᄒᆞᆫ졍보를거ᄒᆞᆫ즉회인현의젹은외연히이쳔너와인티다른청상이업스며동화현에ᄂᆞᆫ이삼ᄇᆡᆨ에불과ᄒᆞ며광졍산부근에ᄂᆞᆫ티란천괴가량이주둔ᄒᆞ엿더라

○회의모채 본일일본츄밀원에셔임시회의를기ᄒᆞ고외채모집안을가결ᄒᆞᆫ다ᄒᆞ고

○서대장출향 요동일본군ᄉᆞ령관서대장이본일동경을출발ᄒᆞ야임디로향ᄒᆞᆫ다ᄒᆞ고

○가상승셩 작일에일본대죠계신대신이예궐ᄒᆞ야경부텰도전통된실황을상주ᄒᆞ미텬황폐하셰서크게가ᄒᆞᆫ공ᄉᆞ가속히셩취됨을칭ᄒᆞ가상히너기셧다ᄒᆞ엿더라

○시졍방침 인쳔샹보의십일월ᄉᆞᆷ이일에발ᄒᆞᆫ동경뎐보를거ᄒᆞᆫ즉일본총리대신계태랑씨는작야에관저에서종의원각파의대의ᄉᆞ들을불너명년도계정계획과및외채방침과대한방침에대ᄒᆞ야셜명ᄒᆞ엿다더라

○의용함대 로국의의용함대의괴선아로스라우호는셔관과롤을신고셰칙함대와합ᄒᆞ기로위ᄒᆞ야샌ᄊᆞ후라ᄉᆞ히졍을동과ᄒᆞ엿다고론돈발뎐에운ᄒᆞ엿더라

○토이기허가 토이기졍부에셔는로국의용함대의쳘졔이다빌쓰희형을통과ᄒᆞᆷ을허가ᄒᆞ엿다고동보에운ᄒᆞ엿더라

○희샹위견빙 희샹위ᄂᆞᆫ변셔견빙ᄒᆞ엿다ᄂᆞᆫ뎐보가잇더라

○대통령션거 미국대통령은누스벨트씨가다시쳔거가되엿더라

○희샹위로군 북도에셔경셩모쳐에달ᄒᆞᆫ뎐보를거ᄒᆞᆫ즉희샹위와고리쌰코간에잇는라쌰를누이에셔로군은귀화ᄒᆞᆫ한인으로본디방에잇는로인들을모집ᄒᆞ야군대에편입ᄒᆞᆫ다ᄒᆞ엿더라

관보

동경뎐 십일월십ᄉᆞᆷ일에일본공ᄉᆞ관착뎐

○려슌젼황 십일월구일려슌공위군보고에그ᄂᆞᆫ티십일월륙일밤에대구경포와및치구포로ᄊᆡ려슌시가의북단무긔고를사격ᄒᆞ야화재를이르키고동일오후이시반에송슈산구포티에서약고는이본대포탄환에쪽밧이되엿다더라

론셜

젼쟁ᄉᆞ진

일젼에봉쳔으로브터젼ᄒᆞᄂᆞᆫ소문과갓흔진대탕국군병이봉쳔남방종산근처에셔로용거ᄒᆞ야잇는모양인즉그동안에탕진에서군ᄉᆞ를셔로조발ᄒᆞ야수일젼에필경풍경이되엿슬듯ᄒᆞ지라구로파트킨장군이자차나라명령을좃지안코사호셔져지군ᄉᆞ를거ᄂᆞ리고드러갑온군ᄉᆞ히알렉시푸총독을반티ᄒᆞ야토반ᄒᆞᄂᆞᆫ주의가잇셔그리ᄒᆞᆷ이런니이제당ᄒᆞ야셔는알렉시푸총독은괴국보로서소환이되엿는지라종금이후로ᄂᆞᆫ제반군무가구로파트킨장중에달녓스니족히동ᄒᆞ기가리오조ᄒᆞᆯ듯ᄒᆞ나그러ᄒᆞ나당초브터구로파트킨씨로ᄒᆞ여곰사령장관의직권을주어횡군ᄒᆞ케ᄒᆞ지안키에그동안조ᄒᆞᆫ긔회를만히일헛슨즉이ᄂᆞᆫ도티여번시지련이불무ᄒᆞ도다

요ᄉᆞ이최근ᄒᆞᆫ보고를거ᄒᆞᆫ즉봉쳔방면에ᄂᆞᆫ괴후가고르지못ᄒᆞ우대우가쪽주ᄒᆞ며안키는사방으로가리며지척을분변키어려운종량국진세ᄂᆞᆫ막샹막하ᄒᆞ야괴왕젼쟁결국된거스로논ᄒᆞ면쟁ᄒᆞ야말ᄒᆞ기어렵드라ᄒᆞ며

ᄯᅩᄒᆞᆫ공보를거ᄒᆞᆫ야려슌소문을드른즉아병의외쳐ᄂᆞᆫ일병의게모도쎄앗기고이제다만남아잇ᄂᆞᆫ거슨ᄒᆞ구안에잇ᄂᆞᆫ포티ᄲᅮᆫ인티날마다일병이화포로공격ᄒᆞ야견단을넌티ᄒᆞᆫ즉셰퇴함티나도착ᄒᆞ게되면훕부지ᄒᆞᆯᄂᆞᆫ지모로겟고ᄯᅩᄒᆞᆫ뒤로는젼봉티함락ᄒᆞᄂᆞᆫ거시우금까지연타ᄒᆞ여온좌셜이될쟁ᄒᆞᆯ수ᄂᆞᆫ업스되엇지ᄒᆞᆫ던지이번ᄊᆞ홈이다시이러만나ᄂᆞᆫ지경이면괴초에샐유지번이무쌍ᄒᆞᆫ리이며ᄯᅩᄒᆞᆫ섯을맛치고아말듯ᄒᆞ도다

잡보

○영씨젼향 월젼에일본으로젼왕ᄒᆞ엿든학부대신리지용씨동행중에군부협판리근튁씨ᄂᆞᆫ작일에발졍ᄒᆞ엿다더라

○파원상보 일젼회에셔각도에진보회를시찰ᄎᆞ로회원을파송ᄒᆞ엿단말은젼보에괴지ᄒᆞ엿거니와상로ᄒᆞᆫ즉광원남북도에ᄂᆞᆫ홍긍셥씨오황히도에ᄂᆞᆫ윤길병씨오경긔도와및충청북도에ᄂᆞᆫ윤갑병씨오충청남도와및경샹남도에ᄂᆞᆫ김규창씨가발졍ᄒᆞ엿더라

○창암포민소 창암포민리상슈외등소니에본포젼부들이일본인복젼구를의게방미ᄒᆞᆫ젼후ᄉᆞ셜은다문관령을봉향ᄒᆞᄂᆞᆫ티ᄂᆞᆫ지아니ᄒᆞ엿고ᄯᅩ오륙삭을제슈ᄒᆞ야주리죽기를면치못ᄒᆞ겟시니쾡리원에이조ᄒᆞ야고토에도라가게ᄒᆞᆷ을복망이라ᄒᆞ엿더라

○귀승쇼고 현인수승이외부로등쇼ᄒᆞ기를일본인중산등이본수금향지티에쳔립ᄒᆞ야최금코자ᄒᆞ오니이조일괄ᄒᆞ야영금만츄케ᄒᆞ기를복망이라ᄒᆞ엿더라

○등디셜치 경부에셔거문도와및쳥발도탕쳐에등디를셜치ᄒᆞᆯ츠로일본사름셔곰기수의게공수를담임ᄒᆞ야목하에공역중인티쳥발도에공역은항일귀로귀후가험악ᄒᆞ고풍낭이도도ᄒᆞᆷ으로공역ᄒᆞ기에심히곤란중이라방금역ᄉᆞ를졍지ᄒᆞ고그셤에파견ᄒᆞᆫ역부는항일거문도로입시이송ᄒᆞ고그역ᄉᆞ에티ᄒᆞ야ᄂᆞᆫ젼여히은씨슬히진취ᄒᆞᆯ계획중이라더라

○북쳥하괴 북쳥셩외남방에셔무ᄒᆞ야병양천괴가주둔ᄒᆞ온확실ᄒᆞᆫ티츠병졸들은탕미들은관젼키위ᄒᆞ야마츠수오십괴티로힐이분이잇고원왕대분명과ᄒᆞ중원디방에경담티들과견ᄒᆞ야영중히경케ᄒᆞᄂᆞᆫ모양이라더라

○조쳥견원 외부에셔경위원에조회ᄒᆞ되작항구에경찰셔셜치ᄒᆞᆫ겻은다문인민보호ᄒᆞ는티빗고지이쇼송ᄒᆞ야논지괏쇼가잇거ᄂᆞᆯ근쟈에경관이지휘를ᄒᆞ야지안코장고눗기를자의로ᄒᆞ야민폐가헌비잇스니각항구경찰셔에훈령ᄒᆞ야장졍티로시항케ᄒᆞ라ᄒᆞ엿더라

TELEGRAMS.

(FROM JAPAN PAPERS).

London, November 6th.

The Baltic Squadron, consisting of five battleships, five cruisers, two transports, and a hospital ship, has left Tangier and is steering for the Atlantic.

London, November 6th.

The international tribunal, which is to enquire into the North Sea outrage, will meet at Paris.

CORRESPONDENTS' EXPERIENCES.

Mr. Edwin Emerson, the correspondent of the "Chicago Daily News," has arrived at Nagasaki from Sasebo, where he has been detained for some time by the Japanese authorities. Mr. Emerson has seen the war from both the Russian and Japanese sides, and is probably the last American who will visit Port Arthur before its occupation by the Japanese. In company with a French correspondent, Mr. Emerson left Chefoo in a ship's lifeboat and, after some difficulty, succeeded in reaching Port Arthur. Their stay in the besieged fortress was very brief, as, after two days, they were sent adrift again by the Russian authorities. Whilst in Port Arthur they were treated very well and were allowed to see the defence. A narrow escape from drowning marked the exit from Port Arthur, due to their boat being swamped. A Japanese picket-boat captured them and, after a compulsory visit to the Japanese forces besieging Port Arthur and to Dalny, they were brought to Sasebo. At the latter place both were striken with typhoid fever; during Mr. Emerson's illness the order for their release came from Tokyo. Upon recovery, both were brought here and handed over to their respective Consuls. The Japanese medical service is highly praised by them, every care and attention possible having been bestowed by the Japanese surgeons.

CRUDELY PUT.

Japan wants to conquer Korea for the purpose of oppressing its people and of exploiting its resources.—Strannik, St. Petersburg.

The longest name in the world is to be found in the Honolulu Post Office Directory. It is that of Miss Annie Keohoanaakalaiuhueakaweloaikanaka.

Increased activity, according to native reports, is apparent in the northeast. The Russians have considerably increased their force there, and now have some 5,000 troops south of the Tumen river.

It appears that recently the police in the open ports have exceeded their duties, whether owing to excess of zeal or to outside pressure is not known. In the meantime we hear that the Foreign Office has requested them to adhere strictly to their own duties.

It is reported that a certain foreign firm in Shanghai has received an order for 50,000 cotton quilt winter blankets for the troops of one of the powers operating in Manchuria. It is believed that the power is Russia. The order stipulates that 10,000 blankets must be delivered on or before the 26th inst.

It is reported there has been a sudden change of attitude at Peking and the ultimate outcome of the Baltic Squadron is the direct cause of it. The pro-Russia party is gaining ascendency. Even Yuan Shih Kai, who is an ardent admirer of Japan, is gradually losing faith in the prowess of that island. He is said to have deputed a Taotai to interview Chang Chih Tung as to the advisability of forming an alliance with Russia.—Shanghai Times.

COLLIER'S EXPERIENCE AT VLADIVOSTOCK.

Mr. William Raine, late chief engineer of the steamship Tiberius, of Hamburg, has just arrived at his home at Seaham Harbour, after a trying experience at Vladivostock. The vessel, which had a carrying capacity of 7,000 tons was a new ship built on Tyne and engined on the Wear, Mr. Raine being the guarantee engineer of the Sunderland firm. The vessel left the Tyne last November for New York. Thence she proceeded again over the Atlantic and through the Mediterranean and Suez Canal to the Far East with a general cargo. She discharged the last of it at Yokohama, after which she went to Newcastle, New South Wales, and loaded a full cargo of coal for Tsingtau, to which, Mr. Raine, who was the only Englishman on board, and the crew, who were Germans, believed they were going. The ship, though loaded at Newcastle, was bunkered at Sydney. She left the last-named port on May 14, but by May 29 land was sighted, to the great suprise of the ship's company. The land was Guam, one of the Ladrones, and here fresh orders were received to take the ship to Olga Bay, Siberian port North of Vladivostock. Olga Bay was reached in due course, but, instead of discharging, the crew were again surprised to find that the ship was still further ordered to Vladivostock.

When the head-quarters of the Russian Pacific Fleet was reached on June 10, the Tiberius stopped a mile and a half out, and received a signal telling her not to enter as it was dangerous. The captain thought it prudent to get even a little further away, and gave orders for the ship's head to be turned. The vessel was just starting, the engines scarcely having moved, when a terrific explosion occured. The water rose in a volume to a height of about sixty feet, and then decended on the ship, while a portion of the mine, rivets from the hull and coal from the hold were thrown on the deck from the outside. Boats were ordered out and signals for assistance at once hoisted. A pinnace from the Fleet then came out, and the Tiberius, which was settling down gradually by the head, was ordered, if she could possibly be kept afloat, to follow in the wake of the Russian craft into the harbour. She was, therefore, put full speed ahead for the harbour. She had then three feet of water in the engine-room, and the main deck was only six inches above water. On passing the Vladivock Squadron the cruisers Russia, Gromovoi, and Rurik, had their boats out, and the Russian sailors cheered. The Siberius was run speed on the beach and no lives were lost. She was struck by the mine on the starboard quarter, and subsequent inspection showed that the hole torn in the hull thirty feet long by eighteen feet high, and six feet below the water-line. The portion of the mine which came on deck had part of the brass cap attached, and the Russian officers pronounced it it to be Japanese. The coal, of course was for the Russian Fleet, and the Czar's Government purchased both ship and cargo, the crew proceeding from Vladivostock, on July 20 to Hamburg by train, via the Trans-Siberian Railway, Moscow, and St. Petersburg, a journey which took twenty-five days, the distance covered being about 8,500 miles. At Vladivostock there were three other German steamers which had taken coal from England to the Russian warships.

A resident of the Kwaksan district has been arrested by the Japanese on a charge of wrecking the telegraph lines.

The Governors of Munchou and Kowon have been instructed by the Japanese military authorities to provide a census of the population in their districts.

The priests of the Ha-in-sa monastery are greatly incensed against a Japanese named Nagayama. This gentleman recently arrived at their monastery and commenced to stake out ground in the estate of the monastery. This sacrilege, they greatly resent.

Russia has asked for its liberal constitution, and in Copenhagen such a document really exists and is considered of high value. Russia had in 1879 drawn up a sketch of a constitution providing for the summoning of a consultative chamber, and preparing for the introduction of liberal institutions. The Tsar Alexander II. had approved of the sketch with several alterations, and it was also approved by the then Hereditary Grand Duke, who later became Alexander III., and by several Ministers. But the murder of Alexander II. in 1881 stopped every approach to a liberal policy, and the document referred to seemed to have disappeared. Now the Russian Government, remarkably enough, appears to have interested itself in the outlined constitution, for, learning that the son of the man who drafted it lives in Copenhagen, it invited him to search his father's papers. There after 25 years has been found the paper in question containing both the marginal notes of Alexander II and also the names of those statesmen who had read it. The document has now, through the Russian Embassy at Copenhagen, been sent to the Government: and there is a great deal of excitement and expectation concerning its further fate.—China Review.

Many stories are current regarding the recent flight of Major Yi Kui Chau, the Chief of the Electrical Bureau. That he committed a murder and fled before his crine was discovered, there seems no room for doubt, but the causes which led up to his crime have not yet been clearly ascertained. Kyeng-Sun-Hang was the name of the victim between whom and Major Yi some differences appear to have existed the nature of which however have been reported in such varied shapes, that they appear to have been mere conjectures. Major Yi has disappeared entirely, taking with him his family and as many of his possessions as his hurried flight would permit. His elder brother Mr. Yi-Kiu-Won, the director of the Agricultural Bureau, is also in hiding.

Thirty two graduates of the Hupeh Military Academy have been sent to Japan by Viceroy Chang Chih-tung to pursue a post-graduate course in one of the Japanese Military Colleges. This party of young military officers was to have left Wuchang for Tokyo on 28th October.

Major-General Kodama, who sustained a wound in the Shaho battle, returned on Nov. 2nd to Hiroshima.

The Governor of Kiaochau was a guest at the German Legation on Saturday evening.

The Korea Daily News.

Issued at 5 P. M. daily except Sundays.

Rate of Subscription:—
Per Year,............Yen 25.
Per Quarter,..........Yen 7.
Per Month,..........Yen 2.50.

Postage in Korea not charged extra.
Postage abroad charged extra.

Advertisements, 50 sen per day for 1 inch or less.
5 yen per month per inch.
50 yen per year per inch.

All communications to
E. T. BETHELL,
Editor and Publisher,
Pak-tong, Seoul.

KOREA'S FUTURE.

When Japan commenced the war she explained to the world that she was "fighting for her national existence." The expression "took on" and has become a catch phrase, apparently escaping any searching criticism.

We find it hard to believe that Japan's "National existence" ever was threatened. However aggressive Russia might in the future have become, it is absurd to suggest that she would ever attempt active aggression in Japan itself. Japan is, and always will be, perfectly secure from unprovoked invasion, protected as she is by a strong army and a country abounding in natural defenses, and safeguarded by the heavy interests held by other Powers in the Pacific.

No, what Russia threatened was Japan's expansion; not Japan's existence. Japan and Russia are fighting for the possession of Korea and Manchuria, although of course it is an open question whether the victor will be allowed to retain the spoils. Still: this is what the war is about, and it is quite as absurd to describe the Japanese cause as a wholly righteous one, as it is to totally condemn Russia's action.

Severe strictures were passed upon Russia's repeated failures to evacuate Manchuria in accordance with her promises, and yet Japan has promised to respect and maintain the independence and integrity of Korea, while it is an open secret that if she gets the opportunity, a very different course will be taken. Both nations are tarred with the same brush, and it is well therefore to discard the idea that either is right or either is wrong, and take an entirely dispassionate view of the probabilities of the future.

The result of the war it is impossible to foretell. Whether it will be fought on until one side or the other is in a position to dictate terms of peace, whether the belligerents will agree to mediation, or whether intervention will be forced upon them, are all purely matters for conjecture.

Japan's objective is, clearly enough, the acquisition of Korea, and Manchuria is only of secondary importance to her, while Russian designs are the exact converse. Undoubtedly Russia was greedy and wanted everything; otherwise an agreement could have been arrived at which would at least have satisfied Japan and Russia.

Now a word as to Korea's future. As we have said before, we do not believe that other Powers will allow either belligerent, even if completely victorious, to do as it likes with this country. Its possession by aggressive nations like Japan or Russia would hopelessly upset the balance of power in the Far East. However in the remote contingency of Korea falling into the hands of one of these Powers, it is as well to consider the lines of policy likely to be pursued.

Broadly contrasted, Russia's designs may be described as primarily strategic, while Japan's object is commercial expansion and colonization. A good deal has been said of the Russification of Manchuria but we are in a position to state that this is a fallacy and owes its origin to the statements of superficial observers whose vision was limited to the country immediately contiguous to the railway. The rest of Manchuria remains as Manchurian as ever. There is no reason to suppose that Russia would pursue a different course in Korea. Korean agriculture would probably prosper under her protection in the same way as the Korean settlements in Siberia have prospered.

With Japan the case is different. Although we sympathise with Japan and admire her courage in embarking on this war in defense of what she considers, rightly or wrongly, to be her rights, we cannot conceal our opinion that there is no room, in Korea, for both Koreans and Japanese. There is too little sympathy between the two nations for Korea to submit quietly to Japanese domination, while the existence side by side in this country of both nationals on apparently equal terms, would undoubtedly end in the effacement of the Koreans.

KUK'S TOUR

It appears that the expedition of officials, headed by Mr. Yi-Chai-Kuk, to Japan, is not to come to such a speedy end after all. It will be remembered that on hearing of the death of the Crown Princess, they announced their intention of leaving for Korea immediately. Now it seems that they will not be permitted to return before December at the earliest.

A London "Express" correspondent learns on very high authority that the result of the royal meeting at Marienbed will be the conclusion of an arbitration treaty between Great Britain and Austria. It was well known in official circles here that the meeting between King Edward and the Emperor Francis Joseph was far more than a merely formal return call. Through the usual diplomatic channels King Edward had made known his desire that his work in the interests of the peace of the world, already so fruitful in the arbitration treaties with France, Italy, Spain, and Germany, should be completed by a similar treaty with Austria. Draft proposals had already been drawn up, and at the meeting at Marienbed the two monarchs were able to discuss the matter finally. As the result of this discussion the treaty is soon to be an accomplished fact. An official announcement to this effect will be made in the near future. Since King Edward came to the throne four treaties of arbitration with European Powers have been signed, as follows:—

Country.	Where Signed.	Date.
France	London	Oct. 15, 1903
Italy	Rome	Feb. 1, 1904
Spain	London	Feb. 27, 1904
Germany	London	July 11, 1904

There can now be no doubt of the opening up of China. The "Shanghai Mercury" reports that on September 26th a Chinese funeral procession was seen passing along, and that the deceased's bicycle was a conspicuous object therein.

Some 50 wounded soldiers who are undergoing treatment at the Uyeaoya Hotel, at Yugawera, Hakone, on the 20th ult. invited a few sword dancers to give an exhibition of their skill. The entertainment took place in an upper room, and when it was in full swing the floor suddenly collapsed. Four of the men received slight injuries.

THE TROOPS AT THE IMPERIAL JAPANESE BIRTHDAY REVIEW.

A valued correspondent, says the "Eastern World," sends us the following account of the troops who participated in the Review of the 3rd inst.:—

INFANTRY.

Guards, 3 battalions à 500 men	1,500
Line, 6 " " 600 "	3,600
	5,100

ENGINEERS.

Guards 1 company	80
Line 2 companies à 80 men ..	160
	240

MOUNTED ARTILLERY.

Guards, 2 batteries Line 3 " Indep. Brigades 5 "	10 batteries à 6 guns= 60 guns à 10 men ..	600

CAVALRY.

Guards, 1 squadron 60 men Line 2 squadrons à 60 men 120 men Indep. Brigades 4 squadrons à 80 men 320 men	500

MOUNTED TRAIN.

Guards, 1 company 40 men Line, 2 " 60 "	100
Total.......	6,540

To the above number of effectives would have to be added about 10% for fatigue and police duty.

The company officers were nearly all very old or very young, retired officers unattached or young recently promoted lieutenants and sub-lieutenants, at least for the infantry. In the ranks there was a mixture of recruits of the class 1904 and of members of the territorial army, many of whom wore the China-Japanese War medal. It must be admitted then that marching units have been formed of men of all categories of the army, and one can no longer distinguish between the active army and a second army, which might be called a reserve army, or an army of the second line, and which contains all the units that can be formed of disposables of all classes.

It was to be noted that the infantry guards had a new flag, whilst the infantry battalions of the line had another flag. It appears that two new marching regiments have been formed which may soon go to the front.

Here follow a few observations which, to be on the safe side of the press regulations, we do not feel at liberty to publish, although they will probably be published in European papers. We may only say, therefore, that they serve to confirm us in our opinion that this war should never have taken place and that it can not be brought to an end too soon.

The four doctors who attended the late Crown Princess have been sent to the Law Department to receive punishment for there want of skill in dealing with the case. Mr. Yun Yong Sun, the chief of the Medical Department, has requested that he may also undergo punishment, but His Majesty is understood to have refused this rather peculiar request. It would seem that the way to avoid punishment, in Korea, is to ask for it.

The Financial Department being rather short of funds, the expenses for the funeral of the late Crown Princess will be paid by the Household Bureau. Mr. Megeta has complained that he was not consulted about the disbursement of such a large sum of money, and draws the attention of the Finance Department to the fact that he is their adviser and must be consulted on all such occasions.

A despatch from Mexico City announces that the title to the summit of the Mexican extinct volcano Popocatepelt has passed by purchase to a syndicate of American capitalists after long negotiations. The crater of the volcano contains mines in which it is estimated there are 60,000,000 tons of sulphur. The Americans have bought the mines for several million dollars, and will spend vast sums in working them.

The Korea Daily News.

VOL. I, MONDAY, NOVEMBER 14, 1904. No. 100

HONGKONG & SHANGHAI BANKING CORPORATION.

Paid-up Capital $10,000,000
Reserve Fund:—Sterling Reserve... 10,000,000
Silver Reserve..... 7,000,000

27,000,000
Reserve Liability of Proprietors... 10,000,000

HEAD OFFICE, HONGKONG.

London Bankers, London and County Banking Company Limited.

Branches and Agencies, London.

Amoy,	Hankow	Penang,
Bangkok,	Hiogo,	Rangoon,
Batavia,	Iloilo,	Saigon,
Bombay,	Lyons,	San Francisco,
Calcutta,	Manila,	Singapore,
Colombo,	Nagasaki,	Sourabaya,
Foochow,	New York,	Tientsin,
Hamburg,	Peking,	Yokohama,

Credits granted on approved Securities, and every description of Banking and Exchange business transacted.

Drafts granted on London and the chief Commercial places in Europe, India, Australia, America, China and Japan.

HOLME RINGER & CO., AGENTS, CHEMULPO.

ON CHEONG & CO., SEOUL.

GENERAL STORE KEEPERS.
Imported provisions, Cooking Utensils Crockery, etc.
FRESH BREAD DAILY.

MITSU BISHI DOCKYARD & ENGINE WORKS, NAGASAKI.

CODE WORD, "DOCK."

A. 1, A. B. C., and Engineering Codes used.

DOCK No. 1 (at Tategami).

Extreme Length .... 523 feet
Length on blocks .... 513 ,,
Width of Entrance on Top...... 89 ,,
,, ,, Bottom.... 77 ,,
Water on Blocks at Spring Tide 26½ ,,

DOCK No. 2 (Mukaijima).

Extreme Length .... 371 feet
Length on Blocks .... 360 ,,
Width of Entrance on Top...... 66 ,,
,, ,, Bottom 53 ,,
Water on Blocks at Spring Tide 22 ,,

PATENT SLIP (at Kosuge).

Can take vessels up to 1,000 tons gross

THE WORKS are well equipped with the LATEST IMPROVEMENTS, and can execute any kind of work in SHIPBUILDING and MARINE ENGINEERING, as well as in REPAIRING of SHIPS.

The COMPANY'S new powerful steamer OURA-MARU (712 tons, 700 I.H.P.), specially built for SALVAGE PURPOSES, and equipped with necessary gear, is always READY at SHORT NOTICE.

CHARTERED BANK OF INDIA AUSTRALIA & CHINA.

INCORPORATED BY ROYAL CHARTER 1853

HEAD OFFICES:—LONDON.

Paid-up Capital £800,000
Reserve Liability of Shareholders 800,000
Reserve Fund 800,000

Drafts granted upon all the principal places in the world and every description of Exchange and banking business transacted.

E. MEYER & Co., Agents, Chemulpo.

E. MEYER & CO.
Chemulpo.

SOLE AGENTS IN KOREA FOR:

A. T. Morse, Sons & Co's "Fresco" Distemper

In all colours ready for use on walls, Ceilings etc.

and

AVENARIUS CARBOLINEUM

A wood-preserving and antiseptic oil preparation

Against decay, dry-rot, fungus and wood-destroying insects.

A large supply always in Stock. Prices upon application.

E. MEYER & Co., Chemulpo.

THE METHODIST PUBLISHING HOUSE.
Little West Gate, Seoul.

JOB PRINTING, TYPEWRITER PAPER
CARBON PAPER, VISITING CARDS
STATIONERY, BOOK BINDING
BOOK PUBLISHERS
AMERICAN SCHOOL BOOKS
SPENCERIAN COPY BOOKS
PEN CARBON LETTER AND BILL BOOKS

S. A. BECK, Manager.

HOKURKU DOBOKU KAISHA.

Branch office in Chong Dong, Seoul.

Japanese telephone No. 165

CONTRACT DEPARTMENT.

We can contract to build any building or construction.

MERCHANDISE DEPARTMENT.

We can provide any building material. We have just contracted to build the new Belgian Legation.

DAI-ICHI GINKO.

LIMITED.

(Formerly the First National Bank)

ESTABLISHED 1873

INCORPORATED UNDER PRESENT LAW 1896

Capital - - - - - - - - Yen 5,000,000
Reserve Fund - - - - - 1,500,000

HEAD OFFICE:—TOKIO.

President: Baron SHIBUSAWA.

BRANCHES AND CORRESPONDENTS In the Principal Cities and Towns of Japan.

Interest Allowed on

Fixed deposits 1 year - - - 6¼ per cent
" " 6 months - - - 6 per cent

Special current accounts 1½ sen daily per Y 100
General " " 1 " " " 100

M. TANAKA, Manager, Chemulpo.

HOLME RINGER & Co.
Chemulpo.

General Merchants and Government Contractors.

Agents for the leading Banks
Steamship Companies
and
Insurance Companies

Importers of Merchandise of every description.

KAMEYA & CO.

GENERAL STOREKEEPERS

Chinkokai - - Seoul

(Established 1895, Tokyo)

Confectionery, Hams, Canned Goods, Cutlery, Hirano & Tansan Water. Provisions, Gents, Furnishing goods, Toilet Articles, Travelling Bags, Tobacco, Cigars & Cigarettes Kitchen Utensils. Coffee, Biscuits.

Fresh Goods always kept in Stock.

Prices Moderate

Please come and inspect our goods

NIPPON YUSEN KAISHA.

JAPANESE MAIL STEAMSHIP CO.

DEA MAIL CONTRACT WITH THE IMPERIAL JAPANESE GOVERNMENT.

European Line

Regular Fortnightly Service between Yokohama Kobe, Moji, Shanghai, Hongkong, Singapore, Penang Colombo, Port Said, Marseilles, London and Antwerp

American Line

Regular Fortnightly Service between Hongkong and Seattle, calling at Shanghai, Moji, Kobe, Yokohama and Victoria, B. C.

Australian Line

Regular weekly Service betwen Japan Ports and Australia, calling at Hongkong and Manila.

(Above Three Lines Suspended until further notice).

Shanghai Line

Weekly Service between Shanghai and Japan Ports

Korea Line

Service Kobe, Moji, Nagasaki, Fusan, Chemupo, Chefoo, Taiku.
S. S. Bahelsberg, 2181 tons.
Service Kobe, Moji, Fusan, Chemulpo, Chinnampo
S. S. ARGO, S. S. Ohio.

BORDEN'S CONDENSED MILK CO.

New York, U. S. A.

ALWAYS IN STOCK

Eagle Brand Condensed Milk.

Gold Seal Condensed Milk.

Peerless (Family) Evaporated Cream.

Borden's Malted Milk.

E. MEYER & CO. Chemulpo, Korea,
Sole Agents

ROYAL INSURANCE COMPANY,
Funds exceed £10,000,000
FIRE
AT CURRENT RATES.
LIFE
REDUCED PREMIUM.
HOLME RINGER & Co., Agents, Chemulpo.

HOTEL DU PALAIS
SEOUL.

The only first class Hotel in Seoul. Situated in the centre of the city opposite the palace.

Cuisine under the supervision of an experienced French Chef.

Well ventilated and furnished throughout.

TARIFF UPON APPLICATION

L. MARTIN
Proprietor and Manager.

大韓每日申報
대한미일신보

(뎨일빅일호) (슈요일) 일쳔구빅사년십일월십륙일

본샤고빅

이신보는영어와한어로셔져미일출판홈

신문가

한쟝 엽뎐두돈오푼

일삭료 엽뎐두량닷돈

우표가미삭닷돈

다닷돈으로밧숩

광고료는

귀한의쟝단과주힝의다쇼로ᄌᆞ감ᄒᆞ되혐가로밧을터이오며오리지아녀대한사람마다다이신문을보실터이니광고내시기를원ᄒᆞ시는이들은우리신문사에와셔면약ᄒᆞ심을희망ᄒᆞ웁

○발힝소 박동대한미일신보샤범어학교엽헤젼영국인셜필립졍자리오

샤쟝 영국인 (비셜)

평양 퇴리졈

○평양효동사는권미보씨로우리신문관퇴리인을뎡ᄒᆞ엿ᄉᆞ오니평양에계신구람코져ᄒᆞ시는 쳠군ᄌᆞ는퇴리졈에왕림ᄒᆞ와면의ᄒᆞ시옵

샤고

○우리대한미일신보의목뎍은대한의안녕질셔에관ᄒᆞᆫ모든뎨목에뎌ᄒᆞ야는공평ᄒᆞᆫ변론을쥬쟝홈이라우리동신원의탐보는신문보시는쳠군ᄌᆞ의게ᄒᆞᆼ샹보도ᄒᆞ리며편지를긔셔ᄒᆞ여주시는이는셩명과번디를젹어붓치시기를희망ᄒᆞ오나이거슨신문샹에긔ᄌᆡᄒᆞ란거시아니오디만근히신용ᄒᆞ는증거를삼고쟈홈이라긔ᄌᆞ는아모긔셔던지긔ᄌᆡᄒᆞᆷ을퇴각ᄒᆞ는권리를가젓ᄉᆞ오나퇴각ᄒᆞ는리유를말홀터이오며공중광회를문란케ᄒᆞ는듯ᄒᆞᆫ긔셔는의례히밧지안켓ᄉᆞᆸ나이다

●본샤셜시이릭로신문을미양우톄로발젼ᄒᆞ와톄젼부의임의로젼ᄒᆞ든ᄉᆞ로면곳에는혹늣게젼ᄒᆞ기도ᄒᆞ며혹밋쳐가슬ᄒᆞᆫ곳에젼ᄒᆞ기도ᄒᆞ며혹이나젼ᄒᆞ는곳도잇다ᄒᆞ와우리신문을ᄉᆞ랑ᄒᆞ야구람ᄒᆞ시는 쳠군ᄌᆞ의게ᄃᆡ단ᄒᆞ야미우미안ᄒᆞ옵기로지금은분젼인을두고미일일ᄌᆞ이젼ᄒᆞ며아니젼ᄒᆞ거나늣게거나ᄒᆞ온치가잇도록ᄒᆞ라ᄒᆞ오니혹ᄒᆞ야니젼ᄒᆞ거나늣게젼ᄒᆞ거나ᄒᆞᆫ일이잇스면본샤로통긔ᄒᆞ야주심을희망ᄒᆞᆸ

본샤광고

○본샤신문중에긔지ᄒᆞᆫ호수를소용ᄒᆞᆯ데가잇셔이에광고ᄒᆞ오니누구시던지그중에아모호수던지가져오시는이는미쟝에빅수젼두푼식드리리다

뎨이호 뎨삼호 뎨이십호 뎨ᄉᆞ십이호 뎨ᄉᆞ십삼호 뎨오십삼호 뎨ᄉᆞ십ᄉᆞ호와뎨오십오호 뎨륙십이호

관보

뎨이쳔구빅팔십일호광무팔년십일월십이일

셔임급ᄉᆞ령

○명공니부특진관셔칙임관일등 졍이품 리완용

○명공니부특진관셔칙임관삼등 종이품 김영덕 종이품 리용션

○임홍문관학ᄉᆞ셔주임관이등 종이품 윤길구

○의원면졍임례의원소경 비셔원승 신셕균

○졍임례의원소경 비셔원승 리셕종

이샹십일월구일

궁내부대신ᄉᆞ

○국장도감별단

○시칙문제술관 봉조하 김병국 예차 교훈원총쟤 조병식 셔사관 시종무관쟝 민영환 예차 궁니부특진관 조병필

○의칙문제술관 영돈령원ᄉᆞ 심순택 예차 궁니부특진관 박뎡양 셔사관 종일품 김셩근 예차 종일품 김종한

○힝쟝제술관 의졍부참졍 신긔션 예차 홍문관학ᄉᆞ 김학진

○지문제술관 궁니부특진관 윤용션 예차 태의원경 민영규 셔사관 종일품 셔졍순 예차 관돈령원ᄉᆞ 홍순형

○개명졍셔사관 의졍부찬졍 민병셕 예차 궁니부특진관 박용대

○하현궁명졍셔사관 중추원의쟝 민영소 예차 종일품 리경직

○표셕대ᄌᆞ젼문셔사관 궁니부특진관 윤용구 예차 궁니부특진관 리근슈

○보젼문셔사관 궁니부특진관 조병세 예차 졍일품 리슌익

○총호ᄉᆞ신리근명근 쥬 원소도감도청랑쳥이원별단을써드림ᄃᆡ로근샹 쥬ᄒᆞ와광무팔년십일월륙일에봉 지의쥬ᄒᆞ다

○원소도감별단 도쳥이망국시죵관 리인규 룽품 리의

○쟝례원경신윤덕영이근 쥬ᄒᆞ되금차 샹례시에 황뎨 황태ᄌᆞ룽졔올금음력십월초ᄉᆞ일셩복으로브터동월십륙일셔지삼삭ᄉᆞ일이라각아문ᄀᆡ좌와밋형샹문셔잉 쥬잉 계울ᄎᆞᆷ월ᄉᆞ칠일로시힝홈ᄉᆞᆺ으로쥬 위ᄒᆞᆷ이하여ᄒᆞ올지근샹 쥬ᄒᆞ와광무팔년십일월구일에봉 지의쥬ᄒᆞ다

뎨이쳔구빅팔십이호 광무팔년십일월십이일

셔임급ᄉᆞ령

○임니부관졔국쟝셔주임관일등 종이품 리용세

십일월십일

○명 빈뎐립번중샹 의양군 리지ᄀᆞ

○명 빈뎐립번향관 중추원의쟝 민영소 교육부총감 리지용 비셔원경 리지현 궁니부특진관 민영린 황태ᄌᆞ비궁대부 민충식

이샹십일월십일

궁내부대신ᄉᆞ

○총호ᄉᆞ신리근명근 쥬 빈뎐도감감조관구품리두용구품빈윤룡식구품신승균구품강돈희구품윤교홍구품리종악으로차하ᄒᆞ야ᄎᆞ임케홈이하여ᄒᆞ올지근샹 쥬ᄒᆞ와광무팔년십일월십일에봉 지의쥬ᄒᆞ다

○교육부관졔 속

뎨ᄉᆞ됴 교육총감은 대황뎨폐하씌셔직예ᄒᆞ야부무를총리ᄒᆞ며뎨국군교육에관ᄒᆞᆫ졔반됴규와법령의교졍과됴사를힝ᄒᆞ고뎨국군무관학교와연셩학교와유년학교와하ᄉᆞ학교와군악학교를관할홈이라

뎨오됴 교육총감은뎨국군군ᄃᆡ의졍셜됴례를의ᄒᆞ야 칙명을봉승ᄒᆞ고검열ᄒᆞᆯ수가잇ᄂᆞ니군ᄃᆡ의검열을힝홈이라

뎨륙됴 부감은총감을보좌ᄒᆞ야부니셔무를쥬쟝홈이라

뎨칠됴 참모쟝은부니직원을통할ᄒᆞ며교육총감부감을찬ᄒᆞ야부니ᄉᆞ무를졍리홈이라

뎨팔됴 참모관은참모쟝의감시를밧다부무를담임홈이라

뎨구됴 부관은부니일반ᄉᆞ무를쥬쟝ᄒᆞ며회계번역과밋문부됴사와긔쥬등ᄉᆞ무를감시홈이라

뎨십됴 긔치병과쟝은긔병과밋치중병ᄃᆡ의본과젼문교육샹에졔일치진보케ᄒᆞ는칙을입ᄒᆞ고ᄯᅩ본과에관ᄒᆞᆫ수홍을됴사연구ᄒᆞ야샹의도ᄒᆞ고혹긔안ᄒᆞᆯ수를쥬쟝홈이라

뎨십일됴 포공병과쟝은포병과밋공병ᄃᆡ의본과젼문교육샹에졔일치진보케ᄒᆞ는칙을입ᄒᆞ고ᄯᅩ본과에관ᄒᆞᆫ수홍을됴사연구ᄒᆞ야샹의도ᄒᆞ고혹의안도ᄒᆞᆯ수를쥬쟝홈이라

뎨십이됴 과쟝은교육총감의명령을의ᄒᆞ야긔병포병공병치중병각ᄃᆡ를검열ᄒᆞᄂᆞ니검열을힝ᄒᆞ시는그셩젹을보고홈이라

뎨십삼됴 과원은각기과쟝아릭잇셔ᄉᆞ무를난화담당홈이라

뎨십ᄉᆞ됴 향관은부니금젼물품의회계ᄉᆞ무를쥬쟝홈이라

뎨십오됴 번역관은번역과밋통역ᄉᆞ무를담임홈이라

뎨십륙됴 셔긔는졔반문부의긔쥬보존을담임홈이라

뎨십칠됴 본부에소속ᄒᆞᆫ참모쟝교를졔ᄒᆞᆫ외에군인군속의임면진급등의관ᄒᆞ야쟝교회의소의가부졍의를취ᄒᆞ야교육총감이군부대신과의론셔홈이라

뎨십팔됴 본관졔는반포일로시힝홈이라

UNION INSURANCE SOCIETY OF CANTON.

ead office Hongkong.
larine risks und-rwritten at current rates.

Agents in Chemulpo.
E. MEYER & Co.

COMPAGNIE DES MESSAGERIES MARITIMES.

Fortnightly Direct Service.

For Marseilles
via Ports.
Sailing from Yokohama
Calling at Kobe,
Shanghai, Hongkong, Saigon, Singapore, Colombo, Djibonti, Suez, Port Said and Marseilles.

For particulars apply to
HOLME RINGER & Co.,
Chemulpo.

HAYASHIDA & Co.,

16 MYENG DONG, CHIN KO KAI, SEOUL.
BRANCH OFFICE AT CHEMULPO.

Money changers, Coal and Wood Merchants, Express Agents.

We are agents for the Pyeng-yang Coal Company and the Karazu Coal Company of Japan. We have the best quality of both anthracite and bituminous coal, and prompt execution of orders is our speciality. Firewood of all kinds kept in stock. Full weight guaranteed. Money of all denominations exchanged at current rates. Parcels received for all parts.

CHINA MUTUAL LIFE INS. CO.

Most favourable terms to policy holders.

Benefit system unsurpassed.

HOLME RINGER & Co.
Agents, Chemulpo.

C. P. R.

CANADIAN PACIFIC RAILWAY COMPANY'S ROYAL MAIL STEAMSHIP LINE.

THE FAST ROUTE BETWEEN CHINA, JAPAN, AND EUROPE VIA CANADA AND THE UNITED STATES.

Route from Hongkong via Shanghai, Nagasaki (Inland Sea of Japan) Kobe, Yokohama Victoria and Vancouver.

Twin Screw Empress Steamship 6,000 Tons—Speed 19 knots.

PROPOSED SAILING FROM YOKOHAMA.
R. M. S. Empress of India.
R. M. S. Empress of Japan.
R. M. S. Empress of China.
R. M. S. Athenian.
R. M. S. Tartar.

Special reduction (first class only) granted to members of the Military, Naval, Diplomatic and Civil services and to Missionaries.

Passengers have choice of ten routes across the Continent of America and have privilege of travelling by any Atlantic Steamship Line.

Round the World passage tickets in connection with the P. and O. S. N., North German Lloyd and Messageries Co.'s **£125.**

All rates payable at current rate of exchange.

For further information, Tickets, Guide Books, etc., apply to

HOLME, RINGER & Co., AGENTS,
Chemulpo.

Grand Hotel,

(Formerly the Station Hotel)

Near the Railway Terminus, West Gate Seoul.

The Best Hotel in Korea
Handsome new Building.
Fine Airy Rooms
Excellent Cuisine.
Terms Moderate.
Special terms to Missionaries
and to permanent boarders.

Electric cars within 2 minutes' walk.

W. H. EMBERLEY,
Proprietor

EVERY FACILITY.

In connection with Life Assurance Business is afforded by

The Standard Life Assurance Co.,

One of the largest and wealthiest of the Provident Institutions of the United Kingdom Forms of Application and all information will be promptly afforded on application.

10 CENTS A DAY.

Not a very large expenditure is it? But it is sufficient to secure for a man of 30 a policy with the STANDARD LIFE OFFICE for

$1323.

For all particulars of rates, etc., apply to

Holme, Ringer & Co.,
Agents, Chemulpo.

THE NEW YORK LIFE INSURANCE COMPANY.

Have you ever been declined by any Company?

Are you engaged in a specially hazardous occupation?

Have you heard of the New York Life Insurance Company's New Classifications for this class of Risks?

If not, send your date of birth, occupation and particulars of rejection, if any to

E. MEYER & Co.,
Agents, Chemulpo.

MITSUI BUSSAN KAISHA.
(MITSUI & Co.)

MITSUI GINKO.
(MITSUI BANK.)

The Bank is owned by the members of the Mitsui Family, who, as partners, assume an unlimited responsibility for all liabilities of the Bank:—

Capital..................... Yen 5,000,000
Reserve Fund .... " 5,600,000

HEAD OFFICE, TOKYO.
LONDON OFFICE, 34 LIME ST., E. C.

BRANCHES AND AGENCIES:—
New York, San Francisco, Hamburg, Bombay, Singapore, Manila, Hongkong, Amoy, Chefoo, Tientsin.
Kobe, Hakodate, Yokohama, Kure, Yokosuka, Moji, Shimonoseki, Miike, Wakamatsu, Nagasaki, Kuchinotsu, Karatsu, Sasebo, Misume, Taipeh, &c.

Telegraphic Address for all the Offices:
"MITSUI."
A. B. C. AND A. 1 CODES USED.

Contractors of Coal
To the Imperial Japanese Navy. Arsenals and Railway Bureau, Principal Railway Companies and Industrial Work, Home and Foreign Mail and Freight Steamers.

Sole Proprietors
Of the famous Miike, Tagawa and Yamano Coal Mines.

Sole Agents
For the sale of Fukumo, Hokoku, Ichimura, Kanoda, Mannoura, Onoura, Ostuji, Sonoda, Tsubaruro, Yoshinotani, Yoshio, Yurokibura and other coals.

YANGTSE INSURANCE ASSOCIATION, LTD.

The undersigned, having been appointed agents for the above company, are prepared to issue policies and pay losses on marine risks at regular rates.

E. MEYER & Co.,
Agents, Chemulpo.

AMERICAN KOREAN ELECTRIC CO.

Light and Power.

Main Office: Electric Building, Chong No.

RAILWAY DEPARTMENT.

OPERATING CARS BETWEEN EAST AND WEST GATE, EVERY TEN MINUTES:—

First Car leaves East Gate at 6:30 A. M. First Car leaves West Gate at 6:55 A. M
Last Car " East Gate at 10:40 P. M. Last " " West Gate at 11:00 P.M

OPERATING CARS BETWEEN EAST GATE AND IMPERIAL TOMB TERMINUS, EVERY TWENTY MINUTES:—
CONNECTING WITH EVERY ALTERNATE CAR ARRIVING AT EAST GATE FROM CHONG NO.

First Car leaves East Gate for Tomb at 6:50 A. M.
" " " Tomb for East Gate at 7:10 A. M.
Last " " East Gate for Tomb at 9:50 P. M.
" " " Tomb for East Gate at 10:10 P. M.

OPERATING CARS BETWEEN CHONG NO AND YUNG SAN RIVER EVERY TWELVE MINUTES:—

First Car leaves Chong No for South Gate at 6:48 A. M.
" " " Chong No for Yung San at 7:24 A. M.
" " " South Gate for Chong No at 6:56 A. M.
" " " Yung San for Chong No at 7:57 A. M.
Last " " South Gate for Chong No 11:00 P. M.
" " " Yung San for Chong No at 10:11 P. M.

SPECIAL PRIVATE CARS FURNISHED TO SUIT CONVENIENCE OF PATRONS. PRICES ON APPLICATION AT HEAD OFFICE.

LIGHTING DEPARTMENT.

Where less than 250 candle power of light is used, the rate per month will be
Per 16 candle power incandescent lamp,—All night.—Yen 2.50.
32 candle power incandescent lamp:—All night:—Yen 4.00.
50 candle power incandescent lamp:—All night:—Yen 6.00.
150 " " " " — " " " 10.00.
1200 " " enclosed arc " " " " 20.00.

Where more than 250 candle power of light is used, a Meter will be installed, if requested:—Rent of Meter Yen 2.00 per month. Rate of charges by meter reading:—Two Sen per Ampere per hour. (Approximately this is equal to about One Sen per 16 C. P. lamp per hour) Minimum monthly charge where meter is installed, Yen 20.00 per month, which includes rental of meter.

Estimates for installing lights furnished on application.

An assortment of chandeliers always on hand.

K. Murakami.
Photograph Studio
Chinkokai, Seoul.

Printing, Developing and Enlargement, of Photographs always Undertaken.

Korean Views and Pictures Illustrating Native Customs always on Sale,

---

THE OSAKA SHOSEN KAISHA.

Boats frequently on the berth for Chinnampo.

REGULAR SAILINGS BETWEEN JAPAN AND KOREAN PORTS.

FUSAN AND KOBE VIA SHIMONOSEKI.

OSAKA VIA MOKPO, FUSAN, SHIMONOSEKI AND KOBE.

MOJI DIRECT.

OSAKA VIA KUNSAN, MASANPO, FUSAN, SHIMONOSEKI AND KOBE.

CHEMULPO KUNSAN LINE,
Every three days.

CHEMULPO CHINNAMPO LINE.
Every three days.

For Freight and passage and further particulars apply to

THE OSAKA SHOSEN KAISHA,
Chemulpo.

RONDON, PLAISANT & CO.

General Storekeepers and Merchants, Ships Contractors, Tobacconists, Commission and Forwarding Agents, Coal Merchants

IMPORTERS AND EXPORTERS

Seoul & Chemulpo.

W. D. WENTWORTH.

LANDING
AND
SHIPPING AGENT
AND
CUSTOMS BROKER.

12 OURA, NAGASAKI.

STEWARD & CO.

Chemulpo.

Shipchandlers and Storekeepers, Naval and Mercantile Contrrctors, Landing and Shipping Agents.

STEWARD'S HOTEL

Chemulpo.

Best accommodation in the port for travellers. Clean and well-aired rooms, good cuisine prompt attendance, moderate tariff.

론셜

한국의리두형편

일아기젼될ᄯᆡ에일본셔각국에향ᄒᆞ야셜명ᄒᆞ기를이번싸홈은자긔나라의ᄉᆞ존지도를위ᄒᆞ야ᄒᆞᆷ이라고ᄒᆞ엿스되이는일본셔용언ᄒᆞᆫ말로ᄒᆞ는줄로알아세상공론에는버셔나는지라

긔왕에도일본이남의나라의경동ᄒᆞ야위협ᄒᆞᆷ을당ᄒᆞᆫ것ᄀᆞᆺᄒᆞ면우리나라도밋기가용ᄒᆞ무ᄒᆡ이며젼후일에라도아라사이쳥보ᄒᆞᆯ것ᄀᆞᆺ흘진ᄃᆡ유ᄒᆞ가야ㅣ로되이졔일본셔먼져금조히일을이근킹은을치아니ᄒᆞᆫ의사인둣ᄒᆞᆫ거시

일본은강병이잇서능히나라를보호ᄒᆞᆯ만도ᄒᆞ며방어지쵝이유죡ᄒᆞ야쳥노ᄒᆞᆷ을밧지도아니ᄒᆞᆯ터이오ᄯᅩᄒᆞᆫ티평양안에다른권력으로방조ᄒᆞᆷ도잇ᄉᆞᆫ즉아라사이무단히일본의밧ᄂᆞᆫ망ᄒᆞᆷ과나라의ᄉᆞ존ᄒᆞᆫ바를위협ᄒᆞᆯ리유가만무ᄒᆞᆫ지라

이는모도당치못ᄒᆞᆫ말이라일아젼쟁됨은실로한국과및만쥬로말미암아남의인ᄌᆞ무론어느나라이던지ᄐᆞᆨ승ᄒᆞ는자는그괴폐ᄒᆞᆷ을보존케ᄒᆞ고ᄌᆞᄒᆞᆷ이어늘이계차ᄶᅡ홈ᄒᆞ는자리에일본셔젼수히올타는것도불가ᄒᆞᆫ말이오ᄯᅩᄒᆞᆫ아라사를그르다고ᄒᆞ는것도리치에당치아니ᄒᆞᆫ거시

아라사에서는만쥬쳘병ᄒᆞᆫ다칭ᄒᆞ고여러번약조를어긴일이잇스며일본셔는한국의독립과강토를보호ᄒᆞᆫ다ᄒᆞ엿ᄂᆞᆫᄃᆡ그중에로츌된일도잇고아즉저지도은밀ᄒᆞᆫ일도잇ᄉᆞᆫ즉만일이일이밧고여되엿던들무상다른곡졀이잇셧슬는지오히려알수업ᄂᆞᆫ지라

이제ᄒᆞ린ᄒᆞᆫ일을가지고엿저분명히누구를지목ᄒᆞ야칙망ᄒᆞ련오ᄉᆞ시ᄉᆞ비는ᄎᆔᄒᆞ지사를보고야ᄌᆞ셰히알터인지라더옥말ᄒᆞᆯ거시업스며

ᄯᅩᄒᆞᆫ젼쟁결국으로말ᄒᆞ드리도두나라중에어느나라이던지ᄒᆞᆨ화ᄒᆞ자고먼저청구ᄒᆞᆫ다던지혹다른나라이량국에힝ᄒᆞ도록중재를식인다던지ᄯᅩᄒᆞᆫ어느나라이일아량국을모도압제ᄒᆞᆯ권리가잇서위협으로ᄡᅥᄒᆞᆷ을졍지ᄒᆞ게ᄒᆞᆫ다던지ᄒᆞ세가지중에ᄒᆞᆫ가지라도필경생겨야귀졍이날터인즉이는미리말ᄒᆞ기어려운일이며

잡보

○리씨도주 면화과장참령리규찬씨가수일젼에샹인ᄒᆞ고죄가발각되기젼에쳐조권속파가장즁물을가지고황망히도주ᄒᆞ엿다는소문이랑자ᄒᆞ더니그죄안에대ᄒᆞ야는엇지된원인지아직명ᄇᆡᆨ히알수업스나여러가지로소문이나는ᄃᆡ당초에괴샹ᄒᆞᆫ셔갈사는경셩힝이란ᄒᆞ는자와젼랑샹관으로그리되엿다ᄒᆞ는거시젹확무의ᄒᆞᆫ둣ᄒᆞ나더시듯는ᄃᆡ로ᄌᆞ세히보도ᄒᆞ리며그ᄇᆡᆨ써농무국장리규원씨도ᄯᅩᄒᆞᆫ괴신ᄒᆞ엿다더라

○ᄒᆞᆷ금쳥부 원산근쳐잇는진보회장한남규씨가등회ᄃᆡ표ᄒᆞ야일본군ᄉᆞ를빙금빅원을산슈ᄇᆡ티에부치기를쳥원ᄒᆞ엿더라

○이황탄신 작일은이ᄐᆡ리황뎨탄신인고로각국공ᄉᆞ이하문무관이이ᄐᆡ리공ᄉᆞ관에진왕하례ᄒᆞ는뜻을표ᄒᆞ엿더라

○청죠경과 외부에서법공관에조회ᄒᆞ되우리동군법원공문닉기에김병도양교일ᄉᆞ를사실ᄒᆞᆫ즉김병도가이우리나라사름인즉악장에샹관샹항을의지ᄒᆞ아관결ᄒᆞᆯ것이오이교일ᄉᆞᆫ제본ᄒᆞᆯ빈아니라히법이문시일의게관계가잇스니귀경ᄒᆞᆯ일ᄌᆞ을못공포ᄒᆞ야귀관과원의심판ᄒᆞ인ᄒᆞ는ᄃᆡ편케ᄒᆞ라ᄒᆞ엿기죠차죠회ᄒᆞ야쳥ᄒᆞ노니죠량편리케ᄒᆞ라ᄒᆞ엿더라

○회원샤별 작쟉일에안쥬군쥬차ᄃᆡ에서군부로면회ᄒᆞ기를별소위진보회원쳔여명이일제단발ᄒᆞ엿다더라

○가계퍼가 탁지부에서히군슈가아평외에는외획을영영허락지아니ᄒᆞᆫ다ᄒᆞ더니대신쳥과셰가그사는대ᄃᆡ쟝리ᄒᆞ과계결ᄒᆞ야남도외획샴만원의젼문을닉인지라남도에서결젼을영젼으로슈봉ᄒᆞ야빗동젼과샹환ᄒᆞ면가게가배나되는지라샴식만원외획이롱샴만원이라ᄒᆞ는ᄃᆡ민ᄃᆡ신이샴쳥동근쳐에ᄒᆞᆫᄯᅢ가를식팔만량에샷다더라

○ᄉᆞ긔분견 참쳔ᄌᆞ위ᄊᆡ는칭병ᄒᆞ고안에누어손님을ᄉᆞ례ᄒᆞ고보지아니ᄒᆞ더라

○횡리젼방 작작일에ᄒᆞᆫ시골손이ᄒᆞ문동리규쳔가에쇼챤ᄉᆞ가잇기로사ᄒᆞᆫ즁로써의샹ᄒᆞ야지라이사ᄒᆞ던중의문괴가엉는방곡슌검의게무론즁슌검이희롱ᄒᆞ여ᄃᆡ닙ᄒᆞ여왈관쳥령이시방슈평관을임ᄒᆞ엿다ᄒᆞ는지라의싱엇시드리챠터니슌검과현병이졍에ᄀᆞ둥ᄒᆞ고로그쥬인령감잇고업는것을무론즁슌검이죵시포박ᄒᆞ야남셔로장아가서심문ᄒᆞ거늘그위젼을듯고방곡슌검의게방문ᄒᆞ던젼후ᄉᆞ졍을명ᄇᆡᆨ히말ᄒᆞᆫᄃᆡ경무관이슌검을불너징벌ᄒᆞᆫ후에그사름은빅방ᄒᆞ고슌검은죄롱ᄒᆞᆫ죄로파면ᄒᆞ엿다더라

○개욕단샹 빈ᄒᆞᆼ의국븍을과년으로반포가되엿더니외국인의물문이불일ᄒᆞ다지파탄ᄉᆡᆼᄒᆞ기로다시반포가된다더라

○일셜일과 국쟝과원쇼도감이ᄯᅩ셜시가된지라 ᄒᆞᆫ룽을외봉ᄒᆞ야금곡으로쳔릉ᄒᆞ란드도감은쳘파ᄒᆞ엿다더라

○외문수환국 일본만쥬군위문수도한경에서파견ᄒᆞ엿든권즁헌씨일ᄒᆡᆼ은수일젼에환국ᄒᆞ엿더라

○젼ᄌᆞ경계 평양감리가외부로보고ᄒᆞ기를일본인이본군닉젼방에드러와병원을셜시ᄒᆞᆫ다칭ᄒᆞ고민젼일쳔이ᄇᆡᆨ묘를덩케로ᄎᆞᆷ아우리졍부쥰허엽시ᄌᆞ의로쳔힝ᄒᆞ는일이심이피당ᄒᆞ기에이에ᄎᆞᆨ보ᄒᆞ노라ᄒᆞ엿더라

○북쳥아경 북쳥군슈가외부로보고ᄒᆞ되아병샹쳔여귀는동으로향ᄒᆞ야젼진ᄒᆞ고쳔여귀는현금본군당포에류ᄒᆞᆫ다고ᄒᆞ엿더라

○진보회연셜 안변군슈히원의보고닉기에샹월이십구일에소위진보회가본군에모혀연셜ᄒᆞ야왈 황실을존즁케ᄒᆞ고독립과ᄌᆞ유를권고ᄒᆞ고시졍기션ᄒᆞ기를권고ᄒᆞ야일본군ᄉᆞ샹방희가업게ᄒᆞ고ᄯᅩ각국죵교의지회가엄케ᄒᆞ자는ᄉᆞ인ᄃᆡ그셰일본군병오ᄇᆡᆨ명이와참관ᄒᆞ고본군슈가만단효유ᄒᆞ되가히히산치못ᄒᆞᆫ다ᄒᆞ엿더라

○경죠도양 일본ᄉᆞ령관랍영승샹공이외부로공함ᄒᆞ되본년이월에우리군ᄉᆞ슈비이당디에도챡ᄒᆞ엿슬ᄯᅢ에귀국 대황뎨폐하께셔원자ᄒᆞ신지명으로룩군부령에칙회두비하샤룩명이졍대위원이되여우리군ᄉᆞ로ᄒᆞᆫ야공휴양ᄒᆞ기를엇엇기로본관이ᄭᅡ이ᄯᅳᆺ으로빙희우리졍부에보ᄒᆞ엿스니히원등에ᄒᆞᆫ로도ᄯᅩᄒᆞᆫ귀졍부로통변이교양ᄒᆞ기를찬졀이ᄇᆞ라고귀국대황뎨젼에표리셔일쟝을슈지쳥ᄒᆞ니청권ᄃᆡ드려보시게ᄒᆞ라ᄒᆞ엿더라

○면방피챡 일진회에서작일경긔관찰수리근교씨가에총ᄃᆡ원을파숑ᄒᆞ야원쥬ᄃᆡ에셔장아뷔변진보회원샹명을엇지ᄒᆞ야쳐슈ᄒᆞᆯ진문ᄒᆞ고지슈된ᄌᆞ즉을방숑ᄒᆞ란신 죠칙을이즉시방숑ᄒᆞ라ᄂᆞᆫ면ᄒᆞᆫ을ᄡᅢ숑ᄒᆞ엿다더라

○한관계시 한셩관윤민경식씨가졍부훈령을봉승ᄒᆞ야각방곡에게시ᄒᆞᆫ기요는든즉국쟝졍이라도인민의쟝수는지나고귀졔샹계외에우계는지지ᄒᆞ북에는방잉ᄒᆞ고귀지말나ᄒᆞ엿더라

○회사부숙경계 농샹공부에셔평안북도판찰부로훈령ᄒᆞ기를운산미국인금광회사경계외에수방삼십리는농샹공부회샤의속ᄒᆞᆫ다ᄒᆞ엿더라

○가산젹몰 황실지경리규찬의계임쳐ᄒᆞ엿더니리규찬이가샹인ᄒᆞᆫ후에경보는죄가지고도망ᄒᆞᆫ고로리ᄡᅥ의가산과중블완젹몰ᄒᆞ엿서도오히려부족ᄒᆞᆷ을ᄯᅢᄆᆡ리리ᄡᅥ가경쳥과ᄃᆡ부ᄒᆞᆯ것을만히거리ᄒᆞ엿다ᄒᆞ는고로경ᄡᅥ의가산도경리원에셔분수히젹몰ᄒᆞ엿다더라

○셔임금면관 리규찬이가샹인도쥬ᄒᆞᆫ이후에그힝농무국장국쟝도잘나ᄂᆞᆫ도피ᄒᆞ엿ᄂᆞᆫ지라참셔관셔병슉씨가그ᄃᆡ에농샹공부참서관군수리탁씨는농샹공부참서관을피임ᄒᆞ엿다더라

○원소지샹 황ᄐᆡᄌᆞ비궁원소지로왕심리에잇는이젼유릉구지와쟝례ᄒᆞ는지라원소도감뎨신과원소도감계원들이경리원에ᄯᅩ나가셔간심ᄒᆞ엿다더라

○공수젹계 각부부원에셔는공용젼계와ᄉᆞ수젹계를쳐ᄒᆞ야무졍가를ᄒᆞ게공납ᄒᆞ라ᄒᆞ엿더라

○방비티군 마산포에주져ᄒᆞᆫ일본병수가방비ᄃᆡ군평을반ᄌᆞᆺᄂᆞᆫ의예ᄒᆞ기를외부에거졀ᄒᆞ고이쟝과ᄎᆔ조ᄒᆞᄂᆞᆫ자는마산에셔방비ᄒᆞ게ᄒᆞᆫ다ᄒᆞ엿더라

○북쳥리신 북쳥리신을거ᄒᆞᆫ즉셩진이북에는아병이곳곳이병참소를셜시ᄒᆞ고보병과긔병이합오ᄇᆡᆨ명ᄒᆞᆯ쳔여명이주둔ᄒᆞ엿ᄉᆞᆫ즉그실수는몃쳔명인지진젹히알수업고함관령이남서지는일병이젼진ᄒᆞ엿ᄂᆞᆫᄃᆡ쳔여명에불과ᄒᆞ고아병은촌간에아즉의셜ᄒᆞᆫ것도업다ᄒᆞ며관찰ᄉᆞ가슈령ᄒᆞᆫ즉왕림ᄒᆞᆫ시무ᄒᆞ기를쳥ᄒᆞ되관찰ᄉᆞ는말ᄒᆞ되신잉리도슈평은단일낭으로아병의군졍을졍탐ᄒᆞ는자ㅣ니가히부임케못ᄒᆞ겟시요인민의보호ᄂᆞᆫ우리가스ᄉᆞ로담당ᄒᆞ겟다ᄒᆞ더라

○열샹교후 강화ᄃᆡᄃᆡ쟝리동휘씨가그ᄯᅳᆯ리ᄒᆞᆫ공히에자긔수비로쇼학교를사로세우고하스병즁에ᄌᆞ졔와평민에ᄌᆞ졔이십여명을모집ᄒᆞ야본국디지와외국디지와산슐과역ᄉᆞ와만국력ᄉᆞ로열심교육ᄒᆞ는ᄃᆡ분부거ᄒᆞ는ᄌᆞ뎨와교원이이러ᄒᆞᆫ공익ᄉᆞ업에열심ᄒᆞᄂᆞᆫ자ㅣ라유리ᄒᆞ고ᄯᅩᄒᆞᆫ공익으로열심ᄒᆞᆷ을외국인이다칭찬ᄒᆞ엿더라

TELEGRAMS.

Nov. 5th.

General Sakharoff reports that the Japanese appear to be preparing to take up the offensive against the Russian right and left wings,—L'Echo de Chine.

Shanghai, Nov. 9th.

At the conference in Paris, relative to the Hull affair, Admiral Fournier will represent France and Admiral Dewey America.—Tsingtauer Nachrichten.

Shanghai, Nov. 9th.

The Herreros insurrection in German South-west Africa is ended.

Tokyo, Nov. 13th.

Field Marshal Oyama reports that in the direction of the Japanese left wing the enemy made an attack at midnight on the 11th inst. but were repulsed.

On the 9th inst. the enemy, numbering 500 infantry and cavalry, attacked the Japanese at Sosaiton, but were repulsed and retreated towards Bakyeusi. The Russian casualties were over 60. The Japanese not more than 6 or 7.

Tokyo, Nov. 13th.

The Russians attacked our left wing at Wuchatze, but being repulsed they retreated to Tahantaitze.

THE IMPORTANCE OF TEHLING.

The real Russian position, recently wrote Mr. Whigham, one of the "Morning Post" correspondents, is Tehling. It is the one place on the railway in Southern Manchuria which differs materially from all the rest, and it is the spot which General Kuropatkin chose as his real base long ago when he first came to Manchuria. The defence of Teh-ling is of far more importance than the holding of any position like Liaoyang or Hai-cheng, because Tehling is the natural fortress of Southern Manchuria. Once it is lost, the Russians will not only have lost their hold on the Mukden and Kirin Province, but also the vast granary which lies between Teh-ling and Harbin, and which is practically essential to the existence of their Army in the Far East. It does not, of course, follow that even if they were driven from Teh-ling they would retreat nearly 300 miles to Harbin without offering battle again. But since Tehling is the strongest position south of Harbin, it is certain that if the Russians cannot defend it they cannot make a successful stand anywhere else. On the left or north bank of the river, as it comes towards Teh-ling, there is a long range of hills, forming, with the river at their base, a splendid protection for the right flank of a Russian Army resting at Teh-ling, while on the eastern side of the town there are the usual hills of Eastern Manchuria. The position is the strongest that can be found anywhere on the railway between Harbin and Newchwang, and it is not to be easily outflanked. The right is especially well protected; for, instead of the open plain which extends to the west of Liaoyang and Mukden, there is here the Liao River, with a high bluff on its northern bank and on the left flank there are far fewer roads than there are to the east of Liaoyang or Mukden. Not only is Teh-ling itself a great centre of supplies, but less than 30 miles to the north there is the town of Kai-yuan, which is one of the chief agricultural centres of Manchuria. Teh-ling is, therefore, not only a place which can be defended, but one which the Russians must at all costs retain. As long as Kuropatkin's Army is there, it dominates Southern Manchuria. The position of the Japanese Army at the Manchurian capital can never be secure as long as there is an unbeaten Russian Army at Teh-ling. In the second place, it is absolutely necessary that the Russians should hold as much of Southern Manchuria as they can, in order, as far as possible, to feed their Army on the country. As long as they hold Teh-ling they have the chief wheat-producing districts of Manchuria behind them, and they still can draw on Mongolia for ponies and cattle.

A PLEA FOR PEACE.

It is with the greatest reluctance that we read or think about it. In sacrifice of life, human and bestial, it exceeds in horror all wars of modern times. The daring of the Japanese, the dogged and invincible bravery of the Russians, bring back the days of Attila and Genghis Khan, of Tamerlane, and the succession of Mahomet. Assailants dash themselves against forts, entrenchments, mines, with a disregard of life never surpassed; and the defenders meet the onset with equal courage and resolution. From one point of view the heroism displayed by both sides kindles enthusiasm, from another it excites despair. Why should two peoples, both so brave, hurl themselves at each other and strive to accomplish each other's destruction? Surely a better way might be found, even at this late hour, the way of amity and peace. Foemen so well matched display qualities which should make them friends for all time. Do they hate each other now, these enemies pitted against each other, slaying and striving to slay? Oh, no; they respect and admire each other, and amid all the booming of artillery and clashing of steel, there is a longing for peace. A faint hope held us that peace might have been near had the Japanese strategy been successful in rounding up Kuropatkin's army, and forcing it to surrender. But that hope, never high, must, now be abandoned. The Japanese have failed in their master stroke of tractics, as they have failed in their assaults upon Port Arthur, and the Emperor of Japan and his Ministers know it. "The war will be a long one," he is reported to have told his people, in the very hour when they were rejoicing over the great victory of Liaoyang. It might have been short had that victory been complete. Alas! it was so far from complete, that the substantial results of the fighting are with the Russians. Kuropatkin has extricated his army, thanks to the sublime heroism with which the troops, told off by him to delay the Japanese, threw their lives away. Much war material and food may have been abandoned, lives in tens of thousands have been sacrificed on both sides, but the bulk of the Russian army has escaped, and lives to fight another day. And as it withdraws towards Harbin, fighting desperately at every step, it draws nearer its base. At the same time, the exhaustion of the Japanese increases. Their long marches through a flooded country nearly roadless—altogether roadess in the Eurorean sense of the word—must have impaired their staying power and weakened their capacity to deliver effective blows at the Russian rear guard. The war may for this very reason splutter away into desultory engagements, or die down into something like winter quarters, an unbearable cost to both belligerents, to be renewed next year with greater fury than ever. And Port Arthur holds out resourceful, heroic, undaunted. Is there no-hope of peace? Must two such valiant nations go on until they have compassed each other's destruction and until economic impotence compels them to lay down their arms, losers both? Intervention has been talked of, but Japan knows what "friendly intervention" by European Powers involves, and will have none of it. Russia also has little cause to love her neighbours. Why cannot the combatants come to terms themselves, disregarding every interest except their own?—Investors Review.

Mr. Yi Kiu-won has been dismissed from his post as Director of the Agricultural Bureau on account of his brother's (Yi Kiu-Chan) crime.

The difficulty of getting homing pigeons to carry messages outwards has been surmounted. They are to be crossed with parrots, so that they can ask the way!

The Japanese Consul at Masanpo has announced that in future martial-law will obtain in that district. Permission must be obtained from the military authorities by fishermen wishing to fish near certain islands on the coast

A COMING CAUSE CELEBRE.

London, Sept. 27,—The cause célèbre par excellence of the coming legal year is the action pending in the King's Bench against the Secretary of State for India brought by the trustee in bankruptcy of Prince Victor Albert Jay Duleep Singh. The pecuniary part of the claim is rather a complicated one. It includes a sum of £25,000, the value of a house belonging to the Maharajah Duleep Singh (Prince Victor's father) in 1857 and destroyed that year by the East India Company's soldiers. But the bulk of the claim (which runs into hundreds of thousands of pounds not yet calculated by the plaintiff) refers to the difference between the actual pension allowed to the Maharajah by the Indian Government down to his death and to his son Prince Victor afterwards, and the pension of £30,000 (between four and five lacs of rupees) covenanted to be paid by the East India Company in 1849 in return for the Maharajah's renunciation "for himself, his heirs and his successors, all right, title, and claim to the sovereignty of the Punjab or to any sovereignty power whatever." It is interesting to note that this Agreement of March 29, 1849, contained the famous clause:—The gem called the Koh-i-noor, which was taken from Shah Shooja-ool-Moolk by Maharajah Runjeet Singh (father of the Maharajah Duleep Singh), shall be surrendered by the Maharajah of Lahore to the Queen of England.

A Korean engineer is shortly to be despatched to Japan to undergo a course of practical study on Japanese railways.

The president of the Gensan branch of the Chin Po Hoi has presented Y1,000 to the relief of the families of Japanese soldiers in the field.

According to a medical report, the number of Scarletina cases in Seoul from Oct. 14th to the 10th inst. were 3,329. Only 10 deaths are recorded.

Upon Siberian borders
Stood a Russian, ill at ease,
He said: "Do I hear orders,
Or did the general sneeze?"

It is said that owing to outside pressure, the term of mourning for the late Crown Princess, already fixed at one year, will be slightly shortened.

Doctor—Well, Mr. Jenkins, did you follow my prescription? Jenkins—No. If I had, I should have broken my neck. Doctor—Why, what do you mean? Jenkins—I threw the prescription out of the window.

The Foreign Office are in receipt of a letter, from the Japanese military authorities, eulogising the conduct of 16 Korean officers, who were "told off" in February to look after the comfort of the Japanese officers, when marching through Korea.

According to a despatch, from Dukchong, the Russians have established military posts everywhere north of Songchin. It is difficult to estimate the number of Russian troops as they are placed in small bodies all over the country. Their Commanders refuse to allow newly appointed Korean officials to take up their positions in that district, as, they consider it not improbable that they may be Japanese spies.

The "Novoe Vremya" announces the despatch of 350 experienced ship's mechanics of various kinds, but chiefly builders, smiths, and boilermakers, from St. Petersburg to Vladivostock on Sept. 15. They each received a premium of 25 roubles (£2. 12.s), an allowance of 60 kopecks (1s.3d.) daily for expenses on the journey, and a free passage. They are to receive double the wages they would receive in St Petersburg free rations with a daily allowance of vodky, and the days spent on the journey out or home to, count as full days of work.

A private letter to the "China Review," from Japan says:—At this period of the year large quanties of merchandise are usually brought to the commercial centres from the rural districts of the country. The conditions are different, however, this year. Owing probably to the scarcity of transport facilities, there is no accumulation of goods in the Tokyo warehouses, and, to cite one instance, the amount of stores at the Tokyo Soko Kaisha shows a decrease of a million "yen" in value. A similar state of affairs prevails in Osaka and Kobe.

The Tokyo correspondent of the "Japan Herald" says:—I referred in my last letter to some peculiar means employed by the authorities to get the people to subscribe to the loans. A paragraph which, with slight modifications, appeared in the "Jiji," the "Kokumin" and other papers shows other methods at work. According to it, many families who have received compensation from the Government for the loss of their sons killed in the war have decided to consecrate that money (from Y200 to Y400 in the case of privates) to the purchase of war loan bonds, and animosity against the enemy has been so powerfully aroused by the sight of the wounded sent home that country people show a much greater disposition to invest their savings in the loans. So far, however, as I have been able to observe, the effect of the return of so many men wounded and maimed for life is quite different.

The Korea Daily News.

Issued at 5 P. M. daily except Sundays.

Rate of Subscription :—
Per Year,............Yen 25.
Per Quarter,..........Yen 7.
Per Month,..........Yen 2.50.

Postage in Korea not charged extra.
Postage abroad charged extra.

Advertisements, 50 sen per day for 1 inch or less.
5 yen per month per inch.
50 yen per year per inch.

All communications to
E. T. BETHELL,
Editor and Publisher,
Pak-tong, Seoul.

PROPHETS.

Prophets are always with us. In days of yore they were men "without honour in their own country," but prophets like other people have moved with the times and it appears that now-a-days they have just as strong a hold upon the credulous as ever they had.

In connection with horse-racing, prophets still do a thriving trade, weather prophets continue to beguile us into going out without our umbrellas, financial prophets continue to wax rich by sitting tight and ignoring all prophesies (their own included), and last but not least there is the war prophet.

The profession of prophesy is no longer the crude thing it used to be: it has made great strides and has called other sciences to its aid. First and foremost among these is the operation known as "hedging." Should we have any readers so unsophisticated as to be unaware of the meaning of this expression we may say that it corresponds, almost exactly, to the American expression "Sitting on the fence."

With this difference; A man "sitting on the fence" stays there until he decides which side it is safest to jump to, while a man who "hedges" jumps at once but is careful to provide himself with a means of making a dignified retreat if occasion arises.

Such are our modern prophets. Their moment of triumph comes when they are able to arise, point to an event and say, impressively, "I TOLD YOU SO."

To achieve this end they "hedge," and in this connection we quote the following from the "Times" (London) military correspondent on September 23rd, written after the battle of Liaoyang but before the Shaho engagement. The military correspondent says:—

"The Russians still retain their card of re entry so long as they hold Tie-ling, and Tie-ling is not an easy place to take. Moreover, we have long ago pointed out that Prince Khilkoff, the Russian Minister of Ways and Communications was a more dangerous enemy for Japan than Kuropatkin himself. Khilkoff could get his ideas carried out; Kuropatkin, with inferior tools, could not.

"This Minister, very early in the war, displayed intelligent energy, and we had to label him dangerous. He not only knew what to do, but—rarest of gifts—he knew how to do it, and the railway troops and employes under him proved their competence from the very start. The railway administration has entirely disabused our minds of faith in the very misleading assurances given before the war by a British officer of engineers, of some experience in railway work, to the effect that the Trans-Siberian would break down under the stress of continuous traffic. On the contrary, it has steadily improved. Many months ago we had to point out that, although our estimate of from four to six military trains a day represented, so far as we could judge, the actual traffic on the line, we should be compelled continually to alter these figures owing to the work in progress, and we mentioned the month of August as the time when Japan would be compelled to increase largely her military forces in Manchuria in order to cope successfully with the growing facilities of Russian transport. Official estimates are wanting, but it will have been remarked some weeks ago, when some of the officers and men of the "Knight Commander" were sent home by rail from Vladivostock, and that the estimate of the through traffic they gave exceeded all previous calculations upon which trust could be placed. If this opinion was unskilled, it was at least unprejudiced and independent. No other opinion was vouchsafed until a few days ago when our Paris correspondent quoted M. Marcel Hutin of the "Echo de Paris," as sending word from St. Petersburg that 1,700 men with guns and ammunition were passing Kharbin daily. On the whole, we are disposed to believe that this information is correct and that it must represent a through traffic of 12 military trains a day.

We have also to consider that the harvest throughout Manchuria has been exceptionally abundant, and that Kuropatkin at Tie-ling has still a rich country at his back, even though he has lost the lower valley of the Liao and cannot rely upon easy means of communication with Pechili. All the circumstances combine to improve Russia's chance and to require a much greater effort on the part of Japan than has hitherto been necessary. If we were prepared to allow that 6 trains a day could, on an average and continuously, reinforce the army by 800 to 1,000 men a day, and maintain an army of 250,000 men efficient, we must naturally admit that double the number of trains can double the out put "of reinforcements and supply" "double the previous effectives" though also at double the cost when they are on the field.

It is also certain that, when once the maximum strength of the army has been reached and all the units have been provided with transport, the subsequent despatch of drafts to maintain the corps and services at full strength should present no insuperable difficulties. Given that this improved situation was reached about the end of July, the full fruits cannot, of course, be gathered for some months to come, and in the interval Japan must make a corresponding effort, and must suit her strategy to the changing circumstances.

Here we have a typical instance of how "hedging" is accomplished. The "Times" military correspondent is saying "I told you so." A search through all his previous writings would take a very long time, so we are content to accept his word for it that he did tell us so, but we are equally satisfied with our conviction that his opinions in this connection are being prominently put forth for the first time.

The "Times" military correspondent is apparently ill-pleased with his position of having to admit that the Russians can place men and supplies in the field to double the amount originally estimated by him, as he points out that the cost will also be double! We may add that they will take up double the room, breathe double the amount of air and take double the amount of killing, burial and praying for.

Poor old prophet! We are neither pro-Russian nor pro-Japanese; our sympathies are confined to Korea; but we cannot help being amused at this *volte-face* on the part of the critically judicious, cocksure military correspondent of the London "Times."

At the beginning of the war Japan came in for so many columns of sickening adulation written for the home papers by men who took the Japanese at their own valuation that we are glad to see praise being more equally divided. It will do Japan no harm, as men who have held Japan in esteem have been driven to dislike the very name on account of the nauseating eulogies which have until recently intruded upon the space of almost every magazine and newspaper in England. A little adverse criticism will do Japan no harm and will lose her none of her friends.

STEEL PLATES FOR HONGKONG.

According to the Portland, Ore., "Telegram," Mr. James J. Hill has asked Mr. E. H. Harriman to transport 3,000 tons of steel plates to Hongkong. The plates were shipped from Eastern mills to Puget Sound, and were to have been sent from the Northern Pacific terminal on Hill steamers to the Orient. The reason for the Northern Pacific's action in desiring the steel re-shipped from Portland to the Orient, is not clear to shipping men, but it is believed that the war situation has influenced the action of the Northern Pacific. It cannot be learned what action the Harriman interests will take in the matter.

GETTING EVEN WITH THE LANDLORD.

A man recently took a house upon a lease in a certain crescent in London without examining the terms of his agreement as closely as he should. After a time the landlord called upon him and pointed out that he was bound to do all the outside painting at certain intervals. He protested, but it was "so nominated in the bond," and there was no help for him. After a good deal of thought he hired the painters and directed them to paint the whole of the front of the house red, white and blue—in stripes. When it was finished, the neighborhood—it was rather a fashionable part—was up in arms, and the landlord was frantic. The tenant politely explained to him that there was nothing in the agreement about the colour and that red, white and blue, in stripes, was his favourite combination, but he thought he might, perhaps, be better pleased with the painting of the back, which he proposed to colour green, with yellow spots.

The landlord, who well knew that not another house could be let in the crescent if he carried out his threat, nearly had a fit at the idea, and within a week the tenant had a new lease, in which the landlord undertook to do all the outside painting himself.

Work on the new lighthouse, in the course of construction on Chil Pal Do, has been temporarly suspended owing to the rough weather at sea.

The Japanese soldier reiceives forty-five cents a month. Cannot something be done to protect Russia against the pauper labour of Asia?—The Louisville Courier-Journal.

The British torpedo boat destroyer "Chamois" has been lost off the Island of Cephalonia, in the Mediterranean. All on board were saved. While going at full speed on a trial, a screw blade came off and pierced the bottom of the destroyer. Two stokers were scalded.

The Korea Daily News.

VOL. I, TUESDAY, NOVEMBER 15, 1904. No. 101

HONGKONG & SHANGHAI BANKING CORPORATION.

Paid-up Capital..... ....$10,000,000
Reserve Fund:—Sterling Reserve... 10,000,000
Silver Reserve..... 7,000,000

27,000,000
Reserve Liability of Proprietors... 10,000,000

HEAD OFFICE, HONGKONG.

London Bankers, London and County Banking Company Limited.
Branches and Agencies,
London.

Amoy,	Hankow	Penang.
Bangkok,	Hiogo,	Rangoon,
Batavia,	Iloilo,	Saigon,
Bombay,	Lyons,	San Francisco,
Calcutta,	Manila,	Singapore,
Colombo,	Nagasaki,	Sourabaya,
Foochow,	New York,	Tientsin,
Hamburg,	Peking,	Yokohama,

Credits granted on approved Securities, and every description of Banking and Exchange business transacted.

Drafts granted on London and the chief Commercial places in Europe, India, Australia, America, China and Japan.

HOLME RINGER & Co., AGENTS,
CHEMULPO.

ON CHEONG & CO.,
SEOUL.
GENERAL STORE KEEPERS.
Imported provisions, Cooking Utensils Crockery, etc.
FRESH BREAD DAILY.

MITSU BISHI DOCKYARD & ENGINE WORKS,
NAGASAKI.

CODE WORD, "DOCK."

A. 1, A. B. C., and Engineering Codes used.

DOCK No. 1 (at Tategami).

Extreme Length..............523 feet
Length on blocks..............513 ,,
Width of Entrance on Top......89 ,,
,, ,, Bottom....77 ,,
Water on Blocks at Spring Tide 26½ ,,

DOCK No. 2 (Mukaijima).

Extreme Length..............371 feet
Length on Blocks.............360 ,,
Width of Entrance on Top......66 ,,
,, ,, Bottom 53 ,,
Water on Blocks at Spring Tide 22 ,,

PATENT SLIP (at Kosuge).

Can take vessels up to 1,000 tons gross

THE WORKS are well equipped with the LATEST IMPROVEMENTS, and can execute any kind of work in SHIPBUILDING and MARINE ENGINEERING, as well as in REPAIRING of SHIPS.

The COMPANY'S new powerful steamer OURA-MARU (712 tons, 700 I.H.P.), specially built for SALVAGE PURPOSES, and equipped with necessary gear, is always READY at SHORT NOTICE.

CHARTERED BANK OF INDIA AUSTRALIA & CHINA.

INCORPORATED BY ROYAL CHARTER 1853

HEAD OFFICES:—LONDON.

Paid-up Capital £800,000
Reserve Liability of Shareholders 800,000
Reserve Fund 800,000

Drafts granted upon all the principal places in the world and every description of Exchange and banking business transacted.

E. MEYER & Co., Agents,
Chemulpo.

E. MEYER & CO.

Chemulpo.

SOLE AGENTS IN KOREA FOR:

A. T. Morse, Sons & Co's "Fresco" Distemper

In all colours ready for use on walls, Ceilings etc.
and
AVENARIUS CARBOLINEUM

A wood-preserving and antiseptic oil preparation

Against decay, dry-rot, fungus and wood-destroying insects.

A large supply always in Stock.
Prices upon application.

E. MEYER & Co.,
Chemulpo.

THE METHODIST PUBLISHING HOUSE.
Little West Gate, Seoul.

JOB PRINTING, TYPEWRITER PAPER
CARBON PAPER, VISITING CARDS
STATIONERY, BOOK BINDING
BOOK PUBLISHERS
AMERICAN SCHOOL BOOKS
SPENCERIAN COPY BOOKS
PEN CARBON LETTER AND BILL BOOKS

S. A. BECK, Manager.

HOKURKU DOBOKU KAISHA.

Branch office in Chong Dong, Seoul.

Japanese telephone No. 165

CONTRACT DEPARTMENT.

We can contract to build any building or construction.

MERCHANDISE DEPARTMENT.

We can provide any building material. We have just contracted to build the new Belgian Legation.

DAI-ICHI GINKO.

LIMITED.

(Formerly the First National Bank)

ESTABLISHED 1873

INCORPORATED UNDER PRESENT LAW 1896

Capital - - - - - - - - - Yen 5,000,000
Reserve Fund - - - - - 1,500,000

HEAD OFFICE:—TOKIO.

President: Baron SHIBUSAWA.

BRANCHES AND CORRESPONDENTS
In the Principal Cities and Towns of Japan.

Interest Allowed on
Fixed deposits 1 year - - - 6½ per cent
" " 6 months - - - 6 per cent

Special current accounts 1½ sen daily per Y 100
General " " 1 " " " 100

M. TANAKA,
Manager, Chemulpo.

HOLME RINGER & Co.

Chemulpo.

General Merchants and Government Contractors.

Agents for the leading

Banks

Steamship Companies

and

Insurance Companies

Importers of Merchandise of every description.

KAMEYA & CO.

GENERAL STOREKEEPERS
Chinkokai - - Seoul
(Established 1895. Tokyo)

Confectionery, Hams, Canned Goods, Cutlery, Hirano & Tansan Water. Provisions, Gents, Furnishing goods, Toilet Articles, Travelling Bags, Tobacco, Cigars & Cigarettes Kitchen Utensils. Coffee. Biscuits.

Fresh Goods always kept in Stock.
Prices Moderate
Please come and inspect our goods

NIPPON YUSEN KAISHA.

JAPANESE MAIL STEAMSHIP CO.

UNDER MAIL CONTRACT WITH THE IMPERIAL JAPANESE GOVERNMENT.

European Line

Regular Fortnightly Service between Yokohama Kobe, Moji, Shanghai, Hongkong, Singapore, Penang Colombo, Port Said, Marseilles, London and Antwerp

American Line

Regular Fortnightly Service between Hongkong and Seattle, calling at Shanghai, Moji, Kobe, Yokohama and Victoria, B. C.

Australian Line

Regular weekly Service betweu Japan Ports and Australia, calling at Hongkong and Manila.

(Above Three Lines Suspended until further notice).

Shanghai Line

Weekly Service between Shanghai and Japan Ports

Korea Line

Service Kobe, Moji, Nagasaki, Fusan Chemulpo Chefoo, Taiku.
S. S. Babelsberg, 2151 tons.
Service Kobe, Moji, Fusan, Chemulpo, Chinnampo
S. S. Argo, S. S. Ohio

BORDEN'S CONDENSED MILK CO.

New York, U. S. A.

ALWAYS IN STOCK

Eagle Brand Condensed Milk.

Gold Seal Condensed Milk.

Peerless (Family) Evaporated Cream.

Borden's Malted Milk.

E. MEYER & CO.
Chemulpo, Korea,
Sole Agents

ROYAL INSURANCE COMPANY,
Funds exceed £10,000,000
FIRE
AT CURRENT RATES.
LIFE
REDUCED PREMIUM.
HOLME RINGER & Co.,
Agents, Chemulpo.

HOTEL DU PALAIS

SEOUL.

The only first class Hotel in Seoul. Situated in the centre of the city opposite the palace.

Cuisine under the supervision of an experienced French Chef.

Well ventilated and furnished throughout.

TARIFF UPON APPLICATION

L. MARTIN
Proprietor and Manager.

大韓每日申報
대한미일신보

(뎨일빅이호) (목요일) 일쳔구빅사년십일월십칠일

본사고빅

이신보는영어와한어로셔계리
일츌판ᄒᆞ웁
신문갑
한쟝 엽두돈오푼
일삭도 엽두량엿돈
우표가미삭닷돈
다엿돈으로밧숩
광고료는
귀한의쟝단과ᄎᆞ흥의디쇼로중
감ᄒᆞ되혐가로밧을터이오며오
리지아니ᄒᆞ야대한사람마다다이신
문을보실터이니광고ᄒᆞ시기를
원ᄒᆞ시는이들은우리신문사에
와셔면약ᄒᆞ심을희망ᄒᆞ웁
◯발힝소 박동대한미일신보
사벽여학교압헤젼영국인셰필
림쟝자리오
사쟝 영국인 (베셜)
평양 디리졈
◯평양효동사는 권미보씨로우
리신문판매디리인을뎡ᄒᆞ엿
ᄉᆞ오니평양에계신구람코져ᄒᆞ
시는 쳠군ᄌᆞ는권씨디리졈에왕
림ᄒᆞ와면회ᄒᆞ시ᄋᆞ웁

사고

◯우리대한미일신보의목뎍은
대한의안녕질서에관ᄒᆞᆫ모든대
목에디ᄒᆞ야는공평ᄒᆞᆫ변론을주
쟝ᄒᆞᆷ이라우리동신원의탐보는
신문보시는쳠군ᄌᆞ의게ᄒᆞᆼ샹보
도ᄒᆞ려니와편지들과셔ᄒᆞ며주사
논이는셩명과반ᄃᆞ시뎍어보내치
시기를희망ᄒᆞ오나비ᄅᆞ게슴신문
샹에게뎨ᄒᆞ라는거시아니오타
만국공신ᄒᆞ논증거를숨고자
ᄒᆞᆷ이라과자는아모과서든지과
저ᄒᆞᆷ을뢰각ᄒᆞ는권리를가젓ᄉᆞ
나뢰ᄎᆞᆨᄒᆞ는리유를말ᄒᆞᆯ터이오
며공중평론을문란케ᄒᆞ는듯ᄒᆞᆫ
귀셔는의례히밧지안켓ᄉᆞ나이
다

●본사셜시이리로신문을미양
우례로분젼ᄒᆞ와례젼부의임의
로젼ᄒᆞ든ᄃᆞ시로번곳에는ᄒᆞ는듯게
젼ᄒᆞ기도ᄒᆞ며ᄒᆞ면칠거슬ᄒᆞᆫ집
에젼ᄒᆞ기도ᄒᆞ며ᄒᆞ아니젼ᄒᆞ는
곳도잇다ᄒᆞ시와우리신문을ᄉᆞ랑
ᄒᆞ야구람ᄒᆞ시는 쳠군ᄌᆞ의게
미ᄒᆞ야미우미안ᄒᆞ온바기로지금
은분젼인을두고미일즉이젼
ᄒᆞ며아니젼ᄒᆞ거나늣게거나ᄒᆞᆫ
가엽도록ᄒᆞ랏ᄒᆞ오니ᄒᆞ야니
젼ᄒᆞ게는ᄒᆞᆯ듯게젼ᄒᆞ거나ᄒᆞᆫ일
이잇스면본사로통긔ᄒᆞ여주심
을희망ᄒᆞ웁

관보

뎨이쳔구빅팔십삼호
광무팔년십일월십ᄉᆞ일
셔임급ᄉᆞ령
◯궁내부참봉 니부종두ᄉᆞ의ᄉᆞ
박형리
십일월십일일
◯임피지부ᄌᆞ셔관입판홍등
챵릉참봉 리지근
죵뎡부ᄉᆞ
◯총호소ᄉᆞ셔리군명근 주원
소봉상령산ᄉᆞ를평관상소로궁
속거힝ᄉᆞ로쟝예원으로 주하
의리니간신ᄎᆞ로본감제됴리주
명과쟝예원소경민영돈과합과
대신일시셔리리진하가상디관
등을게는리교금일츌거ᄒᆞᆯ뜻으
로군상 주ᄒᆞ와
광무팔년십일월십일일에봉 지
의주ᄒᆞ다
◯총호소ᄉᆞ셔리군명근 주국
장도감을금일에이믜시역ᄒᆞ엿
승으로당쳥과감조관등일원으
로의례은회상디ᄒᆞᆯ뜻으로감
주ᄒᆞ와
광무팔년십일월십일일에봉
지의주ᄒᆞ다
◯륙군무관학교관제
뎨일됴 륙군무관학교는륙군
각병과무관학도의게초급무
관됨에필요ᄒᆞᆫ교육을힝ᄒᆞᆷ이
라
뎨이됴 학도의교육은이거슬
교슈와훈육에분ᄒᆞ니그강령
은교육총감이뎡ᄒᆞᆷ이라
뎨삼됴 학도교육에실시ᄒᆞ는교
쟝이구안ᄒᆞ야교육총감의인
가를쳥ᄒᆞ야뎡ᄒᆞᆷ이라
뎨ᄉᆞ됴 본교의직원은여좌ᄒᆞᆷ
이라
교쟝 일인 참쟝흑졍령
부관 일인 졍위
교관 십팔인 부참령샹인
각병과졍위십인외국어학과
에오인 주판임문관
의관 일인 일이등군의
슈의 일인 일이등슈의
향관 일인 일이등군ᄉᆞ
주번역관 이인 주임
슈ᄉᆞ 삼인 판임
학도디쟝 교관중겸임
일인 부참령
학도디부관 일인 부위
학도디중디쟝 삼인 졍
위
학도디부 십이인 각병
과부참위
륙무졍교 삼인
조교 삼십오인 각병과
졍부교
뎨오됴 교쟝은교육총감의게
예ᄒᆞ야교무를총리ᄒᆞ며학도
를교육ᄒᆞ는직칙에임ᄒᆞᆷ이라
뎨륙됴 부관은교니셔무를주
쟝ᄒᆞᆷ이라
뎨칠됴 군ᄉᆞ학교관은군ᄉᆞ학
각과의슈업을담ᄒᆞ야밋교련
관교관은각과의교쟝이됨이
라
뎨팔됴 마술교관은학도의마
술훈련ᄒᆞ는디임ᄒᆞ고쇼학교
마구일졀ᄉᆞ무와마필의교도
를주쟝ᄒᆞᆷ이라
뎨구됴 문관교관은외국어학
의슈업을담ᄒᆞ야맛ᄒᆞᆷ이라
뎨십됴 의관은교니위싱ᄉᆞ무
를주쟝ᄒᆞᆷ이라
뎨십일됴 슈의는교니마필위
싱ᄉᆞ무를주쟝ᄒᆞᆷ이라
뎨십이됴 향관은회계ᄉᆞ무를
주쟝ᄒᆞᆷ이라
뎨십삼됴 번역관은번역과통
역의ᄉᆞ무를주쟝ᄒᆞᆷ이라
뎨십ᄉᆞ됴 쥬ᄉᆞ는부관의지휘
를밧아문부셔긔의ᄉᆞ무에맛
ᄒᆞᆷ이라
뎨십오됴 학도디쟝은학도디
를거ᄂᆞ려학도의훈육을감독
ᄒᆞ고각중디쟝으로ᄒᆞ여곰각
기훈육을맛게ᄒᆞ며교쟝의게
디ᄒᆞ야이를쳬진보케ᄒᆞ는직칙
에맛ᄒᆞᆷ이라
뎨십륙됴 중디쟝은학도디부
위관을지휘ᄒᆞ야중디학도의
훈육을담임ᄒᆞ고그셩젹에칙
ᄒᆞ야는면디맛ᄒᆞᆷ이라
뎨십칠됴 학도디부위관은학
도교육의제과목을나노와맛
고ᄒᆞᆼ샹학도의근힝을감시ᄒᆞ
며분담ᄒᆞᆫ훈육에칙ᄒᆞ야는그
직칙에임ᄒᆞᆷ이라

뎐보

십일월십삼일일본공ᄉᆞ관
착뎐
대산만주군총ᄉᆞ령관보고
가좌와ᄀᆞᆺᄒᆞ니
◯로병격퇴 군의좌익방면에
는십일월십일밤중에무진티
젼면에적병이와서음습ᄒᆞ엿스
나일본군ᄉᆞ의게격퇴되엿다ᄒᆞ
고 ᄯᅩ십일월구일에는소ㅣ시
둔방면에쳥츌ᄒᆞᆫ적군은보병이
빅과긔병샹빅인디일본슈비디
의게격퇴되야마ᄎᆞᆷ조로퇴각ᄒᆞ
엿는디적의손상은흑십여명이
오일본군의손상자는륙칠명에
지나지아니ᄒᆞ엿다ᄒᆞ엿더라
동일만주군총ᄉᆞ령부발경
셩ᄉᆞ령부착공보
◯샹동 군의좌익방면오가ᄌᆞ
에적병이쳥로ᄒᆞ야드러왓셧스
나격퇴ᄒᆞᆷ이되야대한티ᄌᆞ로퇴
각ᄒᆞ엿다ᄒᆞ엿더라
동일동경발
◯참호졈령 이통신과ᄉᆞ슈산
젼면에잇는대규모의히ᄌᆞ논일
군의게졈령ᄒᆞᆫ비되엿는티로군
의셜비ᄒᆞᆫ대포는소구경포외에
는스케되지못ᄒᆞ엿더라
동일동뎐
◯로병압ᄉᆞ 이통신과ᄉᆞ수산
후면의히ᄌᆞ논일군포탄에히파
ᄒᆞᆷ이되야흠탕ᄒᆞ리가헤여져ᄂᆞᆫ
논교로로군의슈비병이만히압
ᄉᆞᄒᆞ엿다ᄒᆞ엿더라

잡보

◯슈도ᄉᆞ건리쟝 일본인조쳔
쳥번씨도금은로담당ᄒᆞᆫ궁중슈
도ᄉᆞ논미국놈ᄉᆞ가지샹ᄎᆞ외부
대신의게향ᄒᆞ야ᄒᆞ더니금번에외
부대신이미용수와교셥ᄒᆞᆫ거ᄉᆞᆯ과
로휘수건에두어가지됴약을부
쳐됴쳔씨의공역ᄉᆞ안을승인ᄒᆞᆯ
모양이잇더라
◯치젹힝자 평북티인ᄋᆞ젼셜
을ᄃᆞ로죵관챨ᄉᆞ쟝승원씨는도
임ᄒᆞᆫ후로민ᄉᆞ를죵ᄉᆞᆨ거ᄅᆞᆯ쳐ᄒᆞ고
힝링ᄒᆞᆯ졈ᄌᆞᄒᆞ야쳥촉이힝ᄒᆞᆯ아
니ᄒᆞ고관사송과소지를일졀듬소
싱야부치ᄒᆞ기셩빙ᄒᆞ며부중
에붓잡아ᄒᆞᆫ기영금ᄒᆞ미인민
수가헌젹이으로습집ᄒᆞᆫ는
자ㅣ마는지비하ᄒᆞᆫ셔ᄂᆞᆫ아셔로
젼ᄒᆞ야외오기들이잡민이도안
ᄒᆞ로쳥펀지도쓸티업고쥬ᄉᆞ셔

UNION INSURANCE SOCIETY OF CANTON.

Head office Hongkong.
Marine risks underwritten at current rates.
Agents in Chemulpo,
E. MEYER & Co.

COMPAGNIE DES MESSAGERIES MARITIMES.

Fortnightly Direct Service.

For Marseilles
via Ports.
Sailing from Yokohama
Calling at Kobe,
Shanghai, Hongkong, Saigon, Singapore,
Colombo, Djibouti, Suez, Port Said
and Marseilles.

For particulars apply to
HOLME RINGER & Co.,
Chemulpo.

HAYASHIDA & Co.,

16 MYENG DONG, CHIN KO KAI, SEOUL.
BRANCH OFFICE AT CHEMULPO.

Money changers, Coal and Wood Merchants, Express Agents.

We are agents for the Pyeng-yang Coal Company and the Karazu Coal Company of Japan. We have the best quality of both anthracite and bituminous coal, and prompt execution of orders is our speciality. Firewood of all kinds kept in stock. Full weight guaranteed. Money of all denominations exchanged at current rates. Parcels received for all parts.

CHINA MUTUAL LIFE INS. CO.

Most favourable terms to policy holders.

Benefit system unsurpassed.

HOLME RINGER & Co.
Agents, Chemulpo.

C. P. R.

CANADIAN PACIFIC RAILWAY COMPANY'S ROYAL MAIL STEAMSHIP LINE.

THE FAST ROUTE BETWEEN CHINA, JAPAN, AND EUROPE VIA CANADA AND THE UNITED STATES.

Route from Hongkong via Shanghai, Nagasaki (Inland Sea of Japan) Kobe, Yokohama Victoria and Vancouver.

Twin Screw Empress Steamship 6,000 Tons—Speed 19 knots.

PROPOSED SAILING FROM YOKOHAMA.

R. M. S. Empress of India.
R. M. S. Empress of Japan.
R. M. S. Empress of China.
R. M. S. Athenian.
R. M. S. Tartar.

Special reduction (first class only) granted to members of the Military, Naval, Diplomatic and Civil services and to Missionaries.

Passengers have choice of ten routes across the Continent of America and have privilege of travelling by any Atlantic Steamship Line.

Round the World passage tickets in connection with the P. and O. S. N., North German Lloyd and Messageries Co.'s £125.

All rates payable at current rate of exchange.

For further information, Tickets, Guide Books, etc., apply to

HOLME, RINGER & CO., AGENTS,
Chemulpo.

Grand Hotel,

(Formerly the Station Hotel)

Near the Railway Terminus, West Gate Seoul.

The Best Hotel in Korea
Handsome new Building.
Fine Airy Rooms
Excellent Cuisine.
Terms Moderate.
Special terms to Missionaries
and to permanent boarders.

Electric cars within 2 minutes' walk.

W. H. EMBERLEY,
Proprietor

EVERY FACILITY.

In connection with Life Assurance Business is afforded by

The Standard Life Assurance Co.,

One of the largest and wealthiest of the Provident Institutions of the United Kingdom Forms of Application and all information will be promptly afforded on application.

10 CENTS A DAY.

Not a very large expenditure is it? But it is sufficient to secure for a man of 30 a policy with the STANDARD LIFE OFFICE for

$1323.

For all particulars of rates, etc., apply to

Holme, Ringer & Co.,
Agents, Chemulpo.

THE NEW YORK LIFE INSURANCE COMPANY.

Have you ever been declined by any Company?

Are you engaged in a specially hazardous occupation?

Have you heard of the New York Life Insurance Company's New Classifications for this class of Risks?

If not, send your date of birth, occupation and particulars of rejection, if any to

E. MEYER & Co.,
Agents, Chemulpo.

MITSUI BUSSAN KAISHA.
(MITSUI & Co.)

MITSUI GINKO.
(MITSUI BANK.)

The Bank is owned by the members of the Mitsui Family, who, as partners, assume an unlimited responsibility for all liabilities of the Bank:—

Capital .... Yen 5,000,000
Reserve Fund .... " 5,600,000

HEAD OFFICE, TOKYO.
LONDON OFFICE, 34 LIME ST., E. C.

BRANCHES AND AGENCIES:—
New York, San Francisco, Hamburg, Bombay, Singapore, Manila, Hongkong, Amoy, Chefoo, Tientsin.

Kobe, Hakodate, Yokohama, Kure, Yokosuka, Moji, Shimonoseki, Miike, Wakamatsu, Nagasaki, Kuchinotsu, Karatsu, Sasebo, Misume, Taipeh, &c.

Telegraphic Address for all the Offices:
"MITSUI."
A. B. C. AND A. 1 CODES USED.

Contractors of Coal
To the Imperial Japanese Navy. Arsenals and Railway Bureau, Principal Railway Companies and Industrial Work, Home and Foreign Mail and Freight Steamers.

Sole Proprietors
Of the famous Miike, Tagawa and Yamano Coal Mines.

Sole Agents
For the sale of Fukumo, Hokoku, Ichimura, Kanoda, Mannoura, Onoura, Ostuji, Sonoda Tsubaruro, Yoshinotani, Yoshio, Yurokibura and other coals.

YANGTSE INSURANCE ASSOCIATION, LTD.

The undersigned, having been appointed agents for the above company, are prepared to issue policies and pay losses on marine risks at regular rates.

E. MEYER & Co.,
Agents, Chemulpo.

AMERICAN KOREAN ELECTRIC CO.

Light and Power.

Main Office: Electric Building, Chong No.

RAILWAY DEPARTMENT.

OPERATING CARS BETWEEN EAST AND WEST GATE, EVERY TEN MINUTES:—

First Car leaves East Gate at 7:00 A. M. First Car leaves R. R. Station at 7:25 A. M
Last Car " East Gate at 10:05 P. M. Last " " R. R. Station at 9:40 P.M

OPERATING CARS BETWEEN EAST GATE AND IMPERIAL TOMB TERMINUS, EVERY TWENTY MINUTES:—
CONNECTING WITH EVERY ALTERNATE CAR ARRIVING AT EAST GATE FROM CHONG NO.

First Car leaves East Gate for Tomb at 7:10 A. M.
" " " Tomb for East Gate at 7:35 A. M.
Last " " East Gate for Tomb at 7:50 P. M.
" " " Tomb for East Gate at 8:10 P. M.

OPERATING CARS BETWEEN CHONG NO AND YUNG SAN RIVER EVERY TWELVE MINUTES:—

First Car leaves Chong No for South Gate at 7:12 A. M.
" " " Chong No for Yung San at 7:36 A. M.
" " " South Gate for Chong No at 7:20 A. M.
" " " Yung San for Chong No at 8:09 A. M.
Last " " South Gate for Chong No 10:00 P. M.
" " " Yung San for Chong No at 9:33 P. M.

SPECIAL PRIVATE CARS FURNISHED TO SUIT CONVENIENCE OF PATRONS. PRICES ON APPLICATION AT HEAD OFFICE.

LIGHTING DEPARTMENT

Where less than 250 candle power of light is used, the rate per month will be
Per 16 candle power incandescent lamp,—All night.—Yen 2.50.
32 candle power incandescent lamp:—All night:—Yen 4.00.
50 candle power incandescent lamp:—All night:—Yen 6.00.
150 " " " " " " 10.00.
1200 " " enclosed arc " " " 20.00.

Where more than 250 candle power of light is used, a Meter will be installed, if requested:—Rent of Meter Yen 2.00 per month. Rate of charges by meter reading:—Two Sen per Ampere per hour. (Approximately this is equal to about One Sen per 16 C. P. lamp per hour) Minimum monthly charge where meter is installed, Yen 20.00 per month, which includes rental of meter.

Estimates for installing lights furnished on application.

An assortment of chandeliers always on hand.

K. Murakami,
Photograph Studio
Chinkokai, Seoul.

Printing, Developing and Enlargement, of Photographs always Undertaken.

Korean Views and Pictures Illustrating Native Customs always on Sale,

---

THE OSAKA SHOSEN KAISHA.

Boats frequently on the berth for Chinnampo.

REGULAR SAILINGS BETWEEN JAPAN AND KOREAN PORTS.

FUSAN AND KOBE VIA SHIMONOSEKI.

OSAKA VIA MOKPO, FUSAN, SHIMONOSEKI AND KOBE.

MOJI DIRECT.

OSAKA VIA KUNSAN, MASANPO, FUSAN, SHIMONOSEKI AND KOBE.

CHEMULPO KUNSAN LINE,
Every three days.

CHEMULPO CHINNAMPO LINE.
Every three days.

For Freight and passage and further particulars apply to

THE OSAKA SHOSEN KAISHA,
Chemulpo.

LONDON, PLAISANT & CO.

General Storekeepers and Merchants, Ships Contractors, Tobacconists, Commission and Forwarding Agents, Coal Merchants

IMPORTERS AND EXPORTERS

Seoul & Chemulpo.

W. D. WENTWORTH.

LANDING
AND
SHIPPING AGENT
AND
CUSTOMS BROKER.

12 OURA, NAGASAKI.

STEWARD & CO.

Chemulpo.

Shipchandlers and Storekeepers, Naval and Mercantile Contractors, Landing and Shipping Agents.

STEWARD'S HOTEL

Chemulpo.

Best accommodation in the port for travellers. Clean and well-aired rooms, good cuisine prompt attendance, moderate tariff.

긔노쓸ᄃᆡ엄고숀진경ᄉᆞ도쓸ᄃᆡ엄고기셩도쓸ᄃᆡ엄다고ᄒᆞᄂᆞᆫ동요가파다ᄒᆞ더라

○리병ᄌᆞ됴사 한셩니에셔풍열병에방위원이오셔니에병든자치료ᄒᆞᆫ슈ᄅᆞᆯ위원장의게보고ᄒᆞ엿ᄂᆞᆫᄃᆡ십월십ᄉᆞ일로ᄇᆡ로븟소본월십일ᄭᆞ지병든자삼쳔삼ᄇᆡᆨ이십구인ᄂᆡ에죽은자ㅣ일쳔명이라더라

○션쳔보관 종졍원에셔ᄂᆡ부로조회ᄒᆞ기ᄅᆞᆯ금번션쳔보관계ᄉᆔ졍ᄒᆞᆯ됴진이실노만하ᄒᆞᆫ권에ᄉᆡ분의이나되니진에잇든됴진을반드시기졍ᄒᆞᆫ연후에아가히취용완셩ᄒᆞ겟스니외각군에잇ᄂᆞᆫ됴진을모도모화올녀보ᄂᆡ게ᄒᆞ라ᄒᆞᆫ지라ᄂᆡ부에셔십삼도관찰부로훈령ᄒᆞ엿더라

○문쳔진보회 문쳔군수명우셥씨가ᄂᆡ부로보고ᄒᆞ엿ᄂᆞᆫ니기에음력구월이십삼일졍오에ᄃᆡ양븍납우자몃사ᄅᆞᆷ이진보회회쟝이라칭ᄒᆞ고단발ᄒᆞᆫ자과ᄇᆡᆨ명을ᄋᆞᆸ니로모화노코기명ᄒᆞ며나라ᄒᆞᆯ도를을ᄂᆞᆫ등수로써의쟝쥬연셜ᄒᆞ고각기도라갓다ᄒᆞ엿더라

○슈립일어학교 회동사ᄂᆞᆫ최등셥씨가사립일어학교ᄅᆞᆯ셜시ᄒᆞ고학도를모집ᄒᆞ야졔쟉십오일브터기학ᄒᆞ엿더라

○사찰위원젼졍 일진회에셔ᄉᆞ찰위원ᄇᆡᆨ이십오명을션졍ᄒᆞ야동셔남븍중오셔에각기이십오명식파츌ᄒᆞ야수찰케ᄒᆞ엿더라

○의관조현 궁ᄂᆡ부에셔졍빅ᄒᆞ든의관들쟝죠ᄎᆞᆯᄒᆞᆫ츠로 주본월드리 지가나린지라 의관유풍경씨등ᄉᆞ인이광리원에조현취슈ᄒᆞᆫ고로광리원에셔ᄇᆞᆸ부로보고ᄒᆞ엿더라

○원소광구 졔쟉십오일에샹티관들이 원소ᄅᆞᆯ넙니구ᄎᆞ로동대문밧그로ᄊᆞ나갓다더라

○비왕명명일 졔쟉십오일은비ᄅᆞ시국대군쥬명명ᄒᆞ신날인ᄃᆡ일본국영국법국덕국쳥국이ᄐᆡ리국공ᄉᆞ와령ᄉᆞ들과한뎡각ᄃᆡ관들이샹오열두시에비국공관에일졔이가셔츅하ᄒᆞ엿더라

○쟝괴군효슈 셔소문안븍차다리셔ᄉᆞᄂᆞᆫ쳥인쟝가의집에셔한국ᄇᆡᆨ뎡들과몃쳥민몃ᄎᆡ모혀샹작일밤에잡긔ᄒᆞ쇼ᄇᆡ리교ᄒᆞᄂᆞᆫ고로일본헌병과한국순검이곳드러가붓들어잡아노코호유ᄒᆞᆫ후에곳다방숑ᄒᆞ엿더라

○역부티젼 탁지부에셔각부부원쳥ᄇᆡᆫ인의게미명하에역부ᄇᆡ로티젼을이원오십젼식지발ᄒᆞ엿더라

○면죠잉유 이졔동졍에졔지ᄒᆞᆫᄒᆞ부대신리지국씨의귀국ᄒᆞ기ᄂᆞᆫ상이월셔지언괴ᄒᆞ엿다ᄒᆞ더니겡눈ᄒᆞᆫ즉동씨가본월이십ᄉᆞ오일즘ᄒᆞ야동경발ᄒᆞᆫ다고면보가왓스며ᄯᅩ쳥영운씨의게셔도이졔 황태ᄌᆞ비ᄒᆞ셔ᄒᆞ신에티ᄒᆞ야슉히귀국ᄒᆞ겟스니 폐하셰 샹쥬ᄒᆞ라고 궁ᄂᆡ부셔에 면보가도달ᄒᆞ엿ᄂᆞᆫᄃᆡ취히부에셔 셩지를봉승ᄒᆞ야취씨의게도로면보ᄒᆞ기ᄅᆞᆯ졍이원에국쟝을거ᄒᆡᆼᄒᆞᆯ터이니급히귀국ᄒᆞ지말고시찰임무를완젼히맛치라고ᄒᆞ엿더라

○회규졍돈 한셩신보에ᄀᆡ졔ᄒᆞ기를티사동일공졔ᄒᆞᄂᆞᆫ위원회의ᄒᆞ고일진회원을다쟝아국면으로처리ᄒᆞ고다시유지조슈ᄒᆞᆫ사ᄅᆞᆷ으로ᄯᅳᆺ을밧ᄒᆞᆫ회규를졍ᄒᆞ야쥬고권한을졍ᄒᆞ야졍부와즁츄원에헌의케ᄒᆞᆯ터인ᄃᆡ회쟝의은죠ᄇᆡᆨ식씨ᄂᆞᆫ졍ᄒᆞ고회원은견부게셔뢰사ᄒᆞᆫᄂᆡ원중이로졍ᄒᆞᆫ다더라

○원소탁졍 원소를동관외쟝리로졍ᄒᆞᆫ지라졔쟉일에ᄂᆞᆫ졔마이슈학부대신셔리와궁ᄂᆡ부관인이지샤ᄎᆞ로츌거ᄒᆞ엿ᄂᆞᆫᄃᆡ히소ᄂᆞᆫ유릉구쾌라니히조의사분묘ᄂᆞᆫ젼브터금지ᄒᆞᆫ고로과을길분묘가샹여쳐에불ᄊᆞᄒᆞᆫ다더라

○쳥관연회 졔쟉십오일은쳥국셔태후만쳘슌경졀이라한셩ᄂᆡ에거류ᄒᆞᄂᆞᆫ쳥샹ᄂᆞᆫ국긔와등으로써경츅ᄒᆞ고쳥국관에셔ᄂᆞᆫᄂᆡ외신ᄉᆞ가연회ᄒᆞ엿다더라

○망야공역 인산을티월로셩ᄒᆡᆼᄒᆞᆯ지라국쟝도감에셔쟝셩을드리졔반공역을망야공역ᄒᆞᆫ다더라

○쳑간슈셰 쳥경회사에셔ᄂᆡ하젼수만원으로자본숨고쳑간ᄒᆞ야예미샤에열람식슈세ᄒᆞᆫ다ᄒᆞᄂᆞᆫ고로셩ᄂᆡ민심이일졀불안ᄒᆞᆫ지라만약실시ᄒᆞ면셩중이ᄐᆡ단소요ᄒᆞᆯ귀미가잇다니라

○관찰보납 금번국쟝도감에모든경비가군신ᄒᆞᆫ지라각관찰수가수ᄇᆡᆨ원이상을보죠샹납ᄒᆞᆯ터이라더라

○회원셜교 일진회원최도셥씨가쟉일브터경셩회동에일어학교ᄅᆞᆯ셜립ᄒᆞ고츄즁ᄌᆞ뎨를교육ᄒᆞᄂᆞᆫᄃᆡ일어교ᄉᆞᄂᆞᆫ중왕부본에유학ᄒᆞ든신의승씨를고빙ᄒᆞ엿다더라

○츄회처ᄅᆞᆯ 쟉일ᄂᆡ부에셔의졍부조회ᄅᆞᆯ드인ᄒᆞ야십삼도에훈령ᄒᆞ되근ᄅᆡ도젹의번이졈졈더ᄒᆞ야ᄇᆡᆨ셩과쟝ᄉᆞ를온을ᄐᆞ셔ᄒᆞᆫ단말이죵죵들니니만약이런ᄒᆞᆫ변이잇거든젼졔를쥬지말고도젹을괴어ᄒᆞ착ᄒᆞ되돈을쥬고힘을ᄡᅳ을찻ᄂᆞᆫ자ㅣ잇스면샹당ᄒᆞᆫ률에쳐ᄒᆞᆫ다ᄒᆞ엿더라

○셩남난쳐 셩진감리셔리죵우씨가구월십일일에외부로보고ᄒᆞᆫ니기에셩금에로군이며과류쥬ᄒᆞᆫ것과밋졍진ᄒᆞᆫ군ᄉᆞ합계가삼쳔여명인대로국쳠쟝을인과부령일인과밋김인슈가본시ᄃᆡ에와셔거처ᄒᆞ며쳥구ᄒᆞᄂᆞᆫ거어ᄅᆞᆷ이변ᄒᆞᆫ간다ᄒᆞ미과연잡음ᄒᆞ기ᄃᆞᆼ에드려가고각군에노약을슈히마도ᄒᆞᄂᆞᆫᄃᆡ관란ᄒᆞ고그중피샹ᄒᆞᆫ치바ᄂᆞᆫ사바다엇은지표ᄂᆞᆫ비록샹으ᄯᅡᆫ로ᄒᆡᆼ용ᄒᆞ고부녀를ᄲᅢ앗셔량나도죠흠도겁ᄂᆡᄂᆞᆫ일이엽고민카슈잔이야ᄒᆞ기를비며분변등슈인은안졋고분셔하ᄯᅳᆺ들은쥬졍홀츠이엽고ᄯᅩᄒᆞᆫ방ᄉᆞᆺ흘슈도엽스민베슬을버린고카기ᄅᆞ결단ᄒᆞᆫ논ᄯᅩ이어련일이아님미아니요것감히조하로쳔권ᄒᆞ지못ᄒᆞ겟기로써ᄒᆞ시ᄒᆞᆫ심을기다릴ᄡᅳᆯ이라ᄒᆞ엿더라

○법관힘쳥 법광관과외부간에김병도ᄉᆞ건으로루ᄎᆞ교셥ᄒᆞᆫ일은본보에임의긔ᄌᆡᄒᆞ엿거니와졔쟉일셔로이ᄯᅩ공힘ᄒᆞ기를김병수도를본셔번ᄒᆞ야국문ᄒᆞᆯ일병ᄒᆞᆫ을엇지못ᄒᆞ엿시니다스ᄒᆞ약을경ᄒᆞ야의론키를바란다ᄒᆞ엿더라

○조쳥감독 일공ᄉᆞ가외부로조회ᄒᆞ기를귀국칙쥬연광도부근계도ᄂᆡ에우리칙임ᄉᆞ소용건츅룰보호ᄒᆞ여곱이졔감독ᄒᆞᄂᆞᆫ사ᄅᆞᆷ이학디방관의계신칙ᄒᆞ기를쳥ᄒᆞ니임시감독ᄒᆞᆯ케ᄒᆞ라ᄒᆞ엿더라

○경수경임 녀수ᄃᆡ쟝본쟝신즁으로경무수를에경ᄒᆞ야거ᄒᆡᆼᄒᆞᄂᆞᆫ젼레인티헌금경무수양셩환씨ᄂᆞᆫ일죵쟝신을지니지못ᄒᆞ엿ᄂᆞᆫ고로부쟝리죵건씨로습임ᄒᆞ야ᄇᆡ왕ᄃᆡ쟝을명ᄒᆞ신터이라더라

○사금미반 쳥계회ᄉᆞ를명동에셜시ᄒᆞ고ᄂᆡ하젼수쳔원을교티중인티부ᄃᆡ신리용ᄐᆡ씨가공졔젼에ᄂᆞᆫ귀잉ᄒᆞ야시무홀수엽다ᄒᆞ고탁지부에쳥구명령셔를쳐판치아니ᄒᆞ야죵지발치못ᄒᆞ엿더라

○회원문례 일진회쟝윤시병부회쟝유학쥬량씨가회원이삼인을드리고졔쟉일에의졍부근명세를방문ᄒᆞ고국가다간ᄒᆞᆫ ᄯᅢ에명망이놉흔각하가유샹이팀우동회원의만죵ᄒᆞᆫ빈라ᄒᆞ고ᄯᅩ환ᄃᆡᄌᆞ비젼하ᄒᆞ셔ᄒᆞ신ᄉᆔ에티ᄒᆞ야본졔귀한을일기보으로결졍ᄒᆞᆷ은엇더ᄒᆞᆫ연례인지신민의분의로황실의상례귀ᄒᆞᆫ볼회쟝부니이하젼국회원이감히마좀흘비나에셔이계인죡이쳔만동포가쟝아란에셔ᄲᅢ져분원ᄒᆞᆷ이젼국에봉관ᄒᆞᆫ고ᄯᅩ일향졍경이방쟝ᄒᆞ야일반인민이다국가젼도를근심ᄒᆞᄂᆞᆫ티이졔의외번을만나오ᄇᆡᆨ년리인들지인뎐레를반포ᄒᆞ야아민의괴로움을도라다보지아니ᄒᆞᆫ죡우티인민들은그쟝ᄎᆞ어ᄂᆞ셔에편안이거ᄒᆞ리오소눈과곳ᄒᆞᆫ진ᄂᆡ샹례귀한일귀넌ᄂᆞᆫ셜로명외문ᄐᆡᄌᆞ의면례의지ᄒᆞᆷ이나산졀이셩각긴티이졔한국은숩젼ᄒᆞᆫ동랍방국이니그면례고셕은일졀우리나라고리더례에의지ᄒᆞᆯ거시요만일그리치아니ᄒᆞᆫ죽시방을ᄡᅳᆯ거시어ᄂᆞᆯ하필명나라고례를인용ᄒᆞᆫ리요이런ᄒᆞᆫ일은국계을손상ᄒᆞᆷ이요각ᄇᆞᆨ가보필의직칙에잇셔젼국여졍을갑취동츅ᄒᆞ야귀졍ᄒᆞᆯ도리ᄂᆞᆫ강구ᄒᆞᆫ셩ᄋᆞᆼ복망이라ᄒᆞ야리의졍이삼괴여셩각ᄒᆞ기를갑동케ᄒᆞ엿ᄂᆞᆫ티리의졍은이의견에ᄃᆡ단히감동된모양이라더라

론셜

전호련속

○일본의목뎍인즉첫재한국을어든경륜이요만쥬ᄂᆞᆫ오히려둘재인즁아라사의계획ᄒᆞᄂᆞᆫ바와ᄂᆞᆫ셔로다른거시아라사에셔ᄂᆞᆫ한국을두지아니ᄒᆞᆷ은아니로되아라사에셔ᄂᆞᆫ반분지일이라도일아량국간에셔로합당ᄒᆞ도록ᄒᆞ엿ᄂᆞᆫ도다

한국의리두쳥편은긔왕신문에도보도ᄒᆞᆫ바어니와일아량국중에필경어ᄂᆞ나라이던지완젼히승쳡을ᄒᆞᄂᆞᆫ경우라도ᄯᅩᄒᆞᆫ고외에다른나라이잇슨즉한국을조귀의마음ᄃᆡ로ᄒᆞ라고둘리가만무ᄒᆞ며동양의권리를잡아번복ᄒᆞ도록만달리ᄎᆡ가쇠ᄒᆞᆫ엿스나그런ᄒᆞ나셜혹어느나라쟝중에든지드리갈지경에아면보죠ᄒᆞᆫ졍칙을인도ᄒᆞ야잘되여갈방침을싱각ᄒᆞ여야홀터이어ᄂᆞᆯ두나라의목적이모도그리치아니ᄒᆞ야일본은자긔의샹업분획쟝ᄒᆞ며셔민홀의사가진중ᄒᆞ고아라사에셔ᄂᆞᆫ군략샹일을필요ᄒᆞ게넉이며만쥬로분터필도ᄅᆞᆯ부셜ᄒᆞ야연속ᄒᆞ랴ᄒᆞᆯ터인즉아라사에셔ᄂᆞᆫ비록이러케ᄒᆞᆫ다ᄒᆞ드ᄅᆡ도다른사건은엽슬터인ᄃᆡ지라아라사ᄂᆞᆫ한국에ᄃᆡᄒᆞ야샹관ᄒᆞᆷ이만쥬안에아ᄂᆞᆫ상관ᄒᆞᆷ과갓치ᄒᆞ며셔빅리아ᄇᆡᆨ셩과챳취농업이ᄒᆞ왕ᄒᆞᆯ터이되일본에셔샹관ᄒᆞᆷ은쟝ᄎᆞ코ᄀᆡ다른지라우리도일본으로더브리강졍이불무ᄒᆞᆫ즉다만그나라의열심으로전쟁을니르키감졍ᄒᆞ게방비ᄒᆞᆷ을쳥ᄒᆞ야니ᄒᆞ며ᄯᅩᄒᆞᆫ시시비비간에을티고만ᄒᆞᆯ터이나그리ᄒᆞ나

져ᄃᆡ신민ᄒᆞ야ᄂᆞᆫ한국안에두나라ᄇᆡᆨ셩이거쥬ᄒᆞ기도쳠쳠ᄒᆞᆯᄲᅮᆫ더러량국간에ᄭᅬᆨ쳐가게이저은지라셜혹한국ᄇᆡᆨ셩이일본의관활ᄒᆞᄂᆞᆫ바를슌종ᄒᆞ드ᄅᆡ도필경져샹으로말ᄆᆡ암아불ᄒᆞᆫ셩경이뎡녕날터이로다

TELEGRAMS.

Army head quarters, Seoul.

Field-Marshal Oyama reports that on the morning of the 14th inst. two companies of Russian cavalry with a reserve of infantry advanced towards Setintun and Fuchachwang, but were repulsed by the Japanese outposts.

FROM JAPAN PAPERS.

London, Nov. 9th.

In view of the passage of a portion of the Baltic Fleet through the Suez Canal, elaborate precautions are being taken, guards being posted along the banks.

Berlin, Nov. 9th.

The Russian Government has made satisfactory arrangements with the Suez Canal Company for the passage of the Baltic Fleet through the Canal.

Berlin, Nov. 9th.

Several colliers belonging to the Volunteer Fleet have passed the Bosphorus since Monday last.

Berlin, Nov. 8th.

It is reported from Paris that Russia has placed orders to the value of 200 million francs with French shipbuilding yards for the restoration of her fleet.

London, Nov. 9th.

Admiral Sir Cyprian Bridge, G. C. B., and Mr. Butler Aspinall, K. C., have opened the British enquiry at Hull.

London, Nov. 9.

The officials at the Democratic headquarters admit that Mr. Roosevelt has been elected by an overwhelming majority and has carried every doubtful State. His plurality vote in New York State was over 200,000, thus exceeding the plurality vote obtained by the late President McKinley at the election in 1900.

Judge Parker, the Democratic candidate, telegraphed to President Roosevelt: "The people, by their votes, have emphatically approved of your Administration, and I congratulate you."

London, Nov. 10.

Mr. Higgins, the Republican nominee, has been elected Governor of New York State.

The majority of the Republican Party in the House of Representatives has been increased from thirty to about fifty.

London, Nov. 7.

An immense Japanese order for khaki cloth and blankets has been placed in England.

Krupp's Works are supplying Russia with fresh guns for her Manchurian Army.

Berlin, Nov. 7.

The French Ambassador to St Petersburg, M. Bompard, states in the Paris paper "Le Gaulois" that he is certain Russia in the end will be victorious. He says that Japan is already weakened and Russia will not give way before victory is assured. Japan wanted war and therefore bears the responsiblity.

THE SITUATION IN THE NORTHEAST.

The acting Kamni of Song-chin, wiring on the 30th inst. reports that the number of Russians at Song-chin and to the south is about 3,000. A Russian Major-General, a Lieut-Colonel and Kim In Su, formerly of the Korean army, are staying in the Kamni's office. They have set the people to work repairing roads and bringing in grain, for which they are paid in roubles. The women seem to have no fear of the Russians; on the contrary they appear to enjoy their society.

The sum of $2.50 has been paid to each official for expenses incurred in buying mourning clothes.

Viscount Hisamatsu died on Nov. 2nd in Tokyo. He was ex-feudal lord of the district of Nako in Shimosa province.

At Munchon a large demonstration of the Chin-po-hoi has taken place. The meeting was led by two men, clothed in European attire, evidently delegates from Seoul.

The Japanese soldiers' and Sailors' Widows and Families' Fund which is being raised by the Japanese ladies in London up to the end of September amounted to £20,208 14s. 3d.

On the 4th instant the Western Hongwanji of Kyoto applied for Y800,000 worth of the new Domestic Bonds. Mr. Tsuji Chuhei, of Kyoto, applied for Y130,000 worth, and Mr. Tsukamoto Yosoji of the same city for Y100,000.

A number of settlers at the Shimshu island, one of the Kurile group, have determind to pass the winter there. The steamer "Owari Maru," which had been despatched thither to bring these men away, has had a fruitless journey.

Lieut-General Sakai left Hiroshima on Nov. 7th for the front. An Osaka telegram reports that the condition of Lieut-General Baron Ogawa, who is under treatment in consequence of a wound sustained at Liaoyang, is improving.

The British steamer "Kaisow," under charter to the Nippon Yusen Kaisha, was scheduled to sail from Yokohama on the 5th inst. for Europe. It is reported that foreign underwriters have all refused to insure the goods shipped on the vessel.

Mr. J. D. Rockefeller is laying out at his magnificent new residence at Pocantico Hills, U. S., a rose garden, upon which £10,000 will be spent. Europe, as well as America, will be ransacked for the finest specimens.

The N.Y.K. steamer "Hokkai Maru," while lying at Hakodate was driven from her anchorage during the gale on the morning of the 7th, and struck a rock. She went to the bottom shortly afterwards. All hands were saved.

It is stated that during the past 3 days a violent storm of wind and rain has prevailed at Port Arthur, effectually interrupting all operations We do not know exactly what three days are referred to, but presumably they are the 4th, the 5th and the 6th, or possibly the 5th, 6th and 7th.—Japan Mail.

Mrs. Nicolson, widow of the Major-General Nicolson, of the Bombay Army, committed suicide on October 5 by poisoning herself with perchloride of mercury. Mrs. Nicholson was the author of two clever volumes of verse, "The Garden of Kama" and "Stars of the Desert." She wrote under the pen-name of Laurence Hope.

A picture collector tells of a comment he heard in a gallery. He stood behind two young women from the country, one of whom called attention to an atrocious animal picture labelled "Two Dogs: After Landseer?" The other young woman studied the picture closely. Where is he? she said; "I guess this must be one of them puzzle pictures."

Finding themselves at leisure from their duty of steering the ship of State. Mr. Balfour and Mr. Lyttelton on a Monday in last September took part in a spirited rescue of a party of boys who were being swept out to sea near Aberlady, Firth of Forth. The Cabinet Ministers were playing at golf when the boys' cries for help were heard, and wading into the sea, they launched fishing-boat. Mr. Lyttelton took an oar, and Mr. Balfour would have entered the boat also, but it was then fully manned.

Mr. Saionji, one the directors of the First Bank, Tokyo, died on the morning of Nov. 7th. The funeral will take place on the 9th at Yanaka.

The wedding ceremony between Princess Mitsuko of Kitashirakwa no-miya and the heir of Count Kanroji will take place on the 14th inst., when the bride will leave the princely mansion at Kioicho at 1 P. M. for the Count's residence at Sendagaya. A body of cavalry is to be attached to the bride's cortege as a guard of honour. Princess Mitsuko is the eldest daughter of the late General Prince Kitashirakawa.—Japan Gazette.

Students who speak Japanese and are fairly well educated are being selected to go to Fengtien and assist the Japanese municipal arrangements in the varicus places they are controlling, everything being done through Chinese officials under Japanese directions. The Wai Wu Pu has wired to the Tartar General at Fengtien to ask the Japanese not to institute their municipal government in any of the cities taken, as the Chinese can govern themselves. The Japanese absolutely refuse to entertain the request.—Peking Times.

A report from the district of Taipeh, Formosa, to the Tokio Home Department, says the "Kobe Herald," states that a severe earthquake occurred there on the 6th inst, at 4 30 in the morning At Kagi and its vicinity, where the shock was severest, one hundred and fifty-four houses were entirely destroyed, and thirty-three others partially demolished, while seventy-eight persons were killed and twenty-three others (including one Japanese) wounded. The damage to property is now being investigated.

In honour of the birthday of the King of the Belgians, a dinner was given yesterday evening, at the residence of Miss Sontag, by Mr. Delcoigne. The toast of "His Majesty, the King of the Belgians," was enthusiasatically received. Owing to illness Mrs. De Vos was unfortunately unable to attend; the guests present were Miss Sontag, Mr. and Mrs F Eckert, Misses Amalie, Irène and Lisbeth Eckert, Mr De Vos (Belgian Vice Consul), Dr. Ney (German Vice Consul), Dr. Wunsch, Messrs. Bolljahn, Koen and Stender, Lieut. Pak and Mr. Ko Hei-kong.

FREED AFTER TWENTY YEARS.

One of the most dramatic stories in the annals of crime is recalled by the impending release, after nearly twenty years' penal servitude, of John Lee, who, sentenced to death for murder, stood three times on the scaffold, which on each occasion would not act.

Lee was tried and found guilty of murdering Miss Keyse, an elderly lady who lived in a lonely thatched cottage at Babbacombe, near Torquay. He was one the servants, and the motive for the crime was said to exist in the fact that his wages had been reduced by sixpence a week.

Miss Keyse's body was discovered in the early morning. The head was nearly cut off, she had terrible wounds on the skull, and her clothes were smouldering.

Lee persisted in declaring his innocence, but the jury thought otherwise, and one bleak morning in February he stood on the scaffold in Exeter Gaol awaiting the pulling of the bolt that would send him to sudden death. Berry was the executioner. He had previously tested the levers and the trap door, and they had worked properly.

But now, when the lever was drawn, the platform stuck fast, despite the weight of the condemned man, and it could not be forced.

Lee, with the rope still round his neck, was marched away. The trapdoor then opened easily. He was brought back. Again it would not move. He was taken away once more, and yet again returned. But the result was the same. The Under-Sheriff came post-haste to London, and the Home Secretary commuted the sentence to penal servitude for life.

At his trial a letter from Lee's sweet-heart was read. It ran: "If it was your lot to crack stones in the street, and you will still take me to be your wife, I will not say no....I shall never be tired of waiting for you, Jack ....Perhaps if I had loved you less you would have loved me more."

That letter was written nearly twenty years ago. It is not known whether the writer is still living.

The Korea Daily News.

Issued at 5 P. M. daily except Sundays.

Rate of Subscription:—
Per Year............Yen 25.
Per Quarter,..........Yen 7.
Per Month,..........Yen 2.50.

Postage in Korea not charged extra.
Postage abroad charged extra.

Advertisements, 50 sen per day for 1 inch or less.
5 yen per month per inch.
50 yen per year per inch.

All communications to
E. T. BETHELL,
Editor and Publisher,
Pak-tong, Seoul.

THE INTERNAL CONDITION OF RUSSIA.

The following letter, which appeared in the London "Times," will come as a surprise to many who have believed in the stories of disaffection which have been so rife lately:—

TO THE EDITOR OF "THE TIMES."

Sir,—I have just completed my three months of travel through the north and centre of Russia in Europe. May I add a few words to my last letter?

My previous impressions have been further confirmed on these two points—that Russians are practically united in the determination to bring the war to a successful end and that they are confident that this end will be attained.

We should be more ready to understand this if we knew more of the remarkable advance which is being made in the development of the life of the peasants. Wallace's great book tells the beginning of this story. The progress which has been made since its publication has been described to me as nothing less than extraordinary. My informants were those best acquainted with the country life—landowners, priests schoolmasters, doctors, and the peasants themselves. I travelled through three country districts—that of Kashin which may be considered an average district of Great Russia; that of Rostoff, which is one of the very best: and parts of the Smolensk government, where the peasant life is much more backward. There were great differences; but, when my informants compared the present state of things with that of ten or 15 years ago, I could not fail to see that the same strong advance is going on everywhere and that the differences are much more of degree than of kind. The character of this advance is not at all what we should call political. It is the will, the personal initiative, what Russians call "the consciousness," that is being developed. It is a great moral advance, with, of course, many phases which may cause temporary disappointment, but always, on the whole, a great advance. It concerns itself with the personal affairs of the peasants. As to politics, it may fairly be questioned whether the local government of the peasants is, on the whole, inferior to the local government of the same class in England. I saw no indications—though I always looked for them—that the peasants as a class wish to claim a share in the central government. Meanwhile, we quite misunderstand the effects of the reign of Alexander III., unless we see in that reign a great development of national solidarity amongst the Great Russians. It is thus that I would account for the present strong development of patriotism—that is, by the combination of the local personal initative Developed by Alexander II. with the encouragement of national solidarity by Alexandar III. In a word, now that the peasants have much more interest in their own affairs, they are much more able to feel the solidarity of their country, As to the fact itself I stand in no doubt. Three times ignorant peasants have threatened to hand me over to the authorities as a Japanese. In nearly every case of political agitation in the country of which I have heard the peasants have taken up the same attitude. "Go away," they would say, "we have more serious things to think of now." No one can say that the war is popular, but every reverse it is becoming more and more national. In many parts the peasants are sending with their own horses every day for newspapers. Of course, there must be malinerers in all armies; I have seen everywhere a readiness and generally a keen desire for service at the war. The Vilna military district cannot be considered exceptionally patriotic, yet lots had to be cast between the many volunteers for service. Most interesting is the attitude of the aliens and the students. I have had long private conversations with some of them. A military student expelled from Kharkoff tells me that his friends are all anxious to go to the war, not, it is true, to kill the Japanese, but to help in healing the Russian wounded. A Pole who had likewise got into trouble even apologized for the mildness of his compatriots, but explained that their only chance of bettering their lot was to give all possible help to Russia in her time of difficulty. He strongly denied that there was any kind of antipathy between the Polish and Russian characters. A Jew, with more personal grievances and therefore more bitterness, still took the same line.

Few try to explain how success is to come. All hopes are generally dependent on the Baltic fleet, which is to arrive intact, win command of the seas, and starve out the Japanese army, and even, if necessary, a Japanese Port Arthur. These hopes, will, of course, be destroyed if England were drawn into the war.

There is no national spite against the Japanese. But everywhere there is strong irritation against England. Russians think that her moral support of Japan alone make a war possible. After very many talks on the subject I am convinced that this irritation, as natural as our own attitude toward Germany after the Kaiser's telegram, will not lead to any serious action.

To sum up, I would advise Englishmen to take it for granted that the spirit in which Russians look at the war is in the main the same as that which dominated England during our own black fortnight not very long ago.

BERNARD PEARS.

University Club, Liverpool.

JAPANESE TRAVEL IN KOREA.

We learn from a Japan paper that the Korean Vice-Minister for Foreign Affairs, has issued an intimation to the Governors of cities and prefectures in Korea announcing that Japanese visiting Korea need no longer obtain passports, unless they desire to have them.

The Il Chin Hoi have announced their intention of forming patrols to guard their interests in the city; 125 of their number have already been "told off" for this duty.

Admiral Sir Cyprian Bridge, in the "Cornhill Magazine," has been making some remarks on the lessons to be learnt from the naval performances of Japan in the present war. On the whole, he comes to the conclusion that no startling revelations have been given to the world as a result of the different operations on sea. In naval circles, and also amongst the general public, some disappointment exists because there has not been a good face-to-face battle on the sea, but this of course is a poor compliment to strategy. The main object of belligerent fleets at the present day is to intercept their opponent's ships and prevent them from forming up for a general engagement, and in this object the Japanese have been eminently successful in the present war. The Russians have never been able to collect their ships and offer the Japanese a sound battle: the mistake of the Muscovites in having their vessels scattered in all directions is now patent to everyone. In Admiral Bridge's opinion, as well as that of the majority of naval experts, the Japanese strategy has been admirable. On the subject of mines, and torpedoes, Admiral Bridge does not wax enthusiastic. Commenting on the sinking of the "Petropavlovsk," and, Hatsuse," each through contact with a submarine mine laid by its own friends, he says we did not require the present war to tell us that the detonation of a certain quantity of explosive material within a certain distance from the hull of a ship and at a certain depth below the surface of the water, will inflict terrible damage on it, practically amounting to its distruction. The locomotive torpedo has not been successful in sinking warships, though it has seriously damaged some of the Russian vessels. Admiral Bridge considers that the old rule that naval actions are decided by superiority of gunfire has been fully verified, and cites the case of "Varyag" to bear him out. Though, however, many of the ten shot that hit her were theoretically capable of sinking her, she was really sunk by her own crew. "The point worth noting," adds the writer, "is that it was on account of the size of her butcher's bill" that she was defeated. She had rather over a hundred killed and wounded, and gave up the fight just as the English "Java" or the French "Sybille" had to do in the old days."

Science, it is said, has no nationality. In existing circumstances, observes a London journal, it is at least courteous on the part of the Imperial Russian Geographical Society to present to the Geographs Society of Lhassa and other places in Tibet, taken by Russian subjects during 1900 and 1901. The photographs were placed on exhibition in London.

It is reported in mandarin circles, states the N.-C. Daily News, that the Ministers of the Waiwupu have been lately conferring almost daily with Sir Ernest Satow with reference to the changing of the Younghusband Treaty at Lhassa. The reply of the British Minister, it is stated, was that the clauses in that Treaty referring to railways, mines and foreign intercourse were now so well Known in Europe and Asia that it would be difficult to change them, but with regard to other clauses his diplomatic answer was that if he could do anything to modify them in accordance with the wishes of the Chinese Government he would do so with pleasure.

Some days ago we published the information that the scheme of renewing the N. Y. K. service between Bombay and Japan will be dropped for the present. We now learn from the "Japan Times" that the reason of this is that the different marine insurance companies either decline to accept risks for cotton, the principal cargo on the line, or else ask for almost prohibitory rates, thus rendering the prospect of the service extremely gloomy. Mr. Kinnosuke Harada, manager of the Osaka Branch of the Company, and Mr. Takeo Yamabe, President of the associated cotton mills, are now in the capital, but according to our contemporary it seems doubtful whether the resumption of the service will take place in the near future.

The Korea Daily News.

VOL. I, WEDNESDAY, NOVEMBER 16, 1904. No. 102

HONGKONG & SHANGHAI BANKING CORPORATION.

Paid-up Capital..... ....$10,000,000
Reserve Fund:—Sterling Reserve... 10,000,000
Silver Reserve..... 7,000,000

27,000,000
Reserve Liability of Proprietors... 10,000,000

HEAD OFFICE, HONGKONG.

London Bankers, London and County Banking Company Limited
Branches and Agencies,
London.

Amoy,	Hankow	Penang,
Bangkok,	Hiogo,	Rangoon,
Batavia,	Iloilo,	Saigon,
Bombay,	Lyons,	San Francisco,
Calcutta,	Manila,	Singapore,
Colombo,	Nagasaki,	Sourabaya,
Foochow,	New York,	Tientsin,
Hamburg,	Peking,	Yokohama,

Credits granted on approved Securities, and every description of Banking and Exchange business transacted.

Drafts granted on London and the chief Commercial places in Europe, India, Australia, America, China and Japan.

HOLME RINGER & CO., AGENTS,
CHEMULPO.

ON CHEONG & CO.,
SEOUL.

GENERAL STORE KEEPERS.
Imported provisions, Cooking Utensils Crockery, etc.
FRESH BREAD DAILY.

MITSU BISHI DOCKYARD & ENGINE WORKS,
NAGASAKI.

CODE WORD, "DOCK,"

A. 1, A. B. C., and Engineering Codes used.

DOCK No. 1 (at Tategami).

Extreme Length..............523 feet
Length on blocks .... 513 ,,
Width of Entrance on Top......89 ,,
,, ,, Bottom....77 ,,
Water on Blocks at Spring Tide 26½ ,,

DOCK No. 2 (Mukaijima).

Extreme Length..............371 feet
Length on Blocks............360 ,,
Width of Entrance on Top......66 ,,
,, ,, Bottom 53 ,,
Water on Blocks at Spring Tide 22 ,,

PATENT SLIP (at Kosuge).

Can take vessels up to 1,000 tons gross.

THE WORKS are well equipped with the LATEST IMPROVEMENTS, and can execute any kind of work in SHIPBUILDING and MARINE ENGINEERING, as well as in REPAIRING of SHIPS.

The COMPANY'S new powerful steamer OURA-MARU (712 tons, 700 I.H.P.), specially built for SALVAGE PURPOSES, and equipped with necessary gear, is always READY at SHORT NOTICE.

CHARTERED BANK OF INDIA AUSTRALIA & CHINA.

INCORPORATED BY ROYAL CHARTER 1853

HEAD OFFICES:—LONDON.

Paid-up Capital £800,000
Reserve Liability of Shareholders 800,000
Reserve Fund 800,000

Drafts granted upon all the principal places in the world and every description of Exchange and banking business transacted.

E. MEYER & Co., Agents,
Chemulpo.

E. MEYER & CO.
Chemulpo.

SOLE AGENTS IN KOREA FOR:

A. T. Morse, Sons & Co's "Fresco" Distemper

In all colours ready for use on walls, Ceilings etc.
and

AVENARIUS CARBOLINEUM

A wood-preserving and antiseptic oil preparation

Against decay, dry-rot, fungus and wood-destroying insects.

A large supply always in Stock.
Prices upon application.

E. MEYER & Co.,
Chemulpo.

THE METHODIST PUBLISHING HOUSE,
Little West Gate, Seoul.

JOB PRINTING, TYPEWRITER PAPER
CARBON PAPER, VISITING CARDS
STATIONERY, BOOK BINDING
BOOK PUBLISHERS
AMERICAN SCHOOL BOOKS
SPENCERIAN COPY BOOKS
PEN CARBON LETTER AND BILL BOOKS

S. A. BECK, Manager.

HOKURKU DOBOKU KAISHA.

Branch office in Chong Dong. Seoul.
Japanese telephone No. 165

CONTRACT DEPARTMENT.

We can contract to build any building or construction.

MERCHANDISE DEPARTMENT.

We can provide any building material.
We have just contracted to build the new Belgian Legation.

DAI-ICHI GINKO
LIMITED.
(Formerly the First National Bank)

ESTABLISHED 1873

INCORPORATED UNDER PRESENT LAW 1896

Capital - - - - - - - - - Yen 5,000,000
Reserve Fund - . - - - 1,500,000

HEAD OFFICE:—TOKIO.

President: Baron SHIBUSAWA.

BRANCHES AND CORRESPONDENTS
In the Principal Cities and Towns of Japan.
Interest Allowed on
Fixed deposits 1 year - - - 6½ per cent
" " 6 months - - - 6 per cent

Special current accounts 1½ sen daily per Y 100
General " " 1 " " " 100

M. TANAKA,
Manager, Chemulpo.

HOLME RINGER & Co.
Chemulpo.

General Merchants and Government Contractors.

Agents for the leading
Banks
Steamship Companies
and
Insurance Companies

Importers of Merchandise of every description.

KAMEYA & CO.
GENERAL STOREKEEPERS
Chinkokai - - Seoul
(*Established 1895, Tokyo*)

Confectionery, Hams, Canned Goods, Cutlery, Hirano & Tansan Water. Provisions, Gents, Furnishing goods, Toilet Articles, Travelling Bags, Tobacco, Cigars & Cigarettes Kitchen Utensils. Coffee. Biscuits.

Fresh Goods always kept in Stock.
Prices Moderate
Please come and inspect our goods

NIPPON YUSEN KAISHA.
JAPANESE MAIL STEAMSHIP CO.
DER MAIL CONTRACT WITH THE IMPERIAL JAPANESE GOVERNMENT.

European Line

Regular Fortnightly Service between Yokohama Kobe, Moji, Shanghai, Hongkong, Singapore, Penang Colombo, Port Said, Marseilles, London and Antwerp

American Line

Regular Fortnightly Service between Hongkong and Seattle, calling at Shanghai, Moji, Kobe, Yokohama and Victoria, B. C.

Australian Line

Regular weekly Service betwen Japan Ports and Australia, calling at Hongkong and Manila.
(Above Three Lines Suspended until further notice).

Shanghai Line

Weekly Service between Shanghai and Japan Ports

Korea Line

Service Kobe, Moji, Nagasaki, Fusan Chemupo Chefoo, Taiku.
S. S. Bahrisberg, 2181 tons,
Service Kobe, Moji, Fusan, Chemulpo, Chinnampo
S. S. ARGO, S. S. Ohio.

BORDEN'S CONDENSED MILK CO.
New York, U. S. A.

ALWAYS IN STOCK
Eagle Brand Condensed Milk.
Gold Seal Condensed Milk.
Peerless (Family) Evaporated Cream.
Borden's Malted Milk.

E. MEYER & CO.
Chemulpo, Korea,
Sole Agents

ROYAL INSURANCE COMPANY,
Funds exceed £10,000,000
FIRE
AT CURRENT RATES.
LIFE
REDUCED PREMIUM.
HOLME RINGER & Co.,
Agents, Chemulpo.

HOTEL DU PALAIS
SEOUL.

The only first class Hotel in Seoul. Situated in the centre of the city opposite the palace.

Cuisine under the supervision of an experienced French Chef.

Well ventilated and furnished throughout.

TARIFF UPON APPLICATION

L. MARTIN
Proprietor and Manager.

大韓每日申報
대한ᄆᆡ일신보

(뎨일빅삼호) (금요일) 일쳔구빅사년십일월십팔일

본샤고빅

이신보는영국ᄉᆞ와한어로셔ᄆᆡ
일출판ᄒᆞ옵

신문가

한장 엽푼오푼
일삭도 엽두량닷돈
우표가ᄎᆡ삭닷돈
다밧돈으로밧숩

광고로는

귀한의장단과ᄌᆞ칭의다쇼로종
감ᄒᆞ되렴가로밧올터이오며오
리지아녀대한사람마다다이신
문을보실터이니광고버시기를
원ᄒᆞ시ᄂᆞᆫ이들은우리신문사에
와서면약ᄒᆞ심을희망ᄒᆞ옵

○발힝소 박동대한ᄆᆡ일신보
사범어학교압헤젼영국인셜필
림졍자리오

사쟝 영국인 (ᄇᆡ셜)

평양 디리졈

○평양효동사는권ᄇᆡ보씨로우
리신문관ᄇᆡ티리인을뢰졍ᄒᆞ얏
스오니평양에계신구람코저ᄒᆞ
시는 쳠군ᄌᆞ는ᄒᆞ티리졈에왕
림ᄒᆞ와면의ᄒᆞ시옵

사고

○우리대한ᄆᆡ일신보의목뎍은
대한의안녕질서에관한모든데
목에ᄃᆡᄒᆞ야는공평한변론을주
쟝홈이라우리동신원의답보는
신문보시는쳠군ᄌᆞ의게ᄒᆞ상보
도ᄒᆞ리며편지를귀셔ᄒᆞ여주시
는이는셩명과반ᄃᆡ를젹어붓치
시기를희망ᄒᆞ오니이거슨신문
샹에긔ᄌᆡᄒᆞ랴는거시아니오다
만극히신용ᄒᆞ는증거를숨고자
ᄒᆞᆷ이라귀자는아모귀셔던지귀
ᄌᆡᄒᆞᆷ을되쟈ᄒᆞ는권리를가졋스
나되쟈ᄒᆞ는리우를말ᄒᆞᆯ터이오
며공중광화를문란케ᄒᆞ는듯ᄒᆞᆫ
귀셔는의례히밧지안켓숩나이
다

●본사셜시이래로신문을ᄆᆡ양
우례로분젼ᄒᆞ와레젼부의입의
로젼ᄒᆞ듯스로번곳에는혹늣게
젼ᄒᆞ기도ᄒᆞ며혹벗칠거슬ᄒᆞᆫ졉
에젼ᄒᆞ기도ᄒᆞ며혹아니젼ᄒᆞ는
곳도잇다ᄒᆞ와우리신문을슈탕
ᄒᆞ야구람ᄒᆞ시는 쳠군ᄌᆞ의게금
티ᄒᆞ야ᄆᆡ우미안ᄒᆞ옵기로지
운분젼인을두고ᄆᆡ일일즉이젼
ᄒᆞ며아니젼ᄒᆞ거나늣게거나ᄒᆞᆫ
치가업도록ᄒᆞ랴ᄒᆞ오니혹아니
젼ᄒᆞ거나혹늣게젼ᄒᆞ거나ᄒᆞᆫ일
이잇스면본사로통긔ᄒᆞ여주심
을희망ᄒᆞ옵

관보

뎨이쳔구ᄇᆡᆨ팔십ᄉᆞ호
광무팔년십일월십오일
셔임급ᄉᆞ령

○임법부참서관주임관오등
농상공부샹공국쟝 박규병
○임의효젼참봉서관임관륙등
서졍관 리희명
○임의효젼참의서관임관팔등
리시용 리창원 윤긔츈 빅
남션
○임원소참봉서관임관팔등
리희창 김용긔
○임원소충의서관임관팔등
유면

이상십일월십일

○명공니부등진관서쳐임관일
등 경효젼제조 리간휘
○명경효젼제조서쳐임관일등
태의원경 민영규
○명태의원경서쳐임관삼등
궁니부특진관 박용대
○의원면경임시장원시곡관
쟝례원샹례 리인규
○임시장원시곡관서관임관ᄉᆞ
등 규장각직각 리범소
○경임규장각직각 기로소슈
직관 김조현
○임창릉참봉서관임관팔등
영희젼참봉 리원영
○임영희젼참봉서관임관륙등
사직서참봉 허졍
○임사직서참봉서관임관칠등
의릉참봉 리덕주
○임의릉참봉서관임관팔등
박영희

이상십일월십이일

궁뎐휼사

○춍호ᄉᆞ신리근명군 주 훈
전분 문경젼으로ᄒᆞ라교죠칙
이ᄂᆞ리사신등이샹가나가셜괴
온즉젼빈제도가쳥착ᄒᆞ야 훈
적비셜에준비치못ᄒᆞ와ᄉᆞ케에
만만황송이온신등이감히ᄌᆞ하
쳔편치못ᄒᆞ오니엇지ᄒᆞ을지감
주ᄒᆞ와 광무팔년십일월십이
일봉 지니에젼작제도는령궁
니부에션ᄉᆞ로죵편마련슈기ᄒᆞ
라ᄒᆞ셧더라

○총호ᄉᆞ신리근명군 주 국
쟝도감당쳥남만희가신병이잇
ᄊᆞ와켸임키를빌기에ᄎᆞ차ᄒᆞ고
그티에젼셔쟝관에윤병구로차
하ᄒᆞ야찻임케홈이하여ᄋᆞᆸ을지
감쥬ᄒᆞ와 광무팔년십일월십
삼일에봉 지의주ᄒᆞ다

교육부관제 속

뎨십팔됴 학도는유년학교졸
업한ᄌᆞ로뎡홈이라
다만유년학교학도가졸업
ᄒᆞ기젼십년간은이한계잇
지아니홈이라
뎨십구됴 학도의년령은십팔
세로만이십삼세ᄭᆞ지한홈이
라
뎨이십됴 학도는ᄆᆡ년ᄇᆡᆨ명식
모집ᄒᆞ야립학케홈이라
뎨이십일됴 학도의슈학긔한
은만삼기년으로뎡홈이라
뎨이십이됴 학도를립학슌셔
에좃차ᄎᆞ례로졸업케홈이라
뎨이십삼됴 학도는졍원을인
ᄒᆞ야뢰교홈을허락지아니홈
이라
뎨이십ᄉᆞ됴 학도중에좌긔혼
수항에관ᄒᆞᆫ자는뢰교케홈이
라
일 학슐의예습이온젼치못
ᄒᆞᆫ야슈학의진보ᄒᆞᆯ미홈평ᄒᆞ야
졸업홀긔망이업는자
이 군긔를문란이ᄒᆞ며혹벌
츅을여러번범ᄒᆞᆫ자
삼 픔힝이부졍ᄒᆞ야가죠ᄒᆞᆯ
긔망이업는자
ᄉᆞ 샹리질병을인ᄒᆞ야슈학
에감당치못ᄒᆞᆫ자
오 졸업시험에낙뎨ᄒᆞᆫ자
뎨이십오됴 젼됴뎨일뎨오항
에ᄃᆡ당ᄒᆞ야뢰교케ᄒᆞᆫ자중에오
히려귀망이잇는자와질병과
밋기타ᄉᆞ고를인ᄒᆞ야슈학긔
한니에뎡ᄒᆞᆫ바학슐을ᄆᆞᆺ지못
ᄒᆞᆫ자와졸업시험을슈치못ᄒᆞᆫ
자는다시ᄒᆞᆫ학을명ᄒᆞ는수가
잇슴이라
뎨이십륙됴 우이됴에당ᄒᆞᆫ자
가잇슬ᄯᆡ에는교쟝이그ᄉᆞ유
를교육총감의게신보ᄒᆞ야교
육총감이ᄎᆞ를관뎡홈이라
뎨이십칠됴 학도의슈학과말
이지ᄒᆞ면교쟝이졸업시험의
규겨을셜명ᄒᆞ야교육총감의
게신보ᄒᆞ고그가ᄂᆞᆫ처뎡홈을
엇어졸업시험을힝홈이라
뎨이십팔됴 졸업시험을맛친
면교쟝이각교관과학도티쟝
과밋증티쟝을모와회의를기
ᄒᆞ고셩젹을됴사ᄒᆞ야학과의
ᄎᆞ례를샹고ᄒᆞ야뎡ᄒᆞ고교육
총감의게신보ᄒᆞ고그인가를
엇어금뎨자의게졸업증셔를
여홈이라
뎨이십구됴 졸업증셔을부여
ᄒᆞᆫ자의게는임관서무를명홈
이라
뎨삼십됴 쳬항을당ᄒᆞᆫ학도가
슈학을맛치면전졔됴에준ᄒᆞ
야조뎡홈이바
뎨삼십일됴 학도의게는졀쥬
일간이니에하긔휴업을여홈
을득홈이라
뎨삼십이됴 본관졔는반포일
로시힝홈이라
뎨삼십삼됴 광무ᄉᆞ년구월ᄉᆞ
일반포ᄒᆞᆫ무관학교관졔는폐
지홈이라

잡보

○과견시찰 텬도원괴ᄉᆞ취범
셕을명ᄒᆞ야일본에젼왕케ᄒᆞ고
텬도규졍뎨도와밋ᄉᆞ무을시찰
케ᄒᆞᆫ다더라

○무고취역 곡산군에셔역부
ᄉᆞ로민요가니러나일인을살희
ᄒᆞᆫ수진으로일병도파견ᄒᆞ고량
국쟈에샹지ᄒᆞ더니히군에셔ᄌᆞ
원ᄒᆞ야경의텰도역ᄉᆞ에역부ᄒᆞᆫ
쳔명에역부를ᄌᆞ비ᄒᆞ야응역ᄒᆞ
기로작뎡이되엿더라

○면쟝보호 일진회에셔각도
관찰부로면보ᄒᆞ기를국샹용제
젼이라도진보회원의싱명지산
을보호ᄒᆞ야거졍이업게ᄒᆞ라ᄒᆞ
엿다더니츙쳥북도관찰ᄉᆞ가회
면ᄒᆞ기를 국샹은보통이라가각
군진보회원는누구며싱명지산
은하필공제젼에만보호ᄒᆞ리요
ᄒᆞ엿더라

○면셜츄보 함경도로좃차온
사ᄅᆞᆷ의젼셜을드른즉근리영흥
덕원등디에서진보회민들이다
츈야간에셔밧갈아먹는사ᄅᆞᆷ이
란일조에홀연쟝시ᄂᆞ도회쳐로
슈빅호샹ᄉᆞ빅명식취집ᄒᆞ야일
쟝연셜을ᄒᆞ야굴ᄋᆞ되니싱강에
본리죠죠ᄒᆞ고무샤ᄒᆞᆫ우밍이라
이왕에는외국인을비쳑ᄒᆞ기로
쥬의를숨앗더니근일시세소문

UNION INSURANCE SOCIETY OF CANTON.

Head office Hongkong.
Marine risks underwritten at current rates.
Agents in Chemulpo,
E. MEYER & Co.

COMPAGNIE DES MESSAGERIES MARITIMES.

Fortnightly Direct Service.

For Marseilles
via Ports.
Sailing from Yokohama
Calling at Kobe,
Shanghai, Hongkong, Saigon, Singapore,
Colombo, Djibonti, Suez, Port Said
and Marseilles.

For particulars apply to
HOLME RINGER & Co.,
Chemulpo.

HAYASHIDA & Co.,
16 MYENG DONG, CHIN KO KAI, SEOUL.
BRANCH OFFICE AT CHEMULPO.

Money changers, Coal and Wood Merchants, Express Agents.

We are agents for the Pyeng-yang Coal Company and the Karazu Coal Company of Japan. We have the best quality of both anthracite and bituminous coal, and prompt execution of orders is our speciality. Firewood of all kinds kept in stock. Full weight guaranteed. Money of all denominations exchanged at current rates. Parcels received for all parts.

CHINA MUTUAL LIFE INS. CO.

Most favourable terms to policy holders.

Benefit system unsurpassed.

HOLME RINGER & Co.
Agents, Chemulpo.

C. P. R.

CANADIAN PACIFIC RAILWAY COMPANY'S ROYAL MAIL STEAMSHIP LINE.

THE FAST ROUTE BETWEEN CHINA, JAPAN, AND EUROPE VIA CANADA AND THE UNITED STATES.

Route from Hongkong via Shanghai, Nagasaki (Inland Sea of Japan) Kobe, Yokohama, Victoria and Vancouver.

Twin Screw Empress Steamship—6,000 Tons—Speed 19 knots.

PROPOSED SAILING FROM YOKOHAMA.
R. M. S. Empress of India.
R. M. S. Empress of Japan.
R. M. S. Empress of China.
R. M. S. Athenian.
R. M. S. Tartar.

Special reduction (first class only) granted to members of the Military, Naval, Diplomatic and Civil services and to Missionaries.
Passengers have choice of ten routes across the Continent of America and have privilege of travelling by any Atlantic Steamship Line.
Round the World passage tickets in connection with the P. and O. S. N., North German Lloyd and Messageries Co.'s £125.
All rates payable at current rate of exchange.
For further information, Tickets, Guide Books, etc., apply to

HOLME, RINGER & Co., AGENTS,
Chemulpo.

Grand Hotel,
(Formerly the Station Hotel)

Near the Railway Terminus.
West Gate Seoul.

The Best Hotel in Korea
Handsome new Building.
Fine Airy Rooms
Excellent Cuisine.
Terms Moderate.
Special terms to Missionaries
and to permanent boarders.

Electric cars within 2 minutes' walk.

W. H. EMBERLEY,
Proprietor

EVERY FACILITY.

In connection with Life Assurance Business is afforded by

The Standard Life Assurance Co.,

One of the largest and wealthiest of the Provident Institutions of the United Kingdom Forms of Application and all information will be promptly afforded on application.

10 CENTS A DAY.

Not a very large expenditure is it? But it is sufficient to secure for a man of 30 a policy with the STANDARD LIFE OFFICE for

$1323.

For all particulars of rates, etc., apply to

Holme, Ringer & Co.,
Agents, Chemulpo.

THE NEW YORK LIFE INSURANCE COMPANY.

Have you ever been declined by any Company?

Are you engaged in a specially hazardous occupation?

Have you heard of the New York Life Insurance Company's New Classifications for this class of Risks?

If not, send your date of birth, occupation and particulars of rejection, if any to

E. MEYER & Co.,
Agents, Chemulpo.

MITSUI BUSSAN KAISHA.
(MITSUI & Co.)
MITSUI GINKO.
(MITSUI BANK.)

The Bank is owned by the members of the Mitsui Family, who, as partners, assume an unlimited responsibility for all liabilities of the Bank:—

Capital........................Yen 5,000,000
Reserve Fund.................. " 5,600,000

HEAD OFFICE, TOKYO.
LONDON OFFICE, 34 LIME ST., E. C.

BRANCHES AND AGENCIES:—
New York, San Francisco, Hamburg, Bombay, Singapore, Manila, Hongkong, Amoy, Chefoo, Tientsin.
Kobe, Hakodate, Yokohama, Kure, Yokosuka, Moji, Shimonoseki, Miike, Wakamatsu, Nagasaki, Kuchinotsu, Karatsu, Sasebo, Misume, Taipeh, &c.

Telegraphic Address for all the Offices:
"MITSUI."
A. B. C. AND A. I CODES USED.

Contractors of Coal
To the Imperial Japanese Navy. Arsenals and Railway Bureau, Principal Railway Companies and Industrial Work, Home and Foreign Mail and Freight Steamers.
Sole Proprietors
Of the famous Miike, Tagawa and Yamano Coal Mines.
Sole Agents
For the sale of Fukumo, Hokoku, Ichimura, Kanoda, Mannoura, Onoura, Ostuji, Sonoda, Tsubaruro, Yoshinotani, Yoshio, Yurokibura and other coals.

YANGTSE INSURANCE ASSOCIATION, LTD.

The undersigned, having been appointed agents for the above company, are prepared to issue policies and pay losses on marine risks at regular rates.

E. MEYER & Co.,
Agents, Chemulpo.

AMERICAN KOREAN ELECTRIC CO.

Light and Power.

Main Office: Electric Building, Chong No.

RAILWAY DEPARTMENT.

OPERATING CARS BETWEEN EAST AND WEST GATE, EVERY TEN MINUTES:—
First Car leaves East Gate at 7:00 A. M. First Car leaves R. R. Station at 7:25 A. M
Last Car " East Gate at 10:05 P. M. Last " " R. R. Station at 9:40 P.M

OPERATING CARS BETWEEN EAST GATE AND IMPERIAL TOMB TERMINUS, EVERY TWENTY MINUTES:—
CONNECTING WITH EVERY ALTERNATE CAR ARRIVING AT EAST GATE FROM CHONG NO.
First Car leaves East Gate for Tomb at 7:10 A. M.
" " " Tomb for East Gate at 7:35 A. M.
Last " " East Gate for Tomb at 7:50 P. M.
" " " Tomb for East Gate at 8:10 P. M.

OPERATING CARS BETWEEN CHONG NO AND YUNG SAN RIVER EVERY TWELVE MINUTES:—
First Car leaves Chong No for South Gate at 7:12 A. M.
" " " Chong No for Yung San at 7:36 A. M.
" " " South Gate for Chong No at 7:20 A. M.
" " " Yung San for Chong No at 8:09 A. M.
Last " " South Gate for Chong No 10:00 P. M.
" " " Yung San for Chong No at 9:33 P. M.

SPECIAL PRIVATE CARS FURNISHED TO SUIT CONVENIENCE OF PATRONS. PRICES ON APPLICATION AT HEAD OFFICE.

LIGHTING DEPARTMENT.

Where less than 250 candle power of light is used, the rate per month will be
Per 16 candle power incandescent lamp,—All night.—Yen 2.50.
32 candle power incandescent lamp:—All night:—Yen 4.00.
50 candle power incandescent lamp:—All night:—Yen 6.00.
150 " " " —" " " 10.00.
1200 " " enclosed arc " " " 20.00.

Where more than 250 candle power of light is used, a Meter will be installed, if requested:—Rent of Meter Yen 2.00 per month. Rate of charges by meter reading:—Two Sen per Ampere per hour. (Approximately this is equal to about One Sen per 16 C. P. lamp per hour) Minimum monthly charge where meter is installed, Yen 20.00 per month, which includes rental of meter.
Estimates for installing lights furnished on application.
An assortment of chandeliers always on hand.

K. Murakami,
Photograph Studio
Chinkokai, Seoul.

Printing, Developing and Enlargement, of Photographs always Undertaken.

Korean Views and Pictures Illustrating Native Customs always on Sale,

---

THE OSAKA SHOSEN KAISHA.

Boats frequently on the berth for Chinnampo.

REGULAR SAILINGS BETWEEN JAPAN AND KOREAN PORTS.

FUSAN AND KOBE VIA SHIMONOSEKI.

OSAKA VIA MOKPO, FUSAN, SHIMONOSEKI AND KOBE.

MOJI DIRECT.

OSAKA VIA KUNSAN, MASANPO, FUSAN, SHIMONOSEKI AND KOBE.

CHEMULPO KUNSAN LINE,
Every three days.

CHEMULPO CHINNAMPO LINE.
Every three days.

For Freight and passage and further particulars apply to
THE OSAKA SHOSEN KAISHA,
Chemulpo.

RONDON, PLAISANT & CO.

General Storekeepers and Merchants, Ships Contractors, Tobacconists, Commission and Forwarding Agents, Coal Merchants
IMPORTERS AND EXPORTERS

Seoul & Chemulpo.

W. D. WENTWORTH.

LANDING
AND
SHIPPING AGENT
AND
CUSTOMS BROER.

12 OURA, NAGASAKI.

STEWARD & CO.
Chemulpo.

Shipchandlers and Storekeepers, Naval and Mercantile Contrrctors, Landing and Shipping Agents.

STEWARD'S HOTEL
Chemulpo.

Best accommodation in the port for travellers. Clean and well-aired rooms, good cuisine, prompt attendance, moderate tariff.

을드ᄂᆞᆫ 중에 인민이 불가불 기화ᄒᆞ여야 국가를 평안이 ᄒᆞ고 신민의 성명 재산을 보젼ᄒᆞᆯ 터이기로 시방으로브터 이후 셔지ᄂᆞᆫ 일제 단발ᄒᆞ고 일본 사ᄅᆞᆷ을 친절이 교셥ᄒᆞ며 야기 명신보의 힘을 힘닙을 텬디나 아모조록 우리 이쳔만 동포ᄂᆞᆫ 일본 사ᄅᆞᆷ을 친밀히 사귀여 기화ᄒᆞ기를 힘쓰ᄌᆞᄒᆞᄂᆞᆫ 지라 그 회민이 모여 연셜ᄒᆞᆫ 세마다 일병이 가셔 참예ᄒᆞ다가 연셜ᄒᆞᆷ을 듯고 일병도 다 치하ᄒᆞ야 ᄀᆞᆯᄋᆞᄃᆡ 귀국 사ᄅᆞᆷ이 이ᄀᆞᆺ치 기화ᄒᆞ기에 ᄌᆞ쥬 귀의ᄒᆞ니 미우 고맙소 ᄒᆞ며 셔로 호ᄒᆞ더라 ᄒᆞ고 젼ᄒᆞᄂᆞᆫᄃᆡ 일회민은 평ᄉᆡᆼ에 일자 무식으로 세계 형편이 엇더ᄒᆞᆫ지 기화가 무어신지 아지도 못ᄒᆞ던 붕두 란발로 ᄉᆡᆼ이 나 파망ᄒᆞᆫ 자ㅣ라 ᄌᆞ긔의 머리털을 ᄭᅡᆨ사기를 쳔금ᄀᆞᆺ치 녀기고 머리 ᄭᅡᆨ근 ᄉᆞᄅᆞᆷ을 보면 왜놈이라 ᄒᆞ고 욕ᄒᆞ던 인물뎐이 일조일셕에 삭발ᄒᆞ고 회중에 참예ᄒᆞ야 셔로 놀납다 ᄒᆞᆫ 일이라고 괴이ᄒᆞ던 사ᄅᆞᆷ들이 만흔지라 황셩신문에 긔재ᄒᆞ엿기에 그 대지만 말ᄒᆞ노라

○보쳥원류 함경남도 관찰ᄉᆞ 김가진 씨가 작일에 내부로 보고ᄒᆞ기를 덕원 군슈 리종원의 일은 임의 보ᄒᆞ엿거니와 귀뎍이 혼란ᄒᆞ오니 원류ᄒᆞᄂᆞᆫ 자가 단지 ᄒᆞ오니 일졍 천동치 말고 셰민망을 위ᄒᆞ야 계ᄒᆞ고 곳 시명ᄒᆞ라 ᄒᆞ엿더라

○분참셜시 대구 관찰ᄉᆞ 리용익 씨가 내부에 보고ᄒᆞ기를 관하 각 군에 근일 일본 병참소 즁대 쟝관이 군졔를 보ᄂᆞᆫ 말ᄒᆞ기를 경산 군수가 금번 분참 티와 셩곡 군 삼산 동 등디에 분참을 셜시ᄒᆞ겟스니 가옥을 셰를 엇지 조처ᄒᆞ올는지 시명ᄒᆞ라 ᄒᆞ엿더라

○일미시힝 참정 신긔션 씨가 내외지셔 임을 간칙ᄒᆞ임관이 보ᄒᆞ기로 상 쥬지 가ᄒᆞ야 반포ᄒᆞ고 그 ᄆᆡᆫ이 일쟉 시오 일ᄒᆞ나 드러셔 힝치 못ᄒᆞ고 공쳔이 ᄌᆞ니 로 물시 되엿다더라

○학ᄌᆞ금쳥구 학교 ᄉᆞ무를 시찰ᄎᆞ로 일본에 젼왕ᄒᆞ야 잇ᄂᆞᆫ 리지국 씨가 재작일에 학부로 편보ᄒᆞ기를 류학ᄉᆡᆼ의 학ᄌᆞ금이 임의 졀핍ᄒᆞ엿스니 탁지부에 쳥구ᄒᆞ야 죡속히 지발ᄒᆞ게 ᄒᆞ라 ᄒᆞ엿더라

○단쳔군 금동학 단쳔 군슈 리현졔 씨가 작월 십일에 내부로 보고ᄒᆞᆫ 보고 내기에 운ᄒᆞ엿스되 우리 대한 ᄃᆞᆫ 동이 으로 일본 놈 나 옷ᄒᆞ고 북으로 로국에 잣가오니 로 국에 든지 일본에 든지 ᄒᆞ하후 하 발으로 ᄒᆞ리 오 지금 병마가 맘 뒤 쇼 아 니 가 며 말 밋 암 아 드 리 오 ᄂᆞᆫ 조 음에 평 졍 ᄒᆞᆫ 듯 ᄒᆞᆷ 불 가 불 히 ᄃᆡ 방에 쳥구ᄒᆞ올 ᄃᆡ 이 죠 교 런 지 의 에 누구든 능히 괴 ᄃᆡ ᄒᆞ리 오 그 런 ᄒᆞᆫ 티 관 국 이 지 쟝 ᄒᆞᆫ 후 에 일 병 은 단 쳔 에 ᄒᆞ나 도 며 괴 ᄋᆞᆫ 거 시 엽 고 본 군 은 수 일 브 터 양 무 셔 지 본 군

ᄲᅮ 지 나 남 으 로 나 간 쟈 가 광 이 수 쳔 명 이 나 되 고 보 병 은 불 과 빅 여 명 이 라 본 군 ᄃᆡ 경 남 북 에 광 활 ᄒᆞ 고 초 원 ᄒᆞᆫ 빅 ᄯᅥ 리 시 비 에 ᄒᆞᆨ 류 수 도 ᄒᆞ 며 ᄒᆞᆷ 쥬 둔 노 ᄒᆞᆫ 병 참 이 태 장 ᄃᆡ 셧 곳 이 나 되 ᄂᆞᆫ 티 쵸 마 와 ᄒᆞᆼ 샹 류 ᄒᆞᄂᆞᆫ 자 가 각 기 이 싱 여 괴 식 ᄒᆞ 기 이 심 며 과 시 잇 셔 셔 로 왕 리 ᄒᆞ ᄂᆞᆫ 대 기 이 아 잇 ᄂᆞᆫ 보 리 이 다 른 쥬 류 일 쇤 더 러 며 희 항 위 가 일 인 만 곳 지 못 ᄒᆞ 야 보 ᄂᆞᆫ 자 가 다 ᄂᆞᆫ 니 여 다 라 나 지 안 ᄂᆞᆫ 이 가 업 셔 열 졍 이 면 아 ᄒᆞᆷ 이 나 빈 엇 수 오 며 군 량 미 와 마 량 쵸 를 다 민 간 에 셔 사 드 리 며 구 ᄒᆞᄂᆞᆫ 티 로 공 급 ᄒᆞ 여 주 되 며 회 ᄂᆞᆫ 오 히 려 위 령 ᄒᆞ 야 소 ᄉᆞ 로 수 탐 ᄒᆞ 며 겸 탈 ᄒᆞ 고 주 ᄂᆞᆫ 사 이 나 갑 슨 시 가 에 비 교 ᄒᆞ 면 무 비 락 가 가 되 옵 고 가 셩 졍 에 류 주 ᄒᆞᄂᆞᆫ 로 군 의 슈 관 과 며 브 러 경 무 관 은 월 경 ᄒᆞ 며 칭 탁 ᄒᆞ 야 빅 셩 의 모 믹 을 어 지 로 산 거 시 ᄯᅡ ᄒᆞᆫ 수 빅 석 이 되 고 보 로 빈 면 담 을 몰 을 노 화 ᄌᆞ 발 아 브 랄 며 디 가 업 게 ᄒᆞ 엿 스 니 경 황 ᄒᆞᆫ 남 아 에 잔 민 이 엇 지 써 ᄉᆡᆼ 존 ᄒᆞ 오 릿 가 면 잔 목 을 가 셜 ᄒᆞᆷ 과 평 진 을 리 치 ᄒᆞᆷ 과 최 종 을 수 운 ᄒᆞᄂᆞᆫ ᄃᆡ 취 지 으 로 치 기 를 탕 쟈 히 ᄒᆞ 빈 방 금 이 가 을 쳘 의 농 민 들 이 쥭 으 라 도 ᄒᆞᆫ 수 업 고 부 역 ᄒᆞᄂᆞᆫ 쟈 ᄂᆞᆫ 쇠 ᄒᆞᆫ 부 ᄒᆞᆫ 거 시 만 고 ᄯᅩ 샹 대 쳔 의 드 린 록 ᄇᆡᆨ 간 을 건 조 ᄒᆞᆯ 츄 로 송 판 을 쳐 어 슈 운 ᄒᆞᄂᆞᆫ 역 수 에 인 민 이 부 샹 ᄒᆞ 여 지 ᄒᆞ 엿 스 니 이 거 슨 엇 더 연 고 인 지 알 지 못 ᄒᆞ 겟 고 관 원 과 ᄇᆡᆨ 셩 이 등 에 ᄌᆞ 리 를 ᄯᅥ 지 못 ᄒᆞ 고 빗 은 쌍 에 붓 치 지 못 ᄒᆞ 고 도 오 히 려 ᄯᅢ 회 의 칙 망 을 밧 을 가 두 려 워 ᄒᆞ 야 제 반 수 에 응 남 ᄒᆞ 기 를 진 ᄉᆡᆼ 길 탄 ᄒᆞ 지 아 님 이 업 스 되 군 슈 가 불 셜 게 힝 ᄒᆞᆫ 다 고 ᄒᆞ 야 군 중 에 압 도 ᄒᆞ 기 쳐 지 에 니 르 렷 다 가 요 힝 무 ᄉᆞ 히 면 ᄒᆞ 엿 수 오 며 소 위 동 학 은 ᄭᅳᆺ 도 가 에 셔 등 금 ᄒᆞᄂᆞᆫ 바 이 어 ᄂᆞᆯ 이 무 리 가 엇 지 ᄒᆞ 야 로 군 진 중 에 붓 칭 호 왈 진 의 일 진 소 ᄒᆞ 고 소 위 회 쟝 ᄒᆞᆫ 놈 셔 ᄂᆞᆫ 진 소 위 ᄃᆡ ᄒᆞᆫ 령 을 가 지 고 드 러 와 서 셩 문 에 방 을 붓 치 고 당 류 를 취 집 ᄒᆞ 미 일 도 취 ᄂᆞᆫ 거 시 구 름 ᄀᆞᆺ 치 ᄒᆞ 야 일 간 에 쟉 기 량 이 면 되 셔 가 지 고 와 서 모 히 ᄂᆞᆫ 쟈 가 거 의 쳔 여 명 에 니 르 미 곳 단 쳔 과 갑 산 과 길 쥬 와 병 쳔 과 경 셩 등 디 사 ᄅᆞᆷ 으 로 셔 무 빈 우 죠 ᄒᆞᄂᆞᆫ 민 이 오 죵 ᄎᆞ 로 참 회 ᄒᆞᆯ 쟈 가 ᄯᅩ 면 쳔 빅 명 이 니 될 넌 지 알 지 못 ᄒᆞ 겟 스 오 며 이 수 방 에 일 이 만 ᄒᆞᆫ 빅 를 남 ᄒᆞ 와 셔 소 잇 칙 망 은 빈 에 편 키 어 려 운 바 이 오 니 본 군 슈 를 밧 비 로 감 ᄒᆞ 여 면 ᄒᆞ 라 ᄯᅥ 주 샹 을 쳔 만 복 망 이 라 ᄒᆞ 엿 더 라

○죠칭과졔 미 용 수 가 외 부 로 죠 회 ᄒᆞ 되 근 ᄂᆡ 부 슈 ᄃᆡ 쟈 로 본 샤 가 구 ᄃᆡ 신 으 로 더 브 러 면 회 ᄒᆞᆫ 후

예 ᄒᆞᆫ 공 ᄉᆡᆨ 을 일 인 죠 쳔 의 게 ᄒᆞᆯ 금 ᄒᆞᆯ 식 으 로 신 문 에 게 지 ᄒᆞ 엿 스 니 즉 본 샤 와 밋 귀 대 신 간 에 면 의 ᄒᆞᆫ 일 이 도 모 지 업 고 다 만 ᄒᆞᆫ 미 면 괴 회 샤 소 관 ᄉᆞ 로 ᄒᆞᆫ 번 죠 회 ᄒᆞ 엿 거 늘 이 곳 치 과 ᄌᆡ ᄒᆞᆷ 이 심 이 괴 란 ᄒᆞᆫ 지 라 드 시 츌 보 치 말 나 ᄒᆞ 엿 더 라

○문 우 도 약 평 하 군 수 윤 괴 셥 씨 가 외 부 로 보 고 ᄒᆞ 기 를 평 의 턴 도 션 이 본 군 을 지 나 이 믜 기 동 ᄒᆞ 엿 ᄂᆞᆫ 티 본 군 니 에 졍 거 쟝 이 두 곳 이 오 졍 렁 ᄒᆞᆫ 빈 신 이 별 고 곤 쥭 련 이 도 를 허 란 ᄒᆞᆯ 세 에 이 러 ᄒᆞᆫ 죠 약 이 잇 셧 ᄂᆞᆫ 지 ᄒᆞᆫ 시 ᄒᆞ 야 셔 교 셥 ᄒᆞᄂᆞᆫ 티 편 케 ᄒᆞ 기 를 바 란 다 ᄒᆞ 엿 더 라

○졔쥬보고 졔 쥬 군 수 가 외 부 로 보 고 ᄒᆞ 기 를 음 력 칠 월 이 십 ᄉᆞ 일 에 일 본 ᄉᆞ 션 일 쳑 이 본 군 좌 면 포 에 리 박 ᄒᆞ 야 목 쥐 와 괴 ᄌᆡ 를 하 륙 ᄒᆞ 니 건 츅 ᄒᆞᆯ 뜻 이 잇 다 ᄒᆞ 엿 고 대 졍 군 보 고 내 에 음 력 칠 월 이 십 오 일 에 일 본 ᄉᆞ 션 일 쳑 이 본 군 우 면 포 구 에 리 박 ᄒᆞ 야 목 ᄌᆡ 와 밋 괴 계 를 하 륙 ᄒᆞ 야 모 슬 봉 우 희 다 건 츅 ᄒᆞ 기 에 기 ᄒᆞᆼ 치 아 니 ᄒᆞᆫ 구 안 에 외 인 이 건 츅 ᄒᆞᆷ 이 이 쟝 졍 에 금 ᄒᆞᆫ 바 이 와 엄 금 ᄒᆞᆯ 뜻 으 로 이 믜 지 령 ᄒᆞ 엿 더 니 회 랑 군 에 셔 ᄯᅩ 보 고 ᄒᆞ 기 를 일 인 이 티 답 ᄒᆞ 야 ᄀᆞᆯ 아 ᄃᆡ 우 리 ᄂᆞᆫ 비 칙 군 소 속 으 로 어 괴 와 셔 진 츅 ᄒᆞᆷ 은 다 만 다 른 병 참 티 왕 ᄒᆞᄂᆞᆫ 것 만 보 라 ᄂᆞᆫ 니 가 히 ᄃᆡ 리 말 할 고 ᄯᅩ 일 한 량 국 이 동 명 ᄒᆞᆫ 본 인 즉 반 드 시 이 갓 치 금 ᄒᆞ 지 말 나 ᄒᆞ 엿 더 라

○회관귀복 동 신 원 회 관 강 인 규 씨 가 당 고 ᄒᆞ 고 부 령 본 졔 로 ᄂᆞ 려 갓 더 니 ᄒᆞ 원 에 셔 말 ᄒᆞ 기 를 이 사 ᄅᆞᆷ 이 아 니 면 시 무 ᄒᆞᆯ 수 업 다 ᄒᆞ 야 괴 복 이 된 다 더 라

○거졔순환 공 졔 후 에 ᄂᆞᆫ 각 관 직 의 차 함 이 다 시 발 ᄒᆞ 야 거 ᄃᆡ ᄒᆞᆫ 졔 쟝 이 순 환 될 터 이 라 더 라

○ᄒᆞᆨᄉᆡᆼ열회 일 쟉 에 어 비 신 씨 졔 중 원 ᄒᆞᆨ ᄉᆡᆼ 연 에 참 예 ᄒᆞᆫ 양 인 은 부 장 남 녀 ᄒᆞᆸ 오 십 여 명 이 오 한 인 은 부 관 반 윤 용 텰 부 령 리 인 영 ᄒᆞ 니 부 령 법 원 쟝 화 ᄂᆞᆫ ᄉᆡᆼ ᄒᆞᆸ 관 리 근 ᄉᆡᆼ 육 군 장 신 티 후 외 부 협 판 윤 치 호 와 대 국 신 문 ᄉᆞ 쟝 리 종 일 졔 씨 인 ᄃᆡ 윤 치 호 씨 ᄂᆞᆫ 동 부 인 ᄒᆞ 야 참 예 ᄒᆞ 야 영 어 로 연 셜 ᄒᆞ 엿 다 더 라

○국졔미결 금 번 국 졔 를 강 봉 ᄒᆞᆯ 티 인 티 레 셜 이 분 일 ᄒᆞ 야 혹 은 대 공 소 봉 이 라 ᄒᆞ 며 혹 은 시 봉 이 가 라 ᄒᆞ 야 아 직 결 졍 치 못 ᄒᆞ 엿 다 더 라

○하 방 령 관 호 위 총 관 리 근 퇴 씨 ᄂᆞᆫ 일 본 군 ᄉᆞ 령 관 을 자 조 심 방 ᄒᆞᆫ 다 더 라

론셜

아라사의 내지 동졍

영국 인ᄑᆡ어 ᄉᆞ세가 아라사를 유람ᄒᆞ고 ᄂᆡ디 형편을 긔록ᄒᆞ야 론 ᄐᆡᆷᄉᆞ 신문샤 쟝의게 긔셔ᄒᆞᆫ 바를 동보히 계지ᄒᆞ엿기로 좌에 번등ᄒᆞ노라

북이 아라사 북방과 및 구라파 아라사 중앙으로 도라ᄃᆞᆫ이며 유람ᄒᆞᆫ 배에 그 나라 학교 교ᄉᆞ와 회당 목ᄉᆞ이며 지에 농부셔 지란 도친견ᄒᆞ야 셔로 계분이 잇게 지니엿ᄂᆞᆫᄃᆡ 이 사ᄅᆞᆷ들과 ᄒᆞᆷ게 ᄒᆞᆨ동ᄒᆡᆼᄒᆞ야 방조ᄒᆞᄂᆞᆫ 바를 밧히 알엇ᄂᆞᆫ지라

소경 각쳐 중에 가쟝 ᄒᆞᆫ 이라 ᄒᆞᄂᆞᆫ 곳은 아라사 안에 즁등되ᄂᆞᆫ ᄃᆡ 방이요 르로스트포라 ᄒᆞᄂᆞᆫ ᄉᆡᆼ은 국중에 뎨일가ᄂᆞᆫ ᄃᆡ 쳐이며 스몰렌스코라 ᄒᆞᄂᆞᆫ 곳은 그 중에 ᄎᆞᄎᆞ ᄒᆞᆫ 도방인ᄃᆡ 동힝ᄒᆞ엿든 사ᄅᆞᆷ들이 말ᄒᆞ기를 이곳이 귀왕수 ᄉᆡᆼ 년젼에 비교ᄒᆞᆯ진ᄃᆡ 크게 발달이 된 거시 만타 ᄒᆞ고 ᄃᆞᆫ ᄒᆞᄂᆞᆫ지라 그 ᄉᆞ유인 즉 젼쟈에ᄂᆞᆫ 이곳에 사ᄂᆞᆫ 우쥰ᄒᆞᆫ ᄇᆡᆨ셩들이 불학무식ᄒᆞ야 졍치가 무엇인지 법률이 무엇인지 모르고 지ᄂᆡ더니 근일에 이르러ᄂᆞᆫ 크게 지명이 되여 ᄉᆞᄉᆞ로 관장을 두고 치민ᄒᆞᄂᆞᆫ 법을 연구ᄒᆞ야 법졔가 잇게 지니ᄂᆞᆫᄃᆡ 도리여 즁앙 졍부로 더브러 난호여 각각 셜입ᄒᆞᆷ의 ᄉᆞ와 명을 논ᄒᆞᄂᆞᆫ 중 각쳐에셔 신문을 발간ᄒᆞ야 우마에 시리 ᄀᆡ인이 다 열람ᄒᆞ도록 ᄒᆞᄂᆞᆫ지라 ᄇᆡᆨ셩들이 모도 슌박ᄒᆞ야 나라에 충셩ᄒᆞ며 괴쵸를 공교ᄒᆞ게 ᄒᆞ란ᄒᆞᆯ 조음에 일아 긔쟝이 된 고로 분격ᄒᆞᄂᆞᆫ 마음들과 진츙ᄒᆞᄂᆞᆫ 졍셩들이 일층 더옥ᄒᆞ야 ᄌᆞ원 츌젼ᄒᆞ라 ᄒᆞᄂᆞᆫ 자ㅣ 불가승수인ᄃᆡ

만일 혹 그 중에 친졀ᄒᆞᆫ 교구가 잇서 츌젼ᄒᆞᆷ을 면ᄒᆞ여 ᄒᆞ면 ᄃᆡ단히 칙망ᄒᆞ야 도리여 구박ᄒᆞ고 ᄒᆞᄂᆞᆫ 말이 우리ᄂᆞᆫ 일본 군ᄉᆞ들을 괴여 치죽이고 ᄯᅡ라 사외 병상ᄒᆞᆫ 군졸을 치료ᄒᆞ야 구완ᄒᆞ여야 ᄒᆞ겟다 ᄒᆞ며 면력 합의 ᄒᆞᆷ이 과연 위 ᄒᆞᆫ 중에 본은 실로 황의 치 안코 영국을 더욱 편중히 녀이ᄂᆞᆫ지라

이ᄂᆞᆫ 다른 ᄭᅡ닭이 아니라 다만 이 ᄇᆡᆨ셩들의 소견에ᄂᆞᆫ 영국의 방조ᄒᆞᆷ만 아니면 엇지 일본이 감히 ᄃᆡ젹ᄒᆞ리오 ᄒᆞ야 영국으로 ᄒᆞ야곰 포장화심ᄒᆞᄂᆞᆫ 뜻이 만흔 즉 쳥컨ᄃᆡ 영국 ᄇᆡᆨ셩들은 아모조록 아라사 ᄉᆞ셰의 리ᄒᆡ 귀의ᄒᆞᄂᆞᆫ 마음을 범연히 알지 말고 졍신을 ᄎᆞ려 아라사의 젼쟁 결국 되ᄂᆞᆫ 바를 주목ᄒᆞ야 보기를 권고ᄒᆞᆫ다고 ᄒᆞ엿다더라

뎐보

만쥬군총ᄉᆞ령부발 ᄯᅢ
일본ᄉᆞ령부착뎐

○봉텬젼황 십ᄉᆞ일조에 후원ᄒᆞᆫ 보병이 잇ᄂᆞᆫ 젹과 병이 중ᄃᆡ가 령이ᄒᆞᆨ림ᄯᅩᆫ과 밋 부가졍에 향ᄒᆞ야 젼진ᄒᆞ야 왓스나 우리 젼조의 격퇴ᄒᆞᆫ 바 되엿다더라

TELEGRAMS.

Head Quarters Seoul.

At 1:40 A. M. on the 15th inst. reports Field Marshal Oyama one company of cavalry attacked our garrison at Shinglungtun but were repulsed.

Tokyo, Nov. 15th.

The Japanese loan has been very successfully floated, being oversubscribed 8 or 9 times in London and New York.

Tokyo Nov. 16th.

According to a telegram from Chefoo one Russian destroyer has escaped from Port Arthur and arrived at that port.

Later.

A despatch from Chefoo states that a very heavy snowfall has occurred there. The Russian destroyer, which escaped from Port Arthur, is the (name unrecognizable K. D. N.)

Head Quartors Seoul.

A report from Songchin states that the Russians are buying quantities of provisions and fuel. Prices have consequenty risen and the people are in want.

FROM JAPAN PAPERS.

London, Nov. 11.

The Republican majority in the House of Representatives will be 100. The remarkable triumph of Mr. Roosevelt is ascribed to the popular admiration of him as a typical American, and also to the country's approval of his Imperialistic policy.

At Washington it is stated that Congress will be asked to vote the sum of eight and a quarter millions sterling for the building of new men-of-war, including three battleships and five fast cruisers.

Berlin, Nov. 10.

M. Etienne, speaking in the French Chamber, expressed the hope that while the alliance betwoen France and Russia is strengthened, France would cultivate the friendship of Great Britain. He hoped that in time an Anglo Russsian Alliance would be concluded.

Berlin, Nov. 10.

The Russian Government has promised to remunerate those who are able to give any particulars regarding the suspicious vessels which were present during the recent incident in the North Sea.

The following British colliers are now employed in conveying coal for the Baltic Fleet:—"Roddam," "Cheviotdale," "Japton," "Aberlour," "Conway," "Frankby," "Ninian Stuart," St. Leonards," St. Nioholas," "Yedo," "Hursdale," "William Storrs," and "Oceano."

London, Nov. 10.

Lord Lansdowne, Secretary for Foreign Affairs, speaking at the Lord Mayor's banquet at the Guildhall, said he believed the Convention recently concluded was most friendly to the French Republic. It had established most intimate and cordial relations between Great Britain and France which would enable the two nations to exercise a useful and pacific influence over the other Powers. His lordship instanced the assistance given by France in effecting an amicable settlement between Great Britain and Russia with reference to the recent incident in the North Sea. The attack on British citizens in the North Sea was an affront to the British flag, the consequences of which, if it had been intentional, he would rather not contemplate. Recent evidence had, however, satisfied him that the Russian Government believed in all good faith that the facts of the case were contrary to what the British public supposed.

Paris, Nov. 11.

The difficulties as to the constitution of the Commission of Inquiry into the North Sea incident have now been settled, and the Commission will commence its work at the Quai d'Orsay at the end of November.

THE JAPANESE ASSAULT ON THE BALTIC FLEET.

Under the above heading the "Tsingtauer Neueste Nachrichten" has the following article (freely translated). From latest reports to us and from Reuter's telegrams relative to the so-called Hull incident, it appears that the officers of the Russian Baltic Fleet were convinced that they were attacked by the Japanese before they opened fire, and through this deplorable belief wounded and killed a number of English fishermen. The forthcoming international enquiry will doubtless throw light on how far the statements of the Russian Admiral agree with the facts as already stated.

Anyone, who has voyaged through the North Sea and knows how the English fishermen follow thefr calling, most nights fishing without lights in the path of big steamers and that they can have scarcely any idea of international affairs, can scarcely be surprised at the occurrence.

When one further sees that the British Government, in direct contrast to the views of the English Press, does not entertain the idea of resorting to arms, but places the matter before an international board of enquiry, one can also not deny that in Downing Street the matter is not considered to be so simple as stated by theHull fishermen. As we have said, the forthcoming enquiry will throw light on this.

In the meantime, from several quarters, the question is asked whether the Japanese are not attempting secretly to attack the Baltic Fleet.

We cannot close our eyes to the fact that many circumstences during the past few months have tended to make the Russians at least extremely suspicious. In the middle of September a Japanese was arrested in deserted Skagen, where he said he had gone on a visit of pleasure.

As he afterwards gave proof that he was a Naval officer Captain Takikawa, attaché to the Japanese Legition at Berlin, he was released, but kept under strict surveillance of the Danish police until he crossed the German border. That, at a time where his country is engaged in war, Captain Takikawa should have undertaken a voyage of pleasure through Stohckholm, Malmoe, Copenhagen, Karsor and Kyborg seems at least a little suspicious. One can well understand that in St Petersburg it is thought that something more than pleasure brings a large number of Japanese naval officers to Europe and England at the time when the Baltic Fleet is starting. It is well known that during the last few months a large number of Japanese, naval officers, torpedo officers and engineers have taken passage from the east in the European bound liners. Seemingly their destination has been England, Denmark and Sweden. Further, news comes from Bombay that Japanese naval officers bought a schooner there and set sail for the Cape of Good Hope. It is scarcely probable that they have also gone on a voyage of pleasure. It is at least more probable that a torpedo or mine attack has been planned on the fleet. That a stir has been made in St. Petersburg by this view, the official newspaper "Journal de St. Petersburg" clearly shows, in the following telegram sent through the "ostasiatsche Lloyd" service.

"The 'Nipponismus' knows no bounds set by military honor. A result of this is the Hull affair. The only remedy for the 'Nipponismus' is to set a ban on the Japanese."

If we throw a glance at the events of the present struggle between Russia and Japan, the one thing, which strike's us most of all, is the unexpectedness of the blows struck, which has assured them so many victories over their enemies. In Japan comprehensive preparations have been made to conquer the Baltic Fleet, if possible to destroy it, at any rate to weaken it.

The Baltic Fleet has no distance to go before it finds itself on the field of battle against Japan. If the Japanese can attack them in the Mediterranean so much the better for Japan. On the other hand it is also natural that the Russian ships journey with decks cleared for action, so as to be prepared to attack the enemy, when they meet.

Admiral Roschdjestwensky telegraphed to St. Petersburg from Vigo that he was attacked by two torpedo boats, one of which he sank. the other escaping.

One will grant the Russian Naval officers sufficient knowledge to distinguish even at night, a torpedoboat from a fishing trawler. If they had been torpedoboats of other nations who had by accident crossed the path of the fleet, then they would have immediately declared their nationality. Besides the loss of one of the vessels would have been made known, when the other reached home.

There therefore is absolutely no occasion to doubt the evidence of Admiral Roschdjestwensky. It will not surprise us if we hear a great deal more of Japanese attacks on the Batlic Fleet before it reaches the orient. On the contrary, we expect them as a matter of course.

The Standard's correspondent with General Kuroki's forces wiring from Liao yang on September 21st says, in reference to the Liao-yang battle,:—The Japanese must have realised that there would be no repetition by them of the German "Itatic" at Sedan the moment the Russians abandoned their first line of defence at Anshentien, when General Kuroki had forced his way through the line of defence to the East, on the Tang-ho, and threatened the Russian rear. It is possiblethat even a leader more daring and resourceful then Marshal Oyama might have inflicted a decisive defeat on his opponents. As it was, the Japanese Commander was overborne by fear for his own communications.

Governed by this consideration, he concentrated his forces for their protection, hurled himself headlong against fortifications thrown up for the express purpose of detaining him, reduced the troops under General Kuroki, on whose movement everything depended, to one Division and a-half, and made a feeble demonstration against the railway. One is tempted to ask whether, when the enemy was escaping by the window after having bolted the door, it was really worth while to waste strength in breaking open the latter, intead of running round to the former.

I had ventured to embody these comments on the Japanese tactics in two of my previous messages, but they were struck out and returned to Yin-Kow, in accordance with those restrictions by the Censorship which have driven some of my colleagues at the Front to leave the Japanese Heardquarters for the comparative freedom of China.

The cablegrams I have seen from Europe appear to present the position of the Japanese in a worse light than is warranted by the circumstances. They are fully prepared, as a matter of fact, to advance to Mukeu, or even, if necessary, to Kharbin, and their confidence in themselves and their leaders is, as it should be, wholly unshaken.

The funeral of the late Crown Princess will take place next mouth. Preparations are being actively pushed forward.

Mr. Choi Dong-sup, a member of the Il-chin-hoi, has established a Japanese school for Korean students (presumably of the Il-chin-hoi faith) at Hoi-dong.

Mr. Yi Chai-kuk wires from Tokyo that the Korean students in Japan are already out of funds. He asks the Financial Department to settle this difficulty for them as speedily as possible.

Truly we have to go abroad for news. This is the latest. A telegram from the "N. C. Daily News" correspondent at Tokyo says that Korea will, it is expected, adopt the gold standard.

We find that our contemporary from whom we elicited the information (as published yesterday) that the Korean Vice Minister of Foreign Affairs had issued instructions dispensing with passports for Japanese in Korea, was mistaken. The Japanese Vice Minister of Foreign Affairs was responsible for the order.

Immense quantities of cargo are lying along the bund at Newchwang, chiefly imports by Japanese steamers. Vessels from that port state that the piled-up cargo stretches for miles. On the other hand the bean cake export from Newchang is practically at a stand still, and want of beans is greatly felt in Japan.—China Gazette

---

We call our readers' attention to the advertisement of an auction which will take place at the residence of Mr. H. G. Brand tomorrow.

The Korea Daily News.

Issued at 5 P. M. daily except Sundays.

Rate of Subscription:—
Per Year............Yen 25.
Per Quarter..........Yen 7.
Per Month..........Yen 2.50.

Postage in Korea not charged extra.
Postage abroad charged extra.

Advertisements. 50 sen per day for 1 inch or less.
5 yen per month per inch.
50 yen per year per inch.

All communications to
E. T. BETHELL,
Editor and Publisher,
Pak-tong, Seoul.

THE IL CHIN HOI.

From comments made from time to time by our contemporaries abroad, we notice that many misconceptions exist as to the "personnel" and objects of the "Ilchiu hoi," and its country cousin the "Chin-po Hoi."

It will be remembered that in July last many societies were formed amongst the Koreans, with the object of presenting memorials to the throne protesting against the granting of the demands for the cession of something more than half Korea presented by the Japanese Government in the name of Mr. Nagamori. The opinions of these societies were naturally anti, Japanese, and the Japanese Military authorities, in addition to adopting sternly repressive measures, decided to encourage an opposition society. Through a tool of theirs a certain Mr. Komochi, a former minor Korean official, at that time "out of work" was approached with the suggestion that he should get together a society pledged to support Japanese interests in Korea.

The result is the "Il-chin-hoi," a society pretending to have lofty aims for the betterment of Korea, but in reality owing its existence to financial support from the Japanese Headquarters. Its members have distinguished themselves by close-cropping their hair and wearing foreign-style headgear so that they are conspicuous in the streets. This does their cause no good as they are a particularly dirty and ill-favoured lot and a glance at them is sufficient to dispel all illusions that they are "out" for anything except the "stuff."

Their procedure hitherto has been to pester high officials with senseless memorials calling for impossible reforms, and they appear to have hoped to gain something by trading on the Emperor's well-known dislike of public demonstrations. Yesterday it was reported that they had told off some 120 of their number to parade the streets of Seoul, and today we learn that they are discussing the formation of a Japanese language school.

It seems now that their Japanese employers have found them somewhat out of hand, and for the sake of peace and quietness it is to be hoped that they will withdraw their protection and allow the Korean authorities to deal with these vagabonds as they deserve.

The Il-chin-hoi is a two-edged weapon; if men can be bought for one purpose they can be bought for another, and unless the army headquarters are careful they will find themselves with another foe on their hands. We have already received news from the north that a large number of the Chin-po-hoi people have gone over to the Russians, and we fully expect to hear of other similar occurrences. Under these circumstances it would seem advisable to immediately withdraw all support from these societies. Whatever purpose they were originally intended to serve they do not appear to have accomplished anything, good or bad, and if payment is withheld the societies will speedily be no more.

The whole incident is a discreditable one, and the sooner we are given an opportunity of forgetting it, the better.

MARTIAL LAW.

The following additional proclamation has been issued by General Hasegawa. It will be seen the object is to prevent communication between that part of Korea occupied by the Russians and that held by the Japanese

1.—Persons who intend to proceed by water to the part of Ham Gyongdo occupied by the Russians, or to Usuri, from Gensan, must apply for permission to the Commander of the Japanese garrision, at Gensan, submitting a written petition mentioning the destination and object of the voyage, and the length of the journey.

2.—Owners or Captains of ships wishing to proceed to the places mentioned must submit a written statement, giving the name of the ship and the amount of tonnage, also the nature and amount of the cargo, and the ports to be touched at.

3.—If necessary, the Commander may prohibit any persons or ship from proceeding to the places mentioned.

4.—No arms, ammunition, explosives, or the like, may be convoyed to the places mentioned.

5.—Penalties will be inflicted under Martial Law in the case of above regulations not being obeyed.

We learn from the "Chefoo Daily News" that wounded and otherwise incapacitated soldiers have been brought in to Dalny from Port Arthur, according to various Chinese reports, at the rate of from four hundred to one thousand per day.

A St. Petersburg telegram, dated Oct. 13. states that five Japanese cruisers are in the vicinity of Vladivostock and that the Japanese troops in North Korea are expected to be conveyed to Vladivostock in the near future. The story about the cruisers may be correct but we certainly do not believe that the Japanese intend transporting troops to Vladivostock via North Korea.

The following paragraph is from the "Japan Gazette." It has a very ancient smell and we wonder where the "Japan Gazette" got it from. A Korean politician is alleged to have drawn from the Imperial Treasury Y20,000 or Y30,000 a year in order to oppose the policy proposed by Count Okuma in respect to Korea. It is said the money was hitherto obtained on the pretext of being for the deal with Marquis Ito.

The "Chugai Shogyo" states that the last of the Nippon Yusen Kaisha's steamers to sail for North China this year will probably be the "Independent," which will leave Japan on the 23rd inst., as those waters it is expected, will be closed to navigation about the 5th prox. During the last winter the Company, by order of the military authorities, ran its steamers as far as Tsinhwangtao, near Shanhaikwan, making connection with the railway at the latter place. Whether similar measures will be taken this year is not yet known.

The Governor-General of French Indo-China has given orders for the work of fortifying Port Courbet to be begun at once, so that, in case of war, that port may serve as a refuge and meeting centre for the mobile defence on the coast of Tonquin. Barracks for the Field Artillery have just been built at a great cost at Sontay, but only on their completion, says the "Hong Kong Telegraph," did the authorities become aware of the fact that the architect had forgotten to provide stables for the horses and mules.

MUKDEN.

Advices from the north state that General Rennenkampf's Cossacks have been annoying the Japanese troops in their successful raids on the enemy's flank. These Cossacks move about very quickly, and carry some artillery with them. Their forte seems to be to make quick strikes at lines of communication. Swooping down on their adversaries, the latter are usually thrown into confusion from which they do not recover quickly enough to do the attacking party much injury. One or two Russian surgeons captured by the Japanese state that the Japanese suffer somewhat from dysentery, and have asked their prisoners' assistance in combating the disease.

THE NEW JAPANESE LOAN.

Particulars are now to hand of the new loan which was floated in London and New York on the 10th inst.

Altogether the conditions are far from favourable to Japan, and the inferences to be drawn are not pleasant. It will be remembered that the issue of this loan has been hanging fire for some weeks and that we were told that the Japanese were awaiting a victory in order to obtain favourable terms. That investors at home do not think much of the prospects is evidenced by the fact that the present issue price is £3 less than that of the last loan. The Tokio authorities also recognise that the terms are not favourable. The following were the conditions as given in the "Kobe Chronicle" That bonds for the total amount required, £12,000,000, are to be floated in London and New York, £6,000,000 in each city, the rate of interest to be 5 per cent. per annum, and the issuing price £90 10s. per £100 face value. The actual amount receivable by the Government is £86 15s., a commission of £3 15s. being paid to the underwriters. The Customs revenue of the Empire is pledged as security.

The Bonds must be subscribed and paid up in four months between the present month and February next, and they will be redeemed in four years and a half, from April 5th, 1907, to October 5th, 1911. After April 5th, 1907, the Government may redeem any amount at option, the amount to be redeemed on every occasion to be advertised in the newspapers six months previously.

The interest on the bonds will be paid half-yearly, on April 5th, and October 5th. Interest coupons in arrear and bonds drawn will be accepted as payment of Customs duty at the rate of 2s. 0½. per yen.

It is stated that arrangements for floating the loan are already completed in London and New York. The syndicate undertaking the flotation is composed of the Hongkong and Shanghai Bank, the Yokohama Specie Bank, and Parr's Bank.

As will be remembered, the Government was authorised to issue bonds to the amount of Y380,000,000 by an Urgent Imperial Ordinance and Law No. 1 of this year, which were approved by the Diet during the special session in April last. The bonds are now being issued to the above amount, namely, Y280,000,000 in Japan, and Y100,000,000 in London and New York. The bonds now to be issued in those cities are said to be a portion of the Y570,000,000 which it is proposed to raise next year. The present issue is intended chiefly to strengthen the reserve of gold in the Bank of Japan.

The "Tokyo Asahi's" Takeshiki correspondent wires under date of the 8th inst. that, according to a report, Vladivostock is already icebound.

The Japanese army is subsisting principally on rice and preserved foods, but is comfortably equipped. Their principal fear is for forage for their horses, for during the winter the country is swept clean on both sides of the railway, and the inhabitants are reluctant to sell anything.—Chefoo Daily News.

The Korea Daily News.

VOL. I, THURSDAY, NOVEMBER 17, 1904. No. 103

HONGKONG & SHANGHAI BANKING CORPORATION.

Paid-up Capital....................$10,000,000
Reserve Fund:—Sterling Reserve... 10,000,000
Silver Reserve..... 7,000,000

27,000,000
Reserve Liability of Proprietors... 10,000,000

HEAD OFFICE, HONGKONG.

London Bankers, London and County Banking Company Limited.

Branches and Agencies,
London.

Amoy,	Hankow	Penang,
Bangkok,	Hiogo,	Rangoon,
Batavia,	Iloilo,	Saigon,
Bombay,	Lyons,	San Francisco,
Calcutta,	Manila,	Singapore,
Colombo,	Nagasaki,	Sourabaya,
Foochow,	New York,	Tientsin,
Hamburg,	Peking,	Yokohama,

Credits granted on approved Securities, and every description of Banking and Exchange business transacted.

Drafts granted on London and the chief Commercial places in Europe, India, Australia, America, China and Japan.

HOLME RINGER & CO., AGENTS,
CHEMULPO.

ON CHEONG & CO.,
SEOUL.

GENERAL STORE KEEPERS.
Imported provisions, Cooking Utensils Crockery, etc.
FRESH BREAD DAILY.

MITSU BISHI DOCKYARD & ENGINE WORKS,
NAGASAKI.

CODE WORD, "DOCK."

A. 1, A. B. C., and Engineering Codes used.

DOCK No. 1 (at Tategami).

Extreme Length..............523 feet
Length on blocks............ 513 „
Width of Entrance on Top......89 „
„ „ Bottom....77 „
Water on Blocks at Spring Tide 26½ „

DOCK No. 2 (Mukaijima).

Extreme Length..............371 feet
Length on Blocks.............360 „
Width of Entrance on Top......66 „
„ „ Bottom 53 „
Water on Blocks at Spring Tide 22 „

PATENT SLIP (at Kosuge).

Can take vessels up to 1,000 tons gross

THE WORKS are well equipped with the LATEST IMPROVEMENTS, and can execute any kind of work in SHIPBUILDING and MARINE ENGINEERING, as well as in REPAIRING of SHIPS.

The COMPANY'S new powerful steamer OURA-MARU (712 tons, 700 I.H.P.), specially built for SALVAGE PURPOSES, and equipped with necessary gear, is always READY at SHORT NOTICE.

CHARTERED BANK OF INDIA AUSTRALIA & CHINA.

INCORPORATED BY ROYAL CHARTER 1853

HEAD OFFICES:—LONDON.

Paid-up Capital £800,000
Reserve Liability of Shareholders 800,000
Reserve Fund 800,000

Drafts granted upon all the principal places in the world and every description of Exchange and banking business transacted.

E. MEYER & Co., Agents,
Chemulpo.

E. MEYER & CO.
Chemulpo.

SOLE AGENTS IN KOREA FOR:
A. T. Morse, Sons & Co's "Fresco" Distemper

In all colours ready for use on walls, Ceilings etc.

and

AVENARIUS CARBOLINEUM

A wood-preserving and antiseptic oil preparation

Against decay, dry-rot, fungus and wood-destroying insects.

A large supply always in Stock. Prices upon application.

E. MEYER & Co.,
Chemulpo.

THE METHODIST PUBLISHING HOUSE,
Little West Gate, Seoul.

JOB PRINTING, TYPEWRITER PAPER
CARBON PAPER, VISITING CARDS
STATIONERY, BOOK BINDING
BOOK PUBLISHERS
AMERICAN SCHOOL BOOKS
SPENCERIAN COPY BOOKS
PEN CARBON LETTER AND BILL BOOKS

S. A. BECK, Manager.

HOKURKU DOBOKU KAISHA.

Branch office in Chong Dong, Seoul.

Japanese telephone No. 165

CONTRACT DEPARTMENT.

We can contract to build any building or construction.

MERCHANDISE DEPARTMENT.

We can provide any building material. We have just contracted to build the new Belgian Legation.

DAI-ICHI GINKO
LIMITED.
(Formerly the First National Bank)

ESTABLISHED 1873

INCORPORATED UNDER PRESENT LAW 1896

Capital - - - - - - - - Yen 5,000,000
Reserve Fund - - - - - 1,500,000

HEAD OFFICE:—TOKIO.

President: Baron SHIBUSAWA.

BRANCHES AND CORRESPONDENTS
In the Principal Cities and Towns of Japan.

Interest Allowed on
Fixed deposits 1 year - - - 6½ per cent
" " 6 months - - - 6 per cent

Special current accounts 1½ sen daily per Y 100
General " " 1 " " " 100

M. TANAKA,
Manager, Chemulpo.

HOLME RINGER & Co.
Chemulpo.

General Merchants and Government Contractors.

Agents for the leading Banks
Steamship Companies
and
Insurance Companies

Importers of Merchandise of every description.

KAMEYA & CO.
GENERAL STOREKEEPERS
Chinkokai - - Seoul
(*Established 1895, Tokyo*)

Confectionery, Hams, Canned Goods, Cutlery, Hirano & Tansan Water. Provisions, Gents, Furnishing goods, Toilet Articles, Travelling Bags, Tobacco, Cigars & Cigarettes Kitchen Utensils. Coffee. Biscuits.

Fresh Goods always kept in Stock.
Prices Moderate
☞ *Please come and inspect our goods*

NIPPON YUSEN KAISHA.

JAPANESE MAIL STEAMSHIP CO.

UNDER MAIL CONTRACT WITH THE IMPERIAL JAPANESE GOVERNMENT.

European Line

Regular Fortnightly Service between Yokohama Kobe, Moji, Shanghai, Hongkong, Singapore, Penang Colombo, Port Said, Marseilles, London and Antwerp

American Line

Regular Fortnightly Service between Hongkong and Seattle, calling at Shanghai, Moji, Kobe, Yokohama and Victoria, B. C.

Australian Line

Regular weekly Service betwen Japan Ports and Australia, calling at Hongkong and Manila.
(Above Three Lines Suspended until further notice).

Shanghai Line

Weekly Service between Shanghai and Japan Ports

Korea Line

Service Kobe, Moji, Nagasaki, Fusan Chemupo Chefoo, Taiku.
S. S. Bahelsberg, 2181 tons.
Service Kobe, Moji, Fusan, Chemulpo, Chinnampo
S. S. ARGO, S. S. Ohio.

BORDEN'S CONDENSED MILK CO.
New York, U. S. A.

ALWAYS IN STOCK
Eagle Brand Condensed Milk.
Gold Seal Condensed Milk.
Peerless (Family) Evaporated Cream.
Borden's Malted Milk.

E. MEYER & CO.
Chemulpo, Korea,
Sole Agents

ROYAL INSURANCE COMPANY,
Funds exceed £10,000,000
FIRE
AT CURRENT RATES.
LIFE
REDUCED PREMIUM.
HOLME RINGER & Co.,
Agents, Chemulpo.

HOTEL DU PALAIS
SEOUL.

The only first class Hotel in Seoul. Situated in the centre of the city opposite the palace.

Cuisine under the supervision of an experienced French Chef.

Well ventilated and furnished throughout.

TARIFF UPON APPLICATION

L. MARTIN
Proprietor and Manager.

大韓每日申報
대한미일신보

(뎨일ᄇᆡᆨᄉᆞ호) (토요일) 일쳔구ᄇᆡᆨᄉᆞ년십일월십구일

본샤고ᄇᆡᆨ

이신보ᄂᆞᆫ영어와한어로셔거미일츌판ᄒᆞᆸ

신문가

한쟝 엽두돈오푼
일삭됴 엽두량닷돈
우표가ᄆᆡ삭닷돈
다맛돈으로밧솝

광고료ᄂᆞᆫ

긔한의쟝단과ᄌᆞ힝의다쇼로즁감ᄒᆞ되렴가로밧을터이오며오ᄅᆡ지아녀대한사람마다다이신문을보실터이니광고내시기를원ᄒᆞ시ᄂᆞᆫ이들은우리신문샤에와셔면약ᄒᆞ심을희망ᄒᆞᆸ

○발힝소 박동대한미일신보샤법어학교압헤젼영국인셜필림집자리오

샤쟝 영국인 (비셜)

평양 ᄃᆡ리점

○평양효동사ᄂᆞᆫ권미보씨로우리신문관ᄃᆡ리인을ᄐᆡᆨ정ᄒᆞ엿ᄉᆞ오니평양에계신구람코져ᄒᆞ시ᄂᆞᆫ 쳠군ᄌᆞᄂᆞᆫ히ᄃᆡ리졈에왕림ᄒᆞ와면외ᄒᆞ시옵

샤고

○우리대한미일신보의목뎍은대한의안녕질셔에관한모든데목에ᄃᆡᄒᆞ야ᄂᆞᆫ공평한변론을쥬쟝ᄒᆞᆷ이라우리동신원의탐보ᄂᆞᆫ신문보시ᄂᆞᆫ쳠군ᄌᆞ의계흥상보도ᄒᆞ리며편지를긔셔ᄒᆞ여주시ᄂᆞᆫ이ᄂᆞᆫ셩명과반ᄃᆡ를젹어붓치시기를희망ᄒᆞ오니이거슬신문샹에긔ᄌᆡ코져ᄒᆞ라ᄂᆞᆫ거시아니오다만극히신용ᄒᆞᄂᆞᆫ증거를삼고쟈ᄒᆞᆷ이라긔쟈ᄂᆞᆫ아모긔셔던지긔ᄌᆡᄒᆞᆷ을되각ᄒᆞᄂᆞᆫ권리를가졋ᄉᆞ나되각ᄒᆞᄂᆞᆫ리유를말ᄒᆞᆯ터이오며공즁평화를문란케ᄒᆞᄂᆞᆫ듯ᄒᆞᆫ긔셔ᄂᆞᆫ의례히밧지안켓ᄉᆞᆸ나이다

●본샤셜시이ᄅᆡ로신문을ᄆᆡ양우례로분젼ᄒᆞ와례젼부의임의로젼ᄒᆞᆫ듯스로먼곳에ᄂᆞᆫ혹늣게젼ᄒᆞ기도ᄒᆞ며혹몃칠거슬ᄒᆞᆫ겁에젼ᄒᆞ기도ᄒᆞ며혹아니젼ᄒᆞᄂᆞᆫ곳도잇다ᄒᆞ와우리신문을ᄉᆞ랑ᄒᆞ야구람ᄒᆞ시ᄂᆞᆫ쳠군ᄌᆞ의게ᄃᆡᄒᆞ야ᄆᆡ우미안ᄒᆞ옵기로지금은분젼인을두고ᄆᆡ일일즉이젼ᄒᆞ며아니젼ᄒᆞ거나늣게거나ᄒᆞᆫ치가업도록ᄒᆞ랴ᄒᆞ오니혹아니젼ᄒᆞ거나혹늣게젼ᄒᆞ거나ᄒᆞᆫ일이잇스면본샤로통긔ᄒᆞ여쥬심을희망ᄒᆞᆸ

관보

뎨이쳔구ᄇᆡᆨ팔십오호

광무팔년십일월십륙일

셔임급ᄉᆞ령

○명젼왕일본국시찰텰도규정급ᄉᆞ무이리 텰도원긔ᄉᆞ 최번셕 십원십구일

○의원면본관 농샹공부긔슈 김셩쵸

○임농샹공부긔슈셔판임관일등 륙품 리샹연

이샹십일월오일

○승셔관임관삼등 평리원쥬ᄉᆞ 박유관 십일월팔일쥬

궁뎡록ᄉᆞ

○총호ᄉᆞ신리근명근 쥬금차국츌시에삼도감슈용이만분급박ᄒᆞ고현금물가가쳑등ᄒᆞ와비젼현슈ᄒᆞ오니위션은화삼십오만원을령탁지부에산외에지츌ᄒᆞ야불일획송ᄒᆞ야ᄒᆞ여곰긔한에밋쳐비용케ᄒᆞᆷ이 하여ᄒᆞ올집근샹 쥬ᄒᆞ와광무팔년십일월십ᄉᆞ일에봉 지의쥬ᄒᆞ다

고시

○통신원고시뎨삼호 진위면보샤를셜치ᄒᆞ고본월십이일브터면보를통신ᄒᆞ니인민은통실ᄒᆞᆯᄉᆞ

위치ᄂᆞᆫ직산군삼셔면셩환에아직권셜ᄒᆞᆷ이라

광무팔년십일월십이일

통신원총관 민샹호

륙군연셩학교관졔

뎨일됴 교육부니에연셩학교를치ᄒᆞᆷ이라

뎨이됴 연셩학교ᄂᆞᆫ륙군의교육을데일케ᄒᆞ며또ᄀᆡ양ᄒᆞ거위ᄒᆞ야둠어니학원과학도의계젼술사격술과졔죠금술의학술를련슉케시힝ᄒᆞ며또그연습에관ᄒᆞᆫ교측을일졍케ᄒᆞ고졔과학술의원리를연구진셩케ᄒᆞᆷ이라

뎨삼됴 연셩학교학원과밋학도ᄂᆞᆫ좌의삼과에분ᄒᆞᆷ이라

기일 젼술과

본과학원은각ᄃᆡ현역예지ᄒᆞᆫ위관을ᄐᆡᆨ파ᄒᆞ야긔에처우며혹령관을ᄐᆡᆨ파ᄒᆞ야학원에취ᄒᆞᆷ도잇스니슈학긔한은일ᄀᆡ년이샹혹일ᄀᆡ년반이니로졍ᄒᆞᆷ이라

기이 사격과

본과학원과밋학도ᄂᆞᆫ보병ᄃᆡ의현역에지ᄒᆞᆫ위관파밋하ᄉᆞ를ᄐᆡᆨ파ᄒᆞ야이위에취우나니혹긔병과포병과공병각ᄃᆡ의현역에지ᄒᆞᆫ위관과밋학ᄉᆞ를ᄐᆡᆨ파ᄒᆞ야슈학케ᄒᆞᆷ도잇스니슈학긔한은모다륙ᄀᆡ월이니샹으로졍ᄒᆞᆷ이라

기삼 졔죠금술과

본과학원과밋학도ᄂᆞᆫ보병과긔병과포병과공병각ᄃᆡ의현역에지ᄒᆞᆫ위관과밋하ᄉᆞ를ᄐᆡᆨ파ᄒᆞ야이에취우ᄂᆞ니슈학긔한은모다륙ᄀᆡ월이샹으로졍ᄒᆞᆷ이라

뎨ᄉᆞ됴 군ᄃᆡ교육을ᄒᆞᆫ골ᄀᆞᆺ치ᄀᆡ양ᄒᆞ며또학원과밋학도의연슉케ᄒᆞ며졔반연구에취우기위ᄒᆞ야본교니에교셩ᄃᆡ를두고보병각ᄃᆡ의현역즁에ᄃᆡ지를ᄒᆞᆫ하ᄉᆞ병졸을션ᄐᆡᆨᄒᆞ야차를편셩ᄒᆞᆷ이라

뎨오됴 본교의직원은좌와ᄀᆞᆺᄒᆞᆷ이라

교쟝 일인 참쟝혹졍령
부관 일인 졍위
교관 삼십일인 령관삼인 졍위팔인부위이십인
의관 일인 이등군의
교관겸무
향관 일인 일이등군ᄉᆞ
번역관 이인 쥬관
셔긔 삼인 어ᄉᆞ혹판임문관
교셩ᄃᆡ쟝 일인 부참령
부관 일인 부위
즁ᄃᆡ쟝 ᄉᆞ인 졍위
교셩ᄃᆡ부 십륙인 부위
특무정교 ᄉᆞ인 졍부교
죠교 ᄉᆞ십인

뎨륙됴 교셩ᄃᆡ장부관즁ᄃᆡ쟝소ᄃᆡ쟝은교관으로겸임ᄒᆞᆷ이라

뎨칠됴 교쟝은교륙총감에예ᄒᆞ야학술을발달케ᄒᆞᄂᆞᆫ직쳑에임ᄒᆞᆷ이라

뎨팔됴 부관은교니일반ᄉᆞ무를쥬쟝ᄒᆞᆷ이라

뎨구됴 교관은젼술과사격과체죠금술과등학술의교슈를분담ᄒᆞ며또각과의학술을연구죠사ᄒᆞ고령관교관은각과의과쟝이됨이라

뎨십됴 교셩ᄃᆡ의쟝이하졔직원의직무ᄂᆞᆫ군ᄃᆡ니무의졍칙을젹용ᄒᆞᆷ이라

뎨십일됴 의관은교니위싱ᄉᆞ무를쥬쟝ᄒᆞᆷ이라

뎨십이됴 향관은회계서무를쥬쟝ᄒᆞᆷ이라

뎨십삼됴 번역관은번역통역의ᄉᆞ무를쥬쟝ᄒᆞᆷ이라

뎨십ᄉᆞ됴 셔긔ᄂᆞᆫ부관의지휘를밧다문부셔긔의ᄉᆞ무에임ᄒᆞᆷ이라

뎨십오됴 학원과밋학도의원슈와입교시일은교육총감과군부대신이이것을졍ᄒᆞᆷ이라

뎨십륙됴 학원과밋학도를ᄐᆡᆨᄒᆞ야입교의명령이잇ᄂᆞᆫ때ᄂᆞᆫ그각ᄃᆡ쟝은슈학의젹당ᄒᆞᆫ쟈를션졍ᄒᆞ야입긔한이쥬일젼에그군젹과고과표의죠ᄉᆞ건을연셩학교쟝의게보냄이라

뎨십칠됴 학원은학교밧게거쥬케ᄒᆞ며학도ᄂᆞᆫ학교안에거쥬케ᄒᆞ고슈학에긴요ᄒᆞᆫ병긔탄약셔유와긔구쇼모품등은차여혹지급ᄒᆞᄂᆞᆫᄉᆞ가잇스니다만학도ᄂᆞᆫ무긔피복쟝구를휴ᄃᆡ케ᄒᆞᆷ에라

뎨십팔됴 학원과밋학도즁에졍원급기타업무에관ᄒᆞᆫ졔건은총히교쟝의쳐판에속ᄒᆞᆷ이라

뎐보

만쥬군총ᄉᆞ령부발 당디군ᄉᆞ령부착젼

○홍릉소젼 십오일오젼일시ᄉᆞ십분에젹보병일즁ᄃᆡ와긔병일즁ᄃᆡ가홍릉돈에와셔엄습ᄒᆞ엿스ᄂᆞ즉시우리슈비ᄃᆡ의격퇴ᄒᆞᆫ비되엿다ᄒᆞ엿더라

(십륙일오후일시신눈특발)

○지척불변 지부항에ᄂᆞᆫ어제아츰브터큰눈이와셔지쳑을변치못ᄒᆞ더라

○로함일츌 로국구축함라ᄶᅳ도로부누이호가작일셔시에지부항으로도망ᄒᆞ야왓다ᄒᆞ엿더라

십일월십오일경셩착면

○시량쥰비 셩진부근에셔너도ᄒᆞᆫ졍보를거ᄒᆞᆫ즉동지부건에로병이목하의양식과나무와숫

UNION INSURANCE SOCIETY OF CANTON.

Head office Hongkong.
Marine risks underwritten at current rates.
Agents in Chemulpo,
E. MEYER & Co.

COMPAGNIE DES MESSAGERIES MARITIMES.

Fortnightly Direct Service.

For Marseilles
via Ports.
Sailing from Yokohama
Calling at Kobe,
Shanghai, Hongkong, Saigon, Singapore,
Colombo, Djibonti, Suez, Port Said
and Marseilles.

For particulars apply to
HOLME RINGER & Co.,
Chemulpo.

HAYASHIDA & Co.,

16 MYENG DONG, CHIN KO KAI, SEOUL.
BRANCH OFFICE AT CHEMULPO.

Money changers, Coal and Wood Merchants, Express Agents.

We are agents for the Pyeng-yang Coal Company and the Karazu Coal Company of Japan. We have the best quality of both anthracite and bituminous coal, and prompt execution of orders is our speciality. Firewood of all kinds kept in stock. Full weight guaranteed. Money of all denominations exchanged at current rates. Parcels received for all parts.

CHINA MUTUAL LIFE INS. CO.

Most favourable terms to policy holders.

Benefit system unsurpassed.

HOLME RINGER & Co.
Agents, Chemulpo.

C. P. R.

CANADIAN PACIFIC RAILWAY COMPANY'S ROYAL MAIL STEAMSHIP LINE.

THE FAST ROUTE BETWEEN CHINA, JAPAN, AND EUROPE VIA CANADA AND THE UNITED STATES.

Route from Hongkong via Shanghai, Nagasaki (Inland Sea of Japan) Kobe, Yokohama, Victoria and Vancouver.

Twin Screw Empress Steamship—6,000 Tons—Speed 19 knots.

PROPOSED SAILING FROM YOKOHAMA.
R. M. S. Empress of India.
R. M. S. Empress of Japan.
R. M. S. Empress of China.
R. M. S. Athenian.
R. M. S. Tartar.

Special reduction (first class only) granted to members of the Military, Naval, Diplomatic and Civil services and to Missionaries.

Passengers have choice of ten routes across the Continent of America and have privilege of travelling by any Atlantic Steamship Line.

Round the World passage tickets in connection with the P. and O. S. N., North German Lloyd and Messageries Co.'s **£125.**

All rates payable at current rate of exchange.

For further information, Tickets, Guide Books, etc., apply to

HOLME, RINGER & Co., AGENTS,
Chemulpo.

Grand Hotel,

(Formerly the Station Hotel)

Near the Railway Terminus, West Gate Seoul.

The Best Hotel in Korea
Handsome new Building.
Fine Airy Rooms
Excellent Cuisine.
Terms Moderate.
Special terms to Missionaries and to permanent boarders.

Electric cars within 2 minutes' walk.

W. H. EMBERLEY,
Proprietor

EVERY FACILITY.

In connection with Life Assurance Business is afforded by

The Standard Life Assurance Co.,

One of the largest and wealthiest of the Provident Institutions of the United Kingdom Forms of Application and all information will be promptly afforded on application.

10 CENTS A DAY.

Not a very large expenditure is it? But it is sufficient to secure for a man of 30 a policy with the STANDARD LIFE OFFICE for

$1323.

For all particulars of rates, etc., apply to

Holme, Ringer & Co.,
Agents, Chemulpo.

THE NEW YORK LIFE INSURANCE COMPANY.

Have you ever been declined by any Company?

Are you engaged in a specially hazardous occupation?

Have you heard of the New York Life Insurance Company's New Classifications for this class of Risks?

If not, send your date of birth, occupation and particulars of rejection, if any to

E. MEYER & Co.,
Agents, Chemulpo.

MITSUI BUSSAN KAISHA.
(MITSUI & Co.)
MITSUI GINKO.
(MITSUI BANK.)

The Bank is owned by the members of the Mitsui Family, who, as partners, assume an unlimited responsibility for all liabilities of the Bank:—

Capital.......................Yen 5,000,000
Reserve Fund....................." 5,600,000

HEAD OFFICE, TOKYO.

LONDON OFFICE, 34 LIME ST., E. C.

BRANCHES AND AGENCIES:—
New York, San Francisco, Hamburg, Bombay, Singapore, Manila, Hongkong, Amoy, Chefoo, Tientsin.
Kobe, Hakodate, Yokohama, Kure, Yokosuka, Moji, Shimonoseki, Miike, Wakamatsu, Nagasaki, Kuchinotsu, Karatsu, Sasebo, Misume, Taipeh, &c.

Telegraphic Address for all the Offices:
"MITSUI."
A. B. C. AND A. I CODES USED.

Contractors of Coal
To the Imperial Japanese Navy. Arsenals and Railway Bureau, Principal Railway Companies and Industrial Work, Home and Foreign Mail and Freight Steamers.

Sole Proprietors
Of the famous Miike, Tagawa and Yamano Coal Mines.

Sole Agents
For the sale of Fukumo, Hokoku, Ichimura, Kanoda, Mannoura, Onoura, Ostuji, Sonoda, Tsubaruro, Yoshinotani, Yoshio, Yurokibura and other coals.

YANGTSE INSURANCE ASSOCIATION, LTD.

The undersigned, having been appointed agents for the above company, are prepared to issue policies and pay losses on marine risks at regular rates.

E. MEYER & Co.,
Agents, Chemulpo.

AMERICAN KOREAN ELECTRIC CO.

Light and Power.

Main Office: Electric Building, Chong No.

RAILWAY DEPARTMENT.

OPERATING CARS BETWEEN EAST AND WEST GATE, EVERY TEN MINUTES:—

First Car leaves East Gate at 7:00 A. M. First Car leaves R. R. Station at 7:25 A. M
Last Car " East Gate at 10:05 P. M. Last " " R. R. Station at 9:40 P.M

OPERATING CARS BETWEEN EAST GATE AND IMPERIAL TOMB TERMINUS, EVERY TWENTY MINUTES:—
CONNECTING WITH EVERY ALTERNATE CAR ARRIVING AT EAST GATE FROM CHONG NO.

First Car leaves East Gate for Tomb at 7:10 A. M.
" " " Tomb for East Gate at 7:35 A. M.
Last " " East Gate for Tomb at 7:50 P. M.
" " " Tomb for East Gate at 8:10 P. M.

OPERATING CARS BETWEEN CHONG NO AND YUNG SAN RIVER EVERY TWELVE MINUTES:—

First Car leaves Chong No for South Gate at 7:12 A. M.
" " " Chong No for Yung San at 7:36 A. M.
" " " South Gate for Chong No at 7:20 A. M.
" " " Yung San for Chong No at 8:09 A. M.
Last " " South Gate for Chong No 10:00 P. M.
" " " Yung San for Chong No at 9:33 P. M.

SPECIAL PRIVATE CARS FURNISHED TO SUIT CONVENIENCE OF PATRONS. PRICES ON APPLICATION AT HEAD OFFICE.

LIGHTING DEPARTMENT.

Where less than 250 candle power of light is used, the rate per month will be
Per 16 candle power incandescent lamp,—All night.—Yen 2.50.
32 candle power incandescent lamp:—All night:—Yen 4.00.
50 candle power incandescent lamp:—All night:—Yen 6.00.
150 " " " " — " " " 10.00.
1200 " " enclosed arc " " " " 20.00.

Where more than 250 candle power of light is used, a Meter will be installed, if requested:—Rent of Meter Yen 2.00 per month. Rate of charges by meter reading:—Two Sen per Ampere per hour. (Approximately this is equal to about One Sen per 16 C. P. lamp per hour) Minimum monthly charge where meter is installed, Yen 20.00 per month, which includes rental of meter.

Estimates for installing lights furnished on application.
An assortment of chandeliers always on hand.

K. Murakami,
Photograph Studio
Chinkokai, Seoul.

Printing, Developing and Enlargement, of Photographs always Undertaken.

Korean Views and Pictures Illustrating Native Customs always on Sale,

---

THE OSAKA SHOSEN KAISHA.

Boats frequently on the berth for Chinnampo.

REGULAR SAILINGS BETWEEN JAPAN AND KOREAN PORTS.

FUSAN AND KOBE VIA SHIMONOSEKI.

OSAKA VIA MOKPO, FUSAN, SHIMONOSEKI AND KOBE.

MOJI DIRECT.

OSAKA VIA KUNSAN, MASANPO, FUSAN, SHIMONOSEKI AND KOBE.

CHEMULPO KUNSAN LINE,
Every three days.

CHEMULPO CHINNAMPO LINE.
Every three days.

For Freight and passage and further particulars apply to
THE OSAKA SHOSEN KAISHA,
Chemulpo.

RONDON, PLAISANT & CO.

General Storekeepers and Merchants, Ships Contractors, Tobacconists, Commission and Forwarding Agents, Coal Merchants

IMPORTERS AND EXPORTERS

Seoul & Chemulpo.

W. D. WENTWORTH.

LANDING
AND
SHIPPING AGENT
AND
CUSTOMS BROER.

12 OURA, NAGASAKI.

STEWARD & CO.
Chemulpo.

Shipchandlers and Storekeepers, Naval and Mercantile Contrrctors, Landing and Shipping Agents.

STEWARD'S HOTEL
Chemulpo.

Best accommodation in the port for travellers. Clean and well-aired rooms, good cuisine prompt attendance, moderate tariff.

무역ᄒᆞ기에분망ᄒᆞ니필시엄동쥰비얀티이것으로연ᄒᆞ야셩진부건에제반물가가비상히올나디방인민이대단곤란ᄒᆞ다ᄒᆞ엿더라

외보

○극독도경 극동총독아렉시후장군이본월십일일에아라ᄉᆞ셔울에도착ᄒᆞ엿더라

○발표예액 일본정부에셔본월십이일에예산을발표ᄒᆞ되세입익삼익오빅칠십팔만일쳔팔빅구십팔원에세출액일억팔쳔이빅삼십오만구쳔구십오원을타제ᄒᆞ고그잉여익은군ᄉᆞ비에츙용ᄒᆞᆫ다ᄒᆞ엿다더라

○정령피회 아라ᄉᆞ정령보스도후씨가아렉식후장군의명을인ᄒᆞ야표면샹에담금ᄒᆞᆫ목적이라칭ᄒᆞ고몽고로발왕ᄒᆞ엿더니히디에셔피살ᄒᆞ엿더라

○아션파피 악국장갑슌양함구로보호가울산히면에셔일본함디의게피상ᄒᆞ야히삼위에셔슈리ᄒᆞ더니슈리후에운젼ᄒᆞ다가돌모롱이에셔부듸져침몰ᄒᆞ엿다더라

○정당결정 일본헌정부본당에셔관쥬에디ᄒᆞᆫ정칙을협의결뎡ᄒᆞ엿ᄂᆞᆫ디만쥬ᄂᆞᆫ일아량국이평화ᄒᆞᆫ후에청국으로돌려보니고기왕에아국이만쥬에셔어든차됴권과그다른권리ᄂᆞᆫ일본이가지고만쥬에부셜ᄒᆞᆫ동청텰도ᄂᆞᆫ군ᄉᆞ샹에ᄉᆞ용ᄒᆞᆯ거신고로일본이가지쟈ᄒᆞ엿더라

○실업쟈연의금 아라파른디방에셔극동젼쟁으로말미암아노동ᄒᆞ던쟈가업을이허ᄇᆞ리고싱활에곤란ᄒᆞᆫ쟈가심이만ᄒᆞᆫ고로파란군무총독쟈션가에셔의연금을모집ᄒᆞ야이러ᄒᆞᆫ곤란쟈를나노와주랴ᄒᆞᆫ다더라

○황망퇴각 봉텬텰령간에잇ᄂᆞᆫ마젹이근쟈에그세력이듸셩ᄒᆞ야여러번아라ᄉᆞ군ᄉᆞ의병참션ᄂᆞᆯ에침입ᄒᆞ고ᄯᅩ텰령이북의텰도부근에도마젹이횡힝ᄒᆞ야여러번텰도를파피ᄒᆞ고ᄯᅩ쟝츈부회덕현이북합맹과산디방에도마젹삼빅여명이텰도를파피ᄒᆞ랴ᄒᆞᆷ으로아라ᄉᆞ군ᄉᆞ가마딕슈빅명을파송ᄒᆞ야공격케ᄒᆞ엿더니마젹이즁로에잠복ᄒᆞ엿다가아라사군ᄉᆞ를공격ᄒᆞᆷ으로아라ᄉᆞ군ᄉᆞ이황망히퇴각ᄒᆞ엿더라

잡보

○우유일진회 윤시병의일진회를쎄트려업시ᄒᆞᆯᄎᆞ로죠병식씨가회장이되여ᄯᅩ일진회를셜시ᄒᆞᆫ다ᄂᆞᆫ말이랑자ᄒᆞᆫ디회원은증ᄭᅥ관인으로만션정ᄒᆞᆫ다ᄒᆞ며오륙일후에대일회ᄀᆡ회를ᄒᆞᆫ다운운ᄒᆞ더라

○법관죠회 법국공ᄉᆞ가작일에ᄯᅩ외부로죠회ᄒᆞ기를김병도를압교ᄒᆞ라ᄂᆞᆫ일ᄉᆞ로발셔여러번죠쳥ᄒᆞ엿거니와김병도의션부가입의로국원적에입적ᄒᆞ엿슨즉김병도의게니르러ᄂᆞᆫ벌셔량디나되엿ᄂᆞᆫ지라로국법률디로ᄒᆞᄂᆞᆫ거시가ᄒᆞ거놀이곳처압교ᄒᆞ지아니ᄒᆞ니국제샹교셥에쟝ᄎᆞ관싱경지폐가잇스리에고ᄒᆞ엿더라

○면훈령찰 니부에셔대구관찰부로면훈ᄒᆞ기를니디에셔외국인이집을사거나ᄯᅩ니지못ᄒᆞᄂᆞᆫ거슨약장에ᄭᅵ지ᄒᆞ야잇스미관찰부에셔맛당히조량ᄒᆞ여빌녀쥬게ᄒᆞ라ᄒᆞ엿더라

○면훈합찰 니부에셔함흥관찰부로면훈ᄒᆞ기를관하각군슈가공ᄉᆞ던지ᄉᆞ송던지무ᄉᆞᆫ일을위ᄒᆞ야디경을써나게된즉곳관찰부에보ᄒᆞ야써ᄉᆞ령부로통지ᄒᆞ게ᄒᆞᆷ이맛당ᄒᆞ다ᄒᆞ엿더라

○면훈평찰 니부에셔평양관찰부로면훈ᄒᆞ기를안쥬읍에형세가심히급박ᄒᆞᆫ디지금만일군슈를갱차ᄒᆞ면도리여더욱지완ᄒᆞᆯ지니김광현의게엄히신칙ᄒᆞ야즉각으로부임케ᄒᆞᆯᄉᆞ로쳐분을봉승ᄒᆞ엿스미이럿트시엄칙지하에다시혹ᄉᆞ양ᄒᆞ거든피ᄒᆞ거ᄂᆞᆫᄒᆞ면압샹ᄒᆞ야징관케ᄒᆞᆯᄉᆞ라ᄒᆞ엿더라

○진회질문 평안도에셔동학당을포살ᄒᆞᆫ고로일진회에셔작일에참모부장윤웅렬씨의게공함ᄒᆞ고총디원윤정식씨를파송ᄒᆞ야질문ᄒᆞ기를대감ᄭᅦ셔도이젼에독립협회회쟝으로츙군의국ᄒᆞᄂᆞᆫ마ᄋᆞᆷ이다른사ᄅᆞᆷ보다빅가되엿거니와동학당이라ᄒᆞᄂᆞᆫ거시곳진보회오진보회가칭ᄒᆞ시ᄂᆞᆫ일진회라충의ᄒᆞᄂᆞᆫ마음으로단톄를일웟거ᄂᆞᆯ듯ᄒᆞ니이라ᄒᆞ야면훈ᄒᆞ야포살케ᄒᆞ니이거시엇전몸술정ᄉᆞ오니가ᄒᆞ미육웅렬ᄡᅵ가되답ᄒᆞ야글오디이거ᄉᆞᆫ정부에셔처관ᄒᆞ야면치ᄒᆞ야면훈ᄒᆞᆫ일이오본시참모부에셔ᄌᆞ유ᄒᆞ여ᄒᆞᆫ일은아니어니와히도의보고를거ᄒᆞᆫ즉히도등의주문이조지ᄒᆞᆯᄲᅮᆫ더러 죠칙즁에션왕이라ᄒᆞᆫ왕조를션싱이라ᄂᆞᆫ싱조로위죠ᄒᆞ야즁인에마ᄋᆞᆷ을현혹게ᄒᆞᆫ고로포살ᄒᆞᆷ이라ᄒᆞ엿더라

○동지회원 경셩에잇ᄂᆞᆫ진보회원이근일에합ᄒᆞᆫ진보회를향ᄒᆞ야동지ᄒᆞ엿다ᄂᆞᆫ디그대요ᄂᆞᆫ정부에셔불가불진보회를박멸코자ᄒᆞ야근쟈에니르러ᄂᆞᆫ단발ᄒᆞᆫ쟈오륙빅명을교용ᄒᆞ야이것들로ᄒᆞ야곰진보회원이라칭ᄒᆞ야함흥으로파견ᄒᆞ야도쳐에셔민가에불도노코슈량ᄒᆞᆫ빅셩을사납게되졉ᄒᆞ며혹은군ᄉᆞ샹에방헤ᄒᆞ야졔반슈단으로써더방인민이진보회를협의ᄒᆞ고원망케ᄒᆞᆫ후에자연이업셔지개ᄒᆞ랴ᄒᆞ니쥬의ᄒᆞ라ᄒᆞ엿더라

○샹쥬쳥체 고양군슈리쥬현씨ᄂᆞᆫ니부로청원ᄒᆞ야샹쥬허체키를청ᄒᆞ엿더라

○법ᄉᆞ힐문 법공ᄉᆞ가ᄯᅩ외부에가셔대신을보고담판ᄒᆞ기를김병도를귀국인이라칭ᄒᆞ야그법률에쳐ᄒᆞ고잡아보니지아니ᄒᆞ면쟝ᄎᆞᆺ큰싱경이날터이니깁히싱각ᄒᆞ야쳐관ᄒᆞ라ᄒᆞ엿더라

○당샹천입 천릉도감은혁파ᄒᆞᆫ지라도감당샹리봉의씨도히임이되엿더라

○학비금지 발리지국씨가오십명유학싱학쟈비를지발ᄒᆞ라ᄒᆞ엿더니대니에셔니하젼으로ᄉᆞ쳔원을나리샤즉시지발ᄒᆞ엿다더라

○공천오유오 음력본월십륙이즉공제일이라공제후에군슈셔임을쥬본ᄒᆞᆯ터인디제소위공쳔으로되기ᄂᆞᆫ고ᄉᆞᄒᆞ고유젼쟈만셔임된다더라

○륙혈포환슈 경무청에셔각슌산슌검의게혹불우지경이잇슬ᄭᅡᄒᆞ야륙혈포를주엇더니일병이군ᄉᆞ경찰놀힝ᄒᆞᆫ후에슌검을슈험ᄒᆞ야샹지ᄒᆞᄂᆞᆫ고로도로허유익ᄒᆞᆯ거시업다ᄒᆞ야각기본셔에셔륙혈표를본쳥으로거두어드렷다더라

○론복쟈피착 과년복에디ᄒᆞ야격례가아니라고말ᄒᆞ고삼ᄀᆡ월로정ᄒᆞ기를건의ᄒᆞ던박지용등이인은이로말미암아피착ᄒᆞ야옥에구슈가되엿다더라

○식민회샤 대륙식민회샤ᄂᆞᆫ일향휘무와임겸길랑외에이십ᄉᆞ명이합자금빅만원으로셜시ᄒᆞᄂᆞᆫ무한칙임대회샤인디묵셔가와포아와남아미리가등디와셔기타체에디리졈을셜치ᄒᆞ고병원과운힝소와그다른긔관어완젼이쥰비ᄒᆞ야다시아미리가와비률빈등디에도확장ᄒᆞ기위ᄒᆞ야위션리년이월니로한인삼빅의가족을모집ᄒᆞ야묵셔가에식민ᄒᆞᆯ계획이라더라

○셩은보급 법부에셔작일에의정부죠회를인ᄒᆞ야십삼부지관소에훈령ᄒᆞ되죵리로가친죄인의셩명을낫낫치죠사보고ᄒᆞ야본군에셔그정형을슈작ᄒᆞ야공평쳐판ᄒᆞ야 셩은을널게펴라ᄒᆞ엿더라

론셜

우리ᄂᆞᆫ외국으로단인이후에눈으로본바도만흐며입으로가히칭셔ᄒᆞ야평론ᄒᆞᆫ쟈도잇스되오즉풀기어렵고알수업ᄂᆞᆫ쟈ㅣ잇스니이ᄂᆞᆫ다만일진회와진보회의목적이로다

지나간칠월에한국빅셩들이몃몃회를창셜ᄒᆞ야 황위를안령케ᄒᆞᆫ다고도칭ᄒᆞ며장삼씨의황무지ᄀᆡ간사건에디ᄒᆞ야인허치못ᄒᆞ게ᄒᆞᆫ다고물의가불동ᄒᆞ며박론이이러나일본사ᄅᆞᆷ으로ᄒᆞ며여금실로반디ᄒᆞ며ᄯᅩᄒᆞᆫ일본사ᄅᆞᆷ들은군력을합셰ᄒᆞ야민회명셕ᄀᆞᆷ과여히압제ᄒᆞ야셔로반디ᄒᆞ기로작정ᄒᆞ더니

맛참그러ᄒᆞᆯ즈음에이왕버슬도지낸고모처씨라ᄒᆞᄂᆞᆫ미셩년훈한국량반훈분이의견을특별히니여한국의리익을일본사ᄅᆞᆷ의게부조ᄒᆞ도록만드려한회를갱셜ᄒᆞ엿ᄂᆞᆫ디이회인즉일진회인지라

이회의목적은아모조록나라를진보ᄒᆞ게ᄒᆞᆫ다ᄂᆞᆫ조흔말노칭탁ᄒᆞ야창언ᄒᆞ기ᄂᆞᆫᄒᆞ나그실상인즉일본사령부로셔경비를주어지탕ᄒᆞ게ᄒᆞ야보존ᄒᆞᄂᆞᆫ쟈인디소위회원들은셔로분변ᄒᆞ기위ᄒᆞ야머리를밧삭삭근우에외국모자만쓰고길로번득거리며단이ᄂᆞᆫ지라

그츄ᄒᆞᆫ모양과병든형용이며허탕ᄒᆞᆫ고불사ᄒᆞᆷ이비ᄒᆞᆯ디업거ᄂᆞᆯ그즁에ᄒᆞᆫ다ᄂᆞᆫ일은지각업ᄂᆞᆫ의샤로되지못ᄒᆞᆯ마량ᄒᆞᆫ다칭ᄒᆞ고대관들의게무랍업시소요ᄒᆞ게구ᄂᆞᆫ일이며

대황뎨폐하의밝히통촉ᄒᆞ옵시고블긍히녁이시ᄂᆞᆫ바를말ᄉᆞᆷᄒᆞ야혹될가헛도히바라ᄂᆞᆫ바일ᄲᅮᆫ일러니

작일소문을드른즉회원즁에사찰명식일빅여십인을ᄲᅡᆸ아셔울로샹으로단이며자량을식이게ᄒᆞᆫ다ᄒᆞ더니ᄯᅩ어제소문에ᄂᆞᆫ일어학교를셜시ᄒᆞᆫ다ᄒᆞᆫ즉

이ᄂᆞᆫ다름이아니라이왕에브호ᄒᆞ든일본사ᄅᆞᆷ들이무삼미흡ᄒᆞᆫ바를보왓든지조ᄀᆡ들의보호ᄒᆞᆫ든바를은근히환철ᄒᆞ야무사ᄒᆞᆫ도록만들고은영즁한국관리로ᄒᆞ여곰이쟈들을엇더케쳐치ᄒᆞ던지ᄒᆞ게버려둔모양인지라

그회인즉립지가견확지못ᄒᆞ야셔로규각이나셔ᄒᆞᆫ사ᄅᆞᆷ은동으로가라면ᄯᅩ다른사ᄅᆞᆷ은셔으로향ᄒᆞᆫ즉만일병참부에셔조쳐ᄒᆞ지아니ᄒᆞ면자중지란이이러날터이며

ᄯᅩ북도로젼ᄒᆞᄂᆞᆫ소문을드른즉진보회당수빅명이아인의게로붓쫏쳐나ᄒᆞᆯ즉ᄯᅩᄒᆞᆫ무삼다른일이싱길듯ᄒᆞᆫ지라

이러ᄒᆞᆫ일을보드리도그회에지탕ᄒᆞ게공급ᄒᆞ든바를당장이라도환수ᄒᆞ야상관치말미조흔듯ᄒᆞᆫ거시져히들이당초에무삼목젹이든지션악간에미사에셩취치못ᄒᆞᆯ거ᄉᆞᆫ블언가샹ᄒᆞᆫ일이며ᄯᅩᄒᆞᆫ회비만되여쥬지아니ᄒᆞ면스ᄉᆞ로환산ᄒᆞ야칩식이될터인지라

이공연ᄒᆞᆫ쓸디업ᄂᆞᆫ일로명예만손샹이되게ᄒᆞᆫ즉엇더케ᄒᆞ던지아모조록속속히귀정을내여잇고말게되엿스면데일조흘듯ᄒᆞ도다

TELEGRAMS.

Tokyo, Nov. 17th.

The Russian destroyer, which entered Chefoo harbor, was blown up after her crew had been landed. The masts are visible above water.

MASTER OF THE SEA

("EXPRESS" SPECIAL CORRESPONDENT.)

Paris, Thursday, 15th Sept.

"Do you not think it probable, Cavaliero Pino, that in a short while you will become the richest man alive?"

It was the first question that I put to the inventor. Pino latterly has been a much-sought-after and a seldom seen individual. The fame of his inventions—his hydroscope, which allows him to view the bottom of the sea at any depth, and elevator, which allows him to raise any sunken object by the power of compressed air—spread far abroad after the first account of them appeared in the "Express" some time ago.

Then at once shoals of letter, poured upon him; people sought him out in Italy from all parts of the world. Editors craved articles; salvage companies, pearl fishers, sponge fishers, and fishermen proper clamoured for the right to use his invention. One Englishman offered Pino £5,000 for the use of a hydroscope for a limited time off the Northumberland coast. An Italian newspaper offered to pay the price of a new hydroscope—some £2,000—if only a reporter might be allowed to investigate and describe the work in Vigo Bay. But Pino refused to hear any one.

Only when business called him to Paris the other day did he remember to send a telegram to the writer making an appointment in fulfillment of an old promise.

UNTOLD WEALTH.

He did not answer at once when I asked the harvest of wealth he might reap; by nature he is the most unassuming of men. Then he said;

"The answer must depend somewhat on the concessions that I am able to gain. Sea treasure is not common property; every sunken ship has an owner somewhere. But if I have luck, if no mistakes are made in my business arrangements, I answer, Yes, I think I shall become the richest man. For I am certain of the power of my instruments; I am convinced that I hold the secret not only for finding all the treasures of the sea, but for recovering them also.

"At Vigo alone," he went on, "twenty-eight milion pounds' worth of gold and silver is to be picked up with the Spanish treasure fleet that sank there in 1702. So the Spanish Government estimates. To recover this is the beginning, but not the end of my work.

"My business manager, Dr. Carlo Iberti, has made contacts with the Spanish officials, giving us the right to seek for lost treasure in five other places—Trafalgar among them. Then we are thinking of sending an elevator quite soon to Port Arthur, to raise the ironclads lost there, valued even now at £20,000,000, I am told. Then, when I consider the fish in the sea that my hydroscope can reveal to us, the pearls, the coral banks, the sponges—when I remember the three ships, one big and two small, that go down in the world's waters every day—I confess I can see no limit to future possibilities.

"But at present the treasure fleet at Vigo is our one aim."

THE VIGO GALLEONS.

Then Pino went on to describe how in April last he set sail from Italy to Vigo on his fine steamer, the San Clemente. On board was the first big hydroscope—a beautiful instrument that had just been built to the order of the Italian company that has floated his inventions. Several smaller hydroscopes were on board, too, and a number of elevators, for these are very simple machines. Accommodation was found for a crew of forty-five picked men.

Arrived at Vigo, no time was lost in getting to work. Under the eyes of a warship, which watches the search on the Spanish Government's behalf, for the State is to receive 20 per cent. of all treasure recovered, the preliminary survey work has been going steadily forward since the beginning of May. And the work has prospered, for nine of the ancient galleons already have been identified.

Of course, long before the search actively began, every known fact concerning the treasure ships had been collected for Cavaliere Pino. There is not a scrap of evidence in Spain bearing on the history of Vigo Bay that has not been sifted by Dr. Carlo Iberti, the manager of Pino's company. He learnt the whole story of the lost treasure fleet, the names of the ships and their captains, and the amount of the treasure and the number of guns each carried.

BAFFLED BY SAND.

Had the waters of Vigo Bay been clear instead of sandy, Pino's great hydroscope would nave discovered the ships long since. For the lenses of this sea telescope reflect all the objects in clear water within a wide range, at whatever depth. Even after the hydroscope had revealed a tell-tale mast projecting from the sea-bed, or the corner of a wooden bulwark, it was a slow business clearing away the sand to make measurement and survey. Special instruments had to be employed, for the sand rises in clouds when divers descend, obliterating their view. In these circumstances, Pino wisely decided against any premature attempt to raise a galleon until the preliminary survey work had been completed.

At the present moment while this general survey goes forward, a separate search party is seeking to locate one of the ships known to have been sunk in clear water. Probably she could be raised with far less difficulty than could the others, and if all goes well and she is successfully discovered by the hydroscope and raised by the power of the elevators, then a grand assault will be organised on the other identified ships, and every effort will be redoubled to secure the treasure.

"I seek to find the easiest task to begin upon," said Cavaliere Pino, having explained the situation. "With that once accomplished, we shall know how to overcome the difficulties of the other cases. We have made a very good beginning, and I am more than satisfied, and more hopeful than ever."

Pino has the most implicit confidence in his companion inventions for exploring the sea. Should he be successful at Vigo Bay as he hopes, and should a few of the millions of money lying beneath the waves pass into his pocket, he will become a power in the world that will cause a good many peaceful revolutions. If his hydroscopes do nothing more than to make fish the cheapest and commonest of all foods, that will be something.

It is rumoured that the Il-chin-hoi society will shortly be broken up, and that a new society will be established with Mr. Cho Byeng-sik as president.

Reports from Paris state that the Russian troops occupying trenches on the Shaho have been without shelter since Oct. 15th. Communication between the various detachments is impossible owing to the vigilance of the Japanese.

Two venturesome Koreans have made a suggestion to the Government that the term of mourning for the late Crown Princess should be shortened to three months. This is evidently considered as rank heresy for the two gentlemen have been imprisoned.

Captain Gundersen of the "Ohio" which steamer arrived in Chemulpo yesterday, reports very bad weather outside. Heavy seas were running and snow and sleet falling. Off Mokpo the weather was so rough and the ship rolling so heavily that a quantity of coal, which was carried on deck, went overboard.

VLADIVOSTOCK.

The master of a vessel which has just reached Chefoo from Vladivostock, reports that the defences at the latter place are in a very complete state. Ships with provisions, ammunition and other necessaries arrive constantly. Five were unloading at the time when this informant left the port. The European residents, confident in the safety of the place, are remaining there placidly. Several submarines are said to have recently arrived, though the fact is kept very secret. At a distance of 7 miles from the shore lines of torpedo-mines are laid and 3 miles further inland there are lines of electric mines. The garrison do not expect either to be attacked by the Japanese this winter or to be marched into Korea.

AN EXCISE OFFICER'S TRICK.

A story which goes to show the depravity of some Chinese officials was told at the Magistracy, on Nov. 4. The defendant in the case in question was an excise officer, and it was shown that some time ago he had a quarrel with a Chinese woman, in whose house a girl he was paying his addresses to lived. He determined to have revenge on the woman for quarrelling with him, and at once asked another officer to take out a warrant to search her house for opium. This was done and on the day fixed for the raid the excise officer visited the house and asked his girl to place some opium he had brought under the woman's bed. She refused and was thrashed by the defendant who then hid the opium himself, it being done up in a box with a number of cigars. Another girl in the house, however, saw what was going on and informed her mistress, and together they recovered the opium and took it to the police station before the defendant had made the raid. The police allowed him to make the raid, which was, of course, fruitless, and then arrested him. Mr. Hazeland considered that the case was the worst of its kind he had been called upon to deal with. The law only allowed a maximum penalty of $500, or three months' gaol. He did not think this was a case in which a fine should be imposed and sentenced the defendant to three months' gaol with six hours in the stock, without the option of a fine. He was sorry he could not make the sentence six months.—Overland Mail.

The Magistrate of Dan Chon, reporting to the Home Office on October 10th, asks to be relieved from his post. He says Korea is a neighbour of Japan on one side, of Russia on the other. On Korea devolves the task of assisting the passage of the troops of both nations. Both Russian and Japanese troops require labour, provisions, etc., from the Koreans. Since the beginning of the war no Japanese troops have been seen in his district, but some 4,000 Russians have arrived since April and have established five military stations, for which they require provisions. Also the people have to labor on the roads, felling trees for building bridges. Over the Sam Dai Chon river, they commenced to build a bridge 600 *kans* in length but this has, for some reason, not been completed. The Russian military commander and a police officer recently visited his district and ordered the people to sell them rice and barley. The people are afraid of the Russians, so many have run away and their houses are empty. The Tonghaks have now joined forces with the Russians, so it is impossible to prohibit their meetings as the Government has ordered. Recently the Tonghak leader posted a proclamation on the walls of the magistracy calling for volunteers for the society, so many people are coming in to join him. The Magistrate winds up his report with the plea that he be dismissed as he is unable to carrry out his duties properly in such disturbing times.

The Daily Mail states that Lloyd's will shortly pay £1,000,000 for losses at sea, such losses being mostly due to seizure during the present war.

The financial condition of the Korean students in Japan, has now been improved. His Majesty has kindly contributed $4,000 towards their support.

The police patrols, in the neighbouring country have hitherto carried revolvers in case of emergency. Now, we understand, the Japanese have lodged an objection against their carrying firearms.

After being employed for one day recently in the women's camp on the Humboldt River, Elko, Nevada, a Chinaman hanged himself. According to the New York American, his suicide was "due to fright through being alone with so many women."

The "Tageblatt für Nord China," giving some details of the Novik's last voyage, states that before Saghalien was reached, everything inflammable on board, fittings, furniture etc., had to be burnt as the ship was almost entirely out of coal.

A Mukden letter says that the natives suffered the most at the Shaho River, for when the Japanese pursued the Russians, many of the refugees were mistaken for Russians in ambush and were therefore fired upon. A large number of them were drowned in the Shaho River.

Mr. Kim Kwang Kyun, the magistrate of Anju finds himself in rather an unfortunate predicament. Owing to a state of unrest in his district, he recently resigned and left his post. Now he has been ordered by the Government to return, or if he still persists in resigning he will be brought up to Seoul and be severely punished.

The shooting of some Tonghaks in Pyeng-An province has provoked an attack on the parties responsible from the Il Chin Hoi society. They have written to General Yun Woong Nyul stating that the men were members of the Chin Po Hoi (and consequently under the protection of the Il Chin Hoi) and demanding a reason for what they term an outrage. The General replies that it is none of his business but Tonghaks or Chin Po Hoi people they deserved their punishment for publishing inflammatory proclamations which were likely to incite the people to revolt.

All vessels arriving from the North have experienced rough weather and captains report that the northeast monsoon is now in full blast. The weather is particularly rough between here and the Paracels and further south bad weather is also being experienced. Advantage is being taken of this, according to recent arrivals from the vicinity of Port Arthur, by blockade runners. One gentleman states that he saw a number of vessels sheltering close in some island, and, within easy run of Port Arthur, and when the weather became too rough for the Japanese destroyers to venture out they at once steamed off in that direction.—Overland Mail.

The Korea Daily News.

Issued at 5 P. M. daily except Sundays.

Rate of Subscription:—
Per Year,............Yen 25.
Per Quarter,..........Yen 7.
Per Month,..........Yen 2.50.

Postage in Korea not charged extra.
Postage abroad charged extra.

Advertisements, 50 sen per day for 1 inch or less.
5 yen per month per inch.
50 yen per year per inch.

All communications to
E. T. BETHELL,
Editor and Publisher,
Pak-tong, Seoul

THE BALTIC SQUADRON.

Now that several weeks have elapsed since the "North Sea incident," it becomes possible to make a calm review of the whole affair and the incidents that led up to it.

Our readers may remember that we have, from the first, refrained from joining in the wholesale condemnation of Russia, indulged in by most of the British newspapers. While thoroughly agreeing that the incident itself, without explanation, was a gross outrage and an insult to British honour calling for severe reprisals, we have never been able to believe that the Russian action was entirely unprovoked.

That the Russians believe in their own explanation that there were hostile vessels amongst the trawlers there is no reason to doubt. In reference to this, Lord Lansdowne, speaking at the Guildhall, said "Recent evidence had, however, satisfied him that the Russian Government believed in all good faith that the facts of the case were contrary to what the British public supposed." The mere assurance to this effect would hardly have justified Lord Lansdowne in speaking as he did, and it seems probable that the Russian Government has confidentially laid before the British Government, evidence showing that they had good reason to fear an attack in the North Sea. The fact that the Russian Government is now offering rewards for information concerning suspicious vessels which were in the North Sea at the time, serves to strengthen this view.

Yesterday we published a translation of an article from our Tsingtau contemporary which would carry much more conviction did it not display such strong anti-Japanese bias. Still we think it is fair enough in its contention that the Baltic fleet has to expect attacks from the Japanese at every stage of its journey. We have received information that it has even been thought necessary to post guards along the banks of the Suez Canal.

Truly the enterprise of the Baltic squadron is a desperate one. Their voyage to the East will be marked by continual alarms and unceasing vigilance, and even if they safely arrive in these waters, it is hard to say where a harbour will be found to shelter them and enable them to refit. Neutral harbours are not available, Japan is certain to protect all her own and Formosan ports with mines, and even if Port Arthur should accomplish the apparently impossible and hold out, it will be of no use as a naval base until the investing army has been dislodged by a long land campaign. There remain Vladivostok and the Korean ports, and in order to reach Vladivostok and Eastern Korea the fleet would have to run the gauntlet of the Tsushima Straits—a task which it would hardly be equal to after a long and exhausting voyage. In addition to this, Vladivostok and the Northern Korean ports will be ice-bound and the restrictions recently placed by the Japanese military authorities upon navigation in the neighbourhood of Gensan seem to indicate that some defenses are to be arranged in that harbour. There only remain the harbours on the south and west coasts of Korea; those on the south have been fortified by the Japanese and those on the west are, to say the least of it, ill-adopted as naval bases.

On the whole the outlook for the Baltic squadron is a very gloomy one, and the enterprise is, as we have said, a desperate one. They who have undertaken it are brave men, and it behooves us to suspend judgment upon apparent outrages until all the facts are known to us.

BLOCKADE RUNNING.

Two stories of contraband cruises are told in the "South China Morning Post." The "Lady Mitchell" seems to be in trouble but the "Ellamy" has apparently provided against all contingencies.

The Lady Mitchell, which left Hong Kong on Nov. 1st for Tsingtau, has returned to that port through, it is said, a breakdown in her machinery. It is also rumoured that the crew refused to proceed in the ship.

It is said that the steamer Lady Mitchell was purchased in Singapore by the same company who purchased the Sishan. She loaded a full cargo of tinned meats, flour, etc., here and cleared for Tsingtau. The master had great difficulty in getting a crew to proceed in the vessel, but they were eventually got together by an advance on the regular wages.

The captain of the s.s. Lady Mitchell was charged on Nov. 3rd at the Hong Kong Police Court, by the boarding officer, for having no port of registry on his vessel's stern. He was finded $5.

Singapore was formerly painted on her, but since the vessel left the port a day or two ago, this name had been removed. The maximum penalty for this is £100. So that Captain Daniels appears to have got off lightly. It is reported that the crew have again left the vessel, it having been made known to them that they were bound, not to Tsingtau, but to Port Arthur. For reasons unknown the Harbour Office authorities are holding back her register.

Of the "Ellamy," the same paper says:—The blockade runner Ellamy cleared Manila on Oct. 27 for Astoria and sailed for Vladivostock presumably. A new crew consisting of anything that could be scraped up, was signed on at the British Consulate. A 2nd mate, and a 2nd and a 3rd engineer, firemen, and sailors were signed on, as the others had refused to go. Mr. Riodan was the second engineer and he and all of the others who signed the articles received an advance of six months wages. The crew all proceeded to get drunk after receiving their advances and it was then that the mate who had taken too much cargo on, told one of the officers of the transport service whom he was trying to induce to join the expedition that the vessel came in here for bunker coal, and while the vessel was in port the crew decided that they would leave the ship or obtain higher wages. He added that the cargo of the ship consists almost entirely of ammunition, field guns, quick firers, rifles, and other munitions of war. This is all covered by about two feet of coal.

The entire cargo of the ship has been sold to both of the combatants pending delivery, and the cost of the vessel has also figured in with the price for which the cargo is to be sold. In this way the owners and shippers have combined their interests, so that if the vessel was captured by either of the belligerents there would be no danger of confiscation, two sets of papers having been made out.

THE GENERAL SLOCUM.

The finding of the Board who investigated the circumstances attending the fire on the "General Slocum" and the attendent awful loss of life comes somewhat as a surprise.

In their official report the Local Board of Steamboat Inspectors hold that the negligence and incompetence of the crew were responsible for the disaster on the excursion steamer Slocum, which was burned last June, when 959 lives were lost.

The report declares that, contrary to the general belief, the life-saving appliances were adequate, but the ignorance of the crew and a total lack of discipline prevented their proper use. It is recommended that the licenses of the captain, pilot, and chief engineer be revoked.

BRISK BUSINESS IN SHIPPING.

The Norwegian steamer "Borg," has been sold to Mr. Tanaka of Tokyo for Yen 140,000. She is of 1,168 gross and 738 reg. tons, and was built by Messrs. Nyiands, Verksted at Christiana in 1896. The Dutch steamer "Meddan," 653 tons, has also changed hands, the purchaser being Mr. Ishikaki of Hakodate. The steamer was constructed at Amsterdam in 1889, and has been transferred for Yen 60,000.

The British steamer "Dean," 1,538 tons, has been purchased by Mr. Hashimoto of Nagasaki, the price paid, according to the vernacular papers, being Y105,000. Another British steamer, the "Saladin," has been bought by Mr. Kawasaki Shozo, of Kobe, for Y80,000; and the Norwegian steamer "Herme" by Mr. Okazaki of Kobe. All these vessels are at present in Kobe harbour. And from Hongkong we learn that the British steamer "Bentego," 2,400 tons, and "Nonkin," 4,000 tons, are reported as sold to Japanese.

JAPANESE BONDS.

During the operations immediately preceding the flotation of the last issue of Japanese war bonds in London, all Japanese securities seem to have been having a rather unsettled time of it. Just previous to the flotation of the second instalment of bonds preferentially secured upon H. I. J. M's customs, at £90.10.0 the first issue had been quoted in London at £93.12.6.

So far as we can gather, the term "preferential" means that the interest on these bonds has first call upon the revenue of the Japanese customs, and that the bond-holders can take no action so long as their interest is forthcoming.

It will now be interesting to note whether the second issue will rise in price and take its place with the first or whether the tendency will be the other way about. In view of the excellence of the security, the lowness of the price and the high rate of interest, it seems unlikely, unless unexpected disaster occur, that Japanese bonds can decline much further, but at the same time it must be remembered that the conditions of this last loan seem particularly adverse to Japan when viewed in the light of such knowledge as we have of the present state of affairs.

Several steamers cruising in the Baltic under the Danish flag belong to Russia, and are used for service between Sweden and Norway. In the Great Belt the steamers Frigga, Dragor, and Turist have on board members of the Russian police, who are watching all passenger boats, and a sharp watch is kept on the few Japanese known to them.

The Hamburg-American Line, it is stated, has decided to bring at once into service 12 steamers which had been withdrawn from traffic for some time. These steamers are said to be bound for the Far East. This is a variation of another statement that twelve colliers of the mentioned line have received sealed orders to sail for Cardiff to load 50,000 tons of coal for the Baltic Fleet.

The Korea Daily News.

VOL. I, FRIDAY, NOVEMBER 18, 1904. No. 104

HONGKONG & SHANGHAI BANKING CORPORATION.

Paid-up Capital....................$10,000,000
Reserve Fund:—Sterling Reserve... 10,000,000
Silver Reserve..... 7,000,000

27,000,000
Reserve Liability of Proprietors... 10,000,000

HEAD OFFICE, HONGKONG.

London Bankers, London and County Banking Company Limited.
Branches and Agencies,
London.

Amoy,	Hankow	Penang,
Bangkok,	Hiogo,	Rangoon,
Batavia,	Iloilo,	Saigon,
Bombay,	Lyons,	San Francisco,
Calcutta,	Manila,	Singapore,
Colombo,	Nagasaki,	Sourabaya,
Foochow,	New York,	Tientsin,
Hamburg,	Peking,	Yokohama,

Credits granted on approved Securities, and every description of Banking and Exchange business transacted.

Drafts granted on London and the chief Commercial places in Europe, India, Australia, America, China and Japan.

HOLME RINGER & Co., AGENTS,
CHEMULPO.

ON CHEONG & CO.,
SEOUL.
GENERAL STORE KEEPERS.
Imported provisions, Cooking Utensils Crockery, etc.
FRESH BREAD DAILY.

MITSU BISHI DOCKYARD & ENGINE WORKS,
NAGASAKI.

CODE WORD, "DOCK."

A. 1, A. B. C., and Engineering Codes used.

DOCK No. 1 (at Tategami).

Extreme Length..............523 feet
Length on blocks .... 513 ,,
Width of Entrance on Top......89 ,,
,, ,, Bottom....77 ,,
Water on Blocks at Spring Tide 26½ ,,

DOCK No. 2 (Mukaijima).

Extreme Length..............371 feet
Length on Blocks............360 ,,
Width of Entrance on Top......66 ,,
,, ,, Bottom 53 ,,
Water on Blocks at Spring Tide 22 ,,

PATENT SLIP (at Kosuge).

Can take vessels up to 1,000 tons gross.

THE WORKS are well equipped with the LATEST IMPROVEMENTS, and can execute any kind of work in SHIPBUILDING and MARINE ENGINEERING, as well as in REPAIRING of SHIPS.

The COMPANY'S new powerful steamer OURA-MARU (712 tons, 700 I.H.P.), specially built for SALVAGE PURPOSES, and equipped with necessary gear, is always READY at SHORT NOTICE.

CHARTERED BANK OF INDIA AUSTRALIA & CHINA.

INCORPORATED BY ROYAL CHARTER 1853

HEAD OFFICES:—LONDON.

Paid-up Capital £800,000
Reserve Liability of Shareholders 800,000
Reserve Fund 800,000

Drafts granted upon all the principal places in the world and every description of Exchange and banking business transacted.

E. MEYER & Co., Agents,
Chemulpo.

E. MEYER & CO.

Chemulpo.

SOLE AGENTS IN KOREA FOR:

A. T. Morse, Sons & Co's "Fresco" Distemper

In all colours ready for use on walls, Ceilings etc.

and

AVENARIUS CARBOLINEUM

A wood-preserving and antiseptic oil preparation

Against decay, dry-rot, fungus and wood-destroying insects.

A large supply always in Stock.
Prices upon application.

E. MEYER & Co.,
Chemulpo.

THE METHODIST PUBLISHING HOUSE,
Little West Gate, Seoul.

JOB PRINTING, TYPEWRITER PAPER
CARBON PAPER, VISITING CARDS
STATIONERY, BOOK BINDING
BOOK PUBLISHERS
AMERICAN SCHOOL BOOKS
SPENCERIAN COPY BOOKS
PEN CARBON LETTER AND BILL BOOKS

S. A. BECK, Manager.

HOKURKU DOBOKU KAISHA.

Branch office in Chong Dong, Seoul.

Japanese telephone No. 165

CONTRACT DEPARTMENT.

We can contract to build any building or construction.

MERCHANDISE DEPARTMENT.

We can provide any building material. We have just contracted to build the new Belgian Legation.

DAI-ICHI GINKO.

LIMITED.

(Formerly the First National Bank)

ESTABLISHED 1873

INCORPORATED UNDER PRESENT LAW 1896

Capital - - - - - - - - Yen 5,000,000
Reserve Fund - - - - - 1,500,000

HEAD OFFICE:—TOKIO.

President: Baron SHIBUSAWA.

BRANCHES AND CORRESPONDENTS
In the Principal Cities and Towns of Japan.
Interest Allowed on
Fixed deposits 1 year - - - 6½ per cent
" " 6 months - - - 6 per cent

Special current accounts 1½ sen daily per Y 100
General " " 1 " " " 100

M. TANAKA,
Manager, Chemulpo.

SINGER SEWING MACHINES

씽거ᄌᆞ봉침

SOLE AGENTS FOR KOREA
젼매소

HOLME RINGER & CO.
Chemulpo.
졔물포 함릉거양ᄒᆡᆼ

KAMEYA & CO.

GENERAL STOREKEEPERS

Chinkokai - - Seoul

(Established 1895, Tokyo)

Confectionery, Hams, Canned Goods, Cutlery, Hirano & Tansan Water. Provisions, Gents, Furnishing goods, Toilet Articles, Travelling Bags, Tobacco, Cigars & Cigarettes Kitchen Utensils. Coffee, Biscuits.

Fresh Goods always kept in Stock.
Prices Moderate
Please come and inspect our goods

NIPPON YUSEN KAISHA.

JAPANESE MAIL STEAMSHIP CO.

DER MAIL CONTRACT WITH THE IMPERIAL JAPANESE GOVERNMENT.

European Line

Regular Fortnightly Service between Yokohama Kobe, Moji, Shanghai, Hongkong, Singapore, Penang Colombo, Port Said, Marseilles, London and Antwerp

American Line

Regular Fortnightly Service between Hongkong and Seattle, calling t Shanghai, Moji, Kobe, Yokohama and Victoria, B. C.

Australian Line

Regular weekly Service betwen Japan Ports and Australia, calling at Hongkong and Manila.
(Above Three Lines Suspended until further notice).

Shanghai Line

Weekly Service between Shanghai and Japan Ports

Korea Line

Service Kobe, Moji, Nagasaki, Fusan Chemupo Chef foo, Taiku.
S. S. Bahelsberg, 2181 tons.
Service Kobe, Moji, Fusan, Chemulpo, Chinnampo
S. S. ARGO, S. S. Ohio.

BORDEN'S CONDENSED MILK CO.

New York, U. S. A.

ALWAYS IN STOCK
Eagle Brand Condensed Milk.
Gold Seal Condensed Milk.
Peerless (Family) Evaporated Cream.
Borden's Malted Milk.

E. MEYER & CO.
Chemulpo, Korea,
Sole Agents

ROYAL INSURANCE COMPANY,
Funds exceed £10,000,000
FIRE
AT CURRENT RATES.
LIFE
REDUCED PREMIUM.
HOLME RINGER & Co.,
Agents, Chemulpo.

HOTEL DU PALAIS

SEOUL.

The only first class Hotel in Seoul. Situated in the centre of the city opposite the palace.

Cuisine under the supervision of an experienced French Chef.

Well ventilated and furnished throughout.

TARIFF UPON APPLICATION

L. MARTIN
Proprietor and Manager.

大韓每日申報

대한매일신보

(뎨일빅오호) (일요일) 일쳔구빅사년십일월이십일일

본사고빅

이신보는영국와한국으로셔거믹일출판ᄒᆞᆷ

신문갑

ᄒᆞᆫ쟝 엽뎐두돈오푼

일삭됴 엽뎐팔량닷돈

우표가리삭닷돈

다ᄉᆞᆺ돈으로밧숩

광고료는

긔ᄒᆞᆫ의쟝단과ᄌᆞᄒᆡᆼ의다쇼로ᄎᆞ등잇게ᄒᆞ되렴가로밧을터이오며오리지아녀대한사ᄅᆞᆷ마다다이신문을보실터이니광고내시기를원ᄒᆞ시ᄂᆞᆫ이들은우리신문사에와셔면약ᄒᆞ시기를희망ᄒᆞᆷ

○발ᄒᆡᆼ소 박동대한ᄆᆡ일신보사 법어학교압희 젼영국인셜필림 졍자리오

사쟝 영국인 (빅셜)

평양 ᄃᆡ리졈

○평양효동사ᄂᆞᆫ권미보씨로우리신문ᄃᆡ리졈을ᄃᆡ리인을뒤졍ᄒᆞ엿ᄉᆞ오니평양에계신구람코져ᄒᆞ시ᄂᆞᆫ 쳠군ᄌᆞᄂᆞᆫ흥ᄃᆡ리졈에왕림ᄒᆞ와면의ᄒᆞ시옵

사고

○우리대한미일신보의목뎍은대한의안녕질서에관한모든대목에ᄃᆡᄒᆞ야ᄂᆞᆫ공평한변론을쥬쟝ᄒᆞᆷ이라우리동신원의ᄇᆞ람ᄂᆞᆫ신문보시ᄂᆞᆫ쳠군ᄌᆞ의게ᄒᆞᆼ상보도ᄒᆞ리며편지를긔셔ᄒᆞ여주시ᄂᆞᆫ이ᄂᆞᆫ셩명과반ᄃᆡ를ᄌᆡ어봇치시기를희망ᄒᆞ오나이거슨신문상에긔ᄌᆡᄒᆞ랴ᄂᆞᆫ거시아니오다만그ᄒᆡ신실ᄒᆞᆫᄌᆞ거를숨고자ᄒᆞᆷ이라긔쟈ᄂᆞᆫ아모긔셔던지긔ᄌᆡᄒᆞᆯ뒤ᄎᆞᄒᆞᄂᆞᆫ권리를가졋ᄉᆞ오나리ᄎᆞᆨᄒᆞᄂᆞᆫ리유를말ᄒᆞᆯ터이오며공즁평화를문란케ᄒᆞᄂᆞᆫ듯ᄒᆞᆫ긔셔ᄂᆞᆫ의례히반지안켓숩나이다

●본사셜시이래로신문을미양우례로분젼ᄒᆞ와례젼부의임의로젼ᄒᆞᄂᆞᆫᄉᆞ로만곳에ᄂᆞᆫ혹늣게젼ᄒᆞ기도ᄒᆞ며혹멋칠거슬ᄒᆞᆫ꺼번에젼ᄒᆞ기도ᄒᆞ며혹아니젼ᄒᆞᄂᆞᆫ곳도잇다ᄒᆞ와우리신문을ᄉᆞ랑ᄒᆞ야구람ᄒᆞ시ᄂᆞᆫ 쳠군ᄌᆞ의계ᄃᆡᄒᆞ야미우피안ᄒᆞ옵기로지금은분젼인을두고미일일즉이젼ᄒᆞ며아니젼ᄒᆞ거나늣게젼ᄒᆞ거나ᄒᆞᆫ일가잇도록ᄒᆞ랴ᄒᆞ오니혹아니젼ᄒᆞ거나혹늣게젼ᄒᆞ거나ᄒᆞᆫ일이잇ᄉᆞ면본사로통긔ᄒᆞ여주시기를희망ᄒᆞᆷ

관보

뎨이쳔구빅팔십륙호

광무팔년십일월십칠일

셔임급ᄉᆞ령

○의원면본관 쟝례원샹례 리인규

○의원면겸임 규쟝각직각 긔로쇼슈직관 김죵한

○명시종원경셔칙임관삼등 쟝례원경 윤덕영

○명쟝례원경셔칙임관삼등 궁ᄂᆡ부특진관 조졍희

○임쟝례원샹례셔주임관륙등 시강원시독관 서샹훈

○임규쟝각직각셔칙임관륙등 륙픔 리의국

○겸임시강원시독관 긔로쇼슈직관 김죵한

○승셔칙임관오등 쥬젼ᄉᆞ주ᄉᆞ 노인뎍

이상십일월십오일

궁뎡록ᄉᆞ

○죠칙의졍부찬졍민영셰은희졍임시종원경ᄒᆞ라

○죠칙명쟝례원경윤덕영으로위시종원경ᄒᆞ고궁ᄂᆡ부특진관조졍희로위쟝례원경ᄒᆞ라

○죠칙빈뎐도감제조윤덕영과궁쟝도감제조리용딕ᄂᆞᆫ샹환ᄒᆞ라ᄒᆞ셧더라

○츙효ᄉᆞ신리근명은 쥬원소도감감동을쳑샹ᄑᆞᆷ긔진우박명환으로ᄎᆞ하ᄒᆞ야보샬피계홈이하여ᄒᆞᆫ지근상 주ᄒᆞ와광무팔년십일월십ᄉᆞ일에봉지의주ᄒᆞ다

륙군연셩학교관제 속

뎨십구됴 학원과밋학도ᄂᆞᆫ쟝쳥을인ᄒᆞ야긔친후퇴교ᄒᆞᆷ을허락지아니ᄒᆞ되질병과혹ᄉᆞ고를인ᄒᆞ야학슐을슈업ᄒᆞᆯ희망이무ᄒᆞᆫ이ᄂᆞᆫ퇴교케ᄒᆞ미ᄒᆞᆷ이라

뎨이십됴 교쟝은슈학과말에각교관을모ᄒᆞ고회의를거ᄒᆞ야슈학의셩젹을조ᄉᆞᄒᆞ야학원과관에졔ᄒᆞ야ᄂᆞᆫ슈학증명셔를졔ᄒᆞ고학도ᄒᆞᄉᆞ에졔ᄒᆞ야ᄂᆞᆫ학슐슈업증을졔ᄒᆞ야교졍의고열을지ᄂᆞᆫ후에ᄎᆞ를본인의게줌이라

뎨이십일됴 교쟝은학원과밋학도의슈학긔말에슈학근만과학슐의우렬을조사ᄒᆞ야교관렬셔표를민드러교육총감의게보ᄒᆞ고교육총감은ᄎᆞ를군부대신과밋소속ᄃᆡ쟝의게젼지ᄒᆞᆷ이라

뎨이십이됴 교셩ᄃᆡ의퇴과ᄒᆞᆫ하ᄉᆞ병졸은현역일긔년이샹에부역ᄒᆞᆫ후참교와밋병졸즁에셔션발ᄒᆞᆷ이라

뎨이십삼됴 교셩ᄃᆡ의편입ᄒᆞᆫ하ᄉᆞ병졸은무긔피복장구를휴ᄃᆡ케ᄒᆞ고교셩ᄃᆡ의ᄎᆔ쟝을부착케ᄒᆞᆷ이라

뎨이십ᄉᆞ됴 연습상필요ᄒᆞᆫ물인ᄒᆞ야긔병ᄃᆡ마필을ᄉᆞ용ᄒᆞᆷ을득ᄒᆞᆷ이라

뎨이십오됴 본관제ᄂᆞᆫ반포일로시ᄒᆡᆼᄒᆞᆷ이라

륙군유년학교관제

뎨일됴 륙군유년학교ᄂᆞᆫ무관학도될쟈ᄅᆞᆯ요ᄒᆞᆫ보통학과와밋군인의예비교육을ᄒᆡᆼᄒᆞ야륙군각병과무관학도될인원을양셩ᄒᆞᆷ이라

뎨이됴 학도의교육은교슈와밋훈육에분ᄒᆞ니그강령은교육총감의인쟝ᄒᆞᆷ을엇어ᄒᆡᆼᄒᆞᆷ이라

뎨삼됴 본교학도ᄂᆞᆫ년령십오세로십팔세ᄭᆞ지자ᄅᆞᆯ모집ᄒᆞ야이에젹용이라

뎨ᄉᆞ됴 본교에학도ᄃᆡ를셜ᄒᆞ고ᄒᆞᆨ도ᄃᆡ쟝은교쟝이예겸ᄒᆞᆷ이라

뎨오됴 본교의직원은좌와ᄀᆞᆺ치졍ᄒᆞᆷ이라

교쟝 일인 졍부령

부관 일인 졍위

교관 십칠인 마슐과졍부참위일인 무학습보조과십일인 외국어학과륙인

학도ᄃᆡ즁ᄃᆡ쟝 삼인 졍위

학도ᄃᆡ부 십이인 부위혹참위

의관 일인 일이등군의

향관 일인 일이등군ᄉᆞ

듕무졍교 삼인

죠교 이십구인 마슐 삼인

죠교의인병 졍부교

뎨륙됴 교쟝은교육총감의게예ᄒᆞ야교무를총리ᄒᆞ고학도교육의책에임ᄒᆞᆷ이라

뎨칠됴 부관은교쟝의명을밧ᄋᆞ셔무를주쟝ᄒᆞᆷ이라

뎨팔됴 마슐과교관은학도의마슐훈련에임ᄒᆞ고생학교마구일졀ᄉᆞ무와마필의죠교를맛ᄒᆞᆷ이라

뎨구됴 문관교관은각학과의교슈를분담ᄒᆞᆷ이라

본교관즁직임자일인을션뎡ᄒᆞ야교두를명ᄒᆞ고교슈젼반의슈업을감시ᄒᆞ며교쟝의게ᄃᆡᄒᆞ야일졔히진보케ᄒᆞᄂᆞᆫ칙에임ᄒᆞᆷ이라

뎨십됴 즁ᄃᆡ쟝은즁ᄃᆡ부위관을지휘ᄒᆞ야즁ᄃᆡ학도의훈육을담임ᄒᆞ고군인졍신을겸념ᄒᆞ학도로ᄡᅥ군긔에관슉케ᄒᆞ며고셩젹에취ᄒᆞ야ᄂᆞᆫ젼담ᄒᆞᄂᆞᆫ직칙에임ᄒᆞᆷ이라

뎨십일됴 즁ᄃᆡ부위관은학도훈육의제과목을분담ᄒᆞ며학도의긍ᄒᆡᆼ을날마다감시ᄒᆞ고ᄌᆞ긔가모범이되야ᄎᆞ를ᄀᆞᄅᆞ쳐인도ᄒᆞ며분담ᄒᆞᆫ훈육에나가셔ᄂᆞᆫ그직칙에임ᄒᆞᆷ이라

뎨십이됴 학도의인원은민즁ᄃᆡ에일빅인으로편셩ᄒᆞ되민년에일긔즁ᄃᆡ식츙원ᄒᆞᆯᄎᆞᄅᆞᆯ좃차모집ᄒᆞᆷ이라

잡보

○투쟝가즁 셔셔금계졍은ᄌᆞ긔로분명ᄒᆞᆫ금산ᄌᆞ니이ᄂᆞᆫ죵죵ᄒᆞᆫ구식지빈ᄀᆞ승야투쟝ᄒᆞ야북망산을면ᄃᆞ니그형셰가그지ᄂᆞᆯ슈업ᄂᆞᆫ지라불가불과음기리니와진죵금지치못ᄒᆞᆫ죄칙으로히셔경찰관도상ᄒᆞᆫ반다시벌이잇스리라ᄒᆞ더라

○일진시찰 일진회에셔각회원의ᄒᆡᆼ위와가칭일진회원이라ᄒᆞ고ᄒᆡᆼ픽ᄒᆞᄂᆞᆫ거슬시찰ᄒᆞ기위ᄒᆞ야작일에시찰원일빅오십명을티젼ᄒᆞ야한셩오셔에분파ᄒᆞ야주야시무ᄒᆞᆫ다더라

○삼국교셥 파리에셔발간ᄒᆞᄂᆞᆫ고로아신문에빅림뎐에긔ᄅᆞᆯ의ᄃᆡ에다게루란도신문에보ᄒᆞᆫ바를게ᄒᆞᆫ즉구동에참혹ᄒᆞᆫ젼쟁을졍지ᄒᆞ기와ᄒᆞ야영미법삼국이셔로교셥ᄒᆞ엿ᄂᆞᆫᄃᆡ그교셥의긔초ᄂᆞᆫ일본으로ᄒᆞ야곰한국을유지케ᄒᆞᄂᆞᆫᄃᆡ셔ᄂᆞᆫ만쥬젼쳥평ᄒᆞᆷ을단렴케ᄒᆞᆷ에잇다ᄒᆞ엿더라

UNION INSURANCE SOCIETY OF CANTON.

Head office Hongkong.
Marine risks underwritten at current rates.
Agents in Chemulpo,
E. MEYER & Co.

COMPAGNIE DES MESSAGERIES MARITIMES.

Fortnightly Direct Service.

For Marseilles
via Ports.
Sailing from Yokohama
Calling at Kobe,
Shanghai, Hongkong, Saigon, Singapore,
Colombo, Djibonti, Suez, Port Said
and Marseilles.

For particulars apply to
HOLME RINGER & Co.,
Chemulpo.

HAYASHIDA & Co.,

16 MYENG DONG, CHIN KO KAI, SEOUL.
BRANCH OFFICE AT CHEMULPO.

Money changers, Coal and Wood Merchants, Express Agents.

We are agents for the Pyeng-yang Coal Company and the Karazu Coal Company of Japan. We have the best quality of both anthracite and bituminous coal, and prompt execution of orders is our speciality. Firewood of all kinds kept in stock. Full weight guaranteed. Money of all denominations exchanged at current rates. Parcels received for all parts.

CHINA MUTUAL LIFE INS. CO.

Most favourable terms to policy holders.

Benefit system unsurpassed.

HOLME RINGER & Co.
Agents, Chemulpo.

C. P. R.

CANADIAN PACIFIC RAILWAY COMPANY'S ROYAL MAIL STEAMSHIP LINE.

THE FAST ROUTE BETWEEN CHINA, JAPAN, AND EUROPE VIA CANADA AND THE UNITED STATES.

Route from Hongkong via Shanghai, Nagasaki (Inland Sea of Japan) Kobe, Yokohama Victoria and Vancouver.

Twin Screw Empress Steamship—6,000 Tons—Speed 19 knots.

PROPOSED SAILING FROM YOKOHAMA.
R. M. S. Empress of India.
R. M. S. Empress of Japan.
R. M. S. Empress of China.
R. M. S. Athenian.
R. M. S. Tartar.

Special reduction (first class only) granted to members of the Military, Naval, Diplomatic and Civil services and to Missionaries.

Passengers have choice of ten routes across the Continent of America and have privilege of travelling by any Atlantic Steamship Line.

Round the World passage tickets in connection with the P. and O. S. N., North German Lloyd and Messageries Co.'s **£125.**

All rates payable at current rate of exchange.

For further information, Tickets, Guide Books, etc., apply to

HOLME, RINGER & Co., AGENTS,
Chemulpo.

Grand Hotel,

(Formerly the Station Hotel)

Near the Railway Terminus, West Gate Seoul.

The Best Hotel in Korea
Handsome new Building.
Fine Airy Rooms
Excellent Cuisine.
Terms Moderate.
Special terms to Missionaries
and to permanent boarders.

Electric cars within 2 minutes' walk.

W. H. EMBERLEY,
Proprietor

EVERY FACILITY.

In connection with Life Assurance Business is afforded by

The Standard Life Assurance Co.,

One of the largest and wealthiest of the Provident Institutions of the United Kingdom Forms of Application and all information will be promptly afforded on application.

10 CENTS A DAY.

Not a very large expenditure is it? But it is sufficient to secure for a man of 30 a policy with the STANDARD LIFE OFFICE for

$1323.

For all particulars of rates, etc., apply to

Holme, Ringer & Co.,
Agents, Chemulpo.

THE NEW YORK LIFE INSURANCE COMPANY.

Have you ever been declined by any Company?

Are you engaged in a specially hazardous occupation?

Have you heard of the New York Life Insurance Company's New Classifications for this class of Risks?

If not, send your date of birth, occupation and particulars of rejection, if any to

E. MEYER & Co.,
Agents, Chemulpo.

MITSUI BUSSAN KAISHA.
(MITSUI & Co.)

MITSUI GINKO.
(MITSUI BANK.)

The Bank is owned by the members of the Mitsui Family, who, as partners, assume an unlimited responsibility for all liabilities of the Bank:—

Capital.......................Yen 5,000,000
Reserve Fund..................." 5,600,000

HEAD OFFICE, TOKYO.
LONDON OFFICE, 34 LIME ST., E. C.

BRANCHES AND AGENCIES:—
New York, San Francisco, Hamburg, Bombay, Singapore, Manila, Hongkong, Amoy, Chefoo, Tientsin.

Kobe, Hakodate, Yokohama, Kure, Yokosuka, Moji, Shimonoseki, Miike, Wakamatsu, Nagasaki, Kuchinotsu, Karatsu, Sasebo, Misume, Taipeh, &c.

Telegraphic Address for all the Offices:
"MITSUI."
A. B. C. AND A. I CODES USED.

Contractors of Coal
To the Imperial Japanese Navy. Arsenals and Railway Bureau, Principal Railway Companies and Industrial Work, Home and Foreign Mail and Freight Steamers.

Sole Proprietors
Of the famous Miike, Tagawa and Yamano Coal Mines.

Sole Agents
For the sale of Fukumo, Hokoku, Ichimura, Kanoda, Mannoura, Onoura, Ostuji, Sonoda, Tsubaruro, Yoshinotani, Yoshio, Yurokibura and other coals.

YANGTSE INSURANCE ASSOCIATION, LTD.

The undersigned, having been appointed agents for the above company, are prepared to issue policies and pay losses on marine risks at regular rates.

E. MEYER & Co.,
Agents, Chemulpo.

AMERICAN KOREAN ELECTRIC CO.

Light and Power.

Main Office: Electric Building, Chong No.

RAILWAY DEPARTMENT.

OPERATING CARS BETWEEN EAST AND WEST GATE, EVERY TEN MINUTES:—

First Car leaves East Gate at 7:00 A. M. First Car leaves R. R. Station at 7:25 A. M
Last Car " East Gate at 9:40 P. M. Last " " R. R. Station at 10:05 P. M

OPERATING CARS BETWEEN EAST GATE AND IMPERIAL TOMB TERMINUS, EVERY TWENTY MINUTES:—
CONNECTING WITH EVERY ALTERNATE CAR ARRIVING AT EAST GATE FROM CHONG NO.

First Car leaves East Gate for Tomb at 7:10 A. M.
" " " Tomb for East Gate at 7:35 A. M.
Last " " East Gate for Tomb at 7:50 P. M.
" " " Tomb for East Gate at 8:10 P. M.

OPERATING CARS BETWEEN CHONG NO AND YUNG SAN RIVER EVERY TWELVE MINUTES:—

First Car leaves Chong No for South Gate at 7:12 A. M.
" " " Chong No for Yung San at 7:36 A. M.
" " " South Gate for Chong No at 7:20 A. M.
" " " Yung San for Chong No at 8:09 A. M.
Last " " South Gate for Chong No 10:00 P. M.
" " " Yung San for Chong No at 9:33 P. M.

SPECIAL PRIVATE CARS FURNISHED TO SUIT CONVENIENCE OF PATRONS. PRICES ON APPLICATION AT HEAD OFFICE.

LIGHTING DEPARTMENT.

Where less than 250 candle power of light is used, the rate per month will be
Per 16 candle power incandescent lamp,—All night.—Yen 2.50.
32 candle power incandescent lamp:—All night:—Yen 4.00.
50 candle power incandescent lamp:—All night:—Yen 6.00.
150 " " " " — " " 10.00.
1200 " " enclosed arc " " " " 20.00.

Where more than 250 candle power of light is used, a Meter will be installed, if requested:—Rent of Meter Yen 2.00 per month. Rate of charges by meter reading:—Two Sen per Ampere per hour. (Approximately this is equal to about One Sen per 16 C. P. lamp per hour) Minimum monthly charge where meter is installed, Yen 20.00 per month, which includes rental of meter.

Estimates for installing lights furnished on application.
An assortment of chandeliers always on hand.

K. Murakami,
Photograph Studio
Chinkokai, Seoul.

Printing, Developing and Enlargement, of Photographs always Undertaken.

Korean Views and Pictures Illustrating Native Customs always on Sale.

THE OSAKA SHOSEN KAISHA.

Boats frequently on the berth for Chinnampo.

REGULAR SAILINGS BETWEEN JAPAN AND KOREAN PORTS.

FUSAN AND KOBE VIA SHIMONOSEKI.

OSAKA VIA MOKPO, FUSAN, SHIMONOSEKI AND KOBE.

MOJI DIRECT.

OSAKA VIA KUNSAN, MASANPO, FUSAN, SHIMONOSEKI AND KOBE.

CHEMULPO KUNSAN LINE,
Every three days.

CHEMULPO CHINNAMPO LINE.
Every three days.

For Freight and passage and further particulars apply to
THE OSAKA SHOSEN KAISHA,
Chemulpo.

RONDON, PLAISANT & CO.

General Storekeepers and Merchants, Ships Contractors, Tobacconists, Commission and Forwarding Agents, Coal Merchants

IMPORTERS AND EXPORTERS

Seoul & Chemulpo.

W. D. WENTWORTH.

LANDING
AND
SHIPPING AGENT
AND
CUSTOMS BROER.

12 OURA, NAGASAKI.

STEWARD & CO.

Chemulpo.

Shipchandlers and Storekeepers, Naval and Mercantile Contrrctors, Landing and Shipping Agents.

STEWARD'S HOTEL

Chemulpo.

Best accommodation in the port for travellers. Clean and well-aired rooms, good cuisine prompt attendance, moderate tariff.

○로협세력 근리에 보도를 거ᄒᆞᆫ즉 동양에 출릭ᄒᆞᆫ 파라협티의 셰력이 젼투ᄒᆞᆷ칠쳑과 ᄉᆞ찬양ᄒᆞᆷ둘쳑과 구축ᄒᆞᆷ칠쳑과 의용ᄒᆞᆷ티이쳑파 공작션일쳑파 병원션일쳑파 운송션오쳑비오쏘이ᄒᆞᆷ티와 연합ᄒᆞ기 위ᄒᆞ야 방금 츄즁ᄒᆞ는 군ᄒᆞᆷ이 ᄉᆞ찬양ᄒᆞᆷ이쳑과 구축ᄒᆞᆷ오쳑파 보조ᄉᆞ찬양ᄒᆞᆷ룩쳑과 운송션삼쳑이오 또 흑히에서 출릭ᄒᆞ야 졍졍ᄒᆞᆷ ᄒᆞ란는 군ᄒᆞᆷ이 의용ᄒᆞᆷ티ᄉᆞ쳑파 운송션륙쳑과 쇄빙션일쳑이오 히오처비쏘 석탄션대탁이 심쳑이 각처에 빅치되엿는티 우제ᄒᆞᆷ즁에 무순ᄒᆞᆷ은 소사를 경과ᄒᆞ고 무손ᄒᆞᆷ은 회망붕을 지나는지 아직 자세치 못ᄒᆞ더라

○충남위계 공쥬관찰ᄉᆞ가 니부로 보고ᄒᆞ기를 향니에 탁지부ᄒᆞ 훈령을 승젼ᄒᆞ야 특별히 사름을 파송ᄒᆞ야 원근에 볼니 탐지ᄒᆞ며 각군에 훈ᄒᆞ야 몸소 심찰ᄒᆞ야 제며견을 수실ᄒᆞ야 ᄒᆞ여곰 실수를 아제들여 보고ᄒᆞ게 ᄒᆞ엿더니 각양제결ᄒᆞᆷ이 ᄒᆞ야 일만삼쳔ᄉᆞ빅팔십오결이십일부 구속인고로 수쳔오빅팔십칠결ᄉᆞ실일부는 퇴감ᄒᆞ야 주고 팔쳔팔빅구십이결팔십부 구속으로 경탕히 결총으로 장앗ᄉᆞ온바 공쥬등 이십팔군은 덕욱 심ᄒᆞ고 제ᄉᆞ등 칠군은 그 다음이오 셔셩등 삼군은 저괴ᄒᆞᆫ신ᄒᆞ오니 제결을 제표로 등긔ᄒᆞ야 ᄒᆞᆫ다ᄒᆞ엿다더라

○도별연부 경상남도관찰ᄉᆞ 셩기운씨의 보고니기에 관하창원군의 향교와 긱사지쳐지티에 일본군용뎐도를 부셜ᄒᆞ는 일은 젼에 임의 보고ᄒᆞ엿거니와 역부들이 자세ᄒᆞ고 아로ᄒᆞ는 겻파괴 아인간에 서로 구타ᄒᆞ는 변이 출일ᄒᆞ야 싱겨나 민혤난ᄒᆞ며 평방홈이 곳초 싱긴쌘더러 황차 히감부에셔 히군경니에 호송이 수쳔일빅구십여호에서 민호에 인부를 조발시혀 부역ᄒᆞ게 ᄒᆞᆷ쯧ᄉᆞ로 말ᄒᆞ며 반일 모집ᄒᆞ는티 응거 아니ᄒᆞ면 맛당히 군병을 발ᄒᆞ야 로력으로 쵸모ᄒᆞ기를 경영ᄒᆞᆫ다ᄒᆞ엿더라

○원소황경 원소긔니들 동대문밧 마장리로 왕경ᄒᆞ야 지심자싱셕지잉의지변는지라 지작 싱팔일에 양쥬군슈 ᄒᆞ티운파 한셩윤 소운방 승조와 니부토목국장 유진석샹씨가 별인ᄒᆞᆷ 도로들 적간ᄒᆞᆯᄎᆞ로 나가서 답ᄉᆞᄒᆞ엿더라

○별젼 신림 지작일은 비궁뎐하 ᄒᆞ옹셔ᄒᆞ옵신데 이칠 비란 대황뎨폐하와 황티ᄌᆞ뎐하계옵셔 친림ᄒᆞ사 별뎐을 셜힝ᄒᆞ옵시는티 빅관이 외레히 입참ᄒᆞ엿더라

○국장태일 국장길일은 음력 십일월이십구일노 쵸뎡일ᄒᆞ엿더라

○빙펀공함 빙공관에셔 외부로 조회ᄒᆞ되 김병도 양교일수로 여러번 봉함ᄒᆞ야 청ᄒᆞ엿고 본일에도 쏘훈낭이다 ᄒᆞ도롱교티ᄒᆞ야도 맛참니 소식이 엽기에 쏘 이굿치 통교ᄒᆞ노라 ᄒᆞ엿고 쏘 조회ᄒᆞ되 김병도가 아라사에 입젹훈 리유를 입의 전에 셜명ᄒᆞ엿는티 엇지ᄒᆞ야 분셔로 장아보니지 아니ᄒᆞ나바 이것으로 ᄒᆞ여곰 우리 졍부에 보고ᄒᆞ야 써 회지를 기다려 조처ᄒᆞᆯ터이니 쳥컨티 조량ᄒᆞ라 ᄒᆞ엿고 쏘 조회ᄒᆞ되 김병도는 아라사에 입젹훈 사름이라 귀졍부에셔 이굿치 오릭 가두어스니 부득불 귀졍부에 향ᄒᆞ야 손히빈상금을 요구ᄒᆞᆯ터이니 조량ᄒᆞ라 ᄒᆞ엿더라

○미관조회 미공관에셔 외부로 조회ᄒᆞ되 각신문에 긔ᄌᆡᄒᆞᆫ중 한셩부에서 각디ᄇᆡ에 훈칙ᄒᆞ기를 일본사름은 비록 리힝권이 업드리도 거쥬ᄒᆞᆯ시니티에 등힝ᄒᆞᆫ다ᄒᆞ니 이일에 올코 그른 것을 확실이 시명ᄒᆞ라 ᄒᆞ엿는티 외부에셔 미관으로 조복ᄒᆞ기를 일인이란 힝권업시 니티에 등힝ᄒᆞᆫ다는 사는 본티의 린이 엽고 히신문에 괴지ᄒᆞᆫ 거시 잘못 드름이니 죽히 밋지 못ᄒᆞᆯ 거이라 ᄒᆞ엿더라

○쳥구셜명 일본졍부에셔 거월 이십오일에 졍말국과 서반아와 법국과 화란에 티ᄒᆞ야 중입위반수로 등친ᄒᆞ엿더니 우ᄉᆞ국중에서 차등친에 티ᄒᆞ야 회답홈이 엽다ᄒᆞᆫ티 그후 파란합티가 서반아뷔이고 써와 밋 법평차홈반에셔 중입을 어괴며 힝동홈이 잇숨으로 일본졍부에서 이ᄉᆞ건으로 법국과 서반아 량국에 셜명ᄒᆞ기를 청구ᄒᆞ엿더니 서반아에서 답ᄒᆞ되 우리졍부에서 중립에 무릇 구지ᄒᆞ며 교전국 군함의 투힝외를 조치ᄒᆞ는 일을 힝치 아니ᄒᆞ겟고 일본졍부가 셜명을 쳥구ᄒᆞᆫ 수실에 티ᄒᆞ야는 다시 자세히 조사ᄒᆞ겟다 ᄒᆞ엿더라

○귀쥬린신 일본졍토종교쟝 송강빅웅씨와 등변에 양쳔환씨와 히쥬거ᄒᆞ는 젼쥬수 우티졍 최양엽 제씨가 동평청의ᄒᆞ야 히쥬부너에 근정을 명ᄒᆞ고 본월 싱이일 오후 일시에 랑국국긔를 놉히 달고 기회식을 힝ᄒᆞ는티 당디 일본거류민과 대한인민 쳔여명이 제회ᄒᆞ야 당일 교사 송강씨가 연셜ᄒᆞ기를 종교는 닐너괴고 쳥년을 회집ᄒᆞ야 일어와 외교학문을 교슈ᄒᆞ야 일한량국간 교린ᄒᆞ는티는 무궤ᄒᆞ자는 의지로 셜명ᄒᆞ고 이인ᄋᆞᆫ 비답수ᄒᆞᆫ후에 일한 량국 대황뎨폐하를 위ᄒᆞ야 만세를 서로 부르고 등상시에 진취ᄒᆞ엿는티 삼수일간에 종교신도와 쳥년회원이 수오십인에 이르럿다더라

식김제ᄒᆞ량씨가 덕셜군에 잇는 젼답을 니슈수서 공토란ᄒᆞ고 슈셰과 원젼 상국의게 젼답ᄒᆞᆫ수로 궁니부에 누츠 호소ᄒᆞ더니 일작에 최김량씨가 회원 ᄒᆞᆫ종규씨로 동힝ᄒᆞ야 궁니부대신서리 용태씨 사저에 젼왕ᄒᆞ야 히졍도ᄉᆞ진을 질문ᄒᆞᆫ스로 작일의 진회에서 평의회를 긔ᄒᆞ고 사법위원 염중모 양재익씨가 최김홍샹씨 수인에 티ᄒᆞ야 셜명ᄒᆞᆫ대개른드로즉 인민의 싱명재산을 보호ᄒᆞᆷ은 본회의 목젹이라 비런ᄉᆞ진이 잇스면 회중에서 궁니대신의게 공함도 ᄒᆞ겟고 위원을 파송ᄒᆞ야 젼문ᄒᆞᆷ이 가ᄒᆞ거늘 슈빅명중에 최김량원이 본회에 입참ᄒᆞᆫ 본의가 히졍토만 위ᄒᆞ야 회원을 빙ᄌᆞᄒᆞ고 이런 일을 힝ᄒᆞᆷ이 창회ᄒᆞ는 목젹이 아니라ᄒᆞ야 최명식 김제홍 량씨는 출회ᄒᆞ고 홍종규씨는 가칭작인ᄒᆞ고 동힝ᄒᆞᆫ 죄로 중견책에 시벌ᄒᆞ야 회중에 공포ᄒᆞ엿다더라

○쳥요교비 외부에셔 궁니부로 공함ᄒᆞ기를 아라사사롬 틱이로와 밋 구린쳔의 귀룩ᄒᆞᆫ 단ᄌᆞ니에 일너스되 대한졍부에 유리제조기수에는 민이로요 졔조기쇼에는 구린쳔으로 교방ᄒᆞ야 일쳔구빅삼년에 일을 인연ᄒᆞ야 한성으로 좃차 아라사에 갓고 그 다음히 도륙을 셰에려숩에서 젼쟁을 맛나 도칭ᄒᆞ지 못ᄒᆞ고 히량원이 싱각ᄒᆞ기를 힝함동이 스수로 폐지ᄒᆞᆫ줄 알고 단니는 돈이며 좌ᄒᆞ니은 본년도 월봉과 밋 쥬졉비가 항오쳔수빅원이요 들지ᄂᆞᆫ 한셩으로브터 아라사지 러비 일쳔오빅원은 항동니에서 괴ᄌᆡᄒᆞᆫ바요 셰젓지는 힌셩에서 버린고 잔물수로 갑시 일쳔원이요 젼ᄌᆡ는 아픔블리원쉼지간런비 오빅원을 곳지 발ᄒᆞᆯ리라 ᄒᆞᆫ기에 빅란양포ᄒᆞ니 조량ᄒᆞ시며 ᄒᆞ에엿더라

외보

○일본사금광 일본인 슈쳔욱 젼국에 잇는 사금광은 대장싱소관인대 그 젹부의 수분일을 조사ᄒᆞᆫ즉 싱억원이 싱ᄒᆞᆯ만ᄒᆞ다 ᄒᆞ는티 그 실샹은 수싱억원이 출ᄒᆞᆯ자라 가령 금번 젼정 오렌지라도 경비는 걱정ᄒᆞᆯ거시 죠곰도 엽다ᄒᆞ더라

○파란함대 빅입면우거ᄒᆞᆫ즉 현금 파란함대를 위ᄒᆞ야 셕탄은 젼에 죵수ᄒᆞ는 영국괴션중에 그 샹합대일ᄒᆞᆷ을 합셜이 아는 것이 싱쳑이라더라

론셜

셰틱함티

수싱일젼에 아라사 셰틱함티가 동양으로 향ᄒᆞ야 출발ᄒᆞ다가 복ᄒᆞ에서 영국어럽티를 징겻파격ᄒᆞ야 의외의 일을 이로커장히며 잇는 사진이 비계 아비로소 탄쳥에 되엿는딕 고세에 비헐로 말믹앙아 영국 모든 신문에서 홍의가 불등ᄒᆞ야 란사로함을 돌련보낭으로 엇지ᄒᆞᆯ수 업시 장히여 잇섯스며

아라사이 영국에 되ᄒᆞ야 비되도록 종대히 진합ᄒᆞᆫ 일을 힝ᄒᆞᆯ지경이면 영국이 안령히 보고 잇서 원수를 갑ᄒᆞ리 아니ᄒᆞ리가 업슬은 우쥰ᄒᆞᆫ 사듬이라도 다 ᄌᆞ셔히 알벼미어는 문득 이리ᄒᆞᆫ 일에 범ᄒᆞᆯ은 아라사가 화를 자취ᄒᆞ려 ᄒᆞᆷ이로다

아라사에서 당초에 빙ᄌᆞᄒᆞ는 말인즉 일본뇌가 어뢰티중에 써여 잇기에 파격ᄒᆞᆷ이라고 셜명ᄒᆞ나 그러ᄒᆞ나 영국귀족 젠스샌니씨가 졀드원에서 이 사실에 티ᄒᆞ야 연셜ᄒᆞ기를 죵이가 분명ᄒᆞᆫ넘에 아라사졍부에서 자괴의 싱각티로만 죳케 셜명ᄒᆞᆷ은 영국의 공동지론을 반티ᄒᆞᆷ이라고 동의ᄒᆞᆫ후 이 사연으로 당장ᄒᆞ엿더니

아라사에서 다시 셜명ᄒᆞ야 왈 우리가 당초브터 북히에서 무삼 공격이 잇슨가 염며가 불무ᄒᆞᆫ 조음에 과연 히지에 이르러 의혹나는 션격이 현출됨으로 파격ᄒᆞᆷ이라고 ᄒᆞ야 그 실샹을 자셰히 셜명ᄒᆞ포 비상금을 영국졍부로 보냇다ᄒᆞ는지라

이 말을 듯드티도 셰틱함티가 출발ᄒᆞ는 중로에서도 일방의 계공격을 당ᄒᆞᆯ가 ᄒᆞ는 넘녀가 잇는 모양인즉 우리는 괴왕 듯기에 쉬시히 쳥에 디쟝츳 죵박ᄒᆞᆷ이 필요ᄒᆞ겟다ᄒᆞ는 말뿐 드리는티 만일 이러ᄒᆞᆯ지경이면 대단히 위티ᄒᆞᆫ거시 동쟁으로 발힝ᄒᆞ는 동안에는 항샹 조심ᄒᆞ야 경겁ᄒᆞ는 마음을 놋키 어려우며 셜혹 무사히 지너나온다ᄒᆞ드리도 죵박ᄒᆞᆯ곳이 졍령 업슬지라

중립ᄒᆞᆫ 나라 항구에는 갑불싱의인즉 일본쥬방은 자괴가 굿게 보호ᄒᆞ야 포모사ᄒᆞᆫ 항구에는 지퇴포셔지 무뎌스며 라숩ᄒᆞᆫ 항구에는 일병이 수룩으로 병진ᄒᆞ야 모도 잇슨즉 특별히 무삼 변동이 잇기전에는 디옥 싱각이 어려운즉

이외의 생으로 말ᄒᆞ면 디반히 삼위와 한국ᄒᆞᆫ구쌘인티 만일 그로력ᄒᆞ는 군사들로 ᄒᆞ야 공히 상위에 이르럿다가 다시 동방으로 향발ᄒᆞ게 ᄒᆞ면 악형을 힝ᄒᆞ는거와 갓ᄒᆞ여 모도 도망ᄒᆞᆯ터이은쌘더러 겸병도 될터이요 쏘ᄒᆞᆫ 일본군사가 원산항구 근쳐에 주둔ᄒᆞ야 엄숙히 방비ᄒᆞ는 모양이며

남방히면에도 일본병함이 번여잇고 셔편히안에는 당초에 히군 중박ᄒᆞᆯ곳이 못된즉 셰틱함티의 소젼히 싱히 모호ᄒᆞᆫ지라 그런고로 우리는 셰틱함티의 위티ᄒᆞᆷ이 블무염려라 ᄒᆞ노라

TELEGRAMS.

Headquarters, Seoul.

Field Marshal Oyama reports that on the 16th inst. a body of Russian cavalry and infantry attacked the Japanese force on the right bank of the Hunho, their principal force however retiring at dusk. During an artillery duel the next day 3 Japanese were wounded. The Russian casualties could not be clearly ascertained, but they seemed to be excessive of the Japanese.

Tokyo, Nov. 17th.

The new Japanese loan in London has been succefully floated, the amount having been over subscribed many times.

Tokyo, Nov. 17th.

The Russian Government has bought up large quantities of Chinese cloth, for the use of the troops during the winter.

HOW GOVERNMENTS KEEP THEIR TELEGRAMS SECRET.

SOME INTRICATE CODES.

Every day, says Answers, messages of the most important and secret character pass between the British Government and its diplomatic and consular agents abroad, which it is a matter of supreme importance should be kept absolutely secret, except from those for whom such messages are directly intended. The secrecy is preserved by the use of various codes, the key to which is known to very few persons, and in some instances the precaution is observed of changing the code once every six months. The four great departments of the British Government possessing codes are the Foreign and Colonial Offices the War Office, and the Admiralty. The code in use at the Foreign Office is by far the the most intricate, and consists, in fact, of two different codes, which are altered at least twice a year. There are two officials at the Foreign Office who are continually employed in revising the codes and altering the keys. The Foreign Office codes are made out in two languages, English and French, and a code message has to be despatched in both languages. For instance, supposing a code message is being despatched to our Ambassador of Paris by wire—the first part of it if transmitted in English, is what is officially known as the "shell" of the code. The message to the uniniated individual leads exactly like an ordinay commnunciation relating to the every-day business of our foreign affairs, but certain placing of the words informs the Ambassador that the message is a code one. The other message then arrives in French and the two together are then read by means of the key, which the Ambassador of his secretary holds. If a reply is necessary, it can be sent either in French of English alone. However, as a matter of fact, it is rarely that messages of very grave importance are sent by wire, except under very special circumstances. One of the King's foreign messengers, of whom there are ten employed at the Foreign Office, is generally despatched to carry a code message, and must deliver it in person to the individual to whom it is addressed. For messages of less importance, the Foreign Office uses a cipher code which is changed about once in three years. The code to use at the Colonial Office is made out altogether in French, and is of a very complicated character. Officials in the Government secret service are continually at work testing the secrecy of the various codes. Fictitious messages of an apparently highly important character are despatched to these officials at different places all over the world in various codes, which are purposely allowed to pass through the hands of a number of persons, and it is the business of the secret service officials to ascertain if there is a "leakage" anywhere—that is to say, if the real meaning of these messages appears to be known to anyone not in possesion of the keys of the different codes. This sometimes happens, and the particular code in which a "leakage" is reported, is promptly put out of use until it has been revised and the key altered. The code service of this country costs about £50,000 a year to maintain, and is infinitely the cheapest service of the character among European nations. France spends £100,000 per annum on her code service, and Russia, two years ago, paid £250,000 for the maintenance of her code service for twelve months. The Russian code service is the most elaborate and intricate in the world. It is made out by dozens of experts, each of whom works independently of the other, so that none of them has the remotest idea of what the final code is like. The work of each of these experts is taken in hand by two officials, occupying high places in the Russian government, who, between them, complete the official secret language and the keys to it. The secrecy of the code is guarded with the utmost care, and a person suspected of giving the key away promptly disppears, together with the individual suspected of receiving it. Yet, in spite of all the most elaborate precautions, the code service of Russia is more frequently tampered with than that of any other nation.

FOREIGN LITERATURE IN JAPAN.

An article in a recent number of "Harper's Weekly" written by a Japanese, gives some interesting details of the state of foreign literature in Japan. Until she broke loose from her exclusively Oriental past some forty years ago, the only foreign element in the life and thought of Japan was Chinese.

The first European language that the Japanese set themselves to grapple with after the revolution was Dutch. It speaks well for their determination to Westernize themselves that they were still able to persevere.

To-day, "while the English is the most common among our people and is studied by all high school pupils, German and French are favoured generally by our scholars and physicians." Of the tongues taught in the foreign language school at Tokio, Russian, curiously enough, is the favourite.

The most widely known English writer in Japan is Carlyle. Next to him comes Macaulay. Emerson is admired by some of the English students, and we see the influences of his writings among many Japanese journalists to-day."

Mill and Herbert Spencer "have had a tremendous influence upon the thought of modern Japan." In poetry Tennyson Longfellow—his "Evangeline" is heard from the lips of any little girl in a girl's seminary in Japan—Wordsworth, Byron and Milton, and in fiction Irving, Thackeray and Dickens are the best known.

"Othello," "Macbeth," and the "Merchant of Venice" have been translated by Professor Yuzo Tsubouchi. Tolstoy has many worshippers, and no one who is not acquainted with German is regarded as a scholar.

Rousseau's "Contract Social" was the book which "first taught the Japanese the idea of civil right and liberty." A translation of it "has been circulated in every Japanese home." The writers of French fiction and drama, on the other hand do not seem to find many friends in Japan.

THE STAYING POWER.

The most remarkable instance of the display of the power of national perseverance and endurance in modern times, says the "Jiji," is that of England during the Napoleonic wars, which lasted on and off for twenty years, and during which time that country expended 830 million pounds. The more remarkable was the way in which England came out of the war practically richer and stronger. This wonderful feat encompassed by England is ascribed to the fact that the British nation as a whole worked hard toward extending her trade and developing new sources of wealth by applying scientific discoveries to new enterprises and under takings, all which circumstances were made possible for her by securing the control of the sea at the early atage of the war. This shows that a mere policy of negative economy cannot of itself be of much use when a nation is engaged in an exhaustive war of long duration: a nation must be in possession of means of regeneration and wealth-creating mechanism. The "Jiji" would consequently denounce the contentions of a coterie of men who insist on the nation practising a do-nothing economy, so as to increase the people's savings with which to carry on the war. Japan's position is similar to that of England's a century ago, in so far as we are in command of the sea; and the journal would appeal to the patriotism of our business, industrial, and capitalistic circles for the extension of our trade and the opening of new sources of wealth by the fearless investment of their money.—Japan Times.

DRINK SOUR MILK.

There should be a premium on sour milk, if Prof. Elie Metehnikoff, of the Pasteur Institute, is to be believed. He declares that, to follow the example of the Bulgarians and drink large quantities of such milk, will make for longevity. As the Professor explains the matter in the "Pall Mall Magazine," sour milk contains a large bacillus, remarkable for the amount of lactic acid it can produce. This microbe can be introduced into the body with great benefit to health, at it preys on myriads of its harmful fellows.

According to a Shanghai despatch, the Captain of the Russian destroyer Reshiteljui, which was captured by the Japanese in Chefoo harbor, has disappeared. It is thought, that he may have left secretly on a German Mail steamer.

A site for the Crown Princess' tomb has been finally selected at Mackang Ni outside the East Gate. Yesterday a party of officials visited the place and made arrangements for the roads to be repaired in view of the funeral procession. The funeral will probably take place early in January.

Since the news was announced that anyone capable of dispersing the. Il Chin Hoi would be appointed Chief of Police, many swindlers have applied, says the Kanjo Shimpo."The best man so far, continues the same journal, is Mr. Yi Myeng Sang, but have you, Mr. Yi, the power to disperse this strong Gathering?

Some friction has occured between the French Legation and the Foreign Office, owing to the persistent refusal of the latter to hand over Lieut. Kim Byung Do to justice. Lieut. Kim is a Russian subject and is wanted to answer a charge of assault, brought against him in the French court. Very strong representations, we understand, have been made by the French Minister, to obtain possession of him, but apparently without avail.

Two Russians, formerly employed by the Korean Government in the munufacture of glass and weaving, have now filed a claim for araears of salary and travelling expenses. It appears that before war broke out they had been on leave in Russia and had reached as far as Port Arthur, when hostilities prevented them from returning to Seoul. Their claim, the total of which amounts to $8,400, includes the price of furniture abandoned in Seoul.

It is said that Mr. Cho Byung-sik's announcement of a new society to be formed has been received with disapproval by the Japanese Military authorities and consequently the proposal has fallen through. General Yi Keun Pak, the chief of the Imperial guard, however has stated his intention of going into the society business and will open up with the announcement of his proposed society's views in a few days. In connection with this we were interested to hear from our reporter yesterday that general Yi Keun Pak is a frequent visitor at the Japanese Head Quarters.

On the banks of the Teluga River, in Cutch, there was recently killed a crocodile, and the following inventory was made of the contents of the brute's stomach: A half-digested little calf, a human skull, a silver bangle, some brass ornaments, a little tin box containg tobacco, a lime case, a nut-cracker, a horn case containg twelve annas, six pies in copper and a soda water bottle containing some mustard oil.

Germans have long since accustomed us to the edible fork, and now, says a contemporary, English hotel-keepers have started an edible menu card. It is made of biscuit, and not meant to be eaten, of course, until the end of the meal. A menu card and a glass of wine will, however, it is thought, satisfy many who like a quick lunch. If progress is made along these lines we shall soon have edible waiters.—The Bystander.

The building of the railway close to the sacred precincts of the temple at Chang Won has led to serious trouble, reports the Governor of South Kyengsang Province. Fights occur daily between the Japanese railway coolies and the Korean inhabitants of the district. Moreover the railway authorities have announced their intention of collecting Korean coolies to assist in the work. If they do not come willingly, Japanese soldiers will collect them by force.

A Korean newspaper office was visited on Thursday evening by a young man, who expressed a desire to receive information about advertisement rates. On being enlightened, he deposited sixty Yen and a weighty looking document on a table and went off "at the double." Upon investigation, the document turned out to be a lengthy Tonghak proclamation, declaiming against the Government. The editor of the newspaper in question found himself unable to insert the advertisement in his columns and is looking for the owner of the money, so that he may return it.

We have just received two interesting stories from our Korean reporter, whose particular style it seems a pity to spoil by alteration. The first story calls for no particular comment, but it occurs to us with regard to the second that the relationship between the Kamni of Chemulpo and the curious box (via the dreamer and the faun) would be a fruitful subject for investigation.

* * *

On the day before yesterday there was a Japanese cake-maker commencing his business directly at front of turnip heaps on Chong No where turnip merchants sell turnips. So the Korean who is owner of turnips told the Jap to remove little way from the heap of turnips, but the Jap said the Korean must go to other place with turnips. At this time one of Korean, respectators scolded the Jap what his bad action. Then that Jap at once struck the Korean near to dead, at last other Koreans carried him in chair to his house.

* * *

In one night that Mr. Chi Woon-yung, the former privy councillor, has got one curious box in his dream which was given by a faun; when he awakened he found the same box at front of him. At once that Mr. Chi Woon-yung presented that box to Emperor and the Emperor himself opened the box, and when looked in, he found the 4 words "big rain, heavy fall" and other 4 words "Ul Sa 3rd month," and some more other words which recorded the future fortune of Mr. Ha Sang-ki, the Kamni of Chemulpo.

The Korea Daily News.

Issued at 5 P. M. daily except Sundays.

Rate of Subscription:—
Per Year,............Yen 25.
Per Quarter,..........Yen 7.
Per Month,..........Yen 2.50.

Postage in Korea not charged extra.
Postage abroad charged extra.

Advertisements. 50 sen per day for 1 inch or less.
5 yen per month per inch.
50 yen per year per inch.

All communications to

E. T. BETHELL,
Editor and Publisher.
Pak-tong, Seoul

SCAVENGERS.

We note the formation of a new scavenging company which has applied to the Government for encouraging money. By this we presume a subsidy is meant, and we note that in addition to this the company proposes to charge each house 40 cents monthly for removing night-soil and refuse.

It is certainly time that something in this way was done. In Seoul where the closets are for the most part built over the roadside gutters, the condition of the streets is too disgusting for words and is a serious menace to health. In Japan things are certainly much better managed and as we believe the new company is a Japanese enterprise, there is reason to hope for an improved order of things.

At the same time we suggest to the Government that before a subsidy of any kind is granted, some guarantee be obtained that the work will be systematically and thoroughly done.

It will be remembered that it was only in July last that a similar company was formed which went out of business after pocketing the Government subsidy and making one or two vexatious regulations which put the householders to unnecessary expense.

Therefore it will be advisable for the government, before granting any finance to the new venture, to appoint an official to see that the money is properly applied and the work efficiently done. We should think that the matter could very conveniently be placed under the control of the police, but there must at any rate be someone to superintend the work and to whom people can make complaints when necessary.

THE PASSPORT QUESTION.

There seems to be some misunderstanding somewhere on this subject. A Japan contemporary published the information that the Korean Vice Minister for Foreign Affairs had issued a notice that Japanese desiring to travel in the interior of Korea would not, in future, require passports. We reproduced the item and promptly received a contradiction from the Korean Foreign Office and it now seems that it was the Japanese Vice Minister for Foreign Affairs who issued the notice.

Failing explanation, the whole affair is extraordinary, as Japanese officials have no control over Korean internal affairs, and it is not for them to say whether their nationals require passports or not when travelling in Korea. It may of course be possible that hitherto a Japanese passport has been necessary in addition to the one issued by the Korean Government and that this is what has now been dispensed with.

MR. DOOLEY ON THE BRINGING UP OF CHILDREN.

BY F. P. DUNNE.

"Did ye iver see a man as proud iv annything as Hogan is iv that kid iv his?" said Mr. Dooley.

"Oh, iv coorse," said Mr. Dooley, "ye have contimpt f'r an amachoor father that has on'y wan offspring. An ol' profissyonal parent like ye that's practically done nawthin all ye'er life but be a father to helpless childher don't understand th' emotions iv th' author iv a limited. But Hogan don't care. So far as I am able to judge fr'm what he says, his is th' on'y perfect an' complete child that has been projooced this cinchry. He looks on you th' way Hinnery James wud look on Mary Jane Holmes.

"I wint around to see this here projidy th' other day. Hogan met me at th dure. Wipe o ffye'er feet, says he. 'Why,' says I. 'Baby,' says he. 'Microbes,' he says. He thin conducted me to a basin iv water an' insthructed me to wash me hands in a preparation iv carbolic acid. Whin I was th'rly perfumed, he inthrajoced me to a toothless ol' gintleman, who was settin' up in a cradle atin' his right foot. 'Ain't he fine?' says Hogan.

'Wondherful,' says I. 'Did ye iver see such an expressyon?' says he. 'Niver,' says I. 'as Hiven is me judge, niver.' 'Look at his hair,' he says. I will,' say I. 'Ain't his eyes beautiful?' 'They ar're,' I says. 'Ar-re they glass or onl'y imitation?' says I. 'An' them cunning little feet,' says he. 'On close inspiction,' says I, 'yes they ar-re they ar-re feet. Ye'er offspring don't know it though. He thinks that wan is a 'doughnut,' 'He's not as old as he looks,' says Hogan. 'He cudden't be,' says I. 'He looks old enough to be a Dimmycratic candydate f'r Vice President. Why, he's lost most iv his teeth,' I says. 'Go wan,' says he, 'he's just gettin' thim. He has two uppers an' four lower,' he says, 'If he had a few more, he'd be a sleepin' car,' says I. 'Does he speak?' says I. 'Sure,' says Hogan. 'Say pappa.' he says. 'Gah,' says young Hogan. 'Hear that?' says Hogan; 'that's poppa,' Say momma,' says he. 'Gah,' says th' projidy. 'That's momma,' says Hogan. 'See, here's Misther Dooley,' says he. 'Blub,' says th' phenomynon. 'Look at that,' says Hogan, 'he knows ye,' he says.

"Well, ye know, Hinnissy, wan iv th' things that has made me popular in th' ward is that I make a bluff at adorin' childher. Between you an' me I'd as lave salute a dish rag as a recent infant, but I always do it. So I put on an alurin' smile an' says I, 'Well, little ol' goozy goo, will give his Dooleyums a kiss?' At that minyit Hogan seized me be th' collar an' dhragged me away fr'm th' cradle. 'Wud ye kill me child?' says he. 'How?' says I. 'With a kiss,' says he. 'Am I that bad,' says I. 'Don't ye know that there ar-re mickrobes that can be transmitted to an infant in a kiss?' says he 'Well,' say I with indignation, 'I'm not proud iv mesilf as an antiseptic American,' I says, 'but in an encounter between me an' that there young cannibal,' 'I'll lave it to th' boord iv helth who takes th' biggest chance,' I says, an' we wint out followed be a howl fr'm th' projidy. 'He's singin,'' says Hogan. 'He has lost his notes,' says I.

"Whin we got downstairs, Hogan give me a lecture on th' bringin' up iv childher. As though I needed it, me that's been consulted on bringin' up half th' childher in Archey road. 'In the ol' days,' says he, 'childher was brought up catch as catch can,' he says. But it's different now. They're as carefully watched as a geeranyum in a consarvatory he says. 'Here it is.T h' first thing that should be done f'r a child is to deprive it iv its parents. Th' less th' infant sees iv poppa an' momma, th' betther f'r him. If they ar-re so base as to want to look at th' little darling,' they shud first be examined be a competent physician to see that there is nawthin' wrong with thim that they cud give th' baby. They will thin take a bath iv sulphuric acid, an' havin' carefully attired thimselves in a sturlized rubber suit, they will approach within eight feet iv th' object iv their ignoble affection an' lave at wanst. In no case mus' they kiss, hug or fondle their projeny. Many diseases, such as lumbago, pain in th' chist, premachoor baldness, senile decrepitude which are privilent among adults, can be communicated to a child fr'm th' parent. Besides it is bad f'r th' moral nature iv th' infant. Affection f'r its parents is wan iv th' mos' dangerous symptoms iv rickets. Th' parents may not be worthy iv th' love iv a thurly sturlized child. An' infant's first jooty is to th' doctor to whom it owes its bein' an' stavin.' Childher ar-re imitative an' if they see much iv their parents they may grow up to look like thim. That wud be a great misfortune. If parents see their childher befure they enther Harvared, they ar-re forbidden to teach thim foolish wurruds like "poppa,' an' "momma." At two a properly brought up child shud be able to articulate indistinctly th' wurruds "Docthor Bolt on th' Care an' Feedin' iv Infants," which is betther thin sayin' "momma" an' more exact.

"'Gr-reat care shud be taken iv th' infant's food, Durin' th' first two years, it shud have nawthin' but milk. At three a little canary bur-rd seed can be added. At five an egg ivry other Choosdah. At siven an orange. At twelve th' child may ate a shredded biscuit. At forty th' little tot may have stewed prunes. An' so on. At no time, however, shud th' child be stuffed with green gages, pork an' beans, onions, Boston baked brown bread, saleratus biscuit or other food.

"'It's wonderful,' says Hogan," how they-ve got it rayjooced to science. They can almost make a short baby long on rayjucin' th' amount of protides an caseens in th' milk,' he says. 'Haven't ye iver kissed ye'er young?' say I. 'Wanst in awhile,' he says, 'whin I'm thurly disinfected, I go up an' blow a kiss at him through th' window,' he says.

"'Well,' says I, 'it may be all right,' I, says, but if I cud have a son an' heir without causin' talk I bet ye I'd not apply f' a permit fr'm th' Health Board f'r him an' me to come together. Parents was made befure childher annyhow, an' they have a prire claim to be considhered. Sure, it may be a good thing to bring thim up on a sanitary plan, But it seems to me that they got all right in th' ol' days whin number two had just larned to fall down stairs at th' time number three enthered th' wurruld. May be they were stronger thin they ar-re now. Th' docthor niver pretinded to see whether th' milk was proprly biled. He cudden't very well. Th' childher was allowed to set up at th' table an have a good cup iv tay an' a pickle or two. If there was more thin enough to go around, they got what nobody else wanted. They got plinty iv fresh air playin' in allays an' vacant lots an' ivry wanst in awhile they were allowed to go down an' fall into te' river. No attintion was paid to their dite. Th' prisint race iv nayroes who are now startlin' th' wurru'd in finance, polytics, th' arts an' sciences, burglay an lithrachoor, was brought up on wathermillen rinds, speckled apples, raw onions, stolen fr'm th' grocer, an' cocoanut pie. Their nursery was th' back yard. They larned to walk as soon as they were able an' if they got bow legged ivryobody said they wud be sthrong men. As f'r annybody preventin' a fond parent fr'm comin' home saturdah night an' wallowin' in his beaucheous child, th' docthor that suggisted it wud have to move. 'No' sir,' say I, 'get as much amusement as ye can out iv ye'er infant,' says I. 'Teach him to love ye now,' I says, before he knows. Afther awhile he'll get onto ye an' it'll be too late.'"

'Ye know a lot about it," said Mr. Hennessy.

"I do." said Mr. Dooley. "Not bein' an author, I'm a gr-reat critic."—The Call.

A branch of the Korean Emigration company has been established in Mexico. The first batch of emgirants, 300 men, with their families, will be sent there in February.

The Korea Daily News.

VOL. I, SATURDAY, NOVEMBER 19, 1904. No. 105

HONGKONG & SHANGHAI BANKING CORPORATION.

Paid-up Capital..... ....$10,000,000
Reserve Fund:—Sterling Reserve... 10,000,000
Silver Reserve..... 7,000,000

27,000,000
Reserve Liability of Proprietors... 10,000,000

HEAD OFFICE, HONGKONG.

London Bankers, London and County Banking Company Limited.
Branches and Agencies,
London.

Amoy,	Hankow	Penang,
Bangkok,	Hiogo,	Rangoon,
Batavia,	Iloilo,	Saigon,
Bombay,	Lyons,	San Francisco,
Calcutta,	Manila,	Singapore,
Colombo,	Nagasaki,	Sourabaya,
Foochow,	New York,	Tientsin,
Hamburg,	Peking,	Yokohama,

Credits granted on approved Securities, and every description of Banking and Exchange business transacted.

Drafts granted on London and the chief Commercial places in Europe, India, Australia, America, China and Japan.

HOLME RINGER & CO., AGENTS,
CHEMULPO.

ON CHEONG & CO.,
SEOUL.

GENERAL STORE KEEPERS.
Imported provisions, Cooking Utensils Crockery, etc.
FRESH BREAD DAILY.

MITSU BISHI DOCKYARD & ENGINE WORKS,
NAGASAKI.

CODE WORD, "DOCK."

A. 1, A. B. C., and Engineering Codes used.

DOCK No. 1 (at Tategami).

Extreme Length..............523 feet
Length on blocks .... 513 „
Width of Entrance on Top......89 „
„ „ Bottom....77 „
Water on Blocks at Spring Tide 26½ „

DOCK No. 2 (Mukaijima).

Extreme Length..............371 feet
Length on Blocks.............360 „
Width of Entrance on Top......66 „
„ „ Bottom 53 „
Water on Blocks at Spring Tide 22 „

PATENT SLIP (at Kosuge).

Can take vessels up to 1,000 tons gross.

THE WORKS are well equipped with the LATEST IMPROVEMENTS, and can execute any kind of work in SHIPBUILDING and MARINE ENGINEERING, as well as in REPAIRING of SHIPS.

The COMPANY'S new powerful steamer OURA-MARU (712 tons, 700 I.H.P.), specially built for SALVAGE PURPOSES, and equipped with necessary gear, is always READY at SHORT NOTICE.

CHARTERED BANK OF INDIA AUSTRALIA & CHINA.

INCORPORATED BY ROYAL CHARTER 1853

HEAD OFFICES:—LONDON.

Paid-up Capital £800,000
Reserve Liability of Shareholders 800,000
Reserve Fund 800,000

Drafts granted upon all the principal places in the world and every description of Exchange and banking business transacted.

E. MEYER & Co., Agents,
Chemulpo.

E. MEYER & CO.
Chemulpo.

SOLE AGENTS IN KOREA FOR:

A. T. Morse, Sons & Co's "Fresco" Distemper

In all colours ready for use on walls, Ceilings etc.

and

AVENARIUS CARBOLINEUM

A wood-preserving and antiseptic oil preparation

Against decay, dry-rot, fungus and wood-destroying insects.

A large supply always in Stock. Prices upon application.

E. MEYER & Co.,
Chemulpo.

THE METHODIST PUBLISHING HOUSE,
Little West Gate, Seoul.

JOB PRINTING, TYPEWRITER PAPER
CARBON PAPER, VISITING CARDS
STATIONERY, BOOK BINDING
BOOK PUBLISHERS
AMERICAN SCHOOL BOOKS
SPENCERIAN COPY BOOKS
PEN CARBON LETTER AND BILL BOOKS

S. A. BECK, Manager.

HOKURKU DOBOKU KAISHA.

Branch office in Chong Dong, Seoul.
Japanese telephone No. 165

CONTRACT DEPARTMENT.

We can contract to build any building or construction.

MERCHANDISE DEPARTMENT.

We can provide any building material.
We have just contracted to build the new Belgian Legation.

DAI-ICHI GINKO.

LIMITED.

(Formerly the First National Bank)

ESTABLISHED 1873

INCORPORATED UNDER PRESENT LAW 1896

Capital - - - - - - - - - Yen 5,000,000
Reserve Fund - . - - - 1,500,000

HEAD OFFICE:—TOKIO.

President: Baron SHIBUSAWA.

BRANCHES AND CORRESPONDENTS
In the Principal Cities and Towns of Japan.

Interest Allowed on
Fixed deposits 1 year - - - 6½ per cent
" " 6 months - - - 6 per cent

Special current accounts 1½ sen daily per Y 100
General " " 1 " " " 100

M. TANAKA,
Manager, Chemulpo.

SINGER SEWING MACHINES

씽거ᄌᆞ봉침

SOLE AGENTS FOR KOREA
젼매쇼

HOLME RINGER & CO.
Chemulpo.
제물포 함릉거양힝

KAMEYA & CO.

GENERAL STOREKEEPERS
Chinkokai - - Seoul
(Established 1895, Tokyo)

Confectionery, Hams, Canned Goods, Cutlery, Hirano & Tansan Water. Provisions, Gents, Furnishing goods, Toilet Articles, Travelling Bags, Tobacco, Cigars & Cigarettes Kitchen Utensils. Coffee. Biscuits.

Fresh Goods always kept in Stock.
Prices Moderate
Please come and inspect our goods

NIPPON YUSEN KAISHA.

JAPANESE MAIL STEAMSHIP CO.

DER MAIL CONTRACT WITH THE IMPERIAL JAPANESE GOVERNMENT.

European Line

Regular Fortnightly Service between Yokohama Kobe, Moji, Shanghai, Hongkong, Singapore, Penang Colombo Port Said, Marseilles, London and Antwerp

American Line

Regular Fortnightly Service between Hongkong and Seattle, calling at Shanghai, Moji, Kobe, Yokohama and Victoria, B. C.

Australian Line

Regular weekly Service betwen Japan Ports and Australia, calling at Hongkong and Manila.
(Above Three Lines Suspended until further notice).

Shanghai Line

Weekly Service between Shanghai and Japan Ports

Korea Line

Service Kobe, Moji, Nagasaki, Fusan Chemupo Chef foo, Taiku.
S. S. Bahelsberg, 2181 tons.
Service Kobe, Moji, Fusan, Chemulpo, Chinnampo
S. S. ARGO, S. S. Ohio.

BORDEN'S CONDENSED MILK CO.

New York, U. S. A.

ALWAYS IN STOCK
Eagle Brand Condensed Milk.
Gold Seal Condensed Milk.
Peerless (Family) Evaporated Cream.
Borden's Malted Milk.

E. MEYER & CO.
Chemulpo, Korea,
Sole Agents

ROYAL INSURANCE COMPANY,
Funds exceed £10,000,000
FIRE
AT CURRENT RATES.
LIFE
REDUCED PREMIUM.
HOLME RINGER & Co.,
Agents, Chemulpo.

HOTEL DU PALAIS
SEOUL.

The only first class Hotel in Seoul. Situated in the centre of the city opposite the palace.

Cuisine under the supervision of an experienced French Chef.

Well ventilated and furnished throughout.

TARIFF UPON APPLICATION

L. MARTIN
Proprietor and Manager.

(호륙빅일뎨)　(일요화)　일이십이월일십년사빅구천일

본샤고빅

이신보는영ㅅ와한어로셔가티
의출판홈
신문가
한쟝　엽두돈오픈
일삭도　엽두량닷돈
우표가티샤닷돈
다밧돈으로밧숩
광고료는
귀한의장단과ᄌ힝의다쇼로ᄎ
관홍되혐가로밧을터히오매오
티지하내대한사람바다다이신
문을보실터이니광고버시기를
원ᄒ시는이들은우리신문사에
와셔면약ᄒ시믈희망ᄒ옵
○발힝소　바동대한미일신보
사법이학교엽희전영국인셔필
림집자리오
사쟝 영국인 (비셜)
광양 티리졍
○평양효동사는권네보써로우
리신문광티티리인을뎡ᄒ였
스오니평양에계신구람코져ᄒ
시는 쳠군ᄌ는혁티리졍에왕
림ᄒ와면의ᄒ시옵

사고

○우리대한미일신보의목뎍은
대한의인민결셔에관한모든대
목에티ᄒ야는공평한번론을쥬
쟝홈이라우리동신원의탐보는
신문보시는쳠군ᄌ의게ᄒ샹보
도ᄒ리며편지들과셔ᄒ여주시
는이는쳥명과번디를쟥이불치
시기를희망ᄒ오니이거슨신문
샹에과쳐ᄒ란는거시아니오단
반드히신용ᄒ는증거를숨고자
홈이라귀자는아모귀셔던지과
재홈을퇴각ᄒ는권리를가졋스
니회각ᄒ는리유는말ᄒ터이오
며공중평화를문란케ᄒ는듯ᄒ
귀셔는의례히밧지안켓숩니다

◎본사셰셔엇더케신문을뎌양
우리로분젼ᄒ와레젼ᄂ의잉의
로젼ᄒ든것스로번곳에는홍붓게
젼ᄒ기도ᄒ며혹면칠거슬ᄒ던
에젼ᄒ기도ᄒ며혹아니젼ᄒ는
곳도잇다ᄒ와우리신문을ᄉ랑
ᄒ야구람ᄒ시는 쳠군ᄌ의계
디ᄒ야미우미안ᄒ옵거로지금
은분젼인을두고미일에는의젼
ᄒ며아니젼ᄒ거나뉴계거나ᄒ
는거ᄉ있스면본샤로긔별ᄒ시
면즉시조ᄉᄒ야다시잘ᄒ기로
젼ᄒ기는혹시못ᄒ는ᄃ홀이잇
ᄂ니이거슨니ᄒ야니ᄒᄂ고년
ᄌ의ᄃ옹ᄒ오니ᄒᄂ의편리를
취ᄒ시옵

젼ᄒ기는혹ᄉ계젼ᄒ기나ᄒᆫ일
거잇스면본샤로ᄐ계ᄒ여주심
을희망ᄒ옵

관보

뎨이쳔구빅팔십실호
광무팔년십일월십팔일
서임급ᄉ령
○의원면본관 대구면보ᄉ쥬
ᄉ 최승철
○임대구면보ᄉ쥬ᄉ셔판임관
ᄉ등 한셩면보ᄉ쥬ᄉ 리귀
쇼
○임한셩면보ᄉ쥬ᄉ셔판임관
ᄉ등 젼쥬ᄉ 최승철
○금이금봉 한셩면보ᄉ쥬ᄉ
최승철
○금샹금봉 대구면보ᄉ쥬ᄉ
리귀쇼
이상십일월십오일
○명동신사면회회문부조사위
원 경샹룡 박용규
피셔원쥬ᄉ 한병구
샹일월십륙일
육군 연셩학교관제 속
뎨십삼됴 학도의슈학긔한삼
개년으로졍ᄒ고차를샹학년
에분홈이라
뎨십ᄉ됴 학도의슈학에긴요
ᄒᆫ긔구와밋그림과글시등은
차례ᄒ거ᄂ혹지급ᄒ는ᄉ무
가잇숩니라
뎨십오됴 학도는졍원을인ᄒ
퇴교홈을허락지아니ᄒ지라
뎨십륙됴 학도중에학술우등
이요공힝방졍ᄒᆫ자면시험을
션발ᄒ야사쟝을명ᄒ고특별
ᄒᆫ휘쟝을부치게홈이라
뎨십칠됴라 학도중에좌게항을
범ᄒᆫ자는퇴교케홈이라
일 학술의슈득이오졍치못ᄒ
야졸업ᄒᆯ가망이업는자
이 군긔를문란케ᄒ며법측을
여러번범ᄒᆫ자
삼 ᄉ힝이부졍ᄒ야긔조ᄒᆯ가
망이업는자
ᄉ 질병을인ᄒ야슈학에불감
ᄒᆫ자
오 졸업시험에낙제ᄒᆫ자
뎨십팔됴 학도중에학년에졍
ᄒᆫ바학술을진슈치못ᄒᆫ자와
질병ᄉ고등을인ᄒ야졸업시
험을 치못ᄒᆫ자와졸업시험
에낙ᄌᄒᆫ자는이라도오히려

귀망이잇는자는계학보ᄉ케
ᄒᆫ후에졸업케ᄒ고또일학년
을연긔슈학케홈을득ᄒᄂ니
단번케학일슈는무관ᄒ도교
육에쟝의가엽게ᄒ며연긔는
젼학긔
를ᄒ야일회에한홈이라
뎨십구됴 학도중졸업시험에
급계ᄒᆫ자라도샹리질병등을
인ᄒ야무관ᄒ도됨을엇지못
ᄒᆯ자의게는졸업증셔만쥬어
퇴교케홈이라
뎨이십됴 우십됴에관ᄒᆫ자가
잇슬째에는교쟝이그ᄉ유를
갓쵸어교육총감의게신보ᄒ
야츄후쳐분홈이라
뎨이십일됴 학도에슈학긔말
비이로면교쟝이졸업시험에
규졍을셜졍ᄒ야교육총감의
게신보ᄒ고그인죵을득ᄒ야
졸업시험을힝홈이라
뎨이십이됴 졸업시험을죵ᄒ
면교쟝은각교관과밋죵티쟝
을모티ᄒ야회의를기ᄒ고셩젹
을조사ᄒ야열셔를졍ᄒ고교
과표를제ᄒ야교육총감의게
차를진달ᄒ고그인가를득ᄒ
야급계ᄒᆫ자의게교육과졍과
졸업증셔를급여홈이라
뎨이십삼됴 교육총감은졸업
ᄒᆫ학도중에무관ᄒ도될만ᄒᆫ자
는군부대신과협의ᄒᆫ후에무
관학도를명ᄒ야교셩ᄃ에부
치되티부군무는동긔월이남
으로졍홈이라
뎨이십ᄉ됴 례하을남ᄒᆫ학도
가보ᄉ슈를맛쳐면젼졔죠를죤
ᄒ야조쳐ᄒ야졍홈이라
뎨이십오됴 학도의게난벌에
쳥쥬건이나의ᄂᆫ귀흉가ᄂᆫ군
ᄒ미이라
뎨이십륙됴 본관졔는반포일
시힝홈이라
륙군헌병됴례
뎨일쟝 총측
뎨일됴 륙군헌병ᄉ령부는군
부대신관할에쇽ᄒ야군ᄉ경
찰힝졍경찰ᄉ법경찰을관할
ᄒ야맛홈이라
뎨이됴 륙군헌병은그직무집
힝에당ᄒᄂ야군ᄉ경찰에관ᄒᆫ
ᄉ는군부대신에오쳥에응ᄒ
고힝졍경찰에관ᄒ야는내부
대신과각관찰ᄉ의요쳥을응
ᄒ고ᄉ법경찰에관ᄒ야는법
부대신과평리ᄉ의요쳥을응

홈이라
뎨삼됴 헌병은그직무에관ᄒ
야쟈긔의견으로는즉시병긔를
사용홈을득ᄒ되ᄉ의가급박
지안코디방에통신ᄒᆯ만ᄒᆫ경
우에는ᄉ령부에셔티보를기
ᄒ야군부에졍보ᄒ야 쳐명
을봉승ᄒᆫ후에사용홈이라
일 쟝형ᄒᄂᆫ포힝을슈ᄒᆯ세
이 졍슈ᄒᆫ토디와위쟝ᄒᆫ쳐
소를방힝이아니면슈호ᄒ기
어려운세
삼 인명을방희ᄒᆯ째에병력
이아니면구호ᄒ기어려운세
ᄉ 직무로써사름으로더브
러져ᄒᆯ째에병력이아니면
제승ᄒ기어려운때
뎨ᄉ됴 본령은반포일로시힝
홈이라
뎨오됴 광무ᄉ년륙월샹십일
칙령뎨이십삼호륙군헌병됴례
뎨일쟝총측은폐지홈이라

잡보

○의샹의힝악　지작일죵로에
셔쳥군쟝ᄉ가쳥군을방비ᄎ로
써온양회다가뻑쟝ᄉ일인이양
홀박고가기를나히는교로쳥군
쟝ᄉ가조곰자리를옴기라ᄒᆫ죽
일샹이라치에온당치못ᄒ게말
ᄒ야골으ᄃ비의쳥군을리치로
옴기라ᄒᆫ쥭결희잇던한일인명
이그무리홈을보고희혈인의무
리홈을설명ᄒᆫ죽일인이홀디에
구타ᄒ야과졀ᄒ야방에엉드리
지미과리ᄒᆫ한인을ᄌ귀의쟝으
로미여브니진가에셔보는사
름들이일인의힝악을미워ᄒ지
아니리업더라
○원소간샹　지작일에　원소
간셩을맛겻는티ᄎ호ᄉ리근명
과원일매션운용션과의쟝민병
소졔씨가계진ᄒ엿더라
○시샹샹경　참쟝신샹ᄒᆫ씨는
자귀셔산회픔을쳔당의계비리
버리고랑규무지ᄒ더니돈을주
고희픔을차자도로쟝ᄉ지니고
일작칙팔엄에샹경ᄒ야등문밧
왕샹비계셔쟝잔유ᄒᆫ다더라
○조요회리진　조병식씨가을진
회돌다시설시ᄒᆫ다ᄒ더니일본
ᄉ령부에셔쾌이히락지아니ᄒ
는지라도로중지ᄒ고호위총관
리근퇴씨가운동ᄒ야ᄒᆫ회를셜

코자훈티판찰이노흥야삭지처
굴은인티살반회판훈오랑캐갓튼
놈이랑반을보와서무엇흥리요
라흥고거절흥고보지아니흥다더라

○의졍부조복 의졍부에서외
부로조복흥기를안변등디에일
인이벌목수는본티일본수에조
쳥흥반도엽순죠가취쥬흥치못
흥게시요산합흥부에잇는일본
군병포고중에겸령둥차는그군
수상판리흥기위흥으로써비록
경술흔데셔나온말이나국계상
사헤에흥용순홍이잇스니취부에
신칙흥야비리몬자감군인민의
게고시흥야셔로엄숙히경계흥
야군수상방히가업게흥야죄를
범치안케흥을보른다흥엿더라

TELEGRAMS.

(FROM JAPAN PAPERS).

London, Nov. 12.

The Paris journal the "Temps" states that the Japanese Minister to France has called on M. Delcasse, the Minister for Foreign Affairs, in reference to certain points relating to the observance of neutrality, on the ground that there was reason to believe that there at present existed a divergence of interpretation which, however, should not be exaggerated. This, said the Minister, could soon be removed, France having hitherto reconciled her duties as Ally of Russia with those incumbent upon her as a neutral Power. Japan, the Minister added, appreciated the uprightness of the intentions of France in this delicate situation.

Explanations regarding the affair are proceeding amicably.

London, Nov. 13.

On the 12th instant the French Chamber of Deputies approved of M. Declasse's declaration anent the Anglo-French Agreement by 436 to 94 votes.

Berlin, Nov. 13.

The London "Times" states that British manufacturers may supply all kind of war material to Russia and Japan, the Government having no intention of disturbing a lucrative business.

Viscount Hayashi, Japanese Minister in London, is said to have mentioned to representatives of the Press in London that Japan does not consider coal to be contraband of war, nor the supplying of coal to be a violation of the laws of neutrality.

Tokyo, Nov. 18th.

The Taotai of Chefoo has requested the Russian Consul to hand over the weapons and ammunition of the Russian destroyer. The officers will be received on board the Chinese cruiser Heiyen. The Russian Consul had agreed to do this on the 17th inst.

Tokyo, Nov. 18th.

One section of the Baltic Fleet left Dakar (Senegal) on the 16th inst. The other section has left Suda Bay.

Army Headquarters Seoul, Nov. 19th.

On the 16th inst. 150 men of the Russian cavalry were seen advancing north of Kanotinenhowling. An ambush was prepared and the enemy retreated. Their Casualties were 2 wounded.

Since the morning of the 18th inst, the Russian artillery has been cannonading near Shaho-po and about 1 batallion of their infantry were posted near Saolintse; our artillery however engaged them and caused them to retreat.

Later.

On the afternoon of the 17th inst, 400 or 500 Russian infantry and cavalry with a few guns arrived near the right bank of the Hun ho and bombarded our positions near Korotaisi, setting fire to this village and some others to the south-east.

Later.

On the 17th inst, our scouts came in collision with 20 Russians near the right bank of the Taitse-ho, but repulsed them. The Russian casulties were small.

Later.

On the 18th inst. a small body of Russian infantry advanced on Sinlingtun, but were repulsed.

Berlin, Nov. 13.

Both Russia and Japan have declined to take part in the Peace Conference at The Hague proposed by President Roosevelt.

London, Nov. 15.

The French Chamber has ratified the Anglo-French Agreement.

London, Nov. 14.

The "Temps" learns from St. Petersburg that Vice-Admiral Beaumont has been appointed the British representative on the Commission of Inquiry into the North Sea incident.

London, Nov. 15.

The appointment of Vice-Admiral Beaumont as British representative on the International Commission is confirmed.

[Vice-Admial Beaumont is Commander-in-Chief on the Australian Station, being previously in command of the Pacific Station.]

London, Nov. 13.

The "Echo de Paris" publishes a St. Petersburg message stating a Russian loan for fifty-three millions sterling is being arranged with German and Dutch Banks.

London, Nov. 13.

A tremendous blizzard has been experienced in America, as a result of which New York has been cut off from communication with the west and south.

Shin-min-tun, Nov. 7.

A European just down from Tiehlin states that the Russians expect a second main attack in force by the Japanese in a short time.

It is the opinion of many Russian officers that they can hold out for at least a mouth in their present position, keeping the Japanese at bay; and then retire, if necessary, on Tiehlin; where there is a very strong position, and a large stock of munitions and supplies.

The success of the operations have been entirely so far due to the superior fire of both guns and rifles; and they are much helped by their search-lights, of which the Russians have none.

Owing to the danger caused thorugh so many Chinese spies entering the Russian lines for the Japanese, General Kuropatkin has issued orders that no more Chinese are to be allowed in the camp at all. Any disobeying will be shot summarily.

The railway from Harbin to Moukden is well working day and night, and is used entirely for military purposes; the reinforcements arriving at Moukden at the rate of about 5,000 daily.

It is definitely decided that the Russians will not go into any winter quarters, but will continue fighting right through the cold weather, until the Japanese are driven back; the latter are beginning already to find out the severity and difficulties of a winter campaign so far away from their base.

The Russians soldiers are now fully provided with their winter clothing, including skin coats and fur-boots.

The spirits of both officers and men are good; and they have the greatest confidence in their generals.—China Review.

The Vice Minister of the War Office has telegraphically notified the Government that he has finished his inspection of matters in Japan. The Government has ordered him to return.

The Il Chin Hoi society has despatched two envoys to each of the 13 provinces to preach their creed to the natives.

It is rumoured that the Peddlars are about to reorganize their society, their excuse being that "trade is so bad in Seoul at present."

By hitting the target 127 times out of 189 the Cæsar, Lord Charles Beresford's flagship, has made a world's record for the 12-pounder gun.

Lieutenant Yun Chi Sung has completed his course of military education in Japan and is to return immediately to take up a position in the Korean army.

JAPAN AND KOREA.

Politicians in Japan are still cooking their hare before they have caught it. The "Japan Mail" says:—

We gather from Tokyo journals a summarized idea of the speech made by Baron Komura at the meeting of politicians on the 11th instant in the residence of the Prime Minister. His Excellency said that in spite of her repeated defeats Russia showed no sign of yielding. She had declared, on the contrary, that unless her enemy yieded, she would absorb the whole of Manchuria, would annex Korea, would destroy the Japanese fleet, and would never allow a Japanese to set foot on the continent of Asia. Japan therefore, knew what Russia's ideas were; she had herself declared them. With regard to Manchuria, the Minister said that any utterance of his on such a subject would assuredly be taken up by the foreign public and made the theme of discussion such as was to be deprecated at this juncture. Therefore he would ask permission to remain silent. Concerning Korea, however, he did not hesitate to say that Japan's policy remained unchanged. She was determined to maintain the integrity and the independence of the peninsular empire. For that object she had fought ten years ago, and for that object she was fighting to-day. So far as forms were concerned, they had been satisfied the treaties and conventions she had already concluded with Korea would suffice. Everything now depended on the manner of giving effect to them. Korea's finances must be regulated, her foreign policy must be watched and, if necessary, even her domestic affairs might require management. Japan could not shrink from her duty in these matters.

At the conclusion of this speech Mr. Oishi Masami, the Progressist leader, rose and said that, so far as he could gather, the policy of his Party differed somewhat from the policy af the Government with regard to Manchuria and Korea. Possibly, however, a frank interchange of views might remove the points of difference, and he asked, therefore that a time convenient should be appointed for such interchange. The Premier and the Foreign Minister replied that they too approved and desired that method of procedure, and that a time should be fixed.

RUSSIAN AMAZON'S ADVENTURES IN MANCHURIA.

Mr. F. von Jessen, a special correspondent of the Daily Graphic, has given the following curious account of a Russian woman scout whom he met at the station at Liaoyang:—"There by the window is a peculiar little man—smooth, plump, beardless, and curly-headed. If he did not carry a revolver and a sword in his belt, if he did not wear high boots and an officer's blouse and cap, upon my honour I should take him for a woman. My neighbour smiles at this remark, and offers to introduce me. 'Alexander Ivanovitch, will you allow me?' The name is sufficiently masculine, and so is the dress; but I will be hanged if Alexander Ivanovitch, in spite of his revolvea, his sword, his bright new St. George's cross, and his medals, is not a woman! Well, in the course of our conversation, after the first few formalities, she admits the correctness of my surmise. It is, indeed, too obvious for concealment. Alexander Ivanovitch should be Alexandra Ivanovna. She is a student from one of the Siberian High Schools. She has for a couple of terms studied Eastern languages at the University of Tomsk, and she speaks Chinese and Japanese fluently. She has already during the Boxer rising, followed the Russian troops disguised as a man. She admits that her love of adventure is so strong that she cannot control it; and when the present war broke out she again offered her services as a scout. The high millitary authorities did not receive her very graciously, although she wore her medal for services reneered during the Boxer war, and although she was able to prove that she had a complete knowledge of the Manchurian and of the enemy. It was only after having given the General information about the Russian and Japanese positions, information which could have been obtained only but to a few at headquarters, that her services were accepted. She received a certificate of identity, which, in accordance with her wishes, was made out in the name of a man (the name I have used here is ficitious), and a couple of horsemen were given here for an escort. Since then she has been all over the country lying between the opposing armies and she has rendered such great service, and has displayed such skill and daring, that General Kuropatkin has decorated her with the Cross of St. George."

A BRAVE SOLDIER'S TRAGIC FATE.

(Concluded from page 2.)

You are a brave and honorable soldier, and I admire you from the bottom of my heart and in my unofficial capacity, and bemoan the hard fate which has overtaken you. Imperial Japan demands your life, as she believes for her own best interests; therefore my duty is plain. However, if you have any property which you wish to leave to your wife and family, or any last message which you would wish sent to them, I will be only too glad to do what I can for you."

These kind words so affected the prisoner that he was again forced to tears, and great sobs shook his frame. Then remembering this, to be a womanish action, he gnashed his teeth in the vain effort to keep back the tears. Poor man! He was not a coward. He cared nothing for the death so close at hand, but for this family in distaut Russia he thought much. Between his sobs he said to Captain Hamono:—

"When I was arrested I was prepared in mind for this fate. Had you not spoken to me in so sympathetic a manner I would not have displayed this grief over my family, which I beg you not to attribute to any cowardly motive on my part. As for property, I have none. God help my wife and little children. Will you shake hands with me, Sir?

Stern faced Hamano clasped the outstretched hand and then drew away. A Gensdarme stepped smartly forward and bound a white cotton cloth over the prisoner's eyes. A young officer of the infantry drew his sword. The Osaka rifles clicked and the fatal word was spoken. It was all over before any of us appreciated the fact. The doctor ran to the side of the postrate body and pronounced life gone. So died Ryaboff, a Russian private of the 28th Khambarsky regiment of the 71st division of the 5th Corps.

We understand that the attitude taken up by the French Legation, in the matter of Kim Byung Do, will shortly lead to the giving up of that individual to justice.

Sixty-six Koreans, who had been residing in Manchuria, arrived in Chemulpo on the 18th inst. and immedially repaired to their native townships and villages.

The time of departure and arrival of trains on the Seoul-Chemulpo railroad has been altered. The same schedule is retained but the time in use for the future will be Japanese time; i.e. thirty-five minutes earlier than the standard hitherto in use.

The Korea Daily News.

Issued at 5 P. M. daily except Sundays.

Rate of Subscription :—
Per Year,.............Yen 25.
Per Quarter,...........Yen 7.
Per Month,...........Yen 2.50.

Postage in Korea not charged extra.
Postage abroad charged extra.

Advertisements, 50 sen per day for 1 inch or less.
5 yen per month per inch.
50 yen per year per inch.

All communications to

E. T. BETHELL,
Editor and Publisher,
Pak-tong, Seoul

CIVILIZATION, ET CETERA.

Under this caption the "Japan Mail" of November 15th has the following:—

Some time ago three Koreans were apprehended in the act of removing the rails or otherwise damaging the Seoul-Wiju line. The region through which this line runs is under martial law, and in consequence of frequent attempts made by Koreans to commit outrages of the above nature, outrages not merely against property but also against life, the three culprits were condemned to be shot, and accordingly, having been bound to crosses fixed upright, they were fusilladed, while in order that their fate might deter others, the corpses were left hanging on the crosses for some time. In all that there is not the smallest iota inviting condemnation. The criminals were justly punished; they did not deserve any kind of sympathy, and the exposure of their bodies was a natural measure under the circumstances. But it appears that some enterprising photograher succeeded in taking photographs of the execution, and this fact evoked from the Korea Daily News an article so foolish that it would have raised a laugh could such a subject be mirth-provoking. Few took any notice of this article, and its scanty readers probably set it down as a shallow attempt to court notoriety.

The "Japan Mail," continuing, strongly condemns the view taken by the "Echo de Chine" that the tying of the Koreans to crosses was a deliberate sneer at the Christian religion, being a parody of the crucifixion of Jesus Christ. On this point we agree with the "Mail," we are quite convinced that nothing of the kind was intended or even thought of.

But we should like to know what we have done that the "Japan Mail" should be so angry with us. In his wrath the Editor of the "Japan Mail" loses either his head or his honesty, for he altogether misrepresents the facts of the case. What we condemned and still condemn as revolting, brutal and disgraceful was the method of execution. The facts of the case were very plainly set forth in our article. The condemned Koreans were "potted at" at distance of about 40 yards. The soldiers did not fire volleys and one of the Koreans was shot seven times and another five times before they were put out of agony.

And of this the "Japan Mail" says "there is not the smallest iota inviting condemnation," and that "the criminals were justly punished." The "Japan Mail" owes its existence to Japanese bounty and it is therefore natural enough for it to enter the lists as champion of everything Japanese and it does this in a way which commands some sort of admiration, if only for its thoroughness. We believe the editor was formerly a British military officer, but if he can bring himself to condone such a piece of cold blooded butchery as was the excution of the three Koreans, we can only say that he is well out of the British army.

PORT ARTHUR.

There is practically no news from Port Arthur. The outer ditches of the forts Sunsushan and Urlungshan are said to have been captured by the Japanese but there is no official confirmation of this. The Japanese newspapers seem at last to be realizing the magnitude of the task which still lies before General Nishi. The forts and the main *enciente* are still intact and the besiegers are making but slow progress.

Reports have it, that trains will be running from Fusan to Pyengyang in January next.

Mr. Chi Woon-yung (the dreamer of fauns and boxes) has gone on a visit to China. We presume he has gone to unravel the mysteries contained in the words found in his box.

The Il-chin-hoi are about to make another of their futile requests to Government officials to resign their posts. We understand that the Il-chin-hoi will shortly be ordered to vacate theirs.

There seems to be some difficulty experienced by magistrates in distinguishing between Tonghaks and Chin-po-hoi people. The president of the Il-chin-hoi has another complaint to make that a Chin-po-hoi man has been arrested at Yensan in mistake for a Tonghak.

Interviewing the war correspondent of "Le Journal," after Liaoyang, General Kuropatkin indulged in a safe prophecy: "Ah, monsieur, you have already witnessed many terrible events" said the Genralissimo, with the most complete serenity, "but if you stay on with the Russian army you will see a good many more. That I can promise you."

A BRAVE SOLDIER'S TRAGIC FATE.

(FROM THE CHEFOO DAILY NEWS.)

It was recently my fortune to witness the execution of a young Russian private of infantry who had been captured within the lines near Yentai disguised as a Chinese. I was so impressed by the superb conduct of the ill-fated man during his captivity and even on the execution field itself, that I have decided to tell the story so that others besides the few who gathered at the place of his death may know how a Russian can die for his country's sake. To me he compared favorably with the patriot Seizo Yokogawa, who, it will be remembered, sent this message to his little daughter before the rifles spoke: "Papa dies by the order of His Majesty, the Emperor."

It was while a portion of the invading army was encamped near the Yentai Colliery that this young Russian, Ryaboff by name, volunteered to penetrate Japanese camps, and ascertain what he might about the disposition of the troops, their condition, number, etc. His instructions were to reconnoitre the positions in the distance of ten versts North-east of Yentai Station. Being unusually short for a Russian and having a face burned a deep brown by the Manchurian sun there was nothing incongruous about his disguise. The guards, sentries and patrols permitted him to pass without question, never dreaming he was a Russ. Being a man of quick perception he readily secured a fund of information which had it ever reached General Kuropatkin's headquarters would have been of inestimatable disadvantage to Japanese military operations of the immediate future. His capture however was brought about by the merest freak of fortune.

One evening the spy was making his way through a millet field near Yentai with a sickle over his shoulder. He wished to give the impression that he was a reaper returning homewards after his day's work. Near the Colliery he happened to pass a Japanese soldier, cooking supper, who in a manner customary with all soldiers in a hostile country cried "Here you, fetch a pail of water from the river there!" Fearful of betraying himself, the Russian apparently paid no heed to the soldier's command. Angered by this the latter sprang from his pots and pans to punish him. Now thoroughly frightened the Russian took to his heels. A race began which was eagerly watched by a number of soldiers ready to welcome any relief to the monotony of camp life. Suddenly a gust of wind carried away the spy's Chinese hat and false queue and he was immediately recognized. A great shout went up from the soldiers and every one now joined in the pursuit of the fugitive who ran until he fell prone upon the earth totally exhausted. An hour later he was standing in the presence of the commandant. Sorely disheartened by his misfortune he made no secret of the purpose that had brought him into the camp. He was finally remanded to the guard house and preperations were at once begun for his court-martial.

The court assembled on the thirtieth day of the ninth moon. The members were Major Tetsutato Fukuwara, Captain Matasuke Hamano and Judge Advocate Koozoo Namai. As the prisoner entered he bowed respectfully to the court and stood at attention. It is safe to presume that he felt reasonably certain that death could be his only punishment. Nevertheless his face gave no indication of the tumult raging in his heart. A silence, such as I never knew before, fell in the court-room, when Major Fukuwara, chief justice, arose and read the allegations in a low but distinct voice. Witnesses were sworn as a mere matter of form, the accused having confessed his guilt. Little time, however, was devoted to their examination. Finally Judge Hamano arose and read the sentence. It was a shortly worded document and ended up with these words: "I sentence him to death."

There is an awful fascination about a man's face when he knows he is near death. Every spectator morbidly watches it, attributing this that and the other thing to every twitch of its muscles. Ryaboff, however, listened to the words of the sentence, which must have sunk like knife thrusts into his heart, without betraying the least agitation. Then when it was over and the judge was reseated the prisoner said in a steady voice: "I am satisfied."

At evening a few days later the execution took place. The accused took his stand near a Mara tree in a wild rocky valley. Four soldiers were drawn up in a line facing him. The judges of the court were present, also a large concourse of soldiers and civilians. The condemned was placed in position by Lieutenant Fugita of the Gendarmes, the chief executioner. As is customary with Japenese military executions, the prisoner's wrists were unbound upon his arrival upon the execution ground. Two gendarmes even stepped forward and rubbed the flesh where it had been chafed by the ropes.

"May I pray to my God?" queried the prisoner, looking up at Lieutenant Fugita who readily assented. Then there was a great silence while the Russian knelt and offered his last prayer to the God in whom he believed so well. When it was over Captain Hamano said to the condemned:—

"Have you a wife?"

"Yes, I have a wife" answered the prisoner "and also two little children," Here his voice broke, his lips trembled and great tears flooded his eyes. It was a trying moment for everybody present. Even the stong-hearted gendarmes, to whom executions were matters of frequent occurrence, looked ill at ease. Say what you will, it is a dreadful strain to watch a big, strong man weep for his family and keep the tears from coming to one's own eyes. Captain Hamano then said to the prisoner:—

(Continued on 3rd page.)

The Korea Daily News.

VOL. I, MONDAY, NOVEMBER 21, 1904. No. 106

HONGKONG & SHANGHAI BANKING CORPORATION.

Paid-up Capital..........................$10,000,000
Reserve Fund:—Sterling Reserve... 10,000,000
Silver Reserve..... 7,000,000

27,000,000
Reserve Liability of Proprietors... 10,000,000

HEAD OFFICE, HONGKONG.

London Bankers, London and County Banking Company Limited.

Branches and Agencies,

London.

Amoy,	Hankow,	Penang,
Bangkok,	Hiogo,	Rangoon,
Batavia,	Iloilo,	Saigon,
Bombay,	Lyons,	San Francisco,
Calcutta,	Manila,	Singapore,
Colombo,	Nagasaki,	Sourabaya,
Foochow,	New York,	Tientsin,
Hamburg,	Peking,	Yokohama,

Credits granted on approved Securities, and every description of Banking and Exchange business transacted.

Drafts granted on London and the chief Commercial places in Europe, India, Australia, America, China and Japan.

HOLME RINGER & Co., AGENTS,
CHEMULPO.

ON CHEONG & CO.,
SEOUL.

GENERAL STORE KEEPERS.
Imported provisions, Cooking Utensils Crockery, etc.
FRESH BREAD DAILY.

MITSU BISHI DOCKYARD & ENGINE WORKS,

NAGASAKI.

CODE WORD, "DOCK."

A. 1, A. B. C., and Engineering Codes used.

DOCK No. 1 (at Tategami).

Extreme Length..............523 feet
Length on blocks .... 513 „
Width of Entrance on Top......89 „
„ „ Bottom....77 „
Water on Blocks at Spring Tide 26½ „

DOCK No. 2 (Mukaijima).

Extreme Length..............371 feet
Length on Blocks............360 „
Width of Entrance on Top......66 „
„ „ Bottom 53 „
Water on Blocks at Spring Tide 22 „

PATENT SLIP (at Kosuge).

Can take vessels up to 1,000 tons gross.

THE WORKS are well equipped with the LATEST IMPROVEMENTS, and can execute any kind of work in SHIPBUILDING and MARINE ENGINEERING, as well as in REPAIRING of SHIPS.

The COMPANY'S new powerful steamer OURA-MARU (712 tons, 700 I.H.P.), specially built for SALVAGE PURPOSES, and equipped with necessary gear, is always READY at SHORT NOTICE.

CHARTERED BANK OF INDIA AUSTRALIA & CHINA.

INCORPORATED BY ROYAL CHARTER 1853

HEAD OFFICES:—LONDON.

Paid-up Capital £800,000
Reserve Liability of Shareholders 800,000
Reserve Fund 800,000

Drafts granted upon all the principal places in the world and every description of Exchange and banking business transacted.

E. MEYER & Co., Agents,
Chemulpo.

E. MEYER & CO.

Chemulpo.

SOLE AGENTS IN KOREA FOR:

A. T. Morse, Sons & Co's "Fresco" Distemper

In all colours ready for use on walls, Ceilings etc.

and

AVENARIUS CARBOLINEUM

A wood-preserving and antiseptic oil preparation

Against decay, dry-rot, fungus and wood-destroying insects.

A large supply always in Stock. Prices upon application.

E. MEYER & Co.,
Chemulpo.

THE METHODIST PUBLISHING HOUSE,

Little West Gate, Seoul.

JOB PRINTING, TYPEWRITER PAPER
CARBON PAPER, VISITING CARDS
STATIONERY, BOOK BINDING
BOOK PUBLISHERS
AMERICAN SCHOOL BOOKS
SPENCERIAN COPY BOOKS
PEN CARBON LETTER AND BILL BOOKS

S. A. BECK, Manager.

HOKURKU DOBOKU KAISHA.

Branch office in Chong Dong, Seoul.

Japanese telephone No. 165

CONTRACT DEPARTMENT.

We can contract to build any building or construction.

MERCHANDISE DEPARTMENT.

We can provide any building material. We have just contracted to build the new Belgian Legation.

DAI-ICHI GINKO.

LIMITED.

(Formerly the First National Bank)

ESTABLISHED 1873

INCORPORATED UNDER PRESENT LAW 1896

Capital - - - - - - - - Yen 5,000,000
Reserve Fund - - - - - 1,500,000

HEAD OFFICE:—TOKIO.

President: Baron SHIBUSAWA.

BRANCHES AND CORRESPONDENTS

In the Principal Cities and Towns of Japan.

Interest Allowed on

Fixed deposits 1 year - - - 6½ per cent
" " 6 months - - - 6 per cent

Special current accounts 1½ sen daily per Y 100
General " " 1 " " " 100

M. TANAKA,
Manager, Chemulpo.

SINGER SEWING MACHINES

씽거즈봉침

SOLE AGENTS FOR KOREA

전매쇼

HOLME RINGER & CO.
Chemulpo.

졔물포 함릉거양힝

KAMEYA & CO.

GENERAL STOREKEEPERS

Chinkokai - - Seoul

(*Established 1895, Tokyo*)

Confectionery, Hams, Canned Goods, Cutlery, Hirano & Tansan Water. Provisions, Gents, Furnishing goods, Toilet Articles, Travelling Bags, Tobacco, Cigars & Cigarettes Kitchen Utensils. Coffee. Biscuits.

Fresh Goods always kept in Stock.

Prices Moderate

☞ *Please come and inspect our goods*

NIPPON YUSEN KAISHA.

JAPANESE MAIL STEAMSHIP CO.

UNDER MAIL CONTRACT WITH THE IMPERIAL JAPANESE GOVERNMENT.

European Line

Regular Fortnightly Service between Yokohama Kobe, Moji, Shanghai, Hongkong, Singapore, Penang Colombo, Port Said, Marseilles, London and Antwerp

American Line

Regular Fortnightly Service between Hongkong and Seattle, calling at Shanghai, Moji, Kobe, Yokohama and Victoria, B. C.

Australian Line

Regular weekly Service betwen Japan Ports and Australia, callingiat Hongkong and Manila.

(Above Three Lines Suspended until further notice).

Shanghai Line

Weekly Service between Shanghai and Japan Ports

Korea Line

Service Kobe, Moji, Nagasaki, Fusan Chemulpo Chefoo, Taiku.

S. S. Bahelsberg, 2181 tons.

Service Kobe, Moji, Fusan, Chemulpo, Chinnampo

S. S. ARGO, S. S. Ohio.

BORDEN'S CONDENSED MILK CO.

New York, U. S. A.

ALWAYS IN STOCK

Eagle Brand Condensed Milk.

Gold Seal Condensed Milk.

Peerless (Family) Evaporated Cream.

Borden's Malted Milk.

E. MEYER & CO.
Chemulpo, Korea,
Sole Agents

ROYAL INSURANCE COMPANY,

Funds exceed £10,000,000

FIRE

AT CURRENT RATES.

LIFE

REDUCED PREMIUM.

HOLME RINGER & Co.,
Agents, Chemulpo.

HOTEL DU PALAIS

SEOUL.

The only first class Hotel in Seoul. Situated in the centre of the city opposite the palace.

Cuisine under the supervision of an experienced French Chef.

Well ventilated and furnished throughout.

TARIFF UPON APPLICATION

L. MARTIN

Proprietor and Manag'r.

大韓每日申報

대한매일신보

(뎨일빅칠호) (슈요일) 일쳔구빅사년십일월이십삼일

본샤고빅

이신보는영어와한어로셔거빅일출판홈

신문가

한쟝 엽두돈오푼

일삭표 엽두량닷돈

우표가ᄂᆞᆫ 샤닷돈

다ᄆᆞᆺ돈으로밧숩

광고료는

귀한의장단과ᄌᆞ힝의다쇼로종갑ᄒᆞ되뎡가로밧을터이오매오리지아녀대한사람마다다이신문을보실터이니광고버시기를원ᄒᆞ시ᄂᆞᆫ이들은우리신문사에와셔면약ᄒᆞ심을희망ᄒᆞᆷ

○발힝소 박동대한매일신보사 발힝겸인쇄쟈 영국인 셔셜빌 발쟝자리오

사쟝 영국인 (빅셜)

평양 디리졈

○평양효동사ᄂᆞᆫ권티보씨로우리신문관ᄒᆡ티리인을뎡ᄒᆞ엿ᄉᆞ오니평양에계신구람코져ᄒᆞ시ᄂᆞᆫ쳠군ᄌᆞᄂᆞᆫ디리졈에왕림ᄒᆞ와면의ᄒᆞ시옵

샤고

○우리대한매일신보의목뎍은대한의안녕질셔에관한모든대목에디ᄒᆞ야ᄂᆞᆫ공평한번론을주장홈이라우리동신원의탐보ᄂᆞᆫ신문보시ᄂᆞᆫ쳠군ᄌᆞ의게ᄒᆞ샹보도ᄒᆞ리며편지를긔셔ᄒᆞ여주시ᄂᆞᆫ이ᄂᆞᆫ셩명과번디를져어붓치시기를희망ᄒᆞ오나이거슨신문상에긔재ᄒᆞ란ᄂᆞᆫ거시아니오다만긔히ᄌᆞ셔알ᄒᆞᄂᆞᆫ즁거를숨고자ᄒᆞᆷ이라긔자ᄂᆞᆫ아모긔셔던지과지ᄒᆞᆷ을퇴각ᄒᆞᄂᆞᆫ권리를가졋스나퇴각ᄒᆞᄂᆞᆫ리유ᄂᆞᆫ말ᄒᆞᆯ터이오며공즁평화를문란케ᄒᆞᄂᆞᆫ듯ᄒᆞᆫ긔셔ᄂᆞᆫ의례히밧지안켓ᄉᆞᆸ나이다

●본샤셜시이릭로신문을미양우레로본쟈ᄒᆞ와레쟌부의양의로젼ᄒᆞᄂᆞᆫ것스로번곳에ᄂᆞᆫ혹늣게젼ᄒᆞ기도ᄒᆞ며혹멋칠거슬ᄒᆞᆫ번에젼ᄒᆞ기도ᄒᆞ며혹아니젼ᄒᆞᄂᆞᆫ곳도잇다ᄒᆞ와우리신문을ᄉᆞ랑ᄒᆞ야구람ᄒᆞ시ᄂᆞᆫ쳠군ᄌᆞ의게금티ᄒᆞ야민우미안ᄒᆞ옵기로지금이젼은분젼인을두고미일죵이나졈ᄒᆞ며아니젼ᄒᆞ거나늣게거나ᄒᆞᄂᆞᆫ치가업도록ᄒᆞ란ᄒᆞ오니혹아니젼ᄒᆞ거나늣게젼ᄒᆞ거나ᄒᆞᆫ일이잇스면본샤로통긔ᄒᆞ여주심을희망ᄒᆞᆷ

잡보

○슌안금광 슌안금광에ᄂᆞᆫ사금이만히나ᄂᆞᆫ고로시방취금에죵ᄉᆞᄒᆞᄂᆞᆫ광부가수쳔여명이라더라

○류민귀향 만쥬방면에거쥬ᄒᆞ든한인류식쳔명이작년이래의샹린호환편으로인ᄒᆞ여귀착ᄒᆞ야ᄌᆞ의로각기향리로도라갓다더라

○평양진보회 평양동신들이ᄒᆞᆫ쥬형금에진보회가각디방에셔평양으로회집ᄒᆞ야수무소를졍ᄒᆞ고긔회ᄒᆞᆯ조ᄂᆞᆫ데지아니ᄒᆞ엿ᄂᆞᆫ디죵로예포고문을써셔방ᄒᆞ며로샹에삼삼오오로작반ᄒᆞ야단니ᄂᆞᆫ자ㅣ불가승슈오무비진보회원이라ᄒᆞ더라

○가산군슈 평안도로온사룸의젼셜을드른즉가산군슈최지호씨ᄂᆞᆫ역부를모집ᄒᆞᆫ다고빈잔ᄒᆞᆫ에오빅명을쟉졍ᄒᆞ야응모케ᄒᆞᆫ다ᄒᆞ야슈쳡을파셔ᄌᆞ귀가다맥고이른본병참소에ᄂᆞᆫ일빅오십명가평만보너기로ᄒᆞ엿다ᄒᆞ며무고히빅셩을잡아드려라탄ᄒᆞ며수령들도거힝을잘아니ᄒᆞ야셧리ᄂᆞᆫ쳥을만ᄒᆞᆫ다더라

○텰령쥬둔 텰령에잇ᄂᆞᆫ아라사군슈ᄂᆞᆫ근일동문외십리허에참호를기착ᄒᆞ며또셔남간쳐에포대를더세우며신과ᄒᆞᆫ즁원병은태반이나이곳에유쥬케ᄒᆞ며또텰령셩북방일빅이십리되ᄂᆞᆫ쳥하구와셔남편일빅오십리되ᄂᆞᆫ방하구와셔샹쳐에도다유쥬ᄒᆞ얏더라ᄒᆞ며군슈가쥬ᄒᆞ든둔ᄒᆞ고봉쳔으로보터남으로ᄂᆞᆫ려간다ᄒᆞ엿더라

○디리쳘폐 려슌셔항쳘거부근에로병이셜비ᄒᆞᆫ디뢰를일병이쳘폐ᄒᆞ엿다ᄒᆞᄂᆞᆫ디그리유ᄂᆞᆫᄌᆞ귀국병이죵망히도쥬ᄒᆞᆯ때에디뢰를범ᄒᆞᆯ가두려워ᄒᆞᄂᆞᆫ바ㅣ라더라

쳥국판리부아셜 샹히면을거ᄒᆞᆫ즉아라ᄉᆞ국쟁탈힝티가동양으로츌리ᄒᆞᆫ다ᄂᆞᆫ보가잇ᄉᆞᆫ후로쥬쳥아공ᄉᆞ가거예외보문로ᄒᆞᆷ셔례후와각태신의게ᄋᆞᆫ돈ᄒᆞᆷ으로원세기씨도아라수에부쳘의향이잇셔향자에그말로를쟝졔동씨의게파송ᄒᆞ야비밀히샹의ᄒᆞᆯ수가잇다ᄂᆞᆫ말이젼파ᄒᆞᄂᆞᆫ티사건에진젹ᄒᆞ며아니ᄒᆞᆫ것은조셰치못ᄒᆞ나대저쳥국관민의셩각이번젼홈은젹확ᄒᆞ다더라

○쟝교류학 영국죵구셩에셔류민한변룬군쟝교즁으로사명식류학싱을션뎡ᄒᆞ야일본에파송ᄒᆞᆯ아이기년간쥐학ᄒᆞ고일본말을학습케ᄒᆞᆫ다더라

○보호릉디 아라사달력으로십월십오일에로국황뎨가후구쟝군의게쳐면을보니여왈쳥국사이즁립을능히지히니우리군사가봉텬에잇ᄂᆞᆫ릉침디를손히ᄒᆞᄂᆞᆫ폐가업게ᄒᆞ기위ᄒᆞ야그디오를보호케ᄒᆞ라ᄒᆞ엿다더라

○봉공즁포 금월칠일에발ᄒᆞᆫ셔분돈면을거ᄒᆞᆫ즉구문파회사에셔만쥬로군에티ᄒᆞ야시로빌든즁포를공급ᄒᆞᆫ다ᄒᆞ엿더라

○일로사샹의비교 오월일일로샹십월십오일간젼투에일로량군의사샹ᄒᆞᆫ비교가여좌ᄒᆞ니일본군ᄉᆞ의사샹자ᄂᆞᆫ합계수만삼쳔구빅명이오아라ᄉᆞ군ᄉᆞ사샹자ᄂᆞᆫ십이만수쳔팔빅구명의이라더라

뎐보

만쥬군총ᄉᆞ령부발 당디부ᄉᆞ령부착

○ᄒᆞᆫ하쇼젼 십륙일대포슈문이잇ᄂᆞᆫ젹의보긔병은ᄒᆞᆫ하우안을공격ᄒᆞ야왓ᄉᆞ나황혼시에그쥬력은북방에퇴각ᄒᆞ엿고이날이포격을위ᄒᆞ야우리하사졸삼명이부샹ᄒᆞ고젹의손히ᄂᆞᆫ자셰히알지못ᄒᆞ나우리의ᄉᆞ샹보담슈빅나되겟더라

(십칠일오후팔시ᄉᆞ십분발)

○외쳐셩홍 론돈에셔우리공최예응모일은십삼빅에달ᄒᆞ엿더라

십일월십구일평셩군ᄉᆞ령부뎐챡

○회인쇼젼 십륙일에우리쳑후ᄂᆞᆫ잔연구령(회인남방빅리)의북방에셔젹긔병오십긔가젼진ᄒᆞ야옴을알아써격퇴ᄒᆞ고미격긔ᄒᆞᆫ것을기다려젹을습격ᄒᆞ야격퇴ᄒᆞ엿ᄂᆞᆫ티젹은부샹쟈이명이셩ᄒᆞ엿고그후에우리의부티ᄂᆞᆫ우모(회인남방ᄉᆞ십리)ᄭᆞ지뎐진ᄒᆞ엿스나젹병을보지못ᄒᆞ엿더라

만조군총ᄉᆞ령부발 당디ᄉᆞ령부착뎐

○티ᄌᆞ하쇼젼 십칠일에우리근젹후ᄂᆞᆫ티ᄌᆞ하좌안의외티이촌부샹이ᄌᆞ긔슬격퇴ᄒᆞ고젹은약간의사자를싱ᄒᆞ야격퇴ᄒᆞ엿더라

○ᄒᆞ룽쇼젼 십팔일야츙미명에동에젹의보병부티ᄂᆞᆫᄒᆞᆼ부근의ᄒᆞ자군은ᄌᆞ왓스나이것을격퇴ᄒᆞ엿더라

○도쥬촌락 시이야린사부근에ᄂᆞᆫ젹보병일대티가진향ᄒᆞ야잇ᄂᆞᆫ고로우리포병이이를노ᄒᆞ야사격으로ᄒᆞ엿ᄂᆞᆫ티젹은퇴퇴ᄒᆞ야촌락으로도망ᄒᆞ엿더라

○ᄒᆞᆫ하포격 십칠일오후에젹의보긔병수오빅과대포슈문이ᄒᆞᆫ하우안에셔고ㅣ바고대이레이시부근을포격ᄒᆞᆷ은우리로ᄒᆞ여곰이를가히되와닛그도ᄒᆞ엿더라

관보

뎨이쳔구빅팔십삼호

광무팔년십일월십구일

셔임급ᄉᆞ령

○의원면본관 비셔원승 김

○졔셔 홍문관시독 김졔수

○임비셔원승셔 괸임판칠등 조남일

○임홍문관시독셔 괸임판수등 리범셜

이샹십일월십칠일

육군법원관제 ᄉᆞ

뎨일됴 육군법원은군부대신의관할에속ᄒᆞ야육군군인의범죄ᄒᆞᆫ형ᄉᆞ를심판ᄒᆞ며감옥을총독홈이라

뎨이됴 육군법원에좌기직원을치홈이라

원쟝 일인 육군참쟝

리ᄉᆞ 삼인 칙임일인샹

이등이샹 쥬ᄉᆞ 일인 주임

쥬ᄉᆞ 구인 판임

뎨삼됴 원쟝은원니ᄉᆞ무를관리ᄒᆞ고소속직원을지휘감독홈이라

뎨ᄉᆞ됴 리ᄉᆞᄂᆞᆫ원쟝의명을승ᄒᆞ야고쥬임ᄉᆞ무를담임홈이라

뎨오됴 리ᄉᆞᄂᆞᆫ죄범의구인과

심판과 집행과 과정챵 감옥에 임검ᄒᆞᄂᆞᆫ 졔ᄉᆞ무를 힝ᄒᆞᆷ이라

뎨륙됴 원장이 ᄉᆞ고가 잇ᄂᆞᆫ ᄯᆡ에ᄂᆞᆫ 슈반리ᄉᆞ가 그 ᄉᆞ무를 셔리ᄒᆞᆷ이라

뎨칠됴 주ᄉᆞᄂᆞᆫ 상관의 지휘를 승ᄒᆞ야 셔무에 종ᄉᆞᄒᆞᆷ이라

뎨팔됴 주ᄉᆞᄂᆞᆫ 일졀 심판의 공슐을 필긔ᄒᆞ며 쇼송ᄉᆞ건에 관ᄒᆞᆫ 셔류를 조졔보존ᄒᆞ고 그 다른 셔셔에 관ᄒᆞᆫ ᄉᆞ무를 힝ᄒᆞᆷ이라

뎨구됴 륙군법원에셔 특지로 하부ᄒᆞ신 죄인을 심판ᄒᆞᄂᆞᆫ ᄉᆞ가 잇슴이라

뎨십됴 륙군법원에셔 쳥주임관을 구락ᄒᆞ야 심판ᄒᆞᄂᆞᆫ ᄯᆡᄂᆞᆫ 군부대신의 계가를 ᄎᆞ보ᄒᆞᆷ이라

뎨십일됴 륙군법원ᄂᆡ에 군법회의를 치ᄒᆞ야 군인의 류형명 형ᄉᆞ샹의 죄를 판결ᄒᆞᆷ이라

뎨십이됴 륙군법원ᄂᆡ에 주임관과 판임관의 임면진퇴ᄂᆞᆫ 군부대신이 힝ᄒᆞᆷ이라

뎨십삼됴 륙군법원 직원의 년봉과 밋 관직 등은 개국오빅ᄉᆞ년 칙령 뎨오십칠호 관등봉급령에 의지ᄒᆞᆷ이라

뎨십ᄉᆞ됴 본관제ᄂᆞᆫ 반포ᄒᆞᆫ 날로부터 시힝ᄒᆞᆷ이라

뎨십오됴 광무ᄉᆞ년 구월 십팔일 칙령 뎨삼십삼호 륙군법원관제ᄂᆞᆫ 폐지ᄒᆞᆷ이라

군긔창관졔

뎨일됴 군긔창은 군부대신 관할에 속ᄒᆞ야 륙군의 슈요ᄒᆞᄂᆞᆫ 병긔와 탄약과 긔구와 지료를 졔조슈리ᄒᆞ며 ᄒᆡ군의 슈요ᄒᆞᄂᆞᆫ 화약을 졔조ᄒᆞ고 ᄯᅩ 졔혁과 졔융과 밋 군용ᄒᆡᆼ구와 피복졔의 ᄉᆞ무를 맛ᄒᆞᆷ이라

뎨이됴 군긔창은 경셩에 치ᄒᆞ고 창ᄂᆡ에 좌기 졔조소를 비치ᄒᆞᆷ이라

총포졔조소
탄환졔조소
화약졔조소
졔혁소
직조소

뎨삼됴 군긔창의 직원은 좌와 ᄀᆞᆺᄒᆞᆷ이라

관리 일인 참쟝 혹 졍령
부관리 일인 포병졍부령
부관 일인 포병참령 혹 졍위
금수관 이인 포병참령
향관 이인 이샹등ᄉᆞ계
의관 일인 일이삼등군의
주ᄉᆞ 삼인 판임본관
졔조소쟝 오인 참령 혹 졍위
기ᄉᆞ 팔인 주임 판임

뎨ᄉᆞ됴 관리ᄂᆞᆫ 창ᄂᆡᄉᆞ무를 총리ᄒᆞ고 소속직원을 지휘감독ᄒᆞ며 특히 졔조근에 관ᄒᆞᆫ ᄉᆞ무를 맛ᄒᆞᆷ이라

뎨오됴 부관리ᄂᆞᆫ 관리를 보좌ᄒᆞ야 창ᄂᆡᄉᆞ무를 리졍ᄒᆞᆷ이라

뎨륙됴 부관은 창ᄂᆡ일반셔무를 주쟝ᄒᆞᆷ이라

뎨칠됴 금수관은 졔조ᄒᆞᆫ 병긔 탄약과 긔구지료와 밋 그 지료 본졀의 금수ᄂᆞᆫ 주쟝ᄒᆞᆷ이라

뎨팔됴 향관은 창ᄂᆡ일졀회계 ᄉᆞ무를 주쟝ᄒᆞᆷ이라

뎨구됴 의관은 창ᄂᆡ일졀위싱 ᄉᆞ무를 주쟝ᄒᆞᆷ이라

뎨십됴 주ᄉᆞᄂᆞᆫ 샹관의 지휘를 승ᄒᆞ야 문부긔쥬 등 ᄉᆞ무에 종ᄉᆞᄒᆞᆷ이라

뎨십일됴 총포졔조소ᄂᆞᆫ 군용ᄒᆞᄂᆞᆫ 총포를 졔조슈리ᄒᆞ기 위ᄒᆞ야 치ᄒᆞᆷ이니 ᄒᆞᆯ 소쟝은 포병참령 혹 졍위로 치ᄒᆞ고 기ᄉᆞ 이인과 기슈 오인을 치ᄒᆞ야 각기 업무를 분담ᄒᆞᆷ이라

뎨십이됴 탄환졔조소ᄂᆞᆫ 군용에 슈요ᄒᆞᆫ 탄환을 졔조ᄒᆞ기 위ᄒᆞ야 치ᄒᆞᆷ이니 ᄒᆞᆯ 소쟝은 포병참령 혹 졍위로 치ᄒᆞ고 기ᄉᆞ 일인과 기슈 ᄉᆞ인을 치ᄒᆞ야 각기 업무를 분담ᄒᆞᆷ이라

론셜

○금월 십오일에 발간ᄒᆞᆫ바 일본 ᄆᆡ일신문에 게ᄌᆡᄒᆞᆷ이 여좌ᄒᆞ기에 좌에 번등ᄒᆞ노라

이왕에 한국빅셩 삼명이 경의쳘도에 작간ᄒᆞᆷ으로 포착이 되여 포형에 처ᄒᆞᆷ은 죵왕에도 한국빅셩이 죵죵 쳘도에 작간ᄒᆞ야 다만 긔차에 방ᄒᆡ를 밧을 ᄲᅮᆫ아니라 ᄒᆞ인명도 손샹이 되ᄂᆞᆫ 고로 경의간 쳘도에ᄂᆞᆫ 범간ᄒᆞᄂᆞᆫ 쟈 잇ᄉᆞ면 군률로 시힝ᄒᆞ게 ᄒᆞ야 그 작간ᄒᆞᆫ 쟈로 ᄒᆞ여곰 십조목에 ᄆᆡ여 달고 포형을 힝ᄒᆞᆷ이요 ᄯᅩᄒᆞᆫ 죽은 후에라도 몃날 동안을 외구ᄒᆞ미 ᄆᆡ여 달아둠은 다른 빅셩으로 ᄒᆞ여곰 이러ᄒᆞᆫ 참혹ᄒᆞᆫ 경샹을 뵈여 징계ᄒᆞᄌᆞᄒᆞᆷ이 본의인지라

이거시 여간 젹은 죄가 아니오 죽을 범ᄒᆞᆫ 쟈로 ᄒᆞ여곰 죄 당ᄒᆞᆫ 거시 올케 된 일이나 그러ᄒᆞ나 대한ᄆᆡ일신보에셔ᄂᆞᆫ 이 일을 조계ᄂᆞ이며 사진을 박아도 죵동ᄒᆞ야 사진 박이ᄂᆞᆫ 사ᄅᆞᆷ들이 이 사진을 만히 리셔 엇다 ᄒᆞᆫ즉 심히 우습고 파연 어리셕은 일인지라

이러ᄒᆞᆫ 론셜은 주의ᄒᆞ여 볼 사ᄅᆞᆷ도 젹고 ᄯᅩᄒᆞᆫ 보ᄂᆞᆫ 사ᄅᆞᆷ으로 말ᄒᆞ여도 대단히 명예가 업셔지겟다 ᄒᆞ엿스며 ᄯᅩ 말ᄒᆞ기를 한국빅셩들로 ᄒᆞ여곰 조목에 ᄆᆡ단 계손아소를 위ᄒᆞᄂᆞᆫ 나라에 대단히 수치가 되게 ᄒᆞᆷ이요 예수그리스도계셔 십ᄌᆞ가에 못박혀 도라가셧다 ᄒᆞᄂᆞᆫ 이 두어 마ᄃᆡ를 젹이 우리의 싱각에ᄂᆞᆫ 말치 합당타고 ᄒᆞᆯ 수 업ᄂᆞᆫ 거시 아닌가 ᄒᆞᆷ도 아니요 ᄯᅩᄒᆞᆫ 조롱이라고 마음에 둔 듯ᄒᆞᆫ 거시엿시되

대저 우리가 일본 ᄆᆡ일신문에 ᄃᆡᄒᆞ야 계로ᄒᆞ도록 ᄒᆞᆫ 말이 무엇시 잇ᄂᆞᆫ지 게에 이ᄃᆡ도록 샹ᄒᆞᆫ 말ᄒᆞ엿ᄂᆞᆫ지 ᄂᆞᆫ지를 원ᄒᆞᄂᆞᆫ 바이며 아모리 분쟁소ᄅᆡ를 ᄆᆡ말이라도 엇지 이러케 손샹례면 되ᄂᆞᆫ 줄을 모르리오 우리 신문에 이왕 게ᄌᆡᄒᆞᆫ 바ᄂᆞᆫ 그 빅셩 삼명이 시ᄒᆞᆫ 참악ᄒᆞ야 금수와 ᄀᆞᆺᄒᆞᆫ 곳으로 ᄃᆡ강 말ᄒᆞ엿슬 ᄲᅮᆫ인ᄃᆡ 려ᄯᅩᄒᆞᆫ 죠이ᄂᆞᆫ 거ᄉᆞ로 말ᄒᆞ드ᄅᆡ도 분원지지에 다 ᄆᆡ여 다리 놋코 일졔히 방총ᄒᆞ여 포살치 못ᄒᆞ야 오륙ᄎᆞ 륙칠ᄎᆞ에 간신이 목숨을 ᄭᅳᆫ는 고로 그 참은ᄒᆞᆫ 바를 말ᄒᆞᆷ이어ᄂᆞᆯ

ᄆᆡ일신문에ᄂᆞᆫ 그 빅셩들의 범죄ᄒᆞᆫ 것도 젹지 안코 찰벌도 잘 당ᄒᆞ엿다 ᄒᆞ엿스니 이ᄂᆞᆫ 무리ᄒᆞᆫ 말이라 일본의 보조로써 신문을 유지ᄒᆞ여 가ᄂᆞᆫ 셔담에 엇더ᄒᆞᆫ 일이든지 다만 친일만 ᄒᆞ기 위ᄒᆞ야 ᄆᆡ양 셜명ᄒᆞᆷ이로ᄃᆡ 이 신문과 쟈인즁 죵왕에 영국셔무관이든 사ᄅᆞᆷ인지라 이 사ᄅᆞᆷ이 악ᄒᆞᆫ 참혹ᄒᆞ고 피샹ᄒᆞᆫ 일을 당ᄒᆞᄂᆞᆫ 리도가 치 용셔ᄒᆞᆯ만ᄒᆞ엿슬러이어ᄂᆞᆯ 도리여 이 사ᄅᆞᆷ에 비리케 말ᄒᆞᆷ은 젼증ᄒᆞᆯ 수 업게 너이노라

잡보

○아국류학싱 한아됴약을 쳬결ᄒᆞᆫ 후에 아국에 산류학싱을 쇼환ᄒᆞ엿스되 ᄆᆡᆺ치 소셔이 엇던니 ᄯᅥᄂᆞ 아공ᄉᆞ 리범진씨가 류학싱 이삼명을 ᄆᆡ명에 일빅원식 버여주어 회국ᄒᆞᄂᆞᆫᄃᆡ 뎡샹진씨의 아들과 안중환씨의 아들은 죵로에셔 치ᄉᆞᄒᆞᆫ 고로 학샹위로 시러다가 평ᄒᆞᆫ긔 시쟝에 나 그리미 쟝빈을 쳥구ᄒᆞ엿고 그 여에ᄂᆞᆫ 산지ᄉᆞ방ᄒᆞ야 류리ᄒᆞ야 샹경ᄒᆞᄂᆞᆫᄃᆡ 김ᄀᆞ연씨ᄂᆞᆫ 지작일에 그 중 몬져 드러왓더라

○모군회국 밀양사ᄂᆞᆫ 김승이라 ᄒᆞᄂᆞᆫ 쟈가 일본군ᄉᆞ에 종군ᄒᆞ야 모군으로 부역ᄒᆞ야 쳥국셔지 드리갓더가 군중에셔 울ᄒᆞ든 ᄯᅢ에 탄환을 맛져 부샹ᄒᆞ야 회국ᄒᆞ야ᄂᆞᆫᄃᆡ 일젼에 보각군에셔 련ᄎᆞ 치승ᄒᆞ야 일작에 양셩ᄒᆞ엿더라

○원소봉표 지작이십일일 오후ᄒᆞᆫ시쯤에 원소를 봉표ᄒᆞᄂᆞᆫᄃᆡ 총호ᄉᆞ 리하영씨와 원임대신과 경긔관찰ᄉᆞ와 양쥬군슈가 ᄒᆞᆫ가지로 나아갓더라

○발쳔면보 대구관찰ᄉᆞ가 ᄂᆡ부로 면보ᄒᆞ기를 젼 대구군슈가 관찰ᄉᆞ셔리로 잇슬 ᄯᅢ에 경쥬군에셔 작폐ᄒᆞ든 리병구를 ᄂᆡ부에 보ᄒᆞ고 ᄒᆞᆫ 후에 압샹시여 경무셔에 보되슈ᄒᆞ엿더니 지금에 ᄒᆞᆫ영을 봉승ᄒᆞ야 쳥하군수로 쟝수ᄒᆞᆫ 후 멍구를 본군으로 환ᄒᆞ엿스오나 못 회면ᄒᆞ엿다 ᄒᆞ엿더라

○총금요샹 일본수가 외부로 조회ᄒᆞ되 곡산군민요 죄인 챵이 싱명증 최경로ᄂᆞᆫ 샹인은 피슈가 되고 셩룡현은 졍범이 되고 일안은 종범이 되엿ᄂᆞᆫᄃᆡ 우리 수령부 취조셔가 본져온 고로 조회ᄒᆞ니 샹ᄒᆡ 본방사ᄅᆞᆷ 쳥원의 유죡구휼금을 요쳥ᄒᆞᆯ터이니 쳥컨ᄃᆡ 조량ᄒᆞ라 ᄒᆞ엿더라

○병수방문 지작일 하오삼시량에 병용ᄉᆞ가 외부를 방문ᄒᆞ엿더라

○법관우합 법부관에셔 외부로 공함ᄒᆞ기를 김병도 일교 일수로 공함으로써 조회ᄒᆞ고 ᄯᅩ 법의도 ᄒᆞ엿스되 오히려 일교치 아니ᄒᆞ니 심히 아혹ᄒᆞ고 본관에셔 일시 지관소를 베풀고 본시 일수들 심문ᄒᆞᄂᆞᆫᄃᆡ 히 김병도가 진중이 된고로 이에 일교ᄒᆞ기를 쳥ᄒᆞ고 ᄯᅩ 김병도가 아라ᄉᆞ에 릴적ᄒᆞᆫ 톄 확실ᄒᆞᆫ 증거가 두 가지가 잇스니 첫지ᄂᆞᆫ 아라ᄉᆞ 공관에 답인ᄒᆞᆫ 문서 젹이 잇고 둘지ᄂᆞᆫ 본수가 아라ᄉᆞ 졍부에 ᄃᆡ답ᄒᆞᆫ 조회답ᄒᆞ기를 아라ᄉᆞ 사에 릴젹ᄒᆞ엿다 ᄒᆞ엿더라

○과쟝문쳔 면화과쟝 리규찬의 뒤를 박용규가 피임ᄒᆞᆫ 뒤 첨분이ᄂᆞᆫ 리샤ᄒᆡ 과쟝은 아죽 쳔동치 말나 ᄒᆞ엿다 ᄒᆞ엿더라

○공계후시무 금월 이십이일은 공제일이라 이 십삼일로부터 각부부원쳥에셔 기인 시무ᄒᆞᆫ다더라

○우셜일회 근일운효쟝가 씨부샹을 조직ᄒᆞ야 일회를 셜립ᄒᆞᆯᄎᆞ로 취지셔를 발간 공포ᄒᆞᄂᆞᆫᄃᆡ 그 주의ᄂᆞᆫ 일진회와 ᄀᆞᆺ다더라

○귀샹티진츅 한셩ᄂᆡ에 귀샹티를 진츅ᄒᆞᆯᄎᆞ로 쳥금티단을 쳐량ᄒᆞᄂᆞᆫ 중인ᄃᆡ 쟝광은 룡쳔 평위 이 한ᄒᆞ고 경비ᄂᆞᆫ 일화 십만원가량이라더라

○리세포착 일진회를 ᄇᆡ멸ᄒᆞ기 위ᄒᆞ야 비밀운동ᄒᆞ던 리방형씨를 지작일 경성일본헌병이 포착ᄒᆞ야 일본군수령부에셔 심사ᄒᆞᆫ 즁 동씨ᄂᆞᆫ 비린일이 업셧다고 발명ᄒᆞ엿더라

○원소시역 원소를 미의 완홍지라 음력 본월이십샹일로 브터 시역ᄒᆞᆫ다더라

○예산표조사 탁지부에셔 명년도 예산을 편셩ᄒᆞ기 위ᄒᆞ야 각부부원쳥으로 통첩ᄒᆞ기를 각히 관쳥으로 츙애 산표를 조사ᄒᆞ야 보ᄂᆡ 로교송ᄒᆞ라 ᄒᆞ엿더라

○무쳐샹납 밀양군수 조종셔씨 가공납젼 이십오만량을 탁지부로 샹랍ᄒᆞᆫ 즉 히부에셔 말ᄒᆞ기를 ᄂᆡ쟝원에 리획ᄒᆞ엿스니 히원에 가서 봉납ᄒᆞ라 ᄒᆞᄂᆞᆫ고로 ᄂᆡ쟝원으로 간즉 히원에셔 말ᄒᆞ기를 봉셰관 리금ᄒᆞ엿스니 히관의게 봉납ᄒᆞ라 ᄒᆞᆫ지라 셰부득이 ᄒᆞ야 하히 젼을 가지고 다시 히군으로 하거ᄒᆞ엿다더라

TELEGRAMS.

Tokyo Nov. 21st.

A Russian powder magazine situated near the Arsenal at Port Arthur was struck by a shell from our naval guns on the 19th inst. and exploded. The attack is gradually progressing.

Tokyo, Nov. 21st.

A Japanese force stationed near Kianchang attacked the Russians at Pingchiangsan and drove them from their position. The Japanese captured a flag some horses and weapons and took six prisoners, including one officer.

Army Head Huarters, Seoul.

Field Marshal Oyama reports that at noon on the 19th inst, two sections of Russian infantry supported by one company were seen, east of Luchiangtun. The Japanese artillery opened fire on them and dispersed them.

The Russians on the Liaoyang-Mukden road opened a slow cannonade with siege guns on the evening of the 18th continuing the firing till next morning.

Tokyo, Nov. 20th.

According to a private report, the Japanese on the 18th inst. made a desperate attack on the Sungsushan fort and finally succeeded in occupying it.

Tokyo, Nov. 20th.

According to a Reuter telegram, General Stoessel has reported to the Czar that Port Arthur can hold out for a few months longer. He had been slightly wounded on the head,

HYPNOTISM IN JUGGLERY.

In a paragraph in a recent issue of the "Straits Times," the theory, supported by Captain James Parker, was advanced that hypnotism is the means by which Hindu Fakirs accomplish their most startling illusions. These travelling jugglers certainly perform some wonderful tricks, and the article referred to recalls to memory an interesting perfomance which was given in Lipis some time ago by a party of Brahmins. Among their tricks were swallowing pieces of white cloth and unrolling through the mouth several yards of thread of different colours; this thread would then be again swallowed by another man, and then a friend of his would take a knife and make a puncture in the other's skin above the ribs and pull out all the thread through it; the thing looked so real that one could see the blood trickle down the man's side. One of the men would put some flour into his mouth, and the next moment he started expectorating nails, needles and stones! Another introduced telegraph wire into his mouth and pulled it out through his nose; this trick probably needed a deal of effort, as one could see the man shiver as if in pain. Another marvellous feat was that of the man who appeared to be fast asleep suspended in mid-air, one of his hands clasping at arm's length from him an ordinary bamboo, about five feet long which was not even imbedded in the ground. An enclosure 6' x 4' was curtained off and the man walked into it and lay down on the floor, in full view of the audience; but for the man, the enclosure was quite empty; the curtain of heavy cloth was then drawn down, and we waited for perhaps 10 minutes; then up went the curtain on all sides, and the man asleep in the air, six feet above the ground and supported by nothing visible. Several people went up to the man and felt him; his body was perfectly rigid. After another ten minutes or so, the curtain suddenly fell, and the man emerged shortly afterwards from the enclosure; he complained of great weakness and immediately applied himself to a brass bowl which was said to contain "holy water." This feat ended the performance, which was a very remarkable one. There was a large crowd of Malays present, and they put it all down to the Devil, to whom nothing was impossible, and who, according to them, was introduced by the Brahmins concealed in the hollow of the bamboo! So firmly were they convinced of this, that nothing would induce them to touch that bamboo, the idea being that the devil like the cobra, is harmless so long as you do not interfere with him.

JAPANESE SPIES IN RUSSIA.

A despatch from St. Petersburg to the Manchurian Army "Daily News" says: On September 19th in St. Petersburg, two Japanese naval officers were arrested, charged with espionage. Both had resided in this city under the guise of modest shopmen in a tea store. One of them, called Saratori, up to the beginning of the war had served as merchant's clerk in the warehouse of Messrs. Vasilieff, Dementjeff and Co. (Nevsky Prospect); and being discharged immediately after the villainous Japanese attack upon the Russian fleet, he expressed a desire to remain forever in Russia and to embrace Orthodoxy, under the pretence of his affection for a Russian girl and his intention to marry her. The change of his religion and the marriage were as a matter of fact carried out. Saratori received at the baptismal font the name of Constantine, and at the end of April was living with his wife in a boarding-house in No. 15, Italian Road. A short time after this they were joined by another Japanese from Tokyo, called Tokki Mamatzu, a Buddhist, according to his passport, who also pretended to be an ex-clerk thrown out of his situation owing to the war. Saratori and Mamatzu lived in one room, for which they paid about 60 roubles; they lived in easy circumstances and were well supplied with money. From the beginning of the war a watch on both was instituted and despite the great prudence of Saratori and Mamatzu this surveillance brought them to arrest. On a sudden swoop being made, they were found in their room along with several documents, which proved their criminal intent and their real status as Japanese naval officers.

A LIBERAL OFFER.

A Chinese vernacular journal states that Messrs. L Spitzel & Co., of Shanghai, have sent in a proposal to the Chinese authorities that the said company will undertake to raise a loan amounting to five million taels in order to establish an arsenal for the Chinese Government for manufacturing rifles, guns and ammunitions with the most modern machinery. Again the same foreign firm has stated that as the firm has a stock of Mauser rifles of the most modern type of German make if any of the provincial government wishes to buy the same the firm can supply the same within seven weeks. The loan can be arranged at six per cent. interest per annum without any other conditions. However, that Chinese authorities are not taking the proposal is very suspicious.

ENTERPRISE IN CHINA.

Chang Chi-tung, Viceroy of Hukwang, seems to be going ahead. The "Sinwanpao" says that he has entered into an agreement with the Kawasaki Dockyard at Kobe to build six light draft river gunboats each with 13 knots speed, at 455,000 yen and also for second class torpedo boats with a speed of 23 knots at 3,930,000 yen paying 560,000 yen in advance. The ships have to be handed over to the Chinese authorities at Kobe within 26 months from the date of contract which was signed on the 24th October.—Sinwanpao.

RUSSIA BUYING FAST CRUISERS.

According to the Daily Telegraph correspondent at St. Petersburg, who states that he has received the information from a trustworthy quarter, Russia has recently purchased seven fast cruisers —six from Chili and the Argentine and one from Brazil.

JAPANESE BONDS IN LONDON.

There is again an advance in the price of Japanese securities. Tokyo newspapers are manifesting considerable dissatisfaction with the lowness of the price at which the last loan was floated, pointing out that the rise in price already shows the underwriters a profit of nearly two per cent.

The following are quotations received by the Yokohama Specie Bank last week:—4-per-cent Bonds at £75 10s., an advance of 15s. over the last quotation; the War Loan Bonds at £89 6s 5d., an advance of £1 0s. 5d.; 5 per cents. unchanged at £16 16s. 5d.; while 6 per cents rose by 10s. and stood at £95 5s.

Major-General Beruno in command of the Russian troops in north-east Korea has issued a procalmation announcing that, in future the taxes in the northern districts will be under Russian control.

From the "South China Post" we learn that five vessels have been lost by Japan in the last six months, and the Government has, it is reported, decided, at a Cabinet Meeting held recently, to construct two battle-ships of 18,000 tons displacement each, two first class cruisers of 14 or 15,000 tons each, and a number of smaller vissels, commencing the work at come in the course of next year.

A Korean from the Mil Yang district, who was among the first batch of coolies collected by the Japanese and sent to Manchuria, has been wounded on the battle-field. He experienced great difficulty in returning to Korea as his leg was broken and he could find no one to assist him. He begged his way as far as the Korean frontier where a Magistrate found him and sent him on to Seoul.

The Vicomte de Fontenay, French Chargé d'Affaires at Seoul, left Paris on Oct. 1st for St. Petersburg, according to the "Temps," for the two-fold purpose of giving the Czar information on the events which have taken place in Korea during the last six months, and of thanking His Majesty for the Cross of Commander of the Order of St. Anne. The Vicomte, as French Chargé d'Affaires at Seoul, recently was in charge of Russian interests in the Korean capital.

It is announced that an Italian colonel, who has invented a very practicable device for cutting the wires connecting a fortress with mines laid outside, is in negotiation with a foreign Power for the sale of the invention. The inventor claims that by his system a few soldiers can without danger, and in prefect silence, cut some thousands of wires in a few minutes. The device was tried recently near Rome before a committee of general officers with much success. It is thought that the foreign Power in question is Japan.

A merchant steamer with a 4-funnel torpedo destroyer in tow was observed on Sunday off Warren island near Chemulpo, proceeding in a Northerly direction. The merchantman was apparently Japanese, but whether the destroyer was Japanese or a prize taken from the Russians is not known.

Hitherto it has always been the custom for the Korean Government to maintain a certain number of students in St. Pertersburg. When war broke out only twelve were there, but the lot of these has been rendered miserable through the cutting off of funds by the Korean Government. Finding themselves destitute, they applied to Mr. Yi Pum Chin, Korean Minister to St. Petersburg, for pecuniary aid. He readily gave them $100 each and advised them to return to Korea immediately. Following his advice, they set out on the Siberian railroad for Vladivostok, where only ten of them recently arrived, two of their number having died on the Journey. From Vladivostok they set out, once more penniless, on foot for Seoul, begging food on the road. The first to reach Seoul was Mr. Kim Ki Yun who arrived on Sunday.

THE CZAR INTERVIEWED.

Mr. Melville Stone, the manager of the assoceated Press, describes in the "Daily Chronicle" an audience which has been granted to him by the Czar of Russia, and in which he touched on the intelligence service and the censorship of foreign newspapers; after having submitted his views on the subject to His Imperial Majesty, it is understood that the abolition of the grievances is now assured. Mr. Stone says:—

"No Sovereign of Europe probably is more misunderstood than the Emperor of Russia. The fact that by reason of the Russian scheme of government he is an autocrat, head of the Greek Church, and is, therefore, by his own people accounted a holy person, has led to the impression that he is difficult of access, most reserved, and even austere. On the contrary, he is one of the most democratic Sovereigns in the world. During a recent visit to St. Petersburg, without any warning, I received a command to an audience. There was no indication, as is usual at the European Courts, of the costume to be worn; but the messenger advised me that the costume expected would consist of the ordinary American evening dress, with waistcoat replaced by gold ones."

After a short description of his reception at the Winter Palace, Mr. Stone proceeds:—

"A door was then opened, and a servant announced that the Emperor awaited me. Upon entering the room, which seemed to be a library or study, I found His Majesty alone standing by the table. I attempted to follow the prescribed regulations for addressing a Sovereign, which call for three formed bows, one upon entering the room, one as you approach him, and a third as you address him. After the first salutation, however, he stepped forward, extended his hand, and said pleasantly: 'I am glad to see you, Mr. Stone'

"Emperor Nicholas II. is a man something under medium height, well proportioned, and bears a striking resemblance to his cousins, Prince Henry and the Prince of Wales. He wears a full sandy beard, cut rather short. He has a most kindly impressive, mild, blue eye, betokening at once great kindness, and a great discernment. He was dressed in the blue trousers of an army officer, with white duck fatigue jacket, trimmed in blue braid.

"During the whole of the audience, which lasted over an hour, he remained standing.

"I asked after some introductory words His Majesty whether he desired me to speak with frankness, and being given that assurance I did so.

"His attitude was entirely favourable, and he said that he saw no reason why Russia should not be put upon the same basis as the other Governments mentioned. When I suggested putting th facts in the form of a written memorandum, he said he would be pleased if would do so, as he then could discuss the matter more intelligently with his Ministers. He gave me to understand that unless some obstacle then unforeseen should arise all the privileges asked for would be extended.

"Instead of terminating the interview, he continued to talk on other topics, including the traditional good relations between the United States and Russia. He impressed me as a man sincerely purposing to do whatever lay i his power for the betterment of the condition of his people. He is not in an way a weakling, as has been repeated declared in print, but a man of stro constitution and great poise. It h been my good fortune to meet in audience several Sovereigns, and I believe that, with the possible exceptions of the Emperor of Germany and the King of England, he is the strongest monarch in Europe.

"The conversation was in Englis which he speaks without any trace foreign accent, his tutor having been English clergyman. It is also ... prescribed language of the household, order having been issued while I was St. Petersburg that all the attendan upon the Royal Family should spe that language."

The Korea Daily News.

Issued at 5 P. M. daily except Sundays.

Rate of Subscription:—
Per Year,............Yen 25.
Per Quarter,.........Yen 7.
Per Month,........ .Yen 2.50.

Postage in Korea not charged extra.
Postage abroad charged extra.

Advertisements, 50 sen per day for 1 inch or less.
5 yen per month per inch.
50 yen per year per inch.

All communications to
E. T. BETHELL,
Editor and Publisher,
Pak-tong, Seoul

REACTION IN JAPAN.

From time to time in the Japanese press there appear articles which, as straws show which way the wind blows, give indications that although the people of Japan realize that now the country hopelessly committed to war there is no help but to go through with it, there are many who are by no means so optimistic about the result and consequences of the war as are the jingoes who brought it about. It is realized that success is by no means certain, and that a victory, even if achieved, may be a barren one.

Commenting upon some remarks made by the "Japan Mail," the "Eastern World" says:—

Russia does not, as the "Mail" pretends to believe, *simulate* determination, she *is* determined, and the war, as we said before it began, *will* be a protracted one. Brilliant as the Japanese successes have been they have been only *tactical* successes which have not materially affected the *strategical* issues of the war. We quite agree with the "Mail," however, when it says that the prospect of a war of exhaustion is a gloomy one. It is, but no gloomier than, with our more correct appreciation of the dynamic factors entering the issue, it presented itself to us at the outset. Upon the heads of all who in the press or on the platform helped to bring about this war then be the blood of its victims, between them and happiness be for ever the stream of the tears of the widows and orphans they helped to make, when, as honest, well meaning men, they should have cried out against this war from the housetops.

This is a very powerful protest against the war on humanitarian grounds, while the "Jidai Shicho," as translated by the "Kobe Chronicle," deals in a very pessimistic humour with the economic aspect of the situation. It says:—

"It is well to bear in mind that although the actual enemy to be beaten is Russia, yet when the profits of victory are to be reaped, it will no more be Russia that we shall have as an opponent, but England and America. After triumphing over Russia on the field of battle, we shall have to wrestle with the two Powers named on the economic field. The idea is expressed that the English and Americans who have shown sympathy with us during this war will not fail to assist us in dealing with the financial problems which will arise in regard to the administration of Manchuria and Korea, and indeed it is not entirely unreasonable to suppose that the sympathy now shown by the two great Powers will be a warrant of their sympathy in the future. But one must not forget that sympathy and the calculations of self-interest do not always go hand in hand, especially in the relations of civilised countries. If it is necessary to give an example, it may be pointed out that when our Government was about to launch a loan of one hundred million yen in London and New York, all the world thought that in virtue of the sympathy shown towards us the British and American bankers would subscribe this loan on not too onerous terms. In reality, what happened? Simply that British and American bankers exacted a rate of interest amounting (when the selling price is calculated) to more than eight per cent., and in addition demanded our Customs as guarantee against the loan. The fact alone of being compelled to hypothecate our Customs places us on the level of Egypt and the South American republics; and, moreover, British and American bankers demanded in addition a rate of interest which would not have been exacted even from those countries. On consideration it must be admitted that we have no reason to consider ourselves much flattered. No doubt the ill success of this loan is due partly to the shortcomings of our diplomacy; but it has at the same time afforded us a clear proof that sympathy is not exactly ready money.

"Now when, after the war, it will be necessary to develop railways, mines, industries, agriculture, and forestry (in Manchuria and Korea), it will be very difficult for us to find the necessary funds to spend upon such undertakings. Thereupon British and American companies, able to obtain capital at comparatively low interest, will throw themselves into the new field of exploitation. We shall have opened up Manchuria to them at the price of our blood and treasure. We shall look on with folded arms, while the English and Americans, who during the war remained quiet spectators of the fight, and from whom we obtained the favour of loans at high interest, reap the profits of our labours."

The "Jidai" then looks for reasons for this deplorable state of affairs. It says:—

"We are justly proud of our loyalty to the Emperor and of the patriotism of our nation; even foreigners recognise these qualities in us, and some exalt them. But neither loyalty nor patriotism are titles to confidence when commercial and industrial questions are concerned. One's breast may be covered with decorations, but will these decorations procure us an ounce of credit? The credit which is necessary to attract capital comes from perseverance; and unfortunately in this quality, notwithstanding our military abilities, we are sadly lacking. For example, foreigners who for many years past have built up commerce in our open ports are unanimous in saying that in point of commercial probity the Japanese are decidedly below the Chinese. Moreover, if one considers the doings of our compatriots who have gone to trade in China and Korea, it must be admitted that though some are doubtless honest men, the larger part are unfortunately simply vagabonds (gorotsuki) who, armed with iron sticks, intimidate the Koreans, or with lying speeches take advantage of the implicity of the Chinese. It is by conduct very different from this—by the display of honesty and the exhibition of kindness,—that we can gain the confidence of Koreans and Chinese, and it is only the same qualities and by conscientious work that we can hope to attract foreign capital and operate the field of exploitation which will open to our efforts. But first of all we must deliberately determine on one thing which seems to greatly frighten some of our compatriots,—that is, we must give foreigners the right to own land. Mining rights will not suffice to encourage the inflow of foreign capital: it is landed property alone that offers the necessary guarantee.

Japanese advisers press the Korean Government to concede land-owning rights to us in Korea; but what would they have to say if the Koreans replied: 'How is that you find this thing good for us when you regard it as so bad for yourselves?' If we do not know how to attract foreign capital by liberal concessions, we shall have to send to Korea and Manchuria only poor devils of emigrants who in those places will become the slaves of foreign capitalists; and the present war will merely result in a deplorable financial set-back to Japan." There is nothing new in all this. To those who have given any thought to the subject, the remarks of the 'Jidai Shicho" come as a string of platitudes but the fact remains that these subjects, which ought to have been exhaustively dealt with before war was even thought of, are only just beginning to receive consideration in Japan.

The Chin Po Hoi people are reported to be preparing for a monster meeting to be held at Pyeng Yang.

The Governor of North Ham Kyeng province some time ago was dismissed from his post and ordered to return to Seoul. The Russian troops however have requested him to remain as he has proved himself extremely useful to them.

The Japanese Minister has informed the Korean officials that before raising a foreign loan to meet the expenses of the Crown Princess' funeral, they must consult with him. Furthermore he considers that one year is much too long a period for mourning.

A report is current that the Household Department sent $400,000 nickel money to the Finance Department for circulation. We give the report for what it is worth as it might easily be a story circulated with a view to causing a fluctuation in the money market.

A new submarine has been designed by M. Laubeuf, Chief Naval Architect of the French Government, and designer of the Narval, perhaps the most successful type of submarine in the French Navy. In general shape the new vessel resembles former models, but she is provided with special mechanism which enables her to be completely submerged within two minutes of the first manoeuvres being started. The old models take seven or eight minutes to disappear. The new vessel's motors developed 250-h.p., and her speed is 16 knots.

Many great battles have been fought in the snow. Eylau and Hohenlinden being familiar examples. Austerlitz was fought in intensely cold weather and the Russian losses were increased by Napoleon turning the fire of his artillery on the frozen lakes over which the Russians sought to retreat. In the U. S. Civil War, Fort Donnelson was captured in February Fredericksburg was fought in December, Stone River on December 31, 1862, January 2, 1868, and Thomas defeated and ruined Hood's army at Nashville on the 15th and 16th of December, 1864. Hence it will be seen that history does not warrant us in believing that the war in the East will pass into an unofficial truce when the snow begins to drift.—Boston Transcript.

The Korea Daily News.

VOL. I, TUESDAY, NOVEMBER 22, 1904. No. 107

HONGKONG & SHANGHAI BANKING CORPORATION.

Paid-up Capital	$10,000,000
Reserve Fund:—Sterling Reserve	10,000,000
Silver Reserve	7,000,000
	27,000,000
Reserve Liability of Proprietors	10,000,000

HEAD OFFICE, HONGKONG.

London Bankers, London and County Banking Company Limited.

Branches and Agencies,

London.

Amoy,	Hankow	Penang,
Bangkok,	Hiogo,	Rangoon,
Batavia,	Iloilo,	Saigon,
Bombay,	Lyons,	San Francisco,
Calcutta,	Manila,	Singapore,
Colombo,	Nagasaki,	Sourabaya,
Foochow,	New York,	Tientsin,
Hamburg,	Peking,	Yokohama,

Credits granted on approved Securities, and every description of Banking and Exchange business transacted.

Drafts granted on London and the chief Commercial places in Europe, India, Australia, America, China and Japan.

HOLME RINGER & Co., AGENTS, CHEMULPO.

ON CHEONG & CO., SEOUL.

GENERAL STORE KEEPERS.

Imported provisions, Cooking Utensils Crockery, etc.

FRESH BREAD DAILY.

MITSU BISHI DOCKYARD & ENGINE WORKS,

NAGASAKI.

CODE WORD, "DOCK."

A. 1, A. B. C., and Engineering Codes used.

DOCK No. 1 (at Tategami).

Extreme Length	523 feet
Length on blocks	513 ,,
Width of Entrance on Top	89 ,,
,, ,, Bottom	77 ,,
Water on Blocks at Spring Tide	26½ ,,

DOCK No. 2 (Mukaijima).

Extreme Length	371 feet
Length on Blocks	360 ,,
Width of Entrance on Top	66 ,,
,, ,, Bottom	53 ,,
Water on Blocks at Spring Tide	22 ,,

PATENT SLIP (at Kosuge).

Can take vessels up to 1,000 tons gross.

THE WORKS are well equipped with the LATEST IMPROVEMENTS, and can execute any kind of work in SHIPBUILDING and MARINE ENGINEERING, as well as in REPAIRING of SHIPS.

The COMPANY'S new powerful steamer OURA-MARU (712 tons, 700 I.H.P.), specially built for SALVAGE PURPOSES, and equipped with necessary gear, is always READY at SHORT NOTICE.

CHARTERED BANK OF INDIA AUSTRALIA & CHINA.

INCORPORATED BY ROYAL CHARTER 1853

HEAD OFFICES:—LONDON.

Paid-up Capital	£800,000
Reserve Liability of Shareholders	800,000
Reserve Fund	800,000

Drafts granted upon all the principal places in the world and every description of Exchange and banking business transacted.

E. MEYER & Co., Agents, Chemulpo.

E. MEYER & CO.

Chemulpo.

SOLE AGENTS IN KOREA FOR:

A. T. Morse, Sons & Co's "Fresco" Distemper

In all colours ready for use on walls, Ceilings etc.

and

AVENARIUS CARBOLINEUM

A wood-preserving and antiseptic oil preparation

Against decay, dry-rot, fungus and wood-destroying insects.

A large supply always in Stock. Prices upon application.

E. MEYER & Co., Chemulpo.

THE METHODIST PUBLISHING HOUSE,

Little West Gate, Seoul.

JOB PRINTING, TYPEWRITER PAPER
CARBON PAPER, VISITING CARDS
STATIONERY, BOOK BINDING
BOOK PUBLISHERS
AMERICAN SCHOOL BOOKS
SPENCERIAN COPY BOOKS
PEN CARBON LETTER AND BILL BOOKS

S. A. BECK, Manager.

HOKURKU DOBOKU KAISHA.

Branch office in Chong Dong, Seoul.

Japanese telephone No. 165

CONTRACT DEPARTMENT.

We can contract to build any building or construction.

MERCHANDISE DEPARTMENT.

We can provide any building material. We have just contracted to build the new Belgian Legation.

DAI-ICHI GINKO.

LIMITED.

(Formerly the First National Bank)

ESTABLISHED 1873

INCORPORATED UNDER PRESENT LAW 1896

Capital	Yen 5,000,000
Reserve Fund	1,500,000

HEAD OFFICE:—TOKIO.

President: Baron SHIBUSAWA.

BRANCHES AND CORRESPONDENTS.

In the Principal Cities and Towns of Japan.

Interest Allowed on

Fixed deposits 1 year	6½ per cent
" " 6 months	6 per cent
Special current accounts 1½ sen daily per Y	100
General " " " " "	100

M. TANAKA, Manager, Chemulpo.

SINGER SEWING MACHINES

씽거조봉침

SOLE AGENTS FOR KOREA

전매쇼

HOLME RINGER & CO. Chemulpo.

제물포 함릉거양힝

KAMEYA & CO.

GENERAL STOREKEEPERS

Chinkokai - - Seoul

(*Established 1895, Tokyo*)

Confectionery, Hams, Canned Goods, Cutlery, Hirano & Tansan Water. Provisions, Gents, Furnishing goods, Toilet Articles, Travelling Bags, Tobacco, Cigars & Cigarettes Kitchen Utensils. Coffee. Biscuits.

Fresh Goods always kept in Stock.

Prices Moderate

☞ *Please come and inspect our goods*

NIPPON YUSEN KAISHA.

JAPANESE MAIL STEAMSHIP CO.

DER MAIL CONTRACT WITH THE IMPERIAL JAPANESE GOVERNMENT.

European Line

Regular Fortnightly Service between Yokohama Kobe, Moji, Shanghai, Hongkong, Singapore, Penang Colombo, Port. Said, Marseilles, London and Antwerp

American Line

Regular Fortnightly Service between Hongkong and Seattle, calling at Shanghai, Moji, Kobe, Yokohama and Victoria, B. C.

Australian Line

Regular weekly Service betwen Japan Ports and Australia, callingat Hongkong and Manila.

(Above Three Lines Suspended until further notice).

Shanghai Line

Weekly Service between Shanghai and Japan Ports

Korea Line

Service Kobe, Moji, Nagasaki, Fusan Chemupo Chef foo, Taiku.

S. S. Bahelsberg, 2181 tons.

Service Kobe, Moji, Fusan, Chemulpo, Chinnampo S. S. ARGO, S. S. Ohio.

BORDEN'S CONDENSED MILK CO.

New York, U. S. A.

ALWAYS IN STOCK

Eagle Brand Condensed Milk.

Gold Seal Condensed Milk.

Peerless (Family) Evaporated Cream.

Borden's Malted Milk.

E. MEYER & CO. Chemulpo, Korea, Sole Agents

ROYAL INSURANCE COMPANY,

Funds exceed £10,000,000

FIRE

AT CURRENT RATES.

LIFE

REDUCED PREMIUM.

HOLME RINGER & Co., Agents, Chemulpo.

HOTEL DU PALAIS

SEOUL.

The only first class Hotel in Seoul. Situated in the centre of the city opposite the palace.

Cuisine under the supervision of an experienced French Chef.

Well ventilated and furnished throughout.

TARIFF UPON APPLICATION

L. MARTIN

Proprietor and Manager.

大韓每日申報
대한매일신보

(뎨팔빅일호) (목요일) 일천구빅사년십일월이십사일

본샤고빅

오신보는영어와한어로석거미
익츌판ᄒᆞᆸ

신문가

한쟝 엽두돈오푼
일삭됴 엽두량닷돈
우표가미삭닷돈
다맛돈으로밧ᄉᆞᆸ

광고료는

긔한의쟝단과ᄌᆞ힝의다쇼로즁
감ᄒᆞ되렴가로밧을터이오며오
리지아녀대한사람마다다이신
문을보실터이니광고내시기를
원ᄒᆞ시는이들은우리신문샤에
와셔면약ᄒᆞ심을희망ᄒᆞᆸ

○발힝소 박동대한미일신보
샤법어학교압헤젼영국인셜필
림집자리오

사쟝 영국인 (비셜)

평양 디리점

○평양효동사는권미보씨로우
리신문관미디리인을뎡ᄒᆞ엿
ᄉᆞ오니평양에계신구람코져ᄒᆞ
시는 쳠군ᄌᆞ는히디리점에왕
림ᄒᆞ와면의ᄒᆞ시옵

사고

○우리대한미일신보의목뎍은
대한의안녕질서에관한모든대
목에디ᄒᆞ야는공평한변론을쥬
쟝ᄒᆞᆷ이라우리동신원의담보는
신문보시는쳠군ᄌᆞ의계ᄒᆞᆼ샹보
도ᄒᆞ리며편지를긔셔ᄒᆞ여주시
는이는셩명과반디를적어붓치
시기를희망ᄒᆞ오니이거슬신문
샹에긔지ᄒᆞ라는거시아니오다
만극히신용ᄒᆞ는증거를삼고쟈
ᄒᆞᆷ이라긔쟈는아모긔셔던지긔
ᄌᆡᄒᆞᆷ을되각ᄒᆞ는권리를가졋ᄉᆞ
나되각ᄒᆞ는리유를말ᄒᆞᆯ터이오
며공즁평화를문란케ᄒᆞ는듯ᄒᆞᆫ
긔셔는의례히밧지안켓ᄉᆞᆸ나이
다

●본사셜시이래로신문을미양
우례로분젼ᄒᆞ와례젼부의임의
로젼ᄒᆞᆫ듯스로면곳에는혹늣게
젼ᄒᆞ기도ᄒᆞ며혹멋칠거슬ᄒᆞᆫ겁
에젼ᄒᆞ기도ᄒᆞ며혹아니젼ᄒᆞ는
곳도잇다ᄒᆞ와우리신문을ᄉᆞ랑
ᄒᆞ야구람ᄒᆞ시는 쳠군ᄌᆞ의계
되ᄒᆞ야미우미안ᄒᆞ옵기로지금
은분젼인을두고미일일즉이젼
ᄒᆞ며아니젼ᄒᆞ거나늣게거나ᄒᆞᆫ
치가업도록ᄒᆞ라ᄒᆞ오니혹아니
젼ᄒᆞ거나혹늣게젼ᄒᆞ거나ᄒᆞᆫ일
이잇스면본샤로통긔ᄒᆞ여쥬심
을희망ᄒᆞᆸ

뎐보

군ᄉᆞ령부착뎐

○졈령평졍산 본월십칠일에
함창부근에잇든우리군ᄉᆞ의일
부디가평졍산부근을직히는바
뎍을공격ᄒᆞᆫ다가이것을격퇴ᄒᆞ
야평졍산을졈령ᄒᆞ엿더라젼리
품은즁디과와무렁ᄒᆞ와마필등이
요사로잡은바는대위일명과하
ᄉᆞ이하오명이잇더라

○유쟁돈소젼 십구일오시량
에유쟁돈의동방에셔젹보병약
이쇼디가역ᄉᆞ를ᄒᆞ며그후방에
약일즁디보병이잇셧기로우리
포병이이것을향ᄒᆞ야사격ᄒᆞ고
피란케ᄒᆞ엿더라

○화약고폭발 십일월십구일
우리히군포의포격으로긔계국
부근에지ᄒᆞᆫ바젹의화약고를폭
발ᄒᆞ엿고또공격ᄒᆞ는일은미리
졍ᄒᆞᆫ것ᄀᆞᆺ치진보ᄒᆞᆫ다ᄒᆞ엿더라

〔이십일오후일시ᄉᆞ십분발

○송슈산졈령 확실ᄒᆞᆫ보고를
거ᄒᆞᆫ즉송슈산포디의폭발은쥬
공이극히큰지라본월십팔일에
우리군ᄉᆞ는크게돌격을힝ᄒᆞ야
동포디의외안을굿세게엄습ᄒᆞ
야확실히졈령홈을엇엇더라

〔이십일오후구시발

○로쟝뎐쥬 론돈로이데루뎐
보를거ᄒᆞᆫ즉려슌의슈쟝스뎃셰
루는로데셰면쥬ᄒᆞ야골ᄋᆞ디려
슌은오히려두어달을지팅ᄒᆞ야
가지겟고신은머리에조곰샹홈
을가졋다ᄒᆞ엿더라

○로데송별 빅임면을거ᄒᆞᆫ즉
아라ᄉᆞ황뎨셔셔파란로우잇지
ᄯᅡ에셔만쥬로발왕ᄒᆞᆯ군디이만
인에게송별ᄒᆞ엿는디히군디에
디포ᄉᆞ십팔문이잇더라

외보

○미국죠합비 론돈뎐을거ᄒᆞᆫ
즉미국국회에셔셔로민든군함
비(그즁에젼투함삼쳑과밋슌
양함오쳑졔죠비도잇슴)로팔
빅이십오만방을쳥구ᄒᆞ는의안
이졔츌되리라더라

○로함명운 려슌을공위ᄒᆞᆫ일
본군ᄉᆞ가재번브터대구경포로
써려슌을포격홈으로항구니에
지ᄒᆞᆫ아라ᄉᆞ군함이여러번피샹
ᄒᆞ야이제는빅옥산포디하에업
듸여일본군ᄉᆞ의포격을피ᄒᆞᆫ다
는디만약빅옥산포디가함낙이
되면일본군ᄉᆞ의공격홈을모폐
키어렵고항외로도츌ᄒᆞ거나불
연ᄒᆞ면일본군ᄉᆞ의란환에ᄀᆞ루
가될지라고로아라ᄉᆞ군ᄉᆞ가셜
혹ᄂᆞᆫ철산으로되각ᄒᆞᆫ드리도일
본군ᄉᆞ가빅옥산포디를졈령ᄒᆞ
면아라ᄉᆞ군함이심히어려울터
이라ᄒᆞ엿더라

○유태인참경 로국에셔군디
동원령을힝ᄒᆞ는때에유태사름
에디ᄒᆞ야포학ᄒᆞᆷ이자심ᄒᆞ야웟데
부스구져자에셔는십일월이십오
일로이십팔일ᄭᆞ지삼일간에유
태인의창표와밋가옥등을샹달
ᄒᆞ는디사샹쟈슈명이잇다더라

○거졀평화 미국대통령루스
벨트씨졔의ᄒᆞᆫ바히아신평화회
의에관ᄒᆞ야일로량국이그동참
ᄒᆞ기를거졀ᄒᆞ엿다더라

○영법협약 금월십이일에발
ᄒᆞᆫ론돈뎐에왈법국대의원에셔
외무경뗼루갓세씨션언ᄒᆞᆫ빠영
법협약에관ᄒᆞ야젼회원ᄉᆞ분에
삼이샹이결의ᄒᆞ엿다더라

○파작함 론돈뎐에왈파
라작함디의일부가구리트도스
셔만에니르럿다ᄒᆞ엿더라

○긔시허셜 빅임에셔발ᄒᆞᆫ뎐
보에왈려슌함락후에일본이영
미법삼국에디ᄒᆞ야즁지ᄒᆞᆷ을구
ᄒᆞᆫ다ᄂᆞᆫ풍셜과밋미국대통령이
졔의ᄒᆞᆫ바평화회의에참동홈을
일로량국이거졀ᄒᆞ엿다ᄂᆞᆫᄉᆞᄂᆞᆫ
다허셜이라ᄒᆞ엿더라

○슈뢰발견 병원션죠어산환
이금월팔일에산동고각등디로
브터북방ᄉᆞ십일도십분되는히
면동방십삼히리쳐에셔긔계슈
뢰를발견ᄒᆞ야직기시에왕리쟈
로ᄒᆞ야곰쥬의케ᄒᆞ기위ᄒᆞ야표
목을셰웟다더라

○미국히군확쟝 론돈에셔발
ᄒᆞᆫ뎐보에왈미국에셔히군인원
을륙만ᄉᆞ쳔ᄉᆞ빅ᄉᆞ십오인으로
확쟝ᄒᆞᆫ다ᄒᆞ엿더라

관보

뎨이쳔구빅팔십구호
광무팔년십일월이십일일
셔임급ᄉᆞ령

○의원면본관 돈령원쥬ᄉᆞ
홍승범 샹의ᄉᆞ쥬ᄉᆞ 김교헌
비셔원랑 죠남일 혜릉참봉
리더웅

○임돈령원쥬ᄉᆞ셔관임관륙등
봉샹ᄉᆞ쥬ᄉᆞ 쟝필원

○인샹의ᄉᆞ쥬등셔판임관륙등
봉샹ᄉᆞ쥬ᄉᆞ 박긔덕

○임봉샹ᄉᆞ쥬ᄉᆞ셔관임관ᄉᆞ등
륙픔 김교헌

○임봉샹ᄉᆞ쥬ᄉᆞ셔판임관칠등
륙픔 홍승범

○임비셔원랑셔관임관칠능
구품 뎡홍셕

○임혜릉참봉셔관임관팔능
리홍쥬

○명분비셔원랑 륙픔 김지
ᄉᆞ

미샹십일월십팔일
궁뎡록ᄉᆞ

○죠왈금번간심지힝온중츄원
의쟝민영쇼로ᄀᆞᆺ치진거ᄒᆞ라
십일월십일일

○죠왈륙군부장리봉의는히
쳑봉시비왕대쟝ᄒᆞ라
십일월십삼일

○죠왈원소자심도감당샹이하
는림시ᄒᆞ라 십일월십팔일

○총호ᄉᆞ신리근명근쥬 원소
져잔심시에시원임대신총호ᄉᆞ
이하진거ᄉᆞ로죠칙이ᄂᆞ리샤
국ᄂᆡ부특진관윤용션은신병이
잇ᄉᆞ와신근명과본도감졔죠민
영달과 궁ᄂᆡ부대신임시셔
리리용태와학부대신임시셔리
박졔슌과쟝례원경죠졍희가모
든디ᄉᆞ를거ᄂᆞ리고명일에츌거
홀뜻으로근샹 쥬ᄒᆞ와광무
팔년십일월십팔일에봉 지
의쥬ᄒᆞ다

군긔창관졔 속

뎨십삼됴 화약졔죠소는륙히
군의슈요ᄒᆞᆫ화약을졔죠ᄒᆞ기
위ᄒᆞ야치홈이니졔죠소장은
포병참령혹졍위로츼우고긔
ᄉᆞ이인과긔슈팔인을치ᄒᆞ야
각기임무를분담홈이라

뎨십ᄉᆞ됴 졔혁소는졔혁ᄉᆞ무
와또군용에슈요ᄒᆞᆫ혁구를졔
죠ᄒᆞ기위ᄒᆞ야치홈이니졔혁
소장은각병과참령졍위혹긔
ᄉᆞ로츼우고긔ᄉᆞ일인파긔슈
ᄉᆞ인을치ᄒᆞ야각기업무를분
담홈이라

뎨십오됴 직죠소는군용의슈

UNION INSURANCE SOCIETY OF CANTON.

Head office Hongkong.
Marine risks underwritten at current rates.
Agents in Chemulpo
E. MEYER & Co.

COMPAGNIE DES MESSAGERIES MARITIMES.

Fortnightly Direct Service.

For Marseilles
via Ports.
Sailing from Yokohama
Calling at Kobe,
Shanghai, Hongkong, Saigon, Singapore,
Colombo, Djibonti, Suez, Port Said
and Marseilles.

For particulars apply to
HOLME RINGER & Co.,
Chemulpo.

HAYASHIDA & Co.,

16 MYENG DONG, CHIN KO KAI, SEOUL.
BRANCH OFFICE AT CHEMULPO.

Money changers, Coal and Wood Merchants, Express Agents.

We are agents for the Pyeng-yang Coal Company and the Karazu Coal Company of Japan. We have the best quality of both anthracite and bituminous coal, and prompt execution of orders is our speciality. Firewood of all kinds kept in stock. Full weight guaranteed. Money of all denominations exchanged at current rates. Parcels received for all parts.

CHINA MUTUAL LIFE INS. CO.

Most favourable terms to policy holders.

Benefit system unsurpassed.

HOLME RINGER & Co.
Agents, Chemulpo.

C. P. R.

CANADIAN PACIFIC RAILWAY COMPANY'S ROYAL MAIL STEAMSHIP LINE.

THE FAST ROUTE BETWEEN CHINA, JAPAN, AND EUROPE VIA CANADA AND THE UNITED STATES.

Route from Hongkong via Shanghai, Nagasaki (Inland Sea of Japan) Kobe, Yokohama Victoria and Vancouver.

Twin Screw Empress Steamship—6,000 Tons—Speed 19 knots.

PROPOSED SAILING FROM YOKOHAMA.
R. M. S. Empress of India.
R. M. S. Empress of Japan.
R. M. S. Empress of China.
R. M. S. Athenian.
R. M. S. Tartar.

Special reduction (first class only) granted to members of the Military, Naval, Diplomatic and Civil services and to Missionaries.

Passengers have choice of ten routes across the Continent of America and have privilege of travelling by any Atlantic Steamship Line.

Round the World passage tickets in connection with the P. and O. S. N., North German Lloyd and Messageries Co.'s **£125.**

All rates payable at current rate of exchange.

For further information, Tickets, Guide Books, etc., apply to

HOLME, RINGER & Co., AGENTS,
Chemulpo.

Grand Hotel,

(Formerly the Station Hotel)

Near the Railway Terminus.
West Gate Seoul.

The Best Hotel in Korea
Handsome new Building.
Fine Airy Rooms
Excellent Cuisine.
Terms Moderate.
Special terms to Missionaries
and to permanent boarders.

Electric cars within 2 minutes' walk.

W. H. EMBERLEY,
Proprieto

EVERY FACILITY.

In connection with Life Assurance Business is afforded by

The Standard Life Assurance Co.,

One of the largest and wealthiest of the Provident Institutions of the United Kingdom. Forms of Application and all information will be promptly afforded on application.

10 CENTS A DAY.

Not a very large expenditure is it? But it is sufficient to secure for a man of 30 a policy with the STANDARD LIFE OFFICE for

$1323.

For all particulars of rates, etc., apply to

Holme, Ringer & Co.,
Agents, Chemulpo.

THE NEW YORK LIFE INSURANCE COMPANY.

Have you ever been declined by any Company?

Are you engaged in a specially hazardous occupation?

Have you heard of the New York Life Insurance Company's New Classifications for this class of Risks?

If not, send your date of birth, occupation and particulars of rejection, if any to

E. MEYER & Co.,
Agents, Chemulpo.

MITSUI BUSSAN KAISHA.
(MITSUI & Co.)

MITSUI GINKO.
(MITSUI BANK.)

The Bank is owned by the members of the Mitsui Family, who, as partners, assume an unlimited responsibility for all liabilities of the Bank:—

Capital ....Yen 5,000,000
Reserve Fund .... " 5,600,000

HEAD OFFICE, TOKYO.

LONDON OFFICE, 34 LIME ST., E. C.

BRANCHES AND AGENCIES:—
New York, San Francisco, Hamburg, Bombay, Singapore, Manila, Hongkong, Amoy, Chefoo, Tientsin.

Kobe, Hakodate, Yokohama, Kure, Yokosuka, Moji, Shimonoseki, Miike, Wakamatsu, Nagasaki, Kuchinotsu, Karatsu, Sasebo, Misume, Taipeh, &c.

Telegraphic Address for all the Offices:
"MITSUI."

A. B. C. AND A. 1 CODES USED.

Contractors of Coal
To the Imperial Japanese Navy. Arsenals and Railway Bureau, Principal Railway Companies and Industrial Work, Home and Foreign Mail and Freight Steamers.

Sole Proprietors
Of the famous Miike, Tagawa and Yamano Coal Mines.

Sole Agents
For the sale of Fukumo, Hokoku, Ichimura, Kanoda, Mannoura, Onoura, Ostuji, Sonoda, Tsubaruro, Yoshinotani, Yoshio, Yurokibura and other coals.

YANGTSE INSURANCE ASSOCIATION, LTD.

The undersigned, having been appointed agents for the above company, are prepared to issue policies and pay losses on marine risks at regular rates.

E. MEYER & Co.,
Agents, Chemulpo.

AMERICAN KOREAN ELECTRIC CO.

Light and Power.

Main Office: Electric Building, Chong No.

RAILWAY DEPARTMENT.

OPERATING CARS BETWEEN EAST AND WEST GATE, EVERY TEN MINUTES:—

First Car leaves East Gate at 7:00 A. M. First Car leaves R. R. Station at 7:25 A. M
Last Car " East Gate at 9:40 P. M. Last " " R. R. Station at 10:05 P.M

OPERATING CARS BETWEEN EAST GATE AND IMPERIAL TOMB TERMINUS, EVERY TWENTY MINUTES:—

CONNECTING WITH EVERY ALTERNATE CAR ARRIVING AT EAST GATE FROM CHONG NO.

First Car leaves East Gate for Tomb at 7:10 A. M.
" " " Tomb for East Gate at 7:35 A. M.
Last " " East Gate for Tomb at 7:50 P. M.
" " " Tomb for East Gate at 8:10 P. M.

OPERATING CARS BETWEEN CHONG NO AND YUNG SAN RIVER EVERY TWELVE MINUTES:—

First Car leaves Chong No for South Gate at 7:12 A. M.
" " " Chong No for Yung San at 7:36 A. M.
" " " South Gate for Chong No at 7:20 A. M.
" " " Yung San for Chong No at 8:09 A. M.
Last " " South Gate for Chong No 10:00 P. M.
" " " Yung San for Chong No at 9:33 P. M.

SPECIAL PRIVATE CARS FURNISHED TO SUIT CONVENIENCE OF PATRONS. PRICES ON APPLICATION AT HEAD OFFICE.

LIGHTING DEPARTMENT.

Where less than 250 candle power of light is used, the rate per month will be
Per 16 candle power incandescent lamp,—All night.—Yen 2.50.
32 candle power incandescent lamp:—All night:—Yen 4.00.
50 candle power incandescent lamp:—All night:—Yen 6.00.
150 " " " " — " " " 10.00.
1200 " " enclosed arc " " " 20.00.

Where more than 250 candle power of light is used, a Meter will be installed, if requested:—Rent of Meter Yen 2.00 per month. Rate of charges by meter reading:—Two Sen per Ampere per hour. (Approximately this is equal to about One Sen per 16 C. P. lamp per hour) Minimum monthly charge where meter is installed, Yen 20.00 per month, which includes rental of meter.

Estimates for installing lights furnished on application.
An assortment of chandeliers always on hand.

K. Murakami,
Photograph Studio
Chinkokai, Seoul.

Printing, Developing and Enlargement, of Photographs always Undertaken.

Korean Views and Pictures Illustrating Native Customs always on Sale.

THE OSAKA SHOSEN KAISHA.

Boats frequently on the berth for Chinnampo.

REGULAR SAILINGS BETWEEN JAPAN AND KOREAN PORTS.

FUSAN AND KOBE VIA SHIMONOSEKI.

OSAKA VIA MOKPO, FUSAN, SHIMONOSEKI AND KOBE.

MOJI DIRECT.

OSAKA VIA KUNSAN, MASANPO, FUSAN, SHIMONOSEKI AND KOBE.

CHEMULPO KUNSAN LINE,
Every three days.

CHEMULPO CHINNAMPO LINE.
Every three days.

For Freight and passage and further particulars apply to
THE OSAKA SHOSEN KAISHA,
Chemulpo

RONDON, PLAISANT & CO.

General Storekeepers and Merchants, Ships Contractors, Tobacconists, Commission and Forwarding Agents, Coal Merchants

IMPORTERS AND EXPORTERS

Seoul & Chemulpo.

W. D. WENTWORTH.

LANDING
AND
SHIPPING AGENT
AND
CUSTOMS BORDER.

12 OURA, NAGASAKI.

STEWARD & CO.

Chemulpo.

Shipchandlers and Storekeepers, Naval and Mercantile Contractors, Landing and Shipping Agents.

STEWARD'S HOTEL

Chemulpo.

Best accommodation in this port for travelers. Clean and well-aired rooms, good cuisine pompt attendance, moderate tariff.

요ᄒᆞᆫ응속직죠와피복을제죠ᄒᆞ기위ᄒᆞ야처ᄒᆞᆷ이니직죠소쟝은갑벽과참령과졍위혹긔소로ᄎᆞ우고긔ᄉᆞ이인과긔슈십인을ᄎᆞᄒᆞ야각기임무를분담ᄒᆞᆷ이라

뎨십륙됴 각소에긔소ᄂᆞᆫ각소쟝의게며긔슈ᄂᆞᆫ긔ᄉᆞ에게각기지휘를슈ᄒᆞ야소무에종ᄉᆞᄒᆞᆷ이라

뎨십칠됴 군용제식의병긔란약긔구지료ᄂᆞᆫ군용을위ᄒᆞ야제죠ᄒᆞᄂᆞᆫ외에ᄂᆞᆫ군부대신의허가를밧지못ᄒᆞ면제죠ᄒᆞᆷ을부득ᄒᆞᆷ이라다만타관청혹인민이물픔의제죠를쳥탁ᄒᆞᆫ셰ᄂᆞᆫ군용제죠ᄉᆞ업에방ᄒᆞ가업슴을한ᄒᆞ야응작ᄒᆞᄂᆞᆫ수를득ᄒᆞ되군부대신의인허를쳥ᄒᆞᆷ이라

뎨십팔됴 본관제ᄂᆞᆫ반포일로브터시힝ᄒᆞᆷ이라

뎨십구됴 광무팔년칠월륙일칙령뎨십팔호군긔창관제ᄂᆞᆫ폐지ᄒᆞᆷ이라

륙희군쟝교분한령

뎨일됴 쟝교ᄂᆞᆫ종신토록그관직을보유ᄒᆞ고그복쟝을착ᄒᆞ고그관직에딕ᄒᆞᆫ례우를향ᄒᆞᄂᆞ니이것을쟝교의분한이라ᄒᆞᆷ이라

뎨이됴 쟝교ᄂᆞᆫ좌에게ᄒᆞᆫ일ᄉᆞᄒᆞᆼ을언ᄒᆞᆷ이아니면그분한을실ᄒᆞᆷ이무이ᄒᆞᆷ이라

뎨일 본인의쳥원을허용ᄒᆞ야그벼슬을면ᄒᆞᆫ셰

뎨이 뎨국인된분한을이러번린때

뎨삼 즁죄의형벌에쳐ᄒᆞᆫ때

뎨ᄉᆞ 삭관션고를바든때

뎨오 금고에쳐ᄒᆞ야그관직을이러버린때

뎨륙 무관된본직분에위빈ᄒᆞ야척지에의지ᄒᆞ야면관된셰

뎨삼됴 쟝교에위쳐를분ᄒᆞᆷ이좌와ᄀᆞᆺᄒᆞᆷ이라

뎨일 현역

뎨이 예비

뎨삼 후비

뎨ᄉᆞ 퇴역

뎨ᄉᆞ됴 현역은현금군무를봉ᄒᆞᄂᆞᆫ쟈와슈학을피명ᄒᆞᄂᆞᆫ쟈와밋륙희군쟝관이각기부니문관을피임ᄒᆞᆫ쟈를칭ᄒᆞᆷ이라륙희군쟝관이졍부니문관을피임ᄒᆞᆫ쟈ᄂᆞᆫ특지로현역에복케ᄒᆞᄂᆞᆫ수가잇슴이라

휴직과밋졍직에지쟈ᄂᆞᆫ현ᄒᆞᆫ역에쥰ᄒᆞᆷ이라

휴직은좌에게ᄒᆞᆫ일ᄉᆞᄒᆞᆼ에인ᄒᆞ야직무가무ᄒᆞᆫ때를이름이라

일 휘딕

이 폐직

삼 졍원지졍

ᄉᆞ 만긔휘임

오 부노되엿든쟈가국긔ᄒᆞ엿스나다른관원이그직위를되임ᄒᆞᆫ때

륙 특별ᄒᆞᆫ임무를종ᄒᆞ엿거나밋슈학만긔된후에취직의명이업ᄂᆞᆫ때

칠 샹리질병이륙ᄀᆡ월에이르도록오히려쾌복이못된때에다만본인에쳥원이잇거ᄂᆞ혹직무에말미암아되월ᄒᆞᆯ필요가잇ᄂᆞᆫ때ᄂᆞᆫ륙ᄀᆡ월을기다리지아니ᄒᆞᆷ이라

팔 본인의쳥원을인ᄒᆞ야슈학을허용ᄒᆞᆫ때

졍직은그힝위가즁계ᄒᆞᆯ만ᄒᆞᆫᄉᆞ가잇거ᄂᆞ그졍상이쵸경ᄒᆞ야지직혹취직ᄒᆞᆷ을그치ᄂᆞᆫ쟈를칭ᄒᆞᆷ이니다문졍직ᄒᆞᆫ쟈ᄂᆞᆫ일ᄀᆡ년이아니면취직ᄒᆞᆷ을엇지못ᄒᆞᆷ이라

뎨오됴 예비ᄂᆞᆫ좌에게ᄒᆞᆫ일ᄉᆞᄒᆞᆼ에당ᄒᆞᆫ쟈를칭ᄒᆞᆷ이라

뎨일 셩지로현역되ᄒᆞᆫ때

뎨이 휴직에지ᄒᆞ야오년에이르도록취직지못ᄒᆞᆫ때다문뎨ᄉᆞ됴뎨이ᄒᆞᆼ의뎨팔뎨구에당ᄒᆞᆫ쟈ᄂᆞᆫ이한에잇지아니ᄒᆞᆷ이라

뎨삼 졍직에지ᄒᆞ야이년에지ᄒᆞ도록취직되지못ᄒᆞᆫ때

뎨ᄉᆞ 륙군각부의외문관에젼임ᄒᆞᆫ때

뎨오 일년지원병으로ᄉᆞ관에피임ᄒᆞᆫ때

뎨륙 예비준ᄉᆞ관하ᄉᆞ로위관에피임ᄒᆞᆫ때

뎨륙됴 후비ᄂᆞᆫ좌의게ᄒᆞᆫ일ᄉᆞᄒᆞᆼ에당ᄒᆞᆫ쟈를칭ᄒᆞᆷ이라

뎨일 일년ᄀᆡ만한되야현역에되ᄒᆞᆫ때

뎨이 예비만긔된때

뎨삼 후비쥰ᄉᆞ관하ᄉᆞ로위관에승임ᄒᆞᆫ때

잡보

○다슈퇴임 셔임ᄒᆞᆯ군슈과궐이이십군이나되ᄂᆞᆫ지라공제가이믜지ᄂᆞᆫ고로니부대신리용태씨가공천즁으로그다슈를퇴ᄒᆞ야죠사ᄒᆞ고슈졍ᄒᆞᄂᆞᆫ즁이라더라

○립표졈딕 남문외도화동한월명가되에일본ᄉᆞ령부로셔긔를세우고터를졈령ᄒᆞ엿다고서셔에셔경무쳥에보고ᄒᆞ엿더라

○현씨셔신 일본에시찰로갓든현영운씨의셔신이 궁니부로츌림ᄒᆞ엿다더라

○심샹립씨 심샹훈씨ᄂᆞᆫ작쟈일밤에립셩ᄒᆞ야쟉일밤에립시ᄒᆞ엿ᄂᆞᆫ뒤근일잔에참졍을피임ᄒᆞᆫ다ᄂᆞᆫ풍셜이잇스며또일변으로ᄂᆞᆫ리근호씨가피임ᄒᆞᆫ다ᄂᆞᆫ말도잇스니좌우간체임이되겟다더라

○ᄉᆞ령관고시 함흥에쥬차ᄒᆞᆫ일본ᄉᆞ령관의고시를히도관찰ᄉᆞ가졍부로벳겨보고ᄒᆞ엿ᄂᆞᆫ딕여좌ᄒᆞ니

대일본한국쥬차군ᄉᆞ령관은함경남북도모든빅셩의게널니포고ᄒᆞ노니우리군ᄉᆞ의젹군된쟈ᄂᆞᆫ아국군딕라너희등죄업ᄂᆞᆫ모든빅셩의게니르러ᄂᆞᆫ츄호도불범ᄒᆞᆯ뿐더러이거슬무휼ᄒᆞ미조익ᄒᆞᄂᆞᆫ어미가ᄉᆞ랑ᄒᆞᄂᆞᆫ아희를보ᄂᆞᆫ것과갓치ᄒᆞᆷ은너희도ᄯᅩᄒᆞᆫ아ᄂᆞᆫ바이라젹군의지나간디방을조셰히시찰ᄒᆞᆫ즉흉포ᄒᆞᆷ이더옥심ᄒᆞ야혹량민을살히도ᄒᆞ며부녀를릉욕식이며민가를불살로며지물을겁탈ᄒᆞ니그참담ᄒᆞᆫ샹은가히형언ᄒᆞᆯ수엄ᄂᆞᆫ지라그런고로젹군을구축ᄒᆞ야다시ᄯᅩ오지못ᄒᆞ게ᄒᆞ야너희를도탄지즁에셔구원ᄒᆞ여내랴ᄒᆞ노니이거시본관의직칙이라함경남북도에군령을포고ᄒᆞ야군ᄉᆞ샹의일체ᄉᆞ건을관리ᄒᆞ니너희가집에잇ᄂᆞᆫ쟈ᄂᆞᆫ그긔거ᄒᆞᆷ을편안히ᄒᆞ고피란ᄒᆞ야리산ᄒᆞᆫ쟈ᄂᆞᆫ즉속히도라옴이가ᄒᆞ고만약우리군딕의치하에잇ᄂᆞᆫ빅셩을가히ᄒᆞᄂᆞᆫ쟈가잇거든너희등은쳔히와셔호소ᄒᆞ야원통ᄒᆞᆷ이업시공편되이판결케ᄒᆞ고우리의게보호를밋고의탁ᄒᆞ야좌긔ᄒᆞᆫ소건을엄히직희라

일은 군졍디역안에셔우리군ᄉᆞ샹힝동을방히ᄒᆞᄂᆞᆫ쟈ᄂᆞᆫ가령도로와교량과텰도와면션등을파피ᄒᆞ며ᄯᅩ그운ᄉᆞᆼᄒᆞᆷ을방히ᄒᆞ며병긔와탄약과량식과기타군슈픔과우편물과또군용건셜물과몃비와슈례등을훼손ᄒᆞ거나파피ᄒᆞ거나혹도젹ᄒᆞ여가져가ᄂᆞᆫ쟈ᄂᆞᆫ군률에쳐벌ᄒᆞᆯᄉᆞ

일은 군졍디역안에셔젹군의힝동ᄒᆞᆷ에편리케ᄒᆞᄂᆞᆫ쟈ᄂᆞᆫ등률에쳐벌ᄒᆞᆯᄉᆞ

일은 군졍디역안에셔보안에히롭게ᄒᆞᆷ이잇ᄂᆞᆫ쟈ᄂᆞᆫ군률에쳐벌ᄒᆞᆯᄉᆞ

일은 본ᄉᆞ령관과쟝관이발ᄒᆞᆫ군ᄉᆞ샹명령을억의ᄂᆞᆫ쟈ᄂᆞᆫ군률에쳐ᄒᆞᆯᄉᆞ

명치삼십칠년십월일

한국쥬차군ᄉᆞ령관

○경졀휴간 본일은미국경졀이라본샤사무에미국인과계관이잇ᄂᆞᆫ고로일일ᄂᆞᆷ뎡보ᄒᆞ오니죠량ᄒᆞ시옵

론셜

일본의반동력

○자초로일본신문에ᄂᆞᆫ바롬부ᄂᆞᆫ뒤로좃차이현령비현령으로계지ᄒᆞᄂᆞᆫ셔론에빅셩들도자긔나라에셔싸홈시작ᄒᆞᄂᆞᆫ거시여당이업ᄂᆞᆫ일로자셔히들알되엇지ᄒᆞᆯ수업시걸어여간거서요ᄯᅩᄒᆞᆫ그즁여러사롬의소견에ᄂᆞᆫ확실히승쳡ᄒᆞᆯ줄로만알아츙동ᄒᆞᆷ으로그리됨에로딕아모리셩취ᄒᆞᆯ줄을졍령알아스며셜혹승쳡ᄒᆞ야셩용ᄒᆞᄂᆞᆫ경우라도망망무여ᄒᆞ야불셩모양일지라

일본메일신문과이스턴월드라ᄒᆞᄂᆞᆫ두신문에게지ᄒᆞ야셜명ᄒᆞᆫ바를본즉아라사에셔ᄂᆞᆫ실샹으로싸호랴ᄒᆞᄂᆞᆫ마음은업고긔왕우리의말ᄒᆞᆫ바와ᄀᆞᆺ치다만연타ᄒᆞ기로만작졍ᄒᆞᆫ듯ᄒᆞ며일본셔ᄂᆞᆫ그동안승쳡ᄒᆞᆷ으로써일ᄒᆞᆷ은빗나스되이ᄂᆞᆫ다만군략샹으로자연히됨이요실샹돗ᄒᆞᆷ에긔이ᄒᆞᆫ병법으로탄복ᄒᆞ도록만단거손업다ᄒᆞ엿ᄂᆞᆫ지라

이졔이신문들에계지ᄒᆞᆫ이과연우리의뜻과합당ᄒᆞᆯ뿐더러ᄯᅩᄒᆞᆫ우리의셜명ᄒᆞᆫ바를면져ᄒᆞ엿슨죡별노히갱언ᄒᆞᆯ거시업스되엇지던지이번싸홈에쇠진케될일이실로밍랑ᄒᆞᆫ자라당초브터신문에계지ᄒᆞ며빅단으로용ᄒᆞ계여란리를이르켜싱명을죽이계ᄒᆞᄒᆞ고과부들과어린자식들로ᄒᆞ야곰눈물을흘녀가되게ᄒᆞ며ᄯᅩᄒᆞᆫ지각잇ᄂᆞᆫ사롬들은참아견되지못ᄒᆞ야눈물을먹음고츌젼케ᄒᆞ기를뉘라셔만드라ᄂᆞᆫ뇨실로칙은ᄒᆞᆫ일이며

ᄯᅩᄒᆞᆫᄶᅵ되쉬조신문을거ᄒᆞᆫ즉신호크로늬클신문에지졍샹형편계지ᄒᆞᆫ거슬번등ᄒᆞᆷ이여좌ᄒᆞ니

우리ᄂᆞᆫ마음을깁히싱각ᄒᆞ여둘일이잇ᄂᆞᆫ지라우리나라이만일아라사를격멸ᄒᆞᆯ지경이면이ᄂᆞᆫ우리의젹국인죡말ᄒᆞᆯ거시업스되지어영국과미국두나라ᄒᆞ야ᄂᆞᆫ불가불승쳡ᄒᆞᆫ리익을ᄒᆞᆷ셰ᄒᆞ여야ᄒᆞᆯ지라영미량국이이반젼쟁에우리나라를방조ᄒᆞ야감졍을뵈일뿐더러한국과만쥬를관리ᄒᆞᆯ일에되ᄒᆞ야차관문뎨에실신치가니ᄒᆞᄂᆞᆫ경우어면균쳠리익놈싱각지아니ᄒᆞᆯ수가업ᄂᆞᆫ거시이졔우리가이두나라로더브력감졍놀힝ᄒᆞᆷ어쟝리에감졍을바를즁거가분명히잇ᄂᆞᆫ지라그러ᄒᆞ나ᄒᆞᆼ샹감졍만싱각ᄒᆞ야나라의리의되ᄂᆞᆫ거슬ᄒᆞᆷ셰난ᄒᆞᆯ거손아니로되ᄯᅩᄒᆞᆫ긔명ᄒᆞᆫ나라들로더부려특별히쳔결ᄒᆞ자ᄒᆞᆷ이로다

근일에위션즁거ᄒᆞ야불일이한가지가잇셧스니만일우리나라졍부에셔론돈과혹축에향ᄒᆞ야일만만원을차관ᄒᆞ야달나ᄒᆞ엿손즉셰샹에셔ᄂᆞᆫ웅당싱각ᄒᆞ기에영미량국이우리나라로더브러감졍이잇손즉은힝영업ᄒᆞᄂᆞᆫ사롬이라도이의리를싱각ᄒᆞ여경변으로말ᄒᆞᆯ쥴로안바이어ᄂᆞᆯ도리혀약차ᄒᆞᆫ거관의팔분이리가더되게강박ᄒᆞᆫ요구ᄒᆞᆯ뿐더러우리나라히관들을보즁ᄒᆞ고방치ᄒᆞ기로ᄒᆞᆫ즉우리나라히관들ᄒᆞᆯ면당으로잡으랴ᄒᆞᄂᆞᆫ거시괴왕에남아므리가와의급나라에공화ᄒᆞᆯ때라도이러케리익오즁쳠ᄒᆞ샹강박히ᄒᆞ지아니ᄒᆞ엿슬더인지라우리ᄂᆞᆫ영미량국에딕ᄒᆞ야아쳠ᄒᆞᆯ리유가실로업스며ᄯᅩᄒᆞᆫ차관사건에잘못됨은무타ㅣ라우리나라외교관들이수단이부죡ᄒᆞ야그리됨일뿐더러아모리감졍올포ᄒᆞᄂᆞᆫ분의라도돈올이왕예비치아니ᄒᆞ엿슬터임올그리됨이여그러ᄒᆞ되[미완]

TELEGRAMS.

Army He-d Quarters Seoul.

On the 20th inst. about 600 Russian cavalry and infantry with 4 guns entered Weitzeko but were attacked by our troops and dislodged from their position at 9 P. M. on the 21st.

FROM JAPAN PAPERS.

Berlin, Nov. 16.

It is reported from Paris that M. Andre, the Minister for War, has resigned, and is to be succeeded by M. Berteaux, a Radical Deputy and broker.

Berlin, Nov. 15.

The Japanese Minister in Paris has complained to the French Government of the frequency with which Russian war vessels visit French harbours (en route to the Far East).

It is stated London that M. Delcasse, Minister for Foreign Affairs, has given an evasive answer to Japan's protest.

Berlin, Nov. 15.

The symptoms signifying an improvement in Anglo-German relations on the part of the Press is heartily welcomed in Germany.

Berlin, Nov. 16.

The Board of Trade inquiry into the damage done the Hull trawling fleet in the North Sea by the Baltic Fleet has commenced at Hull.

London, November 17.

The Earl of Northbrook, P.C., D.C.L., L.L.D., F.R.S., is dead.

Lo November 17.

Admiral Alexeie... been received in audience by H.I.M. the Czar of Russia.

London, November 17.

Mr. Gwynne, of Reuter's Agency, has been appointed editor of the "Standard," consequent upon the change in proprietorship.

Tokyo, November 17.

The Governor of Suez has ordered all traffic northward to be stopped during the passage of the Baltic Squadron through the Suez Canal. Merchantmen have been ordered to refrain from throwing anything in the Canal and to abstain from demonstrations.

London, Nov. 16.

The Russian Minister at Washington, referring to certain vague reports in regard to mediation, declared that Russia would fight to the bitter end, and would listen to no suggestion of mediation.

Berlin, Nov. 15.

A report is current in Paris that Russia will take part in a new Peace Conference such as is proposed by the United States, if held after the present war.

M. Nelidoff, Russian Minister in Paris, states that Russia will not think of making peace with Japan at present.

London, Nov. 16.

Prince Fushimi has called on President Roosevelt and conveyed to him good wishes and friendship of the Emperor of Japan, and hoped there would be still closer relations between the United States and Japan.

President Roosevelt in reply assured the Prince that the sentiments to which he had given expression were shared by the American people, who wished the people of Japan prosperity.

. Later.

President Roosevelt yesterday afternoon returned Prince Fushimi's call, being accompanied by his secretary and military and naval aides-de-camp.

In the evening Prince Fushimi dined at the white House with the President, the staff of the Japanese Legation in Washington, members of the Cabinet, and of the Diplomatic Corps being present.

THE PROBLEM OF WIRELESS TELEGRAPHY.

What remains to be done to make wireless telegraphy a commerical as it is already a practical success? It does not seem necessary to ensure the secrecy of its communications, because inviolable secrecy—as has many times been pointed out—is enjoyed neither by the ordinary telegraph nor the telephone. Any enemy who can "tap" it so as to intercept the message, and, having mastered it can send it on or suppress it as he pleases, and, with a little scientific knowledge, the same trick can be played with even greater ease on a telephone. But the receiving station of neither telegraph nor telephone is sensitive to messages sent out by stations not connected with them, and in this respect they enjoy at present a most enviable advantage over all systems of wireless telegraph. Electric waves or ripples in the ether will set in activity all sufficiently sensitive appliances within their range, whether intended for them or not, and this at once annuls a great part of the benefit that we expected to derive from them. The French have already complained that the great waves sent out by the Poldhu station will prevent them corresponding with ships off their Atlantic coasts, and the complaint seems well founded. How to obviate such objections is the remaining difficulty in the way of the free use of wirelss telegraphy.

That some part of this may disappear in practice seems possible. The operators on the ship lately employed by the "Times" in the Far East seem to have said that they learned in time to distinguish the Russian from the Japanese signals that they unintentionally picked up. They were, in fact, in the postion of a talkative crowd who yet contrives to confine his attention to only those voices that interest him. But this would soon cease to be the case in the presence of an overpowering noise, to which the great waves used in long distance work seem to correspond, and would, of course, be impossible if other waves were flying about, as they would be if the system ever came into general use, simultaneously and in all directions. Hence Mr. Marconi, Sir Oliver Lodge, and their Continental and American rivals have all turned their attention to some system of "syntony," or tuning by which their receiving instruments can be prevented from responding to any impulses but those coming from their own sender; but all such attempts have hitherto failed. It is quite true that an electric circuit can be so arranged as to be in tune with another in the same way as a tuning fork tuned to a certain note will respond when this note is struck on a neighbouring instrument; but the analogy, as is so often the case with experiments on the ether, is not so close as it looks. The tuning fork will respond to the required note and to none other; but the electric circuit, though responding most readily to the one with which it is, as electricians say, "in resonance," will yet respond, even if somewhat less well, to any other within a somewhat wide range. If a tuning fork emitted its peculiar note in response to every piano or brass band that was displaying its noisy activity within hearing, one can imagine how untrustworthy it would be; and the same thing is true, within limits, of wireless telegraphy. Professor Fleming, who has for long been associated with the Marconi experiments, at one time thought that the difficulty had been surmounted, but we fancy he must have been disagreeably undeceived when a rival expert most unkindly contrived to introduce the contumelious word Rats! into the messages which he was receiving from Cornwall before a scientific audience in Piccadilly. That the means of overcoming it will eventually be discovered, or may even now be locked within the bosom of some scientific experimenter, we may all hope. But, so far as can be seen, it has not yet been brought forward.—F. L. in "T.P.'s Weekly."

Kim Byong-do, the captivity of whom has proved quite a serious bone of contention was handed over to the French Legation on Monday.

An observatory is shortly to be erected at Seoul at a cost estimated at Y100,000, says the "Daihan Ilpo.

Yesteaday afternoon a meeting was held in the Finance Department to discuss next year's budget.

A proposition has been made by the Japanese in Fusan for the building of an Electric Railway to run in conjunction with the Seoul-Fusan line.

Ordinary business has been resumed in the Government Departments, official mourning for the Crown Princess being ended yesterday.

Mr. Min Hyung-sik, one of Mr. Yi Chai-kuk's brigade has announced that he is satisfied with his inspection of affairs in Japan and will return to Korea by the first steamer.

Following upon the efforts of his concubine, we are now told that General Hyon Yung-woon has despatched a weighty message to the Palace. The despatch was received on the 19th. inst.

A story is current that a secret Meeting was held by certain officials, when it was decided to request the Minister of a certain Foreign Power to assist in the task of breaking up the Il Chin Hoi society. It seems hardly likely that there will be any outcome of this.

According to the Cleveland Leader, a missionary who has returned to the United States from Jerusalem says that Dowie has flooded the Holy City with circulars announcing that he will enter it riding on a white donkey, and will make the greatest proclamation ever heard on earth.

A Paris physician has designed a house on a rotating platform so as to permit any side of it to be brought into the sunlight at any time of the day. A gas engine moves the platform in conjunction with clockwork mechanism, which enables the house to follow the movement of the sun.

The question of Lieut. Kim Byung Do being handed over to the French Legation for trial becomes more and more serious. It appears that he is now wanted as witness in a case against a French subject. The French Minister has received telegraphic advice from St. Petersburg that Kim Byung Do is really a Russian subject.

The Magistrate of Mil Yang considers himself hardly dealt with and no wonder. Recently he made his annual trip to Seoul with the amount of taxes collected in his district viz: $10,000. The Finance Department refused to receive it however and passed him out to the Household Bureau, where he was told he ought to have paid it to the tax-collector. He has returned to his district to find that gentleman and unburden himself of his treasure, which he has carried some thousand li in a vain endeavour to dispose of it.

Minot, N. D., Oct. 11.—A Great Northern freight train carrying two "knocked down" torpedo boats consigned to Japan was wrecked east of here yesterday. There is talk of spies of the Russian Government doing it. A car journal was tampered with while the train was at the station of Rugby. Two suspected section hands have disappeared. The steel of the torpedo boats was not much damaged, but the woodwork will have to be rebuilt. The material of the wrecked boats is piled up here. That is awkward. But for that Dakota accident those little war canoes might have got here as canned goods, or hardware unenumerated. It was not to be, and now Dakota, for the first time in her existence, will have the uncommon experince of having a temporary naval shipyard established on her soil.—Eastern World.

The two delegates of the Il Chin Hoi Society have a tale of woe to unfold as a result of their mission to the north. The climax of their sorrows was reached, when on arriving in the Whanghai province and being told that the Governor had been freely carrying out his orders to disperse the Chin Po Hoi meetings, they sent a message to him asking for an interview. His reply was brief, but doubtless galling; "Tell the savages with shaved heads that they cannot speak with a Korean nobleman."

In spite of the great pains taken by the Japanese to ensure, a pro-Japanese Government in Korea, there is evidence of the existence of a party, which is not pledged to Japan. How this comes within the scope of military affairs we do not know but the fact remains that General Hasegawa has written to the government complaining that a strong Russian party still exists. Perhaps the Japanese still think that a complaint emanating from military head-quarters will carry more weight than a diplomatic representation.

The Japanese do not seem to be acting up to the high standard, which they set for themselves, in protecting the Koreans. They seem, on the contrary, to be protecting themselves at the expense of those, whom they promised to protect. We hear that the Japanese Minister has informed the Foreign Office that the riot of Kioksan was caused by 20 men, 3 of whom were the leaders, 16 criminals and one doubtful. Seven Japanese were killed in the same affray and the Korean Government is to be held responsible for the relief of their families. Who is to relieve the families of the Koreans, we are not told.

Paris, Oct. 5.—The latest thing in Paris journalism, a paper bearing the title of L'Invisible, made its appearance on the boulevards to-day. The newspaper, which is a decidedly funereal-looking production, is unlike anything that has ever been seen before, for it is printed on black, carbonised paper with white ink. It well deserves its title, The Invisible, for it is almost impossible to read it. It is published at a penny, consists of four pages, and is to be issued on the 5th and 20th of each month. The editor informs his readers that his contributors, unlike those of other journals, will not sign their articles. The staff will be absolutely free, independent, and invisible. Prominence is given on the first page to an "interview with the Pope" by the "Invisible's" special correspondent, who, it is stated, in the momentary absence of Cardinal Merry del Val, imitated his Eminence's voice, and had a conversation on the telephone with Pius X. The other pages are devoted to contributions of a not too interesting nature, news which is not fresh, and a feuilleton. Prizes of £40, £20 and £10 are offered by the editor for the best articles on the subject of social reform.

The Korea Daily News.

Issued at 5 P. M. daily except Sundays.

Rate of Subscription :—
Per Year,............Yen 25.
Per Quarter,..........Yen 7.
Per Month,...........Yen 2.50.

Postage in Korea not charged extra.
Postage abroad charged extra.

Advertisements, 50 sen per day for 1 inch or less.
5 yen per month per inch.
50 yen per year per inch.

All communications to

E. T. BETHELL,
Editor and Publisher,
Pak-tong, Seoul

Tomorrow being an American National Holiday (Thanksgiving Day), there will be no issue of the Korea Daily News.

PORT ARTHUR.

The telegram which we published yesterday purporting to be a message sent by General Stoessel to the Czar to the effect that Port Arthur can hold out for some months longer will come as a surprise to many. Although the Japanese have given up-speculating as to the probable date of the fall of the fortress, all the reports from the front are still couched in terms of optimism and satisfaction with the progress made.

Depending, as we do, upon Japanese sources for most of our news, it is only natural that we receive somewhat one-sided impressions of the conditions and course of events. It is only recently that we have known for certain that the main defenses are still intact and the stories that reached us months ago that Port Arthur would soon be starved into submission or would be compelled to capitulate through lack of ammunition and water have proved incorrect.

Under these circumstances it is hard to know what to believe and the interesting question as to the safety of the warships still in the harbour must for the present remain unanswered. There seems to be no doubt that parts of the harbour are exposed to Japanese fire but as we have of late heard no further reports of damage to the warships we assume that a safe anchorage has been found somewhere.

Now that the Baltic fleet is well on its way, the destruction of the Port Arthur squadron is of the utmost importance to Japan. As will be seen from the following tables Admiral Togo's squadron is not greatly superior to the Baltic fleet and if the Port Arthur squadron remains effective Admiral Togo's task will be a much heavier one.

The following is from the "London Times":—

THE SECOND PACIFIC SQUADRON.

BATTLESHIPS.

Name.	Displacement	L.H.P.	Nominal Speed.	Gun Protection.	Weight of Broadside Fire
Kniaz Suaroff. ….. } Alexander III… Borodino… Orel ……	13,516	16,800	18.0	11,6	4,426
Ossliabia ..	12,674	14,500	19.0	10.5	2,672
Sissot Veliky.	8,880	8500	16.0	12.5	3,186
Navarin	9,476	9,000	16.0	12.6	3,404
ARMOURED CRUISERS					
Dmitri Donskoi	5,893	7,000	15.0	12.2	444
Admiral Nakhimoff....	8,500	9,000	19.0	6.0	944

PROTECTED CRUISERS

Name.	Dis.	L H.P.	N.S.	G.P.	W.B.F.
Oleg........	6,675	19,500	23.9	4.0	872
Aurora.....	6,630	11,600	20.0	4½	632
Svietlana....	3,828	8,500	20.0	4.0	476
Almaz......	3,285	7,500	19.0	—	184
Jemtchug } Izumrud }	3,200	17,000	25.0	—	184

Of the seven battleships in this list, the four first named are of the same class, and are modern vessels. They are unquestionably powerful in every respect. Two were launched in 1901 and two in 1902. They may be compared not unfavourably with our own "Formidable" type af battleship, for, although the latter have a displacement of about 1,500 tons to their advantage, the armament is similar in the two classes. With regard to protection, the Russian ships have a complete belt, and the principal armour is of the same thickness in both types, but the Russians sre lacking somewhat in the protection afforded to their secondary batteries and to the channels for the provision of ammunition. The weight of armour carried by the ships of each class is estimated to be about 4,000 tons. In regard to the disposition of the guns the principal difference is that the 6in. guns are carried in pairs in secondary turrets on the bow, beam, and quarter of the Russian vessels, whereas the secondary armament of the "Formidable" class is in casemates; the Russians in this respect may be said to follow the French system, indeed the ships of the "Borodino" class are not unlike the "Cesarevitch," which was built at La Seyne. The speed of the "Borodino" class is estimated at 18 knots. The other battleships are the "Ossliabia," launched in 1898, a sister ship to the "Peresviet" and "Pobieda," which have been frequently described in the columns of "The Times," the "Sissoi Veliky," a still older vessel and the "Navarin," which dates back to 1891. It will be noticed that this is a very heterogeneous battle squadron, and although the four first named vessels are fairly equal on paper to the Japanese ships they would have to meet, they would be sadly hampered in manoeuvring power and in other respects by their consorts.

To turn to the cruisers, the two vessels classed as "armoured" scarcely deserve this distinction. They have, it is true, both of them been rehabilitated recently and supplied with fresh boilers and engines, but they are far from a match for any of the armoured cruisers of Japan. Of the protected cruisers, the "Oley" is a sister to the "Bogatyr," but a Russian built ship, while the latter was constructed at Stettin. The "Aurora" is a sister to the "Diana," at present laid up at Saigon, and to the "Pallada," which returned to Port Arthur after the battle of Shan-tung. The "Svietlana" is a French built cruiser launched at Havre in 1896. The "Almaz" was originally intended to act as a yacht in the service of Admiral Alexieff, but, like most of the yachts of foreign navies, she carries an armament and her guns have some protection. The "Jemtchug" and "Izumrud" are similar in most of their particulars to the "Novik," detroyed at Korsakovsk. If these six cruisers have not a formidable fighting capacity, they make a fairly useful list of scouts, most of the ships having good steaming capacity, provided their machinery has not been allowed to deteriorate by incompetency or inexperience on the part of the engineers.

Of the remaining vessels attached to the squadron, the 30 torpedo-boats which it was originally stated would accompany the force have apparently dwindled down to seven destroyers. These, however, are all new, are about 216ft. in length, of 27-knot speed, and were constructed in Russia on a design originally supplied by Laird of Birkenhead. In addition there are a number of armed transports, some of which may carry torpedo-boats, a repairing ship, a hospital ship, and various other auxiliary vessels, the services of which will no doubt be found useful during such a voyage.

Opposed to these vessels there is the Japanese fleet which Admiral Togo has so ably commanded, and of which the following is a tabular statement :—

JAPANESE FLEET.

BATTLESHIPS.

Name.	Displacement.	H. I. P.	Nominal Speed.	Gun Protection.	Weight of Broadside Fire.
Asahi...... } Shikishima. }	15,000	15,000	18.0	14.6	4,232
Mikasa....	15,200	16,000	18.0	14.6	4,232
Yashima.. } Fuji ...... }	12,300	13,000	18.0	14.6	4,005
ARMOURED CRUISERS.					
Tokiwa...... } Asama....... }	9,750	18,000	21.5	6.6	1,778
Yakumo......	9,850	16,000	20.0	6.6	1,679
Azuma.... ...	9,436	17,000	21.0	6.6	1,679
Idzumo ... } Iwate ..... }	9,800	15,000	24.7	7.6	1,777
Kasuga ... } Nisshin ... }	7,583	14,000	20.0	6.6	1,686
PROTECTED CRUISERS.					
Takasugo..	4,300	15,500	24.0	4½-2	804
Kasagi.... } Chitose... }	4,784	15,500	22.5	4½	804
Itsukushima } Hashidate.. } Matsushima }	4,277	5,400	16.7	11.4	1,260
Naniwa	3,727	7,120	10.0	0.0	1,200
Takachiho...	3,727	7,120	10.5	0.0	1,200
Akitsushima	3,150	8,400	18.0	—	380
Nitaka......	3,420	9,500	20.0	—	466
Tsushima ...	3,420	9,500	20.0	—	466
Suma	2,700	8,500	20.0	—	335
Akashi.......	2,700	8,500	20.0	—	335
Idzumi......	3,000	6,000	18.0	—	330

A CUSTOMS UNION.

The "Kokumin Shimbun," a well informed Tokio newspaper, says there is talk of establishing a customs union between Korea and Japan. No particulars are given as to its purpose or scope.

An enterprising gentleman named Kim Yong Chon has established a society at Yeung Heung with the object of opposing the Chin Po Hoi. About 100, so far, have enrolled themselves under his standard.

The disastrous fire in the military storehouses at Antung seems to have set the authorities thinking, as we learn that it has now been decided that all the arsenals, factories, etc., belonging to the Imperial Navy, will be closed for the present to any visitors, whether Japanese or foreign.

The Japanese railway between Seoul and Fusan being completed, negotiations are proceeding between the Government Railway Bureau, and the Sanyo and Seoul-Fusan Railway Companies, to inaugurate a through service between Tokyo and Seoul. The distance between the termini and the number of hours computed for the service, are as follows :—

	Miles.	Hrs. Mts.
Tokyo to Kobe	375	16.30
Connection at Kobe ...	—	.30
Kobe to Shimonoseki.	329.	12.00
Connection at Shimo.	—	1.00
Shimonoseki to Fusan, Steamship Intermediary.	140	10.00
Connection at Fusan.	—	1.00
Fusan to Seoul..........	268	15.00
Total	1,112	56.00

The Korea Daily News.

VOL. I, WEDNESDAY, NOVEMBER 23, 1904. No. 108

HONGKONG & SHANGHAI BANKING CORPORATION.

Paid-up Capital..............................$10,000,000
Reserve Fund:—Sterling Reserve... 10,000,000
Silver Reserve..... 7,000,000

27,000,000
Reserve Liability of Proprietors... 10,000,000

HEAD OFFICE, HONGKONG.

London Bankers, London and County Banking Company Limited.

Branches and Agencies,

London.		
Amoy,	Hankow	Penang,
Bangkok,	Hiogo,	Rangoon,
Batavia,	Iloilo,	Saigon,
Bombay,	Lyons,	San Francisco,
Calcutta,	Manila,	Singapore,
Colombo,	Nagasaki,	Sourabaya,
Foochow,	New York,	Tientsin,
Hamburg,	Peking,	Yokohama,

Credits granted on approved Securities, and every description of Banking and Exchange business transacted.

Drafts granted on London and the chief Commercial places in Europe, India, Australia, America, China and Japan.

HOLME RINGER & Co., AGENTS, CHEMULPO.

ON CHEONG & CO., SEOUL.

GENERAL STORE KEEPERS.

Imported provisions, Cooking Utensils Crockery, etc.

FRESH BREAD DAILY.

MITSU BISHI DOCKYARD & ENGINE WORKS, NAGASAKI.

CODE WORD, "DOCK."

A. 1, A. B. C., and Engineering Codes used.

DOCK No. 1 (at Tategami).

Extreme Length..............523 feet
Length on blocks............ 513 ,,
Width of Entrance on Top......89 ,,
,, ,, Bottom....77 ,,
Water on Blocks at Spring Tide 26½ ,,

DOCK No. 2 (Mukaijima).

Extreme Length..............371 feet
Length on Blocks.............360 ,,
Width of Entrance on Top......66 ,,
,, ,, Bottom 53 ,,
Water on Blocks at Spring Tide 22 ,,

PATENT SLIP (at Kosuge).

Can take vessels up to 1,000 tons gross.

THE WORKS are well equipped with the LATEST IMPROVEMENTS, and can execute any kind of work in SHIPBUILDING and MARINE ENGINEERING, as well as in REPAIRING of SHIPS.

The COMPANY'S new powerful steamer OURA-MARU, (712 tons, 700 I.H.P.), specially built for SALVAGE PURPOSES, and equipped with necessary gear, is always READY at SHORT NOTICE.

CHARTERED BANK OF INDIA AUSTRALIA & CHINA.

INCORPORATED BY ROYAL CHARTER 1853

HEAD OFFICES:—LONDON.

Paid-up Capital £800,000
Reserve Liability of Shareholders 800,000
Reserve Fund 800,000

Drafts granted upon all the principal places in the world and every description of Exchange and banking business transacted.

E. MEYER & Co., Agents, Chemulpo.

E. MEYER & CO. Chemulpo.

SOLE AGENTS IN KOREA FOR:

A. T. Morse, Sons & Co's "Fresco" Distemper

In all colours ready for use on walls, Ceilings etc.

and

AVENARIUS CARBOLINEUM

A wood-preserving and antiseptic oil preparation

Against decay, dry-rot, fungus and wood-destroying insects.

A large supply always in Stock. Prices upon application.

E. MEYER & Co., Chemulpo.

THE METHODIST PUBLISHING HOUSE, Little West Gate, Seoul.

JOB PRINTING, TYPEWRITER PAPER
CARBON PAPER, VISITING CARDS
STATIONERY, BOOK BINDING
BOOK PUBLISHERS
AMERICAN SCHOOL BOOKS
SPENCERIAN COPY BOOKS
PEN CARBON LETTER AND BILL BOOKS

S. A. BECK, Manager.

HOKURKU DOBOKU KAISHA.

Branch office in Chong Dong, Seoul.

Japanese telephone No. 165

CONTRACT DEPARTMENT.

We can contract to build any building or construction.

MERCHANDISE DEPARTMENT.

We can provide any building material. We have just contracted to build the new Belgian Legation.

DAI-ICHI GINKO, LIMITED.

(Formerly the First National Bank)

ESTABLISHED 1873

INCORPORATED UNDER PRESENT LAW 1896

Capital - - - - - - - - Yen 5,000,000
Reserve Fund - - - - - 1,500,000

HEAD OFFICE:—TOKIO.

President: Baron SHIBUSAWA.

BRANCHES AND CORRESPONDENTS In the Principal Cities and Towns of Japan.

Interest Allowed on

Fixed deposits 1 year - - - 6½ per cent
" " 6 months - - - 6 per cent

Special current accounts 1½ sen daily per Y 100
General " " 1 " " " 100

M. TANAKA, Manager, Chemulpo.

SINGER SEWING MACHINES

씽거조봉침

SOLE AGENTS FOR KOREA

전매쇼

HOLME RINGER & CO. Chemulpo.

제물포 함릉거양힝

KAMEYA & CO.

GENERAL STOREKEEPERS

Chinkokai - - Seoul

(Established 1895, Tokyo)

Confectionery, Hams, Canned Goods, Cutlery, Hirano & Tansan Water. Provisions, Gents, Furnishing goods, Toilet Articles, Travelling Bags, Tobacco, Cigars & Cigarettes Kitchen Utensils. Coffee, Biscuits

Fresh Goods always kept in Stock.

Prices [illegible]

Please come and inspect our goods

NIPPON YUSEN KAISHA.

JAPANESE MAIL STEAMSHIP CO.

UNDER MAIL CONTRACT WITH THE IMPERIAL JAPANESE GOVERNMENT.

European Line

Regular Fortnightly Service between Yokohama Kobe, Moji, Shanghai, Hongkong, Singapore, Penang Colombo, Port Said, Marseilles, London and Antwerp

American Line

Regular Fortnightly Service between Hongkong and Seattle, calling at Shanghai, Moji, Kobe, Yokohama and Victoria, B. C.

Australian Line

Regular weekly Service betwen Japan Ports and Australia, calling at Hongkong and Manila.

(Above Three Lines Suspended until further notice).

Shanghai Line

Weekly Service between Shanghai and Japan Ports

Korea Line

Service Kobe, Moji, Nagasaki, Fusan Chemupo Cheffoo, Taiku.

S. S. [illegible]berg, 2181 tons.

[illegible] Kobe, Moji, Fusan, Chemulpo, Chinnampo

S. S. ARGO, S. S. Ohio.

BORDEN'S CONDENSED MILK CO.

New York, U. S. A.

ALWAYS IN STOCK

Eagle Brand Condensed Milk.

Gold Seal Condensed Milk.

Peerless (Family) Evaporated Cream.

Borden's Malted Milk.

E. MEYER & CO. Chemulpo, Korea, Sole Agents

ROYAL INSURANCE COMPANY,

Funds exceed £10,000,000

FIRE

AT CURRENT RATES.

LIFE

REDUCED PREMIUM.

HOLME RINGER & Co., Agents, Chemulpo.

HOTEL DU PALAIS

SEOUL.

The only first class Hotel in Seoul, Situated in the centre of the city opposite the palace.

Cuisine under the supervision of an experienced French Chef.

Well ventilated and furnished throughout.

TARIFF UPON APPLICATION

L. [illegible]

Proprietor and Manager.

大韓每日申報

대한미일신보

(뎨일빅구호) (일요일) 일쳔구빅ᄉᆞ년십일월이십륙일

본사고빅

이 신보는 영어와 한어로 셕지 미일 출판ᄒᆞᆷ

신문가

한쟝 엽뎐두돈오푼

일삭도 엽뎐두량닷돈

우표가 미삭 닷돈

다 엽뎐으로 밧숩

광고료는

귀한의 쟝단과 ᄌᆞ항의 다쇼로 종감ᄒᆞ되 렴가로 밧을터이오며 오린지 아니ᄒᆞ야 대한사람마다 다 이 신문을 보실터이니 광고내시기를 원ᄒᆞ시는이들은 우리 신문샤에 와셔 면약ᄒᆞ심을 희망ᄒᆞᆷ

○발ᄒᆡᆼ소 박동 대한미일신보샤 법어학교 앏헤 젼 영국인 셜필림 집자리오

샤쟝 영국인 (비셜)

평양 디리졈

○평양 효동 사는 권미보씨로 우리 신문 관미 디리인을 뎡ᄒᆞ엿스오니 평양에 계신 구람코져ᄒᆞ시는 쳠군ᄌᆞ는 항 디리졈에 왕림ᄒᆞ와 면의ᄒᆞ시옵

샤고

○우리 대한미일신보의 목뎍은 대한의 안녕질셔에 관한 모든 대목에 되ᄒᆞ야는 공평한 변론을 쥬쟝ᄒᆞᆷ이라 우리 동신원의 탐보는 신문보시는 쳠군ᄌᆞ의 계ᄒᆞᆫ 샹보도ᄒᆞ리며 편지를 긔셔ᄒᆞ며 주시는이는 셩명과 번디를 젹어 붓치시기를 희망ᄒᆞ오니 이 긔슨 신문샹에 긔졔ᄒᆞ란는거시 아니오 다만 극히 신용ᄒᆞ는 증거를 숨고자ᄒᆞᆷ이라 긔자는 아모 긔셔던지 긔지ᄒᆞᆷ을 퇴각ᄒᆞ는 권리를 가젓스나 퇴각ᄒᆞ는 리유를 말ᄒᆞᆯ터이오며 공중 광고를 문란케ᄒᆞ는 듯ᄒᆞᆫ 긔셔는 의례히 밧지 안켓숩나이다

●본사셜시 이러로 신문을 미양 우리로 분젼ᄒᆞ와 리젼부의 일의로 젼ᄒᆞ든 것ᄉᆞ로 민곳에는 ᄒᆞᆼ늣게 젼ᄒᆞ기도ᄒᆞ며 혹 면칠 긔슬ᄒᆞᆫ 겁에 젼ᄒᆞ기도ᄒᆞ며 혹 아니 젼ᄒᆞ는 곳도 잇다ᄒᆞ와 우리 신문을 ᄉᆞ랑ᄒᆞ야 구람ᄒᆞ시는 쳠군ᄌᆞ의게 티ᄒᆞ야 미우 미안ᄒᆞ옴기로 지금은 분젼인을 두고 미일 조이 젼ᄒᆞ며 아니 젼ᄒᆞ거나 늣게 거나ᄒᆞᆫ 치가 엽도록ᄒᆞ란ᄒᆞ오니ᄒᆞ야니 젼ᄒᆞ거나 혹 늣게 젼ᄒᆞ거나ᄒᆞᆫ 일이 잇스면 본샤로 통긔ᄒᆞ여 주심을 희망ᄒᆞᆷ

관보

뎨이쳔구빅구십ᄉᆞ호

광무팔년십이월이십이일

셔임급ᄉᆞ령

○명례궁원도졔조셔칙임관일등 궁내부특진관 죠병세

○의원면본관 혜릉참봉 리ᄒᆞᆼ쥬

○혜릉참봉셔판임관팔등 륙품 리뎡응

○임등신ᄉᆞ 면화과쥬ᄉᆞ셔판임관팔등 쟝릉참봉 남뎡칠

○임쟝릉참봉셔판임관팔등 신영셥

○승셔판임관오등 샹의ᄉᆞ쥬ᄉᆞ 박귀틱 면션ᄉᆞ쥬ᄉᆞ 박용구

이샹십이월십구일

○명궁내부특진관셔칙임관삼등 경효뎐졔조 죠종필

십이월이십일

륙군쟝교분한령 속

뎨칠됴 퇴역은후비만긔에지ᄒᆞᆫ자와밋샹리질병으로영구국역을쳔티지못ᄒᆞ야현역이나예비나후비에퇴ᄒᆞᆫ쟈를칭ᄒᆞᆷ이라

뎨팔됴 예비후비는층히소집에응ᄒᆞᆷ이라

뎨구됴 분령은쟝교샹당관에도젹용ᄒᆞᆷ이라

륙군무관진급령

뎨일됴 륙군무관의진급은급을ᄯᆞ라챠뎨진ᄒᆞᆷ이니견원이업는셰는보셔ᄒᆞᆷ을엇지못ᄒᆞᆷ이라

뎨이됴 륙군무관의진급은실역졍년최하긔한을지나지아니ᄒᆞ면진급ᄒᆞᆷ을엇지못ᄒᆞᆷ이라

뎨삼됴 실역졍년최하긔한을졍ᄒᆞᆷ이여좌와ᄀᆞᆺᄒᆞᆷ이라

참교에셔부교에진ᄒᆞᆷ은반년이오부교로졍교에진ᄒᆞᆷ은일년이오졍교로특무졍교에진ᄒᆞᆷ은이년이오특무졍교로참위에진ᄒᆞᆷ은이년으로졍ᄒᆞᆷ이라

다만헌병졍교리등참위에진ᄒᆞᆷ은수년으로졍ᄒᆞᆷ이라

참위로부위와부위로졍위에진ᄒᆞᆷ은각이년이오졍위로참령에진ᄒᆞᆷ은ᄉᆞ년으로졍ᄒᆞᆷ이라

참령으로부령에진ᄒᆞᆷ은삼년이오부령으로졍령과졍령으로참쟝에진ᄒᆞᆷ은각이년으로졍ᄒᆞᆷ이라

참쟝으로부쟝에진ᄒᆞᆷ은삼년이오부쟝으로디쟝에진ᄒᆞᆷ은뎡젼쟈의취ᄒᆞ야 특지로써쳠림ᄒᆞ는례가됨으로실역뎡년최하긔한으로졍치아니ᄒᆞᆷ이라

뎨ᄉᆞ됴 젼시에졔ᄒᆞ야는각관의실역뎡년을반감ᄒᆞᆷ을엇음이라

뎨오됴 휴직과밋졍직의년월은실역졍년에산립지아니ᄒᆞᆷ

다만졍에계조되기뢰ᄒᆞ야휴직ᄒᆞᆫ자가졍당ᄒᆞᆫ리[illegible]잇는쟈는그년월을실역졍년에산립ᄒᆞᆷ을득ᄒᆞᆷ이라

뎨륙됴 륙군무관진급방이셔두가지가잇스니일은뎡년보셔보셔라ᄒᆞᆷ이ᄉᆞ

뎨칠됴 뎡년보셔는실역뎡년최하긔한을지난슈챠에죵ᄒᆞ야진급케ᄒᆞᆷ을이름이오발탁보셔는실역뎡년최하긔한을지나지아니ᄒᆞ야도발탁진급케ᄒᆞᆷ을이름이니그구별이좌와ᄀᆞᆺᄒᆞᆷ이라

참교로부교로졍교와졍교로특무졍교에진ᄒᆞᆷ은다발탁으로ᄒᆞᆷ이라

참위로부위에진ᄒᆞᆷ은뎡년샹분지이발탁삼분지일이오부위로졍위에진ᄒᆞᆷ은뎡년과발탁이샹반이오졍위로참령과참령으로부령과부령으로졍령에진ᄒᆞᆷ은다발탁으로ᄒᆞᆷ이라

젼시ᄒᆞᆫ수번에졔ᄒᆞ야동원을힝ᄒᆞᆫ각부대에속ᄒᆞᆫ부참위의진급은다발탁으로ᄒᆞᆷ이라

뎨팔됴 특무졍교와헌병졍교가참위에진급ᄒᆞᆷ은젼시에공젹이발군ᄒᆞ고쟝교에젹당ᄒᆞᆫ학력이잇는쟈만한ᄒᆞᆷ이라

뎨구됴 쟝교는직권에의지ᄒᆞ야부하를발탁ᄒᆞ는권이잇스나다만직속쟝관이잇는쟈는그뎜을특히예졔ᄒᆞ야비로힝ᄒᆞᆷ이라

뎨십됴 쟝관의진급과밋쟝관에진ᄒᆞᆷ은 샹지로ᄒᆞᆷ이나몬져니지를군부대신에게일음을에로ᄒᆞᆷ이라

뎨십일됴 군부대신은미년쟝교의실역뎡년평부를작ᄒᆞ야샹쥬ᄒᆞᆷ이라

뎨십이됴 쟝교의발탁진급ᄒᆞᆯ보와밋좌ᄉᆞ관의쟝교에진급ᄒᆞ는후보는 샹쥬로졍ᄒᆞ나니군부대신은 샹지를봉ᄒᆞ야견졍후보명부를조졔ᄒᆞᆷ이라

뎨십삼됴 하ᄉᆞ가준ᄉᆞ관에진급과밋하ᄉᆞ에진급ᄒᆞ는후보는수단쟝과밋차외동등이샹권이잇는쟝관과병경리국쟝과밋외무국쟝이차를졔견ᄒᆞ야견졍후보명부를조졔ᄒᆞᆷ이라

뎨십ᄉᆞ됴 견졍후보명부는고조졔일로브터차년견졍후보명부조졔일ᄭᆞ지쓸미라

뎨십오됴 좌의경우에졔ᄒᆞ야는젼조례에의지아니ᄒᆞ고진급케ᄒᆞᆷ을득ᄒᆞᆷ이라

일 젹젼에졔ᄒᆞ야슈훈을쥬ᄒᆞ야슈쟝이젼군에포고ᄒᆞᆫ자

이 군디가젹젼에졔ᄒᆞ야인원이결핍ᄒᆞ야보셔졍규를반부미능치못ᄒᆞᆫᄯᆡ

뎨십륙됴 발군일에당ᄒᆞ야젼디에림ᄒᆞ는슈쟝의게는특히보셔ᄒᆞ는권리를증미ᄒᆞᆷ이라

뎨십칠됴 쟝교샹당관병위셩부경리부군악부하ᄉᆞ와밋계용쟝의진급은쟝교와밋졍병과하ᄉᆞ진급례에의지ᄒᆞᆷ이라

뎨십팔됴 졍교가특무졍교에진급ᄒᆞᆷ은긔ᄅᆞᆯ디후팔긔년이샹복역ᄒᆞᆫ쟈에만한ᄒᆞᆷ이라

졔조공병졍교와밋조공병일등졔공쟝의조공병샹등공쟝에진급ᄒᆞᆷ은ᄃᆡ로ᄒᆞ후 (조병공쟝후보ᄒᆞᆯ도출신ᄒᆞᆫ쟈로ᄒᆞ림교후) 팔긔년이샹복역ᄒᆞ고실역뎡년이이년을과ᄒᆞᆫ쟈에만한ᄒᆞᆷ이라

젼항조공병졍교의진급에되ᄒᆞ야는그복역년증군긔창출셩부에셔이긔년이샹복역ᄒᆞᆷ을가ᄒᆞᆷ이라

뎨십구됴 일등군악슈의군악쟝보에진급ᄒᆞᆷ은실역뎡년최하한을이년으로졍ᄒᆞᆷ이라

UNION INSURANCE SOCIETY OF CANTON.

Head office Hongkong.
Marine risks underwritten at current rates.
Agents in Chemulpo.
E. MEYER & Co.

COMPAGNIE DES MESSAGERIES MARITIMES.

Fortnightly Direct Service.

For Marseilles
via Ports.
Sailing from Yokohama
Calling at Kobe,
Shanghai, Hongkong, Saigon, Singapore,
Colombo, Djibonti, Suez, Port Said
and Marseilles.

For particulars apply to
HOLME RINGER & Co.,
Chemulpo.

HAYASHIDA & Co.,

16 MYENG DONG, CHIN KO KAI, SEOUL.
BRANCH OFFICE AT CHEMULPO.

Money changers, Coal and Wood Merchants, Express Agents.

We are agents for the Pyeng-yang Coal Company and the Karazu Coal Company of Japan. We have the best quality of both anthracite and bituminous coal, and prompt execution of orders is our speciality. Firewood of all kinds kept in stock. Full weight guaranteed. Money of all denominations exchanged at current rates. Parcels received for all parts.

CHINA MUTUAL LIFE INS. CO.

Most favourable terms to policy holders.

Benefit system unsurpassed.

HOLME RINGER & Co.
Agents, Chemulpo.

C. P. R.

CANADIAN PACIFIC RAILWAY COMPANY'S ROYAL MAIL STEAMSHIP LINE.

THE FAST ROUTE BETWEEN CHINA, JAPAN, AND EUROPE VIA CANADA AND THE UNITED STATES.

Route from Hongkong via Shanghai, Nagasaki (Inland Sea of Japan) Kobe, Yokohama Victoria and Vancouver.

Twin Screw Empress Steamship—6,000 Tons—Speed 19 knots

PROPOSED SAILING FROM YOKOHAMA.
R. M. S. Empress of India.
R. M. S. Empress of Japan.
R. M. S. Empress of China.
R. M. S. Athenian.
R. M. S. Tartar.

Special reduction (first class only) granted to members of the Military, Naval, Diplomatic and Civil services and to Missionaries.

Passengers have choice of ten routes across the Continent of America and have privilege of travelling by any Atlantic Steamship Line.

Round the World passage tickets in connection with the P. and O. S. N., North German Lloyd and Messageries Co.'s **£125.**

All rates payable at current rate of exchange.

For further information, Tickets, Guide Books, etc., apply to

HOLME, RINGER & CO., AGENTS,
Chemulpo.

Grand Hotel,

(Formerly the Station Hotel)

Near the Railway Terminus, West Gate Seoul.

The Best Hotel in Korea.
Handsome new Building.
Fine Airy Rooms
Excellent Cuisine.
Terms Moderate.
Special terms to Missionaries
and to permanent boarders.

Electric cars within 2 minutes' walk.

W. H. EMBERLEY,
Proprietor

EVERY FACILITY.

In connection with Life Assurance Business is afforded by

The Standard Life Assurance Co.,

One of the largest and wealthiest of the Provident Institutions of the United Kingdom Forms of Application and all information will be promptly afforded on application.

10 CENTS A DAY.

Not a very large expenditure is it? But it is sufficient to secure for a man of 30 a policy with the STANDARD LIFE OFFICE for

$1323.

For all particulars of rates, etc., apply to

Holme, Ringer & Co.,
Agents, Chemulpo.

THE NEW YORK LIFE INSURANCE COMPANY.

Have you ever been declined by any Company?

Are you engaged in a specially hazardous occupation?

Have you heard of the New York Life Insurance Company's New Classifications for this class of Risks?

If not, send your date of birth, occupation and particulars of rejection, if any to

E. MEYER & Co.,
Agents, Chemulpo.

MITSUI BUSSAN KAISHA.
(MITSUI & Co.)

MITSUI GINKO.
(MITSUI BANK.)

The Bank is owned by the members of the Mitsui Family, who, as partners, assume an unlimited responsibility for all liabilities of the Bank:—

Capital....................Yen 5,000,000
Reserve Fund .... " 5,600,000

HEAD OFFICE, TOKYO.
LONDON OFFICE, 34 LIME ST., E. C.

BRANCHES AND AGENCIES:—
New York, San Francisco, Hamburg, Bombay, Singapore, Manila, Hongkong, Amoy. Chefoo, Tientsin.

Kobe, Hakodate, Yokohama, Kure, Yokosuka, Moji, Shimonoseki, Miike, Wakamatsu, Nagasaki, Kuchinotsu, Karatsu, Sasebo, Misume, Taipeh, &c.

Telegraphic Address for all the Offices:
"MITSUI"
A. B. C. AND A. 1 CODES USED.

Contractors of Coal

To the Imperial Japanese Navy. Arsenals and Railway Bureau, Principal Railway Companies and Industrial Work, Home and Foreign Mail and Freight Steamers.

Sole Proprietors

Of the famous Miike, Tagawa and Yamano Coal Mines.

Sole Agents

For the sale of Fukuno, Hokoku, Ichimura, Kanoda, Mannoura, Onoura, Ostuji, Sonoda Tsubaruro, Yoshinotani, Yoshio, Yurokibura and other coals.

YANGTSE INSURANCE ASSOCIATION, LTD.

The undersigned, having been appointed agents for the above company, are prepared to issue policies and pay losses on marine risks at regular rates.

E. MEYER & Co.,
Agents, Chemulpo.

AMERICAN KOREAN ELECTRIC CO.

Light and Power.

Main Office: Electric Building, Chong No.

RAILWAY DEPARTMENT.

OPERATING CARS BETWEEN EAST AND WEST GATE, EVERY TEN MINUTES:—

First Car leaves East Gate at 7:00 A. M. First Car leaves R. R. Station at 7:25 A. M
Last Car " East Gate at 9:40 P. M. Last " " R. R. Station at 10:05 P.M

OPERATING CARS BETWEEN EAST GATE AND IMPERIAL TOMB TERMINUS, EVERY TWENTY MINUTES:—

CONNECTING WITH EVERY ALTERNATE CAR ARRIVING AT EAST GATE FROM CHONG NO.

First Car leaves East Gate for Tomb at 7:10 A. M.
" " " Tomb for East Gate at 7:35 A. M.
Last " " East Gate for Tomb at 7:50 P. M.
" " " Tomb for East Gate at 8:10 P. M.

OPERATING CARS BETWEEN CHONG NO AND YUNG SAN RIVER EVERY TWELVE MINUTES:—

First Car leaves Chong No for South Gate at 7:12 A. M.
" " " Chong No for Yung San at 7:36 A. M.
" " " South Gate for Chong No at 7:20 A. M.
" " " Yung San for Chong No at 8:09 A. M.
Last " " South Gate for Chong No 10:00 P. M.
" " " Yung San for Chong No at 9:33 P. M.

SPECIAL PRIVATE CARS FURNISHED TO SUIT CONVENIENCE OF PATRONS. PRICES ON APPLICATION AT HEAD OFFICE.

LIGHTING DEPARTMENT.

Where less than 250 candle power of light is used, the rate per month will be
Per 16 candle power incandescent lamp,—All night.—Yen 2.50.
32 candle power incandescent lamp:—All night:—Yen 4.00.
50 candle power incandescent lamp:—All night:—Yen 6.00.
150 " " " " — " " 10.00.
1200 " " enclosed arc " " " " 20.00.

Where more than 250 candle power of light is used, a Meter will be installed, if requested:—Rent of Meter Yen 2.00 per month. Rate of charges by meter reading:—Two Sen per Ampere per hour. (Approximately this is equal to about One Sen per 16 C. P. lamp per hour) Minimum monthly charge where meter is installed, Yen 20.00 per month, which includes rental of meter.

Estimates for installing lights furnished on application.

An assortment of chandeliers always on hand.

K. Murakami.

Photograph Studio
Chinkokai, Seoul.

Printing, Developing and Enlargement, of Photographs always Undertaken.

Korean Views and Pictures Illustrating Native Customs always on Sale.

THE OSAKA SHOSEN KAISHA.

Boats frequently on the berth for Chinnampo.

REGULAR SAILINGS BETWEEN JAPAN AND KOREAN PORTS.

FUSAN AND KOBE VIA SHIMONOSEKI.

OSAKA VIA MOKPO, FUSAN, SHIMONOSEKI AND KOBE.

MOJI DIRECT.

OSAKA VIA KUNSAN, MASANPO, FUSAN, SHIMONOSEKI AND KOBE.

CHEMULPO KUNSAN LINE,
Every three days.

CHEMULPO CHINNAMPO LINE.
Every three days.

For Freight and passage and further particulars apply to

THE OSAKA SHOSEN KAISHA,
Chemulpo

LONDON, PLAISANT & CO.

General Storekeepers and Merchants, Ships Contractors, Tobacconists, Commission and Forwarding Agents, Coal Merchants

IMPORTERS AND EXPORTERS

Seoul & Chemulpo.

W. D. WENTWORTH.

LANDING
AND
SHIPPING AGENT
AND
CUSTOMS BORDER.

12 OURA, NAGASAKI.

STEWARD & CO.

Chemulpo.

Shipchandlers and Storekeepers, Naval and Mercantile Contractors, Landing and Shipping Agents.

STEWARD'S HOTEL

Chemulpo.

Best accommodation in the port for travelers. Clean and well-aired rooms, good cuisine and prompt attendence, moderate tariff.

군악쟝보가군악쟝에진급홈은실역뎡년오년을지니고공뵈가발군ᄒᆞᆫ자에ᄒᆞᆫᄒᆞᆷ이라

뎨이십됴 젼됴에외지ᄒᆞ야진급홈은다반탁으로홈이라

뎨이십일됴 단과하수된참교ᄂᆞᆫ평시제지ᄒᆞ야부교에진급홈이업슴이라

뎨이십이됴 긔국오빅수년칙령뎨구십오호륙군무관진급령은본령반포일로브터폐지홈이라

잡보

○당파조직 근일졍부에ᄒᆞᆫ당파가새로조직이되야신긔션을ᄃᆞᆫ명리용리리근호리근퇴리근샹뎨셰가단톄로졍권을쥬쟝ᄒᆞᆫ다더라

○경수신임 리근호씨ᄂᆞᆫ경무수를피임ᄒᆞ엿더라

○션분진불 리근호씨가모외국인에게지화삼쳔원을션분으로보닌ᄂᆞᆫ티원동모대신이즁간에진불ᄒᆞᆫ지라리씨간에ᄂᆞᆫ싸홈이ᄂᆞᆫ걱ᄒᆞᆫ즁이라더라

○민공사발명 쥬쳥ᄒᆞ수민영쳘씨회면을거ᄒᆞᆫ즉 비공홍셔ᄂᆞᆫ됴핀을의지ᄒᆞ야아라사공관에셔명ᄒᆞ엿고연회에ᄂᆞᆫ참예치아니ᄒᆞ엿다ᄒᆞ엿스되일본공ᄉᆞ가이사진에티ᄒᆞ야권고홈이잇ᄂᆞᆫ지라민공사를면관ᄒᆞᆫ다더라

○일진회고시 일진회에서연 [illegible]

TELEGRAMS.

FROM JAPAN PAPERS.

Berlin, November 17.

The Russian Government has refused to accept offers by several British and American firms to undertake the work of doubling the line on the Siberian railway, preferring to carry out the task itself.—Mainichi.

The Tokio Foreign Department has received a telegram stating that the auxiliary cruisers Oleg, Izumrud, Lion, Donie Isle, and Nielegg, and eight destroyers, belonging to the Baltic Squadron, left Libau on the 16th inst. According to a later report, the Russian cruiser Oleg, four auxiliary cruisers, and six torpedo-boats, passed the southern point of Sweden on the 17th, at 3 p. m. It is believed that they will join the portion of the Baltic Squadron which is to pass through the Suez Canal.

London, Nov. 16.

Rumours are again being spread that Russia has purchased four Chilian armoured cruisers and three Argentine protected cruisers Asahi.

"London, November 18th."

At a banquet given by King Edward at Windsor in honour of H.M. the King of Portugal, who is now making a return-visit to England, the King in toasting his guest announced that an Anglo-Portuguese Arbitration Treaty was signed yesterday at Windsor.

Tokyo, November 23rd.

On the 21st inst, one force of the Japanese troops attacked the enemy at Weitzeko and dispersed them. A superior force of Russians repulsed the attack of the Japanese left, but the latter being reinforced drove the Russians back to Kanholing. The enemy left 39 dead on the field and six prisoners were taken; also 30 rifles and 50 cartridges were captured. The Japanese losses were 3 wounded.

Tokyo, Nov. 23rd

On the night of the 21st inst. the Russians made a sortie from the east Kikwansan fort, but were repulsed. On the afternoon of the 22nd, a fire broke out near the arsenal situated near the harbour. This was due to the bombardment by our naval guns.

Berlin, Nov. 17.

The port of St. Petersburg has been closed to shipping for the present.

A Dutch steamer has sailed, conveying the body of the late Paul Kruger to South Africa. Wreaths were sent by the Royalties of the Netherlands.—Sinpapore Free Press.

Professor McAlister told the students of Guy's Hospital recently that he had decovered in the British Museum a hair restorer invented by a King of Egypt. The ingredient are calves' feet and dogs' claws boiled in oil.

Thomas Melville, of St. Andrews, and his brother, George Melville, of Cupar, who have just celebrated their ninety-fourth birthday are said to be the oldest twins in Great Britain. An American pair of twins not long ago attempted to dance a hornpipe on their 115th birthday.

ENGLAND AND THE WAR.

The following is an extract from a letter to the "Spectator" and is said to voice the opinions of a growing section of the British public:—

I hope no one will accuse me of raising an unnecessary note of alarm if I point out that the close of the Russo-Japanese War may find this country in a very unpleasant predicament. You have shown much cautious wisdom in your comments on the war but the general view of the public, taught by most of its newspapers, is that Japan will, by a series of brilliant victories, after at most two campaigns, force Russia to accept a humiliating peace, and that England, as Japan's ally, will share in the moral, and perhaps the substantial, fruits of her victory.

"This is a pleasing prospect, but it may fail of realisation. I have never been able to find substantial grounds for the almost universal expection of a complete Russian defeat. Journalists are creatures of impulse of the hour, and military experts are like most experts,—utterly untrustworthy. That a great Christian Power, full of pride and resources and with her future at stake, should accept defeat from an Asiatic race without a prolonged struggle is incredible. That she should be completely defeated in the end is almost as incredible. The Japanese have certainly won the first round. The Russians, unprepared and outnumbered, have been forced to play a waiting and retreating game, but the battles have really been rearguard actions on a large scale and Kuropatkin has probably done all along that which he intended to do. The next six months may alter the face of things. It is useless to dogmatise. The war may close in three ways,—by a Japanese victory, by a Russian victory, or by a drawn game. The last may possibly be the end; but if the war is to end in the decisive victory of one side, I should place my money on the Russian horse. Whatever hopes of a speedy victory the Japanese had two months ago, they have lost them now; even though they summon China to their side. The Russian armies will grow stronger every day. They are learning their lesson under the best of teachers, and they have behind them the resources of an immense Empire which has never known defeat as other Empires have known it.

A few days ago a Japanese was sent by his legation to inspect the court's of law and government prisons.

A robbery on a large scale occurred on the 20th inst, at the village Keumchuk-ni in the Muchu district. Twenty-four houses were burnt and their occupants robbed of their valuables.

The Mayor of Milwaukee has accepted an invitation from the Under and Over Sea Navigation Company of St. Louis to travel from Milwaukee to the Exhibition in a submarine boat and return in an air-ship.

Mr. Yi Chai Kuk has telegraphed that all the members of his committee have satisfied themselves that their mission to Japan has been successfully accomplished and they will consequently return by the first opportunity.

A prophet has declared that if the remains of the Crown Princess be interred outside the East Gate, great trouble will come to the Imperial family in three years' time. He is now in jail and his "confreres" have posphesied that he is likely to remain there until his prophecy is fulfilled.

The family of the late Rev. H. G. Appenzeller, who, it will be remembered, met his death through the collision of two steamers near Chemulpo in June 1902, have brought an action for damages against the Osaka Shosen Kaisha of Osaka. The amount claimed is $55,425 U. S. gold.

THE JUMPING BEETLE GAME.

Have you ever played Halticoridæ? The chances are against the fact, for it was only introduced into England a few evenings ago by American visitors, who discovered in the pretty little beetle a new source of innocent amusement.

It is a game of chance that is played with Halticoridæ, and it is safe to say that it is unlikely to be introduced anywhere except where the game is played simply as an amusement, where the stakes are only for added interest, not for gain.

Its introduction into London was through the agency of Colonel H. C. Duval, who, in New York, represents the allied Vanderbilt interests. Colonel Duval while staying at the Savoy Hotel received business communications from Mexico, and with them came the little bug, or beetle, which his business associates in Mexico sent for his amusement, Halticoridæ being a game greatly enjoyed by the Mexican senors and senoritas.

Halticoridæ is a beautiful electrical prismatic bug or beetle. Its colours change almost every second—now it is a gold, now silver, now heliotrope—in fact, right through the programme of colours, shades, and tints does it go as you gaze upon it.

When you touch it gently, the beetle jumps into the air with the ease of an acrobat, changing its colours, and alighting on the table in exactly the place you would say it was not falling to again, for when descending it changes its course at a distance of possibly two inches from the table.

Americans are not slow to make some use of anything, and so the Mexican bug became the principal element in the new game "Halticoridæ."

A lasrge piece of cardboard is taken and in the centre a ring is pencilled. From this towards the players lines are drawn and each space numbered. The bug is placed in the ring and touched by one of the players, after all have selected the spaces they think the strange insect will drop into.

A party of Americans, including a former Mayor of New York, a Brooklyn District Attorney, a General, and others of Colonel Duval's guests, spent an exciting evening at the game, and now importation of Halticoridæ is being anxiously awaited. It is all that is needed say those who know the game, to make London on a dull day glow with enjoyment.—Free Press.

The Foreign Office have telegraphed to the Korean Minister at Peking ordering him to return immediately to Korea.

A dispute as to the possession of an island near Wiju has arisen between the Korean and Chinese Governments. The former seems to be in the right in claiming it as Korean territory.

Mr. Chai Bum Suk, an engineer of the Korean Railway Department has been ordered, by His Majesty, to go to Japan to study the railway system in vogue there.

The Il Chin Hoi have issued another inflammatory proclamation. This time their efforts are directed against taxation; presumably their wages have been reduced.

The present Commander of the Vladivostock cruiser "Gromoboi" has been transferred to another post and been succeed by Captain von Jessen of the lately sunken "Novik."

A magistrate named Kim Chul Whan has been detected by the people of Chang Yun in defrauding them in connection with payments for coolies taken by the Japanese. He succeeded in escaping to Chinnampo, where he laid false accusations against those, who had detected him in his swindle. These were arrested and imprisoned by the Japanese, while the evil-doer Kim Chul Whan evades justice.

On the 23rd inst. His Majesty held a long session with all his Ministers.

The touring craze has evidently caught on in Seoul, for we are told that 17 more officials are shortly to visit Japan with a view to inspecting various branches of Japanese administration.

Eight native chiefs of the Carolina Islands, brought to California to be impressed with the country, were induced to "shoot the chute." Immediately after they hurried back to their hotel, and locked themselves in their rooms, refusing to leave except on condition that they be at once sent home. They declare America is "too big."

The Finance Department has informed all the other branches of the Korean Government that it is essential, this year, that the budget should be prepared by Japanese. The interest of all officials is solicited in bringing this to a happy consummation.

In connection with this it is interesting to learn from the Kobe Herald that, The Jiji has received a Seoul despatch, dated 6th inst., stating that the Korean Budget for next year is now being compiled under the superintendence of Mr. Megata, the Japanese financial adviser to Korea, and will probably be finished during the present year. The Korean fiscal year commences in the month of January, but owing to the irregular manner in which the compilation has hitherto been conducted, the Budget was seldom completed until the following March or April. This year all the necessary preparations are expected to be made before the end of December, so that the Budget for the next fiscal year may be put into operation in Janusry next.

Since news of the active operations round Port Arthur and in Manchuria have been received, says the "Rangoon Gazette," excitement has again sent its thrill through the "Japanese party" amongst the Burmans and their heated discussions with the Russian side have taken a new, but not unexpected, development in the form of betting. Burmese are very fond of betting and the craze exists amongst women as well as men. They are fond of lotteries and do not consider money badly invested which is spent in buying tickets in various race sweeps. They are, as a rule, very sanguine of success, and not a few whose means are inadequate borrow from the Chetties and risk their all in betting. They have, too, their national lottery. "The thirty-six animals," where they sometimes win, but more frequently lose, a good deal of money. Again, it is not rare, in the districts, for two villages to train each one or two buffaloes to fight, and there is heavy betting when the fight takes place. The date of the fall of Port Arthur is now the object of a good deal of betting. Some place it at a few months' distant, some at a few days; and the Russian fortress is a strong "competitor at present" with the paddy market and the speculation in land and houses. It may be noted that for some time past many Chinese, who are betting heavily on the fall of Port Arthur, backed their opinion that Sept. 15th would see its fall.

The Korea Daily News.

Issued at 5 P. M. daily except Sundays.

Rate of Subscription :—
Per Year,............Yen 25.
Per Quarter,..........Yen 7.
Per Month,..........Yen 2.50.

Postage in Korea not charged extra.
Postage abroad charged extra.

Advertisements. 50 sen per day for 1 inch or less.
5 yen per month per inch.
50 yen per year per inch.

All communications to
E. T. BETHELL,
Editor and Publisher,
Pak-tong, Seoul

THE BALTIC FLEET AND THE SUEZ CANAL.

(FROM THE JAPAN HERALD).

The question whether the Balitc Fleet would be permitted to pass the Suez Canal in view of existing international arrangements must be answered in the affirmative, but since the public cannot be expected to know the particulars it may be of some interest to give a brief outline of the conditions which govern the passage of the Canal. The Canal was built by the Compagnie Universelle by virtue of a concession granted by the Khedive which was ratified by a Firman of the Suzerain, the Sultan of Turkey, and in accordance with that concession the Canal is worked, under the territorial supremacy of Egypt in whose territories it lies, and its waters form a part of the territorial waters of Egypt. On account of its paramount international importance and of its objects a special regulation of its juridical condition became necessary, and the Sultan's Firman of the 22nd February, 1866, already contained the clause that the Canal should be opened to merchant ships of all nationalities. An international commission which met in Constantinople in 1883, upon the invitation of the Sultan, declared that navigation through the Canal was open to men-of-war and vessels chartered as troopships. The Declaration of the 6, 14th December, 1873, was accepted by the Porte, by nearly all naval Powers and by the Director to the Compagnie Universelle. The Suez Canal, therefore, was under the protection of all Europe. The Declaration of 1873, however, had not considered the position in which merchant ships in the case of a war in which the Porte might be involved would find themselves. It showed a loophole, in so far as it did not secure the freedom of navigation unconditionarily and completely. During the Russo-Turkish war, therefore, the European merchants and shareholders of the Canal were very much disquieted. England, however, in February, 1877, declared that it would consider every attempt to block the Canal or its approaches, or to impede its traffic, as a threat to her Indian possessions, and that any attempt of the kind would make its further neutrality impossible. Earl Derby made a similar declaration to the Russian Ambassador in May, 1877, and Russia replied that it was not her intention to block the Canal or to impede or threaten navigation through it. The events which took place in Egypt in 1882 led to its occupation by England and showed the pressing necessity of an international protection on a clear basis which would bind all states alike. On the 30th March, 1885, a Conference was opened in Paris, and Spain and the Netherlands were invited to participate Nine states were represented, and Egypt, as a vassal vote. The conference passed without result, and long diplomatic negotiations ensued. Finally, after all difficulties were settled a Convention was signed at Constantinople on the 29th October, 1888, by Germany, Austria, England, Spain, France, Italy, the Netherlands, Russia and Turkey.

The object of the Convention was to secure the free use of the Canal both in peace and war. The Canal must be open to ships of all nations at all times. It must not be blocked under any circumstances. No acts of war must take place either in the Canal nor in the port at its entrance, nor within a distance of three nautical miles, not even if Turkey herself should be one of the belligerent Powers. The passing through of warships of the belligerent Powers must take place in the shortest possible time. Their stay at Port Said, and in the roads at Suez except in cases of peril of the sea is forbidden. An interval of twenty-four hours must lie between the passage of two hostile ships. The belligerents may not embark or disembark in the Canal in the entrance ports either troops or war material. At no time must war ships be stationed in the Canal. Only non-belligerent Powers may keep at the most two warships stationed at the entrance ports. The Sweetwater Canal is under the same guarantees as the Sea Canal, as well as the material of both canals. The Sultan and the Khedive may enact general police measures, provided that the freedom of navigation is respected. The Suez Canal has not been "neutralised" by the Convention of Constantinople. That term is not adapted to Characterise the international legal position of the Canal. The Canal would only then be neutralised if it had been closed for warships of belligerent parties, and neither England nor France, nor any other state, which, like Spain (at that time) and Holland, had possessions in Eastern Asia, would have co-operated. That would have been a retrograde step. The Russian Delegate had expressed the desire that the arrangements made should be extended to the Red Sea, so that the approach to the Canal from the South should be secured under all circumstances, but the Italian Delegate opposed the proposition and it fell through. It will be seen, therefore, that the Baltic fleet has nothing to fear in the Suez Canal, which, above all, must be also considered as the British road to India, but in all probability its dangers from torpedo attack will begin in the Red Sea, as the Japanese could easily keep torpedo boats and colliers to supply them with coal there, and the probability is that will be done.

MR. DOOLEY ON THE WAR AGAIN.

"This is a tur-rble war," said Mr. Hennessey.

"Nawthin' tur-ible about it," said Mr. Dooley. "It's a war. I can't say more thin that. All th' other wars ye've iver shone in his been ayther German wars, which is carried on be markin' examination papers, or English wars, which is th' same as stealin' money from childher, or our own late gloryous war, which is like gettin' dhrunk an' bein' fined twinty millyod dollars or hundred years in the Philippeens. But this is a rale war. It's a gloryous war. What cud be finer to th' iditor iv a London newspaper thin th' spictacle which he can well imagine iv th' dauntless Jap'nese hurlin' thimsilves their gijiantic foe an' recklessly layin' down their lives that England may live? An' what cud be more sublime to a warlike banker in Paris thin th' thought iv th' increase activity on th' banks iv th' Loyang? It ought to stir th' blood in th' heart of iv'ry American citizen." "Now, if I had me way, Hinnessy, I wudden't let th' common people fight at all. That's th' way it used to be. Whin wan iv th' ol' kings in Brian Boru's day had a spat with a neighbor, both iv them ordhered hats at th' hardware store an' wint out an' pounded thim till their head ached. That's th' way it ought to be. Supposin' th' Czar iv Rooshya an th' Mikado iv Japan fell out. What wud be dacinter f'r thim thin to have a gintlemanly mix-up? Nick Romanoff, th' Rushyan champeen, an' Mike Adoo, th' cillybrated Jap'nese Jiu Jitsu bantam, come togither las night before a crowd iv ripresentative sports in a barn on th' outskirts iv th' city. Th' Rooshyan was seconded by Faure, th, Frinch light-weight, an Bill Honezollern, th' Prooshyan whirlwind. In th' Jap's corner was Al Guelph, who bate th' Llama iv Thibet las' week, an' Rosenfelt, th' American champeen, who has issued a defi to th' wurruld. Before th' gong sounded th' Jap rushed over an' sthruck th' Rooshyan a heavy blow beneath th' belt. A claim iv foul was enthered but not allowed, an at th' tap iv th' gong both boys wint at it hammer an' tongs, but it was soon apparent that th' Rooshyan, though heavier, was not in as good condition as his opponent. It was Walcott an Choynski all over, on'y th' Rooshyan hung on with gr'reat courage. At th' end iv th' twintieth round, whin both boys were on th' ropes, th' ref'ree, th' well known fight promoter, Misther Rothschild, declared th' bout a dhraw. Considerable bad blood was aroused be a claim be th' fighters that durin' th' battle they were robbed iv' their clothes be their seconds. As a financial entherprise th' fight was a frost. Th' box official's receipts did not akel th' rent iv th' barn an' thrainin' expinses, an' th' referee decided that as th' fight was a dhraw he was entitled to th' stakes. "Wudden't it be fine? Who wudden't walk to Bloomington Illinye, to see that sturdy but prodent warryor, th' King iv England, mixin' it up with the Llama iv Thibet, or our own invincible champeen takin' on th' Emp'ror iv Germany? If they didn't like th, weepins, they'd have me permission to use axes. I'd go further. I wudden't bar anybody fr'm ffghtin' who wanted to fight. If anybody felt th' martial spirit in time, he wud have a place to use it up. I'd have armies composed on'y iv officers. It wud be gr-reat. D'ye s'pose they'd iver get near enough to each other to hurt? They'd complain that th' throuble with th' long distance guns was that they cudden't be made distant enough. Supposin' Gin'ral Kurypotkin had to do all th' fightin' f'r himsilf. It wud be betther f'r him, becaueses thin he cud ordher an advance without bein' so crowded comin' back. Supposin,' to gratify his heeryoic spirit, he had to ordher himself to carry a thrunk, a cook stove, a shovel, a pickaxe, an ikon an' a wurrurd iv good cheer fr'm th' Czar two hundhred miles over a clay road an' if he did it successfully an' didn't spill annything, he might hope to be punctured by a bayonet. An' suppose Gin'ral Oyama had to walk barefooted accrost Manchuria an' subsist f'r four months be whainin' his beak on a cuttle-fish bone. How soon d'ye think there wud be a battle? War wud be wan contiuyous manoover-with wan iv thim manooverin' west, an' th, other manooverin' east. They'd niver meet till years afteer th' gloryous sthruggle."

"They'll niver do it," said Mr. Hennessy. "There have always been wars."

"An' fools," said Mr. Dooley.

"But wudden't ye defend y'r own fireside?"

"I don't need to," said Mr. Dooley. "If I keep on coal enough, me fireside will make t too hot f'r annywan that invades it,"

The Korea Daily News.

VOL. I, FRIDAY, NOVEMBER 25, 1904. No. 109

HONGKONG & SHANGHAI BANKING CORPORATION.

Paid-up Capital..... ....$10,000,000
Reserve Fund:—Sterling Reserve... 10,000,000
Silver Reserve..... 7,000,000

27,000,000

Reserve Liability of Proprietors... 10,000,000

HEAD OFFICE, HONGKONG.

London Bankers, London and County Banking Company Limited.
Branches and Agencies,
London.

Amoy,	Hankow	Penang,
Bangkok,	Hiogo,	Rangoon,
Batavia,	Iloilo,	Saigon,
Bombay,	Lyons,	San Francisco,
Calcutta,	Manila,	Singapore,
Colombo,	Nagasaki,	Sourabaya,
Foochow,	New York,	Tientsin,
Hamburg.	Peking,	Yokohama,

Credits granted on approved Securities, and every description of Banking and Exchange business transacted.

Drafts granted on London and the chief Commercial places in Europe, India, Australia, America, China and Japan.

HOLME RINGER & CO., AGENTS,
CHEMULPO.

ON CHEONG & CO.,
SEOUL.
GENERAL STORE KEEPERS.
Imported provisions, Cooking Utensils Crockery, etc.
FRESH BREAD DAILY.

MITSU BISHI DOCKYARD & ENGINE WORKS,
NAGASAKI.

CODE WORD, "DOCK."

A 1, A. B. C., and Engineering Codes used.

DOCK No. 1 (at Tategami)

Extreme Length..............523 feet
Length on blocks............513 ,,
Width of Entrance on Top......89 ,,
,, ,, Bottom....77 ,,
Water on Blocks at Spring Tide 26½ ,,

DOCK No. 2 (Mukaijima).

Extreme Length..............371 feet
Length on Blocks............360 ,,
Width of Entrance on Top......66 ,,
,, ,, Bottom 53 ,,
Water on Blocks at Spring Tide 22 ,,

PATENT SLIP (at Kosuge).

Can take vessels up to 1,000 tons gross.

THE WORKS are well equipped with the LATEST IMPROVEMENTS, and can execute any kind of work in SHIPBUILDING and MARINE ENGINEERING, as well as in REPAIRING of SHIPS.

The COMPANY'S new powerful steamer OURA-MARU (712 tons, 700 I.H.P.), specially built for SALVAGE PURPOSES, and equipped with necessary gear, is always READY at SHORT NOTICE.

CHARTERED BANK OF INDIA AUSTRALIA & CHINA.

INCORPORATED BY ROYAL CHARTER 1853

HEAD OFFICES:—LONDON.

Paid-up Capital £800,000
Reserve Liability of Shareholders 800,000
Reserve Fund 800,000

Drafts granted upon all the principal places in the world and every description of Exchange and banking business transacted.

E. MEYER & Co., Agents,
Chemulpo.

E. MEYER & CO.
Chemulpo.

SOLE AGENTS IN KOREA FOR:
A. T. Morse, Sons & Co's
"Fresco" Distemper

In all colours ready for use on walls, Ceilings etc.
and
AVENARIUS CARBOLINEUM

A wood-preserving and antiseptic oil preparation
Against decay, dry-rot, fungus and wood-destroying insects.

A large supply always in Stock.
Prices upon application.

E. MEYER & Co.,
Chemulpo

THE METHODIST PUBLISHING HOUSE.
Little West Gate, Seoul.

JOB PRINTING, TYPEWRITER PAPER
CARBON PAPER, VISITING CARDS
STATIONERY, BOOK BINDING
BOOK PUBLISHERS
AMERICAN SCHOOL BOOKS
SPENCERIAN COPY BOOKS
PEN CARBON LETTER AND BILL BOOKS

S. A. BECK, Manager.

HOKURKU DOBOKU KAISHA.
Branch office in Chong Dong. Seoul.
Japanese telephone No. 165
CONTRACT DEPARTMENT.
We can contract to build any building or construction.
MERCHANDISE DEPARTMENT.
We can provide any building material.
We have just contracted to build the new Belgian Legation.

DAI-ICHI GINKO.
LIMITED.
(Formerly the First National Bank)

ESTABLISHED 1873

INCORPORATED UNDER PRESENT LAW 1896

Capital - - - - - - - - Yen 5,000,000
Reserve Fund - , - - - 1,500,000

HEAD OFFICE:—TOKIO.

President: Baron SHIBUSAWA.

BRANCHES AND CORRESPONDENTS
In the Principal Cities and Towns of Japan.
Interest Allowed on
Fixed deposits 1 year - - - 6½ per cent
" " 6 months - - - 6 per cent

Special current accounts 1½ sen daily per Y 100
General " " 1 " " " 100

M. TANAKA,
Manager, Chemulpo.

SINGER SEWING MACHINES
씽거즈봉침

SOLE AGENTS FOR KOREA
젼매쇼

HOLME RINGER & CO
Chemulpo
졔물포 함릉거양힝

KAMEYA & CO.
GENERAL STOREKEEPERS
Chinkokai - - Seoul
(*Established 1895, Tokyo*)

Confectionery, Hams, Canned Goods, Cutlery, Hirano & Tansan Water. Provisions, Gents, Furnishing goods, Toilet Articles, Travelling Bags, Tobacco, Cigars & Cigarettes Kitchen Utensils. Coffee, Biscuits.

Fresh Goods always kept in Stock.
Prices Moderate
Please come and inspect our goods

NIPPON YUSEN KAISHA.
JAPANESE MAIL STEAMSHIP CO.
DER MAIL CONTRACT WITH THE IMPERIAL JAPANESE GOVERNMENT.

European Line

Regular Fortnightly Service between Yokohama Kobe, Moji, Shanghai, Hongkong, Singapore, Penang Colombo, Port Said, Marseilles, London and Antwerp

American Line

Regular Fortnightly Service between Hongkong and Seattle, calling at Shanghai, Moji, Kobe, Yokohama and Victoria, B. C.

Australian Line

Regular weekly Service betwen Japan Ports and Australia, calling at Hongkong and Manila.
(Above Three Lines Suspended until further notice).

Shanghai Line

Weekly Service between Shanghai and Japan Ports

Korea Line

Service Kobe, Moji, Nagasaki, Fusan Chemupo Chefoo, Taiku.
S. S. Bahelsberg, 2181 tons.
Service Kobe, Moji, Fusan, Chemulpo, Chinnampo
S. S. ARGO, S. S. Ohio.

BORDEN'S CONDENSED MILK CO.
New York, U. S. A.

ALWAYS IN STOCK
Eagle Brand Condensed Milk.
Gold Seal Condensed Milk.
Peerless (Family) Evaporated Cream.
Borden's Malted Milk.

E. MEYER & CO.
Chemulpo, Korea,
Sole Agents

ROYAL INSURANCE COMPANY,
Funds exceed £10,000,000
FIRE
AT CURRENT RATES.
LIFE
REDUCED PREMIUM.
HOLME RINGER & Co.,
Agents, Chemulpo.

HOTEL DU PALAIS
SEOUL.

The only first class Hotel in Seoul. Situated in the centre of the city opposite the palace.

Cuisine under the supervision of are experienced French Chef.

Well ventilated and furnished throughout.

TARIFF UPON APPLICATION
L. MARTIN
Proprietor and Manager.

大韓每日申報
대한매일신보

(호십빅일몌)　　(일요월)　　일팔십이월일십년사빅구천일

본샤고빅

오신보는영어와한국문셔계의
일출판ᄒᆞᆷ
신문가
한장　엽두돈오푼
일삭도　엽두량엿돈
우표가디삭다섯돈
다엿돈으로밧습
광고료는

귀한외쟝단과ᄌᆞ항의다쇼로ᄒᆞ
감ᄒᆞ되렴가로밧을터이오며오
터지아니ᄒᆞ대한사람마다이신
문을보실터이니광고내시기를
원ᄒᆞ시는이들은우리신문사에
와셔편약ᄒᆞ심을회망ᄒᆞᆷ

◯발힝소　박동대한미일신보
샤발힝ᄒᆞ교영해전셩국인셜필
됨쟝자리오
샤쟝 영국인 (비셜)
평양 디리졈
◯평양호동샤는권미보셔로우
리신문쵸비터리인을뎡ᄒᆞ엿
스오니평양에계신구람코져ᄒᆞ
시는 첨군ᄌᆞ는터리졈에왕
림ᄒᆞ와편의ᄒᆞ시옵

샤셜

◯우리대한미일신보의목뎍은
대한의인민뎐셔에반한모든리
롭게터ᄒᆞ야는공평한변론을쥬
쟝ᄒᆞ이라우리동양익원의릐을보는
신문보셔는쳠군ᄌᆞ의계ᄒᆞ엿보
도ᄒᆞ리며편지를귀셔ᄒᆞ매주시
는이는셩명과밧디를젹어보치
시기를희망ᄒᆞ오니이기슬신문
상에귀졔ᄒᆞ라는거시아니오다
만구ᄒᆞ신용ᄒᆞ는증거를삼고자
홈이라귀자는아모귀셔터가귀
지홈을되각ᄒᆞ는권리를가졋스
나되각ᄒᆞ는리유를말ᄒᆞ터이오
며공평한론문과쳔계ᄒᆞ는긋흔
다귀셔는의퇴치못지안켓습니이

◉본샤셜시이리로신문을미일
우례로분젼ᄒᆞ와례졍부의양의
로쳠ᄒᆞ는듯스로면굿에는혹굿계
전ᄒᆞ기도ᄒᆞ며혹맛젹거을도형
에젼ᄒᆞ기도ᄒᆞ며혹아니젼ᄒᆞ는
곳도잇다ᄒᆞ오와우리신문을슈팀
ᄒᆞ야구람ᄒᆞ시는 쳠군ᄌᆞ의계
되ᄒᆞ야되우미안ᄒᆞ옵기로디금
은분젼인을두고미일일즉이젼
ᄒᆞ며아니젼ᄒᆞ거나늦게거나ᄒᆞ
거가엽도록ᄒᆞ라ᄒᆞ오니ᄒᆞ야나

젼ᄒᆞ거나죠흔긋계젼ᄒᆞ거나혼일
외잇스면본샤로통긔ᄒᆞ여주심
을회망ᄒᆞᆷ

잡보

◯동문셔답　영국공관가리
는곽우산군으로미셥리되는무
인지경이라금일평양셩에촌전졍
영쇼에셔쥬일군슈ᄌᆞᆼ으로가
가는돈샹법금을슈운ᄒᆞ는데봉
슈리로고쥬에서계ᄒᆞ셥영아인
츌ᄒᆞ야는ᄒᆞ기를엇지ᄒᆞ야계
오나우리가발셔보셔계가서
엇다ᄒᆞ고쳬하셧다ᄒᆞᆫ즉도젹놈
이문귀회를터셔그리ᄒᆞ이라
그쇠에셔을셔를하나히가는티
옷도셔로엿고몸이가진돈긴도
젹지아니ᄒᆞ되미쇼문을듯고미
우렴려ᄒᆞ야가미를쳔셩에셔어
로가나모는자ㅣ잇스면통으
로가면셔으로젼다ᄒᆞ고도형ᄒᆞ
기를청ᄒᆞ여지아니ᄒᆞ고완산을무
수이ᄒᆞ엿다ᄒᆞ더라

◯일계공셩　평양에계일병오뫼
명이북도로셔샹졍ᄒᆞ는디김셩
동기쥬막에셔듬한마리를쟝아
먹고오는지라그쥬인김진텬이
분로ᄒᆞ야듬기일병에두목이되로
가는디그쥬인이고ᄒᆞ기를지금
귀병정이우리듬한마리를쟝아
먹고갑슬주지아니ᄒᆞ고곳스니
이런법은귀국에나대한에나엇
스니공평이주고가라ᄒᆞ즉그쟝관
이되답ᄒᆞ기를그디가우리계셔
한마리갑슬밧으라면네리라ᄒᆞ산
즉김진텬이알고귀국ᄒᆞ는야그는
쟝과샹치가로버셔기로쟝그쉬
을밧으라ᄒᆞ엿ᄉᆞ니셔잡혀ᄒᆞ였다
이나라계ᄒᆞ는사름이쇼는거시쇼
벼슬ᄒᆞ는사름은졈쟈는사름이쇼
졈쟈는사름이엇지오만ᄒᆞᆫ마
리갑슬밧으냐ᄒᆞ고즉일이ᄒᆞ엿
더니그만두엇다더라

◯농샹무츅　일젼에농샹무보
과셔ᄒᆞ로옹이순에평지츅ᄒᆞ얏을가
지고오는되라그동지ᄒᆞ는사름
이무파반옥니편지논뉘케로가
나ᄒᆞ엿는ᄃᆡ고중의터디명이목함ᄒᆞ
셩이만원ᄉᆞ중의계ᄒᆞ는관지라
ᄒᆞ기에쳔못ᄒᆞ기를무산졉티이라
ᄒᆞ엿ᄉᆞ터니ᄒᆞ기를맛인동군을ᄒᆞ
ᄒᆞ엿ᄉᆞ외상ᄒᆞᆫ지지세롱ᄒᆞ야ᄒᆞ
부관ᄒᆞ얏스보터ᄒᆞ도록기의리
이엿ᄉᆞ인다ᄒᆞ고우ᄒᆞ계한거시ᄒᆞ
다시리라ᄒᆞ엿다ᄒᆞ더라

◯동학견집　함경남도관찰사
가동학당이셩에평을셥슈ᄒᆞ엿
다가기아병의셰ᄌᆞ이엇업ᄒᆞᆫ다니
부부의셔계명이칙도안공ᄒᆞ기를
벌리히셥셔물과출ᄒᆞ야인귀이
고쟝ᄒᆞ야무로의죠ᄒᆞ셔ᄒᆞ엿
더라

◯무쥬젹당　무쥬군수보틀게
쥬음리구월이십일야에젹당오
십여명이불돈를도에집허터에
돌역ᄒᆞ야븐가새리유경혼호적
ᄒᆞ야일반운슐을을슈히쇼할화ᄒᆞ
엿더ᄒᆞᆫ다ᄒᆞ엿더라

가산화젹　가산군보고를게
ᄒᆞ쥬읍면구월이십ᄒᆞ발에에가
산군관셔성에에사는김녕ᄒᆞ얘엉
에셔셔셩화ᄒᆞ여쳡신은조ᄒᆞ화
우셔아와계 천골몸수 터 ᄒᆞ엿더다ᄒᆞ
엿더라

◯란지조회　탁지부에셔장부
부원방에조희ᄒᆞ기를계샹에다
의가기젼셔보로권혼규례가잇셔
호엽히리로ᄂᆞᆫ소ᄌᆞ가나로나커나
ᄒᆞ거자못ᄒᆞ는데인터ᄒᆞ혼법일지
라도무셔보디셔이단지면일에
이안셔형리의독회를가뇌형명지
ᄒᆞ였슈연ᄂᆞᆫ지라셔훈바로다부터
본며도죠에에ᄂᆞ살을ᄌᆞ셰세 각판량
ᄒᆞᆫ거버니을하이스로써경ᄒᆞ고혼
고ᄂᆞᆫ셰구벼희를잇되도로ᄌᆞᆫ인의
고서와라ᄒᆞ남셔반본젼홈이셔도
맛당이계ᄒᆞ엿시ᄋᆞ 쥬귀관경에 셔
져ᄒᆞᆫ쇼명라로류되ᄒᆞ아ᄒᆞ일러로졀
의외계쵸갑주ᄒᆞ이ᄋᆞ터ᄒᆞ엿지ᄒᆞ야
이에져조가위셥ᄒᆞ 아청샹시비룽예
셔에선돈외이지반을경구ᄒᆞᆫ의
ᄒᆞ곳ᄒᆞᆫ관셩넘셔 나누ᄒᆞ구며리이용
ᄒᆞ며대증갑쟁논ᄂᆞᆫ시문동ᄒᆞ다회메
됨젼되로ᄒᆞᆫ권ᄒᆞ승인골을미ᄒᆞ앗
지아니ᄒᆞ고아뢰를ᄒᆞ로벼에의
지도로밧죵거ᄂᆞ로써 만원ᄉᆞᆫ고ᄒᆞ
에바감ᄂᆞᆫ거시ᄒᆞ증ᄒᆞ엿서영노
수엽ᄒᆞ야 ᄌᆞ에 바리ᄃᆞᆫ가고문부롤
산외묘ᄒᆞ슐ᄒᆞ엿스 가번ᄒᆞ코에
으로ᄂᆞᆫ 아외ᄒᆞ 짐종ᄌᆞ구ᄂᆞᆫ이왕
견승이인ᄒᆞ쥬ᄒᆞ다ᄒᆞ엿고ᄉᆞ이ᄂᆞᆫ
번돈의셥ᄒᆞ가련ᄉᆞ미뎐면도ᄒᆞ
혀리이ᄋᆞ증계ᄒᆞ대ᄒᆞ구를회일고ᄉᆞ
ᄂᆞᆫᄒᆞ로ᄃᆞ이가보ᄒᆞ버ᄌᆞ미금ᄌᆞ계ᄂᆞᆫ
계ᄒᆞ외ᄒᆞ가ᄒᆞ다ᄒᆞ엿더라

◯경편회의　경무관한최셔는
신교ᄒᆞ고그터에셥셔고셰가파
일ᄒᆞ엿더라

◯비셔하교　평양도정ᄒᆞᆫ보고
ᄒᆞᆫ이야상평ᄒᆞ야남촌산ᄒᆞᆯ리동보
형궐주예동ᄒᆞ는터방에이미이
ᄒᆞ야아그주인이그ᄒᆞ계을가져나
답ᄒᆞ고오이그사름이금일산쇼에
셔즁ᄒᆞ실명은공부ᄒᆞ야지금출세
ᄒᆞ야상경ᄒᆞ엿ᄂᆞᆫ더보로져계샹
이　황샹계젼거ᄒᆞ엿대ᄒᆞ무샹
쥬밍ᄒᆞᆫ엣이잇던지로티ᄒᆞ외계
을밝ᄒᆞᆫ다ᄒᆞ는되그사름의슈쳥
리ᄒᆞ로ᄒᆞ션거ᄉᆞ니말ᄒᆞ엿고호동
ᄒᆞᆯ량ᄒᆞ니쟈조가잇ᄂᆞᆫ듯ᄒᆞ다ᄒᆞ
더라

◯정연군민소　정연군민등이
외부에호소ᄒᆞ기를본군향쟝김
쳥ᄒᆞ이가본디간졍ᄒᆞ으로지ᄂᆞᆫ
쳥일본영부로셩졉ᄒᆞ에예보청
빌렴이로졍ᄒᆞ으로셔샹ᄒᆞ리셔
에셔일본병참소에회외ᄒᆞ야셩
감ᄒᆞ야이빌셩명으로정ᄒᆞ엿
미니김쳥ᄒᆞ이가졍계졍ᄒᆞ엿스료
셰샹ᄒᆞ뎡에벼졍ᄒᆞ고민쳔에수
렴ᄒᆞ기을에죵졍이결로ᄒᆞ아본
군으로졍이라ᄒᆞ쥬죵로에셔도
쥬ᄒᆞ야죵샹포로가셔동샤로ᄒᆞ
야금졍졍혼겻슨병졍소에무소
ᄒᆞ야일본헌병셥오뎡이본군에
와셔본군민죠진셩등이인되및
외물거ᄒᆞ는사름한이의졍회가
케엽ᄒᆞ지수삭이로라오히려노
외외본니지아니ᄒᆞ니랴지되엿
셔사뎡권의계ᄒᆞ죠ᄒᆞ야무희ᄒᆞ
세샤름은노의보니케한엉케ᄒᆞ
코김쳥ᄒᆞ을쳐치ᄒᆞ야셔와셥을
중쳐ᄒᆞ계ᄒᆞ라ᄒᆞ엿더라

◯헉부대면보　헉부대신이동경
에셔외부로뎐보ᄒᆞ기를쳐쟝믈
이미밋것스나회주ᄒᆞ겟다ᄒᆞ엿
더라

◯쳔셔뎐경　쥬뎡공샤가쳔셔
를이미밧엇다고뎐보ᄒᆞ엿더라
◯셔리의뎐보　쥬미공ᄉᆞ셔리
귀일ᄒᆞ죵무셔가일본동졍에셔
외부로뎐보ᄒᆞ기를금일에동셜
을따고미국으로향ᄒᆞᆫ다ᄒᆞ엿더
라

◯면회쳥구　오부에셔쥬졍공
샤의계면회ᄒᆞ기를본일회국공
교방티에영을밧ᄒᆞ야리케혼다
ᄒᆞ엿더라

◯외죠일관　외부에셔일본공관
에죠회ᄒᆞ되우리외셩부공관니
계에일본쳠도셔무샤갈샹트릴
도원기사치뎡이이가계　뎡ᄒᆞ

UNION INSURANCE SOCIETY OF CANTON.

Head office Hongkong.
Marine risks underwritten at current rates.
Agents in Chemulpo:
E. MEYER & Co.

COMPAGNIE DES MESSAGERIES MARITIMES.

Fortnightly Direct Service.

For Marseilles via Ports.

Sailing from Yokohama

Calling at Kobe,

Shanghai, Hongkong, Saigon, Singapore, Colombo, Djibonti, Suez, Port Said and Marseilles.

For particulars apply to
HOLME RINGER & Co.,
Chemulpo.

HAYASHIDA & Co.,

16 MYENG DONG, CHIN KO KAI, SEOUL.
BRANCH OFFICE AT CHEMULPO.

Money changers, Coal and Wood Merchants, Express Agents.

We are agents for the Pyeng-yang Coal Company and the Karazu Coal Company of Japan. We have the best quality of both anthracite and bituminous coal, and prompt execution of orders is our speciality. Firewood of all kinds kept in stock. Full weight guaranteed. Money of all denominations exchanged at current rates. Parcels received for all parts.

CHINA MUTUAL LIFE INS. CO.

Most favourable terms to policy holders

Benefit system unsurpassed.

HOLME RINGER & Co.
Agents, Chemulpo.

C. P. R.

CANADIAN PACIFIC RAILWAY COMPANY'S ROYAL MAIL STEAMSHIP LINE.

THE FAST ROUTE BETWEEN CHINA, JAPAN, AND EUROPE VIA CANADA AND THE UNITED STATES.

Route from Hongkong via Shanghai, Nagasaki (Inland Sea of Japan) Kobe, Yokohama Victoria and Vancouver.

Twin Screw Empress Steamship—6,000 Tons—Speed 19 knots.

PROPOSED SAILING FROM YOKOHAMA.
R. M. S. Empress of India.
R. M. S. Empress of Japan.
R. M. S. Empress of China.
R. M. S. Athenian.
R. M. S. Tartar.

Special reduction (first class only) granted to members of the Military, Naval, Diplomatic and Civil services and to Missionaries.

Passengers have choice of ten routes across the Continent of America and have privilege of travelling by any Atlantic Steamship Line.

Round the World passage tickets in connection with the P. and O. S. N., North German Lloyd and Messageries Co.'s £125.

All rates payable at current rate of exchange.

For further information, Tickets, Guide Books, etc., apply to

HOLME, RINGER & Co., AGENTS,
Chemulpo.

Grand Hotel,

(*Formerly the Station Hotel*)

Near the Railway Terminus, West Gate Seoul.

The Best Hotel in Korea
Handsome new Building.
Fine Airy Rooms
Excellent Cuisine.
Terms Moderate.
Special terms to Missionaries and to permanent boarders.

Electric cars within 2 minutes' walk.

W. H. EMBERLEY,
Proprietor

EVERY FACILITY.

In connection with Life Assurance Business is afforded by

The Standard Life Assurance Co.,

One of the largest and wealthiest of the Provident Institutions of the United Kingdom Forms of Application and all information will be promptly afforded on application.

10 CENTS A DAY.

Not a very large expenditure is it? But it is sufficient to secure for a man of 30 a policy with the STANDARD LIFE OFFICE for

$1323.

For all particulars of rates, etc., apply to

Holme, Ringer & Co.,
Agents, Chemulpo.

THE NEW YORK LIFE INSURANCE COMPANY.

Have you ever been declined by any Company?

Are you engaged in a specially hazardous occupation?

Have you heard of the New York Life Insurance Company's New Classifications for this class of Risks?

If not, send your date of birth, occupation and particulars of rejection, if any to

E. MEYER & Co.,
Agents, Chemulpo.

MITSUI BUSSAN KAISHA
(MITSUI & Co.)

MITSUI GINKO.
(MITSUI BANK.)

The Bank is owned by the members of the Mitsui Family, who, as partners, assume an unlimited responsibility for all liabilities of the Bank:—

Capital.......................Yen 5,000,000
Reserve Fund.................. " 5,600,000

HEAD OFFICE, TOKYO.

LONDON OFFICE, 34 LIME ST., E. C.

BRANCHES AND AGENCIES:—
New York, San Francisco, Hamburg, Bombay, Singapore, Manila, Hongkong, Amoy, Chefoo, Tientsin.

Kobe, Hakodate, Yokohama, Kure, Yokosuka, Moji, Shimonoseki, Miike, Wakamatsu, Nagasaki, Kuchinotsu, Karatsu, Sasebo, Misume, Taipeh, &c.

Telegraphic Address for all the Offices:
"MITSUI."

A. B. C. AND A. 1 CODES USED.

Contractors of Coal

To the Imperial Japanese Navy. Arsenals and Railway Bureau, Principal Railway Companies and Industrial Work, Home and Foreign Mail and Freight Steamers.

Sole Proprietors

Of the famous Miike, Tagawa and Yamano Coal Mines.

Sole Agents

For the sale of Fukumo, Hokoku, Ichimura, Kanoda, Mannoura, Onoura, Ostuji, Sonoda. Tsubaruro, Yoshinotani, Yoshio, Yurokibura and other coals.

YANGTSE INSURANCE ASSOCIATION, LTD.

The undersigned, having been appointed agents for the above company, are prepared to issue policies and pay losses on marine risks at regular rates.

E. MEYER & Co.,
Agents, Chemulpo.

AMERICAN KOREAN ELECTRIC CO.

Light and Power.

Main Office: Electric Building, Chong No.

RAILWAY DEPARTMENT.

OPERATING CARS BETWEEN EAST AND WEST GATE, EVERY TEN MINUTES:—

First Car leaves East Gate at 7:00 A. M. First Car leaves R. R Station at 7:25 A. M
Last Car " East Gate at 9:40 P. M. Last " " R. R. Station at 10:05 P. M

OPERATING CARS BETWEEN EAST GATE AND IMPERIAL TOMB TERMINUS, EVERY TWENTY MINUTES:—

CONNECTING WITH EVERY ALTERNATE CAR ARRIVING AT EAST GATE FROM CHONG NO.

First Car leaves East Gate for Tomb at 7:10 A. M.
" " " Tomb for East Gate at 7:35 A. M.
Last " " East Gate for Tomb at 7:50 P. M.
" " " Tomb for East Gate at 8:10 P. M.

OPERATING CARS BETWEEN CHONG NO AND YUNG SAN RIVER EVERY TWELVE MINUTES:—

First Car leaves Chong No for South Gate at 7:12 A. M.
" " " Chong No for Yung San at 7:36 A. M.
" " " South Gate for Chong No at 7:20 A. M.
" " " Yung San for Chong No at 8:09 A. M.
Last " " South Gate for Chong No 10:00 P. M.
" " " Yung San for Chong No at 9:33 P. M.

SPECIAL PRIVATE CARS FURNISHED TO SUIT CONVENIENCE OF PATRONS. PRICES ON APPLICATION AT HEAD OFFICE.

LIGHTING DEPARTMENT.

Where less than 250 candle power of light is used, the rate per month will be
Per 16 candle power incandescent lamp,—All night.—Yen 2.50.
32 candle power incandescent lamp:—All night:—Yen 4.00.
50 candle power incandescent lamp:—All night:—Yen 6.00.
150 " " " " " " 10.00.
1200 " " enclosed arc " " " " 20.00.

Where more than 250 candle power of light is used, a Meter will be installed, if requested:—Rent of Meter Yen 2.00 per month. Rate of charges by meter reading:—Two Sen per Ampere per hour. (Approximately this is equal to about One Sen per 16 C. P. lamp per hour) Minimum monthly charge where meter is installed, Yen 20.00 per month, which includes rental of meter.

Estimates for installing lights furnished on application.
An assortment of chandeliers always on hand.

K. Murakami.

Photograph Studio
Chinkokai, Seoul.

Printing, Developing and Enlargement, of Photographs always Undertaken.

Korean Views and Pictures Illustrating Native Customs always on Sale,

THE OSAKA SHOSEN KAISHA.

Boats frequently on the berth for Chinnampo.

REGULAR SAILINGS BETWEEN JAPAN AND KOREAN PORTS.

FUSAN AND KOBE VIA SHIMONOSEKI.

OSAKA VIA MOKPO, FUSAN, SHIMONOSEKI AND KOBE.

MOJI DIRECT.

OSAKA VIA KUNSAN, MASANPO, FUSAN, SHIMONOSEKI AND KOBE.

CHEMULPO KUNSAN LINE,
Every three days.

CHEMULPO CHINNAMPO LINE.
Every three days.

For Freight and passage and further particulars apply to

THE OSAKA SHOSEN KAISHA,
Chemulpo.

RONDON, PLAISANT & CO.

General Storekeepers and Merchants, Ships Contractors, Tobacconists, Commission and Forwarding Agents, Coal Merchants

IMPORTERS AND EXPORTERS

Seoul & Chemulpo.

W. D. WENTWORTH.

LANDING
AND
SHIPPING AGENT
AND
CUSTOMS BORDER.

12 OURA, NAGASAKI.

STEWARD & CO.

Chemulpo.

Shipchandlers and Storekeepers, Naval and Mercantile Contractors, Landing and Shipping Agents.

STEWARD'S HOTEL

Chemulpo.

Best accommodation in this port for travellers. Clean and well-aired rooms, good cuisine and prompt attendence, moderate tariff.

봉승ᄒᆞ고 일은에왕ᄒᆞ엿ᄂᆞᆫ디일로써일본공관에죠회ᄒᆞ라ᄒᆞ엿더라

◯회조졍계 작이십오일에ᄂᆞᆫ한셩소윤박승죠양쥬군슈홍티윤고양군슈리죠현졔씨가회동ᄒᆞ야 유강원닉외히ᄌᆞ를젹간졍계ᄒᆞ엿더라

◯뎨일ᄎᆞ기회 라유셕씨등이일진회와동일ᄒᆞᆫ목젹으로취지셔를반포ᄒᆞ고샹민을발긔ᄒᆞ야샹업회를죠직ᄒᆞᄂᆞᆫ디뎨일ᄎᆞ회를십륙일에션젼도가에셔긔회ᄒᆞ엿더라

◯민씨계획 쥬쳥공ᄉᆞ민영철씨ᄂᆞᆫ졍부에셔면칙ᄉᆞ한ᄒᆞ엿스나씨가당쵸에평안관찰ᄉᆞ로평안남북도인민을할육거피ᄒᆞ야자긔의몸을살찌우고히도민인이경부에호소ᄒᆞ면자긔의궁흉극악ᄒᆞᆫ죄샹이탈로ᄒᆞᆯᄭᅡ렴녀ᄒᆞ야쥬쳥공ᄉᆞ를도독ᄒᆞ야탈신ᄒᆞ엿ᄂᆞᆫ디슈다ᄒᆞᆫ직산을쳥국에슈입ᄒᆞ야일후안신지방을마련ᄒᆞ엿더니지금졍부에득죄ᄒᆞ엿슨즉결단코회국지아니ᄒᆞ고쳥국에가산을셜치ᄒᆞᆯ계획이라더라

◯돈체ᄉᆞ피명 닉부대신리용틱씨ᄂᆞᆫ안산시돈체ᄉᆞ를피명ᄒᆞ엿더라

◯대관파송셜 졍부에셔일본에파견ᄒᆞᆫ시찰을소환ᄒᆞᆯ긔약이묘연ᄒᆞᆫ디대관즁에십칠명을ᄯᅩ파송ᄒᆞᆫ다ᄒᆞᆷ으로한셩졍계가ᄆᆡ우공구ᄒᆞᆫ즁이라더라

◯졍계샹쥬 텰도원총지심샹훈씨ᄂᆞᆫ샹경이후지작이십ᄉᆞ일에립디ᄒᆞ야졍계형편을샹쥬ᄒᆞ엿다더라

◯량대신샹소 의졍대신리근명참졍신긔션량씨ᄂᆞᆫ소직샹소를ᄒᆞ엿더라

관보

뎨이천구빅구십이호

광무팔년십일월이십ᄉᆞ일

셔임급ᄉᆞ령

◯승셔관암관오등 군긔창기슈 황은쳘

십일월이일

●승셔판임관오등 군부쥬ᄉᆞ 심샹휘

십일월십륙일

◯의원면본관 옥구항공립소학교교원 심긔셥 륙군법원쥬ᄉᆞ 박죵국

◯임옥구항공립소학교교원셔원판임관륙등 리광리

◯임경긔관찰부공립소학교교셔판임관륙등 무교원 신현졍

◯승셔판임관ᄉᆞ등 관립소학교교원 쥬졍균

◯임륙군법원쥬ᄉᆞ셔판임관륙등 라샹면

이샹십일월이십이일

뎨이천구빅구십삼호

광무팔년십일월이십오일

셔임급ᄉᆞ령

승셔관임관ᄉᆞ등 챵원감리셔쥬ᄉᆞ 홍슌규

구월이십ᄉᆞ일

◯승셔관임관ᄉᆞ등 닉부쥬ᄉᆞ 리티영 닉부쥬ᄉᆞ 윤명셥

십일월구일

◯임한셩우체ᄉᆞ쥬ᄉᆞ셔관임관륙등 한셩우체지ᄉᆞ쥬ᄉᆞ 원경샹

◯임한셩우체지ᄉᆞ쥬ᄉᆞ셔관임관륙등 히쥬우체ᄉᆞ쥬ᄉᆞ 윤병한

◯급삼급봉 한셩우체사쥬사 원경상 한셩우체지사쥬사 윤병한

이샹십일월이십이일

◯의관면본관 비셔원승 졍슈 홍문관시독 임빅영

◯명궁닉부특진관셔칙임관이등 태의원경 박용대

◯임홍문관시독셔판임관칠등 비셔원랑 신영학

◯임비셔원랑셔관임관륙등 륙품 뎡현

◯명분비셔원랑 홍문관시독 신영학

◯임장릉참봉셔관임관팔등

◯명태의원경셔칙임관삼등 종일품 민영규

◯명 경효전제죠셔칙임관일등 종일품 김셩근

◯임비셔원승셔쥬임관륙등 정삼품 리법인

창릉참봉 리원영

◯임창릉참봉셔관임관팔등 온릉참봉 김진슈

◯임온릉참봉셔관임관팔등 김샹필

◯임소영원슈봉관셔판임관팔등 휘경원슈봉관 셔학보

◯임휘경원슈봉관셔관임관팔동 박회쥰

◯명인산시돈체ᄉᆞ 닉부대신 리용티 ◯명인산시비왕대쟝 경무사 박셩긔 ◯임히쥬우체사쥬사셔판임관륙등 히쥬우체쥬사 강만형 ◯급삼급봉 히쥬우체쥬사 강만형

이샹십일월이십삼일

잡보

◯죠쳥전칙 외부에셔쳥공관에죠회ᄒᆞ기를우리룡천군신도강황쵸평사관위원김샹학의보고ᄂᆡ기에본원이당디에리도ᄒᆞ야히디평을답사ᄒᆞᆫ즉이것이우리나라속디라확신ᄒᆞ야의심이업ᄂᆞᆫ고로회동ᄒᆞ야심판ᄒᆞᆯ뜻으로쳥공관에죠회ᄒᆞ야안동지현의게쳥ᄒᆞ엿더니곳죠복ᄒᆞ기를한국에쥬차ᄒᆞᆫ우리공사의훈칙으리도ᄒᆞᆫ후에야맛당이심판ᄒᆞᆫ다ᄒᆞᄂᆞᆫ고로히디도한벌을그려써보ᄂᆡ고ᄒᆞᄂᆞᆫ디부치오니곳쳥관에이죠ᄒᆞ야안동지현에젼칙ᄒᆞ야회동심판케ᄒᆞ라ᄒᆞ엿기에이것을거ᄒᆞ야죠회ᄒᆞ니쳥컨디시힝ᄒᆞ라ᄒᆞ엿더라

◯어전회의 작이십삼일밤에의졍이하각부부대신이립디ᄒᆞ야각기관쳥ᄉᆞ흉을시졍긔션ᄎᆞ로어전회의를ᄒᆞ엿더라

◯대관전임 리근호씨가경무사를피임ᄒᆞᆫ다ᄒᆞ더니엇지ᄒᆞ야피임치못ᄒᆞ고헌병디ᄉᆞ령관원우샹씨ᄂᆞᆫ즁츄원의관으로젼임ᄒᆞ고경무ᄉᆞ양셩환씨ᄂᆞᆫᄉᆞ령관으로젼임ᄒᆞ고교육부참모빅셩긔씨가경무ᄉᆞ를겸임ᄒᆞ야임산시에비왕대쟝을피명ᄒᆞᆫ다더라

◯가가훼쳘 국쟝도감뎨죠민영환씨가닉부로죠회ᄒᆞ기를이번 국쟝을모실대에대쇼여를봉츌ᄒᆞᆯ직로를북궐궁셩에셔셔편큰길노좃차힝ᄒᆞ야셔십ᄌᆞ각모퉁이에니르러ᄂᆞᆫ맛당히여를돌닐터인디셔남모퉁이에잇ᄂᆞᆫ가가몃잔은부득불훼쳘ᄒᆞ여옴겨야ᄒᆞ겟슨즉회여ᄒᆞᄂᆞᆫ곳에셔브터히연로의가가를슈리ᄒᆞᆯ등졀은사셰가미리긔약ᄒᆞ야ᄒᆞᆯ거시니형편을간심ᄒᆞ야미리슈리ᄒᆞ야ᄒᆞ여곰림시ᄒᆞ야미급ᄒᆞᆷ이업게ᄒᆞ라ᄒᆞ엿더라

뎐보

작일당공ᄉᆞ관면착

◯위ᄌᆞ곡젼황 십일월이십일일우리군ᄉᆞ의일부지디ᄂᆞᆫ위ᄌᆞ곡[이양변문북편ᄉᆞ십리]에젹ᄒᆞᆫ젹의야영디의일부대를격퇴ᄒᆞ고졈령ᄒᆞ엿ᄂᆞᆫ디우세ᄒᆞᆫ젹은졈ᄎᆞ우리좌칙비에입박ᄒᆞ엿스나일부디의즁원을득ᄒᆞ야건합령방향으로퇴격ᄒᆞᆫ지라젹은예비대칠십일ᄉᆞ단이빅팔십삼ᄉᆞ연디에속ᄒᆞᆫ바보병약륙빅명과밋긔병삼빅명과대포ᄉᆞ문인디젹의버린바신체삼십구명과ᄉᆞ로잡은쟈ㅣ륙명이요우리ᄂᆞᆫᄯᅩ소총삼십병과탄약오십발과ᄒᆞᆰ으로만든그릇사십기등을엇엇ᄂᆞᆫ디우리군사의부샹ᄒᆞᆫ쟈ᄂᆞᆫ졍샹소위와하사이하이명이더라

작일당디공ᄉᆞ관착면

◯공위군공보 십일월이십일일밤동계관산북포디젼의우리공위부디에디ᄒᆞ야젹병이엄습ᄒᆞ야왓스ᄂᆞ즉시격퇴ᄒᆞ엿고십일월이십이일오후몃시반씀우리히군포의포격을피ᄒᆞ야홍닉긔긔극부근에큰화지를니르켜오후구시ᄭᆞ지연ᄒᆞ야소화ᄒᆞ엿다더라

론셜

수스히협에ᄊᆞᆯ릭함ᄃᆡ

일본허랄드실문역등이라

ᄊᆞᆯ릭함ᄃᆡ가수스히협을지ᄂᆞ나올셰에응당만국[illegible] 디로인어ᄒᆞᆷ을쳥ᄒᆞᆯ[illegible] 락은ᄒᆞᆯ터이나그[illegible] 의되기예도달ᄒᆞᆫ[illegible] 을관리ᄒᆞᄂᆞᆫ나라에[illegible] 취치안코젼폐되[illegible] 지오히려모를거시 당초에그ᄯᅡ인즉[illegible] 며히협부셜ᄒᆞ기ᄂᆞᆫ[illegible] 가ᄒᆞᆷ으로써금[illegible] 로합결ᄒᆞ야토이[illegible] ᄒᆞ야싸은고로각국사[illegible] ᄒᆞᄂᆞᆫ증셔ᄂᆞᆫ토이기[illegible] 가ᄒᆞ기로작졍이되[illegible]

일쳔팔빅륙십륙년 [illegible] 일에토이기국황뎨가[illegible] 각국에디단히긴즁ᄒᆞᆫ[illegible] 각ᄒᆞ고특별ᄒᆞᆫ규칙을[illegible] 언ᄒᆞ되이히협은각국샹젼[illegible] 에됴흥을만드라편입ᄒᆞ야법률[illegible] ᄒᆞ기위ᄒᆞ야만든바이라[illegible] 과다름이업시시행이[illegible] 그후일쳔팔빅팔십삼년에[illegible] 국황뎨가각국위원들[illegible] 말ᄒᆞ기를만일이히협으로[illegible] 어느나라병합이던지단이[illegible] 거든먼져우리나라에쳥ᄒᆞ야[illegible] 허쟝을어든후에힝ᄒᆞ게ᄒᆞ자ᄒᆞ야작졍이되엿고ᄯᅩ토이기국졍부에셔공회ᄒᆞ기를이히협[illegible] 로흥ᄒᆞᄂᆞᆫ권리ᄂᆞᆫ금픽ᄒᆞ[illegible] 버ᄉᆡᆯ리감독으로ᄒᆞ야곰관리케ᄒᆞ자고타졍이되엿ᄂᆞᆫ고로구라파졔국애셔이히협을극진히보호ᄒᆞ더니

일쳔팔빅칠십삼년에젼쟁에ᄊᆞ관되ᄂᆞᆫ샹션츌입밋쳐싱각지못ᄒᆞᄉᆞ닭에자의로츌힝케ᄒᆞ야가만히도망ᄒᆞ야나가ᄂᆞᆫ지라이때에는맛춤아라사와토이기량국에젼갱될때인고로구라파에모든샹고들과히협건츅ᄒᆞᆯ셰에고본금낸사ᄅᆞᆷ들의의론이불둥ᄒᆞ야크게소요ᄒᆞ엿스며

일쳔팔빅칠십칠년이월에ᄂᆞᆫ영국셔인도국에혹무삼히가밋칠가염녀ᄒᆞ야그히협을봉폐ᄒᆞ야션복도단이지못ᄒᆞ게ᄒᆞ도록ᄒᆞ라ᄒᆞ엿스되오히려자의로못ᄒᆞ고아라사대사의게사연으로말ᄒᆞ엿더니아라사에셔디답ᄒᆞ기를영국셔그히협을봉폐ᄒᆞ야남의나라흥히ᄒᆞᆷ을위협ᄒᆞᆯ리유가업다ᄒᆞ으로못되엿고

일쳔팔빅팔십이년에이르러급나라에향ᄒᆞ야이러ᄒᆞᆫ사졍을의말ᄒᆞᆫ후영국에셔졈령ᄒᆞ야자긔나라일과갓치만국보호에필요ᄒᆞᆫ바를자의로압제ᄒᆞᄂᆞᆫ고로일쳔팔빅팔십오년삼월삼십일에법국파리에셔공회를열고셔반아국과뇌더랜국도함셰쳥ᄒᆞ야의론ᄒᆞ엿ᄂᆞᆫ디그때에ᄂᆞᆫ귀정이되지못ᄒᆞ고비로소일쳔팔빅팔십팔년십월이십구일에야덕국과오지리와영국과셔반아국과법국과이태리국과뇌더랜국과아라사국과토이국과아흡나라이모혀회의ᄒᆞᆫ후결안이되여과왕토이기국황뎨의통힝인허쟝주던거손물시ᄒᆞ게작졍ᄒᆞ고특별히각국에셔서로만드려조인ᄒᆞ엿ᄂᆞᆫ디 미완

TELEGRAMS.

Tokyo, Nov. 25th.

The attack on Port Arthur is progressing extremely well. There is reason to believe that rejoicing will take place in a few days.

These joyful tidings from Port Arthur are becoming rather chronic. We seem to remember a similar telegram on August 12, and subsequent months have also proved fertile with news of the projected fall of the citadel.—K. D. N.

EXPERTS' OPINIONS ON THE WAR.

The following are the opinions of three experts, two Russian and one French, on the war, as published by the London "Times" in October.

An interesting interview with General Romanoff, late commander of the 16th Division at the front, is published in the "Novosti Dnya." General Romanoff was severely injured by a fall from his horse on the Yan-tzu-ling heights some weeks ago and is at present en route to a Crimean health resort. In the course of this interview he declared that the perfection attained in quick-firing artillery and long distance rifles had revolutionized battlefield work. There was no comparing even the Russo-Turkish war with the war in Manchuria. "What is wanted to-day is an overwhelming weight of artillery, with an enormous reserve of gun ammunition, and great skill in masking gun positions, together with alertness in shifting them from one point to another." The Russian troops forming the wing operating on the Russian left, and comprising among others the division under General Romanoff, "did what they could to check the advance of the Japanese, who undoubtedly reckoned on occupying Liaoyang earlier." General Romanoff went on to say:—"The present big war has really begun with Liao-yang. We may now expect a series of bloody engagements, and in my opinion it is the coming period of Russian advance which will prove the more complicated and difficult half of the campaign."

This opinion is known to be largely held in competent Russian quarters. Even should the Japanese be beaten below Kharbin, responsible Russian soldiers already entertain few delusions in regard to the inevitable difficulty of any such task as that of driving the Japanese, acting on the defensive, step by step out of Manchuria. This point deserves to be emphasized, as the only argument, to-day as six months ago, which will carry conviction in responsible Russian circles and make for peace is the argument of physical force. The mandate is still to spare no expense and lose no time in pushing out good troops and plenty of them so as to bring the campaign to a successful conclusion for Russia with all possible speed. But the feasibility of campaigning "for years" in Manchuria is already seriously discounted. There are significant indications in certain Government circles here that in the event of the Japanese attaining successfully their northernmost objective and saddling Russia with the very difficult task of assuming the offensive, Russia will be more inclined to hasten the end of the war than seems to be generally supposed. The formation of a second Russian grand army notwithstanding, it is becoming increasingly apparent to Staff Departments here that Japan on the defensive can reply to Russia in the way of reinforcements man for man.

To return to General Romanoff, he frankly admits that "the mountainous country which has hitherto helped the defence will now cease to be our ally and will prove a boon to the enemy acting in his turn on the defensive." He admits that the Japanese outflanked Russia divisions "with ease," and asks pessimistically, "How are we to outflank or surround the enemy with an army of 300,000?" General Romanoff, however, hastens to declare that he is not absolutely despondent in regard to the further course of the campaign. All the same, the tone of his remarks is the reverse of optimistic. He says,—"We all believe we shall win, but, looking at the roof of the matter, I say that, whilst we shall win, the war will be a severe one, since the enemy has turned out to be a most brave and capable one. Besides having to fight with the enemy proper we have to contend with the difficulties of our own base. The Japanese can risk employing whatever and as much gun ammunition as they wish, for a week suffices to replenish their supplies. We can only do this after an interval of a month and a half." What follows is of especial interest. "I strongly believe that had Kuropatkin not been haunted by fears for position of an army gathered together after such a superhuman effort from a distance of 10,000 versts, he would have given decisive battle at Liau-yang and, what is more, he would in all probability have won. But to have done that would have been to risk all. And if something serious had happened? Suppose a defeat? What then? That defeat would have told on the whole future course of the campaign. It might indeed, have been the end of the war."

The second opinion comes from Moscow under date of the October 5th:—

General Velichko, under whose direction the fortifications of the Russian positions at the seat of war in the Far East were carried out, has arrived here. He states that, thanks to these fortifications, General Kuropatkin was able to leave comparatively few troops in Liau-yang and to attack General Kuroki with the bulk of his army. "The wonderful retreat upon Mukden," adds the General, "had no kind of influence upon the strategical position of the Russian army. I do not believe in a turning movement of the Japanese in the direction of Tieling. The prolonged inactivity of the Japanese is to be ascribed to the enormous losses, estimated at 30,000 sustained by them at Liau-yang. The Russians had 3,000 killed and 13,000 wounded at Liau-yang. I think it impossible for the Japanese to form new corps; they will have to confine themselves to replacing the men they have lost."

(To be continued.)

The Minister of Foreign Affairs has been an absentee from his post for some days.

Wireless telegraphy is to be introduced in Switzerland to furnish distress signals for too venturesome Alps climbers.

Thirty-two American students who are taking advantage of the legacy of the late Mr. Cecil Rhodes to complete their educational training at Oxford arrived on the Ivernia at Queenstown from Boston recently.

A fatal accident occurred yesterday outside the South Gate. While working on the new railway embankment, a Korean coolie was crushed to death under a mass of earth dislodged by the sudden collapse of part of the embankment.

Boasting of his English nationality a South Sea Islander was rebuked by one of his friends. "Bah," said he, "you haven't got a drop of English blood in you." The South Sea Islander sniffed. "My dear good friend, said he, "my great-grandfather helped to eat Captain Cook."

A few days ago Mr. Min Yung Son was the recipient of a visit from a stranger from the country, who brought a sealed and mysterious looking letter, which he handed to Mr. Min and then suddenly took his departure. The letter was found to contain a message from Major Kim In Su (late of the Korea army and now with the Russians at Songchin) to the effect that 20,000 Russians are now preparing to march on Seoul. Mr. Min handed the letter over to the Japanese Military authorities, and commenced a search for the bearer of the missive, who has however mysteriously disappeared.

GOOD RIDDANCE

The news of the down fall of mischief makers is always good news. General Hyon Yung-won and his concubine between them have made more mischief than would have been thought possible of such transparent conspirators. What claim to influence the General ever had we do not know, but his concubine (we will call her this in our reluctance to apply a stronger word) seems by dint of unscrupulous enterprise to have at one time placed herself and her nominal protector in positions of power.

That these positions were gained on the understanding that "Lady" Hyun had considerable influence with influential Japanese is certain, and it is therefore very gratifying to find that the Japanese are now repudiating both the concubine and the "gentleman" who has been content to bask in her favour.

When Japanese power in Korea appeared to be on the wane, general and "Lady" Hyon promptly left this country and took refuge in Japan and "Lady" Hyon subsequently had the effrontery to telegraph to the Palace that she had "arranged" that all Japanese, objectionable to the Emperor of Korea, would be recalled.

How have the mighty fallen! The "Daihan Ilpo" which is the mouthpiece of official Japanese opinion in Korea, and which, in the early stages of the war chronicled the doings of this dissolute pair as important, now says:—

"General Hyŏn Yung-woon who went to Japan to study military affairs now stays there with his concubine in the hope of being able to get himself reinstated in position in Korea, but these hopes will not be realised. At first, when he left Korea on the pretence of investigating military affairs in Japan, he took with him the sum of $50,000 and his real object was to ascertain the intentions of the progressist party with regard to Korea. He has been assiduously calling on Japanese politicians, but even the youngest of them has concluded that general Hyŏn is a person of no importance and he is accordingly making no headway. Recently he called on Count Okuma but was refused admission and it now seems that his quest is a hopeles one."

Let us now hope that we have now heard the last of this traitor and his officious concubine.

RETIREMENT OF MR. SHERLOCK HOLMES.

AN INTERVIEW WITH SIR A. CONAN DOYLE.

The world will learn with very great regret that December next will mark the final retirement from public life of the eminent detective, Sherlock Holmes. Despite his iron constitution and nerves of steel, Mr. Holmes is at last feeling the strain of his great achievements. He will take a little place in the country and with his magnificent record behind him will settle down to enjoy the remainder of his days in the simple pleasures of the idyllic life. The bold announcement of his retirement is chronicled in "The Bookman" as follows: "We hear that Sir Arthur Conan Doyle has written for the Christmas number of the Strand Magazine the last adventure of the famous Sherlock Holmes which he will ever chronicle. It is said to be "The Adventure of the Second Stain."

Last month a representative of the Daily Mail journed to the lovely Hindhead home of Sir Arthur Conan Doyle to ascertain, if possible, the reasons and circumstances of the famous detective's retirement.

"A man must retire some time," he said; "he can't go on for ever. Yes his retirement is now absolute and final, So far as I know there is not the slightest intention of his ever again entering on the work of the detection of crime. His last adventure will be a strenuous one, and will, I think, be on a level with some of his higher achievements. After it, he retires for good. For a long time he nursed the idea of a country life with its simply delights. He will take a little place and will go in for bee-keeping."

"Is there not a probability that a period result in a reaction and throw him once more into the consideration of complex and dangerous problems?"

"From what I know," replied Sir Arthur emphatically, "Sherlock Holmes's retirement will be final. He will not again emerge."

It was pointed out to Sir Arthur that some years ago, after the memorable occasion of his encounter with Moriarty on the mountain side, the detective was lost to veiw for a considerable time; was, indeed, believed to be dead.

"Yes," said the author thoughtfully, "and I, for one, firmly believed that he was dead. It was merely by accident that I didn't chronicle the finding of his body. This time, however, his exit will be final.

"No, he won't marry. You will remember he has always wanted time to write a work on the scientific side of his experiences. It is possible that in his retirement he will put his mind on that."

Speaking of incidents in the life of Sherlock Holmes, Sir Arthur recalled Mr. Gillette's preparation for the presentation of the famous detective on the stage. "Mr. Gillette," he said, "wired to me from America asking if he might marry Sherlock Holmes in the play. I replied at once, "Marry him, kill him, or do what you like with him!"

"Yes," added Sir Arthur, "I am rather tired of Sherlock Holmes. I expect the public is too. My first idea of him sprang from Dr. Bell, of Edinburgh University, whom I knew was a medical student there. He had the clear-cut mind of Sherlock Holmes. He would tell the trade of a patient by little signs about him, and would often state what a person was suffering from before a word passed. Thinking of a detective story, I decided that reasoning rather than coincidence should from its basis. Then my experience of Dr. Bell suggested Sherlock Holmes to me.

"'A Study in Scarlet was the first book I published. It made no particular stir. Sherlock Holmes caught on when I began to write the short stories which appeared month by month. I had taken rooms in Wimpole-street with the idea of becoming a consultant on eye troubles. I used to wait there three or four hours every day for the patients who didn't turn up. I utilised my time in writing the first of the Sherlock Holmes short stories."

From that casual beginning sprang the prominent public life of the renowned detective, who makes his farewell bow at Christmas.

The Il Chin Hoi's touring committee have wired news of another alleged case of oppression by a Governor on Chin Po Hoi people. The Governor of Chon Chu, they say, has arrested and beaten two members of that loyal band, nearly killing them. The Il Chin Hoi have announced their intention of obtaining reparation from the Government.

A meeting was held in Manila recently for the purpose of organizing a new bank which is to be known as the Banco de Filipinas. It is to be a purely Filipino institution founded upon Filipino capital with $300,000 Philippine currency. Later the capital will be increased to $3,000,000 and the bank will be made a strictly agricultural bank. This question of an agricultural bank has been before the minds of the Filipino people for a long time, says the "Cablenews." Aguinaldo having been very much interested in the scheme, asking the United States government an immense sum of money, several millions, at one time for the foundation of a bank of that description.

The Korea Daily News.

Issued at 5 P. M. daily except Sundays.
Rate of Subscription :—
Per Year............Yen 25.
Per Quarter,..........Yen 7.
Per Month,..........Yen 2.50.

Postage in Korea not charged extra.
Postage abroad charged extra.

Advertisements, 50 sen per day for 1 inch or less.
5 yen per month per inch.
50 yen per year per inch.

All communications to
E. T. BETHELL,
Editor and Publisher,
Pak-tong, Seoul

WHAT KOREA MUST DO.

In consequence of her geographical situation Korea has always been in the unfortunate position of being the Tom Tiddler's ground of the Far East. Unable to stand up for her own rights she has successively been compelled to herself under the wings of China, Japan Russia and now Japan again.

That of all her "protectors" Japan is the one Korea likes least is absolutely certain. If she dared, Japan would annex Korea tomorrow, but not daring she leaves no stone unturned, short of actual annexation, to forward her designs and establish her influence in this country.

Fortunately for Korea, Japan by withholding land-owning rights from foreigners in her own country has not impressed the great commercial nations as being the best power to control Korea and on purely commercial grounds it is practically certain that Great Britain and the United States, in spite of the friendship for Japan, will allow her no privileges which they do not share. In fact if England and America are well advised and have correctly assessed the present position they will demand that the Japanese government exercises, in future, more efficient control over the commercial peculiarities of its subjects than has hitherto been the case. Fair trading has at present no chance when it comes into conflict with the methods pursued by Japanese merchants here.

Therefore it would appear to be at least very probable that Korea will not have to face the unwelcome prospect of a Japanese protectorate and will, for a time at least, be left alone to direct her own affairs, internal and international.

The Korean Government, however, must not take too much comfort from this reflection, but must look upon her escape as a warning, and so govern her country as to afford no excuse for outside interference in future.

At present Korea is probably the worst governed country in the world, and it is only her immense natural wealth that keeps her from a condition of hopeless insolvency. There are swarms of useless underpaid officials who have to resort to corrupt practises in order to live, and there are millions of idle people who would work hard enough had they any hope of being allowed to retain the fruits of their labour.

A complete revision of the laws of the country and the establishment of a system of taxation free from corruption are two reforms which must be instituted at once. To effect this, Korea, for a time at least, must employ foreign advisers of experience in these matters and must give them greater powers than she has been in the habit of permitting to foreign advisers.

The efforts of Japan's nominees, however well intentioned, we look upon as foredoomed to complete failure. What ever confidence the Korean Government ever had in Japan's intentions has been long ago destroyed. Had it not, the recent pleasant statement of the "Japan Mail," to the effect that in the wrecking of Korea lay Japan's opportunity, would have dealt it its death-blow.

So, to effect anything really useful, Korea must pull herself together, assert her undoubted right to employ what advisers she pleases, and put the adjustment of her affairs in the hands of experienced men known to have no other interests to serve.

If any argument be needed, it is only neccessary to point to the splendid results obtained, both here and in China, by the placing of the Imperial Customs under foreign control.

LEFT FLANK ATTACK.

The following taken from the "Brigadezeitung," a paper edited in Tientsin by a German military officer, is interesting:

The lines of the two opposing Manchurian armies extend over a distance of fifty kilometres, and this front has probably not been reduced since the arrival of reinforcements on the Russian side. That the Russians have been able, ever after the battle of Yentai, to get a foothold on the banks of the Shaho, and to assume the offensive with portions of their army, is proof of their staying qualities and ability of their commander. It is to be presumed that the Japanese will attempt to bring about a decisive engagement with the left flank of Kuropatkin's forces. The soil of the great Liao plain is becoming more suitable day by day for the movement of great bodies of soldiers, and especially for manoeuvers of cavalry. Consequently here before their right flank, will the Russians be able to use their superior cavalry with telling effect. Of quite another character is the country opposite the Russian left flank. A flank movement in this direction is much more feasible for the Japanese. The Russian cavalry up to date has been of little use over this ground. However, previous battles have shown that General Kuropatkin has concentrated a great force on the left of his line, knowing this to be the probable point of Japanese attack, and this force has made victory possible. The fact that Kuropatkin has been called to the supreme command of the army in East Asia will prove a telling factor in the campaign.

THE DEAD AT LIAOYANG.

He had no quarrel with any man,
He knew not what they called him for:
Yet, roll and pack upon his back,
Ivan, the peasant, went to war.
"The Little Father calls," he said,
And followed, followed as he sang.
Till on a trampled trench he lay
Among the dead at Liaoyang.

Not his the dream of land and power,
The greed of gain; the dread of loss:
He marched with orders to the field
To bear his rifle—and his cross.
God had ordained it, so he faced
The pelting hail that snarled and sang
And gave his patient blood a way
Among the dead at Liaoyang.

Among the glitter of his court
In safety sat the mystic Czar!
Safe sat the scheming Minister
Who cast a careless die for war;
They could not hear the shattered groan,
The horrid chant of death that rang
Where unconsulted thousands lay,
Among the dead at Liaoyang.

He had no quarrel with any man,
He had no cause to battle for:
Yet, roll and pack upon his back,
Ivan, the peasant, went to war.
A minister had made a map
From which a deadly army sprang.
So Ivan fell and made no sign
Among the dead at Liaoyang.

New York Globe.

[Those whose opinions do not fall in line with those of the poet, can, if they please, substitute Japanese names for Czar and Ivan and Port Arthur for Liaoyang.]

Ed. K. D. N.

IRON DUKE DERIDED IRON ROAD.

It was in 1830 that the opening of the railway between Liverpool and Manchester was celebrated. The Duke of Wellington's ideas concerning the iron road of seventy-eight years ago are thus described by Chaplain Gleig. "The Duke of Wellington was invited in his capacity of Prime Minister to take part in the opening journey. It chanced that he was at Walmer and surrounded by a large company of guests when the invitation reached him, and not a few, especially his lady friends, were urging him to decline. No great or permanent good could come of the invitation, because stage coaches already travelled at the rated of eight or ten miles in the hour, and if any attempt were made to exceed that pace the respiration of the passengers would become painful, perhaps impossible. The duke would listen to no remonstrances. He thought, as others did, that the experiment was risky, and derided the idea of accelerating the pace, as was promised, to twenty miles an hour. Even a twelve-mile pace he regarded as excessive, because difficult, if not impossible, to control, and agreed in the opinion that the iron way would never, for general traffic, supersede our macadamised roads, then brought to perfection."—Chicago News.

The Foreign Office have telegraphically ordered Mr. Yi Chai Kuk to return with his party of sight seers.

The President and Vice-President of the Council of State, together with the Ministers of Finance and Agriculture have sent in their resignations.

A Japanese syndicate have obtained a concession from the Acting Minister of the Household Department, for the construction of water works in Chemulpo.

The Governor of North Chulla province has been instructed by the Home Office to release 3 men belonging to the Chin Po Hoi, whom he recently imprisoned.

The Korean Minister to Peking says he will return, according to instructions as soon as he can get a steamer, but no money has been sent him for his travelling expenses and he is unfortunately out of funds.

The national Education Society will shortly hold their opening meeting at the young men's association club. Mr. Hidewara, a Japanese teacher in the Korean middle school, has been invited to attend and make the opening speech.

A Korean non-commissioned officer and two soldiers, despatched from Chong Sung to Yeung Heung on military affairs has been arrested and imprisoned by the Japanese, on the grounds that Chong Sung is occupied by the Russians and they cannot permit the men to return after visiting territory in Japanese occupation.

A correspondent at Dortmund states that Krupps's of Essen, are working day and night in manufacturing new guns for Japan and Russia. There are two special rooms, one for the Russian and another for the Japanese officers and designers or draughtsmen. Several new patterns of guns are in process of manufacture, one of a calibre hitherto unknown, and with a special arrangement for accelerating the speed of the projectile.

The Korea Daily News.

VOL. I, | SATURDAY, NOVEMBER 26, 1904. | No. 110

大韓每日申報
대한미일신보

(뎨일빅십일호) (화요일) 일쳔구빅사년십일월이십구일

본샤고빅

으신보논영어와한어로셕거미일츌판ᄒᆞᆸ

신문가

한쟝 엽두돈오푼
일삭됴 엽두량닷돈
우표가미삭닷돈
다맛돈으로밧습

광고료논

귀한의쟝단과ᄌᆞ힝의다쇼로즁감ᄒᆞ되렴가로밧을터이오며오릭지아녀대한사람마다다이신문을보실터이니광고내시기를원ᄒᆞ시는이들은우리신문샤에와셔면약ᄒᆞ심을희망ᄒᆞᆸ

○발힝소 박동대한미일신보샤법어학교압헤젼영국인셜필림집자리오

샤쟝 영국인 (비셜)

평양 디리졈

○평양효동사ᄂᆞᆫ권미보씨로우리신문관디리인을턱졍ᄒᆞ엿ᄉᆞ오니평양에계신구람코져ᄒᆞ시는쳠군ᄌᆞ는히디리졈에왕림ᄒᆞ와면의ᄒᆞ시옵

사고

○우리대한미일신보의목뎍은대한의안녕질셔에관한모든대목에ᄃᆡᄒᆞ야ᄂᆞᆫ공평한변론을쥬쟝ᄒᆞᆷ이라우리동신원의담론은신문보시ᄂᆞᆫ쳠군ᄌᆞ의계흥상보도ᄒᆞ리며편지를긔셔ᄒᆞ여주시ᄂᆞᆫ이ᄂᆞᆫ셩명과반ᄃᆡ를젹어붓치시기를희망ᄒᆞ오니이거슬신문샹에긔ᄌᆡᄒᆞ라ᄂᆞᆫ거시아니오다만극히신용ᄒᆞᄂᆞᆫ증거를숨고쟈ᄒᆞᆷ이라긔쟈ᄂᆞᆫ아모긔셔던지긔ᄌᆡᄒᆞᆷ을되각각ᄒᆞᄂᆞᆫ권리를가젓스나되각ᄒᆞᄂᆞᆫ리유를말ᄒᆞᆯ터이오며공즁평화를문란케ᄒᆞᄂᆞᆫ듯ᄒᆞᆫ긔셔ᄂᆞᆫ의례히밧지안켓ᄉᆞᆸ나이다

●본샤셜시이리로신문을미양우례로분젼ᄒᆞ와뎨젼부의임의로젼ᄒᆞᆫ듯ᄉᆞ로면곳에ᄂᆞᆫ혹늣게젼ᄒᆞ기도ᄒᆞ며혹몃칠거슬ᄒᆞᆫ겁에젼ᄒᆞ기도ᄒᆞ며혹아니젼ᄒᆞᄂᆞᆫ곳도잇다ᄒᆞ와우리신문을ᄉᆞ랑ᄒᆞ야구람ᄒᆞ시ᄂᆞᆫ 쳠군ᄌᆞ의게되ᄒᆞ야미우미안ᄒᆞ옵기로지금은분젼인을두고미일일즉이젼ᄒᆞ며아니젼ᄒᆞ거나늣게거나ᄒᆞᆫ치가업도록ᄒᆞ랴ᄒᆞ오니혹아니전ᄒᆞ거나혹늣게젼ᄒᆞ거나ᄒᆞᆫ일이잇스면본샤로통긔ᄒᆞ여쥬심을희망ᄒᆞᆸ

잡보

○쥽포관쳥원 쥽포관의홍군슈죠병유씨가내부로훈쳥원셔에운ᄒᆞ엿스되본관이그지지가이소입을감당치못ᄒᆞ겟ᄉᆞ오니쥽포관의소입을곳 주면ᄒᆞ라ᄒᆞ엿고또의견셔에운ᄒᆞ엿스되업디여싱각건대쥽포관은쥽ᄒᆞᆫ소임이라지략과담용이잇슨연후에야가히션졍ᄒᆞᄂᆞᆫ디맛당ᄒᆞᆫ지라무롯뎐하의일이근본이잇고씃치잇ᄂᆞ니현금디방관리즁에혹광젼인쥭쥭독히빗드리고샹납인쥭건쳬ᄒᆞᄂᆞᆫ쟈잇셔만일즁간에셔리를놈기지못ᄒᆞᆯ것ᄀᆞᆺᄒᆞ면젼슈히건몰ᄒᆞ니막즁ᄒᆞᆫ공납을경변월세로록ᄉᆞ채와ᄀᆞᆺ치보와국고에샹납지아니ᄒᆞ니이ᄂᆞᆫ나라의도적이오무죄ᄒᆞᆫ량민을억지로죄를얽어악형을버플며몰닉뢰물을만히토석ᄒᆞ니이ᄂᆞᆫ빅셩의도적이라도적으로써말ᄒᆞᆯ양이면도적은이도적에셔더큰거시업거ᄂᆞᆯ이거ᄉᆞᆫ쥽포ᄒᆞ라고허락지아니ᄒᆞ고도로혀절도의무리를칙망ᄒᆞ니엇지근본을버리고씃출다ᄉᆞ림이아니리오도적도ᄯᅩᄒᆞᆫ사ᄅᆞᆷ이라지금이러케도적질ᄒᆞᆷ을엇지ᄒᆞᆷ기를즐겨ᄒᆞᆯ비리오졍소를싸다롭게ᄒᆞᄂᆞᆫ듯스로직업을편안이ᄒᆞᆯ슈업셔셔류리ᄒᆞ야쥭게되미반ᄃᆞ시쥭을ᄶᅡᆼ에라도드러가니던디에셔품부ᄒᆞᆫ셩질과부모의게셔밧ᄎᆞᆫ신례로엇지도적의게만ᄊᆞ로죵조가잇리오지그도적을싱각건ᄃᆡ극히의궁ᄒᆞᆫ지라정샹지가히일일베혀죽이리오감엇식히고회기식혀귀화케ᄒᆞᄂᆞᆫ거동시요긴ᄒᆞᆫ길이라첫재무엇신고ᄒᆞ니담탑ᄒᆞᄂᆞᆫ거술징계ᄒᆞᆯ지니관리되고셔도적질ᄒᆞ자아니ᄒᆞ면빅셩도ᄯᅩᄒᆞᆫ도적질ᄒᆞ지아니ᄒᆞᄒᆞᆯ지라사건쟝졍모든됴목즁에운ᄒᆞ엿스되쥽포ᄒᆞᄂᆞᆫ디잘방죠쳐아니ᄒᆞ면도러보고ᄒᆞ야벌을쳥ᄒᆞ라ᄒᆞ니비록방죠를잘ᄒᆞ라다손쳐드릭도젹슈공권으로총과칼을가진젹당을엇지써딕젹ᄒᆞ릿가그윽히어리셕은소견을쳡부ᄒᆞ오니졍부에이죠ᄒᆞᆫ와쥽포관의소임을급히례면ᄒᆞ여주시기를복망이라ᄒᆞ엿더라

○죄슈압거 경위원에셔법부로죠회ᄒᆞ기를례산사ᄅᆞᆷ김현귀가풍슈로라고칭탁ᄒᆞ고파쥬군슈신셕효를반연ᄒᆞ야감히요언망셜노씨막즁ᄒᆞᆫ국사에현란케ᄒᆞᆫ온바졍괴렵과최돈샹과리죵우동이ᄯᅩᄒᆞᆫ사환으로셔작반ᄒᆞ야정셔ᄒᆞᄂᆞᆫᄃᆡ역사ᄒᆞ엿습기에이샹죄범오인을일병압교ᄒᆞ오니심관ᄒᆞ시기를위요라ᄒᆞ엿더라

○면조송피 경샹북도관찰ᄉᆞ쟝승원씨ᄂᆞᆫ참졍신긔션씨의게면조일빅근을송피ᄒᆞ엿더라

○인홍슈도 인허 궁니부대신셔리리용ᄐᆡᆨ씨가인쳔홍슈도부셜권을일본사ᄅᆞᆷ의게인허ᄒᆞ엿다더라

○고시총지청연 일젼에경부텰도회샤총지고시공위씨가구락부에셜연ᄒᆞ고각부대신을쳥요ᄒᆞ엿더라

○대관사소 의졍리근명씨와참졍신긔션씨와탁지대신민영긔씨와농샹대신리도재씨졔씨가사직소를올넛더라

○회국칙교 외부에셔쥬일공관에면보ᄒᆞ기를학부대신이하졔원을속히회국ᄒᆞᆯ사로봉지ᄒᆞ엿다더라

○하이위지 쥬쳥공사가외부로면보ᄒᆞ되션편을기ᄃᆡ려셔발졍ᄒᆞ겟스나회환비를보ᄂᆡ지아니ᄒᆞ니엇지ᄒᆞᆯᄂᆞᆫ지회면ᄒᆞ라ᄒᆞ엿더라

○제봉ᄎᆞ발환 양복졈쥬인일본인원등복송씨가외교관대례복지봉ᄎᆞ로견양을가지고금일에동경으로발환ᄒᆞᆫ다더라

○대신결셕 외부대신이쟉금량일에히부에사진치아니ᄒᆞ엿더라

○굴토압사 남문밧텰도역소에셔역부리진술이가구명이를파다가ᄌᆞ이문어져즉시치사ᄒᆞ엿더라

○국사봉립표 지쟉일에일인이남산봉화지국사당압헤표목을셰우표과ᄡᆞᆯ에쓰기롤한국쥬챠군사령부라ᄒᆞ엿더라

○황간회적 음구월이십일밤에화적오십명이황잔등디로종ᄒᆞ야무쥬군풍동면금쳑리에돌립ᄒᆞ야사십이호를츙화ᄒᆞ야일반가산이몰소ᄒᆞ엿다고ᄒᆞ더라

○진명회공함 진명회회쟝라유셕씨가일본헌병부ᄃᆡ쟝과한국경무쳥과경위원에공함ᄒᆞᆫ젼문이여좌ᄒᆞ니

경계쟈ᄂᆞᆫ라유셕이가광무이년독립협회시에그릇우리졍부에간사ᄒᆞᆫ쎄에속아수만샹민을영솔ᄒᆞ고문명의사회를단타ᄒᆞ야스ᄉᆞ로야만의힘실에빠져ᄂᆡ외국인의침밧고ᄯᅡ지즘이되야스니붓그러뉘우침이어ᄃᆡ밋치리오다힝이오늘날문명의제회를당ᄒᆞ니비록유셕의우미로도젹이마음에ᄭᆡ다름이잇셔동지쟈약간인으로더브러금월하오일졈에면동션면도가에셜회ᄒᆞ고동포를권유ᄒᆞ며졍부를츙고ᄒᆞ야쟝ᄎᆞᆺ혼가지로문명의지경에나가고쟈ᄒᆞᄂᆞᆫ뜻인고로구회를일홈ᄒᆞ야진명이라ᄒᆞ엿스니싱각건ᄃᆡ각하ᄂᆞᆫ직칙이경찰ᄒᆞᄂᆞᆫᄃᆡ잇슨즉인민취회ᄒᆞᄂᆞᆫᄃᆡ맛당

관보

뎨이천구빅구십ᄉᆞ호

광무팔년십일월이십륙일

셔임급ᄉᆞ령

○승셔관임관오등 경위원쥬ᄉᆞ 한대원
십월이십삼일
○승셔관임관ᄉᆞ등 경위원총슌 리덕슌
십월이십ᄉᆞ일
○승셔관임관삼등 인천항총슌 박연규
십일월십팔일
○명규쟝각학ᄉᆞ셔칙임관삼등 경효뎐졔죠 김셩근
○명경효뎐졔죠셔칙임관일등 종일품 김규홍
○겸임쟝례원쟝례 비셔원승 신셩균
○의원면본관 온릉참봉 김샹필
숙릉참봉 리희명
○임온릉참봉셔판임관팔등 통신ᄉᆞ면회과쥬ᄉᆞ 남뎡칠
○임슉릉참봉셔판임관팔등 리강년
○승셔쥬임관ᄉᆞ등 텰도원문셔과쟝 김남집
○승셔관임관삼등 텰도원쥬ᄉᆞ 리용셕
○승셔판임관오등 쟝례원쥬ᄉᆞ 쟝셰영

UNION INSURANCE SOCIETY OF CANTON.

Head office Hongkong.
Marine risks underwritten at current rates.
Agents in Chemulpo,
E. MEYER & Co.

COMPAGNIE DES MESSAGERIES MARITIMES.

Fortnightly Direct Service.

For Marseilles
via Ports.
Sailing from Yokohama
Calling at Kobe,
Shanghai, Hongkong, Saigon, Singapore,
Colombo, Djibouti, Suez, Port Said
and Marseilles.

For particulars apply to
HOLME RINGER & Co.,
Chemulpo.

HAYASHIDA & Co.,

16 MYENG-DONG, CHIN KO KAI, SEOUL.
BRANCH OFFICE AT CHEMULPO.

Money changers, Coal and Wood Merchants, Express Agents.

We are agents for the Pyeng-yang Coal Company and the Karazu Coal Company of Japan. We have the best quality of both anthracite and bituminous coal, and prompt execution of orders is our speciality. Firewood of all kinds kept in stock. Full weight guaranteed. Money of all denominations exchanged at current rates. Parcels received for all parts.

CHINA MUTUAL LIFE INS. CO.

Most favourable terms to policy holders.

Benefit system unsurpassed.

HOLME RINGER & Co.
Agents, Chemulpo.

C. P. R.

CANADIAN PACIFIC RAILWAY COMPANY'S ROYAL MAIL STEAMSHIP LINE.

THE FAST ROUTE BETWEEN CHINA, JAPAN, AND EUROPE VIA CANADA AND THE UNITED STATES.

Route from Hongkong via Shanghai, Nagasaki (Inland Sea of Japan) Kobe, Yokohama to Victoria and Vancouver.

Twin Screw Empress Steamship—6,000 Tons—Speed 19 knots.

PROPOSED SAILING FROM YOKOHAMA.
R. M. S. Empress of India.
R. M. S. Empress of Japan.
R. M. S. Empress of China.
R. M. S. Athenian.
R. M. S. Tartar.

Special reduction (first class only) granted to members of the Military, Naval, Diplomatic and Civil services and to Missionaries.
Passengers have choice of ten routes across the Continent of America and have privilege of travelling by any Atlantic Steamship Line.
Round the World passage tickets in connection with the P. and O. S. N., North German Lloyd and Messageries Co.'s £125.
All rates payable at current rate of exchange.
For further information, Tickets, Guide Books, etc., apply to
HOLME, RINGER & Co., AGENTS,
Chemulpo.

Grand Hotel,

(Formerly the Station Hotel)

Near the Railway Terminus,
West Gate, Seoul.

The Best Hotel in Korea
Handsome new Building.
Fine Airy Rooms
Excellent Cuisine
Terms Moderate.
Special terms to Missionaries
and to permanent boarders.

Electric cars within 2 minutes' walk.

W. H. EMBERLEY,
Proprietor

EVERY FACILITY.

In connection with Life Assurance Business is afforded by

The Standard Life Assurance Co.,

One of the largest and wealthiest of the Provident Institutions of the United Kingdom Forms of Application and all information will be promptly afforded on application.

10 CENTS A DAY.

Not a very large expenditure is it? But it is sufficient to secure for a man of 30 a policy with the STANDARD LIFE OFFICE for

$1323.

For all particulars of rates, etc., apply to

Holme, Ringer & Co.,
Agents, Chemulpo.

THE NEW YORK LIFE INSURANCE COMPANY.

Have you ever been declined by any Company?

Are you engaged in a specially hazardous occupation?

Have you heard of the New York Life Insurance Company's New Classifications for this class of Risks?

If not, send your date of birth, occupation and particulars of rejection, if any to

E. MEYER & Co.,
Agents, Chemulpo.

MITSUI BUSSAN KAISHA.
(MITSUI & Co.)
MITSUI GINKO.
(MITSUI BANK.)

The Bank is owned by the members of the Mitsui Family, who, as partners, assume an unlimited responsibility for all liabilities of the Bank:—

Capital .... Yen 5,000,000
Reserve Fund .... " 5,600,000

HEAD OFFICE, TOKYO.
LONDON OFFICE, 34 LIME ST., E. C.

BRANCHES AND AGENCIES:—
New York, San Francisco, Hamburg, Bombay, Singapore, Manila, Hongkong, Amoy, Chefoo, Tientsin.
Kobe, Hakodate, Yokohama, Kure, Yokosuka, Moji, Shimonoseki, Miike, Wakamatsu, Nagasaki, Kuchinotsu, Karatsu, Sasebo, Misume, Taipeh, &c.

Telegraphic Address for all the Offices:
"MITSUI."
A. B. C. AND A. 1 CODES USED.

Contractors of Coal
To the Imperial Japanese Navy. Arsenals and Railway Bureau, Principal Railway Companies and Industrial Work, Home and Foreign Mail and Freight Steamers.

Sole Proprietors
Of the famous Miike, Tagawa and Yamano Coal Mines.

Sole Agents
For the sale of Fukumo, Hokoku, Ichimura, Kanoda, Maunoura, Onoura, Ostuji, Sonoda, Tsubaruro, Yoshinotani, Yoshio, Yurokibura and other coals.

YANGTSE INSURANCE ASSOCIATION, LTD

The undersigned, having been appointed agents for the above company, are prepared to issue policies and pay losses on marine risks at regular rates.

E. MEYER & Co.,
Agents, Chemulpo.

AMERICAN KOREAN ELECTRIC CO.

Light and Power.

Main Office: Electric Building, Chong No.

RAILWAY DEPARTMENT.

OPERATING CARS BETWEEN EAST AND WEST GATE, EVERY TEN MINUTES:—

First Car leaves East Gate at 7:00 A. M. First Car leaves R. R Station at 7:25 A. M
Last Car " East Gate at 9:40 P. M. Last " " R. R. Station at 10:05 P.M

OPERATING CARS BETWEEN EAST GATE AND IMPERIAL TOMB TERMINUS, EVERY TWENTY MINUTES:—

CONNECTING WITH EVERY ALTERNATE CAR ARRIVING AT EAST GATE FROM CHONG NO.

First Car leaves East Gate for Tomb at 7:10 A. M.
" " " Tomb for East Gate at 7:35 A. M.
Last " " East Gate for Tomb at 7:50 P. M.
" " " Tomb for East Gate at 8:10 P. M.

OPERATING CARS BETWEEN CHONG NO AND YUNG SAN RIVER EVERY TWELVE MINUTES:—

First Car leaves Chong No for South Gate at 7:12 A. M.
" " " Chong No for Yung San at 7:36 A. M.
" " " South Gate for Chong No at 7:20 A. M.
" " " Yung San for Chong No at 8:09 A. M.
Last " " South Gate for Chong No 10:00 P. M.
" " " Yung San for Chong No at 9:33 P. M.

SPECIAL PRIVATE CARS FURNISHED TO SUIT CONVENIENCE OF PATRONS. PRICES ON APPLICATION AT HEAD OFFICE.

LIGHTING DEPARTMENT

Where less than 250 candle power of light is used, the rate per month will be
Per 16 candle power incandescent lamp,—All night.—Yen 2.50.
32 candle power incandescent lamp:—All night:—Yen 4.00.
50 candle power incandescent lamp:—All night:—Yen 6.00.
150 " " " " — " " " 10.00.
1200 " " enclosed arc " " " " 20.00.

Where more than 250 candle power of light is used, a Meter will be installed, if requested:—Rent of Meter Yen 2.00 per month. Rate of charges by meter reading:—Two Sen per Ampere per hour. (Approximately this is equal to about One Sen per 16 C. P. lamp per hour) Minimum monthly charge where meter is installed, Yen 20.00 per month, which includes rental of meter.

Estimates for installing lights furnished on application.
An assortment of chandeliers always on hand.

K. Murakami,
Photograph Studio
Chinkokai, Seoul.

Printing, Developing and Enlargement, of Photographs always Undertaken.

Korean Views and Pictures Illustrating Native Customs always on Sale.

THE OSAKA SHOSEN KAISHA.

Boats frequently on the berth for Chinnampo.

REGULAR SAILINGS BETWEEN JAPAN AND KOREAN PORTS.

FUSAN AND KOBE VIA SHIMONOSEKI.

OSAKA VIA MOKPO, FUSAN, SHIMONOSEKI AND KOBE.

MOJI DIRECT.

OSAKA VIA KUNSAN, MASANPO, FUSAN, SHIMONOSEKI AND KOBE.

CHEMULPO KUNSAN LINE,
Every three days.

CHEMULPO CHINNAMPO LINE.
Every three days.

For Freight and passage and further particulars apply to
THE OSAKA SHOSEN KAISHA,
Chemulpo

RONDON, PLAISANT & CO.

General Storekeepers and Merchants, Ships Contractors, Tobacconists, Commission and Forwarding Agents, Coal Merchants

IMPORTERS AND EXPORTERS

Seoul & Chemulpo.

W. D. WENTWORTH.

LANDING
AND
SHIPPING AGENT
AND
CUSTOMS BORDER.

12 OURA, NAGASAKI.

STEWARD & CO.

Chemulpo.

Shipchandlers and Storekeepers, Naval and Mercantile Contractors, Landing and Shipping Agents.

STEWARD'S HOTEL

Chemulpo.

Best accommodation in this port for travellers. Clean and well-aired rooms, good cuisine and prompt attendence, moderate tariff.

○금일문봉 ᄂ부관졔국장
리용세
이샹십일월이십ᄉ일
궁내부록ᄉ
○조셔ᄒ야 골ᄋ샤ᄃᆡ 향쟈비창
ᄒᆫ중의 관의쳥죄ᄒ뎨읍죵ᄒᆫ졋
은다믄ᄉ면과극졔에잇슴쎈아
니요셜ᄒᆫ젼례에가히빙쟈ᄒᆯ이
잇스니모든의관은특별히분간
ᄒ야방송ᄒ라ᄒ셧더라
○조셔ᄒ야 골ᄋ샤ᄃᆡ 국쟝도감
졔조윤덕영을명ᄒ샤빈젼도감
졔조를샹으시고빈종무관쟝조
동윤으로국쟝도감졔조를샹으
시다
이샹십일월이십삼일
○조셔ᄒ야 골ᄋ샤ᄃᆡ 경효젼졔
조김셩근을명ᄒ샤규쟝각학ᄉ졔
를샹으시고김규홍으로경효젼
졔조를샹으시다
십일월이십ᄉ일

론셜

슈ᄉ히헌텹에 쉘릐헙티
일본헤랄드신문에등 (속)

○고조인ᄒᆫ글에ᄒ엿스되평란
지시와젼쟁지ᄎ를무론ᄒ고그
히헝에ᄌ유로통힝ᄒ야편리ᄒ
도록ᄒ엿고이히헝인즉각국에
셔션쳑을죵발ᄒ기위ᄒ야긔통
ᄒᆫ바인즉무론어ᄂ나라이던지
하며ᄒᆫᄉ건이거나봉폐치못ᄒᆯ
일이며ᄯᅩᄒᆫ젼쟁이될셰에ᄂᆞᆫ이
히헝근쳐어ᄂ셔이던지샹명히
리안에ᄂ병뎡든디라ᄃ지못ᄒ게
ᄒᆯ일괘비롯ᄒ이기국에서어ᄂ
나라로ᄃ부러젼쟁이되든지도
임ᄒ죵바ᄒ을일의로못ᄒ게ᄒ
고ᄯᅩᄒᆫ젼투함들은이히헝으로
지니가기ᄂᆞᆫᄒ드ᄃ도졍시간ᄉ
숙ᄒ히ᄒ쟈ᄒ엿더니
그항구안에서ᄂᆞᆫ뵈셩들이맘ᄒ
기를다ᄒ고바다에ᄃ방함을ᄆ
다리검속ᄒᆯ일아니라수ᄉ통지
예도이빙을시힝ᄒ계ᄒ며무론
어ᄂ나라이던지기젼ᄒᆫ나라빈
논이히헝에이르러이셩수시
간에외에ᄂ더지톄치못ᄒ게ᄒ
며교젼ᄒᄂ나라병함은이항구
에드리와군ᄉ던지군물을탐지
치못ᄒ게ᄒ는거시조금ᄲ시이
법을졍ᄒ야분진ᄒ병함이일홈
ᄒ야오리죵박지아니ᄒ리ᄒ셤리
이며ᄯᅩᄒᆫ싸ᄒ아니ᄒᄂ나라병
함들로ᄒ여곰일ᄒᆼᄒ야직히게
ᄒ는거시조리ᄒ야그리케되엿
ᄂᆞᆫ지라
이외에대양히헝과갑ᄉ히헝은
토이기국황뎨외의금국군주가
ᄒᆼ히ᄒᆷ을ᄌ유로ᄒ엿셧스나그
리ᄒ나교스탄빈씨에셔구대강
국이모혀의결ᄒᆫ이후로통립이
못되엿ᄂᆞᆫ디
만일에당ᄒ초부터젼국병함의엉
ᄒᆼᄒᆷ을금지ᄒ엿슬진ᄃᆡ응당영
국과법국은교사ᄒ고서반아국
파화란국과이태리국에서라도
이일에ᄃᆡᄒ야동샹ᄒᆷ력ᄒ야쳥
조ᄒ엿슬지라
죵왕에아라사와젼위원이이법
을ᄒᆼ히에셔지쓰자ᄒ엿더니이
티리국위원이이일에ᄂᆞᆫ반ᄃᆡᄒ
야되지못ᄒ엿스죠이번에쉘릐
헙티가나올ᄯᅢ에수스히헝지니
기ᄂᆞᆫ아모렴녀도업슬터이되ᄒ
히헝에이르러서ᄂᆞᆫᄒ이른셔수되
야정이던지운송션을파송에비ᄒ
야무슴권계이잇슬가불무렴녀
일듯ᄒ다고ᄒ엿더라 (완)

잡보

히젼쟝총ᄒᆯ리유가잇ᄂᆞᆫ고로이에
모될귀양을미리고ᄒ고ᄎ취ᄌ서
일환을알보ᄒ오니조량ᄒ샤싱을
보란다ᄒ엿더라
광무팔년십일월이십륙일
ᄃᆡ유셕

○이쟝치지졍 궁내부에셔내
부로조회ᄒ기를 원소내외히
조내사무ᄃᆡ를 ᄒ등례들의
지ᄒ야과음기라신 치분을봉
승ᄒ왓스니이쟝치소를곳가ᄅ
쳐졍케ᄒ고히디방관의게훈칙
ᄒ야불일거ᄒᆼ되ᄒ라ᄒ엿더라
○리씨귀송 빈명화씨가평양
관찰사로지임시에리갑씨도ᄃᆡ
들탈취ᄒ엿던지참위리경씨가
우금십오년을엉울이너이다가
일작에빈명화씨를가셔보고일
쟝ᄒ파를지엇ᄂᆞᆫ티리갑씨가일
간송사ᄒ논다더라
○수부교편 ᄃᆡ운학교ᄂᆞᆫ학도
가졸업ᄒ면교편을곳불칫다가
켤을기다려ᄎ우ᄂᆞᆫ티스범학교
ᄂᆞᆫ그리치아니ᄒ야비록학원이
졸업을ᄒ엿드리도다시켤잇ᄂᆞᆫ
것을기티려ᄎ운죵학원이소망
이업셔쳥탕팔탁ᄒ야졍졍조잔
ᄒᆫᄂᆞᆫ고로교쟝김명진씨가다른
학교규뎨들의지ᄒ야졸업ᄒ면
곳교관으로불쳐쟈고의정부의
안건을학부에졔출ᄒ엿더라
○신챵경미안 ᄃᆡ관김쳔구등
조롤ᄉ진에티ᄒ야신챵경도무
소셜업ᄒᆫ수가잇던지ᄯᅩᄒᆫ미안
ᄒᆫ중에잇다더라
○회보간츌 일진회에셔회보
를발간ᄒᆯᄃᆡ인테활판과쥬ᄌᄂᆞᆫ
젼광문사것을비용ᄒ리라더라
○권고방송 젼라북도관찰부
에셔진보회원삼인을챠슈ᄒᆼ영
ᄒᆫ다ᄒᆷ으로일진회에셔내부에
권고ᄒ기를히삼인을불일즉방
ᄒ야셩경이업게ᄒ라ᄒ엿다더
라
○내대수적 ᄂ부대신리용
티씨ᄂᆞᆫ쟝츳ᄉ직샹소를ᄒᆫ다ᄒ
더라
○군비츄감 탁지부에셔명년
도예산표를방금조ᄉ중인데군
부예산이만이츄감이될듯ᄒ
다더라

○쳘졍비지 ᄉ참졍비지내에
곳시무ᄒ라ᄒ셧더라
○한병구류 죵셩에잇ᄂᆞᆫ한국
디방티에서졍평영ᄒ부군으로
하ᄉ일명샹등병일명병졍일명
을파견ᄒ야군비금을죵발ᄒ엿
거니와우리군졍구역내에서이
러ᄒᆫ일을쟝쟈고지내지못ᄒᆯ쌘
아니라방금아라사군ᄉ가졈령
ᄒᆫ디역내에지ᄒᆫ한국병졍이우
리군ᄉ가졈령ᄒᆫ디역내로리도
ᄒ야ᄯᅩ도라갑이우리군ᄉ샹에
유익ᄒ지못ᄒᆷ으로히병졍삼인
을구류ᄒ엿다더라
○면ᄒᆫ젼북 내부에서젼라북
도관찰부로면ᄒᆫᄒ기를곳드른
즉진보회미명을챠슈ᄒ고형벌
을폐ᄒᆫ다ᄒ니십월이십구일법
조칙중에지슈ᄒᆫ자를방셕ᄒ야
써츅단ᄒᆫ뜻을뵈ᄒ되조치안코
션동ᄒᄂᆞᆫ자ᄂᆞᆫ가히용티치못ᄒᆯ
지라ᄒ엿시니이거순과연가히
용티치못ᄒᆯ죄가잇ᄂᆞᆫ가그러치
아니ᄒ면엇지가히창슈ᄒ고형
벌을베풀리오ᄉ실을곳회면ᄒ
라ᄒ엿더라
○슈산회사계약 일공ᄉ가외
부로조회ᄒ기를쟝긔도포경합
자회사쟝림포명이가귀국슈산
회사뎌표인민병한으로더부러
계약을셩립ᄒ고슈산회사소유
케권을포경회사에위임ᄒ야졍
허ᄒᆫ지라포경회사위ᄉ엽을경샹
히관쟝에셔비ᄒᆯ터이니졍권티츙
원산히관쟝의계신칙ᄒ야부산과
평양의계젼조ᄒ야시힝
ᄃᆡ홈을바라ᄂᆞᆫ이다ᄒ엿ᄂᆞᆫ데별지
한슈산란ᄒ다ᄒ엿ᄂᆞᆫ뎨경부등비
슈회사에셔졍부에허락ᄒᆷ에
엇어셔사가지도표목을셩립ᄒ고
그일졀슈엽을포경회사에위임
ᄒ고그표ᄂᆞᆫ좌곳치졍ᄒᆷ
일대한슈산회사ᄂᆞᆫ룩도표취지소
유를인ᄒ야일졀슈엽을포계소
회사에젼임ᄒ고졍힝ᄒ되그
리약손히ᄂᆞᆫ슈산회사에서간
셥지못ᄒᆯᄉ
일에ᄂᆞᆫ계약셩립이십년이차기젼
에ᄂᆞᆫ졔반비용이심이만ᄒ니
곳치이를엇지못ᄒ고슈산회
사보조금을비년일빅원식교
급ᄒᆯᄉ
일이계약이십년이찬후에ᄂᆞᆫ교
리금미두수에오원식슈산회사에
교급ᄒᆯᄉ
일이계약중에기졍ᄒᆫ표긴이잇
스면쌍방사티표자가서로협의
ᄒ야ᄒ되십년이차기젼에기
졍치못ᄒᆯᄉ
우계약을두벌을민드러량사
스로포자가보젼ᄒ고ᄯᅩᄒᆫ후에각각
ᄒ야일본공ᄉ관에ᄋ뎡을등인ᄉ
○곽쳔조회 쟝곽쳔ᄉ령관이
일군부에조회ᄒᆫ니기에
일은죠셩북쳥랑대에
당ᄒᆫ처분을베플사티쟝의게상
한국디방티비치ᄂᆞᆫ본관의

동의를말미암지아니ᄒ면엇
지못ᄒᆯ사
얀은현재사관이아라사에귀화
사ᄒᆫ자ᄂᆞᆫ일병면관ᄒ고츌젹ᄒᆯ
○라유셕교시 ᄯᅢ기쟝사린셔
ᄉᆫ비가지빅쟝유ᄒ나히라쟝사
로써산뎡유ᄒᄂᆞᆫ거ᄉ각국의통ᄒ
뎡ᄒᄂᆞᆫ규례어ᄂᆞᆫ지어우리나라
ᄒ여서ᄂᆞᆫ오빅년리로쟝사규칙
을폐ᄒ시봉힝ᄒ다가근리에ᄂᆞᆫ
임원들이쳥쟝ᄒ며탐학ᄒᄂᆞᆫ류
가만히잇서우ᄒ므로ᄂᆞᆫ국가의보
호ᄒᄂᆞᆫ은턱을닙지못ᄒ고아래
로ᄂᆞᆫ셩령의조잔ᄒᄂᆞᆫ폐를도라
보지아니ᄒ야자로침학ᄒᆫ을당
ᄒᄂᆞᆫ거슨진실노그ᄅᆡᄒᆯ빈라가
히이여탄식ᄒᆯ진뎌쳔금에갈
국에일이반고졍부의치교가불
지못ᄒ야이쳔만동포가빈ᄉ되
경에니르럿스니수해와츈리가
곳ᄒᆫ바에엇지가히슈슈방관ᄒ
고말리오써ᄒᆫ바로쟝사규례를
별노뎡ᄒ야우ᄒ로 황실을존
중히ᄒ고아래로셩민을보호ᄒ
ᄂᆞᆫ목적으로써교셥쳥셩으로등
히샹회소를셜시ᄒ고샹업을흥
왕케ᄒ야문명카젼ᄒᄂᆞᆫ디발
달ᄒ야 황실을존중히ᄒ며생
민을보호ᄒᄂᆞᆫ셩심으로어리셕
은충졍이잇ᄂᆞᆫ바에어와곳치앙
고ᄒ오니유지ᄒᆫ쳠군ᄌᄂᆞᆫ금음
력이십일하오한뎜죵에션젼도
가로일졔히리회ᄒ야써큰일을
돈독히ᄒ기를힝심이라ᄒ엿더
라
○진명회긔회 지난토요일하
오한시에라유셕과원진광인이
쳔젼도가에츌셕ᄒ엿ᄂᆞᆫ티방관
ᄒᄂᆞᆫ자가대단히만코내국순검
과헌병이뤼도ᄒ엿고일인과및
헌병슈샹인이와서관광ᄒᄂᆞᆫ디
경위원에서ᄂᆞᆫ별순검을파송ᄒ
야히회의쥬쟝ᄒᄂᆞᆫ수샹인의셩
명을적어가고ᄉ무원이아직모
히지아ᄒ니아일병쟝ᄒ여오ᄂᆞᆫ
티회쟝등의명목은기히ᄒᆫ후에
아션졍ᄒᆫ다ᄒ고라유셕씨가본
회의취지셔를팔계인의계ᄒᆫ
쟝셔ᄂᆞᆫ회쥬고본회의목적을대
강연셜ᄒ고세시쯤에폐회ᄒ엿
더라
○쟝덕 사급 궁내부에서내
부로조회ᄒ기를시종원봉시리
용션의가묘가양쥬등마산아래
빈봉산에잇ᄂᆞᆫ티시 원소히ᄌ
안에드럿ᄂᆞᆫ고로즉각에파셔옴
길터인테가히쟝봉ᄒᆯ만ᄒᆫ쌍이
엄ᄂᆞᆫ즉양근북면불리리에잇ᄂᆞᆫ
뎐마산아래삼쳔뇽과계우동ᄉ
이에잇ᄂᆞᆫ혼ᄉ산등을특별히 ᄉ
급ᄒ신수로 지의를봉승ᄒ왓
스니ᄒ부와히군에훈칙ᄒ야시힝
케ᄒᆯ사ᄅᆞᆷ이라ᄒ엿더라

TELEGRAMS.

FROM JAPAN PAPERS.

London, Nov. 17.

Despatches have been published in St. Petersburg from General Stoessel, commanding the beleaguered garrison at Port Arthur. The messages, which were sent *viâ* Chefoo by the destroyer "Rastoropny," and bear date of October 25th, October 26th, and November 2nd, show that the Russians had five hundred casualties in repelling an assault on the fortress by the Japanese on the 25th and 26th ultimo. The last dispatch, dated Tsar's Accession Day (November 3rd), is couched in a tone of most fervent loyalty and is jubilant with triumph because of the fact that nine days' continuous assault had been finally repulsed on this great day on which the Japanese swore they would take the fortress. The last message contained no hint of impending disaster, but the fact that nothing has been published from the garrison later than November 3rd is regarded as significant.

Berlin, Nov. 20.

Mexico is about to introduce reform in her currency, by which the Mexican dollar will be valued at half the American dollar. The coining of silver for private individuals, except for purposes of export, is to be stopped.

Berlin, Nov. 20

A statue of the late Emperor Frederick of Germany (presented by the Kaiser) has been unveiled in Washington.

President Roosevelt and Baron Stern berg, German Ambassador to the United States, attended the unveiling ceremony, and in their speeches dwelt on the friendly relations existing between the two nations, the President referring particularly to the negotiations now pending with reference to a German-American Arbitration Treaty.

London, Nov. 18.

General Sakharoff wires to St. Petersburg that last night the Japanese attacked one of the Russian advanced positions at Puteloff, formerly known as Lone Tree Hill, but were repulsed.

Berlin, Nov. 20.

The refusal by Russia to give any promise to punish those responsible for the recent outrage in the North Sea has delayed the signing of the Agreement drawn up between Russia and Great Britain for the settlement of the difficulty.

The Board of Trade investigation at Hull has been concluded, Russia having acceded to the demands made by Great Britain.

Berlin, Nov. 20.

Reports circulated that a Russian loan is to be raised in Germany this year are incorrect. There is, however, a possibility of a loan being raised next year if application is made.

London, Nov. 18.

The American Consul General at Chefoo, telegraphing to the State Department at Washington, says the situation at Port Arthur is extremely critical, the outer forts having fallen into the possession of the Japanese.

London, Nov. 19.

General Stoessel telegraphs to the Tsar that the garrison at Port Arthur can hold out for several months.

London, Nov. 20.

A section of the Baltic Fleet is expected at Port Said on Wednesday *en route* to the Far East.

London, Nov. 20.

The United States Naval Estimates for 1905 amount to $114,590,000.

Berlin, Nov. 20.

The supplementary Baltic Squadron has been sighted off the Danish coast.

Berlin, Nov. 20.

A new battleship for the German Navy has been launched at Kiel. The launching ceremony was performed by the Kaiser, who named the new vessel the "Deutschland."

Count von Buelow, the Imperial Chancellor, who was present at the launch, dwelt in the course of a speech on the peaceful tendency of German foreign policy.

PEACE PROSPECTS.

Commenting upon an article on Peace, in the "New York Sun," the "Eastern World" says; we quite agree with the proposition that the cession of "Saghalien, much less of Vladivostock, or a square mile of inland territory, which is acknowledged to be Russian" should not be asked for. For these reasons: Saghalien, it is true, is reported to possess much natural wealth, but it will be ample time to think of Saghalien when Japan has educated sufficient skilled labour to fill the most elementary requirements for the rational development of the national resources of the Hokkaido, and that will not be for the next twenty or thirty years, for, so far, no one in Japan, neither inside nor outside of the ranks of the Government, has recognized the fact that the true and only source of a country's strength, lies, and must lie, in an army of highly trained and intelligent artisans and tradesmen of all kinds of trades, and that without such an army "and its reserves," the military and naval forces will sooner or later be found to be standing on air. The daily work of Japan cannot be done by any one, nor anyhow and at any time. One of the reasons why these facts are not understood, perhaps, is that the majority of journalists who for some inscrutable reason felt themselves called upon to discuss them, were the more or less legitimate or illegitimate offspring of paste pots and inkstands, reared in the incubator of musty offices into which the fresh breezes of hardworking every day life, with and under all sorts and conditions of men, never penetrate. We may be pardoned therefore a little impatience with that class of handfed journalists.

In the meantime Saghalien would be no more than a happy hunting ground for speculators, swindlers and idle and dissolute characters generally of the same type which has brought discredit upon Japan in Korea, opened to them through an expensive and practically useless and unprofitable sentiment, not even a popular sentiment, but a sentiment of a few Tokyo journalists of the class just referred to. That is all. Any demand for Vladivostock, or any portion of as yet unconquered and unoccupied territory would simply be laughed at and the Japanese Government would have sufficient common sense not to make it.

A request for Russian recognition, of Japanese suzerainty over Korea, on the other hand would be superfluous. Japan, by the right of the stronger—a not very moral but generally very effective right—now holds Korea as firmly as she will ever hold it. She has simply to continue to hold it, and to fortify the northern frontier of Korea, a course which we strongly advocated after the war with China, and which, if adopted, would have forestalled the present war. This is very bad for Korea, of course, from a purely national standpoint, but the question is whether the Koreans can be considered as a nation that can take a national standpoint, since so far they have given no evidence whatsoever of national aims and ideas. After some years of Japanese rule, of here and there misrule perhaps, national aims and ideas may spring into existence, and then perhaps there would be a general rebellion. That would be Russia's opportunity to break a lance and, incidentally a few Japanese heads, in the cause of the famous "independence" of Korea, Until then Japan would be quite safe in Korea, and it is quite certain that in the meantime she will not drill Korean armies, and that she will not teach the Koreans to make guns, rifles, Shimose power or similar chemical preparations of well known medicinal effects. Japan would have to eat her words, of course, in that event, but Baron Komura has already begun to show us how that may be done without causing any very general comment, and the portion of the British press that is, let us says, under Japanese "influence" will do the rest. The public at large does not require any very fine spun arguments. Type, a size or two larger than that ordinarily used, will do very good service instead. Mr. Hearst in the New York "Journal" even considers it necessary to appeal to—or to reach?—the intellect of his readers with type three inches high, and with red type, and there is no evidence that they consider that fact as an insult.

Next, the restoration of Manchuria and Liaotung to China, is, in the first place, the business of China. At all events a Chinese request to that effect should precede any Japanese demand, but, as a sovereign state, China may make what arrangements she pleases with Russia. She may favourably receive any Russian "Nagamori plan" she pleases, and no country in the would would have the right to prevent her from doing so. That is a point that has to be considered, and if Japan should find it incumbent upon herself to go to war with China because China has the idea that she can do what she pleases with her own, she would receive a very peremtory mandate from the world at large to keep the peace. That is another point to be considered.

In the event of Russia succumbing to Japan in the end, Japan would have an unquestionable right to demand an indemnity, but the request might as well not be made because Russia would not comply with it, and Japan has no means to make her do so. That fact is recognized in Tokyo. There would be very little generosity, therefore, in not making the request, if there "were" such a thing as international generosity, which there in not, and what is the principal point to be considered, in the event of Japan being victorious, there is the "second" war with Russia for which immediate preparations would have to be made and carried on with all possible speed.

But what is to be the outcome then, it may be asked. Frankly, we do not know, and we shall not indulge in idle prophecies. The best answer perhaps is to be found in Mr. Dooley's opinions on the war which, to some extent and in other words have also appeared in these columns. Mr. Dooley says:—

"It 'was Walcott an' Choynski all over, on'y th' Rooshyan hung on with gr'reat courage. At th' end iv th' twintieth round, whin both boys were on th' ropes, th' ref'ree th' well known fight promoter, Misther Rothschild, declared th' bout a dhraw. Considerable bad blood was aroused be a claim be th' fighters that durin' th' battle they were robbed iv' their clothes b' their seconds. As a financial eutherprise th' fight was a frost. Th' box official's receipts did not akel th' rent iv th' barn an' thrainin' expinses, an' th' referee decided that as the' fight was a dhraw he was entitled to th' stakes.

Japan would, however, be in a little better position than either of the two bruisers in so far as she would attempt to get her expenses out of Korea. With what success, and whether undisturbed or not, remains to be seen.

THE WAGES OF SIN

Mr. Yun Si-byung, the President of the Il Chin Hoi society, has made himself objectionable in many quarters, but his latest achievements have so roused the ire of two students of the Confucian college that they have requested the government to execute him and hang up his head on the streets as a warning to his followers. They also recommend a like punishment to a few of his friends.

Mr. Hayashi was received in audience by His Majesty at 3.30 p. m. today.

The Superintendent of the Seoul Fusan railway, Mr. Haruichi left for Japan yesterday.

Mr. Stevens accompanied by Mr. Hagiwara (Secretary of the Japanese Legation) is due here by the "Ohio" on her next trip from Japan.

The Imperial Household Department have ordered the removal of the graves, situated on the hill-side chosen for the burial-place of the Crown Princess.

The Korean Minister, to Paris telegraphs that his *confrere* at the Hague informs him that a convention will be called there in December to make some necessary alteration in the rule Governing the Naval Red Cross.

This morning an aspiring candidate for Il Chin Hoi honours entered the establishment of a Korean barber with the object of having his crown shaved, but was prevented from accomplishing his desire by a Korean gendarme, who took him into custody.

Whaling rights on the coast of Korea have been given to a Korean Japanese combine. The Japanese Minister has requested the Foreign Office to ask the Chief Commissioner of Customs to notify the Commissioners at Fusan and Gensan of this fact.

The Il Chin Hoi are said to have recently enrolled over 20,000 new recruits in their ranks. This addition to their numbers, however, does not seem to have increased their wisdom, or led to the accomplishment of any of their self-imposed tasks.

More disappointments have met the Il Chin Hoi delegates in there tour through the country. At Hoing Sung they heard that 20 members of the Chin Po Hoi were languishing in jail. They attempted to interview the Major in command of the local troops, with the object of obtaining the release of their country cousins, but without success.

The War Office have received from General Hasegawa the following requests: Firstly, the punishment of the Commanders of the Korean troops at Chong Sung and Puk Chong. Secondly, That the disposal of military guards thoughout the country must be submitted to the Japanese Headquarters before any change is made. Thirdly, The dismissal from the army of any officers who may be Russian subjects.

From the North of Pyeng Yang comes a story to the effect that a number of that branch of the Chin Po Hoi have offered their services to the Japanese on the railroad, free, gratis, and for nothing. This is rather too tall a story to swallow without a severe gulp. The Chin Po Hoi is recruited from a class of people, who are generally too lazy to work at all, and they certainly would not work without payment; therefore one can be perfectly sure that, if they are working on the railway, they are being uncommonly well paid or are doing their workunder compulsion.

As a proof of the amount of reliability which can be placed on their protestations of loyalty to Japan and her causes by the Chin Po Hoi, is evinced by a report in the Daito Shimpo (a Japanese contemporary) to the effect that a body of people belonging to this society recently visited the Russian General in Songchin, and offered, for a price, to transfer their support and influence. However, the Russian General's duty seemed to him to lie more in the path of fighting than intriguing, and the Chin Po Hoi's offer was summarily declined. Presumably now, the Chin Po Hoi will be more fervent than ever in their allegiance to Japanese. Cannot the Japanese realise that the support of a pack of scoundrels is something to be ashamed of? For our part, we are looking forward to a time when the Korean Government will be in a position to deal with these renegades according to their deserts.

The Korea Daily News.

Issued at , daily except Sundays.

Rate of Subscription:
Per Year,.
Per Quarter,........Yen 25.
Per Month,.........Yen 7.
Yen 2.50.

Postage in Korea not charged extra.
Postage abroad charged extra.

Advertisements, 50 sen per day for 1 inch or less.
5 yen per month per inch.
50 yen per year per inch.

All communications to
E. T. BETHELL,
Editor and Publisher,
Pak-tong, Seoul

JAPAN AND HER FRIENDS.

Because we refrain from colouring our news and views with the pro-Japanese tint so lavishly used by many newspapers in the Far East; we frequently find ourselves accused of adopting an anti-Japanese policy.

Well, by having refused to believe that the recent Hull affair was a "deliberate outrage" or a "drunken freak," or by having been sceptical about the imminent fall of Port Arthur, or by having pointed out that there is room for improvement in Japanese behaviour in Korea,—if by publishing our opinions upon these subjects we are "ante-Japanese" then we plead guilty and are hardened sinners, inasmuch as we are not ashamed and shall do it again.

In the same way as the doctor who prescribes coloured water and complete rest soon has a bigger banking account than the practitioners who bluntly orders more exercise and less to eat, so do the newspapers who carefully, exclude from their columns anything likely to offend Japan, grow in favour with the Japanese at the expense of their more honest contemporaries. And in the same way as the invalid finally discovers that his complaint is only getting worse under the "rose-water" treatment so will Japan eventually realize that the "bouquets" now being handed her by a servile and subsidized press are doing her more harm than good.

We shall presently argue that, in spite of all her "fashionable physicians" may say to the contrary, Japan has brought many of her troubles upon herself; but in the meantime we digress in order to point out how badly Japan is sometimes served.

On September 30th we had occasion to make some strong comments upon the execution, by matial law, of three Koreans for an alleged tampering of the railway. Into the merits of the case we did not enter, but the method of execution was such as to make it impossible to pass the incident by in silence. However, having said our say we had hoped to forget the whole affair but the "Japan Mail" which is paid to serve Japan's interests will not let it be forgotten. After waiting for six weeks the "Japan Mail" in an article hopelessly misrepresenting the facts of the case reopens the whole question by compelling us to put it right. So far as the part of the incident originally dealt with by us (i.e., the manner of execution) was concerned, we did so on November 15th, but it has since been pointed out to us that there were other statements in the "Mail" calling for correction. The "Japan Mail" implies that the acts of these Koreans were outrages against property and life. We have never been able to get at the truth of the matter but the probabilities strongly indicate that the offence was only a technical one, but even had a rail been removed there was no menace to life as with the exception of very light construction trucks there was at that time no traffic on the line. This is the way in which Japan's *paid* friends reopen painful subjects, which her *real* friends would be glad to forget.

And now, with reference to our opinions on the war we should like to quote from our brilliant contemporary, the Easten World. The Editor says that a friend remarked that "it seemed as "though we were pleased that Port Arthur was not yet taken."

"We offered to declare in the present issue, and we now do so, that we would be glad to see Port Arthur taken to-day, so that there would be an end to the carnage that has been going on there for so many months, but we have no reason to wish the Russians "jolly well licked," because they have never, individually or collectively, done us any wrong, and we are neutral.

The "Eastern World" concuides its article as follows :—

"When Port Arthur finally does fall its brave defenders ought to be allowed to march out with flying colours and sidearms, attended by a Japanese guard of honour."

In all this we are in exact agreement with the "Eastern World" and shall continue to give honour where honour is due, be it to Kuropatkin or Kuroki, Nogi or Stoessel.

There is no doubt that in Russia's repeated failures to keep her promises to evacuate Manchuria and her aggressive attitude in Korea, Japan had a sufficiently good *casus belli*, but it by no means follows that she was justified in going to war. In fact events have already proved that she was not justified. A perusal of the article on "peace prospects" which we print in another column will convince our readers that Japan will get nothing out of the war except the credit for military skill and bravery which is undoubtedly her due. Of course she hoped to get more but this only goes to show that she entered into the war without a proper estimate of her own or Russia's capacities. Japan is already hard put to it to find money and men, while Russia has an apparently inexhaustable supply of both.

It seems very likely that there were causes contributing to Japan's declaration of war which have not yet received due attention. It must be remembered that less than forty years ago Japan was a feudal, i. e. essentially military, nation; her favourite stories were those of battle and her heroes were fighting men. Then the feudal system was abolished in favour of Constitutional Government, the old feudal fighting men went to form the Imperial army and this faction has always been more powerful than any other in Japan.

It is well known that the war with China was entered into upon very flimsy pretexts and was, as a matter of fact, forced upon the Government by the military faction. The same may be the case this time; at all events it is safe to say that the military party was more than willing to go to war.

The war may be said to be due to a bellicose disposition and overconfidence on the part of Japan's leaders and military men and if the consequences were to be confined to them we should have nothing to say.

As it is the burden will fall on the shoulders of Japan's peaceful working population.

EXPERTS' OPINIONS ON THE WAR.

(Continued from last issue.)

Continuing, the General said that the outbreak of the war had found Russia so unprepared that there were no defences nor even roads or bridges on the scene of hostilities. Consequently these had to be hastily constructed wherever it was thought that the enemy might be expected. Events showed that part of the work was absolutely wasted., but the efficacy of the defences thrown up had been shown on more than one occasion, and especially at Liao-yang. In the actual defence of the fortifications there the Russians lost only 300 men. The 1,200 casualties sustained by General Levestan's division were suffered while it was fighting outside the fortifications.

Although he did not believe that the Russians would retire to Tie-ling, General Velichko said that in any case Liao-yang, Mukden, and Tie-ling were only names on the map and were of small importance from the military point of view. The line of the Hun-ho, on the other hand, was of great stretegic value and offered splendid facilities for defence. There was no possible reason why the operations should be interrupted during the winter. In Manchuria there was hardly any snow, and the roads in winter were in capital condition.

General Velichko antcipated that the Russians would very soon be in a position to assume the offensive. Port Arthur, he was convinced, would hold out to the last biscuit and cartridge. He believed that there were still several months' provisions in the fortress, and as to the water supply, not only were there several wells in Port Arthur, but there was also a small lake.

The third opinion is from General Moulin and is dated October 7th:—

In the absence of any contradiction from General Moulin, the French Military Attaché in St. Petersburg, of the criticism attributed to him by the correspondent of the "Petit Parisien," it is worth while noting some furthur remarks of this officer, which are not less significant and which appear in the form of an interview with the St. Petersburg correspondent of the "Journal."

General Moulin is reported to have unshaken confidence in the success of the Russians, provided only that they stick to their guns. They have but to persevere. Russia can send 10 more army corps to Manchuria with 1,000 guns. Her mountain artillery is twice as strong as that of the Japanese. The quality of the Japanese troops is now going to decline rapidly. They have only officers enough to take the place of the dead ones. The moment is at hand when all the advantages will be on the side of the Russians. They are strengthening their General Staff, and learning rapidly by experience. They have money enough. All the probabilities are on their side, and they will shortly have the upper hand. Before the end of 1905 they will have seized such territorial guarantees as will permit the negotiation of an honourable peace. The war will not last so long as the Transvaal war, and the crisis will not have been so severe for Russia as it was for England. A new era will open for Russia and "les Janues," said General Noulin, "seront les Jaunes a leur tour."

Yesterday afternoon Messrs. Na Yu Suk and Won Chik, the promoters of the new society Chin Myung Hoi, held an opening meeting at Chong No. Very little interest was evinced in the proceedings, only about 200 people, mostly non-participants, being present. Both Korean and Japanese police had their eye on the speech-makers, but did not interfere.

The Korea Daily News.

VOL. I, MONDAY, NOVEMBER 28, 1904. No. 111

大韓每日申報

대한미일신보

(뎨일빅십삼호) (목요일) 일쳔구빅사년십이월일일

본샤고빅

이신보는영어와한어로셕거미
일츌판ᄒᆞᆸ
신문가
한장 엽두돈오푼
일삭됴 엽두량닷돈
우표가미삭닷돈
다맛돈으로밧ᄉᆞᆸ
광고료는
긔한의장단과ᄌᆞ힝의다쇼로ᄌᆞ
감ᄒᆞ되렴가로밧을터이오며오
릭지아녀대한사람마다다이신
문을보실터이니광고내시기를
원ᄒᆞ시는이들은우리신문샤에
와셔면약ᄒᆞ심을희망ᄒᆞᆸ
○발힝소 박동대한미일신보
샤법어학교압헤젼영국인셜필
림집자리오
샤쟝 영국인 (비셜)

평양 ᄃᆡ리뎜

○평양효동사는권미보씨로우
리신문관ᄃᆡ리인을뎡ᄒᆞ엿
ᄉᆞ오니평양에계신구람코져ᄒᆞ
시는쳠군ᄌᆞ는ᄃᆡ리뎜에왕
림ᄒᆞ와면의ᄒᆞ시ᄋᆞᆸ

사고

○우리대한미일신보의목뎍은
대한의안녕질셔에관한모든데
목에ᄃᆡᄒᆞ야는공평한변론을쥬
장ᄒᆞᆷ이라우리통신원의탐보는
신문보시는쳠군ᄌᆞ의계ᄒᆞᆼ상보
도ᄒᆞ리며편지를긔셔ᄒᆞ여주시
는이는셩명과반ᄃᆡ를젹어붓치
시기를희망ᄒᆞ오니이거슬신문
상에긔ᄌᆡᄒᆞ라는거시아니오다
만극히신용ᄒᆞ는증거를숨고쟈
ᄒᆞᆷ이라긔자는아모긔셔던지긔
ᄌᆡᄒᆞᆷ을되각ᄒᆞ는권리를가졋스
나되각ᄒᆞᆫ리유를말ᄒᆞᆯ터이오
며공즁평회를문란케ᄒᆞ는듯ᄒᆞᆫ
긔셔는의례히밧지안켓ᄉᆞᆸ나이
다

●본샤셜시이리로신문을미양
우례로분젼ᄒᆞ와례젼부의임의
로젼ᄒᆞᆫ듯ᄉᆞ로먼곳에는혹늣게
젼ᄒᆞ기도ᄒᆞ며혹몃칠거슬ᄒᆞᆫ겁
에젼ᄒᆞ기도ᄒᆞ며혹아니젼ᄒᆞ는
곳도잇다ᄒᆞ와우리신문을ᄉᆞ랑
ᄒᆞ야구람ᄒᆞ시는쳠군ᄌᆞ의게
되ᄒᆞ야미우미안ᄒᆞᆸ기로지금
은분젼인을두고미일일즉이젼
ᄒᆞ며아니젼ᄒᆞ거나늣게거나ᄒᆞᆫ
치가업도록ᄒᆞ랴ᄒᆞ오니혹아니
젼ᄒᆞ거나혹늣게젼ᄒᆞ거나ᄒᆞᆫ일
이잇스면본샤로통긔ᄒᆞ여쥬심
을희망ᄒᆞᆸ

관보

뎨이쳔구빅구십륙호
광무팔년십일월이십구일
셔임급ᄉᆞ령
○중종이품가션대부니부협판
동훈대부힝종친부면부 리하
젼
정삼품통정대부한셩부판
윤리히창의교의법면츄
중 십월십팔일
○의원면본관 시흥면보ᄉᆞ쥬
ᄉᆞ 박형셕
○임시흥면보ᄉᆞ쥬ᄉᆞ셔판임관
륙등 김셩면보ᄉᆞ 쥬ᄉᆞ 셩
두식
○임김셩면보ᄉᆞ쥬ᄉᆞ셔판임관
륙등 셩진면보ᄉᆞ쥬ᄉᆞ 한쟝
현
○급삼급봉 시흥면보ᄉᆞ쥬ᄉᆞ
셩두식 김셩면보ᄉᆞ쥬ᄉᆞ 한
쟝현
이샹십일월십구일
○의원면본관 규쟝각직학ᄉᆞ
홍슌구 털도원기ᄉᆞ 한긔쥰
털도원쥬ᄉᆞ 죠용구
○임규쟝각직학ᄉᆞ셔쥬임관륙
등 정삼품 셔긍슌
○임털도원기ᄉᆞ셔쥬임관륙등
젼쥬ᄉᆞ 졍관영
○임털도원쥬ᄉᆞ셔판임관륙등
김덕졔
○증종이품가션대부니부협판
학싱 김병호
○증종이품가션대부니부협판
학싱 김쥬규
○증종삼품통훈대부쟝례원좌
쟝례 학싱 김즁근
이샹종이품가션대부젼한
셩부판윤 김대진의 고조고
○증조고의법면츄 증
○임즁츄원의관셔칙임관삼등
종이품 김즁환
이샹십일월이십륙일
○명비궁우쥬셔ᄉᆞ관 정삼
품 셔상교
○명비궁우쥬셔ᄉᆞ관 정삼
품 뎡인표
○명비궁지문초도셔셔ᄉᆞ관
오품 리인규
○명비궁지문초도셔셔ᄉᆞ관
예ᄎᆞ 륙품 리원세
○명비궁만쟝졔술관 봉죠
하 김병국
령돈령원ᄉᆞ 심슌턱
태의원도졔죠 죠병세
의졍부의졍 리근명
즁츄원의쟝 민영쇼
궁ᄂᆡ부특진관 윤용션
완슌군 리지완
표훈원총지 죠병식
시종무관쟝 민영환
졍일품 리슌익
궁ᄂᆡ부특진관 박졍양
태의원경 민영규
궁ᄂᆡ부특진관 죠병필
경효뎐졔죠 김규홍
종일품 셔졍슌
궁ᄂᆡ부특진관 죠병호
규쟝각학ᄉᆞ 김셩근
종일품 리유승
궁ᄂᆡ부특진관 리건하
털도원총지 심샹훈
의졍부참졍 신긔션
궁ᄂᆡ부특진관 김셕진
종일품 셔샹죠
의졍부찬졍 민병셕
판돈령원ᄉᆞ 홍순형
종일품 김종한
례식원쟝 민종묵
종일품 리헌직
종일품 리졍노
종일품 쟝셕룡
궁ᄂᆡ부특진관 윤용구
궁ᄂᆡ부특진관 리근슈
궁ᄂᆡ부특진관 박용대
교육부총감 리지용
법부대신 김가진
궁ᄂᆡ부특진관 민영달
궁ᄂᆡ부특진관 남뎡철
졍이품 박긔양
졍이품 리헌영
쟝례원경 조졍희
의졍부찬졍 박제슌
궁ᄂᆡ부특진관 리쥬영
지돈령원ᄉᆞ 김학슈
궁ᄂᆡ부특젼관 죠종필
졍이품 리원일
졍이품 리병익
경효뎐졔죠 김학진
궁ᄂᆡ부특진권 죠동희
농샹공부대신 리도지
졍이품 민영우
궁ᄂᆡ부특진관 리완용
비종무관쟝 죠동윤
졍이품 졍한죠
회계원경 리지곤
궁ᄂᆡ부특진관 윤용식
졍이품 조희일
기로소비셔쟝 조졍구
궁ᄂᆡ부특진관 서신보
궁ᄂᆡ부특진관 김ᄉᆞ철
시종원경 윤덕영
홍문관경연관 송병션
종이품 민졍식
종이품 민종식
궁ᄂᆡ부특진관 김영덕
종묘셔재됴 윤티홍
궁ᄂᆡ부특진관 조한국
비셔원경 리지현
궁ᄂᆡ부특진관 민경호
평리원지관쟝 민병한
홍문관부학ᄉᆞ 윤길구
종이품 김종규
종이품 정인승
영희뎐제됴 죠동면
궁ᄂᆡ부특진관 김만슈
통신원총관 민샹호
궁ᄂᆡ부특진관 남규회
궁ᄂᆡ부특진관 김석규
한셩부관윤 민경식
경효뎐제됴 윤달영
봉샹ᄉᆞ제됴 민영국
봉샹ᄉᆞ제됴 민형식
궁ᄂᆡ부특진관 리용선
궁ᄂᆡ부특진관 민영린
시강원첨사 죠동완
쟝례원소경 민영돈
궁ᄂᆡ부특진관 심샹황
궁ᄂᆡ부특진관 홍승목
궁ᄂᆡ부특진관 오정근
궁ᄂᆡ봉특진관 홍종영
봉샹사제됴 리호석
창산군 리희창
홍문관경연관 곽종석
졍삼품 민영슈
졍삼품 리됴영
졍삼품 뎡규년
졍삼품 리순ᄒᆞ
○명비궁만쟝졔술관예차 봉
샹ᄉᆞ제됴 리지덕 외부교섭
국정 리샹설 종이품 강우
형 종이품 윤긔원
○명비궁만쟝셔사관시강원시
독관 리병소 시강원시독관
심쥬틱 시강원시독관 박졔
황 기로소슈직관 김쥰한
규쟝각직각 리의국 쟝례원샹
례 셔샹훈 비셔원랑 리문
구 비셔원랑 허만필 홍문
관시독 리범셜 비셔원랑
정 현
명비궁만쟝셔ᄉᆞ관예차 홍문
관시독 정현지 홍문관시독
박영대
○의원면본관 광릉령 유
휘

◯임츄등현셔 판임관칠등 ᄐᆡ복ᄉᆞ쥬ᄉᆞ 김봉쥬

◯임ᄐᆡ복ᄉᆞ쥬ᄉᆞ 셔판임관칠등 경릉참봉 민회식

◯임경릉참봉 셔판임관팔등 목릉참봉 리ᄂᆞᆫ필

◯임목릉참봉 셔판임관팔등 리은샹

◯임농샹사 면화과쥬ᄉᆞ 셔판임관륙등 윤 셩

◯임농샹사 면화과쥬ᄉᆞ 셔판임관팔등 홍승겨

◯증종이품가션대부 니부협판 학셩리샹도

◯증졍삼품통졍대부비셔원승 증통훈대부사헌부 지평 리긔부

◯증종삼품통훈대부장례원좌쟝례 통훈대부형칠원협감 리우원

이샹종이품가션대부니장원경 리병규의 고조고 증조고의 별면츄 중

◯증종이품가션대부니부협판 부사져 윤듕연

◯증졍삼품통졍대부비셔원승 션교랑 윤셕쳘

◯증종삼품통훈대부장례원좌쟝례 부사직 윤취은

이샹종이품가션대부니쟝원경 윤기명의 고조고 증조고의 별면츄증　　이샹십이월이십칠일

　궁뎐록사

◯의졍부참졍신긔션사직소 비지니에 소를 살피고 경의 간구홈을 갓초 살핀지라 바야흐로 이간회의퇴흥이 ᄂᆞᆺ화히 일젼티 가로써 당ᄒᆞ고 그 다시 번거치 말고 곳이러나 시무홀사로 부탕을 보니여 션유ᄒᆞ시다

◯탁지부대신민영긔사직소 비지니에 소를 살피고 경의 간구홈을 갓초 살핀지라 샹ᄒᆞᆫ 사무에 엇나기를 기다려 보더니 엇지 거연이 가기를 말ᄒᆞᄂᆞᆫ뇨 경은 그 사양치 말고 힝공홀 사로 부탕을 보니여 션유ᄒᆞ시다

　이샹십이월이십오일

논셜

려슌형편

려슌에 잇ᄂᆞᆫ 아라사 스도셀쟝군이 아황ᄭᅴ 쥬달ᄒᆞ기를 려슌은 아즉도 몃달동안을 지탱ᄒᆞ여 가ᄀᆡᆺ다ᄒᆞ엿다고 일젼 우리 신문에 긔ᄌᆡᄒᆞ엿더니 중에도 보도ᄒᆞᆫ 비 이로되 사실ᄒᆞᆫ 확실히 알슈 업ᄂᆞᆫ 말인 거시 일본셔 어느 날에 려슌을 분명코 함낙홀ᄂᆞᆫ지ᄂᆞᆫ 알슈 업스되 히지로부터 젼ᄒᆞᄂᆞᆫ 소문을 드른즉 티 우금ᄭᅡ지도 일본 군사를 졈령ᄒᆞ야 졈졈 진보만 되ᄂᆞᆫ 모양인지라 그러ᄒᆞ나

그 곳 소문은 다 만일 본사ᄅᆞᆷ의게로만 조차 젼파가 된즉 우리ᄂᆞᆫ 려슌 소문과 사졍을 알아 변여지홀슈 업시 일본사ᄅᆞᆷ의 말만 밋을 밧게 업ᄂᆞᆫ티

몃달젼부터 이 ᄅᆞ기를 려슌에 잇ᄂᆞᆫ 아라사 군사로 ᄒᆞ여곰 주려 죽게 만드러 복종을 ᄒᆞ게 ᄒᆞᆫ다지 군비가 핍진ᄒᆞ야 스ᄉᆞ로 항복을 ᄒᆞᆫ케 ᄒᆞᆫ다지 좌우간 무삼 법ᄅᆞᆼ이 날줄로 밋ᄂᆞᆫ더니 우금ᄭᆞ지 일본셔 밧어ᄒᆞᆫ 기에도 소희가 불소홀 ᄲᅮᆫ더러 항구 밧그로 만응게ᄒᆞ야 잇ᄂᆞᆫ 모양인즉 엇던 말을 젹확히 죠신ᄒᆞ여야 올흘ᄂᆞᆫ지 모르겟다 ᄒᆞ요 사이도 일병이 항구 밧그로 에워싸고 련속ᄒᆞ야 포격ᄒᆞᄂᆞᆫ 모양이로되 어느 나라 병함과 손되엿다ᄂᆞᆫ 힝도 ᄒᆞᆯ 후ᄂᆞᆫ 엽스ᄂᆞᆫ즉 곳을ᄂᆞᆫ지도 쎗지 안코 죵용히 졈령ᄒᆞ엿ᄂᆞᆫ지 그리ᄒᆞᄂᆞᆫ 자셔히ᄂᆞᆫ 알슈 엽스되

이제 당ᄒᆞ야셔ᄂᆞᆫ 아라사 셰틱 함ᄃᆡ가 무사히 발힝ᄒᆞ야 나오ᄂᆞᆫ 모양인즉 이 함ᄃᆡ의 권셰홈이 일본 동향함ᄃᆡ의 죠직홈에 ᄃᆡᄒᆞ야 조곰도 불하ᄒᆞᆫ 즁 려슌에 잇ᄂᆞᆫ 아병파함셰ᄒᆞᄂᆞᆫ 경우 이 며동향ᄃᆡ로 외로 력홈이 오히려 오날날 배ᄃᆡ 더ᄒᆞᆯ지니

려슌을 공격ᄒᆞ야 파멸홈이 일본의게ᄂᆞᆫ 심히 긴급ᄒᆞᆫ 일이로다

아라사의 뎨이 ᄐᆡ평양 함ᄃᆡ에 편셩ᄒᆞᆫ 바 ᄃᆡ론돈 ᄃᆡ타임스 신문에 게ᄌᆡᄒᆞ엿기로 좌에 등보ᄒᆞ노라

　젼투함

ᄭᅳ니아스슈로푸　알렉산더　뎨삼

보로듸노　오렐　오슬리바

시소이벨리키　나바린

합팔쳑이오

　쳘갑션

키쏜　드미추리쏜스코이　아드미랄나

키모푸　합이쳑이오

　구원션

올레그　오로라　스비트라나

알마스　졈트쳉　이스므럭드

합륙쳑이니 총계 십오쳑 중에 우ᄒᆞᆫ 고로 잇ᄂᆞᆫ 젼투함 비쳑은 돈슈민와 속력과 졔반 셜장이 동일ᄒᆞᆫ 쥬오죠ᄒᆞᆫ 군함일 ᄲᅢ더러 다시 ᄒᆞᆫ 말홀것 업시 유력ᄒᆞᆫ 군함인 듯ᄒᆞᆫ 거로시 두쳑은 일쳔구빅일년에 비로소 사용ᄒᆞ엿고 ᄯᅩ 두쳑은 일쳔구빅이년에 범슈ᄒᆞᆫ 자인즉 이 비쳑은 셰로 가히 비교홀 만ᄒᆞ되 그 남아지 세쳑은 미쳑에 일쳔오빅 돈 가식이 나 ᄃᆡᄒᆞ야 말ᄒᆞᄂᆞᆫ 즁 함비가 불션ᄒᆞ야 이상 비쳑으로 ᄒᆞ여곰 현슈히 등분이 잇스며　미완

잡보

◯우비불균 탁지대신 민영긔씨ᄂᆞᆫ 외획ᄉᆞ건으로 고문관의게 크게 힐칙을 당ᄒᆞ야 일젼 샹소에 비우로써 윤허치 아니ᄒᆞ셧스나 퇴평제 임홀 터이오 그 후임은 박제슌씨가 단망이라더라

◯충청쳥원위원 충청북도관찰사 리승우씨의 보고를 거ᄒᆞᆫ즉 음셩 본월삼칠일에 일진회원의 원군과 잡병이 본부에 리도ᄒᆞ야 등ᄌᆞᄒᆞ고 본기를 칭ᄒᆞᄂᆞᆫ 고로 더부러 젹칩ᄒᆞ고 돈이ᄂᆞᆫ 소유를 무른즉 ᄃᆡ답ᄒᆞᄃᆡ 흑 회원 용할디홈이 잇슬가 념녀홈이오 ᄯᅩ 관리와 더브러 사죡들이 불법힝위로 힝픠ᄒᆞᄂᆞᆫ 거슬 탐지ᄒᆞ러 버려 왓노라 ᄒᆞ고 곳 청쥬로 향ᄒᆞ야 갓다 ᄒᆞ엿더라

◯면훈압샹 최봉ᄐᆡ라ᄒᆞᄂᆞᆫ 위명인이 진보회원이로라고 칭ᄒᆞ고 원산등디에셔 불법힝위를 ᄒᆞᄂᆞᆫ고로 진보회에셔 착지ᄒᆞ야 문ᄎᆞᄒᆞᆫ즉 최가 ᄇᆡᆨᄒᆞ기를 졍부에셔 식인바로써 진보회를 방해홀ᄎᆞ로 니러와 이러홈이라 ᄒᆞ엿ᄂᆞᆫ티 문쳔군슈 명유셥씨가 최가를 세엇셔 찻더니 지작일에 일진회원 여면사름이 니부에 젼왕ᄒᆞ야 회군슈를 면관ᄒᆞ라ᄒᆞᆫ고로 니부에셔 문쳔군으로 면훈ᄒᆞ기를 최봉ᄐᆡᄂᆞᆫ 습교를 졍ᄒᆞ야 망야압샹ᄒᆞ고 회문ᄎᆞ를 ᄌᆞ세히 면보ᄒᆞ라 ᄒᆞ엿더라

◯일사폐현 거 이십팔일하오 세시반에 일본공사가 폐현ᄒᆞ엿더라

◯죠셰불응 모쳐에셔 죠병식씨를 교츅ᄒᆞ야 승후ᄒᆞᄂᆞᆫ 샹소를 니라고 권ᄒᆞ엿더니 죠씨가 시세를 본즉 진소홈이 불가타ᄒᆞ야 불응ᄒᆞ엿다더라

◯회산방셕 평북관찰ᄉᆞ 리용관씨가 보고ᄒᆞ기를 강계에 취당ᄒᆞᄂᆞᆫ 자들은 다 효유ᄒᆞ야 회산케ᄒᆞ고 이왕 착슈ᄒᆞ엿든 자들은 방송ᄉᆞ혓노라ᄒᆞ엿더라

◯살인범금 진남포에 잇ᄂᆞᆫ 일본사ᄅᆞᆷ 경뎐죠의 공용인 육면중티랑이가 안쥬등디로 려힝ᄒᆞᄂᆞᆫ중에 본월이일에 ᄌᆞ막에셔 류숙ᄒᆞᄂᆞᆫ티 한인삼명이 방으로 드러와서 일인의 가진 돈 칠빅 보자ᄒᆞ며 그 ᄎᆞᆼ 쏫ᄂᆞᆫ 변안기를 원ᄒᆞᄂᆞᆫ지라 기시에 그 일인이 목쳘포에 칸환든 ᄭᅥ슬 니져ᄲᅡ리고 방포ᄒᆞᆫ기를 시험ᄒᆞ다가 한인일명이 탄환을 마져 죽엇ᄉᆞᆫ고로 일본경찰셔에셔 심사ᄒᆞᆫ 후에 당초에 일인이 총노은 것이 아니고 ᄒᆞᆫ 일이 아닌고로 벌금 사십원에 쳐ᄒᆞ엿다더라

◯셔긔관귀임긔 일본공관일등셔긔관 츄원슈일씨가 본월삼십일경에ᄂᆞᆫ 한셩에 귀도ᄒᆞᆯ 터인티 외부고문관 스지븐씨와 동힝이 되리라더라

◯계류비분급 근리 일진회 총이반이 엄졍ᄒᆞ야 거진 만여명에 달ᄒᆞ단 말은 본보에 이미 긔ᄌᆡᄒᆞ엿거니와 그 회원의 계류비가 불소ᄒᆞᆫ지라 동회에셔 회원미명하에 한화 삼십젼식 매일 분급ᄒᆞᆫ다더라

◯슈령칙굴 졍쥬슈 졍셕운씨국에 고리ᄅᆞ 유명ᄒᆞᆫ 안졍석로 츌샹ᄒᆞᄂᆞᆫ 바 ㅣ 리니 근리에 대구에서 일본사ᄅᆞᆷ 약쟝사로써 카휘슈명을 칠굴흠세횡 종인대 이젓슨별본케 슈출흠진티 고가액이엘지에 사빅원가량이라더라

◯칭셤참형 갸니ᄒᆞᄂᆞᆫ 츙향돈슈가 오시비이돈이오 승탑원이 심일명되ᄂᆞᆫ 조고마ᄒᆞᆫ 지션이오 션쥬ᄂᆞᆫ 런인영바형리량세인티인ᄒᆞ얏본인가 리샹젼에서 차일ᄒᆞ야 인ᄒᆞᆫ과 하쥬간ᄒᆞ로 세사용ᄒᆞ엇ᄂᆞᆫ티 거비실흠이오 젼패시반에 히쥬를 받ᄒᆞ야 황강으로 향ᄒᆞ야 ᄒᆞᆼ히ᄒᆞᄂᆞᆫ즁 오후오시이십분경에 황강셔 관셥리되ᄂᆞᆫ셔에셔 불형히 암초에 부듸져 순식간에 침몰되야 승긱의 젼부와 일인이명과 한인삼십이삼명이 몰슈이 히즁에 침몰ᄒᆞ야 션긱즁 세일인 일명만 다힝이 진젼다더라

◯비밀샹쥬 일쟉에 일공사의 패쳔호 일볼다시 드른즉 패쳔시에 좌우를 물니치고 두시간동안 무슨 중대사건을 샹쥬ᄒᆞ엿더라

◯낙셩연셜힝 탁지고문관 관틱을 탁지부니에 건축ᄒᆞᄂᆞᆫ티 일간 쥰공이 되야 낙셩연을 셜힝ᄒᆞᆫ다더라

외보

◯덕함진슈식 빅림뎐보를 거ᄒᆞᆫ즉 덕국진홍에셔 대젼투함의 진슈식을 거힝ᄒᆞ엿ᄂᆞᆫ티 덕뎨께셔ᄂᆞᆫ 이 대젼투함을 도이치란도호라 명명ᄒᆞ고 슈샹 ᄇᆞ로빅쟉은 그 연셜즁에 덕국의 함ᄃᆡ를 졔조홈이 평화목젹이라고 셩명ᄒᆞ엿더라

◯함ᄃᆡ릭착긔 목하 동양으로 츌ᄅᆡᄒᆞᄂᆞᆫ 파라자함ᄃᆡ의 동졍을 확실이 드른즉 아비리가 셔부를 도라오ᄂᆞᆫ 자ᄂᆞᆫ 의연히 ᄒᆞᆼ히ᄒᆞ고 쇼함 오리샥호와 이스볼도호 셩ᄒᆞᆫ 후 발ᄐᆡᄂᆞᆫ 쳠금ᄅᆡᆼ 말국ᄒᆡ뎐에셔 ᄒᆞᆼ힝ᄒᆞ고 소 운하를 지나ᄂᆞᆫ 자ᄂᆞᆫ 상금 구리도에 졍박ᄒᆞᆫ즉 일로ᄡᅥ 볼진ᄃᆡ 이 함ᄃᆡ가 후 발ᄐᆡ를 기다려 힝홀 것이오 리년 일월 중슌즘에ᄂᆞᆫ 동양에 도착ᄒᆞ리라더라

뎐보

군사령부착

◯샹도강ᄌᆞ소젼 금월이십칠일 오후륙시반에 젹의 보병약 이즁ᄃᆡ가 샹도강ᄌᆞ에 엄습ᄒᆞ야 왓스나 팔시반에 이것을 격퇴ᄒᆞ엿다ᄒᆞ엿더라

◯젹병난사 동월이십칠일 오후삼시반에 사하 우안 림쟝보부근의 젹 보병이 우리 군사의게 ᄃᆡᄒᆞ야 어지러이 사격ᄒᆞ엿스나 우리ᄂᆞᆫ 응사치 아니ᄒᆞ엿더니 오후십일시반에 고요ᄒᆞ엿다ᄒᆞ엿더라

TELEGRAMS.

Army Headquarters, Seoul.

At 6.30 p. m. on the 29th inst 2 Companies of Russian infantry attacked the Japanese position at Santaokiangtze. Fighting continued until 8.30 p m. when the Russians were repulsed

Later.

At 10.20 p. m. on the same day, the Russian infantry on the right bank of the Shaho opened a desultory rifle fire on the Japanese, who did not reply. The Russians ceased firing at 11.30 p.m.

Later.

A Japanese force from Kwantien occupied Ho In Shen on the 26th inst. The Russians, numbering only 800, removed the telegraph instruments before evacuating the place.

(FROM CHINA PAPERS.)

London, Nov 22.

The meeting of the Hague Tribunal to decide the question of the Japanese House Tax dispute opened yesterday.

Berlin, Nov. 21.

The Reichstag will meet again on Tuesday, the 29th inst. The new commercial treaties will be submitted at once.

Berlin, Nov. 21.

The steamer Gertrud Woermann, transporting troops to German Southwest Africa, has been wrecked north of Swakopmund. All officers and men have been saved, also three hundred horses were recovered during good weather.

Chefoo, Nov. 21.

The crew of the Rastoropny which is for the time being on board of the Chinese cruiser Hai-yung, is waiting further orders.

Peking, Nov. 21st.

Chou Fu, Acting Viceroy of the Liang Kiang Provinces, in addressing his subordinate official in Shantung said he was about to take his departure, but that he could not leave without giving them a grave warning, as to what lay before them, after his departure. He told his hearers that Germany and German merchants desire to monopolize the commercial interest of the province. He considered they were justified in this if the native merchants through slackness in trade permitted it. The natives had everything in their favour to improve their trade but if they neglected their opportunities then they were playing into the hands of the Germans. He exhorted the officials to insist on Chinese merchants improving their interests at the new treaty towns Choutsan and Weihsien. These would be great centres of trade and unless Shantung merchants exerted themselves German traders would acquire the chief interests of these towns. He said, China, must maintain herself by commerce and not arms, this was the true spirit of reform.

Chefoo, Nov. 21st.

The German steamer Progress and the English steamer Kai-ping have arrived here from Vladivostock. They report, that the harbour of Vladivostock is systematically mined and that the town is strongly fortified and almost impregnable. There are plenty of provisions. Especially large quantities of coal have been stored. The cruisers Rossia, Bogatyr and Gromoboi were, when the two steamers left, in good condition. The customs office in Vladivostock is closed. The shipping is placed under the control of a naval officer.

The Japanese Minister claims from the Foreign Office Y255.70, damages for the wounding of a Japanese subject in the riot at Kongchu. Previous claims of this nature have, we understand, been satisfied out of the deposit in the Dai Ichi Ginko.

VOYAGE IN A SUBMARINE.

In the October Woman's Home Companion, Moran Robertson, the well-known writer of sea stories, describes as follows a trip in a submarine:

"You are not aware of any sensation different from that of normal life in the open. There is none of the sinking, gone and empty feeling that you expected. In spite of what you have read and imagined, there are no sensations to afflict you.

"The flooring beneath you has taken an inclination of ten degrees, which continues for a few moments; then the man watching the depth indicator again moves his wheel, and the floor becomes horizontal. You are twelve feet beneath the surface, and the man watching the depth indicator, by occasional shifting of the wheel keeps the boat at this depth, while the commander, standing on the platform at the lower end of the coning tower steps, alternately scanning the compass and the eyepiece of the periscope, steers the course that will bring you to that far away battleship, and seeks through the reflected haze for some sign of the world above. But there is none in that haze, nor will be for an hour, and as collisions are possible at twelve feet of submergence, the man at the dividing gear again moves his wheel, which sends the boat deeper—to twenty foot depth, which immerses the lens of the periscope and keeps the captain's eyes fixed only upon the compass.

"Twent minutes go by and the commander motions to his aid at the diving gear. The boat approaches the surface lifts the lens of the periscope out of the water, and resumes the horizontal, while the captain searches the periscope. Nothing but haze, and a dim line of horizon on which are a few sails and columns of smoke—nothing of that doomed battleship. Again the boat sinks, and goes on for another twenty minutes, and again she rises for a peep, to no results—she has gone but half the distance, and it is too soon to expect them. Thirty minutes later she rises again, and nothing shows; but another peep ten minutes later discloses an anchored boat flying a flag, and soon the other is seen. They are a little to one side, and the course is changed until they bear ahead.

"Now the torpedo tube in the bow is manned, and the disturbance of trim must be counteracted by the inclination of the driving rudder. The torpedo carried in the tube is always ready; all that is required to discharge it is to open the bow port and to eject compressed air into the breech. The torpedo does the rest."

THE WELCOME SOCIETY.

We have been requested to insert the following:—The object of the Society is to welcome foreign visitors to Japan and to render them every assistance during their stay. The Imperial Household, patronising the objects of the Society, has honored it with a substantial contribution. The Society aims uniquely at bringing within tourists' reach means of accurately observing the features of the country and the characteristics of the people; aiding them to visit spaces specially interesting or famous for scenic beauties; enabling them to view objects of art and enter into social or commercial relations with the people; in short, affording them all facilities and conveniences toward the accomplishment of their several aims, thus indirectly promoting, in however small a degree, the cause of international intercourse and trade. Nearly all the Foreign Ministers in Japan and many distinguished Japanese are honorary members. The subscription to obtain membership in the case of foreign visitors is only five yen, which payment entitles them and their families to receive all the services of the Society without further charge.

If a tourist applies to the Society, the latter will gladly secure for him the services of a trustworthy guide or interpreter. If a tourist place himself in communication with the Society, the latter will spare no pains to supply full information with regard to any route, furnishing details as to distances, the character of hotels and other matters of interest or convenience; and will employ every available means to add to the security and comfort of his journey. Visitors may be introduced by the Society to the following places:—Private Houses and Landscape Gardens; the Houses of Parliament; the Governmental and other Schools and Universities; the Prisons; the Hospitals; the Principal Factories; the Castles; the Mint; the Fencing and "Jujutsu" Saloons etc., etc. On a request from a tourist, the Society is ready to serve as a medium for introducing him to any one, should the circumstances seem to warrant such introduction. If a tourist desires to buy Japanese articles and wishes to know the best places for procuring them, the Society will direct him to manufacturers and dealers whom it considers trustworthy.

It should be clearly understood that the Society is in no sense a money-making corporation. On the contrary, its promoters and supporters contribute periodically, without receiving or expecting any return, such sums as are needed to maintain the organization and defray current expenditures; their unique purpose being to promote and facilitate between Japan and foreign peoples such intimate intercourse as will tend to dispel racial prejudice and to break down the barriers between East and West.

The above is merely an outline of the Society's prospectus. Those desirous of obtaining further or special information, are requested to write to

THE WELCOME SOCIETY
at the Chamber of Commerce,
Tokyo, Japan.

SOCIALISM DISCOURAGED.

The "Yorodzu" says it is evident that the Government is determined to nip socialism in Japan in the bud before it bears any fruit. In a recent issue, the "Heimin Shimbun," which is a weekly organ of the radical Japanese socialists, published some inflammatory articles, and in its lattest issue a translation of a Communist declaration. The sale of both issues was forbidden and the editor and publisher have been prosecuted on charge of having published articles with the intention of causing a change in the form of government. Not only that; on Sunday last a social gathering of socialists, which was held at Oji in the suburb of Tokyo under the auspices of the "Heimin Shimbun" in commemoration of the first anniversary of its birth, was summarily dispersed by the police. Many of the socialists, some of whom had come up to the capital from distant places with the sole object of attending the meeting, repaired to the office of the journal and intended to meet there, but were again ordered to disperse. They then proceeded to Hibiya Park in order to have their photograph taken, but the police still interfered and dispersed them.

In spite, however, of such severe measures taken by the Government against socialists, they appear to be steadily gaining in influence and force. In consequence of the spread of education, a considerable number of young Japanese are yearly turned out from school, and not a few of them are unable to find work and positions. The result is that they are mostly converted to socialism and hope for a reorganization of society. —Japan Advertiser.

The cost of coolie's wages alone at the funeral of the Crown Princess is estimated at the sum of $40,000.

The Governor of North Chong Chung reports having been visited by Il Chin Hoi delegates from Seoul. They warned him against oppressing Chin Po Hoi people.

A new society, ostensibly on the lines of the Il Chin Hoi but said to be in direct opposition to their views, will shortly be started. The new society has, for its promoters, a number of well known officials.

The French gun-boat "Kersaint" arrived in Chemulpo on Sunday.

Yesterday afternoon a Korean soldier was arrested at Chong No by the police on a charge of theft.

The remainder of the Marine Guard of the Italian Legation are to leave Seoul on the 2nd prox.

The Japanese Minister is said to have requested the dismissal of Mr. Min Yung Chul, Korean Minister to Peking, on the grounds that he still Communicates with the Russian Minister to China.

The British steam-launch "Wangfat," trading between Wuchou and Konghao, was captured by pirates as she was leaving Wuchou, and beached 20 miles below the port. She was recaptured by Chinese soldiers, and two of the pirates loaded with booty, were made prisoners.

From the telegrams appearing in our columns yesterday anent a general assault on the Port Arthur forts, we expected to have some more definite news to-day. With the exception of one telegram (so censored that it is almost unintelligible), appearing in one of our Japanese contemporaries, there is absolutely nothing new from that quarter.

A person by the name of Choi Bongdai, calling himself a member of the Chin Po Hoi has been arrested near Gensan by the leaders of that society on account of his evil behaviour and rowdiness. An investigation of the matter led them to believe that he was not a Chin Po Hoi man at all and he subsequently confessed this to be the truth and stated that he had been sent by certain parties to make trouble in the ranks of the Chin Po Hoi.

It has struck many observers, says a home journal, that the Hereros have displayed unwonted military skill in the struggle in South-West Africa, and it is a fact that their tactics are greatly superior to those of the Kaffirs in general. The Hereros are not a puely Kaffir race, but are dashed with Hottentot blood. It is, however, not to this cause that their military ability is attributable, but to the presence among them of numerous Griquas, who have in them more than a trace of their Boer descent—men who speak Cape Dutch, have learned from the Rhenish missionaries much of the arts of civilisation, and who are anything but untutored savages. They mix the vigour of the Dutch with the cunning of the Hottentot, and, operating in a hilly country which they know perfectly, have hitherto held their own better than most people anticipated.

The Korea Daily News.

Issued at 5 P. M. daily except Sundays.

Rate of Subscription :—
Per Year,............Yen 25.
Per Quarter,..........Yen 7.
Per Month,..........Yen 2.50.

Postage in Korea not charged extra.
Postage abroad charged extra.

Advertisements, 50 sen per day for 1 inch or less.
5 yen per month per inch.
50 yen per year per inch.

All communications to
E. T. BETHELL,
Editor and Publisher,
Pak-toug, Seoul.

PARTICULARS OF THE OCCUPATION OF PANLUNGSHAN.

(Continued.)

The proposal was heartily agreed to and a reconnaissance was commenced. At 10 a. m., it was observed that the enemy's vigilance was relaxing. Meanwhile two or three hand grenades with fuses attached were hastily made, and the task of throwing them into the casemate was entrusted to Sergeant Himeno and two soldiers. The hand grenade was small enough to enter the loophole, whence the muzle of the machine gun protruded.

At first it was intended that the explosive should be thrown on the roof of the casemate, but the plan was afterwards abandoned, owing to the doubtfulness of its efficiency.

Sergeant Himeno started on his mission with a light heart. He ordered the two soldiers attached to him to lie down in a crevice, and he alone worked his way up the slope, persistently keeping to the cover of the furrows created by shells. At times he feigned death, lying with his face upward. The disguise was so skilful that one of his two companions hastened back to the trench and reported him dead. The sergeant, however, steadily approached the enemy's citadel, and passed the last wire entanglement by creeping under the wires. Then having reached the foot of the outer slope of the casemate, he ignited the fuse, and running up to the casemate threw the grenade through the loophole. By the time he regained a crevice down the slope, an explosion took place in the casemate. Looking back, he saw that a small breach had been made in the wall on the right-upper part of the loophole, but the extent of the damage to the interior was not known. He then returned to the trench and reported the matter.

By that time some more handgrenades had been prepared. Sergeant Himeno and three soldiers were then given grenades, which they were to throw into the casemate and caponiere. The four men took the same route and advanced one by one. They were seen to assemable at a small furrow, where they lay down awaiting an opportunity to proceed farther. But they did not move for some time. Captain Sugiyama therefore dispatched two more soldiers, each with a bamboo pole, five inches in circumference and 10 feet in length. The poles were filled with explosives specially suited for the destruction of the caponiere. These soldiers also conveyed to Sergeant Himeno a request from Captain Sugiyama that matters should be expedited. It was at about 10:30 A. M. The five soldiers under the sergeant then proceeded in single file towards the fort, halting and crawling from time to time. One of them threw an explosive through the loop hole of the casemate, while the four others placed explosives up the caponiere, and the next moment they were running back to the crevice. The explosion of the machine-gun was the first to take place. With a tremendous force, the casemate was blown up, its roof flying high into the air, and the machine-gun was shattered to pieces. Terrific explosions then followed one after another, destroying the greater part of the caponiere. At this sight our troops in the trench clapped their hands and shouted "Banzai for the Sappers." But one of the explosives in the bamboo pole had not exploded, even after the lapse of five minutes since the ignition of its fuse. It had been placed on the caponiere at the projected angle of the fort, on the left side of the casemate, by private Nakajima, who was called to account by his daring comrades for his failure.

Mortified by his non-success, Nakajima rushed straight towards the fort, and calmly examining the deadly explosive, discovered that the fuse had been extinguished. He struck a match, again lit the fuse, and placed the explosive in position. An explosion took place instantly, and the caponiere was smashed to pieces and another shot of banzai from our trench greeted this gallant feat. Nagajima was, however, wounded during the accomplishment of this task.

The main defence of the fort being pierced by the gallant pioneers, Captain Sugiyama detected signs of wavering on the part of the Russians and urged Captain Kayukawa to effect a charge. This proposal was at once carried out, and all the infantry and sappers, less than 70 in all, were hurled upon the strong fort. Captain Kayukawa was soon wounded and his place taken by Lieut. Tanaka. The flag of the Ouchi Regiment was borne by a Sub-Lieutenant Tanaka. They swept up the slope like a hurricane, and drove off the enemy from the fort at 11 A. M. when every soldier produced the Rising Sun from his pocket and waved it high on the fort, with lusty shouts of banzai, and beckoned to the other troops far below the hill. The Orishita Regiment and Yamamoto battalion also soon arrived in the fort.

A portion of the Russion garrison fled in the direction of Wangtai, but the main force still held the western slope. Taking cover in the outer embankment of the fort, the Russians not only severely fired on the fort but also obstructed the advance of the Japanese. Moreover the neighbouring forts showered a hail of shells on the fort.

The Japanese, though fully exposed to gun and rifle fire, fought desperately, some of them using their rifles and others hurling stones on the Russians. The sappers hastened to reconstruct a parapet from the debris.

Major-General Ichinohe seeing the critical situation at the fort, ordered a body of troops commanded by a sub-lieutenant to attack the rear of the Russians clinging to the slope, and dispatched a body of sappers to the fort; at the same time ordering two Japanese machine guns to proceed forward.

On the hill the ammunition was running short and the soldiers were losing heart. Lieut-Colonel Orishita and Major Nakanishi were running to and fro, threatening to shoot any man who turned his back to the enemy. Before long, however, a shell fired by the enemy killed these two officers.

Major-General Ichinohe then determined to proceed to the fort in person, and, accompanied by Lieut-Colonel Serizawa, Captain Sugimoto and some troops, he ascended the slope, where shells were bursting everywhere. The two officers accompanying him fell on the way. The Major-General was fortunate enough to reach the fort.

The Commander of the Central Column then having assured the Commander of the Investing Army that the fort could be retained, ordered the Mikami Regiment to reinforce the fort. Major-General Takenouchi assumed the command of the Regiment, which after sustaining severe losses, reached the fort.

Fighting of a desperate nature continued on the hill till 1.30 P. M. The casualties were heavy on both sides. At times the issue of the day hung in the balance, but finally the Russians were completely routed, mainly due to the fire ot the Japanese machine guns.

OCCUPATION OF THE WEST PANLUNGSHAN FORT.

Meanwhile Colonel Sunaga, who was standing beside the Commander of the Central Column, believed that the garrison of the West Panlungshan fort was showing signs of weakening and addressed the Commander to that effect. The latter at once suggested to Major-General Ichinohe that two companies under Captain Hamaguchi should be sent to his assistance. At the same time he summoned Captain Hamaguchi and instructed him to proceed first to the East Panlungshan fort and reconnoitre the west fort, and then if possible to charge the latter. Before the departure the Commander addressed the companies, urging them to fight to the last man, as the issue of the battle depended on this particular enterprise.

The companies reached the east fort at 5 p. m. and at once charged the west forts under cover of the bombardment from the east fort. The gallant attack proved successful and the first line of defence was quickly carried. The enemy, however, offered a stubborn resistance on the second and third lines, so that our troops had to effect several disastrous assaults before they could capture the west fort, which was finally carried at 8 p. m. This was not, however, the end of the battle. Under cover of darkness, the enemy delivered desperate counter-attacks on our troops holding the west fort. Captain Hamaguchi was seriously wounded, and the retention of the fort seemed again precarious. It was solely due to the fierce attack on the flank and rear of the Russians by the Mikami Regiment and Yamamoto Battalion despatched from the east fort, that the fort was saved. At 11 p. m. the Russians finally withdrew from the field.

Subsequently it was arranged that Major-General Ichinohe should hold the east, and Major-General Takenouchi the west fort of Panlungshan.

THE "EASTERN WORLD" ON THE LAST LOAN.

Quite a number of telegrams have been sent from London to Japan to announce that the new loan has been a great success, that it has been subscribed ten or thirteen times over, etc., etc. No wonder it was, for it is not often that an 8% plum falls into the lap of European financiers. Japan is quite good enough for 220 million yen, and what risk there is to be taken is balanced by the high interest. But the interest is only 6%. Quite so, but let us see how it works out.

For every £100 bond the Goverment gets £86.15.0 net, a difference of £13.5.0 per 100, which the Government, that is, as a matter of fact, not the *Government* but the *people* of Japan and foreign residents in Japan *also*, will have to pay after 7 years on redemption. The Government, that is, its members, who just now contracted the loan, by that time will be Privy Councillors, retired statesmen with pensions and grants, or something of the kind, and better able to pay *their* share than any one else. The interest on £100 at 6% p. a. amounts to £42.—.—. for seven years. At the end of 7 years then the Government, that is the people, and we and you, will have paid in all £13.5—plus £42.—.— =£55.5.—. or, within an unappreciable fraction, 8% per annum.

No wonder then that the loan was a great success. The wonder is why it was not taken up in Japan at only *five* per cent, on much better terms, and, last but not least, *without* the security of the Customs.

Erkläret mir Prinz Oerindanz
Dieses Räthsel der Finanz.

Not only, then, has Japan to pay a very high interest, but she had to give a second mortgage on her Customs, and it would be of interest to many if the terms of that mortgage were to be published.

The Magistrate of Dan Chon was also arrested and is still detained in the Russian camp at Puk Chong.

The Magistrate of Pu Riong, returning to his district from Seoul, was arrested by a party of Russians and taken to Songchin, where he speedily obtained his release and returned to the capital.

The Magistrate of Man Kyung reports that his district is infested day and night by bands of armed robbers. He says the people are in great terror and he proposes as a remedy, to form armed patrols to protect lives and property.

The Korea Daily News.

VOL. I, WEDNESDAY, NOVEMBER 30, 1904. No. 113

HONGKONG & SHANGHAI BANKING CORPORATION.

Paid-up Capital.....................$10,000,000
Reserve Fund:—Sterling Reserve... 10,000,000
Silver Reserve..... 7,000,000

27,000,000
Reserve Liability of Proprietors... 10,000,000

HEAD OFFICE, HONGKONG.

London Bankers, London and County Banking Company Limited
Branches and Agencies,
London.

Amoy,	Hankow	Penang,
Bangkok,	Hiogo,	Rangoon,
Batavia,	Iloilo,	Saigon,
Bombay,	Lyons,	San Francisco,
Calcutta,	Manila,	Singapore,
Colombo,	Nagasaki,	Sourabaya,
Foochow,	New York,	Tientsin,
Hamburg,	Peking,	Yokohama,

Credits granted on approved Securities, and every description of Banking and Exchange business transacted.

Drafts granted on London and the chief Commercial places in Europe, India, Australia, America, China and Japan.

HOLME RINGER & Co., AGENTS,
CHEMULPO.

ON CHEONG & CO.,
SEOUL.
GENERAL STORE KEEPERS.
Imported provisions, Cooking Utensils Crockery, etc.
FRESH BREAD DAILY.

MITSU BISHI DOCKYARD & ENGINE WORKS,
NAGASAKI.

CODE WORD, "DOCK."

A 1, A. B. C., and Engineering Codes used.

DOCK No. 1 (at Tategami).

Extreme Length..............523 feet
Length on blocks .... 513 ,,
Width of Entrance on Top......89 ,,
,, ,, Bottom....77 ,,
Water on Blocks at Spring Tide 26½ ,,

DOCK No. 2 (Mukaijima).

Extreme Length..............371 feet
Length on Blocks............360 ,,
Width of Entrance on Top......66 ,,
,, ,, Bottom 53 ,,
Water on Blocks at Spring Tide 22 ,,

PATENT SLIP (at Kosuge).

Can take vessels up to 1,000 tons gross.

THE WORKS are well equipped with the LATEST IMPROVEMENTS, and can execute any kind of work in SHIPBUILDING and MARINE ENGINEERING, as well as in REPAIRING of SHIPS.

The COMPANY'S new powerful steamer OURA-MARU (712 tons, 700 I.H.P.), specially built for SALVAGE PURPOSES, and equipped with necessary gear, is always READY at SHORT NOTICE.

CHARTERED BANK OF INDIA AUSTRALIA & CHINA.

INCORPORATED BY ROYAL CHARTER 1853

HEAD OFFICES:—LONDON.

Paid-up Capital £800,000
Reserve Liability of Shareholders 800,000
Reserve Fund 800,000

Drafts granted upon all the principal places in the world and every description of Exchange and banking business transacted.

E. MEYER & Co., Agents,
Chemulpo.

E. MEYER & CO.
Chemulpo

SOLE AGENTS IN KOREA FO. .
A. T. Morse, Sons & Co's "Fresco" Distemper

In all colours ready for use on walls, Ceilings etc.

and

AVENARIUS CARBOLINEUM

A wood-preserving and antiseptic oil preparation

Against decay, dry-rot, fungus and wood-destroying insects.

A large supply always in Stock.
Prices upon application.

E. MEYER & Co.,
Chemulpo.

THE ETHODIST PUBLISHING HOUSE,
Little West Gate, Seoul.

JOB PRINTING, TYPEWRITER PAPER
CARBON PAPER, VISITING CARDS
STATIONERY, BOOK BINDING
BOOK PUBLISHERS
AMERICAN SCHOOL BOOKS
SPENCERIAN COPY BOOKS
PEN CARBON LETTER AND BILL BOOKS

S. A. BECK, Manager.

HOKURKU DOBOKU KAISHA.
Branch office in Chong Dong, Seoul.
Japanese telephone No. 165
CONTRACT DEPARTMENT.
We can contract to build any building or construction.
MERCHANDISE DEPARTMENT.
We can provide any building material. We have just contracted to build the new Belgian Legation.

DAI-ICHI GINKO
LIMITED.
(Formerly the First National Bank)

ESTABLISHED 1873

INCORPORATED UNDER PRESENT LAW 1896

Capital - - - - - - - - - Yen 5,000,000
Reserve Fund - . - - - 1,500,000

HEAD OFFICE:—TOKIO.

President: Baron SHIBUSAWA.

BRANCHES AND CORRESPONDENTS
In the Principal Cities and Towns of Japan.
Interest Allowed on
Fixed deposits 1 year - - - 6½ per cent
" " 6 months - - - 6 per cent

Special current accounts 1½ sen daily per Y 100
General " " 1 " " " 100

M. TANAKA,
Manager, Chemulpo.

SINGER SEWING MACHINES
씽거조봉침

SOLE AGENTS FOR KOREA
전매쇼

HOLME RINGER & CO.
Chemulpo.
졔물포 함릉거양힝

KAMEYA & CO.
GENERAL STOREKEEPERS
Chinkokai - - Seoul
(*Established 1895, Tokyo*)

Confectionery, Hams, Canned Goods, Cutlery, Hirano & Tansan Water. Provisions, Gents, Furnishing goods, Toilet Articles. Travelling Bags, Tobacco, Cigars & Cigarettes Kitchen Utensils. Coffee, Biscuits

Fresh Goods always kept in Stock.
Prices Moderate
Please come and inspect our goods

NIPPON YUSEN KAISHA.
JAPANESE MAIL STEAMSHIP CO.
DER MAIL CONTRACT WITH THE IMPERIAL JAPANESE GOVERNMENT.

European Line
Regular Fortnightly Service between Yokohama Kobe, Moji, Shanghai, Hongkong, Singapore, Penang Colombo, Port Said, Marseilles, London and Antwerp.

American Line
Regular Fortnightly Service between Hongkong and Seattle, calling at Shanghai, Moji, Kobe, Yokohama and Victoria, B. C.

Australian Line
Regular weekly Service betwen Japan Ports and Australia, callingat Hongkong and Manila.
(Above Three Lines, Suspended until further notice).

Shanghai Line
Weekly Service between Shanghai and Japan Ports

Corea Line
Service Kobe, Moji, Nagasaki, Fusan Chemulpo Chefoo, Taiku.
S. S. Bahelsberg, 2181 tons.
Service Kobe, Moji, Fusan, Chemulpo, Chinnampo
S. S. ARGO, S. S. Ohio.

BORDEN'S CONDENSED MILK CO.
New York, U. S. A.

ALWAYS IN STOCK
Eagle Brand Condensed Milk.
Gold Seal Condensed Milk.
Peerless (Family) Evaporated Cream.
Borden's Malted Milk.

E. MEYER & CO.
Chemulpo, Korea,
Sole Agents

ROYAL INSURANCE COMPANY,
Funds exceed £10,000,000.
FIRE
AT CURRENT RATES.
LIFE
REDUCED PREMIUM.
HOLME RINGER & Co.,
Agents, Chemulpo

HOTEL DU PALAIS
SEOUL.

The only first class Hotel in Seoul. Situated in the centre of the city opposite the palace.

Cuisine under the supervision of re experienced French Chef.

Well ventilated and furnished throughout.

TARIFF UPON APPLICATION
L. MARTIN
Proprietor and Manager.

報申日每韓大

보신일ᄆᆡ한대

(호ᄉ십빅일뎨)　(일요금)　일이월이십년사빅구쳔일

본샤고빅

오신보는영어와한국문셔계미 일출판홈읍

신문가

한쟝　영푼돈오푼
일삭됴　영푼팔돈

우표가미샤닷돈
다밧돈으로밧숩

광고료는

귀한의장단과ᄌ항의다쇼로죵 갑ᄒᆞ되명가로밧을터이오매오 티지아녀ᄃᆡ한사람마다다이신 문을보실터이니광고내시기를 원ᄒᆞ시는이들은우리신문샤에 와서면약ᄒᆞ심을희망ᄒᆞᆸ

○발항소　비동ᄃᆡ한ᄆᆡ일신보 샤발힝쇼

샤고

○우리ᄃᆡ한ᄆᆡ일신보의목뎍은

관보

잡보

[illegible] INSURANCE SOCIETY
[illegible] CANTON.

[illegible] underwritten at current rates.
Agents in Chemulpo.
E. MEYER & Co.

COMPAGNIE DES
MESSAGERIES MARITIMES.

[illegible]ghtly Direct Service.

For Marseilles
via Ports.
Sailing from Yokohama
Calling at Kobe,
Shanghai, Hongkong, Saigon, Singapore,
Colombo, Djibonti, Suez, Port Said
and Marseilles.

For particulars apply to
HOLME RINGER & Co.,
Chemulpo.

HAYASHIDA & Co.,

[illegible] MYENG DONG, CHIN KO KAI, SEOUL.
BRANCH OFFICE AT CHEMULPO.

Money changers, Coal and Wood Merchants, Express Agents.

We are agents for the Pyeng-yang Coal Company and the Karazu Coal Company of Japan. We have the best quality of both anthracite and bituminous coal, and prompt execution of orders is our speciality. Firewood of all kinds kept in stock. Full weight guaranteed. Money of all denominations exchanged at current rates. Parcels received for all parts.

CHINA MUTUAL LIFE INS. CO.

Most favourable terms to policy holders.

Benefit system unsurpassed.

HOLME RINGER & Co.
Agents, Chemulpo.

C. P. R.

CANADIAN PACIFIC RAILWAY COMPANY'S ROYAL MAIL STEAMSHIP LINE.

THE FAST ROUTE BETWEEN CHINA, JAPAN, AND EUROPE VIA CANADA AND THE UNITED STATES.

Route from Hongkong via Shanghai, Nagasaki (Inland Sea of Japan) Kobe, Yokohama Victoria and Vancouver.

Twin Screw Empress Steamship—6,000 Tons—Speed 19 knots.

PROPOSED SAILING FROM YOKOHAMA.
R. M. S. Empress of India.
R. M. S. Empress of Japan.
R. M. S. Empress of China.
R. M. S. Athenian.
R. M. S. Tartar.

Special reduction (first class only) granted to members of the Military, Naval, Diplomatic and Civil services and to Missionaries.
Passengers have choice of ten routes across the Continent of America and have privilege of travelling by any Atlantic Steamship Line.
Round the World passage tickets in connection with the P. and O. S. N., North German Lloyd and Messageries Co.'s **£125**.
All rates payable at current rate of exchange.
For further information, Tickets, Guide Books, etc., apply to
HOLME, RINGER & CO., AGENTS,
Chemulpo.

Grand Hotel,

(Formerly the Station Hotel)

Near the Railway Terminus, West Gate Seoul.

The Best Hotel in Korea
Handsome new Building.
Fine Airy Rooms
Excellent Cuisine.
Terms Moderate.
Special terms to Missionaries
and to permanent boarders.

Electric cars within 2 minutes' walk.

W. H. EMBERLEY,
Proprietor

EVERY FACILITY.

In connection with Life Assurance Business is afforded by

The Standard Life Assurance Co.,

One of the largest and wealthiest of the Provident Institutions of the United Kingdom Forms of Application and all information will be promptly afforded on application.

10 CENTS A DAY.

Not a very large expenditure is it? But it is sufficient to secure for a man of 30 a policy with the STANDARD LIFE OFFICE for

$1323.

For all particulars of rates, etc., apply to

Holme, Ringer & Co.,
Agents, Chemulpo.

THE NEW YORK LIFE INSURANCE COMPANY.

Have you ever been declined by any Company?

Are you engaged in a specially hazardous occupation?

Have you heard of the New York Life Insurance Company's New Classifications for this class of Risks?

If not, send your date of birth, occupation and particulars of rejection, if any to

E. MEYER & Co.,
Agents, Chemulpo.

MITSUI BUSSAN KAISHA.
(MITSUI & Co.)
MITSUI GINKO.
(MITSUI BANK.)

The Bank is owned by the members of the Mitsui Family, who, as partners, assume an unlimited responsibility for all liabilities of the Bank:—

Capital..................... .....Yen 5,000,000
Reserve Fund .... " 5,600,000

HEAD OFFICE, TOKYO.
LONDON OFFICE, 34 LIME ST., E. C.

BRANCHES AND AGENCIES:—
New York, San Francisco, Hamburg, Bombay, Singapore, Manila, Hongkong, Amoy, Chefoo, Tientsin.
Kobe, Hakodate, Yokohama, Kure, Yokosuka, Moji, Shimonoseki, Miike, Wakamatsu, Nagasaki, Kuchinotsu, Karatsu, Sasebo, Misume, Taipeh, &c.

Telegraphic Address for all the Offices:
"MITSUI."
A. B. C. AND A. I CODES USED.

Contractors of Coal
To the Imperial Japanese Navy. Arsenals and Railway Bureau, Principal Railway Companies and Industrial Work, Home and Foreign Mail and Freight Steamers.
Sole Proprietors
Of the famous Miike, Tagawa and Yamano Coal Mines.
Sole Agents
For the sale of Fukumo, Hokoku, Ichimura, Kanoda, Mannoura, Onoura, Ostuji, Sonoda, Tsubaruro, Yoshinotani, Yoshio, Yurokibura and other coals.

YANGTSE INSURANCE ASSOCIATION, LTD.

The undersigned, having been appointed agents for the above company, are prepared to issue policies and pay losses on marine risks at regular rates.

E. MEYER & Co.,
Agents, Chemulpo.

AMERICAN KOREAN ELECTRIC CO.

Light and Power.

Main Office: Electric Building, Chong No.

RAILWAY DEPARTMENT.

OPERATING CARS BETWEEN EAST AND WEST GATE, EVERY TEN MINUTES:—

First Car leaves East Gate at 7:00 A. M. First Car leaves R. R. Station at 7:25 A. M
Last Car " East Gate at 9:40 P. M. Last " " R. R. Station at 10:05 P.M

OPERATING CARS BETWEEN EAST GATE AND IMPERIAL TOMB TERMINUS, EVERY TWENTY MINUTES:—

CONNECTING WITH EVERY ALTERNATE CAR ARRIVING AT EAST GATE FROM CHONG NO.

First Car leaves East Gate for Tomb at 7:10 A. M
" " " Tomb for East Gate at 7:35 A. M.
Last " " East Gate for Tomb at 7:50 P. M.
" " " Tomb for East Gate at 8:10 P. M.

OPERATING CARS BETWEEN CHONG NO AND YUNG SAN RIVER EVERY TWELVE MINUTES:—

First Car leaves Chong No for South Gate at 7:12 A. M.
" " " Chong No for Yung San at 7:36 A. M.
" " " South Gate for Chong No at 7:20 A. M.
" " " Yung San for Chong No at 8:09 A. M.
Last " " South Gate for Chong No 10:00 P. M.
" " " Yung San for Chong No at 9:33 P. M.

SPECIAL PRIVATE CARS FURNISHED TO SUIT CONVENIENCE OF PATRONS. PRICES ON APPLICATION AT HEAD OFFICE.

LIGHTING DEPARTMENT.

Where less than 250 candle power of light is used, the rate per month will be
Per 16 candle power incandescent lamp,—All night.—Yen 2.50.
32 candle power incandescent lamp:—All night:—Yen 4.00.
50 candle power incandescent lamp:—All night:—Yen 6.00.
150 " " " " — " " " 10.00.
1200 " " enclosed arc " " " " 20.00.

Where more than 250 candle power of light is used, a Meter will be installed, if requested:—Rent of Meter Yen 2.00 per month. Rate of charges by meter reading:—Two Sen per Ampere per hour. (Approximately this is equal to about One Sen per 16 C. P. lamp per hour) Minimum monthly charge where meter is installed, Yen 20.00 per month, which includes rental of meter.

Estimates for installing lights furnished on application.
An assortment of chandeliers always on hand.

K. Murakami.

Photograph Studio
Chinkokai, Seoul.

Printing, Developing and Enlargement, of Photographs always Undertaken.

Korean Views and Pictures Illustrating Native Customs always on Sale,

---

THE OSAKA SHOSEN KAISHA.

Boats frequently on the berth for Chinnampo.

REGULAR SAILINGS BETWEEN JAPAN AND KOREAN PORTS.

FUSAN AND KOBE VIA SHIMONOSEKI.

OSAKA VIA MOKPO, FUSAN, SHIMONOSEKI AND KOBE.

MOJI DIRECT.

OSAKA VIA KUNSAN, MASANPO, FUSAN, SHIMONOSEKI AND KOBE.

CHEMULPO KUNSAN LINE,
Every three days.

CHEMULPO CHINNAMPO LINE.
Every three days.

For Freight and passage and further particulars apply to
THE OSAKA SHOSEN KAISHA,
Chemulpo.

RONDON, PLAISANT & CO.

General Storekeepers and Merchants, Ships Contractors, Tobacconists, Commission and Forwarding Agents, Coal Merchants

IMPORTERS AND EXPORTERS

Seoul & Chemulpo.

W. D. WENTWORTH.

LANDING
AND
SHIPPING AGENT
AND
CUSTOMS BORDER.

12 OURA, NAGASAKI.

STEWARD & CO.

Chemulpo.

Shipchandlers and Storekeepers, Naval and Mercantile Contrrctors, Landing and Shipping Agents.

STEWARD'S HOTEL

Chemulpo.

Best accommodation in this port for travellers. Clean and well-aired rooms, good cuisine and prompt attendence, moderate tariff.

○샹례경임 닉부대신리용티
씨는궁내부대신을겸임ᄒᆞ고샹례
원젼도감졔됴를괴명ᄒᆞᆫ고로사
무가호번ᄒᆞ야닉부에는사진치
못ᄒᆞ고궁닉부에셔닉부공문을
드린다가쳐판ᄒᆞᆫ다더라

○헌병착병 재작일하오
랑에대광교에셔헌병들이
ᄒᆞ나흘잡아가는ᄃᆡ관광ᄒᆞ는자
ㅣ수빅명이라그리ᄒᆞᆫ무슨죠
병명이도적질ᄒᆞᆫ고로잡아간
다ᄒᆞ는ᄃᆡ챵병명인지도적이병
뎡복색을ᄒᆞ엿는지알수업다ᄒᆞ
더라

○부속타지 빅룡회지기를뎡
지ᄒᆞ고뎐환국을타지부로부속
ᄒᆞᆫ후에히국소속관리는ᄎᆞ연봉
시ᄒᆞ엿다더라

○시찰환국 부산감리의뎐보
를거ᄒᆞᆫ즉일본에갓든시찰의일
ᄒᆡᆼ이거월이십구일에본항에도
박ᄒᆞ야삼십일괴차로발졍ᄒᆞᆫ다
ᄒᆞ엿더라

○관찰부임쳐탐 닉부에셔함
경남도관찰부로뎐훈ᄒᆞ기를함
경북도새관찰사김로규의부임
ᄒᆞᆫ써부를탐보ᄒᆞ라ᄒᆞ고창자에도
뎐칙을ᄒᆞ엿거니와비룡뎐션이
나우계가업슬지라도신편에과
이히별반칙탐ᄒᆞ야호신일닉로
회뎐케ᄒᆞ라신 지의를봉승ᄒᆞ
엿다ᄒᆞ엿더라

○원수록표 관계리졍소에셔
각부부원쳥에통쳡ᄒᆞ기를귀부
부원쳥의칙주관임관과밋소속
각관쳥의칙주관임관외원수와
고원이하리예속의익수를ᄒᆞ나도
빠지말고죠ᄉᆞᆼ일닉로일일히밧겨
버의졍부안에노패소로긔록ᄒᆞ여보
신ᄒᆞᆷ을바라노라ᄒᆞ엿더라

○쳔왕쳔셔 덕국황리쳔왕의
계대한 황뎨폐하게셔금쳑대
훈쟝을사급ᄒᆞ신지라헌쳔왕의
감은ᄒᆞ는쳔셔가왓는고로외부
대신이봉졍ᄒᆞ고재작일에덕국
공관으로죠회ᄒᆞ엿더라

○무료퇴거 진보회는죽동향
여회라셔즁ᄒᆞ는힝동이발각된
고로경무부훈령을인ᄒᆞ야진위디
에셔쳐벌ᄒᆞ고또원산에셔최봉
태가경부명령으로진보회를방
츙히ᄒᆞᆫ다ᄒᆞ야재작일진회에셔
후사쟝을질문ᄒᆞ엿더니참졍의게
이ᄃᆡ답ᄒᆞ야ᄀᆞᆯᄋᆞᄃᆡ최회가동
도의힝동이분명ᄒᆞᆫ지라병뎡으
로써진압ᄒᆞ엿거니와소위회중
에셔시방졍부는밍세코ᄒᆞᆫ가지
아니ᄒᆞᆫ다ᄒᆞ더니시방졍부를엇
지ᄒᆞ야방무ᄒᆞᄂᆞ뇨ᄒᆞᆫ즉참졍이위
원이무료히퇴거ᄒᆞ엿다더라

○한대영졉 한부대신일힝이
삼십일하오팔시에입셩ᄒᆞᆫ다ᄒᆞᆷ
으로한부에셔각한도를지휘ᄒᆞ
야새문밧영뎐거쟝에셔영졉ᄒᆞ기
로쥬션ᄒᆞ더니경부를도가영동
군에셔ᄒᆞ로밤을지내고일일에
샹경ᄒᆞᄂᆞᆫ지라모든한도가그리
회를기드려뎡거장으로영졉ᄒᆞ
엿다더라

○월봉어음 각부월급을어음
으로분급ᄒᆞ엿는ᄃᆡ오날셔지찻
지못ᄒᆞᆫ병뎡이잇다더라

○외함립통 지난일요일에법
국포함거보상이인항에도박ᄒᆞ
엿더라

○외병쟝발 의대리공관보호
ᄒᆞᆫ군은리월이일에모다셔울을
써나다더라

○쳥죠보호 쳥국공관에셔외부
로죠회ᄒᆞ기를쳥샹손연방이가
힝쥬에잇셔피힝ᄒᆞᆫ일ᄉᆞ영국공
관죠회를인ᄒᆞ야본관에셔ᄒᆞᆫ인
쳔쟝영사관번역관소가인을파
송ᄒᆞ야마부등이명으로더브러
함게가니호죠ᄒᆞᆫ빙을보내여ᄃᆡ
방관으로ᄒᆞ야곰보호케ᄒᆞ오며
ᄯᅩ귀부과원을어ᄂᆞ날에보내ᄂᆞᆫ
지죠시시명ᄒᆞ야동왕ᄒᆞᄂᆞᆫᄃᆡ편
리케ᄒᆞᆷ이가ᄒᆞ다ᄒᆞ엿더라

○량사방외대 재작일하오이
시에의대리공사가외부에젼왕
ᄒᆞ야대신을방문ᄒᆞ엿고동일하
오삼시에쳥국공사도외대를방
문ᄒᆞ엿더라

○죠쳥시명 외부에셔농상공
부에죠회ᄒᆞ되일공사가죠회ᄒᆞ
기를슈산회사ᄃᆡ표인민병한과
일본쟝긔포경회사에셔계약을
셩립ᄒᆞ고슈산회사소유ᄒᆞᆫ권리
를젼혀포경회사에맛기ᄂᆞᆫ계약이던지
국인ᄒᆞᆫ일이업스면시힝치못ᄒᆞᄂᆞᆫ
은법뎐에ᄌᆞ졔ᄒᆞ거ᄂᆞᆯ슈산회사
와포경회사에셔셩약ᄒᆞᆫ것이
면예어긔엿ᄉᆞᆫ니라슈산회사
맛은본대신이금시초문인고로
귀부에죠회ᄒᆞ오니ᄒᆡ회사시
부로셔인허ᄒᆞ엿ᄂᆞᆫ지못시부ᄂᆞᆫ명
ᄒᆞᆷ을바란다ᄒᆞ엿더라

○뇌죨샹빗만금 남대문밧뎡
거쟝으로브터셔빙고지지원산
텰도긔디로표목을세웟다ᄒᆞ는
고로셔빙민인등이일진회에쳥
죡ᄒᆞ기를텰도를다른ᄃᆡ로옴겨
노케ᄒᆞ야주면우리가샹빗만량
을드리겟다ᄒᆞᆫ즉일진회에셔ᄃᆡ
답ᄒᆞ기를우리회는젼국인민을
도탄중에셔건지고져ᄒᆞ거ᄂᆞᆯ엇
지이곳ᄒᆞᆫ일동인민의사졍을도
라보리요ᄒᆞ엿다더라

○지회셜치 일진회에셔각도
각군에회원을파송ᄒᆞ야지회를
셜치ᄒᆞᆫ다더라

론셜

젼호련쇽

쳘ᄉᆞᆸ션으로말ᄒᆞᆯ진ᄃᆡ자괴보호
ᄒᆞ기만위ᄒᆞ야그젼셜ᄒᆞᆫ파죵요
로운졔도는진션진미ᄒᆞ나그러
ᄒᆞ나아병들은그죵반ᄒᆞᆯ곳에셔
먹을군량과시료는항샹부족ᄒᆞ
계랍졔ᄒᆞ나니이는무타ㅣ라쳘
갑의돈수가원시중ᄒᆞᆫ중군함
에ᄃᆡ포셜치함과긔계쟉홈이안
법국량자를모방홈이만아셔그
리홈이니
샹로되노젼투함은법국라세
이싹혜셔사리빗치군함파지은바
이며그남아지오셰리이하젼투
함들은일쳔팔빅구십팔년브터
사용ᄒᆞ야포리스비드와포비다
군함으로더브러항샹홈께단니
던자ㅣ며시오ᄃᆡ빌리키와나바
린젼투함은일쳔팔빅구십일년브
에제죠ᄒᆞᆫ자ㅣ인ᄃᆡ여러히가되여
못쓰게되엿다고론ᄒᆞ든ᄯᅡ임쓰신
문에왕왕히게ᄌᆡᄒᆞ든바인즉이
런ᄒᆞᆫ군함들로ᄒᆞ여곰편셩ᄒᆞ야
함ᄃᆡ라칭홈이실로우수은일쌘
더러비록젼투함비쳑은건셜ᄒᆞᆫ
고우뎡ᄒᆞᆫ다ᄒᆞ드리도일본을당
ᄒᆞ지못ᄒᆞᆯ거시요
구원션으로말ᄒᆞ드리도울레이
는당쵸에아라사람이졔죠ᄒᆞᆫ
엿다가츄후로스틔린ᄊᆡ에셔수
보ᄒᆞ야샐가드린션에부속ᄒᆞ엿
든바이오로라는신동젼쟁이
후에란슌ᄒᆞᆫ구로챳슨죡세곤이
나흥펠라드ᄊᆡ에바리두엇슬뿐
ᄒᆞᆫ거시고스비들라는일쳔팔빅
구십륙년에법국셔졔죠ᄒᆞᆫ배로
마하부리에셔사용ᄒᆞ든빈이며
마스는알벽시포수사메독의션
유ᄒᆞ든빈로셔군량과긔계를젹
지ᄒᆞᆫ바이며졍쟝이수미리드
는노빅셔에셔고셕과보슈의게
결단ᄒᆞ남자인즉만일견단이나
아니나되고원젼홈것갓드면엇지
이리유가잇스리오이번젼쟁에다
서쓰자홈진ᄃᆡ중수의과파모든지
물픔이젼명ᄒᆞ야쓰게되엿는지
는쏘ᄒᆞᆫ알수업스되번번치못ᄒᆞᆫ
과판수로써부리며더욱손ᄒᆡᄒᆞ나
되게아니ᄒᆞᄂᆞᆫ지가히밋지못ᄒᆞᆯ
것고이함ᄃᆡ에부속ᄒᆞᆫ수뢰졍삼
ᄉᆞ쳑중에일곱쳑은과와겟ᄉᆞ되
의게파손이되엿다ᄒᆞ엿스나즉그
동안에수보ᄒᆞ야나오는지는알
수업겟고그남아지운송션과군
의ᄃᆡ션은오리홍히ᄒᆞ든바인즉
이도쏘ᄒᆞᆫ쓰게되엿슬는지ᄂᆞᆫ히
란모들지라
그러ᄒᆞ나일본함ᄃᆡ에ᄃᆡᄒᆞ야수사
뎨독의게명령ᄒᆞ야관활ᄒᆞ는함
쳑에수효는여좌ᄒᆞ노니

젼투함

아사히 시기시마 미카사
야수마 류지 함오쳑이오

쳘갑션

도기와 아사마 야구모
수모 잇슈모 이와데 가슈가
니쉰 함팔쳑이요

구원션

다가슈시 카사기 치드쓰
수마 아가시 잇수미 하시다
잇쓰구시마 니리가 숫시마
뎨 맛수쉬마 난뷔와 타가
치오 아기수시마 항샹사쳑
인죵도함이십칠쳑인지라
이러ᄒᆞᆫ즉아라사ᄃᆡ평양함ᄃᆡ가
일본함ᄃᆡ에비교ᄒᆞ면진ᄃᆡ셜로일
본셔조곰도위구ᄒᆞᆯ이업슬리이
로다
(완)

뎐보

○로국의죠합 아라사에셔현
금잇는함션외에도젼투함오쳑
칭반이쳔이빅사십이돈과쟝쳐
갑슌양함일등슌양함등삼쳑과
슌양함륙쳑과포함일쳑과구츅
함십오쳑과쟝슈뎡십삼쳑을계
죠중이오ᄯᅩ아라사에셔각죵쟝
슈뎡과구츅함이십일쳑을계죠
중이라더라

○모살괴착 상히에셔발ᄒᆞᆫ뎐
보를거ᄒᆞᆫ즉왕지츈이가로졍쳥
함셜을주쟝ᄒᆞᆫ다ᄒᆞ야금월십구
일밤에엇던오리졍에셔ᄒᆞᆫ셔쳥
이단총으로왕지츈을암살코져
ᄒᆞ다가포박이되엿는ᄃᆡ히셔쳥
은젼자에일본셔류학ᄒᆞᆫ자ㅣ러
라

로돈발 십월이십일일

○히아기회 히아평화회는일
본가우세문졔들의졍ᄒᆞ기위ᄒᆞ
야작일에기회ᄒᆞ엿더라

빅림발 동일

○덕국신약 덕국의회는리쟈
요일이십구일에다시기회ᄒᆞᆫ다
ᄒᆞᄂᆞᆫᄃᆡ새로계결ᄒᆞᆫ샹업됴약을쥰
시취결ᄒᆞᆯ터이라더라

동디발 동일

○덕함쳥몰 덕국군함계토루
드위란은덕령셔남아프리카에
군사를운송ᄒᆞ는길에샤옵덴드
븍방에셔파션이되엿는ᄃᆡ군사
와탑샹빅여명은구원ᄒᆞ야냇다
더라

븍경발 동일

○총독죵곡 쳥국량강총독츄
후뵈가샹동관하각군에명령ᄒᆞᆫ
ᄃᆡ귀계에ᄒᆞ엿스되덕국이샨동신
긔항ᄃᆡ에샹업권을독졈ᄒᆞ랴ᄒᆞ
는의향이니쳥국샹민이샹업에
ᄂᆞ타ᄒᆞ면권리를외인의게다쎗
길것이니아모조록샹민을권고
ᄒᆞ고쟝려ᄒᆞ야샹업이일진ᄒᆞ게
ᄒᆞ라ᄒᆞ엿더라

지부발 동일

○포항군항 덕함프로그렛스
와병함가이광이포렴사덕항으
로브터왓는ᄃᆡ젼ᄒᆞᄂᆞᆫ말을드른
니그항구는견고히방어ᄒᆞ고식
료와셕탄을만이싸코회판은닷
쳣는ᄃᆡ션박츌입은히군이감독
ᄒᆞ더라ᄒᆞ더라

TELEGRAMS.

(FROM JAPAN PAPERS.)

Berlin, Nov. 22.

Vessels belonging the to Baltic fleet have proceeded on their voyage from Candia and Suez.

London, Nov. 22.

Viceroy Alexeieff has been appointed a member of the Council of Empire and of the Committee of Ministers.

Berlin, Nov. 22.

Viceroy Alexeieff has been appointed a member of the Ministers' Council.

Berlin, Nov. 22.

Russia has bought the Danish steamer "Siam."

The London "Standard confirms the report that several torpedo destroyers built at Yarrow have been delivered to the Russian Government.

Berlin, Nov. 22.

The Arbitration Treaty between Great Britain and Germany is expected to be signed shortly.

Berlin, Nov. 22.

The German transport "Gertrud Woermann," which was wrecked north of Swakopmund while carrying reinforcements for German Africa, has become a total loss. Most of the cargo, however, has been saved.

Berlin, Nov. 22.

The proposal made by President Roosevelt to hold another Peace Conference shortly has been accepted by all the European Powers, reservations being made as to the time and programme.

Berlin, Nov. 24.

A better feeling is now prevalent in the writings of the British Press towards Germany, due to the attitude adopted in Government circles in London.

Berlin, Nov. 23.

The London "Daily Express" publishes details of a destroyer built at Yarrow and delivered to the Baltic Fleet on October 15th

Berlin, Nov. 23.

The Japanese Government has bought 10,000 tons of coal at Cardiff, and has chartered a steamer at San Francisco to carry rails and waggons to be used in Manchuria

London, Nov. 23.

A public memorial will be erected in Hull to the victims of the recent disaster in the North Sea.

London, Nov. 23.

The St. Petersburg journal "Rus" urges Russia to defend her interests in the Near and Middle East with greater vigour than ever; otherwise Southeastern Persia and the Gulf will soon be British possessions.

A telegram received by the Tokio Foreign Department states that the report that the Russian bluejackets of the Baltic Squadron created serious disturbances in Crete, killing and wounding many inhabitants, under the influence of drink, is not correct. The troubles were confined to the sailors thamselves, one of these being killed by his comrades.

London, Nov. 22.

The "Rion" (late Volunteer Fleet steamer "Petersburg") and other vessels, on November 18th anchored off Skaw Bay, and are awaiting repairs which are to be effected on the screws of the destroyers by a salvage company, Denmark refusing any use of port facilities at Frederikshaven.

London, Nov. 24.

Reuter's correspondent at Canea, Crete, partly confirms the reports of disgraceful conduct on the part of members of the Baltic Fleet. There were constant scenes of drunkenness wherein several officers participated. One Russian was killed by his comrades; others were severely wounded. The commands of the officers were entirely disregarded and there is no discipline. Many seamen have been left behind, lost or deserted.

Berlin, Nov. 24.

According to the Novoe Vremya, the third Russian Fleet for the Far East, has now been formed.

Berlin, Nov. 25.

The Russian warships are now taking in provisions and water at Port Said.

London, Nov. 23.

It is reported that a Russian Five per cent, loan of £48,000,000 sterling is to be issued at 96 in Germany in January next, France participating. £11,600,000 is to be expended in Germany on Russian warships and Russia also abandons her opposition to the Bagdad railway.

London, Nov. 25.

A disastrous storm has taken place in the North Sea, many ships being wrecked. There has also been a severe snowstorm in the Northern Midlands of England. The snow, which fell with blinding force, destroyed a number of telegraph wires. Their Majesties the King and Queen of Portugal, who have been staying at Chatsworth as guests of the Duke of Devonshire, are unable to return to London on account of the snowdrifts.

London, Nov. 24.

The House Tax tribunal at The Hague has adjourned, having given the parties till the 15th of December to present their cases, and till the 15th of February to lodge replies thereto.

Paris, Oct. 25.

A sequel to the Dreyfus case was the opening of a court-martial to-day of four prominent officers of the War Minister-Cols. Dautrich, Rollan, Francois and Marechal—charged with using military funds and otherwise influencing witnesses against Dreyfus at Rennes. The previous ministerial investigation partially vindicated the accused, who demanded a court-martial. Col. Dautrich testified that during the entire course of the proceedings at Rennes he followed the orders of his superiors. The indictment charges Col Dautrich, while custodian of the military archives in 1899, with mutilating books and making erasures for the purpose of shielding a diversion of the funds by Cols. Francois and Marechal. The three are specifically charged with appropriating $4,000 when the prosecution of Dreyfus was going on. A large crowd attended the trial, including Maitre Labori, Col. Picquart, Joseph Reinach, the biographer of Dreyfus, and other notabilities of the Dreyfus case. The testimony was largely technical and concerned the methods of handling war archives and funds. The trial went over to to-morrow. The four accused officers are detained in prison.—Kobe Herald.

AN EPISODE OF THE SHAHO BATTLE.

St. Petersburg, Oct. 10.

Nemirovich Danchenko, the well-known Russian war correspondent, telegraphs a description of the recapture of Lone Tree hill, which fell into the hands of the Japanese during a night attack while the Russians slept. He says:

"General Kuropatkin the following day ordered the hill to be retaken, and the whole Russian aritillery concentrated at 5 in the morning and showered the hill with projectiles, the awful spectacle lasting the entire day. It seemed that no human being could outlive such an ordeal, yet the defenders remained manfully at their posts.

"The sun was already declining when Kuropatkin gave the orders to storm. Six regiments advanced, fording the river in the face of a murderous fire. The enemy determined to make us pay dearly for it. He poured a hail of gun and rifle fire on our advancing columns, but nothing could stop them. They reached the other side, clambered up, and at 11 o'clock at night the position was in our hands. I have just visited the scene of our triumph. The trenches are filled with dead Japanese and Russians clutched in a death embrace.

"I saw no such ghastly sight at Shipka or at Plevna. The credit for the achievements belongs chiefly to the Thirty-sixth and Nineteenth rifles. Four other regiments participated. The Thirty-sixth attacked from the East and the Nineteenth from the West. Poutiloff, leading the brigade and personally directing the attack, was the first to reach the summit, and was in the thick of the fiercest fighting around the Japanese guns. The Japanese gunners died at their guns. Kuropatkin personally thanked the heroes for their gallant exploit. The captured guns were brought to Moukden."

The general staff believes that the storming of Lone Tree hill, for valour and slaughter, will occupy a place by itself in military annals. Kuropatkin, under whose eye the assault was made, rechristened it Poutiloff hill, in honour of the man who led the attack at the head of the Second brigade of the East Siberian Rifle Division, and who was subsequently decorated on the field with the St. George's Cross.

The hill is a precipitous rocky height; and, although the Japanese had occupied it only a short time, they had thrown up very strong defenses. The river running at its foot increased the difficulty of the task, but it was scaled and carried successfully against the unprecedented opposition of a Japanese division, 14,000 men, with many guns. The Russian losses were terrible. The fighting on the crest of the hill was altogether with cold steel. The Russian officers, with swords aloft, leading the scaling column, were literally lifted in the air by the Japanese bayonets, and the Japanese then bayoneted the first of the Russian soldiers who lay piled in the tenches. All the dead in the trenches were bayoneted, their weapons bearing marks of the dreadful combat.

A lot of bad-feeling is said to exist between the Korean and Chinese merchants at Mokpo, in consequence of which trade is at a dead lock.

A Korean military officer has been arrested by the Japanese in Gensan, on suspicion of being a Russian spy. He is being brought up to Seoul for trial.

A Korean lady, according to the Daito Shimpo, has presented 10 pieces of fur to the Japanese Army Head Quarters to be forwarded to the troops in Manchuria.

The Magistrate of Kamsung reports that a Japanese captain of a small sailing vessel has applied to him for permission to cut ice from the river at Whachinpo.

The Ottawa correspondent of the "Daily Mail" states that Captain Low, the leader of the Neptune expedition to the Artic regions, found five graves on Beechy Island. The inscriptions on these graves show that two are the graves of Sir John Franklin and some of his men of the Erebus and Terror, and that three are those of a later expedition.

Three of the largest cargo-carrying Steamers of the Hamburg-American Line arrived at Barry on the 12th ult. to load Welsh coal for the Russian Fleet. The "Balavia" a twin screw steamer of 11,000 tons register will take 9,000 tons cargo of the Rhymney Company's coal, while the steamships "Bethania" and "Bosnia" will carry 8,800 and 6,000 tons respectively of Powell-Dufferyn coals. All the coal has to be double-screened before being shipped.

The road between Gensan and Ham heung has now been completely repaired by the Japanese. In addition to the facilities for transport thus effected, a Japanese steamer is to ply between Gensan and the seaport nearest Hamheung.

Two steamers which are under construction at the Mitsu Bishi Shipbuilding Yard have been named the Tsushi Maru and Iki Maru. The work will be complete in June next. They will be employed on the service between Shimonoseki and Fusan to make connection between the Sanyo Railway and the Seoul-Fusan Railway.

A launch from the "Retvizan" succeeded in sinking a four funnelled Japanese destroyer in Tahe Bay on November 3rd. From the accounts to hand it appears that three Japanese torpedo boats or destroyers were at work in Tahe Bay attempting to pick up mines. A small launch from the "Retvizan" put out and got quite close to the vessels without being observed. A torpedo was discharged at the destroyer, striking her and sinking her quickly. Apparently those on board the Japanese vessels thought they had struck a mine, for no effort was made to chase the launch and the latter got back safely.—Chefoo Daily News.

A scene probably without its parallel in theatrical annals occurred at the Grand Theatre, Swansea, on October 1st. at the conclusion of Sir Henry Irving's farewell performance. After the curtain had fallen on the act the veteran actor was called before the curtain, and was greeted with great cheering. Then some one in the gallery commenced the hymn "Lead, kindly" light, and the strain was taken up by his companions, and in a few seconds the whole audience had risen and was fervently singing Newman's beautiful hymn. Sir Henry expressed his delight with the singing, which, he said, would be forever engraved on his memory. Then another Welshman, with a full rich voice, struck up "God be with you till we meet again," and the audience joined in heartily. Sir Henry Irving stood with bowed head, and was deeply moved by the remarkable demonstration.

The Korea Daily News.

Issued at 5 P. M. daily except Sundays.

Rate of Subscription :—
Per Year,............Yen 25.
Per Quarter,..........Yen 7.
Per Month,..........Yen 2.50.

Postage in Korea not charged extra.
Postage abroad charged extra.

Advertisements, 50 sen per day for 1 inch or less.
5 yen per month per inch.
50 yen per year per inch.

All communications to

E. T. BETHELL,
Editor and Publisher,
Pak-tong, Seoul.

THE JAPAN MAIL ON PORT ARTHUR.

It appears probable that the plan laid out by the General and the Admiral at Port Arthur, and endorsed—if not suggested—by St. Petersburg, is that the remaining vessels of the squardron should cling to the shelter of the harbour and the forts until the Baltic Fleet arrives in the immediate neighbourhood of the Liaotung Peninsula, when they could sally out, the Japanese squadrons being thus caught between two fires. Evident ly that would be an ideal manoeuvre from the Russian point of view. Admiral Togo would find himself assailed simultaneously by 12 line-of-battle ships, to say nothing of cruisers and torpedo-craft and his position would be at best highly critical. But the consummation of such a scheme depends wholly on the security of the harbour. For the past month there has been only one part of the harbour where even tolerable safety can be enjoyed by war-ships, and that part is the estuary of the river under the hill called Pehyushan. The attack of the besiegers is now directed mainly against the north and east sectors, namely, Sunshushan, Urluagshan and Keekwanshan. These forts captured, Pehyushan could probably be reduced without great difficulty. The final real key of the situation so far as concerns the harbour, is Hwangkinshan (Golden Hill). If Hwangkinshan were in Japanese possession no Russian ship could lie in the harbour for an hour. The forts on Tiger's Tail also would be untenable for they are completely commanded from Hwangkinshan. The problem for the ships therefore is, can Hwangkinshan hold out until the Baltic Fleet arrives. General Stoessel is represented as having reported to St. Petersburg that the fortress may count on several months of life still. Yet he is busily preparing a citadel at Liaotishan, whereas to retire to Liaotishan would mean the abandonment of all the permanent forts, including Hwangkinshan, as well as of the two harbours. What would then become of the fleet? It is doubtful whether a more interesting or momentous situation ever occurred in any war. Immense issues depend upon the garrison's capacity of resistance and upon the besiegers' potentiality of attack. The question must be settled in the course of the next two months.

The "Japan Mail" also says; a danger exists for Japan; the danger of having her sea-communications cut. Could Russia accomplish that the situation would be changed at once. In land-fighting Japan is absolutely safe, but in sea-fighting she labours under the disadvantage of possessing a limited number of ships, which can not be reinforced while the war lasts. There lies the only element of peril.

NAVAL CONSTRUCTION.

A very interesting comparative table has been published in Tokyo showing the programmes of ship-building which the various Powers have laid out for themselves. The following are the figures:—

BATTLE-SHIPS.		Tons.
England	10	163,800
America	13	110,200
Russia	5	72,242
France	5	87,770
Germany	6	77,950
Italy	4	49,760
PROTECTED CRUISERS.		
England	11	35,080
America	5	17,450
Russia	2	13,290
France	—	—
Germany	4	12,792
Italy	—	—
ARMOURED CRUISERS.		
England	16	204,500
America	13	140,600
Russia	14	210,800
France	7	88,447
Germany	3	29,512
Italy	2	7,234

With regard to the figures for Russia in this table, it has to be noted that nothing absolutely certain is known. Rumour says that the Russian Government has determined to build 10 armoured cruisers of 18,000 tons, each the most powerful vessels of their kind in the world, and 4 armoured cruisers of 7,700 tons each, of the "Bayan" type.

DESTROYERS.	
England	29
America	—
Russia	15*
France	12
Germany	6

*(In addition to 21 said to have been ordered in a foreign country).

GUNBOATS.		
England	—	—
America	2	2,170
Russia	1	1,316
France	—	—
Germany	—	899

TORPEDO BOATS.	
England	4
America	0
Russia	12*
Germany	1
Italy	5

*(In addition to others building elsewhere).

COUNTERFEITING IN JAPAN.

Fujita Jitsutaro, thirty-four years of age, of Okayama prefecture, was arrested on Tuesday in Osaka, where he has been living, and charged with counterfeiting Korean nickel currency. Fujita is an old hand at the business. Since the 6th September last he is believed to have turned out nearly four thousand coins. At the beginning of the year he was sentenced to four months' imprisonment for a similar offence.

A Russian passenger on the Gaelic, from Shanghai, received considerable attention from the police on the vessel's arrival at Nagasaki. It is stated that an examination of his papers showed him to be the former manager of the Chinese Eastern Railway's agency at Korsakoff. He was on the Argun at the time of her capture by the Japanese and, with the other passengers, was taken to Sasebo and released. His present destination is San Francisco, and the authorities discovered that he is now employed by Messrs. Semeloff & Co.. of Shanghai, who have received an order from Major-General Dessino for from 7,000 to 10,000 casks of salt beef, and have sent him to superintend the shipment of the order. Although he is engaged in obtaining supplies for the enemy, the authorities allowed him to proceed on his journey, possibly owing to the difficulty of interfering with a passenger, not an actual combatant, on a neutral vessel.—Nagasaki Press.

According to a report from Songchin the Russians have laid up a large store of flour and are evidently preparing to spend the winter there. Some of the men have gone into winter clothing.

China has declared her intention of joining The Hague Arbitration Convention.

The Kamni of Fusan telegraphs that Mr. Yi Chai Kuk and party have arrived there safely and were to leave by train for Seoul at 2 P. M. today.

A Chinese named Sonlingfang, a British subject, was recently killed by Koreans near Haiju. The secretary of the Chinese Legation in Chemulpo is to be despatched to that place to enquire into the matter and assist in securing justice on the perpetrators of the murder.

The two houses on the hill-side of Namsan immediately above the German Legation recently advertised in our columns "to let," have been respectively occupied by Mr. E. T. Bethell and Mr. H. J. Mühlensteth, who wish to notify their friends of their change of residence.

The Anglo-Russian Agreement drawn up with regard to the North Sea incident contains a clause providing that the investigation held at Hull shall state whether the responsibility for the disaster rests upon British subjects or others.

Yesterday a committee from the Il Chin Hoi was despatched to Mr. Yi Kyeun Meung, the President of the Council of State, to enquire what term of mourning for the Crown Princess had been fixed. Mr. Sin Ki Sou, the Vice President, was also visited by these gentry, and requested to resign. What success crowned their efforts we are unable to state.

Four thousand Japanese prisoners of war are now interned in the Kieff Military District; 1,000 are at Kieff, 1,000 at Kremenchug, and 2,000 at Poltava. The soldiers are lodged in the barracks left vacant by the troops who have gone to the front, and the officers are quartered in private lodgings, which are looked after by the municipal authorities.—Shanghai Times.

Enquiries are being made in London and New York by the Siamese Government for the supplying of 50,000 rifles of the latest pattern. It appears that the King of Siam has been much occupied since the present war opened with the arrangements for defending his country in case of need, and he is far from satisfied with the situation. His military advisers have advised him to have his army completely re-armed.

The Foreign Office has declared the contract entered into between a Korean styling himself the head of the Korean Fisheries Co., and a Japanese whaling syndicate at Nagasaki for whaling rights on the Korean coasts, null and void. The Foreign Office is unaware of the existence of a "Korean Fisheries Co." and moreover cannot endorse any such contract, which was made without it's knowledge.

The following letter has been received by the United States Department of Agriculture:—"My wife had a Tame cat that dyd. For the enrichment of the soil I had the Carkis deposited under the roots of a Gooseberry Bush. (The Frute being up to then of the smooth varriety.) But the next Seson's Frute, after the Cat was berred, the Gooseberrys was all Hairy—and more Remarkable, the Catapilers of the Same Bush was All of said Hairy description."

The hunger for statistics has induced the French "Monde Artiste" to pay into the secret of the number of musical notes which the eye of the pianist has to take in. Also, into the number of movements which his hands have to make in the course of a minute. The result is that henceforth the poor pianist will feel he has fallen short of the ideal unless his eyes have absorbed 1,500 notes per minute and his fingers have excuted the 2,000 movements which are the ordinary allowance of the aspiring and piano-practising musician.

The Korea Daily News.

VOL. I, THURSDAY, DECEMBER 1, 1904. No. 114

大韓每日申報
대한매일신보

(뎨일빅오십호) (토요일) 일쳔구빅사년십이월이일

본샤고빅

이신보는영어와한국문으로셕거민일출판홈

신문가

한쟝 엽젼두돈오푼

일삭표 엽젼두량닷돈

우표가미삭닷돈

다밧돈으로밧숨

광고료는

귀한의쟝단과즈항의다쇼로증감홀터명가로밧을터이오매오리자하너대한사람마다다이신문을보실터이니광고내시기를원흐시는이들은우리신문사에와셔편약흐심을희망흐옵

○발행소 박동대한미일신보사발이하교압혜젼영국인셜필림쟝자리오

사쟝 영국인 (비셜)

평양 테리졈

○평양효동사는권미보씨로우리신문관티테리인을퇴쟝흐엿스오니평양에계신구람흐고져흐시는 쳠군즈는위티리졈에왕림흐와편의흐시옵

사고

○우리대한미일신보의목뎍은대한의인념젼셔에관한모든뎨목에티흐야는공평한변론을쥬쟝홈이라우리동신원의탐보는신문보시는쳠군즈의계홍샹보도흐리며펀지들귀셔흐며주시는이는셩명과번디들젹어붓치시기를희망흐오니이거슨신문샹에긔재흐란는거시아니오다만국휘신용흐는즁거를숨고자홈이라귀자는아모귀셔던지고귀지흐올퇴가흐는권리를가젓스나며공즁평화를문란케흐는듯흐오이셔는의편히밧지아니켓숩나이다

●본사셜시이리로신문을미양우혜로분젼흐와레젼부의임의로젼흐든굿스로번곳에는후눈게젼흐기도흐며혹멋칠거슬혼섭곳에젼흐기도흐며혹아니젼흐는곳도잇다흐와우리신문을슈랑흐시는 쳠군즈외계랑되흐야구람흐시는미우미안흐옵기로지금은분젼인을두고미일일즉이젼흐게흐엿스오니혹늣게젼흐거나혹아니젼흐는

젼흐거는혹늣게젼흐거나흔일이잇스면본사로통긔흐여주시믈희망흐옵

관보

뎨이쳔구빅구십팔호

광무팔년십이월일일

셔임급사령

○면본관 진위대오연디대대쟝홍군보병참령 심홍택 진위대오연디대상대대쟝홍군보병참령 김명환

○승셔원일관신상등 탁지부쥬사 리셕구 조중익 탁지부쥬사 리

○의원 면본관 승령젼참봉 김창유 진쟝 홍효창 원공영 과쥬사

○관찰 임시종원 한셩 김풍 등 현

○하 임덕승 평젼참봉 서 관임 관팔등

○동 임명왕 참봉 조경 관팔등

○임등이상 사면 회 과쥬사 셔 관임

○구 임효창 원참봉 서관 임관팔등

○의원 면본관 덕원감리서쥬사 권현섭 상회 감리서쥬사

○일 임덕원 감리서쥬사 서 관임 관팔등

○임상화 감리서쥬사 서 관임 관팔등

○부모 공명이 쟝부 군부총쟝대신 리쥬관 참모부쟝 육군부쟝 군부참

○○○ 재(대)요 ○구 임호 리방 군부

구규압 진쟝부 모 (rest of this passage illegible)

면사 라 구잇터교도빈대압진쟝부모 이 이이교이젼로 ... 권셔 판셔 쥬사 ...

면본관 진위대 ... 구경 ...

는흐약셔엽지나도는일에다를탄량부군참

(논셜)

압고셔취진티에흰금쳥편이로 샹샹흐오면고위치와규제가시 방에방흐되이잇사온즉가히변 동이엄지못흘터이오나일비샹 히긴즁흐와신이감히쳔편치못 흐오니엇지흐올는지감쥬흐와 광무팔년십일월이십팔일에 봉지의주방편의도는란샹회의 흐야드리라흐옵셧더라

○의졍부참졍신기션이곤 주 광안남도관찰사리중하가셔 리 외부대신사무서에미국인거렴 의하고귀국흐는길에주미공사 외계흔쳑홈이잇는티사의는비 록별반조어가엽사오나교제소 진에샴가지못흔최망을면흐기 어렵운지라이귀월감봉흠이엇 더흐올는지곤 상 주흐와 광무팔년십일월이십구일에봉 지의주흐다

○궁니부대신리용틱곤 주래 식원번역관엄달환이가방금게 샹즁에잇서히원사무가긴즁흐 와셩슈에붓치기어렵사오니귀 봉셔무케홈이엇더흐올는지곤 샹 주흐와 광무팔년십일월이 십구일에봉 지의주흐다

잡보

○한셩부보고 한셩부에셔니 부로보고흔긔의들거흔즉향자 에외국인등의샨빠집문권을빗 고아닙나쳥흔일노써임의어리 변보고흐엿거니와그욕이사실 흐온즉근리에한셩니에커류흐 는외국인의호수총액이히로더 흐고드론로더흐야그믜흔바가 옥에티흐야문권을쳥흐는일도 쏘흔이거스사세라부리만하가 용는거스사셰에진실로그러흘 비라면저본부로셔그실디의방 의됨이엽슬거시주획흔거슬조 믜이흔거시긔부에플흐고인가 흘쏘흔후에야바아흐로문권을 발급흐엿논티미샹슨인흐는거 슬반드시급속히홈을과약흐기 어려운으로인흐야쎄각히령사 외독최흐며청나홈을밧사오니 대기이문권을발급홈을회탁지 안는것도진실노씨 가옥을미 밉흐는권흔는불졔이 수엽고만 일샹저흐야큐안흐여두 신으 련가는것도사리의타방치아닐

가져취홀뿐아니라혼것이웃슬 돈몽흐며친구를회목흐는의분 을일흔쎼들이온쥬이거슨불가 불특별이방편지도를연구흐야 써션후지칙을도모흘지니조량 흐와신속히판리흐야흐여곰이 웃에칙망을면케흐심을보라다 흐엿더라

○운동임방 진명회도시방쟝 부는명셰코한가지아니흔디 흐고공포흐더니부샹에죳기를 원흐는자ㅣ흐나토영셔회원이 명셩홈의회쟝과유셩씨가경향 각젼임방에게로통문을돌녓다 더라

○주쟝무인 리규원리규찬형 데가샬옥사건으로피신흐는티 리씨션샨셩며쟝이 원소히조 니에잇셔파게되는지라주쟝흐 는사롬이엄셔곤막샹업이라더 라

○쳔림곡레 음력십일월이십 구일 빈궁하현시에쳔림곡레 흐옵시기로마련흐옵셧다더라

○졍부조회니부 졍부에셔니 부로조회흐기를근일에탐랑이 즈샹흐야티방인민들이류리흐 고탕패흐야호읍지셩이날마다 들니며아니들니는곳이엄스니 진실노만만히참흔지라탐화민 쇼로말흘진티흔즁에흔조코민 샹에셔민제를탈취흐는거시지 어디샹의리가쇼망홈이오 버쳥명으로흡흐오니 (rest of passage illegible)

빅셩의정지 가비록샹분무훌홀 지라도모옹을편안히흐고지버 기를보젼키어렵거든흐물며특 탐흐며엑속어 쎄잇셔 하항에젼 빙으로흐며곰쳔리에파죡흐고 평부에달아와호소흐기셔지에 니르니그졍상을싱각흔티츔하 리말을안코져홀지라디샹히 쳐치홀수업는고로히민소를보 버니두판찰부에는는듯시신칙 흐오셔별노수검판을쟝흐야도 져히수칙흐야 연호소흔것과 곳거든히부음판근슈는곳주풍 시흥흐야금히탐쟝흔을흐는을 빈창자주어쎄증민의원을쓰셔게 흐시고곳회시흐란흐엿더라

UNION INSURANCE SOCIETY OF CANTON.

Head office Hongkong.
Marine risks underwritten at current rates.
Agents in Chemulpo,
E. MEYER & Co.

COMPAGNIE DES MESSAGERIES MARITIMES.

Fortnightly Direct Service.

For Marseilles
via Ports.
Sailing from Yokohama
Calling at Kobe,
Shanghai, Hongkong, Saigon, Singapore,
Colombo, Djibonti, Suez, Port Said
and Marseilles.

For particulars apply to
HOLME RINGER & Co.,
Chemulpo.

HAYASHIDA & Co.,

6 MYENG DONG, CHIN KO KAI, SEOUL.
BRANCH OFFICE AT CHEMULPO.

Money changers, Coal and Wood Merchants, Express Agents.

We are agents for the Pyeng-yang Coal Company and the Karazu Coal Company of Japan. We have the best quality of both anthracite and bituminous coal, and prompt execution of orders is our speciality. Firewood of all kinds kept in stock. Full weight guaranteed. Money of all denominations exchanged at current rates. Parcels received for all parts.

CHINA MUTUAL LIFE INS. CO.

Most favourable terms to policy holders.

Benefit system unsurpassed.

HOLME RINGER & Co.
Agents, Chemulpo.

C. P. R.

CANADIAN PACIFIC RAILWAY COMPANY'S ROYAL MAIL STEAMSHIP LINE.

THE FAST ROUTE BETWEEN CHINA, JAPAN, AND EUROPE VIA CANADA AND THE UNITED STATES.

Route from Hongkong via Shanghai, Nagasaki (Inland Sea of Japan) Kobe, Yokohama Victoria and Vancouver.

Twin Screw Empress Steamship 6,000 Tons Speed 19 knots.

PROPOSED SAILING FROM YOKOHAMA.
R. M. S. Empress of India.
R. M. S. Empress of Japan.
R. M. S. Empress of China.
R. M. S. Athenian.
R. M. S. Taatar.

Special reduction (first class only) granted to members of the Military, Naval, Diplomatic and Civil services and to Missionaries.

Passengers have choice of ten routes across the Continent of America and have privilege of travelling by any Atlantic Steamship Line.

Round the World passage tickets in connection with the P. and O. S. N., North German Lloyd and Messageries Co.'s **£125.**

All rates payable at current rate of exchange.

For further information, Tickets, Guide Books, etc., apply to

HOLME, RINGER & Co., AGENTS,
Chemulpo.

Grand Hotel,

(Formerly the Station Hotel)

Near the Railway Terminus, West Gate Seoul.

The Best Hotel in Korea
Handsome new Building.
Fine Airy Rooms
Excellent Cuisine.
Terms Moderate.
Special terms to Missionaries
and to permanent boarders.

Electric cars within 2 minutes' walk.

W. H. EMBERLEY,
Proprietor

EVERY FACILITY.

In connection with Life Assurance Business is afforded by

The Standard Life Assurance Co.,

One of the largest and wealthiest of the Provident Institutions of the United Kingdom Forms of Application and all information will be promptly afforded on application.

10 CENTS A DAY.

Not a very large expenditure is it? But it is sufficient to secure for a man of 30 a policy with the STANDARD LIFE OFFICE for

$1323.

For all particulars of rates, etc., apply to

Holme, Ringer & Co.,
Agents, Chemulpo.

THE NEW YORK LIFE INSURANCE COMPANY.

Have you ever been declined by any Company?

Are you engaged in a specially hazardous occupation?

Have you heard of the New York Life Insurance Company's New Classifications for this class of Risks?

If not, send your date of birth, occupation and particulars of rejection, if any to

E. MEYER & Co.,
Agents, Chemulpo.

MITSUI BUSSAN KAISHA.
(MITSUI & Co.)

MITSUI GINKO.
(MITSUI BANK.)

The Bank is owned by the members of the Mitsui Family, who, as partners, assume an unlimited responsibility for all liabilities of the Bank:—

Capital........................Yen 5,000,000
Reserve Fund.................. " 5,600,000

HEAD OFFICE, TOKYO.
LONDON OFFICE, 34 LIME ST., E. C.

BRANCHES AND AGENCIES:—
New York, San Francisco, Hamburg, Bombay, Singapore, Manila, Hongkong, Amoy, Chefoo, Tientsin.
Kobe, Hakodate, Yokohama, Kure, Yokosuka, Moji, Shimonoseki, Miike, Wakamatsu, Nagasaki, Kuchinotsu, Karatsu, Sasebo, Misume, Taipeh, &c.

Telegraphic Address for all the Offices:
"MITSUI."

A. B. C. AND A. I CODES USED.

Contractors of Coal
To the Imperial Japanese Navy. Arsenals and Railway Bureau, Principal Railway Companies and Industrial Work, Home and Foreign Mail and Freight Steamers.

Sole Proprietors
Of the famous Miike, Tagawa and Yamano Coal Mines.

Sole Agents
For the sale of Fukumo, Hokoku, Ichimura, Kanoda, Mannoura, Onoura, Ostuji, Sonoda, Tsubaruro, Yoshinotani, Yoshio, Yurokibura and other coals.

YANGTSE INSURANCE ASSOCIATION, LTD.

The undersigned, having been appointed agents for the above company, are prepared to issue policies and pay losses on marine risks at regular rates.

E. MEYER & Co.,
Agents, Chemulpo.

AMERICAN KOREAN ELECTRIC CO.

Light and Power.

Main Office: Electric Building, Chong No.

RAILWAY DEPARTMENT.

OPERATING CARS BETWEEN EAST AND WEST GATE, EVERY TEN MINUTES:—

First Car leaves East Gate at 7:00 A. M. First Car leaves R. R. Station at 7:25 A. M
Last Car " East Gate at 9:40 P. M. Last " " R. R. Station at 10:05 P.M

OPERATING CARS BETWEEN EAST GATE AND IMPERIAL TOMB TERMINUS, EVERY TWENTY MINUTES:—
CONNECTING WITH EVERY ALTERNATE CAR ARRIVING AT EAST GATE FROM CHONG NO.

First Car leaves East Gate for Tomb at 7:10 A. M.
" " " Tomb for East Gate at 7:35 A. M.
Last " " East Gate for Tomb at 7:50 P. M.
" " " Tomb for East Gate at 8:10 P. M.

OPERATING CARS BETWEEN CHONG NO AND YUNG SAN RIVER EVERY TWELVE MINUTES:—

First Car leaves Chong No for South Gate at 7:12 A. M.
" " " Chong No for Yung San at 7:36 A. M.
" " " South Gate for Chong No at 7:20 A. M.
" " " Yung San for Chong No at 8:09 A. M.
Last " " South Gate for Chong No 10:00 P. M.
" " " Yung San for Chong No at 9:33 P. M.

SPECIAL PRIVATE CARS FURNISHED TO SUIT CONVENIENCE OF PATRONS. PRICES ON APPLICATION AT HEAD OFFICE.

LIGHTING DEPARTMENT.

Where less than 250 candle power of light is used, the rate per month will be
Per 16 candle power incandescent lamp,—All night.—Yen 2.50.
32 candle power incandescent lamp:—All night:—Yen 4.00.
50 candle power incandescent lamp:—All night:—Yen 6.00.
150 " " " " " " ,, 10.00.
1200 ,, ,, enclosed are ,, ,, ,, ,, 20.00.

Where more than 250 candle power of light is used, a Meter will be installed, freqvedted:—Rent of Meter Yen 2.00 per month. Rate of charges by meter reading:—Two Sen per Ampere per hour. (Approximately this is equal to about One Sen per 16 C. P. lamp per hour) Minimum monthly charge where meter is installed, Yen 20.00 per month, which includes rental of meter.

Estimates for installing lights furnished on application.
An assortment of chandeliers always on hand.

K. Murakami.

Photograph Studio
Chinkokai, Seoul.

Printing, Developing and Enlargement, of Photographs always Undertaken.

Korean Views and Pictures Illustrating Native Customs always on Sale,

---

THE OSAKA SHOSEN KAISHA.

Boats frequently on the berth for Chinnampo.

REGULAR SAILINGS BETWEEN JAPAN AND KOREAN PORTS.

FUSAN AND KOBE VIA SHIMONOSEKI.

OSAKA VIA MOKPO, FUSAN, SHIMONOSEKI AND KOBE.

MOJI DIRECT.

OSAKA VIA KUNSAN, MASANPO, FUSAN, SHIMONOSEKI AND KOBE.

CHEMULPO KUNSAN LINE,
Every three days.

CHEMULPO CHINNAMPO LINE.
Every three days.

For Freight and passage and further particulars apply to

THE OSAKA SHOSEN KAISHA,
Chemulpo.

RONDON, PLAISANT & CO.

General Storekeepers and Merchants, Ships Contractors, Tobacconists, Commission and Forwarding Agents, Coal Merchants

IMPORTERS AND EXPORTERS

Seoul & Chemulpo.

W. D. WENTWORTH.

LANDING
AND
SHIPPING AGENT
AND
CUSTOMS BORDER.

12 OURA, NAGASAKI.

STEWARD & CO.

Chemulpo.

Shipchandlers and Storekeepers, Naval and Mercantile Contrrctors, Landing and Shipping Agents.

STEWARD'S HOTEL

Chemulpo.

Best accommodation in the port for travelers. Clean and well-aired rooms, good cuisin and prompt attendence, moderate tariff.

◯굴도압수 공쥬사ᄂᆞᆫ림경현이가남대문밧렬도역수ᄒᆞᄂᆞᆫᄃᆡ셔흙을파다가눈녀즉수ᄒᆞ엿더라

◯졍부통쳡니부 졍부에셔니부로통쳡ᄒᆞ기를경샹북도슌찰ᄉᆞ홍우셕의주본을본즉대구군슈류승영의젼후불법ᄒᆞᆫ힝위ᄂᆞᆫ손가락으로세기어려오미이ᄀᆞᆺ흔혼암ᄒᆞ고탐람ᄒᆞᆫ슈령은ᄒᆞ로를머물너도ᄒᆞ로의히잇슬지라비로봉고파직ᄒᆞ엿다ᄒᆞ엿스니류군슈ᄂᆞᆫ면관 주본에련ᄒᆞ야셔명ᄒᆞ라ᄒᆞ엿더라

◯명찰면보 경샹북도관찰ᄉᆞ의면보를거ᄒᆞᆫ즉슌찰ᄉᆞ홍우셕의죠회니긔에쟝긔군문챵은봉고파직ᄒᆞᆫ다고ᄒᆞ엿다ᄒᆞ엿더라

◯청축고문관 거삼십일에일본공관셔긔관국분샹티랑씨가학부대신을박문ᄒᆞ고권고ᄒᆞ기를귀국에각학교가미비ᄒᆞ니각디방디를에감액ᄒᆞ야그경비써학교를쳐쳐에셜시ᄒᆞ고즁학교교ᄉᆞ폐원란으로고문관을합동ᄒᆞ고국니학무를확쟝ᄒᆞ라ᄒᆞ엿더라

◯엄립규령 관졔리졍소에셔각관졔를긔졍ᄒᆞᄂᆞᆫ즁인ᄃᆡ소무를대단히비밀히ᄒᆞ야본소관원즁에셔다른ᄃᆡ루셜ᄒᆞ면벌반쳐분ᄒᆞ기로엄히규졍을세웟다더라

◯외획물시 탁지대신민영긔씨가남도외획젼삼십만원으로미안ᄒᆞᆫ신 처분ᄭᆞ지니르럿더니히외획은물시되엿더라

◯시찰일힝입셩 일본에시찰원리지국엄쥬의민형식리샹쳔황신틔현빅운일힝이하오구시량에새문밧뎡거쟝에도착ᄒᆞ야입셩ᄒᆞᄂᆞᆫᄃᆡ영졉ᄒᆞᄂᆞᆫ자가부지기수라ᄒᆞ며리용익현영운량씨ᄂᆞᆫ회국ᄒᆞᆯ긔한이묘연ᄒᆞ다더라

론셜

청국즁립

일본이즁립셩명ᄒᆞᆫ청국ᄂᆡ지에다젼졍터를만들믄올치아니ᄒᆞᆫ줄을모로ᄂᆞᆫ비가아니언마ᄂᆞᆫ만일그러치아니ᄒᆞᆯ지경이면아라사의침로ᄒᆞᆷ으로써청국이긔왕원수를일본의게갑프려ᄒᆞᆯ염녀도불무ᄒᆞ며ᄯᅩᄒᆞᆫ즁립셩명ᄒᆞᆷ을파약지아니케ᄒᆞ랴면관계가크게될터인고로부득이그리ᄒᆞᆷ인지라

청국셔즁립ᄒᆞᄂᆞᆫ셩명은아모리ᄒᆞ엿드러도일아량국의유익ᄒᆞ게될때에ᄂᆞᆫ엇지ᄒᆞᆯ수업시위격ᄒᆞᆷ을당ᄒᆞ게되엿슴이라고ᄒᆞ야일본조일신문에계지ᄒᆞᆷ이여좌ᄒᆞ기에번등ᄒᆞ노라

반일우리나라이청국의즁립셩명ᄒᆞᆫ바를관계ᄒᆞ야샹관치아니ᄒᆞ엿든덜아병들이져희의마음ᄃᆡ로만주도ᄯᅥ옥조케반다려슬더이요봉쳔과신민둔등지에셔도청민의게수합되ᄂᆞᆫᄃᆡ로군량을더옥쥰비ᄒᆞ엿슬듯ᄒᆞᆫ거시멀니불거시아니라월젼연ᄃᆡ에셔아라사으르스텔늬병함만불지라도연ᄃᆡ와대련만등지로단니며곡식을젹지ᄒᆞ야필요ᄒᆞᆫ도록은ᄒᆞ엿스나은피ᄒᆞᆯ곳이업서공교히연ᄃᆡ에셔격침ᄒᆞᆯ빈되엿슨즉이거스로만말ᄒᆞ여도두강대ᄒᆞᆫ락들에셔ᄒᆞᄂᆞᆫ일을청국이감히엇지ᄒᆞᆯ수업ᄂᆞᆫ연고ㅣ니라ᄒᆞ엿ᄂᆞᆫ지라

일아량국이청국의방조ᄒᆞ여주기를바람은고사ᄒᆞ고아라사에셔ᄂᆞᆫ병란ᄒᆞᆯ욕심이츙만ᄒᆞ며일본셔ᄂᆞᆫ슌망지려를싱각ᄒᆞ야그리ᄒᆞᆷ이라고ᄒᆞ되우리의싱각에ᄂᆞᆫ심히아혹ᄒᆞᆫ자ㅣ잇스니이제이말ᄒᆞᄂᆞᆫ거손공연ᄒᆞᆫ변론인것갓트되청국은어좌어우에필경유익ᄒᆞᆷ이조곰도업슬지라

아라사ᄲᅡᆯ틱함ᄃᆡ가동양으로나오게되면필경청국어느항구에즁박ᄒᆞᆯ터인즉그때에만일외국에셔관셥ᄒᆞ야말ᄒᆞ지아니ᄒᆞ면청국에셔ᄂᆞᆫ능히금지ᄒᆞᆯ권리가업슬지니

사셰가이러ᄒᆞᆫ즉즁립셩명ᄒᆞᆫ바를엇지ᄒᆞᆯ수업시파약된양으로아라사의게향ᄒᆞ야불가불변명ᄒᆞᆯ터이니이러ᄒᆞᆯ지경이면북경에잇ᄂᆞᆫ일본공사도심히괴로올듯ᄒᆞ도다

잡보

◯의졍피임 박졔슌리지국량씨ᄂᆞᆫ리졍소의졍관을피임ᄒᆞ엿더라

◯어업벌빙청구 간셩군슈리준구씨의보고를거ᄒᆞᆫ즉음력구월초이일에일인들이본군화진포구에셔어업ᄒᆞᆯ추로부산흥공문을가지고와셔어업을시작ᄒᆞ기를청ᄒᆞ더니음력구월십ᄉᆞ일에션쟝문협샤틔랑이가본군오현면쟝평리화진포에셔어름을쓰기를청원ᄒᆞ오니엇지ᄒᆞ올지오ᄒᆞ엿더라

◯감봉즁계 외부에셔미국공관에죠회ᄒᆞ기를평양감리셔주ᄉᆞ원용덕이가감리셔에잇슬때에리일영ᄉᆞᆯ구지잡고ᄂᆞᆺ치아니ᄒᆞᆫ소로사실ᄒᆞᆫ즉히원이쟝졍을몰나외교샹에문란케ᄒᆞᆷ이니일ᄀᆡ월감봉에쳐ᄒᆞ야도츅히써즁계가되겟다ᄒᆞ엿더라

◯죠청젼주 덕공관에셔외부에조회ᄒᆞ되현금우리외부면보ᄂᆡ미에우리대황뎨ᄭᅴ셔귀국황태조비홍셔ᄒᆞ심을드르시고블승경악ᄒᆞ샤일로말매암아귀국 대황뎨ᄭᅴ와 황태ᄌᆞᄭᅴ젼주ᄒᆞ라ᄒᆞ엿기에조회ᄒᆞ니쳥컨ᄃᆡ젼쥬ᄒᆞ라ᄒᆞ엿더라

◯리씨감봉 외부에셔미공관에용합ᄒᆞ되귀국인거렴이히고ᄒᆞ고귀국ᄒᆞᆯ때에본부에셔ᄂᆞᆫ위임ᄒᆞᆫ일업스나히인이일을ᄒᆞᆫ다빙자ᄒᆞ고교제샹에손실ᄒᆞᆷ이잇기에그새본부셔리대신리즁하ᄂᆞᆫ삼가지못ᄒᆞᆫ죄칙으로일긔월감봉에처ᄒᆞ엿스니칭컨ᄃᆡ죠량ᄒᆞ라ᄒᆞ엿더라

◉출급처분 리규찬외게괴살ᄒᆞᆫ경션힝은리규찬과거리ᄒᆞ괴든공젼흠표가잇다ᄒᆞ고빅ᄆᆡ칠십여셕을경우원으로슈입ᄒᆞ며ᄯᅩ잡곡칠필빅셕을집류ᄒᆞᆫ고로 처분ᄂᆡ에경원지로질변ᄒᆞ고야집류ᄒᆞᆫ곡식은도로ᄂᆡ여쥬라ᄒᆞ옵셧더라

외보

◯미소항의 로국에쥬차ᄒᆞᆫ미국대ᄉᆞᄂᆞᆫ로병이만쥬에셔청인의의복을입ᄂᆞᆫᄉᆞ건에관하야로국졍부에되ᄒᆞ야ᄒᆞᆼ의를졔츌ᄒᆞ엿더라

◯로국독병상보 빅림면보를거ᄒᆞᆫ즉로국셔ᄂᆞᆫ좌개ᄒᆞᆷ과ᄀᆞᆺ치동병ᄒᆞ엿ᄂᆞᆫᄃᆡ

기에후군관구에셔ᄂᆞᆫ
뎨구군단과뎨십군단과뎨십일군단과뎨십이군단과뎨이십일군단과

고삭극군관구에셔ᄂᆞᆫ
뎨이혼셩ᄉᆞ단과신광려단과

막사과군단에셔ᄂᆞᆫ
특무려단과뎨십삼군단과뎨십칠군단과보충려단과

와루쏘뷔야군관구에셔ᄂᆞᆫ
뎨오군단과뎨륙군단과뎨십ᄉᆞ군단뎨십오군단과뎨십륙군단과뎨십ᄉᆞ군단뎨십오군단뎨십구군단과근위보병삼ᄭᅴᄉᆞ단과뎨일긔병군단과뎨이긔병군단과보충려단과

우위루나군관구에셔ᄂᆞᆫ
뎨이군단과뎨삼군단과뎨ᄉᆞ군단과뎨십륙군단과뎨이십군단과보충군단인ᄃᆡ동계가십구군단이더라

뎐보

십일월삼십일경셩공ᄉᆞ관착공보

◯송수산공격 송수산과밋그동방에잇ᄂᆞᆫ포대를되ᄒᆞ야그외안의비탈언덕과밋그부근디를견확히졈령ᄒᆞ엿스나아직돌입ᄒᆞᆯ긔회에니르지못ᄒᆞ엿고목하에궁곡과기타측방긔관을파괴ᄒᆞᄂᆞᆫ즁이오이빅ᄡᅡᆷ쳐의놉흔ᄡᅡᆼ에되ᄒᆞ야공젹ᄒᆞᆫ거ᄉᆞᆫ세번공격ᄒᆞᆷ을인ᄒᆞ야그우회부근에잇ᄂᆞᆫ젹군의ᄒᆡ조를탈취ᄒᆞ고목하에이거슬보존ᄒᆞ여잇고더옥나아가그포ᄃᆡ를탈취ᄒᆞ기에로력ᄒᆞᄂᆞᆫ즁이라ᄒᆞ엿더라

◯회인방면젹졍 회인현파변셕합달파륙도하조부근에잇ᄂᆞᆫ젹군은되각ᄒᆞ고ᄯᅩ목하 경고셩방면에잇ᄂᆞᆫ젹군의병ᄒᆞᆫ은보괴병을합ᄒᆞ야일쳔명이오대포가감소ᄒᆞ야이문만되엿다더라

빅림발 십일월이십이일

◯로함진발 볼틱함대ᄂᆞᆫ캔듸아와스웨쓰로브터진발ᄒᆞ엿다더라

동디발 동일

◯로쟝입관 젼관등총독알넥시푸씨ᄂᆞᆫ의졍부참졍을임명ᄒᆞ엿더라

동디발 동일

◯로국매함 로국이단국륜션사얌을샷다ᄒᆞ며야로에셔졔죠ᄒᆞᆫ수뢰파괴함몃쳑을로국졍부에보냇다고론돈스텐다드신문에확실이말ᄒᆞ엿더라

동디발 동일

◯영덕약죠 영덕즁지죠약은미구에라인된다더라

동디발 동일

◯우일평화 미국대통령루스벨트씨가창론ᄒᆞᆫ평화회ᄂᆞᆫ구주졔국이찬셩ᄒᆞ야그시긔와졀ᄎᆞ를졍ᄒᆞ랴고예비ᄒᆞᆫ다더라

동디발 동월이십ᄉᆞ일

◯영덕호의 영국각신문이덕국을향ᄒᆞ야호의를표ᄒᆞᄂᆞᆫ지라그ᄉᆞ둙은영국졍부의의향을ᄡᅥ름이더라

동디발 동월이십삼일

◯일본젼비 일본졍부가카듸푸에셔셕탄일만돈을사고만쥬에털로지료와슈레를운송ᄒᆞ기위ᄒᆞ야미국샹항에셔륜션일쳑을고입ᄒᆞ엿더라

론돈발 동일

◯북히긔렴 북히에셔비명에ᄉᆞ망ᄒᆞᆫ자를위ᄒᆞ야영국에셔혈이라ᄂᆞᆫᄡᅥ에긔렴쇼돌건츅ᄒᆞᆫ다더라

동디발 동일

◯로보권됴 로국승피득보신문롯스ᄂᆞᆫ졍부를권고ᄒᆞ되동방구라파와즁앙아시아에로국의리익을젼보다더용밍스럽게보호ᄒᆞᆯ거시니만일그럿치아니ᄒᆞ면동남파샤와파샤만은미구에영국의졈령ᄒᆞᆷ이되리라ᄒᆞ엿더라

광고

THE IL CHIN HOI.

This society still flourishes. Recently by bullying the Home Office they succeeded in procuring the release of two of their adherents who were imprisoned in North Chulla province. Another report says that they are now making arrangements to establish branches throughout the Empire. No wonder the Japanese "War expenses" mount up. A story reaches us from Sŏ Bing Ko which makes us suspect that the inhabitants of that district have been indulging in a little fun at the expense of the noble society. It appears that, finding that the whole of the ground from the South Gate down to the river, including their district, had been staked out by the Seoul-Fusan Railway Company, the people of Sŏ Bing Ko approached the "Il Chin Hoi" and offered them $120,000 if they could persuade the Railway Company to expand in some other direction. The "Il Chin Hoi" grandiloquently replied that their attention was occupied with far weightier matters than the tribulations of a pettifogging village.

BEFORE MOUKDEN.

The "Brigadezeitung" has the following editorial on the situation in Manchuria:

The fight in Manchuria has been continued about three weeks without bringing decided advantage to either of the antagonists. The wounds given and received are deep, and both sides seem to be exhausted. This standstill in the operations, however, is only indicative of important events. It is known that the Russians, at the news of the battle of Liaoyang, commenced a second large mobilization. The extent of this mobilization, as given by the press, may be exagerated, but in any event, the arrival of the fresh troops will weigh heavily in the scale.

The first columns of the additional troops must have reached Moukden by this time. Why has Marshal Oyama, however, not pushed on to the next attack? Perhaps because he also expects considerable reinforcement. Perhaps he is waiting for the arrival of the army now before Port Arthur, which he believes will have such success as to enable it to join him. Perhaps the difficulties of supplying his present large army have delayed operations. These difficulties are bound to increase as his army pushes forward. The Japanese line of communication has been considerably shortened since the fall of Newchwang, but the distance from Newchwang to Shaho is great; and as the Russians succeeded in retreating with the locomotives, the railway has been of no use to the Japanese as a means of transport. This has undoubtedly given much trouble to them.

The difficulties with which the Russians have had to contend are comparatively greater. The enormous length of their line of communication makes one admire the skill of their commissary department, which has up to date met the demands of a great army in a most satisfactory way.

The "Daito Shimpo's" liver must be out of order. It suffers from a "sense of impending disaster." We are mysteriously told that a "bolt from the blue" will before long descend into our midst, but the "Daito" refuses to give any particulars.

With regard to the protest lodged by the American Minister against the imprisonment of one Yi Il-yung for selling some land to a missionary in Ping Yang, the Foreign Office has notified the American Minister that the acting-Kamni of Ping Yang was responsible for the outrage and that he has been fined one month's salary by way of punishment.

Mr. Kokubo, acting-Secretary of the Japanese Legation, yesterday visited the Acting Minister of the Korean Education Department and unfolded a plan for increasing the Educational facilities of Korea. Mr. Kokubo's newly-born solicitude for Education is explained by the fact that he suggested the reduction of the army as a means of providing the money.

THE END OF KUK'S TOUR.

The Committee of Inspection, headed by Mr. Yi Chai Kuk, which has been on a visit to Japan, arrived in Seoul last night, having come overland from Fusan.

WINTER AT THE FRONT.

The two following extracts serve to give an idea of the climatic conditions which will prevail at the seat of war for the next four months. No one will envy either soldiers or sailors.

There was no autumn in Manchuria, the summer changing to winter all at once. The Hun-ho, the upper part of the Liaoho, has not yet frozen, and it is believed that it will be some little time before the troops are able to walk over the ice. The thermometer registered 10° on the morning of the 19th, being the lowest since the 1st. The average temperature is about 28°, the glass rising to 30° when the sun is warmest. The wind blows very strongly day after day. There was a light snow on the 13th and the natives state that the wind is keeping away the snow. The force of the wind is very great, scarcely concievable by those who have not been outside of the islands of Japan. Since the maize was cut the velocity of the wind is belived to have considerably increased. The winter clothings for the Japanese troops have all been supplied and no protection against the cold has bee over-looked.

Hard northerly and northwesterly winds are now prevalent outside Port Arthur, accompanied by heavy falls of snow. The snow as a rule falls so thickly that everything is effectually hidden. These storms last about two hours, followed by spells of fine weather. Hard winds often carry away to sea the mines laid at the entrance of Port Arthur harbour, and these are a constant menace to the Japanese blocking squadron. At daytime they can be easily discovered, but are a peril at night, especially when seas are running high and navigation near Port Arthur is dangerous. Recently one of these mines was discovered and blown up by a transport.

The Asahi regrets that the Japanese military notes which are now being circulated on the continent to the extent of 63 million yen, have begun to show a depreciation of about 10 per cent. at Yinkow. This depreciation was brought about by occasional delay in complying with the demand for their conversion into silver, a circumstance unavoidable at times in the midst of the great turmoil of battle-fields. The advantages of employing these notes being obvious, the journal hopes that the authorities will take immediate steps to supply the Japanese administration quarters at Dalny, Yinkow and other places of importance with sufficient reserves of silver, so that their credit may be recovered and maintained at par throughout Manchuria.

"There is a young man in England" says "The Dietetic and Hygienic Gazette" who at the age of twenty-four is developing at the rate of only one sixth of that of the average human being. At present he is learning his alphabet and can count up to ten only. During the last nineteen years he has eaten but three meals a week, has slept twenty-hours, without the slightest variation. In spite of his twenty-four years he looks no older then a boy of four or five and is only thirty-six inches in height. For the same period his development physically has been at only one-sixth the ordinary rate, while absolutely regular and perfect in every other way. At his birth this child weighed ten pounds and in no way differed from any other child. He grew and thrived in the usual way until he attained the age of five. Then his progress was suddenly and mysteriouly arrested, and since then six years have been the same to him as one year to the normal person. He has attracted the attention of many medical and scientific men, more than one of whom has expressed the conviction that this remarkable man will live to be no less than three centuries old."

RELIEF FOR THE AMERICAN GUARD.

The "Chefoo Daily News" of Nov. 29th says:—

The U. S. Collier, "Nanshan," arrived in the harbor yesterday from the South and immediately engaged in coaling the "New Orleans." Both vessels are expected to leave for Chemulpo to-day. On board the "Nanshan" are twenty eight American marines under Captain Broach who are en route to relieve the legation guard at Seoul. Since her last visit to this port the "Nanshan" has been back to Cavite. Her commander, Captain Prideaux, is at present in Australia where he expects to marry. His leave is of three months duration, and during this time his vessel will be under command of Captain Maxwell.

The is a dignified resident in Hongkong who chews tobacco. One day he was coming down from the Peak in a tram. He needed a chew and took a liberal one from a plug that was black and expansive. A man sitting next to him leaned over and said:

"Sir, I am surprised that a person of your evident intellience should chew tobacco. It is a filthy habit. You are a hog, sir, a hog!" and much more to the same effect.

The resident listened for a minute or two. Then he unlimbered. He told the meddling person exactly what he thought of him, and he used none of the graces of oratory in so doing. He "cussed" him up hill and down dale.

The man sat unmoved. After the resident had exhausted himself in his effort to squelch his neighbour, that person dragged a little pad of paper out of his pocket and said mildly:

"Would you mind writing down what you have said? I am very deaf."

THE PROBLEM OF WIRELESS TELEGRAPHY.

What remains to be done to make wireless telegraphy a commerical as it is already practical success? It does not seem necessary to ensure the secrecy of its communications, because inviolable secrecy—as has many times been pointed out—is enjoyed neither by the ordinary telegraph nor the telephone. Any enemy who can get hold at a telegraph wire can "tap" it so as to intercept the message, and, having mastered it, can send it on or suppress it as he pleases, and, with a little scientific knowledge, the same trick can be played with even greater ease on a telephone. But the receiving station of neither telegraph nor telephone is sensitive to messages sent out by stations not connected with them, and in this respect they enjoy at present a most enviable advantage over all systems of wireless telegraphy. Electric waves or ripples in the ether will set in activity all sufficiently sensitive appliances within their range, whether intended for them or not, and this at once annuals a great part of the benefit that we expected to derive from them. The French have already complained that the great waves sent out by the Poldhu station will prevent them from corresponding with ships off their Atlantic coasts, and the complaint seems well founded. How to obviate such objection is the remaining difficulty in the way of the free use of wireless telegraphy.

That some part of this may disappear in practise seems possible. The operators on the ship lately employed by the "Times" in the Far East seem to have said that they learned in time to distinguish the Russian from the Japanese signals that they unintentionally picked up. They were in fact, in the position of a man in a talkative crowd who yet contrives to confine his attention to only those voices that interest him. But this would soon cease to be the case in the presence of an overpowering noise, to which the great waves used in long distance work seem to correspond, and would, of course, be impossible if other waves were flying about, as they would be if the system ever came into general use, simultaneously and in all directions. Hence Mr. Marconi, Sir Oliver Lodge, and their Continental and American rivals have all turned their attention to some system of "syntony," or tuning, by which their receiving instruments can be prevented from responding to any impulses but those coming from their own senders; but all such attempts have hitherto failed. It is quite true that an electric circuit can be so arranged as to be in tune with another in the same way as a tuning fork tuned to certain note will respond when this note is struck on a neighbouring instrument; but the analogy, as is so often the case with experiments on the ether, is not so close as it looks. The tuning fork will respond to the required note and to none other; but the electric circuit, though responding most readily to the one with which it is, as electricians say, "in resonance," will yet respond, even if somewhat less well, to any other within a somewhat wide range. If a tuning fork emitted its peculiar note in response to every piano or every brass band that was displaying its noisy activity within hearing, one can imagine how untrustworthy it would be; and the same thing is true, within limits, of wireless telegraphy. Professor Fleming, who has for long been associated with the Marconi experiments, at one time thought that the difficulty had been surmounted, but we fancy he must have been disagreeably undeceived when a rival expert most unkindly contrived to introduce the contumelious word Rats! into the messages which he was receiving from Cornwall before a scientific audience in Piccadilly. That the means of overcoming it will eventually be discovered, or may even now be locked within the bosom of some scientific experimenter, we may all hope. But, so far as can be seen, it has not yet been brought forward.—F. L. in T. P.'s weekly.

The press boat "Samson" says the "Chefoo Daily News" is reported to have had a little tilt with the Japanese squadron on her last trip. The story goes that she was hailed with a blank shot, and politely but firmly informed that if she was caught within twenty miles of Port Arthur she would be put into Davy Jones' locker. No doubt Bennet Burleigh, with his well known geniality, stroked the ruffled feathers of his tormentors and assured them that he couldn't swim—a plea sufficient to insure his craft against harm.

The Korea Daily News.

Issued at 5 P. M. daily except Sundays.

Rate of Subscription:—
Per Year,............Yen 25.
Per Quarter,..........Yen 7.
Per Month,..........Yen 2.50.

Postage in Korea not charged extra.
Postage abroad charged extra.

Advertisements, 50 sen per day for 1 inch or less.
5 yen per month per inch.
50 yen per year per inch.

All communications to

E. T. BETHELL,
Editor and Publisher,
Pak-tong, Seoul.

EDUCATION AND REFORM.

That there is a lack of educational facilities in Korea goes without saying. There are the old schools where musty-fusty classics are half heartedly imparted to a lot of inattentive students, and there are some primary and middle schools where a perfunctory sort of educational system prevails. In addition there are the English, German, French and Japanese schools where knowledge is dispensed according to the nationality of the instructors. Furthermore there are the missionary schools where the curriculum includes various religious propaganda. But a purely Korean advanced school free from bias, religious or political, does not at present exist, while there is a great necessity for not only one but many schools of this kind.

By failing to provide them, Korea is only laying up trouble for herself. At present her students go to Japan to finish their education; what happens to them there we cannot say, but they return to Korea with that little knowledge which is a dangerous thing, and ideas which the words Radical, Socialistic or Nihilistic, only half describe.

An incident recently occurred in Shanghai which, in this connection, is worth recounting. It appears that an ex-Governor named Wang Chih-chun received an invitation to go to a certain house in the Shanghai settlement on November 14th to have a private conversation with a Mr. Wu Pao-chu. He did not avail himself of the invitation but was persuaded to go to a native restaurant on the following Saturday, the 19th. Arriving at the restaurant, his original host was not to be seen but he found himself in the company of a man bearing the unmistakeable ear-marks of a student newly returned from Japan. The ex-Governor, not liking his surroundings, left the premises and was entering his carriage when he was fired at, but fortunately not injured. All concerned in the plot have been arrested and it appears that at least some of them are students recently returned from Japan. Their grievance seems to be that the ex-Governor was a man of reactionary and pro-Russian ideas. Commenting upon the episode the "China Gazette" speaks of "the presence in the Settlement of large numbers of dangerous characters who have returned from Japan, thoroughly imbued with the most revolutionary ideas and filled with murderous plots to carry out their own project of assisting the Japanese by "removing" all those Chinese officials who have not been won over to see in Japan the real and only regenerator of China."

The comment of the "China Gazette" may be a little too severe, and the same danger probably does not threaten Korea, but facts are facts and the incident may serve as an object lesson.

Japan has at present none too much money to spend, and no time at all to devote, to barren enterprises and it is therefore safe to assume that in undertaking the rôle of "teacher" to large numbers of aliens, Chinese and Korean, she has some ulterior motive. It is as well to remember, in this connection, that Japanese students, to finish their education, invariably go to Europe or America.

We are far from suggesting that Japan ever intends that the foreign students turned out in her schools should become assassins, but the fact remains that the students return to their countries filled with revolutionary ideas.

Thus is mischief made; and in the present state of affairs, when a few sparks will set the whole of the Far East ablaze, the fewer Korean students who go to Japan and return with half disgested ideas, the better.

Korea has the remedy in her own hands. Let her organize a proper educational establishment, and keep her students at home for a while. It is no use tearing down a house until you know how to build a better one, yet this is the thing that all young reformers want to commence by doing.

THE JAPANESE PRESS AND THE WAR.

As the following extracts will show, the Japanese press still maintains an attitude of cheerful optimism. We do not share it. In spite of the recent astonishing assertion of the "Times" military correspondent that the attacking army has an advantage, it is evident that the commanders of the two armies at the Shaho think differently and each is waiting for the other to assume the offensive. This the Japanese will be compelled ultimately to do and the result of those operations is by no means the foregone conclusion that the "Jiji" pretends to believe it is.

The "Nichi Nichi" speaks of the "fatalistic belief," on the part of the Russians, in the ultimate relief of Port Arthur. The "Nichi Nichi" must remember that it has, in common with all other Japanese newspapers, been confidently predicting the fall of the stronghold ever since July, and we advise them to prepare for more disappointments.

As regards the Baltic fleet, we have no very high opinion of its chances, but this war has been full of surprises and there may be more in store. Japanese reports confirm the statement that the Port Arthur squadron is in good fighting trim while it is certain that Admiral Togo's squadron, powerful as it looks on paper, cannot have been through its many engagements without some loss in efficency.

The "Nichi Nichi" says that judged by the public utterances of the Tsar and the commanders of his armies, on the occasion of the formation of the second and third armies and of the departure of the Baltic fleet, Port Arthur still forms for Russia the life and *raison d'etre* of the campaign. This fatalistic belief in the ultimate rescue of Port Arthur can only multiply political and strategical blunders on the part of Russia; and viewed in this light the delay in the fall of the isolated enemy is not necessarily an unmixed evil to us; for it will make worse the confusion which is to overtake the Russian forces on land and sea, the moment his reduction is accomplished, as either will then have lost the main cause to fight for.

The "Jiji" ventures to predict another great battle, in a very short while, between the hostile armies now facing each other with the Shaho between them; because the opposing forces being, as they are, entrenched in open and exposed country, neither is in the position to winter through the months of inclement weather, so that it is as much a matter of necessity for our forces to drive the enemy before them and occupy Mukden and Tielling, as it is for the Russians to make every effort to recover Liaoyang before the cold sets in in earnest, while it is out of the question for them to retreat to Kharbin, for such alternative if adopted would entail on them consequences which they would rather not conceive. Hence the inevitability and imminence of a fierce encounter. The "Jiji" would welome such an encounter, for whatever may be the enemy's strength with all his newly arrived reinforcements, our armies have already received their fresh recruits, and the conflict can end only in one way, and that in our victory. As for the naval situation, let it be supposed that the Baltic fleet succeeds in reaching Far Eastern waters before the fall of Port Arthur. Where will it establish its base? To attempt to enter that harbour will be suicidal. It will probably seek shelter at Vladivostock and content itself at making thence occasional piratical excursions of short duration. But all this is based on supposition. As a matter of fact, it will be safe to say that the fleet will not arrive in these seas for two months hence, and in the meantime Port Arthur will be taken as surely as any human event can be foreseen. In that event it will be an easy task to seal up the fleet in Vladivostock, if not to annihilate its warships. The "Jiji" is as strongly certain of our naval supremacy in the Eastern seas as it is astonished at the complete lack of judgment on the enemy's part in sending out hither his only available naval force, only to be exterminated.

EARLY USE OF COAL IN CHINA.

Marco Polo, the Portuguese, was the first European since the days of Greek and Roman ascendancy, to explore the remote parts of Asia. This was in the latter part of the thirteenth century. A correspondent of the "Bulletin," in looking through Marco Polo's account of his travels, found the following reference to "stones which are burnt instead of wood." "It may be observed, also, that throughout the whole province of Cathay there is a kind of black stones cut from the mountains in veins, which burn like logs. They maintain the fire better than wood. If you put them on in the evening they will preserve it the whole night and will be found burning in the morning. Throughout the whole of Cathay this fuel is used. They have also wood indeed, but the stones are much less expensive. This early reference to coal is of especial value because it shows that the Chinese possessed a knowledge of its use 600 years ago, before coal was much used in Europe.

The German Minister has sent a despatch to the Foreign Office asking that the Emperor and Crown Prince be informed that he has received from the Kaiser a telegraphic message of sympathy on the death of the Crown Princess.

The Korea Daily News.

VOL. I, FRIDAY, DECEMBER 2, 1904. No. 115

HONGKONG & SHANGHAI BANKING CORPORATION.

Paid-up Capital..... ....$10,000,000
Reserve Fund:—Sterling Reserve... 10,000,000
Silver Reserve..... 7,000,000

27,000,000
Reserve Liability of Proprietors... 10,000,000

HEAD OFFICE, HONGKONG.

London Bankers, London and County Banking Company Limited
Branches and Agencies,
London.

Amoy, Hankow, Penang,
Bangkok, Hiogo, Rangoon,
Batavia, Iloilo, Saigon,
Bombay, Lyons, San Francisco,
Calcutta, Manila, Singapore,
Colombo, Nagasaki, Sourabaya,
Foochow, New York, Tientsin,
Hamburg, Peking, Yokohama,

Credits granted on approved Securities, and every description of Banking and Exchange business transacted.

Drafts granted on London and the chief Commercial places in Europe, India, Australia, America, China and Japan.

HOLME RINGER & Co., AGENTS,
CHEMULPO.

ON CHEONG & CO.,
SEOUL.
GENERAL STORE KEEPERS.
Imported provisions, Cooking Utensils Crockery, etc.
FRESH BREAD DAILY.

MITSU BISHI DOCKYARD & ENGINE WORKS,
NAGASAKI.

CODE WORD, "DOCK."

A 1, A. B. C., and Engineering Codes used.

DOCK No. 1 (at Tategami).

Extreme Length..............523 feet
Length on blocks .... 513 ,,
Width of Entrance on Top......89 ,,
,, ,, Bottom....77 ,,
Water on Blocks at Spring Tide 26½ ,,

DOCK No. 2 (Mukaijima).

Extreme Length..............371 feet
Length on Blocks..............360 ,,
Width of Entrance on Top......66 ,,
,, ,, Bottom 53 ,,
Water on Blocks at Spring Tide 22 ,,

PATENT SLIP (at Kosuge).
Can take vessels up to 1,000 tons gross.

THE WORKS are well equipped with the LATEST IMPROVEMENTS, and can execute any kind of work in SHIPBUILDING and MARINE ENGINEERING, as well as in REPAIRING of SHIPS.

The COMPANY'S new powerful steamer OURA-MARU (712 tons, 700 I.H.P.), specially built for SALVAGE PURPOSES, and equipped with necessary gear, is always READY at SHORT NOTICE.

CHARTERED BANK OF INDIA AUSTRALIA & CHINA.

INCORPORATED BY ROYAL CHARTER 1853

HEAD OFFICES:—LONDON.

Paid-up Capital £800,000
Reserve Liability of Shareholders............................. 800,000
Reserve Fund 800,000

Drafts granted upon all the principal places in the world and every description of Exchange and banking business transacted.

E. MEYER & Co., Agents,
Chemulpo.

E. MEYER & CO.
Chemulpo.

SOLE AGENTS IN KOREA FOR:
A. T. Morse, Sons & Co's "Fresco" Distemper

In all colours ready for use on walls, Ceilings etc.
and
AVENARIUS CARBOLINEUM

A wood-preserving and antiseptic oil preparation

Against decay, dry-rot, fungus and wood-destroying insects.

A large supply always in Stock.
Prices upon application.

E. MEYER & Co.,
Chemulpo.

THE METHODIST PUBLISHING HOUSE,
Little West Gate, Seoul.

JOB PRINTING, TYPEWRITER PAPER
CARBON PAPER, VISITING CARDS
STATIONERY, BOOK BINDING
BOOK PUBLISHERS
AMERICAN SCHOOL BOOKS
SPENCERIAN COPY BOOKS
PEN CARBON LETTER AND BILL BOOKS

S. A. BECK, Manager.

HOKURKU DOBOKU KAISHA.
Branch office in Chong Dong, Seoul.
Japanese telephone No. 165

CONTRACT DEPARTMENT.
We can contract to build any building or construction.

MERCHANDISE DEPARTMENT.
We can provide any building material. We have just contracted to build the new Belgian Legation.

DAI-ICHI GINKO.
LIMITED.
(Formerly the First National Bank)

ESTABLISHED 1873

INCORPORATED UNDER PRESENT LAW 1896

Capital - - - - - - - - - Yen 5,000,000
Reserve Fund - . - - - 1,500,000

HEAD OFFICE:—TOKIO.

President: Baron SHIBUSAWA.

BRANCHES AND CORRESPONDENTS
In the Principal Cities and Towns of Japan.
Interest Allowed on
Fixed deposits 1 year - - - 6½ per cent
" " 6 months - - - 6 per cent

Special current accounts 1½ sen daily per Y 100
General " " 1 " " " 100

M. TANAKA,
Manager, Chemulpo.

SINGER SEWING MACHINES
씽거ᄌᆞ봉침

SOLE AGENTS FOR KOREA
전매쇼

HOLME RINGER & CO.
Chemulpo.
졔물포 함릉거양힝

KAMEYA & CO.
GENERAL STOREKEEPERS
Chinkokai - - Seoul
(Established 1895, Tokyo)

Confectionery, Hams, Canned Goods, Cutlery, Hirano & Tansan Water, Provisions, Gents, Furnishing goods, Toilet Articles, Travelling Bags, Tobacco, Cigars & Cigarettes Kitchen Utensils. Coffee, Biscuits.

Fresh Goods always kept in Stock.
Prices Moderate
☞ *Please come and inspect our goods*

NIPPON YUSEN KAISHA.
JAPANESE MAIL STEAMSHIP CO.
UNDER MAIL CONTRACT WITH THE IMPERIAL JAPANESE GOVERNMENT.

European Line
Regular Fortnightly Service between Yokohama Kobe, Moji, Shanghai, Hongkong, Singapore, Penang Colombo, Port Said, Marseilles, London and Antwerp

American Line
Regular Fortnightly Service between Hongkong and Seattle, calling at Shanghai, Moji, Kobe, Yokohama and Victoria, B. C.

Australian Line
Regular weekly Service betwen Japan Ports and Australia, calling at Hongkong and Manila.
(Above Three Lines Suspended until further notice).

Shanghai Line
Weekly Service between Shanghai and Japan Ports

Korea Line
Service Kobe, Moji, Nagasaki, Fusan Chemupo Chef foo, Taiku.
S. S. Bahelsberg, 2181 tons.
Service Kobe, Moji, Fusan, Chemulpo, Chinnampo
S. S. ARGO, S. S. Ohio.

BORDEN'S CONDENSED MILK CO.
New York, U. S. A.

ALWAYS IN STOCK
Eagle Brand Condensed Milk.
Gold Seal Condensed Milk.
Peerless (Family) Evaporated Cream.
Borden's Malted Milk.

E. MEYER & CO.
Chemulpo, Korea,
Sole Agents

ROYAL INSURANCE COMPANY,
Funds exceed £10,000,000
FIRE
AT CURRENT RATES.
LIFE
REDUCED PREMIUM.
HOLME RINGER & Co.,
Agents, Chemulpo.

HOTEL DU PALAIS
SEOUL.

The only first class Hotel in Seoul. Situated in the centre of the city opposite the palace.

Cuisine under the supervision of an experienced French Chef.

Well ventilated and furnished throughout.

TARIFF UPON APPLICATION

L. MARTIN
Proprietor and Manager.

大韓每日申報

대한ᄆᆡ일신보

(뎨일ᄇᆡᆨ십륙호)　　(월요일)　　일쳔구ᄇᆡᆨ사년십이월삼일

본샤고ᄇᆡᆨ

이신보는영어와한어로셔지미
금출판ᄒᆞᆷ

신문가

한쟝　엽뎐오푼
일삭됴　엽두량닷돈
우표가ᄆᆡ삭닷돈
다ᄆᆡᆺ돈으로밧숨

광고료는
귀한의쟝단과ᄌᆞ항의다쇼로즁
감ᄒᆞ되ᄒᆞᆫ번가로밧을터이오며오
리지아니ᄒᆞ야대한사람마다다이신
문을보실터이니광고내시기를
원ᄒᆞ시는이들은우리신문사에
와셔면약ᄒᆞ심을희망ᄒᆞᆷ

○발ᄒᆡᆼ소　박동대한ᄆᆡ일신보
사법어학교압헤젼영국인셜필
립자리오

사쟝 영국인 (ᄇᆡ셜)

평양　ᄃᆡ리졈

○평양효동사는권미보씨로우
리신문과ᄃᆡ리인을뎡ᄒᆞ엿
ᄉᆞ오니평양에계신구람코져ᄒᆞ
시는　쳠군ᄌᆞ는ᄃᆡ리졈에왕
림ᄒᆞ와면의ᄒᆞ시옵

샤고

○우리대한ᄆᆡ일신보의목뎍은
대한의안녕질서에관한모든데
목에대ᄒᆞ야는공평한변론을주
쟝홈이라우리통신원의탐보는
신문보시는쳠군ᄌᆞ의게ᄒᆞᆼ샹보
도ᄒᆞ리며편지들긔셔ᄒᆞ여주시
는이는셩명과번디를젹어붓치
시기를희망ᄒᆞ오나이거슨신문
샹에긔ᄌᆡᄒᆞ란거시아니오다
만그히신용ᄒᆞ는증거를삼고자
홈이라긔ᄌᆞᄒᆞ는아모긔셔던지긔
ᄌᆡ홈을퇴각ᄒᆞ는권리를가젓소
나퇴각ᄒᆞ는리유를말ᄒᆞᆯ터이오
며공즁평화를문란케ᄒᆞ는듯ᄒᆞᆫ
긔셔는의례히밧지안켓습니이
다

●본사셜시이ᄅᆡ로신문을ᄆᆡ양
우례로분젼ᄒᆞ와뎨젼부의잉의
로젼ᄒᆞ든스로미곳에는ᄒᆞ늣게
젼ᄒᆞ기도ᄒᆞ며혹멋칠거슬ᄒᆞᆫ텹
에젼ᄒᆞ기도ᄒᆞ며혹아니젼ᄒᆞ는
곳도잇다ᄒᆞ와우리신문을ᄉᆞ랑
ᄒᆞ야구람ᄒᆞ시는　쳠군ᄌᆞ의게
ᄃᆡᄒᆞ야미우미안ᄒᆞ옵기로지금
은분젼인을두고ᄆᆡ일일죽이젼
ᄒᆞ며아니젼ᄒᆞ거나늣게거나ᄒᆞᆫ
폐가업도록ᄒᆞ랴ᄒᆞ오니ᄒᆞᆨ아니
젼ᄒᆞ거나혹늣게젼ᄒᆞ거나ᄒᆞᆫ일
이잇스면본사로통긔ᄒᆞ여주심
을희망ᄒᆞ옵

관보

뎨이쳔구ᄇᆡᆨ구십구호　광
무팔년십이월이일

셔임급사령

○승셔판임삼등　청쥬우톄사
쥬사　신ᄐᆡ영　십월이십이일
○승셔판임판사등　슈원우톄
사쥬사　임우순　십일월삼일
○승셔판임판사등．전쥬우톄
쥬사　윤순의　○금이금봉
전쥬우톄사쥬사　윤순의
이상십일월십팔일
○승셔판임판삼등　한셩우톄
쥬사　리슈면　십이월이십이
일
○명판제리경소의정관　의정
부찬졍　박제순　학부대신
리재극
○의원면본관　쟝례원상례
서상훈　봉상사쥬사　홍순병
함경남북분봉상사쥬사　셔봉
슈　챵합평남도분봉상사쥬사　김
두괴　례식원참리관　신ᄒᆡ영
홍쥬군공립소학교교원　박제
현
○임쟝례원상례셔주임관륙등
시강원시독관　박제황　○임
봉상사쥬사셔판임관칠등　돈
령원쥬사　홍진표　○임돈령
원쥬사셔판임관칠등　티봉ᄉᆞ
쥬ᄉᆞ　민회식○임티봉ᄉᆞ쥬ᄉᆞ
셔판임관륙등　류풍　홍승병
○임시강원시독관셔판임관칠
등　류풍　리원세　○함경남
도분봉상사쥬ᄉᆞ셔판임관팔등
한도현　쥬　규　○죵정사품
릉정대부비서원승　고학성
리완용　○죵종삼품릉정대부
쟝례원좌쟝례　고학성　리명
환

이상죵이픔가선대부전한셩
부관윤리용세의조고증조고
의박면추　증

○임례식원참리관셔주임관삼
등ᄂᆡ쟝원공업과쟝　현ᄇᆡᆨ운
○임ᄂᆡ쟝원공업과쟝셔주임관
륙등　탁지부주사부관　최경형
○임릉천감리셔주사셔판임관
륙등　구흥　고은상　○임평
무쳥죵숙셔판임관륙등　박용
순　○승셔판임관오등　외국
어학교부교관　셔병형　○임
홍주군공립소학교교원셔판임
관오등　남양군공립소학교교
원　리필구　○임남양군공립
소학교교원셔판임관오등　젼
교원　박제현　이상십일월삼
십일

궁ᄂᆡ부령사

○총호사신리근명근주　친
젼샹량문제술관과셔사관셜에
차별단을세드림쟉으로근샹
주ᄒᆞ와　광무팔년십일월이십
구일에봉　지의주ᄒᆞ니
○원소도감별단
○친젼샹량문제술관　ᄒᆞ문관
학ᄉᆞ　셔졍순
예차　시종원경　윤덕영
셔ᄉᆞ관　궁ᄂᆡ부특진관　리
완용
예차　궁ᄂᆡ부특진관　조
종필
○죠셔ᄒᆞ야골ᄋᆞ샤ᄃᆡ평토뎐방원
ᄉᆞ신승휘를명ᄒᆞ야샤ᄀᆡ의원도졔
죠를겸잉케ᄒᆞ시다
○중추원의관김중환ᄉᆞ직소
비지셩소구실경은ᄉᆞ양치말고
힝공ᄒᆞ라ᄒᆞ셧더라

뎐보

경셩동사관챡뎐

○련슌젼황　련슌봉위군은십
일월삼십일에바브미이빅삼고
디를티ᄒᆞ야포격ᄒᆞ기시ᄒᆞᆫ다가
ᄒᆞ엿스나저의저항홈이완강ᄒᆞ
야그곳을아직지못ᄒᆞᆫ지라ᄒᆞ오
오시량에동디셔남부에향ᄒᆞᆫ바
부터는돌격을시ᄒᆡᆼᄒᆞ야산악티
기로는련야삼미돌에어ᄋᆡ이되
고ᄒᆞ오청시에중젼티로며보리
산악티기를향ᄒᆞ야돌입ᄒᆞ다가
이것을졈령ᄒᆞ엿고그동북부에
향ᄒᆞᆫ부티도ᄯᅩᄒᆞᆫ돌격을실시ᄒᆞ
야하오팔시에젼혀이빅삼고디
를젼부가우리의졈령ᄒᆞᆫ바ㅣ되지
라이고디의동편에는젹의시체
가ᄊᆞ여그수를죠나치못ᄒᆞ겟더
라

○로병형위　동경외무성에온
뎐보에말ᄒᆞ되로국봉텬함티히
군이크레리에셔착중에오란홈
을지어셔거긔거민들을만이샬
히ᄒᆞ엿다는말을히셜이오그히

군들이저의동료의계교샹ᄒᆞ엿더
라

등디발　십일월이십이일

○로함령뎐　로국군함리온파
쓰다른비들이십일월십팔일에
스코만에셔츌발ᄒᆞ야슈리ᄒᆞ라
ᄒᆞ는티파레드리쉬블항에셔는
못ᄒᆞᆯ줄노단국이거절ᄒᆞ엿더라

등디발　동월이십ᄉᆞ일

○로함항위　크리레잇는쿠티
롱신원이확실이보ᄒᆞ되로국블
틱함티의히군의힝위가블젼ᄒᆞ
야항샹술에취ᄒᆞ고ᄉᆞ관의명령
은복죵치아니ᄒᆞ며히군들이만
이뒤로써리저셔도망ᄒᆞ고저의
쎄리다도아셔ᄒᆞ나는죽고버리
이샹ᄒᆞ엿다더라

ᄇᆡᆨ림발　동일

○로함죠직　로국신문노보브
레ᄆᆡ야의말ᄒᆞᆫ바를거ᄒᆞᆫ즉로국이
극동에파숑ᄒᆞᆯ데삼함ᄃᆡ를죠직
ᄒᆞ엿더라

등디발　동월이십오일

○로함힝지　로국군함들이지
금포트세이드에셔셔로와미올
문을셥는다더라

론돈발　동월이십삼일

○로국외채　로국이래년일월
에미국에셔사쳔사ᄇᆡᆨ만방의국
채를일년오푼변리오ᄇᆡᆨ에구십
륙으로모집ᄒᆞᆫ다는ᄃᆡ그즁에일
쳔오ᄇᆡᆨ만방은로국이군함
갑으로미국에셔쓸터이오쏘로
국이미국을위ᄒᆞ야ᄇᆡᆨ뎌질로에
티ᄒᆞ야반ᄃᆡᄒᆞ던것을그만둔다
더라

잡보

승후ᄉᆞ윤동　황귀비뎐하승
후ᄒᆞᆯᄉᆞ진에ᄃᆡᄒᆞ야리근틱씨가
열심으로ᄒᆞ는중이라더라
○망명자특사셜　지난이십팔
일에일본ᄉᆞ가좌우틍물이지고
비밀히샹　쥬ᄒᆞ엿는ᄃᆡ근일
논쟝계에망명자을특사ᄉᆞ용ᄒᆞᆫ다
는젼셜이파다ᄒᆞ더라
○흥화원ᄂᆡ하　금번여사군이
괴후ᄒᆞᆫ평　벼에블쥬ᄒᆞᆷ으로블
별이　　하례ᄒᆞ샤특히원을충
호샤의게느리샤로양ᄒᆞ야블급
ᄒᆞ라ᄒᆞ옵셧더라
○경사발제　경무사는여사ᄃᆡ
쟝을경임ᄒᆞ엿는ᄃᆡ쟈일하오사

UNION INSURANCE SOCIETY OF CANTON.

Head office Hongkong.
Marine risks underwritten at current rates.
Agents in Chemulpo,
E. MEYER & Co.

COMPAGNIE DES MESSAGERIES MARITIMES.

Fortnightly Direct Service.

For Marseilles
via Ports.
Sailing from Yokohama
Calling at Kobe,
Shanghai, Hongkong, Saigon, Singapore,
Colombo, Djibouti, Suez, Port Said
and Marseilles.

For particulars apply to
HOLME RINGER & Co.,
Chemulpo.

HAYASHIDA & CO.,

16 MYENG DONG, CHIN KO KAI, SEOUL.
BRANCH OFFICE AT CHEMULPO.

Money changers, Coal and Wood Merchants, Express Agents.

We are agents for the Pyeng-yang Coal Company and the Karazu Coal Company of Japan. We have the best quality of both anthracite and bituminous coal, and prompt execution of orders is our speciality. Firewood of all kinds kept in stock. Full weight guaranteed. Money of all denominations exchanged at current rates. Parcels received for all parts.

CHINA MUTUAL LIFE INS. CO.

Most favourable terms to policy holders.

Benefit system unsurpassed.

HOLME RINGER & Co.
Agents, Chemulpo.

C. P. R.

CANADIAN PACIFIC RAILWAY COMPANY'S ROYAL MAIL STEAMSHIP LINE.

THE FAST ROUTE BETWEEN CHINA, JAPAN, AND EUROPE VIA CANADA AND THE UNITED STATES.

Ro[illegible] Hongkong via Shanghai, Nagasaki (Inland Sea of Japan) Kobe, Yokohama Victoria and Vancouver.

Twin Screw Empress Steamship—6,000 Tons—Speed 19 knots.

[illegible] SED SAILING FROM YOKOHAMA.
R. M. S. Empress of India.
R. M. S. Empress of Japan.
R. M. S. Empress of China.
M. S. Athenian.
R. M. S. Tartar.

Special reduction (first class only) granted to members of the Military, Naval, Diplomatic and Civil services and to Missionaries.
Passenges have choice of ten routes across the Continent of America and have privilege of travelling by any Atlantic Steamship Line.
Round the World passage tickets in connection with the P. and O. S. N., North German Lloyd and Messageries Co.'s £25.
All rates payable at current rate of exchange.
For further information, Tickets, Guide Books, etc., apply to

HOLME, RINGER & Co., AGENTS,
Chemulpo.

Grand Hotel,

(Formerly the Station Hotel)

Near the Railway Terminu ,
West Gate Seoul.

The Best Hotel in Korea
Handsome new Building.
Fine Airy Rooms
Excellent Cuisine.
Terms Moderate.
Special terms to Missionaries
and to permanent boarders.

Electric cars within 2 minutes' walk.

W. H. EMBERLEY,
Proprietor

EVERY FACILITY.

In connection with Life Assurance Business is afforded by

The Standard Life Assurance Co.,

One of the largest and wealthiest of the Provident Institutions of the United Kingdom Forms of Application and all information will be promptly afforded on application.

10 CENTS A DAY.

Not a very large expenditure is it? But it is sufficient to secure for a man of 30 a policy with the STANDARD LIFE OFFICE for

$1323.

For all particulars of rates, etc., apply to

Holme, Ringer & Co.,
Agents, Chemulpo.

THE NEW YORK LIFE INSURANCE COMPANY.

Have you ever been declined by any Company?

Are you engaged in a specially hazardous occupation?

Have you heard of the New York Life Insurance Company's New Classifications for this class of Risks?

If not, send your date of birth, occupation and particulars of rejection, if any to

E. MEYER & Co.,
Agents, Chemulpo.

MITSUI BUSSAN KAISHA.
(MITSUI & Co.)

MITSUI GINKO.
(MITSUI BANK.)

The Bank is owned by the members of the Mitsui Family, who, as partners, assume an unlimited responsibility for all liabilities of the Bank:—

Capital.................... .....Yen 5,000,000
Reserve Fund.................... " 5,600,000

HEAD OFFICE, TOKYO.
LONDON OFFICE, 34 LIME ST., E. C.

BRANCHES AND AGENCIES:—
New York, San Francisco, Hamburg, Bombay, Singapore, Manila, Hongkong, Amoy, Chefoo, Tientsin.
Kobe, Hakodate, Yokohama, Kure, Yokosuka, Moji, Shimonoseki, Miike, Wakamatsu, Nagasaki, Kuchinotsu, Karatsu, Sasebo, Misume, Taipeh, &c.

Telegraphic Address for all the Offices:
"MITSUI."
A. B. C. AND A. 1 CODES USED.

Contractors of Coal
To the Imperial Japanese Navy. Arsenals and Railway Bureau, Principal Railway Companies and Industrial Work, Home and Foreign Mail and Freight Steamers.
Sole Proprietors
Of the famous Miike, Tagawa and Yamano Coal Mines.
Sole Agents
For the sale of Fukumo, Hokoku, Ichimura, Kanoda, Mannoura, Onoura, Ostuji, Sonoda. Tsubaruro, Yoshinotani, Yoshio, Yurokibura and other coals.

YANGTSE INSURANCE ASSOCIATION, LTD.

The undersigned, having been appointed agents for the above company, are prepared to issue policies and pay losses on marine risks at regular rates.

E. MEYER & Co.,
Agents, Chemulpo.

AMERICAN KOREAN ELECTRIC CO.

Light and Power.

Main Office: Electric Building, Chong No.

RAILWAY DEPARTMENT.

OPERATING CARS BETWEEN EAST AND WEST GATE, EVERY TEN MINUTES:—

First Car leaves East Gate at 7:00 A. M. First Car le[illegible] Station at 7:25 A. M
Last Car " East Gate at 9:40 P. M. Last " " R. R. Station at 10:05 P. M

OPERATING CARS BETWEEN EAST GATE AND IMPERIAL TOMB TERMINUS, EVERY TWENTY MINUTES:—

CONNECTING WITH EVERY ALTERNATE CAR ARRIVING AT EAST GATE FROM CHONG NO.

First Car leaves East Gate for Tomb at 7:10 A. M.
" " " Tomb for East Gate at 7:35 A. M.
Last " " East Gate for Tomb at 7:50 P. M.
" " " Tomb for East Gate at 8:10 P. M.

OPERATING CARS BETWEEN CHONG NO AND YUNG SAN RIVER EVERY TWELVE MINUTES:—

First Car leaves Chong No for South Gate at 7:12 A. M.
" " " Chong No for Yung San at 7:36 A. M.
" " " South Gate for Chong No at 7:20 A. M.
" " " Yung San for Chong No at 8:09 A. M.
Last " " South Gate for Chong No 10:00 P. M.
" " " Yung San for Chong No at 9:33 P. M.

SPECIAL PRIVATE CARS FURNISHED TO SUIT CONVENIENCE OF PATRONS. PRICES ON APPLICATION AT HEAD OFFICE.

LIGHTING DEPARTMENT.

Where less than 250 candle power of light is used, the rate per month will be
Per 16 candle power incandescent lamp,—All night.—Yen 2.50.
32 candle power incandescent lamp:—All night:—Yen 4.00.
50 candle power incandescent lamp:—All night:—Yen 6.00.
150 ,, ,, ,, ,, ,, ,, ,, 10.00.
1200 ,, ,, enclosed are ,, ,, ,, ,, 20.00.

Where more than 250 candle power of light is used, a Meter will be installed, freqvedted:—Rent of Meter Yen 2.00 per month. Rate of charges by meter reading:—Two Sen per Ampere per hour. (Approximately this is equal to about One Sen per 16 C. P. lamp per hour) Minimum monthly charge where meter is installed, Yen 20.00 per month, which includes rental of meter.

Estimates for installing lights furnished on application.
An assortment of chandeliers always on hand.

K. Murakami.

Photograph Studio
Chinkokai, Seoul.

Printing, Developing and Enlargement, of Photographs always Undertaken.

Korean Views and Pictures Illustrating Native Customs always on Sale,

---

THE OSAKA SHOSEN KAISHA.

Boats frequently on the berth for Chinnampo.

REGULAR SAILINGS BETWEEN JAPAN AND KOREAN PORTS.

FUSAN AND KOBE VIA SHIMONOSEKI.

OSAKA VIA MOKPO, FUSAN, SHIMONOSEKI AND KOBE.

MOJI DIRECT.

OSAKA VIA KUNSAN, MASANPO, FUSAN, SHIMONOSEKI AND KOBE.

CHEMULPO KUNSAN LINE,
Every three days.

CHEMULPO CHINNAMPO LINE.
Every three days.

For Freight and passage and further particulars apply to

THE OSAKA SHOSEN KAISHA,
Chemulpo.

RONDON, PLAISANT & CO.

General Storekeepers and Merchants, Ships Contractors, Tobacconists, Commission and Forwarding Agents, Coal Merchants

IMPORTERS AND EXPORTERS

Seoul & Chemulpo.

W. D. WENTWORTH.

LANDING
AND
SHIPPING AGENT
AND
CUSTOMS BORDER.

12 OURA, NAGASAKI.

STEWARD & CO.

Chemulpo.

Shipchandlers and Storekeepers, Naval and Mercantile Contrrctors, Landing and Shipping Agencs.

STEWARD'S HOTEL

Chemulpo.

Best accommodation in this port for traveler s. Clean and well-aired rooms, good cuisin and prompt attendence, moderate tariff.

시반에뢰젼병문을지내ᄂᆞᆫ데ᄇᆡᆨ제쇼리가엄숙ᄒᆞ며도로힝인이듯고말ᄒᆞ기를다른대관힝차에ᄂᆞᆫ벽제셩이업더니싱살지권울가진광반인죽벽제ᄒᆞᆫ다ᄒᆞ더라

○골화위사 칙원항철도에범입된산소를파옴기ᄂᆞᆫ데무덤을과고빅골을모흐랴ᄒᆞᆫ즉빅골은업고비암다숫만잇다가다르ᄂᆞᆫ지리그뫼조손이그것을보고곤ᄋᆞᆫ디산리가업다ᄒᆞ고웃고갓다더라

○독츌빅원 지ᄂᆞᆫ화요일만국청연회에방청ᄒᆞᆫ평양친구졍모씨가제즁원병상연보젼으로일빅원을독츌ᄒᆞ엿다더라

○파송사핵 공쥬병요ᄉᆞ건으로그사핵ᄒᆞ기위ᄒᆞ야법부에셔한셩지관소금ᄉᆞ홍죵한씨를파송ᄒᆞ고히쥬군쳥인산옥ᄉᆞ에ᄂᆞᆫ평리원판ᄉᆞ태명시씨를파송ᄒᆞᆫ다더라

○의장조고 즁츄원의장민영소ᄂᆞᆫ그자친상을당ᄒᆞ야의장을체임ᄒᆞ고젼관셔죠희일씨도일에졸셔ᄒᆞ엿더라

○잠상확장 농상공부에셔각도에잠상을확장ᄒᆞᆫ다ᄒᆞ야죵상위원삼십구인을차츌ᄒᆞ엿ᄂᆞᆫ디츙쳥남북도와황히도에만위션쎵나무십오만칠쳔쥬를하송ᄒᆞ고히관찰부로훈뎡ᄒᆞ엿더라

○각부관제등송 관제리졍소에셔각관쳥에통쳡ᄒᆞ기를각부부의현힝ᄒᆞᄂᆞᆫ관제와밋분과규졍과일체규측을즉일니로ᄡᅥ지말고벗겨보냄을ᄇᆞ란다ᄒᆞ엿더라

○ᄂᆡ부면훈 ᄂᆡ부에십삼도로면훈ᄒᆞ기를쳔임ᄒᆞᄂᆞᆫ규측중에시찰ᄉᆞ를본도인ᄡᅥ지말나ᄒᆞᆷ은거쳔ᄒᆞᄂᆞᆫ즁에본도인도참입ᄒᆞ라ᄂᆞᆫ뜻이오본도인만젼히거쳔ᄒᆞ라ᄂᆞᆫ뜻이아니라ᄒᆞ엿더라

○미인연회 지작야에셔쇼문안에사ᄂᆞᆫ미국인보시옥씨집에셔법덕량풍ᄉᆞ와미국신샹들이연회ᄒᆞ엿더라

○헌병파송 헌병ᄉᆞ령부와밋참모부에셔함경북도디방대댱을압샹ᄒᆞᆯ초로헌병을파송ᄒᆞ엿다더라

○ᄂᆡ부면훈젼북 ᄂᆡ부에셔젼라북도순찰의게면훈ᄒᆞ기를회민을방셕ᄒᆞ라신ᄉᆞ로죠칙이잇섯고진보회민에안순집과김쥬ᄉᆞᄂᆞᆫ엇지ᄒᆞ야착슈되엿스며만일완강히나라법을좃지아님이아니어던곳방송ᄒᆞ고회던ᄒᆞ라ᄒᆞ엿더라

○죠쳥치도비 지발ᄂᆡ부에셔탁지부에죠회ᄒᆞ기를 소침젼아리로외홍젼문안ᄉᆞ지젼답을흙으로메우고평란ᄒᆞ게치도ᄒᆞᄂᆞᆫ역ᄉᆞ가호번ᄒᆞᆫ고로ᄒᆞ야잔역ᄉᆞ시급ᄒᆞ와위원을파송ᄒᆞ야쳐심ᄒᆞᆫ후에희역비예산셔를ᄡᅥ여보ᄂᆡ니이만칠쳔오빅구십일원을금년도치도비로더지츌ᄒᆞᆷ을ᄇᆞ란다ᄒᆞ엿고또죠회ᄒᆞ기를원소에도로와교량슈츅ᄒᆞᄂᆞᆫ역ᄉᆞ가만분셔급ᄒᆞ와위원을파송ᄒᆞ야잔심ᄒᆞᆫ즉이십리신작로가다ᄉᆞ답인ᄃᆡ도모지메여슈츅ᄒᆞᆯ벽오놉흔언덕을평탄케ᄒᆞ기와교량시로건츅ᄒᆞᆯ역ᄉᆞ가심히호ᄃᆡᄒᆞ니히역비삼만일쳔일빅십칠원을지발ᄒᆞ야불일시역케ᄒᆞ라ᄒᆞ엿더라

○휴쟝하ᄉᆞ 일본에시찰로갓던리지국민형식엄쥬의리샹하황신티현빅운제씨가지작일하오구시에입셩ᄒᆞ엿ᄂᆞᆫ대리지극에게ᄂᆞᆫ욱일대슈쟝을하ᄉᆞᄒᆞ시고그다른관원들은셔보쟝을하ᄉᆞᄒᆞ옵셧더라

○대관잡기 졍부에셔법부와경위원과경무쳥에죠회ᄒᆞ기를거월삼십일에본참졍이상쥬ᄒᆞ기를잡괴ᄒᆞ며괴인편지ᄒᆞᄂᆞᆫ거슨나라의큰금법이라비록려염의필부라도진실노판을버리고돈내기를ᄒᆞᆷ이잇스면반드시뵈이ᄂᆞᆫ디로단단히금ᄒᆞ야즁ᄒᆞᆫ쟈ᄂᆞᆫ도적을드ᄉᆞ리ᄂᆞᆫ률노ᄡᅥ시힝ᄒᆞᄂᆞ니대기ᄡᅥᄒᆞᆫ바풍속을돈독히ᄒᆞ고빅셩의지산을보호홈이라근리에드른즉칙임과등관들이또ᄒᆞᆫ만히무리로모혀잡기ᄒᆞ야ᄒᆞᆫ케에승부가루만금이동ᄒᆞ며혹은우벽처로청ᄒᆞ야몰내와굴을짓고혹은외치를모집ᄒᆞ기를시약심상ᄒᆞ야속여ᄡᅥ앗ᄂᆞᆫ힝습이번동록림객이나달지아니ᄒᆞ야부요ᄒᆞᆫ든집이일죠에젹슈가되여도붓그려옴도업고뉘웃침도업서침익ᄒᆞᆷ이날노심ᄒᆞ야랄연ᄒᆞ고혼연ᄒᆞᆷ이귀신의게홀닌것ᄀᆞᆺ치되여죠뎡체면을손상ᄒᆞ야외인의슈모를씻치고지산을탕픽ᄒᆞ야인심을피란케ᄒᆞ니히탄ᄒᆞᆫ기가극진ᄒᆞᆷ은이무가론이어니와법맛ᄒᆞᆫ관원은그위엄을두려워ᄒᆞ야감히누구던지엇지ᄒᆞ지못ᄒᆞ니나라히장ᄎᆞᆺ엇지ᄡᅥ법을벼플며빅셩은엇지ᄡᅥ금ᄒᆞᄂᆞᆫ바가잇ᄂᆞᆫ거슬알니오급히법부와경위원과경무쳥에훈령ᄒᆞ와법을벼플어괴찰ᄒᆞ야칙임관이하를현로되ᄂᆞᆫ디로주츰ᄒᆞ고구라ᄒᆞ야죵률로ᄡᅥ벼플고붓잡은바장젼은다과를물론ᄒᆞ고일일히포착ᄒᆞᆫ관리의게주어ᄡᅥ격동ᄒᆞ야권면케ᄒᆞ옴이엇더ᄒᆞ올넌지ᄒᆞ고삼가 샹주ᄒᆞ와봉 지의주라ᄒᆞ옵셧시니흠쥰ᄒᆞ야시힝ᄒᆞ라ᄒᆞ엿더라

론셜

일본셔붕우의게ᄒᆞᄂᆞᆫ일

동양에셔발간ᄒᆞᄂᆞᆫ각쳐신문에ᄂᆞᆫ모도일본의게만듯기죳토록찬양ᄒᆞ야부일ᄒᆞᄂᆞᆫ태도가잇스되우리신문에ᄂᆞᆫ왕왕히일본졍책의잘못ᄒᆞᄂᆞᆫ바로ᄡᅥ반ᄃᆡᄒᆞᆫ즉우리도역시스스로범파ᄒᆞᆷ을모르ᄂᆞᆫ바아니로되이ᄂᆞᆫ엇지ᄒᆞᆯ수업서그리ᄒᆞᆷ인거시근일에일본셔한국에ᄃᆡᄒᆞ야ᄒᆞᄂᆞᆫ일이모도잔학무도ᄒᆞ며여취여광ᄒᆞᆫ즉려순을합낙ᄒᆞᆫ다ᄂᆞᆫ것도밋울수가업스며한국을진보가되게ᄒᆞᆫ다ᄂᆞᆫ것도또ᄒᆞᆫ알수업ᄂᆞᆫ지라그러ᄒᆞ나만일우리의싱각에잇ᄂᆞᆫ디로이러ᄒᆞᆫ여러가지를모도로츌ᄒᆞ야신문상에게지ᄒᆞᆯ것갓트면일본의게ᄂᆞᆫ독죄만ᄒᆞᆯᄲᅮᆫ아니라큰죄인이될러이여그러ᄒᆞ되우리의게당ᄒᆞ여셔ᄂᆞᆫ조곰도수치ᄒᆞᆯ거시업고또ᄒᆞᆫ이후에라도불법ᄒᆞᄂᆞᆫ일만잇게되면련쇽ᄒᆞ야게지ᄒᆞᆯ터인지라

이ᄂᆞᆫ엇지ᄒᆞᆫ닭이뇨ᄒᆞᆯ진ᄃᆡ비컨ᄃᆡ한의원이잇셔약방문을아모커나속히녀여당장에만낫도록만달고돈만만히밧은후그병인이다시와셔문병ᄒᆞ게만ᄒᆞ니버다의셔에ᄒᆞᆫ슉ᄒᆞᆫ의원이방문은지원ᄒᆞ게ᄂᆡ며론병은변변치못ᄒᆞ게ᄒᆞ드리도병이완젼히패복되게ᄒᆞ니만갓지못ᄒᆞ나니신문도역시이와갓타여당장에만아유구용ᄒᆞ야좃케만ᄒᆞᄂᆞᆫ거시일후에ᄂᆞᆫ죠곰도죠ᄒᆞᆯ거시업ᄂᆞᆫ지라그런고로우리ᄂᆞᆫ공평ᄒᆞᆫ의론으로다른신문과갓치아첨ᄒᆞᆯ거시아니오무론무삼일에던지잘못ᄒᆞᄂᆞᆫ일만잇슬지경이면오직게지ᄒᆞ겟노라

구월슴십일우리신문에보도ᄒᆞ기를한국빅셩슴명이털도에작간ᄒᆞᆫ죄로군률노시힝ᄒᆞ야포살ᄒᆞᆷ을당ᄒᆞ엿다ᄒᆞ엿거니와당초에이러ᄒᆞᆫ사실은게지ᄒᆞᆯ거업서그러ᄒᆞ되포형ᄉᆞ지힝ᄒᆞᆫ일을우연지사로돌여침묵ᄒᆞ고잇기어려운고로게지ᄒᆞ엿스나즉시잇고만일이러니

일본신문에셔ᄂᆞᆫ이일이무슴조ᄒᆞᆫ일로만녁여잇지아니ᄒᆞ고두엇다가사실도자셰히알지못ᄒᆞ고달포만에우리ᄒᆞᆫ말ᄒᆞᆫ바를핑박ᄒᆞ야자긔가올흔모양으로셜명ᄒᆞ엿ᄂᆞᆫ지라

그런고로우리도역시그ᄯᅢ포형ᄒᆞᆫ사실을소샹히게지ᄒᆞ야ᄃᆡ답ᄒᆞ엿더니일본신문에셔또번복ᄒᆞ야셜명ᄒᆞ기를그털도에작잔ᄒᆞᆫ한국빅셩들은집줏인명과긔차에탑지ᄒᆞᆫ물건을히ᄒᆞ려ᄒᆞᆫᄭᅡᄃᆞᆰ에악형을베풀미라ᄒᆞ엿ᄂᆞᆫ지라그러ᄒᆞ나우리의생각에ᄂᆞᆫ어불셩셜인거시그ᄯᅢ에다만쳘도면젼긔만를나노왓슬ᄲᅮᆫ이오사람과물건은탑지치아니ᄒᆞ엿슨즉이일로인연ᄒᆞ야이ᄃᆡ도록심히말ᄒᆞᆷ은혹다른친졀ᄒᆞᆫ붕우의게도힝ᄒᆞᆯᄂᆞᆫ지진실로아혹ᄒᆞ노라

외보

○가옥폭발 론돈면을거ᄒᆞᆫ즉아라사구로바도긴쟝군의보고에굴으ᄃᆡ아라사결사ᄃᆡ수명이십일월십륙일밤에아라ᄉᆞ군사좌익방면에일본병뎡이십오명이점령ᄒᆞᆫ디나ᄉᆞᄅᆞᆷ에가옥을폭발케ᄒᆞ엿ᄂᆞᆫ디일본병뎡이다죽엇다ᄒᆞ엿더라

○우양견탈 아라시군사가근쟈에광령파밋의쥬등디방에셔우양능오빅여두를봉텬으로슈송ᄒᆞ다가즁로에셔마젹의습격을피ᄒᆞ야물수히견탈ᄒᆞ엿고또ᄑᆡ색국긔병쳔오빅명이안즈보에셔마젹파젼투ᄒᆞᆫ후에ᄯᅩ격긔원으로되각ᄒᆞ엿ᄂᆞᆫ디그ᄯᅢ고식국긔병슴사십명이죽엇다더라

○셤라병비 셤라젼부ᄂᆞᆫ신식춍오만병을론돈뉴윤등디에맛츄엇ᄂᆞᆫ디이ᄂᆞᆫ셤라왕이일로긔젼이후에쟈긔나라를방슈ᄒᆞᆯ계척에진력ᄒᆞᆷ이오셤나국군부고문관이셤나국륙군무쟝을일신이ᄒᆞ라권고ᄒᆞᆷ이러라

TELEGRAMS.

Army Headquarters, Seoul.

The Japanese army attacking Port Arthur opened a heavy bombardment on the citadel from daylight on November 30th, and also made an assault on the forts, but the Russians repulsed the attack. At 5 P. M. a detachment to the Southwest of the Russian trenches on the hill-side made a sudden attack and reached a position under cover a short distance from the trenches. At 7 P. M. they were reinforced and succeeded in occupying the position.

(This telegram is very obscure. The trenches and positon carried are denominated, in the despatch, position No. 203.—Ed.K. D. N.

Tokyo, Dec. 2nd.

The Russians have made several attempts to retake the positions occupied by the Japanese on Nov. 30th, but without success. The slaughter has been terrible.

(FROM JAPAN PAPERS.)

London, Nov. 25.

Public attention has been attracted to the recent passage through the Suez Canal southwards of three yachts—the "Fiorentina," "Catarina," and "Emerald."

The London agents of the "Fiorentina," and "Catarina" decline to disclose the names of the charterers and the mysterious mission of the yachts, but it is supposed they are for the purpose of exploring the reefs in the Red Sea on behalf of the Baltic Squadron.

London, Nov. 25.

The Hon. Charles Hardinge, British Ambassador at St. Petersburg, and Count Lamsdorff, the Russian Minister of Foreign Affairs, have signed the Convention fixing the arrangements of the inquiry into the North Sea incident.

Berlin, Nov. 25.

The Russian papers give details of the friendly reception accorded the crew of the Russian cruiser "Lena" at San Francisco.

London, Nov. 25.

Viscountess Hayashi, wife of the Japanese Minister in London, leaves for Japan on Tuesday. The return of the Viscountess is due to the fact that the English climate does not agree with her health.

London, Nov. 25.

The Russian correspondents at Mukden dwell on the difficulties of obtaining food, forage, and fuel, especially fuel, without which the huge blocks of ice from the river wells cannot be melted, rendering the supply of water all insurmountable problem.

London, Nov. 24.

Under the auspices of the German Colonial Society, on the 16th instant a traveller delivered a lecture in Berlin in which he called attention to the ubiquitous activity of Japanese traders in China who were menacing German trade. The speaker pointed out that even in the province of Shautung it was the Japanese and not the Germans who benefited by increase of trade.

INTERNAL RUSSIA.

Mr. McCormick, the American Ambassador at St. Petersburg, sailed from Cherbourg for New York on the steamer Deutchland; but before his departure, Mr. McCormick talked with a representative of the Associated Press concerning the general conditions in Russia. He said:

"It is difficult for anyone not living in Russia to realize the complete calm prevailing notwithstanding the tremendous struggle in which Russia is engaged. St. Petersburg has the same outward appearance as before the war. There is the same social activity and business is going on as usual, and the people do not show any deep anxiety as to the progress or results of the war. I made a trip into the interior, where there was the same calm and absence of excitement.

"This calmness is the complete confidence of the people and the government. There are some elements of agitation and opposition in Russia, as in other countries, but the great bulk of the people are devotedly loyal to the Emperor and government, and they have implicit confidence that the ruling powers will take the steps necessary to bring the war to a successful conclusion."

Asked concerning Russia's economic conditions, the Ambassador said; "I see no evidence that the war is seriously affecting Russia's trade, business or finances. The war naturally disarranges and depresses some lines of business, but there is nothing like a panicky sentiment. Russian finances seem equal to all present and future requirements. The status of the latest issue of Russian bonds shows this. Beginning at par, they rapidly advanced, despite the early discouragements of the war, until they reached 521 last Wednesday."

Asked relative to the rumours of internal troubles in Russia, Ambassador McCormick said he had not observed any indication of serious unrest or agitation. Once in a while, there was some local disorder, without significance, which the foreign opponents of Russia magnified into a general movement, whereas no such movement existed.

Mr. McCormick said the appointment of Prince Viatopolk-Mirsky as Minister of the Interior, in succession to M. Von Plehve, promises to exert an important influence upon Russian internal affairs, mainly toward moderating the severity of old Russian traditions.

Mr. McCormick expresses satisfaction at the recent action of the government in referring the American communication relative to Jews to a commission which was to study the subject.

Speaking generally, the Ambassador said the relations between the United States and Russia continue most satisfactory.

Mr. McCormick will go to Washington to report to the President and Secretary Hay, and later will visit Chicago before returning to Russia.

THE MIDDLE AGES REVIVED.

The penance imposed by the Pope Pius X upon Prince Frederick of Schönburg-Waldenburg and his divorced wife, the Princess Alice of Bourbon, who is so well known in Paris and at French watering places, came as a severe shock to the princely pair. To start off humbly on a pilgrimage to Rome as a condition of the reconciliation brought about by the efforts of his Holiness, travelling without any state or circumstance, simply clad—the Prince is shod with sandals, as an extra touch of mediævalism—and staying only at the more modest hotels on their road, evinces a certain amount of fortitude in these days of luxurious travelling. The frequent spells of wet weather during the present season were admitted as a pretext for a day's rest. The journey must be made without a break. Nevertheless, an intimate friend of the Princess announces that these quiet hours on the road to Rome were the calmest and most peaceful of an otherwise stormy married life. The Princess should be morally better equipped to face the storms of life than most women. A very perfunctory acquaintance with the annals of the family of her father, Don Carlos should suffice to convince a prince, of the Spanish branch of the houses of Bourbon that the uneventful happiness of mediocrity would scarcely be possible for her. Born in 1876, the princess Alice was married in her twenty-first year to the Prince of Schonburg—Waldenburg at Venice, the ceremony being performed by the Pope himself, then Cardinal Sarto. The marriage did not prove a happy one, however, and after nearly six years of a checkered existence the princess ran away from her home, alleging her husband's ill treatment as the cause of the step. Her flight laid her open to the attacks of a certain part of the German press, reports having been spread about that she had gone off with her own coachman. It speedily became known, however, that the princess had gone to Italy and was occupying a villa near Genoa belonging to her brother, Don Jaime, which had been at once placed at her disposal by his secretary, the afterwards notorious Comte de Spa. It was this individual who, a few months ago, was the means of bringing the princess' name and private affairs once more into public notice, by pledging the celebrated necklace known as the Queen's necklace which has been the property of the Spanish Bourbons since the Revolution. Taking advantage of his employer's departure for Manchuria, the Comte de Spa (a Belgian adventurer, masquerading under this name) raised a large sum of money in Paris upon Queen Marie Antionette's necklace, and went off to London with the booty. He was speedily tracked and the necklace restored to its present holder, the Princess Alice. The pilgrimage of the now reunited pair seems to be a return to the mental attitude of the faithful of the Middle Ages to their spirtual head. It has nothing in common with the yearly pilgrimages to Lourdes, when special trains convey thousands of invalids and cripples to the healing waters of the famous spring. The object of such pilgrims as those is a purely utilitarian one. But a tedious and probably inconvenient stroll through Southern Europe, undertaken as a public recognition of past errors, and further enhanced by a voluntary renunciation of modern comforts, is a new form of penance that meets great favour at the Vatican, and is likely to be prescribed quite frequently in future by Pius X. Princess Alice, in a letter to a young lady friend in Paris, states that she has only three books with her—viz., the Holy Bible the "Narrative of Jane Shore," who atoned for her sins by walking through the streets of London, garbed in a winding sheet and holding in her hand a lighted taper; and a guide book with a map of the country. In French Catholic circles admiration is expressed for the moral courage of the Pope in putting so severe a test upon the illustrious couple, and also for the humble devotion of the Prince of Schönburg-Waldenburg and of his recalcitrant wife Princess Alice of Bourbon.

A visit to the War Office was the greater feature of yesterday's Il Chin Hoi programme.

All members of the committee of inspection, returned from Japan, have received decorations from the Mikado.

The President of the Privy Council has resigned his post, but whether he will be permitted to leave is not yet known.

A report from Chulla Province states that some Japanese have arrived there and have attempted to levy so-called taxes from the Koreans.

The officers of the local guard of Pukchong have been dismissed on account of their inability to prevent the Russians from removing the rifles of their troops.

The Home Office informs the Finance Department that $50,000 will be required for the repair of roads and bridges on the road to the tomb of the Crown Princess.

Another fatality occurred, on the new railway works near the South gate, yesterday. A coolie named Im Kyeng Hun was crushed to death by a mass of falling earth.

A vernacular contemporary remarks that although the committee of inspection has arrived from Japan, it is hopeless to expect the return of Yi Yong-ik and General Hyou Yong-woon.

The Agricultural Department is paying particular attention, for the present, to the growth of mulberry trees. One hundred and fifty thousand cuttings have been sent to north Choong Chong province.

Some surprise was evinced, on the return of the Inspection Committee, when it was discovered that with one exception the members had shaved their heads. Mr. Yi Sang Chon was the notable exception.

His Majesty has presented $6,000 to the coolies who will take part in the funeral procession of the Crown Princess, so that they may be able to provide themselves with warm and suitable clothing in advance.

Mr. Kokobu of the Japanese Legation visited the acting Minister of the Education Department on Wednesday last and requested him to appoint Mr. Hitewara (the Japanese teacher in the middle school) educational adviser to the Government

We learn from a recent visitor from Newchwang says the "China Review" that last week Lt. Colonels Haldane and Tulloch British Military Attaches with the Japanese armies at Yeutai, arrived in Newchwang on a short stay, in order to purchase necessaries. They returned three days after

INDEPENDENCE AND INTEGRITY.

It seems that the Japanese authorities here have not got their servants under proper control. We hear of an incident to-day to which we respectfully call the attention of the army headquarters. At about noon a house in the occupation of a foreigner was entered by a couple of soldiers, one of whom bore the silver stripe indicating promotion from the ranks. These soldiers carried nothing to show their authority, but said that they wished to arrest a certain person. Although it was pointed out to them that they had no right in a foreigner's house they still refused to take their departure. We are glad to say that they eventually left without having succeeded in their quest. We shall have a good deal more to say on this subject on Monday. In the meantime we are sorry to see signs of proposed reductions in any of the Legation Guards.

The Korea Daily News.

Issued at 5 P. M. daily except Sundays.

Rate of Subscription:—
Per Year............Yen 25.
Per Quarter..........Yen 7.
Per Month..........Yen 2.50.

Postage in Korea not charged extra.
Postage abroad charged extra.

Advertisements, 50 sen per day for 1 inch or less.
5 yen per month per inch.
50 yen per year per inch.

All communications to

E. T. BETHELL,
Editor and Publisher,
Pak-tong, Seoul.

PROBABILITIES OF THE WAR.

SPECIAL TO THE "CHEFOO DAILY NEWS."

The Japanese infantry man is a wonder, and has on many occasions sacrificed himself in carrying out the plans of those who are running the campaign, thereby extricating from many a serious dilemma the genius who fights battles within the headquarters tent.

The leaders in the Japanese army have made some blunders, and it is only the private soldier's blind patriotism and recklessness that has enabled his commanding generals to make the showing they have made up to date. He is absolutely regardless of his life. Neither bullets nor shells stop him. That is why he has died in battle in overwhelming numbers. One day I was accompanying a Japanese infantry column. My horse started bucking and kicking, frightened by the shrieking of the shells and the whizzing of the bullets. The air was full of exploding shrapnel, the fragments falling all around us. A soldier seized the animal's bridle and led him along in a perfect rain of shot and shell.

Japanese artillery is on a par with others. Japanese cavalry is useless. The horses are weak and bad-tempered, and do not think much of their riders.

The commissary and quartermaster departments of the Japanese army work excellently. Two or three times a day trains come up to the front from Newchwang and Dalny, loaded with troops and provisions.

The soldiers are well fed. Their ration consists of rice, corned beef, pickles, "saki," and sometime cigarettes. The troops have not sufficient tents or barracks, and a portion of the army is still camping in the open air on the bare ground, with the temperature getting lower every day. Suffering is bound to come. Not long since the men experienced great inconvenience and even hardship during a snow storm. The correspondents believe that the increasing cold weather will prove disastrous to them.

The Japanese are learning gradually to respect the great bravery and skill of their enemy. Before the first battle of Liaoyang they underrated the Russians. It was the general opinion among the soldiers that the Russians were afraid of them and were flying before the victorious arms of the Mikado.

Just before the battle I was standing with a Japanese officer watching the Russian lines with aid of glasses. My companion remarked in a somewhat sneering way that he wondered if the great General of the Russians would let himself be seen this time.

After the battle the same officer expressed his admiration for the strategist and his brave soldiers, saying he had certainly performed a great feat in getting his whole army away in perfect order.

Since the battle the Japanese have become thoroughly convinced of the endurance of their antagonists, and every advance has been performed with the utmost care and caution.

Practically no progress has been made since October 19th. In fact the Russians have gained some ground. My opinion is that the Japanese are falling back, and that their first stand will be made at Liaoyang. However, the military and strategical value of this place has been exaggerated. It will be difficult for the Japanese to hold the position against an attack by the Russians. The taking of Liaoyang is only a question of numbers. It may be a second Plevna. I believe the Japanese will be forced to retreat, and will not be able to make much of a stand before reaching Ichang, where the ground will be more in their favor.

NEW CRETAN COMPLICATIONS.

There is no doubt that the elements which are favourable to the annexation of Crete to Greece are making an immense effort to hasten the solution of a problem which, in many ways, may be considered dangerous. The matter is made acute by the fact that Prince George of Greece, high commissioner of the powers in Crete, recently commenced a tour of Europe, which tour has a clearly defined political character. At Rome Prince George had an interview with Signor Tattoni, the minister of foreign affairs, and at Paris he has had conferences with M. Delcasse. While the prince is thus working in Europe the Cretan opposition is active in Greece this opposition being in full agreement with Prince George, that Crete should be annexed. The government of Crete, on the othar hand, desires the maintenance of the "status quo." The heads of this Cretan opposition, M. M. Benizelos, Manos, and Foumis, recently went to Athens in order to explain their standpoint to the Greek authorities. These men declare that the reunion of Crete with Greece has become indispensable, and that a protectorate similar to that applied in Bosnia or Herzegovnia, which has been recommended, is absolutely inacceptable. The Cretans wish to be united to Greece on a basis of equality and fulness of rights, and, if the powers refuse to give them satisfaction, the Cretans will themselves solemnly proclaim the union with Greece; they will send deputies to the Hellenic parliament, and will invite the king of Greece to recognize the island as a portion of his dominions.

This menace, however, should not be considered too seriously, for the reason that the thing is not so simple as the Cretans think. As a matter of fact they have not the right thus to dispose of their destinies, for the reason that Turkey is, in a nominal sense, master of Crete, and there is no doubt that the Sultan will not easily renounce the rights which were guaranteed by the powers at the time of the settlement of the Cretan question. Turkey will never consent to the radical separation of any portion of her territory, and if the king of Greece recognizes Crete as a portion of the dominions of Greece a conflict between Athens and Constantinople will be inevitable.

Prince George does not wish any complications of this sort. The prince desires that the reunion of Crete with Greece shall be the work of the powers, before whose wish Turkey will not dare to protest. The impatience of the Cretan opposition may, however, jeopardize this accomplishment, and, while it is certain that some day Crete will be annexed to Greece, attempts to precipitate matters will not only do harm, but will also prejudice the interests which the Greeks have in Macedonia. There is little doubt that these many considerations will be evident to the Greek authorities and that moderation will prevail.—China Review.

BAIKAL RING-RAILWAY.

St. Petersburg, October 2nd.

The importance of the newly-built railway round the southern end of Lake Baikal was shown by the inscription "Lisbon and Vladivostock," which was displayed on a very beautiful triumphal arch under which the first train ran on September 25th. The work of building this line was begun in 1899. The difficulties that had to be overcome were enormous. The total length of the line is 163 miles, and the cost, so far, has been £5,678,260, or £34,906 per mile. The line starts from Irkutsk station, and runs thence for 56 miles along the rocky shore of Lake Baikal, where the mountain spurs, inlets, and other natural hindrances, had to be overcome by means of tunnels, bridges, and viaducts. The western section of the line contains 22 tunnels, from the mouths of which nearly 400,000 cubic fathoms of rock have been blasted by dynamite. The permanent way is 2 3-5th fathoms wide, and the rails weigh 24 pounds per foot run, as against the very light rails of the Siberian Railway, for the latter were only 18 pounds to the foot. The permanent way required 16,500 acres of surface, of which 3,754 acres were covered by a thick forest growth, and no less than 1,005,000 cubic fathoms of earth were used in making the track; 461,700 cubic fathoms of rock had to be blasted by dynamite in order to lay down the permanent way. Great care has been taken with the gradients and curves. The gradients do not exceed anywhere 1 in 7,000, while no curve is less than 150 fathoms. Some work remains to be finished, but it is not important, and will not affect the temporary running of ordinary trains. All the station buildings are completed. As the line has been built so solidly the first train to run upon it was able to attain a very good speed.

The Americans continue to show us the way, remarks the London "Globe." When our ships are stopped on the high seas we make a fuss and begin taking off our coats. Not so the shrewd man from the States. An American ship, carrying stores for the Russians, was stopped the other day by the Japanese. The captain received boarders very politely, mentioned that the weather held up nicely, and in a rich nasal twang tried to sell them the cargo.

On the 19th inst., at 3 a. m., the Port Arthur blockading squadron discovered a steamer, near Yentao, apparently making for Port Arthur. The Japanese cruiser "Tatsuta" gave chase and overhauled her at 5 a. m. Upon examination she proved to be the German steamer "Peteran," with a cargo of winter clothing, blankets, medical necessaries, and preserved meat. A prize crew was put on board the vessel and she was taken to Sasebo, to undergo examination by the Prize Court there.

The Chinese Foreign Office has, says the Peking correspondent of the "Tokyo Asahi," recently requested Mr. Uchida, our Minister, to prohibit the Japanese pawnbrokers at Peking from carrying on their business, the reason being that no native with a capital of less than 100,000 taels was allowed to become a pawnbroker and that this privilege should not be enjoyed by the Japanese to the detriment of the natives. In reply, Mr. Uchida stated that there were also German and Korean pawnbrokers at Peking, who are in similar circumstances as the Japanese, and that, should the veto be also imposed on these men, the Japanese pawnbrokers should be ordered to discontinue their occupation. Thereupon the Chinese authorities forwarded a similar request to the German and Korean Representatives, but no answer has yet been received from the latter.

The Korea Daily News.

VOL. I, SATURDAY, DECEMBER 3, 1904. No. 116

HONGKONG & SHANGHAI BANKING CORPORATION.

Paid-up Capital..... ....$10,000,000
Reserve Fund:—Sterling Reserve... 10,000,000
Silver Reserve..... 7,000,000

27,000,000
Reserve Liability of Proprietors... 10,000,000

HEAD OFFICE, HONGKONG.

London Bankers, London and County Banking Company Limited
Branches and Agencies,
London.

Amoy,	Hankow	Penang,
Bangkok,	Hiogo,	Rangoon,
Batavia,	Iloilo,	Saigon,
Bombay,	Lyons,	San Francisco,
Calcutta,	Manila,	Singapore,
Colombo,	Nagasaki,	Sourabaya,
Foochow,	New York,	Tientsin,
Hamburg,	Peking,	Yokohama,

Credits granted on approved Securities, and every description of Banking and Exchange business transacted.

Drafts granted on London and the chief Commercial places in Europe, India, Australia, America, China and Japan.

HOLME RINGER & Co., AGENTS,
CHEMULPO.

ON CHEONG & CO.,
SEOUL.

GENERAL STORE KEEPERS.
Imported provisions, Cooking Utensils Crockery, etc.
FRESH BREAD DAILY.

MITSU BISHI DOCKYARD & ENGINE WORKS,
NAGASAKI.

CODE WORD, "DOCK."

A 1, A. B. C., and Engineering Codes used.

DOCK No. 1 (at Tategami).

Extreme Length..............523 feet
Length on blocks .... 513 ,,
Width of Entrance on Top......89 ,,
,, ,, Bottom....77 ,,
Water on Blocks at Spring Tide 26½ ,,

DOCK No. 2 (Mukaijima).

Extreme Length..............371 feet
Length on Blocks.............360 ,,
Width of Entrance on Top......66 ,,
,, ,, Bottom 53 ,,
Water on Blocks at Spring Tide 22 ,,

PATENT SLIP (at Kosuge)

Can take vessels up to 1,000 tons gross.

THE WORKS are well equipped with the LATEST IMPROVEMENTS, and can execute any kind of work in SHIPBUILDING and MARINE ENGINEERING, as well as in REPAIRING of SHIPS.

The COMPANY'S new powerful steamer OURA-MARU (712 tons, 700 I.H.P.), specially built for SALVAGE PURPOSES, and equipped with necessary gear, is always READY at SHORT NOTICE.

CHARTERED BANK OF INDIA AUSTRALIA & CHINA.

INCORPORATED BY ROYAL CHARTER 1853.

HEAD OFFICES:—LONDON.

Paid-up Capital £800,000
Reserve Liability of Share-holders 800,000
Reserve Fund 800,000

Drafts granted upon all the principal places in the world and every description of Exchange and banking business transacted.

E. MEYER & Co., Agents,
Chemulpo.

E. MEYER & CO.
Chemulpo.

SOLE AGENTS IN KOREA FOR:
A. T. Morse, Sons & Co's "Fresco" Distemper

in all colours ready for use on walls, Ceilings etc.

and

AVENARIUS CARBOLINEUM

A wood-preserving and antiseptic oil preparation

Against decay, dry-rot, fungus and wood-destroying insects.

A large supply always in Stock.
Prices upon application.

E. MEYER & Co.,
Chemulpo.

THE METHODIST PUBLISHING HOUSE.
Little West Gate, Seoul.

JOB PRINTING. TYPEWRITER PAPER
CARBON PAPER, VISITING CARDS
STATIONERY, BOOK BINDING
BOOK PUBLISHERS
AMERICAN SCHOOL BOOKS
SPENCERIAN COPY BOOKS
PEN CARBON LETTER AND BILL BOOKS

S. A. BECK, Manager.

HOKURKU DOBOKU KAISHA.

Branch office in Chong Dong, Seoul.

Japanese telephone No. 165

CONTRACT DEPARTMENT.

We can contract to build any building or construction.

MERCHANDISE DEPARTMENT.

We can provide any building material. We have just contracted to build the new Belgian Legation.

DAI-ICHI GINKO.
LIMITED.
(Formerly the First National Bank)

ESTABLISHED 1873

INCORPORATED UNDER PRESENT LAW 1896

Capital - - - - - - - - - Yen 5,000,000
Reserve Fund - . - - - 1,500,000

HEAD OFFICE:—TOKIO.

President: Baron SHIBUSAWA.

BRANCHES AND CORRESPONDENTS
In the Principal Cities and Towns of Japan.

Interest Allowed on
Fixed deposits 1 year - - - 6½ per cent
" " 6 months - - - 6 per cent

Special current accounts 1½ sen daily per Y 100
General " " 1 " " " 100

M. TANAKA,
Manager, Chemulpo.

SINGER SEWING MACHINES

씽거조봉침

SOLE AGENTS FOR KOREA
젼매쇼

HOLME RINGER & CO.
Chemulpo.
졔물포 함릉거양힝

KAMEYA & CO.
GENERAL STOREKEEPERS
Chinkokai - - Seoul
(Established 1895, Tokyo)

Confectionery, Hams, Canned Goods, Cutlery, Hirano & Tansan Water. Provisions, Gents, Furnishing goods, Toilet Articles, Travelling Bags, Tobacco, Cigars & Cigarettes Kitchen Utensils. Coffee. Biscuits.

Fresh Goods always kept in Stock.
Prices Moderate
Please come and inspect our goods

NIPPON YUSEN KAISHA.
JAPANESE MAIL STEAMSHIP CO.
UNDER MAIL CONTRACT WITH THE IMPERIAL JAPANESE GOVERNMENT.

European Line

Regular Fortnightly Service between Yokohama Kobe, Moji, Shanghai, Hongkong, Singapore, Penang Colombo, Port Said, Marseilles, London and Antwerp

American Line

Regular Fortnightly Service between Hongkong and Seattle, calling at Shanghai, Moji, Kobe, Yokohama and Victoria, B. C.

Australian Line

Regular weekly Service betwen Japan Ports and Australia, calling at Hongkong and Manila.
(Above Three Lines Suspended until further notice)

Shanghai Line

Weekly Service between Shanghai and Japan Ports

Korea Line

Service Kobe, Moji, Nagasaki, Fusan Chemupo Chefoo, Taiku.
S. S. Bahelsberg, 2181 tons.
Service Kobe, Moji, Fusan, Chemulpo, Chinnampo
S. S. ARGO, S. S. Ohio.

BORDEN'S CONDENSED MILK CO.
New York, U. S. A.

ALWAYS IN STOCK
Eagle Brand Condensed Milk.
Gold Seal Condensed Milk.
Peerless (Family) Evaporated Cream.
Borden's Malted Milk.

E. MEYER & CO.
Chemulpo, Korea,
Sole Agents

ROYAL INSURANCE COMPANY,
Funds exceed £10,000,000
FIRE
AT CURRENT RATES.
LIFE
REDUCED PREMIUM.
HOLME RINGER & Co.,
Agents, Chemulpo.

HOTEL DU PALAIS
SEOUL.

The only first class Hotel in Seoul. Situated in the centre of the city opposite the palace.

Cuisine under the supervision of an experienced French Chef.

Well ventilated and furnished throughout.

TARIFF UPON APPLICATION
L. MARTIN
Proripetor and Manager

大韓每日申報

대한미일신보

(뎨일빅십칠호) (화요일) (일쳔 … 년 십이월 륙일)

본샤고빅

이신보는 일요와 한영으로 셔거미 일츌판ᄒᆞᆸ

신문가

한쟝 엽두돈오푼

일삭됴 엽두량닷돈

우표가리 샥닷돈

다엿돈으로밧ᄉᆞᆸ

광고료는

귀한외쟝단과 ᄌᆞ힝의다쇼로쥬 강ᄒᆞ되평가로밧을터이오며오 리져아니ᄒᆞᄂᆞᆫ대한사람마다다이신 문을보셔야ᄒᆞ니광고내시기를 원ᄒᆞ시ᄂᆞᆫ이들은우리신문샤에 와셔편약ᄒᆞ심을희망ᄒᆞᄋᆞᆸ

○발힝소 박동대한미일신보 사발힝겸편집인 영국인셜필 림졍자리오

사쟝 영국인 (비셜)

평양 디리졈

○평양홍동사는 권미보씨로우 리신문총디리인을뎡ᄒᆞ엿 스오니평양에계신구람코져ᄒᆞ 시는 첨군ᄌᆞ는 디리졈에와셔 쳥ᄒᆞ와뎡약ᄒᆞ시ᄋᆞᆸ

샤고

○우리대한미일신보의목뎍은 대한의안녕질셔에관한모든 …

관보

외보

잡보

논셜

려슌에일본통신

만일아라사괴릉보에셔별로히 등츌ᄒᆞᆫ의견이엇고려순에잇는 장관과수사뎨독계에회훈ᄒᆞᆫ바 와갓흔진ᄃᆡ요동반도에셰력향 ᄃᆡ도쳐되기까지는다만려순항 구안에장괴여잇슬터이로되만 일고려치아니ᄒᆞ야츙돌ᄒᆞ야나 오는경우이면일본함ᄃᆡ의형셰 가심히위급ᄒᆞᆯ터이요ᄯᅩᄒᆞᆫ아라 사에셔는군함으로써큰사진되 홈이더욱필요ᄒᆞ게될터인즉 현금소견으로는동향졔독이순 양함과수뢰졍들은치지ᄒᆞ고려 도젼투함셩비쳑만거나리고승 격ᄒᆞᆯ지경이면죠흔위치라도졈 령ᄒᆞᆯ지라그러ᄒᆞ나이계획ᄃᆡ로 ᄒᆞ라면항구를불가불방비ᄒᆞ야 긴즁히져ᄒᆞ야ᄒᆞᆯ거시

거월에는비유산하에병향죵박 ᄒᆞ기에조흔항구가잇는셔닭에 무사히지닉엿스되지금은일본 군사가동북으로들너싸고졀수 산과여락산과기관산을향ᄒᆞ유 용격ᄒᆞᆫ즉이산샹들에잇는모든 진루는졈령이되엿슬터이나그 러ᄒᆞ나아죵결국은비유산졈령 여부에다만달녓고ᄯᅩᄒᆞᆫ황금산 진루은젼ᄒᆞ기에오죽지탕이될 지라

만일황금산셔지일병의게쇄아 겻던들아국병함이잠시라도그 항구에졍박지못ᄒᆞ게되엿고ᄯᅩ ᄒᆞᆫ황금산샹에운거ᄒᆞ야명령홈 으로써크게외뢰가된즉엇지던 지쌍ᄃᆡ합ᄃᆡ도착될세쳐지는무 사히경과ᄒᆞᆫ듯ᄒᆞᆫ거시스트셀장 군이괴릉보로귀별ᄒᆞ기를려순 은수삭동안을가히지보ᄒᆞ여가 겟다고ᄒᆞ엿슴쎤터러니ᄃᆡ산진 망즁이라ᄒᆞ는ᄃᆡ

나ᄃᆡ산이라ᄒᆞ는산은황금산으 로더브러연ᄒᆞ엿는고로만일황 금산에셔불ᄒᆡᆼᄒᆞᆫ일이잇슬지경 이면나ᄃᆡ산으로퇴거ᄒᆞ야괴ᄒᆞ 기에도심히조흘쎤터러항구가 암ᄒᆞᆫ로잇서셔함ᄃᆡ죵박ᄒᆞ기에 도ᄯᅩᄒᆞᆫ필요ᄒᆞᆫ고로아라사에셔 는이곳에다군사를셜치ᄒᆞ야아 모조록공고히유지ᄒᆞ도록ᄒᆞᆫ다 ᄒᆞᆫ즉이와갓흔진ᄃᆡ다시수삭동 안은자연연ᄃᆡ가될지라이거시 큰염녀라ᄒᆞ엿고

일본신문에는계진ᄒᆞᆫ바를본즉 일본셔론졈에는조금도염녀가 업스되지어회젼ᄒᆞ야는크게걱 졍인거시병함이라ᄒᆞ는거시원 릭수효가잇는ᄃᆡ만일츌항ᄒᆞ는 ᄃᆡ로파손이나되고즉시졈령ᄒᆞ 야귀졍이아니불지경이면ᄃᆡ단 히염녀되는바라ᄒᆞ엿더라

잡보

○교숀릉립 일본에셔챵론컷 [illegible]

든졔관인들은다만발ᄒᆞ엿스되 리라샹관셰는사발치아니ᄒᆞ엿는 지라폐젼ᄒᆞᆯ셰에머리를푸럿는 니고로폐복을입고입ᄃᆡᄒᆞᆫ후에회 국ᄒᆞ엿는ᄃᆡ작일평남녁친구들 이모혀말ᄒᆞ기를긴머리로츌입 홈이장ᄒᆞᆫ마음이라ᄒᆞ는지라셔 로반ᄃᆡᄒᆞ야결으ᄃᆡ찬아리폐 머리안ᄒᆞᆯ지언졍그복장을위ᄒᆞ야 리루계시단반ᄒᆞᆫ거보다ᄒᆞ야 다ᄒᆞ고일장젼화를ᄒᆞ엿다더라

○평양병작폐 북도로파송ᄒᆞᆫ병 뎡의계셰거필금롤졍양쥬든이 되에셔두류ᄒᆞ는ᄃᆡ작폐가무쌍ᄒᆞ ᄃᆡ군부에셔죠쳐아니ᄒᆞ고소환 치도아니홈으로민원이자자ᄒᆞ다 더라

○죠졍사유 비국공관에셔 부로죠회ᄒᆞ기를무릉샬졍에도에 셰잇논츅ᄒᆞᆫ만국회판회총지장이관에외 에죠회ᄒᆞ고보니경젼ᄃᆡ죠사 ᄒᆞ야밧으라ᄒᆞ엿더라

○청죠회왕 외부에셔령국공 관에죠복ᄒᆞ기를귀국에엽젹ᄒᆞᆫ 샹손연밧의치명ᄒᆞᆫ일사는우 리변부항문을검ᄒᆞ엿거니와죠 북니기에샹 쥬ᄒᆞ야평리원관 사뎨명식을파송ᄒᆞ야위임사판 ᄒᆞᆫ다ᄒᆞ엿기에본부에셔도ᄯᅩᄒᆞᆫ관 번역관리근춘을파송ᄒᆞ야한셩에 동변김셕졍을티동ᄒᆞ고불일등 졍흥리인즉귀셔빅위원도ᄯᅩᄒᆞᆫ 곳갓치감이가다ᄒᆞ엿더라

○유표회원 작일하오이시에 진교기로일진회원ᄒᆞ니히지나 논티머리에는학도쓰는수포를 쓰고몸에는양복입고두루막이 를입고발에는비단티수혜를신 어스니비록대한복과셔이나보는 사람마다다시보고단시보니아 마이샹ᄒᆞᆫ가보더라

○일신락당 작일하오 삼시 에진명회에셔면동연면도가셔 가모연셜ᄒᆞ기를비유ᄒᆞᆯ것이세 상지가잇는ᄃᆡ권졔는쌍별이비 동젹은물건이로ᄃᆡ체징이나로 몸을근ᄃᆡ리면여러히일신으로 고와분고쌍면근사름이라도쏫 이바놀이젹은쇠엿치로ᄃᆡ큰사기 름이라도ᄶᅵ로면젼ᄃᆡ지못ᄒᆞ고 쥬조시에왈샤름이부를아니 ᄒᆞ면쵸목금슈와분로에도비ᄒᆞ 지못ᄒᆞᆫ다ᄒᆞ엿스니나라히갈되 는거시대소강약에잇지안코쥬 우리이쳔만동포논일심으로나 아가면잘되겟다ᄒᆞ엿더라

○관수전임 한셩지판소쥬 관수김연식씨는슌찰소로전임 ᄒᆞ고그티에김졔슌씨가피임ᄒᆞ 고관수하규일씨는등쥬관으로 젼임ᄒᆞ고그티에는이외 리용구씨가피임ᄒᆞ 엿더라

○전답환츄 룡군참위리경 의가젼답사셕여일경을민영휘 씨게젼탈ᄒᆞᆫ바수ᄇᆡᆨ으로리참위가 민씨를걸보고희젼답을도로니 라ᄒᆞᆫ즉민보국이도뢰여위협ᄒᆞ 며리참위를잡아가두다ᄒᆞ더니 이본수령관장곡쳔씨가민영휘 씨의게공함ᄒᆞ고희도ᄃᆡ를도로

쥬고엇다수히츄슈ᄒᆞ드논미변ᄒᆡ 셕시쟝니로갑ᄒᆞ라ᄒᆞ엿더라

○어평미안 전북순찰사박졔 슌씨가죄인을졍부로보리ᄒᆞ는 ᄃᆡᄒᆞᆼ벙의셩명이어소최로등죠 인ᄃᆡ신참졍이그ᄃᆡ로샹 쥬ᄒᆞ엿다가하슌ᄒᆞ시논ᄃᆡ셕 이븐지라신참졍이방금미안즁 이라더라

○운산군슈보고 운산군슈가 외부로보고ᄒᆞ기를본군초리에 잇는바미국금광으로빅셩의 빗을긔계ᄒᆞ고빅셩의젼을회졍 ᄒᆞ야빅셩으로ᄒᆞ여곰회산케ᄒᆞ 야가히졍쥬ᄒᆞᆯ수가업스니호포 외겔계는가히밧을곳이업논지 라츅감ᄒᆞᆯ뜻으로보ᄒᆞ야라지부 에쳥ᄒᆞ엿더니지령니에외부에 셔죠졍ᄒᆞᆫ후에야츅감ᄒᆞ겟다ᄒᆞ 엿기에이보고ᄒᆞ니탁지부에면 죠ᄒᆞ기를보란다ᄒᆞ엿더라

○령국사관연셩 십이월이일 샹오십이시에령국함쟝삼원파일 외사관오인이연셩ᄒᆞ엿더라

○쳐분등군 쳐분을경무쳥으 로논리사 ᄒᆞᆼ릉화즈니에잇는 브티규쳔의분총십삼쟝을그친 쇽이라도쟝아다가분일등군케 ᄒᆞ라ᄒᆞ엿셧더라

○샹쥬규정 외부에셔샹 쥬 ᄒᆞ고외교관사진규칙을졍ᄒᆞ야 ᄃᆡ명공사와밋령사가미쥬일에 일차식외부로사진회동ᄒᆞ기로 작뎡ᄒᆞ엿더라

○권교면관 십이월샹일샹오 에일진회에셔신참졍의게총ᄃᆡ 를파송ᄒᆞ야총하사저ᄒᆞ기를권 고ᄒᆞ고하오에는신여명을니부 로파송ᄒᆞ야회원을밧ᄃᆡᄒᆞᆫ황히 도관찰사을면관ᄒᆞ라ᄒᆞ엿더라

○한어교사신교 쳥국공사의 티신씨가외부로죠회ᄒᆞ기를한 어교사호문휘의가쇽의말을드 른즉회교사가죄셔츙로슈유를 엇어귀국ᄒᆞᆫ후에병이나셔즉엇 다ᄒᆞ니귀부ᄃᆡ신은학부에젼칙 ᄒᆞ여귀별ᄒᆞ와은봉외에이기월 월봉을지발ᄒᆞ여주어히가죡을 귀국ᄒᆞ게홈을보란다ᄒᆞ엿더로

○사진시간 외부에셔사진시 간을미일샹오열시로작뎡ᄒᆞ고 사퇴시간은하오네시반으로작 뎡ᄒᆞ야오는월로일ᄇᆡ터실시ᄒᆞ 논ᄃᆡ사진시간을엄이여념으면 월봉을날노써계산ᄒᆞ야일봉에 셔죵분의오를감ᄒᆞ기로겨뎡 ᄒᆞ엿더라

○젼북회면 젼라북도관찰부 에셔진보회원최슌셩과김쥬사 봉우를착슈ᄒᆞ고항묘ᄒᆞᆫ다홈이 로일진회에셔니부에루츠젼보 ᄒᆞ야즉시방셕홈을쳥ᄒᆞᆫ고로니 부에셔회도로무숀일노착슈ᄒᆞ

○졍부회의 작일하오훈시에 졍부에셔회의ᄒᆞ고 참졍이츌 셕ᄒᆞ엿더라

엿는지면담ᄒᆞ엿더니작일에회 면ᄒᆞ기를김봉우의죄샹은방쟝 ᄒᆞ고관쟝의계범ᄒᆞ엿다ᄒᆞ엿다 더라

○면훈경임 니부에셔젼남관 찰부로면훈ᄒᆞ기를흥양군민소 를졉ᄒᆞᆫ즉본부쥬사김샹두가흥 양군슈셔리와동쇄관을졈ᄃᆡᄒᆞ 야슌교를ᄃᆡ리고는리와작폐을 ᄒᆞᆫ다ᄒᆞ니심히기란ᄒᆞᆫ지라히군 셔리경등쇄관을히남군슈로차 졍ᄒᆞ야시무ᄒᆞ고곳회면ᄒᆞ라ᄒᆞ 엿더라

○진명회문졔 진명회에셔삼 일하오일시에기회ᄒᆞ엿는ᄃᆡ회 원은불과이십여명이오방쳥ᄒᆞ 논사름은불가승슈오문뎨는샹 무ᄒᆞ기는국민부강이니샹무를 발달ᄒᆞ라면졍치문명자을등흥 즘로밋음이라ᄒᆞ엿더라

○순찰계임 젼남순찰수리시 명씨는계임ᄒᆞ고그ᄃᆡ는리시져 씨가피임ᄒᆞ엿다더라

○광쥬젹경 충쥬로오는사람 의젼셜을드른즉거월삼십일밤 에광쥬군지쥬막에젹한사십명 이돌입ᄒᆞ야쥬막졍파ᄒᆞᆫ과의졔 물을탈취ᄒᆞ엿스나다힝이사람 은샹치아니ᄒᆞ엿더라

면보

륜돈발 십일월이십오일

○북희수진 령국쥬로ᄃᆡ수하 뎡씨와로국외부ᄃᆡ신람스도푸 씨가북희수진됴사ᄒᆞ는ᄃᆡᄒᆞ 야죠약을라인ᄒᆞ엿더라

[동디발 동일]

○샹항로함 로국각신문들은 미국샹항에셔로국슌양함레나 를젼ᄃᆡᄒᆞ엿다는말을발표ᄒᆞ엿 더라

동디발 동일

○로인곤란 국뎐에잇는로국 동신쟈들이셔물파쟉식ᄒᆡᆼ용빗 믈이졀핍ᄒᆞ고먹을물이젹어셔 ᄃᆡ단곤란ᄒᆞ다더라

동디발 동월이십수일

○리귀일샹 덕국신민회사감 독하에관ᄒᆞᆼᄒᆞ는자가계월십륙 일에빅림에셔연셜ᄒᆞ되쳥국에 셔도쳐에일본샹민이활동ᄒᆞ야 덕국샹업과경쟁홈을쥬의ᄒᆞ라 ᄒᆞ고산동셩에셔도샹업이흥왕 ᄒᆞ는리익이일본사름의게로도 라가고덕국사름은리익이업계 된다ᄒᆞ엿더라

광고

TELEGRAMS.

(LATEST NEWS FROM TSINGTAO.)

Dec. 1st.

The Japanese attack on Port Arthur on Nov 30th resulted in failure. They were repulsed in every direction and retreated, with heavy loss, at noon.

Later.

Admiral Dewey has refused to act on the Hull disaster enquiry committee.

Later.

The chief positions at Port Arthur are still in the hands of the Russians, the Japanese attacks on the 28th and 29th ult, having been repulsed.

Later.

From the 24th to 27th Nov. General Rennenkampf repulsed all the Japanese attacks made on his force, although the Japanese greatly outnumbered the Russians.

Later.

General Kuropatkin has been appointed Commander-in-Chief of Russian foces, both on land and sea.

Later.

A Russian lifeboat, which left Port Arthur on Nov. 16th, arrived near Weihaiwei on Nov. 22nd. The boat was taken in charge by the British authorities. The officer in charge is believed to be the bearer of important despatches.

FROM JAPAN PAPERS

London, 25th November.

The Berlin bankers have taken up twenty and the Paris bankers thirty millions of the Russian five per cent. War Loan of fifty million sterling, redeemable in five and seven years, to be issued in January.—Reuter.

London, Nov. 27, 8.10 P. M.

The supplemental vessels of the Baltic Squadron are now at Cherbourg. It is reported that the Orel has been damaged and consequently returned to Libau.

London, Nov. 26.

Two battleships and three cruisers, with nine transports, belonging to the Baltic Fleet anchored last night in the Bitter Lakes, seven destroyers remaining at Suez.

While the Squadron was passing through the Canal men were stationed at the guns and torpedo-tubes.

The anchorage of the Fleet at Suez is being patrolled by police boats.

London, Nov. 27.

The remaining vessels of the Baltic Squadron have arrived at Suez, but have been ordered to leave within twenty-four hours.

The vessels have not been allowed to coal at the port.

Later.

The vessels belonging to the Baltic Fleet have left Suez after coaling from transports.

London, Nov. 25.

The warships Sissoi Veliky, Navarin, Jemtchug, Svietlana, Almaz, seven destroyers, and nine Volunteer ships have arrived at Port Said, where they were supplied with fresh water and provisions, but they were refused coal. Seven destroyers have already reached Suez, and other ships will arrive there an hour later. The Suez Canal Company is taking strict measures as to the Russian warships. The Commander of the Russian squadron has paid a visit to the British warship Furious, where he asserted that the reported disturbances of the Russian sailors were baseless. A portion of the fleet has left Skaw.—"Asahi."

London, Nov. 27.

In connection with the removal of Viceroy Alexieff from the chief command of the Russian forces in the Far East, an Imperial Rescript expresses satisfaction at the services rendered by the Viceroy, and confers upon him the Order of St. George of the Third Class.

Peking, Nov. 28.

M. Lessar, Russian Minister at Peking has asked the Chinese Government to recall Chung-Shakulan, Taotai of Mukden on the ground of incompetence.—Mainichi.

London, Nov. 27, 8.10 P. M.

Interviewed with regard to the supplies of coal to the Baltic Squadron, Viscount Hayashi and Bron Suyematsu have given expression to the indignation among the Japanese concerning the material assistance which Russia is obtaining from Europe in general.

London, Nov. 27.

The Supreme Prize Court at St. Petersburg has confirmed the decision of the Vladivostok Court ordering the confiscation of the British steamer "Cheltenham," which was captured by the Vladivostok Squadron while on the voyage from Japan to Korea with railway material.

COUNT OKUMA'S SPEECH.

Count Okuma's speech delivered on the occasion of the general meeting of the Progressives on Saturday was as follows:—

"Gentlemen,—In these days of great national events, I deem it an honour to be thus afforded an opportunity of placing my views before you. It is also with a sense of responsibility that I take up the task. But before proceeding to that object, permit me to make known the sincere joy I felt when I saw our party expressing its deepest gratitude to our soldiers and sailors fighting at the front and its fullest sympathy with their bereaved families. Our forces are achieving glorious successes, which are of course due to the illustrious virtue of the Emperor and to the intense patriotism of our people. But think of it! Our men are perishing daily in great numbers for the sake of their country. No human incident is so terrible and so destructive as a battle. When I think of the terrible sacrifice of life in this war, I cannot help sympathizing with our brave soldiers and sailors. This feeling is strengthened when we remember that the world's recognition of our worth as a nation has been earned by the blood of our loyal and gallant troops.

"The war with Russia is a great struggle, and the world's attention is riveted to it. The nation which has launched in this great war shall not hope for its termination until its object has been attained. We ought to recognize the fact that the attainment of our object will depend upon the power of self-control and perseverance of the nation. Some military critics have indulged themselves in enumerating the weak points of our enemy and in exalting our strength. In Russia the bureaucracy and people are not united. The nation is composed of heterogeneous races, and a popular uprising is not impossible. The people are poor, and internal loans cannot be easily raised. An irrefutable instance of her weakness is that her authorities are experiencing great difficulty in drawing up her financial programme. But her strenth has been undisputed in Europe for a long time. It is therefore too rash a conclusion to hope for her defeat by seeing her weak side only, and we must never allow ourselves to underestimate our enemy's strength. It would appear that a section of our countrymen is inclined to think that Russia, after a crushing defeat, will ultimately be reduced into insignificance and will be expelled from the comity of European nations. This is really an absurd notion. We must, at the present juncture, spare ourselves no pains in endevouring to secure the continuation of foreign respect and sympathy as hostilities drag on. When I reflect on this point, I am led to believe that diplomacy is as important a factor as troops in the attainment of the object of the present war.

"Whilst that section of our people above referred to was thinking light of the enemy, his Baltic squadron is just on the point of passing the Suez Canal—an event hitherto deemed impossible by our easy-going folks. Then, several instances of the violation of neutrality have occurred since the departure of that squadron for the Far East, and yet nothing has definitely been known as to what steps have been taken by our Government.

"Let us now turn our eyes upon our diplomacy in Peking. There Russia, in spite of her defeat in arms, is apparently achieving diplomatic successes. What is the reason of all this? It is a source of profound regret that China's recent actions are such that one is led to doubt the extent of our diplomatic activity in that country. We cannot help feeling doubtful, nay, even apprehensive, not only as regards China but also Korea. Korea is already within the sphere of our influence, so that Japan must not act in such a way as to prejudice this privilege. The facts seem, however, contrary. And what is the cause of all this? I deeply regret that Japan should have been placed in such a position as to have to give one of her victorious Generals a sort of Governor-Generalship in Korea, in spite of the fact that there is our Minister Plenipotentiary in that country. In short, our diplomacy is characterized with inactivity.

"Outside of diplomacy, I find domestic administration in an equally unsatisfactory condition, quite inconsistent with the progress of the war. The present war is a war of the nation united as a whole. This is why the people are endeavouring to increase their productive power so as to meet the future demands from the country, and are also displaying their enthusiasm even by disposing of their ancestral property.

"Under the circumstances, the Government ought to be careful how it goes about securing the funds required for military purposes; otherwise unexpected consequences may follow. The utmost attention must be paid in order that the producing power of the nation be not impaired. There are, however, some who, taking unfair advantage of the deeply-stirred spirit of patriotism, defend the imposition of injurious taxes. I regret this most deeply. In view of the present situation, I see no reason whatever to offer any opposition to the increase of taxes. We must, however, oppose most stoutly any proposal that may tend to the impairment of the people's productive power. I need scarcely say that should taxation be wantonly increased year after year, the result would be a serious injury to the national interests. A glance at the increased taxation programme mapped out by the government will reveal the fact that some of the taxes proposed therein are unduly heavy. I am completely at a loss to understand why the people who are so loyally making sacrifices for the carrying out of the present struggle should be burdened with a taxation which is sure to be unnecessarily irksome and vexatious. I therefore ask all of you—the representatives of the nation—to reject all taxation proposals of this description.

"Generally speaking, the administration of a country is greatly governed by the wishes of its people. Should a Government attempt to conduct national affairs independently of people's desires, it is inevitable that bad effects will follow. It appears that the Government fails adequately to recognize the loyalty and patriotism thus far shown by the nation. Otherwise, how should we explain the Government's conduct in connection with the One Hundred and Thirtieth Bank case, for the Government wasted a large sum of money that had been obtained from the people? Is this not proof positive that the Goverment has failed to properly appreciate the disinterested patriotism with which the people are supporting the war? Such being the case, I fear that the people will not only place no confidence in the Government's procedure but that a reaction will occur amongst them in the future. I do not want to attack the present Ministry, but I would not remain behind others in guarding the interests of the country. I should not have made such utterance as the above had I not been impressed by the gravity of the situation and by my anxiety to witness the State emerge victorious in the present struggle."

The Chinese Minister has informed the Foreign Office that the teacher of the Chinese school died, while on leave in China. He trusts that two months extra salary will be paid to the deceased's relatives, so that they may return home.

The "Daito Shimpo" informs it's readers that the Russians at Songchin are sorely afraid of a Japanese bombardment from the sea. This priceless gem of information emanates from a "Korean who has been to Songchin."

Mr. Sin Ki Son, the Vice President of state is endeavouring to induce the other ministers to resign and offers to set the ball rolling by vacating his post. The Il Chin Hoi are said to be responsible for this peculiar attitude taken by Mr. Sin.

The Governor of Pyeng Yang has been accused of excessive methods in his taxation of the people. His victims assert that not less than $120,000 is the amount squeezed. The Government have decided to recall him and appoint a court to investigate his case.

Justice in a case, which has been dragging on for 15 years, has at last been arrived at by the intervention of General Hasegawa, who has ordered the defendant, an army officer accused of stealing a junior's property of rice-fields, to make restoration. He is to pay the plaintiff 1,500 bags of rice, the estimated yearly harvest being 100 bags, plus interest for 15 years.

NOTICE.

The power of attorney granted to Mr. Walter George Bennett to sign the name of our firm per procuration has this day been withdrawn.

Nagasaki, 30th November, 1904.

HOLME, RINGER & Co.

The Korea Daily News.

Issued at 5 P. M. daily except Sundays.

Rate of Subscription :—
Per Year.............Yen 25.
Per Quarter,..........Yen 7.
Per Month,..........Yen 2.50.

Postage in Korea not charged extra.
Postage abroad charged extra.

Advertisements, 50 sen per day for 1 inch or less.
5 yen per month per inch.
50 yen per year per inch.

All communications to

E. T. BETHELL,
Editor and Publisher,
Pak-tong, Seoul.

THE SINEWS OF WAR.

Count Okuma, addressing the progressists in Tokio has made a speech which will call forth surprised comment from a good many quarters. While praising unreservedly Japan's conduct of the war from the purely Military and Naval point of view, the state of affairs in the other two services most concerned, viz, the Financial and Diplomatic, receive anything but indulgent treatment at the hands of Count Okuma.

It will be remembered that the two factors which we have always been told would largely assist in Russia's downfall were (1) Financial weakness (2) Disaffection and Revolt in her own country. These are the very two evils which now seem to threaten Japan. It will be seen from the speech which we reproduce in another column that Count Okuma and his party strongly oppose the increased taxation proposed by the Government and prophesy a "reaction" in the country should these proposals be persisted in. This attitude places the Government in a quandary, as in order to meet with any success in raising loans abroad, it is necessary for Japan to show that she has also plenty of resources at home. That this view is at any rate held by the financial authorities in Japan is evidenced by the desperate measures which have been adopted in order to make a good showing in the estimated revenue for the coming year. As an instance we may note a considerable increase in the import duty on telephones, which are practically all for Government use. Then again, there is the proposed tax on salt. Salt is neccessary to human health and there is no substitute for it and as rich and poor alike need the same amount of salt, the burden of this tax will fall most heavily on the shoulders of those least able to bear it.

Yet it is difficult to see how either the Government or the progressist will find a way out of it. We have received the news that Berlin and Paris bankers have arranged to lend Russia fifty million pounds sterling at five per cent and when the recent Japanese loan of twelve million at nearly eight per cent is compared with this, it becomes, very certain that Japan's "Promises to pay" are not looked upon as desirable security in London and New York.

A good deal has been made of the fact that the recent Japanese loan was subscribed many times over, but it must be borne in mind that because an issue of £12,000,000 is over-subscribed ten times, it by no means follows that an issue of £120,000,000 would have been fully subscribed. Investors who want £2,000 of a certain issue, if they see a probability of over-subscription, apply for a larger amount in order to get the desired amount allotted to them.

Japan's prospects are far from rosy, financially at any rate, and if her efforts at raising money in her own country are to result, as Count Okuma foreshadows, in distrust of the Government and "reaction," it is hard to see how she can continue this war much longer.

Japan's real friends have for some time been advising her to signify her willingness to discuss terms of peace and we are also of the opinion that there is no time like the present.

NETHERLANDS INDIA.

Of late, there has been an increasing emigration of people from certain districts in Java to Singapore without any adequate reason for the outflow. The Netherlands Consul-General at Singapore was directed to inquire into the matter, with the result that the emigration was traced to the action of crimps. It seems that some persons from Singapore, with the aid of confederates in Java, had set about persuading Javanese, by deceitful means, to leave their homes. The emigrants are misled by promises that they would find plenty of work at Singapore, and would make so much money thereby that a pilgrimage to Mecca would come within easy reach. On arrival at Singapore, however, they find that the persons who had recruited them had been paid for it by their employers. The employers cut the amount from the wages due to the labourers. The result is that the latter have to work for a year or two without pay. Of this arrangement they were quite ignorant on quitting Java. The Java Government has instructed the district authorities there to warn the people against these crimps.

Much false coin in now circulating in Java in the shape of half-guilder pieces. The latter are so well turned out that only a practised eye can make them out. The ring is good and clear. These pieces are made out of Singapore dollars worth 1.20 guilders each. Out of every dollar the coiners turn out five half guilder pieces, the profit being about one hundred per cent.

The Batavia "Nieuwsblad" has it that the N. I. Government intends to establish at Batavia, Samarang, and Sourabaya—the three principal ports of Java —departments for managing Chinese affairs after the model of the Chinese Protectorates in the Straits Settlements. The head of each department will have a staff of Chinese clerks. The department duties will comprise keeping registers of births, deaths, and marriages for Chinese, besides supplying passes and residence permits to persons of that nationality.—China Review.

MURDEROUS SUN.

The "Novoye Vremya" correspondent quotes the following conversation with a particpant in the battle of Taschichao:

"Where were the Japanese stationed?"

"There were none, as far as we could see. Dozens of shells and thousands of bullets fell near our company. But we couldn't see one Jap."

Another soldier said :—

"Half a company of Siberian Rifles suddenly came under rifle fire without seeing a single Japanese. Many men were killed and wounded. The soldier beside me suddenly staggered and fell. We turned him over, but there was no trace of a wound. The Manchurian sun had killed him."

Another "Novoye Vremya" correspondent describes a man whose skin was actually scorched off by the heat.

The "Daito Shimpo" publishes a eulogistic article on the coolie volunteers (?) from the ranks of the Cina Po Hoi. Our contemporary says that contrary to the habits of ordinary Koreans, these marvellous beings actually commence work before daybre and continue till after dark, wh the ordinary paid coolie belives in nencing work late and finishing ear. Does our contemporary really expect people to believe that a Korean coolie will work *without payment* from dewy morn till dusky eve?

A PROPOSED UNIVERSAL ALPHABET.

Boston University is arranging to call a world's conference of philologists and university professors to take steps for the establishment of a "universal alphabet" and the institution of some reforms in spelling, which will form the basis for a universal language, the need of which has long been felt, and for which the many attempts to provide, including Volapuk and Esperanto, have so far proved inadequate. An universal alphabet under the plan proposed by Boston University would indicate the pronunciation of all words in the leading European languages. The twenty-six letters of the Roman alphabet are known all over the world, and probably 90 per cent. of the world's printing is done with those letters. Thus the basis of a "universal alphabet" already exists; it only remains to remove a few differences. For the most part, the twenty-six letters represent the same sounds in all languages. Write such words as arm, brick, past, black, harmony, individuality and others, and they will be pronounced alike, or nearly alike, by all Europeans, even though they may not know a word of English. However, as the value of the letters is not quite the same in all languages, or even within one language, it becomes necessary to resort to dictionaries and language manuals for keys of pronunciation. As the scientific study of pronunciation is of comparatively recent development, no uniformity has yet been attained in its notation. Almost every dictionary uses a key of its own, which is useful only to the reader of that particular dictionary. Whoever wishes to consult several dictionaries has to learn as many different keys, and whenever he wishes to ascertain the pronunciation of a word he has to consult the key at the bottom of the page or in the beginning of the book.

MADMEN AT THE FRONT.

The Moscow press continues to publish painful stories of lunacy and mania at the front. The "Sibirsky Viestnik" prints the following picture of a soldier driven mad by horror:—

"Into the Tomsk Municipal Hospital is carried a wounded man of middle age. He is covered with knife wounds, one in the chest, another in the side, and two in the stomach, the latter so deep that his internal organs are visible.

"Paying no attention to his injuries he continues to relate triumphantly how he has destroyed a whole Japanese corps. He looks fearfully around.

"'What are you afraid of?' asks the doctor.

"'The Japanese army is after me, they want vengeance. Save me!'

"Another madman thinks he is the Czar, and bestows decorations of tinfoil on his keeper. This man rushed into battle at Wafangtien shouting, "Follow your Czar—Batiushka, brave subject!"

"During the earlier fighting around Liaoyang, two lunatics escaped and went over to the Japanese. They were sent back next morning under the white flag."

In the last number of La Revue a writer proves to his own satisfaction by an ample genealogical table that the Emperor William is descended from the Admiral de Coligny on his father's side, and from the Duc de Guise on that of his mother. The Kaiser is therefore, on both sides of his family, says the genealogist, of good French origin.

The correspondents of the "Nippon," "Hochi," and "Osaka Mainichi" with the Port Arthur Army have been ordered to leave the peninsula, permission to follow the army having been withdrawn in consequence of the correspondents having dispatched letters without first submitting them to the censor. The correspondent of the "Kokumin" with the Second Army Corps has also been ordered back on a similar charge.

The Korea Daily News.

VOL. I, MONDAY, DECEMBER 5, 1904. No. 117

大韓每日申報
대한매일신보

(뎨일빅십팔호) (슈요일) 일쳔구빅사년십이월칠일

본사고빅

이신보는영어와한국문로셔계디일출판ᄒᆞ옴

신문가

ᄒᆞᆫ쟝 엽젼두돈오푼

일삭됴 엽젼두량닷돈

우표가디삭디닷돈

다엇돈으로밧숩

광고료ᄂᆞᆫ

귀한의장단과조ᄒᆞᆼ을ᄯᅡ라쇼로ᄒᆞᆷ 갑ᄒᆞᆫ되명가로밧을터이오매오 린지아니ᄒᆞᆫ대한사람마다이쳔 문을보실터이니광고내시기를 원ᄒᆞ시ᄂᆞᆫ이들은우리신문사에 와서면약ᄒᆞ심을희망ᄒᆞᆷ

○발행소 남부동대한매일신보 사셔울편전영국인셜렐 평장자리오

샤쟝 영국인 (비셜)

평양 디리졍

○평양을통ᄒᆞ는권리보씨로우 리신문을미디리인용되게ᄒᆞ엿 시스오니평양에게신구람졔ᄌᆞᄒᆞ 시ᄂᆞᆫ 쳠군ᄌᆞ는그이리졍에왕 림ᄒᆞ와면의ᄒᆞ시옴

샤고

○우리대한매일신보의목뎍은 대한의일반젹셔에관ᄒᆞᆫ모든대 쇼에티ᄒᆞ야는공평ᄒᆞᆫ번론을쥬 쟝ᄒᆞᆷ이라우리동신원의리본는 신문보시는쳠군ᄌᆞ의게ᄒᆞᆼ상보 도ᄒᆞ리며편지를긔셔ᄒᆞ여주시 는이는셩명과번디를졔어붓치 시기를희망ᄒᆞ오나미게승신문 샹에긔졔ᄒᆞ랴는거시아니오다 만극히신용ᄒᆞ는증거를숨고쟈 ᄒᆞᆷ이라긔쟈는아모긔셔든지긔 쟤ᄒᆞᆷ을되쟈ᄒᆞ는권리를가졋스 나되쟈ᄒᆞ는리유를말ᄒᆞᆯ터이오 며공즁평화를문란케ᄒᆞ는듯ᄒᆞᆫ 긔셔는의폐히밧지안켓숩나이 다

●본사졔셔이리로신문을미양 우히로분젼ᄒᆞ와히젼부의임의 로젼ᄒᆞ는듯스로민곳에는ᄒᆞ늣게 젼ᄒᆞ기도ᄒᆞ며ᄒᆞ면쳘거슬ᄒᆞᆫ결 에젼ᄒᆞ기도ᄒᆞ며ᄒᆞ아니젼ᄒᆞ는 곳도잇다ᄒᆞ와우리신문을수탕 ᄒᆞ야구람ᄒᆞ시는 쳠군ᄌᆞ의게긍 티ᄒᆞ야미우미안ᄒᆞ옵기로지금 은본젼인을두고미일죵이젼 ᄒᆞ며아니젼ᄒᆞ거나늣게ᄒᆞ거나ᄒᆞᆫ 폐가잇도록ᄒᆞ라ᄒᆞ오니ᄒᆞ야나 젼ᄒᆞ거는흐줏게젼ᄒᆞ는혹뉴시 실이잇스면본사로통긔ᄒᆞ여주심을희망ᄒᆞ옴

관보

메샹쳔일호 평무관뎐신

이월오일

셔 원봉슈범

○승경샹쥬 츅중 리답용

슈원이셔오일

승흥증이흥 정샹표증 벽봉쥬

승경샹표증 동국표증 김병관

승경샹표증 동국표증 리완슈

승경샹표증 동국표증 유흥쥴

승경샹표증 ᄉᆞ표증 김윤비

승경샹표증 동국표증 최샹필

승경샹표증 동국표증 조동쥴

승경샹표증 동국표증 리귀현

이샹오월십일일

○의원면본관 황려조비궁베

○부 민즁식

○형 황려조비궁대부셔쥬임

관ᄉᆞ등 경샹표증 송티현

이샹십일월오일

○의원면본관 북청면보ᄉᆞ쥬

ᄉᆞ 리병즁

○일븍경면보ᄉᆞ쥬ᄉᆞ셔관임관

ᄉᆞ등 ○임황흥면보ᄉᆞ쥬ᄉᆞ김인

빈 ○임흥면보ᄉᆞ쥬ᄉᆞ셔

임관ᄉᆞ등 젼쥬ᄉᆞ 리병즁

○금인 북경면보ᄉᆞ쥬ᄉᆞ

김빈이 흥흥면보ᄉᆞ쥬사 리

병종 이샹십일월이십오일

○의원면본관 동신ᄉᆞ면회과

쥬ᄉᆞ 흥승각

○명공니부등진관셔칙임관일

등경효젼쳬조서칙임관 김규흥

경니부등진관 조병호 ○명

리쟝원셰경제 ○쳑임관ᄉᆞ등

쳑임관ᄉᆞ등 ○명공니부등진관

영돈임관 샹등 ○명쟝례원소경

관ᄉᆞ등 종이표증 조용하 칙임

쳑임관

이샹십일월이십일일

○의원면본관 비셔원승

승규화 동신ᄉᆞ면회과쥬ᄉᆞ

쥬ᄉᆞ 동신ᄉᆞ면회과쥬ᄉᆞ

등신ᄉᆞ면회과쥬ᄉᆞ

ᄉᆞ 김조리

○임비셔원승 과쥬ᄉᆞ

김ᄉᆞ 서쥬판임관륙등

구품규신 ○임등신ᄉᆞ

면회과쥬ᄉᆞ 판임관륙등

조승구 ○명시종원분쥬

구품 ᄒᆞᆼ셕유 구품

김유봉 면경

○명니쟝원소관경샹남도등쳐

티쟝토군보병졍위 리영관

○명니쟝원소관젼라북도등쳐

관 진위대이히트대샹대티대

티쟝토군보병참령 빅남신

○명니쟝원소관젼라남도등쳐

관 한셩졔관소관ᄉᆞ 하규일

○명경샹남도순찰ᄉᆞ 한셩졔

관소슈반관ᄉᆞ 김연식

이샹십이월이일

공뎐등ᄉᆞ

○조서ᄒᆞ야갈아샤디이졀용에 ᄒᆞ번ᄒᆞ고거대ᄒᆞᆫ티탁지ᄉᆞ세예 간중ᄒᆞᆷ을가히칭각지아니ᄒᆞᆯ수 업셔ᄒᆞ이나퇴젼샹만원을ᄂᆞ리 노니샹도감에나노와보니여보 용케ᄒᆞ라ᄒᆞ엿더라

○조셔ᄒᆞ야갈아샤디 경효젼 졔조김규흥을명ᄒᆞ사궁니부등 진관을삼으시고궁니부등진관 조병호를명ᄒᆞ사경효젼제조를 삼으시다

○조셔ᄒᆞ야갈아샤디즁이품리 셰직를명ᄒᆞ사니쟝원경을삼으 시고쟝례원소경민영돈을명ᄒᆞ 사궁니부등진관을삼으시고종 이품조용하를명ᄒᆞ사쟝례원소 경을삼으시다

이샹십이월일일

외보

○경금면당 일본동경조일신 에말ᄒᆞ엿스되청국총리아문에 셔일본녀젼공ᄉᆞ의게조회ᄒᆞ되 북경에서청국샹민중에면당포 를ᄒᆞ는자는자본금십만량이하 가젼자는리탑ᄒᆞ지아니ᄒᆞ는되 이계일본샹민이북경에셔면당 영업을ᄒᆞ야본국샹민의게방히 되니청컨되금ᄒᆞ라ᄒᆞ엿거놀너 젼셰가대답ᄒᆞ되북경에셔한국 사름과며국사름도그와갓흔샹 영에종ᄉᆞᄒᆞ는자잇스나반일그 것을금ᄒᆞ면나도비록샹의면당 영업을금ᄒᆞ겟다ᄒᆞ는고로총 리아문에셔한국공ᄉᆞ와며국공 ᄉᆞ의게그것을금ᄒᆞ라고조회ᄒᆞ 엿는대두곳에셔아즉대답이업 다ᄒᆞ엿더라

○일로뎐쳔 금월십구일샹오 삼시에일본리슌함대가 언티군 티에셔리슌구로가 로젼쳔을 발쥬ᄒᆞ야일본슌양ᄒᆞ 쌍다가 츳차가셔그날샹오시에젼쳐 셔겸수ᄒᆞ니그빈는며국도셤쾨 히관연티거울의블과냥탄즈의

약제로와등이남은고기를실엇 는지라일본사세보라는셔에로 보냇다더라

○일사쳐변 영국돈에글농 신문에말ᄒᆞ엿스되우리영국빈 는청샹에셔졍류될배면모든사 름들이다항망ᄒᆞ거는미국사롬 들은그럿치아니ᄒᆞ지라젼일에 ᄒᆞᆫ미국빈가로국을위ᄒᆞ야몰진 을실고가다가일본사름의게잡 류ᄒᆞᆷ이되엿는되그미국빈의합 쟝이그일본사름을용ᄉᆞ히령젹 ᄒᆞ고그일귀가되우줏소인수ᄒᆞ 며그빈의실은물긴을도로버일 본사름의게엇지찻관리를가ᄒᆞ 더라더라

론셜

교휵을귀랑ᄒᆞᄂᆞᆫ일

○한국에소위인민교휵이라ᄒᆞ 는거시셩취ᄒᆞ엿ᄉᆞ야만흘수업 논지라년구ᄒᆞ엿다는학교에셔 논히티ᄒᆞ는항도들로ᄒᆞ여곰구로 치논바이오즉쓸더업논곳에사 졔ᄒᆞ이요소ᄒᆞᆫ학교라ᄒᆞᄂᆞᆫ학교리켱 ᄒᆞ는것도명식으로만셜시ᄒᆞ야 다만ᄉᆞ쳑만되게ᄒᆞ엿슬ᄲᅮᆫ이요 ᄯᅩ이외에영어와덕어와법어와 일어도각각이학교가잇스되그 교ᄉᆞ된샤름의나라흥ᄉᆞ만ᄒᆞ고방 ᄒᆞ야진보되엿다는학교에셔는 피샹ᄒᆞᆫ셩젼로자유항동ᄒᆞᆯ다ᄒᆞᆯ 이요국중에죵교라던지경치라 던지ᄀᆞᄅᆞ치는학교는우금것업 슨즉그중에중대ᄒᆞ고긴요ᄒᆞᆫ학 교가업게되면아모리ᄒᆞᆫ다ᄒᆞᆫ학 교가잇다ᄒᆞ드티도가히무엇에 쓰리요이날다만학교유지ᄒᆞ기 에수고만될터인즁

근일에소위일본으로유학ᄒᆞᆫ리 보냇다는학도들은관경공부를 을엇더케셩취ᄒᆞ고을는지에인 ᄒᆞᆯ수는업스되응당환국ᄒᆞᄂᆞᆫ날 에는여간학문이라고비ᄒᆞᆫ거시 도리여화가될듯ᄒᆞ지라

일젼에청국신문을본즉샹히에 셔ᄒᆞᆫ피샹ᄒᆞᆫ일이잇기엿는티관 찰수로잇는왕지츈씨가거월십 오일에유로쥬씨의쳥쳡으로모 처에가셔담화ᄒᆞ고도라온일이 잇섯는지라

그후삼구일에ᄒᆞᆫ토리ᄀᆞ졍을드리 간즁그리관쥬인은엽교다만일 본디며운한셩ᄒᆞ나이잇게놀왕

씨의싱각에그사ᄅᆞᆷ잇ᄂᆞᆫ거시조
치아니ᄒᆞ야즉시마차를타고회
졍ᄒᆞ라ᄒᆞᆯ즈음에그학싱이왕씨
의게로향ᄒᆞ야총을노앗ᄂᆞᆫ데다
힝히맛지아니ᄒᆞ야상ᄒᆞᆫ지경은
면ᄒᆞ엿고
그후에그놈을잡아곡절을심사
ᄒᆞᆫ즉이놈이외에도일본단여온당
이여러히잇ᄂᆞᆫ데다른ᄭᅡ닭이아
니라왕씨가아라사를도와반동
ᄒᆞᆫ다ᄂᆞᆫ의사를둠으로죽이랴ᄒᆞᆷ
이라ᄒᆞ고ᄒᆞ엿다ᄒᆞ엿스며
ᄯᅩ계지ᄒᆞᆫ기를젼후로일본가셔
단여온사ᄅᆞᆷ이만ᄒᆞ되이사ᄅᆞᆷ들
은모도일본만도아혁명당의ᄯᅳᆺ
을두며만복경륜이음모비계로
써상인히물을ᄒᆞ랴ᄒᆞᆫ즉이ᄂᆞᆫ당
초에가지아니ᄒᆞᆷ만못ᄒᆞ다ᄒᆞ엿
슨즉
이일은과연엇지ᄒᆞᆫ곡절인지모
를거시구라파나아미리가로가
셔공부ᄒᆞ고온사ᄅᆞᆷ들을불젼ᄃᆡ
모도공부에만쥬의ᄒᆞ야셩취된
사ᄅᆞᆷ이만ᄒᆞ되오즉일본셔공부
ᄒᆞ고온사ᄅᆞᆷ들은자긔노르시나
ᄒᆞ여사ᄅᆞᆷ이나질녀죽인다던지
공연ᄒᆞᆫ혁명ᄒᆞᆯ외차나둘ᄲᅮᆫ인즉
실노한국학싱을일본에유학ᄒᆞᆫ
다ᄂᆞᆫ거시심히위티ᄒᆞᆫ일인지라
아모죠록국중에다엇더케적당
히교휵ᄒᆞᆯ방침을싱각ᄒᆞᄂᆞᆫ거시
대단히죠ᄒᆞᆯ듯ᄒᆞᆫ지라미셩년ᄒᆞᆫ
어린사ᄅᆞᆷ들이다만혈긔소발로
집을엇더케죳토록건축ᄒᆞᆯ생각
은차치ᄒᆞ고회철면져ᄒᆞᆷ파다름
이업슨즉유학ᄒᆞ러보낸거시과
연쓸디업ᄂᆞᆫ일인듯ᄒᆞ도다

잡보

○회민히산 전라북도관찰ᄉᆞ
의면보를거ᄒᆞᆫ즉단발ᄒᆞᆫ자ᄇᆡᆨ여
명이부하에취집ᄒᆞ엿기로본ᄉᆞ
가효유ᄒᆞ야ᄒᆡ산ᄒᆞ게ᄒᆞ엿다ᄒᆞ
엿더라

○슌찰보고 경상북도슌찰ᄉᆞ
홍우셕의보고를거ᄒᆞᆫ즉봉고파
츌ᄒᆞᆫ대구군슈류승영의장젼이
삼만삼쳔팔ᄇᆡᆨ량이오ᄯᅩ슈셰를
람징ᄒᆞ야보고에는제감ᄒᆞᆷ을청
ᄒᆞ고민간에는주지아니ᄒᆞ며온
젼히제몸에만리익ᄒᆞ기를일삼
아만인산을문드니무손공을나
타내고져ᄒᆞᆷ이몃쳔금이나되
논돈을맛츔니혼ᄌᆞ먹어버리고
말만ᄒᆞᆫ죠고ᄒᆞᆫ고을에셔잔민
의지산을휘쓰러먹다가봉고당
ᄒᆞᆯ거슬면키어려오미괴미를면
져알고도망ᄒᆞ니더옥히파당
ᄒᆞᆫ고로방붓쳐ᄇᆡᆨ셩의게효유
ᄒᆞ고그간리들을티벌식여가두
워두엇다ᄒᆞ엿더라

○봉고주본 전라북도슌찰ᄉᆞ
박졔빈씨의주본을거ᄒᆞᆫ즉졍읍
군슈윤익의병은일ᄒᆞᄂᆞᆫ거슬다쳡
의게셔드러병고위령은간리들
의게맛겨ᄒᆞ야졍례가훼손ᄒᆞᆫ민
위션봉ᄒᆞ고니급히면관ᄒᆞ고죠
쳐ᄒᆞ라ᄒᆞ고부안군슈장영의씨
도봉고파직ᄒᆞ엿다ᄒᆞ엿더라

○위원미졍 법부에셔외부에
죠회ᄒᆞ되원히판ᄉᆞ에셔외국인치폐
ᄉᆞ로평리원ᄒᆞᆫ엿더니태명시를파송
ᄒᆞ야심평리원ᄒᆞ엿더니명의병
이홀연위ᄌᆞ케ᄒᆞ야뎡졍키어렵기
에본부참셔관죠회영을쥬픔
ᄒᆞ고원으로졍ᄒᆞ야장찻불일
등졍ᄒᆞ겟기이에죠회ᄒᆞᆫ다ᄒᆞ엿
더라

○훈칙보호 외부에셔젼라경
샹량도각군슈의게훈령ᄒᆞ기를
경셩에쥬차ᄒᆞᆫ일공ᄉᆞ공합니ᄀᆡ
에농샹무기ᄉᆞ본젼힝ᄀᆡ와삼셩
문일랑등륙인은젼라경샹량도
로더와밋농산시찰로농무기ᄉᆞ
에졍샹회지죠와공학ᄉᆞ에신산
민죠이인은히량도광산시찰ᄎᆞ
로히디에젼왕ᄒᆞᆯ터이니만일히
원등이히디경에도달ᄒᆞ거든보
호ᄒᆞ라ᄒᆞ엿더라

○경산군슈보고 경산군슈가
외부로보고ᄒᆞ기를귀부훈령을
졉ᄒᆞᆫ즉닉기에경부텰도션이경
산만촌과ᄆᆡᆺ신동등디로지나ᄂᆞᆫ
바큰돌을길가온디다가뎌져위
협ᄒᆞᆯ셔두려우니각면인민의게
신칙ᄒᆞ야텰도샹에손히ᄒᆞᆷ이업
게ᄒᆞ라ᄒᆞ엿기만촌파신동을죠
사ᄒᆞᆫ즉만촌파신동이본군디경
이아니오만촌은대구에미엿고
신촌은쳥도군에미인고로이에
보고ᄒᆞᆫ다ᄒᆞ엿더라

○대관소슈 젼쥬ᄉᆞ김졍호씨
가승 후ᄉᆞ운동을열심쥬션ᄒᆞ더
일잔모대관이소슈가되야샹소
ᄒᆞᆫ다더라

○리씨거송 참위리갑씨가부
쟝민영휘씨와젼답ᄉᆞ건으로륙
군법원에거졍ᄒᆞᆯ러인ᄃᆡ법원에
셔ᄂᆞᆫ민씨가문관시에샹관ᄒᆞᆫ일
이오ᄯᅩ민ᄉᆞ인즉본원에셔밧을
리유가업다ᄒᆞ엿더라

○량관젼임 탁지참셔관민영
오씨ᄂᆞᆫ지무관으로젼임ᄒᆞ고그
ᄃᆡ에젼참리관신히영씨가피임
ᄒᆞ엿더라

○관졔리졍 관졔리졍소에셔
ᄂᆞᆫ졔를밧장리졍즁인ᄃᆡ닉부에
ᄂᆞᆫᄉᆞ십명쥬ᄉᆞ를십팔인만두고
탁지부쥬ᄉᆞᄂᆞᆫ칠십명을이십명
만두고농샹공부ᄂᆞᆫ혁파ᄒᆞ야농
무일국만락지부에부치고법부
쥬ᄉᆞ이십인은십인으로두고군
부에ᄂᆞᆫ쥬ᄉᆞ오인만두고각진위
ᄃᆡᄂᆞᆫ폐ᄒᆞ야버리고경각ᄃᆡ에ᄂᆞᆫ
궐을ᄯᅡ라보직치말기로ᄒᆞ고각
관쳥속ᄉᆞᄂᆞᆫ폐지ᄒᆞ고 궁닉부
소쇽관졔ᄂᆞᆫ아즉착슈치못ᄒᆞ엿
다더라

○디방졔도 디방졔도리졍셜
도리졍ᄒᆞ야십ᄇᆡᆨ륙십군을일ᄇᆡᆨ
오십군으로감ᄒᆞ야졍ᄒᆞ고관찰
부ᄂᆞᆫ동ᄉᆞ남북즁앙으로셜치ᄒᆞ
기로회의ᄒᆞᆫ다더라

○졍계ᄎᆞ회동 원소화소구역
을졍계ᄒᆞᆯᄎᆞ로오일에닉부대신
파경긔관찰ᄉᆞ와한셩판윤과양
쥬군슈가원소로회동ᄒᆞ엿다더
라

○졍부회의안건 오일하오훈
시에졍부에셔회의ᄒᆞᆫ안건은각
쥬임관임면과각경비예산외지
츌ᄉᆞ건파인쇄국을탁지부에셜
립ᄒᆞᆯᄉᆞ건이라더라

○공진회광고문 동양학문에
왈ᄇᆡᆨ셩이나라에근본이니근본
이굿어야나라가편안ᄒᆞ다ᄒᆞ엿
고서양학문가에셔말ᄒᆞ기를인
민은정부에본체라ᄒᆞ며ᄯᅩ골ᄋᆞ
ᄃᆡ인민은정부에예비라ᄒᆞ엿스
니인민의즁ᄒᆞᆷ은일로미루여가
히싱각ᄒᆞᆯ터이온ᄃᆡ향일본회지
취를쳐음에ᄂᆞᆫ상민취지라ᄒᆞ고
최종에ᄂᆞᆫ진명회취지라ᄒᆞ엿스
니외면으로보면샹민진명이
오기타ᄉᆞ룡공병은서로간셥아
니ᄒᆞᄂᆞᆫ듯의심ᄒᆞ야혐의홈이불
무ᄒᆞ고본회문명ᄒᆞ라든처음마
암이크게유감ᄒᆞ옵기본회일홈
을공진이라개졍ᄒᆞ야ᄉᆞ룡공샹
병으로ᄒᆞ야곰합셰문명ᄒᆞᄂᆞᆫᄃᆡ
나가게ᄒᆞ노니ᄯᅳᆺ잇ᄂᆞᆫ모든군ᄌᆞ
ᄂᆞᆫ이회에명의을죠량ᄒᆞ야다본
회에드시기를바란다ᄒᆞ엿ᄂᆞᆫᄃᆡ
륙일하오일시에특별회를셜힝
ᄒᆞ엿다더라

뎐보

청도최근발 십이월일일

○일병퇴각 거월삼십일에일
병이려슌구룰엄습ᄒᆞ다가ᄉᆞ방
으로몰녀셔오졍새에일병이대
패ᄒᆞ야퇴각ᄒᆞ엿더라

동디발 동일

○려슌형편 려슌의긴요ᄒᆞᆫ쳐
쇼ᄂᆞᆫ아즉로인의슈즁에잇ᄂᆞᆫ지
라거월이십팔구일에일병이엄
습ᄒᆞ다가물니침이되엿더라

동디발 동일

○이소젹즁 거월이십ᄉᆞ일노
브터이십칠일ᄭᆞ지로쟝렌벤캄
푸씨가쟈긔진즁에엄습ᄒᆞ야오
ᄂᆞᆫ일병을물니첫ᄂᆞᆫ대로병보다
일병이대단이만엇다더라

동디발 동일

○히륙겸임 구로파도긴대쟝
이로국륙히군총ᄉᆞ령관에피임
ᄒᆞ엿더라

동디발 동일

○로션피집 로국의훈싱명구
졔션이거월십륙일에려슌구에
셔ᄲᅥ나셔이십이일에위히위에
도박ᄒᆞ엿ᄂᆞᆫ대영국사람이그비
들잡은지라잡혀잇ᄂᆞᆫ그비의ᄉᆞ
관이긴요ᄒᆞᆫ통신을가진줄노밋
ᄂᆞᆫ다더라

론돈발 십일월이십오일

덕법분담 ᄇᆡᆨ림은ᄒᆡᆼ가들은
이쳔만파리은ᄒᆡᆼ가들은삼쳔만
방의로국외채를ᄇᆡᆨ오변에담당
ᄒᆞ야오쳔만방놀오년과칠년에
필보ᄒᆞ기로ᄒᆞ고닉년일월브터
모집ᄒᆞᆫ다더라

동디발 동월이십칠일

○로션환귀 불티함디종션들
은지금쳐벅이라ᄂᆞᆫᄯᅡ에잇ᄂᆞᆫ대
오랜이라ᄂᆞᆫ비가샹ᄒᆞᆫᄭᆞ닭에리
보로도라간다더라

북경발 동월이십팔일

○로ᄉᆞ쳥구 쥬쳥로국공ᄉᆞ렛
사씨가쳥졍에쳥구ᄒᆞ되봉텬도
대졍셔란의위인이부죡ᄒᆞ니불
너오라ᄒᆞ엿더라

당디군ᄉᆞ령부착뎐

○평졍산소젼 십이월일일오
젼구시에평졍산에셔흥왕묘에
향ᄒᆞ야젹귀병이ᄇᆡᆨ명이공격ᄒᆞ
야왓스나우리군ᄉᆞ의일부ᄂᆞᆫ즉
시격퇴ᄒᆞ엿더라

○범구쇼젼 십이월ᄉᆞ일오젼
륙시ᄉᆞ십분에젹보병약일쇼ᄃᆡ
가닉구ᄌᆞ[함챵셔북편이라]부
근에잇ᄂᆞᆫ우리부ᄃᆡ에ᄃᆡᄒᆞ야ᄆᆡᆼ
렬ᄒᆞᆫ샤격을시작ᄒᆞ엿스나교젼
후에이거슬격퇴ᄒᆞ엿다더라

○왜두산쇼젼 십이월삼일밤
에왜두산날ᄌᆞ보부근에젹보병
약이삼즁ᄃᆡ가와셔엄습ᄒᆞ엿스
나이거슬격퇴ᄒᆞ엿더라

○고가자졈령 동일오젼이시
에우리군ᄉᆞ에일부ᄂᆞᆫ고가자의
젹을북방으로격퇴ᄒᆞ고이거슬
졈령ᄒᆞ야동디촌락을불티버리
엿ᄂᆞᆫᄃᆡ동디ᄂᆞᆫ괴관포약일문을
가진젹의보병약일즁ᄃᆡ의졈거
ᄒᆞ던쳐소러라

TELEGRAMS.

Tokyo, Dec. 5.

A two days armistice has been arranged at Port Arthur to enable both forces to bury their dead.

Tokyo, Dec. 5th.

At Vladivostok, although the harbor has frozen over, it has not yet been found necessary to use ice breakers. It is said that the report that the "Gromovoi" had struck a rock and been partially disabled is confirmed.

Army Hedquarters.

At 9 a. m. on December 1st about 100 Russian cavalry attacked the Japanese force near Pingchiangsan, but were immediately repulsed.

At 6. 40 a. m, on the 4th inst a body of Russian infantry opened a rifle fire on the Japanese force near Kiauchang, but after a sharp fight were repulsed.

At night on the 3rd inst two companies of Russian infantry attacked the Japanese force near Waitusan and were also repulsed.

At 2 a. m. on December 3rd, the Japanese force drove the Russians out of Hochatze and burnt down that village.

(These reports all refer to skirmishes on the Japanese lines of communication, south of their main army in Manchuria. Ed. K. D. N.)

Tokyo. Dec. 5th.

Six Russian men-of-war, seven destroyers and nine transports have anchored outside the harbor of Djibouti.

THE JAPANESE IN CHINA.

FROM CHINA PAPERS.

The Japanese Minister has sent a despatch to the Minister of the Board of Foreign Affairs complaining of the numerous complaints which have been received against the doings of certain Koreans, who have cut their hair short and, in European dress, have been posing as Japanese.

The Japanese Minister requests that a census of those Koreans be taken by the Chinese Government in order to prevent trouble and misidentification in the future.

The Japanese Minister has asked permission of the Wai Wu Pu for a certain Japanese official to investigate the office for the Control of Mongolian Affairs.

Owing to the complaints which have been received regarding the conduct of the Japanese in the employment of the camphor monopolists of Fokien province it is reported that the Central Government is about to cancel the agreement with the Japanese, and undertake the management and control of this lucrative business itself assisted by Japanese experts.

It is reported that the Central Government proposes to introduce changes in the Government similar to those of Korea. All Ministers to foreign countries and all the Ministers and officials of boards who have dealings with foreigners will, it is said, be ordered to dress in foreign style. This change will not affect the other Ministers and officials.

In addition to their desire to appoint Mr. Hitewara adviser to the Educational Department, the powers that be are now said to be endeavouring to appoint Mr. Takahashi assistant adviser.

Owing to the persistent efforts of the Il Chin Hoi to obtain the release of two Chin Po Hoi people, imprisoned by the governor of North Chulla province, the Home Office have at last caved in and ordered the governor to let them go. The worthy governor however is made of sterner stuff and positively refuses to release one of the men, who, he asserts, threatened one of his officers with a drawn sword.

The "Japan Mail" says the "Japan Herald" is very angry because one of "our Yokohama contemporaries" recently declared that Prince Fushimi had gone to America to arrange a foreign loan. We wonder which paper it was? "It is," the "Mail" gracefully adds, "occasionally very difficult to fathom the depths of silliness in which some of the news mongers of this Settlement wallow, but we doubt whether the record is not permanetly broken by this fiction of an Imperial Prince going abroad to raise a loan." This is a very fine sentence, worthy of the "Mail" at its best, but is not the metaphor a little over drawn? What is a depth of silliness, and how do you wallow in it when it is so difficult to fathom it? Wallowing, we thought, was generally conducted in shallow water and not in places where you can break records in fathoming depths. Moreover is not the "Mail" rather confused in its grammar? According to its statement a record in fathoming the depths of silliness in which the journalists (for this is how we translate "news-mongers") of this city wallow has been broken. This is what the "Mail" says, but we have an idea it is not what it intended to say. Logically the sentence has no subject because the "Mail" does not tell us who has broken the record. The journalists of this town wallow in depths of silliness, and somebody has obligingly come forward and fathomed these depths. Can it be the "Mail" itself? It certainly displays a curiously complete knowledge of the subject. Who, moreover, was the gentleman who established the record? Probably the "Mail" does not include itself among the "news-mongers" and in this it will find many to agree with it. At all events one of the newspapers of this city has made the "Mail" very angry, and not being able to reply directly it has got in a kick under the table. This will teach our contemporary, whoever it may be, to be more careful, and to pay more attention to the guaranteed information which is served up daily to the readers of the "Mail," The "Mail," as is well known, is the only true source of information, and the other Yokohama papers would do well to sit at its feet, or lie in its eyes, or whatever other metaphor is most suitable, and humbly repeat the crumbs of wisdom that appear in its sheets. They will thus learn that it is only a pure coincidence that Prince Fushimi happened to be in America at the time a loan was being floated, and that it is only another coincidence that the encouraging words of President Roosevelt to Japan were published at the time the lists were open.

His Majesty has paid Y5,000 towards compensation to the owners of houses, which may have to be removed to facilitate the progress of the Crown Princess' funeral procession.

The "Daito Shimpo" is still managing the Russian invasion in the northeast. Our Japanese contemporary has now dispensed with Russian scouts and has put Russian soldiers into winter clothing, and quarters.

If there in one thing the Russians know how to do well it is to keep warm in the winter. A St. Petersburg despatch announces that 225,000 sheep skin and fur suits for the troops in Manchuria have already reached the front.

The Foreign Office have instructed the Magistrates of all districts in the Chulla and Kyeungsang provinces to afford special facilities to six Japanese engineers, who are shortly proceeding north to inspect the agricultural and mining possibilities of the country.

An unexpected "denouement" was arrived at today in the case of the Prefect of Kangwha, who it will be remembered was charge with oppression and excessive taxation of the people of his district. Last night 50 countrymen from Kangwha arrived in Seoul and begged that the Prefect should not be dismissed, asseverating that the charges against him are entirely false and that he is the best man they have ever had.

APPALLING SLAUGHTER AT PORT ARTHUR

The subject of Port Arthur has dropped almost completely out of the Japanese inspired papers to-day, writes the last "China Gazette." There is no mention of it in either the foreign or Chinese press, and we are left in complete darkness as to how long the Japanese remained on the "crest of the counterscarp" after they had reached it on the 30th ult. But this painful silence on the subject ever since certainly goes to show that they did not stay there for long, having been doubtless blown to pieces by the Russian guns in the impregnable forts, not one of which was reached by the Japanese and which stand as strong, and proudly defiant as ever today.

From an authoritative quarter, whose sources of information are unique and undoubted, we learn to-day that the grand birthday attack upon the Russian fortress has cost the besieging forces the heaviest losses they have yet sustained in the war, almost as much as Liaoyang and the Shaho combined. Indeed the figures are so enormous that without knowing the unlimited resources in means for destroying human life possessed by this grim outpost of Russian power, one could hardly credit such losses as we are assured the Japanese sustained before they gave up in blank despair on the night of the 2nd inst. the terrific and useless waste of their best troops, who were mowed down by the sheltered Russians or blown up by mines for seven days and nights, almost without intermission.

We are assured that from the commecement of the attack up to the time when our informant's advices left Dalny the Japanese had lost the enormous number of 42,000 men in killed and wounded. And all without taking a single fort of permanent construction or making any real progress with the task in hand.

Our informant had no means of getting even the roughest idea of Russian losses.

So discouraged were the Japanese with this result that they slackened their fire and rested from further attacks early on the morning of the 3rd—the Emperor's birthday—which was ushered in upon a scene of carnage and a half of their number.

The wearied troops then rested from sheer exhaustion, having lost between a third and a half of their number.

The news is confirmed by advices which reached us yesterday from Japan, to the effect that reinforcements to the strength of over two divisions, or more than 40,000 men have been hurried off in the last couple of days from Japan to Dalny to fill up the gaps caused by the terrific slaughter of the previous week. These reserves consist of the last veterans of the Chino-Japan war i. e. men between 34 and 42 years of age.

The tenth anniversary of the taking of Port Arthur by the Japanese from the Chinese and is now past and gone (21st) we have no news of any great feat in the present war to commemorate that memorable date. The difference between then and now is remarkable.

The Chin Myeng Hoi society held a meeting on Saturday, when it was discovered that they really mean business. Some really sensible measures of reform were put forward, which seem far more practical and pleasant than the empty vapourings of the Il Chin Hoi Society.

One of the Il Chin Hoi's shining lights, Mr. Kang Chai In, has despatched a weighty letter to the President of state, advising him to resign, as the attitude taken up by the Government in certain matters does not meet with the wishes of the Il Chin Hoi. Presumably Mr. Kang means that his and the Il Chin Hoi's "employers" are not exactly pleased with the fact that the Government does not always do everything that they are told to by the powers that reign over the Il Chin Hoi.

It is some three years ago that ping-pong was devastating London, and now it has so utterly disappeared that perhaps it may be necessary to state that the queer compound word was the name of a sort of indoor lawn tennis played upon a table. Three years ago every home was littered with little hollow celluloid balls which were never to be found when wanted, and which invariably got trodden upon by the heads of the family at the most unexpected moments. Not only young men and maidens, but middleaged celebrities who had lost whatever Apollo-like grace they once possessed, used to grovel under the tables, or fish with landing-nets for the elusive balls. Every third shop was full of immature rackets and inflated quinine pills, and from every open window came the monotonous ping-pong from which the occupation derived its name. Every parish had its champion, but now all these heroes are, in their ping-pong incarnation, as dead as Julius Cæsar, and have vanished like the snows of yester year. But all rackets and balls cannot have dissolved into thin air. Somewhere beyond the outermost ring of London there must be a rubbish heap where the tons of indestructible celluloid which went to make up the myriads of balls must be slowly turning into dust. Ping-pong was the lion of a season, and then disappeared, leaving, like Swedish Charles, "the name at which the world grew pale, to point a moral or adorn a tale."—The Globe.

The Railway Bureau is collecting assistant engineers, firemen, etc., among employees of the Government and private railways. These men, say Tokyo papers, will be employed on the East China, Seoul-Fusan and Seoul-Wiju Railways.

The "Messenger of the Manchurian Army" states that the report, in the foreign press, that the Russian war-correspondent W. Nemirovitch-Dantchenko received orders to leave the seat of war, is without any foundation.

Mr. Stevens is to leave Kobe for Seoul on the 12th inst. He will be accompanied by Mr. Hagiwara, who leaves, Tokyo on the 10th

The Korea Daily News.

Issued at 5 P. M. daily except Sundays.

Rate of Subscription:—
Per Year,............Yen 25.
Per Quarter,..........Yen 7.
Per Month,..........Yen 2.50.

Postage in Korea not charged extra.
Postage abroad charged extra.

Advertisements,, 50 sen per day for 1 inch or less.
5 yen per month per inch.
50 yen per year per inch.

All communications to

E. T. BETHELL,
Editor and Publisher,
Pak-tong, Seoul.

SECRET SOCIETIES.

Yesterday we discussed Count Okuma's speech in so far as his remarks had any bearing upon the conditions inside Japan. Today we will deal with his strictures upon her Diplomatic progress; that is to say the progress that Japanese Ambassadors, Ministers, Consuls, other representatives and common people have made in countries other than their own.

Let us commence with Great Britain. "Peace with honour" was the way in which one of Great Britain's greatest statesman laid down the policy of the greatest Empire the world has yet seen. Off and on with varying success Great Britain has followed the policy laid down by Disraeli. When Great Britain entered into the arrangement which is now known in the Far East as the Anglo-Japanese alliance it is quite certain that Peace was Great Britain's object, and it seems equally certain that, at that time, Great Britain thought that Japan's ideas corresponded. So far as that agreement is concerned Japan has already violated it, and, if on apportunity occurs she will violate it still further, in Korea. In the meantime Great Britain has done more for Japan than she was compelled to do and we find that, still unsatisfied, Viscount Hayashi and Baron Suyematsu are now informing the world that they are not satisfied with the behavior of the rest of Europe.

The protest of course amounts to nothing because it bore upon the accommodation afforded to the Baltic Fleet and the Baltic Fleet is already clear of Europe.

Regarding America little has to be said; America promised nothing but has, from the outset of the war, made it very clear that she has certain commercial rights which she wishes to remain intact. Prince Fushimi's visit was of no significance so far as any alteration in America's diplomatic attitude to the belligerents was concerned. America fortunately is only a spectator of this war and it is certain now that she will continue to be a spectator.

The Japanese press, aided by the "London Times," "Japan Mail" and other interested newspapers have been busy discovering "bogeys" all over Europe, and whatever friends Japan may have had to start with are probably now alienated by her petulant protests when ever everything does not go quite according to her liking.

Now let us turn our attention to Asia; to the seat of war. Of Japan's diplomacy in Korea we can only say—and we speak advisedly and after consideration —nothing could be worse. Whose fault it is we cannot say, but between the people who originally guaranteed the Independence and Integrity of this Empire and the progressists who now almost openly advocate the annexation of Korea by Japan there are many parties which hold and proselitize views widely divergent from Japan's original promises. Count Okuma criticizes Japanese diplomacy in Korea but it is not clear whether his remarks were aimed at Japan's past, present or future policy. Still it does not matter much, as so far as we can see, all are equally mistaken, fundamentally rotten and futile.

There is another point which is daily growing more significant. We have from time to time written about the Il-chin-hoi which is a Society of vagabonds fostered and fed by the Japanese army headquarters here. We take some credit to ourselves for having taken at least some of the wind out of the sails of these professional agitators, but we regret to find that Mr. Komochi (or somebody like him) is not confining his energies to Korea.

A similar society flourishes in China and the name of it is the Ai-kok-hui. Ai-kok-hui means League of Patriots, and there is little difference between this society and the one which is being so tenderly nursed by the Japanese authorities in Korea. Infact there is very little difference, andthe two societies seem to be on the same level of mercenary subserviency to their paymasters.

Speaking of the Ai-kok-hui the "China Gazette" says:—It is an organised society of revolutionists, composed principally of the returned students from Japan. The society, according to the documents seized by the Police, is intensely anti-foreign and anti-dynastic. It aims at the destruction by force and a sudden rising, of all white men in China, as well as the overturning of the Mauchu rule. It was organized in Tokyo with the assistance and guidance of the party in Japan which has done so much for the extension of Japanese interest in Peking, Shanghai and varions parts of China. Almost every one, without evception, of the Chinese students sent in recent years to Japan by the Chinese provinces is a member of the society, which has a throughly military organization. Some of its members in the Foreign Settlement in Shang-hai go openly about in a semi-foreign military uniform, many of them wearing breeches with the broad yellow or gold stripe of the Japanese military pattern. So far as we can gather the place raided in Avenue Road is only one of the very small centres, the larger being situated in Park Road and other places. Our information goes to show that they have accumulated large quantities of arms, especially revolvers imported through an American house, and rifles sold by a well, known Japanese commercial firm. And again referring to a raid on a house in the Shanghai settlement used as a rendezvous by the society the "China Gazette" continues;—

It is understood that documents of a very compromising character have since been found by the Police in the house, connecting its occupants with the secret society known as the "Ai Koh hui" (League of Patriots) who recently caused disturbances in Honan from which the foreign missionaries had to flee, while some documents in Japanese written by some unknown Japanese organiser laying down the rules of the Society and giving instructions to its members, were also discovered by the Police in their search in connection with the case. But great pressure will no doubt be exerted quietly to hush up this phase of the business. The search was made yesterday about noon by Mr. McEuen of the Police.

It is reported among rhe natives that the men at present in custody of the Police belong to the same gang that caused a lot of trouble to Viceroy Chang Chih Tung in 1900 and again quite recently. Several of them were caught, including the son of the Governor Tan of Honan and were executed in 1900 in Hankow. The headquart ers of the Society are here in Shanghai, with branches all along the Yangtse River.

Now whatever purposes the "Il-Chin-hoi in Korea and the Ai-kok-hui in China may be ultimately intended to serve, it must be very plain to all that they accomplish at least one thing, and that is the destruction of all confidence in Japan's protecstions of sincerity in dealings with Korea and China.

Even if by the aid of the machinations of these Societies, Japan succeeds in gaining some sort of temporary foothold in China and Korea, it can surely be only a temporary one and as soon as Japan's power is felt to be on the wane, China and Korea will both turn and stamp out these pestilential Societies and Japanese Diplomacy will be discredited for ever. So that it is not a matter for surprise when we find Count Okuma apprehensive with regard to Japan's prospects in China and Korea.

The "oldest man in the world" is one Bruno Cotrim, who has drowsed away 150 of the most stirring and eventful years in the history of mankind down in sleepy old Rio Janeiro, Brazil. He was a boy of 11 years when the first colonial congress assembled, 14 when Cook circumnavigated the globe; a young man of 20 when Watt produced the first practical steam engine; 21 when it ended; 42 when Washington declined a third term; 50 when the first locomotive was put in use and when Napoleon reached the zenith of his glory, and was crowned emperor of the French; 53 when Fulton was running his first steamboat; 60 when Waterloo was fought; 80 when Spain abolished the Inquisition; 83 when Texas became independent, Morse took out his patent for an electric telegraph and Victoria was made queen of England; 85 when photography was invented; 103 when the first Atlantic cable was laid; 106 when the Lincoln was elecfed president, 107 when the civil war broke out: and 122 when Bell was showing the telephone at the centennial in Philadelphia

---

The Army Reorganisation Department is considering the suggestion from certain quarters that the troops should be educated. It is said that there will be no true patriotism until this is done, and that the quickest way to attain the desired end is to write a special book on military matters and the Russo-Japan war for circulation amongst the troops.

A general resignation of cabinet Ministers is prophesied to take place in a few days. The ubiquitous Vice President of State, Mr. Sin Ki Son, is said to be the puller of wires, which will bring about this event.

The Finance Department have requested all government offices to hand in the orignal copies of their compilations for next year's budget before the 5th inst.

The Il Chin Hoi have instructed the Chin Po Hoi to alter their name to Il Chin Hoi branch society, as these two illustrious concerns are now amalgamated.

The Korea Daily News.

VOL. I, TUESDAY, DECEMBER 6, 1904. No. 118

HONGKONG & SHANGHAI
BANKING CORPORATION.

Paid-up Capital.....	$10,000,000
Reserve Fund:—Sterling Reserve...	10,000,000
Silver Reserve.....	7,000,000
	27,000,000
Reserve Liability of Proprietors...	10,000,000

HEAD OFFICE, HONGKO G

London Bankers, London a unty
Banking Company Li ite
Branches and Ager es
London.

Amoy,	Hankow	Penang,
Bangkok	Hiogo,	Rangoon,
Batavia,	Iloilo,	Saigon,
Bombay,	Lyons,	San Francisco,
Calcutta,	Manila,	Singapore,
Colombo,	Nagasaki,	Sourabaya,
Foochow,	New York,	Tientsin,
Hamburg,	Peking,	Yokohama,

Credits granted on approved Securities, and every description of Banking and Exchange business transacted.

Drafts granted on London and the chief Commercial places in Europe, India, Australia, America, China and Japan.

HOLME RINGER & CO., AGENTS,
CHEMULPO.

ON CHEONG & CO.,
SEOUL.
GENERAL STORE KEEPERS.
Imported provisions, Cooking Utensils
Crockery, etc.
FRESH BREAD DAILY.

MITSU BISHI DOCKYARD & ENGINE WORKS,
NAGASAKI.

CODE WORD, "DOCK."

A 1, A. B. C., and Engineering Codes used.

DOCK No. 1 (at Tategami)

Extreme Length...............	523 feet
Length on blocks	513 ,,
Width of Entrance on Top......	89 ,,
,, ,, Bottom....	77 ,,
Water on Blocks at Spring Tide	26½ ,,

DOCK No. 2 (Mukaijima).

Extreme Length..............	371 feet
Length on Blocks.............	360 ,,
Width of Entrance on Top......	66 ,,
,, ,, Bottom	53 ,,
Water on Blocks at Spring Tide	22 ,,

PATENT SLIP (at Kosuge)

Can take vessels up to 1,000 tons gross.

THE WORKS are well equipped with the LATEST IMPROVEMENTS, and can execute any kind of work in SHIPBUILDING and MARINE ENGINEERING, as well as in REPAIRING of SHIPS.

The COMPANY'S new powerfu steamer OURA-MARU (712 tons, 700 I.H.P.), specially built for SALVAGE PURPOSES, and equipped with necessary gear, is always READY at SHORT NOTICE.

CHARTERED BANK OF INDIA
AUSTRALIA & CHINA

INCORPORATED BY ROYAL CHARTER 1853

HEAD OFFICES:—LONDON.

Paid-up Capital	£800,000
Reserve Liability of Shareholders	800,000
Reserve Fund	800,000

Drafts granted upon all the principal places in the world and every description of Exchange and banking business transacted.

E. MEYER & CO., Agents,
Chemulpo.

E. MEYER & CO.
Chemulpo.

SOLE AGENTS IN KOREA FOR:

A. T. Morse, Sons & Co's
"Fresco" Distemper

In all colours ready for use on walls, Ceilings etc.

and

AVENARIUS CARBOLINEUM

A wood-preserving and antiseptic oil preparation

Against decay, dry-rot, fungus and wood-destroying insects.

A large supply always in Stock.
Prices upon application.

E. MEYER & CO.,
Chemulpo.

THE METHODIST
PUBLISHING HOUSE,
Little West Gate, Seoul.

JOB PRINTING, TYPEWRITER PAPER
CARBON PAPER, VISITING CARDS
STATIONERY, BOOK BINDING
BOOK PUBLISHERS
AMERICAN SCHOOL BOOKS
SPENCERIAN COPY BOOKS
PEN CARBON LETTER AND BILL BOOKS

S. A. BECK, Manager.

HOKURKU DOBOKU KAISHA.

Branch office in Chong Dong, Seoul.

Japanese telephone No. 165

CONTRACT DEPARTMENT.

We can contract to build any building or construction.

MERCHANDISE DEPARTMENT.

We can provide any building material. We have just contracted to build the new Belgian Legation.

DAI-ICHI GINKO.

LIMITED.

(Formerly the First National Bank)

ESTABLISHED 1873

INCORPORATED UNDER PRESENT LAW 1896

Capital - - - - - - - - - -	Yen 5,000,000
Reserve Fund - . - - -	1,500,000

HEAD OFFICE:—TOKIO.

President: Baron SHIBUSAWA.

BRANCHES AND CORRESPONDENTS
In the Principal Cities and Towns of Japan.
Interest Allowed on

Fixed deposits 1 year - - -	6½	per cent
" " 6 months - - -	6	per cent

Special current accounts 1½ sen daily per Y 100
General " " 1 " " " 100

M. TANAKA,
Manager, Chemulpo.

SINGER
SEWING
MACHINES

씽거조봉침

SOLE AGENTS
FOR KOREA
젼매쇼

HOLME RINGER & CO.
Chemulpo.

졔물포 함릉거양힝

KAMEYA & CO.
GENERAL STOREKEEPERS
Chinkokai - - Seoul

(Established 1895, Tokyo)

Confectionery, Hams, Canned Goods, Cutlery, Hirano & Tansan Water. Provisions, Gents, Furnishing goods, Toilet Articles, Travelling Bags, Tobacco, Cigars & Cigarettes Kitchen Utensils. Coffee, Biscuits

Fresh Goods always kept in Stock.
Prices Moderate
Please come and inspect our goods

NIPPON YUSEN KAISHA.

JAPANESE MAIL STEAMSHIP CO.

UNDER MAIL CONTRACT WITH THE IMPERIAL JAPANESE GOVERNMENT.

European Line

Regular Fortnightly Service between Yokohama Kobe, Moji, Shanghai, Hongkong, Singapore, Penang Colombo, Port Said, Marseilles, London and Antwerp

American Line

Regular Fortnightly Service between Hongkong and Seattle, calling at Shanghai, Moji, Kobe, Yokohama and Victoria, B. C.

Australian Line

Regular weekly Service betwen Japan Ports and Australia, calling at Hongkong and Manila.

(Above Three Lines Suspended until further notice).

Shanghai Line

Weekly Service between Shanghai and Japan Ports

Korea Line

Service Kobe, Moji, Nagasaki, Fusan Chemulpo Chefoo, Taiku.
S. S. Babelsberg, 2181 tons.
Service Kobe, Moji, Fusan, Chemulpo, Chinnampo
S. S. ARGO, S. S. Ohio.

BORDEN'S
CONDENSED
MILK CO.
New York, U. S. A.

ALWAYS IN STOCK

Eagle Brand Condensed Milk.

Gold Seal Condensed Milk.

Peerless (Family) Evaporated Cream.

Borden's Malted Milk.

E. MEYER & CO.
Chemulpo, Korea,
Sole Agents

ROYAL INSURANCE COMPANY,
Funds exceed £10,000,000
FIRE
AT CURRENT RATES.
LIFE
REDUCED PREMIUM.
HOLME RINGER & CO.,
Agents, Chemulpo.

HOTEL DU
PALAIS
SEOUL.

The only first class Hotel in Seoul Situated in the centre of the city opposite the palace.

Cuisine under the supervision of an experienced French Chef.

Well ventilated and furnished throughout.

TARIFF UPON APPLICATION

L. MARTIN
Proripetor and Manager

大韓每日申報
대한매일신보

(뎨일백십구호)　　(목요일)　　(일천구백사년십이월팔일)

본사고백

이신보ᄂᆞᆫ영어와한어로셔거리
일출판ᄒᆞᆷ
신문가
한장　엽두돈오푼
일삭표　엽두량닷돈
우표가리삭닷돈
다닷돈으로밧습
광고료ᄂᆞᆫ
귀한의쟝단과ᄎᆞ항의다쇼로중
감ᄒᆞ되렴가로밧을터이오며오
리지아녀대한사람마다다이신
문을보실터이니광고내시기를
원ᄒᆞ시ᄂᆞᆫ이들은우리신문사에
와서면약ᄒᆞ심을희망ᄒᆞᆷ
○발힝소　뎐동대한미일신보
사발힝과편집ᄒᆞᄂᆞᆫ쳥영국인셜필
림쟝자리오
사쟝 영국인 (비셜)
평양 티리졈
○평양효동사ᄂᆞᆫ권미보씨로우
리신문관미티리인을뒤졍ᄒᆞ엿
시ᄉᆞ오니평양에계신구람코져ᄒᆞ
시ᄂᆞᆫ　쳠군ᄌᆞᄂᆞᆫ히티리졈에왕
림ᄒᆞ와면의ᄒᆞ시옵

사고

○우리대한미일신보의목뎍은
대한의안녕질서에관한모든대
목에티ᄒᆞ야ᄂᆞᆫ공평한변론을쥬
장홈이라우리동신원의담보ᄂᆞᆫ
신문보시ᄂᆞᆫ쳠군ᄌᆞ의게ᄒᆞᆼ상보
도ᄒᆞ리며편지ᄒᆞᆫ귀서ᄒᆞ며주시
ᄂᆞᆫ이ᄂᆞᆫ성명과반ᄃᆞᆫ뎌어붓치
시기를희망ᄒᆞ오니비거슨신문
상에귀졔ᄒᆞ란ᄂᆞᆫ거시아니오다
만국ᄒᆞ신용ᄒᆞᄂᆞᆫ증거를숨고자
홈이라귀자ᄂᆞᆫ아모귀서던지과
치ᄒᆞᆷ을되각ᄒᆞᄂᆞᆫ권리를가졋스
나되각ᄒᆞᄂᆞᆫ리유ᄂᆞᆫ말ᄒᆞᆯ터이오
며공중평화를문란케ᄒᆞᄂᆞᆫ듯ᄒᆞᆫ
귀서ᄂᆞᆫ의례히밧지안켓ᄉᆞ나이
다
●본사셜시이리로신문을미양
우레로본젼ᄒᆞ와레젼부의임의
로젼ᄒᆞᆫ듯스로면곳에ᄂᆞᆫ후ᄂᆞᆫ듯케
젼ᄒᆞ기도ᄒᆞ며ᄒᆞ며첩거슬ᄒᆞᆫ접
에젼ᄒᆞ기도ᄒᆞ며ᄒᆞ아니젼ᄒᆞᄂᆞᆫ
곳도잇다ᄒᆞ와우리신문을수랑
ᄒᆞ야구람ᄒᆞ시ᄂᆞᆫ　쳠군ᄌᆞ의게
뒤ᄒᆞ야미우미안ᄒᆞ옵기로지금
은본젼인을두고면일즉이젼
ᄒᆞ며아니젼ᄒᆞ거나늣게ᄒᆞ거나호
폐가업도록ᄒᆞ라ᄒᆞ오니혹아니
젼ᄒᆞ거나ᄂᆞᆫ쳥늣게젼ᄒᆞ거나ᄒᆞᆫ일
이잇스면본사로통괴ᄒᆞ여쥬심
을희망ᄒᆞᆷ

관보

광무팔년십
이월륙일　호외
셔임급ᄉᆞ령
○승종이품 정삼품 오현근
○승종이품 정삼품 최유옥
○승정삼품 륙품 신석영
이상오월십일
○임경무청경무관셔쥬임관이
등○종이품 조규하
○의원면본관 봉상군수 홍
세영
이상십이월ᄉᆞ일
○승서관임관삼등 탁지부주
ᄉᆞ○최석두
회대○면본관 진위대오련티
티향관륙군이등군ᄉᆞ 강대
이
이상십이월이일
○임법관양셩ᄉᆞ쇼반ᄉᆞ서판임관
륙등 길경학
○셩명양근군임시우체주ᄉᆞ 오
호○셔면임괴군임시우체주사 오
병○명인천군임시우체주사 리
쥬
이상십이월이일
○임중추원부의쟝셔칙임관일
등○리종건
○리종셥의원면본관 비서원승
쥬종원시종 비서원승 박준쳔
○윤　리경ㅜ 쟝례원쟝 봉시신
○오힝시종원분시어 정삼품
일영
○종○임비서원승셔주임관이등
종이품 윤상학
○정○임비서원승셔주임관륙등
정삼품 박제셩
○경○임시종원시종셔주임관륙등
경삼품 리필하
쟝례원쟝례 비서원승
○윤○임쟝례원쟝례셔주임관팔등
윤상학 남뎡철
○김○임봉시셔주임관팔등
김용달
○죠○명시종원분시어 정삼품
죠두현 정삼품 한창교
이상십이월삼일
공덕륙사
○의○죠셕ᄒᆞ야글ᄋᆞ사ᄃᆡᄒᆞᆫ부등
진관리중간을명ᄒᆞ사중추원부
의쟝을삼으시다
○군부대신륙군부쟝리윤용창
모부쟝종쟝셔리참모부쟝륙군
부장윤웅렬교육부총감륙군부
장리지용군　주ᄒᆞ되진위대오
련티대이대티쟝륙군보
병참령신ᄐᆡ휴의본년구월삼십
일츌ᄒᆞᆫ대ᄉᆞ실상호보고서를
쥬졍ᄒᆞᆫ즉본티향관륙군이등
군사강필회가신병이잇다이로
코면직ᄒᆞ기를쳥원ᄒᆞ고곳아라
사진중에드러갓다ᄒᆞ오니군법
으로헤아리건티파송홈이맛당
ᄒᆞᆫ지라위선면본관ᄒᆞ고인ᄒᆞ
야헤티에신칙ᄒᆞ와ᄒᆞ야공법을
배품리쟝아울너써죠률죵판홈
이엇더ᄒᆞ올지군　쥬ᄒᆞ와　광
무팔년십이월일일에봉　지의
쥬라ᄒᆞ옵심다라
○의졍부찬졍최익현ᄉᆞ직소
비지셩소구실경비라경숭헤
길훈로부와지도에졍ᄒᆞ고효실
홈은바쳐기다리ᄂᆞᆫ자ㅣ한곳이
계훈번호유ᄒᆞ셔등이아니라또
말에올홈이그비을당ᄒᆞᆫ지라차
우홈이졈졈극진홈이기다리고
기다림이더욱간졀ᄒᆞᆫ지라그변
거이ᄉᆞ양ᄒᆞ야말고곳을나오라ᄒᆞ
시고디방관을보내여젼유ᄒᆞ시
다
십이월ᄉᆞ일

뎐보

발뎐돈론　십이월이십륙일
○봉텬함대　봉텬함대의젼투
함이쳑과쇼슌양함삼쳑과운송션두
구쳑은간밤에빗터호에피박ᄒᆞ
고수뢰파괴함쳑은스웻스에
머믈다더라
그함대가그운하에지날때에ᄂᆞᆫ
대포들파수뢰통들을젼징ᄒᆞᆯ배
에와굿치예비ᄒᆞ더라
스웻스에피박ᄒᆞ야잇ᄂᆞᆫ함대ᄂᆞᆫ
쇼경션으로쇼경ᄒᆞ고잇더라
발뎐동　십이월이십칠일
○로함부리　봉텬함의나머지
비들이스웻스에도박ᄒᆞ엿ᄂᆞᆫ대지
이셩사시안으로세나라고명령
ᄒᆞ고그항구에셔ᄂᆞᆫ셕탄실기를
허락지아니ᄒᆞ엿다더라
발뎐동　동일
○로함츌발　봉텬함대에쇽ᄒᆞᆫ
비들은그운송션으로브터셕탄
을실은후에스웻스를떠낫다더
라
발뎐돈론　십이월이십오일
○로함군박　로국군함오쳑과
수뢰파괴함칠쳑이ᄃᆞᆫ세이트에도박ᄒᆞ야거긔
셔며율을파세로ᄂᆞᆫ실엇스나셕
탄은거졀ᄒᆞ엿고수뢰파괴함쳘
쳑은벌셔스웻스에왓고다른비
들은훈셔귀에온다ᄒᆞ며그함대
수령관이영국군함류렷스에차
저와서져의회군의무한한곤난
을셜명ᄒᆞ더라그함대의ᄒᆞᆫ부분
은스코라는쌍에셔쎄낫다더라
발뎐동　동월이십칠일
○로장명에　할페시파총독이
국동로로군총수령관을갈넌후에
로황이조칙을나리셔아써외수
영을칭찬ᄒᆞ고삼등센죠지훈쟝
을하수ᄒᆞ엿다더라
발뎐동　동일
○일인격로　본티ᄒᆞᆫ대에셔탄
을풍금ᄒᆞᄂᆞᆫ대티ᄒᆞ야일본하야
시ᄎᆞ쟉과수에마쌍남쟉이구라
파에셔로국을도아쥬다고일본
인사회에분로홈을격동ᄒᆞ엿더
라
발뎐동　동일
○영션몰수　일본으로브터한
국에쳘로지료를실고가다가로
국히삼위항대에붓잡힌영국륜
션첼텐함은히삼위에서판결홈
을의ᄒᆞ야몰수ᄒᆞ라고셩괴득보
에셔명령ᄒᆞ엿더라

잡보

○리마교인횡폐　가평등디에
셔리마교인이횡악이대단홈으
로빅셩이견티지못ᄒᆞ야두사람
이일젼에샹경ᄒᆞ야쥬교졔호소
ᄒᆞ라다가도로나려갓다더라
○자용단번　작일십이시량에
근광교아리모문젼에멸일ᄒᆞᄂᆞᆫ
자ㅣ븡봉ᄒᆞᆫ가지믄듣고가다가
그주인이붓잡고쎄아슨즉그사
람이무류ᄒᆞ야말ᄒᆞ기를벼가도
적질ᄒᆞᆫ것이아니라파라도말
ᄒᆞ엿다ᄒᆞᆫ즉그주인은히랍ᄒᆞᆫ일
이업다ᄒᆞ야혼쳐시비ᄒᆞ엿다더
라
○셩가횡퇴　졍인학은본리숍
검인티원신사ᄂᆞᆫ예수교인최장
숀과쟝간면분이잇서최쟝숀의
양복을파라주마ᄒᆞ고오원에결
가ᄒᆞ야가져갓ᄂᆞᆫ티갑도아니주
고분건도아니주고건몬ᄒᆞᄂᆞᆫ지
고라최쟝숀인즉그사람이숩졈
로의상엽시주엇ᄂᆞᆫ티지금은인

UNION INSURANCE SOCIETY OF CANTON.

Head office Hongkong.
Marine risks underwritten at current rates.
Agents in Chemulpo,
E. MEYER & Co.

COMPAGNIE DES MESSAGERIES MARITIMES.

Fortnightly Direct Service.

For Marseilles
via Ports.
Sailing from Yokohama
Calling at Kobe,
Shanghai, Hongkong, Saigon, Singapore,
Colombo, Djibonti, Suez, Port Said
and Marseilles.

For particulars apply to
HOLME RINGER & Co.,
Chemulpo.

HAYASHIDA & CO.,

16 MYENG DONG, CHIN KO KAI, SEOUL.
BRANCH OFFICE AT CHEMULPO.

Money changers, Coal and Wood Merchants, Express Agents.

We are agents for the Pyeng-yang Coal Company and the Karazu Coal Company of Japan. We have the best quality of both anthracite and bituminous coal, and prompt execution of orders is our speciality. Firewood of all kinds kept in stock. Full weight guaranteed. Money of all denominations exchanged at current rates. Parcels received for all parts.

CHINA MUTUAL LIFE INS. OC.

Most favourable terms to policy holders.

Benefit system unsurpassed.

HOLME RINGER & Co.
Agents, Chemulpo.

C. P. R.

CANADIAN PACIFIC RAILWAY COMPANY'S ROYAL MAIL STEAMSHIP LINE.

THE FAST ROUTE BETWEEN CHINA, JAPAN, AND EUROPE VIA CANADA AND THE UNITED STATES.

Route from Hongkong via Shanghai, Nagasaki (Inland Sea of Japan) Kobe, Yokohama Victoria and Vancouver.

Twin Screw Empress Steamship 6,000 Tons Speed 19 knots.

PROPOSED SAILING FROM YOKOHAMA.

R. M. S. Empress of India.
R. M. S. Empress of Japan.
R. M. S. Empress of China.
R. M. S. Athenian.
R. M. S. Taatar.

Special reduction (first class only) granted to members of the Military, Naval, Diplomatic and Civil services and to Missionaries.

Passengers have choice of ten routes across the Continent of America and have privilege of travelling by any Atlantic Steamship Line.

Round the World passage tickets in connection with the P. and O. S. N., North German Lloyd and Messageries Co.'s £125.

All rates payable at current rate of exchange.

For further information, Tickets, Guide Books, etc., apply to

HOLME, RINGER & Co., AGENTS,
Chemulpo.

Grand Hotel,

(Formerly the Station Hotel)

Near the Railway Terminus, West Gate Seoul.

The Best Hotel in Korea
Handsome new Building.
Fine Airy Rooms
Excellent Cuisine.
Terms Moderate.
Special terms to Missionaries
and to permanent boarders.

Electric cars within 2 minutes' walk.

W. H. EMBERLEY.

Proprietor.

EVERY FACILITY.

In connection with Life Assurance Business is afforded by

The Standard Life Assurance Co.,

One of the largest and wealthiest of the Provident Institutions of the United Kingdom Forms of Application and all information will be promptly afforded on application.

10 CENTS A DAY.

Not a very large expenditure is it? But it is sufficient to secure for a man of 30 a policy with the STANDARD LIFE OFFICE for

$1323.

For all particulars of rates, etc., apply to

Holme, Ringer & Co.,
Agents, Chemulpo.

THE NEW YORK LIFE INSURANCE COMPANY.

Have you ever been declined by any Company?

Are you engaged in a specially hazardous occupation?

Have you heard of the New York Life Insurance Company's New Classifications for this class of Risks?

If not, send your date of birth, occupation and particulars of rejection, if any to

E. MEYER & Co.,
Agents, Chemulpo.

MITSUI BUSSAN KAISHA.
(MITSUI & Co.)
MITSUI GINKO.
(MITSUI BANK.)

The Bank is owned by the members of the Mitsui Family, who, as partners, assume an unmited responsibility for all liabilities of the Bank:—

Capital ....Yen 5,000,000
Reserve Fund .... " 5,600,000

HEAD OFFICE, TOKYO.

LONDON OFFICE, 34 LIME ST., E. C.

BRANCHES AND AGENCIES:—
New York, San Francisco, Hamburg, Bombay, Singapore, Manila, Hongkong, Amoy, Chefoo, Tientsin.

Kobe, Hakodate, Yokohama, Kure, Yokosuka, Moji, Shimonoseki, Miike, Wakamatsu, Nagasaki, Kuchinotsu, Karatsu, Sasebo, Misume, Taipeh, &c.

Telegraphic Address for all the Offices:
"MITSUI."
A. B. C. AND A. 1 CODES USED.

Contractors of Coal
To the Imperial Japanese Navy. Arsenals and Railway Bureau, Principal Railway Companies and Industrial Work, Home and Foreign Mail and Freight Steamers.

Sole Proprietors
Of the famous Miike, Tagawa and Yamano Coal Mines.

Sole Agents
For the sale of Fukumo, Hokoku, Ichimura, Kanoda, Mannoura, Onoura, Ostuji, Sonoda, Tsubaruro, Yoshinotani, Yoshio, Yurokibura and other coals.

YANGTSE INSURANCE ASSOCIATION, LTD.

The undersigned, having been appointed agents for the above company, are prepared to issue policies and pay losses on marine risks at regular rates.

E. MEYER & Co.,
Agents, Chemulpo.

AMERICAN KOREAN ELECTRIC CO.

Light and Power.

Main Office: Electric Building, Chong No.

RAILWAY DEPARTMENT.

OPERATING CARS BETWEEN EAST AND WEST GATE, EVERY TEN MINUTES:—

First Car leaves East Gate at 7:00 A. M. First Car leaves R. R. Station at 7:25 A. M
Last Car " East Gate at 9:40 P. M. Last " " R. R. Station at 10:05 P.M

OPERATING CARS BETWEEN EAST GATE AND IMPERIAL TOMB TERMINUS, EVERY TWENTY MINUTES:—
CONNECTING WITH EVERY ALTERNATE CAR ARRIVING AT EAST GATE FROM CHONG NO.

First Car leaves East Gate for Tomb at 7:10 A. M.
" " " Tomb for East Gate at 7:35 A. M.
Last " " East Gate for Tomb at 7:50 P. M.
" " " Tomb for East Gate at 8:10 P. M.

OPERATING CARS BETWEEN CHONG NO AND YUNG SAN RIVER EVERY TWELVE MINUTES:—

First Car leaves Chong No for South Gate at 7:12 A. M.
" " " Chong No for Yung San at 7:36 A. M.
" " " South Gate for Chong No at 7:20 A. M.
" " " Yung San for Chong No at 8:09 A. M.
Last " " South Gate for Chong No 10:00 P. M.
" " " Yung San for Chong No at 9:33 P. M.

SPECIAL PRIVATE CARS FURNISHED TO SUIT CONVENIENCE OF PATRONS. PRICES ON APPLICATION AT HEAD OFFICE.

LIGHTING DEPARTMENT.

Where less than 250 candle power of light is used, the rate per month will be
Per 16 candle power incandescent lamp,—All night.—Yen 2.50.
32 candle power incandescent lamp:—All night:—Yen 4.00.
50 candle power incandescent lamp:—All night:—Yen 6.00.
150 " " " " " " 10.00.
1200 " " enclosed arc " " " " 20.00.

Where more than 250 candle power of light is used, a Meter will be installed, freqvedted:—Rent of Meter Yen 2.00 per month. Rate of charges by meter reading:—Two Sen per Ampere per hour. (Approximately this is equal to about One Sen per 16 C. P. lamp per hour) Minimum monthly charge where meter is installed, Yen 20.00 per month, which includes rental of meter.

Estimates for installing lights furnished on application.

An assortment of chandeliers always on hand.

K. Murakami.

Photograph Studio
Chinkokai, Seoul.

Printing, Developing and Enlargement, of Photographs always Undertaken.

Korean Views and Pictures Illustrating Native Customs always on Sale,

THE OSAKA SHOSEN KAISHA.

Boats frequently on the berth for Chinnampo.

REGULAR SAILINGS BETWEEN JAPAN AND KOREAN PORTS.

FUSAN AND KOBE VIA SHIMONOSEKI.

OSAKA VIA MOKPO, FUSAN, SHIMONOSEKI AND KOBE.

MOJI DIRECT.

OSAKA VIA KUNSAN, MASANPO, FUSAN, SHIMONOSEKI AND KOBE.

CHEMULPO KUNSAN LINE, Every three days.

CHEMULPO CHINNAMPO LINE. Every three days.

For Freight and passage and further particulars apply to

THE OSAKA SHOSEN KAISHA,
Chemulpo.

LONDON, PLAISANT & CO.

General Storekeepers and Merchants, Ships Contractors, Tobacconists, Commission and Forwarding Agents, Coal Merchants

IMPORTERS AND EXPORTERS

Seoul & Chemulpo.

W. D. WENTWORTH.

LANDING
AND
SHIPPING AGENT
AND
CUSTOMS BORDER.

12 OURA, NAGASAKI.

STEWARD & CO.

Chemulpo.

Shipchandlers and Storekeepers, Naval and Mercantile Contractors, Landing and Shipping Agents.

STEWARD'S HOTEL

Chemulpo.

Best accommodation in the port for travellers. Clean and well-aired rooms, good cuisine and prompt attendence, moderate tariff.

빅셩ᄒ엿스니 엇지 통분치 아니ᄒ리오

○강화 … 강화부윤이 …

룡관에 호산ᄒ다더라

○청쥬폐현 … 외부로 조회ᄒ기를 우리나라 왕폐하ᄭ 진강ᄒ신 … 로 조회ᄒ엿거니와 …

론셜

잡보

광고

TELEGRAMS.

Tokyo, Dec. 5th.

Owing to the occupation by the Japanese of 203 metre hill, and the subsequent bombardment of the harbour, the shipping has been greatly damaged. Some Russians, who were secretly entrenched on the hill, were discovered and dislodged.

FROM JAPAN PAPERS.

Berlin, Nov. 30.

The portion of the Russian Squadron proceeding to the Far East *via* the Cape has arrived at one of the ports in German Africa, but the Squadron will receive no coal there.

Berlin, Nov. 30.

A Russian torpedo-boat, somewhat damaged, has arrived at Brest.

London, Nov. 30.

In the Australian House of Representatives, Mr. Bruce Smith on December 8th will move an amendment to the Immigration Restriction Law to the effect that the entrance of Japanese into the Commonwealth be permitted on the ground that the Japanese nation has placed itself in the front rank (by the present war), has granted the fullest freedom of religious belief, and has become the honoured ally of Great Britain. [Mr. Bruce-Smith was one of the strong opponents of the passage of this Immigration Restriction Law a year or two ago, upon which occasion, however, he was in a very small minority.]

Berlin, Nov. 30.

An interview with Count von Buelow appears in the current issue of the "Nineteenth Century," in the course of which the Chancellor makes some friendly remarks concerning Anglo-German relations, and expresses a hope that any misunderstandings will disappear.

Berlin, Nov. 30.

The negotiations recently entered into in Vienna for the conclusion of a Commercial Treaty between Austria and Germany have not been successful. There was, however, no rupture.

LOSS OF THE JAPANESE BATTLE-SHIP "YASHIMA."

In reply to a telegram to the Naval Department at Tokyo, says the "Kobe Herald," we were to-day informed that there was no objection to the publication of the following Associated Press cable, which appeared in the American papers of Nov. 4th :—

Paris, Nov. 3.

The Associated Press was put in a position to-day to state positively that despatches from Chefoo, Port Arthur and Tokio last June to the effect that the Japanese battleship Yashima had been sunk by a mine off Dalny, which despatches were denied by the Japanese authorities at the time, have finally been officially confirmed. The Japanese Government has notified foreign governments of the loss of the ship. The number of men who went down with the vessel is not known, but it is believed to have been small. The official details show that the Yashima struck a Russian mine and later attempted to make Daily harbour, but this proved impossible and she sank in deep water. The Yashima was one of the finest battleships of the Japanese navy. Her displacement was 12,300 tons, about the size of the American battleship Maine, and she had a speed of nineteen knots. She carried a heavy battery of four 12-inch., ten 6-inch and 24 other guns of smaller calibre.

It is rumoured that the Magistrate of Ho In has been captured by bandits, and is being held captive for ransom.

AN IMPROVED BATTLESHIP.

The conclusion drawn by the writer of an article in the "Marine Francaise," the organ of the French Ministry of Marine, is to decry the utility of the battleship. His contention that the warship of the future is the swift cruiser, is vigorously challenged in German naval circles. The Russo-Japanese war, it is asserted, by no means proves the failure of the battleship, although the value the cruiser and the destroyer has certainly been demonstrated.

It is pointed out that the British Admiralty, whose experience and technical skill is admitted to be the first in the world, is devoting all its energies to perfecting the battleship, giving it a greater speed, greater fighting radius, and more powerful armament. It is thought here that the reasons which led the Minister of Marine to prefer the cruiser to the ironclad are more of a financial than of a naval order.

The Magistrate of Su An reports more troubles arising in his district owing to the frequent visits of robbers and Tonghaks.

The Italian Minister has requested the Foreign Office to obtain him an audience with His Majesty, so that he may personally present an autograph letter from his Sovereign.

The following European telegram has been received by the Foreign Department at Tokio:—General Kaulbars, Commander of the 3rd Russian Army in Manchuria, and his staff, left home on November 28th. They are expected at Mukden on December 24.

Really our Japanese contemporary the "Daito Shimpo," possesses a fund of information regarding the sentiments of the Russians in the North-East. According to this journal, even the poor whales, which abound off that coast, and are now, by the way, enjoying a well-earned respite from the unwelcome attentions of Russian and Japanese whalers, have come under suspicion of being Japanese torpedo-boats in disguise.

The following telegram has been received by the Tokyo Foreign Department:—In connection with the attack on the Hull fishing fleet, Rear-Admiral Cholky, of the Baltic Squadron, has made the following statement:—The incident originated in a misunderstanding of signals by the Russian warships. A little before the departure of the Squadron new signals were adopted, and it was owing to these being unfamiliar that the mistake occurred.

The Seoul Fusan railway has proved rather a failure to would be travellers to Fusan, as it has now been notified that no passengers will be accepted before January 1st. Even then owing to the rapidity, with which the track has been laid the instability of the wooden bridges erected, the journey from Seoul to Fusan will occupy more than 24 hours. It is hoped that at some future date, when the wooden bridges will be replaced by iron structures, the distance of 275 miles, will be covered in a little over 10 hours.

A department inquiry is proceeding at the Admiralty, in which some of the most distinguished authorities in the Service are taking part, as to the relative advantages of a battle-ship and a first-class cruiser. The point is what superiority the battle-ship, with its slow movement, would have with its heavier armament, against that alert and mobile cruiser? The cruiser would probably have a quicker delivery of fire to the extent of at least two to one. Would this equalise the weight of metal thrown by the battleship? Upon the answers to this question the future of shipbuilding to a large extent depends. It is at least an evidence of the trend of opinion that we are building more first-class cruisers than before.

The Chin Myeng Hoi have for certain reasons, altered the name of their society to Kong Chin Hoi. Yesterday, under their new title they held a large meeting at Chong No and decided to send a committee to the Government with the object of ascertaining details of Agricultural and Industrial rights in the interior.

MR. DOOLY ON THE COMFORTS OF TRAVEL.

BY F. D. DUNNE.

D'ye know," said Mr. Hennessy, "ye can go fr'm Chicago to New York in twenty hours? It must be like flyin."

"It is something like flyin'," said Mr. Dooley, "but it's also like fallin' off a roof or bein, clubbed by a polisman."

"It's wonderful how luxuryous modhern thravel is," said Mr. Dooley. "It's almost a dhream. Ye go to bed a night in Kansas City an'ye ar-re still awake in Chicago in th' mornin'. Ye have New York to-day an' nex' Thursdah ye rr-re in San Francisco an' can't get back. An' all th' time ye injye such comforts an' iligances as wud make th' Shah iv Persha invious if he heerd iv thim. I haven't thravelled much since I hastily put four thousan' miles iv salt wather an' smilin' land between me an' the constabulary, but I've always wanted to fly through space on wan iv them place cars with th' beautiful names. Th' man that names te' Pullman cars an' th' pa-aper collars iv this counthry is our greatest pote, whoiver he is. I cud see mesilf steppin' aboard a palace on wheels called Obulula or Onarka an' bein' fired fr'm wan Union deepo to another, So las' month whin a towny iv mine in Saint Looey asked me down there I determined to make' th' plunge. With th' invitation come a fine consarvitive article be th' gin'ral passenger agent indivrin,' Hinnissy, to give a faint idee iv th' glories iv th' thrip. There was pitchers in this little pome showin' how th' thrain looked to th'passenger agent. Iligantly dhressed ladies an' gintlemen set in th' handsomely upholstered seats, or sthrolled through th' broad aisles. Pierpont Morgan was disclosed in a corner dictatin a letther to Andhrew Carnaygie.

(To be continued.)

NOTICE.

The power of attorney granted to Mr. Walter George Bennett to sign the name of our firm per procuration has this day been withdrawn.

Nagasaki, 30th November, 1904.

HOLME, RINGER & Co.

PROSPECTUS.

The Chemulpo Electric Company, Limited.

REGISTERED IN JAPAN

Capital Yen 125,000.00

Divided into 2,500 Shares of Yen 50.00 each.

Of this number 1,230 Shares have been subscribed for and will be allotted, the remaining 1,270 Shares are now offered for subscription by the Public.

Payable 20 per cent on Application
20 " " " 15 Feb. 1905.
30 " " " 15 June 1905.
30 " " " 15 Sept. 1905.

PROVISIONAL DIRECTORS.

C. WOLTER.
KAKU EITARO.
TANAKA SASHICHIRO.
HORI RIKITARO.

BANKERS.

Dai-ichi Ginko, Chemulpo and Seoul.
Juhachi Ginko, Chemulpo.
Gojuhachi Ginko, Chemulpo and Seoul.

This Company is formed to supply the town of Chemulpo with an Electric Plant for Light and Power.

With the different Municipalities favorable contracts have been secured.

An Electric Plant for 3,000 Lamps of 16 C. P. burning simultaneously, of the best make will be installed, which is capable of supplying the necessary light and power for years to come. Provision has also been ma'e to easily enlarge this installation should this become necessary.

The General Management of the Company will be in the hands of a Board of Directors (three Japanese and two foreigners) to be elected at the meeting of the Shareholders.

Application for Shares should be forwarded to the Bankers of the Company together with the amount payable on application.

If the number of Shares applied for by any one applicant be not allotted, the surplus of the amount paid on Deposit will be appropriated toward the sum due on allotment, unless the person who has made the deposit in question applies for the return of such surplus.

As it is desired not to disappoint smaller applicants, they shall, if possible, receive proportionate allotments out of the number of shares over and above 10 applied for by any one applicant.

Share list will close at noon on January 10th, 1905.

The Korea Daily News.

Issued at 5 P. M. daily except Sundays.

Rate of Subscription:—
Per Year,............Yen 25.
Per Quarter,..........Yen 7.
Per Month,..........Yen 2.50.

Postage in Korea not charged extra.
Postage abroad charged extra.

Advertisements, 50 sen per day for 1 inch or less.
5 yen per month per inch.
50 yen per year per inch.

All communications to
E. T. BETHELL,
Editor and Publisher,
Pak-tong, Seoul.

EXTRACTS FROM A LETTER FROM RUSSIA.

(WRITTEN TO THE SINGAPORE FREE PRESS BY JOHN DILL ROSS).

The British press generally is sadly ill informed about Russia and the Russians, and the attitude adopted by our newspapers during the present war does them no credit. Instead of a dispassionate record of events, with fair and enlightened comment on a war which is of peculiar interest to us as a nation, we have had a torrent of laudation and of hyperbolical hysterics concerning all that is Japanese, accompanied by an equally one-sided and unsparing condemnation of everything Russian. Our journalists at home and abroad seem to have lost all sense of proportion, and their central idea is to twist facts to suit their own views. The "Times" is notoriously lopsided in its pronouncements about Russia. The proprietors of this great journal are probably busy at this time of the year with some such scheme as the "Times" Goose Club. (The "Times" Goose with the "Times" stuffing delivered at your door for sixpence-halpenny, to be followed by monthly instalments of one shilling for the next seventeen years. Weigh in with the cash to-day! No time to be lost, etc.) This sort of thing seems to be more in accordance with the traditions of the "Times" of to-day than any serious attempt to educate the British public in the lessons of the war. It is really sad, however, to see such a respectable and well-written paper as the "Morning Post" publishing telegrams announcing the suicide of General Stoessel and the execution of Admiral Ouchtomsky, both of which tragic events were averred to have taken place at Port Arthur. This is not journalism, neither is it cricket. I have no idea who the Shanghai correspondent of the "Morning Post" may be, except than his confiding editor vouched for him as being a gentlemen possessed of exceptional facilities for acquiring valuable information. It is to the "Morning Post" journalist-diplomat to whom the world is indebted for the items of news already mentioned, together with many other interesting details, such as the blowing up by the Russians of their own fleet at Port Arthur some weeks before they fought their last general action with Admiral Togo. It is to be hoped that the citizens of Shanghai will set about putting up a statue of the "Morning Post" gentleman without delay. There is plenty of room on the Bund for such a statue, and somehow the site seems suitable. Somewhere in front of the Club for instance.

These misleading reports trouble men's minds, causing them to prophesy things which do not come to pass. Thus in an August issue of the "Singapore Free Press" your Military Editor confidently announced the fall of Port Arthur within ten days. Well, there seems to be a bit of a mistake somewhere—but then, those there Russians!

Much more distressing, however, is it to see a prominent London paper solemnly declaring that the naval engagement of the 10th August altogether throws into the shade the battles of Trafalgar and Lepento. Is it not possible to beland Togo without belittling Nelson? Now that the smoke of action has cleared away a little, it would hardly seem that the action off Round Island does much credit to either side. If it is true that the Russians lost their Admiral early in the fight, but even that unhappy circumstance hardly explains the events which followed. But still more inexplicable is the failure of Admiral Togo, with his immense superiority in ships and guns to account for the whole Russian fleet. He ought to have sunk or captured every one of the Russian ships without exception. Would our Nelson have been satisfied with anything less? And again, what business had Admiral Kamimura with his six heavy cruisers to allow two out of the three Vladivostock ships to escape after he had succeeded in briuging them to action? I cannot but believe, that if British admirals had been in command under similiar circumstances, they would have given a very different account of the enemy.

Much has been said in your own columns and elsewhere about the constant defeats and retreats of the Russian army. Is it not fair to assume that, after having suffered all these consecutive reverses, the magnificent stand made by General Kuropatkin at Liaoyang entitles his army to respect? Here, in Russia, we firmly believe that General Kuropatkin had actually won the battle of Liaoyang when General Orloff threw the victory away. The retreat to Mukden was one of the finest in history and could only have been carried out by a fine army under a great general.

We, of all people, should have some sympathy with soldiers who will fight well after repeated defeats and retreats. Our own military operations generally commence with reverses and "unfortunate incidents" although it has been our good fortune, hitherto, to "muddle through" to a more or less successful conclusion.

Not to know when he is beaten, has always been the finest characteristic of the British soldier, and it is just as well he possesses it, because it is often his luck to get soundly whacked when we start him on one of our blessed wars.

We ought to be able to appreciate the rare fighting qualities of the Russian soldiers without in the least detracting from the brilliant performances of his Asiatic enemy. But before we are to judge the Japanese soldier we ought to see how he stands up to adverse fortune. It is a comparatively easy matter to fight enthusiastically on the winning side.

Another piece of claptrap which has been very hardworked in the British press, is the sentimental business about colossal Russia wilfully attacking "Little Japan." The population of Japan is actually greater than that of the United Kingdom, but in the event of an enemy attempting a landing on our shores, should we set up a shout about "Little England?" Not unless we were very "little Englanders" indeed. The Japanese are fighting it out practically on their own base and have secured the command of the sea, while the Russians are involved in a purely colonial war at an enormous distance. Of the difficulties of such a war we ought to have some conception, considering that it took us three years to knock out some sixty thousand Boers—after a fashion. The spirit of the Boers is anything but broken yet, and they are only waiting for the ministry to be formed by "C-B" and his friends, to see if they cannot get rid of Lord Milner—and others. I think we must all acknowledge that "Little Japan" is a very big thing indeed.

Russian corruption is another favourite theme of our enlightened press. Corruption was to have curled up the Siberian Railway within three weeks from the commencement of the war. Indeed the railway was a somewhat mythical affair, the entire line having been practically stolen by unscrupulous contractors and officials. Similarly corruption had stolen all the money for the coals, stores, and ammunition for Port Arthur. The fact remains that the Siberian railway is working splendidly, and reflects the greatest credit on Prince Khilkoff and his staff, while the defence of Port Arthur is daily proof that skilful and honest work has been done in that direction. Doubtless there has been some corruption and mismanagement, but on nothing like the vast scale supposed, or the war would necessarily have been ended before now.

It is of course a relief to turn from the Siberian Railway to the working of our Remount Department during the Boer War, and to the management of our Departments which loaded up our infantry with 6lb. tins of meat which the poor fellows threw away at the first chance, and provided them with leaky cartridge belts which strewed the veldt with ammunition as they trailed across it. The Royal Patriotic Fund is another source of legitimate pride to every respectable Briton. The money subscribed for the widows and orphans of the Crimean War is still in the Bank, thank goodness, and must have been accumulating a fair amount of interest since 1855 or thereabouts. Well the widows must be dead for the most part by now, so that there is no need to trouble about *them* but it is rather rough on the bald-headed Crimean Orphan that he should be treated as an "ankle-biter" and a "get-a-bit" when he endeavours to trouser a trifle on account from the funds of this carefully administered charity. The matter was brought up in parliament after the Boer War, and it was put right by changing the name of the Fund.

We are in a position therefore to say hard things of the Russians, and we are availing ourselves of the privilege most heartily. We did not quite enjoy all that was printed and pictured of us in France, Holland and Germany during the Boer War, but that may be an additional reason for writing acres of unkind prose about the Russians.

But on the other hand, our press excels itself in worshipping Japan and all that therein is. I have seen a good deal about Japan myself, and now read with surprise, that this interesting country is populated by a host of angels in arms, and that my old friend the Jap, who certainly appeared to me to have his little failings (especially in business matters) is none other than the just man made perfect. To me all this is incomprehensible, and I do not see the good of it. Beyond leading some millions of untravelled people at home into forming very wrong estimates of Japanese character, the fulsome adulation of Japan which is being turned out by the ton may do no especial harm, unless indeed, our Japanese friends find it a bit trying to their well known modesty.

Let us therefore print all that is bright and beautiful about Japan, whether it happen to be true or not, though it would best suit our interests as a nation to study the actual facts of the war, and make some practical use of the tremendous object lesson which is being worked out before us. But let us have a little sanity, a little common sense and fairness when we seriously *think* about Russia and Japan.

Not all the articles ever printed can shape the course of a shell, or deflect the flight of a bullet. It is not for newspapers to win or lose battles, but they can sow the seeds of illfeeling and national enmities which may end in hating other countries, rather than in loving one's own.

It is a point to be considered whether a weak Russia and a powerful Germany works out to the advantage of Great Britain. The German danger is one which strikes much nearer home than the Far East. This is a very large question, however, and one not to be lightly approached.

My own sympathies in the present crisis are wholly Russian, but I have always known the "Free Press" to extend fair treatment to a political opponent, and certainly to possess the courage to afford the consideration of an important question from the other point of view.

The Japanese Consul at Bombay wires under date of the 21st inst. that Aden has been proclaimed a pest-infected port.

Of late from 15 to 21 trains a day laden with fresh troops have been arriving at Harbin; the capacity of the railway has proved to be from four to five times greater than the Japanese and the "Times" specially despatched expert calculated. Hence the upsetting of all the Japanese plans and calculations!

The Korea Daily News.

VOL. I, WEDNESDAY, DECEMBER 7, 1904. No. 119

HONGKONG & SHANGHAI BANKING CORPORATION.

Paid-up Capital..... ....$10,000,000
Reserve Fund:—Sterling Reserve... 10,000,000
Silver Reserve..... 7,000,000

27,000,000
Reserve Liability of Proprietors... 10,000,000

HEAD OFFICE, HONGKONG.

London Bankers, London and County Banking Company Limited
Branches and Agencies,
London.

Amoy,	Hankow	Penang,
Bangkok,	Hiogo,	Rangoon,
Batavia,	Iloilo,	Saigon,
Bombay,	Lyons,	San Francisco,
Calcutta,	Manila,	Singapore,
Colombo,	Nagasaki,	Sourabaya,
Foochow,	New York,	Tientsin,
Hamburg,	Peking,	Yokohama,

Credits granted on approved Securities, and every description of Banking and Exchange business transacted.

Drafts granted on London and the chief Commercial places in Europe, India, Australia, America, China and Japan.

HOLME RINGER & Co., AGENTS,
CHEMULPO.

ON CHEONG & CO.,
SEOUL.

GENERAL STORE KEEPERS.
Imported provisions, Cooking Utensils Crockery, etc.
FRESH BREAD DAILY.

MITSU BISHI DOCKYARD & ENGINE WORKS,
NAGASAKI.

CODE WORD, "DOCK."

A 1, A. B. C., and Engineering Codes used.

DOCK No. 1 (at Tategami).

Extreme Length..............523 feet
Length on blocks............. 513 „
Width of Entrance on Top......89 „
„ „ Bottom....77 „
Water on Blocks at Spring Tide 26½ „

DOCK No. 2 (Mukaijima).

Extreme Length..............371 feet
Length on Blocks.............360 „
Width of Entrance on Top......66 „
„ „ Bottom 53 „
Water on Blocks at Spring Tide 22 „

PATENT SLIP (at Kosuge).
Can take vessels up to 1,000 tons gross

THE WORKS are well equipped with the LATEST IMPROVEMENTS, and can execute any kind of work in SHIPBUILDING and MARINE ENGINEERING, as well as in REPAIRING of SHIPS.

The COMPANY'S new powerful steamer OURA-MARU (712 tons, 700 I.H.P.), specially built for SALVAGE PURPOSES, and equipped with necessary gear, is always READY at SHORT NOTICE.

CHARTERED BANK OF INDIA AUSTRALIA & CHINA.

INCORPORATED BY ROYAL CHARTER 1853

HEAD OFFICES:—LONDON.

Paid-up Capital £800,000
Reserve Liability of Shareholders 800,000
Reserve Fund 800,000

Drafts granted upon all the principal places in the world and every description of Exchange and banking business transacted.

E. MEYER & Co., Agents,
Chemulpo.

E. MEYER & CO.
Chemulpo.

SOLE AGENTS IN KOREA FOR:
A. T. Morse, Sons & Co's
"Fresco" Distemper

In all colours ready for use on walls, Ceilings etc.

and

AVENARIUS CARBOLINEUM

A wood-preserving and antiseptic oil preparation

Against decay, dry-rot, fungus and wood-destroying insects.

A large supply always in Stock.
Prices upon application.

E. MEYER & Co.,
Chemulpo.

THE METHODIST PUBLISHING HOUSE,
Little West Gate, Seoul.

JOB PRINTING, TYPEWRITER PAPER
CARBON PAPER, VISITING CARDS
STATIONERY, BOOK BINDING
BOOK PUBLISHERS
AMERICAN SCHOOL BOOKS
SPENCERIAN COPY BOOKS
PEN CARBON LETTER AND BILL BOOKS

S. A. BECK, Manager.

HOKURKU DOBOKU KAISHA.

Branch office in Chong Dong, Seoul.

Japanese telephone No. 165

CONTRACT DEPARTMENT.
We can contract to build any building or construction.

MERCHANDISE DEPARTMENT.
We can provide any building material.
We have just contracted to build the new Belgian Legation.

DAI-ICHI GINKO.
LIMITED.
(Formerly the First National Bank.)

ESTABLISHED 1873

INCORPORATED UNDER PRESENT LAW 189

Capital - - - - - - - - Yen 5,000,000
Reserve Fund - - - - - 1,500,000

HEAD OFFICE:—TOKIO.

President: Baron SHIBUSAWA.

BRANCHES AND CORRESPONDENTS
In the Principal Cities and Towns of Japan.
Interest Allowed on
Fixed deposits 1 year - - - 6½ per cent
" " 6 months - - - 6 per cent

Special current accounts 1½ sen daily per Y 100
General " " 1 " " " 100

M. TANAKA,
Manager, Chemulpo.

SINGER SEWING MACHINES

씽거조봉침

SOLE AGENTS FOR KOREA
젼매쇼

HOLME RINGER & CO.
Chemulpo.
졔물포 함릉거양힝

KAMEYA & CO.
GENERAL STOREKEEPERS
Chinkokai - - Seoul

(Established 1895, Tokyo)

Confectionery, Hams, Canned Goods, Cutlery, Hirano & Tansan Water. Provisions, Gents, Furnishing goods, Toilet Articles, Travelling Bags, Tobacco, Cigars & Cigarettes Kitchen Utensils. Coffee. Biscuits

Fresh Goods always kept in Stock.
Prices Moderate
Please come and inspect our goods

NIPPON YUSEN KAISHA.

JAPANESE MAIL STEAMSHIP CO.

UNDER MAIL CONTRACT WITH THE IMPERIAL JAPANESE GOVERNMENT.

European Line

Regular Fortnightly Service between Yokohama Kobe, Moji, Shanghai, Hongkong, Singapore, Penang Colombo, Port Said, Marseilles, London and Antwerp

American Line

Regular Fortnightly Service between Hongkong and Seattle, calling at Shanghai, Moji, Kobe, Yokohama and Victoria, B. C.

Australian Line

Regular weekly Service betwen Japan Ports and Australia, calling at Hongkong and Manila.
(Above Three Lines Suspended until further notice).

Shanghai Line

Weekly Service between Shanghai and Japan Ports

Korea Line

Service Kobe, Moji, Nagasaki, Fusan Chemulpo Chefoo, Taiku.
S. S. Bahelsberg, 2181 tons.
Service Kobe, Moji, Fusan, Chemulpo, Chinnampo
S. S. ARGO, S. S. Ohio.

BORDEN'S CONDENSED MILK CO.
New York, U. S. A.

ALWAYS IN STOCK
Eagle Brand Condensed Milk.
Gold Seal Condensed Milk.
Peerless (Family) Evaporated Cream.
Borden's Malted Milk.

E. MEYER & CO.
Chemulpo, Korea,
Sole Agents

ROYAL INSURANCE COMPANY,
Funds exceed £10,000,000
FIRE
AT CURRENT RATES.
LIFE
REDUCED PREMIUM.
HOLME RINGER & Co.,
Agents, Chemulpo.

HOTEL DU PALAIS
SEOUL.

The only first class Hotel in Seoul. Situated in the centre of the city opposite the palace.

Cuisine under the supervision of an experienced French Chef.

Well ventilated and furnished throughout.

TARIFF UPON APPLICATION

L. MARTIN
Proprietor and Manager

大韓每日申報
대한미일신보

(뎨일빅이십호) (금요일) 일쳔구빅사년십이월구일

본사고빅

이신보는영어와한어로셕거미일츌판ᄒᆞᆸ

신문가

한쟝 엽두돈오푼

일삭됴 엽두량닷돈

우표가미삭닷돈

다맛돈으로밧숩

광고료는

긔한의쟝단과ᄌᆞᄒᆡᆼ의다쇼로즁감ᄒᆞ되렴가로밧을터이오며오리지아녀대한사람마다다이신문을보실터이니광고내시가돌원ᄒᆞ시는이들은우리신문샤에와셔면약ᄒᆞ심을회망ᄒᆞᆸ

○발힝소 박동대한미일신보샤법어학교압헤젼영국인셜필림집자리오

샤쟝 영국인 (비셜)

평양 디리점

○평양효동사는권미보씨로우리신문관미디리인을뎡ᄒᆞ엿ᄉᆞ오니평양에계신구람코져ᄒᆞ시는쳠군ᄌᆞ는히디리점에왕림ᄒᆞ와면의ᄒᆞ시ᄋᆞᆸ

사고

○우리대한미일신보의목뎍은대한의안녕질셔에관한모든뎨목에디ᄒᆞ야는공평한변론을쥬쟝홈이라우리동신원의탐보는신문보시는쳠군ᄌᆞ의계ᄒᆞᆼ상보도ᄒᆞ리며편지를긔셔ᄒᆞ여주시는이는셩명과반ᄃᆡ를젹어붓치시기를회망ᄒᆞ오니이거슬신문샹에긔ᄌᆡᄒᆞ랴는거시아니오다만국히긔자는신용ᄒᆞ는증거를숨고쟈홈이라긔자는아모긔셔던지긔지홈을퇴각ᄒᆞ는권리를가졋ᄉᆞ나퇴각ᄒᆞ는리유를말홀터이오며공즁평화를문란케ᄒᆞ는듯ᄒᆞᆫ긔셔는의례히밧지안켓ᄉᆞᆸ나이다

●본사셜시이리로신문을미양우례로분젼ᄒᆞ와례젼부의임의로젼ᄒᆞᆫ듯스로뎐곳에는혹늣게젼ᄒᆞ기도ᄒᆞ며혹몃칠거슬훈겁에젼ᄒᆞ기도ᄒᆞ며혹아니젼ᄒᆞ는곳도잇다ᄒᆞ와우리신문을ᄉᆞ랑ᄒᆞ야구람ᄒᆞ시는쳠군ᄌᆞ의계ᄃᆡᄒᆞ야미우미안ᄒᆞ옵기로지금은분젼인을두고미일일즉이젼ᄒᆞ며아니젼ᄒᆞ거나늣게거나ᄒᆞᆫ폐가업도록ᄒᆞ랴ᄒᆞ오니혹아니젼ᄒᆞ거나혹늣게젼ᄒᆞ거나ᄒᆞᆫ일이잇스면본샤로통긔ᄒᆞ여쥬심을회망ᄒᆞᆸ

외보

○대외씨연셜 일젼에일본진보당총회에셔빅작대외즁신씨가연셜ᄒᆞ엿는ᄃᆡ미우볼만ᄒᆞ기로이아래긔지ᄒᆞ노라

여러분드르시오국민의대소가잇는이날에여러분압헤늬의견을늬놀긔회를주심은늬의게영광이오또그뿐아니라늬가말ᄒᆞ는대디ᄒᆞ야잘못잔칙임도잇슬듯ᄒᆞ오그러ᄒᆞ나늬의목적에나아가셔말ᄒᆞ기젼에늬가ᄒᆞᆯ말이잇소우리진보당이지금압헤셔싸우는우리륙히군에디ᄒᆞ야깁히감ᄉᆞᄒᆞᆷ을표ᄒᆞ고또그륙히군들의가속에디ᄒᆞ야가득ᄒᆞᆫ졍렴을뵈이는거슬보면늬가실노깃붐을이긔지못ᄒᆞ오우리텬황의셩덕과우리인민의이국열셩으로우리륙히군이영광스러운승젼을엇엇소그러ᄒᆞ나싱각ᄒᆞ야보시오우리인민들이져의나라ᄯᅢ문에미일만이죽소인류의위험ᄒᆞᆷ이ᄒᆞᆫ젼정ᄀᆞᆺ치무셥고말살스러운것은업지요이젼징에싱명의샹히ᄒᆞ는거슬싱각ᄒᆞ면늬가우리용밍ᄒᆞᆫ륙히군에디ᄒᆞ야갑ᄒᆞᆫ정렴이졀노소ᄉᆞ나오또우리츙용ᄒᆞᆫ군인의피로우리국민이국민된공효를엇엇다ᄒᆞ고세계에셔말ᄒᆞ는거슬싱각ᄒᆞ면나의싱각이더욱엇더타말ᄒᆞᆯ수업소이번일로젼쟁이ᄒᆞᆫ큰경쟁이오세계에셔쥬목ᄒᆞ는비라이큰싸홈에착수ᄒᆞᆫ국민은그목적을달ᄒᆞ기ᄭᆞ지는그싸홈의즁지ᄒᆞ기를바랄수업는ᄃᆡ우리의목적을달ᄒᆞ기는우리국민의쟈립심과인력심에달닌거슬우리가알미가ᄒᆞ오엇던군인들의언론은ᄃᆡ젹의약ᄒᆞᆫ거와우리의강ᄒᆞᆫ거슬료량ᄒᆞ고스ᄉᆞ로죠아ᄒᆞ되로국은졍부와인민이합심이못되고그국민이다른인죵들이셕겻스니민요나기가쉬으며그인민들이빈궁ᄒᆞ니늬쳬들모집ᄒᆞ기어렵고그정부에셔지정예산에크게곤난ᄒᆞ야실노약ᄒᆞᆫᄯᅢ이만타ᄒᆞ나그러ᄒᆞ나로국의강력을오리구라파에셔반대치못ᄒᆞ엿는지라그럼으로로국의지금약ᄒᆞᆫ편만보고로국이픽ᄒᆞ기를바라는거슨너무소홀ᄒᆞ니우리는반다시대젹의강력을오히ᄒᆞ지아니ᄒᆞᆯ거시오우리인민의ᄒᆞᆫ소샹은로국이ᄒᆞᆫ번대픽ᄒᆞᆫ후면무여지ᄒᆞ게되야셔구라파각국샤회즁에셜녀날수노싱각ᄒᆞ나기거슨츰지각업는의견이오이교ᄃᆡ에우리는반다시우리나라에ᄃᆡᄒᆞ야외국의졍렴과공경ᄒᆞ는ᄯᅳᆺ슬강력으로만보젼ᄒᆞ랴고의쓸것아니오나는지금젼쟁에긴ᄒᆞᆫ일이외교가군ᄉᆞ만못지안타고밋소우리인민은대젹을가비엽게아는즁에그쉽게아는사룸들이지금ᄭᅡ지못오리라싱각ᄒᆞ든대젹의불특함대는스웨스운하를지나온다ᄒᆞ오그함대의ᄯᅢ남으로브터각즁립국의수ᄎᆞ반대는잇셧스나우리졍부에셔는무숨계획이잇는지아직확실히알일이업소 미완

관보

뎨삼쳔삼호 광무팔년십이월칠일

셔임급사령

○히셔리총지사무 렬도원부총지최영하

십일월이십사일

○ᄉᆞ셔관임관오등 경위원총슌리응진 심이월삼일

○의원면본관 온릉참봉 김용달

○입온릉참봉셔관임관팔등 슌창원참봉 리두노○임슌창원참봉셔관임관팔등 남찬회

○명시종원부시어 정삼품 리슌휘 정삼품 빅윤긔

이상십이월사일

○히시종원분시어 정삼품 리승휘 정삼품 빅윤긔

○명시종원부시어 종삼품 유셕관 사픔 빅남승 홍지

칠빅경긔계슌 유졍희

○중종이품가션대부 늬부협판

고학싱 리규노 ○중졍삼품

통졍대부비셔원승 고학싱

리동션 ○중종삼품통졍대부

쟝례원좌쟝례 고학싱 리두연

이샹젼늬쟝원경리셰지의고죠고증죠고의법면추 중

○면본관 탁지부쥬사 리종쥰 탁지부쥬ᄉᆞ 김정진 탁지부쥬ᄉᆞ 리회영

우는히원등이히세검ᄉᆞ위임으로비단ᄌᆞ세치못ᄒᆞᆯ뿐아니라도로혀싱폐가되야원망이잇기에면본관ᄒᆞ소

이샹십이월오일

궁명록사

○군부대신륙군부장리윤용참모부총쟝셔리참모부부장륙군부장윤웅렬 교육부총감륙군부장리지용근 쥬ᄒᆞ되젼쟈북관광지ᄃᆡ에지위와다못규졔는시의에맛당치못ᄒᆞᆫ즉가히변통을아니치못ᄒᆞᆯ뜻으로샹쥬ᄒᆞ와방핀지도를란샹회의ᄒᆞ야ᄡᅥ드리라ᄒᆞ신 명을복승ᄒᆞ와신등이회동ᄒᆞ야강확ᄒᆞ온즉잔졀이복렴ᄒᆞ옵건ᄃᆡ히진ᄃᆡ의졔쳐ᄒᆞ옴이진실노변방지경의민졍의진압홈이가쟝근일일로보건ᄃᆡ방슈홈이임이허슈홈이만코진무홈이막기에맛기ᄯᅩᄒᆞᆫ어려운지라ᄒᆞᆫ갓거지의거리를허비ᄒᆞᆯᄯᅡ름인즉히량진ᄃᆡ를둠이유익홈이업는지라이제아죽폐지ᄒᆞ옵고힘드려방략을궁구ᄒᆞ와종금이후에다시베플미시의에맛당홈가ᄒᆞ와근쥬ᄒᆞ오니셩지를업드려기다리옵는이다

광무팔년십이월삼일에봉 지

ᄒᆞ와제왈가라ᄒᆞ옵시다

○의졍부찬졍신긔션궁니부대신임시셔리니부대신륙군부장리용태근쥬ᄒᆞ되아젼에치젹을규졍ᄒᆞ와빅셩에근심을도와줌이어늬ᄯᅢ에급무가아니리오마는근쟈에슈령에탐학홈과이혼포홈이날로심ᄒᆞᆫ지라싱령들이다도탄에ᄲᅡ지고법강이ᄶᅥ녀진지라현금에팔도인민의물실듯ᄒᆞ고미ᄀᆞᆺ치모혀소란ᄒᆞᆫ만가지형샹은진실로일로말미암이라진실로별로이판결ᄒᆞ는법을니여대단이즁치홈을더ᄒᆞ지아니ᄒᆞ면고기ᄀᆞᆺ치발딱거리는인정을위로ᄒᆞᆯ길이업고나라에명을기여미을수업는지라평양군슈평한쥬는탐학ᄒᆞ는소리가길에실여쓰미민쟝과부보를참상ᄒᆞ옵건ᄃᆡ근년에빙공영수ᄒᆞ야가결을비렴ᄒᆞᆫ거시누십만량에안를지아니ᄒᆞ오니진실로젼고에업는바ㅣ라위션면본관ᄒᆞ옵고법으로ᄒᆞ야곰구라ᄒᆞ와궁진이핵실ᄒᆞ옵고그쟝젼은차자민간에환퇴ᄒᆞ오며인ᄒᆞ야죠률엄판ᄒᆞ오며밝히사보ᄒᆞ지못ᄒᆞᆫ평안남도관찰ᄉᆞ리쥬

UNION INSURANCE SOCIETY OF CANTON.

Head office Hongkong.
Marine risks underwritten at current rates.
Agents in Chemulpo,
E. MEYER & Co.

COMPAGNIE DES MESSAGERIES MARITIMES.

Fortnightly Direct Service.

For Marseilles
via Ports.
Sailing from Yokohama
Calling at Kobe,
Shanghai, Hongkong, Saigon, Singapore,
Colombo, Djibouti, Suez, Port Said
and Marseilles

For particulars apply to
HOLME RINGER & Co.,
Chemulpo.

HAYASHIDA & CO.,

16 MYENG DONG, CHIN KO KAI, SEOUL.
BRANCH OFFICE AT CHEMULPO.

Money changers, Coal and Wood Merchants, Express Agents.

We are agents for the Pyeng-yang Coal Company and the Karazu Coal Company of Japan. We have the best quality of both anthracite and bituminous coal, and prompt execution of orders is our speciality. Firewood of all kinds kept in stock. Full weight guaranteed. Money of all denominations exchanged at current rates. Parcels received for all parts.

CHINA MUTUAL LIFE INS. OC.

Most favourable terms to policy holders.

Benefit system unsurpassed.

HOLME RINGER & Co.
Agents, Chemulpo.

C. P. R.

CANADIAN PACIFIC RAILWAY COMPANY'S ROYAL MAIL STEAMSHIP LINE.

THE FAST ROUTE BETWEEN CHINA, JAPAN AND EUROPE VIA CANADA AND THE UNITED STATES.

Route from Hongkong via Shanghai, Nagasaki (Inland Sea of Japan) Kobe, Yokohama Victoria and Vancouver.

Twin Screw Empress Steamship—6,000 Tons—Speed 19 kn

PROPOSED SAILING FROM YOKOHAMA.
R. M. S. Empress of India.
R. M. S. Empress of Japan.
R. M. S. Empress of China.
R. M. S. Athonian.
R. M. S. Tastar.

Special reduction (first class only) granted to members of the Military, Naval, Diplomatic and Civil services and to Missionaries.

Passengers have choice of ten routes across the Continent of America and have privilege of travelling by any Atlantic Steamship Line.

Round the World passage tickets in connection with the P. and O. S. N., North German Lloyd and Messageries Co.'s £125.

All rates payable at current rate of exchange.

For further information, Tickets, Guide Books, etc., apply to

HOLME, RINGER & Co., AGENTS,
Chemulpo.

Grand Hotel,

(Formerly the Station Hotel)

Near the Railway Terminus, West Gate Seoul.

The Best Hotel in Korea
Handsome new Building.
Fine Airy Rooms
Excellent Cuisine.
Terms Moderate.
Special terms to Missionaries
and to permanent boarders.

Electric cars within 2 minutes' walk.

W. H. EMBERLEY.
Proprietor.

EVERY FACILITY.

In connection with Life Assurance Business is afforded by

The Standard Life Assurance Co.,

One of the largest and wealthiest of the Provident Institutions of the United Kingdom Forms of Application and all information will be promptly afforded on application.

10 CENTS A DAY.

Not a very large expenditure is it? But it is sufficient to secure for a man of 30 a policy with the STANDARD LIFE OFFICE for

$1323.

For all particulars of rates, etc., apply to

Holme, Ringer & Co.,
Agents, Chemulpo.

THE NEW YORK LIFE INSURANCE COMPANY

Have you ever been declined by any Company?

Are you engaged in a specially hazardous occupation?

Have you heard of the New York Life Insurance Company's New Classifications for this class of Risks?

If not, send your date of birth, occupation and particulars of rejection, if any to

E. MEYER & Co.,
Agents, Chemulpo.

MITSUI BUSSAN KAISHA.
(MITSUI & Co.)

MITSUI GINKO.
(MITSUI BANK.)

The Bank is owned by the members of the Mitsui Family, who, as partners, assume an unlimited responsibility for all liabilities of the Bank:—

Capital .... Yen 5,000,000
Reserve Fund .... " 5,600,000

HEAD OFFICE, TOKYO.

LONDON OFFICE, 34, LIME ST., E. C.

BRANCHES AND AGENCIES:

New York, San Francisco, Hamburg, Bombay, Singapore, Manila, Hongkong, Amoy, Chefoo, Tientsin.

Kobe, Hakodate, Yokohama, Kure, Yokosuka, Moji, Shimonoseki, Miike, Wakamatsu Nagasaki, Kuchinotsu, Karatsu, Sasebo, Misume, Taipeh, &c

Telegraphic Address for all the Offices:
"MITSUI."
A. B. C. AND A. 1 CODES USED.

Contractors of Coal

To the Imperial Japanese Navy. Arsenals and Railway Bureau, Principal Railway Companies and Industrial Work, Home and Foreign Mail and Freight Steamers.

Sole Proprietors

Of the famous Miike, Tagawa and Yamano Coal Mines.

Sole Agents

For the sale of Fukumo, Hokoku, Ichimura, Kanoda, Mannoura, Onoura, Ostuji, Sonoda, Tsubaruro, Yoshinotani, Yoshio, Yurokibura and other coals.

YANGTSE INSURANCE ASSOCIATION, LTD.

The undersigned, having been appointed agents for the above company, are prepared to issue policies and pay losses on marine risks at regular rates.

E. MEYER & Co.,
Agents, Chemulpo.

AMERICAN KOREAN ELECTRIC CO.

Light and Power.

Main Office: Electric Building, Chong No.

RAILWAY DEPARTMENT.

OPERATING CARS BETWEEN EAST AND WEST GATE, EVERY TEN MINUTES:—

First Car leaves East Gate at 7:00 A. M. First Car leaves R. R. Station at 7:25 A. M
Last Car " East Gate at 9:40 P. M. Last " " R. R. Station at 10:05 P.M

OPERATING CARS BETWEEN EAST GATE AND IMPERIAL TOMB TERMINUS, EVERY TWENTY MINUTES:—

CONNECTING WITH EVERY ALTERNATE CAR ARRIVING AT EAST GATE FROM CHONG NO.

First Car leaves East Gate for Tomb at 7:10 A. M.
" " " Tomb for East Gate at 7:35 A. M.
Last " " East Gate for Tomb at 7:50 P. M.
" " " Tomb for East Gate at 8:10 P. M.

OPERATING CARS BETWEEN CHONG NO AND YUNG SAN RIVER EVERY TWELVE MINUTES:—

First Car leaves Chong No for South Gate at 7:12 A. M.
" " " Chong No for Yung San at 7:36 A. M.
" " " South Gate for Chong No at 7:20 A. M.
" " " Yung San for Chong No at 8:09 A. M.
Last " " South Gate for Chong No 10:00 P. M.
" " " Yung San for Chong No at 9:33 P. M

SPECIAL PRIVATE CARS FURNISHED TO SUIT CONVENIENCE OF PATRONS. PRICES ON APPLICATION AT HEAD OFFICE.

LIGHTING DEPARTMENT

Where less than 250 candle power of light is used, the rate per month will be
Per 16 candle power incandescent lamp,—All night.—Yen 2.50.
32 candle power incandescent lamp:—All night:—Yen 4.00.
50 candle power incandescent lamp:—All night:—Yen 6.00.
150 " " " " " " " 10.00.
1200 " " enclosed are " " " " 20.00.

Where more than 250 candle power of light is used, a Meter will be installed, irequvedted:—Rent of Meter Yen 2.00 per month. Rate of charges by meter reading:—Two Sen per Ampere per hour. (Approximately this is equal to about One Sen per 16 C. P. lamp per hour) Minimum monthly charge where meter is installed, Yen 20.00 per month, which includes rental of meter.

Estimates for installing lights furnished on application
An assortment of chandeliers always on hand.

K. Murakami.
Photograph Studio
Chinkokai, Seoul.

Printing, Developing and Enlargement, of Photographs always Undertaken.

Korean Views and Pictures Illustrating Native Customs always on Sale.

THE OSAKA SHOSEN KAISHA.

Boats frequently on the berth for Chinnampo.

REGULAR SAILINGS BETWEEN JAPAN AND KOREAN PORTS.

FUSAN AND KOBE VIA SHIMONOSEKI.

OSAKA VIA MOKPO, FUSAN, SHIMONOSEKI AND KOBE.

MOJI DIRECT.

OSAKA VIA KUNSAN, MASANPO, FUSAN, SHIMONOSEKI AND KOBE.

CHEMULPO KUNSAN LINE,
Every three days.

CHEMULPO CHINNAMPO LINE.
Every three days.

For Freight and passage and further particulars apply to
THE OSAKA SHOSEN KAISHA,
Chemulpo.

ONDON, PLAISANT & CO.

General Storekeepers and Merchants, Ships Contractors, Tobacconists, Commission and Forwarding Agents, Coal Merchants

IMPORTERS AND EXPORTERS

Seoul & Chemulpo.

W. D. WENTWORTH.

LANDING
AND
SHIPPING AGENT
AND
CUSTOMS BORDER.

12 OURA, NAGASAKI.

STEWARD & CO.

Chemulpo.

Shipchandlers and Storekeepers, Naval and Mercantile Contrrctors, Landing and Shipping Agents.

STEWARD'S HOTEL

Chemulpo.

Best accommodation in the port for travellers. Clean and well-aired rooms, good cuisine and prompt attendence, moderate tariff.

하는죵젼칙으로베프며명ᄉᆞ를
한만이ᄒᆞᆫ삼등군슈민졍식은삼
ᄀᆡ월감봉에쳐ᄒᆞ와이죡죄를
지고거헝ᄒᆞᆫ계ᄒᆞ오며초산군슈
윤션던은사소ᄒᆞᆫ집불츄심ᄒᆞᆫ는
ᄉᆞ건으로군민를혹힝ᄒᆞ야세인
명의죽음에이루어포병ᄒᆞᆫ부녀
가쳔리에다라와졍쇼ᄒᆞ니빅셩
의자목의관원이되야엇지참아
이리ᄒᆞ리요박비ᄒᆞᆫ부로ᄒᆞ여곰
압상심관ᄒᆞ오며젼평강군슈죠
셩지는탐학ᄒᆞᆷ으로민효를이루
엇소죠가망칙ᄒᆞ되져오의원면
본관ᄒᆞ고말아싸온즉가ᄒᆞ괴왕
으로물론ᄒᆞᆯ슈업는지라가ᄒᆞ또ᄒᆞᆫ법
부로ᄒᆞ야곰구리ᄒᆞ야증관ᄒᆞ오
며공쥬군슈죠쥰회는올여름에
리료가비록관가에실슈가업다
ᄒᆞᆯ지나평일에힝졍ᄒᆞᆷ이진실로
능히민을심복ᄒᆞ엿스면엇지
이법분에괴변을당ᄒᆞ엿스리오
달신상경ᄒᆞ와다시쓸듸업싸오
니큰고을에급ᄒᆞᆫ소무가여러달
광폐ᄒᆞ와스니또ᄒᆞᆫ면관중판ᄒᆞ
오며당초에샹부에보ᄒᆞ지아니
ᄒᆞᆫ츙남관찰ᄉᆞ리항의는또ᄒᆞᆫ즁
젼칙에쳐ᄒᆞ옵고평강공쥬두고
을긔료ᄒᆞᆫ리민은닉부로훈령을
발ᄒᆞ와법부에이죠ᄒᆞ야법듸로
슈범을판결ᄒᆞ야ᄒᆞᆫ법률에쳐ᄒᆞ
와써빅셩에원망을씻치오며써
빅샹의쯧을진졍ᄒᆞ와법강의만
일을진동ᄒᆞᆯᄭᅥᄒᆞ와근 샹쥬ᄒᆞ
와붕지의쥬라ᄒᆞ옵셧더라

론셜

일본의빅작이여러가지사실에
대ᄒᆞ야가히경탄ᄒᆞᆯ만ᄒᆞᆫ일로써
졔출ᄒᆞ야 연셜ᄒᆞᆫ바를동경에
잇는진보당들의게괴셔ᄒᆞ엿는
듸일본이쟝수와군ᄉᆞ는유여ᄒᆞ
야가히다른나라로더부러싸
홈만ᄒᆞᆫ즉이는파연찬양ᄒᆞᆯ만
ᄒᆞᆫ일이로되오즉크게관계되는
바자는다만지졍파외교수단이
오히려부족ᄒᆞ야ᄀᆞ젼ᄒᆞᆷ을ᄒᆞᆼ샹
실심으로염려ᄒᆞᆷ이잇는ᄭᅡ닭에
유독대외씨는진실로근지ᄒᆞ다
가엇지ᄒᆞᆯ수업시허락ᄒᆞᆫ양으로
셜명ᄒᆞ엿슨즉
이거스로써볼진듸지졍에부족
ᄒᆞᆷ으로말ᄆᆡ암아젼국에반대가
ᄆᆡ러날모양인즉만일이지졍만
아니엿드면아라사를멸망ᄒᆞ엿
슬거시여놀이졔이지경에이름
은실로일본에지앙인거시로다
빅작대외씨의이사건으로연셜
ᄒᆞᆫ일관ᄒᆞ장ᄎᆞ다른날에계지ᄒᆞᆯ
터이로되대강사실인즉졍부에
셔군비의부족ᄒᆞᆷ으로써세랍을
증가ᄒᆞ려ᄒᆞ는고로대외씨와동
써당파에셔는이러ᄒᆞᆫ긔미를알
고미리반대ᄒᆞ야고집ᄒᆞᆫ즉만일
이러ᄒᆞᆷ을불계ᄒᆞ고괴여히ᄒᆞ려
ᄒᆞᆯ진대젼국인민의반동ᄒᆞᆯ염려
가불무ᄒᆞᆫ지라
그런고로졍부에셔는이후에환
보ᄒᆞᆯ죠ᄒᆞᆫ도리가잇는ᄭᅡ닭에외
국에차관을ᄒᆞ라ᄒᆞ되우리의싱
각에는그리ᄒᆞᆯ거시아니라면화
비를증첨ᄒᆞ는거시대단히조흔
방침일듯ᄒᆞᆫ거시면화는졍부에
셔부셜ᄒᆞᆫ자인즉이일은ᄒᆞᆫ조면
심히쉰편ᄒᆞᆯ듯ᄒᆞ며또ᄒᆞᆫ럼세를
증가ᄒᆞ는거슨무론빅셩의빈부
귀쳔ᄒᆞ고평균이만졍세ᄒᆞ엿스
면이는사룸마다모도먹고쓰는
물건인즉세랍ᄒᆞ기에도응당어
렵지안케싱각ᄒᆞᆯ지라
그러ᄒᆞ 세랍증가ᄒᆞᆯ방칙은이
두가지밧게업거놀요ᄉᆞ이소문
을드른즉덕국빅림과법국파리
에셔은히ᄉᆞ업ᄒᆞ는쥬인들이아
라사로더부러체결ᄒᆞ야오쳔만
박올오푼변리에차관ᄒᆞ기로중
약이되엿다는듸일본셔는영국
룬돈과미국육츅에셔일쳔오빅
만원을팔푼리자에어드랴ᄒᆞ되
마음과갓치괴왕말ᄒᆞᆫ티로되지
아니ᄒᆞᆫ는모양인즉
만일치급ᄒᆞ는사룸이차관ᄒᆞ야
지발ᄒᆞ라는마음만잇슬지경이
면그동안에몃쳔만방의거관이
라도여러번되엿슬지라이졔일
본형편이차관ᄒᆞᆷ에티ᄒᆞ야이대
도록대외빅작의반티가어러는
즉만일이지경으로결과가되면
전쟁결말나기ᄭᅡ지엇더케련속
ᄒᆞ야지탕ᄒᆞ여갈는지모를지라
젼후사세가이러ᄒᆞᆫ즉일본의쳔
졀ᄒᆞᆫ친구가잇게되면아모쪼록
이일을화평ᄒᆞ야취셔가되도록
권면ᄒᆞ고근일형편듸로론란만
ᄒᆞ지만케ᄒᆞ기를바라노라

잡보

○면교발뎡 십이월칠일에쟝
연군슈가외부로면보ᄒᆞ기를삼
화항병참소에셔본관을청ᄒᆞ야
모도여의론ᄒᆞ자기에금일에발
뎡ᄒᆞᆫ다ᄒᆞ엿더라

○죠쳥교ᄉᆞ퇴셜 학부에셔외
부에죠회ᄒᆞ기를한어교ᄉᆞ호문
휘이미신료ᄒᆞ야히교ᄒᆞ엿슨즉
쳥컨듸쳥공ᄉᆞ의게이죠ᄒᆞ야학
문이고명ᄒᆞ고픔힝이단아ᄒᆞᆫ사
람으로그자리를치우게ᄒᆞ라ᄒᆞ
엿더라

○면훈히찰 에부에셔히쥬관
찰ᄉᆞ의게면보ᄒᆞ기를청샹치명
ᄒᆞᆫᄉᆞ로본부에셔위원을파송ᄒᆞ
야영공관위원파쳥공관파원을
듸동ᄒᆞ고금일에발졍ᄒᆞ니히원
등이디경에도달ᄒᆞᆫ후슈ᄉᆞ등졀
을각별관급ᄒᆞ라ᄒᆞ엿더라

○일ᄉᆞ리방외부 쟉칠일하오
삼시에일공ᄉᆞ가외부에젼왕ᄒᆞ
야리시도록담화ᄒᆞ엿더라

○공찰면보 공쥬관찰ᄉᆞ가일
쟉일에닉부로면보ᄒᆞ기를진보
회원십여인이부하에리도ᄒᆞ야
류ᄒᆞ며또일진회쟝의면보가잇
셔ᄀᆡ회ᄒᆞᆫ다ᄒᆞ오니엇지죠쳐ᄒᆞ
올넌지곳회면ᄒᆞ라ᄒᆞ엿더라

○량ᄉᆞ죠회 영국공ᄉᆞ가외부
로죠회ᄒᆞ기를황히도슈안금광
[illegible]샹지ᄒᆞ야인허치아니ᄒᆞ면본
공ᄉᆞ는철관ᄒᆞ고귀국ᄒᆞᆯ터이라
ᄒᆞ엿고 외티리국공ᄉᆞ는본졍
부의훈령을접쥰ᄒᆞ야외부로죠
회ᄒᆞ기를금광일ᄉᆞ로죠회ᄒᆞᆫ지
가이믜경년ᄒᆞ엿셔도오히려쥰
허치아니ᄒᆞ니이번에샹지ᄒᆞ면
쳘관ᄒᆞ고귀국ᄒᆞ겟노라ᄒᆞ엿더
라

○잡세혁파 경위원에셔오강
잡세를관할ᄒᆞ야슈세ᄒᆞ는고로
일진회에셔총디위원을경위원
총관권중석씨의게보내여잡세
를혁파ᄒᆞ라ᄒᆞ고ᄉᆞ직퇴거ᄒᆞ라
ᄒᆞ엿더니경위원에셔고시ᄒᆞ야
잡세는혁파ᄒᆞ엿더라

○여ᄉᆞ티젼독봉 각방곡슌검
이믜호에여ᄉᆞ티젼을독촉ᄒᆞ야
슈봉ᄒᆞ는듸대소호에협잡이불
일ᄒᆞ다더라

○합쳥훈칙 일공관에셔외부
에공함ᄒᆞ기를징남포와긔진포
쟈에도로슈기ᄉᆞ로이믜죠쳥ᄒᆞ
야맛당히히디방관의게훈칙ᄒᆞ
라ᄒᆞ엿고이도로가군용샹에급
무여늘이제ᄭᆞ지훈칙ᄒᆞ지안ᄒᆞᆫ
다고히디ᄉᆞ령관이보고ᄒᆞ엿스
니쳥컨듸속히훈칙ᄒᆞᆫ후그일조
를시명ᄒᆞ라ᄒᆞ엿더라

○관인의기회 각대관의잡기
가대쳐ᄒᆞᆷ으로신참졍이샹쥬
엄금ᄒᆞ엿는듸근일에그이하중
관등이잡기회를삼여경위원총
관권중석궁닉부협판박용화한
셩판윤민경식부장리지용모모
제씨가화투회를셜시ᄒᆞ고츈회
로셜국ᄒᆞ는듸그즁에독실이파
다ᄒᆞ다더라

○쳐분히산 승후샹소ᄉᆞ로각
쳐에셔사룸마다운동ᄒᆞ는데
쳐분을느리사무론모ᄉᆞᄒᆞ고회
등ᄒᆞ는쟈는일제히산ᄒᆞ라ᄒᆞ옵
셧다더라

○습의겸힝 인산쵸도습의를
음력본월초오일로택뎡ᄒᆞ엿더
니여ᄉᆞ군도오히려쥰비치못ᄒᆞ
고졔반ᄉᆞ무가미비ᄒᆞᆷ으로여ᄉᆞ
대쟝빅셩긔씨가샹 쥬ᄒᆞ고쵸
도습의를십칠일지도습의로겸
힝ᄒᆞᆫ다ᄒᆞ더라

○여ᄉᆞ티젼 금번인산여ᄉᆞ군
티젼을대중쇼삼등에분등ᄒᆞ엿
는듸불계빈부관인ᄒᆞ고중셔만
비ᄒᆞ는듸집간수로대가는빅
량중가는오십량쇼가는이십오
량식밧는듸중셔호수가만여호
라합오륙십만량가령이된다ᄒᆞ
는듸군인인즉빅팔명이라쓰는
예산은십만량가량이라더라

○슌검월봉 ᄎᆞ시에슌검월급
이적어거힝ᄒᆞᆯ슈가업는고로조
되ᄒᆞ는폐가만흔지라하등슌검
은십팔원이오일등슌검은이십
원을쥬기로회외ᄒᆞ엿다더라

○아동잡기 쟉일하오이시에
아희세시남촌어두목팔일본마
티영문압에잇는밧진흙구덩이
에셔화투로써잡기를ᄒᆞ다가별
슌검의게잡혓는듸ᄒᆞᆫ놈은도망
ᄒᆞ고두놈만잡아갓다더라

○병욕탈총 지작일밤에진골
포막에파수ᄒᆞ는병뎡의총을병
뎡놈이ᄲᅢ아스랴고무한힐난ᄒᆞ
는듸동리사룸이모히미그만두
고갓다는듸병뎡의총을ᄲᅢ아셔
무엇ᄒᆞ랴넌지알수업다고ᄒᆞ더
라

뎐보

지작야팔시동경발

○졈령후포격 어빅삼고디를
졈령ᄒᆞᆫ결과로려슌항니에쇠잔
ᄒᆞᆫ군함을포격ᄒᆞ고큰손히를죠
엇고또동디구확안에잠복ᄒᆞᆫ젹
의쇠잔ᄒᆞᆫ군ᄉᆞ를발견ᄒᆞ야이계
을다쓰러버렷더라

○소ᄉᆞ의즁립 파라작함듸에
속ᄒᆞᆫ잔부군함이소ᄉᆞ항에도착
ᄒᆞᆫ배에동항으로브터이십사서
간니에출거ᄒᆞ라명ᄒᆞ고셕탄실
기를허락지아니ᄒᆞ엿더라

○로국식언 구론스닷트에셔
발ᄒᆞᆫ룡신을거ᄒᆞᆫ즉금년이월에
인쳔에셔격침ᄒᆞᆫ와리약호와고
쓰호의쟝교슈병과밋화병과그
다른승긱우지차젼투에참가치
안는다맹세ᄒᆞ고히방ᄒᆞ기를독
ᄒᆞ엿는듸금에히군인등이로재
스도렌스기ㅣ함디에참가ᄒᆞ야
동으로향ᄒᆞ야항히ᄒᆞ는즁이라
ᄒᆞ더라

〔경셩일본공ᄉᆞ관면챠〕

○려슌픽함상보 대본영공보
에왈려슌공위군은십이월삼일
에히군포를가지고젹함을사격
ᄒᆞ야 젹의젼투함일만이쳔톡
빅칠십ᄉᆞ돈되는보비에단군함
울여셧발맛치고 젹의젼투함
일민이쳔구빅룩돈과굿혼 ᄅᆡ
도위싼 군함을여덜발이맛고
기타군함에는열여셧발이마졋
고또십이월오일에또동포함으
로사격ᄒᆞ야 보미에다 호에
일곱발이맛고 젼투함일만구
빅룩십돈되는볼다와호 에열
훈번이맛고오례도위싼에열훈
발이마졋고하오삼시ᄭᆞ지우리
포듸에ᄒᆞᆫ란환이빅옥산남방화
약고에대폭연을발ᄒᆞ게ᄒᆞ고다
음에화저가이려나두시잔이되
도록불을ᄭᅳ지아니ᄒᆞ엿고또동
일에즁포를가지고젹함을사격
ᄒᆞ야비례슈위도 젼투함일만
이쳔룩빅칠십ᄉᆞ돈 에두발이
맛고그다른군함에두발이마졋
는듸군함은약ᄒᆞᆫ시간ᄭᆞ지대폭
연을날녓더라

〔군ᄉᆞ령부면챠〕

광고

TELEGRAMS.

Japanese Legation.

The Russians at Chihfansan were unable to withstand the bombardment of the Japanese troops on 203 metre hill, so on Dec. 6th, they evacuated that position, which the Japanese then occupied at 1 p. m.

At 2 p. m. the Japanese drove the Russians from Sitzekao (1500 metres west of Etzeshan) and at 3 p. m. drove them from their position on rising ground north of Saulicho (northeast of Etzeshan.) The Japanese then occupied those places

For the past few days, the Russian ships have been continually bombarded, with the result that the Poltava has taken a big list to port and is nearly submerged, the Retvisan has taken a list to starboard and the Bayan appears to be on the rocks.

At 4 p. m. on December 6th the Russians despatched a messenger under a white flag with a proposal for a 5 hours armistice to bury the dead. This was agreed to.

London, Dec. 1.

The Russian Government has applied to the Washington Government to postpone the session of the Second Hague Conference until the end of the war.—*Kobe Simbun.*

Shanghai, Dec. 2.

Shanghai appears to be a market for the Russian Army and Navy. Two German butcheries here have received orders from the Russians to provide several million "kins" of beef for the Baltic Squadron. The Russian naval officers here are often seen in the same carriage with Mr. Spitzer, who is believed to have conveyed large quantities of stores to Port Arthur.—*Mainichi.*

Army Headquarters.

In the forenoon of the 6th inst, the Japanese scouts north of Kianchang fell in with 20 Russian Cavalry; two of the latter were killed and the remainder retreated.

A report from the main army in Manchuria states that at 2 a. m. on the 6th inst, two companies of Russian infantry attacked Potzeho, where a small Japanese garrison was stationed. These retreated leaving the position in the hands of the Russians, but being reinforced later retook the place.

Japanese Legation.

The Japanese Naval Commander of naval fort No. 89 attacking Port Arthur, reports that the ships Poltava and Retvisan can be clearly seen. The former is nearly submerged and the latter has taken a very heavy list to starboard. It is his opinion that these ships are now entirely out of action.

London, Nov. 30.

It is reported that an American shipbuilder has arranged to construct at Sebastapol (Crimea) 100 Russian warships.—Asahi.

London, Nov. 30.

With respect to the speech of Lord Lansdowne, British Secretary for Foreign Affairs, the coal merchants at Cardiff declare that under existing circumstances it is impossible for them to stop the export of coal to either of the belligerents, and that the coal purchased for Russia is for the most part shipped through the medium of German merchants, who decline to disclose the cargoes.—Asahi.

The Italian Minister was received in audience today at 2 P. M. by His Majesty. The Japanese Minister was received at 4 P M.

The Education Department have requested the Foreign Office to fill up the post of teacher in the Chinese School, made vacant by the death of Mr. Ho Mun Wi.

Yesterday, the Japanese Minister paid a long visit to the Foreign Office, to discuss various matters.

The new society Kong-chin-hoi is making a dead set against Government tax-collectors.

The War Office have abolished the local guard of Pukchong and Chong Sung and sent back the soldiers there to their homes.

The Foreign Office have drawn up a contract for their agreement with Mr. Stevens. His salary and term of engagement are the principal items included.

A taxation on the houses of Seoul has been levied with the object of securing sufficient funds to pay for coolie hire on the occasion of the funeral of the Crown Princess. The taxes vary between $1.00 and $4.00 according to the status of the Citizens.

The Governor of North Kyengsang province states that the Japanese have placed flags in numerous villages in his district. On enquiry, he was told by the Japanese military authorities that they were making a survey of his province. No better explanation being forthcoming, he had the flags removed by his own officials.

The Il-chin-hoi have increased the number of men serving on each of their so-called investigation committees to ten. One of these bodies is despatched daily to the Vice President of State, requesting him to resign; another visits the Home Office with the object of obtaining the dismissal of the Governors of the Whanghai and Chulla provinces.

Hector Fuller of the Indianapolis "News," the first correspondent to run the blockade into Port Arthur, has written an account of his experiences while in the beleagured city. According to the "Novi Krai," he has depended more on imagination than fact for his details. A Russian officer, recently arrived here from the fortress, states Mr. Fuller was kept a close prisoner while in the city, and that a court was organized to try him under charge of being a spy. Subsequently, and before a verdict could be rendered, General Stoessel squashed the proceedings, saying to the members of the court—"I am satisfied this man is harmless." The officer further states that Mr. Fuller's nerve was badly shaken by the sweat-box proceedings, and that he broke into tears in the presence of General Stoessel. One who has never gone an examination at the hands of the military police should not judge too hastily in this case.—Chefoo Daily News.

The most mysterious man on the China coast is Mr. Bennet Burleigh of the London "Daily Telegraph." If the North American Indians of thirty years ago had known Mr. Burleigh they would have promptly named him The-Man-Who-Comes-And-Goes-In-The Night. It was but the other day that Mr. Burleigh and Mr. Lawton mysteriously disappeared from Chefoo on that most mysterious of craft, the "Samson." Some said that they had gone to Shanghai, while others where sure that the running of the Port Arthur blockade was contemplated. Those who know Mr. Burleigh best are satisfied that danger would not deter him in any enterprise which promised news. However the "Samson" did not go to Shanghai. Neither did it go to Port Arthur Where it went no one seems to know—even Mr. Burleigh.

With bated breath a captain of a coasting steamer told me yesterday that he had seen Mr Burleigh on the streets of Newchwang during the time he was popularly supposed to be en route to either Shanghai or Port Arthur. Of course the captain may have been mistaken—there are so many Japanese officers who look, talk and act like Mr. Burleigh. However the question no longer is—Where has Mr. Burleigh gone?, but—Where will Mr. Burleigh go? He will certainly not submit to a trip to Sasebo.—Chefoo Daily News.

That the canal as a means of inland communication is by no means obsolete is well demonstrated, remarks Harper's Weekly, by the fact that there is at present under discussion a project for a ship canal from the Rhine to the Danube, which, if constructed, will prove the most important waterway in Europe. The proposition involves the dredging of the Neckar from Mannheim, where it flows into the Rhine, to Heilbronn, and thence to Cannstatt or Essingen and Neckarems, so that it would be navigable for steamers and barges of considerable draught. The distances would be 110 miles, and the expense is estimated at about $10,000,000. From Neckarems to the Danube, a distance of seventy-one and one-half miles, the beds of the Rems, Kocher, and Brenz, all small streams, would be followed, and there would be required a considerable amount of excavation and engineering work, such as lock construction, which is expected to cost about $25,000,000. There would be a certain amount of water power available from the various locks and feeders of the canal. The commercial advantages following the construction of such a canal are readily apparent—it would bring the various States of Germany and other parts of Europe into much closer relation. For example, Bavaria would be connected not only with the Upper Rhine district, but also with French and Alsace-Lorraine canal system, while to the east it would gain access to Russia, Austria Hungary, and the Balkan Peninsula.

The trial of Count von Baudissin on the charge of insulting the Army in his book, "First Class Men," has ended in his being sentenced to a fine of £15, or in default thirty days' imprisonment, while his publisher is fined £10, or twenty days' imprisonment. The publisher is fined a further £10 for contravention of the Press Laws. The whole of the book was read in court. The Count, in his defence, said he wished to show how society petted and spoiled young officers, who were often very ignorant, thereby making the young men absurdly conceited; how people fed the officers on champagne and caviare, while at home they were contented to make a dinner off threepennyworth of sausage. Owing to the poverty of the families of many officers and the growing luxury of the Army, about 15 per cent. of the officers coming from the cadet schools went wrong through debt.

The above-mentioned book has been published in London by Fisher Unwin. It is the remorseless story of the ill-fortune of a manufacturer's son drafted by the Kaiser into a crack regiment where hitherto only the "best" families had been represented.

The Korea Daily News.

Issued at 5 P. M. daily except Sundays.

Rate of Subscription:—
Per Year,............Yen 25.
Per Quarter,..........Yen 7.
Per Month,..........Yen 2.50.

Postage in Korea not charged extra.
Postage abroad charged extra.

Advertisements, 50 sen per day for 1 inch or less.
5 yen per month per inch.
50 yen per year per inch.

All communications to

E. T. BETHELL,
Editor and Publisher,
Pak-tong, Seoul.

AN ALLEGED JAPANESE PLOT.

St. Petersburg, Nov. 5.—A sensational report is current here, attributed to a high authority, that Russia will undertake before the international commission to prove that the Japanese Minister at The Hague actually organized an attack on the Russian squadron, and will produce a message sent by the Minister containing complete evidence that such was the case. The Associated Press has not obtained official confirmation of the sensational report that an intercepted despatch from the Japanese Minister at The Hague would be produced in the court of enquiry into the recent North Sea affair to prove the existence of a plot to destroy the Russian Baltic fleet. There is alleged to be good ground for believing the report true and that there are many indications that the Russian Government has been long in possession of strong evidence of a Japanese plan to intercept all Admiral Rojestvensky's warships. This is held to explain the willingness of Russia to submit the case to international arbitration. Emperor Nicholas, during an audience with British Ambassador Harding last Sunday, declared in the most positive terms that there were Japanese torpedo boats in the North Sea. Apparently, Denmark was impressed by the same belief. The Russian Empress Dowager, who was then in Copenhagen, did not fail to communicate to her father the communication received by her from St. Petersburg. This might account for the extraordinary precautions adopted by the Danish Government in detailing warships to escort the Baltic Sea fleet through Danish waters. Another remarkable story is current in well informed circles, to the effect that two baloons were seen hovering over the Skagerack while the Russian fleet entered the North Sea. These were said to have been manned by Japanese with the object of watching the Russians and possibly dropping explosives. No hint of suspicion is expressed in any responsible quarter that the British Government was in the slightest degree in any way responsible for the alleged machinations of the Japanese agent. On the contrary, official circles express the highest praise for the conduct of the British Government throughout the North Sea incident.

The Japanese Minister announces that his request to have the road between Chinnampo and Ki Chinpo repaired, having been ignored, he must insist on the local authorities being immediately instructed to commence work.

The Magistrate of Chang Nyon reports that he has been requested by the Japanese Military authorities at Chinnampo, to proceed there for a personal interview with the Japanese commander.

MR. DOOLY ON THE COMFORTS OF TRAVEL.

BY F. D. DUNNE.

(Continued from yesterday.)

In th' barber shop Jawn D. Rockyfeller was bein' shaved. In th' smokin' car ye cud see a crowd iv jolly men playin' poker; near by sat three wags tellin' comic stories, while a naygur waither dashed to an' fro an' pushed mint juleps into the fash'nable comp'ny. Says I to myself; 'Here is life. They'll have to dhrag me fr'm that rollin' home iv bliss feet formost,' says I. An' I wint boundin' down to th' deepo. I slung four dollars at th' prisidint iv th' road when he had con-cluded some important business with his nails, an' he slung back a yard iv green paper by which I surrindered me rights as an American citizen. With this here deed in me hand I wint through a line iv haughty gintlemen in unyform, an' wan afther another looked at th' ticket an' punchea a hole in it. Whin I got to th' thrain th' last iv these gr-reat men says: 'Have Ye got a ticket? I had,' says I. 'This porous plasther was a ticket three minyits ago!' 'Get aboard,' says he, givin' me a short, frindly kick, aa' an' in a minyit I found mesilf amid a scene iv Oryentel splendhor an' no place to put me gripsack.

I shtud dhrinkin in th' glories iv th, scene until a proud man who cud qualify on color f'r all his meals at th' White House come up an, ordhered me to bed. Fond as I am iv th' colored man, Hinnissy, I wud sometimes wish that th' summer styles in Pullman porters was more light an' airy. It is thrue that th' naygur porter is more durable an' doesn't show the th' dirt, but on th' other hand, he, shows th' heat more. Where,' says I, 'do I sleep? I don't know where ye sleep, cap., says he, 'but ye'er ticket reads f'r an upper berth.' 'I wud prefer a thrapeze,' says I, but if ye'll call out th' fire department, may be they can help me in,' I says. At that he projooced a scalin' laddher an' th' thrain goin' around a curve at that minyit, I soon found mesilf on me hands an' knees in wan iv th' coziest little upstairs rooms ye iver saw. He dhrew th' curtains, an' so will I. But some day whin I am down town I am goin' to dhrop in on me frind th' prisident iv the Pullman company an' ask him to publish a few hints to th' wayfarer, I wud like to know how a gintleman can take off his clothes while settin' on thim. It wud help a good deal to know what to do with th' clothes whin ye have squirmed out iv thim. Ar-re they to be rolled up in a ball an' placed undher th' head or dhropped into th' aisle? Again, in th' mornin' how to get into th' clothes without throwin' th' thrain off th' thrack? I will tell ye confidiutially, Hinnissy, that not bein a accntortionist th' on'y thing I took off was me hat.

"Th' thrain sped on an' on. I cud not sleep. Th' luxury iv thravel kept me wide awake. Who wud coort slumber in such a cosy little bower? There were some that did it; I heerd thim coortin.' But not I. I lay awake while we flew, or, I might say bumped, through space. It seemed hardly a minyit befure we were in Saint Looey. It seemed a year. On an' iver on we flew past forest, river an' plain. Th' lights burned brightly just over me left ear, th' windows open an' let in th' hoarse, exultant shriek iv th' locymotive, th' conversation iv th' baggage-man to th' heavy thrunk, th' bammy night air an' gr-reat purple clouds iv Illinye coal smoke. I took in enough iv th' splindid product iv our prairie soil to qualify as a coal-yard. Be th' time th' sun peeked, or I may say jumped, into me little roost, I wud've made a cheerful grate fire an' left a slight deposit iv r-red ashes. Th' mornin' came too soon.

"What hasn't American ingenuity done f'r th' wurruld? Here we were fairly flyin' through space or stoppin' f'r wather at polo, Illinye, an' ye cud wash ye'ersilf as comfortably as ye cud in th' hydrant back iv th' gashouse. There was three handsome wash-basins, wan piece iv shy, evasive soap, an' towels galore—that is, almost enough to go round. In front iv each wash-basin was a dilicately nurtured child iv luxury cleansin' himself an' th' surroundin' furniture at wan blow. Havin' injyed a very refreshin' attimpt at a bath, I sauntered out into th' car. It looked almost like th' pichers in th' pamphlet, or wud've if all th' boots had been removed. Th' scene was rendered more attharctive be th' prisince iv th' fair sect. A charmin' wom n is always charmin,' but niver more so thin on a sleepincar in th' mornin' afther a hard night's rest an' forty miles fr'm a curlin' ir'n. With their pretty faces slightly sthreaked be the right iv way, their eyes dancin' with suppressed fury an' their hair almost straight, they make a pitcher that few can f'rget—an' they're lucky. But me eyes were not f'r thim. To tell ye th' truth, Hinnissy, I was hungry. I thought to find a place among th' coal in me f'r wan iv thim sumchous meals I had r-read about, an' I summoned th' black prince, who was foldin' up th' beddin, with his teeth. 'I wud like a breakfast fr'm ye'er superbly equipped buffay,' says I. 'I got ye,' says he. 'We have canned asparygus, an' wather fresh fr'm th' company's own spring at th' Chicago wahter-wurruks,' he says. 'Have ye anything to eat?' says I. 'Sind me th' cook,' I says. 'I'm th' cook,' says he, wipin' a pair iv shoes with his sleeve. 'What do ye do ye'er cookin' with?' says I. "With a can-opener,' says he, givin' a hearty laugh.

"An' so we whiled th' time away till Saint Looey was reached. O'Brien an' his wife nursed me back to life, I rayturned on th' canal-boat an' here I am almost as well as befure I made me pleasure jaunt. I'm not goin' to do it again. Let thim that will bask in their comforts. I stay at home. Whiniver I feel th' desire to fly through space, I throw four dollars out iv th' window, put a cinder into me eye, an' go to bed on a shelf in th' closet.

"I guess, Hinnissy, whin ye come to think iv it, they ain't anny such thing as luxury in thravel. We was meant to stay where we found oursilves first an' thravellin' is conthry to nature. I can go fr'm Chicago to New York in twinty hours, but what's th' matter with Chicago? I can injye places bether be not goin' to thim. I think iv Italy as th' home iv th' Pope, but Hogan, who has been there, thinks iv th' flea. I can see th' dome iv St. Pether's risin against th' sky, but he can on'y see th' cabman that charged him eighty liars or thirty cents iv our money to carry him around th' block. I think iv New York as a place where people set shinin' their dimonds with satin napkins at th' Waldrof an' dhrinkin' champagne out iv goold coal-scuttles with Jawn W. Gates, But I know a man down there that dhrives a dhray.

"They ain't anny easy way iv thravellin.' Our ancesthors didn't have anny fast thrains, but they didn't want thim. They looked on a man thravellin' as a man dead, an' so he is. Comfort is in havin' things where ye can reach thim. A man is as comfortable on a camel as on a private car, an' a man who cud injye bouncin' over steel rails at sixty miles an hour cud go to sleep on top iv a donkey injine. Th' good Lord didn't intind us to be gaddin' arount th' wurruld. Th' more we thry to do it, th' harder its made f'r us. A man is supposed to take his meals an' his sleep in an attichood iv repose. It ain't nachral to begin on a biled egg at Galesburg an' end on it at Bloomington. We weren't expicted to spread a meal over two hundherd miles an' our snores over a thousand. If th' Lord had wanted San Francisco to be near New York he'd have put it there. Th' railroads haven't made it any nearer. It' still tin thousan' miles, or whativer it is, an' ye'd be more tired if ye reached it in wan day thin ye wud if ye did it in two months in a covered wagon an' stopped f'r sleep an' meals. Man was meant to stay where he is or walk. If Nature had intinded us to fly, she wud've fixed us with wings an' taught us to ate chicken food."

"But th' railroods assists Nature," said Mr. Hennessy.

"They do," said Mr, Dooley. "They make it hard to thravel."—Westminister Budget.

The Korea Daily News.

VOL. I, THURSDAY, DECEMBER 8, 1904. No. 120

HONGKONG & SHANGHAI BANKING CORPORATION.

Paid-up Capital..... ... .$10,000,000
Reserve Fund:—Sterlin , Reserve... 10,000,000
Silver Reserve..... 7,000,000

27,000,000

Reserve Liability of Proprietors... 10,000,000

HEAD OFFICE, HONGKONG.

London Bankers, London and County Banking Company Limited.

Branches and Agencies, London.

Amoy,	Hankow	Penang,
Bangkok,	Hiogo,	Rangoon,
Batavia,	Iloilo,	Saigon,
Bombay,	Lyons,	San Francisco,
Calcutta,	Manila,	Singapore,
Colombo,	Nagasaki,	Sourabaya,
Foochow,	New York,	Tientsin,
Hamburg,	Peking,	Yokohama,

Credits granted on approved Securities, and every description of Banking and Exchange business transacted.

Drafts granted on London and the chief Commercial places in Europe, India, Australia, America, China and Japan.

HOLME RINGER & Co., AGENTS, CHEMULPO

ON CHEONG & CO., SEOUL.

GENERAL STORE KEEPERS.

Imported provisions, Cooking Utensils Crockery, etc.

FRESH BREAD DAILY.

MITSU BISHI DOCKYARD & ENGINE WORKS, NAGASAKI.

CODE WORD, "DOCK."

A 1, A. B. C., and Engineering Codes used.

DOCK No. 1 (at Tategami).

Extreme Length..............523 feet
Length on blocks .... 513 ,,
Width of Entrance on Top......89 ,,
,, ,, Bottom....77 ,,
Water on Blocks at Spring Tide 26½ ,,

DOCK No. 2 (Mukaijima).

Extreme Length..............371 feet
Length on Blocks..............360 ,,
Width of Entrance on Top......66 ,,
,, ,, Bottom 53 ,,
Water on Blocks at Spring Tide 22 ,,

PATENT SLIP (at Kosuge).

Can take vessels up to 1,000 tons gross

THE WORKS are well equipped with the LATEST IMPROVEMENTS, and can execute any kind of work in SHIPBUILDING and MARINE ENGINEERING, as well as in REPAIRING of SHIPS.

The COMPANY'S new powerful steamer OURA-MARU (712 tons, 700 I.H.P.), specially built for SALVAGE PURPOSES, and equipped with necessary gear, is always READY at SHORT NOTICE

CHARTERED BANK OF INDIA AUSTRALIA & CHINA.

INCORPORATED BY ROYAL CHARTER 1853

HEAD OFFICES:—LONDON.

Paid-up Capital £800,000
Reserve Liability of Shareholders 800,000
Reserve Fund 800,000

Drafts granted upon all the principal places in the world and every description of Exchange and banking business transacted.

E. MEYER & Co., Agents, Chemulpo.

E. MEYER & CO.

Chemulpo.

SOLE AGENTS IN KOREA FOR:

A. T. Morse, Sons & Co's "Fresco" Distemper

In all colours ready for use on walls, Ceilings etc.

and

AVENARIUS CARBOLINEUM

A wood-preserving and antiseptic oil preparation

Against decay, dry-rot, fungus and wood-destroying insects.

A large supply always in Stock. Prices upon application.

E. MEYER & Co., Chemulpo.

THE METHODIST PUBLISHING HOUSE, Little West Gate, Seoul.

JOB PRINTING, TYPEWRITER PAPER
CARBON PAPER, VISITING CARDS
STATIONERY, BOOK BINDING
BOOK PUBLISHERS
AMERICAN SCHOOL BOOKS
SPENCERIAN COPY BOOKS
PEN CARBON LETTER AND BILL BOOKS

S. A. BECK, Manager.

HOKURKU DOBOKU KAISHA.

Branch office in Chong Dong. Seoul.

Japanese telephone No. 165

CONTRACT DEPARTMENT.

We can contract to build any building or construction.

MERCHANDISE DEPARTMENT.

We can provide any building material. We have just contracted to build the new Belgian Legation.

DAI-ICHI GINKO

LIMITED.

(Formerly the First National Bank)

ESTABLISHED 1873

INCORPORATED UNDER PRESENT LAW 1896

Capital - - - - - - - - - Yen 5,000,000
Reserve Fund - - - - - 1,500,000

HEAD OFFICE:—TOKIO.

President: Baron SHIBUSAWA.

BRANCHES AND CORRESPONDENTS

In the Principal Cities and Towns of Japan.

Interest Allowed on

Fixed deposits 1 year - - - 6½ per cent
" " 6 months - - - 6 per cent

Special current accounts 1½ sen daily per Y 100
General " " 1 " " " 100

M. TANAKA, Manager, Chemulpo.

SINGER SEWING MACHINES

씽거즈봉침

SOLE AGENTS FOR KOREA

젼매쇼

HOLME RINGER & CO. Chemulpo.

졔물포 함릉거양힝

KAMEYA & CO.

GENERAL STOREKEEPERS

Chinkokai - - Seoul

(Established 1895, Tokyo)

Confectionery, Hams, Canned Goods, Cutlery, Hirano & Tansan Water, Provisions, Gents, Furnishing goods, Toilet Articles, Travelling Bags, Tobacco, Cigars & Cigarettes Kitchen Utensils. Coffee. Biscuits

Fresh Goods always kept in Stock.

Prices Moderate

Please come and inspect our goods

NIPPON YUSEN KAISHA.

JAPANESE MAIL STEAMSHIP CO.

UNDER MAIL CONTRACT WITH THE IMPERIAL JAPANESE GOVERNMENT.

European Line

Regular Fortnightly Service between Yokohama Kobe, Moji, Shanghai, Hongkong, Singapore, Penang Colombo, Port Said, Marseilles, London and Antwerp

American Line

Regular Fortnightly Service between Hongkong and Seattle, calling at Shanghai, Moji, Kobe, Yokohama and Victoria, B. C.

Australian Line

Regular weekly Service betwen Japan Ports and Australia, calling at Hongkong and Manila.

(Above Three Lines Suspended until further notice).

Shanghai Line

Weekly Service between Shanghai and Japan Ports

Korea Line

Service Kobe, Moji, Nagasaki, Fusan Chemupo Chefoo, Taiku.

S. S. Babelsberg, 2181 tons.

Service Kobe, Moji, Fusan, Chemulpo, Chinnampo

S. S. ARGO, S. S. Ohio.

BORDEN'S CONDENSED MILK CO.

New York, U. S. A.

ALWAYS IN STOCK

Eagle Brand Condensed Milk.

Gold Seal Condensed Milk.

Peerless (Family) Evaporated Cream.

Borden's Malted Milk.

E. MEYER & CO. Chemulpo, Korea,
Sole Agents

ROYAL INSURANCE COMPANY,

Funds exceed £10,000,000

FIRE

AT CURRENT RATES.

LIFE

REDUCED PREMIUM.

HOLME RINGER & Co., Agents, Chemulpo.

HOTEL DU PALAIS

SEOUL.

The only first class Hotel in Seoul, Situated in the centre of the city opposite the palace.

Cuisine under the supervision of an experienced French Chef.

Well ventilated and furnished throughout.

TARIFF UPON APPLICATION

L. MARTIN

Proprietor and Manager

報申日每韓大
보신일ᄆᆡ한대

(호일십이ᄇᆡᆨ일뎨) (일요토) 일십월이십년사ᄇᆡᆨ구쳔일

본사고ᄇᆡᆨ

이신보는영어와한어로셕거ᄆᆡ
일츌판ᄒᆞᆷ

신문가
한쟝 엽두돈오푼
일삭도 엽두량엿돈
우표가ᄒᆞᆫ삭닷돈
다엽돈으로밧숩
광고료ᄂᆞᆫ

귀한의쟝단과ᄌᆞ항의다쇼로죵
감ᄒᆞ되렴가로밧을터이오며오
ᄅᆡ지아녀대한사람마다다이신
문을보실터이니광고내시기를
원ᄒᆞ시는이들은우리신문사에
와셔편아ᄒᆞ신ᄃᆡ로회명ᄒᆞᆷ

○발ᄒᆡᆼ소 박동대한ᄆᆡ일신보
사ᄇᆡᆨ이한교앙쇄 젼영국인셜필
립쟝자리오
사쟝 영국인 (ᄇᆡ셜)
평양 ᄃᆡ리졈
○평양효동사는권미보씨로우
리신문판ᄆᆡᄃᆡ리인을뎡ᄒᆞ엿
시니평양에계신구람ᄒᆞ고져ᄒᆞ
시는 쳠군ᄌᆞ는그ᄃᆡ리졈에왕
림ᄒᆞ와편의ᄒᆞ시옵

샤고

○우리대한ᄆᆡ일신보의목뎍은
대한의안녕질셔에관한모든ᄃᆡ
목에ᄃᆡᄒᆞ야는공평한변론을주
쟝홈이라우리동지원의ᄃᆡ보는
신문보시는쳠군ᄌᆞ의게ᄒᆞᆼ샹보
도ᄒᆞ려며편지를긔셔ᄒᆞ여주시
는이는ᄉᆡᆼ명과반ᄃᆡ를져어보치
시기를희망ᄒᆞ오나미거슨신문
샹에긔ᄌᆡᄒᆞ랴는거시아니오다
만극히신용ᄒᆞ는증거를숨고자
ᄒᆞᆷ이라긔ᄌᆡ는아모긔셔던지긔
ᄌᆡᄒᆞᆷ을퇴각ᄒᆞ는권리를가졋스
나퇴각ᄒᆞ는리유를말홀터이오
며공중평화를문란케ᄒᆞ는듯ᄒᆞᆫ
긔셔는의례히밧지안켓숩나이
다

●본사셜시이ᄅᆡ로신문을ᄆᆡ양
우톄로분젼ᄒᆞ와톄젼부의임의
로젼ᄒᆞ는것스로면곳에는혹늣게
젼ᄒᆞ기도ᄒᆞ며혹면칠거슨ᄒᆞᆫ겹
에젼ᄒᆞ기도ᄒᆞ며혹아니젼ᄒᆞ는
곳도잇다ᄒᆞ오와우리신문을ᄉᆞ랑
ᄒᆞ야구람ᄒᆞ시는 쳠군ᄌᆞ의게당
ᄃᆡᄒᆞ야면우미안ᄒᆞ옵기로지금
은분젼인을두고ᄆᆡ일조이젼
ᄒᆞ며하나젼ᄒᆞ거나늣게거나ᄒᆞᆫ
폐가엽도록ᄒᆞ랴ᄒᆞ오나혹아니
젼ᄒᆞ거나혹늣게젼ᄒᆞ거나ᄒᆞᆫ일
이잇스면본사로통긔ᄒᆞ여주심
을희망ᄒᆞᆷ

관보

례셩칙ᄉᆞ호 광무팔년십
이월팔일
셔 임금사령
○승셔원판임관오등 한셩우톄
지사주사 윤병한
신십월십륙일
○승셔원판임관삼등 통신원주
사○김쳘현 신이월이일
쥬○의 원면본관 통신사면회과
쥬사사 유봉규 통신사면회과
인쥬쥰 문규가신 쟝통쳠봉 유
○등칙쟝임봉쳠봉셔 판임관팔등
○임봉 리원영 ○임쟝통쳠쟝
봉쥬사 판임관팔등 구포 유린
사셔 ○승셔판임관삼등 부무
관쥬셔 유중렴 ○임탁지부법
셔쥬민영오 임탁지부쥬사
제신관 판임관사셔 탁지부쳠셔
○셔 영임관삼등 임젼 탁지부
히의 원면본관 비이월쳥원오일
[illegible]

샹용○쥰○임리쥬○위쥬○
[illegible]
○의 졍부쳠쟝신과셔군 쥬ᄒᆞ

되경괴순찰ᄉᆞ구연하와츙쳥도
순찰ᄉᆞ리시영이가단 칙지를
밧숩고신병이잇다ᄒᆞ고횡연
이ᄉᆞ직단ᄌᆞ를졍ᄒᆞ니방강지년
에근로ᄒᆞ기를ᄉᆞ양치아니홀ᄇᆡ
여늘무고히면관ᄒᆞ기를도모ᄒᆞ
야규측폐ᄒᆞ는뜻이나타나니사
톄로헤아리건ᄃᆡ만만히연ᄒᆞᆫ지
라가히오리킬지못ᄒᆞ겟다숨기
부득이ᄒᆞ와의면ᄒᆞ왓스나고리
ᄒᆞ나지금사롬슈용ᄒᆞᆯ지음을당
ᄒᆞ야이풍속을쇄ᄒᆞᆫ가히징구케
ᄒᆞᆫ슈영사오니다즁견ᄎᆡᆨ을ᄇᆡ풀
어경괴순찰사의ᄃᆡ에쟝삼등리
용구츙쳥남도슌찰사의ᄃᆡ에경
삼품리시직로ᄎᆡ하ᄒᆞ와분일등
경케ᄒᆞ옵고산홈부임치아니ᄒᆞᆫ
논폐가잇거든벌반경칙ᄒᆞ냐써
ᄆᆡ부리논ᄃᆡ즁홈을뵈임이엇더
ᄒᆞ올지근샹 츄ᄒᆞ와광무팔년
십이월륙일에 봉 지의주라
ᄒᆞ옵셧더라

외보

○대외셰연셜(속) 지금북쳥
에셔우리외교ᄒᆞ는것을도라보
시다로국은싸홈은피ᄒᆞ면셔도
이북경에셔외교는현재이잘되오
셔우리외교샹ᄒᆞᆫ쟝이못됨이오
쳥국ᄲᆞᆫ아니라한국에도ᄯᅩᄒᆞᆫ그오
러ᄒᆞ오한국은벌셔우리세력범
위안에잇스니우리가반드시져
러케아권리를순히ᄒᆞ지안토록
ᄒᆞ야되겟소그러ᄒᆞ나고실샹ᄒᆞ
는일을보면다번ᄃᆡ요외것ᄒᆞ다
무숨일이오이론본이젼권ᄒᆞᆫ수
를한국에두어잇스며셔ᄒᆞᆫ편으
로이번승젼ᄒᆞᆫ대쟝의게한국에
츙돌보앙것ᄒᆞᆫ권리를준것이나
는갑ᄒᆞᆫ이셔ᄒᆞ야오ᄃᆡ졔엿는말
ᄒᆞ자변우리외교가활동ᄒᆞ지못
ᄒᆞ오외교외에도나쟝이그와ᄀᆞᆺ
치만죡지못ᄒᆞ오지금싸홈의진
보ᄒᆞ야나아가는것과는반대요
이번싸홈은국민의젼쳬가항샹
ᄒᆞᆫ번ᄡᅳ라그럼으로인민이저의들
의치샨을아모ᄯᅩ록느려셔쟝리
국용에응ᄒᆞ랴고ᄒᆞ며저의들의
죠샹브터젼ᄒᆞ오는가산이라도
드릴열심이오이런ᄉᆞ괴에그졍
부는군비에디ᄒᆞ야죠심홈이가
ᄒᆞ니그럿치아니ᄒᆞ면외외ᄒᆞᆯ이
잇슬는지알슈업소아모죠록국
민의ᄌᆡ산권을샹히ᄒᆞ지아니ᄒᆞ
도록ᄒᆞ되셔지던지주의홀것이
어늘이졔인국심이갑히발동ᄒᆞᆫ계국
민들의셔국민의게희로운셰금을
ᄐᆞ기를쳥ᄒᆞ오니가이것을민
우밧갑히셔ᄒᆞ녀이오지금쳐ᄃᆡ
가셰금의ᄂᆞ리는것을반ᄃᆡᄒᆞ리
유가죠곰도업소마는우리가불
가불인민의ᄌᆡ산권에ᄒᆡ로을것
은엇던린지우리국셰계반ᄃᆡᄒᆞ
야겟소셰금을맛당히ᄒᆞᆯ마다ᄃᆡ
종업시ᄂᆞ리는것이올은지비
가말ᄒᆞᆯ것도업소그결과는국민
의리익의비샹ᄒᆞᆫ손ᄒᆡ가될터이
오졍부의예산표를쟝차보면그
즁에엇던셰는ᄃᆡ종업시증ᄒᆞᆫ되
다나논엇지ᄒᆞ야지금젼쟁에츙
샹ᄒᆞ랴계공급ᄒᆞᆫ논우리인민이
맛당히부진ᄒᆞ고피로운셰금을
담당ᄒᆞᆯ것을원홈모로겟소그럼
으로나논국민의ᄃᆡ표자된여러
분의게이런셰금의ᄂᆞ리는법안
은거역ᄒᆞ기를쳥홈니이다
(미완)

뎐보

ᄇᆡᆨ림발 십이월십일
○로황원횡 극동에오는로국
함대의ᄒᆞᆫ부분은아프리카희망
봉으로지나셔마다가스가의
ᄒᆞᆫ항구에도박ᄒᆞ엿는ᄃᆡ거긔셔
셕탄을엇지못ᄒᆞ리라ᄒᆞ더라
동ᄃᆡ발 동일
○로황우리 아잔파샹ᄒᆞᆫ로국
슈뢰졍일쳑이부례스트에도착
ᄒᆞ엿다더라
론돈발 동일
○호주와일인 호대리즁의원
에셔금월팔일에의원부루쓰스
미쓰씨가식민졔한법의긔졍안
을졔츌ᄒᆞ엿는ᄃᆡ그긔졍안
은지금일본국민이ᄒᆞ번젼쟁으
로일본국민이되엿고죵교의자
유를회탁ᄒᆞ엿고영국과평에스
런ᄉᆞ동밍국이되엿스니일본사
롬을회탁ᄒᆞ야우리공화권에참
예ᄒᆞ게ᄒᆞ자는일이라스미쓰씨
는년젼에식민졔한법을의졍ᄒᆞᆯ
ᄯᅢ에ᄀᆞᆼ경이반ᄃᆡᄒᆞ다가소슈로
젹던사롬이더라
ᄇᆡᆨ림발 동일
○영덕관계 나인뎐쓰셰류리
리는신문에덕국외부대신불노
씨와슈쟈ᄒᆞᆫ말을긔ᄌᆡᄒᆞ엿는ᄃᆡ

UNION INSURANCE SOCIETY OF CANTON.

Head office Hongkong.
Marine risks underwritten at current rates.
Agents in Chemulpo,
E. MEYER & Co.

COMPAGNIE DES MESSAGERIES MARITIMES.

Fortnightly Direct Service.

For Marseilles
via Ports.
Sailing from Yokohama
Calling at Kobe,
Shanghai, Hongkong, Saigon, Singapore,
Colombo, Djibonti, Suez, Port Said
and Marseilles.

For particulars apply to
HOLME RINGER & Co.,
Chemulpo.

HAYASHIDA & CO.,

16 MYENG DONG, CHIN KO KAI, SEOUL.
BRANCH OFFICE AT CHEMULPO.

Money changers, Coal and Wood Merchants, Express Agents.

We are agents for the Pyeng-yang Coal Company and the Karazu Coal Company of Japan. We have the best quality of both anthracite and bituminous coal, and prompt execution of orders is our speciality. Firewood of all kinds kept in stock. Full weight guaranteed. Money of all denominations exchanged at current rates. Parcels received for all parts.

CHINA MUTUAL LIFE INS. OC.

Most favourable terms to policy holders.

Benefit system unsurpassed.

HOLME RINGER & Co,
Agents, Chemulpo.

C. P. R.

CANADIAN PACIFIC RAILWAY COMPANY'S ROYAL MAIL STEAMSHIP LINE.

THE FAST ROUTE BETWEEN CHINA, JAPAN, AND EUROPE VIA CANADA AND THE UNITED STATES.

Route from Hongkong via Shanghai, Nagasaki (Inland Sea of Japan) Kobe, Yokohama Victoria and Vancouver.

Twin Screw Empress Steamship—6,000 Tons—Speed 19 knots.

PROPOSED SAILING FROM YOKOHAMA.
R. M. S. Empress of India.
R. M. S. Empress of Japan.
R. M. S. Empress of China.
R. M. S. Athenian.
R. M. S. Tartar.

Special reduction (first class only) granted to members of the Military, Naval, Diplomatic and Civil services and to Missionaries.

Passengers have choice of ten routes across the Continent of America and have privilege of travelling by any Atlantic Steamship Line.

Round the World passage tickets in connection with the P. and O. S. N., North German Lloyd and Messageries Co.'s **£125.**

All rates payable at current rate of exchange.

For further information, Tickets, Guide Books, etc., apply to

HOLME, RINGER & Co., AGENTS,
Chemulpo.

Grand Hotel,

(Formerly the Station Hotel)

Near the Railway Terminus,
West Gate Seoul.

The Best Hotel in Korea
Handsome new Building.
Fine Airy Rooms
Excellent Cuisine.
Terms Moderate.
Special terms to Missionaries
and to permanent boarders.

Electric cars within 2 minutes' walk.

W. H. EMBERLEY.
Proprietor.

EVERY FACILITY.

In connection with Life Assurance Business is afforded by

The Standard Life Assurance Co.,

One of the largest and wealthiest of the Provident Institutions of the United Kingdom Forms of Application and all information will be promptly afforded on application.

10 CENTS A DAY.

Not a very large expenditure is it? But it is sufficient to secure for a man of 30 a policy with the STANDARD LIFE OFFICE for

$1323.

For all particulars of rates, etc., apply to

Holme, Ringer & Co.,
Agents, Chemulpo.

THE NEW YORK LIFE INSURANCE COMPANY.

Have you ever been declined by any Company?

Are you engaged in a specially hazardous occupation?

Have you heard of the New York Life Insurance Company's New Classifications for this class of Risks?

If not, send your date of birth, occupation and particulars of rejection, if any to

E. MEYER & Co.,
Agents, Chemulpo.

MITSUI BUSSAN KAISHA.
(MITSUI & Co.)

MITSUI GINKO.
(MITSUI BANK.)

The Bank is owned by the members of the Mitsui Family, who, as partners, assume an unmited responsibility for all liabilities of the Bank:—

Capital .... Yen 5,000,000
Reserve Fund .... " 5,600,000

HEAD OFFICE, TOKYO.
LONDON OFFICE, 34 LIME ST., E. C.

BRANCHES AND AGENCIES:—
New York, San Francisco, Hamburg, Bombay, Singapore, Manila, Hongkong, Amoy, Chefoo, Tientsin.
Kobe, Hakodate, Yokohama, Kure, Yokosuka, Moji, Shimonoseki, Miike, Wakamatsu, Nagasaki, Kuchinotsu, Karatsu, Sasebo, Misume, Taipeh, &c.

Telegraphic Address for all the Offices:
"MITSUI."
A. B. C. AND A. I CODES USED.

Contractors of Coal
To the Imperial Japanese Navy. Arsenals and Railway Bureau, Principal Railway Companies and Industrial Work, Home and Foreign Mail and Freight Steamers.

Sole Proprietors
Of the famous Miike, Tagawa and Yamano Coal Mines.

Sole Agents
For the sale of Fukumo, Hokoku, Ichimura, Kanoda, Mannoura, Onoura, Ostuji, Sonoda. Tsubaruro, Yoshinotani, Yoshio, Yurokibura and other coals.

YANGTSE INSURANCE ASSOCIATION, LTD.

The undersigned, having been appointed agents for the above company, are prepared to issue policies and pay losses on marine risks at regular rates.

E. MEYER & Co.,
Agents, Chemulpo.

AMERICAN KOREAN ELECTRIC CO.

Light and Power.

Main Office: Electric Building, Chong No.

RAILWAY DEPARTMENT.

OPERATING CARS BETWEEN EAST AND WEST GATE, EVERY TEN MINUTES:—

First Car leaves East Gate at 7:00 A. M. First Car leaves R. R. Station at 7:25 A. M
Last Car " East Gate at 9:40 P. M. Last " " R. R. Station at 10:05 P.M

OPERATING CARS BETWEEN EAST GATE AND IMPERIAL TOMB TERMINUS, EVERY TWENTY MINUTES:—

CONNECTING WITH EVERY ALTERNATE CAR ARRIVING AT EAST GATE FROM CHONG NO.

First Car leaves East Gate for Tomb at 7:10 A. M.
" " " Tomb for East Gate at 7:35 A. M.
Last " " East Gate for Tomb at 7:50 P. M.
" " " Tomb for East Gate at 8:10 P. M.

OPERATING CARS BETWEEN CHONG NO AND YUNG SAN RIVER EVERY TWELVE MINUTES:—

First Car leaves Chong No for South Gate at 7:12 A. M.
" " " Chong No for Yung San at 7:36 A. M.
" " " South Gate for Chong No at 7:20 A. M.
" " " Yung San for Chong No at 8:09 A. M.
Last " " South Gate for Chong No 10:00 P. M.
" " " Yung San for Chong No at 9:33 P. M.

SPECIAL PRIVATE CARS FURNISHED TO SUIT CONVENIENCE OF PATRONS. PRICES ON APPLICATION AT HEAD OFFICE.

LIGHTING DEPARTMENT.

Where less than 250 candle power of light is used, the rate per month will be
Per 16 candle power incandescent lamp,—All night.—Yen 2.50.
32 candle power incandescent lamp:—All night:—Yen 4.00.
50 candle power incandescent lamp:—All night:—Yen 6.00.
150 " " " " " " 10.00.
1200 " " enclosed are " " " 20.00.

Where more than 250 candle power of light is used, a Meter will be installed, freqvedted:—Rent of Meter Yen 2.00 per month. Rate of charges by meter reading:—Two Sen per Ampere per hour. (Approximately this is equal to about One Sen per 16 C. P. lamp per hour) Minimum monthly charge where meter is installed, Yen 20.00 per month, which includes rental of meter.

Estimates for installing lights furnished on application

An assortment of chandeliers always on hand.

K. Murakami.
Photograph Studio
Chinkokai, Seoul.

Printing, Developing and Enlargement, of Photographs always Undertaken.

Korean Views and Pictures Illustrating Native Customs always on Sale,

THE OSAKA SHOSEN KAISHA.

Boats frequently on the berth for Chinnampo.

REGULAR SAILINGS BETWEEN JAPAN AND KOREAN PORTS.

FUSAN AND KOBE VIA SHIMONOSEKI.

OSAKA VIA MOKPO, FUSAN, SHIMONOSEKI AND KOBE.

MOJI DIRECT.

OSAKA VIA KUNSAN, MASANPO, FUSAN, SHIMONOSEKI AND KOBE.

CHEMULPO KUNSAN LINE,
Every three days.

CHEMULPO CHINNAMPO LINE.
Every three days.

For Freight and passage and further particulars apply to
THE OSAKA SHOSEN KAISHA,
Chemulpo

RONDON, PLAISANT & CO.

General Storekeepers and Merchants, Ships Contractors, Tobacconists, Commission and Forwarding Agents, Coal Merchants

IMPORTERS AND EXPORTERS

Seoul & Chemulpo.

W. D. WENTWORTH.

LANDING
AND
SHIPPING AGENT
AND
CUSTOMS BORDER.

12 OURA, NAGASAKI.

STEWARD & CO.

Chemulpo.

Shipchandlers and Storekeepers, Naval and Mercantile Contrrctors, Landing and Shipping Agents.

STEWARD'S HOTEL

Chemulpo.

Best accommodation in the port for travellers. Clean and well-aired rooms, good 'cuisine' and prompt attendance, moderate tariff.

불노씨는영덕관계에호의를표ᄒ고량국간에셔로오히홈이업셔지기를바란다ᄒ더라ᄒ엿더라

○오덕관계 (동디발 동일) 오디리셔울부업나에셔의론ᄒ던오덕샹업약죠는셩립되지못ᄒ엿다더라

○로청졍회 (론돈발 십이월일일) 로국졍부는히아뎨이평화회를전장의뭇나기ᄭ지연긔ᄒ기를미국졍부에말ᄒ엿다더라

○샹히로인 (샹히발 동월) 샹히는로국륙히군의무역쟝곳치되엿는지라샹히에잇는고기쟝사덕국사롬들이슈빅만근의고기를블틱합ᄃ를위ᄒ야공급ᄒ기로ᄒ고로국히군사관들이려순구에각물을만이슈응ᄒ다고말긔잇는스핏쓰씨와곳치슈레타고단니는것을쟈로볼녀라

○미일과로합 (론돈발 십일월삼십일) 비짓는미국사롬ᄒ나이로로국세바스타풀이라는싸에셔로국군함빅쳑을짓는ᄃ지휘ᄒ다더라

○젼쟁과셕란 (동디발 동일) 영국외부대신랜스다운씨의연셜애디ᄒ야영국가되푸셕란장사를이지금사세로는져교전ᄒ는두나라즁에어ᄃ로던지셕란을슈출홈을정지흘슈업다ᄒ고로국을위ᄒ야사는셕란은만이덕국장사의거잔ᄒ이라ᄒ엿더라

○송슈전황 본월륙일샹오에우리장교척후가송슈구 함창복방삼십한리부근에셔젹긔병약이십명을만낫다ᄆ그즁에이명을죽이고이것을격퇴ᄒ엿더라

○만쥬군보 만쥬군보고에왈륙일샹오두시량에대용진영의보병약이즁ᄃ가포조연으로와엄습ᄒ엿는ᄃ히다에잇는쇼초는일시에그위치를철퇴ᄒ엿스나다시증원ᄃ를득ᄒ다가히디를회복ᄒ엿더라

〔일본공ᄉ관뎐착〕

○젹관산점령 젹관산의젹병이이빅삼고디를점령ᄒ고잇는ᄇ우리군사의사격ᄒ는것을익이지못ᄒ고십이월륙일에그젼다를철퇴ᄒ니우리군ᄉ는하오일시에그전부를졈령ᄒ엿고그다음하오두시량에ᄉ조구의조산오셔편으로일쳔오빅미돌하오삼시에삼리교의조슈의동북편북방면고디의젹을격퇴ᄒ야우리군ᄉ가잇기를졈령ᄒ엿고수일리에속ᄒᆫ적함ᄉ격을유ᄒ야불다와호는우편이기우러져샹갑판ᄭ지침슈ᄒ고레도위싼 호는합체의좌편이기우러젓고 바야안호는걸인것과곳더라

○시체슈습 십이월륙일오후사시에젹의군사가리ᄒ야약오시간의휴전을힝ᄒ야피차의시체를슈습ᄒ는고로우리는이것을허락ᄒ엿다ᄒ엿더라

〔십이월륙일발〕

대히포디팔십구호히군포디지휘관보고대ᄀ가좌와곳더라

○히군공보 본일이빅삼고디에이르러항ᄂ를관측ᄒ즉풀다호는침몰ᄒ야바다밋헤잡히드라간자라 레도위싼 호는삼히좌편으로기우는지라우이함으아모리ᄒ야도젼투ᄒ기어려운쟈라확신ᄒ지라우는금죠에발현ᄒ것인ᄃ작일포격ᄒ효과라고밋겟다ᄒ엿더라

론셜

비밀사회

일본대외빅작이연셜ᄒ일로말미아마일본국ᄂ에형편된바는어제우리신문에대강셜명ᄒ엿거니와동씨의말ᄒ바와갓치외교수단의진보됨으로말ᄒ진ᄃ과연일본의대사와공사와령사와밋ᄃ표자와평민ᄭ지라도나라를셩양되게홈이오히려다른나라로써비교ᄒ것갓트면진실로부족홈이잇슨즉대외씨의변론ᄒ바를파연칙망키어렵도다영국으로말ᄒ드리도그외교의진보됨이다시말홀것업는거시정부에ᄒ낫관인의정칙으로써전국에반포ᄒ야그경중히녁이고화평ᄒ계지ᄂ는바는세샹이다아는지라그런고로그동안에혹변긔ᄒ자도잇셧스되다만씌스랠리씨의정약으로반포홈만전국이순종ᄒ엿나니당초에영국셔일본으로더브러동맹ᄒ기도전국이좃케녁이는ᄭ닭에흠이니이는무라-라그표에영국셔생각ᄒ가를일본의주견이영국으로더브러동일ᄒ모양이며또ᄒ영국의화평ᄒ뜻만확실히홀로밋고ᄒ바는동양에셔도아는바이어니와맹약긔한이아즉ᄭ지도남아잇거늘일본셔는만일조흔긔회만잇게되면약죠를어기여지어ᄒ국사건에도위약ᄒ랴논일이잇손즉만일영국셔이러케ᄒ랴ᄒ엿드면일본의게ᄂ향ᄒ야더옥합당치못ᄒ일이만아슬더인지라빅작ᄒ야쉬써와남작수예마슈씨가쌜틱합ᄃ의출향홈으로써세계에포고ᄒ야구라파의힘위가대단히올치아니ᄒ양으로말ᄒ엿스나그러나쌜틱합ᄃ는긔왕구라파로셔출항ᄒ는허가를어더슨즉이제론란ᄒ야탄핵홀거시업스며미국으로말홀진ᄃ미국셔는당초에일본으로더브러아모약죠홈도업셔그러ᄒ되혹이번젼쟁에자긔나라샹업권이손ᄒ가될가다만염여ᄒ엿슬ᄲᅮᆫ인지라고로푸쉬미친왕이미국에방견ᄒ엿슬ᄯᆡ에도교전지국에관계되는바는미국외교가에셔일절기구치아니ᄒ야다힝이여번젼쟁오수수방관홀다름이로다요사이일본각쳐에모든유력ᄒ신문들과재어영국타임쓰신문의힘ᄭ지비러셔자긔의조흘ᄃ로슌종케아니된다교분격ᄒ티도로각국을론박ᄒ셔닭에조흔친구와돈목ᄒ든나라에셔들도점점셩분ᄒ야소원ᄒ야쟈는고로다시발명ᄒ노라고무어플물이며 (미완)

잡보

○강청방미 와부에셔알공관에죠회ᄒ기를니쟝원공문니ᄀ에황히도봉세관이보고ᄒ되황주에주차ᄒ일본병참관이히군로하면칠방에잇는비둔전밧미ᄒ가를청ᄒ는지라문셔를삼이여억지로나쟝ᄒ엿스니참컨대일공사의계지죠ᄒ야사령부에전죠ᄒ야이러ᄒ힝위를잔압케ᄒ라ᄒ엿기사실ᄒ즉막중둔전이비록군용디에관계가되드리도본정부승인업시억지로사라고홈이비단리치가아닐ᄲᅮᆫ아니라본대신도일로써근심ᄒ니청컨ᄃ사령부에죠회ᄒ야곳다첩ᄒ야관단홈을바란다ᄒ엿더라

○의사폐현 지작일하오삼시에의태리공사가부인과녀식울다리고 폐현ᄒ는ᄃ국셔를봉정ᄒ엿다더라

○통상회설힝 젼션젼관리쥰씨가공진회쟝으로피천ᄒ야금일에통상회를설힝ᄒ다ᄒ고쟉팔일에는정부에쟝셔ᄒ야정처의업더케홀방침을시명ᄒ엿더라

○농학량부잉치 리졍[illegible]에셔농상공부와학부를폐지ᄒ다ᄒ더니의정관가등중웅씨등이반론ᄒ야왈젼국의부강ᄒ논근원과지식의발달ᄒᆞᆫ거시어마을오인ᄂ고로가히폐지치못ᄒ다ᄒ야그져두엇다더라

○고문관겸임 중학교교사폐원탄씨는학부고문관을겸임ᄒ가ᄂ합동ᄒ교교교씨는학부보좌원으로작정ᄒ다더라

○전북관찰금면 팔일하오훈시에전라북도관찰사가ᄂ부로급히면보ᄒ기를회원천여명이효유ᄒ야도혜여지지아니ᄒ야인민이크게소요ᄒ니엇지죠처ᄒ는지곳회면ᄒ라ᄒ엿더라

○죠청연셔 외부에셔ᄂ부에죠회ᄒ기를룡천감리겸군수윤용구가임의감리셔에부임ᄒ엿는ᄃ감리셔근축ᄒ기젼에히관으로셔월봉을지발ᄒ다ᄒ니히원에록업시공무에종사홈이이공파사에낭핍가되는고로권세를좃차월봉지발홀사로청의셔을이에보니니연명셔인ᄒ야작환ᄒ야주시기를바란다ᄒ엿더라

○청즉지명 군부에셔외부에죠복ᄒ기를공쥬일샹의손히비샹일사검사ᄎ로본부에셔헌병부위권중협ᄒ파송ᄒ야자실ᄒ즉다만관진태량의가옥물픔손히금일천칠빅여원만보명ᄒ엿고송원우ᄎ랑등손ᄒ사로ᄒ야는도모자듯자도못ᄒ엿는ᄃ그물픔을가라쳐ᄇ히지도안코훔연이ᄇ샹을청ᄒ나일야심야온당치못흘지라청컨ᄃ일공사의게죠회ᄒ야다시히샹민등의게훈칙ᄒ야물픔을지명ᄒ후에다시죠회홈이가ᄒ다ᄒ엿더라

○회원상원 일진회원중ᄒ분은봉시츙쥬사는디자거집에셔떠날ᄯ에로조팔빅원을가지고오며동리사롬이십오명을다라고왓는디지금여러날두류홈으로로조가핍진ᄒ지라식쥬인아밥을아니ᄒ야쥬며다리교온사롬이십오인은청원을ᄒ고ᄌ긔는공연이팔빅원만썻다더라

○양쥬잔직 양쥬군슈는지금원소역소를죰간ᄒ는더역군거처홀방침ᄭ지모다담당ᄒ고쥬식가ᄭ지헐가로정ᄒ야그역소장식이며모든사롬이다칭송ᄒ다더라

○량소폐현 의태리공소가금광소로와부에죠회ᄒ고폐현홈을청ᄒ엿다더니팔일오후두시에폐현ᄒ고소시에는알공소가폐현ᄒ다더라

○혁파량진디 군부에셔샹쥬ᄒ야종셔북청량진위디를혁파ᄒ고허오연ᄃ로훈련ᄒ기를ᄉ졸은히송ᄒ고군물나마지는봉치ᄒ고처보ᄒ라ᄒ엿다더라

광고

TELEGRAMS.

Army Headquarters.

At night on the 6th inst a detachment of Japanese infantry attacked 200 Russian infantry near Tungchau (about 230 li north of Pingtiengsen), and after a sharp fight forced them to retreat. The Russians left 6 dead on the field as well as 22 rifles, 4 swords, 500 cartridges, 34 knapsacks and 3 horses.

A report from the Manchurican army near the Shaho states that at 2 a. m. on the 6th, some Russian infantry attacked Fangsin, but were repulsed.

At 4 30 A. M. one company of Russian infantry drove back the Japanese patrols near Sehlintun, but a larger Japanese force coming up, the position was reoccupied.

Japanese Legation.

A report from the besieging army at Port Arthur states that the bombardment on the Russian men-of-war resulted in the Pallada, Peresviet and Pobieda being struck several times, causing conflagrations on board. The Pobieda has taken a list to starboard.

The Foreign Office yesterday transmitted a report from the Household Bureau to the Japanese Legation. The taxcollector of Whanghai wired to the Bureau that he had been forced by the Japanese military authorities at Whangchu to sell Government property at Nohamyun. The Foreign Office request the Japanese Legation to telegraph the Whangchu authorities, forbidding them to adopt these measures. The Foreign Office, in their despatch, add a reminder that property cannot be sold to foreigners without the consent of the Government, and in this case permission is not forthcoming.

Miss Daisy Devoe presided at the piano and bautifully played Mendel & Sons' wedding-march.—Clear Lake Correspondence.

We understand that the S. S. Calchas, the capture of which by the Russians has caused so much discussion, has left Vladivostock. It will be remembered that the principal Russian Prize Court recently ordered her release.

The French Representative in Peking is reported to have addressed a species of ultimatum to the Wai-wu-pu, in the sense that unless effective steps be taken within a hundred days to quell the Kwansi insurgents, France will assume the initiative with her own troops. M. Dubail is also reported to have demanded an indemnity of 100,000 taels for the warehouses destroyed by these insurgents in Kwangchou Bay.

Messrs. Vickers Sons, and Maxim have produced in Manxman the fastest turbine-driven merchant steamer afloat. This vessel completed recently a two days' trial in the Firth of Clyde, in which she attained a maximum speed of 23½ knots, which is about 1½ knots faster than any turbine-driven merchant vessel yet constructed. The Manxman is over 2,000 tons. and will carry 1,500 passengers in all.

It is announced that an Italian colonel, who has invented a very practicable device for cutting the wires connecting a fortress with mines laid outside, is in negotiations with a foreign Power for the sale of the invention. The inventor claims that by his system a few soldiers can without danger, and in perfect silence, cut some thousands of wires in a few minutes. The device was tried recently near Rome before a committee of general officers with much success.

On account of the financial stress of the Shangtung province, every effort is being put forth towards the use of public funds. The local authories have ordered that all those who are identified as Boxers at one time or another during 1900 shall be subject to investigation, and their property to confiscation. This is apparently an excellent way to discourage Boxerism.—Eastern Times.

THE CENTENARY OF SHRAPNEL.

The tremendous losses and the painful carnage of which we read so frequently in the reports from the front in the present struggle between Japan and Russia are most certainly chiefly due to the artillery employed by both combatants, remarks the N.-C. Daily News. Of the different kinds of shell and shot fired from modern guns, shrapnel has the redoubtable distinction of being the most effective against whatever foe it may be used in battle on terra firma. It is a grim coincidence that this deadly carrier of destruction should be able to look back upon a century of its existence during a time when it is being employed to such a gruesome extent, but such is actually the case. The time of its invention at the beginning of the nineteenth century corresponds with the commencement of the war at the beginning of the present century. The bullets being thrown in conical formation on the adversary, they are not distributed over any larger space, but kept closely together and consequently whole ranks are simply mown down within range of the explosion.

UNLUCKY NAMES.

If one should be so bold as to characterize the superstitious sailor as silly, he would at once declare that there is sufficient reason for his belief, and would proceed to prove that war vessels named after stinging and venomous things have been unlucky, and that the country should not be so indifferent to the men who follow "a life on the ocean wave" as to organize a mosquito fleet. That Snake is regarded as an unfortunate name for a vessel is shown by the fact that two of that name have been lost, one in 1781 and the other in 1847; but no vessel bearing that name now appears although that of Serpent, which is only a substitute name for Snake, is an unlucky one also, for the one wrecked in 1892 was the fourth British war vessel of that name to meet the same fate. Viper has been an unlucky name in the British navy. The first one was wrecked in 1780, but the admiralty would not swerve, and so kept the name on the list, each vessel meeting its doom, and the fourth was lost only recently. The French navy has also been unlucky with vessels so named. The Viper, used in the British service after she became a prize from the French, was lost in 1793. The second was lost a year later, the third in 1797 and the fourth was recently lost in a collision off Guernsey.

The Cobra, another British war vessel, was lost recently at the same time as the Viper. Among other vessels similarly named and which met fates other than in battle are the Rattle-snake, in 1781; the Alligator, in 1782; the Crocodile, in 1784; the Adder in 1846; three Lizards, two Dragons and one Basilisk. All of these were of the British navy. The list could be made larger by citing the records of other navies. The Norsemen, who were so fond of naming their veesels against the laws of superstition, and using hideous heads of dragons and reptiles on their high prows, were less unfortunate and these did not meet with frequent disastars. They did have a belief, however that it was unlucky and a sacrilege to select such a name as did Lord Dunraven for his first yacht to challenge for the America's cup, the Valkyrie. And this belief was strengthened when she was sunk by the Satanita. The second challenger, with the same name, gave trouble, and she was broken up after only a short existence.—"Navy League Journal."

The Kamni of Yong Chon complains that the Customs have refused payment of his salary until his office has been built and he enters on his duties there.

The Japanese who was the victim of the soldiers' riot at Kongchu has filed a claim for $1,700 damages. This amount, he asserts, was the value of the goods in his house, when the place was stormed by the infuriated soldiers, and everything was destroyed.

The Governor of North Ham Kyeng province reports that the new Magistrate of Pu Riong was arrested by the Russians and detained at Songchin pending instructions from Russia. Orders have now been received to send him back to Seoul.

On the afternoon of the 7th inst, the Japanese Minister held a long interview with the Minister of Foreign Affairs, and at it's conclusion requested an immediate audience with His Majesty. This was however, postponed till yesterday afternoon, when, it is said, extremely important matters were discussed.

The Vienna "Volksblad" says that there is in a hospital at Tomsk, Siberia, a man who is 200 years of age. This is proved by his birth certificate and other documents, including a passport issued to him in 1763, in which his age is given as 60. He is said to be mentally sound though bed-ridden and to remember having seen Peter the Great and his wife Catherine. "Old Parr," England's nearest approach to Methuselah, died in 1635 aged 153, although Stow, in his "Chronicles" speaks of a certain Johannes de Temporibus who lived 361 years!

General Balashoff is one of the most pronounced characters in the Russian Empire. His pre-emienent characteristic is an extraordinary sanguinity. He writes to Chefoo that work on the new three story hospital at Port Arthur is rapidly progressing, the carpenters at work on the third story having long since grown accustomed to shell fire. Already the lower story of the hospital is occupied with wounded. General Balashoff says that he hopes the hospital will be completed by February, and immediately after its completion work will commence on a new church.

There is a report about town, says the "Chefoo Daily News," that the traffic in provisions and other army supplies carried in Japanese ships from Chefoo to Dalny via Weihaiwei, is to be suspended. It is not quite clear as yet what influence has been brought to bear upon the Japanese authorities to cause them to arrive at this decision. Those who might be able to inform the public in the premises could not be interviewed yesterday, but information as to the reasons for such action, if the report be true, will probably be forthcoming quickly.

The Korea Daily News.

Issued at 5 P. M. daily except Sundays.

Rate of Subscription:—
Per Year,............Yen 25.
Per Quarter,..........Yen 7.
Per Month,..........Yen 2.50.

Postage in Korea not charged extra.
Postage abroad charged extra.

Advertisements, 50 sen per day for 1 inch or less.
5 yen per month per inch.
50 yen per year per inch.

All communications to
E. T. BETHELL,
Editor and Publisher,
Pak-tong, Seoul.

RUMOURS OF CHANGES.

Korea's position with regard to the belligerents in the present war has from the first been an anomalous one, and it seems that her troubles are by no means at an end.

The air here has always been full of rumours and as there is an exceptionally heavy crop at the present time, we will on the presumption that there can be no smoke without some fire, give an outline of what Japan's intentions with regard to the Government of Korea are said to be.

It is rumoured that from the first of January next, the whole of Korea will be placed under martial law with General Hasegawa as a sort of Military Governor. It is also reported that the Japanese Legation will be closed, and that Mr. Hayashi will assume control of the Korean Home Office, while the various other Departments are to be allotted as follows:—

Education	Mr. Kokubo
Military	Major Nodzu
Household	Mr. Kato
Finance	Mr. Megata
Foreign	Mr. Stevens

Rumour goes on to say that pressure will be brought on the Emperor to recall all his plenipotentiaries from abroad with the hope that this will induce the various treaty Powers to withdraw their representatives from Korea.

We give these stories for what they are worth. The programme involves riding rough-shod through and over both the spirit and letter of several treaties, and had recent events not considerably shaken our faith in the purity of Japan's intentions, we would not for a moment believe these rumours, still less give currency to them. As it is we reserve our opinion.

Of course there is still something to be done before these dreams can become realities. Korea has to be forced to consent, and the other Powers have to be persuaded.

It may be news to some that Russia has all along refused to regard Korea as an ally of Japan, having probably good reason to believe that the agreement signed by Korea and Japan in February last was only instrumented after considerable pressure had been brought to bear. The Japanese were very wroth when the Russian Minister at Peking half-masted his flag on receipt of the news of the death of the Crown Princess. However as Russia still regards Korea as a friendly Power, the action was only proper.

We now await with considerable interest the developement of events during the next month or so. That something is afoot is certain, but whether events will take the course outlined above and expected by many Korean officials, it is impossible to say.

In the meantime the general opinion is that Japan is in too much of a hurry, and would do better to wait until after the war.

When the British ship Gothland, belonging to Messrs. Donald Currie and Co., was making for Hamburg, having been three days at sea, an alarm of fire was raised. Thin pungent wreaths of smoke aroused the suspicion of the second mate, Mr. J. P. Sewart, and when a hatch was removed flames burst forth. The hands were called on deck, the boat's nose was turned towards the distant Netherland coast, and the hosepipe was brought into play. When the fire was at length got under it was found to have originated in a large wooden packing-case, which was still burning, and which was filled with an assortment of inflammatory articles. Suspicion fell upon the consignor, a former sea captain, named John W. Jago, who was afterwards arrested at his house in Seacombe, on the Cheshire side of the Mersey, and yesterday charged at Liverpool with maliciously setting fire to the ship. It was stated that the packing-case, which had been heavily insured, was carefully stowed, according to special instructions, with a mark uppermost. Mr. H. E. Davies, an analyst, told the magistrates that the box contained a heap of clothing, papers and magazines, fire lighters, sulphur, resin, nitre, and a fine powder consisting of a mixture of charcoal, resin, nitre, and sulphur all soaked in creosote oil. Had the box got blazing properly, he said, there would probably have been a terrific explosion. While expressing himself puzzled as to how the fire started, the analyst offered an ingenious theory. There was not the slightest evidence of any machinery or clockwork contrivance for firing a fuse, but in the bottom of the box there were some charred remains of rubber tubing, broken bits of tubing, and a small triangular piece of wood with a hinge upon it. He suggested that the rubber tubing had been filled with strong sulphuric acid and the end tied up. After eating its way through the rubber the sulphuric acid would come in contact with the glass tubing, containing a mixture of potassium chlorate and sugar, causing an autburst of flames. The prisoner, who reserved his defence, was committed for trial.

Yesterday, a special session was held by the Government to discuss matters of special importance.

It is said that an agreement has been drawn up, by which Messrs. Hitewara and Takahashi will be appointed respectively Adviser and Assistant Adviser of the Educational Department.

Mr. Yi Chun has been appointed the President of the new society, Kong-chin-hoi. Yesterday he made several proposals of reform to the Government and to-day he will hold a meeting at Chongno.

The Governor of North Chulla province, whose districts seem to be infested by Chin-po-hoi-ites, wired that 1,000 of these gentry had collected and were causing a disturbance. He was powerless to control them.

Simla, Oct. 20.—Mr. Louis Dane, Foreign Secretary here, will be in charge of the British mission to Kabul which starts about November 25. He will be accompanied by a small party which may include Mr. Dobbs, who recently returned from his adventurous trans-Afghan journey. No newspaper correspondents will be allowed to accompany the party. The mission is expected to occupy about two months. The attitude of the Amir is exceedingly friendly, as shown by the arrangements he has just made for a party of Europeans, including Major Cleveland, of the Indian Medical Service, Mrs. Cleveland and Miss Brown, both lady doctors, and Mr. Finlayson, an engineer, to proceed unofficially to Kabul, starting next week.

AN ENTERPRISING LIEUTENANT.

Things seem to be fairly slack in the Japanese commissariat department here just now. At all events Lieutenant Kurushima has found time to write a long letter to the "Chuo Shimbun" (Tokio) denouncing the Editor of the "Korea Daily News" as a Russian spy. The whole article is charming but perhaps the nicest bit is the description of the Editor's personal appearauce;—"He is an Englishman, but his appearance is very disgraceful broker-like fellow, his eyes are always turning." We shall immediately consult an oculist, but in the meantime, returning good for evil, we will say that Mr. Kurushima is a Japanese but his appearance is not disgraceful.

There is one matter upon which we wish to correct the talented and charming correspondent of the "Chuo Shimbun." The Editor did not drink any whiskey in the train from Chemulpo to Seoul. It was beer, and Mr. Kurushima ought to remember this as he drank half of it. The Editor is quite sure of this as he remembers paying for it.

Finally the Editor of this paper is not a Russian spy. If he were, he would take good care not to inform Lieutenant (late Sergeant) Kurushima of the fact.

THE LATEST CLASS OF BRITISH BATTLESHIPS.

Naval experts were lately afforded an opportunity of seeing the plans for the new Lord Nelson class of battleships shortly to be laid down. Although the view that these vessels mark a mistaken policy by reason of their enormous displacement seems to be growing in naval circles, the designs promise a most formidable and efficient type of battleship. Some very important new features are to be introduced, in which the influence of the war lessons from the Far East is clearly apparent. Chief among these is a determined attempt to neutralise the deadly efficacy of torpedo attack. It had been in contemplation originally to armour these new ships under water with four-inch Krupp plating, but this intention was abandoned—first, on account of the excessive weight imposed, and, secondly, because the protection imparted against torpedoes by light armour is very problematical. The plan that Mr. Philip Watte has adopted consists of a novel development of the double bottom. In all existing battleships this double bottom extends the whole length of the ship, and is carried in armoured vessels to the height of the lower edge of the armour belting, which rests upon its shoulder. The distance between the inner and outer skin has heretofore been only a few inches. Mr. Philip Watts hopes that by building the inner wall of stouter plating, and allowing a considerable space between it and the outer bilge of the ship, the explosion of a torpedo outside the vessel will not suffice to fracture both skins.

To minimise the risk of this still further it is intended to fill the intervening space between the inner and outer walls with some loose material that will "take up" much of the concussion.

A longitudinal bulkhead will run fore and aft at some little distance inside the shell plating, and this is expected to offer an effectual resistance to the explosion of a torpedo on impact with the outer wall. It will furthermore exclude any inrush of water into the interior.

Another striking departure in design is afforded by the midship cross-section of these new battleships. They will have virtually no curve at all to the bilge, being very nearly square. The idea is that in a hull of this shape the bottom is less likely to be affected by torpedoes.

The walls of the magazines are to be very much more massive than in any preceding type. This is due to the fact that in some of the Russian warships the magazine walls are known to have split in action.

The Korea Daily News.

VOL. I, FRIDAY, DECEMBER 9, 1904. No. 121

HONGKONG & SHANGHAI BANKING CORPORATION.

Paid-up Capital..... ....$10,000,000
Reserve Fund:—Sterling Reserve... 10,000,000
Silver Reserve..... 7,000,000

27,000,000
Reserve Liability of Proprietors... 10,000,000

HEAD OFFICE, HONGKONG.

London Bankers, London and County Banking Company Limited.
Branches and Agencies,
London.

Amoy,	Hankow	Penang,
Bangkok,	Hiogo.	Rangoon,
Batavia,	Iloilo,	Saigon,
Bombay,	Lyons,	San Francisco,
Calcutta,	Manila,	Singapore,
Colombo,	Nagasaki,	Sourabaya,
Foochow,	New York,	Tientsin,
Hamburg,	Peking,	Yokohama,

Credits granted on approved Securities, and every description of Banking and Exchange business transacted.

Drafts granted on London and the chief Commercial places in Europe, India, Australia, America, China and Japan.

HOLME RINGER & CO., AGENTS,
CHEMULPO.

HOKURKU DOBOKU KAISHA.

Branch office in Chong Dong, Seoul.

Japanese telephone No. 165

CONTRACT DEPARTMENT.

We can contract to build any building or construction.

MERCHANDISE DEPARTMENT.

We can provide any building material. We have just contracted to build the new Belgian Legation.

E. MEYER & Co.,
Agents,
Chemulpo.

CHARTERED BANK OF INDIA AUSTRALIA & CHINA.

INCORPORATED BY ROYAL CHARTER 1853

HEAD OFFICES:—LONDON.

Paid-up Capital £800,000
Reserve Liability of Shareholders 800,000
Reserve Fund 800,000

Drafts granted upon all the principal places in the world and every description of Exchange and banking business transacted.

E. MEYER & Co., Agents,
Chemulpo.

MITSU BISHI DOCKYARD & ENGINE WORKS,
NAGASAKI.

CODE WORD, "DOCK."

A 1, A. B. C., and Engineering Codes used.

DOCK No. 1 (at Tategami).

Extreme Length..............523 feet
Length on blocks .... 513 ,,
Width of Entrance on Top......89 ,,
,, ,, Bottom....77 ,,
Water on Blocks at Spring Tide 26½ ,,

DOCK No. 2 (Mukaijima).

Extreme Length..............371 feet
Length on Blocks.............360 ,,
Width of Entrance on Top......66 ,,
,, ,, Bottom 53 ,,
Water on Blocks at Spring Tide 22 ,,

PATENT SLIP (at Kosuge).

Can take vessels up to 1,000 tons gross

THE WORKS are well equipped with the LATEST IMPROVEMENTS, and can execute any kind of work in SHIPBUILDING and MARINE ENGINEERING, as well as in REPAIRING of SHIPS.

The COMPANY'S new powerfu steamer OURA-MARU (712 tons, 700 I.H.P.), specially built for SALVAGE PURPOSES, and equipped with necessary gear, is always READY at SHORT NOTICE.

THE METHODIST PUBLISHING HOUSE,
Little West Gate, Seoul.

JOB PRINTING, TYPEWRITER PAPER
CARBON PAPER, VISITING CARDS
STATIONERY, BOOK BINDING
BOOK PUBLISHERS
AMERICAN SCHOOL BOOKS
SPENCERIAN COPY BOOKS
PEN CARBON LETTER AND BILL BOOKS

S. A. BECK, Manager.

DAI-ICHI GINKO,

LIMITED.

(Formerly the First National Bank)

ESTABLISHED 1873

INCORPORATED UNDER PRESENT LAW 1896

Capital - - - - - - - - Yen 5,000,000
Reserve Fund - - - - - 1,500,000

HEAD OFFICE:—TOKIO.

President: Baron SHIBUSAWA.

BRANCHES AND CORRESPONDENTS
In the Principal Cities and Towns of Japan.
Interest Allowed on

Fixed deposits 1 year - - - 6½ per cent
" " 6 months - - - 6 per cent

Special current accounts 1½ sen daily per Y 100
General " " 1 " " " 100

M. TANAKA,
Manager, Chemulpo.

SINGER SEWING MACHINES

씽거즈봉침

SOLE AGENTS FOR KOREA

젼매쇼

HOLME RINGER & CO.
Chemulpo.

졔물포 함륭거양힝

KAMEYA & CO.

GENERAL STOREKEEPERS

Chinkokai - - Seoul

(*Established 1895, Tokyo*)

Confectionery, Hams, Canned Goods, Cutlery, Hirano & Tansan Water. Provisions, Gents, Furnishing goods, Toilet Articles, Travelling Bags, Tobacco, Cigars & Cigarettes Kitchen Utensils. Coffee. Biscuits

Fresh Goods always kept in Stock.
Prices Moderate
☞ *Please come and inspect our goods*

NIPPON YUSEN KAISHA.

JAPANESE MAIL STEAMSHIP CO.

UNDER MAIL CONTRACT WITH THE IMPERIAL JAPANESE GOVERNMENT.

European Line

Regular Fortnightly Service between Yokohama Kobe, Moji, Shanghai, Hongkong, Singapore, Penang Colombo, Port Said, Marseilles, London and Antwerp

American Line

Regular Fortnightly Service between Hongkong and Seattle, calling at Shanghai, Moji, Kobe, Yokohama and Victoria, B. C.

Australian Line

Regular weekly Service betwen Japan Ports and Australia, calling at Hongkong and Manila.
(Above Three Lines Suspended until further notice).

Shanghai Line

Weekly Service between Shanghai and Japan Ports

Korea Line

Service Kobe, Moji, Nagasaki, Fusan Chemupo Cheffoo, Taiku.
S. S. Bahelsberg, 2181 tons.
Service Kobe, Moji, Fusan, Chemulpo, Chinnampo
S. S. ARGO, S. S. Ohio.

BORDEN'S CONDENSED MILK CO.

New York, U. S. A.

ALWAYS IN STOCK

Eagle Brand Condensed Milk.

Gold Seal Condensed Milk.

Peerless (Family) Evaporated Cream.

Borden's Malted Milk.

E. MEYER & CO.
Chemulpo, Korea,
Sole Agents

ROYAL INSURANCE COMPANY,
Funds exceed £10,000,000
FIRE
AT CURRENT RATES.
LIFE
REDUCED PREMIUM.
HOLME RINGER & Co.,
Agents, Chemulpo.

HOTEL DU PALAIS
SEOUL.

The only first class Hotel in Seoul. Situated in the centre of the city opposite the palace.

Cuisine under the supervision of an experienced French Chef.

Well ventilated and furnished throughout.

TARIFF UPON APPLICATION

L. MARTIN
Proripetor andM anager

大韓每日申報

대한미일신보

(뎨일빅이십이호) (일요일) 일쳔구빅사년십이월십삼

본샤고빅

이신보는영어와한어로셕거미일츌판ᄒᆞ옵

신문가

한쟝 엽두돈오푼

일삭료 엽두량닷돈

우표가미삭닷돈

다맛돈으로밧숩

광고료는

긔한의쟝단과ᄌᆞ힝의다쇼로증감ᄒᆞ되렴가로밧을터이오며오리자아녀대한사람마다다이신문을보실터이니광고내시기를원ᄒᆞ시는이들은우리신문샤에와셔면약ᄒᆞ심을희망ᄒᆞ옵

○발힝소 박동대한미일신보샤법어학교압헤젼영국인셜필림집자리오

샤쟝 영국인 (비셜)

평양 디리졈

○평양효동사는권미보씨로우리신문관미디리인을뎡ᄒᆞ엿ᄉᆞ오니평양에계신구람코져ᄒᆞ시는쳠군ᄌᆞ는히디리졈에왕림ᄒᆞ와면의ᄒᆞ시옵

샤고

○우리대한미일신보의목뎍은대한의안녕질셔에관한모든데목에디ᄒᆞ야는공평한변론을쥬쟝홈이라우리동신원의담보는신문보시는쳠군ᄌᆞ의게항상보도ᄒᆞ리며편지를긔셔ᄒᆞ여주시는이는셩명과반디를젹어붓치시기를희망ᄒᆞ오니이거슬신문샹에긔지ᄒᆞ라는거시아니오다만극히신용ᄒᆞ는증거를숨고쟈홈이라긔쟈는아모긔셔던지긔지홈을되각ᄒᆞ는권리를가졋ᄉᆞ나되각ᄒᆞ는리유를말홀터이오며공즁평화를문란케ᄒᆞ는듯ᄒᆞᆫ긔셔는의례히밧지안켓숩나이다

●본사셜시이리로신문을미양우례로분젼ᄒᆞ와례젼부의임의로젼ᄒᆞᆫ듯스로면곳에는혹늣게젼ᄒᆞ기도ᄒᆞ며혹몃칠거슬ᄒᆞᆫ겁에젼ᄒᆞ기도ᄒᆞ며혹아니젼ᄒᆞ는곳도잇다ᄒᆞ와우리신문을ᄉᆞ랑ᄒᆞ야구람ᄒᆞ시는 쳠군ᄌᆞ의게디ᄒᆞ야미우미안ᄒᆞ옵기로지금은분젼인을두고미일일즉이젼ᄒᆞ며아니젼ᄒᆞ거나늣게거나ᄒᆞᆫ폐가업도록ᄒᆞ라ᄒᆞ오니혹아니젼ᄒᆞ거나혹늣게젼ᄒᆞ거나ᄒᆞᆫ일이잇스면본샤로통긔ᄒᆞ여쥬심을희망ᄒᆞ옵

관보

뎨삼쳔오호 광무팔년십이월구일

셔임급ᄉᆞ령

○승종이픔 졍삼픔 윤원구

○승졍삼픔 륙품 리인슈

○승졍삼품 륙품 박티양

이샹오월십일일

○셔판임관오등 진위뎨삼연디뎨삼디대륙군군의보 손혁규

○셔판임관일등 경무쳥총슌 안영희 경무쳥총슌 젼화셔 경무쳥총슌 리헌무 경무쳥총슌 리지관

십일월삼일

○임한셩지판소판ᄉᆞ셔쥬임관ᄉᆞ등 졍삼품 리경구

십이월삼일

○면중계 젼디계아문위원 김셕현

○임법부회계국쟝셔쥬임관이등 졍삼품 셔샹우

○임곽산군공립소학교교원셔판임관륙등 리쥰호

○강원도관찰부공립소학교교원셔판임관륙등 신지균

○겸임황히도슌회지판소판ᄉᆞ 법부참셔관 윤셔보

이샹십월륙일

○명궁닉부특진관셔칙임관일등 종일품 졍락용

○명궁닉부특진관셔칙임관삼등 종이픔 김병익 종이픔 김완슈 종이픔 황기연 홍문관부학ᄉᆞ 윤길구

○명궁닉부특진관셔칙임관ᄉᆞ등 종이픔 졍우묵

○의원면본관 비셔원랑 허만필 혜릉참봉 리인구

○히시종원분시어 구품 홍지칠 구품 양지하 구품 리죵셕 구픔 김세룡 구품 최현기

○임비셔원랑셔판임관륙등 륙품 임빅영

○임혜릉참봉셔판임관팔등 륙품 리던응

○임통신ᄉᆞ면화과쥬ᄉᆞ셔판임관팔등 오창영 안승긔 리치졍

○명시죵원분시어 구픔 민우식 김영모 유셕셕 리또긔 리시영 젼긔보

○중종이픔가션대부닉부협판 고통덕랑 리염

죵이픔가션대부닉장원경 리명식의고의법면츄 중

○중종이품가션대부닉부협관 고졍삼픔젼의관 졍대권

○중졍삼픔통졍대부비셔원승 고사과 리현셩

○중구품죵사랑즁학교교관 고학싱 강의힝 고학싱 록티

이샹효힝이탁이ᄒᆞ야병시중직

이샹십이월칠일

궁뎡록사

○죠셔ᄒᆞ야갈아샤딕죵일픔졍락용졍이픔김병익종이품김완슈황기연졍우묵홍문부학사윤길구를명ᄒᆞ샤궁닉부특진관등삼으시다

○의졍부참졍신긔션탁지부대신민영긔군쥬ᄒᆞ되젼지계아문위원김셕현의힝위가미당ᄒᆞ야가히그져둘슈가업ᄉᆞ와젼디계아문으로부터샹쥬면ᄒᆞ엿더니히원의졍적을미루어궁구ᄒᆞ온즉가히용셔홀것이잇는고로면즁계ᄒᆞ기로써삼가갓츄록지를여러셩재를업디여기다리와 광무팔년십이월륙일에봉 제제왈가타ᄒᆞ시다

잡보

○슈원군공보 슈원군슈가공보ᄒᆞ기를본월오일에단발ᄒᆞᆫ자가어디로조ᄎᆞ오는지삼삼오오로옵져에회집ᄒᆞ야본일모헌쟈ㅣ합위일 오십여명인디각셩문에계방ᄒᆞ기를본회를음력본월초ᄉᆞ일오졍에죵각에셔긔회ᄒᆞ고연셜ᄒᆞᆫ다ᄒᆞ엿는디히인등이각각산지쥬막ᄒᆞ야혹당쟝에삭발ᄒᆞ는쟈도잇다더라

초산슈의젹악 의졍부에셔닉부로죠회ᄒᆞ기를초산군거ᄒᆞ는리소사의청원니의져의남편리승진이가을부에고용ᄒᆞ더니거삼월분에아라사병뎡이고을에드러옴으로군슈윤셕뎐이가도타ᄒᆞ미히향쟝이조긔남편을불너군슈의옷상조를십리밧신셕관의집에져다두라ᄒᆞ야거힝ᄒᆞ엿더니그후에군슈와향쟝이히의샹을이십리밧게문소집이다옴겨두엇다가아라사병뎡이물너간후에군슈가환관ᄒᆞ야의복을견실ᄒᆞ엿다ᄒᆞ고져의남편과시형데를착형ᄒᆞ야져의남편은즉ᄉᆞᄒᆞ고문소집에셔고용ᄒᆞ는사룸김원복도소형을뵈ᄒᆞ고의녀는나티ᄒᆞ야일문이혹화를당ᄒᆞ엿다ᄒᆞ니히군슈들즉각압샹ᄒᆞ야쳣지는국법을베폴고둘지는원통ᄒᆞᆫ것을보샹ᄒᆞ라ᄒᆞ엿더라

긴급회의 지작일하오ᄒᆞᆫ시에졍부에셔각부로통쳡ᄒᆞ야무숩긴급ᄒᆞᆫ사건이잇는지동일셰시에임시회의를홀터이니긔한에밋쳐곳회동ᄒᆞ라ᄒᆞ엿더라

○송현적경 지작일밤에송현김관셔의ᄌᆞ뎨집에셔수쳔금을도젹마젓다ᄒᆞ고작일밤ᄌᆞ시량에는송현민승지집에화적이츙화ᄒᆞ야사랑십여간이몰슈히닷는되방셰간즁ᄒᆞ나토못구ᄒᆞ고오쳔량ᄌᆞ리슈병서지닷더라

망로츄죵 근일셩즁에일본광디뇨름구경ᄒᆞ리고청ᄒᆞ는쟈ㅣ긔를들고북를치며거리로단이미아회들과시끌사룸이옹위ᄒᆞ야ᄊᆞ라단이되힘듦고수고로운줄을모르고츄죵ᄒᆞ며구경ᄒᆞᆫ다더라

○인장분급 일진회에셔각군에파송ᄒᆞᆫ회원의도장아모군일진회지회장지장이라ᄒᆞ야각각삭여쥬엇다더라

○고시부동 지관소압헤고시ᄒᆞ기는미일샹오젼에민소를밧는다ᄒᆞ고관ᄉᆞ는오후셔지ᄉᆞ진치니ᄒᆞ야송ᄉᆞᄒᆞ는빅셩이문압헤셔그다리게ᄒᆞᆫ다더라

뎐보

군ᄉᆞ령부착면

○습격쟈격퇴 우리군ᄉᆞ의일부디가륙일밤에동챵부근「평뎡산의북편약삼십리」에잇든젹의보긔병약이빅을밤에엄습ᄒᆞ야이것을격퇴ᄒᆞ엿는디젹의버린시톄가륙이요편리픔은쇼총이십이기와군도ᄉᆞ기와락약오빅기와외투삼십ᄉᆞ와마삼필파기타약간이라더라

○만쥬군보고 만쥬군ᄉᆞ하방면보고에왈본월륙일샹오이시에젹의보병약일쇼디가방신의동방에와엄습ᄒᆞ엿스나이것을격퇴ᄒᆞ엿더라

UNION INSURANCE SOCIETY OF CANTON.

Head office Hongkong.
Marine risks underwritten at current rates.
Agents in Chemulpo,
E. MEYER & Co.

COMPAGNIE DES MESSAGERIES MARITIMES.

Fortnightly Direct Service.

For Marseilles
via Ports.
Sailing from Yokohama
Calling at Kobe,
Shanghai, Hongkong, Saigon, Singapore, Colombo, Djibouti, Suez, Port Said and Marseilles.

For particulars apply to
HOLME RINGER & Co.,
Chemulpo.

HAYASHIDA & CO.,

16 MYENG DONG, CHIN KO KAI, SEOUL.
BRANCH OFFICE AT CHEMULPO.

Money changers, Coal and Wood Merchants, Express Agents.

We are agents for the Pyeng-yang Coal Company and the Karazu Coal Company of Japan. We have the best quality of both anthracite and bituminous coal, and prompt execution of orders is our speciality. Firewood of all kinds kept in stock. Full weight guaranteed. Money of all denominations exchanged at current rates. Parcels received for all parts.

CHINA MUTUAL LIFE INS. OC.

Most favourable terms to policy holders.

Benefit system unsurpassed.

HOLME RINGER & Co.
Agents, Chemulpo.

C. P. R.

CANADIAN PACIFIC RAILWAY COMPANY'S ROYAL MAIL STEAMSHIP LINE.

THE FAST ROUTE BETWEEN CHINA, JAPAN, AND EUROPE VIA CANADA AND THE UNITED STATES.

Route from Hongkong via Shanghai, Nagasaki (Inland Sea of Japan) Kobe, Yokohama Victoria and Vancouver.

Twin Screw Empress Steamship—6,000 Tons—Speed 19 knots.

PROPOSED SAILING FROM YOKOHAMA.
R M S Empress of India
R M S. Empress of Japan
R M S Empress of China
R. M. S. Athenian.
R. M. S. Taatar.

Special reduction (first class only) granted to members of the Military, Naval, Diplomatic and Civil services and to Missionaries.

Passengers have choice of ten routes across the Continent of America and have privilege of travelling by any Atlantic Steamship Line.

Round the World passage tickets in connection with the P. and O. S. N., North German Lloyd and Messageries Co.'s **£125.**

All rates payable at current rate of exchange.

For further information, Tickets, Guide Books, etc., apply to

HOLME, RINGER & Co., AGENTS,
Chemulpo.

Grand Hotel,

(*Formerly the Station Hotel*)

Near the Railway Terminus, West Gate Seoul.

The Best Hotel in Korea.
Handsome new Building.
Fine Airy Rooms
Excellent Cuisine.
Terms Moderate.
Special terms to Missionaries and to permanent boarders.

Electric cars within 2 minutes' walk.

W. H. EMBERLEY.

Proprietor.

EVERY FACILITY.

In connection with Life Assurance Business is afforded by

The Standard Life Assurance Co.,

One of the largest and wealthiest of the Provident Institutions of the United Kingdom Forms of Application and all information will be promptly afforded on application.

10 CENTS A DAY.

Not a very large expenditure is it? But it is sufficient to secure for a man of 30 a policy with the STANDARD LIFE OFFICE for

$1323.

For all particulars of rates, etc., apply to

Holme, Ringer & Co.,
Agents, Chemulpo.

THE NEW YORK LIFE INSURANCE COMPANY.

Have you ever been declined by any Company?

Are you engaged in a specially hazardous occupation?

Have you heard of the New York Life Insurance Company's New Classifications for this class of Risks?

If not, send your date of birth, occupation and particulars of rejection, if any to

E. MEYER & Co.,
Agents, Chemulpo.

MITSUI BUSSAN KAISHA.
(MITSUI & Co.)
MITSUI GINKO.
(MITSUI BANK.)

The Bank is owned by the members of the Mitsui Family, who, as partners, assume an unlimited responsibility for all liabilities of the Bank:—

Capital...................... .....Yen 5,000,000
Reserve Fund.................... " 5,600,000

HEAD OFFICE, TOKYO.
LONDON OFFICE, 34 LIME ST., E. C.

BRANCHES AND AGENCIES:—
New York, San Francisco, Hamburg, Bombay, Singapore, Manila, Hongkong, Amoy, Chefoo, Tientsin.
Kobe, Hakodate, Yokohama, Kure, Yokosuka, Moji, Shimonoseki, Miike, Wakamatsu, Nagasaki, Kuchinotsu, Karatsu, Sasebo, Misume, Taipeh, &c.

Telegraphic Address for all the Offices:
"MITSUI."
A. B. C. AND A. 1 CODES USED.

Contractors of Coal
To the Imperial Japanese Navy. Arsenals and Railway Bureau, Principal Railway Companies and Industrial Work, Home and Foreign Mail and Freight Steamers.

Sole Proprietors
Of the famous Miike, Tagawa and Yamano Coal Mines.

Sole Agents
For the sale of Fukumo, Hokoku, Ichimura, Kanoda, Mannoura, Onoura, Ostuji, Sonoda, Tsubaruro, Yoshinotani, Yoshio, Yurokibura and other coals.

YANGTSE INSURANCE ASSOCIATION, LTD.

The undersigned, having been appointed agents for the above company, are prepared to issue policies and pay losses on marine risks at regular rates.

E. MEYER & Co.,
Agents, Chemulpo.

AMERICAN KOREAN ELECTRIC CO.

Light and Power.

Main Office: Electric Building, Chong No.

RAILWAY DEPARTMENT.

OPERATING CARS BETWEEN EAST AND WEST GATE, EVERY TEN MINUTES:—

First Car leaves East Gate at 7:00 A. M. First Car leaves R. R. Station at 7:25 A. M
Last Car " East Gate at 9:40 P. M. Last " " R. R. Station at 10:05 P.M

OPERATING CARS BETWEEN EAST GATE AND IMPERIAL TOMB TERMINUS, EVERY TWENTY MINUTES:—
CONNECTING WITH EVERY ALTERNATE CAR ARRIVING AT EAST GATE FROM CHONG NO.

First Car leaves East Gate for Tomb at 7:10 A. M.
" " " Tomb for East Gate at 7:35 A. M.
Last " " East Gate for Tomb at 7:50 P. M.
" " " Tomb for East Gate at 8:10 P. M.

OPERATING CARS BETWEEN CHONG NO AND YUNG SAN RIVER EVERY TWELVE MINUTES:—

First Car leaves Chong No for South Gate at 7:12 A. M.
" " " Chong No for Yung San at 7:36 A. M.
" " " South Gate for Chong No at 7:20 A. M.
" " " Yung San for Chong No at 8:09 A. M.
Last " " South Gate for Chong No 10:00 P. M.
" " " Yung San for Chong No at 9:33 P. M.

SPECIAL PRIVATE CARS FURNISHED TO SUIT CONVENIENCE OF PATRONS. PRICES ON APPLICATION AT HEAD OFFICE.

LIGHTING DEPARTMENT

Where less than 250 candle power of light is used, the rate per month will be
Per 16 candle power incandescent lamp,—All night.—Yen 2.50.
32 candle power incandescent lamp:—All night:—Yen 4.00.
50 candle power incandescent lamp:—All night:—Yen 6.00.
150 " " " " " " " 10.00.
1200 " " enclosed are " " " " " 20.00.

Where more than 250 candle power of light is used, a Meter will be installed, freqvedted:—Rent of Meter Yen 2.00 per month. Rate of charges by meter reading:—Two Sen per Ampere per hour. (Approximately this is equal to about One Sen per 16 C. P. lamp per hour) Minimum monthly charge where meter is inStalled, Yen 20.00 per month, which includes rental of meter.

Estimates for installing lights furnished on application
An assortment of chandeliers always on hand.

K. Murakami.

Photograph Studio
Chinkokai, Seoul.

Printing, Developing and Enlargement, of Photographs always Undertaken.

Korean Views and Pictures Illustrating Native Customs always on Sale,

---

THE OSAKA SHOSEN KAISHA.

Boats frequently on the berth for Chinnampo.

REGULAR SAILINGS BETWEEN JAPAN AND KOREAN PORTS.

FUSAN AND KOBE VIA SHIMONOSEKI.

OSAKA VIA MOKPO, FUSAN, SHIMONOSEKI AND KOBE.

MOJI DIRECT.

OSAKA VIA KUNSAN, MASANPO, FUSAN, SHIMONOSEKI AND KOBE.

CHEMULPO KUNSAN LINE, Every three days.

CHEMULPO CHINNAMPO LINE. Every three days.

For Freight and passage and further particulars apply to

THE OSAKA SHOSEN KAISHA,
Chemulpo.

RONDON, PLAISANT & CO.

General Storekeepers and Merchants, Ships Contractors, Tobacconists, Commission and Forwarding Agents, Coal Merchants

IMPORTERS AND EXPORTERS

Seoul & Chemulpo.

W. D. WENTWORTH.

LANDING
AND
SHIPPING AGENT
AND
CUSTOMS BORDER.

12 OURA, NAGASAKI.

STEWARD & CO.

Chemulpo.

Shipchandlers and Storekeepers, Naval and Mercantile Contrrctors, Landing and Shipping Agents.

STEWARD'S HOTEL

Chemulpo.

Best accommodation in the port for travelers. Clean and well-aired rooms, good cuisine and prompt attendence, moderate tariff.

○감시병철퇴 동일샹오소시반에적의보병약일즁되가흑림듄부근으로공격ᄒᆞ며왓스미우리감시병은잠시후방으로철퇴ᄒᆞ엿스ᄂᆞ샹오칠시에이것을회복ᄒᆞ엿더라

(일본공ᄉᆞ관착뎐)

○려슌공위군보고 려슌공위군보고요령에왈슈요일젹합포격은조못효험이잇셔발나다호(슌양함륙쳔칠빅삼십일돈)과(비레수위도)호와 (보비에다호등이모다슈다ᄒᆞᆫ탄환을밧앗고(비레슈위도)등은ᄒᆞ오삼시십오분에화지를이르켜좌편으로기우러ᄯᅥ럿더라

(일본공ᄉᆞ관착뎐)

○려슌지휘관보고 려슌히군포디지휘관의보고요령에왈슈요일하오에이빅삼고디에셔관측ᄒᆞᆫ바를거ᄒᆞᆫ즉(레도위싼)호ᄂᆞᆫ(슈다안워구)셕지침슈ᄒᆞ야바다밋헤가라안진것갓고 (고비예다)호ᄂᆞᆫ현저히좌현으로기우러져셔방으로쒸여낫다더라

외보

○대외써연셜[속] 대체국가외죠직됨이만이민망을ᄯᅡ려셔다ᄉᆞ리나니만일한정부가민망을어긔여셔국ᄉᆞ를ᄒᆞ랴ᄒᆞ면좃치못ᄒᆞᆫ일이곳이러나기를면ᄒᆞ기어려울지라지금우리정부ᄂᆞᆫ국민의이국심을졍당히아려주지못ᄒᆞ오지금우리가뎨일빅삼십은힝에뎌ᄒᆞᆫ관계에정부의힝위ᄅᆞᆯ셜명ᄒᆞ면정부가인민의게엇은금젼을엇더케만이쓸디업시엿섯쇼이것이정부가인민이이번젼쟁에뎌ᄒᆞ야협력ᄒᆞᄂᆞᆫ이국심을정당이아려쥬지못ᄒᆞᄂᆞᆫ확실ᄒᆞᆫ증거가아니오넛가이것이다니가그인민이정부에뎌ᄒᆞ야신임만아니ᄒᆞᆯ섇아니라쟝릭에무ᄉᆞᆷ힝동이잇슬ᄂᆞᆫ지두려워ᄒᆞᄂᆞᆫ셔돍이오나ᄂᆞᆫ지금닉각을공격ᄒᆞ기를원ᄒᆞ지아니ᄒᆞ오마ᄂᆞᆫ그나라의리익을보호ᄒᆞᄂᆞᆫ디ᄂᆞᆫ다른사ᄅᆞᆷ의게뒤지지아니ᄒᆞ겟소닉가만일지금ᄉᆞ셰의근심됨과이번젼쟁의승리룰보라ᄂᆞᆫ디감발되지아니ᄒᆞ면이런셜명을아니ᄒᆞ겟ᄉᆞᆸᄂᆞ이다 [완]

잡보

○폐현후문 수일젼에일본공ᄉᆞ가 폐현ᄒᆞᆫ말ᄉᆞᆷ은이왕긔지ᄒᆞ엿거니와 샹주ᄒᆞᆫ말ᄉᆞᆷ을다시드른즉평양군슈팽한쥬ᄂᆞᆫ잉임ᄒᆞ고창원군슈권익샹은텰로에방히ᄒᆞᆫ일노면관ᄒᆞ고그디에ᄂᆞᆫ빅남쥰씨로셔임ᄒᆞ기ᄅᆞᆯ 샹주ᄒᆞ엿더라

○부임부득 단쳔군슈김유직씨ᄂᆞᆫ아병이샹지ᄒᆞᄂᆞᆫ고로부임ᄒᆞ지못ᄒᆞᆫ다더라

○디관쳐역 원소긔지를불길ᄒᆞ다ᄒᆞ야피슈ᄒᆞ엿든풍슈김현귀ᄂᆞᆫ징역종신에쳐ᄒᆞ고신석효ᄂᆞᆫ역십오년에쳐ᄒᆞ고기여리종우정긔렵은티팔십에방송ᄒᆞ엿더라

○회의안건 거팔일하오셰시에정부에셔림시회의를ᄒᆞ엿ᄂᆞᆫ디그안건인즉젼라북도회민을히산ᄒᆞᆯ방침을샹의ᄒᆞ유긔어히효유ᄒᆞ야히산케ᄒᆞ되호원ᄒᆞᄂᆞᆫ쟈부를질문ᄒᆞ고되송케ᄒᆞ라고젼라북도관찰ᄉᆞ의게면훈ᄒᆞ엿더라

○완찰면보 젼라관찰ᄉᆞ가일쟉일에닉부로면보ᄒᆞᆫ기를회민이점점나아와그수를아지못ᄒᆞ겟고대단히소요ᄒᆞ오니진위디로더브러ᄯᅩ차보님이엇더ᄒᆞ올지오ᄒᆞ엿더라

○불허부임 고원군슈가닉부로면보ᄒᆞᆫ기를본군슈가원산항에니른즉일본사령부에셔말ᄒᆞ기를쥬경군사령부의인가가잇기젼에ᄂᆞᆫ부임ᄒᆞ지못ᄒᆞ리라ᄒᆞ오니군사령부로젼죠ᄒᆞ와인가들엇은후에곳하답ᄒᆞ시기를복망이라ᄒᆞ엿더라

○교쳥숭등 쥬쳥공사가외부로보고ᄒᆞᆫ기를본관참셔관김필희가셜관ᄒᆞᆫ처음으로브더지금셕지수년에미양교셥ᄒᆞᄂᆞᆫ데외국말이숙습효로가파다ᄒᆞ니히원의숭등긔한은비록명년이월어나그효로를위ᄒᆞ야어에실상을들어보고ᄒᆞ오니그자격에부비ᄒᆞ야승등케ᄒᆞ심을브란다ᄒᆞ엿더라

○합쳥폐현 영풍관에셔외부에공함ᄒᆞᆫ기를금광인허쳥훈일사ᄂᆞᆫ이믜일쥬일젼에 귀부대신으로더브러면의ᄒᆞ야ᄀᆞᆺ추말ᄒᆞ엿스되오히려엇더탄회시가업기에두번재면의ᄒᆞ기를쳥ᄒᆞ야도ᄯᅩ엇지못ᄒᆞ니본사ᄂᆞᆫ이사졍으로써 폐현ᄒᆞ기를원ᄒᆞᆫ니쳥권되디신샹 쥬ᄒᆞ야그일ᄌᆞ를시명ᄒᆞ라ᄒᆞ엿더라

○독쥰금광 지쟉일외공사폐현ᄒᆞᆯᄯᅢ에금광ᄒᆞᆫ곳을엇어다더라

○졍부죠회 닉부 졍부에셔닉부에죠회ᄒᆞ되치졍에잘ᄒᆞ며못ᄒᆞᄂᆞᆫ것과싱민에편ᄒᆞ고아니편ᄒᆞᆫ것이다빅셩갓가운관원의게미이고그써권ᄒᆞ고중계ᄒᆞ고닉치고울니ᄂᆞᆫ것이ᄯᅩᄒᆞᆫ오직파법에엄ᄒᆞᆫ되잇나니엄ᄒᆞ지아니ᄒᆞ면엇지홀고만근이리로슌량홈은드물고담학홈이셩풍ᄒᆞ야박할흠이갈슈록더ᄒᆞᆫ지라과셰ᄒᆞᄂᆞᆫ정사가걸니고막히여간악ᄒᆞᆫ아젼이환룡ᄒᆞ묘빅셩의지산이탕셕ᄒᆞ고도적이층만ᄒᆞ야궁고ᄒᆞ고근심ᄒᆞᄂᆞᆫ형샹을참아듯고불슈업ᄂᆞᆫ되근리규칙이미비ᄒᆞ야관찰사ᄂᆞᆫ출척ᄒᆞᆫ다ᄒᆞ야도내게ᄉᆞ지안다ᄒᆞ야졀례를안음ᄒᆞ야슈보홀쎄에ᄂᆞᆫ그죵출이ᄂᆞᆫ다빅교귀부에셔ᄂᆞᆫ임시ᄒᆞ야폄ᄒᆞᆫ것이미양의심이만을섇더라졍ᄒᆞ고등분ᄒᆞᄂᆞᆫ지음에샹량ᄒᆞ노라고만이허비ᄒᆞ야게보홈이긔한을어긔미분경ᄒᆞᄂᆞᆫ것이일로말미암아포폄이밝지못홈이오날날ᄀᆞᆺ흔지라일로써본월륙일에ᄀᆡ국오빅오년 칙령뎨삼십칠호디방관리직제뎨륙됴즁관찰사ᄂᆞᆫ관하부목ᄉᆞ와군슈의치젹을미년량ᄎᆞ일월칠월십오일로정긔ᄒᆞ야하에샹쥬하삼등을정ᄒᆞ야구자를첨입ᄒᆞ야기부표ᄒᆞᄂᆞᆫ일로써반포ᄒᆞ되협금긔한쟝ᄎᆞᆺ갓가온디도로가멀므로ᄯᅢ가지나도록못ᄒᆞ기쉬우니각관찰부에비식ᄒᆞ야샹즁하삼등으로일일이다시곳쳐경부에보ᄒᆞ게ᄒᆞ시고금번포폄은각별엄쥰케ᄒᆞ야써츌쳑ᄒᆞᄂᆞᆫ졍ᄉᆞ에븕게ᄒᆞ심을바란다ᄒᆞ엿더라

○민씨피신 민대신병셕씨가평양관찰ᄉᆞ지임시에그영리박찬규의수만금지산을륵탈ᄒᆞᆫ일로년젼에박찬규가샹경ᄒᆞ야그돈을차지랴고호소ᄒᆞᆫ일은닉외국이아ᄂᆞᆫ바ㅣ라지금다시운동ᄒᆞᄂᆞᆫ디저작일에일본인들과룽ᄉᆞᄒᆞ나히민대신집에간즉숨고보지아니ᄒᆞᆫ다ᄂᆞᆫ디필경은그돈을물어쥬고말이라더라

○별슌담긔 쇼안동근쳐에져작일브터경위원별슌검이담긔ᄒᆞᆫ다더라

○필유곡졀 지작일하오두시에양복ᄒᆞᆫ쟈ᄒᆞ나히옥관ᄌᆞ붓친량반ᄒᆞ나흘손목을서로붓잡고풍우ᄀᆞᆺ치모라평리원으로드러가ᄂᆞᆫ디대한사ᄅᆞᆷ이양복을ᄒᆞ엿다고도ᄒᆞ고일인이라고도ᄒᆞᄂᆞᆫ디알수업다더라

론셜

젼호련속

○ᄯᅩᄒᆞᆫ아셰아로말ᄒᆞ진디란리거리를만들게ᄒᆞᄂᆞᆫ자ㅣ잇ᄂᆞ니이ᄂᆞᆫ무어시뇨한국에잇ᄂᆞᆫ일본외교관들이모조록한국에잘될일을권면ᄒᆞ야셩취됨이엇슬줄로안바이어ᄂᆞᆯ이금소견으로ᄂᆞᆫ이왕보다오히려망칙ᄒᆞᆫ즉이거시다뉘의허물인지우리ᄂᆞᆫ참아말홀수업스나그러ᄒᆞ나당초에한국외독립과강토를보젼ᄒᆞ게ᄒᆞᆫ다보증ᄒᆞ더니필경진보쟈들의실샹ᄒᆞᄂᆞᆫ바ᄂᆞᆫ점점이왕약조홈파어기여변심이되ᄂᆞᆫ모양인지라

대외빅작도한국사건에일본외교관들의ᄒᆞᄂᆞᆫ일을평론ᄒᆞ엿스나그러ᄒᆞ나우리의보기에ᄂᆞᆫ일본사ᄅᆞᆷ의날로ᄒᆞᄂᆞᆫ바니이왕에ᄒᆞᆫ일이던지방금ᄒᆞᄂᆞᆫ일이던지리두에쟝ᄎᆞᆺᄒᆞᆯ일이던지그실샹디로좃차분명히로츌ᄒᆞ게ᄂᆞᆫ말을아니ᄒᆞ엿슨즉동씨의셜명ᄒᆞᆫ것도오히려유익ᄒᆞᆯ거시업스며

ᄯᅩᄒᆞᆫ요사이날로셩대ᄒᆞ여가ᄂᆞᆫ쟈ㅣ잇ᄂᆞᆫ지라소위일진회라ᄒᆞᄂᆞᆫ바로써우리신문에왕왕히보도ᄒᆞᆫ바ㅣ어니와이회ᄂᆞᆫ당초에파락호된란봉류들로ᄒᆞ여곰조직ᄒᆞ야일본병참사령부로셔경비를디여먹여살이ᄂᆞᆫ회인지라그라ᄒᆞ나그즁에도후명예나ᄂᆞᆫ일을힝ᄒᆞᆯ가우리ᄂᆞᆫ밋엇더니당초에소지ᄡᅥ라ᄒᆞᄂᆞᆫ량반이자긔의마음대로한국을위ᄒᆞ여쳐사치못ᄒᆞ며

청국에도소위의국회라ᄒᆞᄂᆞᆫ거시싱기엿ᄂᆞᆫ디이회인즉일진회와갓치일본사령부에셔경비를디여쥼은아니로되은령즁어ᄂᆞ곳에셔유지ᄒᆞ도록ᄒᆞ게만ᄒᆞᄂᆞᆫ사ᄅᆞᆷ이잇셔지탕ᄒᆞᆫ즉실샹갓흔형편이오크게ᄂᆞᆫ다를거시업ᄂᆞᆫ지라

청국게이셔트신문을거ᄒᆞ여의국회의소문을쟈셰히드른즉그회ᄂᆞᆫ일본가셔단여온청인들이혁명ᄒᆞᆯ의사로조직ᄒᆞ엿ᄂᆞᆫ디년젼슌검의게포착되엿슬셔에그회즁문부들수협ᄒᆞ여본즉외국을반디ᄒᆞ며저히나라정부를반디ᄒᆞᆫ다홈이러니홀연봉긔ᄒᆞ여청국에잇ᄂᆞᆫ구라파빅인종들을살히ᄒᆞ며만쥬법률을번갱ᄒᆞ려드ᄂᆞᆫ디

당초근인인즉일본셔교준ᄒᆞ여방조ᄒᆞᄂᆞᆫ당파가잇ᄂᆞᆫ지라북경파샹히와모든각디방으로쳐쳐이유인ᄒᆞ여단니ᄂᆞᆫ디근년에일본으로유학ᄒᆞ고온사ᄅᆞᆷ들은일본무관복쟝과갓치만다려금실로줄과동을다라입고륙혈포와총파혹다른병긔들도가지고도라단니면셔노략이무쌍ᄒᆞᆫ디샹히에잇ᄂᆞᆫ인가하나을억지로ᄂᆞᆨ탈ᄒᆞ여도회처를만달고호난셔에셔ᄂᆞᆫ의국회원의작요홈으로ᄡᅥ외국교회식이ᄂᆞᆫ사ᄅᆞᆷ이모도다도망ᄒᆞᆫ일이잇셧다ᄒᆞᄂᆞᆫ지라

모든형편이이러ᄒᆞᆫ즉

한국에일진회와청국의의국회잇ᄂᆞᆫ거시한가지일이라도셩취ᄒᆞ랴홈은고사ᄒᆞ고다만일본의호홈을자셰ᄒᆞ여한국량국의가히ᄒᆞᆯ만ᄒᆞᆫ일도방히가되게ᄒᆞᆫ즉이두나라에셔일본외교수단으로되ᄂᆞᆫ거슬볼진디모도명예가손히가되게만홈이오ᄯᅩᄒᆞᆫ대외빅작의한청량국을위ᄒᆞ여셜명ᄒᆞᆫ디도이러ᄒᆞᆫ말은업슨즉실로긔이ᄒᆞ녀이러ᄒᆞ여감복ᄒᆞᆯ거시업노라

광고

TELEGRAMS.

Japanese Legation.

The naval artillery commander with the forces at Port Arthur states that at 2:30 P. M. on Thursday the condition of the Russian men-of-war was as follows:

The Peresviet list to starboard. Poltava, Retvisan and Pobieda submerged to upper deck. Pallada list to starboard, Bayan on fire.

The Sevastopol was anchored out of sight near the east harbour. On Thursday the fire was directed on the three last named vessels.

Army Headquarters.

On the 8th inst., a Japanest force encountered 40 Russian cavalry near Sungsukow (30 *li* north of Kianchang). The Russians lost half their force in killed, but the Japanese suffered no casualties.

Shanghai, Dec. 9th.

The Russian cruiser "Askold" secretly took in coal to-day and is prepared to weigh anchor and join the Baltic squadron.

FROM JAPAN PAPERS.

London, Dec. 2.

Russia has suggested to the United States Government that the second Peace Conference be postponed until the conclusion of the war.

London, Dec. 3.

It is stated officially at Washington that Russia's suggestion to postpone the Hague Convention necessarily prevents the United States taking further steps in the matter, as it is desirable that Russia should participate in the Convention when held.

London, Dec. 2.

Rear-Admiral Davies, U.S.N., has accepted the position of American representive at the International Enquiry.

London, Dec. 3rd.

General Kuropatkin reports that the Japanese rearguard (? advanced guard) is retreating upon Shinkhechau, having been driven,on the 29th ult., from a pass. the Russian losses were slight.

The Japanese retired to another fortified pass one mile-and-a-half away and this position was also captured by the Russians after a short and stubborn resistance.

London, Dec. 2nd.

The Bulgarian Chamber has adopted an extraordinary credit of one and three-quarters million sterling (£1,750,-000) in order to purchase ninety batteries of quick-firers. The guns are required for extending the Black Sea coast defences.

London, Decembe r 3rd.

The supplementary portion of the Baltic Fleet has reached Tangier.

Three large and two small Russian warships have passed Perim (Red Sea), going southwards.

The Japanese Minister received in audience the day before yesterday, strongly urged His Majesty to retain the present magistrate of Pyeng Yang at his post and to dismiss the magistrate of Chang Won, who has placed many difficulties in the way of the railway authorities. It is said that His Majesty agreed and will appoint Mr. Paik Nam Chun, in the place of Mr. Kwon Ik Sang, in charge of Chang Won.

Señor Anasagasti, the Argentine Commissioner to the St. Louis Expoition, confirms the old rumour that the greatest cataract in the would exists on the Iguazu River, between Brazil and Argentina, about 700 miles north of Buenos Aires. The Iguazu Falls are 210ft. high, 13,000ft. wide, and are half again as great in volume as those of Niagara.

DESTROYER REPORTED STRANDED.

The reported stranding of a Japanese destroyer with four funnels between Chefoo Bluff and Chefoo cape has apparently been verified, a Chinese having returned from the Bluff with the news that he sighted a Japanese cruiser towing a destroyer with four funnels in the direction of Port Arthur yesterday afternoon. He says that the cruiser and his story in other ways bears the stamp of truth.

It is said that the Chinese was sent to the Bluff for the purpose of ascertaining whether or not the destroyer was there.

The story of the stranding originated with members of the crew of the "Rastoropini," who said they were chased to the mouth of the harbor by a four funnelled destroyer which suddenly disappeared in the snow storm.

While the Japanese destroyers were in sight from the beach on Thursday a loud explosion was heard from the direction of the Bluff. This fact taken in connection with the rumour of the stranding of the destroyer led to the supposition that the latter had been blown up rather than have the news of the disaster get abroad.

It is now supposed that the explosion was that of a mine washed ashore by the heavy sea.—Chefoo Daily News.

[In all probability, this is the destroyer, which we recently reported as having been sighted in tow off Chemulpo.—K. D. N.]

THE TERRORS OF RONTGEN RAYS.

There are in London, it is estimated, a score of X-ray operators suffering from that mysterious disease which proved fatal in the case of Mr. Clarence Dally, Mr. Edison's assistant. The disease, which is apparently incurable, is set up as a direct result of the manipulation of the Rontgen rays; and the hands of the operator appear to be the most vulnerable part. A fortnight ago, one well-known doctor, who is in charge of the X-ray department at one of the largest of the London hospitals, had the first two joints of the forefinger of his right hand amputated, and last Thursday it was necessary to take the remainder of the finger away.

"You can see from the fingers of the right hand how the trouble has develop ed," he remarked to a Weekly Dispatch interview. The hand seemed as though it had been severely scalded. It was covered with an ulcerous eruption, and the nails looked as though they had been crushed and torn to pieces.

"Have you suffered much pain during the progress of the malady?"

The doctor's face clouded over at the recollection of his sufferings. "My dear sir," he said, "I have suffered the torments of the damned! From last June onward, until I had my finger amputated, I scarcely knew what sleep was. Night after night I rolled about in agony.

"All the earlier workers," proceeded the doctor, "are suffering in greater or less degree: and this is due solely to the fact that we did not know what we were working with, and took no precautionary methods against possible danger."

Mr. Harry Cox, of Rosebery-avenue, who supplies the Admiralty and the War Office with X-ray apparatus, is another of the victims. He carries his left arm in a sling as the result of his injuries.

The Gentlemen, who prophesied dark happenings if the remains of the late Crown Princess should be interred at the spot chosen, have now been sentenced to punishment. Yi Chong and Ching Ki Yup are to received 80 blows. Sin Suk Hio will be imprisoned for 15 years and Kim Hyun Ku has received a life sentence with hard labour. The latter Gentleman is considered to be responsible for a plot to change the site of the tomb to one of his own choosing; his profession being the selection of graves for deceased members of the Imperial family, it is thought that professional jealousy led him to denounce the selection of another member of his fraternity.

At an audience on Thursday, the Italian Minister obtained from His Majesty, the promise of a goldi-mining concession.

It is stated in Tientsin that the Peking Government has decided to cancel the Hankow Canton railway concession, in consequence of the Americans having virtually sold it to the Belgians.

The Korean Minister at Peking has applied to the government for some recognition of the services of Mim Pil Hi, the first secretary of the Legation, who filled his post excellently for some years.

A special session was called yesterday to discuss ways and means of dealing with the Chin Po Hoi in the North Chulla province. The Governor was telegraphically instructed to ask them what grievance they entertained and then disperse them.

Mr. Kim Yu-chik, recently appointed Magistrate of Danchon finds himself unable to reach his post, owing to the reluctance of the Russian troops to permit the passage of Korean officials from territory in Japanese military occuption to places under their control.

With the return of the winter gales the arduous nature of the work of the Japanese blockading squadron in the Gulf has been much increased. There is very little abatement in the activity of the attempts to run the blockade, since enormous profits are to be made from shipping stores to forbidden ports.

Work on the construction of the trans-Formosan Railway is now being pushed forward for military reasons. A length of 118 miles. on the railway's northers section and that of 86 miles on the Southern section have already been completed. The southern line is expected to be extended by 8 miles by the 15th inst.

The "Nichi Nichi's" Nagasaki correspondent learns from a person who has arrived there from the Tumen, that there are indications that the Russian forces at Possiet Bay have been greatly increased this month. The Russians are constructing permanent defensive works on the northern bank of the Tumen River. It has hitherto been believed that the construction ,of a bridge across river was impossible but according to reports this feat can be accomplished.

A report from the Japanese Consul at Vancouver dated October 5 states that Japanese emigrants to Canada have hitherto been subjected only to the emigration law of District of Columbia, but that the Dominion Government has recently declared that the Emigration Law promulgated by the federal authorities in 1880 and amended in 1902 should be enforced against all emigrants arriving there from Far Eastern countries. For this purpose an inspector has been newly appointed at Vancouver and Victoria, as is the case at the various ports on the Atlantic coast. The delay in the enforcement of the Federal Emigration Law was due to the fact that the necessary preparations had not been effected until quite recently.

The Korea Daily News.

Issued at 5 P. M. daily except Sundays.

Rate of Subscription:—
Per Year,............Yen 25.
Per Quarter,..........Yen 7.
Per Month,...........Yen 2.50.

Postage in Korea not charged extra.
Postage abroad charged extra.

Advertisements, 50 sen per day for 1 inch or less.
5 yen per month per inch.
50 yen per year per inch.

All communications to

E. T. BETHELL,
Editor and Publisher,
Pak-tong, Seoul.

A DEADLOCK.

Although we have so often received news of the destruction of Russian men of war which has since turned out to be incorrect, we think that this time the news will prove to have been well founded.

Two hundred and three metre hill, although not one of the inner ring of forts commands, by its eminence, that part of the harbour where the Russian battleships have hitherto taken refuge from the Japanese shells and if as seems to be the case, the Japanese have undisputed possession of this hill and have mounted heavy guns there, Port Arthur, as a harbour is now lost to the Russians.

If General Stoessel adheres to his brave determination to go on fighting to a finish, it will yet be several months before the stronghold can be completely taken by the Japanese; possibly two months, possibly more. If it be true, as the reported destruction of the Russian war-ships would indicate, that Japanese artillery now commands the whole harbour there is reason to hope that the Japanese will now abandon the storming tactics which have proved so costly in lives and be content to adopt less heroic measures for the final subjugation of Port Arthur.

What her attack on the stronghold has cost Japan in life will probably never be known. Even if the figures are given out, there will always be the suspicion that the Japanese Government is not taking the world entirely into its confidence. Taking into consideration the formidable nature of the defenses, the number of attacks, successful or unsuccessful, that have been reported, and the inevitable prevalence of disease, 100,000 would appear to be a conservative estimate of the Japanese losses to date.

This alone is a sufficient argument against the continuance of hostilities but when it is remembered that 100,000 families in Japan are deprived of their breadwinners and subjected to increased taxation at the time the same argument becomes overwhelming.

Home newspapers, which have from the first taken a more optimistic view of Japan's prospects in Northern Manchuria than has been justified by events, now begin to give expression to the opinion that operations there can at the best only result in a deadlock. Such an opinion is not a cheerful one but it is founded on reason. Russia's resources and capacity to continue this war have from the first been consistently underestimated while laudatory articles have been written about Japan, which, while having no direct bearing upon the war, have led the world to believe that she goes to battle equipped with qualifications such as have never been previously possessed by any fighting force.

The intense patriotism and courage of the Japanese has never been doubted; had it been, this war has amply demonstrated that in devotion to their country and personal valour the Japanese have no superiors in the world. The completeness of the equipment of her soldiers and sailors and the systematic manner in which every contingency has been provided, show that that genius which is described as "an infinite capacity for taking pains" is a national characteristic.

But the end of the war seems no nearer and if some steps are not taken towards a pacific settlement of the dispute we have before us the prospect of the continuance of the awful expenditure of life and treasure for many months to come.

Let us hope that the deadlock now reached may serve as an excuse for the commencement of peace negotiations The ill-effects of war are far-reaching and in these days of enlightenment it should surely be possible to arrive at a less evil way of settling disputes.

THE CAPE TO CAIRO RAILWAY.

IMPORTANT LAND SETTLEMENT SCHEME.

Sir Charles Metcalfe, who is leaving direct for the Victoria Falls in order to superintend the extension of the Cape to Cairo Railway from the Zambesi to Barotseland, will on his arrival in South Africa begin work upon a scheme which is about to be inaugurated for the settlement of colonists along the railway. In the course of an interview with Reuter's representative before his embarkation for the Cape, Sir Charles Metcalfe said:—

"One of the greatest needs of South Africa is an increased white population. With the object of inducing colonists to come into the country now being tapped by the Cape to Cairo Railway, land is being surveyed which will be given out in free grants of 160 acres each to "bona fide" settlers. At the present moment we are reserving plots along the line from Bulawayo to Salisbury. No piece of land will be more than three miles distant from the railway. This scheme will be carried out north of Bulwayo right up to the Zambesi and beyond as the railway progresses, and judging from last year's favourable results of cotton and tobacco cultivation settlers should have a prosperous future before them I expect that some settlers will begin taking up these grants in November. With £100 capital intending settlers ought to be able to support themselves until their first crops are saleable. If after a year's experience these settlers find the country and the prospects satisfactory, money will probably be advanced, where necessary, to enable them to send for their families and continue work on a larger scale.

"Good progress is being made with the Cape to Cairo Railway north of the Zambesi on the section known as the northern extension from Victoria Falls Kalomo, the administrative centre of Barotseland, a disance of 100 miles..... At the Victoria Falls, the engineers are hard at work at the culiver bridge which is to span the Zambesi. The bridge work is ready and is being shipped out in sections as wanted. The foundations are all in hand on the south side of the river; two of the bays are already erected. Work is in progress simultaneously from both banks of the Zambesi. The bridge will have ten bays in all, and the rate of progress is expected to be two bays a month. Immense quantities of material are already on the spot, An electric motor cable with a span of over 900 ft.—the largest thing of its kind which has been attempted—carries the material from one bank of the Zambesi to the other. This is a new experiment and cheapens considerably the cost of erection. By next spring, when the line reaches Kalomo, the question will arise of the further extension of the rail towards Tanganyika.

"I know there are people who think the Cape to Cairo line mythical. There are others who shrug their shoulders at this railway development and say, "Will it pay?" I am firmly of the opinion that there will be not merely one line in this region, but that it will become a network of railways. I base this opinion on the productiveness of the soil and the immense population there will be in that territory, now that we have absolutely stopped the slave trade."—The Times.

THE SIBERIAN RAILWAY.

A Special Commission has been sitting at the Ministry of Finance for the purpose of considering the financial side of the work involved in doubling the track of the Siberian Railway. According to the estimates presented by Prince Khilkoff, the cost of laying down a second track as far as Lake Baikal would amount to £10,588,235, and of carrying a second track round Lake Baikal and of adding another line of rails to the Manchurian Railway would amount to £5,294,118 in each case; that is, a total of 200,000,000 roubles, or £21,176,470. It is reported that an English syndicate has offered to lay down the second line of rails as far as Lake Baikal in one year for the sum of £21,176,470. This offer has been rejected by the Minister of Ways of Communication, Prince Khilkoff, as he is of opinion that he can lay down the second line throughout its entire length for the same outlay and in the space of two years.

The *P. & T. Times* says:—Queues are in great demand in Peking just now, certain Chinese stating they have got large orders to fill for people of "a certain country."

At a ball given by the Mayor and Mayoress of Hanley, at the Victoria Hall, the Mayor and town clerk danced a cakewalk in their official robes. The "turn" was a great success.

The *P. T. Times* of the 19th ultimo gives the curious information that seven hundred and sixty-two packages of guns and fittings arrived at Tientsin from Osaka, the consignees of which were unknown.

It appears that the Japanese authorities have arranged to work the Yentai colliery near Liaoyang, which was under Russian management before its capture by the Japanese Army. Mr. Ghyaki, a senior mining expert of the Government Department of Agriculture and Commerce, is leaving Tokyo in a few days to superintend the work in the mine.

It is reported that a second Boxer rebellion is brewing in North China. Incendiary hand bills are being widely distributed, and so apparent is the popular unrest that the situation is causing the Peking officials the greatest anxiety. The former movement was pro-Manchu and anti-foreign, but the present movement is both anti-foreign and anti-Manchu. It is feared that if the movement is not immediately quashed the results will be serious.

Recent issues of the Port Arthur "Novi Krai" "reports the Chefoo Daily News, received by the "Rastorupnui" contain a number of advertisements which are extremely out of keeping with the supposed nervous strain under which the inhabitants of Port Arthur are laboring. For example one "ad" reads as follows: "The undersigned desires to take lessons in the English language, apply to Kuntz & Albers. The General Staff informs the public that some of the officers of the garrison, especially those serving in the trenches, are without field glasses and requests that all civilians having good glasses present them for sale at the general staff headquarters. Messrs. Kuntz & Albers state that until further notice their store will be open to trade between eight A. M. and five P.M.

The Korea Daily News.

VOL. I, SATURDAY, DECEMBER 10, 1904. No. 122

大韓每日申報
대한매일신보

(뎨일빅이십삼호) (화요일) 일쳔구빅사년십이월십삼일

사고뵉

이신보는영어와한국문셕거러
일츌판홉
신문가
한쟝 엽젼두돈오푼
일삭표 엽젼두량닷돈
우표가미삭닷돈
다닷돈으로밧숩
광고료는
귀한의쟝단과즈항의다쇼로쥰
감홍되몃가로밧을티이오며오
리지아녀대한사람마다다이신
문을보실터이니광고내시기를
원흐시는이들은우리신문사에
와셔면약흐심을희망흡
○발횡소 박동대한미일신보
사벽이한교옆히젼명국인셜립
림정자리오
사쟝 영국인 (빅셜)
평양 디리졈
○평양효동사는권미보씨로우
리신문판매디리인을디졍흐엿
시니오니평양에계신구람코져흐
시는 쳠군즈는히디리졈에와졍
탐흐와면회흐시옴

사고

○우리대한매일신보의목뎍은
대한의안녕질서에관한모든데
목에디흐야는공평한법론을쥬
쟝홈이라우리동신원의탐보는
신문보시는쳠군즈의게흐상보
도흐리며편지들귀셔흐며주시
는이는성명과번디들쟉이붓처
시기를희망흐오니이거슨신문
상에긔쟤흐란는거시아니오다
만극히신용흐는증거를숨고자
홈이라귀자는아모귀셔던지귀
쟤홈을되쟈흐는권리들가졋스
나되쟈흐는리유를말홀터이오
며공즁평화들문란케흐는듯훈
귀셔는의례히밧지안켓숩나이
다
●본사셜시이라로신문을미양
우례로분젼흐와례젼부의안의
로젼흐든것스로면곳에는흐늣게
젼흐기도흐며흐면칠거슬흐엿집
에젼흐기도흐며흐아니젼흐는
곳도잇다흐와우리신문을수탕
흐야구람흐시는 쳠군즈의게
디흐야미우미안흐옵기로지금
은분젼인을두고미일엄즁이젼
흐며아니젼흐거나늣게거나흐
폐가엄도륵흐라흐오니흐아니

젼흐거는흐늣게젼흐거나흐일
이잇스면본사로통긔흐여주심
을희망흐옵

관보

대삼쳔륙호 광무팔년
십이월십일
셔임급수령
○임중추원의관셔칙임관수등
종이품 홍병덕
○임경위원총순셔판임관륙등
구품 김티원
의원면본관 중추원의관
고영철 중추원의관 리의향
중추원의관 유형구 중추원
의관 김영호 중추원의관
오구영 중추원의관 리은호
○임중추원의관셔주임관륙등
경위원총슌 문홍셥
정삼품 리근용 정삼품 김
현덕 정삼품 장근식 륙품김
김병수 구품리교항
이상십이월칠일
○히시종원분시어 구품 빅
정괴 구품 리계순 구품
김영모 구품 리시영
○명장례원쇼경셔칙임관삼등
종이품 죠동완
○명시강원첨수셔칙임관삼등
종이품 윤우식
○명시종원분시어 륙품 리
규익 륙품 리종호
○명시종원분시어 구연티
○승셔판임관오등 육구갑리
셔쥬수 리면승
○의원면본관 군부쥬수 손
쥰모 의학교교관 면홍규
○임군부쥬수셔판임관륙등
셔수근
○임의학교교관셔판임관륙등
의학교서긔 리우승
○임의학교서긔셔판임관일등
전교관 면홍규
금삼급봉 의학교교관 리유
승
이상십이월팔일
○죠서흐야골으샤디종이품홍
병덕을명흐샤중추원의관을삼
으시다
광무팔년십이월칠일
중추원의장디판부의장록군
부쟝 리종건
○죠서흐야골으샤디종이품죠
동완을명흐샤장례원쇼경을삼

으시고종이품윤우식으로시강
원첨수를삼으시다

외보

○션동뎨쟝 쳥국션동셩계
이쓰이군즁흐야고무쇄모젹흐는뎨의
셔쟈는러지라그디방관이명령흐되
쟈에훈쟈는사실종관흐거시오에그참
니혼자등의의져산은젹몰흐다흐며스죠
훈방법이시의회단을금흐기는엿
○의쟝발명 의대리에쟝령흐
나이이포대에걸넌젼과셜즁을
약금흐는당흐방이밟을신발명흐야관
가한죠흐외국에그발명권을판라자
분흐말흐되이상이벡으로흐면군사
셕군동위흐매젼코리우죠용히명
라엿는인안흐아셔미디천기들니
다티그모와셔그랍근세에여리흐
셩정이방호흐시더라
○아렌불불이등 대리지
구는유형병라흐비아아죠렌향
동흔다뎌라
○표쟈귀오희 로국불틔
군는참쟝흠킈씨 가말흐되헙에
이군흠에셔니러논사건진은로국
흐에셔그표귀틀오희흔연코라
○부오권평화 신일이
거부다폐스단디에셔밥일이에
당수두즁이흐하의원에셔신이
흐흐가동홍국즈상의계권교흐논
흐며곰동국즈상의계권교흐논
안군은인계즁흐엇논히겨의
을중지케흐키는외교수단에죠
○평화회의 아라사니각의
우잇디씨가미국대통령이케의장
훈평과셔회의사진으로미국신문
에빅셔희흐여월너논대통령무스
빅셩은의의를찬셩흐나아라사
훈즁노회아라사국미코코죤영
흐라흐엽이흐기를오디리서를드
흐즁성흡비 이혼교슈국족씨
흐교숑희생흐엇말흐다더라
○중립원뷘 모처에온보고를
드르니회많봉으로도라오논아
라사헙디가지금덕국
코셔후세셕가젼을셀논이
러요에케엉탈운에잇논ノ레당
신비셩엽일렬이 신디

일에면보흡을거훈죽로국헙디
가디국평디안구라파폐구미만
에셔셕탄을싣논중이라흐엿더
라

잡보

○칙치동군 삼작일경무쳥에
셔리규찬외죵승리규익을칙치
흐야 흥릉히즈닉에잇논분
묘를동군흐엿더라
○위문수복 명 복정군위문
대스켜즁헌씨가회국흐후에빗
선을보티복 명흐고아죵일티
흐지못흐야복정군의회경을상
주흐지못흐지라소신을과송흐
야위문흠이외신에지나지못흐
다고일인의공론시비가분분흐
다더라
○순쳔발쟝 평샹남도순쳔소
김연식씨는십일일에발쟝훈다
더라
○쳥슈죵납 김관서종헌씨가
츄슈죠들션복흐야슈운샹리흐
다가양쳔젼강에셜화흐야젼인
이교화흐륵흐엿더니항쥬거흐
논김슈산등이음거셜어멋셕을
겸어간지라젼쥬등이일로셔졍
탈흐야고소흐미김판셔가히인
등을경무쳥에쳑슈흐고쟝죠일
빗오십셕을물녀밧논다더라
○지쟝금광쳐소 의공수모탁
고씨가일작 폐현흐빅에샹히
주흐야금광흐곳을엇은지라히
금광을지쟝흡추로용관위원을
파송훈다흐며금광회사 난은명
흔에출리훈다더라
○쟝씨셜회 덕산군계흐는쟝
졍환씨등이동지인샹빅여인을
모와히군에진보회를셜시흐야
부근쥬군에포고셔들광포흐고
일진회쟝윤시병씨의게공함흐
아지회들쳥인흐엿논디그목적
은일진회와동일흐다더라
○진위판방셔 젼자에죵셩파
및북쳥의진위디위판을피임흐
야경셩에셔발흐야부임흐다가
빈쳔산일본수비디에서일본군졍
디에니을경파흐야로군의졍거
디로부임흠은일본군수의게리
치안란흔리유로그위관등을류
케케흐엿더니지작일에경셩으
로송환흐야작일에방셕흐엿논
디그셩명이좌와곳더라
졍위김광수 참위최영슈 등

박현병 동리준현 동명규국
동유범수 동신석구 임참위
박회순외에병명이명이더라

○졍문군머 원산항에셔일본
수명부에졍류되엿든북관진위
티소관관인이양샹이되엿더니
일작에몽방이되엿는디졔작샹
일에일졔히군부로가셔태신우
졍견ᄒᆞ고졍문군ᄒᆞ기를북관은일
본과아라사가셔로진치고경계
ᄒᆞ는셔이ᄂᆡ왕티치못ᄒᆞ게ᄒᆞᆷ은계
쟈ᄒᆞ지못ᄒᆞᆷ이아니어늘나고ᄂᆡ남보
직ᄒᆞ여두고무슴일노무단히환
티들식혀이지경에니르러군졸
나라스수로멸서케ᄒᆞ고졍ᄒᆞ는
되리에폐를셩치케ᄒᆞ엿느뇨ᄒᆞ
되리대신은무부답이라더라

○회민불산 공쥬관찰ᄉᆞ가ᄂᆡ
부로보ᄒᆞ기를부하에회민수
빅명가량이회집ᄒᆞ엿는디만
으로효유ᄒᆞ여도히산치아니ᄒᆞ단
니엇지조쳐ᄒᆞ올지못회시ᄒᆞ
라ᄒᆞ엿더라

○면훈문쳔 ᄂᆡ부에셔문쳔군
슈의게면훈ᄒᆞ기를원항에잇든
최봉태를당초에무슴일노인연
ᄒᆞ야월경ᄒᆞ야착거ᄒᆞ엿스며경
부에셔비밀히파송ᄒᆞ엿다ᄒᆞ고가
칭ᄒᆞ는자를엇지영슈ᄒᆞ야보지아냇관
ᄒᆞ고회민의게도보ᄂᆡ지아니ᄒᆞ
ᄒᆞ엿스며곳쌍ᄒᆞ기도아니ᄒᆞ
커ᄒᆞ고세무소이젼실ᄒᆞ엿다칭ᄒᆞ
야후회ᄒᆞ고발손ᄒᆞᆫ일지시죵각을에보샹이
ᄒᆞ엿더라

○졍문면관 외부에셔졍부로
죠회ᄒᆞ기를일본공ᄉᆞ가셩명ᄒᆞ
기를평양군슈평쥬ᄒᆞᆫ주는일죵우
리가귀군수샹에공로가잇스미본수
가담화ᄒᆞ엿는일인티회젼ᄒᆞ고
귀졍부에셔는이군슈를무지못
샹이잇서파면ᄒᆞ엿는지회시ᄒᆞ
라ᄒᆞ엿기로비에죠회ᄒᆞ오니곳
시명ᄒᆞ야써명빅히보고ᄒᆞᆷ을
케ᄒᆞ기를바란다ᄒᆞ엿더라

론셜

변동되는풍셜

○일아량국의긔젼됨으로써한
국의형편은당초보다도변ᄒᆞ야
괴샹ᄒᆞᆫ폐되엿슴은셰샹이다아는바
기에도각국이ᄌᆞ못경ᄯᅥᆺᄒᆞᆫ
엿는지라
이에ᄅᆞᆯ당ᄒᆞ야무근지셜도만코
난신지어도ᄉᆡᆼ긔ᄂᆞᆫ것도가하고
수는엇스나그런ᄒᆞ나요ᄉᆞ이
풍셜을드른즉일본셔한국졍부
반드리권고ᄒᆞᆷ의ᄉᆞ를ᄃᆡ다ᄂᆞᆫ니티
이말도엿시즌신키는어렵우나
그런ᄒᆞ나분세지아니ᄒᆞᆫ군등에
서공연이엄ᄒᆞᆫ리치가엇지잇
스리요
과쟝명년일월브리는쟝곡쳔대
가관리ᄒᆞ야다군법을ᄒᆞ리라는자
도잇스며조ᄒᆞᆫ일본공ᄉᆞ일권말
서는공관을쟝츗봉폐ᄒᆞ고한국
며부를관활ᄒᆞᆫ다는소문도잇스

그외에각부에도각각분비ᄒᆞ야
관리케ᄒᆞᆫ다는ᄃᆡ궁ᄂᆡ부에는가
등세요외부에는스틔븐스씨요
탁지에는목하면씨요군부에는
야진씨요학부에는국분씨라ᄒᆞ
며샤ᄒᆞᆫᄯᅢ황뎨폐하ᄭᅴ셔주달ᄒᆞ야
각국에주차ᄒᆞᆫ한국공사들을모
도소환ᄒᆞ게ᄒᆞᆫ다는ᄃᆡ이는다름
이아니라밧일이런ᄒᆞᆯ지경이면
한국에잇는각국대표자들도자
연히철환ᄒᆞ겟는고로그런ᄒᆞᆷ이
라ᄒᆞ는지라
이소문이가히드를만ᄒᆞ기에신
문에게진ᄒᆞ야셜명ᄒᆞ기는ᄒᆞ나
요사이말들은실로히황ᄒᆞᆫ바이
만ᄒᆞᆫ즉분명히밋을수가업는거
시일본셰력형공졔ᄒᆞ게쳐ᄉᆞᄒᆞ
는자리에엇지그런케ᄒᆞᆯ리치가
잇스리요
우리는호말만치도붕신히너이
나그런ᄒᆞ나셜ᄒᆞᆷ이만이진젹ᄒᆞ
야된다ᄒᆞ드ᄅᆡ도져ᄭᅡ지에되는밧
자ㅣ몃가지가잇느니한국에서
엇지ᄒᆞᆯ수업시암졔ᄒᆞᆷ으로써응
락ᄒᆞ는수도잇스며ᄒᆞᆷ쟝ᄃᆡᄒᆞᆫ나
라의셰권ᄒᆞᆷ으로도ᄒᆞ는수가쏘
ᄒᆞᆫ잇는지라
금년이월에한국이일본으로더
브러밍약ᄒᆞ야서로조인ᄒᆞᆷ이암
졔에견ᄃᆡ지못ᄒᆞ야ᄒᆞᆫ줄로알아
ᄯᅥᆫ지당초에는아라사에셔한국
을도모지ᄉᆡᆼ각지아니ᄒᆞ야거졀
ᄒᆞᆫ다ᄒᆞ엿더니금번 황뎨ᄭᅴ승
하ᄒᆞ옵셧다는긔별은듯고북경
에주차ᄒᆞᆫ아국공ᄉᆞ가반괴를다
라도폐를ᄒᆡᆼᄒᆞ엿다ᄒᆞ는고로일
본셔는이소문을듯고ᄃᆡ단히불
로ᄒᆞ엿다ᄒᆞᆫ지라
그런ᄒᆞ나엇졔던지아라사에셔
는한국을아쥬ᄌᆞ지도ᄉᆡᆼ각ᄒᆞ야
친졀ᄒᆞᆫ권리를뵈이며ᄯᅩᄒᆞᆫ황위
를졍ᄃᆡᄒᆞ게ᄒᆞᄂᆞᆫ도라
리월브리일본셔한국을아모조
록박ᄂᆡᆫ케ᄒᆞ야크게유의ᄒᆞ도록
ᄒᆞᆯ는지우리는지금브리옹망ᄒᆞ
는바어니와이우의말ᄒᆞᆫ바와갓
치진졍ᄇᆞᆸ외의일로만ᄒᆡᆼᄒᆞᆯ지경
이면한국관리들의긔왕바라던
바와엇더ᄒᆞᆯ는지우리는발ᄒᆞᆯ수
업는지라
일본셔주의ᄒᆞ는바ㅣ심히속급
ᄒᆞᆫ즉우리ᄉᆡᆼ각에는젼졍ᄌᆡ국되
노기를기다리ᄂᆞᆫ거시조ᄒᆞᆯ듯ᄒᆞ
다라

뎐보

[경셩공ᄉᆞ관챠뎐]

○포티지휘관보고 히군포티
지휘관요평에일복요일하오이
시반의로항현샹이좌와여ᄒᆞ니
비레슈위토호는 슈다아워구
셔지몰에쟝기고발나다호는좌
편으로기우리지고 비아안
호는좌졔를괴ᄒᆞ고 셰바수도
보리 호는 졘투함일만구빅
톤식은 동항괴중의겻히횡
ᄒᆞ엿스니몹오일에는 빌나간다
ᄒᆞ오와 비아안호 와 셰바수
도부리 보오들위쥬ᄒᆞ야포격ᄒᆞ
엿노라ᄒᆞ엿더라

당디군슈평부챠뎐

○송슈구쇼젼 본월팔일에우
리군ᄉᆞ가송슈구 함챵을븍으
로약ᄉᆞ십을만나비것을쳐그십
여명을죽엿는ᄃᆡ우리는손샹이
업다더라

십이월십일 일본공ᄉᆞ관
챠뎐보

○졔함포격ᄒᆞ문 십이월팔일
에의런슌공위군히군참모의보고
ᄒᆞᆫ온ᄒᆞ엿스되
[illegible]

○대포격별보 려슌히군포티
지휘관의보고에운ᄒᆞ엿스되십
이월팔일아무ㅣ르ᄂᆞᆫ명중환
을밧아비오산동남샹록파멸ᄒᆞ고
기타빗유ᄉᆞ시조공쟝것다ᄒᆞ고
국부근에는창고와건츅물등이
큰손히를쥬엇다ᄒᆞ엿더라

십이월구일 동경발

○광화회의쳥동 일본졍부에
셔는미국졍부에셔뎨의ᄒᆞᆫ광화
회의에일로젼국에는관계가업
다는됴건에티ᄒᆞ야찬셩ᄒᆞᄂᆞᆫ뜻
스로회답ᄒᆞ엿더라

십이월십일 동경발

○젹함파난 려슌구에잇는젹
함세바수도불호는우리군ᄉᆞ의
위력이잇는포격을익ᄅᆞ지못ᄒᆞ
야큰손히를밧고항구밧만두샨
리로피ᄒᆞ여숨엇다ᄒᆞ엿더라

잡보

○거샹자무별 이왕단발ᄒᆞ던금
ᄒᆞᆯ빈에쟝ᄒᆞᆫ자마다ᄒᆞ등인예인
력거군이나교군군이나말군이
오쌍근일에회투노름을금ᄒᆞ는
티쟝혐가는자마다교군군아니
면지계군비나아회들이라실샹
으로말ᄒᆞ자ᄒᆞ면모모ᄃᆡ관졀에
셔는관원으로쟝기를ᄒᆞ미거ᄒᆞ
는슌검파병뎡이파슈를ᄒᆞᄂᆞᆫ지
라병슌검이감히드리가지도못
ᄒᆞᆫ다더ᄒᆞ니그런ᄒᆞᆫ쥴ᄒᆞ등샤회
인덥죄쳐이잇고샹등샤회에는
쟝기를ᄒᆞ야도관계치아니ᄒᆞᆫ다
고들ᄒᆞᆫ더라

군부동쳠회의 참쟝단
태신참부쟝이청군로병수
이동쳠ᄒᆞ야각로

장관이회의ᄒᆞ기를종금이후로
북관수령을평위관으로택차ᄒᆞ
승ᄒᆞ야겨젼을수쇄ᄒᆞ다가아라
사병뎡이과시상형ᄒᆞ거든다시
회티병을모집ᄒᆞ야격퇴ᄒᆞ면복
방을가히보젼ᄒᆞ리라ᄒᆞ야일쟈
다시회의ᄒᆞᆫ다더라

○거졀부등 일공ᄉᆞ가외부로
죠회ᄒᆞ유죵남표와경이포도로
들수츅ᄒᆞ라ᄒᆞ엿더니부에셔거
졀ᄒᆞ고못ᄒᆞ게ᄒᆞ어히관찰ᄉᆞ의
게훈령ᄒᆞ기를연로각군슈가죵
남표일령ᄉᆞ와셔로디관ᄒᆞ야쳥
로를수츅케ᄒᆞ라ᄒᆞ엿더라

○청금직죵 옥구감리가외
부로보고ᄒᆞ기를셔쳔두무고리
기는곳본항샹류화금춘하미리
로션세위원이사름을칙쳐이파
송ᄒᆞ야리왕ᄒᆞ는션샹의게세과
를ᄂᆡ며빗으티빗셩의원만파샹
민의호소가답지ᄒᆞ는고로이에
쳐보ᄒᆞ니이죠등신원ᄒᆞ야젼샤
의게과세를두번밧지못ᄒᆞ게ᄒᆞ
라ᄒᆞ엿더라

○죠회샹립치변 일공ᄉᆞ가외
부로죠회ᄒᆞ기를귀국양등두만
탕강샹림이우리군티소용을위
ᄒᆞ야쟝ᄎᆞᆺ쳐슈ᄒᆞ야치벌ᄒᆞ겟ᄉᆞᆸ
이오히디가쟈귀국국방샹관계
가되깃기일한의졍셔주지를좃
차ᄒᆞᆷ이오그규측인즉귀졍부에
셔죵망쳥쟝ᄒᆞᆯ수로우리졍부ᄭᅴ
펑이잇스니졍컨티죠량ᄒᆞ라ᄒᆞ
엿더라

○졍ᄒᆞᆫ감리젼관 외부에셔니
쟝원에죠회ᄒᆞ기를의쥬는한
쳥교계에쳐ᄒᆞ야통샹쟝졍을
졍립ᄒᆞ야과세를증강에베픈
지가미여러히오기국오빅샹년
에편지ᄒᆞ야분시케ᄒᆞ엿더니졍
금의쥬감리셔셜시ᄒᆞ야등샹쟝
졍을다시졍립ᄒᆞ고히감리티민
박이가쟝츗부임ᄒᆞᆫ다ᄒᆞ니귀원
에셔티쳔군슈죠졍윤의게부탁
ᄒᆞ야과원수세ᄒᆞ는것은보다의
주감리의게돌려보니여관할ᄒᆞ
야졍세로써수송ᄒᆞ라ᄒᆞ니이ᄉᆞ
의로써히군수의게훈칙ᄒᆞ기를
바란다ᄒᆞ엿더라

○죠졍향죤거항 원소도감에
셔니부로죠회ᄒᆞ되 원소화소
구역을이미졍ᄒᆞ미민가를회철
ᄒᆞ고수총을파올거수숙히거형
ᄒᆞᆯ스로니부로ᄒᆞ야픔결과관찰
수의게지위ᄒᆞ야디방관을거느
리고나가거힝ᄒᆞ라ᄒᆞ엿기로도
감에셔제도도졍감일원이곳쳐
나가간심ᄒᆞᆯ뜻으로미리문졉신
칙ᄒᆞᆯ수로이미주하 를경ᄒᆞ
엿스니흠죤거힝ᄒᆞᆷ을바란다ᄒᆞ
엿더라

○경리반포 관졔리졍이요감
편지리져작일에는코게회동ᄒᆞ
야다시리졍반포ᄒᆞᆫ다더라

TELEGRAMS.

Japanese Legation.

A report received from the Commander of the naval force attacking Port Arthur states that the bombardment on the 8th inst. resulted in the Pallada being set on fire and later sinking. The Giriak was struck by 11 shells and crippled. The Bayan was hit 22 times and set on fire, which lasted for 5 hours. Later the Japanese directed their fire on the Sevastapol and the transports.

Tokyo, Dec. 9.

The Japanese Government have signified their willingness to take part in a peace conference at the conclusion of the present war.

Tokyo, Dec. 10.

The Sevastopol, unable to withstand the Japanese bombardment, has sought refuge under the lee of the hill at the harbour's mouth.

Army Headquarters.

At 3 A. M. on the 9th inst. a small force of Russians attacked the Japanese outposts near the railway, but were repulsed. Later, being reinforced, they returned and drove back the Japanese outposts to a distance of 400 metres. At the same time they shelled the Japanese positions near Hanchaiow, Sinfantai and Lamuntun, but retired at daybreak. The Russians appeared to have suffered great damage, leaving many dead in front of the Japanese outposts.

FROM JAPAN PAPERS.

Berlin, Dec. 4.

One portion of the Baltic Squadron has passed Perim.

Berlin, Dec. 4.

The proposed Peace Conference at The Hague has been postponed till the close of the present war.

Berlin, Dec. 4.

The Russian Government has suspended the more liberal Press Law recently instituted, on the ground that its management is open to criticism and that the public is likely to be excited under its provisions.

London, Dec. 3.

The "Novoye Vremya" again strongly urges the Russian Government to dispatch a third squadron to the Far East, because, it says, the mastery of the sea is necessary, and the Baltic Fleet is too weak in comparison with the forces by which it will be opposed.

A branch of the Il-chin-hoi, with 300 supporters, has been established at Doksan.

It is again rumoured in China that, owing to existing state of affairs and hard pressure from outside, there will be a change of the capital from Peking to somewhere else.

It is reported in a China paper that the Central Government at Peking is in receipt of telegraphic despatches from two of its Ministers abroad announcing the end of the war is near at hand, and advising that the Government should have experienced and qualified officers in readiness for negotiations with the different Powers.

A revival of anti-foreign placards is reported from Peking. The language used on these follows the general expressions of the Boxer placards of 1900, but has one vital difference which has set the Manchus and Chinese officials in the North seriously thinking. This is that, whereas the Boxers of 1900 declared as an article of faith that they would loyally support the Manchu Dynasty in their crusade against the Western barbarians, the present placards in the North make mention of the Manchu dynasty only in an inimical sense and hinting that "the Tartar must also go."

REINFORCEMENTS.

A San Francisco telegram to the Manila Cablenews says:

Russia has purchased four ships from the Argentine Republic to augment the Baltic fleet now en route to the Far East.

The ships will be despatched at once to join the squadron near the Cape of Good Hope, South Africa.

From the same source we also learn that twenty thousand additional troops have been added to the army of investment at Port Arthur.

This assignment has been made to cover the recent losses from the ranks on account of death, sickness and disability, and with the further view of increasing the pressure already exerted on the besieged fort.

Should the severe weather continue at Shaho and vincinity, several regiments will be withdrawn from that section to augment the forces operating at Port Arthur.

THE HISTORICAL INTEREST OF THE 203 METRE FORT.

The 203 metre height, which was permanently occupied by the Japanese in the fourth general attack on the Port Arthur main defence line, is an historical point in modern warfare. It was on this hill that the late General Yamaji established his headquarters on the occasion of the capture of Port Arthur in the Chino-Japanese war. On the night of Nov. 20th, 1894, the Japanese troops of the First Division, under the famous General, bivouacked on the western side of Itzushan, arriving by way of Louisa Bay, and at 6 o'clock on the following morning they commenced firing on the Itzushan fort and after a general charge lasting only two hours that strong fort fell into their hands. Soon afterwards the Japanese stormed the town and the fall of the entire fortress was quickly effected. That morning General Yamaji ascended a hill and, commanding the whole situation, directed the operations. The hill was indeed the present 203 metre height, which has just been carried by the officers and men of the right wing of the Investing Army, who are also enjoying the historical honour gained ten years ago, says the "Kokumin."

The work of a pickpocket is done in a moment of abstraction.

The Wai Wu-pu has wired to the provincial authorities of Honan and Anhui to suppress the revolutionary society, the Ai How-hui, and at the same time, to give due protection to the missionaries and their properties.—Sin Wan-pao.

A despatch from St. Petersburg to the "San Francisco Chronicle" says that Russia probably will decide to ignore the Japanese protest regarding Russian troops wearing Chinese clothes, as Japan did in the case of the Russian protest in regard to the Russian torpedo boat destroyer "Reshitelni" cut out of Chefoo harbour by the Japanese.

Russian Headquarters, 28th November.—From the 24th to the 27th November detachments of General Rennenkampf's corps withstood the attacks of superior forces of the enemy near Zinche-chen. All the attacks of the Japanese were repulsed with great losses to them. Our casualities were about seventy killed and wounded.—Shanghai Times.

The secret societies of Hunan are planning rebellion, and since the arrest of a few of their leaders the returned student teachers of the Hunan Government schools are scared owing to the circulation of rumours that they are connected with the movement. Many have fled in sheer fright. It is also reported that the Viceroy at Wuchang is in receipt of urgent telegraphic despatches from the Governor of Hunan, and it is believed that they are in connection with this rebellious movement.

The removal of the sand and silt from the after portion of the Chinese crusiser Haitien, wrecked on Elliot Island, shows that her bottom is split open along the keel for a considerable distance, and there is practically no hope of saving her.

A short time ago Prince Pu Lun memorialised the Throne advising the creation of an admiralty department and the reorganisation of the navy, but owing to the lack of funds and the absence of a suitable natural harbour, the Government has been obliged to shelve the scheme for the present. It is said that the scheme will be revived on the conclusion of the war, and after Port Arthur and Wei-hai-wei have been returned to China.

The following paragraph which has been going the round of far-eastern journals comes as news to us: "The Japanese are reported to be enlisting one-third of Korean soldiers in their army in Korea."

Manila editors evidently imagine that they will gain the same distinction by going to Bilibid, as old Dorritt did by his residence in the Marshalsea. The latest to qualify for a term is Mr. Chauncey Mc-Govern, of the "Gossip."

The Japanese have always taken a very definite stand with regard to the use of opium. No opium is imported into any part of the Japanese Empire by private individuals; it must all pass through Government officials, who only allow it to be used for medical purposes, under very strict regulations. Opium-smoking and opium-dealing is a crime for which Japanese citizens in Japan, and Formosa as well, are punished with penal servitude of varying degrees. In Formosa only confirmed opium-smokers are able to obtain the drug, and that under the strictest surveillance. At the same time, as we learn from "Engineering," moral pressure is brought to bear on the younger generations, and there can be no doubt that, under this wise policy, the opium habit will rapidly diminish.

The Marquis of Anglesey's occupation at Dinard, where he is recruiting his health, are driving and poker-work. "I must apologise," he said to a "Mail" interviewer, "for not appearing before you in peacock-blue plush, wearing a diamond and sapphire tiara, a turquise dog-collar, ropes of pearls, and slippers studded with Burma rubies; but I prefer, and always have preferred, Scotch tweed." "I'm writing a book—on myself," he added. "It will probably consist of a series of essays on humanity—as I have known it. I may have something to say about some of my friends. I don't think I shall act again just yet. I've had the usual offer from America, but my health wouldn't stand it. Just to amuse myself I'm adapting plays. When things get right again—in two or three years from now—I shall have my own theatre once more." Lord Anglesey, adds the correspondent, leaves one with the impression of a man whose tastes and lack of intellect have been enormously exaggerated.

The Korea Daily News.

Issued at 5 P. M. daily except Sundays.

Rate of Subscription:—
Per Year,............Yen 25.
Per Quarter,..........Yen 7.
Per Month,..........Yen 2.50.

Postage in Korea not charged extra.
Postage abroad charged extra.

Advertisements, 50 sen per day for 1 inch or less.
5 yen per month per inch.
50 yen per year per inch.

All communications to
E. T. BETHELL,
Editor and Publisher,
Pak-tong, Seoul.

MARQUIS SAIONJI AND THE WAR.

The most powerful faction in the Tokio Diet is that of the Constitutionalists, and therefore some remarks made to his followers by Marquis Saionji, the leader of the party, are of great interest.

The keynote of Marquis Saionji's discourse was economy. He impressed upon his hearers that the end of the war was still a long way off, and that in order to be able to bring it to a successful issue, careful conservancy of funds was essential. He pointed out that in time of war there is always a tendency to reckless expenditure of money, and argued that Japan must not, in her enthusiasm for the war, throw financial prudence to the winds.

Continuing, the Marquis said:—

"We trust the authorities will be genuinely earnest and honest in administering the native affairs. Now I purposely use these two terms, though it may seem needless to do so. For I must say that, in my judgment, we have recently had cases of very careless administration, as, for instance, the demand made by our Government for securing the right of developing waste lands in Korea, or that other case of subsidising a certain bank with Government funds."

Now it is clear that the Marquis implies that considerable unnecessary expense was gone to in the efforts to obtain the waste lands concession, and we think that if investigation were made, it would be found that a good deal of precious money was still being wasted in Korea. The subsidisation of the Il-chin-hoi is an unwarrantable use to put funds intended for war purposes. Had it not become public who the real promoters of the Il-chin-hoi were, the society might, being given credit for disinterestedness, have been able to further Japanese aims in Korea, but now that it is known to consist of a lot of disreputable paid agitators, content to sell their country for a monthly pittance, the Il-chin-hoi is discredited and its actions only serve to bring the name of Japan into disrepute.

That the Japanese do not confine their subsidising operations to Korea is shown by the following paragraph about the Ai How-hui which appears in the "China Gazette" of November 30th:—

"The ex-Governor Wang Chih-chuen, who accompanied the new Viceroy Choufu to tiffin at the Japanese Consulate General on Monday, has, we hear from Chinese sources, determined to give evidence at the Mixed Court against his would-be assassins, and some revelations of a very startling character, the nature of which we are not at liberty to disclose at the moment, will in all likelihood be given at the next hearing, which will go much further than anything we have written in establishing the fact that the new anti-foreign and anti-dynastic movement, whose headquarters in China are in Shanghai, is essentially of Japanese origin."

The maintainance of these societies must be a costly business and we suggest to the Japanese Government thet it is hardly a proper use to make of public money.

There are two other directions in which retrenchment would be desirable; the blindly pro-Japanese attitude taken up by so mamy newspapers must be the result of considerable wire-pulling and palm-oiling, and there will probably come a time when Japan will wish that she still had at her disposal the enormous sums of money which she spends in sending news of her victories all over the world.

In our opinion Japan manifests too great a partiality for methods which cannot be described as exactly straight. forward, and it is extremely doubtful whether the canvss of the good-opinion of the world which she is conducting through the press is worth its cost. The extremely able and vigourous defense of Russia by John Dill Ross, which we reproduced a few days ago, would, its author implied, never have been written had he not been moved to it by the unfairly pro-Japanese attitude of most of the press.

A VISIT TO THE CHINESE EMPRESS.

Lady Susan Townley's recently published "Chinese Note-book" contains the following interesting account of a visit to the Chinese Dowager Empress:—

"In front of her was a high table covered with yellow silk on which were set two vases filled with chrysanthemums, and between them a glass containing a carved coral sceptre of exquisite workmanship. It was not until the Empress-Dowager pushed aside this glass, in order to stretch forward her hands across the table to the ladies who were presented to her, that I had an opportunity of really studying this remarkable woman, of whom I have heard and read so much. She sat upon a kind of Turkish divan covered with figured Chinese silk of a beautiful yolk of egg colour; being low of stature, her feet (which are of natural size, she being a Manchu) barely touched the ground and only her head and shoulders were visible over the table placed in front of her. She wore a Chinese coat, loose and hanging from the shoulders, of a diaphanous pale blue silk material, covered with the most exquisite Chinese embroidery of vine leaves and grapes. Round her neck was a pale blue satin ribbon about an inch and a half wide, studded with large lustrous pearls pierced and sewn to the ribbon. Her head was dressed according to the Manchu fashion, the hair being parted in front and brushed smoothly over the ears, to be afterwards caught up at the back and draped high and wide over a kind of paper-cutter of dark green jade set, like an Alsatian bow, crosswise on the summit of the head. The ends of this paper-cutter were decorated with great bunches of artificial flowers, butterfles and hanging crimson silk tassels. Her complexion is that of a North Italian, and, being a widow, both cheeks are unpowdered according to Chinese custom in such cases. Her piercing dark eyes, when not engaged looking at the ladies, roved curiously about amongst her surroundings. Her age is sixty-eight, as she told us herself, but her hair being dyed jet black, and most of it artificial, her appearance is that of a much younger woman. Her hands are long and tapering, and like those of many Chinese women, very prettily shaped, but they are disfigured by the curious national custom of letting the nails grow inordinately long. The nails of the two smaller fingers of the right hand were protected by gold shields which fitted to the finger like a lady's thimble and gradually tapered off to a length of three or four inches."

"COLLIER'S" ON PATENT MEDICINE.

The sins of alcohol are often celebrated, but usually the alcohol so vituperated is in the form of whiskey, gin or other compound intended ostensibly for pleasure. It is a satisfaction, therefore, to see the evil assailed in a form which wears the garb of virtue. Mr. Bok, famous purveyor of manners and morality, is a man of contrast. Not long ago he published as essay on extortion in New York, which from end to end was undiluted "fake." Now, however, he appears with an article of which any journalist might be proud, attacking an outrage with truth and potency. The people who drink or eat patent medicines number millions. Some do it to save doctors' bills, others because they find the patent medicine more effective, since no reputable doctor would give in quantity and kind what the patent medicine contains. Beer contains from 2 to 5 per cent. of alcohol. Lydia Pinkham's Vegetable Compound contains 20.6 per cent. of alcohol, Paine's Celery Compound 21, Ayer's Sarsaparilla 26.2, Hood's Sarsaparilla 18 8, Vinol 28.5, Parker's Tonic 41.6, Boker's Stomach Bitters 42.6, Hostetter's Stomach Bitters 44.3, Warner's Safe Tonic Bitters 35.7, and so on, through a long list given by Mr. Bok, which all who are their own doctors may read in the "Ladies' Home Journal" for May. Opium, digitalis and other powerful drugs also add to the power of these "medicines," by which drunkards are formed and babies are poisoned at the breast. Nothing succeeds like success, and a person who has been cheered by one of these compounds goes about enthusiatically urging it on his friends. Much virtue in a name. Call a mixture by some moral title and thousands will swallow and advocate it who would hesitate at absinthe or raw gin. The law, which forbids harmless oleomargarine to be sold as butter, does not prevent these poisons from being sold as "non-alcoholic." The Woman's Christian Temperance Union busies itself with such important matters as christening ships with wine. Life insurance companies, more intelligent, have begun to ask their applicants whether they have the bahit of using patent medicine. The preparations are popular in prohibition States.—Collier's Weekly

NEW NAGASAKI STEAMSHIP SERVICE.

The committee appointed by Governor Arakawa to forward the scheme for a new Nagasaki Steamship Company, assembled at the International Club on Monday evening, says the "Nagasaki Press" They estimate that Y 400,000 will be required to commence operations and they suggest that, with this sum, two or more second-hand steamers be purchased in order to open a Korean service. A meeting will be held in a few days to discuss the suggestions of the Committee.

It is reported that both the Emperor and the Crown Prince are suffering from a slight indisposition.

Forty-two Chin-po-hoi people, recruits for the Il-chin-hoi, arrived in Seoul on Friday night and were duly enrolled in the ranks of that society.

Eight military officers, recently drafted to the Puk-chong and Chong-sung districts, were arrested recently by the Japanese at Gensan and brought up to Seoul. They were released on Friday and immediately visited the Minister of War, demanding an explanation of the indignity put upon them.

The Korea Daily News.

VOL. I, MONDAY, DECEMBER 12, 1904. No. 123

大韓每日申報
대한미일신보

(뎨일빅이십ᄉᆞ호) (슈요일) 일쳔구빅ᄉᆞ년십이월십ᄉᆞ일

샤고빅

이신보는영어와한어로셕거미일츌판ᄒᆞ옵

신문가

한쟝 엽두돈오푼
일삭됴 엽두량닷돈
우표가미삭닷돈
다맛돈으로밧숩

광고료는

긔한의쟝단과ᄌᆞ힝의다쇼로즘감ᄒᆞ되렴가로밧올터이오며오리지아녀대한사람마다다이신문을보실터이니광고내시기를원ᄒᆞ시는이들은우리신문샤에와셔면약ᄒᆞ심을희망ᄒᆞ옵

○발힝소 박동대한미일신보샤법어학교압헤젼영국인셜필림집자리오

샤쟝 영국인 (비셜)

평양 디리점

○평양효동사는권미보씨로우리신문관미디리인을뎡ᄒᆞ엿ᄉᆞ오니평양에계신구람코져ᄒᆞ시는쳠군ᄌᆞ는히디리점에왕림ᄒᆞ와면의ᄒᆞ시옵

샤고

○우리대한미일신보의목뎍은대한의안녕질셔에관한모든데목에디ᄒᆞ야는공평한변론을쥬쟝홈이라우리톻신원의탐보는신문보시는쳠군ᄌᆞ의게홍상보도ᄒᆞ리며편지를긔셔ᄒᆞ여주시는이는셩명과반디를젹어붓치시기를희망ᄒᆞ오니이거슨신문샹에긔진ᄒᆞ랴는거시아니오다만국히신용ᄒᆞ는증거를숨고쟈홈이라긔자는아모긔셔던지긔지홈을되되각각ᄒᆞ는권리를가졋스나되각ᄒᆞ는리유를말홀터이오며공즁평화를문란케ᄒᆞ는듯혼긔셔는의례히밧지안켓숩나이다

●본사셜시이릭로신문을미양우례로분젼ᄒᆞ와례젼부의임의로뎐ᄒᆞᆫ듯스로면곳에는혹늣게젼ᄒᆞ기도ᄒᆞ며혹몃칠거슬훈겁에젼ᄒᆞ기도ᄒᆞ며혹아니젼ᄒᆞ는곳도잇다ᄒᆞ와우리신문을ᄉᆞ랑ᄒᆞ야구람ᄒᆞ시는쳠군ᄌᆞ의게디ᄒᆞ야미우미안ᄒᆞ옵기로지금은분젼인을두고미일일즉이젼ᄒᆞ며아니젼ᄒᆞ거나늣게거나혼폐가업도록ᄒᆞ랴ᄒᆞ오니혹아니젼ᄒᆞ거나혹늣게젼ᄒᆞ거나ᄒᆞᆫ일이잇스면본샤로통긔ᄒᆞ여쥬심을희망ᄒᆞ옵

관보

뎨삼쳔칠호 광무팔년십이월십이일

셔임급사령

○승종이품 졍삼품 김회원
○승졍삼품 륙품 강일
○승졍삼품 륙품 리유뎡
○승졍삼품 륙품 김병단
이샹오월십일
○탁지부인쇄국쟝셔칙임관ᄉᆞ
등즁츄원의관 최셕조
[illegible]
○임평리원관ᄉᆞ셔칙임관ᄉᆞ등
평리원관ᄉᆞ 리샹던
졍삼품 김지슌
이샹십이월팔일
○임즁츄원의관셔칙임관ᄉᆞ등
졍례원소경 죠용하
○의원면본관 비셔승 리셕종
동신사면화과쥬사 오창영
동신사면화과쥬사 김영진
동신사면화과쥬사 안승긔
동신사면화과쥬사 리치졍
닉장원긔록과쥬사 홍사셜
○임비셔원승셔쥬임관 오등
○시강원부쳠사 민봉식 임시강원시강 ... 종이품 김종한 ... 쥬사 박근호 ... 궁닉부특진관 윤용션 ... 의졍부참찬 ... 군부 ... 리근셩 ... 의원면본관 ... 비셔원승 ... 룩군법원쥬사 홍원 ... 팔일 ... 정리경등의잡은

(칙령)

바는대례니토셩의의론을가히어길수업스니원소곡림의병은부득이환침ᄒᆞ되비창훈희포는더욱지억ᄒᆞ기어려운사로비셔량을보니여전유ᄒᆞ시다

칙령 십이월구일

○칙령뎨십십호

인쇄국관졔

뎨일됴 인쇄국은셔룡산방에셜시ᄒᆞ고탁지부대신의관리에속ᄒᆞ야인쇄와밋죠지도판회동사무를마타관리홀사

뎨이됴 인쇄국은일등국이니좌기직원을치홀사

국쟝 일인 칙임혹쥬임
기사 삼인 쥬임
쥬사 사인 판임
기슈 팔인 판임

뎨삼됴 국쟝은탁지부대신의지휘감독을승ᄒᆞ야인쇄국즁일졀사무를통리홀사

뎨사됴 기사는국쟝의지휘를승ᄒᆞ야국닉공무를감리홀사

뎨오됴 쥬사는샹관의지휘를승ᄒᆞ야회계와셔무에종사홀사

뎨륙됴 기슈는샹관의지휘를승ᄒᆞ야공무에종사홀사

뎨칠됴 쥬판임관의년봉과밋관등은긔국오빅사년칙령뎨오십칠호관등봉급령에의지홀사

다만국쟝의년봉은긔국오빅사년칙령뎨일빅륙십칠호국쟝봉급령에의지홀사

뎨팔됴 본령은반포일로부터시힝홀사

광무팔년십이월륙일

어압 어새 봉

칙 의졍부참졍 신긔션

탁지부대신 민영긔

뎐보

론돈발 십이월이일

○미샹임명 미국히군참쟝대비씨가만국담지회에미국디표쟈로임명ᄒᆞ엿더라

동디발 동일

○비국군비 비리시의원에셔속발대포구십좌를사라고이빅칠십오만방의공채를모집ᄒᆞ기로작뎡ᄒᆞ엿는디그대포들은북히방슈로확쟝ᄒᆞ는디소용이라더라

동디발 동월삼일

○로미관계 로국이평화회의로물니자고동의홈은미국으로ᄒᆞ야금그사건에더착슈치못ᄒᆞ게홈이니로국을이번평화회에쎄는것이좃타고화승돈에셔공포ᄒᆞ엿더라

동디발 동일

○로함근항 불특함디에딸닌부분이대기어에도착ᄒᆞ엿고대합삼쳑과소함이쳑이홍히번폐림항에지냇다더라

동디발 동일

○로국공보 구로핏긴대쟝의공보에말ᄒᆞ되거월이십구일에신계찬이라는ᄯᅡ에셔일병을격퇴ᄒᆞ엿는디로병의살샹은젹엇고일병이일영리반밧게물너간것을로병이츄격ᄒᆞ야잠시샹지훈후에그진을졈령ᄒᆞ엿다더라

외보

○철로확쟝 로국탁지부에셔시베리아철로를두줄노홀예산을샹량ᄒᆞ기위ᄒᆞ야특별위원을두엇는디길고푸천왕의예산훈거슬거ᄒᆞᆫ즉바이갈호ᄭᆞ지데이션로를쌀라면그경비가일천오십팔만팔천이빅삼십오방이들겟고바이갈호로브터만쥬ᄭᆞ지는일천오십팔만팔천이빅삼십륙방이들겟스니도합이이천일빅십칠만륙천사빅칠십일방이니즉이억만루불이라훈영국회샤가예산이천일빅십칠만륙천사빅칠십방에일년긔한으로바이갈호ᄭᆞ지션로를맛터노켓다쟈원ᄒᆞ엿더니로국통신부대신이불허ᄒᆞ엿다는디길고푸친왕은쟈긔예산디로ᄒᆞ야만쥬ᄭᆞ지이년만이면젼톻ᄒᆞ게ᄒᆞ다ᄒᆞ더라

유물무쥬 거월십구일파앤드릐타임산신문에샹훈소문을긔지ᄒᆞ엿는디대판으로브터뎐진에총칠빅륙십이샹과ᄯᅩ그부속물이낫왓는디그물건의쥬인은아즉아지못훈다더라

엔타이탄광 일본이료양을함락ᄒᆞ기젼에로국이관할ᄒᆞ든료양근쳐에잇는엔타이셕탄광을일본사룸이홀게회으로일본

UNION INSURANCE SOCIETY OF CANTON.

Head office Hongkong.
Marine risks underwritten at current rates.
Agents in Chemulpo,
E. MEYER & Co.

COMPAGNIE DES MESSAGERIES MARITIMES.

Fortnightly Direct Service.

For Marseilles
via Ports.

Sailing from Yokohama
Calling at Kobe,
Shanghai, Hongkong, Saigon, Singapore,
Colombo, Djibouti, Suez, Port Said
and Marseilles.

For particulars apply to
HOLME RINGER & Co.,
Chemulpo.

HAYASHIDA & CO.,

16 MYENG DONG. CHIN KO KAI, SEOUL.
BRANCH OFFICE AT CHEMULPO.

Money changers, Coal and Wood Merchants, Express Agents.

We are agents for the Pyeng-yang Coal Company and the Karazu Coal Company of Japan. We have the best quality of both anthracite and bituminous coal, and prompt execution of orders is our speciality. Firewood of all kinds kept in stock. Full weight guaranteed. Money of all denominations exchanged at current rates. Parcels received for all parts.

CHINA MUTUAL LIFE INS. OC.

Most favourable terms to policy holders.

Benefit system unsurpassed.

HOLME RINGER & Co.
Agents, Chemulpo.

C. P. R.

CANADIAN PACIFIC RAILWAY COMPANY'S ROYAL MAIL STEAMSHIP LINE.

THE FAST ROUTE BETWEEN CHINA, JAPAN, AND EUROPE VIA CANADA AND THE UNITED STATES.

Route from Hongkong via Shanghai, Nagasaki (Inland Sea of Japan) Kobe, Yokohama Victoria and Vancouver.

Twin Screw Empress Steamship—6,000 Tons—Speed 19 knots.

PROPOSED SAILING FROM YOKOHAMA.

R. M. S. Empress of India.
R. M. S. Empress of Japan.
R. M. S. Empress of China.
R. M. S. Athenian.
R. M. S. Tartar.

Special reduction (first class only) granted to members of the Military, Naval, Diplomatic and Civil services and to Missionaries.

Passengers have choice of ten routes across the Continent of America and have privilege of travelling by any Atlantic Steamship Line.

Round the World passage tickets in connection with the P. and O. S. N., North German Lloyd and Messageries Co.'s **£125.**

All rates payable at current rate of exchange.

For further information, Tickets, Guide Books, etc., apply to

HOLME, RINGER & Co., AGENTS,
Chemulpo.

Grand Hotel,

(Formerly the Station Hotel)

Near the Railway Terminus,
West Gate Seoul.

The Best Hotel in Korea;
Handsome new Building.
Fine Airy Rooms
Excellent Cuisine.
Terms Moderate.
Special terms to Missionaries
and to permanent boarders.

Electric cars within 2 minutes' walk.

W. H. EMBERLEY.
Proprietor

EVERY FACILITY.

In connection with Life Assurance Business is afforded by

The Standard Life Assurance Co.,

One of the largest and wealthiest of the Provident Institutions of the United Kingdom Forms of Application and all information will be promptly afforded on application.

10 CENTS A DAY.

Not a very large expenditure is it? But it is sufficient to secure for a man of 30 a policy with the STANDARD LIFE OFFICE for

$1323.

For all particulars of rates, etc., apply to

Holme, Ringer & Co.,
Agents, Chemulpo.

THE NEW YORK LIFE INSURANCE COMPANY.

Have you ever been declined by any Company?

Are you engaged in a specially hazardous occupation?

Have you heard of the New York Life Insurance Company's New Classifications for this class of Risks?

If not, send your date of birth, occupation and particulars of rejection, if any to

E. MEYER & Co.,
Agents, Chemulpo.

MITSUI BUSSAN KAISHA.
(MITSUI & Co.)

MITSUI GINKO.
(MITSUI BANK.)

The Bank is owned by the members of the Mitsui Family, who, as partners, assume an unlimited responsibility for all liabilities of the Bank:—

Capital.......................Yen 5,000,000
Reserve Fund .... " 5,600,000

HEAD OFFICE, TOKYO.

LONDON OFFICE, 34 LIME ST., E. C.

BRANCHES AND AGENCIES:—
New York, San Francisco, Hamburg, Bombay, Singapore, Manila, Hongkong, Amoy, Chefoo, Tientsin.

Kobe, Hakodate, Yokohama, Kure, Yokosuka, Moji, Shimonoseki, Miike, Wakamatsu, Nagasaki, Kuchinotsu, Karatsu, Sasebo, Misume, Taipeh, &c.

Telegraphic Address for all the Offices:
"MITSUI"
A. B. C. AND A. 1 CODES USED.

Contractors of Coal
To the Imperial Japanese Navy, Arsenals and Railway Bureau, Principal Railway Companies and Industrial Work, Home and Foreign Mail and Freight Steamers.

Sole Proprietors
Of the famous Miike, Tagawa and Yamano Coal Mines.

Sole Agents
For the sale of Fukumo, Hokoku, Ichimura, Kanoda, Mannoura, Onoura, Ostuji, Sonoda, Tsubaruro, Yoshinotani, Yoshio, Yurokibura and other coals.

YANGTSE INSURANCE ASSOCIATION, LTD.

The undersigned, having been appointed agents for the above company, are prepared to issue policies and pay losses on marine risks at regular rates.

E. MEYER & Co.,
Agents, Chemulpo.

AMERICAN KOREAN ELECTRIC CO.

Light and Power.

Main Office: Electric Building, Chong No.

RAILWAY DEPARTMENT.

OPERATING CARS BETWEEN EAST AND WEST GATE, EVERY TEN MINUTES:—

First Car leaves East Gate at 7:00 A. M. First Car leaves R. R. Station at 7:25 A. M
Last Car " East Gate at 9:40 P. M. Last " " R. R. Station at 10:05 P.M

OPERATING CARS BETWEEN EAST GATE AND IMPERIAL TOMB TERMINUS, EVERY TWENTY MINUTES:—

CONNECTING WITH EVERY ALTERNATE CAR ARRIVING AT EAST GATE FROM CHONG NO.

First Car leaves East Gate for Tomb at 7:10 A. M.
" " " Tomb for East Gate at 7:35 A. M.
Last " " East Gate for Tomb at 7:50 P. M.
" " " Tomb for East Gate at 8:10 P. M.

OPERATING CARS BETWEEN CHONG NO AND YUNG SAN RIVER EVERY TWELVE MINUTES:—

First Car leaves Chong No for South Gate at 7:12 A. M.
" " " Chong No for Yung San at 7:36 A. M.
" " " South Gate for Chong No at 7:20 A. M.
" " " Yung San for Chong No at 8:09 A. M.
Last " " South Gate for Chong No 10:00 P. M.
" " " Yung San for Chong No at 9:33 P. M.

SPECIAL PRIVATE CARS FURNISHED TO SUIT CONVENIENCE OF PATRONS. PRICES ON APPLICATION AT HEAD OFFICE.

LIGHTING DEPARTMENT.

Where less than 250 candle power of light is used, the rate per month will be
Per 16 candle power incandescent lamp,—All night.—Yen 2.50.
32 candle power incandescent lamp:—All night:—Yen 4.00.
50 candle power incandescent lamp:—All night:—Yen 6.00.
150 " " " " " " ,, 10.00.
1200 ,, ,, enclosed are ,, ,, ,, ,, 20.00.

Where more than 250 candle power of light is used, a Meter will be installed, freqvedted:—Rent of Meter Yen 2.00 per month. Rate of charges by meter reading:—Two Sen per Ampere per hour. (Approximately this is equal to about One Sen per 16 C. P. lamp per hour) Minimum monthly charge where meter is installed, Yen 20.00 per month, which includes rental of meter.

Estimates for installing lights furnished on application
An assortment of chandeliers always on hand.

K. Murakami.
Photograph Studio
Chinkokai, Seoul.

Printing, Developing and Enlargement, of Photographs always Undertaken.

Korean Views and Pictures Illustrating Native Customs always on Sale,

---

THE OSAKA SHOSEN KAISHA.

Boats frequently on the berth for Chinnampo.

REGULAR SAILINGS BETWEEN JAPAN AND KOREAN PORTS.

FUSAN AND KOBE VIA SHIMONOSEKI

OSAKA VIA MOKPO FUSAN, SHIMONOSEKI AND KOBE.

MOJI DIRECT.

OSAKA VIA KUNSAN, MASANPO, FUSAN, SHIMONOSEKI AND KOBE.

CHEMULPO KUNSAN LINE,
Every three days.

CHEMULPO CHINNAMPO LINE.
Every three days.

For Freight and passage and further particulars apply to
THE OSAKA SHOSEN KAISHA,
Chemulpo

LONDON, PLAISANT & CO.

General Storekeepers and Merchants, Ships Contractors, Tobacconists, Commission and Forwarding Agents, Coal Merchants

IMPORTERS AND EXPORTERS

Seoul & Chemulpo.

W. D. WENTWORTH.

LANDING
AND
SHIPPING AGENT
AND
CUSTOMS BORDER.

12 OURA, NAGASAKI.

STEWARD & CO.

Chemulpo.

Shipchandlers and Storekeepers, Naval and Mercantile Contractors, Landing and Shipping Agents.

STEWARD'S HOTEL

Chemulpo.

Best accommodation in the port for travellers. Clean and well-aired rooms, good cuisine and prompt attendence, moderate tariff.

농샹무셩기ᄉ가아기셰가고일
을겁뎍ᄒ갓ᄉ로슈일간에ᄃ경을
셰는다더라

○의회단결과 북청디방에의
확던이더시이러나란ᄒ는티고
인셩외쇼요ᄒ거ᄒ슬북경관인들
은비우념전ᄒ며이전에는의회
단외쥬의가외국은반티ᄒ나만
쥬는복종ᄒ러니이번은만쥬셔
지반티ᄒ다ᄒ니이운동을만일
못진압ᄒ지못ᄒ면그결과가미
우죵치못ᄒ리라더라

잡보

특명환임 경무부에셔 부로
죠회ᄒ기를경찰부운운졍규의
쟝졍이상거ᄉ샹만려환은ᄃ사관
을경ᄒ야ᄒ며긔비하편ᄒ고일과
못ᄒ면죠ᄒ는지라ᄒ는니녀지
작일에외부로 쳐분을셰리시
기를참강ᄒ부운운 졍규는못환임
ᄒ아시무케ᄒ라ᄒ엿다더라

○공진회의 삼작일도공요일
공진회에셔긔회ᄒ고회장각쟐유에
셔셰가긔츌ᄒ셰ᄒ아셔명ᄒ기를ᄌ
긔의ᄒ분이부족ᄒ즁은ᄒᄂ지잇다은
고ᄉ룸의게회장을ᄉᄒ고ᄋ던쟈은
아리빌죠셰로더경ᄒ고뭇회쟝의
김명죠를회로션경ᄒ고평의원은
윤효졍윤하영이하계셔로션졍
ᄒ고이후부회쟝과ᄂ셰는공무원
으로볼경ᄒ엿는티윤효졍씨가
츌셕ᄒ야동양대셰와졍부부의실
과민영환의셔ᄒ뎡을일봉연셜
ᄒ고기타경항모제셰가시국관
계에티ᄒ야연셜ᄒ고폐회ᄒ엿
ᄂ에회쟝졍죠씨가회즁에공포
아을면ᄒ만ᄒ에회가다시셜립
ᄒ흔죡의만속증이ᄒᄂ가다ᄂ회
광샹ᄒᄂ면셰를샹샹ᄒ엿다더라

함경환임 일쟉스가니부에
공함ᄒ되 경계쟈는광양에쥬
지ᄒ얀계국령ᄉ의면보를ᄂᄒ죽
평양군수변관흔리유를관찰ᄉ
의게부쥬ᄒ죡관찰ᄉ의인너시에
군수가경셰를ᄇ유령ᄒ곳이다
이삼년젼덕국시관찰ᄉ의소위오
본관찰ᄉ도와압ᄒ엿소에는경ᄒ엿
부문를보지못ᄒ엿ᄂ니강원찰ᄉ
의말미러ᄒ죽가망ᄒ지진효던은
진셩노신관찰ᄉ의잇슴을가히
알거시오이본군수의면관ᄒ것은
그리우가경술듯ᄒ니ᄒ히면관의
명운긋에셰ᄒ야쥬치ᄒ군티의
편케ᄒ라ᄒ엿더라

○향교쥬졍 단쳔군보고에야
박ᄉ국잠이죵운ᄒ기를각셩
유셰등아다ᄉ병참에셔구관ᄒ
야유셰를ᄒ되ᄒᄂ지라경부에셔신
창경이계의ᄒ야일본헌병보를드
러죡쥭관은빈방쇼유니가야니
라히ᄉ진이엿ᄂ계ᄒ중미ᄒ계ᄒ
는나부대신은듯고도가가마ᄒ두엇
기즉그징이연슬수업ᄂᄒ야기을
졍졍샹 죵졍쳰는교회히소진을
회의는니더라

○경부회의 경부에셔작
군효협ᄒ야국ᄉ회의ᄒ엿ᄂᄃ셰는단
요쵸셰ᄒ수유셰슝쳐ᄒᄂ에로ᄒ니련
시계ᄉ졍개의셩ᄒ엿다더라

○시진회경 일진회에셔는
졍부에셔진고ᄒ는슈셔경문의ᄌ유
공권을이셩ᄒ야엿슴으로경축ᄒ
에기위ᄒ야특별ᄒ주회ᄒ고 시
며리가ᄒ즁에엿더라

○나면경쳡 경무부에셔
셔는단젼간슈인진을진조용의
못ᄒ일노이번은경부회의에졍
을무기어면이엿다더라

○회원외국 경부에셔는규
로졔보는의ᄉ기를너진길에빅부
은분ᄂ승ᄒ야드리오비곳ᄉ셔명
고ᄉ노승ᄉ의ᄒ는ᄉ기곳ᄒ셔효유ᄒ
셔쳑ᄒ에효유를은ᄉ기아ᄋ나ᄒ면
셔ᄉ도빗고로는ᄉ셩이지나ᄒ금슈
셔는젼으로는셩노ᄒ야지긋ᄒ의
ᄀ니드리가곳ᄉ이노ᄂ회ᄐ셩ᄒ의
곳ᄒ쥬니예이ᄉ리만ᄒ이다을셰의
ᄉᄒ아머분쇼관리가곳의셔엿ᄂ셔
만쳐비ᄒ머도부ᄅᄉ긍셰젼ᄋ득
올셰흔진이영수오시긔바리ᄒ
엿ᄒ리라

○경찰경기 음력일월이
일발일에계동셩ᄂ보빈ᄒ인
에동명ᄒ전을ᄂ노화위에연일
진도물ᄋ유ᄉ셰ᄒ셰곳고군ᄉ리
전을ᄉ지주ᄉ엿ᄂᄀ고수가국
ᄂ셰ᄋ보ᄒᄂ소ᄂ셰ᄂ루ᄂᄂ셰
셩양ᄂ동ᄀ도ᄂ고ᄂ못ᄂ회ᄂ가
ᄀᄂᄀᄃ다ᄂᄆᄂᄋ리엿ᄂ가니ᄐ

○공쟝우편 공쥬관찰ᄉ
부로보고ᄒ기를본ᄉ진ᄉ월
다ᄉ쵸우ᄂ도ᄋ셰ᄐᄉ아부ᄂ
ᄂᄒᄋᄂ라

○단일경하 거셰일ᄅ은쥬관
이비랍ᄉ의단일ᄂ그날은ᄌ일
이라엿더ᄒ아도ᄋ의ᄋᄂ시ᄂ
일곤ᄒ기는ᄐᄂᄉᄂ회ᄂ

○로변리속 장진군ᄉ가외부
로보고ᄒ기를음력일월ᄉ삼일
에아라사병ᄉ의보ᄒ는ᄉᄂᄂ쥬
고스로의ᄉ리ᄉᄋᄂᄀᄂᄉᄂ
고그이는난도로반ᄂᄒ쥬ᄉ갓ᄂ
ᄒ엿더라

○우편보경 우구편니가외부
에보고ᄒ기를본관경ᄉ헌병셩ᄒ
일에경ᄒ으로로보리ᄒ비경ᄂ지음
에ᄉ쥬ᄂ이ᄉᄂ쥬ᄂᄀ구오ᄐ로
쥬쟝ᄉᄀ시수가ᄃᄆ고보로ᄀᄂ로
ᄂ는지류ᄂᄋ뭇ᄂᄆ고ᄀ로ᄂᄋᄂ
지유가표ᄂᄂᄂᄀᄋᄐᄂᄂᄂᄂ
진이ᄋᄀᄂ로ᄂᄂᄂᄂᄀᄂᄂ
뵌뇌ᄉ의ᄂᄂᄂᄂᄂᄂᄂᄂ
은ᄐ오바ᄐᄋᄂᄀᄂᄂᄂ
치쥬ᄒ아ᄂᄂᄂᄂᄂ
○심샹우편 ᄂᄂᄂ
상셔ᄂᄂᄂᄂ

지금의경무ᄉ를   ᄒ기
스ᄂᄂᄂ졍ᄂᄂ엿ᄂ
라

○혼인진쇽   돈령원에셔
각부부원경에공ᄒ엿ᄂ기를비
공졍ᄒ의셔ᄂᄂᄂᄂ
샹ᄉᄂᄂᄂᄂ
인ᄂᄂᄂ라

○셩ᄂᄂ과 셩ᄂ에무ᄂᄂ
도ᄂᄂᄂ는ᄂᄂ뎡ᄂ
교ᄂᄂᄂ

○지관쇼화쟝   ᄂ계지ᄂ
셔지ᄂᄂᄂ
도ᄂᄂᄂ
면ᄂᄂ라

○괴이ᄂ회   강화부ᄂ
수ᄂᄂᄂ
경이ᄂᄂ
ᄂᄂᄂ
시ᄂᄂᄂ
수지ᄂᄂᄂ라

론셜

한션정ᄒ는일

○비록우리는아라사병함이겁
단ᄂ보다ᄒ는소를ᄂᄂᄂ그
리ᄒ되고ᄂᄂᄂᄂ
이셩ᄂᄂᄂᄂ
면ᄂᄂᄂᄂ
를ᄂᄂᄂ라

ᄂᄂᄂᄂ

히반포치아니ᄒ야멋지못ᄒ도
록만드는지라
우리의정작으로셩각건ᄃ그방
어ᄒ는군ᄉ들의광장홈과승리
지간에싸홈된수효는잇ᄉ근듯
ᄂ거셔소연ᄒ며산ᄒ은유힝ᄒ는
병의죽은자ㅣ불부ᄒ엿슬터인
죵이거슬통계ᄒ야가량ᄒ면일
본군수의손히가셩만명에불하
ᄒ지도다
그러ᄒ나다시젼쟝을련숙ᄒ야
ᄒ다ᄒ드리도이외에군ᄉ로라
도죡죡유여ᄒ듯ᄒ되샤만명죽
은이사름들의권쇽들로ᄒ여곰
셰남을죵가ᄒ리ᄒ지경이면셜
경교못될듯ᄒ거시일본셔는당
ᄒ ᄂ ᄂ 라

광고

○광양군수ᄂ에셔의셩명ᄃ쟝
을위ᄒ야ᄂ표ᄂᄂ
무ᄂ소부지ᄒ오니ᄂ
에셔ᄂᄂᄂ
을ᄂᄂᄂ

덕국아셰아은힝
본점ᄂᄂ향
지점ᄂ지ᄂ소
인쳔셰창양ᄂ

차ᄂ우힝
본점ᄂ
지점ᄂ
인쳔셰ᄂ

TELEGRAMS.

(FROM JAPAN PAPERS.)

London, Dec. 3.

The whole of Admiral Foelkersahm's squadron has passed Perim, making for Aden.

The "Catarina," one of the three yachts mentioned in a dispatch of the 25th ultimo as having passed through the Canal southward, and whose mission aroused a good deal of speculation, left Massowah on the 30th ultimo.

Berlin, Dec. 4.

It has transpired that a Russian torpedo-boat dispatched from the Yarrow Iron Works to Libau succeeded in passing through the German Baltic Canal on October 8th under false pretences. The German authorities were deceived as to the mission of the boat, as the officials of the Canal state that those on board declared the vessel to be the yacht "Caroline." She flew the British commercial flag and carried a British certificate.

London, Dec. 5.

The Japanese Minister at Madrid has asked the Spanish Foreign Minister for explanations regarding the supply of coal and provisions to the Baltic Fleet during its stay at Vigo. The Foreign Minister in reply states that Spain has strictly observed neutrality.

London, Dec. 3.

The Russian Press is agitating for the opening of the Dardanelles to the Black Sea Fleet, for which, the "Novoye Vremya" contends, only the consent of the Porte is necessary.

Berlin, Dec. 4.

The deaths are announced from Munich of Prince Frederick of the House of Hohenzollern, and from Vienna of Count Kapnist, the Russian Ambassador to Austria-Hungary.

(Prince Frederick of the House of Hohenzollern is an uncle of Prince Carl Anton of Hohenzollern, who is now with the Japanese Headquarters Staff in Manchuria.)

Tokyo, Dec. 12th.

A London telegram of the 10th inst, states that the news of the destruction of the Port Arthur squadron has caused a panic in St. Petersburg. The Japanese loan is receiving increased support in England and America. The Russian third Eastern squadron will leave in January.

Tokyo, Dec. 12th.

The Japanese vessel Saiyen, engaged in the blockade of Port Arthur, struck a mine on the 30th ult and sank. The Captain and 38 men were drowned.

London, December 5th.

The reform movement in Russia is spreading rapidly throughout the country.

London, Dec. 2.

The St. Petersburg correspondent of the London "Daily Telegraph" reiterates, with unimpeachble confirmation, that Russian diplomacy contemplates a lasting peace with Japan, with a view to an offensive and defensive alliance, which is indispensable to Russia's Eastern policy.

London, December 5th.

The annual report of the Secretary of the United States' Navy recommends the formation of such a navy as no other power would desire to engage.

Berlin, Dec. 4.

Russia has declared that she is willing to consent to the proposed American Arbitration Treaty in principle.

The Reform office have signified their intention of extending the duties of the Supreme Court to all provincial towns.

THE BALTIC FLEET.

The following particulars of the units composing the Russian fleet, appear in the "Ostasiatiche Lloyd;"

Commander-in-Chief; Rear-Admiral Roschdestwensky.

Chief-of-Staff, Captain Pamjatni.

A. Fleet.

First Division.

Imperator Alexander III. (Flagship.)
Borodino Kniaz Suwarov
Orel

All four built during 1902 and 1901. 13,516 tons.

Armament, 4 30.5 centimeter turret guns,
12 15 centimeter guns.
56 small calibre quick-firers.

Engines, 16,300 horse-power, speed 18 knots, coaling capacity 2,000 tons, sufficient for 4,600 knots.

Crew, 650 men.

Second Division.

Commander, Rear-Admiral Wirenius.
Chief-of-Staff, Captain Slipjanow.
Osliabija (Flagship of the Division).
Sissoi Velicki, Navarin
Imperator Alexander II.

Ships built in 1898, 1894, 1891 and 1887, tonnage from 9,000 to 12,600. Armament 4 25 and 30.5 centimetre turret guns, and a somewhat weaker quick firing battery than the First Division. Steaming capacity of 6,000 knots, maximum 17.16 knots. Crew 720 men.

Third Division.

Commander: Commodore Schiyjagin.
Dinitri Donskoi (Flagship of the Division).
Oleg

First class cruisers of 6,600 and 5,800 tons. 16 guns and 30 and 34 quick firers. Speed 17 and 19 knots.

Aurora Izumrud
Zemeng Almas

Second class cruisers 3,800 to 6.600 tons, armament of 14 guns, 16 small calibre quickfirers and four topedo-tubes. Speed of 20 knots, specially built for scouting work. Crew of 400 men.

C. Torpedo Fleet.

Swjetlana (Commodore's ship)

Cruiser of 3,860 tons. 6 15 and 10 4.7 milimetre quickfirers, 4 torpedo-tubes. Speed 20 knots, steaming capacity 7,000 knots, Crew 320 men.

Wojwoda Posadnik Abreck

Cruisers of 400 to 900 tons, armament 6 quick firing guns, speed 21 Knots. Crew of 300 men.

Twenty torpedo-craft, each of 320 tons displacement, speed from 21 to 29 Knots; armament of eight torpedoes, and 7.6 and three 3.7 millimetre quick-firers. Crew of 20 men.

D. Transports.

Kanschatka Ozean
Europa Samojed

CRUISERS OF THE VOLTUTEER FLEET.

Cherson Wladimir
Kostrama Saratow
Petersburg Smolensk
Moskwa Poltava

Reports from the north-east state that the Russians are preparing for an advance southwards. Increased activity is apparent at Songchin.

The Society fever is evidently in the air. Yet another society, to be formed by people belonging to the Japanese monastery in Seoul, is now discussed.

An order has been made against Sir Frank Swettenham, late Governor of the Straits Settlements, on a petition for the restitution of conjugal rights on the part of his wife, whom he left in 1894.

It is reported that Chang Chih Tung has memorialised the Throne advising that China should endeavour to end the war between Russia and Japan, and that she should pay the war indemnity exacted from Russia by Japan. He further advises that after peace has been declared China should devote her whole attention to the reorganisation of her army as a precaution against the future aggression of Russia.

INTERVIEW WITH PRINCE KHILKOFF.

A representative of the "Birzheviya Viedomosti" has had an interview with Prince Khilkoff, Minister of Ways of Communication, who is represented as having declared that all the unfavourable reports circulated abroad with regard to the Circum-Baikal railway were incorrect. The Minister, admitted, however, that the pioneer train, by which he himself travelled, took four days to cover a distance of twenty versts (thirteen miles). It was also true that the train was derailed no fewer than four times during the journey, but no further accidents of a similar nature had since occurred. Trains were now running at a speed of twenty versts (thirteen miles) an hour, and it was possible to dispatch sixteen trains daily along the lake, and also across it on icebreakers. The Trans-Baikal and Siberian lines were also capable of dealing with that amount of traffic.

Prince Khilkoff laid stress on the fact that, as long as the transport of troops continued, the forwarding of private goods beyond Yakutsk would be attended with great difficulty. The sole means of remedying this state of affairs was to make use of the Siberian waterways, particularly those of the Obi and Yenisei systems, and a plan with this end in view, the carrying out of which would cost about 12,000,000 roubles, had already been drafted.

In conclusion, the Minister declared that if the transport of troops were to go on for any length of time, it would scarcely be possible to open the Siberian railway to commercial traffic even a year hence.

The Government, yesterday afternoon, held a reception at which several members of the Il Chin Hoi, including the President, were present.

On the 1st inst, says the Magistrate of Tai An, his office was attacked by a band of robbers armed with rifles. They entered his premises and seized many thousands of dollars, representing taxes collected; they then carried the magistrate and his secretary away with them to a distance of 40 *li*, but released them next day, when they returned and telegraphed their report to the Government.

With kindly consideration for the nerves of his distinguished guest, Mr. J. P. Morgan yesterday showed the Archbishop of Canterbury nothing more disturbing than the wreck of a train. Some day, when the Archbishop is more acclimated Mr. Morgan may take him into the gallery of the Stock Exchange and let him watch the wreck of a whole railroad.—New York World.

Military officials of the the Japanese Headquarters Staff at Liaoyang have assured Viceroy Yuan Shi Kai that on their approaching Mukden a special force will be detailed to protect the city and the ancestral tombs of the reigning dynasty. A certain Japanese general, however, pointed out to Viceroy Yuan's representative that the troops were being obstructed and inconvenienced by the behaviour of certain of the inhabitants, in great contrast to the time when they were under the influence of the Russians.

The Kamni of Kunsan report to the Foreign Office that he has been robbed by a Japanese official of the Seoul-Fusan railway. He left Seoul on the 16th ult. with five packages of luggage, which, when he arrived at Yongtongpo, he duly registered and had placed in the luggage van of a southward bound train. On arrival at Daichon he presented his receipt for five packages to the official in charge of the luggage, but was only handed four. When he asked for the other one the official snatched the receipt from him and ordered him away. The contents of the package missing, he estimates at over 100 yen.

The formation of a league in Algeria for the prevention of malaria has moved some ardent unbelievers in the mosquito theory of the origin of that disease to issue a challenge to the promoters of the movement. Drs. Legrain and Treille, both retired medical officers of French army, offer themselves as the subjects of experiment. They will submit, states the "British Medical Journal," to be bitten by mosquitoes fed on a patient suffering from quartan ague, "the only type of fever on which one can count for an accurate and protracted observation." They undertake to use no preventive treatment beforehand, to take no bark or quinine in any form, and to use no anti-pyretic medicine. They consider Dr. Manson's experiments unscientific and inconclusive, and are anxious that the question may be tested on their persons before a campaign, "as useless as it is likely to be costly," is entered upon in Algeria.

General Dessino, at Shanghai announces an official report to the effect that on Nov 27th at a village located between Russian volunteer and engineering troops and a Japanese position the Russians blew up a tower, which had been employed by the Japanese as a redoubt. Subsequently a body of scouts, belonging to General Rennenkamp's detachment, was posted on the site. On Nov. 28th, the Japanese tried an attack on the Russian position near Jichen, but were repulsed with heavy losses. On the 28th and 29th General Rennencamp assumed the offensive and dislodged the enemy from two fortified positions on the top of a hill and pursued him. The enemy took flight, leaving 230 dead on the field. The Russians caputred enormous quantities of arms, tools, and other articles. According to Chinese residents, the enemy carried away a large number of dead and wounded by carts. The Russians secured seven prisoners. The enemy burnt a large quantity of provisions at a village on the Taitzuho plain on the occasion of his retreat.

The Korea Daily News.

Issued at 5 P. M. daily except Sundays.

Rate of Subscription:—
Per Year,............Yen 25.
Per Quarter,..........Yen 7.
Per Month,..........Yen 2.50.

Postage in Korea not charged extra.
Postage abroad charged extra.

Advertisements, 50 sen per day for 1 inch or less.
5 yen per month per inch.
50 yen per year per inch.

All communications to
E. T. BETHELL,
Editor and Publisher,
Pak-tong, Seoul.

NORTH SEA INCIDENT.

The following are the main features of the Russian explanation of the North Sea incident.

1. Information which reached Vice-Admiral Rojestvensky as he was leaving British waters showed that suspicious vessels were in the North sea, navigating first under one flag and then under another.

2. The transport "Kamtchatka" reported by wireless telegragh some time before the incident occurred that she had seen two torpedo boats (the "Kamtchtka being then thirty miles behind the squadron.)

3. Later the receipt of a suspicious wireless message signed "Kamtchatka," asking for the exact latitude and longitude of the squadron, a message which it was afterward ascertained was never sent by the "Kamtchatka."

4. Then the appearance of two torpedo boats alongside the squadron, which could not have been Russians, as all the Russian topedo boats were then in the English channel. The squadron did not fire until the torpedo boats were seen.

NARROW ESCAPE OF PRESIDENT ROOSEVELT.

Washington, Nov. 3.

President Roosevelt had an escape from death so narrow that it was almost miraculous, by being thrown from a horse while he was riding through the country near Washington a few days ago.

The President was approaching a high fence at top speed, when the horse stumbled and fell, throwing Mr. Roosevelt off forward. He struck squarely on his head, and was so severely stunned that he was unconscious for some time, just how long he does not know, as he was riding entirely alone. When he regained his senses he found his horse standing near him.

The President tried to mount, but was so dizzy from the shock that he could not stand. It was some time before he ragained full control of his legs and arms. He then remounted and rode along. There was a great lump on the right side of the President's head and blood trickling from a long but shallow scalp wound above the right ear. The cut extended down into the the forehead and evidences of it still are there; the earth was soft or the President would have been killed.

The Governor of Kongchu reports himself as suffering from the unwelcome attentions of the Chin Po Hoi.

The Reform Office having regulated the affairs of Council of State, has now turned its attention towards the Home Office.

Two junks with provisions on board were captered off Port Arthur by a Japanese warship on the 28th ult., and immediately conveyed to Dalny.

Owing to strong Japanese demands, the Foreign Office have instructed the officials at Chinnampo to repair the roads between Chinnampo and Kyem-I-po.

The steamers Ramnoor, Saladin and Hermes have been sold to Japanese shipowners. They have become the property of Mr. Matsumoto, Mr. Kawasaki, and Mr. Okazaki, respectively, of Kobe.

THE JIJI ON FINANCE.

The "Jiji" has on more than one occasion referred to different individual impositions proposed by the Government, which it considers ill-advised. It would now find fault with the general policy which guides the Government in its endeavour to raise an augmented revenue of 82,720,000 yen. In the first place it suspects that, in choosing the sources of revenue, the Government has been guided by no other consideration but that of making up for the amount required, without, therefore, paying any attention to the question of how any particular tax will affect the national economics, and quotes the case of the proposed salt monopoly in support of the charge. In the second place, the journal thinks that it perceives traces of interested motives on the part of the Government who have discriminating tendencies, as in the case of a customs duty on rice, which cannot but prove a measure of great benefit to the farming class. Lastly, the "Jiji" thinks the Government's disregard of the economic side of the question has led it to proposing too many new and small taxes, a circumstance which may always be regarded as a sign of lack of judgment. It has nothing whatever to quarrel about so far as the amount of the campaign appropriation is concerned, but it thinks the Government should not be allowed to indulge in persecutory taxes, just because the country is engaged in a momentous foreign war. —Japan Times.

The announcement by the Russians that they would in future control the taxation in the districts under their occupation, has caused somewhat of a flutter in certain official circles. The War Office is especially active and certain Generals are discussing the advisability of mobilising the disbanded soldiers.

Owing to the representations of the Japanese Minister, the Government have decided to withdraw their order of dismissal of Pang Han Chu, the Magistrate of Pyeng Yang. Mr. Pang was accused of levying excessive taxation, and only owes his retention in office to the assiduous assistance which he has rendered to the Japanese Military authorities at Pyeng Yang.

Tseng Chi, Military Governor of Fengtien, wired to Peking requesting the government to send relief to the natives who are suffering on account of the war. The Japanese Minister advised the latter not to do anything of the sort, fearing that these will eventually go to the hands of the Russians instead of to the sufferers. The Peking government has ordered 3,000 suits of winter clothes and food to be forward to Mukden, placing them at the disposal of Tseng Chi.

In spite of the flattering article on Japanese colonising methods in Formosa, which recently appeared in the London Times, the following paragraph from the Japan Mail indicates that things are not all as they should be. "A telegram from Taipeh, dated the 3rd instant, says that on the morning of the 1st, 200 insurgents attacked Seisuiko in the Byoritsu jurisdiction. The police fought stoutly, but their communications were severed, and together with the inhabitants they had 40 wounded. On the night of the 2nd the fighting was renewed."

According to the annual report of the Interstate Commerce Commission, 9,984 persons were killed on American railroads during the last fiscal year ending July 1st. In the last ten years 78,152 persons have been killed in accidents on American railroads. Here is the table of the slaughter by years:

1895	6,136
1896	5,845
1897	6,437
1898	6,859
1899	7,123
1900	7,865
1901	8,455
1902	8,588
1902	9,840
1904	9,984
Total for ten years	78,152

A San Francisco telegram states that General Kodama declares that the Japanese will winter in Port Arthur.

President Roosevelt has ordered the Interstate Commerce Commission to make a full and complete investigation into the business and methods of the Standard Oil Company.

After fifty years' consideration the law officers of the United States decided that tomatoes are fruit. Twenty-five years' further pondering has placed the cocoa-nut in the same category.

The Shungte-pao, a Japanese paper published in Peking in the vernacular, has been circulating reports to the effect that the foreign ministers are about to urge the reinstatement of the Emperor and the consequent retirement of the Empress Dowager. There is however nothing in the story which, says the Universal Gazette, is circulated for some mischievous purpose.

The following telegram has been received by the South China Morning Post from its Shanghai correspondent. Application has been lately make by the pro-Russian party through the Japanese Consulate at Shanghai for permission to send a specially chartered steamer to Port Arthur with medicines and medical appliances. The Consulate replied yesterday stating that Headquarters, whilst appreciating the humanity of the proposal, declined to entertain it. If it were necessary to forward medicines to Port Arthur, they would do so themselves.

It is reported that the Szechuan students in Japan have telegraphed to Viceroy Sic Liang, of Szechuan, urging him not to grant any railway concessions to French or British syndicates, and informing him that they have raised amongst themselves over $300,000 as a nucleus of a fund to be employed in the building of the necessary provincial railways. They inform the Viceroy that their telegram will be followed by a memorial giving full particulars of their scheme for railway building based upon the system of Japan. They ask for 5 per cent. interest on their subscribed capital, and advise the Viceroy to start work at once by provisionally drawing upon the revenue of the province for expenses. In order to raise further capital they request to be furnished with plans, etc., of the proposed railways.

The Universal Gazette learns that the Governor of Hunan wired to Peking that three of the leading members of the Ai Kow-hui, a revolutionary society had been captured. Two of them were decapitated, one of them being let off, as a witness against some students from Japan who are also implicated in the movement. The progressive officials at Peking do not like to see the students getting into trouble, especially President Chao Erh-sen, who is doing everything to save them. Commenting upon this the China Gazette says. The progressive officials do not wish the Central Government to know that the chief thing which the Chinese students sent to Japan have learnt so far is to conspire by every means in their power to overturn the Manchu government and place China under Japan's leadership."

Under the auspices of the Colonial Society, the traveler, Herr Wons, in a lecture in Berlin drew attention to the ubiquitous activity of Japanese traders in China, which ubiquity "was menacing German trade, even in our Shantung; where the Japanese and not the Germans had benefited by the increase of trade resulting from the Tsingtau-Tsinanfu railway." He contrasted, unfavourably to the Japanese, their commercial morality against that of the Chinese, and complained that the Japanese Courts were prejudiced against foreigners. He believed that the real object of the war was the commercial and industrial expansion of Japan, and warned his hearers that if the Japanese were victorious the Chinese would give increased support to Japanese trade and German trade would be stranded "high and dry."

The Korea Daily News.

VOL. I, TUESDAY, DECEMBER 13, 1904. No. 124

HONGKONG & SHANGHAI BANKING CORPORATION.

Paid-up Capital..... ....$10,000,000
Reserve Fund:—Sterling Reserve... 10,000,000
Silver Reserve..... 7,000,000

27,000,000
Reserve Liability of Proprietors... 10,000,000

HEAD OFFICE, HONGKONG.

London Bankers, London and County Banking Company Limited

Branches and Agencies,

London.		
Amoy,	Hankow	Penang,
Bangkok,	Hiogo,	Rangoon,
Batavia,	Iloilo,	Saigon,
Bombay,	Lyons,	San Francisco,
Calcutta,	Manila,	Singapore,
Colombo,	Nagasaki,	Sourabaya,
Foochow,	New York,	Tientsin,
Hamburg,	Peking,	Yokohama,

Credits granted on approved Securities, and every description of Banking and Exchange business transacted.

Drafts granted on London and the chief Commercial places in Europe, India, Australia, America, China and Japan.

HOLME RINGER & Co., AGENTS, CHEMULPO.

HOKURKU DOBOKU KAISHA.

Branch office in Chong Dong, Seoul.

Japanese telephone No. 165

CONTRACT DEPARTMENT.

We can contract to build any building or construction.

MERCHANDISE DEPARTMENT.

We can provide any building material. We have just contracted to build the new Belgian Legation.

E. MEYER & Co., Agents, Chemulpo.

CHARTERED BANK OF INDIA AUSTRALIA & CHINA.

INCORPORATED BY ROYAL CHARTER 1853

HEAD OFFICES:—LONDON.

Paid-up Capital £800,000
Reserve Liability of Shareholders 800,000
Reserve Fund 800,000

Drafts granted upon all the principal places in the world and every description of Exchange and banking business transacted.

E. MEYER & Co., Agents, Chemulpo.

MITSU BISHI DOCKYARD & ENGINE WORKS, NAGASAKI.

CODE WORD, "DOCK."

A 1, A. B. C., and Engineering Codes used.

DOCK No. 1 (at Tategami).

Extreme Length..............523 feet
Length on blocks .... 513 ,,
Width of Entrance on Top......89 ,,
,, ,, Bottom....77 ,,
Water on Blocks at Spring Tide 26½ ,,

DOCK No. 2 (Mukaijima).

Extreme Length..............371 feet
Length on Blocks..............360 ,,
Width of Entrance on Top......66 ,,
,, ,, Bottom 53 ,,
Water on Blocks at Spring Tide 22 ,,

PATENT SLIP (at Kosuge).

Can take vessels up to 1,000 tons gross

THE WORKS are well equipped with the LATEST IMPROVEMENTS, and can execute any kind of work in SHIPBUILDING and MARINE ENGINEERING, as well as in REPAIRING of SHIPS.

The COMPANY'S new powerfu steamer OURA-MARU (712 tons, 700 I.H.P.), specially built for SALVAGE PURPOSES, and equipped with necessary gear, is always READY at SHORT NOTICE.

THE METHODIST PUBLISHING HOUSE,

Little West Gate, Seoul.

JOB PRINTING, TYPEWRITER PAPER
CARBON PAPER, VISITING CARDS
STATIONERY, BOOK BINDING
BOOK PUBLISHERS
AMERICAN SCHOOL BOOKS
SPENCERIAN COPY BOOKS
PEN CARBON LETTER AND BILL BOOKS

S. A. BECK, Manager.

DAI-ICHI GINKO LIMITED.

(Formerly the First National Bank)

ESTABLISHED 1873

INCORPORATED UNDER PRESENT LAW 1896

Capital - - - - - - - - Yen 5,000,000
Reserve Fund - - - - - 1,500,000

HEAD OFFICE:—TOKIO.

President: Baron SHIBUSAWA.

BRANCHES AND CORRESPONDENTS

In the Principal Cities and Towns of Japan.

Interest Allowed on

Fixed deposits 1 year - - - 6½ per cent
" " 6 months - - - 6 per cent

Special current accounts 1½ sen daily per Y 100
General " " 1 " " " 100

M. TANAKA, Manager, Chemulpo.

SINGER SEWING MACHINES

씽거조봉침

SOLE AGENTS FOR KOREA

젼매쇼

HOLME RINGER & CO.
Chemulpo.

졔물포 함릉거양힝

KAMEYA & CO.

GENERAL STOREKEEPERS

Chinkokai - - Seoul

(Established 1895, Tokyo)

Confectionery, Hams, Canned Goods, Cutlery, Hirano & Tansan Water. Provisions, Gents, Furnishing goods, Toilet Articles, Travelling Bags, Tobacco, Cigars & Cigarettes Kitchen Utensils. Coffee, Biscuits.

Fresh Goods always kept in Stock.

Prices Moderate

Please come and inspect our goods

NIPPON YUSEN KAISHA;

JAPANESE MAIL STEAMSHIP CO.

DER MAIL CONTRACT WITH THE IMPERIAL JAPANESE GOVERNMENT.

European Line

Regular Fortnightly Service between Yokohama Kobe, Moji, Shanghai, Hongkong, Singapore, Penang Colombo, Port Said, Marseilles, London and Antwerp

American Line

Regular Fortnightly Service between Hongkong and Seattle, calling at Shanghai, Moji, Kobe, Yokohama and Victoria, B. C.

Australian Line

Regular weekly Service betwen Japan Ports and Australia, calling at Hongkong and Manila.

(Above Three Lines Suspended until further notice).

Shanghai Line

Weekly Service between Shanghai and Japan Ports

Korea Line

Service Kobe, Moji, Nagasaki, Fusan Chemupo Cheffoo, Taiku.

S. S. Bahelsberg, 2181 tons.

Service Kobe, Moji, Fusan, Chemulpo, Chinnampo

S. S. ARGO, S. S. Ohio.

BORDEN'S CONDENSED MILK CO.

New York, U. S. A.

ALWAYS IN STOCK

Eagle Brand Condensed Milk.

Gold Seal Condensed Milk.

Peerless (Family) Evaporated Cream.

Borden's Malted Milk.

E. MEYER & CO.
Chemulpo, Korea,
Sole Agent

ROYAL INSURANCE COMPANY

Funds exceed £10,000,000

FIRE

AT CURRENT RATES.

LIFE

REDUCED PREMIUM.

HOLME RINGER & Co., Agents, Chemulpo.

HOTEL DU PALAIS

SEOUL.

The only first class Hotel in Seoul. Situated in the centre of the city opposite the palace.

Cuisine under the supervision of an experienced French Chef.

Well ventilated and furnished throughout.

TARIFF UPON APPLICATION

L. MARTIN

Proripetor and Manager

大韓每日申報
대한ᄆᆡ일신보

(뎨일ᄇᆡᆨ이십오호)　(목요일)　일쳔구ᄇᆡᆨ사년십이월십오일

사고ᄇᆡᆨ

이신보ᄂᆞᆫ영어와한어로셔계ᄆᆡ
일출판ᄒᆞᆸ

신문가
ᄒᆞᆫ장　엽두돈오푼
일삭표　엽두량닷돈
우표가ᄆᆡ삭닷돈
다맛돈으로밧ᄉᆞᆸ

광고료ᄂᆞᆫ
귀ᄒᆞᆫ의쟝단과ᄌᆞ항의다쇼로죵
감ᄒᆞ되령가로밧을터이오ᄆᆡ오
ᄅᆡ지아녀대한사람마다다이신
문을보실터이니광고ᄇᆡ시기를
원ᄒᆞ시ᄂᆞᆫ이들은우리신문사에
와서면약ᄒᆞ심을희망ᄒᆞᆸ

○발ᄒᆡᆼ소　박동대한ᄆᆡ일신보
사발ᄒᆡᆼ소겸인쇄소젼영국인셜필
립졍자리오
사쟝 영국인 (ᄇᆡ셜)

평양　ᄃᆡ리졈
○평양죵로사ᄂᆞᆫ권ᄆᆡ보씨로우
리신문ᄃᆡ리인을ᄐᆡᆨ졍ᄒᆞ엿
ᄉᆞ오니평양에계신구람코자ᄒᆞ
시ᄂᆞᆫ　쳠군ᄌᆞᄂᆞᆫᄒᆡᄃᆡ리졈에왕
림ᄒᆞ와면의ᄒᆞ시옵

사고

○우리대한ᄆᆡ일신보의목뎍은
대한의안녕질서에관ᄒᆞᆫ모든데
목에ᄃᆡᄒᆞ야ᄂᆞᆫ공평ᄒᆞᆫ변론을주
쟝ᄒᆞᆷ이라우리통신원의탐보ᄂᆞᆫ
신문보시ᄂᆞᆫ쳠군ᄌᆞ의게ᄒᆞᆼ상보
도ᄒᆞ리며편지를귀셔ᄒᆞ며주시
ᄂᆞᆫ이ᄂᆞᆫ셩명과번디를젹어붓치
시기를희망ᄒᆞ오나이거슨신문
상에긔ᄌᆡᄒᆞ란ᄂᆞᆫ거시아니오다
만극히신용ᄒᆞᄂᆞᆫ증거를숨고자
ᄒᆞᆷ이라긔쟈ᄂᆞᆫ아모귀셔던지긔
ᄌᆡᄒᆞᆷ을퇴각ᄒᆞᄂᆞᆫ권리를가졋소
나퇴각ᄒᆞᄂᆞᆫ리유를말ᄒᆞᆯ터이오
며공즁평화를문란케ᄒᆞᄂᆞᆫ듯ᄒᆞᆫ
귀셔ᄂᆞᆫ의례히밧지안켓ᄉᆞᆸ나이
다

●본사셜시이ᄅᆡ로신문을ᄆᆡ양
우톄로분젼ᄒᆞ와ᄒᆡ젼부의임의
로젼ᄒᆞᄂᆞᆫ것스로번곳에ᄂᆞᆫ호늣게
젼ᄒᆞ기도ᄒᆞ며혹면졀거숨ᄒᆞᆫ겁
에젼ᄒᆞ기도ᄒᆞ며혹아니젼ᄒᆞᄂᆞᆫ
곳도잇다ᄒᆞ와우리신문을ᄉᆞ랑
ᄒᆞ야구람ᄒᆞ시ᄂᆞᆫ　쳠군ᄌᆞ의게
ᄃᆡᄒᆞ야ᄆᆡ우미안ᄒᆞ옵기로지금
은본젼인을두고ᄆᆡ일ᄆᆡ즁이젼
ᄒᆞ며아니젼ᄒᆞ거나늣게거나ᄒᆞᆯ
폐가업도록ᄒᆞ랴ᄒᆞ오니ᄒᆞ야ᄂᆡ
젼ᄒᆞ거나혹늣게젼ᄒᆞ거나ᄒᆞᆫ일
이잇ᄉᆞ면본사로통긔ᄒᆞ여주심
을희망ᄒᆞᆸ

관보

뎨삼쳔괄호
광무팔년십이월십삼일

○명경효젼졔됴셔칙임관이등
죵이품　리졍노
○ᄒᆡ시죵원분시어　졍삼품
최중연　륙품　김셕됴　륙품
리규의　륙품　리죵호
○ᄒᆡ시죵원분시어　졍삼품
죠두환　졍삼품　한창교　구
품　민우식　구품면관보
○ᄒᆡ시죵원분쥬ᄉᆞ　구품　죠
슌구
○명시죵원분쥬ᄉᆞ　륙품　셔
쥬학
이상십이월구일
○면본관　통신ᄉᆞ면회과쥬ᄉᆞ
고샹후　통신ᄉᆞ면회과쥬ᄉᆞ　송
명셕　통신ᄉᆞ면회과쥬ᄉᆞ　셜
인셕　통신ᄉᆞ면회과쥬ᄉᆞ　엄
필규　통신ᄉᆞ면회과쥬ᄉᆞ　김
죵권　통신ᄉᆞ면회과쥬ᄉᆞ　리
병현　통신ᄉᆞ면회과쥬ᄉᆞ　김
슌젼　ᄂᆡ쟝원봉엽과쥬ᄉᆞ　송
셩욱　슌쳔군슈봉　노찬셕
○ᄒᆡ시죵원분시어　구품　진
호쳥　구품　김ᄐᆡ경　구품
남샹필　구품　민영근　구품
리희진　구품　리긔복　구품
쟝지한　구품　박규현　구품
김대낙　구품　오두화　구품
심샹찬
○ᄒᆡ시죵원분쥬ᄉᆞ　륙품　셔
쥬학
○명ᄂᆡ쟝원경셔칙임관샹등
죵이품　오현근
○명궁ᄂᆡ부특진관셔칙임관샹
등　시강원쳠사　윤우식
○명시강원쳠사셔칙임관샹등
쟝례원소경　죠동완
○임비셔원승셔주임관오등
졍삼품　셔병션
○임통신사면회과주사셔판임
관팔등　공셩지　김셩용　김
진오　박창록　강긔현　박긔
보　죠병이　셜창호
○임ᄂᆡ쟝원공엽과쥬사셔판임
관팔등　남즁식
○임　슌창원참봉셔판임관팔
등　쟝릉참봉　유린죠
○쟝릉참봉셔판임관팔등　효
릉참봉　김경진
○임효릉참봉셔판임관팔등
통신사면회과주사　홍사철
○임슌릉참봉셔판임관팔등
박봉진
○명평안남북도징세관　구품
오규희
이상십이월십일
○명경효젼졔됴셔칙임관삼등
궁ᄂᆡ부특진관　김병익
○명쟝례원소경셔칙임관ᄉᆞ등
비셔원승　윤샹학
○임비셔원승셔주임관륙등
졍삼품　권영슈
○겸임쟝례원쟝례　비셔원승
권영슈
○겸임쟝례원소경　비셔원승
죠병구
○의원면본관　통신ᄉᆞ면회과
쥬ᄉᆞ　공셩지　통신ᄉᆞ면회과
쥬ᄉᆞ　김셩용　통신ᄉᆞ면회과
쥬ᄉᆞ　김진오　통신ᄉᆞ면회과
쥬ᄉᆞ박창록　통신ᄉᆞ면회과쥬
ᄉᆞ　강긔현　통신ᄉᆞ면회과쥬
ᄉᆞ　죠병이　통신ᄉᆞ면회과쥬
ᄉᆞ　셜창호
○죵이품긔션대부ᄂᆡ부협판
학셩　ᄇᆡ지홍
○죵졍삼품통졍대부비셔원승
학셩　ᄇᆡ도견
○죵죵삼품통훈대부쟝례원좌
쟝례　학셩　ᄇᆡ이견
이상졍삼품통졍대부진헌
셩부관윤ᄇᆡ국ᄐᆡ의고죠고
증죠고의벼면츄　증
이상십이월십이일
○의졍부참졍신긔션　궁ᄂᆡ부
대신임시서리ᄂᆡ부대신특진관
장리용ᄐᆡ근　주ᄒᆞ되곳엿티이
평샹북도슌찰ᄉᆞ홍우셕오　주
본오ᄃᆡ하ᄒᆞ신을보온즉쟝과군
슈를칭셕이가부임ᄒᆞ야졍치를
도란보지아니ᄒᆞ고ᄇᆡᆨ셩의피를
긁거쟈안봄을삼ᄯᆞ온고로곳봉
고ᄒᆞ엿다ᄒᆞᆸ엇숩기차졍이사실
ᄒᆞᆫ즉이러ᄒᆞᆫ탐오불법ᄒᆞᄂᆞᆫ군수
ᄂᆞᆫ가히그쟈를슈가잇ᄉᆞ오위선
면관ᄒᆞ옵고법부로ᄒᆞ여곰구ᄅᆞ
증징ᄒᆞᆷ이엇더ᄒᆞ올지근샹　주
ᄒᆞ외광무팔년십이월팔일에봉
지의주ᄒᆞ란ᄒᆞ옵시다

외보

○항로셩긔　남아셰아기포런스
오말ᄒᆞᆫ바를거ᄒᆞᆫ즉아라가와지
수가쟝과과션회사를죠직ᄒᆞ란
ᄒᆞᄂᆞᆫᄃᆡ자본금사십만원으로부
리도든ᄇᆡ두어쳑을사셔한국에항
로를열리이라ᄒᆞ엿더라
○로국젼비　로국이아직ᄐᆡᆫ인
공화국에셔빈사척을사셔남아
푸리가희망봉근쳐에셔극동에
나오ᄂᆞᆫ불특항티에항ᄒᆞᆫ다ᄒᆞ여
려슌구오셔쥬고병들고싸ᄒᆞ요
지못ᄒᆞ게된군사를보ᄒᆞ기위
ᄒᆞ야이만명의병수를ᄂᆡ보낸다
ᄒᆞ며사홀에호셔만일괴가연속
ᄒᆞ야후독ᄒᆞᆫ디경이면몃엿티의
구군ᄉᆞ를그곳으로운송ᄒᆞ야려슌
구에더듸다더라
○진졍비교　일본젼탁지쳥관
쳠평슈일씨가본월오일에리졔
학회에셔일로량국의지졍을연
구셜ᄒᆞ되로국탁지부에셔ᄂᆞᆫ구
본은이억만원의지졍이잇슨즉일
억만원을더ᄒᆞ기ᄂᆞᆫ용이ᄒᆞ며ᄯᅩ로
노국젼비ᄂᆞᆫ일본젼비에비ᄒᆞ면
만원을지출ᄒᆞ야ᄒᆞᆯ것이오로국은
은인민의분광ᄒᆞ기어려운즉
을ᄂᆡ외채로모집ᄒᆞᄂᆞᆫᄃᆡ
외국에셔신용을엇기어려우나
ᄂᆡ일본은국ᄂᆡ공채도모집이잘되
잇스며일본지졍은로국보다유여ᄒᆞ다ᄒᆞ
엿더라

뎐보

샹ᄒᆡ오후십일시발
○로함뎐몰　려슌함ᄃᆡ가젼몰
ᄒᆞ엿기로로국셔울에셔ᄂᆞᆫ크게
공황을ᄀᆡᆨᄒᆞ고명미인은열셩으
로츅하ᄒᆞᄂᆞᆫ뜻을표ᄒᆞ고일본공
ᄉᆞ최ᄂᆞᆫ쪽ᄂᆞᆼᄒᆞ엿고로국뎨삼동양
함ᄃᆡᄂᆞᆫ리일월에발졍ᄒᆞᆯ터이라
더라
●원죠ᄒᆞ조란　공보를거ᄒᆞᆫ즉
우리졔원호ᄂᆞᆫ십이월십일일려
슌부근에셔우리륙군에ᄒᆡᆼ동을
방조ᄒᆞ고봉쇄감시ᄒᆞᄂᆞᆫ즁에긔
계수뢰를부디치쳠몰ᄒᆞ야함쟝
ᄒᆞᆫ단마ᄃᆡ좌이하삼십팔명은젼ᄉᆞ
ᄒᆞ고기타ᄂᆞᆫ구ᄒᆞ엿도라
○평화회의연긔　ᄇᆡᆨ림뎐을거
ᄒᆞᆫ즉미국이뎨의ᄒᆞᆫ바평화회의
가일아젼쟁이긋ᄂᆞᆫ후ᄭᆞ지연
긔되엿더라

○셔반아외대회답 두리면본거혼즁셔반아에주차ᄒᆞᆫ일본공ᄉᆞ가부이고향오셔파라작협디의계셔탄과밋식료품을슈응ᄒᆞᆫ고ᄉᆞ건으로셔반아외부대신의게셜명을쳥구ᄒᆞ엿더니동외부대신이엄졍중립을유지ᄒᆞᆫ뜻으로회답ᄒᆞ엿더라

빅림발 십이월ᄉᆞ일

○로함근도 불틱함디의ᄒᆞᆫ부분이폐림올지낫다더라

동디발 동일

○평화졍회 헤아평화회의는이번젼쟁의숫나기ᄭᆞ지연긔ᄒᆞ엿더라

동디발 동일

○로국신문 로국신문이근릭졍부에디ᄒᆞ야자유로평론ᄒᆞ야셰론이심히격앙홈으로로국졍부에셔향자에신문조례에자유언론을허락ᄒᆞ엿다가이번에다시금지홈에니르럿더라

론돈발 십이월삼일

○신문소론 로국신문노보보평아가다시졍부를권고ᄒᆞ되극동에대ᄒᆞᆫ함디를파송ᄒᆞᆯ거시아니라샹에셔우승ᄒᆞᆫ권리를잇슴이필요ᄒᆞ고또불틱함디의셰력이일본함디보다약ᄒᆞᆫ셔동이라ᄒᆞ엿더라

잡보

○유자불취 남촌인셩부지사는모군군ᄒᆞ나히잇는티소경자식ᄒᆞ나홀두고그쳐가죽으미쏘후취ᄒᆞ야자식ᄒᆞ나홀나흔지라그후취ᄒᆞᆫ쳐가불량ᄒᆞ야그병신자식을죳차버니고병신자식이거리로단니며ᄒᆞᆫ풀식구걸ᄒᆞ야셩명을보젼ᄒᆞ더니ᄒᆞ로는그아비가보고츄은이녁여다리다가그졔웃슬입히고졍에두엇더니그후쳐가제자식을향ᄒᆞ야말ᄒᆞ기를젼쳐소싱만슈랑ᄒᆞ니이자식은진쟉죽여엽시깃다ᄒᆞ고쏘악ᄒᆞ미그아비된자ㅣ마음이편치못ᄒᆞ야엇지홀는지답답히녁이는티그병신자식이훈졍에서살슈업슬모양이라ᄒᆞ더라

○회민소요 남으로좃차온사름의젼셜을드른즉젼라도익산군에진보회와일진회원이멋천명식돈취ᄒᆞ야민심이대단소요ᄒᆞ야환산티경이라더라

○진퇴랑란 근티고을을주린다ᄒᆞ미군슈셔임된자ㅣ날마다남북으로분주이단니나인력거삭만히비ᄒᆞᆫ다더라

○단발층생 일젼에종로면긔회사압해셔엇던단발ᄒᆞᆫ사름이오좀을누는티평거슈가맛츔보고말ᄒᆞ되단발은긔명의목적이라ᄒᆞ면서기나도야지곳치아모티나오좀을누니이무삼목적인고ᄒᆞ니그단발ᄒᆞᆫ자ㅣ무료히퇴거ᄒᆞ엿다더라

○경셰불시 민병한씨가슈삭회사를셜시ᄒᆞ고일인림포명의곳경회사와자유로계약ᄒᆞᆫ수건으로외부와농상공부에서민씨와샹지ᄒᆞᆫ다는말은이왕게진ᄒᆞ엿거니와일젼에림공ᄉᆞ가다시셩명ᄒᆞ기를곳인쥰ᄒᆞ고ᄎᆞ히관에ᄒᆞᆫ젹ᄒᆞ야히관에셔이왕슈쇄ᄒᆞ든고린셰는불시ᄒᆞ라ᄒᆞ는고로수이을젼에외부에셔그말대로히관에공함ᄒᆞ고신칙ᄒᆞ엿더라

○청풍슈파직 경상북도관찰ᄉᆞ가니부로면보ᄒᆞ기를순창군수ᄒᆞᆼ우셕의죄회를거ᄒᆞᆫ즉음력싱월초ᄉᆞ일에청풍군슈안영중을봉ᄒᆞ고ᄒᆞᆫ고칠곡군슈류응렬로써서리를차졍ᄒᆞ엿다ᄒᆞ엿더라

○한풍슈면보 청풍군슈안영중씨가니부로면보ᄒᆞ기를순찰ᄉᆞ홍우셕이가죵인을만히거느리고각군에드니며자폐ᄒᆞ미도젹이디웅치셩ᄒᆞ고리민이보젼ᄒᆞ기가어렵기로죵인을칙슈ᄒᆞ고순찰ᄉᆞ는곳쳘경식엿노라ᄒᆞ엿더라

○청풍슈힝괴 경상북도관찰ᄉᆞ가산니부로면보ᄒᆞ기를초닷셋날져녁에드른즉군슈가포군을거ᄒᆞ고풍군에니르러본즉군수가리와포군이든부리며거죠가괴악ᄒᆞ다ᄒᆞ는고로순찰ᄉᆞ를보호ᄒᆞᆫ초로순검과순교를엄히병망아발송ᄒᆞ엿다ᄒᆞ엿더라

○문쳔슈면보 문쳔군슈민영유셩씨가최봉대를원산항에셔월경ᄒᆞ야착거ᄒᆞ엿다가방송ᄒᆞ엿다고일진회셔니부에젼보ᄒᆞ엿미니부에셔는사실ᄒᆞ야보ᄒᆞ라ᄒᆞ고면보ᄒᆞ엿더니문쳔군슈가니부로면보ᄒᆞ기를최봉대ᄒᆞᆫ죽진보회인으로삼파빅숩일등이관졍ᄒᆞ에곳ᄒᆞᆫ야빅쳔거시오당초에근슈가쟝어온거슨아니오문샹등이쟝셔셩쳠어너뷔무로양샹ᄒᆞ기를원ᄒᆞ기에니어밋거곳평슐ᄒᆞᆫ고갓디ᄒᆞ엿더라

○ᄒᆞᆫ쟝반사 경셩에쥬졉ᄒᆞ엿든일본소쟝산근씨가일간회국ᄒᆞ는고로포ᄒᆞᆫ원에서 쳐분을봉승ᄒᆞ야친근소장이하이십오졍인의계각각기그ᄒᆞᆫ등을셔랴펠괘티국쟝을반사ᄒᆞ엿다더라

○리써불쳥 참위리갑씨가부쟝민영휘씨의게수빅셕식미변츄수ᄒᆞ는쟝젼을십오년젼에견탈ᄒᆞ고헌금도로차조런ᄒᆞᆫ단말은본보에임의긔재ᄒᆞ엿거니와민부쟝이리치와경위에쌔지는지라ᄒᆞᆯ수업시로지는의례히너여노코리민변ᄒᆞᆯ빗셕식분쌕으로가롱쳔셕을곳쥬마ᄒᆞ도리갑씨가리등져아니ᄒᆞ는고로민씨가관박싱중이라더라

○진퇴랑란 금츈에평양디병명룡빅명을평승ᄒᆞ고북관아병을밧어츳로함경북도에출슈ᄒᆞᆫ

흿티챵평김쳔쥬씨가원산예류진ᄒᆞ고동씨가근일에샹경ᄒᆞ엿스나회군ᄒᆞ라는명령이아직엽는고로립셩치못ᄒᆞ고진퇴랑란이라더라

○평양리신 평양디신을거혼즉진보회에셔음력시월이십칠일오후두시에평양셩니웃밧제에셔기회ᄒᆞ고사대강령을포고ᄒᆞ며회원은이쳔명가량이라ᄒᆞ며시국에급엽ᄒᆞᆫ말로연셜ᄒᆞ엿고평양셩니경년유지ᄒᆞᆫ사름멧십명이면합회를챵립ᄒᆞᆫ지슈삼삭에회원이빅여인이요민목요일오후칠시에회동기회ᄒᆞ고학문샹유죠ᄒᆞᆫ말로셔로권면ᄒᆞ는티대단이발달되며일셩증인민이며합회를대단이앙모ᄒᆞ고평양군슈팽한쥬씨가학문샹유죠ᄒᆞᆫ말로찬셩ᄒᆞ고보조금이십원을보니엿다ᄒᆞ더라

○청원불허외인 젼군슈쟝괴흥이가쳥원셔니에본인이숑화군슈지임시에슈안근홍동에잇는바셕광혼곳을본군몽젼중으로슈도소등ᄒᆞ기위ᄒᆞ야이십만원의다액을허비ᄒᆞ고히공젼미납죠건으로광리원에퇴슈ᄒᆞ엿는티이제신문을본즉영공ᄉᆞ가이셔광을쳥구ᄒᆞᆫ다ᄒᆞ는고로이에앙소ᄒᆞ오니사죠ᄒᆞ신후빗셩이으로ᄒᆞ여금셔광을두계ᄒᆞ야다외국인의게젼셜치말기를보라ᄒᆞ엿더라

○회진외부 작일은화요일이란외부쇼속디명외교관등이또외부에수진ᄒᆞ야회동ᄒᆞ엿더라

○면고긔명셩문 외부파원리긴츙이가면보ᄒᆞ기를작일브티긔명ᄒᆞ야쳥샹치명수 긴을셩문ᄒᆞᆫ다더라

○보리후조처 일젼단쳔군아병수빈으로신참졍은됴모지듯지못ᄒᆞ엿다ᄒᆞ고니부대신리용틔씨를면관ᄒᆞᆫ다고계쥴ᄒᆞ엿더니참쳔ᄒᆞ위씨가왈니는본지가오린라이미나졍계쟝ᄒᆞ엿다ᄒᆞᆫ가의신참졍이도로허샬피지못ᄒᆞᆫ칙망으로히쥬본안을문시ᄒᆞ고함흥관찰부로훈령ᄒᆞ야이리수병뎡의힝동을다시사실ᄒᆞ야보리ᄒᆞᆫ후에다시조처ᄒᆞ자ᄒᆞ엿더라

○총감수직 교육부총감리지용씨는ᄉᆞ직샹소ᄒᆞ엿더라

○처분앙샹 한풍군슈안영중씨가봉고ᄒᆞ고셔지당ᄒᆞ고순찰ᄉᆞ를거ᄒᆞ야 대니에ᄎᆞ지면보ᄒᆞᆫ지라 처분을하ᄒᆞ사곳압샹ᄒᆞ라ᄒᆞᆫ올셧다더라

○왕쳥나힌 일젼일진회에셔졍부명령으로드린갓디니쳥쳔흐리위씨가때표자가되야슈작ᄒᆞᆫ는테운시변이월우리회민은황실을오히리발ᄒᆞ지아니ᄒᆞ고

인면지산민보호ᄒᆞᆫ면우리바라는이가히항당ᄒᆞᆫ다ᄒᆞ고참졍공ᄒᆞ에나인ᄒᆞᆫ면중민의게보이고빅셩을가히히산ᄒᆞ리란ᄒᆞᆫ티졍부에셔반쇼ᄒᆞ야왈나쟝이죽인이라엇지ᄒᆞ야상지ᄒᆞ리오마는시골사름들이졍이나젼쟝을파란다만일진회에명령만듯고샹졍ᄒᆞ야두류ᄒᆞᆫ니자긔의제산을보젼치못ᄒᆞ리라다ᄒᆞᆫ송ᄒᆞ고당초회규를외지ᄒᆞ야셔로쟝구ᄒᆞᆫ것을죳차죠쳐ᄒᆞ면국수들위ᄒᆞ야만힝이라ᄒᆞ엿는티결과를엇지못ᄒᆞ고각각도라갓다더라

외보

○통령중상 미국대통령루스벨트씨가거월에화승돈근방에셔처마ᄒᆞ다가탈마ᄒᆞ야중상ᄒᆞ엿는티그샹처는우편머리로귀와우편이마에티단ᄒᆞ고타마ᄒᆞᆫ후에는혼층동안이나졍신을일코누엇섯는티밤일그셔히단단ᄒᆞ엿더면루스벨트씨는죽슈ᄒᆞᆯ엿슬번ᄒᆞ엿다더라

○북히수진 로국이북히수진을셜명ᄒᆞ엿는티그대ᄀᆞ가이와곳더라

대일 회군부쟝로제스트벤스기씨가영국히변을세나란홀조음에북히에슈쌍ᄒᆞᆫ빈두척이잇는티괴호들이젼도다펏다가쏘저것도다펏다ᄒᆞᆫ다는보고를보앗고

대이 그수진나기젼에그함디의샹싱령리키에잇는운송선이굿가가무션젼으로보고ᄒᆞ되엿던슈뢰졍두척을보앗다ᄒᆞ고

대삼 종잇다가운송션함쟝가가보니는것곳ᄒᆞᆫ슈샹ᄒᆞᆫ무션면이왓스니그함디의잇는경위션을무펏는티그후에아리본슈갑쳣가는그뢰면븐을ᄒᆞᆫ일아엽다ᄒᆞ고

대ᄉᆞ 그때에그함디의영ᄒᆞᆫ로슈뢰졍수척이뵈이는티그것이로국의것은아닌것이분명ᄒᆞᆫ것이로국수뢰졍은그때에다영길리히협에잇섯는지라그럼으로자세ᄒᆞᆫ후에조격ᄒᆞ엿다ᄒᆞ엿더라

○쳘로샹인 미국에서금년일년니에지번쳘셔지쳘로에치어죽은사름이구쳔구빅팔십ᄉᆞ명인티지번십년동안에미국쳘로에서죽은인명이칠만팔쳔일빅오십이명이더라

광고

○광양군슈됴에셔의셩명도장을위됴ᄒᆞ야위됴표제도빈홀고무소부지ᄒᆞ오니이런놈은밥도에서싱혼지라본도장은회폐불용ᄒᆞ오니너외국인은속지마음

됴예셔 고빅

TELEGRAMS.

Toko Dec. 11th.

The Mikado has forwarded a present of biscuits to General Hasegawa for the Japanese troops in Korea

Tokyo Dec. 11th.

According to a London telegram, the Czar has presented the officers of the British cruiser Talbot with some silver bowls and spoons, in recognition of their services rendered to the crews of the Varyag ank Koreetz.

Army Head quarters.

On the 11th inst, 2 companies of Russian infantry and 3 of cavalry attacked the Japanese near Tiensuibatze, but were repulsed owing to a heavy shell fire.

Japanese Legation.

An official report from Port Arthur states that on the 11th inst, the Russian wireless telegraph station was badly damaged and an arsenal set on fire.

FROM JAPAN PAPERS.

London, Dec. 5.

Reuter's correspondent at Perim states that Admiral Foelkersahm's squadron is coaling from colliers off Mushah Island, between Obok and Jibutil.

London, Dec. 5

The British Foreign Office late on Saturday night instructed the authorities at Cardiff, under the Foreign Enlistment Act, to prohibit the German steamer "Captain W. Newgell" from coaling at the port, the Government having received proof that a previous cargo of coal shipped by the vessel had been delivered to the Baltic Fleet.

Four hundred tons had already been taken on board when coaling operations were stopped.

It is understood that the Government is investigating the case.

Later.

Coaling operations have been stopped on another German collier at Cardiff. The shipper in this case is stated to be the German honorary Consul at Cardiff.

Berlin, Dec. 5.

Much discussion is taking place in the British, French, and Russian papers regarding the Russian suggestion that the Dardanelles be opened to the Black Sea Fleet.

The European Governments, however, have not yet approached the question, and the general opinion is that the prospects of their doing so are now remote owing to the premature pulication of the Russian proposals.

London, Dec. 6.

The Naval headquarters at St. Petersburg announces that supplementary information has been received from Admiral Rohjestvensky, in command of the Baltic Squadron, relative to the recent incident in the North Sea.

The Admiral states that the order to "Cease fire" was signalled ten minutes after the attack in order to prevent the hindmost vessels of the Squadron hitting their own ships.

The "Aurora" was struck by five projectiles, and as a result the Chaplain of the ship and a petty officer were wounded. The Chaplian died at Tangier from the injuries received.

Later.

The English papers regard the belated statement that has been received from Admiral Rohjestvensky, which is somewhat obscurely worded, as virtually admitting that the Russians fired upon one another.

London, dec. 7.

The report that Russia intends sending a third squadron to the Far East is st ated to be unfounded.

Berlin, Dec. 7.

The "Lokalanzeiger" publishes a telegram from St. Petersburg to the effect that Russia has bought from Chile and Argentine war-ships to the value of sixty million roubles. The vessels, it is stated, are to join the Baltic Squadron, but will fly the Chinese flag until they have arrived at St. Petersburg (!).

London, Dec. 7.

With regard to the Dardanelles question, the British Government has informed the Russian Government that it is impossible under any circumstances that the passage through the Dardanelles of the Black Sea Squadron can be allowed.

London, Dec. 7.

The cruisers "Oleg" and "Izumrud," forming the vanguard of Admiral Bobrovosky's Supplementary Squadron of the Baltic Fleet, has left Tangier, proceeding in the direction of Suez.

These vessels are accompained by the cruiser "Rion," formerly the Volunteer Fleet steamer "Smoiensk," and two torpedo destroyers.

Later.

The rest of the vessels of Admiral Bobrovosky's Squadron, consisting of the cruiser "Dnieper," formerly the Volunteer Fleet steamer "Petersburg," and two torpedo-destroyers, with transports, have left Tangier eastwards.

Berlin, Dec. 6.

The Baltic Squadron is being supplied with provisions at Jibutil from its own transports.

It is announced from St. Petersburg that a third Baltic Squadron is being prepared for the Far East, consisting of seven batteships, four cruisers, and forty torpedo-boats.

DISMISSED MAGISTRATE.

We find that a statement which appeared in our columns yesterday, to the effect that the Government had decided, owing to Japanese representations, to reinstate the dismissed magistrate of Pyengyang, was incorrect.

The magistrate had already been dismissed after conclusive proof, of his oppression of the people, had been obtained, when the Japanese filed a complaint against his dismissal on the grounds that he was of invaluable assistance to the Japanese military authorities.

The Home office replied that the man had been dismissed for criminal oppression of the people after due consideration had been given to his case. The Korean Government having come to this decision they add, they fail to see that the Japanese have any say in the matter.

It certainiy seems, to us, that things have come to a sorry pass when the Japanese, knowing full well that the man is a criminal and that thousands of people are suffering under his oppression, desire to reverse the just decision of his own Government and keep him in office, because it suits their military affairs.

A telegram from the representative of the Foreign Office, despatched to Haiju in connection with the murder of the Chinese, a British subject, states that the trial opened yesterday. Mr. Porter of the British Legation is there on behalf of British interests.

At a special session held by the government on Monday, it was finally decided to despatch 3,000 Korean soldiers to resist the Russians in the northeast. It will be remembered that, last spring, 600 Korean soldiers, under Major Kim Won-kiu, were despatched from Pyeng-yang to north Ham Kyeng province for the same purpose, but speedily found their way to Gensan not relishing an encounter with the Russians.

DASTARDLY ASSAULT ON FOREIGNER BY JAPANESE SOLDIERS.

On Monday night Mr. Gorschalki, an old Seoul resident, was assulted in his own house by two Japanese soldiers.

Mr. Gorschalki states that while sitting in his house at 8:30 P. M., he became aware of strange voices in his garden. On going to his front door, he was confronted by two Japanese soldiers, who appeared to be in a state of intoxication; they advanced on the verandah, and despite Mr. Gorschalki's remonstrances attempted to force an entrance into the house. Mr. Gorschalki then peremptorily ordered them away, when one suddenly drew his side-arm from its scabbard and made a vicious slash at him cutting him severely on the hand. They then took to their heels.

Mr. Gorschalki states that this is not the first time that he has received a visit from Japanese soldiers. On two previous occasions he has found soldiers in his garden and experienced difficulty in getting them to leave. We sincerely trust that the Japanese military authorities will lose no time in taking steps to secure these miscreants and mete out proper justice to them. Although Mr. Gorschalki has only received a slight wound on the hand, had he not quickly stepped back when he was struck at, he might have been very severely wounded or even killed.

This case should be sufficient to force the military authorities to adopt some measures to secure both foreigners and Koreans from any furthur occurrences of this nature, and place some restriction on irresponsible soldiers.

The Chinese Consul at Chemulpo has gone, on furlongh, to China.

Mr. Stevens, in company with Mr. and Mrs. Hagiwara is due to leave Kobe by the "Ohio" on Friday next.

Major General Yamane who has been staying in Seoul, will shortly leave for Japan. He has been decorated by His Majesty.

The Il Chin Hoi have decided to send committees to invistigate the cases of the Prefect of Kangwha and the Magistrate of Pyeng Yang, both of whom have been excessively oppressing the people in their districts.

The Japanese Minister has applied to the Government for permission for the military authorities to make use of the timber from the forests on the Tumen and Yalu rivers. For military purposes, he adds it is essential that the authorities should be given supreme control in this matter.

The Korea Daily News.

Issued at 5 P. M. daily except Sundays.

Rate of Subscription:—
Per Year,............Yen 25.
Per Quarter,..........Yen 7.
Per Month,..........Yen 2.50.

Postage in Korea not charged extra.
Postage abroad charged extra.

Advertisements, 50 sen per day for 1 inch or less.
5 yen per month per inch.
50 yen per year per inch.

All communications to

E. T. BETHELL,
Editor and Publisher,
Pak-tong, Seoul.

A NEW ASPECT.

Mr. F. A. Mackenzie who was with General Kuroki's forces as special correspondent for the "London Daily Mail" has given it as his opinion that the troubles of the Japanese are only just commencing. He gives as reasons the slowness of their advance in Manchuria and their failure to adopt a policy acceptable to the Koreans.

The situation in the neighbourhood of Liaoyang is certainly obscure at present. It is seldom possible to make any comparison between the Russian and Japanese reports as the respective generals adopt entirely different nomenclature in discribing actions. However, it seems clear that the Russians have had time to organize their forces so that not only can they not be counted upon to retreat as heretofore but they are able to make an independent advance threatening the Japanese communications between Liaoyang and the Yalu river.

Whether this advance is only a diversion or flanking movement or whether it is the pioneer of the descent of the army of 50,000 which is reported to be assembled at Kirin is at present only a subject for speculation, but there are many circumstances which lend colour to the view that the second Manchurian army was to push southward from Kirin.

If a Russian army can gain control of the Yalu river, the railways in Korea which have been pushed forward by Japan at so much trouble and expense will become useless as communications. As in the winter a port in Korea is the only available base besides Dalny the necessity of Japan's maintaining these communications becomes apparent, and there is a corresponding certainty of a Russian attack whenever and wherever possible.

Herein the folly of the over-bearing policy which Japan has pursued in this country becomes apparent. Their sole friends are a lot of paid agitators who will, on the first signs of trouble leave them as rats leave a sinking ship and Japan's lines of communications through Korea will be as great an anxiety to her as the trans-Siberian Railway is to the Russians.

STOLEN SIGNAL BOOKS.

A report comes from the Mediterranean, says the naval correspondent of "The Globe, that the signal-book which was missed from its appointed place in the "Prince George" at the beginning of February, and which was afterwards stated to have been found, was not found; and that an offcer now serving in the Mediterranean Fleet says that he has reason to know that the book is now in the hands of a foreign Admiralty. This tale is sufficiently unpleasant, but on the top of it comes another from China to the effect that a similar signal-book has within the past two months disappeared from the battleship "Centurion. The later story goes that the signal crew, being under suspicion with regard to the alleged loss of the book, were greatly relieved, individually, when one of their number voluntarily stated that he threw the book overboard. Such a statement was naturally followed by the immediate arrest of the self-accuser; and at the time the letter containing this informatin was written, he was awaiting trial by court-martial. The man has refused to assign any reason for his action—which is not generally believed—and no steps are being neglected to find the missing signal-book. Diving operations are being prosecuted with the utmost energy, in order to ascertain the truth or otherwise of the man's statement, it being pretty certain that if it was thrown overboard it will be found in close proximity to the place where the "Centurion" was then anchored, since these books are bound in leaden covers, for the express purpose of ensuring their immediate descent to the bottom when thrown overboard, as they would be in the event of defeat by an enemy, in order to prevent such invaluable information from falling into the enemy's hands.

PICTURES OF CAMP AND BATTLE.

Russian newspapers to-day like their English contemporaries during the Boer War, print large numbers of interesting extracts from letters of soldiers at the front. The Russian "Tommy Atkins" takes war seriously. The following extract, culled from an exchange, of a Cossack named Korniloff to his mater at Stavropol is highly interesting:—

"We had an awful fight to-day with about twice as many Japs, and before we had to clear off stuck a score of them. I myself killed two, running the second through the body so hard that he slipped halfway up my lance. Finally the Japs shelled us, and drove us off. It's an awful thing to retreat before these heathens. Still, when we got back, I prayed and thanked God for making me brave, and His instrument in slaying His enemies. One of our men said, 'Why do you pray?' I answered, 'I killed two heathens.' He laughed, and said, 'Don't tell those yarns. Our old Cossack, who chopped up the French, used to bring back their ears to prove it.'"

Apparently slight wounds do not trouble "Private Ivan." Mikhail Dubovsky, an infantryman, wounded at Wa-fang-tien, is quoted in the "Sibirskiya Viedomosti" as follows:

"I have seven wounds, all bullets, yet can write to you, my dear mother, just like a whole man. The Jap bullets are small, and don't hurt. . . . In our big battle, where we cut the whole Japanese Army to pieces, and captured thousands of prisoners (!), we never minded bullets. Stchuka, who is well, and sends his bow to the starosta, got a shot in his left arm, and up he takes a handful of wet mud, and plastered it on, and that stopped the bleeding. In fact, we like to be wounded, as we get a rest, and Captain Sukharin call us 'molodtsi' (fine fellows), and gives us money. It only hurts if you get one in the heart. The brain doesn't matter."

Dubovsky's ideas of medicine are, however not more primitive than Kniazeff, an artilleryman, who, writing of the Motienling fight, said:

"Our men have got a grand way of curing wounds. You cut off the 'gaolan' (millet) ears, chew them into a paste, and bind it on. If you can wet it first in vodka, so much the better, but our chaps would rather drink the vodka."

A letter from another private, written from Haicheng over two months ago, relates the following tragic story;

"One of our Poles, who was called 'Razboinik' (the Robber) was shot to-day. He deserved it, too. His real name was Pier. [illegible]s good Pier was set to guard ov[illegible] Japanese. They said they were [illegible]rs, but they looked like privates, and dirty privates, too. They were no sort of men. Anyway, they escaped, and next day there was a row. Pier says, 'I don't know how they escaped. There's a hole cut in the side of the house.'

"When they searched Pier, he had two twenty-rouble notes in his boot. 'Where did you get them?' asks the colonel. 'I got them from my father. Didn't I, Prokhor?'—turning to me. Now I knew that he had got money from his father, and said 'Yes.' But the colonel asks, as cold as ice, 'Does your father forge notes? These are forged and, what's more, they're forged in Japan. You'll hang.' And so he was tried, but shot, not hanged. However, Poles don't count for much, and no Russian ever turned traitor."

"We Siberians were going to manage the war all alone," wrote Piotr Khrebtoff; "but now our Government is sending out men from Mother Russia. We think we're the best, and wait till it comes for sticking Japs, and see who can stick hardest. The Russians are well set up, and drilled like ants; but our men could beat them in strength as easily as they could beat the Japs. The Russians bring lots of tobacco, and have better bayonets than we, so we're glad to see them."

Acting Viceroy Tuan Fang has received instructions from the Central Government to start a mint for making copper cents at Shanghai.

The chief Chinese local official at Hsinmintun is alleged to be working strenuously in Russian interests so far as concerns the transport of cereals to Mukden.

General Skrydloff is reported to have reached Mukden from Vladivostock on the 30th of November, and he is said to believe that the relief of Port Arthur is still possible.

It is reported that Prince Ching has been in secret conference with the Ministers of the Grand Council regarding the probable outcome of the war between Russia and Japan.

The Russians are said to have despatched 15 heavy guns to the Shaho by train from Tiehling, and to have received a re-inforcement of 20,000 men, supposed to be particularly brave troops. There was already bravery enough on the Russian side.

It is said remarks the "Japan Mail" that there are 50,000 Russian troops in Kirin and that they are preparing to advance south. There might be some idea of utilizing the Zungari for an expedition from Kirin, but confirmation of the rumour is needed.

It has been mentioned in connection with the attempt on the life of ex-Governor Wang Chih-chun that the Chinese authorities are endeavouring to have the men arrested transferred to the native city for trial. The "N. C. D. News" learns that the Senior Consul has informed the Taotai that the offence having been committed within the Settlement, the trial must be at the Mixed Court.

In the "Nichi Nichi Shimbun" there appears an account showing the terrible sufferings of those whose duty holds them in the trenches. The fighting is mere child's play compared with the nervous strain of hiding day after day in holes in the ground with the certainty that if one raises one's head it will be a mark for many rifles. The cold and discomfort are intensified by inundations of rain water and snow water mingled with blood.

The two following reports have been received simultaneously from the North Kyeng Song province. The Governor states that the special overseer, appointed by the government to look into affairs in that province, has dismissed the Magistrate of Hyon Poong. The Magistrate of Hyon Poong reports that the overseer, Hong Woo Suk, accompained by many servants, had been causing disturbances in his district, so he imprisoned all the servants and drove the overseer away.

The Korea Daily News.

VOL. I, WEDNESDAY, DECEMBER 14, 1904. No. 125

HONGKONG & SHANGHAI BANKING CORPORATION.

Paid-up Capital..... ....$10,000,000
Reserve Fund:—Sterling Reserve... 10,000,000
Silver Reserve..... 7,000,000

27,000,000
Reserve Liability of Proprietors... 10,000,000

HEAD OFFICE, HONGKONG.

London Bankers, London and County Banking Company Limited.
Branches and Agencies,
London.

Amoy,	Hankow	Penang,
Bangkok,	Hiogo,	Rangoon,
Batavia,	Iloilo,	Saigon,
Bombay,	Lyons,	San Francisco,
Calcutta,	Manila,	Singapore,
Colombo,	Nagasaki,	Sourabaya,
Foochow,	New York,	Tientsin,
Hamburg,	Peking,	Yokohama,

Credits granted on approved Securities, and every description of Banking and Exchange business transacted.

Drafts granted on London and the chief Commercial places in Europe, India, Australia, America, China and Japan.

HOLME RINGER & Co., AGENTS,
CHEMULPO.

HOKURKU DOBOKU KAISHA.

Branch office in Chong Dong, Seoul.
Japanese telephone No. 165

CONTRACT DEPARTMENT.

We can contract to build any building or construction.

MERCHANDISE DEPARTMENT.

We can provide any building material. We have just contracted to build the new Belgian Legation.

E. MEYER & Co.,
Agents,
Chemulpo.

CHARTERED BANK OF INDIA AUSTRALIA & CHINA.

INCORPORATED BY ROYAL CHARTER 1853

HEAD OFFICES:—LONDON.

Paid-up Capital £800,000
Reserve Liability of Shareholders 800,000
Reserve Fund 800,000

Drafts granted upon all the principal places in the world and every description of Exchange and banking business transacted.

E. MEYER & Co., Agents,
Chemulpo.

MITSU BISHI DOCKYARD & ENGINE WORKS,
NAGASAKI.

CODE WORD, "DOCK."

A 1, A. B. C., and Engineering Codes used.

DOCK No. 1 (at Tategami).

Extreme Length..............523 feet
Length on blocks .... 513 ,,
Width of Entrance on Top......89 ,,
,, ,, Bottom....77 ,,
Water on Blocks at Spring Tide 26½ ,,

DOCK No. 2 (Mukaijima).

Extreme Length..............371 feet
Length on Blocks.............360 ,,
Width of Entrance on Top......66 ,,
,, ,, Bottom 53 ,,
Water on Blocks at Spring Tide 22 ,,

PATENT SLIP (at Kosuge).

Can take vessels up to 1,000 tons gross.

THE WORKS are well equipped with the LATEST IMPROVEMENTS, and can execute any kind of work in SHIPBUILDING and MARINE ENGINEERING, as well as in REPAIRING of SHIPS.

The COMPANY'S new powerfu steamer OURA-MARU (712 tons, 700 I.H.P.), specially built for SALVAGE PURPOSES, and equipped with necessary gear, is always READY at SHORT NOTICE.

THE METHODIST PUBLISHING HOUSE,

Little West Gate, Seoul.

JOB PRINTING, TYPEWRITER PAPER
CARBON PAPER, VISITING CARDS
STATIONERY, BOOK BINDING
BOOK PUBLISHERS
AMERICAN SCHOOL BOOKS
SPENCERIAN COPY BOOKS
PEN CARBON LETTER AND BILL BOOKS

S. A. BECK, Manager.

DAI-ICHI GINKO.

LIMITED.

(Formerly the First National Bank)

ESTABLISHED 1873

INCORPORATED UNDER PRESENT LAW 1896

Capital - - - - - - - - - Yen 5,000,000
Reserve Fund - - - - - 1,500,000

HEAD OFFICE:—TOKIO.

President: Baron SHIBUSAWA.

BRANCHES AND CORRESPONDENTS
In the Principal Cities and Towns of Japan.
Interest Allowed on
Fixed deposits 1 year - - - 6½ per cent
" " 6 months - - - 6 per cent

Special current accounts 1½ sen daily per Y 100
General " " 1 " " " 100

M. TANAKA,
Manager, Chemulpo.

SINGER SEWING MACHINES

씽거ㅈ봉침

SOLE AGENTS FOR KOREA

전매쇼

HOLME RINGER & CO.
Chemulpo.

제물포 함릉거양힝

KAMEYA & CO.

GENERAL STOREKEEPERS

Chinkokai - - Seoul

(Established 1895, Tokyo)

Confectionery, Hams, Canned Goods, Cutlery, Hirano & Tansan Water, Provisions, Gents, Furnishing goods, Toilet Articles, Travelling Bags, Tobacco, Cigars & Cigarettes Kitchen Utensils. Coffee. Biscuits

Fresh Goods always kept in Stock.
Prices Moderate
Please come and inspect our goods

NIPPON YUSEN KAISHA.

JAPANESE MAIL STEAMSHIP CO.

DER MAIL CONTRACT WITH THE IMPERIAL JAPANESE JVERNMENT

European Line

Regular Fortnightly Service between Yokohama Kobe, Moji, Shanghai, Hongkong, Singapore, Penang Colombo, Port Said, Marseilles, London and Antwerp

American Line

Regular Fortnightly Service between Hongkong and Seattle, calling at Shanghai, Moji, Kobe, Yokohama and Victoria, B. C.

Australian Line

Regular weekly Service betwen Japan Ports and Australia, calling at Hongkong and Manila.
(Above Three Lines Suspended until further notice)

Shanghai Line

Weekly Service between Shanghai and Japan Ports

Korea Line

Service Kobe, Moji, Nagasaki, Fusan Chemulpo Chefoo, Taiku.
S. S. Bahelsberg, 2181 tons.
Service Kobe, Moji, Fusan, Chemulpo, Chinnampo
S. S. ARGO, S. S. Ohio.

BORDEN'S CONDENSED MILK CO.

New York, U. S. A.

ALWAYS IN STOCK

Eagle Brand Condensed Milk.

Gold Seal Condensed Milk.

Peerless (Family) Evaporated Cream.

Borden's Malted Milk.

E. MEYER & CO.
Chemulpo, Korea,
Sole Agent

ROYAL INSURANCE COMPANY.
Funds exceed £10,000,000
FIRE
AT CURRENT RATES.
LIFE
REDUCED PREMIUM.
HOLME RINGER & Co.,
Agents, Chemulpo.

HOTEL DU PALAIS

SEOUL.

The only first class Hotel in Seoul. Situated in the centre of the city opposite the palace.

Cuisine under the supervision of an experienced French Chef.

Well ventilated and furnished throughout.

TARIFF UPON APPLICATION

L. MARTIN
Proripetor and Manage,

大韓每日申報

대한ᄆᆡ일신보

(뎨일빅이십륙호) (금요일) 일천구빅사년십이월십륙일

사고빅

이신보는영어와한어로셕거ᄆᆡ일츌판ᄒᆞᆷ

신문갑

한쟝 엽두돈오푼

일삭표 엽두량닷돈

우표가미삭닷돈

다맛돈으로밧숩

광고료는

귀한의쟝단과ᄌᆞᄒᆡᆼ의다쇼로죵가ᄒᆞ되ᄆᆡ일가로밧을터이오ᄆᆡ오ᄅᆡ지아녀ᄐᆡ한사람마다다이신문을보실터이니광고내시기를원ᄒᆞ시ᄂᆞᆫ이들은우리신문샤에와셔편약ᄒᆞ심을희망ᄒᆞᆷ

○발힝소 [illegible]

사쟝 영국인 (빈셜)

평양 [illegible]

○평양[illegible]ᄂᆞᆫ [illegible]

사고

○우리대한ᄆᆡ일신보의목뎍은 [illegible]

●본샤에셔 [illegible]

관보

셔임급ᄉᆞ령

○ [illegible]

잡보

○ [illegible]

UNION INSURANCE SOCIETY OF CANTON.

Head office Hongkong.
Marine risks underwritten at current rates.

Agents in Chemulpo,
E. MEYER & Co.

COMPAGNIE DES MESSAGERIES MARITIMES.

Fortnightly Direct Service.

For Marseilles
via Ports.
Sailing from Yokohama
Calling at Kobe,
Shanghai, Hongkong, Saigon, Singapore,
Colombo, Djiboti, Suez, Port Said
and Marseilles.

For particulars apply to
HOLME RINGER & Co.,
Chemulpo.

HAYASHIDA & CO.,

16 MYENG DONG, CHIN KO KAI, SEOUL.
BRANCH OFFICE AT CHEMULPO.

Money changers, Coal and Wood Merchants, Express Agents.

We are agents for the Pyeng-yang Coal Company and the Karazu Coal Company of Japan. We have the best quality of both anthracite and bituminous coal, and prompt execution of orders is our speciality. Firewood of all kinds kept in stock. Full weight guaranteed. Money of all denominations exchanged at current rates. Parcels received for all parts.

CHINA MUTUAL LIFE INS. OC.

Most favourable terms to policy holders.

Benefit system unsurpassed.

HOLME RINGER & Co.
Agents, Chemulpo.

C. P. R.

CANADIAN PACIFIC RAILWAY COMPANY'S ROYAL MAIL STEAMSHIP LINE.

THE FAST ROUTE BETWEEN CHINA, JAPAN, AND EUROPE VIA CANADA AND THE UNITED STATES.

Route from Hongkong via Shanghai, Nagasaki (Inland Sea of Japan) Kobe, Yokohama Victoria and Vancouver.

Twin Screw Empress Steamship—6,000 Tons—Speed 19 knots.

PROPOSED SAILING FROM YOKOHAMA.

R. M. S. Empress of India.
R. M. S. Empress of Japan.
R. M. S. Empress of China.
R. M. S. Athenian.
R. M. S. Tartar.

Special reduction (first class only) granted to members of the Military, Naval, Diplomatic and Civil services and to Missionaries.

Passengers have choice of ten routes across the Continent of America and have privilege of travelling by any Atlantic Steamship Line.

Round the World passage tickets in connection with the P. and O. S. N., North German Lloyd and Messageries Co.'s **£125.**

All rates payable at current rate of exchange.

For further information, Tickets, Guide Books, etc., apply to

HOLME, RINGER & Co., AGENTS,
Chemulpo.

Grand Hotel,

(Formerly the Station Hotel)

Near the Railway Terminus.
West Gate Seoul.

The Best Hotel in Korea;
Handsome new Building.
Fine Airy Rooms
Excellent Cuisine.
Terms Moderate.
Special terms to Missionaries
and to permanent boarders.

Electric cars within 2 minutes' walk.

W. H. EMBERLEY.

Proprietor

AMERICAN KOREAN ELECTRIC CO

Light and Power.

Main Office: Electric Building, Chong No.

RAILWAY DEPARTMENT.

OPERATING CARS BETWEEN EAST AND WEST GATE, EVERY TEN MINUTES:—

First Car leaves East Gate at 7:00 A. M. First Car leaves R. R. Station at 7:25 A. M
Last Car " East Gate at 9:40 P. M. Last " " R. R. Station at 10:05 P. M

OPERATING CARS BETWEEN EAST GATE AND IMPERIAL TOMB TERMINUS, EVERY TWENTY MINUTES:—

CONNECTING WITH EVERY ALTERNATE CAR ARRIVING AT EAST GATE FROM CHONG NO.

First Car leaves East Gate for Tomb at 7:10 A. M.
" " " Tomb for East Gate at 7:35 A. M.
Last " " East Gate for Tomb at 7:50 P. M.
" " " Tomb for East Gate at 8:10 P. M.

OPERATING CARS BETWEEN CHONG NO AND YUNG SAN RIVER EVERY TWELVE MINUTES:—

First Car leaves Chong No for South Gate at 7:12 A. M.
" " " Chong No for Yung San at 7:36 A. M.
" " " South Gate for Chong No at 7:20 A. M.
" " " Yung San for Chong No at 8:09 A. M.
Last " " South Gate for Chong No 10:00 P. M.
" " " Yung San for Chong No at 9:33 P. M.

SPECIAL PRIVATE CARS FURNISHED TO SUIT CONVENIENCE OF PATRONS. PRICES ON APPLICATION AT HEAD OFFICE.

LIGHTING DEPARTMENT

Where less than 250 candle power of light is used, the rate per month will be
Per 16 candle power incandescent lamp,—All night.—Yen 2.50.
32 candle power incandescent lamp:—All night:—Yen 4.00.
50 candle power incandescent lamp:—All night:—Yen 6.00.
150 " " " " " " ,, 10.00.
1200 ,, ,, enclosed are ,, ,, ,, ,, 20.00.

Where more than 250 candle power of light is used, a Meter will be installed, freqvedted:—Rent of Meter Yen 2.00 per month. Rate of charges by meter reading:—Two Sen per Ampere per hour. (Approximately this is equal to about One Sen per 16 C. P. lamp per hour) Minimum monthly charge where meter is installed, Yen 20.00 per month, which includes rental of meter.

Estimates for installing lights furnished on application

An assortment of chandeliers always on hand.

EVERY FACILITY.

In connection with Life Assurance Business is afforded by

The Standard Life Assurance Co.,

One of the largest and wealthiest of the Provident Institutions of the United Kingdom Forms of Application and all information will be promptly afforded on application.

10 CENTS A DAY.

Not a very large expenditure is it? But it is sufficient to secure for a man of 30 a policy with the STANDARD LIFE OFFICE for

$1323.

For all particulars of rates, etc., apply to

Holme, Ringer & Co.,
Agents, Chemulpo.

THE NEW YORK LIFE INSURANCE COMPANY.

Have you ever been declined by any Company?

Are you engaged in a specially hazardous occupation?

Have you heard of the New York Life Insurance Company's New Classifications for this class of Risks?

If not, send your date of birth, occupation and particulars of rejection, if any to

E. MEYER & Co.,
Agents, Chemulpo.

K. Murakami.

Photograph Studio
Chinkokai, Seoul.

Printing, Developing and Enlargement, of Photographs always Undertaken.

Korean Views and Pictures Illustrating Native Customs always on Sale.

THE OSAKA SHOSEN KAISHA.

Boats frequently on the berth for Chinnampo.

REGULAR SAILINGS BETWEEN JAPAN AND KOREAN PORTS.

FUSAN AND KOBE VIA SHIMONOSEKI.

OSAKA VIA MOKPO, FUSAN, SHIMONOSEKI AND KOBE.

MOJI DIRECT.

OSAKA VIA KUNSAN, MASANPO, FUSAN, SHIMONOSEKI AND KOBE.

CHEMULPO KUNSAN LINE,
Every three days.

CHEMULPO CHINNAMPO LINE.
Every three days.

For Freight and passage and further particulars apply to

THE OSAKA SHOSEN KAISHA,
Chemulpo

MITSUI BUSSAN KAISHA.
(MITSUI & Co.)

MITSUI GINKO.
(MITSUI BANK.)

The Bank is owned by the members of the Mitsui Family, who, as partners, assume an unlimited responsibility for all liabilities of the Bank:—

Capital...................... .....Yen 5,000,000
Reserve Fund.................... " 5,600,000

HEAD OFFICE, TOKYO.

LONDON OFFICE, 34 LIME ST., E. C.

BRANCHES AND AGENCIES:—

New York, San Francisco, Hamburg, Bombay, Singapore, Manila, Hongkong, Amoy, Chefoo, Tientsin.

Kobe, Hakodate, Yokohama, Kure, Yokosuka, Moji, Shimonoseki, Miike, Wakamatsu, Nagasaki, Kuchinotsu, Karatsu, Sasebo, Misume, Taipeh, &c.

Telegraphic Address for all the Offices:

"MITSUI."

A. B. C. AND A. I CODES USED.

Contractors of Coal

To the Imperial Japanese Navy. Arsenals and Railway Bureau, Principal Railway Companies and Industrial Work, Home and Foreign Mail and Freight Steamers.

Sole Proprietors

Of the famous Miike, Tagawa and Yamano Coal Mines.

Sole Agents

For the sale of Fukumo, Hokoku, Ichimura, Kanoda, Mannoura, Onoura, Ostuji, Sonoda, Tsubaruro, Yoshinotani, Yoshio, Yurokibura and other coals.

YANGTSE INSURANCE ASSOCIATION, LTD.

The undersigned, having been appointed agents for the above company, are prepared to issue policies and pay losses on marine risks at regular rates.

E. MEYER & Co.,
Agents, Chemulpo.

RONDON, PLAISANT & CO.

General Storekeepers and Merchants, Ships Contractors, Tobacconists, Commission and Forwarding Agents, Coal Merchants

IMPORTERS AND EXPORTERS

Seoul & Chemulpo.

W. D. WENTWORTH.

LANDING
AND
SHIPPING AGENT
AND
CUSTOMS BORDER.

12 OURA, NAGASAKI.

STEWARD & CO.

Chemulpo.

Shipchandlers and Storekeepers, Naval and Mercantile Contrrctors, Landing and Shipping Agents.

STEWARD'S HOTEL

Chemulpo.

Best accommodation in the port for travellers. Clean and well-aired rooms, good cuisin and prompt attendence, moderate tarif.

론셜

시로난광경

일본흑목대장으로더브러ᄒᆞᆷ께단이든론돈미일신문샤특별통신원맥칸쓰씨의말을드른즉동씨의생각에는일병의계쟝ᄎᆞ격졍거리가생기게시작이된다ᄒᆞ며또ᄒᆞᆫ만쥬에도젼진ᄒᆞᆷ을지원ᄒᆞ게ᄒᆞ며손히가되여가면서한국사람들의게는졍권을힝ᄒᆞ려ᄒᆞᆫ다고ᄒᆞ는뒤현금요양근지졍항은대단히불분명ᄒᆞᆫ지라아라사이던지일본의보동으로ᄒᆞ는보고는쥰신ᄒᆞ여서로비교치못ᄒᆞᆯ거시그사실됨이문조로계지ᄒᆞᆫ바와는대샹불동ᄒᆞ도다그러ᄒᆞ나엇지던지아병들은일병으로더브러격리ᄒᆞᆫ조음에자긔의힘것조직ᄒᆞᆯ동안이릉준ᄒᆞ엿슨즉긔왕픠거ᄒᆞᆫ거스로는말ᄒᆞᆯ거시아니요다만독립으로젼진ᄒᆞ야요양과압록강사이에잇는일본동신을공동케ᄒᆞᆯᄎᆞ로출발ᄒᆞᆫ다는뒤군사들의수효인즉현금기린짱에오만명이모혀잇서계교를여러가지로싱각ᄒᆞ는쥬이며또ᄒᆞᆫ만쥬에잇는데이군을기린으로브터남으로향ᄒᆞ야니여모랏다고ᄒᆞ는말도잇스니만일아병이득승ᄒᆞ야압록강만관활ᄒᆞ는지경이면일본셔수고를드리며지물을허비ᄒᆞ야한국에부셜ᄒᆞᆫ털도도필경통ᄒᆞ지못ᄒᆞ야쓸뒤업시될터이며또ᄒᆞᆫ동졀에는일본셔엇지ᄒᆞᆯ수업시대련만외에한국ᄒᆞᆫ어느항구에다든지불가불근거지를만다라동신ᄒᆞᆷ에아모쏘록필요ᄒᆞᆫ도록ᄒᆞᆯ지니그러ᄒᆞᆯ지경이면무론어느쎄던지어느곳에서아병으로더브러공격이되엿다는소문이응당잇슬지라그때에는일본셔한국에졍젼을압제ᄒᆞ며힝ᄒᆞ든일도도리여ᄒᆞᆫ어리셕은일이분명히될터이며또ᄒᆞᆫ아라사의셔빅리아털도가잇슨즉한국으로교통ᄒᆞᆫ일본통신이쟝ᄎᆞ큰걱졍거리가될듯ᄒᆞ다고ᄒᆞ더라

잡보

○치도최촉 한셩부에셔닉부로보고ᄒᆞ기를현금에일본병참ᄉᆞ량부의공합을졉숭ᄒᆞᆫ온즉량털리에셔브터관터고지와관골등디에도로를슈축ᄒᆞᆷ이군ᄉᆞ샹에필요ᄒᆞᆷ이잇는뒤현금에결빙ᄒᆞᆯ시거가림박ᄒᆞ엿슨즉지급히조처ᄒᆞ라ᄒᆞ엿ᄉᆞ오니즉속히판리ᄒᆞ라ᄒᆞ엿더라

○봉고 쥬본 젼라북도슌찰ᄉᆞ박제빈씨가 쥬본ᄒᆞ기를부안군슈쟝영익이는쇠잔ᄒᆞᆫ고을을리나는구멍으ᄉᆞᆷ고조코만빅셩을됴흔지물ᄀᆞᆺ치녁여뢰물이아니면민송을판결ᄒᆞ여쥬지아니ᄒᆞ고의례히돈을내지아니ᄒᆞ면리임을차졍치아니ᄒᆞ는고로위션봉고ᄒᆞ오니그죄샹은법부에령ᄒᆞ야죠률ᄒᆞ야감처ᄒᆞ게ᄒᆞ고장젼은일일히슈쇄ᄒᆞ여밧게ᄒᆞᆯ소로분부ᄒᆞ옵이엇더ᄒᆞ올는지요ᄒᆞ야 주ᄒᆞ엿는지라졍부와닉부에셔련명셔인ᄒᆞ야면관 쥬본을ᄒᆞ엿더라

○물시파병ᄉᆞ 단쳔이북에아병ᄉᆞ건으로졍부에셔는파병ᄒᆞ야격퇴ᄒᆞᆫ다더니그의안이곳쳐변ᄒᆞ야아국ᄉᆞ관이필시조하로ᄒᆞ는힝위니히군슈의계령ᄒᆞ야진력ᄒᆞ야담판ᄒᆞ야그불법힝위를긔어히금단ᄒᆞ는거시가ᄒᆞ다ᄒᆞ야함경남도관찰부로훈령ᄒᆞᆫ다더라

○면훈젼북 닉부에셔젼라북도관찰부로면훈ᄒᆞ기를금구군에지슈ᄒᆞᆫ김쥬ᄉᆞ진화를슌찰ᄉᆞ가람형ᄒᆞ야치ᄉᆞᄒᆞ엿다ᄒᆞ고청문이랑쟈ᄒᆞᆫ고로향쟈에면훈ᄒᆞ엿더니슌찰ᄉᆞ가답면ᄒᆞᆫ거를김가가인병치ᄉᆞᄒᆞ엿다ᄒᆞ니심히아혹ᄒᆞᆫ지라관찰부로셔별노사롬을보내여김민의치ᄉᆞᄒᆞᆫ위졀을별노담지ᄒᆞ야곳보고ᄒᆞ라ᄒᆞ엿더라

○폭발약슈입 덕국공ᄉᆞ가외부로죠회ᄒᆞ기를금광에소용ᄒᆞᆯ폭발약을졍ᄎᆞ슈입ᄒᆞᆯ터이니허관으로훈칙ᄒᆞ야달나ᄒᆞ엿더라

○젼죠관리시명 압록두만량강샹하삼림을군ᄉᆞ샹소용이라ᄒᆞ고일공ᄉᆞ가외부로죠회ᄒᆞ야인쥰ᄒᆞᆷ을쳥ᄒᆞ더니외부에셔ᄉᆞ계즁대ᄒᆞᆫ즉가히쳔편치못ᄒᆞ겟다ᄒᆞ야작일의졍부로젼죠ᄒᆞ기를이안건의인쥰여부를죵속히판리ᄒᆞ야곳시명ᄒᆞ라ᄒᆞ엿더라

○고미결졍 각쳐금광에작폐가대단ᄒᆞᆷ으로졍부에셔샹쥬ᄒᆞ고금광일관은모다혁파ᄒᆞᆫ다더니닉장원경셔리김영진씨가저극히반ᄃᆡᄒᆞ야금광ᄉᆞ로군슈가피히ᄒᆞᆫ직산군에금광을다시셜사ᄒᆞᆫ다더라

○고문리긔 외부고문관스틔분씨는일본공ᄉᆞ관츄원셔긔관과밋동부인과동반ᄒᆞ야이십륙일신호에셔[요와요]호를탑승ᄒᆞ고리한ᄒᆞᆯ뜻으로공면이잇더라

○훈령사보 강계진위뒤츌쥬병이진보회원이명을포살ᄒᆞ엿단말은이왕에긔지ᄒᆞ엿거니와현금히ᄉᆞ건을륙군법원에사힉ᄒᆞᆯ터인뒤히뒤에훈령ᄒᆞ야사실ᄒᆞ야보고ᄒᆞ라ᄒᆞᆫ즉츌쥬병이조하로쳐단ᄒᆞᆷ이아니오지휘관의명령으로포형ᄒᆞᆫ지라고로지휘관과평북관찰ᄉᆞ리용관씨를압샹ᄒᆞᆯ터이라더라

○타죠이익 닉장원소봉각둔토를년젼에는도죠로슈세ᄒᆞ더니금년에도죠관을파송ᄒᆞ야분반으로타죠ᄒᆞ야수만셕의리익을엇엇다더라

○곤란슈응 일본병참소에셔경셩으로브터평양ᄭᆞ지도로를슈축ᄒᆞ는뒤각군에공문ᄒᆞ야셔슈이십명식등뒤ᄒᆞ라ᄒᆞᆷ으로대단곤란즁이더라

○쳥관죠회 쳥공관에셔외부로죠회ᄒᆞ기를룡쳔황초평사실을일사로본대신이귀부죠회사의를졉쥰ᄒᆞ여우리동병도ᄃᆡ에젼죠ᄒᆞ야봉텬군독부에셔안동현에훈칙ᄒᆞ야귀부파원김샹학으로더브러셔로사실료감ᄒᆞᆫ란훈령을봉승ᄒᆞ엿스니쳥컨ᄃᆡ죠량ᄒᆞ라ᄒᆞ엿더라

○연산군슈보고 연산군슈가외부에보고ᄒᆞ기를본군셔면마구평일인송본구의가옥이십일간과작농ᄒᆞᆯ십오두락사로히면에셔보ᄂᆡ지가잇기에별반젹간ᄒᆞᆯ차로보낸즉파연보고ᄒᆞᆫ것과ᄀᆞᆺ혼지라외국인이닉디에집진는거시장뎡이아니라고셜명ᄒᆞ여도맛참닉듯지아니ᄒᆞ는지라본군슈의힘으로는검지ᄒᆞ기가심히어려기에이에치보ᄒᆞᆫ다ᄒᆞ엿더라

○쳥공사체임 쳥공사허틔신의셔임이만한된지라히임ᄒᆞ고경찬왕번역관즁광면씨가습임ᄒᆞ엿다더라

○덕사방외부 지작일샹오십일시에덕공사가외부를리방ᄒᆞ엿다더라

○확졍회국 일본에유력ᄒᆞ는리용익씨는인산젼에회국ᄒᆞ기로확졍ᄒᆞ엿더라

뎐보

론돈발 십이월삼일

○로함졉근 포엘거삼ᄲᆡ쟝의함ᄃᆡ가폐림을지니셔아덴을향ᄒᆞᆫ다더라

빅림발 동월ᄉᆞ일

덕국견ᄀᆡ 영국야로죠션쇼에셔제죠ᄒᆞᆫ로국슈뢰졍일쳑이십이월팔일에덕국불특운하를경과ᄒᆞᆯ시그때덕국관리에ᄃᆡᄒᆞ야말ᄒᆞ되그빈는ᄉᆞ쥬션키놀나인이라ᄒᆞ고또영국샹션긔를달고영국즁명셔로가졋는ᄃᆡ덕국관리가속앗다더라

동디발 동월오일

○미국히군 미국히군대신의년죵보고에말ᄒᆞ엿스되미국히군을확장ᄒᆞ야다른나라예셔감이법졉ᄒᆞᆯ무옴이못나게ᄒᆞ쟈ᄒᆞ엿더라

빅림발 동월ᄉᆞ일

○미국죵지 로국에셔공언ᄒᆞ되미국에셔제의ᄒᆞᆫ죵지죠약의대지는허락ᄒᆞ기됴죠와ᄒᆞᆫ다ᄒᆞ엿더라

동경발 십이월십이일

○문칙결의 졍우회와헌졍본당이합심ᄒᆞ야졍부의힝졍졍리의단힝ᄒᆞᆷ을쳥ᄒᆞ고대일빅삼십힝사건에대ᄒᆞ야무러척망ᄒᆞ기로결의ᄒᆞ엿다더라

동디발 동일

○함대즁지 불틱함ᄃᆡ는동으로힝션ᄒᆞᆷ을즁지ᄒᆞ엿다는ᄃᆡ이것은려슌함ᄃᆡ가다멸ᄒᆞᆫ고로일본졍부에셔법덕량국과강졍ᄒᆞᆫ교셥을ᄯᅡ결과라더라

관에온면보

홍룡둔의동편젼슈하자라는셔에로국보병이즁ᄃᆡ와긔병삼즁ᄃᆡ가침노ᄒᆞ야드러오거ᄂᆞᆯ일병이포격ᄒᆞ야물니쳣다더라

○면신화지 십이월십이일동디에온면보십이일포격에황금산줄기에잇는무선뎐신국에현저ᄒᆞᆫ손히가잇셧고또긔계국에화지가낫다ᄒᆞ엿더라

론돈발 십이월삼일

○로보연론 로국신문들은혹히합ᄃᆡ를우ᄒᆞ야다다넬쓰를ᄭᅵ방ᄒᆞ기를지축ᄒᆞ더라

동디발 동월오일

○로국닉요 로국에셔혁명운동이젼국에퍼진다더라

동디발 동월이일

○평화예산 론돈딜늬텔네그릭프신문의셩피득보통신원이확실이보고ᄒᆞ되로국외고가가후일에일본과화친ᄒᆞᆯ것을미리개량ᄒᆞ는뒤로국의국동졍칙에방히가업시ᄒᆞᆫ다ᄯᅥ라

론돈발 십이월오일

○로함지탄 폐림에잇ᄂᆞᆫ루터동신원의보고를거ᄒᆞᆫ즉로국히군대쟝표엘거삼씨의함ᄃᆡ가오복과지부릴사이에잇는무사도에셔탄쟝사의게셕탄을사셔실엇다ᄒᆞ엿더라

동디발 동일

○덕슈로탄 덕국륜션킵흰뉴젤호가셕탄을카듸프에셔실어셔로합에공급ᄒᆞ는징거가잇는고로영국외부에셔카듸프관리의게그덕국비가그항구에셔셕탄을실는거슬금ᄒᆞ라명령ᄒᆞ엿는뒤금령이나리기젼에그비에벌셔ᄉᆞ빅돈의셕탄을실엇는지라영국졍부에셔이사건을사실ᄒᆞᆫ다더라

동디발 동일

○덕우슈탄 카듸프에셔또다른덕국비ᄒᆞ나를셕탄실지못ᄒᆞ게금ᄒᆞ엿는ᄃᆡ그셕탄실는사롬은카듸프에잇는덕국명예령사각더라

빅림발

○로국쳥구 로국이구쥬각국에ᄃᆡᄒᆞ야흑히함ᄃᆡ롤위ᄒᆞ야다다넬쓰를ᄭᅵ방ᄒᆞ야달나ᄒᆞ는일노영법로각신문에언론이쟈쟈ᄒᆞᆫᄃᆡ구쥬각국졍부는아즉이문제에ᄃᆡᄒᆞ야의론이업는지라그러ᄒᆞ나각국공론이이문제는되기어려운것이로국에셔너무죠급히이문졔를쳥구ᄒᆞ엿다ᄒᆞ더라

TELEGRAMS.

(FROM JAPAN PAPERS.)

Berlin, Dec. 6.

A German commercial expedition under the leadership of Herr Rosen, a Privy Councillor, is going to Abyssinia. The expedition will depart on the 26th instant by the "Genoa" for Jibutil.

Hongkong, Dec. 8.

A private telegram received here today ordering certain arrangements to be made discloses the fact that the immediate objective of the Baltic Fleet is Formosa.

Berlin, Dec. 6.

Count von Buelow, the Imperial Chancellor, speaking in the Reichstag, strongly condemned the provocative tone adopted by the Socialist (in their condemnation of Russia) in regard to the Hull case, and repudiated the possibility of a conflict between Great Britain and Germany.

The Chancellor also announced that various reforms were contemplated in German Colonial policy, especially in regard to South-West Africa, where a Civil Governor and a local Government administrating its own finances would be sanctioned. The Colonial Office, added the Count, would also probably be reorganised.

Berlin, Dec. 6.

The Madrid journed "Liberal" announces that Japan's protest against the supply of coal and provisions to the Baltic Fleet at Vigo has been presented to the Spanish Government.

Berlin, Dec. 7.

The Krupp Works, out of its balance of the net profit of 11, 562, 762 mark, pays a dividend of 6 per cent.

Berlin, Dec. 7.

Prince Adalbert of Prussia, a son of the Kaiser, who is now serving in the German Fleet on the China station, has visited the King of Siam.

His Highness was accorded a very cordial reception, and on leaving was the recipient of valuable presents from his Majesty.

London, Dec. 7.

The French Senate has adopted the Anglo-French Convention by 215 votes to 37.

Berlin, Dec. 6.

The Moscow correspondent of the London "Standard" says it is reported that a division of Russian troops has been ordered to march on Afghanistan.

[The London "Standard," formerly a most trustworthy journal, has recently come into the hands of the proprietor of the "Daily Express," and is presumably run on the same senational lines.]

Berlin, Dec. 7.

Prince Albrecht of Prussia has paid a visit to the Pope. The visit, which was made merely an act of courtesy, was very brief, as the Pope was evidently suffering from a cold, his voice being hoarse.

A milder course, than the despatch of the three thousand Korean warriors, has been decided upon, in dealing with the Russians in the north-east. The governor of Hamheung has been instructed to interview the Russian officers in command and settle any difficulties there may be.

An investigation into the case of the Magistrate of Pyeng Yang has led the Government to believe that the amount of his "squeezes" from the people is upward of $400,000. They have instucted the Foreign Office to inform the Japanese Minister, who wished to keep him in Office, of this fact and state that under no consideration can he retain his post.

MISSION TO TIBET.

A telegram has been received from Peking stating that H.E. Tang Shao-Yi has recently received a hint from Prince Ching that he may not have to go to Tibet after all as the scene of negotiations will probably be transferred to London. It is quite possible that H. E. Wu Tiag-fang may go to London instead of H. E. Tang Shao-yi.

Peking, October 30.—The German Minister at Peking is reported to be most strongly opposed to the Anglo-Tibetan treaty. It is said that he warned the Chinese Minister for Foreign Affairs to the effect that if China consent to Article 9 of the Treaty, the other Powers would prefer dremands for equal Privileges. The French Representative is also reported to be opposing the treaty.

The influential Englishmen at Peking hold the view that Germany is not interested either in Tibet or in Manchuria. Consequently they insist that even if the German opposition gain the goodwill of Russia at the cost of provoking British resentment, it will prove highly disadvantageous to her. They state that the Chinese Court has no material influence over Tibet, but England listened as a matter of courtesy to the Chinese proposal and afforded China a chance to sign the treaty, so that if the Chinese Court refuse to entertain the British demand, it will naturally lead to the self-abnegation of China's claim for sovereignty. They understand that the proposed revision of the treaty will be impossible.

Peking, Oct. 30.—The report published about eight days ago, first by the "Tsung-Wei-Ji-Pao" and lately also by some English papers at Shanghai, according to which the United States, Germany and Italy have jointly protested against the Lhassa treaty, is a pure invention, spread apparently for the purpose of sowing mistrust against Germany with the Chinese. It is especially untrue that Baron Mumm, the German Minister at Peking, had made any threats at the Waiwupu with regard to this treaty, and that on his instigation France and Russia had also protested against the treaty. It is well-known that Germany has no political interest whatever in Tibetan affairs.—"Der Ostasiatische Lloyd."

PRESIDENT ROOSEVELT AND THE PEACE CONFERENCE.

SPEECH TO THE DELEGRATES OF THE INTER-PARLIMENTARY.

American papers to hand give particulars of the recent speech by President Roosevelt in which he announced that at an early date he would ask the nations of the world to join in a second cong ess at The Hague for the promotion of arbitration. The occasion for the announcement was the reception by the President of the delegates to the Inter-Parliamentary Union, which recently held a session at St. Louis. At that session the following resolution was unanimously adopted :—

Whereas, enlightened public opinion and the spirit of modern civilisation alike demand that controversies between nations be settled in the same manner as disputes between individuals are settled that is, by the judgment of courts in accordance with recognised principles of law ; therefore,

This congress requests that the several Governments send delegates to an international conference to the convened at a time and place to be agreed on by them, for the consideration of the following questions :—

First—Questions for the consideration of which the conference at The Hague expressed the wish that a future conference be called.

Second—The negotiation of arbitration treaties between the nations represented at the conference to be convened.

Third—The advisability of creating a congress of nations to convene periodically for the discussion of international questions.

And respectfully and cordially requests the President of the United States to invite all the nations to send representatives to such conference.

The delegates were received at the White House, where the resolution was formally presented to the President by Dr. Albert Gobat, of Switzerland, General Secretary of the Inter-Parliamentary Union.

President Roosevelt, in addressing the delegates, said:—

I greet you with profound pleasure as representatives in a special sense of the great international movement for peace and goodwill among the nations of the world. It is a matter of gratification to all Americans that we have had the honour of receiving you here as the nation's guests. You are men skilled in the practical work of government in your several countries, and this fact adds weight to your championship of the cause of international justice. I thank you for your kind allusions to what the Government of the United States has accomplished for the policies you have at heart, and I assure you that this Government's attitude will continue unchanged in reference thereto. We are even now taking steps to secure arbitration treaties with all other Governments which are willing to enter into them with us.

In response to your resolution I shall at an early date ask the other nations to join in a second Congress at the Hague. (Applause.) I feel, as I am sure you do, that our efforts should take the shape of pushing forward toward completion the work already begun at the Hague, and that whatever is now done should appear, not as something divergent therefrom, but as a continuance thereof. At the first conference at the Hague several questions were left unsettled, and it was expressly provided that there should be a second conference A reasonable time has elapsed, and I feel that your union has shown sound judgment in concluding that a second conference should now be called to carry some steps farther toward completing the work of the first. It would be visionary to expect too immediate success for the great cause you are championing, but very substantial progress can be made if we strive with resolution and good sense toward the goal of securing among the nations of the earth, as among the individuals of each nation, a just sense of responsibility in each toward others and a just recognition in each of the rights of others. The right and the responsibility must go hand in hand. Every effort must be unceasing both to secure in each nation full acknowledgement of the rights of others and to bring about in each nation an ever-growing sense of its own responsibility. At an early date I shall issue the call for the conference you request. I again greet you and bid you welcome in the name of the American people, and wish you God-speed in your efforts for the common good of mankind.

THE GERMAN ADMINISTRATION. OF KIAOCHAU.

The leased territory of Kiaochau is on an entirely different footing from the other German Protectorates, and is mainly a naval station for the German Squadron in the Far East. As Mr. J. B. Whitehead, Councillor to His Majesty's Embassy at Berlin, explains in his annual report on the German colonies, it consists of the harbour and town of Tsingtau and its environs, which are directly administered by the German authorities, and connected with which are certain treaty rights and privileges over the whole province of Shantung. The administration of Kiaochau is exercised by the German Admiralty, and not by the Colonial Department of the Foreign Office; and Herr von Liebert states that this has been a fortunate dispensation for the Protectorate, as the Admiralty does not show the diffidence in dealing with the Imperial Parliament which is characteristic of the Colonial Department. The result is that Kiaochau since its occupation cost the Imperial Treasury almost as much per annum as all the other German colonies taken together, but that on the other hand the advance made has been most striking. Kiaochau has in fact developed with surprising rapidity; the Shantung railway has now reached Tsinanfu, the capital of the Province of Shantung, and has tapped the productive coalfields in that neighbourhood, thus diverting the trade of the province from Chefoo to the German port. By the construction of breakwater, which is to be 1½ miles in length, when completed, an excellent inner harbour has been created, in which the largest vessels can lie alongside the quay and load directly from railway trucks; a whole quarter of European villas has been created, and two new Chinese towns have come into existence in its vicinity. On the outer beach a large hotel has been opened for the reception of summer residents from Hongkong, Chefoo, and Shanghai. In 1902-03 the trade of the port had increased by 100 per cent. as compared with that of the preceding year. The system of land tenure by which the township was to be insured has undergone considerable modification since it was first established in 1898. According to the original scheme land was sold by the Government on condition that the purchaser should within a given time construct buildings or otherwise make profitable use of the ground in a manner approved by the Government. If he failed to do so the land reverted to the State, the actual owner being returned one-half of the price paid by the first purchaser. In April, 1903, the General German laws regulating land tenure were introduced in the Protectorate, and consequently this system, which was not consonant with them, had to be abolished. In order, however, to prevent speculative purchases, and consequent waste of useful land, an arrangement was made by which a penaty, secured by a mortgage, was imposed on a purchaser who failed to build on or otherwise use the land bought. This again, was found inconvenient because it curtailed the purchaser's borrowing powers, and a new scheme has consequently been worked out according to which a purchaser of land shall within the time allowed for the construction of building or other utilisation of the ground pay 6 per cent. land tax, after that period 9 per cent, after three years or more 12 per cent., and so on till, a maximun of 24 per cent. is reached. As soon as the approved plan of utilisation has been executed the land tax will again fall to 6 per cent. This scheme has been accepted by the landowners, and seems to afford sufficient security against purchases merely intended as a speculation on rise in value. The Government continues to purchase land from Chinese owners without encountering difficulties. In the year under review about 484 acres were bought by the Government mostly for purposes of forestry and similar objects, the sales to Europeans for building purposes amounting to about 37 acres. When land originally purchased from Government is resold by the first or a later owner, one-third of any unearned increase in value is claimed by the State.

The Governor of Seoul reports to the Home Office that the Japanese military authorities nave demanded the repair of the roads through the village of Yang Chul Ni, Kwan Ki Hyun and Rwandoug, envirous of the city.

The Korea Daily News.

Issued at 5 P. M. daily except Sundays.

Rate of Subscription:—
Per Year............Yen 25.
Per Quarter..........Yen 7.
Per Month,..........Yen 2.50.

Postage in Korea not charged extra.
Postage abroad charged extra.

Advertisements. 50 sen per day for 1 inch or less.
5 yen per month per inch.
50 yen per year per inch.

All communications to
E. T. BETHELL,
Editor and Publisher,
Pak-toug, Seoul.

DISCIPLINE.

It cannot be expected that large bodies of soldiery can pass through a country without some discomfort and unpleasantness being inflicted upon the residents.

Here in Seoul we have had large numbers of men arrive, stop for a while, and pass on in quick succession, and a feature of their visits which has impressed everyone is the admirable discipline which has been maintained, reducing cases of rowdyism to a minimum.

Because of this we should prefer to say nothing of the few cases of friction which have arisen in Seoul, and we should say nothing did we not believe that a large proportion of these cases originate in the same way, and that when the attention of the military authorities has been drawn to it a recurrence will be provided against.

We refer to trespass. It is not to be expected that the soldiers at present billeted here, belonging as they do to the Reserves or Territorial Army will be so well disciplined as regular troops, but at least some steps can be taken to prevent them from invading private property.

We could cite several instances of wanton trespass where foreigners have been the victims, and the recent shameful attack on Mr. Gorschalki originated in the same way. Koreans are long-suffering people and not much given to complaining, but it is safe to assume that many of them have suffered from the same cause.

The fact that Mr. Gorschalki's house is directly opposite the former army headquarters, where a sentry always stands lends colour to the supposition that the soldiers believe they may commit these raids with impunity.

This is far from a pleasant state of affairs and we sincerely trust that now the attention of the authorities has been drawn to it we shall have no more of such cases to report.

Liquid fuel is so admirably suited to many purposes that some people appear to jump to the conclusion that it is adapted to every purpose to which coal is put. That its use may be very greatly extended cannot be doubted, because of many good points which it has; but when we consider, says Engineering, that the present annual output of oil-fuel in the world does not exceed 20,000,000 tons, while the world's production of coal is about 773,000,000 tons, it is at once clear that, unless vast supplies of oil are discovered, of which at present we know nothing, we need hardly expect that the use of oil fuel will materially affect the quantity of coal consumed.

The Magistrate of Tai Chon has been ordered to come up to Seoul to be tried for the shooting of two Chin Po Coi agitators. The Government have taken this step to quiet the Il Chin Hoi, who have been clamouring for this punishment.

THE BALTIC FLEET.

A Tokyo telegram which appears in the "Dai han Ilpo" says that, consequent upon the annihilation of the Port Arthur squadron, the Baltic squadron has abandoned its voyage to the Far East and that the Japanese Government has made strong representations to France and Germany on the subject.

What these representations can be we do not know. Does the Japanese Government expect France and Germany to insist on the Baltic fleet continuing?

On the whole we regard the message as a silly and groundless piece of sensationalism. In the first place, we do not believe in the story of the destruction of the Port Arthur fleet; some very considerable damage has doubtless been done but the minute reports of how many times the vessels have been hit and what condition they are in, are rather bewildering in view of the fact that most of the ships are invisible from 203 metre hill and of the others only the masts can be seen.

It must be remembered that the failure of the operations against the Erlungshan Sungsuhan and Kikwan shan forts has been a great disappointment to the Japanese and there is therefore at least a strong probability that we are being given a highly coloured version of successes in other directions.

BIG BATTLES AND RAINFALL.

The United States War and Navy Departments are close observers of events at the front, and among other points which attract their particular attention is, according to the "New York Tribune," that of the weather conditions accompanying the operations of the two forces. Official records show that almost every important action since gun, cannon, and morter have become factors in warfare was accompanied or followed by thunderstorms or heavy rainfalls. In fact, the continuous discharge of firearms and heavy ordnance is said to be the direct cause of this natural phenomenon.

In the last war between France and Germany the occurrence of storms of rain after battles was specially noticeable, and the accounts from the battlefields contained many allusions to the subject. An article in a German newspaper, dated Frankfort-on-the-Main, September 14, 1870, says: "Since the commencement of actual hostilities between Germany and France—that is, from about the first week in August to the present time—we have had in this part of Germany scarcely a day without rain, generally continuous, and often accompanied by thunderstorms. There is little doubt that the many storms and rains which we have had in Germany for the last six weeks—a most unusual thing at this season here—have been brought on by the cannonading and firing of small arms in Alsace and Lorraine." The same phenomenon has been observed in many parts of the world.

It is refreshing to hear that a place exists where the Chin Po Hoi microbe cannot live. The people of Hong Chon have proclaimed that they will kill the first man, who comes to their village discussing shaved heads.

His Majesty is reported by the "Kanjo Shimpo" to have recenty closely questioned the minister of war concerning the fortifications at Port Arthur and the possibilities of the Russian defence. General Yi gave a detailed report of operations and his opinion that the defenders could hold out for at least two months.

At the reception accorded the Il Chin Hoi by the Government a few days ago, Mr. Ho Wi the Vice President of State advised them to send back the deluded countrymen who had spent their little all to come up and join tne society, to their homes. When this was done, and a reasonable attitude adopted by the Il Chin Hoi, affairs of interest to the people in general might then be discussed.

CANTON-HANKOW RAILWAY.

The struggle for the control of this great railway is being carried on with unabated energy, writes the Canton correspondent of the "North China Daily News," and, we may add, unabated bitterness. The whole question is very mixed. It is now well-known that, because the American syndicate trembled for the stability of China, in the year of her uprising for liberty, 1900, the manager sold a large number of the shares to the Belgians. The financiers of China have now become alarmed, because they saw, and still see, and also fear, the influence of France and Russia behind the scenes. They have come to comprehend, moreover, that there is money in the concern, because the Canton-Fatshan branch pays well. They want to regain control and keep it in their own hands. They are, therefore, agitating, and affirming that because the Americans sold the shares without consultation with the Chinese, they, the former, have broken the agreement and therefore it is annulled. The whole question seems to be very complicated. Some Hunanese sent a bogus telegram to the Foreign Office, Peking, urging that the American syndicate be still retained, and that the transactions with the Belgians be allowed to stand. Whilst all this was being brought to light, the correspondence between Sheng or Shanghai, and Wu, the late Chinese Minister at Washington, has been published in the native papers here, as well, I believe, as in Shanghai. From the gist of these documents, it would appear that Sheng delayed his reply to the dispatch of the Chinese Minister for six months, although he was informed of what was going on, and it was his duty immediately to vote it. Such are some of the facts and statements concerning this complicated question, as they have appeared here in the native Press and are being discussed by the local Chamber of Commerce. A Canton paper does not hesitate to place Sheng in this dilemma. He knew the facts. By delaying his reply, he was either under the influence of the Belgians, or else he was culpably negligent. The editor indeed tells him that he played the part of Punch and Judy to attract the attention of others, whilst the control of the line was sold to those whom the Chinese distrusted. How far all this represents the actual truth, the man in the street, of course, cannot say. There must be something in it, seeing that the most sober, fair, and reliable of the Canton dailies publishes the information, and then ventures on such stinging criticism. Meanwhile it appears that the work on the main line has, for the time, been discontinued. The branch line is kept open and is apparently a paying concern. In all this we seem to see once more the Chinese vociferously shouting to close the stable door after the proverbial horse has left the building. It is, however, unfortunate that this important work has received a temporary check.

It is said that Yi Yong Ik will return to Korea in time to be present at the funeral of the Crown Princess.

In view of the revolution in field hospital methods which has marked the present war, the United States General Staff has decided to send surgeons as attaches to the Japanese and Russian armies, if the necessary permission from the belligerent Powers can be obtained.

H.M.S. "Aurora" arrived at Plymouth on November 2nd from Las Palmas. The "Aurora," which is a training ship for cadets belonging to H.M.S. "Britannia," was cleared for action, and had been so all the way home, as at Las Palmas it was stated that hostilities had broken out between Great Britain and Russia. Great excitement had prevailed on board, the searchlights being regularly worked at night, whilst all the guns were loaded and projectiles in position at the mouth of the ammunition hoists. The "Aurora steamed home at a speed of 14 knots, and on arrival at Plymouth the crew were surprised to hear there was no war.

The Korea Daily News.

VOL. I, THURSDAY, DECEMBER 15, 1904. No. 126

大韓每日申報
대한ᄆᆡ일신보

(뎨일빅이십칠호) (토요일) (일쳔구빅사년십이월십칠일)

사고빅

이신보는영어와한어로섞거ᄆᆡ일츌판ᄒᆞ옵

신문가

한쟝 엽두돈오푼

일삭됴 엽두량닷돈

우표가ᄆᆡ삭닷돈

다맛돈으로밧습

광고료는

긔한의쟝단과ᄌᆞ힝의다쇼로즁감ᄒᆞ되렴가로밧을터이오며오리지아녀대한사람마다다이신문을보실터이니광고내시기를원ᄒᆞ시는이들은우리신문샤에와셔면약ᄒᆞ심을희망ᄒᆞ옵

○발힝소 박동대한ᄆᆡ일신보샤법어학교압헤젼영국인셜필립집자리오

샤쟝 영국인 (비셜)

평양 ᄃᆡ리졈

○평양효동사는권미보씨로우리신문관ᄃᆡ리인을ᄐᆡᆨ졍ᄒᆞ엿ᄉᆞ오니평양에계신구람코져ᄒᆞ시는쳠군ᄌᆞ는희ᄃᆡ리졈에왕림ᄒᆞ와면의ᄒᆞ시옵

사고

○우리대한ᄆᆡ일신보의목뎍은대한의안녕질셔에관한모든뎨목에ᄃᆡᄒᆞ야는공평한변론을쥬쟝홈이라우리통신원의탐보는신문보시는쳠군ᄌᆞ의게ᄒᆞᆼ샹보도ᄒᆞ리며편지를긔셔ᄒᆞ여주시는이는셩명과반ᄃᆡ를젹어붓치시기를희망ᄒᆞ오니이거슬신문샹에긔지ᄒᆞ랴는거시아니오다만극히신용ᄒᆞ는증거를숨고쟈홈이라긔쟈는아모긔셔던지긔지홈을퇴각ᄒᆞ는권리를가졋스나퇴각ᄒᆞ는리유를말홀터이오며공즁평화를문란케ᄒᆞ는듯ᄒᆞᆫ긔셔는의례히밧지안켓습나이다

●본사셜시이리로신문을ᄆᆡ양우례로분젼ᄒᆞ와례젼부의임의로젼ᄒᆞᆫ듯스로먼곳에는혹늣게젼ᄒᆞ기도ᄒᆞ며혹몃칠거슬ᄒᆞᆫ겁에젼ᄒᆞ기도ᄒᆞ며혹아니젼ᄒᆞ는곳도잇다ᄒᆞ와우리신문을ᄉᆞ랑ᄒᆞ야구람ᄒᆞ시는쳠군ᄌᆞ의게ᄃᆡᄒᆞ야ᄆᆡ우미안ᄒᆞ옵기로지금은분젼인을두고ᄆᆡ일일즉이젼ᄒᆞ며아니젼ᄒᆞ거나늣게거나ᄒᆞᆫ폐가업도록ᄒᆞ랴ᄒᆞ오니혹아니젼ᄒᆞ거나혹늣게젼ᄒᆞ거나ᄒᆞᆫ일이잇스면본샤로통긔ᄒᆞ여쥬심을희망ᄒᆞ옵

관보

뎨삼쳔[illegible]호 광무팔년십이월십오일

셔임급사령

○셔훈일등ᄉᆞ팔괘쟝 일본국임시군용텰도감륙군쇼쟝 산근무량 ○셔훈삼등ᄉᆞ태극쟝 일본국임시텰도대ᄃᆡ쟝륙군공병즁좌 정샹일랑 일본국임시군용텰도감부기사쟝텰도기사 셕쳔셕ᄃᆡ ○셔훈삼등ᄉᆞ팔괘쟝 일본국임시군용텰도감부부원 륙군공병쇼좌 도변겸이 일본국임시군용텰도감부원 륙군공병쇼좌 셔원무ᄐᆡ랑 일본국임시군용텰도감부건축반쟝텰도기사 가등용 ○셔훈ᄉᆞ등ᄉᆞ팔괘쟝 일본국임시군용텰도감부경리과원륙군일등쥬계 흑소은태랑 ○셔훈오등ᄉᆞ팔괘쟝 일본국임시군용텰도감부부륙군삼등쥬계 슈도연일랑

이샹십이월십이일

○의원면본관 즁츄원의관 김병원 즁츄원의관 정의동 즁츄원의관 오병션 즁츄원의관 허일 즁츄원의관 최형건 즁츄원의관 리규협 즁츄원의관 김현ᄐᆡ

○임즁츄원의관셔쥬임관륙등 정삼품 최셕죠 정삼품 쟝긔원 정삼품 정창묵 륙품 리희샹 륙품 김영두 륙품 김연치 구품 허현

○급일급봉 탁지부인쇄국쟝 최셕죠

이샹십이월십이일

뎐보

론돈발 동일

○로함우발 젼의용함ᄃᆡ에부쇽ᄒᆞ엿던순양함니에페와슈뢰파괴함이쳑과운송션들노죠작ᄒᆞᆫ보브로스기대쟝의함ᄃᆡ가탱기어를ᄯᅥ나셔동으로향ᄒᆞ야온다더라

빅림발 동월륙일

○로함소식 지부틔에셔불란셔함ᄃᆡ가져의운송션으로브터식물을실엇다ᄒᆞ며숭피독보에셔공포ᄒᆞᆫ말을드른즉극동에보낼뎨삼볼틱함ᄃᆡ를죠직ᄒᆞ는ᄃᆡ젼두함칠쳑과순양함ᄉᆞ쳑과슈뢰정ᄉᆞ십쳑이라더라

동경발 동월십삼일

○학싱야료 로국셔울셩피득보에셔학생들이대회를열고젼제압제ᄒᆞ는폭정을힝ᄒᆞ는귀족정치를무너트리고일본과젼쟁을즁지홀일을챵론ᄒᆞ야대단히분란홈을이러켯다더라

론돈발 동월륙일

○로함샹격 로국히군부에셔북히ᄉᆞ건에ᄃᆡᄒᆞ야볼틱함ᄃᆡᄉᆞ령관로졔스트밴스기대쟝의속보를공포ᄒᆞ엿는ᄃᆡ그대쟝이북히ᄉᆞ건의이러날ᄯᅢ에포격ᄒᆞᆫ지십분후에곳정지ᄒᆞ라명령ᄒᆞᆫ것아그함ᄃᆡ의뒤에잇는비의놋는대포가쟈긔비에맛는ᄭᅡ닭이라그함ᄃᆡ즁에아로라는비에란환다섯이마져셔그비의셜교ᄉᆞ와아리ᄉᆞ관ᄒᆞ나이샹ᄒᆞ엿는ᄃᆡ그셜교ᄉᆞ는샹쳐로ᄒᆞ야탱기어에셔죽엇다ᄒᆞ엿더라

동디발 십이월륙일

○로함샹격과영국공론 로함이서로포격ᄒᆞ엿다는로졔스트밴스기대쟝의보고는말이피샹ᄒᆞ고져의비ᄭᅵ리셔로포격이되엿다는말이밋기어렵다고영국각신문에말ᄒᆞ엿더라

○뎨삼함ᄃᆡ허언 로국이극동에뎨삼함ᄃᆡ를파송ᄒᆞᆫ다는말은알슈업다ᄒᆞ엿더라

빅림발 동일

○로국매함 셩피득보면보를거ᄒᆞᆫ즉로국이륙쳔만루불을드리여남미칠리와아젠타인국으로브터군함들을놀샷는지라이군함들은볼틱함ᄃᆡ에부쇽홀터인ᄃᆡ이군함들을셩피독보에가져오기ᄭᆞ지는쳥국긔호를단다ᄒᆞ엿스니미샹ᄒᆞᆫ말이더라

론돈발 동월칠일

○다다넬쓰문제와영국 다다넬쓰를기방ᄒᆞ야달나는로국쳥구에ᄃᆡᄒᆞ야영국졍부에셔ᄃᆡ답ᄒᆞ되ᄉᆞ셰가어덧던지흑히함ᄃᆡ의다다넬산협의길을여러쥬기를허락지못ᄒᆞ겟다ᄒᆞ엿더라

동디발 동일

○로함속리 볼틱함ᄃᆡ에부쇽ᄒᆞᆫ순양함올넥과이숨루드가랭기어를지나셔스웻스로향ᄒᆞ는ᄃᆡ젼의용함ᄃᆡ에부쇽ᄒᆞ엿던슌양함리온과슈뢰파피함이쳑이동힝ᄒᆞᆫ다더라

외보

○영국류학생 영국졍부에셔는ᄌᆞ금이후로ᄆᆡ년사명식륙군ᄃᆡ위나혹즁위쇼위즁에셔연구류학싱을션정ᄒᆞ야일본에파견ᄒᆞ야류학ᄒᆞ게ᄒᆞᆫ다고십일월사일론돈발면에운ᄒᆞ엿더라

○영국황ᄐᆡᄌᆞ 영국황ᄐᆡᄌᆞ면하는본년즁에일본국에유람ᄒᆞ랴ᄒᆞ엿더니ᄯᅢ가맛참젼징이되여유예즁인ᄃᆡ평화극복이되면곳유람ᄒᆞᆫ다더라

○이ᄐᆡ리황족 일본에유람홀ᄎᆞ로군함리구모시아호를타고목하에히샹에셔체류ᄒᆞ는이ᄐᆡ리국황족아불지공작면하는국왕폐하의죵뎨요년셰는삼십이셰인ᄃᆡ북극을탐졍ᄒᆞ야검사홈으로유명ᄒᆞᆫ난센박사보담수년을먼쳠북극을탐졍검사ᄒᆞ야복위션필십륙도사십륙분되는곳ᄭᆞ지드러갓드라ᄒᆞ며동면하는이번에신호에샹륙ᄒᆞ야동으로향홀터이라더라

잡보

○졍부죠복 의졍부에셔외부에죠복ᄒᆞ기를귀부죠회너에일공사가면의ᄒᆞ기를평양젼군슈팽한쥬가일본군사샹에근로가잇다ᄒᆞ여일직이귀대신을향ᄒᆞ여공함ᄒᆞ고무손죄과로파면ᄒᆞᆫ다ᄒᆞ며엇지ᄒᆞ여면관ᄒᆞᆫ거슬시명ᄒᆞ라ᄒᆞ엿스니이죠회를인ᄒᆞ여곳회답ᄒᆞ야시명ᄒᆞ라ᄒᆞ엿기에히군민소를사실ᄒᆞᆫ즉임인년에가결를늑봉ᄒᆞ고셕고젼을잠식ᄒᆞ고향록원죠젼을잠식ᄒᆞ고역부삭젼즁ᄡᅥ러먹은거시합일빅사십여만량이오ᄯᅩ탐확홈이망유기극ᄒᆞᆫ고로이죠너부ᄒᆞ여위원을파송ᄒᆞ여사실ᄒᆞ라ᄒᆞ엿더니그사실ᄒᆞ여보고ᄒᆞᆫ너ᄀᆡ에비록가리고보호홈이만ᄒᆞ나그가결남즁ᄒᆞᆫ거시합십륙만이쳔일빅이십량이니이거시진젹ᄒᆞᆫ쟝물이라그죄과가시각이라도용ᄃᆡ치못ᄒᆞ겟기현금사법에붓쳐죠률즁판홀터이어늘비록군사샹에사소ᄒᆞᆫ근로가잇드ᄅᆡ도그엇지용셔홈을엇으리오이공문으로ᄡᅥ일사의게셩명홈이가ᄒᆞ다ᄒᆞ엿더라

UNION INSURANCE SOCIETY OF CANTON.

Head office Hongkong.
Marine risks underwritten at current rates.
Agents in Chemulpo,
E. MEYER & Co.

COMPAGNIE DES MESSAGERIES MARITIMES.

Fortnightly Direct Service.

For Marseilles
via Ports.
Sailing from Yokohama
Calling at Kobe,
Shanghai, Hongkong, Saigon, Singapore,
Colombo, Djibonti, Suez, Port Said
and Marseilles.

For particulars apply to
HOLME RINGER & Co.,
Chemulpo.

HAYASHIDA & CO.,

16 MYENG DONG, CHIN KO KAI, SEOUL.
BRANCH OFFICE AT CHEMULPO.

Money changers, Coal and Wood Merchants, Express Agents.

We are agents for the Pyeng-yang Coal Company and the Karatsu Coal Company of Japan. We have the best quality of both anthracite and bituminous coal, and prompt execution of orders is our speciality. Firewood of all kinds kept in stock. Full weight guaranteed. Money of all denominations exchanged at current rates. Parcels received for all parts.

CHINA MUTUAL LIFE INS. OC.

Most favourable terms to policy holders.

Benefit system unsurpassed.

HOLME RINGER & Co.
Agents, Chemulpo.

C. P. R.

CANADIAN PACIFIC RAILWAY COMPANY'S ROYAL MAIL STEAMSHIP LINE.

THE FAST ROUTE BETWEEN CHINA, JAPAN, AND EUROPE VIA CANADA AND THE UNITED STATES.

Route from Hongkong via Shanghai, Nagasaki (Inland Sea of Japan) Kobe, Yokohama Victoria and Vancouver.

Twin Screw Empress Steamship—6,000 Tons—Speed 19 knots.

PROPOSED SAILING FROM YOKOHAMA.
R. M. S. Empress of India.
R. M. S. Empress of Japan.
R. M. S. Empress of China.
R. M. S. Athenian.
R. M. S. Taatar.

Special reduction (first class only) granted to members of the Military, Naval, Diplomatic and Civil services and to Missionaries.

Passengers have choice of ten routes across the Continent of America and have privilege of travelling by any Atlantic Steamship Line.

Round the World passage tickets in connection with the P. and O. S. N., North German Lloyd and Messageries Co.'s **£125.**

All rates payable at current rate of exchange.

For further information, Tickets, Guide Books, etc., apply to

HOLME, RINGER & Co., AGENTS,
Chemulpo.

Grand Hotel,

(*Formerly the Station Hotel*)

Near the Railway Terminus, West Gate Seoul.

The Best Hotel in Korea.
Handsome new Building
Fine Airy Rooms
Excellent Cuisine.
Terms Moderate.
Special terms to Missionaries
and to permanent boarders.

Electric cars within 2 minutes' walk.

W. H. EMBERLEY.
Proprietor

EVERY FACILITY.

In connection with Life Assurance Business afforded by

The Standard Life Assurance Co.,

One of the largest and wealthiest of the Provident Institutions of the United Kingdom Forms of Application and all information will be promptly afforded on application.

10 CENTS A DAY.

Not a very large expenditure is it? But it is sufficient to secure for a man of 30 a policy with the STANDARD LIFE OFFICE for

$1323.

For all particulars of rates, etc., apply to

Holme, Ringer & Co.,
Agents, Chemulpo.

THE NEW YORK LIFE INSURANCE COMPANY.

Have you ever been declined by any Company?

Are you engaged in a specially hazardous occupation?

Have you heard of the New York Life Insurance Company's New Classifications for this class of Risks?

If not, send your date of birth, occupation and particulars of rejection, if any to

E. MEYER & Co.,
Agents, Chemulpo.

MITSUI BUSSAN KAISHA.
(MITSUI & Co.)

MITSUI GINKO.
(MITSUI BANK.)

The Bank is owned by the members of the Mitsui Family, who, as partners, assume an unlimited responsibility for all liabilities of the Bank:—

Capital.................... .....Yen 5,000,000
Reserve Fund...................." 5,600,000

HEAD OFFICE, TOKYO.

LONDON OFFICE, 34 LIME ST., E. C.

BRANCHES AND AGENCIES:—
New York, San Francisco, Hamburg. Bombay, Singapore, Manila, Hongkong, Amoy, Chefoo, Tientsin.

Kobe, Hakodate, Yokohama, Kure, Yokosuka, Moji, Shimonoseki, Miike, Wakamatsu, Nagasaki, Kuchinotsu, Karatsu, Sasebo, Misume, Taipeh, &c.

Telegraphic Address for all the Offices:
"MITSUI."

A. B. C. AND A. I CODES USED.

Contractors of Coal

To the Imperial Japanese Navy. Arsenals and Railway Bureau, Principal Railway Companies and Industrial Work, Home and Foreign Mail and Freight Steamers.

Sole Proprietors

Of the famous Miike, Tagawa and Yamano Coal Mines.

Sole Agents

For the sale of Fukumo, Hokoku, Ichimura, Kanoda, Mannoura, Onoura, Ostuji, Sonoda, Tsubaruro, Yoshinotani, Yoshio, Yurokibura and other coals.

YANGTSE INSURANCE ASSOCIATION, LTD.

The undersigned, having been appointed agents for the above company, are prepared to issue policies and pay losses on marine risks at regular rates.

E. MEYER & Co.,
Agents, Chemulpo.

AMERICAN KOREAN ELECTRIC CO.

Light and Power.

Main Office: Electric Building, Chong No.

RAILWAY DEPARTMENT.

OPERATING CARS BETWEEN EAST AND WEST GATE, EVERY TEN MINUTES:—

First Car leaves East Gate at 7:00 A. M. First Car leaves R. R. Station at 7:25 A. M
Last Car " East Gate at 9:40 P. M. Last " " R. R. Station at 10:05 P. M

OPERATING CARS BETWEEN EAST GATE AND IMPERIAL TOMB TERMINUS, EVERY TWENTY MINUTES:—

CONNECTING WITH EVERY ALTERNATE CAR ARRIVING AT EAST GATE FROM CHONG NO.

First Car leaves East Gate for Tomb at 7:10 A. M.
" " " Tomb for East Gate at 7:35 A. M.
Last " " East Gate for Tomb at 7:80 P. M.
" " " Tomb for East Gate at 8:10 P. M.

OPERATING CARS BETWEEN CHONG NO. AND YUNG SAN RIVER EVERY TWELVE MINUTES:—

First Car leaves Chong No for South Gate at 7:12 A. M.
" " " Chong No for Yung San at 7:36 A. M.
" " " South Gate for Chong No at 7:20 A. M.
" " " Yung San for Chong No at 8:09 A. M.
Last " " South Gate for Chong No 10:00 P. M.
" " " Yung San for Chong No at 9:33 P. M.

SPECIAL PRIVATE CARS FURNISHED TO SUIT CONVENIENCE OF PATRONS. PRICES ON APPLICATION AT HEAD OFFICE.

LIGHTING DEPARTMENT

Where less than 250 candle power of light is used, the rate per month will be
Per 16 candle power incandescent lamp,—All night.—Yen 2.50.
32 candle power incandescent lamp:—All night:—Yen 4.00.
50 candle power incandescent lamps—All night:—Yen 6.00.
150 " " " " " " " 10.00.
1200 " " enclosed arc " " " " 20.00.

Where more than 250 candle power of light is used, a Meter will be installed, freqvedted:—Rent of Meter Yen 2.00 per month. Rate of charges by meter reading:—Two Sen per Ampere per hour. (Approximately this is equal to about One Sen per 16 C. P. lamp per hour) Minimum monthly charge where meter is installed, Yen 20.00 per month, which includes rental of meter.

Estimates for installing lights furnished on application

An assortment of chandeliers always on hand.

K. Murakami.
Photograph Studio
Chinkokai, Seoul.

Printing, Developing and Enlargement, of Photographs always Undertaken.

Korean Views and Pictures Illustrating Native Customs always on Sale.

THE OSAKA SHOSEN KAISHA.

Boats frequently on the berth for Chinnampo.

REGULAR SAILINGS BETWEEN JAPAN AND KOREAN PORTS.

FUSAN AND KOBE VIA SHIMONOSEKI.

OSAKA VIA MOKPO, FUSAN, SHIMONOSEKI AND KOBE.

MOJI DIRECT.

OSAKA VIA KUNSAN, MASANPO, FUSAN, SHIMONOSEKI AND KOBE.

CHEMULPO KUNSAN LINE,
Every three days.

CHEMULPO CHINNAMPO LINE.
Every three days.

For Freight and passage and further particulars apply to

THE OSAKA SHOSEN KAISHA,
Chemulpo.

RONDON, PLAISANT & CO.

General Storekeepers and Merchants, Ships Contractors, Tobacconists, Commission and Forwarding Agents, Coal Merchants

IMPORTERS AND EXPORTERS

Seoul & Chemulpo.

W. D. WENTWORTH.

LANDING
AND
SHIPPING AGENT
AND
CUSTOMS BORDER.

12 OURA, NAGASAKI.

STEWARD & CO.

Chemulpo.

Shipchandlers and Storekeepers, Naval and Mercantile Contrrctors, Landing and Shipping Agents.

STEWARD'S HOTEL

Chemulpo.

Best accommodation in the port for travelers. Clean and well-aired rooms, good cuisine and prompt attendence, moderate tariff.

○기졍가궁 화쳔군사ᄂᆞᆫ 물장사가 권모의게 견실ᄒᆞᆫ 말은 작보에 긔지ᄒᆞ엿거니와 그 자초리유를 드른즉 당초에 샹납젼을 엇어 쌀을 사가지고 온거시 ᄃᆡ허무ᄒᆞ게 ᄡᅥ 잇긴지라 집에 도라갈슈도 업고 또 업부형시하라 만일 뷘손으로 드러가면 그 부모의 걱졍이 무셥고 또ᄒᆞᆫ 샹납젼을 감보ᄒᆞᆯ길이 업ᄂᆞᆫ지라 서울셔 아모버리라도 ᄒᆞ여 그 돈을 충납ᄒᆞ라 ᄒᆞᆫ다 ᄒᆞ니 참 가여운 일이오 또 그 권가의 힝위ᄂᆞᆫ 가히 증감ᄒᆞᆯ만ᄒᆞᆫ 일이라더라

○염쳔위원의견 근일관졔의졍소에셔 츅일회의ᄒᆞᄂᆞᆫᄃᆡ 위원 염쳔씨의 제츌ᄒᆞᆫ 의견이 좌와 ᄀᆞᆺᄒᆞ니

일 ᄂᆡ장원을 혁파ᄒᆞ야 탁지부에 부속ᄒᆞᆯ사

일 경위원을 폐지ᄒᆞ야 경무쳥에 합부ᄒᆞᆯ사

일 각쥬외공사를 소환ᄒᆞᆯ사이라더라

○션하심후하심 김포사ᄂᆞᆫ 사ᄅᆞᆷ 하나히 쌀 닷셤을 싯고 오다가 비에 불이 나미 이웃비를 부르며 인명을 구ᄒᆞ라 ᄒᆞ야 다른 비에을 나셔 비에 불을 잡은 후에 가본즉 쌀 닉셤은 타지 안코 ᄒᆞᆫ셤은 반이 나란지라 쌀임자가 그 반셤 탄 쌀은 션인을 주어 먹으라 ᄒᆞ고 닉셤만 싯고 와셔 지판소에 졍ᄒᆞ야 그 쌀 ᄒᆞᆫ셤을 밧아 달나고 ᄒᆞ야 그 션인은 지금 감옥셔에 갓쳣ᄂᆞᆫᄃᆡ 대단 억울ᄒᆞ다더라

○인장환취 원산항일본사령부에셔 문쳔군슈의게 죠회ᄒᆞ기를 고원군슈ᄂᆞᆫ 쥬경사령관의 인허가 내려오기 젼에ᄂᆞᆫ 부임치 못ᄒᆞᆯ터인즉 교구ᄒᆞᄂᆞᆫ 인장을 도로 쳐즈되 만일 도로 찻지 아니ᄒᆞ면 싱경와 남을 일면키 어려우리라 ᄒᆞᆫ지라 히군슈가 ᄂᆡ부로 젼치ᄒᆞ야 면보ᄒᆞ엿더라

○인부슈응 경셩병참사령관 목하츙신씨가 고양군슈의게 죠회ᄒᆞ기를 본군 숫돌고개에셔 그 아래 도로를 슈츅ᄒᆞᄂᆞᆫᄃᆡ 셕슈와 밋 인부를 공급ᄒᆞ라 ᄒᆞᆫ지라 셕슈ᄂᆞᆫ 본군에 본ᄅᆡ 업슨즉 인부만 의례히 슈응ᄒᆞ마 ᄒᆞ엿더라

○안셩지회 안셩군슈 리죵응씨가 ᄂᆡ보로 보고ᄒᆞ기를 본월 십삼일에 삭발ᄒᆞᆫ 쟈 빅여명이 슈원으로 좃차 본군에 ᄅᆡ도ᄒᆞ야 읍뎌에셔 일진회를 셜립ᄒᆞ고 총대위원 강슈셕 셔샹욱 량인이 군슈를 드러와 보고 지회장 장긔환의 통쳡을 젼ᄒᆞ되 일젼회 목뎍을 셩취ᄒᆞ기 젼에ᄂᆞᆫ 히산치 아니ᄒᆞ다 ᄒᆞ오니 엇지 죠쳐ᄒᆞ올넌지오 ᄒᆞ엿더라

○우쳥금광 덕국공사가 외부로 죠회ᄒᆞ기를 금셩당고ᄀᆡ 금광우 설시ᄒᆞᆫ지 다년에 손히가 불소ᄒᆞ니 히금광은 장찻 귀졍부에 부ᄒᆞᆯ터이오니 영국의 국량공사가 귀졍부에 금광을 쳥구ᄒᆞ야 엇은ᄃᆡ로 이젼례를 의지ᄒᆞ야 됴흔 금광ᄒᆞᆯ곳을 다시 인허ᄒᆞ라 ᄒᆞ엿더라

○일ᄉᆞ쳥구 여의 일본공사가 외부로 죠회ᄒᆞ야 창원군슈 권익샹은 텰도샹 사무에 방히ᄒᆞᆫ 거시 만흐니 면관ᄒᆞ고 그ᄃᆡ에ᄂᆞᆫ 윤ᄐᆡ홍으로 셔임ᄒᆞ라 ᄒᆞ엿ᄂᆞᆫᄃᆡ 거십사일 밤에 ᄂᆡ부에셔 주본ᄒᆞ야 권군슈ᄂᆞᆫ 허체ᄒᆞ고 윤ᄐᆡ홍씨로 셔임ᄒᆞ엿더라

○미국박람회 미국공관에셔 외부로 죠회ᄒᆞ기를 미국 루위쓰에셔 빅년에 일ᄎᆞ식ᄒᆞᄂᆞᆫ 박람회를 ᄅᆡ년 오월 일일에셔브터 동년 십월 오일ᄭᆞ지 ᄀᆡ회ᄒᆞ야 미동양거민의 활동ᄒᆞᄂᆞᆫ 의사가 잇ᄂᆞᆫ지라 히회사쟝의 쳥쳡이 ᄅᆡ도ᄒᆞ엿기로 이에 히쳥쳡을 송교ᄒᆞ고 죠회ᄒᆞ오니 귀졍부에셔도 파원ᄒᆞ야 참회케ᄒᆞ라 ᄒᆞ엿더라

○공진회장셔 거십오일하오 두시에 공진회에셔ᄂᆞᆫ 특별회를 ᄀᆡ셜ᄒᆞ엿ᄂᆞᆫᄃᆡ 슉쳥궁금ᄒᆞ고 시졍ᄀᆡ션을 실시ᄒᆞ야 궁중에 츌입ᄒᆞ며 요언망셜노 옹폐총명ᄒᆞᄂᆞᆫ 좌도군쟝 강홍대 김대진 무녀슈련 등 수십인을 문죄ᄒᆞ야 구축ᄒᆞ긔를 졍부에 권고ᄒᆞᄂᆞᆫ 쟝셔를 ᄡᅥ셔 총대위원 삼인을 파송ᄒᆞ야 신참졍의게 권고ᄒᆞ엿고 니쟝원에 독쇄관을 디방으로 파송ᄒᆞ야 민간에 협잡이 층생ᄒᆞ야 인민이 보존ᄒᆞ기 어려오민 독쇄관을 파견ᄒᆞᆫ 일에 ᄃᆡᄒᆞ야 질문ᄒᆞ며 또 곳 소환케ᄒᆞ라고 총대 삼인을 과송ᄒᆞ야 ᄂᆡ쟝원경 셔리 김영진씨의게 질문ᄒᆞ엿더라

○쳔셔이졍 쥬일공관에셔 외부로 일작일에 면보ᄒᆞ기를 황샹폐하의 쳔셔를 이믜 일본황뎨폐하ᄭᅴ 드렷다 ᄒᆞ엿더라

○셔긔싱도임 쥬미공관에셔 외부로 일작일에 면보ᄒᆞ기를 셔긔싱 홍죵무가 작십ᄉᆞ일에 본셔에 리착ᄒᆞ엿다 ᄒᆞ엿더라

○리씨학민 젼판셔 리졍노씨가 광쥬사ᄂᆞᆫ 윤광오씨의 젼답을 무리히 탈취ᄒᆞᄂᆞᆫ 고로 윤씨가 관찰부에 졍소ᄒᆞ엿더니 리씨가 관찰사와 부동ᄒᆞ야 윤씨를 착슈ᄒᆞ엿다 ᄒᆞ니 여차ᄒᆞᆫ 불법힝위가 지금도 만이 잇나보더라

○훈칙량군 외부에셔 룡쳔의쥬 량군슈의게 훈령ᄒᆞ되 귀군부근 황쵸평과 밋 제도 사실ᄒᆞᆯ소로 젼위원 김샹학이를 다시 파송ᄒᆞ야 쳥관으로 더브러 쟝ᄎᆞᆺ 회동ᄒᆞ야 심판ᄒᆞᆯ터인 고로 이에 훈령ᄒᆞ니 도착ᄒᆞ거든 곳 동변 일명과 셔긔 일명과 ᄉᆞ령 일명을 파송ᄒᆞ야 두호ᄒᆞᆯ이가 ᄒᆞ다 ᄒᆞ엿더라

●훈칙사감위원 위부에셔 황쵸평사감위원 김샹학의게 훈령ᄒᆞ되 황쵸평 사실ᄒᆞᆯᄉᆞ로 이믜 쳥공ᄉᆞ의게 죠회ᄒᆞ엿거니와 히공ᄉᆞ가 쳥국 동변도ᄃᆡ에 가ᄂᆞᆫ 바 공함을 보낸 고로 이에 훈령에 부치노니 히공문을 히도ᄃᆡ에 젼치케ᄒᆞ야 사실ᄒᆞᄂᆞᆫᄃᆡ 지졀이 나게ᄒᆞ지 말나 ᄒᆞ엿더라

○일ᄉᆞ예겸 쥬외각공ᄉᆞ를 쇼환ᄒᆞ쟈ᄂᆞᆫ 물론이 잇셔 명년도 예산에ᄂᆞᆫ 히경비를 편입지 아니ᄒᆞᆫ다 ᄒᆞᄂᆞᆫᄃᆡ 그ᄃᆡ신에ᄂᆞᆫ 각히국에 쥬차ᄒᆞᆫ 일공ᄉᆞ가 예겸ᄒᆞ기로 쟉졍이 된다더라

셜론

셔원사후작의 연셜과 또ᄒᆞᆫ 란리라

○일본에 헌졍당이라 ᄒᆞᄂᆞᆫ 거슨 동경안에 ᄒᆞᆫ 유력ᄒᆞᆫ 국회인ᄃᆡ 히회령수로 잇ᄂᆞᆫ 셔원사후작이 모든 회원들의게 ᄃᆡᄒᆞ야 죵ᄃᆡ 히리익될 사건을 연셜ᄒᆞ엿ᄂᆞᆫᄃᆡ 동씨의 담론ᄒᆞᆫ 본의인즉 경제ᄒᆞᆫ자ᄂᆞᆫ 목젹이 최긴ᄒᆞ야 말ᄒᆞᆷ인지라 젼쟁은 점점 묘연ᄒᆞ야 오래모양이니 군비지발ᄒᆞᆷ도 련속슈응ᄒᆞ야 랑ᄑᆡ가 되지 안토록 ᄒᆞ자ᄂᆞᆫ 뜻이며 또ᄒᆞᆫ 이ᄯᅢ를 닷ᄒᆞ야 젼지를 주의치 아니ᄒᆞ고 쌀수가 업ᄂᆞᆫ 거시 다만 ᄡᅡᄒᆞᆷ에만 열심으로 ᄒᆞ고 지졍에ᄂᆞᆫ 등한ᄒᆞ게 ᄒᆞᆫ다고 ᄒᆞ야 그 듯ᄂᆞᆫ 사ᄅᆞᆷ들로 ᄒᆞ여곰 일ᄭᆡ여 명심ᄒᆞ도록 ᄒᆞᆫ바이며 동씨가 이 연셜ᄒᆞᆯᄯᅢ에 또 말ᄒᆞ기를 우리나라의 주무ᄒᆞᄂᆞᆫ 관리들이 불가불 국무에 조심ᄒᆞ야 렬심으로 ᄒᆞ여야 ᄒᆞᆯ지라 나의 싱각ᄀᆞᆺ타여셔ᄂᆞᆫ 이 두가지ᄂᆞᆫ 거시 보기에ᄂᆞᆫ 필요치 아니ᄒᆞᆯ것 ᄀᆞᆺ트여 그러ᄒᆞ되 지졍관리ᄒᆞᆷ에 당ᄒᆞ야 졍부로셔 주의치 아니ᄒᆞᄂᆞᆫ 비 잇ᄂᆞ니 이ᄂᆞᆫ 한국에 황무지간ᄒᆞᆯ 권리도 요구ᄒᆞᆯ만ᄒᆞᆫ 일이며 또ᄒᆞᆫ 졍부자본으로ᄡᅥ 은힝도 가히 셜립ᄒᆞᆯ 일이라고 ᄒᆞ엿ᄂᆞᆫ지라 동씨가 자긔나라의 지졍을 불긴ᄒᆞᆫᄃᆡ 허비ᄒᆞᄂᆞᆫ 바로ᄡᅥ 연셜ᄒᆞᆷ애 ᄃᆡᄒᆞ야 한국황무지 요구ᄒᆞᆷ을 흔합ᄒᆞ야 말ᄒᆞ엿슨즉 이 일을 깁히 궁구ᄒᆞᆫ진ᄃᆡ 황무지를 요구ᄒᆞ야 리익되게 ᄒᆞᆷ은 고사ᄒᆞ고 근일에 한국에다 조흔 일본지물을 날로 허비ᄒᆞᆷ이 잇ᄂᆞ니 이ᄂᆞᆫ 다른 거시 아니라 소위 일본셔 ᄃᆡ여주ᄂᆞᆫ 일진회 경비ᄂᆞᆫ 중거도 ᄒᆞᆯ수 업시 자본을 드리ᄂᆞᆫ 란리거리를 만달야고 ᄒᆞᄂᆞᆫ 거시 일진회라 ᄒᆞᄂᆞᆫ 거시 싱기여 그 회원즁에 혹 무삼일에 진보가 되도록 ᄒᆞᆫ 사ᄅᆞᆷ이 잇ᄂᆞ뇨 다만 명예에만 유익지 안케 ᄒᆞᄂᆞᆫ도다 셜회된 이후로 공연히 션동ᄒᆞᄂᆞᆫ 자ㅣ 몃치 잇셔셔 일본사ᄅᆞᆷ의 뜻에만 합당ᄒᆞ게 ᄒᆞ며 또ᄒᆞᆫ 자긔들의게 미삭주ᄂᆞᆫ 바를 위ᄒᆞ야 장ᄎᆞ 나라를 파라먹게 되드ᄅᆡ도 마음에 깃부게 녁이며 뜻에 흡족ᄒᆞ게 아ᄂᆞᆫ지라 이희에 명예와 힝위의 조치못ᄒᆞᆷ으로ᄡᅥ 일본셔지 명예가 손샹이 되게 만ᄃᆞᆯ며 십일월 삼십일에 발간ᄒᆞᆫ 쳥국게이시트신문을 볼진ᄃᆡ 한국에 보조금ᄃᆡ여 죰을 방한지 아니ᄒᆞᄂᆞᆫ 거시 량이 치야니지라 쳥국에 잇ᄂᆞᆫ 의국회라 ᄒᆞᄂᆞᆫ 것도 역시 일본셔 쳥비를 ᄃᆡ여주어 상히와 쳥국ᄂᆡ지에다 도회쳐를 만ᄃᆞᆯ고 외국도 반ᄃᆡᄒᆞ며 져히나라 정부도 반ᄃᆡᄒᆞᆫ나ᄂᆞᆫ 사실은 괴왕에도 계지ᄒᆞ엿거니와 근일에ᄂᆞᆫ 더욱 강셩ᄒᆞ야 관찰사 왕지츈씨를 자살ᄒᆞ라고 ᄒᆞ며 모든 놀니온 일만 힝ᄒᆞᄂᆞᆫᄃᆡ 점점 갈사록 드를만ᄒᆞᆫ 일이 또ᄒᆞᆫ 불무ᄒᆞ겟다고 ᄒᆞ엿ᄂᆞᆫ지라 일본셔 이 두회를 유지ᄒᆞ게 ᄒᆞᆷ이 쟝차 위험ᄒᆞᆷ을 만ᄃᆞᆯ어 ᄒᆞᄂᆞᆫ 일인즉 우리ᄂᆞᆫ 쳥컨ᄃᆡ 일본정부에셔ᄂᆞᆫ 지물을 당연히 쌀만ᄒᆞᆫ 곳에나 ᄡᅥ셔 국지가 되게 ᄒᆞ엿스면 조흘듯ᄒᆞ도다

뎐보

[십오일공ᄉᆞ관착뎐]

일본히군포ᄃᆡ지휘관의 보고가 여좌ᄒᆞ더라

○호미포격 히군포ᄃᆡ가 십이월 십삼일노 호미괴국 어뢰영과 그 부근에 미인비을 포격ᄒᆞ야 어뢰영은 화지를 이르켜 약 일시간을 연소ᄒᆞ고 또 비에도 대포 여섯발이 맛고 또 잠역션 삼척을 과괴ᄒᆞ고 기타 일척은 화지를 이르켜 침몰ᄒᆞ고 건축물에 ᄃᆡᄒᆞ야 포격ᄒᆞᆫ 것도 큰 손히를 쥬엇고 또 세바슈도보리호에 향ᄒᆞ엿고 또 셰바슈도보리호에 향ᄒᆞ야 간접사격을 힝ᄒᆞ엿ᄂᆞᆫᄃᆡ 뎐괴불량ᄒᆞ야 충분과측키 어려음으로 즁지ᄒᆞ엿더라

광고

덕국아세아은힝
본졈은 덕국빅림에 잇고 향항지졈은 샹히등지에 잇소
인천셰창양힝ᄃᆡ리졈

차터드은힝
자본금총액은 이천오빅만원
본졈은 영국론돈에 잇고 지졈은 각ᄃᆡ도회처에 잇소
인천셰창양힝ᄃᆡ리졈

뎨일은힝[뎨일국립은힝]
본뎜은 일본동경에 잇고
ᄌᆞ본금총익 륙빅이십오만원
리식은 ᄆᆡ빅원에 삼젼오리에셔 륙젼오리ᄭᆞ지인테
뎡긔훈ᄃᆡ로 계산홈
경셩뎨일은힝지졈쟝 면죵

향항샹히은힝
조원금총익 숨천륙빅오십만원
본졈은 향항에 잇고
지졈은 쳥국 일본 기타 각국ᄃᆡ쳐에 잇소
인천셰창양힝ᄃᆡ리졈

TELEGRAMS.

Japanese Legation.

A report from the officer commanding the naval brigade at Port Arthur states that on the 13th inst, the cannonade was principally directed on the fish torpedo arsenal at Tiger's Tail and the ships anchored in the vicinity. The arsenal was set on fire, the conflagration lasting two hours. One ship was struck six times, three transports were sunk and another ship was set on fire and sank. The several buildings were also damaged. The Sevastopol was subjected to high angle fire, but as the weather was stormy and it was impossible to see clearly firing was soon suspended.

[The distance from 203 metre hill, behind which are situated the Japanese batteries, is 8,500 metres.—[Ed. K. D.N.]

Army Headquarters.

Admiral Togo sends the following reports of torpedo attacks made on the Sevastopol.

On the 12th inst, the squadron commanded by Captain Kasama attacked the Russian vessel, but without result. Later Captain Masada's squadron under a fire from the enemy, which however took no effect, discharged several torpedoes but nothing was accomplished and the next morning the ship was observed to be anchored in the same place. On the 13th inst. Captain Arakawa's flotilla fired on the shipping but without inflicting much damage; one vessel's funnel was carried away and another's engines were temporarily disabled. At 4 P. M. Captain Andashi's flotilla attacked but were forced to retreat owing to the heavy fire of the enemy; two of his vessels were hit and three men killed.

(FROM JAPAN PAPERS.)

London, Dec, 8, 5:55 P. M.

The warships of the Baltic Squadron are still taking in coal and provisions at Jibutil. Some of the supplementary vessels are at Malaga.

London, Dec. 8, 5:55 P. M.

General Gripenberg has arrived at Mukden.

London, Dec. 8, 5:55 P. M.

It is reported from St. Petersburg that the Czar has ordered the formation of another squadron for the Far East.

Berlin, Dec. 8.

The Czar issued an Imperial Decree on the 7th, directing the formation of a third naval squadron for despatch to the Far East.—"Mainichi."

London, Dec. 8, 5:50 P. M.

The persons implicated in the navigation of the Russian torpedo boat to Liban under the pretext that it was a yacht are absent on the Continent.

The following telegram has been received by the Tokyo Foreign Department:—

The British Government is now making an investigation concerning the Yarrow Company's proceedings. A representative of the firm is said to have stated that the vessel was sold to a French merchant without any idea that it would be delivered to the Russians. But the Frenchman sold it to Russia and it was sent to Libau for the purpose of being used as a torpedo destroyer.

Berlin, December 8.

The German steamer Captain W. Menzell, which was stopped from coaling at Cardiff, has been ordered by the owners to return to Hamburg. The coal question will not cause any trouble between Britain and Germany, neither will it cause any diplomatic difficulty, the German Government being unwilling to allow any serious international crisis to arise through the action of private firms.—"Mainichi."

Berlin, Dec. 8.

The Morning Post states that several Cardiff merchants have hired colliers with a view to sending coal to chinese ports for Japan.—"Mainichi."

By some new and mysterious arrangement now in force any Chinese apparently living in his native land, who sends his name to Japan and pays a small fee, can become a Japanese subject and obtain effective registation at the nearest consulate. It will be well for the other powers and the Chinese authorities to enquire into the meaning of this extraordinary procedure which rests we believe upon a very transparent trick of impersonation in Japan by Chinese kept for that purpose.—China Gazette.

THE JAPANNING OF KOREA.

From an exchange we learn that it is notable that in the Seoul-Fusan Railway, the traffic of which will be officially opened on January 1st, the trains from Seoul to Fusan are called the up-trains and those from Fusan to Seoul down-trains, as Tokyo is regarded as the centre. The passenger and freight fares are all to be received in Japanese currency. The topographical nomenclature is to be all in the Japanese style.

It was also notable that about one month ago the authorities of the Seoul-Chemulpo Railway elected to adopt Japan time, despatching their trains some 35 minutes earlier than had been previously the case. No notice of this change had been given to foreigners with the result that several intending passengers were subjected to considerable inconvenience.

ALFRED AUSTEN'S LATEST.

We are ashamed to say that the British Poet Laureate is responsible for the following.

NEMESIS.

(LONDON STANDARD.)

Still moving onward, onward, onward,
wave after wave before,
Living breaker battalions rolling to
War's insatiate shore:
Forward, backward, forming, re-forming, ever-replenished tide,
Wending they know not whither, to die
as their fathers died;
To wailing mother and weeping maid
leaving famishing homes afar,
Voiceless, sleepless, lifeless, graveless,
doing the Will of the Tsar.

II.

For, sloughing the garment of graceful
Peace, and winged with the scales of
War.
And grating, on thoughts and things
that were, the things and the thoughts
that are,
An Island People who swarm over sea
to undo a triple wrong.
Than the dauntlessly brave yet dauntless more, than colossal strength more
strong.
Scale passes and peaks, and storm the
cliffs, that only the thunders know,
Till the granite Muscovite rank are
shattered, and scattered like drifting
snow.

III.

And the strong young Child of a yet
young Sire keeps watch, but with war-flag furled,
And British sentinels motionless stand
at the fortress gates of the world;
And the raveuing sloth slinks snow-ward more, with the fact of Fate on
its heel,
While Nemesis nears fraud-pilfered
Port narrowing knots of steel,
And still up in Heaven reigns Right
Divine still wields the sceptre and rod,
And worshippers throng to Buddhist
shrines, praising the will of God.

A gentleman Kuk In Ku belonging to the Il Chin Hoi fraternity, died a few days ago and on his death-bed implored his friends to hold a feast at his grave on the day when the society will be successful.

THE FRENCH GREAT SEAL.

It has been discovered, somewhat late in the day, that the Third Republic has no Great Seal of its own, and an artist has been commissioned to design one. There are, however, six Great Seals of one sort or another in the museum of the French Foreign Office, representing not only the previous republics but also the regimes of the Bourbons and the Bonapartes. The most interesting is that of Napoleon I, which is mutilated. The mutilation was effected with a chisel by order of Louis XVIII., who feared lest it should be stolen and treacherously used against him. His own seal bore the date 1795—the year of the death of his nephew, Louis XVII., in the Temple. One of Danton's services to the Republic was to give instructions for the designing of a seal. The idea which he communicated to the artist was "a Hercules knocking down a King." This design, however' though approved by a committee, was never executed.

The campaign of the Il-Chin-hoi goes on apace. The "Dai Han Ilpo" and "Kanjo Shinpo" both write editorially lauding the doings of the infamous Society.

The French demands in connection with acquiring Luchow, or its vicinity, as a concession, is becoming more urgent, to which effect the Viceroy of Canton has informed the Wai Wu Pu by wire. The later replied, giving instructions to lodge a protest and to vindicate China's rights, but hitherto there has been no fruitful result.—Ex.

At a Reform Committee meeting held yesterday, Mr. Shiogawa a Japanese member, proposed the following clauses.

1. The abolishment of the Household Bureau, its affairs to be connected by the finance Department.
2. The junction of the special police with the general Police Department.
3. The recall of all Ministers abroad.

A foreign war correspondent writes, no description of the Japanese soldier would be just which failed to mention his courtesy and his honesty. Living in the midst of the army, displaying many luxuries which must be tempting to soldiers kept on a most economical basis, the correspondents leave their effects about the camps without fear for the safety of them. Nothing is stolen, not even tobacco or food. The same thing could hardly be said of other soldiers.

About two years ago a discussion arose concerning the site of the Queen's tomb, when it was decided to remove the coffin and inter it in a more suitable spot. This was never carried out, but nevertheless a sum varying from 20 cents to 8 dollars, according to the status of the person, was collected from householders in Seoul towards the cost of the removal. Now that a like sum is being levied for the funeral of the Crown Princess, enquiries are being made as to the disposal of the money previously collected. General Yi Chong Keun was in charge of the obsequies on the first occasion.

The Korea Daily News.

Issued at 5 P. M. daily except Sundays.
Rate of Subscription:—
Per Year............Yen 25.
Per Quarter..........Yen 7.
Per Month...........Yen 2.50.

Postage in Korea not charged extra.
Postage abroad charged extra.

Advertisements, 50 sen per day for 1 inch or less.
5 yen per month per inch.
50 yen per year per inch.

All communications to
E. T. BETHELL,
Editor and Publisher,
Pak-tong, Seoul.

DISSENTION IN THE JAPANESE DIET.

That Japan is by no means of one opinion regarding this war is evident from the following report from the Kobe Herald of the 8th inst. Further, the fact that the Government answers to the principal questions were given behind closed doors is far from reassuring.

The Budget Committee of the House of Representatives met at 10:30 A. M. yesterday. The Premier (Count Katsura) and all the other Ministers were present. Mr. Kurihara, Chairman of the Committee, declared the meeting open, and Mr. Shigeoka Kungoro then made a speech in which he complained of the difficulty of obtaining explanations as to the Budget from the Ministers. "When we ask questions about the Budget," he declared, "all the Ministers seek to evade answering by pronouncing the word 'war.' The Ministers of the War and Naval Departments insisted upon making their statements with closed doors, but all they had to say was that war is expensive and that the Government is not permiting any waste of money. The Foreign Minister adopts the same attitude." No reply was accorded to this speech, and it was followed by a long discourse by Mr. Oishi, a prominent member of the Progressive party, who criticised the policy of the Government in regard to foreign countries. In the course of his observations he spoke as follows:—

"As to the measures taken by France and Germany in connection with the Baltic Squadron, what protest have you (the Japanese authorities) made? If satisfactory replies are received what steps are you going to take? What is the attitude of Great Britain, which is our only ally at the present juncture? With regard to Korea, you have succeeded in making an agreement and have sent two Advisers, but what advantages have you secured by these steps? In our opinion the measures taken are no better than matters of form. Even the Japanese Minister at Seoul is extremely inactive. As for Manchuria, why do you prohibit the entrance into that country of any Japanese with the exception of those who are connected with the Army? It is true that Manchuria is the seat of war, but that is not a sufficient explanation. The Chinese Government is said to be applying to the Powers for assistance in regaining Manchuria, quite regardless of the fact that we are now fighting for their cause. What steps are you going to take to enable us to hold our own?" Baron Komura then replied to the above criticisms, but insisted upon doing so with closed doors. His explanations are stated to have been only partially satisfactory to the Opposition.

The Committee resumed its proceedings in the afternoon, when Count Katsura, the Premier, spoke as follows:—

"As several questions have been put concerning the reduction of administrative expenditure, I feel I am under an obligation to say a few words. Since I became Prime Minister, I have heard much about this matter and I have been paying much attention to it, the result of which you can clearly see in the present Budget. We have curtailed all branches of expenditure as much as possible and we will continue this policy in the future. But it must be remembered that, although Japan is now carrying on a great war, she cannot neglect her home administration, which also requires money. If you consider the matter from our point of view you will readily see that we are effecting all possible economies." Baron Sone, the Financial Minister, then delivered a lengthy speech in explanation of the advance of Y6,000,000 to the 130th Bank, the gist of which was that the Government was obliged to go ot the rescue of the Bank in order to prevent a great commercial disaster, and if they had not taken this action eight other Banks would have failed. Mr. Sakurai asked the Minister to explain why the Government directed the Yokohama Speice Bank to lend Y1,000,000 to the 130th Bank.—Mr. Sakaya, Vice Financial Minister, said they had to prevent the Bank from becoming bankrupt in view of the flotation of the Japan loan in London, Mr. Matsumoto Kumpei asked the Minister why there is so great a difference in value between the Russian and Japanese Stocks in London, the former standing at above £90. The Minister asked for the room to be cleared of the public and then gave what is stated to have been a full explanation on this subject. The Committee adjourned at 4 in the afternoon.

JAPANESE REFUGEES FROM SIBERIA.

Amongst the arrivals in port says the "China Overland Mail" of Hongkong, on Dec. 2 was the German steamer "Willehad," which has been chartered by the Japanese Government to convey Japanese refugees from Bremen to their homes in Japan. The steamer on arrival took up a berth in sight of Blake Pier, and it was at once seen that her decks were lined with passengers, there being no less than 853 on board, mostly men, but also including women and children. The refugee are mostly from Siberia and have been waiting ever since the war broke out for transportation, but owing to the pressure on the ships chartered by the Japanese Government this was the opportunity that presented itself of bringing them home after they had been transported from Russia to Germany.

They all look well and happy and express themselves as being delighted to be on their way home again. The men evinced the keenest interest in the progress of the war but are quite out of touch with recent events. They nearly all have adopted the European style of dress, but notwithstanding this very few of them understood any English while some spoke German and others Russian.

Amongst the refugees are 58 men who have been engaged as merchants while resident in Russia, and they are travelling as cabin passengers but the remainder are not of the moneyed class and for their accommodation practically the whole of their vessel has been fitted up as one class.

The voyage across from Bremen was a pleasant one, the weather being calm until a few days before Hongkong was reached when the monsoon was encountered and made the sea somewhat rough, but this did not greatly trouble the refugese, who, for the most part, proved themselves to be good sailors. Port Said and Singapore were the only ports of call.

On November 3 a very pleasant ceremony took place on board to celebrate the anniversary of the Emperor of Japan's birthday, and an excellent dinner was served on board in honour of the occasion for which a unique menu in German and Japanese was made out. All of the passengers held high carnival during the day and were joined in the evening by the officers of the ship in drinking the health of their Emperor.

After a short stay in port, to take in provisions and other stores, the "Willehad" proceeds to Nagasaki, Yokohama and other Japanese ports.

We have received from Messrs. Rondon plaisant Co. samples of "Biscuits Pernot." Enticing in appearance these biscuits are the most delicious we have ever tasted and we can most heartily recommend them as adjuncts to dessert or afternoon tea.

The biscuits are nicely packed in useful air-tight boxes.

The Japanese Military authorities have requested the services of 20 men, from each district between Seoul and Pyeng Yang, to assist in repairs on the road.

Yuan Taotai's second son and his wife are going to travel and study in England. They were offered free tuition and enterainment in Japan but declined the kind offer.

H.E. Tuan Fang, Governor of Soochow, has raised a large sum of money for educational purposes and is about to send some 100 students to study in Europe and America. It is worthy of note that this enlightened Manchu official does not select the cheaper and nearer Japanese as the scene of his young proteges' studies.

A Peking dispatch reports that the Grand Council received recently a long telegram from Lu Yuan-ting, Governor of Hunan, to the effect that he has discovered a conspiracy amongst the students of the newly-established Provincial College of Hunan, at Changsha, whose object is to overturn the Manchu dynasty, and that the students arrested have also confessed the names of certain Chinese students now studying in Japan, as fellow-conspirators. In reply to the Governor of Hunan's telegram, the Empress Dowager issued a Rescript commanding the summary execution of two of the chief conspirators and releasing the others who had been arrested.

One of the most comical results of a printer's error which has been reported for some time is recorded in the British Medical Journal—"In Section I, (Physiology) of the British Association, a paper by Doctor Adamkiewiez with the title 'Ist der Krebs erblich?'—that is, 'Is Cancer Hereditary?'—was on the programme. 'Erblich' was misprinted 'erdlich,' meaning earthly, and the Times announced that a paper had been read by Doctor Admkiewiz on 'Is the Crab a Sea or Land Animal?'"

Polish papers have made an estimate of the officers of Polish birth who have fallen in the war, and declare that no fewer than 110 Roman Catholic Poles were killed at Liaoyang of whom forty-five were of the rank of Captain or higher. Among the number were two Major-Generals. It is also noted that Poles of the highest distinction are taking an active part in the most dangerous operations, such as the carrying of despatches to and from Port Arthur by Prince Radziwill. Another member of the highest Polish aristocracy, allied with the Imperial House of Austria, Count Wielopolski, is also serving as an officer in a Cossack regiment at the front. The papers contrast the activity of Polish nobles with the scarcity of great Russian names among the officers at the front.

The Korea Daily News.

VOL. I, FRIDAY, DECEMBER 16, 1904. No. 127

大韓每日申報

대한미일신보

(뎨일빅이십팔호)　　(일요일)　　일쳔구빅사년십이월십구일

사고 빅

이 신보는 영어와 한어로 셔계뎨
일출판ᄒᆞᆷ

신문갑

한장　엽두돈오푼
일삭료　엽두팔돈

우표가되 사다돈
다섯돈으로밧슴

광고료는
귀한의 쟝단과 ᄌᆞ흥의 다쇼로 종
감ᄒᆞ되 렴가로 밧을터이오며 오
리지 아녀 대한사람마다 다 이 신
문을 보실터이니 광고내시기를
원ᄒᆞ시ᄂᆞᆫ이ᄂᆞᆫ 우리 신문사에
와서 면약ᄒᆞ심을 희망ᄒᆞᆷ
○발형소　남동대하뎐일신보
사별이학교 양회 전영국인셜필
평경자리오

사장 영국인 (비셜)

평양　티리졈

○평양효동사는 권미보씨로 우
리신문판미티리인을 퇴졍ᄒᆞ엿
사소오니평양에계신구람코져ᄒᆞ
시는　쳠군ᄌᆞ논칭티리졈에왕
림ᄒᆞ와면의ᄒᆞ시옵

사고

○우리대한미일신보의본뎐은
대한의인명쟈셔에관한모든뎨
목에티ᄒᆞ야논공평한번론을쥬
쟝ᄒᆞᆷ이라우리동신ᄒᆞᆫ의탐보논
신문보시논쳠군ᄌᆞ의게ᄒᆞ상보
도ᄒᆞ리며펵지들귀셔ᄒᆞ며주시
논이논셩명과번디를ᄌᆡ여녹치
시기들희망ᄒᆞ오니이귀승신문
샹에긔지ᄒᆞ관논지시아니오다
만국희신용ᄒᆞ논ᄌᆞ기들숨고자
ᄒᆞᆷ이라귀자논아모귀셔던지과
지ᄒᆞᆷ을되ᄌᆞᄒᆞ논귀리들가졋스
나되쟈ᄒᆞ논리유들말ᄒᆞᆯ터이오
며공쥥평화들문란케ᄒᆞ논듯ᄒᆞᆫ
귀셔논의례히밧지안켓슴나이
다
●본사셜시이리로신문을미당
우레두분젼ᄒᆞ와레젼두의일의
로젼ᄒᆞᆫ곳스도머곳에논ᄒᆞᆨ눗지
젼ᄒᆞ기도ᄒᆞ며ᄒᆞ먹칠거슬ᄒᆞᆫ법
에젼ᄒᆞ기도ᄒᆞ며ᄒᆞ아나젼ᄒᆞ논
곳도잇더ᄒᆞ와우리신문을수랑
ᄒᆞ야구람ᄒᆞ시논　쳠군ᄌᆞ의게
티ᄒᆞ야미두마안ᄒᆞ옵기로지금
은본젼인을두교미일일숨이젼
ᄒᆞ며아니젼ᄒᆞ거나늣게거나ᄒᆞᆫ
폐가엽도록ᄒᆞ라ᄒᆞ오니ᄎᆞ아니

젼ᄒᆞ거나ᄒᆞᆨ늣게젼ᄒᆞ거나ᄒᆞᆫ일
이잇스면본사로통귀ᄒᆞ며쥬심
을희망ᄒᆞ옵

관보

뎨삼쳔삼일호
광무팔년십이월십륙일

서임급ᄉᆞ령

○의원면본관　쟝례원우쟝례
조진셜　ᄒᆞᆷ문관서독　박영대
효릉참봉　ᄒᆞᆷ수쳘
○희시종원분서어　구픔　구
연티
○임쟝례원우쟝례서주임관륙
등　ᄒᆞᆷ문관시독　리범셜
○임ᄒᆞᆷ문관시독서주임관오등
종삼픔　유면호
○임ᄒᆞᆷ문관시독서주임관ᄉᆞ등
규쟝각직각　리외국
임규쟝각서주임관ᄉᆞ등　륙
픔　서상훈
○임효릉참봉서판임관팔등
쟝릉참봉　김병진
○임쟝릉참봉서판임관팔등
희릉참봉　윤즁구
○임희릉참봉서판임관팔등
구픔　ᄒᆞᆷ수쳘
○명시종원분서어　구셜화
○조종이픔가션대부너부협판
리학성　윤덕션
○증졍삼픔통졍대부비서원승
고성군　진수윤쳘호
○증종삼픔통훈대부쟝례원좌
쟝례　고성군진ᄉᆞ　윤극경
이상종이픔가션대부너장원
경　윤필구의고조고증조고
의ᄇᆞᆯ면추증

상ᄉᆞ십이월십ᄉᆞ일
○궁너부대신임시서리너부대
신통군부쟝리용티근　주ᄒᆞ되
곳엽티여비서원승관영슈의보
고를보온즉　영릉참고유제대
축문태도원문서과쟝김남졍이
가모든집ᄉᆞ적찬ᄒᆞᆯ때에진즉티
령취아니ᄒᆞ교추후　향ᄉᆞᄒᆞᆯ세
에진참ᄒᆞ엿다ᄒᆞ기에적찬ᄒᆞ논
티진참치아니ᄒᆞᆫ것과권참ᄒᆞᆫ것
이다르오나그리ᄒᆞ나ᄉᆞ례로써
헤아리진ᄃᆡ그쟈들수가엽ᄉᆞ오
나써종견취을베플미엇더ᄒᆞ올
지근　상주ᄒᆞ와　광무팔년십
이월십ᄉᆞ일에봉　지의주ᄒᆞ라
ᄒᆞ옵시다

면보

십오일　공ᄉᆞ관챡
일본동향ᄉᆞ령쟝관의보고가

며좌ᄒᆞ니
○슈뢰디ᄉᆞ격　십이월십이일
오젼○시반에영갈종좌의지휘
ᄒᆞ논슈뢰뎡티가려슌항외에졍
박ᄒᆞᆫ세바수보리들습격ᄒᆞ엿스
나그효과논확실이알기어려우
며그다음에졍호쇼좌의지휘ᄒᆞ
논슈뢰뎡티논맹렬ᄒᆞᆫ젹의방어
포화들무릅스고그중가ᄎᆞ운거
리에달ᄒᆞ야슈추발수ᄒᆞ야그쪽
발진동ᄒᆞᆷ을보와스나그이튼날
아ᄎᆞᆷ에젹함은의연히그위치에
진ᄒᆞ고우리함티논손히가엽셧
스며십이월십삼일오젼의시반
에확천쇼좌의지휘ᄒᆞ논슈뢰뎡
티도젹을습격ᄒᆞ야젹의포화하
에슈추사격을시힝ᄒᆞ엿스나효
과가확졍키란ᄒᆞ며이습격에ᄒᆞᆫ
슈뢰뎡은엄돌에ᄒᆞᆫ관환을밧고
ᄒᆞᆫ슈뢰뎡은귀관실에ᄒᆞᆫ탄환을
밧아진퇴에자유을이랏슴으로
로효험이구ᄒᆞ야귀착ᄒᆞ엿논티
슈뢰뎡에사상이엄고또오젼륙
시에과쇼쟝의지휘ᄒᆞ논슈뢰뎡
티도습격ᄒᆞᆷ을시칭ᄒᆞ엿스나포
화로인ᄒᆞ야젹의형젹을엇지못
ᄒᆞ고동시에쏘안뎝티위의지휘
ᄒᆞ논슈뢰뎡은젹함의게거진도
착ᄒᆞ야슈뢰들발사ᄒᆞ야쪽발ᄒᆞᆫ슈
연외남잉을보왓스나효과논분
지못ᄒᆞ며이때에청이다맹렬ᄒᆞᆫ
젹의포화들무릅서걱포란약을
상빗고얼쳑에논하ᄉᆞ졸삼명의부
자가잇다ᄒᆞ엿더라

빅림발　십이월륙일

○덕국의상엄담팡　덕국츄밀
칙관로셴싸가거나린상엄담합
티논아비사나아로향ᄒᆞ야갈터
인티금월이십구일에쳬노아란
논비로지부린에향ᄒᆞ야떠논다
더라

향항발　동월팔일

○로함파티만　향항에ᄒᆞᆫ슈ᄉᆞ
뎐보가왓논티불퇴함티의갈가
온목젹티논티만이라ᄒᆞ엿더라

빅림발　동월륙일

○덕상연셜　덕국졔상빅작뷸
에노씨가연셜ᄒᆞ되서남아푸리카
에덕국신민쟝취을기랑ᄒᆞ교식
민부관계도리쟝ᄒᆞ야ᄒᆞ겟다ᄒᆞ
엿더라

빅림발　십이월륙일

○일본과서반아　마덕리신문
리부렬오말ᄒᆞ되셔반아비교에

서붙잡힘티오서신란과서분을
용금ᄒᆞᆷ에티ᄒᆞ야일본이반티ᄒᆞ
논의론을서반아정부에제츌ᄒᆞ
엿더라

동디발　동월칠일

○친왕셔방　덕국황뎨의아들
아달버트친왕이덕국동양함티
에서수무를보논티셔나왓을ᄎᆞ
져가서티젼을찰밧고셰남젹에
셔나왕으로브티강진션물을만
이밧엇다더라

론돈발　동일

○영법협약　법국상의원에서
법뎡표삼십칠에티ᄒᆞ야이빅십
오표의다슈로영법협약을통과
ᄒᆞ엿더라

빅림발　십이월륙일

○로국동병　론돈스틴다드신
문의모스코통신원이말ᄒᆞ되로
국에서군ᄉᆞᄒᆞᆫ사ᄅᆞᆷ을아푸가니
스탄에힝군ᄒᆞ라명령ᄒᆞ엿다더
라

론돈스틴ᄃᆞ신문은젼에논밋
을만ᄒᆞᆫ신문이더니지금은쥬
히이밧귀여서젼만못ᄒᆞ다더
라

동디발　동월칠일

○친왕이방교왕　덕국알브레
트친왕이라마교왕을심방ᄒᆞ엿
논티교왕이참귀로일논서듕에
졉시면회ᄒᆞ엿더라

외보

○로국의뎐보　상히뎐보에말
ᄒᆞ되로국대본영에서십이월이
일에샹히에잇논뎨스시노참쟝
의게사ᄒᆞ우편의싸홈ᄒᆞᆫ것을뎐
보ᄒᆞ엿논티십일월이십칠일에
논로국의의용병과ᄆᆞᆼ병이일군
의망티들쫓발시기교이십팔일
에논일병이지쥔셴근방에서친
어논것을격퇴ᄒᆞ야큰손히를엽
게ᄒᆞ엿고이십구일과삼십일은
로국레비강포쟝군이일병을두
곳포티에서쫓ᄎᆞ서공격ᄒᆞ엿논
티일병은젼쟝에시케이빅삼십
을버리교그들넘길때에티자보
쳔쥰에잇편창고와랑식을불살
낫교로병은총과칼과티론물품
을만이엇고또드인의말을드론
즉일병의수샹이심이만ᄒᆞ야서
마ᄎᆞ로운송ᄒᆞ더라ᄒᆞ엿다더라

UNION INSURANCE SOCIETY OF CANTON.

Head office Hongkong.
Marine risks underwritten at current rates.

Agents in Chemulpo,
E. MEYER & Co.

COMPAGNIE DES MESSAGERIES MARITIMES.

Fortnightly Direct Service.

For Marseilles
via Ports.
(Sailing from Yokohama
Calling at Kobe,
Shanghai, Hongkong, Saigon, Singapore,
Colombo, Djibonti, Suez, Port Said
and Marseilles.

For particulars apply to
HOLME RINGER & Co.,
Chemulpo.

HAYASHIDA & CO.,

16 MYENG DONG, CHIN KO KAI, SEOUL.
BRANCH OFFICE AT CHEMULPO.

Money changers, Coal and Wood Merchants,
Express Agents.

We are agents for the Pyeng-yang Coal Company and the Karazu Coal Company of Japan. We have the best quality of both anthracite and bituminous coal, and prompt execution of orders is our speciality. Firewood of all kinds kept in stock. Full weight guaranteed. Money of all denominations exchanged at current rates. Parcels received for all parts.

CHINA MUTUAL LIFE INS. OC.

Most favourable terms to policy holders.

Benefit system unsurpassed.

HOLME RINGER & Co.
Agents, Chemulpo.

C. P. R.

CANADIAN PACIFIC RAILWAY COMPANY'S ROYAL MAIL STEAMSHIP LINE.

THE FAST ROUTE BETWEEN CHINA, JAPAN, AND EUROPE VIA CANADA AND THE UNITED STATES.

Route from Hongkong via Shanghai, Nagasaki (Inland Sea of Japan) Kobe, Yokohama Victoria and Vancouver.

Twin Screw Empress Steamship 6,000 Tons. Speed 19 knots.

PROPOSED SAILING FROM YOKOHAMA.

R. M. S. Empress of India.
R. M. S. Empress of Japan.
R. M. S. Empress of China.
R. M. S. Athenian.
R. M. S. Tartar.

Special reduction (first class only) granted to members of the Military, Naval, Diplomatic and Civil services and to Missionarias.

Passengers have choice of ten routes across the Continent of America and have privilege of travelling by any Atlantic Steamship Line.

Round the World passage tickets in connection with the P. and O. S. N., North German Lloyd and Messageries Co.'s **£125**.

All rates payable at current rate of exchange.

For further information, Tickets, Guide Books, etc., apply to

HOLME, RINGER & Co., AGENTS,
Chemulpo.

Grand Hotel,

(Formerly the Station Hotel)

Near the Railway Terminus,
West Gate Seoul.

The Best Hotel in Korea;
Handsome new Building.
Fine Airy Rooms
Excellent Cuisine.
Terms Moderate.
Special terms to Missionaries
and to permanent boarders.

Electric cars within 2 minutes' walk.

W. H. EMBERLEY.
Proprietor

EVERY FACILITY.

In connection with Life Assurance Business is afforded by

The Standard Life Assurance Co.,

One of the largest and wealthiest of the Provident Institutions of the United Kingdom Forms of Application and all information will be promptly afforded on application.

10 CENTS A DAY.

Not a very large expenditure is it? But it is sufficient to secure for a man of 30 a policy with the STANDARD LIFE OFFICE for

$1323.

For all particulars of rates, etc., apply to

Holme, Ringer & Co.,
Agents, Chemulpo.

THE NEW YORK LIFE INSURANCE COMPANY.

Have you ever been declined by any Company?

Are you engaged in a specially hazardous occupation?

Have you heard of the New York Life Insurance Company's New Classifications for this class of Risks?

If not, send your date of birth, occupation and particulars of rejection, if any to

E. MEYER & Co.,
Agents, Chemulpo.

MITSUI BUSSAN KAISHA.
(MITSUI & Co.)
MITSUI GINKO.
(MITSUI BANK.)

The Bank is owned by the members of the Mitsui Family, who, as partners, assume an unlimited responsibility for all liabilities of the Bank:—

Capital.................. .....Yen 5,000,000
Reserve Fund .... " 5,600,000

HEAD OFFICE, TOKYO.
LONDON OFFICE, 34 LIME ST., E. C.

BRANCHES AND AGENCIES:—
New York, San Francisco, Hamburg, Bombay, Singapore, Manila, Hongkong, Amoy, Chefoo, Tientsin.

Kobe, Hakodate, Yokohama, Kure, Yokosuka, Moji, Shimonoseki, Miike, Wakamatsu, Nagasaki, Kuchinotsu, Karatsu, Sasebo, Misume, Taipeh, &c.

Telegraphic Address for all the Offices:
"MITSUI."
A. B. C. AND A. I CODES USED.

Contractors of Coal
To the Imperial Japanese Navy. Arsenals and Railway Bureau, Principal Railway Companies and Industrial Work, Home and Foreign Mail and Freight Steamers.

Sole Proprietors
Of the famous Miike, Tagawa and Yamano Coal Mines.

Sole Agents
For the sale of Fukumo, Hokoku, Ichimura, Kanoda, Mannoura, Onoura, Ostuji, Sonoda, Tsubaruro, Yoshinotani, Yoshio, Yurokibura and other coals.

YANGTSE INSURANCE ASSOCIATION, LTD.

The undersigned, having been appointed agents for the above company, are prepared to issue policies and pay losses on marine risks at regular rates.

E. MEYER & Co.,
Agents, Chemulpo.

AMERICAN KOREAN ELECTRIC CO.

Light and Power.

Main Office: Electric Building, Chong No.

RAILWAY DEPARTMENT.

OPERATING CARS BETWEEN EAST AND WEST GATE, EVERY TEN MINUTES:—

First Car leaves East Gate at 7:00 A. M. First Car leaves R. R. Station at 7:25 A. M.
Last Car " East Gate at 9:40 P. M. Last " " R. R. Station at 10:05 P.M.

OPERATING CARS BETWEEN EAST GATE AND IMPERIAL TOMB TERMINUS, EVERY TWENTY MINUTES:—

CONNECTING WITH EVERY ALTERNATE CAR ARRIVING AT EAST GATE FROM CHONG NO.

First Car leaves East Gate for Tomb at 7:10 A. M.
" " " Tomb for East Gate at 7:35 A. M.
Last " " East Gate for Tomb at 7:50 P. M.
" " " Tomb for East Gate at 8:10 P. M.

OPERATING CARS BETWEEN CHONG NO AND YUNG SAN RIVER EVERY TWELVE MINUTES:—

First Car leaves Chong No for South Gate at 7:12 A. M.
" " " Chong No for Yung San at 7:36 A. M.
" " " South Gate for Chong No at 7:20 A. M.
" " " Yung San for Chong No at 8:09 A. M.
Last " " South Gate for Chong No 10:00 P. M.
" " " Yung San for Chong No at 9:33 P. M.

SPECIAL PRIVATE CARS FURNISHED TO SUIT CONVENIENCE OF PATRONS. PRICES ON APPLICATION AT HEAD OFFICE.

LIGHTING DEPARTMENT

Where less than 250 candle power of light is used, the rate per month will be
Per 16 candle power incandescent lamp,—All night.—Yen 2.50.
32 candle power incandescent lamp:—All night:—Yen 4.00.
50 candle power incandescent lamp:—All night:—Yen 6.00.
150 " " " " " " ,, 10.00.
1200 ,, ,, enclosed are " " " ,, 20.00.

Where more than 250 candle power of light is used, a Meter will be installed, freqvdted:—Rent of Meter Yen 2.00 per month. Rate of charges by meter reading:—Two Sen per Ampere per hour. (Approximately this is equal to about One Sen per 16 C. P. lamp per hour) Minimum monthly charge where meter is installed, Yen 20.00 per month, which includes rental of meter.

Estimates for installing lights furnished on application
An assortment of chandeliers always on hand.

K. Murakami.

Photograph Studio
Chinkokai, Seoul.

Printing, Developing and Enlargement, of Photographs always Undertaken.

Korean Views and Pictures Illustrating Native Customs always on Sale.

THE OSAKA SHOSEN KAISHA.

Boats frequently on the berth for Chinnampo.

REGULAR SAILINGS BETWEEN JAPAN AND KOREAN PORTS.

FUSAN AND KOBE VIA SHIMONOSEKI.

OSAKA VIA MOKPO, FUSAN, SHIMONOSEKI AND KOBE.

MOJI DIRECT.

OSAKA VIA KUNSAN, MASANPO, FUSAN, SHIMONOSEKI AND KOBE.

CHEMULPO KUNSAN LINE,
Every three days.

CHEMULPO CHINNAMPO LINE.
Every three days.

For Freight and passage and further particulars apply to

THE OSAKA SHOSEN KAISHA,
Chemulpo.

LONDON, PLAISANT & CO.

General Storekeepers and Merchants, Ships Contractors, Tobacconists, Commission and Forwarding Agents, Coal Merchants

IMPORTERS AND EXPORTERS

Seoul & Chemulpo.

W. D. WENTWORTH.

LANDING
AND
SHIPPING AGENT
AND
CUSTOMS BORDER.

12 OURA, NAGASAKI.

STEWARD & CO.

Chemulpo.

Shipchandlers and Storekeepers, Naval and Mercantile Contrrctors, Landing and Shipping Agents.

STEWARD'S HOTEL

Chemulpo.

Best accommodation in the port for travellers. Clean and well-aired rooms, good cuisine and prompt attendence, moderate tariff.

론셜

교쥭ᄒᆞ는법

무릇 어느 나라에던지 일진대병이 지나갈 ᄯᅢ에 져경도식이 지안코 송구ᄒᆞ게 도굴지 아니ᄒᆞ야 거안생ᄒᆞ는 ᄇᆡᆨ셩의게셔 지란도 다당치 지안키는 바라지 못ᄒᆞᆯ지라 우리는 이나라에 잇셔셔 히다ᄒᆞᆫ 군병이 한셩으로 도착ᄒᆞ야 열마 동안을 두류ᄒᆞ는것과 신속히 발졍ᄒᆞ는것도 보앗스되 거기 졀묘ᄒᆞᆷ이 파연 교쥭바든 군사 갓트ᄆᆡ 요ᄒᆞᆫ 말 맛치도 소요ᄒᆞ게 ᄒᆞ는 일이 엇셧ᄂᆞᆫ지라

그런고로 우리가 한셩안에셔는 이러ᄒᆞᆫ 일에 ᄃᆡᄒᆞ야 말ᄒᆞᆯ 거시 도모지 업스며 셜혹 무삼 관일이 잇셧드ᄅᆡ도 ᄃᆡ리여 우리는 밋지 아니ᄒᆞ야 말하지 아니케 되엿스며 ᄯᅩᄒᆞᆫ 군ᄃᆡ 쟝관들이라도 이모조록 군병의게 주의ᄒᆞ야 아모일도 엉시 방어ᄒᆞᆯ 줄로 만일 아깃부게 녀인바이어늘

이제 당ᄒᆞ야셔는 그 범과ᄒᆞᆷ을 가히 말ᄒᆞᆯ자ㅣ 잇나니 현금 한셩에 잇는 병졍들은 모도 예비병과 지방ᄃᆡ 병졍인즉 진픙범제 잇는 군ᄃᆡ와 갓치 만들야 면야 조조록 교ᄒᆞᆨ을 잘 시여야 흘리 이나고 리ᄒᆞ나 위션 남의 집에 돌입ᄒᆞ야 침어ᄒᆞ는 폐단을 막아야 ᄒᆞᆯ지니 귀왕에도 후외국 사람들이 음란 방사ᄒᆞᆫ 일로써 죽엿다는 말을 드럿더니 근일에도 ᄯᅩ 이란ᄒᆞᆫ 일이 고 샹기씨 집에셔 싱기여 대단ᄒᆞᆫ 수치를 당ᄒᆞ엿는ᄃᆡ 봉ᄒᆞᆫ 한국 ᄇᆡᆨ셩들은 비록 갑히 호소ᄒᆞ는 못ᄒᆞ며 그러ᄒᆞ되 이러ᄒᆞᆫ 일에 곤란들을 종종 밧는도다 고 샹기씨의 집은 맛참이 본병참 사령부 건너집인고로 대문에 파수 보는 병졍ᄭᆞ지 잇셔스되 오히려 죄를 당ᄒᆞ지 아니ᄒᆞᆯ줄을 알고 남의 집에 돌입ᄒᆞ야 범죄ᄒᆞ엿스니

이는 직분을 지히여 복무ᄒᆞ는 모양에 ᄃᆡ단히 들인지라 우리는 모건ᄃᆡ 군ᄃᆡ 쟝관들은 아모조록 이런ᄒᆞᆫ 일에 주의ᄒᆞ야 단속ᄒᆞ기를 밋나니 만일 그러ᄒᆞᆯ지경이면 다시 이런 소문이 들니지 아니ᄒᆞᆯ듯ᄒᆞ도다

외보

○졔황죵병 덕국정부에서 명년에 쳔구ᄇᆡᆨ년의 졔함계획을 실시ᄒᆞ려는고로 의회에서는 히군에 관ᄒᆞ야 시로 료구ᄒᆞ지 아니ᄒᆞ며 ᄯᅩ 륙군의 평시 인원은 이만인으로 증가ᄒᆞ엿다더라

○포렴함ᄃᆡ근경 향일에 쟝시 일본 군함에 츙돌ᄒᆞ야 상존함ᄃᆡ를 곤란케ᄒᆞᆫ 포렴함ᄃᆡ도 거괄월 십ᄉᆞ일을 산히 변에셔 [리우리이쓰구]는 격침ᄒᆞ엿스며 [구른보이]와 밋 [로시아]의 이함ᄃᆡ도 큰 손ᄒᆡ를 밧고 겨우 포렴에 도망ᄒᆞᆫ 슬픈 ᄃᆡ경에 ᄲᅡ져 드러갓스며 고후 량함이 갓추 슈리ᄒᆞ는ᄃᆡ 착슈ᄒᆞᆫ다 ᄒᆞ니 모쳐에 말ᄒᆞᆫ 경보를 거ᄒᆞᆫ즉 근자에 [구른보이]는 슈리가 죤공되야 운젼ᄒᆞ는 시험ᄒᆞᆫ 항ᄒᆞᆯ ᄯᅢ에 손상ᄒᆞ엿다는 소는 진덕ᄒᆞᆫ 스실이 [며로시야]는 도저히 슈리ᄒᆞ엿스며 [본가지루]의 손상은 확실ᄒᆞ더라

잡보

○면쟝초치 윤셩보와 리근쥰이 가외부에 면보ᄒᆞ기를 사관ᄉᆞ로 ᄀᆡ명신문ᄒᆞᆫ지 이믜 ᄉᆞ일이 지나되 량편의 공초가 ᄃᆡ단이 샹좌가 되야 ᄒᆞᆫ곳시 간과날만히 비ᄒᆞ엿고 자하로는 가히 쳔단치 못ᄒᆞ겟스니 평리원으로 붓니다가 귀결ᄒᆞ기를 엄ᄃᆡ 바란다 ᄒᆞ엿더라

○경관불부 룡쳔과 의쥬 감리는 이미 부임ᄎᆞ로 발졍ᄒᆞ엿스되 히항 경무관 등은 관졔 리졍에 경부무관을 불시ᄒᆞᆫ다 ᄒᆞᆷ으로 아즉 부임치 못ᄒᆞᆫ다더라

○졍부졔의 졍부에서 쥬외공사를 소환ᄒᆞ기로 졔의 중이라더라

○파츌쥬본샹송 젼라남도관찰ᄉᆞ 김셰긔씨가 본직을 민듯ᄒᆞᆫ고로 쳐음 부임ᄒᆞᆯ ᄯᅢ에 여로이 병과ᄒᆞ더니 작ᄉᆞ룩일 상오 십점에 히도 슌찰ᄉᆞ 안죵덕씨가 니부로 면보ᄒᆞ기를 본도 관찰ᄉᆞ 파직 쥬본을 샹송ᄒᆞᆫ다 ᄒᆞ엿더라

○셜영신문간힝 일본인이 대구 관찰부 동문밧게 ᄃᆡ구 실업신문을 셜립ᄒᆞ고 음력 본월 십오일븟터 간힝ᄒᆞᆫ다고 관찰소 가니부로 보고ᄒᆞ엿더라

○부윤급면 강화부윤 윤쳘규씨가 장젼이 삼십삼만량이 되는고로 쥬본ᄒᆞ여 면관ᄒᆞᆫ다는 소진으로 인ᄒᆞ야 샹경ᄒᆞ엿다가 도로 환임ᄒᆞ엿더니 저작 십륙일에 부로 급히 젼보ᄒᆞ기를 본관이 공스에 도원군계홈이 업고 사사에 도슈령이 업는ᄃᆡ 십오일 샹오 세시에 본부 진위ᄃᆡ 참령 리동휘가 샹문을 파쇄ᄒᆞ며 무수ᄒᆞᆫ 병졸이 옹위ᄒᆞ야 모혀 셧는ᄃᆡ 리동휘가 앙셔셔 검을 두르며 일소ᄃᆡ 수졸이 담총ᄒᆞ고 돌입ᄒᆞ더니 너이 쓸 총을 들고 란확ᄒᆞ야 너희 총을 노토록ᄒᆞ고 셩명을 ᄃᆡ호ᄒᆞ며 글오ᄃᆡ 너를 죽이고 나도 죽겟다 ᄒᆞ고 발창 노창분을 차고 경ᄂᆡ에 돌입ᄒᆞ야 창호를 타파ᄒᆞ며 집과 총으로써 곳곳와셔 셰로 러ᄒᆞ며 ᄃᆡ당 창평은 모픈 이송엄ᄒᆞᆫ지라 그 ᄒᆞᆼᄒᆞᆫ 칼날을 피ᄒᆞ야 월장ᄒᆞ야 도망ᄒᆞ야 금방 샹경ᄒᆞ오며 이 거시 무슴 심장으로 ᄇᆡᆫ병ᄒᆞ여 돌입ᄒᆞ야 본관을 죽이고자 ᄒᆞ는지 젼명은 비록 보존ᄒᆞ엿스나 리씨는 반다시 몸을 당ᄒᆞᆯᄃᆡ이니 군부에 이조ᄒᆞ와 리동휘를 붓잡아 샹ᄒᆞ야 도덕ᄒᆞᆫ 소힝ᄒᆞ야 복슈ᄒᆞᆷ을 갑는 놀노 시ᄒᆡᆼᄒᆞ라 ᄒᆞ엿더라

○쳥졔임후소환 외부에서 군부에 조회ᄒᆞ기를 룩군참위 윤치셩 소환일ᄉᆞ는 임의 일공ᄉᆞ의게 공ᄒᆞ엿거니와 이에 조복을 젼조ᄒᆞᆫ즉 니기에 우리 졍부 훈령에 이르기를 본방류학ᄉᆡᆼ 룩군참위 윤치셩 협금 등 여관으로 이믜 죵군ᄒᆞ엿스니 히 등 여 졔임ᄒᆞᆫ 후에 히 소환ᄒᆞᆫ 탕을 맛당히 히원의게 교부ᄒᆞ야 곳 츌졍지로브터 귀국케ᄒᆞ라 ᄒᆞ엿스니 쳥컨ᄃᆡ 사조ᄒᆞ라 ᄒᆞ엿더라

○리씨회국긔 용익씨의 환국ᄒᆞᆫ 사는 작보에 긔지ᄒᆞ엿거니와 동씨가 작일 동경에셔 발졍ᄒᆞ엿는ᄃᆡ 귀로에 강쳐에셔 광산을 시찰ᄒᆞ려 인ᄒᆞ고로 경셩에 도착ᄒᆞ기는 금월 회간이 되겟다더라

○민총졍류 작일 하오 ᄒᆞᆫ시량에 동ᄃᆡ문안 두리목에셔 총가진자를 잡아노코 누가 총을 보ᄂᆡ며 어ᄃᆡ로 가져가나 무른즉 가사의 룽으로 보ᄂᆡᆫ다 ᄒᆞ고 [illegible]

○원졍롬젼함 군자에 ᄂᆡ장원경에 젼함이 발미 되엿는ᄃᆡ 원미자ㅣ 연속ᄒᆞ야 셔임ᄒᆞ고 면관ᄒᆞ는ᄃᆡ 견들이 업다ᄒᆞ엿더라

○민씨셜명 젼보에 긔재ᄒᆞᆫ 잡보 즁 리씨 불쳥이란 문졔에 ᄃᆡᄒᆞ야 민영휘씨가 본사에 사름을 보ᄂᆡ여 셜명ᄒᆞ야 왈 리참씨와 샹면ᄒᆞᆫ 젼도는 방초에 ᄂᆡ가 평양 거ᄒᆞ는 졍회 조의게 믹득ᄒᆞᆫ 거시 ᄂᆡ리참씨와는 샹관이 초무ᄒᆞ고 그 젼도와 미변 사ᄇᆡᆨ셕 심오년 츄슈조를 ᄂᆡ여주마 ᄒᆞ엿단 말은 모다 허셜이라고 ᄒᆞ더라

○젼문키결 평셩황후 쳔릉ᄒᆞ오다 든시에 여사ᄃᆡ젼을 오셔ᄂᆡ 사만오 젼여호에셔 히호에 오량으로 샹호에 칠관 원셕지 거두엇더니 현금 쳔릉을 영위 덕지ᄒᆞ고 슌명비 인산에 여사ᄃᆡ젼은 의례히 쇄납ᄒᆞ는지라 젼에 슈납ᄒᆞᆫ 돈으로 쓰라ᄒᆞ고 ᄂᆡ일 호ᄯᆡ가 ᄒᆡ회에셔 젼 여사ᄃᆡ쟝 리죵빈씨의게 젼ᄃᆡ젼의 엇지ᄒᆞᆫ 거슬 진문ᄒᆞᆫ다더라

○ᄂᆡᄃᆡ파송관인 관졔리졍소에셔 각 관졔를 리졍ᄒᆞ야 관인을 감셩ᄒᆞ는ᄃᆡ 각 쟝관이 참셕ᄒᆞ야 졍당케 리졍ᄒᆞ엿시되 ᄂᆡ부대신 리ᄌᆡ씨는 심샹이 보왓더니 ᄐᆡ반이나 방ᄒᆞᆷᄒᆞ야 금 반포는 ᄃᆞᆺ지라 니ᄃᆡ가 자리졍관의게 관인을 파송ᄒᆞ야 말ᄒᆞ기를 니부 관졔는 본ᄃᆡ신이 샹쥬ᄒᆞ야 졍졍ᄒᆞᆫ 후에 반포케 ᄒᆞ자 ᄒᆞ야 시비가 쟁싱ᄒᆞᆫ다더라

○승총단발회 일진회원을 각군에 파송ᄒᆞ엿단 말은 본보에 이왕 긔재ᄒᆞ엿거니와 지금 다시 드른즉 셔울셔 ᄂᆡ려간 ᄇᆡ에 단발ᄒᆞᆫ는 가위들 사가지고 가는ᄃᆡ ᄇᆡᆨ셩들이 말ᄒᆞ기를 일진회가 곳 삭발회라고 들ᄒᆞ더라

○룽가생젼 송현 망건방에셔 아희들이 모혀 노는ᄃᆡ ᄒᆞᆫ 아희가 목도리ᄒᆞᆫ 아희의 목도리를 쟝아다 ᄅᆡᆫ지라 그 아희가 츙은 줄이며 너머져 죽은 모양이 뵈지라 숨이 막히여 ᄂᆡ며 진죽이 상ᄒᆞ엿던지 삼ᄉᆞ일을 누어 ᄭᆡ나지 못ᄒᆞ는ᄃᆡ 만일 죽으면 그 목도리 쟝아다 ᄅᆡᆫ 아희는 무사치 못ᄒᆞᆯ라 ᄒᆞ고 지금 약을 쓰는 중이라더라

외보

○로군쾌몽교 북경면을 거ᄒᆞᆫ즉 아라사 군수이 마젹을 사드리여 ᄇᆡ몽고 가루진ᄃᆡ에 쳥일ᄒᆞ야 중립ᄃᆡ를 버리고 군슈품을 보충ᄒᆞ기 위ᄒᆞ야 여러히 말과 양과 도야지와 보리와 셔속등 물을 량탈ᄒᆞ더니 근일에는 그 량탈ᄒᆞ던 욱심ᄒᆞ야 마젹의 란을 만나는 자ㅣ 샹히 만타는ᄃᆡ 몽고 왕등이 열하 도춍의게 급히 고ᄒᆞᆷ으로 열하 도춍이 히ᄃᆡ방에 병뎡을 파송ᄒᆞ야 마젹을 토벌ᄒᆞ고 ᄯᅩ 군긔쳐소에 ᄃᆡᄒᆞ야 아라사국의 불법힝위와 마젹을 토벌키 관란ᄒᆞᆷ을 ᄌᆞ조 급보ᄒᆞ엿다 ᄒᆞ고 ᄯᅩ 몽고 왕등의 면보를 거ᄒᆞᆫ즉 히ᄃᆡ방에 횡ᄒᆡᆼᄒᆞ는 마젹은 그 복쟝이 로병과 동일ᄒᆞ야 로병과 마젹을 분별키 어렵다 ᄒᆞ엿더라

○슈비병송교 향일 쟝긔에 도챡ᄒᆞᆫ 덕국 긔션의 온 젼션을 드른즉 덕국 신진 군인 회사에셔는 다 로국 군ᄃᆡ의 ᄇᆡᆺ방을 엿시 녀기며 로국이 덕국 국졍의 슈비병을 쿠동으로 보별 숫에 ᄃᆡᄒᆞ야 외교가는 관찰ᄒᆞ는 바이 잇스며 ᄯᅩ 파리에셔는 일본 진쟝의 시용이 샹히 듯렵더라

○로군세력 로군이 대코싱오문 쑨 대평으로브터 사하에 운송ᄒᆞ고 특별히 용빙스리온 군수이 만명을 넌ᄒᆞ엿다더라

○로군남하의 풍셜 길림에 잇는 로병 오만명이 남으로 향ᄒᆞ야 셰 남쥰비를 ᄒᆞ는ᄃᆡ 아직 확실ᄒᆞᆫ 보고는 업다더라

○미송군의 이번 平졍에야 젼병원의 방법에 숫밧괘 방히가 잇슬듯ᄒᆞᆫ 렴려가 잇는고로 미국 군부에셔 두 교젼국의 인가를 엇으면 군의들 ᄂᆡ보ᄂᆡ야 일로 량진에 ᄯᅡ리 단니게 ᄒᆞ기로 작정ᄒᆞ엿다더라

TELEGRAMS.

Army Headquarters.

At 10 A. M. on the 15th inst. 15 Russian cavalry-men appeared 20 li north of Kienchang. Two of them were picked off by Japanese sharp shooters. At 10.30 A. M. on the 15th inst. the Japanese scouts attacked four Russians and killed them all. The Russians according to their shoulder straps belonged to the 37th Division.

A report received from Captain Yamada of the 3rd naval squadron gives the follow details of attacks by the Japanese fleet on Port Arthur:

At 3.30 A. M. on the 14th inst. the torpedo squadrons commanded by Captain Otaki and Miyamoto made an attack on the shipping. The first-named squadron failed owing to the search lights of the Sevastopol discovering it, but Miyamoto's flotilla got within range and managed to discharge two torpedos. A heavy snow storm was raging at the time and the boats became separated, that under the command of Lieutenant Tagata not yet having returned. It is thought that she sank with all hands.

Continual attacks have since been made and it is ascertained that the Sevastopol is slightly down by the bows, the forward torpedo tubes being submerged.

(FROM JAPAN PAPERS.)

Berlin, Dec. 9.

M. Syvetou, the French Deputy who during a recent debate in the Senate made an attack on General Andre, the Minister for War, and struck him in the face, has died suddenly, having been poisoned by gas.

Berlin, Dec. 9.

The Anglo-German Commercial Treaty will probably be signed about the beginning of next week.

We regret to hear of the death of Mr. G. C. Byng, of Messrs Samuel Samuel Co. & Moji. No particulars are at hand.

Natung, President of the Wai-Wu Pu, has called for a list of the foreign hongs at Peking, as Peking is not an open port and China objects to the presence of so many foreign hongs.

The Japanese military authorities in Gensan have informed the Magistrate of Munchon that the Magistrate of Kuwon will not be permitted to go to his post, and the magistrate of Munchon must immediately recover the official seals from him.

The Japanese military authorities of Seoul having ordered the magistrate of Koyang to supply a number of stone masons and coolies to repair the roads, this gentleman finds himself in somewhat of a quandary. Stone masonry is unknown in his district!

Leaving aside their Excellencies Soeng Kung-pao and Lu Hai-huan, Treaty Commissioner and President of the Board of Work, Says an exchange, there are now residing in Sanghai two-ex-governors, Teng Huahsi of Kueichow, and Wang Chich-chun of Kuangsi, and an Ex-Provincial Treasurer, Jui Chang of Kiangning. This shows that Chinese officials of high rank appreciate the benefits of civilised and enlightened Municipal Government in Shanghai, and yet they appear chary of introducing such in the interior, and do not try to impress on the younger generation of mandarins, whom they see about them, the value of following such good examples. Since the attack on his life, we are not so sure that ex-governor Wang Chich-chun will be quite so appreciative of "the benefits of civilized and enlightened municipal government in Shanghai."

CORRESPONDENCE.

The Editor

KOREA DAILY NEWS,

SEOUL.

DEAR SIR:—

It may interest your readers to receive some hints so that they are not misled by the recent Japanese telegrams regarding 203 metre hill.

It is probable that there are very few European residents in Korea who know very much about the Geographical positions of Port Arther and its surroundings but I have known these particulars ever since 1874 and as what I am now writing is for the sole object of clearing away some of the sand which has been thrown into people's eyes, I am sure that the Russians will excuse me if I give away any military secrets.

There are three lines of fortifications surrounding Port Arthur on the land side. Beyond the inner, or main line of forts there is some three or four kilometres away, a line of secondary defenses and beyond these again at about the same interval there was another line of temporary defenses. These last are what the Japanese succeedeed in taking some two or three months ago, while the middle or secondary line of forts comprises those which they are now bringing, or trying to bring under their subjugation but up to date not all of them have been taken and among those is the so much quoted 308 metre hill. But this hill so given is a "bluff" as the reports of it would imply that it was one of the main fortifications only distant from the harbour about two miles in a direct line, and ignorant people are led to believe that the Japanese could shell the harbour from there.

Now if this hill and its fortifications had been occupied by the Japanese it would actually mean the taking or fall of port Arthur, (although there is at least one more fort having a greater altitude than 204 metre hill and that fort is not far from it). It would mean that the Japanese army had surrounded and completely subjugated every one of the Russian forts.

But, even if we imagine that this much talked of fort has been taken, and we also imagine that the vessels whose names have been given as sunk would remain in the direct line of fire? Would they not get under shelter? (Which they would be able to do).

Again, supposing that the Japanese had taken this position, would the Russians on giving up such an important position leave large guns in a state to be made use of by their enemy and at the same time oblige them with the ammunition for them also? It can hardly be believed that they would and even if, for instance, we grant that they did, would the Japanese be able to train those guns from an elevation of 203 metres so as to fire effectively and damage and sink ships as reported? I think not. In the first instance direct fire c[illegible]'d not be effected and a fire which only exploded over them would not sink these vessels. We have an instance in the "Isarewich," which after having been fired at for 2½ hours by eleven vessels, is, although much damaged, still afloat

We know that the sinking of the Port Arthur ships is much desired and as every day brings the Balfic fleet nearer these reports ar quite natural.

It is amusing that we at last are told that the Battle-ship "Yashima" has been sunk. It may be worthy of comment that she was sunk two or three months ago but that the name of a gun-boat was given instead of her. It may be still more interesting to your readers to hear that the guns (Naval guns) now made use of at the siege against Port Arthur belonged to this vessel as she was sunk in no great depth of water.

It was reported from Tokio that the "Pallada" had got away from Port Arthur and nothing more was heard of her. Now we are being told that she lies to starboard and that others are submerged!

A later report mentions the sinking of the Chinese Cruiser "Saiyen," taken by the Japanese during the China-Japan war, there was also another vessel lost which was taken from the Chinese. There is still the "Chinyen" battleship left and the Chinese prophecy that she will also be sunk as the sinking of the other two is Joss-Pidgin.

Along with the foregoing it may be interesting to know that a "Koku" of rice leaving Chemulpo at Liaoyang costs Yen 132.00 and a battle of Asahi beer sells at Dalny for Yen 1.80.

Yours truly,

"STRICT OBSERVER."

CHEFOO NEWS.

The following paragraphs are taken from the "Chefoo Daily News" of December 1st:—

A junk arrived yesterday morning from Laotishan. It left at seven-thirty on the evening of the twenty-second inst. En route to Chefoo it was stopped by six Japanese torpedo boats, but after a brief examination, allowed to proceed. Its captain reports that four days ago a pile of coal near the railway station at Port Arthur was hit by a Japanese shell and set on fire. The conflagration lasted a whole day. From other Chinese he learned that the Russians had buried some of their dead near Pai-lan.

According to the captain there had been no heavy fighting or bombarding at Port Arthur for several days when he sailed the last time from Laotishan.

About the first of the month the attacking forces made an attempt to cross a moat near Pigeon Bay with the idea of attacking fortifications on Laotishan. The attempt was a complete failure.

When the junk left Laotishan the Japanese were still in strong force at Shan li Kian, vainly striving to advance along the main road to Port Arthur. According to passengers on the vessel more than sixty per cent of the houses in Port Arthur have been seriously damaged by Japanese shells.

Yesterday afternoon another junk arrived from the besieged fortress. On board were six Indian watchmen. This junk was also stoped by six Japanese torpedo boats and searched.

A large junk arrived yesterday afternoon from We-haiwei, loaded with a cargo of bones. The vessels might have been a floating slaughter house, if the odor emanating from her vicinity was any indication. The enterprising crew chose a most convenient but objectionable spot for the dumping of their freight—the shore in front of the Beach Hotel.

The Japanese auxiliary cruiser "Hong-Kong Maru" was reported to have been just without the harbor limits yesterday morning, busily engaged in signalling, presumably to Chefoo. What was the purpose of her presence no one was quite able to say. That she was close to Chefoo is impossible of dispute, as she was observed by several persons.

The old Toyo Kisen Kaisha liner has changed somewhat since she plied between Hongkong and San Franciscon. Her immaculate white dress has been changed to a coat of leaden hue, and her decks are graced with numerous guns which lend a war-like air to her graceful lines. She is fitted out with a wireless telegraph outfit, and at a distance appears like a "sure enough" man-of-war. She is at present performing the duties of a scouting ship, intercepting the peaceful progress of various merchantmen plying along the China coast, examining their papers and cargo, and genetally making herself a nuisance.

The Japanese are said to be buying a quantity of "cayuse" ponies from Canada and the "Wild West." These beasts are hard, weight carriers, and forage for themselves. They are not for the Government stud farms, but for the winter campaign in Manchuria.

The German Minister has informed the Foreign Office that the gold mine in Kim Sung district having proved a failure it will shortly be returned to the Government. When this is effected, he trusts that a concession on a more favourable site will be granted in the same manner as recently Obtained by the British and Italian minister.

We have much pleasure in noting another addition to the few British enterprises in Korea. Messrs Bennett & Co. have established themselves as General Merchants and Commission Agents in Chemulpo. Their offices will be immediately opposite the Japanese Post and Telegraph Office and the new firm commences operations from January 1st 1905.

A new society called the Kong Chin Hoi has been formed and the opening meeting was held on Thursday afternoon at Chong No. It was then decided to send a letter to the Government suggesting, as a commencent of reforming policy, the dismissal of 15 sourcerers from the Palace. We hear that the society is supported by the Palace and its initial step would seem to show that its members really have reform at heart.

Judging from the contents of the "Japan Mail" of December 10th, the Editor was at that time in a particularly truculent humour. Apparently Mr. Yi Yong Ik has been proof against Japanese blandishments. The "Japan Mail" concludes an aspersive but incorrect article by saying: "The public used to give Mr. Yi Yong Ik credit for some shrewdness." Then Korean politics come in for attention and the "Mail" plaintively says that Japan "has to be perpetually on her good behauior" in Korea. How annoying! The "Mail" particularly shines in its commemt upon the Italian claim upon the Korean Government for the fulfilment of a former promise of a mining concession. The "Japan Mail" calls it "an undignified "attempt to subject Korea to inconvenience in the sequel of her own generosity," and yet the "Japan Mail" did not even condemn the Nagamori scheme!

The Korea Daily News.

Issued at 5 P. M. daily except Sundays.

Rate of Subscription:—
Per Year,............Yen 25.
Per Quarter,..........Yen 7.
Per Month,..........Yen 2.50.

Postage in Korea not charged extra.
Postage abroad charged extra.

Advertisements, 50 sen per day for 1 inch or less.
5 yen per month per inch.
50 yen per year per inch.

All communications to
E. T. BETHELL,
Editor and Publisher,
Pak-tong, Seoul.

POLITICS AND THE TRUTH.

As will have been seen from the report of the meeting of the Budget committee in Tokio which we published yesterday, the administration of recent affairs by the Government is meeting with a good deal of disapproval.

And indeed the position of the Government does not seem to be a strong one. When an admission so damaging as the one relative to the affairs of the 130th Bank, wherein the Government stated that this Bank was bolstered up because the news of its true condition would have adversely affected the flotation of the foreign loan, is not withheld from the public, it would certainly appear that the replies to the other questions which were given behind closed doors must have been of a very unsatisfactory nature indeed.

We understand, from other sources, that the reply of the Government in explanation of the assistance given to the 130th Bank is looked upon as unsatisfactory and incomplete, but in the meantime there is another feature of the case which cannot remain unnoticed.

We have been told, with many flourishes of trumpets, that Japan's financial position is an unassailable one and that she can provide the funds to carry on this war for several years yet, but how can we reconcile this optimistic statement with the Government admission that the failure of a comparatively unimportant bank like the 130th would have interfered with the issue of the relatively trifling loan of £12,000,000 carrying interest at the rate of 8 per cent? What was expected to happen if the news of the 130th Bank failure had become public? Would interest at a higher rate than 8% have had to be given or would it have been found impossible to float the loan at any price?

And again, if the Japanese Government considers itself justified in hushing up any matters which might adversely affect its schemes are we not logically correct in going a little farther and assuming that all the news which is disseminated from Tokio is given for the furtherance of political ends?

There is, at any rate, considerable justification for this view. The correspondent of the "Daily Telegraph" was undoubtedly correct when he telegraphed home that political neccessities would compel the Japanese to strain every nerve to effect the speedy capture of Port Arthur. This of course meant that the Government urgently wanted the news of some signal successes in order to disarm opposition on the occasion of the meeting of the Diet.

The news from the Shaho is distinctly unfavourable to Japan. Oyama is obviously unable to carry out his projected advance on Moukden; on the contrary, it appears that he will have his hands full in repulsing Russian advances into territory he has already occupied. Port Arthur has not fallen, indeed the attacks on the forts of the main *enciente* viz: Erlungshan, Suusushan and Kikukshan, have so far resulted in disastrous failure.

Therefore it is only natural to expect that such successes as there are, viz; the capture of 203 metre hill, have been made a good deal more of than the achievement warrants.

If the reports of the resistance offered by the Russians are correct the hill must have been regarded by them as of considerable strategic importance, but it is by no means certain that the position will be of equal advantage to the Japanese, and all the stories of the destruction of the fleet, although of course not without some foundation may prove to have been highly coloured owing to the exigencies of the political situation.

MR. D. W. STEVENS.

From the last number of "The Journal of the American Asiatic Association" the "North China Daily News" quotes some statements by the editor, Mr. John Foord, adding, as will be seen, some comments of its own:—

Mr. Foord congratulates Korea on securing Mr. D. W. Stevens as diplomatic adviser of her Government. Mr. Foord mentions the criticisms that have been made recently of some of Japan's methods of administration at Seoul, and says that "there is certainly no man whose presence at the Korean capital could be a safer guarantee against a repetition of the policy of ten years ago than that of Mr. Stevens," and that the Japanese Government should have recommended him to Korea is a proof of Japan's sincerity. More than twenty-five years ago Mr. Stevens went to Tokyo as second Secretary of the U. S. Legation; he subsequently entered the Japanese service, and has been for many years Counsellor of the Japanese Legation at Washington. "In every respect Mr. Stevens brings to the discharge of his duties as diplomatic adviser to the Korean Department of Foreign Affairs qualifications which it is given to very few men to acquire or possess. No one at all familiar with the facts will be disposed to minimise the difficulties of his new position and no greater tribute could be paid to Mr. Stevens than is involved in the assumption that he will be found able to discharge its responsibilities with satisfaction to both Governments. It offers a great opportunity for the conduct of what is essentially a work of national regeneration, and while replete with possibilities of incessant worry and profound discouragement, one is tempted to believe that in the rare combination of qualities which Mr. Stevens will bring to its discharge, there is the potentiality and the promise of a brilliant success." We have given what may possibly at first sight be thought unnecessary prominence to this appointment, because the intrinsic weakness and misgovernment of Korea have made her the shuttlecock of the adjacent Powers, and the resurrection and maintainence of peace in the East will be markedly assisted by the influence which it is hoped Mr. Stevens will promptly acquire and retain in the counsels of the Emperor Yi.

The editor of the "Journal" makes one error. Mr. Stevens was Secretary, not Second Secretary, of the United States Legation at the time he entered the Japanese service.

An international guarantee has been signed at Peking that Mukden and the Imperial Tombs shall not be bombarded.

The Hunghutse carried off a drove of cattle which some Mahomedan dealers were taking to the Russians, and handed them over to the Japanese.

NOTES FROM CHINA PAPERS.

It is reported that Yuan Taotai of Shanghai has received a telegraphic order from the Acting Viceroy at Nanking to the effect that Magistrate Huang of the Mixed Court in Shanghai is not proving a competent official and that Magistrate Kwan will take over the Magistrate of the Mixed Court—Sinwanpao.

CHINA TO ASK FOR AN ARMISTICE DURING WINTER

According to a Peking despatch to the "Osaka Mainichi," dated the 6th inst., a rumour is current at the Chinese capital to the effect that the Viceroys and Governors of the different provinces in China have recently presented to the Emperor a joint memorial urging the latter to request both belligerents to suspend hostilities during the winter, the interval to be utilized for asserting China's sovereignty over Manchuria and invoking the assistance of foreign Powers for mediation.

Yuan Taotai has communicated with the Japanese Consul General that Japanese have been selling to the Chinese machines for counterfeiting coins and requests the latter to stop it.

The Board of Commerce has summoned a Chinese multi-millionaire to consider the construction of railways in Fokien to prevent the concession falling into the hands of foreigners.

THROWING STONES AND GLASS HOUSES.

The following is from the "Eastern World:"—We had occasion to be invisibly present for a moment at a recent interview between the Spanish Minister and Baron Komura on the subject of Spanish neutrality at Vigo. We shall not report all we heard, but in the course of the interview the Spanish Minister pertinently refreshed the memory of Baron Komura with the fact that, in spite of neutrality, Nagasaki served the American warships as a naval basis in the Spanish American war.

There was the sound of breaking glass, and our astral body being very sensitive to noises floated away on the breeze.

GENERAL STOESSEL

The "Jiji's" Yingkow correspondent learns from a person who has arrived from Port Arthur that General Stoessel, on receipt of the invitation of surrender from the Japanese Army, declared that as the life of every soldier in his garrison belonged to the Tsar, no lives would be spared by surrender. He was determined to see whether a stronghold constructed on the most scientific system would be able to maintain itself for a pre-arranged period. He had therefore absolutely no reason to accept the invitation to surrender. General Stoessel has his Headquarters at Laohuwei and visits the forts every day on a white horse, encouraging his troops.

A Shimonoseki despatch transmits a statement by another person from the front to the effect that General Stoessel regrets having allowed the Chinese to remain in Port Arthur, as he finds that through them certain military secrets have leaked out, eventually leading to the occupation of important positions by the Japanese.—Japan Times.

Yi Yong Ik has left Tokyo on a tour of inspection of the mines of Japan. When this is completed he will come on to Seoul without returning to Tokyo.

The following advertisement of a local Japanese outfitting establishment has been sent us, presumably for insertion in our columns. "The textures of cloth are very fashionable and the mechanics are very skinful at their works. Moreover as all my members are honest and careful in all, we hope that customers will order without doubt."

The Korea Daily News.

VOL. I, | SATURDAY, DECEMBER 17, 1904. | No. 128

大韓每日申報
대한ᄆᆡ일신보

(뎨일ᄇᆡᆨ이십구호)　(화요일)　일쳔구ᄇᆡᆨ사년십이월이십일

사고ᄇᆡᆨ

이신보는영어와한어로셔거ᄆᆡ일츌판ᄒᆞᆸ

신문가

한쟝　엽두돈오푼

일삭됴　엽두량닷돈

우표가ᄆᆡ삭닷돈

다맛돈으로밧습

광고료는

과한의쟝단과조힝의다쇼로즁감ᄒᆞ되렴가로밧을터이오며오ᄅᆡ지아녀대한사람마다다이신문을보실터이니광고내시기돌원ᄒᆞ시는이들은우리신문샤에와셔면약ᄒᆞ심을희망ᄒᆞᆸ

○발힝소　박동대한ᄆᆡ일신보샤법어학교압헤젼영국인셜필림집자리오

샤쟝　영국인　(비셜)

평양　ᄃᆡ리점

○평양효동사는권미보씨로우리신문관ᄃᆡ리인을뎡ᄒᆞ엿ᄉᆞ오니평양에계신구람코져ᄒᆞ시는쳠군ᄌᆞ는히ᄃᆡ리점에왕림ᄒᆞ와면의ᄒᆞ십

사고

○우리대한ᄆᆡ일신보의목뎍은대한의안녕질셔에관ᄒᆞᆫ모든뎨목에ᄃᆡᄒᆞ야논공평한변론을쥬쟝ᄒᆞᆷ이라우리통신원의탐보는신문보시는쳠군ᄌᆞ의게ᄒᆞᆼ상보도ᄒᆞ리며편지를긔셔ᄒᆞ여주시는이논셩명과반ᄃᆡ를젹어븟치시기를희망ᄒᆞ오니이거슨신문상에긔ᄌᆡᄒᆞ랴는거시아니오다만극히신용ᄒᆞ는증거를숨고쟈ᄒᆞᆷ이라긔쟈는아모긔셔던지긔ᄌᆡᄒᆞᆷ을되각ᄒᆞ는권리를가졋스나되각ᄒᆞ는리유를말ᄒᆞᆯ터이오며공즁평화를문란케ᄒᆞ는듯ᄒᆞᆫ긔셔는의례히밧지안켓ᄉᆞᆸ나이다

●본샤셜시이리로신문을ᄆᆡ양우례로분젼ᄒᆞ와례젼부의입의로젼ᄒᆞᆫ듯스로먼곳에는혹늣게젼ᄒᆞ기도ᄒᆞ며혹몃쳘거슬ᄒᆞᆫ겁에젼ᄒᆞ기도ᄒᆞ며혹아니젼ᄒᆞ는곳도잇다ᄒᆞ와우리신문을수당ᄒᆞ야구람ᄒᆞ시는　쳠군ᄌᆞ의게ᄃᆡᄒᆞ야ᄆᆡ우미안ᄒᆞ옵기로지금온분젼인을두고ᄆᆡ일일즉이젼ᄒᆞ며아니젼ᄒᆞ거나늣게거나ᄒᆞᆫ폐가업도록ᄒᆞ랴ᄒᆞ오니혹아니젼ᄒᆞ거나혹늣게젼ᄒᆞ거나ᄒᆞᆫ일이잇스면본샤로통긔ᄒᆞ여쥬심을희망ᄒᆞᆸ

관보

뎨삼쳔십이호

광무팔년십이월십칠일

셔임급사령

○승셔관임관오등　한셩면보지사쥬사　졍한벽

십이월십삼일

○승셔판임관삼등　한셩우체샤쥬사　젼규환

십이월십이일

○승셔판임관삼등　한셩우체사쥬사　리원상

십이월십삼일

○명경샹남도종두사무위원　츙청북도종두사무위원　죠필하

○명츙청북도종두사무위원　평안북도종두사무위원　리셰용

○명평안북도종두사무위원　리명은

○히제쥬목종두사무위원　리희경

○명제쥬목종두사무위원　안ᄐᆡᆨ슈

○면본관　챵원면보사쥬사　리츈복

○우는챵원면보사쟝셔샹셕의보고셔를거ᄒᆞᆫ즉히원이쳔리지소ᄒᆞ고고등한이시무ᄒᆞ와여러번효유ᄒᆞ오나일향부츔이라ᄒᆞ엿기일로써면본관ᄒᆞ는사

○임부산면보사쥬사셔관임관륙등　시흥면보샤쥬사　셩두

○급삼급봉　부산면보샤쥬사　셩두식

이샹십이월십사일

○명관제리졍소의졍관　외부협관　윤치호　통신원회관　쟝화식

○의원면본관　비셔승　셔병션

봉샹사부졔됴　신헌균

니장원공업파쥬사　남쥰식

○임비셔원승셔쥬임관사등　졍삼품　리범인

○임니장원공업파쥬사셔판임관륙등　김원셕

○명시종원분시어　죠병셩

○임샹의샤쟝셔쥬임관륙등　봉샹샤부졔됴　심구ᄐᆡᆨ

○임봉샹사부졔됴셔쥬임관오등　비셔원승　죠범구　면셔샤쟝　리룡상

○임비셔원승셔쥬임관삼등　졍삼품　신헌균

○임면션샤쟝셔쥬임관삼등　졍삼품　리근목

○겸임래의원쇼경　비셔원승　신헌균

○증츄이품가션대부니부협판　교학셩　죠병칠

○증졍삼품통졍대부비셔원승　교학셩　죠윤영

○증츄삼품통훈대부쟝례원좌쟝　고둥더랑　죠진쥬

이샹종이픔가션대부쟝례원소경　죠용하의고조고증조고의법면츄　증

이샹십이월십오일

뎐보

○불틱함ᄃᆡ의즁지ᄒᆞᆫ다는허셜　대한일보에긔ᄌᆡᄒᆞᆫ동경뎐보에말ᄒᆞ되려쇼구의ᄑᆡᄒᆞᆷ으로ᄒᆞ야불틱함ᄃᆡ가극동으로나옴을즁지ᄒᆞ고일본졍부가법덕량국에ᄃᆡᄒᆞ야강경히교셥햇다ᄒᆞ엿스니그교셥ᄒᆞ엿다ᄒᆞᆷ은무삼ᄉᆞ건인지우리는알슈업스나일본졍부는법국덕국이불틱함ᄃᆡ를항샹핍박ᄒᆞᆷ을바라는지대한일보에난말은웬통지각업고허무ᄒᆞᆫ보고로우리는ᄉᆡᆼ각ᄒᆞ노라대일우리는려쇼함ᄃᆡ의멸망ᄒᆞ엿다는말을밋지아니ᄒᆞ는것이그함ᄃᆡ에젹지아니ᄒᆞᆫ손ᄒᆡ가잇게ᄒᆞ엿다는말은피ᄒᆡ치아니ᄒᆞ거니와이ᄇᆡᆨ삼미돌고디나다른곳으로브터로국군함의돗ᄃᆡ만뵈이지그군함의젼톄는보지못ᄒᆞᆯ터인ᄃᆡ그군함에ᄃᆡ포알이몃치맛젓스니그군함들의근경이엇더ᄒᆞ니ᄒᆞ는력력ᄒᆞᆫ보고는그ᄉᆞ실샹으로보면희미ᄒᆞᆫ말이로다이룡산과숑슈산과계관산포ᄃᆡ를공격ᄒᆞᆯ세에일본군사가실ᄑᆡᄒᆞᆷ은우리가잇지아니ᄒᆞ엿스니다른방향에셔일본들이승젼ᄒᆞ일이잇셧슴이미우근사ᄒᆞᆫ일이로다

(십이월십오일오젼십시삼십오분발뎐)산젼뎨삼함ᄃᆡ사령관보고

○습격단힝　작일십사일오젼십일시반브터금죠삼시ᄭᆞ지룩긔슈뢰뎡ᄃᆡ와밋특종슈뢰뎡등은잔단이업시〔세ᄲᅡ스도보리〕〔오도쓰뉘〕와밋군용션에ᄃᆡᄒᆞ야습격을결단코힝ᄒᆞ엿는ᄃᆡ아즉샹보는졉ᄒᆞ지못ᄒᆞ엿스나그러ᄒᆞ나금죠오젼구시망누의보고를거ᄒᆞᆫ즉〔세ᄲᅡ스도보리〕는함슈가작일브터침하ᄒᆞ야거히함슈슈뢰발사관샹ᄭᆞ지면혀슈즁에침ᄒᆞ엿다ᄒᆞ엿더라

〔작일당디사령관챡뎐〕

○하변소젼　십오일오젼십시경에적긔병약십오명이하협〔하합창셔북삼십리허〕에현츌ᄒᆞ야우리군사의사격을의지ᄒᆞ야부샹ᄒᆞᆫ자삼명을츌ᄒᆞ고퇴격ᄒᆞ엿다ᄒᆞ엿더라

○젹초젼몰　십오일오젼일시반에우리쳑후는흥륭돈의동북방ᄃᆡ에잇는적의사인초를습격ᄒᆞ야놉슈히이거슬죽엿는ᄃᆡ견쟝번호를거ᄒᆞᆫ즉적은삼십칠사단에속ᄒᆞᆫ쟈ㅣ라더라

론돈발

○론돈면보　로국긔혁운동이뎐국에확쟝ᄒᆞ야더방집회는쇼녀져써헌법을요구ᄒᆞ고

○진히경뎐　려슌함ᄃᆡ젼몰의보가발표되야국니일반이진히경뎐ᄒᆞ고

○로함ᄃᆡ역항　로세쓰도의령솔ᄒᆞᆫ함ᄃᆡ는량부아불리가의〔못쭈시메쩨수〕에역항ᄒᆞ엿더라

○슈뢰습격　십사일미명에비샹ᄒᆞᆫ장셜을범ᄒᆞ고〔세ᄲᅡ스도보리〕와군용션에ᄃᆡᄒᆞ야슈뢰습격을힝ᄒᆞ고또십사일밤브터익죠ᄭᆞ지간단이업시〔세ᄲᅡ스도보리〕와〔오도와쓰뉘〕를습격ᄒᆞ엿는ᄃᆡ〔세ᄲᅡ스도보리〕는함슈가슈뢰사관의샹ᄭᆞ지침몰ᄒᆞ엿더라

일작일히군관사챡뎐

○슈뢰습격공보　십이월십오일오젼○시삼분발산젼뎨삼함ᄃᆡ사령관보고에말ᄒᆞ엿스되십사일오젼삼반히군소좌대룡염지죠의거나린슈뢰뎡ᄃᆡ와밋히군대위궁본송태랑의지휘ᄒᆞᆫ슈뢰뎡ᄃᆡ는다〔세ᄲᅡ스도보리〕와밋군용션을습격ᄒᆞ엿는ᄃᆡ대룡ᄃᆡ는밀렬ᄒᆞᆫ눈의방ᄒᆡᄒᆞᆫ미되야목젹을달치못ᄒᆞ엿스나궁본ᄃᆡ는대륙ᄃᆡ가담히등의계비샹ᄒᆞᆫ

UNION INSURANCE SOCIETY OF CANTON.

Head office Hongkong.
Marine risks underwritten at current rates.
Agents in Chemulpo,
E. MEYER & Co.

COMPAGNIE DES MESSAGERIES MARITIMES.

Fortnightly Direct Service.

For Marseilles
via Ports.
Sailing from Yokohama
Calling at Kobe,
Shanghai, Hongkong, Saigon, Singapore,
Colombo, Djibonti, Suez, Port Said
and Marseilles.

For particulars apply to
HOLME RINGER & Co.,
Chemulpo.

HAYASHIDA & CO.,

16 MYENG DONG, CHIN KO KAI, SEOUL.
BRANCH OFFICE AT CHEMULPO.

Money changers, Coal and Wood Merchants, Express Agents.

We are agents for the Pyeng-yang Coal Company and the Karazu Coal Company of Japan. We have the best quality of both anthracite and bituminous coal, and prompt execution of orders is our speciality. Firewood of all kinds kept in stock. Full weight guaranteed. Money of all denominations exchanged at current rates. Parcels received for all parts.

CHINA MUTUAL LIFE INS. OC.

Most favourable terms to policy holders.

Benefit system unsurpassed.

HOLME RINGER & Co.
Agents, Chemulpo.

C. P. R.

CANADIAN PACIFIC RAILWAY COMPANY'S ROYAL MAIL STEAMSHIP LINE.

THE FAST ROUTE BETWEEN CHINA, JAPAN, AND EUROPE VIA CANADA AND THE UNITED STATES.

Route from Hongkong via Shanghai, Nagasaki (Inland Sea of Japan) Kobe. Yokohama Victoria and Vancouver.

Twin Screw Empress Steamship—6,000 Tons—Speed 19 knots.

PROPOSED SAILING FROM YOKOHAMA.
R. M. S. Empress of India.
R. M. S. Empress of Japan.
R. M. S. Empress of China.
R. M. S. Athenian.
R. M. S. Tartar.

Special reduction (first class only) granted to members of the Military, Naval, Diplomatic and Civil services and to Missionaries.

Passengers have choice of ten routes across the Continent of America and have privilege of travelling by any Atlantic Steamship Line.

Round the World passage tickets in connection with the P. and O. S. N., North German Lloyd and Messageries Co.'s **£125.**

All rates payable at current rate of exchange.

For further information, Tickets, Guide Books, etc., apply to

HOLME, RINGER & Co., AGENTS,
Chemulpo.

Grand Hotel,

(Formerly the Station Hotel)

Near the Railway Terminus, West Gate Seoul.

The Best Hotel in Korea
Handsome new Building.
Fine Airy Rooms
Excellent Cuisine.
Terms Moderate.
Special terms to Missionaries
and to permanent boarders.

Electric cars within 2 minutes' walk.

W. H. EMBERLEY.
Proprietor

EVERY FACILITY.

In connection with Life Assurance Business is afforded by

The Standard Life Assurance Co.,

One of the largest and wealthiest of the Provident Institutions of the United Kingdom Forms of Application and all information will be promptly afforded on application.

10 CENTS A DAY.

Not a very large expenditure is it? But it is sufficient to secure for a man of 30 a policy with the STANDARD LIFE OFFICE for

$1323.

For all particulars of rates, etc., apply to

Holme, Ringer & Co.,
Agents, Chemulpo.

THE NEW YORK LIFE INSURANCE COMPANY.

Have you ever been declined by any Company?

Are you engaged in a specially hazardous occupation?

Have you heard of the New York Life Insurance Company's New Classifications for this class of Risks?

If not, send your date of birth, occupation and particulars of rejection, if any to

E. MEYER & Co.,
Agents, Chemulpo.

MITSUI BUSSAN KAISHA.
(MITSUI & Co.)

MITSUI GINKO.
(MITSUI BANK.)

The Bank is owned by the members of the Mitsui Family, who, as partners, assume an unlimited responsibility for all liabilities of the Bank:—

Capital.................... .....Yen 5,000,000
Reserve Fund.................. " 5,600,000

HEAD OFFICE, TOKYO.
LONDON OFFICE, 34 LIME ST., E. C.

BRANCHES AND AGENCIES:—
New York, San Francisco, Hamburg, Bombay, Singapore, Manila, Hongkong, Amoy, Chefoo, Tientsin.

Kobe, Hakodate, Yokohama, Kure, Yokosuka, Moji, Shimonoseki, Miike, Wakamatsu, Nagasaki, Kuchinotsu, Karatsu, Sasebo, Misume, Taipeh, &c.

Telegraphic Address for all the Offices:
"MITSUI."
A. B. C. AND A. 1 CODES USED.

Contractors of Coal
To the Imperial Japanese Navy. Arsenals and Railway Bureau, Principal Railway Companies and Industrial Work, Home and Foreign Mail and Freight Steamers.

Sole Proprietors
Of the famous Miike, Tagawa and Yamano Coal Mines.

Sole Agents
For the sale of Fukumo, Hokoku, Ichimura, Kanoda, Mannoura, Onoura, Ostuji, Sonoda, Tsubaruro, Yoshinotani, Yoshio, Yurokibura and other coals.

YANGTSE INSURANCE ASSOCIATION, LTD.

The undersigned, having been appointed agents for the above company, are prepared to issue policies and pay losses on marine risks at regular rates.

E. MEYER & Co.,
Agents, Chemulpo.

AMERICAN KOREAN ELECTRIC CO.

Light and Power.

Main Office: Electric Building, Chong No.

RAILWAY DEPARTMENT.

OPERATING CARS BETWEEN EAST AND WEST GATE, EVERY TEN MINUTES:—

First Car leaves East Gate at 7:00 A. M. First Car leaves R. R. Station at 7:25 A. M
Last Car " East Gate at 9:40 P. M. Last " " R. R. Station at 10:05 P.M

OPERATING CARS BETWEEN EAST GATE AND IMPERIAL TOMB TERMINUS, EVERY TWENTY MINUTES:—

CONNECTING WITH EVERY ALTERNATE CAR ARRIVING AT EAST GATE FROM CHONG NO.

First Car leaves East Gate for Tomb at 7:10 A. M.
" " " Tomb for East Gate at 7:35 A. M.
Last " " East Gate for Tomb at 7:50 P. M.
" " " Tomb for East Gate at 8:10 P. M.

OPERATING CARS BETWEEN CHONG NO AND YUNG SAN RIVER EVERY TWELVE MINUTES:—

First Car leaves Chong No for South Gate at 7:12 A. M.
" " " Chong No for Yung San at 7:36 A. M.
" " " South Gate for Chong No at 7:20 A. M.
" " " Yung San for Chong No at 8:09 A. M.
Last " " South Gate for Chong No 10:00 P. M.
" " " Yung San for Chong No at 9:33 P. M.

SPECIAL PRIVATE CARS FURNISHED TO SUIT CONVENIENCE OF PATRONS. PRICES ON APPLICATION AT HEAD OFFICE.

LIGHTING DEPARTMENT.

Where less than 250 candle power of light is used, the rate per month will be
Per 16 candle power incandescent lamp,—All night.—Yen 2.50.
32 candle power incandescent lamp:—All night:—Yen 4.00.
50 candle power incandescent lamp:—All night:—Yen 6.00.
150 " " " " " " ,, 10.00.
1200 " ,, enclosed are ,, ,, ,, ,, 20.00.

Where more than 250 candle power of light is used, a Meter will be installed, freqvedted:—Rent of Meter Yen 2.00 per month. Rate of charges by meter reading:—Two Sen per Ampere per hour. (Approximately this is equal to about One Sen per 16 C. P. lamp per hour) Minimum monthly charge where meter is installed, Yen 20.00 per month, which includes rental of meter.

Estimates for installing lights furnished on application

An assortment of chandeliers always on hand.

K. Murakami.

Photograph Studio
Chinkokai, Seoul.

Printing, Developing and Enlargement, of Photographs always Undertaken.

Korean Views and Pictures Illustrating Native Customs always on Sale,

---

THE OSAKA SHOSEN KAISHA.

Boats frequently on the berth for Chinnampo.

REGULAR SAILINGS BETWEEN JAPAN AND KOREAN PORTS.

FUSAN AND KOBE VIA SHIMONOSEKI.

OSAKA VIA MOKPO, FUSAN, SHIMONOSEKI AND KOBE.

MOJI DIRECT.

OSAKA VIA KUNSAN, MASANPO, FUSAN, SHIMONOSEKI AND KOBE.

CHEMULPO KUNSAN LINE,
Every three days.

CHEMULPO CHINNAMPO LINE.
Every three days.

For Freight and passage and further particulars apply to

THE OSAKA SHOSEN KAISHA,
Chemulpo

RONDON, PLAISANT & CO.

General Storekeepers and Merchants, Ships Contractors, Tobacconists, Commission and Forwarding Agents, Coal Merchants

IMPORTERS AND EXPORTERS

Seoul & Chemulpo.

W. D. WENTWORTH.

LANDING
AND
SHIPPING AGENT
AND
CUSTOMS BORDER.

12 OURA, NAGASAKI.

STEWARD & CO.

Chemulpo.

Shipchandlers and Storekeepers, Naval and Mercantile Contractors. Landing and Shipping Agents.

STEWARD'S HOTEL

Chemulpo.

Best accommodation in the port for travellers. Clean and well-aired rooms, good cuisine and prompt attendence, moderate tariff.

강셜을무릅스고드듸여옥젹에
달ᄒᆞ야젹합유셕종에랑뎡이셔
로견실ᄒᆞ엿스나오젼사시경에
ᄒᆡ군대위중모젼부빈의뎡은군
용함에향ᄒᆞ고궁본대위의뎡은
[세싸스도보리]에향ᄒᆞ야슈뢰
를사격ᄒᆞᄂᆞᆫ듸중모뎐뎡우그폭
발ᄒᆞᆷ을칭탄ᄒᆞ고이뎡이함셕지
몰너갓스되ᄒᆡ군대위영면즁ᄎᆞ
랑의뎡과ᄂᆞᆫ드듸여상회치못ᄒᆞ
엿ᄂᆞᆫ듸동뎡은지이금ᄒᆞ야도귀
ᄒᆡ치아니ᄒᆞ니고운ᄒᆡᆼ에판ᄒᆞ야
우편함을금치못ᄒᆞᆫ지라금죠에
나로라망누와소함에셔ᄂᆞᆫ함셕
지[세싸스도보리]의함슈가상을
쳥ᄉᆞᆼ을칭하ᄒᆞᆫ상태에잇ᄂᆞᆫ쥴을
보고ᄒᆞ엿더라

론돈발 십이월팔일

◯로함슈ᄎᆞᆫ 불틱함대의군함
들은아죠지브틸에셔셕탄과식
물을싣고쏘약간죵선들은말나
가에잇다더라

동디발 동일

○로쟝신린 로쟝그린펜벅쟝
군이봉텬에도착ᄒᆞ엿더라

빅림발 동일

○로국데삼함디 본월칠일에
로국황뎨가쳐평으로ᄀᆞ동에보
낼뎨삼함디를죠직ᄒᆞ라명령ᄒᆞ
엿다더라

◯아로제션소의ᄉᆞ실 동경외
무셩에온뎐보에말ᄒᆞ엿스되영
국졍부에셔아로제션소의ᄒᆡᆼ동
에디ᄒᆞ야방쟝사실ᄒᆞᄂᆞᆫ중인듸
그제션소의디표자가말ᄒᆞ되그
ᄇᆡ를로국사ᄅᆞᆷ의게보닐싱각은
아니ᄒᆞ고ᄒᆞᆫ법국쟝사에셔팔랏
ᄂᆞᆫ듸그법국사ᄅᆞᆷ이로국에파랏
셔편보에보넛ᄂᆞᆫ듸그ᄇᆡᄂᆞᆫ슈뢰
파괴함으로쓸것이라ᄒᆞ엿다더
라

빅림발 십이월팔일

◯셕탄사건과영뎍 카듸푸에
셔셕탄실키를금ᄒᆞᆫ덕국론셜감
ᄐᆡᆫ몐셰호ᄂᆞᆫ그ᄇᆡ쥬인들이힘벅
으로도라가라고명령ᄒᆞ엿ᄂᆞᆫ듸
그셕탄사건으로ᄒᆞ야영덕사이
에무숨갈등이날리도업고또무
숨외교상에말이되지도아니홀
것이며덕국졍부에셔ᄒᆞᆫ사사회사
의ᄒᆡᆼ위로국제문제될이리키지
아니홀예졍이라더라

동디발 동일

◯욕슈일탄 론잉포쓰드에발
ᄒᆞᆫ뢰카듸푸챵ᄉᆞ들이일본을위
ᄒᆞ야셕탄을쳥국항구에보니랴
고그곳셕탄쟝사를고용ᄒᆞ엿다
더라

외보

◯쳥인번젹 근일에일본이쳥
인의일본에림젹ᄒᆞᄂᆞᆫ규칙을새
로치이샹ᄒᆞ게ᄀᆞ쟝ᄒᆞ엿ᄂᆞᆫ듸쳥
국닉디에잇ᄂᆞᆫ쳥인이자긔의셩명
을일본으로보니고랩젹비죠곰
만드리면일본빅셩이되ᄂᆞᆫ듸림
젹죵셔ᄂᆞᆫ그림젹ᄒᆞᄂᆞᆫ쳥인의잇
ᄂᆞᆫ곳으로셔로그중갓가온일본령사
관에셔타가진다더라

◯한국에일본셰력 경부텰로
가닉년일월일일에기회식을ᄒᆡᆼ
ᄒᆞᆯ터인듸셔울에셔부산에가ᄂᆞᆫ
슈레ᄂᆞᆫ올나간다ᄒᆞ고부산에셔
셔울에오ᄂᆞᆫ슈레ᄂᆞᆫ닉려간다ᄒᆞᆫ
다ᄂᆞᆫ듸그것은동경을즁심을삼
ᄂᆞᆫ연고라ᄒᆞ고차셰ᄂᆞᆫ일본돈
으로밧게ᄒᆞ고쳘로변에디명은
다일본말노부르게ᄒᆞᆫ다ᄒᆞ며일
샤젼에경인쳘로회사에셔일본
시간을쓰기로쟉뎡ᄒᆞ엿스니그
젼보다삼십오분이늘게되엿ᄂᆞᆫ
듸외국사ᄅᆞᆷ들에게이말을미리
통긔ᄒᆞ지아니ᄒᆞ야셔차타려나
아갓다가낭패ᄒᆞᆫ자도잇고더러ᄂᆞᆫ
불편ᄒᆞᆫ일이만히잇셧다더라

◯압졔탄로 로군이봉쳔에셔
쳥국황뎨죠릉에보물을북평으
로보낸다ᄒᆞ고함삼빅기안에다
가탄환과화약을만히시러셔금
쥬로보니다가즁로에셔일본군
사의게슈색을당ᄒᆞ야몰슈히젼
탈ᄒᆞ엿ᄂᆞᆫ듸이탄환과화약은려
슌으로비밀히슈운ᄒᆞ려다가탈
로된것이라더라

론셜

일본국회의의견이다른일

◯금월팔일신호칭랏드신문에
게재ᄒᆞᆫ바죠지홈과갓틀진뎐일
본셔젼쟁은괘렴ᄒᆞ야ᄒᆞ나도의
졔츌ᄒᆞᄂᆞᆫ사ᄅᆞᆷ이업슴은분명
ᄒᆞ며또ᄒᆞᆫ갈수록졍부로셔특별
ᄒᆞᆫ수건에ᄃᆡᄒᆞ야ᄃᆡ답ᄒᆞᄂᆞᆫ거슨
가불명ᄒᆞ야그사리로써결원ᄒᆞ야
가ᄂᆞᆫ도다
작일샹오십시 샹셥불에듸의원
에대신사무원들이모혓ᄂᆞᆫ듸총
리대신계빅작이하각대신이모
도참례ᄒᆞ엿ᄂᆞᆫ지라
의회의쟝을아씨가지회홈을셜
명ᄒᆞᆫ후번쟝ᄒᆞᆫ오랑씨가연셜ᄒᆞ
기를각대신들은예산사건으로
써셜명ᄒᆞ기가어려울듯ᄒᆞ거시
우리가예산문제로말ᄒᆞᄂᆞᆫ자리
인즉젼쟁일수로ᄂᆞᆫ기구ᄒᆞ야ᄃᆡ
답ᄒᆞ기를모피ᄒᆞᆯ터이라ᄂᆞᆫ뜻으
로셜명ᄒᆞ며
목군과회군량대신은자긔들의
말ᄒᆞᄂᆞᆫ바를모호ᄒᆞ게홈으로써
주쟝ᄒᆞ나그러ᄒᆞ나모든모힌사
ᄅᆞᆷ들의말은젼쟁되기ᄲᆡ저졍만
크게칭비ᄒᆞ엿다ᄒᆞ며또ᄒᆞᆫ졍부
에셔ᄂᆞᆫ무삼쓸돈이던지회락ᄒᆞ
지아니ᄒᆞᆫ다고들말ᄒᆞ며
외부대신도역시갓튼ᄃᆡ도로써
ᄒᆞ고묵묵히들잇더니
진보당원대셕씨가졍부에셔외
국에ᄃᆡᄒᆞ야졍략힝홈을평론ᄒᆞ
야자긔의긔왕보고ᄒᆞ야온바사
샹을셜명ᄒᆞᆫ즉모든의원들은동
도씨의말홈이합당ᄒᆞ야모다응답
ᄒᆞ엿셧다ᄂᆞᆫ듸그셜명홈이여좌ᄒᆞ
우리나라졍략으로써말ᄒᆞᆫ진듸
덕국과법국이아라사셰력합ᄒᆞᆫ듸
로더부러련결ᄒᆞ엿스되졍부계
공ᄉᆞ들은이일에ᄃᆡᄒᆞ야론박ᄒᆞᆫ거
시무엇시뇨만일합당ᄒᆞᆫ듸답을
봇지경이면쟝ᄎᆞᆺ엇더케드ᄒᆞ랴
ᄒᆞ오ᄒᆞ며
영국은로뎌브리동밍ᄒᆞ엿다ᄒᆞ
되이ᄲᆡ를당ᄒᆞ야그나라에셔ᄃᆡ
도보이ᄂᆞᆫ거시무엇이잇스며
한국으로말ᄒᆞ드리도일한약졍
ᄒᆞᆫ후에두어고문관을보니엿스
나희셜ᄒᆡ취ᄒᆞᆯ리익이무엇이뇨
우리의싱각갓ᄒᆞ여셔ᄂᆞᆫ이러ᄒᆞᆫ
졍칙은아니홈만갓지못ᄒᆞ며ᄒᆞᆫ
국에주차ᄒᆞᆫ공ᄉᆞ도심히칭ᄃᆡᄒᆞ
고
만쥬로말ᄒᆞ드리도무론엇더ᄒᆞᆫ
일본사ᄅᆞᆷ이던지군ᄃᆡ에샹관이
업ᄂᆞᆫ자ㅣ면일졀금지ᄒᆞ고드리
지아니ᄒᆞ니이ᄂᆞᆫ엇지ᄒᆞᆫ리유이
뇨싸홈인즉만쥬셔담이어그러
니되이것도말아니되ᄂᆞᆫ자ㅣ잇
ᄂᆞᆫ니
쳥국졍부에셔ᄂᆞᆫ말ᄒᆞ기를만쥬
희복홈에방조ᄒᆞ기위ᄒᆞ야권리
들을부린다고ᄒᆞᄂᆞᆫ듸
우리나라에셔ᄂᆞᆫ이일로말ᄆᆡ아
마싸홈즉이러케싸호ᄂᆞᆫ거시우
리의게릉ᄒᆞ야우리를진졍케셔
무엇시뇨ᄒᆞᆫ즉
소촌남쟉은이평론ᄒᆞᄂᆞᆫ말을듯
고ᄃᆡ답ᄒᆞ기ᄂᆞᆫᄒᆞ나그러ᄒᆞ나셜
명ᄒᆞᄂᆞᆫ바ㅣ다만불공평ᄒᆞᆫ반ᄃᆡ
로만쥬쟝ᄒᆞ야협당ᄒᆞ도록만ᄒᆞ
엿ᄂᆞᆫ지라
시이날오후에위원들이다시모
작ᄒᆞᆯᄯᆡ에총리대신계빅쟉모
말ᄒᆞ야왕ᄒᆡᆼᄒᆞᆷ이감손된다ᄂᆞᆫ
문제에ᄃᆡᄒᆞ야ᄂᆞᆫ나의게ᄃᆡ답ᄒᆞ
야샹관되ᄂᆞᆫ말인즉두어마듸말
ᄒᆞ노라ᄒᆞ며
ᄂᆡ가총리대신ᄒᆞᆫ이후로이사건
을듯기도만히ᄒᆞ엿고또ᄒᆞᆫ슈의
에도만히ᄒᆞ엿슨즉그결과ᄂᆞᆫ이번
리가모든홀일을극력히ᄒᆞᆫ지라우
도록ᄒᆞ엿스니쟝ᄎᆞ졍략을이ᄃᆡ
각ᄒᆡᆼᄒᆞᆯ터이나그러ᄒᆞ나ᄯᅩᄒᆞᆫ싱
에셔방금큰젼쟁이되ᄂᆞ니졍은
소홈이ᄒᆞ지못ᄒᆞᆯ거시며져졍쳥
구홈도또ᄒᆞᆫ그러ᄒᆞᆫ즉만일우리
의ᄒᆞᄂᆞᆫ광경을주목ᄒᆞ야볼진댄
가모도평졔ᄒᆞᄂᆞᆫ바로써가히셜효
가잇슴을알터이라ᄒᆞ며
대쟝대신조녜남쟉의연셜에ᄂᆞᆫ
륙빅만원을일빅삼십은ᄒᆡᆼ에미
리엇게ᄒᆞᆫ거슨무리ㅣ라졍부주
의에ᄂᆞᆫ은ᄒᆡᆼ을위ᄒᆞ야부지ᄒᆞ도
록홈이요또ᄒᆞᆫ샹업에도크게히
됨을막자고ᄒᆞ야불가불ᄒᆞᆫ바이
어늘만일그사ᄅᆞᆷ들이이ᄒᆞᄂᆞᆫ바
를취치아니ᄒᆞᆯ지경이면다른여
러은ᄒᆡᆼ이모도결단이날터이라
고ᄒᆞᆫ즉
녕졍씨가견문ᄒᆞ되엇지ᄒᆞ야졍
부에셔횡빈졍금은ᄒᆡᆼ에향ᄒᆞ야
일빅만원을일빅삼십은ᄒᆡᆼ에뎌
어ᄒᆞ도록ᄒᆞ엿ᄂᆞ뇨ᄒᆞᆫ즉
대쟝셩ᄎᆞ관과곽씨가ᄃᆡ답ᄒᆞ기
를이ᄂᆞᆫ그은ᄒᆡᆼ이파산됨으로써
곤돈에일본국ᄎᆡ의표부홈을방
도비ᄒᆞ자고홈이로라ᄒᆞᆫ즉맛수모
엇지ᄒᆞ야론돈은수식이괴ᄒᆡᆼ에
ᄂᆞᆫ구식방으로뎡ᄒᆞ엿거ᄂᆞᆯ지금
에ᄂᆞᆫ일본과아라사사이에차등
이잇ᄂᆞ뇨ᄒᆞᆫ즉
그대신이말ᄒᆞ기를이목젹에ᄃᆡ
ᄒᆞ야ᄂᆞᆫ셜명을다ᄒᆞ엿다ᄒᆞ며방
을쳥결케ᄒᆞ여야ᄒᆞ겟다ᄒᆞ고하
오비시에폐회ᄒᆞ엿다더라

잡보

◯부윤참령상지 강화부윤윤
철규씨를회부진위ᄃᆡ대장리
동휘씨가무단히병뎡을거ᄂᆞ리
고즁이라ᄒᆞᄂᆞᆫ고로도망ᄒᆞ야올
나왓다ᄒᆞ며니외졍계에젼파ᄒᆞ
야리동휘를모살ᄒᆞᆯ에쳐ᄒᆞ라ᄒᆞ
기에그사실을다시탐지ᄒᆞᆫ즉윤
부윤의탐쟝삼십만량이리동
휘로ᄒᆞ야곰발각되야신문에셔
지뎌젼포ᄒᆞ엿다ᄒᆞ야셔로의심
ᄒᆞ니윤부윤이일로써평의를막
어리동휘가아라사국간쳡ᄒᆞᄂᆞᆫ
자ㅣ라ᄒᆞ고향일일신문에괴
셔ᄒᆞ야포고ᄒᆞᆫ것이화셜이즁거
가잇ᄂᆞᆫ고로리창평이견문ᄎᆞ로
십오일밤에윤부윤을심방ᄒᆞᆫ즉
윤씨가가히ᄃᆡ답ᄒᆞᆯ말이업셔도
망ᄒᆞ야올나와이리케운동ᄒᆞᄂᆞᆫ
중이라더라

공진회쳥원 공진회에셔외
졍부에쳥원ᄒᆞ기를회명을공진
이라ᄒᆞᆷ은샹하공지ᄒᆞ고진어문
명ᄒᆞᄂᆞᆫ목젹이라우의셔나가고
자ᄒᆞ나아리셔나가지아니ᄒᆞᆫ즉
귀로며브리나가며아리셔나가
고져ᄒᆞ나우의에셔나가지아니
ᄒᆞᆫ즉뀌로며브리나가리요이러
홈으로본회가젼국샹하가ᄒᆞᆫ가
지로문명에나감이라그도리에
바ᄅᆞᆷ이이깃고그ᄒᆡᆼᄒᆞᄂᆞᆫ듸쉬움
이이깃고그효험에곰이또이깃
ᄒᆞᆫ니이ᄂᆞᆫ동양에고유ᄒᆞᆫ문명이
요겨를단코오날날셔으로브터동
에이른것이아니라이에본회의
표준세가지근강령을들어좌에
긔렬ᄒᆞ오니본회취지를통촉ᄒᆞ
시와샹 주하의ᄒᆞ신후셰니공
인ᄒᆞ와민국의다ᄒᆡᆼ홈을바란다
ᄒᆞ엿더라

일 황실위권이뎐법에졍ᄒᆞᆫ바
안에잇ᄂᆞᆫ자를존즁케ᄒᆞᆯ수

일 졍부명령이법률규측안에
잇ᄂᆞᆫ자를복죵ᄒᆞᆯ수

일 인민의권이고유ᄒᆞᆫ법한안
에등ᄒᆞᆫ자를자유ᄒᆞᆯ수

광무팔년십이월십칠일공진회
쟝리준
외졍부참졍신긔션 각하

TELEGRAMS.

Army Headquarters.

On the 15th inst. 600 Russian infantry and cavalry attacked the Japanese position near Pingchunsan. After a fight lasting for 3½ hours, they were repulsed.

(FROM JAPAN PAPERS.)

London, Dec. 10.

During the debate in the Reichstag on the Budget and Army Bills, the Socialists opposed any increased grants on behalf of the Army on the ground that Russia has been crippled by the present war and there was no necessity for such heavy burdens for purposes of defence. The Socialists again renewed their charges that the Government had shown partiality towards Russia in the present war.

Count von Buelow, the Imperial Chancellor, in reply, deprecated the holding of sentimental views on delicate questions of international policy. It was this which caused the people to take the wrong road in regard to the war with the Boers in South Africa. He reasserted that Germany had observed the most complete neutrality in the dispute between Japan and Russia, and he ridiculed the suggestion that there existed a secret Russo-German Treaty.

Berlin, Dec. 11.

The shipbuilding company of Macfie and Levy, of Philadelphia, has become bankrupt.

Berlin, Dec 11.

Naval experts in London express the belief that the destrnction of the Russian warships at Port Arthur has rendered the voyage of the Baltic Fleet wholly futile, and prophesy that the latter will ultimately be obliged to seek refuge in a neutral port and be dismantled.

Berlin, Cec. 11

The German troops have stormed the chief position occupied by the Witboys, causing them to retreat eastwards in wild confusion.

Berlin, Dec. 11.

Count von Buelow, referring in the course of a debate in the Reichstag to the present situation in international affairs, that the complete observaance of neutrality by Germany in the present war was such as could not be called in question by any friendly Power. The Chancellor again re-asserted that no secret Treaty exists between Germany and Russia.

London, Dec. 12.

The Admiralty announces that henceforth the reserve fleet will remain in constant commission, ready for immediate service and exercising at sea periodically.

There will be manœuvres in 1905—6, when the navy throughout the world will assume that war has broken out.

According to reports from Constantinople, the Sultan issued an Irade, on lately, sanctioning the construction of the proposed railway from Jeddah to Mecca. "Die Ziet's" correspondent learns that the Khedive who is now at Constantinople, told the Sultan about the large number of murders and robberies of Egyptian pilgrims to Mecca committed by the Bedouins, and declared that, as the Turkish authorities could not protect them, it might be advisable for pilgrims from Egypt to select another route to Mecca. This seems to have determined the Sultan to allow the new railway line. In a letter to the "Standard," Mr. Archibald Dunn recently pointed out the great importance for England and Egypt, as well as for Turkey, of a line from Jeddah to the Cities, and he quoted a report from the British Consul at Jeddah stating that in 1904 44,718 pilgrims arrived by the Red Sea there and proceeded across the mountains and desert to Mecca, a most adngerous and exhausting journey

THE HEATHEN CHINEE.

A difficulty has arisen between the governments of China and Portugal in regard to the treatment of Chinese who have become naturalized Portuguese It appears that throughout the Canton province there is a considerable number of these men, who have become naturalized at Macao and other Portuguese settlements. Many are charged with seeking and obtaining naturalization papers, after they have committed some offence against Chinese law and thereby they attempt to avoid punishment. When naturalized they are furnished with the necessary papers and a passport, and when they travel in the interior of China, they expect the treatment which is supposed to be accorded to foreigners minus the abuse.

According to the report of the Viceroy of the Fukien province, there are some tens of thousands there. The charge brought against these men is that they are obstreperous, that they rely on the prestige of a Western power to bully the mandarins, that they are quarrelsome and overbearing amongst the people with whom they associate, and that generally speaking they command all the privileges that Chinese law offers, and towards these privileges they pay little or nothing.

Sundry communications have passed between the Viceroys of these two provinces, at Pekin, so the "Yeung Shing Times" here says but no solution of the difficulty has yet been found, which shall be satisfactoty to both parties.

One suggestion offered by the Viceroy of the Canton province is this: Whenever a Chinese becomes a naturalized Portuguese, before his application is settled, a communication should be sent to the Viceroy, who shall say whether he is an unimpeachable character or not.

It does not yet appear how the question will be settled. No doubt there have been those who have relied on these powers to do things that they had better left undone, and then have tried to escape the justice which their misdeeds have deserved.—China Overland Mail.

Kwangchu reports itself, through its Magistrate, as suffering from Il-chin-hoi-itis.

The Governor of South Hamkyeng, according to his confrere of the northern province, died on the 3rd instant.

The Belgian Minister has renewed his application, made to the Government three years ago, for a gold-mining concession.

A report is current to the effect that the "Righteous Army" are re-gathering with a view to the overthrow of the Il-chin-hoi.

The Il-chin-hoi people in Pyengyang are being put to a new use. They now take the place of the coolies, which the Japanese military authorities find so hard to obtain.

Replying to the complaint of the Foreign Office that several Japanese have seized ground and are building houses near Yonsan, the Japanese Minister states that the local Magistrate and the nearest Japanese Consul can settle the matter between them.

It is wonderful how things adjust themselves. The Japanese papers have wounded Stoessel killed him and then wounded him again; they have captured Mitschenko and got rid of General Grippenberg by means of an apoplectic fit. These people are still actively opposing Japan's progress. Now from America comes a long story about the death of General Kuroki at the Shaho battle. We reserve our obituary notice until we have better evidence.

THE MISSING ATTACHES.

Lieutenant Roques, commander of the French gunboat "Surprise", is in Chefoo on a special mission, seeking information of the missing naval attache Lieutenant de Cuverville, who left Port Arthur in a junk in August and mysteriously disappeared. Lieutenant Roques has come from Shanghai, where his ship now is, by command of the Admiral commanding the French Asiatic squadron.

Lieutenant de Cuverville, it will be remembered, set sail with Lieutenant von Gilgenheimb, German attache at Port Arthur, about the middle of August, since which nothing has been heard of either of them, or of the junk which carried them out.

Lieutenant Roques visited the Taotai yesterday in his search for information bearing upon the mission with which he has been entrusted. He will proceed to Tientsin, where he will conduct further investigation.

Lieutenant Roques is the officer who escorted Dreyfus from his place of imprisonment on Devil's Isle to France. The Lieutenant states that the French have at present four submarine vessels in Saigon, and that there will be several more at that place by February next.—Chefoo Daily News.

General Hasegawa was yesterday afternoon received in audience by His Mjesty.

On the 16th inst, Mr. An Chong Dok, special superintendent of the South Chulla province, telegraphed the announcement that he had dismissed the Governor of the province. The Governor is much incensed, as only recently he paid a very stiff price for his appointment.

The Russian advance towards Saimachi is probably responsible for General Hasegawa's departure from Seoul. A descent upon Motienling is not impossible, and General Hasegawa, as a prudent general should, is presumably making his head-quarters somewhere nearer the field of probable operations.

Mr. Gorschalki this morning underwent a slight operation for the removal of the thumb nail of his right hand, which was recently wounded by Japanese soldiers. We understand that the German Consulate has his case in hand and will endeavour to bring his assailants to justice.

On Saturday afternoon Colonel Kil Yong Su and Mr. Yun Yong Sik obtained their release from the Japanese headquarters. Arrested some three months ago under suspicion of being Russian spies, these gentlemen have, at last, been found innocent. Immdiately on gaining his freedom, Colonel Kil Yong Su was received by His Majesty in audience.

At the supper at the Hongkong Club which followed the fete on the Cricket Ground there, the Hongkong Umpire, Mr. A. G. Ward, acknowledged with hearty apologies and regrets that two mistaken decisions on his part gave the match to Hongkong which would otherwise have been won by Shanghai. Twice he gave Hongkong batsmen "not out' when they were really "out," and this gave Hongkong 80 runs which these batsmen subsequently compiled—N. C. D. News.

The Dai-Han Ilpo is continuing its campaign against the Korean Government. Writing editioirally on Friday it warned the world that unless appointment to government permission met with the approval of the Japanese Minister and the Korean populace, there would be trouble. On Saturday the Dai Han Ilpo likened Korea to Russia, and, speaking of the popular rising in Russia, prophesies the same conditions here unless the government acts according to the will of the people. We may point out that while the country is full of noisy agitators in the employ of the Japanese, it is impossible for the government to know what the wishes of the people really are.

SIX THOUSAND LIVES SAVED BY A HORSE.

Far from Nepera, quietly munching her oats in the stable of the largest biological laboratory on earth, stood a gentle white mare, unmindful of the fact that a miracle had been worked through her, or what would have been regarded as one in the olden days. She had saved the lives of 6,000 disease-stricken children, writes Hugo Ericksen, since she had entered the mammoth establ'shthat had been her home during the past two years, and would soon be retired to the country to recover from the debilitating effect of the repeated blood letting to which she had been subjected in the interests of humanity.

The substance obtained from her blood that counterbalanced the diphtheria toxin, or poison, was prepared by a method consisting of a number of steps. The horse is immune to diphtheria by nature, and this immunity is greatly increased by the treatment to which he is subjected. Hence scientists agreed upon the horse as the most suitable animal for the production of antidiphtheritic serum. He stands the injection of the diphtheria toxin without any apparent discomfort, and furnishes great amounts of serum from time to time.

The horses selected for the purpose are all between four and six years old when purchased, and perefectly healthy. Wholesome food is of the utmost importance to the proper execution of the immunizing process. The more invigoroting the diet, the greater is the animal's tolerance of the dipththeria poison or toxin, and the more potent the serum it eventually produces. The horses are carefully groomed and exercised every day.

In the establishment sheltering the white horse, to which this narrative pertains, large, sunny paddocks rejoin the stables, giving the animals ample room and exercise; on stormy days a covered space, sufficient for sixty horses at a time, is used for this purpose. The operating room is a light, airy, aseptic and capacious chamber. The cement floors and painted and varnished brick walls are readily and thoroughly sterilized with carbolic acid solution. Heavy, close-fitting double doors render this apartment practically air-tight and germ-proof.

The Korea Daily News.

Issued at 5 P. M. daily except Sundays.

Rate of Subscription:—
Per Year,............Yen 25.
Per Quarter,..........Yen 7.
Per Month,..........Yen 2.50.

Postage in Korea not charged extra.
Postage abroad charged extra.

Advertisements, 50 sen per day for 1 inch or less.
5 yen per month per inch.
50 yen per year per inch.

All communications to
E. T. BETHELL,
Editor and Publisher,
Pak-tong, Seoul.

MR. YI YONG-IK.

It is of course well known that the "Japan Mail" is a newspaper subsidised by the Japanese and it is therefore only natural that it should deal with every thing from a Japanese point of view.

There are always two sides to a question and the Editor of the "Japan Mail" is perfectly justified in writing upon events as they present themselves to him. Every newspaper does this and although we seldom find ourselves in agreement with the "Japan Mail" upon Korean questions, we should have no fault to find with that newspaper did it not so often resort to what are, apparently, deliberate mis-representations.

Mr. Yi Yong-ik is shortly to leave Tokio for Korea, and it would appear that the Japanese have not found him so complaisant and amenable to their blandishments as some of his nationals have been. Therefore the "Japan Mail" deems it its duty to attack him which it does as follows:—

"Yi Yong-ik, who is now a refugee in Japan and who enjoys the distinction of being at one moment regarded as pro-Russian, at another as pro-Japanese, is said to have telegraphed to Seoul that four Japanese members of the Diet, now on a visit to the Korean capital, are working with the new reform party for the overthrow of the Korean Government. Mr. Yi is a remarkable person in one respect—his complete reliance on Japanese long-suffering. The cause of his flight to Japan was that he busied himself over much in an essay to oppose the conclusion of the last convention between Korea and Japan, and finding things too hot for him in Seoul, he judged it expedient to take his departure. Coming to Japan, then, as political enemy of this country, he enjoys, Japanese hospitality and protection in that character, and he repays the benevolence by attempting to create trouble between Japan and Korea. It is in the last degree improbable that four members of the Diet are now in Seoul, at the very moment when the Diet is sitting in Tokyo, and it is even less improbable that they would associate themselves with any such wild enterprise. The public used to give Mr. Yi Yong-ik credit for some shrewdness."

Now it is a matter of common knowledge that Mr. Yi Yong-ik was deported from Korea by the Japanese whether with or without his consent we do not know, but either is possible.

The more one studies the "Japan Mail's" article the more inconsequent does it appear. It is admitted that Mr. Yi Yong-ik opposed the Japan-Korea convention, and therefore those he had to fear were the Japanese or pro-Japanese party. His departure to Japan was probably made a condition of his safety, and he went to Japan as a political enemy of Japan that country and he enjoyed "Japanese hospitality and benevolence in that character."

That is to say that Mr. Yi Yong-ik made no secret of his anti-Japanese opinions and it is probable that if he had had his own way he would have chosen some other asylum than Japan. However he was sent to Japan and it is sheer can't for the "Japan Mail" to talk about "protection hospitality" and "benevolence."

The Japanese evidently hoped, by some means or other to convert him to their way of thinking. They have apparently failed and we are glad to see it, for although there are many stories of oppressive acts committed by him when in power, Mr. Yi Yong-ik is admitted on all sides to be a man of great strength of will, and a devoted and faithful servant to the Emperor of Korea.

No one therefore has a right to blame him when, hearing of something that seems to threaten the safety of his master, he sends a message of warning.

As to the truth of the story of the intrigues of four members of the Diet in Seoul we know nothing, but we differ from the "Japan Mail" when it calls it improbable. Japanese of much greater eminence than the four members of the Diet have been mixed up in much more discreditable enterprises in this country.

So long as the Japanese persist in their lamentbale policy of encouraging the Il Chin Hoi we shall not be surprised at any other charges which are brought against them

A STORY OF LIAOYANG.

The soldiers were pouring across the bridge. They were muddy and bedraggled and so tired they could hardly walk. A big, whiskered captain, his uniform stained with mud and half torn off, his sword gone and his brave gold braid hanging by one cord and trailing to his heels, turned as he reached the north side of the bridge to take a last look toward Liaoyang. Then he sat down and cried as I have seen a child cry, writes Richard H. Little, war correspondent for the "Chicago Daily News," who is with the Russian Army. A half hundred straggling soldiers who were standing by uncovered their heads. The officer looked up and saw them and huskily repeated the phrase with which the Russian officers always address the men: "How are you, my children?" Always before I have heard the men repeat in a well-drilled chorus: "We are quite well, your excellency." A few of them started to say it this time but they broke down. Then one of them spoke. There was a man with me who spoke Russian. He said that the soldier answered: "We beat them, excellency." "Yes, yes," said the captain. "We beat them, children, but we will beat them again." "We beat them," broke in another soldier, excitedly. "Why must we go back?" "It is so ordered, my children," said the officer. "It is necessary; but we shall come this way again." As the men turned and walked away I saw that many of them were crying. The officer turned to us and said, wearily: "We beat them. For four days they pounded us with their whole strength, but our line held. This very day they hurled at us another great assault, the general assault of the battle. We broke them up and sent them back with an awful loss. They could not have come again. Our brave soldiers were beside themselves with joy. Our turn had come and we waited for the command to go forward. The Japanese were terribly used up. We would have driven them back to Haicheng, but instead the order came for us to give up the intrenchments that we would have died in rather than have let the Japanese drive us out of. Victory was ours, It is heart.breaking."

Hong Kong papers write with strong approval of the interest taken by H. E. the Governor in the sports of the Colony. Major Sir Matthew Nathan is a clever polo player, has shown great interest in Cricket, Football and Gymkhanas, and now announces his intention of "going in" actively for rowing. He intends to pull with a crew of Royal Engineers in a four oared race against Royal Artillerymen. He will also present prizes for other events.

An amusing story, says the China Review illustrative of the wily and not always scrupulous attitude of the Japanese trader towards European patents, is going the rounds of the Berlin press. Many German articles bear the letters "D. R. M. S.," which stand for "Deutscher Reichs-Muster-Schutz," or, literally, German Imperial Sample Protection. It occurred to a Japanese to register these letters as his trade mark; and now he is bringing actions against German importers, whose wares bear them! ! !

Serious trouble has arisen between the Prefect of Kangwha and the officer commanding the local military guard. Major Yi Dong Whi recently accused the Prefect of unduly extorting money from the people, whereupon this gentleman immediately replied by denouncing the Major, to the Japanese, as a Russian spy. Hearing of this Major Yi collected a body of men, armed with rifles, and attacked the Prefect's office, the Prefect himself narrowly escaping chastisement by climbing over the wall at the rear of the premises. Both gentlemen are on their way to Seoul to demand satisfaction.

Many great battles have been fought in the snow. Eylau and Hohenlinde being familiar examples. Austerlitz was fought in tensely cold weather and the Russian losses were increased by Napoeon turning the fire of his artillery on the frozen lakes over which the Russians sought to retreat. In the U. S. Civil War, Fort Donnelson was captured in February, Fredericksburg was fought in December, Stone River on December 31, 1862, January 2, 1863, and Thomas defeated and ruined Hood's army at Nahville on the 15th and 16th of December, 1864. Hence it will be seen that history does not warrant us in believing that the war in the East will pass into an unofficial truce when the snow begins to drift.—Boston Transcript.

Those who scouted the Russian suggestion that there were Japanese torpedo boats amongst the Hull fishing fleet as ridiculous and preposterous, must find the news that recently reached us of the purchase, by Russian agents, of a torpedo boat from an English firm, very disconcerting. How, it was asked could a Japanese torpedo boat possibly be in English waters? One could not have been sent from Japan and no English builder would commit such a breach of neutrality as to sell a war vessel to a belligereut. Yet a few weeks afterwards, Russia, the enemy of Englands' ally, succeeds, by resorting to a very transparent subterfuge, effecting the purchase of a torpedo boat from one of England's biggest ship-building firms. If Russian could do this, why not Japan. The transaction will at any rate serve to show that Russia was not entirely unjustified in her suspicions.

The China Gazette, in the course of a leading article says; the Japanese people are in such straits that as we learn upon undoubted authority, the arrears of taxes in Tokyo alone amounted, at the beginning of the month, to fifteen million yen. The difficulty of collecting the taxes is everywhere increasing in the country, and people are presenting themselves in crowds to the authorities in many places, declaring their inability to pay any more money and asking the Government to take themselves instead of trying to squeeze any further taxes where no process of official pressure and no feelings of patriotism can extract anything in hard cash. It is all very pitiful, very patriotic, and alas very hopeless, for we do not see any way out of the terrible straits into which the war party have plunged their unfortunate country.

The Korea Daily News.

VOL. I, MONDAY, DECEMBER 19, 1904. No. 129

HONGKONG & SHANGHAI BANKING CORPORATION.

Paid-up Capital..... ....$10,000,000
Reserve Fund:—Sterling Reserve... 10,000,000
Silver Reserve..... 7,000,000

27,000,000
Reserve Liability of Proprietors... 10,000,000.

HEAD OFFICE, HONGKONG.

London Bankers, London and County Banking Company Limited.
Branches and Agencies,
London.

Amoy,	Hankow	Penang,
Bangkok,	Hiogo,	Rangoon,
Batavia,	Iloilo,	Saigon,
Bombay,	Lyons,	San Francisco,
Calcutta,	Manila,	Singapore,
Colombo,	Nagasaki,	Sourabaya,
Foochow,	New York,	Tientsin,
Hamburg,	Peking,	Yokohama,

Credits granted on approved Securities, and every description of Banking and Exchange business transacted.

Drafts granted on London and the chief Commercial places in Europe, India, Australia, America, China and Japan.

HOLME RINGER & Co., AGENTS,
CHEMULPO.

HOKURKU DOBOKU KAISHA.

Branch office in Chong Dong, Seoul.
Japanese telephone No. 165

CONTRACT DEPARTMENT.

We can contract to build any building or construction.

MERCHANDISE DEPARTMENT.

We can provide any building material. We have just contracted to build the new Belgian Legation.

E. MEYER & CO.

Chemulpo.

SOLE AGENTS IN KOREA FOR.

A. T. Morse, Sons & Co.'s

"Fresco" Distemper

In all colours ready for use on walls, Ceilings etc.

and

AVENARIUS CARBOLINEUM

A wood-preserving and antiseptic oil preparation

Against decay, dry-rot, fungus and wood-destroying insects.

A large supply always in stock.
Prices upon application.

E. MEYER & Co.,
Chemulpo.

CHARTERED BANK OF INDIA AUSTRALIA & CHINA.

INCORPORATED BY ROYAL CHARTER 185

HEAD OFFICES:—LONDON.

Paid-up Capital £800,000
Reserve Liability of Share-holders 800,000
Reserve Fund 800,000

Drafts granted upon all the principal places in the world and every description of Exchange and banking business transacted.

E. MEYER & Co., Agents,
Chemulpo.

MITSU BISHI DOCKYARD & ENGINE WORKS,
NAGASAKI.

CODE WORD, "DOCK."

A 1, A. B. C., and Engineering Codes used.

DOCK No. 1 (at Tategami).

Extreme Length.............523 feet
Length on blocks .... 513 „
Width of Entrance on Top......89 „
„ „ Bottom....77 „
Water on Blocks at Spring Tide 26½ „

DOCK No. 2 (Mukaijima).

Extreme Length.............371 feet
Length on Blocks.............360 „
Width of Entrance on Top......66 „
„ „ Bottom 53 „
Water on Blocks at Spring Tide 22 „

PATENT SLIP (at Kosuge).
Can take vessels up to 1,000 tons gross

THE WORKS are well equipped with the LATEST IMPROVEMENTS, and can execute any kind of work in SHIPBUILDING and MARINE ENGINEERING, as well as in REPAIRING of SHIPS.

The COMPANY'S new powerful steamer OURA-MARU (712 tons, 700 I.H.P.), specially built for SALVAGE PURPOSES, and equipped with necessary gear, is always READY at SHORT NOTICE.

THE METHODIST PUBLISHING HOUSE,

Little West Gate, Seoul.

JOB PRINTING, TYPEWRITER PAPER
CARBON PAPER, VISITING CARDS
STATIONERY, BOOK BINDING
BOOK PUBLISHERS
AMERICAN SCHOOL BOOKS
SPENCERIAN COPY BOOKS
PEN CARBON LETTER AND BILL BOOKS

S. A. BECK, Manager.

DAI-ICHI GINKO

LIMITED.

(Formerly the First National Bank)

ESTABLISHED 1873

INCORPORATED UNDER PRESENT LAW 189

Capital - - - - - - - - - Yen 5,000,000
Reserve Fund - - - - - 1,500,000

HEAD OFFICE:—TOKIO.

President: Baron SHIBUSAWA.

BRANCHES AND CORRESPONDENTS
In the Principal Cities and Towns of Japan.
Interest Allowed on
Fixed deposits 1 year - - - 6½ per cent
" 6 months - - - 6 per cent

Special current accounts 1½ sen daily per Y 100
General " " 1 " " " 100

M. TANAKA,
Manager, Chemulpo.

SINGER SEWING MACHINES

싱거즈봉침

SOLE AGENTS
FOR KOREA
전매쇼

HOLME RINGER & CO.
Chemulpo.

졔믈포 함릉거양힝

KAMEYA & CO.

GENERAL STOREKEEPERS

Chinkokai - - Seoul

(Established 1895, Tokyo)

Confectionery, Hams, Canned Goods, Cutlery, Hirano & Tansan Water. Provisions, Gents, Furnishing goods, Toilet Articles, Travelling Bags, Tobacco, Cigars & Cigarettes Kitchen Utensils. Coffee, Biscuits

Fresh Goods always kept in Stock.
Prices Moderate
☞ *Please come and inspect our goods*

NIPPON YUSEN KAISHA.

JAPANESE MAIL STEAMSHIP CO.

UNDER MAIL CONTRACT WITH THE IMPERIAL JAPANESE GOVERNMENT.

European Line

Regular Fortnightly Service between Yokohama Kobe, Moji, Shanghai, Hongkong, Singapore, Penang Colombo, Port Said, Marseilles, London and Antwerp

American Line

Regular Fortnightly Service between Hongkong and Seattle, calling at Shanghai, Moji, Kobe, Yokohama and Victoria, B. C.

Australian Line

Regular weekly Service betwen Japan Ports and Australia, calling at Hongkong and Manila.
(Above Three Lines Suspended until further notice).

Shanghai Line

Weekly Service between Shanghai and Japan Ports

Korea Line

Service Kobe, Moji, Nagasaki, Fusan Chemupo Chef foo, Taiku.
S. S. Bahelsberg, 2181 tons.
Service Kobe, Moji, Fusan, Chemulpo, Chinnampo
S. S. ARGO, S. S. Ohio.

BORDEN'S CONDENSED MILK CO.

New York, U. S. A.

ALWAYS IN STOCK

Eagle Brand Condensed Milk.

Gold Seal Condensed Milk.

Peerless (Family) Evaporated Cream.

Borden's Malted Milk.

E. MEYER & CO.
Chemulpo, Korea,
Sole Agents

ROYAL INSURANCE COMPANY,
Funds exceed £10,000,000

FIRE

AT CURRENT RATES.

LIFE

REDUCED PREMIUM.
HOLME RINGER & Co.,
Agents, Chemulpo.

HOTEL DU PALAIS

SEOUL.

The only first class Hotel in Seoul. Situated in the centre of the city opposite the palace.

Cuisine under the supervision of an experienced French Chef.

Well ventilated and

TARIFF UPON APPLICATION

L. MARTIN
Proripetor and Manager

報申日每韓大
보신일ᄆᆡ한대

(호십삼빅일뎨)　(일요쉬)　일일십이월이십년사빅구쳔일

본사고빅

이신보ᄂᆞᆫ영어와한어로셔再 뮈
일출판ᄒᆞᆷ
신문가
한쟝　엽두돈오푼
일삭됴　엽두량닷돈
우표가미삭닷돈
다닷돈으로밧슴
광고료ᄂᆞᆫ
귀한의쟝단과ᄌᆞ힝의다쇼로ᄌᆞᆼ
감ᄒᆞ되랍가로밧을터이오ᄆᆡ오
리.티지아녀대한사람마다다이신
문을보실터이나광고버시기롤
원ᄒᆞ시ᄂᆞᆫ이들은우리신문사에
와셔면약ᄒᆞ심을희망ᄒᆞᆷ
○발힝소　박동대한ᄆᆡ일신보
사별어학교엽헤젼영국인셜필
림졍자리오
사쟝 영국인 (빅셜)
평양 티리졈
○평양효동사ᄂᆞᆫ권미보씨로우
리신문괄매티리인을뎡ᄒᆞᆫᆞ엿
시ᄉᆞ오니평양에계신구람코져ᄒᆞ
시ᄂᆞᆫ 쳠군ᄌᆞᄂᆞᆫ히티리졈에왕
림ᄒᆞ와면의ᄒᆞ시옵

사고

○우리대한ᄆᆡ일신보의목뎍은
대한의안녕질셔에관한모든대
복에티ᄒᆞ야ᄂᆞᆫ공평한변론을ᄌᆞ쥬
쟝ᄒᆞᆷ이라우리동신원의담보ᄂᆞᆫ
신문보시ᄂᆞᆫ쳠군ᄌᆞ의게ᄒᆞᆼ상보
도ᄒᆞᆯ리매편지를귀셔ᄒᆞ여주시
ᄂᆞᆫ이ᄂᆞᆫ성명과번디를젹어붓치
시기를희망ᄒᆞ오니이거슨신문
상에긔쟤ᄒᆞ란ᄂᆞᆫ거시아니오다
만구히신용ᄒᆞᄂᆞᆫ증거를숨고자ᄒᆞᆷ
ᄒᆞᆷ이라귀쟈ᄂᆞᆫ아모귀셔던지귀
쉬ᄒᆞᆷ을퇴각ᄒᆞᄂᆞᆫ권리를가졋스
나퇴각ᄒᆞᄂᆞᆫ리유를발ᄒᆞᆯ터이오
며공중평화를문란케ᄒᆞᄂᆞᆫ듯ᄒᆞᆫ
귀셔ᄂᆞᆫ의례히밧지안켓슴나이
다
●본사셜시이리로신문을미양
우레로분젼ᄒᆞ와레젼부의임의
로젼ᄒᆞᆫ듯스로던곳에ᄂᆞᆫᄒᆞᆨ늣게
젼ᄒᆞ기도ᄒᆞ며ᄒᆞᆨ면젼치슴ᄒᆞᆫ곕
에젼ᄒᆞ기도ᄒᆞ며ᄒᆞᆨ아니젼ᄒᆞᄂᆞᆫ
곳도잇다ᄒᆞ와우리신문을수랑
ᄒᆞ야구람ᄒᆞ시ᄂᆞᆫ 쳠군ᄌᆞ의게
되ᄒᆞ야면우미안ᄒᆞ옵기로지금
은분젼인을두고민일조이젼
ᄒᆞ며아니젼ᄒᆞ거나늣게거나ᄒᆞᆫ
폐가업도록ᄒᆞ라ᄒᆞ오니ᄒᆞᆨ아니

젼ᄒᆞ거ᄂᆞ ᄒᆞᆨ늣게젼ᄒᆞ거나ᄒᆞᆫ일
이잇ᄉᆞ면본사로통긔ᄒᆞ여주심
을희망ᄒᆞᆷ

잡보

○쳥평보고　강화쳥평리ᄂᆞᆫ휘
씨가군부로보고ᄒᆞ기를부윤윤
졀규가쟝젼밧ᄌᆞ리ᄉᆞ로의셤ᄒᆞᆫ지
아니ᄒᆞᆷ사롬의게의산을두어사
롬으로ᄒᆞ야곰봉츅ᄒᆞᆫ세에세지
계ᄒᆞ야아라사국간쳡자로본관
을모함ᄒᆞ니일아과젼지간에우
쳡자가그죄사ᄒᆞ기가어려우니
윤부윤으로더브리지ᄌᆞ쾌ᄒᆞ야유
죄무죄자를변명케ᄒᆞ라ᄒᆞ엿더
라
○청풍군슈장젼　청풍군슈안
영중을봉고ᄒᆞ고파직ᄒᆞᆫ일은이
왕괴졔ᄒᆞ엿거니와숩졀ᄉᆞᄒᆞᆼ우
셕씨가그쟝젼롤만롤쳔칠량닷
돈을사출ᄒᆞ야닉부로보고ᄒᆞ엿
더라
○용진항졍정부　공진회에셔
거상쳘이하오ᄂᆞ시에동상회를
기셜ᄒᆞ고젼번에회도군ᄃᆞᆯ을법
ᄉᆞ에붓쳐슈졍　공금ᄒᆞᆯᄉᆞ
데로이믜창칭ᄒᆞ엿거니와아직엇
더케조쳐ᄒᆞᆫ다ᄂᆞᆫ말이업스니지파
연조쳐ᄒᆞ기어렵거든본회에셔
조힝쳐단ᄒᆞᆯ터이라고며의ᄒᆞ야
정부에총티를파송ᄒᆞ엿더라
○여사티젼　여사쳥에셔며사
티젼을구별ᄒᆞ야교시ᄒᆞ엿ᄂᆞᆫ티
와가사셤일간이샹에ᄂᆞᆫ영젼스
믈닷량이오오　샥셤간이샹에ᄂᆞᆫ
열닷량이오오　싀일간이샹에ᄂᆞᆫ
닐곱량이오오　오간이샹에ᄂᆞᆫ셕
량셕이오　ᄎᆞ가열ᄒᆞᆫ간이샹에
ᄂᆞᆫ영젼두량이오　여셧간이샹
에ᄂᆞᆫᄒᆞᆫ량식을수렴ᄒᆞ기로작졍
ᄒᆞ엿더라
○경찰즐셔　함경남도관찰사
가닉부로면보ᄒᆞ기를함경북도
관찰사김로규의셩사여부를탐
지ᄒᆞ라ᄒᆞ엿삽ᄂᆞ오나도로가불통
되여연케ᄒᆞ엿스며그간에진졀
히탄쳔군슈의계답지ᄒᆞᆫ증거성
원조사음에즐셔ᄒᆞ엿다ᄒᆞ엿더
라
○공쥬공연　거섭홍일에공쥬
관찰사가닉부로면보ᄒᆞ기를감
쳐회원이부하에와셔모혓ᄂᆞᆫ티
부지기슈오명일에기회ᄒᆞ코연
셜ᄒᆞᆫ다ᄒᆞ미민셩이대단히소요
ᄒᆞ오니엇지ᄒᆞ오리잇가히졍부
시ᄒᆞᆯ라ᄒᆞ엿더라
○닉부답면　거섭쳘에닉부에
서공쥬관찰부로답면ᄒᆞ기를
조칙사의티로효유ᄒᆞ야히산케
ᄒᆞ되위령ᄒᆞᄂᆞᆫ자ᄂᆞᆫ가히용티치못
ᄒᆞᆯ지라ᄒᆞ엿더라
○순찰보고　경상북도순찰사
ᄒᆞ우셕씨가닉부로보고ᄒᆞ기를
성주군슈김창슈가부임ᄒᆞᆫ이후
로졍치가션ᄒᆞ지못ᄒᆞ고탐학ᄒᆞᆫ
거시여러가지라듯기에히연ᄒᆞᆫ
고로방쟝회군으로순힝ᄒᆞ야사
실ᄒᆞᆫ즉ᄒᆞᆯᄌᆞ음에동군슈가마춤
관찰부에가셔아니잇기로히군
일을사실ᄒᆞ기를인ᄒᆞ야그슈비
아젼을착슈ᄒᆞ엿더니김창슈가
관찰사의게청원ᄒᆞ고ᄌᆞ일에인
장을버려바리고기차로환향ᄒᆞ
엿ᄂᆞᆫ지라본사가쟝츳히군에답
녀가셔히군문부와군슈의힝위
를사실ᄒᆞ야면츅ᄒᆞ여보고ᄒᆞᆯ터
이니그군슈의소임을위션주면
ᄒᆞ라ᄒᆞ엿더라
○은진젹당　음력십월이십륙
일밤에젹당쳘팔십명이홍양총
과탄환도가지고홍됴총파군도
도가지고회인군에셔브터은진
군산니면종곡에리도ᄒᆞ야징을
다과ᄒᆞ며졔물을겁탈ᄒᆞᄂᆞᆫ티가
사셜ᄒᆞ호롤총화ᄒᆞ고길에마져
즉사ᄒᆞᆫ자가일명이오중샹ᄒᆞ여
거진죽게된자가셤명이오블에
타셔죽은소가일젹이라히군슈
김괴운씨가가셔조셰히젹간ᄒᆞ
야닉부로보고ᄒᆞ엿더라

관보

대한광무팔
년십이월십구일
셔임즙수령
○종즁이품가션대부닉부협판
교한셩 오수영
종이품가션대부닉장원경오쳔
군의고의변면츄　종
○의원면본관　비셔원승 민
봉식　뎡흥형　성주목 지롱
참봉 유명제　농샹공부기슈
김교필
○히시종원분시어　구품 죠
병셩
○명궁닉부특진관셔쳐엄관일
등　태의원경　민영규
○명태의원경셔쳐임관삼등

궁닉부특진관　박용대
○임비셔원승셔주임관오등
졍샹홍　리셕종
○임덕릉령셔관임관칠등　의
릉참봉　최영렬
○임의릉참봉셔관임판팔등
박계호
○임지릉참봉셔판임관팔등
한즁샹
○임농샹공부기슈셔판임관수
등　농샹공부주ᄉᆞ　리즁구
○임농샹공부주ᄉᆞ셔판임관오
등구품　김교필
광무팔년십이월십구일
궁닉부대신민영휘
○죠셔ᄒᆞ야ᄀᆞᆯᄋᆞ샤ᄃᆡ태의원경
민영기를명ᄒᆞ샤궁닉부특진관
을삼으시고궁닉부특진관박용
대로태의원경을삼으시다
○총호ᄉᆞ신리근명ᄋᆞᆫ　쥬ᄒᆞ되
원소도감낭청샹픔오셩무을
이더차하ᄒᆞ와닉ᄉᆞ를보살피게홈
이엇더ᄒᆞ올지ᄋᆞᆫ샹ᄋᆞᆫ샹
쥬ᄒᆞ와광무팔년십이월십륙일
에봉　지의쥬ᄒᆞᆫ라ᄒᆞ옵시다
○총호ᄉᆞ신리근명ᄋᆞᆫ　쥬ᄒᆞ되
국장도감낭샹과랑쳥이　대
여모신길에행편을간심ᄒᆞ온쥭
대여길이초원ᄒᆞ옵고오리
쳐도치못ᄒᆞ와퇴탈ᄒᆞ야힘축ᄒᆞ
온즉민가가막당이반이회졀홈
이온티신재로ᄂᆞᆫ보계원으로
터리곳마쟝리교기로향ᄒᆞ야화
향졍ᄉᆞ지ᄂᆞᆫ이　원소동두가
되와여간젼답에ᄒᆞᆫ입ᄒᆞᆯ두어곳
파교량을신죠ᄒᆞᆯ터이오나일로
쎄졍ᄒᆞ오면모다편의ᄒᆞᆯ샛호티
ᄉᆞ세가신중ᄒᆞ와감히쳔단치못
ᄒᆞ겟슴으로감쥬ᄒᆞ와　광무
팔년십이월십수일에봉　지
의쥬닉에중민의폐가젹고쌴도지
로에편ᄒᆞ고찻ᄎᆞ온니신재로써
졍ᄒᆞ라ᄒᆞ옵시다

뎐보

빅림발　십이월구일
○타셜대신　법국의회에서의
원시베톤씨가의회에셔토론ᄒᆞ
다가군부대신앙드르씨의엽뿔
을쳐셔당쟝에중엇ᄂᆞᆫ티셰쓰둑
으로치둑ᄒᆞ엿더라
동디발　동일
○영벌상엽죠약　영벌상엽죠
약은슈일후에할동과인ᄒᆞᆫ다더
라

UNION INSURANCE SOCIETY OF CANTON.

Head office Hongkong.
Marine risks underwritten at current rates.

Agents in Chemulpo,
E. MEYER & Co.

COMPAGNIE DES MESSAGERIES MARITIMES.

Fortnightly Direct Service.

For Marseilles
via Ports.
Sailing from Yokohama
Calling at Kobe,
Shanghai, Hongkong, Saigon, Singapore,
Colombo, Djibonti, Suez, Port Said
and Marseilles.

For particulars apply to
HOLME RINGER & Co.,
Chemulpo.

HAYASHIDA & CO.,

16 MYENG DONG, CHIN KO KAI, SEOUL.
BRANCH OFFICE AT CHEMULPO.

Money changers, Coal and Wood Merchants, Express Agents.

We are agents for the Pyeng-yang Coal Company and the Karazu Coal Company of Japan. We have the best quality of both anthracite and bituminous coal, and prompt execution of orders is our speciality. Firewood of all kinds kept in stock. Full weight guaranteed. Money of all denominations exchanged at current rates. Parcels received for all parts.

CHINA MUTUAL LIFE INS. OC.

Most favourable terms to policy holders.

Benefit system unsurpassed.

HOLME RINGER & Co.
Agents, Chemulpo.

C. P. R.

CANADIAN PACIFIC RAILWAY COMPANY'S ROYAL MAIL STEAMSHIP LINE.

THE FAST ROUTE BETWEEN CHINA, JAPAN, AND EUROPE VIA CANADA AND THE UNITED STATES.

Route from Hongkong via Shanghai, Nagasaki (Inland Sea of Japan) Kobe, Yokohama Victoria and Vancouver.

Twin Screw Empress Steamship—6,000 Tons—Speed 19 knots.

PROPOSED SAILING FROM YOKOHAMA.

R. M. S. Empress of India.
R. M. S. Empress of Japan.
R. M. S. Empress of China.
R. M. S. Athenian.
R. M. S. Tartar.

Special reduction (first class only) granted to members of the Military, Naval, Diplomatic and Civil services and to Missionaries.

Passengers have choice of ten routes across the Continent of America and have privilege of travelling by any Atlantic Steamship Line.

Round the World passage tickets in connection with the P. and O. S. N., North German Lloyd and Messageries Co.'s **£125.**

All rates payable at current rate of exchange.

For further information, Tickets, Guide Books, etc., apply to

HOLME, RINGER & Co., AGENTS,
Chemulpo.

Grand Hotel,

(Formerly the Station Hotel)

Near the Railway Terminus, West Gate Seoul.

The Best Hotel in Korea,
Handsome new Building.
Fine Airy Rooms
Excellent Cuisine.
Terms Moderate.
Special terms to Missionaries
and to permanent boarders.

Electric cars within 2 minutes' walk.

W. H. EMBERLEY.
Proprietor

EVERY FACILITY.

In connection with Life Assurance Business is afforded by

The Standard Life Assurance Co.,

One of the largest and wealthiest of the Provident Institutions of the United Kingdom Forms of Application and all information will be promptly afforded on application.

10 CENTS A DAY.

Not a very large expenditure is it? But it is sufficient to secure for a man of 30 a policy with the STANDARD LIFE OFFICE for

$1323.

For all particulars of rates, etc., apply to

Holme, Ringer & Co.,
Agents, Chemulpo.

THE NEW YORK LIFE INSURANCE COMPANY.

Have you ever been declined by any Company?

Are you engaged in a specially hazardous occupation?

Have you heard of the New York Life Insurance Company's New Classifications for this class of Risks?

If not, send your date of birth, occupation and particulars of rejection, if any to

E. MEYER & Co.,
Agents, Chemulpo.

MITSUI BUSSAN KAISHA.
(MITSUI & Co.)

MITSUI GINKO.
(MITSUI BANK.)

The Bank is owned by the members of the Mitsui Family, who, as partners, assume an unlimited responsibility for all liabilities of the Bank:—

Capital.................... .....Yen 5,000,000
Reserve Fund.................. " 5,600,000

HEAD OFFICE, TOKYO.

LONDON OFFICE, 34 LIME ST., E. C.

BRANCHES AND AGENCIES:—
New York, San Francisco, Hamburg, Bombay, Singapore, Manila, Hongkong, Amoy, Chefoo, Tientsin.

Kobe, Hakodate, Yokohama, Kure, Yokosuka, Moji, Shimonoseki, Miike, Wakamatsu, Nagasaki, Kuchinotsu, Karatsu, Sasebo, Misume, Taipeh, &c.

Telegraphic Address for all the Offices:
"MITSUI."

A. B. C. AND A. 1 CODES USED.

Contractors of Coal

To the Imperial Japanese Navy. Arsenals and Railway Bureau, Principal Railway Companies and Industrial Work, Home and Foreign Mail and Freight Steamers.

Sole Proprietors

Of the famous Miike, Tagawa and Yamano Coal Mines.

Sole Agents

For the sale of Fukumo, Hokoku, Ichimura, Kanoda, Mannoura, Onoura, Ostuji, Sonoda, Tsubaruro, Yoshinotani, Yoshio, Yurokibura and other coals.

YANGTSE INSURANCE ASSOCIATION, LTD.

The undersigned, having been appointed agents for the above company, are prepared to issue policies and pay losses on marine risks at regular rates.

E. MEYER & Co.,
Agents, Chemulpo.

AMERICAN KOREAN ELECTRIC CO.

Light and Power.

Main Office: Electric Building, Chong No.

RAILWAY DEPARTMENT.

OPERATING CARS BETWEEN EAST AND WEST GATE, EVERY TEN MINUTES:—

First Car leaves East Gate at 7:00 A. M. First Car leaves R. R. Station at 7:25 A. M
Last Car " East Gate at 9:40 P. M. Last " " R. R. Station at 10:05 P.M

OPERATING CARS BETWEEN EAST GATE AND IMPERIAL TOMB TERMINUS, EVERY TWENTY MINUTES:—

CONNECTING WITH EVERY ALTERNATE CAR ARRIVING AT EAST GATE FROM CHONG NO.

First Car leaves East Gate for Tomb at 7:10 A. M.
" " " Tomb for East Gate at 7:35 A. M.
Last " " East Gate for Tomb at 7:50 P. M.
" " " Tomb for East Gate at 8:10 P. M.

OPERATING CARS BETWEEN CHONG NO AND YUNG SAN RIVER EVERY TWELVE MINUTES:—

First Car leaves Chong No for South Gate at 7:12 A. M.
" " " Chong No for Yung San at 7:36 A. M.
" " " South Gate for Chong No at 7:20 A. M.
" " " Yung San for Chong No at 8:09 A. M.
Last " " South Gate for Chong No 10:00 P. M.
" " " Yung San for Chong No at 9:33 P. M.

SPECIAL PRIVATE CARS FURNISHED TO SUIT CONVENIENCE OF PATRONS. PRICES ON APPLICATION AT HEAD OFFICE.

LIGHTING DEPARTMENT.

Where less than 250 candle power of light is used, the rate per month will be
Per 16 candle power incandescent lamp,—All night.—Yen 2.50.
32 candle power incandescent lamp:—All night:—Yen 4.00.
50 candle power incandescent lamp:—All night:—Yen 6.00.
150 " " " " " " " 10.00.
1200 " " enclosed are " " " " 20.00.

Where more than 250 candle power of light is used, a Meter will be installed, freqvedted:—Rent of Meter Yen 2.00 per month. Rate of charges by meter reading:—Two Sen per Ampere per hour. (Approximately this is equal to about One Sen per 16 C. P. lamp per hour) Minimum monthly charge where meter is installed, Yen 20.00 per month, which includes rental of meter.

Estimates for installing lights furnished on application

An assortment of chandeliers always on hand.

K. Murakami.
Photograph Studio
Chinkokai, Seoul.

Printing, Developing and Enlargement, of Photographs always Undertaken.

Korean Views and Pictures Illustrating Native Customs always on Sale,

---

THE OSAKA SHOSEN KAISHA.

Boats frequently on the berth for Chinnampo.

REGULAR SAILINGS BETWEEN JAPAN AND KOREAN PORTS.

FUSAN AND KOBE VIA SHIMONOSEKI.

OSAKA VIA MOKPO, FUSAN, SHIMONOSEKI AND KOBE.

MOJI DIRECT.

OSAKA VIA KUNSAN, MASANPO, FUSAN, SHIMONOSEKI AND KOBE.

CHEMULPO KUNSAN LINE,
Every three days.

CHEMULPO CHINNAMPO LINE,
Every three days.

For Freight and passage and further particulars apply to

THE OSAKA SHOSEN KAISHA,
Chemulpo.

RONDON, PLAISANT & CO.

General Storekeepers and Merchants, Ships Contractors, Tobacconists, Commission and Forwarding Agents, Coal Merchants

IMPORTERS AND EXPORTERS

Seoul & Chemulpo.

W. D. WENTWORTH.

LANDING
AND
SHIPPING AGENT
AND
CUSTOMS BORDER.

12 OURA, NAGASAKI.

STEWARD & CO.

Chemulpo.

Shipchandlers and Storekeepers, Naval and Mercantile Contractors, Landing and Shipping Agents.

STEWARD'S HOTEL

Chemulpo.

Best accommodation in the port for travellers. Clean and well-aired rooms, good cuisine and prompt attendence, moderate tariff.

일본으로도망ᄒᆞ여온리유인즉

논셜

잡보

TELEGRAMS.

Army Headquarters.

At 6 A. M. on the 17th inst. about 100 Russian infantry attacked Lichiawafung, and at 2 A. M. on the 18th a body of infantry attacked Tungwaisunkow, but both were repulsed.

On the evening of the 17th inst. the Russian scouts appeared several times close to Santaskangtze and later a small force attacked the Japanese patrols west of Shinlungtun, but were repulsed.

At 2.20 P. M. on the 18th inst, the Russian artillery at Sefangtai fired 80 shells at the Japanese positions near the railway bridge, but effected no casualties

COMPARISON OF THE ARTILLERY FORCES.

FROM THE CHEFOO DAILY NEWS.

Moukden, November 20.

Much has been said and written about the superiority of the Japanese artillery, as demonstrated from the time the troops left the Yalu and began to push on into Manchuria. The press has been filled with columns of comment on the scientific marksmanship of daring gunners, and the illustrated periodicals have presented for the edification of their readers full page reproductions from photographs by their special correspondents, aimed to show the prowess of the little men behind the guns.

But the Japanese artillerymen seem to be losing their cunning, and it is no longer easy to detect their much heralded superiority. This is evident every day at the front. It is also noticeable that the Russians are improving in their artillery fire in the same degree in which the Japanese are deterioriating, not alone in the accuracy of their fire, but in the knack with which they move and place their guns. In the beginning the Russians failed to conceal their batteries, contenting themselves with following the old tactics of mounting them in commanding but exposed places, where they were easily detected and sometimes silenced by the enemy.

The reason for the apparent failure of the Japanese to continue the brilliant artillery record which they inaugurated at the beginning of the war seems to be found in the fact that many of the well schooled and drilled gunners who first took the field have been killed in the fierce artillery duels which have always preceded the battles from the Yalu to Shaho. The standing army of Japan was comparatively small, and the trained men in the artillery arm were consequently few. The campaign has been characterized by hard artillery fighting, and with the heavy losses that have resulted, it has been difficult to replace the experienced gunners with men who are able to maintain the high standard established at the outset. Losses among the officers have been particularly heavy.

On the other hand, as the Russians have had but a fraction of their effective field artillery in action, and as they have had, and still have, numbers of trained men in reserve, who have been constantly augmenting the original forces, the matter of replacing their losses has not been so serious a question with them.

A CENSUS OF KOREA.

A census of the population of Korea has been drawn up by the Home Office from the reports of the Governers of all provinces, with the exception of north Ham Kyeng.

Seoul,	Houses	42,730	Population	192,304.
Kyeug Ki Province	Houses	170,424	Population	672,636.
South Cnoong Chong	"	124,370	"	474,312.
North " "	"	76,877	"	300,345.
South Chulla	"	124,310	"	490,054.
North "	"	110,835	"	440,901.
South Kyeng Sang	"	131,487	"	569,967.
North " "	"	161,522	"	601.163.
KangWon Province	"	82,154	"	301,885.
Whang Hai "	"	96,466	"	382,230.
South Pyeng An	"	97,332	"	392,572.
North " "	"	97 534	"	420,725.
South Ham Kyong	"	58,928	"	450,693.

PRIZE ESSAY COMPETITION.

There is no limit to the enterprise of Lord Charles Beresford. He is ever devising means for popularising the Navy, of bringing about the feeling between officers and men, and of improving the training of both.

With the object of collecting the views of his officers in the Channel Fleet and of promoting discussion on the subject of the lessons of the Russo-Japanese war, he has just promoted an essay competition. Officers of all ranks in the Channel Fleet are invited to write a short essay under the following heading;

"With reference to the present war in the East, what are the lessons to be learnt by the British Empire, and more particularly by the British Navy as regards: (a) organisation and training for war; (b) conduct of a war especially as regards naval strategy and tactics?"

The Vice-Admiral and Captain Hope-Robertson of the "Theseus" and Commander Fuller of the "Majestic," will judge the essays, which are limited to 2,500 words, and were to be sent the flag-commander of the "Cœsar," by October 15. Each essay is to be headed by a motto, and accompanied by a sealed envelope with the motto written outside, and the name of the author inside. These envelopes will not be opened until after the essays have been judged.

The author of the best essay will be presented with a copy of Captain Mahan's works, and towards the end of November, Lord Charles Beresford will deliver a lecture on board the "Cœsar" giving his own views on the subject, together with a resume of the principal points of the competing essays.

General Hyon Yung-woon, whose projected return to Japan has been much discussed, is reported to be now returning before the end of the year.

A telegram to the "Nichi Nichi" from Shanghai says that the Chinese Government has borrowed six millions of taels from the Hongkong and Shanghai Bank to pay the installment of the Indemnity due at the close of this year. The rate of interest is said to be five per cent.

The following original translation from the pen of our Korean "man who knows" may be of interest. "The Seoul Fusan Railway is now completed. It is said that the men, who were students in Japan, will be appointed Magistrates near both sides of that railway line. At formerly the men who could speak hardly "Good-bye" were appointed clerks in Departments, and now everyone who can only speak "Sayonara" will be appointed Magistrate of a southern district.

We regret to learn that the leading lights of the great Il Chiu Hoi society, yesterday evening gave themselves up to an evening of (questionable) enjoyment. It appears that the chief agent of this society in the country, yesterday met the President of the society in the Capital, the occasion was made one of rejoicing. People residing in the neighbourhood of the Palace, were astonished to see some 40 or 50 Koreans, minus topknots, rolling home in the early hours this morning.

The Daily Telegraph of Nov. 8th has the following from its Hull correspondent.

"An official communication has been received from the Japanese Legation by the Hull coroner, stating that no Japanese war vessels were within 200 miles of the scene of the Russian attack on British fishing vessels in the North Sea."

The Japanese statement that there were no vessels within 200 miles, seems to show that there were some within 250 miles doubtless for the purpose of attacking the Baltic Fleet. This is surely sufficient evidence that the Russians were warranted in their belief that an attack on the squadron was imminent.

THE THIRD RUSSIAN SQUADRON.

According to an official telegram published elsewhere the Russian Government has decided to send a third squadron to the Far East. As to the components of this squadron, the information furnished by publications in our possession is as follows writes the "Japan Mail."

The "Admiral Oushakoff," the "Admiral Seniavine" and the "General Admiral Apraksin" are three ironclads launched respectively in 1893. 1894 and 1896. They have a displacement of 4,126 tons and a nominal speed of 16 knots, probably now 15 at most. Their chief armour is a steel belt The "Apraksin" has three 10-inch guns and the other two have four 9-inch guns.

The "Imperator Nicolai I." and the "Imperator Alexander II. are battle-ships of 9,700 tons displacement and 16.5 and 15.9 knots speed respectively. They were launched the former in 1889 the latter in 1887 and are therefore old ships. They have complete compound belts of armour, 6 to 14 inches thick, 8 feet wide in the "Nicolai and 9 feet wide in the Alexander, and they each carry two 12-inch and four 9-inch guns.

The Slava is a battle-ship of 13,516 tons and 18 knots speed. She was laid down in 1901 and was still unfinished at the date of latest advices. When finished she is to carry four 12 inch and twelve 6-inch guns. She is of the "Borodino" type.

As to the "Pole" (?) we have no certain information, but she is probably of the "Sevastopol" type.

The "Admiral Oushakoff," the "Admiral Seniavine" and the "General Apraksin were all built for service in the Caspian Sea, according to the Naval Pocket Book.

The "Minin" we do not know.

The "Pamyat Azova" and the "Vladimir Monomach" are old friends, having been on the Far-Eastern station for saveral years. The former was launched in 1888; the latter in 1881. The "Pamyat Azova" has a displacement of 6,700 tons, a nominal speed of 18.8 knots and an armament of two 8-inch and thirteen 6 inch guns; while the corresponding figures for the "Vladimir Monomach" are 5.754 tons, 15 knots and five 6-inch quick-firers.

LIBERAL PARDON FOR LESE MAJESTE.

It is announced that Emperor William has decided to hereafter use the pardoning power liberally in cases of lese majeste. This is a radical departure from the previous practice. It heretofore had been practically unknown for the emperor to pardon a person convicted of this offence. It is now stated that he intends to pardon almost without exception when the offender is shown to belong to the uneducated classes, or to be incapable of weighing the consequces of a hasty word.

Also offences committed during drunkenness or while in an excited condition, rendering deliberation impossible, will constitute the basis for pardon. The emperor has directed the ministry of justice to deal liberally with all persons convicted of an insult to his majesty who petition for pardon and show penitence,

It is expected that the new practice will greatly reduce the number who will serve out sentences for this offence, since the impression is general that many offenders have been convicted n many cases through overofficious state's attorneys and judges.

In view of the protests made by the people against the heavy taxes levied to meet the forthcoming funeral expenses, the Funeral Bureau have slightly reduced the amounts to be collected and have issued the following table, showing the ratios of taxation; Owners of tile roofed houses covering more than 41 kan will pay $5.00. Owners of tile-roofed covering over 21 kans will pay $3.00. Owners of thatch-roofed houses over 21 kans $0.40. Over 6 kans $0.20.

Mr. Yi Yong Ik has telegraphed the information that he will return to Seoul. in company with Mr. D. W. Steuens.

The Chinese Minister has informed the government that the Chinese authorities in Peking demand the recall of Mr. Yi Pum Yun, who, with a following of troops, has caused much trouble on the "Korean Chinese frontier."

A Tientsin native newspaper learns that the Army Reorganisation Department of Peking has ordered from certain German firms Tls. 2,000,000 worth of 7½ centimetre field-guns, 6,000 magazine rifles, 1,000 magazine carbines, 600 revolvers, 4,000 cartridge boxes and 40,000 smokeless cartridges, all to be delivered at Tientsim by the mouth of March next.

A curious experiment has been carried out at Copenhagen, with a vessel built in the Royal Dockyard on the lines of Noah's Ark. Professor D. Simonsen, the Chief Rabbi, furnished the engineers with the dimensions of the original Noah's Ark, making a opecial translation from Hebrew Scriptures relating thereto. As a result, what is believed to be an exact model was constructed. After the Ark had been launched a number of Danish scientists made a trip in the strange craft, which proved quite seaworthy. The exports on board declared that the model was the steadiest vessels ever seen on the hige seas.

The Korea Daily News.

Issued at 5 P. M. daily except Sundays.

Rate of Subscription :—
Per Year,............Yen 25.
Per Quarter,..........Yen 7.
Per Month,..........Yen 2.50.

Postage in Korea not charged extra.
Postage abroad charged extra.

Advertisements, 50 sen per day for 1 inch or less.
5 yen per month per inch.
50 yen per year per inch.

All communications to

E. T. BETHELL,
Editor and Publisher,
Pak-tong, Seoul.

CHINA'S NEUTRALITY.

From the "Japan Times" we learn that, referring to the rumour that the Russian dismantled cruiser at Shanghai, the "Askold," is secretly taking in coal, besides being furnished with a new steering gear, apparently for the purpose of making her escape and eventually joining the Baltic fleet, the "Jiji" says, judging by the enemy's conduct in the past, there is a possibility of the report being well founded. If the latter should prove to be the case, Japan should not remain passive, but at once take steps to suit herself. When at first China failed to enforce the 24-hour rule on that warship, Japan could with every right have dealt with her in a manner she deserved. But Japan took pity on China's insufficiency of power, besides being anxious not to cause disturbances in an international trade mart as Shanghai is, and allowed the ship to be finally dismantled, overlooking the delay of time. But China should not be permitted to plead inability for every form of neutrality-destroying irregularites. We have had enough of the "Askold's" crew's disquieting conduct on land, the escape of the "Riesitelini's" commander, and that sort of thing. When it comes to the prospect of the enemy's fugitive warship committed to Chinese custody taking French leave, the matter is too serious to be winked at. Consequently should there be found any truth in the rumour under consideration, we should no longer be trammelled by the considerations of pity on China or deference to the foreign communities, but should adopt measures on the basis that China's neutrality is no longer a thing of reliability.

This is all very well, China, during this war, has never been in a position to "enforce" her neutrality, and even if she had been, it seems to us that it was solely for China to decide whether or no she should resort to force. So far, China belongs to China, and if she does not choose to actively resent encroachments upon her territory or waters by the belligerent it seems to be entirely her own affair and we cannot perceive where Japan will find a remedy.

The "Jiji" in advocating that all pretense that China is a power likely to enforce her neutrality be thrown to the winds, is in our opinion treading upon dangerous ground. That the "Askold" is at present in Chinese custody goes without saying, but so was the Rieshetelini when the Japanese towed her out of Chefoo harbour. On that occasion it was Japan who committed the breach of neutrality and if any similar measures are taken with regard to the "Askold," Japan will again be in the wrong and the consequences will be far more serious.

Even if the unexpected were to happen and other foreign powers offered no opposition to the Japanese capture of the "Askold," Japan would in taking this action, be providing Russia with a fine excuse for making a naval base of any port in China she chose to select.

This would, it appears to us, be a particularly disastrous state of affairs for Japan and it is far better for her to face the possibility of the "Askold" joining the approaching Russian fleet, than it would be to place herself absolutely in the wrong by such a flagrant breach of neutrality as the forcible interference with the "Askold" in a treaty port would be.

ELECTRIC TRACTION IN RUSSIA.

Two rather ambitious schemes for electric traction on a large scale have recently been brought before the Electrotechnical Association of St. Petersburg. The first is no less than the electrofication of the Trans-Siberian Railway, a project considered by Count A. F. Lubieuski as not only desirable, but necessary. The transportation of passengers and goods on this railway has developed to such an extent that it will soon become necessary to increase the number of trains which at the present time amount to forty or fifty per day. Owing to several circumstances, particularly the lightness of the rails and the insufficiency of water, the existing trains are said to have reached their practical limit of speed; and though the water difficulty might be met by canalisation or other means, the relaying of the track would entail enormous expenditure of money and time. The Count maintains that the most rational and economical way of meeting the case is by the introduction of electric traction on some parts of the line at least: The existing track would be made use of, and the many sharp curves and heavy gradients would not limit the speed of a multiple-unit eletric train to the same extent as in the case of a train drawn by a steam locomotive. It is proposed to make use of the rivers and waterfalls along the course of the line for the supply of electric energy, which would be generated at power-stations from 100 to 200 kilometres apart, and distributed in both directions to trans, former sub-stations at a pressure of 100,000 volts. It must be evident, we think, to the most sanguine of engineers that the scheme outlined above, even if possible, could not be realised in time to meet the present traffic difficulties, though it appears to have been seriously considered as a desirable alternative to the relaying of the track. The second project was brought forward by Mr. G. O. Graftis, and is rather more modest in its scope. He proposes the electrification of the Caucasian railways on the grounds that electric traction is particularly adapted to a mountainous country, and that abundance of power is at hand in the waterfalls of the Caucasus. The large number of rivers and mountain torrents watering the district through which the railway runs, and supplying up to 80 cubic metres of water per second constitute an ideal source of power, which could be turned to account with little difficulty. As to the expense of constructing a line along the rocky coast of the Black Sea, the speaker adduced figures showing the cost of the Italian Lecco-Sondrio-Chiavenna elecric railway and Vladikavkase steam railway. He estimated that the establishment of central stations and substations equipped with plant for producing three-phase current at 30,000 volts would entail an expense of 1,000,000 above the cost of a steam service. On the other hand, the working expenses of the electric service with the same amount of passengers and goods carried would show an annual saving of 800l. per mile as compared with steam. It is also claimed that, as the electric service would admit of heavier gradients, the construction of the permanent way would be cheapened. After the meeting, in consequence of the importance of schemes of this nature to a district well suppied with water power, the Electrotechnical Association appointed a committee to make an exhaustive investigation of the subject.—"Engineering.

A JAPANESE VIEW OF THE CANTON-HANKOW LINE.

The most important railway in China is of course the trunk line that traverses the empire from north to south, and which consists of two separate lines under different managements, namely the Peking-Hankow line belonging to a Belgian syndicate, and the Canton-Hankow line controlled by an American syndicate. The "Asahi" (according to translation in the "Japan Times") says that the Belgian syndicate, as is well known, is in name only, the controlling power behind it being a Russo-French combination. It was to counteract this combination that China granted the Canton-Hankow concession to the American syndicate; but latterly, says the journal, that syndicate, or rather the portion of the trunk road under its nominal control, has also come to be practically under the same management as its northern half. The journal sees a serious danger for China in leaving a great railway in the heart of the empire in the hands of so undesirable a combination as of French and Russian shareholders. As for the American syndicate, the "Asahi" considers the transfer of the control of the road to the hands of the Belgo-Russo-French shareholders a virtual defeat for the American syndicate, because it was the careless and indifference of the latter that caused the transfer in question, which when accomplished, has robbed it of its power to manage the concern. It happens, however, that the American syndicate, owing no doubt to its internecine dissensions, has arbitrarily suspended the building of the road, and China is inclined to cancel its concession for that reason, an intention which, it is reported is supported by the U. S. Government. The journal hopes that China will carry out her intention and re-grant the concession to a syndicate purely and truly American, for it is essential that this should be so; while the concession if properly exploited will create in China a valuable vested interest for the United States.

The result of the first fire at annual cock-crowing competition in Paris is that a bird named Tannhauser has taken first prize by crowing sixty-six times in half an hour. Toreador, the first day's champion, was second with thirty-eight crows, and Santos Dumont third with thirty-six crows.

Owing to a prosperous export trade in coal, the stock of the fuel at Moji is gradually decreasing, and the price has now gone up by two yen per 100 piculs, compared with that at the beginning of this month. There are signs, a Moji telegram says, that the price will not come down for some time to come. —Nagasaki Press.

A definite treaty of peace between Chili and Bolivia has been signed. The German Emperor is appointed arbiter in case of difficulty. Bolivia renounces all rights to a port in the Pacific, and Chili guarantees the construction of a railroad between La Paz, Bolivia, and the Chilian port of Arica.

The projected visit of the Prince and Princess of Wales to India next autumn is already arousing much interest in Anglo-Indian circles. The tour is not to include Ceylon, and in all probability will not even involve formal visits to Mediterranean stations. It is understood that no merchant liner will be chartered for the occassion, as in the case of the "Ophir" cruise, but that the precedent established thirty years ago by the King will be followed. In that event the Prince will hoist his pennant as an Admiral of the Royal Navy, and service discipline will prevail. The expectation is, according to a London correspondent, that after a visit to Karachi the Royal party will make for Bombay, and will cross the peninsula to Madras, travelling thence to Calcutta, or perhaps also Rangoon, and continuing the tour across the northern plains to the remotest frontiers.

The Korea Daily News.

VOL. I, TUESDAY, DECEMBER 20, 1904. No. 130

大韓每日申報
대한ᄆᆡ일신보

(뎨일빅삼십일호) (목요일) 일쳔구빅ᄉᆞ년십이월이십이일

본샤고

이신보는영어와한어로셕거ᄆᆡ일츌판ᄒᆞᆸ

신문가

한장 엽두돈오푼

일삭됴 엽두량닷돈

우표가ᄆᆡ삭닷돈

다맛돈으로밧ᄉᆞᆸ

광고료는

긔한의장단과ᄌᆞ힝의다쇼로즁감ᄒᆞ되렴가로밧을터이오며오ᄅᆡ지아녀대한사람마다다이신문을보실터이니광고내시기를원ᄒᆞ시는이들은우리신문샤에와셔면약ᄒᆞ심을희망ᄒᆞᆸ

○발힝소 박동대한ᄆᆡ일신보샤법어학교압헤젼영국인셜필림집자리오

샤쟝 영국인 (비셜)

평양 ᄃᆡ리뎜

○평양효동사는권미보씨로우리신문관ᄃᆡ리인을뎡ᄒᆞ엿ᄉᆞ오니평양에계신구람코져ᄒᆞ시는쳠군ᄌᆞ는ᄒᆡᄃᆡ리뎜에왕림ᄒᆞ와면의ᄒᆞ시ᄋᆞᆸ

샤고

○우리대한ᄆᆡ일신보의목뎍은대한의안녕질셔에관ᄒᆞᆫ모든데목에ᄃᆡᄒᆞ야논공평ᄒᆞᆫ변론을쥬쟝홈이라우리동신원의탐보ᄒᆞᆫ신문보시는쳠군ᄌᆞ의게홍샹보도ᄒᆞ리며편지를긔셔ᄒᆞ여주시는이는셩명과반디를젹어붓치시기를희망ᄒᆞ오니이거슨신문샹에긔ᄌᆡᄒᆞ라는거시아니오다만국히신용ᄒᆞ논즁거를숨고쟈홈이라긔쟈는아모긔셔뎐지긔지홈을되각ᄒᆞ논권리를가졋ᄉᆞ나되각ᄒᆞᆫ리유를말홀터이오며공즁평화를문란케ᄒᆞ는듯ᄒᆞᆫ긔셔는의례히밧지안켓ᄉᆞᆸ나이다

●본샤셜시이릭로신문을ᄆᆡ양우례로분젼ᄒᆞᆫ와례젼부의임의로젼ᄒᆞᆫ듯ᄉᆞ로면곳에는혹늣게젼ᄒᆞ기도ᄒᆞ며혹멋칠거슬ᄒᆞᆫ겁에젼ᄒᆞ기도ᄒᆞ며혹아니젼ᄒᆞ는곳도잇다ᄒᆞ와우리신문을ᄉᆞ랑ᄒᆞ야구람ᄒᆞ시는 쳠군ᄌᆞ의계ᄃᆡᄒᆞ야ᄆᆡ우미안ᄒᆞᆸ기로지금은분젼인을두고ᄆᆡ일일즉이젼ᄒᆞ며아니젼ᄒᆞ거나늣게거나ᄒᆞᆫ폐가업도록ᄒᆞ랴ᄒᆞ오니혹아니젼ᄒᆞ거나늣게젼ᄒᆞ거나ᄒᆞᆫ일이잇스면본샤로통긔ᄒᆞ여쥬심을희망ᄒᆞᆸ

잡보

○졍부총회 각판졔리졍사건으로십팔일샹오열두시에졍부에셔총회를ᄒᆞ엿더라

○광쥬회민 젼라남도슌찰사가ᄂᆡ부로뎐보ᄒᆞ기를일진회원ᄇᆡᆨ여명이젼쥬로브터ᄂᆡ려와셔련락부졀ᄒᆞ는ᄃᆡ아직작폐는업고위션ᄃᆡ면ᄒᆞ야효유ᄒᆞ고면져보고ᄒᆞ오니안무홀넌지소멸홀넌지량됴간회면를기다려거힝ᄒᆞ겟노라ᄒᆞ엿는고로ᄂᆡ부에셔회면ᄒᆞ기를죠칙ᄃᆡ로효유ᄒᆞ야긔허이히산케홈이가ᄒᆞ다ᄒᆞ엿더라

○비쳔슈파직 황ᄒᆡ도슌찰사뎡규회씨가비쳔군슈유긔쥰을봉고파직ᄒᆞ고졍부로보고ᄒᆞ엿더라

○평산셔리도망 평산군슈셔리금쳔군슈김현ᄐᆡ가일안의치도비륙십여만량을표를써낸일노써거졍ᄒᆞ야이에탈신지계를내여인쟝을다보내고거연이발졍ᄒᆞ엿다고황ᄒᆡ관찰사가ᄂᆡ부로보고ᄒᆞ엿더라

○탁훈각도 탁지부에셔각도로훈령ᄒᆞ기를근ᄅᆡ에각군슈가각등공젼을쳬납ᄒᆞ기를아니ᄒᆞ는사ᄅᆞᆷ이업스니만일쟝졍을엄히세우지아니ᄒᆞ면이셰졍을졍리홀슈업스니지금실시ᄒᆞ는날에ᄒᆞᆫ나히라도혹쥰힝치안는폐가잇스면규칙ᄃᆡ로률을시힝홀뜻으로관하각군에젼칙ᄒᆞ야신칙홈이가ᄒᆞ다ᄒᆞ엿더라

○결젼졍긔 각군에각년결젼미납됴를양력십이월ᄂᆡ로몰슈히필납ᄒᆞ고신결젼은양력십이월이듬히삼월ᄂᆡ로긔한을졍ᄒᆞ되처음긔한젼에반액을미납ᄒᆞᆫ군슈는곳맛당히쥬면ᄒᆞ고룰올시힝ᄒᆞ기로ᄒᆞ엿더라

○결젼독봉엄금 의졍부에셔각도관찰부로훈령ᄒᆞ기를각ᄃᆡ방결셰를음십월에시작ᄒᆞ야십일월에슈납ᄒᆞ는거시스스로젼례가되엿스니한젼에독봉ᄒᆞ는폐는일일히엄금ᄒᆞ는거시가ᄒᆞ다ᄒᆞ엿더라

○금광복셜 ᄂᆡ장원경셔리김영진씨가봉폐ᄒᆞᆫ금광을복셜ᄒᆞ고황ᄒᆡ도로훈령ᄒᆞ기를금쳔토산에셔로ᄀᆡ셜ᄒᆞᆫ금광의범졀을ᄒᆡ금광감리의ᄀᆡ죠ᄒᆞ는ᄃᆡ로거힝케ᄒᆞ라ᄒᆞ엿더라

○복졔샹소 황태자비복졔사건으로원로와밋산림학자의게하슌ᄒᆞ옵셧더니옥쳔군사는송산림병션씨가십팔일에샹소ᄒᆞ엿더라

○합복호젹불납 각도호젹을ᄂᆡ부에다필납ᄒᆞ엿스되합경북도에셔는금년도호젹을십이월이되도록밧치지안는고로젼관찰사리윤직와ᄂᆡ부판적국쟝리용세씨는일삭감봉에쳐ᄒᆞᆫ다더라

○질문여사대쟝 여사대쟝빅셩긔씨가고시ᄒᆞ고여사ᄃᆡ젼을슈렴ᄒᆞ는고로일진회에셔고시ᄒᆞ고빅씨의게질문ᄒᆞ기를쳔룡도감시에여사ᄃᆡ젼을이믜슈봉ᄒᆞ엿는도감을쳘폐ᄒᆞ엿슨즉희슈봉ᄒᆞᆫ젼이ᄌᆞ지ᄒᆞ거늘엇지ᄒᆞ야이용ᄒᆞ지아니ᄒᆞ고ᄯᅩ슈렴ᄒᆞ며ᄯᅩᄂᆡ하젼이유족ᄒᆞ니슈젼고시를물시ᄒᆞ라ᄒᆞ엿더라

○피슈도비도타 지령황쥬에셔동도ᄉᆞ십여명을봉산일본병참소에셔압슈ᄒᆞ엿는ᄃᆡ송화군에피슈ᄒᆞ엿던동도피슈강덕지는도타ᄒᆞ엿다더라

○호구총슈 광무팔년갑진도즁인민호구총슈를각관찰부에셔ᄂᆡ부에보고ᄒᆞ엿는ᄃᆡ그호구슈효가좌와ᄀᆞᆺ더라

한셩부 호슈는 ᄉᆞ만이쳔칠빅삼십
인구슈는 십구만이쳔삼빅ᄉᆞ

경긔도 호슈는 십칠만ᄉᆞ빅이십ᄉᆞ
인구슈는 륙십칠만이쳔륙빅삼십륙

츙쳥남도 호슈는 십이만ᄉᆞ쳔삼빅칠십
인구슈는 ᄉᆞ십칠만ᄉᆞ쳔삼빅십이

츙쳥북도 호슈는 칠만륙쳔팔빅칠십칠
인구수는 삼십만삼빅ᄉᆞ십오

젼라남도 호수는 십이만ᄉᆞ쳔삼십
인구수는 ᄉᆞ십구만오십ᄉᆞ

젼라북도 호수는 십일만팔빅삼십오
인구수는 ᄉᆞ십ᄉᆞ만구빅일

경샹남도 호수는 십삼만일쳔ᄉᆞ빅팔십칠
인구수는 오십만구쳔구빅륙십칠

경샹북도 호수는 십륙만일쳔오빅이십이
인구수는 륙십만일쳔일빅륙십삼

강원도 호수는 팔만이쳔일빅오십ᄉᆞ
인구수는 삼십만일쳔팔빅팔십오

황ᄒᆡ도 호수는 구만륙쳔ᄉᆞ빅륙십륙
인구수는 삼십팔만이쳔이빅삼십

평안남도 호수는 구만칠쳔삼빅삼십이
인구수는 삼십구만이쳔이빅칠십이

평안북도 호수는 구만칠쳔오빅삼십ᄉᆞ
인구수는 ᄉᆞ십이만칠빅이십오

함경남도 호수는 오만팔쳔구빅이십팔
인구수는 ᄉᆞ십오만륙빅구십삼

이샹호수에총합은일빅삼십칠만ᄉᆞ쳔구빅륙십구오
인구에총합은오빅륙십이만구쳔ᄉᆞ빅팔십칠이더라

○이셩지합 지금국즁에두회가잇스니한회는일진회오ᄯᅩᄒᆞᆫ회는공진회라그목적인즉다ᄒᆞᆫ가지오그일홈으로말ᄒᆞ면두글ᄌᆞ뜻도ᄯᅩᄒᆞᆫᄀᆞᆺᄒᆞ나조곰ᄀᆞᆺ지아니ᄒᆞᆫ것을비유ᄒᆞ면리판셔와김팔셔라고ᄒᆞ는말과ᄀᆞᆺᄒᆞᆫ데두회가쟝찻일홈을ᄀᆞᆺ치짓는다더라

○풍셜란신 지금경부텰도를거진다통ᄒᆞ엿는ᄃᆡ연로젼답이텰도에드러간지라경부텰도좌우ᄀᆞᆺ가온군읍군수는일본유학싱으로ᄐᆡᆨ용ᄒᆞᆫ다는ᄃᆡ여항유지쟈ㅣ왈이젼에는삭ᄊᆡ이만알면각아문쥬ᄉᆞ를ᄒᆞ엿거니와지금은사요나라만알면남도군슈를ᄒᆞ겟다더라

UNION INSURANCE SOCIETY OF CANTON.

Head office Hongkong.
Marine risks underwritten at current rates.

Agents in Chemulpo,
E. MEYER & Co.

COMPAGNIE DES MESSAGERIES MARITIMES.

Fortnightly Direct Service.

For Marseilles
via Ports.
Sailing from Yokohama
Calling at Kobe,
Shanghai, Hongkong, Saigon, Singapore,
Colombo, Djibonti, Suez, Port Said
and Marseilles.

For particulars apply to
HOLME RINGER & Co.,
Chemulpo.

HAYASHIDA & CO.,

16 MYENG DONG, CHIN KO KAI, SEOUL.
BRANCH OFFICE AT CHEMULPO.

Money changers, Coal and Wood Merchants, Express Agents.

We are agents for the Pyeng-yang Coal Company and the K--azu Coal Company of Japan. We have the best quality of both anthracite and bituminous coal, and prompt execution of orders is our speciality. Firewood of all kinds kept in stock. Full weight guaranteed. Money of all denominations exchanged at current rates. Parcels received for all parts.

CHINA MUTUAL LIFE INS. OC.

Most favourable terms to policy holders.

Benefit system unsurpassed.

HOLME RINGER & Co.
Agents, Chemulpo.

C. P. R.

CANADIAN PACIFIC RAILWAY COMPANY'S ROYAL MAIL STEAMSHIP LINE.

THE FAST ROUTE BETWEEN CHINA, JAPAN, AND EUROPE VIA CANADA AND THE UNITED STATES.

Route from Hongkong via Shanghai, Nagasaki (Inland Sea of Japan) Kobe, Yokohama Victoria and Vancouver.

Twin Screw Empress Steamship—6,000 Tons—Speed 19 knots.

PROPOSED SAILING FROM YOKOHAMA.
R. M. S. Empress of India.
R. M. S. Empress of Japan.
R. M. S. Empress of China.
R. M. S. Athenian.
R. M. S. Tartar.

Special reduction (first class only) granted to members of the Military, Naval, Diplomatic and Civil services and to Missionaries.

Passengers have choice of ten routes across the Continent of America and have privilege of travelling by any Atlantic Steamship Line.

Round the World passage tickets in connection with the P. and O. S. N., North German Lloyd and Messageries Co.'s £125.

All rates payable at current rate of exchange.

For further information, Tickets, Guide Books, etc., apply to

HOLME, RINGER & Co., AGENTS,
Chemulpo.

Grand Hotel,

(Formerly the Station Hotel)

Near the Railway Terminus, West Gate Seoul.

The Best Hotel in Korea;
Handsome new Building.
Fine Airy Rooms
Excellent Cuisine.
Terms Moderate.
Special terms to Missionaries
and to permanent boarders.

Electric cars within 2 minutes' walk.

W. H. EMBERLEY.
Proprietor

EVERY FACILITY.

In connection with Life Assurance Business is afforded by

The Standard Life Assurance Co.,

One of the largest and wealthiest of the Provident Institutions of the United Kingdom Forms of Application and all information will be promptly afforded on application.

10 CENTS A DAY.

Not a very large expenditure is it? But it is sufficient to secure for a man of 30 a policy with the STANDARD LIFE OFFICE for

$1323.

For all particulars of rates, etc., apply to

Holme, Ringer & Co.,
Agents, Chemulpo.

THE NEW YORK LIFE INSURANCE COMPANY.

Have you ever been declined by any Company?

Are you engaged in a specially hazardous occupation?

Have you heard of the New York Life Insurance Company's New Classifications for this class of Risks?

If not, send your date of birth, occupation and particulars of rejection, if any to

E. MEYER & Co.,
Agents, Chemulpo.

MITSUI BUSSAN KAISHA.
(MITSUI & Co.)

MITSUI GINKO.
(MITSUI BANK.)

The Bank is owned by the members of the Mitsui Family, who, as partners, assume an unlimited responsibility for all liabilities of the Bank:—

Capital........................Yen 5,000,000
Reserve Fund.................. " 5,600,000

HEAD OFFICE, TOKYO.
LONDON OFFICE, 34 LIME ST., E. C.

BRANCHES AND AGENCIES:—
New York, San Francisco, Hamburg, Bombay, Singapore, Manila, Hongkong, Amoy, Chefoo, Tientsin.

Kobe, Hakodate, Yokohama, Kure, Yokosuka, Moji, Shimonoseki, Miike, Wakamatsu, Nagasaki, Kuchinotsu, Karatsu, Sasebo, Misume, Taipeh, &c.

Telegraphic Address for all the Offices:
"MITSUI."
A. B. C. AND A. 1 CODES USED.

Contractors of Coal
To the Imperial Japanese Navy. Arsenals and Railway Bureau, Principal Railway Companies and Industrial Work, Home and Foreign Mail and Freight Steamers.

Sole Proprietors
Of the famous Miike, Tagawa and Yamano Coal Mines.

Sole Agents
For the sale of Fukumo, Hokoku, Ichimura, Kanoda, Mannoura, Onoura, Ostuji, Sonoda, Tsubaruro, Yoshinotani, Yoshio, Yurokibura and other coals.

YANGTSE INSURANCE ASSOCIATION, LTD.

The undersigned, having been appointed agents for the above company, are prepared to issue policies and pay losses on marine risks at regular rates.

E. MEYER & Co.,
Agents, Chemulpo.

AMERICAN KOREAN ELECTRIC CO.

Light and Power.

Main Office: Electric Building, Chong No.

RAILWAY DEPARTMENT.

OPERATING CARS BETWEEN EAST AND WEST GATE, EVERY TEN MINUTES:—

First Car leaves East Gate at 7:00 A. M. First Car leaves R. R. Station at 7:25 A. M
Last Car " East Gate at 9:40 P. M. Last " " R. R. Station at 10:05 P. M.

OPERATING CARS BETWEEN EAST GATE AND IMPERIAL TOMB TERMINUS, EVERY TWENTY MINUTES:—

CONNECTING WITH EVERY ALTERNATE CAR ARRIVING AT EAST GATE FROM CHONG NO.

First Car leaves East Gate for Tomb at 7:10 A. M.
" " " Tomb for East Gate at 7:35 A. M.
Last " " East Gate for Tomb at 7:50 P. M.
" " " Tomb for East Gate at 8:10 P. M.

OPERATING CARS BETWEEN CHONG NO AND YUNG SAN RIVER EVERY TWELVE MINUTES:—

First Car leaves Chong No for South Gate at 7:12 A. M.
" " " Chong No for Yung San at 7:36 A. M.
" " " South Gate for Chong No at 7:20 A. M.
" " " Yung San for Chong No at 8:09 A. M.
Last " " South Gate for Chong No 10:00 P. M.
" " " Yung San for Chong No at 9:33 P. M.

SPECIAL PRIVATE CARS FURNISHED TO SUIT CONVENIENCE OF PATRONS. PRICES ON APPLICATION AT HEAD OFFICE.

LIGHTING DEPARTMENT.

Where less than 250 candle power of light is used, the rate per month will be
Per 16 candle power incandescent lamp,—All night.—Yen 2.50.
32 candle power incandescent lamp:—All night:—Yen 4.00.
50 candle power incandescent lamp:—All night:—Yen 6.00.
150 ,, ,, ,, ,, ,, ,, ,, 10.00.
1200 ,, ,, enclosed are ,, ,, ,, ,, 20.00.

Where more than 250 candle power of light is used, a Meter will be installed, freqvedted:—Rent of Meter Yen 2.00 per month. Rate of charges by meter reading:—Two Sen per Ampere per hour. (Approximately this is equal to about One Sen per 16 C. P. lamp per hour) Minimum monthly charge where meter is installed, Yen 20.00 per month, which includes rental of meter.

Estimates for installing lights furnished on application

An assortment of chandeliers always on hand.

K. Murakami.
Photograph Studio
Chinkokai, Seoul.

Printing, Developing and Enlargement, of Photographs always Undertaken.

Korean Views and Pictures Illustrating Native Customs always on Sale.

THE OSAKA SHOSEN KAISHA.

Boats frequently on the berth for Chinnampo.

REGULAR SAILINGS BETWEEN JAPAN AND KOREAN PORTS.

FUSAN AND KOBE VIA SHIMONOSEKI.

OSAKA VIA MOKPO, FUSAN, SHIMONOSEKI AND KOBE.

MOJI DIRECT.

OSAKA VIA KUNSAN, MASANPO, FUSAN, SHIMONOSEKI AND KOBE.

CHEMULPO KUNSAN LINE,
Every three days.

CHEMULPO CHINNAMPO LINE.
Every three days.

For Freight and passage and further particulars apply to

THE OSAKA SHOSEN KAISHA,
Chemulpo

RONDON, PLAISANT & CO.

General Storekeepers and Merchants, Ships Contractors, Tobacconists, Commission and Forwarding Agents, Coal Merchants

IMPORTERS AND EXPORTERS

Seoul & Chemulpo.

W. D. WENTWORTH.

LANDING
AND
SHIPPING AGENT
AND
CUSTOMS BORDER.

12 OURA, NAGASAKI.

STEWARD & CO.

Chemulpo.

Shipchandlers and Storekeepers, Naval and Mercantile Contrrctors, Landing and Shipping Agents.

STEWARD'S HOTEL

Chemulpo.

Best accommodation in the port for travellers. Clean and well-aired rooms, good cuisin and prompt attendence, moderate tariff.

론셜

정략과샹ᄒᆞᆫ실샹리허

지작일우리신문에게지ᄒᆞᆫ바동경셔예산회의되엿다ᄂᆞᆫ소문으로볼진딕정부로셔근일힝정홈에딕ᄒᆞ야불긍히들넉이ᄂᆞᆫ바를회의ᄒᆞᆫ듯ᄒᆞ며정부일관도역시보기에강경치못ᄒᆞᆫ듯ᄒᆞᆫ거시결단나ᄂᆞᆫ일빅삼십은힝은외국국치의표부됨으로써빅셩들도엇지ᄒᆞᆯᄉᆞ업시반딕ᄒᆞ야금지치못ᄒᆞᄂᆞᆫᄉᆞ건에ᄂᆞᆫ정부로셔셜명ᄒᆞ여그러ᄒᆞ되일절다른문제에듸ᄒᆞ야ᄂᆞᆫ듸답들이심히모호ᄒᆞ야불합ᄒᆞᆫ게된모양이분명ᄒᆞᆫ지라또ᄒᆞᆫ다른곳으로브터젼ᄒᆞᄂᆞᆫ말을드른즉일빅삼십은힝을방죠ᄒᆞ야정부로셔셜명ᄒᆞ야듸답홈에도심히불합ᄒᆞ며또ᄒᆞᆫ귀정이나지못ᄒᆞᆫ모양이중저간에주의아니치못ᄒᆞᆯ사건으로다른형편이잇드라ᄒᆞᆫ즉우리ᄂᆞᆫ불명히ᄶᅢ다를지라

긔왕에우리ᄂᆞᆫ일본을칭도ᄒᆞ야포양ᄒᆞ기를일본셔ᄂᆞᆫ이번젼쟁에지졍으로ᄂᆞᆫ곤난을당ᄒᆞ지아니ᄒᆞ겟고또ᄒᆞᆫ군비의쓸자본이아직도수년은지당ᄒᆞ여가리라고ᄒᆞ엿거ᄂᆞᆯ이제팔리번에일쳔이빅만방의약간금액을ᄭᅮ러닉ᄂᆞᆫ딕로결단이나ᄂᆞᆫ이엇지ᄒᆞᆫᄂᆞ니ᄒᆞ야정부로더브러구익가삼히되게되ᄂᆞᆫ바약ᄎᆞᄒᆞᆫ일빅삼십은힝으로써우리ᄂᆞᆫ무엇시라고다시다른사ᄅᆞᆷ의게딕ᄒᆞ야밋도록말을ᄒᆞ며만일히은힝이결단이나셔공립이되게되엿슬진딕무엇을밋고당ᄒᆞ여가랴ᄒᆞ엿스며또ᄒᆞᆫ리익이팔리번에셔더옥만케되엿드면국치를표부치못ᄒᆞ게될번ᄒᆞ엿스며외에일본정부로셔ᄂᆞᆫ반딕가응당잇슬일일로써다만자긔의ᄉᆡᆼ각딕로죵이만ᄒᆞᆫ자ᄒᆞᆫ나자연히동경으로셔필경정략샹의일홈으로말미암아소문이젼파가되여우리의게도들인즉우리ᄂᆞᆫ엇지이일올론리ᄒᆞ야교정치아니ᄒᆞ려ᄒᆞ리요엇지던지이관경에딕ᄒᆞ야긴즁히연명ᄒᆞᆯ빅잇ᄂᆞ니데일리ᄲᅧᆯ리그리푸동신원이자긔의집으로면보ᄒᆞᆯ때에의신업시교정ᄒᆞ야말ᄒᆞ기를정략샹필요ᄂᆞᆫ려순을신속히포획ᄒᆞ도록진력ᄒᆞ야ᄒᆞ겟다고ᄒᆞ여순즉이ᄂᆞᆫ일본정부의셔급속히ᄒᆞ려홈을알고셔로응ᄒᆞ야국회에셔반딕홈을막조교홈인지라

ᄉᆞ호소문을드른즉그곳은일본의게딕단히불리ᄒᆞ게됨이분명ᄒᆞᆫ거시대산암군은봉쳔으로돌출ᄒᆞ야젼진ᄒᆞᆫ바를도로퇴보치못ᄒᆞᆯ뿐더러도리혀퇴각ᄒᆞ엿든야병들이일본셔거우점령ᄒᆞᆫ고합락만ᄒᆞ지못ᄒᆞ려순디방으로젼진ᄒᆞ야츙만ᄒᆞ엿ᄂᆞᆫ고로어령산과순수산과긔각산진루도공격ᄒᆞ야결단넨지가임의오래거슬못ᄒᆞ엿다ᄒᆞ니이ᄂᆞᆫ관계되지아니ᄒᆞᆯ거시이빅삼쳑되ᄂᆞᆫ산을점령ᄒᆞ엿슨즉다른산버다셩공홈이오히려비승ᄒᆞᆫ지라그러ᄒᆞ나아병들이져항ᄒᆞᆫ다ᄂᆞᆫ소문이과연진젹ᄒᆞᆫ말일진댄응당그산을회복ᄒᆞ라고군략을베풀터이니그러ᄒᆞᆯ지경이면일병의게ᄂᆞᆫ그와갓치져 곳이업슬지며샹ᄒᆞᆫ함딕의 되엿다ᄒᆞᄂᆞᆫ말도잇슨즉이연빙거업ᄂᆞᆫ말을ᄒᆞᆯ리가업ᄂᆞ니이거시모도정략샹졍홍에심히급박홈을나타여닉임이로다

관보

뎨삼쳔십ᄉᆞ호 샹무팔

십이월이십일

셔임급ᄉᆞ령

○승종이픔 정삼픔 유정슈

○승종이픔 정삼픔 리샹규

○승정삼픔 ᄉᆞ픔 피희두

○승정삼픔 오픔 리지철

○승정삼픔 륙픔 차효슌

○승정삼픔 륙픔 서샹규

○승정삼픔 륙픔 김용제

○승정삼픔 륙픔 심인턱

○승정삼픔 륙픔 김용규

○승정삼픔 륙픔 죠규하

○승정삼픔 륙픔 김영두

○승정삼픔 륙픔 오덕근

○승정삼픔 륙픔 김세교

○승정삼픔 륙픔 김봉남

○승정삼픔 륙픔 리일령

○승정삼픔 륙픔 박진영

○승정삼픔 륙픔 리경용

○승정삼픔 륙픔 윤신모

이샹오월십일일

○의원면본관 황태ᄌᆞ비궁대부 민충식

○겸임 황태ᄌᆞ비궁대부 법부참셔관 송대현

이샹십월이ᄉᆞ일

○의원면본관 즁츄원의관 장건식 즁츄원의관 김병슈 즁츄원의관 문홍셥 즁츄원의관 정창묵 즁츄원의관 리교항

○임즁츄원의관셔쥬임관륙등 종이픔 비영진 정삼픔 송익현 정삼픔 리덕우 정삼품 양명슈 정삼품 안긔양

이샹십이월십오일

○의원면본관 장례원상례 박제황 홍문관시독 유면호 광학국쥬ᄉᆞ 윤턱셥 통신ᄉᆞ면화과쥬ᄉᆞ 하덕성 졔릉참봉 윤종현 후릉참봉 홍덕쥬 목릉참봉 유셕근 즁츄원의관 리희상

○임장례원상례셔쥬임관륙등 홍문관시독 리의국

○임홍문관시독셔판임관칠등 시강원시독관 리원셰 륙품 죠남일

○임시강원시독관셔판임관ᄉᆞ등 륙품 박제황

○임광학국쥬ᄉᆞ셔판임관륙등 고희등

○임졔릉참봉셔판임관팔등 유티린

○임후릉참봉셔판임관팔등 김지규

○임목릉참봉셔판임관팔등 윤병규

○임즁츄원의관셔칙임관ᄉᆞ등 샹의ᄉᆞ쟝 민강호

○임즁츄원의관셔쥬임관오등 창원군슈 권익샹

○승셔판임관삼등 닉부쥬ᄉᆞ 승

이샹십이월십칠일

의원면본관 졔릉참봉 유티인 후릉참병 김지규 목릉참봉 윤병규 홍문관시독 리원셰

○임홍문관시독셔판임관륙등 륙품 허만필

○임졔릉참봉셔판임관팔등 구픔 윤종헌

○임후릉참봉셔판임관팔등 구품 홍덕쥬

○임목릉참봉셔판임관팔등 구픔 유셕근

○임통신ᄉᆞ면화과쥬ᄉᆞ셔판임관팔등 김연건 서병죠 박긔챵 최영쥰 김영셥 셔병문 졍신턱

○명시종원분시어 정삼품 김익우

○승셔쥬임관오등 례식원번역관 박긔쥰

○명닉장원경셔칙임관삼등 종이품 박봉쥬

이샹십이월십팔일

뎐보

론돈발 십이월십일

○덕국의회 덕국의회에셔샤회당들이군ᄉᆞ비에딕ᄒᆞ야반딕ᄒᆞ되로국이지금젼쟁에힘을쓰니우리가군ᄉᆞ비를늘일필요가업다ᄒᆞ고또이번일로젼쟁에딕ᄒᆞ야덕국에셔로국에호의를보이ᄂᆞᆫ것을척망ᄒᆞ니지샹불노씨가딕답ᄒᆞ되덕국은일로젼쟁에엄정즁립을직혓고덕로비밀죠약의젼셜은허무ᄒᆞᆫ말이라ᄒᆞ엿더라

빅림발 동월십일일

○졔션소과산 미국필나피아에잇ᄂᆞᆫ맥파이레비졔션회사가파이낫다더라

빅림발 십이월십일일

○로함의쟝릭 론돈히군샤회에셔말ᄒᆞ되려슌구에셔로국군함들의멸망홈으로볼틱함딕ᄂᆞᆫ웬둥쓸딕업시되엿다ᄒᆞ고또세탁ᄒᆞ되볼틱함딕가즁립항구에폐ᄒᆞ야드러가셔필경멸망ᄒᆞᆫ다ᄒᆞ엿더라

동디발 동일

○덕병득승 덕국군ᄉᆞ가윗보이사ᄅᆞᆷ들이ᄎᆞ지ᄒᆞᆫ긴요ᄒᆞᆫ쳐소를엄습ᄒᆞ야그것들이동편으로어즈러이도망ᄒᆞ엿더라

론돈발 동월십이일

○영국히군예비 영국히군부에셔예비함딕에명령ᄒᆞ야ᄒᆞᆫ번호령이면곳젼디에나아갈져긋치예비ᄒᆞ고자죠히샹연습ᄒᆞ라ᄒᆞ엿더라

십구일군ᄉᆞ령부착뎐

○습리퇴격 십칠일아춤여섯시에젹의보병약일빅이리가와봉에습리ᄒᆞ고이튼날오젼두시후에젹의보병약일소딕가동왜승구부근에리습ᄒᆞ엿스나우리젼초가즉시이것을격퇴ᄒᆞ엿다ᄒᆞ며

○홍릉소젼 십칠일오후팔시브터십일시ᄭᆞ지젹의척후가십오명식젼후삼ᄎᆞ를삼도강조우리젼초에향ᄒᆞ야젼진ᄒᆞ고또밤ᄒᆞᆫ시경에약일소딕가홍릉돈셔방우리소초에향ᄒᆞ야젼진ᄒᆞ엿스나모다이것을격퇴ᄒᆞ엿더라

○사방딕사격 ᄉᆞ방딕부근에지ᄒᆞᆫ적이포병십팔일오후이시삼십분경에텰도교부근에향ᄒᆞ야약팔십발의사격을ᄒᆡᆼᄒᆞ엿스나우리의손히가업다ᄒᆞ엿더라

잡보

○부쟈동곡 셩안에ᄒᆞᆫ부쟈가잇ᄂᆞᆫ딕이부쟈의규모가삼동이라도방에불을때지안코지닉ᄂᆞᆫ쟈ㅣ라작일에대관ᄒᆞᆫ분이그부쟈의게쳥쳬를ᄒᆞ라고언변잇ᄂᆞᆫ쟈를보닉여말ᄒᆞ기를내집이슈십만량아치오또나의부조월급이미삭에ᄉᆞ오쳔량인즉달마다일쳔오백량식변리로제ᄒᆞ야줄터이니돈을몃쳔원을쉬이라ᄒᆞᆫ즉그부쟈가이말을듯고이우히잇다가대셩통곡ᄒᆞ며말ᄒᆞ기를지금내아달이감옥셔에갓쳐잇ᄂᆞᆫ딕이것이웬일이나ᄒᆞ고눈물이비오듯ᄒᆞᄂᆞᆫ지라말ᄒᆞ든쟈ㅣ어이가업셔작별도못ᄒᆞ고도로왓다ᄒᆞᄂᆞᆫ딕그부쟈의셩은신씨오그대관의셩은김씨라더라

○일병과양인 작일에로계원일본병참소에셔원산으로수운ᄒᆞᄂᆞᆫ탄환바리가길에결진ᄒᆞ엿ᄂᆞᆫ딕맛참양인ᄒᆞᆫ아이지나가다가길이막힘을보고마부를집힝이로셔리며지나가ᄂᆞᆫ지라일병이붓잡고힐란ᄒᆞᆫ즉양인이일병을ᄲᅮ리치며말ᄒᆞ기를우리ᄂᆞᆫ그딕와샹관이업다ᄒᆞ고오미또다른일병이ᄶᅩᆺ차가다가그만두고도라갓다ᄒᆞ엿더라

○량씨입셩 외부고문관스틔분씨와일본공관셔긔관쥬원슈일씨가작일하오다셧시에입셩ᄒᆞ엿더라

TELEGRAMS.

Army Headquarters.

At 3 P. M. on the 18th inst. the Russian artillery northeast of Taosan dropped a few shells into the Japanese positions, but they did not take effect.

At midnight on the same day, thirty Russian infantry attacked a Japanese patrol, but were repulsed with a small loss.

Japanese Legation.

A report from the Army investing Port Arthur states that an explosion was effected at the north fort of East Kikwanshan at 2.05 P. M. on the 18th inst. and subsequently an assault was made on the fort. Owing to the stubborn resistance of the Russians no ground was gained until 7:00 P. M. when Lieut-General Yoshima bravely leading a reserve force reached the outer trenches. A continuous assault was then made which led to the final occupation of the fort at 11.15 P.M. The Japanese then immediately commenced building additional defense works.

When the Russians retreated they exploded 4 mines, which had been laid at an important place. They left behind them two 9-inch guns and two machine guns, a quantity of ammunition and 40 or 50 dead. The Japanese casualties have not yet been counted, but they do not appear to be very great.

Shanghai, Dec. 13.

The Captain of the Askold is still coaling his vessel. Over 1,000 tons have already been shipped, but the work will not be finished before tomorrow. The accuracy of the steering gear is doubtful.—Mainichi.

London, Dec. 13, 5.35 P. M.

The portion of the Baltic Squadron which is proceeding *via* the Cape is nearing Simon's Bay. It is making slow progress.

Berlin, Dec. 14.

A part of the Baltic Squadron is expected to arrive off Madagascar within a week.—Mainichi.

London, Dec. 12, 6.45 p. m.

The Russian Admiralty states that the Baltic Squadron is accompanied by ice-breaking vessels which will render the harbour at Vladivostock available.

London' Dec. 12, 6.45 p.m.

Two of the warships of Rojestvensky's Squadron have passed the Cape of Good Hope. The hospital-ship Orel is coaling there. The cruisers Oleg and Dnieper and the torpedo destroyer Grosny have arrived in Suda Bay, Crete. Admiral Rojestvensky will assemble the entire fleet, including the supplementary vessels, in the Indian Oecan.

Shanghai, Dec. 13.

Maojr-General Dessino has been decorated with the insignia of St. Vladimir. General Kuropatkin wired him his congratulations.—Mainichi.

Berlin, Dec. 12.

The "Neue Freie Press" of Vienna publishes a report from London to the effect that a complete plan for mediation between Japan and Russia will be put forward (by the Powers) after the fall of Port Arthur.

London, Dec. 13, 5.35 p. m.

Lord Curzon has arrived at Calcutta. He has resumed office as Viceroy of India.

London, Dec. 13.

The Chinese attacked the Kaffirs at the Witwatersrand gold mines. Four were killed and 33 wounded.

Mr. D. W. Stevens and Mr. Hagiwara are due to arrive this afternoon by train from Chemulpo.

THE IMPERIAL TOMBS AT MUKDEN.

General Kuropatkin, in a despatch to the Czar, makes the following statement about the Imperial Tombs at Mukden.

"On September 22, having had an enquiry addressed to me regarding a complaint made by the Chinese Government that our troops had felled trees in the sacred groves of the Imperial tombs at Fuling, I paid a visit to the groves and the tombs. The complaint was without foundation, not a tree having been touched by the troops within the bounds of the park where all the buildings and tombs are situated. Our sentries are stationed at the gates and allow no soldiers to enter. When qustioned by me the Chinese officials in charge of the tombs made no charge against the troops.

"While preparing positions our troops had some trees cut down to form firing platforms, mainly on the left bank of the Hunho. Some dozen trees were felled. Roads already existing were repaired, and for that several dozen trees were felled on waste places about the Imperial tombs' enclosure. Before clearing the roads the Corps Commandant, Lieutenant-General Baron Stackelberg, consulted the guardian of the tombs, who only begged him not to touch the trees in the enclosure.

"In order to throw a clear light on the complaint put forward by the Chinese Government, I report that—as appeared from my own examination—the Imperial tombs at Fuling are negligently kept up; the enclosing wall has in several places collapsed, and I found Chinese horses and mules that had got through the breaches in the wall grazing within the sacred groves. Besides this—as was afterwards ascertained—the guardian of the sacred groves, the Manchu Fuyam, who has long exercised these functions, is at the present time in prison for having sold wood stuff from the sacred groves to the inhabitants of Mukden." Kobe Herald.

General Hasegawa's residence is shortly to be communicated with the Palace by telephone.

A track of ground in four districts has been sold to the Japanese military authorities for the sum of $17,270.

A rather curious story is unfolded in the following despatch from the Foreign Office to the Household Department; The Foreign Office are in receipt of a report, from the Kamni of Mokpo, stating that the special superintendent of that province, appointed last year, Mr. Yun Woo Byung pawned his official seal and certificate, in a Japanese pawnshop, for $1,200. He was unable to repay the amount before the term expired, and last autumn he died. Now the Japanese Consul demands the amount advanced on the security, which had Mr. Yun lived would have been good, but now is valueless.

The "Straits Times" learns that Messrs Boutead and Co. and Messrs. Huttenbach Bros.—the two firms who up till now have stood out of what is known among local shipping people as the Americn Shipping Conference—have given in their allegiance to this organization, and it is understood that rates to America will go up at once from 20-to-25-per cent of 50 cubic feet. There is also reason to believe that the American Conference means to enforce a sliding scale on the same lines as that operated by the Homeward Shipping Conferece.

All of which means, of course, that local shippers are now entirely bound down to book in Conference ships at whatever rate the Conference may think fit to charge for freight,—in other words that the only outlet for goods from this port, shipped free of the Conference, is blocked, and that the whole of the freightage to European and American ports is now controlled entirely, so far as rates are concerned, by these two Conference.—Hongkong Telegraph.

PALMIST SPY.

An Austrian officer, Baron von Weigel, who served against the Turks in the war of 1788, gives the most thrilling account I have ever read of an escape from the enemy. He was warned three times in the most solemn tones by a gipsy palmist to beware August 20, months before that date, and the warning so impressed him that he was immeasurably relieved to find, when the fatal day came, that, though it was the turn of his regiment to furnish a picket for the night, two other officers were down on the roster to go on duty before him. One of them, however, was taken suddenly ill, and when the other proceeded to mount his horse the usually gentle creature reared and threw him, breaking his leg, The baron therefore had to go, not without a presentiment of certain death. He escaped it by a miracle, with eight sabre wounds, and after a night of such horrors as even in that ferocious war (where the Turks gave no quarter, but offered a ducat for every Austrian head brought in) must have been unprecedented. Some time after his recovery from his wounds the gipsy was condemned to be hanged as a Turkish spy, and the baron, on the eve of her execution, asked for an explanation of her prediction that August 20 would be for him a fatal day. She then confessed to him that, acting as a spy for both sides, she had made use for her prophecies and her heavy bets on her prophecies, of the information thus obtained. In order to secure the fulfilment of her prediction with regard to the baron, she had instigated the Turks to make an overwhelming night attack on his picket, and she had contrived that he should be the officer in command by disabling the two on the roster before him—the one by an overdose of drugged wine, and the other by thrusting a piece of burning tinder up the nostrils of his horse. She had been at all this trouble because not only her reputation as a palmist, but also a big bet, depended upon the baron's being killed on the day she had predicted for his death.—From "T. P. in his Anecdotage in "T.P.'s Weekly.

A POST OFFICE GROUSE.

The following excerpt from a home journal to hand by last mail, will be found interesting. In point of "red tape" and a limitless vocabulary of "terms to suit occasions," it stands out bravely as hard to beat!

Returned Letter Office, Mount Pleasant, Clerkenwell, London, E. C.,
Oct. 13, 1904.

Sir—I am directed by the Postmaster-General to inform you that the grouse (for which you inquire) posted at Dundee on September 15th, sent by——, which could not be delivered because it escaped from the parcel during transit, has been sold, in accordance with the regulations of the department, to avoid total loss, and having realised 9d a warrant for that amount will be forwarded to you by the Comptroller and Accountant-General.—I am, sir, your obedient servant,

——, Controller.

[Reply.]
London, Oct. 18, 1904.

The Controller, Returned Letter Office, Mount Pleasant, Clerkenwell.

Sir—I beg to acknowledge with thanks your letter of the 13th instant, and am pleased to learn that I am to receive 9d. for the grouse which "escaped during transit" from the parcel of game sent me from Dundee on September 15th.

I hope the purchaser of this extraordinary and phenomenal bird has preserved it—if such an elusive entity, a veritable feathered De Wet—could possibly be materialised sufficiently and pinned down for such a purpose.

A fowl capable, although dead, of escaping from its parcel, and which you have been able (apparently without recapture) to sell for 9d. "to avoid total loss," deserves, if not preserved, a place at least in the historical records of the Post Office and a niche in history by the side of Boyle Roche's famous bird.

NOT A CHEAP HORSE.

(From "Lippincott's Magazine.")

That Confederate money was never taken seriously is well illustrated in the following story told by the late Gen. John B. Gordon:

One day, during a temporary cessation of hostilites between the opposing forces, a tall, strapping Yankee rode into the Confederate camp on a sorry looking old horse to effect a trade for some tobacco.

"Hullo, Yank," hailed one of a number of Confederate soldiers lolling about on the grass in front of a tent, "that's a right smart horse you got there."

"Think so?" returned the Yank.

"Yes; what'll you take for him?"

"Oh, I don't know."

"Well, I'll givo you $700 for him," bantered the Confederate.

"You go to blazes!" indignantly returned the Yank. "I've just paid $10,000 of your money to have him curried."

A NEW ANÆSTHETIC.

A new local anæsthetic of the cocaine order has been discovered. It is called "eucaine," and the use of the drug will permit the carrying out of operations on patients who cannot take chloroform, owing to heart weakness. It will also enable the surgeon to take more time over his work. Although scarcely adaptable for amputations, it will be useful for treatment of the thyroid glands. The eucaine is injected by means of a hypodermic needle under the skin at the place where the incision is to be made. After a few moments the skin may be cut without the patient feeling anything. As different and independent parts are exposed, the drug is dropped at intervals of a few minutes. A highly-successful operation with anæsthetic was recently carried out in a London hospital, the operation lasting one and a half hours.

Kang Yu Wei, the leading Chinese reformer, arrived in Vancouver on November 22nd and after a stay of a week or so was to visit the principal centres of the United States in the interests of the Chinese Empire Reform Association.

The Korea Daily News.

Issued at 5 P. M. daily except Sundays.

Rate of Subscription:—
Per Year,............Yen 25.
Per Quarter,..........Yen 7.
Per Month,..........Yen 2.50.

Postage in Korea not charged extra.
Postage abroad charged extra.

Advertisements, 50 sen per day for 1 inch or less.
5 yen per month per inch.
50 yen per year per inch.

All communications to
E. T. BETHELL,
Editor and Publisher,
Pak-tong, Seoul.

PORT ARTHUR FROM THE INSIDE.

Mr. Ernest Brindle has telegraphed to the Daily Mail from Chefoo the contents of a letter which he received on Nov. 3 from a Russian in the besieged fortress. It reads as follows:— Since I saw you I have been in the depths of hell, but still hope to reach a haven of deliverance. You remember the first bombardment of Port Arthur and the treacherous attack of the Japanese, when several splendid ships were damaged and brave men killed, and also the subsequent naval bombardments which cost our foes thousands of pounds, but caused us little injury. Often did I watch those fierce attacks from the tops of the hills, and saw the shells dropping into the town and the waters of the harbour and on the sides of the hills. Although the fright of the Chinese was great, we Russians laughed and considered the matter a joke. I remember when you approached close to Port Arthur in a despatch boat, and gave to the captain of the destroyer Skori, which was afterwards destroyed, some photographs of the sunken Varyag and Korietz in the harbour of Chemulpo—pictures which were examined with the greatest eagerness by naval and military officers at the fortress. At that time we believed in the strength of our warships and the valour of our seamen. Soon afterwards gallant Admiral Makaroff met his death in a sortie through the diabolical cunning of the Japanese in sinking the battleship Petropavlovsk. The deaths of our admiral and of that genius of the brush, Verestchagin, who stirred the whole world by his realistic pictures, led to forebodings of the inferiority of our fleet to that of the Japanese.

That night a [illegible]umber of friends dined together, ar[illegible] memory of the dead was drunk [illegible]ce, but a vow of revenge was sw[illegible]n. A few days later the Japanese battleship Hatsuse was sunk by one of our mines, and also the Yoshino.

After the capture of Kinchau and Naushan the investment by the Japanese on the land side of the fortress ever narrowed, until after weeks of sanguinary fighting they reached and captured the last positions, which act as watch towers to the lines of forts, known now by name in every part of the world. Those victories were won at a tremendous cost by the Japanese. We can afford the lost fortifications, which are now mostly possessed by the Japanese, but at what a fearful cost to our yellow foe! Several redoubts once occupied by us, and protected by electric wires and land mines innumerable, are now in the hands of the Japanese, who sacrifice whole regiments of men in their steady advance. For weeks we retired before the irresistible valour and superiour number of the enemy to the great forts. It was now that there began the real awfulness of the siege, which would require the pen of a Zola or the brush of a Verestchagin to picture. The forts were protected by mines, wire entanglements and trenches, and to capture these our foes devoted time and concentrated effort. By day a furious bombardment, with its merciless rain of shells, strewed the ground with dead and filled our already crowded hospitals with men suffering from sickening wounds, while by night a stealthy advance took place marked by the blue flicker of electric wires as they sent scores of the advancing enemy to meet their gods. The uncanny part of all this is that these men meet death in utter silence. One sees the fiercest fights, but hears no sound. One moonlight night at Etseshan I watched the assault of a ghostly mass of moving figures, through which continual lanes were made by our guns, admitting glimpses of the scenes behind. These gaps were closed up as if by magic, and the masses surged onward, while our men, forsaking the trenches, sought the shelter of the forts. On they came until close up to us. The mines exploded, and the earth opened; bodies were hurled high into the air and then sank again to earth. Hands clutched rifles, and in the moonlight bayonets looked like fireworks shooting upwards and descending point downwards into the body of a man. I dream of the sight even now. I believe that all the inventions of military genius are unable to daunt these heroes, who are incapable of recognising that so long as we have ammunition the fortress is impregnable, for still they come against us. During the long, burning days of the summer and pleasant nights marked by the coolness of early autumn, they came against us, and we repulsed them. It has been mainly fighting in the trenches. Our principal forts are uninjured, but the houses in the town are badly damaged. Most of them are in ruins and the harbour works are in a sad plight. Some of our ships have been injured by falling shells, and it is impossible with our scant resources to repair them. We have not a single bottle left of anæsthetics. Just think what agony the wounded must endure. The food is of the coarest, and even that beginning to be scarce, while there is much disease.

But we are all animated with the resolve to hold out, come what will. Our trials, hardships, and terrors are indescribable evils which have made us something more than human. We are still in possession of all the forts, and each day and night expect to hear the boom of the guns of the relieving host far northward, or the sight of the vanguard of the fleet from home coming by sea. In that belief, and in the confidence of our own strength, we fight for the flag. The Japanese round us often fight with Titanic energy, but for every man we lose our foes bemoan the loss of a hundred. We have left behind us the memories of civilisation, and live now in caves like prehistoric men—in bombproof shelters which ever and anon are penetrated by shells. Our soldiers are gladiators and great-hearted heroes. Disasters by land and worse disasters by sea do not affect them except for a moment. Their numbers are thinned, but they are not afraid that relief will not come. The last sortie of the fleet was a failure, because of the inability to repair the vessels damaged in the previous engagements. But there will come a time when there will be no bearing the inconveniencs of the siege due to sickness, scarcity of food, and cramped quarters, no enduring the unceasing hell of bursting shells shattering houses, killing unfortunate friends, and tearing huge holes in the ground, to say nothing of the miasma arising from a thousand corpses rotting on the hills and in the ravines. Round the forts, the stenchbred flies, the "red heads," whose bite is poisonous, are increasing in number. Lately the bombardments have increased in fury, and the fiery messengers of hate and destruction greet us every minute. If I live to be a hundred there will always be in my ears the solemn music of whistling shot and savage shell. A few days ago there was a new development, and our whole garrison sallied forth. It was evident that the Japanese were making another fanatical attempt to capture the fortress, but they cannot succeed—they only add to the terrible number of their dead. God be with us. Farewell.

THE CASE OF GENERAL ORLOFF.

The Russian defeat at Liaoyang has been hitherto attributed to a serious blunder by General Orloff, and he was cashiered, but according to a St. Petersburg correspondent of the Echo de Paris, Orloff has just been given another command. The St. Petersburg correspondent of the "Matin" adds the information that it has been decided to attach Orloff to the General Staff at St. Petersburg, with the rank of General of a division, and that Kuropatkin is anxious to make reparation for his treatment of him after Liaoyang by attaching him to his own staff. He gives a detailed account of what (as he says) really happened, with the aim of showing Orloff did all, and more than he could be expected to do, and that the responsibility for the defeat rests on General Stackelberg, and the contradictory and dilatory orders of the General Staff. It was, according to this story, Stackelberg who, by not arriving in time, left a gap between the troops of Bilderling and the troops of Orloff, and the Japanese, pouring through this gap, got behind the Russians. When at last Orloff, retreating, did join hand with Stackelberg, the latter, misunderstanding the situation, covered him with insults and abuse for his inevitable retreat, and, as Orloff's superior officer, ordered him to attack at once, but only with a single battalion (which Orloff, acquainted with the position—as Stackelberg was not—knew to be quite ridiculous), and to lead the attack in person. This last order, of course, was a gratuitous reflection on Orloff's personal courage. Orloff, however, obeyed the order to the letter. He led a single battalion to the attack through the millet, which hid the men but allowed himself, who was mounted, to be a clear mark above it for the enemy. Then Stackelberg, seized with remorse, sent orders forward that Orloff was to dismount. Orloff paid no attention to this order. Three times he was wounded, but still advanced. At last a bullet hit him in the stomach, and he fell off his horse. His men picked him up, the tears pouring down their cheeks, and the General made a desperate effort to remount, but fell back in a faint. He has only recently come out of the hospital.

In one point Mr. Balfour's recent speech showed weakness and want of courage. He capitulated unconditionally in face of "Rojestvensky," and referred to him throughout as "the Russian Admiral."

The Korea Daily News.

VOL. I, WEDNESDAY, DECEMBER 21, 1904. No. 131

大韓每日申報
대한미일신보

(뎨일빅삼십이호) (금요일) 일쳔구빅ᄉᆞ년십이월이십삼일

본샤고빅

이신보는영어와한어로셔계리
일출판ᄒᆞ옵
신문가
한쟝 엽두돈오푼
일삭도 엽두량닷돈
우표가미삭닷돈
다밧돈으로밧솜
광고료는
귀한의쟝단과ᄌᆞ힝의다쇼로죵
감ᄒᆞ되한가로밧을터이오매오
리지아녀대한사람마다이신
문을보실터이니광고내시기를
원ᄒᆞ시는이들은우리신문샤에
와서편약ᄒᆞ심을희망ᄒᆞ옵
○발힝소 박동대한미일신보
샤번버항교압헤젼영국인셜펠
림젼자리오
샤쟝 영국인 (비셜)
평양 디리졈
○평양효동사는김미보씨로우
리신문관미디리인을뎡ᄒᆞ엿
시ᄉᆞ오니평양에계신구람ᄒᆞ실
는 쳠군ᄌᆞ는헝티리졈에왕ᄒᆞ
림ᄒᆞ와면의ᄒᆞ시옵

샤고

○우리대한미일신보의목뎍은
대한의안녕질서에관한모든대
목에뎨ᄎᆞ야는공평한변론을쥬
쟝홈이라우리동신원회탐보는
신문보시는쳠군ᄌᆞ의게ᄒᆞ샹보
도ᄒᆞ리며편지를긔셔ᄒᆞ며주시
는이는셩명과번디를젹어붓치
시기를희망ᄒᆞ오니비커슨신문
샹에긔ᄌᆡᄒᆞᆯ는거시아니오다
만국히신용ᄒᆞᄂᆞᆫ죵거를숨고자
홈이라긔자는아모긔셔던지긔
지홈은되각ᄒᆞᄂᆞᆫ권리를가젓스
나리가ᄒᆞᄂᆞᆫ리유를말홀터이오
며공중평화를문란케ᄒᆞᄂᆞᆫ듯훈
긔셔는의례히밧지안켓습나이
다

●본샤셜시에리로신문을미양
우레로분젼ᄒᆞ와례젼부의임의
로젼ᄒᆞᄂᆞᆫ곳ᄉᆞ로면곳에는홀숫게
젼ᄒᆞ기도ᄒᆞ며혹멋칠거슬ᄒᆞᆫ겹
에젼ᄒᆞ기도ᄒᆞ며혹아니젼ᄒᆞᄂᆞᆫ
곳도잇다ᄒᆞ와우리신문을ᄉᆞ랑
ᄒᆞ야구람ᄒᆞ시는 쳠군ᄌᆞ의계
되ᄒᆞ야면우미안ᄒᆞ옵기로지금
은분젼인을두고미일죠이젼
ᄒᆞ며아니젼ᄒᆞ거나늣게거나ᄒᆞᆫ
폐가업도록ᄒᆞ랴ᄒᆞ오니ᄒᆞᆫ아니
젼ᄒᆞ거나ᄒᆞ옵ᄂᆞᆫ계젼ᄒᆞ거나ᄒᆞᆫ일
이잇스면본샤로통긔ᄒᆞ여쥬심
을희망ᄒᆞ옵

관보

뎨삼쳔십오호 광무팔년
십이월이일
셔임급ᄉᆞ령
○금일금봉 법부회계국쟝
셔상우
○금일금봉 평리원판ᄉᆞ 김
계순
한셩지판소수반판ᄉᆞ 리샹린
한셩지판소판ᄉᆞ 리경구
이샹십이월십일
○승셔주임관오등 경위원경
무관 김윤영
십이월십칠일
○명셔리호위티쟝판ᄉᆞ무 표
훈원부참모쟝경임경무ᄉᆞ총관창
쟝 백셩긔
십이월십팔일
○의원면본관 비서원승 권
영수 시종원좌시어 김챵진
홍문관시독 죠남일 동신ᄉᆞ
면화과쥬ᄉᆞ 김연진 동신ᄉᆞ
면화과쥬ᄉᆞ 서병죠 동신ᄉᆞ
면화과쥬ᄉᆞ 박귀창 동신ᄉᆞ
면화과쥬ᄉᆞ 최영준 동신ᄉᆞ
면화과쥬ᄉᆞ 김영셥 동신ᄉᆞ
면화과쥬ᄉᆞ 서병문 동신ᄉᆞ
면화과쥬ᄉᆞ 졍식퇴
○힝시종원분시어 졍상풍
김영우 구품 유석관
○임비서원승서주임관륙등
졍삼품 신석균
○경임장례원장례 비서승
리범인
○임시종원좌시어서판임관팔
등 구품 리헌용
○임홍문관시독서판임관칠등
륙품 신용우
○명시종원분시어 륙품 송
창호 구품 홍종헌 리티영
죠중길 채명석
○임내부광제원쥬ᄉᆞ서판임관
륙등 젼교관 강대창
이상십이월십구일

외보

○로병의비교 지부미일신문
에말ᄒᆞ엿스되이번일로젼쟁에
일봉강싸홈으로브터만쥬에서
지모라드리길벼에일본로병의
지능을세상에셔칭찬ᄒᆞ엿스나
지금은일본로병들이그지릉을
이렷다고ᄒᆞᆯ만ᄒᆞ도다대로ᄂᆞᆫ
방법샐아니라대포를운동ᄒᆞ고
실ᄂᆞᆫ대셔지로국포병만못ᄒᆞ며
라그셔들은처음에젼쟝에나왓
든잘교련ᄒᆞᆫ일본포병들은만히
죽음이니일본의샹비병은비교
젹으로적은셔들에교련잘된포
병의슈효도셔리젹은티이번싸
홈에포젼이만ᄒᆞ엿던교로그ᄂᆞᆫ수
들이만이쥭엇고포병ᄉᆞ관들은
특별히민이쥭엇ᄂᆞᆫ지라그티셰ᄉᆞ
교련잘ᄒᆞ고지릉잇ᄂᆞᆫ군ᄉᆞ와ᄉᆞ
관을치우기극난ᄒᆞ며로국은쳐
음에저의포병의일부분만가지
고싸우고다슈의예비포병이잇
서서항샹더나아오ᄂᆞᆫ교로그포
병의죽은티에치우기가그럿케
어렵지아니ᄒᆞᆫ셔들이다ᄒᆞ엿더
라

○힝ᄉᆞ진과일본용ᄉᆞ공함 로
돈뎐보에됴비고리포신문에샹일
월팔일힝ᄉᆞ신을계지ᄒᆞ엿ᄂᆞᆫ티
칠ᄉᆞ진금ᄉᆞ관이론돈잇ᄂᆞᆫ일본
공ᄉᆞ관의용함을졉ᄒᆞᆫ죽고공함
에말ᄒᆞ기를복히에셔영국이션
을로국이습격ᄒᆞᆫ곳으로브터이
빅여리안에ᄂᆞᆫ일본군함이업셧
다ᄒᆞᆫ지라지금일본사름저의들
말이빅여리안에ᄂᆞᆫ셧다ᄒᆞ
니그러면로국분릐ᄒᆞᆫ티를습격
ᄒᆞᆫ라고이빅오십영리안에ᄂᆞᆫ잇
셧ᄂᆞᆫ것이외삼영슬듯일노분티
경이면로국사름들이저의힘티
에습격ᄒᆞᆷ이잇슬줄안것이증거
업ᄂᆞᆫ말이아니로다

○분수항쟁풍 일본문ᄉᆞ항에
ᄂᆞᆫ하마다거울에ᄂᆞᆫ폭풍이대단
ᄒᆞ여고히를밧지안님젹이드문
티금년에ᄂᆞᆫ더욱심ᄒᆞ야거월이
십구일아춤에항구밧게잇든일
본호마신이오젼세시브터다숫
시셔지두시간에열여덟척이칭
물ᄒᆞ엿ᄂᆞᆫ티비사공들과부인ᄒᆞ
나계졍아희ᄒᆞ나히새저죽엇다
더라

○사쟈칭쟈사 젼일에일본
신문들은로국대쟝스토에셀씨
를샹힝엿다가죡엿다가다시샹
그림펀미스취ㄴ교를사로잡고사
른들이지금대쟝을엿ᄉᆞ더니고의
젼진을막고잇스며이제미국으
로브터사하싸홈에일본흑목대
쟝의죽은진비아기가왓스나우
리ᄂᆞᆫ이것도아마성ᄉᆞ름죽이ᄂᆞᆫ
줄노회샹ᄒᆞ노라

○표쟝부아쟝부 토국이헝씨
에셔고기장ᄂᆞᆫ빈중에일본슈퇴
쟝비셕거잇다가교ᄒᆞᄂᆞᆫ말을듯
고이샹이넉이ᄂᆞᆫ사름들은근리
에우리가드ᄅᆞᆫ죽로국이영국회
사에서슈퇴쟝ᄒᆞᆫ젹을숭며셔샷
다ᄂᆞᆫ소문을드릐보시면일본슈
퇴쟝이영국히샹에엇지잇겟나
나ᄒᆞᄂᆞᆫ말을못ᄒᆞ겟소일본이슈
퇴쟝을영국히샹에보냇다거나
영국제셕자가증립셩명ᄒᆞᆫ중에
젼쟁국에빈을퍄랏다고ᄂᆞᆫ말ᄒᆞᆯ
슈업스나그러ᄒᆞ나엿마아니되
국아셔영국동맹국의티쳑되ᄂᆞᆫ로
국이영국의대일쳔계쳔소로브
터무샹계쳑으로던지슈퇴정ᄒᆞᆫ
쳑을샅사갓ᄂᆞᆫ지라만일로국이
이런일을ᄒᆞᆯ때에엇지일본은ᄒᆞ
지말나ᄂᆞᆫ리치가잇ᄂᆞᆫ가그럼으
로형싸에서브러나사진은로국
이졍탐으로소홀이ᄒᆞ엿다고말
ᄒᆞᆯ계아니라ᄒᆞ노라

뎐보

군ᄉᆞ령부착뎐
○사하방면사격 본월십팔일
하오삼시가지날시럼산동북방
의젹포병이우리젼초를향ᄒᆞ야
수실발을사격ᄒᆞ엿ᄉᆞ나우리군
ᄉᆞ에는손히가업셧다ᄒᆞ엿더라
○습리자격퇴 십팔일밤반에
림복둔의동북방으로젹보병이
샹십이평이우리젼초압헤와음
홈이샹ᄎᆞ로티우리젼초에는습
다이것을격퇴ᄒᆞ야젹의게로약
간손히ᄅᆞᆯ이여보냇다ᄒᆞ엿더라
교동항연합함티수령쟝관보
젹함파괴샹보 려순구항
니의젹함은향ᄒᆞ야군항외에셔
흠은의셔치아니ᄒᆞ교항외에지못
ᄒᆞᆫ[셰바쓰도쌕리]ᄂᆞᆫ우리수뢰
공격으로임의항히력을이ᄅᆞᆯ아
죡히실이관단ᄒᆞᆯ형상을보지못
ᄒᆞ고묵하각방면에셔죠사ᄒᆞᆫ
이오그다ᄅᆞᆫ구츅함통쳑이젼존ᄒᆞᆷ
이확실ᄒᆞ다ᄒᆞ엿더라
경셩공수관착뎐
○졍평동계관산 리순용위군
보교에왼군의부ᄂᆞᆫ십이월십
팔일하오이십오분에동계관산

UNION INSURANCE SOCIETY OF CANTON.

Head office Hongkong.
Marine risks underwritten at current rates.
Agents in Chemulpo,
E. MEYER & Co.

COMPAGNIE DES MESSAGERIES MARITIMES.

Fortnightly Direct Service.

For Marseilles
via Ports.
Sailing from Yokohama
Calling at Kobe,
Shanghai, Hongkong, Saigon, Singapore,
Colombo, Djibonti, Suez, Port Said
and Marseilles.

For particulars apply to
HOLME RINGER & Co.,
Chemulpo.

HAYASHIDA & CO.,

16 MYENG DONG, CHIN KO KAI, SEOUL.
BRANCH OFFICE AT CHEMULPO.

Money changers, Coal and Wood Merchants, Express Agents.

We are agents for the Pyeng-yang Coal Company and the Karazu Coal Company of Japan. We have the best quality of both anthracite and bituminous coal, and prompt execution of orders is our speciality. Firewood of all kinds kept in stock. Full weight guaranteed. Money of all denominations exchanged at current rates. Parcels received for all parts.

CHINA MUTUAL LIFE INS. OC.

Most favourable terms to policy holders.

Benefit system unsurpassed.

HOLME RINGER & Co.
Agents, Chemulpo.

C. P. R.

CANADIAN PACIFIC RAILWAY COMPANY'S ROYAL MAIL STEAMSHIP LINE.

THE FAST ROUTE BETWEEN CHINA, JAPAN, AND EUROPE VIA CANADA AND THE UNITED STATES.

Route from Hongkong via Shanghai, Nagasaki (Inland Sea of Japan) Kobe, Yokohama Victoria and Vancouver.

Twin Screw Empress Steamship—6,000 Tons—Speed 19 knots.

PROPOSED SAILING FROM YOKOHAMA.
R. M. S. Empress of India.
R. M. S. Empress of Japan.
R. M. S. Empress of China.
R. M. S. Athenian.
R. M. S. Tartar.

Special reduction (first class only) granted to members of the Military, Naval, Diplomatic and Civil services and to Missionaries.

Passengers have choice of ten routes across the Continent of America and have privilege of travelling by any Atlantic Steamship Line.

Round the World passage tickets in connection with the P. and O. S. N., North German Lloyd and Messageries Co.'s **£125**.

All rates payable at current rate of exchange.

For further information, Tickets, Guide Books, etc., apply to

HOLME, RINGER & Co., AGENTS,
Chemulpo.

Grand Hotel,

(Formerly the Station Hotel)

Near the Railway Terminus,
West Gate Seoul.

The Best Hotel in Korea;
Handsome new Building.
Fine Airy Rooms
Excellent Cuisine.
Terms Moderate.
Special terms to Missionaries
and to permanent boarders.

Electric cars within 2 minutes' walk.

W. H. EMBERLEY.
Proprietor

AMERICAN KOREAN ELECTRIC CO.

Light and Power.

Main Office: Electric Building, Chong No.

RAILWAY DEPARTMENT.

OPERATING CARS BETWEEN EAST AND WEST GATE, EVERY TEN MINUTES:—

First Car leaves East Gate at 7:00 A. M. First Car leaves R. R. Station at 7:25 A. M
Last Car " East Gate at 9:40 P. M. Last " " R. R. Station at 10:05 P.M

OPERATING CARS BETWEEN EAST GATE AND IMPERIAL TOMB TERMINUS, EVERY TWENTY MINUTES:—

CONNECTING WITH EVERY ALTERNATE CAR ARRIVING AT EAST GATE FROM CHONG NO.

First Car leaves East Gate for Tomb at 7:10 A. M.
" " " Tomb for East Gate at 7:35 A. M.
Last " " East Gate for Tomb at 7:50 P. M.
" " " Tomb for East Gate at 8:10 P. M.

OPERATING CARS BETWEEN CHONG NO AND YUNG SAN RIVER EVERY TWELVE MINUTES:—

First Car leaves Chong No for South Gate at 7:12 A. M.
" " " Chong No for Yung San at 7:36 A. M.
" " " South Gate for Chong No at 7:20 A. M.
" " " Yung San for Chong No at 8:09 A. M.
Last " " South Gate for Chong No 10:00 P. M.
" " " Yung San for Chong No at 9:33 P. M.

SPECIAL PRIVATE CARS FURNISHED TO SUIT CONVENIENCE OF PATRONS. PRICES ON APPLICATION AT HEAD OFFICE.

LIGHTING DEPARTMENT.

Where less than 250 candle power of light is used, the rate per month will be
Per 16 candle power incandescent lamp,—All night.—Yen 2.50.
32 candle power incandescent lamp:—All night:—Yen 4.00.
50 candle power incandescent lamp:—All night:—Yen 6.00.
150 " " " " " " " 10.00.
1200 " " enclosed are " " " " 20.00.

Where more than 250 candle power of light is used, a Meter will be installed, freqvedted:—Rent of Meter Yen 2.00 per month. Rate of charges by meter reading:—Two Sen per Ampere per hour. (Approximately this is equal to about One Sen per 16 C. P. lamp per hour) Minimum monthly charge where meter is installed, Yen 20.00 per month, which includes rental of meter.

Estimates for installing lights furnished on application

An assortment of chandeliers always on hand.

EVERY FACILITY.

In connection with Life Assurance Business is afforded by

The Standard Life Assurance Co.,

One of the largest and wealthiest of the Provident Institutions of the United Kingdom Forms of Application and all information will be promptly afforded on application.

10 CENTS A DAY.

Not a very large expenditure is it? But it is sufficient to secure for a man of 30 a policy with the STANDARD LIFE OFFICE for

$1323.

For all particulars of rates, etc., apply to

Holme, Ringer & Co.,
Agents, Chemulpo.

THE NEW YORK LIFE INSURANCE COMPANY.

Have you ever been declined by any Company?

Are you engaged in a specially hazardous occupation?

Have you heard of the New York Life Insurance Company's New Classifications for this class of Risks?

If not, send your date of birth, occupation and particulars of rejection, if any to

E. MEYER & Co.,
Agents, Chemulpo.

K. Murakami.
Photograph Studio
Chinkokai, Seoul.

Printing, Developing and Enlargement, of Photographs always Undertaken.

Korean Views and Pictures Illustrating Native Customs always on Sale,

---

THE OSAKA SHOSEN KAISHA.

Boats frequently on the berth for Chinnampo.

REGULAR SAILINGS BETWEEN JAPAN AND KOREAN PORTS.

FUSAN AND KOBE VIA SHIMONOSEKI.

OSAKA VIA MOKPO, FUSAN, SHIMONOSEKI AND KOBE.

MOJI DIRECT.

OSAKA VIA KUNSAN, MASANPO, FUSAN, SHIMONOSEKI AND KOBE.

CHEMULPO KUNSAN LINE,
Every three days.

CHEMULPO CHINNAMPO LINE.
Every three days.

For Freight and passage and further particulars apply to
THE OSAKA SHOSEN KAISHA,
Chemulpo.

MITSUI BUSSAN KAISHA.
(MITSUI & Co.)

MITSUI GINKO.
(MITSUI BANK.)

The Bank is owned by the members of the Mitsui Family, who, as partners, assume an unlimited responsibility for all liabilities of the Bank:—

Capital..........................Yen 5,000,000
Reserve Fund.................. " 5,600,000

HEAD OFFICE, TOKYO.

LONDON OFFICE, 34 LIME ST., E. C.

BRANCHES AND AGENCIES:—
New York, San Francisco, Hamburg, Bombay, Singapore, Manila, Hongkong, Amoy, Chefoo, Tientsin.

Kobe, Hakodate, Yokohama, Kure, Yokosuka, Moji, Shimonoseki, Miike, Wakamatsu, Nagasaki, Kuchinotsu, Karatsu, Sasebo, Misume, Taipeh, &c.

Telegraphic Address for all the Offices:
"MITSUI."

A. B. C. AND A. 1 CODES USED.

Contractors of Coal

To the Imperial Japanese Navy. Arsenals and Railway Bureau, Principal Railway Companies and Industrial Work, Home and Foreign Mail and Freight Steamers.

Sole Proprietors

Of the famous Miike, Tagawa and Yamuno Coal Mines.

Sole Agents

For the sale of Fukumo, Hokoku, Ichimura, Kanoda, Mannoura, Onoura, Ostuji, Sonoda, Tsubaruro, Yoshinotani, Yoshio, Yurokibura and other coals.

YANGTSE INSURANCE ASSOCIATION, LTD.

The undersigned, having been appointed agents for the above company, are prepared to issue policies and pay losses on marine risks at regular rates.

E. MEYER & Co.,
Agents, Chemulpo.

RONDON, PLAISANT & CO.

General Storekeepers and Merchants, Ships Contractors, Tobacconists, Commission and Forwarding Agents, Coal Merchants

IMPORTERS AND EXPORTERS

Seoul & Chemulpo.

W. D. WENTWORTH.

LANDING
AND
SHIPPING AGENT
AND
CUSTOMS BORDER.

12 OURA, NAGASAKI.

STEWARD & CO.

Chemulpo.

Shipchandlers and Storekeepers, Naval and Mercantile Contrrctors, Landing and Shipping Agents.

STEWARD'S HOTEL

Chemulpo.

Best accommodation in the port for travellers. Clean and well-aired rooms, good cuisine **and prompt attendence, moderate tariff.**

아조회ᄒᆞᆫ단ᄒᆞ엿기히에조회ᄒᆞ
녀조량시복ᄒᆞ신을보난다ᄒᆞ엿
더라

○경의지가 의정부에서룡천
감리경균수봉급을쳥발ᄒᆞ기로
쳥의ᄒᆞ던수ᄂᆞᆫ미회의를쳥ᄒᆞ
야 지가ᄒᆞ엿더라

○제진외부 지쟉일은화요일
히라각외교관들이외부에제진
ᄒᆞ엿더라

○단결젼부관제 신구일졍부
에서회의ᄒᆞ야관제리졍을의결
ᄒᆞ엿다더니졍부관제만가결ᄒᆞ
엿더라

○곡산민소 곡산민리병호등
이외부에등장ᄒᆞ기를인부모졍
홀베예일인이사을ᄒᆞ표도주지
아니ᄒᆞᄂᆞᆫ고로다부역ᄒᆞᄂᆞᆫ되원
ᄒᆞ지아니ᄒᆞ고일인이본군에다
팔뵈명을비쟝ᄒᆞᄂᆞᆫ고로부득이
가ᄒᆞ야팔뵈명을미명에샹뵈량교
로가조회ᄒᆞ기에차셔가잇슴을
아렷더니본군민회경로등이
민회라쳥ᄒᆞ고관리들을배에일인
이항쟝과쇽쇼ᄒᆞ고료리를바더본부동ᄒᆞ야
아군을두교피빗셩을란탁ᄒᆞ야
쳥인은즉수ᄒᆞ고피샹쟈사명도
이예치사ᄒᆞ고도피샹쟈벗사봉
이시방즉을디경이오일인의죽
불과쳘인만지사ᄒᆞ엿고디쟝인교
리봉웅리과반이인은리쟝인교
로다만빙관찬ᄒᆞ엿ᄂᆞᆫ디를보군
사가쟝잔지수삼이으로봉오히
리방쳥ᄒᆞ지아니ᄒᆞᄂᆞᆫ고로부원
쳥리ᄒᆞ고쳐ᄒᆞ쇼ᄒᆞ오니쳔일군관
에지조ᄒᆞ야회쳥이으로졍인두사
들은곳고로여빙쳔케ᄒᆞ시고그
남아지죄범은쏘ᄒᆞᆫ일쳥중징흠을
디쳐단케ᄒᆞ시기를보란다ᄒᆞ엿
더라

평양통신

○젹쟝승수 평양셩니에스승
지라ᄒᆞᄂᆞᆫ셔지ᄂᆞᆫ이젼에지원된
이불쳥ᄒᆞ야시비가만하뢰지된
지가오리더니금번히도관찰수
리중하가부하수빌이계ᄒᆞ항
흠ᄉᆞ으로효유ᄒᆞ미수멀을이합
동ᄒᆞ야밋인이위빙관셔흘럼을ᄒᆞ야
다시중샹ᄒᆞ고위젼셔지귀럼지
란쳥ᄒᆞ고제수ᄒᆞ엿ᄂᆞᆫ지라셔지
ᄂᆞᆫ슌젼ᄒᆞ방교인디과명은만
국젹수비의각국법률로쳥ᄒᆞ
아사문에고시ᄒᆞ엿ᄂᆞᆫ디본군수
괭찬쥬씨ᄂᆞᆫ이젼당항ᄒᆞ던수단
으로졍민심을이므로만저
아된다ᄒᆞ고각방유림의게발문
ᄒᆞ야시송케ᄒᆞ고훈졍케ᄒᆞ고가쟝
흥항ᄒᆞᄂᆞᆫ모양이로만일ᄒᆞᄂᆞᆫ디니쳔
만의외에면관이되다ᄒᆞᄂᆞᆫ소문을
을듯교회유시ᄒᆞ도자라군유림들
은사송케로회쳡ᄒᆞ야본군수유림
원쥬를ᄒᆞ야달니고희의유림으로쳔
사허부디회수공뵉여뎡이로쳥쳡
쳘셔가교로희유림통을며니만도뎨
최망ᄒᆞ엿다더라

느리교부분셔쟝ᄋᆞ쳥젼로도향ᄒᆞ
아니리쳔회우로송관을발여코고우
에ᄂᆞᆫ디지진훔으로며디리지도ᄒᆞᆫ다니
라

○명인승이셩인 지작일상오
십시에남촌사ᄂᆞᆫ장남하나히비
우기에와서나무를사란ᄂᆞᆫ데디비
나무ᄒᆞᆫ빅리를맛낫치만져셔보고그
중에표ᄒᆞᄂᆞᆫ나무를잡고사쳔팔솜
에흥졍ᄒᆞᄂᆞᆫ즁디져즌잇논시롬도
나무하사기가극란ᄒᆞᆫ덕쟝남빅ᄂᆞᆫ솜
으로만져고도헌사나쟝남빅ᄂᆞᆫ솜
일수가엽더교ᄒᆞ엿더라

○판광쟈태운 지작일에외외
궁승위인이로로도로생에판광쟈
ㅣ구름곳더라

○일번일젼 입선시에ᄂᆞᆫ비왕
디쟝이오외칭관을세경ᄒᆞᄂᆞᆫ교
로되교리르케ᄂᆞᆫ됴리ᄒᆞᆫ용ᄒᆞ교뵈
셩디계가경엄ᄒᆞ엿더라

○조쳥ᄒᆞ오죠 미국공수가외부
로조회ᄒᆞ기를본국인셕궐이가
각도로셔쳔을펴더이니ᄒᆞ죠쟝을
세보내라ᄒᆞ엿더라

○광쥬일진회 젼라남도광쥬
수가내부로지쟉일에며보ᄒᆞ기
를단발ᄒᆞᆫ쟈가빅여명이일진회라
칭ᄒᆞ고강일에부하여티도회치쇼
효유ᄒᆞ엿도회셩샌지안ᄂᆞᆫ다ᄒᆞ엿
더라

○군용디단가 거졔등수군에
일인군용디단쟝일만칠쳔이빅
칠십엿원수쳔광을내부에서졍부
회의에데츌ᄒᆞ야경의ᄒᆞᆫ후에
주계ᄒᆞ엿더라

○회쳡답청 외부에셔슈상회
샤의쳥원을볼경ᄒᆞ야교리쟝늦리
번녀에디답ᄒᆞᄂᆞᆫ일노총회관에
ᄒᆞ셩ᄒᆞ엿더니빅탁에만셰가답쳥
ᄒᆞ기를교리셰를면ᄒᆞ여달라니ᄂᆞᆫ
일은가히쥰힝치못ᄒᆞ겟기서오히
셤의에ᄂᆞᆫ다라가조약를도숟을시
명흥문면분회관애셔인위일관송
ᄒᆞ야사무케ᄒᆞ되이며ᄒᆞᆫ일명의원
봉ᄒᆞ회사에셔지발케ᄒᆞ라ᄒᆞ
엿더라

○졍쥬사복 외부에셔궁니부
로조회ᄒᆞ기를무안감리보고니
게히경엇니부에셔파송ᄒᆞᆫ젼리
유송이빙이가본항에외잇셔파이
우세를알본상민상권금쟝의게
면지ᄒᆞ야삼만이쳔량을최용ᄒᆞ
고환이지나도오히려갑치아니
ᄒᆞ고유쟝셥을가불힝이쟉궤가유
에본항에도차흉쳥수가무리교유
람ᄂᆞᆫ쥬으로졍부이젼조회로교
조회ᄒᆞ엿기이유셔죠의웃계야
셔록조회에쳥부ᄒᆞ오니조량히
분ᄒᆞ신욕을보난다ᄒᆞ엿더라

○조쳥참회 외부에서궁니부샹
부에조회ᄒᆞ기를미공수가조회
ᄒᆞ되며회번답리희초회를미티엿던

녓일에홍가셩진이라ᄂᆞᆫ인도잇
나소즁다만봉샹노만돌일나시아
일슨진디갈히셩각ᄒᆞ야ᄒᆞ즐기서
가진ᄒᆞᆫ쳥국의게도오리랏토롤
을잡히며잇슨가시아니오또ᄒᆞᆫ
외국사회에도쳥ᄒᆞ야경향혀빈
아닌즉쳥국에소위즁립이란ᄒᆞ
ᄂᆞᆫ거슨미구에밋지ᄒᆞᆫ셰시졀을
노앗고션계를ᄒᆞ여야ᄒᆞᆫ지라쳥
국셔쟈의리난즉즁립홈이르셰이
번싸홈에아쳐ᄒᆞᄂᆞᆫ권리를도모
지쳥ᄒᆞ쟈아니ᄒᆞᆫ거시만오쟐된
일인거시만잇슨가니만흔졀리던
쟈리가좌우간엇슴이며즁립이된
을쓰라아쳥국은쟈쳥국이라

TELEGRAMS.

Army Headquarters.

At 10 A. M. the 20th inst. the Japanese outposts encountered 30 Russian scouts in the Hongwon district and caused them to retire, leaving one dead and a few rifles on the field.

Army Headquarters.

On the 20th inst. a body of Japanese infantry attacked a Russian cavalry force near Huatsentze and dispersed about 100 Russian infantry near Lakuenkoling. The Japanese casualitiese were nil, but they captured one prisoner and one horse.

At 5 P. M. on the 19th inst. the Russian artillery opened fire on the Japanese position near Shinlingtun, but inflicted no damage.

At 1 A. M. on the 20th inst. a section of Russian infantry attacked Naolopao and another force Tatzepao, but both were repulsed.

At 4:30 A. M. Kinsantun and Selintun were also attacked, the fighting lasting for one hour, but the Japanese suffered no casualties and the Russians were repulsed.

(FROM JAPAN PAPERS)

London, Dec. 15.

Admiral Rohjestvensky's squadron arrived at Angra Pequena (on the west coast of Namaqualand) on the 11th instant, and is reported to be coaling from colliers.

Reuter's correspondent at Aden reports that Admiral Foelkersahm's squadron is still at Jibutil, awaiting the arrival of the supplementary squadron under Admiral Bebrovosky.

Later.

Admiral Foelkersahm's squadron has quitted Jibutil waters.

London, Dec. 16.

The growth of the Liberal movement in Russia is daily manifested by the newspapers, which contain outspoken articles advocating the far-reaching reforms which the students and the educated classes are emphatically demanding.

RUSSIA'S NAVAL CONSTRUCTION PLANS.

St. Petersburg, November 19th.

America is likely to profit, both directly and indirectly, from the execution of the large naval programme which Russia is now elaborating.

The vital importance of sea power has been Russia's bitterest lesson of the war and the Government is fully determined that the maintenance of the empire's future position as a first-class power will be impossible without an adequate navy. If the losses the Pacific fleet has already sustained should be followed by disaster to Vice-Admiral Rojestvensky's squadron it will be necessary not only to rebuild the whole navy, but to increase its strength. The immensity of the task seems to be fully appreciated. While some of the contracts will be placed abroad, owing to the limited facilities of Russian yards (and it is expected that at least one big ship will be constructed in America), the Admiralty's plans will be directed toward ultimate divorce from dependence upon foreign shipbuilders by the organization at home of vast shipbuilding, armour plate, orduance and kindred industries.

For this purpose it is realized, however, that foreign builders and specialists must be attracted, and some alluring prospects are likely to present themselves. English builders have already made advances, but, owing to the anti-English sentiment, British firms are not meeting with a very cordial reception. The disposition is to turn toward France, Germany or the United States.

Among the Americans here negotiating with the Russian Government is J. Wilson, who is trying to sell an invention of smokeless powder. The particular merit of the powder, it is claimed, which is adapted to heavy artillery, is a quick-drying quality, ordinary smokeless powder taking several months to dry.

Theodore S. Darling, who has options on the dynamite guns at San Francisco which were recentiy sold by the United States, is trying to negotiate their sale to Russia with a view to their shipment to Vladivostock.

Emperor Nicholas will leave for Caucasus on December 3rd to bid farewell to the Circassian Cavalry.

VISCOUNT HAYASHI'S VIEWS.

In an interview with Viscount Hayashi, the Japanese Minister in London which appears in the "Standard," his Excellency is reported as having said:—We hold to our promise to China to return Manchuria to her when we have recovered it. The Japanese Government intedend to carry that out in every way. The case of Korea is very different; it is in so helpess a state that we must look after it to protect our own interests. The peninsula is one with which the nation has long been associated, and has proved, and is likely to prove, a good field of emigration for our crowded people. The climate suits us well. We can only say that, in view of the existing treaies, we find such statements simply amazing. Viscount Hayashi clearly implies that Japan does not intend to keep her promise to uphold Korea's autonomy.

THE QUESTION OF ARGENTINE'S NEUTRALITY.

A telegram received at the Foreign Office, Tokio, says:—With regard to the rumour that negotiations have been in progress between the Argentine Republic and Russia for the purchase by the latter of the former's warships, the Argentine Minister at London has announced through the British press that he has been ordered by his Government to positively state there is no truth in the rumour.

A PLEA FOR JUSTICE.

The latest despatch from the Law Department to the Foreign Office is a complaint from the Magistrate of Anju that the Japanese are not being properly punished for their offences against Korean life and property. A native of Anju, named Im Dong-hun, was recently shot by a Japanese called Okuta, who was subsequently arrested by Japanese gendarmes, but has not yet been sentenced to any punishment whatever. The Law Department trusts that the Japanese Legation will see that justice is done.

Mr. Yun Yong-sun, former Prime Minister, died yesterday.

A UNITED AMERICA.

The Ottawa "Express" has published an article by Mr. Andrew Carnegie, who says that those born north and south of the imaginary line between Canada and the United States, being all Americans, must soon merge. He continues:—

"It were as great a folly to remain divided as for England and Scotland to have done so. Native-born Canadians and Americans are a common type indistinguishable one from the other. Nothing is surer in the near future than that they must unite. It were criminal for them to stand apart. It need not be feared that force will ever be used or required to accomplish this union. It must come in the natural order of things. Political as well as material bodies obey the law of gravitation. Canada's destiny is to join the Republic as Scotland did England; then, taking the hand of the rebellious big brother and mother, placing them in each other's thus reuniting the happy family, that should never have known separation."

MILITARY OCCUPATION OF PYENG YANG CAUSES DISTRESS.

Although the recent departure of Japanese soldiers from Seoul has relieved this city of a certain amount of congestion our neighbours in Pyeng-yang do not seem to be so well off. From there we learn that many of the poorer population have been turned out of their houses to make room for the troops and that consequently much distress exists, particularly in the district of the city called Yi Mun Dong. It appears that the majority of the householders there having been ejected from their homes, are wandering through the streets in a pitiable state, made worse by the inclemency of the weather.

Some cases of violence are also reported notably that of Kim Yong-whan. Kim was sitting quietly in his house, when a drunken soldier entered and, without provocation, stuck his sword into him, killing him immediately. Kim's wife, although panic stricken, rushed after the murderer and succeeded in securing his arrest by Japanese gendarmes.

MAJOR-GENERAL DESSINO.

A Nagasaki message of the 12th inst. states that, according to a person who has recently returned from Shanghai, Major-General Dessino, Russian Agent at the latter port, has received a present from his Government in appreciation of his services since the outbreak of hostilities. The Russian officer in question will shortly leave Shanghai for Chefoo.

DEATH OF GENERAL NOGI'S SONS.

We receive with sincere regret the news of the death before Port Arthur of the Lieutenant Nogi the second son of the gallant General commanding the Japanese attacking forces. It will be remembered that when he lost his first son at Nanshan, general Nogi ordered the funeral service to be deferred, quietly saying that if he failed to take Port Arthur, he and his remaining son would lose their lives, and three services could then be held in one. The Japanese warrior is made of stern stuff.

The Korea Daily News.

Issued at 5 P. M. daily except Sundays.

Rate of Subscription :—
Per Year,............Yen 25.
Per Quarter,..........Yen 7.
Per Month,..........Yen 2.50.

Postage in Korea not charged extra.
Postage abroad charged extra.

Advertisements, 50 sen per day for 1 inch or less.
5 yen per month per inch.
50 yen per year per inch.

All communications to

E. T. BETHELL,
Editor and Publisher,
Pak-tong, Seoul.

PORT ARTHUR.

The latest news from Tokio seems to indicate that Russia has for the present at least, lost all power of assuming the offensive at Port Arthur. As so little had been heard of 203 metre hill previous to its capture by the Japanese we were inclined to think that the Tokio enthusiasts had given this position a fictitious importance but we now learn from one who knows Port Arthur well that artillery mounted on this hill really dominates the greater part of the harbour and town.

The performances of the Port Arthur squadron have never been such as to command a word of praise. With the exception of the gallant little "Novik" and one or two destroyers the fleet has throughout the war given an exhibition of pitiable helplessness, and its end which seems to be *un fait accompli* is a fitting termination to its career.

This helplessness is all the more surprising when we remember the great bravery everywhere shown by the Russians on land, and the explanation seems to be that there is something lacking in Russian nature or training which is essential in the making of a good fighting sailor.

Now taking it for granted as the news justifies us in doing, that the Port Arthur squadron is now a thing of the past, and that the harbour is no longer available as a refuge for Russian ships, it is interesting to speculate upon what General Stoessel's next move will be. He seems to have lately made several ineffectual and disastrous attempts to recapture 203 metre hill but as every day that the Japanese have been left in possession has enabled them to make their position more secure, it is probable that Stoessel has now abandoned all hope of driving them out of it.

Another Japanese succees is the capture of one of the Kikwanshan forts. This Fort is one of the series in which Erlungshan and Sunseushan are situated and is protected by at least one of them, which makes the apparent ease with which it was captured somewhat puzzling.

There are however many forts where General Stoessel can, if he chooses, make stand after stand against the Japanese advance and while he holds even one of them with a sufficiency of supplies and ammunition, Port Arthur cannot be said to have fallen. It hardly seems, however, that the game would be worth the candle. The harbour is useless to Russia while Japanese artillery dominates it. Nothing short of a land attack which cannot, under even the most favourable circumstances, be made for at least six months, would be successful in recapturing the positions now held by the Japanese.

It certainly appears, now that the Port Arthur squadron has been rendered useless, there is no valid reason why Stoessel should continue his valiant, but costly defense. It is true that with a very inconsiderable force he is keeping a large Japanese army occupied, but he is at the same time hampering General Kuropatkin who, so long as the Russian flag flies over Port Arthur, is in duty bound to make that place his objective and is precluded from making advances in other directions which although victorious would bring him no nearer Port Arthur.

With regard to the stories of peace which are going the rounds of the press, we are unable to believe that the fall of Port Arthur will bring that desirable state of affairs any nearer. In fact we are inclined to take the opposite view and think that the prospects of Russia listening to peace proposals would be more remote than ever.

As things stand at present there is little likelihood of either side being able to strike a decisive blow and the end of the war seems as far off as ever.

THE REBELLION IN KUANGSI.

The "Sinwênpao" publishes a telegram from Kueilin, the provincial capital of Kuangsi, to the effect that the Government troops under General Huang Chung-li obtained a great victory on the 9th inst. near Liuchoufu over a large body of well-armed insurgents under the leadership of a well-known rebel called Lu A-fa, and that, after a battle which was maintained with great determination on both sides, the insurgents were defeated with much slaughter and their leader captured. This Chief is an important man to capture, as he and his followers surrendered last spring to the Government, and after having been furnished with new arms and ammunition and transformed into Government "braves," Lu A-fa suddenly mutinied, slew the mandarins placed over him, plundered the Government stores and made off to the hills. There is, however, another side to the shield, for it is stated that Governor Ko, having had his suspicions raised concerning the loyalty of the newly-made troops had given secret order three months ago to the military officers commanding other troops encamped in the vicinity suddenly to attack the suspects and slaughter them without mercy. The insurgent Chief heard of this and turned the tables on the mandarins before the latter had had their plans anywhere matured. The capture of Lu A-fa and some of his lieutenants on the 9th instant is therefore hailed by the Kuangsi officials as very joyous news, with promotions, as well, before them.

THE STRENGTH OF THE KUANGSI ARMY.

A military officer in Kuangsi, writing to his friends in Shanghai, states that including the contingents sent by the Liangkiang, Hukuang, Min-Che and Kuangtung provinces, there are now in Kuangsi province fighting the insurgents no less than ninety-nine full battalions of 500 men each, or 49,500 men, and twenty-six incomplete battalions, or "Ch'i" of 350 men each, or 9,100 men, making a total of 58,600 men of all arms, all of whom are equipped with modern weapons of precision. Of this number there are only about 1,500 mounted troops, and the army possesses about forty-eight field guns and sixty mountain guns, one half of which are muzzle-loaders.—N.-C. D. News.

We learn from the "Nagasaki Press" that the estimate for the construction of the Japanese military railway between Seoul and Wiju amounts, according to the statement made by General Terauchi at a meeting of the Budget Committee, to yen 16,000,000. This amount has been appropriated from the War Funds. Two-thirds of the length of the line is to be completed by the end of this month.

The Japanese Minister has been granted an audience for tomorrow at 2 P. M.

The Japanese have ordered 2 million Dutch cheeses from Gouda. They are required for food, not ammunition.

A reduction in the number of officials for next year is rumoured, while it is said that the ranks of the tax-collectors will be augmented by over 100.

The Japanese Minister has requested the Foreign Office to in future appoint only Japanese speaking officials to magistracies in the Ham Hyeng Province.

The "Daihan Ilpo" learns that the officers and soldiers of the local guard at Chongsung have thrown in their lot with the Russians and enrolled themselves under the banner of the Czar.

It is said that a company is being formed to start a general motor car service to run in various parts of Colombo. The cars will run daily through certain specified routes on a fixed scale of fares. It is to be worked with ordinary kerosene oil instead of petrol.

Rear-Admiral von Moltke arrived at Shanghai on the 12th inst last from home to relieve Rear-Admiral Holtzendorf as Second-in-Command of the German Asiatic squadron. The new Commander will fly his flag on the cruiser Hansa.

Mr. Stevens and Mr. Hagiwara arrived yesterday afternoon at 5 P. M. Mr. Stevens will reside at Miss Sonntag's house. It is understood that his agreement with the government is practically identical with that of Mr. Megata.

Mr. Kim Du Won, a salt merchant, whose goods had been stolen by some Japanese and who had been imprisoned for attempting to lay hands on the Japanese Minister, was released a few days ago. He now requests the Foreign Office to press his claim on the Japanese Legation for $1,000, the amount of the goods stolen.

We understand that there will shortly be some changes in the British consular service here. Mr. Hyde-Lay who is now in Chemulpo, goes home on leave, and Mr. Harrington is to be transferred from Seoul to take his place. Mr. Holmes will come from Japan to fill the vacancy thus caused. Mr. Porter, of the Seoul consulate, also shortly leaves for home but it is not yet known who his successor is to be.

The Korean Government will probably close its Legation in Peking after the return of the Korean Minister who is expected to arrive at Seoul from Peking shortly.—Japan Gazette. Rumours of the above nature are being industriously circulated by the Japanese, but we have excellent authority for stating that so long as Korea is allowed to retain her promised Independence, no such changes will be made.

Regarding the departure for Japan of Mr. Uchida, the Japanese Minister at Peking, it is stated among the foreign community at Tientsin and also in the "China Review" that the Japanese Minister is going to negotiate with the Tokyo Government as to Japanese foreign policy in view of of the approaching arrival of the time when Russia will listen to peace. The "China Times" says that the Japanese Government has summoned Mr. Uchida to instruct him as to Japan's diplomatic attitude after the fall of Port Arthur and also to give him some confidential instructions dealing with the disquiet in the interior of China. This report has been wired by the "Asahi's" Tientsin correspondent.

The Korea Daily News.

VOL. I, | THURSDAY, DECEMBER 22, 1904 | No. 132

大韓每日申報
대한ᄆᆡ일신보

(뎨일빅삼십삼호) (도요일) 일쳔구빅ᄉᆞ년십이월이십ᄉᆞ일

본샤고빅

이신보는영어와한어로셕거미일츌판ᄒᆞᄋᆞᆸ

신문가

한쟝 엽두돈오푼

일삭됴 엽두량닷돈

우표가미삭닷돈

다맛돈으로밧솜

광고료는

긔한의쟝단과ᄌᆞ힝의다쇼로즁감ᄒᆞ되렴가로밧을터이오며오리지아녀대한사람마다다이신문을보실터이니광고내시기를원ᄒᆞ시ᄂᆞᆫ이들은우리신문샤에와셔면약ᄒᆞ심을희망ᄒᆞᄋᆞᆸ

○발힝소 박동대한미일신보샤법어학교압혜젼영국인셜필림집자리오

샤쟝 영국인 (비셜

평양 디리졈

○평양효동사는권미보씨로우리신문관디리인을뎡ᄒᆞ엿ᄉᆞ오니평양에계신구람코져ᄒᆞ시는 쳠군ᄌᆞ는히디리졈에왕림ᄒᆞ와면의ᄒᆞ시ᄋᆞᆸ

샤고

○우리대한미일신보의목뎍은대한의안녕질셔에관한모든ᄆᆡ녹에디ᄒᆞ야는공평한변론을쥬쟝홈이라우리동신원의탐보ᄂᆞᆫ신문보시는쳠군ᄌᆞ의게홍샹보도ᄒᆞ리며편지를긔셔ᄒᆞ여주시는이는셩명과반디를젹어붓치시기를희망ᄒᆞ오니이거슨신샹에긔지ᄒᆞ라는거시아니오다만극히신용ᄒᆞᄂᆞᆫ증거를숨고쟈홈이라긔자는아모긔셔던지긔ᄌᆡ홈을되각ᄒᆞᄂᆞᆫ권리를가졋ᄉᆞ나되각ᄒᆞᄂᆞᆫ리유를말홀터이오며공즁평화를문란케ᄒᆞᄂᆞᆫ듯ᄒᆞᆫ긔셔는의례히밧지안켓ᄉᆞᆸ나이다

●본사셜시이릭로신문을미양우례로분젼ᄒᆞ와례젼부의임의도집ᄒᆞᆫ듯ᄉᆞ로먼곳에는혹늣게젼ᄒᆞ기도ᄒᆞ며혹몃칠거슬ᄒᆞᆫ겁에젼ᄒᆞ기도ᄒᆞ며혹아니젼ᄒᆞ는곳도잇다ᄒᆞ와우리신문을ᄉᆞ랑ᄒᆞ야구람ᄒᆞ시는 쳠군ᄌᆞ의게되ᄒᆞ야미우미안ᄒᆞᄋᆞᆸ기로지금은분젼인을두고미일일즉이젼ᄒᆞ며아니젼ᄒᆞ거나늣게거나ᄒᆞᆫ폐가업도록ᄒᆞ랴ᄒᆞ오니혹아니젼ᄒᆞ거나혹늣게젼ᄒᆞ거나ᄒᆞᆫ일이잇스면본샤로통긔ᄒᆞ여쥬심을희망ᄒᆞᄋᆞᆸ

잡보

○닉감외대 근일에각부에는인원을감액ᄒᆞ며ᄯᅩ각군에는봉세관빅명을가셜ᄒᆞ여둔다더라

○일진회원 일진회에단발ᄒᆞᆫ고결심ᄒᆞᆫ쟈가경향간에합ᄒᆞ여십삼만명이라ᄒᆞ며먹을량식은가히넉달을지낼거시유족ᄒᆞ다ᄒᆞ더라

○여사군미비 금번슌명비인산시에동대문밧각동에셔모화낼거시여동사군이삼쳔명이오등롱군이삼쳔명인디지금여사청에셔는여사군삼쳔명을내라ᄒᆞ고내라ᄒᆞ고영문에셔는이젼원등롱군삼쳔명을내라ᄒᆞ니도합륙쳔명이잇셔야되겟는디지금심쳔명만잇스미내라는디로츙수ᄒᆞᆯ도리가업는지라동민들이호소ᄒᆞᆫ다더라

○일병집류양인 일젼에미국령사가산양ᄒᆞ러동족으로가다일본병참소에붓들녀ᄒᆞ로밤을집류ᄒᆞ엿다가셔울셔편지가내려간후에야노혀왓고ᄯᅩ수삼일젼에미국션교사ᄒᆞᆫ사ᄅᆞᆷ이지나오다가일병의게힐난을당ᄒᆞ고왓다ᄒᆞ미일공사가이일을알고그병참소에별반죠쳐ᄒᆞᆫ다더라

○군슈난쳐 함경도군슈들은부임ᄒᆞᆯ수도업고아니ᄒᆞᆯ수도업는거시일본사령부의인가가업는즉부임ᄒᆞᆯ수가업고셜혹사령부인가를엇어부임을ᄒᆞ드리도ᄯᅩ아병이핍박ᄒᆞ니시로부임ᄒᆞᆫ는군슈들은진퇴유곡이라더라

○필유봉일 히쥬사는쟈ᄒᆞ나히저희일가의면답수만량아치를팔아가지고샹경ᄒᆞ야셩안ᄂᆞᆼ셥자각근쳐에셔산다ᄒᆞ는고로그일가십여명이올나와셔차지나알수업셔셔로의론ᄒᆞ기를물쟝사를ᄒᆞ면찻기가쉬우리라ᄒᆞ며만일찻기곳ᄒᆞ면살녀두지안는다고별은다더라

○완찰보고 젼라북도관찰사가닉부로보고ᄒᆞ기를현금각군에봉세ᄒᆞᆯ거시당두ᄒᆞ엿고회민은만히모혀소요를니르키는디관하에금구임실익산부안졍읍오군에는오리광관이되여민망ᄒᆞ오니곳샹주ᄒᆞ고셔임ᄒᆞ여최촉ᄒᆞ여곳내려보내라ᄒᆞ엿더라

○예쳔화젹 예쳔군슈가닉부로보고ᄒᆞ기를본월초사일에화젹십구명이각기긔계를가지고본군양산면에돌입ᄒᆞ여인가륙호를즁화ᄒᆞ여가쟝즙물을몰수히소화ᄒᆞ엿다ᄒᆞ엿더라

○일병힝ᄒᆡ 향일에시로평양에드러온일병이리문골빅셩의가ᄉᆞ를젼슈히엇고류쥬ᄒᆞᆯ시히동빅셩들은셜뎡에셔방황ᄒᆞ더니음력십일월초오일에하허일병이술에취ᄒᆞ야히동 거김룡한에집에돌립ᄒᆞ야무고히칼노김씨의다리를ᄶᅵ루미김씨가즉ᄉᆞᄒᆞᄂᆞᆫ지라김씨의쳐가통곡ᄒᆞ며히일병을맛나도망ᄒᆞ던일병이헌병의게잡힘을보고그사실을고ᄒᆞᆫ즉히일병을헌병부에가두고김씨의시신을일졀검사ᄒᆞᆫ다ᄒᆞ며동일하허교군일명도일병의칼에피샹ᄒᆞ엿다ᄒᆞ는고로근일평양셩닉에셔는밤이면한인은출립ᄒᆞ기대단이극난ᄒᆞ다ᄒᆞ더라

○총순담지 평양지시쟝총순리건영씨는본셔심사가불량ᄒᆞ야일졀경찰샹에말못되는일이빅셩의게크게셩판되야원셩이랑ᄌᆞᄒᆞᆫ지라향쟈에본시쟝감리신대균씨가샹경ᄒᆞ엿슬때에순검이십여명을가셜ᄒᆞ고만단도적에슈단으로샹민의지산을침탈ᄒᆞ더니하힝신감리가다시ᄂᆞ려와경무관리의독으로빅셩이수화의ᄲᅡ진거슬구ᄒᆞ랴홈으로본감리와경무서간에원수ᄀᆞᆺ치샹지가되엿다더라

○샹무회셜립 평양대동학교찬셩원뎡지명김대윤김윤화졔씨가본리교육샹에쥬의ᄒᆞ다ᄒᆞ더니근일대동학교로학교찬셩회를권셜ᄒᆞ고일반교육가계찬셩ᄒᆞ기를ᄒᆞᆷ스홀다ᄒᆞ며리덕환김룡홍옥경슈졔씨는본시샹민으로샹무흥왕ᄒᆞ기를위ᄒᆞ야샹업회의쇼를셜립ᄒᆞ고일반샹민을모집ᄒᆞ야쥬야열심홈으로샹무회가점점흥왕ᄒᆞᆫ다더라

○특별판사차츌 평안북도지휘관의용관씨는강계디병뎡이인민을포형ᄒᆞᆫ사건과강화부윤윤철규씨와대디장리동휘씨사건을지관ᄒᆞ기위ᄒᆞ야륙군법원에셔특별판사를차츌ᄒᆞᆫ다더라

○쟝셜회의 북쳥이북으로는아라사병뎡이과시수쇄결셰ᄒᆞ야ᄯᅡ를졈령ᄒᆞᆫ다는고로발병ᄒᆞ다든것이즁지되엿는디각디위관은조원츌젼ᄒᆞᄂᆞᆫ고로군부에셔히사안에디ᄒᆞ야ᄯᅩ회의가된다더라

○안산후반포 관졔리졍안을슈졍ᄒᆞ엿는디그반포는인산후에야힝ᄒᆞᆫ다더라

○회의셩안 졍부에셔외국공사의금광쳥구ᄒᆞᄂᆞᆫ사건으로일공사의권력을경유ᄒᆞ기위ᄒᆞ야회의결졍ᄒᆞ야셩안ᄒᆞᆫ다더라

○군수과궐 군수과궐이삼십여명인데셔임쥬본은신년일월에나시힝ᄒᆞᆫ다더라

론셜

러슌아진으로셔나온소문

○십일월삼십일일에어닉스트쌕린씨가현금일병의게에워싸여잇는한아라사사람의게셔온편지를바다본후동씨가연티로셔미일신문샤로면보ᄒᆞ엿다는디그마쪽장서에긔록ᄒᆞᆫ수연이여좌ᄒᆞ니

우리셔로만는이후로나는죽을광경에드러잇스되오히려면치못ᄒᆞ엿ᄂᆞᆫ즉이항구버셔나기를바라노라ᄒᆞ고ᄒᆞ며ᄯᅩ말ᄒᆞ야왈형은려슌셔쳐음ᄒᆞᆫ든ᄡᅡ홈과일병이흘계로써공격ᄒᆞᆫ바를긔억ᄒᆞᆯ는지알수업셔그려ᄒᆞ되그때에는조ᄒᆞᆫ군함도수삼쳑이샹ᄒᆞ고담략잇는사ᄅᆞᆷ들도죽엇스나그러ᄒᆞ나그츄후젼쟁에는일병이도리여여러쳔명이죽엇고우리는략간손상이되엿는디이러케밍렬ᄒᆞᆫ공격이가조될때마다나는산샹으로올나가그광경을살펴본즉탄환이폭발ᄒᆞ야항구와동리와산과물속으로방향업시ᄯᅥ러지는지라비록쳥국사ᄅᆞᆷ들은경겁ᄒᆞ야두려워들ᄒᆞ여그러ᄒᆞ되우리아라사사ᄅᆞᆷ들은냉소ᄒᆞ고도리여롱판으로싱각들을ᄒᆞ엿스며

형이긔왕려슌근쳐에도착ᄒᆞ엿

UNION INSURANCE SOCIETY OF CANTON.

Head office Hongkong.
Marine risks underwritten at current rates.
Agents in Chemulpo,
E. MEYER & Co.

COMPAGNIE DES MESSAGERIES MARITIMES.

Fortnightly Direct Service.

For Marseilles
via Ports.
Sailing from Yokohama
Calling at Kobe,
Shanghai, Hongkong, Saigon, Singapore,
Colombo, Djibouti, Suez, Port Said
and Marseilles.

For particulars apply to
HOLME RINGER & Co.,
Chemulpo.

HAYASHIDA & CO.,

16 MYENG DONG, CHIN KO KAI, SEOUL.
BRANCH OFFICE AT CHEMULPO.

Money changers, Coal and Wood Merchants, Express Agents.

We are agents for the Pyeng-yang Coal [Com]pany and the Karazu Coal Company of [Japa]n. We have the best quality of both an[thraci]te and bituminous coal, and prompt ex[ecution] of orders is our speciality. Firewood of all kinds kept in stock. Full weight guaranteed. Money of all denominations exchanged at current rates. Parcels received for all parts.

CHINA MUTUAL LIFE INS. OC.

Most favourable terms to policy holders.

Benefit system unsurpassed.

HOLME RINGER & Co.
Agents, Chemulpo.

C. P. R.

CANADIAN PACIFIC RAILWAY COMPANY'S ROYAL MAIL STEAMSHIP LINE.

THE FAST ROUTE BETWEEN CHINA, JAPAN, AND EUROPE VIA CANADA AND THE UNITED STATES.

Route from Hongkong via Shanghai, Nagasaki (Inland Sea of Japan) Kobe, Yokohama Victoria and Vancouver.

Twin Screw Empress Steamship—6,000 Tons—Speed 19 knots.

PROPOSED SAILING FROM YOKOHAMA.
R. M. S. Empress of India.
R. M. S. Empress of Japan.
R. M. S. Empress of China.
R. M. S. Athenian.
R. M. S. Tartar.

Special reduction (first class only) granted to members of the Military, Naval, Diplomatic and Civil services and to Missionaries.

Passengers have choice of ten routes across the Continent of America and have privilege of travelling by any Atlantic Steamship Line.

Round the World passage tickets in connection with the P. and O. S. N., North German Lloyd and Messageries Co.'s **£125.**

All rates payable at current rate of exchange.

For further information, Tickets, Guide Books, etc., apply to

HOLME, RINGER & Co., AGENTS,
Chemulpo.

Grand Hotel,

(Formerly the Station Hotel)

Near the Railway Terminus, West Gate Seoul.

The Best Hotel in Korea;
Handsome new Building.
Fine Airy Rooms
Excellent Cuisine.
Terms Moderate.
Special terms to Missionaries
and to permanent boarders.

Electric cars within 2 minutes' walk.

W. H. EMBERLEY.
Proprietor

EVERY FACILITY.

In connection with Life Assurance Business is afforded by

The Standard Life Assurance Co.,

One of the largest and wealthiest of the Provident Institutions of the United Kingdom Forms of Application and all information will be promptly afforded on application.

10 CENTS A DAY.

Not a very large expenditure is it? But it is sufficient to secure for a man of 30 a policy with the STANDARD LIFE OFFICE for

$1323.

For all particulars of rates, etc., apply to

Holme, Ringer & Co.,
Agents, Chemulpo.

THE NEW YORK LIFE INSURANCE COMPANY.

Have you ever been declined by any Company?

Are you engaged in a specially hazardous occupation?

Have you heard of the New York Life Insurance Company's New Classifications for this class of Risks?

If not, send your date of birth, occupation and particulars of rejection, if any to

E. MEYER & Co.,
Agents, Chemulpo.

MITSUI BUSSAN KAISHA.
(MITSUI & Co.)

MITSUI GINKO.
(MITSUI BANK.)

The Bank is owned by the members of the Mitsui Family, who, as partners, assume an unlimited responsibility for all liabilities of the Bank:—

Capital.......................Yen 5,000,0[00]
Reserve Fund..................." 5,600,0[00]

HEAD OFFICE, TOKYO.

LONDON OFFICE, 34 LIME ST., E. C.

BRANCHES AND AGENCIES:—

New York, San Francisco, Hamburg, Bombay, Singapore, Manila, Hongkong, Amoy, Chefoo, Tientsin.

Kobe, Hakodate, Yokohama, Kure, Yokosuka, Moji, Shimonoseki, Miike, Wakamatsu, Nagasaki, Kuchinotsu, Karatsu, Sasebo, Misume, Taipeh, &c.

Telegraphic Address for all the Offices:
"MITSUI."

A. B. C. AND A. 1 CODES USED.

Contractors of Coal

To the Imperial Japanese Navy. Arsenals and Railway Bureau, Principal Railway Companies and Industrial Work, Home and Foreign Mail and Freight Steamers.

Sole Proprietors

Of the famous Miike, Tagawa and Yamano Coal Mines.

Sole Agents

For the sale of Fukumo, Hokoku, Ichimura, Kanoda, Mannoura, Onoura, Ostuji, Sonoda, Tsubaruro, Yoshinotani, Yoshio, Yurokibura and other coals.

YANGTSE INSURANCE ASSOCIATION, LTD.

The undersigned, having been appointed agents for the above company, are prepared to issue policies and pay losses on marine risks at regular rates.

E. MEYER & Co.,
Agents, Chemulpo.

AMERICAN KOREAN ELECTRIC CO.

Light and Power.

Main Office: Electric Building, Chong No.

RAILWAY DEPARTMENT.

OPERATING CARS BETWEEN EAST AND WEST GATE, EVERY TEN MINUTES:—

First Car leaves East Gate at 7:00 A. M. First Car leaves R. R. Station at 7:25 A. M
Last Car " East Gate at 9:40 P. M. Last " " R. R. Station at 10:05 P.M

OPERATING CARS BETWEEN EAST GATE AND IMPERIAL TOMB TERMINUS, EVERY TWENTY MINUTES:—

CONNECTING WITH EVERY ALTERNATE CAR ARRIVING AT EAST GATE FROM CHONG NO.

First Car leaves East Gate for Tomb at 7:10 A. M.
" " " Tomb for East Gate at 7:35 A. M.
Last " " East Gate for Tomb at 7:50 P. M.
" " " Tomb for East Gate at 8:10 P. M.

OPERATING CARS BETWEEN CHONG NO AND YUNG SAN RIVER EVERY TWELVE MINUTES:—

First Car leaves Chong No for South Gate at 7:12 A. M.
" " " Chong No for Yung San at 7:36 A. M.
" " " South Gate for Chong No at 7:20 A. M.
" " " Yung San for Chong No at 8:09 A. M.
Last " " South Gate for Chong No 10:00 P. M.
" " " Yung San for Chong No at 9:33 P. M.

SPECIAL PRIVATE CARS FURNISHED TO SUIT CONVENIENCE OF PATRONS. PRICES ON APPLICATION AT HEAD OFFICE.

LIGHTING DEPARTMENT

Where less than 250 candle power of light is used, the rate per month will be
Per 16 candle power incandescent lamp,—All night.—Yen 2.50.
32 candle power incandescent lamp:—All night:—Yen 4.00.
50 candle power incandescent lamp:—All night:—Yen 6.00.
150 " " " " " " " 10.00.
1200 " " enclosed are " " " " 20.00.

Where more than 250 candle power of light is used, a Meter will be installed, freqvested:—Rent of Meter Yen 2.00 per month. Rate of charges by meter reading:—Two Sen per Ampere per hour. (Approximately this is equal to about One Sen per 16 C. P. lamp per hour) Minimum monthly charge where meter is installed, Yen 20.00 per month, which includes rental of meter.

Estimates for installing lights furnished on application

An assortment of chandeliers always on hand.

K. Murakami.
Photograph Studio
Chinkokai, Seoul.

Printing, Developing and Enlargement, of Photographs always Undertaken.

Korean Views and Pictures Illustrating Native Customs always on Sale,

---

THE OSAKA SHOSEN KAISHA.

Boats frequently on the berth for Chinnampo.

REGULAR SAILINGS BETWEEN JAPAN AND KOREAN PORTS.

FUSAN AND KOBE VIA SHIMONOSEKI.

OSAKA VIA MOKPO, FUSAN, SHIMONOSEKI AND KOBE.

MOJI DIRECT.

OSAKA VIA KUNSAN, MASANPO, FUSAN, SHIMONOSEKI AND KOBE.

CHEMULPO KUNSAN LINE,
Every three days.

CHEMULPO CHINNAMPO LINE.
Every three days.

For Freight and passage and further particulars apply to
THE OSAKA SHOSEN KAISHA,
Chemulpo.

RONDON, PLAISANT & CO.

General Storekeepers and Merchants, Ships Contractors, Tobacconists, Commission and Forwarding Agents, Coal Merchants

IMPORTERS AND EXPORTERS

Seoul & Chemulpo.

W. D. WENTWORTH.

LANDING
AND
SHIPPING AGENT
AND
CUSTOMS BORDER.

12 OURA, NAGASAKI.

STEWARD & CO.

Chemulpo.

Shipchandlers and Storekeepers, Naval and Mercantile Contrrctors, Landing and Shipping Agents.

STEWARD'S HOTEL

Chemulpo.

Best accommodation in the port for travellers. Clean and well-aired rooms, good cuisine and prompt attendence, moderate tariff.

슬때에제물포셔우리나라함쳑의격침ᄒᆞᆫ바ㅣ되야그호와코리스호의사진박인거슬과피된스코리호함장의게보니엿든거슬려슌셩칙안에잇는룩히장관이모도모혀분격ᄒᆞ야살펴보기는ᄒᆞ엿스되

그때에는우리나라병함의유력함과히군들의호용ᄒᆞᆫ자ㅣ잇슴으로튼튼히밋엇더니그리ᄒᆞᆫ지미구에우리나라의영걸ᄒᆞᆫ수사뎨독마칼로푸씨가일본놈의흉악ᄒᆞᆫ흉계에ᄲᅡ져에워싸임을헛치고나오다가(피추로파물로비스크)전투함의격침홈으로말미아마세상을리별ᄒᆞ엿는지라

쎄리스트최긴씨가우리수사뎨독의죽은모양과또ᄒᆞᆫ궤이ᄒᆞᆫ솔ᄒᆞ나를그리고그엽헤다가실상형편을론리ᄒᆞ기를우리나라군함이일본으로너브러비교홀진ᄃᆡ변변치못ᄒᆞ다고미리말ᄒᆞ야세샹에다돌니여소요ᄒᆞ게만단일이잇셧는지라

그날밤에여러친구들이모도모혀야찬을홈ᄭᅴ먹는ᄃᆡ죽은사룸들을추억ᄒᆞ고술은모도만취ᄒᆞ엿스되종용이들잇셧스나그러ᄒᆞ나다만복수ᄒᆞ기로밍셔ᄒᆞ야셔로결심ᄒᆞ엿더니

과연수일후에일본전투함하수셰와요쉬노가우리의무든바지되포의폭발홈으로써파침이되엿스며

금주와남산을어덧다가일병의게에워싸여공격을당ᄒᆞᆫ거슨셩칙에엽길이심히협착홈으로말미아마엇지홀수업시당ᄒᆞ엿스나그러ᄒᆞ나일병들은이곳에셔몃공일동안을싸와허다ᄒᆞᆫ싱령을잔학ᄒᆞ게죽이여피가흘너ᄂᆡ가되게된후우리의최후진터ᄭᆞ지이르러포획ᄒᆞ엿는ᄃᆡ이는황연히드러난일인즉그진터의일홈들ᄭᆞ지라도역역히세샹에셔다알터인지라

셜옥저히가승첩은ᄒᆞ엿다ᄒᆞ드리도

(미완)

잡보

○영졉차하거 외부고문관이이십일일상오에인쳔항으로셔입셩ᄒᆞᄂᆞᆫ고로외부협판윤치호씨번역관어윤젹씨가영졉ᄎᆞ로인쳔항에ᄂᆞ려갓다더라

○일ᄉᆞ죠회외부 일공ᄉᆞ가외부로공문ᄒᆞ기를함경도각군슈는그일어를아는쟈로퇴차ᄒᆞ라ᄒᆞ엿다더라

○염샹청원 원산염샹김두원이가일공ᄉᆞ의게손씨검ᄒᆞ고증역방면이되엿더니또외부에청원ᄒᆞ기를일공ᄉᆞ의게죠회ᄒᆞ야염가전이만오천구빅여령을곳차자달나ᄒᆞ엿더라

○츅일회의 관졔리정건을확정ᄒᆞ기위ᄒᆞ야이십삼일보터츅일총회가된다더라

○과장피임 면화파쟝은오리관이되엿더니병참소에구슈증역ᄒᆞ다가일쟉에몽방된길영슈씨가피임ᄒᆞ엿더라

○반급불공 여ᄉᆞ대쟝빅청긔씨는여ᄉᆞ군의게반급ᄒᆞ라신ᄂᆡ쥬젼을각시젼에는화주는ᄃᆡ공평히ᄒᆞ지못ᄒᆞᆫ탓스로민원이랑자ᄒᆞᆫ지라황샹폐하ᄭᅦ옵셔동촉이되샤하순ᄒᆞ옵셧는고로황송ᄒᆞ옵이라더라

○고빙합동 외부고문관수지분씨는정동손탁집에류ᄒᆞ는ᄃᆡ외부에셔는히원의고빙홀합동을셩립ᄒᆞ엿는ᄃᆡ년한과월봉은탁지고문관의례를의ᄒᆞ여문들엇다더라

○법대반론 법부대신김가진씨는신병으로집에잇셔관졔리정소에불참ᄒᆞ엿더니정소에셔법부관원을대단히감액ᄒᆞᆫ지라김대신이반대ᄒᆞ야굴ᄋᆞᄃᆡ본대신은가히이거슬쥰힝치못홀지니다시의견을뎨츌ᄒᆞ야가결ᄒᆞᆫ후에야본부관계는시힝ᄒᆞᆫ다ᄒᆞ엿더라

○고양군민등소 ᄂᆡ쟝원에셔구관슈쇄ᄒᆞ는역둔토도죠젼을금년위시ᄒᆞ야분쟉슈쇄ᄒᆞ는고로빅셩이지탱ᄒᆞ야보젼ᄒᆞ기가어려운지라고양거민ᄉᆞ빅여명이ᄂᆡ쟝원과ᄂᆡ부에등소ᄒᆞᆫ다더라

○강화부윤보고 강화부윤윤철규씨가또ᄂᆡ부에보고ᄒᆞ기를현금본부셔긔의고목을졉ᄒᆞᆫ온즉음력십월십이일미시량에진위ᄃᆡ즁ᄃᆡ장소ᄃᆡ장각일명이동헌에올나와셔ᄂᆡ외문짝을간심ᄒᆞᆫ후에곳나려가더니죠곰잇다가대ᄃᆡ장분부를인ᄒᆞ야각청두목을대령ᄒᆞ라ᄒᆞ기에ᄂᆡ의ᄉᆞ또가군부에보고ᄒᆞ기를동헌문짝을파쇄홈뜻으로말ᄒᆞ기에ᄉᆞ룸을보ᄂᆡ여검ᄉᆞᄒᆞᆫ즉샹ᄒᆞᆫ곳은ᄒᆞᄂᆞ토업스니녀의들이다짐ᄒᆞᆫ다ᄒᆞ엿기다짐ᄒᆞ오며별슌검ᄒᆡᆼ슈를병뎡으로ᄒᆞ야곰갑아갈즈음에ᄶᅡ린거슨가히이로말홀수가업스며부속빅가다피신ᄒᆞ야각청이뷔엿다ᄒᆞ니그러ᄒᆞᆫᄒᆡᆼ위는다만직분에만를릴뿐아니라공변된격식에비ᄒᆞ면더욱히탄이오며부ᄂᆡᄉᆞ무로맙홀지라도쥬관무인ᄒᆞ고각항직역을거힝ᄒᆞ기가어려우니이것도또ᄒᆞᆫ낭픠라더옥잔절이두렵고민망ᄒᆞ다ᄒᆞ엿더라

○죠청중계악습 양근군슈가외부로보고ᄒᆞ기를본군셔시면거ᄒᆞ는안관셕과김억쇠가서로송샤ᄒᆞ는젼답사로재판ᄒᆞᆫ즉안관셕의말이무리홈으로재판에락졔ᄒᆞᆫ후에교인이라자중ᄒᆞ고본관을구욕홈이망유기극ᄒᆞ기에그심샹을들어보고ᄒᆞ오니법공사와죵현교당에지죠ᄒᆞ야안관셕의악습을증계케ᄒᆞ고또명리로ᄒᆞ야곰정사베프는ᄃᆡ편케홈을바란다ᄒᆞ엿더라

○죠청샹명 법부에셔외부에죠회ᄒᆞ되평남지관소판소보고ᄂᆡ기에안쥬군슈보고를거ᄒᆞᆫ즉본군갈화면룡연리거ᄒᆞᄂᆞᆫ림동휘가본년정월에령변으로이사ᄒᆞ고구월순간에츄수ᄎᆞ로히동리에와셔류ᄒᆞ더니동월이십륙일에오면즁태랑이가삼화로브터와셔림죵홈집에셔류ᄒᆞ매림동휘가일인을보고셩명을문답홀지음에일인이륙혈포로써헷방을ᄒᆞ고둘재번에ᄂᆞᆫ곳노와동휘에오른눈원편이마져즉사ᄒᆞᆫ지라오면이를일본군ᄃᆡ로잡아감으로심판홀수가업다ᄒᆞ기에이에보고ᄒᆞ니외부에지죠ᄒᆞ야일공사의게젼죠ᄒᆞ야교셥샹명케ᄒᆞ라ᄒᆞ엿기이에죠회ᄒᆞᆫ다ᄒᆞ엿더라

○량사방외대 재작일하오두시에의공사가외부대신를방문ᄒᆞ고또삼시에영공사가외대를방문ᄒᆞ엿더라

○고문입셩 외부고문관수지분씨는작일하오에입셩ᄒᆞ야졍동손택의집으로드러갓다더라

○슌찰사거죠 젼남관찰사김셰긔씨가ᄂᆡ부로면보ᄒᆞ기를순찰사안죵덕씨가부에드려와결젼가계부획사로장찻파면훈령를ᄒᆞᆫ다ᄒᆞ고각군결세가대탕감야이십량에ᄒᆞ고긔세가대창ᄒᆞ야관찰부쥬에사와셔긔를모다슌검의게미루에잡아가고일장풍파에출도봉고ᄒᆞᄂᆞᆫ모양으로공동홈이위렵ᄒᆞ고거죠가히피ᄒᆞ기에보고를샹송ᄒᆞ고쳐분만바란다ᄒᆞ엿더라

관보

데삼천십륙호 광무팔년십이월이십이일

셔임급ᄉᆞ령

○승가의 종이품 박의병

○승정삼품 륙품 심샹각

○의원면본관 종츄원의관 김연칙 김영두 종츄원의관 허현 종츄원의관 비영진 종츄원의관 송익현

○임종츄원의관셔쥬임관륙등 정삼품 윤병렬 륙품 박영대필 구품 한인수 구품 김동필 젼윤셕

이샹십이월십구일

○히시종원분시어 륙품 송창호 구품 홍종원 구품 죠중길 구품 리티영

○명시종원분시어 리시용 홍재현 뎡환봉 송문현

○즁구품종사랑즁학교교관 고학싱 구영셕 효행이탁이ᄒᆞ야시이 중직

이샹십이월이십일

뎐보

군ᄉᆞ령부착뎐

○합북소젼 본월이십일샹오십시에우리척후병이홍원에셔적긔병약삼십명과츙돌ᄒᆞ야이것을격퇴ᄒᆞ엿는ᄃᆡ우리군ᄉᆞ에는손샹이업고적의버린시체가한나며소총과다른약자젼리픔이잇더라

○함창소젼 이십일우리군ᄉᆞ의일부가화쳠ᄌᆞ부근에셔적긔병약수십명을격양ᄒᆞ고락권구혀부근에셔적의보병약일빅을북방으로퇴격ᄒᆞ엿는ᄃᆡ우리군사에는손샹이업고적일명은사로잡혓고엇은바는마일필파그다른약간이더라

○홍룡소포젼 십구일하오오시량에적포병이홍룡둔부근을포격ᄒᆞ엿스나우리군사에는손히가업다ᄒᆞ엿더라

○흑림둔뇽젼 이십일샹오일시에적보병약일소ᄃᆡ가남부변우록보에동사시량에보병일즁ᄃᆡ가달ᄌᆞ보에리습ᄒᆞ엿스나이것을격퇴ᄒᆞ엿고동샹오사시반에적보병이약일즁ᄃᆡ는금삼둔부근이오또적은수의적병이흑림둔부근에와엄습ᄒᆞ엿스나이것을격퇴ᄒᆞ엿는ᄃᆡ금삼둔부근에셔는전투ᄒᆞ기를거진ᄒᆞᆫ시간이ᄂᆞᄒᆞ엿스나우리군사에는손샹이업다ᄒᆞ엿더라

광고

TELEGRAMS

Japanese Legation.

Latest investigations of the war material left by the Russians in the north fort of East Kikwansan show the following results:

Two 47 milimetre quick firing guns, one of which is in good condition.

Two 24 milimetre quick firers, one of which can be made use of.

Four machine guns, all good.

Five 8 in. field guns, which are now being examined.

450 47 milimetre shells.

240 24 milimetre shells.

1150 machine gun shells.

Also a quantity of rifles, cartridges etc., have been captured.

REPRIMANDING AN OFFICER.

Washington, November 17.

Secretary Taft sent a letter to-day to Lieutenant-Colonel W. L. Pitcher, Twenty-eighth Infantry at the Presidio, which will make that officer's ears tingle. The letter is the closing incident in a case which attracted much attention some months ago, in which Colonel Pitcher was accused of having heartlessly jilted Miss Caroline Harold, to whom he was engaged to be married. When called upon for an explanation, Colonel Pitcher tartly informed the department that it had nothing to do with his love affairs.

Secretary Taft in dignified, but extremely pointed language, reviews Colonel Pitcher's actions. He says there is not sufficient evidence at hand to prove Pitcher guilty of similar acts toward other women, but that the conclusion is irresistible that such was the case and that the department might make an example of Pitcher were it not for the fact that Miss Harold urgently requested that the matter be dropped without further publicity. On this account, Colonel Pitcher is let off with a sharp reprimand. Secretary Taft decided not to make the letter public, as he is anxious that the matter should be dropped for the good of all concerned.

Pitcher was engaged to marry Miss Harold, who was a clerk in the War Department. She resigned her place in anticipation of the wedding, and for some unknown reason Pitcher broke the engagement in such a manner as to bring forth strong criticism from the department and his brother officers. When called to account for his action Pitcher wrote the letter for which Secretary Taft reprimanded him severely, on account of its impertinent and defiant tone.

An accident occurred yesterday on the Seoul-Fusan Railway. When a train was passing the Chupunguyung Mountain pass, a part of the embankment gave way and the entire train was precipitated from the track. Fortunately the casualties were small, only two Japanese being killed and three wounded.

The "Daito Shimpo" learns that the Russians at Songchin have been compelled to supply their comrades at Pukchong, owing to the unpreparedness of the latter, with provisions. There are 3 or 4 Russian patrols at the Daimunliung pass, and the Russians, who encountered a Japanese force recently, come undoubtedly from this force.

"In the Navy are you, my friend?" inquired a man with mutton-chop whiskers to his neighbour in a 'bus. The sailor nodded.

"Well," said the other, "I'm not exactly in the Navy, but I'm a naval contractor—that is, I furnish the cheese for the Navy."

"Oh, ye do, do ye?" shouted the sailor, jumping up suddenly. "You are the blanketty blank son of a marlinespike I've been looking for these twenty years." Saying that Jack brought his mighty fist down on the contractor's shiny hat, butted him in the chest, and landed him neatly into a passing mud cart. "Now," he roared, looking round with a glare, "show me the cove as furnishes the butter, and I'll bury ye ogether!"

NEW BRITISH CRUISERS.

The three armoured cruisers of the current shipbuilding programme which are to be laid down at Portsmouth, Devonport, and Pembroke will reach the high water-mark in cruiser construction.

The new vessels, which will be named the "Minotaur," "Shannon," and "Defence," will practically be battleships.

In both power and size they will exceed anything of their class afloat. The following are the particulars of the ships:—

Guns: Four 9.2 inch; ten 7.5 inch.
Shells: 380 lbs. and 200 lbs.
Rate: Four shells per minute.
Penetration: 2½ ft. of iron.
Armour belt: 300 ft. of 6 in. steel.
Gun protection: 8 in. steel.
Speed: Twenty-three knots.
Horse-power 27,000.
Boilers: Water-tube.
Displacement: 14,600 tons.
Cost: About £800,000.-Japan Gazette.

UNREST IN CHINA.

Mr. Bennet Burleigh wired last month from Shanghai to the Daily Telegraph: The political outlook in China is worse to-day than it was in 1900, prior to the Boxer outbreak. The widespread operations, of the socret societies show a most dangerous recrudescence of the anti-foreign feeling and the agitators are not invariably Chinese, although they may pass as such.

British officers who have returned from a tour of observation, state that the drilling of large bodies of well equipped troops is going on night and day in many districts of the Southern and Middle Northern Provinces. The soldiers are being taught by trained officers, who are not all Chinese. Field evolutions and firing practice are proceeding constantly. The Chinese authorities have bought up all European provisions offered wholesale at Shanghai, particularly flour and tinned meats, besides quantities of arms, ammunition, clothing and military equipment generally.—China Gazette.

Philadelphians were amazed recently to see a goat dashing through the streets bleating out the first notes of the "Star-Spangled Banner." As it appeared to be in pain, the animal was stopped, and was found to have swallowed an automatic mouth-organ, which had stuck in its windpipe.

Mr. Yun Kil Byung, a philantropic member of the Il Chin Hoi society, who recently went to the north Pyeng An province, to alleviate the imaginary sufferings of some members of the country branch of the society, has been arrested and placed in jail at Wiju, under suspicion of being a Tonghak.

The British Minister reports to the Foreign Office that their repesentative, supposed to be attending the Haiju, case continually reports himself to the British representative as being sick and refuses to attend. The latter gentleman is unable to proceed with the case without his cooperation and as the weather is becoming bitterly cold, he finds himself greatly inconvenienced.

In order to raise funds for the reorganisation of the Chinese Navy, Prince Pu Lun is of the opinion that if an able and "smooth-mouthed" official were sent abroad he would be able to collect a considerable amount of money from the Chinese residents in foreign countries. Prince Pu Lun has visited many places in his recent tour of the world, and relies upon the patriotism of Chinese who welcomed him.

A Mainichi telegram from Fusan, of Thursday's date, states that on the 4th inst, at five o'clock in the afternoon, Mr. Hidaka Tomojiro, a member of Messrs. Harada & Company of Fusan, who had gone to Sokei district, Kyong-Sang-Do, to collect money from the farmers for agricultural instruments which they had bought from the firm on credit, was attacked by about eighty natives and returned home severely wounded. The incident was at once reported to the Japanese Consulate.

SANDOW IN CALCUTTA.

A LOCAL OPINION.

The Calcutta correspondent of the "Rangoon Times" writes thus of Sandow the "strong man," who is now exhibiting in that city:—Sandow has descended on us, as "the Perfect Man" and as a smart boomster of himself and his goods. Assisted by a troupe of variety show artistes of more or less merit, chiefly more, he opened to a very big house, and made a favourable impression on the Calcutta public. I see some of the papers describe it as the biggest house the Royal has ever held, but to one who can remember the palmy days of good old George Lewis and the phenomenal season of the first little Pollards during the Exhibition year, not to mention other houses, crammed to suffocation, comes readily the indulgent smile. Sandow has placarded the town liberally, he has advertised judiciously, he has been given columns of interview and anecdote, and he has put before us a first-class entertainment; all of which proves that he is a first-class showman. He is a little inclined to take himself too seriously, we think, and seems to be under the pleasing delusion that his visit to India is to be reckoned among the most astounding things of the present century; but bless you, we all know Sandow, we are most of us thoroughly well acquainted with his system and his methods together with those of dozens of other rival strong men and muscle professors, and when we read that his chief object in coming here is to preach the gospel of physical culture, we smile again. There can be no doubt, however, that he is the king of weight-lifters, and an attractive personality, and although he rides a very high gear, as a Yankee friend of mine expressed it, he is well worth seeing and will doubtles make a profitable tour in this country.

A later report regarding the Haiju affair, comes from the representative of the Law Department, who states that the Chinaman was only beaten by the Koreans and not killed.

The Kamni of Masanpo reports that the Japanese Consul has demanded the sale of plot No. four of the Foreign settlement. The Foreign Office have instructed the Commissioner of Customs to have the ground surveyed.

The Foreign Office have telegraphed the investigation committee at Haiju, requesting an immediate report of their proceedings, as conflicting rumours are current anent the death of the Chinaman supposed to have been murdered by Koreans.

The Governor of Kongchu reports that a great disturbance suddenly arose in his town on the 21st inst. On proceeding to investigate the cause, he found that the people were forcibly ejecting a large number of Il Chin Hoi people, who had found their way into the town. The police soon restored order but not until some of the Il Chin Hoi had been roughly handled and the rest had fled in terror.

The other day, coming up in a coasting steamer, a passenger related an interesting occurrence, says the China Mail. It appears that there were only a few first class passengers, but many Chinese in the third class. On arrival at the Taku bar, however, much to his surprise, about 25 of these Chinese appeared in quite a transformation scene, as Japanese officers, having discarded their queues and Chinese garments, and were apparelled in all the pomp and glory of lace bedecked and much decorated uniforms, swords and plumed kepis. Of course to those 'in the know' the explanation was simple; but to casual and nervous visitors the protean change might have been considered alarming. They were only propogandists of the new method of 'Japaning China.

TOMMY ATKINS AT HOME.

Last night the guard of the British Legation provided the foreign Community with a very pleasant evening. The proceedings opened with a "Nigger Show" but where everything was excellent detailed criticism would be out of place. The performance gave evidence of careful rehearsal and good management throughout and if we selected one item for particular praise, it would be the "whistling song." The jokes kept the audience in a ripple of laughter and we were all sorry when the curtain fell. Herr Eckert's band next discoursed pleasant harmony and after an encore had been given, several local residents "contributed." Miss Scranton and Captain Phillips R. M. L. I. both sang charmingly and Bishop Corfe gave an amusing reading. The proceedings were brought to a close with a "screaming" farce dealing with the adventures a charming girl, her father, and a cab man who disguises himself as a spiritualist. From first to last everything was a success and we hope the men of the "British Legation guard" will be encouraged to Provide another show before Spring. The Chair was taken by Mr. Mc Leavy Brown, C. M. G. and Captain Phillips presided at the piano.

The "man in the street" says that all the rice in Japan having been finished Japan now intends to recover all the flour which Koreans have imported from Japan. Consequently many thousand Japanese will shortly come to Korea from Japan and the inhabitants of the latter country will have to seek a fresh asylum, possibly in Hawaii, possibly in Mexico.

General Cronje, who is still taking part in the Boer war show at St. Louis, is reported to have said on a recent interview: "Though silence reigns in South Africa and all may appear calm, yet there is no peace in the hearts of the Boers. When the great day comes, when the skeletons will crawl to one another and the limbs rejoin, and when South Africa lifts her voice against oppression, then I trust that the echo of sympathy and assistance from America will be more forcible than in the past."

The Korea Daily News

Issued at 5 P. M. daily except Sundays.

Rate of Subscription:—
Per Year,............Yen 25.
Per Quarter,..........Yen 7.
Per Month,..........Yen 2.50.

Postage in Korea not charged extra.
Postage abroad charged extra.

Advertisements, 50 sen per day for 1 inch or less.
5 yen per month per inch.
50 yen per year per inch.

All communications to

E. T. BETHELL,
Editor and Publisher,
Pak-tong, Seoul.

FORTIFIED TIEHLING.

(SPECIAL TO THE SHANGHAI TIMES).

Tiehling, 15th November.

The Russian forces here and at Mukden are being considerably augmented. There are now enormous forces at both these places which require feeding. There was very little done in the way of cultivation of crops since the war broke out and the Russians took care to purchase all the available stores of wheat barley, oats, beans and peas. There are very few cattle in these regions of Manchuria which do not belong to the Russians, who have either purchased or seized the same wherever they were procurable. At first the local natives were quite content with the purchases made by the Russians, but as time began to show there was likelihood of an early cessation of hostilities, discontent spread and swelled the ranks of the Hunghutze with these who had no other means of subsistance. Prices have in most cases increased by something between 50 and 200 per cent. The frequent raids of the Hunghutze gangs on the Russian grain depots and cattle droves keep the natives fairly well supplied with the necessaries of life at the top price of the markets. Were it not for these raids man of the natives who are peacefully inclined would starve. As a result those who have interest in neither the Russians or Japanese, have very interested sympathy with the Hunghutze, who will raid both belligerents for the purpose of providing food for the people.

The Russians are paying very big wages for coolie labourers, for defence works, road leveling, carters, drovers, and general camp hands. These coolies, ignorant as they seem, are full of information which they supply to the bandits in the ranks of whom are many of their relations. Any drover who brings in from Mongolia ponies, cattle, pigs, sheep or goats obtains 5 to 10 times the price they received during peace. This is a big inducement to Mongolia to such an extent that it will be years before prices in the cattle and pony raising districts become normal. In reality the Russians are paying far more than 5 or 10 times the peace [illegible] for these animals, as within the [illegible] few nights a large percentage are raided, pass again into the hands of the dealers who resell them to the Russians or carry them back. The Russians have tried to put a stop to this traffic by branding all cattle or ponies purchased with the army brand or chop.

Reverting to another aspect of the situation, namely that of local defence, I gather from those coversant with military councils, that the Russians are considering the advisability of building semi-permanent defences here in Tiehling and employing Chinese coolies to do the work. The main defences will be situated about 5 miles west of the city. Emplacements are being erected all along the rivers Hunho at Mukden and Tiehling-ho. The environs of the positions have been well sapped, with a trench twenty-five feet deep surmounted by an embankment 8 feet high. These are further protected by a number of powerful batteries, pitfalls and wire entanglements similar to those which were found at Nan Shan in the Liao Tung. The whole of the Tiehling-ho to the south of the city gives the appearance of a virtual fortress. The Russians are constructing a magnificent military road about 100 feet wide on the flat and 60 feet wide in the passes. This is expected to be completed in a month or two. To the west and southwest of the city, when I visited that vicinity, I found work was being carried out on the undulating soil. Deep trenches are being cut in the hills on the southern side after the fashion employed by the Boers in the South African war. These defences to the west are somewhat curved and are designed to protect the city position from a flanking movement on that side. They are very powerful particularly about 5 miles to the west of the Railway Station, which is considered to be of vital importance in the defence. Formidable but only a little less powerful defences are being constructed in a semicircle from this point to one 8 miles further west extending in the direction of the Liao river, which is expected to be the cover of the right flank.

In all the positions occupied by the field batteries straw and tall dead grasses have been utilized as excellent masks and most of these places are given the appearance of Chinese graves.

If I had not visited this region for a long time I would hardly recognise it. Instead of the old cart roads, that took any convenient route across the nearest fields, the Russians have built a splendid military main road from Mukden to Tiehling with a strong bridge crossing the Tiehling-ho. From this main road several branches have been built to the various strategic positions to the east and west, on which it will be easy to move artillery at all seasons of the year. A perfectly level road runs along the side of the Tiehling-ho and instead of transporting supplies with great inconvenience over the old rubble bed of the stream, these are now moved rapidly along the new road with the greatest facility. A strong detachment of Russians occupy Fahkoumen and examine all travellers, Chinese, Mongolians and others. These soldiers, who have been left without their winter clothes, have been forced to take to the Mongolian sheepskin coat and it is hard to distinguish between them and Chinese or Mongolian carters.

The Liao River is now completely frozen over in places, but not sufficiently to bear heavy traffic. It has, however, barred any river transport up or down. Independantly of river transport, I have an impression, which I believe is generally borne out by those most conversant with this country, that there are greater facilities for transit in winter than in summer. I am therefore opposed to the view that either of the armies will go into winter quarters during this season. On the contrary I expect a much more vigorous compaign in the vicinity of Tiehling and Mukden than this war has yet seen. Both armies are straining to their utmost to concentrate for a decisive move in the next few weeks. The Russians here feel confident that when the ground is sufficiently hard to permit of cavalry movements, then the tide of war will turn in their favour. The time they consider theirs is now on us if they are capable of doing anything and certainly they are doing everything to ensure success.

At the present time there are not 1,000 men inside the wall of Tiehling. Near the railway station and along the line of the river, which is now the base of the Russian campaign, there is an enormous concentration and great activity. In the vicinity of the station alone there are some five thousand men maintained. Daily as each trainload of freshly arrived troops reaches the station those previously encamped move on to the front. On some days 3,000 to 5,000 fresh arrivals are counted. Much artillery and cavalry are being sent back here from Mukden, which would indicate that the great fight will be in this neighbourhood, and on the level ground to the west of the railway. If Russia is going to gain a victory at all it must be here where her arrangements are as perfect as a hasty concentration can make them.

THE WAR AND THE HUMOURISTS.

Recent events have provided the "funny" men and joke editors with material which they have not been slow to make use of. Here are a few of their productions:—

Japan's first serious reverse in Manchuria has come in the departure of Viceroy Alexieff.—The Detroit Free Press.

Carrie Nation would be doing the world a favour if she could manage to get at the vodka supply of the Russian Navy.—The Washington Evening Star.

It is reported that Kuropatkin's charger deserted to the Japanese in the last battle. There's horse sense for you.—The Philadelphia North American.

It is difficult to imagine the extent of the disaster which would ensue if one-half of the Russian navy should unexpectedly meet the other half on a dark night.—The New York Sun.

"What is the the meaning of 'contraband of war'?" asked the man in search of information.

"It all depends," said the man with information on tap. "For instance, if you are at war and some country wants to sell coal to your enemy, coal is contraband. If you are at peace and want to sell coal to some country that's at war, it isn't contraband. See?"—Chicago Tribune.

Tomorrow an audience will be given to the Japanese Minister and Messrs Stevens and Hagiwara, as well as all Ministers of Departments.

The Kamni of Pyeng-yang and the Chief of Police there, are reported to be at loggerheads, owing to the latter's excessive "squeezes." The Kamni is said to be taking the part of the people against their oppressor.

The three first members of the Po An Hoi society to be arrested by the Japanese, were released yesterday, after a promise has been extracted from them not to be naughty again. They spent their time, in jail, in learning Japanese, and are now quite fluent speakers of that language.

The Korea Daily News.

VOL. I, FRIDAY, DECEMBER 23, 1904. No. 133

HONGKONG & SHANGHAI BANKING CORPORATION.

Paid-up Capital	$10,000,000
Reserve Fund:—Sterling Reserve	10,000,000
Silver Reserve	7,000,000
	27,000,000
Reserve Liability of Proprietors	10,000,000

HEAD OFFICE, HONGKONG.

London Bankers, London and County Banking Company Limited.

Branches and Agencies, London.

Amoy,	Hankow	Penang,
Bangkok,	Hiogo,	Rangoon,
Batavia,	Iloilo,	Saigon,
Bombay,	Lyons,	San Francisco,
Calcutta,	Manila,	Singapore,
Colombo,	Nagasaki,	Sourabaya,
Foochow,	New York,	Tientsin,
Hamburg,	Peking,	Yokohama,

Credits granted on approved Securities, and every description of Banking and Exchange business transacted.

Drafts granted on London and the chief Commercial places in Europe, India, Australia, America, China and Japan.

HOLME RINGER & CO., AGENTS, CHEMULPO.

HOKURKU DOBOKU KAISHA.

Branch office in Chong Dong. Seoul.

Japanese telephone No. 165

CONTRACT DEPARTMENT.

We can contract to build any building or construction.

MERCHANDISE DEPARTMENT.

We can provide any building material. We have just contracted to build the new Belgian Legation.

E. MEYER & CO.

Chemulpo.

SOLE AGENTS IN KOREA FOR.

A. T. Morse, Sons & Co.'s "Fresco" Distemper

In all colours ready for use on walls, Ceilings etc.

and

AVENARIUS CARBOLINEUM

A wood-preserving and antiseptic oil preparation

Against decay, dry-rot, fungus and wood-destroying insects.

A large supply always in stock.

Prices upon application.

E. MEYER & CO.,

CHARTERED BANK OF INDIA AUSTRALIA & CHINA.

INCORPORATED BY ROYAL CHARTER 1853

HEAD OFFICES:—LONDON.

Paid-up Capital	£800,000
Reserve Liability of Shareholders	800,000
Reserve Fund	800,000

Drafts granted upon all the principal places in the world and every description of Exchange and banking business transacted.

E. MEYER & CO., Agents, Chemulpo.

MITSU BISHI DOCKYARD & ENGINE WORKS, NAGASAKI.

CODE WORD, "DOCK."

A 1, A. B. C., and Engineering Codes used.

DOCK No. 1 (at Tategami).

Extreme Length	523 feet
Length on blocks	513 ,,
Width of Entrance on Top	89 ,,
,, ,, Bottom	77 ,,
Water on Blocks at Spring Tide	26½ ,,

DOCK No. 2 (Mukaijima).

Extreme Length	371 feet
Length on Blocks	360 ,,
Width of Entrance on Top	66 ,,
,, ,, Bottom	53 ,,
Water on Blocks at Spring Tide	22 ,,

PATENT SLIP (at Kosuge).

Can take vessels up to 1,000 tons gross.

THE WORKS are well equipped with the LATEST IMPROVEMENTS, and can execute any kind of work in SHIPBUILDING and MARINE ENGINEERING, as well as in REPAIRING of SHIPS.

The COMPANY'S new powerfu steamer OURA-MARU (712 tons, 700 I.H.P.), specially built for SALVAGE PURPOSES, and equipped with necessary gear, is always READY at SHORT NOTICE.

THE METHODIST PUBLISHING HOUSE.

Little West Gate, Seoul.

JOB PRINTING, TYPEWRITER PAPER
CARBON PAPER, VISITING CARDS
STATIONERY, BOOK BINDING
BOOK PUBLISHERS
AMERICAN SCHOOL BOOKS
SPENCERIAN COPY BOOKS
PEN CARBON LETTER AND BILL BOOKS

S. A. BECK, Manager.

DAI-ICHI GINKO.

LIMITED.

(Formerly the First National Bank)

ESTABLISHED 1873

INCORPORATED UNDER PRESENT LAW 1896

Capital	Yen 5,000,000
Reserve Fund	1,500,000

HEAD OFFICE:—TOKIO.

President: Baron SHIBUSAWA.

BRANCHES AND CORRESPONDENTS

In the Principal Cities and Towns of Japan.

Interest Allowed on

Fixed deposits 1 year	- - -	6½ per cent
" " 6 months	- - -	6 per cent

Special current accounts 1½ sen daily per Y 100
General " " 1 " " " 100

M. TANAKA, Manager, Chemulpo.

SINGER SEWING MACHINES

씽거조봉침

SOLE AGENTS FOR KOREA

전매쇼

HOLME RINGER & CO. Chemulpo.

졔물포 함룽거양힝

KAMEYA & CO.

GENERAL STOREKEEPERS

Chinkokai - - Seoul

(Established 1895, Tokyo)

Confectionery, Hams, Canned Goods, Cutlery, Hirano & Tansan Water. Provisions, Gents, Furnishing goods, Toilet Articles, Travelling Bags, Tobacco, Cigars & Cigarettes Kitchen Utensils. Coffee, Biscuits

Fresh Goods always kept in Stock.

Prices Moderate

☞ *Please come and inspect our goods*

NIPPON YUSEN KAISHA.

JAPANESE MAIL STEAMSHIP CO.

DER MAIL CONTRACT WITH THE IMPERIAL JAPANESE GOVERNMENT.

European Line

Regular Fortnightly Service between Yokohama Kobe, Moji, Shanghai, Hongkong, Singapore, Penang Colombo, Port Said, Marseilles, London and Antwerp

American Line

Regular Fortnightly Service between Hongkong and Seattle, calling at Shanghai, Moji, Kobe, Yokohama and Victoria, B. C.

Australian Line

Regular weekly Service betwen Japan Ports and Australia, calling at Hongkong and Manila.

(Above Three Lines Suspended until further notice).

Shanghai Line

Weekly Service between Shanghai and Japan Ports

Korea Line

Service Kobe, Moji, Nagasaki, Fusan Chemupo Cheffoo, Taiku.

S. S. Bahelsberg, 2181 tons.

Service Kobe, Moji, Fusan, Chemulpo, Chinnampo

S. S. ARGO, S. S. Ohio.

BORDEN'S CONDENSED MILK CO.

New York, U. S. A.

ALWAYS IN STOCK

Eagle Brand Condensed Milk.

Gold Seal Condensed Milk.

Peerless (Family) Evaporated Cream.

Borden's Malted Milk.

E. MEYER & CO. Chemulpo Korea, Sole Agents

ROYAL INSURANCE COMPANY,

Funds exceed £10,000,000

FIRE

AT CURRENT RATES.

LIFE

REDUCED PREMIUM.

HOLME RINGER & CO., Agents, Chemulpo.

HOTEL DU PALAIS

SEOUL.

The only first class Hotel in Seoul Situated in the centre of the city opposite the palace.

Cuisine under the supervision of an experienced French Chef.

Well ventilated and furnished throughout.

TARIFF UPON APPLICATION

L. MARTIN

Proripetor and Manager

大韓每日申報
대한ᄆᆡ일신보

(뎨일빅삼십ᄉ호) (월요일) 일쳔구빅ᄉ년십이월이십륙일

본샤고빅

이 신보는 영어와 한어로 셔 ᄆᆡ일 츌판ᄒᆞ옴

신문가

한쟝 엽두돈오푼

일삭됴 엽두량닷돈

우표가미 삭당닷돈

다섯돈으로밧숨

광고료논

귀한의쟝단과조항의다쇼로ᄒᆞ 강ᄒᆞ되ᄒᆡᆼ가ᄂᆞᆫ밧을터이오ᄆᆡ오 린지아녀ᄯᅢ한사람마다다이신 문을보실터이니광고버서기를 원ᄒᆞ시ᄂᆞᆫ이들은우리신문사에 와셔번약ᄒᆞ심을희망ᄒᆞ옴

○발ᄒᆡᆼ소 박동대한ᄆᆡ일신보 사발어학교앙쾌젼영국인셜필 ᄒᆡᆼ쟝자킈오

사쟝 영국인 (비셜)

평양 디리졍

○평양효동사ᄂᆞᆫ쥐미보셰로우 쾌 신문좌ᄆᆡ다리인을퇴졍ᄒᆞᆫ엿 시스오니평양에계신구람코져ᄒᆞᆫ ᄂᆞᆫ 쳠군ᄌᆞᄂᆞᆫ힝디리졍에왕 림ᄒᆞ와번회ᄒᆞ시옴

사고

○우리대한ᄆᆡ일신보의목덕은 대한의안녕질셔에관한모든대 목에ᄃᆡᄒᆞ야ᄂᆞᆫ공평한변론을쥬 쟝ᄒᆞᆷ이라우리동신원외탐보ᄂᆞᆫ 신문보시ᄂᆞᆫ쳠군ᄌᆞ의계ᄒᆞ상보 도ᄒᆞ려ᄒᆞᆷ편지든귀셔ᄒᆞ여주시 ᄂᆞᆫ의ᄂᆞᆫ셩명과번디든ᄌᆡ어붓쳐 시기를희망ᄒᆞ오니미거슨신문 상에긔ᄌᆡᄒᆞ라ᄂᆞᆫ거시아니오다 만극히신용ᄒᆞᄂᆞᆫ증거를숨코자 ᄒᆞᆷ이라귀자ᄂᆞᆫ아모귀셔든지귀 쥐ᄒᆞᆷ을되쟝ᄒᆞᄂᆞᆫ권리든가졋스 나되쟝ᄒᆞᄂᆞᆫ리유를말ᄒᆞᆯ터이오 며공중평쥭등론란케ᄒᆞᄂᆞᆫ듯ᄒᆞᆫ 귀셔ᄂᆞᆫ의례히밧지안케ᄉᆞᆸ나이 다

●본사셜시이리로신문을ᄃᆡ양 우혜로분젼ᄒᆞ와혜젼부의양의 로젼ᄒᆞᆫ듯스로번곳에ᄂᆞᆫ혹늣게 젼ᄒᆞ기도ᄒᆞ며혹면쳔키숨ᄒᆞᆫ텹 에젼ᄒᆞ기도ᄒᆞ며ᄒᆞ아니젼ᄒᆞᄂᆞᆫ 곳도잇다ᄒᆞ와우리신문을수탕 ᄒᆞ야구람ᄒᆞ시ᄂᆞᆫ 쳠군ᄌᆞ의계 티ᄒᆞ야면우미안ᄒᆞ옵기로지금 은분젼인을두고ᄆᆡ일일즉이젼 ᄒᆞ며아니젼ᄒᆞ거나늣게거나ᄒᆞᆫ 폐가잇도록ᄒᆞ란ᄒᆞ오니혹아니 젼ᄒᆞ거ᄂᆞ혹늣게젼ᄒᆞ거나ᄒᆞᆫ일 이잇스면본사로통긔ᄒᆞ여주심 을희망ᄒᆞ옴

잡보

○대됴양면 원로대신윤용션 씨가츌셔ᄒᆞᆫ고로빈면대됴윤덕 영씨ᄂᆞᆫ궤임ᄒᆞ고기되에ᄂᆞᆫ샹용 부대신리도지씨가잉피ᄒᆞ엿더 라

졍부리졍안 일젼에관계리 졍소에셔회의ᄒᆞ엿ᄂᆞᆫ되외졍부 리졍안진만의결비되엿ᄂᆞᆫ지라 의졍은총졍으로ᄒᆞ고찬졍은불 시ᄒᆞ야각부대신이피졈ᄒᆞ기로 결졍이되엿더라

○대사되젼 어ᄉᆞ쳥에셔대ᄉᆞ 되젼을탐붕ᄒᆞᄂᆞᆫ고로일젼회에 셔만찬에고시ᄒᆞ고회쳥에권고 ᄒᆞ야되젼을분시ᄒᆞ라ᄒᆞ엿더니 이퇴밧은서에ᄂᆞᆫ분문ᄒᆞ고남셔 에ᄂᆞᆫ분시가되엿더라

○방원회의 동군방원에서각 되죄인을평리ᄒᆞ기위ᄒᆞ야금일 에각관ᄉᆞ쟝이하회ᄉᆞ를이회의 ᄒᆞᆫ다더라

○순쳥원구류 일진회순쳥원 윤길병씨ᄂᆞᆫ평안북도일되를순 챨ᄒᆞ러도니든로ᄎᆞ에의주에셔 진쇄되에구류가되엿다고면보 ᄒᆞ엿더라

○샴쳬몽방셜 보안회ᄉᆞ로일 병의계피착ᄒᆞ엿던원세셩리범 셕신힝규샹씨가안주일병참에 셔오록삭ᄒᆞᆷ신ᄒᆞ니군헌일본군 ᄉᆞ령부에셔면쳑방숑ᄒᆞᆫ엿단말 이잇더라

○진회공합 작일일진회에셔 군부대신의공함ᄒᆞᆷ이좌와곳ᄒᆞᆫ 니경계자ᄂᆞᆫ작일에본회진주지 회의보쳥을젹준ᄒᆞᆫ즉힝디ᄎᆞᆫ쥬 디방되가포함비자샹ᄒᆞ야회민 으로ᄒᆞ야곰능히힝디에셔젼보 치못ᄒᆞ게ᄒᆞ니대저본회의지회 를디방에셜시ᄒᆞᆷ미무허시각하 의게손히가잇진되광민을모히 ᄒᆞ야금구들이지리지게ᄒᆞᄂᆞᆫ뇨 이ᄂᆞᆫ졍부가본회인힉ᄒᆞᆫ후로ᄂᆞᆫ 터며옥샹ᄒᆞᆫ것은쟝하기쟈되에 가만이동ᄒᆞ야다만그칭명죄산 을힉ᄒᆞ랴ᄒᆞ니이졋비무순싱술 이보리오디방쟝퇴에ᄒᆞ민ᄒᆞᆫ다ᄂᆞᆫ 고코가남마다이로고면보눈남 이듯ᄒᆞ니이졋싱쟈ᄒᆞ고말ᄒᆞ란 면ᄒᆞ욕쟈졉ᄒᆞᆫ아이에공합으로 졍ᄒᆞ노나죠광ᄒᆞᆫ신후에각디방 니로ᄒᆞ야쾌회믹음젼ᄒᆞᆫ세ᄂᆞᆫ 리유를시명ᄒᆞ라ᄒᆞ엿더라

○포진일진회 포진군수리희 셰쳘씨가니뷔로보로ᄒᆞᆫ기를보빔 자오인에이일진회라칭ᄒᆞᄂᆞᆫ단밧ᄒᆞᆫ 졍부로올며보ᄂᆞᆫ발나ᄒᆞ며숑양 졍에미이보되ᄂᆞᆫ자가지금수빗 명비나되고ᄉᆞ무소를셜시ᄒᆞ란 ᄒᆞ디효유ᄒᆞ에도힉쳔지아니ᄒᆞ 니엇지ᄒᆞ리오ᄒᆞ엿더라

○홍인수재 근일에함경북도 종두위원이이희성경ᄒᆞ야친구 한아훙민나수재ᄒᆞ다가종두위 원의ᄆᆡ되ᄂᆞᆫ이위원을갈고복영 사도왜쟝교쾌믿쳔군유토쟝로 다ᄒᆞᆷ즉고친구의되당이조비ᄂᆞᆫ 돈아직도킈화를모른다ᄒᆞ고버ᄂᆞᆫ 훙모음이잇스면외국에ᄉᆞ람의 원비곳지안타ᄒᆞ고두사ᄅᆞᆷ의쏘 를쳔디죡위ᄒᆞ고본국에셔엿ᄒᆞ니 라

○오쟝인귀오 일본이핼야진 우졍이후로란이나셔궁중에서ᄂᆞᆫ 작ᄒᆞ여ᄒᆞ셧든밀후ᄅᆞᆯ앙ᄒᆞ니 ○원돈되에셔ᄂᆞᆫ주셩과불도 ᄒᆞ엿ᄂᆞᆫ힝으로환관의 며동도 ᄒᆞ노니

○고이환역 어졈역의ᄒᆞᆫ모 의가ᄂᆞᆫ되우리ᄂᆞᆫ길되엿스니쑈 을ᄒᆞ려니와셔가로갈슈빗게엇다 ᄒᆞ엿더라

○신동ᄒᆞᆫ녀인 셰분밧팔ᄎᆞ졍 근치에나히ᄒᆞᆫᄉᆞ싱이나되녀인 이잇ᄂᆞᆫ디무론모힌ᄒᆞ고손금ᄒᆞ 번만보면그사름의궝셩질ᄒᆞᆷ을 판단ᄒᆞᄂᆞᆫ고로고븍차ᄂᆞᆫ열한왕젹 이오계번일을모다아ᄂᆞᆫ고로포 아에은빌비힝ᄒᆞᆫ이리이라도발ᄒᆞ 고논지라도젹놈곳ᄒᆞᆫ자ᄂᆞᆫ가지안 코그외에ᄂᆞᆫ만ᄂᆞᆫ차자다니ᄂᆞᆫ티 벽시연즁이잇셔아챵본디디 라

○중동신화 작일남촌즁동에 셔신화ᄒᆞ엿ᄂᆞᆫ되디힝히일본사 름이쳐셔쵸가칠팔간이소화ᄒᆞ엿 라

○병원연회 제작야동경빈예 남대문밧시로지은병원에셔일 회ᄒᆞ엿ᄂᆞᆫ되고병원쟝에비신씨 가연셜ᄒᆞ야왈비졍근미국인이 대한사름을위ᄒᆞ야일화수만원 을보니여지엇스니대한동포ᄂᆞᆫ 병엇거든와셔치료ᄒᆞ라ᄒᆞ고ᄒᆞ엿 다더라

○원봉순금 법부관인들 을감영ᄒᆞᄂᆞᆫ되군경원봉을졍월 분터흘림다ᄒᆞᄂᆞᆫ고로쟝원을리 우기다린다ᄒᆞ더라

○코루계약 외부와일본공사 셔쵸진등슈경ᄒᆞ엿ᄂᆞᆫ되외아에 ᄒᆞ더라

일 원봉이ᄇᆡᆨ원

일 가ᄉᆞ비가로사빅원

일 본국회활시비실비와혜찰 빅원을가급ᄒᆞ고

일 안용ᄒᆞ야회힝ᄒᆞᆷ셰에ᄂᆞᆫ실 비외에일비금신지시지급 ᄒᆞᆯ슈라ᄒᆞ엿더라

○최홍슈파직 황히도송화군 명규회씨가너부로면보ᄒᆞ기를 셔흥군슈리범홍이가결세를취 징ᄒᆞ야탐학ᄒᆞᆷ이평군에석지못 ᄒᆞ지금이회봉고파츌ᄒᆞ고희 쥬군슈다인국으로셔리를버엿 ᄒᆞ엿더라

○숨옥쳔졀히 종친부쟝상ᄉᆞ 진회회가본원이신일발행에발 ᄒᆞᆫ면보에온든번스되금ᄒᆞᆫ신시 랑에박인간현회지셩이나미궁 ᄂᆞᆫ숀흰직둉ᄒᆞᆫ뫼쾌춘박셔쳔예 명이회순괴향ᄒᆞ야일진회춘셔샹 ᄒᆞ고ᄒᆞ되ᄉᆞ삭ᄒᆞ아진ᄒᆞ희를빈ᄒᆞᆫ 졀ᄒᆞ되회로쟝을시닷ᄒᆞ고ᄃᆞ ᄒᆞ엿더라

○조계ᄎᆞ흥 창원흥리현협무 ᄉᆞ쟈가외부로보고ᄒᆞ기를일본영 ᄉᆞ가조회ᄒᆞ기를죡조계일본이 ᄂᆞᆫ 사회되단을쟝졋빈ᄒᆞ고로외 자공하ᄎᆞ탐ᄒᆞ라ᄒᆞ고로의계호 셔총세무사빈닉와ᄉᆞ팡에ᄉᆞ 랑ᄒᆞ야쳥ᄉᆞ를ᄉᆞ 에 ᄒᆞ엿더라

○보쳥구라 평주젼군슈빅병 의을란쳥ᄎᆞ얌샹ᄒᆞᆫ히ᄒᆞ다가괴경 은문시가되엿더니경샹북도슌 챵사ᄒᆞ유셔ᄒᆡ기박군슈의쟝젼 을로면ᄒᆞ야졍부로보ᄒᆞ고ᄒᆞ던 케ᄒᆞ야샹부로상ᄒᆞᆫ을쳥ᄒᆞ지라 에셔방부로쵸회ᄒᆞ기를보병익 을곳ᄎᆞ라귀ᄒᆞᄐᆡᆨᄒᆞ엿더라

○쳥샹의탁 회셔 ᄒᆞᆫ쥬평셰포 에서청국샹샹순평빙이리셔괴 셩ᄒᆞ셔ᄌᆞ으로영경빙ᄒᆞ ᄉᆞ롤가 회ᄒᆞ고외방받후에셔도라가 역판비방부과현정에셔의공 차샹ᄒᆞᆫ즈ᄂᆞᆫ잇소되ᄒᆞ야곳치ᄂᆞᆫ 에야ᄇᆞ우ᄒᆞ니희울오ᄒᆞ시란 비되한부ᄎᆞ다라

UNION INSURANCE SOCIETY OF CANTON.

Head office Hongkong.
Marine risks underwritten at current rates.

Agents in Chemulpo,
E. MEYER & Co.

COMPAGNIE DES MESSAGERIES MARITIMES.

Fortnightly Direct Service.

For Marseilles
via Ports.
Sailing from Yokohama
Calling at Kobe,
Shanghai, Hongkong, Saigon, Singapore,
Colombo, Djibonti, Suez, Port Said
and Marseilles.

For particulars apply to
HOLME RINGER & Co.,
Chemulpo.

HAYASHIDA & CO.,

16 MYENG DONG, CHIN KO KAI, SEOUL.
BRANCH OFFICE AT CHEMULPO.

Money changers, Coal and Wood Merchants, Express Agents.

We are agents for the Pyeng-yang Coal Company and the Karazu Coal Company of Japan. We have the best quality of both anthracite and bituminous coal, and prompt execution of orders is our speciality. Firewood of all kinds kept in stock. Full weight guaranteed. Money of all denominations exchanged at current rates. Parcels received for all parts.

CHINA MUTUAL LIFE INS. OC.

Most favourable terms to policy holders.

Benefit system unsurpassed.

HOLME RINGER & Co.
Agents, Chemulpo.

C. P. R.

CANADIAN PACIFIC RAILWAY COMPANY'S ROYAL MAIL STEAMSHIP LINE.

THE FAST ROUTE BETWEEN CHINA, JAPAN, AND EUROPE VIA CANADA AND THE UNITED STATES.

Route from Hongkong via Shanghai, Nagasaki (Inland Sea of Japan) Kobe, Yokohama Victoria and Vancouver.

Twin Screw Empress Steamship—6,000 Tons—Speed 19 knots.

PROPOSED SAILING FROM YOKOHAMA.

R. M. S. Empress of India.
R. M. S. Empress of Japan.
R. M. S. Empress of China.
R. M. S. Athenian.
R. M. S. Tartar.

Special reduction (first class only) granted to members of the Military, Naval, Diplomatic and Civil services and to Missionaries.

Passengers have choice of ten routes across the Continent of America and have privilege of travelling by any Atlantic Steamship Line.

Round the World passage tickets in connection with the P. and O. S. N., North German Lloyd and Messageries Co.'s £125.

All rates payable at current rate of exchange.

For further information, Tickets, Guide Books, etc., apply to

HOLME, RINGER & Co., AGENTS,
Chemulpo.

Grand Hotel,

(Formerly the Station Hotel)

Near the Railway Terminus.
West Gate Seoul.

The Best Hotel in Korea.
Handsome new Building.
Fine Airy Rooms
Excellent Cuisine.
Terms Moderate.
Special terms to Missionaries
and to permanent boarders.

Electric cars within 2 minutes' walk.

W. H. EMBERLEY.
Proprietor

EVERY FACILITY.

In connection with Life Assurance Business is afforded by

The Standard Life Assurance Co.,

One of the largest and wealthiest of the Provident Institutions of the United Kingdom Forms of Application and all information will be promptly afforded on application.

10 CENTS A DAY.

Not a very large expenditure is it? But it is sufficient to secure for a man of 30 a policy with the STANDARD LIFE OFFICE for

$1323.

For all particulars of rates, etc., apply to

Holme, Ringer & Co.,
Agents, Chemulpo.

THE NEW YORK LIFE INSURANCE COMPANY.

Have you ever been declined by any Company?

Are you engaged in a specially hazardous occupation?

Have you heard of the New York Life Insurance Company's New Classifications for this class of Risks?

If not, send your date of birth, occupation and particulars of rejection, if any to

E. MEYER & Co.,
Agents, Chemulpo.

MITSUI BUSSAN KAISHA.
(MITSUI & Co.)

MITSUI GINKO.
(MITSUI BANK.)

The Bank is owned by the members of the Mitsui Family, who, as partners, assume an unlimited responsibility for all liabilities of the Bank:—

Capital.......................Yen 5,000,000
Reserve Fund.................." 5,600,000

HEAD OFFICE, TOKYO.

LONDON OFFICE, 34 LIME ST., E. C.

BRANCHES AND AGENCIES:—
New York, San Francisco, Hamburg, Bombay, Singapore, Manila, Hongkong, Amoy, Chefoo, Tientsin.

Kobe, Hakodate, Yokohama, Kure, Yokosuka, Moji, Shimonoseki, Miike, Wakamatsu, Nagasaki, Kuchinotsu, Karatsu, Sasebo, Misume, Taipeh, &c.

Telegraphic Address for all the Offices
"MITSUI."

A. B. C. AND A. I CODES USED.

Contractors of Coal

To the Imperial Japanese Navy. Arsenals and Railway Bureau, Principal Railway Companies and Industrial Work, Home and Foreign Mail and Freight Steamers.

Sole Proprietors

Of the famous Miike, Tagawa and Yamano Coal Mines.

Sole Agents

For the sale of Fukumo, Hokoku, Ichimura, Kanoda, Mannoura, Onoura, Ostuji, Sonoda, Tsubaruro, Yoshinotani, Yoshio, Yurokibura and other coals.

YANGTSE INSURANCE ASSOCIATION, LTD.

The undersigned, having been appointed agents for the above company, are prepared to issue policies and pay losses on marine risks at regular rates.

E. MEYER & Co.,
Agents, Chemulpo.

AMERICAN KOREAN ELECTRIC CO.

Light and Power.

Main Office: Electric Building, Chong No.

RAILWAY DEPARTMENT.

OPERATING CARS BETWEEN EAST AND WEST GATE, EVERY TEN MINUTES:—

First Car leaves East Gate at 7:00 A. M. First Car leaves R. R. Station at 7:25 A. M
Last Car " East Gate at 9:40 P. M. Last " " R. R. Station at 10:05 P.M

OPERATING CARS BETWEEN EAST GATE AND IMPERIAL TOMB TERMINUS, EVERY TWENTY MINUTES:—

CONNECTING WITH EVERY ALTERNATE CAR ARRIVING AT EAST GATE FROM CHONG NO.

First Car leaves East Gate for Tomb at 7:10 A. M.
" " " Tomb for East Gate at 7:35 A. M.
Last " " East Gate for Tomb at 7:50 P. M.
" " " Tomb for East Gate at 8:10 P. M.

OPERATING CARS BETWEEN CHONG NO AND YUNG SAN RIVER EVERY TWELVE MINUTES:—

First Car leaves Chong No for South Gate at 7:12 A. M.
" " " Chong No for Yung San at 7:36 A. M.
" " " South Gate for Chong No at 7:20 A. M.
" " " Yung San for Chong No at 8:09 A. M.
Last " " South Gate for Chong No 10:00 P. M.
" " " Yung San for Chong No at 9:33 P. M.

SPECIAL PRIVATE CARS FURNISHED TO SUIT CONVENIENCE OF PATRONS. PRICES ON APPLICATION AT HEAD OFFICE.

LIGHTING DEPARTMENT.

Where less than 250 candle power of light is used, the rate per month will be

Per 16 candle power incandescent lamp,—All night.—Yen 2.50.
32 candle power incandescent lamp:—All night:—Yen 4.00.
50 candle power incandescent lamp:—All night:—Yen 6.00.
150 " " " " " " " 10.00.
1200 " " enclosed are " " " " 20.00.

Where more than 250 candle power of light is used, a Meter will be installed, freqvedted:—Rent of Meter Yen 2.00 per month. Rate of charges by meter reading:—Two Sen per Ampere per hour. (Approximately this is equal to about One Sen per 16 C. P. lamp per hour) Minimum monthly charge where meter is inStalled, Yen 20.00 per month, which includes rental of meter.

Estimates for installing lights furnished on application

An assortment of chandeliers always on hand.

K. Murakami.

Photograph Studio
Chinkokai, Seoul.

Printing, Developing and Enlargement, of Photographs always Undertaken.

Korean Views and Pictures Illustrating Native Customs always on Sale,

THE OSAKA SHOSEN KAISHA.

Boats frequently on the berth for Chinnampo.

REGULAR SAILINGS BETWEEN JAPAN AND KOREAN PORTS.

FUSAN AND KOBE VIA SHIMONOSEKI.

OSAKA VIA MOKPO, FUSAN, SHIMONOSEKI AND KOBE.

MOJI DIRECT.

OSAKA VIA KUNSAN, MASANPO, FUSAN, SHIMONOSEKI AND KOBE.

CHEMULPO KUNSAN LINE,
Every three days.

CHEMULPO CHINNAMPO LINE.
Every three days.

For Freight and passage and further particulars apply to

THE OSAKA SHOSEN KAISHA,
Chemulpo.

RONDON, PLAISANT & CO.

General Storekeepers and Merchants, Ships Contractors, Tobacconists, Commission and Forwarding Agents, Coal Merchants

IMPORTERS AND EXPORTERS

Seoul & Chemulpo.

W. D. WENTWORTH.

LANDING
AND
SHIPPING AGENT
AND
CUSTOMS BORDER.

12 OURA, NAGASAKI.

STEWARD & CO.

Chemulpo.

Shipchandlers and Storekeepers, Naval and Mercantile Contrrctors, Landing and Shipping Agents.

STEWARD'S HOTEL

Chemulpo.

Best accommodation in the port for travelliers. Clean and well-aired rooms, good cuisine and prompt attendence, moderate tariff.

관보

뎨삼쳔삭칠호 광무팔년
십이월이십삼일
서임급ᄉ령

○임농상공부상공국장서주임관일등 졍삼품 송리헌
십이월십칠일

○임탁지부인쇄국기수서주임관삼등 젼뎐환국기수 리티응○임탁지부인쇄국기수서주임관오등 젼뎐환국기수 유진호 ○임탁지부인쇄국기ᄉ서주임관륙등 젼뎐환국기ᄉ 리상졀 ○임탁지부인쇄국주ᄉ서판임관일등 젼뎐환국주ᄉ 리용팔○임탁지부인쇄국주사서판임관삼등 젼뎐환국주사 쟝후 ○임탁지부인쇄국주사서판임관ᄉ등 젼뎐환국주사 안봉흠 젼뎐환국주사 안승렬 ○임탁지부인쇄국기수서판임관일등 젼뎐환국기수 리항일 ○임탁지부인쇄국기수서판임관이등 젼뎐환국기수 박두희 ○임탁지부인쇄국기수서판임관사등 젼뎐환국기수 김익종 젼뎐환국기수 박셩우 젼뎐환국기수 최호원 젼뎐환국기수 림시틱 젼뎐환국기수 조종욱 젼뎐환국기수 오대근
이상십이월십구일

○명시종원경서칙임관삼등 궁내부특진관 남뎡쳘 ○명쟝례원소경서칙임관삼등 시강원참사 조동완 ○명궁내부특진관서칙임관사등 종이품 윤상학 ○명경영시강원첨사 비서원겸 리지현
이상십이월이십일

○의원면본관 후릉참봉 홍덕주 영릉참봉 홍문관시독 신용우 안릉참봉 리승회 경릉참봉 송대진 화릉참봉 김석하 귀ᄌ릉참봉 윤자익○면본관 졍릉령 리종셕

○희시종원분시어 리시용 홍치련 덕환봉 송문현

○임홍릉신사면화파주사서판임관팔등 최귀승 유홍시 송병구 박병치 안종유 ○임평도원주사서판임관팔등 최응렬 황석연 신병익 윤병석 박지규 됴병호 한상니 리교우 박셩우 강주훈 김종빈 리홍치

○임후릉참봉서판임관팔등 윤종을 ○임영릉참봉서판임관팔등 허진구 ○임경릉면참봉서판임관팔등 김준희 ○임화릉참봉서판임관팔등 김영표 ○임귀ᄌ릉참봉서판임관팔등 김상형 ○임졍릉령서판임관칠등 창릉령 김히수 ○임창릉령서판임관칠등 효릉령 유희종

○임효릉령서판임관칠등 명릉령 윤교셩

○임영릉령서판임관칠등 태릉수주수 홍승범

○임태릉수주수서판임관칠등 돈령원주수 민회식
임홍문관시독서판임관수등 륙품 박희쳘

○임돈령원주수서판임관칠등 교방수주수 홍진표

○임안릉참봉서판임관팔등 리영관

○의원면본관 농상공학교셔긔 송무용

○임농상공학교서긔서판임관륙등 김영션

○급안릉봉 농상공부상공국쟝 송리헌
이상십이월이십일일

론셜

젼호련쇽

○군ᄉ롤은무수히죽이고엇더ᄒᆞᆫ족지금우리의잇ᄂᆞᆫ셩칙을ᄯᅩ다시ᄲᅢ아ᄉᆞ랴ᄒᆞᆯ진ᄃᆡ우리ᄂᆞᆫ주린ᄒᆞᆯ터이나그러ᄒᆞ나그황인종젹군의무섭게죽ᄂᆞᆫ거슬엇지츙아보리오만일병이우리의잇ᄂᆞᆫ곳을졈령ᄒᆞ려ᄒᆞᆯ지경이면불가불우리의보호ᄒᆞ랴고반드리노ᄒᆞᆫ연고권셜과ᄉᆡᆼ에무든히다ᄒᆞᆫ지라포가모도일병의수중에드러가야ᄒᆞᆯ터인ᄃᆡ

만일이문건들을취ᄒᆞ랴고ᄒᆞᆯ진ᄃᆡ젼진ᄒᆞᄂᆞᆫ동안에일부장즁이번져모도죽을터인지라젹병들은호욕ᄒᆞᆷ이비ᄒᆞᆯ터엿스며ᄯᅩᄒᆞᆫ세계에상등군병일죵이리케ᄒᆞ고라도취ᄒᆞᆫ조ᄂᆞᆫ외사가잇슬진ᄃᆡ우리ᄂᆞᆫ셔로ᄃᆡ젹ᄒᆞ야항거ᄒᆞ기젼에번져되게ᄒᆞ여야ᄒᆞᆯ터인ᄃᆡ이제일병들은우리를포회ᄒᆞ라고ᄒᆞᄂᆞᆫ모양인죽이ᄂᆞᆫ실로위름ᄒᆞᆫ경광을당ᄒᆞ랴고자취ᄒᆞᆯ인지라필경당ᄒᆞᆫ후에야귀왕비ᄅᆞ스최긴써의문리ᄒᆞ고그린슐이미이일을즁조ᄒᆞ야졈감지젼으미리뵈난쥴로셰덧고응당그리ᄒᆞᆯ무른터인지라

그ᄯᅢ에동ᄉᆡ가그린거랑인죵우리나라성취들을모도지뢰포를무터보호ᄒᆞ게ᄒᆞ고면귀련션을사방으로느리노와젹병들로ᄒᆞ여여금흠셰웅취ᄒᆞ여죽ᄂᆞᆫ모양으로그리ᄒᆞ엿ᄂᆞᆫᄃᆡ

낫에ᄂᆞᆫ폭발ᄒᆞᄂᆞᆫ탄환이비오듯ᄒᆞᄂᆞᆫ중에죽은자ᄂᆞᆫ길이메여장바젓고병상ᄉᆞ졸들은우리진중병원에셔치료ᄒᆞ기에수고롤도리여밧ᄂᆞᆫ모양과

밤에ᄂᆞᆫ젹병들이비밀히우리의진을범ᄒᆞ랴ᄒᆞ야젼진ᄒᆞ다가면귀뢰션과운에모도몰즁으로셰을나가하ᄂᆞᆯ에게신ᄒᆞᄂᆞᆫ념을ᄒᆞᆷ셰뵈옹케될터인ᄃᆡ아모소리도못ᄒᆞ고죽어무론아모라도ᄊᆡ홈ᄒᆞᄂᆞᆫ거ᄉᆞᆫ보되듯나ᄂᆞᆫ소리ᄂᆞᆫ도모지업ᄂᆞᆫ양으로ᄒᆞ엿ᄂᆞᆫ지라

하로ᄂᆞᆫ명랑ᄒᆞᆫ달밤인ᄃᆡ벼가엣수산이라ᄒᆞᄂᆞᆫ곳에을나우리나라군ᄉᆞ들의공격ᄒᆞᆷ으로써젹병들의죽ᄂᆞᆫ모양을살펴본즉ᄃᆡ포로발사ᄒᆞᆷ에죽ᄂᆞᆫ자ㅣ련쇽ᄒᆞ야길이메엿ᄂᆞᆫᄃᆡ그참광의셤요ᄒᆞᆷ은가히ᄒᆞᆫ경치를이롤만ᄒᆞ며ᄯᅩᄒᆞᆫ우리의쳘션ᄂᆞ린노ᄒᆞᆫ우ᄒᆞ로졈졈찻가히젼진ᄒᆞᆯ수룩죽ᄂᆞᆫ거슨볼진ᄃᆡ우리나라군병이요슐부리ᄂᆞᆫ깃곳흔거시우리의게로찻가히발ᄒᆡ들수륙지뢰포가터지며쌍이ᄊᆡ지며공중으로불ᄭᅵᄂᆡ올나갓다가다시ᄶᅡ우ᄒᆞ로ᄯᅥ러지ᄂᆞᆫᄃᆡ [미완]

잡보

○경졀졍보 작일로일은예수탄일인고로경츅ᄒᆞ기위ᄒᆞ야량일간뎡간ᄒᆞ엿다가수요일부터속간ᄒᆞᆯ터이오니죠량ᄒᆞ시오

○하불기셩 송현에사ᄂᆞᆫ엄씨한아히잇ᄉᆡ부모를떠의교수양부의게ᄌᆞ라ᄂᆞᆫ지라지금사ᄉᆡᆼ며ᄲᅢ가되도록수양부양ᄉᆡᆼ으로힝세ᄒᆞᆫ다더라

○의졍쟉교 상대쟝일하오세시에윤의졍이쟉교ᄒᆞ엿ᄂᆞᆫᄃᆡ년세가팔순이라더라

○일관공함 일공관에서외부로공함ᄒᆞ되쟝간귀죠ᄒᆞ엿든본관일등셔긔관츄원과및시로퇴명ᄒᆞᆫ본관외교관보소아인래량이가쟈이십일에챵임ᄒᆞ엿기에공포ᄒᆞᆫ다ᄒᆞ엿더라

○영관공함 영공관에서외부로공함ᄒᆞ되본관과송ᄒᆞᆫ빗위원의면보니기에귀부파원이연일방쳥ᄒᆞ고긔옥심ᄒᆞ지아니ᄒᆞ니다시리지못ᄒᆞ갯다ᄒᆞ엿기에포ᄒᆞ고ᄒᆞ노나쳥컨ᄃᆡ죠량관리ᄒᆞ라ᄒᆞ엿더라

○쳥숙불쟝 비지발 주미공관에셔외부로보고ᄒᆞ기를외교관보쟝비규츅을실시ᄒᆞᆫ지오린로ᄃᆡ본관셔긔졍김윤창이가시무ᄒᆞᆫ지여러날이로ᄃᆡ봉쟝비를일ᄐᆡ셔지주지아니ᄒᆞ니회가엣일빗이십원을곳지발ᄒᆞ야부쳐보니라ᄒᆞ엿더라

○면ᄒᆞᆫ휘주파원 외부에셔휘주파원리근츈의게면훈ᄒᆞ기를즁민이쳥원을써렷다ᄒᆞ고ᄯᅩ쳥인이죽지아니ᄒᆞ엿다ᄒᆞ니과연시뢰가잇ᄂᆞ냐엇지ᄒᆞ야자셰히보고치아니ᄒᆞᄂᆞ냐ᄒᆞ엿더라

○일사폐현 금일에일공사가각부대신과외부고문관스티분씨와츄원슈일셰들듸동ᄒᆞ고폐현ᄒᆞᆫ다더라

○상업상회설시 일본죠계민유명과밋김영진씨등이통동ᄒᆞ야상업상회라명칭ᄒᆞ고창고회사경미소를남분졍거쟝일ᄉᆞ너딕단에서셜치ᄒᆞᄂᆞᆫᄃᆡ쳥금김영진씨가이만오천원을지츌ᄒᆞᆫ다더라

○샹죵주ᄉᆞ교육의견 교원리승교씨포의방셩신공우세ᄂᆞᆫ본시지쳥에셔렬분명쟝수영병학교와식발달시연구ᄒᆞ야전국권면동유교ᄒᆞᆫ덕니금추관계리명쇼에서들에셔국ᄒᆞᆫ번엿ᄂᆞᆫ졔티들경항ᄒᆞᆯ의전호에학비금을순츄로빈졍ᄒᆞ고향ᄒᆞ야민간중에학교를각읍에젼국광셜ᄒᆞᆫ고녀교령지학비로ᄂᆞᆫ강자형ᄒᆞᆫ상페하의교로문교육명에치를티양ᄒᆞ엿더라

○단상상소 국제강등수로송쳥병셜위과종써가상소가ᄉᆞᆼ이소ᄒᆞ엿다니젼참일쥬젼에서외수시동노ᄂᆞᆫ각티위에관오인ᄉᆞ에셔슬구라ᄒᆞᄂᆞᆫ코로남셔오다가정의징이에단ᄒᆞᆫ조현병을ᄯᅩ구라ᄒᆞᄂᆞᆫ병기평이금벌사령부로보ᄒᆞ야히위관오인을원에쳑수ᄒᆞ엿다ᄒᆞ엿더라

외보

○로국인돈엽지부 금신륙일지부에셔발ᄒᆞᆫ면보를거ᄒᆞᆫ즉금인오후두시에모포와식요셔류등을휴티ᄒᆞᆫ로국인쳘명이ᄊᆞᆫ데빈다란본향에원은에동데드린고로드리ᄂᆞᆫ것이잇ᄂᆞᆫ밤을탄지라셔도망ᄒᆞ야국원이군관ᄒᆞᆫ등에의론ᄒᆞ엿다더라

○영국무관보고 본돈셔발ᄒᆞᆫ면보를거ᄒᆞᆫ즉일본군에종수ᄒᆞᆫ영국무관의보고ᄒᆞᆫ바에일영국군이잇ᄂᆞᆫ곳쳬ᄒᆞᆯ지칭ᄒᆞ엿ᄂᆞᆫ티모ᄒᆞ야다ᄒᆞ엿다더라

○영국취군 영국군귀항의관병ᄒᆞᆫ바청국의포진ᄒᆞ고의죠사를기록케ᄒᆞᆫ바는의흉관리신천ᄒᆞᆫ엿더라

ᄒᆞᆫ이에병과창셜립 쳥국에셔금회밋귀공고쳥동하셔남제도오셩목하게ᄂᆞᆫ횡중이다히창으로공금과져셔부ᄂᆞᆫ가히알ᄂᆞᆫ슈엽다ᄒᆞ고결과셕이라ᄒᆞ엿더라

뎐보

(련순공위군보고공사관챵뎐)

희서등젼리공능계관산복포디여니ᄋᆞ이셔ᄆᆡᆷ적가히미리ᄉᆡᆼ은이셜사미가포착ᄂᆞᆫ엇ᄉᆞᆫ것이좌와이믄것상ᄒᆞᆫ다ᄉᆞ용미리ᄉᆞ에가당ᄒᆞ며과군중만ᄒᆞᆫ헤포사일문이문은ᄉᆞᆫ만ᄒᆞ셤을빅사쇼ᄉᆞ와과이ᄉᆞ만ᄉᆞ포ᄉᆞ오ᄉᆞ미문쇼다온ᄒᆞ고셜오맛ᄒᆞᆫ이빅과그다ᄒᆞ고과귀포이뎐과밋소츙이라ᄒᆞ엿더라

TELEGRAMS.

Japanese Legation.

Admiral Togo reports that he personally made an inpection of the condition of the Sevastapol on the 21st inst. She was then lying at anchor under Chengtusan about 400 metres from the shore. Her pumps were being busily worked as the damage done by the Japanese torpedoes was great. She is evidently incapacitated from navigation or further fight. One destroyer was also badly damaged.

According to a prisoner captured. eight torpedoes struck the torpedo nets but one struck the hull of the Sevastopol on the starboard quarter. She has taken a list to starboard of at least 10 degrees and her gun ports on the middle deck are nearly submerged.

Japanese Legation.

A report from Port Arthur states that the left wing of the besieging army on Thursday morning occupied a small hill north of Sanyangtu and later after a spirited attack gained some hilly ground near Kinwan (Pigeon Bay) and captured one gun. The Russians made a counter attack, which was however repulsed.

(It is rather difficult to explain the appearance of the *left* wing at Pigeon Bay—Ed. K.D.N.

AMENITIES AT PORT ARTHUR.

An "Osaka Mainichi" correspondent with the Investing Army has sent the following interesting account of the proceedings during the truces for the collection of the dead and wounded on Dec. 2nd and 3rd:—It had been arranged between the Japanese and the Russians that there should be a temporary cessation of hostilities in the direction of the left flank of the Japanese Army, in the neighbourhood of the outer trench of the north battery on Touchikwanshan, but as the Russians were seen to be engaged in preparing embrasures on the top of the inner slope of the trench, the Japanese asked the enemy to abandon the proposed truce. However, after a short time, a Russian soldier appeared in the entrance of the battery and called out in Japanese "Anata oidenasai uchimasen kara." (Please come along as we will not shoot at you). Major Gondo, Commander of the battallion, and several other Japanese officers then ascended the slope to the top. They were there received by the Commander of a Russian Regiment and a number of other officers, who were much pleased at the confidence the Japanese had displayed in thus venturing into their midst, and greeted them with smiles and handshakes. Judging from the cordiality of the meeting, it might have been thought that it was between old friends who had met again after a long separation. The Russians congratulated the Japanese on their healthy appearance after the long investment, and said that the bravery shown by them during the last engagement was almost superhuman. The calmness with which the Japanese met death, they continued, could not be equalled by any other nation. They also thanked the visitors for coming up to their quarters, and offered them some wine. Major Gondo heartily expressed his pleasure at the hospitality of the Russians and chatted with them concerning the severity of the recent fighting. The Japanese then drank the health of the Russian officers, the latter returning the compliment, and they eventually separated with promises to meet again under fire. In the meantime both the Japanese and Russian troops had been actively engaged in carrying away their dead. On December 3rd a similar truce was observed in the vicinity of the main battery on Touchikwashan, a point between the Russian skirmishers' trench and the Japanese advanced trench appointed as a meeting place. From the Russian side, a medical staff officer of the rank of General, who is also a Russian Court Councillor, and over twenty other officers, proceeded to the place of meeting whilst Major Kuwada, Captain Hayashida, and over ten other officers attended there on behalf of the Japanese. They exchanged cards, shook hands, and cordially drank each other's health in bottles of wine with which both the Japanese and the Russians had provided themselves. All appeared to be glad beyond measure to have such an opportunity of clearing away the dead bodies and were anxious to set the world an example of mutual sympathy and good will in the midst of hostilities. They talked together most cordially and a photograph of the group was taken as a souvenir of the unique occasion. If any outsider had been there, he would not have been able to suppose that those present had been fighting against one another. In parting, one of the Russian officers said to the Japanese:—

"The fortress of Port Arthur will not be easily captured. You must be prepared for it to be covered with the corpses of Japanese and Russians before it falls. We, Russians, shall do our best to defend the fortress, and we shall not let you have 203 metre hill without paying very highly. It will be defended to the last man. We are still well provided with wine, provisions and ammunition." He concluded by exclaiming: "God bless you, Japanese." The Japanese officers returned a cordial answer and promised to prove, under fire, how brave and persistent the Japanese can be. Just then Mr. Shiga, a prominent member of the Kenseihonto, who is now with the Investing Army, arrived on the scene and addressed both the Japanese and Russian officers, jocosely, as follows:—"If, after the present war, Japan and Russia should form an alliance, they would not be afraid to fight any Power in the world. Japan could take the aggressive against the enemy while Russia defended the two countries against the foe. Thus the two nations would be able to divide the world between them." Both the Japanese and the Russian officers shouted. "Hear, hear," and clapped their hands at this speech. In the meantime Russian soldiers carried the Japanese dead bodies from the Russian trench to the Japanese lines, and the Japanese conveyed the Russian corpses to the enemey's quarters. Mr. Shiga remarked that it would be impossible to see a more humane and touching spectacle. All the dead bodies having been removed, the Russian and Japanese officers parted on the most friendly terms.—Kobe Herald.

MILITARY SERVICE NOT AN EVIL.

The common impression that the German military system is harmful in its effects and generally opposed by the German people is contradicted by J. L. Bashford in the October "Nineteenth Century." This author regards the German army as an admirable training school for the soldiers:

In addition to their ordinary drill they get plenty of instruction about matters of every-day life, and this serves to sharpen their wits and their memory. They leave their regiment with a stock of increased knowledge, and are physically stronger; and the common soldiers can, if they desire it, acquire a little knowledge of geography, history, and arithmetic; and other instruction is open to them also. If a man capitulates and serves for twelve years, obtaining a good conduct certificate, he is sure of a good appointment in the public service or in private service. Should he prefer to quit at the termination of his two or three years' service, it is quite certain that he will have acquired habits of order and regularity which will serve him in good stead all his life. The experience gained in maneuver time will have widened his vision of things and sharpened his intellect. On return to the occupation of a civilian he is in every sense a more useful man. Every employer of labor will tell you so. The man who has served in the army is preferred to the man who has not served.

It is a matter of common experience that weakly recruits grow strong through the daily training, the regular life, and the good and abundant food they enjoy with the regiment. This applies especially to those who come from the confined occupations of town life. The constant movement in the fresh air restores them to health and strength.

The belief that compulsory service is a serious obstacle to the industrial progress of a nation is also contradicted by Mr. Bashford. He says:

"Admitting to the full that compulsory service entails a certain amount of dislocation in industrial life, it is quite absurd to say that the manhood of the nation is paralyzed in Germany, or that the activity of the whole people is arrested in its development during the time of service. If one goes into the question in an unprejudiced frame of mind, it will be found that, though the workers from the factories and the numerous trades and professions of the country are called upon to interrupt their life's work, every workman stands in this regard on an equality with his fellows. Further, although he is not earning wages for two years when with the colors, he is being kept well in every respect at the expense of the state, and is acknowledged to be acquiring qualities which render him afterwards a more acceptable worker, so that his capital value is substantially greater at the end of his time of service than it was when he joined as a raw recruit. In many cases this capital value becomes considerably enhanced.

The "Eastern World" gives the Russian estimate of casualties in the war as follows:—

Battle places.	Russians.	Japanese.
May 1st Yalu	2,398	1,039
10th Lu-sanli-pan	300	146
26th Kinchow	3,370	4,207
June 1st Tehlitzs	9,270	1,163
27th Fenshui-lien	430	171
July 8th Kaiping	201	153
17th Motienlin	1,000	299
19th Kiao-tan	1000	423
25th Tashi-kiao	2,000	1,077
31st Homuching	4,250	860
Aug 1st Yushu-iintzs and Yantzs-lin	2,000	946
Sept. 4th Liaoyang	25,000	17,537
14 Shaho	49,201	15,879

In round numbers, the Russian casualties accumulate a hundred thousand, while that of the Japanese forty-four thousand.

The Japanese losses at Port Arthur are not mentioned but will amount to fully 50,000 with a large percentage of killed, so that the losses on both sides will be about equal.

Japanese official reports to the contrary notwithstanding, says the "Chefoo Daily News" a great many people are disinclined to give credence to the rumor of the sinking of the Russian ships at Port Arthur by Japanese shells. The feeling prevails here to some extent that the Russians may have seen fit to open the seavalves of vessels with the idea of temporarily submerging them that they might not offer such good targets for the Japanese gunners. This is as popular and common recourse in modern warfare, the majority of the latter-day warships being so built, that they can be submerged and raised without great difficulty. The raising of the Spanish ships at Manila by the Americans was a good example of how easily this can be done. Had the work been accomplished a year earlier all the ships raised, with the exception of those that were sunk by shells, would have been fit for re-entering the service. In the case of the Russian vessels at Port Arthur, they might be sunk and raised three times a month.

Discussing the possibility of peace negotiations between Russia and Japan, the "Eastern World" says:—The question perhaps is as to which of the two is to take the first step. It is very evident that Russia, which was attacked in the middle of the night, can not do so, and the Japanese Government which prepared for this war and opened hostilities as soon as it was ready, does not see its way to face its own people with offers of peace to Russia, for it would probably ask for much more than it would be willing to accept, so that its propositions would be curtly rejected and no second offer could be made.

From a Japan exchange we learn that according to an investigation made by the "Issinkai," the number of Koreans in Seoul who have cut off their top-knots is 168,062. The odd 62 carries conviction, otherwise we should be more sceptical than we are. As it is we think the investigations of the "Issinkai" (whatever it or they may be) are probably not more than 160,000 wide of the mark.

The report that the "Askold" was preparing to escape from Shanghai must be pigeon-holed along with the accounts of the death of Stoessel and like stories, as we learn that a Shanghai telegram states that on the 14th instant the Chinese officials inspected the Russian warships detained at Shanghai and found everything in order. There was no sign of the vessels attempting to make their escape, as had been freely rumoured was the case.

The Il Chin Hoi society, on hearing that the Righteous Army was rising, immediately telegraphed their leaders, endeavouring to secure their support to the Il Chin Hoi cause. The message ran somewhat as follows. "The swindlers of the Government are collecting insurgents to kill all members of our society. We are afraid that you will quarrel with those insurgents, so please come up to Seoul, where you will be safe under our wing, and can assist us in our glorious cause."

This is a world of ups and downs. Just as we hear of the adoption by the Russian Government of a much more liberal attitude toward the press of that country, we hear of the suppression of two Japanese newspapers within a mouth. The latest to go is the "Shakai Shugi," a weekly paper, an organ of the socialists which was suppressed by the Minister for Home Affairs on the ground that it published statements injurious to social order.

In was evening time in a childrens' hospital, and the nurse on duty was giving the little ones their last meal for the day, All, save one, were patiently waiting their turn to be served, the one in question being a little rosy-cheeked convalescent, who was calling lustily for her portion.

"Aren't you just a little impatient, Dorothy?" inquired the kindly nurse, with just a tinge of correction in her tone.

"No, I'm a little she patient."

The Korea Daily News.

Issued at 5 P. M. daily except Sundays.

Rate of Subscription:—

Per Year,............Yen 25.
Per Quarter,..........Yen 7.
Per Month,..........Yen 2.50.

Postage in Korea not charged extra.
Postage abroad charged extra.

Advertisements, 50 sen per day for 1 inch or less.
5 yen per month per inch.
50 yen per year per inch.

All communications to

E. T. BETHELL,
Editor and Publisher,
Pak-tong, Seoul.

NOTICE.

Monday and Tuesday, Dec. 26th and 27th, will be observed as holidays by the Korea Daily News. On these days, the office will be closed and there will be no issue of the paper.

THE BALTIC FLEET.

It is conceded on all sides that the key to success in this war lies in naval supremacy: without a powerful fleet to obstruct Japanese transports Russia will find it difficult, if not impossible, to drive the Japanese out of Manchuria, and on the other hand should Japan lose the absolute command of the sea which she now possesses, she will find her Manchurian Army in the position which Napoleon saw would be his should he undertake an invasion of England. Napoleon said that it would be easy enough to get into England but extremely difficult to get out of it again.

Therefore the arrival of the Baltic squadron in these waters will mark a crisis in the war. The crisis will be a graver one for Japan than for Russia, for in the event of defeat she will have to face the problem of getting her army out of a country which she has invaded by sea, a problem which even Napoleon confessed himself unable to solve. A defeat would be to Russia simply a negative one; leaving Port Arthur out of the question command of the sea would only avail her for offensive tactics, so that even should the whole of the Baltic Squadron be sent to the bottom, Kuropatkin's power of resistance would not be affected.

According to her politicians and newspapers, Japan is only too anxious to try conclusions with the coming fleet, but the frequent attempts to hinder its progress by protests against alleged breaches of neutrality rather incline one to be sceptical on this subject. From such reports as have hitherto been available it has certainly appeared that Japan has all the best of it and the despatch of the Baltic fleet partook more of the nature of a forlorn hope than anything else.

This view, however, is not held by naval experts, and the following extracts from a comparison of the two fleets based upon Jane's War Game, throws new light upon the subject. We may say that this War Game is a kind of chess with warships for pieces. Each warship has a value given to it according to its effectiveness, and can be moved about the table at a rate in strict relation to the speed of the actual vessel which it represents. The Game is played in all the navies of the world and is admittedly a criterion of actual warfare.

The extracts are as follows:—

Now that the Baltic Fleet has made a start for the Far East it may not be without interest to try and arrive at some sort of estimate of how it compares with the hostile fleet it is perhaps destined to meet. But as "counting heads" is about as misleading a method of estimating navies or squadrons as can be devised, it is necessary to employ some other standard of comparison. A classification based on the number of guns or the amount of armour carried is almost equally misleading; but by taking into account the whole of the offensive and defensive qualities of ships of different classes, and giving marks accordingly, it is possible to arrive at a fairly sound basis for comparison. This system has been worked out most carefully and there are tables, which are used by all the navies in the War Game designed by Jane, and it is on these figures that the calculation will be based.

It must, however, be premised that supposing a particular battleship's figure or rating to be expressed as 1, it does not follow that five cruisers whose rating is, 2 would be the equivalent of it; it would be as rational to compare, say, the tactical values of a cavalry and an infantry unit on the basis of their respective weights or speed. The comparison only holds between ships of the same type, i.e., between battleships and battleships, or cruisers and cruisers. The Baltic Fleet then consists—or probably consisted when it started—of seven battle ships, two so-called belted cruisers, and six protected cruisers. Of the battleships four are probably of the new Borodino type, extremely good ships in every way, and they are represented in Jane's table as representing a value of 1 each. Then there is the Osliabya with a value of .9, the Sissoi Veliki .6, and the Navarin .5. The battle squadron then is theoretically capable of being represented when compared with other battle squadrons by the figure 6. If we take it as at least probable that by the time they reach the Far East Port Arthur and the ships lying there can be disregarded, and that the whole Japanese fleet will be available to meet the Russian reinforcements we can compare the value of the opposing forces. The Mikasa, Asahi and Shikshima are worth 1 each, the Fuji and Yashima .8 each—a total of 4.6. The comparison so far is unfavourable to the Japanese. But apart from the indeterminable value of war training and *morale* there is another factor to be taken into consideration, viz., the armoured cruisers on both sides, for, as we know, two at least of the Japanese cruisers took part in the big battle of the 10th August. Now the Russians have two indifferent ships of this classs in the Baltic Fleet, the "Admiral Nakhimoff" and the "Demitri Donskoi," dating back to the 80's and represented numerically by the figure .25. Even supposing them to be foolish enough to take part in an engagement they would only bring up the fighting figure to 6.5; and the Japanese on the other hand possess not only the two really modern cruisers purchased this year from Argentina with a figure of .6, but the six "Asamas" worth the same. Some of these would no doubt be employed in keeping watch over the Vladivostock squadron, but as any one of them is worth as much as the Sissoi Veliki and more than the Navarin they may fairly be expected to be represented in any action. Four of these eight ships being present would at once turn the scale in favour of the Japanese, bringing their figure up to 7 as against the Russian 6.5. The Russian protected cruisers may be left out of consideration altogether, as far as fleet actions are concerned; for experience has shown what fate is likely to befall ships like the Novik, Varyag and Askold in the presence of armoured vessels. But stress must be laid on the fact that Russian gunnery is bad, the crews are new to the ships, some of the latter are certain to break down, and that the whole will be foul with the long sea voyage.

It will be seen from the above that the writer assesses the value of the Russian and Japanese fleet as 6.5 and 7 respectively, but as since the article was written the news of the "Yashima" has been confirmed, the figures now stand at 6.5 for the Russian and 6.2 for the Japanese fleet. There are of course many other factors to be taken into consideration. The Japanese crews have had valuable experience of actual war and the Russian fleet will be perpetually in difficulties owing to the absence of a naval base.

Still the encounter should not be the one-sided affair we have been led to expect; the Russians evidently intend to make a good fight of it or an extremely capable admiral like Rodjestvensky would not be bringing the fleet out to these waters. Some allowance must also be made for damage to Japanese ships of which the world has not been informed.

The Magistrate of Yehchon reports that robbers have burnt down the village of Somangkok in his district.

The Korean Railway office is shortly to be abolished and a Railway Bureau will be established in the Agricultural Department.

On Thursday the Government held a special session to discuss the advisability of appointing military instead of civil magistrates to the northern districts.

At Ibrox Park recently, A. Shrubb, the champion long-distance runner, established two new amateur records. He ran 10 miles in 50 min. 40¼ sec., and covered 11 miles 1137 yards in the hour.

The Government have issued a mandate to the Il Chin Hoi ordering the breaking up of the society on the grounds that its members have committed criminal offences against the Government.

Rumours of a society to be formed by the Japanese Monastery have recently been current and it is now stated that General Yi Chi Yong has been requested to preside over a gathering in connection with this.

A curious error was made in Tokio when the telegram announcing the loss of the "Saiyen" was sent off. The tonnage was given as 1344 tons whereas it is really about 2500. We first noticed the error in the local papers and thought it probably originated locally but as we find the same mistake in China papers, Tokio must be responsible.

The Governor of Chong Chu yesterday telegraphed that 500 members of the Il Chin Hoi society, armed with rifles and swords, entered the town and endeavoured to force a way into the Governor's office. The people are terrorised and are running away from these marauders, who are making senseless demands of the officials.

The Korea Daily News.

VOL. I, SATURDAY, DECEMBER 24, 1904. No. 134

HONGKONG & SHANGHAI BANKING CORPORATION.

Paid-up Capital	$10,000,000
Reserve Fund:—Sterling Reserve	10,000,000
Silver Reserve	7,000,000
	27,000,000
Reserve Liability of Proprietors	10,000,000

HEAD OFFICE, HONGKONG.

London Bankers, London and County Banking Company Limited.

Branches and Agencies, London.

Amoy,	Hankow	Penang,
Bangkok,	Hiogo,	Rangoon,
Batavia,	Iloilo,	Saigon,
Bombay,	Lyons,	San Francisco,
Calcutta,	Manila,	Singapore,
Colombo,	Nagasaki,	Sourabaya,
Foochow,	New York,	Tientsin,
Hamburg,	Peking,	Yokohama,

Credits granted on approved Securities, and every description of Banking and Exchange business transacted.

Drafts granted on London and the chief Commercial places in Europe, India, Australia, America, China and Japan.

HOLME RINGER & Co., AGENTS, CHEMULPO.

HOKURKU DOBOKU KAISHA.

Branch office in Chong Dong, Seoul.

Japanese telephone No. 165

CONTRACT DEPARTMENT.

We can contract to build any building or construction.

MERCHANDISE DEPARTMENT.

We can provide any building material.

We have just contracted to build the new Belgian Legation.

E. MEYER & CO.

Chemulpo.

SOLE AGENTS IN KOREA FOR.

A. T. Morse, Sons & Co.'s "Fresco" Distemper

In all colours ready for use on walls, Ceilings etc.

and

AVENARIUS CARBOLINEUM

A wood-preserving and antiseptic oil preparation

Against decay, dry-rot, fungus and wood-destroying insects.

A large supply always in stock. Prices upon application.

E. MEYER & Co., Chemulpo.

CHARTERED BANK OF INDIA AUSTRALIA & CHINA.

INCORPORATED BY ROYAL CHARTER 1853

HEAD OFFICES:—LONDON.

Paid-up Capital	£800,000
Reserve Liability of Shareholders	800,000
Reserve Fund	800,000

Drafts granted upon all the principal places in the world and every description of Exchange and banking business transacted.

E. MEYER & Co., Agents, Chemulpo.

MITSU BISHI DOCKYARD & ENGINE WORKS, NAGASAKI.

CODE WORD, "DOCK."

A 1, A. B. C., and Engineering Codes used.

DOCK No. 1 (at Tategami).

Extreme Length	523 feet
Length on blocks	513 ,,
Width of Entrance on Top	[illegible] ,,
,, ,, Bottom	77 ,,
Water on Blocks at Spring Tide	26½ ,,

DOCK No. 2 (Mukaijima).

Extreme Length	371 feet
Length on Blocks	360 ,,
Width of Entrance on Top	66 ,,
,, ,, Bottom	53 ,,
Water on Blocks at Spring Tide	22 ,,

PATENT SLIP (at Kosuge).

Can take vessels up to 1,000 tons gross

THE WORKS are well equipped with the LATEST IMPROVEMENTS, and can execute any kind of work in SHIPBUILDING and MARINE ENGINEERING, as well as in REPAIRING of SHIPS.

The COMPANY'S new powerfu steamer OURA-MARU (712 tons, 700 I.H.P.), specially built for SALVAGE PURPOSES, and equipped with necessary gear, is always READY at SHORT NOTICE.

THE METHODIST PUBLISHING HOUSE,

Little West Gate, Seoul.

JOB PRINTING, TYPEWRITER PAPER
CARBON PAPER, VISITING CARDS
STATIONERY, BOOK BINDING
BOOK PUBLISHERS
AMERICAN SCHOOL BOOKS
SPENCERIAN COPY BOOKS
PEN CARBON LETTER AND BILL BOOKS

S.A. BECK, Manager.

DAI-ICHI GINKO.

LIMITED.

(Formerly the First National Bank)

ESTABLISHED 1873

INCORPORATED UNDER PRESENT LAW 1896

Capital	Yen 5,000,000
Reserve Fund	1,500,000

HEAD OFFICE:—TOKIO.

President: Baron SHIBUSAWA.

BRANCHES AND CORRESPONDENTS In the Principal Cities and Towns of Japan.

Interest Allowed on

Fixed deposits 1 year	6½ per cent	
" " 6 months	6 per cent	

Special current accounts 1½ sen daily per Y 100
General " " 1 " " " 100

M. TANAKA, Manager, Chemulpo.

SINGER SEWING MACHINES

씽거즈봉침

SOLE AGENTS FOR KOREA

젼매쇼

HOLME RINGER & CO. Chemulpo.

졔물포 함릉거양힝

KAMEYA & CO.

GENERAL STOREKEEPERS

Chinkokai - - Seoul

(Established 1895, Tokyo)

Confectionery, Hams, Canned Goods, Cutlery, Hirano & Tansan Water, Provisions, Gents, Furnishing goods, Toilet Articles, Travelling Bags, Tobacco, Cigars & Cigarettes Kitchen Utensils. Coffee, Biscuits

Fresh Goods always kept in Stock.

Prices Moderate

Please come and inspect our goods.

NIPPON YUSEN KAISHA.

JAPANESE MAIL STEAMSHIP CO.

UNDER MAIL CONTRACT WITH THE IMPERIAL JAPANESE GOVERNMENT.

European Line

Regular Fortnightly Service between Yokohama Kobe, Moji, Shanghai, Hongkong, Singapore, Penang Colombo, Port Said, Marseilles, London and Antwerp

American Line

Regular Fortnightly Service between Hongkong and Seattle, calling at Shanghai, Moji, Kobe, Yokohama and Victoria, B. C.

Australian Line

Regular weekly Service betwen Japan Ports and Australia, calling at Hongkong and Manila.

(Above Three Lines Suspended until further notice).

Shanghai Line

Weekly Service between Shanghai and Japan Ports

Korea Line

Service Kobe, Moji, Nagasaki, Fusan Chemupo Cheffoo, Taiku.

S. S. Bahelsberg, 2181 tons.

Service Kobe, Moji, Fusan, Chemulpo, Chinnampo

S. S. ARGO, S. S. Ohio.

BORDEN'S CONDENSED MILK CO.

New York, U. S. A.

ALWAYS IN STOCK

Eagle Brand Condensed Milk.

Gold Seal Condensed Milk.

Peerless (Family) Evaporated Cream.

Borden's Malted Milk.

E. MEYER & CO. Chemulpo Korea, Sole Agents

ROYAL INSURANCE COMPANY.

Funds exceed £10,000,000

FIRE

AT CURRENT RATES.

LIFE

REDUCED PREMIUM.

HOLME RINGER & Co., Agents, Chemulpo.

HOTEL DU PALAIS

SEOUL.

The only first class Hotel in Seoul Situated in the centre of the city opposite the palace.

Cuisine under the supervision of an experienced French Chef.

Well ventilated and furnished throughout.

TARIFF UPON APPLICATION

L. MARTIN

Proripetor and Manager

大韓每日申報
대한ᄆᆡ일신보

(뎨일빅삼십오호) (목요일) 일쳔구빅사년 십이월 이십구일

본샤고빅

이신보는영어와한국문로셔계리
헐츌판ᄒᆞᆸ

신문가
한쟝 엽젼두돈오푼
일삭됴 엽젼팔냥닷돈
우표가ᄆᆡ삭닷돈
다맛돈으로밧ᄉᆞᆸ

광고료는
귀한의쟝단과조항의다쇼로즁간ᄒᆞᆫ되쳥가로밧을터이오며오린지아녀대한사람마다이신문을보실터이니광고내시기를원ᄒᆞ시는이들은우리신문샤에와셔변약ᄒᆞ심을희망ᄒᆞᆸ

○발ᄒᆡᆼ소 박동대한ᄆᆡ일신보사무아하무료합희젼영국인셜필림졍자리오
사쟝 영국인 (비셜)

평양 ᄃᆡ리졈

○평양효동사는권미보씨로우리신문판매ᄃᆡ리인을뎡ᄒᆞ엿시ᄂᆞ오니평양에계신구람ᄒᆞ는 쳠군ᄌᆞ는ᄒᆞ됴ᄃᆡ리졈에왕림ᄒᆞ와면의ᄒᆞ시옵

사고

○우리대한ᄆᆡ일신보의목뎍은대한의인민젼톄에관한모든ᄃᆡ목에ᄃᆡᄒᆞ야는공평한변론을쥬쟝홈이라우리통신원의탐보는신문보시는쳠군ᄌᆞ의게ᄒᆞᆼ샹보도ᄒᆞ리며편지들귀셔ᄒᆞ며주시는이는셩명과번디를젹어붓치시기를희망ᄒᆞ오니이거ᄉᆞᆫ신문샹에게ᄌᆡᄒᆞ라는거시아니오다만귀ᄒᆞᆫ신용ᄒᆞ는증거를삼고자홈이라귀자는아모귀셔던지괴지ᄒᆞᆷ을퇴각ᄒᆞ는권리를가졋스나퇴각ᄒᆞ는리유를말ᄒᆞᆯ터이오며공즁광고ᄂᆞᆫ문란케ᄒᆞ는듯ᄒᆞᆫ귀셔는의례히밧지안케ᄉᆞᆸ나이다

●본샤셜시이래로신문을ᄆᆡ냥우편로분젼ᄒᆞ와혜젼부의일의로젼ᄒᆞᆫ즉스로번곳에는혹늣게젼ᄒᆞ기도ᄒᆞ며혹멋칠지ᄂᆞᆺ혼일에젼ᄒᆞ기도ᄒᆞ며혹아니젼ᄒᆞᆫ는곳도잇다ᄒᆞ와우리신문을ᄉᆞ랑ᄒᆞ야구람ᄒᆞ시는 쳠군ᄌᆞ의게ᄃᆡᄒᆞ야ᄆᆡ우미안ᄒᆞ옵기로지금은분젼인을두고ᄆᆡ일일즉이젼ᄒᆞ며아니젼ᄒᆞ거나늣게거나ᄒᆞᄂᆞᆫ폐가업도록ᄒᆞ라ᄒᆞ오니혹아니젼ᄒᆞ거ᄂᆞ혹늣게젼ᄒᆞ거나ᄒᆞᆫ일이잇스면본샤로통긔ᄒᆞ여주심을희망ᄒᆞᆸ

잡보

○장진진보회 장진군슈리종션씨가ᄂᆡ부로보고ᄒᆞ기를소위진보회원이빅여명이본군에리도ᄒᆞ야일졔히단발ᄒᆞ고귀회ᄒᆞ야연셜ᄒᆞ는ᄃᆡ 황실을존즁히ᄒᆞ며독립긔초를견고케ᄒᆞ며졍치를기션ᄒᆞ며인민의싱명과ᄌᆡ산을보호ᄒᆞᆫ다ᄒᆞ엿다더라

○호례졍쳡 덕국인의거덕이가한졍갑대관의계졍쳡ᄒᆞ기를금이십구일목요일에북의녀셔이ᄂᆡ부고문관ᄃᆡ일광의계츌가ᄒᆞ는ᄃᆡ당일상오열졈에죵현텬쥬교당에셔셩례ᄒᆞ고열ᄒᆞᆫ졈에졍동손탁부인집에셔진치를베셜ᄒᆞ오니계귀ᄒᆞ야광림ᄒᆞ심을바라노라ᄒᆞ엿더라

○좌도구라 졍부에셔경무쳥으로훈령ᄒᆞ야좌도요술로혹세무민ᄒᆞ는자를무론남녀ᄒᆞ고착치ᄒᆞ야엄징ᄒᆞ라ᄒᆞᆫ지라즁ᄎᆡ츄원칙임의관강홍대최병쥬셩광호샹인을경무쳥에셔장ᄎᆡ뎍치ᄒᆞᆯ수로법부에셔구라 쥬본ᄒᆞ엿는ᄃᆡ희샹인은미리알고이믜피신ᄒᆞ엿더라

○슉청공금 뎨실졔도졍리국으로령ᄒᆞ사 궁금을슉쳥ᄒᆞ야듀뱔이방법을세우라신지죠칙을나리신지라경위원총쇼관이강졍문에셔츌립ᄒᆞ는ᄃᆡ쇼리들엄히수힘ᄒᆞ는다ᄒᆞ더라

○샹젼회사쳥원 ᄂᆡ부과슈리호영등이농샹공부에쳥원ᄒᆞ기를랑샹원동포에샹젼회사를셜치ᄒᆞ고샹민과셥쳑을신칙ᄒᆞ야졈찰ᄒᆞ겟다ᄒᆞ엿는ᄃᆡ그됴목은좌와굿ᄒᆞ니

일은 원동셰소에셔는ᄂᆡ장원편할노소금과쌀과콩에ᄃᆡ셕에엽엿돈만슈쇄홀ᄉᆞ

이ᄂᆞᆫ 세감이가세라칭ᄒᆞ는ᄆᆡ셕ᄒᆞᆫ량ᄂᆡ에ᄂᆡ돈을갑ᄒᆞ고엿돈은본샤로부속ᄒᆞ야일년에ᄉᆞ쳔원은샹납ᄒᆞ고ᄉᆞ쳔원은ᄌᆞ본ᄒᆞ고이쳔원은ᄉᆞ즁경비로쓸ᄉᆞ

삼은 ᄆᆡᆫ양슈샹포와샹탕포와의랑박진포와깁히ᄉᆞ항포와츄계물지포에셔쳥세밧는거ᄉᆞᆫ혁파홀ᄉᆞ

ᄉᆞ은 샹납은ᄆᆡ년으로위시ᄒᆞ야ᄉᆞ쳔원을츈츄량등으로샹납홀ᄉᆞ

오ᄂᆞᆫ 세감이ᄆᆡ셕엿돈외에만일ᄒᆞᆫ닙이라도더밧으면엄징ᄒᆞ며금단ᄒᆞᆯ거시오본셰샹납은봉츄ᄒᆞ야거힝ᄒᆞᆯ사

○리씨도경 리용익씨가미샹사일에부산에도박ᄒᆞ야긔초를밧타고이싱동일하오팔시에문밧뎡거장에도착ᄒᆞ미그집안사룸들이영졉ᄒᆞ러만히나갓더라

○일진회경계 일진회에셔는각ᄃᆡ방에의병이니러나일진회를방히ᄒᆞ러홈을알고이번에각ᄃᆡ방지회에ᄃᆡᄒᆞ야훈령ᄒᆞ기를만일의병이쟉동ᄒᆞ야우리회원의계위티홈을ᄭᅵ치려ᄒᆞ는경우에ᄂᆞ니르거든각ᄃᆡ방지회회원를이ᄃᆡ오를편셩ᄒᆞ야엄슉ᄒᆞᆫ진셔를보젼ᄒᆞ야셩경ᄒᆞ라ᄒᆞ고려ᄒᆞᆫ번본회에셔는각회원을신분보호홀방칙을취ᄒᆞ겟노라ᄒᆞ엿더라

○평도수샹 경부텰도준거가츄풍령을지나니디가케도밧고로셰력져일은이명은즁샤ᄒᆞ고샴명은부샹ᄒᆞ엿다더라

○군인군슈 일젼에졍부에셔회의ᄒᆞᆫ기를북도ᄃᆡ방관은군인으로써임명ᄒᆞ야군졍과민졍을통할케ᄒᆞᆫ다더라

○고문방문 거이십샹일하오이두시에외부고문관슈지분씨가외부에처음으로방문ᄒᆞ엿더라

○젼주회민 젼라북도관찰ᄉᆞ가거이십이일에ᄂᆡ부로뎐보ᄒᆞ기를작일에회민ᄉᆞ오빅명이혹총도베ᄒᆞ고혹검도가지고혹말도ᄐᆞ고몃포졍문으로드러와셔화당으로드러오라고ᄒᆞ며ᄯᅩ작쳥에셔두류ᄒᆞ려ᄒᆞ기로응치아니ᄒᆞᆫ즉도로나갓는ᄃᆡ민졍이ᄃᆡ단히쇼요ᄒᆞ다ᄒᆞ엿고

그잇흔날에ᄯᅩ뎐보ᄒᆞ기를리병원이가회쟝이라칭ᄒᆞ고수ᄃᆡ쟝령을샹부로보고ᄒᆞ야셜시케ᄒᆞ죠라ᄒᆞ고셔함으로쳥ᄒᆞ엿스니엇지쳐ᄒᆞ릿가ᄒᆞ엿더라

○희주회민 희주관찰사가ᄂᆡ부로뎐보ᄒᆞ기를음력본월십사일에관하각군인민사오빅명이일진회라칭ᄒᆞ고부하에취회ᄒᆞ엿기로비진히신칙ᄒᆞ야효유ᄒᆞᄆᆡ지금은이믜다히산ᄒᆞ엿다ᄒᆞ엿더라

○졍부조회 의졍부에셔ᄂᆡ부로조회ᄒᆞ기를ᄃᆡ방관을졔잇는ᄃᆡ로취위셔임ᄒᆞ는거시어ᄂᆞ셰인들굽무가아니리오마ᄂᆞᆫᄒᆞᆫ불며오ᄂᆞᆯ날이리오민ᄉᆡᆼ이탕퇴ᄒᆞ고ᄉᆞ번비츄싱ᄒᆞ며ᄯᅩ견셰를슈봉ᄒᆞᄂᆞᆫ배를당ᄒᆞ야과궐된고을에어리들이지니고ᄒᆞ박년이되도록차ᄃᆡ를ᄇᆡ지아니ᄒᆞ고봉고파직된슈령의ᄃᆡ의ᄂᆞᆫ더욱일시가위급ᄒᆞᆫ거ᄂᆞᆯ비록국샹즁에ᄒᆞ교가잣슴을인ᄒᆞ야용무에거를치못ᄒᆞᆫ다ᄒᆞ나민졍과국ᄉᆞ에엇지민망치아니리오현금에궐난군슈들을일ᄂᆡ로셔임ᄒᆞ고쳥의셔를므ᄂᆞᆫ리보ᄂᆡ시고비록쳔에든ᄯᅳᆺ사룸이진지라도불가불경의ᄒᆞᆫ뜻으로일젼괴졔리졍ᄒᆞ는회의셕에셔결졍이되엿시니죠량ᄒᆞ라ᄒᆞ엿더라

○공쥬셔리죠츌 츙쳥남도슌찰ᄉᆞ리시직씨가협도관찰ᄉᆞ의게조회ᄒᆞ기를목쳔군슈박졍빈이가공쥬군슈셔리로잇셔탐학불법ᄒᆞ야졍문이희리ᄒᆞ니위션쵹츌경외ᄒᆞ라ᄒᆞ엿더라

○쳥송화빈낭 쳥송군슈리세영씨가ᄂᆡ부로보고ᄒᆞ기를음력십월십일일광명에화빈당이라칭ᄒᆞ는젹당오륙십명이본군문거동에돌입ᄒᆞ야남녀이십여인을타상ᄒᆞ며지산을탈취ᄒᆞ고곳도쳥으로가셔열아홉집을츙화ᄒᆞ고ᄯᅩ거쳥으로가셔열비집을쇼화ᄒᆞ고ᄯᅩ우미곡으로가셔호집을불질너ᄐᆡ웟고음력십월초십일에는부남면에셔살화ᄒᆞ야일등에십칠호가진쇼ᄒᆞ엿다ᄒᆞ엿더라

○연일화적 연일군슈박민쥰씨가ᄂᆡ부로보고ᄒᆞ기를본월칠일에됴젼리에셔살화ᄒᆞ야십이호가련ᄒᆞ야타ᄂᆞᆺ다ᄒᆞ엿더라

○함창화적 함창군슈김귀수씨가ᄂᆡ부로보고ᄒᆞ기를음력십월초륙일에우연비살화ᄒᆞ야졍쳥외온쾌열세간이몰수히타ᄂᆞᆺ다ᄒᆞ엿더라

○함양화적 함양군슈박졍규씨가ᄂᆡ부로보고ᄒᆞ기를음력구월이십오일에갈쳐동에셔살화ᄒᆞ야여듧집이몰수히타ᄂᆞᆺ다ᄒᆞ엿더라

UNION INSURANCE SOCIETY OF CANTON.

Head office Hongkong.
Marine risks underwritten at current rates.

Agents in Chemulpo,
E. MEYER & Co.

COMPAGNIE DES MESSAGERIES MARITIMES.

Fortnightly Direct Service.

For Marseilles
via Ports.
Sailing from Yokohama
Calling at Kobe,
Shanghai, Hongkong, Saigon, Singapore,
Colombo, Djibonti, Suez, Port Said
and Marseilles.

For particulars apply to
HOLME RINGER & Co.,
Chemulpo.

HAYASHIDA & CO.,

16 MYENG DONG, CHIN KO KAI, SEOUL.
BRANCH OFFICE AT CHEMULPO.

Money changers, Coal and Wood Merchants, Express Agents.

We are agents for the Pyeng-yang Coal Company and the Karazu Coal Company of Japan. We have the best quality of both anthracite and bituminous coal, and prompt execution of orders is our speciality. Firewood of all kinds kept in stock. Full weight guaranteed. Money of all denominations exchanged at current rates. Parcels received for all parts.

CHINA MUTUAL LIFE INS. OC.

Most favourable terms to policy holders.

Benefit system unsurpassed.

HOLME RINGER & Co.
Agents, Chemulpo.

C. P. R.

CANADIAN PACIFIC RAILWAY COMPANY'S ROYAL MAIL STEAMSHIP LINE.

THE FAST ROUTE BETWEEN CHINA, JAPAN, AND EUROPE VIA CANADA AND THE UNITED STATES.

Route from Hongkong via Shanghai, Nagasaki (Inland Sea of Japan) Kobe, Yokohama Victoria and Vancouver.

Twin Screw Empress Steamship—6,000 Tons—Speed 19 knots.

PROPOSED SAILING FROM YOKOHAMA.
R. M. S. Empress of India.
R. M. S. Empress of Japan.
R. M. S. Empress of China.
R. M. S. Athenian.
R. M. S. Tartar.

Special reduction (first class only) granted to members of the Military, Naval, Diplomatic and Civil services and to Missionaries.

Passengers have choice of ten routes across the Continent of America and have privilege of travelling by any Atlantic Steamship Line.

Round the World passage tickets in connection with the P. and O. S. N., North German Lloyd and Messageries Co.'s £125.

All rates payable at current rate of exchange.

For further information, Tickets, Guide Books, etc., apply to

HOLME, RINGER & Co., AGENTS,
Chemulpo.

Grand Hotel,

(Formerly the Station Hotel)

Near the Railway Terminus, West Gate Seoul.

The Best Hotel in Korea.
Handsome new Building.
Fine Airy Rooms
Excellent Cuisine.
Terms Moderate.
Special terms to Missionaries
and to permanent boarders.

Electric cars within 2 minutes' walk.

W. H. EMBERLEY.
Proprietor

EVERY FACILITY.

In connection with Life Assurance Business is afforded by

The Standard Life Assurance Co.,

One of the largest and wealthiest of the Provident Institutions of the United Kingdom Forms of Application and all information will be promptly afforded on application.

10 CENTS A DAY.

Not a very large expenditure is it? But it is sufficient to secure for a man of 30 a policy with the STANDARD LIFE OFFICE for

$1323.

For all particulars of rates, etc., apply to

Holme, Ringer & Co.,
Agents, Chemulpo.

THE NEW YORK LIFE INSURANCE COMPANY.

Have you ever been declined by any Company?

Are you engaged in a specially hazardous occupation?

Have you heard of the New York Life Insurance Company's New Classifications for this class of Risks?

If not, send your date of birth, occupation and particulars of rejection, if any to

E. MEYER & Co.,
Agents, Chemulpo.

MITSUI BUSSAN KAISHA.

(MITSUI & Co.)

MITSUI GINKO.

(MITSUI BANK.)

The Bank is owned by the members of the Mitsui Family, who, as partners, assume an unmited responsibility for all liabilities of the Bank:—

Capital........................Yen 5,000,000
Reserve Fund.................. " 5,600,000

HEAD OFFICE, TOKYO.

LONDON OFFICE, 34 LIME ST., E. C.

BRANCHES AND AGENCIES:—
New York, San Francisco, Hamburg, Bombay, Singapore, Manila, Hongkong, Amoy, Chefoo, Tientsin.

Kobe, Hakodate, Yokohama, Kure, Yokosuka, Moji, Shimonoseki, Miike, Wakamatsu, Nagasaki, Kuchinotsu, Karatsu, Sasebo, Misume, Taipeh, &c.

Telegraphic Address for all the Offices:
"MITSUI."
A. B. C. AND A. 1 CODES USED.

Contractors of Coal
To the Imperial Japanese Navy. Arsenals and Railway Bureau, Principal Railway Companies and Industrial Work, Home and Foreign Mail and Freight Steamers.

Sole Proprietors
Of the famous Miike, Tagawa and Yamano Coal Mines.

Sole Agents
For the sale of Fukumo, Hokoku, Ichimura, Kanoda, Mannoura, Onoura, Ostuji, Sonoda, Tsubaruro, Yoshinotani, Yoshio, Yurokibura and other coals.

YANGTSE INSURANCE ASSOCIATION, LTD.

The undersigned, having been appointed agents for the above company, are prepared to issue policies and pay losses on marine risks at regular rates.

E. MEYER & Co.,
Agents, Chemulpo.

AMERICAN KOREAN ELECTRIC CO.

Light and Power.

Main Office: Electric Building, Chong No.

RAILWAY DEPARTMENT.

OPERATING CARS BETWEEN EAST AND WEST GATE, EVERY TEN MINUTES:—

First Car leaves East Gate at 7:00 A. M. First Car leaves R. R. Station at 7:25 A. M
Last Car " East Gate at 8.40 P. M. Last " " R. R. Station at 9.05 P.M

OPERATING CARS BETWEEN EAST GATE AND IMPERIAL TOMB TERMINUS, EVERY TWENTY MINUTES:—

CONNECTING WITH EVERY ALTERNATE CAR ARRIVING AT EAST GATE FROM CHONG NO.

First Car leaves East Gate for Tomb at 7:10 A. M.
" " " Tomb for East Gate at 7:30 A. M.
Last " " East Gate for Tomb at 7:50 P. M.
" " " Tomb for East Gate at 8:10 P. M.

OPERATING CARS BETWEEN CHONG NO AND YUNG SAN RIVER EVERY TWELVE MINUTES:—

First Car leaves Chong No for South Gate at 7:12 A. M.
" " " Chong No for Yung San at 7:36 A. M.
" " " South Gate for Chong No at 7:20 A. M.
" " " Yung San for Chong No at 8:09 A. M.
Last " " South Gate for Chong No 9:00 P. M.
" " " Yung San for Chong No at 8.45. P. M.

SPECIAL PRIVATE CARS FURNISHED TO SUIT CONVENIENCE OF PATRONS. PRICES ON APPLICATION AT HEAD OFFICE.

LIGHTING DEPARTMENT.

Where less than 250 candle power of light is used, the rate per month will be
Per 16 candle power incandescent lamp,—All night.—Yen 2.50.
32 candle power incandescent lamp:—All night:—Yen 4.00.
50 candle power incandescent lamp:—All night:—Yen 6.00.
150 " " " " " " " 10.00.
1200 " " enclosed are " " " " 20.00.

Where more than 250 candle power of light is used, a Meter will be installed, freqvedted:—Rent of Meter Yen 2.00 per month. Rate of charges by meter reading:—Two Sen per Ampere per hour. (Approximately this is equal to about One Sen per 16 C. P. lamp per hour) Minimum monthly charge where meter is installed, Yen 20.00 per month, which includes rental of meter.

Estimates for installing lights furnished on application

An assortment of chandeliers always on hand.

K. Murakami.

Photograph Studio
Chinkokai, Seoul.

Printing, Developing and Enlargement, of Photographs always Undertaken.

Korean Views and Pictures Illustrating Native Customs always on Sale,

---

THE OSAKA SHOSEN KAISHA.

Boats frequently on the berth for Chinnampo.

REGULAR SAILINGS BETWEEN JAPAN AND KOREAN PORTS.

FUSAN AND KOBE VIA SHIMONOSEKI.

OSAKA VIA MOKPO, FUSAN, SHIMONOSEKI AND KOBE.

MOJI DIRECT.

OSAKA VIA KUNSAN, MASANPO, FUSAN, SHIMONOSEKI AND KOBE.

CHEMULPO KUNSAN LINE,
Every three days.

CHEMULPO CHINNAMPO LINE.
Every three days.

For Freight and passage and further particulars apply to

THE OSAKA SHOSEN KAISHA,
Chemulpo.

RONDON, PLAISANT & CO.

General Storekeepers and Merchants, Ships Contractors, Tobacconists, Commission and Forwarding Agents, Coal Merchants

IMPORTERS AND EXPORTERS

Seoul & Chemulpo.

W. D. WENTWORTH.

LANDING
AND
SHIPPING AGENT
AND
CUSTOMS BORDER.

12 OURA, NAGASAKI.

STEWARD & CO.

Chemulpo.

Shipchandlers and Storekeepers, Naval and Mercantile Contrrctors, Landing and Shipping Agents.

STEWARD'S HOTEL

Chemulpo.

Best accommodation in the port for travelliers. Clean and well-aired rooms, good cuisin and prompt attendence, moderate tariff.

○보정법률채 진남군수박일헌씨의보고를거ᄒᆞᆫ즉본군이진위대와병대보린곳치잇서병뎡과빅셩이병뎡의의ᄉᆞ중ᄒᆞᆫ줄을알지못ᄒᆞ고린변양시셔로닷토와일에조예뎜이변하병뎡과빅셩이서로갈등이되고서야마오니셤후지계온군의빅셩의ᄌᆞ대로ᄒᆞ며쥴법률을밧습ᄒᆞ야등효케ᄒᆞᆫ연후에야잇는바권한을가히위월치못ᄒᆞᆯ지니통군법률한신오권을비러보내여분파케ᄒᆞ라ᄒᆞ엿더라

○일진고시 일진회에서고시ᄒᆞᆫ기를참찬회위의종형회경이가모처에서운동비수만원을밧아가지고셩남으로내려가서패류들회동ᄒᆞ야본회를다파ᄒᆞ려ᄒᆞ니다알아추려라ᄒᆞ엿더라

○북도류민 함경남도관찰소가내부로보고ᄒᆞᆫ기를근자에교ᄅᆞᆫ죵단쳔이북각군인민이어린거슬신올고늘근이를붓들고류리ᄒᆞ야더경봄지나남으로향ᄒᆞ는자가날노멋빅명이된다ᄒᆞ기로함흥군남편디경은남으로나가는요로인고로회동존위와두민의게고시ᄒᆞ야류리ᄒᆞ는빅셩이어느고을에서기주ᄒᆞ든지몃ᄒᆞ나나아오는리유와어느곳으로[illegible]열이되도록보티지나가게시티엇빅명이나되는디기시셩진과밋단쳔빅셩으로서아병의경향흥을의외지못ᄒᆞ야쟝챳경원도등디로향ᄒᆞ여간다고ᄒᆞ엿더라

외보

○영군승의 영국히군셩고시에말ᄒᆞ엿스되금후로에비함디의젼부는항상ᄒᆞᆫ평을유ᄒᆞ는상티를가져어느때던지실무에복ᄌᆞᆼᄒᆞᆯ준비를ᄒᆞ며또경괘로히상에항동ᄒᆞ며또세중에영국히군은일쳔구빅오륙년에연습ᄒᆞᆯ기항ᄒᆞᆯ리비빈연습중에는기젼홍파곳치가량ᄒᆞ라ᄒᆞ엿더라

○덕국총리즁셔 덕국자유당의총리후리도리히 함마쓰헨씨가즁셔ᄒᆞ엿는디동씨는일쳔팔빅이십사년에(희쓰센)에서츌싱ᄒᆞᆫ사름이라더라

○평대계획 아메리카시후는아란사국합디편셩ᄒᆞᆫ계획을아메계출ᄒᆞ엿다더라

○량국평화의 아무셴진국과빗아라셰이국은평화회의를ᄒᆞ엿더라

○신조과션 일본과션중사회사의과션긴세환이분원일일브터마산포부산간을격일ᄒᆞ여졍긔항ᄒᆞ기를기시ᄒᆞ엿는티두수는고거우사실사돈미나계조홈이더ᄒᆞ고ᄒᆞᆫ과셤이리계승리단편리ᄒᆞ다더라

○군사비경쟁 일젼일본에비위원데사분과회에셔림시군사비쳥의만원에티ᄒᆞ여일린일호도사갑이무ᄒᆞ게젼원이ᄒᆞ셔지소색을쳐겨쟝ᄒᆞ되엿고고베에대셕쟁과씨는죵리에통ᄒᆞ군의룡쟉이국민으로ᄒᆞ여공뎌욱만죵케ᄒᆞᆫ지라오히려또쟝리의큰항동을반란다ᄒᆞ고쾌탁ᄒᆞᆫ마음으로쳔셩ᄒᆞ엿고산본회샹은회원졔씨의발셩을총찬ᄒᆞ고이후에셩지를봉계ᄒᆞ여국민의외퇴를빈반쳐아니ᄒᆞ고졍졍분려ᄒᆞᆯ뜻스로답사ᄒᆞ엿더라

○로표제쟝예산 로국대쟝신은공표홀예산안건과비밀대산안두번을계죠ᄒᆞ여공표예산안은그진젹ᄒᆞᆫ관계가잇는쟈지외에는고린허를알기능치못ᄒᆞᆫ라에는민일고진안의니면을탐로ᄒᆞᆫ진티로국지졍은용비치광졔일류부에티ᄒᆞ여알지라쳥금에로국찬ᄒᆞ는가격은젼쟁의영향이셔국운항가와결탁ᄒᆞ고종리외동일국ᄒᆞᆫ가격을지보ᄒᆞ기위ᄒᆞ여비밀히가계를샹급ᄒᆞ고민슈ᄒᆞ구제나이능히쳐못ᄒᆞᆯ러이라ᄒᆞ엿더라

○사젼공판 한보아미리가귀셤회사의보고ᄒᆞᆫ바를거ᄒᆞᆫ즉덕국과일본에티ᄒᆞ야셩회사가영국에셔관업ᄒᆞ엿는디일본이비밀리에그것을사셔진영에셔원쟝ᄒᆞ엿다더라

○려순위형지 려순군형히모쳐구역밧긔는이거슬위형ᄒᆞ라ᄒᆞ엿난아셔병의ᄒᆞᆼ을ᄒᆞᆫ편ᄒᆞᆫ후에는오항ᄒᆞ야간지고위쳥계에ᄃᆞ리가는쟈ㅣ잇는지라양자에엇던이ᄅᆞᆫ쳔이그셧는너기에는리봉쇄ᄒᆞᆷ의포격을슈ᄒᆞ여쥬밀슈조는아간이나홀엘과볼ᄒᆞᆯ벼에는그방향을고못ᄒᆞ야위쳐에리ᄒᆞ야일본봉쇄함을바라보고황망히도망ᄒᆞ는쟈ㅣ잇다더라

론셜

젼호련쇽

손에는총을잡고공중으로소사을나갈때에보면총삼에ᄭᅧ인창들은맛치불노리ᄒᆞ는거와곳치번방에빗치며섬요ᄒᆞ다가세리젼빠에는일병ᄒᆞ나식이죽어나려지는티지금싱각ᄒᆞ여도맛치샴군거와흡사ᄒᆞ지라이거슨우리나라군티에셔신츌피몽ᄒᆞᆫ졔죠로셰로발명ᄒᆞᆫ몽긴미나그러ᄒᆞ나영웅ᄒᆞ호걸곳ᄒᆞᆫ일본수즁들은두려워ᄒᆞ지아니ᄒᆞᆯ준으로알아며니저리켸영등ᄒᆞᆫ수즁들도이거순무어ᄉᆞᆫ지오히려아직못ᄒᆞ야우금결우리들향ᄒᆞᆫ쎄야달녀들기는ᄒᆞ되우리의게이런ᄒᆞᆫ군물이잇는쳐뎌에명쳐은쎄잇기지아니ᄒᆞ며나니화왕지견보티싱양뎔세셔지련속ᄒᆞ야싸호지아니ᄒᆞᆫ날이오히련희활ᄒᆞ며또ᄒᆞᆫᄒᆞᆼ샹우리를향ᄒᆞ야젼진ᄒᆞ야그런ᄒᆞ되우리는젹병을퇴각ᄒᆞ고또ᄒᆞᆫ진루안에셔싸홈은ᄒᆞ히ᄒᆞ기에싱샹병최은손히홈이엇서스나그런ᄒᆞ나그건쳐동리에잇는졍들이며항구에셔공역ᄒᆞ는바들은모도손샹ᄒᆞ야결단이남으로써우리의함쳐들도후란환의폭발ᄒᆞ야ᄭᅢ여린징으로말미암아샹ᄒᆞᆫ자ㅣ슐미스되수보치못ᄒᆞ엿스며병이나잇스민먹계스되술도ᄒᆞᆫ등이업서먹지못ᄒᆞ고그샹쳐에어구ᄒᆞᆫ바를젼티ᄒᆞ여참기가실로손허우며소위음식이라ᄒᆞ는거슨번번치못ᄒᆞ야병이싱길거곳ᄒᆞᆫ거시여러번이되이역간신히호구ᄒᆞᆯ뿐이지라

그러ᄒᆞ나무셤일이잇술지경이면우리군ᄉᆞ들은지탕ᄒᆞ여가기로서로면려ᄒᆞ는거시미샹불이러운뻬도만코또ᄒᆞᆫ위등ᄒᆞᆫ뻬도반하여십로사름은당키구난ᄒᆞᆯ경우가잇스나그런ᄒᆞ나우금셔지셩쳑을굿게직히여잇술뿐더러도리여지금은매로쇼리듯기로바라는지라

ᄃᆡ란에ᄒᆞ야알ᄒᆞ야병ᄃᆡ주은의가우리도리를이ᄒᆞᆫ듯ᄒᆞᆫ고셔극력ᄒᆞ야싸와그런ᄒᆞ되우리는젹병들의슐폰항ᄅᆞᆯ보고오히려분ᄒᆞᆫ마음으로참아못ᄒᆞ야거짓싱슈ᄒᆞᆷ과것치용셔ᄒᆞᆷ바잇더니지금당ᄒᆞ여서는그런ᄒᆞᆫ마음을둘수가업는거시군ᄉᆞ에잇는거슬대포로방격ᄒᆞᆷ과갓흔여수ᄒᆞᆯ술으로병진ᄒᆞ는환란이당두ᄒᆞ엿슨즉장시라도젹병의게히젼홀들수업는고로우리군ᄉᆞ들의답대ᄒᆞᆷ과굿셈으로써조롬도두렵ᄒᆞ계너이지아니ᄒᆞ고ᄃᆡ젹ᄒᆞ라ᄒᆞ는지라

아종ᄶᅡ홈ᄒᆞᆯ때에함티의손히됨은무티ㅣ라하왕표젼ᄒᆞᆯ때에샹ᄒᆞᆫ빈들수보치못ᄒᆞᆷ으로써그런뎡이나그런ᄒᆞ나이제당ᄒᆞ여서는젹병의계에위ᄶᅡ이며싱병지경에이르ᄂᆞᆫ일이며서로의부족ᄒᆞᆷ과란환의폭발ᄒᆞᆷ으로써불힝ᄒᆞᆫ사름들만공연히죽이며무이ᄒᆞᆫ지옥에잇는거와갓치한량업는수고도밧기가과연지리ᄒᆞᆫ싱덕러샹곽과도로에종이쟝반진시레에서죽ᄒᆞᆫ병들이싱기여젼령ᄒᆞ케되기는이무가론인즁군일에는싸홈들을열심으로ᄒᆞ야방포ᄒᆞ는소티들이로쳔티여듯기어려운지라

수일젼브터는우리진중에서로발명ᄒᆞᆫ자ㅣ잇서일진사즁을모도들ᄒᆞ야응젹ᄒᆞ엿수즁일병들은아모리우리샹쳑을포획ᄒᆞ라고젼력ᄒᆞ야도필경쥐치못ᄒᆞᆯ티이요다만군병에샹ᄒᆞᆫ쳠가ᄒᆞᆯ티이라고ᄒᆞ엿다더라

(완)

관보

뎨삼쳔삼ᄇᆡᆨ호

광무팔년십이월이십ᄉᆞ일

서임급ᄉᆞ령

○희법부법률긔초위원 법부참서관 리종셩

십이월이십일일

○의원면본관 평남도원쥬ᄉᆞ 최응렬 평남도원쥬ᄉᆞ 황서연 평남도원쥬ᄉᆞ 신병익 평남도원쥬ᄉᆞ 윤병식 평남도원쥬ᄉᆞ 박지규 평남도원쥬ᄉᆞ 도표병호 평남도원쥬ᄉᆞ 리교우 평남도원쥬ᄉᆞ 한상니 평남도원쥬ᄉᆞ 박셩우 평남도원쥬ᄉᆞ 김쥬쥰 평남도원쥬ᄉᆞ 김종빈 평남도원쥬ᄉᆞ 리홍졔 경리원참봉 김쥰희 화릉참봉 김영표 후릉참봉 윤종을 영릉참봉 진구 귀ᄌᆞ능참봉 김셩용 시종원좌시어 리헌용

○임경리원참봉 서판임관팔등 구품 송대진

○임화릉참봉 서판임관팔등 구품 김셕하

○임후릉참봉 서판임관팔등 구품 홍덕쥬

○임영릉참봉 서판임관팔등 구품 조만희

○임귀ᄌᆞ능참봉 서판임관팔등 구품 윤자익

○임명릉뎨우부참서 셔판임관팔등 뎡이품 리유인

○임시종원좌시어 셔판임관팔등 뎡이품 김창진

십이월이십이일

광무팔년십이월이십ᄉᆞ일

서임급ᄉᆞ령

○희법부법률긔초위원 법부참서관 김낙헌

십이월이십구일

광고

우리신문을구람ᄒᆞ시는 쳠군자의게티ᄒᆞ야대단이감사ᄒᆞ오나신문값을혹종이되야도아니보내시는곳이잇사오니종금이후로는미월초싱에너로아니보내시면신문을분젼ᄒᆞ지아니ᄒᆞ겟사오니애독쳠군자는조량ᄒᆞ시와속히보내주시기를바라압

잡보

○무거오문 근일졔비가창궐ᄒᆞ야멸군에문젼도능탈ᄒᆞ며군수도피접ᄒᆞ는자ㅣ죵죵잇는고로만경군수명인희씨가계포예척임을당ᄒᆞ야방비홀츠로음하예주창을신쳥ᄒᆞ고포군을설시ᄒᆞᆯ을경부에경구ᄒᆞ는중이미좌셜은일진회원박명호츠로의병을빙쟈ᄒᆞᆫ다ᄒᆞ니이것은진거짓말이라더라

TELEGRAMS.

Japanese Legation.

Marshal Oyama reports that fighting has been proceeding in the direction of the Japanese left wing for the past few days. The Japanese on the 24th inst, drove the Russians out of the villages behind Sanyungten and Saofangchen. They also occupied a Russian position at the extremity of their right wing.

Army Aeaaquarters.

On the 22nd, inst a Japanese force attacked 20 Russian cavalrymen on the left bank of the Taitse-ho near Saimachi and put them to flight. On the 22rd inst, 50 Russians were encountered near Sangsukao and were defeated. They left 4 killed and 4 wounded on the field.

At noon on the 25th inst, 32 Russian infantry made an attack on Honan a village near Taochatse but were quickly repulsed.

At 4 p. m. on the same day, a Company of Russian Cavalry attacked Peitikao but were defeated after a brisk fight. Their casualties were two killed one of them an officer. Twelve dead horses were also left on the field.

Japanese Legation.

On the 22nd inst, the besieging army at Port Arthur opened a heavy bombardment on the Russian defence works on the small hill Goyochi and fire was also directed on the Sunsushan and Urlungshan fort, causing much damage. Early on the 23rd, a detachment of the left wing attacked Goyochi and carried the position at 7-30 a. m. The hill was them subjected to a heavy fire from the Russian batteries and a counter attack made at 8.20 but it was unsuccessful and the position still remains in hands of the Japanese.

Owing to the heavy bombardment the north fort of West Tayangkan* was set on fire and some of the guns badly damaged.

According to a prisoner captured, two Russian Generals were killed and one wounded during the fight on 203 metre hill.

*(West Tayangkan is one of the main defences about 1000 metres distant from 203 metre hill.)

(FROM JAPAN PAPERS)

London, Dec. 22.

According to the newspapers, it has been ascertained that the secret agents mentioned in yesterday's message as supposed to be acting in the interests of Russia are two English seafaring men of the better class named Walsh and Beckett. These men, when interviewed, admitted that they were in the Russian employ, and had got four statements from Hull fishermen confirming the reports that there were torpedo-boats among the trawling fleet at the time of the attack by the Baltic Squadron in the North Sea. These statements had been signed before the Russian Consul at Hull. The men denied that they had resorted to bribery to obtain these statements; they had only compensated their informants for loss of time.

The Russian Consul at Hull, who is an Englishman, interviewed, said he anticipated that an official statement would be issued shortly, and it was only his duty to take the statements laid before him.

Berlin, Dec. 21st.

Troops are being mobilised in many districts in Russia, while officers on the reserve list are also being called up.

Berlin, Dec. 21.

The "Frankfort Gazette" publishes a report stating that anxiety prevails in Paris in consequence of a demand made by Japan to be allowed to participate officially in the inquiry by the International Commission at the Quai d'Orsy into the conduct of the Baltic Fleet in sinking British trawlers in the North Sea.

London, Dec. 21.

The North Sea Commision is to meet at Paris on Thursday.—Reuter.—Japan Mail

London, Dec. 20.

Admiral Kanakoff and other Russian commissioners have left for Paris to be present at the international conference with regard to the Hull affair.—Asahi.

London Dec. 21.

It is announced that Canada is about to establish, in agreement with the British Admiralty, a Canadian Squadron. The formation of the squadron will begin with the construction of three cruisers, which will be manned by the Canadian Naval Militia.

THE NORTH SEA INCIDENT.

The report of the Commission enquiring into the North Sea incident should make interesting reading when it is published. Evidence in support of the Russian contention that hostile warships were about is continually coming to light and the following letter, published by an Amsterdam paper, written by a Dutch engineer named Kooy, who is connected with the wireless telegraph system on board the Russian transport "Kamchatka" belonging to Admiral Rojestvensky's divison of the second Pacific fleet is intructive. The letter says that shortly after the "Kamchatka anchored at Skagen for coal, a wireless message was received stating that four torpedo boats which had been purchased by Japan had left the Danish fjords. When the "Kamchatka" left Skagen she was convoyed by two cruisers, but lost them on the first night during a fog. The weather cleared on the second night, and shortly after 8 o'clock four vessels were sighted steaming rapidly. An order was given to man the guns and the "Kamchatka fired blank shells as a warning to the vessels to change their course. They continued to approach, however, whereupon the "Khamchatka" commenced a furious cannonade. Two torpedo boats crossed the line of fire.

Under the searchlight, Kooy in his letter, says, he clearly saw two torpedo boats, and he is certain they were not Russian vessels. One of the torpedo boats launched a torpedo, but the "Kamchatka" changed her position and no damage was done. The torpedo boat then slackened speed, and Kooy thinks she was damaged by the fire from the "Kamchatka." It is stated that the second torpedo boat also launched a torpedo, but he did not see them. The other torpedo boats disappeared and he believes they attacked Vice-Admiral Rojestvensky. The "Kamchatka" sent a wireless warning to Rojestvensky. The writer says that every one in Kronstadt knows when and where the Japanese purchased the torpedo boats.

The Roman Catholie Cathedral will be the scene of a very interesting function at ten o'clock tomorrow morning when the wedding will take place of Mr. A Delcoigne, adviser to the Home Department, and Miss Irene Eckert. The witnesses for the bride will be H. E. Herr von Saldern and Dr. Wunsch, while Mr. R de Vos, Belgian Vice Consul and Mr. U Bolljahn will act in the same capacity for the bridegroom. During the ceremony the Imperial band will discourse appropriate music. Both bride and groom are very popular and highly esteemed and the best wishes of the whole community will go with them in their new life.

The Household Bureau has dismissed the claim, recently made by two Russian employees of the Government on the grounds that the men left for Russia without first obtaining leave.

The Kamni of Pyengyang telegraphs that a Japanese soldier has murdered a Korean, named Kin Yong Han by running him through with his bayonet.

The Japanese Minister has obtained permission for an Audience with His Majesty for tomorrow afternoon.

MILITARY PROGRESS IN CHINA.

A Peking despatch states that H. E. Viceroy Yuan Shih-kai, who is a member of the Committee on Army Reorganization of which Prince Ching is the President, has ordered the establishment of a School of Military Strategy and Tactics in connection with the Military Academy to be started next spring by the Army Re-organization Department in Peking, The principal instructors of this School are to be engaged from Japan and the Japanese Government will be asked to select the necessary officers for the Chinese Government.

It is reported from Tientsin that no less than forty-eight twelve-centimetre (4½-inch) guns with sufficient ammunition have lately arrived at Tangku from Europe and that thirty-six of them are to be for the forces stationed in the vicinity of Yungpingfu, near the Great wall, while the remaining twelve guns are destined for the troops at Paoting. The Northern Army, under the supreme command of Viceroy Yuan Shih-kai, we hear therefore, now possesses no less than one hundred and eight of these guns.—N.-C. D. News.

FINACE IN JAPAN.

The Tokyo press is in a by no means complaisant mood at present. Feelings of patriotism apparently prevent the publication of any adverse criticism about the war itself, but the amount of agitation on subjects bearing a very close relation to the war clearly indicates a strong undercurrent of dissatisfaction somewhere.

The recent action of the Bank of Japan in raising the rate of interest provokes some adverse comment from the "Tokyo Asahi" which points out that although a similar proceeding by the Bank of England during the Boer War had the effect of attracting foreign capital into the country. Japan can hope for [illegible] result, as is evidenced by the fact that the government was compelled to pledge the Customs revenue in order to obtain the loans recently floated.

The "Asahi," while admitting that the amount of paper money in circulation is much in excess of what it should be, says that the raising of the rate of interest will not correct this inasmuch as the principal borrower is the government itself, and foresees as a consequence a general congestion of the economics of the country which will increase the difficulties of the people in responding to calls upon them for funds for the continuance of the war.

Mr. Yi Yong Ik returned to Seoul on Monday.

The Governor of North Chulla reports that the local members of the Il Chin Hoi have again begun to riot and he has ordered the Police to disperse them.

The family of the Chinese teacher Ho Mun Wi whose death was recently announced have received a present of $120,00 from the Education Department.

The Foreign Office have informed the Japanese Legation that it is absolutely imperative that Lientenant Yun Chi Sung, who is with the Japanese forces at the front, should return at once.

We are requested to announce that the following ladies will receive New Year's calls with Mrs. Allen at the American Legation, from 3 to 5 P. M. on Monday January 2nd: Mrs. Bostwick; Mrs. Bunker; Mrs. Elliott; Mrs. McLellen Mrs. Scranton; Mrs. Dr. Scranton and Miss Scranton.

From the "Japan Times" we learn that a Seoul despatch of the 19th itst. says that Major-General Bernar, commander of the Russian force at Songjin, North-eastern Korea, has recently reported to the St. Petersburg Government to the effect that the districts north of Pukchhong have been successfully occupied. The despatch adds that a telegram of congratulation has consequently been received by the Russian officer from the Russian authorities at home.

IL CHIN HOI IN DISGRACE.

Trouble in the ranks of the Il Chin Hoi, which had been brewing for some days culminated in an outburst on Monday when many of their members created a disturbance outside the main gate of the Palace.

The new society, the Kong Chin Hoi was the original cause of the trouble. Its members on Saturday held a meeting and decided to assert themselves by forcibly abducting two prominent officials, Messes Yi Yu-in and Ku Pon-sun, both of whom are professedly fortune tellers. This was duly carried out and these gentlemen were locked up in the society's meeting place and harangued by the President as follows.

"You two men, a few years ago, were low people in the country, but you came up to Seoul and swindled the Emperor with your tales of fortune telling. You are now rich and each of you has ten wives. This is the result of much swindling. A clear proof that you are not really able to tell fortunes is shown by the fact that you were unaware that we were going to arrest you today."

The President then asked the meeting what punishment the men deserved. The majority of the members were in favour of killing them, but wiser counsel prevailing, they were marched off to the Supreme Court and handed over to the Chief Judge. The matter was reported to His Majesty, who immediately ordered the release of the prisoners. The Police authorities then made several arrests of the leaders of the Kong Chin Hoi, with the result that the Il Chin Hoi, as stated above, despatched a body of their members to create a disturbance outside the Palace on Monday and demand the release of those arrested. At one time it looked as though there might be serious trouble and the guards around the Palace were considerably strengthened, but after a great deal of shouting and hand-clapping the mob dispersed.

Speaking of the recent armistice at Port Arthur and the attendant exchange of amenities between the garrison and the besiegers, the "Japan Mail," in execrable taste, delivers itself of the following:"—Naturally one asks, what had produced this change of mood on the side of the Russians. Had they been softened by what they saw of Japanese valour and humanity, or did they act in obedience to that wonderful injunction —wonderful because of the source from which it emanated—"Make to yourselves friends of the mammon of unrighteous ness that when ye fail they may receive you into their houses?" Were the Russians beginning to apprehend failure? The armistice being mutual, the same remark would apply with equal force to the Japanese, but we venture to say that even the most rabid Russophile would not be quilty of such an ungenerous insinuation.

The Korea Daily News.

Issued at 5 P. M. daily except Sundays.

Rate of Subscription :—
Per Year,............Yen 25.
Per Quarter,..........Yen 7.
Per Month,...........Yen 2.50.

Postage in Korea not charged extra.
Postage abroad charged extra.

Advertisements, 50 sen per day for 1 inch or less.
5 yen per month per inch.
50 yen per year per inch.

All communications to

E. T. BETHELL,
Editor and Publisher,
Pak-tong, Seoul.

OURSELVES AND THE JAPANESE PRESS.

Our contemporary the "Daihan Ilpo," in its issue of December 23rd devotes a long article to a criticism of the attitude taken up by us in dealing with affairs in this country and the war. We are pleased to notice a considerable diminution in the abuse which generally falls to our lot when Japanese newspapers refer to us; true, the "Daihan" still calls us "the organ of the pro-Russian party" but in view of the fact that it is characteristic of the Japanese that they seem honestly to believe that anyone refusing to swallow whole the pabulum of news daily doled out from Tokio, and exercises instead a right to independent criticism must of neccessity be pro-Russian, we are neither surprised nor hurt by this. The Japanese always go to extremes and do not seem to see the possiblity of anyone else adopting a middle course.

The "Daihan Ilpo," quoting various articles which have appeared in the "Korea Daily News" charges us with having said (1) that Japan intends to disregard the terms of the Anglo-Japanese Alliance with regard to Korea if she sees the opportunity (2) That the Il-chin Hoi society is a collection of rascals and the Japanese Army Headquarters in Seoul pays its expenses (3) That the Russian Minister to Peking was justified in half-masting his flag on receiving the news of the death of the Crown Princess of Korea (4) that in the event of her being forced to retreat and depend entirely upon Korea for her communications Japan would realize the unwisdom of the policy she is now pursuing in this country.

There are trifling inaccuracies in these extracts from our columns but they are substantially correct, and we still adhere to the opinions there set forth. We have given our reasons so often that it would be wearisome to recount them, but we may say that since they were written nothing has occurred to change our views.

Proceeding, the "Daihan Ilpo" demands to know what we have to say about the Russian depredations in North Korea and their action in arrogating to themselves the right to collect taxes. There are several things to be said to this; if, as its criticism of the Peking flag incident would indicate, the "Daihan" thinks that Russia should look upon Korea as an ally of Japan then the "Daihan" must admit that the Russians in the north have a right to look upon the occupied territory as conquered ground and administer it how they like. We do not, however think that this is the Russian view, we do not believe that they recognize the validity of the last Japan-Korea convention, and look upon Korea as a neutral power. Some incidents of harshness and unavoidable injustice are inevitable but the Japanese have also offended in this respect and it appears that the Russian action in undertaking the civil administration of the occupied districts has its exact paralled in the Japanese proceedings at Newchwang and many other places in Manchuria. What is sauce for the goose is sauce for the gander.

A STRANDED WHALE.

Mt Lavinia Hotel at Colombo has been going through a servere crisis, owing to the decomposition of a stranded whale close by. The aroma "arrived and knocked loudly" about 10 P. M. on a Saturday night. One sufferer wrote, after the stench broke up a bridge party:—

We sought, alas, without success, to evade that awful smell. But it grew almost visibly. It penetrated the most inaccessible quarters. It clung to one with the grim tenacity of the octopus. We sought relief in sleep, but that escape was denied us. A feverish night ensued, and we had a battle royal for breath. Some of the Boarders took refuge in the billiard room, while the tennis court, from its favourable situation proved a popular rendezvous. The following day, Sunday, brought no relief, but rather the horrible stench was intensified."

The radius of the smell is put at three miles.

(By way of coincidence a personal paragragh in the adjoining column records the departure to Rangoon of a gentleman named S. Tench.)

TWO HUNDRED AND THREE METRE HILL.

Much has been said in recent official messages about "203 Metre Hill," a position in the defence line at Port Arthur. The location of this hill is not generally well known. It can be located by the following bearings:

Four miles N. W. from the entrance to the harbor.

Three miles N. E. from a central point on the coast of Pigeon Bay.

Five and one half miles almost due north from the most southern point of the West Basin.

Four miles from the most northern point of the West Basin.

Five and one quarter miles N. W. from the east extreme of the East Basin.

Eight and three quarter miles N. N.E. from Laotishan Point.

Four milies S. E. from the most southern point of Luisa Bay.

It is an outer position in Port Arthur's defences, at an elevation of 691 feet, and the Russians had but one gun mounted on it.

It took the Japanese five days of severe fighting to drive the Russians from "203 Metre Hill." Some very hard fighting took place at this point. General Stoessel took occasion to compliment his men upon their success in repulsing the Japanese here.

The Russians call this position "High Hill." This is the largest hill close to the fortifications on the west flank. Just beyond it are "Long Hill" and "Corner Hill" forming a line between Pigeon Bay and Luisa Bay. At these places the attacking troops have lost many men. "Chefoo Daily News..

GOVERNMENT PRINTING OFFICE.

A Seoul despatch dated the 7th inst., received by the "Osaka Mainichi," states that, in accordance with the advice of Mr. Megata, financial adviser to Korea, the Korean Treasury has decided to establish a Printing Office for the issue of notes, and has appointed former chief of the Mint, the Director of the same.

An immense pig, weighing over five hundred and thirty pounds was slaughtered at Penang the other night. Some idea of the size of the animal may be gathered from the fact that seven coolies failed to lift it on to the hooks in the cooling room.

Reuter informs us that the Reform movement in Russia is spreading. It has a big area to cover.

We read that removal of the appendix has been successfully accomplished without surgical aid. It was performed by a committee of clergy, operating on Hymns Ancient and Modern.

It is reported from Peking that Finance Minister Chin Yee Shun is negotiating with the Belgian Minister for a loan of $10,000,000. The security for this loan has not yet been arranged

---

There are over 100 Japanese at Paotingfu busily occupied in making investgations and studying Chinese methods of government. It is said that the services of these Japanese will be employed in the administration of the territory at present occupied by the Japanese troops.

The Tokio Government has received information to the effect that owing to the difficulties experinced in mobilising the men and in obtaining arms and clothing, it is not expected that the organisation of General Gripenberg's army will be completed before the end of February next.

"I am writing to you in pencil," says a Russian officer at Port Arthur, "as our commander is at present writing with the only pen we have here." The pen may be mightier than the sword, but clearly those who planned the defence of the "fraud-pilfered port," as Alfred Austen designates it did not think so.

Says "Indian Engineering"—There *ought* to be only one time kept over the whole of the world, without any adjustment whatever. What would it matter if at certain places the sun was said to rise at 12 o'clock? Or would the labourer enjoy his midday meal the less because his watch showed half-past six?

It is always sad to see the taking of a strong valuable life in its early vigour. If the untimely end is due, either wholly or in part, to the use of tobacco or alcohol, we naturally feel still more sorry to see such an unworthy shipping out of a useful and potentially great life. We note that Noah Raby, of Eatontown, N. J., recently died, and under circumstances that makes his death particularly sad. Mr. Raby according to his own statements, which seems to be pretty well confirmed, was but 136 years old, and there can be little doubt that his untimely death was due to his consumption of liquor during 120 years of that time. He was a constant user of alcoholic beverages and tobacco, and had it not been for the deadly effect of these poisons upon his strong and vigorous system, Mr. Raby might have lived to a good old age. Too bad!—California on Medicine.

Russia's intention to despatch a third squadron so soon is probably due says the *Eastern World* to the destruction of the Port Arthur fleet since the occupation by the Japanese of 203 meter hill. The inglorious end of those warships is an event so far as we know unparaled in history, and whilst we may not rashly condemn their commanders, we may say that had the writer been in command of one of them, either every Japanese ship would have been at the bottom of the sea, or his own, or he would have been shot for disobedience of orders to remain in harbour.

As it is, the destruction of that ingorious fleet with which the heroic conduct of the Russian land forces forms such a pleasing contrast, makes the reduction of Port Arthur of secondary importance and it is to be hoped that the besieging army will get a brief respite from its arduous work. It sorely needs such a respite and a brief armistice now, as already suggested in another column, should be equally welcome to both sides.

The Korea Daily News.

VOL. I, | WEDNESDAY, DECEMBER 28, 1904. | No. 135

HONGKONG & SHANGHAI BANKING CORPORATION.

Paid-up Capital.................... $10,000,000
Reserve Fund:—Sterling Reserve... 10,000,000
Silver Reserve..... 7,000,000

27,000,000

Reserve Liability of Proprietors... 10,000,000

HEAD OFFICE, HONGKONG.

London Bankers, London and County Banking Company Limited.

Branches and Agencies,
London.

Amoy,	Hankow	Penang,
Bangkok,	Hiogo,	Rangoon,
Batavia,	Iloilo,	Saigon,
Bombay,	Lyons,	San Francisco,
Calcutta,	Manila,	Singapore,
Colombo,	Nagasaki,	Sourabaya,
Foochow,	New York,	Tientsin,
Hamburg,	Peking,	Yokohama,

Credits granted on approved Securities, and every description of Banking and Exchange business transacted.

Drafts granted on London and the chief Commercial places in Europe, India, Australia, America, China and Japan.

HOLME RINGER & CO., AGENTS,
CHEMULPO.

HOKURKU DOBOKU KAISHA.

Branch office in Chong Dong, Seoul.

Japanese telephone No. 165

CONTRACT DEPARTMENT.

We can contract to build any building or construction.

MERCHANDISE DEPARTMENT.

We can provide any building material. We have just contracted to build the new Belgian Legation.

E. MEYER & CO.

Chemulpo.

SOLE AGENTS IN KOREA FOR.

A. T. Morse, Sons & Co.'s

"Fresco" Distemper

In all colours ready for use on walls, Ceilings etc.

and

AVENARIUS CARBOLINEUM

A wood-preserving and antiseptic oil preparation

Against decay, dry-rot, fungus and wood-destroying insects.

A large supply always in stock.

Prices upon application.

E. MEYER & Co.,
Chemulpo.

CHARTERED BANK OF INDIA AUSTRALIA & CHINA.

INCORPORATED BY ROYAL CHARTER 1853

HEAD OFFICES:—LONDON.

Paid-up Capital £800,000
Reserve Liability of Shareholders 800,000
Reserve Fund 800,000

Drafts granted upon all the principal places in the world and every description of Exchange and banking business transacted.

E. MEYER & Co., Agents,
Chemulpo.

MITSU BISHI DOCKYARD & ENGINE WORKS,

NAGASAKI.

CODE WORD, "DOCK."

A 1, A. B. C., and Engineering Codes used.

DOCK No. 1 (at Tategami).

Extreme Length.............. 523 feet
Length on blocks .... 513 ,,
Width of Entrance on Top...... 89 ,,
,, ,, Bottom.... 77 ,,
Water on Blocks at Spring Tide 26½ ,,

DOCK No. 2 (Mukaijima).

Extreme Length.............. 371 feet
Length on Blocks............. 360 ,,
Width of Entrance on Top...... 66 ,,
,, ,, Bottom 53 ,,
Water on Blocks at Spring Tide 22 ,,

PATENT SLIP (at Kosuge).

Can take vessels up to 1,000 tons gross.

THE WORKS are well equipped with the LATEST IMPROVEMENTS, and can execute any kind of work in SHIPBUILDING and MARINE ENGINEERING, as well as in REPAIRING of SHIPS.

The COMPANY'S new powerfu steamer OURA-MARU (712 tons, 700 I.H.P.), specially built for SALVAGE PURPOSES, and equipped with necessary gear, is always READY at SHORT NOTICE.

THE METHODIST PUBLISHING HOUSE,

Little West Gate, Seoul.

JOB PRINTING, TYPEWRITER PAPER
CARBON PAPER, VISITING CARDS
STATIONERY, BOOK BINDING
BOOK PUBLISHERS
AMERICAN SCHOOL BOOKS
SPENCERIAN COPY BOOKS
PEN CARBON LETTER AND BILL BOOKS

S.A. BECK, Manager.

DAI-ICHI GINKO.

LIMITED.

(Formerly the First National Bank)

ESTABLISHED 1873

INCORPORATED UNDER PRESENT LAW 1896

Capital - - - - - - - - Yen 5,000,000
Reserve Fund - . - - - 1,500,000

HEAD OFFICE:—TOKIO.

President: Baron SHIBUSAWA.

BRANCHES AND CORRESPONDENTS In the Principal Cities and Towns of Japan.

Interest Allowed on

Fixed deposits 1 year - - - 6½ per cent
" " 6 months - - - 6 per cent

Special current accounts 1½ sen daily per Y 100
General " " 1 " " " 100

M. TANAKA,
Manager, Chemulpo.

SINGER SEWING MACHINES

씽거ᄌᆞ봉침

SOLE AGENTS FOR KOREA

젼매쇼

HOLME RINGER & CO.
Chemulpo.

제물포 함릉거양힝

KAMEYA & CO.

GENERAL STOREKEEPERS

Chinkokai - - Seoul

(*Established 1895, Tokyo*)

Confectionery, Hams, Canned Goods, Cutlery, Hirano & Tansan Water. Provisions, Gents, Furnishing goods, Toilet Articles, Travelling Bags, Tobacco, Cigars & Cigarettes Kitchen Utensils. Coffee, Biscuits

Fresh Goods always kept in Stock.
Prices Moderate
☞ *Please come and inspect our goods.*

NIPPON YUSEN KAISHA.

JAPANESE MAIL STEAMSHIP CO.

DER MAIL CONTRACT WITH THE IMPERIAL JAPANESE GOVERNMENT.

European Line

Regular Fortnightly Service between Yokohama Kobe, Moji, Shanghai, Hongkong, Singapore, Penang Colombo, Port Said, Marseilles, London and Antwerp

American Line

Regular Fortnightly Service between Hongkong and Seattle, calling at Shanghai, Moji, Kobe, Yokohama and Victoria, B. C.

Australian Line

Regular weekly Service betwen Japan Ports and Australia, calling at Hongkong and Manila.

(Above Three Lines Suspended until further notice).

Shanghai Line

Weekly Service between Shanghai and Japan Ports

Korea Line

Service Kobe, Moji, Nagasaki, Fusan Chemupo Chef foo, Taiku.

S. S. Bahelsberg, 2181 tons.

Service Kobe, Moji, Fusan, Chemulpo, Chinnampo

S. S. ARGO, S. S. Ohio.

BORDEN'S CONDENSED MILK CO.

New York, U. S. A.

ALWAYS IN STOCK

Eagle Brand Condensed Milk.

Gold Seal Condensed Milk.

Peerless (Family) Evaporated Cream.

Borden's Malted Milk.

E. MEYER & CO.
Chemulpo Korea,
Sole Agents

ROYAL INSURANCE COMPANY,

Funds exceed £10,000,000

FIRE

AT CURRENT RATES.

LIFE

REDUCED PREMIUM.

HOLME RINGER & Co.,
Agents, Chemulpo.

HOTEL DU PALAIS

SEOUL.

The only first class Hotel in Seoul Situated in the centre of the city opposite the palace.

Cuisine under the supervision of an experienced French Chef.

Well ventilated and furnished throughout.

TARIFF UPON APPLICATION

L. MARTIN
Proripctor and Manager

大韓每日申報
대한매일신보

(뎨일빅삼십륙호) (금요일) 일천구빅사년십이월삼십일

본사고빅

이신보는병오와한일조석거리월출판ᄒᆞᄋᆞᆸ

신문가

한쟝 엽뎐돈오푼

일삭표 엽뎐팔십돈

우표가리삭닷돈

다엿돈으로밧ᄉᆞᆸ

광고료는

귀한회쟝단과ᄌᆞ항의디쇼로즁감ᄒᆞ되ᄒᆞᆫ번가로밧을터이오며오릭지아니ᄒᆞ매대한사람마다이신문을보실터이니광고바시기를ᄇᆞ람웰ᄒᆞ시는이들은우리신문사에와서편야ᄒᆞ심을희망ᄒᆞᄋᆞᆸ

○발힝소 박동대한매일신보사발이ᄒᆞᆫ보엄해전영국인셜핑령정자리오

사쟝 영국인 (빅셜)

평양 디리졈

○평양졈동사는권미보씨로우리신문광미디리인을뎡ᄒᆞ엿시ᄉᆞ오니평양에계신구람코져ᄒᆞ시는 쳠군ᄌᆞ는허디리졈에왕림ᄒᆞ와면의ᄒᆞ시ᄋᆞᆸ

사고

○우리대한매일신보의목뎍은뎌한의인녕졍셔에편한모든데목에되ᄒᆞ야논공평한법률을쥬쟝ᄒᆞᆷ이라우리동신원의ᄒᆞᆸ보는신문보시는쳠군ᄌᆞ의게ᄒᆞ샹보도ᄒᆞ리며편지들귀서ᄒᆞ여주시논이는셩명과번디들쟈이붓치서기를희망ᄒᆞ오니이거슨신문샹에귀졔ᄒᆞ란는거시아니오다만긔히신용ᄒᆞ논증거를삼고자ᄒᆞᆷ이라귀자는아모귀서던지귀진ᄒᆞᆷ을되갸ᄒᆞ논권리든가젓스나되갸ᄒᆞ논리유든말ᄒᆞᆯ터이오며공즁평화든문란케ᄒᆞ논듯ᄒᆞᆫ귀서는의례히밧지안켓ᄉᆞᆸ나이다

●본사셰시이리로신문을미양우례로분전ᄒᆞ와혜젼부의엄의로젼ᄒᆞ든ᄌᆞ소로번곳에는흑늣게젼ᄒᆞ기도ᄒᆞ며흑멋쳘거슬ᄒᆞᆫ꺼번에젼ᄒᆞ기도ᄒᆞ며흑아니젼ᄒᆞ논곳도잇다ᄒᆞ와우리신문을ᄉᆞ랑ᄒᆞ야구람ᄒᆞ시는 쳠군ᄌᆞ외계금티ᄒᆞ야미우미안ᄒᆞ옵기로지금은분젼인을두고미일일즉이젼ᄒᆞ며아니젼ᄒᆞ거나늣게거나ᄒᆞᆫ폐가업도록ᄒᆞ란ᄒᆞ오니ᄒᆞ야이니젼ᄒᆞ거는흑늣게젼ᄒᆞ거나ᄒᆞᆫ일이잇스면본샤로통긔ᄒᆞ여주시믈희망ᄒᆞᄋᆞᆸ

관보

젼호 속

○의원면본관 쟝례원샹례 리외국 ᄒᆞ등참봉 ᄒᆞ명쥬 사릉참봉 구논셔 온릉참봉 리두노 쟝릉참봉 남덕철 동신ᄉᆞ면회과주ᄉᆞ 최귀승 동신사면회과주사 유ᄒᆞᆼ식 동신사면회과쥬사 송영구 동신사면회과쥬사 박병쥐 동신사면회과쥬사 안종유

○임쟝례원샹례서주임관륙등 시강원시독관 리병소 ○임후릉참봉서판임관팔등 윤샹훈 ○임사릉참봉서판임관팔등 김형익 ○임온릉참봉서판임관팔등 리규원 ○임철도원주사서판임관팔등 한규셜 구명서 봉문셕 ○임장릉참봉서판임관팔등 리셕영

○임동신사면회과주사서판임관팔등 김병셕 리귀휘 문쟝후 김세종 권용국 ○경임시강원시독관 쟝례원샹례 리병소 ○승서판임관일등 궁내부주사 김헌비

○중종이품가선대부니부형환 표종이품가선대부비서원승 박형명 ○중정삼품통정대부부비서원승 중등용표판죠봉대대부 박리후 ○중종삼픔통훈대부쟝례원좌쟝례 표등덕랑 박효죠

이상종이픔가선대부니쟝혁

면츄 경박봉주뮈고조교중조교의병

이상중

이상셩이월이십삼일

잡보

○공진회면말 거ᄂᆞ요일본월이십수일은곳공진회통샹회인디당일오후두시에통별회를경힝ᄒᆞᆯ시젼법부대신리유인씨복송자] 외비부참셔관구본숩씨(샹송자 량인을쳐거ᄒᆞ야계하에쟝ᄇᆞ니고량씨외죄들이일히셜명ᄒᆞ야골오디법ᄒᆞ는본사하향쟈인으로서술수를빙쟈ᄒᆞ고경셩에올나와홍세무민ᄒᆞ며웅폐 런츄ᄒᆞ야부귀ᄒᆞᆷ이지극ᄒᆞ고쳐쳠이셩여명이나되논거시단뇨ᄒᆞᆯ죄어니와오놀날에귀장ᄒᆞ혀오논것도모든거슬보면다빈궤군망상ᄒᆞᆫ죄악을볼론가샹이라ᄒᆞ고일쟝연셜ᄒᆞᆫ후에종회원과방관쟈의게향ᄒᆞ야미두사를의죄악이약초ᄒᆞᆫ너주며맛당ᄒᆞᆫ나ᄒᆞᆫ디모든사ᄅᆞᆷ이다일졔히손바닥을치며갈치ᄒᆞ여ᄀᆞᆯ오디죽여맛당ᄒᆞ다ᄒᆞ니또문의ᄒᆞ기를그러면이당쟝에서만민이공동ᄒᆞᆫ가온디죽여버림이엇더ᄒᆞ나ᄒᆞ고무수히헐문ᄒᆞᆯ때에리구팡씨논박답샹ᄒᆞᆫᄒᆞ야룸을셰리안졍치못ᄒᆞᆫ데회쟝이광씨의계뭇기를너희는죄가잇ᄂᆞ냐엽ᄂᆞ냐ᄒᆞᆫ죽리씨가디답ᄒᆞ되여귀장헌은쟈엿지죄가엽다ᄒᆞ리오ᄒᆞᆫ지라필경에는견쟝ᄒᆞ기를나라에법수가범관이잇스니법ᄉᆞ로양부ᄒᆞ야재판ᄒᆞ야죄를다스림이올타ᄒᆞ고리유셕등샹인미량씨들평리원으로신을고가서제판관의게압부ᄒᆞᆫ디쳐음에논밧지안인으리ᄒᆞ다가나죵에ᄒᆞᆯ수엽시병야두고

당일에평리원에서법부로보고ᄒᆞ기를쳥금에공진회에서회쟝리준과부회쟝김명준과총무원라유셕과평의쟝윤효졍광한뭉등이등진편리유인과니부참서관구본승광원미죄도로웅폐련츄ᄒᆞ야나라훈칙를폐ᄒᆞ고빅셩을범ᄒᆞ게ᄒᆞᆫ죄들괴고등이ᄌᆞ복ᄒᆞ온고로이에쳥원ᄒᆞ오니등벌히심편ᄒᆞ외국법을분히졔을부망이라ᄒᆞ고소쟝을가지고와서쳥ᄒᆞ며더리고왓스온바ᄒᆞᆫ탕원비이미중민외괴고인미되엿논고로아직졉류ᄒᆞ여두엇고미에보고ᄒᆞ오니사죠ᄒᆞ라ᄒᆞ엿는디법부대신갑가진쎄게이언규로샹 쥬ᄒᆞ엿고

당야에졍부에서는공진회를죠쳐ᄒᆞ기위ᄒᆞ야긴급회의ᄒᆞ엿논디회석에서군부대신리용파니부대신리용티량씨가발론ᄒᆞ기를경무청으로지휘ᄒᆞ야숩젼을몯수히파출ᄒᆞ야회원을힝착ᄒᆞ다가못되면헌병을모도발ᄒᆞ고헌병도유위부족ᄒᆞ거든각티병뎡을모도발ᄒᆞ야회를타멸ᄒᆞ쟈ᄒᆞ디가

황샹폐하계옵서는그리케ᄒᆞᆷ이불가ᄒᆞ다ᄒᆞ옵시고 죠칙을버리셔귈으샤티드ᄅᆞ존쥬샹민비가스수로친단히회를셜시ᄒᆞ야수ᄉᆞ로미명칭을세우고졍부를능평ᄒᆞ야싱지어대신을쟝아욕뵈고범ᄉᆞ에어지로압부ᄒᆞ니이논젼에엽는변이라졍부계신이능히거조를잘ᄒᆞ여민폐를엽시ᄒᆞ고민싱을진졍ᄒᆞ야그지취을그릇치지아녓든들귀강의회괴ᄒᆞᆷ이엿지이러ᄒᆞ리오지되엿스리오진셜노귀탄ᄒᆞ도다본시금단치못ᄒᆞᆫ경임평무수빅셩괴논위션히임ᄒᆞ고경무쳥으로엄칙ᄒᆞ야피슈를힝포ᄒᆞ야법부로ᄒᆞ여곰조률징판ᄒᆞ고여당은효유ᄒᆞ야히산식여다시취회ᄒᆞ지못ᄒᆞ게ᄒᆞ라ᄒᆞᄋᆞᆸ시고또 칙령을경무쳥으로버리사순검을만히파송ᄒᆞ야리유인과구본슌량인을근구ᄒᆞ야보호ᄒᆞ야집으로돌녀보내라ᄒᆞᄋᆞᆸ셧더라

교당야에경무ᄉᆞ빅셩귀씨는갈니고티에참쟝김평근씨가퇴임ᄒᆞ야각방곡에 조칙을인ᄒᆞ야야계시ᄒᆞᆫ후에슌검을파송ᄒᆞ야회쟝이하오륙명을잡착ᄒᆞ는디익일이십오일조죠에회쟝리쥰광총무라유셕과평의쟝윤효졍과샹쇼를착ᄒᆞ엿고그츄후에윤하는지라부회장김명준씨이ᄒᆞ계회원들이무청ᄭᅵ진졍에회ᄒᆞ야귀회ᄒᆞᆫ호젼경언셜ᄒᆞᆫ후에텁시티파회쟝전경무관김경식씨와회원량한뭉홍모졔씨가일졔히경무쳥계쥐슈ᄒᆞ기를ᄌᆞ원ᄒᆞ는디경무관쳠량이히칙ᄒᆞ라신 칙령을괴봉승ᄒᆞ고수삼ᄎᆞ쳔유ᄒᆞᆷ으로회원등이동의ᄒᆞ고 황칙을봉힝ᄒᆞ야아직되귀ᄒᆞ엿다가명일다시모히자ᄒᆞ고퇴귀ᄒᆞ야죵로수무소로회동ᄒᆞ야경야ᄒᆞ엿고동야에는회민이쭉동ᄒᆞᆷ으로인ᄒᆞ야졍부에서는회의가되엿는디각대신이 젼나에서경야ᄒᆞ고나아오지못ᄒᆞ엿고각셔숩검은협빈ᄒᆞ야회민의쭉동ᄒᆞᆷ을명계ᄒᆞ엿고각별이시군들은회민이ᄌᆞᆸ으란ᄒᆞᆷ으로모도모도피신ᄒᆞ엿더니당일에는모도모혀스쳔ᄒᆞ엿더라

이십륙일샹오열시증에경무쳥에착슈된회쟝리쥰이하수인을평리원에압표ᄒᆞ엿는디공진회원들은쇼광리원문젼에계회ᄒᆞ

UNION INSURANCE SOCIETY OF CANTON.

Head office Hongkong.
Marine risks underwritten at current rates.
Agents in Chemulpo,
F. MEYER & Co.

COMPAGNIE DES MESSAGERIES MARITIMES.

Fortnightly Direct Service.

For Marseilles via Ports.

Sailing from Yokohama Calling at Kobe, Shanghai, Hongkong, Saigon, Singapore, Colombo, Djibonti, Suez, Port Said and Marseilles.

For particulars apply to
HOLME RINGER & Co.,
Chemulpo.

HAYASHIDA & CO.,

16 MYENG DONG, CHIN KO KAI, SEOUL.
BRANCH OFFICE AT CHEMULPO.

Money changers, Coal and Wood Merchants, Express Agents.

We are agents for the Pyeng-yang Coal Company and the Karazu Coal Company of Japan. We have the best quality of both an thracite and bituminous coal, and prompt ex ecution of orders is our speciality. Firewood of all kinds kept in stock. Full weight guaranteed. Money of all denominations exchanged at current rates. Parcels received for all parts.

CHINA MUTUAL LIFE INS. OC.

Most favourable terms to policy holders.

Benefit system unsurpassed.

HOLME RINGER & Co.
Agents, Chemulpo.

C. P. R.

CANADIAN PACIFIC RAILWAY COMPANY'S ROYAL MAIL STEAMSHIP LINE.

THE FAST ROUTE BETWEEN CHINA, JAPAN, AND EUROPE VIA CANADA AND THE UNITED STATES.

Route from Hongkong via Shanghai, Nagasaki (Inland Sea of Japan) Kobe, Yokohama Victoria and Vancouver.

Twin Screw Empress Steamship—6,000 Tons—Speed 19 knots.

PROPOSED SAILING FROM YOKOHAMA.
R. M. S. Empress of India
R. M. S. Empress of Japan.
R. M. S. Empress of China.
R. M. S. Athenian.
R. M. S. Tartar.

Special reduction (first class only) granted to members of the Military, Naval, Diplomatic and Civil services and to Missionaries.
Passengers have choice of ten routes across the Continent of America and have privilege of travelling by any Atlantic Steamship Line.
Round the World passage tickets in connection with the P. and O. S. N., North German Lloyd and Messageries Co.'s **£125**.
All rates payable at current rate of exchange.
For further information, Tickets, Guide Books, etc., apply to
HOLME, RINGER & CO., AGENTS, Chemulpo.

Grand Hotel,

(Formerly the Station Hotel)

Near the Railway Terminus, West Gate Seoul.

The Best Hotel in Korea;
Handsome new Building.
Fine Airy Rooms
Excellent Cuisine.
Terms Moderate.
Special terms to Missionaries and to permanent boarders.

Electric cars within 2 minutes' walk.

W. H. EMBERLEY.
Proprietor

EVERY FACILITY.

In connection with Life Assurance Business is afforded by

The Standard Life Assurance Co.,

One of the largest and wealthiest of the Provident Institutions of the United Kingdom Forms of Application and all information will be promptly afforded on application.

10 CENTS A DAY.

Not a very large expenditure is it? But it is sufficient to secure for a man of 30 a policy with the STANDARD LIFE OFFICE for

$1323.

For all particulars of rates, etc., apply to

Holme, Ringer & Co.,
Agents, Chemulpo.

THE NEW YORK LIFE INSURANCE COMPANY.

Have you ever been declined by any Company?

Are you engaged in a specially hazardous occupation?

Have you heard of the New York Life Insurance Company's New Classifications for this class of Risks?

If not, send your date of birth, occupation and particulars of rejection, if any to

E. MEYER & Co.,
Agents, Chemulpo.

MITSUI BUSSAN KAISHA.
(MITSUI & Co.)
MITSUI GINKO.
(MITSUI BANK.)

The Bank is owned by the members of the Mitsui Family, who, as partners, assume an unlimited responsibility for all liabilities of the Bank:—

Capital.......................... Yen 5,000,000
Reserve Fund .... " 5,600,000

HEAD OFFICE, TOKYO.
LONDON OFFICE, 34 LIME ST., E. C.

BRANCHES AND AGENCIES:—
New York, San Francisco, Hamburg, Bombay, Singapore, Manila, Hongkong, Amoy, Chefoo, Tientsin.
Kobe, Hakodate, Yokohama, Kure, Yokosuka, Moji, Shimonoseki, Miike, Wakamatsu, Nagasaki, Kuchinotsu, Karatsu, Sasebo, Misume, Taipeh, &c.

Telegraphic Address for all the Offices:
"MITSUI."
A. B. C. AND A. 1 CODES USED.

Contractors of Coal
To the Imperial Japanese Navy, Arsenals and Railway Bureau, Principal Railway Companies and Industrial Work, Home and Foreign Mail and Freight Steamers.
Sole Proprietors
Of the famous Miike, Tagawa and Yamano Coal Mines.
Sole Agents
For the sale of Fukumo, Hokoku, Ichimura, Kanoda, Mannoura, Onoura, Ostuji, Sonoda, Tsubaruro, Yoshinotani, Yoshio, Yurokibura and other coals.

YANGTSE INSURANCE ASSOCIATION, LTD.

The undersigned, having been appointed agents for the above company, are prepared to issue policies and pay losses on marine risks at regular rates.

E. MEYER & Co.,
Agents, Chemulpo.

AMERICAN KOREAN ELECTRIC CO.

Light and Power.

Main Office: Electric Building, Chong No.

RAILWAY DEPARTMENT.

OPERATING CARS BETWEEN EAST AND WEST GATE, EVERY TEN MINUTES:—

First Car leaves East Gate at 7:00 A. M. First Car leaves R. R. Station at 7:25 A. M
Last Car " East Gate at 8.40 P. M. Last " " R. R. Station at 9.05 P.M

OPERATING CARS BETWEEN EAST GATE AND IMPERIAL TOMB TERMINUS, EVERY TWENTY MINUTES:—
CONNECTING WITH EVERY ALTERNATE CAR ARRIVING AT EAST GATE FROM CHONG NO.

First Car leaves East Gate for Tomb at 7:10 A. M.
" " " Tomb for East Gate at 7:30 A. M.
Last " " East Gate for Tomb at 7:50 P. M.
" " " Tomb for East Gate at 8:10 P. M.

OPERATING CARS BETWEEN CHONG NO AND YUNG SAN RIVER EVERY TWELVE MINUTES:—

First Car leaves Chong No for South Gate at 7:12 A. M.
" " " Chong No for Yung San at 7:36 A. M.
" " " South Gate for Chong No at 7:20 A. M.
" " " Yung San for Chong No at 8:09 A. M.
Last " " South Gate for Chong No 9:00 P. M.
" " " Yung San for Chong No at 8.45 p. M.

SPECIAL PRIVATE CARS FURNISHED TO SUIT CONVENIENCE OF PATRONS. PRICES ON APPLICATION AT HEAD OFFICE.

LIGHTING DEPARTMENT.

Where less than 250 candle power of light is used, the rate per month will be
Per 16 candle power incandescent lamp,—All night.—Yen 2.50.
32 candle power incandescent lamp:—All night:—Yen 4.00.
50 candle power incandescent lamp:—All night:—Yen 6.00.
150 " " " " " " 10.00.
1200 " enclosed are " " " " 20.00.

Where more than 250 candle power of light is used, a Meter will be installed, freqvedted:—Rent of Meter Yen 2.00 per month. Rate of charges by meter reading:—Two Sen per Ampere per hour. (Approximately this is equal to about One Sen per 16 C. P. lamp per hour) Minimum monthly charge where meter is installed, Yen 20.00 per month, which includes rental of meter.
Estimates for installing lights furnished on application
An assortment of chandeliers always on hand.

K. Murakami.
Photograph Studio
Chinkokai, Seoul.

Printing, Developing and Enlargement, of Photographs always Undertaken.

Korean Views and Pictures Illustrating Native Customs always on Sale,

THE OSAKA SHOSEN KAISHA.

Boats frequently on the berth for Chinnampo.

REGULAR SAILINGS BETWEEN JAPAN AND KOREAN PORTS.

FUSAN AND KOBE VIA SHIMONOSEKI.

OSAKA VIA MOKPO, FUSAN, SHIMONOSEKI AND KOBE.

MOJI DIRECT.

OSAKA VIA KUNSAN, MASANPO, FUSAN, SHIMONOSEKI AND KOBE.

CHEMULPO KUNSAN LINE,
Every three days.

CHEMULPO CHINNAMPO LINE.
Every three days.

For Freight and passage and further particulars apply to
THE OSAKA SHOSEN KAISHA,
Chemulpo.

RONDON, PLAISANT & CO.

General Storekeepers and Merchants, Ships Contractors, Tobacconists, Commission and Forwarding Agents, Coal Merchants

IMPORTERS AND EXPORTERS

Seoul & Chemulpo.

W. D. WENTWORTH.

LANDING
AND
SHIPPING AGENT
AND
CUSTOMS BORDER.

12 OURA, NAGASAKI.

STEWARD & CO.

Chemulpo.

Shipchandlers and Storekeepers, Naval and Mercantile Contrrctors, Landing and Shipping Agents.

STEWARD'S HOTEL

Chemulpo.

Best accommodation in the port for travellers. Clean and well-aired rooms, good cuisine and prompt attendence, moderate tariff.

흥원ᄒ니졍권티젼 쥬흥란흥엿더라

론셜

우리의자유와 셩흔일본신문

○금월이십삼일에발간흔대한일보에우리가한국사졍과젼국형편을말흔나교쟝황히평론ᄒ엿는지라일본신문들이우리의게되ᄒ야비방ᄒ는말이심히패다ᄒ며셔흔빈샤ᄒ여그러ᄒ되우리는다만죠케블써롤이러니이제대한일보에는심지어우리다려아당의괴괴이라ᄒ고셔지목ᄒ야칭호ᄒ엿슨즉이는일본지사름의등별흔쟝셜로써다른사름으로ᄒ야곰자귀의말흔바를신쳥ᄒ도록ᄒ야우리의독립으로평론ᄒ는바를아당이라ᄒ고셜명ᄒ엿스나그러ᄒ나우리의계는샹실로경겁ᄒᆯ것도업스며또흔ᄒ뵐자도업는지라우리신문에괴왕계제흔바몃조법ᄒ고각국인졍ᄒ야등보ᄒ기를일본은한국사건과갓치무샹케를회만어를티평이면일명ᄒ며형홈진윤쾌려쳐ᄒ나흔다ᄒ엿스며일한회논라봉들의취징ᄒ미어놀한셩의주찰흔일본사령부에셔경비를티여죠단ᄒ엿다ᄒ며쳥국에잇는아라샤ᄉ사는한국황뎨자비면하ᄉ하ᄒ음셧다는귀변을듯고반괴들다라죠례를힝ᄒ엿다ᄒ며일본이한국에다동신을느리는것과및불명ᄒ졍칙으로써시힝이되도록앙이제ᄒ는일이필경셩취치못ᄒ엿괴라ᄒ고우리신문에계ᄒ엿스니교흥진티크게착오됨은엿스ᄒ엿슨즉이로영량홀수남엿손즁졍수히벌ᄒ야게지ᄒ기순엿스되아병를운복도디방에드러와노란흠이무쌍ᄒ며셰렴을마음디로밧아의취ᄒ는일이만흐되는말ᄒ지아니흔다ᄒ고ᄒ엿스니이는대한일보에셔이러케흔말자ㅣ아니며또흔두어ᄒ셰티셜명흔자ㅣ잇스며쥬쳥아샤가발계조폐흔일로평론흔바는일흔챵국한의약홈과갓치아라사에셔도한국을고렴ᄒ는듯ᄒ는셩칭이도잇서그러홈이로되우리는아라사사름들이이흔관계ᄒ엿다고한국을즁립ᄒ는권리가잇는냐라로알는지도오히려밋지못ᄒ는바일듯ᄒ며그리홈인듯ᄒ며리또흔북도에노란흠으로말ᄒ드리도티방을보도쟈히가졈령ᄒ아마음티로힝쟝ᄒ는거슬대한일보에셔는엇더ᄒ다고말ᄒ리오실로아인들의불법흔일과가흔흔힝위가업는바는아니로되가흔번으로싱각ᄒ진대일본사름이나일반인거시일본사름들도우쟝과흉만쥬등디에서힝쟝ᄒ야착수ᄒ는바에갓흔일이만흔즉수지오지자웅이리요ᄒ노라

ᄒ야곳인명치 수흥을빈샹ᄒ란ᄒ엿더라

○쳥죠범관 니쟝원에셔외부에복함ᄒ기를아라사사람에직무죠위원과류리기슈와샹등으로졍ᄂ일인니원리쳥유도여시귀국흔교로히합동이ᄉ수로폐지ᄒ엿교하등공졍일명ᄃ비긔잇서시무ᄒ지연마ᄃ되야이에죵은지라히기스등일봉과한샹니벌리교간문긴샹슈쳔원을지발ᄒ라ᄒ호되일이싱이죵거가엿스니일로써법공ᄉ에지죠흠이가ᄒ다ᄒ엿더라

○졉티외관 지쟉양샹신이시예외부에셔오쳔회를빈셜ᄒ고교문판과일공ᄉ와영공ᄉ를졉티ᄒ엿더라

○죠쳥존안 영국공ᄉ가일젼에외부로죠회ᄒ기를작일에귀대신으로더브러방면ᄒ야담화흔배에ᄋ의대금흔바이어니와귀국에셔우리샹민을보호ᄒ미소용되는화물의폐와호는원리영샹과한샹이리닉갓치엇는것미라만일귀국민이후와죠ᄒ는폐가잇스면귀졍부로엄졀이나실ᄒ야금지흔다ᄒ엿는티이것에티ᄒ야귀대신으로더브러피차예죤안비잇셔야ᄒ깃기에비문으로죠회ᄒ니쳥컨티죠량ᄒ라ᄒ엿더라

○죠쳥졍치딕방관 청공관에셔외부에죠회ᄒ되히쥬관셔포에잇는영국에잉져흔쳥국샹민치명스로외차에위원을파송ᄒ야심ᄉᄒ는티쟉일영공관에셔사름을파송ᄒ야외셔말ᄒ기를히쥬에파송홀영관위원빅이의면보니기에머리빅셩이돌로써영쳥관위원우거흔쳐소에던져교쏘아을니ᄉ소리지르기를쳥인타샹흔것은무죄흔말이라ᄒ니사셜흔즉히디방관보호도ᄒ지아니ᄒ고로히평을드니쳥컨티귀대신은히디방관과위원의게면칙ᄒ야못관계ᄒ기를바란다ᄒ엿더라

○면결소환 과원리진츈의가외부에면보ᄒ기를영국평사가회셩ᄒ지아니ᄒ기로관계ᄒ게약이엉코한곳금액만히비ᄒ니이곳에언셔유이ᄒᆯ겻이업스니다란진티곳조환ᄒ라ᄒ엿더라

○쥬쳥공ᄉ면보 쥬쳥공관에셔면보ᄒ기를쳥국외무부죠회니기에쥬한쳥ᄉᄉ대신허티신은케잉과한이된고로그티에후보오픔경당증광젼이가츌사대신이되야귀국경셩에쥬차흔다ᄒ엿기에보고흔다ᄒ엿더라

○죠쳥젼쥬 일공관에셔외부로죠회ᄒ기를이번에경셩에도착흔본방신사ᄉ죵오위흔샹등에태창희발랑이가 폐현ᄒ기

디에밧승의고취임ᄒ기를기드리귀국케ᄒ란는수로 지의원ᄒ니다시일공ᄉ의게가죠의아가소환ᄒ라ᄒ엿기이에죠회흔다ᄒ엿더라

○죠복영관 외부에셔영공관에죠복ᄒ기를영샹에소용되는화물의피와호블위조젼용ᄒ는폐가잇스면조례즁치ᄒ다는수는본대신은이론이업깃다ᄒ엿더라

○김뎨슈파직 젼라북도관찰사박제빈씨가금뎨군슈평옥씨를봉고파직ᄒ엿더라

○슌검파송젼북 젼라북도관찰ᄉ의면보니에회민이흉담총ᄒ고흉티검ᄒ고포졍문으로곳드러왓다ᄒ엿더니졍부의죠회를등인ᄒ야닉부에셔경무쳥으로훈령ᄒ기를일이심샹치아니ᄒ니병졍은ᄒ야히산케ᄒ고그ᄒ지죵두는거술가히쟝시라도검을ᄂ지ᄒ니총순파슌검을지완치못ᄒ야엄칙ᄒ야죤힝케ᄒ며거힝ᄒ는졍지를곳시명라ᄒ엿더라

○보호병명 거이십오일에경부에셔긴급흔회의를ᄒ엿는티회민이수수로히챵거홈을방흠츄로각대신가에병뎡륙명식파송ᄒ야보호ᄒ다더라

○참모부죠회 참모부에셔닉부와군부로죠회ᄒ기를졍부참졍찬졍참찬과각부대신즁에군위인죵보호병를명을친위티에서파송ᄒ고군인이나니이는헌병샹명파순검샹명식파송ᄒ엿사로셩지등봉송ᄒ엿시니파송홀베예등병이영칙ᄒ야극력보호ᄒ되소홀홈이엽게ᄒ라ᄒ엿더라

○취곤발차 샹작일젼시반에느리를병문에셔취곤ᄒ니히면차에례리잿는티비사름이셔다셜넘ᄒ쟁으로드린다뉘엿고다형에면ᄎ에는눈니지아니ᄒ엿다더라

○경수신업 샹작일에경무수는케잉ᄒ고김쟁근씨가셔임ᄒ엿는티그수셜은회원이무란ᄒ이관인을ᄌ앗가둔일이오경무수는불셜신칙ᄒᆫ차ᄃ이라더라

○신임경수교시 신임경무수가고시ᄒ기를경부죠회를인ᄒ야샹민이무란히회를셜시ᄒ야대관을능욕ᄒ며무란이관인을착슈ᄒ니블가블시샹흔일이ᄋ회니죵간별히ᄉ람ᄒ야범과ᄒ는ᄒ야ᄒ쥐ᄂ죠를ᄒ는고며당은효유ᄒ야산케ᄒ라ᄒ엿다더라

○평감보고 평양감리가외부에보고ᄒ기를본월십일일재너부에일본병일명이술이취ᄒ야리부동김용한의집에돌입ᄒ야창느로써용한의좌편다리를질너당장에죽은지라극히참혹ᄒ기에보고ᄒ오니일공ᄉ의게젼죠

치회연셜ᄒ엿고공진일젼량취가동ᄋ에는셔로회합ᄒ야오후두시증에랑회회원수쳔명이죵로에회집ᄒ미관평자가구름굿치모혀죵로동셔남북에구등차셔사름만는닐수업슬뿐더러면거ᄌ블통이되엿고그때에경무쳥에셔총순이ᄒᆫ일과순검오륙명을파송ᄒ야순검이발검ᄒ고회원을홋치려ᄒ다가흔사름이드리를쎄넘샹흔지라회원들이분개막심ᄒ야연셜ᄒ야왈우리대황뎨폐하ᄭᅴ셔는이젹ᄌ를샹휼ᄒ라셜리가업는티나라에역젹이잇서빅셩을살휘ᄒ려ᄒ니빅셩이엇지살니오사름이지원극통ᄒ면하는님을불너호소ᄒ는니우리가이굿치통분흔일이엿스니머리셔흔번하는님쎄소사ᄒ고일제히대안문압헤가셔쏘하는님쎄망소사ᄒ자고ᄒ니만민이기원셜타ᄒ야일졔히죵로에셔써나대안문압흐로가셔일제히하는님ᄭᅴ소사ᄒ고엇던회원들은티밧임이나대셩통곡ᄒ고두어시동안후에는이마곤ᄒ엿스면우리의지원흠을 대황뎨폐하ᄭᅴ셔 통측ᄒ셧스리라ᄒ며고명일ᄯᅩ모히기로ᄒ고퇴거ᄒ엿고

등야네평리원에셔는리쥰용효졍라유셕윤하영사인을심판ᄒ엿고참졍신긔션씨는민회를회산홀ᄎ로죵각에고시ᄒ엿고경위원총관권중석씨는봉 칙ᄒ야순검을단속ᄒ고각민회사무소에젼왕ᄒ여회민을쥰출ᄒ고회가사에대문을봉쇄ᄒ엿고이십칠일에경무쳥에셔는각방곡과리막에순검을파송ᄒ야시봉사름이류경ᄒ는자를일일히젹간ᄒ야축출ᄒ더라

○좌명비시제 승명비시제ᄒ기위ᄒ야 공니닌인비졍로수라예출거ᄒ야샹일을셜힝ᄒ엿더라

○회쟝쳔졍 경셩일힌졍도죵교회에셔회원과를계셜ᄒ다ᄒ며니리지용영쥬의써로회쟝과부회쟝을쳔졍ᄒ엿다더라

○부승농부 관제리쟝소에셔탐도원은폐지ᄒ야농샹공부에탐도국을의젼셜시ᄒ다더라

○수죄자처판 금이십ᄉ일륙군법원에서장관이회의ᄒ야여신로범이하수죄자를처판ᄒ엿더라

○죠회쳥관 외부에셔청공관에죠회ᄒ기를향부공ᄉ니기에그한어교ᄉ호문취의졍슐회국ᄒ기위ᄒ야일빅이십원을지발ᄒᆫ다ᄒ엿기이에죠회ᄒᆫ다ᄒ엿더라

○우졍ᄂ환 외부에셔일공관에죠회ᄒ기를참모부공ᄉ니기에통군창위원좌셩이가헌금젼

SERIOUS RIOT IN SEOUL.

That aggregation of lazy, mischievous ne'er-do-wells made up from the Il Chin hoi and kindred organizations, seems bent on wreaking serious mischief in Korea.

As we have repeatedly said the Il Chin hoi has been maintained by the Japanese army Headquarters here from whom the members have received "encouraging money" at the rate of sixty cents a day, payable every five days when the agitators receive three dollars all at once

Naturally enough all the workings of the organization are not made known to us, but there undoubtedly exists a good understanding between these anarchists and the Japanese.

The neighbourhood of the palace was again to-day the scene of uproar and anarchy. Shortly after 12 o'clock a band of disreputable Koreans, wearing the frowsy European cap which is the insignia of a "reformer," held a meeting in a building at the back of the Continental Hotel.

A number of Korean soldiers remained in the neighbourhood to maintain order, and presently for some reason or other a disturbance arose which culminated in a riot.

The affair was somewhat "Irish" in character and up to the time we go to press our information only says that several people were wounded.

When our reporter arrived upon the scene the Japanese Gendarmerie and Military were in charge, and were searching the Korean barracks for officers, several of whom had already been arrested.

In case the "Japan Mail" should call this "restoring order" we point out that all this trouble would never have occurred if the Japanese had not encouraged and paid these renegade agitators.

NEWS FROM RUSSIAN SOURCES.

The "Tokyo Asahi's" Shanghai correspondent reports that the Russian organ at Shanghai has published a telegram from Chefoo, the gist of which is that in the last assault on the 203-metre height the Japanese lost 12,000 men during the first two hours, and that even with these heavy sacrifices they were unable to occupy the position permanently, but were compelled to retire at last. Neither party therefore is in possession of the height at present. The message adds that since the 15th November the Japanese have lost three torpedo-boats, and that two steamers, one carrying provisions and the other munitions, have arrived at Port Arthur since the 1st instant.

Last night a body of the Il-chin hoi marched to the central police station and effected the release of Mr. Yun Si Byung, their president and several of his assistants

---

Mr. Chalmers, British Consul, who has been transferred from Shimonoseki to Tansui, Formosa, left for Kobe on the 20th inst. on his way home on leave.

Mr. Playfair, the late Vice-Consul at Kobe, has succeeded Mr. Chalmers and has arrived at Shimonoseki.

The telegram received here to the effect that a Japanese squadron consisting of 2 battleships 1 cruiser 12 destroyers together with the "Nippon Maru" and "Hongkong Maru" had been seen off Singapore going Westwards seems to be founded on fact as long ago as December 13th the "Universal Gazette" published the following Tokio telegram:—

The second Japanese fleet has been got ready. Everything is done in absolute secrecy. It is decided that as soon as the Baltic fleet reaches a certain point, the Japanese fleet will proceed to meet it.—

DIFFICULTIES AT PORT ARTHUR.

General Kodama's Chief of Staff General Nogi, in the course of an interview with a "London Daily News" correspondent, is reported to have said :—"Our blockade is perfect. The Russian forts are well built on the Belgian model. The general situation of the forts also is similar to the Belgian forts. They are iron plated toward the sea; toward the land they are only earthworks, with some masonry and a little concrete. A clever engineer designed them. We find them absolutely changed since the China war, when we took Port Arthur in one day. Then one fort, Tseshan, was the key of the whole position. Once that had been taken all the others fell. Now we can not say any single fort is the key. All are so arranged that we must take them in detail. The capture of one means only the capture of that individual fort, not of a series as formerly. Study as we may, we find it difficult to locate their weakness, they have carried fortification to such an extent."

KOREAN NEWS IN JAPAN.

The following, which we take from the "Kobe Herald" is a fair specimen of the "news" transmitted to Japanese newspapers by their Seoul correspondents:—

A Mainichi telegram from Seoul, Dated Dec. 29, states that, in response to an invitation from the Korean Emperor, General Hasegawa paid a visit to His Majesty on the 18th at three o'clock in the afternoon, accompanied by Major Kaidzu, who is well acquainted with the Korean language, and some other officers. The Korean officials report that, in reply to questions put by the Emperor, the General explained the changes that are being made in the Korean military system. When he stated that he would take full charge of the measures for the security of the Imperial Household, the Emperor was extremely pleased, and expressed a wish that the General should have a conversation with the Crown Prince, who was thereupon called into the room. Both the Emperor and the Prince talked freely with the General. Telephone communication will be established shortly between General Hasegawa's official residence and the Palace and Imperial Household Department.

It seems that the China Inland Mission has decided that its members should discontinue wearing Chinese clothes and queues. For many years it has been argued by a considerable number of thoughtful observers, that the native "disguise" did more harm than good, because its use was misinterpreted by the majority of the populace. While a few could understand the idea, most of them were firmly convinced that the foreigners were masquerading under false pretences, and so on. Even at best, the Chinese did not respect or esteem the Chinese clothed missionary more than the one who appeared plainly as his natural self. The C. I. Mission is therefore to be congratulated on the change.—The China Times.

That corruption is not confined to Russia is shown by the following. An officer and twenty-five non-commissioned officers belonging to the Kure Naval Station are reported by the "Jiji" to have been punished with between one month and one year's imprisonment with hard labour. They had received bribes from merchants patronized by the office.

The New York Sun states that Mr. Whitelaw Reid, the well-known editor of the New York "Tribune, will succeed Mr. J. H. Choate as United States Ambassador to the Court of St. James.

The Tokio "Asahi" has reported that an American shipbuilding firm has contracted to build a hundred Russian men-of-war at Sebastopol!

IS THIS A JOKE?

At the instance and expense of Mr. Kokei Kuwada, and ex-Army Surgeon, a religious service for the Japanese and Russian horses killed in the war has been held at the Kwannon temple at Asakusa, over 100 priests being present. Surgeon-General Baron Ishiguro, Lieutenant-General Okosai, several military surgeons and many others attended the ceremony.

THE IL-CHIN-HOI.

Not content with their foolish outburst on Monday, the Il-chin-hoi society held another large meeting on Tuesday afternoon. The Chief of Police on being informed led a force of gendarmes to the meeting place on Chong-no and quickly dispersed the mob, later effectually closing up the premises of the society.

His Majesty has ordered that the society shall be broken up as speedily as possible and until this is effected he has authorised the military authorities to furnish body-guards of soldiers to all high officials. A strengthening of the Palace guards has also been advised.

The Shanhaikwan authorities have applied to the Throne for permission to restrain merchants and cargo from proceeding Northward.

The "Chefoo Daily News" has received an emphatic denial of the statement there is friction between General Stoessel and Admiral Wirin.

The employees at Krupp's ordnance works at Essen are working double relays. One order is for 200,000 shells of a completely new make, and probably intended for Russia or Japan.

It is announced that three sorcerers Messrs. Kang Hong Tai, Choi Byung Chu and Sung Kwang Ho have found it advisable to efface themselves for a while owing to the intention of the Law Department to have them arrested.

The following terse but alarming paragraph has been handed in by our city reporter ; "The Il Chin Hoi society has prepared 6 straw trays to carry away some Ministers etc." This is rather a large order and who or what are the etceteras?

After the President of the Kong Chin Hoi had been arrested on Monday, his wife visited the quarters of the society and harangued, the crowd in bold and fearless terms exhorting them to be brave in the face of their difficulties. No lamentations for the temporary loss of her husband were expressed.

A Japanese officer, stopping at Chefoo is according to the "Chefoo Daily News," given as authority for the statement that Nogi has had nearly one hundred thousand casualties at Port Arthur. The officer is also reported to have said that the wounds inflicted by the bullets of the regulation Russian rifle are much more severe than the ones made by the Osaka bullet.

Sentence of punishment has been passed very speedily on four of the Kong-chin-hoi people arrested last Saturday. Na Yu-suk, the principal offender, has been condemned to death while Yi Chun, Yun Hio-chung and Yun Ha-yun will each serve a life sentence with hard labour. The Law Department have requested His Majesty's consent.

The Magistrate of Kyong Sang reports that the Russians, numbering about 2,000 now staying in his district, are extremely particular in their inspection of new arrivals from the south, fearing Japanese espionage. A despatch from another quarter states that the Russians knowing nothing about the Il Chin Hoi society, it is extremely inadvisable for any members of that fraternity to be found in the north as with their cropped hair they are liable to be mistaken for Japanese in disguise.

CONDITIONS TO CEASE HOSTILTIES.

A telegram from Paris in Canadian papers, dated Nov. 26th, said:—

The report of the Committee on the Foreign Budget contains the following special statement in connection with the Russo-Japanese War.

"Already Japan has made known the conditions on which she is ready to close hostilities. These consist in the return of Manchuria to China, the dismantling of Port Arthur and the establishment of Korean independence, with the right of Japanese to acquire land. Russia's refusal of the foregoing conditions shows that it is her purpose to carry on the conflict to the end."

When the correspondent of the Associated Press enquired at the Foreign Office what authority there was explained that the conditions were not officially made known by the Japanese Government, but by the Japanese Commercial Association, representing the powerful progressive element, and having influence with the Government. Therefore it was believed to reflect Japanese official wishes.

Referring again to the recent rise in the bank rate in Japan we find that the present rates of interest work out at from 7.36 per cent for loans against gilt-edged securities to nearly 8½ per cent for ordinary commercial advances. This rate of interest but adversely affects the commerce of the country and in explanation of it the "Japan Times" says:—"The enhancement of the bank rates has been necessitated by the inflating tendency of the Japanese currency. The amount of money in circulation at the end of November showed an increase of about 46 million yen as compared with the corresponding period of last year, and an increase of 7 million yen over the previous month. At the end of November the total amount of convertible notes issued stood at 248 million yen, which after wards decreased to 233 million yen. But according to the latest returns, these figures have again risen to 244 million yen, so that the raising of the bank rates is considered necessary in order to check the inflation of the currency."

Among the passengers who recently passed through Singapore "en route" to the Farthest East was, says the "Straits Times," one whose advent was, for obvious reasons, unheralded. That was Mr. Orlan C. Cullen, the American inventor of the ball-bearing rifled gun, who left here on Saturday for Tokyo. Mr. Cullen's marvellous invention practically gives double power—weight for weight, and calibre for calibre—to all artillery built according to its plans. The Japanese Government is understood to have contracted for all the guns that Mr. Cullen can turn out during the next few years. An illustrated article on the principle of the gun appears in this month's Knowledge.

From all accounts Saigon seems now to be the shipping rendezvous for Port Arthur and Vladivostock. A steamer recently bought in Bombay has just completed loading a full cargo of tinned meat and rice and has cleared for Newchwang, which port everyone knows closes the first week of this month. Large quantities of provisions are being shipped from Hongkong to Saigon and there loaded by vessels, which clear for any port. It is surmised that a quantity of provisions will be shipped from there to meet the Baltic fleet.

His Majesty has ordered the War Department to post guards at the City Gates to prevent the ingress of undesirable country folk. He also commands the Police to eject all suspicious looking people from the capital.

The Korea Daily News.

Issued at 5 P. M. daily except Sundays.

Rate of Subscription:—
Per Year,............Yen 25.
Per Quarter,..........Yen 7.
Per Month,..........Yen 2.50.

Postage in Korea not charged extra.
Postage abroad charged extra.

Advertisements, 50 sen per day for 1 inch or less.
5 yen per month per inch.
50 yen per year per inch.

All communications to

E. T. BETHELL,
Editor and Publisher,
Pak-tong, Seoul.

ADVISERS IN KOREA.

Anyone attempting to reform Korea must look forward to many hours of heart sickness and despondency. If active opposition were encountered it might be overcome, but instead of that the would-be reformer finds himself confronted with a heavy, soggy, unimpressionable barrier of passive resistance against which he beats in vain.

Japan is at present filling the role of regenerator of Korea, and the task of effecting reforms is probably many times more difficult for her than it would be for anyone else. The Koreans are filled with a profound distrust of her intentions and a deep-roofed dislike of her people. Korea's suspicions and fears are not unfounded, and if she believes that the independence which was given to her with such a flourish of trumpets some years ago is but an incident in the transference of suzerainty from China to Japan, it must be admitted that she has many good reasons for that belief.

Thus it is that the Koreans are disposed to suspect a sinister motive behind every proposal for reform emanating from the Japanese or the pro-Japanese party, and as in place of a renewal of the former protestations of a determination to uphold the integrity and independence of this unfortunate country we find the Tokio press continually urging its Government to adopt stronger measures in Korea. It is not to be wondered at that all proposals for an alteration in the present *regime*, whether advanced by H. E. Mr. Hayashi or by General Hasegawa, are not received with a very hearty welcome.

Korea's army, for instance, is at present worse than useless. As it is too small to be of any account against another country and much larger than is necessary for police purposes in Korea, the money spent upon it is, rightly enough, said by the Japanese to be wasted. Yet in view of the fact, that it is not so long ago that by the provision of instructors and other measures the Japanese assisted and encouraged the maintainence of this army, it is not surprising if the Emperor is disposed to regard any reduction of it as a dimunition of his body-guard and a potential menace to the safety of himself and his people.

And so it is through every Department of the Korean Government service. Even when the Koreans, on their own initiative, have appointed foreign advisers, they have never given them any real power, and but seldom manifested much desire for their advice. The position of advisers, Japanese nominees, who were not spontaneously appointed by the Korean Government is still more difficult. They will not be actively opposed, but their advice will have as little effect on its recipients as water on a duck's back, and it will be only by the exercise of great patience and earnest endeavour in restoring the confidence of the Koreans in Japan's good intentions, that any headway may ultimately be made.

TWO HUNDRED AND THREE METRE HILL.

The "Tokyo Asahi's" correspondent at Chefoo wires that a two-masted boat belonging to the Port Arthur Harbour Office arrived at Chefoo from Port Arthur on the 17th inst., carrying on board a Russian Lieutenant-Commander, another officer and six blue jackets. The first-mentioned is stated to be the officer second in command of the battleship "Poltava" and also to be in charge of a secret message from Lieutenant-General Stoessel. The boat is only 20 feet long, and is specially equipped to make her seaworthy.

The "Asahi's" correspondent further transmits what purports to be the story of the Russian Lieutenant-Commander. His statement must apparently be received with some allowance, but as it is nevertheless interesting in several respects, we translate it in substance as follows:—

At 7 p. m. on the 16th inst., says the Russian officer, our boat left Loatiehshan, and after struggling through a heavy snowstorm for 15 hours, at last succeeded in reaching Chefoo. I was wounded in the right leg while attacking the 203-metre height on the 15th inst. The majority of the crews of all the Russian warships, except the battleship "Sevastopol," have landed and taken their place in the fighting line. No calls have been made either on the crew or armament of the "Sevastopol," but all the heavy guns of the other warvessels have been landed according to orders from Stoessel, in spite of the remonstrances of Rear-Admiral Viren. The fighting on the 203-metre hill lasted a fortnight, during which time the position was taken and retaken three times. This engagement was of the severest description. The hill was literally covered with the bodies of the dead and almost all the rocks were smeared with blood. The Russians had placed no great value on that eminence, which was only provided with temporary defensive works. It was only for Russia's prestige and the safer retention of the fortress that we Russians fought so desperately on that hill. The latter is at present occupied by neither army. Nor is Stoessel willing to retake the height at the risk of further casualties. The Japanese have retired to an adjoining elevation called Long Hill (which is probably the same hill known to our army as Akasakayama), but their officers are occasionally seen ascending the 203-metre eminence, presumably for the purpose of making observations. Whenever these officers appear on the summit they are subjected to the fire of some 500 rifles from the neighbouring Russian positions, but the officers are admirably self-possessed and appear to take no notice of their danger. During the first Japanese attack on the 203-metre height, a Russian corporal named Peter Constantinoti wrested the Japanese standard from the hands of an ensign and was on the point of tearing it with his sword, when he was struck by seven bullets and killed. The second assault was the severest of all the engagements, the conflicting forces being so close to each other that they were able to fire their rifles point blank at one another. The third Japanese assault was fatal to the Russians, the Japanese having set fire to wood sprinkled with kerosene oil and other inflammable materials, which were piled up windward. The Russians were consequently swept by the furious flames and had to abandon the position. After the fighting was over, an armistice of five hours was agreed upon between the opposing forces in order to collect the bodies of their respective dead. During the final assault by the Japanese, the latter displayed exceptional intrepidity. One of them attempted to plant the flag of the Rising Sun on the parapet, only to meet with instantaneous death, a bullet piercing his head. He was succeeded by a second, who also fell. A third man immediately took his turn, but met a similar fate. Nothing daunted, one after another the Japanese gallantly endeavoured to hoist their standard, but in vain, altogether eight men falling dead upon the ground. The Russian commander was so impressed with the spectacle that he ordered his men to refrain from picking off those gallant foes, who would never stop until they succeeded in their attempt, however perilous it might be.

In this connection, the "Asahi's" correspondent states that our Consul at Chefoo has forwarded a communication to the local taotai, asking the latter to take immediate steps for the detention of the Russian officers and men mentioned above. The Chinese authorities are consequently negotiating with the Russian Consul in this connection.—Japan Times.

Mr. Steven's contract with the Government was duly signed on the 27th inst.

It is announced at Portsmouth that King Edward starts on a cruise in the Mediterranean early in February.

We learn from New York, that a group of financiers have decided to open a bank there that will run night and day.

Two police inspectors from the North-east have been dismissed on account of their handing over their swords to Russian officers.

A Chinese native reporter says that there are scarcely any Japanese troops left at Kinchow, Fuchow, Haechen or Kaiping,—only a few soldiers remain at each place to act as guards and patrols.

"Puck" says that missionary effort in Japan has received a fresh impetus from the fact that some of the recent naval victories of the Mikado's forces have been won by converted cruisers.

Yesterday afternoon the Il Chin Hoi society held a special meeting in a house close to the Palace, but the Police getting wind of it quickly had the meeting broken up, and the President and a few leaders arrested.

S. Takno, of the Kure Naval station, was arrested on Dec. 5th on a charge of fraud. He will be tried by Court-Martial. It is reported by the "Yoroezu" that from April 1st, 1901, to July 18th this man stole yen 7,547 belonging to the office, having forged receipts from meat merchants who were patronized by the naval station.

The appeal of the Japanese authorities to retain the Magistrate of Pyeng-yang in office has apparently been finally rejected, for in the latest of the Home Office to the Law Department, the latter are authorised to arrest and punish the Magistrates of Pyeng-yan Chosan and Hyeng Kang. "Squeezing" is the cause of each man's downfall.

We hear, says the "China Gazette," that Mr. Prest, late of the Shanghai Police force, who has for some time past been in charge of the Viceroy Chang Chih-tung's police at Wuchang, has been supplanted by a Japanese Chang is now the most completely Japped of all the high Chinese officials and openly declares he has no further use for white men!

A telegram from the capital, dated December 9th, says the "China Gazette" reports that Tsĕng Chun has been appointed Chinese Minister to Korea, and that Yin Chang has been ordered to remain at his post in Berlin for another three years. Tsĕng Cheu is the owner of the Universal Gazette and a 'persona grata' naturally of the Japanese. Hence his appointment to Korea by Chinese.

The Korea Daily News.

VOL. I, THURSDAY, DECEMBER 29, 1904. No. 136

HONGKONG & SHANGHAI BANKING CORPORATION.

Paid-up Capital	$10,000,000
Reserve Fund:—Sterling Reserve	10,000,000
Silver Reserve	7,000,000
	27,000,000
Reserve Liability of Proprietors	10,000,000

HEAD OFFICE, HONGKONG.

London Bankers, London and County Banking Company Limited.

Branches and Agencies,

London.

Amoy,	Hankow	Penang,
Bangkok,	Hiogo,	Rangoon,
Batavia,	Iloilo,	Saigon,
Bombay,	Lyons,	San Francisco,
Calcutta,	Manila,	Singapore,
Colombo,	Nagasaki,	Sourabaya,
Foochow,	New York,	Tientsin,
Hamburg,	Peking,	Yokohama,

Credits granted on approved Securities, and every description of Banking and Exchange business transacted.

Drafts granted on London and the chief Commercial places in Europe, India, Australia, America, China and Japan.

HOLME RINGER & Co., AGENTS, CHEMULPO.

HOKURKU DOBOKU KAISHA.

Branch office in Chong Dong. Seoul.

Japanese telephone No. 165

CONTRACT DEPARTMENT.

We can contract to build any building or construction.

MERCHANDISE DEPARTMENT.

We can provide any building material. We have just contracted to build the new Belgian Legation.

E. MEYER & CO.

Chemulpo.

SOLE AGENTS IN KOREA FOR.

A. T. Morse, Sons & Co.'s "Fresco" Distemper

In all colours ready for use on walls, Ceilings etc.

and

AVENARIUS CARBOLINEUM

A wood-preserving and antiseptic oil preparation

Against decay, dry-rot, fungus and wood-destroying insects.

A large supply always in stock.

Prices upon application.

E. MEYER & Co.,

Chemulpo.

CHARTERED BANK OF INDIA AUSTRALIA & CHINA.

INCORPORATED BY ROYAL CHARTER 1853

HEAD OFFICES:—LONDON.

Paid-up Capital	£800,000
Reserve Liability of Shareholders	800,000
Reserve Fund	800,000

Drafts granted upon all the principal places in the world and every description of Exchange and banking business transacted.

E. MEYER & Co., Agents,

Chemulpo.

MITSU BISHI DOCKYARD & ENGINE WORKS,

NAGASAKI.

CODE WORD, "DOCK."

A 1, A. B. C., and Engineering Codes used.

DOCK No. 1 (at Tategami).

Extreme Length	523 feet
Length on blocks	513 "
Width of Entrance on Top	89 "
" " Bottom	77 "
Water on Blocks at Spring Tide	26½ "

DOCK No. 2 (Mukaijima).

Extreme Length	371 feet
Length on Blocks	360 "
Width of Entrance on Top	66 "
" " Bottom	53 "
Water on Blocks at Spring Tide	22 "

PATENT SLIP (at Kosuge).

Can take vessels up to 1,000 tons gross.

THE WORKS are well equipped with the LATEST IMPROVEMENTS, and can execute any kind of work in SHIPBUILDING and MARINE ENGINEERING, as well as in REPAIRING of SHIPS.

The COMPANY'S new powerful steamer OURA-MARU (712 tons, 700 I.H.P.), specially built for SALVAGE PURPOSES, and equipped with necessary gear, is always READY at SHORT NOTICE.

THE METHODIST PUBLISHING HOUSE,

Little West Gate, Seoul.

JOB PRINTING, TYPEWRITER PAPER
CARBON PAPER, VISITING CARDS
STATIONERY, BOOK BINDING
BOOK PUBLISHERS
AMERICAN SCHOOL BOOKS
SPENCERIAN COPY BOOKS
PEN CARBON LETTER AND BILL BOOKS

S.A. BECK, Manager.

DAI-ICHI GINKO.

LIMITED.

(Formerly the First National Bank)

ESTABLISHED 1873

INCORPORATED UNDER PRESENT LAW 1896

Capital	Yen 5,000,000
Reserve Fund	1,500,000

HEAD OFFICE:—TOKIO.

President: Baron SHIBUSAWA.

BRANCHES AND CORRESPONDENTS

In the Principal Cities and Towns of Japan.

Interest Allowed on

Fixed deposits 1 year	6½ per cent
" " 6 months	6 per cent

Special current accounts 1½ sen daily per Y 100

General " " 1 " " " 100

M. TANAKA,

Manager, Chemulpo.

SINGER SEWING MACHINES

싱거조봉침

SOLE AGENTS FOR KOREA

전매쇼

HOLME RINGER & CO.

Chemulpo.

제믈포 함릉거양힝

KAMEYA & CO.

GENERAL STOREKEEPERS

Chinkokai - - Seoul

(*Established 1895, Tokyo*)

Confectionery, Hams, Canned Goods, Cutlery, Hirano & Tansan Water. Provisions, Gents, Furnishing goods, Toilet Articles, Travelling Bags, Tobacco, Cigars & Cigarettes Kitchen Utensils. Coffee, Biscuits

Fresh Goods always kept in Stock.

Prices Moderate

Please come and inspect our goods.

NIPPON YUSEN KAISHA.

JAPANESE MAIL STEAMSHIP CO.

UNDER MAIL CONTRACT WITH THE IMPERIAL JAPANESE GOVERNMENT.

European Line

Regular Fortnightly Service between Yokohama Kobe, Moji, Shanghai, Hongkong, Singapore, Penang Colombo, Port Said, Marseilles, London and Antwerp

American Line

Regular Fortnightly Service between Hongkong and Seattle, calling at Shanghai, Moji, Kobe, Yokohama and Victoria, B. C.

Australian Line

Regular weekly Service betwen Japan Ports and Australia, calling at Hongkong and Manila.

(Above Three Lines Suspended until further notice).

Shanghai Line

Weekly Service between Shanghai and Japan Ports

Korea Line

Service Kobe, Moji, Nagasaki, Fusan Chemupo Chef foo, Taiku.

S. S. Bahelsberg, 2181 tons.

Service Kobe, Moji, Fusan, Chemulpo, Chinnampo

S. S. ARGO, S. S. Ohio.

BORDEN'S CONDENSED MILK CO.

New York, U. S. A.

ALWAYS IN STOCK

Eagle Brand Condensed Milk.

Gold Seal Condensed Milk.

Peerless (Family) Evaporated Cream.

Borden's Malted Milk.

E. MEYER & CO.

Chemulpo Korea,

Sole Agents

ROYAL INSURANCE COMPANY

Funds exceed £10,000,000

FIRE

AT CURRENT RATES.

LIFE

REDUCED PREMIUM.

HOLME RINGER & Co.,

Agents, Chemulpo

HOTEL DU PALAIS

SEOUL.

The only first class Hotel in Seoul Situated in the centre of the city opposite the palace.

Cuisine under the supervision of an experienced French Chef.

Well ventilated and furnished through-out.

TARIFF UPON APPLICATION

L. MARTIN

Proripetor and Manager

大韓每日申報

대한매일신보

(뎨일빅삼십칠호)　(토요일)　일쳔구빅사년 십이월 삼십일일

본샤고빅

뎐보

잡보

UNION INSURANCE SOCIETY OF CANTON.

Head office Hongkong.
Marine risks underwritten at current rates.
Agents in Chemulpo,
E. MEYER & Co.

COMPAGNIE DES MESSAGERIES MARITIMES.

Fortnightly Direct Service.

For Marseilles
via Ports.
Sailing from Yokohama
Calling at Kobe,
Shanghai, Hongkong, Saigon, Singapore,
Colombo, Djibouti, Suez, Port Said
and Marseilles.

For particulars apply to
HOLME RINGER & Co.,
Chemulpo.

HAYASHIDA & CO.,

16 MYENG DONG, CHIN KO KAI, SEOUL.
BRANCH OFFICE AT CHEMULPO.

Money changers, Coal and Wood Merchants, Express Agents.

We are agents for the Pyeng-yang Coal Company and the Karazu Coal Company of Japan. We have the best quality of both anthracite and bituminous coal, and prompt execution of orders is our speciality. Firewood of all kinds kept in stock. Full weight guaranteed. Money of all denominations exchanged at current rates. Parcels received for all parts.

CHINA MUTUAL LIFE INS. OC.

Most favourable terms to policy holders.

Benefit system unsurpassed.

HOLME RINGER & Co.
Agents, Chemulpo.

C. P. R.

CANADIAN PACIFIC RAILWAY COMPANY'S ROYAL MAIL STEAMSHIP LINE.

THE FAST ROUTE BETWEEN CHINA, JAPAN, AND EUROPE VIA CANADA AND THE UNITED STATES.

Route from Hongkong via Shanghai, Nagasaki (Inland Sea of Japan) Kobe, Yokohama Victoria and Vancouver.

Twin Screw Empress Steamship—6,000 Tons—Speed 19 knots.

PROPOSED SAILING FROM YOKOHAMA.

R. M. S. Empress of India.
R. M. S. Empress of Japan.
R. M. S. Empress of China.
R. M. S. Athenian.
R. M. S. Tartar.

Special reduction (first class only) granted to members of the Military, Naval, Diplomatic and Civil services and to Missionaries.

Passengers have choice of ten routes across the Continent of America and have privilege of travelling by any Atlantic Steamship Line.

Round the World passage tickets in connection with the P. and O. S. N., North German Lloyd and Messageries Co.'s £125.

All rates payable at current rate of exchange.

For further information, Tickets, Guide Books, etc., apply to

HOLME, RINGER & CO., AGENTS,
Chemulpo.

Grand Hotel,

(Formerly the Station Hotel)

Near the Railway Terminus, West Gate Seoul.

The Best Hotel in Korea;
Handsome new Building.
Fine Airy Rooms
Excellent Cuisine.
Terms Moderate.
Special terms to Missionaries
and to permanent boarders.

Electric cars within 2 minutes' walk.

W. H. EMBERLEY.
Proprietor

EVERY FACILITY.

In connection with Life Assurance Business is afforded by

The Standard Life Assurance Co.,

One of the largest and wealthiest of the Provident Institutions of the United Kingdom Forms of Application and all information will be promptly afforded on application.

10 CENTS A DAY.

Not a very large expenditure is it? But it is sufficient to secure for a man of 30 a policy with the STANDARD LIFE OFFICE for

$1323.

For all particulars of rates, etc., apply to

Holme, Ringer & Co.,
Agents, Chemulpo.

THE NEW YORK LIFE INSURANCE COMPANY.

Have you ever been declined by any Company?

Are you engaged in a specially hazardous occupation?

Have you heard of the New York Life Insurance Company's New Classifications for this class of Risks?

If not, send your date of birth, occupation and particulars of rejection, if any to

E. MEYER & Co.,
Agents, Chemulpo.

MITSUI BUSSAN KAISHA.
(MITSUI & Co.)

MITSUI GINKO.
(MITSUI BANK.)

The Bank is owned by the members of the Mitsui Family, who, as partners, assume an unlimited responsibility for all liabilities of the Bank:—

Capital.................... .....Yen 5,000,000
Reserve Fund .... " 5,600,000

HEAD OFFICE, TOKYO.

LONDON OFFICE, 34 LIME ST., E. C.

BRANCHES AND AGENCIES:—
New York, San Francisco, Hamburg, Bombay, Singapore, Manila, Hongkong, Amoy, Chefoo, Tientsin.

Kobe, Hakodate, Yokohama, Kure, Yokosuka, Moji, Shimonoseki, Miike, Wakamatsu, Nagasaki, Kuchinotsu, Karatsu, Sasebo, Misume, Taipeh, &c.

Telegraphic Address for all the Offices:

"MITSUI."

A. B. C. AND A. 1 CODES USED.

Contractors of Coal

To the Imperial Japanese Navy. Arsenalr and Railway Bureau, Principal Railway Companies and Industrial Work, Home and Foreign Mail and Freight Steamers.

Sole Proprietors

Of the famous Miike, Tagawa and Yamano Coal Mines.

Sole Agents

For the sale of Fukumo, Hokoku, Ichimura, Kanoda, Mannoura, Onoura, Ostuji, Sonoda, Tsubaruro, Yoshinotani, Yoshio, Yurokibura and other coals.

YANGTSE INSURANCE ASSOCIATION, LTD.

The undersigned, having been appointed agents for the above company, are prepared to issue policies and pay losses on marine risks at regular rates.

E. MEYER & Co.,
Agents, Chemulpo.

AMERICAN KOREAN ELECTRIC CO.

Light and Power.

Main Office: Electric Building, Chong No.

RAILWAY DEPARTMENT.

OPERATING CARS BETWEEN EAST AND WEST GATE, EVERY TEN MINUTES:—

First Car leaves East Gate at 7:00 A. M. First Car leaves R. R. Station at 7:25 A. M
Last Car " East Gate at 8.40 P. M. Last " " R. R. Station at 9.05 P.M

OPERATING CARS BETWEEN EAST GATE AND IMPERIAL TOMB TERMINUS, EVERY TWENTY MINUTES:—

CONNECTING WITH EVERY ALTERNATE CAR ARRIVING AT EAST GATE FROM CHONG NO.

First Car leaves East Gate for Tomb at 7:10 A. M.
" " " Tomb for East Gate at 7:30 A. M.
Last " " East Gate for Tomb at 7:50 P. M.
" " " Tomb for East Gate at 8:10 P. M.

OPERATING CARS BETWEEN CHONG NO AND YUNG SAN RIVER EVERY TWELVE MINUTES:—

First Car leaves Chong No for South Gate at 7:12 A. M.
" " " Chong No for Yung San at 7:36 A. M.
" " " South Gate for Chong No at 7:20 A. M.
" " " Yung San for Chong No at 8:09 A. M.
Last " " South Gate for Chong No 9:00 P. M.
" " " Yung San for Chong No at 8.45. P. M.

SPECIAL PRIVATE CARS FURNISHED TO SUIT CONVENIENCE OF PATRONS. PRICES ON APPLICATION AT HEAD OFFICE.

LIGHTING DEPARTMENT.

Where less than 250 candle power of light is used, the rate per month will be
Per 16 candle power incandescent lamp,—All night.—Yen 2.50.
32 candle power incandescent lamp:—All night:—Yen 4.00.
50 candle power incandescent lamp:—All night:—Yen 6.00.
150 " " " " " " " 10.00.
1200 ,, ,, enclosed are ,, ,, ,, ,, 20.00.

Where more than 250 candle power of light is used, a Meter will be installed, freqvedted:—Rent of Meter Yen 2.00 per month. Rate of charges by meter reading:—Two Sen per Ampere per hour. (Approximately this is equal to about One Sen per 16 C. P. lamp per hour) Minimum monthly charge where meter is inStalled, Yen 20.00 per month, which includes rental of meter.

Estimates for installing lights furnished on application
An assortment of chandeliers always on hand.

K. Murakami.

Photograph Studio
Chinkokai, Seoul.

Printing, Developing and Enlargement, of Photographs always Undertaken.

Korean Views and Pictures Illustrating Native Customs always on Sale,

---

THE OSAKA SHOSEN KAISHA.

Boats frequently on the berth for Chinnampo.

REGULAR SAILINGS BETWEEN JAPAN AND KOREAN PORTS.

FUSAN AND KOBE VIA SHIMONOSEKI.

OSAKA VIA MOKPO, FUSAN, SHIMONOSEKI AND KOBE.

MOJI DIRECT.

OSAKA VIA KUNSAN, MASANPO, FUSAN, SHIMONOSEKI AND KOBE.

CHEMULPO KUNSAN LINE,
Every three days.

CHEMULPO CHINNAMPO LINE.
Every three days.

For Freight and passage and further particulars apply to
THE OSAKA SHOSEN KAISHA,
Chemulpo,

RONDON, PLAISANT & CO.

General Storekeepers and Merchants, Ships Contractors, Tobacconists, Commission and Forwarding Agents, Coal Merchants

IMPORTERS AND EXPORTERS

Seoul & Chemulpo.

W. D. WENTWORTH.

LANDING
AND
SHIPPING AGENT
AND
CUSTOMS BORDER.

12 OURA, NAGASAKI.

STEWARD & CO.

Chemulpo.

Shipchandlers and Storekeepers, Naval and Mercantile Contrrectors, Landing and Shipping Agents.

STEWARD'S HOTEL

Chemulpo.

Best accommodation in the port for travellers. Clean and well-aired rooms, good cuisine and prompt attendence, moderate tariff.

○김세원의 엄샹긔두원씨가 일본대쟝 쟝곡쳔씨와 젼권공ᄉᆞ 림권죠씨와 평ᄉᆞ샹 지구미견씨와 번역관 염쳔ᄉᆞ씨의게 엄가영이 만오쳔구빅구십여량을 ᄎᆞ자 달나고 호소ᄒᆞ야 일본우편으로 편지를 부쳐지 오륙일이 지나도 아모 소식이 업다ᄒᆞᄂᆞᆫᄃᆡ 김씨ᄂᆞᆫ 일본사ᄅᆞᆷ으로 ᄒᆞ야곰 가망신ᄒᆞ고 져금 일본사ᄅᆞᆷ의 ᄃᆡ표ᄒᆞᄂᆞᆫ 관인들의게 억울ᄒᆞᆷ을 호소ᄒᆞ야도 쳥약불문ᄒᆞᆷ으로 김씨가 도로에서 셔셜ᄒᆞ야 경샹이 가긍ᄒᆞ더라

○명년도예산 탁지부고문관 목하뎐씨가 명년도 각부부원쳥 부금을 작졍ᄒᆞ야 예산에 편셩ᄒᆞ라ᄒᆞ엿ᄂᆞᆫᄃᆡ ᄯᅢ기를 거ᄒᆞᆫ즉 관임관등 합년봉은 [illegible]만이쳔원이오 주임관의 등합년봉은 일만원이오 칙임관은 팔쳔원으로 작졍ᄒᆞ라ᄒᆞ고 관원의 액수 다소ᄂᆞᆫ 가히 샹관치 아닐거시라고 ᄒᆞ엿더라

○관ᄉᆞ뎐보 희쥬에서 쳥인샹 욱ᄉᆞ진에 ᄉᆞᆫ희져관소 관ᄉᆞ윤셩보씨가 법부로 뎐보ᄒᆞ기를 영평ᄉᆞ가 당초에 톰문을 아지 못ᄒᆞ고 한ᄒᆡ의 공ᄎᆞ도 ᄯᅩᄒᆞᆫ 공ᄇᆞᆫ되지 안타ᄒᆞ며 관수ᄅᆞᆯ 져희ᄒᆞ고 희싱ᄒᆞ지 안코져ᄒᆞ오ᄆᆡ 가히 속히 결말ᄒᆞ지 못ᄒᆞ겟다 ᄒᆞ엿더라

○인ᄎᆞᆼ샹쾌 샹자일에 동ᄃᆡ문안으로 가ᄂᆞᆫ 뎐거ᄅᆞᆫ자ㅣ 졀문소년인ᄃᆡ 술이 취ᄒᆞ야 아모ᄃᆡ 지향란ᄒᆞ더니 맛ᄎᆞᆷ 그 뎐거에 ᄂᆡ인ᄒᆞ나 취ᄒᆞᆫᄂᆞᆫ지라 얼골이 묘ᄒᆞ야 샹미야ᄅᆞ다우믜 그 취ᄀᆡᆨ이 그 녀인을 보고 무슈 힐란ᄒᆞᄂᆞᆫ지라 그 쟝거슈가 보다가 졍거ᄒᆞᆫ후 ᄇᆞᆯ길로 그 취ᄀᆡᆨ을 차ᄂᆞᆫᄃᆡ 쳐ᄂᆡ여런 사ᄅᆞᆷ이 그 거죠를 보고 샹쾌ᄒᆞ다 ᄒᆞ엿더라

○김화회원 김화ᄃᆡ인의 젼셜을 드른즉 거샹오일에 일진회원 팔빅명이 김화군에 모혀 ᄀᆡ회ᄒᆞ엿ᄂᆞᆫᄃᆡ 당일에 ᄌᆞ원샤ᄇᆞᆫᄒᆞᆫ자ㅣ 슈샥빅명이오 ᄯᅩᄒᆞᆫ 군슈를 무슈히 ᄂᆞᆫ박ᄒᆞᄆᆡ 군슈가 황겁ᄒᆞ엿다더라

○셔임쳥의 ᄂᆡ부에셔 젼쳥원군슈 권익샹씨로 부안군슈를 셔잉ᄒᆞᆯᄎᆞ로 졍부에 쳥의ᄒᆞ엿다더라

○죠쳥사관 ᄂᆡ부에셔 법부로 죠회ᄒᆞ기를 평양군슈 팽한쥬와 초산군슈 윤셕린과 평강젼군슈 죠셩졔를 면관ᄒᆞ고 미귀 쥬졔서지 되엿고 졍부죠회가 연ᄒᆞ야 니로 비일병라치ᄒᆞ야 구별ᄒᆞ야 사관ᄒᆞ고 회쟝젼을 져져히 도로 밧고 시병ᄒᆞ여 달나ᄒᆞ엿더라

○면훈회민히산 ᄂᆡ부에셔 각도관찰부에 면훈ᄒᆞ기를 관하 각군에 의병이라 칭ᄒᆞ고 민일취회ᄒᆞᄂᆞᆫ자 잇거든 엄칙ᄒᆞ야 히산ᄒᆞ고 ᄯᅩ 회민이 발향ᄒᆞ야 샹경ᄒᆞᄂᆞᆫ자 잇거든 디경에 지나감을 엄히 금ᄒᆞ되 만일 소홀ᄒᆞᆷ이 잇스면 중칙을 면키 어려우리니 곳 거ᄒᆡᆼᄒᆞ고 형디를 뎐보ᄒᆞ라 ᄒᆞ엿더라

○뎐훈엄금샹경 지작이십팔일에 ᄂᆡ부에셔 ᄯᅩ 십삼도관찰부로 뎐보ᄒᆞ기를 소위 회민이 지금 인의 법을 범ᄒᆞ엿스니 각군에ᄂᆞᆫ 다시 신칙ᄒᆞ야 방곡에 게시ᄒᆞ야 ᄒᆞ여곰 각각 스ᄉᆞ로 쉬룸케ᄒᆞ고 대로와 밋 요로에 막고 직혀 취당ᄒᆞ며 샹경ᄒᆞᄂᆞᆫ거슬 엄금ᄒᆞ고 만일 완패ᄒᆞ야 좇지 안ᄂᆞᆫ자 잇거든 착슈ᄒᆞ고 사실ᄒᆞ야 보ᄒᆞ야 ᄡᅥ 법으로 다사리게 ᄒᆞ라 ᄒᆞ엿더라

○량세샹판 거이십륙일에 륙군법원에서 강화부윤 윤철규와 동부대ᄃᆡ쟝 리동휘를 심판ᄒᆞ엿더라

○회원션고 평리원에 지수ᄒᆞᆫ 공진회쟝 리준과 회원 윤효정은 하명샹인은 징역종신에 쳐ᄒᆞ고 리유셕은 교에 쳐ᄒᆞ기로 션고ᄒᆞ엿ᄂᆞᆫᄃᆡ 법부에셔 일간 샹쥬ᄒᆞᆫ다더라

론셜

한국에 고문관

○아모던지 지금 한국을 기량ᄒᆞ란면 불가불 ᄒᆞᆫ 참셕이라고 숙샹ᄒᆞᄂᆞᆫ 일이 얼마 잇슬것이니 그 기량ᄒᆞᄂᆞᆫᄃᆡ ᄃᆡᄒᆞ야 활동ᄒᆞᆫ 반ᄃᆡ가 잇스면 그 반ᄃᆡᄒᆞᄂᆞᆫ 것을 ᄒᆡ칠듯ᄒᆞ나 차졈으로 반ᄃᆡᄒᆞᆷ은 헷되만 쓸ᄯᅢ름이오 분ᄂᆞᆫ라고 ᄒᆞᆷ이 쓸ᄃᆡ 업슬지라 지금 일본이 한국에 기량자가 되엿스나 한국을 기량ᄒᆞ기에ᄂᆞᆫ 일본이 다른 나라보다 멋빈나 더 어려울듯ᄒᆞ도다 일본의 ᄒᆞ고자ᄒᆞᄂᆞᆫ 일은 한국사ᄅᆞᆷ들이 밋지 아니ᄒᆞ고 일본사ᄅᆞᆷ들을 갑히 미워ᄒᆞ야서 의심과 공구심이 잇스며 슈년젼에 일본이 승젼ᄒᆞ야 한국을 독립시겻다ᄒᆞᄂᆞᆫ 것은 지금 와서ᄂᆞᆫ 한국을 독립시긴것이 아니라 일본이 한국을 청국으로 ᄲᅢ리지게ᄒᆞ야 져의가 그젼 청국이 한국에 ᄃᆡᄒᆞ던 권리를 ᄎᆞ지ᄒᆞ란고 ᄒᆞᄂᆞᆫ줄노 싱각ᄒᆞ니 그런케 밋을 리유가 만이 잇ᄂᆞᆫ지라 그런고로 일본사ᄅᆞᆷ이나 소위 일본당들이 권고ᄒᆞᄂᆞᆫ 기량안은 그 일에 ᄃᆡᄒᆞ야 속에 무ᄉᆞᆷ 샥셔둠이 잇ᄂᆞᆫ줄노 한인은 의심ᄒᆞ며 일본이 한국의 독립을 보젼ᄒᆞᆫ다ᄂᆞᆫ 빙셰에 ᄃᆡᄒᆞ야ᄂᆞᆫ 듯경신문들이 져의 졍부에 권고ᄒᆞ되 한국에 강경슈단을 쓰라ᄒᆞ니 지금 한국에셔 일본공ᄉᆞ나 쟝곡쳔대쟝이 죵교ᄒᆞᄂᆞᆫ 것을 신심으로 죠와셔 밧지 아니ᄒᆞᄂᆞᆫ 것이 ᄯᅩᄒᆞᆫ 고이치 아니ᄒᆞ도다

가령 한국 륙군으로 말ᄒᆞ면 지금은 쓸ᄃᆡ업ᄂᆞᆫ 것이 그 군ᄉᆞ로ᄂᆞᆫ 다ᄅᆞᆫ 나라에 ᄃᆡᄒᆞ야 항거ᄒᆞ기ᄂᆞᆫ 너무 젹고 ᄂᆡ국에셔 진압ᄒᆞ기에ᄂᆞᆫ 너무 번ᄒᆞᆫ지라 군ᄃᆡ에 드ᄂᆞᆫ 경비ᄂᆞᆫ 거져 ᄂᆡ버리ᄂᆞᆫ 것이라고 일본사ᄅᆞᆷ이 말ᄒᆞᄂᆞᆫ 것이 졍당ᄒᆞ도다 그런ᄒᆞ나 그 ᄉᆞ샹으로 볼것 ᄀᆞᆺᄒᆞ면 얼마 오ᄅᆡ기 젼에 일본이 한국 군ᄃᆡ의 소용될 물품을 공급ᄒᆞ며 교ᄉᆞ를 ᄂᆡ보ᄂᆡ고 ᄯᅩ 그 외 다른 일노도 한국군ᄃᆡ의 유지ᄒᆞᆷ을 찬셩ᄒᆞ다가 지금 쥬린다ᄒᆞ니 한국 황뎨 계셔ᄂᆞᆫ 당신의 시위군병을 쥬리고 당신과 당신 인민의 안녕보호ᄒᆞᆷ을 방히ᄒᆞᄂᆞᆫ줄노 아시ᄂᆞᆫ 것이 ᄯᅩᄒᆞᆫ 이샹히 너일것이 아니로다

그ᄲᅮᆫ 아니라 졍부의 각부도 그런ᄒᆞ도다 한국사ᄅᆞᆷ들이 자긔들의 마ᄋᆞᆷ으로 번 외국고문관도 츙권력을 주지 아니ᄒᆞ고 고문관의게 고문ᄒᆞᄂᆞᆫ 일이 드믈거든 지금 일본사ᄅᆞᆷ이 쳔거ᄒᆞᆫ 고문관들은 한국졍부에서 자의로 ᄲᅡᆫ 사ᄅᆞᆷ들도 의나 오더 어려움을 일비 잇슬지라 그 사ᄅᆞᆷ들을 쾌 놋코 반ᄃᆡᄂᆞᆫ 아니ᄒᆞ켓지마ᄂᆞᆫ 그 사ᄅᆞᆷ들의 한국졍부에 ᄃᆡᄒᆞ야 권고ᄒᆞᄂᆞᆫ 것이 맛치 오리등의 물붓ᄂᆞᆫ것 ᄀᆞᆺᄒᆞᆯᄐᆡ이니 한국이 일본의 충고들의 ᄉᆡᆼ엽게 ᄒᆞ란면 그게 인ᄃᆡᄒᆞ고 ᄆᆡ우 진력ᄒᆞ여야 될것이라 그리ᄒᆞᆫ 후에야 일을 가히 시작ᄒᆞ리라 ᄒᆞ노라

관보

뎨삼쳔이십호 광무팔년 십이월이십칠일

서임급사령

○명유향병에 방림시위원 학교교관 유세환 의학교교관 윤샹만 의학교교관 김샹진 ○임경무쳥경무관 서주임관일등 종이품 엄셕호

이샹 십이월십구일

○임의학교교관 서주임관륙등 의학교교관 안샹호

십이월이십일일

○승서판임관오등 탁지부주사 유근

십이월이십이일

○임교방사주사 서판임관팔등 윤경석 ○서칙임관삼등 계용수장 엄쥰원 ○명대구군림시우체주사 리귀슈 ○명당진군림시우체주사 고덩희

이샹 십이월이십삼일

○임경무사 서칙임관이등 륙군참쟝 김경근

○면본관 통신ᄉᆞ뎐화과쟝 리규쳔 의원면본관 비서원승 신셕균 교방ᄉᆞ주ᄉᆞ 윤경석 텰도원주ᄉᆞ 한규셩 텰도원주ᄉᆞ 구명서 텰도원주ᄉᆞ 봉문셕 덕릉령 최영렬 후릉참봉 윤샹훈 사릉참봉 김헌이 온릉참봉 리규현 쟝릉참봉 리셕영 취릉참봉 한의원 순창원참봉 유인쥰

○임통신사뎐화과쟝 서주임관오등 졍삼픔 박용규 ○임비서원승 서주임관이등 뎐셩사장 리근목 ○임통신사뎐화과기사 서주임관륙등 시종원시종 소회영 ○임시종원시종 서주임관오등 졍삼픔 죠존중 ○임덕릉령 서판임관륙등 션원젼참봉 리귀승 ○임션원젼참봉 서판임관팔등 젼참령 ○임후릉참봉 서판임관팔등 구픔 홍덕쥬 ○임사릉참봉 서판임관팔등 구픔 구돈서 ○임온릉참봉 서판임관팔등 구픔 리두노 ○임쟝릉참봉 서판임관팔등 구픔 남명철 ○임취릉참봉 서판임관팔등 강호 ○임순창원참봉 서판임관팔등 한종환

○임텰도원주사 서판임관팔등 교명관 신광국 리진션 김교현 김용헌

○명경긔남북도사검위원 구픔 리종구

○명강원도사검위원 구픔 김평영

○명황히도사검위원 구픔 김셕창

○명시종원분시어 구픔 남중회 명딘셰 리승노 계찬묵 민치운 윤승노 곤 박영진 리진구 김셕범 의학교교관 안샹호

이샹 십이월이십일

○의원면본관 덕주 통신ᄉᆞ뎐화과주ᄉᆞ 김홍영셕 통신ᄉᆞ뎐화과주ᄉᆞ 리귀회 통신ᄉᆞ뎐화과주ᄉᆞ 문긔쟝후 통신ᄉᆞ뎐화과주ᄉᆞ 김세중 통신ᄉᆞ뎐화과주ᄉᆞ 최용무 텰도원주ᄉᆞ 고영필 텰도원주ᄉᆞ 신광국 텰도원주ᄉᆞ 리진션 텰도원주ᄉᆞ 김교헌 텰도원주ᄉᆞ 김용헌 취릉참봉 강호 순창원참봉 한종환

○임후릉참봉 서판임관팔등 리규원

○임뎐셩사장 서주임관이등 비서원승 리근목

○임비서원승 서주임관륙등 졍삼픔 리귀승

○임통신사뎐화기사 서주임관륙등 구픔 한진구 구픔 윤종율

○임교방사주사 서판임관팔등 신셩희

○임취릉참봉 서판임관팔등 구픔 한의원

○임순창원참봉 서판임관팔등 구픔 유인쥰

TELEGRAMS.

(FROM JAPAN PAPERS)

Berlin, Dec. 23.

The former Crown Princess of Saxony recently arrived at Dresden and endeavoured to see her children. Her request was refused, and she then left the town.

London, Dec. 24.

The fog which has paralysed London for two days has lifted, but is still general throughout England, and shipping is at a standstill.

London, Dec. 23.

With reference to statements made in the Press that Russia had resorted to bribery in order to obtain statements from Hull fishermen as to the presence of torpedo-boats with the trawling fleet in the North Sea, the Russian Consul at Hull now declares that only the boatswain of the "Avas" signed a sworn statement. Asked as to the man's condition, the Consul said he did not think the man was drunk at the time.

The Consul added that other fishermen had made statements, but they were afraid to sign them.

The boatswain of the "Avas," interviewed later, declared that he was drunk when taken to the Russian Consulate to make his statement.

London, Dec. 24.

The situation in Morocco is creating much uneasiness. The unrest there is increasing, and it is feared that France will find great difficulty in pursuing its policy of peaceful penetration without a display of force.

A SUCCESSFUL TURBINE TRIP.

The success of the turbine principle of propulsion has just been proved, by voyage, to Melbourne of the Loongana, the first turbine steamer that has made a long sea voyage. The advantages of the turbine compared with the ordinary method of steam propulsion are great. It is smaller, lighter, and simpler than the steam-engine, and requires much less coal, while there is an absence of the vibration that is such an unpleasant feature of the ordinary screw propeller. Greater speed is another advantage of the turbine steamer. The actual steaming time of the Loongana from Greenock to Fremantle was only a trifle over 32 days, the average speed being 15 knots an hour. But between Greenock and Port Said the average was 16 knots, this being the longest continuous voyage ever made by a steamer of this class. During the 24 hours before her arrival at Fremantle, the vessel covered a distance of 410 miles. The run from Fremantle to Williamstown was slightly quicker than the record run of the Bombala a short time ago. The turbine principle is very simple. It is based on the fact that steam rushing through a nozzle along a movable drum or cylinder, in which are fixed a number of projecting blades, causes the drum to rotate with great rapidity. In the Parsons turbine, with which the Loongana is fitted, the drum is placed inside a cast-iron or steel barrel, the internal diameter of which is a little greater than that of the drum. In this barrel are a similar series of projecting blades, fixed so as to be opposite the spaces between the blades in the drum. The steam passing along the barrel rushes through the spaces between the fixed blades, and, striking the blades of the drum, makes it revolve with high velocity. Both sets of blades act as nozzles, and the steam, rushing from between the revolving blades in turn, strikes against the fixed blades and increases the impetus. The steam is thus directed alternately to the fixed and the revolving blades, so keeping up a constant rotation of the drum that carries the shaft. This is the essential principle of the turbine, which is evidently destined to work a revolution in dteam navigation.

THE ST. LOUIS EXHIBITION.

The total attendance at the Louisiana Purchase Exposition has been 19,000,000, the expenditure $22,000,000 the receipts from admissions and concessions $10,000,000 and the subscriptions $12,000,000. There will be a small amount left for the stockholders. The Exposition just closed was undoubtedly the most colossal undertaking of its kind ever attempted. The total cost of the fair, including the outlay for State and foreign government buildings and private concessions is estimated at between forty and fifty millions. At one time there was a bad financial outlook and a big loan had to be solicited from the government but the last months of the fair proved to be record breakers in point of attendance and all obligations were promptly met.

SOUTH AMERICAN WARSHIPS.

A London message of November 19th says that the Japanese diplomatic representatives in Europe, at the request of Tokyo, have made inquiries into a report that Russia is acquiring a new fleet from Chile and Argentina. The Tokyo Government was recently informed that Chile and Argentina between them had sold or optioned to Colombia six or seven war vessels which Colombia intends to turn over to Russia. Inquiries carried on here and in South America by Japanese agents have elicited an emphatical denial from both Chile and Argentina. These governments are said to have stated that they are anxious to sell certain vessels, but not at the risk of being heavily mulcted for breach of neutrality. Despite the official denials which have been transmitted to Tokyo, more than one Japanese diplomat in Europe is apprehensive that in some way or other these half dozen war vessels may shortly pass under the control of Russia.

Japanese independent inquiries confirm the published statement that an American house is concerned in negotiations looking to some such acquisition on the part of Russia. The efforts of Russia to stimulate shipbuilding within her territory, as detailed in the press dispatch from St. Petersburg last night, have been known to leading firms for some time. An agent of the Russian Admiralty recently made an offer here to one of the largest British shipbuilding firms in which he guaranteed a certain number of orders and a form of subsidy if the firm would open a navy yard on the Baltic. The terms were unsatisfactory and the offer was refused. A somewhat similar suggestion is now under consideration by the Vickers-Maxim Company, but it is not likely to be accepted.

The Il Chin Hoi are said to have received a telegram from their *confreres* in the North Chulla province, informing them that 20,000 men are marching to their assistance.

On the 19th inst. at 3.30 p. m. the Japanese cruiser "Tsushima" overhauled the British steamer "Negretia, off Ulsan, Korea, and discovered on board a considerable quantity of contraband goods consigned to Vladivostock. The vessel was consequently seized and brought to Sasebo.

The Governor of north Chulla Province telegraphs that on asking some of the Il Chin Hoi people why they were armed with rifles and swords, they replied that they were not sent by the society but had joined the Japanese as police officers.

A merchant of Riga, named Hirrow, has been placed in prison for a curious offence. He had missed his last train home, but, finding that a goods train was shortly to start, he bought a fowl and booked it by the train, at the same time obtaining a ticket for himself as attendant on live stock. He reached his destination, but is now being prosecuted by the railway company for fraud.

MR. DOOLEY ON PORT ARTHUR.

"'Answers to Corryspondints—Mayski: Take half a pound iv tar, a quart iv cookin' sherry, two pints iv vinegar an' a pound iv potash, an' apply to th' face with a paint brush befure retirin'.

"'Arthurski Lumleyvitch: No, Arthur, it is not considered in good form, whin walkin' with a lady, to run whin a bomb dhrops in ye'er neighbourhood. Seize ye'er fair companyon be th' elbows an' place her in front iv ye. Th' rule iv all pilite circles is, "Ladies first."

"'Timothyvitch K.: Jeffreys in th' sicond round.

"'Anxious. We don't know.'

"Sure, Hinnissy, it's always th' same way. Wan iv th' sthrangest things about life is that it will go on in onfav'rable circumstances an go out whin ivrything is aisy. A man can live an' have a good time, no mather what happens to him. I lived here durin th' cholery. I didn't like it, but they was on'y wan other thing to do, an' I didn't care f'r that. If ye're livin' in a town that's bein' bombarded, ye don't like it at first, but afther a while ye begin to accomydate ye'ersilf to it, an' by an' by, whin a shell dhrops near ye while ye're argyin' about th' tariff, ye step aside, an' if ye're still there afther th' smoke is cleared away, ye raysume th' argymint. Ye have to make new frinds, but so ye do in Chicago. A man iv me age loses more frinds in a year an' is in more danger thin a defender iv Port Arthur at twinty wan. Bustin' shells is on'y wan iv th' chances iv life like pnoomony an' argyin with a polisman.

"Besides, I bet ye no garrison iver rayfused to surrinder whin it wa starvin onless it was afraid th' inimy wud shoot th' man with th' white flag. A garrison begins to think iv surrindherin' whin it can't get pie at ivry meal. Cut out wan iv its meals an, it begins to wondher what's th' use iv fightin' a lot iv nice fellows. Rayjooce it more, an' some iv th' sojers will say to th' gin'ral: 'If ye haven't got a sheet or a pillowslip handy f'r a flag, ye can use our shirts.' Ye may change th' dite to horse meat, but horse meat rayminds a European sojer iv what his mother used to call beef. But he's got to have enough. A hungry man won't fight excipt f'r food, an' he'd follow a beefsteak twice as far as he wud th' flag iv anny Imp'ror or Tsar.

"Why don't Gin'ral Stoessel surrinder, annyhow?" asked Mr. Hennessy.

"No wan has told him to. He's a German," said Mr. Dooley.

"No, sir; if I ain't far out iv th' way, Port Arthur ain't sufferin' nearly as bad as I am abot it. It wud prob'bly be th' place to spind th' winther if ye didn't mind livin' in a fallen city—a quiet life, conjaynal people, comfortable an' safe homes, little wurruk an' some fightin. Its always th' same way. I've wept me last weep over th' sufferit' iv th' besieged. I shed manny tears on account iv' th' poor Spanyards in Sandago, but whin th' Amercan sojers got into th' town they were almost suffycated be th' smell iv garlic cookin' with omelttes. I raymimber how pained I was over th' disperate plight iv th' sojers an' diplomats at Pekin. I rushed an army over there. They kilt Chinymen be th' thousands an' in th' face iv incredible misstatments fought their way to th' dures iv th' palace, where their starvin' brothers were imprisoned. What did they find? They found th' diplomats in their shirt sleeves fillin' packin' cases with th' undherwear iv th' Chinese Imp'oy an' th' spoons iv th' Chinese Impress. Th' air was filled with cries iv, 'Hinnery, won't ye set on this thrunk? I can't get the lid down since ye put in that hatefull idol.'

"So I'll save me tears about Port Arthur till all th' rayturns are in. I'd like to get hold iv a copy iv th' "Port" Arthur Melojeen." I Wondher where I cud subscribe to it. I'd bet ye'd find it cheerful: 'Yisterdah was univintful. Th' Japs threw a few shells befure breakfast an' thin retired. This thing has got to stop. Friday we had a dog banded, an if this occurs again we will appeal to th' authorlties. Th' Eschemojensky band give a concert on th' public square, an' manny iv th' towns-people tu out to hear it. John Smithinsky was t. befure Judge Hoganenski on th' family change. He was sentenced to twenty knouts or fifty days. Main Sthreet is torn up again. How long will this condition last befure th' people iv our fair city rise in their might against th' corruptionists at th' city hall? Closin' quotations on th' Port Arthur Board iv Thrade: Caviar, 16 asked, 14 bid; candles, quiet an' unchanged, with a fair demand f'r light upland tallow.

PRIZE COURT DECISIONS.

The Supreme Prize Court at St. Petersburg has decided that the sinking of the German steamer "Thea" in July last was unjustified. The owners claim £39,000 sterling, but as no appeal was made regarding the cargo, the Vladivostock judgment stands.

The court has justified the seizure of the "Arabia," upheld Messrs. Dodwell and Co.'s appeal regarding the flour for Kobe, and confirmed the confiscation of the rest of the cargo, seeing that no appeals were lodged.

The quashing of the Vladivostock decision in the Dodwell case is most important, involving as it does the whole question of conditional contraband. —N. C. D. News.

The magistrate of Choong Chu reports that a band of robbers are carrying on depredations in his district.

The Righteous Army have apparently refused the offer of the Il Chin Hoi's protection, for latest advices from the north state that they are gathering with the intention of breaking up the Il Chin Hoi.

Reuter reports that Count Bulow, speaking in the "German Reichstag" said that there were undercurrents in Europe impelling toward warlike complications; Germany being the bulwark of peace, solely because of its strenght.

A salt merchant named Kim Tu Won has been robbed of $6,000 worth of merchandise by a Japanese and although he has addressed letters to the Japanese Consulate and the Japanese Legation, he has been unable to recover his goods. He and his family are left destitute in consequence.

A proclamation from the Il Chin Hoi, society was yesterday posted on the streets. It informed the public in general that as it was impossible to gain the ear of the Government they proposed in future to make known any misdeeds of Government officials, by Proclaiming them on the streets.

Mr. Megata has fixed the amounts which may be expended next year on salaries of high officials at $8,000; of 2nd class officials at $10,000; of lower grade officials at $12,000. No limit will be made to the number of officials employed, but their total salaries must not exceed the limits mentioned.

The Korea Daily News.

Issued at 5 P. M. daily except Sundays.

Rate of Subscription:—
Per Year,............Yen 25.
Per Quarter,..........Yen 7.
Per Month,..........Yen 2.50.

Postage in Korea not charged extra.
Postage abroad charged extra.

Advertisements, 50 sen per day for 1 inch or less.
5 yen per month per inch.
50 yen per year per inch.

All communications to

E. T. BETHELL,
Editor and Publisher,
Pak-tong, Seoul.

THE IL-CHIN-HOI.

As we briefly reported yesterday the Il-chin-hoi meeting which was held at noon resulted in bloodshed. The facts of the matter appear to be as follows. Finding the Il-chin-hoi becoming daily more turbulent, the Emperor had given orders that in future all meetings were to be dispersed. Accordingly, when the disreputable mob commenced to assemble yesterday a detachment of Korean soldiery appeared upon the scene and advised them to make themselves scarce. This they failed to do and the soldiers then resorted to force.

Some four or five of the agitators were slightly wounded and then the Japanese soldiers interfered on behalf of the Il-chin-hoi, disarmed the Korean soldiers and arrested their officers.

What excuse will be made by the Japanese for their highhanded proceedings we do not know but the fact remains that the Japanese authorities are responsible for all the trouble, from beginning to end. By the aid of subsidies they get together a society composed of all the riff-raff of Seoul which does not include a single respectable Korean. This society assembles and talks sedition yet when the Korean Government takes steps to suppress the meetings the Japanese step in and prevent them.

What are we coming to? The real purpose which the Il Chin Hoi is intended to serve has not yet leaked out but we should not be surprised if the ultimate design of the Japanese is the substitution of Japanese for Korean soldiers as palace guard.

However a little cold steel will damp the ardour of the Il-Chin hoi patriots and we regret that they did not get a severer taste yesterday. A very valuble member of the society told us that there were twelve severely injured but from personal observation we should say that there were 2 or 3 slightly injured and a large number severely frightened. We ourselves saw some of the wounded "making up" previous to getting into their ambulances to be paraded through the streets. One lout with absolutely nothing the matter with him smeared some blood on his clothes, wrapped a dirty rag round his head, and then entered the ambulance and looked the picture of a martyred patriot.

DELCOIGNE-ECKERT WEDDING.

The Roman Cathedral, Seoul, was today the scene of a very impressive ceremony, when Mr. Adhemar Delcoigne (late of His Belgian Majesty's Diplomatic service and now Adviser to the Korean Home Office) was united in the holy bonds of matrimony with Anna Irene the second daughter of Herr and Frau Eckert, of Seoul.

The Cathedral had been beautifully decorated for the occasion. Crosses and loops in harmonies of rose, pink and white lined the walls and the effect was here and there heightened by swinging festoons of evergreen.

Punctually at ten o'clock the wedding party entered the Church and to the strains of the "Marche d'Athalie," the bride and bridegroom, followed by their witnesses, advanced to the altar rails. The service was conducted by "pere" Poisnel, the dean of Seoul, and was presided over by Monseignor Mutel, Bishop of the Roman Church in Korea.

After the happy twain had been made one and a blessing had been bestowed upon the union, Mass was celebrated, rendered additionally impressive by the strains of the Imperial band, whose stirring music filled the lofty cathedral with beautiful melody.

Mass being over, the new couple to the strains of Mendelssohn's Wedding march proceeded to the vestry to sign the register, and were shortly followed by a host of friends anxious to lose no time in presenting their congratulations.

A reception was afterwards held at the house of Miss Sontag where the well-wishers of the happy couple again had an opportunity of offering felicitations and pledging them. The bride, who looked very charming in a dress of white crêpe-de-chine and tulle veil with orange blossoms was the recepient of many good wishes while the bridegroom accepted the hearty handshakes of all his friends.

It would be impossible to give the name of all those present but amongst the campany we noticed most of the ladies of Seoul and the members of the Diplomatic and consular corps in Seoul. The Ministers present were H. E. Mr. Hayashi, Dr. Allen, Mr. Shu Iai Sen, U. Collin de plancy, Sir John Jordan, Herr Von Saldern and U. Monaco while the Consular services were represented by Mr. Mimashi, Mr. Paddock, the Chinese Consul, M. Berteaux and Dr. Ney. Miss Sontag's spacious house was thronged with callers; many Korean officials were present, including the Minister for Foreign Affairs, while M. Delcoigne's Chief, the minister for Home affairs had written expressing his regret that he had been prevented, by pressure of public business, from attending.

Mr. McLeavy Brown, commissioner for the Imperial Customs was present and Mr. Megata, finance adviser to the Korean Government and Mr. Hagiwara, the Secretary to the Japanese Legation also called to offer their congratulations.

All the arrangements were excellent and if the newly married couple's progress through life runs as smoothly as its beginning then the good wishes of all their friends will not have been bestowed in vain.

* * *

Since the above was written we have obtained a full list of those present. Dr. Allen, Mr. Gordon Paddock, Mr. and Mrs. Bostwick, Mrs. Elliott, Mrs. McLellan. Mr. Stevens, Mr. Koen, Mr. and Mrs. Hulbert, H. E. Herr von Saldern, Dr. Wünsch, Dr. Ney, Herr and Frau Eckert and the Misses Amalie and Lisbeth Eckert, Sir John Jordan, Captain Phillips, Messrs. Bolljahn, Stender, Chalmers, Davidson and Frampton, Mr. and Mrs. Halifax, Mr. and Mrs. Bethell, H. E. Mr. Collin de Plancy, Dr. and Mrs. Avison, Mr. and Mme Berteaux, Mr. and Mme Clemencet, Mr. and Mme Cuvillier, Mr. and Mme Remion, Mr. and Mme Monaco, Mr. and Mme R. de Vos, Messrs. Martel, Cremazy, Tremoulet, Muhlensteth and Rabec, H. E. Mr. Hayashi, Mr. Hagiwara, Mr. Furuya, Mr., Mrs. and Miss Mimashi, Mr. Debouchi Mr. and Mrs. Kato, Mr. Kuroda and Mr. Megata, H. E. the Chinese Minister with secretaries Woo and Lu Tzecheong.

A BRITISH NURSE IN CABUL.

London, Nov. 8.

Owing to the fact that she has been engaged uninterruptedly for eight years in medical work in Afghanistan, Mrs. K. Daly, who recently resigned her position as medical officer to the Queen of that country, has had exceptional opportunities for studying affairs in that quarter. She is now in England and has been interviewed with regard to her experiences.

Concerning life in the harem and the court, Mrs. Daly said that next to the Amir himself the chief political factor in the country is the royal wife of the late Amir, who is known as the Queen. She is about forty years of age, of considerable beauty, and particularly intelligent and well-informed. She is virtually a prisoner in her palace, which is regarded with almost as much suspicion as the British Agency owing to her pronounced British sympathies. The Amir's wives and other royal ladies do not live in the voluptuous and idle state usually associated with a harem. They take a great interest in knitting, embroidery, and other feminine pursuits, and the chief wife has a sewing machine, with which she makes her children's clothes. One of the Amir's wives, who is of royal birth, wears English dresses of the style fashionable thirty years ago. An atmosphere of espionage pervades Kabul, said Mrs. Daly, interviewed by a representative of Reuter's Agency. The natives are extremely suspicious, and to be seen speaking to any of the staff of the British Agent (who is virtually a prisoner), means instant banishment. No Afghan is allowed to visit the Agency. Russian influence, said Mrs. Daly, is not much in evidence at Kabul. The court and the common people are anti-Russian, and the latter favour a closer connection with the British.

"It was generally believed last year that there was a Russian emissary in Kabul," said Mrs. Daly, "and soon after the Amir came to the throne presents of Russian guns and ammunition were refused by the Afghan Government. From my own knowledge and observation I should say that the Russian advances meet with no favourable response from the Amir or his advisers."

Lieut.-General Kaulbars arrived on December 16th at General Kuropatkin's headquarters.

A battle is reported to have taken place recently near Pyengyang the contestants being Il Chin Hoi people and Peddlers. No details are to hand.

The captain of this vessel recently summoned his crew at Hong Kong for refusing to proceed in the ship. In the course of the hearing he stated that his cargo was Kerosine oil.

Over three hundred Japanese schooners, says the "Chefoo Daily News" at Hope Sound, in one of the Miautau Islands, loaded with supplies ready to be run into Port Arthur upon the reduction of the fortress by the Japanese.

According to a Moji despatch. The crew of a steamer, just returned from the front, state that Dalny is now infested with Russian spies and that incendiarism is repeatedly committed by the natives.

According to members of the Iron and Steel Institute, says the New York Press, a gigantic steel combination, which is being secretly formed in Great Britain, will shortly be completed with a capital nearly as large as that of the United States Steel Corperation.

The Korea Daily News.

VOL. I, FRIDAY, DECEMBER 30, 1904. No. 137

HONGKONG & SHANGHAI BANKING CORPORATION.

Paid-up Capital......	$10,000,000
Reserve Fund:—Sterling Reserve...	10,000,000
Silver Reserve.....	7,000,000
	27,000,000
Reserve Liability of Proprietors...	10,000,000

HEAD OFFICE, HONGKONG.

London Bankers, London and County Banking Company Limited.

Branches and Agencies,
London.

Amoy,	Hankow	Penang,
Bangkok	Hiogo,	Rangoon,
Batavia,	Iloilo,	Saigon,
Bombay,	Lyons,	San Francisco,
Calcutta,	Manila,	Singapore,
Colombo,	Nagasaki,	Sourabaya,
Foochow,	New York,	Tientsin,
Hamburg,	Peking,	Yokohama,

Credits granted on approved Securities, and every description of Banking and Exchange business transacted.

Drafts granted on London and the chief Commercial places in Europe, India, Australia, America, China and Japan.

HOLME RINGER & CO., AGENTS,
CHEMULPO.

HOKURKU DOBOKU KAISHA.

Branch office in Chong Dong. Seoul.

Japanese telephone No. 165

CONTRACT DEPARTMENT.

We can contract to build any building or construction.

MERCHANDISE DEPARTMENT.

We can provide any building material. We have just contracted to build the new Belgian Legation.

E. MEYER & CO.

Chemulpo.

SOLE AGENTS IN KOREA FOR.

A. T. Morse, Sons & Co.'s

"Fresco" Distemper

In all colours ready for use on walls, Ceilings etc.

and

AVENARIUS CARBOLINEUM

A wood-preserving and antiseptic oil preparation

Against decay, dry-rot, fungus and wood-destroying insects.

A large supply always in stock.
Prices upon application.

E. MEYER & CO.,
Chemulpo.

CHARTERED BANK OF INDIA AUSTRALIA & CHINA.

INCORPORATED BY ROYAL CHARTER 1853

HEAD OFFICES:—LONDON.

Paid-up Capital	£800,000
Reserve Liability of Shareholders	800,000
Reserve Fund	800,000

Drafts granted upon all the principal places in the world and every description of Exchange and banking business transacted.

E. MEYER & Co., Agents,
Chemulpo.

MITSU BISHI DOCKYARD & ENGINE WORKS,

NAGASAKI.

CODE WORD, "DOCK."

A 1, A. B. C., and Engineering Codes used.

DOCK No. 1 (at Tategami).

Extreme Length..............	523 feet
Length on blocks	513 ,,
Width of Entrance on Top......	89 ,,
,, ,, Bottom....	77 ,,
Water on Blocks at Spring Tide	26½ ,,

DOCK No. 2 (Mukaijima).

Extreme Length..............	371 feet
Length on Blocks............	360 ,,
Width of Entrance on Top......	66 ,,
,, ,, Bottom	53 ,,
Water on Blocks at Spring Tide	22 ,,

PATENT SLIP (at Kosuge).

Can take vessels up to 1,000 tons gross.

THE WORKS are well equipped with the LATEST IMPROVEMENTS, and can execute any kind of work in SHIPBUILDING and MARINE ENGINEERING, as well as in REPAIRING of SHIPS.

The COMPANY'S new powerful steamer OURA-MARU (712 tons, 700 I.H.P.), specially built for SALVAGE PURPOSES, and equipped with necessary gear, is always READY at SHORT NOTICE.

THE METHODIST PUBLISHING HOUSE,

Little West Gate, Seoul.

JOB PRINTING, TYPEWRITER PAPER
CARBON PAPER, VISITING CARDS
STATIONERY, BOOK BINDING
BOOK PUBLISHERS
AMERICAN SCHOOL BOOKS
SPENCERIAN COPY BOOKS
PEN CARBON LETTER AND BILL BOOKS

S.A. BECK, Manager.

DAI-ICHI GINKO.

LIMITED.

(Formerly the First National Bank)

ESTABLISHED 1873

INCORPORATED UNDER PRESENT LAW 1896

Capital - - - - - - - -	Yen 5,000,000
Reserve Fund - - - - -	1,500,000

HEAD OFFICE:—TOKIO.

President: Baron SHIBUSAWA.

BRANCHES AND CORRESPONDENTS
In the Principal Cities and Towns of Japan.

Interest Allowed on

Fixed deposits 1 year - - -	6½ per cent	
" " 6 months - - -	6 per cent	

Special current accounts 1½ sen daily per Y 100
General " " 1 " " " 100

M. TANAKA,
Manager, Chemulpo.

SINGER SEWING MACHINES

씽거조봉침

SOLE AGENTS FOR KOREA

전매쇼

HOLME RINGER & CO.
Chemulpo.

제물포 함릉거양힝

KAMEYA & CO.

GENERAL STOREKEEPERS

Chinkokai - - Seoul

(*Established 1895, Tokyo*)

Confectionery, Hams, Canned Goods, Cutlery, Hirano & Tansan Water, Provisions, Gents, Furnishing goods, Toilet Articles, Travelling Bags, Tobacco, Cigars & Cigarettes Kitchen Utensils. Coffee, Biscuits

Fresh Goods always kept in Stock.
Prices Moderate
Please come and inspect our goods.

NIPPON YUSEN KAISHA.

JAPANESE MAIL STEAMSHIP CO.

DER MAIL CONTRACT WITH THE IMPERIAL JAPANESE GOVERNMENT.

European Line

Regular Fortnightly Service between Yokohama Kobe, Moji, Shanghai, Hongkong, Singapore, Penang Colombo, Port Said, Marseilles, London and Antwerp

American Line

Regular Fortnightly Service between Hongkong and Seattle, calling at Shanghai, Moji, Kobe, Yokohama and Victoria, B. C.

Australian Line

Regular weekly Service betwen Japan Ports and Australia, calling at Hongkong and Manila.

(Above Three Lines Suspended until further notice).

Shanghai Line

Weekly Service between Shanghai and Japan Ports

Korea Line

Service Kobe, Moji, Nagasaki, Fusan Chemupo Chef foo, Taiku.
S. S. Bahelsberg, 2181 tons.
Service Kobe, Moji, Fusan, Chemulpo, Chinnampo
S. S. ARGO S. S. Ohio.

BORDEN'S CONDENSED MILK CO.

New York, U. S. A.

ALWAYS IN STOCK

Eagle Brand Condensed Milk.

Gold Seal Condensed Milk.

Peerless (Family) Evaporated Cream.

Borden's Malted Milk.

E. MEYER & CO.
Chemulpo Korea,
Sole Agents

ROYAL INSURANCE COMPANY,

Funds exceed £10,000,000

FIRE

AT CURRENT RATES.

LIFE

REDUCED PREMIUM.

HOLME RINGER & CO.,
Agents, Chemulpo

HOTEL DU PALAIS

SEOUL.

The only first class Hotel in Seoul Situated in the centre of the city opposite the palace.

Cuisine under the supervision of an experienced French Chef.

Well ventilated and furnished throughout.

TARIFF UPON APPLICATION

L. MARTIN
Proripetor and Manager

大韓每日申報
대한미일신보

(뎨일빅삼십팔호) (월요일) 일쳔구빅오년팔월이일

본샤고빅

이 신보는영어와한어로셔계빅
셜 츌판홈

신문가

한장 엽두돈오푼
일삭표 엽두량닷돈
우표가미삭닷돈
다 맛돈으로밧숩

광고료는

귀한의쟝단과ᄌ힝의다쇼로즁
감ᄒ되한번가로밧을터이오며오
리지아니ᄒ때한사람마다다이신
문을보실터이니광고내시기롤
원ᄒ시는이들은우리신문사에
와셔편야ᄒ시물희망ᄒ옵

○발힝소 박동대한미일신보
사 법어학교압희젼영국인셜필
링집자리오

사쟝 영국인 (비셜)

평양 디리졈

○평양효동사는권미보씨로우
리신문관미디리인을뎡ᄒ엿
시ᄂ오니평양에계신구람코자ᄒ
시는 첨군ᄌ는히디리졈에왕
림ᄒ와면의ᄒ시옵

샤고

○우리대한미일신보의목뎍은
대한의안녕질셔에관한모든데
목에디ᄒ야는공평한변론을쥬
쟝ᄒᆞ이라우리동신원의탐보는
신문보시는첨군ᄌ의게ᄒᆞ샹보
도ᄒᆞ리며편지를귀셔ᄒ여주시
는이는셩명과번디를쟤어붓치
기를희망ᄒ오니이거슨신문
에긔진ᄒ란는거시아니오다
이신용ᄒᆞ는증거를숨고자
ᄒ고자ᄂ아모과셔던지긔
ᄂ되작ᄒᆞ는권리를가젓소
ᄒᆞᄂ리유를말ᄒ터이오
ᄒᆞ광고문란케ᄒᆞᄂᆞᆫ듯혼
는의례히밧지안켓숩나이

사셜시이리로신문을티양
레로분전ᄒ와레젼부의잇의
도젼ᄒ는스로번곳에는ᄒ눗게
젼ᄒ기도ᄒ며ᄒ먹칠거슨ᄒ겹
에젼ᄒ기도ᄒ며ᄒ야니젼ᄒ는
곳도잇다ᄒ와우리신문을ᄉ랑
ᄒ야구람ᄒ시는 첨군ᄌ의게
되ᄒ야미우미안ᄒ옵기로지금
은분젼인을두고미일중이젼
ᄒ며아니젼ᄒ거나늣게거나ᄒ
폐가엽도록ᄒ란ᄒ오니ᄒ야니

젼ᄒ거ᄂᆞ홈늣게젼ᄒ거나ᄒ혼일
이잇스면본샤로통긔ᄒ여주싱
을희망ᄒ옵

잡보

○대동협의 일젼에단쳔군슈
보고ᄒᆞ바를본즉의병이조세를륵탈ᄒ
고군긔를탈취ᄒ수로리친셔를
샹펼손ᄒᆞ샹의스황용셩제씨가
대동협의쇼를셜립ᄒ엿스나셩
직지하에회집ᄒ지는못ᄒ고졍
부에쟝셔만ᄒ엿다더라

○일인진옥 인셩부쳬뵈밧에
다일인이집을지으란고리를단
논티반걸가량이나셕축을싸며
평쟝ᄒ게짓는모양인티영문이
라ᄒ며남마다수상뎡이역스를
ᄒ다더라

○쥬경야죽 남촌에ᄒ는스싱며
세된교관이잇는티낫이면학교
학도를영으로밧잘고밤이면ᄌ
과가영어를공부를ᄒᆞ는지라외
국사름과약조ᄒ기를ᄒᆞ시숍은대
영어를ᄀ르쳐쥬면ᄒᆞ시숍을ᄒ
한말을ᄀ르쳐쥬마고미일한오
간쳥시숍ᄒ야는외국인의집으로
다닌다더라

○영평젹경 근일에영평도셩
이 교리에셔도젹이소장ᄉ들을
ᄒ싸리고소쾌돈을탈취ᄒ엿는
티아ᄒ고ᄂᆞ주고ᄒᆞ사름은아죵티
재ᄂ니ᄒ엿스나죽기가십다
에ᄒᆞ는티그소쟝ᄉ는참혹히
사ᄂ사ᄅᆷ이라더라

○청셕포군 쟝진군수리죵션
이 가군부에보고ᄒ기를아라사
과병이이디경을지날세본군쳔
의괴밋숩집청에츙화ᄒ야군긔
문일숩을ᄒ낫도놈아지엽시다
티왓단말은이왕에보도ᄒ엿거
니와수면갹군에는쥬티를셜
시ᄒ고쟈은수포도셜시ᄒ야급
ᄒ는것을방비흠이잇스나본군
덕도ᄒ시는굴비셜립흠이가ᄒ다ᄒ엿
라수로들셜립ᄒᆞ미가ᄒ다ᄒ엿더

○봉 칙쥬훈 쟈조관소에
ᄒ죄범으로지쟈야에 죠칙이슈
싼결업이ᄂ빈사금일밥부에셔
광리원과한셩지판소로위션훈
령ᄒ엿더라

○죠칭용결 법공관에셔외부
로죠회ᄒ기를본국상민동동이
가인쳔츅에잇는디단민등ᄒ는수
는당쵸에쳠리셔디권을귀국인
의게발급ᄒ훈것을통ᄒ이가젼미
ᄒ엿고츄후에감리셔에셔단시

신권을일인오와다라의게발급
ᄒ고로본관부영ᄉ가일본영ᄉ
와여러번교셥을ᄒ엿스나결말
이도나지아니ᄒ고인쳔감리가이
미발급ᄒ디권을다시일인의게
발급ᄒ라ᄒ니무리ᄒ일이라이
에죠회ᄒ니쳥컨티사실ᄒ야공
변되게결졍홈이가ᄒ다ᄒ엿더
라

외보

○로국션언 아라사국의룩군
대장이자가션언ᄒ되구로셰도진
쟝군이그병력을싱ᄒ보충ᄒ고
로쟝츠전진ᄒ다ᄒ엿고산길ᄋ
디희리가ᄒ돈를는딜도가왼셩
ᄒ이리로일에능히이쳔오빅
인을슈운ᄒ다ᄒ나국민이보다
헌언이라ᄒ야호발도죵신치아
니ᄒ다ᄒ엿더라

ㄴ과란인죄회 로국파란디
스도죠와씨에셔동병령미츌홀
베예과란인샹쳔명이그국가를
노티부ᄅ고시장으로진힝ᄒ는
중에아라사국보병이부세가츙
돌ᄒ야과란사롬오명이피샹ᄒ
고비샹명이피샹ᄒ엿더라

○증립위관ᄉ건 유아립젼을
거ᄒ즉일본졍부에셔증립위관
ᄉ건으로법국셔반아화란등중립
국졍부가샹금교셥ᄒ는티ᄒ증립
중ᄒ이자괴나라에힘반깃교유
이ᄒ이엇는죠올깨닷고각기평
졍의졍사쳥에혼뎡ᄒ야증립규
쟝을엄슈ᄒ고편파훈ᄒ위가엽
게ᄒ는방칭을취ᄒ엿더라

○렴도관통과 일본졍부에셔
경의렴도가리년오륙월경에기
통되면의쥬에셔만쥬디방을관
통ᄒ야동청렴도연락ᄒ렴도
그리ᄒ죠뎡년중에는긔케ᄒ게
시ᄒ도록ᄒ기위ᄒ여셔산브기는고
통청렴도와연락ᄒ소위대록렴
도가관통될러인티그벼에는일
명에셔경부렴도를미슈ᄒ기로
약졍ᄒ엿다더라

관보

뎨삼쳔이빅일호 광무팔
년삼월이십칠일

서임급사령
○승셔원승관오등 농샹공부
쥬ᄉ 김병관

삼월이십삼일

○의원면본관 중츄원찬의
윤병렬 중츄원의관 곽샹
중츄원의관 안귀랑 쥬원
의관 약명슈 중츄원의관
리명우

○임중츄원의관셔쥬임관륙등
졍샹풍 졍린슈 졍상풍 김
샹열 홍풍 리용의 홍
양경오 홍풍 김명권

삼월이십수일

○의원면본관 훈릉참봉 리
규원 숭션젼참봉 김민
○명슌명비발인시 졔조관
의정부의정 리근명
○임동신사면화과쥬사셔임
관팔등 김남익 강노직 젼
환원 김셩귀 강한영 송원
참봉 유린쥰
○임 후릉참봉셔판임관등
구품 홍덕쥬
○임 숭창원참봉셔판임관팔
등 쟝릉참봉 남명철
○임 쟝릉참봉셔판임관등
한경귀
○임 숭션젼참봉셔판임관팔
등 김종도

이상삼월이십륙일
뎨삼쳔이빅이호 광무팔
년삼월이십구일

서임급사령
○승셔원승관오등 함용언보
사 쥬사 김일졔

구월사일

○승셔원승관오등 태구면보
사 쥬사 리과쇼

삼월사일

○승셔원승관삼등 북청면보
사 쥬사 김인빈

삼월칠일

○명시종원분시어 심경찬

삼월구일

○승셔원승관삼등 함경우졔
사 쥬사 리긍만

삼월이십오일

○임렴도원쥬사셔판임관팔등
뎡셕조 한승교 강노연 빅
낙원 오홍근

○명시종원분시어 리한구
뎡셕창 신창균 리용징 구
픔 박도순 민세호 졍티션
박지창 빅영준

리참원 ○의원면본관 의효전참봉이

ᄂᆞᆸ 의효젼ᄎᆞ의셔 관임관팔
등 리명ᄀᆞ
이샹십이월이십륙일

○명ᄂᆡ쟝원경셔칙임관삼등
죵이품 리명쳘
○의원면본관 비셔원승 리
규승 교방사주사 심셩턱
○비셔원승셔주임관륙등 쟝
샹룡 신셩균 ○임즁추원의
관셔주임관사등 졍삼품 리
규항 ○임한셩부주사 셔관임
관륙등 리명환
이샹십이월이십칠일

대 샹찬이십삼호 광무팔년
십이월십삼일
셔임급사령

○승졍삼품 륙품 리승두
오월십일일
○면본관 함경북도 번계경무
셔총슌 송의식
우ᄂᆞᆫ회원의ᄇᆡ셜이 번계경무
지셔총슌에잇셔슌검의군도이
셩오병을외국병뎡의게전탈홈
은방약이무동이나관계가경ᄒᆞ
지아니ᄒᆞ야즁경에쳐ᄒᆞᆯ것이나
면본관ᄒᆞᄂᆞᆫ사라
십이월이십칠일

○의원면본관 주뎐사슈봉관
리우룡 ○위시종원분시어
륙품 남즁희 구품 뎡관셕
구품 리승도 구품 최춘룡
구품 윤치운 구품 윤 문
구품 박영진 구품 리진구
구품 김셩범
○임 주뎐사슈봉관셔판임관
팔등 리원용 ○임농상공부면
직과주사셔판임관팔등 명국
진 리셩엽 김병문 명규셕
함혁니 리병구 리범하
○위충청북도즁두사무위원
명편셕 ○명충청북도즁두사무
위원 전라북도즁두사무위원
박희면 ○명전라북도즁두사
무위원 구표은 ○명평안북
도즁두사무위원 리희계
○명허쳥향종두지소사무위원
윤봉현 ○승셔원일관오품등
한셩부주사 장춘영
이샹십이월이십칠일

론셜

일진회

○지나간봉요에일진회에셔
기회ᄒᆞ엿다가목관이당자ᄒᆞᆫ지
경이이롬이이결ᄒᆞᆫ니
일진회에셔ᄂᆞᆫ마다모히쟝결명
을으관ᄒᆞ비구ᄂᆞᆫ로로
ᄃᆡ회에ᄒᆡ하ᄒᆞ게슌셔공을ᄒᆞ엿시
교즁금이후로ᄂᆞᆫ모든회원들결
힘산개ᄒᆞ다고 쳐평을나라셔
ᄂᆞᆫ되그회원들은일향쳐셔ᄒᆞᄂᆞᆫ
지라과송ᄒᆞ여ᄃᆞᆫ병뎡들은회원
들모형곳에잇셔셔운업슌시도
갓권ᄒᆞ며쇼수로히ᄂᆞᆫ지도륙ᄒᆞ
나그리ᄒᆞ나종리쳥죵치아니홈
이로셔지ᄒᆞᆫ수업시위란으로홈

에이르러회원즁에사ᄒᆞᆫ이
[illegible]

잡보

[illegible]

원과순검을거느리고작일신시경
에미동리ᄌᆞ에이르러회민의게
ᄒᆞ야별로손을범ᄒᆞᆫ이업ᄂᆞᆫ
티흘티에헌병이취수ᄒᆞ부로착
ᄒᆞ야순검의군도여셔롤전탈
ᄒᆞ고셔순검등이업드러셔기쳔
에셔다ᄒᆞ엿기에조회ᄒᆞ니청
ᄒᆞ엿더라
○윤씨몽방 공진회원윤하영
씨가경리원에착수ᄒᆞ엿더니재
작일에몽방되엿더라
○회민쟝황경셩 일진회중으
로온전북면보등트등죽ᄒᆞ민수
만명이양복을입고분일ᄒᆞ제ᄒᆞ
야경셩으로드러간다ᄒᆞ엿더라
○진회계방 작일에진회에셔
각방곡에게방ᄒᆞ엿ᄂᆞᆫᄃᆡ무도
금평부가인민의게티ᄒᆞ며무도
ᄒᆞᆫ죵경이잇ᄂᆞᆫ고로당샹ᄒᆞ야각
부ᄃᆡ신의게공함ᄒᆞ고보ᄂᆡ여
아니ᄒᆞ면흉ᄒᆞᆫ뒤로ᄇᆡ도도켜쟝
계ᄒᆞ고로소ᄒᆞ엿도다ᄒᆞ엿더라
○신법츄간 신법률을거월
추가ᄒᆞ야의법ᄒᆞ기로ᄒᆞ엿더라

외보

○쥬명연수외의젼 론ᄃᆞᆫ스틴
티하ᄃᆞᆫ신문에론ᄒᆞᆫ것ᄂᆞᆫ일본이
그만에ᄒᆞ엿다ᄒᆞᆯ뒤ᄂᆞᆫ
ᄃᆡ한회복ᄒᆞᆯ것이라
[illegible]

본사고빅

○우리신문을구람ᄒᆞ시ᄂᆞᆫ
쳠군ᄌᆞ의게고ᄒᆞ노니
[illegible]

RESURRECTED ON A DISSECTING TABLE.

The medical students and the surgeon at the Grenoble School of Medicine had a serious fright on November 2nd, for they narrowly escaped dissecting a living woman. The woman had been arrested for drunkennes on the previous day and taken to the police station. Next morning she was found stiff and cold in the cell, and the doctor pronounced her to have been dead for two hours. In due course she was laid out for a postmortem examination. But while the surgeon was getting his instruments ready, the supposed corpse sat up and asked for a glass of water, to the horror of the medical man and his students. The woman was subject to epileptic fits, during which her body assumed a corpse-like rigidity.

In North Pyeng Yang Province the Tong Haks (or Righteous Army) are reported to be assembling with the object of suppressing the Il-chin Hoi agitators. Many officials are said to have joined the movement.

In adition to those mentioned as being present at the reception held at Miss Sontag's residence on Thursday, there were also Messrs Ko Hei Kiong, Kim Tjo Hyon, Ko Hei Sung, Gin Hak Sin and Ko Hai Tong.

A Japanese newspaper states that some 20 or 30 Russian soldiers at Kyeng-wŏn are laying waste the country and violating the women. From the same source we also learn that 200 Russians at Sung-chin are without supplies and are consequently commandeering the stores of the natives. There is absolutely no official confirmation for these and many similar stories which frequently appear in the Japanese newspapers.

Cases have been recorded in India from time to time of a flight of locusts "holding up" His Majesty's Mail until such time as they were brushed away and the train could proceed, but for frogs to behave in such a fashion is a novelty. An American paper states that myriads of frogs covering the railway line stopped a heavy goods train near Spokane, Washington. The rails became so slippery that 287lbs. of sand and an extra engine were required before the train could be restarted.

The Police Department have a serious complaint to make against the Japanese gendarmes. A body of 6 Korean police were despatched on the 6th inst., to the meeting place of the Il Chin Hoi to keep order. On their arrival they were set upon by Japanese gendarmes and after being roughly handled were disarmed and placed under arrest. They had committed no offence or even attempted to arrest any of the Il Chin Hoi people,—a proceeding to which the would have been perfectly entitled.

Some remarks about the work of war-dogs with the Russian Army are communicated by Captain Persidsky to the "Kölnische Zeitung." He writes:—"For the search of wounded men, lying in the maize or kaoling fields, our seven dogs have most remarkably stood the test. Their intelligence is suprising, the English dogs being especially very clever. They have been trained in Harbin and sent out to discover wounded men, lying in cover, by means of scent. In consequence they never err in mistaking a Japanese for a Russian. During the last fight, wounded soldiers were found by this means, where they never would have been looked for. All the 23 men thus found were Russians only. This fact is perhaps regrettable for the Japanese; but these dogs, grown familiar to Europeans alone, do not like or approach Asiatics. We also sent our dogs to a spot. where we supposed there were bodies of Japanese wounded, but, upon their return, we found their water bottles untouched, a proof that they had not come near the enemy's wounded."

A CONSULATE IN A DESERT.

A writer in the World's Work describes the building of a consular post in Persia. After seven months of patient waiting permission to start building at length reached Seistan from Teheran, and work was begun. Two sheep, presented by the Consul, were dragged to the spot as a sacrifice to the Almighty. In the twinkling of an eye the animals were on their backs, their throats were cut, and midst the murmur of a fervent "Bismillah" from the assembled crowd the first brick of the British Consulate in Seistan was laid upon the ground. The ceremony cannot be called the laying of the "foundation stone," for neither foundations nor stones exist in Seistan. All houses are built flush with the ground, the reason for this being that Seistan is practically water-logged, and water is invariably found from two to nine feet below the surface of the ground, thus rendering foundations impracticable. This subsoil water is generally briny and undrinkable. The British Consulate is built on a solid plinth of "pucca" burnt brick, raised 3¼ft. above the ground, and faces south in order that the back of the building may receive the force of the terrible Seistan wind, which blows unceasing night and day for 120 days during the hot months of the year. The labour employed on the Consulate, from the head mason to the coolie, was entirely indigenous, and might almost be described as prehistoric in its nature. The Seistan mason has no idea whatever of a straight line, a right angle, or a perpendicular. One has only to look at the local houses—not excepting the Governor's palace or the city walls—to see that the Seistan is innocent of any idea of symmetry or proportion. A more irregular, misshapen mass of buildings than those to be seen in Seistan it would be difficult to find anywhere. Every Seistan mason is an inveterate opium smoker, and one coolie in ten is the same. Nor is this to be wondered at, for nearly every Seistan mother among the lower classes is wont not only to indulge in this habit herself, but to solace the child at her breast with the same seductive opiate—the panacea of all Seistani ills, bodily and mental.

The tobacco interests of the Philippines are said to be preparing to make a hard fight in the coming Congress for the entire abolition of the tariff. President Roosevelt and Secretary Taft are afraid that 25 per cent. is the limit.

The Chinese Minister to Korea has sent a derspatch to the Foreign Office stating that having resided in Seoul for three years he is now about to retun to China. He will be succeeded by Mr. Tseng Chun.

At the French penal colony, Noumea, New Caledonia, the convicts have organised a band. The leader is a notorious murderer. The cymbal player killed a subpoena-server, and the drum player has murdered his landlord with a hammer. The assistant bandmater was convicted of having cut his wife to pieces.

A remarkable and unnerving experience was that of the Duc de Brissac and Jacques Faure recently, who went up in a balloon from the Park of Saint Cloud, near Paris. As soon as the balloon had risen well over the Aero Club grounds at Saint Cloud it started off in a southerly direction at the rate of seventy miles an hour. When above Troyes the aeronauts entered a snowstorm, and in a short time the balloon was covered with a thick coating of crystals, weighing in all nearly 200 pounds, and forcing the air-ship to the earth. The voyagers landed at the village of Lenglay, near Chatillon. A violent gale was blowing and the night was pitch dark. When news of the arrival was spread the entire population of the village hurried to the spot. The Duke and Faure were carried, half frozen, to the nearest house, where restoratives were applied, and they were put up for the night. The balloon travelled nearly 300 miles in four hours.

NEWS FROM PYENG-YANG.

(FROM A CORRESPONDENT.)

On the 26th ult. a double murder was committed here by a Japanese. Mr. Yi Sung Whan was in his house when a Japanese, armed with a hunting rifle, entered and demanded the immediate supply of some eggs. Mr. Yi was unable to supply him and apologised for this state of affairs, but the Japanese became enraged and struck him. a fatal blow on the forehead. Mr. Yi's son then struck at the Japanese with a stick, but the latter turned round and shot him with his rifle, killing him immediately.

* * *

The people of Pyeng-yang are extremely joyful over the news that their Magistrate is to be tried in Seoul on a charge of oppressing the people. It is hoped that an example will be made of him.

* * *

On the 19th inst., a Korean fisherman engaged in his occupation on the bank of the Taidong river was accosted by a Japanese, who asked him for his haul. Upon his refusal and reqnest for payment, the Japanese drew his sword and struck him, wounding him very severely. The Japanese was subsequently arrested and fined $10. and forced to pay the doctor's charges for the cure of his victim.

* * *

It is stated here that the Kong-chin-hoi are in secret communication with Peddlers, many of whom have recently arrived here with the avowed intention of breaking up the Il-chin-hoi. The Japanese gendarmes however are preparing to protect the latter.

The British steamer "Quito" with 4500 tons of Railway material arrived at Chemulpo on the 29th instant. Ship and cargo are consigned to Messrs Bennett and Co.

Many persons think that the punishment of allowing the Russian Squadron to go on to meet the Japanese is more severe than the occasion warrants.—Punch.

The "smart set" is now getting tiresome. After all, there are but ten Commandments that can be broken, and we have been repeatedly told that these very bad people have simply shattered them several times over. Now we want to hear about some one else.—The world.

Apparently killed by being run over by a train at Leghorn, Italy, Giovanni Crispi was removed to an undertaker's shop. At daybreak the following morning his "corpse" came to life, and, disgusted with the dreary surroundings, picked up a hat and walked home.

A New York man wagered that if President Roosevelt was not re-elected he would let his hair grow until 1908. Judge Parker's supporter, on his part, undertook that if the Democratic candidate was not returned, he would stand barefooted on a cake of ice weighing 300lbs, until it melted. We trust he has been let off.

MAJOR-GEN. NAKAMURA ON THE SIEGE OF PORT ARTHUR.

Continued from 2nd page.

Our men threw themselves flat on the ground, where they remained. A few men entered the enemy's fort, only to be instantly killed. Major-General Nakamura, Lieut.-Col. Okubo, and many other officers were killed or wounded. **Our men struggled** and persevered **from 10 p. m. to 1 a. m.,** but the situation **did not improve.** Finally General **Nogi recalled the** detachment and effected **a modification** in the general plan of **attack.**

VOTE OF CENSURE ON THE JAPANESE GOVERNMENT

The Tokio House of Representatives met on the 17th, a 1.10 p. m., all the Ministers of State being present. The resolution of censure proposed by the Seiyukai and Kenseihonto in connection with the advance of money to the 130th Bank was submitted by the Committee to which it had been referred' and was adopted by a large majority. Premier Katsura repeated his former explanation, but it was received with cries of "No, No." Both the War and Civil Budgets were sanctioned in the forms suggested by the Budget Committee.

The Korea Daily News.

Issued at 5 P. M. daily except Sundays.

Rate of Subscription :—
Per Year,............Yen 25.
Per Quarter,..........Yen 7.
Per Month,...........Yen 2.50.

Postage in Korea not charged extra.
Postage abroad charged extra.

Advertisements, 50 sen per day for 1 inch or less.
5 yen per month per inch.
50 yen per year per inch.

All communications to

E. T. BETHELL,
Editor and Publisher,
Pak-tong, Seoul.

NOTICE.

Monday and Tuesday January 2nd and 3rd will be observed as holidays by the Korea Daily News. On these days the offices will be closed and there will be no issue of the paper.

THE WAR.

The year 1904 closes and 1905 opens upon a glooomy prospect indeed. Whatever hope we had of a peaceful settlement of the troubles in the Far East we have reluctantly abandoned, and there seems little prospect but that the coming year will see a continuation of the wicked waste of blood and treasure which has left such a black mark on the record of the year 1904.

It is only reasonable to suppose that the erstwhile bellicose and aggressive Government of Japan has by now realized the futility of its undertaking, and would be willing to listen to proposals for a peaceful settlement could terms be devised which would involve no loss of face. But, in view of the fact that Japan was the original aggressor, and chose hrr own time and place for the making of the "coup" which was to "Prick the bubble" of Russia's reputation, it can hardly be expected that Japan will obtain by diplomacy anything which she shown her inability to take by force at a time when all the circumstances were in her favour.

Anyone reading the story of Major General Nakamura, which appears in another column, cannot fail to be struck with the note of pessimism which pervades it. The true state of affairs is now being "broken gently" to the people of Japan, but General Nakamura is only saying what we brought so much abuse about our ears by saying on several occasions, even so long ago as September last. The Japanese public, having been misled by an unduly optimistic press and carefully edited official reports, will not take kindly to the course of disillusionment now in store for them, and although the press has been kept well supplied with stories of discontent in Russia, we shall expect presently to hear of an equally undesirable state of affairs in Japan.

The position North of Liaoyang is obscure, but there are indications that the scale is turning in Russia's favour. Had Field Marshal Oyama been in a position to strike the overwhelming blow which we have heard so much about, it would have been struck ere now so that the good news could have come to palliate the dismay caused by the damaging admission of costly failure at Port Arthur. If the news be true—and there is good reason to believe it to be—that Kuropatkin is gradually evacuating Mukden, we take this to be another sign of improvement in the Russian position. It shows that Kuropatkin is now able to pay some attention to a matter of sentiment, and has made himself so strong elsewhere that the tenure of the Manchu holy city is no longer essential to the success of his plans.

The approach of the first Baltic Fleet, the despatch of the second Baltic Fleet, and the possibility of the despatch of the Black Sea Fleet, are factors which must be taken into consideration, while we are told that in another month the organization of the second Manchurian army will be complete and General Grippenberg's command will take the field, operating, probably, from Kirin.

So that it is evident that Russia intends to carry the war through to a finish, and that a peaceful settlement can no longer be hoped for.

MAJOR-GEN. NAKAMURA ON THE SIEGE OF PORT ARTHUR.

(FROM THE JAPAN TIMES.)

Major-General Nakamura, who is now undergoing treatment at the Tokyo Reserve Hospital, has been interviewed by a "Kokumin" representative. The General is progressing favourably, though some time must elapse before he completely recovers. The officer does not speak much of the assault on the Sungshushan Fort, of which he was the leader. After expressing his high opinion of the valour and endurance of the Russians at Port Arthur, the General says:—

"The siege of Port Arthur is more difficult in its execution than has generally been expected by the outside public. In addition to the natural and artificial defences, we have to fight against desperate troops who willingly lay down their lives for the sake of their country. It is true that the 203-metre height and the North Fort of Tungkikwanshan have, though at a heavy cost, already fallen into our hands. But considering the fortress as a whole, the former, whatever value it has with regard to the siege, is no more than an outer fort, while the North Fort of Tungkikwanshan cannot, properly speaking, be regarded as one of the enemy's principal forts. The only forts which have a claim as such are those at Sungshushan, Erhlungshan and some other places. These two forts had once been taken by us, but were recovered by the enemy afterwards. The fact that, in spite of the rapid progress made in our siege work, these forts still defy our assaults, only testifies to the immense difficulties of the task our army is engaged in. Then I discredit any suggestion that the Russian rank and file have been decidedly thinned due to our sustained siege. I would estimate their present number at some 10,000, as it is very likely that the majority of the Russians who were wounded a few months ago have already returned to their ranks. There are moreover quite a large number of sailors, who, as the result of the sinking of their warships, may have been compelled to land and assist in the operations on shore.

Next, the report that the Russians have run short of ammunition can, I think, scarcely be receievd as true. Compared with the enemy's lavish use of ammunition during July and August when he always returned three to one of our shots, it is apparent that he has now become very cantious in this connection. This, however, cannot afford any ground for supposing that the enemy's stock of ammunition has been falling off. On the contrary, he has of late given ample proof whenever the opposing forces have exchanged fire that this is not the case. It is certain that he has no boundless supply of ammunition, but it is also beyond doubt that he can in some measure rely on his own productive power as well as on possible supplies smuggled in from the outside world. With regard to provisions it will be safe to surmise that their stocks are even more plentiful than ammunition. It seems beyond question that the Russans at Port Arthur are communicating with the home authorities' by means of wireless telegraphy, though important messages are often carried to Chefoo through the instrumentality of small war-ships such as destroyers. It is, however, almost impossible for the Russians to send communications from land. It is true that the enemy still employs the Chinese for that purpose, but there is little chance for the latter to succeed in their mission, as no natives are ever allowed to pass the fighting line by either belligerent. It short, it will be no easy task to completely occupy th fortress; the more our siegeworks pro gress, the more stubborn the Russians will become. They will no doubt fight to the last man in defence of the fortress as well as Russia's prestige. Lastly, I deprecate the insinuation that the recent message from Stoessel requesting our army to refrain from firing on the new town and a portion of the old one, shows how hard pressed is the enemy. I think that this idea is not a new one but was formulated by the enemy some time in July or August last and actually proposed to our Army only recently. We have of course never deliberately fired on the buildings flying the Red Cross flag, as stated in Stoessel's messages. Since our occupation of the 203 metre height, we have been sending a fierce fire on to the town and harbour with the result already known, and this may have been sorely felt by the Russians, who were thus compelled to make the above proposal, ostensibly on behalf of the Red Cross."

Apropos of General Nakamura, our local contemporaries publish an account of his achievement during the fourth general attack on Port Arthur, which began on November 26 and culminated in the occuption of the 203-metre height. At first the height was not the object of our attack, which was mainly directed to the forts east of Sungshan. The assult by infantry began at 1 p. m., but as at sunset they had not been able to achieve any palpable success. Major General Nakamura was to carry out another assault during the night.

His troops constituted the special reserves of the Investing Army and consisted of the elite of all the regiments. Before proceeding to the attack, Major-General Nakamura issued the following instructions:

"The object of our detachment is to cut the Port Arthur fortress into two. No one is to entertain the hope of returning alive. Should I fall, Colonel Watanabe will take my place, and should a similar fate befall him, Lieut-Colonel Okubo will then take charge. Every officer in each rank shall appoint his successor. The attack shall be chiefly effected with the bayonet. However severe the enemy's fire, our men must not return a single shot until we have first established a footing. The officers are authorized to kill those men who, without proper reason, straggle behind or separate themselves from the ranks or who retreat."

In other to facilitate recognition, each man was given a white "tasuki" or band crossing on the back. General Nogi in person gave a hearty "send-off" to the detachment.

The detachment proceeded along the main road on the western side of Sungshushan and at 9 p. m. had drawn up in a crevice below the old fort of Sungshushan. The moon was just then rising over the ridge on the east. Our troops gallantly rushed up the slope. The enemy's fort remained silent, but the new fort of Sungshushan poured a scathing fire upon our troops. The search light from Itszshan lit up the advance of our troops. At a distance of 20 metres from the enemy's fort, two mines blew up with a tremendous explosion. This was a signal for the enemy's fort to open a heavy rifle fire.

(Continued on page 3.)

The Korea Daily News.

VOL. I, SATURDAY, DECEMBER 31, 1904. No. 138

大韓每日申報
대한매일신보

(뎨이권일호) (목요일) 일쳔구빅오년일월오일

본샤고빅

이신보는영어와한어로셔계린
월츌판ᄒᆞᆷ
신문가
한쟝 엽두돈오푼
일삭됴 엽두량닷돈
우표가리 삭닷돈
다팟돈으로밧숩
광고료는
귀쳔의쟝단과ᄌᆞᄒᆡᆼ의다쇼로죵
량ᄒᆞ되렴가로밧을터이오며오
릭지아니ᄒᆞ야대한사람마다다이신
문을보실터이니광고내시기를
원ᄒᆞ시는이들은우리신문사에
와서면약ᄒᆞ심을희망ᄒᆞᆷ

○발힝소 박동대한매일신보
사번역하교엽헤젼영국인셜필
립졍자리오
사쟝 영국인 (비셜)
평양 티리졈
○평양효동사는권피보씨로우
리신문관비티리인을뎡ᄒᆞ엿
시ᄉᆞ오니평양에계신구람코자ᄒᆞ
는 쳠군ᄌᆞ는칭티리졈에왕
림ᄒᆞ와면회ᄒᆞ시옵

샤고

○우리대한매일신보의목뎍은
대한의인민졍셔에관한모든대
목에티ᄒᆞ야논공평한번론을쥬
쟝ᄒᆞᆷ이라우리동신원의팀보논
신문보시는쳠군ᄌᆞ의게ᄒᆞ샹보
도ᄒᆞ리며펴지들리서ᄒᆞ매주시
는이논셩명과번디들젹어붓치
시기를희망ᄒᆞ오니하기슴신문
샹에귀졔ᄒᆞ라는거시아니오다
만규히신용ᄒᆞ논증거를숨고자
ᄒᆞᆷ이라귀자논아모귀서던지과
지ᄒᆞᆷ을퇴각ᄒᆞ논권리를가졋소
나퇴각ᄒᆞ논리유를말ᄒᆞᆯ티이오
며공중광고들문란케ᄒᆞ논듯ᄒᆞᆫ
귀서논의례히밧지안켓숩나이
다

●본샤셜시이리로신문을미양
우레로부쳐ᄒᆞ와레젼부의일의
로쳔ᄒᆞ든ᄌᆞ스로면곳에논ᄒᆞ늣게
젼ᄒᆞ기도ᄒᆞ며ᄒᆞ멋첩거슬ᄒᆞᆫ졉
에젼ᄒᆞ기도ᄒᆞ며ᄒᆞ야나젼ᄒᆞ논
곳도잇다ᄒᆞ와우리신문을수랑
ᄒᆞ야구람ᄒᆞ시논 쳠군ᄌᆞ의게
티ᄒᆞ야미우미안ᄒᆞ옵기로지금
은분젼인을두고미일죠이젼
ᄒᆞ며아니젼ᄒᆞ거나늣게거나ᄒᆞᆫ
폐가업도록ᄒᆞ라ᄒᆞ오니ᄒᆞ야니

젼ᄒᆞ거논ᄒᆞ늣게젼ᄒᆞ거나ᄒᆞᆫ일
이잇스면본샤로통긔ᄒᆞ여주심
을희망ᄒᆞᆷ

관보

뎨삼쳔이십ᄉᆞ호
광무팔년십이월삼십일일
셔 일긔슈청
○의원면본관 중츄원의관
면윤셰 중츄원의관 김상열
중츄원의관 리용의 중츄원
의관 양경오 중츄원의관
김명진
○임중츄원의관셔주임관륙등
구품 신상오 구품 유졍렬
구품 김창렬 구품 리용셕
구품 박경노
이샹십이월이십칠일
○히궁니부특진관 종이품박
졔빈
○의원면본관 텰도원쥬ᄉᆞ
뎡셕조 텰도원쥬ᄉᆞ 한승교
텰도원쥬ᄉᆞ 강노진 텰도원
쥬ᄉᆞ 박남원 텰도원쥬ᄉᆞ
오ᄒᆞᆼ근 통신ᄉᆞ면화과쥬ᄉᆞ
뎡국진 통신ᄉᆞ면화과쥬ᄉᆞ
리샹엽 통신ᄉᆞ면화과쥬ᄉᆞ
김영문 통신ᄉᆞ면화과쥬ᄉᆞ
뎡규셕 통신ᄉᆞ면화과쥬ᄉᆞ
한틱린 통신ᄉᆞ면화과쥬ᄉᆞ
리명구 통신ᄉᆞ면화과쥬ᄉᆞ
리병하
○히시종원분시어 구품 리
숭구 구품 뎡석창 구품
신창균 구품 리용샹 구품
박도순 구품 민세호 구품
권틱션 구품 곽지창 구품
림명준
이샹십이월이십구일
○임니부대신셔칙임관일등
표훈원총지 조병식
○임의졍부참졍셔칙임관이등
비셔원경 리지용
○명임시서리궁니부대신ᄉᆞ무
학부대신 리지용
이샹십이월삼십일일
○임의졍부참졍셔칙임관일등
종이품 김셩근
○임법부대신셔칙임관일등
의졍부참졍 권중현
○임의졍부참졍셔칙임관일등
궁니부특진관 리근호
이샹광무팔년십이월삼십
일일

샹쳔이십ᄉᆞ호
광무구년일월이일
셔 남금슈청
○승졍삼품 륙품 리규의
○승졍삼품 륙품 최셕민
이샹광무팔년오월십일일
○셔훈오등ᄉᆞ팔괘쟝 일본국
부령슈 신졍슌졍
○셔훈륙등ᄉᆞ팔괘쟝 일본국
셔긔싱 쳔샹팀일랑
일본국셔긔싱 다뎐환
일본국셔긔싱 중촌졍ᄎᆞ랑
일본국셔긔싱 대포무인
일본국셔긔싱 고응경삼
일본국경찰셔쟝 경부평곡
용
일본국경부 도변응태랑
이샹광무팔년십이월이십
팔일
○임학부주ᄉᆞ셔판임관륙등
중학교교관 임신졔
이샹광무팔년십이월이십
구일
○의원면본관 비셔원승 리
셕종 종묘서령 김용완 숙
릉령 조철호
○히경임종졍분쥬ᄉᆞ 홍문관
시독 신영학
○히분비서랑 홍문관시독
신학영
○티의원도졔됴셔칙임관일등
궁니부특진관 조병세
○명시강원첨ᄉᆞ셔칙임관ᄉᆞ등
종이품 윤샹학
○궁니부특진관셔칙임관일등
졍이품 리용틱
○임비서원승서주임관륙등
중학교쟝 리덕용
○임 종묘서령셔판임관ᄉᆞ등
영희젼령 쟝철상
○임 영희젼령셔판임관오등
사직셔령 조병의
○임 사직셔령셔판임관칠등
틱복ᄉᆞ주ᄉᆞ 민회식
○임 틱복ᄉᆞ주ᄉᆞ셔판임관칠
등 사직셔참봉 리덕주
○임 사직셔참봉셔판임관팔
등 김용오
○임통신ᄉᆞ면화과쥬ᄉᆞ셔판임
관팔등 구품 최상의
○임 슉릉령셔판임관칠등
구품 마항달
○임농상공학교교관셔판임관
륙등 김대희

○임의학교교관셔판임관륙등
슈창경
이샹광무팔년십이월삼십일
○명 인천셰무ᄉᆞ 니부대
신 조병식
이샹광무팔년십이월삼십
일일

잡보

○쳥경소명 쳥경최익현씨
가누수불괴ᄒᆞ던니일젼에상리
ᄒᆞ야문밧게잇슴으로 조칙을
뎌듸혀니리샤곳드리오라ᄒᆞ셧
다라

○회원지송 일진회에셔는국
쟝가젼에후제빈수무리지졍ᄒᆞ엿다
셔작일은국쟝부기회ᄒᆞ논티
지송ᄒᆞ기위ᄒᆞ야인제고로회회에
계(쟝서)모자에곰자영문[퀘]일
자로표ᄒᆞᆫ것을쓰고동대문밧셔
지이지송ᄒᆞ더라는틱회원이수쳔

○명양근계경랴 힝셩샨면리게ᄒᆞ
는김덕화라사롬이셩잇는티고아ᄒᆞ
동비일젼회원으로샹경ᄒᆞ야의
부파직비가군을ᄒᆞ다ᄒᆞᆷ으로면
일포들광아돈이쳔오빅랑과의복
을습을ᄒᆞ야가지고오다가향근
바빙이쥬막에서봉젹ᄒᆞ고춘춘
길식ᄒᆞ야왓는티그아들의슈운
ᄒᆞ다던일은남귀가됨으로또가
졍티팔나고ᄒᆞᆫ다더라
월게약등 칭셩셥드리계
셔졔ᄒᆞ는부인을멱비돌졀ᄒᆞ야근쳔에
ᄒᆞ는카는부인을밋나가지고카
는술과셰을세서빅을지음에강
졍군수의봉분ᄒᆞ논쟉광을쏘삐
셔녕결벽고부인을겁욕ᄒᆞ지ᄒᆞ
열다논티ᄒᆞ고ᄒᆞ귀예도파쇼병뎡
이잇스면ᄒᆞ리케ᄒᆞ지는아비
ᄒᆞ리에횡인며그렬셩ᄒᆞ니ᄒᆞ
슈덕라라ᄒᆞ이션치리라고면
다 쳐등

뎐보

○영국괴후 론돈발
쳥한금에셔ᄒᆞᆫ죵이대단ᄒᆞᆫ이
항에지논은게열쳐
ᄒᆞᆫ이자아쳑ᄒᆞ야섬이
칭이못ᄒᆞ고잇닥터라
○모륵코와근상 모륵코에서
불은ᄒᆞᆫ조지방이잇서서남다
요ᄒᆞᆷ이더ᄒᆞᆫ지라법국이그에가
셔평화를보젼ᄒᆞ랴면병력을
지안국논어렵겟다더라

UNION INSURANCE SOCIETY OF CANTON.

Head office Hongkong.
Marine risks underwritten at current rates.
Agents in Chemulpo,
E. MEYER & Co.

COMPAGNIE DES MESSAGERIES MARITIMES.

Fortnightly Direct Service.

For Marseilles
via Ports.
Sailing from Yokohama
Calling at Kobe,
Shanghai, Hongkong, Saigon, Singapore,
Colombo, Djibonti, Suez, Port Said
and Marseilles.

For particulars apply to
HOLME RINGER & Co.,
Chemulpo.

HAYASHIDA & CO.,

16 MYENG DONG, CHIN KO KAI, SEOUL.
BRANCH OFFICE AT CHEMULPO.

Money changers, Coal and Wood Merchants, Express Agents.

We are agents for the Pyeng-yang Coal Company and the Karazu Coal Company of Japan. We have the best quality of both anthracite and bituminous coal, and prompt execution of orders is our speciality. Firewood of all kinds kept in stock. Full weight guaranteed. Money of all denominations exchanged at current rates. Parcels received for all parts.

CHINA MUTUAL LIFE INS. OC.

Most favourable terms to policy holders.

Benefit system unsurpassed.

HOLME RINGER & Co.
Agents, Chemulpo.

C. P. R.

CANADIAN PACIFIC RAILWAY COMPANY'S ROYAL MAIL STEAMSHIP LINE.

THE FAST ROUTE BETWEEN CHINA, JAPAN, AND EUROPE VIA CANADA AND THE UNITED STATES.

Route from Hongkong via Shanghai, Nagasaki (Inland Sea of Japan) Kobe, Yokohama Victoria and Vancouver.

Twin Screw Empress Steamship—6,000 Tons—Speed 19 knots.

PROPOSED SAILING FROM YOKOHAMA.
R. M. S. Empress of India.
R. M. S. Empress of Japan.
R. M. S. Empress of China.
R. M. S. Athenian.
R. M. S. Tartar.

Special reduction (first class only) granted to members of the Military, Naval, Diplomatic and Civil services and to Missionaries.

Passengers have choice of ten routes across the Continent of America and have privilege of travelling by any Atlantic Steamship Line.

Round the World passage tickets in connection with the P. and O. S. N., North German Lloyd and Messageries Co.'s **£125**.

All rates payable at current rate of exchange.

For further information, Tickets, Guide Books, etc., apply to

HOLME, RINGER & CO., AGENTS,
Chemulpo.

Grand Hotel,

(Formerly the Station Hotel)

Near the Railway Terminus, West Gate Seoul.

The Best Hotel in Korea;
Handsome new Building.
Fine Airy Rooms
Excellent Cuisine.
Terms Moderate.
Special terms to Missionaries
and to permanent boarders.

Electric cars within 2 minutes' walk.

W. H. EMBERLEY.
Proprietor

EVERY FACILITY.

In connection with Life Assurance Business is afforded by

The Standard Life Assurance Co.,

One of the largest and wealthiest of the Provident Institutions of the United Kingdom Forms of Application and all information will be promptly afforded on application.

10 CENTS A DAY.

Not a very large expenditure is it? But it is sufficient to secure for a man of 30 a policy with the STANDARD LIFE OFFICE for

$1323.

For all particulars of rates, etc., apply to

Holme, Ringer & Co.,
Agents, Chemulpo.

THE NEW YORK LIFE INSURANCE COMPANY.

Have you ever been declined by any Company?

Are you engaged in a specially hazardous occupation?

Have you heard of the New York Life Insurance Company's New Classifications for this class of Risks?

If not, send your date of birth, occupation and particulars of rejection; if any to

E. MEYER & Co.,
Agents, Chemulpo.

MITSUI BUSSAN KAISHA.
(MITSUI & Co.).
MITSUI GINKO.
(MITSUI BANK.)

The Bank is owned by the members of the **Mitsui Family, who,** as partners, assume an unmited **responsibility** for all liabilities of the **Bank:—**

Capital.......................Yen 5,000,000
Reserve Fund..................." 5,600,000

HEAD OFFICE, TOKYO.

LONDON OFFICE, 34 LIME ST., E. C.

BRANCHES AND AGENCIES:—

New York, San Francisco, Hamburg, Bombay, Singapore, Manila, Hongkong, Amoy, Chefoo, Tientsin.

Kobe, Hakodate, Yokohama, Kure, Yokosuka, **Moji, Shimonoseki,** Miike, Wakamatsu, **Nagasaki, Kuchinotsu,** Karatsu, Sasebo, **Misume, Taipeh, &c.**

Telegraphic Address for all the Offices:

"MITSUI."

A. B. C. AND A. I CODES USED.

Contractors of Coal

To the Imperial Japanese Navy. Arsenals **and Railway Bureau, Principal** Railway Com**panies and Industrial** Work, **Home** and For**eign Mail and Freight Steamers.**

Sole Proprietors

Of the famous Miike, Tagawa and Yamano Coal **Mines.**

Sole Agents

For the sale of Fukumo, Hokoku, Ichimura, Kanoda, **Mannoura,** Onoura, Ostuji, Sonoda, Tsubaruro, **Yoshinotani, Yoshio, Yurokibura** and other **coals.**

YANGTSE **INSURANCE ASSOCIATION, LTD.**

The undersigned, **having been appointed** agents for the above **company, are prepared to** issue policies and pay **losses on marine risks at** regular rates.

E. MEYER & Co.,
Agents, Chemulpo.

AMERICAN KOREAN ELECTRIC CO.

Light and Power.

Main Office: Electric Building, Chong No.

RAILWAY DEPARTMENT.

OPERATING CARS BETWEEN EAST AND WEST GATE, EVERY TEN MINUTES:—

First Car leaves East Gate at 7:00 A. M. First Car leaves R. R. Station at 7:25 A. M.
Last Car " East Gate at 8.40 P. M. Last " " R. R. Station at 9.05 P. M.

OPERATING CARS BETWEEN EAST GATE AND IMPERIAL TOMB TERMINUS, EVERY TWENTY MINUTES:—

CONNECTING WITH EVERY ALTERNATE CAR ARRIVING AT EAST GATE FROM CHONG NO.

First Car leaves East Gate for Tomb at 7:10 A. M.
" " " Tomb for East Gate at 7:30 A. M.
Last " " East Gate for Tomb at 7:50 P. M.
" " " Tomb for East Gate at 8:10 P. M.

OPERATING CARS BETWEEN CHONG NO AND YUNG SAN RIVER EVERY TWELVE MINUTES:—

First Car leaves Chong No for South Gate at 7:12 A. M.
" " " Chong No for Yung San at 7:36 A. M.
" " " South Gate for Chong No at 7:20 A. M.
" " " Yung San for Chong No at 8:09 A. M.
Last " " South Gate for Chong No 9:00 P. M.
" " " Yung San for Chong No at 8.45. P. M.

SPECIAL PRIVATE CARS FURNISHED TO SUIT CONVENIENCE OF PATRONS. PRICES ON APPLICATION AT HEAD OFFICE.

LIGHTING DEPARTMENT.

Where less than 250 candle power of light is used, the rate per month will be
Per 16 candle power incandescent lamp,—All night.—Yen 2.50.
32 candle power incandescent lamp:—All night:—Yen 4.00.
50 candle power incandescent lamp:—All night:—Yen 6.00.
150 " " " " " " " 10.00.
1200 ,, ,, enclosed are ,, ,, ,, ,, 20.00.

Where more than 250 candle power of light is used, a Meter will be installed, freqvedted:—Rent of Meter Yen 2.00 per month. Rate of charges by meter reading:—Two Sen per Ampere per hour. (Approximately this is equal to about One Sen per 16 C. P. lamp per hour) Minimum monthly charge where meter is in-Stalled, Yen 20.00 per month, which includes rental of meter.

Estimates for installing lights furnished on application

An assortment of chandeliers always on hand.

K. Murakami.

Photograph Studio
Chinkokai, Seoul.

Printing, Developing and Enlargement, of Photographs always Undertaken.

Korean Views and Pictures Illustrating Native Customs always on Sale,

---

THE OSAKA SHOSEN KAISHA.

Boats frequently on the berth for Chinnampo.

REGULAR SAILINGS BETWEEN JAPAN AND KOREAN PORTS.

FUSAN AND KOBE VIA SHIMONOSEKI.

OSAKA VIA MOKPO, FUSAN, SHIMONOSEKI AND KOBE.

MOJI DIRECT.

OSAKA VIA KUNSAN, MASANPO, FUSAN, SHIMONOSEKI AND KOBE.

CHEMULPO KUNSAN LINE
Every three days.

CHEMULPO CHINNAMPO LINE.
Every three days.

For Freight and passage and further particulars apply to
THE OSAKA SHOSEN KAISHA,
Chemulpo

RONDON, PLAISANT & CO.

General **Storekeepers and Merchants, Ships Contractors, Tobacconists, Commission and Forwarding Agents, Coal Merchants**

IMPORTERS AND, **EXPORTERS**

Seoul & Chemulpo.

W. D. WENTWORTH.

LANDING
AND
SHIPPING AGENT
AND
CUSTOMS BORDER.

12 OURA, NAGASAKI.

STEWARD & CO.

Chemulpo.

Shipchandlers and Storekeepers, **Naval and** Mercantile Contrrctors, **Landing and Shipping** Agents.

STEWARD'S HOTEL

Chemulpo.

Best accommodation in the port for travelers. Clean and well-aired rooms, good cuisine and prompt attendence, moderate tariff.

론설

전쟁

○금년은다가고러시아가벌서오ᄂᆞᆫ뒤모든일이참담ᄒᆞ도다극동의전쟁에뒤ᄒᆞ야우리ᄂᆞᆫ평화되기를바라나ᄂᆞ그러ᄒᆞ나모다가망이업고리년에도파와지산을악ᄒᆞ게허비ᄒᆞᆫ금년의불힝ᄒᆞᆫᄉᆞ적을연속홈을또보겟도다

다만가망이잇ᄂᆞᆫ것은지금일본정부가전에ᄒᆞᆫ일의몰지각홈을ᄭᅢ닷고평화죠약이일본에뎨면이나일치아니ᄒᆞ게되면쟝ᄎᆞᆺ화친ᄒᆞ기를허락홀듯ᄒᆞᆫ지라그러ᄒᆞ나ᄉᆞ실샹으로보면일본이젼쟁의션발자가되야ᄃᆡ국은예비도ᄒᆞᆫ기전에ᄯᅢ와쳐소를자긔ᄆᆞ옴ᄃᆡ로ᄆᆞ려서전쟁을시쟉ᄒᆞ엿스니평화될ᄯᅢ에ᄂᆞᆫ일본이자긔의ᄆᆞ옴ᄃᆡ로강력으로취ᄒᆞ든것ᄀᆞᆺ치외교샹으로ᄂᆞᆫ능히엇겟다말ᄒᆞ기어렵도다

일본인민을위ᄒᆞ야ᄂᆞᆫ일이점점글너가ᄂᆞᆫᄃᆡ일본사ᄅᆞᆷ들은말ᄂᆞᆯ그러케아니ᄒᆞ며로국에분요ᄒᆞᆫ막을일본신문지에말ᄒᆞ기를죠와ᄒᆞ나일본에도그와ᄀᆞᆺᄒᆞᆫ불온ᄒᆞᆫᄉᆞ샹이잇ᄂᆞᆫ것을우리가미구에드를듯ᄒᆞ도다

료양이북은ᄉᆞ세가난칙ᄒᆞ나그러ᄒᆞ나로국의형편이됴하잔다ᄂᆞᆫ말이잇ᄂᆞᆫ지라일본총ᄉᆞ령관오구마씨의경영ᄒᆞᄂᆞᆫ일대타격은우리가듯기ᄂᆞᆫ만이ᄒᆞ엿지마ᄂᆞᆫ경영만홀것이아니라지금맛당이ᄒᆞᆫ번대타격을힝ᄒᆞ야그리셔그죠ᄒᆞᆫ소식이나와셔려슌함락되엿다ᄂᆞᆫ허셜에실망ᄒᆞᆫ것을위로ᄒᆞ게홀지로다구로팟긴대쟝이점점봉텬을ᄯᅥ나랴ᄒᆞᆫ다ᄂᆞᆫ말이츰말ᄀᆞᆺᄒᆞ면우리ᄂᆞᆫ그것이또ᄒᆞᆫ로국군ᄉᆞ샹에ᄒᆞᆫ진보ᄒᆞᄂᆞᆫ표로아노라그일에ᄃᆡᄒᆞ야구로팟긴대쟝이지금은정신을정돈ᄒᆞ고자긔의병력이각쳐에강ᄒᆞ게되야셔만쥬에ᄒᆞᆫ도회된봉텬을교슈ᄒᆞᄂᆞᆫ것이자긔의계척에합당치못ᄒᆞ야그리ᄒᆞ랴ᄒᆞᄂᆞᆫ것을가이볼지로다

뎨일불틱함ᄃᆡ의오ᄂᆞᆫ것과뎨이불틱합ᄃᆡ의죠직파혹히합ᄃᆡ의죠직ᄒᆞᆫ다ᄂᆞᆫ말이다싱각홀일이오또이다음달에ᄂᆞᆫ뎨이만쥬군의죠직이쇽나셔그립펜벅대쟝이령솔ᄒᆞ고길림에셔브터힝군ᄒᆞᆫ다ᄒᆞᄂᆞᆫ지라

그러케로국이이젼쟁을쇽ᄒᆞ지보랴ᄒᆞᄂᆞᆫ것이분명ᄒᆞ니평화ᄒᆞ기ᄂᆞᆫ브랄슈업로다

잡보

○쥬일공관면보 일월이일에쥬일공ᄉᆞ가외부로면보ᄒᆞ기를작일에려슌함락ᄒᆞ엿다ᄒᆞ엿고또면보ᄒᆞ기를일본륙군생면화ᄂᆡ에려슌이쟝찻함락ᄒᆞ겟단말온오문이어놀일작에면보ᄒᆞ엿스니죄송ᄒᆞᆫ다ᄒᆞ엿더라

○임치중디발 일공관에셔외부로면보ᄒᆞ기를공쥬ᄃᆡ가폭힝ᄒᆞ야우리샹민에관진태랑의손히비샹일ᄉᆞ로여러번죠청ᄒᆞ야도샹완지아니ᄒᆞ니본ᄉᆞ가불가불남문밧경부텰도뎡거쟝긔디가뎨일은힝에임치ᄒᆞᆫ중에셔디발홀터이니청컨ᄃᆡ죠량ᄒᆞ라ᄒᆞ엿더라

○건긔디영 지작일슌명비궁발인시에일진공진량회가긔를세우고죵로에셔디영ᄒᆞ엿더라

○리쳥지관 평리원에피슈ᄒᆞ엿던공진회장리쥰과윤효정라유셕삼인을거월삼십일일에죠률ᄒᆞ엿ᄂᆞᆫᄃᆡ리윤량인은종진중역을감이등ᄒᆞ야역십년에쳐ᄒᆞ고라유셕은쳐교를감이등ᄒᆞ야십오년증역에쳐ᄒᆞ엿ᄂᆞᆫᄃᆡ히회원이비단그최를항복지아니홀쑨아니라일본변호ᄉᆞ가법ᄉᆞ시무ᄒᆞᄂᆞᆫ날에와셔지판ᄒᆞ기를청ᄒᆞ고또즁민이법부에일제청원ᄒᆞ야지관쟝민병한으로지관ᄒᆞ기를쳥ᄒᆞ엿다더라

○근긔젹경 근긔에젹경이대단ᄒᆞ야시흥과과천과인천과부평등디에쥬야로륙혈포나칼을가지고슈삼인식촌마다초요ᄒᆞᆫ자의계면만량식그럿치안으면문즁이나동즁으로거어라ᄒᆞ고되아모날셔울뎡거쟝이나혹종로ᄀᆞᆺᄒᆞᆫᄃᆡ로가지고오라고표를밧아가지고간후에ᄂᆞᆫ하향물졍이엇지홀슈업셔돈얼마식가지고져오라ᄂᆞᆫ곳에가셔군우ᄃᆡ로김셔방이나리셔방을차즈면의심업시밧아가지고가ᄂᆞᆫᄃᆡ그런일여종종잇다ᄒᆞ더라

○차옥회원 청국신ᄉᆞ모씨가일진회의취지를가샹히녀여대안문압이층양옥을회원의게차급ᄒᆞ고집쥬인청샹의게부탁ᄒᆞ야집세젼ᄉᆞ십원은민의월보죠로물시ᄒᆞ라ᄒᆞ엿더라

○회민샹경 젼라도에셔일진회민이만이군산항으로회집ᄒᆞ야단발ᄒᆞ고양복ᄭᅵ고입일졔히샹경ᄒᆞᆫ다ᄂᆞᆫ면고가ᄂᆡ부에달ᄒᆞ엿더라

○방어계책 근일평양셔ᄂᆞᆫ셔울공진회원의비밀ᄒᆞᆫ통문을발홈으로부샹슈빅명이일변황히도황쥬에모집되고오십명은평양으로드러왓다ᄒᆞᄂᆞᆫᄃᆡ쟝찻일진회지회를방히코져ᄒᆞᆫ다ᄒᆞᄂᆞᆫ고로비밀ᄒᆞᆫᄉᆞ실를방금일본헌병부에셔도사실ᄒᆞᄂᆞᆫ중인ᄃᆡ일진회지회에셔ᄂᆞᆫ십분방어홀계책을도모ᄒᆞᆫ다더라

이샹평양통신

○치료비샹 중 대동강변농봉리사ᄂᆞᆫ한인어부가음력십일월십삼일에강변에셔고기를잡ᄂᆞᆫᄃᆡ하허일인이와셔잡은고기를달나ᄒᆞᆫ즉어부가갑업시ᄂᆞᆫ아니쥰다말ᄒᆞᆫ즉일본인이가진칼노어부의허리를질너중샹된소문을평양일본헌병파츌소에셔듯고히일인을착치ᄒᆞ야사실ᄒᆞᆫ후에어부에치료비를담당케ᄒᆞ며비샹금ᄉᆞ지십원ᄭᆞ지쥬게ᄒᆞ엿다더라

평양통신

○긔션정박 평양은지나간음력십일월초팔일에일긔가극한ᄒᆞ여중남포와대동강으로리왕ᄒᆞᄂᆞᆫ소중긔션은뎡박이되엿더라

○리씨권력 평양ᄀᆡ시쟝총슌리건영씨가향일에슌검이십여명을가셜ᄒᆞ고로곤경을당ᄒᆞᆫ사실은본보에이왕긔지ᄒᆞ엿거니와근일에또슌검을가셜ᄒᆞᄂᆞᆫ고로히시감리도엇지홀수업ᄂᆞᆫ모양인가보더라

○의병운동 평안북도각군에소위의병이라ᄒᆞᄂᆞᆫ당이도쳐에셔봉긔ᄒᆞᄂᆞᆫ모양인ᄃᆡ그즁에이젼관인도혹림참ᄒᆞ엿ᄂᆞᆫᄃᆡ그목젹인즉일진회반ᄃᆡᄒᆞ기위ᄒᆞ야운동ᄒᆞᆫ다더라

○체문방미 평안남도관찰사리중하씨가히디ᄉᆞ숭학교긔부금을모집ᄒᆞ기위ᄒᆞ야각면류림의게쟝의체문을관ᄒᆞ다ᄂᆞᆫ말이잇다더라

○평슈담학 평양군슈팽한쥬씨ᄂᆞᆫ담학슈단으로일군빅셩을모다환산디경을문다라노코도도로혀빅셩을죽인다ᄒᆞᆯ다무한이위엄을뵈이며빅방묘계로협잡류로ᄒᆞ야곰일번상경ᄒᆞ야원류ᄒᆞ려ᄒᆞᄂᆞᆫᄃᆡ별안간강동군슈셔샹쥰씨가평양군에겸관이되고샹원군슈민건식씨ᄂᆞᆫ팽군슈를구인ᄒᆞ야일간압샹케ᄒᆞᆫ다ᄒᆞᆫ민히디인민들은 대황뎨폐하ᄭᅴ만세를부른다더라

○위부피살 평양남도중화군영진방륙리거ᄒᆞᄂᆞᆫ리셩환의아오가거음력십이월일에일본인의게피살ᄒᆞᆫ사실은하허일인이산양ᄎᆞ로히ᄃᆡ에리왕다가리가의집에돌입ᄒᆞ야계란를쳥구ᄒᆞ미리가가듯지아니ᄒᆞᆫ즉부지불각에칼노리가의이마를쳐셔유혈이낭자ᄒᆞᆫ즉그아들이분홈을이긔지못ᄒᆞ야히일본인를구타ᄒᆞᆫ즉일본인이즉시륙혈포로그아들을포살ᄒᆞ엿다더라

외보

○영왕항히 영국대군쥬에드워ー드뎨ᄂᆞᆫ이월초싱에ᄒᆞᆫ슌양함을타고디즁히로향ᄒᆞᆫ다고포트스마우쓰에셔공포ᄒᆞ엿더라

○쥬야은힝 미국뉴욕에셔쟈본가들이은힝ᄒᆞ나를셜시ᄒᆞ야밤낫업시ᄉᆞ무를보게홀계획이라더라

○일인졀도 일본구레히군항에셔거월오일에다가노ᄅᆞᄂᆞᆫᄉᆞ룸이졀도죄로잡혓ᄂᆞᆫᄃᆡ이ᄉᆞ룸이일천구빅일년ᄉᆞ월일일브터칠월십팔일ᄭᆞ지히군항에소속금칠천오빅ᄉᆞ십칠원을졀취ᄒᆞ엿다더라

○샹히신문소보 동경죠일신문에샹히에잇ᄂᆞᆫ로국긔관신문에게지ᄒᆞᆫ지부면보를등지ᄒᆞ엿ᄂᆞᆫᄃᆡ이빅삼미돌고디젼쟁에쳐옴두시간동안에일병일만이천명이죽엇ᄂᆞᆫᄃᆡ그러케만이죽은후에도쟝구히그싸돌점령처못ᄒᆞ고다시물니침이되야셔지금은그고디ᄂᆞᆫ셔로차지ᄒᆞ지못ᄒᆞ고잇스며거십일월십오일이후로일본의슈뢰졍삼척과식물이각항물품을실은륜션두척이침몰ᄒᆞ엿다고ᄒᆞ엿더라

○로쟝리착 로국륙군참쟝플발쓰씨ᄂᆞᆫ거십이월십륙일에구로팟긴대쟝의영문에도착ᄒᆞ엿다더라

○일션예비 지부미일신문에말ᄒᆞ엿스되일본풍범션삼빅여쳑이각식슈용물품을실고려슌합락후면곳려슌으로향ᄒᆞ랴고지금미아우로에잇다더라

○션교ᄉᆞ외번복 청구에셔ᄂᆡ디션교회션교ᄉᆞ들이젼에ᄂᆞᆫ청국복식을입고잇더니근리에공론이다시되여셔청인이그것을의심ᄒᆞ고공경ᄒᆞ지도아니ᄒᆞᄂᆞᆫᄉᆞ독에져의나라복색ᄃᆡ로ᄒᆞ기로결졍ᄒᆞ엿다더라

TELEGRAMS.

(FROM JAPAN PAPERS)

London, Dec. 24.

The British colliers "Yeddo" and "Claveley," bound from Cardiff for Mozambique with 10,000 tons of coal have discharged their cargo at Port Said. A German steamer is now taking part of the cargoes to an unknown destination.

London, Dec. 24.

News has been received that the Venezuelan authorities have planted guns at La Guayra and Puerto Cabello. It is supposed this action has been taken in view of the strong intimation from Washington that Venezuela must mend her ways and discharge her obligations to foreigners residing within her territory

Berlin, Dec. 25.

Report received from Capetown state that Samuel Maherero, one of the Hottentot chiefs who have risen in revolt in German South-West Africa, has fled to British Bechuanaland, where he sought permission to remain.

The Governor of Ngami Land had, however been instructed to prevent fugitives from entering British territory, and if this was found to be impossible he was to disarm and detain them. Latest information states that the chief Samuel Maherero and his followers have already been disarmed, and will be detained in Bechuanaland.

Berlin, Dec. 27.

According to news from Portuguese sources portion of the Baltic fleet arrived at Great Fish Bay, in Portuguese West Africa, on the 26th instant, being accompanied by colliers.

Berlin, Dec. 27.

The Tsar has issued a long Ukase to the Senate announcing certain reforms in the Empire's administration on eight particular points.

The Government organs now begin to critise the Zemstvo agitation in an increasing Liberal spirit.

London, Dec. 27.

The Tsar has issued a Decree declaring that in conjunction with the undeviating maintenance of the immutability of the fundamental laws, it is the duty of the Government to meet any change in the needs of the people which is proved to be mature, even though it involves essential innovations in legislation. His Majesty directs his Ministers to consider the means and possibility of introducing various administrative reforms, and to report to him thereon as soon as possible.

London, Dec. 28.

The St. Petersburg newspapers profess almost unqualified satisfaction at the Decree issued by the Tsar, which the "Novoye Vremya" describes as second only to the enfranchisement of the peasants.

Hongkong is determined to remain strictly neutral in the present war says the "China Mail," and will not allow an ounce of coal to leave the harbour if there is any doubt of its destination. A day or two ago a police officer boarded the Italian cruiser "Liguria" while she was taking on a supply of coal:

'How much coal are you loading?' asked the police officer.

'One thousand tons,' was the reply.

'Well, you must discontinue coaling until I investigate the matter,' remarked the police officer.

He left the ship, returned shortly afterwards and allowed the "Liguria" to continue her coaling operations. Surely it is stretching a point too far to stop a cruiser taking on board 1,000 tons of coal. Even if destined for the Baltic fleet it would not carry them far, and by the time the "Liguria" met the fleet, if she proposed to meet them, she would have but little left, if any at all. However. the cruiser got the coal.

JAPAN AND RUSSIA.

(Continued from 2nd page).

Russia, alarmed by the dominant position which Japan thus secured in the Far East, appealed to the British Liberal Government to join her in settling affairs on a safer basis. The British Government refused, and Germany immediately stepped into a place which we declined to occupy. France joined her, and Japan was forced to give up Port Arthur, but allowed to retain Formosa, in addition to a handsome indemnity. Its independence was at the same time restored to Korea. I fail to understand the sympathy expressed for Japan in being thus "robbed of the fruit of her victory." Her victory was that of a free-booter in a war of aggression without any legitimate provocation, and I have yet to learn that sympathy is due to a freebooter when forced to restore some portion of his booty. Sympathisers with Japan quite forget that the wronged Power was China.

But, I may be told, Russia, having ousted Japan, seized Port Arthur for herself. Let us look at the facts. Five years after the restoration of Port Arthur to China two Roman Catholic missionaries were murdered in China. The German Emperor demanded a compensation of 200,000l. for their relations, in, addition to the erection, at the cost of the Chinese Government, of a memorial cathedral in Pekin. This served a double purpose—the conciliation of the Catholic party in the German Parliament and the beginning of a footing in China. To the evident chagrin of the Kaiser the Chinese Government granted both demands, and Germany was thus balked of a quarrel with China. Three weeks afterwards a powerful German squadron appeared in the harbour of Kiao-Chau and demanded the immediate surrender of that fine port on pain of bombardment in forty-eight hours Again China yielded. In a few days Germany demanded a ninety-nine years lease of Kiao-Chau with thirty miles territory beyond it, and the immediate departure of all Chinese officials and insignia of sovereignty. China yielded again. Russia made overtures to us to join her in checking this buccaneering policy of Germany. On the contrary, we volunteered our good will to Germany and offered to demand no concession of railways or anything else in the rich province of Shantung, of which Kiao-Chau was the port. Russia, fearing a combination of Germany, Japan, and England against her, obtained a twenty-five years' lease of Port Arthur, which commands Talien-wan, the port of outlet for her Siberian trade. We followed by obtaining a lease of Wei-hai-Wei and the free hold of a strip of territory behind Hong-Kong. Italy then made a demand of another slice of Chinese territory, and China, seeing her empire dismembered before her eyes, let loose the Boxer rising on her despoilers.

This led to the occupation of Manchuria by Russia. By treaty with China she had already a railway through that province, with the possession of fifteen miles of country on each side of it, and permission to guard it with a military force. She promised to evacuate it in a given time, and excused hereself for not doing so on the plea that organised brigands—now known as Chunchuses fighting against her under Japanese officers—were raiding her railway and subjects. The raids of the dervishes have kept us in Egypt in violation of repeated promises to retire; and I have no reason to suppose that the one plea is less valid than the other. Certainly Japan had no special right to make war on Russia for remaining in Manchuria. My conclusion of the whole matter is that Russia is morally on the same plane as other Christian nations, but that Japan is morally in a different category. I believe, too, that her victory in this war would be a calamity for England. Her intention is tersely expressed in the following quotation from "Japan by the Japanese:—

"We possess every qualification of the development of our country into a great nation—namely, the commercial supremacy of the Pacific and of the Asiatic continent."

MALCOLM MACCOLL.

IL CHIN HOI NOTES.

The Home Office have received a despatch informing them that large numbers of Il Chin Hoi people in Kunsan have donned European clothes and have announced their intention of marching up to Seoul.

* * *

It is said that a recent rumour to the effect that the Il Chin Hoi would combine with the Kong-chin-hoi is without foundation. The latter society does not show a friendly attitude to the other organisation.

* * *

The "Kanjo Shimpo" learns that the Governor of Kongchu is supposed to be collecting the "Righteous Army" with a view to dispersing the Il Chin Hoi people in his district.

* * *

Reports from the Hamkyeng and Kyengsang provinces state that the numbers of the Il Chin Hoi in Seoul will shortly be augmented by 60,000 people from the north who are preparing to march up to the Capital.

* * *

One of the leading Chinese in this city is said by the "Daihan Ilpo" to be a staunch supporter of the society. His benevolence has led him to order the Chinese, who own the house now used as a meeting place by the Il Chin Hoi, to let them have it free of charge.

BIG GUNS FOR THE NORTHERN ARMY

It is reported from Tientsin that no less than forty-eight twelve-centimetre (4½-inch) guns, with sufficient ammunition, have lately arrived at Tangku from Europe, and that thirty-six of them are to be for the forces stationed in the vicinity of Yungpingfu, near the Great Wall, while the remaining twelve guns guns are destined for the troops at Paoting The Northern Army under the supreme command of Viceroy, Yuan Shih-kai, we hear therefore now possesses no less than one hundred and eight of these guns.

'The coming of spring, says the Chefoo paper, 'will be coincident with the arrival of the Nipponese at the coast, vainly looking for transports to carry hem back to Japan.

The three beachcombers in Hongkong two Americans and one Finn, charged with drowing a sampan woman, with the intention of stealing her boat, have been sentenced to death. The Jury recommended them to mercy.

A rather unpleasant experience fell to the lot of a Missionary yesterday. While he was selling tract calendars at Pil Dong some Japanese soldiers passed, and apparently thinking that their barrack walls needed some adornment. they took three calendars and made off without paying for them.

The Korean officers and soldiers, who were arrested by the Japanese gendarmes when carrying out their duty against the Il Chin Hoi, have been handed over to the Korean Government with a request for their punishment. The "Daito Shimpo" learns that one of the men arrested was an officer disguised in a private's uniform.

The Japanese Minister has informed the Foreign Office that the claim of the sufferers of the Kongchu riot not yet having been settled, he will recover the amount by drawing on the money deposited, as guarantee of payment for the ground in use for railway operations, in the Dai Ichi Bank. It would be interesting to know how much of the money originally deposited now remains, so many claims having been settled in a like manner.

Yesterday's passenger traffic on the Electric Railway broke all previous records. Thirty-four thousand six hundred fifty-four people were carried without an accident in spite of the congested condition of the streets. The highest record heretofore was 28,746 passengers on the Empress Dowager's funeral day last Winter.

Chang Chen-hsuan, the wealthy Singapore merchant in Singapore, who was recently appoited Commercial Superintendent of the Treaty Ports and Director-General of agriculture, mining and railways in Fukien and Canton, will start his work in Canton, as he is most familiar with that port. He will leave Peking after the birthday celebrations.

Four resignations of leading Government Officials have been recorded. Mr. Yi Yong Tai, the Minister of Home Affairs, has resigned and will be succeeded by Mr. Cho Byung Sik. Mr. Kim Ki Chin, the Minister of Law vacates his post, which will be taken by Mr. Kwon Chung Hyun, Mr. Sin Ki Son, the vice President of state, hands over his billet to Mr. Kim Sung Kun, and Mr. Kwon Chung Suk. the chief of the Special Police staff, will be succeeded by Mr. Yang Sun Whan.

No definite news is yet to hand of the situation at Port Arthur. From telegrams yesterday we learn that General Stoessel had opened negotiations with the besieging force and a later message asserted that terms for surrender had been arranged. Prior to this the Urlungshan fort had been captured by the Japanese, who also secured a number of guns. The Foreign Office here received a message on Monday cancelling a previous telegram sent by the Korean Minister in Tokyo, to the effect that Port Arthur had actually fallen.

The Japanese Minister had a long audience with His Majesty on Thursday last. The matters, which came up for discussion were principally the Il Chin Hoi question, the advisability of selecting capable officials and the return of Mr. Yi Yong Ik. Referring to the first question Mr. Hayashi maintained that the Korean troops were guilty of an outrageous action in attacking the Il Chin Hoi mob who had done nothing offensive. With regard to the officials, he contended that the Government was incapable and he urged His Majesty to select capable men of mature age to fill important positions. Referring to Mr. Yi Yong Ik, he requested His Majesty to have this gentleman instructed in the condition of affairs as although a good man, he was ignorant of the present political situation. His Majesty referred Mr. Hayashi to the Minister of Foreign Affairs, who next day received him and discussed the Il Chin Hoi question.

The Korea Daily News.

Issued at 5 P. M. daily except Sundays.

Rate of Subscription:—
Per Year,............Yen 25.
Per Quarter,..........Yen 7.
Per Month,..........Yen 2.50.

Postage in Korea not charged extra.
Postage abroad charged extra.

Advertisements, 50 sen per day for 1 inch or less.
5 yen per month per inch.
50 yen per year per inch.

All communications to

E. T. BETHELL,
Editor and Publisher,
Pak-tong, Seoul.

JAPAN AND HER METHODS.

We are inclined to attach but little importance to that pet bogey of sensation-mongering journals the Yellow Peril, as we believe that at any rate for many years to come China will not be persuaded to put sufficient trust in Japan to place herself at Japan's disposal by entering into an alliance.

Still, incidents daily occur in China which lead one to the conclusion that this alliance is what the Japanese are aiming at, and that their ultimate ambition is summed up in the cry "Asia for the Asiatics. This is clearly indicated by the quotation with which Canon MacColl concludes the able letter reproduced in another column. "Commercial supremacy" sounds very nice and peaceful but military, naval, and political supremacy are its inevitable accompaniments.

Most of the great powers have at one time or another grabbed slices of territory from China, and Japan can hardly be blamed for taking part in the game by trying to get Korea for herself, and at the same time doing all she can to prevent a further division of China. We should have far less to say against this if only we found ourselves able to approve of Japanese methods.

In Shanghai are the headquarters of a Chinese secret society having for its objects the expulsion or extirmination of all foreigners, and the downfall of the Manchu dynasty. Its leading members are young men who have been "educated" in Japan, and their inflammatory literature is largely printed in Tokio. Their propaganda might be regarded as the irresponsible vapourings of a lot of hot-headed young men possessed of that little knowledge which is such a dangerous thing, were it not for the fact that the Il-chin-hoi, which is the revolutionary society of Korea, is admittedly subsidised and directed by the Japanese authorities.

There is therefore some reason to believe that the Japanese may be engineering this secret society in China, and it will be easily seen how much greater would be the power of the Japanese Minister at Peking, when he had at hand an army of fanatical "reformers" ready to do his bidding.

Therefore it may be that Russia, by the failure to evacuate Manchuria which brought the wrath of the world upon her, only sinned in being a little more far-seeing than the rest of us.

Japan's ambition is boundless and there is a certain absence of-let us say-squeamishness in her methods which justifies the suspicion that if she were not opposed she would go a long way before she stopped.

JAPAN AND RUSSIA.

(A LETTER WRITTEN BY CANON MACCOLL TO THE GUARDIAN)

SIR—Entire fairness in controversy is rare virtue, and especially in a controversy in which keen prejudices and sympathies are hotly engaged. I do not pretend to be less prejudiced than others; all I claim is that I have devoted some of the leisure of the last twenty-seven years to a careful study of foreign politics, especially as they regard the mutual relations of Russia and England, and their conduct respectively in the Far and Near East: I began my study with a strong bias against Russia. But an exhaustive study of our Blue-books, together with other literature, from 1844 till now, as well as a year's residence at the British Embassy in St. Petersburg and subsequent visits to Russia, have convinced me that my bias was ill-founded. My sympathies have been on the Russian side in the present war; but before joining in the correspondence in your columns I read the case for Japan as published by the Japanese Government, and I read in addition "Japan by the Japanese," recently published. It is a picture of Japanese policy and character written up to date by leading Japanese statesmen and publicists, and I am content to draw my conclusions from the data supplied by that book alone. I admire the attractive qualities which the Japanese possess, but the question now in debate is, on which side of the quarrel ought our sympathies to lie, first, on ethical grounds; secondly, on grounds of policy? The limits of space preclude the possibility of my doing more than offering typical examples on the Japanese and Russian side. I begin with Japan.

In the year 1881 the man in China, Li-Hung-Chang, wrote a warning letter to a member of the Korean Government, from which I quote the following extract as given in "Japan by the Japanese." The italics are in the original:—

"Japan has in recent years adopted the manners and customs of the European nations, and begun hundreds of new works calculated to increase her wealth and power. But really her treasury is empty, and her debts accumulate from year to year, so that she is forced to pursue a policy of aggrandisement in order to make up for the deficit. Hence the nations neighbouring on her must be extremely vigilant. Korea lies to the north of Japan, as Formosa does to the south of her; and these two lands are just what Japan covets the most. The rapacity of Japan, "relying on her skill in fraud," is well illustrated in the affair of Liukiu, which she has at last absorbed. Your countrymen had better be on the look-out."

Liukiu is a group of islands between Japan and Formosa, and formed an independent State under its own king. Its independence was recognised by the European Powers, and by America. Japan determined to annex it, and the volume before me describes the long series of political trickery, falsehood, and fraud by means of which Japan succeeded first in establishing a protectorate over it, and then in annexing it in 1872.

Japan next turned its covetous eyes on Formosa, a rich island belonging to China. "Japan by the Japanese" describes the extraordinarily clever diplomacy and cunning intrigues by which Japan fastened a quarrel on China in regard to Formosa, which she wrested from China after the war. But Japan's ambition aimed at much higher game than Liukiu and Formosa. The goal of her ambition was the possession of Korea and the subjugation of China, leading up to the hegemony of the yellow race and the proclamation, after organising the forces and material resources of China into a huge military power, of a Monroe doctrine for Asia. The means which Japan adopted to achieve her purpose have been seldom paralleled in the annals of political treachery and crime, and they are described in the volume before me with a frankness which seems to show that the Japanese consider any means justifiable which may be profitable to Japan. When the ground was ripe for a quarrel with China Count Ito was sent to Pekin to claim copartnership with China in Korea. Here is the case for Japan as formulated by Count Ito and related in this volume:—

"The claims of China over Korea were historical only—"i. e., as the history of China reckons Korea among her tributaries, and as China had greatest repugnances of changing the face of history as the worthy legacy of ancestral Emperors, so she was intent on claiming Korea as her vassal State. The claims of Japan over Korea, were economical—i. e., she did not clim any legal authority over Korea, but, from her geographical position and the necessity of providing for her constantly increasing population, she was intent on utilising Korea as the best source from which the defect in the home produce of rice was to be supplied, as well as the nearest field in which the future sons of Japan might find employment."

Was there ever a more barefaced claim to override confessedly legal and political right in favour of national greed? The doctrine is one of indefinite application, and may be advanced, when circumstances are favourable, as a justification for the annexation of Australia—a project incuded among the schemes of Japanese ambition, and regarded as by no means chimerical by the people of Australia.

To carry out its designs on Korea the Japanese Government formed a Japan party in Korea. It had its paid partisans in Court and in the palace. This culminated in a conspiracy, engineered by the Governmsnt of Japan to murder the leading Ministers in the capital of Korea, and establish the creatures of the Japanese in their place. How this atrocious crime was carried out is related in the volume before me as a clever expoit, evidently without the slightest idea that there was anything blameworthy in it. Again, I quote the words of one of the Japanese writers in the volume before me:—

The Japanese and the Korean soldiers "[i. e.," in the pay of Japan] were stationed at the principal posts, and commanded by the Japanese officer, Captian Murakami. Within a few hours the assassins did their work, and killed six or seven of the Ministers of the Chinese ["i. e.," the Government] party. The Chinese solders were stationed in a village at some distance from the capital, and care was taken that nobody should communicate to them what was taking place in the city till all was over."

If I am to take the evidence of this volume, written by Japanese of eminence and learning, I must conclude that the Japanese do not recognise a moral sense in their dealings with foreign nations. For them the end justifies the means, however immoral, when the end is the aggrandisement of Japan. And this entire absence of the idea of sin from the character and policy of the Japanese pervades even their internal legislation. The able writer of the chapter on Religion in this volume is careful to note that adultery in the code of Japan differs essentially from adultery in the codes of Christendom:—

"In the eyes of the Taiho Code," he says, "it was not the immorality of the act, but rather the apprehended danger of the confusion of blood, whereby a person not in reality related to the ancestor might succeed to the worship."

Meanwhile, Japan was recently organizing her military and naval forces for the war against China, which she intended from the first; and when her armaments were ready, while China was unprepared, Japan suddenly attacked China, as Russia afterwards, a month before her formal declaration of war. Your readers may remember how a Japanese ironclad torpedoed and sent to the bottom at close quarters a British ship, under a British captain, carrying Chinese troops to Korea, while the Japanese fired on the wretches struggling in the water. China was conquered with comparative ease, and the victor extorted Port Arthur, with adjacent territory, from her victim, and pratically annexed Korea and Formosa.

(Continued on 3rd page.)

The Korea Daily News.

VOL. II, WEDNESDAY, JANUARY 4, 1905. No. 1

HONGKONG & SHANGHAI BANKING CORPORATION.

Paid-up Capital.................... $10,000,000
Reserve Fund:—Sterling Reserve... 10,000,000
Silver Reserve..... 7,000,000

27,000,000

Reserve Liability of Proprietors... 10,000,000

HEAD OFFICE, HONGKONG.

London Bankers, London and County Banking Company Limited.

Branches and Agencies, London.

Amoy,	Hankow	Penang,
Bangkok,	Hiogo,	Rangoon,
Batavia,	Iloilo,	Saigon,
Bombay,	Lyons,	San Francisco,
Calcutta,	Manila,	Singapore,
Colombo,	Nagasaki,	Sourabaya,
Foochow,	New York,	Tientsin,
Hamburg,	Peking,	Yokohama,

Credits granted on approved Securities, and every description of Banking and Exchange business transacted.

Drafts granted on London and the chief Commercial places in Europe, India, Australia, America, China and Japan.

HOLME RINGER & Co., AGENTS, CHEMULPO.

HOKURKU DOBOKU KAISHA.

Branch office in Chong Dong, Seoul.

Japanese telephone No. 165

CONTRACT DEPARTMENT.

We can contract to build any building or construction.

MERCHANDISE DEPARTMENT.

We can provide any building material. We have just contracted to build the new Belgian Legation.

E. MEYER & CO.

Chemulpo.

SOLE AGENTS IN KOREA FOR.

A. T. Morse, Sons & Co.'s "Fresco" Distemper

In all colours ready for use on walls, Ceilings etc.

and

AVENARIUS CARBOLINEUM

A wood-preserving and antiseptic oil preparation

Against decay, dry-rot, fungus and wood-destroying insects.

A large supply always in stock. Prices upon application.

E. MEYER & Co., Chemulpo.

CHARTERED BANK OF INDIA AUSTRALIA & CHINA.

INCORPORATED BY ROYAL CHARTER 1853

HEAD OFFICES:—LONDON.

Paid-up Capital £800,000
Reserve Liability of Share-holders 800,000
Reserve Fund 800,000

Drafts granted upon all the principal places in the world and every description of Exchange and banking business transacted.

E. MEYER & Co., Agents, Chemulpo.

MITSU BISHI DOCKYARD & ENGINE WORKS, NAGASAKI.

CODE WORD, "DOCK."

A 1, A. B. C., and Engineering Codes used.

DOCK No. 1 (at Tategami).

Extreme Length.................... 523 feet
Length on blocks .... 513 ,,
Width of Entrance on Top...... 89 ,,
,, ,, Bottom.... 77 ,,
Water on Blocks at Spring Tide 26½ ,,

DOCK No. 2 (Mukaijima).

Extreme Length.................... 371 feet
Length on Blocks.................... 360 ,,
Width of Entrance on Top...... 66 ,,
,, ,, Bottom 53 ,,
Water on Blocks at Spring Tide 22 ,,

PATENT SLIP (at Kosuge).

Can take vessels up to 1,000 tons gross.

THE WORKS are well equipped with the LATEST IMPROVEMENTS, and can execute any kind of work in SHIPBUILDING and MARINE ENGINEERING, as well as in REPAIRING of SHIPS.

The COMPANY'S new powerfu steamer OURA-MARU (712 tons, 700 I.H.P.), specially built for SALVAGE PURPOSES, and equipped with necessary gear, is always READY at SHORT NOTICE.

THE METHODIST PUBLISHING HOUSE,

Little West Gate, Seoul.

JOB PRINTING, TYPEWRITER PAPER
CARBON PAPER, VISITING CARDS
STATIONERY, BOOK BINDING
BOOK PUBLISHERS
AMERICAN SCHOOL BOOKS
SPENCERIAN COPY BOOKS
PEN CARBON LETTER AND BILL BOOKS

S.A. BECK, Manager.

DAI-ICHI GINKO.

LIMITED.

(Formerly the First National Bank)

ESTABLISHED 1873

INCORPORATED UNDER PRESENT LAW 1896

Capital - - - - - - - - Yen 5,000,000
Reserve Fund - - - - - 1,500,000

HEAD OFFICE:—TOKIO.

President: Baron SHIBUSAWA.

BRANCHES AND CORRESPONDENTS

In the Principal Cities and Towns of Japan.

Interest Allowed on

Fixed deposits 1 year - - - 6½ per cent
" " 6 months - - - 6 per cent

Special current accounts 1½ sen daily per Y 100
General " " 1 " " " 100

M. TANAKA, Manager, Chemulpo.

SINGER SEWING MACHINES

씽거즈봉침

SOLE AGENTS FOR KOREA

젼매쇼

HOLME RINGER & CO. Chemulpo.

졔물포 함릉거양힝

KAMEYA & CO.

GENERAL STOREKEEPERS

Chinkokai Seoul

(Established 1895, Tokyo)

Confectionery, Hams, Canned Goods, Cutlery, Hirano & Tansan Water, Provisions, Gents, Furnishing goods, Toilet Articles, Travelling Bags, Tobacco, Cigars & Cigarettes Kitchen Utensils. Coffee, Biscuits

Fresh Goods always kept in Stock.

Prices Moderate

Please come and inspect our goods.

NIPPON YUSEN KAISHA.

JAPANESE MAIL STEAMSHIP CO.

UDER MAIL CONTRACT WITH THE IMPERIAL JAPANESE GOVERNMENT.

European Line

Regular Fortnightly Service between Yokohama Kobe, Moji, Shanghai, Hongkong, Singapore, Penang Colombo, Port Said, Marseilles, London and Antwerp

American Line

Regular Fortnightly Service between Hongkong and Seattle, calling at Shanghai, Moji, Kobe, Yokohama and Victoria, B. C.

Australian Line

Regular weekly Service betwen Japan Ports and Australia, calling at Hongkong and Manila.

(Above Three Lines Suspended until further notice).

Shanghai Line

Weekly Service between Shanghai and Japan Ports

Korea Line

Service Kobe, Moji, Nagasaki, Fusan Chemupo Chef foo, Taiku.

S. S. Bahelsberg, 2181 tons.

Service Kobe, Moji, Fusan, Chemulpo, Chinnampo

S. S. ARGO, S. S. Ohio.

BORDEN'S CONDENSED MILK CO.

New York, U. S. A.

ALWAYS IN STOCK

Eagle Brand Condensed Milk.

Gold Seal Condensed Milk.

Peerless (Family) Evaporated Cream.

Borden's Malted Milk.

E. MEYER & CO. Chemulpo Korea,

Sole Agents

ROYAL INSURANCE COMPANY,

Funds exceed £10,000,000

FIRE

AT CURRENT RATES.

LIFE

REDUCED PREMIUM.

HOLME RINGER & Co., Agents, Chemulpo.

HOTEL DU PALAIS

SEOUL.

The only first class Hotel in Seoul Situated in the centre of the city opposite the palace.

Cuisine under the supervision of an experienced French Chef.

Well ventilated and furnished throughout.

TARIFF UPON APPLICATION

L. MARTIN

Proripetor and Manager

大韓每日申報
대한미일신보

(뎨이권이호) (금요일) 일쳔구빅오년일월륙일

본샤고빅

이신보는령어와한어로셔미
일츌판ᄒ옵

신문가

한쟝 엽두돈오푼
일삭도 엽두량닷돈
우표가미삭닷돈
다엿돈으로밧숨

광고료는

귀한의쟝단과ᄌ항의다쇼로증
감ᄒ되한쟝가로밧을터이오며오
릭지아니ᄒ여대한사람마다이신
문을보실터이니광고버시기를
원ᄒ시는이들은우리신문사에
와서편약ᄒ심을희망ᄒ옵

○발힝소 박동대한미일신보
샤법어학교압해젼영국인셜필
립졍지뢰오

사쟝 영국인 (비셜)

평양 뒤리졍

○평양효동사는츄계비보셰로우
린신문관미티리인을퇴졍ᄒ엿
시ᄉ오니평양에계신구람코져ᄒ
는 쳠군ᄌ는뒤리졍에왕
림ᄒ와면의ᄒ시옵

사고

○우리대한미일신보의목뎍은
대한의안녕질서에관한모든대
목에티ᄒ야는공평한변론을쥬
쟝ᄒ올이라우리통신원의탐보는
신문보시는쳠군ᄌ의게ᄒ샹보
도ᄒ리며편지를긔서ᄒ여주시
는이는셩명과반티를젹어붓치
시기를희망ᄒ오나비거슨신문
샹에긔재ᄒ라는거시아니오다
만긔하신용ᄒ는증거를숨고자
홈이라긔자는아모긔서던지긔
지ᄒ올퇴각ᄒ는권리를가졋스
나퇴각ᄒ는리유를말ᄒ터이오
며공중평론이른문란케ᄒ는듯ᄒ
긔서는의례히밧지안켓습나이
다

●본샤셜시이뤼로신문을미양
우례로분젼ᄒ와레젼부의일의
로젼ᄒ든것스로먼곳에는ᄒ늣게
젼ᄒ기도ᄒ며ᄒ며ᄉ쳘귀슴ᄒ엿
에젼ᄒ기도ᄒ며ᄒ야니젼ᄒ는
곳도잇다ᄒ와우리신문을ᄉ랑
ᄒ야구람ᄒ시는 쳠군ᄌ의게
티ᄒ야미우미안ᄒ옵기로지금
은분젼인을두고미일오죵이젼
ᄒ며아니젼ᄒ거나늣게거나ᄒ
면가영도록ᄒ라ᄒ오니ᄒ아니
젼ᄒ거나늣게젼ᄒ거나ᄒ면일
이잇스면본샤로통긔ᄒ여주심
을희망ᄒ옵

잡보

○진회호위 작일인산시에일
진회원빅명식작티ᄒ야목뎍히
서서호위ᄒ는티문안문밧협신
쳘쳐오인원슈효는혜쳔쳘빗명
가광이나되더라

○광쥬일진회 광쥬군슈권중
은씨가닉부에면보ᄒ되샹이월
이십일일진회원칠십여인이
본군공북루하에회집ᄒ야효유
ᄒ야도헤여지지아니ᄒ고날마
다셩ᄒ야지금슈쳔인이온티감
세사로시쟝에셔창도ᄒ며가로
에셔연셜ᄒ야경닉민심이쳘동
ᄒ야세랍졀목차연이히리ᄒ다
ᄒ엿더라

○졍부통쳡 샹작일에의졍부
에서각부에통쳡ᄒ되졍부에날
마다사진ᄒ야서무를강구홈이
조리로졍ᄒ규측인티근릭에는
결석홈이만아로의가결경치못
홈이만흔지라금일로브터구규
측을봉ᄒ준ᄒ일하오두시브터졍
부에의회ᄒ시사진ᄒ라ᄒ엿더라

○교상자면사 일젼풍파에일
진회원샹쟈십명이샹ᄒ엿는티에
대한셩병원에셔치료ᄒ야죽기
를면ᄒ엿다더라

○셔불관광 평산샹월사는로
파하나히잇는티나히근륙십에
셔울말만듯고ᄒᆞᆫ번구경은못ᄒ샹
[illegible]

○경위원회 [illegible]

○송티에 [illegible]

○ᄌ힝ᄌ지 일젼일진회에셔시졍
[illegible]

[illegible]

○일병힝위 작일하오샹시에
편동군쳐에셔슈교인ᄒ야회
가양덕면을ᄉ는티일병몃치지
나다가달평셔쟝을거져졍이가
는지라그달평파는사람은쟝슐
쥬고가져가라ᄒ온즉돈업다ᄒ고
물갑을주어야노코간다ᄒ니
일이잇스리오마는그달평임ᄌ
는그리ᄒ는무리ᄒ병명ᄒ고티격
ᄒ길미엿서그뒤만두엇다더라

회원둘만샹경셜 일진회원
셔이쟝챳샹경ᄒ티인티함경도에
셔샹만명이오경샹도에셔샹만
명합ᄒ면명비미구에샹경ᄒ다
ᄒ더라

외보

○일본닉각의불신임투표 일
본국회가거월심칠일하오일졈
에모혓는티각대신이다출셕ᄒ
지콰위원회에셔죠사ᄒ든예산
빌샹신을힝사진에티ᄒ야졍우
회와헌졍본당이불신임투표를
뎡동의ᄒ야다수가되지라총리
신갓수라씨가그일에닉원들이
명ᄒ엿스나여러의원들이아니
오아니오부른지지ᄒ고군사비와
형젼비는국회에셔여원회에서
청구ᄒ되로쥬찬ᄒ엿다더라

○만국평화회 미국졍부에서
각국에향ᄒ야연츳회고를발ᄒ
야뎌이회만국평화회에관ᄒ사로
셜명ᄒ고피차에잇는평화회의
ᄎ체셔를각국에졍부송치ᄒ고
동회의에참동졍쳡는후일에화
란졍부에서열강국에발송ᄒ다
ᄒ더라

○남생거힝 로군비퇴거ᄒ때
에퇴와버린가옥사십여호를슈
츅ᄒ야그공역이완젼이마츰으
거로거월십오일에병대ᄒ납생을
거힝ᄒ엿다더라

○츈쳔일진회 거비십오일에
츈쳔부에서일진회원슈쳔명이
회집ᄒ야사대강령을셜시ᄒ고츄
로한군에청원ᄒ엿다더라

뎐보

이십칠일군수됨부쳑뎐

○함창츙면 포ᄌ언(함창셔
북샹십리허) 부근에셔이십륙
일오쟝식시량에계병샹십명가
량과강도예이셩명가병이남젼
조에칭입ᄒ야우리관됴시초와젼
두호후에오후호시에쥬가셩ᄌ
방면으로퇴각ᄒ엿다더라

거월이십구일공ᄉ관챵뎐

○이통산젼평 리순용씨군의
좌종티는신이월이십팔일오젼
칠시탕에이통산포티졍면ᄒ빅
을그계쪽발ᄒ고동시에돌격을
힝ᄒ야동ᄒ쟝을졈령ᄒ고ᄒ코
와멋아젼포에슴격을외지ᄒ야
젹의포화를무릅쓰고졈령ᄒ슈
확들셜시ᄒ엿는티그졈령이티단
ᄒ부즁포션을포격ᄒ야즉시졈령
ᄒ고ᄉ나아가서인ᄒ부에항ᄒ
야그곳에굿게지히는군수를쳐
물니치고오후칠시반에드되여
그포티의젼부를졈령ᄒ엿다ᄒ
엿더라

거월삼십일경셩일본공ᄉ
관착

○비통산젼평후소식 신이월
평비샹팔일밤에이통산포티를졍
로ᄒ에는쇼수에적병이잇서셔조
공항거ᄒ엿스나오젼삼시에원
[illegible]

관보

대한광무구년일월삼일
셔임급ᄉ령

○의원면본관 륙군법원쥬ᄉ
김하경 군기창기ᄉ 츄시안
○임륙군법원쥬ᄉ 셔판임관륙
등 구표즁 셩규휘
○임군기창기ᄉ 셔판임관륙등
우즁모

이샹광무구년일월이일

○히시종원분쥬ᄉ 구흥 홍일
즁유 구표즁 김효상 구흥
홍승유
○명비서원경셔초 임윤재이흥
뤼의원경 박용대
○명뤼의원경셔초 임관샹등
흥닉부특진관 김규홍

○병경위원총관셔칙임관삼등
헌병ᄉ령관 양셩환
○승셔칙임관이등 비원쟝
김가진
○임교방ᄉ쥬ᄉ셔판임만ᄉ등
봉상ᄉ쥬ᄉ 김교헌
○임봉상ᄉ쥬ᄉ셔관임관륙등
륙픔 신용우
○명시종원분쥬ᄉ 구픔 듀
관홍 슌강원슈봉관 쳔궁식
농상공부쥬ᄉ 송국린
○명경긔사검위원 졍삼픔
홍지덕
○명경샹남북도사검위원 구
픔 김광규
○명임시셔리텰도원총재ᄉ무
농상공부대신 리도재
○즁죵이픔가션대부군부협판
고령관 염도희
○중정삼픔통정대부농상공부
참셔관 고티판 리죵구
○중구픔종ᄉ랑군부쥬ᄉ 고
교쟝 박츈변
이상츙졀이탁이ᄒᆞ야특시
증직
○중죵이픔가션대부닉부협판
고가션대부 허혁
○중정삼픔통정대부비셔원승
표지평 뎡제호
이상효힝이탁이ᄒᆞ야 증직
을베플다
○의원면본관 즁추원의관
한인슈 즁추원의관 김동필
즁추원의관 리용셕 덕원항
총슌 유진세
○임즁츄원의관셔쥬임관륙등
졍삼픔 리죵원 졍삼픔 심
리셥 졍삼픔 김지슌
○임덕원항총슌셔판임관오등
무안항총슌 강진필
○임무안항총슌셔관임관륙등
륙픔 유진세
이샹광무팔년십이월삼십
일일
○의원면본관 시종원시종
죠존층
○명궁닉부특진관셔칙임관삼
등황히도관찰ᄉ 김학슈 종
이픔 리셩렬
○임시종원시종셔쥬임관륙등
동신ᄉ면화과기ᄉ 오화영
○명시종원분시어 구픔 젼
우셕 구픔 죠광리 김밀제
리병션 김현룡 김병일 리
규일 리봉영 최영죠 박지
관 상린식 윤영비
이샹일월일일

론셜

일본의힝동

○황인죵의연합은아즉되지못
홀것이여러히될지니기젼에는
청국이일본을신임ᄒᆞ야일본과
합심동밍되지아니홀줄노우리
는아노라
그럿치마는청국에셔미일낫타
나는일을보면일본사름들이황
인죵동밍을쥬션ᄒᆞ는ᄃᆡ아세아
는아세아ᄉᆞ름을위훈것시라는
말을표준을삼는지라일본이샹
업샹특권을엇는다ᄒᆞ는것은말
이죠코화평ᄒᆞ나그러ᄒᆞ나졀노
륙히군과졍치샹에도특권을갓
케될지라
젼에나지금에나세계강국들이
만이청국으로브터ᄯᅡᆼ죠각들을
ᄯᅦ아셧스니일본이한국을취ᄒᆞ
랴ᄒᆞ는것과다시청국의토디분
할홈을금ᄒᆞ랴고진력ᄒᆞ는것으
로일본을칙망홀수업도다만일
일본의힝동이우리의ᄆᆞ옴에맛
기만ᄒᆞ면우리가반ᄃᆡ홀일이업
슬지라
샹히에청국ᄉᆞ름의훈비밀회가
잇셔셔그목젹은외국ᄉᆞ름들을
다ᄶᅩᆺ차버리고만쥬황질을젼복
하쟈홈인ᄃᆡ그회의쥬쟝ᄒᆞ는ᄉᆞ
름들은일본에셔교육밧은소년
들이오그회의분격훈셔칙들을
만이동경에셔츌찬훈지라이회
논몸이달고피가끌는학문젹은
쇼년들의모힌곳이니ᄆᆡ우위ᄐᆡ
ᄒᆞ도다이런회들일본ᄉᆞ름에찬
셩ᄒᆞ는ᄉᆞ실이분명훈것이그럿
치아니ᄒᆞ면한국에혁명당이라
고홀만훈일진회를보죠ᄒᆞ고지
회ᄒᆞ기를허락ᄒᆞ엿슬리가잇스
리오
그럼으로일본ᄉᆞ룸이청국에셔
이비밀회를찬셩ᄒᆞ는것을밋을
리유가잇는지라이비밀회원들
이북경에잇는일본공ᄉ의명령
ᄃᆡ로셔행ᄒᆞ게될셰는일본의셰
력이얼마큼강대ᄒᆞ야질것을우
리가쟝ᄎᆞ보게되리로다
일노볼ᄃᆡ경이면로국이세계에
미움밧던만쥬졈령은우리들보
다압일을더발게본죄밧게업도
다
일본의욕심이한이업스며일본
의힝동을보면그범위가좁지아
니ᄒᆞ니만일금지ᄒᆞ지아니ᄒᆞ면
어ᄃᆡᄭᆞ지갈는지알수업다ᄒᆞ노
라

잡보

○아경ᄃᆡ죄 지쟉일묘시하현
궁시망곡홀ᄯᅢ에빈관을입참ᄒᆞ
라ᄒᆞ옵시고 황샹폐하동궁젼
하셰셔영셩문닉의효젼으로어
림ᄒᆞ신즉곡반참원이불과삼ᄉᆞ
인이라 샹이진로ᄒᆞ샤빈관의
참불참을봉현ᄒᆞ라ᄒᆞ옵심의
아경이샹은황숑홈을익이지못
ᄒᆞ야평리원문젼에ᄃᆡ죄ᄒᆞ며일
병자인샹쇼ᄒᆞ는고로특별이분
간ᄒᆞ신다더라
○함락축하 려슌함락지경에
로쟝이투항하야확보가리도훈고
로쟉금쥬야에진고기거류ᄒᆞ는
일인들이경하ᄒᆞ는ᄃᆡ일진회원
이셔로쟉ᄃᆡᄒᆞ야비나더축하ᄒᆞ
엿더라
○일ᄉ셩명 경셩경찰을일본
헌병ᄉ령부에셔쥬권확장훈단
말은젼보에이믜긔지ᄒᆞ엿거니
와재쟉ᄉ일에군ᄉ령부에셔거
류디에포고ᄒᆞᆫ기를경셩급부근
에치안에샹관훈경찰은한국경
찰을ᄃᆡ신ᄒᆞ야헌병ᄃᆡ에셔담당
실시케ᄒᆞ엿는ᄃᆡ히ᄉ안을일공
ᄉ가외부에셩명ᄒᆞ엿더라.
○견톄후방숑 울산거ᄒᆞ는심
뎡턱씨가타인의슈령자본젼구
쳔여원을데일은힝쇼에임치ᄒᆞ
엿다가츄후로파의ᄒᆞ야히젼을
환츄ᄒᆞ엿는ᄃᆡ권즁셕씨가일로
써집단ᄒᆞ야심씨를경위원에착
슈ᄒᆞ엿다가젼이십만량을탈취
ᄒᆞ고경위총관갈인후에방숑ᄒᆞ
엿더라
○대관젼임 경무ᄉ김졍근씨
는헌병ᄉ령관으로젼임ᄒᆞ고그
ᄃᆡ를빅셩긔씨가겸임ᄒᆞ엿는ᄃᆡ
여ᄉ대쟝을겸훈지라금일에곳
파츌ᄒᆞ고그ᄃᆡ는륙군법원쟝신
ᄐᆡ휴씨가젼임훈다더라
○신임참졍샹쥬 참졍김셩근
씨가여졍도처홀ᄎᆞ로위션샹
쥬ᄒᆞ야슌찰ᄉ를쇼환ᄒᆞ고ᄯᅩ리
졍훈관제를물치ᄒᆞ기로써샹
쥬ᄒᆞ엿다더라
○의쥬군슈보고 의쥬군슈가
외부에보고ᄒᆞᆫ기를쇼위진보회
쟝안홍익쥬창건등이읍즁에다
기회ᄒᆞ고연셜ᄒᆞ는고로약간회
시ᄒᆞ야즁계ᄒᆞ고ᄯᅩ일진회원윤
길병이가본군에리도ᄒᆞ야긔회
연셜ᄒᆞᆫ후에본관보기를청ᄒᆞ는
고로거졀ᄒᆞ고드리지아니ᄒᆞ고
병뎡륙칠명으로축츌경외ᄒᆞ엿
더니다른군으로향ᄒᆞᆫ다ᄒᆞ엿더
라
○면고발졍 쥬청공ᄉ민영쳘
이가외부에뎐보ᄒᆞᆫ기를친셔를
밧첫단편지는이믜알아고션편
이업셔일이란쳐ᄒᆞ나쟝ᄎᆞᆺ뎐진
으로발졍ᄒᆞ겟다ᄒᆞ엿더라
○법관죠회 법공관에셔외부
로공함ᄒᆞᆫ기를아산민박영보가
교민의게피살ᄒᆞ야히군으로이
믜착슈ᄒᆞ야죠률ᄒᆞ고자ᄒᆞ는ᄃᆡ
드른즉히군ᄉᆞ림이ᄉᆞ쳐에발통
ᄒᆞ야작변ᄒᆞᆫ즉민요를ᄯᅩ시이르
킨다ᄒᆞ니바라건ᄃᆡ곳히군에훈
칙ᄒᆞ야젼과ᄀᆞᆺ치다시요란치못
ᄒᆞ게ᄒᆞ라ᄒᆞ엿더라
○교육방침 리용익씨는일본
을유력ᄒᆞᆫ후에일층긔명ᄒᆞ야ᄉᆞ
환은영영자되ᄒᆞ야 샹쥬ᄒᆞ고
시졍긔션에유의ᄒᆞ셔칙륙빅여
권을일본에셔사드려인민을교
육ᄒᆞᆯ차로방금인원을고용ᄒᆞ야번
역ᄒᆞ는즁이라더라
○일ᄉ폐현후보 일젼에일공
ᄉ가대창회필량씨를ᄃᆡ동ᄒᆞ고
폐현홀때에샹쥬ᄒᆞ기를일진회
원이아즉은범위밧게일을힝훈
것이업시니관리의학ᄃᆡ를금지
홀일과리용익이가ᄌ격은죠ᄒᆞ
나ᄉ긔를동달치못ᄒᆞ니쥬의ᄒᆞ
실ᄉ요정부에잇는ᄃᆡ판들이불
법힝위를바리지아니ᄒᆞ니로셩
훈원로대신즁에셔퇴용ᄒᆞ야졍
부를죠직홀ᄉ와기타즁대ᄉ건
도잇다는ᄃᆡ일진회를죠쳐홀ᄎᆞ
로외부대신과일공ᄉ가일젼에
회동ᄒᆞ야오ᄅᆡ샹의ᄒᆞ엿다더라
○곽씨샹소 젼참찬곽죵석씨
가샹소ᄒᆞᆫ기를 슌명비복제를
긔년으로마련훈것이본ᄃᆡ뎐례
에업는바ㅣ니졸곡후에는ᄉ셔
인이곳히샹홈이가ᄒᆞ오이다ᄒᆞ
엿더라
○술긱운동긔미 졍부에셔쥬
본ᄒᆞ야잡술긱을착지ᄒᆞᆫ다홈으
로무당과복술과샹쟝이들이다
피신ᄒᆞ엿다ᄒᆞ며강홍대셩관호
쇠병쥬제씨는구라쥬본이된고
로무수히운농ᄒᆞ야구라를물시
케ᄒᆞᆫ다더라
○윤리량씨재판결과 강화부
윤윤쳘규씨와참졍리동휘씨가
샹혈ᄒᆞ야재판훈다는말은이왕
게재ᄒᆞ엿거니와윤쳘규씨가닉
부에뎨삼차보고ᄒᆞᆫ기를리동휘
의힝위가파시불법ᄒᆞ야관사문
을다파쇄ᄒᆞ고관속을위협ᄒᆞ는
고로다도망ᄒᆞ엿다ᄒᆞ더니륙군
법원에셔그판속등을압샹ᄒᆞ야
삼죠ᄃᆡ질훈즉윤씨의말이다허
언이라윤씨가락과ᄒᆞ야죠률차
로구라쥬본이된다ᄒᆞ며윤씨는
졍령인데리참령이착호셩명훈
죄로리참령도죠률이된다더라
○일공사훈령 일본공사훈령
젼문이여좌ᄒᆞ니한국디방관찰
사와밋군슈와기타관리가일반
인민에ᄃᆡᄒᆞ야학정을감힝홈으
로인민이질고가잇셔시정개선
을요구ᄒᆞ는쟈ㅣ축일증가ᄒᆞ는
사실은일반인민의아는바이어
이와일본공사는이샹졍ᄐᆡ을참
아목도홀슈가업고한국에쥬지
훈각령사에ᄃᆡᄒᆞ야디방관찰사
군슈등관리가관법을무란이ᄒᆞ
야학민의힝위가잇스면ᄃᆡ방인
민은이사실을구습ᄒᆞ야일본공
사외게고소홀지요그업무를도
라다보지아니ᄒᆞ고안연히집회
를긔최ᄒᆞ며혹입셩ᄒᆞ야질셔에
히가엇다는취지로한국일반인
민의게고시를결졍ᄒᆞ고히훈령
은발포ᄒᆞ엿더라

광고

TELEGRAMS.

Japanese Legation.

The terms of surrender of Port Arthur are as follows:—

1. The straits and harbour, navy, army (including all men and material) and all the volunteer force shall be handed over to the Japanese.
2. All fortresses and forts of Port Arthur, ships, provisions, ammunition, horses and all official buildings and materials to be handed over.
3. As a guarantee of good faith, before noon on Jan. 3rd the garrisons of Etzeshan, Saoansau, Taiansau and the hilly ground to the southeast must be withdrawn and placed under the surveillance of the Japanese.
4. If any members of the Russian navy or army break any article of the agreement, Japan will be at liberty to resume hostilities.
5. All maps of forts, mines, etc., are to be handed over. Also lists of officials in the army navy and Government offices together with civilians must be prepared. The names of the ships with their crews are to be given as well.
6. Weapons, ammunition, war material, buildings of every description and Government properties are to be left as they stand, so that the distribution of these may be easily carried out by Japanese and Russian committees appointed to this duty.
7. The Japanese force have nothing but praise for the gallant defence of the Russians, consequently the officers will be permitted to wear swords and take some of their private effects with them. Further if the officers and men guarantee not to engage in hostilities again, they will be permitted to return to Russia.

Each officer will be allowed to have one soldier as servant, who will be released when his master has signed his guarantee.

8. All the noncommissioned officers and men must wear a certain distinctive uniform and must wait for the command of their officers, who will be instructed on the subject by the Japanese.
9. The Russians connected with the Red Cross and commisariat departments will be placed under the control of the Japanese Red Cross.

This agreement was duly signed at 9:45 P. M. on the 2nd inst. and the terms are now being carried out. The Emperor of Japan has sent a message to General Nogi, requesting him to do all in his power for General Stoessel who must be admired for his gallant defence.

(FROM JAPAN PAPERS.)

Berlin, Dec. 29.

General Meyendorff has been recalled from Manchuria to be Governor of Warsaw.

Berlin, Dec. 29.

The German Red Cross Society is fitting out an expedition to join the Japanese Army at the front. The party, which will leave Genoa in January, will be under the leadership of Professor Heuler of Breslau.

Berlin, Dec. 29.

Most of the German and French papers are sceptical regarding the reform manifesto issued by the Tsar, which it is thought will not satisfy the reformers. The "Kreuz Zeitung," however expresses the hope that the proposed reforms will prove a successful solution, and thinks it possible that a compromise will be effected between the Government and the advocates of reform.

London, Dec. 29.

Admiral Skrydloff, now in command of the Russian naval forces at Vladivostok, is returning to Europe.

Berlin, Dec. 29.

The Tsar has ordered the mobilisation of the Fourth and Seventh Army Corps, with their Reserve divisions, numbering altogether some eighty thousand men, who will be despatched to Manchuria in detachments.

London, Dec. 28.

The assemblage at Pavloff Hall, St. Petersburg, on the 26th inst., which was widely representative, was called a banquet in order to evade the order regarding the prohibition of public meetings. The meeting only concluded at half-past two the following morning. The speeches delivered were of a most fervid character. A resolution was passed denouncing the present war and demanding a Legislature elected by ballot.

The President and forty members of the Chernigoff Zemstvos have resigned in consequence of the Tsar's "communique," and the Association has therefore been dissolved.

Prince Galitzin, the Mayor of Moscow, has resigned for the same reason.

These and other incidents of a similar character indicate the growing ferment throughout the country.

REFORM OR RETROGRESSION?

Whoever is responsible for the last order issued by the Education Department has nothing to be proud of. It appears that an instruction has been sent round to foreign schools that the Government will discontinue its practise of supplying the students with stationery and that the students must in future fill their own needs in this respect.

We suppose this measure is part of Mr. Megata's scheme of retrenchment, or at least a result of it, but it seems to us that this should be the last direction in which a sane man should intrude a cheese-paring policy. How many hundred dollars will be saved annually by this brilliant financial stroke we do not know, but we do know that, in Korea where it is difficult enough to get students to school under even the most favourable circumstances, a measure of this kind savours of deliberate retrogression. Whether it applies to all the schools or not, this measure will, so far as the foreign language schools are concerned lead to a diminution of the attendance, and as education is the crying need of Korea it is simply scandalous that any step should be taken to place obstacles in the way of students.

THE IL-CHIN-HOI.

We live in hourly expectation of a demonstration from these traitors. For the past few days the streets have been placarded with warnings that after the funeral the Il-chin-hoi would "do something."

We are not told what shape their operations will take but it will probably be the usual one which has been repeated with such regularity that it is evidently part of a cut and dried programme. The Il-chin-hoi assemble and make seditious speeches, the Korean soldiers attempt to disperse them, and then the Japanese soldiers "restore order," this consisting in driving off the Korean soldiers and arresting their leaders.

It will be seen that in this combination there is at any time material for a very serious riot and the Il-chin-hoi people are so persistent and the Japanese people so consistently support them, that it cannot be long before affairs come to a head.

It seems useless to protest against this gross abuse of ill-gotten power, but it is certain that this course of conduct is alienating from Japan whatever respect and sympathy foreigners may have had for her.

The sentences passed on the three men belonging to the Kong Chin Hoi, who were recently arrested and tried by the Supreme Court, have now been commuted to shorter terms of imprisonment. Na Yu Suk who was condemned to death will now serve 15 years rigorous imprisonment. Yi Chun and Yun Hio Chung who originally received a life sentence, will serve 10 years. The Kong Chin Hoi people however are not satisfied and have appealed to the Law Department for another trail of the case when they will be represented by a Japanese attorney.

A WORD OF COUNSEL TO JAPAN.

(Continued from 2nd page.)

Neither Western Europe not the United States are particulaly the friends of either. The Japanese should be all the more ready to come to an agreement with their adversary because their triumph would be sure to awaken jealousies and perhaps stir up hostile action on the part of some of the Powers now professing to be their friends, people who admire their military valour and capacity beyond measure. Do not let the Japanese deceive themselves upon this point either. The English-speaking peoples everywhere are not really in the mass delighted at their success. In the Australian colonies and in Canada that success is viewed not only with suspicion but with dread and often positive aversion. Even here there is probably only a minority of the people anxious for the triumph of Japan, and on the Continent no great Power is definitely on her side Japanese statesmen ought, therefore, to consider in the light of this fact what the position of their country will be at the end of a tremendous war. Let them assume that their confidence in their ability to defeat Russia and drive her troops from Manchuria will be justified by the events and even then they surely cannot help seeing that the triumph will leave their country exhausted, prostrate after the stupendous exertions involved, prostrate and debt fettered, unable therefore to face another enemy forthwith. They must not imagine that they have no other enemies than Russia, or that there is such magnanimity among European Powers as would induce them singly or altogether, to hold their hands and claim no advantage to themselves whatever from the results of Japan's victory. The Japanese must not forget what happened after their triumph over China. Did not the European Powers then step in and snatch the fruit, of victory from their tired hands with an eagerness ominous of events to come? By every honourable means, we repeat and insist, Japan ought to strive to put an end to this war before her strength is so far exhausted as to make her an object of covetousness to Powers in Europe, cursed by the earth hunger, unaffected by scruples. The Japanese dream of regenerating China and we believe them to be the one race in the world best fitted to undertake this magnificent enterprise. But do they suppose that Germany will allow them to carry out this great work of reformation unmolested if her interests in Shantung are likely to be interfered with? Is France going to stay quiet and see a China armed, capable of sending drilled and efficient troops to dispute her possession of Tongking? Will the United States have no anxiety about the Philippines, and will England fold her hands, indifferent to the fate of her commerce? Japan may say "We will interfere with nothing, trade is free to all, any country may come and build railways in China or open up her mines," but she will not be believed. Our Press will be filled with stories of Chinese armies armed and weaponed in the most scientific modern style, and the fears thus evoked will prompt the Powers to again step in and unite to prevent Japan from gathering the harvest of her great scarifices and loss of blood.

These are but a few of the reasons which might be advanced, all tending to impose upon Japanese statesmen the duty of striving now to put an end to the war. They can do so with magnanimity and by giving up something of their ideal, should they take the initiative the moment that Port Arthur is in their hands, nay even if it be only "in extremis." By offering generous terms to Russian—and the Japanese by no means hate the Russian people—they might attain to a lasting peace before exhaustion overtakes them. before the Baltic fleet comes out to break through or at least weaken the blockade of the fortress so, long defended with such heroism. To carry on the war for another year might easily come to imply disasters for which it will take generations to repair, let alone the danger of that dominance of European Powers swayed by their usurers which we dread for her most of all. In examining their position let not Japanese statesmen forget that their foreign debt is already about £1 per head of their population and that, for a people so poor in money and money's equivalents, it is a heavy debt.
—Investors Review.

THE EASTERN WORLD OR THE WAR.

Speaking of the possibilities of a termination of the war the "Eastern World" says:—

"How is the war to end then? Either by intervention, mediation or exhaustion. Intervention is out of the question; mediation offers but small prospect of success unless supported by pressure that would bring it dangerously close to intervention, so that the issue is reduced to the question as to which country will be exhausted first, and there it is evident, from the financial measures to which Japan has already had to resort that the limits of her financial powers of endurance are in sight. In competent local circles, indeed, it is apprehended that gold standard cannot be maintained if the war lasts for six months longer. The Japanese parliament, it is true has granted the war expenditure almost without a question, and has been duly complimented on its patriotism, and so on, but what else could it do? No opposition would have had any effect, or could have done any good. It would only have led to a fresh dissolution.

The Korean Minister at Peking has telegraphed the Foreign Office that he has presented His Majesty's autograph letter at the Chinese Court and will now although there are difficulties in the way, return to Korea.

The Magistrate of Wiju reports that the Il Chin Hoi have been very busy in his district of late and recently they made an attempt to obtain an interview with him, but with the help of the soldiers he managed to evade them.

We are very pleased to hear of the engagement which has been announced of Miss Amalie Eckert and Mr. E. Martel. We add our congratulations and good wishes to those which will have already been showered on the popular couple.

Mr. Yi Yong Ik is said to have announced his intention of refusing any official position which may be offered him, devoting his time instead to the reform question. He has brought back from Japan a large number of books dealing with this matter and he proposes to have them translated into Korean for the benefit of the people in general.

The Korea Daily News.

Issued at 5 P. M. daily except Sundays.

Rate of Subscription:—

Per Year,............Yen 25.
Per Quarter,..........Yen 7.
Per Month,..........Yen 2.50.

Postage in Korea not charged extra.
Postage abroad charged extra.

Advertisements, 50 sen per day for 1 inch or less.
5 yen per month per inch.
50 yen per year per inch.

All communications to

E. T. BETHELL,
Editor and Publisher,
Pak-tong, Seoul.

PORT ARTHUR.

Port Arthur is now for the second time in Japanese hands and one of the bloodiest campaigns in history has been brought to a close. Although at the time of writing the terms of General Stoessel's surrender have not been made known, his valiant defense has entitled him to every consideration and there is no doubt that the Japanese will accord it to him.

Although the frequency of desperate encounters have accustomed us to tales of slaughter, there can be no doubt that the world will receive the news of the settlement with a deep sigh of genuine relief. In the light of past events it would certainly appear that, had the defenders chosen, they could have kept the besiegers at bay for several more months and it would seem that it was just as much motives of humanity as neccessity which prompted General Stoessel's surrender.

This is, however, a point of no importance now. The Japanese were determined to take Port Arthur and they have succeeded and in the joy of victory the terrible cost will be for the time forgotten.

The fall of the fortress will not have any material effect on the rest of the war. Probably some 30,000 Japanese soldiers will be released and be available for operations in other directions, but as Kuropatkin has been steadily receiving reinforcements for the past two months it is more than probable that even this large addition will not give the Japanese a very great numerical superiority over him. A tremendous amount of Artillery will of course be released but we have not heard that there has been any shortage of this Arm at Liao Yang.

On the other hand, Port Arthur has been a millstone around Kuropatkin's neck; so long as Port Arthur stood he was precluded from moving in any other direction and with his object so well known to the Japanese he must have been at a great disadvantage.

Rumours of mediation and stories of peace will doubless fill the air for a while but we are afraid that there is little hope of any solution being arrived at, which would be satisfactory to both parties. Russia is in a better position now than she has been since the outbreak of war, and it is unlikely that she will listen to peace proposals until she has in some measure recovered her lost prestige.

There is however one aspect of the case which all Europeans will welcome. With the fall of Port Arthur and the return of the Baltic Fleet, warlike operations will for the present be confined to Manchuria and there will consequently be a cessation of Japan's charges against other nations of breaches of neutrality. Tokio newspapers and politicians have of late been freely urging that if these alleged breaches of neutrality continued it would be England's duty to come to her assistance and we are sure that all Englishmen will rejoice that the occasion for interference is now unlikely to arise.

A WORD OF COUNSEL TO JAPAN.

Cable messages from Tokio indicate that the Japanese people are far from satisfied with the terms upon which their new foreign loan has been sold. We gather that they think their credit should have risen rather than gone down owing to the magnificent fight they have maintained against Russia. Perhaps also they may have an idea that the benevolent spirit displayed towards them by the official classes and many of the citizens in the two great English-speaking countries should have moved investors therein to something benevolence. We can quite understand the perplexity of the Japanese people who find English and American newspapers full of praise for the prowess and magnificent fighting qualities and yet discover that when it comes to lending money they exact the uttermost farthing. Greater experience of the habits of the money-lending nations would disabuse them of any such confusion of mind and teach that there is no such thing as philanthropy in money-lending. The Japanese have contracted to pay, we estimate, quite 8½ per cent. for their new foreign loan of £12,000,000 nominal, now placed half in London and half in New York. At the issue price the invester gets about eight per cent. for his money, allowing for the premium on redemption at an early date, and if we add in the underwriting commission and the charges of the banks in whose hand the loan was placed for emission it is quite within the mark to put the cost of the money to the Japanese people at 8½ per cent. The terms are severe without question, but it would be doing the Japanese no kindness to lead them to think that they have been over-reached. Their agents, they may rest assured, have done the best possible for them and they must not think that because the loan has been quoted at a premium in the market a higher price could have been exacted from the first subscribers. Without that premium as a bait the loan would probably have been a failure, and the banks who had it in hand were therefore compelled to throw out the attraction of a low issue price so as to attract subscribers. At the very most they could not have got 91½ from the public for this loan. Proof that this is true is furnished by the instability of the market premium. Let dear money touch our market and the scrip would go to a discount.

The £10,000,000 loan recently issued cost the investor three per cent. more than this new issue. When the next loan has to be placed upon the market it is by no means improbable that he will get it three per cent. cheaper than the loan subscribed this week. The longer the war goes on, in other words, the more difficult will it be for Japan to place loans in foreign markets and the Japanese Government ought not to forget that outside England and the United States there are no European money markets really open to it to borrow in. France is too deeply committed to Russian finance to have anything to say to Japanese, and it is a serious loss to a borrowing country to be unable to appeal to the thriftiest and richest population in the world. This being so, would it not be both prudent and in the highest sense patriotic on the part of the Japanese Government to endeavour to come to an arrangement with its great adversary before arriving at the point when yet another foreign war loan will have to be raised? The Japanese Cabinet ought to keep in mind the attitude of Western Powers States towards that fall into difficulties and take the utmost care not to extend their pledges to foreign creditors to a degree which would place them at the mercy of England and the United States or any white Power whatsoever.

Japanese statesmen can surely already see that the money-lending classes have no bowels of compassion, and were the war to go on until the Japanese debt abroad amounted to a total which might throw the finances of Japan into confusion for years peace had returned, they may be quite certain that England and the United States would have no scruple in proposing some arrangement such as exists in Turkey, Egypt and China with a view to make sure that the money lent is paid back. Japan cannot want an "Imperial Martime Customs" administration in the Chinese manner, wholly officered by foreigners and drawing the substance of the nation away in order to fulfill the obligations entered into the European creditor; but a continuance of the war, involving as it must, a succession of foreign loans, will bring her in sight of this danger, and at the very best must embarrass and retard our internal development for many a year to come. Therefore, in all friendliness, and with a sincere admiration for the many high qualities displayed by the Japanese people, not only in the arts of war but in the arts of peace, we counsel their statesmen to pause now and consider whether the present conflict cannot be brought to an end when Port Arthur has fallen if not before. Until then we quite admit that possibly nothing can be done, but after that event it should not be difficult for Russia and Japan to settle their differences and put an end to the slaughter. They respect each other now as they never did before.

Russia also is suffering from exhaustion, and as the weeks and months pass the stability of her present Government is increasingly endangered by outbreaks of popular discontent. During the winter, moreover, it will be well nigh impossible to carry on a campaign in the open. For the next three months at least the armies facing each other just south of Mukden must confine their efforts to petty skirmishes, to desultory attacks upon each other's trenches, to shellings of each other's positions and minor annoyances of the usual war-appetising kind. In a country where the winter temperature sometimes falls to 25 degrees below zero Fahr., it is simply impossible for troops to move away from their shelters and camp out in the open. They can march over the country but they cannot sleep exposed to the night air on the bare ground, and if either army attempted long marches with the view of outflanking the other it would probably suffer a far greater loss of men from cold than from another such battle as that at Liao-yang. The pause thus imposed upon the contending forces by the climate should be seized by the lovers of peace in both Empires to try and bring about an accord. Already the war has gone on long enough to convince Russian statesmen that Manchuria will cost more to reconquer and keep than it can ever be worth. Why let obstinacy inter fere with self interest?

With each pause in the fighting we have a revival of rumours about intervention, and the Washingtion Cabinet is said to be particularly busy in this direction. But both combatants are quite right in suspecting the motives of the Powers fussily ready to play peacemaker. They are selfish motives so far as their Governments go. It is not so with the more enlightened section of men and women throughout Europe and the United States. They hate bloodshed and would welcome any arrangement calculated to put an end to the horrible carnage at which they stand aghast and overwhelmed with pity; but Governments as such must be distinguished from benevolent people in transactions of this kind and it would be easy to bring into relief the underlying motives of self-interest impelling ourselves and the United States, France and Germany to intervene in order to stop the war. We content ourselves now with insisting that Russia and Japan must make their own bargain.

(Continued on 3rd page.)

The Korea Daily News.

VOL. II, THURSDAY, JANUARY 5, 1905 No. 2

HONGKONG & SHANGHAI BANKING CORPORATION.

Paid-up Capital........................	$10,000,000
Reserve Fund:—Sterling Reserve...	10,000,000
Silver Reserve....	7,000,000
	27,000,000
Reserve Liability of Proprietors...	10,000,000

HEAD OFFICE, HONGKONG.

London Bankers; London and County Banking Company Limited.

Branches and Agencies,

London.

Amoy,	Hankow	Penang,
Bangkok,	Hiogo,	Rangoon,
Batavia,	Iloilo,	Saigon,
Bombay,	Lyons,	San Francisco,
Calcutta,	Manila,	Singapore,
Colombo,	Nagasaki,	Sourabaya,
Foochow,	New York,	Tientsin,
Hamburg,	Peking,	Yokohama,

Credits granted on approved Securities, and every description of Banking and Exchange business transacted.

Drafts granted on London and the chief Commercial places in Europe, India, Australia, America, China and Japan.

HOLME RINGER & Co., AGENTS,
CHEMULPO.

HOKURKU DOBOKU KAISHA.

Branch office in Chong Doug, Seoul.

Japanese telephone No. 165

CONTRACT DEPARTMENT.

We can contract to build any building or construction.

MERCHANDISE DEPARTMENT.

We can provide any building material. We have just contracted to build the new Belgian Legation.

E. MEYER & CO.

Chemulpo.

SOLE AGENTS IN KOREA FOR.

A. T. Morse, Sons & Co.'s

"Fresco" Distemper

In all colours ready for use on walls, Ceilings etc.

and

AVENARIUS CARBOLINEUM

A wood-preserving and antiseptic oil preparation

Against decay, dry-rot, fungus and wood-destroying insects.

A large supply always in stock.

Prices upon application.

E. MEYER & Co.,
Chemulpo.

CHARTERED BANK OF INDIA AUSTRALIA & CHINA.

INCORPORATED BY ROYAL CHARTER 1853

HEAD OFFICES:—LONDON.

Paid-up Capital	£800,000
Reserve Liability of Shareholders	800,000
Reserve Fund	800,000

Drafts granted upon all the principal places in the world and every description of Exchange and banking business transacted.

E. MEYER & Co., Agents,
Chemulpo.

MITSU BISHI DOCKYARD & ENGINE WORKS,

NAGASAKI.

CODE WORD, "DOCK."

A 1, A. B. C., and Engineering Codes used,

DOCK No. 1 (at Tategami).

Extreme Length..............	523 feet
Length on blocks	513 ,,
Width of Entrance on Top.....	89 ,,
,, ,, Bottom....	77 ,,
Water on Blocks at Spring Tide	26½ ,,

DOCK No. 2 (Mukaijima).

Extreme Length..............	371 feet
Length on Blocks.............	360 ,,
Width of Entrance on Top......	66 ,,
,, ,, Bottom	53 ,,
Water on Blocks at Spring Tide	22 ,,

PATENT SLIP (at Kosuge).

Can take vessels up to 1,000 tons gross.

THE WORKS are well equipped with the LATEST IMPROVEMENTS, and can execute any kind of work in SHIPBUILDING and MARINE ENGINEERING, as well as in REPAIRING of SHIPS.

The COMPANY'S new powerful steamer OURA-MARU (712 tons, 700 I.H.P.), specially built for SALVAGE PURPOSES, and equipped with necessary gear, is always READY at SHORT NOTICE.

THE METHODIST PUBLISHING HOUSE,

Little West Gate, Seoul.

JOB PRINTING, TYPEWRITER PAPER
CARBON PAPER, VISITING CARDS
STATIONERY, BOOK BINDING
BOOK PUBLISHERS
AMERICAN SCHOOL BOOKS
SPENCERIAN COPY BOOKS
PEN CARBON LETTER AND BILL BOOKS

S.A. BECK, Manager.

DAI-ICHI GINKO.

LIMITED.

(Formerly the First National Bank)

ESTABLISHED 1873

INCORPORATED UNDER PRESENT LAW 1896

Capital - - - - - - - -	Yen 5,000,000
Reserve Fund - - - - -	1,500,000

HEAD OFFICE:—TOKIO.

President: Baron SHIBUSAWA.

BRANCHES AND CORRESPONDENTS In the Principal Cities and Towns of Japan.

Interest Allowed on

Fixed deposits 1 year - - -	6½	per cent
" " 6 months - - -	6	per cent

Special current accounts 1½ sen daily per Y 100
General " " 1 " " " 100

M. TANAKA,
Manager, Chemulpo.

SINGER SEWING MACHINES

씽거즈봉침

SOLE AGENTS FOR KOREA

젼매쇼

HOLME RINGER & CO.
Chemulpo.

졔물포 함룽거양힝

KAMEYA & CO.

GENERAL STOREKEEPERS

Chinkokai - - Seoul

(*Established 1895, Tokyo*)

Confectionery, Hams, Canned Goods, Cutlery, Hirano & Tansan Water, Provisions, Gents, Furnishing goods, Toilet Articles, Travelling Bags, Tobacco, Cigars & Cigarettes Kitchen Utensils. Coffee. Biscuits

Fresh Goods always kept in Stock.

Prices Moderate

Please come and inspect our goods.

NIPPON YUSEN KAISHA.

JAPANESE MAIL STEAMSHIP CO.

UNDER MAIL CONTRACT WITH THE IMPERIAL JAPANESE GOVERNMENT.

European Line

Regular Fortnightly Service between Yokohama Kobe, Moji, Shanghai, Hongkong, Singapore, Penang Colombo, Port Said, Marseilles, London and Antwerp

American Line

Regular Fortnightly Service between Hongkong and Seattle, calling at Shanghai, Moji, Kobe, Yokohama and Victoria, B. C.

Australian Line

Regular weekly Service betwen Japan Ports and Australia, calliugiat Hongkong and Manila.

(Above Three Lines Suspended until further notice).

Shanghai Line

Weekly Service between Shanghai and Japan Ports

Korea Line

Service Kobe, Moji, Nagasaki, Fusan Chemupo Chefoo, Taiku.

S. S. Bahelsberg, 2181 tons.

Service Kobe, Moji, Fusan, Chemulpo, Chinnampo

S. S. ARGO, S. S. Ohio,

BORDEN'S CONDENSED MILK CO.

New York, U. S. A.

ALWAYS IN STOCK

Eagle Brand Condensed Milk.

Gold Seal Condensed Milk.

Peerless (Family) Evaporated Cream.

Borden's Malted Milk.

E. MEYER & CO.
Chemulpo Korea,
Sole Agents

ROYAL INSURANCE COMPANY,

Funds exceed £10,000,000

FIRE

AT CURRENT RATES

LIFE

REDUCED PREMIUM.

HOLME RINGER & Co.,
Agents, Chemulpo.

HOTEL DU PALAIS

SEOUL.

The only first class Hotel in Seoul Situated in the centre of the city opposite the palace.

Cuisine under the supervision of an experienced French Chef.

Well ventilated and furnished throughout.

TARIFF UPON APPLICATION

L. MARTIN
Proripetor and Manager

大韓每日申報
대한미일신보

(뎨이권삼호)　　(토요일)　　일쳔구빅오년일월칠일

본샤고빅

이신보는영어와한어로셔계미
일출판ᄒᆞ옵
신문가
일장 한푼오리
일삭표 엽두량닷돈
우표가미삭닷돈
다밧는이로밧숩
광고료는
긔힝의쟝단과ᄌᆞ힝의다쇼로좃
차ᄒᆞ되ᄃᆡ략가로받을터이오며오
리지아니ᄒᆞᆫ사람마다이신
문을보실터이니광고가시기를
원ᄒᆞ시는이들은우리신문샤에
와셔면약ᄒᆞ심을희망ᄒᆞ옵
○발힝소 박동대한미일신보
샤법어학교압헤젼영국인셜필
림자리오
샤쟝 영국인 (비셜)
평양 디리졈
○평양효동사는권비보씨로우
리신문관디리인을뎡ᄒᆞ엿
사오니평양에계신구람ᄒᆞ시
는 쳠군ᄌᆞ는디리졈에와ᄒᆞ
림ᄒᆞ와면의ᄒᆞ시옵

샤고

○우리대한미일신보의목뎍은
대한의안녕질셔에관한모든대
목에ᄃᆡᄒᆞ야는공평한번론을쥬
장홈이라우리동신원의담보는
신문보시는쳠군ᄌᆞ의계ᄒᆞ샹보
도ᄒᆞ리며원지를귀셔ᄒᆞ며주서
는이는셩명과번디를젹어붓치
서기를희망ᄒᆞ오나이게승신문
샹에게ᄌᆡᄒᆞ란는거시아니오다
만국회신용ᄒᆞ는종거를숨고자
홈이라귀자는아모귀셔던지귀
저ᄒᆞᆯ을되쟈ᄒᆞ는권리를가졋스오
나되쟈ᄒᆞ는리유를말ᄒᆞᆯ터이오
며공중평화를문란케ᄒᆞ는듯ᄒᆞᆫ
귀셔는의례히밧지안켓숩나이
다

●본샤셜시이리로신문을미양
우례로발젼ᄒᆞ와례젼부의입의
로젼ᄒᆞᆫ듯ᄉᆞ로면곳에는ᄒᆞᆨ뇨게
젼ᄒᆞ기도ᄒᆞ며ᄒᆞᆨ면쳘거승ᄒᆞᆫ법
에젼ᄒᆞ기도ᄒᆞ며ᄒᆞᆨ아니젼ᄒᆞ는
곳도잇다ᄒᆞ와우리신문을ᄉᆞ랑
ᄒᆞ야구람ᄒᆞ시는 쳠군ᄌᆞ의계
디ᄒᆞ야미우미안ᄒᆞ옵기로지금
은본젼인을두고미일죵이젼
ᄒᆞ며ᄒᆞ니젼ᄒᆞ거나늣게거나ᄒᆞᆫ
폐가업도록ᄒᆞ라ᄒᆞ오니ᄒᆞᆨ아니

젼ᄒᆞ거나ᄒᆞᆨ늣게젼ᄒᆞ거나ᄒᆞᆫ일
이잇스면본샤로통긔ᄒᆞ여쥬심
을희망ᄒᆞ옵

뎐보

이일오후삼시이십분발
○뤼순일군중 이월일일오후
구시에러순로쟝수뎨세루가희
셩에관ᄒᆞᆫ셔면을일본군사의게
보냇다ᄒᆞ엿더라
이일오후오시오분발
○작슈쪽칭 쟉야셕시반에
이동계관산과및구포루를자슈
쪽발ᄒᆞ고쳘뢰홈으로일군이
거슨졈령ᄒᆞ엿다ᄒᆞ고젹의항셜
ᄋᆞᆫ금죠에모다자슈쪽칭이라ᄒᆞ
엿다더라
이일일본공사관착
○항셔슈취 일월일일낙복사
령관이(슈테셔루)쟝군의항복
ᄒᆞ기를쳥원ᄒᆞ는셔면을밧아다
ᄒᆞ엿더라
삼일졔등참모발이일공사관
착면
○규약톄결 려순항셩규약은
작야에톄결됨으로군의목젹은
젼달ᄒᆞ엿더라
삼일공사관착뎐
○항복됴건승락 항복됴건에
관ᄒᆞᆫ담판은일월이일오후사시
에결뇨ᄒᆞ엿는ᄃᆡ낙복대쟝의요
구ᄒᆞᆫ죠목은총히젹이승락ᄒᆞ엿
고상세ᄒᆞᆫ보고는아즉도달치못
ᄒᆞ엿더라
일월이일공사관착
○항셩폭발 비목쟝군의보고
에밀ᄒᆞ엿스되젹이작일오젼
벗시삼십분에동계관산과구포
ᄃᆡ에서ᄉᆞ사로되겨ᄒᆞ야비거승
폭발ᄒᆞ지라우리군사비두포ᄃᆡ
와ᄃᆡ못남방엣파엔두고ᄃᆡ들졈
령ᄒᆞ엿다ᄒᆞ며젹이항셔와밋항
구에잇는모든비를폭발ᄒᆞᆫ지라
우리군사는일요일아참브터항
동을중지ᄒᆞᆫ항복담판의졀요
홈을기ᄃᆞ린다더라
일월사일히군관샤착
○려순항복도약셔 일월이일
에발ᄒᆞᆫ려순공위일본군의보고
를거ᄒᆞᆫ즉거일일오후구시샤십
오분에됴인된항셩규약의본문
이여좌ᄒᆞ더라
뎨일됴 려순요시와및항졍에
잇는로국륙히군군인과및의

용병과기타관리는총히이젼을
포로ᄒᆞᆯ수
뎨이됴 려순구에잇는젼포루
포ᄃᆡ함션병션과병긔탄약과말과
기타일졔군용샹제지료관ᄉᆞ
관유제물건은현샹으로이젼
을일본군에양도ᄒᆞᆯ수
뎨삼됴 젼이긔됴를승락ᄒᆞᆯ때
에는그담보로리일월삼일졍
오저지의조산쇼안조산대안
조산과및그동남일ᄃᆡ고ᄃᆡ에
고잇는포루포ᄃᆡ의슈비를쳘ᄒᆞ
고일본군의게교부ᄒᆞᆯ수
뎨수됴 로국륙군히군중에본
규약됴인ᄒᆞᆯ때에현존ᄒᆞᆫ뎨이
됴의게물건을파괴ᄒᆞ과손ᄒᆞ
며다른방법으로현샹을변경
ᄒᆞᆫ줄로인뎡ᄒᆞᆯ때에는담판을
폐지ᄒᆞ고일본군은자유힝동
을취ᄒᆞᆯ수
뎨오됴 려슌에잇는로국륙히
군관리는려순요시디뢰슈뢰
기타위험물의부셜도와및려
순에잇는륙히군관제표와륙
히군장교관직등급명부와문
관지셔명부와군ᄃᆡ함션명부
와밋그승탑인원명부와보
통인민의남녀인죵직업원부
표를도제ᄒᆞ야일본군의게교
부ᄒᆞᆯ수
뎨륙됴 병긔(각진ᄒᆞᄃᆡ병
긔를병ᄒᆞᆫ)탄약ᄒᆞᆫ용제지료관수
관유의제물건과마필함션병과
및그나부의제물건(ᄉᆞ물을제
ᄒᆞ고)은다이것을일뎡ᄒᆞᆫ위치
에졍치ᄒᆞ고그슈수방법에관
ᄒᆞ야는일을ᄒᆞᆫ량군위원이규졍
ᄒᆞᆯ수
뎨칠됴 일본군은로국군의용감
ᄒᆞᆫ방어를명예로ᄃᆡ졉ᄒᆞ야로국
륙히군의쟝교와및소속관리
의쳔갈과밋ᄌᆞ긔쟐싱활에필요
ᄒᆞᆫ물픔의휴ᄃᆡ를허락ᄒᆞ고쓰
던과ᄒᆞᆫ쟝교와관리와밋의용병
이취ᄒᆞᆫ본젼역의종국ᄭᆞ지무귀
긔인ᄒᆞᆫ니ᄒᆞ고종국셔지무긔를
ᄒᆞ기로ᄒᆞ고일본군의이
ᄒᆞ야기를밧지아니ᄒᆞ기로ᄒᆞ
승락ᄒᆞ는ᄌᆞ는그본국으로도
라가게ᄒᆞ고위부ᄒᆞ는자에게는
ᄒᆞ야는ᄒᆡᆼ세ᄒᆞᆯ비ᄃᆡ는ᄒᆞ
ᄒᆞ는ᄌᆞ는로국군ᄆᆞᆨ귀를벗
아니ᄒᆞᆯ수
뎨팔됴 무쟝을ᄒᆡ졔ᄒᆞᆫ륙군ᄒᆞᆫ

하사병졸의용병은ᄒᆞ노이뎡
ᄒᆞᆫ로지에일졍ᄒᆞᆫ보ᄃᆡᄅᆞᆯ엽ᄒᆞᆫ
구병은경ᄎᆞᆯ을갈케ᄒᆞᆯ시
이것을지시ᄒᆞᆷ
뎨구됴 려순구에잇는로국륙
히군의위싱부원과밋경리부
원은병샹ᄌᆞ와부로의구호급
양ᄒᆞ기위ᄒᆞ야일본이필요로
인뎡ᄒᆞᆯ때ᄭᆞ지일본군의위싱
부원과경리부원지휘하에쥬
ᄒᆞ야업슈ᄒᆞ게ᄒᆞᆯ수
뎨십됴 보통인민의죠쳐와져
자에힝정과회샤에관ᄒᆞᆫ셰무
와밋기타본규약집힝에관ᄒᆞᆫ
ᄌᆞ셰ᄒᆞᆫ은본규약부록에규뎡ᄒᆞᆯ
수
우부록은본규약과동일ᄒᆞᆫ
효력이잇슴이라
뎨십일됴 본규약은일아량국
이각각일견식계조ᄒᆞ야됴인
ᄒᆞᆫ때브터효력이잇슴을수라ᄒᆞ
엿더라
론돈발 십이월삼십일
○영국셕탄쟝사의금지 영국
셕탄쟝사엣도클나발비회사가
카듸프로브터모쌍빅에셕탄일
만돈을실코가다가포르세이드
에서그졍야졍류되엿는ᄃᆡᄒᆞᆫ덕
국쟈견셩이그지졍의ᄒᆞᆫ부분을지금
셜는지라고항ᄒᆞ는곳스이ᄃᆡ인
지모른다더라
빅림발 동월삼십일일
○로함의소식 포도아사름의
젼ᄒᆞ는소식을드른즉불란셔
의ᄒᆞᆫ부분이금월이십륙일에포
도아령디셔방아푸리카그럿쐬
쉬만에도착ᄒᆞ엿는ᄃᆡ셕탄쟝사
들과동힝ᄒᆞᆫ다더라

잡보

○죠뎡의관리일진회원과평양병
뎡의대한문젼에셔츙돌ᄒᆞᆫ사건
으로일병이챠거ᄒᆞ엿는ᄃᆡ위관
이하이십팔인을군부에로
압리ᄒᆞ야작일졔자일량쥬야를
궁지관ᄒᆞ야방송이되엿는ᄃᆡ
오샹ᄒᆞ야하ᄒᆞ로방송이되엿는ᄃᆡ
이는군부ᄃᆡ신리윤용씨가그죄
를소사로진고로위관이하가죠
○경칭교분 경무청고분관장
츳일본인으로방ᄒᆞᆫ다더라

◯특별 쳐분 일젼공고에불참ᄒᆞᆫᄉᆞ로봉현고ᄂᆞᆫ죵지ᄒᆞ고지삼우재횡윤의례입참ᄒᆞ라신쳐분을ᄂᆞ리셧다더라

◯신경ᄉᆞ횡졍예비 경무ᄉᆞ신틔휴시가칠일브터횡공ᄒᆞᆯ터인ᄃᆡ그예졍ᄒᆞᄂᆞᆫ횡졍이좌와여ᄒᆞ니

일 오셔를단쇽ᄒᆞ야싱명지산을더욱보호ᄒᆞᆯᄉᆞ

일 각젼시졍의횡화어음을실시ᄒᆞᆯᄉᆞ

일 잡기와밋한산비를엄금ᄒᆞᆯᄉᆞ

일 각방곡경찰을다시더엄졍케ᄒᆞᆯᄉᆞ

일 무복금잡술쟈를뵈ᄂᆞᆫᄃᆡ로엄죵ᄒᆞᆯᄉᆞ

일 오셔호구표사쟉ᄅᆞᆼ과인민의싱ᄉᆞ를일일히보명ᄒᆞᆯᄉᆞ

일 오셔쳥결을계쇽실시ᄒᆞᆯᄉᆞ

이라더라

◯리씨피임셜 군부대신리윤용씨ᄂᆞᆫᄉᆞ직상쇼를ᄒᆞ엿ᄂᆞᆫᄃᆡ그ᄃᆡᄂᆞᆫ농부대신리도지씨가피임ᄒᆞᆫ다더라

◯리씨시휼 고양군수리쥬현씨가금번 원소별감동으로사ᄅᆞᆷ을파음기ᄂᆞᆫᄃᆡ그총쥬의계가난ᄒᆞᆷ을쓰라ᄒᆞᆯ금을베플고쳔이힝ᄒᆞ야감동ᄒᆞᆫ지라화양뎡에셔졍비를세웟ᄂᆞᆫᄃᆡ쳔이보고쳔이거두니ᄉᆞ졍도업고원망도업도다졍셩을다ᄒᆞ야죠쳐ᄒᆞ니찬숑ᄒᆞᄂᆞᆫ말이구원에밋쳣다ᄒᆞ엿더라

◯인쳔감리면보 인쳔감리면보니에법국군함일쳑이쟉일에드러왓다가쟉일에나갓다ᄒᆞ엿더라

◯최빅량씨공쳔 함경북도변경무관김병약최남륭이가군물을아라ᄉᆞ사ᄅᆞᆷ의게견실ᄒᆞᆫᄉᆞ건으로면관쥬본이되더니경무쳥에셔그ᄃᆡ를젼ᄎᆞᆼ쥬최병찬빅낙헌으로공쳔ᄒᆞ야니부로보고ᄒᆞ엿다더라

◯일진회면칙 니부에셔각도로면훈ᄒᆞ야일진회원의셩경을방슈ᄒᆞ야엄금ᄒᆞ라ᄒᆞ더니일진회에셔각관찰부로면칙ᄒᆞ기를니부대신리용틱ᄂᆞᆫ미국ᄒᆞᆯ마음으로본회목젹을무수히방히ᄒᆞ야디방에면훈으로다회를타파ᄒᆞ니각하ᄂᆞᆫ깁히싱각ᄒᆞ야란신리용틱의훈령을물시ᄒᆞ야회원을구축말기를ᄇᆞ란다ᄒᆞ엿더라

◯안변군슈보고 안변군슈허원씨가외부에보고ᄒᆞ되원산일본군졍시횡관공함니에본군현지가호와뎐답결총파남녀우마졔반물건을됴사ᄒᆞ야보니라ᄒᆞ엿기에이에치보ᄒᆞᆫ다ᄒᆞ엿더라

◯신계군보 신계군슈김두환씨가외부에보고ᄒᆞ되음력십이월이십팔일에평산남천졈감독

빅우졍길이가본군에리도ᄒᆞ야렬도쇼용지목일빅이십륙티를쟉벌ᄒᆞ야실어갓다ᄒᆞ엿더라

관보

뎨삼쳔이십칠호 광무구년일월사일

셔임급사령

◯히니부광제원위원 황셕쥬 신괴셩

◯명니부광제원위원 리승교 팍죵한

이상광무팔년십이월십구일

◯증죵이픔가션대부니부협판 둉졍대부힝구례현감 김영돈

죵이픔가션대부니장원경김윤환의고의법젼츄 증

광무팔년십이월삼십일일

◯임황히도관찰사셔칙임관삼등 죵일픔 죠병호

일월일일

◯명비셔원승셔칙임관ᄉᆞ등 경효젼제됴 김틔졔

◯명경효젼제됴셔칙임관ᄉᆞ등 궁니부특진관 민영돈

◯의원면본관 비셔원승 리달용

◯임비셔원승 신헌균 홍문관시독 졍현지

◯임비셔원승셔칙임관오등 졍삼픔 리셕죵

◯겸임틔의원소경 비셔원승 리셕죵

◯임홍문관시독셔판임관칠등 비셔원랑 졍홍셕

◯임비셔원랑셔판임관칠등 륙픔 죠남일

◯명분비셔원랑 홍문관시독 졍홍셕

◯명임셔리표훈원총재ᄉᆞ무 니부대신 죠병식

◯임헌병ᄉᆞ령관 경무ᄉᆞ륙군참쟝 김뎡근

◯히셔리호위티총관ᄉᆞ무 교육부참모쟝경무ᄉᆞ임시셔리륙군참쟝 빅셩긔

이상일월이일

◯명림시셔리시죵무관부무관쟝ᄉᆞ무 호위티총관륙군부쟝 리근틱

◯명림시셔리비죵무관부무관쟝ᄉᆞ무 경위원총관륙군참쟝 량셩환

이상일월삼일

뎨삼쳔이십팔호 광무구년일월오일

셔임급ᄉᆞ령

◯승셔판임관삼등 니부죵두ᄉᆞ의ᄉᆞ 셩락춘

일월일일

◯의원면겸임쟝례원쟝례 비셔원승 리범인

◯겸임쟝례원쟝례 비셔원승 신셩균

◯명경무ᄉᆞ림시셔리ᄉᆞ무 교육부참모쟝 빅셩긔

이상일월이일

론셜

려슌구

◯려슌구가지금두번재일본사ᄅᆞᆷ의쟝즁에도라갓스니려ᄉᆞ샹에ᄒᆞᆫ잔인ᄒᆞᆫ싸홈이잇섯도다비록스토셀대쟝의항복ᄒᆞᄂᆞᆫ죠약을보낸때ᄂᆞᆫ모로나그대쟝의굿세게방어ᄒᆞ든것을보면그대쟝이무삼싱각을아니ᄒᆞ엿스리오쟝ᄎᆞᆺ일본사ᄅᆞᆷ이다쳥죵ᄒᆞ기가의심업도다

비록이잔인ᄒᆞᆫ싸홈에인명살히ᄒᆞᄂᆞᆫ소식을자죠드려셔도로혀심샹히녁엿스나세계에셔려슌합락ᄒᆞᆫ소식을드르면뉘아니칭탄ᄒᆞ리오지낸일노보면만일스톳셀대쟝이결심ᄒᆞ면몃달이라도더샹지ᄒᆞ게될터이지마ᄂᆞᆫ지금항복ᄒᆞᆫ은ᄉᆞ세부득이ᄒᆞᆯ뿐아니라인의심에셔나온것이로다

대저이일은지금와셔ᄂᆞᆫ별노긴요ᄒᆞᆯ것이업도다일본사ᄅᆞᆷ들이려슌구돌취ᄒᆞ랴고ᄒᆞ다가지금그목적에달ᄒᆞ엿스니승젼ᄒᆞᆫ죠흔마ᄋᆞᆷ에그시이의쓰고인명과지물을업시ᄒᆞᆫ것은혼춤이질ᄃᆞᆺᄒᆞ도다

ᄒᆞᆫ군항의함락됨이이다음다른젼쟁에무삼큰관계가잇스리오일본군ᄉᆞ삼만명쯤려슌함락ᄒᆞᆫ결과로다른곳으로젼력ᄒᆞ게되겟스나그러ᄒᆞ나지낸ᄀᆞ달을두고구로퀴긴대쟝이군ᄉᆞ를더ᄒᆞ엿스니일본군사가삼만명은말고그브다더만이늘더라도구로퓌긴보다더만이되지못ᄒᆞᆯ듯ᄒᆞ며려슌함락ᄒᆞᄀᆞ에일본포병이미우만이늘터이나우리ᄂᆞᆫ젼브터료양에포병이젹어셔될일이못된다ᄂᆞᆫ말을듯지못ᄒᆞ엿노라ᄯᅩ일변으로보면려슌구가구로퓌긴대쟝의게맛처몸에미인사실곳ᄒᆞ야셔려슌구가무양ᄒᆞ면언졔ᄭᆞ지라도구로퀴긴은다른디방으로동ᄒᆞ야드러가지못ᄒᆞᆯ터인ᄃᆡ그런목젹은일본사ᄅᆞᆷ들도다아럿든ᄭᆞ닭에미우난쳐ᄒᆞ게지낸슬듯ᄒᆞ도다

즁지된다ᄂᆞᆫ풍셜과평화된다ᄂᆞᆫ니야기가쟝ᄎᆞᆺᄒᆞᆫ층승힝ᄒᆞᆯ터이나그러ᄒᆞ나량편이다만족히갑화되기ᄂᆞᆫ가망이젹다ᄒᆞ노라지금로국은기젼이후로뎨일죠흔게제를제음ᄒᆞ야져의이러버린명예와위엄을회복ᄒᆞ기젼에ᄂᆞᆫ평화ᄒᆞ기를허락ᄒᆞᆯ듯습지아니ᄒᆞᆫ지라

엇더ᄒᆞᆫ지구쥬시ᄅᆞᆷ들은죠아ᄒᆞᆯ일이ᄒᆞᆫᄀᆞ지가잇도다려슌함락ᄒᆞᆫ기에불틱ᄒᆞᆫ터가도라가며지금은젼쟁이만쥬에만될터이오다른나라에ᄃᆡᄒᆞ야즁립위반ᄒᆞᆫ다고일본이항의ᄒᆞ던것은업슬지라

동경신문들과졍치가들이펴노코발ᄒᆞ되만일각국에셔즁립위반ᄒᆞᆷ이굿쳐지아니ᄒᆞ면영국이일본을도아쥬ᄂᆞᆫ것이영국에직척이라ᄒᆞ엿스니지금은영국이관계ᄒᆞᆯ일이업슬듯ᄒᆞ게된고로영국사ᄅᆞᆷ들이다죠아ᄒᆞᆯ슐노우리ᄂᆞᆫ확실히밋노라

뎐보

빅림발 십이월이십구일

◯로국동병 로국황뎨셔셔칙령으로데사뎨칠군단의동병ᄒᆞᆷ을명ᄒᆞ엿ᄂᆞᆫᄃᆡ예비병을합ᄒᆞ야팔만명가량이라쟝ᄎᆞ여러ᄃᆡ로난화셔만쥬로보낸다더라

론돈발 동월이십팔일

◯로국분란 금월이십륙일에셩피득보에셔대회를열고밤시도록열심으로연셜ᄒᆞ고이번젼쟁의졍지와립법단례의표션ᄒᆞᆷ을동의결졍ᄒᆞ엿ᄂᆞᆫᄃᆡ처니고푸셥스트보샤회쟝과회원사십명이로황의명령으로퇴회ᄒᆞ야그회가헛쳐젓다ᄒᆞ며모쓰고ᄃᆡ슈길닛신친왕은그분요ᄒᆞᆫ연유로사직ᄒᆞ엿고젼국에이런분란이쳐쳐에이러난다더라

빅림발 십이월이십구일

◯로국긔량과법덕 로국황뎨의긔량죠칙에ᄃᆡᄒᆞ야덕법신문들이만이의심ᄒᆞ며이런긔량으로ᄂᆞᆫ그긔량과의마음에만족치못ᄒᆞ리라ᄒᆞ엿더라

크류쓰제이통신문은말ᄒᆞ되그긔량이잘되그를바란다고로국졍부와긔량파사이에협의가되리라고ᄒᆞ엿더라

론돈발 동일

◯로장회국 히삼위함ᄃᆡ사령관스크리드로푸대쟝은구쥬로도라간다더라

빅림발 십이월이십칠일

◯로국긔량 로국황뎨ᄭᅴ셔원로원에죠칙을ᄂᆞ리여셔데국데도에여ᄃᆞᆲ가지특별죠목을긔량ᄒᆞ라ᄒᆞ엿더라

졍부긔관신문은자유권의느ᄂᆞᆫ것을박론ᄒᆞ더라

동지발 동월이십구일

◯덕국젹십자샤 덕국젹십자샤에셔사ᄅᆞᆷ들을보니셔일본군ᄃᆡ에ᄯᅡ라다니게ᄒᆞᆫ다ᄂᆞᆫᄃᆡ그사ᄅᆞᆷ들이일월안으로이ᄃᆡ리국졔노아쿠ᄂᆞᆫᄯᅡ에셔ᄯᅥ난다ᄒᆞ며그사ᄅᆞᆷ들을령솔ᄒᆞ기ᄂᆞᆫᄒᆞᆯ너써라더라

광고

TELEGRAMS.

(FROM JAPAN PAPERS)

London, Dec. 28.

It is reported that the Japanese military authorities intend to place some 500,000 troops at the disposal of Marshal Oyama, Commander-in-Chief-of the Manchurian Armies, and also to considerably increase the number of artillery corps.

London, Dec. 28.

In view of the belief that Russia will attempt to establish a base at Formosa, or other southern islands, for the Baltic Fleet, Japan has strengthened the defence of her territory in those quarters and has also provisioned her garrisons there.

REPORT FROM MR. SIN TAI-HYU.

In direct opposition to General Hasegawa's proclamation comes the following report from Mr. Sin Tai-hyu, the newly appointed Commissioner of Police. Mr. Sin states that he will take up office to-morrow and make a point of seeing the following police rules enforced.

1. Great attention to be given to the protection of lives, and property of the people in Seoul.
2. Strict attention to be paid to loafers and gamblers.
3. The police sentries at street corners must be more vigilant.
4. All sorcerers to be arrested and punished.
5. Immediate reports to be made of births and deaths.
6. Sanitary work in Seoul to be resumed.

A rumour is current to the effect that a Japanese will be employed as adviser to the Police Department.

The Chinese Minister has requested to be received in audience by His Majesty as he is shortly returning to China.

It is said that the daughter of Mr. So Byong-son has been chosen as a fitting mate for the Crown Prince. The lady is 18 years of age.

The Magistrate of Sinkyeh reports that the Japanese have felled trees and taken away 126 pony loads of timber from his district for use on the railroad.

The Il-chin-hoi have once more had to shift their quarters. They are now located at the premises formerly occupied by the Indepeudent Club outside the West Gate.

His Majesty has graciously commanded the Governor of Kyengki province not to collect any house tax from his people for the latter half of the year, 1904. This is as recognition of the service rendered by the Kyengki people, to the funeral arrangements of the late Crown Princess.

A proclamation, which has been issued by the Japanese Minister, runs as follows:—"The Korean local Governors Magistrates and other officials oppress the people outrageously; so the people are in great trouble and the numbers desiring a reforming policy are increasing daily. The Japanese Minister sympathises greatly with the people in their time of sorrow, therefore, in future, when such cases of oppression arise, the victims may draw up a petition to be forwarded through the consuls to the Japanese Minister." It was only some few days ago that we had to report a case in which the Japanese Minister was making every endeavour to prevent justice being done on the Magistrate of Pyengyang, one of the worst, if not *the* worst, of these "local Magistrates, who oppress the people outrageously."

LANDSLIP AT CHINKIANG.

Incoming river-steamers, says the Shanghai Times, report that a serious landslide occurred at Chinkiang on Friday last, the 23rd ult., causing great loss to life and property. Subsidences of the river bank are to be expected as this period of the year when the water is low, but nothing like the one reported has occurred since the land slip at Nanking in which the godowns of Messrs. Butterfield and Swire disappeared.

The loss of life is estimated to be from 60 to 70 persons, all of which are Chinese and who were either in the buildings, or walking upon the bund at the time of the catastrophe There were several narrow escapes, and several natives are suffering from injuries caused by the falling house-beams, bricks, falling masonry, and debris.

The buildings which collapsed were owned by Chinese and were for the most part utilised as godowns and storehouses. The local Chinese hong of Y. Ching Chong suffered the greatest loss, the whole of the offices, dwelling house, cotton and sugar godowns having been completely wrecked together with their occupants and contents.

An eyewitness describes the "tidal wave" which was caused by the debris falling into the river, as being nearly 7 feet and which caused the moorings of the Standard Oil Co's hulk to carry away and wash the hulk into the middle of the river. The other hulks stood the strain but rolled and pitched considerably for some time after the accident. A steam launch sank but fortunately the passengers had got safely ashore or the loss of life would have been considerably augmented.

The scene of the catastrophe presents a curious sight; of many of the houses on the bund, half only remains and portions of the ruins overhang the water and are expected to collapse.

The Japanese military authorities have commanded the tax collector of South Hamkyeng province to take all monies collected from the people to the magistrate of Kilchu.

The new Minister for Home Affairs has commenced to attend office. His first instructions were to prohibit any officials of his Department from entering his office on any but public affairs.

The Magistrate of Anbyun has been ordered by the Japanese military authorities to prepare a census of the population of his district, together with the number of houses and acreage of fields.

The Police inspector of Mapo reports that the Japanese have requested him to furnish dwellings and supplies for 1,000 coolies, who will shortly come to work on the railroad. He finds himself unable to do this, as there are not sufficient houses, and further complains that the Japanese are cutting timber on the hills at Hung-nye-dong with the purpose of building a railway station.

The Commander-in-Chief of the Japanese forces in Korea has issued a notification that, in future, the policing of the city of Seoul and vicinity will be carried out by Japanese gendarmes. The Korean gendarmes and guards will furthermore have no powers or responsibilities. It is stated that information to this effect will reach the Korean Government and foreign legations through the Japanese Legation.

Why is it that the number of sentences to imprisonment have increased during the last three years? In the absence of any other cause it is exceedingly probable that the recent Transvaal war has produced the same effects in this country, so far as regards the increase of crime, as Continental wars have produced on Continental communities. We cannot with impunity familiarise a population with the horrors of war.—Rev. W. D. Morrison, in Law Magazine.

CHINA NOTES.

Of all the birthday presents received by the Empress Dowager, it is reported that none pleased her so much as the one from Prince Ching. Prince Ching is regarded with so much esteem by the Empress Dowager that she shares her delicacies with him.

It is reported that railway operations are about to be commenced in Kiangsi province. The Provincial Treasurer has been appointed superintendent on the recommendation of the Governor.

Viceroy Shum Chun Huen telegraphs to Peking that Lu A Fa, the leader of the Kwangsi rebels, has been captured and executed, and that as a consequence the rebellion is now on the wane. He prays that the deserving officials be promoted and rewarded.

General Ma Yuk Kwan has sent a lengthy telegraphic despatch to the Grand Council asking for permission to proceed to Kiuliencheng with his troops for the purpose of protecting the inhabitants of Fengtien. In reply, the Grand Council has refused General Ma permission to proceed, saying that instructions have already been sent to Tartar General Tseng Chi to afford the inhabitants his protection. General Ma has been greatly displeased with this reply.

A Nanch'ang, capital of Kiangsi province, despatch states that the Chinese authorities have at last given formal consent to the making of the well-known summer resort of Kuling into an International Settlement, on payment to the Chinese Government of the sum of Tls, 30,000. A Chinese officer, graduate of a military academy, has been recently sent by the Governor of Kiangsi to Kuling to make a topographical map of the place, and mark out the boundaries of the Settlement.

General Kuropatkin's lost charger has come into the possession of Major-General Okazaki, who proposes to present it to the Mikado. The Czar himself gave it to General Kuropatkin.

A Chefoo despatch to the "Osaka Mainichi" states that all the British battleships and cruisers at Wei-hai-wei sailed for Hongkong, the former on 28th ult. and the latter on the 29th.

The Japanese Government has just issued to the public a notification to the effect that the service of postal money orders between Japan and Russia proper, with Great Britain as intermediary, has been opened.

According to a telegram received by the "Tokio Asahi" opinion in London is beginning to reciprocate the desire expressed in Japan for an extension of the scope of the Anglo-Japanese Alliance. It is suggested that, in order to prevent Russian aggression and afford mutual relief, the British Fleet should in case of need guard the shores of Japan, while Japanese troops should be similarly available for the Indian frontier.

Here is a Philippine yarn:—A gentleman staying on business in the Philippine Islands told his servant, a negro, to fill an empty pepper cruet, and waited for the pepper to arrive before commencing his luncheon, which had been served.

The servant, however, was such a long time carrying out his instructions that he at last went out into the kitchen to remonstrate with him for the unnecessary delay.

'How long is it going to take you to do that job?' he asked

'Not much longer,' answered the negro, in his own language; 'but you must remember that it is no small task to force the pepper through these little holes.

Professor Assmann, one of the German Government meteorological experts, says that lightning seldom strikes in a forest where the trees are dense and of about the same height. Danger exists only where isolated trees rise high above their surroundings.

The Korea Daily News.

Issued at 5 P. M. daily except Sundays.

Rate of Subscription:—
Per Year,............Yen 25.
Per Quarter,..........Yen 7.
Per Month,..........Yen 2.50.

Postage in Korea not charged extra.
Postage abroad charged extra.

Advertisements, 50 sen per day for 1 inch or less.
5 yen per month per inch.
50 yen per year per inch.

All communications to

E. T. BETHELL,
Editor and Publisher,
Pak-tong, Seoul.

DIPLOMATIC REPRESENTATIVES.

Among the many misleading stories about Korea for which irresponsible Japanese Correspondents at Seoul are responsible is one which has recently gone the rounds of the Tokio press to the effect that the Korean Diplomatic representatives abroad will have to be recalled as the Commissioner of Customs has declined to pay the money neccessary for their salaries and expenses.

This assertion, so freely made, rests upon the slenderest possible foundation of fact. Mr. McLeavy Brown administers, with great skill and advantage to the Government, the Imperial Korean Customs, and we are sure he would be the last to arrogate to himself the right of vetoing any expenditure sanctioned by the Government.

Mr. McLeavy Brown's advice however carries great weight with His Majesty and his ministers and as there are certain abuses in connection with the Korean Diplomatic Service, Mr. McLeavy Brown has on several occasions protested against what he very properly regards as an unjustifiable waste of public money.

While it is, as at present it is, the will of the Emperor that Korea should be represented at the Foreign Courts, the Customs Service will continue to supply sufficient funds. Mr. McLeavy Brown, however, as is his practise in regard to all expenditure, sets his face against wanton extravagance, and it is this which has probably given rise to the *Canard* circulating in Japan.

Korea's interests abroad are almost *nil* and the principal reason for the despatch of Representatives to other countries is as a token of her independence and an assertion of her Diplomatic equality with other Powers. Of real business there is very little and all there is could easily be transacted in Seoul without the assistance of Ministers abroad. As a matter of fact the sending of these representatives is only a matter of form and great expenditure is therefore unjustifiable.

There have been occasions when Korean Ministers to Foreign Courts have drawn salaries and expenses when they have not been at their posts and there have also been instances when their suites have not been so numerous as they have been represented to be.

A Minister and a Secretary at each Court should be ample for all purposes and the expense would then be an item which no one would object to.

ADMIRAL TOGO

Admiral Togo was to have returned to Tokio on December 30th and great preparations were being made to give Japan's naval hero a fitting reception. Although it is a mystery how the "Cesarevitch"—crippled as she was—was permitted to escape to Tsingtau there is no doubt that Admiral Togo has carried out the work entrusted to him with results which are a great credit to himself and his country.

THE QUESTION OF REFORM.

From a Seoul despatch of the 26th inst., received by the "Kokumin" we learn that the Korean Emperor has rejected the scheme of reform passed by the recent Cabinet Council. It is also feared that it will be impossible under existing circumstances to effectively carry out Mr. Megata's financial scheme. It appears that the Treasury is nearly empty and to make matters worse the expectation of the Government with regard to the taxes has not been realized, due to the mismanagement of officials. The message adds that the recent Cabinet meeting decided that the sum of one million "yen" should be retrenched from the Budget and a further saving of four million "yen" be effected in connection with military reforms. This scheme, however, has now been rejected by the Emperor.

After serving four months and three days improsonment, Fred. Dorr and Edward F. O'Brien, the proprietor and editor, respectively, of the "Manila Freedom," who have been serving sentence for libel on Commissioner Legarda, have been liberated by the authority of President Roosevelt.

A Shanghai despatch states that Mr. John Goodnow, the former U. S. Consul-General at Shanghai, has been succeeded by Mr. J. W. Davidson, U. S. Consul at Antung, China, as the result of which Dr. W. Knappe, German Consul-General, has now become the *doyen* of the Consular body at Shanghai.

A dispatch to the "Asahi" dated Peking Dec. 20th reports that the Chinese Ministers at Paris, London and Washington, who with their colleagues at other courts had been instructed to sound foreign Powers as to the intermediation for the Japan Russia complication, have replied telegraphically to the effect that the foreign views entertain the possibility of an intermediation upon the fall of Port Arthur.

The British War Office has refused the application received from the American Ambassador, requesting that permission be granted to certain British subjects, 356 in number, to wear the "Military Order of the Dragon," formed by American officers in the North China Force of 1900, and of which certain qualified British officers were members. Permission was refused in accordance with the decision arrived at in November, 1902, that, eonsidering the number of Powers engaged in the operations in China, each Power should bestow on its own subjects the distinctions to which they were entitled.

When we said good-bye to the Alake of Abeokutu some months ago, we wondered, says a London paper, what would be the next tidings that we should hear of him after he had arrived in his own far country. As soon as he had quietly settled down again in his own swamp—or is it prairie?—which would linger most gratefully in his memory of all the sights he had seen in Happy England? What would he miss most; what most desire? Well, the answer has come. His Highness has sent to London for 25 cases of plum pudding and vast quantities of tinned soups and fish, and has paid for them in good palm oil and solid mahogany logs.

THE FOREIGN POLICY OF PRESIDENT ROOSEVELT.

The Spectator made the following interesting comments in the course of a recent article on President Roosevelt:—

In the domain of foreign affairs, and in that which concerns the American possessions beyond the sea, we believe that President Roosevelt will show himself neither a braggart nor a poltroon. He will not be afraid to insist that America shall hold her own among the Great Powers of the world, but he will seek no foreign entanglements. It is certain that he wil maintain the Monroe doctrine in the letter and in the spirit, as the American people unquestionably desire that is shall be maintained. But the President is not one of those men who imagine that policies can be based on Fourth of July orations, or on the rhetorical resolutions of deliberative assemblies. If the Monroe doctrine is not to be consigned to the political waste-paper basket, it must rest, in the last resource, upon naval and military power. If America has not a fleet strong enough to say, "Thus far, and no further!" to those who challenge the doctrine, that doctrine in the future will not prove worth the paper on which the Presidential Message of 1823 was written.

That the President will finish the Panama Canal we do not doubt. Nor shall we be surprised if he is able eventually to obtain from Denmark those West Indian islands which she so nearly ceded to the United States, and would, indeed, have ceded but for the secret intervention of Germany to prevent the completion of the bargain. In the Far East, and in all that concerns the future of China, we may expect the President, acting under the advice of Mr. Hay, his Secretary of State—who is now unquestionably one of the ablest, if not the ablest, of living diplomatists—to maintain the attitude already adopted. As regards the Philippines, we may feel sure that the President will do his best to established and maintain administration the first object of which will be, not an adherence to any paper theories or abstract sentiments in regard to popular government, but rather the government of the islands in the true interests of their inhabitants. He will strive to give them just, pure and progressive, which shall seek, that is, the welfare of the Filipinos rather than their so called consent,—a consent which, in truth, would not be that of the people as a whole, but only of certain noisy and self-constituted leaders.

We shall, perhaps, be accused of drawing too optimistic a picture of what President Roosevelt may do, and will do. Time will show. For ourselves, we believe him to have sincerity and absolute common sense,—two qualities which are combined in every ruler whose schemes and policies come to fruition. We believe that his administration will leave indelible traces on the large half of the English-speaking race, and that for the whole of that race it will be a lesson and an example in sound and sane government.

GOLD MINES IN KOREA.

The "Jiji" states that the demands preferred to the Korean Gevernment by the Representatives of England, France and Italy for concessions of gold mines in Korea will be shortly granted. The Cabinet has not yet passed any decision on this question, but the attitude of the Court seems to assure the success of the demands of the foreign Representatives.

A SECOND SUEZ CANAL PROPOSED

London, December 17.—Sir T. V. S. Angier announces that owing to the high tarff charged, he offers matured plans to cut a second Suez Canal.

A big contractor, familiar with work in Egypt, is ready to finance and carry out the undertaking.

The proposal has excited considerable interest in mercantile circles.

The Korea Daily News.

VOL. II, FRIDAY, JANUARY 6, 1905. No. 3

大韓每日申報
대한매일신보

(뎨이권ᄉᆞ호) (월요일) 일쳔구빅오년일월구일

본사고빅

이신보는영어와한어로셔거리
일츌판ᄒᆞᆸ

신문가

한쟝 엽두돈오푼
일삭표 엽두량닷돈
우표가미 삭당닷돈
다밧돈으로밧ᄉᆞᆸ

광고료는

기한의쟝단과ᄉᆞ항의다쇼로죵갑ᄒᆞ되뎡가로밧을터이오며오리지아녀대한사ᄅᆞᆷ마다다이신문을보실터이니광고내시기를원ᄒᆞ시는이들은우리신문사에와서편약ᄒᆞ심을희망ᄒᆞᆸ

○발ᄒᆡᆼ소 박동대한매일신보사 발ᄒᆡᆼ겸편즙인 영국인 셜필립쟝자리오

사쟝 영국인 (ᄇᆡ셜)

평양 ᄃᆡ리뎜

○평양효동사는권ᄉᆞ미보씨로우리신문관ᄃᆡ리인을뎡ᄒᆞ엿사오니평양에게신구람코져ᄒᆞ시는쳠군ᄌᆞ는ᄃᆡ리뎜에왕림ᄒᆞ와편의ᄒᆞ시옵

샤고

○우리대한매일신보의목뎍은대한의안녕질서에관한모든대봉에대ᄒᆞ야는공평한변론을쥬쟝ᄒᆞᆷ이라우리통신원의탐보는신문보셔는쳠군ᄌᆞ의계ᄒᆞᆷ샹보도ᄒᆞ리며편지를긔셔ᄒᆞ여주시는에는셩명과번디를젹어붓치시기를희망ᄒᆞ오니비계술신문샹에긔ᄌᆡᄒᆞ라는거시아니오다만극히신용ᄒᆞ논증거를숨코자ᄒᆞᆷ이라긔쟈논아모긔셔던지긔ᄌᆡᄒᆞᆯ퇴각ᄒᆞ논권리를가졋ᄉᆞ나퇴각ᄒᆞ는리유는발ᄒᆞᆯ터이오며공중평화를문란케ᄒᆞ는듯ᄒᆞᆫ긔셔는외람히밧지안켓ᄉᆞᆸ나이다

●본사셜시이리로신문을미량우리로분젼ᄒᆞ와리젼부의임의로젼ᄒᆞ든스로번곳에는혹늣게젼ᄒᆞ기도ᄒᆞ며혹며칠거슬ᄒᆞᆫ번에젼ᄒᆞ기도ᄒᆞ며혹아니젼ᄒᆞ는곳도잇다ᄒᆞ와우리신문을ᄉᆞ랑ᄒᆞ야구람ᄒᆞ시는 쳠군ᄌᆞ의계뒤ᄒᆞ야미우미안ᄒᆞ옴기로지금은본젼인을두고미일일ᄌᆞ이젼ᄒᆞ며아니젼ᄒᆞ거나늣게거나ᄒᆞᆫ폐가업도록ᄒᆞ란ᄒᆞ오니혹아니젼ᄒᆞ거나혹늣게젼ᄒᆞ거나ᄒᆞᆫ일이잇스면본사로통긔ᄒᆞ여주심을희망ᄒᆞᆸ

잡보

○죠쳥젼죠의관 닉장원에셔외부에죠회ᄒᆞ기를젼에함남봉세위원밧승렬의보고를거ᄒᆞᆫ즉본도각군의도젼을슈봉ᄒᆞ야가지고원산에티도ᄒᆞᆫ즉일본사령부로브터히도젼을길쥬군에젼납ᄒᆞ고너여주지아니ᄒᆞᆫ다ᄒᆞ엿기사실ᄒᆞᆫ즉함남북슈세감리가젼쥬슈군슈를차하ᄒᆞ야ᄒᆞ여곰슈세ᄒᆞᆫ다ᄒᆞ고헌금도로가막히고막히여다시박위원을파송ᄒᆞ야쟝찻함남을슈세ᄒᆞ라ᄒᆞ엿더라일ᄃᆡ의뎨회ᄒᆞᆷ을맛남이심이와홍ᄒᆞ니쳥컨ᄃᆡ일공관에죠회ᄒᆞ와야히사령부에젼죠ᄒᆞ야이쟝공에뎨의홍이업게ᄒᆞᆷ을바란다ᄒᆞ엿더라

○쳥죠쳐관 경무쳥에셔외부로죠회ᄒᆞ기를셔셔쟝의보고니기에작일신시경에일인샹본이가공덕리ᄒᆞ계동마빅쟝등디에리도ᄒᆞ야쳘도작로ᄒᆞᆫ다칭ᄒᆞ고에민가를붓힘쳥ᄒᆞ고민총쳔여쟝을파괴ᄒᆞ기로어ᄂᆞ니이러ᄒᆞᆫ되져에민졍이가하니다ᄒᆞ기예이본교ᄒᆞ오니죠량쳐판ᄒᆞ심이가ᄒᆞ다ᄒᆞ엿더라

○뎐ᄒᆞ슐쇼환 니부에셔경긔샹남강원ᄒᆞ졔셔관찰의계뎐ᄒᆞ되긔를각도슐찰사를소환ᄒᆞ샤로쳐분을봉승ᄒᆞ엿스니슌찰은사잇는군에곳통지ᄒᆞ야곳올나오라ᄒᆞ엿더라

○고문셜연 금일하오ᄒᆞᆫ시에탁지고문관목하젼씨가남문밧연화봉사저에셔연회를셜ᄒᆞ고각부대관을쳥요ᄒᆞᆫ다더라

○츄원셜연 츄원셔긔관은신후부인이리도ᄒᆞ엿슴으로작일오후륙시에여러친구를쳥ᄒᆞ야본구락부에셔야연회를셜ᄒᆞ엿다더라

○권씨담화 경위원총관권즁셕씨는졔ᄒᆡᆼ된후에빅관을디ᄒᆞ야담화ᄒᆞ기를일젼회의젹은당ᄒᆞᆫ의거이라니가젼일에ᄒᆡᆼᄒᆞᆫ쟈유논아니라금일에권리를쓰엿스면일진회를찬셩ᄒᆞᆯ겟노라ᄒᆞ엿다고대한일보에긔ᄌᆡᄒᆞ엿더라

○셰국통탈 일젼에시골사ᄅᆞᆷᄒᆞ나히셔울와셔텬보괘광을등속을사가지고ᄂᆞ려가다가되게원쥬막에드러인자쉬더니맛춤거긔잇는일본병참소통ᄉᆞ와그쥬막쟝이와셔로쟝기를ᄒᆞ더니고시골사ᄅᆞᆷ의어리셕음을보고돈두냥을주며ᄒᆞ는말이이돈을놋코ᄒᆞᆫ번노름을ᄒᆞ라ᄒᆞᆫ즉그시골자가ᄃᆡ답ᄒᆞ기를나는노름을조도모른다ᄒᆞᆫ즉그쥬막쟝이말술이나평셰돈이니가지고가다가 [illegible] ᄒᆞ엿더라

○비궁잔픽 황티ᄌᆞ비궁이뷔엿스니간픽ᄒᆞᆷ을ᄒᆞ는평랑을 [illegible]

○공ᄎᆞ보리 [illegible]

[illegible] ᄒᆞᆫ즉쳥인즁열명이고욕ᄒᆞ는말을알코모든저포민을쌔흘치티포민이쏘ᄒᆞᆫ분ᄒᆞᆷ으로손으로치고몽둥이로싸리스되다만파가쳥인ᄒᆞᄂᆞᆫ아만맛고소위손연방이는본터간졀이잇셔스사로본병이발ᄒᆞ야츙울ᄒᆞ니고니며져수잇올지난후에쥬고파가쳥인죡피라ᄒᆞ야약간상ᄒᆞ고못ᄂᆡ빅병인을관문합히며여와박게근의징으로드러가치료ᄒᆞ다가곳죽은지라이것이비단우리나라샹졍의용쵸ᄒᆞᆫ아니요일인ᄒᆞ젼상길과밋시도뎡죠의목ᄃᆞᆼ이분명ᄒᆞ거늘병용관셤사관은다만쳥상의무쇼ᄒᆞ는공쵸로맛춤닉[illegible] 보고ᄒᆞ부치노라고ᄒᆞ엿더라

관보

광무구년일월칠일 호외 [illegible]

셔임급ᄉᆞ령

○임함경북도변계순심관셔판임관ᄉᆞ등 김일환 (일월이일)

○의원면본관 비셔원승 리 [illegible]

○희원 비셔원승 리병일

○명비셔원승셔칙임관ᄉᆞ등 죵이품 리명샹

○임비셔원승셔주임관오등 졍삼품 셔병셜

○희림시서리시죵무관부무관쟝 사무 호위티총관륙군부쟝 리근틱

○희림시서리비죵무관부무관쟝 사무 경위원총관륙군참쟝 양셩환 (이샹일월ᄉᆞ일)

○명니쟝원경셔칙관샹등 죵이품 김회원 (일월오일)

○의정부참정김셩근군쥬ᄒᆞ되각도순찰ᄉᆞ의관졔를이미셩립ᄒᆞ되셔의로쎠슌령의치졍ᄒᆞ논것을살피게ᄒᆞᆷ이니 [illegible] 순찰ᄉᆞ리셩우와경긔도순찰ᄉᆞ박졔빈과 [illegible] 를모다곳소환ᄒᆞᆷ이 [illegible] 쥬ᄒᆞ와 지의 광무구년일월ᄉᆞ일에봉쥬라ᄒᆞ옵시다

관쳥사항

[illegible] ᄒᆞ엿더라

UNION INSURANCE SOCIETY OF CANTON.

Head office Hongkong.
Marine risks underwritten at current rates.
Agents in Chemulpo,
E. MEYER & Co.

COMPAGNIE DES MESSAGERIES MARITIMES.

Fortnightly Direct Service.

For Marseilles
via Ports.
Sailing from Yokohama
Calling at Kobe,
Shanghai, Hongkong, Saigon, Singapore,
Colombo, Djibouti, Suez, Port Said
and Marseilles.

For particulars apply to
HOLME RINGER & Co.,
Chemulpo.

HAYASHIDA & CO.,

16 MYENG DONG, CHIN KO KAI, SEOUL.
BRANCH OFFICE AT CHEMULPO.

Money changers, Coal and Wood Merchants, Express Agents.

We are agents for the Pyeng-yang Coal Company and the Karazu Coal Company of Japan. We have the best quality of both anthracite and bituminous coal, and prompt execution of orders is our speciality. Firewood of all kinds kept in stock. Full weight guaranteed. Money of all denominations exchanged at current rates. Parcels received for all parts.

CHINA MUTUAL LIFE INS. OC.

Most favourable terms to policy holders.

Benefit system unsurpassed.

HOLME RINGER & Co.
Agents, Chemulpo.

C. P. R.

CANADIAN PACIFIC RAILWAY COMPANY'S ROYAL MAIL STEAMSHIP LINE.

THE FAST ROUTE BETWEEN CHINA, JAPAN, AND EUROPE VIA CANADA AND THE UNITED STATES.

Route from Hongkong via Shanghai, Nagasaki (Inland Sea of Japan) Kobe. Yokohama Victoria and Vancouver.

Twin Screw Empress Steamship—6,000 Tons—Speed 19 knots.

PROPOSED SAILING FROM YOKOHAMA.
R. M. S. Empress of India.
R. M. S. Empress of Japan.
R. M. S. Empress of China.
R. M. S. Athenian.
R. M. S. Taatar.

Special reduction (first class only) granted to members of the Military, Naval, Diplomatic and Civil services and to Missionaries.

Passengers have choice of ten routes across the Continent of America and have privilege of travelling by any Atlantic Steamship Line.

Round the World passage tickets in connection with the P. and O. S. N., North German Lloyd and Messageries Co.'s **£125**.

All rates payable at current rate of exchange.

For further information, Tickets, Guide Books, etc., apply to

HOLME, RINGER & Co., AGENTS,
Chemulpo.

Grand Hotel,

(Formerly the Station Hotel)

Near the Railway Terminus, West Gate Seoul.

The Best Hotel in Korea.
Handsome new Building.
Fine Airy Rooms
Excellent Cuisine.
Terms Moderate.
Special terms to Missionaries
and to permanent boarders.

Electric cars within 2 minutes' walk.

W. H. EMBERLEY.
Proprietor

EVERY FACILITY.

In connection with Life Assurance Business is afforded by

The Standard Life Assurance Co.,

One of the largest and wealthiest of the Provident Institutions of the United Kingdom Forms of Application and all information will be promptly afforded on application.

10 CENTS A DAY.

Not a very large expenditure is it? But it is sufficient to secure for a man of 30 a policy with the STANDARD LIFE OFFICE for

$1323.

For all particulars of rates, etc., apply to

Holme, Ringer & Co.,
Agents, Chemulpo.

THE NEW YORK LIFE INSURANCE COMPANY.

Have you ever been declined by any Company?

Are you engaged in a specially hazardous occupation?

Have you heard of the New York Life Insurance Company's New Classifications for this class of Risks?

If not, send your date of birth, occupation and particulars of rejection, if any to

E. MEYER & Co.,
Agents, Chemulpo.

MITSUI BUSSAN KAISHA
(MITSUI & Co.)

MITSUI GINKO.
(MITSUI BANK.)

The Bank is owned by the members of the Mitsui Family, who, as partners, assume an unlimited responsibility for all liabilities of the Bank:—

Capital........................Yen 5,000,000
Reserve Fund.................. " 5,600,000

HEAD OFFICE, TOKYO.
LONDON OFFICE, 34 LIME ST., E. C.

BRANCHES AND AGENCIES:—
New York, San Francisco, Hamburg, Bombay, Singapore, Manila, Hongkong, Amoy, Chefoo, Tientsin.

Kobe, Hakodate, Yokohama, Kure, Yokosuka, Moji, Shimonoseki, Miike, Wakamatsu, Nagasaki, Kuchinotsu, Karatsu, Sasebo, Misume, Taipeh, &c.

Telegraphic Address for all the Offices:
"MITSUI."

A. B. C. AND A. 1 CODES USED.

Contractors of Coal.
To the Imperial Japanese Navy. Arsenals and Railway Bureau, Principal Railway Companies and Industrial Work, Home and Foreign Mail and Freight Steamers.

Sole Proprietors
Of the famous Miike, Tagawa and Yamano Coal Mines.

Sole Agents
For the sale of Fukumo, Hokoku, Ichimura, Kanoda, Mannoura, Onoura, Ostuji, Sonoda, Tsubaruro, Yoshinotani, Yoshio, Yurokibura and other coals.

YANGTSE INSURANCE ASSOCIATION, LTD.

The undersigned, having been appointed agents for the above company, are prepared to issue policies and pay losses on marine risks at regular rates.

E. MEYER & Co.,
Agents, Chemulpo.

AMERICAN KOREAN ELECTRIC CO.

Light and Power.

Main Office: Electric Building, Chong No.

RAILWAY DEPARTMENT.

OPERATING CARS BETWEEN EAST AND WEST GATE, EVERY TEN MINUTES:—

First Car leaves East Gate at 7:00 A. M. First Car leaves R. R. Station at 7:25 A. M
Last Car " East Gate at 8.40 P. M. Last " " R. R. Station at 9.05 P.M

OPERATING CARS BETWEEN EAST GATE AND IMPERIAL TOMB TERMINUS, EVERY TWENTY MINUTES:—
CONNECTING WITH EVERY ALTERNATE CAR ARRIVING AT EAST GATE FROM CHONG NO.

First Car leaves East Gate for Tomb at 7:10 A. M.
" " " Tomb for East Gate at 7:30 A. M.
Last " " East Gate for Tomb at 7:50 P. M.
" " " Tomb for East Gate at 8:10 P. M.

OPERATING CARS BETWEEN CHONG NO AND YUNG SAN RIVER EVERY TWELVE MINUTES:—

First Car leaves Chong No for South Gate at 7:12 A. M.
" " " Chong No for Yung San at 7:36 A. M.
" " " South Gate for Chong No at 7:20 A. M.
" " " Yung San for Chong No at 8:09 A. M.
Last " " South Gate for Chong No 9:00 P. M.
" " " Yung San for Chong No at 8.45. P. M.

SPECIAL PRIVATE CARS FURNISHED TO SUIT CONVENIENCE OF PATRONS. PRICES ON APPLICATION AT HEAD OFFICE.

LIGHTING DEPARTMENT.

Where less than 250 candle power of light is used, the rate per month will be
Per 16 candle power incandescent lamp,—All night.—Yen 2.50.
32 candle power incandescent lamp:—All night:—Yen 4.00.
50 candle power incandescent lamp:—All night:—Yen 6.00.
150 " " " " " " ,, 10.00.
1200 " " enclosed are " " " ,, 20.00.

Where more than 250 candle power of light is used, a Meter will be installed, freqvedted:—Rent of Meter Yen 2.00 per month. Rate of charges by meter reading:—Two Sen per Ampere per hour. (Approximately this is equal to about One Sen per 16 C. P. lamp per hour) Minimum monthly charge where meter is installed, Yen 20.00 per month, which includes rental of meter.

Estimates for installing lights furnished on application

An assortment of chandeliers always on hand.

K. Murakami.
Photograph Studio
Chinkokai, Seoul.

Printing, Developing and Enlargement, of Photographs always Undertaken.

Korean Views and Pictures Illustrating Native Customs always on Sale,

---

THE OSAKA SHOSEN KAISHA.

Boats frequently on the berth for Chinnampo.

REGULAR SAILINGS BETWEEN JAPAN AND KOREAN PORTS.

FUSAN AND KOBE VIA SHIMONOSEKI.

OSAKA VIA MOKPO, FUSAN, SHIMONOSEKI AND KOBE.

MOJI DIRECT.

OSAKA VIA KUNSAN, MASANPO, FUSAN, SHIMONOSEKI AND KOBE.

CHEMULPO KUNSAN LINE,
Every three days.

CHEMULPO CHINNAMPO LINE.
Every three days.

For Freight and passage and further particulars apply to

THE OSAKA SHOSEN KAISHA,
Chemulpo

RONDON, PLAISANT & CO.

General Storekeepers and Merchants, Ships Contractors, Tobacconists, Commission and Forwarding Agents, Coal Merchants

IMPORTERS AND EXPORTERS

Seoul & Chemulpo.

W. D. WENTWORTH.

LANDING
AND
SHIPPING AGENT
AND
CUSTOMS BORDER.

12 OURA, NAGASAKI.

STEWARD & CO.

Chemulpo.

Shipchandlers and Storekeepers, Naval and Mercantile Contrrctors, Landing and Shipping Agents.

STEWARD'S HOTEL

Chemulpo.

Best accommodation in the port for travelers. Clean and well-aired rooms, good cuisin and prompt attendence, moderate tariff.

ᄂᆞ쟝이며정삼픔경위원경무관한홍슈와륙픔외국어학교교관죠원규와륙픔농상공학교교관리만규ᄂᆞᆫ일본국훈륙등욱일장이며륙픔공사관참셔관리우영과구품륙곡참위박영철과륙픔경위원총슌리긍슌은일본국훈륙등셔보장이며륙픔즁학교교관박승원은일본국훈칠등동엽쟝이며륙픔군부쥬사뎡윤은일본국훈칠등셔보쟝을령슈ᄒᆞ엿기로표훈원에셔경 쥬지가ᄒᆞ후픠용쥰허ᄒᆞ사

일월이일

론셜

외국에한국의교관

○셔울잇ᄂᆞᆫ실답지아니ᄒᆞᆫ일본통신원들이한국ᄉᆞ건에ᄃᆡᄒᆞ야허황ᄒᆞᆫ말을만히보고ᄒᆞ지마ᄂᆞᆫ그즁에ᄒᆞᆫᄉᆞ건이근릭동경각신문에발포ᄒᆞ엿ᄂᆞᆫᄃᆡ외국에잇ᄂᆞᆫ한국외교관들의월급과경비를ᄒᆡ관총세무ᄉᆞ가지출기를거졀ᄒᆞᄂᆞᆫᄭᅡ닭에그외교관들을불너드리게된다고ᄒᆞ엿ᄂᆞᆫ지라이러케확실ᄒᆞ게발포ᄒᆞᆫ말이그ᄉᆞ실샹으로보면근지ᄂᆞᆫ좀잇슬듯ᄒᆞ도다ᄒᆡ관총세무ᄉᆞᄲᅮ라운씨가한국정부에ᄃᆡᄒᆞ야조흔게졔와비샹ᄒᆞᆫ지룽으로ᄒᆡ관ᄉᆞ무들관리ᄒᆞᄂᆞᆫ지라졍부에셔결졍ᄒᆞᆫ무슴경비던지ᄲᅮ라운씨가참람히반ᄃᆡᄒᆞᆯ리가업슬줄노우리ᄂᆞᆫ확실이깃노라한국황뎨폐하ᄭᅴ셔와각대신들이ᄲᅮ라운씨의권고ᄒᆞᆷ을진즁히아시고한국외교ᄉᆞ무에ᄃᆡᄒᆞ야혹람용ᄒᆞᆷ이잇ᄂᆞᆫ고로ᄲᅮ라운씨가공젼을쓸ᄃᆡ업시허비ᄒᆞᄂᆞᆫ줄노싱각ᄒᆞ야반ᄃᆡᄒᆞᆫ게졔가더러잇셧ᄂᆞᆫ지라지금와셔ᄂᆞᆫ한국대황뎨폐하ᄭᅴ셔외국죠졍에한국ᄃᆡ표쟈를두ᄂᆞᆫ거시맛당ᄒᆞᆫ줄노아시니그러ᄒᆞ면어느ᄯᅢᄭᆞ지라도ᄒᆡ관에셔ᄂᆞᆫ거긔적당ᄒᆞᆫ비용을공급ᄒᆞᆯ지라엇더든지각색비에쓸ᄃᆡ업시람비ᄒᆞᄂᆞᆫ거시잇스면ᄲᅮ라운씨가반ᄃᆡᄒᆞ야버릇을햇던ᄭᅡ닭에일본신문에그런말의발표ᄒᆞᆫ비인가ᄒᆞ노라외국에셔한국의리ᄒᆡ관계ᄂᆞᆫ거의업다고ᄒᆞᆯ만ᄒᆞ나외국에ᄃᆡ표쟈를보니ᄂᆞᆫ쥬의ᄂᆞᆫ독립국을표ᄒᆞᆷ이오타국에ᄃᆡᄒᆞ야외교샹평등권을확실히ᄒᆞᆷ이라졍말ᄉᆞ무ᄂᆞᆫ니우젹을ᄲᅮᆫ아니라잇더라도외국에잇ᄂᆞᆫ공ᄉᆞ의찬죠업시도다셔울에셔능히히갈터이니실샹은ᄃᆡ표쟈들을보니ᄂᆞᆫ거시다만외양을위ᄒᆞᆷ이니경비를만히드리ᄂᆞᆫ거ᄉᆞᆫ쓸대업도다젼에외국가ᄂᆞᆫ한국공ᄉᆞ들이그임디에아니잔ᄯᅢ에ᄂᆞᆫ그월급과경비를도로니논젹도잇셧고그슈원들도원졍ᄒᆞᆫ것보다젹게간ᄯᅢ도잇셧ᄂᆞᆫ지라각공ᄉᆞ관에공ᄉᆞ하나와참셔관하나면각식ᄉᆞ무에족족유여ᄒᆞ고그경비도ᄶᅡ러져어셔아모라도반ᄃᆡᄒᆞᆯ거시업시되리라ᄒᆞ노라

잡보

○평찰보고 평안남도관찰ᄉᆞ리즁하씨가니부로보고ᄒᆞ기를회민이샹경ᄒᆞᄂᆞᆫ거슬금지ᄒᆞ라ᄂᆞᆫ면보가잇ᄉᆞ온바의병과유계가쳐쳐에셔션동ᄒᆞᆫ다ᄂᆞᆫ말은혹젼문이잇스나본도니에ᄂᆞᆫ아직각군에셔확보가업고회민은부하에ᄂᆞᆫ슈회소라칭ᄒᆞ고각군에ᄂᆞᆫ다지회소를셜시ᄒᆞ야렬도에부역ᄒᆞ기를조원ᄒᆞ고왕리부절ᄒᆞ니어ᄂᆞ날에어ᄂᆞ길노샹경ᄒᆞᆯᄂᆞᆫ지과연금지ᄒᆞ기어렵다ᄒᆞ엿더라

○목탄분죠 의쥬군슈구완회씨가외부로보고ᄒᆞ기를현금에안동현에잇ᄂᆞᆫ일본군졍관부원무경의죠회를졉ᄒᆞᆫ즉니기에현금에군용목탄이시급ᄒᆞ야림시축셩단쟝에의합ᄒᆞᆷ을엇어일인궁면졍일을명ᄒᆞ야귀군고셩면등디에셔목탄을급속히구위문ᄃᆞᄂᆞᆫᄃᆡ귀군에셔특별히감관을졍ᄒᆞ야곰구워슈송케ᄒᆞ라ᄒᆞᆫ바사실ᄒᆞ여보건ᄃᆡ히면산림은본시빅마산셩구역니에잇셔조리로수호ᄒᆞ고금양ᄒᆞ든거시나지금군용샹에시급히소용ᄒᆞᆫ다ᄒᆞᄂᆞᆫ고로인원을파송ᄒᆞ야목탄을문드러쥬기로ᄒᆞ엿노라ᄒᆞ엿더라

○공진회공합 작일공진회에셔법부대신의게공합ᄒᆞᆷ이여좌ᄒᆞ니

경계쟈ᄂᆞᆫ현금지슈ᄒᆞᆫ본회회원리쥰과윤효졍과유셩삼인이ᄒᆞᆫ사ᄅᆞᆷ의관계ᄲᅮᆫ아니라이에국민의이천만되ᄂᆞᆫ표어ᄂᆞᆯ억지로ᄡᅥ이셰사ᄅᆞᆷ이쳐역ᄒᆞᄂᆞᆫ데항복지아니ᄒᆞᄂᆞᆫ것을즁역에쳐ᄒᆞ니어것이이에이천만인을합ᄒᆡ쳐역ᄒᆞᄂᆞᆫ것이라이천만인으로ᄒᆞ여곰올치아니ᄒᆞᆫ법에쳐ᄒᆞ고나라가편안ᄒᆞ고ᄇᆡᆨ셩이보젼ᄒᆞᆯᄭᅥ시보오너젼일샹합ᄒᆞᆫ것은직칙이이에잇거ᄂᆞᆯ오히려엇지ᄒᆞ라지휘도업고ᄯᅩ엇지ᄒᆞ라가라침도업스니인민의평실각ᄒᆞ를과망ᄒᆞᄂᆞᆫ것이파연어ᄃᆡ잇스며지관쟝이되야ᄯᅩ이ᄀᆞᆺ치법을그릇치며법샹이되야이ᄀᆞᆺ치안연이안져보면무릇안과밧의평론ᄒᆞᆫ고지관ᄒᆞᄂᆞᆫ쟈ㅣ각하가아니면엇더ᄒᆞᆫ사ᄅᆞᆷ으로ᄡᅥᄒᆞ리오특별이더싱각ᄒᆞ야그른법에이르지말게ᄒᆞ기를바란다ᄒᆞ엿더라

○헌병부죠회 광무팔년일월이십삼일에평택군에사ᄂᆞᆫ류이완이가농샹공부에쳥원ᄒᆞ기를본군남면월미쵸평에ᄉᆡᆼ나무를심을터이니인가ᄒᆞ여달나ᄒᆞᆫ지라농샹공부에셔제ᄉᆞᄒᆞ기를과연소애됨이업거든심으라ᄒᆞ엿더니현금일본헌병ᄉᆞ령부에셔농샹공부로죠회ᄒᆞ기를평택남면에잇ᄂᆞᆫ원야팔빅뎡여보를귀대신이류인완의게인허ᄒᆞ야즁졍ᄒᆞ엿ᄂᆞᆫ지묘ᄉᆞᄒᆞᆷ이요긴ᄒᆞ니속히회시ᄒᆞ라ᄒᆞ엿더라

○일관ᄃᆡ힝군슈 각군슈령의유권물보가삼십여과라일본공ᄉᆞ가니부로공함ᄒᆞ기를관쟝이업ᄂᆞᆫ고을에ᄂᆞᆫᄇᆡᆨ셩이의지ᄒᆞᆯ데가업스니본공ᄉᆞ가일본관리로ᄒᆞ여금치졍을ᄃᆡ힝ᄒᆞᆯ터이니히경비를의례히지발ᄒᆞ라ᄒᆞ엿더라

○군대급원쟝 군부대신리윤용씨ᄂᆞᆫ소쳬가되고그ᄃᆡ에ᄂᆞᆫ리종건씨가피임ᄒᆞ고륙군법원쟝운빅셩과씨가피임ᄒᆞ엿더라

○쟝곡쳔고시 조금이후로ᄂᆞᆫ경셩니외와밋그부근디에쳐안경찰은한국경관에ᄃᆡᄒᆞ야일본군사령부헌병으로ᄒᆞ야곰ᄃᆡ리경찰을담임케ᄒᆞᆫ다ᄒᆞ엿더라

○관광인피효 ᄇᆡᆨ번인산셰에관광자의면차탄수효가삼만륙쳔여명이라더라

○ᄒᆡ셔순찰보고 황ᄒᆡ도순찰ᄉᆞ뎡규회가니부에보고ᄒᆞ기를ᄒᆡ셔각군즁봉산황쥬ᄂᆞᆫ일본병참이잇ᄂᆞᆫ고로일인의슈용이만흔데음력륙월로지우금륙ᄀᆡ월을광관ᄒᆞ야읍무거대ᄒᆞ니재망이잇ᄂᆞᆫ사ᄅᆞᆷ이아니면진무ᄒᆞ기가어려우니이미령위관을지낸관원즁외교에연숙ᄒᆞᄂᆞᆫ사ᄅᆞᆷ을택차ᄒᆞ야보니라ᄒᆞ엿더라

○경긔슈령진참 금번인산에경긔슈령은다샹경ᄒᆞ야공고에진참ᄒᆞ엿더라

○고문힝공 외부고문관스틔분씨가금월초싱브터힝공ᄒᆞ야시무ᄒᆞᆯ터인ᄃᆡ각국에셔균쳠리익으로쳥구ᄒᆞᄂᆞᆫ금광ᄉᆞ건도귀졍ᄒᆞ고갑오이후에각국인이손ᄒᆡ당ᄒᆞᆫᄉᆞ건도죠사ᄒᆞᆯ터이라더라

○긔령화지 긔령군슈가외부로보고ᄒᆞ기를음력십일월이십일밤오시량에본군남면부샹리에잇ᄂᆞᆫ일인에집에셔실화ᄒᆞ야일인의집륙호와우리ᄇᆡᆨ셩의집십사호가모ᄃᆡ연소ᄒᆞ야일인륙명은죽고사인은피샹ᄒᆞ고우리ᄇᆡᆨ셩일명은죽고이명은피샹ᄒᆞ엿스니이러ᄒᆞᆫ엄동에졍경이참혹ᄒᆞ오니룡축ᄒᆞ신후특별히싱각ᄒᆞ야휼금을쥬시기를바란다ᄒᆞ엿더라

○아산민소 아산둔포거ᄒᆞᄂᆞᆫ리덕쥰이가외부에호소ᄒᆞ기를경셩에거ᄒᆞᄂᆞᆫ박형리가본인의쟝형으로더브러무슨거리됴건이잇다가계미년분에쟝형이죽고즁형으로더브러다시거리됴이만삼빅여량이쟝칙에잇ᄂᆞᆫᄃᆡ금년삼월분에박형리가일인삼명을거ᄂᆞ리고저의집의리도ᄒᆞ야굴으ᄃᆡ너의쟝형쳐의밧을됴건이만여량이잇다ᄒᆞᄂᆞᆫ고로리치를들어칙망ᄒᆞᆫ즉ᄃᆡ답ᄒᆞᆯ말이업셔물너가더니ᄯᅩ지난ᄃᆞᆯ초ᄉᆞ일에일인삼명과동ᄉᆞ일명을거ᄂᆞ리고와셔안방으로곳드러와피를ᄡᅥ치고돈이쳔여량과위로문권을ᄲᅢ셔갓스니세샹이엇지이리ᄒᆞᆫ강도가잇스리오곳일공관에지죠ᄒᆞ야히일인등을잡아견달ᄒᆞᆫ물건을찾게ᄒᆞ야ᄡᅥ잔인ᄒᆞᆫᄇᆡᆨ셩을살게ᄒᆞ라ᄒᆞ엿더라

○부지하시귀결 향일대안문압헤셔일진회보호ᄒᆞᄂᆞᆫ일본헌병의게돌을던진ᄉᆞ건으로그ᄯᅢᄉᆞ졸을륙군법원에셔처판ᄒᆞ엿ᄂᆞᆫᄃᆡᄉᆞ령관쟝곡쳔씨ᄂᆞᆫ오히려온히치못ᄒᆞ야그세에ᄉᆞ졸을지휘ᄒᆞ든쟝관을지시ᄒᆞ라ᄒᆞ고군부대신과샹지즁이라이진판이어ᄂᆞᄯᅢ에귀결될ᄂᆞᆫ지모르겟다더라

○지유하슌 ᄉᆞ졸등이돌던진ᄉᆞ건으로일본헌병이잡아간지라황샹ᄭᅴ셔쟝곡쳔의게ᄃᆡᄒᆞ야ᄉᆞ졸잡아간일을하슌ᄒᆞ옵셧더니쟝곡쳔은쥬쳥ᄒᆞ기를이런일을엇던신하신이자세이샹쥬ᄒᆞ엿ᄂᆞᆫ지그신하의셩명을하시ᄒᆞ옵소셔ᄒᆞ엿더라

○공진공함 일작에공진회에셔경무ᄉᆞ신태휴씨의게공함ᄒᆞᆷ이여좌ᄒᆞ니

경계쟈ᄂᆞᆫᄇᆡᆨ셩이가진물건을관가에셔ᄲᅢ앗ᄂᆞᆫ것파민회사무소를억지로봉쇄ᄒᆞᄂᆞᆫ거시만국통규에대단히격외여ᄂᆞᆯ사무소를누번이나봉쇄ᄒᆞᄂᆞᆫ거시무슨별ᄒᆞᆫ률례를의거ᄒᆞᆷ이며본회에셔쓰든쟝작삼원어치와기타사션샹과밋교의등즙물을귀쳥으로셔륙박ᄒᆞ야졈득ᄒᆞ엿스니ᄯᅩᄒᆞᆫ무ᄉᆞᆫ가거ᄒᆞᆯ공법이잇습나잇가어ᄂᆞ법에근리ᄒᆞᆷ이만무ᄒᆞ니귀쳥에셔힝졍ᄒᆞ며시무ᄒᆞᄂᆞᆫ거시모다이러ᄒᆞᆫ고로외국슈모가날노니르고니치가날노어조려우미ᄒᆞ오직각하ᄂᆞᆫ특별히세번싱각ᄒᆞ야본회사무소ᄂᆞᆫ곳ᄀᆡ통케ᄒᆞ고우희말ᄒᆞᆫ즙물도ᄯᅩᄒᆞᆫ곳환완ᄒᆞ야공규에억입이업게ᄒᆞ심을바란다ᄒᆞ엿더라

광고

TELEGRAMS.

Tokyo, Jan. 6th.

On the morning of the 5th inst., General Nogi had an interview with General Stoessel at Suishing. Yesterday the 5,000 surrendered combatants arrived at the appointed place.

Jan. 6th.

The Czar has supended his inspection of the troops in southern Russia and returned to St. Petersbug.—Daihan Ilpo.

Jan. 6th.

The Japanese squadron are cruising in the vicinity of Singapore and the straits of Java, Sumatra and Borneo. There are also a few ships near Amoy and Hongkong. France is preparing to prevent the Baltic Feet passing Madagascar.

Tokyo, Jan. 4th.

General Nogi reports that after the Etzeshan and some neighbouring forts had been handed over as a guarantee of good faith, the city of Port Arthur was entered, and it was then seen that the city was in fairly good condition, but the sanitary conditions were horrible. There were 10,000 noncombatants and 25,000 combatants, but of the latter 20,000 were either sick or wounded Every assistance is now being rendered to these.

OPEN DOOR FOR MANCHURIA.

Paris, November 19.—The Chinese Minister in Paris, Souen Packi, has come out as an advocate of applying Secretary Hay's open door policy to Manchuria. The Minister belongs to the Liberal-Progressive element, and has recently addressed a memorial to the Throne urging the gravity of the question which will arise when the present war ends, particularly the maintenance of Chinese sovereignty over Manchuria. In the course of an interview to-day the Minister said: "Whether Russia or Japan is victorious, it will be essential that the victor recognise China's complete authority over Manchuria. It will be natural for the victor to expect special privileges within the territory forming the theatre of the conflict, but China's rights in Manchuria being unquestionable, neither belligerent can claim privileges growing out of coming to fight upon our territory. If any single Power gains special privileges in Manchuria it will operate against the interests of all the other Powers. Therefore, it is to the interest of the world at large to foresee the conclusion of the war and guard against either of the Powers obtaining a privileged position in Manchuria. The Court at Peking is now considering certain measures for reform, and it is just possible that one of the chief results will be an extension of the open door policy to Manchuria and certain other parts of the empire, which thus far have been outside the range of the open door."

The Korean soldiers who were arrested at the time of the Il-Chin Hoi disturbance have been punished according to Korean military laws, but General Hasegawa has announced that he considers the punishment insufficient.

A complaint with the Foreign Office has been lodged by a Korean named Yi Duk Chun, a resident of Asan. This gentleman asserts that for many years, his brothers and he have been carrying on business with a Seoul man named Pak Hyung Nai. Recently his elder brother died and Pak made a false claim against the brothers for a large sum of money, but on the books being shown, Pak announced himself satisfied. However a few days ago he returned, accompanied by three Japanese, and broke into the house, carrying away $1,000 in cash and the title deeds of some fields. Yi requests the Foreign Office to secure, through their Legation, justice on the three Japanese, who assisted in the robbery.

EDUCATING HER EMIGRANTS.

Germany's new move to establish schools for the instruction of intending emigrants will doubtless be carried through with the thoroughness characteristic of every educational move in that country. After a study of history and economic conditions of the land he proposes to settle in, it is to be expected that the emigrant will be better fitted for his new life there. German solidity and steady agressiveness and a stand-pat-to-the-fatherland attitude is now in various Brazilian settlements, giving rise to speculation among American public men. The Germans now exercise a commerical supremacy in South Brazil, and in addition hold tenaciously to the customs, language and traditions of their fatherland.

In the Far East an analogous condition exists, which will presently draw the interested attention of Japanese statesman. Kiaochow Bay, which the Germans occupied temporarily in 1898, has since been quietly leased from China for a term of 99 years. It is now a highly prosperous, fortified German colony, with roads branching out through the Shantung province. The work was undertaken with the persevering thoroughness and ability of the Teuton, and now Germany has not only a small Colony, but a coaling station and harbour for its fleet of warships in the East.—Montreal Daily Star.

Permission was granted last year to a man named Yu In Wan to plant mulberry trees on certain waste lands at Wolmi and Cho Pyeng. Japanese gendarmes are now making enquiries from the Agricultural Department as to the truth of this, but for what reason is not known.

The Japanese Minister has informed the Home Office that there are over 30 districts in the country without magistrates, and the people of these places find themselves consequently much embarrased. He states that in future, Japanese Authorities will administer these districts, but the Korean Government will have to pay the expenses.

A Swatow despatch dated December 29, received by the "Tokyo Asahi," states that on the 24th inst. the British steamer "Wakefield," while steaming in the neighbourhood of Turtle rock, near Swatow, China, ran on to an uncharted rock and became a total wreck. The Captain and 28 of the crew were saved. No futher particulars concerning the accident have been yet received.

The Magistrate of Wiju reports that he has received instructions, from the Japanese military authorities at Autungsen, to send someone to cooperate with a Japanese, who has been sent to Paikmasen to prepare a large quantity of charcoal to be sent to Autungsen. The Magistrate states that he finds himself in a quandary as this proceedure is entirely against the laws of the government, but the charcoal is urgently needed by the Japanese troops.

The Governor of Pyengyang replying to instructions received from the Home Office to prohibit Il Chin Hoi people from leaving for Seoul, states that the headquarters of the society are in his city but there are many branches of the society scattered throughout the country which he finds himself unable to control. Further many of the society's members are working on the railway, and these would be able to leave at any time without his knowledge.

The "Sporting Times" has discovered Ipoh. It says, at Ipoh, which is somewhere in the Malay States, a Protestant padre sometimes turns up to hold service. Before he arrives a native orderly goes the rounds of the whites in the district with a paper, announcing time, &c., of the service, and each European initials the paper to show that he has seen it. The padre scratched his head and then laughed when he found that a polite new-comer had put against his initials "Very sorry, Roman Catholic."

TWO SISTERS WHO ARE PHYSICALLY ONE.

There have arrived in London from Liege the Misses Rosa and Josefa Blazek, who are, no doubt, the most extraordinary examples of human abnormality in existence.

Probably no physiological curiosity of equal interest has been seen in England since Eng and Chang, the Siamese Twins, visited London in 1869 before settling down in a Southern State of American, where they married two sisters, who reared healthy, normal families.

The physical condition of the Misses Blazek differs little from that of the late Siamese Twins. The bodies of the latter were connected near the chest; in the case of these young women the adhesion occurs for some distance up the side, terminating slightly above the waist. Their heads are not quite on a level, Josefa being somewhat the taller of the two. Although the girls of necessity spend their lives side by side, they cannot look into each other's faces. The most that is possible is a sidelong glance that Rosa is enabled to take of her interdependent, but mentally the girls have a separate existence. Nor do their tastes, inclinations, or temperaments coincide. Consequently, they live in a state of constant compromise. The couple—if the plural be permissible—appear very happy and contented, or, as Rosa explained, "We are very much attached to each other in every respect.

The sisters enjoy the usual complement of limbs. They walk with a sprightly, nimble movement, but, of course, four feet are seen in operation, and when the necessity arises for them to lift a heavy article four arms and hands are extended for the purpose.

Born in Prague, the capital of Bohemia, the twins are twenty-six years of age. They speak no language save their native Czech. Mr. Franz Blazek, the father, is a successful farmer. His eldest daughter, who is quite normal, married some years ago, and has now four children. Mr. Blazek has also a son, seventeen years of age.

Through Mr. B. Sherek, who acted as interpreter, the remarkable twins explained that this was their first visit to London.

"It is all very wonderful," said Rosa, and she slipped off the chair in which both sisters had seated themselves, and ran towards the window to take another peep at the ceaseless stream of vehicles. Josefa, who is much the stouter of the two, betrayed by her looks a reluctance to share the restless animation of the more enthusiastic twin; but Rosa's is the dominating character, the stronger mind, and the sister had perforce, if unwillingly, to participate in her actions.

"I am always the victim," said Josefa smiling. "Some time ago Rosa had influenza, and I, although perfectly well, had to lie in bed for a whole week. And I received none of the champagne and other luxuries that were given to Rosa! Night and day I had to lie there, expecting every moment to catch Rosa's influenza; but, like the other things, she kept it to herself."

(To be continued)

KOREAN NEWS IN JAPAN.

The following, taken from the "Japan Ma'li' is a fair average specimen of Korean news as published in Japan:—

Riots of a somewhat serious nature are reported from Seoul. It is already known to the public that two parties in the capital, who claim to be inspired by motives of refrom, recently joined hands for the purpose of procuring the expulsion of the band of necromancers and soothsayers whose pernicious counsels are believed to have much influence on the Court. Recently the police arrested two prominent men of these parties, whereupon a large crowd of their followers repaired to the policestation, and loudly demanded that the trial of the prisoners should be conducted in public. Presently a strong force of constables mustered, and resorting to force, they dispersed the mob causing several casualties among the latter. Thereafter the people repaired to the Palace and cried for justice. They were induced to disperse in consideration of the fact that the "convenances" were violated by such a demonstration at the Palace gates while the Court was still in mourning. But although they left the Palace it was only to proceed to the Bell Tower, where, in the main square of the city, they listened to harangues by their officers. Presently the police again appeared upon the scene, and again hadrecourse to the strong hand, with the result that there were futher casualties. The Emperor is reported to be consulting with General Hasegawa as to the most effective method of restoring tranquility.

THE BURMESE OATH.

"As is well known, perjury," says a Rangoon paper, "is rife in the Courts of Burma generally and in Rangoon in particular," because no form of oath exists which the Burman regards as binding on his conscience. This question having discussed in the vernacular papers, the Government after much consideration has published in the Burmese edition of the "Burma Gazette" a formula of oath to be administered to all Burmese Buddhists in future. It is described by the "Rangoon Gazeette" as "a queer admixture of Buddhism, Brahmanism and Shamanism," which will be unintelligible to nine Burmans out of ten, and "the teuth would not care a jot for half its contents." The oath which should take not less than 15 minutes to recite, is a string of damnatory clauses, very creepy and blood-curdling. Three of them are picked at random:—"If I do tell a lie let the Nat who guards the relics of Sariputra........ kill and pulverise me," If an untruth passes my lips, may all the Nats of the five great rivers of India . . Destroy me. May curdled blood pass my lips rather than a lie, and may I die vomiting blood, my body bent in two."

There will be another celebration of the taking of Port Arthur in the Japanese club this evening.

The Korea Daily News.

Issued at 5 P. M. daily except Sundays.

Rate of Subscription:—
Per Year,............Yen 25.
Per Quarter,..........Yen 7.
Per Month,..........Yen 2.50.

Postage in Korea not charged extra.
Postage abroad charged extra.

Advertisements, 50 sen per day for 1 inch or less.
5 yen per month per inch.
50 yen per year per inch.

All communications to
E. T. BETHELL,
Editor and Publisher,
Pak-tong, Seoul.

AFTER THE WAR.

The "Daily Mail" (Japan) in concluding an article on affairs in China says "We cannot but speculate what the Wai-wu-pu would do in the presence of any symptoms of Japanese discomfiture." Those whose mental horizon is limited may also exercise their brains in speculating what the Koreans will do in like case.

We lay claim to no more than ordinary intelligence, but it is to us as plain as a pikestaff that the Japanese have put all their eggs into one basket and staked everything upon their success in the war.

We have repeatedly urged upon the Japanese authorities that the present is no time for a policy of aggression such as they seem bent on pursuing in Korea, and we are perfectly confident that, brilliant soldiers as the Japanese are, a day will inevitably come when they will wish they had made friends of the Korean people instead of enemies. People in Japan have only a vague idea of the situation here. Their information comes from correspondents who get their "news" from Japanese officials upon whose favour they are absolutely dependent. The Japanese journals accuse us of pro-Russian tendencies and we can certainly reply by calling them pro-Japanese, to and beyond, a fault. Nothing reflecting adversely on the Japanese or their protegees is allowed to leave Korea.

But the indisputable fact remains that whatever the Koreans, under intimidation may say to the contrary, there will be a great shout of the Korean equivalent for "Banzai" when the exodu of their oppressors begins. We do not expect to see any obstacles placed in the path of departing Japanese.

Of China we are not so sure, but a few paragraphs, taken from China papers, may serve to show which way the wind blows:—

"Since the discovery that certain students have been connected with the Hunan revolutionary party, the Government has instructed Na Tung and a certain Minister to interview the Japanese Minister regarding the control of the students in Japan."

"The Board of Foreign Affairs have telegraphed to the Chinese Minister in Japan ordering him to send a monthly list of the names of those students who are being privately educated in the schools and colleges of Japan."

"The Grand Council has been personally instructed by the Empress Dowager to telegraph to the different Viceroys and Governors instructing them to be carefnl in the future in the selection of students for education abroad."

It may be remembered that some time ago a Chinese of some prominence in official circles was, by misrepresentations, lured to a place in Shanghai, and on his endeavouring to make his way out of the house again he was shot at. The Japan Mail, speaking of this, says that "he escaped assassination or at any rate assault" Now "assault" is a nice expression for being shot at, and to our mind the apologies of the "Japan Mail" only add significance to the incident.

With two previsions, the article in the "Japan Mail" is worth reproduction. We would first remind our readers that in its pro-Japanese views the "J. M." out Herods Herod and secondly we wish to call attention to the amusing way in which the "Japan Mail" refuses to commit itself to any statement as to what Japan would do if she *did* get Manchuria. The "J. M." says "the case will be very different." However here is the article:—

The unwarlike Chinese Government naturally has frequent fits of trembling when it looks abroad and observes the menaces growing on the horizon of the empire. Should Russia emerge victorious from the present war, what will be her attitude towards the Middle Kingdom, then lying completely at her mercy, She will have under her hand an immense instrument of coercion. No outside Power will possess the means or the inclination to stand between her and the *spolia opima* of so costly a war, and China herself cannot project any wiser role than feeble acquiescence in everything dicated. The permanent addition of Manchuria to the Russian empire will be the smallest part of the results. If Japan wins, the case will be very different, but what troubles China is the other contingency, and well it may trouble her; for in the constant remonstrances addressed to her by Russia with reference to Hunghutsz and other complicating factors, she must clearly discern the compilation of an account which, should occasion arise, will show the Middle Kingdom heavily in debt to the Northern Colossus. It appears that Mr. Wang Chih-chung, who recently escaped assassination, or at any rate assault, at Shanghai, has again been playing on these fears, and that he is assisted by Mr. Yang, the adopted son of the late Li Hung-chang and inheritor of his eminent father's political beliefs. These two men have been urging upon Peking that Russia must win in the long run; that her might is irresistible, and that the only wise course for China is to agree with her enemy quickly while he is in the gate. The Peking statesmen are reported to have been thrown into a state of considerable trepidation by these counsels, conveyed again and again by letter and by telegram, the latter medium being adroitly used by Wang and Yang, who have cleverly gauged the disturbing influence exercised on an ordinary mind by the receipt of a telegraphic message. But rumour says that some degree of serenity has been restored in the Chinese capital by the report of a high official of the Board of Records—we can not identify his transliterated name—who recently returned from a tour of inspection in the Mukden district, and who declares, as the result of his own personal observation, that the Russians can not win. We wonder whence the nex alarm will come to Peking, and we can not but speculate what the Wai-wu-pu would do in the presence of any symptoms of Japanese discomfiture.

THE SINKING OF THE "SAIYEN."

The following details of the sinking of the cruiser "Saiyen" in Shuangteu bay, as translated by the "Japan Times," are furnished by Lieut-Commander Okuda, second in command of the ill-starred vessel, and one of the survivors of the accident:—

It was at 2.24 P. M. on the 30th ult. when our vessel struck an enemy's mine I was ordered by Captain Tajima to take the necessary steps to save her, but I was powerless, the vessel having heavily listed to the starboard side in less than two minutes after the explosion of the mine. Meanwhile the vessel was fast going down, but the Captain still remained at his post, rejecting all my remonstrances to take to the boat. Finally the vessel sank, the Captain, 18 other officers (including myself), six quasi-officers, and over 140 petty officers and men being whirled into the waves. After a short while, several of us came up to the surface of the water and then there arose a chorus of cries, "Captain!" But there was no reply; the Captain was nowhere to be seen. Meanwhile the merciless enemy on Laotiehshan was pouring a deadly fire upon us, and it was with great difficulty that our warships in the neighbourhood engaged in our rescue. The search was continued even during the night, but no trace could be seen of the Captain and 31 others. The work was resumed the next day, only to end in the same result.

The vessel having been struck below the front engine-room, five men working there were instantly killed, while only three effected their escape from the back engine-room. At the time of the accident the vessel had on board three boats and a steam launch, but only two of the former were lowered, the Chief Paymaster, a Second Sub-Lieutenant and 60 to 70 petty officers and men embarking in them. Just prior to the sinking of the "Saiyen," the Captain was standing on the port and I on the starboard side, so that I must have been the first of the two to fall into the water. When I came to the surface I found and seized a hammock, and was picked up after remaining about half an hour in the water. The cold was not specially felt whilst we were in the water, but once taken into the boat, the cold was most severe, five of the rescued succumbing.

At the last moments of the sinking vessel, Sub-Lieutenant Yasuji Naritomi ran down from the upper deck and succeeded in taking out H. M. the Emperor's photograph, which he left in charge of Chief Signalman Shingo Yamaguchi, and again rushed down and brought out that of H. I. H. the Crown Prince. But he was unable to reach the deck again, for the Vessel was being rapidly flooded, and he therefore jumped into the sea in order to save the photograph and himself. Fortunately he found a board in the water, to which he clung until he was rescued.

SILVER SUITE FOR A PRINCE.

An extraordinary suite of furniture, the sumptuousness of which recalls a scene from the "Arabian Nights," has just been made in London. Constructed throughout of soild silver, it is destined for the Eastern palace of an Indian prince. A massive four-post bedstead, which has absorbed a ton of silver, twelve dining-room chairs, four tables, two divans, a lady's dressing-table, and a cabinet made up the suite, which took nearly a year to make. Weighing altogether over four tons, its value is estimated at £15,000. Over the bed is an allegorical panel symbolising "Sleep."

His Excellency Chou-fu has advised the Chinese Government to employ more British for financial, and Japanese for miliary, reforms. The compliment is almost a double-edged one.

The Korea Daily News

VOL. II, SATURDAY, JANUARY 7, 1905. No. 4

大韓每日申報
대한미일신보

(뎨이권오호) (화요일) 일쳔구빅오년일월십일

본샤고빅

이신보는영어와한어로셔거미일슐판ᄒᆞᄋᆞᆸ

신문가

한장 엽두돈오푼
일삭료 엽두량닷돈
우표가미 삭닷돈
다맛돈으로밧슴

광고료는

긔한의쟝단과ᄌᆞ힝의다쇼로죵감ᄒᆞ되렴가로밧을터이오며오리지아니ᄒᆞ여대한사람마다다이신문을보실터이니광고내시기를원ᄒᆞ시ᄂᆞᆫ이들은우리신문샤에와셔면약ᄒᆞ심을희망ᄒᆞᄋᆞᆸ

○발힝소 박동대한미일신보샤법어학교압헤젼영국인셜필림집자리오
사쟝 영국인 (비셜)

평양 디리뎜

○평양효동사ᄂᆞᆫ권미보씨로우리신문판매디리인을뎡ᄒᆞ엿ᄉᆞ오니평양에계신구람코져ᄒᆞ시ᄂᆞᆫ쳠군ᄌᆞᄂᆞᆫ히디리뎜에왕림ᄒᆞ와면의ᄒᆞ시ᄋᆞᆸ

사고

○우리대한미일신보의목뎍은대한의안녕질셔에관한모든뎨목에디ᄒᆞ야ᄂᆞᆫ공평한변론을쥬쟝홈이라우리통신원의탐보ᄂᆞᆫ신문보시ᄂᆞᆫ쳠군ᄌᆞ의게항상보도ᄒᆞ리며편지를긔셔ᄒᆞ여주시ᄂᆞᆫ이ᄂᆞᆫ셩명파반디를젹어붓치시기를희망ᄒᆞ오니이거슬신문샹에긔지ᄒᆞ라ᄂᆞᆫ거시아니오다만극히신용ᄒᆞᄂᆞᆫ증거를숨고자홈이라긔쟈ᄂᆞᆫ아모긔셔던지긔지홈을되각ᄒᆞᄂᆞᆫ권리를가졋스나되각ᄒᆞᄂᆞᆫ리유를말홀터이오며공즁평화를문란케ᄒᆞᄂᆞᆫ듯ᄒᆞᆫ긔셔ᄂᆞᆫ의례히밧지안켓ᄉᆞᆸ나이다

●본샤셜시이ᄅᆡ로신문을미양우례로분젼ᄒᆞ와례젼부의임의로젼ᄒᆞᆫ즛스로먼곳에ᄂᆞᆫ혹늣게젼ᄒᆞ기도ᄒᆞ며혹몃칠거슬ᄒᆞᆫ겁에젼ᄒᆞ기도ᄒᆞ며혹아니젼ᄒᆞᄂᆞᆫ곳도잇다ᄒᆞ와우리신문을ᄉᆞ랑ᄒᆞ야구람ᄒᆞ시ᄂᆞᆫ 쳠군ᄌᆞ의게디ᄒᆞ야미우미안ᄒᆞᄋᆞᆸ기로지금은분젼인을두고미일일즉이젼ᄒᆞ며아니젼ᄒᆞ거나늣게거나ᄒᆞᆫ폐가업도록ᄒᆞ랴ᄒᆞ오니혹아니젼ᄒᆞ거나늣게젼ᄒᆞ거나ᄒᆞᆫ일이잇스면본샤로통긔ᄒᆞ여쥬심을희망ᄒᆞᄋᆞᆸ

관보

뎨삼쳔삼십호 광무구년
일월칠일
셔임급ᄉᆞ령
○히위문ᄉᆞ 의졍부찬졍륙군
부쟝 권즁현
광무팔년십이월삼십일일
○히분비셔원랑 홍문관시독
졍홍셕
일월사일
○명궁니부특진관셔칙임관일
등 졍일픔 민영휘
○명궁니부특진관셔칙임관이
등 비셔원경 박용대
○명비셔원경셔칙임관이등
의졍부찬졍 리지현
○명궁니부특진관셔칙임관사
등 봉샹사졔됴 민영국
○명봉샹사졔됴셔칙임관사등
비셔원승 김태제
○의원면본관 홍문관시독 박
히철 홍문관시독 졍홍셕
죵묘셔령 쟝길샹
○히시종원분시어 륙군삼등
군사 홍건 죵삼픔 유셕관
사픔 빅남승 구픔 유정희
구픔 구상회 구픔 채명셕
구픔 젼우셕 구픔 김필제
구픔 리병션 구픔 김현룡
구픔 김병일 구픔 리규일
구픔 리봉영 구픔 최영죠
구픔 조광리 구픔 박재관
구픔 샹린식 구픔 윤영비
구픔 원경
○히시종원분쥬사 슌강원슈
봉관 쳔궁식 농샹공부쥬사
송국리 구픔 쥬판홍
○임홍문관시독셔판임관륙등
비셔원랑 리문구 륙픔 양
재팔
○임비셔원승셔주임관오등
졍삼픔 신헌균
○임비셔원랑셔판임관칠등
륙픔 김재사
○임죵묘셔령셔판임관사등
교방사쥬사 김교헌
○임교방사쥬사셔판임관사등
태복사쥬사 리호집
○임태복사쥬사셔판임관사등
륙픔 쟝길샹
이샹일월오일

궁뎐록사

○죠서ᄒᆞ야갈아샤ᄃᆡ황히도황쥬군철도류비십오년죄인신셕효ᄂᆞᆫ방송ᄒᆞ라ᄒᆞ시다

광무구년일월오일
의졍부참졍 김셩근

외부대신리하영사직소 비지
셩소구실경간이라이때에병말ᄒᆞᄂᆞᆫ것이이엇지분의ᄭᅥ보녀그다시번거치말고곳시무ᄒᆞ라ᄒᆞ시고부랑을보니여션유ᄒᆞ시다

군부대신리윤용ᄌᆞ렬쇼비지셩쇼구실경간이라임이지난지라반다시기리홀것이업스니사양ᄒᆞᆫ바ᄂᆞᆫ의시라ᄒᆞᄋᆞᆸ시고부랑을보니여션유ᄒᆞ시다

이샹일월오일

뎐보

사일일본공사관착

긔셩실힝 려슌공위일본군ᄉᆞ목대쟝의보고요령에여좌ᄒᆞ니의조산파기타수긔포디ᄂᆞᆫ오후일시삼십분에긔셩규약실힝ᄒᆞᄂᆞᆫ담보로우리군사의게줌이되엿더라

○젼력구죠 져자와가로ᄂᆞᆫ평온ᄒᆞ며현금잇ᄂᆞᆫ인원은젼투ᄒᆞᆫ지아니ᄒᆞᆫ인원이거진일만명이나되며젼투ᄒᆞᄂᆞᆫ인원이이만오쳔인ᄂᆡ에이만은병든쟈이며식료ᄂᆞᆫ도모지업스며우리군사ᄂᆞᆫ힘을다ᄒᆞ야구죠ᄒᆞᄂᆞᆫ즁이라ᄒᆞ엿더라

론돈발 십이월이십팔일

○일본증병 일본군사쥬무쟈가만쥬군총사령관오야마원슈의휘하에오십만명의군사를두고ᄌᆞ병도미우만이느릴계확이라더라

론돈발 십이월이십팔일

○일본엄방 로국히군이디만에나다른남방셔음볼틱함ᄃᆡ를위ᄒᆞ야근거디를졍ᄒᆞᆯ듯ᄒᆞᆫ기로그디방에일본이방슈ᄒᆞ기를엄ᄒᆞ게ᄒᆞ고그곳에잇ᄂᆞᆫ군ᄃᆡ의식물을더슈운ᄒᆞ야보냇다더라

동경발 일월륙일

○법방로함 법국이볼틱함ᄃᆡ의마다가스갈을통과홈을예방ᄒᆞᆫ다더라

동디발 동일

○량쟝회견 본월오일오젼에려슌공위군사령관노기대쟝과로국대쟝스텟셀씨가슈사문안에셔회견ᄒᆞ엿다더라

외보

○동향대쟝의회국 일본히군대쟝동향씨가거월삼십일에동셩에회환홈에졍이잇셧ᄂᆞᆫᄃᆡ이히군영웅을영졉ᄒᆞ기위ᄒᆞ야그곳에셔미우분쥬ᄒᆞ게예비ᄒᆞ엿다ᄂᆞᆫᄃᆡ로함셋사크빗취호ᄂᆞᆫ엇더케비밀히ᄒᆞ엿던지쳥도로도망ᄒᆞ게되엿지마ᄂᆞᆫ동향대쟝의쟈긔에당ᄒᆞᆫ사무에힘쓴것과그결과가쟈긔의게와쟈긔나라에큰명예가되엿다고홀만ᄒᆞ더라

○뎨이소사운하의창셜ᄒᆞᆫ다ᄂᆞᆫ말 론돈에셔거월십칠일에앤지어씨가말ᄒᆞ되지금소사운하회샤에셔셰금을너무즁ᄒᆞ게바드니다시다른운하하나를ᄯᅳᆯ게회을경영ᄒᆞ쟈ᄒᆞ엿다ᄂᆞᆫᄃᆡ젼브터익급에셔실을만히ᄒᆞ던근츅가하나히그일을맛터ᄒᆞ랴고예비ᄒᆞᄂᆞᆫ잇다더라

잡보

○가소담화 작일오후에남촌산림동으로지나다가본즉맛춤병뎡ᄒᆞ나히오다가쟝님ᄒᆞ나흘맛나병뎡이부러쟝님향ᄒᆞᄂᆞᆫᄃᆡ로길을막으며힐란ᄒᆞᆫ즉그쟝님이셔셔말ᄒᆞ기를네가무어시나ᄒᆞ니그병뎡이ᄃᆡ답ᄒᆞ기를네가신쟝님이니졈을처셔내가무어신지알나ᄒᆞᆫ즉그쟝님이왈네가병뎡일다그병뎡이ᄯᅩ말ᄒᆞ기를올타내가과연병뎡일다마ᄂᆞᆫ병뎡도여러층이니무슨병뎡이겟ᄂᆞ냐그쟝님이왈네가하ᄉᆞ로다ᄒᆞᆫ즉그병뎡이웃고말ᄒᆞ기를쟝님이과연귀신ᄀᆞᆺ치아시니내가말슴ᄒᆞ리다내가아직하ᄉᆞᄂᆞᆫ못ᄒᆞ엿고샹등병으로잇ᄉᆞ나쟝님말슴이이ᄀᆞᆺᄒᆞ니미구에하ᄉᆞ를홀줄노아노라ᄒᆞ고다졍이작별ᄒᆞ고가더라

●량씨ᄉᆞ직 참찬허위씨ᄂᆞᆫ금칠일에ᄉᆞ직샹소ᄒᆞ고탁지대신민영긔씨ᄂᆞᆫ명일에ᄉᆞ직샹소ᄒᆞᆫ다더라

○고문제의 탁지고문관목하뎐씨가각도각군호구를졍실이됴사ᄒᆞ기위ᄒᆞ야일인일명식각군에파송ᄒᆞ로제의즁이라더라

UNION INSURANCE SOCIETY OF CANTON.

Head office Hongkong.
Marine risks underwritten at current rates.
Agents in Chemulpo,
E. MEYER & Co.

COMPAGNIE DES MESSAGERIES MARITIMES.

Fortnightly Direct Service.

For Marseilles
via Ports.
Sailing from Yokohama
Calling at Kobe,
Shanghai, Hongkong, Saigon, Singapore,
Colombo, Djibonti, Suez, Port Said
and Marseilles.

For particulars apply to
HOLME RINGER & Co.,
Chemulpo.

HAYASHIDA & CO.,

16 MYENG DONG, CHIN KO KAI, SEOUL.
BRANCH OFFICE AT CHEMULPO.

Money changers, Coal and Wood Merchants, Express Agents.

We are agents for the Pyeng-yang Coal Company and the Karazu Coal Company of Japan. We have the best quality of both an thracite and bituminous coal, and prompt ex ecution of orders is our speciality. Firewood of all kinds kept in stock. Full weight guaranteed. Money of all denominations exchanged at current rates. Parcels received for all parts.

CHINA MUTUAL LIFE INS. OC.

Most favourable terms to policy holders.

Benefit system unsurpassed.

HOLME RINGER & Co.
Agents, Chemulpo.

C. P. R.

CANADIAN PACIFIC RAILWAY COMPANY'S ROYAL MAIL STEAMSHIP LINE.

THE FAST ROUTE BETWEEN CHINA, JAPAN, AND EUROPE VIA CANADA AND THE UNITED STATES

Route from Hongkong via Shanghai, Nagasaki (Inland Sea of Japan) Kobe, Yokohama, Victoria and Vancouver.

Twin Screw Empress Steamship—6,000 Tons—Speed 19 knots.

PROPOSED SAILING FROM YOKOHAMA.
R. M. S. Empress of India.
R. M. S. Empress of Japan.
R. M. S. Empress of China.
R. M. S. Athenian.
R. M. S. Tastar.

Special reduction (first class only) granted to members of the Military, Naval, Diplomatic and Civil services and to Missionaries.

Passengers have choice of ten routes across the Continent of America and have privilege of travelling by any Atlantic Steamship Line.

Round the World passage tickets in connection with the P. and O. S. N., North German Lloyd and Messageries Co.'s **£125.**

All rates payable at current rate of exchange.

For further information, Tickets, Guide Books, etc., apply to

HOLME, RINGER & CO., AGENTS,
Chemulpo.

Grand Hotel,

(Formerly the Station Hotel)

Near the Railway Terminus, West Gate Seoul.

The Best Hotel in Korea.
Handsome new Building.
Fine Airy Rooms
Excellent Cuisine.
Terms Moderate.
Special terms to Missionaries
and to permanent boarders.

Electric cars within 2 minutes' walk.

W. H. EMBERLEY.

Proprietor

EVERY FACILITY.

In connection with Life Assurance Business is afforded by

The Standard Life Assurance Co.,

One of the largest and wealthiest of the Provident Institutions of the United Kingdom. Forms of Application and all information will be promptly afforded on application.

10 CENTS A DAY.

Not a very large expenditure is it? But it is sufficient to secure for a man of 30 a policy with the STANDARD LIFE OFFICE for

$1323.

For all particulars of rates, etc., apply to

Holme, Ringer & Co.,
Agents, Chemulpo.

THE NEW YORK LIFE INSURANCE COMPANY.

Have you ever been declined by any Company?

Are you engaged in a specially hazardous occupation?

Have you heard of the New York Life Insurance Company's New Classifications for this class of Risks?

If not, send your date of birth, occupation and particulars of rejection, if any to

E. MEYER & Co.,
Agents, Chemulpo.

MITSUI BUSSAN KAISHA.
(MITSUI & Co.)

MITSUI GINKO.
(MITSUI BANK.)

The Bank is owned by the members of the Mitsui Family, who, as partners, assume an unmited responsibility for all liabilities of the Bank:—

Capital........................Yen 5,000,000
Reserve Fund.................. " 5,600,000

HEAD OFFICE, TOKYO.
LONDON OFFICE, 34 LIME ST., E. C.

BRANCHES AND AGENCIES:—
New York, San Francisco, Hamburg, Bombay, Singapore, Manila, Hongkong, Amoy, Chefoo, Tientsin.

Kobe, Hakodate, Yokohama, Kure, Yokosuka, Moji, Shimonoseki, Miike, Wakamatsu Nagasaki, Kuchinotsu, Karatsu, Sasebo, Misume, Taipeh, &c.

Telegraphic Address for all the Offices:
"MITSUI."

A. B. C. AND A. I CODES USED.

Contractors of Coal

To the Imperial Japanese Navy. Arsenals and Railway Bureau, Principal Railway Companies and Industrial Work, Home and Foreign Mail and Freight Steamers.

Sole Proprietors

Of the famous Miike, Tagawa and Yamano Coal Mines.

Sole Agents

For the sale of Fukumo, Hokoku, Ichimura, Kanoda, Mannoura, Onoura, Ostuji, Sonoda, Tsubaruro, Yoshinotani, Yoshio, Yurokibura and other coals.

YANGTSE INSURANCE ASSOCIATION, LTD.

The undersigned, having been appointed agents for the above company, are prepared to issue policies and pay losses on marine risks at regular rates.

E. MEYER & Co.,
Agents, Chemulpo.

AMERICAN KOREAN ELECTRIC CO.

Light and Power.

Main Office: Electric Building, Chong No.

RAILWAY DEPARTMENT.

OPERATING CARS BETWEEN EAST AND WEST GATE, EVERY TEN MINUTES:—

First Car leaves East Gate at 7:00 A. M. First Car leaves R. R. Station at 7:25 A. M
Last Car " East Gate at 8.40 P. M. Last " " R. R. Station at 9.05 P.M

OPERATING CARS BETWEEN EAST GATE AND IMPERIAL TOMB TERMINUS, EVERY TWENTY MINUTES:—

CONNECTING WITH EVERY ALTERNATE CAR ARRIVING AT EAST GATE FROM CHONG NO.

First Car leaves East Gate for Tomb at 7:10 A. M.
" " " Tomb for East Gate at 7:30 A. M.
Last " " East Gate for Tomb at 7:50 P. M.
" " " Tomb for East Gate at 8:10 P. M.

OPERATING CARS BETWEEN CHONG NO AND YUNG SAN RIVER EVERY TWELVE MINUTES:—

First Car leaves Chong No for South Gate at 7:12 A. M.
" " " Chong No for Yung San at 7:36 A. M.
" " " South Gate for Chong No at 7:20 A. M.
" " " Yung San for Chong No at 8:09 A. M.
Last " " South Gate for Chong No 9:00 P. M.
" " " Yung San for Chong No at 8.45. p. M.

SPECIAL PRIVATE CARS FURNISHED TO SUIT CONVENIENCE OF PATRONS. PRICES ON APPLICATION AT HEAD OFFICE.

LIGHTING DEPARTMENT.

Where less than 250 candle power of light is used, the rate per month will be
Per 16 candle power incandescent lamp,—All night.—Yen 2.50.
32 candle power incandescent lamp:—All night:—Yen 4.00.
50 candle power incandescent lamp:—All night:—Yen 6.00.
150 " " " " " " ,, 10.00.
1200 ,, ,, enclosed are ,, ,, ,, ,, 20.00.

Where more than 250 candle power of light is used, a Meter will be installed, freqvedted:—Rent of Meter Yen 2.00 per month. Rate of charges by meter reading:—Two Sen per Ampere per hour. (Approximately this is equal to about One Sen per 16 C. P. lamp per hour) Minimum monthly charge where meter is installed, Yen 20.00 per month, which includes rental of meter.

Estimates for installing lights furnished on application

An assortment of chandeliers always on hand.

K. Murakami.

Photograph Studio
Chinkokai, Seoul.

Printing, Developing and Enlargement, of Photographs always Undertaken.

Korean Views and Pictures Illustrating Native Customs always on Sale,

THE OSAKA SHOSEN KAISHA

Boats frequently on the berth for Chinnampo.

REGULAR SAILINGS BETWEEN JAPAN AND KOREAN PORTS.

FUSAN AND KOBE VIA SHIMONOSEKI.

OSAKA VIA MOKPO, FUSAN, SHIMONOSEKI AND KOBE.

MOJI DIRECT.

OSAKA VIA KUNSAN, MASANPO, FUSAN, SHIMONOSEKI AND KOBE.

CHEMULPO KUNSAN LINE,
Every three days.

CHEMULPO CHINNAMPO LINE.
Every three days.

For Freight and passage and further particulars apply to

THE OSAKA SHOSEN KAISHA,
Chemulpo

RONDON, PLAISANT & CO.

General Storekeepers and Merchants, Ships Contractors, Tobacconists, Commission and Forwarding Agents, Coal Merchants

IMPORTERS AND EXPORTERS

Seoul & Chemulpo.

W. D. WENTWORTH.

LANDING
AND
SHIPPING AGENT
AND
CUSTOMS BORDER.

12 OURA, NAGASAKI.

STEWARD & CO.

Chemulpo.

Shipchandlers and Storekeepers, Naval and Mercantile Contrrctors, Landing and Shipping Agents.

STEWARD'S HOTEL

Chemulpo.

Best accommodation in the port for travelers. Clean and well-aired rooms, good cuisine and prompt attendence, moderate tariff.

론셜

젼쟁의 ᄭᅳᆺᄂᆞᆫ 후

○일본셔 패덴늬 메일신문에 청국ᄉᆞ건을 말ᄒᆞ엿ᄂᆞᆫᄃᆡ 그 말에 ᄒᆞ엿스되 일본이 ᄭᅢ홀 죠짐이 잇스며 청국외무부에셔 엇지홀 것을 우리가 샹샹ᄒᆞᆫ다 ᄒᆞ엿스니 만일 일본이 ᄭᅢ홀 죠짐이 잇슬 경우에ᄂᆞᆫ 아모리 소견이 젹은 사ᄅᆞᆷ이라도 한국의 엇지홀 것을 ᄯᅩᄒᆞᆫ 싱각홀 듯ᄒᆞ도다

우리의 소견이 다른 사ᄅᆞᆷ보다 더 낫지 못ᄒᆞ지마ᄂᆞᆫ 일본이 전승ᄒᆞᄂᆞᆫ 즁에 각색 일을 쟈긔의 죠흔ᄃᆡ로 쟈긔의 압졔로 잡아 당긔ᄂᆞᆫ 것을 분명이 보겟ᄂᆞᆫ지라

우리ᄂᆞᆫ 일본이 한국에 ᄃᆡᄒᆞ야 ᄒᆞᄂᆞᆫ 것 ᄀᆞᆺ흔 침략ᄒᆞᄂᆞᆫ 정책을 쓸 ᄯᅢ가 지금은 아니라 ᄒᆞ고 여러 번 권고ᄒᆞ엿고 일본 군ᄉᆞ샹으로 말ᄒᆞ드ᄅᆡ도 아모 ᄯᅢ라도 일본이 한국 사ᄅᆞᆷ들과 교외ᄅᆞᆯ 잘 보전ᄒᆞ엿더면 죠앗슬 걸 ᄒᆞᄂᆞᆫ 날이 졍령히 잇슬 것을 우리ᄂᆞᆫ 밋ᄂᆞᆫᄃᆡ 일본인민은 여과ᄉᆞ졍에 ᄃᆡᄒᆞ야 다만 분명치 못ᄒᆞᆫ 소견만 잇도다 일본인민의 듯ᄂᆞᆫ 소문은 여긔 잇ᄂᆞᆫ 통신원들이 보ᄒᆞᄂᆞᆫ 것이오 여긔 잇ᄂᆞᆫ 통신원들은 져의 들의 민인 바 일본관리의 게로브터 소문을 듯ᄂᆞᆫ지라 일본신문들은 우리를 로국당이라 고ᄒᆞ지마ᄂᆞᆫ 우리ᄂᆞᆫ 그것들을 잘못된 일본당이라 고부르겟노라 일본 사ᄅᆞᆷ들과 일본 사ᄅᆞᆷ들의 게 보호 밧ᄂᆞᆫ 쟈들이 한국을 ᄯᅥ나게 될 일은 도리켜셔 뵈여지 아니ᄒᆞᄂᆞᆫ지

그러ᄒᆞ나 엇더ᄒᆞᆫ지 한국 사ᄅᆞᆷ들이 져의 들의 압졔쟈들이 가기를 시작홀 ᄯᅢ에 만세를 크게 부르ᄂᆞᆫ 소ᄅᆡ를 드를 일이 확실히 잇슬지라 일본 사ᄅᆞᆷ 든의 ᄯᅥ나가ᄂᆞᆫ 길에 무슴 방애가 잇ᄂᆞᆫ 것을 보기를 우리ᄂᆞᆫ 바라지 아니ᄒᆞ노라

청국에셔ᄂᆞᆫ 엇지 될ᄂᆞᆫ지 우리ᄂᆞᆫ 확실히 아지 못ᄒᆞ나 그러ᄒᆞ나 청국신문지들의 게지ᄒᆞᆫ 몃ᄃᆡ 문은 벳겨 노코 보면 바ᄅᆞᆷ이 어ᄃᆡ로 불ᄂᆞᆫ지 가히 볼지라 그 신문지에 말ᄒᆞ엿스되

호남혁명당에 학싱 몃몃이 관계된 것을 안후로 청국정부에셔 나동씨와 ᄯᅩ 엇던 대관ᄒᆞᆫ나의 게 명령ᄒᆞ야 일본에 잇ᄂᆞᆫ 청국류학생들을 관할ᄒᆞᆯ 일에 ᄃᆡᄒᆞ야 일본공사를 맛나 보라 ᄒᆞ엿고

청국외무부에셔 일본에 잇ᄂᆞᆫ 청국공사의 게 면보ᄒᆞ되 일본각학교에셔 사사로 공부ᄒᆞᄂᆞᆫ 청국류학싱들의 셩명을 매삭 사실ᄒᆞ야 보니라 ᄒᆞ엿고

청국황태후 ᄯᅢ셔 친히 군긔무처에 명령ᄒᆞ시되 각셩춍독과 순무에셔 면보ᄒᆞ야 이다음에ᄂᆞᆫ 외국에 보니ᄂᆞᆫ 류학싱들을 미우 조심ᄒᆞ야 ᄲᅢᆸ으라 신칙ᄒᆞ라 ᄒᆞ엿다 고ᄒᆞ엿더라

ᄒᆞᆫ동안 젼에 청국에 ᄒᆞᆫ 유명ᄒᆞᆫ 관인이 속가셔 샹히 어ᄂᆞ 곳에 갓쳐 셧ᄂᆞᆫᄃᆡ 그 사ᄅᆞᆷ이 그 집으로브터 ᄲᅢ져 나오랴고 ᄒᆞ엿더니 다시 그 사ᄅᆞᆷ을 춍으로 노앗ᄂᆞᆫ지라 이일에 ᄃᆡᄒᆞ야 ᄶᅢ 팬델늬 메일이 말ᄒᆞ되 그 사ᄅᆞᆷ이 샹ᄒᆞ기ᄂᆞᆫ 면ᄒᆞ엿다 ᄒᆞ니 춍으로 노은 일에 ᄃᆡᄒᆞ야 샹ᄒᆞ기ᄂᆞᆫ 면ᄒᆞ엿다 ᄒᆞ니 참 조흔 말이로다 그런 말이 우리의 싱각에 더 의심이 드러 가게 되ᄂᆞᆫ지라 〔미완〕

외보

○니목쟝군ᄉᆞ젹 니목쟝군이 려슌구에 츌졍이리로 그 간란으로 고ᄂᆞᆫᄒᆞᆫ 붓으로 다 긔록키 어려운지라 젼후 격젼에 그 쟝남 파ᄎᆞ남이 ᄉᆞᄒᆞ엿스니 그 범샹ᄒᆞᆫ 사ᄅᆞᆷ ᄀᆞᆺᄒᆞ면 참쳑샹의 눈물로 갑옷을 젹실 것이오 긔의 과ᄌᆞ연쇼침ᄒᆞᆯ터이나 동장군은 미양국란에 힘쓰믄 무ᄉᆞ의 쟝죠ᄒᆞᆫ 면목이라 ᄒᆞ야 원긔가 졈졈 더 셩ᄒᆞ야 평시에도 군복을 벗지 안코 비록 삼복셩졀에 모긔ᄶᅢ가 와셔 피롭게ᄒᆞ드ᄅᆡ도 부하쟝의 곤ᄒᆞᆷ을 싱각ᄒᆞ야 모긔쟝을 쓰지 아니ᄒᆞ고 엄동셜한에 삭풍이 잇드리도 쟝군 거ᄒᆞᄂᆞᆫ 방에 화로를 보지 못ᄒᆞ고 향샹 츄ᄒᆞᆫ 쳐쇼을 멱어써 소졸로 더브러 달고 쓴 것을 ᄀᆞᆺ치ᄒᆞ니 그 부하ᄉᆞ졸이 감격ᄒᆞ지 아니홀이 업다고ᄒᆞ더라

○디하텰로 죵리셰계에 디하텰로 잇ᄂᆞᆫᄃᆡᄂᆞᆫ 론돈과 (긔라스고)와 피리와 홍아리의 부다폐스ᄉᆞ쳐ᄲᅮᆫ이러니 거년 십월에 셰계뎨일 되ᄂᆞᆫᄃᆡ 하텰도가 츅육에 죵셩된지라 죵리 셰계뎨일이리 층ᄎᆞ든 바 론돈 디하텰도ᄂᆞᆫ 공긔유통과 광션공급이 부족ᄒᆞ고로 불편ᄒᆞ더니 금번 츅육 디하텰도ᄂᆞᆫ 공긔와 광션이 유통ᄒᆞ야 잘되고 그 분지션을 합ᄒᆞ면 장이 십여리요 뎡거장이 ᄉᆞ십팔ᄀᆡ쇼인ᄃᆡ 그 삼십삼ᄀᆡ쇼ᄂᆞᆫ 디하에 잇다ᄒᆞ고 이 텰도ᄂᆞᆫ 일쳔팔ᄇᆡᆨ구십ᄉᆞ년에 긔공ᄒᆞ야 최쵸에ᄂᆞᆫ 츅육시민이 담당ᄒᆞ야 경영ᄒᆞ더니 그 후에 이것을 속셩코져ᄒᆞ야 일쳔구ᄇᆡᆨ년에 마크드날ᄯᅳ씨로ᄒᆞ야곰 쥬임기ᄉᆞ를 임ᄒᆞ고 건셜비총액 ᄉᆞ쳔만불ᄂᆡ에 ᄀᆡᄇᆡᆨ칠십오만불은 뎡거장 파츄도 건셜비로 분획ᄒᆞ야 일쳔구ᄇᆡᆨ년 오월 이십오일에 착슈ᄒᆞ야 일쳔이ᄇᆡᆨ칠십오일 후에 쥰공되엿ᄂᆞᆫᄃᆡ 미일 역부 ᄉᆞ쳔륙ᄇᆡᆨ륙십일명식 사역ᄒᆞ엿고 금에 그 승직은 일ᄀᆡ년에 이억만인 가량이라더라

잡보

○보쳥쳘환광군 협쳔군슈가 외부에 보고ᄒᆞ기를 히인ᄉᆞ니에 일인이 금광 치굴ᄒᆞᄂᆞᆫ 소로 향쟈에 부훈을 밧드러 여러 번 금ᄒᆞ야도 듯지 아니ᄒᆞᄂᆞᆫᄃᆡ 파원은 경셩에 거ᄒᆞᄂᆞᆫ 김교면인ᄃᆡ 니장원면쳑을 인ᄒᆞ야 곳 샹경ᄒᆞ고 현금 쥬장ᄒᆞᄂᆞᆫ 사ᄅᆞᆷ은 일인에 죵산회현이온ᄃᆡ 히 일인이 ᄉᆞ환 일인 십일명을 거ᄂᆞ리고 방금 빅셩의 면답과 히인ᄉᆞ 산독을 치굴홈으로 손히가 만이 되ᄂᆞᆫ고로 군민의 호원과 즁들의 울고 호소ᄒᆞᄂᆞᆫ 것이 츅일 답지ᄒᆞ되 일이 외국인의 게 관계가 됨으로 본군으로ᄂᆞᆫ 가히 금홀 슈 업스니 일공관에 면조ᄒᆞ야 광군을 쳘환ᄒᆞ야 빅셩과 즁의 편케ᄒᆞ심을 바란다 ᄒᆞ엿더라

○쳥요대관 지ᄂᆞᆫ 토요일 하오 두시에 일본구락부에셔 려슌함락 츅하회를 관인과 인민이 병셜ᄒᆞ고 각부대신과 협관을 쳥요ᄒᆞ엿더라

○김씨피임 참찬 허위씨ᄂᆞᆫ 체임ᄒᆞ고 그 ᄃᆡᄂᆞᆫ 평리원판ᄉᆞ 김지슌씨가 피임ᄒᆞ엿더라

○최찬졍샹쥬ᄉᆞ건 찬졍 최익현씨가 입시ᄒᆞ고 샹쥬ᄒᆞᆫ ᄉᆞ를 거ᄒᆞᆫ즉 인지를 슈용ᄒᆞ고 면례을 쥰힝ᄒᆞ고 태묘롤 현알ᄒᆞᆫ 후에 민회롤 친히 효유히 송ᄒᆞ고 교린을 신으로 세우고 시졍긔션을 텬하에 포고홀 소인되 죠위에 물너가 포덕문에 쳐ᄒᆞ야 굴아되 우 다셧가지 됴목을 곳 죠쳐이나 리샤 실시ᄒᆞ시면 이어니와 그러치 아니ᄒᆞ면 찰아리 죽드리도 물너가지 아니ᄒᆞ야 국은을 머리로써 되신드리기로 작졍이라더라

○회민입셩 일작일에 동소문으로 단발ᄒᆞᆫ 쟈 몃십명식 쟈되ᄒᆞ야 드러오ᄂᆞᆫᄃᆡ 언어ᄂᆞᆫ 모다 함경도 말이요 ᄒᆞᆫ 오륙십명이나 되엿고 ᄎᆞᄎᆞ 련ᄒᆞ여 드러온다더라

○쳐쳐긔회 조금으로ᄂᆞᆫ 일진회인이 시문밧 독립관으로 모혀 긔회ᄒᆞᆫ다ᄒᆞ며 ᄯᅩ 경셩부근 각디 요ᄒᆡ쳐에셔 회원 삼ᄇᆡᆨ명식 파송ᄒᆞ야 긔회ᄒᆞᆫ다더라

○면쟝혈가 젼라도에셔ᄂᆞᆫ 단발ᄒᆞᆫ 쟈가 도죠를 주지 안ᄂᆞᆫ 고로 답주를이 면장을 팔고져ᄒᆞ나 사ᄂᆞᆫ 사ᄅᆞᆷ이 업셔 지금 모도 헐가로 판다더라

○경무ᄉᆞ연셜 경무ᄉᆞ 신틱휴씨ᄂᆞᆫ 일반경리를 회동ᄒᆞ야 연셜ᄒᆞ야 골오ᄃᆡ 현금 일본ᄉᆞ령부에셔 경셩부근에 안령질셔를 온화케ᄒᆞ기 위ᄒᆞ야 경찰령을 고시ᄒᆞ엿스니 이ᄂᆞᆫ 우리 졍부에셔 조취ᄒᆞᆫ 일이라 샹하일반경리가 진심갈력ᄒᆞ야 경찰ᄒᆞ엿스면 일본이 엇지ᄒᆞ야 지물을 허비ᄒᆞ며 경찰ᄒᆞ라 ᄒᆞ리오 그러ᄒᆞᆫ즉 우리ᄂᆞᆫ 힘졍ᄒᆞᄂᆞᆫᄃᆡ 더욱 신실히 ᄒᆞ야 니외인민이 안령ᄒᆞᆫ즉 피ᄎᆞ 경찰이 스ᄉᆞ로 귀졍이 잇슬지니 일노써 쥬독ᄒᆞ야 극력ᄒᆞ야 ᄒᆞ여가ᄂᆞᆫ 거시 가ᄒᆞ다 ᄒᆞ고 합번ᄒᆞ야 힝졍ᄒᆞᆫ다더라

○남화위녀 작일 삼간동에셔 웬 녀인이 사나회와 셔로 싸호ᄂᆞᆫᄃᆡ 그 리유를 드른즉 본ᄅᆡ 그 녀인 부부ㅣ 빈한무의ᄒᆞᆫ 즁 ᄒᆞᆫ 아들아회가 잇ᄂᆞᆫ지라 ᄒᆞ로ᄂᆞᆫ 그 동리 사ᄂᆞᆫ 자ㅣ 와셔 말ᄒᆞ기를 지금 경샹도 사ᄅᆞᆷ이 와셔 게집아회를 사가라 ᄒᆞ니 네 아ᄃᆞᆯ을 녀복을 식혀 관후에 즁로에 갓다가 도로 ᄲᅢ앗쟈 ᄒᆞ고 돈이 쳔여량의 관후에 젼별ᄎᆞ로 동젹강을 건너더니 맛츰 그 계집아회가 비젼에셔 오좀을 누ᄂᆞᆫ지라 쥬즁지인이 보고 이샹이 너여 살펴보니 과연 산아회라 여러 사ᄅᆞᆷ이 남화위녀ᄒᆞᆫ ᄉᆞ닭이 웬 일이냐고 ᄯᅥ든즉 그 사기든 쥬ㅣ ᄯᅩ ᄒᆞᆫ 긔가 막혀 ᄌᆞ초지종을 셜명ᄒᆞᆫ 후에 도로 입셩ᄒᆞ야 한셩부에 호소ᄒᆞ야 그 부모와 즁미쟈를 잡아 ᄃᆡ질ᄒᆞᆫ 후에 즁미ᄒᆞᆫ 쟈ᄂᆞᆫ ᄃᆡ 몃도에 방송ᄒᆞ고 그 아비ᄂᆞᆫ 입ᄯᅢ 감옥셔 갓쳣ᄂᆞᆫᄃᆡ 지금 그 어미가 그 즁매ᄒᆞᆫ 쟈를 보고 폭악ᄒᆞ기를 이일이도 모지네가 홍화 죠ᄉᆞᄒᆞᆫ 일인ᄃᆡ 녀ᄂᆞᆫ 무ᄉᆞᄒᆞ고 내의 남편은 옥즁에셔 죽게ᄒᆞ니 녀와 나와 죽쟈ᄒᆞ고 싸혼다더라

○죠쳥쳘표 궁ᄂᆡ부에셔 외부에 죠회ᄒᆞ되 현금 운현궁 편지를 졉ᄒᆞᆫ즉 ᄂᆡ긔에 셔공덕리에 잇ᄂᆞᆫ 바 홍셥대원묘소 일인 텰도부셜ᄒᆞᆫ다 충ᄒᆞ고 묘소 지쳑지에 표를 세우고 바야흐로 나무를 베원다ᄒᆞ니 막즁슈호ᄒᆞᄂᆞᆫ ᄶᅡ에 일인이 표를 세우고 벌목홈이 진실노 심이 피당ᄒᆞᆫ지라 곳 일공ᄉᆞ의게 쵸회ᄒᆞ야 표를 것어가게 홈을 바란다 ᄒᆞ엿더라

○합쳥다관 ᄂᆡ부에셔 외부에 공합ᄒᆞ되 일공ᄉᆞ 공함ᄂᆡ긔에 함경남북도 광관된 고을에 군슈를 우리 군인으로 ᄒᆞ야곰 군무를 대리케ᄒᆞ고 월봉 일의 뎨히 디발ᄒᆞ라 ᄒᆞ엿기 사실ᄒᆞᆫ즉 디라와 월봉을 가히 의론업시 경솔이 못홀ᄲᅮᆫ 아니라 이믜 차하ᄒᆞᆫ 군슈ᄂᆞᆫ 혹도로의 죠절홈을 인ᄒᆞ야 곳 부임치 못ᄒᆞ엿고 ᄯᅩ 차하ᄒᆞ지 아니ᄒᆞᆫ 관원은 곳 샹쥬 차하ᄒᆞ야 곳 부임케 ᄒᆞᆯ터이니 일로써 일공ᄉᆞ의게 지죠ᄒᆞ야 힘써 다 판ᄒᆞ기를 바란다 ᄒᆞ엿더라

○남원화젹 음력 십월 이십칠일에 화젹 십여명이 남원 사암리에 돌입ᄒᆞ야 츙화ᄒᆞ야 삼십ᄉᆞ호와 가장즙물이 몰수히 소화ᄒᆞ엿더라

광고

TELEGRAMS.

Army Headquarters.

On the 6th inst, 2 companies of Russian infantry attacked a Japanese detachment at Otzeting (30 li north of Kianchang). In the near vicinity the Russian artillery attempted to place 2 guns in position but a heavy fire from a Japanese battery dislodged them and they retreated in the direction of the Shanghea-ho.

Tokyo Jan. 7th.

The flag-ship of the Baltic squadron, the Kniaz Suvaroff, struck a rock and sank near Madagascar.

Later.

According to a reliable telegram from St. Petersburg. received via New York, the Baltic squadron has been recalled.

Later.

The Russian Miliary authorities are resolved as firmly as ever to to bring the war to a successful issue and have decided to despatch 200,000 more troops.

Chefoo Jan. 2.

Four Russian destroyers have run the blockade and arrived here today.

(FROM JAPAN PAPERS.)

London, Dec. 30.

Negotiations for the issue of a Russian oan have lead to a definite arrangement being made, in accordance wherewith Russia will proceed to issue a four-and-half per cent. loan for £25,000,000 sterling, the issuing price being £95.

[According to a St. Petersburg dispatch, received in Tokyo, negotiations for the issue of Russian bonds have come to a successful conclusion. The amount of bonds to be issued is 500,000-000 mark, bearing 4½ percent. interest. A syndicate of Russian and German bankers and a Dutch bank have undertaken the issue, one of the conditions of which is that the bonds will not be redeemed or replaced by bonds of lower interest within twelve years. It is stated that the issuing price is 98 and that the syndicate has undertaken the flotation at 93. The bonds will be placed on the market shortly.]

London, Jan. 2.

Reuter's Agency learns that there is a consensus of opinion in diplomatic circles that the fall of Port Arthur will serve as a fresh incentive to Russia to renew the struggle, and that Russia will not spare any effort to recapture the stronghold or to compel its submission indirectly. The only reservation is thought to be the internal condition of Russia, which is the dominant factor in the situation at the present moment.

London. Jan. 2.

The Dutch battleship "Tera Ruitel" has been ordered to the East Indies (doubtless to protect Dutch neutrality).

London, Dec. 31.

Reuter's correspondent at Port Said wires that Admiral Bebrovosky's Squadron, comprising the cruisers "Oleg," "Izumrud," "Rion," and "Dnieper," and five torpedo detroyers, are expected there early next week.

London, Jan. 2.

Admiral Robjestvensky,s Squadron anchored yesterday off St. Marie, Madagascar, all the vessels being in excellent condition, despite the fact that violent storms were encountered after leaving the Cape.

London, Jan. 2.

M. de Witte has been appointed President of the Committee of Ministers which is actively preparing material for the study of the reforms indicated in the Manifesto recently issued by the Tsar.

The first meeting of the Committee will take place no the 3rd instant.

The Finnish Diet has decided to petition the Tsar to withdraw his ratification of the Decree issued in 1903 and to re-establish legal order throughout Finand.

(SPECIAL TO CHINA GAZETTE).

Chefoo 29th, December.

A Japanese non-commissioned officer arriving to-day from the south of Moukden, invalided, states that his companions are suffering from the winter; many are dying and incapacitated from bronchial and lung troubles. The authorities are realizing that the regulation ration is unsuitable on account of its lack of fats. Many of the troops are living in tents heated from the small ditches surrounding them, which are filled with fuel, but this is insufficient to protect the men from the cold. The result is that the troops become more inefficient daily. He states that the Russian flanks are being extended and that larger detachments are posted in the flank positions.

JAPANESE REINFORCEMENT.

A telegram dated December 10th at Moukden says:

Well authenticated reports have reached here that the Japanese forces have received additions of from forty to sixty thousand men. Kuropatkin's task is thereby rendered much more difficult. The belligerents probably must for some time be content to hold their present positions. Even though great reinforcements continue to reach him, Kuropatkin's task is a difficult one. The Japanese have built strong and almost impregnable fortifications which will not be easy to attack. These fortifications will have to be flanked to be successfully attacked, and to perform this, great numerical strength will be necessary. The Russian central army will of necessity be as strong as that of the Japanese.

Kuroki's flank has been constantly reinforced, chiefly with artillery. It is not known whether these reinforcements arrived from Port Arthur, or came direct from Japan. Yesterday the Japanese artillery fired during the whole day. A serious fight was expected, but did not come off. The Japanese observed the Russians from their advance positions. The Russian troops stand ready for the fight.—Tageblatt fur Nord-China.

EUROPEANT LOAFERS AS BUDDHIST PRIESTS.

LIGHT AND LUCRATIVE OCCUPATON.

The Eurpean loafer in Burma, according to the "Rangoon Times," commonly becomes a Buddhist priest. As such his occupation is light and lucrative. An angry correspondent writing on the subject says:—"Any one may be accepted as a novice for the Buddhist priesthood, provided he is of good character, is willing to renounce the world, and earnestly and truly seeks the life of the ascetic. But actions speak louder than words, and the actions of some European novices, going round the houses of the faithful Buddhists, gathering hundreds of rupees, under the pretence of founding a library, are eloquent of the real motives that inspired them to enter the order. And not content with exploiting the Rangoon Buddhists, they now contemplate a grand tour in Upper Burma, there to repeat their nefarious performance. A healthy stomach and Hibernian bravado seem to be all that are required to make one a comfortable member of the Sangha."

The Novoe Vremya publishes a telegram received from a trustworthy correspondent at Sofia, to the effect that the Japanese Government has been at work by means of its diplomatic representatives in Western Europe, in sounding the authorities in Constantinople with regard to the establishing of a Japanese Embassy at the Porte, and that although Turkey has agreed to the proposal as a matter of principle, yet the request is regarded as inopportune at this moment. The rumour of Japan being about to establish diplomatic relations with Turkey comes, says a St. Petersburg correspondent, as a great surprise to Russia, as it is scarcely like ly that Russia will succeed in prevent ing Japan sending a diplomatic representative to Turkey.

WITH THE "BLUE AND BUFF."

[The Duke of Beaufort's hounds last year established a record for having killed the largeset number of foxes in one season.]

Innocent Stranger (excitely): "I've just seen seven foxes cross that ride!"

Whip: "Oh, that's only a few of the stragglers, Sir. The main body's gone away at the top—"Punch."

A CHEST EXERCISE.

Grasp an ordinary walking-stick firmly, with the arms hanging down at the sides perfectly straight, Then raise it straight above the head and bring it down the back to the shoulder-blades and on to the waist. At first it may be necessary to grasp the stick almost at both ends, but with practice it can be accomplished with a very small margin beyond the actual width of the shoulders. This is an excellent exercise for any one with a weak chest, and strengthens both throat and lungs.—C Lang Neil., in "Modern Physical Culture."

Mr. Yi Chong Keun has been appointed Minister of War.

His Majesty has sanctioned the execution of 72 criminals, sentenced, for various crimes, to death by the Supreme Court.

His Majesty has been inquiries of General Hasegawa as to the reason of the arrest of Korean soldiers at the time of the Il Chin Hoi riot.

Mr. Megata, the Financial adviser, proposes the despatch of Japanese, to all districts, to form an accurate census of houses and population.

Mr. Min Yung Ki, Minister of Finance, has announced his intention of resigning. Mr. Ho Wi, the assistant councilor of state sent in his resignation on the 7th inst.

The Indian Government has, writes a correspondent of a home paper, decided to spend the large sum of fifty lacs of rupees (£333,000) upon the construction of a good permanent road to Tibet.

On Saturday the Il Chin Hoi society held a meeting outside the East Gate, when it was resolved to combine with the Chemulpo faction and hold a bumper meeting at the former Independent Club's premises today.

Mr. Sin Tai Hyn the newly appointed commissioner of Police, has issued an order prohibiting any one from wearing silk clothes. Another order states that no women may appear on the streets after 9 P. M.

His Majesty has ordered the terms of the three Kong Chin Hoi people, sentenced to imprisonment, to be commuted and the men to be banished instead.

The Kong Chin Hoi society have claimed the sum of Y700 and $300 from the Police Department, asserting that this was the amount of notes and nickels lying in the society's rooms, when these were closed by the police.

Mr. Cnoi Ik Hyun, Councilor of State, recently received in audience by His Megesty made some very strong representations concerning affairs of state. He cautioned His Majesty against appointing incapable officials and requested him to find a way to make amicable arrangements with the neighbouring countries and get rid of the Il Chin Hoi society by friendly means and an announcement of a change of the government's policy. Mr. Choi has announced his intention of waiting outside the Palace Gates until he sees that his recommendations have had effect.

COLDS AND SORE THROATS.

Hartshorr and oil is an excellent remedy for cold on the chest. It should be well rubbed into the chest, and, if the cold is severe, between the shoulders as well, a piece of new flannel (white) being placed over the chest afterwards. The flannel should not be dipped into hartshorn and oil and put on the chest, as it will act as a blister if this is done. A remedy for the chest much used by Germans is tallow. The addition of nutmeg grated over is said to be beneficial. Spread the tallow on linen and put on the chest. For external use, in sore throat, take a piece of lint doubled (eight inches by two). Wring it out of hot water; sprinkle over it a tea-spoonful of eau de Cologne and wrap it round the thoat; cover it with oiled silk of the same size, and tie it all on with a light silk handkerechief.—Health.

FRIENDLY TIBET.

Neither the Lhasa official, nor the common people seem to bear any ill-will towards the British Government for all that has happened. It was the man of Kham who bore the brunt of the fighting, and it is said that the Lamas were not much displeased at the thinning out of these rude but turbulent levies.—"Pioneer," Allahabad.

The Chinese, says a Formosa despatch, a people notoriously subject to panics and sensational alarms, generally originating and mostly merely existent in their own minds, are now in a fearful state of ferment and distraction in the north end of this Island. "They are to be forcibly taken from their homes and fields with out a moment's warning or an hour's respite to take leave of their friends, and shipped off to Manchuria there to be slaughtered by Russian guns." There is literally weeping and wailing in the land and no number of official assurances can make them believe that this is not really true.

The Korea Daily News.

Issued at 5 P. M. daily except Sundays.
Rate of Subscription:—
Per Year,............Yen 25.
Per Quarter,..........Yen 7.
Per Month,..........Yen 2.50.

Postage in Korea not charged extra.
Postage abroad charged extra.

Advertisements, 50 sen per day for 1 inch or less.
5 yen per month per inch.
50 yen per year per inch.

All communications to
E. T. BETHELL,
Editor and Publisher,
Pak-tong, Seoul.

JAPAN AND DIPLOMACY.

The "Chefoo Daily News," which is, to the best of our belief, an independent journal, says that the Japanese are making too much political capital out of the fact that they are "yellow" people.

There is a good deal in this. When the diplomatic correspondence with Russia was published, the world was surprised at the studied moderation of its tone and Baron Suyematsu's able defence of his country in the London press, also created a very favourable impression. The world first under-estimated Japan's capability and then flew to the other extreme with the result that every little country newspaper in England patronisingly talks of "Our brave little yellow friends," "plucky little Japs," and so on *ad nauseam*.

Probably because it suits her purposes Japan submits to all this patronage but an acquantance with her recent history will convince any one that her elder statesmen have no superiors in diplomacy while the skill and valour of her fighting men have never been called into question.

Were these the only two elements to be taken into account we should expect great things from Japan, but there is a very powerful faction of younger politicians in Tokio who bid fair to seriously injure Japan's good name and prestige. We refuse to believe for instance that Mr. Hayashi is acting in accordance with his own wishes when he attempts to force measures on the Korean Government which are in direct opposition to the promises made by him in the earlier stages of the war.

It appears that the Japanese Government is in the hands of a lot of unthinking young men who imagine that Japan's hope of future greatness lies in territorial expansion, and urge this course without stopping to reflect that the end of this war will find Japan without the means to exploit any territory she might acquire.

MINING IN KOREA.

Possession is nine points of the law, and with Japan daily adding to her possessions in Korea on the score of railway extension or accommodation for troops, or gianing control of her coasts by dint of fishing concessions, observation stations, fortifications and what not, it would now be foolish for the Koreans ever to hope to regain entire possession of their kingdom.

Of course in saying this we are leaving the fortunes of war out of our calculations but we are quite sure that nothing short of force will persuade the Japanese to yield any of the privileges which they have lately acquired.

We do not, however, see any great element of danger in this provided the Korean Government goes the right way to work. We note from a Tokio paper, with great satisfaction, that it is considered probable that the Korean Government will assent to the demands for mining concessions made by the Italian, British, German and Belgian Ministers.

This we think is good policy, as the greater the interest held by other powers in Korea, the greater will be their opposition to the assumption of suzerainty by Japan.

There is however considerable room for improvement in the present *modus operandi* and the introduction of a good system of mining laws would be at once a splendid source of revenue and a protective measure.

TWO SISTERS WHO ARE PHYSICALLY ONE.

(Concluded from last issue.)

"You have no cause to complain," rejoined Rosa, laughing heartily in turn. "We used to eat exactly the same amount of food before I had influenza. Now I eat only half the quantity, but you take your usual share and half mine as well."

This discussion apparently reminded Josefa that she had left a box of chocolates in her music-case, and the four legs began to trip along towards the receptacle, into which four hands tried playfully to delve simultaneusly. Rosa, however, secured the prize, and shared the dainties equally.

"We have only one taste in common," said Josefa, "and that is for sweets. In dress, for instance, we quite disagree, though of course, we have to wear the same gown. Three days out of the seven we wear my favourite dress, and on the other four days we don those which Rosa prefers. Rosa has the extra day, because she is cleverer than I."

Then Rosa told a story of how on a recent visit to Paris they took only one ticket for a railway journey.

"We did not know whether the officials would regard us as one passenger or two passengers. So to test the matter I took one ticket. But, the company evidently decided that we were two persons, and they sued 'my better half'—as I call Josefa, because she is the bigger of the two—for her fare. And the judge decided against her—or us which ever you prefer.

"In this hotel also we rank as two persons, for the reason, I suppose, that although we are only one body we have two mouths.".

The movements of this human freak were strange to watch. Instinctively one brain seemed to appreciate the line of thought followed by the other. There was no hesitancy in the combined action. "Occasionally," said Rosa, "when we are in doubt as to what direction, we stop and discuss the matter, thus settling it between us."

Rosa is credited with being the more intelligent half of the whole, and exhibits a remarkable fine sense of humour. She related how they attended a Paris ball dressed as an angel. "A queer angel," she added, "with two heads!"

Before bidding the visitor adieu, Rosa and Josefa cleverly performed a violin duet.

ARRESTED.

Acting Viceroy Tuan Fang, of the Liang Kiang provinces, telegraphs to the Viceroys of the different maritime provinces informing them that through certain arrests of secret society men having been made in Hunan, a plot has been unearthed for the overthrow of the Tartar dynasty.

He futher states that the members of the secret societies are in league with certain students in Japan, and that arrests should be made secretly and quietly. It is rumoured that a rising was planned to take place on the Empress Dowager's birthday.

MINING DEVELOPMENTS IN CHINA.

During last year, says "Engineering," little was done towards exending existing mining concessions or obtaining new grants in China. The Peking Syndicate has not yet commenced to lay down coal at Tientsin, and may find themselves forestalled by German concessionaires in Western Chihli. It has lately come to an arrangement with the owners of the iron deposits in Shanshi for smelting ore on a joint-account basis. A British syndicate has acquired rights to work coal and iron over some 50 square miles in Anhui, about 300 miles from the mouth of the Yangtzu, and is said to be very satisfied with the bargain. Experts have proceeded to the Upper Yangtzu to bore for petroleum on behalf of a foreign syndicate. Antimony continues to come down from the native mines in Hunan. Last year there were delivered fully 3,000 tons of antimony and a similar amount of antimony ore. An installation, under German management, has been put up at Wuch'ang to concentrate lead and zinc ores, and is capable of working 75 tons of ore daily. The Iron-mines at Ta-yeh shipped 50,000 tops of ore (300 tons more than in 1902) to Japan, and, as the iron works at Hanyang increased their output of pig from 75 to 120 tons a day, they must have been supplied with 30,000 additional tons of ore and limestone. In return for a loan of 3,000,000 yen at 6 per cent., these mines have now been mortgaged to a Japanese syndicate for a period of thirty years. A Japanese engineer is to be engaged, and the Imperial Iron Foundry undertakes to purchase 70,000 to 100,000 tons of ore annually at a price which, from now till August, 1915, shall be at the rate of three gold yen per ton for first-class ore, and two yen 20 sen for second class. Coal mines, continues "Engineering," are being developed in different parts of the country, and this is leading to the extension of industrial enterprise. At the end of 1902 Provincial Government granted exclusive mining rights in the north-west of Fukien to certain Chinese French concessionaries, and a French mining engineer of high repute, who has been prospecting there during 1903, has obtained a careful survey of the gold-fields, in the Shro-wu Prefecture. These are described as very valuable and worth working, and it is proposed to form a company with a capital of 1.250,000 dols. to commence operations.

MORE REBELS.

The Governor of Hunan telegraphs that the returned students are planning rebellion, and he has made thirteen arrests. He further states that the students in Japan are connected with this movement, and that the organisation has its headquarters in Tokyo. The Throne has ordered that two of the prominent leaders be executed as an example, and that the others be liberated with a caution.

Mr. Matsumoto Kumpei, supported by 36 members of the House of Representatives Tokio, has introduced the following Representation:—"Treaties of amity and commerce should be concluded with Turkey, Servia and Roumania, and a diplomatic official should be posted in Constantinople. "The Balkan Peninsula is a link in the foreign policy of Europe, and as the tranquillity or otherwise of the Far East is connected with the state of European politics, this country must not neglect to inform itself about Balkan affairs. It is a defect in our foreign relations that we have no intercourse with the above countries."

According to Japanese official investigations at the end of June, Japanese carrying on business in Korea numbered 7,951.

It is stated that the Chinese Government has issued orders for the abolition of German military drill in all the provincial armies of the Empire, and the substitution of Japanese drill.

The Korea Daily News.

VOL. II, MONDAY, JANUARY 9 1905 No. 5

HONGKONG & SHANGHAI BANKING CORPORATION.

Paid-up Capital $10,000,000
Reserve Fund:—Sterling Reserve... 10,000,000
Silver Reserve..... 7,000,000

27,000,000
Reserve Liability of Proprietors... 10,000,000

HEAD OFFICE, HONGKONG.

London Bankers, London and County Banking Company Limited.
Branches and Agencies,
London.

Amoy,	Hankow	Penang,
Bangkok,	Hiogo,	Rangoon,
Batavia,	Iloilo,	Saigon,
Bombay,	Lyons,	San Francisco,
Calcutta,	Manila,	Singapore,
Colombo,	Nagasaki,	Sourabaya,
Foochow,	New York,	Tientsin,
Hamburg,	Peking,	Yokohama,

Credits granted on approved Securities, and every description of Banking and Exchange business transacted.

Drafts granted on London and the chief Commercial places in Europe, India, Australia, America, China and Japan.

HOLME RINGER & Co., AGENTS,
CHEMULPO.

HOKURKU DOBOKU KAISHA.

Branch office in Chong Dong, Seoul.
Japanese telephone No. 165

CONTRACT DEPARTMENT.

We can contract to build any building or construction.

MERCHANDISE DEPARTMENT.

We can provide any building material. We have just contracted to build the new Belgian Legation.

E. MEYER & CO.

Chemulpo.

SOLE AGENTS IN KOREA FOR.

A. T. Morse, Sons & Co.'s

"Fresco" Distemper

In all colours ready for use on walls, Ceilings etc.

and

AVENARIUS CARBOLINEUM

A wood-preserving and antiseptic oil preparation

Against decay, dry-rot, fungus and wood-destroying insects.

A large supply always in stock.
Prices upon application.

E. MEYER & Co.,
Chemulpo.

CHARTERED BANK OF INDIA AUSTRALIA & CHINA.

INCORPORATED BY ROYAL CHARTER 1853

HEAD OFFICES —LONDON.

Paid-up Capital £800,000
Reserve Liability of Shareholders 800,000
Reserve Fund 800,000

Drafts granted upon all the principal places in the world and every description of Exchange and banking business transacted.

E. MEYER & Co., Agents,
Chemulpo.

MITSU BISHI DOCKYARD & ENGINE WORKS,

NAGASAKI.

CODE WORD, "DOCK."

A 1, A. B. C., and Engineering Codes used.

DOCK No. 1 (at Tategami).

Extreme Length.............. 523 feet
Length on blocks .... 513 ,,
Width of Entrance on Top...... 89 ,,
,, ,, Bottom.... 77 ,,
Water on Blocks at Spring Tide 26½ ,,

DOCK No. 2 (Mukaijima).

Extreme Length.............. 371 feet
Length on Blocks............. 360 ,,
Width of Entrance on Top...... 66 ,,
,, ,, Bottom 53 ,,
Water on Blocks at Spring Tide 22 ,,

PATENT SLIP (at Kosuge).
Can take vessels up to 1,000 tons gross.

THE WORKS are well equipped with the LATEST IMPROVEMENTS, and can execute any kind of work in SHIPBUILDING and MARINE ENGINEERING, as well as in REPAIRING of SHIPS.

The COMPANY'S new powerfu steamer OURA-MARU (712 tons, 700 I.H.P.), specially built for SALVAGE PURPOSES, and equipped with necessary gear, is always READY at SHORT NOTICE.

THE METHODIST PUBLISHING HOUSE,

Little West Gate, Seoul.

JOB PRINTING, TYPEWRITER PAPER
CARBON PAPER, VISITING CARDS
STATIONERY, BOOK BINDING
BOOK PUBLISHERS
AMERICAN SCHOOL BOOKS
SPENCERIAN COPY BOOKS
PEN CARBON LETTER AND BILL BOOKS

S.A. BECK, Manager.

DAI-ICHI GINKO.

LIMITED.

(Formerly the First National Bank)

ESTABLISHED 1873

INCORPORATED UNDER PRESENT LAW 1896

Capital - - - - - - - - Yen 5,000,000
Reserve Fund - . - - - 1,500,000

HEAD OFFICE:—TOKIO.

President: Baron SHIBUSAWA.

BRANCHES AND CORRESPONDENTS
In the Principal Cities and Towns of Japan.
Interest Allowed on

Fixed deposits 1 year - - - 6½ per cent
" " 6 months - - - 6 per cent

Special current accounts 1½ sen daily per Y 100
General " " 1 " " " 100

M. TANAKA,
Manager, Chemulpo.

SINGER SEWING MACHINES

씽거ᄌᆞ봉침

SOLE AGENTS FOR KOREA
전매쇼

HOLME RINGER & CO.
Chemulpo.
제물포 함룽거양힝

KAMEYA & CO.

GENERAL STOREKEEPERS
Chinkokai - - Seoul
(Established 1895, Tokyo)

Confectionery, Hams, Canned Goods, Cutlery, Hirano & Tansan Water. Provisions, Gents, Furnishing goods, Toilet Articles, Travelling Bags, Tobacco, Cigars & Cigarettes Kitchen Utensils. Coffee, Biscuits

Fresh Goods always kept in Stock.
Prices Moderate
☞ *Please come and inspect our goods.*

NIPPON YUSEN KAISHA.

JAPANESE MAIL STEAMSHIP CO.

DER MAIL CONTRACT WITH THE IMPERIAL JAPANESE GOVERNMENT.

European Line

Regular Fortnightly Service between Yokohama Kobe, Moji, Shanghai, Hongkong, Singapore, Penang Colombo, Port Said, Marseilles, London and Antwerp

American Line

Regular Fortnightly Service between Hongkong and Seattle, calling at Shanghai, Moji, Kobe, Yokohama and Victoria, B. C.

Australian Line

Regular weekly Service betwen Japan Ports and Australia, calling at Hongkong and Manila.
(Above Three Lines Suspended until further notice).

Shanghai Line

Weekly Service between Shanghai and Japan Ports

Korea Line

Service Kobe, Moji, Nagasaki, Fusan Chemupo Chef foo, Taiku.
S. S. Bahelsberg, 2181 tons.
Service Kobe, Moji, Fusan, Chemulpo, Chinnampo
S. S. ARGO, S. S. Ohio.

BORDEN'S CONDENSED MILK CO.

New York, U. S. A.

ALWAYS IN STOCK

Eagle Brand Condensed Milk.

Gold Seal Condensed Milk.

Peerless (Family) Evaporated Cream.

Borden's Malted Milk.

E. MEYER & CO.
Chemulpo Korea,
Sole Agents

ROYAL INSURANCE COMPANY,
Funds exceed £10,000,000
FIRE
AT CURRENT RATES
LIFE
REDUCED PREMIUM.
HOLME RINGER & Co.,
Agents, Chemulpo.

HOTEL DU PALAIS

SEOUL.

The only first class Hotel in Seoul Situated in the centre of the city opposite the palace.

Cuisine under the supervision of an experienced French Chef.

Well ventilated and furnished throughout.

TARIFF UPON APPLICATION

L. MARTIN
Proripetor and Manager

大韓每日申報
대한매일신보

(뎨이권륙호) (슈요일) 일쳔구빅오년일월십일일

본샤고빅

이신보는영어와한국문셔계리
일출판ᄒᆞᆸ

신문가

한쟝 엽두돈오푼
일삭료 엽두량닷돈
우표가리삭닷돈
다닷돈으로밧숩

광고료는

귀한의장단과ᄌᆞ힝의디쇼로죵
갑ᄒᆞ되혐가로밧을터이오며오
ᄅᆡ지아니ᄒᆞ야대한사람마다다이신
문을보실터이니광고버시기를본샤에
원ᄒᆞ시는이들은우리신문사에
와셔뎡약ᄒᆞ심을희망ᄒᆞᆸ

○발힝소 박동대한매일신보
사발형ᄒᆞᆫ표양쉬젼영국인셜필
림정자리오

사쟝 영국인 (빈셜)

평양 디리졈

○평양효동사는권미보씨로우
리신문관ᄆᆡ티리인을뎡ᄒᆞ엿
시스오니평양에계신구람코쟈ᄒᆞ
는 쳠군ᄌᆞ는칭뎌리졈에왕
림ᄒᆞ와면희ᄒᆞ시옵

사고

○우리대한매일신보의목뎍은
대한의안녕질셔에관한모든대
목에뎌ᄒᆞ야논문평한번론을쥬
쟝홈이라우리동신원의탐보는
신문보시는쳠군ᄌᆞ의게ᄒᆞᆼ샹보
도ᄒᆞ리며혹지든귀셔ᄒᆞ며주시
는이는셩명과번디든젹어붓치
시기를희망ᄒᆞ오니비기슨신문
샹에긔재ᄒᆞ란는거시아니오다
만극히신용ᄒᆞ논주거든솜고자
홈이라긔자는아모긔셔던지긔
재홈을뢰각ᄒᆞ논권리든가졋스
나뢰각ᄒᆞ논리유든말ᄒᆞᆯ터이오
며공중평화든문란케ᄒᆞ는듯ᄒᆞᆫ
긔셔는의빈ᄒᆞ지발지한켓숩나이
다

●본사셰시이리로신문을디양
우헤로분젼ᄒᆞ와헤젼부의일의
로젼ᄒᆞᆫ듯스로먼곳에는혹늣게
젼ᄒᆞ기도ᄒᆞ며혹먹칠ᄒᆞ기슴ᄒᆞᆫ녑
에젼ᄒᆞ기도ᄒᆞ며혹아니젼ᄒᆞ는
곳도잇다ᄒᆞ와우리신문을수탕
ᄒᆞ야구람ᄒᆞ시는 쳠군ᄌᆞ의게
티ᄒᆞ야ᄆᆡ우미안ᄒᆞ옵기로지금
은분젼인을두고ᄆᆡ일일주이젼
ᄒᆞ며아니젼ᄒᆞ거나늣게거나ᄒᆞ올
폐가업도록ᄒᆞ란ᄒᆞ오니혹아니
젼ᄒᆞ거나혹늣게젼ᄒᆞ거나ᄒᆞᆫ일
이잇스면본샤로통긔ᄒᆞ여주심
을희망ᄒᆞᆸ

관보

뎨사쳔삼십일호 광무구
년일월구일
셔임급ᄉᆞ령

○임경무ᄉᆞ서칙임관이등 롱
군법원쟝 신태휴
일월오일

○의원면본관 비서원승 서
병션 비서원랑 김셰수 숙
릉령 마형달

○힝궁니부특진관 종일품
일품 졍낙용 종일품 리건슈 종
이품 죠동희 졍이품 죠병필 졍이품 리지용 종이품 리유
구 종이품 김학슈 종이품 리용션 종이품 김영
덕 종이품 남규희 종이품 졍우묵 종
이품 근 종이품 황기연 종이품 오
윤우 셕

○뎡관돈령원ᄉᆞ서칙임관일등
궁니부특진관 민영규

○병궁니부특진관서칙임관삼등
시강원쳠ᄉᆞ 윤상학

○평시강원쳠ᄉᆞ서칙임관삼등
궁니부특진관 민형식

○임비서원승서쥬임관오등
졍삼품 신필희

○임비서원랑서판임관칠등
구품 졍홍셕

○임 슉릉령서판임관칠등
륙품 리응국

○임릉참봉슈면화과쥬ᄉᆞ서판임
관륙등 노덕셕

○임릉참봉면화과쥬ᄉᆞ서판임
관팔등 리방형

○임니부종두ᄉᆞ의ᄉᆞ서판임관
륙등 졍위헌 송영진
이상일월륙일

○임군부대신서칙임관일등
중츄원의쟝 리종건
일월오일

○임중츄원의쟝서칙임관일등
판돈령원ᄉᆞ 박졍양
궁니부특ᄉᆞ

○농샹공부대신리도재ᄉᆞ직쇼
비지셩쇼구실경간이라쇼임맛
긴것은이셩비번거ᄒᆞᆫ것이아니
오병졍세는또ᄒᆞᆫ가히강잉ᄒᆞᆯ것
비니경은ᄉᆞ양치말고힝공ᄒᆞ라
신일로부랑을보니여셩유ᄒᆞ시
다

○의졍부참졍민병셕ᄉᆞ직쇼
비지셩쇼구실경간이라엇지금
칙갈이기를구ᄒᆞ리오마는거듭
비는것이바에이르럿스니졍ᄒᆞᆫ
바를의시ᄒᆞ라ᄒᆞ시다
이상일월륙일

뎐보

(군ᄉᆞ령부착)

○함창졍보 금월륙일에젹의
보병약이중티가오자평(함창
북으로삼리)부근에서우리군
사부티에티ᄒᆞ야공격ᄒᆞ고오후
일시사십분가량에젹이포이븐
왕쟝평ᄌᆞ(오자평북방이쳔미
돌 남방약일쳔미돌)처평디에
펴두란고ᄒᆞᆫ지음에우리포병이
이것을향ᄒᆞ야맹렬ᄒᆞᆫ사격을힝
ᄒᆞᆫ고로젹이근근히포티를나렬ᄒᆞ야두
고스우리포병의게향ᄒᆞ야포격을
기시ᄒᆞ엿더니오후삼시사십분
에젹이샹쳥하방면으로퇴각ᄒᆞ
엿다ᄒᆞ더라

잡보

○종야지관 참졍김셩근씨가
평리원판ᄉᆞ셩진관소로뎐화ᄒᆞ
기를죄인을못잡았는데ᄒᆞ라ᄒᆞᆷ으로
근일지관쇼판검ᄉᆞ가밤이맛도
록지관ᄒᆞᆫ다더라

○류빈쳐분 평리원에서룡
진회원을관결ᄒᆞ야류셔은역
ᄉᆞ오년이요윤효졍리즁은역신
년에쳐고ᄒᆞ고법부대신이샹
쥬ᄒᆞ엿더니 쳐분으로등감
등ᄒᆞ야류빈로써밧구라ᄒᆞ옵셧
더라

○피임원장 룡군법원쟝은양
셩환씨가운동중이라더라

○처교죄인수효 법부에서츄
본을드릿는ᄃᆡ각지판소에쳐교
로쳐하ᄒᆞᆫ죄인이칠십이명이라
더라

○금지분화자 경무ᄉᆞ신티휴
씨가명을발ᄒᆞ야무론남녀ᄒᆞ고
단속으로옷을입은자는일졀엄
금ᄒᆞ라ᄒᆞ고밤아홉시이후에는
녀인은길에단이지못ᄒᆞ게금지
ᄒᆞᆫ다더라

○공진회경원 공진회에서경
위원에청원ᄒᆞ기를수무쇼봉쇄
ᄒᆞᆫ바에이르화쳘빗원ᄒᆞᆫ화삼빗원
을이러ᄒᆞ니곳출급ᄒᆞ라ᄒᆞᆫ지라
종관양셩환씨가히수건을곳샹
쥬ᄒᆞ엿더라

○양쥬군수시은 양쥬군슈홍
티운씨는금번하 현궁시에드
롱군삼쳔인의게형미오십셕을
특별이분급ᄒᆞ엿다더라

○대흥화젹 대흥군니면사는
리슌하의쳔과가지는딤이심륙
일인데그날밤에화젹수삼명이
륙혈포을가지고돌입ᄒᆞ야용길
ᄒᆞ기를우리가세가지권세가잇
는것은죽이며ᄯᆞᆯ화ᄒᆞ며부녀겁
탈ᄒᆞᆷ이라ᄒᆞ고돈일쳔오빅량을
쎄아셔찻다더라

○왕실리언셜 쟝일에일진회
에서왕실리셰셔가회ᄒᆞ엿는ᄃᆡ
그목젹은수태장령실시ᄒᆞᆯ일인
ᄃᆡ원양자ㅣ쳘샹여명이라더라

○흥의졀금 지금신임경무ᄉᆞ
의힝졍은세샹사ᄅᆞᆷ들이희망ᄒᆞ
논바어니와쟈이ᄂᆞᆫ보리졍은바지
잉ᄂᆞᆫ쟈들을포승으로뢰여ᄂᆞᆫᄃᆡ
젼에서졈은바지를버셔뒤졍어
입고찻다ᄒᆞ니 국샹에졈은바
지잉ᄂᆞᆫ것이불쾌ᄒᆞ미비미더니창
샹쾌ᄒᆞ다고들두에실샹엽시다이
찻치ᄒᆞᄂᆞᆫ쟈와사ᄅᆞᆷ을속여외식
요리집에단이는쟈와칭녀가에
젼황ᄒᆞᄂᆞᆫ자와잡기ᄒᆞᄂᆞᆫ자와
긔와ᄡᅥ쳠ᄒᆞᄂᆞᆫ자와귀신가에뫼문로
다면긔타잡샹ᄒᆞᄂᆞᆫ자와졈치ᄂᆞᆫ자와
고검쇼ᄒᆞᄂᆞᆫ슐쟈와보는자와
등을ᄒᆞ다ᄒᆞᄂᆞᆫ고슈ᄇᆞᆨ화ᄒᆞᆫ동ᄉᆞᆨ이쳑ᄒᆞᆫ켓
ᄒᆞ더라

○경셩총순보고 함경북도관
찰부총순리응규가경무쳥으로
보고ᄒᆞ기를너ᄃᆡ경찰과외국인
을티졉ᄒᆞ며취ᄒᆞᄂᆞᆫ기슈원리
분셔의의무이온바군티가리왕
ᄒᆞ며거류홈으로브리도로가죠
졀ᄒᆞ야너어보고ᄒᆞ지못ᄒᆞ엿사
오니황ᄒᆞ오와뒤좌ᄒᆞ오며본부
관찰ᄉᆞ리윤직는케임된관보가
리도ᄒᆞᆫ날에본군슈로써셔리들
니고쥬시ᄎᆞᆯ셩ᄒᆞ야환죠ᄒᆞ란
조음에로국쟈관제인이비단군
수들결진ᄒᆞ고길을막을ᄉᆡᆼ아
란문밧긔셔파수ᄒᆞᄂᆞᆫ고로몸을
빼여나지못ᄒᆞᆫ을터니쟈넌싱월

에 ᄂᆡ부훈령을 봉승ᄒ와 당 인장을 본군슈 샹헌ᄃᆡ외게 면ᄃᆡᄒ여 표부ᄒ고 셔울에 발졍ᄒ란 든조음에 로진쟝관이 ᄇᆡᆨ명을 령솔ᄒ고 경셩군슈를 위협ᄒ야 당쟝 광경이 여ᄃᆡ가 업ᄉ온바 군슈가 부득이ᄒ야 히인장을 로국쟝관의게 ᄂᆡ여준즉 그 쟝관이 엇지 로란ᄒᆫ 젹의 을ᄒᆫ 팔에 걸고 결으ᄃᆡ 만일 이 을 쓸일이 [illegible] ᄒ여 가변인장을 파쇄ᄒ여 ᄇᆡ리라ᄒ고 ᄂᆡ부에서 온 훈령을 ᄲᆡ앗서가고 셩문을 파슈ᄒ며 리두ᄉ를 츌입치 못ᄒ게 ᄒ기로 보고ᄒ노라ᄒ엿더라

○조쳥젼조친관 일본사외부로 조회ᄒ기를 경셩과 밋 그 부근디에 고치안 유지ᄒᆷ을 위ᄒ야 우리 사령부에서 경찰사무를 담임거ᄒᆡᆼᄒ노니 청컨ᄃᆡ 귀정부에 당ᄒᆫ 관헌의게 젼지ᄒᆷ이 가ᄒ다ᄒ얏더라

○덕관조회 덕공관에서 외부로 조회ᄒ되 젼에 한국에 쥬차ᄒᆫ 우리 령사와 이번의 게ᄒᆫ 쟝을 한황폐하께서 보버셧더니 지금 범국과리로 브터 령슈증이 왓고 쥬샤 황룡괴감ᄒᆫ 셩의로 써 젼쥬ᄒ기를 쳥ᄒ엿기 ᄒ 령슈증셔를 보ᄂᆡ니 쳥컨ᄃᆡ 젼쥬ᄒ라ᄒ엿더라

○쥬쳥룡관면보 작일에 쥬쳥공관에서 외부에 면보ᄒ기를 본공사가 작일에 발환ᄒ엿다더라

○조쳥영방 연산군슈가 외부로 보고ᄒ기를 본군 별곡면 거ᄒᄂᆞᆫ 리등셔가 샹주 거ᄒᄂᆞᆫ 리관쳘 쳐에 돈 진됴건이 엉으로 심샹량인ᄃᆡ 신오랑은 지논 봄에 잉의 보금ᄒ엿고 거월 륙일에 그나마 지신오랑을 다ᄇᆡ 보ᄒ엿ᄂᆞᆫᄃᆡ 리관쳘이가 한젼령도 역부 젹숑장샹탄을 다리고 와서 가슈를 츄셕ᄒᄂᆞᆫ가라고 본관이 그리 쳐를 [illegible] 녀가라고 쳐망ᄒ엿더니 그 잇ᄂᆞᆫ 날밤에 일인 쳡여명을 거나리고 리도ᄒ야 충을 노코 동ᄂᆡ 빗셩 리권만 등 ᄉᆡᆼ인을 잡아갓스니 셰샹에 엇지 이런ᄒᆫ 변이 잇스리오 일본사의게 젼조ᄒ야 곳 엄졍이 방어케ᄒ시기를 바란다ᄒ엿더라

○경흥감리보고 경흥감리가 외부로 보고ᄒ기를 거십일월일일에 아라사 부령 일인이 병뎡이 ᄇᆡᆨ명을 거ᄂᆞ리고 부령으로브터 본셔 각공히와 밋 민가에 리도ᄒ야 쟝츗과 동ᄒ라ᄒᆫ다ᄒ엿더라

○경령회민 향회에서 경셩일진회소셔 만듯고 샹경ᄒ더니 일본헌병이 조화 경찰을 곤공표 실시ᄒ니 회원소동이 안평젼셔에 방해가 될듯ᄒ지라 고로 열쟉동립셔 기회ᄒ고 헌병ᄒᄂᆞᆫᄃᆡ 경관 [illegible]

강가 진라위 깁졍근을 다 슴어바린ᄃᆡ 뒤에 과ᄎᆞ가 평고ᄒᆞᆷ티이라ᄒ고 연셜을 맛치ᄃᆡ 일본헌병사령부에서 명령ᄒ기를 시골회원은 각각 도라가서 취업ᄒ라ᄒ엿ᄂᆞᆫᄃᆡ 그날 회중에ᄂᆞᆫ 한졍부에서 보호슌병을 파송치 말고 일헌병이 담당ᄒ겟노라ᄒ고 쟝곡쳔대쟝이 졍부로 통보ᄒ엿다더라

○쟝곡쳔의견 쟝곡쳔씨가 한국군사 비치에 ᄃᆡᄒ야ᄂᆞᆫ 십대ᄃᆡ로 ᄆᆡ ᄃᆡ에 사ᄇᆡᆨ명식 셜치ᄒ기로 의견셔를 졍부에 제츌ᄒ엿다더라

○ᄂᆡ부면훈젼북 ᄂᆡ부에서 젼라북도관찰부로 면훈ᄒ기를 드론즉 옥과군슈가 회민 일명을 탐샬ᄒ엿다ᄒ니 과연 젹확ᄒᆫ진ᄃᆡ 진샬노 극히 히연ᄒᆫ지라 별노이 목을 보ᄂᆡ여 탐지ᄒ야 회사진의 면말을 샹확곳치 치보ᄒ라ᄒ엿더라

○담포군보 담포군슈가 ᄂᆡ부로 보고ᄒ기를 진보회로라고 칭ᄒᄂᆞᆫ 엇던 사ᄅᆞᆷ이 삼ᄇᆡᆨ명이 읍ᄂᆡ에 모혀드러와 총을 사발ᄒ고 탕진을 ᄡᅦ고 총은 잡순 옷슬 닙고 ᄒᆡᆼ이를 집ᄒ엿고 말인즉 보국안민ᄒ다 칭ᄒ고 사ᄅᆞᆷ을 ᄃᆡᄒ야 연셜ᄒ기를 읍ᄃᆡ에 사무소를 셜치ᄒ다ᄒ야 쳥문이 회파ᄒ고로 불너드러 무른즉 본군에 ᄇᆡᆨ셩이 구명이 되ᄂᆞᆫ지라 [illegible] ᄒ엿더라

○쟝류괴착 근일에 아편연 [illegible]

○ᄆᆡ쟝ᄃᆡ졍계 미국공사가 외부로 조회ᄒ야 양화도에 외국인 ᄆᆡ쟝ᄃᆡ를 확쟝ᄒᆷ은 사건으로 루차 ᄒ셥ᄒ더니 지작구일에 미국공사와 외부협판과 ᄂᆡ부ᄃᆡ방국쟝 제씨가 ᄆᆡ쟝ᄃᆡ를 졍계ᄒᆷ은ᄎᆞ로 츌왕ᄒ엿더라

○일관연회 지작구일에 일본공사가 각ᄃᆡ관을 쳥요ᄒ야 본공관에서 오찬회를 셜ᄒᆡᆼᄒ엿더라

○공진공함 공진회에서 공함ᄒ기를 ᄂᆡ부ᄃᆡ신 조병식은 ᄉ시 도라가서 샹십년 동셔ᄒᆫ후에 나와 츌사ᄒ고 군부대신 리종건은 갑오년에 도망ᄒ엿든 남촌리대쟝이니 진죽 도라갑이 가ᄒ다ᄒ엿더라

○조률무률 시흥군에 민요건으로 압샹ᄒᆫ 졍범 하규명을 조사ᄒ던ᄃᆡ 인ᄃᆡ 본리 젹당ᄒᆫ 률문이 업스미 평리원에서 각법률가에셔 외론을 거둔다더라

별보

론돈발 십이월삼십일

○로국의외채 로국의외채조약이 샹립되엿ᄂᆞᆫᄃᆡ [illegible] 빗반이오 실샹갑은 ᄇᆡᆨ에 구십오로ᄒ야 이쳔오ᄇᆡᆨ만방을 모집ᄒ게 되엿다더라

동디발 일월이일

○화란과협 화란국이 동인도셔읍에 군함네쳑을 이리로 파송ᄒ엿ᄂᆞᆫᄃᆡ 중립을 직히기 위ᄒᆷ이라더라

동디발 동일

○로함소식 로국 힝군대쟝 로졔스트벤스기씨의 함ᄃᆡ가 작일에 마다가스카에 셴마리에셔 ᄯᅥ낫ᄂᆞᆫᄃᆡ 희망봉을 셰ᄂᆞᆫ 후로 풍파를 맛낫것마ᄂᆞᆫ ᄇᆡ들이 다 무양ᄒ더라

론돈발 일월이일

○로국ᄂᆡ졍 윗트씨를 ᄂᆡ각의쟝에 임명ᄒ엿ᄂᆞᆫᄃᆡ 동씨ᄂᆞᆫ 황뎨께셔 ᄂᆡ리신 긔량조칙을 실시ᄒ기 위ᄒ야 열심으로 예비ᄒᆫ다ᄒ며

뎨일ᄂᆡ각회의ᄂᆞᆫ 일월샹일에 연단ᄒ며

분란의회에서 로국황뎨의게 쳥원ᄒ기를 일쳔구ᄇᆡᆨ삼년에 ᄂᆡ린 분란에 ᄃᆡᄒᆫ 조칙을 환슈ᄒ고 분란에 다시 법률젼여를 회복ᄒ야 달나ᄒ엿더라

동디발 십이월삼십일일

○로함슈리 포트세이드에 잇ᄂᆞᆫ 류리등신원의 보ᄒᆫ바를 거ᄒᆫ즉 ᄇᆡ보로보스키 대쟝의 함ᄃᆡ가 일간에 포트세이드에 올터인ᄃᆡ 그 함ᄃᆡᄂᆞᆫ 슈양함과 사젹과 슈리피할 오쳑으로 조직ᄒᆫ거시라ᄒ엿더라

론셜

젼쟁의 됫ᄂᆞᆫ후 (속)

○우리가 한국과 쳥국이 일본의 패ᄒᆞᆯ 조짐이 잇ᄂᆞᆫᄇᆡ에 엇지ᄒᆞᆯ것을 미리 말ᄒ엿스니 [illegible] 일 신문에 보조가 되깃도다 ᄯᅩ 그 신문에 말ᄒ되 이번 ᄊᆞ홈에 일본이 이긔면 쳥국에 ᄃᆡᄒ야 로국이 이긔ᄂᆞᆫ 것과 ᄆᆡ우 다르다 ᄒ엿스니 ᄆᆡ우 우숩 말이로다 그 신문에 [illegible] ᄒ야 보 쳥국을 ᄉᆞ펴보면 젼국에 핍박ᄒᄂᆞᆫ 위협ᄒᄂᆞᆫ 일이 졈졈 만히 가니 [illegible] ᄒᄂᆞᆫ 쳥국졍부가 [illegible] 이번 ᄊᆞ홈에 반일 로국이 이긔게 되면 로국이 쳥국에 ᄃᆡᄒ야 엇지ᄒᆞᆯ고 그ᄯᅢ에ᄂᆞᆫ 로국이 쳥국을 가지고저 ᄒᄂᆞᆫ 무옴ᄃᆡ로ᄒ야 핍박ᄒᄂᆞᆫ 명령이 반ᄃᆞ시 잇슬것이오 [illegible] 일ᄒ게ᄒ려니와 쳥국에셔도 무숨 슈죵ᄒᄂᆞᆫ 외에 능히 다른 계칙을 ᄂᆡ지 못ᄒ리니 이ᄯᅢ 로국이 만쥬를 영원히 졈령ᄒᆷ은 의례히 ᄒᄂᆞᆫ 것도 [illegible]

흔 일에 뒤ᄒ야 항의ᄒᄂᆞᆫ 것을 보면 이다음에 만일 케제가 잇스면 쳥국이 로국의게 부ᄃᆡ 길을 치부ᄒ야 두ᄂᆞᆫ 것이 분명ᄒ도다 근일에 샹히에서 위경을 지ᄂᆡ왓지 츈씨와 리홍쟝씨의 량ᄌᆞ 양유씨가 쳥평ᄒ야 북경졍부에 권고ᄒ되 오리되면 필경 로국이 의일리이오 로국의 셰력을 빙자ᄒ기 어려우니 지금 쳥국을 위ᄒ야 케획ᄒ면 ᄃᆡ젹이 문에 잇슬ᄯᅢ에 속히 화친ᄒᄂᆞᆫ 것이 샹칙이라ᄒ야 북경졍치가들이 이런 말에 경흥ᄒ다더라 이런 말을 편지로도 ᄒ며 면보로도 ᄒᄂᆞᆫᄃᆡ 왕지츈씨와 양유씨가 ᄉᆡᆼ각ᄒ기를 예사 사ᄅᆞᆷ들은 면보로 무숨 말을 드르면 더 마음이 요동된다ᄒ야 여러번 면보로 용교ᄒ게 권고ᄒᄂᆞᆫ지라 그러ᄒ나 근ᄅᆡ에 쳥국 리부관원 ᄒ나이 봉텬디방에 시찰ᄒ고 도라와서 로국이 능히 일아 지 못ᄒ겟다고 자긔의 의견을 말ᄒ야셔 그러므로 북경에서 지금 중안졍ᄒ게 되엿스나 이다음에 어ᄂᆞᆫᄯᅢ ᄯᅩ 북경이 소요ᄒ게 될는지 우리ᄂᆞᆫ 모르겟도다 만일 일본이 패ᄒᆞᆯ 조짐이 잇스면 쳥국외무부에서 엇지ᄒᆞᆯ것을 우리ᄂᆞᆫ 샹샹ᄒ노라ᄒ엿더라

(완)

잡보

○송씨공쳔 작일에 독립관에셔 일진회원들이 모혀 연셜ᄒᆫ후에 즁회장의 원을 송병쥰씨로 택졍ᄒ엿ᄂᆞᆫᄃᆡ 동씨가 여러히 일본 류람을 ᄒ야 각항지식이 넘고 소위 샹방침이 만ᄒᆷ으로 쳔망이 되엿더라

○우산샹쳔츌티 일본수령부에셔 (국회)라고 쓴 우산 샹쳔 파ᄉᆡᆼ시 삼쳔이 나왓ᄂᆞᆫᄃᆡ 쟝ᄎᆞᆺ 회원즁 유력ᄒᆫ 자의게 반급ᄒᆫ다ᄒᄂᆞᆫᄃᆡ 이 우산에 국회라고 쓴 ᄯᅳᆺ슨 국회를 표ᄒᄂᆞᆫ 고로 우산에 특별히 표ᄒ엿다더라

○항거경관츄리 경무관 ᄇᆡ셔ᄃᆡ씨가 양복을 입고 일진회 긔회ᄒᄂᆞᆫ 독립관을 관광ᄎᆞ로 츌거ᄒ엿더니 일헌병이 방참소로 잡아간지라 한셩소윤 박승조씨가 헌병소령부에 젼왕ᄒ야 담판ᄒ고 ᄇᆡ셔ᄃᆡ씨를 차자왓다더라

광고

○본인의 쟝ᄌᆞ 치뎜이가 본시 부랑패류로 그 부형ᄌᆞ뎨간에 분쟈 뎍ᄒ여 가진 면쟝문권을 슈히 도뎍ᄒ며 ᄂᆡ엿기로 셰부동이ᄒ야 셔문권을 만든 일 엇고 이에 광고ᄒ오니 ᄂᆡ외국인간에 샹가속지 말고 한치뎜의 가진 문권을 면졍케 마옵기를 바라옴

평양셩ᄂᆡ 셔부 한치뎜 고ᄇᆡᆨ

TELEGRAMS.

Chefoo, Jan. 2nd.

Beside, the four torpedo-boats a steam launch from Port Arthur has arrived. Two of the torpedo-boats are anchored in the outside harbor and two in front of the Russian Consulate.

Later.

The torpedo-boats and steam launch are manoeuvering in front of the Russian Consulate.

Jan. 3rd.

During the night everything was quiet. This morning another Russian ship has entered the harbour. Six Japanese torpedo boats are lying outside.

Later.

Two Russian torpedo launches have just arrived. Seven Japanese destroyers and one cruiser can be seen anchored outside. The "Baltimore" and the Japanese cruiser fired salutes.—Tsingtauer Neuste Nachrichten.

Army Headquarters.

In the engagement at Otzeling on the 6th inst. the Russians suffered about 40 casualties, including one officer killed. They have retreated in a northerly direction.

Tokyo, Jan. 8th.

The Japanese have permitted General Stoessel to return to Russia; he will leave Dalny on the 12th inst. Admiral Wiren and the military officers Fock Smiloff and Kolpartsky (?) will be sent to Japan as prisoners.

Japanese Legation.

General Nogi wired to Tokyo on the 8th inst. that the prisoners were handed over as agreed. Their total number is 878 officers and 23,491 men. Of these 441 officers and 229 men have taken the oath not to re-engage in hostilities and they will consequently be allowed to return to Russia. The three officers Fock Smiloff and Kolpatsky as well as Admiral Wiren refused to take the oath and they will be sent to Japan as prisoners. General Stoessel leaves Dalny on the 12th inst. for a certain place,

Japanese Legation.

The Admiralty have announced that as the Japanese have now occupied the whole of the Liaotung peninsula, the proclamation issued by Admiral Togo on July 1st has been annulled. No ships, however, unless in the service of the Japanese Government will be permitted to enter the harbor of Port Arthur.

Tokyo, Jan. 9.

An official report received at the Admiralty yesterday states that all the ships in Port Arthur, including the Sevastopol, were blown up and sunk, but 6 Russian destroyers managed to escape in the night. The Akishima and some destroyers were sent after them to Chefoo, while the Choyoda and the Tatsuta were despatched to Kiaochau with the result that the Russian boats are now disarmed.

London, Dec. 24.

The New York "Sun" strongly urges the necessity of concluding an alliance between England and the United States, similar to the Anglo-Japanese Alliance.

The Home Office, replying to Mr. Hayashi's announcement that the districts without magistrates would be placed under the jurisdiction of Japanese to be paid by the Korean government, state that there is absolutely no necessity for this step. Magistrates have been appointed to all districts but in some cases, owing to the interruption of traffic on the roads, they have been unable to proceed to the country to take up their posts.

JAPANESE DEMAND ON KOREA.

The "Nichi Nichi" learns that Mr. Hayashi, Minister at Seoul, has reopened negotiations with the Korean authorities concerning Japan's claim for a sum of over 220,000 yen as indemnity for the murder of or assault on the Japanese by the Koreans. For some time after the demise of the late Korean Empress, a violent anti-Japanese feeling prevailed among the peninsular people, with the result that several cases of murder, in which the Japanese were the victims, occurred. Owing to the usual procrastination of the Korean authorities, the question has for several years past been in abeyance, but now our Government seems to have decided to settle the matter once and for all. Mr. Hagiwara, First Secretary to our Legation in Korea, when he recently returned to his post, was specially instructed to expedite the negotiations in this connection.—Japan Times.

RUSSIAN OPINION OF JAPANESE TACTICS.

Yes, we were greatly mistaken when we called them "little Japs," says the "Russkoye Slovo." We have never before had to deal with such skillful opponents. They have included in their tactics all modern methods, strictly adapting them to their own national peculiarities. For instance, knowing the weakness of their cavalry, they never allow it to go out unsupported. There is always infantry behind it, and our cavalry often runs against it, not expecting its presence.

The Japanese reconnaissance is effected thus: A compact force of riflemen marches, sustained by screens, and patrols move about five versts ahead. At a distance of three versts the scouts are preceded by a number of Chinese. These last come to the Russian lines, examine the camp, and make signal to the Japanese concerning the whereabouts of the cavalry patrols. As the country is mountainous they advance at the rate of seven versts a day, entrenching and fortifying every step they take. Their path is an uninterrupted row of fortifications. Knowing the excitable, impressionable temper of their soldiers, they never pursue the enemy before settling down in good order upon the position occupied, because during a pursuit troops often become disarranged. Judging by their operations one could imagine they are the most phlegmatic and methodical people in the world—so strong in their military education and their knowledge of the art of war. They very reasonably avoid the bayonet. Their leading ranks run away to the right and left, opening the front for the fire of the succeeding lines. Running round these to the rear, they again form their ranks, thus taking the place of reserves.

If the troops uncovered are unable to stop our attack by fire they repeat the manoeuvre. What self-control, what discipline are required in order to do this, and what a consciousness of strengh! When they are on the march it is all but impossible for them to meet with any surprises. In addition to the men detached for guard, they surround their columns by chains of scouts, who advance along the crests of the elevations. Movement under such conditions may be slow, but it is sure.

The value of mineral products of Great Britain in 1903 was £101,808,400 as compared with £107,104,900 in 1902. A decline in the price of coal from 8s. 3d. to 7s. 8d. per ton accounted for the difference, though the production of coal in 1903 was the largest ever reported, 230,234,500 tons.

The Imperial Household Department have informed the Foreign Office that they have received information that the Japanese railway workers are felling trees in the vicinity of the Dai Won Kun's grave and are staking out ground there. They request that the Japanese Legation will put an immediate stop to this desecration of the hallowed spot.

GOLD MINING IN JAPAN.

The "Chugai Shogyo" reports that Mr. Rutherford Harris (formerly connected with the late Mr. Cecil Rhodes), and Captain King have arrived in Japan, as representatives of a Belgian syndicate, for the purpose of working the Japanese goldfields, in concert with Mr. T. Wada, ex-Director of the Mining Bureau in the Agricultural and Commercial Department, and Mr. Junzo Kawamura. As a preliminary step, these two experts have, according to the same paper, already entered into negotiations with the Government for a charter to work the recently discovered Kesen gold mine.

DEFRAUDING THE REVENUE.

On December 23rd in the Imperial Diet, Tokio, Mr. Kusume (Liberal) introduced an interpellation to the Government with regard to the control of the Imperial customs, which he described as lax as testified to by the clandestine imports of sugar by the Nippon Seiseito Kaisha. According to Tokyo papers and to the result of investigations he had made, he said the Government had been defrauded by the Company of about 1,269,000 a year, and this had been going on for sone five years. The Company imported sugar from Hawaii and Java in boxes of 500 pounds, and while transporting them by boats from steamers to the customs, the Company's officials took away 100 pounds from each box, this quantity being carried direct to the Company's secret tank. Thus it paid customs duty on only 400 pounds for each 500 pounds imported. The result was that the Company, which had been unable to declare any dividend at all, was recently paying 20 per cent. to its shareholders. The Japanese customs, the speaker said, was now the security for the foreign loan, and the Government ought to be specially careful in its control. He wanted to know what steps the Government had taken in this matter.

General Hasegawa proposes to the Government that the Korean army shall be reduced to 10 batallions of 400 men each.

A dispatch to ehe "Frankfurter Zeitung" from Constantinople on Nov. 17th said Turkey is ordering 100 new batteries of artillery from German, French and English factories at the cost of $10,000,000, the Krupp Company gets the largest contracts.

The Kong-chin-hoi society have requested the Minister for Home Affairs to retire into privacy for 30 years and study books dealing with up-to-date affairs. As Mr. Cho Byung-sik has already attained the age of 73 this seems rather a tall request.

Twenty six commissariat officials and stewards belonging to the Kure Naval Station, who have since April last been under trial at the court-martial for having carried on a dishonest trade with contractors, were recently sentenced to various terms of imprisonment ranging from one month to ten years. The cantractors involved in the affair, over 20 in number, are still in prison awaiting judgment.

The meeting held yerterday by the Il chin-hoi was the largest, as far as numbers are concerned held yet. It was decided that the society should use every endeavour to obtain the dismissal from the government of Messrs. Sin Ki-son, Yi Yong-tai, Yi Yun-yong, Kim Kachiu, Ho Wi and Kim Chung-keun. Prior to the meeting General Hasegawa wrote to the Foreign Office telling them to refrain from sending Korean police to the meeting place as Japanese gendarmes would be responsible for order. Mr. Bai Suk-tai a police inspector, went to the meeting, merely as a spectator, and was immediately arrested by the gendarmes, but was soon released owing to strong representations made by Mr. Pak Sung-cho, the Vice Governor of Seoul.

FRANCE AND MOROCCO.

Paris, November 14th.

The "Matin" says it is able to indicate M. Delcasse's programme in regard to the policy of pacific penetration in Morocco. The French Government, it says, will first endeavour to restore the weakened authority of the Sultan, and will then direct its efforts towards grouping the different tribes in a sort of federal union, under the direction of the Sultan.

In order to obtain these results France will content herself with sending two representatives, a schoolmaster and a doctor, to each of the towns on the Algerian frontier, Ujda, Figuig, and Igli. These officials will, it is expected, soon be extraordinarily useful as instruments in promoting the French propaganda and France will also endeavour to earn the gratitude of the population by ensuring honesty in commercial dealings between the tribes.

In each tribe a notable will be appointed to surpervise the carrying out of contracts. He will himself lay before the Djemmas and the Cadies any disputes which may arise between the tribes. In the event of his authority being disregarded. France would intervene in order to ensure the triumph.

A Delimitation Commission will also be appointed to settle difficulties which may arise between the Moroccans and the colonists or tribes of Western Algeria. In the interior of the Empire the French work of gradual infiltration will praceed by not less efficacious means. The Sultan's treasury being exhausted, France will furnish him with the means he requires for the construction of bridges, roads, hospitals, and schools, in exchange for a financial or Customs guarantee.

"There is every reason to believe," the "Matin adds, "that the work undertaken in Morocco will proceed steadily and peacefully, and thus M. Delcasse's programme will be realised. In contrast to what happened in Tunis this result will be attained without friction, and, on the contrary, our relations with the Powers we may meet on our way will become closer and more cordial—Reuter.

The Korea Daily News.

Issued at 5 P. M. daily except Sundays.

Rate of Subscription:—
Per Year,............Yen 25.
Per Quarter,..........Yen 7.
Per Month,..........Yen 2.50.

Postage in Korea not charged extra.
Postage abroad charged extra.

Advertisements, 50 sen per day for 1 inch or less.
5 yen per month per inch.
50 yen per year per inch.

All communications to
E. T. BETHELL,
Editor and Publisher,
Pak-tong, Seoul.

AN ANSWER TO THE KOKUMIN.

The Editor of the "Kokumin Shimbun" has forwarded us a copy of that paper for January 1st. The style of the paper is a credit to all reponsible, the printing and illustrations being excellent.

In the ordinary way it does not come within our scope to comment upon the policy of such a newspaper but as the New Year's issue of the Kokumin contains two colums of English, we should like to make a few remarks on the opinions therein given.

To begin with, none could take exception to the aims of the Kokumin as thus set forth:—

"We take this opportunity to explain the standpoint of the "Kokumin Shimbun. Our cardinal object is to be a national organ. From the outset, it has been the contant endeavour of this paper to exert a potent influence for the sake of social edification and national progress. Especially since the war with China. which has been a turning point in our national life, stress has been laid on the necessity of qualifying our nation for their participation in international development and the onward movement of the civilized world. Japan is now widely recognized to be in the foremost rank of the civilized nations. At the same time, we are particularly glad to be able to note that the circulation of this paper has been increased by five fold since the opening of this war. This, we believe, is due to our constant endeavour for promptness and accuracy in statement."

Neither can one do aught but heartily congratulate a newspaper which has achieved such great success by such unimpeachable methods.

The "Kokumin Shimbun" has an International Department with an Editorial article written in English. For the purpose of criticism we reproduce a part of the article.

"The war is still in its first stage and the final result is yet far distant. On entering into hostilities, we only accepted the challenge of Russia, though in form we assumed the offensive. We are completely prepared to continue the war until our ultimate object is realized. There is nothing more misleading than the idea that the fall of Port Arthur is the virtual end of the war. We continue to stick to our original decision and hold to our policy of a preponderating influence in Korea and the open door in Manchuria. It would still be premature to speak today of the future of Manchuria, but it may be asserted that Japan's policy toward Manchuria has undergone no change. If Japan should act in Manchuria in the same manner as Russia has acted, it would be a deliberate betrayal of the international sympathy which has been shown to us from the beginning of the Japanese negotiations with Russia. Nevertheless, we feel warranted in believing that the Powers would not make any attempt to deprive us of the fruit of our victory, should they understand that, in prosecuting this war, Japan is doing invaluable service for the common cause of the civilized world and is paying a large sacrifice. As for Korea, it is often said that Japan is not treating her as a truly independent nation, despite all pledges to preserve the integrity of the Peninsular Kingdom. The plain fact is that, when a man cannot or will not stand by himself, somebody has to hold him, or he collapses. Japan's policy toward Korea has been fixed and unchanged from the time of the Japan-China War. To maintain the existence of the neighboring Kingdom, Japan takes it upon herself to supervise Korea's financial, military, and diplomatic affairs. The form of this programme is completely exhibited in the defensive alliance of February, 1904, and the subsequent agreement between Japan and Korea; and it is now all the more important to realize the spirit of the above programme. Thus Japan has not only the right, but also the duty, to protect Korea, under the terms of the recent engagements. Moveover, Japan has always to bear in mind that the removal of the neighboring pensula to a foreign Power is a standing menace to her very existence."

This is in our opinion the most temperate defense of Japan's position that has yet been published. Japan's aims are clearly set forth up to a certain point and, *prima facie*, no outsider ought to find fault with them.

Upon investigation, however, we find there are several points inviting comment. To begin with the "Kokumin" says that although Japan began the war, she only accepted Russia's challenge. Most people will agree with the "Kokumin" in this and think the question settled. But there is another point to be considered. Japan was not bound to accept the challenge; she only accepted it because she thought the time and circumstances favourable. So they were; much more favourable than they ever would have been again. Russia was beginning (owing to Kuropatkin's urgent representations) to think about getting ready when Japan commenced fighting.

So that Japan must not ask for sympathy because she accepted Russia's challenge. She simply did what suited her best. The many other alternatives did not commend themselves to Japan.

With regard to Korea, mentioning the alliance of Febuary 23rd 1904, (which was signed by the Emperor of Korea after the occupation of his country by Japanese troops and which has of course received no outside ratification) the "Kokumin" asks us to realise the spirit of the programme.

For our part we can only say that it seems to be our critism upon the absence of anything approaching the realization of the true spirit of that programme which has brought us so hopelessly at loggerheads with the Japanese in Korea.

The programme was a very specious and convincing one, but the subsequent talk about a "man who can not or will not stand by himself" or of Japan's supervising Korea's military financial and diplomatic affairs" in order to "maintain the existence of the" "Empire" (not "kingdom") is—well—another story.

There are other stories and that of the Il Chin Hoi is one of them, but none of them fit in with what appears to us to be the spirit of the programme.

We do not believe that the acquisition of Korea would be of benefit to Japan, and in our opposition to all attempts at unfair encroachment we are acting in accordance with this conviction. Imperialism and expansion are fine sounding terms but it must be remembered that the prosperous Jews have no Country, no Army, no Navy, and best of all, no political programme.

THE WHITE PERIL.

The following, says the Chefoo Daily News, is from the pen of a Japanese writer, in the Ta-Kung-Pao, Tientsin:

"The old yellow peril becomes the present day white peril. But how am I to write of it? The pen drops from my trembling hands, and I arraign the justice of heaven. Alas! Alas! Shall we yellow men ever again be our own masters?

"But I would not by groans and tears discourage the aspirations of my fellow Mongols. On the contrary, I boldly make the startling assertion that if this great dream of a golden age and a universal empire is to be realized, it must be through us Mongols. It wholly depends whether we yellow men can unite or not."

The above is a fair sample of a class of literature now being promulgated by Japanese and Chinese fanatics who are unquestionably in the pay of the Japanese Government, as is demonstrated in a recent report of the Society for the Diffusion of Christian and General Knowledge. It any man acquainted with conditions in China has heretofore doubted the fact that the Japauese Government is engineering the most gigantic attempt to instigate another antiforeign campaign in China, he should read the report of this Society which is too long for use in these columns. However, the revelations made by the report are of such a startling nature that some extracts are given.

The following is a paragraph of the report:

"Whilst inflammatory literature is being scattered broadcast all over the empire, and the tax gatherer is ubiquitous, can we wonder that new societies are being formed to give effect to the feelings of both government and people."

Again the report speaks as follows of the expected uprising:

"It will be a war to the death, as has been the case before in China—against the Mongols in the thirteenth, against the Christians and the Portuguese in the seventeenth century, against the Mohammedans in the nineteenth century and tried against all foreigners in 1900. But it will be on a grander scale than ever before."

His Majesty has telegraphed his congratulations to the Mikado, on the birth of a son to the Crown Prince of Japan.

His Majesty has refused to accept the resignations of the Ministers for Foreign Affairs, Finance and Agricultural Departments.

The commissioner of Police has instructed all his officers to redouble their efforts to maintain law in the city, despite the fact that that Japanese gendarmes are now doing police duty.

The magistrate of Hap Chon reports that he has received instructions to prohibit Japanese from gold mining in his district, but he finds them very difficult to carry out. A man named Nagayama with 11 others have commenced digging in the vicinity of the Hai In Sa monastery, regardless of private or government property, and point blank refuse to cease. He requests that the Japanese Legation will order them to withdraw.

The Korea Daily News.

VOL. II, TUESDAY, JANUARY 10, 1905. No. 6

大韓每日申報
대한ᄆᆡ일신보

(뎨이권칠호) (목요일) 일천구ᄇᆡᆨ오년일월십이일

본샤고ᄇᆡᆨ

이신보는영어와한어로셔계ᄆᆡ일츌판ᄒᆞ옵

신문가

ᄒᆞᆫ쟝 엽두돈오푼

ᄒᆞᆫ삭표 엽두량닷돈

우표가ᄒᆞᆫ삭닷돈

다ᄒᆞᆫ돈으로밧ᄉᆞᆸ

광고료는

긔한의쟝단과ᄌᆞ항의다쇼로즁감ᄒᆞ되헐가로밧을터이오며오ᄅᆡ지아니ᄒᆞ야대한사람마다다이신문을보실터이니광고ᄒᆞ시기를원ᄒᆞ시는이들은우리신문사에와서면약ᄒᆞ심을ᄇᆞ라옵

○발ᄒᆡᆼ소 박동대한ᄆᆡ일신보사 발ᄒᆡᆼ겸편즙인 영국인셜필림 쟝ᄌᆞ리오

사쟝 영국인 (비셜)

평양 디리졈

○평양효동사는권ᄆᆡ보씨로우리신문환ᄆᆡ디리인을뎡ᄒᆞ엿사오니평양에계신구람ᄒᆞ고쟈ᄒᆞ시는 쳠군ᄌᆞ는ᄒᆞᆫ디리졈에왕림ᄒᆞ와면의ᄒᆞ시옵

사고

○우리대한ᄆᆡ일신보의목뎍은대한의안녕질서에관ᄒᆞᆫ모든뎨목에디ᄒᆞ야는공평ᄒᆞᆫ변론을쥬쟝ᄒᆞᆷ이라우리동신원의탐보는신문보시는쳠군ᄌᆞ의게ᄒᆞᆼ샹보도ᄒᆞ리며편지들긔셔ᄒᆞ며주시는이는셩명과번디를젹어보내시기를희망ᄒᆞ오나이거슨신문샹에긔ᄌᆡᄒᆞ랴는거시아니오다만극히신용ᄒᆞ는증거를ᄉᆞᆷ고쟈ᄒᆞᆷ이라긔자는아모긔셔던지긔ᄌᆡᄒᆞᆷ을퇴각ᄒᆞ는권리를가젓ᄉᆞ나퇴각ᄒᆞ는리유를말ᄒᆞᆯ터이오며공즁광회를문란케ᄒᆞ는듯ᄒᆞᆫ긔셔는의례히밧지안켓ᄉᆞᆸ나이다

●본사셜시이ᄅᆡ로신문을ᄆᆡ양우톄로분젼ᄒᆞ와톄젼부의임의로젼ᄒᆞ는듯ᄉᆞ로변곳에는ᄒᆞᆨ늣게젼ᄒᆞ기도ᄒᆞ며ᄒᆞᆨ멋칠거슬ᄒᆞᆫ텹에젼ᄒᆞ기도ᄒᆞ며ᄒᆞᆨ아니젼ᄒᆞ는곳도잇다ᄒᆞ와우리신문을ᄉᆞ랑ᄒᆞ야구람ᄒᆞ시는 쳠군ᄌᆞ의게디ᄒᆞ야ᄆᆡ우미안ᄒᆞ옵기로지금은분젼인을두고ᄆᆡ일즉이젼ᄒᆞ며아니젼ᄒᆞ거나늣게거나ᄒᆞᆫ폐가업도록ᄒᆞ란ᄒᆞ오니ᄒᆞᆨ아니젼ᄒᆞ거는ᄒᆞᆨ늣게젼ᄒᆞ거나ᄒᆞᆫ일이잇스면본사로통긔ᄒᆞ며쥬심을희망ᄒᆞ옵

론셜

일본의외교

○지부에뎨ᄅᆡ뉴스라는신문은ᄒᆞᆫ독립ᄒᆞᆫ신문인즁노오리는밋는데그신문에말ᄒᆞ되일본사람들이황인죵인셔담에쟝치샹에리익을만이엇는다ᄒᆞ엿는지라그말이ᄇᆞᆫ이오른지라일본이로국과교셥ᄒᆞ던외교문ᄌᆞ를발표ᄒᆞᆫ때에셰계에셔그문ᄌᆞ의젹당ᄒᆞᆷ을경탄ᄒᆞ엿고론도신문에게ᄌᆡᄒᆞᆫ말솜남쟉의자긔의나라를위ᄒᆞ야변명ᄒᆞᆫ쟝셔는ᄆᆡ우조ᄒᆞᆫ감졍을이리킷도다셰계에셔처음에는일본의ᄌᆡ능을엽슈히녀엿다가지금은그번디로영국에셔는시끝에조고마ᄒᆞᆫ신문지라도모다우리의조고만ᄒᆞᆫ용ᄆᆡᆼᄉᆞ러온황ᄉᆡᆨ친구니용감ᄒᆞᆫ조교만ᄒᆞᆫ일본사람이니ᄒᆞ야귀가양푸ᄂᆞᆫ게ᄢᅦ드는지라

아마이거시그목젹에맛는셔담ᄋᆞᆫ이라일본사람이이런칭예를밧지마는그리ᄒᆞ나일본의근세력소를자셰히보면일본에로셩ᄒᆞᆫ졍치가들이외교샹에뎨일이오군인들의ᄌᆡ능과용ᄆᆡᆼᄒᆞᆷ은발ᄒᆞᆯ것도업는지라

이런졍치가들과군인들만널을쥬쟝ᄒᆞ엿스면우리는일본으로브터큰닐을바랄터이나그러ᄒᆞ나동경에ᄆᆡ우유셰력ᄒᆞᆫ소년졍치가들의단례가잇셔셔일본의명예와셩망을ᄇᆞᆫ히손샹ᄒᆞ는도다한국에잇는림관ᄉᆞ는젼쟝의반쳐음시작ᄒᆞᆯ셰에악죠ᄒᆞᆫ것과샹반ᄒᆞᆫ한국졍부를위협ᄒᆞ는졍췩을쓰는거슨자긔의ᄉᆞᄉᆞ의권으로ᄒᆞ는거시아닌줄노우리는밋노라

지금일본졍부는성각이젹은소년들의슈즁에잇도다그소년들은일본이쟝ᄅᆡ에강대ᄒᆞ게됨이평도를확쟝ᄒᆞ는데잇는줄노싱각ᄒᆞ야이젼졍의죵말에는일본이엇은드디라도직히갈과력이업게될거슨보지못ᄒᆞ고저의졍부에향ᄒᆞ야쉬이지아니ᄒᆞ고권ᄒᆞ는도다

관보

뎨삼쳔삼ᄇᆡᆨ이호 광무구년일월십일일

서임급ᄉᆞ령

○의원면본관 즁추원의관 리종원 즁추원의관 유쟝렬 즁추원의관 신상오 즁추원의관 김창렬 즁추원의관 박경리 즁추원의관 최영운 즁추원의관 신리셥 즁추원의관 김졔순

○임즁추원의관서주임관륙등 졍삼품 윤명셕 륙품 윤자션 륙품 민동식 륙품 유딘즁 륙품 리근하 륙품 신슈형 구품 주판ᄒᆞ 구품 송긔욱

이상일월륙일

○명궁니부특진관서칙임관일등 졍일품 리근명

○명종졍원경서칙임관삼등 비서원승 리명샹

○희궁니부특진관 종이품 민영국

○임비서원승서주임관륙등 졍삼품 김병년

○의원면본관 동신사면회쌰 쥬사 리방형

이상일월칠일

○승서판임관오등 참모부번역관보 리문명

일월구일

공덕룡사

○조셔ᄒᆞ야골ᄋᆞᄉᆞ티 졍일품리근명을명ᄒᆞ야궁니부특진관을명ᄒᆞ시다

○조셔ᄒᆞ야골ᄋᆞᄉᆞ티 찬졍최익현은엇시ᄒᆞ라ᄒᆞ시다

○조셔ᄒᆞ야골ᄋᆞᄉᆞ티 비서원승리명샹을명ᄒᆞ야죵졍원경을슴이시다

이상일월칠일

○의졍부참졍김셩근사직쇼 비지셩쇼구실경간이라반괴를셩찬ᄒᆞ는칙임이중ᄒᆞ고시세가간극ᄒᆞᆫ티병말ᄒᆞᆫ계ᄉᆞᆯ이아니니경은번거치말고곳시무ᄒᆞ라신사로부당을보니여젼유ᄒᆞ시다

○의졍부참찬최위사직쇼 비지셩쇼구실이라진실로사양홈이어긋ᄒᆞ니쳥ᄒᆞᆫ바는의시ᄒᆞ라ᄒᆞ시다

뎐보

일월구일본공사관착동

군공보

○포로수효 일월팔일에발ᄒᆞᆫ니목대쟝의보고요령에왈로군의포로들은교부ᄒᆞᆷ은긔셩규약의규졍ᄒᆞᆷ과곳치실ᄒᆡᆼ이되며로교일에필ᄒᆞ엿는뎨그총수는쟝교가팔ᄇᆡᆨ칠십팔명이오하사와병졸이이만삼쳔사ᄇᆡᆨ구십일명인뎨그즁에쟝교사ᄇᆡᆨ사십일명과병졸이ᄇᆡᆨ이십구명은일의밍셰를ᄒᆞ엿고ᄒᆞ호ᅵ크와스밀노와밋폰바도ᅵ스키쟝관샹인과밋일반히군쇼쟝은포로가되여일본으로압송ᄒᆞ기를희망ᄒᆞ고스테셀쟝군은일월십이일에모방면으로향ᄒᆞ야쳥리와들츌발ᄒᆞᆯ터이라ᄒᆞ엿더라

일월칠일본공사관착

군용보

○봉쇄희제 로동반도는지금에젼부가우리의졈령ᄒᆞᆷ이되엿기로칠월일일에동향대쟝이션고ᄒᆞᆫᄒᆞᆫ봉쇄는일월일일노희졔가되엿는지라그러나려순항은졍시간은일본졍부의사무에복역ᄒᆞ는션박외에는입항ᄒᆞᆷ을허치아니ᄒᆞᆫ다ᄒᆞ엿더라

잡보

○쟝기엄금 경무쳥에서쟝기ᄒᆞ는자를쟝기위ᄒᆞ야ᄯᅢ다사경찰ᄒᆞ는ᄃᆡ외광ᄒᆞ니에서쟝아왓다ᄒᆞ고운현궁니에셔하예빈등이쟝기을ᄒᆞ는고로범ᄉᆞᆫ쟉샹명을곳파송ᄒᆞ야과찰ᄒᆞ는중이라더라

○일본헌병티교시 ᄌᆞ금이후로는경셩과밋부근디에셔회쟝ᄒᆞ는빅셩의사회를톄결ᄒᆞ고자ᄒᆞ는자는며좌ᄒᆞᆫ됴항을쥰ᄒᆡᆼᄒᆞᆷ이가ᄒᆞᆷ

뎨일됴 졍ᄉᆞ에관계ᄒᆞᆫ사회를쳬결ᄒᆞ고자ᄒᆞ는자는그쥬간쟈가결샤조직ᄒᆞ기샹일젼긔ᄒᆞ야사명과ᄉᆞ무소ᄉᆞ무원등의명부를졍원ᄒᆞ야인가를엇음이라 (긔쥬와신분과직업과년령등을자셰히긔록ᄒᆞᆷ)

뎨이됴 졍ᄉᆞ에관계즁인을회동ᄒᆞ고회집ᄒᆞ는ᄯᅢ는회쟝은발긔ᄒᆞᆫ사름이긔회일젼긔ᄒᆞ야회쟝처소와년월일시와밋회집ᄒᆞ는목젹을쳥원ᄒᆞ야인가를경ᄒᆞᆷ이가ᄒᆞᆷ

UNION INSURANCE SOCIETY OF CANTON.

Head office Hongkong.
Marine risks underwritten at current rates.
Agents in Chemulpo,
E. MEYER & Co.

COMPAGNIE DES MESSAGERIES MARITIMES.

Fortnightly Direct Service.

For Marseilles
via Ports.
Sailing from Yokohama
Calling at Kobe,
Shanghai, Hongkong, Saigon, Singapore,
Colombo, Djibonti, Suez, Port Said
and Marseilles.

For particulars apply to
HOLME RINGER & Co.,
Chemulpo.

HAYASHIDA & CO.,
16 MYENG DONG, CHIN KO KAI, SEOUL.
BRANCH OFFICE AT CHEMULPO.

Money changers, Coal and Wood Merchants, Express Agents.

We are agents for the Pyeng-yang Coal Company and the Karazu Coal Company of Japan. We have the best quality of both anthracite and bituminous coal, and prompt execution of orders is our speciality. Firewood of all kinds kept in stock. Full weight guaranteed. Money of all denominations exchanged at current rates. Parcels received for all parts.

CHINA MUTUAL LIFE INS. OC.

Most favourable terms to policy holders.

Benefit system unsurpassed.

HOLME RINGER & Co,
Agents, Chemulpo.

C. P. R.

CANADIAN PACIFIC RAILWAY COMPANY'S ROYAL MAIL STEAMSHIP LINE.

THE FAST ROUTE BETWEEN CHINA, JAPAN, AND EUROPE VIA CANADA AND THE UNITED STATES.

Route from Hongkong via Shanghai, Nagasaki (Inland Sea of Japan) Kobe, Yokohama, Victoria and Vancouver.

Twin Screw Empress Steamship—6,000 Tons—Speed 19 knots.

PROPOSED SAILING FROM YOKOHAMA.
R. M. S. Empress of India.
R. M. S. Empress of Japan.
R. M. S. Empress of China.
R. M. S. Athenian.
R. M. S. Tartar.

Special reduction (first class only) granted to members of the Military, Naval, Diplomatic and Civil services and to Missionaries.

Passengers have choice of ten routes across the Continent of America and have privilege of travelling by any Atlantic Steamship Line.

Round the World passage tickets in connection with the P. and O. S. N., North German Lloyd and Messageries Co.'s £125.

All rates payable at current rate of exchange.

For further information, Tickets, Guide Books, etc., apply to

HOLME, RINGER & CO., AGENTS,
Chemulpo.

Grand Hotel,

(Formerly the Station Hotel)

Near the Railway Terminus, West Gate Seoul.

The Best Hotel in Korea.
Handsome new Building.
Fine Airy Rooms
Excellent Cuisine.
Terms Moderate.
Special terms to Missionaries
and to permanent boarders.

Electric cars within 2 minutes' walk.

W. H. EMBERLEY.
Proprietor

EVERY FACILITY.

In connection with Life Assurance Business is afforded by

The Standard Life Assurance Co.,

One of the largest and wealthiest of the Provident Institutions of the United Kingdom Forms of Application and all information will be promptly afforded on application.

10 CENTS A DAY.

Not a very large expenditure is it? But it is sufficient to secure for a man of 30 a policy with the STANDARD LIFE OFFICE for

$1323.

For all particulars of rates, etc., apply to

Holme, Ringer & Co.,
Agents, Chemulpo.

THE NEW YORK LIFE INSURANCE COMPANY.

Have you ever been declined by any Company?

Are you engaged in a specially hazardous occupation?

Have you heard of the New York Life Insurance Company's New Classifications for this class of Risks?

If not, send your date of birth, occupation and particulars of rejection, if any to

E. MEYER & Co.,
Agents, Chemulpo.

MITSUI BUSSAN KAISHA.
(MITSUI & Co.)
MITSUI GINKO.
(MITSUI BANK.)

The Bank is owned by the members of the Mitsui Family, who, as partners, assume an unlimited responsibility for all liabilities of the Bank:—

Capital........................Yen 5,000,000
Reserve Fund.................. " 3,600,000

HEAD OFFICE, TOKYO.
LONDON OFFICE, 34 LIME ST., E. C.

BRANCHES AND AGENCIES:—
New York, San Francisco, Hamburg, Bombay, Singapore, Manila, Hongkong, Amoy, Chefoo, Tientsin.

Kobe, Hakodate, Yokohama, Kure, Yokosuka, Moji, Shimonoseki, Miike, Wakamatsu, Nagasaki, Kuchinotsu, Karatsu, Sasebo, Misume, Taipeh, &c.

Telegraphic Address for all the Offices:
"MITSUI."
A. B. C. AND A. 1 CODES USED.

Contractors of Coal
To the Imperial Japanese Navy. Arsenals and Railway Bureau, Principal Railway Companies and Industrial Work, Home and Foreign Mail and Freight Steamers.

Sole Proprietors
Of the famous Miike, Tagawa and Yamano Coal Mines.

Sole Agents
For the sale of Fukumo, Hokoku, Ichimura, Kanoda, Mannoura, Onoura, Ostuji, Sonoda, Tsubaruro, Yoshinotani, Yoshio, Yurokibura and other coals.

YANGTSE INSURANCE ASSOCIATION, LTD.

The undersigned, having been appointed agents for the above company, are prepared to issue policies and pay losses on marine risks at regular rates.

E. MEYER & Co.,
Agents, Chemulpo.

AMERICAN KOREAN ELECTRIC CO.

Light and Power.

Main Office: Electric Building, Chong No.

RAILWAY DEPARTMENT.

OPERATING CARS BETWEEN EAST AND WEST GATE, EVERY TEN MINUTES:—

First Car leaves East Gate at 7:00 A. M. First Car leaves R. R. Station at 7:25 A. M
Last Car " East Gate at 8.40 P. M. Last " " R. R. Station at 9.05 P. M

OPERATING CARS BETWEEN EAST GATE AND IMPERIAL TOMB TERMINUS, EVERY TWENTY MINUTES:—

CONNECTING WITH EVERY ALTERNATE CAR ARRIVING AT EAST GATE FROM CHONG NO.

First Car leaves East Gate for Tomb at 7:10 A. M.
" " " Tomb for East Gate at 7:30 A. M.
Last " " East Gate for Tomb at 7:50 P. M.
" " " Tomb for East Gate at 8:10 P. M.

OPERATING CARS BETWEEN CHONG NO AND YUNG SAN RIVER EVERY TWELVE MINUTES:—

First Car leaves Chong No for South Gate at 7:12 A. M.
" " " Chong No for Yung San at 7:36 A. M.
" " " South Gate for Chong No at 7:20 A. M.
" " " Yung San for Chong No at 8:09 A. M.
Last " " South Gate for Chong No 9:00 P. M.
" " " Yung San for Chong No at 8.45. p. M.

SPECIAL PRIVATE CARS FURNISHED TO SUIT CONVENIENCE OF PATRONS. PRICES ON APPLICATION AT HEAD OFFICE.

LIGHTING DEPARTMENT.

Where less than 250 candle power of light is used, the rate per month will be
Per 16 candle power incandescent lamp,—All night.—Yen 2.50.
32 candle power incandescent lamp:—All night:—Yen 4.00.
50 candle power incandescent lamp:—All night:—Yen 6.00.
150 " " " " " " 10.00.
1200 " enclosed are " " " 20.00.

Where more than 250 candle power of light is used, a Meter will be installed, frequvdted:—Rent of Meter Yen 2.00 per month. Rate of charges by meter reading:—Two Sen per Ampere per hour. (Approximately this is equal to about One Sen per 16 C. P. lamp per hour) Minimum monthly charge where meter is installed, Yen 20.00 per month, which includes rental of meter.

Estimates for installing lights furnished on application
An assortment of chandeliers always on hand.

K. Murakami.
Photograph Studio
Chinkokai, Seoul.

Printing, Developing and Enlargement, of Photographs always Undertaken.

Korean Views and Pictures Illustrating Native Customs always on Sale,

---

THE OSAKA SHOSEN KAISHA.

Boats frequently on the berth for Chinnampo.

REGULAR SAILINGS BETWEEN JAPAN AND KOREAN PORTS.

FUSAN AND KOBE VIA SHIMONOSEKI.

OSAKA VIA MOKPO, FUSAN, SHIMONOSEKI AND KOBE.

MOJI DIRECT.

OSAKA VIA KUNSAN, MASANPO, FUSAN, SHIMONOSEKI AND KOBE.

CHEMULPO KUNSAN LINE,
Every three days.

CHEMULPO CHINNAMPO LINE.
Every three days.

For Freight and passage and further particulars apply to

THE OSAKA SHOSEN KAISHA,
Chemulpo

RONDON, PLAISANT & CO.

General Storekeepers and Merchants, Ships Contractors, Tobacconists, Commission and Forwarding Agents, Coal Merchants

IMPORTERS AND EXPORTERS

Seoul & Chemulpo.

W. D. WENTWORTH.

LANDING
AND
SHIPPING AGENT
AND
CUSTOMS BORDER.

12 OURA, NAGASAKI.

STEWARD & CO.
Chemulpo.

Shipchandlers and Storekeepers, Naval and Mercantile Contrrctors, Landing and Shipping Agents.

STEWARD'S HOTEL
Chemulpo.

Best accommodation in the port for travellers. Clean and well-aired rooms, good cuisine and prompt attendence, moderate tariff.

ㄷ삼됴 공수에관계ᄒᆞᆫ사회계
결과및셩은공수에관계가엄
시회집ᄒᆞ든디도며일됴데이
됴를원인가를결ᄒᆞᆷ이가ᄒᆞ야
의지ᄒᆞᆷ

뎨ᄉᆞ됴 집방계서중인이회ᄒᆞ
ᄒᆞ거ᄂᆞ다수인의운동ᄒᆞᆷ을일
결히탁지아니ᄒᆞᆷ(다만관ᄒᆞᆫ
샹자와그외에결례에치탁ᄒᆞᆯ
것은이한에잇지아니ᄒᆞᆷ

뎨오됴 회집ᄒᆞᄂᆞᆫ듸ᄂᆞᆫ헌병으
로ᄒᆞ야금림감케ᄒᆞ야하헌병
의명령을복종ᄒᆞᆷ이가ᄒᆞᆷ

뎨륙됴 사회계결과및회집의
취지서와및기타엇더ᄒᆞᆫ문자
를뭇지아니ᄒᆞ고회의명칭으
로문서를발표ᄒᆞ고회원을발
송ᄒᆞᄂᆞᆫ셰ᄂᆞᆫ전리ᄒᆞ야금렬을경
ᄒᆞᆷ이가ᄒᆞᆷ이라

뎨칠됴 본령을위범ᄒᆞᄂᆞᆫ자ᄂᆞᆫ
군률로처치ᄒᆞᆷ

한국주차헌병대장

일명광생교

○경사령령 경무사신리휴세
가장방국에고시ᄒᆞᆷ이좌와ᄀᆞᆺᄒᆞ
ᄂᆞ니로러가위급ᄒᆞ고로승속이
부피ᄒᆞ야법을엄ᄒᆞ고도두려워
ᄒᆞ지아니ᄒᆞ고원동ᄒᆞᆷ이잇ᄂᆞᆫ듸
도쳔ᄒᆞ고셜렴ᄒᆞᄂᆞᆫ바ㅣ엄습으로
ᄒᆞᆫ돈으로산ᄒᆞᆷ이ᄌᆞᆫ지어ᄅᆞ리가ᄒᆞ
전셰하여ᄐᆞ우리이갓이다경찰
의볼지아니ᄒᆞᆷ과관민의서로및
지못ᄒᆞᆷ이니ᄉᆞ사로도잇ᄂᆞᆫ적률
도라다보면그욧그리요갓은이
로밀ᄒᆞ기어려우리니이본경이
금계도에ᄂᆞᆫ전후제창이ᄒᆞᆫ두번
뿐이아니라ᄯᆞᆫ당ᄒᆞᄂᆞᆫ겨울에
라형청ᄒᆞ야법의지ᄒᆞ야종전
ᄒᆞ리니와그중에샹에정ᄒᆞᄂᆞᆫ근
관계로나만가령을고웃셤이히
를밧ᄂᆞᆫ자ᄂᆞᆫ물을우가히시금금
ᄒᆞ것기어에쓰이별ᄒᆞᆫ도고시ᄒᆞ
ᄂᆞ니이제소원인민은다유리아이번
쳐하경계ᄒᆞ야스사로죄를드ᄒᆞ이
그지말지어다

광무구년일월구일

광귀

일 화도로경도를어지럽케ᄒᆞ
야난리를되ᄒᆞ게ᄒᆞ고퇴셩을속
이ᄂᆞᆫ자(무슨무기샹을쓰자)

일 일을인ᄒᆞ야가쟈를ᄒᆞ며아ᄒᆞ지
자로일을만드러지산을탈취ᄒᆞᄂᆞᆫ

일 무른귀천ᄒᆞ고잠기로일을
샹아가산을경페ᄒᆞ며남이조례
를그릇치게ᄒᆞᄂᆞᆫ자

일 아편연에침륵ᄒᆞ야스사로
그신명을탕패ᄒᆞ며그몸을망ᄒᆞ고
자퇴ᄒᆞ미ᄒᆞ계ᄒᆞ야셔치지못ᄒᆞᄂᆞᆫ

일 무른남녀ᄒᆞ고셩제무방ᄒᆞᆫ
자로히창샹서치ᄒᆞ야주단등속으
로그옷을입은자(비단비히도
이또이로록에서잇ᄂᆞᆫ) 한은음ᄋᆞᆫ성도
일용조셩엄이라며다

○경대츌현 창ᄒᆞ요근치에ᄒᆞᆫ바

리며ᄂᆞᆫ계졉ᄒᆞ야나히엇ᄂᆞᆫ듸근에
예아참편을항ᄒᆞ야결ᄒᆞ며하날
셰고ᄒᆞ야왈나ᄀᆞᆺᄒᆞᆫ젼은을이죠
리방에거리에서자ᄂᆞ가히경지
를면치못ᄒᆞ리라인ᄃᆡ오주 홍원
의대응을림엉여전평이보졸ᄒᆞ
오ᄂᆞ마비호정지ᄃᆡ기을고셔슈
남에ᄒᆞᆯ이계ᄋᆞ셔이다우버흔젼
ᄂᆞᆫ병이안ᄒᆞᆫ사람이죽ᄂᆞᆫ다ᄒᆞ오
니이ᄀᆞᆺ치젼ᄒᆞᆫ일을노세상에두
지마옵시고 샹필의호셩지락
으로사ᄂᆞᆫ이젼빅성도로의게나리
셩히셩에쳐중ᄒᆞ야우ᄒᆞ오ᄂᆞᆫ 샹필
호셩지락을참고아리도이젼빅
셩으로외외ᄒᆞ든은혜를참계ᄒᆞ소
서ᄒᆞ엿더라

○궁니부조목 궁니부에서외
부에조복ᄒᆞ기를요우병이가무
안ᄒᆞ이잇슨때에ᄂᆞᆫ샹의게마례
와아자이게들전ᄒᆞ고묵희ᄒᆞᄂᆞᆫ수ᄂᆞᆫ
본부에서셩명도아지못ᄒᆞᄂᆞᆫ자
오셔전리의일명엿스나일본서
일로에젼부ᄒᆞᆷ을보니라ᄒᆞ엿
더라

○군수경찰시행세측

우리군수ᄂᆞᆫ군수행동샹에리의
을보호ᄒᆞ고쳐죵ᄒᆞᄂᆞᆫ군수의등
뒤에서공안과질셔를유지ᄒᆞᆯ필
요가잇ᄉᆞ셔ᄒᆞ게번에관구ᄒᆞᄂᆞᆫ니
예일본관인외의계고령을반포ᄒᆞ
아이겻을실셔ᄒᆞ엿ᄂᆞᆫ지라이제
경찰과그부근에서정안에관ᄒᆞᆫ
경찰모한국경찰을디리ᄒᆞ야
우죵관외의엄슴ᄒᆞᆷ은도모ᄒᆞ노니
이에증공의최규정을포ᄒᆞ야
일반인민으로ᄒᆞ며곰과실이엄
게ᄒᆞ

좌의각항의ᄒᆞᄂᆞᆫ죄를범ᄒᆞᆫ자와
및종범자와교죠자와미슈범자
와및비음모자ᄂᆞᆫ젼샹을일ᄒᆞ
교또시행리의필요홈에즁죄수형
감금 츄방 과료와및티형에
쳐ᄒᆞ고범죄를세애수용ᄒᆞᆫ를긴
과법죄를의지ᄒᆞ야엇은물건과
금지물은지산샹을회지ᄒᆞ야이것
을몰수ᄒᆞᆷ이가ᄒᆞᆷ

일 재옴을위ᄒᆞ야간쳡의항위
가잇ᄂᆞᆫ자와이겻을인도ᄒᆞ야잔천
셩ᄒᆞᄂᆞᆫ자

이 적군의항동을방조ᄒᆞ고또
ᄂᆞᆫ그편리홈을도모ᄒᆞᄂᆞᆫ자

삼 우리군수의계로정한자를
도망ᄒᆞ야방케ᄒᆞ고또이것을
엄닉ᄒᆞᆫ자

ᄉᆞ 속으로로ᄒᆞ야방항을바라며
기타우리군ᄉᆞ의이되ᄒᆞ야방계
의항위가잇ᄂᆞᆫ자

오 우리군수의항동을방해ᄒᆞᆫ
자

륙 우리군수에되ᄒᆞ야우리군
자 교히로운티의결ᄒᆞᆷ이잇ᄂᆞᆫ

칠 군용뎐신뎐화와계외및뎐
도와슈되와퇴를계드리비ᄂᆞᆫ
폐단이잇거ᄂᆞ리어을취ᄒᆞ야
그군용을방해ᄒᆞᆫ자

팔 군용쳥송물 도로 교량
등을파괴ᄒᆞᆫ자

구 병기탄약 량식 피복기
타군수픔과및군의우편물을
파기ᄒᆞ거ᄂᆞ도젹질ᄒᆞᆫ자

십 진샹의항오에우리군수상의
등신과및수송을방해ᄒᆞᄂᆞᆫ자

십일 우리군수의리익ᄒᆞ게하
나ᄒᆞᆯ리사되탯괴에의등신을로
표ᄒᆞ고셔ᄒᆞᄂᆞᆫ이ᄀᆞᆺᄒᆞᆫ젼셜을포
고ᄒᆞᄂᆞᆫ자

십이 우리군수의리익ᄒᆞ게하
나ᄒᆞᆫ게시를ᄒᆞᄂᆞᆫ자

십삼 우리군수의증방ᄒᆞᆫ승마
인부교용등을방해ᄒᆞ고또이
것을되ᄒᆞ야걸게ᄒᆞᆫ자

십ᄉᆞ 우리군의 군속의진부
질망ᄒᆞ기를방ᄌᆞᆫᄒᆞᆫ자

십오 징회 결사 신문 잡
지 광고 기타ᄂᆞᆫ수단으로
공안 질셔를문란ᄒᆞᆫ자

십륙 일졍ᄒᆞᆫ디역니에출입ᄒᆞᆫ
자졔를금ᄒᆞ며그금지를범ᄒᆞᆫ

십칠 군수령관의명령에위반
ᄒᆞᆫ자

십팔 범죄자를은닉ᄒᆞ야숨기고
또ᄂᆞᆫ이겻을탈휘코자ᄂᆞᆫ이것
을다망식인자

십구 범죄자를위ᄒᆞ야그증거
를인멸ᄒᆞᆫ자

○리셔번회 젼니장원경리요
이셰가일본에유학ᄒᆞᆫ이후에일
본에서은혜를밧은것도만커니
와또학교도ᄒᆞ든경젼경뎡을
쟝연회를정졍ᄒᆞᆫ다니작일하
오일셧시에과졍관에연회를
비셜ᄒᆞ고니외국관원을정요
ᄒᆞ엿ᄂᆞᆫ듸인원수가삼빅여명이
라더라

○군령경찰소우 대안문밧과
셔한병이들원을디기고셔경경을낸
셰이후에그시에군부대신은용셥
씨가경과권인리셔서보고되셔
편ᄒᆞᆫ결과로수령부에서민회취
산ᄒᆞᄂᆞᆫ듸로조처ᄒᆞ랑정은답청
ᄒᆞ여도민회와기타일진회셔에
관ᄒᆞᆫ일노경찰을즉령ᄒᆞᆫ당ᄒᆞ기
로작령이되엿더라

○일진회원 일본헌병ᄉᆞ령부
에셔무경ᄒᆞ여잇ᄂᆞᆫ시골회원들
을위ᄒᆞ야다고령령ᄒᆞ야에서블
치원은모도버리가고셔을회원
은임엿ᄂᆞᆫ듸로회의ᄒᆞᆫ디인데만
일은문데가잇스면셔골회원을
다시블너올일이라ᄒᆞ고면리회
ᄒᆞᆫ죄목을도사ᄒᆞᆫ주도청이오싱
여만명이더라

○괴화죠방 전시종원부주전
졍관셩샹한전승지박희준장참
셔전참령계셔칠셩과오뎐등이싱
기ᄒᆞ나가정무국에괴화ᄒᆞ야작고
경을당ᄒᆞ얏ᄂᆞᆫ데방면이되엿더라

뎐보

지부발 일월이일

○로합도쥬 로국수뢰졍ᄉᆞ쳑
과토란일쳑이ᄒᆞ쳑구로뵈퇴왓척
ᄂᆞᆫ뎌수뢰졍이척이엄음외에잇더
이졍은로국명수관안에잇다라

고동발 일일

솝뢰졍들과계로졍이로국명수관
항되셔 동해셔셤일

○로함우리 방수이에ᄂᆞᆫ이로
남로명시조용ᄒᆞ며니아침에로로
함일덕이또밋야ᄒᆞ야편고일본수
뢰정두쳑은보구쯧ᄀᆞ게잇더라

일월일일 본리군편산최
룡보

○려관함츄계 광창에샹됴뎌
수령관보고에일월일흔구쇠엣
ᄂᆞᆫ젹군이거일월에우리포위군
이세거셩남ᄒᆞ야기를며이ᄒᆞᆷ후
에동항니에잇든대소군함과셔
항히잇든수로라피ᄒᆞ고 수뢰니
로졍항구밧계잇든세바스드보리
ᄒᆞ와및오로와스누이호도침몰
ᄒᆞ엿고항구밧그로도망ᄒᆞ야감으
로우리함쉐이함디증이일부가이
ᄅᆞᆯ츄격ᄒᆞ야로계ᄒᆞ여스니계이구
진도함(함장은증좌에싼샤울디)
와과한구츄함디 (수령관은
증좌에드온수스당) 와ᄒᆞᆫ수뢰
뎡디 (수령관은증좌에령관지)
ᄂᆞᆫ계부방면이수령관등항령ᄒᆞ며
고또뎨예샴함디수령관등항령ᄒᆞ며
소ᄂᆞᆫ원덕뎐함 (함장은대좌에츈
샹계일) 과룡뎐함 (함장은중
좌에부산준도) 과ᄒᆞᆫ구츄함디
(수령관은중좌에령목관티랑)
를거ᄂᆞ리고ᄒᆞ교쥬만방면으로향
ᄒᆞ야각각격창의수최를셔셔뢰
ᄒᆞ예부장을히세ᄒᆞ기를동셤ᄒᆞ계
ᄒᆞ야계창ᄒᆞ의사의쳐를더욕뎌ᄒᆞ
스마렵ᄒᆞᆫ수레ᄒᆞ아와부불의필
ᄒᆞ겨ᄒᆞ오도용감ᄒᆞ연ᄒᆞᆫ군의공
고셔소가엽계ᄒᆞ예우리흔즉노ᄃᆡ
이ᄀᆞ공ᄋᆞᆫ이히밧교면에서ᄒᆞ고노ᄋᆞ
ᄒᆞ기에쟝잇ᄂᆞᆫ격젹의ᄒᆞᆫ탄ᄃᆡᄋᆞᆫ고
ᄒᆞ에니를보고ᄒᆞ노라ᄒᆞ엿
더라

광고

TELEGRAMS.

Weihaiwei, January 4.

The "Andromeda" left this morning at seven o'clock for Port Arthur, carrying all the medical staff and medical stores available at this place to render assistance to the sick and wounded.

(FROM JAPAN PAPERS.)

London, Jan. 4.

The news of the surrender of Port Arthur has now been published in Russia, where it has had a most depressing effect. The papers, however, exhort the Government by prosecuting the campaign to show that Russia is a great nation.

London, Jan. 4.

It is rumoured in Paris that Rojestvensky, Commander of the Baltic Fleet, has been instructed by the Russian Naval Department to return to Libau to take up the position of Commander-in Chief of the whole Russian Navy, but that he has declined to obey the orders.

London, Jan. 4.

A Dutch vessel which has arrived at Batavia reports that four Japanese warships were cruising off the eastern coast of Sumatra on the 3rd.

London, January 4.

The Chinese Minister at London interviewed Lord Lansdowne, Foreign Minister, to-day, in connection with Wei-hai-wei.

London, Jan. 3.

Japanese bonds are strong. The Five per cents have risen two pounds, Four per cents twenty-five shillings; and Six per cents fifteen shillings.

(Several telegrams have arrived too late for this issue, but will appear tomorrow.)

FROM THE "CHEFOO DAILY NEWS."

January 4th.

It was at four o'clock last Sunday afternoon that General Stoessel sent Ensign Malchenko under a flag of truce to the Japanese lines with a proposal to surrender. This proposal was accompanied by a citation of the terms desired by General Stoessel. The envelope containing the important documents "To the Commander of Port Arthur Siege Army." According to refugees arriving here, the terms requested by General Stoessel, which were drawn up by General Smyrnoff, were as follows:

(1) All able-bodied men and officers and all those so slightly wounded or sick that they are able to travel, shall be allowed to retain their arms and return to Russia by first available transportation for such purpose, with the provision that they will not engage in hostilities during the present war.

(2) That the Japanese shall care for all the Russian wounded and sick in the hospital until their recovery, whereupon they, too, shall return to Russia, retaining their arms.

(3) That all non-combatants, irrespective of nationality, shall be given safe conduct by the victors to the nearest neutral port.

Malchenko crossed over to the Japanese lines near Eagle Hill, and was escorted to General Nogi's headquarters by a detachment of Japanese cavalry, but as the General was absent, the envoy had no recourse but to leave the request in the hands of one of Nogi's aides, and return to Port Arthur.

At six o'clock that evening the Japanese abruptly ceased firing their heavy guns, but they re-opened the bombardment on Monday morning, continuing it until late in the afternoon, when General Stoessel is supposed to have received General Nogi's answer.

It is said that this answer was given to General Stoessel himself on Eagle Hill, where he went to meet the Japanese messenger. At this time hostilities had been practically discontinued, and it is probable that the Japanese now have occupied the ruins of the Russian forts which were blown up by the Russians themselves on Sunday night. It is likely the entry of the Japanese troops into Port Arthur itself will take place to-day or to-morrow, if it has not already occurred.

According to officers who arrived on the torpedo launches this morning, and who left Port Arthur Monday night at eight o'clock, the Russians were at work all Sunday night blowing up their forts, ships and military stores. The destruction of these was most complete. The "Bayan" was the first vessel destroyed, and between six and twelve o'clock all except the "Sevastopol" had gone down in shapelees masses. The "Sevastopol" was then towed to the harbor entrance where she was blown up by a large charge of explosive placed amidships. It is stated that this explosion cut the vessel fairly in two, and she sank in two parts. All small and merchant craft in the harbor with the exception of the torpedo launches which came here, were also destroyed after having been towed to the entrance of the harbor. This step was taken in order to completely block the harbor against the entry of the enemy's large warships.

Despite the Japanese blockade which existed the night before last across the west entrance to Chefoo harbor, the two Russian torpedo launches, by a wonderful streak of luck, succeeded in gaining the inner harbor without drawing their enemy's fire. There can be little doubt but what the Japanese naval authorities felt confident General Stoessel would attempt to send out his last report on the siege and explaining the circumstances necessitating his surrender, and this accounts for the presence of the blockading squadron off Chefoo, and for the chagrin felt by the blockaders this morning when the Japanese Consul informed them that the two Ressian boats had entered the harbor during the night as it were right under their very noses.

(To be continued.)

RUSSIA AND INDIA.

"Public Opinion" translates the following from the "Neue Zürcher Zeitung" a Swiss paper:—"England's threatening attitude against Russia suggested the question whether Russia would not remind the ruffled England that her fleet could avail her nothing at her most vulnerable point. We may yet learn that the mobilisation of the British Fleet has been answered with movements of the Russian army on the Indian frontier......Russia has clearly, from the beginning, reckoned on the possibility of having to take up the contest with the allies of Japan, and it had been folly not to have done so......The Russian army in Central Asia has none of the unreadiness of the forces in the Far East; it is a trained and tried organization. The a very serious danger might suddenly arise for England in India, and this consideration undoubtedly restrained her from touching the Russian fleet on its journey to the East.

"India is the foremost source of wealth, the principal support of the power and significance of England, and the loss of this magnificent colony would entail the loss of the Mother Country's position as a world-Power. The retention is thus a matter of life and death for England....But even if she were able to concentrate her military power in its entirety upon India, this would be totally inadequate against the Russian armies, inadequate to subdue the native population.

"The British are perfectly aware of the threatening danger; this unheard-of outburst of an intelligible hatred is therefore all the more astonishing, as it almost placed England in this dangerous situation in India. Even her diplomatists lost their hereditary *sang-froid*. The jeopardy of India makes it quite clear why, after the first outburst, public opinion in London so quickly calmed down."

The Kamni of Kyeng Heung reports that a Russian Colonel and 100 men have taken up their quarters in the Government buildings and offices.

The Japanese Minister has requested the Foreign Office to obtain an audience with His Majesty for three officers of the Japanese torpedo flotilla, now lying at Chemulpo.

THE COAL PROBLEM IN RUSSIA.

The "Journal de Pétersbourg" summarises a number of articles which have recently appeared in Russian newspapers as to the possibility of reducing the present large import of coal into Russia. It is claimed that, were suitable means of transport devised, coal from the Donetz region might supplant Cardiff coal for naval and industrial purposes. The transport difficulty will be removed when a waterway connects the Baltic and the Black Sea; meanwhile, an attempt to solve the problem has been made by the Technical Committee of the Moscow Administration of Ways of Communication, who have sanctioned a scheme for improving the navigation of the Donetz as far as Gundorovo by the construction of seven dams and as many locks, at a cost of six million roubles.

The "Primorskaya Viedomosti" suggests that ths coal supply of the future may possibly be found in Eastern Siberia. The Governor-General of the Amur Region has deputed M. Pfaffius, a mining engineer, to study the coal beds of that country and of Sakhalin, to form a collection of specimens, and to draw up a detailed report on the physical and chemical qualities of the various species, and the cost of working, rates of labour, conditions of transport, etc.

Another paper remarks that the petroleum wells, rather than the coal mines, of Sakhalin should be developed. These are said to be rich in mineral, at a moderate depth from the surface, and situated at only 10 to 16 miles inland. The cost of working would be small, as convict labour is obtainable for about 15d. a day. In view of the political, commercial, and fiscal benefits to be obtained by emancipating Russia from the necessity of seeking coal supplies abroad, the hope is expressed that the Government may be induced to undertake the cost of developing the mineral wealth of the country.

As a recognition of the services held in the Japanese monastery in Chinkogai at the time of the decease of the late Empress Dowager, a Japanese priest named Inouye has been received in audience by His Majesty.

The Police Department have made a very strong complaint to the Foreign Office concerning the arrest by Japanese Gendarmes, of the police inspector, who was present, as a spectator, at the Il Chin Hoi meeting on Monday.

The Japanese gendarmes headquarters have ordered all Il Chin Hoi people from the country to return home and stay there until their services are required, on which occasion they will be called on by their leaders of the society in Seoul.

The Japanese Consul is discussing with the Governor of Seoul a proposal for the building of a large Notice board on Chong No. The latter gentleman seems to think that locality is too crowded to permit of any large structure being placed there.

News received from Gyantse at Allahabad on December 4th, shows that everything is going smoothly there, and the friendly attitude of the Tibetans remains unchanged. The telegraph line to Chumbi works well and Captain O'Connor and a small garrison are kept in touch with the outer world by the receipt of Reuter's telegrams and regular postal daks. The weather is described as perfect, bright clear days, with very little of the terrible winds which swept Tuna plain unceasingly. The nights are cold, but not excessively so.

According to the "Vorwarts," the cost of the operations against the Hereros and Hottentots has cost Germany twice as much per man as the Boer war cost England, namely, twenty-eight shillings per man a day as against fourteen. No doubt the absence of railways had added to the cost of moving and feeding troops; still the figures corroborate the universal testimony of experts as to the efficiency of the British transport system.

PROCLAMATION.

The Chief of the Japanese Gendarmes in Seoul has issued a proclamation concerning the establishment and proceedings of societies in the city.

1. Any one desiring to establish a society must apply for permission to the Japanese authorities 3 days before the society is organized all the names of intending members, together with a full description of them, must be handed in.

2. When a meeting is to be held, notification of the place and hour must be given.

3. A collection of people in the streets, except for the purpose of weddings or funerals, will be strictly prohibited.

4. All meetings will be under the control of Japanese gendarmes.

5. All documents relating to the affairs of any society must be sent in to be examined.

Any infringement of the above laws with be punished by martial law.

Mr. Yi Yong Ik is giving a banquet tonight at the Hajo hotel. Some 300 guests, both Korean and Japanese have been invited.

The Chinese Minister has notified the Foreign Office that he is now prepared to settle the question of the Chinese murdered at Haiju.

It has now been finally decided that the term of mourning, for the late Crown Princess shall be considerably shortened and will probably be ended about the 15th February.

The Japanese Minister has requested the Government to appoint none but Japanese speaking officials to magisterial positions in the north. His Majesty has ordered that only 5 of the appointments requested shall be made.

Replying to the demands of a Japanese pawnbroker at Mokpo, who claims that a Korean official named Yun Woo Byung pledged his official seal for a sum of money and lied without making restitution, the Imperial Household Department state that no man of this name has ever been employed by them and that they can have no cognizance of the matter.

Bekanntmachung.

Die Bekanntmachungen der Eintragungen in das hiesige Deutsche Handelsregister erfolgen im Jahre 1905 durch den "**Ostasiatischen Lloyd**" und die "**The Korea Daily News.**"

Söul, den 27. Dezember 1904.

Der Kaiserlich Deutsche Minister-Resident und General-Konsul.

(L. S.) gez. von Saldern.

The Korea Daily News.

Issued at 5 P. M. daily except Sundays.

Rate of Subscription:—
Per Year,............Yen 25.
Per Quarter,..........Yen 7.
Per Month,..........Yen 2.50.

Postage in Korea not charged extra.
Postage abroad charged extra.

Advertisements, 50 sen per day for 1 inch or less.
5 yen per month per inch.
50 yen per year per inch.

All communications to

E. T. BETHELL,
Editor and Publisher,
Pak-tong, Seoul.

WITH KUROPATKIN AT MUKDEN.

SPECIAL CORRESPONDENCE.

Moukden, Dec. 20.

The delightful crisp mornings when you have to shiver around the barely furnished room of your second class hotel and break the ice in your wash basin before performing your morning ablutions, are now upon us. The correspondents and the gentlemen who are here for what money they can make out of the merchandise they have to sell are about the only people who have the chilliness of the atmosphere thrust disagreeably upon them. Those whose real business it is to be here through the entire season and prepare for it, i. e. the soldiers, are not badly off. They have comfortable clothing—coats that are made for the specific purpose of resisting the rigors of a Manchurian winter, plenty of good "chow," and sleeping quarters that are designed to keep them warm. I have deserted my ramshackle hostelry on several occasions, and have "turned in," not too conspicuously, of course, with the men of the ranks, satisfied to exchange my aristocratic "lodgings" for quarters decidedly more comfortable.

I believe that at the moment this town is the busiest place on earth. The streets are choked with a jostling crowd of soldiers, and the number is increasing daily. There are soldiers "to burn"—also money. It is impossible to push your way through the thoroughfares at times. A constant effort to elbow a passage from one portion of the town to another will in time make a muscular athlete out of the most chronic dyspeptic. The streets are so congested at times that you simply can't move. It seems as if the whole population of Russia has been turned loose upon Manchuria and is concentrating at Moukden as a rallying place. Trains are rolling in at the rate of ten per day, each made up of from fifty to seventy five cars. Six of these trains are now coming in during the day and four at night. Four locomotives are necessary to pull and push each of these large trains along, one in front, two in the middle and one at the rear.

Army supplies by the thousands of tons are to be seen in every direction. They are coming mostly from the south. A certain amount is coming in over the railway from the north, but it is very small in comparison, the railway facilities being devoted mostly to the transportation of troops. The soldiers are provisioned en route to Manchuria by supplies carried with them. The surplus carried on the road is deposited at Mouken and Harbin.

The men seem to be arriving in very good shape. Care is taken to give them a comfortable journey, at any rate over this end of the line. The cars are well warmed, and are not over-crowded. Frequent stops are made at the numerous stations where immense tanks kept constantly filled with boiling water enable the troops to have hot coffee at close intervals.

Money seems to grow on every bush. A ricksha coolie will not look at you unless you can pay him a rouble for a short ride. In fact, the rouble is the coin of lowest denomination to be found, except among the enlisted men, and I have seen the latter with a roll which must have aggregated at least four or five hundred roubles. The rouble is the unit of value. Everthing costs you a rouble. Ricksha coolies are earning as high as twenty-five and thirty roubles per day, and will soon return to their native heath and become prosperous merchants. I have seen a good deal of the Japanese war notes—not in circulation, for you can't pass them for love or money—but in the hands of various people who sell them as curios. I purchased a thousand dollars worth of the paper for thirty cents the other day, and sent the stuff home to my friends as souvenirs.

Strict military discipline prevails, and martial law and the curfew hours remind the civilian of the good old days of peace. The curfew phase of the provost rule does not affect Europeans and Americans, however, as they are at liberty to pass hither and thither at all hours of the day or night. It is aimed principally at the Chinese, and is vigorously enforced. The Chinaman keeps his head indoors after five o'clock in the afternoon. The army authorities were undoubtedly right in imposing strict regulations in this regard, for it is a notorious fact that the natives delight to rake in the attractive rouble, then gather up their belongings, after making what they consider a "pile," and quietly go over to the enemy where they dispense military information with a free hand. The rigid martial law which confines their business to certain hours and localities, puts them indoors after certain hours, and generally keeps a watchful eye on them, has resulted in reducing this disagreeable feature of campaigning to a minimum.

It is difficult to say when this great number of men now massing at and before Moukden will be thrown into the terrible struggle that is soon to come. I believe that the Russians will take the active offensive before February has passed. Nobody on the outside knows what Kuropatkin intends to do, but it is the general belief of those who are keeping watch of developments, that the southward move will be commenced in February. Several things favor this view. The problem of bringing in supplies to feed the vast army which it has been said all along would be thrown into the field by the Russians, has been solved to some extent. These supplies have been coming in large quantities from the south, thus relieving the Trans-Siberian railway of an immense amount of tonnage which it was said at first it would be necessary to attempt to handle, and which it was thought would tax the railway beyond its possibilities, in conjunction with the movement of the necessary troops. Thus has been removed one of the greatest obstacles which confronted the authorities in their efforts to reinforce Kuropatkin heavily and promptly.

The minimizing of this tonnage has made it possible to utilize the railway for the transportation of a larger number of troops within a given time than was at first thought possible of movement. Kuropatkin finds himself at this date with more troops than were expected to have reached him so promptly, and in fact almost ready for the southward march which he is bound to attempt.

In addition, at this season of the year the movement of this large army over an extensive territory full of waterways and low country is much easier than it will be when the warm season sets in and and the ground begins to thaw. The portion of Manchuria within the theatre of war is for months during the spring and summer a vast morass, to a large extent; the movement of an army over such country is difficult, and an attempt to prosecute a campaign of any magnitude would be attended with disappointments and disastrous delays. When the forces at his disposal are of such strength as the commander-in-chief believes will warrant him in pushing onward, the argument is all in favor of advance and against delay. Therefore it is generally believed by those who have studied the situation with some care, that the long-talked of southward advance is soon to begin, and as said above, probably in February.

The opposing armies are both in readiness for a fight to day. The Japanese have intrenched and fortified themselves, preparatory to a defence of what ground they have succeeded in occupying. Their army has been reinforced. On the Russian side the number of men which it was thought necesssary to have in the field before attempting to dislodge the enemy, has possibly been exceeded at this date. The most modern artillery has arrived at the front, and in many places is in position for the opening of the battle. Should Port Arthur not be able to hold out until the opening of this compaign, it will of course mean the release of a large number of Japanese troops from the siege army, and their probable junction with the army in the north, but it is not thought this will have any effect on Kuropatkin's plans. In fact it does not seem to be the opinion here that the attempted relief of Port Arthur enters into those plans. Port Arthur does not seem to be a factor in Kuropatkin's calculations. Its fall or successful resistance will probably cut no figure in the moves of the upper Manchurian army.—Chefoo Daily News.

The Korean Minister to Peking left for Seoul on the 9th inst.

The Japanese Minister has informed the Foreign Office that the Japanese military authorities will in future be responsible for the policeing of Seoul and vicinity.

Three thousand umbrellas with a like number of caps are said to have arrived from Japan for the use of the more prominent members of the Il Chin Hoi. The umbrellas bear the inscription "National Society."

During an Il Chin Hoi demonstration held recently in the Kang Kye district, the soldiers of the local guard opened fire on the mob, killing several men. The Department have despatched 5 gendarmes to arrest the Governor of North Pyengyang province, who will be held responsible for the matter.

The Korea Daily News.

VOL. II, — WEDNESDAY, JANUARY 11, 1905. — No. 7

大韓每日申報

대한ᄆᆡ일신보

(뎨이권팔호) (금요일) 일쳔구ᄇᆡᆨ오년일월십삼일

본샤고ᄇᆡᆨ

이신보는영어와한어로셔계ᄅᆡ일출판ᄒᆞᄋᆞᆸ

신문가

ᄒᆞᆫ쟝 엽두돈오푼

일삭도 엽두량닷돈

우표가ᄀᆞ치삭닷돈

다ᄆᆡᆺ돈으로밧ᄉᆞᆸ

광고료는

귀한의쟝단과ᄌᆞ힝의다쇼로죵감ᄒᆞ되혐가로밧을터이오며오ᄅᆡ지아녀대ᄒᆞᆫ사ᄅᆞᆷ마다다이신문을보실터이니광고내시기를원ᄒᆞ시는이들은우리신문사에와셔면약ᄒᆞ심을희망ᄒᆞᄋᆞᆸ

○발ᄒᆡᆼ소 박동대한ᄆᆡ일신보사법어학교압희젼영국인셜ᄇᆡᆯ텽자리오

사쟝 영국인 (ᄇᆡ셜)

평양 ᄃᆡ리졈

○평양효동사는권미보씨로우리신문판ᄆᆡᄃᆡ리인을ᄐᆡᆨ졍ᄒᆞ엿사오니평양에계신구람코져ᄒᆞ시는 쳠군ᄌᆞ는ᄒᆞᆫ번ᄃᆡ리졈에왕림ᄒᆞ와면의ᄒᆞ시ᄋᆞᆸ

사고

○우리대한ᄆᆡ일신보의목뎍은대한의인명쟐셔에관한모든대목에ᄃᆡᄒᆞ야는공평ᄒᆞᆫ변론을주쟝홈이라우리는신원의ᄐᆞᆷ보는신문보시는쳠군ᄌᆞ의게ᄒᆞ샹보도ᄒᆞ리며편지ᄅᆞᆯ귀셔ᄒᆞ며주시는이는셩명과번ᄃᆡᄅᆞᆯ젹어붓치시기ᄅᆞᆯ희망ᄒᆞ오니ᄒᆡ거슨신문샹에긔ᄌᆡᄒᆞ라는거시아니오다만극히신용ᄒᆞ는증거ᄅᆞᆯ숨고자ᄒᆞᆷ이라긔자는아모긔셔던지긔ᄌᆡᄒᆞᆷ을퇴각ᄒᆞ는권리ᄅᆞᆯ가젓소나퇴각ᄒᆞ는리유ᄅᆞᆯ말ᄒᆞᆯ터이오며공즁평화ᄅᆞᆯ문란케ᄒᆞ는듯ᄒᆞᆫ긔셔는의례히밧지안켓ᄉᆞᆸ나이다

●본사셜시이ᄅᆡ로신문을ᄃᆡ방우례로분젼ᄒᆞ와ᄅᆡ젼부의임의로젼ᄒᆞ든ᄉᆞ로번곳에는ᄒᆞᆨ늣게젼ᄒᆞ기도ᄒᆞ며ᄒᆞᆨ멋질ᄀᆡ습ᄒᆞᆫ법에젼ᄒᆞ기도ᄒᆞ며ᄒᆞᆨ아니젼ᄒᆞ는곳도잇다ᄒᆞ와우리신문을ᄉᆞ랑ᄒᆞ야구람ᄒᆞ시는 쳠군ᄌᆞ의게금은분젼인을두고ᄆᆡ일죵이젼ᄒᆞ며아니젼ᄒᆞ거나늣게거나ᄒᆞᆫ폐가엽도록ᄒᆞ랴ᄒᆞ오니ᄒᆞᆨ아니젼ᄒᆞ거는ᄒᆞᆨ늣게젼ᄒᆞ거나ᄒᆞᆫ일이잇스면본사로통긔ᄒᆞ여주심을희망ᄒᆞᄋᆞᆸ

잡보

○법대ᄒᆞᆫ령 ᄒᆞᆫ셩재판소ᄅᆡ사이인이분쟝ᄒᆞ야일인은텽사롤들시무ᄒᆞ고일인은민사롤시무ᄒᆞᆷ으로판사ᄒᆞᆫ아만드러오지아니ᄒᆞ면관사가자연졔ᄒᆞ는고로로슈반판사리샹ᄐᆡᆫ씨가직작일법부대신의게그리유ᄅᆞᆯ셜명ᄒᆞ엿더니법부에셔ᄒᆞᆫ령ᄒᆞ기롤무론민형사ᄒᆞ고쳥판사가셔로시무ᄒᆞ야제반송사ᄅᆞᆯ쇼결ᄒᆞ는거시가ᄒᆞ다ᄒᆞ엿더라

○창졍제소 참졍김셩근씨는쏘사직샹소ᄅᆞᆯ봉졍ᄒᆞ엿더라、

○쟝위주본 일공사가외부로공함ᄒᆞ야북도슈령을일어ᄒᆞ는사롬으로셔임ᄒᆞ라ᄒᆞ엿다더니일간슈령주본이되는지라 처분ᄂᆡ에일공사쳥ᄒᆞᆫ바는오인말셜시ᄒᆞ라ᄒᆞᄋᆞᆸ셧더라

○리씨탁과 의양군리지강씨가취도에잇는한영슈씨면답수셕락을탈취ᄒᆞ도로귀송ᄒᆞᆷ이법인소흥씨가샹관ᄒᆞ야법공사가외부에여러번죠회ᄒᆞ고다년샹졍ᄒᆞ야결단치못ᄒᆞ더니일작에법부에셔판결ᄒᆞ는ᄃᆡ의양군이탁과ᄒᆞ엿다더라

○지휘관협샹 평안북도강계진위ᄃᆡ에셔민회중몃명을포살ᄒᆞᆫ사건으로군부에셔샹주ᄒᆞ고지휘관리용관을압샹ᄎᆞ로헌병오명을파송ᄒᆞ엿더라

○사금위원도피 일젼에궁ᄂᆡ부에셔사금위원팔인을각도에파송ᄒᆞ는ᄃᆡ그소쟝졔무는산림쳔텩과면답결복과각양쟝세와우토와공힝와호구와쟝시와기타사소ᄒᆞᆫ사항이라도일일히죠사ᄒᆞᆫ다더라

○김화민인사샹 김화군수가공ᄒᆡ등시로지엇는ᄃᆡ그배에본군민뤄으로역사롤식이고기와쟝수운ᄒᆞᆫᄃᆡ가을아니주어ᄇᆡᆨ셩이쟝첫호소ᄒᆞ기린라더라

○인사황사 남대문밧긔칠패사는사ᄅᆞᆷ이빈양이되엿다고ᄒᆞ는ᄃᆡ그사샹을탐문ᄒᆞᆫ즉빈양이[illegible]미나고젼신이기ᄅᆞᆯ바른것ᄎᆞᆺ치운이ᄒᆞ고ᄂᆞᆫ이누르고며리렬이다ᄲᅢ져병셰에누엇는지라고모양이누른구렁이와ᄀᆞᆺ다ᄒᆞ는말을사ᄅᆞᆷ이빈앙이되엿다ᄒᆞᆷ인ᄃᆡ병인즉손이상ᄒᆞᆫ병이라고들ᄒᆞ더라

○죠졍젼주폐쳥 일공사가외부로죠회ᄒᆞ기ᄅᆞᆯ인항에졍박ᄒᆞᆫ본국구츅ᄃᆡ롤귀군즁졍자등본슈사랑과밋함쟝등샹명이 ᄃᆡ황뎨폐하ᄭᅴ알현코자ᄒᆞ니쳥컨ᄃᆡ신샹 주ᄒᆞ라ᄒᆞ엿더라

○졍관공함 졍부관에셔외부에공함ᄒᆞ기ᄅᆞᆯ히주광셔포영국에입젹ᄒᆞᆫ졍샹치명ᄒᆞᆫ사안은리ᄅᆡ비샹일하오두시에본사가맛당히귀부에가셔타판ᄒᆞᆯ터이니그셰에가다리기ᄅᆞᆯ바란다ᄒᆞ엿더라

○중간건몰 가등죵융씨가농샹공부고문관으로고빙ᄒᆞᆫ후에가옥비도하샹쳔원을ᄯᅩ신에지발ᄒᆞ가로작뎡ᄒᆞ야쟉년도에지발ᄒᆞ엿는ᄃᆡ가등씨의계는일쳔원만령슈ᄒᆞ엿고기여이쳔원은샹중간건몰이되고로탁지부와농샹공부에셔셔로샹지중이라ᄒᆞ더라

○욕렴고시ᄃᆡ 일본ᄉᆞ평가한셩부와교셥ᄒᆞ야죵로에고시ᄃᆡ롤셜립ᄒᆞ려ᄒᆞ는ᄃᆡ그도본을본즉광이팔간이오고가이쟝이라한셩부에셔는ᄃᆡ도중에다가이런케세우는거시불가ᄒᆞ다ᄒᆞ야샹지중이라ᄒᆞ더라

○단샹걸졍 숀명ᄇᆡ의괴넌봉졔ᄅᆞᆯ인민이불복ᄒᆞ고ᄯᅩ샹소가답지ᄒᆞ는고로명년졍월쵸샹일츌각후에는졔복ᄒᆞ기로결졍이되엿더라

뎐보

지부발 일월삼일

○로함승리 로국슈뢰졍이산왓는ᄃᆡ일본슈뢰과피ᄒᆞᆷ쳘젹과숩양ᄒᆞᆷ일쳬은ᄒᆞᆼ구밧게잇는것이뵈인다더라

론돈발 십이월이십수일

○영미동ᄆᆡᆼ셜 미국유욕ᄡᅥ에쌀ᄂᆡ라는신문이권고ᄒᆞ되영미량국수이에도을동맹갓치동맹됴약을밋는것이긴요ᄒᆞ다ᄒᆞ엿더라

외보

○화쟝동ᄆᆡᆼ 쳥국금일영동ᄆᆡᆼ을다시일층확쟝ᄒᆞ야홈은일본외회망ᄒᆞᄂᆞᆫ배아니라영국론ᄌᆞ에규쵸ᄒᆞᄂᆞᆫ일반의견도샤ᄒᆞᆫ츠ᄃᆡ로이에구ᄒᆞᄂᆞᆫ모양인ᄃᆡ미확쟝안은로국의영슴ᄒᆞᆷ을예방ᄒᆞ야일영량국이피차부조ᄒᆞᄂᆞᆫ길을긔셔ᄒᆞᆷ인ᄃᆡ영국협ᄃᆡᄂᆞᆫ일죠계유ᄉᆞ지시ᄅᆞᆯ당ᄒᆞ야일본히안에경비ᄒᆞᆯ지며이에ᄃᆡᄒᆞ야보슈ᄒᆞᆯᄯᅳᆺ으로일본륙군은쳥경인도국경을방어ᄒᆞ리라ᄂᆞᆫ젼셜이잇더라

○로됴등봉쇄 금년일월일일에료동반도봉쇄구역변경의션언ᄒᆞᆫ뜻으로연합함ᄃᆡ동향ᄉᆞ령쟝관미회ᄒᆞᆫ군ᄃᆡ신의게보고ᄒᆞᆫ비ㅣ여좌ᄒᆞ니

본관은대국졍부의명령을졉슈ᄒᆞ야명치삼십칠년오월이십륙일에션언ᄒᆞᆫ료동반도의봉쇄구역을변경ᄒᆞ야동삼십팔년일월일일브터쳥국셩경셩료동반도의남구각텬셩계두에비ᄅᆞ기ᄭᆞ지ᄒᆞᆫ외직션으로봉쇄ᄒᆞ야국군이[illegible]란겻과ᄒᆞᆫ[illegible]로이용ᄒᆞ는[illegible]에취ᄒᆞᆫ[illegible]셔션언ᄒᆞ노라[illegible]ᄒᆞ엿다더라

론셜

일본국민신문의게ᄃᆡ답ᄒᆞᆫ말

○일본국민신문의주필이우리의게일월일일에출간ᄒᆞᆫ국민신문을보냇는ᄃᆡ그모양이조코인쇄ᄒᆞᆫ것과도화ᄒᆞᆫ거시ᄆᆡ우쟝미ᄒᆞᆫ지라

원ᄅᆡ우리가이런신문에주의ᄒᆞ야평ᄒᆞᆯ슈가업스나그신문에뵈인쟝이잇는고로그신문의견에ᄃᆡᄒᆞ야멋마ᄃᆡ를론란ᄒᆞ노라

그신문의지취ᄂᆞᆫ 고란ᄒᆞᆯ것이업거니와 그신문에셔말ᄒᆞᆫ 제목 고 우리가 신문에 제말을 제가ᄒᆞ엿스니 목뎍과쳐지ᄅᆞᆯ셜명ᄒᆞ니우리의목뎍은젼국인민의권리ᄅᆞᆯ보호ᄒᆞ며ᄇᆡᆨ셩의직분을ᄒᆞ는 ...

UNION INSURANCE SOCIETY OF CANTON.

Head office Hongkong.
Marine risks underwritten at current rates.
Agents in Chemulpo,
E. MEYER & Co.

COMPAGNIE DES MESSAGERIES MARITIMES.

Fortnightly Direct Service.

For Marseilles
via Ports.
Sailing from Yokohama
Calling at Kobe,
Shanghai, Hongkong, Saigon, Singapore,
Colombo, Djibonti, Suez, Port Said
and Marseilles.

For particulars apply to
HOLME RINGER & Co.,
Chemulpo.

HAYASHIDA & CO.,

16 MYENG DONG, CHIN KO KAI, SEOUL.
BRANCH OFFICE AT CHEMULPO.

Money changers, Coal and Wood Merchants, Express Agents.

We are agents for the Pyeng-yang Coal Company and the Karazu Coal Company of Japan. We have the best quality of both anthracite and bituminous coal, and prompt execution of orders is our speciality. Firewood of all kinds kept in stock. Full weight guaranteed. Money of all denominations exchanged at current rates. Parcels received for all parts.

CHINA MUTUAL LIFE INS. OC.

Most favourable terms to policy holders.

Benefit system unsurpassed.

HOLME RINGER & Co.
Agents, Chemulpo.

C. P. R.

CANADIAN PACIFIC RAILWAY COMPANY'S ROYAL MAIL STEAMSHIP LINE.

THE FAST ROUTE BETWEEN CHINA, JAPAN, AND EUROPE VIA CANADA AND THE UNITED STATES.

Route from Hongkong via Shanghai, Nagasaki (Inland Sea of Japan) Kobe, Yokohama, Victoria and Vancouver.

Twin Screw Empress Steamship—6,000 Tons—Speed 19 knots.

PROPOSED SAILING FROM YOKOHAMA.
R. M. S. Empress of India.
R. M. S. Empress of Japan.
R. M. S. Empress of China.
R. M. S. Athenian.
R. M. S. Tartar.

Special reduction (first class only) granted to members of the Military, Naval, Diplomatic and Civil services and to Missionaries.

Passengers have choice of ten routes across the Continent of America and have privilege of travelling by any Atlantic Steamship Line.

Round the World passage tickets in connection with the P. and O. S. N., North German Lloyd and Messageries Co.'s **£125.**

All rates payable at current rate of exchange.

For further information, Tickets, Guide Books, etc., apply to

HOLME, RINGER & Co., AGENTS,
Chemulpo.

Grand Hotel,

(Formerly the Station Hotel)

Near the Railway Terminus, West Gate Seoul.

The Best Hotel in Korea.
Handsome new Building.
Fine Airy Rooms
Excellent Cuisine.
Terms Moderate.
Special terms to Missionaries
and to permanent boarders.

Electric cars within 2 minutes' walk.

W. H. EMBERLEY.
Proprietor

EVERY FACILITY.

In connection with Life Assurance Business is afforded by

The Standard Life Assurance Co.,

One of the largest and wealthiest of the Provident Institutions of the United Kingdom Forms of Application and all information will be promptly afforded on application.

10 CENTS A DAY.

Not a very large expenditure is it? But it is sufficient to secure for a man of 30 a policy with the STANDARD LIFE OFFICE for

$1323.

For all particulars of rates, etc., apply to

Holme, Ringer & Co.,
Agents, Chemulpo.

THE NEW YORK LIFE INSURANCE COMPANY.

Have you ever been declined by any Company?

Are you engaged in a specially hazardous occupation?

Have you heard of the New York Life Insurance Company's New Classifications for this class of Risks?

If not, send your date of birth, occupation and particulars of rejection, if any to

E. MEYER & Co.,
Agents, Chemulpo.

MITSUI BUSSAN KAISHA.
(MITSUI & Co.)
MITSUI GINKO.
(MITSUI BANK.)

The Bank is owned by the members of the Mitsui Family, who, as partners, assume an unlimited responsibility for all liabilities of the Bank:—

Capital........................Yen 5,000,000
Reserve Fund .... " 5,600,000

HEAD OFFICE, TOKYO.
LONDON OFFICE, 34 LIME ST., E. C.

BRANCHES AND AGENCIES:—
New York, San Francisco, Hamburg, Bombay, Singapore, Manila, Hongkong, Amoy, Chefoo, Tientsin.
Kobe, Hakodate, Yokohama, Kure, Yokosuka, Moji, Shimonoseki, Miike, Wakamatsu, Nagasaki, Kuchinotsu, Karatsu, Sasebo, Misume, Taipeh, &c.

Telegraphic Address for all the Offices:
"MITSUI."
A. B. C. AND A. 1 CODES USED.

Contractors of Coal
To the Imperial Japanese Navy. Arsenals and Railway Bureau, Principal Railway Companies and Industrial Work, Home and Foreign Mail and Freight Steamers.

Sole Proprietors
Of the famous Miike, Tagawa and Yamano Coal Mines.

Sole Agents
For the sale of Fukumo, Hokoku, Ichimura, Kanoda, Mannoura, Onoura, Ostuji, Sonoda, Tsubaruro, Yoshinotani, Yoshio, Yurokibura and other coals.

YANGTSE INSURANCE ASSOCIATION, LTD.

The undersigned, having been appointed agents for the above company, are prepared to issue policies and pay losses on marine risks at regular rates.

E. MEYER & Co.,
Agents, Chemulpo.

AMERICAN KOREAN ELECTRIC CO.

Light and Power.

Main Office: Electric Building, Chong No.

RAILWAY DEPARTMENT.

OPERATING CARS BETWEEN EAST AND WEST GATE, EVERY TEN MINUTES:—

First Car leaves East Gate at 7:00 A. M. First Car leaves R. R. Station at 7:25 A. M
Last Car " East Gate at 8.40 P. M. Last " " R. R. Station at 9.05 P.M

OPERATING CARS BETWEEN EAST GATE AND IMPERIAL TOMB TERMINUS, EVERY TWENTY MINUTES:—
CONNECTING WITH EVERY ALTERNATE CAR ARRIVING AT EAST GATE FROM CHONG NO.

First Car leaves East Gate for Tomb at 7:10 A. M.
" " " Tomb for East Gate at 7:30 A. M.
Last " " East Gate for Tomb at 7:50 P. M.
" " " Tomb for East Gate at 8:10 P. M.

OPERATING CARS BETWEEN CHONG NO AND YUNG SAN RIVER EVERY TWELVE MINUTES:—

First Car leaves Chong No for South Gate at 7:12 A. M.
" " " Chong No for Yung San at 7:36 A. M.
" " " South Gate for Chong No at 7:20 A. M.
" " " Yung San for Chong No at 8:09 A. M.
Last " " South Gate for Chong No 9:00 P. M.
" " " Yung San for Chong No at 8.45. P. M.

SPECIAL PRIVATE CARS FURNISHED TO SUIT CONVENIENCE OF PATRONS. PRICES ON APPLICATION AT HEAD OFFICE.

LIGHTING DEPARTMENT.

Where less than 250 candle power of light is used, the rate per month will be
Per 16 candle power incandescent lamp,—All night.—Yen 2.50.
32 candle power incandescent lamp:—All night:—Yen 4.00.
50 candle power incandescent lamp:—All night:—Yen 6.00.
150 " " " " " " " 10.00.
1200 " " enclosed are " " " " 20.00.

Where more than 250 candle power of light is used, a Meter will be installed, freqvedted:—Rent of Meter Yen 2.00 per month. Rate of charges by meter reading:—Two Sen per Ampere per hour. (Approximately this is equal to about One Sen per 16 C. P. lamp per hour) Minimum monthly charge where meter is installed, Yen 20.00 per month, which includes rental of meter.

Estimates for installing lights furnished on application
An assortment of chandeliers always on hand.

K. Murakami.
Photograph Studio
Chinkokai, Seoul.

Printing, Developing and Enlargement, of Photographs always Undertaken.

Korean Views and Pictures Illustrating Native Customs always on Sale,

THE OSAKA SHOSEN KAISHA.

Boats frequently on the berth for Chinnampo.

REGULAR SAILINGS BETWEEN JAPAN AND KOREAN PORTS.

FUSAN AND KOBE VIA SHIMONOSEKI.

OSAKA VIA MOKPO, FUSAN, SHIMONOSEKI AND KOBE.

MOJI DIRECT.

OSAKA VIA KUNSAN, MASANPO, FUSAN, SHIMONOSEKI AND KOBE.

CHEMULPO KUNSAN LINE,
Every three days.

CHEMULPO CHINNAMPO LINE.
Every three days.

For Freight and passage and further particulars apply to

THE OSAKA SHOSEN KAISHA,
Chemulpo.

RONDON, PLAISANT & CO.

General Storekeepers and Merchants, Ships Contractors, Tobacconists, Commission and Forwarding Agents, Coal Merchants

IMPORTERS AND EXPORTERS

Seoul & Chemulpo.

W. D. WENTWORTH.

LANDING
AND
SHIPPING AGENT
AND
CUSTOMS BORDER.

12 OURA, NAGASAKI.

STEWARD & CO.

Chemulpo.

Shipchandlers and Storekeepers, Naval and Mercantile Contrrctors, Landing and Shipping Agents.

STEWARD'S HOTEL

Chemulpo.

Best accommodation in the port for travelers. Clean and well-aired rooms, good cuisin and prompt attendence, moderate tariff.

진력ᄒᆞᄂᆞᆫᄃᆡ특별히일쳥젼쟁후로브터ᄂᆞᆫ우리국민의싱ᄋᆡ가밧귀ᄂᆞᆫ때가되야셔우리국민이만국진보샹과ᄀᆡ명셰계의젼진ᄒᆞᄂᆞᆫᄃᆡ참예ᄒᆞᆯ필요가잇ᄂᆞᆫ지라지금은일본이ᄀᆡ명국즁에뎨일등된거슬널니아ᄂᆞᆫ도다이때에우리ᄂᆞᆫ특별히조화ᄒᆞᄂᆞᆫ거시이번젼쟁의이러난후로브터우리신문외발힝이젼보다오비나더ᄂᆞᆫ거시라이거ᄉᆞᆫ우리가항샹민첩ᄒᆞ고진실ᄒᆞ게보고ᄒᆞ기를진력ᄒᆞᄂᆞᆫᄭᆞ닭인줄노밋노라ᄒᆞ엿스니

ᄒᆞᆫ신문이이러케찰되야가ᄂᆞᆫ거을아모라도차하아니ᄒᆞᆯ사람이누가잇스리오

국민신문에만국부라ᄂᆞᆫ편이셔로잇셔셔론셜을영어로지엇ᄂᆞᆫᄃᆡ우리가몃대분을ᄲᅩᆸ아셔평론ᄒᆞ랴고이아래에벳기노라

이번젼쟁이아즉ᄭᅳᆺ지ᄂᆞᆫ시초이니그결과ᄂᆞᆫ미우쟝원ᄒᆞᆫ지라이싸홈에시작홈은외양으로ᄂᆞᆫ우리가션말자가된것ᄀᆞᆺᄒᆞ나실샹은우리ᄂᆞᆫ로국에ᄃᆡᄒᆞ야응젼ᄒᆞᆯ다름이로다우리ᄂᆞᆫ우리의목젹을달ᄒᆞ기ᄭᆞ지젼쟁을연속ᄒᆞ랴고완젼히예비ᄒᆞ엿스니려슌함락홈이젼쟁의실샹결말되ᄂᆞᆫ것스로싱각ᄒᆞᄂᆞᆫ사람은미우오히홈이로다우리ᄂᆞᆫ한국에셔특권을차지ᄒᆞ고만쥬를ᄀᆡ방ᄒᆞᄂᆞᆫ졍칙을고슈히ᄒᆞᄂᆞᆫ본ᄅᆡ목젹을변치아니ᄒᆞ노라지금만쥬의쟝리를말ᄒᆞᄂᆞᆫ거시너무일다ᄒᆞ고도ᄒᆞ겟지마ᄂᆞᆫ그러ᄒᆞ나일본의만쥬에ᄃᆡᄒᆞᄂᆞᆫ졍책이변ᄒᆞ지아니ᄒᆞ엿다ᄒᆞ고확실히말ᄒᆞᆯ것도다만일일본이만쥬에셔로국이ᄒᆞ던것갓치ᄒᆞ면일로담판의시작ᄒᆞᆯ때브터우리의계향ᄒᆞ던만국동졍에ᄃᆡᄒᆞ야속힘이되겟ᄂᆞᆫ지라그러ᄒᆞ나우리ᄂᆞᆫ여러강국이만일일본이이싸홈을ᄒᆞᄂᆞᆫ것이ᄀᆡ명셰계의공동리익을위ᄒᆞ야싱명과지산을업시이면셔즁란ᄒᆞᆫ일을ᄒᆞᄂᆞᆫ것을ᄭᆡ다르면우리의승젼ᄒᆞᆫ후에리익을탈취ᄒᆞ랴ᄑᆡᄒᆞ지아니ᄒᆞᆯ줄을보증ᄒᆞ겟노라한국에ᄃᆡᄒᆞ야ᄂᆞᆫ일본이독립보젼을담보ᄒᆞᆫ것은고ᄉᆞᄒᆞ고일본이한국을졍말독립국으로ᄃᆡ접을아니ᄒᆞᆫ다고말이만ᄒᆞ나그러ᄒᆞ나그것은알기쉬운즁거가잇ᄂᆞᆫ것이ᄒᆞᆫ사람이졔가능히셔지못ᄒᆞ면다른사람이붓드러쥬어야지그러치아니ᄒᆞ면그사람이녀머질터이라일본의ᄃᆡᄒᆞᆫ졍칙은일쳥젼쟁시로브터지금ᄭᆞ지일졍불변ᄒᆞ엿ᄂᆞᆫ지라린국의유지홈을위ᄒᆞ야일본이한국의지졍과군무와외교ᄉᆞ무롤감독ᄒᆞᄂᆞᆫ도다거년이월의의졍셔와그다음일한됴약에그차셔롤자셰히셜명ᄒᆞ엿스니지금은그됴약의졍신을아ᄂᆞᆫ것이뎨일긴요ᄒᆞᆫ지라이러ᄒᆞ니이약됴들노ᄒᆞ야일본이한국을보호ᄒᆞᆯ권리ᄲᅮᆫ아니라직척도잇도다ᄯᅩ더구나한국이다른강국의셰력즁에드러가ᄂᆞᆫ것은일본의현존유지에단단ᄒᆞᆫ협위인줄노항샹쥬의ᄒᆞ노다ᄒᆞ엿스니

이의견이지금ᄭᆞ지공포ᄒᆞᆫ일본을위ᄒᆞ야발명ᄒᆞᆫ말즁에뎨일젹당ᄒᆞ다고우리ᄂᆞᆫ싱각ᄒᆞ노라일본의목젹을어ᄃᆡᄭᆞ지한ᄒᆞ야말ᄒᆞ엿고그말에ᄃᆡᄒᆞ야외인이칙망ᄒᆞᆯ사ᄅᆞᆷ이업겟도다

그러ᄒᆞ나자셰히궁구ᄒᆞ야보니평론ᄒᆞᆯ마듸가몃군ᄃᆡ잇스니쳐음그신문에말ᄒᆞᆫ바일본은로국에ᄃᆡᄒᆞ야응젼ᄒᆞᆯ다름이라말브터시작ᄒᆞ야보노라여러사ᄅᆞᆷ들이국민신문과합의ᄒᆞᆯ터이니그러면그문제가작졍이된줄노싱각ᄒᆞᆯ듯ᄒᆞ나그러ᄒᆞ나ᄯᅩ좀싱각ᄒᆞᆯ리유가잇ᄂᆞᆫ지라일분이부독불응젼ᄒᆞ게된것이아니라그때와ᄉᆞ셰가자긔롤위ᄒᆞ야조ᄒᆞᆫᄭᆞᄃᆞᆰ에응젼ᄒᆞᆫ것이니그때에일본이다시ᄯᅩ못맛날됴ᄒᆞᆫ게제롤엇온지라그때에로국은구로패긴대쟝의말노ᄒᆞ야싸홈ᄒᆞᆯ기롤예비ᄒᆞ랴고시작ᄒᆞᆯ때에일본은벌셔싸홈을시작ᄒᆞ엿도다

그러ᄒᆞ니일본은다만로국에ᄃᆡᄒᆞ야응젼ᄒᆞᆫᄭᆞ닭에동졍을ᄇᆞ라지말지어다일본은자긔의조ᄒᆞᆫᄃᆡ로ᄒᆞᆯ다름이로다

한국에ᄃᆡᄒᆞ야ᄂᆞᆫ거년이월이십삼일의졍셔롤말ᄒᆞ면셔져국민신문이그차셔의졍신을알나고ᄒᆞ엿스니그의졍셔ᄂᆞᆫ한국에일본군ᄉᆞ가드러온후에한국대황뎨폐하ᄭᅴ셔다른나라에샹의도업시됴인ᄒᆞ신것이라우리ᄂᆞᆫ그됴약의졍신을알것업다고평론ᄒᆞᄂᆞᆫ것이글노ᄒᆞ야한국에잇ᄂᆞᆫ일본사ᄅᆞᆷ들은가망업ᄂᆞᆫ어리셕은물건으로우리의게뵈이노라

그런말은외양으로ᄂᆞᆫ그럴듯도ᄒᆞ지마ᄂᆞᆫ능히ᄒᆞᆯ노셔지못ᄒᆞᄂᆞᆫᄉᆞᄅᆞᆷ이니일본이한국의군무와지졍과외교ᄉᆞ무롤감독홈이한국을유지ᄒᆞ기위홈이니ᄒᆞᄂᆞᆫ말은ᄯᅩᄯᅡᆫ이야기로다

ᄯᅡᆫ이야기들이만이잇지마ᄂᆞᆫ그즁에일진회도잇지엇던것이그됴약에졍신인지우리에게ᄂᆞᆫ뵈이지아니ᄒᆞᄂᆞᆫ도다

우리ᄂᆞᆫ일본이한국을란병ᄒᆞᄂᆞᆫ것이일본의힝복일줄노밋지아니ᄒᆞ며바르지아니ᄒᆞᆫ침노에ᄃᆡᄒᆞ야우리가반ᄃᆡᄒᆞᄂᆞᆫ것도그ᄭᆞᄃᆞᆰ이로다뎨국쥬의와토디확쟝이말노ᄂᆞᆫ듯기에굉장ᄒᆞᆫ듯ᄒᆞ나그러ᄒᆞ나저번셩ᄒᆞᆫ유태인들은나라도업고록히군도업고ᄯᅩ뎨일노졍치상차도업ᄂᆞᆫ것을ᄉᆡᆨ잇지말지어다

관보

뎨삼쳔삼십삼호 광무구년일월십일일

셔임급ᄉᆞ령

○의원면본관 황희도관찰부쥬ᄉᆞ 리정구 경샹남도관찰부쥬ᄉᆞ 박졔철

○임황희도관찰부쥬ᄉᆞ셔판임관륙등 김희슈

○임경샹남도관찰부쥬ᄉᆞ셔판임관오등 젼쥬ᄉᆞ 김달희

임츙쳥남도관찰부쥬ᄉᆞ셔판임관일등 구픔 셔병소

이샹광무팔년십이월삼십일

○승셔판임관오등 한셩지판소쥬ᄉᆞ 노즁식

일월팔일

○임의졍부참찬셔칙임관이등 시강원첨ᄉᆞ 민형식

○임시강원첨ᄉᆞ셔칙임관이등 공ᄂᆡ부특진관 조한국

○임림시셔리경위원총관ᄉᆞ무 호위ᄃᆡ총관 리근택

○외원면본관 숙릉참봉 리강년 졔릉참봉 윤죵현 후릉참봉 홍덕쥬 창릉참봉 김진슈

○임슉릉참봉셔판임관팔등 김셩집

○임졔릉참봉셔판임관팔등 림영긔

○임후릉참봉셔판임관팔등 신샹균

○임창릉참봉셔판임관팔등 조한직

이샹일월구일

○의졍부찬졍리근호ᄉᆞ직소 비지셩소구실이라ᄉᆞ졍과다못병을말ᄒᆞᆯ결을이업스니경은ᄉᆞ양치말고힝공ᄒᆞ라ᄒᆞ시다

일월구일

잡보

평양통신

○병참부게시 근일평양일본병참ᄉᆞ령부에셔게방ᄒᆞ엿ᄂᆞᆫᄃᆡ그ᄉᆞ의가여좌ᄒᆞ더라남문과셔문과대동문동문에ᄂᆞᆫ조금위ᄒᆞ야우리군용션로가될터이니좌ᄀᆡᄒᆞᆫᄉᆞᄂᆞᆫ허락시아니ᄒᆞᆯᄉᆞ 일은 죵로시졍을다른곳으로이졍ᄒᆞᆯᄉᆞ 이ᄂᆞᆫ드러ᄂᆞᆫ방옥이며 삼은진렬ᄒᆞᆫ물픔이며ᄉᆞᄂᆞᆫ드러나게건츅ᄒᆞᆫ것이라ᄒᆞᄂᆞᆫᄃᆡ히디감리셔리와ᄒᆞᆫ번교섭도업시자의로게방ᄒᆞ엿더라

○관찰훈령 평양셩ᄂᆡᄉᆞ대문에근일히관찰ᄉᆞ리즁하씨가ᄂᆡ부훈령을등인ᄒᆞ야고시ᄒᆞ엿ᄂᆞᆫᄃᆡ일진회민이법을범ᄒᆞᄂᆞᆫ쟈임이만코ᄯᅩ작당ᄒᆞ야샹경ᄒᆞ며착슈ᄉᆞ보ᄒᆞ라ᄒᆞ엿스니다그러ᄒᆞᆫ줄안후에각각그집을편안케ᄒᆞ라ᄒᆞᆫ고로히디일진회지회에셔즉시본회로면보ᄒᆞᆫ즉ᄂᆡ부대신리용ᄃᆡ씨의훈계라ᄒᆞ고답면보가왓다더라

○죠사ᄎᆞ파송 근일셔울셔평양일진지회를됴사ᄎᆞ로슌검몃명이나려갓다고풍셜이랑자ᄒᆞ엿다더라

○팽씨대담 젼평양군슈팽한쥬씨ᄂᆞᆫ면관된후염녀업시일본사ᄅᆞᆷ의집을싱방ᄒᆞᄂᆞᆫᄃᆡ비록죄즁이라도광망은젼과ᄀᆞᆺ치홍샹말ᄒᆞ기를다시복직된다ᄒᆞ며풍셜로ᄂᆞᆫ졍부에셔슌검을파송ᄒᆞ엿다ᄒᆞᄂᆞᆫᄃᆡ무어시두려워착슈치못ᄒᆞᄂᆞᆫ지압샹될긔한은업다ᄒᆞ더라

○철시손히 지ᄂᆞᆫ음력십일월십칠일경에일병이평양셩즁에드러왓ᄂᆞᆫᄃᆡ치즁병의군마를죵로빅목젼등쳐에다드러ᄆᆡ인고로지금ᄭᆞ지철젼이되야일반샹민에손히젹지아니ᄒᆞ다더라

이샹평양통신

○렬심교육 근자에남문밧약현거ᄒᆞᄂᆞᆫ리교헌리승구졍환벽김인긔김형규김죵건리규복졔씨가렬심합력ᄒᆞ야히동리에온슈의숙이란학교를셜립ᄒᆞ고총쥰ᄌᆞ졔를모집ᄒᆞ야교육ᄒᆞᄂᆞᆫᄃᆡ그과졍은한문을위쥬ᄒᆞ고일영문자들ᄯᅩᄒᆞᆫ교슈ᄒᆞᄂᆞᆫ지라학교가ᄉᆞ와경비가군쥴ᄒᆞᆷ으로우졔씨가보죠금을츌연ᄒᆞ고ᄯᅩ젼판셔리완용씨와젼참판김만슈씨와협판윤치호씨가각각연금을보죠ᄒᆞ야찬셩ᄒᆞᄂᆞᆫ지라그즁한문교ᄉᆞᄂᆞᆫ강석두씨오영어교ᄉᆞᄂᆞᆫ정한벽씨오일어교ᄉᆞᄂᆞᆫ김죵건씨오그학원은관동합ᄒᆞ야이십여명인ᄃᆡ그규칙을졍밀이직힌다ᄒᆞ니우졔씨의게ᄃᆡᄒᆞ야찬송ᄒᆞᆯ만ᄒᆞᆫ일이더라

광고

TELEGRAMS.

Army Headquarters, Seoul.

After the battle near Yaotze-ling on the 6th inst. the enemy with over 100 wounded retreated through Shang-hea-ho. At 10 A.M. on the 10th inst. a small detachment of the enemy again appeared at Shang-hea-ho but was repulsed.

Army Headquarters, Seoul.

At 10:30 A. M. on the 10th inst. our scouts came into collision with 30 of the enemy's cavalry at Hong Wŏu (about 10 miles North of Ham Heung) who were repulsed, leaving nine dead on the field. The Japanese lost one man slightly wounded and captured two horses and some weapons.

Tokio, Jan. 11.

General Okasawa, of the Imperial Guard (?) will leave Tokio on the 20th of this month to enquire after the health of the Japanese Army in Korea, Port Arthur and Manchuria.

(FROM JAPAN PAPERS.)

London, Jan. 5.

The report of the Committee appointed to consider the question of the American Merchant Marine has been submitted to Congress. The proposals made include the granting of subsidies for new mail routes and the adoption of measures for stimulating the American carrying trade to South Africa and the Far East.

London, Jan. 5.

The Cairo correspondent of the "Daily Telegraph" learns that in consquence of the proposal to construct anew Canal, the Suez Canal Company proposes to reduce its present charges by half a franc per ton.

London, Jan. 2, p. m.

The Nove Vremya asserts that Admiral Rojestvensky is still suffering from intense nervous strain and expresses the fear that he may consequently misconstrue the presence of the British warships which are shadowing his fleet. It states that he will await the arrival of the additional squadrons at Madagascar.

London, Jan 4.

Various inspired suggestions in the direction of peace are emanating from Washington, representing President Roosevelt as anxious to mediate but explaining that he cannot move until he is approached by both belligerents.

Nothing whatever confirmatory of these reports has been received in London, and none of the rumours regarding peace at the present moment are credited.

London, Jan, 4.

Admiral Foelkersahm's squadron is now anchored in Passandava Bay (on the northwest coast of Madagascar), while the squadron under Admiral Rohjestvensky is now lying in Antongil Bay (on the east coast of Madagscar). Both squadron ares provisioning from the transports "Nossibe," "Majorga," and "Tamatave."

It is believed the two squadrons will rendezvous at Diego Suarez, on the extreme northeast coast of Madagascar.

London, Jan. 5.

France, in reply to representations from Japan regarding the coaling and victualling of the Baltic Squadron at Madagascar, says there is no danger of the nonobservance of neutrality. The local authorities have received strict instructions as to their duties in this matter.

London, Jan. 5.

The Tsar has returned to St. Petersburg.

The fate of the Japanese protected cruiser "Takasago," says an exchange, seems to be no longer in doubt. She struck a mine and was sunk, half of her crew going down with her.

MARITIME DEFENCE ZONE IN FORMOSAN WATERS.

Notification No. 31 issued by the Minister of the Navy, Tokio, on the 23rd December announces that the seas off the port of Kelung, Formosa, which are involved between a line connecting the highest point on the Kelung island with Robihei promontory and a line drawn to the southwest from the above highest point, shall be regarded as a maritime defence zone on and after the above-mentioned date.

Regulations issued in connection with the above provide among other things that, with the exception of vessels belonging to the Imperial Government and regular mail steamers, other vessels desirous of entering or issuing from the zone must obtain the necessary permission of the proper authorities at the above port, and that similiar permission is also needed for vessels which intend to navigate the zone between sunset and dawn. It is further notified that whilst nagivating this zone vessels must not proceed at a greater speed than five knots an hour.

ABOUT THE IL-CHIN-HOI.

The joint programme of the Japanese officials in Seoul and the riff-raff of Korean cooliedom (designated collectively the Il-chin-hoi), is going along nicely.

The Home Office (acting under compulsion) has telegraphed the Governor of Kyengki to arrest a certain Mang-il-ho who had the temerity to oppose the Il-chin-hoi.

The same office has also wired to the Governor of North Pye gan to enquire whether it can really be true that the magistrates of Kwi Sung and Tai-chun attempted to resist the I. C. H. Patriots.

Further, it appears that the magistrate of Ok Ku struck an Il-chin-hoi member and then locked him up. The Home Office wants to know the exact reason for this but without waiting for it orders the release of the I. C. H. gentleman.

Since Mr. Sin Tai Hyu has been chief of police he has prosecuted a rigourous campaign againt sercerers and all exponents of the "Black arts," with the result that these gentry are at present very scarce.

Yesterday at 2:30 P. M., the British and Chinese Ministers met at the Foreign Office to consider the evidence recently taken by Mr. Porter with regard to the alleged murder of a Chinaman at Haiju. What decision was arrived at is not known.

Yesterday Messrs. Yun Kap Byung and Yung Chung Sik, two shining lights of the Il Chin hoi, called at the police department and demanded the dismissal of Inspector Bai Suk Tai who is a brother of the erstwhile famous "Lady" Hyon.

The Japanese gendarmes in Seoul (many of them newly recruited) seem to be having a good time since they commenced to take charge of the city. His Majesty has heard that people abroad at night are indiscriminately arrested and has ordered an investigation.

The Japanese Minister has written to the Foreign Office demanding that the cow-hide monopoly, which belongs to the Imperial Household Department be immediately abolished. He adds that this is not his first application and says that if it is not immediately complied with "Great things will happen in your Department."

An amusing piece of "Squeeze-pidgin" has just come to light. It appears that it was resolved to pay Mr. Kato the very liberal sum of $3,000 for house rent for the time he has been adviser to the Department of Agriculture, and this sum was duly disbursed by the Finance Department. It appears that Mr. Kato has only received $1,000 and enquiries are now being made as to the direction in which the other $2,000 disappeared.

THE NEEDS OF THE U. S. NAVY.

A telegram from Washington dated November 23rd said:—How badly off the United States Navy is for officers, and how seriously this condition may affect the Navy and the Nation, are plainly told in the annual report of Rear-Admiral George A. Converse, Chief of the Bureau of Navigation, approved by Secretary of the Navy Morton to-day.

Experience, especially in gun-fire, he says, has shown that it is necessary to increase the number of officers assigned to ships. Admiral Converse recommends that the number of lieutenants be increased from 350 to 600, and that the number of lieutenant-commanders be increased from 200 to 300.

Because of the important part played by torpedo-craft in the war in the Far East, it is deemed advisable that the large vessels of this type be commanded by lieutenant-commanders. The report says that the youngest American commander to-day, on the day he attained that rank, was older than the average age of the Japanese captains, and about the same as the average of English and German. He had passed the compulsory retirement age for Japanese captains, and was within six months of the compulsory retirement age for English and German captains. The Admiral remarked that "until a measure is adopted for the compulsory retirement of commodores and captains who do not gain promotion at certain ages, the flow or promotion and the ages of officers in the different grades will not be satisfactory.

Regarding the paramount efficiency of battleships and the part played by them in the Far Eastern War, Admiral Converse wrote:

"Although a hundred odd torpedo-boats and torpedo-boat destroyers have been actually engaged for five months against battleships which have been exposed to attack times without number, we have yet to learn authoritatively of a torpedo from a torpedo-vessel causing the loss of a single battleship. It cannot be claimed, therefore, that there has been so far anything to discredit the battleships, as a type, nor is any such outcome to be expected from this war, whatever may be the casualties among battleships. To wage war succesfully with a naval force requires now, as it has required in all ages, a type of vessel which will combine in the most effective manner the qualities of offense, mobility, defence, endurance and self-maintenance. Such vessels are battleships, and they constitute the main strength and reliance of a navy."

Admiral Converse calls attention to the need of a general staff or board, "an advisory body which shall not be under the control of any bureau, but responsible directly to the Secretary."

MR. MEGATA'S FINANCIAL SCHEME.

The fruits of Mr. Megata's strenuous efforts as Financial Adviser to Korea are just beginning to become apparent. From the "Dai Han Ilpo" we learn that, after much investigation and some thought, Mr. Megata has come to the conclusion that it is essential to Korea's welfare that she should borrow ten million yen from the Japanese government.

In view of the fact that the Japanese Government is now paying 8½ per cent for money barrowed in Europe, we are afraid that Korea would have to pay a pretty stiff interest.

In the meantime we commend to the notice of responsible Koreans some remarks we made on November 3rd when discussing Japan's financial methods in this country. We said:—

"All these transactions are distinctly unfavourable to Korea, and as there is from time to time talk of Korea borrowing money from Japan, we recommend the government to make sure of two things before signing the bond. First that they get the money, and, next, that they will be allowed to have the spending of it.

Mr. Yi Keun-tak, the new police Superintend ant, called at the Japanese Legation yesterday.

FISHERMAN KILLED BY A SHELL.

An accident occurred to a fisherman living near Kowloon Bay some days ago under rather peculiar circumstances which has since resulted in his death. It appears that the deceased picked up a live shell while fishing in Kowloon Bay, in June last, and not knowing what it was stored it away in his house. A few days ago however his curiousity to know what was inside of the shell overcame his prudence, and he proceeded to break the shell open by hammering it on some stones. It exploded and blew his right hand off, and inflicted other injuries. The man was taken by the police to the Government Civil Hospital, where his death occurred.

H. E. Mr. Hayashi obtained an audience of His Majesty yesterday in order to present the Lieut-Commander of a Japanese torpedo boat now in Chemulpo

The Japanese in Chemulpo will hold a celebration on Feb. 9th, this being the first anniversary of the battle (?) of Chemulpo.

The Korea Daily News.

Issued at 5 P. M. daily except Sundays.

Rate of Subscription:—
Per Year,............Yen 25.
Per Quarter,..........Yen 7.
Per Month,..........Yen 2.50.

Postage in Korea not charged extra.
Postage abroad charged extra.

Advertisements, 50 sen per day for 1 inch or less.
5 yen per month per inch.
50 yen per year per inch.

All communications to

E. T. BETHELL,
Editor and Publisher,
Pak-tong, Seoul.

STOESSEL'S SURRENDER.

It is to be noted that the Tokio newspapers while ungrudgingly expressing admiration for General Stoessel's gallant defense of Port Arthur, are very much enraged at his action in destroying his ships, permitting some to escape, blocking the harbour and wrecking fortifications after the despatch of his offer to surrender. General Stoessel's behaviour is described as "mean," "cowardly," "dishonourable" etc., but although the Japanese chagrin at the oss of valuable spoils of war is natural enough, we absolutely fail to see any justification for their abuse.

Stoessel had no guarantee that his terms would be accepted, and as a matter of fact very different terms were imposed, and as the Japanese continued to bombard him, he could hardly be expected to await a reply to his message with folded arms.

From a Japanese point of view, General Stoessel's action was doubtless very annoying, but to an outsider it only appears that destroying everything possible before surrendering was only fittingly concluding his heroic defense and giving further evidence of his loyalty to the Czar, his master.

THE JAPANESE, THE IL-CHIN-HOI AND POLITICS.

The real purpose of the Japanese directors of that organization of hired "men," the Il-chin-hoi to wit, has at last been shown to us.

Without them, things would have been altogether too peaceful and orderly in Seoul.

Now, taking advantage of some very slight disorder for which his vassals, the Il-chin-hoi scallywags, were alone responsible, General Hasegawa has placarded the city with proclamations to the effect that order will in future be maintained by his gendarmerie, who will take precedence of the Korean police force.

Things have come to such a pretty pass since the Japanese have begun to "protect" this country in earnest that we think it advisable not to express our opinion of this latest outrage; otherwise we should treat our readers to some very strong language indeed.

The Il-chin-hoi people, having served their purpose *pro tem* have been ordered to return to their homes until they are again summoned by their leaders. When this happens we shall have another coup.

The aim of the Japanese is evidently to get the direction of affairs in this country in the hands of Japanese or Koreans of pro-Japanese views.

This might be excused if such Koreans were superior to the present lot of officials, but the action of the Japanese minister in protesting against the dismissal of a Pyeng Yang official (who had been proven to have been particularly extortionate and oppressive while in office) is evidence that probity is not essential in order to obtain Japanese support.

The Koreans are powerless against this intriguing at present but a time will come when the Japanese will regret the manner in which they are now overreaching themselves.

FROM THE "CHEFOO DAILY NEWS."

(Concluded from yesterday.)

January 4th.

It is well known here that one of the launches did bring most important dispatches for St. Petersburg which were promptly delivered to Mr. Tiedemann upon the arrival of the messenger, and that the St. Petersberg government now has General Stoessel's version of his surrender. An officer arriving by one of these boats is reported to have spoken to a friend as follows:

"There was nothing left to do but surrender. The garrison was in a pitiable condition. Very little ammunition remained for the heavy guns, although there was an abundance of small-arm ammunition in the arsenals; but of what use are rifle balls against twelve inch shells? Had Stoessel held out much longer it would only have meant the extermination of the garrison. All the men and officers were unanimous in their verdict that surrenderwas the only solution of the terrible problem which confronted them.

"Conditions in the hospitals at Port Arthur are heart-rending. Many of the wounded are dying from sheer want of food. Scurvy is very common and shows itself by developing disgusting ulcers in one's mouth. The complaint is so common in the hospitals that the nurses and doctors have grown so accustomed to human suffering that their minds appear to be upset to a degree where they have lost all compassion. The gentleness of the ladies who volunteered for duty in the hospitals was the best medicine the men received.

"Bands are not playing in Port Arthur any more, and every one is as solemn as if the end of the world was at hand. It is not unusual to see men walking along the streets sobbing and crying like little children.

"According to the registration of wounded and dead sixty-five per cent of the military officers have been killed or wounded. Out of two hundred and seven officers of the navy who served in the encounter on "203 Metre Hill" only twenty escaped uninjured.

"It may be safely said the surrender is more due to a lack of men than anything else. I estimate that of the four thousand men considered fit for duty nearly one half would be sent to the hospitals in time of peace."

* * *

Three men-of-war's launches arrived in Chefoo early yesterday morning, having made the run from Port Arthur. One of them was rigged up with a torpedo tube. In fact they might be designated as torpedo launches. They had been in the harbour but a short time when seven Japanese destroyers made their appearance. The latter also entered the harbours.

The launches brought over only about enough men to navigate them. They were boarded immediately by numbers of persons and by the customs authorities. There were no implements of war about them for the attention of the customs people, except the torpedo tube on the smallest of the three, and possibly some small arms carried by one or two of the men. They had run the blockade as successfully as the torpedo boats preceding them the day before, and had experienced no difficulty in getting to Chefoo.

The men seemed to be tired out and were not in a mood to do much talking. Some of them were willing to relate incidents of the struggle at Port Arthur, which are given elsewhere in these columns. The launches left Port Arthur at eight o'clock Monday night, taking the opportunity to seek shelter in this harbour.

Seven Japanese destroyers visited Chefoo yesterday morning, popping into the harbour not long after the arrival of the launches from Port Arthur. A cruiser or a gunboat accompanied them. The cruiser did not enter the harbour, but majestic and dignified, waited on the outskirts, while she occupied a few of her spare moments in saluting Admiral Folger on the U.S S."Baltimore."

The destroyers came quite well inside the harbour limits and stopped in a bunch, remaining an hour or more. Four of them then departed while the other three took up position in a sort of blockading line across the narrow portion of the harbour off Consulate Hill.

It was stated that the object of the vessels visit was to ascertain whether or not the dismantlement of the Russians torpedoers arriving the day before was complete. The destroyers remained until late in the afternoon, and at six o'clock at least one of them was still in the harbor, and she had shifted her position to the inner basinamidst the bulk of the shipping.

* * *

January 5th.

The deplorable conditions prevailing in Port Arthur during the last days of the siege, with reference to the care of the sick and wounded, will probably never be realized except by those who were there. This phase of the defence of the fortress was one that was calculated to make the hearts of its defenders faint. With the terrific bombardment to which the city was subjected, it was impossible, of course, to conduct the hospitals properly. An eye-witness says that the shrieks and moaning of the wounded, and the roaring and crashing of shells by day and by night, combined to make the hospitals veritable hells for those who were sufficently convalescent to appreciate the true situation.

The number of physicians and surgeons was not large enough to attend to the men who must receive their aid, even when an immediate operation meant life and inattention meant death. Oftentimes, he says, he has seen officers and men who had received wounds which did not incapacitate them for duty, stagger in, throw their arms to one side, aid in the dressing of their own wounds, then grab their accoutrements and hurry back to the fortifications. Such scenes as this were of daily occurrence.

The question of the care of the wounded was a serious one, especially as the number grew day by day, and it was a very potent factor in bringing about the determination not to longer resist the ferocious attacks of the enemy, but to ask for terms and surrender.

* * *

The enemy will find but little property of value when its troops get into Port Arthur. A good deal of the city, of course was badly damaged or totally destroyed during the bombardment, but what was untouched by Japanese shell fire and might prove of value to the victors, was destroyed prior to the final exchange of the terms of surrender.

The Russians destroyed two of the main forts. The residence of the Viceroy was also destroyed. Supplies were burned and the men-of-war in the harbor were made away with. Explosives were used in destroying the greater part of this property. In the case of the ships the explosions caused conflagrations in most instances, and the property was consumed by the flames. The "Retvizan," "Pobieda," "Pallada" and "Bayan" passed out of existence in this way. The "Sevastopol" was towed out to the harbor entrance and a charge of gun-cotton placed amidships. She was fairly blown in two, the bow going down first. The harbor entrance is completely blocked for big ships.

Six of the Chinese apprentices who as announced previously, are to enter the British navy with the consent of the British Government, have arrived at Weihaiwei from Nanking, and have been assigned to three different ships, two men on each. The students have the rank of midshipmen and wear European uniforms. They are said to be promising pupils.

The Korea Daily News.

VOL. II, THURSDAY, JANUARY 12, 1905. No. 8

大韓每日申報
대한미일신보

(뎨이권구호)　　(토요일)　　일쳔구빅오년일월십ᄉᆞ일

본샤고빅

이신보는영어와한어로셔미일출판ᄒᆞᆸ

신문가

한쟝　엽두돈오푼

일삭표　엽두량닷돈

우표가미삭닷돈

다맛돈으로밧ᄉᆞᆸ

광고료논

괴한의쟝단과ᄌᆞ항의다쇼로죵감ᄒᆞ되쳐음에는밧을터이오매오터지아니ᄒᆞ면한사람마다다이신문을보실터이니광고내시기를원ᄒᆞ시는이들은우리신문샤에와셔편약ᄒᆞ심을희망ᄒᆞᆸ

○발힝소　박동대한미일신보샤

발힝겸편집인　영국인셜필립

샤쟝　영국인 (빅셜)

평양　터리졈

○평양종로에사는김미보씨로우리신문을판미ᄒᆞ는터리인을뎡ᄒᆞ엿ᄉᆞ오니평양에계신쳠군ᄌᆞ는이터리졈에와셔보시기를ᄇᆞ라ᄋᆞᆸ

샤고

○우리대한미일신보ᄂᆞᆫ창셜ᄒᆞᆫ거시대한의인민들을위ᄒᆞ야모든대쇼ᄉᆞ를들어공평ᄒᆞᆫ언론을쥬쟝ᄒᆞ는것이라우리신문을보ᄂᆞᆫ쳠군ᄌᆞ는셰계형편을아시고...

○본샤셜시이ᄅᆡ로신문을미일발간ᄒᆞ더니...

잡보

○너부대신　너부에셔각부로됴회ᄒᆞ엿ᄂᆞᆫᄃᆡ...

○너부대신　너부에셔각쳐에됴회ᄒᆞ엿ᄂᆞᆫᄃᆡ...

○과쟝승진　...

○회동사관　...

○외부쳥의　외부에셔...

○탁지쳥의　...

○리셔방변　...

○김세죵씨　...

○원산항긔별　...

외보

○대영신문　...

관보

○궁니부　...

별보

○...

UNION INSURANCE SOCIETY OF CANTON.

Head office Hongkong.
Marine risks underwritten at current rates.
Agents in Chemulpo,
E. MEYER & Co.

COMPAGNIE DES MESSAGERIES MARITIMES.

Fortnightly Direct Service.

For Marseilles via Ports.

Sailing from Yokohama Calling at Kobe, Shanghai, Hongkong, Saigon, Singapore, Colombo, Djibonti, Suez, Port Said and Marseilles.

For particulars apply to
HOLME RINGER & Co.,
Chemulpo.

HAYASHIDA & CO.,

16 MYENG DONG, CHIN KO KAI, SEOUL.
BRANCH OFFICE AT CHEMULPO.

Money changers, Coal and Wood Merchants, Express Agents.

We are agents for the Pyeng-yang Coal Company and the Karazu Coal Company of Japan. We have the best quality of both anthracite and bituminous coal, and prompt execution of orders is our speciality. Firewood of all kinds kept in stock. Full weight guaranteed. Loans at low rates. Money of all denominations exchanged at current rates. Parcels received for all parts.

CHINA MUTUAL LIFE INS. OC.

Most favourable terms to policy holders.

Benefit system unsurpassed.

HOLME RINGER & Co.
Agents, Chemulpo.

C. P. R.

CANADIAN PACIFIC RAILWAY COMPANY'S ROYAL MAIL STEAMSHIP LINE.

THE FAST ROUTE BETWEEN CHINA, JAPAN, AND EUROPE VIA CANADA AND THE UNITED STATES.

Route from Hongkong via Shanghai, Nagasaki (Inland Sea of Japan) Kobe, Yokohama Victoria and Vancouver.

Twin Screw Empress Steamship—6,000 Tons—Speed 19 knots.

PROPOSED SAILING FROM YOKOHAMA.
R. M. S. Empress of India.
R. M. S. Empress of Japan.
R. M. S. Empress of China.
R. M. S. Athenian.
R. M. S. Tartar.

Special reduction (first class only) granted to members of the Military, Naval, Diplomatic and Civil services and to Missionaries.

Passengers have choice of ten routes across the Continent of America and have privilege of travelling by any Atlantic Steamship Line.

Round the World passage tickets in connection with the P. and O. S. N., North German Lloyd and Messageries Co.'s **£125.**

All rates payable at current rate of exchange.

For further information, Tickets, Guide Books, etc., apply to

HOLME, RINGER & Co., AGENTS,
Chemulpo.

Grand Hotel,

(Formerly the Station Hotel)

Near the Railway Terminus, West Gate Seoul.

The Best Hotel in Korea.
Handsome new Building.
Fine Airy Rooms
Excellent Cuisine.
Terms Moderate.
Special terms to Missionaries and to permanent boarders.

Electric cars within 2 minutes' walk.

W. H. EMBERLEY.
Proprietor

EVERY FACILITY.

In connection with Life Assurance Business is afforded by

The Standard Life Assurance Co.,

One of the largest and wealthiest of the Provident Institutions of the United Kingdom Forms of Application and all information will be promptly afforded on application.

10 CENTS A DAY.

Not a very large expenditure is it? But it is sufficient to secure for a man of 30 a policy with the STANDARD LIFE OFFICE for

$1323.

For all particulars of rates, etc., apply to

Holme, Ringer & Co.,
Agents, Chemulpo.

THE NEW YORK LIFE INSURANCE COMPANY.

Have you ever been declined by any Company?

Are you engaged in a specially hazardous occupation?

Have you heard of the New York Life Insurance Company's New Classifications for this class of Risks?

If not, send your date of birth, occupation and particulars of rejection, if any to

E. MEYER & Co.,
Agents, Chemulpo.

MITSUI BUSSAN KAISHA.
(MITSUI & Co.)

MITSUI GINKO.
(MITSUI BANK.)

The Bank is owned by the members of the Mitsui Family, who, as partners, assume an unmited responsibility for all liabilities of the Bank:—

Capital..........................Yen 5,000,000
Reserve Fund.................... " 5,600,000

HEAD OFFICE, TOKYO.

LONDON OFFICE, 34 LIME ST., E. C.

BRANCHES AND AGENCIES:—
New York, San Francisco, Hamburg, Bombay, Singapore, Manila, Hongkong, Amoy, Chefoo, Tientsin.

Kobe, Hakodate, Yokohama, Kure, Yokosuka, Moji, Shimonoseki, Miike, Wakamatsu, Nagasaki, Kuchinotsu, Karatsu, Sasebo, Misume, Taipeh, &c.

Telegraphic Address for all the Offices:
"MITSUI."
A. B. C. AND A. I CODES USED.

Contractors of Coal
To the Imperial Japanese Navy. Arsenalr and Railway Bureau, Principal Railway Companies and Industrial Work, Home and Foreign Mail and Freight Steamers.

Sole Proprietors
Of the famous Miike, Tagawa and Yamano Coal Mines.

Sole Agents
For the sale of Fukumo, Hokoku, Ichimura, Kanoda, Mannoura, Onoura, Ostuji, Sonoda, Tsubaruro, Yoshinotani, Yoshio, Yurokibura and other coals.

YANGTSE INSURANCE ASSOCIATION, LTD.

The undersigned, having been appointed agents for the above company, are prepared to issue policies and pay losses on marine risks at regular rates.

E. MEYER & Co.,
Agents, Chemulpo.

AMERICAN KOREAN ELECTRIC CO.

Light and Power.

Main Office: Electric Building, Chong No.

RAILWAY DEPARTMENT.

OPERATING CARS BETWEEN EAST AND WEST GATE, EVERY TEN MINUTES:—

First Car leaves East Gate at 7:00 A. M. First Car leaves R. R. Station at 7:25 A. M
Last Car " East Gate at 8.40 P. M. Last " " R. R. Station at 9.05 P.M

OPERATING CARS BETWEEN EAST GATE AND IMPERIAL TOMB TERMINUS, EVERY TWENTY MINUTES:—
CONNECTING WITH EVERY ALTERNATE CAR ARRIVING AT EAST GATE FROM CHONG NO.

First Car leaves East Gate for Tomb at 7:10 A. M.
" " " Tomb for East Gate at 7:30 A. M.
Last " " East Gate for Tomb at 7:50 P. M.
" " " Tomb for East Gate at 8:10 P. M.

OPERATING CARS BETWEEN CHONG NO AND YUNG SAN RIVER EVERY TWELVE MINUTES:—

First Car leaves Chong No for South Gate at 7:12 A. M.
" " " Chong No for Yung San at 7:36 A. M.
" " " South Gate for Chong No at 7:20 A. M.
" " " Yung San for Chong No at 8:09 A. M.
Last " " South Gate for Chong No 9:00 P. M.
" " " Yung San for Chong No at 8.45. p. M.

SPECIAL PRIVATE CARS FURNISHED TO SUIT CONVENIENCE OF PATRONS. PRICES ON APPLICATION AT HEAD OFFICE.

LIGHTING DEPARTMENT.

Where less than 250 candle power of light is used, the rate per month will be
Per 16 candle power incandescent lamp,—All night.—Yen 2.50.
32 candle power incandescent lamp:—All night:—Yen 4.00.
50 candle power incandescent lamp:—All night:—Yen 6.00.
150 " " " " " " " 10.00.
1200 " " enclosed are " " " " 20.00.

Where more than 250 candle power of light is used, a Meter will be installed, freqvedted:—Rent of Meter Yen 2.00 per month. Rate of charges by meter reading:—Two Sen per Ampere per hour. (Approximately this is equal to about One Sen per 16 C. P. lamp per hour) Minimum monthly charge where meter is installed, Yen 20.00 per month, which includes rental of meter.

Estimates for installing lights furnished on application
An assortment of chandeliers always on hand.

K. Murakami.
Photograph Studio
Chinkokai, Seoul.

Printing, Developing and Enlargement, of Photographs always Undertaken.

Korean Views and Pictures Illustrating Native Customs always on Sale,

THE OSAKA SHOSEN KAISHA.

Boats frequently on the berth for Chinnampo.

REGULAR SAILINGS BETWEEN JAPAN AND KOREAN PORTS.

FUSAN AND KOBE VIA SHIMONOSEKI.

OSAKA VIA MOKPO, FUSAN, SHIMONOSEKI AND KOBE.

MOJI DIRECT.

OSAKA VIA KUNSAN, MASANPO, FUSAN, SHIMONOSEKI AND KOBE.

CHEMULPO KUNSAN LINE,
Every three days.

CHEMULPO CHINNAMPO LINE.
Every three days.

For Freight and passage and further particulars apply to
THE OSAKA SHOSEN KAISHA,
Chemulpo.

RONDON, PLAISANT & CO.

General Storekeepers and Merchants, Ships Contractors, Tobacconists, Commission and Forwarding Agents, Coal Merchants

IMPORTERS AND EXPORTERS

Seoul & Chemulpo.

W. D. WENTWORTH.

LANDING
AND
SHIPPING AGENT
AND
CUSTOMS BORDER.

12 OURA, NAGASAKI.

STEWARD & CO.

Chemulpo.

Shipchandlers and Storekeepers, Naval and Mercantile Contrrctors, Landing and Shipping Agents.

STEWARD'S HOTEL

Chemulpo.

Best accommodation in the port for traveiers. Clean and well-aired rooms, good cuisin and prompt attendence, moderate tariff.

도셔은려슌구로브리공곳에도
망ᄒ야온사름의말을드른즉ᄉ
며노푸대쟝이귀쵸ᄒᆫ것이라는
티

일 봄이셩ᄒᆫ군ᄉ들과ᄉ관들과
적게샹ᄒ고병든자중에는희
힝ᄒ을흘만ᄒᆫ사름들은다병
귀를ᄒ티ᄒ고죵속히로국에
도라가기를허락ᄒ되이번젼
쟁에는다시참여치아니ᄒ기
로약됴ᄒᆯᄉ

이 일본사름들이로국사름들의
샹ᄒ고병드러셔병원에잇는
자들을소복ᄒ기셔지구조ᄒ
야그리ᄒᆫ후에그사름들의게
병귀를ᄒ티ᄒ고로국에도라
가기를허락ᄒᆯᄉ

샹 어느나라사름이던지물론ᄒ
고비젼투원들은일본사름이
그증거가온증립항구로광인
미ᄒ오송ᄒᆯᄉ

말 쳰고챰위가일본군중으로향
ᄒ야군ᄂ갈시일본괴병의일분
티가뷔록대쟝의영문으로호숑
ᄒ엿는지라그러ᄒ나뷔록대쟝
미맛ᄎ엿셔셔그쳥원셔는뷔록
싸의종관의게맛기고려슌구로
도라왓더라

그 날져녁여섯시에일본군중에
셔즐ᄃ에태포노키를긋치더니
그잇흔날아참에다시포격을셔
작ᄒ야오후에긋치니그세에는
아마스툿셀대쟝이벌셔뷔록대쟝의
회답을본듯ᄒ시라

스툿셀대쟝이일본사자를밧게
로나아가셔바져셔그회답을쳔
히바랏다는데그때에는싸홈이
아조긋치고그젼날밤에로국사
롬들이쪽발셕진로국포ᄃ를일
본사름이졈령ᄒᆫ듯ᄒ며그시이
에벌셔일본군수들이려슌구에
드러가지아니ᄒ엿스면오날에
나너일에는드러갈듯더라

지벤월ᄂ일밤여듧시에려슌구
셔슈퇴쟝을ᄒ고ᄯ나서오날드
참에도박ᄒᆫ관인들에말을드른
즉로국사름들이지변일요일
에발셔도통젹의포대를파ᄒᆫ합
션과군물들을쪽발ᄒ여모다엄
으로엘고거서쪽발시커셔침몰
ᄒ엿는지라그것은일본사름의
군함이항구안으로드러오지
못ᄒ게막음이더라

일본사름들이디부항구의셔편
림구를막엇ᄉ마는로국슈뢰정
이척이요항으로대젹의포화를
피ᄒ야니항으로드러온지라
지금스툿셀쟝군이항복ᄒ라는
소셰에티ᄒ야최후보고가잇는
것은일본군에서관계치아니ᄒ
게아려셔거부에잇는일본피식
합티를것어감인ᄃ오날아참에
일본병ᄉ가로국슈뢰정이챡이
지변밤에딥항ᄒ엿다는것을보
교ᄒ야서그폐쇄됨티에서는밤

인교로대젹의빈가목젼에셔가
는것을못보앗다고울불락ᄒ논다
더라

뎐보

위희위발 일월ᄉ일

○운ᄉ양치 군셔인드로며다
호가오날아참칠시에려슌구로
향ᄒ야세낫는데이곳에셔보도
ᄒ는약ᄒ로글시ᄉ고려슌구에병들
고샹ᄒᆫ자들을구ᄒ기를위홈이
라더라

론돈발 동일

○려슌함락과로국여론 로국
에려슌함락ᄒᆫ소문이젼파ᄒ야
일반인심이대단히격졍ᄒ논모
양인ᄃ각신문들은정부에충고
ᄒ되이젼정을연속히ᄒ야로국
이ᄒᆫ큰국민인것을세계에뵈이
라ᄒ엿더라

동대발 동일

○로쟝불복명 파리에셔젼파
ᄒ는말을거ᄒᆫ즉불퇴협티긔수
령관로제스드벤스기대쟝의보
로국히군부에셔명령ᄒ되리계수
로도라와셔로국젼함티의종수
령관의지위를반ᄒ라ᄒ엿스나
로제스드벤스기대쟝은그명령
을좃지아니ᄒ다고말ᄒ더라ᄒ
엿더라

론돈발 일월ᄉ일

○일본함소식 바리비아에도박
ᄒᆫ화란젼션편에젼ᄒ는말을거
ᄒᆫ즉일본군함사쳑이본월삼일
에수마타드라의동편히변에셔
항션ᄒ야세나더라ᄒ엿더라

동대발 동일

○영청과위히위 론돈에잇는
남청국공ᄉ가위히위수진으로오
영국외부대신랜스다운씨와오
회견ᄒ엿다더라

동대발 동월삼일

○일본채권표등 일본채권이
미우고등ᄒ야빅에오분의리자
로졍ᄒᆫ채권은이방이오큰교빅
에수샵분자리는셥오저가을낫다
라

십일오젼 군ᄉ평부챡

○합창방면젼보 룩일요
부근젼투에셰의부샹ᄒᆫ자는자
[illegible]

○북관젼보 십일오젼시반
외에우리쟝교쳑후가홍원에셔
쥭은자ᅵ구명을류괴ᄒ고젹은
ᄒ엿는ᄃ우리군ᄉ에는일명이
란조금샹ᄒ고마이편과소총과기
무과약샹간이라더라

잡보

○변명원슈 완도군슈우긔동
씨의지젹이샴남에웃듬인고로
희군유쟝명슈바명귀리졍우
이너부에청원휘류ᄒ는ᄃ의
외에고금도인이제국신문사에
두서ᄒ야붇치ᄒᆫ모양으로괴질
ᄒ오즉쟝셩슈등이번명ᄒ로한
셩쥐관소에쳥원ᄒ야징사수무
원을조치ᄒ야젼문ᄒ단더라

○너부면훈젼북 너부에셔일
쟉에젼라북도관찰부로면훈ᄒ
기를지금드른즉옥구군슈가깅
슈제군민회수무원을칙슈ᄒ고무
슈란타ᄒ야방지수경이라ᄒ니
이것이무상위졍인지회군에엄
칙ᄒ야즉시방숑ᄒ고치보ᄒ라
ᄒ엿더라

○경셩군보 경셩군슈싱현퇴
씨가너부로싱이월십삼일에발
숑ᄒ보고를거ᄒᆫ즉본월십일에
본군에류쥬ᄒ는로국쟝관이계
관찰ᄉ의수쳐로곳드러가셔폐
무ᄒᆷ일로써힐란ᄒ다가쓴병뎡
을파숑ᄒ야본군슈를쳥리ᄒ야
말ᄒ기를관찰ᄉ의인장을엇
지ᄒ야경퇴ᄒ엿나냐ᄒ기에퇴
답ᄒ기를관찰은일의갈니고경
부에셔본군슈로셔리ᄒ라는훈
령이잇기로경퇴ᄒ엿노라ᄒᆫ즉
도관이쏘말ᄒ기를키국ᄒᆫ칙이
아모리이러ᄒ드리도일로가휴
란젼ᄒ기젼에는관찰ᄉ도갈녀도
라가지못ᄒᆯ거시오군슈도셔리
를ᄒ지못ᄒᆯ거신즉인쟝을도로
쥬라ᄒ며병뎡을다숑ᄒ고위협ᄒ야
흠을츙양치못ᄒᆯ지라극편ᄒ야
빈명ᄒ여도죵셔쳥죵취이니ᄒ
계고인쟝을엇지로도로쥬게ᄒ야
관찰이지금시무ᄒ논다ᄒ엿더
라

○대너면담 일헌병이경찰을
실시ᄒᆫ이후에범률계출엽ᄒ는
자는일헌병이장아간다ᄒᆷ으로
황샹폐하께셔드르시고쥐ᄉ셜
의유무를각경무셔에면담ᄒ고
흉이진일이잇거든곳보고ᄒ라
ᄒ엿다더라

○광쳐의론 근일젼셜을거ᄒ
즉의정부의정은최익현씨가피
임ᄒ겟다ᄒ며참정은신엽회쥬
관찰ᄉ조병호씨가피임ᄒ겟다
더라

○도츅분경 너부대신조병식
씨는광쥐된군수들을숀쥐히셔
임홀ᄎ로각부부원쳥에구근인
원을션택ᄒ야구쳐홀용의가현
젼ᄒ기로도츅분경ᄒ는관습이
잇서너부대신가문젼이시졍곳
다더라

○차졍너하 남촌사는졍씨가
잇는ᄃ령세가지극히빈한ᄒ야
조셕을보계ᄒ더니맛춤어느친
구의돈만쟉리쁘문셔를비러쟝
혀쓰라ᄒ고한양뿔사는신쥬사
를주고왓더니차일피일ᄒ고돈
을아니주는고로다른사름의게
쟝치란고과의ᄒᆫ후에문셔를도
로차자달나ᄒ즉신모의말이그
문셔는리참셔로주엇고리참셔
[illegible]
리돈을주어야쳣젯다ᄒ즉대뎌
ᄒ돈을쓰지도못ᄒ고빗리를달나
ᄒ니우리제판ᄒ겟다ᄒ즉양인
이라ᄒ눈고로재판ᄒᆯ슈도업고
빗우납납ᄒᆷ이라더라

○등소농부 죵로빅목젼시졍
들이농상공부에등소ᄒ기를희
젼의응역이호대ᄒ야지보ᄒ기
어려워각ᄃ되면에서분을마련
ᄒ야달나고등소ᄒ는ᄃ이지귀
졍이엽스민농상공부대문밧긔
셔기다린다더라

○경찰단속 근일경무쳥에셔
각쳐도로를곳치며오예물을
날마다치우며길바닥에돈지단
지잘쓰러쳥결을실시ᄒ더라

○식상금렵 경무쳥에셔일작
일브터죵로나무바리가셔지못
ᄒ게ᄒ는고로나무쟝ᄉ들이셔
셔잇슬테가업셔셔민우곤난ᄒ
다더라

○학부고문 즁학교ᄉ페원
란씨를학부고문관으로고빙ᄒᆫ
다더니방금협동ᄒ는중이오쟉
식삼일브터학부에ᄉ진ᄒ야시
무ᄒ기로작졍이되엿는ᄃ그ᄉ
무소는학무국으로지졍ᄒ엿더
라

○대신계도 대신제도들이의
졍리ᄒᆫ지라 조칙내에곳반포
ᄒ리라ᄒ논설이잇더라

○경위회관 히주광셕포에셔
쳥인이피회ᄒ논ᄉ안을담판귀졍
ᄒ기위ᄒ야거슈로일에영쳥량
공ᄉ가외부에젼왕ᄒ야대신을
졉견ᄒ고담판ᄒ엿스나결졍이
되지못ᄒ야다시회판ᄒᆫ다더라

○회민탐살사항 너부에셔젼
라남도관찰부로면훈ᄒ기를옥
과군슈가회민을탐살ᄒᆫ스건으
로면칙ᄒ게ᄒ라ᄒ남이되여서
이사실ᄒ보고가열히더되니인명
이소관ᄒᆫ데한반히판ᄒᆫ지라곳
도저히사회ᄒ야번쳐뎡보ᄒ고
후에보고ᄒ라ᄒ엿더라

광고

○본인의쟝ᄌ쳐렴이가본시부
랑패류로고부쳥ᄌ데간에분제
ᄒ여가진면쟝문권을수히도
서적ᄒ여너엿기로세부동이ᄒ야
오서문권을모든이고이에광포ᄒ
고한치렴의가진문권을뎐졍ᄒ
마옵기를바라옴

평양성내쟝계리 한괴쳥
고뷕

○본인의서제진셩이가년이미
만이십에주식잡기로일을삼아
탕패가산ᄒ고괴류들부동ᄒ야
후게명도ᄒ고면답문권과가권
을위조ᄒ야동서로단니며투취
코자ᄒ오니니외국인은젼쳐ᄒ
시옵이ᄉ실을각신문에광고ᄒ
오니조량ᄒ심을쳔망

황두쳔거최셩환 고뷕

TELEGRAMS.

Tokyo Jan. 12th.

Generals Stoessel and Nogi have both been decorated by the German Emperor on account of their gallant defence and capture of Port Arthur.

Tokyo Jan. 12th,

According to a London telegram General Kuropatkin is dangerously ill.

(FROM JAPAN PAPERS.)

London, Jan. 6.

There are conflicting reports as to Rojestvensky's flagship. It was at first stated that she had been sunk, but this has since been denied. Two of the cruisers belonging to Admiral Folkersahm's portion of the Squadron are announced to be in a useless condition and incapable of being repaired. It is again reported that it is intended to recall Rojestvensky's Squadron to Russia immediately.

Berlin, Jan. 6.

The Baltic Squadron has received orders from Russia not to leave Madagascar until further orders.

London, Jan. 6.

The Czar's tour has been abandoned and a Council was yesterday held by His Majesty at Tsarko Seloe. It was decided that General Kuropatkin should at once assume the offensive against Oyama.

The following telegram has been received in official quarters at Tokio:—

A Russian Squadron consisting of the undermentioned ships arrived at the island of Santa Maria on the East coast of Madagascar on the 2nd instant. The ships were in good condition. They appear to have been instructed to remain there until joined by the auxiliary squadron:—

Battleships.—Suvaroff, Alexander III., Borodino, Orel, Ossliabia.

Cruisers—Admiral Nakhimoff, Aurora, Dmitri Donskoi.

Special Steamers—Kamchatka, Anazuilu.

One hospital ship.

Berlin, Jan. 5.

The two torpedo-destroyers which escaped from Port Arthur to Tsingtao have now been disarmed. The crews of the destroyers have also been disarmed and interned.

London, Jan. 6.

The "New York Herald publishes a telegram from St. Petersburg stating that the Russian battleship "Kniaz Suvaroff," the flagship of Admiral Rohjestvensky, which recently arrived at Madagascar, has struck a rock and gone to the bottom.

Later.

The report of the loss of the "Kniaz Suvaroff" is absolutely denied in St. Petersburg.

London, Jan. 6

The St. Petersburg correspondent of the "Standard" states that at a Council of Ministers hold at the Palace, and presided over by the Tsar, it has been decided to energetically prosecute the war, and to provide General Kuropatkin with 200,000 more troops before the end of February.

It was also decided that Admiral Rohjestvensky (and his fleet) be recalled.

London, Jan. 6.

An Imperial Decree has been issued appointing Admiral Skrydloff (until recently in command at Vladivostok) a member of the Council of Admirals.

The Governor of Pyeng Yang has requested the Home Office to recall the Magistrates of Pyeng Yang, Yungyu, Chosan and Dokchon as they are incapable of administering justice in their districts.

COCK-A-DOODLE-DOO.

The Editor of the Kobe Daily News has been safely delivered of the following:—

To-day, last year, the talk of War was little conjectured by the masses, though, in certain quarters, it was surmised that unless the Northern Colossus ceased trifling with the sport in bubbles, the patience of the little Nation of the Island Empire with whom she was playing the game would no longer stand the jest.

Unfortunately for the test of Peace in the Far East, Russia, though the negotiation then proceeding bore no traits of ill-omen, went on with her bluffs, making promises which she never intended to fulfil, as have been proven—and, at last, as the world rejoices,—she saw her bubbles bursting in the air as they were let on floating, and for good or for evil, the War trumpets were sounded by the heralds of this Island Empire! and the world has been told that this Nation's patience having been exhausted, the people of the Land of the Rising Sun saw no other recourse but to unsheath their swords to avenge Russia for the wrong she had suffered her pacific neighbour for so long.

The time came; War was declared against Russia! that great Northern Colossus which has set defiance in the Occident and the Near East for a great length of time since the days of Napoleon the First.

And, Oh! what crowds in every land Have cried that--Man was made to mourn!

What were the suggestions as to the issues of the expected great struggles between a *small* Power, and the *great* Colossus of Plevna fame!

The world had never dreampt then that War against such a great historic nation, the possessor of dominions of ice-bound territories, would ever be waged between the Island Empire, the possessor of *only* a fraction between fifty million souls—and, at that, the same little nation which is, at variance, called the remnant of Darwin's creation of Man!

Well, there are many things which Man, in his primitive state, has never known, and, just for once, the existance of Japanese in their hitherto little known hamlets in the Island Empire, somewhat near 135° off the Great Europa, the great Colossus misjudged its due apportionment as destined by the Great Creator of the Universe!

At last, not the least, the veil of the mist these last three-score years have passed on, has been lifted—and a grand panorama of the things that we must see, to Believe, is being shown!

Oh! Caesar! Caesar! that that which belongs to thee—Thou shall own!

Let us see, if in righteousness, we cannot own what we *possessed*, by oppression we *may* forcibly be dispossessed.

Now as to the War.

Now that the conflict must commence, our Nation having been invoked by the Guiding Star to pay no heed to the much vaunted greatness of the inflated Northern Colossus, the possessors of this little Island Empire have plunged to the War with their hearts and souls.

To Fight for the Little Empire's Right?

That this little Nation was prepared for the struggle, no thinking man who knows of the pilfering of our just possession.

PORT ARTHUR,

can deny, and it goes without saying, the world at large expected that the sport at bubbles as disported by Russia must come to an end. The result of the protracted negotiation at St. Petersburg at last came to the crush!

The world must admit that our Government did not take up the cudgels so plaintively thrust upon us, without having regard to the usage of International intercourse first of all, submitting to all the possible safeguards remaining towards an honourable solution of the question in dispute, *sans rancour* (without possible arrogance, as it were) and without having recourse to *noblesse oblige*—taking up arms for the defence of the cause.

But in the face of the treatment accorded us in our efforts to eliminate any disparagement which might have cropped up in the course of the delicate negotiation towards a peaceful solution of the *disagreement*, we found out that Russia had in mind the delusion that she could still force upon us that incusable flippancy in the shape of her *womanish* game of deception regardless of her *sineerest (?)* assurances vouchsafed in *innumerable instances*, in scores of time, as to her desire to leave her paws off the pie which she had made a hole to abstract the contents of the rich viands we were served by our vanquished foe at the memorable occasion of the grand banquet which we were treated to by our neighbour across Manchuria, in the lands of the Mongols, and which our delighted friends in the Land of the Morning Calm contributed somewhat towards the relish in 1984-95.

Well, so far as we know, Russia has not played the trump card. Far from it; she held a hand only a sharper would take; she thereby concealed her hand and tried to bluff! She dragged in two other Powers and between them they peeped at the card she held.

"Good; hold on to it, said one."

And the other immediately saw a chance for the Roulette.

"Shall we back up?" said no 1.

"Je suit a la pot," said the other.

Russia kept her card, and finally tried to divide the pot.

Japan protested, and waited for these long Ten Years——

And now she is in the pot, holding the very set of cards out of the game in which Russia thought she had bluffed her to obtain the rich stake for good.

* * *

As the war is still progressing now over the spoil in dispute, we think it is premature to "call up" the game in which our interest is still in the stake between the sharper who has played the game of bluff.

Those who have, and are still following the events, must by this time have found out that in this year of grace the game of bluff has bluffed the bluffer; though the pot is eagerly watched for other players—the one holding the best card is playing the game to the chagrin of the two on-lookers whose states have long since been out of their hands.

"The Joker is in the pack," said Madame Chrysanteme, "and the Jewel is mine."

The prisoners in the local jail have had the honour of being inspected by a Japanese officer!

We hear that the branch of the Seoul Fusan Railway which runs from Samnangpo to Masampo will be opened for traffic in a few days.

A Peking telegram to Shanghai states that the Russian Minister has asked the Chinese Government for a lease of an anchorage for warships at Macao and Amoy.

The Japanese have put to death a former collector of taxes near Sing-minfu, on account of an accusation being lodged against him to the effect that he is a Russian sympathizer.

A Yinkow letter says that the Russians have constructed a bridge 1,200 metres in length between Teh Ling and Kaiyuan, on which guns have been posted to prevent obstruction in the progress of the work.

On Wednesday night the "chucker-out" of the Il-chin-hoi discovered, during a seance, a sparrow amongst the larks. The "sparrow" turned out to be a soldier. The manner of his death has not been announced.

The Japanese instructor recently assigned to the Imperial Chinese troops in Nanking has arrived to take up his duties. The present instructor, however, refuses to be superceded, and there is likely to be a tempest in a teapot. It is said the men are averse to losing their old teacher and to having forced on them by recent orders a substitute who was *persona non grata* even before his arrival.

The Japanese adviser to the Education Department commences his duties today.

The first Russian destroyer to reach Chefoo on New Year's day was the "Skori;" the "Vlastni" followed, and then came the "Serditi" and the "Statni."

Yesterday a committee of the Il Chin Hoi visited the Police Department and offered some suggestions to the Chief. This gentleman offered the suggestion in return, that the Il Chin Hoi should look to their own country and refrain from attempting to betray it to another power. The committee retired abashed.

Much is said of the tragic deaths of General Kondrachenko and Colonel Rajhevsky. The former was the highest ranking military officer killed during the siege of Port Arthur. The latter was considered one of the bravest men in the army. He distinguished himself by taking two photographs from the deck of the "Petropavlovsk" as she was going down. General Kondrachenko and Colonel Rejhevsky were members of the council of seventeen which was hastily called during the last attack of the Japanese on Fort No. 2. An eleven-inch shell exploded in their midst, killing and frightfully mangling the two officers.

Bekanntmachung.

Die Bekanntmachungen der Eintragungen in das hiesige Deutsche Handelsregister erfolgen im Jahre 1905 durch den **"Ostasiatischen Lloyd" und** die **"The Korea Daily News."**

Soül, den 27. Dezember 1904.

Der Kaiserlich Deutsche Minister-Resident und Generalkonsul.

(L. S.) gez. von Saldern.

The Korea Daily News.

Issued at 5 P. M. daily except Sundays.

Rate of Subscription:—

Per Year,............Yen 25.

Per Quarter,..........Yen 7.

Per Month,..........Yen 2.50.

Postage in Korea not charged extra.
Postage abroad charged extra.

Advertisements, 50 sen per day for 1 inch or less.
5 yen per month per inch.
50 yen per year per inch.

All communications to

E. T. BETHELL,
Editor and Publisher,
Pak-tong, Seoul.

THE WAR.

There seems to be a considerable division of opinion as to the direction which the next events will take in connection with the war.

The fall of Port Arthur has led to the expected crop of rumours of mediation and official denials thereof. We are still of the opinion, so many times expressed in these columns, that the capitulation of Port Arthur only serves to make the prospect of a peaceful settlement more remote than ever.

The Japanese newspapers are impressing upon their readers that the war has only just begun and cables from London tell us of Russia's renewed determination to prosecute the compaign to a successful issue.

It would therefore seem that we are justified in expecting important developements before long. Vladivostock is frozen up and can therefore for the present be left out of the calculations: it is true that ships can get out by following the icebreakers, but getting in again in a hurry would be quite another matter.

Now that the whole of Admiral Togo's fleet has been released from its vigil at Port Arthur it is hardly likely that the Baltic fleet will risk an encounter, not at any rate until it has been very strongly reinforced. We are by no means in agreement with those who consider the Baltic fleet beneath notice but it is certain that it is not sufficiently strong to justify a pitched battle at the present juncture. There are rumours that this fleet has been recalled, but as the expedition has been the subject of so many *canards*, it is impossible to know what to believe.

The last, and, at the moment the most important, factor is Moukden. It appears that the Japanese are entrenched South of the Hunho in a vast crescent which presents its convex face to the enemy. The Russians are entrenched in a parallel curve with their wings slightly overlapping the Japanese. Both sides are comfortably encamped and, on account of the impossibility of digging new trenches with the ground in its present frozen state, there is little likelihood of either of the main armies assuming the offensive unless it receives reinforcements giving it an overwhelming numerical superiority.

To us it appears that this delay is all in Kuropatkin's favour, for while we have it on very good authority that the reinforcements now reaching the Japanese lines consist chiefly of raw recruits, we hear that Kuropatkin is gradually replacing the inferior Siberian troops with which he started with experienced soldiers from Europan Russia.

The skirmishes which we contiuually hear of in the neighbourhood of Saimachi seem to indicate the existence of a considerable Russian force somewhere North of that place. It is possible that Kuropatkin, finding any offensive movement directly South of Moukden to be inadvisable at the present moment, is contemplating an attack upon the Japanese communications.

Of the Japanese we hear little except that they seem to be on their guard wherever they are attacked.

A NEW ENTERPRISE.

Traffic between Korean ports and abroad presents many difficulties. Chemulpo harbour, owing to the abnormal rise and fall of the tide is only available for steamers of small tonnage, and as a rule, in these waters steamers of small tonnage are built of wood, badly engined, and fitted only a trifle more comfortably than prisons.

Therefore we welcome the advent of the "Medan," a steamer of some 500 tons register, which has just been put on the run between Chemulpo and Shanghai by the Hamburg-Amerika Linie, for which company Messrs E. Meyer & Co. are the agents.

A representative of the "Korea Daily News" visited this vesselo yesterday and was agreeably surprised with everything he saw. Everything on board is as spick and span as on a warship and in spite of her small tonnage the "Medan" has saloon accomodation for 18 or more passengers.

There is, of course, corresponding berthing accomodation and luxurious bath-rooms are provided.

Everything that could be devised to increase the comfort of passengers has been provided. For her size, the "Medan" has an exceptionally large promenade deck and the appointments throughout the ship are of the latest and best.

Captain Stalberg is an excellent host and commands capable officers, so nothing stands in the way of the "Medan" becoming "the boat to travel by"

THE "COLLINS" CASE.

Mr. H. B. Collins has been remanded for trial on a charge of disclosing military secrets. The preliminary tribunal, says the "Japan Mail," has found a "prima facie" case against him under an article of the Criminal Code which prescribes a penalty of 6 years imprisonment. He is stated to have left Japan in 1898 and been employed by the Russians in Port Arthur. On the outbreak of war he proceeded to Tientsin and about June, 1904, was engaged by Colonel Ogorodinkoff to go to Japan, search out Japanese military secrects and report them. He received a letter of introduction to General Dessino, with a sum of 1,000 dollars, and, making his way to Shanghai in July, he was further commissioned by that officer, who give him a copy of a private cipher. He at once crossed to Japan and took rooms in the Hotel de Paris, thenceforth employing himself to discover secrets relating to the war. On the 24th of October he used this cipher to indite a letter to General Dessino in which he gave a full account of the proposed despatch of Japanese troops, of their number, their destination and the purpose for which they were to be employed. On the 29th of October he posted this letter, which was stopped by the military authorities in Nagasaki. These facts are declared to have been clearly proved, and Collins has accordingly been committed for trial.

RUSSION OFFICERS ON BOARD THE "NEGRETIA."

At the time of the capture of the steamer "Negretia," there were on board the vessel two men, professedly Germans, who were in charge of her cargo. As the results of trials subsequently held at the Sasebo Prize Court, one of them admitted that he was Lieutenant Powell Mihailovitch Plen, Commander of the Russian destroyer "Ratstoropny," and the other that he was Clargi Warentinovitch Seriyoff, a Second sub-Lieutenant on board the same craft. Both officers were consequently handed over to the Japanese Naval authorities, who have decided to treat them as prisoners of war.

GOLD STANDARD FOR CHINA.

It being reported that Dr. Jenks, American commissioner, appointed at the request of China to draw up a plan for the adoption of a gold standard in that country, has completed his task and submitted his views on the matter, which are roughly that China should newly issue subsidiary silver and copper coins, at the same time that she creates a bullion gold reserve, which may be obtained by transferring for the purpose the profits accruing from mintage, as well as by floating gold bonds abroad, the "Nichi Nichi" ventures to doubt the feasibility of the scheme. Dr. Jenkes' conclusions may have been formed without his having sufficiently studied the actual needs and established commercial methods of the Chinese people, as has been pointed out by Mr. Jamieson, an English fiancial authority in Peking. Supposing that Dr. Jenks' views are flawless and his suggestions execllent, they may, however, meet with the same objection as those to which Mr. Jerome, British Consul in Mexico, refers with regard to another American scheme for the latter country. Yet it is a mistake to think that no radical reform is practicable in China, for her central authorities have in more than one instance succeeded, with fair results, in enforcing sweeping innovations. The real obstacles, says the journal, may rather be looked for from foreign quarters. To give an example, the Powers some time ago pressed China to adopt trade mark regulations, and succeeded in obtaining from her a treaty for that purpose, but now that China is ready to enforce the regulations the powers, with the exception of Japan, are demanding a delay in putting in operation the same. The same fate will befall the currency proposal, says the journal, unless all the Powers unite in assisting China to carry out the measure.

The "Skori," one of the Russian torpedo boats which escaped to Chefoo, was reported sunk in the European and American press on the sixteenth of last March.

We note that the Court formed to try a Russian sailor for the alleged murder of a Chinaman in Shanghai, includes, as interpreter, M. Kerberg, who is described as Dragoman to the Legation at Seoul.

The Magistrate of Chon Chu reports that his district is greatly suffering from Il-chin-hoi people, who take advantage of the presence of gangs of robbers to create disturbances. He has established a volunteer corps to maintain order.

The supercession of the Korean police by Japanese gendarmes is leading to a good deal of friction. Complaints reach us that the Japanese are interfering with the Korean Police in the ordinary execution of their duties and are arrogating to themselves the right to release arrested criminals. We shall doubtless hear more of this shortly.

News of another projected illicit land deal comes from Whang-hai province. It seems that certain Japanese are urging the people of Kyum-i-po district to part with their birthright. The people are loth to do this and apply to the Governor for protection, and the Governor applies to Seoul for instructions.

General Kuropatkin has telegraphed to the Minister of War denying the Japanese assertion that the Russian troops in the field were often disguised in Chinese costume. "On the contrary," he adds, "on the occasion of the assault on the village of Shahopu on October 14, a Japanese detachment were dressed in the grey coats and caps of the Russian soldiers with white borders, a fact which allowed them to approach quite close to the Russian batteries, and thus to capture several guns of the 38th Brigade."

The Korea Daily News.

VOL. II, | FRIDAY, JANUARY 13, 1905. | No: 9

HONGKONG & SHANGHAI BANKING CORPORATION.

Paid-up Capital..... ....$10,000,000
Reserve Fund:—Sterling Reserve... 10,000,000
Silver Reserve..... 7,000,000

27,000,000
Reserve Liability of Proprietors... 10,000,000

HEAD OFFICE, HONGKONG.

London Bankers, London and County Banking Company Limited.
Branches and Agencies, London.

Amoy,	Hankow	Penang,
Bangkok,	Hiogo,	Rangoon,
Batavia,	Iloilo,	Saigon,
Bombay,	Lyons,	San Francisco,
Calcutta,	Manila,	Singapore,
Colombo,	Nagasaki,	Sourabaya,
Foochow,	New York,	Tientsin,
Hamburg,	Peking,	Yokohama,

Credits granted on approved Securities, and every description of Banking and Exchange business transacted.

Drafts granted on London and the chief Commercial places in Europe, India, Australia, America, China and Japan.

HOLME RINGER & Co., AGENTS, CHEMULPO.

HOKURKU DOBOKU KAISHA.

Branch office in Chong Dong, Seoul.
Japanese telephone No. 165

CONTRACT DEPARTMENT.

We can contract to build any building or construction.

MERCHANDISE DEPARTMENT.

We can provide any building material. We have just contracted to build the new Belgian Legation.

E. MEYER & CO.

Chemulpo.

SOLE AGENTS IN KOREA FOR.

A. T. Morse, Sons & Co.'s "Fresco" Distemper

In all colours ready for use on walls, Ceilings etc.

and

AVENARIUS CARBOLINEUM

A wood-preserving and antiseptic oil preparation

Against decay, dry-rot, fungus and wood-destroying insects.

A large supply always in stock.
Prices upon application.

E. MEYER & Co.,
Chemulpo.

CHARTERED BANK OF INDIA AUSTRALIA & CHINA.

INCORPORATED BY ROYAL CHARTER 1853

HEAD OFFICES.—LONDON.

Paid-up Capital £800,000
Reserve Liability of Shareholders 800,000
Reserve Fund 800,000

Drafts granted upon all the principal places in the world and every description of Exchange and banking business transacted.

E. MEYER & Co., Agents,
Chemulpo.

MITSU BISHI DOCKYARD & ENGINE WORKS,
NAGASAKI.

CODE WORD, "DOCK."

A 1, A. B. C., and Engineering Codes used.

DOCK No. 1 (at Tategami).

Extreme Length..............523 feet
Length on blocks .... 513 ,,
Width of Entrance on Top......89 ,,
,, ,, Bottom....77 ,,
Water on Blocks at Spring Tide 26½ ,,

DOCK No. 2 (Mukaijima).

Extreme Length..............371 feet
Length on Blocks............360 ,,
Width of Entrance on Top......66 ,,
,, ,, Bottom 53 ,,
Water on Blocks at Spring Tide 22 ,,

PATENT SLIP (at Kosuge).

Can take vessels up to 1,000 tons gross.

THE WORKS are well equipped with the LATEST IMPROVEMENTS, and can execute any kind of work in SHIPBUILDING and MARINE ENGINEERING, as well as in REPAIRING of SHIPS.

The COMPANY'S new powerfu steamer OURA-MARU (712 tons, 700 I.H.P.), specially built for SALVAGE PURPOSES, and equipped with necessary gear, is always READY at SHORT NOTICE.

THE METHODIST PUBLISHING HOUSE,

Little West Gate, Seoul.

JOB PRINTING, TYPEWRITER PAPER
CARBON PAPER, VISITING CARDS
STATIONERY, BOOK BINDING
BOOK PUBLISHERS
AMERICAN SCHOOL BOOKS
SPENCERIAN COPY BOOKS
PEN CARBON LETTER AND BILL BOOKS

S.A. BECK, Manager.

DAI-ICHI GINKO.

LIMITED.

(Formerly the First National Bank)

ESTABLISHED 1873

INCORPORATED UNDER PRESENT LAW 1896

Capital - - - - - - - - Yen 5,000,000
Reserve Fund - - - - - 1,500,000

HEAD OFFICE:—TOKIO.

President: Baron SHIBUSAWA.

BRANCHES AND CORRESPONDENTS
In the Principal Cities and Towns of Japan.

Interest Allowed on
Fixed deposits 1 year - - - 6½ per cent
" " 6 months - - - 6 per cent

Special current accounts 1½ sen daily per Y 100
General " " 1 " " " 100

M. TANAKA,
Manager Chemulpo.

SINGER SEWING MACHINES

셩거조봉침

SOLE AGENTS FOR KOREA

전매쇼

HOLME RINGER & CO.
Chemulpo.

제물포 함릉거양힝

KAMEYA CO.

GENERAL STOREKEEPERS

Chinkokai - - Seoul

(*Established 1895, Tokyo*)

Confectionery, Hams, Canned Goods, Cutlery, Hirano & Tansan Water. Provisions, Gents, Furnishing goods, Toilet Articles, Travelling Bags, Tobacco, Cigars & Cigarettes Kitchen Utensils. Coffee, Biscuits

Fresh Goods always kept in Stock.

Prices Moderate

Please come and inspect ourgoods.

NIPPON YUSEN KAISHA.

JAPANESE MAIL STEAMSHIP CO.

DER MAIL CONTRACT WITH THE IMPERIAL JAPANESE GOVERNMENT.

European Line

Regular Fortnightly Service between Yokohama Kobe, Moji, Shanghai, Hongkong, Singapore, Penang Colombo, Port Said, Marseilles, London and Antwerp

American Line

Regular Fortnightly Service between Hongkong and Seattle, calling at Shanghai, Moji, Kobe, Yokohama and Victoria, B. C.

Australian Line

Regular weekly Service betwen Japan Ports and Australia, calling at Hongkong and Manila.
(Above Three Lines Suspended until further notice).

Shanghai Line

Weekly Service between Shanghai and Japan Ports

Korea Line

Service Kobe, Moji, Nagasaki, Fusan Chemupo Chef foo, Taiku.
S. S. Bahelsberg, 2181 tons.
Service Kobe, Moji, Fusan, Chemulpo, Chinnampo
S. S. ARGO, S. S. Ohio.

BORDEN'S CONDENSED MILK CO.

New York, U. S. A.

ALWAYS IN STOCK

Eagle Brand Condensed Milk.

Gold Seal Condensed Milk.

Peerless (Family) Evaporated Cream.

Borden's Malted Milk.

E. MEYER & CO.
Chemulpo Korea,
Sole Agents

ROYAL INSURANCE COMPANY,
Funds exceed £10,000,000
FIRE
AT CURRENT RATES
LIFE
REDUCED PREMIUM,
HOLME RINGER & Co.,
Agents, Chemulpo

HOTEL DU PALAIS

SEOUL.

The only first class Hotel in Seoul Situated in the centre of the city opposite the palace.

Cuisine under the supervision of an experienced French Chef.

Well ventilated and furnished throughout.

TARIFF UPON APPLICATION

L. MARTIN
Proripetor and Manager

大韓每日申報
대한미일신보

(뎨이권십호)　　(월요일)　　일쳔구빅오년일월십륙일

본사고빅

이신보는영어와한국문으로셔계미
일츌판ᄒᆞ옵
신문가
한쟝　엽두돈오푼
일삭표　엽두량닷돈
우표가미삭닷돈
다맛돈으로밧ᄉᆞᆸ
광고료는
귀한의쟝단과ᄌᆞ힝의다쇼로죵
갑ᄒᆞ되평가로밧을터이오며오
린문을제ᄒᆞ야보내셜터이나광고내시기를실
원ᄒᆞ시ᄂᆞᆫ이들은우리신문사에
와셔면약ᄒᆞ심을ᄇᆞ라망ᄒᆞ옵
○발힝소　박동대한미일신보
사법어학교압해젼영국인셜필
립정자리오
사쟝 영국인 (빈셜)
평양 디리졈
○평양효동사ᄂᆞᆫ권미보씨로우
리신문관디리인을뎡ᄒᆞ엿
시ᄉᆞ오니평양에계신구람코져ᄒᆞ
시ᄂᆞᆫ 쳠군ᄌᆞᄂᆞᆫ이디리졈에왕
림ᄒᆞ와면의ᄒᆞ시옵

샤고

○우리대한미일신보의목뎍은
대한의안녕질셔에관한모든대
목에디ᄒᆞ야는공평한변론을주
쟝ᄒᆞᆷ이라우리통신원의탐보는
신문보시ᄂᆞᆫ쳠군ᄌᆞ의게ᄒᆞᆼ샹보
도ᄒᆞ려며편지를귀셔ᄒᆞ며주시
ᄂᆞᆫ이ᄂᆞᆫ셩명과반디를적어붓치
시기를희망ᄒᆞ오니이계ᄉᆞᆫ신문
샹에게제ᄒᆞ라ᄂᆞᆫ거시아니오다
만구히신용ᄒᆞᄂᆞᆫ증거를삼고자
ᄒᆞᆷ이라귀자ᄂᆞᆫ아모괴셔던지괴
제ᄒᆞᆷ을되각ᄒᆞᄂᆞᆫ권리를가젓ᄉᆞ
나되각ᄒᆞᄂᆞᆫ리유를말ᄒᆞᆯ터이오
며공중평론을문란케ᄒᆞᄂᆞᆫ듯ᄒᆞᆫ
괴셔ᄂᆞᆫ의례히밧지안켓ᄉᆞᆸ나이
다
◉본사셜시이리로신문을미양
우리로분젼ᄒᆞ와리젼부의임의
로젼ᄒᆞᄂᆞᆫ것스로번곳에ᄂᆞᆫ혹늣게
젼ᄒᆞ기도ᄒᆞ며혹멋칠거슬ᄒᆞᆫ번
에젼ᄒᆞ기도ᄒᆞ며혹아니젼ᄒᆞᄂᆞᆫ
곳도잇더ᄒᆞ와우리신문을수람
ᄒᆞ야구람ᄒᆞ시ᄂᆞᆫ 쳠군ᄌᆞ의게금
티ᄒᆞ야미우미안ᄒᆞ올기로지금
은분젼인을두고미일일주이젼
ᄒᆞ려아니젼ᄒᆞ거나늣게거나ᄒᆞᆫ
폐가업도록ᄒᆞ라ᄒᆞ오니혹아니

젼ᄒᆞ거ᄂᆞᆫ혹늣게젼ᄒᆞ거나ᄒᆞᆫ일
이잇스면본사로통긔ᄒᆞ여주심
을희망ᄒᆞ옵

잡보

○히쥬보고　황히도관찰사가
외부로보고ᄒᆞ기를황쥬군수보
고니기에본군경이포에쥬차ᄒᆞᆫ
바일인이쟝차본군로하팔방면
도로를분셔ᄒᆞ는되다령영방미ᄒᆞ
리고최죽이날마다니르미이로
하팔방인민들이소고ᄒᆞ기에사
실ᄒᆞᆫ즉막즁국토를가히자의로
쳔단ᄒᆞ야외국인의게팔수업다
ᄒᆞ엿기에이에보고ᄒᆞ오니조사
ᄒᆞ신후지령ᄒᆞ시기를바란다ᄒᆞ
엿더라
○평감보고　평양감리가외부
로보고ᄒᆞ기를본셔주사원용덕
이가졍원ᄒᆞ기를향일관보를본
즉외부에셔본원이쟝졍에소미
ᄒᆞ고외교에위반ᄒᆞᆷ이잇다ᄒᆞ야
일긔원감봉에쳐ᄒᆞ엿스니본원의
이무슨쟝졍에소미ᄒᆞ며무슨외
교에위반ᄒᆞᆷ이잇셔벌봉에쳐ᄒᆞ
엿나뇨바라건대외부에곳츄보
ᄒᆞ야일일히시명ᄒᆞ라ᄒᆞ엿기에
이에보고ᄒᆞ오니사조ᄒᆞ시기를
바란다ᄒᆞ엿더라
○함경리송　함셩지관소졈사
셜시에셔외부로공함ᄒᆞ기를작
일본소졈사시보리편우가외부
를샹방ᄒᆞ고을베에사평등이키
부문니에쟝기를셜ᄒᆞ고로곳쟝
에산가공효를밧은즉이상명외
졉하인일명이잇다ᄒᆞᆫ즉그놈들
을곳부니며중감ᄒᆞᄂᆞᆫ디편케ᄒᆞ
기를바란다ᄒᆞ엿더라
○룬회파슈　귀왕에ᄂᆞᆫ각지소
습검을희쟝니부근에사ᄂᆞᆫ사름미
으로명령파슈ᄒᆞ야시무케ᄒᆞ디
ᄒᆞ쟝니에사ᄂᆞᆫ빅셩이셜홀죄를
범ᄒᆞ드리도안면사졍에거리기
사여참아장아가지못ᄒᆞ더니경무
가이거슬기졍ᄒᆞ야다른지소
로일샤셔룬회ᄒᆞ야시무케ᄒᆞ교
지어보호습검과숀산숀졈이라
도일샤셔룬회파숑ᄒᆞ기로작졍
ᄒᆞ엿다더라
○젼남회면　젼라남도관찰부
에셔니부로회면ᄒᆞ기를옥파경
탐이왕반ᄒᆞ기에지졍가되고젼

문에ᄂᆞᆫ이런일이업다ᄒᆞ미일잔
졍탐이니르거든곳면보ᄒᆞ겟노
라ᄒᆞ엿더라
○평찰면보　평안남도관찰ᄉᆞ
리중하씨가니부로면보ᄒᆞ기를
민심은젼동ᄒᆞ고용ᄉᆞᄂᆞᆫ분란ᄒᆞᆫ
디평양영유조산덕쳔능군에공
관됨이심히민망ᄒᆞ오니불일니
로하송ᄒᆞ라ᄒᆞ엿더라
○젼쥬군보　젼쥬군슈가니부
로면보ᄒᆞ기를병뎡니에쳐경이티
심ᄒᆞ야사ᄅᆞᆷ을샹ᄒᆞ며불흥노ᄒᆞ
미엿더니방티에졍ᄒᆞ야파병ᄒᆞ란ᄒᆞ
엿더니말ᄒᆞ기를군부에셔면ᄒᆞᆫ
ᄒᆞ기를군에셔방죄을베플어도
젹을방비ᄒᆞ라고ᄒᆞ엿다ᄒᆞ오미
방죄을베플도리ᄂᆞᆫ향약을다시
밝히ᄂᆞᆫ것과포군을듕셜ᄒᆞᄂᆞᆫ것
신디일젼회민은더욱히란ᄒᆞᆫ디
니르러온졍히여탈과투럭으로
만일ᄉᆞᆸ고군취ᄒᆞᆫ져도ᄂᆞᆫ가위ᄉᆞ
시ᄒᆞ야갈수록더옥심ᄒᆞ니패ᄉᆞ
가에셔조쳐ᄒᆞᆯ수업고빅셩이졔
산을보젼ᄒᆞ기어려우니목하의
졍형이지극히간졀ᄒᆞ미밧ᄒᆞᆫ지
란별쉽교와별포군을셜시ᄒᆞᆷ을
등허ᄒᆞ야불일니로소멸ᄒᆞ야ᄒᆞ
여쥬셔리가코게된환을면케ᄒᆞ
심을보라며곳회면ᄒᆞ라ᄒᆞ엿더
라
○졍슈기량　오셔니에우물수
효를도교사ᄒᆞᆫ즉도합이샹빅여처
인디신경무ᄉᆞ가위싱을힘쟝ᄒᆞ
기위ᄒᆞ야우물물을기량ᄒᆞ기로
계획ᄒᆞᄂᆞᆫ중이라더라
○흥진비리　포목쟝ᄉᆞᄒᆞᄂᆞᆫ조
가가의쳡소실에아들하나흘두
엇ᄂᆞᆫ디쳡돌을당ᄒᆞ미의복을구
치ᄒᆞ야남혀고유샹포렴으로음
식을셩비히치란노코즐기더니
지에죽어바리미그부모가통곡
이졀ᄒᆞ더라

관보

뎨삼쳔삼십오호　광무구
년일월십삼일
셔임급ᄉᆞ령
○명경입뎨셜제도졍리국총지
안평군 리승응
○명경입뎨셜제도졍리국의졍
관 궁닉부교문관 가등증웅
궁닉부협판 박용화 농샹공

부협판　리근상
○명뎨셜제도졍리국비셔　구
품　유치형　구품　쟝헌식
○명뎨셜제도졍리국긔수　총
품리죵회　권원슈　졍인소
이샹광무팔년십월오일
○임히쥬면보수쥬ᄉᆞ셔판임관
규수등　진위면보수쥬ᄉᆞ　림평
○임시흥면보수쥬ᄉᆞ셔판임판
오등　귀셩면보수쥬ᄉᆞ　유인
슈
○금비금봉　히쥬면보수쥬ᄉᆞ
리형규
○금샹금봉　시흥면보수쥬ᄉᆞ
유한수
이샹일월십일
○의원면본관　비셔원승　김
병년　비셔원승　신성균
샤직셔령　민회식
○임비셔원승셔주임관륙등
졍샹퓸　윤주셩　졍샹퓸　리
민티
○임　사직셔령셔판임관륙등
태복사주ᄉᆞ　쟝길샹
○임태복ᄉᆞ쥬ᄉᆞ셔판임관팔등
륙퓸　민회식
○명졍입뎨셜제도졍리국의졍
관　학부대신　리지용　학부
협판　고영희　법부협판　김
규희
○면증계　젼쥬ᄉᆞ　김졍진
젼쥬ᄉᆞ　리희영
○관졍ᄉᆞ항
졔셜제도졍리국직무쟝졍
뎨일됴　궁중에　졔셜제도졍
리국을셜치ᄒᆞ야　졔셜제도
의졍리에관ᄒᆞᆫ일졀ᄉᆞ무를판
리ᄒᆞᆯ수
뎨이됴　졔셜제도졍리국에좌
기직원을둘수
총지　일인
의졍관　륙인
비셔　이인
긔사　삼인
뎨삼됴　총지ᄂᆞᆫ　졔셜제도졍
리ᄉᆞ항에관ᄒᆞ야　지의를봉
승ᄒᆞ야심의립안과밋등이고
의젼을　쥬문ᄒᆞᆯ수
뎨ᄉᆞ됴　총지ᄂᆞᆫ　졔셜제도졍
리에관ᄒᆞᆫ고ᄉᆞ항을샹고ᄒᆞ야셜
ᄒᆞ되지의를봉승ᄒᆞ야그셜힝
을감독ᄒᆞᆯ수

UNION INSURANCE SOCIETY OF CANTON.

Head office Hongkong.
Marine risks underwritten at current rates.

Agents in Chemulpo,
E. MEYER & Co.

COMPAGNIE DES MESSAGERIES MARITIMES.

Fortnightly Direct Service.

For Marseilles
via Ports.
Sailing from Yokohama
Calling at Kobe,
Shanghai, Hongkong, Saigon, Singapore,
Colombo, Djibouti, Suez, Port Said
and Marseilles.

For particulars apply to
HOLME RINGER & Co.,
Chemulpo.

HAYASHIDA & CO.,

16 MYENG DONG, CHIN KO KAI, SEOUL.
BRANCH OFFICE AT CHEMULPO.

Money changers, Coal and Wood Merchants, Express Agents.

We are agents for the Pyeng-yang Coal Company and the Karazu Coal Company of Japan. We have the best quality of both anthracite and bituminous coal, and prompt execution of orders is our speciality. Firewood of all kinds kept in stock. Full weight guaranteed. Money of all denominations exchanged at current rates. Parcels received for all parts.

CHINA MUTUAL LIFE INS. OC.

Most favourable terms to policy holders.

Benefit system unsurpassed.

HOLME RINGER & Co.
Agents, Chemulpo.

C. P. R.

CANADIAN PACIFIC RAILWAY COMPANY'S ROYAL MAIL STEAMSHIP LINE.

THE FAST ROUTE BETWEEN CHINA, JAPAN, AND EUROPE VIA CANADA AND THE UNITED STATES.

Route from Hongkong via Shanghai, Nagasaki (Inland Sea of Japan) Kobe, Yokohama, Victoria and Vancouver.

Twin Screw Empress Steamship—6,000 Tons—Speed 19 knots.

PROPOSED SAILING FROM YOKOHAMA.
R. M. S. Empress of India.
R. M. S. Empress of Japan.
R. M. S. Empress of China.
R. M. S. Athenian.
R. M. S. Tartar.

Special reduction (first class only) granted to members of the Military, Naval, Diplomatic and Civil services and to Missionaries.

Passengers have choice of ten routes across the Continent of America and have privilege of travelling by any Atlantic Steamship Line.

Round the World passage tickets in connection with the P. and O. S. N., North German Lloyd and Messageries Co.'s £125.

All rates payable at current rate of exchange.

For further information, Tickets, Guide Books, etc., apply to

HOLME, RINGER & Co., AGENTS,
Chemulpo.

Grand Hotel,

(Formerly the Station Hotel)

Near the Railway Terminus, West Gate Seoul.

The Best Hotel in Korea.
Handsome new Building.
Fine Airy Rooms
Excellent Cuisine.
Terms Moderate.
Special terms to Missionaries
and to permanent boarders.

Electric cars within 2 minutes' walk.

W. H. EMBERLEY.
Proprietor

EVERY FACILITY.

In connection with Life Assurance Business is afforded by

The Standard Life Assurance Co.,

One of the largest and wealthiest of the Provident Institutions of the United Kingdom Forms of Application and all information will be promptly afforded on application.

10 CENTS A DAY.

Not a very large expenditure is it? But it is sufficient to secure for a man of 30 a policy with the STANDARD LIFE OFFICE for

$1323.

For all particulars of rates, etc., apply to

Holme, Ringer & Co.,
Agents, Chemulpo.

THE NEW YORK LIFE INSURANCE COMPANY.

Have you ever been declined by any Company?

Are you engaged in a specially hazardous occupation?

Have you heard of the New York Life Insurance Company's New Classifications for this class of Risks?

If not, send your date of birth, occupation and particulars of rejection, if any to

E. MEYER & Co.,
Agents, Chemulpo.

MITSUI BUSSAN KAISHA.
(MITSUI & Co.)
MITSUI GINKO.
(MITSUI BANK.)

The Bank is owned by the members of the Mitsui Family, who, as partners, assume an unmited responsibility for all liabilities of the Bank:—

Capital........................Yen 5,000,000
Reserve Fund.................. " 5,600,000

HEAD OFFICE, TOKYO.
LONDON OFFICE, 34 LIME ST., E. C.

BRANCHES AND AGENCIES:—
New York, San Francisco, Hamburg, Bombay, Singapore, Manila, Hongkong, Amoy, Chefoo, Tientsin.
Kobe, Hakodate, Yokohama, Kure, Yokosuka, Moji, Shimonoseki, Miike, Wakamatsu, Nagasaki, Kuchinotsu, Karatsu, Sasebo, Misume, Taipeh, &c.

Telegraphic Address for all the Offices:
"MITSUI."
A. B. C. AND A. I CODES USED.

Contractors of Coal
To the Imperial Japanese Navy. Arsenals and Railway Bureau, Principal Railway Companies and Industrial Work, Home and Foreign Mail and Freight Steamers.

Sole Proprietors
Of the famous Miike, Tagawa and Yamano Coal Mines.

Sole Agents
For the sale of Fukumo, Hokoku, Ichimura, Kanoda, Mannoura, Onoura, Ostuji, Sonoda, Tsubaruro, Yoshinotani, Yoshio, Yurokibura and other coals.

YANGTSE INSURANCE ASSOCIATION, LTD.

The undersigned, having been appointed agents for the above company, are prepared to issue policies and pay losses on marine risks at regular rates.

E. MEYER & Co.,
Agents, Chemulpo.

AMERICAN KOREAN ELECTRIC CO.

Light and Power.

Main Office: Electric Building, Chong No.

RAILWAY DEPARTMENT.

OPERATING CARS BETWEEN EAST AND WEST GATE, EVERY TEN MINUTES:—

First Car leaves East Gate at 7:00 A. M. First Car leaves R. R. Station at 7:25 A. M
Last Car " East Gate at 8.40 P. M. Last " " R. R. Station at 9.05 P.M

OPERATING CARS BETWEEN EAST GATE AND IMPERIAL TOMB TERMINUS, EVERY TWENTY MINUTES:—

CONNECTING WITH EVERY ALTERNATE CAR ARRIVING AT EAST GATE FROM CHONG NO.

First Car leaves East Gate for Tomb at 7:10 A. M.
" " " Tomb for East Gate at 7:30 A. M.
Last " " East Gate for Tomb at 7:50 P. M.
" " " Tomb for East Gate at 8:10 P. M.

OPERATING CARS BETWEEN CHONG NO AND YUNG SAN RIVER EVERY TWELVE MINUTES:—

First Car leaves Chong No for South Gate at 7:12 A. M.
" " " Chong No for Yung San at 7:36 A. M.
" " " South Gate for Chong No at 7:20 A. M.
" " " Yung San for Chong No at 8:09 A. M.
Last " " South Gate for Chong No 9:00 P. M.
" " " Yung San for Chong No at 8.45. P. M.

SPECIAL PRIVATE CARS FURNISHED TO SUIT CONVENIENCE OF PATRONS. PRICES ON APPLICATION AT HEAD OFFICE.

LIGHTING DEPARTMENT.

Where less than 250 candle power of light is used, the rate per month will be
Per 16 candle power incandescent lamp,—All night.—Yen 2.50.
32 candle power incandescent lamp:—All night:—Yen 4.00.
50 candle power incandescent lamp:—All night:—Yen 6.00.
150 " " " " " " " 10.00.
1200 " " enclosed arc " " " " 20.00.

Where more than 250 candle power of light is used, a Meter will be installed, freqvedted:—Rent of Meter Yen 2.00 per month. Rate of charges by meter reading:—Two Sen per Ampere per hour. (Approximately this is equal to about One Sen per 16 C. P. lamp per hour) Minimum monthly charge where meter is installed, Yen 20.00 per month, which includes rental of meter.

Estimates for installing lights furnished on application

An assortment of chandeliers always on hand.

K. Murakami.

Photograph Studio
Chinkokai, Seoul.

Printing, Developing and Enlargement, of Photographs always Undertaken.

Korean Views and Pictures Illustrating Native Customs always on Sale,

---

THE OSAKA SHOSEN KAISHA.

Boats frequently on the berth for Chinnampo.

REGULAR SAILINGS BETWEEN JAPAN AND KOREAN PORTS.

FUSAN AND KOBE VIA SHIMONOSEKI.

OSAKA VIA MOKPO, FUSAN, SHIMONOSEKI AND KOBE.

MOJI DIRECT.

OSAKA VIA KUNSAN, MASANPO, FUSAN, SHIMONOSEKI AND KOBE.

CHEMULPO KUNSAN LINE,
Every three days.

CHEMULPO CHINNAMPO LINE.
Every three days.

For Freight and passage and further particulars apply to

THE OSAKA SHOSEN KAISHA,
Chemulpo

RONDON, PLAISANT & CO.

General Storekeepers and Merchants, Ships Contractors, Tobacconists, Commission and Forwarding Agents, Coal Merchants

IMPORTERS AND EXPORTERS

Seoul & Chemulpo.

W. D. WENTWORTH.

LANDING
AND
SHIPPING AGENT
AND
CUSTOMS BORDER.

12 OURA, NAGASAKI.

STEWARD & CO.

Chemulpo.

Shipchandlers and Storekeepers, Naval and Mercantile Contrrctors, Landing and Shipping Agents.

STEWARD'S HOTEL

Chemulpo.

Best accommodation in the port for travellers. Clean and well-sized rooms, good cuisin and prompt attendence, moderate tariff.

뎨오됴 총지가잇는때는의졍관즁그직무를ᄃᆡ리홈

뎨륙됴 의졍관은총지의명을승ᄒᆞ야졍리ᄉᆞ무를분쟝홈 다만졍리ᄉᆞ무의필요를죠ᄎᆞ각원ᄉᆞ에림시위원을명홈

뎨칠됴 비셔는총지의명을승ᄒᆞ야문셔를관리홈

뎨팔됴 긔ᄉᆞ는샹관에지휘를승ᄒᆞ야셔무에종사홈

뎨구됴 졔실졔도에관ᄒᆞᆫ심의립안은총히긔밀을엄이직힐사

뎨십됴 의졍관은본관샹당ᄒᆞᆫᄃᆡ우를밧고비셔는쥬임ᄃᆡ우오긔사는판임ᄃᆡ우로홈

론셜

스토셀쟝군의항복

○동경각신문들이 스토셀쟝군의려슌을굿세이게직힌것을대단히칭찬ᄒᆞ면셔그쟝군의항복쳥원셔를보낸후에쟈긔의군함들을훼도망시키고훼셰트리며그항구를메이고그포ᄃᆡ를부신닐에ᄃᆡᄒᆞ야대단히셩닉셔말ᄒᆞ되스토셀쟝군의힘위가비루ᄒᆞ고용렬ᄒᆞ다ᄒᆞ엿스나그러ᄒᆞ나비록일본ᄉᆞ룸들이져의싸홈싸와얻은물건들을이러버린것을답답히넉이는것은예ᄉᆞ어니와스토셀쟝군을칙망ᄒᆞ는리유는우리는모로겟노라

스토셀쟝군이쟈긔의쳥원셔를쟈긔의쳥원ᄒᆞᆫᄃᆡ로용랍ᄒᆞᆯ는지보증을보지못ᄒᆞ엿슬지라필경에는쟈긔의쳥원ᄒᆞᆫ것과대단히다르게일본ᄉᆞ룸이요구ᄒᆞ며ᄯᅩ연속히포격ᄒᆞ니그쟝군은손을미고그하회를기ᄃᆞ리기어려웟슬듯ᄒᆞ도다

일본ᄉᆞ룸의소견으로보면스토셀쟝군의힘위가의심업시피로엇슬터이지마는방관지인으로보면항복ᄒᆞ기전에각색물건을다ᄭᆡ트리고부신것이그쟝군의용밍스럽게려슌을직히든닐과ᄀᆞᆺ치쟈긔의쥬인된로국황뎨에게ᄃᆡ긔의츙심을더표ᄒᆞ는젹당ᄒᆞᆫ일노만뵈이더라

별보

일월사일의지부델늬뉴스신문에셔등지홈 (속)

○그로국슈뢰졍이셩피득보로가는긴ᄒᆞᆫ소문을가지고와셔지부잇는로국령사의에데만씨의계젼ᄒᆞ엿스니지금은로국졍부에셔스테셀쟝군의항복ᄒᆞᆫ논리유셔를볼지라그로국슈뢰졍으로온ᄒᆞᆫ관인이쟈긔의친구의게니야기ᄒᆞᆫ말이라고젼홈을드르니그말에ᄒᆞ엿스되

려슌에형편이항복홀것밧게업는것이그군중에사세가가련ᄒᆞ게된지라대포의탄환은거의다업셔지고비록군긔고안에젹은총의탄환은만히잇스나열두치되는대포의탄환이비오듯ᄒᆞ는ᄃᆡ그것이무엇에쓸ᄃᆡ잇스리오만일스토셀쟝군이더오리직히고잇셧드면그군ᄃᆡ만멸종ᄒᆞ얏슬다름이로다이참혹홈을피ᄒᆞ랴면항복ᄒᆞ는것밧게업다고군사를과쟝관들의소견이다ᄀᆞᆺᄒᆞᆫ지라

려슌안에병원의경황을시찰ᄒᆞ면모옴이샹ᄒᆞᆫ만ᄒᆞ도다그만이샹ᄒᆞᆫ사룸들이ᄒᆞᆫ이식물이업셔셔죽으며토혈병이셩ᄒᆞ야간호부들과의원들이정신이요란ᄒᆞᆫ인ᄃᆡ부인들이쟈원ᄒᆞ야병원에드러가셔그병들고샹ᄒᆞᆫ사룸들을구죠ᄒᆞ는인자심이그병샹쟈들의게대단이위로가되는지라려슌안에는풍악소리돌드를슈업고련ᄃᆡ기벽홀세샹ᄀᆞᆺ치죠용ᄒᆞ며어린아히들ᄀᆞᆺ치길노단니면셔울고ᄒᆞᆯ젹거리는사룸들을혼이보겟도다

죽고샹ᄒᆞᆫ도록을보면육군사관들의빅분지륙십오는죽지아니ᄒᆞ엿스면샹ᄒᆞ엿고이빅삼미돌고ᄃᆡ싸홈에히군쟝관이이빅칠인인ᄃᆡ그즁에샹ᄒᆞ지아니ᄒᆞᆫ쟈는다만이십인뿐이더라

다른것의업는것은고사ᄒᆞ고사룸업는것으로항복홀밧게업겟다고말홀지라지금쓸만ᄒᆞᆫ사룸이사쳔명줌되게는ᄃᆡ그즁에거의반슈는만일평안부사지시ᄀᆞᆺᄒᆞ면병원에보낼사룸들이로다ᄒᆞ더라더라

작일아참에로국군함의종션삼척이지부에일즉드러왓는ᄃᆡ려슌으로브터왓는지라그빅들이항구에드러온지얼마아니되야셔일본슈뢰파피함칠척이와셔항구에ᄯᅩᄒᆞᆫ뜨려왓더라그로국빅들에는그비롤져어을만ᄒᆞᆫ사룸만타고항구에드러온후에다른사룸들과히군관인들이만이을나셔싸홈싸우던곳으로브터온비갓지아니ᄒᆞ며그비예잇는사룸즁에군긔를가진쟈는젹은총갓진쟈일이인샏이고젼일에온슈뢰졍들ᄀᆞᆺ치그비들도요힘으로그픽식홀곳으로ᄲᅡ저나와셔지부ᄭᆞ지오기에별노곤란홈이업셧다더라그비에타고온사룸들이다비곤ᄒᆞ야이야기ᄒᆞ기도어려운모양인ᄃᆡ그즁에몃사룸이려슌구에셔격근닐을말ᄒᆞ야여긔에긔져ᄒᆞ며그빅들은지낸월요일밤여달시에려슌에셔ᄯᅥ낫다더라로국비들의드러온후에곳드러온일본슈뢰졍칠척은슌양함일척과포함일척이등ᄒᆞ엿는ᄃᆡ그슌양함은항구안에드러오지아니ᄒᆞ고외항에셔기다리고셔셔미국히군대쟝쫄져씨의군함불티모에향ᄒᆞ야례포를노터라

그일본슈뢰파피함은항구안에ᄀᆞᆺ가이드러와셔ᄒᆞᆫ시간이나더지체ᄒᆞ야그즁에사척은ᄯᅥ나가고삼척은항구에좁은목으로가셔일자로막어셧더라젼셜은드른즉그일본비들의온목젹은그젼날에온로국슈뢰졍이무쟝을히졔ᄒᆞ엿는지아니ᄒᆞ엿는지됴사홈을위홈이라는ᄃᆡ그남어지슈뢰파피함들은오후ᄭᆞ지잇더니다시니항으로ᄯᅥ드러와셔다른빅들의사이에셧더다 (완)

잡보

○유만취업 경무청에셔노는빅셩들을단속ᄒᆞ야ᄉᆞ농공샹ᄉᆞ업즁에나아가벌어먹게인도ᄒᆞ라는ᄃᆡ 쳐분을내리사ᄉᆞ업을불가불실시홀거시니농샹공부대신과학부대신을대령ᄒᆞ라ᄒᆞ옵셧더라

○관졔쟝포 거번에리졍훈관졔를쟝찻반포홀터인ᄃᆡ 쳐분니에히리졍안을종속히총회ᄒᆞ드리라ᄒᆞ옵셧스나인원이미비ᄒᆞ여회의처못ᄒᆞ엿다더라

○원쟝임 륙군법원쟝김졍근씨신고ᄃᆡ에는참쟝빅셩긔씨가피임ᄒᆞᆫ다더라

○호샹권고 거십이일에일진회에셔총ᄃᆡ고경무ᄉᆞ의게파송ᄒᆞ야긔션ᄒᆞᆯ방침을권고ᄒᆞ미경무ᄉᆞ는총ᄃᆡ의게ᄃᆡᄒᆞ야히회ᄢᅢ다른ᄃᆡ의뢰치말고독립힘동의방침을권고ᄒᆞ미히총ᄃᆡ등이유이되ᄒᆞ더라

○김희셜교 김희군슈리근홍씨가부임ᄒᆞᆫ이후로문명교육을보통홀취지로김희에일어학교를셜립ᄒᆞ엿는ᄃᆡ입학ᄒᆞ는자가축일증가홈의쟝리긔망이잇슴으로공립학교로셜립ᄒᆞ라ᄒᆞ야학부에보고ᄒᆞ고그인가를고ᄃᆡᄒᆞ는즁인ᄃᆡ동군슈는미월에륙십원을답답ᄃᆡ출ᄒᆞ며일본인안거원의ᄉᆞ씨를교ᄉᆞ로고빙ᄒᆞ고조교ᄉᆞ만대진리흥현량씨를입용ᄒᆞ엿는ᄃᆡ우쥬임교ᄉᆞ일본인은명예로찬죠ᄒᆞ야월은을밧지아니ᄒᆞᆫ다더라

○질문군경 일진회에셔총ᄃᆡ윤갑병씨등을군부에파송ᄒᆞ야원쥬ᄃᆡ장리민화가병명을거ᄂᆞ리고지물을ᄲᅢ아슨ᄉᆞ로압샹쟈관ᄒᆞ기를쳥ᄒᆞ엿는ᄃᆡ협판엄쥬익씨가말ᄒᆞ기를곳대신ᄭᅴ품ᄒᆞ고압셩ᄒᆞ겟다ᄒᆞ고뎌텬사는유면슈를임의잡아가두엇다ᄒᆞ고지휘ᄒᆞ관리용관은저작일압샹ᄎᆞ발훈ᄒᆞ엿다ᄒᆞ고경위총관리근틱씨사저에ᄃᆡ를보니여질문ᄒᆞ되종로소무소에셔이러버린지화칠빅원과동화일빅오십원탕건여섯기와숀검의게마져샹ᄒᆞᆫ빅셩틱의치료비일빅원을권즁셕쳐에즁출ᄒᆞ기를쳥ᄒᆞᆫᄃᆡ리씨가말ᄒᆞ기를당당이츄급ᄒᆞ마ᄒᆞ엿다더라

○거류디조사 인쳔외국은거류디에면젹죠사ᄒᆞᆫ것을드른즉일본거류디는륙만ᄉᆞ쳔오빅구십평밧기미돌이오각국거류디는십오십일만팔쳔ᄉᆞ빅구십삼평방미돌이오쳥국인거류디는삼만삼빅평방미돌이라더라

○관쟝보고 셩균관쟝서샹훈씨가학부에보고ᄒᆞ되관일병십여명이남신문원쟝을넘어드러왓기로효유ᄒᆞ야되송ᄒᆞ엿스나막즁셜면에유ᄒᆞ야무숀ᄒᆞ돌립홈이사쳬미안ᄒᆞ니외부로경흥ᄒᆞ야일공관에죠ᄒᆞ야검단케ᄒᆞ라ᄒᆞ엿더라

○포박ᄎᆞ파송 무녀슈연이가ᄂᆡ리젼만여원을도득ᄒᆞ야피진ᄎᆞ로명산에긔도ᄒᆞᆫ다칭ᄒᆞ고일젼에발졍ᄒᆞ엿는ᄃᆡ경무사신ᄐᆡ휴씨가그무녀를포박ᄎᆞ로별슌검을파송ᄒᆞ엿다더라

○관광쟈여운 지작야에련연졍뒤극락암에셔지들올니는ᄃᆡ송속남녀와로소아동이관광ᄎᆞ로구름ᄀᆞᆺ치모엿더라

○도믹유쥬물 양구거ᄒᆞ는김염한이가나무장사ᄎᆞ로류쥬목삼빅여귀를사두엇더니본군사논손가가몰슈히집어다가방뎌훈고로경무쳥에졍소ᄒᆞ엿더라

○김씨활인 회동거ᄒᆞ는김쥬사헌셩씨가섬작일밤에평동근쳐로지는ᄃᆡ엇더ᄒᆞᆫ열셔너살쯤된아ᄒᆡ가우물몰가헤셔올며ᄲᅡ지고저ᄒᆞ거놀동씨가급히붓잡고그리유를무른즉그아ᄒᆡ가말ᄒᆞ되저의계모가술과국슈를사오라고돈열닷량을쥬기로보자에돈을싸가지고오다가일허바렷ᄉᆞᆫ즉그저가면마저죽을디경인고로물에ᄲᅡ저죽고저ᄒᆞᆫ다ᄒᆞ가로동씨가돈이십량을주고효유ᄒᆞ야보냇다ᄒᆞ니김씨의활인ᄒᆞᆫ것은가히치하홀만ᄒᆞ다고들ᄒᆞ더라

광고

○본인의쟝ᄌᆞ쳐멸이가본시무랑패류로그부형ᄌᆞ데간에분쟈ᄒᆞ여가진면장문권욕몰수히도적ᄒᆞ여닉엿기로세부독이ᄒᆞ야시문권을문들엇고이에광포ᄒᆞ오니닉외국인잔에삼가속지말고한치멸의가진문권을면집지ᄲᅡ옵기를바라옵

평양셩닉쌍거리 한긔현 고빅

○본인의셔졔진셩이가년이미만이십에주셕잡긔로일을삼아향곽가산ᄒᆞ고곽류를부동ᄒᆞ야혹기명도ᄒᆞ고면답문권과가권을위조ᄒᆞ야동서로단니며독처코자ᄒᆞ오나닉외국인은견긔치마시옵이ᄉᆞ실를각신문에광고ᄒᆞ엿ᄉᆞ오니조량ᄒᆞ심을절망

황토현거최셩환 고빅

TELEGRAMS.

(Received at the Japanese Legation)

General Nogi's Headquarters, Jan. 12th.

The transfer of all the fortifications, forts, ships, weapons, ammunition, accoutrements etc. at Port Arthur was completed on the 12th inst.

The list is as follows:—

Permanent forts	59
Heavy guns	54
Field "	149
Small " (various)	243
Shells	[illegible]
Torpedos	60
Bombs	1,588
Gunpowder kilos.	30,000
Rifles	35,252
Revolvers	579
Swords	1,891
Rifle cartridges	2,266,800
Ammunition wagons	290
Carts	606
Telephones	134
Horses	1920

There were in addition 4 battleships, 2 cruisers, 14 gunboats and destroyers and a number of small steamers all of which have been rendered useless. There at 35 steam launches which we may be able to repair and use.

Tokio, Jan. 13th.

On the 11th instant one of our men of war captured the British steamer "Rosucho" (?) which was bound for Vladivostok with 6,500 tons of coal.

It is announced that, no danger being apprehended from the Vladivostock fleet, the steamship service between Japan and Gensan, which has been suspended since April last, will now be resumed.

Mr. Siu Tai-hyu is vigorously continuing his commendable campaign against sorcerers and their stock in trade. He has ordered the closing of all devil temples and the destruction of their contents.

The "Daito Shimpo" gives currency to the rumour that the Government, being pressed for money, will presently borrow several million yen from Japan. The Government will be very ill-advised if it ever does any such thing.

An aged Councillor of State, Mr. Choi Ik-hyen, who is a strong advocate of reform, has been sitting outside the Palace gates for the past five days and announces his intention of staying there until the desired reforms have been carried out.

The Il-chin-hoi delegates waited on the new Chief of Police yesterday and requested him to compel his predecessor to disgorge the sum of Y700 Japanese currency and $150 Korean currency together with half a dozen I. C. A. caps which were seized when their headquarters were closed by the police. They also ask for $100 for medical attendance on the wounded. Mr. Yi Kun Tak is reported to have assented to all these demands. We suggest that an enquiry as to where the Y700 Japanese currency came from would be a useful measure.

The China Mail reports that a sad tragedy occurred on board the torpedo boat destroyer "Whiting" on Dec. 30, when it was discovered that Lieutenant Commander Jellicoe, the officer commanding the vessel, had committed suicide. The tragedy was discovered shortly before 9 o'clock when the Lieutenant's body was found lying in his cabin with a bullet wound in the head. There was a weapon with which the wound had apparently been inflicted lying in the cabin, and all indications point to a case of suicide. The news came as a shock to the Fleet and no reason for the rash act can be assigned. The Commodore was at once informed, and the body removed to the Naval Mortuary. An inquiry was held on board of the 2nd class cruiser "Thetis" at 3 o'clock that afternoon.

MR. KRUGER'S FORTUNE.

THE EX-PRESIDENT LEAVES £750,000.

Amsterdam, Nov. 23.—The value of the fortune left by the late Mr. Kruger amounts to no less than £750.000. It has been arranged that on the arrival of the Batavier VI. with the ex-President's remains on board at Capetown, the body will lie in state there for a week, and will then be conveyed to Pretoria by special train. At the Transvaal frontier, General Louis Botha is to receive the body and escort it to the capital, where it will agai, lie in state in what was formerly the United Church, but, is now a Government building. In addition to the £25,000 bequeathed to various societies in Holland, the ex-President has left sums to all the funds opened after the South African war for the support of the widows and orphans of Boers who lost their lives. He has also made bequests for the maintenance of the Dutch language. Full details of Mr. Kruger's testamentary dispositions will only be made known after his burial. The funeral is to take place on December 16, Dingaan's Day, after Divine service has been held in the square opposite the late President's former dwelling.

RUSSIAN OFFICES IN CHEFOO.

Lieutenant Balk, the former commander of the "Silatsch," arrived in Chefoo on one of the steam launches which succeeded in getting away from Port Arthur on January 2nd. The "Silatsch" was a powerful tug boat carrying hydraulic pumps and diving apparatus. Lieutenand Balk had in his charge all the small steam craft belonging to the government in Port Arthur. The "Silatsch" rendered good service during the siege. Her first work was done in assisting the "Retvizan," "Cezarevitch" and "Pallada." Later on she was used as a fire boat during the conflagration in the warehouses and dockyards, accomplishing her task in spite of bursting shells.

Lieutenant Balk was a familiar figure at the famous Port Arthur "Race Course" or "Parade Ground," where his pony "Boxer" was a conspicuous competitor.

Lieutenant Karzow, also in Chefoo, and commander of the "Vlastni," is a son of the Russian Consul General in Paris. His brother was killed during the defence of the Kinchow fortress. Lieutenant Karzow himself was wounded some time ago while serving in the forts with his blue-jackets. A shrapnel pierced his leg and he was laid up for several weeks, on recovery resuming command of the destroyer "Vlastni."

An official letter from the magistrate of Heuichön (North of Pyeng Yang) to the Home Office has been intercepted by the Japanese. The letter was to the effect that the Il Chin Hoi, aided by the Japanese, are rising on all sides with the object of handing this country over to Japan. He advacated the immediate suppression of the society. He has been arrested by the Japanese soldiers stationed in his district and the Japanese Minister has forwarded his letter to the Home Office with the request that the magistrate be dismissed from his post.

Chinese who have recently left Harbin report that the Russian troops are being rapidly reinforced, large numbers of men having arrived at Harbin, Moukden and the front. Some of them state that the Russians apparently intend a movement which will encompass the Japanese army, as the lines of the former are being extended and strong detachments placed at extreme points. No fighting of importance has taken place during the past two months, but defence works of every description are being pushed forward on both sides. The point that seems to be firmly fixed in the minds of these Chinese is that the Russian lines are gradually covering a great extent of territory and advancing to some extent.

PREPARING FOR THF BALTIC FLEET.

ACTIVITY AT SAIGON.

Advices from Saigon state that much activity prevails in anticipation of the possible arrival of the Baltic Fleet in that neighbourhood. While it is difficult to glean any news, the government and all firms being remarkably reticent,—the very whisper of the word contraband," sending all concerned deep into their shells,—it is generally, and commonly, known, that the Russian ships, if they ever get so far, will coal and provision at Cape St. James. For this reason remarkable activity is evident both in Saigon and at the point, where large quantities of coal and provisions are now accumulating. It is stated that there is already between 18,000 and 20,000 tons of coal, besides thousands of barrels of "salt junk" and other supplies in readiness for what may yet prove a "phantom fleet." On her last trip down one of our coasting steamers took a large quantity of casks of salt beef, biscuits and pork, consigned to a private firm in Saigon. The s.s. "Tungchow, formerly on the China coasting run, has been bought by a syndicate in Saigon, for the conveyance of the accumulating supplies of coal and provisions to Cape St. James, while it is understood that another well-known steamer is also ready to load coal for the same port. It will be interesting to note the outcome of all this apparent preparation.

GENERAL NOGI.

It is reported that after the affairs of Port Arthur have been disposed of General Nogi will return to Tokyo by command of the Emperor, and, says the Japan Mail, will be appointed to the position formerly held by the late Count Kawamura in connection with the rearing of the Prince Imperial's children. The nation has evidently a feeling of profound sympathy with General Nogi. Various stories are related about him. It is said that he seemed to be almost unconscious of the need of sleep during the last weeks of the siege and after the death of his second son he maintained a cheerful and even buoyant mien during the hours of daylight or in the presence of others, and he would make his staff lie down to rest at the earliest possible moment, but on more than one occasion when he was supposed to be himself sleeping, his officers observed that he was sitting with his head buried in his hands and evidently weeping. All joy had gone out of the brave old general's life, and to the loss of his own two only sons was added the misery of seeing thousands of brave men under his command struck down fruitlessly. If he had known that those who understood the situation wondered, not at his delay in capturing the fortress, but at the splendid progress he was making, some comfort might have come to him, and now at any rate he has his reward. But to what a desolate home will he return!

It is stated that owing to the persistence of the Ningpo inhabitants of Shanghai and the resolute representations of the Japanese Government, the Russians have at length agreed that the marine who killed a Chinaman in the streets of Shanghai shall be tried at the Russian Consulate in the presence of a Chinese Assessor. The men concerned were to be sent under escort to the municipal jail on the 31st ult, and to be brought up for trial on the 3rd inst. The question turned upon whether extraterritorial jurisdiction could be fully claimed on behalf of men interned as the Russians are in Chinese dominions. It appears that such a claim is practiclly inconsistent with the authority which the Chinese must necessarily exercise in discharging their neutral obligations. The method finally adopted, namely, trial by the Russian Consul in the presence of a Chinese official, is doubtless the best exit from the dilemma.

The King has granted Walter Dening, Esq., his authority to accept and wear the Insignia of the Fifth Class of the Imperial Japanese Order of the Rising Sun, which Decoration his Imperial Majesty the Emperor of Japan has been pleased to confer upon Mr. Dening in recognition of valuable services rendered by him to his Imperial Majesty in his capacity of Professor of English Literature in the Second High School at Sendai.

The Magistrate of Yun San reports an extraordinary occurrence in his district. It appears that a man named Yi Duk So had for some time been indebted, in the sum of $6.00, to a man belonging to the Shangchu district. Half this sum was paid last Spring and the remainder last month, but the Shangchu gentleman announced himsecf dissatisfied and demanded heavy interest. The Magistrate was asked to arbitrate and decided the matter settled. The same night however the man returned, accompanied by 10 Japanese armed with rifles. These, after firing a few times, seized 10 Yunsan men and marched off with them and are still holding them, apparently as hostages. The magistrate begs that the Japanese Legation will immediately investigate the affair.

The Korea Daily News.

Issued at 5 P. M. daily except Sundays.

Rate of Subscription:—

Per Year,............Yen 25.
Per Quarter,..........Yen 7.
Per Month,..........Yen 2.50.

Postage in Korea not charged extra.
Postage abroad charged extra.

Advertisements, 50 sen per day for 1 inch or less.
5 yen per month per inch.
50 yen per year per inch.

All communications to

E. T. BETHELL,
Editor and Publisher,
Pak-tong, Seoul.

THE POSITION AT VLADIVOSTOCK.

The feverish night and day activity which, for the last year, has marked the construction of fortifications at Vladivostock, is about to end, and already the van-guard of the Shantung coolies who have comprised the greatest factor in making the Russian port a second Port Arthur has reached Chefoo. The S. S. "Ellamy" arrived day before yesterday, says the Chefoo Daily News of January 5th, with eight hundred and seventy of these hardy fellows on board and the "Canton" came in yesterday afternoon with six hundred and forty-six more who will winter in the home province. In all there are about five thousand coolies still at work on the Russian fortifications, but they are only putting the finishing touches to the latter, and in a month's time the greater part of them will have arrived in Chefoo to spend their hard-earned roubles as only a coolie can.

"The Russians think the Japanese will never take Vladivostock," said an intelligent Chinese who arrived on the "Canton." "They believe the recently constructed forts have made the town impregnable. Eight miles down the channel, and on the Eastern side of the city, there are six very strong forts which my be seen in the day-time from the deck of any ship passing up or down the channel. The guns of these forts all point to the seaward. There are more than six forts on the Eastern side of the city, but one cannot see them from the channel although their guns doubtless cover it at every point.

Further inquiries elicited the following information from the informant.

On the right side of the channel, going down, and to the South of the city, arise three or four large forts all mounted with large guns. These are also observable on a clear day from the channel, but their guns point to the seaward. There is only one fort on the Western side of the city, but it is a strong one, and mounted with heavy guns. To the North, whence the railway comes, there are no forts. The Eastern forts are decidedly the most formidable, and the range of their gun-fire sweeps all the other forts from superior heights. It is evident that they comprise the key to the situation, and should the Japanese lay siege to the city, they will have to bear the brunt of the attack.

Very few Russian soldiers are seen on the streets of Vladivostock, though the garrison numbers over 20,000, and the town is not so lively and gay as it used to be. Practice with large and small arms takes up the greater part of the time of the troops, who are submitted to the strictest discipline and have little "off duty." The greater part of them live in warm brick houses which have been erected near the forts, and despite the severity of the weather are summoned to the guns at all hours of the day and night by pre-arranged signals for mere practice. To all outward appearances this sort of drill is the "real thing" and when the latter does occur, the garrison will probably not appreciate the fact until the first of the enemy's shrapnel shrieks above their heads.

It was on the twenty-second of December that the channel froze over, and nowadays the ice-breaking vessel is engaged every morning in crushing a passage to the open sea. On both sides of this channel a number of mines have been planted, but at present they are concealed by the ice.

LET EM ALL COME.

Mr. Shigetoyo Maruyama, a police inspector in charge of a section of the Metropolitan Police, is according to the "Nagasaki Press," reported to have accepted an offer by the Korean Government to engage him as police adviser.

FRANCE AND HER ALLY.

The friends whom Russia has in such large numbers in our country may be of good cheer. Let the Russian army maintain full and complete confidence in its eminent Commander-in-chief of which he is at all times worthy, let it keep intact its own twofold faith (in God and country), and better days will not be long in dawning upon it.—"Gaulois," Paris.

THE RUSSIANS NEAR SINMINTUN.

The "Tokyo Asahi's" correspondent at Kenpangtsz, wiring under date of the 2nd inst., states, according to the "Japan Times," that some 30 Russian soldiers were stationed at Sinmintun railway station for the purpose of examining passengers. A German merchant now staying at a Chinese hotel at Sinmintun was secretly engaged in supplying the Russians at Mukden with sugar, liquors and other provisions, which he obtained from Tientsin, 60 or 70 goods carriages being daily used for the transportation to Mukden. Quite recently a large quantity of flour laden in over 200 luggage vans, the flour being the property of Chinese who were forwarding it from Kwanchengtze to Chaoyang, was seized at Taiyangtun by a body of Russians and at once sent to the Russian commissariat at Tiehling. Russian reinforcements were arriving thrice daily at Mukden from the north, each train containing 500 or 600 men. The Russians at Sungari were felling timber for the purpose of fuel, the wood being transported southward.

The correspondent further states that the Russians at Fahkuman were enlisting mounted bandits at a monthly salary of 30 roubles. In the direction of Tingkiatun (north of Tiehling), the Russians were purchasing from natives large quantities of live stock, several hundreds of which were daily conveyed to Mukden under a guard of Chinese soldiers, who were employed for the purpose of providing against a possible attack of bandits *en route*.

The situation with the two armies in Manchuria has not changed during the last week. Telegrams tell us of Russian attacks which have not accomplished anything material, but it appears that these movements have been unimportant reconnoissances, as usual, which have no influence on the general situation.

There is no doubt that the Japanese have been reinforcing themselves considerably, although they keep back all information regarding this point. On the Russian side the reinforcements of the Japanese are estimated at from forty to sixty thousand men. If this estimate is correct, it may take some time before the Russian armies have reached the hoped-for superiority in numbers.—Brigadezeitung.

The railway between Shuntefu in Chihli and Changtefu in Honan has been completed and the trains began to run on the 15th inst.

Professor Joachim has been decorated with the Red Cross Medallion by the Japanese Red Cross Society in recognition of his services at a concert recently given in aid of the Japanese wounded.

Certain kinds of ammunition were somewhat scarce in Port Arthur. According to a Russian, considerable six-inch ammunition was made by the garrison after the opening of the siege. It is also said that over six hundred unexploded shells fired in the town by the Japanese were gathered up by the Russians, new caps and fuses were adjusted and they were then fired at the Japanese.

The trial of four Chinese in Shanghai for being concerned in the dissemination of seditious literature (printed in Tokio) has been concluded in the mixed court. The following sentences were pronounced by the Magistrate:—

Zau Keh-foo of the printing office, Sinze, to be imprisoned for two year.

Per Sze-zeh, broker, of Canton Road, eight months' imprisonment.

Mow Pah-zue, bookseller, of Honan Road, eight months' imprisonment.

Wong Cha-zeh, Rord, three months' imprisonment.

That it was a bitter pill for many of the officers and men to feel that they must give up the fortress of Port Arthur and not fight to the death in its defence, is evident from the remarks of one of the officers who reached Chefoo in the refugee torpedo boats and launches. He says that many of the men who had fought with bull-dog tenacity and grim courage, stared stupidly at one another as if suddenly struck dumb, while their officers moved sadly about like persons experiencing the greatest calamity of their lives. Officers and men, however, fully appreciated that surrender was the only thing left for them.

Over-eating has come to be recognised as the most fertile source of peptic ills. Canton Bristow says:—"Curiously enough, it is the fanatical teetotallers themselves who, as a rule, are the eaters in excess. I never can forget the slow, burning passage down the Indian Ocean, when every one save a band of enthusiastic teetotal ministers confined themselves to the most meagre diet imaginable. But these good men steadily ploughed through the daily menu, fortified now and again by gingerbeer and the hope of ultimate salvation, sternly rebuking myself and others who slaked our thirst at infrequent intervals with the weakest and mildest whiskies and sodas. As a matter of fact we kept fit; they, overladen and dyspeptic, were always in misery."

One of the most remarkable performances in desperadoism that ever passed through the prosaic records of the Assize Courts is now agitating Toulon. In 1897 a young Corsican medical student, named Cesarini, was in Toulon, where he fell in love with the daughter of one Dr. Barnier and was persuaded to let matters alone for a year or two, which he spent in French Africa, returning in 1899 to find the lady just married to somebody else. He twice murderously attacked her father—once as he lay in hospital—was arrested, escaped, was betrayed by a Corsican with a grudge against him, and received a sentence of two years' transportation. He escaped from Devil's Island in 1902, murdered his Corsican betrayer, was condemned to death, had his sentence commuted to transportation for life to New Caledonia, and now has once more escaped even from there. He is believed to be in France, and nobody doubts that his one object in life is to murder Dr. Barnier, whom he regards as having fooled him out of the way for his daughter's marriage.

The Korea Daily News.

VOL. II, SATURDAY, JANUARY 14, 1905. No. 10

HONGKONG & SHANGHAI BANKING CORPORATION.

Paid-up Capital..... ....$10,000,000
Reserve Fund:—Sterling Reserve... 10,000,000
Silver Reserve..... 7,000,000

27,000,000

Reserve Liability of Proprietors... 10,000,000

HEAD OFFICE, HONGKONG.

London Bankers, London and County Banking Company Limited.

Branches and Agencies,
London.

Amoy,	Hankow	Penang,
Bangkok,	Hiogo,	Rangoon,
Batavia,	Iloilo,	Saigon,
Bombay,	Lyons,	San Francisco,
Calcutta,	Manila,	Singapore,
Colombo,	Nagasaki,	Sourabaya,
Foochow,	New York,	Tientsin,
Hamburg,	Peking,	Yokohama,

Credits granted on approved Securities, and every description of Banking and Exchange business transacted.

Drafts granted on London and the chief Commercial places in Europe, India, Australia, America, China and Japan.

HOLME RINGER & CO., AGENTS,
CHEMULPO.

HOKURKU DOBOKU KAISHA.

Branch office in Chong Dong, Seoul.

Japanese telephone No. 165

CONTRACT DEPARTMENT.

We can contract to build any building or construction.

MERCHANDISE DEPARTMENT.

We can provide any building material. We have just contracted to build the new Belgian Legation.

E. MEYER & CO.

Chemulpo.

SOLE AGENTS IN KOREA FOR.

A. T. Morse, Sons & Co.'s

"Fresco" Distemper

In all colours ready for use on walls, Ceilings etc.

and

AVENARIUS CARBOLINEUM

A wood-preserving and antiseptic oil preparation

Against decay, dry-rot, fungus and wood-destroying insects.

A large supply always in stock.
Prices upon application.

E. MEYER & Co.,
Chemulpo.

CHARTERED BANK OF INDIA AUSTRALIA & CHINA.

INCORPORATED BY ROYAL CHARTER 1853

HEAD OFFICES.—LONDON.

Paid-up Capital £800,000
Reserve Liability of Shareholders 800,000
Reserve Fund 800,000

Drafts granted upon all the principal places in the world and every description of Exchange and banking business transacted.

E. MEYER & Co., Agents,
Chemulpo.

MITSU BISHI DOCKYARD & ENGINE WORKS,
NAGASAKI.

CODE WORD, "DOCK."

A 1, A. B. C., and Engineering Codes used.

DOCK No. 1 (at Tategami).

Extreme Length..............523 feet
Length on blocks .... 513 ,,
Width of Entrance on Top......89 ,,
,, ,, Bottom....77 ,,
Water on Blocks at Spring Tide 26½ ,,

DOCK No. 2 (Mukaijima).

Extreme Length..............371 feet
Length on Blocks.............360 ,,
Width of Entrance on Top......66 ,,
,, ,, Bottom 53 ,,
Water on Blocks at Spring Tide 22 ,,

PATENT SLIP (at Kosuge).

Can take vessels up to 1,000 tons gross.

THE WORKS are well equipped with the LATEST IMPROVEMENTS, and can execute any kind of work in SHIPBUILDING and MARINE ENGINEERING, as well as in REPAIRING of SHIPS.

The COMPANY'S new powerful steamer OURA-MARU (712 tons, 700 I.H.P.), specially built for SALVAGE PURPOSES, and equipped with necessary gear, is always READY at SHORT NOTICE.

THE METHODIST PUBLISHING HOUSE,

Little West Gate, Seoul.

JOB PRINTING, TYPEWRITER PAPER
CARBON PAPER, VISITING CARDS
STATIONERY, BOOK BINDING
BOOK PUBLISHERS
AMERICAN SCHOOL BOOKS
SPENCERIAN COPY BOOKS
PEN CARBON LETTER AND BILL BOOKS

S.A. BECK, Manager.

DAI-ICHI GINKO.

LIMITED.

(Formerly the First National Bank)

ESTABLISHED 1873

INCORPORATED UNDER PRESENT LAW 1896

Capital - - - - - - - - - Yen 5,000,000
Reserve Fund - . - - - 1,500,000

HEAD OFFICE:—TOKIO.

President: Baron SHIBUSAWA.

BRANCHES AND CORRESPONDENTS
In the Principal Cities and Towns of Japan.

Interest Allowed on

Fixed deposits 1 year - - - 6½ per cent
" " 6 months - - - 6 per cent

Special current accounts 1½ sen daily per Y 100
General " " 1 " " " 100

M. TANAKA,
Manager, Chemulpo.

SINGER SEWING

MACHINES

씽거즈봉침

SOLE AGENTS
FOR KOREA
전매소

HOLME RINGER & CO.
Chemulpo.

제물포 함릉거양힝

KAMEYA CO.

GENERAL STOREKEEPERS

Chinkokai - - Seoul

(*Established 1895, Tokyo*)

Confectionery, Hams, Canned Goods, Cutlery, Hirano & Tansan Water. Provisions, Gents, Furnishing goods, Toilet Articles, Travelling Bags, Tobacco, Cigars & Cigarettes Kitchen Utensils. Coffee, Biscuits

Fresh Goods always kept in Stock.
Prices Moderate
☞ *Please come and inspect our goods.*

NIPPON YUSEN KAISHA.

JAPANESE MAIL STEAMSHIP CO.

DER MAIL CONTRACT WITH THE IMPERIAL JAPANESE GOVERNMENT.

European Line

Regular Fortnightly Service between Yokohama Kobe, Moji, Shanghai, Hongkong, Singapore, Penang Colombo, Port Said, Marseilles, London and Antwerp

American Line

Regular Fortnightly Sefvice between Hongkong and Seattle, calling at Shanghai, Moji, Kobe, Yokohama and Victoria, B. C.

Australian Line

Regular weekly Service betwen Japan Ports and Australia, calling at Hongkong and Manila.

(Above Three Lines Suspended until further notice).

Shanghai Line

Weekly Service between Shanghai and Japan Ports

Korea Line

Service Kobe, Moji, Nagasaki, Fusan Chemupo Cheffoo, Taiku.

S. S. Bahelsberg, 2181 tons.

Service Kobe, Moji, Fusan, Chemulpo, Chinnampo

S. S. ARGO, S. S. Ohio.

BORDEN'S CONDENSED MILK CO.

New York, U. S. A.

ALWAYS IN STOCK

Eagle Brand Condensed Milk.

Gold Seal Condensed Milk.

Peerless (Family) Evaporated Cream.

Borden's Malted Milk.

E. MEYER & CO.
Chemulpo Korea,
Sole Agents

ROYAL INSURANCE COMPANY,
Funds exceed £10,000,000
FIRE
AT CURRENT RATES
LIFE
REDUCED PREMIUM.
HOLME RINGER & Co.,
Agents, Chemulpo.

HOTEL DU PALAIS

SEOUL.

The only first class Hotel in Seoul Situated in the centre of the city opposite the palace.

Cuisine under the supervision of an experienced French Chef.

Well ventilated and furnished throughout.

TARIFF UPON APPLICATION

L. MARTIN
Proripetor and Manager

大韓每日申報
ᄃᆡ한ᄆᆡ일신보

(뎨이권십일호) (화요일) 일쳔구ᄇᆡᆨ오년일월십칠일

본샤고ᄇᆡᆨ

이신보는영어와한어로셔거ᄆᆡ일츌판ᄒᆞᆸ

신문가

한장 엽두돈오푼
일삭됴 엽두량닷돈
우표가ᄆᆡ삭닷돈
다맛돈으로밧ᄉᆞᆸ

광고료는

긔한의쟝단과ᄌᆞ힝의다쇼로증감ᄒᆞ되렴가로밧을터이오며오리지아녀대한사람마다다이신문을보실터이니광고내시기를원ᄒᆞ시는이들은우리신문샤에와셔면약ᄒᆞ심을희망ᄒᆞᆸ

○발힝소 박동대한ᄆᆡ일신보샤법어학교압헤젼영국인셜필림집자리오

샤쟝 영국인 (비셜)

평양 ᄃᆡ리점

○평양효동사는권미보씨로우리신문관ᄆᆡᄃᆡ리인을뎡ᄒᆞ엿ᄉᆞ오니평양에계신구람코져ᄒᆞ시는쳠군ᄌᆞ는ᄒᆡᄃᆡ리점에왕림ᄒᆞ와면의ᄒᆞ시ᄋᆞᆸ

사고

○우리대한ᄆᆡ일신보의목뎍은대한의안녕질셔에관한모든뎨목에ᄃᆡᄒᆞ야는공평한변론을쥬장ᄒᆞᆷ이라우리동신원의담보는신문보시는쳠군ᄌᆞ의게ᄒᆞᆼ샹보도ᄒᆞ리며편지를긔셔ᄒᆞ여주시는이는셩명과반ᄃᆞ시젹어붓치시기를희망ᄒᆞ오니이거슨신문샹에긔ᄌᆡᄒᆞ라는거시아니오다만극히신용ᄒᆞ는증거를삼고쟈ᄒᆞᆷ이라긔쟈는아모긔셔던지긔ᄌᆡᄒᆞᆷ을되각ᄒᆞ는권리를가졋ᄉᆞ나되각ᄒᆞ는리유를말ᄒᆞᆯ터이오며공즁평화를문란케ᄒᆞ는듯ᄒᆞᆫ긔셔는의례히밧지안켓ᄉᆞᆸ나이다

●본샤셜시이래로신문을ᄆᆡ양우례로분젼ᄒᆞ와례젼부의임의로젼ᄒᆞᆫ듯스로면곳에는혹늣게젼ᄒᆞ기도ᄒᆞ며혹몃칠거슬ᄒᆞᆫ겁에젼ᄒᆞ기도ᄒᆞ며혹아니젼ᄒᆞ는곳도잇다ᄒᆞ와우리신문을ᄉᆞ랑ᄒᆞ야구람ᄒᆞ시는 쳠군ᄌᆞ의게ᄃᆡᄒᆞ야ᄆᆡ우미안ᄒᆞ옵기로지금은분젼인을두고ᄆᆡ일일즉이젼ᄒᆞ며아니젼ᄒᆞ거나늣게거나ᄒᆞᆫ폐가업도록ᄒᆞ라ᄒᆞ오니혹아니젼ᄒᆞ거나혹늣게젼ᄒᆞ거나ᄒᆞᆫ일이잇스면본샤로통긔ᄒᆞ여쥬심을희망ᄒᆞᆸ

잡보

○ᄐᆡ약편당 사평리사는박모의쳐가그남편이먼식골간동안에간부와잠통ᄒᆞ야ᄌᆞ식을밴지라남편이오면죄샹이탈로ᄒᆞᆯ가두려워ᄒᆞ야모야에도망ᄒᆞ야하와이로간지라그후남편이집에도라온즉그쳐는업고자식만잇는지라도망ᄒᆞᆫ리유도모로고답답ᄒᆞᆯ수업서ᄆᆞ옴이자언울울ᄒᆞ야하와이로드러갓더니그안히를만나깃븜으로그일가의게편지ᄒᆞ엿는ᄃᆡ그사연이여좌ᄒᆞ니왈수년을보지못ᄒᆞ엿다가다시맛나스니넷곡조가양양ᄒᆞ다대한세샹리별ᄒᆞ고포아에셔셔로만나니황련긱이던당에셔만난것굿다ᄒᆞ엿다더라

○싱션상의경험 연강에싱션즁샹들이명년에싱션이ᄒᆞᆫᄒᆞ고귀ᄒᆞᆷ을미리의론ᄒᆞ는ᄃᆡ자고이금으로마포와감은돌에합빙아니된겨울에경험이잇는ᄃᆡ명년은싱션이극귀ᄒᆞ리라ᄒᆞ며또ᄒᆞᆫ싱션은만히잡을지라도즁촌브터즁츄ᄭᆞ지싱션비일쳑에어름두비를쓴즉이좁은강에박빙으로엇지지탕ᄒᆞ리오이갓치싱각컨ᄃᆡ명년은좌반은지쳔ᄒᆞ고싱션은극귀ᄒᆞ리라더라

○구종잡기 일젼에포덕문밧긔셔각대관의구종별비들이모혀잡기ᄒᆞ다가경무쳥에피착ᄒᆞ야ᄐᆡ벌오도식밍치ᄒᆞ고방송ᄒᆞ엿더라

○일편단심 최찬졍씨가샹쥬ᄒᆞ고포덕문압헤오일을업ᄃᆡ엿는ᄃᆡ죽을지언졍샹쥬ᄒᆞᆫ사를실시ᄒᆞ야가히물너가겟다고ᄒᆞᆫ다더라

○삼화감리보고 삼화항감리가외부로보고ᄒᆞ기를상원거ᄒᆞ는윤길션이가자긔일가사ᄅᆞᆷ의면답문권으로일본사ᄅᆞᆷ등촌츙조ᄋᆡ게지화일만원에채용ᄒᆞᆫ소는본감리도ᄒᆞ기젼에셔리김익영이가일영소의죠회를인ᄒᆞ야일인을보호ᄒᆞ야츄슈케ᄒᆞᆯ뜻으로즁화와밋상원량군에발훈ᄒᆞ엿더니현금경부훈령니에윤길션이가면답문권을위조ᄒᆞ야면집독채ᄒᆞᆷ이젹확ᄒᆞ니윤가외일가를쵸치ᄒᆞ야공졍지판ᄒᆞ라ᄒᆞ엿ᄉᆞᆸ기일로써량군에발훈ᄒᆞ엿더니답보내에윤길션이가도타ᄒᆞ고윤가의일가도츌타ᄒᆞᆫ고로아즉판결치못ᄒᆞ엿다ᄒᆞ엿더라

○룡쳔감리보고 룡쳔감리가외부로보고ᄒᆞ기를본군룡암포조계ᄂᆡ에외토란세둔면세쳥인패망셰와밋기타잡셰를ᄐᆡ쳔군으로브터파원슈셰ᄒᆞ미민폐가더욱심ᄒᆞ니ᄇᆞ라건ᄃᆡ곳ᄂᆡ쟝원에지죠ᄒᆞ야본감리로ᄒᆞ야곰구관슈셰케ᄒᆞ시면ᄐᆡ쳔이ᄇᆡᆨ여리에셔파원파슌검의리왕부비와민간폐원이일로좃차업슬터이니죠사ᄒᆞ신후쳐판ᄒᆞ시기를ᄇᆞ란다ᄒᆞ엿더라

뎐보

십삼일일본공사관착
일월십이일ᄂᆡ목쟝군공보

○슈획물픔슈효 일월십일ᄉᆞ지포루포ᄃᆡ함션병긔와기타졔물건의령슈ᄒᆞᆷ을필ᄒᆞ엿는ᄃᆡ그긴요ᄒᆞᆫ졔물건의픔목과수량의대개가여좌ᄒᆞ니 영구포루포ᄃᆡ가오십구오대구경포가오십사오즁구경포가구ᄇᆡᆨ사십구요쇼구경포가이ᄇᆡᆨ사십삼이오포ᄃᆡ탄환이팔만이쳔륙ᄇᆡᆨ칠십이오슈뢰가륙십이오폭약이일쳔오ᄇᆡᆨ팔십팔이오화약이삼만괴오쇼총이이만오쳔이ᄇᆡᆨ오십이오권총이삼ᄇᆡᆨ칠십구요군도가일쳔팔ᄇᆡᆨ구십일이오소총실포가이ᄇᆡᆨ이십륙만이쳔팔ᄇᆡᆨ이오탄약슈레가이ᄇᆡᆨ이십이오치즁슈레가륙ᄇᆡᆨ륙십오면화괴가일ᄇᆡᆨ삼십사오마필슈효가일쳔구ᄇᆡᆨ이십이라ᄒᆞ엿고젼투함(베례수우잇도)(세바슈도보리)는젼혀물에잇슴으로이거슬졔ᄒᆞᆫ외에슌양함이쳑포함구축함십사쳑파괴션십쳑과쇼즁괴션팔쳑과잡션십이쳑과기타사유션약간인ᄃᆡ이샹은다파피혹침몰ᄒᆞᆫ쟈이오또기외에다소ᄒᆞᆫ슈리를더ᄒᆞ야사용ᄒᆞᆯ쇼중괴션이삼십오쳑이더라

일월십일오후십시삼십분착뎐

○함ᄃᆡ파피상보 젼ᄃᆡ에파견ᄒᆞᆫ일본대본영히군참모면즁경ᄐᆡ랑의보고에왈로국포함 (지지깃도)는려슌구셔항ᄂᆡ어뢰영동방옴으진곳에도착ᄒᆞ야침몰ᄒᆞ되돗ᄃᆡ을슈면에로츌ᄒᆞ엿는ᄃᆡ그원인은이ᄇᆡᆨ삼고ᄃᆡ졈령ᄒᆞᆫ후우리포환이마졋고(라수보이넛구)는항구등ᄃᆡ에셔통로를방식ᄒᆞ야침몰ᄒᆞ고돗ᄃᆡ를슈면에셔현츌ᄒᆞ엿는ᄃᆡ그비는스스로침몰ᄒᆞᆷ파곳고(샤히야가)는셔항ᄂᆡ반도곡ᄒᆞᆫ쳐에셔남셔약삼ᄇᆡᆨ미돌ᄃᆡ졈에침몰ᄒᆞ야(마수도)와연돌을슈면에현츌ᄒᆞ엿는ᄃᆡ그원인은낭산졈령후우리포격에인ᄒᆞᆷ이라대뎌러슌함ᄃᆡ의말로는죵차명료ᄒᆞᆷ이라ᄒᆞ고또구축함은어뢰영잔교부근에(보에오ㅣ이)(시ㅣ누이) 부지ㅣ쥬리ㅣ누이)삼척은파괴ᄒᆞ엿고또그셔방약일쳔미돌ᄃᆡ잔교부근에(수도로쥬오ㅣ이)(라쟈ㅣ슈지ㅣ어쳔쳑은모다파피ᄒᆞ엿는ᄃᆡ이샹오쳑파도망ᄒᆞᆫ구축함륙쳑을중가ᄒᆞ면잇는곳이명ᄇᆡᆨ지못ᄒᆞ야담지ᄒᆞᆫ다더라

외보

○려슌샹황 일본대본영에달ᄒᆞᆫ면보를거ᄒᆞᆫ즉목하려슌의상항이이져자에질셔를유지ᄒᆞ야관민이정숙ᄒᆞ고인구가약삼만오쳔명즁에이만오쳔명은군인인ᄃᆡ군인즁이만명은병상쟈오기타인민의약식은다쇼간나마지가잇스나육죵과채소가핍절ᄒᆞ고병상쟈의위싱지료가또ᄒᆞᆫ업는고로목하그구제에젼력ᄒᆞᆫ다ᄒᆞ엿더라

○마젹의소식 작년륙월에동부만쥬에봉긔ᄒᆞᆫ마젹의ᄒᆞᆫ떼가그뒤회인 홍경 동화 ᄒᆡ룡 모아산일ᄃᆡ디에세력을베플어로병과교젼함이이믜ᄉᆞ십여ᄎᆞ에밋치고그총슈가보괴병일만삼쳔명이오대포슈문이잇는ᄃᆡ십일월십칠일에는그일부ᄃᆡ쟝졈위이하십여명을포뢰ᄒᆞ고십이월륙일에는다른일부ᄃᆡ가홍경부근에셔흑룡강교셕극뎨륙즁ᄃᆡ를격파ᄒᆞ야무긔탄약을만이엇고또일부ᄃᆡ는회인셩에셔집안현을지나임강현셩을웅거ᄒᆞ엿다더라

UNION INSURANCE SOCIETY OF CANTON.

Head office Hongkong.
Marine risks underwritten at current rates.
Agents in Chemulpo,
E. MEYER & Co.

COMPAGNIE DES MESSAGERIES MARITIMES.

Fortnightly Direct Service.

For Marseilles
via Ports.
Sailing from Yokohama
Calling at Kobe,
Shanghai, Hongkong, Saigon, Singapore,
Colombo, Djibonti, Suez, Port Said
and Marseilles.

For particulars apply to
HOLME RINGER & Co.,
Chemulpo.

HAYASHIDA & CO.,

16 MYENG DONG, CHIN KO KAI, SEOUL.
BRANCH OFFICE AT CHEMULPO.

Money changers, Coal and Wood Merchants, Express Agents.

We are agents for the Pyeng-yang Coal Company and the Karazu Coal Company of Japan. We have the best quality of both anthracite and bituminous coal, and prompt execution of orders is our speciality. Firewood of all kinds kept in stock. Full weight guaranteed. Money of all denominations exchanged at current rates. Parcels received for all parts.

CHINA MUTUAL LIFE INS. OC.

Most favourable terms to policy holders.

Benefit system unsurpassed.

HOLME RINGER & Co.
Agents, Chemulpo.

C. P. R.

CANADIAN PACIFIC RAILWAY COMPANY'S ROYAL MAIL STEAMSHIP LINE.

THE FAST ROUTE BETWEEN CHINA, JAPAN, AND EUROPE VIA CANADA AND THE UNITED STATES.

Route from Hongkong via Shanghai, Nagasaki (Inland Sea of Japan) Kobe, Yokohama, Victoria and Vancouver.

Twin Screw Empress Steamship—6,000 Tons—Speed 19 knots.

PROPOSED SAILING FROM YOKOHAMA.
R. M. S. Empress of India.
R. M. S. Empress of Japan.
R. M. S. Empress of China.
R. M. S. Athonian.
R. M. S. Taatar.

Special reduction (first class only) granted to members of the Military, Naval, Diplomatic and Civil services and to Missionaries.

Passengers have choice of ten routes across the Continent of America and have privilege of travelling by any Atlantic Steamship Line.

Round the World passage tickets in connection with the P. and O. S. N., North German Lloyd and Messageries Co.'s £125.

All rates payable at current rate of exchange.

For further information, Tickets, Guide Books, etc., apply to

HOLME, RINGER & Co., AGENTS,
Chemulpo.

Grand Hotel,

(Formerly the Station Hotel)

**Near the Railway Terminus,
West Gate Seoul.**

The Best Hotel in Korea.
Handsome new Building.
Fine Airy Rooms
Excellent Cuisine.
Terms Moderate.
Special terms to Missionaries
and to permanent boarders.

Electric cars within 2 minutes' walk.

W. H. EMBERLEY.

Proprietor

EVERY FACILITY.

In connection with Life Assurance Business is afforded by

The Standard Life Assurance Co.,

One of the largest and wealthiest of the Provident Institutions of the United Kingdom Forms of application and all information will be promptly afforded on application.

10 CENTS A DAY.

Not a very large expenditure is it? But it is sufficient to secure for a man of 30 a policy with the STANDARD LIFE OFFICE for

$1323.

For all particulars of rates, etc., apply to

Holme, Ringer & Co.,
Agents, Chemulpo.

THE NEW YORK LIFE INSURANCE COMPANY.

Have you ever been declined by any Company?

Are you engaged in a specially hazardous occupation?

Have you heard of the New York Life Insurance Company's New Classifications for this class of Risks?

If not, send your date of birth, occupation and particulars of rejection, if any to

E. MEYER & Co.,
Agents, Chemulpo.

MITSUI BUSSAN KAISHA.
(MITSUI & Co.)

MITSUI GINKO.
(MITSUI BANK.)

The Bank is owned by the members of the Mitsui Family, who, as partners, assume an unmited responsibility for all liabilities of the Bank:—

Capital........................Yen 5,000,000
Reserve Fund.................. " 5,600,000

HEAD OFFICE, TOKYO.

LONDON OFFICE, 34 LIME ST., E. C.

BRANCHES AND AGENCIES:—

New York, San Francisco, Hamburg, Bombay, Singapore, Manila, Hongkong, Amoy, Chefoo, Tientsin.

Kobe, Hakodate, Yokohama, Kure, Yokosuka, Moji, Shimonoseki, Miike, Wakamatsu, Nagasaki, Kuchinotsu, Karatsu, Sasebo, Misume, Taipeh, &c.

Telegraphic Address for all the Offices:
"MITSUI."

A. B. C. AND A. I CODES USED.

Contractors of Coal

To the Imperial Japanese Navy. Arsenals and Railway Bureau, Principal Railway Companies and Industrial Work, Home and Foreign Mail and Freight Steamers.

Sole Proprietors

Of the famous Miike, Tagawa and Yamano Coal Mines.

Sole Agents

For the sale of Fukumo, Hokoku, Ichimura, Kanoda, Mannoura, Onoura, Ostuji, Sonoda, Tsubaruro, Yoshinotani, Yoshio, Yurokibura and other coals.

YANGTSE INSURANCE ASSOCIATION, LTD.

The undersigned, having been appointed agents for the above company, are prepared to issue policies and pay losses on marine risks at regular rates.

E. MEYER & Co.,
Agents, Chemulpo.

AMERICAN KOREAN ELECTRIC CO.

Light and Power.

Main Office: Electric Building, Chong No.

RAILWAY DEPARTMENT.

OPERATING CARS BETWEEN EAST AND WEST GATE, EVERY TEN MINUTES:—

First Car leaves East Gate at 7:00 A. M. First Car leaves R. R. Station at 7:25 A. M
Last Car " East Gate at 8.40 P. M. Last " " R. R. Station at 9.05 P. M

OPERATING CARS BETWEEN EAST GATE AND IMPERIAL TOMB TERMINUS, EVERY TWENTY MINUTES:—

CONNECTING WITH EVERY ALTERNATE CAR ARRIVING AT EAST GATE FROM CHONG NO.

First Car leaves East Gate for Tomb at 7:10 A. M.
" " " Tomb for East Gate at 7:30 A. M.
Last " " East Gate for Tomb at 7:50 P. M.
" " " Tomb for East Gate at 8:10 P. M.

OPERATING CARS BETWEEN CHONG NO AND YUNG SAN RIVER EVERY TWELVE MINUTES:—

First Car leaves Chong No for South Gate at 7:12 A. M.
" " " Chong No for Yung San at 7:36 A. M.
" " " South Gate for Chong No at 7:20 A. M.
" " " Yung San for Chong No at 8:09 A. M.
Last " " South Gate for Chong No 9:00 P. M.
" " " Yung San for Chong No at 8.45. P. M.

SPECIAL PRIVATE CARS FURNISHED TO SUIT CONVENIENCE OF PATRONS. PRICES ON APPLICATION AT HEAD OFFICE.

LIGHTING DEPARTMENT.

Where less than 250 candle power of light is used, the rate per month will be
Per 16 candle power incandescent lamp,—All night.—Yen 2.50.
32 candle power incandescent lamp:—All night:—Yen 4.00.
50 candle power incandescent lamp:—All night:—Yen 6.00.
150 " " " " " " 10.00.
1200 " " enclosed are " " " " 20.00.

Where more than 250 candle power of light is used, a Meter will be installed, freqvedted:—Rent of Meter Yen 2.00 per month. Rate of charges by meter reading:—Two Sen per Ampere per hour. (Approximately this is equal to about One Sen per 16 C. P. lamp per hour) Minimum monthly charge where meter is installed, Yen 20.00 per month, which includes rental of meter.

Estimates for installing lights furnished on application

An assortment of chandeliers always on hand.

K. Murakami.

Photograph Studio
Chinkokai, Seoul.

Printing, Developing and Enlargement, of Photographs always Undertaken.

Korean Views and Pictures Illustrating Native Customs always on Sale,

---

THE OSAKA SHOSEN KAISHA.

Boats frequently on the berth for Chinnampo.

REGULAR SAILINGS BETWEEN JAPAN AND KOREAN PORTS.

FUSAN AND KOBE VIA SHIMONOSEKI.

OSAKA VIA MOKPO, FUSAN, SHIMONOSEKI AND KOBE.

MOJI DIRECT.

OSAKA VIA KUNSAN, MASANPO, FUSAN, SHIMONOSEKI AND KOBE.

CHEMULPO KUNSAN LINE,
Every three days.

CHEMULPO CHINNAMPO LINE.
Every three days.

For Freight and passage and further particulars apply to

THE OSAKA SHOSEN KAISHA,
Chemulpo

RONDON, PLAISANT & CO.

General Storekeepers and Merchants, Ships Contractors, Tobacconists, Commission and Forwarding Agents, Coal Merchants

IMPORTERS AND EXPORTERS.

Seoul & Chemulpo.

W. D. WENTWORTH.

LANDING
AND
SHIPPING AGENT
AND
CUSTOMS BORDER.

12 OURA, NAGASAKI.

STEWARD & CO.

Chemulpo.

Shipchandlers and Storekeepers, Naval and Mercantile Contrrctors, Landing and Shipping Agents.

STEWARD'S HOTEL

Chemulpo.

Best accommodation in the port for travelers. Clean and well-aired rooms, good cuisine and prompt attendence, moderate tariff.

론설

젼쟁의 쟝ᄅᆡ

○지금 젼쟁의 쟝ᄅᆡ 방향에 ᄃᆡᄒᆞ야 의견이 다 다른지라 려슌 함락으로 ᄒᆞ야 ᄯᅢ로 ᄒᆞᆫ 번 종젼지 셜이 셩ᄒᆡᆼᄒᆞ나 그러ᄒᆞ나 우리의 의견으로 논젼에 여러 번 말ᄒᆞᆫ 것과 ᄀᆞᆺ치 려슌 함락으로 ᄒᆞ여 그 평화ᄒᆞᆯ 희망이 더 머러젓다 ᄒᆞ노라

일본 신문들은 말ᄒᆞ되 그 젼쟁이 지금이야 시작이라 ᄒᆞ고 ᄒᆞ고 론돈 면보들은 본 죠국으로 이 젼쟁을 시로이 ᄃᆡ곳 세이계ᄒᆞ기로 결쟁ᄒᆞ엿다 ᄒᆞ논지라

그럼으로 우리는 오ᄅᆡ 기젼에 긴요ᄒᆞᆫ 경쟁을 보기가 확실ᄒᆞ도다 취샹위ᄒᆞ구는 지금 어렷스니 아죵 젼쟁의 범위 안에 넛치 아니ᄒᆞᆯ지라 어렷ᄃᆞ리도 파병과 게로ᄃᆡ들이 능히 나아가겟지마ᄂᆞᆫ 셕다서 ᄃᆞ리가기가 불편ᄒᆞᆯ 듯ᄒᆞ도다 지금 동항ᄃᆡ쟝의 함ᄃᆡ가 려슌 함락홈으로 힘을 낫는 곳시 엽스니 불틱 함ᄃᆡ는 빈와 파게와 군수를 만이 ᄃᆡᄒᆞ기 젼에는 ᄃᆡ젹ᄒᆞ기 어려울 듯ᄒᆞᆫ지라 불틱 함ᄃᆡ가 당초에 ᄒᆞᆫ갈 것이 엽다고 ᄒᆞ는 발이 아니라 지금 계제에 일본 함ᄃᆡ와 ᄃᆡ젹ᄒᆞ기는 강력이 부죡ᄒᆞ리로다 ᄯᅩ 이 함ᄃᆡ들 불너드린다는 풍셜이 셩ᄒᆡᆼᄒᆞ나 그러나 그ᄉᆞ니에 작뎡ᄒᆞᆫ 목적으로 보면 엇던 말을 밋을는지 알 수 엽는지라

봉쟝에셔 젼쟁 최진졈은 봉텬이란 일본군은 ᄒᆞᆫ하 남방에셔 진을 반ᄃᆞᆯ 형용으로 치고 ᄃᆡ젹을 향ᄒᆞ야 잇스며 로군은 일본군의 진과 ᄀᆞᆺ치 되고 그 좌우익이 일본군을 싸고 잇스니 량진이 ᄃᆡ젹ᄒᆞ게 자리를 잡고 ᄯᅩ 지금은 셔치어려셔로히 진을 치기 어려운 ᄃᆡ닭에 엿던 군수던지 이 군수가 져 군수보다 월등이 유ᄒᆞ가 만케 되기 젼에는 누가 면져 싸홈을 시작ᄒᆞ기 어려울 듯ᄒᆞ도다

우리의게는 지금 저켸ᄒᆞ는 것이 다구로팟긴 ᄃᆡ쟝의 마옴ᄃᆡ로 ᄒᆞ는 거스로 뵈이는 거시 이 밋을 만ᄒᆞᆫ 곳으로브터 소문을 드르니 지금 일본군 중에 ᄃᆡᄒᆞ는 군수는 ᄒᆞᆫ미 다 련습지 못ᄒᆞᆫ 군수들이오 구로팟긴 ᄃᆡ쟝은 취음에 ᄃᆡ불교 싸홈을 시작ᄒᆞ던 사이베아의 하동 군수 ᄃᆡ신에 구라파에셔 온 평련 잇는 군수들노 졈졈 치인다는 거슬 우리는 드럿노라

사마ᄃᆡ 근처에셔 연속히 젹은 싸홈이 잇다는 거슨 드르면 고북관으로 어느 곳에던지 로군이 조이 잇는 듯ᄒᆞ도다 지금 구로팟긴 ᄃᆡ쟝은 곳 봉텬 남방으로 향ᄒᆞ야 진젼으로 공격홈은 아죵 ᄇᆡ가 아닌지 즁을 알고 일본군의 동신ᄒᆞ는 길을 엄습ᄒᆞ랴 ᄒᆞ는 듯ᄒᆞ도다

일본군은 만일 ᄃᆡ젹이 엄습ᄒᆞ야 오면 방슈ᄒᆞ랴고 ᄒᆞ는 것 외에는 우리는 다른 말을 듯지 못ᄒᆞ엿노라

관보

뎨삼쳔삼십륙호

광무구년일월십ᄉᆞ일

서임급ᄉᆞ령

○의원면본관 졔쥬목쥬ᄉᆞ 팍인명

○임졔쥬목쥬ᄉᆞ 서판임관륙등 오명후

이상광무팔년구월이십칠일

○의원면본관 ᄂᆡ부쥬ᄉᆞ 김유 ᄂᆡ부쥬ᄉᆞ 젼셕죠

○임ᄂᆡ부쥬ᄉᆞ 서판임관륙등 구픔 하졍식 리인협

이상광무팔년십이월십삼일

○금이금봉 ᄂᆡ부죵두ᄉᆞ의ᄉᆞ 송영진

일월구일

○의원면본관 규장각직학ᄉᆞ 서긍순 옥구항우체ᄉᆞ쥬ᄉᆞ 리쳘호

○임규장각직학ᄉᆞ 서쥬임관이등 죵이픔 남규희

○경임쟝례원쟝례 비서원승 윤쥬셩

○임옥구우체ᄉᆞ쥬ᄉᆞ 서판임관이등 부산우체ᄉᆞ쥬ᄉᆞ 리면젹

○임부산우체ᄉᆞ쥬ᄉᆞ 서판임관륙등 젼쥬ᄉᆞ 리쳘호

○금일금봉 옥구우체ᄉᆞ쥬ᄉᆞ 리면젹

○금삼금봉 부산우체ᄉᆞ쥬ᄉᆞ 리쳘호

이상일월십일일

의원면본관 비서원승 리민ᄯᅴ 홍문관시독 리문구

○홍문관시독 양재팔

○명궁ᄂᆡ부특진관 서칙임관이등 시강원쳠ᄉᆞ 조한국

○명시강원쳠ᄉᆞ 서칙임관이등 비서원경 리재현

○명비서원경 서칙임관이등 궁ᄂᆡ부특진관 박용ᄃᆡ

○임비서원승 서쥬임관륙등 졍삼픔 신셕균

○임홍문관시독 서쥬임관오등 졍삼픔 유명호 죵삼픔 오셩죵

○증죵이픔가션ᄃᆡ부ᄂᆡ부협판 고학셩 김과권

○증졍삼픔통졍ᄃᆡ부비서원승 고학셩 김익경

○증죵삼픔통훈ᄃᆡ부쟝례원좌쟝례 고학셩 김졍구

이상죵이픔가션ᄃᆡ부ᄂᆡ쟝원경 김희원 고조 고증조 고의 법면츄증

○명셔리륙군법원쟝ᄉᆞ무 군법원리ᄉᆞ륙군보병참령 신졔영

○칙관졔리쟝소의쟝판 리비원 김가진 륙군부쟝 리용ᄐᆡ

○명관졔리쟝소의쟝판 의졍부참졍 김셩근 ᄂᆡ부ᄃᆡ신 조병식 군부ᄃᆡ신 리죵건 의졍부참졍 리근호 의졍부참찬 민형식

○임중추원의관 서칙임관삼등 졍이픔 한셩근

○면본관 ᄒᆡ쥬면보ᄉᆞ쥬ᄉᆞ 리죵현

우는 ᄒᆡ원이 막중ᄒᆞᆫ 공회를 파ᄉᆞ나 범ᄒᆞ고 젼ᄉᆞ 면한ᄒᆞ야 샹불쳥감홈은 극섬ᄒᆞᆫ 원이기로 면본관

이상일월십이일

궁뎐륙시

○궁ᄂᆡ부특진관 민영달 ᄌᆞ령소 비지셩소구실이라 하필위인이리오 경은 ᄉᆞ양치 말고 ᄒᆡᆼ공ᄒᆞ라 ᄒᆞ시다

○황ᄒᆡ도관찰ᄉᆞ 조병호 ᄉᆞ직소 비지셩소구실이라 이ᄯᅢ이 ᄀᆞᆺ치 ᄉᆞ양홈이 당치 아니ᄒᆞ니 다시 번거치 말고 곳 등도ᄒᆞ라 ᄒᆞ시다

이상일월십일일

○궁ᄂᆡ부특진관 리쥬영 ᄌᆞ령소 비지셩소구실이라 하필위인이리오 경은 ᄉᆞ양치 말고 ᄒᆡᆼ공ᄒᆞ라 ᄒᆞ시다

○중추원의관 홍병덕 ᄉᆞ직소 비지셩소구실이라 쳥ᄒᆞᆫ 바는 의시ᄒᆞᆫ다 ᄒᆞ옵셧더라

이상일월십이일

잡보

○졍부죠회 의졍부에셔 ᄂᆡ부로 죠회ᄒᆞ기를 디방관을 권ᄂᆞᆫ ᄃᆡ로 칙위셔임ᄒᆞ는 거시 어느 ᄯᅢ든 급젼무가 아니리오마ᄂᆞᆫ 각도에 광겸된 고을이 ᄒᆞ여러 ᄃᆞᆯ도 지벗고 홍 반년도 되엿ᄂᆞᆫᄃᆡ 엇지 췌워셔임치 못ᄒᆞ엿스니 ᄇᆡᆨ셩의 ᄉᆡᆼ계와 나라일에 일시가 위급ᄒᆞ온ᄃᆡ 려ᄒᆞ믈며 시국이 급엽ᄒᆞᆫ ᄯᅢ리오 헝권된 군슈들 불일너로 셔임ᄒᆞᆯ 졍의셔를 ᄯᅡ가 보베여써 경의ᄒᆞᆫ 후에 쥬지ᄒᆞ야 셔임케ᄒᆞ시을 ᄇᆞ라ᄂᆞ라 ᄒᆞ엿더라

○임실화적 음력 십일월 초이일에 임실군 신덕면 고치동에셔 셜화ᄒᆞ야 일동쳘 신상호 가릉슈히 소화ᄒᆞ엿고 림경젼의 세 살 먹은 계집아희도 불에 ᄐᆡ셔 죽엇다더라

○량슈쟝젼 졍평군수 빅병의 쎠희쟝젼은 실수 만쳘젼 오빅칠십삼량이오 범동군슈 구범셔씨의 쟝젼은 ᄉᆞ만쳘쳔량이오 빅미가 상빅ᄉᆞ셤셕이오 슈슈와 죠가이 빅셕이오 닭과 계란은 불가승슈라더라

○초무랍살 광쥬관찰ᄉᆞ가 ᄂᆡ부로 면보ᄒᆞ기를 옥과담보ᄂᆡ가 말ᄒᆞ기를 회민쟝 만영은 본ᄃᆡ 동에셔 항피슈로셔 요헝그룹에 버셔나셔 이변에 음ᄂᆡ에 드러와 ᄒᆡ를 셜시ᄒᆞ고 김이범 리만군 등을 업지로 쳥ᄒᆞ야다가 결박ᄒᆞ고 샥발을 식이빈고 죵슉들이 일졔히 나아와 회민을 구츅ᄒᆞ며 ᄒᆡ산식엿고 아당초에 담샬ᄒᆞᆫ 일은 엉터ᄒᆞ엿고 ᄯᅩ 면보ᄒᆞ기를 회민이 각군에 흣허가셔 지회를 분셜ᄒᆞ고 슈빅명은 그냥 부하에 머믈너 잇셔도 회소들 짓ᄂᆞᆫ다 ᄒᆞ오며 방금 부케서는 ᄉᆞᄉᆞ로 폐무ᄒᆞ고 잇ᄂᆞᆫᄃᆡ 포폄셩취ᄒᆞᆯ 방송ᄒᆞ기는 ᄒᆞ오나 황송ᄒᆞ다 ᄒᆞ엿더라

○참모부죠회 참모부에셔 ᄂᆡ부로 죠회ᄒᆞ기를 삼남각도에 증포관이 잇ᄂᆞᆫ 고을에 약간 병뎡을 파송ᄒᆞ야 방죠ᄒᆞ야 달나고 쳥ᄒᆞᆫ 일로 회칙 각군과 부군에 잇ᄂᆞᆫ 진위ᄃᆡ 병뎡즁에셔 각ᄉᆞ명식 파송ᄒᆞ라 ᄒᆞ고 군부로 지죠ᄒᆞ엿노라 ᄒᆞ엿더라

○룩의젼호소 룩지비젼은 곳 공ᄉᆞ간에 협셜ᄒᆞᆫ 젼이라 경쟝이 젼에ᄂᆞᆫ 각 드림젼문건을 지비젼에셔 ᄉᆞ지ᄒᆞ고 분ᄂᆞᆯ 밧아셔 인샨ᄒᆞᆯ ᄯᅢ가 되면 여ᄉᆞ군을 의뢰ᄒᆞ게 ᄒᆡᆼᄒᆞ더니 드림젼을 임의로 셜립ᄒᆞ야 폐지된 이후에ᄂᆞᆫ 란젼법도 ᄌᆞ연 [illegible] 구젼이 영영 [illegible] ᄒᆞ야 분을 도로 밧게 ᄒᆞ라 ᄒᆞ엿더라

○탁항즁지 젼참졍 신샹훈씨가 [illegible] ᄒᆞ엿더라

○[illegible]

○탁지부훈죠 탁지부셔 각부부원쳥에 훈죠회ᄒᆞ기를 구년도 셰출 예산을 지금 편즁ᄒᆞ엿ᄂᆞᆫᄃᆡ 귀부소관 각년도 경비중에 용하와 밋여에 ᄒᆞ하나로 결산ᄒᆞ지 못ᄒᆞ엿고 세로 편셩ᄒᆞᆫ 비목을 지금 ᄯᅩ 지출ᄒᆞ오면 실딘로 지발ᄒᆞᆫ 거사실ᄒᆞᆯ 문란ᄒᆞ야 부분부를 리졍ᄒᆞᆯ 이 미우 말유ᄒᆞᆯ지니 각년도 부ᄅᆞᆯ 속히 결산ᄒᆞ여 보내라 ᄒᆞ엿더라

광고

○본인의 쟝ᄌᆞ 치렬이가 본시 부랑패류로 그 부형ᄌᆞ데 간에 분쥐도 ᄒᆞ여 가진 면장문권을 수히도 적ᄒᆞ여 너엿기로 세부등이 ᄒᆞ야 시문권을 드른엇고 이에 광포ᄒᆞ오니 ᄂᆡ외국인 간에 샹가 쇽지 말고 한치렬의 가진 문권을 면집지 마옴 기른바라옴

평양셩ᄂᆡ 쌍거리 한과현 고ᄇᆡᆨ

TELEGRAMS.

Army Headquarters, Seoul, Jan. 14th.

On the 12th inst our patrol in the neighbourhood of Honan (Yalu district) discovered a body of 14 Russians approaching. They were fired upon and three were killed.

(FROM JAPAN PAPERS.)

London, Jan. 9.

Reuter's correspondent at St. Petersburg states that the following vessels will leave Libau between January 28th and February 2nd to join Admiral Rohjestvensky's Squadron :—The battleship "Imperator Nicolai I." (9,700 tons); the coast-defence ironclads "General Admiral Apraksin," "Admiral Seniavine," and "Admiral Oushakoff" (all of 4,126 tons), and the armoured cruiser "Vladimir Monomakh" (about 5,600 tons).

London, Jan. 9.

The wave of popular emotion first caused in St. Petersburg by the news of the surrender of Port Arthur has already subsided, the Christmas festival having created a diversion of attention on the part of the public, which is joyously celebrating the festival in theatres, music-halls, restaurants, and taverns.

On the other hand, funeral services held at the Isaac and Kasan Cathedrals in memory of the soldiers and sailors who have fallen at Port Arthur have been very poorly attended.

London, Jan. 5.

Lord Selborne, speaking ot Wolverhampton, said that we must regard both Russians and Japanese with the most profound respect. It is comparatively easy to admire the Japanese; they are our allies, and we do admire them without restraint or reserve, but it would ill become us if we did not admire the Russians equally.

London, Jan. 5.

In reference to the statement that there is to be an inquiry into the surrender of Port Arthur, the "Novoe Vremya" declares :—

"Let us have a court-martial by all means; then we shall discover why the fortress was unsupplied with food and ammunition, and who are Russia's real enemies, infinitely more dangcrous than the Japanese."

The "Melita" is due in Chemulpo from Shanghai on Wednesday the 18th and will sail for Shanghai again or Saturday the 21st inst.

Some members of the Kong-chin-hoi (a society which vainly tried to oppose the favoured Il-chin-hoi) have been sentenced to banishment to the island of Chulto.

The Korean Government apparently finds it impossible to bring the Governor of North Pyeng-yang province to justice. All instuctions to him to return to Seoul are met with the reply that the Japanese will not permit him to leave. There is a warm time in store for the Governor of North Pyeng Yang.

Country members of the Il-chin-hoi, who have not yet heard that their sevices are not wanted for the present are still pouring into Seoul. They are being sent back to their homes but in the meantime it becomes apparent that the Japanese will have a nice white elephant on their hands in the near future.

According to Tokio telegrams the Russian right wing outposts have made a very effective raid down the Hun river. On the 11th inst. a few cavalry, under cover of darkness descended on the Japanese communications between Yinkow and Liaoyang and slightly damaged the railway at Aushantien, Haicheng and Tashicho, while on the 12th 8 companies(?) of Russian cavalry with 12 guns appeared at Ninchiatun. On the 13th the same detachment invaded and occupied Newchwang but were, according to a Japanese report, subsequently driven out again.

SEEING THROUGH TELEPHONES.

Particulars of a long-sought-for invention, whereby a person speaking through the telephone can see the person at the other end of the line, are given by the "New York American." That journal states that a scientist of Portland, Oregon, has succeeded, after years of labour, in perfecting the invention, and incredulous visitors to his house are able to see the features of the people they are talking with by looking into a little arrangement just under the telephone mouthpiece, which looks like the front end of a large camera.

The invention is to be patented all over the world, and until this is done full details of the new telephone attachment will not be made public.

It has new been demonstrated, says the journal, that the mirage rays which convey the reflection are operative for hundreds of miles.

The visible parts of the telephone now in use by the intentor are very similar to those in an ordinary telephone. The only noticeable addition is a camera-like attachment just like the front of a kodak with a magnifying lens in the centre. This lens is about three inches above the telephone mouthpiece, so that a person talking can see his reflection in the lens.

Above the lens there is a small incandescent light, which is only used while the person at the telephone is looking intently at the transmitting lens and getting his reflection into perfect focus. When he has done this he can turn out the light, taking care, however, not to sway or move from his position during the ensuing conversation. If he does so the reflection in the transmitting lens becomes hazy and appears so at the other end. How the image is conveyed is the inventor's secret.

KOREA.

A JAPANESE VIEW OF COLONISATION.

Discussions about Korea are now as plentiful and frequent as cries of "Banzai" in the streets. One of the most interesting of these appears in the last number of the "Jidai Shicho." It is from the pen of Mr. T. Yokoi, who is a graduate of the Doshisha College, and afterwards proceeded to America to complete his education. On his return Mr. Yokoi was for a time Editor of the "Osaka Shimpo." He is now a member of the Diet, and was one of the Commission which visited India on a commercial investigation.

Mr Yokoi says that whether Korea be annexed to Japan or be placed under a Japanese protectorate, it is equally essential that Japan should aim at reaping practical benefits from the present situation and not merely an empty name. The Koreans may be brought under Japanese rule, but that circumstance alone will not much benefit Japan. Not much is to be expected of a people so corrupt and destitute of the spirit of progress as the Koreans have proved themselves to be. In order to make Japan's position in Korea sufficiently strong to successfully resist any encroachment that may be made on the country Japan must take up its defence herself. For this purpose the importance of the colonisation of Korea by Japanese must suggest itself to every thoughtful mind. In Korea there are vast tracts of fertile land lying fallow and uncultivated, while in Japan there is a large surplus population, well adapted to agricultural pursuits, increasing at a considerable rate. Korea is too important a field for the future welfare of Japan to remain a mere hunting ground for reckless speculators and political adventurers. If Japan fail to establish in Korea a system ensuring the future safety of the Empire, the blood of her brave sons will have been shed in vain. The question, then, is how Japan can accomplish the colonisation of the peninsula most successfully.

No reliable statistics are obtainable in Korea, but, in the opinion of Mr. Yokoi, there is at least one million of "Cho" of land suitable for cultivation. Besides, there is a large extent of land under cultivation that may be bought from the natives. As to climate the conditions greatly differ in the north and the south of Korea. Generally speaking, however, the climate is better suited to agriculture than the Hokkaido. In the event of the Japanese taking up the work in earnest and introducing improvements as regards irrigation and drainage, the soil will become more fertile than at present and the production will be proportionately increased. The cultivation of rice, wheat and barley, cotton, millet, and almost any kind of agricultural produce are well adapted to the soil. For instance, the cultivation of "genseng," one of the important products of Korea, is not unsuited to the Japanese farmer, while there is every prospect that agriculture in Korea will prove a success under Japanese management, Supposing an area of five "cho" on an average is placed at the disposal of each Japanese settler, a million "cho" will give room for 200,000 families. Even if the number is cut down to one-half Korea offers a field for 100,000 families. If 100,000 Japanese farming families settle in Korea, it would be safe to assume that there would be about an equal number of families engaged in other lines of occupation. These 200,000 families, assuming each to have inmates on an average, would mean a population of a million people. The presence in Korea of a million of Japanese loyal and devoted to their country, may at least be taken as a substantial guarantee to ensure the "independence" of Korea and be depended upon as a strong bulwark in case of emergency.

Mr. Yokoi then proceeds to consider the best means of colonisation. He urges the Government to do everything in its power to encourage Japanese emigration into Korea. If sufficient inducements are offered there is little doubt, thinks the writer, that Japanese tenant farmers will go over to the peninsula to settle. To begin with, the Government should pay part of the expenses required for emigration, and devise means by which the land allotted to each farmer for cultivation should become his property under certain conditions. It is advisable, says Mr. Yokoi, that the Japanese Government should adopt in this respect a policy similar to that which the German Government is pursuing in Poland. An institution under the special protection of the Government may be started for the purpose of giving practical effect to Japanese emigration. Something after the system of the Reuters' Bank of Germany, which has been conducted with so much success for the last few years, may with advantage be introduced for the encouragement of Japanese emigration into Korea. At first it would be necessary for the Government to lease dwellings to the settlers and assist them with advances of the necessary capital so as to enable them to start in their occupation. And measures should be adopted so that these advances may be refunded within a reasonable period of time in the shape of land rent, after which the land should become the property of the respective cultivators. If the Government could devise such means as are suggested above, there is every probability that many Japanese tenant farmers, whose present lot is by no means good, will be induced to avail themselves of the offer. Every year many Japanese farmers cross the sea to Hawaii and America, not with the object of living permanently in those countries with their families, but in order to save what money they can earn by the sweat of their brow and then return home. Things, however, are greatly different as regards Korea. Not only is the peninsula situated in close proximity to Japan, but the general conditions of life there are well adapted to colonisation by the Japanese. If the Government could accomplish the emigration of Japanese into the peninsula in sufficient force to make their presence a potent factor, a foundation for Japanese supremacy in Korea will be firmly estalished.

(To be Continued.)

The O. S. K. made a net profit of yen 1,052,681 in the five months ending the 30th ult.

Defalcations on the part of several magistrates in the provinces are coming to light. Evidently someone up to their little tricks is giving an eye to things.

On the 12th instant Messrs. Hayashi, Megata and Stevens called on the vice-Minister for Home Affairs and had an interview of several hours duration. It is believed that the consultation arose out of the impending departure of M. Delcoigne, adviser to this department.

Mr. Kanno, a Secretary in the Finance Department, and Mr. Yamagata, a specialist in the Imperial Mint at Osaka, have, says the "Kobe Chronicle" been ordered to visit Korea. The business of Mr. Kanno is to report on the condition of the banking business, while Mr. Yamagata is to make inquiries as to the disposal of the machinery of the Korean Mint, which has recently been closed.

The new Chief of police is certainly going vigourously to work. Following upon his campaign against "Devil" shrines, their proprietors and patrons, he gives notice that all men able to work who are found begging will be taken charge of by the police and provided with sufficient exercise to keep them warm. Consequent upon this, says our Korean reporter, most ot the beggars commenced to work themselves aad some of them became soldiers!

The Korea Daily News.

Issued at 5 P. M. daily except Sundays.

Rate of Subscription:—
Per Year,............Yen 25.
Per Quarter,..........Yen 7.
Per Month,..........Yen 2.50.

Postage in Korea not charged extra.
Postage abroad charged extra.

Advertisements, 50 sen per day for 1 inch or less.
5 yen per month per inch.
50 yen per year per inch.

All communications to

E. T. BETHELL,
Editor and Publisher,
Pak-tong, Seoul.

THE SUBJUGATION OF KOREA.

The Il-chin-hoi is at present fairly quiet; the country members have been ordered to return to their homes and there is no particular activity observable amongst the Seoul contingent.

They have, however, already made themselves of considerable use to the Japanese. Taking advantage of the disturbances of which this society was the cause, General Hasegawa has found an excuse to assume control of the Seoul police administration and has also declared that no further societies may be formed without his consent.

Thus it will be seen that the Japanese have deprived the Koreans of any means of expressing their opinions on current events, and it is safe to say that however disagreeable the measures which Japan may in future ask the Korean Government to adopt or accede to, there cannot be a repetition of the outburst of popular indignation which was evoked some time ago by the attempts to obtain Imperial consent to the Nagamori demands.

We presume we may take the article from the "Jidai Shicho," which we reproduce in another column, as representative of a considerable proportion of Japanese public opinion. At all events we can say this; we go to considerable trouble to keep ourselves posted on all that appears about Korea in the Japanese newspapers, and we never come across an article where the Koreans themselves are taken into account as a factor worth consideration. Sometimes, it is true, the possibility of opposition from the Korean Government is discussed, but the fate of the farmers and others who are to be dispossessed of what the Japanese wish to acquire is but rarely mentioned.

The proposals of the "Jidai Shicho" are on the same lines as those of Nagamori, the essential part of both schemes being the acquisition and complete control by Japan, of vast tracts of agricultural land.

This would of course be in direct opposition to Japan's treaties with both Great Britain and Korea, but as the Japanese seem determined to persevere in their demands until they have "obtained" the consent of the Korean Government it will be interesting to review, briefly, the influences which are, and have been, at work. Last Spring, public attention was directed to a demand which a Mr. Nagamori (formerly a Japanese Government official) was making upon the Korean Government for the cession to him, his heirs or assigns, of all the land in Korea not at that time under cultivation. The area of the proposed concession was not known but, was variously estimated at from one half to two thirds of the whole country. The terms were such that it would have been practically impossible for Korea ever to have recovered the land again.

Finding that Mr. Nagamori was not making much headway, the Japanese Government frankly adopted the scheme as their own and spared nothing and nobody in their efforts to put it into effect.

As soon as the Koreans realized the nature of the demands which were being made upon their country, there was a great outcry, mass meetings were held and protests poured in upon the Government from all quarters.

The meetings were of the most orderly character, their sole purpose being to protest against the granting of the Japanese Government's demands, yet the meetings were dispersed by the Japanese Gendarmerie, martial law was proclaimed by the Japanese, and many of the speakers at the meetings were arrested and some of them have, so far as we know, not since been heard of.

In the meantime a Japanese named Komochi, had got together a few Koreans and made arrangements with them for the formation of Society of Koreans, called the Il-chin-hoi, pledged to support Japanese demands and proposals. This society consists of the riff-raff of Seoul and its neighbourhood and is in Japanese pay and under the protection of Japanese Gendarmerie. The alleged object of the society is reform but its real purpose is to harrass and menace the Government.

Recently, seditious speeches having been made, Korean soldiery made an attempt to disperse one of these meetings but were prevented from achieving their purpose by Japanese Gendarmes. In the fray one or two of the Il-chin-hoi people were wounded.

There have been no other signs of disturbance or disorder in Seoul yet the Japanese took advantage of this incident to proclaim a more rigorous form of martial law, assume control of the Seoul police and promulgate regulations prohibiting the holding of meetings or the establishment of Societies.

It will be seen that the Japanese have now not only effectually provided against any public protest against their schemes, but have at their beck and call a large number of Koreans pledged to support them.

Therefore should the Japanese attempt to obtain the consent of the Korean Government to proposals similar to those of Mr. Nagamori of the "Jidai Shicho" it must not be imagined that the absence of any public demonstration against them indicates any change of public sentiment in Korea.

A LETTER FROM THE FRONT.

[FROM THE "GLOBE'S" ST. PETERSBURG CORRESPONDENT.]

Letters from soldiers at the front continue to find their way into the Russian Press at home. Thus, the "*Moskoffskaya Viedomosti*" publishes some interesting extracts from a private letter sent home by a horse-soldier serving with General Mischtshenko at the end of August.

"It is quite impossible for me to answer all your questions; firstly, because we who are on the flank of our main forces know far less about the general position than you are told by telegrams; and secondly, because there is really no time to carry on a long correspondence. Judge for yourself, how can a man write a letter; I lay in ambush for three days, and yesterday and to-day I have had to ride round with the patrols. And when one can rest a while, one is far too tired to think about taking up a pen. Scouting duty has to be done very often, and the work is hard and full of responsibility. Once I was out with a patrol of line Cossacks for four days hanging on the Japanese flank.

"I must confess that I have known scarely where I was, for the lie of the land is so very confusing; nothing but big hills, and then more big hills; and, to make matters worse, they are of such a kind that you cannot lead along a second horse by its bridle. Our maps are certainly not conspicuous for their accuracy, and it is said that the Japanese possess maps of greater accuracy and made with more care. Still, I do not believe this altogether, for only after many years of serious topographical work could the local peculiarities be studied and reduced to paper. Moreover, that the enemy is not better off in this respect than we are is proved by the fact that photographic enlargements of our two-verst map have been found among the plunder taken from them.

"Our little horses are but very poor things at the best, and I am driven to envy the carriers at home; still, thank God that we have at least some sort of horse. So far we have not been able to get hold of any Japanese horses, for the Japanese cavalry is really too careful for anything, and it never advances one step without being supported by the infantry. However, the greater number of the Japanese horses are quite run down; our regiment has one of these horses which was captured by the Cossacks. It is said that the Japanese are improving their horses. As a matter of fact, I came across half of a Japanese squadron while scouting the other day, so far as I could make out, all their horses were in very good condition. I had only eight Cossacks with me, and only the hills enabled us to escape the foe.

"We had a little fight a few days ago; unfortunately I could not be in it, for I had been told off with a detachment to prevent the Japanese from surprising us on our flank, a movement which they love dearly to make. I really do not know why, to judge from the newspapers that so rarely reach us, our correspondents praise everything that is Japanese, especially their treatment of our wounded and prisoners. According to my observations, they are in many cases, if not in all, no better than the Chunchuses. I am writing this letter to you, but I cannot tell when I shall manage to get it sent off, for the Flying Post comes by us very rarely, and when it does happen to go by, it is quite likely that I may be out scouting somewhere. If you do get this letter, please don't forget us, and do write. But, and this is the great thing, don't drive us wild by your horribly sad letters, which are full of pessimism. Without your doleful lamentations, there is quite enough pessimism which reaches us, and which praises everything Japanese and sees only the bad with regard to Russia. At any rate, most of our men here are young and still novices, for they have arrived but recently from European Russia, and so far the gloomy view of the view of the position which they acquired from you at home has not had time to evaporate yet. Just wait and we shall see what they will say when they have become fully acquainted with the hardships and difficulties to which we have grown accustomed long since. We men who have served in this Cossack detachment almost ever since the war broke out have not given way to pessimism; no, on the contrary, we are quite ready to see a well-thought-out plan of the campaign against the Japanese brought to a brilliant end."

RAILWAY OPEN.

The Chang Teh-fu to Shun Teh-fu section of the Peking-Hankow railway has been completed and opened to traffic.

The British Red Cross Society has sent Sir Claude MacDonald by telegraph a sum of £5,000 for the Japanese sick and wounded, in addition to the £2,000 previously sent.

An important gold discovery is announced by Sir William Milton, Administrator of Southern Rhodesia, about 200 miles south of Salisbury, 200 miles east of Bulawayo, and about 75 miles from the railhead at Selukwe. The company's territory is as large as the whole of Europe, leaving out Russia.

The Korea  

VOL. II, MONDAY, JANUARY 16, 1905. No. 11

大韓每日申報
대한ᄆᆡ일신보

(뎨이권십이호) (슈요일) 일쳔구ᄇᆡᆨ오년일월십팔일

본샤고ᄇᆡᆨ

이신보는영어와한어로섯거ᄆᆡ일츌판ᄒᆞᄋᆞᆸ

신문가

한쟝 엽두돈오푼
일삭됴 엽두량닷돈
우표가ᄆᆡ삭닷돈
다맛돈으로밧ᄉᆞᆸ

광고료는

긔한의쟝단과ᄌᆞ힝의다쇼로증감ᄒᆞ되렴가로밧을터이오며오ᄅᆡ지아녀대한사람마다다이신문을보실터이니광고내시기를원ᄒᆞ시는이들은우리신문샤에와서면약ᄒᆞ심을회망ᄒᆞᄋᆞᆸ

○발힝소 박동대한ᄆᆡ일신보샤법어학교압혜젼영국인셜필림집자리오

샤쟝 영국인 (비셜)

평양 ᄃᆡ리졈

○평양효동사는권ᄆᆡ보씨로우리신문관ᄃᆡ리인을뎡ᄒᆞ엿ᄉᆞ오니평양에계신구람코져ᄒᆞ시는쳠군ᄌᆞ는ᄃᆡ리졈에왕림ᄒᆞ와면회ᄒᆞ시ᄋᆞᆸ

사고

○우리대한ᄆᆡ일신보의목뎍은대한의안녕질서에관한모든대목에ᄃᆡᄒᆞ야는공평한변론을쥬쟝ᄒᆞᆷ이라우리동신원의탐보는신문보시는쳠군ᄌᆞ의게ᄒᆞᆼ상보도ᄒᆞ리며편지를긔셔ᄒᆞ여주시는이는셩명과반디를젹어붓치시기를회망ᄒᆞ오니이거슬신문쟝에긔지ᄒᆞ라는거시아니오다만극히신용ᄒᆞ는증거를숨고쟈ᄒᆞᆷ이라긔쟈는아모긔셔던지긔ᄌᆡᄒᆞᆷ을되각ᄒᆞ는권리를가졋스나되각ᄒᆞ는리유를말ᄒᆞᆯ터이오며공즁평화를문란케ᄒᆞ는듯ᄒᆞᆫ긔셔는의례히밧지안켓ᄉᆞᆸ나이다

●본샤셜시어리로신문을ᄆᆡ양우례로분젼ᄒᆞ와례젼부의임의로젼ᄒᆞᆫ듯ᄒᆞ스로면곳에는혹늣게젼ᄒᆞ기도ᄒᆞ며혹멋칠거슬ᄒᆞᆫ겁에젼ᄒᆞ기도ᄒᆞ며혹아니젼ᄒᆞ는곳도잇다ᄒᆞ와우리신문을ᄉᆞ랑ᄒᆞ야구람ᄒᆞ시는 쳠군ᄌᆞ의게ᄃᆡᄒᆞ야ᄆᆡ우미안ᄒᆞᄋᆞᆸ거로지금온분젼인을두고ᄆᆡ일일즉이젼ᄒᆞ며아니젼ᄒᆞ거나늣게거나ᄒᆞᆫ폐가업도록ᄒᆞ랴ᄒᆞ오니혹아니젼ᄒᆞ거나혹늣게젼ᄒᆞ거나ᄒᆞᆫ일이잇스면본샤로통긔ᄒᆞ여쥬심을회망ᄒᆞᄋᆞᆸ

잡보

○함찰보고 함경관찰사가외부로면보ᄒᆞ기를홍원군슈보고ᄂᆡ개에본군룡쳔샤평포졈에아라사사름이쳐셔윤집에면보샤를셜시ᄒᆞᆫ다ᄒᆞ엿기에이에보고ᄒᆞᆫ다ᄒᆞ엿더라

○고히교 ᄂᆡ부고문관ᄃᆡ일광씨가ᄌᆞ원ᄒᆞᆷ으로쟝찻청원ᄒᆞᆯ터인ᄃᆡ히안건은법국공사와외부에셔교셥ᄒᆞ야관리ᄒᆞᆫ다더라

○일ᄉᆞ합쳥 면관 리용ᄐᆡᆨ씨가ᄂᆡ부대신으로잇슬때에회쳔군슈리ᄐᆡᆨ직씨가ᄂᆡ부로공함ᄒᆞ기를현금일본이일진회를발긔ᄒᆞ야쳐쳐에분요ᄒᆞ야점점ᄌᆞ만ᄒᆞ니이거슨한청량국을병탄ᄒᆞ랴는계교라급속히계교를버프려민회를타파ᄒᆞ자ᄒᆞ고긴밀히붓첫더니히도일본병참소에셔히공함을집류ᄒᆞ고징거를삼아리ᄐᆡᆨ직씨를곳압슈ᄒᆞᆫ지라일본공ᄉᆞ가히공함을쳠련ᄒᆞ야ᄂᆡ부로공문ᄒᆞ고히군슈를면관ᄒᆞ라ᄒᆞ엿더라

○리씨방면 젼라도젼어ᄉᆞ리승욱씨와허도젼관찰ᄉᆞ리완용씨가공납ᄉᆞ건으로셔로취탁ᄒᆞᆫ야샹지ᄒᆞ미리관찰의세력이우승ᄒᆞᆷ으로리어ᄉᆞ가오려감옥셔에가쳐서신원을ᄒᆞ지못ᄒᆞ고여라번지관ᄒᆞ야월젼에리어ᄉᆞ가보방이되엿더니법부에셔히안건을관결ᄒᆞ야리어ᄉᆞ를영영방면ᄒᆞ엿더라

○외합츌입 인쳔감리가외부로ᄒᆞᆫ면보를거ᄒᆞᆫ즉십이일에는덕국병함일쳑이츌항ᄒᆞ엿고십삼일에는미국병함일쳑이입항ᄒᆞ엿다더라

○젼찰면보 젼라북도관찰ᄉᆞ가ᄂᆡ부로면보ᄒᆞ기를김제군교유팔인이의병을이르키고져ᄒᆞᆫ다ᄒᆞ고회민들이착거ᄒᆞ야악형을ᄒᆞᆫ다는본군모이가잇기로회민두목이명을착슈ᄒᆞ엿다ᄒᆞ엿더라

○장명되거 찬졍 최익현씨가소명을승ᄒᆞ야샹경ᄒᆞ야시졍ᄀᆡ션에관ᄒᆞᆫᄉᆞ건을직언으로츙간ᄒᆞ고실시ᄒᆞ기를ᄃᆡ명ᄒᆞ더니근일신병으로흠신ᄒᆞᆫ다ᄒᆞ는데작일에ᄉᆞ직ᄒᆞ고언ᄉᆞ소ᄉᆞ지ᄒᆞᆫ지라향제로되거ᄒᆞ라ᄒᆞᄋᆞᆸ신다더라

○경ᄉᆞ셜명 일진회에셔연삼일총ᄃᆡ를경무청에파송ᄒᆞ야경찰에발으지아니ᄒᆞᆫ일은질문ᄒᆞ고공졍ᄒᆞᆫ일은권고ᄒᆞᆷ이신경ᄉᆞ가리유면말을셰셰설명ᄒᆞ엿더라

○제슈비군졸 경효면조석샹식과 의효면샹식제슈비는ᄆᆡ에일쳔이ᄇᆡᆨ량식이요 효혜젼제슈비는ᄆᆡ일이ᄇᆡᆨ량에불과ᄒᆞ는ᄃᆡ진즉디발치아니ᄒᆞᆷ으로곤란ᄒᆞ다더라

○고문도한 경무청에고문관을셜치ᄒᆞ기로확졍이된지라히고문관의일본사ᄅᆞᆷ이도한ᄒᆞ엿다더라

○갱위리졍 리졍ᄒᆞᆫ관제를샹쥬ᄒᆞ엿더니 샹이불긍ᄒᆞ시는고로아즉반포치못ᄒᆞ고히리졍ᄒᆞᆫ안건을다소간별경ᄒᆞ야다시리졍ᄒᆞᆫ다더라

○김포군보 김포군슈가외부로보고ᄒᆞ기를본군반월포에류목ᄉᆞᄆᆡ가잇서히동리에리박ᄒᆞ엿기그동에류쳐ᄒᆞ엿더니본월십이일밤에일본사ᄅᆞᆷ샹야길ᄃᆡ랑이가우리나라ᄇᆡᆨ셩오륙명을거나리고리도ᄒᆞ야류쥬목을차자가며또돈일만량을요구ᄒᆞ며그힝픽가무소부지ᄒᆞ고로부득이ᄒᆞ여겨우일쳔량을관급ᄒᆞᆫ사로민쇼서지잇스니바라건ᄃᆡ곳일관에지죠ᄒᆞ여샹야길ᄃᆡ랑을잡아다가히류쥬목을차진후에견탈ᄒᆞᆫ일쳔량을곳차자쥬라ᄒᆞ엿더라

○죠쳥즁감 군부에셔외부에죠회ᄒᆞ기를헌병안윤명횡신영이가복차교셔편으로숩힝ᄒᆞ다가본즉쳥인교평의집에기국을설ᄒᆞ고평양병뎡일명과쳔위ᄃᆡ병뎡일명이또ᄒᆞᆫ잡기를ᄒᆞ는고로히병등을잡아오려ᄒᆞᆯ지음에쳥인등이칼노안가헌병을쳐즁샹ᄒᆞ미ᄯᅥ메여왓고황가병뎡도ᄯᅩᄒᆞᆫ샹ᄒᆞ여유혈이랑자ᄒᆞ즁쳥인등이모ᄒᆞ자와군도를탈취ᄒᆞ고주지아니ᄒᆞ나량국교제ᄒᆞ는의에엇지이ᄀᆞᆺ치무리ᄒᆞᆫ일이잇스리오청용사의게지죠ᄒᆞ여히물건을곳차자돌녀보내고히쳠인등을또ᄒᆞᆫ즁감에쳐ᄒᆞᆷ을바란다ᄒᆞ엿더라

○평양민소 평양민리창셜등이외부에등소ᄒᆞ기를무릇셔를건축ᄒᆞ고관원을설치ᄒᆞᆷ은그싱민의보호ᄒᆞ기를위ᄒᆞᆷ이어놀감리셔쥬사원용덕이가본ᄃᆡ간리에나마지솜시ᄅᆞᆫ거관삼년에금십만을엇고또김득슈옥안시에로식ᄒᆞᆫ돈이또ᄒᆞᆫ오쳔여량인ᄃᆡ평양ᄇᆡᆨ셩이무손죄과가잇관ᄃᆡ그허를입으리오이원쥬사를관민다론항구감리셔로이송ᄒᆞ여졍을편케ᄒᆞ심을쳔만바란다ᄒᆞ엿더라

○최씨퇴거 군부대신리죵건씨는ᄯᅩ사직샹쇼ᄒᆞᆫ다ᄒᆞ며찬졍최익현씨는소미에셔샹소를내니밧쳔후에 샹이불윤ᄒᆞ시면몸으로써나라일에죽는다ᄒᆞ여포덕문밧게업ᄯᅳ렷더니십오일에지차사직샹소ᄒᆞ고두셔동사쳐로퇴거ᄒᆞ엿더라

뎐보

론돈발 일월륙일

○로함잡보 로제벤스트벤스기대쟝의긔함은침몰ᄒᆞ엿다고젼파ᄒᆞ더니그후로다시드른즉허언이라ᄒᆞ며풀거삼ᄃᆡ장의령솔ᄒᆞᆫ볼틱함ᄃᆡ의ᄒᆞᆫ부본에쏠닌슌양함이쳑이쏠슈업시파샹ᄒᆞᆫ야곳치게도못ᄒᆞ게되엿다ᄒᆞ고로제스트벤스기ᄃᆡ장의함ᄃᆡ는로국으로곳불너드리라고ᄒᆞᆫ대는말이잇다더라

ᄇᆡᆨ림발 동일

○로함슈명 볼틱함ᄃᆡ는다시명령ᄒᆞ기전에는마가스카을ᄯᅥ나지말나는훈칙을바럿다더라

론돈발 동일

○로장임명 히삽위함대ᄉᆞ령관으로잇던스크리드로프대쟝은척령으로히군ᄃᆡ쟝회의소의위명ᄒᆞ엿다더라

론돈발 일월륙일

○로국결심 로국황뎨ᄭᅴ셔작일에싸고셀노라는ᄯᅡ에셔어젼회의를열고의론ᄒᆞ야구로팟킨대쟝의게명령ᄒᆞ야대산대쟝을공격ᄒᆞ라ᄒᆞ기로결졍ᄒᆞ엿다더라

동더발 동일

○로국의졍 론돈스틘다드신문의셩피득보동신원의보고를

UNION INSURANCE SOCIETY OF CANTON.

Head office Hongkong.
Marine risks underwritten at current rates.
Agents in Chemulpo.
E. MEYER & Co.

COMPAGNIE DES MESSAGERIES MARITIMES.

Fortnightly Direct Service.

For Marseilles
via Ports.
Sailing from Yokohama
Calling at Kobe,
Shanghai, Hongkong, Saigon, Singapore,
Colombo, Djibonti, Suez, Port Said
and Marseilles.

For particulars apply to
HOLME RINGER & Co.,
Chemulpo.

HAYASHIDA & CO.,

16 MYENG DONG, CHIN KO KAI, SEOUL.
BRANCH OFFICE AT CHEMULPO.

Money changers, Coal and Wood Merchants,
Express Agents.

We are agents for the Pyeng-yang Coal Company and the Karazu Coal Company of Japan. We have the best quality of both anthracite and bituminous coal, and prompt execution of orders is our speciality. Firewood of all kinds kept in stock. Full weight guaranteed. Money of all denominations exchanged at current rates. Parcels received for all parts.

CHINA MUTUAL LIFE INS. OC.

Most favourable terms to policy holders

Benefit system unsurpassed.

HOLME RINGER & Co.
Agents, Chemulpo.

C. P. R.

CANADIAN PACIFIC RAILWAY COMPANY'S ROYAL MAIL STEAMSHIP LINE.

THE FAST ROUTE BETWEEN CHINA, JAPAN, AND EUROPE VIA CANADA AND THE UNITED STATES.

Route from Hongkong via Shanghai, Nagasaki (Inland Sea of Japan) Kobe, Yokohama, Victoria and Vancouver.

Twin Screw Empress Steamship—6,000 Tons—Speed 19 knots.

PROPOSED SAILING FROM YOKOHAMA.
R. M. S. Empress of India.
R. M. S. Empress of Japan.
R. M. S. Empress of China.
R. M. S. Athenian.
R. M. S. Tartar.

Special reduction (first class only) granted to members of the Military, Naval, Diplomatic and Civil services and to Missionaries.

Passengers have choice of ten routes across the Continent of America and have privilege of travelling by any Atlantic Steamship Line.

Round the World passage tickets in connection with the P. and O. S. N., North German Lloyd and Messageries Co.'s £125.

All rates payable at current rate of exchange.

For further information, Tickets, Guide Books, etc., apply to

HOLME, RINGER & Co., AGENTS,
Chemulpo.

Grand Hotel,

(Formerly the Station Hotel)

Near the Railway Terminus,
West Gate Seoul.

The Best Hotel in Korea.
Handsome new Building.
Fine Airy Rooms
Excellent Cuisine.
Terms Moderate.
Special terms to Missionaries
and to permanent boarders.

Electric cars within 2 minutes' walk.

W. H. EMBERLEY.
Proprietor

EVERY FACILITY.

In connection with Life Assurance Business is afforded by

The Standard Life Assurance Co.,

One of the largest and wealthiest of the Provident Institutions of the United Kingdom Forms of Application and all information will be promptly afforded on application.

10 CENTS A DAY.

Not a very large expenditure is it? But it is sufficient to secure for a man of 30 a policy with the STANDARD LIFE OFFICE for

$1323.

For all particulars of rates, etc., apply to

Holme, Ringer & Co.,
Agents, Chemulpo.

THE NEW YORK LIFE INSURANCE COMPANY.

Have you ever been declined by any Company?

Are you engaged in a specially hazardous occupation?

Have you heard of the New York Life Insurance Company's New Classifications for this class of Risks?

If not, send your date of birth, occupation and particulars of rejection, if any to

E. MEYER & Co.,
Agents, Chemulpo.

MITSUI BUSSAN KAISHA.
(MITSUI & Co.)

MITSUI GINKO.
(MITSUI BANK.)

The Bank is owned by the members of the Mitsui Family, who, as partners, assume an unlimited responsibility for all liabilities of the Bank:—

Capital.............................Yen 5,000,000
Reserve Fund.................... " 5,600,000

HEAD OFFICE, TOKYO.

LONDON OFFICE, 34 LIME ST., E. C.

BRANCHES AND AGENCIES:—
New York, San Francisco, Hamburg, Bombay, Singapore, Manila, Hongkong, Amoy, Chefoo, Tientsin.

Kobe, Hakodate, Yokohama, Kure, Yokosuka, Moji, Shimonoseki, Miike, Wakamatsu, Nagasaki, Kuchinotsu, Karatsu, Sasebo, Misume, Taipeh, &c.

Telegraphic Address for all the Offices:
"MITSUI."

A. B. C. AND A. I CODES USED.

Contractors of Coal
To the Imperial Japanese Navy. Arsenals and Railway Bureau, Principal Railway Companies and Industrial Work, Home and Foreign Mail and Freight Steamers.

Sole Proprietors
Of the famous Miike, Tagawa and Yamano Coal Mines.

Sole Agents
For the sale of Fukumo, Hokoku, Ichimura, Kanoda, Mannoura, Onoura, Ostuji, Sonoda, Tsubaruro, Yoshinotani, Yoshio, Yurokibura and other coals.

YANGTSE INSURANCE ASSOCIATION, LTD.

The undersigned, having been appointed agents for the above company, are prepared to issue policies and pay losses on marine risks at regular rates.

E. MEYER & Co.,
Agents, Chemulpo.

AMERICAN KOREAN ELECTRIC CO.

Light and Power.

Main Office: Electric Building, Chong No.

RAILWAY DEPARTMENT.

OPERATING CARS BETWEEN EAST AND WEST GATE, EVERY TEN MINUTES:—

First Car leaves East Gate at 7:00 A. M. First Car leaves R. R. Station at 7:25 A. M
Last Car " East Gate at 8.40 P. M. Last " " R. R. Station at 9.05 P. M

OPERATING CARS BETWEEN EAST GATE AND IMPERIAL TOMB TERMINUS, EVERY TWENTY MINUTES:—

CONNECTING WITH EVERY ALTERNATE CAR ARRIVING AT EAST GATE FROM CHONG NO.

First Car leaves East Gate for Tomb at 7:10 A. M.
" " " Tomb for East Gate at 7:30 A. M.
Last " " East Gate for Tomb at 7:50 P. M.
" " " Tomb for East Gate at 8:10 P. M.

OPERATING CARS BETWEEN CHONG NO AND YUNG SAN RIVER EVERY TWELVE MINUTES:—

First Car leaves Chong No for South Gate at 7:12 A. M.
" " " Chong No for Yung San at 7:36 A. M.
" " " South Gate for Chong No at 7:20 A. M.
" " " Yung San for Chong No at 8:09 A. M.
Last " " South Gate for Chong No 9:00 P. M.
" " " Yung San for Chong No at 8.45. P. M.

SPECIAL PRIVATE CARS FURNISHED TO SUIT CONVENIENCE OF PATRONS. PRICES ON APPLICATION AT HEAD OFFICE.

LIGHTING DEPARTMENT.

Where less than 250 candle power of light is used, the rate per month will be
Per 16 candle power incandescent lamp,—All night.—Yen 2.50.
32 candle power incandescent lamp:—All night:—Yen 4.00.
50 candle power incandescent lamp:—All night:—Yen 6.00.
150 " " " " " " " 10.00.
1200 " " enclosed are " " " " 20.00.

Where more than 250 candle power of light is used, a Meter will be installed, freqvedted:—Rent of Meter Yen 2.00 per month. Rate of charges by meter reading:—Two Sen per Ampere per hour. (Approximately this is equal to about One Sen per 16 C. P. lamp per hour) Minimum monthly charge where meter is installed, Yen 20.00 per month, which includes rental of meter.

Estimates for installing lights furnished on application
An assortment of chandeliers always on hand.

K. Murakami.
Photograph Studio
Chinkokai, Seoul.

Printing, Developing and Enlargement, of Photographs always Undertaken.

Korean Views and Pictures Illustrating Native Customs always on Sale,

---

THE OSAKA SHOSEN KAISHA.

Boats frequently on the berth for Chinnampo.

REGULAR SAILINGS BETWEEN JAPAN AND KOREAN PORTS.

FUSAN AND KOBE VIA SHIMONOSEKI.

OSAKA VIA MOKPO, FUSAN, SHIMONOSEKI AND KOBE.

MOJI DIRECT.

OSAKA VIA KUNSAN, MASANPO, FUSAN, SHIMONOSEKI AND KOBE.

CHEMULPO KUNSAN LINE.
Every three days.

CHEMULPO CHINNAMPO LINK.
Every three days.

For Freight and passage and further particulars apply to
THE OSAKA SHOSEN KAISHA,
Chemulpo,

RONDON, PLAISANT & CO.

General Storekeepers and Merchants, Ships Contractors, Tobacconists, Commission and Forwarding Agents, Coal Merchants

IMPORTERS AND EXPORTERS

Seoul & Chemulpo.

W. D. WENTWORTH.

LANDING
AND
SHIPPING AGENT
AND
CUSTOMS BORDER.

12 OURA, NAGASAKI.

STEWARD & CO.
Chemulpo.

Shipchandlers and Storekeepers, Naval and Mercantile Contrrctors, Landing and Shipping Agents.

STEWARD'S HOTEL
Chemulpo.

Best accommodation in the port for travellers. Clean and well-aired [illegible] good [illegible] and prompt attendence, moderate tariff

거ᄒᆞᆫ죡으로국궁즁에셔납하회의를열고로국황뎨게셔츌셕ᄒᆞ셧는데졍을활발ᄒᆞ게ᄒᆞ며이월금은젼으로구로팟긴대쟝의게아셔만대병을더보내주기로결졍ᄒᆞ엿고로졔스드벤스기대쟝과또그공티들소환ᄒᆞ기로ᄒᆞ엿다더라

○로협회쟝(빅탐쟝) 편슌구로브터(동월오일) 쳥도에도망ᄒᆞᆫ로국슈뢰과피학이쳑은무쟝을히제ᄒᆞ엿고그변에란ᄒᆞᆫ군ᄉᆞ들도병긔를거두엇다더라

별보

황샹위ᄒᆞᆫ형편

○거년에발낫엿서일을밧부게ᄒᆞ던히샹위포티는지금일이거의숙나가셔거긔에셔일ᄒᆞ던산동역부들이지부에도라왓는데일월삼일에ᄌᆞᆫ쳔ᄭᅵ럽리희호로팔빅쳘십명일월수일에ᄌᆞᆫ쳔칸돈호로홍빅수십륙명이와셔져의는교향에셔겨울을지내랴ᄒᆞᆫ다ᄒᆞ며히샹위에는아즉오쳔명가량이남아잇셔셔포티역ᄉᆞ를ᄒᆞᆫ다는데포대를맛츄고ᄒᆞᆫ달동안에면지부에도라와셔져의들의어렁케번돈으로지내리이라ᄒᆞ더라

그쳥인역부들즁에ᄌᆞᆫ쳔칸돈호로온ᄒᆞᆫ죵명ᄒᆞᆫ자다이야기ᄒᆞᆫ말을거ᄒᆞᆫ즉그ᄯᅢ에ᄒᆞ엿스되

그로국사ᄅᆞᆷ들은일본사ᄅᆞᆷ들이평셩히샹위는취ᄒᆞ지못ᄒᆞᆯ줄노셩각ᄒᆞ며지금싸아논그포티를노ᄒᆞ야그항구는명영ᄒᆞ되리지못ᄒᆞ게될줄노밋는지라그항구의동편으로희항의팔영리아리에비우견고ᄒᆞᆫ포티여셧시잇는디야모빈던지그희쳥을지나가던지ᄒᆞ려면거긔셔바로뵈이고그포티에잇는대포들은다희면으로향ᄒᆞ야노앗스며ᄯᅩ그편에포티여셧외에도더잇지마는그것들은그희쳥에셔보이지아니ᄒᆞ는데그포티에잇는대포들은사방으로숫을향ᄒᆞ야노은것이분명ᄒᆞ다ᄒᆞ며

그항구의남방으로그희쳥의우편에비우큰대포를노은큰포티삼ᄉᆞ쳐가잇스니쳥명ᄒᆞᆫ날이면그희쳥으로브터보이고그대포들은다희면으로향ᄒᆞ야노앗스며그항구의셔방에는다른포대ᄒᆞ나잇는데비우견고ᄒᆞ고비우큰대포를노앗스며그항구의북방에는쳘도의닷는곳인고로포티가엽는디그즁에그동방에잇는포티들이데일굉쟝ᄒᆞ고그항구의문호가되야다른포대들보다놉히소사서만일일본인이그항구를공격ᄒᆞᆯ디경이면그포티들의밍렬ᄒᆞᆫ포격을밧으리라ᄒᆞ며

그항구안에영문에미만명이샹의륙군이잇스나길가에셔는군ᄉᆞ몃명을슈볼엿고그항구의경황도젼과곳치번화ᄒᆞ고셩긔잇지못ᄒᆞᆫ지라그군ᄉᆞ들은엄명ᄒᆞᆫ군률에복죵ᄒᆞ고대포와총을연습ᄒᆞ기에시간을만이지내며그군ᄉᆞ들의다수는그포대들의근처에지은디운벽돌집들안에잇서셔일긔의혹한ᄒᆞᆷ을무릅스고방비ᄒᆞ기위ᄒᆞ야에나갓에나다만연습ᄒᆞ기간에그대포들영ᄒᆞᆫ군ᄉᆞ로취군ᄒᆞᆫ지라외양으로보면츙공격을시작ᄒᆞᆫ는것곳ᄒᆞ며쟝ᄇᆞᆯ공격이될ᄯᅢ라도그군ᄉᆞ들은티젹외란환소리가져의들의머리우로지너가거젼에는그것이연습인지쟝ᄇᆞᆯ공격인지아지못ᄒᆞᆯ듯ᄒᆞ게되엿더라ᄒᆞ며

거년십이월이십이일에그희쳥에겨빙되야서지금은비일아침에그리진바다로비길을니기위ᄒᆞ야파빙션을부리고그희쳥의광편에는슈뢰를만이뭇엇스나지금은어름에뭇쳐잇다고ᄒᆞ더라ᄒᆞ엿더라

론셜

일본ᄉᆞᄅᆞᆷ들과일진회와경쳥이라

○일본사ᄅᆞᆷ이고용ᄒᆞᆫ회라도홀만ᄒᆞᆫ일진회에티ᄒᆞ는그진의를필경은알깃도다

일본사ᄅᆞᆷ의싱각에그런일이스면셔울에너무티평ᄒᆞ고죠용ᄒᆞᆫ듯ᄒᆞᆫ지라

그러셔저의로보낸일진회원들의죵셔드는것을펑케ᄒᆞ고쟝곡쳔대쟝이고시ᄒᆞ되한국의경찰을셔ᄇᆞᆯ쳔ᄒᆞ야일본헌병이안평졍셔를유지ᄒᆞᆫ다ᄒᆞ엿는지라

일본이이나라를보호ᄒᆞᆫ다ᄒᆞᆫ후로일이잘되야가는모양인지우리는그ᄉᆞ이에야리는분란과양계에티ᄒᆞ야차란리항구를셜ᄒᆞᆷ렴ᄒᆞ노라일진회들리용ᄒᆞᆫ후에시평회원들은다시부르기전에는다도라가셔잇스라명령ᄒᆞ엿다니다시부를ᄯᆡ에는ᄯᅩ다

일본인의목적은이나라에서각항ᄉᆞ무의지위갑들ᄒᆞ는권리를일본사ᄅᆞᆷ이나한인의일본당의쟝즁에주이자는것이라

만일지금일본이보호ᄒᆞ는한인들이졍부관인들보다더나ᄒᆞᆫ인물들갓ᄒᆞ면ᄒᆞ용셔ᄒᆞᆯ되니와ᄒᆞᆫ일본공사가싱취ᄒᆞ고엽건에업게ᄒᆞ는평양군슈의민관ᄉᆞ건에다ᄒᆞ야반티ᄒᆞ던ᄒᆡᆼ위는분명히바르지못ᄒᆞᆫ사ᄅᆞᆷ들이일본에보호를엇는가보더라

한인들이지금은일본인의간흉ᄒᆞᆫ계에티ᄒᆞ야반티ᄒᆞᆯ권력이업지마는일본사ᄅᆞᆷ들이다음에지금져의들이ᄒᆞᆫ일을후회ᄒᆞᆯ가잇스리라ᄒᆞ노라

판보

뎨삼쳔삼십칠호
광무구년일월십륙일
셔임급ᄉᆞ령

○명즁계 졍군슈 박병익 (일월십이일)

의원면본관 법관양셩소교관 신우션 법관양셩소박ᄉᆞ 권티명 법관양셩소박ᄉᆞ 신셔 법관양셩소박ᄉᆞ 졍우흥 법관양셩소박ᄉᆞ 죠동슉 법관양셩소박ᄉᆞ 권즁근 법관양셩소박ᄉᆞ 리현구 법관양셩소박ᄉᆞ 김졍학

○임법관양셩소교관셔판임관륙등 권즁한

이상일월십삼일 궁뎡록ᄉᆞ

○군부대신리종건ᄉᆞ직소빈지 셩소구실이라버리고봇친뜻을셩각ᄒᆞ면맛당히쫏기를비는글쟝이엿슬지라다시번거ᄒᆞ게말고시무ᄒᆞ라ᄒᆞ신수로부탕을보너여젼유ᄒᆞ시다

○의졍부참졍최익현ᄉᆞ소빈지 셩소구실이라경의말ᄒᆞᆫ바가다간졀ᄒᆞᆫ지라집음에깅계ᄒᆞ고샹회셔화ᄒᆞ게빗지아니ᄒᆞᆫ것이아니라금일나라형셰가셸치지못ᄒᆞ는것이오리병든것과지라가히ᄒᆞᆫ달을괴약ᄒᆞ야낫게ᄒᆞ미에는가히ᄒᆞᆫ환약으로써ᄒᆞᆯ에소셩ᄒᆞ지못ᄒᆞᆯ지라바야흐로말ᄒᆞ고그효험을못구ᄒᆞ니그시세에익히싱각지못ᄒᆞᆫ지라그계이간우ᄒᆞᆫ지라비화ᄒᆞ게쳔죠이ᄒᆞ는것을힘써셔ᄒᆞᆫ가지국ᄉᆞ를건지는일로부탕을보너여젼유ᄒᆞ시다

이상일월십ᄉᆞ일

잡보

○군티감ᄒᆡᆨ 각군티를ᄉᆞ쳔명만셜치ᄒᆞᆫ다ᄒᆞᆷ으로각티사졸을젼이잇드ᄃᆡ도취우지아니ᄒᆞᆫ다ᄒᆞ는고로각티에셔그자뢰ᄒᆞ는거슬싸라곳취가ᄒᆞᆫ다더라

○항회원취송 금십륙일일진회에셔독립관에기회ᄒᆞ는데일쟝연셜ᄒᆞᆫ후에항회원은몰수히송ᄒᆞ엿더라

○평정탐셩 경무서에셔진작일에하교와호교쳔변에쟝졍가가수십좌를경각동안에회졀ᄒᆞ고그터를평평이다닷다더라

○경ᄉᆞ아삽 근일에경무ᄉᆞ신티휴씨가평복으로밤마다단니며인민의질고를탐지ᄒᆞᆫ다ᄒᆞᆷ으로칭명이칭식ᄒᆞᆫ리라더라

○일진회고시 일진회에셔고시ᄒᆞ기를본월십륙일에독립관으로모히다시기회ᄒᆞᆫ다더라

○쟝시회졔 졔작일야쳘시에느리골쳔우물골셔회졔가잇섯는디당이일긔도음예ᄒᆞᆫ즁바들이엇셧고ᄯᅩᄒᆞᆫ그졍결ᄒᆡ쳔우불이잇서비우요긴이되엿다더라

○린세탁교 졍샹풍리쟝빈씨가쟉일오초혼시에하교다리에서세린것는티호흉불등월쌍아비라쟝신을차리지못ᄒᆞ야경헤보는사ㅣ낫도일고그거지를아는고로그방곡슌검이샤군을엇어그쟝으로보내지ᄒᆞ동세는아적쟝신을차리지못ᄒᆞ더라더라

○경ᄉᆞ교시 우물을슈츅ᄒᆞ라ᄒᆞ는티우물슈츅비는각동인민이ᄌᆞ판ᄒᆞ는티며즁소샹등으로빈비ᄒᆞ랴ᄒᆞ엿고ᄯᅩ우물잇는집은문에우물잇다ᄒᆞ고(우졍)이라써붓쳐화재가잇스면그우물을쓰게ᄒᆞ랴ᄒᆞ엿더라

○최챵쟝결샹 며항로담에최챵쟝의현씨가본대에서세날배에샨아가셔죽거오기로결심ᄌᆞ관ᄒᆞ고항쟝에슈외만가지고왓는티동세의회갑이임의지지낫지오랜지라비록지금즉드티도번이엿슬거시오이악혁ᄌᆞ로고명이의슈히드리나비슐을티ᄒᆞ야여러번불너을너시니은명을항어스니아마동씨가룡으로쎠나라일에죽드라도그죽는것은영광이라고들ᄒᆞ더라

○불금미ᄌᆞ금 소위원파라ᄒᆞ는리가ᄌᆞ총랑반이라ᄒᆞ며경너에두류ᄒᆞ야모처로담이말ᄒᆞ기를지금신셜ᄒᆞ는모ᄉᆞ셜항쥬ᄉᆞ를ᄒᆞ엿는티금명간에쥬판보에반포가된다ᄒᆞ고도처에식최가잇더니지금신경무ᄉᆞ힝경이후로는힝리가카도퇴쇽ᄒᆞ엿다ᄒᆞ니미린쳥쟝번의피신ᄒᆞ는것으로불진티셰경무ᄉᆞ의힝졍을찬양ᄒᆞᆯ쌘아니라이는불금미ᄌᆞ금이라더라

○슈셰지취 함경남도관찰ᄉᆞ리헌경씨가외부로보고ᄒᆞ기를문쳔군슈명유셥과영흥군슈홍손우과안변군슈리원의보고를거ᄒᆞᆫ즉원산쥬차일본령ᄉᆞ관대쟝죠면만항의공문니에판북각디방에서그고을에세금ᄒᆞ로젼이나면경이나징슈ᄒᆞ기위ᄒᆞ야괴원을보낼ᄯᅢ에는슈취보고ᄒᆞ고지휘ᄒᆞ기를쳥ᄒᆞᆷ이가ᄒᆞ며만약보고ᄒᆞ기를티만히ᄒᆞᆫ는자가잇는ᄯᅢ에는무ᄉᆞᆫ죠쳐를ᄒᆞ리라ᄒᆞ엿다ᄒᆞ엿더라

광고

TELEGRAMS.

Army Headquarters Seoul.

The Russian troops who recently invaded the districts of Haicheng, Tashichao, Newchwang and Yingkow with the object of damaging the railway, consisted of at least one division of cavalry belonging to General Mischenko's brigade. On their retreat from Yinkow they were intercepted by one of our detachments at 8 P. M. on the 14th at a point a little west of Newchwang when they were defeated and compelled to retreat in great disorder in a Northwesterly direction.

Army Headquarters, Seoul.

On the 14th inst our scouts met and repulsed about 80 of the enemy at Ultaochatze.

Army Headquarters, Seoul.

The Russians who were defeated at Yaotzeling on the 6th inst. have retreated to the North of Chang-chung-ling having lost 100 killed and wounded and two guns.

Tokio, Jan. 16.

The following promotions are announced:—Lieut-General Kogawa and Kawamura to be full Generals and Major General Ando to be Lieut-General.

THE SUBMARINE BOAT IN WAR.

The Japanese-Russian war has not yet brought submarine boats to a practical test; but it has been sufficiently well developed and proved to make it certain that it will, at some time, play an important part in naval warfare. It is the next great instrument of destuction to be used, especially since the torpedo boat has, in Japanese hands, proved so effective. The submarine torpedo boat is an enlarged Whitehead torpedo, with human intelligence instead of automatic machinery to guide it, and with a launching tube instead of the charge of gun-cotton in its nose. There are several types in more or less successful operation. Notable is the French type that sinks by filling tanks, which is a slow operation. Then there is the Lake (American) submarine, that hauls itself under by inclined hydro-planes; and the Holland type, recently acquired by the United States Government, that dives while under motion, and is really what the others are not—a mechanical fish.—Morgan Robertson in the November World's Work.

The Russian garrison at Vladivostock consists of 26,000 troops.

Plague has broken out at Bangkok. Six deaths have occurred among native Indians.

A few days ago Mr. Yi Bong Nai, the Vice-Minister for Home Affairs, attended, by invitation at the Japanese Army Headquarters.

Yesterday the Il-chin-hoi patriots held a great meeting. Several speeches were made, and the country members were dismissed to their homes.

We learn from the "Daihan Ilpo" that the Japanese Minister is endeavouring to secure the appointment of a Mr. Hayashida as adviser to the Imperial Household Department. Mr. Hayashida is clerk to the lower house of the Japanese Diet.

There are over 9,000 refugees at Yingkow who are being fed and clothed by the International Red Cross Society. Of this number about 1,000 are wounded, and are being treated in the local hospitals. Many have since been sent to their homes. Besides these, there are over 20,000 refugees in Fengtien who are being fed and clothed by Tartar General Tseng Chi. At Liaovang there are 5,000 refugees.

GERMANY IN CHINA.

The "South China Morning Post" has published a paragraph to the effect that the Deputy Governor of Shantung telegraphs to Peking reporting the sudden arrival of from 3,000, to 4,000 German troops in the country. These troops have been stationed at the different stations of the railway, and at Wei Yuan, Ko Mat Yuan, and On You Yuan. Ordnance stores and powder magazines are being hastily erected. Previous to the arrival of these reinforcements only a few hundred troops were stationed along the railway.

A correspondent writes to them as follows:—Sir,—In your issue of the 28th I read, under the heading "German Demand," a report from "native sources," that the German Minister has demanded the immediate removal of Hu Ting Kow, the newly appointed Governor of Shantung province, and that this action of the German Minister in "interfering with China's internal affairs is evident proof of Germany's aggressive policy in China."

Will you kindly permit me, through the columns of your paper, to point out that the "Ostasiatische Lloyd" has contradicted this report. It says: "Of course there is not a single word of truth in the whole matter; it rests, like all the other reports of an unauthorized interference of Germany with China's internal affairs, upon pure invention."

Most likely the "sudden arrival of from 3,000 to 4,000 German troops" in Chinese territory, along the new railway, of which I read in your paper of this morning, rests upon the same inventive power of the native sources, who rejoice in spreading false reports about Germany and its policy.—Yours, etc.,.

It is reported that no obstacles are at present placed in the way of Koreans wishing to resign from the army

The Governor of North Chulla province telegraphs a complaint to the effect that Il-chin-hoi people are gathering in increasing numbers at all the larger towns and that they are a serious hindrance to the transaction of official business

On the night of the 14th instant someone broke into the headquarters of the Il-chin-hoi and, by way of loot, secured four of the caps which are the uniform of the society. We only hope the thief (or thieves) will not have the bad taste to wear them.

The magistrate of Kimpo asks the Foreign Office to adjust a grievance. It appears that some of his people found some some logs floating on the river and dragged them ashore. On the night of the 12th a Japanese named Myeno with servants put in an appearance, claimed the timber and extorted $40 besides. The people are now clamouring for the restitution of their $40.

A few days ago, says a correspondent of the "Japan Herald," a Japanese friend came on the part of some high official of my acquaintance to ask me for a subscription to the Volunteer Fleet Fund. I asked him in whom the ownership of the fleet was to be vested, how the profits if any would be divided and by whom the losses would be borne. He did not know and was much surprised at the questions. He had not subscribed himself, he acknowledged, and was not sure he would. Another Japanese who was listening volunteered then the information that the call for subscriptions had generally fallen flat and the questions I had put had been asked many times but had failed to elicit satisfactory answers. He added irrelevantly that the consent of an Imperial Prince to be Patron was sufficient guarantee that whatever faults there were in the Constitution of the Company—if it is a company—would soon be corrected. The time, however, seems very ill chosen to ask the nation to disburse fifteen million yen towards so badly engineered an enterprise,

The British steamer "Teucer," 2,564 tons gross' built in 1890, and the Norwegian steamer "Noa, have been sold to Japanese, the former for 100,000, and the latter for 130,000 yen.

On the 13th instant a band of robbers invaded the village of Chung-ni, Kyeng Sang district, and killed one Japanese hunter and wounded another who was staying in the village at the time.

We learn that Mr. Wŏn Seh-sung and two other members of the Po-an-hoi society who were arrested by the Japanese last Summer for protesting against the Nagamori demands, and sent to Anju, have been released and have just returned to Seoul.

At a sesion held by the Government on the 15th it was decided to effect considerable modifications in the rules governing the election of Magistrates. The change is supposed to be intended as a countermove to the efforts of the Japanese to obtain control of the magisterial appointments in many districts.

The Governor of Hupeh province has issued instructions for the suppression of certain revolutionary publications which are forbidden to be sold by the bookstalls. Offenders will be severely punished. Proclamations have been posted up advising the peple not to read such publications, and requesting that they be delivered up to the authorities to be burned.

The office of Kamni or superintendant of trade at the treaty ports is controlled by the Department for Foreign Affairs. Recently this department has received a petition from the people of Pyeng Yang praying for the dismissal of the Secretary to the Kamni of that place. It appears that he has held office for three years and has amassed consideral wealth in this period. In one lawsuit alone he is said to have squeezed over $2,000. The people of Pyeng Yang very rightly remind the authorities that officials are supposed to protect them and demand to know what they have done to deserve a visitation like that of their present secretary.

Three Koreans of good position, named Kang Wŏn-hyung, Woo Yong-tak and Yeu Chung-yong have addressed a letter of reproach to the Japanese Legation. They say that when Japan declared war against Russia she declared that she was fighting for Korea's independence. Instead of this however, Japan has forced a number of laws on the people, made demands for all the waste land, built railways, appropriated ground in Seoul, killed many people, assumed charge of the police, and attempted to control the appointments of magistrates. This is what you have done, say the Koreans, and it is a very different thing to upholding our independence. The writers conclude by suggesting that the Japanese should ease the minds of the people by adopting an attitude more in accordance with their original promises

Knowing so well as we do that the Il-chin-hoi (or "Isshin-Kwai") is a society organized and maintained by the Japanese authorities, the prevalence of paragraphs such as the following in the Japanese press is nothing short of exasperating.

The "Jiji" learns from Seoul that, in view of the increased activity of the members of the "Isshin-kwai," Mr. Hayashi, our Minister at Seoul, has sent a note to our Consuls in Korea, instructing the latter to notify the Korean people that their grievances should in future be communicated to him through the local Japanese Consul, instead of making demonstrations against the Korean authorities. The Minister further assures the natives, that the wrongs complained of will be redressed, should an investigation of the facts prove such to exist.

A report from the Hong Wŏn magistrate says that the Russians have established a telegraph office at Pyengpochun, a village in his district.

A Seoul despatch to the "Osaka Mainichi" says that the large building, formerly occupiud by the German Legation, has now been brought by the Korean Government for yen 80,000. The despatch adds that the building, after being thoroughly repaired, is to be the residence of Mr. Megata, Japanese adviser to the Korean Financial Department.

Bekanntmachung.

Die Bekanntmachungen der Eintragungen in das hiesige Deutsche Handelsregister erfolgen im Jahre 1905 durch den **"Ostasiatischen Lloyd" und** die **"The Korea Daily News."**

Söul, den 27. Dezember 1904.

Der Kaiserlich Deutsche Minister Resident und General-Konsul.

(L. S.) gez. von Saldern.

The Korea Daily News.

Issued at 5 P. M. daily except Sundays.
Rate of Subscription:—
Per Year,............Yen 25.
Per Quarter,..........Yen 7.
Per Month,..........Yen 2.50.

Postage in Korea not charged extra.
Postage abroad charged extra.

Advertisements, 50 sen per day for 1 inch or less.
5 yen per month per inch.
50 yen per year per inch.

All communications to
E. T. BETHELL,
Editor and Publisher,
Pak-tong, Seoul.

A STORMY PETREL.

A certain Mr. Demetrius C. Boulger is apparently in Japanese pay. We recollect having seen in the London reviews, from time to time, articles from his pen exalting the Japanese and decrying the Russians.

As we have pointed out before, the Japanese have wasted a great deal of money in getting themselves admired and although of course we have no means of knowing whether D. C. Boulger is, directly or indirectly in their pay, we will, in case there is anything of the sort going on, reproduce parts of an article of his which appeared in "London Opinion," in order to show that he is even a worse prophet than champion.

Mr. Boulger is evidently disgusted that the "Hull incident" did not lead to immediate war between Great Britain and Russia. Finding that the very sensible course had been taken of appointing a commission to enquire into the affair, he says:—

"But has Peace been secured for more than a brief period while national indignation is cooling down at the attack on the Hull fishing-boats? Is there any sign of genuine regret on the part of the Russians for what they did, or have they adopted fresh principles of conduct that will prevent the recurrence of outrage? Everybody knows that Russia has not tied her hands in any way. Admiral Rojdestvensky's fleet will, no doubt, be well behaved so long as it is shadowed by a British naval force of superior strength, and while it is locked up in the Mediterranean it may refrain from holding up an Indian mail steamer. But when the controlling force has been withdrawn, as it will be after passing Suez Canal—for the Government cannot transfer its Mediterranean fleet to the Red Sea—what will happen then? Will the gallant Russian Admiral prohibit his crews from practising their shooting as the squadron furrows the Indian Ocean?

If they were so fearful of Japanese torpedo-boats in the North Sea, they will probably see Togo's warships in every tramp steamer they pass from Suez to Singapore, and there is no loophole for our authorities to pretend that they do not know how he Russian Navy acts under such circumstances. There will be further assertions of the Russian right to bombard any fishing-boats or liners that come within range of the guns of the Baltic squadron, and, judging by precedent, all the Russian Government has to fear is the diplomatic artillery of Downing Street. Having tolerated one brutal and indefensible outrage, the British Government will scarcely be credited with the intention of resorting to extreme measures when, in all human probability, the further achievements of Admiral Rojdestvensky cannot come up to the level of that associated with the name of the Dogger Bank."

And finally he says:—"While the Russians have been talking of Port Arthur as Admiral Rojdestvensky's goal, they may really have had the Dardanelles in their mind."

Of course, in the light of recent event, the last paragraph suffices to make the whole article ridiculous; it is only a consideration of the object for which the article was probably written which lends it a serious aspect.

The immediate object of the article is to inflame the British public against the Russian Navy and Russia by persuading them that Russian men of war deliberately fired on defenseless fishing boats—presumably because they were British. However his hopless failures in the direction of prophesy are more than sufficient to discredit his views of past events.

It will be some time before we hear the decision of the Commission which is adjudicating upon the incident, but enough has already been made public to show that the Russians had considerable justification for their belief that there were hostile vessels in their neighbourhood and even British warships, during manveures, have made mistakes which, had they occured in war time would have led to a far greater loss of innocent life.

DIGESTION IN FISH.

A singular instance of tenacity in the digestion of fish is reported from Sheffield. The fish, which is a ling, four feet long, had what appeared to be an abnormally hard liver. But the cutting up process revealed something far stranger. The supposed hard liver turned out to be nothing else but a piece of stout netting, over two yards long and fourteen inches wide, which had been strangled into the form of a fundamental football. How this great mass of indigestible material came to be swallowed by the creature is a mystery, and the suggestion that the fish caught in the toils of a fisherman's net solved the problem of how to escape by devouring his prison walls is not considered scientifically practicable.

A rumour is current that the Japanese intend adopting the English alphabet. After having examined the Japanese alphabet we can quite believe it.—The Globe.

A belief prevails in naval circles that the delay in the voyage of the Baltic fleet shows that they are practising manœuvres en route to be ready for the actual fighting.

It is reported from Chang-ka-kou, beyond the Great Wall, that members of the different secret societies are active in the surrounding districts sowing sedition and posting up inflammatory placards. Orders have been issued for the arrest of all suspicious individuals.

The "Osaka Mainichi" says that the Osaka Shosen Kaisha has arranged to re-open its bi-weekly steamship service to Kiaochao Bay, which was discontinued on the outbreak of hostilities. The "Nanyang," under charter to the company, was to have sailed from Osaka for Tsingtao on the 10th inst.

It is reported from China that the United States Minister has sent a despatch to the Minister of the Board of Foreign Affairs informing him that President Roosevelt has taken the lead in a movement for the restoration of peace. The Minister of the Board of Foreign Affairs has reported the news to their Majesties the Emperor and Empress Dowager.

KOREA.

A JAPANESE VIEW OF COLONISATION.

(Continued from yesterday.)

Commenting upon the article from the "Jidai Shicho" which appeared yesterday the "Kobe Chronicle" says:—

The proposal which Mr. T. Yokoi makes is one of many suggestions which are now being advanced in Japan with a view to dealing with Korea. Mr. Yokoi's position is, apparently, that it is hopeless to expect the Koreans to do anything for the advancement of their country, and the Japanese must therefore do it for them. He seems to forget that the indolence and improvidence of the Koreans are due in large measure to evil laws which place the farmers and producers at the mercy of officials whose only interest is to obtain as large a revenue from the peasants as possible. Any improvement in tillage which indicates an increase of prosperity is at once pounced upon by the tax-gatherer as evidence that the unfortunate wight can pay more taxes, and therefore the screw is again turned. When the peasant in Korea finds the fruits of his labour secured to him he will show himself as industrious in Korea as he is in Vladivostok and other places to which he emigrates as labourer. It has been noted that wherever the Korean gets free from the vicious government of his native country, he shows that he is animated by the same instincts of acquisition and desire to improve his condition as other men. Unfortunately too many Japanese politicians look at the peninsula entirely from the standpoint of Japan and not from that of the people of Korea. Practically the scheme outlined by Mr. Yokoi amounts to a proposal to expropriate the Korean farmer, either by purchase or otherwise, in favour of emigrants from Japan, who are to be assisted by the Government both monetarily and by way of protective laws. We cannot imagine any proposal more likely to arouse the deepest resentment among the Koreans than to see themselves dispossessed in this way, or to find themselves subject to the competition of neighbours protected by extra-territoriality against unjust exactions which they themselves will possibly have to pay in still fuller measure. It would be better that Japan should take over the country altogether and administer it than that such a state of things should be set up. Moreover, the people of Japan may very well ask why they should be taxed in order to plant Japanese on Korean soil to become, as it were, in a certain sense their competitors. We venture to say that the scheme as ontlined by Mr. Yokoi is altogether unworkable. It is unjust to the bulk of the population in Korea and it is similiarly unjust to the people of this country.

The St. Petersburg city authorities have decided to grant 100,000 roubles for the defenders of Port Arthur and their families. They further resolved to make an appeal to the whole of Russia to raise funds for this purpose.

Owing to the suspicious behaviour of ex-Governor Wong Chun and the pro-Russian machinations of his friends and partisans at the Capital, says the S. C. Morning post, a certain Minister has advised that he be expelled from Shanghai and be ordered to return to his native village so as to keep him from further mischief.

The real significance of the recent Russian raid in the direction of Haicheng Ninchiatun and Newchwang will probably not be known for some time. The chances are that it was a raid pure, and simple, and is the forerunner of many similar expeditions down the Japanese flanks. This will go a long way to justify the slowness of Kuroki's advance so unanimously condemned by the critics. Kuroki took great pains to leave all his communications in good defensive condition and his division is less exposed to these attacks than is the Japanese left wing.

The Korea Daily News.

VOL. II, TUESDAY, JANUARY 17, 1905. No. 12

大韓每日申報
대한ᄆᆡ일신보

(뎨이권십삼호) (목요일) 일쳔구빅오년일월십구일

본샤고빅

이신보는영어와한영으로셔계리
일츌판ᄒᆞ옵

신문가
한장 엽두돈오푼
일삭도 엽두량닷돈
우표가리 삭닷돈
다맛돈으로밧숩

광고료는
귀한의장단과ᄌᆞ힝의다쇼로즁감ᄒᆞ되ᄒᆞᆫ번가로밧을리이오며오리지아녀대한사람마다다이신문을보실터이니광고내시기를원ᄒᆞ시ᄂᆞᆫ이들은우리신문사에와셔면약ᄒᆞ심을희망ᄒᆞ옵

○발힝소 박동대한ᄆᆡ일신보사범어학교압례젼영국인셜필림졍자리오

사쟝 영국인 (비셜)

평양 ᄃᆡ리졈

○평양효동사는권미보씨로우리신문관ᄃᆡ리인을뎡ᄒᆞ엿시ᄉᆞ오니평양에계신구람코져ᄒᆞᄂᆞᆫ 쳠군ᄌᆞᄂᆞᆫ희ᄃᆡ리졈에왕림ᄒᆞ와면회ᄒᆞ시옵

사고

○우리대한ᄆᆡ일신보의목뎍은대한의안녕질셔에관ᄒᆞᆫ모든대목에ᄃᆡᄒᆞ야는공평ᄒᆞᆫ변론을쥬쟝ᄒᆞᆷ이라우리동신원의탐보ᄂᆞᆫ신문보시ᄂᆞᆫ쳠군ᄌᆞ의게ᄒᆞᆼ샹보도ᄒᆞ리며편지를귀셔ᄒᆞ여주시ᄂᆞᆫ이ᄂᆞᆫ셩명과번디를젹어붓치시기를희망ᄒᆞ오나비거슬신문샹에긔ᄌᆡᄒᆞ라ᄂᆞᆫ거시아니오다만극히신용ᄒᆞᄂᆞᆫ즁거를숨고자ᄒᆞᆷ이라긔자ᄂᆞᆫ아모긔셔던지긔ᄌᆡᄒᆞᆷ을퇴각ᄒᆞᄂᆞᆫ권리를가졋ᄉᆞ나퇴각ᄒᆞᄂᆞᆫ리유ᄂᆞᆫ말ᄒᆞᆯ터이오며공즁평화를문란케ᄒᆞᄂᆞᆫ듯ᄒᆞᆫ긔셔ᄂᆞᆫ의례히밧지안켓ᄉᆞᆸᄂᆞ이다

●본사셜시이ᄅᆡ로신문을ᄆᆡ양우례로분젼ᄒᆞ와례젼부의임의로젼ᄒᆞ든ᄉᆞ소로번곳에ᄂᆞᆫ혹늣게젼ᄒᆞ기도ᄒᆞ며혹벗쳘거슬ᄒᆞᆫ집에젼ᄒᆞ기도ᄒᆞ며혹아니젼ᄒᆞᄂᆞᆫ곳도잇다ᄒᆞ시와우리신문을ᄉᆞ랑ᄒᆞ야구람ᄒᆞ시ᄂᆞᆫ 쳠군ᄌᆞ의게ᄃᆡᄒᆞ야면우미안ᄒᆞ옵기로지금은분젼인을두고ᄆᆡ일아ᄎᆞᆷ이젼ᄒᆞ며아니젼ᄒᆞ거나늣게거나ᄒᆞᆫ폐가업도록ᄒᆞ란ᄒᆞ오나혹아니젼ᄒᆞ거나혹늣게젼ᄒᆞ거나ᄒᆞᆫ일이잇스면본사로통긔ᄒᆞ여주심을희망ᄒᆞ옵

잡보

○문위위졍회민 ᄂᆡ부에셔샹샹도관찰부로훈령ᄒᆞ기를디방관이회민을ᄃᆡᄒᆞ야의병이니동학이니ᄒᆞ고학ᄃᆡᄒᆞᆫ다ᄒᆞ니동학이나의병도귀의ᄀᆞ화ᄒᆞ엿슨즉량민이오또회민은관리의학졍을이긔지못ᄒᆞ야발긔ᄒᆞᆫ자이니위졍ᄒᆞ며진압ᄒᆞ지말고힘써효유ᄒᆞ야ᄒᆞ여곰안도케ᄒᆞ기를도모ᄒᆞ라ᄒᆞ엿더라

○인항샹민쳥원 인항샹민등이외부에쳥원ᄒᆞ기를본항감리하샹긔씨가부임ᄒᆞᆫ지여러ᄒᆡ에셜샹으로다ᄉᆞ리ᄂᆞᆫ고로ᄂᆡ외국샹민이힘입어ᄉᆡ업을편안이ᄒᆞ더니이제신문에말ᄒᆞ기를교체된다ᄂᆞᆫ말이잇스ᄆᆡ일항구만인이차셔ᄒᆞ케ᄒᆞ엿ᄉᆞ오니 디폐에쥬달ᄒᆞ야잉임ᄒᆞ야항구졍형에편안케ᄒᆞ시기를바란다ᄒᆞ엿더라

○경괄구화 셩홍열하오셩시랑예죵로젼지젼뒤길모가에셔실화ᄒᆞ야이십여간이몰슈히소화ᄒᆞ고동리졍ᄉᆞ지런소ᄒᆞᄂᆞᆫᄃᆡ일인은소방조긔계를사용ᄒᆞ고경무사이하일반경찰관리가구화ᄒᆞ엿다더라

○교문 폐현 샹홍일하오사시에일공사가 폐현ᄒᆞ고동시에탁지교문관이 폐현ᄒᆞ여졍졍샹사항을샹 쥬ᄒᆞ엿더라

○쟝곡쳔 폐현 십칠일오후삼시량에는일본군사령관쟝곡쳔씨가 폐현ᄒᆞ엿더라

○농한량대임시 합부대신과농부대신을임시ᄒᆞ라ᄒᆞ시고한업과농업을밧답케ᄒᆞ여분부ᄒᆞ옵셧ᄂᆞᆫᄃᆡ아직셔조치ᄒᆞᆯᄂᆞᆫ지모르겟다더라

○셩원쟝교임 동군범원쟝은빗리과씨가피임ᄒᆞ엿다더라

○쇠수 강화대뎨쟝리동취씨와부윤윤쳘규씨가동군범원에셔재판ᄒᆞ여운분부운이탁군과ᄒᆞᆫ사ᄂᆞᆫ업의괴제ᄒᆞ여거니와탁운ᄡᅥᄅᆞᆯ조톨차로구란주본을드린다더니세락으로써린동쥐씨ᄂᆞᆫ도로험피슈ᄒᆞ고윤부윤ᄒᆞᆫ임시무ᄒᆞᆫ다더라

○랑대신발향메젼 대신샹ᄒᆞᆫ씨ᄂᆞᆫ십삼일항례로발향ᄒᆞ고젼대신신권젼씨ᄂᆞᆫ음력본월망후에항례로나려가기로결졍ᄒᆞ엿더라

○보젼문시 십오일하오두시에군슈들을쥬본차로졍부에셔회의ᄒᆞ엿ᄂᆞᆫᄃᆡ일공사의권고ᄒᆞᆫ슈령을셔임ᄒᆞ기로작졍ᄒᆞ고항자군슈보젼ᄒᆞᄂᆞᆫ규측은문시ᄒᆞ엿다더라

○부속경쳥셜 경위원은경무쳥으로부속ᄒᆞ고호위ᄃᆡ를경위원으로리셜ᄒᆞᆫ다ᄒᆞ며 궁ᄂᆡ에궁닉셔를젼과ᄀᆞᆺ치셜시ᄒᆞ야궁셩을경위케ᄒᆞᆫ다더라

○경슈과원셜명 십오일일진회에셔광고ᄒᆞ기를경무ᄉᆞ신ᄐᆡ휴씨가신임이후에회원박지외ᄒᆞ셔바지와기타쥬단회관ᄒᆞ게붓잡ᄒᆞᆫ자를잡아ᄉᆞ리며비단신금단과신갑지졍ᄒᆞᆷ과나무갑조죵을경쳥에셔벌외힝수로인민의자유권리를손상ᄒᆞᆷ이불소ᄒᆞ기로본회에셔과원질문ᄒᆞᆫ즉경ᄌᆞ가인민의불편ᄒᆞᆫ금령은환셜ᄒᆞ기로ᄀᆞ기승락ᄒᆞ엿다더니신경수가총순졍셔또씨들신불일조조에일진회에파송ᄒᆞ야ᄃᆡ광왈본수가이리ᄒᆞᆫ승락도업시수셜이샹셜ᄒᆞ엿스니이ᄂᆞᆫ경찰에크게방ᄒᆡ가되ᄂᆞᆫ지라본수ᄂᆞᆫ젼과ᄀᆞᆺ치시힝ᄒᆞᆯ터이니회광고ᄂᆞᆫ물시ᄒᆞ라ᄒᆞ엿더라

○몽진회고시 작일몽진회에셔고시ᄒᆞ기를본회에셔당초에지회를인허ᄒᆞᆷ이업셧ᄂᆞᆫᄃᆡ황슈귀ᄒᆞᄂᆞᆫ바졍모가ᄌᆞ칭몽진회디회라ᄒᆞ고ᄒᆡ군민우장에셔기회ᄒᆞ며미명에엽수량오젼식밧으며일진회를손ᄒᆡᄒᆞ니이것은란민이라ᄒᆞ고발명ᄒᆞ엿더라

○일소면훈 일본공ᄉᆞ가각령수관으로면훈ᄒᆞ기를한국즁에파밋ᄃᆡ방졍부의시졍개션ᄒᆞᆷ은일한의졍셔를의방ᄒᆞ야일본졍부에셔극력실힝ᄒᆞᆯ필요ᄒᆞᆫ수항은방쟝착수ᄒᆞᄂᆞᆫ즁이라이ᄯᅢ에한국ᄂᆡ에잇ᄂᆞᆫ일본신민은션셔일본졍부의담당인고로조금이후로ᄂᆞᆫ한국인민이디방과밋즁앙졍부의혐의ᄒᆞ며문식ᄒᆞᆷ을만민임의무슈쳥원ᄒᆞᆫ수졍이잇거든온편ᄒᆞᆫ슈단으로방수ᄒᆞᆯ에졍소ᄒᆞ며혹령수관을경유ᄒᆞ야본공ᄉᆞ의게고소ᄒᆞᆷ이가ᄒᆞ지만아무뢰도모회ᄒᆞ고일노인ᄒᆞ야회를셜시ᄒᆞ고즁인을모ᄒᆞ거나ᄃᆡ표자를경셩에파송ᄒᆞᆷ은단졍코신효가업슬ᄲᅮᆫ더러귀즁ᄒᆞᆫ시간과이뢰ᄌᆞ외ᄌᆡ산만허비ᄒᆞ고필경에ᄂᆞᆫ졍부의안졍ᄒᆞᆷ을요란케ᄒᆞᄂᆞᆫ어리셕은힝동이니디방량민은이ᄀᆞᆺ을몸밧아본을진회회편엽을편안히ᄒᆞ고과어히죄에빗지안케ᄒᆞ라ᄒᆞ엿ᄂᆞᆫ지라각ᄒᆡ령수가각령리의게젼죠ᄒᆞ기를관찰수의게죠회ᄒᆞ야ᄆᆡᄃᆡ로시힝케ᄒᆞ라ᄒᆞ엿다더라

○평북면보 평안북도관찰수리용관씨가ᄂᆡ부로면보ᄒᆞ기를귀셩ᄐᆡ쳔에의병일노볍노히인원을과송ᄒᆞ야회원과안동ᄒᆞ야사실ᄒᆞᆫ즉그ᄐᆡ쳔의반회담등샹인이술을취ᄒᆞ야아뇌ᄒᆞ엿ᄂᆞᆫᄃᆡ관가로셔금송ᄒᆞᆫ후에회인은의구히거졉ᄒᆞ엿고귀세인즉별노야뇨ᄒᆞᆷ이업고회소ᄒᆞᆷ무가부졍지빈을모집ᄒᆞᆫ다표ᄒᆞ엿더라

○경렬부인 김화군사ᄂᆞᆫ남도사ᄂᆞᆫ본군에초 히지난더ᄂᆡ게사년동학챵궐ᄒᆞᆯᄯᅢ에다ᄲᅢ아기고쇼ᄒᆞ고후에동비의협챵으로가산을탕진ᄒᆞ야지금주을디경이로되엿더니작년봄에ᄯᅩ동학으로장ᄂᆞᆫ다ᄂᆞᆫ소문을듯고ᄉᆡᆼ각ᄒᆞ기로를지금사라야모랴도엇시ᄆᆡ로ᄒᆞ을만당ᄒᆞᆯ지라쳘아리즁ᄂᆞᆫ다ᄒᆞ고ᄌᆞ결ᄒᆞ엿더니금번거울에술쳥ᄆᆡ본군에온단말을듯고동세의셔가말ᄒᆞ기를우리남편이사라면이번에피로음을당ᄒᆞᆯ겟ᄂᆞᆫ셔ᄃᆡ쥬어엽라국에간거시다ᄒᆡᆼᄒᆞ다ᄒᆞ고인ᄒᆞ여ᄌᆞ결ᄒᆞ엿다더라

○기부등의 근일에쥬단금란ᄒᆞᆫ후로다시ᄃᆞ른즁챵기의평시세의복에ᄂᆞᆫ약목으로엉고손님불세만쥬단으로ᄒᆞᆫ다ᄒᆞᄂᆞᆫ즁졀엽이이ᄀᆞᆺ치ᄒᆞᆯ진ᄃᆡ고기부만둥히부자되깃고기ᄉᆡᆼ은그ᄒᆞᆫ옷도만히못입고ᄒᆞᆫᄀᆞᆺ미음ᄒᆞᄂᆞᆫ분거반된다더라

관보

뎨삼쳔삼십팔호 광무구년이월십칠일

서임급ᄉᆞ령

○의원면본관 육구면보쥬수

UNION INSURANCE SOCIETY OF CANTON.

Head office Hongkong.
Marine risks underwritten at current rates.

Agents in Chemulpo,
E. MEYER & Co.

COMPAGNIE DES MESSAGERIES MARITIMES.

Fortnightly Direct Service.

For Marseilles
via Ports.
Sailing from Yokohama
Calling at Kobe,
Shanghai, Hongkong, Saigon, Singapore,
Colombo, Djibonti, Suez, Port Said
and Marseilles.

For particulars apply to
HOLME RINGER & Co.,
Chemulpo.

HAYASHIDA & CO.,

16 MYENG DONG, CHIN KO KAI, SEOUL.
BRANCH OFFICE AT CHEMULPO.

Money changers, Coal and Wood Merchants, Express Agents.

We are agents for the Pyeng-yang Coal Company and the Karazu Coal Company of Japan. We have the best quality of both anthracite and bituminous coal, and prompt execution of orders is our speciality. Firewood of all kinds kept in stock. Full weight guaranteed. Money of all denominations exchanged at current rates. Parcels received for all parts.

CHINA MUTUAL LIFE INS. OC.

Most favourable terms to policy holders.

Benefit system unsurpassed.

HOLME RINGER & Co.
Agents, Chemulpo.

C. P. R.

CANADIAN PACIFIC RAILWAY COMPANY'S ROYAL MAIL STEAMSHIP LINE.

THE FAST ROUTE BETWEEN CHINA, JAPAN, AND EUROPE VIA CANADA AND THE UNITED STATES.

Route from Hongkong via Shanghai, Nagasaki (Inland Sea of Japan) Kobe, Yokohama Victoria and Vancouver.

Twin Screw Empress Steamship—6,000 Tons—Speed 19 knots.

PROPOSED SAILING FROM YOKOHAMA.
R. M. S. Empress of India.
R. M. S. Empress of Japan.
R. M. S. Empress of China.
R. M. S. Athenian.
R. M. S. Taatar.

Special reduction (first class only) granted to members of the Military, Naval, Diplomatic and Civil services and to Missionaries.

Passengers have choice of ten routes across the Continent of America and have privilege of travelling by any Atlantic Steamship Line.

Round the World passage tickets in connection with the P. and O. S. N., North German Lloyd and Messageries Co.'s **£125.**

All rates payable at current rate of exchange.

For further information, Tickets, Guide Books, etc., apply to

HOLME, RINGER & Co., AGENTS,
Chemulpo.

Grand Hotel,

(Formerly the Station Hotel)

Near the Railway Terminus,
West Gate Seoul.

The Best Hotel in Korea;
Handsome new Building.
Fine Airy Rooms
Excellent Cuisine.
Terms Moderate.
Special terms to Missionaries
and to permanent boarders.

Electric cars within 2 minutes' walk.

W. H. EMBERLEY.
Proprietor

EVERY FACILITY.

In connection with Life Assurance Business is afforded by

The Standard Life Assurance Co.,

One of the largest and wealthiest of the Provident Institutions of the United Kingdom Forms of Application and all information will be promptly afforded on application.

10 CENTS A DAY.

Not a very large expenditure is it? But it is sufficient to secure for a man of 30 a policy with the STANDARD LIFE OFFICE for

$1323.

For all particulars of rates, etc., apply to

Holme, Ringer & Co.,
Agents, Chemulpo.

THE NEW YORK LIFE INSURANCE COMPANY.

Have you ever been declined by any Company?

Are you engaged in a specially hazardous occupation?

Have you heard of the New York Life Insurance Company's New Classifications for this class of Risks?

If not. send your date of birth, occupation and particulars of rejection, if any to

E. MEYER & Co.,
Agents, Chemulpo.

MITSUI BUSSAN KAISHA.
(MITSUI & Co.)
MITSUI GINKO.
(MITSUI BANK.)

The Bank is owned by the members of the Mitsui Family, who, as partners, assume an unmited responsibility for all liabilities of the Bank:—

Capital........................Yen 5,000,000
Reserve Fund...................." 5,600,000

HEAD OFFICE, TOKYO.
LONDON OFFICE, 34 LIME ST., E. C.

BRANCHES AND AGENCIES:—
New York, San Francisco, Hamburg, Bombay, Singapore, Manila, Hongkong, Amoy, Chefoo, Tientsin.

Kobe, Hakodate, Yokohama, Kure, Yokosuka, Moji, Shimonoseki, Miike, Wakamatsu, Nagasaki, Kuchinotsu, Karatsu, Sasebo, Misume, Taipeh, &c.

Telegraphic Address for all the Offices:
"MITSUI."
A. B. C. AND A. 1 CODES USED.

Contractors of Coal
To the Imperial Japanese Navy. Arsenals and Railway Bureau, Principal Railway Companies and Industrial Work, Home and Foreign Mail and Freight Steamers.

Sole Proprietors
Of the famous Miike, Tagawa and Yamano Coal Mines

Sole Agents
For the sale of Fukumo, Hokoku, Ichimura, Kanoda, Mannoura, Onoura, Ostuji, Sonoda, Tsubaruro, Yoshinotani, Yoshio, Yurokibura and other coals.

YANGTSE INSURANCE ASSOCIATION, LTD.

The undersigned, having been appointed agents for the above company, are prepared to issue policies and pay losses on marine risks at regular rates.

E. MEYER & Co.,
Agents, Chemulpo.

AMERICAN KOREAN ELECTRIC CO.

Light and Power.

Main Office: Electric Building, Chong No.

RAILWAY DEPARTMENT.

OPERATING CARS BETWEEN EAST AND WEST GATE, EVERY TEN MINUTES:—

First Car leaves East Gate at 7:00 A. M. First Car leaves R. R. Station at 7:25 A. M
Last Car " East Gate at 8.40 P. M. Last " " R. R. Station at 9.05 P.M

OPERATING CARS BETWEEN EAST GATE AND IMPERIAL TOMB TERMINUS, EVERY TWENTY MINUTES:—
CONNECTING WITH EVERY ALTERNATE CAR ARRIVING AT EAST GATE FROM CHONG NO.

First Car leaves East Gate for Tomb at 7:10 A. M.
" " " Tomb for East Gate at 7:30 A. M
Last " " East Gate for Tomb at 7:50 P. M.
" " " Tomb for East Gate at 8:10 P. M.

OPERATING CARS BETWEEN CHONG NO AND YUNG SAN RIVER EVERY TWELVE MINUTES:—

First Car leaves Chong No for South Gate at 7:12 A. M.
" " " Chong No for Yung San at 7:36 A. M.
" " " South Gate for Chong No at 7:20 A. M.
" " " Yung San for Chong No at 8:09 A. M.
Last " " South Gate for Chong No 9:00 P. M.
" " " Yung San for Chong No at 8.45. P. M.

SPECIAL PRIVATE CARS FURNISHED TO SUIT CONVENIENCE OF PATRONS. PRICES ON APPLICATION AT HEAD OFFICE.

LIGHTING DEPARTMENT.

Where less than 250 candle power of light is used, the rate per month will be
Per 16 candle power incandescent lamp,—All night.—Yen 2.50.
32 candle power incandescent lamp:—All night:—Yen 4.00.
50 candle power incandescent lamp:—All night:—Yen 6.00.
150 " " " " " " 10.00.
1200 " enclosed are " " " " 20.00.

Where more than 250 candle power of light is used, a Meter will be installed, freqvedted:—Rent of Meter Yen 2.00 per month. Rate of charges by meter reading:—Two Sen per Ampere per hour. (Approximately this is equal to about One Sen per 16 C. P. lamp per hour) Minimum monthly charge where meter is installed, Yen 20.00 per month, which includes rental of meter.

Estimates for installing lights furnished on application
An assortment of chandeliers always on hand.

K. Murakami.
Photograph Studio
Chinkokai, Seoul.

Printing, Developing and Enlargement, of Photographs always Undertaken.

Korean Views and Pictures Illustrating Native Customs always on Sale,

THE OSAKA SHOSEN KAISHA.

Boats frequently on the berth for Chinnampo.

REGULAR SAILINGS BETWEEN JAPAN AND KOREAN PORTS.

FUSAN. AND KOBE VIA SHIMONOSEKI.

OSAKA VIA MOKPO, FUSAN, SHIMONOSEKI AND KOBE.

MOJI DIRECT.

OSAKA VIA KUNSAN, MASANPO, FUSAN, SHIMONOSEKI AND KOBE.

CHEMULPO KUNSAN LINE,
Every three days.

CHEMULPO CHINNAMPO LINE.
Every three days.

For Freight and passage and further particulars apply to
THE OSAKA SHOSEN KAISHA,
Chemulpo

RONDON, PLAISANT & CO.

General Storekeepers and Merchants, Ships Contractors, Tobacconists, Commission and Forwarding Agents, Coal Merchants

IMPORTERS AND EXPORTERS

Seoul & Chemulpo.

W. D. WENTWORTH.

LANDING
AND
SHIPPING AGENT
AND
CUSTOMS BORDER.

12 OURA, NAGASAKI.

STEWARD & CO.

Chemulpo.

Shipchandlers and Storekeepers, Naval and Mercantile Contractors, Landing and Shipping Agents.

STEWARD'S HOTEL

Chemulpo.

Best accommodation in the port for travellers. Clean and well-aired rooms, good cuisine andprompt attendence, moderate tariff.

ᄉᆞ 리종헌

○임한셩면보ᄉᆞ주ᄉᆞ셔판임관오등 시흥면보ᄉᆞ주ᄉᆞ 최봉규

○임옥구면보ᄉᆞ주ᄉᆞ셔판임관륙등 셩진우졔ᄉᆞ주ᄉᆞ 조졔환

○승셥급봉 한셩면보ᄉᆞ주ᄉᆞ 최봉규 옥구면보ᄉᆞ주ᄉᆞ 조졔환

이샹일월십이일

○의원면본관 규쟝각직각 서샹훈 효창원참봉 한봉회

○명규쟝각학ᄉᆞ겸임시긔원일긔관셔칙임관삼등 졍일품 리순익

○임규쟝각직각셔판임관ᄉᆞ등 오픔 리인구

○임효창원참봉셔판임관팔등 면계희

○종종이픔가션대부비부졍관 교항셩 리동희

○조종샹픔통훈대부쟝례원좌쟝례 고셩균진ᄉᆞ 리창원

이샹종이픔가션대부젼니쟝츄원경리종명창교중조교의범면

○명졍포관 안동군수 송종면

○승셔판임관ᄉᆞ등 젼라남도관찰부공립소학교교관 홍병하

○임창원면보ᄉᆞ주ᄉᆞ셔판임관ᄉᆞ등 평양면보ᄉᆞ주사 젼규명

○임평양면보사주사셔판임관륙등 경셩면보사주사 박준쳥

○임희쥬면보사주사셔판임관륙등 셩진면보사주사 윤졍형

○승셔판임관륙등 젼라북도관찰부총순 윤덕근

○급샹급봉 농샹공학교교관 김대휘

○급이급봉 창원면보사주사 젼규명

○급ᄉᆞ급봉 평양면보사주사 박준쳥 희쥬면보사주사 윤졍형

이샹일월십사일

○의원면본관 홍문관시독 유면호 홍문관시독 오셩션

○명시종원경셔칙임관삼등 태의원경 김규홍

○명태의원경셔칙임관삼등 비셔원경 박용대

○명비셔원경셔칙임관이등 시강원첨사 리졔현

○명시강원첨사셔칙임관이등 궁내부특진관 조한국

○명내장원경셔칙임관삼등 종이픔 김중환

○임홍문관시독셔판임관륙등 비셔원랑 임빅영

○임홍문관시독셔판임관칠등 륙픔 졍현지

○임비셔원랑셔판임관칠등 륙픔 김한용

○임농신사면회과주사셔판임관팔등 효창원참봉 면계희 김면우

○임효창원참봉셔판임관팔등 구픔 한봉희

이샹일월십오일

궁내부즉ᄉᆞ

○규쟝각학ᄉᆞ홍승헌ᄉᆞ직소 비지셩소구실이라쳥ᄒᆞᆫ바ᄂᆞᆫ의시ᄒᆞ라ᄒᆞ시다

○평안남도관찰ᄉᆞ리즁하ᄌᆞ벌소 비지셩소구실이라지ᄂᆞᆫ일을엇지ᄒᆞ야이ᄀᆞᆺ치말ᄒᆞ리오경은ᄉᆞ양치말고더욱관찰에힘잉을힘쓰라ᄒᆞ시다

이샹일월십ᄉᆞ일

○시종원경남명쳘ᄉᆞ직ᄒᆞᆫᄉᆞ소 비지셩소구실이라시종원경의임명은의시ᄒᆞ라ᄒᆞ시다

○내장원경김희원ᄉᆞ직소 비지셩소구실쳥ᄒᆞᆫ바ᄂᆞᆫ의시ᄒᆞ라ᄒᆞ시다

이샹일월십오일

론셜

한국을졍복ᄒᆞᆷ

○일진회가지금은조용ᄒᆞ고그식골회원들은저의들의고향으로도라가셔명령ᄒᆞ엿스니서울안에별노일이업도다

엇더ᄒᆞ던지그회원들이별셔일본사ᄅᆞᆷ들의리용ᄒᆞᆫ비되엿ᄂᆞᆫ지라그회에셔비ᄅᆞᆫ진분란을평샹아셔쟝곡쳔대쟝이셔울에셔평장권을티리ᄒᆞ고자귀의인허업시ᄂᆞᆫ회를다시셰ᄂᆞᆯ이모지못ᄒᆞ리라ᄂᆞᆫ고시를반포ᄒᆞᄂᆞᆫ말ᄲᅮᆫ리를엇엇도다

일본사ᄅᆞᆷ들이시사에티ᄒᆞ야한인들은저의들의의견을셜명도못ᄒᆞ게ᄒᆞᄂᆞᆫ것이분명ᄒᆞ고엇더ᄒᆞ던지일후에ᄂᆞᆫ일본이한국졍부에티ᄒᆞ야하여ᄒᆞᆫ불합ᄒᆞᆫ요구를ᄒᆞ드리도한인들은이전장샹사건에티ᄒᆞ야반티ᄒᆞ던것ᄀᆞᆺᄒᆞᆫ분발ᄒᆞᄂᆞᆫ공론을능히니지못ᄒᆞᆯ지라

지금일본사ᄅᆞᆷ들의외론ᄋᆞᆫ드ᄅᆞᆯ디경이면저의나라인민을한국에시식민ᄒᆞ고한국에광대ᄒᆞᆫ농업디를졈령ᄒᆞ라ᄒᆞᄂᆞᆫ지라

그날비일병동맹과일한의정셔에한약됴와ᄂᆞᆫ반티이나그러ᄒᆞ나일본이한국졍부에티ᄒᆞ야인허를엇기ᄭᆞ지져의요구ᄒᆞᆫ사건을고집ᄒᆞᄂᆞᆫ것을볼만ᄒᆞ도다지번분에일본젼대쟝셩관이장샹씨가한국졍부에쳥구ᄒᆞᆫ한국진흰디사건은세샹에셔주의ᄒᆞ던알바이어니와그진황디의디광은수엽셧스나가량이젼국토디의반이나샹분지이가되나ᄒᆞ니만일한국졍부에셔그쳥구ᄒᆞᆷ을허락ᄒᆞ엿더면그토디들영영다

시챵기어려웟슬지라

쟝샹ᄉᆞ건이식원지아니ᄒᆞ게되니일본졍부에셔그ᄉᆞ건쟉티맛티셔강경ᄒᆞ게운동ᄒᆞ엿도다한인들이그ᄉᆞ건에주의ᄒᆞᆯ안후로곳중론이분발ᄒᆞ야대회를열고졍부에향ᄒᆞ야ᄉᆞ방으로그ᄉᆞ건의반티가비셴ᄀᆞᆺ치드리오ᄂᆞᆫ지라

그회ᄂᆞᆫ규측이잇고차셔가밝너서그목젹은다만일본졍부의쳥구ᄒᆞᆷ을퇴락ᄒᆞᄂᆞᆫ거슬반티ᄒᆞᆯᄲᅮᆫ이러니그뎟치마ᄂᆞᆫ그회ᄂᆞᆫ필경일본헌병의게핍박이되엿고일본이군법으로시힝ᄒᆞ야그회에서연셜ᄒᆞ던회원들은만히잡혀가셔그중에몃사ᄅᆞᆷ들은지금것엇지되엿ᄂᆞᆫ지모로겟더라

그시비에ᄒᆞᆫ일본사ᄅᆞᆷ에고모치라ᄒᆞᄂᆞᆫ자가한인몃몃을모아서회ᄒᆞ나를조직ᄒᆞ야일진회라고일ᄒᆞᆷ을짓고일본의쳥구와권고를찬됴ᄒᆞ기로ᄒᆞ엿ᄂᆞᆫ티그회ᄂᆞᆫ서울안에와서울근처에란봉패들을모아ᄂᆞᆫ거시오일본사ᄅᆞᆷ이경비를티주고일본헌병의보호ᄒᆞᄂᆞᆫ아리에잇스며보세우ᄂᆞᆫ복쟉은시졍개션이라ᄒᆞ나그참쥬의ᄂᆞᆫ졍부를핍박ᄒᆞ고피등계ᄒᆞ쟈ᄂᆞᆫ거시러라

근일에그회가인심을션동ᄒᆞ고소요ᄒᆞ게ᄒᆞᄂᆞᆫ연셜을ᄒᆞᄂᆞᆫ지라한국병졍이그회를헷치라ᄒᆞᆯ제음에일본헌병이와서막어셔로다ᄐᆞᆺ도ᄂᆞᆫ시비에일진회원의ᄒᆞᆫ분이샹ᄒᆞ엿ᄂᆞᆫ지라

서울안에다ᄅᆞᆫ요란ᄒᆞᆯ리미ᄂᆞᆫ업것스나그런치마ᄂᆞᆫ일본인은이게졔를티셔군법을더엄ᄒᆞ게시힝ᄒᆞ며서울에서경찰권을티리ᄒᆞ고일본의인허업시ᄂᆞᆫ회를조직ᄒᆞᆷ을금ᄒᆞᄂᆞᆫ규측을반포ᄒᆞᆫ지라

지금은일본인이자의계쳥에티ᄒᆞ야공동반티ᄒᆞᆷ을막을베비를단단히ᄒᆞ엿슴샘이니라저의들을찬됴ᄒᆞ기에미발난한인의더슈들저의들의등뒤에두고임의로수힝ᄒᆞᄂᆞᆫ도다

그런저들에만일일본이한국졍부에향ᄒᆞ야쟝샹ᄉᆞ건ᄀᆞᆺᄒᆞᆫ쳥구를ᄒᆞᆯ베에그일에티ᄒᆞ야한인의인용동반티가엇더리도그거시한국에셔민심이변ᄒᆞᆫ것으로ᄂᆞᆫ알지말지어다

뎐보

셩사일공사관착

○우가둔소젼 일월십이일젹의의과병팔긔중티와대포십이문이우가둔부근에로힝ᄒᆞ야우리병참부를공격ᄒᆞ엿스나우리군사군이이거슬공격ᄒᆞ엿스나우리군이이거슬격퇴ᄒᆞ엿더라

○뎐도소손 젹의소수과병이일월십일일밤에뎐음을습ᄒᆞ야인신졈형혁과밋영구뎨셕교방명으로쟝흥잉야텬도에조곰파손을쥬어스나우ᄂᆞᆫ즉시슈복이라ᄒᆞ엿더라

십사일군사령부착

○섬과폐도 섬이일하남부군(함창에셔북삼십리)에잇ᄂᆞᆫ우리강시병이젼진ᄒᆞ야리도ᄒᆞᄂᆞᆫ젹과약섭사명에티ᄒᆞ야사격을더ᄒᆞ야그섬과를줄어버렷더라

(신복일본군ᄉᆞ령부착)

○젹병퇴란 슈일리로힝셩비셕교우쟝영구부근에출몰ᄒᆞ야텰도와뎐션등에방히ᄒᆞ든젹은쟝관(졔비리후)와쟝관(미슈ᄑᆞᄂᆞᆫ)의령솔ᄒᆞᆫ군인티그병력은젹병일슈단에ᄂᆞ리지아니ᄒᆞ고젹은십이일영구를공격ᄒᆞ야다대ᄒᆞᆫ손히를밧은후십ᄉᆞ일오젼팔시경에우샹셔방에셔우리의게퇴로를단ᄒᆞ고져ᄒᆞᆯ지비샹ᄒᆞᆫ손히를밧아셔북방으로ᄎᆞ퇴게ᄒᆞ엿더라

○퇴각즁령 통일요ᄌᆞ령부군에엄습ᄒᆞ야온젹ᄋᆞᆫ쟝교이하뵉여명의ᄉᆞ샹자들이로퍼고베부ᄂᆞᆫ쟝이문의과피를입은후태부ᄂᆞᆫ쟝즁령비북으로퇴각ᄒᆞ엿더라

○졔후퇴젹 십ᄉᆞ일이도가즈에셔우리졔후ᄂᆞᆫ약팔십명의졔라파즁들ᄒᆞ야이것격퇴라ᄒᆞ엿도라

론돈발 일월구일

○로국인심과젼쟁 셩피득보에셔란슌함락으로ᄒᆞ야처음에격양ᄒᆞ던여론은지금은엇셔지셥ᄒᆞ고소싱일에쟝쟝마다젼쳐들교당에셔란슌구에셔젼망ᄒᆞᆫ휘롯군을위ᄒᆞ야베풀례식에ᄂᆞᆫ참예ᄒᆞᆫ사ᄅᆞᆷ이얼마못되엿더라

동디발 동일

○영국귀족의연셜 영국귀족셜본경이ᄇᆞᆯ버힝ᄒᆞᆫ곳에셔연셜ᄒᆞ되우리가ᄇᆞᆯ다시일본과로국을갓치젼티ᄒᆞ며아ᄒᆞᆯ것이일본은우리의동맹국이니우리가조아ᄒᆞᄂᆞᆫ것이의례ᄉᆞ이지마ᄂᆞᆫ고와갓치로국을조아ᄒᆞ지아니ᄒᆞ엿다가ᄂᆞᆫ우리의게즁치못ᄒᆞ리라ᄒᆞ엿다더라

광고

○본인의쟝ᄌᆞ치렬이가본시부랑패류로고부형ᄌᆞ뎨간에분졔ᄒᆞ며가진면쟝문권을수히도젹ᄒᆞ여니엿기로세부등이ᄒᆞ야시문권을모든엇고혹이광포ᄒᆞ오니니외국인간에사가속지말고한치렬의가진문권을면집지마옵기를바라옵

평양셩니쌍거리 한계쥰 고빅

TELEGRAMS.

(FROM JAPAN PAPERS.)

Berlin, Jan. 9.

The intermediation and peace rumours are now being denied from all quarters.

Prince Adalbert of Prussia, the Kaiser's third son, who was with the German East Asiatic squadron, will visit India as the guest of Viceroy Lord Curzon. He is expected to return to Berlin in the latter part of May, when the wedding of the German Crown Prince will also take place. The intended visit to Japan has consequently been abandoned.

The United States have presented an ultimatum to Venezuela, should their demands not be agreed to.—Deutsche Japan-Post service.

The "Standard" says that Gen. Sir William Nicholson is definitely selected as Governor of Gibraltar (in succession to Sir George White, appointed Governor of Chelsea).

The rumours that the Suez Canal Company will reduce the rates are false.

READY WIT.

Innumerable stories are told illustrating Lord Charles' readiness of wit. For instance, he once had a Chinese servant named Tom Fat, who embezzled quite a large sum before he was discovered. Not long afterwards, Lord Charles was expressing the opinion that Heaven was for good people, whatever their creed, when a friend slily asked, "What about Tom Fat?" Quick as lightning came the retort, "*That* fat will most certainly be in the fire!"

CHEAP BIBLES ILLEGAL.

The British and Foreign Bible Society is involved in a curious dispute with the Ottoman Government over the sale of Bibles at Uskub, in Macedonia, by agents of the society.

It is not that the Turkish authorities fear the sale will aid sedition or spread disaffection among the subjects of the Porte, but that the Bibles are sold at "ridiculously low prices," and that therefore the sale partakes of the character of propaganda. The cheapest Bibles are sold at a sum which represents 3s. 1d. in English money.

This is not the first time that the society has had a dispute with the Porte. Last year the request was gravely made that the words in Acts, "Come over into Macedonia and help us," should be altered into. "Come over into the villages of Salonika and Monastir and help us."

The Turkish Government professed to fear that the words as they stood might be interpreted as an invitation to to help the insurgents!

The British Embassy at Constantinople has entered a strong protest against the action of the Porte.

The well informed Tokio correspondent of the "Japan Herald," writing of the newly imposed tax on Textiles, says:—A distinguished publicist, who has been unsparing in his efforts in Parliament and in the Press to prevent the adoption of that unfortunate measure, tells me the wealthy dealers are so enraged at the passage of the law that they have openly threatened not to subscribe to future domestic loans. There must be some truth in the report, as the "Chugwaa Shogyo" gravely reads those dealers a lecture on their lack of patriotism in putting their interests before those of the nation. The reproach is rather absurd, for unless present appearances are greatly deceptive few of the people connected with the domestic textile industry will have any money to subscribe to bonds next year. Rather a grave financial crisis is to be feared which it will take all the resources and ksill of the Nippon Ginko to avert.

THE BRITISH SUPPLY OF COAL FOR THE NAVY.

Professor Boyd Dawkins need not apologise for urging again and again upon public notice the importance of the British Government, by some means or other, securing a hold upon South Wales steam coal for the use of our own warships. In an article in the "National Review" he goes over the whole ground. After showing that the smokeless coal area is being rapidly depleted, "leaving but a narrow margin for the supply of our navy," he adds:—

On this point, so vital to the navy, we may expect to obtain statistics from the Coal Commission. It is clear, from the evidence which they have published, "that the best Welsh steam coal (Admiralty) is being exhausted at an extraordinarily rapid rate, and that the coalfield has now to depend more upon its second and third class seams." I am informed by a competent authority engaged in the trade that the quality now supplied to the Admiralty is not so good as it was ten years ago—the natural result of the diminishing supply of the better Admiralty fuel. We may well ask ourselves how long is it going to last? Mr. Shaw's estimate that 150 to 200 years will elapse before any area which may be reserved for Admiralty purposes by government will be wanted is useless, because it relates to the whole of the South Welsh steam coals, both Admiralty and non-Admiralty. Twenty-five years is probably nearer the mark.

As a matter of fact, we do not know how long the steam coal of South Wales is going to last. On this point we await the results of the Royal Commission. Still less do we know whether the Admiralty will have any choice at all in the immediate future between smokeless and smoking steam coal. Is it wise for us to shut our eyes to this contingency? It is obviously our duty to face the matter now, whether the time of the exhaustion of Admiralty coal be twenty-five or more years hence. If we do not take every step to ensure the command of the sea we deserve to lose it.

If a strong man armed, and having within his borders warlike stores possessed by none of his neighbours and barely sufficient for his own needs, were to sell them to his rivals and possible enemies in the future, so that they could arm themselves against him, we should think it an act of extraordinary folly, even if he got a good price, cash down. We, as a nation, are doing this very thing.

MEMORIAL ON MANCHURIA.

Viceroy Chang Chih Tung has memorialised the Throne regarding the future administration of Manchuria as follows—That the Government of Manchuria be reformed, and that viceroy, governors, provincial judges, trasurers, taotais, magistrates, etc, be appointed to administer the Government; that the standing and auxiliary forces be thoroughly drilled and organised; that a system of police be introduced for the maintenance of law and order; that the number of treaty ports be increased; that an Imperial Government bank to established in Mukden, and that a paper currency be issued for the convenience of the inhabitants of the three Eastern provinces; that an afforestatfon department be established for the control of the timber-producting districts of the three Eastern provinces, and that fisheries be founded for the exploitation of the fishing grounds of the Ap Luk Kiang and Tsung Fa Kiang. Chang's memorial is said to bave contained over 30,000 characters.—S. C. Morning Post.

CLEARING FOR ACTION.

It is trite to say that a warship in the time of peace carries a number of things which are not only useless but a real danger in time of war. The order is therefore given to "clear for action," and as a result everything that can possibly cause splinters or be set on fire is thrown overboard or stowed away according to circumstances. The decks where wood is unavoidably used are thoroughly wetted and kept wet by means of hose pipes. Everything is done to prevent fire, and to quench fire when it breaks out.

The reason for the order "Clear for action" becomes terribly apparent as the battle proceeds. When it comes to close range action, the vessel which has not time to clear, brings about its own ruin. It is then that the upper works, superstructures, military masts, funnels, ventilators, chart houses, bridges, stacks of boats, and top hamper will be shot to fragments, and it is then that the fire demon plays havoc with the ship.

The wooded companion ladders, mess table, benches, and other impediments found between decks are a source of great danger, and on this account the amount of woodwork in the British vessels has been cut down as far as possible, although we have not gone so far as the Japanese and the Americans, who do without tables.

Small boats, etc, are also a grave danger, and there is little chance of their being able to save life after a battle, for they would be in pieces, and most likely consumed by fire. More than likely the life preservers, too, have fallen victims to fire.

It can easily be seen that clearing for action takes some considerable time, and on the swiftness with which a vessel can be cleared very often depends the result of the battle. Be it remembered, by the way, that the Baltic fleet is cleared for action all the time. With regard to the boats, the French method is to fill them with water and surround them with splinter-proof material.

The presence of the top hamper in battleships is another danger and prevents celerity in clearing for action. According to Lieutenant-Commander Wainwright, of the United State Navy, many of our Mediterranean fleet take as long as twenty-four hours to clear on account of the top-hamper.

In a graphic description of the future naval battle. Mr. H. W. Wilson in his "Ironclads in Action" says, "Upon the upper works of the ships, then, will fall most of the damage inflicted during the preliminary cannonade. They will have been prepared for the strain in every conceivable way. Round the funnels sacks of coal will be placed, and near the quickfirers mantlets to catch the splinters. The conning-tower and the positions from which the ship will be fought will also doubtles receive attention. In this way the injury done may be reduced to a minimum, but it will still be extensive. The effect of even small shell charged with high explosives upon unarmoured structures is very deadly. Great holes will be torn in the outer plating: splinters and fragments of shot and shell sent flying through the confined space within; and any wood that may be about, which has not been thoroughly drenched with water, will be set on fire.

"The funnels and ventilators may be riddled till they come down, and inside them, on the splinter-gratings, which commonly cross them at the level of the armour deck, fragments of iron and wood will collect and obstruct the draught. If the ventilators are blocked and the flow of air to the stokehold stopped, the stokers and engineroom men will be exposed to terrible hardships—gasping in a hot and vitiated atmosphere for the air which cannot reach them. The boiler-fires will fail and steam-pressure sink.

What with the stowing away of boat chains, screws, etc., the work of clearing for action a matter of hours, not minutes.—Ex.

TELEGRAPH COMPANIES AND THE WAR.

The dogs of war have brought a golden harvest to the telegraph companies, more sepecially, the Eastern Telegraph, which has had phenomenal payments from the British and Japanese Governments, as well as from newspapers. During the Dogger Bank crisis our Government had the lines during twenty-four hours, and the Japanese have made constant demands of a remunerative character.

The "Manila Cablenews" publishes a wire from San Francisco stating that Baron Kodama, assistant chief of the headquarters staff of the Japanese army, and who recenly disagreed with the present tactics of Field Marshal Oyama, in Manchuria has been recalled for striking the latter officer.

Rhodesia is again to the fore. Its fortunes are looking up. An unlimited source of wealth is just opened up to the colony. Tobacco can be grown there, and tobacco which is said by London merchants to whom samples were submitted, to be better than the best Virginian. "We will take any amount of this," was the verdict. The discovery opens up an era in Rohodesian annals.

Bekanntmachung.

Die Bekanntmachungen der Eintragungen in das hiesige Deutsche Handelsregister erfolgen im Jahre 1905 durch den **"Ostasiatischen Lloyd"** und die **"The Korea Daily News."**

Söul, den 27. Dezember 1904.

Der Kaiserlich Deutsche Minister-Resident und General-Konsul.

(L. S.) gez. von Saldern.

The Korea Daily News.

Issued at 5 P. M. daily except Sundays.

Rate of Subscription:—
Per Year,............Yen 25.
Per Quarter,..........Yen 7.
Per Month,..........Yen 2.50.

Postage in Korea not charged extra.
Postage abroad charged extra.

Advertisements, 50 sen per day for 1 inch or less.
5 yen per month per inch.
50 yen per year per inch.

All communications to

E. T. BETHELL,
Editor and Publisher,
Pak-tong, Seoul.

JAPANESE MISSIONARIES.

It is often the case that missionary labours do not receive due recognition. In many cases men leave happy and comfortable homes and go abroad under adverse circumstances to teach the uninitiated what they believe to be the Gospel.

Gospels vary according to creeds but it is only fair to credit the missionaries of the various creeds with a belief in their propaganda and an honest desire to do good in accordance with their particular beliefs.

Can the same be said, however, with regard to the present exodus of Buddhist priests from Japan to China. Many stories have been told of "Warships following missionaries," many of them without foundation, but we never saw a catch-phrase so well justified as this one is at present by Japanese activities in China.

Anyone with a knowledge of Japanese character will agree that religion plays a very small part in the routine of their lives. The Shinto is the national religion and Buddhism also has a good hold in as much as the country abounds in temples which belong to one or other of these creeds.

But we should be very loth to say that there is in Japan, any particular enthusiasm for either creed; it is true that the various temple festivals are observed, but they are generally the occasions for sprees among the lower orders, while the more well-to-do Japanese content themselves with frequent subscriptions to the temples in their neighbourhood.

Amongst the Japanese there is never observable any marked desire for the propagation of the Gospel according to Buddhist teachings and it therefore makes us suspicious when we find that in the name of Buddha the Japanese are now actively prosecuting a campaign in China.

It may be that Japanese intrigues in Korea have filled us with a profound distrust of their motives in all they undertake but we can at least claim to be in good company when we suggest that something besides an unselfish desire to spread the Buddhist faith is actuating their latest move in China.

The "China Mail," speaking of the movement, says:—

Yet, within a reasonable time it may develop forces which will be far-reaching, and be pregnant of results. Those who have interests in China will naturally regard the enterprise of the Japanese with suspicion, and, when all is said and done, it might pay them to be watchful. There can be little doubt that the movement is, at least, partially political. It is part of the silent revolution now in progress, and well-informed Chinese to not hesitate to affirm that such is its ultimate aim. A translation of the leading ideas and purposes of this new church have been forwarded to us and we give them in the belief that they will be of more than passing interest to many. They set out that (1) the name shall be the Monastery of the Pun Un of China. A site shall be secured in Canton, on which a college shall be built. Afterwards affiliated branches shall be opened all over China. (2) This Chinese monastery shall be affiliated to a certain monastery in Japan. All who conform to, and promulgate the new doctrines, shall rely upon the aegis of the Japanese flag for protection. (Other clauses follow, but they have no bearing on the subject under notice.) Following upon this the Canton Correspondent of the same newspaper wrote:—

A few days ago you referred in your leading article to the question of Japanese Buddhists in China. But the information contained therein was confined to what is alleged to be taking place in the centre of China.

I now have that Japanese Missionaries are about to commence work in the Kwangtung province, even if they are not already here.

Recently, the Viceroy issued a proclamation, in which he stated that the Japanese are not only not to be molested but they are to be protected.

And in conclusion we note the following paragraph in the "S. C. Morning Post:"—

The Minister of the Board of Foreign Affairs has sent a despatch to the Governor of Chekiang inquiring why he had allowed the monks of the different monasteries to place themselves under the influence and control of Japanese Buddhist priests.

Truly the Japanese are not idle. The Independence (!) of Korea is not the only object they have in view.

A DREAM PRESENTIMEMT.

Emerson in one of his lectures reckons dreams amongst the greatest mysteries of the mind of man. It is not prophetic dreams alone, or even chiefly, perhaps, that are mysterious, though these, of course, are obviously inexplicable; but the ordinary, every-night visions of everyone. I welcome always however, such prophetic dreams as the following, because they call attention to these mysterious phenomena of the mind. A week or two since Walter Furneaux, one of the crew of the Brixham smack Lyra, woke his whole household by a piercing shriek on the night before he was due to join the vessel. He explained to his wife and the others who were roused by his scream that he dreamed the Lyra had been run down by a steamer, and that he and the rest of the crew were drowning. Both himself and his wife were so depressed by the dream that they dreaded his joining his ship, and he would, indeed, have stayed ashore if he could have found a substitute. Failing to find one, he sailed that afternoon in the Lyra, and was drowned as he had dreamed by the running down of the smack off the coast of South Devonshire by the steamer Heathbank.—From "T. P. in His Anecdotage" in T. P.'s Weekly.

It has already been reported in our columns, says the "Kobe Chronicle," that Mr. Uchida, Japanese Minister to Peking, will shortly be transferred to some other post. We now learn that Mr. Yamaza, Director of the Political Affairs Bureau in the Foreign Office, will succed Mr. Uchida as Minister to Peking.

THE ALLEGED ENLISTMENT OF CHINESE RECRUITS BY JAPAN.

We learn from the Hongkong Daily Press that the Petersburgskiy Listok has received from its correspondent at Harbin the following telegram, the publication of which, it says, has been permitted by Lieutenant-Colonel Alexieff:—

"To-day I received important information from an absolutely trustworthy source to the effect that General Okassimo and Colonel Sibato, of the Japanese Army, have opened a recruiting station for Chinese at the village of Shilintin, eighty-five kilometres from the station of Sinmin-ting. With the object of obtaining recruits, the Japanese have circulated hundreds of thousands of copies of a Proclamation calling upon the Chinese to place themselves under the Japanese Flag to fight the Europeans, and pointing out that the Japanese and Chinese have the same religion and speak almost the same language (!) During the first few days after the issue of the Proclamation, as many as 7,000 recruits were enrolled daily, each man immediately receiving a Japanese uniform. The number of applicants subsequently dwindled, however, to 1,000 per day, owing to misunderstanding with the Japanese authorities. The Chinese recruits, who are paid at the rate of 40 diaos a month, are known as Voluntary Militia. They are sent after enrollment to Inkoa, whence they are distributed in small detachments among the regular Japanese regiments in the field."

ROBERTS IN HIS OLD FORM.

HIS LONG AND FINE SHOTS AS GOOD AS EVER.

The billard match of 9,000 up between John Roberts and C. Harverson, in which the latter is allowed 2,250 points start, was continued at Messrs. Orme's Billard Saloon, Manchester, yesterday (Nov. 18). The following notes on the play are contributed by Harverson:—

Referring to the wonderful show that John Roberts made on Thursday evening, F. Bateman and I were sitting together, and we could not help applauding him for his fine play, particularly in the 384 break. I cannot say how many times he was in difficulties, but he was always making marvellous shots, and he carried the spectator clean away with him, and wound the break up with a double baulk.

Before I played Roberts this match several people who pose as critics of billiards told me that he would miss all the very fine shots and also the ones a long way off, but I find him just the opposite. He seems to revel in long shots, and also in fine ones, and his game now is not confined so much to the top of the table as it was five years ago. I think he is just playing himself into form, and fully expect to see him make a 560 break before the New Year.

The thing that seems to trouble him most is having to wait for the other player to break down. He has been used lately to get the table all to himself, having had mostly to meet amateur players to his four-year tour abroad. At times he gets a little irritable when the other man has the table, but that will wear off in a week or so. The scores at the close of the afternoon's play were:—

Harverson 7,152
Roberts 6,750

CLOSING SCORES.

Harverson 7,693
Roberts 7,501

Roberts made a break of 344.

A crofter in Scotland had a horse that was very ill. A veterinary surgeon was sent for, and he ordered the crofter to give it a strong powder, which he would send, and also a tube through which the powder was to be blown down the horse's throat. The next day the "Vet." called, and met the crofter's wife. He asked her how the horse was getting on. She replied that the horse was all right, but her husband was ill. The "Vet." expressed great surprise, and asked how that had happened. "Well, sir," replied the wife, "you see the horse blew first."

The Korea Daily News.

VOL. II, WEDNESDAY, JANUARY 18, 1905. No. 13

HONGKONG & SHANGHAI BANKING CORPORATION.

Paid-up Capital..... ....$10,000,000
Reserve Fund:—Sterling Reserve... 10,000,000
Silver Reserve..... 7,000,000

27,000,000
Reserve Liability of Proprietors... 10,000,000

HEAD OFFICE, HONGKONG.

London Bankers, London and County Banking Company Limited.

Branches and Agencies,
London.

Amoy,	Hankow	Penang,
Bangkok,	Hiogo,	Rangoon,
Batavia,	Iloilo,	Saigon,
Bombay,	Lyons,	San Francisco,
Calcutta,	Manila,	Singapore,
Colombo,	Nagasaki,	Sourabaya,
Foochow,	New York,	Tientsin,
Hamburg,	Peking,	Yokohama,

Credits granted on approved Securities, and every description of Banking and Exchange business transacted.

Drafts granted on London and the chief Commercial places in Europe, India, Australia, America, China and Japan.

HOLME RINGER & Co., AGENTS,
CHEMULPO.

HOPURKU DOBOKU KAISHA.

Branch office in Chong Dong, Seoul.

Japanese telephone No. 165

CONTRACT DEPARTMENT.

We can contract to build any building or construction.

MERCHANDISE DEPARTMENT.

We can provide any building material. We have just contracted to build the new Belgian Legation.

E. MEYER & CO.

Chemulpo.

—

SOLE AGENTS IN KOREA FOR,

A. T. Morse, Sons & Co.'s

"Fresco" Distemper

—

In all colours ready for use on walls, Ceilings etc.

and

AVENARIUS CARBOLINEUM

—

A wood-preserving and antiseptic oil preparation

Against decay, dry-rot, fungus and wood-destroying insects.

—

A large supply always in stock.
Prices upon application.

—

E. MEYER & Co.,
Chemulpo.

CHARTERED BANK OF INDIA AUSTRALIA & CHINA.

INCORPORATED BY ROYAL CHARTER 1853

HEAD OFFICES:—LONDON.

Paid-up Capital £800,000
Reserve Liability of Shareholders 800,000
Reserve Fund 800,000

Drafts granted upon all the principal places in the world and every description of Exchange and banking business transacted.

E. MEYER & Co., Agents,
Chemulpo.

MITSU BISHI DOCKYARD & ENGINE WORKS,

NAGASAKI.

CODE WORD, "DOCK."

A. 1, A. B. C., and Engineering Codes used.

DOCK No. 1 (at Tategami).

Extreme Length..............523 feet
Length on blocks..............513 „
Width of Entrance on Top........89 „
„ „ Bottom.....77 „
Water on Blocks at Spring Tide 26½ „

DOCK No. 2 (Mukaijima).

Extreme Length..............371 feet
Length on Blocks..............360 „
Width of Entrance on Top.......66 „
„ „ Bottom 53 „
Water on Blocks at Spring Tide 22 „

PATENT SLIP (at Kosuge).

Can take vessels up to 1,000 tons gross.

THE WORKS are well equipped with the LATEST IMPROVEMENTS, and can execute any kind of work in SHIPBUILDING and MARINE ENGINEERING, as well as in REPAIRING of SHIPS.

The COMPANY'S new powerful steamer OURA-MARU (712 tons, 700 I.H.P.), specially built for SALVAGE PURPOSES, and equipped with necessary gear, is always READY at SHORT NOTICE.

THE METHODIST PUBLISHING HOUSE,

Little West Gate, Seoul.

JOB PRINTING, TYPEWRITER PAPER
CARBON PAPER, VISITING CARDS
STATIONERY, BOOK BINDING
BOOK PUBLISHERS.
AMERICAN SCHOOL BOOKS
SPENCERIAN COPY BOOKS
PEN CARBON LETTER AND BILL BOOKS

S.A. BECK, Manager.

DAI-ICHI GINKO.

LIMITED.

(Formerly the First National Bank)

ESTABLISHED 1873

INCORPORATED UNDER PRESENT LAW 1896

Capital - - - - - - - Yen 5,000,000
Reserve Fund - - - - - 1,500,000

HEAD OFFICE:—TOKIO.

President: Baron SHIBUSAWA.

BRANCHES AND CORRESPONDENTS
In the Principal Cities and Towns of Japan.

Interest Allowed on

Fixed deposits 1 year - - - 6½ per cent
„ „ 6 months - - - 6 per cent

Special current accounts 1½ sen daily per Y 100
General „ „ 1 „ „ „ 100

M. TANAKA,
Manager, Chemulpo.

SINGER SEWING MACHINES

씽거조봉침

—

SOLE AGENTS FOR KOREA

전매쇼

—

HOLME RINGER & CO.
Chemulpo.

졔믈포 함룽거양힝

KAMEYA CO.

GENERAL STOREKEEPERS

Chinkokai - - Seoul

(Established 1895, Tokyo)

Confectionery, Hams, Canned Goods, Cutlery, Hirano & Tansan Water, Provisions, Gents, Furnishing goods, Toilet Articles, Travelling Bags, Tobacco, Cigars & Cigarettes Kitchen Utensils. Coffee, Biscuits

Fresh Goods always kept in Stock.
Prices Moderate
Please come and inspect our goods.

NIPPON YUSEN KAISHA.

JAPANESE MAIL STEAMSHIP CO.

DER MAIL CONTRACT WITH THE IMPERIAL JAPANESE GOVERNMENT.

European Line

Regular Fortnightly Service between Yokohama Kobe, Moji, Shanghai, Hongkong, Singapore, Penang Colombo, Port Said, Marseilles, London and Antwerp

American Line

Regular Fortnightly Service between Hongkong and Seattle, calling at Shanghai, Moji, Kobe, Yokohama and Victoria, B. C.

Australian Line

Regular weekly Service betwen Japan Ports and Australia, calling at Hongkong and Manila.

(Above Three Lines, Suspended until further notice).

Shanghai Line

Weekly Service between Shanghai and Japan Port-

Korea Line

Service Kobe, Moji, Nagasaki, Fusan Chemupo Cheffoo, Taiku.

S. S. Bahelsberg, 2181 tons

Service Kobe, Moji, Fusan, Chemulpo, Chinnampo
S. S. ARGO, S. S. Ohfo.

BORDEN'S CONDENSED MILK CO.

New York, U. S. A.

ALWAYS IN STOCK

Eagle Brand Condensed Milk.

Gold Seal Condensed Milk.

Peerless (Family) Evaporated Cream.

Borden's Malted Milk.

E. MEYER & CO.
Chemulpo Korea,
Sole Agents

ROYAL INSURANCE COMPANY,
Funds exceed £10,000,000
FIRE
AT CURRENT RATES
LIFE
REDUCED PREMIUM.
HOLME RINGER & Co.,
Agents, Chemulpo.

HOTEL DU PALAIS

SEOUL.

The only first class Hotel in Seoul Situated in the centre of the city opposite the palace.

Cuisine under the supervision of an experienced French Chef.

Well ventilated and furnished throughout.

TARIFF UPON APPLICATION

L. MARTIN
Proprietor and Manager

大韓每日申報
대한ᄆᆡ일신보

(뎨이쳔십오호)　(토요일)　일쳔구빅오년일월이십일일

본샤고ᄇᆡᆨ

이신보ᄂᆞᆫ영어와한어로셕거ᄆᆡ일츌판ᄒᆞᆷ

신문가

ᄒᆞᆫ쟝　엽젼두돈오푼

ᄒᆞᆫᄃᆞᆯ　엽젼두량닷돈

우표가ᄃᆡ삭닷돈

다ᄉᆞᆺ돈으로밧ᄉᆞᆷ

광고료ᄂᆞᆫ

귀한의쟝단과ᄌᆞ항의다쇼로증감ᄒᆞ되렴가로밧을터이오ᄆᆡ오리지아녀대한사ᄅᆞᆷ마다다이신문을보실터이니광고내시기를원ᄒᆞ시ᄂᆞᆫ이들은우리신문사에와셔면약ᄒᆞ심을희망ᄒᆞᆷ

○발힝소　바동대한ᄆᆡ일신보사법어학교엽헤젼영국인셜필립자리오

사쟝　영국인　(ᄇᆡ셜)

평양　디리졈

○평양효동사는권미보씨로우리신문광고디리인을뎡ᄒᆞ엿시오니평양에계신구람코져ᄒᆞ시는　쳠군ᄌᆞ는혀디리졈에왕림ᄒᆞ와면의ᄒᆞ시옵

사고

○우리대한ᄆᆡ일신보의목뎍은대한의안녕질셔에관한모든뎨목에되ᄒᆞ야는공평한변론을쥬쟝ᄒᆞᆷ이라우리등신원의담보는신문보시는쳠군ᄌᆞ의게ᄒᆞᆫ샹보도ᄒᆞ리며편지들괴셔ᄒᆞ며주시는이는셩명과번디를젹어붓치셔기를희망ᄒᆞ오나이거슨신문샹에긔재ᄒᆞ란거시아니오다만극히신용ᄒᆞ는증거를숨고쟈ᄒᆞᆷ이라긔쟈는아모긔셔던지긔재ᄒᆞᆷ을되갸ᄒᆞ는권리를가졋스나되갸ᄒᆞ는리유를말ᄒᆞᆯ터이오며공중평화를문란케ᄒᆞ는듯ᄒᆞᆫ긔셔는의례히밧지안켓ᄉᆞᆸ나이다

●본사셰셔이리로신문을ᄃᆡ양우례로분젼ᄒᆞ와레젼부의잉의로젼ᄒᆞᆫ듯스로면곳에는ᄒᆞᆨ늣게젼ᄒᆞ기도ᄒᆞ며ᄒᆞᆨ멋칠거슬혼겁에젼ᄒᆞ기도ᄒᆞ며ᄒᆞᆨ아니젼ᄒᆞ는곳도잇다ᄒᆞ와우리신문을ᄉᆞ랑ᄒᆞ야구람ᄒᆞ시는　쳠군ᄌᆞ의게되ᄒᆞ야면우미안ᄒᆞ온기로지금은분젼인을두고ᄆᆡ일일즉이젼ᄒᆞ며아니젼ᄒᆞ거나늣게가나ᄒᆞᆫ폐가업도록ᄒᆞ란ᄒᆞ오니혹아니젼ᄒᆞ거나혹늣게젼ᄒᆞ거나ᄒᆞᆫ일이잇스면본사로통긔ᄒᆞ야주심을희망ᄒᆞᆷ

잡보

○부산갑리면보　경무쳥통문관찰산씨가신월일에부산에도박ᄒᆞᆫ지라갑리무영씨가경무쳥으로면보ᄒᆞ엿더라

○우빙향교문　너부에도교문팽을일본에고빙ᄒᆞ다ᄒᆞ며헌병사령부에도교문관을일본에교빙ᄒᆞ기로이미쟝ᄒᆞ엿다더라

○차관계약　제쟝을리쟝ᄒᆞ야운항을셜시ᄒᆞᆯᄎᆞ로차관일쳔만원을계약ᄒᆞᆯ터인ᄃᆡ히차관은일본에셔젼혀담당이라더라

○디환거쟝　주쳥용사민영철씨가평양관찰사재임시에인민의재산을티파ᄒᆞ히탐ᄒᆞᆫ고로그셰력에두려워감히구처못ᄒᆞ고더니엄간에환국ᄒᆞ면쳘교ᄒᆞᆫ나란젼치참예ᄒᆞᆫ사건으로면관이된다ᄒᆞ는지라평양민이만히상경ᄒᆞ야도라오기를기다려거쟝ᄒᆞᆫ다더라

○교문연셜　십팔일에각관아예산을졈졍ᄎᆞ로회계국과쟝관멋쥬사가탁지부에회동ᄒᆞᆫ자라목하던교문관이재졍에관ᄒᆞᆫ사항을연셜ᄒᆞ엿더라

○외조일관　외부에셔일공관에조회ᄒᆞ되우리나라쟝례원공문너게에함경남도에잇는각릉과및　션원전진향괌길ᄒᆞᆫ줄이가쟝챵부업ᄒᆞᆯ터인ᄃᆡ일본ᄒᆞᆫ군티용문이업스면혹쟝류ᄒᆞᄂᆞᆫ군가잇다ᄒᆞ야일공사의게조회폐야사령부에젼측ᄒᆞ야물금ᄒᆞ란공문을금ᄒᆞ며주기를바란다ᄒᆞ엿기에이조회를인ᄒᆞ야쳥ᄒᆞ니시힝ᄒᆞ라ᄒᆞ엿더라

○조쳥엄헝단속　외부에셔일공관에조회ᄒᆞ기를우리학부공문너기에셩균관쟝보교에말ᄒᆞᆫ기를일젼에일병샤여명이남신문을넘어문묘에돌입ᄒᆞᆷ으로슈직이로ᄒᆞ여곰효유ᄒᆞ며보냇ᄉᆞ나막중문묘존엄ᄒᆞᆫ셰에외병이무란이드리옴이지극히황숑ᄒᆞ오니쳥컨ᄃᆡ일본공관에조회ᄒᆞ며사령부에젼측ᄒᆞ며엄졀히단속케ᄒᆞ라ᄒᆞ엿기에이에조회ᄒᆞᆫ다ᄒᆞ엿더라

○외부조복　외부에셔조복ᄒᆞ기를향쟈귀조회와밋각도진을보ᄂᆡ심이아ᄒᆞᆯ중ᄒᆞᆫ지라귀국군사복진ᄒᆞ는로파평샹군사경찰은가히업지못ᄒᆞᆯ거시로ᄃᆡ치안경찰로말ᄒᆞ여는진실로가히아니ᄒᆞ니귀공사는귀군사령부에젼측ᄒᆞ며군사경찰외에는ᄃᆡ관치말게ᄒᆞ며써권한을분히ᄒᆞ라ᄒᆞ엿더라

○중무귀견　직작일하오이시에명쳥란용관공사와및령사가법부참셔관윤셩보로더브러외부에회동ᄒᆞ며손언방의치명ᄒᆞᆫ사안을심사ᄒᆞ는ᄃᆡ이시도록담판ᄒᆞ엿스나맛참니귀결치못ᄒᆞ엿다더라

○경ᄉᆞ사의　일젼에종로지젼뒤김봉슌의집에셔실화ᄒᆞ엿ᄉᆞᆯ새에일본헌병과소방조등이와셔진력ᄒᆞ야불을구ᄒᆞ엿ᄂᆞᆫᄃᆡ경무ᄉᆞ가이일에되ᄒᆞ야감사ᄒᆞᆫ뜻슬표기위ᄒᆞ야남셔쟝리덕응씨를일본헌병사령부로파견ᄒᆞ야치사ᄒᆞ엿더니ᄉᆞ령관이회사ᄒᆞ야길ᄋᆞᆫ티귀국순검들도ᄆᆡ우진력ᄒᆞ엿거니와귀국에는아직소방계가업셔진화ᄒᆞ기가극난ᄒᆞᆫ즉뎨리ᄯᅩ지축ᄒᆞᆫ물이업스미괴계를쓸수도업는지라소방괴계는아직쥰비ᄒᆞᆯ수업거니와물이나잘저축ᄒᆞᆯ방도을ᄒᆞ야만일화재가나거든우리계를가져다가쓰라ᄒᆞ엿다더라

○최씨상소　챵쟝최익현씨의상소ᄃᆡ긔를득문ᄒᆞᆫ즉　폐하께옵셔금년룩월이후로브터신을부르심이엇지신의열끌을보시고져ᄒᆞ심이리오ᄒᆞᆫ가지라도엇는어리셕은의견으로나라를도읍게ᄒᆞᆷ으로써ᄒᆞ심이라신의샹주ᄒᆞᆫ바여러됴건이목하에급ᄒᆞᆫ시무에샹ᄒᆞᆫ조곤이라도음이업지못ᄒᆞᆯ지라오늘이엇던날이오보ᄂᆞᆺ가외국인의슈모ᄂᆞᆫ유쇽힝ᄒᆞ고ᄒᆞ거니와셩지이국ᄂᆡ경찰을담임ᄒᆞ는거슨우ᄒᆞᆫ고로죠뎡이업고약례로인민이업슴이라　폐하ᄂᆞᆫ엇지분발변려ᄒᆞ옵시지아니ᄒᆞ시옵나잇가조ᄒᆞᆫ　폐하께옵셔ᄆᆡᆼ발으로법용ᄉᆞ들보시고낫게는침쇼에드시옵셔음양의셰셰ᄒᆞᆫ일을반복ᄒᆞ고저ᄒᆞ옵시니빅ᄉᆞ의폐란ᄒᆞᆷ이일노말ᄆᆡ암이라죵차이후로는밤에취침ᄒᆞ옵시고낫제근신을젼젼ᄒᆞ신연후에야빅ᄉᆞ가가히홍졍ᄒᆞ지니다ᄒᆞ엿더라

○비밀쟉의　일쟉에졍부에셔비밀회의를ᄒᆞ엿다는ᄃᆡ그안진을드른즉　재졍을리졍ᄒᆞ야빅동화를쳐치ᄒᆞ며일쳔만원을차관ᄒᆞ야중앙과밋외각도에은힝을셜립ᄒᆞ며　관인의봉급을귀졍ᄒᆞᆯ수긴인ᄃᆡ빅동화쳐치는룩월에가셔야실효가잇스리라더라

○졍부죵의　직작십팔일에는졍부에셔죵회의가되엿는ᄃᆡ고안건인즉이왕리졍ᄒᆞᆫ관제를죵의ᄒᆞ야곳반포ᄒᆞ기로ᄒᆞ엿더라

○너부면ᄒᆞᆫ젼복　너부에셔젼라북도관찰부로면ᄒᆞᆫᄒᆞ기를형금에드른즉관찰부에셔관속을다발ᄒᆞ야셰문을과슈ᄒᆞ고회민의츌입ᄒᆞ는거슨금단ᄒᆞᆫ샹셔로되저ᄒᆞ며원슈쳐를보듯ᄒᆞᆫ다ᄒᆞ니더군평히우리빅셩인ᄃᆡ엇지이랍리치가잇스리오다못ᄒᆞ요유말ᄒᆞᆷ이가ᄒᆞ고일졀위협으로ᄒᆞ지낫ᄒᆞ엿더라

외보

○룡구기혁　로국도루벨교으룡은막ᄉᆞ과참ᄉᆞ회의쟝외재겨으로로군니졍의위ᄒᆞᆯ홈에관ᄒᆞ야너무대신의게츙고ᄒᆞᆫ수가잇스며ᄯᅩ동씨가황뎨폐빈알ᄒᆞ고로국사회의쳥금에샹항은다만쇼파란이이리날쌘아니라ᄒᆞᆫ콘이기혁잇다ᄒᆞ고즁샹ᄃᆡ에　미리날셔두란웅쥬ᄒᆞ엿더라

○슌유중지　덕국황뎨폐하항ᄌᆞ로덕국동양함ᄃᆡ에승탑ᄒᆞᆫ아달벨도친왕면하께셔는인도티슈가두순경의빈깃으로인도를방문ᄒᆞ고동면하는오월하슌에그형군황뎨ᄌᆞ면하ᄒᆞᆫ례로빅잉에귀착ᄒᆞᆫ예쟝인고로동면하계셔일본슌유는중지ᄒᆞ엿다더라

○쳥국빈상　쳥국이일본빈샹금샹신쳥년하히반괴로샹히은자구십수만일쳔구빅이십수량룩젼이니죵일화일빅이십수만팔쳔구빅구십이원이젼을갑ᄒᆞ스빅이깃을졍금은힝샹히지졈에임치ᄒᆞ교샹히에잇는쇼면결총령ᄉᆞ가본국에면보ᄒᆞ엿더라

UNION INSURANCE SOCIETY OF CANTON.

Head office Hongkong.
Marine risks underwritten at current rates.
Agents in Chemulpo,
E. MEYER & Co.

COMPAGNIE DES MESSAGERIES MARITIMES.

Fortnightly Direct Service.

For Marseilles
via Ports.
Sailing from Yokohama
Calling at Kobe,
Shanghai, Hongkong, Saigon, Singapore,
Colombo, Djibonti, Suez, Port Said
and Marseilles.

For particulars apply to
HOLME RINGER & Co.,
Chemulpo.

HAYASHIDA & CO.,

16 MYENG-DONG, CHIN KO KAI, SEOUL.
BRANCH OFFICE AT CHEMULPO.

Money changers, Coal and Wood Merchants,
Express Agents.

We are agents for the Pyeng-yang Coal Company and the Karazu Coal Company of Japan. We have the best quality of both anthracite and bituminous coal, and prompt execution of orders is our speciality. Firewood of all kinds kept in stock. Full weight guaranteed. Money of all denominations exchanged at current rates. Parcels received for all parts.

CHINA MUTUAL LIFE INS. OC.

Most favourable terms to policy holders.

Benefit system unsurpassed.

HOLME RINGER & Co.
Agents, Chemulpo.

C. P. R.

CANADIAN PACIFIC RAILWAY COMPANY'S ROYAL MAIL STEAMSHIP LINE.

THE FAST ROUTE BETWEEN CHINA, JAPAN, AND EUROPE VIA CANADA AND THE UNITED STATES.

Route from Hongkong via Shanghai, Nagasaki (Inland Sea of Japan) Kobe, Yokohama Victoria and Vancouver.

Twin Screw Empress Steamship—6,000 Tons—Speed 19 knots.

PROPOSED SAILING FROM YOKOHAMA.
R. M. S. Empress of India.
R. M. S. Empress of Japan.
R. M. S. Empress of China.
R. M. S. Athenian.
R. M. S. Tartar.

Special reduction (first class only) granted to members of the Military, Naval, Diplomatic and Civil services and to Missionaries.

Passengers have choice of ten routes across the Continent of America and have privilege of travelling by any Atlantic Steamship Line.

Round the World passage tickets in connection with the P. and O. S. N., North German Lloyd and Messageries Co.'s **£125**.

All rates payable at current rate of exchange.

For further information, Tickets, Guide Books, etc., apply to

HOLME, RINGER & CO., AGENTS,
Chemulpo.

Grand Hotel,

(Formerly the Station Hotel)

Near the Railway Terminus. West Gate Seoul.

The Best Hotel in Korea;
Handsome new Building.
Fine Airy Rooms
Excellent Cuisine.
Terms Moderate.
Special terms to Missionaries
and to permanent boarders.

Electric cars within 2 minutes' walk.

W. H. EMBERLEY.

Proprietor

AMERICAN KOREAN ELECTRIC CO.

Light and Power.

Main Office: Electric Building, Chong No.

RAILWAY DEPARTMENT.

OPERATING CARS BETWEEN EAST AND WEST GATE, EVERY TEN MINUTES:—

First Car leaves East Gate at 7:00 A. M. First Car leaves R. R. Station at 7:25 A. M
Last Car " East Gate at 8.40 P. M. Last " " R. R. Station at 9.05 P.M

OPERATING CARS BETWEEN EAST GATE AND IMPERIAL TOMB TERMINUS, EVERY TWENTY MINUTES:—

CONNECTING WITH EVERY ALTERNATE CAR ARRIVING AT EAST GATE FROM CHONG NO.

First Car leaves East Gate for Tomb at 7:10 A. M.
" " " Tomb for East Gate at 7:30 A. M.
Last " " East Gate for Tomb at 7:50 P. M.
" " " Tomb for East Gate at 8:10 P. M.

OPERATING CARS BETWEEN CHONG NO AND YUNG SAN RIVER EVERY TWELVE MINUTES:—

First Car leaves Chong No for South Gate at 7:12 A. M.
" " " Chong No for Yung San at 7:36 A. M.
" " " South Gate for Chong No at 7:20 A. M.
" " " Yung San for Choug No at 8:09 A. M.
Last " " South Gate for Chong No 9:00 P. M.
" " " Yung San for Chong No at 8.45. p. M.

SPECIAL PRIVATE CARS FURNISHED TO SUIT CONVENIENCE OF PATRONS. PRICES ON APPLICATION AT HEAD OFFICE.

LIGHTING DEPARTMENT.

Where less than 250 candle power of light is used, the rate per month will be
Per 16 candle power incandescent lamp,—All night.—Yen 2.50.
32 candle power incandescent lamp:—All night:—Yen 4.00.
50 candle power incandescent lamp:—All night:—Yen 6.00.
150 " " " " " " " 10.00.
1200 " " enclosed are " " " " 20.00.

Where more than 250 candle power of light is used, a Meter will be installed, freqvedted:—Rent of Meter Yen 2.00 per month. Rate of charges by meter reading:—Two Sen per Ampere per hour. (Approximately this is equal to about One Sen per 16 C. P. lamp per hour) Minimum monthly charge where meter is installed, Yen 20.00 per month, which includes rental of meter.

Estimates for installing lights furnished on application

An assortment of chandeliers always on hand.

EVERY FACILITY.

In connection with Life Assurance Business is afforded by

The Standard Life Assurance Co.,

One of the largest and wealthiest of the Provident Institutions of the United Kingdom Forms of Application and all information will be promptly afforded on application.

10 CENTS A DAY.

Not a very large expenditure is it? But it is sufficient to secure for a man of 30 a policy with the STANDARD LIFE OFFICE for

$1323.

For all particulars of rates, etc., apply to

Holme, Ringer & Co.,
Agents, Chemulpo.

THE NEW YORK LIFE INSURANCE COMPANY.

Have you ever been declined by any Company?

Are you engaged in a specially hazardous occupation?

Have you heard of the New York Life Insurance Company's New Classifications for this class of Risks?

If not, send your date of birth, occupation and particulars of rejection, if any to

E. MEYER & Co.,
Agents, Chemulpo.

K. Murakami.

Photograph Studio
Chinkokai, Seoul.

Printing, Developing and Enlargement, of Photographs always Undertaken.

Korean Views and Pictures Illustrating Native Customs always on Sale,

THE OSAKA SHOSEN KAISHA.

Boats frequently on the berth for Chinnampo.

REGULAR SAILINGS BETWEEN JAPAN AND KOREAN PORTS.

FUSAN AND KOBE VIA SHIMONOSEKI.

OSAKA VIA MOKPO, FUSAN, SHIMONOSEKI AND KOBE.

MOJI DIRECT.

OSAKA VIA KUNSAN, MASANPO, FUSAN, SHIMONOSEKI AND KOBE.

CHEMULPO KUNSAN LINE,
Every three days.

CHEMULPO CHINNAMPO LINE.
Every three days.

For Freight and passage and further particulars apply to

THE OSAKA SHOSEN KAISHA,
Chemulpo.

MITSUI BUSSAN KAISHA.
(MITSUI & Co.)

MITSUI GINKO.
(MITSUI BANK.)

The Bank is owned by the members of the Mitsui Family, who, as partners, assume an unlimited responsibility for all liabilities of the Bank:—

Capital .... Yen 5,000,000
Reserve Fund .... " 5,600,000

HEAD OFFICE, TOKYO.

LONDON OFFICE, 34 LIME ST., E. C.

BRANCHES AND AGENCIES:—

New York, San Francisco, Hamburg, Bombay, Singapore, Manila, Hongkong, Amoy, Chefoo, Tientsin.

Kobe, Hakodate, Yokohama, Kure, Yokosuka, Moji, Shimonoseki, Miike, Wakamatsu, Nagasaki, Kuchinotsu, Karatsu, Sasebo, Misume, Taipeh, &c.

Telegraphic Address for all the Offices:
"MITSUI."

A. B. C. AND A. 1 CODES USED.

Contractors of Coal

To the Imperial Japanese Navy. Arsenals and Railway Bureau, Principal Railway Companies and Industrial Work, Home and Foreign Mail and Freight Steamers.

Sole Proprietors

Of the famous Miike, Tagawa and Yamano Coal Mines.

Sole Agents

For the sale of Fukumo, Hokoku, Ichimura, Kanoda, Mannoura, Onoura, Ostuji, Sonoda, Tsubaruro, Yoshinotani, Yoshio, Yurokibura and other coals.

YANGTSE INSURANCE ASSOCIATION, LTD.

The undersigned, having been appointed agents for the above company, are prepared to issue policies and pay losses on marine risks at regular rates.

E. MEYER & Co.,
Agents, Chemulpo.

RONDON, PLAISANT & CO.

General Storekeepers and Merchants, Ships Contractors, Tobacconists; Commission and Forwarding Agents, Coal Merchants

IMPORTERS AND EXPORTERS

Seoul & Chemulpo.

W. D. WENTWORTH.

LANDING
AND
SHIPPING AGENT
AND
CUSTOMS BORDER.

12 OURA, NAGASAKI.

STEWARD & CO.

Chemulpo.

Shipchandlers and Storekeepers, Naval and Mercantile Contrrctors, Landing and Shipping Agents.

STEWARD'S HOTEL

Chemulpo.

Best accommodation in the port for travellers. Clean and well-aired rooms, good cuisine and prompt attendence, moderate tariff.

○합리빈소식 합리빈에서근일에ᄯᅥ나온쳥국사ᄅᆞᆷ의말드른죡로병이신속ᄒᆞ게ᄂᆞ려가서다슈의군ᄃᆡ가합리빈과봉텬제쳐에도착ᄒᆞ엿스며로국의진셰를보면좌우로진고등군ᄒᆞ게ᄂᆞ려가서일본군을에워싸랴ᄒᆞᄂᆞᆫ것갓쳐뵈히고지번두달동안에ᄂᆞᆫ별노긴요ᄒᆞᆫ젼쟁은업섯스며량편에서각셰으로방슈ᄒᆞᆯᄲᅮᆫ힘쓰고잇다더라

○일포영션 인월십일일에일본군함상션반호가일본히에서셕탄륙쳔오ᄇᆡᆨ돈을싣고히삼위로향ᄒᆞᄂᆞᆫ영국륜션로슈죠호를장고쌍슈퇴쳥이른쳐을싣고히삼위로향ᄒᆞᄂᆞᆫ영국륜션로친돈호를잡앗다더라

○로국헌법초안 아라사에서(쳄스도우오)ᄃᆡ방회의원미상량ᄒᆞᆫ헌법초안이여좌ᄒᆞ니
황뎨ᄂᆞᆫ국가에원머리오대국의졍원은그보좌로황뎨와동일히국가교등ᄃᆡ위에입ᄒᆞᆯ수
황뎨위계승ᄒᆞᄂᆞᆫᄃᆡ취ᄒᆞ야ᄂᆞᆫ현힝규졍을변치아니ᄒᆞᆯ수
황뎨ᄂᆞᆫ대국의졍회에ᄃᆡᄒᆞ야헌법상에션언ᄒᆞ야맹세ᄒᆞᆯ수
대국의졍회ᄂᆞᆫ헌법가변치못ᄒᆞᆫ법아잇슴세에ᄂᆞᆫ황조대위를스ᄉᆞ로버리며또황뎨도계도를졍ᄒᆞᆯ수
황뎨의일신은범ᄒᆞᆯ은ᄂᆞᆫ치못ᄒᆞᆯ수
국무대신은뎨의힝위의ᄃᆡᄒᆞ야ᄎᆡᆨ임이잇스며뎨의권리ᄂᆞᆫ좌와여ᄒᆞᆷ
션젼　강화계결　뎡국과됴약계결　법률에의ᄒᆞ지아니ᄒᆞᆫ명령을발ᄒᆞᆷ　의회히산
황뎨ᄂᆞᆫ대국히군과밋륙군의최샹쥬로셔립ᄒᆞ니그일부ᄂᆞᆫ셰스도부오의원된지삼ᄀᆡ년이샹자오탈일부ᄂᆞᆫ빈민투표에의지ᄒᆞ야졍졈으로보통션거ᄒᆞᆷ이니셩년남ᄌᆞᄂᆞᆫ현졔ᄒᆞᆫ경찰관을지ᄂᆡ지못ᄒᆞᆫ자ᄂᆞᆫ션거권과밋피션거권을잇고국ᄉᆞ범과밋언론에의지ᄒᆞᆫ범죄자ᄂᆞᆫ이권을손샹치아니ᄒᆞ며의원은로관ᄌᆞ에취ᄒᆞᆯ배에ᄂᆞᆫ의원의지쳑을ᄒᆞᆷ졔ᄒᆞᆯ수 다만국무대신이될셰에ᄂᆞᆫ이한에잇지아니ᄒᆞᆷ이라
의졍회ᄂᆞᆫ공변되게회긔ᄒᆞᆯ수
다만헌법변경의사에관ᄒᆞ야ᄂᆞᆫ의졍회의원은각의안졔출권이잇고비안건은의졍회에셔가히결단ᄒᆞᄂᆞᆫ배에대ᄒᆞ야재가를밧을사
국무대신은명의대권은슈샹이비거슬잇고국무대신은자긔졍사치힝위에ᄃᆡᄒᆞ야ᄎᆡᆨ임을담부ᄒᆞᆯ
뎨자와[쳄스도우오]ᄂᆞᆫ스사로다사리ᄂᆞᆫ권리오이자치졔도에의ᄒᆞᆫ우현은지졍보통션거에의지ᄒᆞ야션거될사
제국은신구슈에의지ᄒᆞ야교육에분별ᄒᆞ며전거ᄂᆞᆫ칙령에의지ᄒᆞ야일로일에졔졍ᄒᆞᆫ사비샹조안의완전치아니ᄒᆞᆷ은가히지로취ᄒᆞᆯ거시며이조안발표ᄒᆞᆫ셰에(모스코ㅣ우에도모우지ㅣ)ᄂᆞᆫ(우리나라에ᄯᅩᄒᆞᆫ사ᄅᆞᆷ의보슈ᄒᆞᆯ자가업스나ᄒᆞᆷ평ᄒᆞ엿슴으로로국중등은급히(루스키이공을쇼멸ᄒᆞ야신문언론의단속을명ᄒᆞ게ᄒᆞ엿더라

론셜

일본승려의전교ᄉᆞ

○원리전교ᄉᆞ들의ᄒᆞᄂᆞᆫᄉᆞ무가다른사ᄅᆞᆷ들이젹당ᄒᆞ게아리쥬지아니ᄒᆞᄂᆞᆫ것이라그사ᄅᆞᆷ들이편ᄒᆞ고졍다온고향을ᄯᅥ나서져의들이복음이라고밋ᄂᆞᆫ것을싱관모로ᄂᆞᆫ사ᄅᆞᆷ들의게가리치랴고외국에나아가ᄂᆞᆫ도다
복음이라ᄒᆞᄂᆞᆫ것은신교에ᄯᅥ러서모다다르지마ᄂᆞᆫ엇던교의젼교ᄉᆞ던지자긔의밋ᄂᆞᆫ교에ᄃᆡᄒᆞ야신앙심과그신앙심에의지ᄒᆞ야조ᄒᆞᆫ일을ᄒᆞ랴고그열심ᄒᆞᄂᆞᆫ것이맛당ᄒᆞᆫ지라
지금쳥국에가ᄂᆞᆫ일본의불교젼교ᄉᆞ에ᄃᆡᄒᆞ야ᄂᆞᆫ엇더타고말ᄒᆞ겟ᄂᆞᆫ가샹당에션교ᄉᆞ들ᄯᅥ러서교도신앙ᄒᆞᆫ다ᄂᆞᆫ이야기가잇더니지금쳥국에잇ᄂᆞᆫ일본젼교ᄉᆞ들두고히비ᄒᆞᆫ말이로다
아모라도일본인의힝위를자세히아ᄂᆞᆫ사ᄅᆞᆷ은일본인의칭찬ᄒᆞᆯᄂᆞᆫ승관에죵교ᄂᆞᆫ별노관계가업ᄂᆞᆫ것을알지니신도ᄂᆞᆫ그국교외오불교ᄂᆞᆫ머리과에나우이셔젼국에사찰이만히잇스니그교도ᄯᅩᄒᆞᆫ셩ᄒᆞ나그러ᄒᆞ나이ᄂᆞᆫ교던지일본인이특별히신심신봉ᄒᆞᆫ다ᄒᆞᄂᆞᆫ말ᄒᆞᆫ슈엄도다가쳐사찰에셔져들을니고숭경ᄒᆞᆷ은ᄒᆞ지마ᄂᆞᆫ그것은하등사회를위ᄒᆞᆫᄯᅢ름이오일본인중에도죰낫게지니ᄂᆞᆫ사ᄅᆞᆷ들은져의근쳐에잇ᄂᆞᆫ사찰에셔시로보조금을보니ᄂᆞᆫ것으로만족ᄒᆞ게아ᄂᆞᆫ지라
일본인중에불교를별노괴란ᄒᆞ고ᄒᆞᄂᆞᆫ소문이별노히엿ᄂᆞᆫ지라그럼으로지금일본인이쳥국에셔가며ᄃᆡ의일ᄒᆞᆷ으로션교ᄉᆞ를열심으로보니ᄂᆞᆫ것이우리에게ᄂᆞᆫ피이ᄒᆞ게뵈ᄂᆞᆫ도다
일본인의한국에셔ᄊᆞᄂᆞᆫ음모찬계로ᄒᆞ야일본인의힝동에ᄃᆡᄒᆞ야우리가다갑히의심ᄒᆞ거니와일본인이쳥국에셔불교를파란코ᄒᆞᆫ다ᄂᆞᆫ공평ᄒᆞᆫ희망에ᄃᆡᄒᆞ야근리우리ᄂᆞᆫ이상ᄒᆞᆫ소식을드럿노라
차이나메일신문에일본인이쳥국에셔져의불교를젼파ᄒᆞᄂᆞᆫ힝동에ᄃᆡᄒᆞ야말ᄒᆞ엿스되
열마아니되야셔세력이졈졈번ᄒᆞ야보니파지고견과가조ᄒᆞᆯ리이나쳥국에관계잇ᄂᆞᆫ다른나라ᄂᆞᆫ지금일본인의힝동을의심ᄒᆞᆯ두고쳥국이ᄒᆞᆯ지라그힝동이션교ᄒᆞᆷ만위ᄒᆞᆯᄲᅮᆫ아니라반은졍치상관계가잇고지금ᄉᆞ으로진보ᄒᆞᄂᆞᆫ혁명운동에관계도잇스니쳥명ᄒᆞᆫ쳥국사ᄅᆞᆷ들은일본인의본리를쳑히그러ᄒᆞ다고말ᄒᆞᄂᆞᆫ지라그시로이러ᄂᆞᆫ교회의취지셔를번력ᄒᆞᆫ거슬엇어셔여긔에게ᄌᆡᄒᆞ노니여러분은ᄌᆡ미잇게보실듯
일본 수찰의명칭은쳥국본원ᄉᆞ라ᄒᆞ고광동에ᄒᆞᆫ쳐소를엇어서대학교를지으며츄후로젼국에지회를기셜ᄒᆞᆯ수
이 이교회ᄂᆞᆫ일본에잇ᄂᆞᆫ교회의지회로ᄒᆞ고이교회에든사ᄅᆞᆷ들은일본국과아리에보호를밧을사
다ᄅᆞᆫ됴목도만히잇스나쥬의ᄒᆞᆯ거ᄉᆞ업ᄂᆞᆫ고로계지ᄒᆞ지아니ᄒᆞᆷ
이일에ᄃᆡᄒᆞ야차이나메일신문에광동통신원이편지로보고ᄒᆞ되수일젼에귀신셜른에쳥국에일본불교션교사사진을말ᄒᆞ엿스ᄆᆡ지방나에게귀말ᄒᆞᆫ소문은쳥국중앙ᄃᆡ셔드ᄅᆞᆫ거시라
지금광에셔ᄂᆞᆫ일본션교사가이ᄯᅡ에아ᄌᆞᆨ오지ᄂᆞᆫ아니ᄒᆞ엿스나쟝차사무를시작ᄒᆞ라ᄒᆞᄂᆞᆫ지라근리쳥국총독이ᄒᆞᆫ령ᄒᆞ야일본인을보호ᄒᆞ라ᄒᆞ엿다ᄒᆞ엿더라
에ᄭᅦ으로차이나모잉포쓰트신문에계ᄌᆡᄒᆞᆫ귀졀을벗겨셔이로셜을건맙ᄒᆞ노니그말에ᄒᆞ엿스되쳥국외무부대신이졔갑슈무의게ᄎᆞᆫ명ᄒᆞ되엇지ᄒᆞ야셔각처에ᄒᆡᆼ의승려들이일본불교젼교사의보호를밧게되엇나교답문ᄒᆞ엿다고ᄒᆞ엿더라
일본인들이쳥쥬의류로지아니ᄒᆞ도다일본인의목뎍이한국등람ᄲᅮᆫ아니로다

관보

뎨삼쳔ᄉᆞ십호　광무구년일월십구일

셔임급ᄉᆞ령

○임단양군슈서주임관이등 법부형ᄉᆞ국쟝　셔상욱
○임음셩군슈서주임관일등 졍삼품　박조셜
○임창원군슈서주임관륙등 졍삼품　윤ᄃᆡ흥
○임의령군슈서주임관이등 궁내부참셔관　리용교
○임자인군슈서주임관륙등 법관양셩소교관　김영슉
○임쟝긔군슈서주임관륙등 졍삼품　임창재
○임청풍군슈서주임관륙등 륙품　ᄇᆡᆨ남쥰
○임익산군슈서주임관륙등 슈품　민영셕
○임금구군슈서주임관륙등 진도군슈　민영진
○임임실군슈서주임관일등 경무쳥경무관　조규하
○임경흥군슈서주임관륙등 졍삼품　송종민
○임진도군슈서주임관일등 졍삼품　권중면
○임부안군슈서주임관오등 졍삼품　권익샹
○임회양군슈서주임관륙등 륙품　윤발영
○임통쳔군슈서주임관ᄉᆞ등 졍삼품　심지승
○의원면본관　리원군슈　ᄇᆡᆨ남쥰　부평군슈　남즁원
이샹이월십륙일
○의원면본관　동신ᄉᆞ면화과쥬ᄉᆞ　면계회　동신ᄉᆞ면화과쥬ᄉᆞ　김면욱
○증종일품승졍대부의졍부참졍　졍이품문관대학ᄉᆞ규쟝각학ᄉᆞ　증리조판서　김병진
○증졍이품자헌대부의졍부찬졍　증리조참판　김대균
이샹종일품숭록대부젼쟝례원경　김종한고조고의범연츄증
○증종이품가션대부니부협판　즁동몽교관　김한영
○증졍삼품통졍대부비서원승　즁시헌부감찰　김지풍
이샹종이품가션대부니장원경　김종헌고조고의범연츄증
○증종이품가션대부니부협판　고현감　김학슈
○증종이품가션대부니부협판　가대부　ᄇᆡᆨ인슈
○증졍삼품통졍대부비서원승　고사헌부감찰　김원식
○증종삼품통훈대부쟝례원좌쟝례　고동몽교관　송계인
이샹효형탁리　증직을비롤다
○임의졍부찬졍서칙임관일등　궁내부특진관　민영린
○명군제의졍관　륙군참쟝　영쥬의　륙군참쟝　김승규
○임샹화우톄사쥬사서판임관륙등　리한승
○금셩금봉　샹화우톄사쥬사　리한승
이샹일월십칠일

광고

○본인의쟝ᄌᆞ쳐변이가본시부랑패류로그부형ᄌᆞ뎨간에분쟈ᄒᆞ여가진면쟝문권을슈히도젹ᄒᆞ여니엇기로세부득이ᄒᆞ야시문권을ᄆᆞᆫ들엇고이에광고ᄒᆞ오니외국인간에샹가속지말고쳐변의가진문권을면셜지마옵기를바라옴
평양셩니쟝거리　한계현
고ᄇᆡᆨ

셔울우션회사
힝ᄒᆞᄂᆞᆫ이는등ᄎᆞᆫ션들인ᄃᆡ쳥국과일본셔양국과각국으로슈리ᄒᆞᆷ
인쳔항룡가양힝ᄃᆡ리졈

TELEGRAMS.

(FROM JAPAN PAPERS.)

Berlin, January 13th.

In Westphalia, Germany, 80,000 coalminers have gone on a strike on account of technical differences. The question regarding wages is only a secondary one. It is feared a general strike will break out.

The British Parliament meets on February 14th. There are persistent rumors in Parliamentary circles that there will be a dissolution in the month of March.

Berlin, January 12th.

According to numerous reports, Prince Sviatopolsk-Mirsky, who quite recently was appointed Minister of Home Affairs as successor to M. de Plehwe, is now to be succeeded by M. de White.

The French paper "Eclair" reported that the Baltic Fleet is anchoring off Madagascar close to an island without owner and is awaiting reinforcements.

Tokyo, Jan. 12th.

Reliable reports from Port Arthur say that, notwithstanding some argument as to the blowing-up by the Russians of forts and ships, simultaneously with an alleged armistice proposed by General Stoessel for arrangements of capitulation, there was no armistice in fact, and negotiations opened at once.

The destruction of remnant articles, pending the negotiations, is not only the enemy's right, but also the proper measure to be taken by any belligerent.

Upon the signature of Capitulation, the Russian Commissioner telegraphically instructed his rear to stop destruction and all proceedings were observed by the Russians quite fairly.

London, January 3rd.

The Earl of Selborne, First Lord of the Admiralty, denies the statement that it had been decided to abandon the Rosyth Naval Base.

London, January 6th.

The Canadian Pacific Railway Company has ordered two steamers of 14,500 tons each to be built at Glasgow.

San Francisco, December 28th.

The refitting, and repairing of the Black Sea fleet is being rushed with all possible speed, and apprehension prevails on the part of England that Russia has prevailed on the Sultan of Turkey to permit the passage of the Black sea fleet through the Bosphorus and Dardanelles.

By the terms of the treaty of Paris the right of entry into and out of the Black Sea through the Dardanelles and the Bosphorus is in the hands of the Sultan, under slight restrictions.

It is believed that the Sultan has been subjected to such pressure that he has agreed to declare the Dardanelles open to the warships of Russia and release the imprisoned fleet.

The squadron will be ready to sail in time to intercept the battleship division of the Baltic fleet that is enroute from Capetown.

San Francisco, December 31.

Lord Roberts has demanded the reorganization of the British Army. In a lengthy communication he points out the defects that still exist which cost England so dearly in South Africa. He emphasizes the fact that England is no better prepared for another struggle than she was at the commencement of the Boer war and regrets the fact that the great lesson so dearly bought, has been ignored.

With but few exceptions the English press endorses the demand of Roberts and the general sentiment is alive to the absolute necessity of better drilled and more efficient troops as well as a more practical establishment throughout.

San Francisco, Dec. 31.

Several Japanese cruisers have been sighted at Anjer, Java, on the Straits of Sunda, and the report has gone forth that other Japanese war vessels are in the vicinity. The authorities at Batavia have been informed and the Dutch Government will take immediate steps to enforce strict neutrality of its ports.

It is reported that Admiral Rohzdestvensky has been notified of the presence of the Japanese ships and will make a detour to the south and pass to the westward of the Philippine Islands, probably with the intention of making Vladivostock—Manila Cablenews.

London, Jan. 12.

The American Government has informed China that it disapproves of the proposed cancellation of the concession of the Hankow-Canton railway. As regards American concessionaires, America considers that they are entitled to the protection of the American Government.

The publication in French of an exhaustive statement written by Baron Kodama in 1902, explaining Japanese ambitions, and setting forth particularly that country's designs against French Indo-China, is creating a sensation in Paris.

The Japanese Legations deny the authenticity of the document, but nevertheless it produces a profound sensation.

London, Jan. 13.

Admiral Bolroosky's squadron has entered the Canal.

Admiral Skrydloff has left Vladivostock for St. Petersburg.

President Roosevelt strongly advocates a special session of Congress for a readjustment of the tariff, but the session is unlikely to open before autumn.

Later.

The subscription to the new Russian loan was opened in Berlin and closed almost immediately, the applications being unusually large.

It is reported from Mukden that Russian paper currency in circulation there and northwards fell about 16 per cent. in value on the day following the surrender of Port Arthur.

It is announced that about 1 P. M. on the 12th the Japanese torpedo-boat No. 72 captured in the Tsushima channel the British steamer "Remington (2,856 tons) destined for Vladivostock with 6,500 tons of Cardiff coal on board.

The Russian newspapers publish details of the proposed re-organisation of the Volunteer Fleet after the war. The number of ships will be largely increased, and new passenger and freight services started, one of the most important of the projected new sailings being from Libau or Windau to America.

It is reported by the "Nichi Nichi" that Japan has strictly questioned the Argentine and Chile Republics of the alleged sale of their warships in favour of Russia. The paper does not enjoy liberty to report the exact substance of the replies from these countries, but believes that they have replied that none of their ships had been sold.

Among the people thronging the Ginza and other main thoroughfares to see the decorations and watch the lantern processions go by, says the "Japan Herald" there are few who have not lost a son, a brother or a friend during the five months of the terrible siege or who have not suffered in their business. All think with dread of the coming Armageddon on the Shaho as soon as the advance is resumed. All those thoughts weigh on the public and nothing except the return of peace will bring back the buoyancy and enthusiasm of the early days of last year.

AT VLADIVOSTOCK.

The steamer "Progress" arrived from Vladivostock at Chefoo on the 9th inst. She carried about three hundred and fifty coolies who have been at work on the fortifications at that port.

The "Progress" had an exceptionally short voyage, being favoured with unusually good weather, which is decidly exceptional in Northern Oriental waters at this time of the year. She was but four and one-half days en route.

A Japanese auxiliary cruiser and a torpedo boat stopped her in the straits of Korea and three officers came on board and carefully examined her papers Finding nothing which would justify her seizure she was permitted to proceed on her voyage to Chefoo.

When the "Progress" left Vladivostock there was still considerable work being done on the fortifications. Her officers report that the "Gromoboi" and the "Rossia" are in good condition and frequently put out of the harbour for short voyages. The "Bogatyr," however, is not at present in perfect condition, but her repairs are being rapidly pushed towards completion.

Captain Bremer of the "Progrees" has now made three trips to Vladivostock on that vessel, and he has consequently seen the Russian cruisers in their condition immediately after Kamimura sunk the "Rurik." He is of the opinion that the Russians have done excellent work in repairing the badly injured vessels, and says that as soon as the "Bogatyr" is repaired the "Flying Squadron" will be in good fighting trim.

The work on the new docks at Vladivostock is rapidly progressing and should be finished at the time of the supposed arrival of the Baltic Sqnadron in February.

At the time Captain Bremer left the Russian port the fall of Port Arthur had not been made public there. However, there can be little doubt that the army and navy officials had been notified.—Chefoo Daily News.

PRINCE FUSHIMI AS A CAVALRY EXPERT.

Prince Fushimi, the Mikado's brother, who is visiting theUnited Sates as the personal representative of the Mikado, was the centre of a remarkable scene at Fort Meyer, Virginia, cavalry barracks on 23rd Nov., says the "L. & C. Express." The cavalry, including many seasoned Indian fighters, gave an exhibition of horsemanship before the Prince and a number of foreign military attachés. They charged madly across the plain and stopped within four feet of the distinguished visitors, yelling fiendishly meanwhile. As the troopers dismounted and stood at attention Prince Fushimi stepped forward and made what was undoubtedly the most thorough inspection any of the cavalrymen had ever undergone. The Prince, says a New York correspondent, suddenly jerked the revolver from a big cavalrymen's holster, opened it, minutely examined the mechanism, ran one white-gloved finger into the barrel and about the other parts, seeking dust, and, finding none, replaced it in the holster. He examined the carbines in the same manner. He then deftly removed the bridle from one of the horses and tested its weight and workmanship. He jerked open the mouth of one of the horses to see whether or not the bit made the mouth sore. He then unsaddled a horse, examined the saddle carefully, passed his hand over the horse's back to see if it was chafed, satisfied himself of the weight of the saddle and the texture of the other gear, and expertly replaced every thing as he had found it. Then the Prince examined the troopers individually as to clothes, teeth, and felt their muscles, all so simply, eagerly, and earnestly that only discipline prevented the cavalrymen from breaking into cheers.

The Russians are increasing in strength on the Japanese, left in the North, especially in the vicinity of Hsienchang and its rear, where the number is between 17,000 and 18,000.

The Foreign Office has sent a despatch to the Japanese Legation protesting against General Hasegawa's action in assuming control of the police of Seoul. It is pointed out that this has nothing whatever to do with military affairs.

A Japanese paper alleges that a Swedish subject, staying at a Yokohama Hotel, is investigating the financial state of Japan at this time by secret order of a certain foreign Government, and that he is expected to remain here for one month.

Mr. Maruyama, who is to be adviser to the Police Department, arrived in Fusan on the 18th instant. It is also said that the gay throng of Japanese advisers with shortly be reinforced by two more, one for the Home Department and one for the gendarmerie. The Japanese are certainly making hay while the sun shines.

The Tokio Correspondent of the "Japan Herald" says that of the local financial and commercial disturbances brought on by the war two striking illustrations have lately appeared in the papers in connection with the notorious One Hundred and Thirtieth Bank of Osaka and the Kigyo Ginko of Kyoto. Both banks to make up losses had to make calls upon shares not fully paid up. The shareholders in both cases could not of would not respond. In consequence, after repeated delays, the shares of defaulted shareholders of the first bank were put up to auction last month. The bids on the twenty-four thousand old shares, Y35 paid up, ranged from Y2.90 to Y3.80. No offers were made for the new shares, Y17.50 paid up. It is clear Osaka has little money to spare or has absolutely no confidence in the success of Mr. Yasuda's attempt to reorganise the bank, even with a loan of six millions at two per cent. interest. The Kyoto Bank is even in worse plight, for out of 12,000 shares no less than eleven thousand will have to be sold on the 15th, the owners having failed to meet the call of Y15.

The British Admiralty are understood to be in negotiation for the purchase of an invention which, if it achieve all that is claimed for it, ought to make the submarine one of the most effective engines of naval war. The precise nature and scope of the invention is naturally being kept a profound secret, but it is said that experiments have already been made on a small scale at Portsmouth, and that they have given all the results claimed for the invention. The inventor is stated to be a young engineer's who has for years shown a special aptitude for submarine and torpedo work.

There is reason to believe that the Government has resolved upon the appointment of a British Resident at Lhasa, and that the officer selected for the post will proceed thither from Calcutta early this year. He will be accompanied and permanently protected by an escort of Indian troops under British officers, and will be housed in a special compound close to the Dalai Lama's monastery. While the necessity for this step is in some quarters regretted, it is considered that no other means are available for the purpose of ensuring not only repected for the terms made by Colonel Younghusband's recent expedition, but for checking the establishment of any foreign influence in Tibet.

The Korea Daily News.

Issued at 5 P. M. daily except Sundays.

Rate of Subscription :—
Per Year,............Yen 25.
Per Quarter,..........Yen 7.
Per Month,..........Yen 2.50.

Postage in Korea not charged extra.
Postage abroad charged extra.

Advertisements, 50 sen per day for 1 inch or less.
5 yen per month per inch.
50 yen per year per inch.

All communications to
E. T. BETHELL,
Editor and Publisher,
Pak-tong, Seoul.

RUSSIAN REFORMS.

The Czar prefaced his Message to the Council of State with reference to the various reform measures, as follows:

"In order to foster the interests of the States in accordance with the plan handed down by my ancestors, to whom by the will of God I have succeeded, the policy of the Empire must be preserved and no change made in it. Nevertheless if there be anything requiring reform in matters of administrative business I will not hesitate to carry out such reform, and to that end I do not object even to large alterations in the legislature. It can not be doubted that men of sense, who appreciate that true prosperity depends upon the preservation of tranquility and on the satisfaction of the people's daily needs, will welcome the procedure here outlined."

The Message then proceeds to marshal numerous measures of reform having for their object the improvement of the condition of the farmers, who constitute the bulk of the people. It then adds the following:

"I desire that the above measures which are to be taken into consideration shall be harmonized with the traditional customs of the State and with the general laws so as to firmly guarantee hereafter the liberty already granted to the agricultural classes. The wishes now declared by the local assemblies have attracted general attention but they are altogether unlawful. Young men, misled by evil-minded persons who are acting in their own interests, have held meetings and have preferred demands to the Government. But such demands are altogther inadmissible under the inviolable polity of the Russian Empire. Movements made in the streets of cities and public demonstrations against offices of the Government, are acts in which Russians truly loyal to the State take no part. Such proceedings are made to assume serious significance, but that is contrary to the truth. For their organizers, forgetting the difficulties our country has to encounter in the present war, and carried away by extreme and alien theories, act in a manner which not only does not conduce to Russia's interest but even benefits the enemy. The Government, in the discharge of the duties for which it is responsible, will restrain any attempts to disturb public peace and good order, and will exhaust all suitable means for checking those that set themselves in opposition to it. No private or public associat on must act in excess of its powers. Its president will be held responsible for this. Newspapers, too, must be circumspect, and, not forgetting their responsibility, must endeavour to tranquilize the people.—Japan Mail.

JOURNALISM IN JAPAN.

Under the heading of "Journalism in Seoul" the "Japan Daily Mail" publishes the following:

"There is published in Seoul an Anglo-Korean journal the title of which is a matter of no consequence. From its recent issues we take two extracts:—

"Some four or five of the agitators were slightly wounded and then the Japanese soldiers interfered on behalf of the Il-chin-hoi, disarmed the Korean soldiers and arrestsd their officers.

"What excuse will be made by the Japanese for their high-handed proceedings we do not know but the fact remains that the Japanese authorities are responsible for all the trouble, from beginning to end. By the aid of subsidies they get together a society composed of all the riff-raff of Seoul which does not include a single respectable Korean. This society assembles and talks sedition, yet when the Korean Government takes steps to suppress the meetings the Japanese step in and prevent them.

"What are we coming to? The real purpose which the Il-chin-hoi is intended to serve has not yet leaked out but we should not be surprised if the ultimate design of the Japanese is the substitution of Japanese for Korean soldiers as Palace guards.

* * *

It is only reasonable to suppose that the erstwhile bellicose and aggressive Government of Japan has by now realized the futility of its undertaking, and would be willing to listen to proposals for a peaceful settlement could terms be devised which would involve no loss of face. But, in view of the fact that Japan was the original aggressor, and chose her own time and place for the making of the "coup" which was to "Prick the bubble" of Russia's reputation, it can hardly be expected that Japan will obtain by diplomacy anything which she has shown her inability to take by force at a time when all the circumstances were in her favour."

It is not, we need scarcely say, with any idea of discussing the opinions expressed in these extracts that we quote them. Our object is to compliment the Japanese on the strength of their position in Korea since they can afford to suffer such journalism, and on their liberality in suffering it. In a country like Korea, where newspapers are comparatively novel affairs, the influence they exercise may be very pernicious, and in such countries it has always been deemed wise to impose some legal restraints upon freedom of speech. But the Japanese apparently think that no need for precaution exists in Korea. This is another interesting parallel between Egypt and the little peninsular empire. In Egypt, after 1881, the efforts of the British Government to re-organise the country and to bring prosperity to the people as well as to obtain for them the blessing of security of life and property, were hampered by the French local press, which could see no good in anything English. France was then England's enemy, so far as concerned Egypt. Therefore it was not unnatural that French journals should take that line. England, on the contrary, is now Japan's friend and ally, so that it is distinctly unnatural for an English paper to take any such line in Seoul. But just as the British in Egypt went on quietly doing the right thing and ignoring newspaper clamour, so the Japanese in Korea are following the dictates of wise statesmanship in paying no attention to scurrilous journ-

* * *

als. It is a good sign."

We have before now been the subject of similar articles in the "Japan Mail." This is the last one we shall take any notice of. Our reply to the "Don't put him under the pump" suggestions of our contemporary is this:

The Japanese have displayed no liberality so far as we are concerned; on the contrary such means as have been available have been employed to our detriment. We have also twice been approached with a view to ascertaining our price for altering our tone. As that would apparently involve our producing a paper similar to the "Japan Mail," and as our conscience is not for sale, we have on both occasions declined to discuss the matter.

THE MILITARY CRITIC.

The "Militar Wochenblatt" has the following on the Manchurian campaign, written by a military expert who has been in the East during the campaign. Among other things, he says:

As far as I can see from the opinions of the press in Europe, Kuropatkin is generally blamed because he did not retire to Moukden and there await the necessary reinforcements.

The Russian leader had chosen other ways, and very likely with good reason. The Asiatics care not a fig for the finesse of strategy, but value an enemy according to the resistance he offers. If the Russian army had retreated to Moukden without fighting, the Japanese offensive would undoubtedly have developed a higher speed and energy, and it might not have been possible to keep the Chinese quiet. The theoretically correct retreat to Moukden would have been in Asiatic eyes, a mistake of incalculable degree. The Russian General knew this, and for this reason he decided to retire from position after position, strongly but not stubbornly resisting at each place. In the retreat he had opportunity of making use of the rich resources of the country about him. He decided upon a thoroughly planned campaign of exhaustion of his enemy. He knew that he could count upon the perfect coolness and calmness with which the Russian soldier accepts defeat.

On these battlefields, and with these troops, General Kuropatkin could adopt a system which would be most dangerous in middle Europe, if not impossible. With a number of troops the smallness of which the world will be astonished to know, if the history of this war shall be written, Kuropakin has forced the Japanese to disastrous attacks, and has made them expend their best force before reaching Moukden, from which place western military ideas advised Kuropatkin not to retreat.

The method with which this plan was carried out must be characterized as masterful. I was at Russian headquarters when it was decided to evacuate Newchwang, and at that time was thoroughly impressed with the military theories of western Europe. Without knowing, of course, the situation in detail, I saw that the Russian army was half surrounded, and that communication with the rear, as well as the railway line, was threatened.. I daresay it was a situation which in a game of war must end in sudden retreat. Consequently, I expected either such retreat or a disaster. But nothing of the kind occurred. The Russian army remained, took up the battle, struck a blow here and there, and stood off the enemy for days and days, and at last evacuated its positions in the best of order and without any considerable losses.

The same tactics were repeated at Liaoyang, where the world, at least the Anglo-Saxon part of it, expected another Sedan. This dilatory battle on the grandest scale gave the Japanese no advantage except a gain of ground. No trophies were taken, and it was a completely fruitless and negative victory, which cost them, however, twenty thousand men.

The new trade marks registration act in China seems likely to hang fire. The Japanese are anxious to have it put into force but as it would probably lead to the registration of many pirated foreign trademarks by Japanese, the other powers do not seem to be in such a hurry. According to the "South China Morning post," it is officially announced that in consequence of the representations of the German, the British, the French, the Austrian-Hungarian, and the Italian Ministers, the Chinese Government has declared itself willing to take into kind consideration the proposals of the foreign Governments with regard to the amendments to the trade-mark law, and has bound itself not to make any registration of trade marks before an agreement has been arrived at.

The Korea Daily News.

VOL. II, FRIDAY, JANUARY 20, 1905. No. 15

大韓每日申報
대한미일신보

(뎨이십륙호) (월요일) (일쳔구빅오년일월이십이일)

본사고빅

이신보는영어와한어로셔계리일츌판ᄒᆞᆷ

신문가

한장 엽두돈오푼

일삭표 엽두량닷돈

우표가리삭닷돈

다밧돈으로밧솜

광고료는

귀즁한의장단과조횡의다쇼로즁감ᄒᆞ되평가로밧을터이오며오리지아니ᄒᆞ야대한사람마다다이신문을보실터이니광고버시기를원ᄒᆞ시는이들은우리신문사에와셔편약ᄒᆞ심을희망ᄒᆞᆷ

○발힝소 박동대한미일신보사발힝ᄒᆞ되 영국인 (베셜) 평정자리오

사쟝 영국인 (비셜)

평양 디리점

○평양효동사는권미보씨로우리신문판미ᄒᆞᆫ디리점을뎡ᄒᆞ엿시오니평양에계신구람코져ᄒᆞ는쳠군ᄌᆞ는디리점에가셔왕림ᄒᆞ야편의ᄒᆞ시옵

사고

○우리대한미일신보의목뎍은대한의안녕질셔에관ᄒᆞᆫ모든ᄉᆞ물에디ᄒᆞ야는공평ᄒᆞᆫ변론을주장ᄒᆞᆷ이라우리동셔양의리왕ᄒᆞ는신문보시는쳠군ᄌᆞ의게ᄒᆞᆼ샹보도ᄒᆞ리며편지ᄒᆞ셔쥬시는이는셩명과번디를자셰히긔록ᄒᆞ야시기를희망ᄒᆞ오니이가셔신문샹에긔재ᄒᆞ랴는거시아니오다만극히신용ᄒᆞ는증거를삼고자ᄒᆞᆷ이라긔자는아모리셔편지긔지ᄒᆞᆷ을된각ᄒᆞ는권리를가졋스나뢰각ᄒᆞᆫ편지는돌녀보내지아니ᄒᆞ고중명ᄒᆞ기를도르키오ᄒᆞ는긔셔는의미ᄒᆞ지못ᄒᆞ계습나이다

●본사셜시ᄒᆞᆫ이래로신문을미일우히로보내던ᄒᆞ와해젼부의임의로젼ᄒᆞ는동스로만잇셔는흑늣게젼ᄒᆞ기도ᄒᆞ며흑아니젼ᄒᆞ기도ᄒᆞ며흑야니젼ᄒᆞ는폐도잇다ᄒᆞ오니우리신문을슈람ᄒᆞ시는 쳠군ᄌᆞ의계셔는아무도엄이젼ᄒᆞ는날ᄌᆞᄅᆞᆯ슈요쥬ᄒᆞ면혹이나젼ᄒᆞ기나ᄒᆞᆫ일이잇스면본사로통긔ᄒᆞ여주시옵을희망ᄒᆞᆷ

관보

광무십년 이월이십삼일

○보힘소식 봉황햠대는긔회작함리대영현ᄒᆞ기로정ᄒᆞ는가쇼리에잇슴으로...

동일

○리젼참판의미가 ...

동월 이십일

○로셰블우 로국이대한에셔...

동일

○자미슈금 미국상항에셔...

동월 이십일

○로일협뎡 로국외교대신...

동일

○로국정부의...

동월 이십일

○로일강화 ...

동일

○황관의 ...

동월 이십일

○일본황뎨의소식 ...

(뎨이쇼가사셰음은...)

잡보

○닉부면훈 닉부에셔...

○닉부우면훈 닉부에셔...

○닉부면훈 닉부에셔...

○닉부면훈 닉부에셔...

○닉부면훈 닉부에셔...

UNION INSURANCE SOCIETY OF CANTON.

Head office Hongkong.
Marine risks underwritten at current rates.
Agents in Chemulpo,
E. MEYER & Co.

COMPAGNIE DES MESSAGERIES MARITIMES.

Fortnightly Direct Service.

For Marseilles
via Ports.
Sailing from Yokohama
Calling at Kobe,
Shanghai, Hongkong, Saigon, Singapore,
Colombo, Djibouti, Suez, Port Said
and Marseilles.

For particulars apply to
HOLME RINGER & Co.,
Chemulpo.

HAYASHIDA & CO.,

16 MYENG DONG, CHIN KO KAI, SEOUL.
BRANCH OFFICE AT CHEMULPO.

Money changers, Coal and Wood Merchants, Express Agents.

We are agents for the Pyeng-yang Coal Company and the Karazu Coal Company of Japan. We have the best quality of both authracite and bituminous coal, and prompt execution of orders is our speciality. Firewood of all kinds kept in stock. Full weight guaranteed. Money of all denominations exchanged at current rates. Parcels received for all parts.

CHINA MUTUAL LIFE INS. OC.

Most favourable terms to policy holders.

Benefit system unsurpassed.

HOLME RINGER & Co.
Agents, Chemulpo.

C. P. R

CANADIAN PACIFIC RAILWAY COMPANY'S ROYAL MAIL STEAMSHIP LINE.

THE FAST ROUTE BETWEEN CHINA, JAPAN, AND EUROPE VIA CANADA AND THE UNITED STATES.

Route from Hongkong via Shanghai, Nagasaki (Inland Sea of Japan) Kobe, Yokohama, Victoria and Vancouver.

Twin Screw Empress Steamship—6,000 Tons—Speed 19 knots.

PROPOSED SAILING FROM YOKOHAMA.
R. M. S. Empress of India.
R. M. S. Empress of Japan.
R. M. S. Empress of China.
R. M. J. Athenian.
R. M. S. Tartar.

Special reduction (first class only) granted to members of the Military, Naval, Diplomatic and Civil services and to Missionaries.
Passengers have choice of ten routes across the Continent of America and have privilege of travelling by any Atlantic Steamship Line.
Round the World passage tickets in connection with the P. and O. S. N., North German Lloyd and Messageries Co.'s **£125.**
All rates payable at current rate of exchange.
For further information, Tickets, Guide Books, etc., apply to

HOLME, RINGER & Co., AGENTS,
Chemulpo.

Grand Hotel,

(Formerly the Station Hotel)

Near the Railway Terminus, West Gate Seoul.

The Best Hotel in Korea.
Handsome new Building.
Fine Airy Rooms
Excellent Cuisine.
Terms Moderate.
Special terms to Missionaries
and to permanent boarders.

Electric cars within 2 minutes' walk.

W. H. EMBERLEY.
Proprietor

AMERICAN KOREAN ELECTRIC CO.

Light and Power.

Main Office: Flectric Building, Chong No.

RAILWAY DEPARTMENT.

OPERATING CARS BETWEEN EAST AND WEST GATE, EVERY TEN MINUTES:—

First Car leaves East Gate at 7:00 A. M. First Car leaves R. R. Station at 7:25 A. M
Last Car " East Gate at 8.40 P. M. Last " " R. R. Station at 9.05 P.M

OPERATING CARS BETWEEN EAST GATE AND IMPERIAL TOMB TERMINUS, EVERY TWENTY MINUTES:—
CONNECTING WITH EVERY ALTERNATE CAR ARRIVING AT EAST GATE FROM CHONG NO.

First Car leaves East Gate for Tomb at 7:10 A. M.
" " " Tomb for East Gate at 7:30 A. M.
Last " " East Gate for Tomb at 7:50 P. M.
" " " Tomb for East Gate at 8:10 P. M.

OPERATING CARS BETWEEN CHONG NO AND YUNG SAN RIVER EVERY TWELVE MINUTES:—

First Car leaves Chong No for South Gate at 7:12 A. M.
" " " Chong No for Yung San at 7:36 A. M.
" " " South Gate for Chong No at 7:20 A. M.
" " " Yung San for Chong No at 8:09 A. M.
Last " " South Gate for Chong No 9:00 P. M.
" " " Yung San for Chong No at 8.45. P. M.

SPECIAL PRIVATE CARS FURNISHED TO SUIT CONVENIENCE OF PATRONS. PRICES ON APPLICATION AT HEAD OFFICE.

LIGHTING DEPARTMENT.

Where less than 250 candle power of light is used, the rate per month will be
Per 16 candle power incandescent lamp,—All night.—Yen 2.50.
32 candle power incandescent lamp:—All night:—Yen 4.00.
50 candle power incandescent lamp:—All night:—Yen 6.00.
150 " " " " " " " 10.00.
1200 " " enclosed are " " " " 20.00.

Where more than 250 candle power of light is used, a Meter will be installed, freqvedted:—Rent of Meter Yen 2.00 per month. Rate of charges by meter reading:—Two Sen per Ampere per hour. (Approximately this is equal to about One Sen per 16 C. P. lamp per hour) Minimum monthly charge where meter is installed, Yen 20.00 per month, which includes rental of meter.

Estimates for installing lights furnished on application

An assortment of chandeliers always on hand.

EVERY FACILITY.

In connection with Life Assurance Business is afforded by

The Standard Life Assurance Co.,

One of the largest and wealthiest of the Provident Institutions of the United Kingdom Forms of Application and all information will be promptly afforded on application.

10 CENTS A DAY.

Not a very large expenditure is it? But it is sufficient to secure for a man of 30 a policy with the STANDARD LIFE OFFICE for

$1323.

For all particulars of rates, etc., apply to

Holme, Ringer & Co.,
Agents, Chemulpo.

THE NEW YORK LIFE INSURANCE COMPANY.

Have you ever been declined by any Company?

Are you engaged in a specially hazardous occupation?

Have you heard of the New York Life Insurance Company's New Classifications for this class of Risks?

If not, send your date of birth, occupation and particulars of rejection, if any to

E. MEYER & Co.,
Agents, Chemulpo.

K. Murakami.

Photograph Studio
Chinkokai, Seoul.

Printing, Developing and Enlargement, of Photographs always Undertaken.

Korean Views and Pictures Illustrating Native Customs always on Sale.

THE OSAKA SHOSEN KAISHA.

Boats frequently on the berth for Chinnampo.

REGULAR SAILINGS BETWEEN JAPAN AND KOREAN PORTS.

FUSAN AND KOBE VIA SHIMONOSEKI.

OSAKA VIA MOKPO, FUSAN, SHIMONOSEKI AND KOBE.

MOJI DIRECT.

OSAKA VIA KUNSAN, MASANPO, FUSAN, SHIMONOSEKI AND KOBE

CHEMULPO KUNSAN LINE,
Every three days.

CHEMULPO CHINNAMPO LINE.
Every three days.

For Freight and passage and further particulars apply to

THE OSAKA SHOSEN KAISHA,
Chemulpo

MITSUI BUSSAN KAISHA.
(MITSUI & Co.)

MITSUI GINKO.
(MITSUI BANK.)

The Bank is owned by the members of the Mitsui Family, who, as partners, assume an unlimited responsibility for all liabilities of the Bank:—

Capital........................Yen 5,000,000
Reserve Fund.................. " 5,600,000

HEAD OFFICE, TOKYO.
LONDON OFFICE, 34 LIME ST., E. C.

BRANCBES AND AGENCIES:—
New York, San Francisco, Hamburg, Bombay, Singapore, Manila, Hongkong, Amoy, Chefoo, Tientsin.

Kobe, Hakodate, Yokohama, Kure, Yokosuka, Moji, Shimonoseki, Miike, Wakamatsu, Nagasaki, Kuchinotsu, Karatsu, Sasebo, Misume, Taipeh, &c.

Telegraphic Address for all the Offices:
"MITSUI."
A. B. C. AND A. 1 CODES USED.

Contractors of Coal
To the Imperial Japanese Navy. Arsenals and Railway Bureau, Principal Railway Companies and Industrial Work, Home and Foreign Mail and Freight Steamers.

Sole Proprietors
Of the famous Miike, Tagawa and Yamano Coal Mines.

Sole Agents
For the sale of Fukumo, Hokoku, Ichimura, Kanoda, Mannoura, Onoura, Ostuji, Sonoda, Tsubaruro, Yoshinotani, Yoshio, Yurokibura and other coals.

YANGTSE INSURANCE ASSOCIATION, LTD.

The undersigned, having been appointed agents for the above company, are prepared to issue policies and pay losses on marine risks at regular rates.

E. MEYER & Co.,
Agents, Chemulpo.

RONDON, PLAISANT & CO.

General Storekeepers and Merchants, Ships Contractors, Tobacconists, Commission and Forwarding Agents, Coal Merchants

IMPORTERS AND EXPORTERS

Seoul & Chemulpo.

W. D. WENTWORTH.

LANDING
AND
SHIPPING AGENT
AND
CUSTOMS BORDER.

12 OURA, NAGASAKI.

STEWARD & CO.

Chemulpo.

Shipchandlers and Storekeepers, Naval and Mercantile Contrrctors, Landing and Shipping Agents.

STEWARD'S HOTEL

Chemulpo.

Best accommodation in the port for travellers. Clean and well-aired rooms, good cuisine and prompt attendence, moderate tariff.

론셜

이 상제원은하 현공 망국시에 불찬흔고로모다중진칙에배
표는시

〔일월십팔일 궁닉부〕

칙령
칙령뎨이호
화폐됴례에관흔됴건
뎨일됴 본국화폐의가격은금으로뎌귀쵸를지어본위화의근거를뎡고케홀사
뎨이됴 샹됴에의지흐야광무오년칙령뎨사호 화폐됴례는본년륙월일일브터실시홀사
어압 어새 봉 칙
칙령뎨삼호
이헌졍례을이좌ᄒᆞᆫ화폐법
뎨일됴 광무오년이월십이일칙령뎨사호화폐됴례는실시
...

뎨이됴 구화은심량(은이원)은신화금일원에샹당ᄒᆞ야졍부의
뎨삼됴 구빅동화폐의교환과밋환슈는광무구년칠월일일브터거시ᄒᆞᆯ사
뎨사됴 구빅동화의교환은...
뎨오됴 구동화폐교환과ᄒᆞᆫ종
뎨륙됴 샹기졔됴에의지ᄒᆞ야환슈와밋교환ᄒᆞᄂᆞᆫ방법과밋그교환처소ᄂᆞᆫ탁지부대신이졍ᄒᆞᆯ사
광무구년일월십팔일
어압 어새 봉 칙

광고

◯본인의쟝ᄌᆞ치변이가본시부랑패류로그부형ᄌᆞ뎨간에분쟈ᄒᆞ여가진던쟝문권을문수히도적ᄒᆞ여닉여셰부동이ᄒᆞ야셔문권을닉인ᄂᆞᆫ지고이에광포ᄒᆞ오니

DELIVERY OF A YARROW TORPEDO BOAT.

Various reports have been current as to the secret sale of a torpedo boat built by Messrs. Yarrow. The boat, which was engined with turbines, and was an experiment, had been tried on the Thames in the early autumn, and a little while afterwards—in September—a gentleman from Paris—said to be a Mr. Sennet—put forward proposals for its purchase, stating that he wished it to be transformed for yachting purposes. Messrs. Yarrow entered into treaty to sell, and ultimately notified the Admiralty of the matter, and the Admiralty at once passed on the facts to the Foreign Office. About ten days later, however, before their inquires could be completed, the boat sailed from the Thames in charge of Mr. Roche, who was supposed to take her over on behalf of her new owner.

Inquiries in various quarters show that Messrs. Yarrow had no reason to suspect that the craft was to be used for any other purpose than that advanced by the purchaser, who bought it as a turbine "yacht," similar to the one which the firm had supplied to the late Mr. McCalmont a few years ago. The "Caroline" is described by a man who worked on her as looking as much like a gentleman's yatch as did the vessel adapted for Mr. McCalmont. She was fitted in the same way, and everyone in the yard believed her to be intended merely for a yacht. The crew numbered 14—four engineers, six stokers, and four sailors, the engineers and stokers being selected from the Yarrow yard. They were engaged, one of them is reported to have said, for a cruise, and had no idea where they were going. They got abroad at Yarrow's at midday, and found Mr. Roche awaiting them. They passed quickly down the river, but there was no excitement, for they did not imagine there was any reason why they should be stopped. During the passage of the Kiel Canal the crew were kept below. At Libau, which was reached in three days, they steamed in just as any other vessel would, and moored alongside a wharf. Then the crew learned where they were. They were well paid, and returned to the Thames on a sailing ship. If Mr. Roche had handed the boat to the Russians, she would be useless to them until armed and fitted with torpedo tubes.

According to the Paris correspondent of the Express the mysterious Mr. Roche—the Captain Kettle of fact, who ran the "Caroline" from the Thames to Libau—has been identified there as none other than the heir to a peerage. He is the Hon. James Burke Boche, brother and heir of Lord Fermoy, of the Irish peerage.

There are also rumours that Russia has acquired a second Thames-built torpedo-boat, but they are rather unsubstantial. Little importance is attached in diplomatic circles to the incident, since the transaction was between a private individual and a private firm, and cannot be considered a national matter at all.

Viscount Hayashi, the Japanese Minister to Great Britain, told a newspaper representative that he was absolutely with any knowledge of the transaction. "The Naval Attache," his Excellency suggested, "may have heard some rumour of it, but I am without information concerning it." Captain Kahuraki, the Japanese Naval Attache, confessed to great surprise at the news.

"I have little doubt," he said, "that it is true. I heard some time ago rumours with regard to two torpedo-boat destroyers on the Thames, but I did not believe at the time that they would be sold to Russia, and I took no step whatever. I am greatly surprised that the rumours have turned out to have truth in them."

A certain railway station is surrounded in all directions with cheap restaurants. Over one of these, in great illuminated letters, could be seen the sign, "Open all night." Next to it was a restaurant bearing in equal prominence the placard, "We never close." Third in order was a Chinese laundry in a little tumble-down hovel, and on the front of this building was the sign, in great scrawling letters, "Me wakee too!"

COLLIERS OFF COCHIN CHINA.

The s.s. "Arratoon Apcar, which arrived at Singapore on 26th ult. reports an interesting "rencontre on Thursday evening while off the Cochin China coast, between Faurang Bay and Cape Paderan. Between the hours of 11 P. M. and 4 P. M. the vessel sighted no less than five large steamers, three of which were near enough for it to be seen that they were heavily laden—seemingly colliers—steaming no the northwards. Two were inshore. Such information is contained in the "Arraton Apcar's regular report. The singular and significant fact about the episode is that such a number of large steamers should be north bound on this particular track during the North-east monsoon, when it is well known to shipmasters that the strongest southerly currents prevail along that coast at this time of the year —some times to the extent of 80 miles a day to the south. The regular passage from Singapore during this monsoon is away out to seaward about 150 miles east of Cape Paderan. The only other Eastern port this fleet of steamers might have sailed from would be Saigon; but an exodus of five large freighters from Saigon, on one day, would be an exceptional event in the history of that port after the rice export season had closed. It is possible that they may be colliers having a rendezvous with the Baltic Fleet in one of the numerous little harbours that abound on the coast of Annam.—Straits Times.

RUSSIA AND THE DARDANELLES.

St. Petersburg Dec. 6.—The "Petersburgskya" Gazeta publishes to-day an interview with Hussni Pasha, the Turkish Ambassador here, on the subject of the Dardanelles question.

"The Paris Treaty" says the Ambassador, "only refers to the rights of sovereignty of Turkey, and does not concern England at all.

"The passage of Russian war vessels through the Dardanelles concerns Turkey alone, and as there is no danger of any sort involved in the passage of the ships, it will be sanctioned by that country.

"Any reference to the Paris Treaty is hereby disposed of."

The "Novoe Vremya" cites the authoritative opinion of Mr. Abramovitch Baraovski, Professor of International Law, who says, "the Paris Treaty is not a compact between seven Powers, but a series of compacts of six Powers individually with the Sultan.

"Nowhere is the right of England to watch over treaties between Russia and Turkey admitted.

"The whole Dardanelles question is a purely private affair between Russia and the Porte."

The Novosti declares that the view that only the Sultan's consent is needed is based on a mistaken interpretation of the text of the Treaty of Paris. "The Powers," says the journal, must be consulted before the fleet can enter the Straits.

"The situation is too serious to allow Russia to commit any imprudence in the sense urged by certain publicists—namely, to ignore the threats of the British Government. We should have thought of modifying the treaty before the war.

The "Chugai Shogyo" reports that the authorities of the Dai Ichi Bank have decided to increase the Bank's capital from 5,000,000 yen to 10,000,000 yen by issuing new shares. An extraordinary meeting of the shareholders will be held on the 28th inst. to consider the above proposal. It is stated that in addition to the present branch offices in Korea, the Bank will shortly establish branches at Gensan, Pyengyang and Taiku.

We most emphatically repudiate the following, which appeared in a recent issue of the "Chefoo Daily News":—

According to the most recent copies of the "Korea Daily News" received at this office, there appears to be no limit to what the arrogant Japanese military authorities would do in order to squeeze the last drop of life blood from the present dynasty of Korea. They are abroad in Chosen with the iron heel of military domination; they are wrenching bread from the lips of the starving; they are occupying land to which they have no right, and for which they refuse to pay a fair price. From Seoul north to Wi-ju tyranny reigns; poor, ignorant Koreans who have families to support are led out and ruthlessly shot by ruffianly gendarmes, because they would stay at home and work, that their families might have food instead of following the Japanese armies in Manchuria as coolies a service for which the Japanese pay in a depreciated currency which even their canteen men refuse to accept.

Of all these facts the home governments are aware. There is not a foreign minister at Seoul who has not importuned his government to come to the rescue of the hopeless Koreans. When will the civilized nations awaken to the urgency of appeal? Japan is playing her cards in Korea in an open and brazen-faced manner. Inflated with the idea that she is invulnerable, she is sowing the whirl-wind. She may have to reap it.

The latest fad of the Japanese in Seoul is to "crucify" Koreans who have fallen under their displeasure. To taunt the missionaries and foreigners in general, the victims are fastened to crosses and the proceeding is derisively referred to by the perpetrators as the crucifixion of biblical record.

MISCHIEF WORKERS IN THE LONDON PRESS.

Mr. Henry Norman, M. P., in The World's Work for December:—"Nobody in this country thinks more highly of our Press than I do, or has its welfare more at heart, yet in the face of such another outburst as we have recently witnessed, I should be compelled to support the establishment of an official censorship in times of international crises. For days, no words of personal insult were too gross or too vulgar to be applied to the Russian Admiral and his officers. It was taken for granted that at least they must all have been intoxicated. Every naval man knows perfectly well that it often happens in our own manoeuvres that a fleet fires upon its own torpedo boats, or upon fishing-boats mistaken for them. Without in the least attempting to detract from the shocking character of the action of the Russian fleet, it might at least, in the absence of evidence to the contrary, have been assumed that a terrible blunder had occurred. Now that the danger is over, recriminations are useless, but as a warning for the future, let us not forget that one London daily paper inflamed opinion for two days in succession with a positive statement of an 'Ultimatum to Russia' which "expires this afternoon,' and 'Time limit expired;' that another said of the Russian Admiral, 'The man must be either mad, or drunk, or is a liar:' and a halfpenny evening paper alluded to the Russian commander, on its contents bills, as the 'Mad Dog Admiral.' One of the most experienced journalists living said to me at that time, 'Unless something is done to stop these people, they will involve us some day in a hideous catastrophe.' It is needless to add that a large number of papers preserved their usual sense and dignity. But at such a crisis the irresponsible and sensational minority evert a disastrous influence at home and abroad."

PEARY'S NEW VESSEL.

A vessel is being built in the old yard upon Verona island, off the coast of Maine, which is not destined for purposes of trade. She is to force her way as far possible into the ice covered seas of the far north, carrying Leutenant Commander Peary in order that he may make another dash for the pole. In the Peary ship, the stern, stern-post, keels, keelson and frames are of carefully selected white oak. The massive frames will be only two feet apart from center to center, and they will be enclosed in a cage of steel made of diagonal straps and covering the inner fabric of the ship from stem to stern. Over the straps will be a double course of five-inch planking of yellow pine and white oak, and between these two courses will be tarred hemp or tarred canvans.

A guard strake of white oak surround, the vessel at the level of the main decke projecting outward for such a distancs that when the ice presses against her sides and is forced upward by the resistance, the ship will actually rest upon the guard strake. More than that, should she be frozen in, it would be possible to break the grip of the ice by the use of hydraulic jacks placed under the strake Naturally, so important a part of the yessel's protection is securely fastened to the hull and in addition it is strengthened by an angle bar of steel on itr under side.

The interior of the ship will be almost completely filled with heavy timbers. Starting at the center of the decks, these braces will entend diagonally downwards and outwards, the lower ends resting against the frames and helping them to withstand the pressure of the ice. With a hull thus filled with timbers, provision must be made for living quarters above decks and here there will be two houses, so constructed that they may be removed and set up on shore. For the rest, the vessel will be rigged as a three-masted schooner with an exceptionally large spread of canvas and will also be provided with steam power. She will be of about 1,500 tons and will be ready for service early next summer. It is the explorer's plan to go in the vessel to the northern shore of Grant land, winter there and make his dash for the pole during the following summer,

SUBMARINE-BOAT FLOTILLA.

Imperial Ordinance No. 15 published in the "Official Gazette" of the 13th inst., announces an amendment to the fleet Regulations in consequence of the organization of, submarine-boat flotillas in the Japanese Navy. It is stated that in addition to those already built, several submarine-boats are now in course of construction at the naval yards.

He was telling a thrilling story of his hair-breadth escape, says the Chicago News, and the young girl leaned forward and hung upon his words breathlessly.

"And they were so near," he said, "that we could see the dark muzzles of the wolves."

"Oh, how lucky!" she gasped. "How glad you must have been that they had their muzzles on!"

It is reported in telegrams from Peking to-day says the China Gazette that Mr. Uchida, the Japanese Minister, who is at present in Japan will not return to the former capital, but will be succeeded by Mr. Hayashi, the present Minister at Seoul. No explanations are given for the change but there has lately been a growing feeling that Japanese diplomacy in China has shown signs of failure. It is believed that Mr. Uchida may be sent to fill Mr. Hayashi's present post in Korea.

We havs had many conflicting report about Mr. Uchida but this is the most amazing one. According to advices from Japan Mr. Uchida has again returned to his post at Peking.

The Korea Daily News.

Issued at 5 P. M. daily except Sundays.

Rate of Subscription:—

Per Year,............Yen 25.
Per Quarter,..........Yen 7.
Per Month,..........Yen 2.50.

Postage in Korea not charged extra.
Postage abroad charged extra.

Advertisements, 50 sen per day for 1 inch or less.
5 yen per month per inch.
50 yen per year per inch.

All communications to

E. T. BETHELL,
Editor and Publisher,
Pak-tong, Seoul.

CHINA IN 1904.

FROM THE "CHINA MAIL."

The flight of years does not leave much of an impress upon the immobile face of China, and the one just passing has been very little different from thousands of others that have gone before it. The Government is the same, and all the methods of administration remain as they were. The antagonistic Dowager Empress has, with unfailing watchfulness, kept a clutch on the reins, and over the hills and dales of time she has driven at her own sweet will. Foreign advice to her is like the switch to the horse, and thus we find little has been tendered her. Corrupt and inept to rule such a vast Empire she has plunged along regardless of all the stir in the world about her. In the early part of the year fears were that she would be induced by Russia to assist in the war against Japan; and again it was felt that she would put her weight in with her nautural ally, Japan. But Japan preferred her negative to her active assistance, and the attitude of the powers upon the neutrality question convinced her Ministers that the safety of China lay in her quiescence. Upon the nation the war has had but little apparent effect. As far as can be gathered by casual observers it has not influenced the individual or the community at all. Phlegmatic and irresponsible, they jogged along the tracks that their ancestors have followed for centuries, looking neither or the right nor to the left, leaving Japan and all others to take care of themselves. Occasionally we have heard of anxiety being felt in Court circles about the safety of the integrity of the Empire, but after a searching out of arsenals and a furbishing of arms the air has become tranquil again. Internal troubles have gone on as of yore, and the never-ending Kwangsi rebellion has divided honours with the attempts in the north to resurrect boxerism. The Viceroy of the Two Kwangs, who came with a flourish of trumpets in 1903 to work peace and industry out of chaos, has failed signally. Though proceeding to the heart of the rebel country at the head of a large force of troops he was unable to do any more than others, who have had badly paid men at their command, have been able to do. He has recognised his weakness and inability, and has petitioned the Throne to recall him, but the Throne has declined to do anything of the kind, and now he is on his way back to Canton with none of the laurels that it was expected he would return with. Though the Two Kwangs have been favoured with good harvest during the year little can be said as to the general trade of China, though there are indications that when the various Customs returns are made out there will be a shortage admitted. The war has done much to check the natural flow of trade, and China has been feeling the effects of it. The most important event in the year's history of China was the launching of the scheme of reorganisation by Sir Robert Hart, a scheme which, though having much to recommend it, was visionary in the extreme. To reorganise the civil, naval and military services of a great Empire like China successfully a better foundation than can be found in China is necessary. To put up-to-date weapons in the hands of a horde of coolies under foreign instructors, and valuable battleships and cruisers in the hands of another horde, will not create an efficient army and navy. What is wanted is natural ability to handle them, and that is what the men of China have never shown. Sir Robert's scheme of taxation, too, though it is consistent with Chinese methods of raising taxes, would provoke hostility. The ideas are too comprehensive, however to discuss here in detail, and we must pass along acknowledging the broad and comprehensive character of the scheme. This year practically marked the first serious steps taken by China to consider the advisability of converting her currency from silver to gold. She entertained Professor Jenks, the commissioner delegated by the United States to confer with the Chinese authorities on the question, and has afforded him every assistance in interviewing the officials in Peking and provincial Viceroys, Governors, Treasurers and Treaty Commissioners. With untiring patience the Professor demonstrated to the Chinese the necessity for reforming the currency and the immense gain that would follow the establishment of a gold standard and also of a national bank. It is to be hoped that his work will bear good friut and that the near future will witness the end of the present cumbrous, antiquated, and ruinous system. If the past year has differed in any respect from its predecessor sit is in the few signs China has shown of awakening. The Dowager, for the first time since she has been responsible for the Government of China, publicly recognised the work of the Protestant Missionaries, contributing Tls. 10,000 (or £1,450) to the Lockhart Medical College at Peking; and she has acquiesced in large measure in the sending abroad of students. There has been more work done in opening up the country by railways, but sad to relate the bungling over the Canton-Hankow line has resulted in the total suspension of operations. Twice in the year this has occurred, in the early and the latter part, and now matters are so bad that a total readjustment will probably have to be undertaken. This is not due, however, to any interference of China. The attitude of the American shareholders in the line is to blame, and China only steps in now to reap whatever benefit she can from the trouble. Generally speaking China has been fairly tranquil—that is, of course, as tranquillity goes in China—and it is to be hoped that 1905, in which there is a double eight lunar month, according to China's calendar, will be as peaceful from the foreigners' point of view. When the double intercalory month happens to be the eighth, very particular significance is attached to the fact, as it is said to portend disaster to either the dynasty or the people, or both, and it must be remembered that the terrible events of 1900 happened in a year in which there was a double eighth month.

JAPAN AND MANCHURIA.

In connection with Japan's right in Manchuria, in which politicians and international jurists in Tokyo have been interested since the opening of hostilities, the "Kokumin" says in a leading article to-day that Manchuria is partly leased by Russia and partly included in the neutral zone, its nature being different in international law according to districts. In the other quarters the region between the Yalu and Shaho has already been occupied by the Japanese but the remainder is either occupied by the Russians still or is not relative to the War. Accordingly it would be a great mistake to deal with Manchuria "en-bloc" in respect of the "right" question. On the fall of Port Arthur, which was the centre of Russia's leased land, Japan has just obtained the right to administer Liaotung. It is now the time for Japan to consider and enforce steps for Russia's leased land and also for China's territory included in the zone of operations. In view of the fact that Manchuria is included in the zone of war though it belongs to China, it seems to be difficult for experts to apply international law to the administration of that region. There is no clause applicable to Manchuria even in the Hague Convention of 1899, which represents the latest regulations relating to land campaigns. Right and obligation of the occupants' army in regulating the enemy's territory are stipulated in detail in the same Convention, but there is no clause providing for the case of hostilities in a neutral territory, Therefore, Japan's present steps in Manchuria or measures to be enforced by her in the future will constitue many new prcedents in international law, and Japan may afford a good subject before the next international Hague conference, having to do with conditions which were unexpected in the conference of 1899. As for the application of Japan's right in Manchuria, the "Kokumin" states that Russia had fortified leased land and been unconditionally enforcing her administrative right there for a long t me, and it has now been occupied by Japan with arms. This being the capture of Russia's occupation right, Japan is able to apply in this leased land the Hague stipulations of 1899 regarding military administrative right in the enemy's territory. The final decision on Russia's leased territory is to be given after the restoration of peace and also in negotiations between Japan, Russia and China, so that the Japanese administration of Liaotung is merely a right based on the occupation of war, while the Liaotung lease convention between Russia and China is still effective, for a revision of which a new treaty is necessitated. With regard to the unleased district in Manchuria our contemporary states that the Hague convention of 1899 is free from stipulations to be adopted for hostilities in a neutral country, and further that the Japanese Government, at the commencement of war, promised the Chinese Government not to encroach upon China's territory or appropriate there any Japanese right other than that required for operations. Japan, who is in such a special position, is able in Manchuria outside Russia's leased land, to take steps necessary for operations only, but is incapable of acting as in the enemy's territory. The "Kokumin" concludes that its opinion agrees with views of the authorities concerned, thus respecting China's integrity.

The opening to traffic of the Seoul-Fusan Railway has so for had no unfavourable effect on the coasting steamship service in Korea, nor is the latter likely to be affected in the future, says the "Osaka Mainichi" which bases this contention on the fact that the opening of the Sanyo Railway has had no palpable effect on the steamship services in the Inland Sea. The net result, however, of the opening of the Seoul-Fusan Railway will be a general reduction of freight rates between Japan and Korea, which event will not fail to promote our trade with the peninsular state,

The Korea Daily News.

VOL. II, SATURDAY, JANUARY 21, 1905. No: 16

HONGKONG & SHANGHAI BANKING CORPORATION.

Paid-up Capital $10,000,000
Reserve Fund:—Sterling Reserve... 10,000,000
Silver Reserve..... 7,000,000

27,000,000

Reserve Liability of Proprietors... 10,000,000

HEAD OFFICE, HONGKONG.

London Bankers, London and County Banking Company Limited.

Branches and Agencies, London.

Amoy,	Hankow	Penang,
Bangkok,	Hiogo,	Rangoon,
Batavia,	Iloilo,	Saigon,
Bombay,	Lyons,	San Francisco,
Calcutta,	Manila,	Singapore,
Colombo,	Nagasaki,	Sourabaya,
Foochow,	New York,	Tientsin,
Hamburg,	Peking,	Yokohama,

Credits granted on approved Securities, and every description of Banking and Exchange business transacted.

Drafts granted on London and the chief Commercial places in Europe, India, Australia, America, China and Japan.

HOLME RINGER & Co., AGENTS,
CHEMULPO.

HOKURKU DOBOKU KAISHA.

Branch office in Chong Dong, Seoul.

Japanese telephone No. 165

CONTRACT DEPARTMENT.

We can contract to build any building or construction.

MERCHANDISE DEPARTMENT.

We can provide any building material. We have just contracted to build the new Belgian Legation.

E. MEYER & CO.

Chemulpo.

SOLE AGENTS IN KOREA FOR.

A. T. Morse, Sons & Co.'s

"Fresco" Distemper

In all colours ready for use on walls, Ceilings etc.

and

AVENARIUS CARBOLINEUM

A wood-preserving and antiseptic oil preparation

Against decay, dry-rot, fungus and wood-destroying insects.

A large supply always in stock. Prices upon application.

E. MEYER & Co.,
Chemulpo.

CHARTERED BANK OF INDIA AUSTRALIA & CHINA.

INCORPORATED BY ROYAL CHARTER 1853

HEAD OFFICES.—LONDON.

Paid-up Capital £800,000
Reserve Liability of Shareholders 800,000
Reserve Fund 800,000

Drafts granted upon all the principal places in the world and every description of Exchange and banking business transacted.

E. MEYER & Co., Agents,
Chemulpo.

MITSU BISHI DOCKYARD & ENGINE WORKS,

NAGASAKI.

CODE WORD, "DOCK."

A 1, A. B. C., and Engineering Codes used.

DOCK No. 1 (at Tategami).

Extreme Length..............523 feet
Length on blocks .... 513 „
Width of Entrance on Top......89 „
„ „ Bottom....77 „
Water on Blocks at Spring Tide 26½ „

DOCK No. 2 (Mukaijima).

Extreme Length..............371 feet
Length on Blocks.............360 „
Width of Entrance on Top......66 „
„ „ Bottom 53 „
Water on Blocks at Spring Tide 22 „

PATENT SLIP (at Kosuge).

Can take vessels up to 1,000 tons gross.

THE WORKS are well equipped with the LATEST IMPROVEMENTS, and can execute any kind of work in SHIPBUILDING and MARINE ENGINEERING, as well as in REPAIRING of SHIPS.

The COMPANY'S new powerful steamer OURA-MARU (712 tons, 700 I.H.P.), specially built for SALVAGE PURPOSES, and equipped with necessary gear, is always READY at SHORT NOTICE.

THE METHODIST PUBLISHING HOUSE.

Little West Gate, Seoul.

JOB PRINTING, TYPEWRITER PAPER
CARBON PAPER, VISITING CARDS
STATIONERY, BOOK BINDING
BOOK PUBLISHERS
AMERICAN SCHOOL BOOKS
SPENCERIAN COPY BOOKS
PEN CARBON LETTER AND BILL BOOKS

S.A. BECK, Manager.

DAI-ICHI GINKO.

LIMITED

(Formerly the First National Bank)

ESTABLISHED 1873

INCORPORATED UNDER PRESENT LAW 1896

Capital - - - - - - - - - Yen 5,000,000
Reserve Fund - - - - - 1,500,000

HEAD OFFICE:—TOKIO

President: Baron SHIBUSAWA.

BRANCHES AND CORRESPONDENTS In the Principal Cities and Towns of Japan.

Interest Allowed on

Fixed deposits 1 year - - - 6½ per cent
" " 6 months - - - 6 per cent

Special current accounts 1½ sen daily per Y 100
General " " 1 " " " 100

M. TANAKA,
Manager, Chemulpo.

SINGER SEWING MACHINES

씽거ᄌᆞ봉침

SOLE AGENTS FOR KOREA

젼매쇼

HOLME RINGER & CO.
Chemulpo.

제물포 함릉거양힝

KAMEYA CO.

GENERAL STOREKEEPERS

Chinkokai - - Seoul

(Established 1895, Tokyo)

Confectionery, Hams, Canned Goods, Cutlery, Hirano & Tansan Water. Provisions, Gents, Furnishing goods, Toilet Articles, Travelling Bags, Tobacco, Cigars & Cigarettes Kitchen Utensils. Coffee, Biscuits.

Fresh Goods always kept in Stock.

Prices Moderate

☞ *Please come and inspect our goods.*

NIPPON YUSEN KAISHA.

JAPANESE MAIL STEAMSHIP CO.

UNDER MAIL CONTRACT WITH THE IMPERIAL JAPANESE GOVERNMENT.

European Line

Regular Fortnightly Service between Yokohama Kobe, Moji, Shanghai, Hongkong, Singapore, Penang Colombo, Port Said, Marseilles, London and Antwerp

American Line

Regular Fortnightly Service between Hongkong and Seattle, calling at Shanghai, Moji, Kobe, Yokohama and Victoria, B. C.

Australian Line

Regular weekly Service betwen Japan Ports and Australia, calling at Hongkong and Manila.

(Above Three Lines Suspended until further notice).

Shanghai Line

Weekly Service between Shanghai and Japan Ports

Korea Line

Service Kobe, Moji, Nagasaki, Fusan Chemupo Chefoo, Taiku.

S. S. Bahelsberg, 2181 tons.

Service Kobe, Moji, Fusan, Chemulpo, Chinnampo

S. S. ARGO, S. S. Ohio.

BORDEN'S CONDENSED MILK CO.

New York, U. S. A.

ALWAYS IN STOCK

Eagle Brand Condensed Milk.

Gold Seal Condensed Milk.

Peerless (Family) Evaporated Cream.

Borden's Malted Milk.

E. MEYER & CO.
Chemulpo Korea,
Sole Agents

ROYAL INSURANCE COMPANY,

Funds exceed £10,000,000

FIRE

AT CURRENT RATES

LIFE

REDUCED PREMIUM.

HOLME RINGER & Co.,
Agents, Chemulpo.

HOTEL DU PALAIS

SEOUL.

The only first class Hotel in Seoul Situated in the centre of the city opposite the palace.

Cuisine under the supervision of an experienced French Chef.

Well ventilated and furnished throughout.

TARIFF UPON APPLICATION

L. MARTIN
Proripetor and Manager

大韓每日申報
대한ᄆᆡ일신보

(뎨이권십칠호) (화요일) 일쳔구ᄇᆡᆨ오년일월이십ᄉᆞ일

본샤고ᄇᆡᆨ

이신보는영어와한어로셔계리
일출판ᄒᆞ옵

신문가
한쟝 엽푼오리
일삭도 엽두량닷돈
우표가리 삭닷돈
다맛돈으로밧ᄉᆞᆸ

광고료는
귀한의쟝단과ᄌᆞ항의다소로중
감ᄒᆞ되평가로밧을터이오며오
리지아녀ᄯᅢ한사람마다다이신
문을보실터이니광고바시기를
원ᄒᆞ시는이들은우리신문사에
와서면약ᄒᆞ심을희망ᄒᆞᆸ

○발힝소 박동대한미일신보
사법어학교압해젼영국인셜필
립졍자리오
샤쟝 영국인 (빅셜)

평양 디리졈
○평양효동사는권미보씨로우
리신문광고디리인을뎡ᄒᆞ엿
시ᄉᆞ오니평양에계신구람코져ᄒᆞ
시는 쳠군ᄌᆞ는히디리졈에왕
림ᄒᆞ와면의ᄒᆞ시옵

사고

○우리대한미일신보의목뎍은
대한의인민젼셔에관한모든대
목에디ᄒᆞ야는공평한번론을쥬
쟝ᄒᆞᆯ이라우리동신원의ᄅᆞᆷ보는
신문보시는쳠군ᄌᆞ의게ᄒᆞ샹보
도ᄒᆞ리며평지를괴셔ᄒᆞ며주시
는이는셩명과번디를쟉이붓치
시기를희망ᄒᆞ오니이기슨신문
샹에괴쟤ᄒᆞ라는거시아니오다
만극히신용ᄒᆞ는증거를숨고자
ᄒᆞᆷ이라괴쟈는아모괴셔던지괴
쟤ᄒᆞᆯ을되갸ᄒᆞ는권리를가졋소
나되갸ᄒᆞ는리유를말ᄒᆞᆯ터이오
며공중평화를문란케ᄒᆞ는듯ᄒᆞᆫ
괴셔는의례히밧지안켓ᄉᆞᆸ나이
다

●본샤셜시이릭로신문을디방
우톄로분젼ᄒᆞ와톄젼부의일의
로젼ᄒᆞ는것ᄉᆞ로번곳에는혹늣게
젼ᄒᆞ기도ᄒᆞ며혹빠친거슨혼졉
에젼ᄒᆞ기도ᄒᆞ며혹아니젼ᄒᆞ는
곳도잇다ᄒᆞ오니우리신문을ᄉᆞ랑
ᄒᆞ야구람ᄒᆞ시는 쳠군ᄌᆞ의게
되ᄒᆞ야미우미안ᄒᆞ옵기로지금
은분젼인을두고미일일즉이젼
ᄒᆞ며아니젼ᄒᆞ거나늣게거나ᄒᆞᆫ
페가업도록ᄒᆞ라ᄒᆞ오니혹아니
젼ᄒᆞ거나늣게젼ᄒᆞ거나ᄒᆞᆫ일
이잇스면본사로통긔ᄒᆞ여주심
을희망ᄒᆞᆸ

관보

뎨삼쳔스십비호 광무구
년일월이십일일

셔임급ᄉᆞ령
○의원면본관 중추원의관
윤명셕 중추원의관 윤자션
중추원의관 민동식 중추원
의관 유티쥰 중추원의관
리근하 중추원의관 신슈형
○임중추원의관서주임관륙등
영월군슈 김봉원 졍삼품
김지션 졍삼품 리명환, 졍
삼품 박교샹 졍삼품 윤괴
쥬 구품 윤형식
○면본관 츈쳔군보병참령 리
규찬
미샹일월십팔일
○임회계원출납과쟝서주임관
샹등 농샹공부회계국쟝 엄
쥬승
○의원면본관 덕릉령 리긔
승 사졔서참봉 김용오 교
방ᄉᆞ주ᄉᆞ 박용쥰 법관양셩
소교관 졍인죠
○임 사졔서참봉서판임관팔
등 쟝릉참봉 최헌졍긔
○임 쟝릉참봉서판임관팔등
리뮈샹
○임교방ᄉᆞ주ᄉᆞ서판임관팔등
서경권
○임 덕릉령서판임관칠등
화릉참봉 김셕하
○임 화릉참봉서판임관팔등
리규영
○임법관양셩소교관서판임관
륙등 리강연
○힝법부법률괴초위원 신악
균 ᄒᆞᆼ슌갸
○명법부법률괴초위원 졍삼
품 윤방현 졍삼품 한동리
미샹일월십구일
○임탁디부대신서칙임관일등
황히도관찰ᄉᆞ 죠병호
일월십구일
궁뇌부특ᄉᆞ
○중추원의관최병쥬ᄉᆞ직소
비지셩소구셜말은을ᄒᆞ나그셜
샹이임의업스니엇지번명ᄒᆞ기
를기다리리오경은ᄉᆞ양치말고
힝공ᄒᆞ라ᄒᆞ시다
일월십구일

잡보

○슈도쟝셜 한미뎐긔회샤
셔한셩닉헤식료슈를한강슈를에
인도ᄒᆞ야셩닉쟈거에슈도를노
황졍졍이고를을먹케경영ᄒᆞ는
지는오랜거니와쟝식괴계와괴
ᄉᆞ들이미구에도챡ᄒᆞ야음력졍
월닉부터는한슈ᄒᆞ리라더라

○쟝미괴계 ᄒᆞᆫ런원죠산밋히
사는박화진씨가년젼에욕쟝ᄒᆞ
는괴계쇼본ᄒᆞᆫ좌를사다가지고
ᄒᆞ엿는티지금동씨가유지군ᄌᆞ
와합동ᄒᆞ야ᄌᆞ본금샹쳔원을가
지고다시큰괴계를사왓는티이
괴계는ᄒᆞᆫ번에몽이다섯시일제
히너런지니미일에상샹셔미나
ᄭᅥ내별지라리월망간에는시쟉
ᄒᆞ란ᄒᆞᆫ다더라

○교수고빙 월젼에슈원부ᄉᆞ
림학교에셔젼군슈오완섭씨를
교ᄉᆞ로교빙ᄒᆞ엿는티동씨는다
문박식ᄒᆞ고번ᄉᆞ란칭ᄒᆞ더라

○ᄉᆡᆼ씨봉방 젼평양군슈신샹
의씨가군슈ᄌᆡ임시에공젼진령
ᄒᆞᆫᄉᆞ로슈너계슈ᄒᆞ엿다가일젼
에보방ᄒᆞ야신픔징으로니허간
다더라

○경무쳥훈령 경무쳥에셔각
셔에훈령ᄒᆞ기를ᄯᅢ지환란샹구
는인졍의가히졍시라도지완치
못ᄒᆞᆯ배란근ᄅᆡ에런엄가에셔실
화ᄒᆞᆫ배에런국병뎡과숀졍은듯
고곳와셔몽에위방ᄒᆞᆷ을무릅쓰
고진심으로힘써구원ᄒᆞ는티오
직우리나라경찰관리는승관이
나티ᄒᆞ야도로혀외국인만도못
ᄒᆞ니샹히지런ᄒᆞ며쇼리인거긔
은모ᄒᆞ셔셔구경만ᄒᆞ며혹세들
마웃기만ᄒᆞ고문훈동의를기리
다가고금히란는거슨구원ᄒᆞ지
아니ᄒᆞ니사름의리치로ᄡᅥ하
런본ᄌᆞ의리가엇슴아막심ᄒᆞ고
슈모가불쇼ᄒᆞᆷ쎤버리샹지이고
불힝ᄒᆞᆷ을다힝으로알고등을타
셔도쟉셜ᄒᆞ는쟈도잇스니사름
의란샹이엇슴이엇지이다지
구흔티니르렷느뇨금히맛당히
이별노조속을더ᄒᆞ여아ᄒᆞ겟기로
에흥흡쳐ᄒᆞ니ᄌᆞ금비후로는
일셜화ᄒᆞᆫ졍이잇거든히쟝과
다른방닉에나몬론ᄒᆞ고셔쟝
ᄒᆞ충슌이슌감을렵슬ᄒᆞ고일졔히
가셔구원ᄒᆞ야ᄒᆞ지완홈이엽게
ᄒᆞ며원군인미이믈소쳐히불을
셔ᄂᆞᆫ쟈외에는일졀한쟝지류는
엄칙ᄒᆞ야ᄎᆞ차보니아우승을셧
치며패를닛는거슬면케호티만
일반ᄒᆞᆯ흔괴단비잇스면본셔쟝
양은챡벽당히분경홈이맛당ᄒᆞ다ᄒᆞ엿더라

○원도츌셔 음력샹이월샹
일에봉죠하긴병국씨가광쥬셩
교면구룡동본게에셔츌셔ᄒᆞ엿
더라

○경쳥공함 경무쳥에셔각국
령ᄉᆞ외계공함ᄒᆞ기를한셩닉에
거류ᄒᆞ는각긔본방인의ᄒᆞ호구를
죠ᄉᆞᄒᆞ야시명ᄒᆞ라ᄒᆞ엿더라

○쥐에샹반 신경무ᄉᆞ의경셩
이힝쟝에티ᄒᆞ야칭녕에공관ᄒᆞ
샹반에티ᄒᆞ야는녀부슌을조챡ᄒᆞᆫ
는티티ᄒᆞ야는쟝교인들과셩셔
귀ᄒᆞᆫ닙즈들은셤기며음양술수
자류를은공평치안타ᄒᆞ며칭찬ᄒᆞ고
가야외봉괘비단쳔힝ᄒᆞ는ᄒᆞ고
퇴ᄂᆞᆫ스부만ᄒᆞ쇼셔와교졍ᄒᆞ니
다ᄒᆞ고셔긔쳔과칙과칙일ᄒᆞᆫ
셔ᄒᆞ고졍부ᄒᆞᆫ쟝을ᄆᆡ집ᄒᆞ니
고쟝가세물에몽ᄒᆞ니셩벽의
쟝쥬엑몽에세울의무리ᄒᆞ니
의부경한부부ᄒᆞ게세의
녀계ᄒᆞ는ᄒᆞᆫ티이라편리ᄒᆞᆫ더
라

외보

○일졍부인괴 덕리슌구요시
뎡쟝관시산씨와참모쟝우리써
씨와괴관쟝휘쳔씨외군의쟝령
쟝의히힝은금월이십일뷔츌발
ᄒᆞ야부임ᄒᆞᆫ다더라

○무용졍샹 법국셔국회쇼집
ᄒᆞᆫ샹의원체년쟝구안씨셩셜
샹요업ᄒᆞ되일아쟝군의무용을칭
찬ᄒᆞ며공졍중에젼쟝즁국흠을
희망ᄒᆞᆫ다ᄒᆞ엿더라

○미국농리 미국농무경과일
년쇼써의공포ᄒᆞᆫ바보를거ᄒᆞᆫ즉거
구에미국농작믈이쳐구ᄇᆡᆨᄉᆞ년도
분일ᄇᆡ도에비ᄒᆞ면소ᄉᆞ칠ᄇᆡᆨ
이가ᄒᆞ엿는티그쳔구ᄇᆡᆨ삼년
도에비ᄒᆞ면ᄉᆞ쳔구ᄇᆡᆨ만원이
더ᄒᆞ고일쳔구ᄇᆡᆨ이년도의일
쳔팔ᄇᆡᆨ구십구년에비ᄒᆞ면
ᄉᆞ십억칠쳔구ᄇᆡᆨ만원이증가
ᄒᆞ엿는티미국농업의발달은
실로놀나온지라이
ᄇᆡᆨ오년에는미국부강이더욱
전보다나을지라ᄒᆞ더라

UNION INSURANCE SOCIETY OF CANTON.

Head office Hongkong.
Marine risks underwritten at current rates.

Agents in Chemulpo,
E. MEYER & Co.

COMPAGNIE DES MESSAGERIES MARITIMES

Fortnightly Direct Service.

For Marseilles
via Ports.
Sailing from Yokohama
Calling at Kobe,
Shanghai, Hongkong, Saigon, Singapore,
Colombo, Djiboti, Suez, Port Said
and Marseilles.

For particulars apply to
HOLME RINGER & Co.,
Chemulpo.

HAYASHIDA & CO.,

16 MYENG DONG, CHIN KO KAI, SEOUL.
BRANCH OFFICE AT CHEMULPO.

Money changers, Coal and Wood Merchants, Express Agents.

We are agents for the Pyeng-yang Coal Company and the Karazu Coal Company of Japan. We have the best quality of both anthracite and bituminous coal, and prompt execution of orders is our speciality. Firewood of all kinds kept in stock. Full weight guaranteed. Money of all denominations exchanged at current rates. Parcels received for all parts.

CHINA MUTUAL LIFE INS. OC.

Most favourable terms to policy holders

Benefit system unsurpassed.

HOLME RINGER & Co.
Agents, Chemulpo.

C. P. R.

CANADIAN PACIFIC RAILWAY COMPANY'S ROYAL MAIL STEAMSHIP LINE.

THE FAST ROUTE BETWEEN CHINA, JAPAN, AND EUROPE VIA CANADA AND THE UNITED STATES.

Route from Hongkong via Shanghai, Nagasaki (Inland Sea of Japan) Kobe, Yokohama, Victoria and Vancouver.

Twin Screw Empress Steamship—6,000 Tons—Speed 19 knots.

PROPOSED SAILING FROM YOKOHAMA.
R. M. S. Empress of India.
R. M. S. Empress of Japan.
R. M. S. Empress of China.
R. M. S. Athenian.
R. M. S. Tartar.

Special reduction (first class only) granted to members of the Military, Naval, Diplomatic and Civil services and to Missionaries.

Passengers have choice of ten routes across the Continent of America and have privilege of travelling by any Atlantic Steamship Line.

Round the World passage tickets in connection with the P. and O. S. N., North German Lloyd and Messageries Co.'s £125.

All rates payable at current rate of exchange.

For further information, Tickets, Guide Books, etc., apply to

HOLME, RINGER & Co., AGENTS,
Chemulpo.

Grand Hotel,

(Formerly the Station Hotel)

Near the Railway Terminus, West Gate Seoul.

The Best Hotel in Korea.
Handsome new Building.
Fine Airy Rooms
Excellent Cuisine.
Terms Moderate.
Special terms to Missionaries
and to permanent boarders.

Electric cars within 2 minutes' walk.

W. H. EMBERLEY.
Proprietor

EVERY FACILITY.

In connection with Life Assurance Business is afforded by

The Standard Life Assurance Co.,

One of the largest and wealthiest of the Provident Institutions of the United Kingdom Forms of Application and all information will be promptly afforded on application.

10 CENTS A DAY.

Not a very large expenditure is it? But it is sufficient to secure for a man of 30 a policy with the STANDARD LIFE OFFICE for

$1323.

For all particulars of rates, etc., apply to

Holme, Ringer & Co.,
Agents, Chemulpo.

THE NEW YORK LIFE INSURANCE COMPANY.

Have you ever been declined by any Company?

Are you engaged in a specially hazardous occupation?

Have you heard of the New York Life Insurance Company's New Classifications for this class of Risks?

If not, send your date of birth, occupation and particulars of rejection, if any to

E. MEYER & Co.,
Agents, Chemulpo.

MITSUI BUSSAN KAISHA.
(MITSUI & Co.)

MITSUI GINKO.
(MITSUI BANK.)

The Bank is owned by the members of the Mitsui Family, who, as partners, assume an unlimited responsibility for all liabilities of the Bank:—

Capital........................Yen 5,000,000
Reserve Fund.................. " 5,600,000

HEAD OFFICE, TOKYO.
LONDON OFFICE, 34 LIME ST., E. C.

BRANCHES AND AGENCIES:—

New York, San Francisco, Hamburg, Bombay, Singapore, Manila, Hongkong, Amoy, Chefoo, Tientsin.

Kobe, Hakodate, Yokohama, Kure, Yokosuka, Moji, Shimonoseki, Miike, Wakamatsu, Nagasaki, Kuchinotsu, Karatsu, Sasebo, Misume, Taipeh, &c.

Telegraphic Address for all the Offices:
"MITSUI."
A. B. C. AND A. I CODES USED.

Contractors of Coal

To the Imperial Japanese Navy. Arsenals and Railway Bureau, Principal Railway Companies and Industrial Work, Home and Foreign Mail and Freight Steamers.

Sole Proprietors

Of the famous Miike, Tagawa and Yamano Coal Mines.

Sole Agents

For the sale of Fukumo, Hokoku, Ichimura, Kanoda, Mannoura, Onoura, Ostuji, Sonoda, Tsubaruro, Yoshinotani, Yoshio, Yurokibura and other coals.

YANGTSE INSURANCE ASSOCIATION, LTD.

The undersigned, having been appointed agents for the above company, are prepared to issue policies and pay losses on marine risks at regular rates.

E. MEYER & Co.,
Agents, Chemulpo.

AMERICAN KOREAN ELECTRIC CO.

Light and Power.

Main Office: Electric Building, Chong No.

RAILWAY DEPARTMENT.

OPERATING CARS BETWEEN EAST AND WEST GATE, EVERY TEN MINUTES:—

First Car leaves East Gate at 7:00 A. M. First Car leaves R. R. Station at 7:25 A. M
Last Car " East Gate at 8.40 P. M. Last " " R. R. Station at 9.05 P.M

OPERATING CARS BETWEEN EAST GATE AND IMPERIAL TOMB TERMINUS, EVERY TWENTY MINUTES:—

CONNECTING WITH EVERY ALTERNATE CAR ARRIVING AT EAST GATE FROM CHONG NO.

First Car leaves East Gate for Tomb at 7:10 A. M.
" " " Tomb for East Gate at 7:30 A. M.
Last " " East Gate for Tomb at 7:50 P. M.
" " " Tomb for East Gate at 8:10 P. M.

OPERATING CARS BETWEEN CHONG NO AND YUNG SAN RIVER EVERY TWELVE MINUTES:—

First Car leaves Chong No for South Gate at 7:12 A. M.
" " " Chong No for Yung San at 7:36 A. M.
" " " South Gate for Chong No at 7:20 A. M.
" " " Yung San for Chong No at 8:09 A. M.
Last " " South Gate for Chong No 9:00 P. M.
" " " Yung San for Chong No at 8.45 P. M.

SPECIAL PRIVATE CARS FURNISHED TO SUIT CONVENIENCE OF PATRONS. PRICES ON APPLICATION AT HEAD OFFICE.

LIGHTING DEPARTMENT.

Where less than 250 candle power of light is used, the rate per month will be
Per 16 candle power incandescent lamp,—All night.—Yen 2.50.
32 candle power incandescent lamp:—All night:—Yen 4.00.
50 candle power incandescent lamp:—All night:—Yen 6.00.
150 " " " " " " " 10.00.
1200 " " enclosed are " " " " 20.00.

Where more than 250 candle power of light is used, a Meter will be installed, if requested:—Rent of Meter Yen 2.00 per month. Rate of charges by meter reading:—Two Sen per Ampere per hour. (Approximately this is equal to about One Sen per 16 C. P. lamp per hour) Minimum monthly charge where meter is installed, Yen 20.00 per month, which includes rental of meter.

Estimates for installing lights furnished on application

an assortment of chandeliers always on hand.

K. Murakami.
Photograph Studio
Chinkokai, Seoul.

Printing, Developing and Enlargement, of Photographs always Undertaken.

Korean Views and Pictures Illustrating Native Customs always on Sale.

THE OSAKA SHOSEN KAISHA.

Boats frequently on the berth for Chinnampo.

REGULAR SAILINGS BETWEEN JAPAN AND KOREAN PORTS.

FUSAN AND KOBE VIA SHIMONOSEKI.

OSAKA VIA MOKPO, FUSAN, SHIMONOSEKI AND KOBE.

MOJI DIRECT.

OSAKA VIA KUNSAN, MASANPO, FUSAN, SHIMONOSEKI AND KOBE.

CHEMULPO KUNSAN LINE,
Every three days.

CHEMULPO CHINNAMPO LINE.
Every three days.

For Freight and passage and further particulars apply to

THE OSAKA SHOSEN KAISHA,
Chemulpo.

RONDON, PLAISANT & CO.

General Storekeepers and Merchants, Ships Contractors, Tobacconists, Commission and Forwarding Agents, Coal Merchants

IMPORTERS AND EXPORTERS

Seoul & Chemulpo.

W. D. WENTWORTH.

LANDING
AND
SHIPPING AGENT.
AND
CUSTOMS BROKER.

12 OURA, NAGASAKI.

STEWARD & CO.

Chemulpo.

Shipchandlers and Storekeepers, Naval and Mercantile Contractors, Landing and Shipping Agents.

STEWARD'S HOTEL

Chemulpo.

Best accommodation in the port for travellers. Clean and well-aired rooms, good cuisine and prompt attendance, moderate tariff.

잡보

○탁대임면 탁지대신민영긔
씨ᄃᆡ에황ᄒᆡ도관찰ᄉᆞ조병호씨
가피임ᄒᆞᆫ다더라

○너죠외부 너부에셔희부고
문관ᄃᆡ일광씨의ᄌᆞ원ᄒᆞ고ᄒᆞᆷ을
의쥰ᄒᆞ야외부로조회ᄒᆞ고비국
평ᄉᆞ의게셩명ᄒᆞ라ᄒᆞ엿더라

○광씨평화 민영휘씨가리감
씨로더브러면담ᄉᆞ로괴송ᄒᆞ던
일은젼보에엉의과진ᄒᆞ엿거니
와지쟉일민씨가리씨를쳥ᄒᆞ야
심오년츄슈도ᄉᆞ쳔셕ᄃᆡ가ᄂᆞᆫ삼
만원으로작졍ᄒᆞ야츌급ᄒᆞᆫ후에
평화ᄒᆞ엿다더라

○쳥폐포군 일진회총ᄃᆡ위원
엄종모씨등이군부대신리종건
씨ᄉᆞ저에젼왕ᄒᆞ야함경평안남
북도포군을폐시ᄒᆞᆷ을쳥ᄒᆞᄂᆞᆫ지라
리군대왈이ᄂᆞᆫ나라에방어ᄒᆞ고
검지ᄒᆞᆷ으로젼브터셜시ᄒᆞᆷ이어
ᄂᆞᆯ동도에힝패가잇ᄂᆞᆫ고로포군이
이위엄을보임이오가히난병이
란ᄒᆞᆯ슈업스니결단코혁파ᄒᆞ지
못ᄒᆞᆫ깃다ᄒᆞ고항거ᄒᆞ엿다더라

○총회미기 거십팔일에관제
리졍ᄒᆞᆫ총회ᄂᆞᆫ인원이미비ᄒᆞ야
기회ᄒᆞ지못ᄒᆞ고후일로연긔ᄒᆞ
엿더라

○수포구류 ᄇᆞᆼ화인민들이부
윤권쳘규씨의탐학ᄒᆞᆫ거슬드러
너부에등소ᄒᆞ고그쟝젼을차저
증을쳥원ᄒᆞ엿더니그아ᄂᆞᆫ운방
현씨가거십구일에너부에셕며
ᄃᆞ리가희소장을문시ᄒᆞ라ᄒᆞ고
장민을ᄉᆞᄉᆞ로이포착ᄒᆞ야구류
ᄒᆞ엿더라

○귀불봉쳑 평리원에셔대
벽부도로회샹ᄒᆞᆫ쟝호익등과동
모ᄒᆞ던무관한도로임참위ᄒᆞᆫ자
졀인이일본에잇ᄂᆞᆫᄃᆡ 샹이탕
쳐ᄒᆞ시ᄂᆞᆫ법을베프사모모위관
을소환ᄒᆞ야부져ᄒᆞ라ᄒᆞ읍셧더
니군부ᄃᆡ리종건씨가반ᄃᆡᄒᆞ야왈
이ᄂᆞᆫ대역부도라나ᄂᆞᆫ가히쥬본
을드릴슈엽다ᄒᆞ고괴어히봉
쳐ᄒᆞ지아니ᄒᆞᆫ다더라

○일승착긴한순 경위원순검
월명이죵로에셔취쥬ᄒᆞ야일본
순ᄉᆞ의게언ᄉᆞ가불공ᄒᆞᆫ다ᄒᆞ야
허순ᄉᆞ가장아갓다더니남셔에
셔일본헌병ᄉᆞ령부와교섭ᄒᆞ야
방송ᄒᆞ엿다더라

○의정상주 이십일밤에의정
리근명씨가등ᄃᆡ입시ᄒᆞ야시졍
기션등ᄉᆞ를샹주ᄒᆞ엿다더라

○김씨하거향ᄃᆡ 김학진김종
한씨등이졍우회를셜시ᄒᆞ고기
션졍치를쇄신케ᄒᆞᆫ다더니 쳐
분너에곳치산ᄒᆞ란ᄒᆞ심으로김
종한씨ᄂᆞᆫ일간슈원향ᄃᆡ로나려
간다더라

○리씨셜교 리용익씨가학엽
샹에유의ᄒᆞᆫ다ᄒᆞ더니소학교ᄂᆞᆫ
린언병으로지졍ᄒᆞ고중학교ᄂᆞᆫ
젼야어학교로셜시ᄒᆞᆫ다더라

○겸무빈중역 경무쳥에셔별
단영이ᄃᆞᆯ몬아중역일밤에죵ᄉᆞ케ᄒᆞ엿
명더니경무ᄉᆞ십일밤에그무리벽
경ᄉᆞᄂᆞᆫ니나ᄌᆞ졍분안에희케진ᄒᆞ야
을부로고도망ᄒᆞᆫ고로쳥금동셔번
중셔에셔별영이중파슈를장아
그교쥰ᄒᆞ던자를사힉ᄒᆞᆫ다더라

○흉복자착거 쟉일에구리기
ᄂᆡ거리에셔졈은바지입은자ᄒᆞᆫ
ㅣ아흉순검이쟝ᄆᆡ아가ᄂᆞᆫᄃᆡ쟝운옷잇자
은말ᄒᆞ기를ᄆᆡ리햇고겸은웃닙나
ᄒᆞᄂᆞᆫ자ᄂᆞᆫ장지안교ᄭᅴᄂᆞᆫ쟝이나
케오ᄂᆞᆫ교로순검방이빅셩이란
다완악ᄒᆞᆫ쥬빅셩ᄂᆞᆷ서위ᄒᆞᆯ슈엽
교ᄒᆞ고ᄂᆡᄂᆞᆫ단단이속이리라ᄒᆞ
쟝아갓다더라

○언쥬유리 근일에나모쟝ᄉᆞ
들이우마가셜곳이엽슴으로미
우곤란ᄒᆞᆫ중인ᄃᆡ셩안으로도다셧
군ᄃᆡ가공터ᄃᆡ가잇ᄂᆞᆫᄃᆡ동에ᄂᆞᆫ
ᄒᆞᆫ련원근쳐와셔에ᄂᆞᆫ공졍밧과
남에ᄂᆞᆫ싱수당앞과북에ᄂᆞᆫ츄셩
문앞과중앙에ᄂᆞᆫ탑동공원담밧
ᄭᅴ다셧군ᄃᆡ로졍ᄒᆞ야쥬면공ᄉᆞ
평편ᄒᆞ겟다고ᄒᆞᆫ다더라

○우두소교시 우리대한이우
무의지극히졍묘ᄒᆞᆫ리치를모로
고류힝ᄒᆞᄂᆞᆫ병에걸녀쳥년에횡
ᄉᆞᄒᆞᄂᆞᆫ폐단이잇ᄂᆞᆫ고로
대황뎨폐하의지인지ᄌᆞᄒᆞ옵신
조칙을봉승ᄒᆞ야지금일본의학
교의ᄉᆞ소쥬무차씨를고빙ᄒᆞ야
일본에셔신발명ᄒᆞᆫ우두약을사
서한셩오셔너에림시우두소를
셜치ᄒᆞ엿스니녀졀을ᄒᆞ지못ᄒᆞᆫ
아희든지쟝셩ᄒᆞᆫ사람이라도와
셔약을시종ᄒᆞ여보라ᄒᆞ엿더라

○조쳥폐현 일공관에셔외부
에조회ᄒᆞ기를경시쳥샹중쥰을
귀졍부에셔고문으로고빙ᄒᆞ야
쟉십구일에도착ᄒᆞ엿슴으로
폐현ᄒᆞ기를쳥ᄒᆞ니쳥컨ᄃᆡ젼
쥬ᄒᆞ라ᄒᆞ엿더라

○조쳥젼쥬 쳥공관에셔외부
에조회ᄒᆞ기를우리졍부면훈을
졉ᄒᆞᆫ즉민공ᄉᆞ조회를인ᄒᆞ야우
리 대황뎨가귀국 황뎨ᄌᆞ비
ᄒᆞ셔ᄒᆞ심을드르시고원셩ᄒᆞᆷ을
익이지못ᄒᆞ야본ᄉᆞ를명ᄒᆞ야곳
귀외부에가셔샹가우문ᄒᆞ고샤
그뜻으로젼 쥬ᄒᆞ기를쳥ᄒᆞ엿
더라

○면쳥잉류 영변군슈가외부
로면보ᄒᆞ기를본군쥬차일본래
ᄃᆡ장래면이가군ᄉᆞ규측을엄이
단속ᄒᆞ야읍촌이보안ᄒᆞ고약으
로써병을치료ᄒᆞ야ᄆᆞᆫ이효험이
잇고학교를베플어공부에효험
이잇더니이제훈련이환계ᄒᆞᆫ다
ᄒᆞᄂᆞᆫ빅셩이다가ᄂᆞᆫ거슬앗기니
일본ᄉᆞ령부에젼조ᄒᆞ야잉이ᄃᆡ
쥬차케ᄒᆞ야빅셩의바라ᄂᆞᆫ거슬
칙ᄒᆞ게ᄒᆞ라ᄒᆞ엿더라

○황쥬군민소 황쥬군민홍셩
호등이외부에호소ᄒᆞ기를본군
로하광방에잇ᄂᆞᆫ던답을일본인
이갓방인민을조치ᄒᆞ야어지로
방미ᄒᆞ기를요구ᄒᆞ야위협이자
심ᄒᆞ와셩문방미ᄒᆞᆫ연유로이에
앙소ᄒᆞᆫ다ᄒᆞ엿더라

○림공ᄉᆞ셜연 이십륙일샹오
십이시에림공ᄉᆞ가오찬회를셜
ᄒᆞ고각대관을쳥요ᄒᆞᆫ다더라

○시찰여거 경무쳥고문관환
산중쥬씨가이십일에평무쳥에
젼왕ᄒᆞ야일반경찰ᄉᆞ무를시찰
ᄒᆞ고갓다더라

론셜

로국의긔랑

○로국황뎨계셔각항긔랑안에
ᄃᆡᄒᆞ야의졍부에조칙을ᄂᆞ리셧
ᄂᆞᆫᄃᆡ그조칙에ᄒᆞ엿스되
텬명으로졍이계승ᄒᆞᆫ조종의너
리신졍칙에의지ᄒᆞ고국가의리
익을위ᄒᆞ야데국의졍치ᄂᆞᆫ일졍
불번ᄒᆞᆯ지라그러ᄒᆞ나만일무엇
시던지힝졍ᄉᆞ무에긔랑ᄒᆞᆯᄉᆞ진
이잇스면졍이런긔랑안을셜
시ᄒᆞ기에쥬져치아니ᄒᆞ겟고림
벌ᄉᆞ무의관치변긔ᄒᆞᄂᆞᆫ일이라
도졍이반ᄃᆡᄒᆞ지아니ᄒᆞ리라안
녕질셔를보젼ᄒᆞ고민원을좃ᄂᆞᆫ
ᄃᆡ힝복이날너거슬귀즁히아ᄂᆞᆫ
지각잇ᄂᆞᆫ사ᄅᆞᆷ들은졍의이조칙
을환영ᄒᆞᆯ게시어신엽겟도다ᄒᆞ
엿스며
그다음에ᄂᆞᆫ군ᄉᆞ상긔랑과인민
의다슈된논빈의쟁형에ᄃᆡᄒᆞ야
긔랑ᄒᆞᆯ일을말ᄒᆞ고그셕혜이ᄒᆞ엿
리ᄃᆡ문이잇스니그ᄃᆡ문에ᄒᆞ엿
스되
졍은이긔랑안들이국가의젼리
승관과헌힝법률에적합ᄒᆞ
야ᄂᆞᆫ영샤회의계획ᄒᆞᆫ자유권
을지금브터영구히보존ᄒᆞ기를
원ᄒᆞ노라다방회의에셔쳥구ᄒᆞ
ᄂᆞᆫ일들은공동쥬의들이고키지
마ᄂᆞᆫ그일들은다법에어그려진
거시라일신샹ᄉᆞ의으로일ᄒᆞᄂᆞᆫ
쟝류들이소년들을ᄭᅬ야셔평슈
ᄒᆞ고회를열고졍부에ᄃᆡᄒᆞ야여
러가지를요구ᄒᆞ나그러ᄒᆞ나이
런요구들은다ᄃᆡ로뎨국의일졍
ᄒᆞᆫ졍치및헤ᄂᆞᆫ리라지못ᄒᆞᆯ지라
대도회의가로샹에셔시위운동
ᄒᆞᄂᆞᆫ졍부관인을반ᄃᆡᄒᆞᄂᆞᆫ중회에
ᄂᆞᆫ국가에향ᄒᆞ야진실노충셩스
런운로국인민들은참여ᄒᆞᆷ이업
도다이러ᄒᆞᆫ위ᄂᆞᆫ외양으로졍중
ᄒᆞᆫ의미를표ᄒᆞᄂᆞᆫ자ᄂᆞᆫ거시지마ᄂᆞᆫ
진실ᄒᆞᆫ일은아니로다그런ᄒᆞ이동
을주장ᄒᆞᄂᆞᆫ사ᄅᆞᆷ들은국가의이
번젼쟁에ᄃᆡᄒᆞ야곤란ᄒᆞᆷ을성각
지아니ᄒᆞ고로국리익을돌지아
니ᄒᆞᆯ샏아니라ᄃᆡ젹의게리롭게
ᄒᆞ지되게ᄒᆞ믈ᄒᆞᄂᆞᆫ지라졍부ᄂᆞᆫ
그일에ᄃᆡᄒᆞ야칙임이잇ᄂᆞᆫ져무
를실힝ᄒᆞ기위ᄒᆞ야안령질셔를
방히ᄒᆞᄂᆞᆫ거슬금ᄒᆞ리니오거과
에ᄃᆡᄒᆞ야반ᄃᆡᄒᆞᄂᆞᆫ자들을막기
위ᄒᆞ야진력ᄒᆞᆯ지로다공ᄉᆞ회를
물론ᄒᆞ고그권력범위안에너며
가저아니ᄒᆞᆫ거시오고회쟝이취
임을담부ᄒᆞᆫ이며신문지들외도
반드시근신ᄒᆞ야져의칙임
을잇지말고인민들을안졍케
ᄒᆞ기를힘쓰라ᄒᆞ엿다ᄒᆞ엿더라

외보

○쳔리면화 동경평셰보간의
쟝거리면화ᄂᆞᆫ구랍이라ᄂᆞᆫ셔에
히셜ᄒᆞ야이미멋쳣고목하에시
험중인ᄃᆡ그셩젹이극히랑호ᄒᆞᆷ
아시쟝너면화에비교ᄒᆞᆯ진ᄃᆡ음
셩은젹고명ᄒᆞ나쟝션이기ᄂᆞᆫ쟝
ᄉᆞ리ᄂᆞᆫ엽스며도뤼ᄂᆞᆫ명랑ᄒᆞᆫ다
ᄒᆞ며거리ᄂᆞᆫ마관히형이리의취
져션을가셜ᄒᆞ야약일천리에탈
ᄒᆞᆫ지라미국시아고와츄특간외
에ᄂᆞᆫ셰계무쌍ᄒᆞᆫ쟝거리라본월
중에ᄂᆞᆫ시험을필요ᄒᆞᆫ터인ᄃᆡ이
ᄂᆞᆫ다만일긔션으로군ᄉᆞ외교동
공무상면화외에ᄂᆞᆫ여ᄉᆞ가무ᄒᆞᆫ
고일반공중의면화ᄂᆞᆫ근간에허
락지아니ᄒᆞᆫ다더라

○국회히산셜 영국국회ᄂᆞᆫ이
월십ᄉᆞ일에소집ᄒᆞᆫ의원사회에
셔말ᄒᆞ되국회가삼월에히산될
이라ᄂᆞᆫ풍셜이파다ᄒᆞᆫ다더라

○로장회국 로쟝(스구도로
후)ᄂᆞᆫ포고엽사ᄃᆡ항을출발ᄒᆞ야
셩피득보에향ᄒᆞ엿다더라

TELEGRAMS.

(FROM JAPAN PAPERS.)

London, Jan. 12.

The "Tley, Izumrud, Rion" (late "Smolensk), Dnieper (late "Petersburg)" and three destroyers have passed the Suez Canal.

London, Jan. 12.

It is rumoured in St. Petersburg that the Russian Government being dissatisfied with the actions of General Kuropatkin has ordered him to return. Another report states that the Commander-in-Chief has asked for further re-inforcements.

London, Jan. 12.

Destroyers belonging to the Baltic Squadron are believed to be concentrating off the Seychelles with a view to encountering Admiral Uriu's scouting vessels, which are now in the neighbourhood of the Chagos Archipelago.

London, Jan. 13.

Rumours are current in St. Petersburg concerning the situation. Kuropatkin, who a month ago had only 170,-000 infantry, with an insufficient number of mountain guns, is being censured for his inactivity.

London, Jan. 13.

The Committee on Commerce of the U. S. Senate has increased the proposed maximum subsidies for transpacific services to £80,000 for a monthly, and £16,000 for a fortnightly sevice.

London, Jan. 13.

M. de Fallières has been re-elected President of the French Senate.

London, Jan. 13.

Bolrovosky's Squadron has left Suez, presumably for Jibutil.

London, Jan. 14.

It is stated that Russia has purchased an island in the Indian Ocean, in order to supply Rojestvensky with a base, pending the arrival of the supplementary squadron.

London, Jan. 14.

Russia's protest against Chinese violations of neutrality is considered a transparent device made at the moment of the raid on Nuchiatung, this raid itself probably involving a violation of Chinese territory, and it is the opinion here that China has more reason to complain of Russia's disregard of neutral rights than has Russia.

Vienna, January 14.

Count Lamsdorff, Russian Minister of Finance, has emphatically informed a certain Ambassador at St. Petersburg that Russia will not accept any mediation by a third party with regard to the Russo-Japanese war. It is considered in Austrian diplomatic circles that there is no possibility of mediation for the present, although President Roosevelt is reported to be desirous of proposing action of this kind.

London, Jan. 14.

The Russian Minister of Finance, in his Budget statement, estimates that that the expenditure for 1905 will show a decrease of 63¼ million roubles compared with 1904, this decrease being chiefly in the Departments of Finance and Communications. Ten million roubles are assigned to the doubling of the Siberian railway and 1,800,000 roubles for extra expenditure on the trans-Baikal line. Everything is calculated to strengthen confidence in the finances of Russia, whose monetary system and national economy remain unshaken after eleven months of war.

Berlin, Jan. 15.

The formation of an Anglo-German Club is expected. Anglo-German friendly sentiments are increasing.

London, Jan. 15.

In an Order of the Day issued to the Army and Navy announcing the fall of Port Arthur, the Tsar eulogizes "the glorious garrison whose heroism Russia has witnessed with pride. Peace be to the ashes of the dead, and glory to the living. Our enemy is bold and strong, and the struggle at such a distance is indescribably hard. But Russia is powerful and has undergone harder trials, always emerging more powerful that before. While lamenting our losses, we must not become distracted. With all Russia, I trust that the hour of victory will soon dawn. I pray God to bless our troops and fleets and enable them to uphold the glory of Russia."

London, Jan. 16.

M. Deloncle, while expressing himself as disbelieving in the authenticity of General Kodama's alleged plan for driving French influence out of Indo-China, declares he is firmly convinced that Japan urgently covets that territory. M. Deloncle insists that the French Government must immediately submit to the Chamber a programme of maritime defence of the French Colonies in the Far East.

London, Jan. 16.

An independent account of General Mistchenko's daring raid on the old city of Newchwang shows that the raid was wholly unsuccessful, the Russian cavalry being powerless against entrenched infantry.

London, Jan. 16.

The "Novoe Vremya publishes a telegram from Java, stating that the Japanese have established a base at Labuan (a British island in the Malayan Archipelago), and that the cable has ceased working for the purpose of concealing the fact.

London, January 17th.

A disorderly debate has taken place in the French Chamber.

The Premier, M. Combes, vigorously repudiated the charge of sowing dissension amongst the Republicans by anticlerical persecutions.

A vote of confidence in the Government was passed by 289 votes against 279.

The Cabinet is expected to resign owing to the smallness of the majority.

EXPLOSION AT MOJI.

A serious explosion took place at the Arsenal on Maruyama at 10.35 on the morning of January 15th. Clouds of black smoke filled the air, and great quantities of fragments of wood and iron fell in the town; much alarm being caused among the public. The explosion resulted in a fire, which was got under control by 11.40 A. M.

The ammunition in the Arsenal belonged to the Okuragumi, a well-known Japanese firm. It is believed that the explosion was occasioned through the point of a nail striking some ammunition when it was being hammered into a box. Three men and three women were burnt to death, and seven persons were injured, while over ten others are missing.

MR. MEGATA AND THE SPURIOUS NICKELS.

If it be true, as reported in Japan papers that Mr. Megata, the financial adviser, has actually proposed that the circulation of the spurious nickel five cent pieces, which were smuggled into this country by the Japanese, be prohibited we can only say that it appears to us to be an extremely dangerous suggestion. Doubtless the question is one incapable of easy solution but Mr. Megata's proposal, if put into effect would cause wide spread misery and make the government the object of great popular resentment. Unless more of these nickels are being imported tne question is not of such urgency that is cannot wait until rational ways and means of dealing with it shall have been found.

It is reported that Mr. Yi Yong-ik intends to establish two schools, one on the premises of the former Russian school, and one in a building autside the West Gate.

SIGNS OF THE TIMES.

On the 20th instant two Japanese, one in uniform and one in kimono, called upon M. Martin, the proprietor of the Hotel du Palais and announced their intention of calling every day.

They expected M. Martin to furnish them with a list of his guests and such information with regard to transient callers as he had at his disposal. The enterprising Japanese drew a blank, but for the benefit of the authorities we give their names. The one in kimono is called S. Maekawa while "K. Akano" is on the card of the gentleman in uniform.

We hear that Mr. Megata is shortly to take a trip to Japan on personal business.

In accordance with a request from the Japanese Minister, the magistrate of Heui Chŏn has been dismissed.

The Il Chin Hoi people in Chi-pyung demanded of the magistrate a list of houses, population and taxation of that district. The demand was not complied with.

It is said that Mr. Megata on returning from his visit to Japan will bring back paper money representing Japan's loan to Korea. This appears to us to be a scandalous arrangement. Japan's paper money will soon be much depreciated.

The Editor regrets to inform the author of the article entitled "Seoul in 1975" that the subject is not of sufficient general interest to warrant the insertion of such a long article, If the author will send his address, his manuscript will be returned to him.

A complaint has been forwarded to the Japanese Minister that the constructors of the Seoul-Wiju Railway have been felling timber in the neighborhood of the tomb of the Tai Won Kun. It is requested that the desecration of this and other graves be put a stop to.

It is reported that the Central Prisoners' Information Bureau in Russia hsa communicated with the Prisoners' Information Bureau in Japan proposing an exchange of prisoners. In reply, the Japanese authorities are reported to have consented to the proposal. It is therefore expected that an exchange will take place shortly.

The local Japanese reproduce at great length the stories of strikes and anarchy in Russia. The wish is probably father to the thought. We are hearing a good deal more about "internal disturbances" in Russia than the occasion seems to warrant. From the prolixity of the despatches which reach Japan on this subject one is warranted in believing that therein lies Japan's lost hope.

At Newchwang it is stated, according to the China Review, that the Japanese are freely offering $1.80 of their own war scrip for one dollar Mexican. All Chinese attempting to take silver coin out of the place are more than gently persuaded not to do so. Contractors paid in the special war notes have experienced a shrinkage in their ready cash which they had not figured on.

Our Korean reporter hands us the following story which we confess ourselv unable to get at the true inwardness ot.

The Kamni of Kun San reports the Foreign Office that, on 12th of this month the Japanese Consul at the same port requested us for few police man who will protect him as he will go to Impi district in some matter, but I refused for it because he goes there not for public affairs Next say he requested again, I sent him one policeman, but the magistrate of Impi wrote me a letter which greatly insult me and said me why I sent police man to him, and why I did not arrest the man named Chai who is hid in Kun San. That magistrate wrote me as above, but I never know what kind man is Chai, and what matter about him at all, and I sent policeman not for that matter, it is great fault that he wrote me so impolite, please send a dispatch to Home Office tell to punish him.

It is reported that the Emperor has ordered the War Department to adopt General Hasegwa's recent suggestions.

Some wild animals from Kang Wŏn province, comprising tiger, elk, bear, and deer were recently brought to the palace.

The latest census of Japanese in Chemulpo shows that there are 1772 houses, with a population of 9984 viz: 5666 male and 3818 female.

Mr. Min Yung Chul, Korean Minister to Peking is on his way back to Seoul. He is at Chefoo, waiting for a steamer to bring him over.

The people of Whang-Chu district have complained to the Government that the Japanese compelled them to sell the fields in the villge of Pal-pang-no.

The Japanese gendarmerie, having taken over the policing of Seoul are endeavouring to make a list of houses and population. We are afraid they will not have time to complete their self appointed task.

Telegraphic advices to the "Daihan Ilpo" state that a big strike, involving some 50,000 men, has taken place among em-the mechanics and other artisans. ployed in Russian government arsenals and shipyards. The rumour of Kuropatkin's recall is denied in St. petersbury.

We regret to record the departure by the S. S. Ohio yesterday of Mr. and Mrs. A. Delcoigne. Mr. Delcoigne, who belongs to the Belgian diplomatic service, was for a time "lent" to the Korean Government for whom he acted as adviser to the Home Department.

Mr. Delcoigne is a very able man, had conditions in this country remained normal he would probable have been instrumental in effecting many useful reforms and innovations. However as things are at present, the Japanese allow none but themselves to be heard, and the Belgian Government, probably realizing this, have recalled Mr. Delcoigne and appointed him to a responsible position in their Legation at Washington.

Both Mr. and Mrs Delcoigne were held in high esteem and the whole community is sorry to lose the them and everyones' wishes for a safe voyage and a happy future go with them.

Bekanntmachung.

Die Bekanntmachungen der Eintragungen in das hiesige Deutsche Handelsregister erfolgen im Jahre 1905 durch den **"Ostasiatischen Lloyd" und** die **"The Korea Daily News."**

Soül, den 27. Dezember 1904.

Der Kaiserlich Deutsche Minister-Resident und General-Konsul.

(L. S.) gez. von Saldern.

The Korea Daily News.

Issued at 5 P. M. daily except Sundays.

Rate of Subscription:—
Per Year,............Yen 25.
Per Quarter,..........Yen 7.
Per Month,..........Yen 2.50.

Postage in Korea not charged extra.
Postage abroad charged extra.

Advertisements, 50 sen per day for 1 inch or less.
5 yen per month per inch.
50 yen per year per inch.

All communications to

E. T. BETHELL,
Editor and Publisher,
Pak-tong, Seoul.

THE WAR.

We have several times commented upon the general inaccuracy of all prophesies concerning the war and the mistake of pinning one's faith to anything in particular.

In view of the immense interests invoived it is not possible for either Japan or Russia to know how and when this war will end: Still less is it possible for mere lookers on to foretell events. An event, insignificant from a military point of view may have a far-reaching political importance, and *vice-versa*, a strategic stroke appealing to none but the anxious Commander-in-chief opposing each other will leave the world unmoved.

And yet the political situation is in reality overwhelmingly important. Whether politicians are the servants of the press or whether the newspapers are servants of the politicians is, in most cases, only a question of money. Thus it is that very often at the behest of, or in spite of politicians, the press largely directs the trend of political events. Now dramatic incidents irresitibly appeal to the press, apart from all other considerations, and thus it is that we find Japan, by virtue of her naval swoops upon Chemulpo and Port Arthur and her final military subjugation of Port Arthur, installed as a high favourite by the the sensation loving press of the whole world.

We are in complete agreement with all the praises that have been bestowed upon Japan's Army and Navy. The latter we consider, except in the matter of tonnage, second to none, and the administration of the army and the valour of the men are both beyond criticism. As a matter of fact we have never seen any of these things doubted by competent observers, and if patriotism and enthusiasm and self-devotion would have won the war, Japan would have won it long ago.

But in this war, the war between Japan and Russia, although patriotism and prowess are of course important factors, either side appears to be equally endowed in these respects and therefore ultimate victory should rest with the power having the advantage in remaining issues.

Putting minor issues on one side the two factors in regard to which the belligerent nations should be compared are (1) finance and (2) political and international security. Taking the latter first, it is certain that the Japanese counted upon two things to help them; first the the much talked of dissention and discontent in Russia, and second, the Anglo-Japanese defensive Alliance.

Of the the internal condition of Russia we have already written; there are clearly many grievances, but is it equally clear that the afflicted people in Russia are as powerless to give effect to their resentment as are the Koreans under the present Japanese domination. Therefore we do not think that Japan can look for much help from this direction. News of unrest or disturbances in Russia is immediately telegraphed to the Tokio Government and then passed on to the press, but nothing seems to come of it. So far as political relations with other countries are concerned, Japan would appear to have decidedly the worst of it. In anticipation of this war, Japan canvassed the great powers for an ally. Apparently the advances of her envoy met with but small encouragement for Marquis Ito returned to Japan after only having succeeded in arranging a qualified Alliance with Great Britain.

Apparently there is a great deal of misconception in Japan as to the true nature of that alliance. We believe, and we hope our belief will be verified, that Great Britain will only be called upon to join in the war when another nation takes up arms to assist Russia. We do not think that merely passive breaches of neutrality will constitute a situation compelling Great Britain to join in this war; it is evident that Russia has no apprehensions, otherwise she would hardly be in such haste to pack off every available vessel of her navy.

Finally we come to the financial question. On this subject, the "Eastern World,"—a remarkably well-informed and accurate journal—after giving facts and figures fully justifying its contention, says:—

"It will not be a very bold prophecy then to predict that the gold standard will disappear towards August-September 1905 if Japan can still get foreign loans, and towards March-April 1905, if not, and that the war could only be continued two or three months after those two extreme date."

And then of course bankruptcy would inevitably overtake the nation. This state of affairs is not entirely a source of weakness as it is possible that Great Britain and America, who are Japan's principal creditors, would intervene (and they could effectively intervene) to prevent all their security being frittered away.

Still all this goes to show in what a hopelessly false position Japan has placed herself and friends. What was to have been a coup is fast becoming a disaster and unless the unexpected happens Japan will have to live on empty glory for many a long year.

AN EXPLORER'S IMPRESSIONS OF KUROPATKIN.

INTERESTING APPRECIATION

BY DR. SVEN HEDIN.

Dr. Hedin, the great Swedish explorer and a friend of General Kuropatkin, gives this estimate of the Russian General in a letter to The Times:

"The first time I personally had the honour to meet General Kuropatkin he was military commander of the new province of Transcaspia. That was in October, 1890, and at Askabad, where he had his headquarters. When I called upon him my overcoat was taken charge of by a Cossack, and I was ushered into a large hall where I was received and my visit announced by an aide-de-camp When I let fall the remark that upon my return home I intended to write a book about Turkestan, Kuropatkin replied humourously that there were no secrets in Askabad. I was at perfect liberty to go where I liked; I might freely visit all the institutions in the town, might count the soldiers in the barracks, as well as the big guns, the rifles and the cartridges in the magazines, sketch whatever I thought fit, and, he added, 'You may even write articles about it all to The Times if you like.' If I met with any difficulty I had only to report the matter to him and he would see me righted.

"In April, 1899, I met Kuropatkin several times. On one of these occasions we were sitting at his writing table discussing my contemplated journey when a Cossack entered bringing a huge bundle of papers in a sealed portfolio. While the General was turning them over I took the liberty of asking him what was the meaning of the peculiar marks in blue pencil which I saw on the margins. Kuropatkin told me that they were the military reports of the week which the Czar had just read, and that the blue pencil marks were made by his Imperial Majesty's own hand. One particular mark meant "I approve," another expressed the opposite, while a third signified "I want further detal," and so on. I gave utterance to my astonishment that the Czar found time to read through all those reports, whereupon Kuropatkin answered: 'Yes, and it is even more astonishing how he finds the time for reading through all the reports of all the other Ministries.'

"Everybody who has been brought into personal contact with General Kuropatkin must acknowledge that it would be difficult to meet with a more amiable and attractive personality. What most impresses one about the powerful yet harmonious nature of the man is the air of unruffled calm and serenity which sits upon his features, His face bears the unmistakable stamp of goodness, consideration, and self-control. At this moment he knows that all his tactical and strategical movements are matters of history and will afford a subject of study and of criticism to numberless eager students. But I am convinced that even amid the thunder of the cannon at Liao-yang he was possessed of the same absolutely unshaken calm with which he reviewed the Turkoman militia on the plains outside of Askabad. Never has a depreciatory word been uttered about him behind his back, and never has a Russian general been regard with greater confidence and love by all, from the Czar himself down to the meanest soldier in the ranks. He will have nothing to do with favouritism or nepotism; he is known for his incorruptible sense of justice, and in making his promotions he has never been guided by any other considerations except those of merit and capacity. If he has any favourites at all in the army they are the simple Cossacks. He has never abused his power. His own brother, whom I met at Osh in 1902, was then filling a very subordinate post as pomoshnik or assistant to the chief of that small and insignificant town, which might indeed almost be regarded as a place of deportation in the heart of Asia. I have heard people express astonishment that General Kuropatkin should carry ikons or sacred images with him to the seat of war in the Far East. But it must not be forgotten that General Kuropatkin is a genuine orthodox Russian of the old stamp, and notwithstanding his intimacy with Western Europeans, especially Frenchmen, he has always remained a Russian. At the same time I believe he is much too practical a man to put his trust in sacred images alone; his position renders it necessary that he should, at all events outwardly show them all reverence, for nothing less than that is demanded of their leader by the Russian soldiers, who are often superstitious and generally have been brought up under the influence of ignorant priests. Nevertheless, Kuropatkin is himself a truly religious man in the best sense of the word; but in war he places his reliance principally upon his men and his own counterstrokes of tactics and strategy."

The three men sentenced to death for murder in Hong Kong, two of them Americans and one a Finn, were hanged at five o'clock on the morning of the 11th inst., in the presence of two clergymen and the prison officials. Death was instantaneous.

The Korea Daily News.

VOL. II, MONDAY, JANUARY 23, 1905. No. 17

大韓每日申報
대한ᄆᆡ일신보

(뎨이쳔십팔호)　(슈요일)　일쳔구빅오년일월이십오일

본샤고빅

이신보는영어와한어로셔계디일츌판홈

신문가

한쟝　엽젼두돈오푼

일삭표　엽젼두량닷돈

우표가리삭닷돈

다맛돈으로밧숨

광고료는

귀한의쟝단과ᄌᆞ힝의다쇼로즁방ᄒᆞ되렴가로밧을터이오매오리지아녀대한사람마다다이신문을보실터이니광고버시기를원ᄒᆞ시는이들은우리신문사에와셔면약ᄒᆞ심을희망ᄒᆞᆸ

○발힝소　박동대한ᄆᆡ일신보사범어학교압희젼영국인셜필림집자리오

샤쟝　영국인　(비셜)

평양　디리졈

○평양효동사는긘미보씨로우리신문좌디리인을뎡ᄒᆞ엿시스오니평양에계신구람코져ᄒᆞ시는　쳠군ᄌᆞ는해디리졈에왕림ᄒᆞ와면의ᄒᆞ시옵

샤고

○우리대한ᄆᆡ일신보의목뎍은대한의인녕재셔에관한모든대목에디ᄒᆞ야는공평한변론을쥬쟝홈이라우리동신원의담보는신문보셔는쳠군ᄌᆞ의게ᄒᆞ샹보도ᄒᆞ리며평지둔귀셔ᄒᆞ며주시는이는셩명과번디를져어보치시기를희망ᄒᆞ오니어거슨신문샹에긔ᄌᆡᄒᆞ란는거시아니오다만극히친용ᄒᆞ는즁거를숨고자홈이라귀자는아모귀셔던지귀지홈을되각ᄒᆞ는권리를가졋스나되쟉ᄒᆞ는리유를말홀터이오며고즁광죄를문란케ᄒᆞ는듯ᄒᆞᆫ귀셔는의례히밧지아니ᄒᆞ겟ᄉᆞᆸ니이다

●본사셜시이리로신문을디방우톄로분젼ᄒᆞ야톄젼부의임의로젼ᄒᆞᄂᆞᆫ것스로편곳에는홀눈게젼ᄒᆞ기도ᄒᆞ며혹못젼ᄒᆞ는폐에젼ᄒᆞ기도ᄒᆞ며혹아니젼ᄒᆞ는곳도잇다ᄒᆞ오니우리신문을ᄉᆞ랑ᄒᆞ야구람ᄒᆞ시는　쳠군ᄌᆞ의게티ᄒᆞ야ᄆᆡ우미안ᄒᆞ오며긔지금은본젼인을두고ᄆᆡ일아츰이젼ᄒᆞ며ᄒᆞ나젼ᄒᆞ지나못케지나ᄒᆞᆫ폐가잇도록ᄒᆞ란ᄒᆞ오니ᄒᆞ야나젼ᄒᆞ거나혹늣게젼ᄒᆞ거나ᄒᆞᆫ일이잇스면본샤로통긔ᄒᆞ여주심을희망ᄒᆞᆸ

잡보

○곽산군보　곽산군수가외부로보고ᄒᆞ기를본군민쟝두형이가본티민요에간셥홈이업는티일본군티에셔쟝아간지며련달에이벼ᄉᆞ지몽방치못ᄒᆞ엿스니일이심이부인디홀지라바라건티일슈평부에교셥ᄒᆞ야곳방환케ᄒᆞ야그구업을편케ᄒᆞ란ᄒᆞ엿더라

○죠졍훈칙　일공관에셔외부에죠회ᄒᆞ기를우리나라히군슈샹로부에셔본년수월샹슌간에경샹도에잇는힝동면일부와강원도회남면의부를쟝츙측량ᄒᆞ겟고샹룡에는표를세우고바위돌에논희게칠홀터이니쳥컨티디방에훈칙ᄒᆞ야빅셩으로ᄒᆞ여곰알게ᄒᆞ야혹케ᄒᆞ지말고셔로등속을도훈ᄒᆞ시가ᄒᆞ야방히홈이가ᄒᆞ다ᄒᆞ엿더라

○젼쥬민면　젼쥬군인민등이탁지부로면보ᄒᆞ기를결젼을빅동화로밧으라고호원홈ᄋᆞ로본부와본군에셔쳥ᄒᆞ야민등을일병착슈ᄒᆞ고순엽젼으로독쇄ᄒᆞ니빅셩이져보ᄒᆞᆯ슈업셔극히원통ᄒᆞ와호소ᄒᆞ오니쳐분ᄒᆞ바라옵니다ᄒᆞ엿더라

○죠졍회양　탁지부에셔내부에죠회ᄒᆞ기를경쥬젼군수박병수의가흰군계묘도공젼쳬남훈이진으로써폐부에셔샹　쥬ᄒᆞ교면본관ᄒᆞ엿더니회원이희콩젼부일로죠납ᄒᆞᆫ바이거순곳휘군이경납을맛나빅셩의게셔슈봉치못ᄒᆞᆫ거슨대신밧칠거시라커늘과공화를분으로체납ᄒᆞ는거시고우흥이바지ᄒᆞ며아리를ᄌᆞ흘ᄒᆞ는셩에극히가샹ᄒᆞ와희원을일의샹　쥬ᄒᆞ고면징계ᄒᆞ엿는티지금과세를독측ᄒᆞ는때를당ᄒᆞ야폐읍에수무룰비이는거시극히민망ᄒᆞ니런손ᄒᆞᆫ이로회임ᄒᆞ라티로시무케홈이ᄉᆞ리에합당ᄒᆞ다ᄒᆞ엿더라

○퇴인젹당　퇴인군수가내부로보ᄒᆞᆫ거를거ᄒᆞᆫ즉음력샹월샹십일에화젹이원평등디로브터본군에침입ᄒᆞᆫ다ᄒᆞ는고로숩교를만치발ᄒᆞ야힝착ᄒᆞ게ᄒᆞ엿더니도라와고관ᄒᆞ기를당일수시량에화젹오십명이각기총파의검을가지고만쳠수곽면김영죠의집에드러가죠팔십샹셕과민관셔집에셔조일빅샹셕과김의관집에셔조일빅오십셕과최경젼의집에셔조이빅팔십셕과김영슌의집에셔돈일빅오십량과리감역집에셔졍조일빅오십셕과돈미빅팔십량을탈취ᄒᆞ야각처외가난ᄒᆞᆫ빅셩의게ᄂᆞᆫ화주고읍으로향력식이월일에다른교을로향ᄒᆞ야발졍ᄒᆞ엿다ᄒᆞ엿더라

○문위간셥　원산항에쥬차ᄒᆞᆫ일본군졍관이문쳔등각군에공문ᄒᆞ야무론아모결세ᄒᆞ고군졍관의게보고ᄒᆞ야인허를엇은후에시힝ᄒᆞ라ᄒᆞᆫ말은비왕본보에긔재ᄒᆞ엿거니와이일에티ᄒᆞ야외부에셔일본공ᄉᆞ의게죠회ᄒᆞ기를군수힝동에결세징봉일관은죠곰도샹관이업거는보교를ᄒᆞ고인허를맛ᄒᆞᆫ후에야슈쇄ᄒᆞ란ᄒᆞ는거시대단이국권에방괴이니일노써군졍관의게젼칙ᄒᆞ야교셥ᄒᆞ야간셥지말게홈이가ᄒᆞ다ᄒᆞ엿더라

○리항공셜　근일빅동화를거두ᄃᆞᆫ다ᄒᆞᆫ쥬ᄒᆞᆫ일사쥬를나가ᄒᆞ여거두는변ᄒᆞᆫ리표를샹메고는러히가불소ᄒᆞ리라더라

○대사증험　대원양혜원대사의증험ᄒᆞᆫ일로발ᄒᆞ기를지는일진년에샹동이지나도셩빙이가되나가고히셧ᄃᆞᆯ이심일에고이등셔귀쳔물이챵이ᄒᆞ엿쓰ᄂᆞᄒᆞ엿스니회붕에딘하가무병ᄒᆞ엿대무병ᄒᆞᆷ을명년도입진년못치터라

○무표난면　작야신이시에ᄒᆞᆫ사롬이이공진로뎐불교를향ᄒᆞ여오며노리ᄒᆞᆫ곡조를ᄒᆞ여왈폐셰춘어세가런가환세도이남춘양츈미라ᄒᆞ는디맛참순검을곡지나범야홈으로힝난ᄒᆞ더니그리이졍도사신표를보여뵈고가더라

○호부방황　김제군사는림도형이라ᄒᆞᄂᆞᆫ사롬이돈젼졍ᄒᆞ여세간을다ᄒᆞ고ᄌᆞ근종계가졍ᄉᆞᆯ지못ᄒᆞ야방문ᄒᆞᆫ지십여일에죵시소식이잇지못ᄒᆞ여울며소회문에방울붓치고로번에셔방황ᄒᆞᆫ다더라

○의쥬근항　의쥬에는작년이리로일본인이졈졈증가ᄒᆞ여사업에종사ᄒᆞ는티목하에그호슈가샹십이오인구가빅여명이라ᄀᆞ영업자중에장화졈이둘이오음식졈이하나오리관이둘이오리발소가하나오과자샹이하나오기타는한인소용쟝화졈과각용달졈이잇다더라

○음흉한샹언　엇더ᄒᆞᆫ사룸이샹소를탐학ᄒᆞᆫ다ᄒᆞ고일젼에내부에구소ᄒᆞᆫ고로칠웅의아들운방형씨가그군인을탐지ᄒᆞ자ᄒᆞ여내부젼에날마다기다리다가구소인삼명이내부제지들치자잡차로을며에곳한셩재판소에교소ᄒᆞ야재판훈즉희소민도회일공초니에이거시파연리참령동휘의게부린바ㅣ오비가참령집식구인교로그지휘ᄒᆞ는거슬발시ᄒᆞ기가어위고리홈이라ᄒᆞ고김셩슈의공초니에참령이돈구빅량으로써저지로말ᄒᆞ기를비가금번에강화부윤을ᄒᆞ리이니도임ᄒᆞ는날에맛당이너로써슈검을식인다홈으로이러케됨이라ᄒᆞ고방외포용초니에참령인너에비가금번재판훈후에부윤을ᄒᆞᆯ터이니도임ᄒᆞ는날에히부부교원과및향쟝을과간에너로써차임ᄒᆞ켓다ᄒᆞ는고로이러케됨이라ᄒᆞ엿스니금년여름이후로부군지셜을쥬츌ᄒᆞ야졍부와너부를속이고각신문에게포ᄒᆞᆫ여사룸의이목을현혹ᄒᆞ미라가젼후교죠미소연탈로홈으로당일법사에서샹한을갑옥셔에이슈ᄒᆞ엿더라

○혼례셩의　륙군참위김응션씨가경무관최혁린씨규슈와결혼ᄒᆞ여작일하오훈시에혼례를거힝ᄒᆞᄂᆞᆫ티무관학교쟝리병무참령리회두표성근참위리찬두령박명쳘류동열남궤창김명현김귀원쟝위로빅린등제씨와일본사령부관샹구씨와기타사관일인이참관ᄒᆞ엿고혼례식을거힝홀때에신랑과신부와참관ᄒᆞ는제원을일제히사진을박앗는티대한에도죵차로혼례의의식이문명긔진홈이라라

UNION INSURANCE SOCIETY OF CANTON.

Head office Hongkong.
Marine risks underwritten at current rates.
Agents in Chemulpo,
E. MEYER & Co.

COMPAGNIE DES MESSAGERIES MARITIMES.

Fortnightly Direct Service.

For Marseilles
via Ports.
Sailing from Yokohama
Calling at Kobe,
Shanghai, Hongkong, Saigon, Singapore,
Colombo, Djibonti, Suez, Port Said
and Marseilles.

For particulars apply to
HOLME RINGER & Co.,
Chemulpo.

HAYASHIDA & CO.,

16 MYENG DONG, CHIN KO KAI, SEOUL.
BRANCH OFFICE AT CHEMULPO.

Money changers, Coal and Wood Merchants, Express Agents.

We are agents for the Pyeng-yang Coal Company and the Karazu Coal Company of Japan. We have the best quality of both anthracite and bituminous coal, and prompt execution of orders is our speciality. Firewood of all kinds kept in stock. Full weight guaranteed. Money of all denominations exchanged at current rates. Parcels received for all parts.

CHINA MUTUAL LIFE INS. OC.

Most favourable terms to policy holders.

Benefit system unsurpassed.

HOLME RINGER & Co.
Agents, Chemulpo.

C. P. R.

CANADIAN PACIFIC RAILWAY COMPANY'S ROYAL MAIL STEAMSHIP LINE.

THE FAST ROUTE BETWEEN CHINA, JAPAN, AND EUROPE VIA CANADA AND THE UNITED STATES.

Route from Hongkong via Shanghai, Nagasaki (Inland Sea of Japan) Kobe, Yokohama, Victoria and Vancouver.

Twin Screw Empress Steamship—6,000 Tons—Speed 19 knots.

PROPOSED SAILING FROM YOKOHAMA.
R. M. S. Empress of India.
R. M. S. Empress of Japan.
R. M. S. Empress of China.
R. M. S. Athenian.
R. M. S. Tartar.

Special reductior (first class only) granted to members of the Military, Naval, Diplomatic and Civil services and to Missionaries.

Passengers have choice of ten routes across the Continent of America and have privilege of travelling by any Atlantic Steamship Line.

Round the World passage tickets in connection with the P. and O. S. N., North German Lloyd and Messageries Co.'s £125.

All rates payable at current rate of exchange.

For further information, Tickets, Guide Books, etc., apply to

HOLME, RINGER & Co., AGENTS,
Chemulpo.

Grand Hotel,

(Formerly the Station Hotel)

Near the Railway Terminus, West Gate Seoul.

The Best Hotel in Korea;
Handsome new Building.
Fine Airy Rooms
Excellent Cuisine.
Terms Moderate.
Special terms to Missionaries
and to permanent boarders.

Electric cars within 2 minutes' walk.

W. H. EMBERLEY.
Proprietor

EVERY FACILITY.

In connection with Life Assurance Business is afforded by

The Standard Life Assurance Co.,

One of the largest and wealthiest of the Provident Institutions of the United Kingdom Forms of Application and all information will be promptly afforded on application.

10 CENTS A DAY.

Not a very large expenditure is it? But it is sufficient to secure for a man of 30 a policy with the STANDARD LIFE OFFICE for

$1323.

For all particulars of rates, etc., apply to

Holme, Ringer & Co.,
Agents, Chemulpo.

THE NEW YORK LIFE INSURANCE COMPANY.

Have you ever been declined by any Company?

Are you engaged in a specially hazardous occupation?

Have you heard of the New York Life Insurance Company's New Classifications for this class of Risks?

If not, send your date of birth, occupation and particulars of rejection, if any to

E. MEYER & Co.,
Agents, Chemulpo.

MITSUI BUSSAN KAISHA.
(MITSUI & Co.)

MITSUI GINKO.
(MITSUI BANK.)

The Bank is owned by the members of the Mitsui Family, who, as partners, assume an unlimited responsibility for all liabilities of the Bank:—

Capital........................Yen 5,000,000
Reserve Fund.................. " 5,600,000

HEAD OFFICE, TOKYO.
LONDON OFFICE, 34 LIME ST., E. C.

BRANCHES AND AGENCIES:—
New York, San Francisco, Hamburg, Bombay, Singapore, Manila, Hongkong, Amoy, Chefoo, Tientsin.
Kobe, Hakodate, Yokohama, Kure, Yokosuka, Moji, Shimonoseki, Miike, Wakamatsu, Nagasaki, Kuchinotsu, Karatsu, Sasebo, Misume, Taipeh, &c.

Telegraphic Address for all the Offices:
"MITSUI."
A. B. C. AND A. I CODES USED.

Contractors of Coal
To the Imperial Japanese Navy. Arsenals and Railway Bureau, Principal Railway Companies and Industrial Work, Home and Foreign Mail and Freight Steamers.

Sole Proprietors
Of the famous Miike, Tagawa and Yamano Coal Mines.

Sole Agents
For the sale of Fukumo, Hokoku, Ichimura, Kanoda, Mannoura, Onoura, Ostuji, Sonoda, Tsubaruro, Yoshinotani, Yoshio, Yurokibura and other coals.

YANGTSE INSURANCE ASSOCIATION, LTD.

The undersigned, having been appointed agents for the above company, are prepared to issue policies and pay losses on marine risks at regular rates.

E. MEYER & Co.,
Agents, Chemulpo.

AMERICAN KOREAN ELECTRIC CO.

Light and Power.

Main Office: Electric Building, Chong No.

RAILWAY DEPARTMENT.

OPERATING CARS BETWEEN EAST AND WEST GATE, EVERY TEN MINUTES:—

First Car leaves East Gate at 7:00 A. M. First Car leaves R. R. Station at 7:25 A. M
Last Car " East Gate at 8.40 P. M. Last " " R. R. Station at 9.05 P.M

OPERATING CARS BETWEEN EAST GATE AND IMPERIAL TOMB TERMINUS, EVERY TWENTY MINUTES:—

CONNECTING WITH EVERY ALTERNATE CAR ARRIVING AT EAST GATE FROM CHONG NO.

First Car leaves East Gate for Tomb at 7:10 A. M.
" " " Tomb for East Gate at 7:30 A. M.
Last " " East Gate for Tomb at 7:50 P. M.
" " " Tomb for East Gate at 8:10 P. M.

OPERATING CARS BETWEEN CHONG NO AND YUNG SAN RIVER EVERY TWELVE MINUTES:—

First Car leaves Chong No for South Gate at 7:12 A. M.
" " " Chong No for Yung San at 7:36 A. M.
" " " South Gate for Chong No at 7:20 A. M.
" " " Yung San for Chong No at 8:09 A. M.
Last " " South Gate for Chong No 9:00 P. M.
" " " Yung San for Chong No at 8.45. P. M.

SPECIAL PRIVATE CARS FURNISHED TO SUIT CONVENIENCE OF PATRONS. PRICES ON APPLICATION AT HEAD OFFICE.

LIGHTING DEPARTMENT.

Where less than 250 candle power of light is used, the rate per month will be
Per 16 candle power incandescent lamp,—All night.—Yen 2.50.
32 candle power incandescent lamp:—All night:—Yen 4.00.
50 candle power incandescent lamp:—All night:—Yen 6.00.
150 " " " " " " 10.00.
1200 " " enclosed are " " " " 20.00.

Where more than 250 candle power of light is used, a Meter will be installed, if requested:—Rent of Meter Yen 2.00 per month. Rate of charges by meter reading:—Two Sen per Ampere per hour. (Approximately this is equal to about One Sen per 16 C. P. lamp per hour) Minimum monthly charge where meter is installed, Yen 20.00 per month, which includes rental of meter.

Estimates for installing lights furnished on application

An assortment of chandeliers always on hand.

K. Murakami.
Photograph Studio
Chinkokai, Seoul.

Printing, Developing and Enlargement, of Photographs always Undertaken.

Korean Views and Pictures Illustrating Native Customs always on Sale,

THE OSAKA SHOSEN KAISHA.

Boats frequently on the berth for Chinnampo.

REGULAR SAILINGS BETWEEN JAPAN AND KOREAN PORTS.

FUSAN AND KOBE VIA SHIMONOSEKI.

OSAKA VIA MOKPO, FUSAN, SHIMONOSEKI AND KOBE.

MOJI DIRECT.

OSAKA VIA KUNSAN, MASANPO, FUSAN, SHIMONOSEKI AND KOBE.

CHEMULPO KUNSAN LINE,
Every three days.

CHEMULPO CHINNAMPO LINE.
Every three days.

For Freight and passage and further particulars apply to

THE OSAKA SHOSEN KAISHA,
Chemulpo

RONDON, PLAISANT & CO.

General Storekeepers and Merchants, Ships Contractors, Tobacconists, Commission and Forwarding Agents, Coal Merchants

IMPORTERS AND EXPORTERS

Seoul & Chemulpo.

W. D. WENTWORTH.

LANDING
AND
SHIPPING AGENT.
AND
CUSTOMS BROKER.

12 OURA, NAGASAKI.

STEWARD & CO.

Chemulpo.

Shipchandlers and Storekeepers, Naval and Mercantile Contractors, Landing and Shipping Agents.

STEWARD'S HOTEL

Chemulpo.

Best accommodation in the port for travellers. Clean and well-aired rooms, good cuisine and prompt attendance, moderate tariff.

○의쥬군보 의쥬군수가외부로보고ᄒᆞ기를본월ᄎᆞ일에부훈령니예의병ᄎᆞ리ᄌᆞ일신ᄂᆞᆫ이유의아니라ᄒᆞᆫ일진회장김도진이가귀셩을ᄒᆞ니모회원셩ᄒᆞᄂᆞᆫ고로신이의ᄌᆞ장아ᄒᆞ야지ᄒᆞ고회시ᄒᆞ엿더니음력ᄉᆞ일원상인일에김도진이가다시지회원ᄌᆞᆼᄒᆞ고슈각ᄌᆞᆼ명을드러간셜시ᄒᆞ다ᄒᆞ니비루원룬은터에셔보고도를ᄒᆞ나원이시이희완ᄒᆞ오니가딕방의엄칙ᄒᆞ야단속케ᄒᆞ라ᄒᆞ엿더라

뎐보

뮈림발 일월십삼일

○로관입례 로국해셔셔로난부대신스바는로국을슈며스기로셩왕은간니교회의이드비가엄명이된다ᄂᆞᆫ말이잇더라

동경발 동일

○로월등경 법국에셔글나야신문에보고ᄒᆞᆫ말을거ᄒᆞᆫ즉본월일향디가타다가쓰기에셔나셔그근처에잇가온주인영ᄂᆞᆫ셔음에셔군함들이ᄯᅥ오기를기다리고잇다더라

돈돈발 동월십삼일

○로함출발 로국흑군에쟝를투스기의함뒤ᄂᆞᆫ스밋스오하에지벗다ᄒᆞ엿더라

○로톄의호견과 뮈림에셔로국신톄권의모집홈을위ᄒᆞ야주셔슷ᄂᆞᆫ톄이음모자커비셩ᄒᆞ편다ᄒᆞ엿다더라

동ᄯᅦ발 동월십삼일

○미국평고 미국졍부에셔쳥국졍부에경고ᄒᆞᆫ되신국문ᄒᆞᆫ관련민토의인릭권을분시ᄒᆞ다ᄂᆞᆫ계소우리졍부에셔불공ᄒᆞᄂᆞᆫ거시니그권리ᄂᆞᆫ미국에잇ᄂᆞᆫ거신고로미국졍부ᄂᆞᆫ그권리를보호홈을노셩각ᄒᆞᆫ다ᄒᆞ엿다더라

뮈림발 동월십삼일

○영국국회소식 영국의국회ᄂᆞᆫ이월십수일에모일터이라ᄂᆞᆫ티오ᄂᆞᆫ사월에ᄂᆞᆫ해산되리라ᄂᆞᆫ말이잇더라

○함쟝쇼견 본월이십일샹오에뎨국쟝일병이데로이분으로로조함부근에출현ᄒᆞ야우리군수들을공격ᄒᆞ엿스나우리지디가죠셰이기술진퇴지벗면으로격퇴ᄒᆞ엿더라

○로국남관귀미 일월십구일샹오쥬에셔발표ᄒᆞᆫ바로국셔울에셔발ᄒᆞᆫ연보를거ᄒᆞᆫ즉셩국관보에셔노동자가대동밍파ᄒᆞᆫ이이러나군함쟝수졍과기타계반셤밧게조ᄒᆞᄂᆞᆫ데와관유계작소와밋기타공회군용병과단야계조ᄒᆞᄂᆞᆫ데리공장이그사업을불슈이즁지ᄒᆞ지라로국평민들은요동과쇼요가쳥치상셰게팀셩을드로키ᄒᆞ눈셰이라나셔오동두와자ᄂᆞᆫ셩귀위예방ᄒᆞ고셔영즁ᄒᆞ야관셩경위ᄒᆞᄂᆞᆫ티쥬요ᄒᆞᆫ공장쇼우자들이

금엽ᄎᆞᆯ구ᄒᆞ엿ᄂᆞᆫᄃᆡ궁병에회의ᄒᆞ야셩졍부지축ᄒᆞ을강경ᄒᆞᆫ듸의오회에자유은ᄃᆡᆼ이로국가티방에이계나혁셰가용이치안타ᄒᆞ엿더라

관보

뎨삼천수십삼호 광무구년일월이십삼일

셔임급ᄉᆞ령

○평리원판ᄉᆞ셔리 평리원검ᄉᆞ 리근명 일월이십수일

○승셔원승지 탁지부쥬ᄉᆞ 김병우 일월이십수일

○승셔원승지 함경북도관찰부쥬ᄉᆞ 현ᄉᆞ영

○군부참령 니부쥬ᄉᆞ의ᄉᆞ 리ᄉᆞ현

이샹일월이십사일

○승셔원승지 부산감리셔리 윤ᄌᆞ용

○승셔원승지 셩진감리셔리 리츈명 창원감리셔리 셔상셕

○군부참령 셩진감리셔리 셔상셕

이샹일월이십삼일

○승셔원승지 탁지부쥬ᄉᆞ 문용우

양원부쥬ᄉᆞ셔리판임관 구릉 리윤용

○군부참령 원산감리셔리 리윤용

이샹일월이십구일

○평리원검ᄉᆞ 법부형ᄉᆞ국 현병석

○의원보조원 비셔원랑 김하용 졍부참찬 리민샹 표방순 쥬임 셔경원 니부쥬ᄉᆞ 현용숙

○궁내부셔리 구룽 리윤구

○일본공ᄉᆞ관셔리 구룽 김용오

○일본공ᄉᆞ관셔리 일본쥬ᄉᆞ 윤진포

○일본공ᄉᆞ관셔리 일본쥬ᄉᆞ 박용균

○즁추원의관 니부참셔관 한성 오상익

○즁추원의관 경무ᄉᆞ 오필균

○즁추원의관 경위원총관 오도학

이샹즁추원의관 리션경 오ᄐᆡ경 조ᄃᆡ고 즁조 고

○즁추원의관 니부협판 셩군련 리용익

○즁추원의관 경위원총관 한셩 리원필

○즁추원의관 경위원총관 동민영 리원필

이샹즁추원의관 리민경 조ᄃᆡ고 즁조 고 의관 츄

○의쥬부 뎌ᄉᆞ 김광균

○평남니부 쥬ᄉᆞ 보지원

이샹일월이십일

○평리원쥬ᄉᆞ 한셩부 리빙우

론셜

쳥국ᄒᆞ는 기왕 본국 ᄇᆞᆼ한

○쳥국관일셰가 뎌국의 쳥관은 변혀가나ᄒᆞ야셔 여러번권ᄒᆞ나 관이진지ᄒᆞ지아니ᄒᆞ고 진다면 일허바치도진치못ᄒᆞᆫ지거디 리ᄒᆞᄂᆞᆫ셰력후ᄂᆞᆫ장샹의열심으로 ᄌᆞ금 이거주 의원쟝의 안ᄒᆞ니 교국의 담보와게 ᄒᆞᆫ ᄎᆞ조관 ᄒᆞ고 그 권리를 국건ᄒᆞᄂᆞᆫ 그 담 셩젹 ᄌᆞ 교와 랴 ᄎᆞ리치샹ᄒᆞᄂᆞᆫ 계 ᄒᆞ야 ...

(이하 본문 판독 곤란)

외보

○북히함ᄃᆡ와 로의기 비월이십팔일미국샹항면보를거ᄒᆞᆫ즉로국이북히함ᄃᆡ를ᄒᆞᆫ되ᄉᆞ이도이가금ᄉᆞ히ᄒᆞᆫ다ᄂᆞᆫᄃᆡ로국이도이가위의지계쳥구ᄒᆞ야보쇼포리쇼의와다더법쇼를통ᄒᆞᄂᆞᆫ북히함ᄃᆡ의경을기ᄒᆞ엿다ᄂᆞᆫ말이영국에서셩ᄒᆞ엿더라

광고

○본인의쟝ᄉᆞ 한셩부

TELEGRAMS.

(FROM JAPAN PAPERS)

London, Jan. 15.

Earl Cairns has been found dead at Cannes.

London, Jan. 15.

The Grand Duke Serge, Governor of Moscow, and Garichin, Governor of the Caucasus, have been dismissed from their positions Prince Sviatopolk Mirski, Minister of the Interior, will discharge their duties for the time being.

London, Jan. 16.

In the explanation of the Russian Budget it is stated that, in accordance with the law of 1890, the Budget does not include the outlays directly incurred for warlike purposes. Up to the close of last year, the extraordinary expenditure made by the various departments totalled 621 million roubles.

In the extraordinary appropriations for railway construction there is a sum of 10 millions of roubles for doubling the Siberian Railway, and a sum of 1,800,000 roubles for the circum-Baikal line.

The hard money in the Treasury at the end of 1903 was 1,058 million roubles and in consequence of the 5-per-cent. foreign loan this amount was increased on the 14th of July, 1904, so that it rose to 1,237 millions, since which time until the 21st of December it had not undergone any diminution.

Berlin, Jan. 16.

The Powers are showing much reserve with regard to the Russian circular complaining of Chinese breaches of neutrality. The German Government has not received the circular. The United States is making enquiries into the matter. The public regard Russia's action as simply a characteristic device necessitated by the situation at the front.

London, Jan. 17.

Mr. John John Hay, U. S. Scretary of State, has cabled to the U. S. Minister at Peking calling attention to the Circular Note issued to the Powers by Russia complaining of China's violation of neutrality since the beginning of the war. Mr, Hay expresses the hope that China will earnestly consider the charges made.

London, Jan. 17.

A blizzard was experienced all over England yesterday. The estuary of the Thames is frozen for a considerable distance from the shore. Showers of ice fell in London, where the traffic is quite disorganised by the conditions prevailing.

The coast of the British Isles is strewn with wrecks, and several deaths from cold are reported.

The Tsar issued a declaration in which he expresses his wish to uphold Russian valour and endurance, and he says that the time of victory for Russia is approaching.

Japanese telegrams report a skirmish near Chupang-new on the 21st resulting in a Russian defeat but no details are given. It is also reported that on the 22nd a Russian infantry lieutenant walked into the Japanese lines and surrendered.

It is given out by the Tokio Naval Department that the Submarine Torpedo Squadron of which the organization was announced in the "Official Gazette" of the 13th instant, comprises ten vessels which were put together in Japanese dock-yards.

Capt. J. H. Rinder, well-known in Japan, has been appointed Captain of the giant "Minnesota, scheduled to leave Seattle for the Orient on the 21st inst. Capt. Troubridge, who previously commanded the Minnesota, will remain in America to take her sister-ship the Dakota.

A SUBMARINE TO CROSS THE ATLANTIC.

At Newport News (Va.) The keel has been laid at the shipyard for a new and larger Lake submarine boat, in which the inventor, Simon Lake, expects to make a trip across the Atlantic, under her own power, in an effort to demonstrate her seaworthiness. The new vessel will be eighty-three feet long, and proportionately large in every way. She will carry four torpedo tubes, ten torpedoes, and, without assistance, will have a cruising radius of 1,000 miles.

"This will be the first submarine boat of any class to attempt a trip across the ocean," said Lake. "There is no reason, however, why she should not cross the ocean in safety. Ordinary torpedo boats have made the voyage without inconvenience, and the craft we are now having built will be more seaworthy than any torpedo boat ever built."

THE INNER HISTORY OF WAR

BY F. A. MACKENZIE IN THE "DAILY MAIL."

The war is now, in my opinion, at a stage more difficult for Japan than at any time since it began.

The long delay in the capture of Port Arthur has injured the Japanese strategic plans; the three armies on the Shaho are for the moment held up by a numerically superior Russian force; and in Japan itself there are now considerably over a hundred thousand wounded men.

The campaign of 1904 has shown that, while the bravery of the Japanese soldiers and the fierce patriotism of the people stand almost unequalled, there are certain serious weaknesses in the position and methods of our allies which give cause for uneasiness.

JAPAN'S CHIEF DANGERS:

Some of the chief dangers to Japan may be summed up thus;

The growing improvement of the Russian morale.

The over-caution of the Japanese generals, and their neglect to follow up their victories fully.

The heavy losses incurred by the Japanese in direct attacks.

The fact that the Russians have now learned the surprise methods of Japanese attacks, and are prepared against them.

Lastly, and for the moment least important, the failure of the Japanese to placate the Koreans.

When Alexeieff's "bluff" was called and war began, he was taken by surprise. He had a phantom army of ill-disciplined soldiers, his stores and armaments existed mainly on paper, his ships were scattered, and the champagne-soaked brains of his officers were attuned to the songs of women rather than to the sound of guns.

The Russians in Manchuria were the rotten apple, waiting to be kicked out of the path by one straight blow. But the blow did not come. Port Arthur could have been taken, and easily taken, by the end of February. Dalny lay ready for seizure. But the Japanese remained passive until Port Arthur's phantom force became a real one, until her qarners were filled, and her magazines stocked with ammunition.

The Japanese plan of campaign was this: The First Army was to land at and near Chinnampo immediately the frost broke, and to advance northwards. After driving the Russians back from the Yalu it was to march on to Liaoyang, the Second and Fourth Armies meanwhile landing on the Liaotung peninsula and advancing in a great line, clearing the Russians before them. The three armies were to reach Liaoyang by not later than the middle of July, the Third Army meanwhile having taken Port Arthur. Liaoyang was to be taken before the rainy season began. In September, assisted by the Third Army, Mukden was to be attacked and captured. The Japanese were than to hold the line of hills for the winter against a Russian advance, and divert a large part of their force to invest Vladivostock. It was hoped that Russia then, in order to save Vladivostock, would ask for peace.

The plan has miscarried. The miscarriage has not been the fault of the Japanese soldiers or sailors, for never have men fought better than they. But their generalship was too slow, and at every point where a bold taking of risk was wanted caution ruled.

But when the blow should have been struck we paused again. The thing looked too easy. Grand Headquarters feared a trap, and before Grand Headquarters was reassured Kuropatkin had thrown fresh forces along our front, and our opportunity had gone, so we waited again, while Liaoyang was being further entrenched, and while fresh troops were being mobilised in Russia and brought against us.

THE RISE OF FIGHTING RUSSIA.

Thus the supreme advantages offered to us by the unreadiness of the Russian and by their unacquaintance with Japanese methods of fighting have been largely lost.

But this miracle has taken place under our eyes. After every defeat the Russians have fought better than before. The Russians as soldiers have many faults. They lack individual initiative; their men in the ranks are not over bright; they are too fond of vodka, champagne, and nerve-wrecking amusements. But they do not want for courage, and with that one virtue, all other things are being added to them.

The severe discipline of Kuropatkin is eliminating the hopeless officers from his service, and the men who six months ago were swilling in the stews of Newchwang or Liaoyang are to-day seriously doing their duty. Japan has now to face not the careless, inefficient mobs of of the springtime, but thorough fighting men.

No army can fight as the Japanese fight without incurring terrible losses. Frontal attacks, whether made during the day or night, cannot be pushed home without fearful slaughter. More than once I have come across instances of whole battalions being wiped out when caught at short range. At least one such instance occurred on our left flank during the battle of Liaoyang.

The question naturally arises—How far can Japan stand this drain of men? The tooth-comb of the conscription has already been drawn very fine through the country. The younger men have all been called to arms. The troops now going to the front are mostly older reservists, who have been longer from the colours. A hundred thousand men may fall in the next two battles around the Shahao. Russia will feel such loss heavily. Can Japan stand the strain? Each battle now grows bloodier than the last. A decisive battle, properly followed up, is worth any loss, but battles such as the last two to the north are a tremendous price paid for nothing.

Korea has, for the moment, largely faded from the public gaze. But the Hermit Kingdom may soon again be a centre of great interest. A Russian invasion of North-Eastern Korea, from Vladivostock, is one of the possibilities of the coming spring. Some malign fate seems to follow Japanese attempts to adminster Korea. The terrible blunder of ten years since, when the Korean Empress was murdered under the direction of the then Japanese Minister, is not yet forgotten. The Japanese Government repudiated it, and punished the Minister, but the memory lingers.

The Korean people as a whole, from members of the Court downwards, believe that the Japanese intend to take everything from them and to make them their hewers of wood and drawers of water.

Eleven months ago, when the Russian cavalry swept down into Northern Korea, the natives lied to them to send them back, and aided the Japanese with information. They are now prepared to hail the Russians.

It is, says the "Japan Mail" stated in well-informed circles in Tokyo that a new first-class armoured cruiser is under construction in Japanese dock-yards.

The "Kokumin" declines to regard the recent Russian cavalry raid on the Liaoho Valley as one of the usual Russian tricks and thinks that it is connected with the Shaho operations to some extent. This Russian surprise so boldly essayed on the Japanese constitutes a violation of the neutrality of the West Liao district. The Tokyo paper instances the Japanese proverb: "Negligence is a great enemy," and hopes that the general operations by the Manchurian Headquarters will not be affected.

It appears that the rumours of peace current in London rest upon very slender foundations. It has been announced that King Edward, the Czar, Emperor Francis Joseph, and the Kaiser will meet at Copenhagen this month and it has been immediately concluded that they are assenbling to discuss the possibility of mediation. If the meeting accomplishes the confinement of the war to the two combatants already engaged, it will have achieved a great deal.

Mr. Uchida, Japanese Minister to Peking, who has been staying in the capital for some weeks past, will leave Shimbashi at 6 P. M. on Wednesday for China. The "Kokumin" believes that he is returning to the post with a definite programme in his pocket for dealing with the subsequent development of the situation. But it is hardly necessary to remark that Japan's policy toward China is not of an aggressive character, but is to safeguard the integrity of the Continent Empire and to maintain an equal opportunity for international commerce and industry. Prognostication is still useless, but it goes without saying that the affairs is the Extreme Orient are not same as prior to the opening of hostilities. Meanwhile, the Tokyo paper feels warranted in saying that Japan has no sinister purpose in China. Her constant endeavour has been and is to be directed toward the extension of the peaceful-interests and the insurance of the welfare of the Far East, on which intention her Continent neighbours can rely.—Japan Gazette.

The Korea Daily News.

Issued at 5 P. M. daily except Sundays.

Rate of Subscription:—
Per Year,............Yen 25.
Per Quarter,..........Yen 7.
Per Month,..........Yen 2.50.

Postage in Korea not charged extra.
Postage abroad charged extra.

Advertisements, 50 sen per day for 1 inch or less.
5 yen per month per inch.
50 yen per year per inch.

All communications to
E. T. BETHELL,
Editor and Publisher,
Pak-tong, Seoul.

STRUGGLE FOR PEACE.

A Tokio report declares that the Japanese people are anxiously awaiting the coming of the Baltic fleet, so that Togo may crush it. Confidence of this sort has its home in Japan. What Togo did to the Port Arthur squadron will be repeated upon the arrival of the Baltic fleet, Tokio believes beyond a doubt. London encourages this belief. Moreover, the view is largely held in America that Japan will preserve her naval supremacy. The reason that Japan is a favorite does not lie in the number and superiority of ships, but in the excellence of their manipulation and in the greater effectiveness of Japanese gunnery. The world at large has a small opinion of the Russians as sea fighters. The North sea incident hurt Russian naval prestige almost as seriously as the dismal show of the Port Arthur squadron against Togo and the Vladivostok fleet againt Kamimura.

Moreover, the Baltic fleet will arrive in Asiatic waters in a fouled and racked condition, and, from all we know, at a time of year when it will be impossible to make Vladivostok for cleaning and repairs. And yet, says a correspondent of the Chicago Daily News, Tokio is wrong to regard the destruction of the Baltic fleet as certain as its arrival within striking distance of the capable Japanese admiral. Togo himself has been weakened by the hard service of the year, and his losses, while small in ratio to the damage administered, are at the same time greater than the world has been given to understand. He will have to face a preponderance of battleships and a sea force that has everything to win and no shores threatened or armies cut off if it lose—a force that has the example of its predecessor by which to profit and a prize of incalculable value for victory.

Tokio believes that the destruction of the Baltic fleet will put Russia in a frame of mind in which she will gladly listen to proposals of peace on terms satisfactory to Japan. The "Jiji Shimpo," highly representative of the Japanese press, urges Japanese arms to push the conflict with such fury that the enemy will have to sue for peace. Tokio prays that the continuation of the battle of the Shaho river will result in the complete shattering of Kuropatkin's forces, so that Russia will be forced to desist from hostilities. Japan wants peace badly. She is terrified as the game unfolds mile after mile. The monster that she has driven and pummeled will not stay whipped, but quietly and without nerves or noise, augments and returns to the fight. Japan perceives the unsubstantiality of England's support; that it is of the press and not of the treasure house. English bankers make her pay exorbitant interest for the money she borrows. England is not yet in her dotage; she is for England still. Japan is fighting for peace, and fighting magnificently; but her enemy, unless rent by civil war, will not be the one to cry "enough!" This is not Russia's way. She knows that years will crush Japan if her troops cannot. She realizes vividly that if she lies down to Japan now the integrity of her domain will not long survive China's.

RUSSIANS PROVISIONING.

It is reported that the Russians, accompanied by interpreters, are buying up all the food and provisions in Shun Yang and the surrounding districts. Natives who are unwilling to sell their winter stores of grain, etc., are obliged to do so under compulsion, and in order to forestall the Japanese the Russians are offering extraordinary prices as an inducement. It is said that in case of retreat the Russians willdestroy all that has been purchased and commandeered.

SHIP'S CARGO CONFISCATED AT HONKONG.

According to a Hongkong despatch which the "Osaka Asahi" has received from Shanghai, says the "Nagasaki Press," the steamer "Tungchow," which took on board a quantity of arms and ammunition from the Russian cruiser "Diana" at Saigon and which sailed from the French port under instructions to await further orders at Gutzlaff Island, outside Shanghai, was, on arrival, ordered to Saigon, presumably on account of the fall of Port Arthur. While on the return trip from the island to Saigon the steamer put into Hongkong to take in coal there on the 13th inst.

The British Authorities found the vessel guilty of a breach of neutrality and all the cargo on board the steamer was confiscated and the Captain fined 250 dollars.

The number of Russian prisoners from Port Arthur, so far quartered in Japan, is 8,108, including 428 at Matsuyama, 2,020 at Dairi (near Moji), 5,000 at Osaka, and 1660 at Himeji.

Arrivals from Dalny state the Japanese troops have recently been landed there and many of them sent northward by rail. The number of the troops is reported to be from twelve to fifteen thousand.

It is stated that from first to last the relations between the Russian army and navy were thoroughly bad at Port Arthur, so bad in fact that some people find herein a sufficient cause for the failure of the defence.

According to a Nagasaki telegram one of the Russian officers who has recently arrived at the above port from Port Arthur, has stated that on the occasion of the surrender of the fortress a telegram from the Empress Dowager of Russia was transmitted to General Stoessel through the courtesy of the Investing Army. The message was very cordially worded. His Majesty expressing her earnest desire to see the gallant soldier as early as possible.

The latest Seoul census has has resulted in the following figures.

	Houses.	Population.
Japanese	1,462	5,785
Chinese	285	2697
American	28	29
English	8	6
German	4	6
French	5	6
Korean	43,350	191,754

From the above statistics it will be noted that the Chinese pack tightest, viz: Something over 9 to a house. The Japanese come next with an average of 4. Koreans only run to 2½ per roof. The English seem to spread themselves most as they have 8 houses amongst 5 people. The French also have a spare house. These tables are, if we may judge from personal observation, absolutely unreliable.

A Peking special to the "Kokumin" says that according to a person returning from Mongolia, a French missionary on the local boundary is handling the supply of ammunition and horses for the Russians.

From a distinguished Russian officer who recently passed throug Shanghai on his way from the front, the "China Gazette" learns that the Russian Commander-in-chief has now under his immediate command a force of no less than 400,000 men.

According to latest telegrams H. M. the Czar and his Ministers have after a council of war determined to send out no less then 200,000 more men before the end of next month, so that the Russian forces opposing Japan's further progress into Manchuria will then not be far short of 600,000 men.

The Household Bureau has transmitted to the Foreign Office a complaint from the Government Tax Collector in South Ham Kyeng province to the effect that the Commander of the Japanese garrison in Gensan has told him that he may not collect taxes without his permission. It is asked that the attention of the Japanese Minister be drawn to this.

A Peking despatch dated the 14th inst., received by the "Tokyo Asahi," states that the Chinese Government having decided to establish a Naval Department and to re-organize the Navy, a proposal is now gaining strength in official circles that Great Britain should be asked to surrender Wei-hai-wei to the Chinese, in order that an arsenal may be established there.

Major-General Wilmann, speaking through the columns of the "Kokumin Shimbun," expresses the highest admiration for the courage of the Japanese artillery and for the skill of their gunnery. His explanation of the surrender is that there were not men enough in the end to defend the forts, and that the number of sick and wounded had become unmanageable. Blood poisoning was above all prevalent.

On Jany 14th the Japanese Army at Port Arthur held a requiem service for the troops killed during the siege. In the course of the reading of a written prayer, General Nogi said:—"In connection with the surrender of the fortress, I received a most gracious message from His Majesty the Emperor, but I feel that the merit ought to be shared among those still in this world and those who are now invisible. I cannot bear to take the glory to myself."

All present were greatly moved, and many sobs were heard.

Press despatches from Takeu (near the Shaho), dated January 13, state that the Russian troops are constantly moving to and fro in groups of one battalion and at times are subjected to drill. The objective of the Russian gunfire seems unchanged, says the Kobe Herald, but during the night the fire often assumes a searching character, directed at the Japanese inner positions. The enemy has been reconnoitering with a balloon in the neighbourhood of Shaho-pao. The weather at the Shaho is at present less cold that formerly the thermometer registering 5.5 degree below zero on the morning of January 13.

It come out at an inquest held in Hongkong on the body of a child drowned in a collision between the steam lunch "Wingloi" and a sampan, that a very gallant attempt to rescue the child had been made by Dr. A. F. Foster, the Assistant Health Officer. Dr. Foster was on another launch when he was informed that two children were under an overturned sampan. He plunged into the water, broke away part of the sampan, which was already damaged, and succeeded in extricating and resuscitating one child. The other was unfortunately dead. The attention of the Royal Humane Society is to be directed to Dr. Foster's exploit. In connection with the collision the master of the "Wingloi was put under arrest.

The Korea Daily News.

VOL. II, TUESDAY, JANUARY 24, 1905. No. 18

大韓每日申報
대한ᄆᆡ일신보

(뎨이쳔십구호) (목요일) 일쳔구빅오년일월이십륙일

본샤고ᄇᆡᆨ

이신보는영어와한어로셕거ᄆᆡ일츌판ᄒᆞᆷ

신문가

한쟝 엽푼오리

일삭도 엽두량닷돈

우표가리삭닷돈

다맛돈으로밧ᄉᆞᆷ

광고료는

긔한의쟝단과ᄌᆞ힝의다쇼로죵갑ᄒᆞ되렴가로밧을터이오며오리ᄌᆞ하녀대한사람마다다이신문을보실터이니광고버시기를원ᄒᆞ시는이들은우리신문사에와서편약ᄒᆞ심을희망ᄒᆞᆷ

○발힝소 ᄇᆡ동대한ᄆᆡ일신보사 발힝겸편집인 영국인 ᄇᆡ셜 필쟝자리오

사쟝 영국인 (ᄇᆡ셜)

평양 디리졈

○평양죵로사는권뎡보씨로우리신문관디디리인을뎡ᄒᆞ엿시오니평양에계신구람코자ᄒᆞ시는 쳠군ᄌᆞ는허디리졈에왕림ᄒᆞ와면의ᄒᆞ시옵

샤고

○우리대한ᄆᆡ일신보의목뎍은대한의안녕질서에관한모든뎨목에ᄃᆡᄒᆞ야는공평한변론을쥬쟝ᄒᆞᆷ이라우리동신원의탐보ᄒᆞ는신문보시는쳠군ᄌᆞ의게ᄒᆞᆼ샹보도ᄒᆞ리며평지를긔셔ᄒᆞ며주시는이는셩명과번디를젹어붓치시기를희망ᄒᆞ오나비거슨신문샹에긔재ᄒᆞ란는거시아니오다만긔허신용ᄒᆞ논ᄌᆞ거를숨고자ᄒᆞᆷ이라귀자는아모긔셔던지긔지ᄒᆞᆷ을되챠ᄒᆞ는권리를가졋소나되쟈ᄒᆞ는리유를말ᄒᆞᆯ터이오며공즁평화를문란케ᄒᆞᄂᆞᆫ듯ᄒᆞᆫ긔셔는의례히밧지아니켓ᄉᆞᆸ나이다

●본샤셜시이리로신문을ᄆᆡ양우례로분젼ᄒᆞ와례젼부의임의로젼ᄒᆞ는듯소로번곳에는후늣게젼ᄒᆞ기도ᄒᆞ며혹먹쳘거슬ᄒᆞᆫ협에젼ᄒᆞ기도ᄒᆞ며혹아니젼ᄒᆞ는곳도잇다ᄒᆞ와우리신문을ᄉᆞ랑ᄒᆞ야구람ᄒᆞ시는 쳠군ᄌᆞ의계ᄃᆡᄒᆞ야ᄆᆡ우미안ᄒᆞ옵기로지금은분젼인을두고ᄆᆡ일일즉이젼ᄒᆞ며아니젼ᄒᆞ거나늣게젼ᄒᆞ거나ᄒᆞᆫ폐가엽도록ᄒᆞ라ᄒᆞ오니혹아니젼ᄒᆞ거나혹늣게젼ᄒᆞ거나ᄒᆞᆫ일이잇스면본샤로통긔ᄒᆞ여주심을희망ᄒᆞᆷ

잡보

○민원쟉폐 강화부윤한쳘규씨는현금에보방이되엿는ᄃᆡ그동안에발셔횡렴ᄒᆞ야학쟝의젼일보담몃빅나징ᄒᆞ야불가형언인고로부하의민원이랑자ᄒᆞ고쎠그아들윤방헌씨가그호원ᄒᆞ는강화빅셩들을잡아지로착슈ᄒᆞᆫ고로민원이새에신이여세부득이ᄒᆞ야일본령ᄉᆞ의게호원ᄒᆞᆫ다더라

○법부괴초즁지 젼법부대신김가진씨가법부를괴초ᄒᆞ시로쟝ᄒᆞ야쟝츳반포ᄒᆞ란다가계엄이되엿디히수염이못ᄒᆞ니귀결이되지못ᄒᆞᄂᆞ즁지가되엿더라

○일슈항쟝 일본공ᄉᆞ가지작일에ᄂᆡ부로공함ᄒᆞ기를현금원산경무관박긔호는경찰ᄉᆞ무에셩격이반이잇셔서반다시됴흔결과로신임ᄒᆞ만ᄒᆞᆫ고로함ᄒᆞ에잇는지딘소쟝이히원을고원군슈직무를직힝케ᄒᆞᆷ을쳥ᄒᆞ엿스니귀졍부에셔히원을곳히군슈로셔임ᄒᆞ고현금고원군슈의가젼인쟝을곳히원의게쥬게ᄒᆞᆷ을비란ᄒᆞᆫ오며이거슨군수평판의제고ᄒᆞᆫ거신고로요쳥ᄒᆞ노라ᄒᆞ엿더라

○경쥬조회 직작일에경무쳥에서한셩부로조회ᄒᆞ기를무릇일졀군물에ᄂᆡ헌거슬ᄉᆞᄉᆞ로ᄆᆡ셔로ᄆᆡᄆᆡᄒᆞ거나혹면당잡지못ᄒᆞᆷ은ᄂᆡ외국의금미온ᄃᆡ우리나라병뎡과순검비ᄂᆞᆫ죵죵홈볼가지기를ᄆᆡ란고편ᄒᆞ게ᄒᆞ야괴롭을엇의여법ᄒᆞ야가진바총과포와칼과졉과복쟝등물을ᄂᆡ외국인면방포에면당잡히ᄂᆞᆫ자가쟉금잇기로ᄆᆡ양군경광ᄎᆞᆼ에셔병뎡과순검을엄히단속ᄒᆞ야그폐를막으며면쥬의게엄ᄎᆡᆨᄒᆞ야일졀관셥지말게ᄒᆞ고젼에면당잡흔거순힝의수실ᄒᆞ야거두어드린것수오나지어일ᄒᆞᆫ의샹젼ᄒᆞ야논소관된규칙이잇지아니ᄒᆞ면비거슬어제ᄒᆞᆯ슈업ᄉᆞ오며금물을쳥ᄒᆞᄂᆞᆫ거순젼히본쳥의최임이기로이에조회ᄒᆞ오논일본령ᄉᆞ의게이조ᄒᆞ야금물을면집ᄒᆞᄂᆞᆫ거슬금지케ᄒᆞ라ᄒᆞ엿더라

○경쳥우조 경무쳥에서쟉한셩부로조회ᄒᆞ기를쳥인이아편연을방ᄆᆡᄒᆞᄂᆞᆫ고로쳥인의샹졈은아편먹ᄂᆞᆫ외굴이되여인민이닷토와가셔먹어파가망신ᄒᆞ되마츰ᄂᆡ세다라곳치지못ᄒᆞ니쳥국령ᄉᆞ와교셥ᄒᆞ야아편약을ᄆᆡᄆᆡᄒᆞᄂᆞᆫ거슬엄금케ᄒᆞ라ᄒᆞ엿더라

○츄쳥슈렴 경무쳥에서우본율슈츅ᄒᆞ츠로그경비를민호에분비ᄒᆞ야슈렴ᄒᆞᄂᆞᆫᄃᆡ와가나초가나다셧간이하ᄂᆞᆫ닷량이오나셧간이샹은열량이오열간이샹은스물닷량비오십간이샹은수삼량이오시간이샹은통쳥셩량셕비령ᄒᆞᆫ다더라

○광협입항 인쳔항감리의보를거ᄒᆞᆫ즉영국군함과덕국군함가일쳑식작일에입항ᄒᆞ엿다더라

○대관입면 샤작일에쳠졍김쟝근씨는소케되고그ᄃᆡ에는탁지부대신조병호씨가승임ᄒᆞ고탁지대신은임시민영귀씨가환임ᄒᆞ엿더라

○죠쳥면세 쳥공관에서외부로조회ᄒᆞ기를신항죵광대신이면보니기에종려본월일일민광이를타고인쳔으로향ᄒᆞᆯ터이니한셩부에조회ᄒᆞ야인쳔총세무스에훈칙ᄒᆞ야항리에세를면케ᄒᆞ라ᄒᆞ엿스니쳥컨ᄃᆡ곳시힝ᄒᆞ라ᄒᆞ엿더라

○주쳥공관보고 주쳥공관에셔외부ᄂᆞᆫ보고ᄒᆞ기를쳥국외부공문을니기에ᄒᆞᆫ작우리황뎨폐하의탄신일경슌기국치하국셔에답셔를ᄂᆡ괴숑ᄒᆞ야한국에주차ᄒᆞᆫ우리공ᄉᆞ로ᄒᆞ야곰뎐졍ᄒᆞ라ᄒᆞ엿스니쳥컨ᄃᆡ귀졍부에젼달ᄒᆞ라ᄒᆞ엿기이에보고ᄒᆞᆫ다ᄒᆞ엿더라

○외조비관 외부에서비국공관에조회ᄒᆞ되니부조회니기에ᄐᆡ일과고문관이쳥원ᄒᆞ기를리미원이삼관에결단코희국ᄒᆞᆫ뒤다ᄒᆞ엿스니쳥컨ᄃᆡ곳희고ᄒᆞᆫ후본년량월봉과및희국비를합동레에의지ᄒᆞ야지발ᄒᆞ야써속히발쟝케ᄒᆞ라ᄒᆞ엿스니일노써비로소의게젼죠ᄒᆞ라ᄒᆞ엿기이에조회ᄒᆞᆫ다ᄒᆞ엿더라

○포아주민쳥원 포아주민은경호등이쳥원ᄒᆞ엿ᄂᆞᆫ긔에일쳥담국에서ᄂᆞᆫ관원을파숑ᄒᆞ야각각칙국인민을보호ᄒᆞᄂᆞᆫ지라우리빅셩도오륙쳔명이로ᄃᆡ의지ᄒᆞᆯ고밋을곳이업스니시무에연숙ᄒᆞᆫ관원으로퇴차파숑ᄒᆞ면허비ᄂᆞᆫ인민즁으로구취ᄒᆞ야본조ᄒᆞᆯ터이오니파쥬차케ᄒᆞ심을바란다ᄒᆞ엿더라

○우위담관 손연방의셔명일소로지각일한호두시에법부대신과외부대신과영쟝통공스가외부에계회ᄒᆞ야담판ᄒᆞ엿다더라

○신문회쟝 미국신문을번명ᄒᆞ야대한국민신문이라ᄒᆞ고ᄂᆡ부에쳥원인가ᄒᆞ엿ᄂᆞᆫᄃᆡ활판긔게ᄂᆞᆫ자샹준금ᄒᆞ야경비멋쳔원을ᄂᆡ히ᄒᆞ옵시고희사ᄒᆞ에서ᄂᆞᆫ작금에발명ᄒᆞ야졔국인민에친호에일쟝식보조게ᄒᆞ고희가의온군슈가슈쇄샹납케ᄒᆞᆫ다더라

○군ᄃᆡ경의예졍 군제를리경ᄒᆞ야경향각ᄃᆡ대병을수쳔명만셜치ᄒᆞᆫ다ᄒᆞ더니다시펵계ᄒᆞ야향ᄃᆡ병은수쳔명이오경ᄃᆡ병은시위쳔위포병공병긔병장쳔명식합오쳔여명을셜치ᄒᆞ기로졍ᄒᆞ엿다더라

●관위시힝 법부에서신법률을괴초ᄒᆞ야쟝츳반포코져ᄒᆞ더니대신이자조갈님으로이룰이반포되기가어렵다더라

관보

뎨삼쳔수십수호 광무구년일월이십사일

셔임급슈령

○승졍삼품 륙품 리경찬

광무팔년오월십일일

○임즁학교쟝셔주임관륙등 졍삼품 리단용

일월십륙일

임의학교교관주임관륙등 륙군삼등군의 유병필

○승셔주임관스등 농상공부참셔관 셔병슈

○승셔주임관오등 농상공부기수 졍룡환

이상일월십구일

○임법관양셩소교관셔주임관륙등 륙품 박희옥

UNION INSURANCE SOCIETY OF CANTON.

Head office Hongkong.
Marine risks underwritten at current rates.
Agents in Chemulpo,
E. MEYER & Co.

COMPAGNIE DES MESSAGERIES MARITIMES.

Fortnightly Direct Service.

For Marseilles
via Ports.
Sailing from Yokohama
Calling at Kobe,
Shanghai, Hongkong, Saigon, Singapore,
Colombo, Djibouti, Suez, Port Said
and Marseilles.

For particulars apply to
HOLME RINGER & Co.,
Chemulpo.

HAYASHIDA & CO.,

16 MYENG DONG, CHIN KO KAI, SEOUL.
BRANCH OFFICE AT CHEMULPO.

Money changers, Coal and Wood Merchants, Express Agents.

We are agents for the Pyeng-yang Coal Company and the Karazu Coal Company of Japan. We have the best quality of both anthracite and bituminous coal, and prompt execution of orders is our speciality. Firewood of all kinds kept in stock. Full weight guaranteed. Money of all denominations exchanged at current rates. Parcels received for all parts.

CHINA MUTUAL LIFE INS. OC.

Most favourable terms to policy holders.

Benefit system unsurpassed.

HOLME RINGER & Co.
Agents, Chemulpo.

C. P. R.

CANADIAN PACIFIC RAILWAY COMPANY'S ROYAL MAIL STEAMSHIP LINE.

THE FAST ROUTE BETWEEN CHINA, JAPAN, AND EUROPE VIA CANADA AND THE UNITED STATES.

Route from Hongkong via Shanghai, Nagasaki (Inland Sea of Japan) Kobe, Yokohama, Victoria and Vancouver.

Twin Screw Empress Steamship—6,000 Tons—Speed 19 knots.

PROPOSED SAILING FROM YOKOHAMA.
R. M. S. Empress of India.
R. M. S. Empress of Japan.
R. M. S. Empress of China.
R. M. S. Athenian.
R. M. S. Tartar.

Special reduction (first class only) granted to members of the Military, Naval, Diplomatic and Civil services and to Missionaries.

Passengers have choice of ten routes across the Continent of America and have privilege of travelling by any Atlantic Steamship Line.

Round the World passage tickets in connection with the P. and O. S. N., North German Lloyd and Messageries Co.'s £125.

All rates payable at current rate of exchange.

For further information, Tickets, Guide Books, etc., apply to

HOLME, RINGER & CO., AGENTS,
Chemulpo.

Grand Hotel,

(Formerly the Station Hotel)

Near the Railway Terminus.
West Gate Seoul.

The Best Hotel in Korea
Handsome new Building.
Fine Airy Rooms
Excellent Cuisine.
Terms Moderate.
Special terms to Missionaries
and to permanent boarders.

Electric cars within 2 minutes' walk.

W. H. EMBERLEY.
Proprietor

EVERY FACILITY.

In connection with Life Assurance Business is afforded by

The Standard Life Assurance Co.,

One of the largest and wealthiest of the Provident Institutions of the United Kingdom Forms of Application and all information will be promptly afforded on application.

10 CENTS A DAY.

Not a very large expenditure is it? But it is sufficient to secure for a man of 30 a policy with the STANDARD LIFE OFFICE for

$1323.

For all particulars of rates, etc., apply to

Holme, Ringer & Co.,
Agents, Chemulpo.

THE NEW YORK LIFE INSURANCE COMPANY.

Have you ever been declined by any Company?

Are you engaged in a specially hazardous occupation?

Have you heard of the New York Life Insurance Company's New Classifications for this class of Risks?

If not, send your date of birth, occupation and particulars of rejection, if any to

E. MEYER & Co.,
Agents, Chemulpo.

MITSUI BUSSAN KAISHA.
(MITSUI & Co.)
MITSUI GINKO.
(MITSUI BANK.)

The Bank is owned by the members of the Mitsui Family, who, as partners, assume an unlimited responsibility for all liabilities of the Bank:—

Capital........................Yen 5,000,000
Reserve Fund................. " 5,600,000

HEAD OFFICE, TOKYO.
LONDON OFFICE, 34 LIME ST., E. C.

BRANCHES AND AGENCIES:—
New York, San Francisco, Hamburg, Bombay, Singapore, Manila, Hongkong, Amoy, Chefoo, Tientsin.

Kobe, Hakodate, Yokohama, Kure, Yokosuka, Moji, Shimonoseki, Miike, Wakamatsu, Nagasaki, Kuchinotsu, Karatsu, Sasebo, Misume, Taipeh, &c.

Telegraphic Address for all the Offices:
"MITSUI."
A. B. C. AND A. I CODES USED.

Contractors of Coal
To the Imperial Japanese Navy. Arsenals and Railway Bureau, Principal Railway Companies and Industrial Work, Home and Foreign Mail and Freight Steamers.

Sole Proprietors
Of the famous Miike, Tagawa and Yamano Coal Mines.

Sole Agents
For the sale of Fukumo, Hokoku, Ichimura, Kanoda, Mannoura, Onoura, Ostuji, Sonoda, Tsubaruro, Yoshinotani, Yoshio, Yurokibura and other coals.

YANGTSE INSURANCE ASSOCIATION, LTD.

The undersigned, having been appointed agents for the above company, are prepared to issue policies and pay losses on marine risks at regular rates.

E. MEYER & Co.,
Agents, Chemulpo.

AMERICAN KOREAN ELECTRIC CO.

Light and Power.

Main Office: Electric Building, Chong No.

RAILWAY DEPARTMENT.

OPERATING CARS BETWEEN EAST AND WEST GATE, EVERY TEN MINUTES:—

First Car leaves East Gate at 7:00 A. M. First Car leaves R. R. Station at 7:25 A. M
Last Car " East Gate at 8.40 P. M. Last " " R. R. Station at 9.05 P.M

OPERATING CARS BETWEEN EAST GATE AND IMPERIAL TOMB TERMINUS, EVERY TWENTY MINUTES:—

CONNECTING WITH EVERY ALTERNATE CAR ARRIVING AT EAST GATE FROM CHONG NO.

First Car leaves East Gate for Tomb at 7:10 A. M.
" " " Tomb for East Gate at 7:30 A. M.
Last " " East Gate for Tomb at 7:50 P. M.
" " " Tomb for East Gate at 8:10 P. M.

OPERATING CARS BETWEEN CHONG NO AND YUNG SAN RIVER EVERY TWELVE MINUTES:—

First Car leaves Chong No for South Gate at 7:12 A. M.
" " " Chong No for Yung San at 7:36 A. M.
" " " South Gate for Chong No at 7:20 A. M.
" " " Yung San for Chong No at 8:09 A. M.
Last " " South Gate for Chong No 9:00 P. M.
" " " Yung San for Chong No at 8.45. p. M.

SPECIAL PRIVATE CARS FURNISHED TO SUIT CONVENIENCE OF PATRONS. PRICES ON APPLICATION AT HEAD OFFICE.

LIGHTING DEPARTMENT.

Where less than 250 candle power of light is used, the rate per month will be
Per 16 candle power incandescent lamp,—All night.—Yen 2.50.
32 candle power incandescent lamp:—All night:—Yen 4.00.
50 candle power incandescent lamp:—All night:—Yen 6.00.
150 " " " " " " " 10.00.
1200 " " enclosed are " " " " 20.00.

Where more than 250 candle power of light is used, a Meter will be installed, if requested:—Rent of Meter Yen 2.00 per month. Rate of charges by meter reading:—Two Sen per Ampere per hour. (Approximately this is equal to about One Sen per 16 C. P. lamp per hour) Minimum monthly charge where meter is installed, Yen 20.00 per month, which includes rental of meter.

Estimates for installing lights furnished on application

An assortment of chandeliers always on hand.

K. Murakami.

Photograph Studio
Chinkokai, Seoul.

Printing, Developing and Enlargement, of Photographs always Undertaken.

Korean Views and Pictures Illustrating Native Customs always on Sale,

---

THE OSAKA SHOSEN KAISHA.

Boats frequently on the berth for Chinnampo.

REGULAR SAILINGS BETWEEN JAPAN AND KOREAN PORTS.

FUSAN AND KOBE VIA SHIMONOSEKI.

OSAKA VIA MOKPO, FUSAN, SHIMONOSEKI AND KOBE.

MOJI DIRECT.

OSAKA VIA KUNSAN, MASANPO, FUSAN, SHIMONOSEKI AND KOBE.

CHEMULPO KUNSAN LINE,
Every three days.

CHEMULPO CHINNAMPO LINE.
Every three days.

For Freight and passage and further particulars apply to

THE OSAKA SHOSEN KAISHA,
Chemulpo

RONDON, PLAISANT & CO.

General Storekeepers and Merchants, Ships Contractors, Tobacconists, Commission and Forwarding Agents, Coal Merchants

IMPORTERS AND EXPORTERS

Seoul & Chemulpo.

W. D. WENTWORTH.

LANDING
AND
SHIPPING AGENT.
AND
CUSTOMS BROKER.

12 OURA, NAGASAKI.

STEWARD & CO.

Chemulpo.

Shipchandlers and Storekeepers, Naval and Mercantile Contractors, Landing and Shipping Agents.

STEWARD'S HOTEL

Chemulpo.

Best accommodation in the port for travellers. Clean and well-aired rooms, good cuisine and prompt attendance, moderate tariff.

◯의원면겸임법관양성소교관
농신원번역관 방승헌
◯임법관양성소교관셔쥬임관
륙등 구픔 원직상
이상일월이십일
◯의원면본관 영릉령 홍승
범 즁츄원의관 쥬관홍 즁
츄원의관 송긔옥 즁츄원의
관 강봉원 즁츄원의관 김
지션 즁츄원의관 리명환
인쳔감리셔쥬사 염완괴 젼
라북도관찰부쥬사 죠병션
◯임즁츄원의관셔쥬임관륙등
륙픔 함션지 구픔 윤현모
구픔 오셩규 구픔 셔현보
◯명문관학사셔칙임관삼등
종일픔 죠병호
◯임영릉령셔판임관칠등 원
구단사졔셔령 황범슈
◯협원구단차졔셔령셔판임관
륙등 시강원시종관 리병철
◯엄셔강원시종관셔판임관륙
등 구픔 리긔용
◯임필도원쥬사셔판임관륙등
리필쥰 윤철구 민병호 윤
긔학 장보연 김현문 리승
구 목의상
◯임인쳔감리셔쥬사셔판임관
륙등 리지영
◯임전라북도관찰부쥬사셔판
임관륙등 한용협
◯승셔관임관오등 너부쥬사
원대규
이상일월이십일일
◯명홍문관학사셔칙임관삼등
종일픔 김셩근
◯의원면본관 비셔원승 신
셩균 후릉참봉 홍덕쥬 지
릉참봉 한쥰상 슌릉참봉
죠일원
◯임비셔원승셔쥬임관륙등
졍삼픔 리경현
◯의원면겸임장례원쟝례 봉
상사부졔됴 죠한원
◯겸임장례원장례 봉상사부졔
됴 서병찬 임후릉참봉셔관
임관팔등 리병근 임지릉참
봉셔판임관팔등 김직병
◯임슌릉참봉셔판임관팔등
셔찬슈
◯임홍신사면화과쥬사셔판임
관팔등 김현목 한인슈 박
셰긔
이상일월이십이일

외보

◯친왕관전 덕국황뎨칙령을
의지ᄒᆞ야일본군을좃차관젼ᄒᆞ
기위ᄒᆞ야작년십이월즁순에동
경을출발ᄒᆞᆫ덕국황족후엔오루
레룬친왕뎐하ᄭᅴ셔는목하한원
궁인지쳔왕뎐하와함ᄭᅴ체지ᄒᆞ
시는ᄃᆡ등디점령젼구로파독긴
의관ᄉᆞ에합ᄯᅢ거ᄒᆞ샤시로승
마ᄒᆞ고젼션에리왕ᄒᆞ야친밀히
만젼ᄒᆞᆫ다더라

◯로뎨찬양 로뎨ᄭᅴ셔는륙히
군에향ᄒᆞ여려슌함락을공시ᄒᆞ
는훈령을발표ᄒᆞ엿는ᄃᆡ로뎨는
명예가잇는포루슈비병의공로
를찬상ᄒᆞ여그용감ᄒᆞᆫ힝위는로
국이스ᄉᆞ로자랑ᄒᆞᆯ바이라ᄒᆞ고
ᄯᅩ싱자의게는평온ᄒᆞ며사쟈의
게는광영이라우리적은용밍ᄒᆞ
고ᄯᅩ강쟝ᄒᆞ여이굿치편거리에
젼쟁의곤란은가히형언못ᄒᆞᆯ지
라쟝ᄅᆡ아국강국으로금일브터
일층곤란ᄒᆞᆫ경쟁쟈와로되여점
점강대ᄒᆞᆯ지라써기는거손가히
쉽ᄒᆞ나우리는아국전토를들어
이거슬어지럽게ᄒᆞ는ᄃᆡ잇지아
니ᄒᆞ겟ᄉᆞ며짐은우리나라승리
가속히홈을밋고샹뎨ᄭᅴ향ᄒᆞ여
군ᄃᆡ와밋함ᄃᆡ에ᄃᆡᄒᆞ야아국명
예를발양ᄒᆞ는축복을쥬셤을변
다ᄒᆞ엿더라

론셜

전쟁의형편

◯우리가전에여러번전쟁에ᄃᆡ
ᄒᆞ야각인의의견을말ᄒᆞ엿져마
는ᄒᆞᆫ사ᄅᆞᆷ의의견을특별히고집
ᄒᆞ야밋는것은오히려ᄒᆞᆷ이라ᄒᆞ노
라
일본이나로국도이전쟁의결말
이어느ᄯᅢ엇더케될는지아지못
ᄒᆞᆯ거서오더구나방관지인이야
그ᄉᆞ건을미리말ᄒᆞᆯ슈업겟도다
군ᄉᆞ상으로는현저ᄒᆞᆫᄉᆞ건을볼
슈업스나셔로ᄃᆡ적으로잇는총
슈령관들만속에계산이잇스리
로다
그러ᄒᆞ나정치상관계가참긴요
ᄒᆞ도다지금일본이재물포히전
과려슌구함락으로세계의신문
지의게칭찬을대단이듯는지라
우리도일본의륙히군을칭찬ᄒᆞᆷ
에동졍을표ᄒᆞ겟도다일본의히
군은우리의성각에는돈슈외다
소는고ᄉᆞᄒᆞ고세계에출저아니
갈터이어륙군의조직과군인의
용감ᄒᆞᆷ이다평론ᄒᆞᆯ것이업스며
만일의국심과열심으로이징을
익일것갓ᄒᆞ면일본이벌셔익인
졔가오래되엿슬터이라
그러ᄒᆞ나이번전쟁에는비록의
국ᄒᆞ는ᄆᆞ옴과무용ᄒᆞᆫ정신이긴
요ᄒᆞ나량편이다그ᄆᆞ옴과그정
신이갓ᄒᆞ니종말에승전ᄒᆞᆷ은오
리지탕ᄒᆞ는힘에달녓는지라
세쇄ᄒᆞᆫ닐은고ᄉᆞᄒᆞ고지금두교
젼국ᄉᆞ이에비교ᄒᆞᆯ두가지긴요
ᄉᆞ건이잇스니
일 지졍
이 정치상과국졔상의보증
데이ᄉᆞ건을면져말ᄒᆞᆯ것갓ᄒᆞ면
일본은도아쥬는닐이두가지가
잇스니로국에셔이젼쟁에ᄃᆡᄒᆞ
야의이와불평론이잇다는것과
ᄯᅩ일영동밍이라
로국의ᄂᆡ디형편은우리가벌셔
말ᄒᆞᆫ것과갓치심란ᄒᆞᆫ닐이만치
마는로국에셔분요롤짓는인민
물은맛쳐현금에한인들이일본
압졔더밋헤잇는겟갓치져의들
의피로온것을발표ᄒᆞᆯ힘이업는
지라그러ᄒᆞᆷ으로우리는일본이글
노ᄒᆞ야일비지력의도음이라도
능히엇을ᄲᅮᆫ싱각지아니ᄒᆞ며로
국의ᄂᆡ란과분요에ᄃᆡᄒᆞ야등경
정부에서면보롤졉슈ᄒᆞ야각신
문에전파ᄒᆞ지마는정말노그러
케된일을보지못ᄒᆞ엿고각국과
관계롤보면일본이되단히좃치
못ᄒᆞ도다이젼쟁을시작ᄒᆞᆫ라고
각강국들에향ᄒᆞ야동맹ᄒᆞᆷ을요
구ᄒᆞ엿논ᄃᆡ대ᄉᆞ롤파송ᄒᆞ야각
국에도라다니다가결과가좃치
못ᄒᆞ고이동후가계우영국파제
ᄒᆞᆫ잇논동맹을의정ᄒᆞ고도라왓
는지라
일본에셔는영일동맹의성질을
만히오히ᄒᆞ는지라우러는밋기
롤영국이다만다른나라가동병
ᄒᆞ야로국을도아줄경우에는일
본을위ᄒᆞ야이전징에참셥ᄒᆞᆯ지
라도잔졉으로즁립위반ᄒᆞ는일
노는영국이전징에참셥ᄒᆞ라
고나셜리가업슬줄로싱각ᄒᆞ노
라로국도그싱각이다잇스니그
렷쳐아너ᄒᆞ면자긔나라에잇는
쓸만ᄒᆞᆫ군함들을모다져러케급
히극동에파송ᄒᆞᆯ리가잇스리어
결말에논쟁졍문제롤론란ᄒᆞᆯ더
이라이문제에ᄃᆡᄒᆞ야이쓰현워
드신문에말ᄒᆞ엿스되
만일일본이능히외채롤연속ᄒᆞ
야엇을것곳더라도금년팔구월
이면그금위본화가업셔질것이
오만일외채롤다시못엇을것갓
ᄒᆞ면삼ᄉᆞ월이면업셔질터이니
이번전쟁은이샹에말ᄒᆞᆫ긔한의
삼ᄉᆞ삭후ᄭᆞ지연속ᄒᆞᆷ을계우엇
으리라예언ᄒᆞ엿스니
그러ᄒᆞ면그ᄯᅢ는국민파산이될
터이나일본의채쥬되는영미량
국에셔나셔셔잔셥ᄒᆞ야그채권
의보중될만ᄒᆞᆫ것이업셔지는것
을막을러이라
그럿치마는그ᄯᅢ에는일본이후
망업는허명무실ᄒᆞᆫᄃᆡ위에잇슬
터이니불의지ᄉᆞ가아니어러난
다ᄒᆞ드ᄅᆡ도일본이실속업는영
광에허구ᄒᆞᆫ세월을보낼터이라
ᄒᆞ노라

뎐보

이십삼일동ᄉᆞ관착)

◯로민의진졍 아국반관작면
보에는동국포병공창긔계제작
쇼와밋기타공쟝의동밍파공은
그셰가더욱즁가ᄒᆞᆷ을승인ᄒᆞᆫ다
ᄒᆞ고
빅림각신문에는히동밍파공이
보통동밍파공이아니라혁명의
셩질을가진자ㅣ라고의론ᄒᆞ엿
고
동밍파공쟈는로국황뎨ᄭᅴ대기
여좌ᄒᆞᆫ청원셔롤샹ᄒᆞ엿스되션
동의경우는전졔졍치에의지ᄒᆞ
야압복ᄒᆞᆷ을피ᄒᆞ는노예의샹ᄐᆡ
에불과ᄒᆞ니궁즁과부즁에는국
가를문란ᄒᆞ고곤란ᄒᆞᆫ상히에ᄲᅡ
지게ᄒᆞ는도적의집합ᄒᆞᆫ단체인
ᄃᆡ필경국가에명예를쥬는전쟁
을담부ᄒᆞ고인민은국무에관ᄒᆞ
야그희망을밋을양달을피ᄒᆞ나
신등은이굿흔샹ᄐᆡ에잇셔셔는
찰아리죽을지언뎡싱존ᄒᆞᆯ뜻이
업는고로신등은황샹폐하가신
등의게민론에ᄃᆡ표ᄀᆡ관을주어
신등의이갓치가련ᄒᆞᆫ경우에잇
슴을청원ᄒᆞᆫ다ᄒᆞ며ᄯᅩ각종환란
의ᄉᆞ실을루술ᄒᆞ고최후에는왈
금신등이가취ᄒᆞᆯ길아두가지가
잇스니쳣재는(쟈유힝복)이둘
재는(불망구하)이라ᄒᆞ엿다라

잡보

◯고문 폐현 삼작일하오네
시에는군부고문관야진진무씨
가쇼졉이되엿고재작일하오베
시에는일본공ᄉᆞ림권죠씨가시
로나온경무청고문관환산즁쥰
씨와탁지고문관목하뎐죵티랑
씨를ᄃᆡ동ᄒᆞ고교수옥헌에셔
폐현ᄒᆞ엿고동일하오다셧시반
에는궁ᄂᆡ부고문관가등중웅씨
가쇼졉이되엿더라
◯협잡현로 전자에민영휘씨
와리갑씨가면답으로샹협ᄒᆞᆫᄉᆞ
는다시드른즉즁간에협잡ᄒᆞᆫ돈
ᄉᆞ샹이달로가된즉량씨는샹협
ᄒᆞᆯᄉᆞ건이업는고로파최예광화
ᄒᆞ엿다더라
◯이장비도사 궁ᄂᆡ부에셔유
강원ᄒᆞᆫ자ᄂᆡ에ᄉᆞ분을파옴긴후
ᄯᅵ비롤도사ᄒᆞ엿는ᄃᆡ 니하
전구십만량ᄂᆡ에유쥬춍오빅이
십장에면장에오빅오십량식쥰
급ᄒᆞ니합이이십팔만량ᄂᆡ에셔
오무쥬춍이천ᄉᆞ빅ᄉᆞ십ᄉᆞ장에
ᄆᆡ장에이빅오십량식출급ᄒᆞ니
합이륙십일만량이오무형
춍일천륙빅팔십일장에미장에
오십오량식출급ᄒᆞ니합이구만
이천ᄉᆞ빅오십오량이라
니하젼즁에부족전이팔만구쳔
ᄉᆞ빅오십오량이라더라
◯쳔왕환국 의친왕뎐하ᄭᅴ셔
현금미국에유학ᄒᆞ시는ᄃᆡ귀국
ᄒᆞ실ᄎᆞ로거이십일일에궁ᄂᆡ부
로뎐보ᄒᆞ셧더라

광고

TELEGRAMS.

(FROM JAPAN PAPERS)

London, Jan. 10.

General Kuropatkin has captured an important Japanese conv...

London, Jan. 17.

According to a St. Petersburg telegram, Admiral Rojestvensky has reported to the Czar that his Squadron has effected a juncture with the Folkersahm Squadron off Madagascar, and that he will proceed at once eastward without waiting for the Botrolosky Squadron, expecting to meet the latter near the equator.

London, Jan. 18.

Correspondents of French papers wire from St. Petersburg that the Baltic Fleet has sailed from Madagascar

Later.

The Russian Squadron has passed Perim.

London, Jan. 18.

The Novoe Vremya complains that Japan obtains telegraphic intelligence of the movements of Rojestvensky's warships, and demands that the British Government shall prevent the transmission of such telegrams. The journal quotes as a precedent the case of the telegrams sent from Jamaica to Santiago during the Spanish-American war.

London, Jan. 18

A great strike on the part of iron workers and kindred trades in St. Petersburg has commenced, and is assuming a threatening aspect. Fifty thousand men are already out, and as a result all works has ceased in the Government Dockyard on the Neva. The whole movement is being directed by most capable organisation.

London, Jan. 18.

The Russian troops in the neighbourhood of the Shaho have been panic stricken by information that the Japanese have laid mines in the vicinity of One Tree Hill (Putiloff). They anticipate that Marquis Oyama will shortly prepare for a general engagement.—Mainichi.

London, Jan. 18.

It is announced from St. Petersburg that General Kuropatkin intends to use cavalry extensively on the plains of the Hunho. General's Gripenberg's force will be entrusted with the direct offensive. General Kaulbars will menace the Japanese right wing. General Linievitch will attack the Japanese communications south of Mukden.

London, Jan. 18.

Botrolosky's Squadron, comprising six vessels, has passed Perim and proceeded in the direction of Jibutil.

Berlin, Jan. 18.

Russian Minister of Finance is arranging for the increase of duties on tobacco and spirits, while the Stamp Duty will also be increased.

Berlin, Jan. 18.

There are indications that the new Russian loan has been a success.—Mainichi.

Berlin, Jan. 18.

The circum-Baikal railway is now open for ordinary passenger traffic.—Mainichi.

London, Jan. 18, 8 P. M.

It is stated that the Czar has accepted the resignation of Prince Sviatopolk Mirski, Minister of the Interior

Berlin Jan. 18th.

In the Ruhrdistrickt in Germany—the largest coal-mining district there—a general strike amongst the coal miners has broken out; so far order is preserved.

London, Jan. 18.

The sudden demand for coal from Germany has resulted in a rise of prices in England, especially for bunker coal. Yesterday there was a rise in some cases to the extent of two shillings per ton.

Berlin via Shanghai, Jan. 18.

General Mischtschenko has returned from his successful raid with his Cossacks and joined the main army again. New skirmishes are reported as taking place near Shing-chang.

Newchwang, Jan. 18

The recent raid made by General Mestchenko with about 20 Sotnias of Cossacks took the Japanese completely by surprise; and had not the General stopped to attack old Newchwang 90 li from here up the river, he could have entirely captured everything and everybody in this place; which contains about 10 million yens' worth of supplies for the Japanese troops in the North. At old Newchwang there were 300 Japanese of which 294 were killed, wounded or taken prisoners; with a loss only of 16 men, whilst 6 got away and gave the alarm; so that, when the Cossacks arrived at Newchuitun (old Russian town) Railway station the Japanese were prepared in ambush and were able to check the raid and hold off the Russian advance guard until reinforcements came up, first 600 from Tashicho, and then another 900 from Haicheng. The artillery duel which ensued and lasted about four hours also gave everyone the alarm and resulted in little damage. The Russians had 12 light field guns with them, on galloping carriages, whilst the Japanese brought into position 18 guns of a heavier calibre. At the attack on the station the Cossacks lost 47 killed and wounded and the Japanese 11. Owing to the success of this Cossack raid, there are now about 4000 men in garrison at Newchwang 10,000 at Tashicho, and about 20,000 at Haicheng and Liaoyang. During the fighting some Russian shells fell near Bush Bros. Godown, and other premises at that end of the town, and the skirmish was witnessed by your correspondent and many others from the top story ofsome buildings near the Railway station. It is also reported here that a Japanese Brigadefrom Liaoyang attempted to make a counter attack upon the Russian extreme right flank between Moukden and Shin-mun-tun but were caught in land mines, broken into disorder by a bayonet charge, and then the remainder cut up by cavalry. The Japanese losses are stated to have been heavy, but the exact number is not known

Berlin Jan. 19.

In Tokio the strength of the Russian troops at the Shaho is calculated to be 370,000 men

Berlin Jan. 19th.

The situation in Russia is almost absolutely quiet and the danger of a revolution seem to be quite removed

WHAT NEXT?

Tokio Telegrams dated January 24th to local Japanese papers, contain the following:-

The Arsenal at Sebastopol has been destroyed by fire.

The present whereabouts of the Czar of Russia are not known. The Empress Dowager of Russia is also in hiding. 40,000 strikers from a neighbouring arsenal have entered St. Petersburg.

* * *

There are also other telegrams announcing strikes and rioting in St. Petersburg but beyond the fact that there is a great deal of internal discontent in Russia, they convey nothing. (Ed.)

Berlin suburbs are now served by a railless electric tramway-car deriving its motive power from overhead wires.

H. I. H. prince Eui-Chin who has been studying in Ameria, telegraphs that he intends to return to Korea shortly

The opium habit is said to be on the increase among Koreans and the police Department has asked that some restraint be placed on the indiscriminate sale, by Chinamen, of this article.

Yesterday at 4 P. M. Mr. Hayashi, the Japanese Minister, accompanied by Mr. Megata and Mr. Maruyama, the new police adviser, was received in audience by His Majesty.

JAPANESE LOAN BLUNDER.

The London issuing banks for the recent Japanese loan have discovered some curious mistakes in the printing of the bonds, which was done in New York. A number of the £100 and £200 bonds have different amounts in the watermark and in the text. The error will cause the banks an immense amount of trouble as the defective bonds will have to be called in and exchanged. The proportion of bonds in which the mistakes have been made is not yet known, but the £200 scrip forms a large proportion of the whole.

The following circular has been issued by the Yokohama Specie Bank and by Parr's Bank:—

"Dear Sir,—Japanese Loan.—We shall be obliged by your carefully examining the bonds delievered to you. We regret to say the printers in New York from whom we receive the bonds appear in some cases to have put amounts both in words and in figures in the text at variance with the denomination as expressed in the lower left-hand corner in the watermark and in the endorsement, and likewise to have made errors in printing the amount of the coupons. Should you find any of the bonds not in order, may we trouble you to return them forthwith for exchange?"

The Koreans in Hawaii have written to complain of their lack of a consul and and have offered to pay the expenses of a capable man.

Mr. Cho Pyŏng Ho, formly Minister for finance has been appointed to succeed Mr. Kim Syŏng Veun as vice president of the cabinet and Mr. Min Yŏng Ki will again become Minister for finance.

Mr. Yu Byung Yul the magistrate of Kŏwon left for his district but was unable to proceed north of Gensan and has in consequence returned to Seoul. Presumably the Japanese would not allow him to pass.

Perhaps the following despatch from the Japanese Minister to the Home Office will help to explain the foregoing paragraph. The Japanese General at Ham-heung requests that Pak Keui Ho, police inspector at Gensan, who is a very capable man be appointed magistrate at Kŏwon.

The Japanese Minister has notified the Foreign Office that a Japanese naval detachment will commence surveying the southeast coast of Korea. Flags will be erected in various places and the rocks will be daubed with white. The Foreign Office is requested to arrange for all possible assistance to be given to the party

It has long been a matter of common knowledge that Japanese pawnbrokers are willing or even anxious to accept from improvident Korean soldiers, as pledges, their arms, ammunition and accoutrements. We are glad to see that this matter has at last been taken official notice of, the chief of police having asked the governor of Seoul to request the Japanese consul to prohibit his subjects from making loans against articles of this nature

MILITARY ORDERS.

On the ground of "military necessity" General Hasegawa has issued the following proclamation with regard to Ham Kyeng province:—

It is forbidden to remove property or to buy, sell or mortgage ground within the following boundaries:—

(1) From the boundary of Sonching Ku to a line at the South of Yeung Heung.

(2) To the East of Yeung Heung, Kowŏn, Sachikpong, Kamochong and No-in-to.

(3) On the north, No-in-ti, An-Byun, and Apnyong Doug.

(4) Baik-kwŏn-li (presumably a Japanese settlement) near Gensan is alone excepted.

Anyone violating these provisions will be punished by martail law.

There seems to be a good deal of friction in the districts north of Gensan on account of the Japanese attempt to control the collection of taxes. What has the "Daihan-Ilpo" to say to this? It was not long ago that it strongly condemned the Russians for doing the same thing.

The magistrate of Wiju, having received instructions to disperse any Tong Haks who might be in his district, reports that there are no Tong Haks but plenty of Il-chin-hoi people whom he is punishing. The Japanese Military authorities are protecting then but the magistrate is still taking measures to disperse them.

The "Chekuk Shimmun" which was once raided by the Japanese for alleged anti-Japanese views is to expand considerably It is said to have the Emperor's support and the paper is to be distributed in the ratio of one copy to every ten houses throughout Korea. The magistrates of the different districts are to collect payment. We do not think much of this arrangement.

Speculation is rife regarding the destination of the tow-boat Kougnam, which left Shanghai on the 6th inst. deeply loaded (presumably coal) and with a large deck cargo of coal. Local opinion has it that she is proceeding to the assistance of a Russian destroyer which was unable to get into Tsingtau owing to the presence of the Japanese fleet outside the harbour and which now lies at anchor somewhere to the northward of Shaweishan. The alternative is, that she is proceeding to look for a dismasted junk.

Bekanntmachung.

Die Bekanntmachungen der Eintragungen in das hiesige Deutsche Handelsregister erfolgen im Jahre 1905 durch den "**Ostasiatischen Lloyd**" und die "**The Korea Daily News.**"

Söul, den 27. Dezember 1904.

Der Kaiserlich Deutsche Minister-Resident und General-Consul.

(L. S.) gez. von Saldern.

The Korea Daily News.

Issued at 5 P. M. daily except Sundays.

Rate of Subscription:—
Per Year,............Yen 25.
Per Quarter,..........Yen 7.
Per Month,..........Yen 2.50.

Postage in Korea not charged extra.
Postage abroad charged extra.

Advertisements, 50 sen per day for 1 inch or less.
5 yen per month per inch.
50 yen per year per inch.

All communications to

E. T. BETHELL,
Editor and Publisher,
Pak-tong, Seoul.

THE COMING BATTLE.

The long period of inactivity on the part of the two main armies facing each, other at the Shaho is now to come to an end. Tokio advices say that Field Marshal Oyama is preparing for a battle on a large scale which he regards as imminent.

We are not told whether the Japanese army is to take the offensive or whether Oyama's preparations are the result of a conviction that the Russians are about to make an attack on a grand scale. Since the capitulation of Port Arthur there has not been time for much in the way of reinforcements to reach the northern army from that direction, and as Kuropatkin has been steadily receiving fresh drafts of men and artillery from Europe it seems likely that the present time for a battle is not Oyama's own choosing.

Had he fought earlier, Kuropatkin would have had fewer men while it is probable that a further delay of two or three weeks would have enabled at least one division from Port Arthur to be added to Oyama's army.

There remains one other explanation of Oyama's decision to attack. It may be that the Russian flanking movements on both wings of his army are of a more serious nature than we have been led to believe and that the Japanese are driven to make a grand attack by way of reply.

Whatever the leading up to it there can be no doubt that the coming battle will be fraught with the gravest consequence. This is not the weather in which to bivouac in the open, yet that will most certainly be the fate of one, if not both, armies. It will be bad enough for uninjured men but the condition of the wounded will be too terrible to think of.

It is impossible to arrive at any idea of what the results of the coming battle will be. The communications of both armies are in excellent order but the Japanese lines seem to be more open to attack than the Russian. In the earlier battles the Russians lost heavily through failing to efficiently mask their batteries thus providing a splendid target for the hidden Japanese artillery. The Japanese also, by their surprise tactics frequently caught the Russians at a disadvantage.

We are now told that in the later engagements the Russians displayed equal skill with the Japanese in masking their batteries and there can be no doubt that experience will have made them more cautious against surprises. Although it is impossible to give either belligerent credit for the greater courage it seems to be agreed on all sides that the Japanese soldier with his greater intelligence and resourcefulness is more efficient than the Russian.

The weather will be a great factor in this battle but victory will probably rest with the biggest battalions and this is a subject upon which there is no reliable information available.

THE RUSSIAN RAID

The Mainichi correspondent at Moji has sent his paper the following statements made by Japanese officers who have just returned there from the front:—The Russians who made a raid on Haicheng through neutral territory attempted to damage a Japanese train between Haicheng and Anshantien by placing explosives on the railway lines. An explosion took place when the train, which was proceeding at full speed, was midway between the above two stations, and the Russians then fired volleys upon it from an ambush. The engine and two cars were damaged a little but the train succeeded in returning. On receiving the news, the Japanese garrisons at Anshantien and Haicheng went in pursuit of the enemy, with the result that three Russian Cavalry were captured by the Japanese, the rest succeeding in effecting their escape. The damage done to the track, which extended over about eighteen feet, was at once repaired. Explosives were found at two other points on the line. The Russians, having met little success in this locality, are believed to have advanced toward Newchwang and Haicheng. Officers who left the Shaho only a few days ago state that the Russians who appeared near Anshanten, Tashichiao and Neuchaton, on the 11th, comprised Infantry, Cavalry and Artillery, and numbered about 3,000. According to the natives, about a brigade of Russian Cavalry was in their rear. They went first to the vicinity of Neuchaton, passing through the neutral district west of the river Liao. Subsequently they appear to have sent a detachment toward Tashichiao for the purpose of destroying the railway, while the main force was concentrated near Inkao. An artillery position was established at a point about 3,000 metres from Inkao, and an attempt was made to cut off the Japanese commissariat quarters. Being repulsed by the Japanese fire, they returned to the neutral district. Another officer who has returned from the front states that the Russians attempted to destroy the Japanese railway and telegraph communications. A number of Cossacks in Chinese costumes have been at Anshantien lately. On the 7th, at 1 A. M., about one hundred and twenty of the enemy suddenly appeared between Anshantien and Haicheng, and attempted to blow up the railway line under cover of the darkness. A train carrying Japanese troops approached at full speed and failed to notice the warning of a labourer, who waved a flag in order to stop it. It consequently ran over the explosives but fortunately sustained little damage.

With regard to the recent attacks by Russian cavalry on the Japanese communications in the Newchwang neighbourhood, reports from Peking state that the Cossacks commenced their ride from Pehchipau, a place about 17 miles west of Sinmintun. They thence travelled down well to the westward of the Liao and they finally crossed the latter river on the ice. It is said that Lieut.-Colonel Miyazaki distinguished himself greatly by his defence of Neuchaton. Had his force, a comparatively small body, been driven from Neuchaton, the Russians might not only have cut the railway between Inkao and Tashichiao but also might have pushed on to Inkao, and possibly scored a signal success by burning the Japanese commissariat station at the latter place. Colonel Miyazaki's men had thrown up entrenchments, and behind these they waited until the Russian cavalry came within a hundred and fifty metres, when they opened a withering fire, emptying some 200 saddles and driving back the Cossacks in confusion.

A NICE MAN.

The infernal machine which John William Jago devised to set fire to the "Gothland" a coasting vessl, when three days out on the high seas, was, according to his own confession at the Liverpool Assizes, conceived in Dartmoor Prison.

Jago is a man into whose eventful past have been crowded bold adventures and audacious crimes. Besides having served a sentence of fifteen months' imprisonment for forgery, he was sentenced to five years' penal servitude for having robbed the mails while acting as chief officer on board an Atlantic liner.

A short, thick-set, bearded man, with a clever face, Jago, who has been a lieutement in the Naval Reserve and a master of many ships, made a clever defence.

The allegation was that, having insured a wooden packing case for £400, he filled it with an inflammable assortment of fire-lighters, charcoal, paper and clothing saturated with creosote oil and sprinkled over with a mixture of sulphur and and nitre. In this he placed an india-rubber tubing containing sulphuric acid and nitre, which gradually ate its way through the rubber and came in contact with a glass tube containing chlorate of potash.

This caused an explosion and set fire to the box in the ship's hold when three days out on the voyage from Liverpool to Hamburg. The fire was put out at sea, and the box, the contents of which were only partly destroyed, was analysed.

Jago's alternative theory was ingenious. It was that when ruminating in his cell in Dartmoor gaol the idea of a non-deviating ship's compass occured to him, and he evolved a new patent which, on coming out of prison, he began to develope. He took a small house at Egremont and lived there alone, finding work as a labourer under the district council, and making, in his spare time, a number of chemical experiments.

He produced letters from foreign legations to show that he had been in correspondence over some patent and said he had been advised not to sell the compass for £1,000. Among other things he had discovered how to preserve milk in fluids by means of charcoal, and called a clerical gentleman to prove that he tasted the preservative.

He determined to take his compass, of which he had now made a working model, to New York, but as, owing to his record, it would be difficult to book a passage from Liverpool, he determined to go via Hamburg, and was sending his packing case on ahead. He placed the working model inside, and threw in the charcoal and the nitre and sulphur simply because they would come in useful for the experiments in America.

As he failed to account for the absence of any tangible sign of mechanism in the box, however, the jury concluded that the much-vaunted working model devised in prison for improving navigation was nothing less than a diabolical instrument of destruction.

Mr. Justice Phillimore, who characterised insurance frauds as the worst kind of frauds because they involved the loss of property and often of life, said that the best service the prisoner could render was to act as a finger-post to warn others. He sentenced him to fifteen years' penal servitude.—"Daily Mail."

COUNT OKUMA ON MEDIATION RUMOURS.

It is stated says the "Kobe Herald" that Count Okuma recently made some observations to a journalist as to the rumours concerning prospects of peace. He is represented to have said that the reports that Russia has made overtures for peace are intrinsically absurd. He stated that even if Russia was anxious for peace, she would not make the fact known herself. Overtures for peace would be tantamount to a proposal to surreuder on Russia's part. Some European countries may be entertaining a desire to try mediation at a favourable opportunity, the Count thought, and they may formulate a plan of trying arbitration for the purpose of enabling Russia to preserve her prestige as a great Power. He added that if by some chance the Powers were placed in the position of interfering, it would prove a serious matter, as it might result in establishing a precedent for deciding all Eastern questions by a conference of the Powers. England, Japan's ally, would never listen to such a proposal, he thought, so that as long as the determination of the Japanese remains firm there is nothing to be feared. He considered it as a reassuring indication that the Japanese people high and low were strongly determined to assail Russia until she sued for peace.

The Korea Daily News.

VOL. II, WEDNESDAY, JANUARY 25, 1905. No. 19

大韓每日申報
대한미일신보

(뎨이권이십호) (금요일) 일쳔구빅오년 일월 이십칠일

본샤고빅

이 신보는 영어와 한어로 셔계 미
일 출판ᄒᆞᆸ

신문가

한쟝 엽두돈오푼
일삭도 엽두량닷돈
우표가미 삭당닷돈
다섯돈으로밧숩
광고료는

귀한의 쟝단과 ᄌᆞ형의 다쇼로 ᄌᆞᆼ
감ᄒᆞ되 렴가로 밧을터이오 며 오
린지 아녀 대한사람마다 다 이 신
문을 보실터이니 광고 내시기를
원ᄒᆞ시는이들은 우리 신문샤에
와서 면약ᄒᆞ심을 희망ᄒᆞᆸ

○발힝소 ᄇᆞ동 대한미일신보
사 발혀한 교 영례 젼 영국인 셜필
림 쟝자 리오

사쟝 영국인 (빅셜)

평양 티리졈

○평양효동사는 권미보씨로 우
리 신문 환매 티리인을 뎡ᄒᆞ엿
시ᄉᆞ오니 평양에 계신 구람 코져 ᄒᆞ
는 쳠군ᄌᆞ는 ᄒᆞᆫ 티리졈에 왕
림ᄒᆞ와 면회ᄒᆞ시ᄋᆞᆸ

사고

○우리 대한미일신보의 목뎍은
대한의 안녕질서에 관ᄒᆞᆫ 모든 대
목에 티ᄒᆞ야 논공평ᄒᆞᆫ 변론을 쥬
쟝ᄒᆞᆷ이라 우리 동신원의 담보는
신문보셔는 쳠군ᄌᆞ의 계ᄒᆞᆫ 샹보
도ᄒᆞ리며 편지를 긔셔ᄒᆞ여 주시
는이 논셩명과 번디를 계이 붓치
시기를 희망ᄒᆞ오니 이 거슨 신문
샹에 긔재ᄒᆞ란 는 거시 아니오 다
만 구히 신용ᄒᆞ는 증거를 숨고자 ᄒᆞ
ᄒᆞᆷ이라 긔자는 아모 긔셔 던지 긔 과
지 ᄒᆞᆷ을 뢰 차 ᄒᆞ는 권리를 가 졋 스
나 뢰 차 ᄒᆞᆫ 는 리유를 말 ᄒᆞᆯ 터 이 오
며 공 중 평 화 를 문 란 케 ᄒᆞ ᄂᆞᆫ 듯 ᄒᆞᆫ
긔 셔 는 의 례 히 밧 지 안 캣 숩 나 이
다

●본샤셜시 이 리로 신문을 미 양
우 례 로 분 젼 ᄒᆞ 와 례 젼 부 의 임 의
로 젼 ᄒᆞ든 ᄉᆞ 로 면 곳 에 는 ᄒᆞ 노 ᄒᆞ 게
젼 ᄒᆞ 기 도 ᄒᆞ 며 ᄒᆞ 면 쳘 거 슬 ᄒᆞ 년 밥
에 젼 ᄒᆞ 기 도 ᄒᆞ 며 ᄒᆞ 야 나 젼 ᄒᆞ 는
곳 도 잇 다 ᄒᆞ 와 우 리 신 문 을 ᄉᆞ 랑
ᄒᆞ 야 구 람 ᄒᆞ 시 는 쳠 군 ᄌᆞ 의 계 랑
티 ᄒᆞ 야 미 우 미 안 ᄒᆞ 음 기 로 지 계 공
은 분 젼 인 을 두 고 미 일 존 이 젼
ᄒᆞ 며 ᄒᆞ 나 젼 ᄒᆞ 거 나 늣 게 거 나 ᄒᆞᆫ
폐 가 엽 도 록 ᄒᆞ 랴 ᄒᆞ 오 니 ᄒᆞ 야 니

젼ᄒᆞ거ᄂᆞᆫ ᄒᆞ 늣게 젼ᄒᆞ거나 ᄒᆞᆫ 일
이 잇스면 본샤로 통긔ᄒᆞ여 주심
을 희망ᄒᆞᆸ

뎐보

비엔나 발 일월십ᄉᆞ일

○로기중계 로국탁지대신렵
스도프빅이 셩괴득보에 잇는 엿
뎐대ᄉᆞ의계 말ᄒᆞ되 로국은 이번
젼쟁에 티ᄒᆞ야 미 삼국의 중계는
밧지 아니ᄒᆞ겟다 ᄒᆞ엿고 오 디 리
외교사회에서는 셩각ᄒᆞ되 비룡
미국 디통령루스벨트씨 가 일로
케젼쟁에 중계ᄒᆞ랴 ᄒᆞ나 능히 그 리
되지 못ᄒᆞ리라 ᄒᆞ더라

론돈 발 동월십륙일

○일본이 히군근거디 를 쟝 ᄒᆞ 엿
단 말 로 국 신 문 노 보 브 레 마 에
자 바 면 보 를 게 제 ᄒᆞ 엿 는 티 일 본
이 말 나 안 제 도 중 에 영 국 령 디 에
린 부 안 서 음 에 히 군 근 거 디 를 쟝
지 ᄒᆞ 고 그 녈 을 숨 기 랴 고 뎐 보 를 쟝
신 엿 다 ᄒᆞ 엿 더 라

동 디 발 동 월 십 칠 일

○ 법 국 니 각 의 불 신 임 법 국 의
회 에 서 니 각 불 신 임 투 표 를 동 의
ᄒᆞ 야 가 란 ᄒᆞᆫ 자 가 이 빅 팔 십 구 인
이 오 부 란 ᄒᆞᆫ 자 가 이 빅 칠 십 구 인
디 라 법 국 니 각 은 ᄉᆞ 직 ᄒᆞ 리 라 ᄒᆞ
라

론 돈 발 일 월 십 이 일

○ 로 쟝 통 쟝 의 풍 셜 셩 피 득 보
에 서 풍 셜 이 젼 파 ᄒᆞ 는 티 로 국 쟝
만 부 종 히 비 이 로 쥣 긴 대 쟝 의 형 등 을
평 을 ᄒᆞ 엿 디 ᄒᆞ 며 또 구 로 팟 긴 대
쟝 은 군 ᄉᆞ 를 디 비 보 니 랍 낫 다 는
말 이 잇 더 라

동 디 발 동 월 십 삼 일

○ 로 함 발 힝 로 국 히 군 대 쟝 불
로 브 스 기 씨 의 함 티 는 소 ᄉᆞ 운 하
를 셔 나 서 지 부 티 로 향 ᄒᆞ 야 발 힝
ᄒᆞ 엿 다 더 라

동 디 발 동 월 십 ᄉᆞ 일

○ 로 국 이 히 군 근 거 디 를 샷 단 말
로 국 이 불 픽 함 디 의 근 거 디 를 사
다 긔 ᄂᆞᆫ 위 ᄒᆞ 야 인 도 양 에 ᄒᆞᆫ 셤 을 샷
린 함 디 가 잇 ᄂᆞᆫ 티 그 서 음 에 서 분 샷
다 더 라 부 속 군 함 들 오 긔 를 기 를

빅 림 발 동 월 십 오 일

○ 영 뎍 호 의 영 뎍 졍 회 의 조 직
에 곳 된 다 는 말 이 잇 스 며 영 뎍 간
뎌 쳔 밀 ᄒᆞᆫ 교 의 가 날 마 다 느 리 간
다 더 라

미 샤 삼 일 오 후 오 시 발

○로국의 대분란 일쟉 아 론 돈
셔 발 ᄒᆞᆫ 뎐 보 에 왈 로 국 셔 울 에 갓
신문샤의 쥐 룡 도 도 쟝 ᄒᆞᆫ 동 맹 파 공
에 중 가 ᄒᆞ 고 (후 로 우 ᄶᅥ 셩) 이 란
자 ㅣ 이 일 만 오 쳔 명 의 운 동 자 를 령
솔 ᄒᆞ 고 교 쇠 구 병 과 충 돌 ᄒᆞ 야 샹
샹 이 만 교 죡 도 는 쟝 히 를 렴 표 망
을 셜 치 ᄒᆞ 고 오 만 명 의 군 티 는 기
힝 당 을 쏘 아 죽 이 는 중 이 라 더 라
(이 십 ᄉᆞ 일 오 후 일 시 ᄉᆞ 십
분 발

○ 젼 로 지 분 격 동 뎐 을 거 ᄒᆞᆫ 즉
본 월 이 십 이 일 에 아 라 사 셔 울 에
셔 로 동 자 와 교 셰 구 병 이 졍 투 ᄒᆞᆫ
결 과 로 죽 은 자 ㅣ 일 쳔 오 륙 빅 명
과 부 샹 ᄌᆞ ᄉᆞ 오 쳔 명 에 이 르 럿 숨
으 로 젼 로 국 의 인 민 은 분 격 젼 로
ᄒᆞᆫ 중 이 라 더 라

외보

○로국에 산 섬오이를본돈서발
ᄒᆞᆫ 뎐 보 를 거 ᄒᆞᆫ 즉 로 국 대 쟝 며 산
이 이 금 년 도 에 샨 표 초 안 을 발 표
ᄒᆞ 엿 는 티 그 초 안 을 거 ᄒᆞᆫ 즉 일 쳔
구 빅 오 년 의 경 비 예 산 액 은 젼 년
도 와 비 교 ᄒᆞ 즉 진 티 륙 쳔 오 빅 오 십
만 류 가 감 쇼 ᄒᆞ 엿 스 며 그 감 ᄒᆞᆷ 은
대 기 대 쟝 셩 과 및 계 신 셩 으 로 편
대 쟝 셩 과 및 계 신 셩 으 로 편
아 계 ᄒᆞ 엿 스 며 일 쳔 만 류 는 서 빅 리
아 텰 도 젼 을 불 젼 으 로 부 셜 ᄒᆞ 기
위 ᄒᆞ 야 편 졔 ᄒᆞ 며 또 빅 팔 십 만 류
는 (바 이 가 루) 붕 젼 의 등 별 경 비
로 에 산 ᄒᆞ 엿 스 니
우 에 산 에 는 츄 경 비 를 산 립 ᄒᆞ 엿
는 티 로 국 졔 졍 과 및 화 폐 계 도 는
심 히 견 고 ᄒᆞ 야 지 나 는 젼 쟁 후 라 도
그 신 용 의 잇 숨 을 명 빅 ᄒᆞ 게 위 ᄒᆞᆷ
이 라 더 라

○ 년 로 무 용 본 월 십 ᄉᆞ 일 일 본
에 포 뢰 된 로 국 (아 례 산 더 우 이
지 나 면 논) 중 쟝 은 쳘 신 여 셰 의
로 쟝 으 로 흔 슈 령 이 셤 히 걷 여 결
곳 교 심 히 곤 핍 ᄒᆞ 야 샴 쳥 리 목 힝
쟝 ᄒᆞ 는 티 두 번 이 나 쉬 더 라 ᄒᆞ 며 동
쟝 군 은 동 부 셔 빅 리 아 조 격 보 병
대 쳘 ᄉᆞ 단 쟝 이 오 그 아 날 은 히 군
군 의 로 쟈 쳔 에 한 국 인 쳔 히 면 에
가 격 침 된 (코 렛) ᄒᆞ 에 승 함 ᄒᆞ 엿
헌 금 은 본 국 에 오 잇 다 더 라

잡보

○ 로 중 셩 남 고 양 군 ᄉᆞ 는 리 소
사 가 로 잉 티 ᄒᆞ 야 말 삭 에 셔 을 을
나 오 는 티 돈 의 문 밧 월 암 동 로 변
에 셔 히 복 셩 남 ᄒᆞ 엿 다 더 라

○송긔도주 졔 작 일 초 혼 에 창
외 동 비 거 리 에 셔 두 사 룸 이 인 력
거 를 라 고 급 히 초 동 근 쳐 에 와 셔
죵 은 뽈 목 에 ᄂᆞ 리 급 히 도 망 ᄒᆞ 엿
는 티 그 빅 는 하 오 쳘 서 나 되 며 사
룸 의 얼 골 도 분 명 치 못 ᄒᆞ 고 공 연
이 멧 시 간 칭 만 히 비 ᄒᆞ 엿 다 더

○ 죵 중 됴 사 작 일 에 경 무 쳥 에
서 슌 검 의 죵 속 과 보 종 과 슌 검 다
란 인 넌 조 됴 를 셩 칙 ᄒᆞ 라 고 ᄒᆞ 엿 디 더

○ 궁 민 진 휼 남 촌 에 빈 한 사 룸
의 졍 을 측 ᄒᆞ 호 ᄒᆞ 야 가 는 티 그 리 유
는 진 휼 금 을 분 급 ᄒᆞᆫ 다 ᄒᆞ 는 티 졍
잇 고 빈 한 ᄒᆞᆫ 자 만 쥬 고 징 엽 는 자
는 셩 최 에 젹 지 도 아 니 ᄒᆞᆫ 다 더 라

○ 리 씨 셜 교 리 용 익 씨 가 학 교
셜 시 ᄒᆞ 기 에 열 심 ᄒᆞ 는 티 히 학 교
의 챤 셩 쟝 은 영 친 왕 뎐 하 계 셔
리 교 서 ᄒᆞ 시 가 챤 셩 부 쟝 은 원 슌 군
지 쥐 완 씨 교 피 쳔 ᄒᆞ 엿 더 라

○ 종 로 시 샹 종 로 에 볼 마 디 나
무 신 섯 고 ᄃᆞ 리 와 종 일 트 록 버 린 서
서 팔 나 고 잇 는 나 무 쟝 ᄉᆞ 들 을 금
ᄒᆞ 야 다 른 티 로 옴 겨 가 서 서 계 ᄒᆞ
엿 더 니 일 분 샹 민 이 와 서 종 로 에
젼 을 버 리 고 잇 스 미 이 거 순 금 지
ᄒᆞᆷ 수 엽 는 지 라 나 무 쟝 ᄉᆞ 들 금 ᄒᆞ
는 거 시 도 로 히 무 의 ᄒᆞ 다 ᄒᆞ 야 나
무 쟝 ᄉᆞ 들 을 도 로 종 로 에 와 서 버
려 셧 게 ᄒᆞ 엿 더 라

○ 닉 디 졔 임 셜 닉 부 티 신 됴 병
식 씨 는 졔 임 된 다 ᄒᆞ 며 그 티 에 는
리 지 용 씨 가 피 임 ᄒᆞᆫ 다 더 라

○ 검 ᄉᆞ 슈 뢰 보 승 교 지 ᄉᆞ 는 쟝
보 형 씨 는 변 단 으 로 졍 쟝 ᄒᆞ 디 가
한 셩 졔 관 소 에 피 착 ᄒᆞ 엿 더 니 보
방 이 되 엿 는 티 검 ᄉᆞ ᄒᆞ 종 환 씨 의
게 뢰 물 을 주 엇 다 ᄒᆞ 야 쟝 가 는 사
헌 중 이 오 ᄒᆞ 검 ᄉᆞ 는 룸 경 이 된 다
더 라

○ 일 쳥 경 관 찬 셩 경 무 쳥 에 서
오 서 닉 에 우 톰 을 외 국 우 톰 모 양
으 로 수 리 ᄒᆞ 기 로 ᄒᆞ 는 티 그 경 비
를 부 득 불 그 톰 을 먹 는 사 룸 들 의 게
계 비 렴 ᄒᆞ 미 일 쳥 량 국 경 무 관 과
교 섭 ᄒᆞᆫ 즉 다 찬 셩 ᄒᆞ 야 비 렴 을 곳
거 비 기 로 ᄒᆞ 엿 다 더 라

○ 고 양 군 슈 츌 빈 고 양 군 에 서
일 젼 에 셜 회 ᄒᆞ 야 빈 가 를 호 가 를
수 휘 티 서 이 동 젼 에 빅 셩 들 이 ᄒᆞᆫ
뎨 에 서 의 지 엽 시 방 황 ᄒᆞ 는 지 라
간 슈 리 쥬 현 씨 가 미 ᄒᆞ 에 오 빅 량
식 츌 금 으 로 주 예 은 졍 이 칭 송 ᄒᆞ
더 라
더 라

UNION INSURANCE SOCIETY OF CANTON.

Head office Hongkong.
Marine risks underwritten at current rates.

Agents in Chemulpo,
E. MEYER & Co.

COMPAGNIE DES MESSAGERIES MARITIMES.

Fortnightly Direct Service.

For Marseilles
via Ports.
Sailing from Yokohama
Calling at Kobe,
Shanghai, Hongkong, Saigon, Singapore,
Colombo, Djibonti, Suez, Port Said
and Marseilles.

For particulars apply to
HOLME RINGER & Co.,
Chemulpo.

HAYASHIDA & CO.,

16 MYENG DONG, CHIN KO KAI, SEOUL.
BRANCH OFFICE AT CHEMULPO.

Money changers, Coal and Wood Merchants, Express Agents.

We are agents for the Pyeng-yang Coal Company and the Karazu Coal Company of Japan. We have the best quality of both anthracite and bituminous coal, and prompt execution of orders is our speciality. Firewood of all kinds kept in stock. Full weight guaranteed. Money of all denominations exchanged at current rates. Parcels received for all parts.

CHINA MUTUAL LIFE INS. OC.

Most favourable terms to policy holders.

Benefit system unsurpassed

HOLME RINGER & Co.
Agents, Chemulpo.

C. P. R.

CANADIAN PACIFIC RAILWAY COMPANY'S ROYAL MAIL STEAMSHIP LINE.

THE FAST ROUTE BETWEEN CHINA, JAPAN, AND EUROPE VIA CANADA AND THE UNITED STATES.

Route from Hongkong via Shanghai, Nagasaki (Inland Sea of Japan) Kobe, Yokohama Victoria and Vancouver.

Twin Screw Empress Steamship—6,000 Tons—Speed 19 knots.

PROPOSED SAILING FROM YOKOHAMA.
R. M. S. Empress of India.
R. M. S. Empress of Japan.
R. M. S. Empress of China.
R. M. S. Athenian.
R. M. S. Tartar.

Special reduction (first class only) granted to members of the Military, Naval, Diplomatic and Civil services and to Missionaries.

Passengers have choice of ten routes across the Continent of America and have privilege of travelling by any Atlantic Steamship Line.

Round the World passage tickets in connection with the P. and O. S. N., North German Lloyd and Messageries Co.'s **£125.**

All rates payable at current rate of exchange.

For further information, Tickets, Guide Books, etc., apply to

HOLME, RINGER & Co., AGENTS,
Chemulpo.

Grand Hotel,

(Formerly the Station Hotel)

Near the Railway Terminus, West Gate Seoul.

The Best Hotel in Korea.
Handsome new Building.
Fine Airy Rooms
Excellent Cuisine.
Terms Moderate.
Special terms to Missionaries
and to permanent boarders.

Electric cars within 2 minutes' walk.

W. H. EMBERLEY.
Proprietor

EVERY FACILITY.

In connection with Life Assurance Business is afforded by

The Standard Life Assurance Co.,

One of the largest and wealthiest of the Provident Institutions of the United Kingdom Forms of Application and all information will be promptly afforded on application.

10 CENTS A DAY.

Not a very large expenditure is it? But it is sufficient to secure for a man of 30 a policy with the STANDARD LIFE OFFICE for

$1323.

For all particulars of rates, etc., apply to

Holme, Ringer & Co.,
Agents, Chemulpo.

THE NEW YORK LIFE INSURANCE COMPANY.

Have you ever been declined by any Company?

Are you engaged in a specially hazardous occupation?

Have you heard of the New York Life Insurance Company's New Classifications for this class of Risks?

If not, send your date of birth, occupation and particulars of rejection, if any to

E. MEYER & Co.,
Agents, Chemulpo.

MITSUI BUSSAN KAISHA.
(MITSUI & Co.)

MITSUI GINKO.
(MITSUI BANK.)

The Bank is owned by the members of the Mitsui Family, who, as partners, assume an unlimited responsibility for all liabilities of the Bank:—

Capital........................Yen 5,000,000
Reserve Fund.................. " 5,600,000

HEAD OFFICE, TOKYO.

LONDON OFFICE, 34 LIME ST., E. C.

BRANCHES AND AGENCIES:-
New York, San Francisco, Hamburg, Bombay, Singapore, Manila Hongkong, Amoy, Chefoo, Tientsin.

Kobe, Hakodate, Yokohama, Kure, Yokosuka, Moji, Shimonoseki, Miike, Wakamatsu, Nagasaki, Kuchinotsu, Karatsu, Sasebo, Misume, Taipeh, &c.

Telegraphic Address for all the Offices:
"MITSUI."
A. B. C. AND A. I CODES USED.

Contractors of Coal
To the Imperial Japanese Navy. Arsenals and Railway Bureau, Principal Railway Companies and Industrial Work, Home and Foreign Mail and Freight Steamers.

Sole Proprietors
Of the famous Miike, Tagawa and Yamano Coal Mines.

Sole Agents
For the sale of Fukumo, Hokoku, Ichimura Kanoda, Mannoura, Onoura, Ostuji, Sonoda Tsubaruro, Yoshinotani, Yoshio, Yurokibura and other coals.

YANGTSE INSURANCE ASSOCIATION, LTD.

The undersigned, having been appointed agents for the above company, are prepared to issue policies and pay losses on marine risks at regular rates.

E. MEYER & Co.,
Agents, Chemulpo.

AMERICAN KOREAN ELECTRIC CO.

Light and Power.

Main Office: Electric Building, Chong No.

RAILWAY DEPARTMENT.

OPERATING CARS BETWEEN EAST AND WEST GATE, EVERY TEN MINUTES:—

First Car leaves East Gate at 7:00 A. M. First Car leaves R. R. Station at 7:25 A. M
Last Car " East Gate at 8.40 P. M. Last " " R. R. Station at 9.05 P.M

OPERATING CARS BETWEEN EAST GATE AND IMPERIAL TOMB TERMINUS, EVERY TWENTY MINUTES:—
CONNECTING WITH EVERY ALTERNATE CAR ARRIVING AT EAST GATE FROM CHONG NO.

First Car leaves East Gate for Tomb at 7:10 A. M.
" " " Tomb for East Gate at 7:30 A. M.
Last " " East Gate for Tomb at 7:50 P. M.
" " " Tomb for East Gate at 8:10 P. M.

OPERATING CARS BETWEEN CHONG NO AND YUNG SAN RIVER EVERY TWELVE MINUTES:—

First Car leaves Chong No for South Gate at 7:12 A. M.
" " " Chong No for Yung San at 7:36 A. M.
" " " South Gate for Chong No at 7:20 A. M.
" " " Yung San for Chong No at 8:09 A. M.
Last " " South Gate for Chong No 9:00 P. M.
" " " Yung San for Chong No at 8.45. P. M.

SPECIAL PRIVATE CARS FURNISHED TO SUIT CONVENIENCE OF PATRONS. PRICES ON APPLICATION AT HEAD OFFICE.

LIGHTING DEPARTMENT.

Where less than 250 candle power of light is used, the rate per month will be
Per 16 candle power incandescent lamp,—All night.—Yen 2.50.
32 candle power incandescent lamp:—All night:—Yen 4.00.
50 candle power incandescent lamp:—All night:—Yen 6.00.
150 " " " " " " " 10.00.
1200 ,, ,, enclosed arc ,, ,, ,, ,, 20.00.

Where more than 250 candle power of light is used, a Meter will be installed, if requested:—Rent of Meter Yen 2.00 per month. Rate of charges by meter reading:—Two Sen per Ampere per hour. (Approximately this is equal to about One Sen per 16 C. P. lamp per hour) Minimum monthly charge where meter is installed, Yen 20.00 per month, which includes rental of meter.

Estimates for installing lights furnished on application

An assortment of chandeliers always on hand.

K. Murakami.
Photograph Studio
Chinkokai, Seoul.

Printing, Developing and Enlargement, of Photographs always Undertaken.

Korean Views and Pictures Illustrating Native Customs always on Sale,

---

THE OSAKA SHOSEN KAISHA.

Boats frequently on the berth for Chinnampo.

REGULAR SAILINGS BETWEEN JAPAN AND KOREAN PORTS.

FUSAN AND KOBE VIA SHIMONOSEKI.

OSAKA VIA MOKPO, FUSAN, SHIMONOSEKI AND KOBE.

MOJI DIRECT.

OSAKA VIA KUNSAN, MASANPO, FUSAN, SHIMONOSEKI AND KOBE.

CHEMULPO KUNSAN LINE,
Every three days.

CHEMULPO CHINNAMPO LINE.
Every three days.

For Freight and passage and further particulars apply to

THE OSAKA SHOSEN KAISHA,
Chemulpo

RONDON, PLAISANT & CO.

General Storekeepers and Merchants, Ships Contractors, Tobacconists, Commission and Forwarding Agents, Coal Merchants

IMPORTERS AND EXPORTERS

Seoul & Chemulpo.

W. D. WENTWORTH.

LANDING
AND
SHIPPING AGENT.
AND
CUSTOMS BROKER.

12 OURA, NAGASAKI.

STEWARD & CO.

Chemulpo.

Shipchandlers and Storekeepers, Naval and Mercantile Contractors, Landing and Shipping Agents.

STEWARD'S HOTEL

Chemulpo.

Best accommodation in the port for travellers. Clean and well-aired rooms, good cuisine and prompt attendance, moderate tariff.

론셜

젼쟁과평화

○동경통신을거ᄒᆞᆫ즉일본인민
들은동향대쟝이곳싸드려부시
게셜틱ᄒᆞᆫ티가숙히나아오기를
열심으로기다린다ᄒᆞ니비쎠위
싱각이일본에쌔리가빗햇도다
동향대쟝이란승함티에티ᄒᆞ야
ᄒᆞᆫ던일을불긔함티의제샨다시
그러케ᄒᆞᆯ줄로동경에서는외싱
엽시및교논돈에서는그밋는마
옴을권쟝ᄒᆞ며샨미국에서는일
본이제히권을영구히보젼ᄒᆞᆯ줄
로만히아는지라일본을칭찬ᄒᆞ
는셔담은그군함들의슈가만코
픔이놉하서그럿타는거시아니
라군함들을부리는방법이졍랑
ᄒᆞ고대포들이조흔연고이라세
계에셔로국인들은슈젼자로는
아지아니ᄒᆞ고븍히수견이로국
힘군명예를손상ᄒᆞ기를커의라
순함티가동향대쟝의채와히샹
위함티가샹촌대쟝의게괘ᄒᆞᆫ바
ᄒᆞ도다
에면구나불긔함티가아세아바다
에도착ᄒᆞ면변들이샹ᄒᆞᆫ곳도잇
슬거시오드러온젓도잇슬거시
니그젓들을수리ᄒᆞ고닥기위ᄒᆞ
야이힘안에히샹위에가기가능
치못ᄒᆞᆯ듯ᄒᆞ도다그러ᄒᆞ나미국
에치카고데빌뉴스신문의ᄒᆞᆫ통
신원이말ᄒᆞ되동경에셔만일불
긔함티가일본히군의포격ᄒᆞᆯ바
ᄒᆞᆫ거리에당도ᄒᆞᆯ더경이면곳과
멸ᄒᆞᆯ줄로확신이아는것은잘못
된싱각이라동향대쟝도금년에
어려운수무와손히로약ᄒᆞ야졋
고그손히는셰샹이아는것보다
심샹은더크게낫는지라지금불
긔함티들그러케쉽게격파ᄒᆞ리
라ᄒᆞᆯ슈업슬듯ᄒᆞ다ᄒᆞ엿더라
동경에서쪽졍랑ᄒᆞ기를만일불
긔함티만쳐멸ᄒᆞ면로국이일본
의게졍ᄒᆞ는평화조약티로쳥죵
ᄒᆞ리라ᄒᆞ며일본인의의수들은
히티표ᄒᆞᆫ시수신문에도티젹이
평화를청ᄒᆞ도록용망을보며싸
우기를원ᄒᆞ고ᄒᆞ도동경에셔사하
젹졍을연속ᄒᆞ야구로팟긘의군
략을젼멸ᄒᆞ야로국이싸홈을졍
지ᄒᆞ게되기를츅슈ᄒᆞ나일본이
츙어리엽게평화를원ᄒᆞ는도다
의본이지금신리번근불진이는
쳐쪽을맛고잇슬거시아니라는
니저도아니ᄒᆞ고세들지도아니
ᄒᆞ고샤죠옹히도라와셔싸홈을
더크게ᄒᆞ리이라일본은영국의
조력을밋으나은힝과신문지와
다른지라영국의은힝가들이일
본에셔샹영는빈으로두울셰며
쥬며영국이아직노흔ᄒᆞ지아니
ᄒᆞ엿스니아쥭저지영국은영국
을위ᄒᆞᆯ다름이로다
일본이평화를위ᄒᆞ야싸호는티
평쟝ᄒᆞ게싸우는도다그러ᄒᆞ나

로국이비난ᄒᆞᆫ만으로방인이가
면ᄒᆞ지아니ᄒᆞᆯ거시아니ᄒᆞ가니되
의버듯이그럿치아니ᄒᆞᆫ지리로국의
면이만일일본을군수로뭇이의면
만세일로의일줄로알고잇스며쟈
두얼지금로국이일본의게드러국
의평도로보다엇마며오리가보젼
치못ᄒᆞᆯ줄을발게보고잇다ᄒᆞ노
라

관보

광무구년일월이십오일
대판젼셔십오호
셔임금사령

○셔대훈사리화쟝 일본국쥬
차군사령부부군대쟝남쟉 쟝
곡쳔호도
○셔훈일등사팔괘쟝 일본국
쥬차군참모쟝륙군소쟝 낙합
풍삼랑
○셔훈이등사태극쟝 일본국
륙군군의감 횡쳔죠쟝
○셔훈이등사팔괘쟝 일본국
륙군일등쥬계졍 초야영항
○셔훈삼등사팔괘쟝 일본국
림시군용텰도티감부륙군소좌
히진샹웅
이샹이월십팔일
○명충쥬군림시우체쥬사 민
계국
○명부안군림시우체쥬사 셔봉
회
이샹일월이십일일
○의원면본관 후릉참봉 리
병군 숙릉참봉 셔챤슈 졍
릉참봉 김제텰
○임후릉참봉셔판임관팔등
구흥룡덕쥬
○임숙릉참봉셔판임관팔등
구흥 죠원일
○임졍릉참봉셔판임관팔등
김쥬환
○면중계 률룡리죵셕
○임중추원의관셔칙임관사등
졍샤흥 리범구
이샹일월이십삼일

잡보

○산슈츙시 지작일에남문안
쟝에오소리셰마리를계속에너
허봉ᄒᆞ야가지온거서티ᄒᆞᆫ사ᄅᆞᆷ
이미마리에샹심랑식견가ᄒᆞ야
계를열고본즉음에ᄒᆞᆫ마리가룩
셔버나와다라나니다가사ᄅᆞᆷ이만
ᄒᆞᆫ고로습포막마루및라히드리가
숨엇는지라그것을보고사ᄅᆞᆷ가
이우ᄅᆞᆷᄒᆞᆫ는죠음에쌘가빠가발
아쌩이다샷다지미쌩쟝수가분
ᄒᆞᆷ을이이지못ᄒᆞ야그오슈리를
이써쥬인과쳐음견슈가ᄒᆞᆫ사로결
말ᄒᆞ기를나는산오슈리티로다
가ᄒᆞ엿더니죠엿스니쓸티엽더
쟝ᄒᆞ고사지아니ᄒᆞ는지라오리
죽쌩쟝수는쌩쟝사의게갑슬답ᄒᆞ
쌩이수는가게오니갑슬님소리
가ᄒᆞ엿소리의게ᄒᆞ는지갑슬받은
되엿스니로ᄒᆞ고손히아나ᄒᆞᆫ
금ᄒᆞ고

을수엽서비ᄒᆞ고셔로ᄒᆞᆫ난ᄒᆞ다가ᄒᆞᆯ
팔고갓다더라ᄒᆞ엿더라

○샨슈다수경무소션티후세는
명빛ᄒᆞ다ᄒᆞ고소문이탕자ᄒᆞᆫ미경녀
향간인민들이왕권세에놀는자
빗쳐못ᄒᆞᆫ돈이며텽쟝ᄒᆞ는
의게숙야손히된일노호소ᄒᆞᆫ는
일이날노더욱만하간다더라

○은힝표위죠 미국젼교소모
목수의말젼싱노릇ᄒᆞ는박쥬스
라ᄒᆞ는자는조리ᄒᆞᆫ인에쓸돈이
부족ᄒᆞ야은힝표빗원을위죠ᄒᆞ
야가지고가셔의싱엽셔돈을차
자왓더니그일이필경탈로되여
셔금가ᄒᆞᆫ인날에불의에일본병
예에쟝쟉갓더니쟝인됨사들이찰
고돈빗원을무리쥬고노하나왓
고광목수의집에문하인노릇ᄒᆞ
는쟈는은힝표벗신원을위조ᄒᆞ
아가지교차지편갓다가은힝소
에서의심이나리돈을주지안코
그놈을쟝으라ᄒᆞᆯ즈음에과미틀
얼고빨셔도망ᄒᆞ야부지거쳐라
더라

○졍죠외부 졍공관에셔죠회
ᄒᆞ기를한어교수츄션일수는이
수비에협당ᄒᆞᆫ사름이엽고오직
북평순단부샹셩두방역이가문
ᄒᆞᆯ가경등ᄒᆞ니후취임을협방ᄒᆞᆯ
는자가부에쳐단을한부대션와
게샹의ᄒᆞ야히대신이자증ᄒᆞᆯ여
가ᄒᆞ다ᄒᆞ엿더라

○영관죠회 영공관에서외부
에죠회ᄒᆞ기를히쥬손연방의명
안수는영쟉예귀부에회동ᄒᆞ야
은이젼쳥빗둥신수원의비샹으
로쟝ᄒᆞᆫ자는오작귀부태샨이졍
혁쥬션ᄒᆞ야화광ᄒᆞ케담판ᄒᆞ야
미일을요졍ᄒᆞ엿스니납수무제
라ᄒᆞ엿더라

○의관공함 의공관에셔외부
에공함ᄒᆞ기를명슈요일하오두
시에본수가귀부를방문ᄒᆞᆯ터이
니바라건티그세을기드려졍견
ᄒᆞ라ᄒᆞ엿더라

○너죵동셩원 너부에서동샨
원으로죠회ᄒᆞ기를린금ᄒᆞᆫ원군라
슈도두편의보고를졍ᄒᆞᆫ즉아라
수 사름들이 면보소를 광포졍
(거리는음예서수샹오리 최셕
운의졍에셜시ᄒᆞᆫ다ᄒᆞ니외병이
면젼을세우고등신ᄒᆞ지못ᄒᆞᆯ은
공법에자계ᄒᆞ거는보고ᄒᆞᆫ보ㅣ
이곳ᄒᆞ나셩이피당ᄒᆞᆫ지라엄졀
히이ᄒᆞᆫ평ᄒᆞ야금단케ᄒᆞ라ᄒᆞ엿더
라

○불합죽퇴거 일쟉야에바셔
승리경현이가엉시ᄒᆞ야사경긔
젼의셜시ᄒᆞᆫ방쳥으로슈차를봉
졍ᄒᆞ고참졍죠병호씨도슈치ᄒᆞ야
도아쟝츳수진ᄒᆞᆯ터인티또ᄒᆞᆫ봉쎄
시졍기젼의슈차를쟝츳봉졍
ᄒᆞᆯ터이라ᄒᆞ며만일말을쓰지
니ᄒᆞ교횡ᄒᆞ는거시협지아니ᄒᆞ
면과이퇴ᄒᆞ기예졍이라ᄒᆞ더라

○덕병입셩 덕국히군륙신대
이입셩ᄒᆞ야덕어학교와각처를
유람ᄒᆞ고법국슈관은동룡관대
궤을관광ᄒᆞ엿더라

○일진회권고 일진회에셔너
부에권고ᄒᆞ기를슈찬수외봉쥬
ᄒᆞᆫ슈령은외룸갑쳐ᄒᆞᆯ수외졍쥬
젼군슈박병의현임은이법외에
임비너위셧면본관ᄒᆞ야그탐쟝
ᄒᆞᆫ죄는의법갑죵ᄒᆞᆯ수와립화부
윤운쳘규의탐학ᄒᆞᆷ을의룡영강ᄒᆞᆯ
슈와게히챤깅하슈의셰젼을간ᄒᆞᆯ
군에외획ᄒᆞᆫ이버요안악군슈
가깅용악의탐쟝을습수형호ᄒᆞᆫ
아보일반오쳔량만쟝연군슈의
외는문셔ᄒᆞ고사힉죠를ᄒᆞᆯ수와
의쥬군슈구완희의탐쟝면관ᄒᆞᆯ
수외슈안박쳔량군슈가교졸파
포군을밧ᄒᆞ야회원을탄티ᄒᆞᆫ수
로사힉ᄒᆞᆯ오룩됴진이라더라

○경의문시 각쥬임관을임면
ᄒᆞ야경탄회면부에셔졍부에졍의ᄒᆞ
탄경의ᄒᆞᆫ후에사횡ᄒᆞ미즈연ᄒᆞᆫ
야가되며수무에방히가된티ᄒᆞᆫ
이종금이후로는각가쥬무쟝관
단이ᄌᆞ던ᄒᆞ야 쥬분ᄒᆞ기로ᄒᆞᆫ
더라

○유권문보 군경찰정경비를
갑ᄒᆞ야인원을티게ᄒᆞ는지라
군경탕졍에서논권나는티로보
용은ᄒᆞᆫ지아니ᄒᆞᆫ다더
○경계쟝번 근일한셩경계
번동ᄒᆞ야로제샹은뢰기ᄒᆞ고신
졍부조제비 졍츠박표된다더

○즁학교수 즁학교교수폐원
탐쎄가학부로문빗으로젼힝ᄒᆞᆯ
이터에일인문학수교교셰가교방
이된다더라

○렵회군보 렵회군슈가외부
로보고ᄒᆞ기를본군빌최 샹등
이동젼을습빗젼으로슈납ᄒᆞᆫ다
츄ᄒᆞ고면납젼셰를졍퇴ᄒᆞ는뜻
서스로면쟝셩과능동ᄒᆞ여방을본교
로슌찰사가며당을졍야증계ᄒᆞ
후에방송ᄒᆞ엿고최가피슈는도
망ᄒᆞ여졍지못ᄒᆞ엿슴으로관속
벽가취가외쟝을희과ᄒᆞ엿더니
홀연본원초괄일에욕구항으로
면티일슘사와면강리세습챨ᄒᆞ며
명야최가의일을두호ᄒᆞᆫ너희가이
본군에와셔적폐를ᄒᆞᆫ니최가빈
당헌의편ᄒᆞᆫ지라이에보ᄒᆞ고ᄒᆞ오니
일샤의계교셜ᄒᆞ여율구향열명
샤의게젹칙ᄒᆞ며월죠ᄒᆞ며간셩
ᄒᆞᆫ지못ᄒᆞ케ᄒᆞ라ᄒᆞ엿더라

광고

○본인의쟝조쳐텰미가본시부
탕폐루토그부형졋데산에분지
ᄒᆞ여가진면쟝문권을수히토
젹ᄒᆞ며너엿기로세부득이ᄒᆞ야
시분권을모든이고이에광포ᄒᆞ
오니너외국인간에샹가속지말
고한쳐텰의가진문권을면졍저
마옹기를바라옴
광양셩너쌩거리 한괴현
고빅

TELEGRAMS.

(FROM JAPAN PAPERS)

THE SHAHO.

London, Jan. 20.

It is officially announced at St. Petersburg that the Russian plan on the Shaho will be as follows: General Kuropatkin will try a movement with a large cavalry corps on the plains of the Hun; General Grippenberg will take the offensive; General Kaulbars will menace the Japanese right wing; and General Linievitch will attack the Japanese (left wing) by the road south of Mukden.

London, Jan. 20.

It is semi-officially announced in St. Petersburg that the scene of the recent raid on Newchwang, made by Russian cavalry under the command of General Mischenko, is specifically included within the area of hostilities, as recognised at the beginning of the war.

THE BALTIC FLEET.

London, Jan. 19.

Fifteen large Hamburg-America steamers were insured in London yesterday for half their value. They are intended to carry cargoes to a certain point west of Ceylon. The premiums were low in spite of the war risks. The inference drawn here is that the Baltic warships are to be recalled and that the vessels referred to will supply them with coal during the homeward voyage. The insurance of only half the value and the lowness of the premiums are explained on the supposition that the Japanese squadrons are not coming west of Colombo.

The following telegrams have been received in official quarters at Tokio:—

Two destroyers belonging to the Baltic Fleet have struck rocks near Madagascar, and are now undergoing repairs in a private dock. It is not true that the flagship sunk. She is said to have collided with one of her consorts.

The flagship of the Baltic Fleet, which was reported to have sunk, was only damaged. She collided with her consort, but is still afloat.

London, Jan. 21.

The Russian and English cases, concerning the attack upon the fishing boats in the North Sea on October 21st, have been read before the International Commission at Paris.

CHINA'S NEUTRALITY.

Washington, Jan. 17.

Mr. Hay, U. S. Secretary of State, has addressed a circular to the Powers, in which he proposes to reassure the Powers' agreement regarding the "open door" and integrity of territory in China,—an agreement which was concluded immediately after the outbreak of the war. Great Britain, Germany and Italy immediately expressed their consent to the proposal. After the other Powers have replied to the circular, Mr. Hay will communicate the result to Japan and Russia, and make arrangements for giving moral support to China for the purpose of maintaining her neutrality.

London, Jan. 17.

It is stated here that the action of the United States implies that the latter disapproves of the Russian Circular as to the alleged Japanese breaches of neutrality in China. Recognising that Russia has actually violated Chinese neutrality, she is not inclined to make much of the Russian protest against Japan, and considers that Russia's action debars her from demanding equal treatment in China.

Berlin, Jan. 18.

The French paper "Le Temps" comments unfavourably on the Russian Circular as to alleged breaches of neutrality by China. "Le Temps" states that the Powers are agreed in desiring to prevent China from interfering in the war.

Berlin, Jan. 19.

The "Journal des Débats," of Paris, publishes the programme of the recently formed Anglo-French Commercial Association with reference to Central China, in which the acquisition by Russia of territory north of the Great Wall is recognised.

London, Jan. 18

It is announced in Washington that China is issuing a general denial to the charges made in the Russian Note to the Powers complaining of the violation of China's neutrality since the begining of the war. The officials in Washington, it is stated, consider joint action on the part of the Powers with a view to preserving China's neutrality to be necessary owing to the danger of another anti-foreign outbreak in China, and have therefore sent a Circular to the Powers suggesting such action if circumstances should compel.

Later.

It is announced in Washington that Russia has thanked Mr. John Hay, the U. S. Secretary of State, for calling the attention of the Chinese Government to the allegation regarding violation of neutrality.

Count Cassini, the Russian Ambassador at Washington, declares that Russia has positive proof of the violation of neutrality, and that unless China mends her ways Russia will be forced to look to her own interests.

London, Jan. 18.

The American reply to the Russian neutrality circular indicates that Russia must observe her engagements equally with China.

It is believed at Washingtion that Russia contemplates the seizure of a Chinese port as a naval base for the Baltic squadron.

GENERAL NEWS.

London, Jan. 19.

The strike in St. Petersburg has ceased to be merely a trade movement, and is now assuming a distinctly political character.

The demands made by the strikers include a recognition of the rights of the people, the remedy of poverty, and redress of oppression by capitalists. Attached to these are large demands for free education, the granting of popular liberties, and representative government.

Other trades beside the cotton operatives and iron workers and kindred occupations are joining in the strike.

Berlin, Jan. 19.

Prince Sergius has been dismissed from the post of Governor of Moscow. This has created a sensation in Russia.

London, Jan. 18.

There has been a severe earthquake in South Russia. Hundreds of persons are entombed in the mines.

Berlin, Jan. 19.

Prince Ferdinand of Bulgaria is to visit Berlin to attend the celebrations in honour of the Kaiers's birthday on the 27th instant.

London, Jan. 17.

It is reported from Rome that the King of Italy is about to decorate Generals Nogi and Stoessel with an Italian Order.

Chungking, Jan. 8.

It is reported here that Viceroy Hsi Liang has been informed from Tokyo that the native Christian converts have bought up land on the track of the Chengtu-Hankow Railway, which line the Japanese hope to obtain as their share of the railway prizes in China. The Viceroy has given orders to the local authorities to stop this practice to avoid complications.—Eastern Times.

London, Jan. 19.

M. Combes, the French Premier, has resigned office.

Berlin, Jan. 18.

The Grand Duchess of Saxe-Weimar has died from the results of a cold.

THE TROUBLES IN ST. PETERSBURG.

London, Jan. 20.

It is officially announced at St. Petersburg that during the firing of the usual salute after the blessing of the waters of the Neva, one of the guns of a battery of artillery stationed near the Bourse fired a shrapnel shell instead of blank, with the result that four windows of the Winter Palace were broken. The Tsar happened to be some distance from the Palace when the incident occurred.

From other accounts of the affair it appears that the charge of shrapnel was inadvertently left in the gun from which it was fired. The battery engaged in firing the salute belonged to the Horse Artillery, the most aristocratic corps in the Russian Army. The shrapnel, it is stated, was left in the gun after practice on Tuesday.

Notwithstanding the incident, the ceremony of blessing the Neva was carried out according to programme.

The occurrence occasioned wild rumours to the effect that the affair was the outcome of a military plot.

The men belonging to the battery firing the salute have been arrested.

London, Jan. 20.

Bands of strikers each consisting of about five thousand men are parading the streets of St. Petersburg enforcing a general strike, even the Government printing works being compelled to stop work.

A petition to the Tsar is being circulated for signature at the workmen's meetings which bitterly complains of the desperate condition of the labourers and the deprivation of human rights to which they are subjected. The petition concludes: "Be compassionate! Let us live! Under present conditions we prefer to die."

The Tsar has departed for his palace at Tsarkoe.

London, January 20th.

The strikes have ceased but the trade movements are assuming a distinctly political character.

The Koreans are excellent couriers, but it is doubted whether they can equal the following performances. Mr. Florence O'Driscoll, who has recently been exploring the great mountain ranges in the north of the Argentine, has discovered that the breed of runners, which were so prominent a feature of the civilization of the Incas, is by no means extinct. In a lecture delivered before the Royal Geographical Society he said:—"I have often had a telegram delivered at the station, 40 miles distant from where sent, and an answer received and brought back by the same man, all, including the journey of 80 miles, not occupying more than eighteen hours; the man was well content to receive two Bolivian dollars, or three shillings in English money, for the service. I saw a man who delivered a message 200 miles away and brought an answer back, covering within six days and nights 400 miles. As he did this work for a native, his charge was five Bolivian dollars (seven and six-pence English money,) out of which he provided his own food." All the people in this region Mr. O'Driscoll found were born runners and mountain climbers. Even the little children climbed mountains without difficulty. If they could not of course, it would be awkward, as the mountains are everywhere in the way

Some one in the Home Office is a humourist. The magistrate of Hong Won, having reported that the Russians have established telegraph offices there the Home Office now informs him that "you may prohibit it."

REPAIRING THE PORT ARTHUR DOCKYARD.

About 1,200 Japanese labourers have arrived at Port Arthur from Dalny and are now repairing the dockyard in the east harbour on which Japanese shell were concentrated for a long time.

THE RUSSIAN POINT OF VIEW.

Persons arriving from Moukden yesterday via Hsimintun and Chingwantao, agree that the Russians are about ready to begin a southerly movement of their entire line. It is their opinion that Kuropaktin will take the aggressive during the latter days of this month, and they are firm in their conviction that victory will crown his efforts.

As for the Japanese, it is reported that they have insufficient men to maintain a solid front to the Russian position, which is being constantly extended. One of the arrivals stated to the "Chefoo Daily News" that the Japanese are freely enlisting the Manchurian bandits whom they keep in the most advanced trenches; but with every bandit there is a Japanese soldier whose business it is to shoot the Manchurian in case he turns tail. These recruits are paid twenty five sen more per day than are the Japanese soldiers. The most of them have cut off their long hair so that in case of their capture the Russian will be unable to distinguish them from Japanese.

The influx of troops from Europe into Moukden continues unabated and, by spring it is likely that Kuropatkin will have a mobile army of one half million men. The troops are well fed and comfortably quartered at the front: the greatest hardship being outpost duty on cold and stormy nights. The men talk about the retaking of Port Arthur and Liaoyang as matters of course.

By the express desire of the King of Portugal, during his recent vist to England, the correspondent of the Press Association and another journalist were presented to his Majesty at Wood Norton, when he expressed his gratification at the warmth of the reception given to himself and his Consort throughout their tour.

The Korea Daily News.

Issued at 5 P. M. daily except Sundays.

Rate of Subscription:—
Per Year............Yen 25.
Per Quarter,..........Yen 7.
Per Month,..........Yen 2.50.

Postage in Korea not charged extra.
Postage abroad charged extra.

Advertisements, 50 sen per day for 1 inch or less.
5 yen per month per inch.
50 yen per year per inch.

All communications to

E. T. BETHELL,
Editor and Publisher,
Pak-tong, Seoul

DISAFFECTION IN RUSSIA.

From the multitudinous telegrams which are now coming to the Far East we conclude that the strikes and general manifestations of disaffection in Russia are regarded by the Japanese as of considerable importance.

It is only to be hoped that they will have, ultimately, considerable effect, for it is certain that, in Russia, the lot of the peasant and artisan is a hard one, and many officials rule by tyranny alone.

But we do not think that the present rebellion, even if it be as serious as the telegrams reaching Japan represent it to be, can be expected to have any influence on the present war; not, at any rate, for some time.

Russia is an immense country and it would take years for any movement of revolt to become a national menace. We shall however probably be right in assuming that when Japan started on her self-appointed task of driving the Russians from Manchuria, she counted largely upon the indirect assistance which she would obtain from anarchists in Russia. We are told that these strikes are well organized, but however perfect their organization may be it does not seem likely that they can have any immediate far-reaching effect.

When we hear of the "muzzling of the Russian press" on the one hand, and agitation against the war on the other, we are driven to the conclusion that the agitation is largely due to ignorance. We never did see any good reason for the press censorship practised in Russia, (and latterly in Japan) and it appears to us that in the present instance Russia is suffering through her own acts. Japan has been represented as the champion of the weak against the strong and the ignorant populace of Russia may believe that Japan is only protecting herself against Russian aggression, but that is a very untenable theory and a few days residence in Korea (for whose independence and integrity Japan started out to fight) would soon dispel that, and many other, illusions about the Japanese.

Russia and Japan are fighting for exactly the same thing viz: Territorial expansion, and both nations are equally right, or wrong, according to the point of view. Japan, foolishly we think, is anxious to add Korea to her Empire and sees in Russia's various attempts to secure a warm water outlet for her Siberian trade, a menace to the success of her project. Russia is not of course, in the abstract, justified in grabbing more land because she has already a good deal, but her action has many precedents.

So far as the war is concerned it appears to us that the Russian people have far less ground for complaint than have the Japanese. The increases of taxation that we hear of, viz: On tobacco, spirits and revenue stamps, are by no means such an infliction on the people as are the new Japanese imposts on rice, cloths and other neccessaries.

Neither does conscription bear so heavily upon them. Russia's population being many times greater than that of Japan, the despatch of a million men from that country would cause less distress in Russia than the mobilization of half that number in Japan.

It is, we think, safe to assume that the present disturbed condition of Russia is only due to the war inasmuch as the agitators have seized upon the war as a favourable opportunity to make themselves heard, and we are not inclined to believe that against the war, as a war, there is any particular outcry in Russia.

We are quite of opinion that the present is a lamentable state of affairs but we do not believe in putting the whole blame upon Russian Autocracy. The Russian Grand-Dukes may have been proud, blind and self-centred but they have their exact protypes among the Japanese, and although we admit that Russia took no steps to avoid this war are quite sure that many people in high positions in Japan would have been sadly disappointed if she had done so.

It now looks as if the war will continue a long time yet and if the belligerents get no other tangible result out of it they will at least have received some lessons which will be useful to them in the future government of their own countries.

THE RESPONSIBILITY FOR THE WAR.

AN ARCHBISHOPS STATEMENT.

A Russian correspondent sends the information to the "Pall Mall Gazette" that in the yearly report of "The Brotherhood of the Orthodox Church in China" an open letter, written by the Russian Archbishop of Manchuria, Innokentyi, has created the greatest sensation throughout Russia. The Archishop declares without hesitation that for the present war, its terrible sacrifices and Russian humiliations, the responsibility lies with the Russian administration in the Far East. When he first arrived at Dalny, the seat of his diocese, he says he was painfully struck and deeply saddened by the carelessness, light-heartedness, and dissoluteness of the Russian officers and the Tchinovniks (the State's employes)

None of them ever thought that the Japanese would dare declare war, but even if they dared do so their army would be annihilated in the very first battle! And the first Japanese cannon shot filled these boasters with astonishment and confusion. The want of organization, general disorder, the unpreparedness, and the differences and disunion among the higher officers could not but bring about defeat and calamities. Carelessness and contempt of the enemy were responsible for the loss of our fleet. The dissolute and simply scandalous life of many Russians in Manchuria had, even before the war, deprived us of the respect and sympathy of the indigenous population, who now on every step show how they hate and despise us. It is time to humiliate ourselves before God and to repent!

Reading this honest and straight-forward statement, adds the correspondent, every Russian feels its inherent truth. More intelligent ones interpret the epistle as saying: "Repentance means Reform!" There is no fear that a revolution will take place in Russia, but the conviction that fundamental reforms are absolutely necessary is rapidly spreading through all classes of the Russian nation.

France has declined to entertain anything about the Japanese complaint as regards a breach of neutrality at Madagascar; assuring Japan that nothing has happened that establishes a breach thereof.

JAPANESE PLANS.

Whatever we may say or think about the Japanese in Korea, the charge of diffidence may never be laid at their door. According to despatches reaching Japan from Japanese correspondents here, Mr. Hayashi is now discussing three important questions with the Korean Government: One is the coastwise carrying trade; another the recall of Korea's foreign representatives; and the third the transfer of the country's machinery of communications to Japanese care and supervision. All these problems says the correspondent, have an intimate connection with the repair of Korean finance, and though some opposition is offered, the present expectation seems to be that the Seoul Government will fall in with Japan's projects. From the same source it is stated that Korea has at length paid over the sum Y240,000 which represents compensation for losses suffered by Japanese subjects in 1895. Furthermore, according to to Japan newspapers, the Mainichi correspondent in Seoul is reponsible for the following:—"The Korean Government is about to dismiss all its foreign officials. The French adviser to the Department of Justice and the Danish adviser to the Imperial Household Department will" leave on the expira- of their terms.

For every one Foreign adviser who leaves about six Japanese advisers arrive. This is somewhat rough on the Financial adviser.

THE SUBMARINE SQUADRON.

A great deal of interest has been excited in Japan by the official announcement of the organization of a squadron of submarines. The squadron is associated with the name of Commander Oguri, who is said to be a firm believer in submarines. What interests the Japanese especally, says the "Japan Mail," is that an opportunity may now perhaps be first furnished for testing the practical efficacy of this type of vessel, which has attracted so much attention and been the subject of much controversy, It would suggest itself, however, that the great potency which has been now demonstrated on behalf of the mechanical mine militates against the use of the submarine, or at any rate, greatly narrows its sphere of action.

NEWS FROM MANILLA.

Anent the visit of Japanese warships to southern waters, the "Manila American" has the following:—

Japanese cruiser "Takansi" approached entrance of north channel at one-fifty P. M., and after spelling out her name turned and went due south until center of south channel was reached, when vessel again turned and headed southwest. Asked her if she was going into port and vessel replied in the negative, she refused to state where she was from, ignoring the signals.

The Captain of the German steamer "Speza," which arrived in port early yesterday morning, reports having sighted, thirty miles off the entrance to Manila bay, a large Japanese cruiser. This was on Thursday afternoon. When the cruiser sighted the German vessel, she put about and bore down on the "Speza," and when within signalling distance, hoisted signals enquiring where the steamer hailed from and where bound. These were answered, and apparently to the satisfaction of the Mikado's war vessel, for she at once put to sea again under a full head of steam.

The captain of the "Speza" describes the cruiser as being a large one with three funnels and two military masts.

This war vessel is evidently the one that has been scouting in the San Bernadino straits and which paid Manilla a short visit on Thursday.

The "Speza" is from Antwerp and Hamburg.

On the 17th instant at 11 A. M. a Japanese war-ship stopped the British steamer "Bawtry" in the Tsushima strait, and finding on examination that she was laden with provisions, machine oil and ship-building material for Vladivostock, arrested her and took her to Sasebo. The "Bawtry" is a steamer of 1,542 tons register.

The Korea Daily News.

VOL. II, THURSDAY, JANUARY 26, 1905. No. 20

HONGKONG & SHANGHAI BANKING CORPORATION.

Paid-up Capital.................£10,000,000
Reserve Fund:—Sterling Reserve... 10,000,000
Silver Reserve..... 7,000,000

27,000,000
Reserve Liability of Proprietors... 10,000,000

HEAD OFFICE, HONGKONG.

London Bankers, London and County Banking Company Limited.
Branches and Agencies,
London.

Amoy,	Hankow	Penang,
Bangkok,	Hiogo,	Rangoon,
Batavia,	Iloilo,	Saigon,
Bombay,	Lyons,	San Francisco,
Calcutta,	Manila,	Singapore,
Colombo,	Nagasaki,	Sourabaya,
Foochow,	New York,	Tientsin,
Hamburg,	Peking,	Yokohama,

Credits granted on approved Securities, and every description of Banking and Exchange business transacted.

Drafts granted on London and the chief Commercial places in Europe, India, Australia, America, China and Japan.

HOLME RINGER & Co., AGENTS,
CHEMULPO.

HOKURKU DOBOKU KAISHA.

Branch office in Chong Dong, Seoul.
Japanese telephone No. 165

CONTRACT DEPARTMENT.

We can contract to build any building or construction.

MERCHANDISE DEPARTMENT.

We can provide any building material. We have just contracted to build the new Belgian Legation.

E. MEYER & CO.
Chemulpo.

SOLE AGENTS IN KOREA FOR.

A. T. Morse, Sons & Co.'s "Fresco" Distemper

In all colours ready for use on walls, Ceilings etc.
and
AVENARIUS CARBOLINEUM

A wood-preserving and antiseptic oil preparation
Against decay, dry-rot, fungus and wood-destroying insects.

A large supply always in stock.
Prices upon application.

E. MEYER & Co.,
Chemulpo.

CHARTERED BANK OF INDIA AUSTRALIA & CHINA.

INCORPORATED BY ROYAL CHARTER 1853

HEAD OFFICES.—LONDON.

Paid-up Capital £800,000
Reserve Liability of Share-holders 800,000
Reserve Fund 800,000

Drafts granted upon all the principal places in the world and every description of Exchange and banking business transacted.

E. MEYER & Co., Agents,
Chemulpo.

MITSU BISHI DOCKYARD & ENGINE WORKS,

NAGASAKI.

CODE WORD, "DOCK."

A 1, A. B. C., and Engineering Codes used.

DOCK No. 1 (at Tategami).

Extreme Length..............523 feet
Length on blocks .... 513 ,,
Width of Entrance on Top......89 ,,
,, ,, Bottom....77 ,,
Water on Blocks at Spring Tide 26½ ,,

DOCK No. 2 (Mukaijima).

Extreme Length..............371 feet
Length on Blocks............360 ,,
Width of Entrance on Top......66 ,,
,, ,, Bottom 53 ,,
Water on Blocks at Spring Tide 22 ,,

PATENT SLIP (at Kosuge).
Can take vessels up to 1,000 tons gross

THE WORKS are well equipped with the LATEST IMPROVEMENTS, and can execute any kind of work in SHIPBUILDING and MARINE ENGINEERING, as well as in REPAIRING of SHIPS.

The COMPANY'S new powerfu steamer OURA-MARU (712 tons, 700 I.H.P.), specially built for SALVAGE PURPOSES, and equipped with necessary gear, is always READY at SHORT NOTICE.

THE METHODIST PUBLISHING HOUSE,

Little West Gate, Seoul.

JOB PRINTING, TYPEWRITER PAPER
CARBON PAPER, VISITING CARDS
STATIONERY, BOOK BINDING
BOOK PUBLISHERS
AMERICAN SCHOOL BOOKS
SPENCERIAN COPY BOOKS
PEN CARBON LETTER AND BILL BOOKS

S.A. BECK, Manager.

DAI-ICHI GINKO.

LIMITED.

(Formerly the First National Bank)

ESTABLISHED 1873

INCORPORATED UNDER PRESENT LAW 1896

Capital - - - - - - - - Yen 5,000,000
Reserve Fund - - - - - 1,500,000

HEAD OFFICE:—TOKIO.

President: Baron SHIBUSAWA.

BRANCHES AND CORRESPONDENTS
In the Principal Cities and Towns of Japan.
Interest Allowed on
Fixed deposits 1 year - - - 6½ per cent
" " 6 months - - - 6 per cent

Special current accounts 1½ sen daily per Y 100
General " " 1 " " " 100

M. TANAKA,
Manager, Chemulpo.

SINGER SEWING MACHINES

싱거즈봉침

SOLE AGENTS FOR KOREA
전매쇼

HOLME RINGER & CO.
Chemulpo.
제물포 함릉거양힝

KAMEYA CO.

GENERAL STOREKEEPERS
Chinkokai - - Seoul
(Established 1895, Tokyo)

Confectionery, Hams, Canned Goods, Cutlery, Hirano & Tansan Water. Provisions, Gents, Furnishing goods, Toilet Articles, Travelling Bags, Tobacco, Cigars & Cigarettes Kitchen Utensils. Coffee, Biscuits.

Fresh Goods always kept in Stock.
Prices Moderate
☞ *Please come and inspect our goods.*

NIPPON YUSEN KAISHA.

JAPANESE MAIL STEAMSHIP CO.

UNDER MAIL CONTRACT WITH THE IMPERIAL JAPANESE GOVERNMENT.

European Line

Regular Fortnightly Service between Yokohama Kobe, Moji, Shanghai, Hongkong, Singapore, Penang Colombo, Port Said, Marseilles, London and Antwerp

American Line

Regular Fortnightly Service between Hongkong and Seattle, calling at Shanghai, Moji, Kobe, Yokohama and Victoria, B. C.

Australian Line

Regular weekly Service betwen Japan Ports and Australia, calling at Hongkong and Manila.
(Above Three Lines, Suspended until further notice).

Shanghai Line

Weekly Service between Shanghai and Japan Ports

Korea Line

Service Kobe, Moji, Nagasaki, Fusan Chemulpo Chefoo, Taku.
S. S. Babelsberg, 2181 tons.
Service Kobe, Moji, Fusan, Chemulpo, Chinnampo
S. S. ARGO, S. S. Ohio.

BORDEN'S CONDENSED MILK CO.

New York, U. S. A.

ALWAYS IN STOCK
Eagle Brand Condensed Milk.
Gold Seal Condensed Milk.
Peerless (Family) Evaporated Cream.
Borden's Malted Milk.

E. MEYER & CO.
Chemulpo Korea,
Sole Agents

ROYAL INSURANCE COMPANY,
Funds exceed £10,000,000
FIRE
AT CURRENT RATES
LIFE
REDUCED PREMIUM.
HOLME RINGER & Co.,
Agents, Chemulpo.

HOTEL DU PALAIS.

SEOUL.

The only first class Hotel in Seoul Situated in the centre of the city opposite the palace.

Cuisine under the supervision of an experienced French Chef.

Well ventilated and furnished throughout.

TARIFF UPON APPLICATION

L. MARTIN
Proprietor and Manager.

大韓每日申報

대한미일신보

(뎨이권이십일호) (토요일) 일쳔구빅오년일월이십팔일

본사고빅

사고

잡보

관보

UNION INSURANCE SOCIETY OF CANTON.

Head office Hongkong.
Marine risks underwritten at current rates.

Agents in Chemulpo,
E. MEYER & Co.

COMPAGNIE DES MESSAGERIES MARITIMES.

Fortnightly Direct Service.

For Marseilles
via Ports.

Sailing from Yokohama
Calling at Kobe,
Shanghai, Hongkong, Saigon, Singapore,
Colombo, Djibouti, Suez, Port Said
and Marseilles.

For particulars apply to
HOLME RINGER & Co.,
Chemulpo.

HAYASHIDA & CO.,

16 MYENG DONG, CHIN KO KAI, SEOUL.
BRANCH OFFICE AT CHEMULPO.

Money changers, Coal and Wood Merchants, Express Agents.

We are agents for the Pyeng-yang Coal Company and the Karazu Coal Company of Japan. We have the best quality of both anthracite and bituminous coal, and prompt execution of orders is our speciality. Firewood of all kinds kept in stock. Full weight guaranteed. Money of all denominations exchanged at current rates. Parcels received for all parts.

CHINA MUTUAL LIFE INS. OC.

Most favourable terms to policy holders.

Benefit system unsurpassed.

HOLME RINGER & Co.
Agents, Chemulpo.

C. P. R.

CANADIAN PACIFIC RAILWAY COMPANY'S ROYAL MAIL STEAMSHIP LINE.

THE FAST ROUTE BETWEEN CHINA, JAPAN, AND EUROPE VIA CANADA AND THE UNITED STATES.

Route from Hongkong via Shanghai, Nagasaki (Inland Sea of Japan) Kobe, Yokohama, Victoria and Vancouver.

Twin Screw Empress Steamship—6,000 Tons—Speed 19 knots.

PROPOSED SAILING FROM YOKOHAMA.
R. M. S. Empress of India.
R. M. S. Empress of Japan.
R. M. S. Empress of China.
R. M. S. Athenian.
R. M. S. Tartar.

Special reduction (first class only) granted to members of the Military, Naval, Diplomatic and Civil services and to Missionaries.

Passengers have choice of ten routes across the Continent of America and have privilege of travelling by any Atlantic Steamship Line.

Round the World passage tickets in connection with the P. and O. S. N., North German Lloyd and Messageries Co.'s **£125.**

All rates payable at current rate of exchange.

For further information, Tickets, Guide Books, etc., apply to

HOLME, RINGER & Co., AGENTS,
Chemulpo.

Grand Hotel,

(Formerly the Station Hotel)

Near the Railway Terminus, West Gate Seoul.

The Best Hotel in Korea]
Handsome new Building.
Fine Airy Rooms
Excellent Cuisine.
Terms Moderate.
Special terms to Missionaries
and to permanent boarders.

Electric cars within 2 minutes' walk.

W. H. EMBERLEY.
Proprietor

EVERY FACILITY.

In connection with Life Assurance Business is afforded by

The Standard Life Assurance Co.,

One of the largest and wealthiest of the Provident Institutions of the United Kingdom Forms of Application and all information will be promptly afforded on application.

10 CENTS A DAY.

Not a very large expenditure is it? But it is sufficient to secure for a man of 30 a policy with the STANDARD LIFE OFFICE for

$1323.

For all particulars of rates, etc., apply to

Holme, Ringer & Co.,
Agents, Chemulpo.

THE NEW YORK LIFE INSURANCE COMPANY.

Have you ever been declined by any Company?

Are you engaged in a specially hazardous occupation?

Have you heard of the New York Life Insurance Company's New Classifications for this class of Risks?

If not, send your date of birth, occupation and particulars of rejection, if any to

E. MEYER & Co.,
Agents, Chemulpo.

MITSUI BUSSAN KAISHA.
(MITSUI & Co.)

MITSUI GINKO.
(MITSUI BANK.)

The Bank is owned by the members of the Mitsui Family, who, as partners, assume an unlimited responsibility for all liabilities of the Bank:—

Capital......................Yen 5,000,000
Reserve Fund.................. " 5,600,000

HEAD OFFICE, TOKYO.

LONDON OFFICE, 34 LIME ST., E. C.

BRANCHES AND AGENCIES:—
New York, San Francisco, Hamburg, Bombay, Singapore, Manila, Hongkong, Amoy, Chefoo, Tientsin.

Kobe, Hakodate, Yokohama, Kure, Yokosuka, Moji, Shimonoseki, Miike, Wakamatsu, Nagasaki, Kuchinotsu, Karatsu, Sasebo, Misume, Taipeh, &c.

Telegraphic Address for all the Offices:
"MITSUI."

A. B. C. AND A. I CODES USED.

Contractors of Coal

To the Imperial Japanese Navy. Arsenals and Railway Bureau, Principal Railway Companies and Industrial Work, Home and Foreign Mail and Freight Steamers.

Sole Proprietors

Of the famous Miike, Tagawa and Yamano Coal Mines.

Sole Agents

For the sale of Fukumo, Hokoku, Ichimura, Kanoda, Mannoura, Onoura, Ostuji, Sonoda, Tsubaruro, Yoshinotani, Yoshio, Yurokibura and other coals.

YANGTSE INSURANCE ASSOCIATION, LTD.

The undersigned, having been appointed agents for the above company, are prepared to issue policies and pay losses on marine risks at regular rates.

E. MEYER & Co.,
Agents, Chemulpo.

AMERICAN KOREAN ELECTRIC CO.

Light and Power.

Main Office: Electric Building, Chong No.

RAILWAY DEPARTMENT.

OPERATING CARS BETWEEN EAST AND WEST GATE, EVERY TEN MINUTES:—

First Car leaves East Gate at 7:00 A. M. First Car leaves R. R. Station at 7:25 A. M
Last Car " East Gate at 8.40 P. M. Last " " R. R. Station at 9.05 P.M

OPERATING CARS BETWEEN EAST GATE AND IMPERIAL TOMB TERMINUS, EVERY TWENTY MINUTES:—
CONNECTING WITH EVERY ALTERNATE CAR ARRIVING AT EAST GATE FROM CHONG NO.

First Car leaves East Gate for Tomb at 7:10 A. M.
" " " Tomb for East Gate at 7:30 A. M.
Last " " East Gate for Tomb at 7:50 P. M.
" " " Tomb for East Gate at 8:10 P. M.

OPERATING CARS BETWEEN CHONG NO AND YUNG SAN RIVER EVERY TWELVE MINUTES:—

First Car leaves Chong No for South Gate at 7:12 A. M.
" " " Chong No for Yung San at 7:36 A. M.
" " " South Gate for Chong No at 7:20 A. M.
" " " Yung San for Chong No at 8:09 A. M.
Last " " South Gate for Chong No 9:00 P. M.
" " " Yung San for Chong No at 8.45. p. M.

SPECIAL PRIVATE CARS FURNISHED TO SUIT CONVENIENCE OF PATRONS. PRICES ON APPLICATION AT HEAD OFFICE.

LIGHTING DEPARTMENT.

Where less than 250 candle power of light is used, the rate per month will be
Per 16 candle power incandescent lamp,—All night.—Yen 2.50.
32 candle power incandescent lamp:—All night:—Yen 4.00.
50 candle power incandescent lamp:—All night:—Yen 6.00.
150 " " " " " " 10.00.
1200 " " enclosed arc " " " 20.00.

Where more than 250 candle power of light is used, a Meter will be installed, if requested:—Rent of Meter Yen 2.00 per month. Rate of charges by meter reading:—Two Sen per Ampere per hour. (Approximately this is equal to about One Sen per 16 C. P. lamp per hour) Minimum monthly charge where meter is installed, Yen 20.00 per month, which includes rental of meter.

Estimates for installing lights furnished on application
An assortment of chandeliers always on hand.

K. Murakami.

Photograph Studio
Chinkokai, Seoul.

Printing, Developing and Enlargement, of Photographs always Undertaken.

Korean Views and Pictures Illustrating Native Customs always on Sale,

---

THE OSAKA SHOSEN KAISHA.

Boats frequently on the berth for Chinnampo.

REGULAR SAILINGS BETWEEN JAPAN AND KOREAN PORTS.

FUSAN AND KOBE VIA SHIMONOSEKI.

OSAKA VIA MOKPO, FUSAN, SHIMONOSEKI AND KOBE.

MOJI DIRECT.

OSAKA VIA KUNSAN, MASANPO, FUSAN, SHIMONOSEKI AND KOBE.

CHEMULPO KUNSAN LINE,
Every three days.

CHEMULPO CHINNAMPO LINE.
Every three days.

For Freight and passage and further particulars apply to

THE OSAKA SHOSEN KAISHA,
Chemulpo,

RONDON, PLAISANT & CO.

General Storekeepers and Merchants, Ships Contractors, Tobacconists, Commission and Forwarding Agents, Coal Merchants

IMPORTERS AND EXPORTERS

Seoul & Chemulpo.

W. D. WENTWORTH.

LANDING
AND
SHIPPING AGENT.
AND
CUSTOMS BROKER.

12 OURA, NAGASAKI.

STEWARD & CO.

Chemulpo.

Shipchandlers and Storekeepers, Naval and Mercantile Contractors, Landing and Shipping Agents.

STEWARD'S HOTEL

Chemulpo.

Best accommodation in the port for travellers. Clean and well-aired rooms, good cuisine and prompt attendance, moderate tariff.

○명봉샹사졔됴셔칙임관삼등 궁니부특진관 윤샹학
○임정릉참봉셔판임관팔등 구픔 김지철
○명궁니부소관각궁각사세부도사의원 궁니부참셔관 홍승연 구픔 유치형 구픔 장헌식 륙픔 리종화
○즁졍삼픔통졍대부비셔원승 고부호군 박인수 고도ᄉᆞ 박졔남 고쳡졍 김샹학
○즁구품종ᄉᆞ랑즁학교교관 고학셩 황문찬 이샹은효행 이탁리ᄒᆞ야병시 증직
○증종삼품통훈대부쟝례원좌 쟝례 고통덕랑 유철영
○즁구품종ᄉᆞ랑즁학교교관 고학셩 박원규 이샹은효힝 이탁리ᄒᆞ야병시 증직
○임시위데일연디데삼대디륙군군의보셔판임관삼등 의학교교관 송챵수
○급삼급봉 의학교교관 유병필 관립소학교교원 김희식 관립소학교교원 남명식
이샹일월이십ᄉᆞ일
○의정부찬정죠병호ᄉᆞ직언ᄉᆞ 소 비지셩소구실경간이라 말훈바는다간절이올흐나경을 기다려써교미코저홈이니엇지 가허소양ᄒᆞ리오부무가바야흐로거챵ᄒᆞ니다시번거처말고곳 힝공ᄒᆞ라고슷혜일절을붓처입의비하홈이락여러번재지말고 힐등홀소로부량을보닉여선유ᄒᆞ시다
일월이십ᄉᆞ일
○구년도예산표 광무팔년십이월이십륙일에정부에셔쥬지훈광무구년도예산표가여좌ᄒᆞ더라
○셰입셰출디죠
셰입총액은일쳔ᄉᆞ빅구십륙만오빅칠십ᄉᆞ원이오
셰출총액은일쳔구빅십일만삼쳔륙빅륙십오원인디 셰입부족액ᄉᆞ빅십오만삼쳔구빅일원
참죠 셰입즁지화가계 팔십륙만오쳔원이오
셰출즁지화가계 일빅칠십구만구빅오십팔원이오
셰츌젼년도보젼ᄉᆞ빅륙십일만ᄉᆞ쳔이빅륙십삼원
○셰입
데일관 죠셰 일쳔이빅삼십오만일쳔팔빅이십ᄉᆞ원
데일항 디셰 구빅칠십ᄉᆞ만삼쳔오빅삼십ᄉᆞ원
데이항 호셰 ᄉᆞ십륙만삼쳔이빅륙십원
데삼항 역도젼 이십일만원
데ᄉᆞ항 어렴곽션셰 팔만오천삼십원
데오항 항셰 팔십오만원
지화
데이관 관업슈입 이십ᄉᆞ만이천오빅원
데일항 뎐보 십팔만일천오빅원
데이항 뎐화 칠천오빅원
데삼항 우편 삼만ᄉᆞ천오빅원
데ᄉᆞ항 인쇄국 일만오천원
지화
데오항 관보 ᄉᆞ천원
데삼관 잡슈입 일천이빅오십원
데일항 잡슈입 일천이빅오십원
데ᄉᆞ관 귀왕년도쇼속미납셰 슈입 이빅오십만원
지화슈입차중 팔십륙만오천원
셰입총계 일천ᄉᆞ빅구십륙만오빅칠십ᄉᆞ원
○셰출경상부
황실비
데일관 황실비 일빅칠만삼빅오십구원
데일항 황실비 일빅칠만삼빅오십구원
데이관 향ᄉᆞ비 이십칠만구천륙빅ᄉᆞ십일원
데일항 향ᄉᆞ비 이십칠만구천륙빅ᄉᆞ십일원
지화지출차증 십오만ᄉᆞ천원
합계 일빅ᄉᆞ십오만ᄉᆞ천원
궁니부쇼관
데일관 철도원본청 일만구천ᄉᆞ빅칠십원
데일항 봉급 일만이천원
데이항 청비 이천구빅오십팔원
데삼항 청ᄉᆞ슈리비 일빅이십원
데ᄉᆞ항 잡급급잡비 일천구빅구십이원
데오항 려비 구빅원
데륙항 외국인제급 일천이빅원 (지화)
데칠항 졉디비 이빅원
데팔항 긔계비 일빅원
데이관 부산출쟝쇼 이천원
데일항 청비 삼빅원
데이항 잡급급잡비 일천오빅원
데삼항 려비 이빅원
궁니부소관
데삼관 서북털도국 이만오천삼빅오십삼원
데일항 봉급 구천원
데이항 청비 삼빅칠십오원
데삼항 청ᄉᆞ슈리비 오십원
데ᄉᆞ항 잡급급잡비 오빅이십팔원
데오항 려비 일천원
데륙항 외국인제급 일만ᄉᆞ천ᄉᆞ빅원 (지화)
데ᄉᆞ관 경위원본청 십륙만이천ᄉᆞ빅칠원
데일항 봉급 일만륙천이십원
데이항 청비 일만륙천륙빅ᄉᆞ십ᄉᆞ원
데삼항 청ᄉᆞ수리비 일천이빅원
데ᄉᆞ항 잡급잡비 십이만오천륙빅이십원
데오항 려비 칠빅원
데륙항 긔밀비 이빅원
데칠항 죄수식비 이천이십삼원
데오관 기항쟝경무셔 륙만구천팔빅삼십팔원
데일항 봉급 일만륙빅이원
데이항 청비 ᄉᆞ천구빅원
데삼항 청ᄉᆞ수리비 륙빅이십원
데ᄉᆞ항 잡급급잡비 삼만구천구빅륙십원
데오항 려비 삼천륙빅원
데륙항 피복비 팔천륙빅삼십팔원
데칠항 죄슈식비 일천오빅원 (미완)

론셜

쟝릭의젼졍

○사하에셔일로량군이셔로향ᄒᆞ고오릭상지ᄒᆞ더니즈금은결말이나게될듯훈것이동경소문을드른즉일본원슈대산씨가미구에크게싸우랴고예비훈다ᄒᆞ엿더라

일본군이먼져공격ᄒᆞ는형세롤취ᄒᆞ는지로국이크게습격ᄒᆞ라ᄒᆞ는디ᄒᆞ야대산원슈가격ᄒᆞ거홀예비롤ᄒᆞ는지알슈업스나일본은려순을함락훈후에진북군에군ᄉᆞ를만히더보낼듯이업셧고나로팟킨은구라파로브터항상싱력군과대포들더밧엇스니지금싸홈을ᄒᆞ랴는것은대산의무옴디로퇴정훈일이아인것갓도다

만일대삭씨가진즉싸왓더면구로팟킨대쟝의군ᄉᆞ는지금보다얼마쯤슈효가적엇슬터인디지금삼쥬일을지체ᄒᆞ엿셔도일본군은려순으로일수단쯤밧게더오지못ᄒᆞ엿슬지라

대산원슈가공격ᄒᆞ는형세롤취홀리류가훈가지엇스니로국군이좌우익으로협공홀길을맹렬히ᄒᆞ는서닭에일본군이세부득이ᄒᆞ야되거로큰공격을시작ᄒᆞ게되는듯훈지라

얼더덧지이번싸홈은참독ᄒᆞ게싸울터인즉지금이한데셔군ᄉᆞ들이밤새울괴후가아니나그러ᄒᆞ나글노ᄒᆞ야엇던군ᄉᆞ던지만이샹훌것이니셩훈ᄉᆞ롬들도못견디려니와샹훈군ᄉᆞ들의정경을싱각ᄒᆞ면참혹ᄒᆞ도다.

이싸홈의결과는엇지될는지알슈업스나량군의룡신긔관은다정미훈중에일본군의룡신긔관이대포의위치롤잘못노아셔일본군의숨겨노은대포의계맛치죠훈관력곳ᄒᆞ셔로국군의손히가심ᄒᆞ엿셧고또일본군이출기불의ᄒᆞ는계칙으로혼이로군을ᄉᆞ로잡엇셧는디근리에는드른즉로국군도일본과갓치대포들을공교ᄒᆞ게노으며일본군의출기불의ᄒᆞ는계칙에티ᄒᆞ야일칭더쥬의훈다ᄒᆞ는지라

비록량군즁에어디로더용맹이잇다는명예가도라갈는지알슈업스나어디로보던지일본군이로국군보다더민쳡ᄒᆞ고실심이잇다고ᄒᆞ겟ᄯᅡ다

이싸홈에괴후가대단히관계되겟스며군ᄉᆞ의슈효가만훈편에셔승전홀듯ᄒᆞ나군ᄉᆞ의슈효에티ᄒᆞ야는밋을만훈소문이업더라

뎐보

빅림발

○도국지졍 로국탁지대신이연초와소쥬의셰롤느리고인지셰도느리기로작졍ᄒᆞ엿다더라 로국의시로이모집홀외채가잘될가량이잇다더라

론돈발 일월십팔일

○도병의젼략 셩피득보에셔공포ᄒᆞ되구로팟긴대쟝이혼하평원에셔긔병을만히리용ᄒᆞ라는디그리편벅대쟝은일본군의젼면을직접으로공격ᄒᆞ고골바쓰대쟝은우편을칠터이오리에빗츠대쟝은봉텬남방에잇는일본군의통신긔관을엄습홀터이라ᄒᆞ더라

동디발。동일

○로국니대의소직 로국황뎨셔셔니부대신스바토폴드머스기친왕의소직홈을허락ᄒᆞ엿다더라

빅림발 동일

○로국텰도의긔통 로국에바이갈호슈롤둘너논텰도는지금보통승객의게도타기를허락ᄒᆞ엿다더라

동디발 동월십구일

○로국니디의형편 로국니디의형편은긔의다죠용ᄒᆞ고혁명운동의위엄홈도쾌히업서졋다더라

광고

○본인의장조치렬이가본시부랑패류로그부형ᄌᆞ데간에분지ᄒᆞ여가진면장문권을몰수히도적ᄒᆞ여니엿기로셰부득이ᄒᆞ야셔문권을만들엇고이에광포ᄒᆞ오니니외국인자에삼가속지말고한치렬의가진문권을면집지마옵기를바라옵

평양성닉쌍거리 한긔현 고빅

TELEGRAMS.

(FROM JAPAN PAPERS)

GENERAL NEWS.

London, Jan. 19.
Admiral Dewey has advised President Roosevelt to increase the U. S. naval force in Chinese waters by two battle ships in view of eventualities.

Berlin, Jan. 20.
The situation in the Balkans is again becoming more serious owing to the activity of the Bulgarian Committee.

Berlin, Jan. 20.
Several of the chiefs of the Hereros who recently rose in rebellion against the German Colonial authorities have now been subdued.

Berlin, Jan. 20.
The German Government is trying to effect an amicable settlement of the miners' strike. Two hundred thousand men are involved.—Mainichi.

Berlin, Jan. 20.
The German Crown Prince, while driving recently, was thrown from his dogcart, but escaped injury.

Berlin, Jan. 20.
In America some 40,000 mill operatives are out on strike.

THE WAR.

Little or nothing of interest appears among the telegrams to the local Japanese papers.

There appears to have been a skirmish at Pao-tze-yuen in which the Japanese were, as usual, victorious, and a Tokio telegram dated Jan. 26th says that Kuropatkin has sent urgent requests for men, ammunition and provisions. The last telegram, about one week ago, to a similar effect which came to Korea from Japan has not yet been confirmed.

On the 23rd inst. per S. S. "Ohio" 92 more Korean coolies left for Hawaii.

It is reported that, acting on the advice of General Hasegawa, the Emperor has decided to retain only two battalions of troops in Seoul while the remaining eight battalions are to be quartered in the provinces.

During the risings subsequent to the murder of the Queen some ten years ago, some Japanese were killed. For this the Japanese Minister has now succeeded in obtaining $180,000 indemnity from the Korean Government. Might is evidently right and the Y10,000,000 loan will, to all appearances, have a short but merry life.

Sir Charles Dilke, in a paper read to the Young Liberal's League recently, said that while all other countries had rearmed their forces there was not, with the exception of fifteen imperfect batteries hurriedly purchased in Germany during the Boer war, a single quick-firing gun in the possession of the British regular field artillery.

The kinky little word, "zemstvo," which appears so frequently in news from Russia these days, is derived from the noun, "zemlia," meaning land, and the verb, "vopeét," to clamor: Thus it signifies "the voice of the land" and is a council of landed proprietors appointed to deliberate and report to the central executive the wants of the rural population. It is something like an English county council without the latter's authority, yet that authority is what it now pleads for. The zemstvo was founded in 1864 and Alexander II. intended it as one of most important of his reforms.

ATTENTION.

We wonder how the Korean "Tommy" would like the following orders which were recently issued by the Home District Headquarters in England.

"For the credit of the Army in general and their own corps in particular," men on furlough, especially those in London, are asked to pay more attention to their dress. The most common complaints are:—

"Wearing caps on the back of the head to display effeminate and unsoldierlike curls on the forehead.

"Carrying a cigarette behind the ear.

"Walking with hands in trousers pockets.

"Wearing civilian boots and mufflers in cold weather."

THE RAILWAY AT PORT ARTHUR.

A Tokio message to the Mainichi states that the Japanese are about to restore the railway lines between Port Arthur and Dalny to the Russian guage, with a view to using the eight engines and three hundred cars received from the Russians at Port Arthur. The lines were reduced to the Japanese guage when the railway fell into the hands of General Nogi's Army. All the Japanese engines and cars used in that vicinity at present will be sent to the north.

In this connection it will be remembered that it has been reported that when adapting Russian railways to their own guage the Japanese have sawn off the sleepers so as to render them useless should the railway again fall into Russian hands, and that, therefore, reinstating the Russian guage will be no light task.

General Kawamura, recently in command of the Tenth Division, has been promoted to the rank of full General and has returned to Tokio from the front. It is reported in Tokio that he is about to undertake some special duty, probably in connection with the new army which is to have its headquarters in the Yalu district.

In the third criminal section of the Tokyo Court of Appeal on Jan. 20th decision was given in the appeal case brought by Mr. S. H. Kuhn against the sentence delivered in the Yokohama District Court. The appellant was absent. The higher tribunal dismissed his appeal Later enquiries have elicited the information that Mr. Kuhn appears to have left Japan.

It may be interesting to stamp collectors says the Japan Gazette, to note that, owing to a scarcity of 2 cent stamps in Korea, the Seoul Post Office has surcharged several sheets of the old 25 Poon stamps, of the 1886 issue, in native characters for 2 cents; and these are being used for a short time on newspapers and other documents requiring a fee of that amount. They promise to become a great rarity.

That arch-conspirator, General Hyŏn, is according to the Daihan Ilpo," still busy. From Japan he has written to the Household Department that, after the fall of Port Arthur, the Japanese decided to annex Korea. General Hyŏn says that this is breaking his heart, and he is urging the Japanese Government to respect Korea's independence. We do not think that General Hyŏn's efforts will make much difference, either way.

The is considerable speculation in Tokio as to what action will be taken to prevent a Russian invasion of Korea. There is a rumour, which is probably true, that another army will be formed with head quarters in the Yalu region. Considerable Japanese reinforcements have recently gone north and wounded men are from time to time being landed at Chemulpo. The general concensus of opinion seems to be that a Russia descent will be attempted very shortly and that the Japanese will not attack Vladivostock until events have more definitely shaped themselves.

HORNY-HANDED TOIL.

[The record for strenuousness among British workmen has just been lowered. A member of the Islington Borough Council states that he recently watched a man working on one of their roads. The honest fellow struck his pick into one hole a hundred and fifty time without moving anything.]

I'm an honest British workman,
And I do whate'er I may
To please my good employers
And to earn my daily pay,
I likes my pipe, I likes my beer,
I rest, like other men;
But when I really gets to work,
My word, you watch me then!

"An' ye're no man, Lord Charles," said the old fellow, regretfully; "Sure, ye're no man."

"Why that?" asked the candidate.

"Arrah, thin"—in the tone of one who hated to have to find fault with a Beresford—"the last toime a Beresford stood, it's up to the knees Oi was in blood and whisky, an'sorra a drop of aythur have Oi seen this toime."

More recently, when Lord Charles was contesting York City, a solemn old clergyman came up to him on the platform, and mouthed out, "Permit me to have the honour of conversing with you. I had the privilege, many years ago, of being confirmed by your venerated uncle, the Primate of all Ireland."

It was a desperate situation, but fortunately Lord William Beresford, most winning, diplomatic, and tactful of men, was in the hall, and Lord Charles hailed him in stentorian tones.

"Bill, Bill! Here's an old parson who says he was confirmed by old Uncle John. Come up here and talk to him.—"Arlington," in "London Opinion."

L'Impartial says that Wang Chih-chun has been banished to his native place, as being generally unpopular. This is the ex-official who was recently nearly assassinated in Shanghai.

It appears that a "claim" in Klondyke given by a generous miner to King Edward some years ago has become valuable, and unless the King goes to work it the claim may be "jumped."

The Russian Raid on Newchiatun on the 12th instant, which followed the destruction of a part of the railway in the districts of Anshantien, Haicheng and Yingkow on the 11th inst. was, in accordance with reports received by the "China Review" from the most reliable sources, far more successful and did much more harm than has been so far stated. The Cossacks did burn and capture lots of stores, and only withdrew when the Japanese got up strong enough reinforcements from Liaoyang and Tashicho. General Mistchenko now threatens the entire Japanese communications from Newchwang to Moukden; and, in consequence, great numbers of Japanese soldiers are being sent to guard the long line of railway at present in Japanese possession.

A Dalny message to "Chefoo Daily News" dated the 15th instant says:—The entry of the Japanese troops into the fortress at Port Arthur is apparently to be followed as quickly by the presence of civilian workmen, to engage in the restoration of such portions of the town as have been injured in the bombardment, as was the case immediately following the seizure of Dalny by the Mikado's soldiers. The first thing to receive the attention of the Japanese in Port Arthur will be the docks and harbor. Twelve hundred Japanese laborers have left here this week for Port Arthur. It is stated that they will at once begin work on the old dock in the East Basin. This dock, while it was used by the Russians in repairing and fitting out their ships of war and other vessels, was never brought to a finished state, and owing to the long siege and bombardment of the town, with the particularly concentrated fire of the Japanese during the latter days of the siege, is in bad repair. It is stated here that the Japanese will bend all their energy toward putting it into perfect shape.

UNDERGROUND HOMES.

In the selection of a building site the Behring Strait Eskimo chooses a bank near the shore, with a gentle slope toward the south. Here he excavates with his whalebone shovel a place ten or twelve feet square and about six feet deep. Level with the floor he digs a tunnel three and one-half or four feet squarr out to the hillside, and here he sets up a driftwood inclosure, with an opening at the top large enough to admit one person at a time. In all the long winter months, when the snowdrifts keep the subterranean resident confined for weeks at a time, but little snow finds its way through this opening. Moreover, as the heat rises to the top, little of it escapes through the tunnel.

The room thus excavated is studded closely with driftwood, of which there is always an abundance; a rafter is placed at each corner, reaching to a square frame or skylight in the center. This is covered with the intestines of seals or walrus, instead of glass. The spaces between the rafters are filed out with brush whalebone, split logs or odds and ends of boards found along the beach. This thatch is covered with sod or loose ground, and the home is complete—a home warm and comfortable, and one that offers no obstruction to the almost cotinual north wind from January to the middle of May.

As a rule no fireplace is found in these underground dwellings. But little cooking is done. The natives live on dry fish, stored up in summer, or on raw frozen tomcods caught through the ice by the women in the winter. This, with seal oil, blubber and seal meat, constitutes the entire diet. Knives, forks, and spoons are unknown. The men find an excellent substitute in their first and second fingers, which they dip into the tray of seal oil and lick with great gusto. The women use three fingers and the childdren all four.

For the young people of the family, or families—for they crowd into one hut as many as possibly can find sleeping room—a platform six feet long is constructed, the entire width of the room, midway between floor and ceiling. Here the boys and girls rest their limbs in months of slumber, the floor being reserved for the old folks.

The French Consul at Hupeh is to receive the Double Dragon order of 1st class, 2nd division for his speedy settlement of the late trouble there with converts.

The Korea Daily News.

Issued at 5 P. M. daily except Sundays.

Rate of Subscription:—

Per Year............Yen 25.

Per Quarter..........Yen 7.

Per Month..........Yen 2.50.

Postage in Korea not charged extra.
Postage abroad charged-extra.

Advertisements, 50 sen per day for 1 inch or less.
5 yen per month per inch.
50 yen per year per inch.

All communications to

E. T. BETHELL,
Editor and Publisher,
Pak-tong, Seoul.

THE SITUATION ON THE SHAHO.

According to the latest intelligence received in official quarters here, says the "Kokumin," there are now some 20,000 Russian in the neighbourhood of Hsiencheng, this force constituting a portion of the left wing of General Kuropatkin's army. In addition, 2,000 Russians are stationed a Hweijan and Tunghwa, east of Hsienchang. The front of the right wing of the Russian Army has been extended to the west of Mukeu. The total strength of the enemy in the direction of the Shaho is roughly estimated at 270,000. The Russian forces at Nicolisk, north of Vladivostock, also now number some 60,000. The transportation of troops from Russia still continues, some 15 trains from the west daily arriving at Kharbin. It seems to be the intention of General Kuropatkin to operate against our positions from the direction of Hsienchang and the Korean boundaries.

A Moji despatch dated the 18th inst., also states that, according to the statement of an officer belonging to the Imperial Guards who has just returned home from the front, the Russians in the direction of the Shaho appear to have already made good the losses sustained in the late battle, having received large reinforcements from home. It is believed that the enemy's main force is stationed in the neighbourhood of Mukden and that General Kuropatkin's headquarters are situated at Tahshan. After the late Battle of the Shaho the enemy in front of our Right Wing was numerically weak, but has since then been reinforced. At Fushun, there is a coal mine worked by the Russians and in consequence of its importance the latter have especially strengthened their defences in that direction. At one time it was supposed that the Russians on the Shaho would withdraw northward when the defensive work at Tiehling had been completed, but no such step under existing circumstances is likely to be taken by the Russians. The officer further stated that the weather at the front was bitterly cold. For instance, in one of the recent skirmishes, which lasted three hours, many soldiers were frostbitten. Such being the situation, it will be almost impossible for the present for the opposing armies commence operations on a large scale.—Japan Times.

RUSSIAN FORCES IN NORTH KOREA.

The "Nichi Nichi's" Shimonoseki correspondent states that, according to an officer who arrived at the above port from North Korea on the 19th inst., the headquarters of the enemy's forces in North Korea are established at Songjin, where there is a Russian force of 3,000 infantry and 12 guns. At Pukchöng, there are 2,000 Russian troops, with four guns.

VLADIVOSTOCK NEWS.

Two German steamers, which have been staying at Vladivostock for about one month after landing Cardiff coal there, arrived at Moji on the 16th, having left the Russian port on the 13th. According to their crews, the harbour of Vladivostock is ice-bound to the depth of about two feet and the cold is intense. The cruiser "Rossia" has her repairs nearly completed. The "Gromoboi" and the "Bogatyr" are still in dock and will be made good in the course of this month. On completion of repairs, the three vessels may be restored to fighting capacity. There are one dozen torpedo boats in the harbour. Admiral Skrydloff left Vladivostock for St. Petersburg on the 12th inst. It is said that be will not return to the port. The Russians are generally dreaming of the arrival of the Baltic Squadron at Vladivostock. The news of the fall of Port Arthur reached there on the 2nd inst. when the residents were greatly disturbed. The Vladivostock garrison is said to be about 35,000 strong. Over ten foreign steamers are now at anchor and some 200,000 tons of coal, principally Cardiff coal, is in stock at Vladivostock.—Japan Gazette.

THE NORTH SEA INCIDENT.

A dispatch from Paris dated the 24th ult. says the Russian defence before the International Commission which is to inquire into the North Sea incident is practically completed. The main features are given as follows:—

First—That the firing by the Russian squadron was justified as a defence against attack. This entails proving the presence of Japanese torpedo-boats. The Russian delegates declare that they have this proof in the most positive and overwhelming form.

Second—That even if the Russians were not attacked, they believed they were attacked, and therefore the defensive measures taken were in absolute good faith.

Third—At most, it was an accident at sea, where the dangers and risks are extreme and analogous to the British battleship "Camperdown" ramming and sinking the British battleship "Victoria" and the recent firing by a British warship upon a coasting vessel during target practice,

RUSSIAN OFFICERS AT MATSUYAMA.

A Tokyo message states that the Russian officers from Port Arthur have only been temporarily allowed to retain their swords. The terms of surrender cannot be interpreted as meaning that the officers are to be allowed to have their swords while detained in prisoners' quarters. A Mainichi telegram from Matsuyama, dated the 20th states that the Committee which has control of the prisoners has decided to keep all the swords in their care. The Russian officers are much incensed. The Japanese troops and police are on the alert. Two Russian officers resisted by force when the Committee's representative requested them to hand over their swords. They were placed under arrest. Among the officers from Port Arthur are a Marquis and a Baron A prisoner tried to escape from Matsuyama on the night of the 18th, but was at once discovered.

THE HANKOW-PEKING RAILWAY.

Viceroy Chang Chih Tung and Sheng Sun Wai have telegraphed to the Chinese Minister at Washington requesting him to explain to the Secretary of the United States Foreign Affairs Department the reasons for the cancellation of the Hankow-Peking Railway concession. They explain that they are the mouthpieces of the inhabitants of three provinces who are unanimous in their desire to have the concession cancelled, and express the hope that the United States Government will not place any obstacles in the way so as to prevent the desire of the people from being realised.

THE NEUTRALITY QUESTION.

The reasons put forward in the Russian Government's circular note charging the Chinese Authorities with neglecting their duties of neutrality are said to be five, namely:—(1) That the Japanese are allowed to made use of the Hunghutzu. (2) That the Chinese Government employs Japanese officers to train its troops. (3) That the Japanese are allowed to have a naval base in the Miao Islands near Chefoo. (4) That the export of contraband of war from Chefoo for Japanese use has been freely permitted. (5) That the Japanese Iron Foundry is supplied with iron are from the Taiya Mine in China.

Reports from the north state that the ice on the Yalu has already commenced to melt. There is evidence however, that another spell of cold weather is about to set in.

The following is from the "Tokio Asahi:"—The term of Mr. J. McLeavy Brown, Chief Commissioner of the Customs, expires in August this year, but his contract will not be renewed.

The Governor of the Straits Settlements has issued a proclamation, operative from the 16th inst., that no Straits dollars shall be exported beyond the limits of the Malay Peninsula, the Dutch East Indies and Borneo.

The far-seeing Japanese are already taking measures for safeguarding the land communications of their army, in prospect of the arrival of the Baltic Fleet putting an end to their exclusive command of the sea.—Novosti, St. Petersburg.

From the "Chefoo Daily News" we learn that telegraph messages for Port Arthur and Dalny may now be sent *via* Newchwang. There is a censorship and telegrams must be marked "via Newchwang" and are only accepted at senders risk.

Viceroy Tsen Chen Hsuen has telegraphed to Peking that, in view of the approach of the Baltic fleet to Far Eastern waters, special attention should be paid to such places af Chusan and Santaochu along the China coast which are important harbours, and that this step should be taken so as to safeguard China's neutrality rights.

A Tokio despatch to the Japan Gazette says it is stated on high authority that the prospects of diplomacy still defy prognostication. The fall of Port Arthur cannot but seriously affect the general situation, but Japan will adhere to her original programme with which international sympathy is increasing more than ever. It is all-important to accomplish the ultimate object without procrastination. General resentment is expressed here at Russia's abuse of Chinese clothes and the employment of Chinese regulars.

Count Reventlow, the well-known German naval expert, recently delivered a lecture on "Great Britain and the German Navy," in the course of which he said that Great Britain could still claim to be "Mistress of the Seas." The naval power of France, Italy and Russia had decreased, and Great Britain was now so strong that she could easily face two, or even three opponents simultaneously. Germany could at present only send 13 battleships to sea; and of this number only two could claim to be completely efficient. Great Britain, on the other hand, could immediately send out 41 battleships independently of the Mediterranean Fleet. In view of those figures, Count Reventlow claimed that British suspicions of Germany's naval ambitions were ridiculous, and that Great Britain had no reason to object to further development of the German navy.

The Korea Daily News.

VOL. II, FRIDAY, JANUARY 27, 1905. No. 21

大韓每日申報

대한ᄆᆡ일신보

(뎨이쳔이십이호) (월요일) 일쳔구ᄇᆡᆨ오년일월삼십일

본샤고ᄇᆡᆨ

이신보ᄂᆞᆫ영어와한어로셕거ᄆᆡ일츌판ᄒᆞᄋᆞᆸ

신문갑

한쟝 엽두돈오푼

일삭됴 엽두량닷돈

우표갑ᄭᆞ지 삭닷돈

다ᄉᆞᆺ돈으로밧ᄉᆞᆸ

광고료ᄂᆞᆫ

귀한의쟝단과ᄌᆞᄒᆡᆼ의다쇼로즁감ᄒᆞ되렴가로밧을터이오며오ᄅᆡ지아녀대한사ᄅᆞᆷ마다다이신문을보실터이니광고내시기를원ᄒᆞ시ᄂᆞᆫ이들은우리신문사에와서면약ᄒᆞ심을희망ᄒᆞᄋᆞᆸ

○발ᄒᆡᆼ소 박동대한ᄆᆡ일신보사발어한교엽해젼영국인셜필림집자리오

사쟝 영국인 (배셜)

평양 디리졈

○평양효동사ᄂᆞᆫ 권미보씨로우리신문관디리인을뎡ᄒᆞ엿시오니평양에계신구람코저ᄒᆞ시ᄂᆞᆫ 쳠군ᄌᆞᄂᆞᆫ해디리졈에왕림ᄒᆞ와면의ᄒᆞ시ᄋᆞᆸ

사고

○우리대한ᄆᆡ일신보의목뎍은대한의안녕질서에관한모든대목에되ᄒᆞ야ᄂᆞᆫ공평한변론을쥬쟝ᄒᆞᆷ이라우리동신원의ᄇᆞ란보ᄂᆞᆫ신문보시ᄂᆞᆫ쳠군ᄌᆞ의게ᄒᆞᆼ상보도ᄒᆞ리며편지들귀셔ᄒᆞ여주시ᄂᆞᆫ이ᄂᆞᆫ셩명과번디를적어붓치시기를희망ᄒᆞ오니벼게ᄉᆞᆯ신문샹에괴제ᄒᆞᆯ란ᄂᆞᆫ거시아니오다만극히신용ᄒᆞᄂᆞᆫ즁거를숨고자ᄒᆞᆷ이라괴자ᄂᆞᆫ아모괴서던지괴쥐ᄒᆞᆷ을되각ᄒᆞᄂᆞᆫ권리를가졋소나되각ᄒᆞᄂᆞᆫ리유ᄂᆞᆫ발ᄒᆞᆯ터이오며공즁평화를문란케ᄒᆞᄂᆞᆫ듯ᄒᆞᆫ괴서ᄂᆞᆫ의뢰ᄒᆞ이밧지안켓ᄉᆞᆸ니이다

●본사셜시이ᄅᆡ로신문을ᄆᆡ양우례로분젼ᄒᆞ와례젼부의임의로젼ᄒᆞᆫ듯ᄉᆞ오로번곳에ᄂᆞᆫ후ᄂᆞᆺ게젼ᄒᆞ기도ᄒᆞ며혹멋칠거슬ᄒᆞᆫ번에젼ᄒᆞ기도ᄒᆞ며혹아니젼ᄒᆞᄂᆞᆫ곳도잇다ᄒᆞ와우리신문을ᄉᆞ랑ᄒᆞ야구람ᄒᆞ시ᄂᆞᆫ 쳠군ᄌᆞ의게되ᄒᆞ야ᄆᆡ우미안ᄒᆞ옵기로지금은분젼인을두고ᄆᆡ일일즉이젼ᄒᆞ며아니젼ᄒᆞ거나늣게거나ᄒᆞ폐가엽도록ᄒᆞ랴ᄒᆞ오니혹아니젼ᄒᆞ거나혹늣게젼ᄒᆞ거나ᄒᆞᆫ일이잇스면본사로통긔ᄒᆞ여주심을희망ᄒᆞᄋᆞᆸ

뎐보

론돈발 일월십일

○로슈일군 구로팟긴대쟝이엇ᄂᆞᆫ뵈긴요ᄒᆞᆫ슈비군을엄습ᄒᆞ야쟝엿다더라

동디발 동이월십칠일

○로함의보고 셩피득보뎐보를거ᄒᆞᆫ즉로졔스ᄐᆡ벤스기대쟝이로국황뎨셔보고ᄒᆞ되자긔의함ᄃᆡ가풀거샹대쟝의함ᄃᆡ와련합ᄒᆞ야마다가스카를떠나서보ᄃᆞ로노스기의함ᄃᆡ를기ᄃᆞ린것엽서동편으로진발ᄒᆞ야젹도근방에서보ᄃᆞ로노스기의함ᄃᆡ를맛낫게희ᄒᆞᆫ이라ᄒᆞ엿다ᄒᆞ엿더라

동디발 동월십팔일

○로함출발 법국신문통신원이셩피득보에서뎐보ᄒᆞᆫ것을거ᄒᆞᆫ즉불ᄅᆡᆨ함대가마다가스카로브터셰나서항쳔ᄒᆞ엿다ᄒᆞ엿더라

동디발 동일

○로함소식 보ᄃᆞ로노스기대쟝의함ᄃᆡ가쾌림을지ᄂᆡ서지부틸로향ᄒᆞ야진발ᄒᆞ엿ᄂᆞᆫ데그함ᄃᆡᄂᆞᆫ비ᄇᆡ셕쳑으로조직ᄒᆞᆫ것이더라ᄒᆞ엿더라

론돈발 일월십팔일

○로국신문과영국관계 로국신문노보브레마ᄂᆞᆫ일본이불릭쳠ᄃᆡ의동쟝을뎐보로소문을듯ᄂᆞᆫ일을론란ᄒᆞ며영국정부에서이런뎐보의젼ᄒᆞᆫ것을맛당히금ᄒᆞᆯᄭᅥ시라고론박ᄒᆞ엿더라

동디발 동일

○로국쳘공의쟝엽 로국쳘공과셩피득보에쳘물무역이거의뎡지ᄒᆞ게되엿ᄂᆞᆫ데그것은혁명파에서운동ᄒᆞᆫ일이라오박명의쳘공이벌서휴엽ᄒᆞ야그결과로졍부소관희군제션소에서정무ᄒᆞ엿다더라

동디발 동일

○로군의경동 사하군방에잇ᄂᆞᆫ로국군ᄃᆡᄂᆞᆫ일본군의그근디에디뢰포를뭇엇다ᄂᆞᆫ풍셜에히졍ᄒᆞ엿고셔대신원슈가곳큰싸홈을시작ᄒᆞ리라ᄒᆞ야예비ᄒᆞᆫ다더라

ᄇᆡᆨ림발 일월십구일

○로군의슈효 동경에서샤호에잇ᄂᆞᆫ로국군수가삼십칠만명가량이라고말ᄒᆞ더라더라

론돈발 동월십팔일

○영국셕탄의고등 덕국셕탄광에서분란이이러난서닭에영국에서셕탄갑이고등ᄒᆞ야작일에ᄂᆞᆫ셕탄ᄆᆡ돈에두실링식이나올낫다더라

잡보

○죠졍고빙 학부에서외부에죠회ᄒᆞ기를즁학교사폐원탄이를본부참예원으로고빙ᄒᆞᄂᆞᆫ합동을청의셔를이에송교ᄒᆞ니쳥컨대연셔ᄒᆞᆫ후작환ᄒᆞ기를바란다ᄒᆞ엿ᄂᆞᆫ티그월봉은지화삼ᄇᆡᆨ원으로작뎡ᄒᆞᆫ다ᄒᆞ엿더라

○쳥의셔인 외부에서졍부에사쳥의ᄒᆞ기를졍삼흠교헌이가무에관등졔ᄒᆞᆫ교로옥구감리셔앙안을이에졔츌ᄒᆞᆫ다ᄒᆞ엿더라

○탐쟝환츌금 ᄇᆡᆨ셩긔씨ᄂᆞᆫ영변관찰사직임시에탐쟝ᄒᆞ엿든돈을취ᄒᆞᆫ인민의게도로ᄂᆡ여주엇다더라

○민씨문외디명 민영린씨가귀국ᄒᆞ여문외에서디명ᄒᆞᄂᆞᆫ티졀교ᄒᆞᆫ아국에교셥홈으로쟝ᄎᆞᆺ면관ᄒᆞᆫ다ᄒᆞ며면관ᄒᆞᆫ후에ᄂᆞᆫ평양민인이곳졍소ᄒᆞ여민씨가평양관찰사직임시에탐쟝ᄒᆞᆫ거슬물슈히환츄ᄒᆞᆯ터이라더라

○탐쟝완거 쳔졍밧긔양리근호씨가우물슈츌비슈렴에완거ᄒᆞ고너지아니ᄒᆞᄂᆞᆫ고로경무에서희가인을챡치ᄒᆞ엿더라

○국쟝피임 법부회계국쟝은참서관리종셩씨가피임ᄒᆞ엿더라

○량경관회견 한셩니쳥경찰범과우물슈츌ᄒᆞᄂᆞᆫ소건에디ᄒᆞ야그엇더케ᄒᆞᆯ방침을샹의ᄒᆞᆯᄎᆞ로일본경부와경무ᄉᆞ가삼오일샹오십일시량에회견ᄒᆞ여담판ᄒᆞ엿더라

○가쥬리 함경남도관찰사리쳔경씨의보고를거ᄒᆞᆫ즉삼슈군슈계슌니가쳥국림강현에서파송ᄒᆞᆫ변군젼관리ᄂᆞᆫ곳랑에ᄇᆡ류ᄒᆞᆫ나서찬무본의국번카슈명ᄒᆞ리홍뎍의외에ᄒᆞᆫ가간도로면에엽거ᄒᆞᆫ향약김상훈과티동면향약인명범이가가종리쟝인죠방칠인을포착ᄒᆞᆫ다칭탁ᄒᆞ고위민을췌동ᄒᆞ야방쟝취당을타살코저ᄒᆞᆫ다ᄒᆞ니취칠인일즉역시대한국민이라진가ᄂᆞᆫ우리게상관이업스나인명을타살ᄒᆞᆫ다ᄒᆞ미듯기에샹ᄒᆞᆫ경취ᄒᆞᆫ지라그명리가되여인명을살취ᄒᆞᆫ다ᄂᆞᆫ말을듯고알고도모른체홈이가ᄒᆞ냐아니ᄒᆞ나바리긴티쥬의죠치ᄒᆞ여ᄒᆞ여공랑국법계의혼단이업케ᄒᆞ라ᄒᆞᆫ지라본군에서곳쟝채를발송ᄒᆞ여쟝인죠와밋동당죠종면을착치ᄒᆞ고며당은도망ᄒᆞᆫ지라취초ᄒᆞᆫ즉쟝가의공초니에본인이본시삼남인물로서금년팔월분에북간도에나ᄂᆞ려리희티를봉착ᄒᆞᆫ즉궐자말이며과환민이드러와사ᄂᆞᆫ거시수쳔호나되매이벽를당ᄒᆞ여호젹을거두고세를거두면소출하수쳔금을싱징ᄒᆞ리라ᄒᆞᄂᆞᆫ고로총리인쟝을무ᄂᆞᆫ고죠종ᄒᆞ여면으로ᄒᆞ여금고시를편간셩ᄒᆞ여위션쥬ᄒᆞ고샹슈원편라ᄒᆞ엿다고삼슈군에서보고ᄒᆞ엿더니ᄒᆡ군에서ᄯᅩ보고ᄒᆞ기를쟝계권관리셔대쟝규와ᄒᆞᆫ평넝ᄒᆞᆫᄉᆞ후에본디에서니쟝죠광한을곳본디로시무ᄒᆞ엿라ᄒᆞᆫ고로관찰부에보고ᄒᆞ여잉송ᄒᆞ엿더니쳐ᄲᅢ고효지ᄒᆞᆫᄉᆞ후에본디에서판결ᄒᆞ기를기다리노라ᄒᆞ고병즁의게ᄒᆞ여죄인을압송ᄒᆞ엿다ᄒᆞ엿더라

○죠졍환권 남셔회동방니의징수싱일호를일본인이미슈ᄒᆞ엿ᄂᆞᆫ티음본령ᄉᆞ가한셩부로죠회ᄒᆞ고가권을밧고야말나고쳥ᄒᆞ엿더라

○차관상지 졍부에서은화삼쳔만원을일본에서차관ᄒᆞᆯ차로탁지고문관과계약즁인티졍부에셔국회관세만담임ᄒᆞᆫ다고일본대표자ᄂᆞᆫ젼국세를담보ᄒᆞ라ᄒᆞ미샹지ᄒᆞ야미결홈으로림공ᄉᆞ가미란대를초쳥ᄒᆞ야샹힐ᄒᆞ다가림공ᄉᆞ가이십륙일에폐현ᄒᆞ야 쥬품ᄒᆞ엿다더라

UNION INSURANCE SOCIETY OF CANTON.

Head office Hongkong.
Marine risks underwritten at current rates.
Agents in Chemulpo,
E. MEYER & Co.

COMPAGNIE DES MESSAGERIES MARITIMES.

Fortnightly Direct Service.

For Marseilles
via Ports.
Sailing from Yokohama
Calling at Kobe,
Shanghai, Hongkong, Saigon, Singapore,
Colombo, Djibonti, Suez, Port Said
and Marseilles.

For particulars apply to
HOLME RINGER & Co.,
Chemulpo.

HAYASHIDA & CO.,

16 MYENG DONG, CHIN KO KAI, SEOUL.
BRANCH OFFICE AT CHEMULPO.

Money changers, Coal and Wood Merchants, Express Agents.

We are agents for the Pyeng-yang Coal Company and the Karazu Coal Company of Japan. We have the best quality of both anthracite and bituminous coal, and prompt execution of orders is our speciality. Firewood of all kinds kept in stock. Full weight guaranteed. Money of all denominations exchanged at current rates. Parcels received for all parts.

CHINA MUTUAL LIFE INS. OC.

Most favourable terms to policy holders.

Benefit system unsurpassed.

HOLME RINGER & Co.
Agents, Chemulpo.

C. P. R.

CANADIAN PACIFIC RAILWAY COMPANY'S ROYAL MAIL STEAMSHIP LINE.

THE FAST ROUTE BETWEEN CHINA, JAPAN, AND EUROPE VIA CANADA AND THE UNITED STATES.

Route from Hongkong via Shanghai, Nagasaki (Inland Sea of Japan) Kobe, Yokohama Victoria and Vancouver.

Twin Screw Empress Steamship—6,000 Tons—Speed 19 knots.

PROPOSED SAILING FROM YOKOHAMA.

R. M. S. Empress of India.
R. M. S. Empress of Japan.
R. M. S. Empress of China.
R. M. S. Athenian.
R. M. S. Tartar.

Special reduction (first class only) granted to members of the Military, Naval, Diplomatic and Civil services and to Missionaries.

Passengers have choice of ten routes across the Continent of America and have privilege of travelling by any Atlantic Steamship Line.

Round the World passage tickets in connection with the P. and O. S. N., North German Lloyd and Messageries Co.'s **£125.**

All rates payable at current rate of exchange.

For further information, Tickets, Guide Books, etc., apply to

HOLME, RINGER & Co., AGENTS,
Chemulpo.

Grand Hotel,

(Formerly the Station Hotel)

Near the Railway Terminus. West Gate Seoul.

The Best Hotel in Korea,
Handsome new Building.
Fine Airy Rooms
Excellent Cuisine.
Terms Moderate.
Special terms to Missionaries
and to permanent boarders.

Electric cars within 2 minutes' walk.

W. H. EMBERLEY.
Proprietor

EVERY FACILITY.

In connection with Life Assurance Business is afforded by

The Standard Life Assurance Co.,

One of the largest and wealthiest of the Provident Institutions of the United Kingdom Forms of Application and all information will be promptly afforded on application.

10 CENTS A DAY.

Not a very large expenditure is it? But it is sufficient to secure for a man of 30 a policy with the STANDARD LIFE OFFICE for

$1323.

For all particulars of rates, etc., apply to

Holme, Ringer & Co.,
Agents, Chemulpo.

THE NEW YORK LIFE INSURANCE COMPANY.

Have you ever been declined by any Company?

Are you engaged in a specially hazardous occupation?

Have you heard of the New York Life Insurance Company's New Classifications for this class of Risks?

If not, send your date of birth, occupation and particulars of rejection, if any to

E. MEYER & Co.,
Agents, Chemulpo.

MITSUI BUSSAN KAISHA.
(MITSUI & Co.)
MITSUI GINKO.
(MITSUI BANK.)

The Bank is owned by the members of the Mitsui Family, who, as partners, assume an unlimited responsibility for all liabilities of the Bank:—

Capital.......................Yen 5,000,000
Reserve Fund...................." 5,600,000

HEAD OFFICE, TOKYO.
LONDON OFFICE, 34 LIME ST., E. C.

BRANCHES AND AGENCIES:—
New York, San Francisco, Hamburg, Bombay, Singapore, Manila, Hongkong, Amoy, Chefoo, Tientsin.

Kobe, Hakodate, Yokohama, Kure, Yokosuka, Moji, Shimonoseki, Miike, Wakamatsu, Nagasaki, Kuchinotsu, Karatsu, Sasebo, Misume, Taipeh, &c.

Telegraphic Address for all the Offices:
"MITSUI."
A. B. C. AND A. 1 CODES USED.

Contractors of Coal.
To the Imperial Japanese Navy. Arsenals and Railway Bureau, Principal Railway Companies and Industrial Work, Home and Foreign Mail and Freight Steamers.

Sole Proprietors
Of the famous Miike, Tagawa and Yamano Coal Mines.

Sole Agents
For the sale of Fukumo, Hokoku, Ichimura, Kanoda, Mannoura, Onoura, Ostuji, Sonoda, Tsubaruro, Yoshinotani, Yoshio, Yurokibura and other coals.

YANGTSE INSURANCE ASSOCIATION, LTD.

The undersigned, having been appointed agents for the above company, are prepared to issue policies and pay losses on marine risks at regular rates.

E. MEYER & Co.,
Agents, Chemulpo.

AMERICAN KOREAN ELECTRIC CO.

Light and Power.

Main Office: Electric Building, Chong No.

RAILWAY DEPARTMENT.

OPERATING CARS BETWEEN EAST AND WEST GATE, EVERY TEN MINUTES:—

First Car leaves East Gate at 7:00 A. M. First Car leaves R. R. Station at 7:25 A. M
Last Car " East Gate at 8.40 P. M. Last " " R. R. Station at 9.05 P.M

OPERATING CARS BETWEEN EAST GATE AND IMPERIAL TOMB TERMINUS, EVERY TWENTY MINUTES:—
CONNECTING WITH EVERY ALTERNATE CAR ARRIVING AT EAST GATE FROM CHONG NO.

First Car leaves East Gate for Tomb at 7:10 A. M.
" " " Tomb for East Gate at 7:30 A. M.
Last " " East Gate for Tomb at 7:50 P. M.
" " " Tomb for East Gate at 8:10 P. M.

OPERATING CARS BETWEEN CHONG NO AND YUNG SAN RIVER EVERY TWELVE MINUTES:—

First Car leaves Chong No for South Gate at 7:12 A. M.
" " " Chong No for Yung San at 7:36 A. M.
" " " South Gate for Chong No at 7:20 A. M.
" " " Yung San for Chong No at 8:09 A. M.
Last " " South Gate for Chong No 9:00 P. M.
" " " Yung San for Chong No at 8.45. P. M.

SPECIAL PRIVATE CARS FURNISHED TO SUIT CONVENIENCE OF PATRONS. PRICES ON APPLICATION AT HEAD OFFICE.

LIGHTING DEPARTMENT.

Where less than 250 candle power of light is used, the rate per month will be
Per 16 candle power incandescent lamp,—All night.—Yen 2.50.
32 candle power incandescent lamp:—All night:—Yen 4.00.
50 candle power incandescent lamp:—All night:—Yen 6.00.
150 " " " " " " 10.00.
1200 " " enclosed arc " " " " 20.00.

Where more than 250 candle power of light is used, a Meter will be installed, if requested:—Rent of Meter Yen 2.00 per month. Rate of charges by meter reading:—Two Sen per Ampere per hour. (Approximately this is equal to about One Sen per 16 C. P. lamp per hour). Minimum monthly charge where meter is installed, Yen 20.00 per month, which includes rental of meter.

Estimates for installing lights furnished on application
An assortment of chandeliers always on hand.

K. Murakami.

Photograph Studio
Chinkokai, Seoul.

Printing, Developing and Enlargement, of Photographs always Undertaken.

Korean Views and Pictures Illustrating Native Customs always on Sale,

---

THE OSAKA SHOSEN KAISHA.

Boats frequently on the berth for Chinnampo.

REGULAR SAILINGS BETWEEN JAPAN AND KOREAN PORTS.

FUSAN AND KOBE VIA SHIMONOSEKI.

OSAKA VIA MOKPO, FUSAN, SHIMONOSEKI AND KOBE.

MOJI DIRECT.

OSAKA VIA KUNSAN, MASANPO, FUSAN, SHIMONOSEKI AND KOBE.

CHEMULPO KUNSAN LINE,
Every three days.

CHEMULPO CHINNAMPO LINE.
Every three days.

For Freight and passage and further particulars apply to
THE OSAKA SHOSEN KAISHA,
Chemulpo.

RONDON, PLAISANT & CO.

General Storekeepers and Merchants, Ships Contractors, Tobacconists, Commission and Forwarding Agents, Coal Merchants

IMPORTERS AND EXPORTERS

Seoul & Chemulpo.

W. D. WENTWORTH.

LANDING
AND
SHIPPING AGENT.
AND
CUSTOMS BROKER.

12 OURA, NAGASAKI.

STEWARD & CO.

Chemulpo.

Shipchandlers and Storekeepers, Naval and Mercantile Contractors, Landing and Shipping Agents.

STEWARD'S HOTEL

Chemulpo.

Best accommodation in the port for travellers. Clean and well-aired rooms, good cuisine and prompt attendance, moderate tariff.

별보

지부데닐늬유스에서듣지홈 대한민일신보의최근보를받아보니한국에서안하무인한일본군디가한국에피를싸란고한는닐비제한이업서서쥬련수름의잉슐로브리방을셋는모양이로다서담업시아모셔이나천량한고잡도잘쥬지아니한란한며셔올에서브리의쥬서지는한쟝이생ᄒᆞ야의식을용금ᄒᆞᆯ권쇽이잇는가난ᄒᆞ고무식ᄒᆞᆫ한인들을잘쓰지도못ᄒᆞᄂᆞᆫ군용슈표를주면서일본군에역부로만쥬에가지란아니ᄒᆞ고쳥에잇서서쳥일보란ᄒᆞᆫ다고진인ᄒᆞᆫ일본헌병들이참혹ᄒᆞ게포살ᄒᆞ엿다ᄒᆞᄂᆞᆫ지라셔울에잇ᄂᆞᆫ외국공ᄉᆞ들중에ᄒᆞᆫ나도자긔의졍부에디ᄒᆞ야이고단ᄒᆞᆫ한인들을구원ᄒᆞ기를쳥ᄒᆞ지아니ᄒᆞᆫ사름이업스나이ᄂᆞᆫ월ᄒᆞᆫ개명ᄒᆞᆫ국민들이이금ᄒᆞ게ᄒᆞ야담나ᄂᆞᆫ소리에귀를세구셰치ᄂᆞᆫ들ᄂᆞᆫ지일본이지금한국을가지고쾌노고ᄂᆞᆫ니면서자긔ᄂᆞᆫ근디릴수름이업슴을로싱각ᄒᆞ니일본이지금바롬을잡ᄂᆞᆫ도다어더먹을것이만이잇슬듯

근리에셔울에셔일본수름들이믜저의계거실닌한인을잡자필수고쥭엿스니외국수름들과쳔에소교수를회통ᄒᆞᄂᆞᆫ양으로맛치야작교경셔에잇ᄂᆞᆫ졍차와갓치실피를수용홈이라ᄒᆞ엿더라

론셜

로국회민원

○근동에오ᄂᆞᆫ뎐보들이만이로국난란의쇼평을젼ᄒᆞ며일본에셔ᄂᆞᆫ심샹치아니ᄒᆞ게싱각ᄒᆞ나지금은그리치아니ᄒᆞ지마ᄂᆞᆫ뎐경은심샹치아니ᄒᆞ게되기를바라노니로국에셔농부들과공쟝들은고셩이자심ᄒᆞ고관인들은만히한졍으로시졍ᄒᆞ엿던고이로다

그러ᄒᆞ나지금로국에혁명운동은셜령일본에오ᄂᆞᆫ뎐보ᄉᆞ의와갓치심샹치아니ᄒᆞ드리도아주운이번젼정에ᄂᆞᆫ영향이밋치지아니ᄒᆞᆯ것이로국은ᄒᆞᆫ광대ᄒᆞᆫ나라이라젼국인민이혁명운동에연합ᄒᆞ게되라면여러ᄒᆡ가될것이며일본이이번젼정을이르킨셰에로국의혁명당이계관졍으로쳔조가만히잇슬줄로혜산ᄒᆞᆫ듯ᄒᆞ고지금로국의혁명운동이조직이잘되엿다ᄒᆞ나그조직이얼마쯤잘되엿다ᄒᆞ드리도로국무슘영향이잇슬듯슬지아니ᄒᆞ리로다

우리ᄂᆞᆫ드르니로국신문들이단슈을바드면셔ᄒᆞᆫ편으로ᄂᆞᆫ젼정에뎌ᄒᆞ야반디를ᄒᆞᆫ다ᄒᆞ나그반디ᄒᆞᆷ은수졍을보로ᄂᆞᆫ셔담이니로국에셔나근리일본에셔나신문단속을잡ᄒᆞᄂᆞᆫ것을보지못ᄒᆞ엿노라현금ᄉᆞ셰로ᄂᆞᆫ로국이자긔의형위로꼬란ᄒᆞᆷ을밧ᄂᆞᆫ것이일본은약국으로강국을디ᄒᆞ야교전ᄒᆞᄂᆞᆫ줄노아러셔로국에무식ᄒᆞᆫ인민들은일본이로국의강박에디ᄒᆞ야자슈자호ᄒᆞᆫ다ᄒᆞ고밋으나이것은교질ᄒᆞᆫ싱각이아니라일본이그ᄃᆞᆨ립과강토보젼을위ᄒᆞ야젼정을시작ᄒᆞ엿다고ᄒᆞᄂᆞᆫ한국에슈일만두류ᄒᆞ야보면그싱각이다업셔질것이오일본의리망ᄒᆞ고간사ᄒᆞᆷ을세ᄃᆞᆯ지라

로국과일본이ᄉᆡᆨ갓ᄒᆞᆫ목적으로싸우나니그목적은평토의확쟝이라두국민이시비간에방관지인이보기에ᄂᆞᆫ다름이업스며일본은우리의싱각에ᄂᆞᆫ여러셔지마ᄂᆞᆫ한국을자긔메국에항부ᄒᆞ라고힘을쓰고로국이사이베리아무역을위ᄒᆞ야얼지아니ᄒᆞᄂᆞᆫ항구를엇으랴고애쓰ᄂᆞᆫ것션즉일본의경영에방히되ᄂᆞᆫ일을셜파ᄒᆞ고잇스며로국은번셔로디를만히가졋스니외레히토디를더욕심낼거시업스나그러나젼일에남의토디를졈령ᄒᆞᆫ힝위가만히잇셧ᄂᆞᆫ지라

지금ᄭᆞ지젼정에디ᄒᆞ야ᄂᆞᆫ우리보기에ᄂᆞᆫ로국인민이일본인민보다원망ᄒᆞᆷ일이더우젹은거시세금의중가ᄒᆞᆫ거슬보면로국에셔ᄂᆞᆫ남조와소주와인지의세를느렷스니일본의미곡과의복가음과다른진요물픔에세를느린것보다인민의게아모히가엿스며동병ᄒᆞᄂᆞᆫ거스로말ᄒᆞ드리도로국인민이일본보다더곤란을밧지아니ᄒᆞᄂᆞᆫ거시로국의인구가일본보다몃ᄇᆡ가더만ᄒᆞ야서그나라로브터오십만병을내여세우기가일본에서이십오만명의동병ᄒᆞ기보다걱정이젹을터이로다

우리의싱각에ᄂᆞᆫ로국의내디와셔우한온치아니ᄒᆞᆫ쳐ᄃᆞᆷ은그반디와ᄒᆞᄂᆞᆫ사름들이이젼정을귀회삼아셔쟈긔의들의말ᄒᆞᆫ거슬평쟝ᄒᆞ게ᄒᆞ노라ᄒᆞ고그러ᄒᆞᆫ거시오이젼졍ᄒᆞᄂᆞᆫ일에디ᄒᆞ야특별ᄒᆞᆫ분란은아니ᄒᆞᆯ줄로밋노라

지금ᄉᆞ셰가모다비참ᄒᆞ게되엿스나로국의젼제졍치만졔망ᄒᆞᆯ거시아니오로국의귀족들이거만ᄒᆞ고탐욕이만ᄒᆞ나일본에도그병통이잇스며로국이이번젼졍을패ᄒᆞᆯ괴미가엿지만ᄂᆞᆫ셜령잇드리도일본이샹등샤회에셔ᄂᆞᆫ크게실망ᄒᆞ리로다

지금이젼정이아직도오릭갈것갓ᄒᆞ나관졍관국이별로죠흔결과가엿슬지라도이다음에자긔들의나라들을다스리ᄂᆞᆫ데로긴요ᄒᆞᆫ공부를밧으리라ᄒᆞ노라

관보

뎨사쳔ᄉᆞ빅칠호 광무구년일월이십칠일

○임외부교셥국쟝서칙임관ᄉᆞ등 졍삼품 리시영

○의원면본관 중추원의관 문귀쥬 중추원의관 박교샹 중추원의관 윤헝식

임중추원의관서칙임관ᄉᆞ등 종이품 리봉호 졍삼품 리종완

○임중추원의관서주임관륙등 구품 리제경 구품 최한우 구품 김진회

○경이등봉 외부교셥구쟝 리시영

이상일월이십ᄉᆞ일

○의원면본관 궁니부대신비서관 김교헌 통신ᄉᆞ면화과주ᄉᆞ 김현몽 통신ᄉᆞ면화과주ᄉᆞ 한인순 통신ᄉᆞ면화과주ᄉᆞ 빅세귀 텰도원주ᄉᆞ 리필준 텰도원주ᄉᆞ 윤친구 텰도원주ᄉᆞ 민병호 텰도원주ᄉᆞ 윤귀학 텰도원주ᄉᆞ 쟝보연 텰도원주ᄉᆞ 김형문 텰도원주ᄉᆞ 리승구 텰도원주ᄉᆞ 목의상

○임 궁니부대신비서관서주임관일등 유구상 졍학죠

○승서관임관오등 주차병국공ᄉᆞ관서기생 강팀현

이상일월이십오일

외보

○한만귀영 동아공ᄉᆞᄂᆞᆫ한만귀엄ᄒᆞᆫ지자회원이발귀ᄒᆞ야셜립ᄒᆞᆫ위탁샹ᄉᆞ회사이니자본금팔십만원중귀위오십만이젼주가모졍되엿ᄂᆞᆫ데그ᄉᆞ업목젹은여좌ᄒᆞ니(일)서쟉 퇴약 교육품의제조판미(이)수출엽셔금위탁판미(삼)젼이항목젹을달ᄒᆞ기에필요ᄒᆞᆫ위탁판미등인데본졈은동경에셜치ᄒᆞ고지졈은쳥국샹히한구북경 텬진 영구 쳥리와급한국경셩과기타디요디에셜치ᄒᆞ고한만귀엉동기관디회의수업을실힝ᄒᆞ기위ᄒᆞᆷ이라더라

○로군기쳥 거십ᄉᆞ일론돈셔발ᄒᆞᆫ뎐보를거ᄒᆞᆫ즉영국츙리대신바루호씨가(구라수고ㅡ)시쟝에셔로군기쳥에관ᄒᆞᆫ졍부ᄉᆞ젹에디ᄒᆞ야연셜ᄒᆞ되영국로군의진정ᄒᆞᆫ문제ᄂᆞᆫ모다로군구과츙돌을요귀ᄒᆞᆯ염여가잇ᄂᆞᆫ영국로군의문제ᄂᆞᆫ(오ㅡ가니ㅡ수단)의방비문제뿐이며또로군싱기협은인도셔북국경에셔엇더ᄒᆞᆫ졍졍이라도이젼보다일층유력ᄒᆞᆫ간셥을엇게ᄒᆞ나ᄉᆞ탕권티인도에잇ᄂᆞᆫ영군은기지에비)쟝군에엄즁ᄒᆞᆫ감독하에그편성을기협ᄒᆞ되병수에중가를불위ᄒᆞ고그실력을크게증가ᄒᆞ엿스며또영국로군이귀용ᄒᆞᄂᆞᆫ졔포ᄂᆞᆫ세계중최량ᄒᆞᆫ것이ᄂᆞᆫ자긔젼ᄒᆞ며또희군에ᄂᆞᆫ기ᄒᆞᆫ혐ᄒᆞᆫ거ᄅᆞᆯ과로히군의젼투력은샹비를중가케ᄒᆞᆷ을엇ᄂᆞᆫ다ᄒᆞ엿더라

○쳥뎡빌명 로국졍부의셔쳥국의중립위반을각국의지죠ᄒᆞᆫ바ㅣ여좌ᄒᆞᆫ디[일]일본군이마젹을조종ᄒᆞᄂᆞᆫᄉᆞ(이 쳥국이일본ᄉᆞ관을교육ᄒᆞᄂᆞᆫᄉᆞ[삼]히군근거디로일본군의표도텰도ᄉᆞ용ᄒᆞᆷ을묵허ᄒᆞᄂᆞᆫᄉᆞ(ᄉᆞ)지부에셔젼지로향ᄒᆞ야금졔픔을슈츌ᄒᆞᄂᆞᆫᄉᆞ[오]먼쳐외쳔지올일본의슈츌ᄒᆞᄂᆞᆫᄉᆞ등인디우에디ᄒᆞ야쳥국졍부에서주외공ᄉᆞ의게ᄒᆞᆫ뎐ᄒᆞ되이샹ᄉᆞ실은젼혀로국졍부의구조ᄒᆞᆫ허흠이오쳥국졍부에셔ᄂᆞᆫ중립을엄슈ᄒᆞ여ᄒᆞ말도위반ᄒᆞᆫ힝위가엽ᄂᆞᆫᄉᆞ를텰국졍부에변명케ᄒᆞ엿더라

○팔괴죠련 목하쳥국보졍부서ᄒᆞᆫ련ᄒᆞᄂᆞᆫ팔괴련군은금셩과원화현ᄉᆞᄋᆞ로쳥귀명병년조춘에거보졍에셔괴견ᄒᆞ고또쾌병식을거힝ᄒᆞᆯ터인디련병소에셔ᄂᆞᆫ히ᄒᆞᆫ련군의복쟝과기타죠계에분망ᄒᆞ며또신식ᄒᆞᆫ련외중가ᄒᆞᆯ쟝뎡샹쳔명을모졍ᄒᆞ엿더라

○영일의세력 영국모ㅣ넝보지도신문에론ᄒᆞ되영국이일본에디ᄒᆞ야학샹이인셰ᄒᆞᆷ이무ᄒᆞᄒᆞ고그희ᄉᆡᆼᄒᆞᆫ신디위를승인ᄒᆞᄂᆞᆫ방침을취ᄒᆞᆯ진디아세아에영국세력도또ᄒᆞᆫ중티에잇지아니ᄒᆞᆫ고도에발ᄒᆞ게고련맹ᄒᆞᆫ일영량국에디ᄒᆞ야다른련동의방국은세력샹에뎨일로공구ᄒᆞᆯ만ᄒᆞᆫ디슈를엇지못ᄒᆞᆷ이라ᄒᆞ엿더라

○텰도진보 뎨반중만텰도ᄂᆞᆫ항일셧시국분요에관ᄒᆞ야쟝셰공사를중지ᄒᆞᆫ다ᄂᆞᆫ풍셜이잇더니금번에또급속히공사진힝ᄒᆞᆷ에결졍ᄒᆞ야목하슈쳔인의공부를중가ᄒᆞ야주야이공사가진보ᄒᆞ야샹월중에ᄂᆞᆫ공사를필요ᄒᆞᆯ목젹인디중차로귀룡브터디남서쥐니르기에거우일쳔도졍에불과ᄒᆞᆫ디이미본도교통샹에일디진보가되리라더라

○중립불슈 거십일일파밋싱일에우쟝파히셔부군에와셔힝슴ᄒᆞ야병은명빅히로셔들경ᄒᆞ야침입ᄒᆞᆫ것으로쳥국중립을파담ᄒᆞᆫ것이라일본졍부에셔ᄂᆞᆫ기젼당시에로국이중립엄슈와한도로일본도또ᄒᆞᆫ중립엄슈의권리를류보ᄒᆞ엿거ᄂᆞᆯ만일로국이그중립을엄슈ᄒᆞᆷ을보지못ᄒᆞᆯ진디일본도또ᄒᆞᆫ이에디ᄒᆞ야이것을준슈치못ᄒᆞᆷ은당연ᄒᆞᆫ지라금에쳥국졍부에디ᄒᆞ야중립유지에관ᄒᆞ야경고ᄒᆞ엿스나필경그효과를보지못ᄒᆞᆯ경우에ᄂᆞᆫ단연코일본졍부도중립준슈권한을응ᄒᆡ키어려울터이라더라

TELEGRAMS.

(FROM JAPAN PAPERS)

RIOTS IN RUSSIA.

London, Jan. 21.

The strike in St. Petersburg is spreading like wild-fire. The police remain passive, apparently fearing to precipitate a conflict but the garrison is standing to arms.

London, Jan. 22.

The situation in St. Petersburg is the most serious ever known. The town is in partial darkness, and everyone is buying candles, anticipating a stoppage of the gas and electric light works. None of the newspapers can be published owing to the strike. The civil employés of the arsenal have also joined the men who have struck work.

Sinister demonstrations took place outside the Winter Palace in the presentation of a petition which is the most remarkable and outspoken document ever presented to an autocratic sovereign. This petition declares that the people of Russia are insulted and treated as slaves, burdened by labour beyond their strength; stifled by despotism and the intolerable yoke of officialism. Injustice, it is declared, has now reached the limit of endurance, and death is preferable to the intolerable sufferings of the people. A national representation, urges the petition, is indispensable, and an immediate convocation of the representatives of all classes is demanded. This will be the sole balm of the people's wounds.

"Satisfy these demands," the petitioners says, "and you will make Russia happy and glorious. If you do not reply to the people's prayer, we shall die in the square before the palace."

A Prefect's notice has been issued, especially in view of the notification that 400,000 men will march to the palace on Sunday afternoon, headed by a young priest named Father Gapon, in full canonicals and with his crucifix, who is heart and soul in the movement.

The workmen insist on seeing the Tsar himself, and therefore a deputation of their number has gone to Tsarskoe-selo to try and deliver to text of the petition, and enable the Tsar to consider it before the monster demonstration is held.

Troops are hurrying up to the capital from all districts.

[A Tokyo dispatch to the "Kobe Shimbun" reproduces a London telegram to the effect that the Priest Gapon, with 15,000 strikers, attempted to present a petition at the palace, when the Cossacks proceeded to use their swords. The strikers are reported to have broken down telegraph lines, and set up steel wire nets and other barriers. In the square fronting the palace a large number of men have been killed or wounded. Fifty thousand troops are fighting with the Revolutionists.]

Berlin, Jan. 21.

It is stated in St. Petersburg that the shot used by one of the guns in firing the salute last week was only a case shot; a fixed case shot, it is pointed out, would have done immense damage.

CHINA'S NEUTRALITY.

London, Jan. 21.

The direct purpose of the Circular issued to the Powers by Mr. John Hay, U. S. Secretary of State, with reference to China, is to prevent land-grabbing at the end of the war, to preserve the "open door," and the old territorial *status quo* of China proper.

The Circular has been formally and warmly accepted by Great Britain, France, and Germany.

It is pointed out that the Circular does not apply to Manchuria, for which Russia and Japan are now fighting.

It is thought in diplomatic circles that the acceptance of the Circular by the Powers mentioned arrests any scheme set afoot for the readjustment of China's boundaries, and removes the potential cause of future friction.

Berlin, Jan. 21.

Great Britain, Germany, and Italy support the attitude taken by the U. S. Government arising out of the Russian circular Note, and in view of later peace negotiations, declare that China proper shall not be included within the belligerent territoy.

GENERAL NEWS.

COAL IN ENGLAND.

Berlin, Jan. 21.

The price of coal in England is advancing.

London, Jan. 20.

The Captain of the Resitelinui, who escaped from Shanghai, has had conferred on him the second class order of St. Stanilaus in appreciation of his bravery.

London, Jan. 19.

The "London Morning Post" affirms that if England is prepared to grant the fullest and most ungrudging recognition of the new position won by Japan, British influence in Asia will be greater than ever. With England and Japan allied, no single nation could be a serious rival.

San Francisco, Jan. 18.

Irving B. Dudley has been appointed by President Roosevelt to confer with President Castro of Venezuela with a view to an amicable settlement of the differences that have incited friction between that country and the United States.

Mr. Dudley will go to Venezuela as the personal representative of President Roosevelt and will investigate the procedure and facts in the case of the confiscation by the Venezuelan government of the American Asphalt Company's property, and will submit his report to the President.

Mr. Dudley was formerly Minister to Peru. His home is at San Diego, California.

AN ALMOST INCREDIBLE DEAL.

If the outcome of Mr. Megata's advice to the Korean Finance Department be correctly reported we can only say that instead of the Korean Government it is the Japanese Government that should pay him and pay him handsomely too.

The new loan is, we are told to be paid in Japanese paper money. It is to be five million yen or ten million dollars.

From Korean sources we learn that the Government is willing to hypothecate the Maritime Customs as security but that the Japanese demand a lien on the whole of the revenue of Korea. This dispute is said to have been dealt with at an audience granted to Mr. Hayashi and Mr. Megata on the 26th instant but the outcome has not transpired.

If this transaction goes through it will be the prettiest example of a "heads I win, tails you lose" scheme that the world has ever seen.

According to the statement of the Bank of Japan, the amount of notes in circulation on Jan. 7th was yen 262,000,000 while the gold reserve amounted only yen 76,000,000 so that Japanese paper money is a far from promising asset.

We learn that the new police adviser, Mr. Maruyama is exerting pressure to have the duties of collecting the taxes added to his Department and we also hear that Mr. McLeavy Brown's contract as Commissioner of Maritime Customs will not be renewed so that it is probable that the Japanese have their covetous eyes on this source of revenue.

So that in return for yen 5,000,000 in paper money of doubtful value Japan asks for the whole of Korea's revenue to do as she likes with.

Directly this proposal of Japan to lend yen 5,000,000 at six per cent was mooted we smelt a rat, but who would have imagined that an extraordinary deal like this was contemplated?

FRANCE'S ALLEGED BREACHES OF NEUTRALTY.

STRONG ARTICLE IN A PARIS JOURNAL.

The Tokio Foreign Department has received the following telegram:—The French paper Le Petit Journal makes the following observations:—According to the Tokio telegrams, some of the Japanese papers assert that France has violated the principles of neutrality. They declare that France has opened her ports to Russian warships destined for the Far East, and has supplied them with military necessaries, thus facilitating the movements of Russia. They contend that these proceedings are obviously violations of the principle of neutrality and cannot be condoned. If Japan, they continue, should be obliged to enlarge the area of the war, France must be held responsible. The Tokio papers also allege that Mr. Motono, Japanese Minister at Paris, has made representations to M. Delcasse, French Foreign Minister, on the matter. Bluster of this kind is, of course, beneath notice. It is natural that Japan should desire to involve another Power in the war in order to lighten the burden under which she is at present suffering. But it is too childish of Japan to abuse France on the pretext that the latter supplied coal to the Russian warships. Japan will not provoke France into war by such childish accusations. The abuse in which the Japanese papers are indulging is altogether without any justification, for France has been very strict in the maintainance of her neutrality. It is certain that if she had behaved toward any other Power as she has toward Russia, complaints of unfriendiness would have been made. One of the provisions of the International Marine Regulations to to the effect that "a warship belonging to any belligerent is entitled to obtain in a neutral port only so much coal as will enable her to reach the nearest home port, and that this assistance should not be given to the same vessel on more than one occasion." Now what has happened in the case of the Russian warships at French Ports? A few Russian destroyers and a collier entered Cherbourg, and the former obtained coal from the collier. Other Russian destroyer and a transport did the same at Brest and Algiers. The Russian warships directly under the command of Admiral Rojestvensky obtained some coal from their own colliers at Dakar. We hear that the Russian warships took in coal from the shore at Vigo, but that port is not in the possession of France. According to the international regulations referred to above, neutral ports are entitled to give a limited quantity of coal to belligerents, but France has had no occasion to take advantage of his permission, thanks to the great precautions adopted by the Russians. In 1897, when war broke out between America and Spain, France made a declaration as to the attitude she would adopt toward the belligerents, and all the French authorities abroad were instructed to take the necessary steps to enforce this declaration. At that time, the Governor of Martinique supplied coal to a destroyer of Admiral Cervera's Squadron, to enable the vessel to reach Havana, the nearest Spanish port, and the United States made no complaint. It is not wise for Japan to show herself more fond of making grievances than the Europeans Powers. If she continues in this course, she must be taught that, after her conduct in regard to the Resitelinui at Chefoo and the Variag at Chemulpo, she has no right to complain of breaches of neutrality on the part of other nations.

An epidemic of Scarletina prevails amongst the Japanese residents of Seoul.

Admirals Togo and Kamimura were to leave Tokio to rejoin their respective fleets on the 23rd inst.

The Il-chin-hoi people are fairly quiet but they are worrying the Government in small ways so that they shall not be entirely forgotten.

BEST BREAK OF THE YEAR.

JOHN ROBERTS MAKES 595 AT MANCHESTER.

John Roberts treated the onlookers to a bright and sparkling exposition of billiards at Manchester on Tuesday afternoon. Not since he commenced his month's visit to Cottonopolis, three weeks ago, has the veteran been so prolific in his scoring. The sitting lasted seventy minutes, Roberts arriving at his proper quota of points—750—in fourteen visits to the table. On the other hand, Bateman, who is receiving 2,500 points start in 9,000, was wofully out of form, and his aggregate points only totalled 180.

In his visits to Manchester John Roberts has seldom left his native town without doing something prodigious in so far as break-making is concerned, and in the evening he accomplished a remarkable performance. Following upon the grand form of Dawson and Stevenson during the last few days, the veteran more than emulated their example by scoring in the evening an unfinished contribution of 592 in thirty-five minutes. In his compilation Roberts was never in difficulties, and his strokes were of a most varied character. He scored in almost every position on the board, and left off with the balls well placed. The ex-champion had thus the distinction of subscribing so far the highest break of the season, with an opportunity still open to him of making if a record.

The next afternoon, however, Roberts added only three to his overnight 592.

A report has been received to the effect that the Korean Post and Telegraph office at Chemulpo was destroyed by fire last night. Incendiarism is suspected.

A Moji correspondent of the "Kokumin" reports that the P. & O. Steamer "Mazagon," of some 5,000 tons, has run on a rock off Fukura, Hikoshima. Detail are not yet to hand.

We understand that the Japanese are pressing for a wholesale discharge of officials, but that Mr. Yi Ha Yung and Mr. Kwong Chung Huh, (Ministers of Foreign Affairs and Law respectively) will not be asked to resign.

We hear that, owing to the absence from his office of Mr. Cho-Byung-ho, the Vice-President of State, several agreements with Japanese advisers, (including a Miss Takahashi whose speciality is not defined) have not yet been instrumented.

The Japanese Minister and advisers are reported to have a scheme on foot whereby the Dai-Ichi Bank will become the Korean National Bank. The Japanese intrigues here have become farcical, and it is not to be for a moment believed that any Foreign Power will acquisce in them. Let the Dai Ichi Bank first bring some money to Korea.

The Korea Daily News.

Issued at 5 P. M. daily except Sundays.

Rate of Subscription:—
Per Year,............Yen 25.
Per Quarter,..........Yen 7.
Per Month,..........Yen 2.50.

Postage in Korea not charged extra.
Postage abroad charged extra.

Advertisements, 50 sen per day for 1 inch or less.
5 yen per month per inch.
50 yen per year per inch.

All communications to
E. T. BETHELL,
Editor and Publisher,
Pak-tong, Seoul

THE TSAR'S REFORM DECREE.

The following communication was issued by the Russian Government on the morning following the publication of the decree by the Tsar.

In the autumn of the year there was a meeting in St. Petersburg, of several Zemstvos of the various governments, who expressed a series of desires concerning what are, in their opinion, indispensable reforms in the different governments of the Empire. These desires were made the subjects of action by members of various other assemblies which met for the purpose, and also, knowing the provisions of law, were considered at the deliberations of several councils and Zemstvos.

Thus, by the action of people who endeavoured to introduce discord into public and State life, excitement arose in the minds of certain sections of society, chiefly among impressionable youths. In certain towns of the Empire there occurred a series of noisy meetings, which demanded the presentation to the Government of certain demands which were inadmissible, in the face of the sacred foundations of the laws of the Empire and the indestructible elements which form the Government. These sections of the public made street demonstrations in bands and openly resisted the police authorities.

Such movements against the existing order of the Government which have fallen adversely upon the bulk of the Russian people, who are loyal to the everlasting foundations of the existing Government, gave to the excitement above referred to an undeserved importance of a general tendency. The Russian people involved in this movement, forgetful of the grievous war which has fallen to the lot of Russia, blinded by chimerical hopes of profits which they might expect from a radical change in the ancient foundations of the Russian State and life, and not knowing what they were doing, acted to the advantage not of the country, but of its enemies.

Now, the duty of the Government is to preserve order in the State and protect the public confidence from all change in the true course of internal life. Therefore any destruction of order and peace and all meetings of an anti-Government character must and will be stopped by all legal means at the disposition of the authorities, and those concerned in those disorders, especially persons employed in the Government service, will be held responsible.

Zemstvo and town statutes and every form of institution and company must not go beyond the limits provided for them and must not concern themselves in questions in the consideration of which they have no legal authority. Presidents of public meetings who allow consideration to take place of matters not in their province on questions of general government are liable under the existing laws: and organs of the Press, with the knowledge of the responsibility which rests upon them, must for their part introduce the necessary calming effect on public life, which has deviated in recent times from its proper course.

THE JAPANESE POINT OF VIEW.

God alone knows when and how the war will be terminated, is practically what the "Kokumin" says on the prospect. It is no doubt a serious thing for Russia, that her *moujik*, who has hitherto been the blind supporter of the bureaucracy, is now going over to the revolutionist side, as the despatches from St. Petersburg indicate. The internal dissensions may grow so great in Russia that they may ultimately compel her government to give up the struggle. They may and they may not; but that has nothing to do with us, for we in no way count on them. Nor are we perturbed in the slightest degree that the fall of Port Arthur has been productive of any change in the situation, contrary to the expectation of some outsiders that it would. We have from the beginning made up our mind that the conflict will be of long duration. We are glad, however, says the journal, that that grand event has filled us with fresh courage and inspiration and re-strengthened our resolution never to stop the war until our object for engaging in it is fully attained.—Japan Times.

Whether the "Tokio Nichi Nichi Shimbun" is unduly optimistic, being cognizant of the present state of affairs at the Shaho or whether it is simply speaking at random, we, of course cannot say, but in its issue of January 20th it adduces three reasons why the Japanese have heretofore failed to inflict a crushing defeat on Kuropatkin and contends that these factors being now eliminated, it only remains for Field Marshal Oyama to march on to Glory. We give the opinions of the Tokio Journal as translated by the "Japan Times." The Nichi Nichi says:—

"The principal reasons why our main force in Manchuria, while scoring splendid victories both at Liaoyang and Shaho, has not in either case been able to give the enemy a disastrous chase are three. First: On both occasions our forces were of just enough strength to defeat the enemy, but not to give him pursuit. Secondly: Our control of the sea was not then as complete as it is now, and the mishaps our transports met affected our supply arrangements to such an extent as to interfere with the work of reinforcement. Thirdly: Our finances had not then been perfected in such way to enable us so carry out a grand movement of desired magnitude. But conditions are different now in all these points: The open route for the concentration of all the required strength in the north, the inexhaustible reinforcements with every facility for their transportation, and the full and adequate financial arrangements. Such being the case, says the journal, there should be no excuse for unnecessarily delaying what should be the decisive and final great battle at the front. The Government and the authorities at the front, it demands, should have the courage to throw themselves into the coming engagement to the entire limit of their power, so as to make either a Metz or a Sedan, and administer on Kuropatkin's armies a blow that will strike them down, to rise no more.

It is perfectly true that the Japanese now have the sea to themselves and that their transport service to Manchuria is free from risk of interruption but most accounts do not appear to ascribe to the Japanese forces any overwhelming superiority in numbers or artillery and we by no means agree with the Nichi Nichi that "Japan's financial arrangements are full and adequate."

All reports agree that the Russian front overlaps the Japanese on both wings and this would hardly be the case unless he had a greater number of men than the Japanese and the Russian movements north of Korea are by no means idle threats.

On the whole we are inclined to agree with the opinion that Japan has allowed her best opportunities to go by and that the prospects of her inflicting a crushing defeat on the Russians are at present very remote.

JAPANESE COMMERCE.

It is reported that in July last year a Japanese merchant, taking with him a quantity of cloisonné, curios, embroideries, etc., proceeded to Sydney. Upon arrival at that port he sold the goods at public auction and reaped a good profit says the Japan Times. He then proceeded to Melbourne, whence he ordered a similar consignment of goods from this country. The goods duly arrived and having passed the Melbourne Customs, were advertised to be sold at public auction on October 25, 26 and 27. On October 25, however, the Superintendent of the Customs, accompanied by several officers, visited the auction room and confiscated the whole of the Japanese goods, this action being taken in accordance with Article 161 of the Federal Customs regulations; in other words, on the ground that the goods had been invoiced at much below their actual value. They were afterwards sold by public auction under the direction of the Customs authorities, who gave the Japanese merchant the money corresponding to the invoice price, with ten per cent. added, the merchant receiving in all £275. It is estimated that the goods actually fetched at auction some £2,000. The merchant in question at once returned to this country, entrusting his interests to his fellow merchants there.

According to the merchant's representative at Melbourne, the invoice value of the first lot of goods was accepted by the Customs, but the latter subsequently found that the actual value was much higher than the invoice price. In view of this, the second consignment was confiscated. The contention brought forward by the merchant in question was that the articles were all manufactured for export purposes, and that owing to the war their prices on the home market had greatly fallen. In spite of these protestations, it is beyond doubt that the invoice price of the second consignment was much lower than the actual value. Transactions of this description will not only impair the credit of our merchants, but will also effect the progress of trade between the two countries. Attention is therefore directed to the fact that dishonorable practices of this nature must in future be discontinued.

Men may glory in the strenuous deeds of Drake and the strenuous diplomacy of "Old Pam," but those who are thoughtful will find equal cause for glorying in the strong self-control which, in the North Sea incident, has enabled England to defer the sword of vengeance to the scales of justice when, as all the world well knows, the former was in her hand and it was within her power to wield it with the fullest effect.—Tribune, New York.

The Korea Daily News.

VOL. II, SATURDAY, JANUARY 28, 1905 No. 22

大韓每日申報

대한미일신보

일쳔구빅오년일월삼십일일 (화요일) (뎨이권이십삼호)

본샤고빅

이신보는영어와한어로셕거ᄆᆡ일츌ᄒᆞᆷ

신문가

한쟝 엽두돈오푼

일삭됴 엽두량닷돈

우표가ᄆᆡ삭닷돈

다맛돈으로밧솜

광고료는

과한의장단과ᄌᆞ힝의다쇼로즁감ᄒᆞ되렴가로밧을터이오며오리지아녀대한사람마다다이신문을보실터이니광고내시기를원ᄒᆞ시ᄂᆞᆫ이들은우리신문샤에와셔면약ᄒᆞ심을희망ᄒᆞᆷ

○발힝소 박동대한ᄆᆡ일신보샤법어학교압헤젼영국인셜필림집자리오

사쟝 영국인 (비셜)

평양 티리졈

○평양효동사ᄂᆞᆫ 권미보씨로우리신문관미티리안을뎡ᄒᆞ엿ᄉᆞ오니평양에계신구람코져ᄒᆞ시ᄂᆞᆫ 쳠군ᄌᆞᄂᆞᆫ히티리졈에왕림ᄒᆞ와면의ᄒᆞ시옵

사고

○우리대한ᄆᆡ일신보의목뎍은대한의안녕질셔에관한모든대목에더ᄒᆞ야ᄂᆞᆫ공평한변론을쥬쟝홈에더라우리통신원의담보는신문보셔ᄂᆞᆫ쳠군ᄌᆞ의게홍샹보도ᄒᆞ리며편지를긔셔ᄒᆞ여주시ᄂᆞᆫ이ᄂᆞᆫ셩명과반드틀젹어붓처시기를희망ᄒᆞ오니아거슬신문샹에긔ᄌᆡᄒᆞ라ᄂᆞᆫ거시아니오다만극히신용ᄒᆞᆯᄂᆞᆫ즁거를숨고쟈홈이라긔쟈ᄂᆞᆫ아모긔셔던지긔ᄌᆡ홈을되각ᄒᆞᄂᆞᆫ권리를가졋스나되각ᄒᆞᄂᆞᆫ리유를말홀터이오며공즁평화를문란케ᄒᆞᄂᆞᆫ듯ᄒᆞᆫ긔셔ᄂᆞᆫ의례히밧지안켓ᄉᆞᆸ나이다

●본샤셜시이릭로신문을ᄆᆡ양우례로분젼ᄒᆞ와례젼부의임의로젼ᄒᆞᆫ듯스로먼곳에ᄂᆞᆫ혹늣게젼ᄒᆞ기도ᄒᆞ며혹몃칠거슬ᄒᆞᆫ겁에젼ᄒᆞ기도ᄒᆞ며혹아니젼ᄒᆞᄂᆞᆫ곳도잇다ᄒᆞ와우리신문을ᄉᆞ랑ᄒᆞ야구람ᄒᆞ시ᄂᆞᆫ 쳠군ᄌᆞ의게티ᄒᆞ야ᄆᆡ우미안ᄒᆞ옵기로지금은분젼인을두고ᄆᆡ일일즉이젼ᄒᆞ며아니젼ᄒᆞ거나늣게거나ᄒᆞᆫ폐가업도록ᄒᆞ랴ᄒᆞ오니혹아니젼ᄒᆞ거나늣게젼ᄒᆞ거나ᄒᆞᆫ일이잇스면본샤로통긔ᄒᆞ여쥬심을희망ᄒᆞᆷ

잡보

○제지쇼셜시 리지현제씨가자본을구취ᄒᆞ야양ᄌᆞ떡쇼에제지쇼를셜시ᄒᆞ고양지를제죠즁이라더라

○환산고문권고 경무쳥고문관환산즁쥰씨가신경ᄉᆞ를졉견ᄒᆞ고권고ᄒᆞ기를경찰이려항간은졈ᄎᆞ취셔가되나고등경찰을아직착슈치못ᄒᆞ엿스니쟝뎡를의지ᄒᆞ야실시ᄒᆞᆫ쟈ᄒᆞ엿ᄂᆞᆫ티만일교등경찰이실시가되면공자왕손이라도법을범ᄒᆞ면혜아리지아니ᄒᆞ고거힝홀터이니쇼위완고ᄒᆞᆫ대관은그즁에만니걸니라더라

○고빙약관 학부대신리지극씨가일본티표자의츄쳔ᄒᆞᆫ동국인폐원탄씨를금번에다시학부참예관으로고빙ᄒᆞᄂᆞᆫ티그졍결ᄒᆞᆫ약관이대기좌와ᄀᆞᆺᄒᆞ니라

뎨일됴 학부대신은계약의쇼뎡됴건을좃차폐원탄을학부참예관으로고빙ᄒᆞ야교육샹ᄉᆞ무에관ᄒᆞᆫ초의안을면관ᄒᆞ야졍부에졔의홀ᄉᆞ

뎨이됴 대한국학부ᄂᆞᆫ일졀교육샹문셔를폐원탄의게긔운ᄒᆞ야폐원탄의동의를경ᄒᆞᆫ후에쳐리홀ᄉᆞ

뎨삼됴 폐원탄의봉급은월익금화삼빅원으로졍ᄒᆞ야ᄆᆡ월말에지급홀ᄉᆞ

대한졍부ᄂᆞᆫ샹당ᄒᆞᆫ관ᄉᆞ를폐원탄의게공급ᄒᆞ되샹당ᄒᆞᆫ관ᄉᆞ를공급지못홀때에ᄂᆞᆫ관ᄉᆞ료로ᄆᆡ삭에금화이십오원식급여홀ᄉᆞ

뎨ᄉᆞ됴 폐원탄ᄉᆞ가귀국홀때에ᄂᆞᆫ션차료외에ᄆᆡ일금화이원을지급홀ᄉᆞ

뎨오됴 본계약을히약ᄒᆞᄂᆞᆫ필요가이러나ᄂᆞᆫ때에ᄂᆞᆫ셔로협의ᄒᆞ야경셩에잇ᄂᆞᆫ일본대국티표쟈의동의를경ᄒᆞ야파약홀ᄉᆞ

○파면ᄐᆡ거 젼셜를거ᄒᆞᆫ즉홍원에잇든로병은졈ᄎᆞ북방으로퇴각ᄒᆞ엿ᄂᆞᆫ티리원이남에ᄂᆞᆫ면션쥬를파피ᄒᆞ고퇴거ᄒᆞ엿더라

○우편지국신셜 일본우편국온일반공무의편리를위ᄒᆞ야셔ᄂᆡ필동에츌지국을셜ᄒᆞ고우편ᄉᆞ무를거시ᄒᆞᆫ다더라

관보

뎨삼쳔ᄉᆞ십팔호 광무구년일월이십팔일

셔임급시령

○명셔리총감ᄉᆞ무 교육부부감륙군참쟝 구영죠

일월십일일

○임철도원쥬ᄉᆞ셔판임관륙등 강희원 리귀식 고원신 강인긔 졍티션 김동헌

일월이십오일

○임즁츄원의관셔칙임관ᄉᆞ등 법부참셔관 리죵셩

○임법관양셩소박ᄉᆞ셔판임관륙등 바뎡환 권즁션 연쥰권흥슈 리연홍 김영묵 리면용 유문규

이상일월이십륙일

○구년도예산표 (속)

뎨륙관 례식원 이만일쳔이빅륙십원

뎨일항 봉급 일만오쳔ᄉᆞ빅삼십원

뎨이항 쳥비 삼쳔삼빅륙십륙원

뎨삼항 쳥ᄉᆞ슈리비 ᄉᆞ빅원

뎨ᄉᆞ항 잡급급잡비 일쳔오빅팔십ᄉᆞ원

뎨오항 려비 삼빅원

뎨륙항 교졉비 일빅팔십원

뎨칠관 광학국 칠쳔륙빅이십팔원

뎨일항 봉급 이쳔ᄉᆞ빅오십원

뎨이항 쳥비 구빅팔십원

뎨삼항 쳥ᄉᆞ슈리비 이빅오십원

뎨ᄉᆞ항 잡급급잡비 일쳔이빅삼십원

뎨오항 려비 이쳔칠빅십팔원

지화지츌차중 일만오쳔륙빅원

궁ᄂᆡ부소관합계삼십이만삼쳔오빅오십륙원

기로소소관

뎨일관 기로소본쳥 이만오쳔구빅이십칠원

뎨일항 봉급 ᄉᆞ쳔구빅팔십원

뎨이항 쳥비 일만구쳔칠빅구십오원

뎨삼항 잡급급잡비 일쳔일빅오십이원

궁ᄂᆡ부소관합계이만오쳔구빅이십칠원

의졍부소관

뎨일관 의졍부본쳥 삼만구쳔륙빅칠십원

뎨일항 봉급 이만구쳔이빅오십원

뎨이항 쳥비 일쳔팔빅원

뎨삼항 쳥ᄉᆞ슈리비 이빅원

뎨ᄉᆞ항 잡급급잡비 삼쳔삼빅륙십원

뎨오항 려비 륙십원

뎨륙항 관보비 오쳔원

뎨이관 사고슈호비 팔빅ᄉᆞ십원

뎨일항 사고슈호비 팔빅ᄉᆞ십원

뎨삼관 표훈원 일만구쳔이빅륙십팔원

뎨일항 봉급 구쳔륙빅삼십오원

뎨이항 쳥비 칠빅원

뎨삼항 쳥ᄉᆞ슈리비 이빅원

뎨ᄉᆞ항 잡급급잡비 일쳔일빅오십이원

뎨오항 려비 일빅오십원

뎨륙항 제장비 칠쳔ᄉᆞ빅삼십일원

의졍부소관합계오만구쳔칠빅칠십팔원

ᄂᆡ부소관

뎨일관 ᄂᆡ부본쳥 ᄉᆞ만ᄉᆞ쳔륙빅십오원

뎨일항 봉급 삼만칠빅팔십원

뎨이항 쳥비 이쳔오빅구십오원

뎨삼항 쳥ᄉᆞ슈리비 삼빅원

뎨ᄉᆞ항 잡급급잡비 삼쳔삼빅ᄉᆞ십원

뎨오항 려비 ᄉᆞ빅원

뎨륙항 외국인졔급 칠쳔이빅원 (지화)

뎨이관 한셩부 륙쳔삼빅칠십원

UNION INSURANCE SOCIETY OF CANTON.

Head office Hongkong.
Marine risks underwritten at current rates.

Agents in Chemulpo,
E. MEYER & Co.

COMPAGNIE DES MESSAGERIES MARITIMES.

Fortnightly Direct Service.

For Marseilles
via Ports.
Sailing from Yokohama
Calling at Kobe,
Shanghai, Hongkong, Saigon, Singapore,
Colombo, Djibonti, Suez, Port Said
and Marseilles.

For particulars apply to
HOLME RINGER & CO.,
Chemulpo.

HAYASHIDA & CO.,

16 MYENG DONG, CHIN KO KAI, SEOUL.
BRANCH OFFICE AT CHEMULPO.

Money changers, Coal and Wood Merchants, Express Agents.

We are agents for the Pyeng-yang Coal Company and the Karazu Coal Company of Japan. We have the best quality of both anthracite and bituminous coal, and prompt execution of orders is our speciality. Firewood of all kinds kept in stock. Full weight guaranteed. Money of all denominations exchanged at current rates. Parcels received for all parts.

CHINA MUTUAL LIFE INS. OC.

Most favourable terms to policy holders.

Benefit system unsurpassed.

HOLME RINGER & Co.
Agents, Chemulpo.

C. P. R.

CANADIAN PACIFIC RAILWAY COMPANY'S ROYAL MAIL STEAMSHIP LINE.

THE FAST ROUTE BETWEEN CHINA, JAPAN, AND EUROPE VIA CANADA AND THE UNITED STATES.

Route from Hongkong via Shanghai, Nagasaki (Inland Sea of Japan) Kobe, Yokohama Victoria and Vancouver.

Twin Screw Empress Steamship—6,000 Tons—Speed 19 knots.

PROPOSED SAILING FROM YOKOHAMA.

R. M. S. Empress of India.
R. M. S. Empress of Japan.
R. M. S. Empress of China.
R. M. S. Athenian.
R. M. S. Tartar.

Special reduction (first class only) granted to members of the Military, Naval, Diplomatic and Civil services and to Missionaries.

Passengers have choice of ten routes across the Continent of America and have privilege of travelling by any Atlantic Steamship Line.

Round the World passage tickets in connection with the P. and O. S. N., North German Lloyd and Messageries Co.'s **£125.**

All rates payable at current rate of exchange.

For further information, Tickets, Guide Books, etc., apply to

HOLME, RINGER & CO., AGENTS,
Chemulpo.

Grand Hotel,

(Formerly the Station Hotel)

Near the Railway Terminus, West Gate Seoul.

The Best Hotel in Korea
Handsome new Building.
Fine Airy Rooms
Excellent Cuisine.
Terms Moderate.
Special terms to Missionaries
and to permanent boarders.

Electric cars within 2 minutes' walk.

W. H. EMBERLEY.
Proprietor

EVERY FACILITY.

In connection with Life Assurance Business is afforded by

The Standard Life Assurance Co.,

One of the largest and wealthiest of the Provident Institutions of the United Kingdom Forms of Application and all information will be promptly afforded on application.

10 CENTS A DAY.

Not a very large expenditure is it? But it is sufficient to secure for a man of 30 a policy with the STANDARD LIFE OFFICE for

$1323.

For all particulars of rates, etc., apply to

Holme, Ringer & Co.,
Agents, Chemulpo.

THE NEW YORK LIFE INSURANCE COMPANY.

Have you ever been declined by any Company?

Are you engaged in a specially hazardous occupation?

Have you heard of the New York Life Insurance Company's New Classifications for this class of Risks?

If not, send your date of birth, occupation and particulars of rejection, if any to

E. MEYER & Co.,
Agents, Chemulpo.

MITSUI BUSSAN KAISHA.
(MITSUI & Co.)

MITSUI GINKO.
(MITSUI BANK.)

The Bank is owned by the members of the Mitsui Family, who, as partners, assume an unlimited responsibility for all liabilities of the Bank:—

Capital........................Yen 5,000,000
Reserve Fund.................. " 5,600,000

HEAD OFFICE, TOKYO.
LONDON OFFICE, 34 LIME ST., E. C.

BRANCHES AND AGENCIES:—
New York, San Francisco, Hamburg, Bombay, Singapore, Manila, Hongkong, Amoy, Chefoo, Tientsin.
Kobe, Hakodate, Yokohama, Kure, Yokosuka, Moji, Shimonoseki, Miike, Wakamatsu, Nagasaki, Kuchinotsu, Karatsu, Sasebo, Misume, Taipeh, &c.

Telegraphic Address for all the Offices:
"MITSUI."
A. B. C. AND A. 1 CODES USED.

Contractors of Coal
To the Imperial Japanese Navy. Arsenals and Railway Bureau, Principal Railway Companies and Industrial Work, Home and Foreign Mail and Freight Steamers.

Sole Proprietors
Of the famous Miike, Tagawa and Yamano Coal Mines.

Sole Agents
For the sale of Fukumo, Hokoku, Ichimura, Kanoda, Mannoura, Onoura, Ostuji, Sonoda, Tsubaruro, Yoshinotani, Yoshio, Yurokibura and other coals.

YANGTSE INSURANCE ASSOCIATION, LTD.

The undersigned, having been appointed agents for the above company, are prepared to issue policies and pay losses on marine risks at regular rates.

E. MEYER & Co.,
Agents, Chemulpo.

AMERICAN KOREAN ELECTRIC CO.

Light and Power.

Main Office: Electric Building, Chong No.

RAILWAY DEPARTMENT.

OPERATING CARS BETWEEN EAST AND WEST GATE, EVERY TEN MINUTES:—

First Car leaves East Gate at 7:00 A. M. First Car leaves R. R. Station at 7:25 A. M.
Last Car " East Gate at 8.40 P. M. Last " " R. R. Station at 9.05 P. M.

OPERATING CARS BETWEEN EAST GATE AND IMPERIAL TOMB TERMINUS, EVERY TWENTY MINUTES:—

CONNECTING WITH EVERY ALTERNATE CAR ARRIVING AT EAST GATE FROM CHONG NO.

First Car leaves East Gate for Tomb at 7:10 A. M.
" " " Tomb for East Gate at 7:30 A. M.
Last " " East Gate for Tomb at 7:50 P. M.
" " " Tomb for East Gate at 8:10 P. M.

OPERATING CARS BETWEEN CHONG NO AND YUNG SAN RIVER EVERY TWELVE MINUTES:—

First Car leaves Chong No for South Gate at 7:12 A. M.
" " " Chong No for Yung San at 7:36 A. M.
" " " South Gate for Chong No at 7:20 A. M.
" " " Yung San for Chong No at 8:09 A. M.
Last " " South Gate for Chong No 9:00 P. M.
" " " Yung San for Chong No at 8.45. p. M.

SPECIAL PRIVATE CARS FURNISHED TO SUIT CONVENIENCE OF PATRONS. PRICES ON APPLICATION AT HEAD OFFICE.

LIGHTING DEPARTMENT.

Where less than 250 candle power of light is used, the rate per month will be

Per 16 candle power incandescent lamp,—All night.—Yen 2.50.
32 candle power incandescent lamp:—All night:—Yen 4.00.
50 candle power incandescent lamp:—All night:—Yen 6.00.
150 " " " " " " " 10.00.
1200 " " enclosed arc " " " " 20.00.

Where more than 250 candle power of light is used, a Meter will be installed, if requested:—Rent of Meter Yen 2.00 per month. Rate of charges by meter reading:—Two Sen per Ampere per hour. (Approximately this is equal to about One Sen per 16 C. P. lamp per hour) Minimum monthly charge where meter is installed, Yen 20.00 per month, which includes rental of meter.

Estimates for installing lights furnished on application

An assortment of chandeliers always on hand.

K. Murakami.
Photograph Studio
Chinkokai, Seoul.

Printing, Developing and Enlargement, of Photographs always Undertaken.

Korean Views and Pictures Illustrating Native Customs always on Sale.

THE OSAKA SHOSEN KAISHA.

Boats frequently on the berth for Chinnampo.

REGULAR SAILINGS BETWEEN JAPAN AND KOREAN PORTS.

FUSAN AND KOBE VIA SHIMONOSEKI.

OSAKA VIA MOKPO, FUSAN, SHIMONOSEKI AND KOBE.

MOJI DIRECT.

OSAKA VIA KUNSAN, MASANPO, FUSAN, SHIMONOSEKI AND KOBE.

CHEMULPO KUNSAN LINE,
Every three days.

CHEMULPO CHINNAMPO LINE.
Every three days.

For Freight and passage and further particulars apply to

THE OSAKA SHOSEN KAISHA,
Chemulpo.

RONDON, PLAISANT & CO.

General Storekeepers and Merchants, Ships Contractors, Tobacconists, Commission and Forwarding Agents, Coal Merchants

IMPORTERS AND EXPORTERS

Seoul & Chemulpo.

W. D. WENTWORTH.

LANDING
AND
SHIPPING AGENT.
AND
CUSTOMS BROKER.

12 OURA, NAGASAKI.

STEWARD & CO.

Chemulpo.

Shipchandlers and Storekeepers, Naval and Mercantile Contractors, Landing and Shipping Agents.

STEWARD'S HOTEL

Chemulpo.

Best accommodation in the port for travellers. Clean and well-aired rooms, good cuisine and prompt attendance, moderate tariff.

뎨일항 봉급 삼쳔팔뵉원
뎨이항 쳥비 일쳔원
뎨삼항 쳥수슈리비 오십원
뎨수항 잡급급잡비 일쳔수뵉수십원
뎨오항 려비 팔십원
뎨삼관 디방재판소 팔만이쳔칠뵉팔십팔원
뎨일항 봉급 수만이쳔팔뵉수십팔원
뎨이항 쳥비 구쳔일뵉원
뎨삼항 쳥수슈리비 륙뵉원
뎨수항 잡급급잡비 이만륙쳔삼뵉수십원
뎨오항 려비 삼쳔구뵉원

잡보

○양계대리 인쳔부치거ᄒᆞᄂᆞᆫ 졍수파ᄂᆞᆫ진쟝을파라동촌잇ᄂᆞᆫ빗 십여간을사고양계ᄒᆞᄂᆞᆫ티시방 오뵉여슈를기르ᄂᆞᆫ지라조미도 잇거니와미일리익이블소ᄒᆞ다 ᄒᆞ며명츈에ᄂᆞᆫ쳔슈를기르겟다 더라

○조쳥상환 일공관에셔외부 에조회ᄒᆞ기를병진이십구년에 본방인키국간디방비도쳐에잇 셔치샹ᄒᆞᆫ손히비샹금ᄉᆞ는여러 번조회ᄒᆞ야최촉ᄒᆞ엿거니와사 실ᄒᆞᆫ즉히비샹금이합삼팔만칠 쳔여원이니쳥컨티곳샹환ᄒᆞᆷ이 가ᄒᆞ다ᄒᆞ엿더라

○주일공ᄉᆞ보고 주일공ᄉᆞ가 외부에보고ᄒᆞ기를슈원리용문 의ᄒᆞᆫ월봉을엇지ᄒᆞ야지발치아니 ᄒᆞᄂᆞᆫ뇨ᄒᆞ며바라건티깁쳘키바 귀죠박졍션의젼례를의지ᄒᆞ야 곳지발ᄒᆞ라ᄒᆞ엿더라

○무츄조회 한셩니가로샹에 셔일인이츌기ᄒᆞᄂᆞᆫ수로경무쳥 에셔ᄂᆞᆫ츌ᄒᆞ고한셩부에셔ᄂᆞᆫ쳥 일병수의게무츄조회ᄒᆞᄂᆞᆫ지라 병수가히안건을조쳐ᄒᆞ기위ᄒᆞ 야경시와무츄회의ᄒᆞ엿더라

○면퇴슌검 경무쳥에셔금번 도졍비만여원이감츅된지라슌 검일뵉명가량을감ᄒᆞ에산이 더니쟉일에과면과자퇴쟈가도합 팔십일명이라각항졍친을환쟝 ᄒᆞ기로경무수가과마슌검도셜시 ᄒᆞ기위ᄒᆞ야가혜졍ᄒᆞ엿다더라

○량부교빙협동 니부에셔ᄂᆞᆫ 본부교문관과경무쳥교문관을 현금협동즁이오학부에셔ᄂᆞᆫ본 부참여관과한어교수를협동즁 이라더라

○쳘가도쥬 일본조계니에 인일인이려기도가에셔셜국잡기ᄒᆞ 논고로남셔슌검이츄착ᄒᆞᆫ즉계 한이도쥬ᄒᆞ야슌검을무수난타 ᄒᆞ야괴지사경이라일본슌사가 히슌검을보호ᄒᆞ야담숑ᄒᆞ고난 타ᄒᆞ던쟈ᄂᆞᆫ일명을챡득ᄒᆞ야 셔로잡아간지라경무쳥에셔ᄂᆞᆫ그 ᄒᆞ여담을과포ᄒᆞᄂᆞᆫ티다쳘가도쥬 ᄒᆞ엿더라

○궁민구휼 경위원에셔궁민 을구휼ᄒᆞ기로각셔빈호를됴사ᄒᆞ 야분등으로반젼ᄒᆞ더라

○회쟝편싱 일진회지회쟝련 평셩씨ᄂᆞᆫ분리조ᄂᆞᆫᄒᆞ야가셰가 분빈ᄒᆞ고제가지졀이유리ᄒᆞ더 니군티일진회에목젹을듯고부 조ㅣ일잠ᄒᆞ야각군지회쟝이되 엿ᄂᆞᆫ티저간일비를자비ᄒᆞ야쓰더 며남의게은ᄒᆞᆫ을이라도먹지 안코자긔와갓치단니ᄂᆞᆫ하인 신이라도셩계ᄒᆞ며ᄯᅩ다른사ᄅᆞᆷ을 티ᄒᆞ야말ᄒᆞ기를우리인민이 문명티치를모르ᄂᆞᆫ고로지금 이갓치비어국에압제를밧ᄂᆞᆫ것 이니어셔부지런이일ᄒᆞ야기명 샹학문을공부ᄒᆞ자고권면ᄒᆞ야 회샤를괴어이계과되기를힘쓴 다더라

○박쳔회인 박쳔군수가이십 칠일에니부로면보ᄒᆞ기를본군 에잇ᄂᆞᆫ회민을효유ᄒᆞ며도히ᄒᆞ여 지지안티니금월에빅셩으로더 브러셔로닷토아공당을피ᄒᆞ 엿다ᄒᆞ엿더라

○참졍계쇼 참졍조병호씨ᄂᆞᆫ 졔ᄒᆞᆫ사직샹쇼를올녓더라

○외부조회 일쟉에외부에셔 함경남도관찰수의보고를등인 ᄒᆞ야일본공ᄉᆞ의게조회ᄒᆞ기 를원산항의주차ᄒᆞᆫ일본군졍관 이명령이라ᄒᆞ고칭ᄒᆞ고각군에 문을ᄂᆞ리워군슈가세금을징슈ᄒᆞᆯ ᄒᆞᆫ베에못보고ᄒᆞ야지휘ᄒᆞ기를 자졍ᄒᆞ되만일보고를티만ᄒᆞᄂᆞᆫ 가잇스면쳐분ᄒᆞ리라ᄒᆞ온운ᄒᆞᆷ 엿고ᄯᅩᄒᆞᆫ세칙ᄒᆞ고신쳬ᄒᆞᆷ이 잇다ᄒᆞ니허군졍관이귀시군랴 샹관요로키졍부명령을밧아북 관에셔군졍을시힝ᄒᆞᆫ즉맛당 시히오이스샹위에진실노힐키거 간셩ᄒᆞᆷ이부당ᄒᆞ게ᄂᆞᆫ론ᄒᆞ며세아 졍은국가의졍령이라각군수가 ᄂᆞᆫ거시에명리로셔ᄌᆞ의로징슈ᄒᆞ 지군졍관계가업ᄂᆞᆫ거시오도모 군수가셜노보고ᄒᆞᆫ리가엄ᄉᆞ피 졍관도ᄯᅩᄒᆞᆫ지휘ᄒᆞᆯ티가업스티 이뮈보고ᄒᆞᄂᆞᆫ자를쳐분ᄒᆞ리라ᄒᆞᆫ ᄂᆞᆫ말은웃ᄒᆞᆫ시리ᄒᆞ며부당ᄒᆞᆫ지라 쇼위ᄒᆞᆫ시리ᄒᆞᆫ즁에ᄒᆞ이일향에티 라말ᄒᆞᄂᆞᆫ기를티방관이우리군티 에블리ᄒᆞᆫ고즉뎍방ᄒᆞᆫ명ᄒᆞᆫ군티 ᄒᆞ여곰티방ᄒᆞᆫ졍을챠지ᄒᆞ야ᄒᆞ 단ᄒᆞ엿스니마지못ᄒᆞ게되러니군졍 관이엇지ᄒᆞᆫ기ᄒᆞᆫ리국명리를조ᄎᆞ외 로명퇴ᄒᆞ며친단ᄒᆞ야처벌ᄒᆞ며 ᄯᅩ후임을스ᄉᆞ로션졍ᄒᆞ야ᄒᆞᆫ다ᄒᆞ니 공군졍을차지ᄒᆞ게ᄒᆞ리오본티 신은회란ᄒᆞᆷ을이괴지못ᄒᆞᆯ꼬ᄒᆞ던 ᄯᅩ명령이ᄒᆞᆫ니시ᄒᆞ야ᄒᆞᄂᆞᆫᄌᆞ의ᄒᆞᆫ 보고ᄒᆞ게ᄒᆞ고지휘ᄒᆞ야ᄒᆞᆫ켓에데 논분ᄌᆞ논심히교셥ᄅᆞᆷ등의도리 가아니ᄒᆞ고군졍관의교전칙ᄒᆞᆫ리 ᄒᆞ야금세ᄒᆞ군졍관의교졍칙ᄒᆞ야권한 을잔셜ᄒᆞ야 옹립ᄒᆞ지 밀게ᄒᆞᆷ이가ᄒᆞ다ᄒᆞ 엿더라

○외부우조 일쟉에외부에셔 셔샹회감리의보고를등인ᄒᆞ야 일본공ᄉᆞ의게조회ᄒᆞ기를삼화 항에잇ᄂᆞᆫ일본령ᄉᆞ가감회쇼동 헌에티ᄒᆞ야광운케ᄒᆞ기위ᄒᆞ야일 한에셩셔를거ᄒᆞ야졈ᄎᆞ셜힝ᄒᆞ시 기를챡슈ᄒᆞ켓다ᄒᆞ고교시ᄒᆞ엿시 니사실ᄒᆞ며보진티긴밀에비 롯ᄒᆞᆷ원등의분요가잇셧스나키 헌병이회복시혓다온운ᄒᆞᆷ은보 티이런일이업ᄂᆞᆫ티아지못게라 무엇ᄉᆞᆯ빙거ᄒᆞ야말ᄒᆞᆷ이며기신 ᄒᆞᆫ다ᄒᆞ고말ᄒᆞᄂᆞᆫ일관은사실치티 한일의정셔에그츙고를용납ᄒᆞᆫ 다ᄂᆞᆫ말은계지ᄒᆞ엿거니와도로 지키정부에셔실힝ᄒᆞᆫ다ᄂᆞᆫ키졀 은엿거ᄂᆞᆫ실힝ᄒᆞ야착슈ᄒᆞᆫ다ᄒᆞᆷ 은실노아지못ᄒᆞᆫ비요본국신민 이만일원등ᄒᆞᆫ수졍이잇스면스 사로본국에사법ᄒᆞᆫ관부가잇서 공쇼를밧아심리ᄒᆞ기ᄂᆞᆫ엿지ᄒᆞ 야귀국령사가월권ᄒᆞ야관리ᄒᆞ 리오비록숑안일지라도각기조 국법관의게도라가심판케ᄒᆞᆷ은 이미한일슈호규례에밝힌명문에 잇ᄂᆞᆫ티이번귀국령사의온운ᄒᆞᆫ 거슨라ᄎᆞ밧기니ᄀᆞ집히힐난ᄒᆞ지 라ᄒᆞ형사의게면칙ᄒᆞ야금히이 런랑동ᄒᆞᆷ이엽시ᄒᆞᆷ이가ᄒᆞ다ᄒᆞ엿 더라

별보

사하의형편

○일본국민신문에긔재ᄒᆞ엿스 되동경관인사회에셔졉슈ᄒᆞᆫ최 근보를거ᄒᆞᆫ즉셕쳔군방에지금 잇ᄂᆞᆫ군티ᄂᆞᆫ쳔창의평화잔파동화 에잇ᄂᆞᆫ이쳔명의로병과련합ᄒᆞ오 아구로팟긴대쟝의좌익군이 로군우익의젼면은봉텬셔방으 지쳇젓스며사하방면에잇ᄂᆞᆫ로 병의도항이이삭쳔만명가량이 오히셥위의북편닉곤니스코 잇ᄂᆞᆫ로병의슈효도지금륙만명 가량이되고구라과로브티군ᄉᆞ 의운송이연쇽ᄒᆞ야형벨에리ᄂᆞᆯ 구로로로엉다셧수레가도챡ᄒᆞᆫ 쟝팟긴대쟝이션창방면과 국티경으로브티일본군에향ᄒᆞ 야긔젼ᄒᆞᆯ의향인듯ᄒᆞ다ᄒᆞ더라 ᄒᆞ엿스며

금월십칠일븟터사하방면에셔발 ᄒᆞᆫ포젼은지도과의온친위티 에쇽ᄒᆞᆫ수편의말을드른즉사하 방면에잇ᄂᆞᆫ로병은젼쟝ᄒᆞᆷ에 망ᄒᆞᆫ군ᄉᆞ의수효를벌셔세로 운ᄒᆞ군ᄉᆞ로충티ᄒᆞ고로군ᄂᆞᆫ본영 을옴겨다군방에잇스며구로팟킨 대쟝의영은ᄋᆞ니산에잇ᄂᆞᆫ듯ᄒᆞᆫ 티젼일사하젼쟝에일본군의우 익에티ᄒᆞ야격렬ᄒᆞᆫ공격ᄒᆞᆫ로병 ᄒᆞ엿고니그후로브티못ᄒᆞᆫ로 셕탄광부술에로병이최근ᄒᆞᆫ 훈ᄌᆞ답에그방면에ᄂᆞᆫ등변히젼 고ᄒᆞ평에방수ᄒᆞ엿스며젼일에ᄒᆞᄂᆞᆫ 대평잇게방슈역ᄉᆞ가숫너면샤하 예잇ᄂᆞᆫ로병들이북방으로몰ᄉᆞ너 갈숄로에샹ᄒᆞ엿더니현금수샹 으로ᄂᆞᆫ그렴듯ᄒᆞ지아니ᄒᆞ다ᄒᆞ 코그ᄉᆞ팔이쇼말ᄒᆞ되젼디에귀 후가미우치위셔근일젹은싸홈 에셰시찬동안에군ᄉᆞ들이만히 어렷스니이러ᄒᆞᆫ형편에엇던군 수던지금은크게긔젼ᄒᆞ기ᄂᆞᆫ 어려우리라ᄒᆞ더라ᄒᆞ엿더라

뎐보

○위조곡쇼젼 일월이십이일 오젼셰시와오시간에우리일부 티가위조곡과밋그셔방부근에 잇ᄂᆞᆫ젹의진디를밤에엄습ᄒᆞ야 도쳐에젹을란동케ᄒᆞ고이것을 북방으로파란케ᄒᆞ엿ᄂᆞᆫ티이때 우리군티의목격ᄒᆞᆫ젹의죽은자 ㅣ님오이나어든밤으로인ᄒᆞ야 우리군티의발견치못ᄒᆞᆫ수샹자 ㅣ가만ᄒᆞ며그밧게포획ᄒᆞᆫ병이 오수휘물품은바펄과그다른잡 품약간이라더라

(이십륙일오치착뎐)

○젹퇴마가방면 이십오일오 후삼시경에젹의보병약이대티 와긔병일중티가포조연부근으 로포격ᄒᆞ티도ᄒᆞ엿스나우리일부 티가이거슬양격ᄒᆞ야젹은다수 ᄒᆞᆫ손히를밧고일몰후에나셔북 방면마가셩조방면으로퇴각ᄒᆞ 엿더라

외보

○려슌샹황 려슌항니에도착 ᄒᆞᆫ군함즁항외에(세바스도보 리)외에ᄂᆞᆫ함은날바다슈리를 요구ᄒᆞᆯ티이일본함티의일부 에편입ᄒᆞᆷ을엇지못ᄒᆞᆯ(ㄷ며항구 도쳐에침몰ᄒᆞᆫ슈뢰가잇슴이위 험이만코쓰항구퇴색젼이잇서 구츅양이자유가못되나슈뢰명 령을합의츌입에ᄂᆞᆫ뒤힘이엄고과 록ᄒᆞ모모뎡이항니를경계ᄒᆞ더 리동항션거ᄂᆞᆫ과다ᄒᆞᆫ손히가엄 시죠곰슈리ᄒᆞᆷ을요구ᄒᆞᆯ진티죽 아리로브리빗옥산아리에이코 리ᄂᆞᆫ빗시가에잇ᄂᆞᆫ(스텐셀)쟝 군이ᄒᆞᆫ의관사정과기타진츅 물과빗시가젼부ᄂᆞᆫ의외로손히 가젹고시시가방면은귀국제 조소에잇ᄂᆞᆫ런관과밋(레루)등 은각포티방비ᄒᆞ기위ᄒᆞ야운커 ᄒᆞ엿스되원료가어제가엄고쓰 운젼ᄒᆞᆫ부로외에귀계국조션소 에잇ᄂᆞᆫ직공이대관오젼인이라 도라

○로국졍황 로국의요란이쟉 디방에젼파ᄒᆞ야각셔부의졍셔 가문란ᄒᆞᆷ에이르고ᄯᅩ과란과분 란에반역운동이셩ᄒᆞ고ᄯᅩ구로 세도긴쟝군이병졸쇄란셔과란 약등의보급ᄒᆞ기를쳥구ᄒᆞ나운 송에극란ᄒᆞ고ᄯᅩ셔빅리아텰도

TELEGRAMS.

(FROM JAPAN PAPERS.)

London, January 22nd.

Serious demonstrations took place on Sunday in St. Petersburg.

Fifteen thousand strikers started for the Winter Palace but the route was barred by Cossacks, who fired on the crowd and drove them back, after which the fighting became general.

The crowd blocked the Nicholas bridge and were attacked by infantry, uhlans, and Cossacks. The strikers appealed to the soldiers not to shoot their brothers. The infantry laid down their rifles but uhlans and Cossacks charged.

Sanguinary conflicts took place all over the city. Father Gapon was wounded and many women and children were killed and wounded.

The scenes which are taking place are indescribable. The mob is tearing down the telegraph poles and making wire entanglements and barricades.

A night of horrors is in prospect.

FROM CHINA PAPERS.

Tokyo, 17th January.

It has been decided that all the Russian men-of-war sunk in Port Arthur harbor and roadsteads are to be raised and used for active service, with the exception of the Sevastopol and one gunboat. Divers have already reported on submerged vessels which are found to be only slightly damaged. This is particularly the case with the Pobieda. Five steamers of varying sizes have already been floated. Of the guns in the various forts it has been found that 540 are in excellent condition and available for immediate service.

London, 18th January.

It is reported that the Russion mobilization of reserves is progressing smoothly in all the districts. There were a few minor disturbances. The Czar has despatched his own officers to the districts to secure accurate information of the disturbances.

London, 18th January.

A telegram from St. Petersburg states that the Czar has ordered General Kuropatkin not to make a general advance movement, until sufficient troops are at his command to effectually crush the Japanese Army in Manchuria. It is the general opinion at the Russian capital that the result of the next battle will decide the fate of the war.

London, 18th January.

The raid made by General Mischenko in the vicinity of Yingkow is regarded as a preliminary movement of the advance of the Third Russian Army between Liaoyang and Yingkow

London, 18th January.

The resentment felt by Japan at the prolonged stay of the Baltic Fleet at Madagascar is, it is averred, based on a misapprehension regarding French neutrality regulations. The latter differ totally from the British regulations, and place no limit on the stay of belligerent vessels in French ports unless they are accompanied by prizes. It is pointed out that Japan may enjoy similar advantages at Saigon.

London, 18th January.

The strikes at Baku are ended, the employers having yielded.

In connection with the recent appointment of Mr. Maruyama as possible adviser to the Korean Government, it is now reported that the latter has provisionally decided to appoint Japanese police inspectors to superintend the provincial police affairs. Referring to this subject, the "Nichi Nichi" says that 13 Japanese police inspectors and 27 assistants will be engaged shortly by the Korean Government.

THE JAPANESE POINT OF VIEW.

SECURITY FOR FOREIGN LOANS.

Blundering as the Government's act was in yielding to the demand of binding the customs duties as security for the foreign loans issued last year, and granted that is would be difficult to raise in the present circumstances further foreign loans without similar pledges, *Jiji* would none the less discourage all unnecessary talk, such as of the Government purchase of the private railways for security purposes. If necessary, securities can be obtained in abundance by the Government's monopolies. In the present calculation, the tobacco, camphor, and salt monopoltes are to yield at the least an aggregate annual income of 41,530,000 yen to the Government, and this amount is obviously enough to pay interest on a foreign loan of several hundred million yen. The journal further dwells on the disadvantage of limiting the maximum of the amount issuable for a single market at 50 or 60 million yen, especially in view of the former instance of 100 million yen in bulk in London.

BALTIC SQUADRON.

While the reported departure of the Baltic Squadron from Madagascar with the Falkersahm detachment may not necessarily mean its direct advent to the Far East, the "Asahi" would on its part withold its view on the point until the combined fleet reaches Reunion, for its eastward departure thence my be taken as a fair test of Rojestvensky's final decision. In the meantime the journal would draw the Government's attention to the manner in which the verification of the prediction of Mr. H. W. Wilson, the naval expert, has become impossible. The naval authority in question was of opinion that the Baltic fleet would be recalled home in the event, either, of the Powers beginning to observe their neutrality with more strictness than before, or of the fall of Port Arthur. Port Arthur has fallen, but, says the journal, the Powers, some of them at least, have not mended their ways, and the fleet will in all probability be enabled to continue. its eastward voyage. For this unsatisfactory trend of affairs, the jounal would hold the inactivity of our Foreign Office as responsible.

WHAT RUSSIA OWES TO JAPAN.

The Russians have been converting themselves into a new army. What was raw material nine months ago has been hammered out by the Japanese on the anvil of war, and has become tempered steel. Nothing, indeed, has been more remarkable than this gradual improvement during the war in the fighting efficiency of the Russians. It is no exaggeration to say that their army is ten times more efficient than it was last spring. The Japanese, on the other hand, though they began so well, have not improved.—Spectator.

The total number of plague cases reported in Formosa during last year was 4,435, of which 3,325 proved fatal.

At Shanghai telegram to the "Tokyo Asahi," states that the U.S. warships are concentrating at Amoy, presumably due to the rumour that the Baltic fleet, on its arrival in these waters, will occupy Amoy or a neighbouring port as its base.

It has been agreed that three Russian naval officers on the retired list who were taken prisoners at the time of the seizure of the "Ekaterinoslav," shall be exchanged for three Japanese naval officers captured by the Russians when the "Kinshu Maru" was sunk.

It is encouraging to learn from the Society of Naval Architects that America is building one merchant vessel. As it is of "moderate size" there is reason to believe that our navy will be strong enough to protect it against everything but Congress.—The New York American.

THE SHAHO.

The "Asahi Shimbun's" correspondent writes that the Russians are extending their wings. The troops hitherto in Mukden have been pushed forward to more advanced positions along the Hun, and those in Fushun have moved out into the Hanchang region, the places of these sections beings taken in Mukden and Fushun by some 30,000 men who have recently arrived from Russia.

It is of course possible that the fall of Port Arthur may have produced an effect upon Kuropatkin's strategy, and that instead of massing his forces along the line of greatest resistance, which is undoubtedly the route from Mukden to Liaoyang, he may now have it in view to strike further eastward, directing his blows at the Korean frontier rather than at the Kwantung Peninsula. But it has long appeared to us, and indeed we have often stated, that such extensions and distributions as are now reported to be taking place, might have been anticipated from the moment when Russia decided to place in the field three armies, which, although coordinated under one leader for general purposes, would move in a large measure independently within their respective fields of operation. Russia has now three objectives. It is true that Port Arthur and Dalny have passed into Japanese hands, as has also Yingkow. But it is equally true that unless these places be recovered, Manchuria becomes a wholly worthlese possession. Here then we have two lines of action clearly indicated. The third line is Korea. For reasons too obvious to need explanation, the advantage of carrying the struggle into Korea would be enormous. These are the broad indications afforded by the situation, and consequently what we anticipate is that Gripenberg will operate towards Yingkow, Kuropatkin towards Liaoyang and Kaulbars toward Korea. Possibly the positions of Kaulbars and Gripenberg may be exchanged, but that does not affect the general plan. And another point concerning which no reasonable doubt seems to offer, is that the southward movement of the Russian right army, whether led by Kaulbars or by Gripenberg, will be largely if not wholly through the territories westward of the Liao. To this army will be attached the main bulk of the Russian cavalry, since the flat lands of the Liao Valley offer good opportunities for utilizing it.

A telegram from Takou says that up to the 20th instant there had been no change in the situation on the Shaho. **The enemy's industry in connexion with defensive works seemed to have abated somewhat. Every second day the Russians send up a balloon. They did so at noon on the 20th, and the Japanese opened fire on a force about a battalion strong which was observed to have assembled at the place of the balloon's ascent, namely Hwangshan. The enemy dispersed, a part—apparently the staff—moving towards Kaukiatun. Two prisoners who came in and gave themselves up on the 18th instant, are reported to have said that a great number of the Russian soldiers are anxious to surrender.**

A despatch to the "Asahi" from the front says that the Russian forces have increased in number, but that a full supply of winter clothing has not yet been received, and many of the men are still in summer costume. The consequence is that numerous cases of sickness from exposure occur. Slight cases are treated at Mukden or Tiehling, the serious ones being sent to Harbin. Food is insufficient, and strenuous exertions are made to obtain supplies of cattle from Kirin and Hsinmuntun. Many of the men wounded in the battle of the Shaho have recovered and rejoined the ranks. In the new lines—presumably the lines recently reported to have been extended along the right bank of the Hun—the troops under the orders of Kaulbars are being posted, and works of defence are under construction in their rear. In these works some 200 guns appear to have been mounted. (Japan Mail)

In view of the approaching marriage of the Crown Prince, the Wedding Hall is to be renovated and re-decorated.

The Russians in North Korea are reported to have made a raid and destroyed the telegraphs as far as Ma-Woo Liung.

The Japanese Minister has reprimanded the Foreign office for engaging a Chinese teacher without first cousulting him.

We hear that the Minister of War has not yet assented to General Hasegawa's plans for the wholesale reduction of the Korean army.

It is reported that on New Year's Day His Majesty the Emperor will proceed in state to the ancestral tombs to offer up the annual sacrifice.

H. E. The Japanese Minister is still seeking to abolish the cowhide monopoly which is, he states, disadvantageous to both the Korean producer and the Japanese dealer.

The magistrate of Yong Chŏu has forwarded to the Foreign office a claim for ground which the Japanesese have staked out for railway and other purposes in his district and asks for payment.

The Korean Home Office is strenuously objecting to paying Mr. Maruyawa, the new Police Inspector, a salary of Y300 PER MENSEM It would indeed be interesting to know how much Mr. Maruyama got in Nagasaki.

Conflicting reports have been received regarding the fighting which is now in progress on the Shaho. We have as yet received no details but understand that both sides claim to have been victorious. According to Japanese messages, a number of Russians have been taken prisoners.

It is stated that steps have been taken to actually commence the line from Gensan to Seoul, a distance of over 140 miles. There are said to be one or two engineering difficulties near the centre of the route, but on the whole the work will be much easier than that on the Seoul-Fusan road.

It now appears that the Japanese loan to Korea will be $3,000,000 in paper money and that the Maritime Customs are to be the security. The Dai Ichi Bank is mixed up in the scheme but there still appears to be a hitch somewhere. We will deal with this at greater length to-morrow, contenting ourselves, for the present, by saying that it is "enough to make a cat laugh."

His Majesty has granted the following audiences:

Jan 30th 3.30 P. M.	The Japanese	Minister
" " 4.30 "	" American	"
" 31st 3.30 "	" Chinese	"
" " 4.30 "	" French	"
Feb. 1st 3.30 "	" English	"
" " 4.30 "	" German	"
" 2nd 3.30 "	" Italian	"
" " 4.30 "	" Bylgian Consul	

The Korea Daily News.

Issued at 5 P. M. daily except Sundays.

Rate of Subscription:—
Per Year,............Yen [illegible]
Per Quarter,..........Yen [illegible]
Per Month,..........Yen 2.50.

Postage in Korea not charged extra.
Postage abroad charged extra.

Advertisements, 50 sen per day for 1 inch or less.
5 yen per month per inch.
50 yen per year per inch.

All communications to

E. T. BETHELL,
Editor and Publisher,
Pak-tong, Seoul.

KOREA'S HOPES.

If the recent acts of the Japanese in regard to the Government of this country gave an evidence of a sincere desire for reform there would be some reason for the haste which is being manifested as of course there is never a moment to be lost in commencing honest reform.

But there is no evidence of this, the motives underlying each separate coup turn out to be entirely selfish and the interests of Korea receive no attention, or are, at any rate, disregarded.

It Japan had acquired Korea by conquest, her present attitude would be just what one would expect but this has not yet happened, nor in our opinion is it likely to happen. If peace were to be made she might, by abandoning all claims to interfere with Russia in Manchuria, obtain recognition of such arrangements as she has persuaded the Korean Government to assent to; or she may entertain the idea, if the worst comes to the worst of handing Port Arthur back to Russia in exchange for a guarantee against interference with her designs in Korea.

Otherwise there is absolutely no explanation for the frantic haste which Japan exhibits to obtain complete control of this country. It is not probable that Japan's actions are the unexpected result of recent circumstances, on the contrary from the time when, immediately after the outbreak of war, Mr. Nagamori came forward with his impudent scheme, the persistency of Japanese intrigues in Korea indicates that virtual possession of this country was part of the war programme.

Looked at in this light Japan's attitude is explicable. Had Japan by now, succeeded in defeating Russia she would certainly have been able to stipulate for non-interference with her projects in Korea, and the presumption is that although the war has not been so successful as was expected, it is thought in Tokio that there is little to lose by persisting in the original schemes with regard to Korea.

In our opinion this is a mistaken idea. Even if Korea retained her independence, Japan could have, without territorial acquisitions, secured control of the greater part of the commerce of this country, if she had displayed the slightest desire to ingratiate herself with the people.

But this she has not done, on the contrary, the interests of the owners of the country have in every instance been made subservient to the ambitions of the intruders and it is unlikely that the Koreans will forget it.

Korea's complaisance with all the recent Japanese demands can only be accounted for by the theory that she is looking forward to the time when she can repudiate the whole lot, lock, stock and barrel, advisers, loans, concessions and all.

Whether such a time will arrive or not, it is certain that the Koreans are devoutly praying for it, and looking upon it as the only thing between themselves and effacement.

It is this that strengthens our conviction that Russia will lose no time in making a demonstration in Korea and it is probable that in addition to her other troubles Korea will soon be the scene of war.

CHINA'S PEACE POLICY

The Chinese Minister at Washington addressed the American Academy of Political and Social Science as follows a short time ago:—

"For 2,000 years China has not swerved an iota from steadily pursuing a consistent policy of peace. This may be put down to the fact that all the men who have played a prominent part in Chinese affairs have invariably been thorough followers of Confucius. It is to-day the scholar who is the ruler of the empire. The soldier holds a lower place.

"It may be urged that the Chinese have brought much unnecessary sufferings upon themselves by their firm adherence to the principles of peace. It is true that this has left their country practically exposed to foreign invasions. China's wonderful recuperative power must be sought in the sterling character of the people themselves. They may be wanting in those showy qualities of mind and body which the people of the West admire and cultivate, but they are endowed to an eminent degree with those hardy virtues which tell most in the struggle for existence, namely, patience, industry and thrift.

"Arbitration is the method now best recommended for the settlement of international disputes. This is a step in the right direction. But so long as nations are armed to the teeth there is always a strong temptation to test the effectiveness of the weapons they possess. As long as there is powder in the magazine there is always danger of an explosion from a flying spark."

NATURE'S AIDS.

Besides being an essential part of the culinary art, salt has many other uses perhaps not generally known. Salt cleanses the palate and furred tongue, and a gargle of salt and water is often efficacious. A pinch of salt on the tongue, followed ten minutes after by a drink of cold water, often cures a sick headache. Salt hardens the gums, makes the teeth white and sweetens the breath. Salt added to the water in which cut flowers stand keeps them fresh. Salt used dry in the same manner as snuff will do much to relieve colds, hay fever, etc. Salt in warm water, if used for bathing tired eyes, will be found very refreshing. Salt and water will stop hemorrhage from tooth-extraction.

Drink a glass of water when you get out of bed in the morning. Never mind the size of the glass. Let the water be cold if you will. Some people prescribe hot water, but that is not necessary. You may have washed your face already and relished the experience. All that is luxurious in the cold bath is artifical. That which should prompt the glass of water after sleeping is natural. Drink a glass of cold water in the name of cleanliness. It becomes one of the shortest and easiest of toilet duties. It is swallowed in a second, and in five minutes it has passed from the stomach, taking with it the clogging secretions of the alimentary tracts. It has left behind the stimulus that goes with cold water, and by filling the arterial system to the normal, it puts a spur to the circulation that has grown sluggish in the night.

Major-General Bahn, retired, writing of the new gun with which the German artillery is being re-armed, says it has a rate of fire, unaimed, of 25 shots a minute, and, well aimed, of 16 shots a minute, so that the new batteries of four guns deliver an accurate fire of 64 shots a minute, against the present six-gun batteries highest average of 72 inadequately aimed shots.

NEW FRENCH GUN.

Great interest has been caused in Paris by recent experiments with a new cannon, a secret invention. The most recent tests were made at Havre last Sunday, in the presence of M. Berteaux, Minister of War, and fifty Deputies and Senators. Three men can operate it—one to sight and one to attend the breech while the duties of the third are a secret depending upon the invention. So powerful is the force of the shot, it is said, that no ship of any navy would be able to withstand it.

French military experts, discussing the new cannon, estimate that 100 such cannon would adequately protect the entire coast of France. The cost of the cannon is said to be $100,000, including its quota of projectiles.

A NEW GIBRALTAR.

It is reported from London that British agents in Arabia are laying plans for a great coup. This is nothing less than acquisition of Shikh-Said, which in Britain's hands would be converted into a Gibraltar on the route to India. Lord Lansdowne has had the scheme developed to him—probably during Curzon's visit to London—and is discussing it with the Porte. Jean Dupuy, discussing the project in the "Petit Parisien," says London aims to dismember the Ottoman States in Arabia and to bring them into vassalage to a new authority, may be Egypt, or more likly British India. British enterprise in that part of the world is traceable to the far-sighted Curzon. The Sultan and Shah are alarmed at the prospect.

NEW ELECTRIC BLANKET.

There is hope for the man or woman who cannot manage to keep warm during cold weather. An Alsation engineer, Camille Hergott, has invented a blanket which is always warm and takes no notice of the weather. The heat is furnished by fine electric wires of special construction, woven into the material and heated by a small battery. The blanket cannot possibly take fire, as the wires would break before the heat became sufficient to cause that. Mr. Herrgott is patenting his blanket in America and Canada, for he believes he will gain a fortune there, especially in the Northwest and West, by the manufacture and sale of the blankets in these regions.

It is reported from Perth Amboy, N. J. that the torpedo boat "Gregory," built for the Russian Government by Lewis Nixon, has been given a trial trip here. Nine other similar boats built by Mr. Nixon for Russia, are awaiting shipment.

According to news received from Gibraltar some of the Channel Fleet battleships are getting but poor results from their long-range firing, "battle practice" as it is termed. The Jupiter only hit the target once with her 12-in. guns, and her average with the 6-in. weapons was poor. From her 12-in guns the battleship Hannibal fired forty-three rounds, and nine of these struck the target. With her 6-in. guns the Hannibal hit the target ninety-three times out of 158 attempts.

If proof were needed of the universal desire for peace, says the Tokio correspondent of the "Japan Herald," the Stock Exchange, that barometer of public hopes and fears, gave it recently. For a long time speculators had been waiting for the fall of Port Arthur, expecting a big jump in all sound stocks. The bulls were disappointed. Quotations when the house met on the 5th barely rose by one point. The next day they dropped again to remain at the December level for a week. But the rumour of peace overtures acted like magic. Immediately buyers came forward while sellers held back, and quotations rose above Port Arthur prices and have remained high ever since.

The Korea Daily News.

VOL. II, MONDAY, JANUARY 30, 1905. No. 23

HONGKONG & SHANGHAI BANKING CORPORATION.

Paid-up Capital $10,000,000
Reserve Fund:—Sterling Reserve... 10,000,000
Silver Reserve..... 7,000,000

27,000,000
Reserve Liability of Proprietors... 10,000,000

HEAD OFFICE, HONGKONG.

London Bankers, London and County Banking Company Limited.

Branches and Agencies,
London.

Amoy,	Hankow	Penang,
Bangkok	Hiogo,	Rangoon,
Batavia,	Iloilo,	Saigon,
Bombay,	Lyons,	San Francisco,
Calcutta,	Manila,	Singapore,
Colombo,	Nagasaki,	Sourabaya,
Foochow,	New York,	Tientsin,
Hamburg,	Peking,	Yokohama,

Credits granted on approved Securities, and every description of Banking and Exchange business transacted.

Drafts granted on London and the chief Commercial places in Europe, India, Australia, America, China and Japan.

HOLME RINGER & CO., AGENTS, CHEMULPO.

HOKURKU DOBOKU KAISHA.

Branch office in Chong Dong. Seoul.

Japanese telephone No. 165

CONTRACT DEPARTMENT.

We can contract to build any building or construction.

MERCHANDISE DEPARTMENT.

We can provide any building material.
We have just contracted to build the new Belgian Legation.

E. MEYER & CO.

Chemulpo.

SOLE AGENTS IN KOREA FOR.

A. T. Morse, Sons & Co.'s
"Fresco" Distemper

In all colours ready for use on walls, Ceilings etc.

and

AVENARIUS CARBOLINEUM

A wood-preserving and antiseptic oil preparation

Against decay, dry-rot, fungus and wood-destroying insects.

A large supply always in stock.
Prices upon application.

E. MEYER & CO.,
Chemulpo.

CHARTERED BANK OF INDIA AUSTRALIA & CHINA.

INCORPORATED BY ROYAL CHARTER 1853

HEAD OFFICES —LONDON.

Paid-up Capital £800,000
Reserve Liability of Shareholders 800,000
Reserve Fund 800,000

Drafts granted upon all the principal places in the world and every description of Exchange and banking business transacted.

E. MEYER & CO., Agents,
Chemulpo

MITSU BISHI DOCKYARD & ENGINE WORKS,
NAGASAKI.

CODE WORD, "DOCK."

A 1, A. B. C., and Engineering Codes used.

DOCK No. 1 (at Tategami).

Extreme Length.... ....523 feet
Length on blocks .... 513 ,,
Width of Entrance on Top......89 ,,
,, ,, Bottom....77 ,,
Water on Blocks at Spring Tide 26½ ,,

DOCK No. 2 (Mukaijima).

Extreme Length..............371 feet
Length on Blocks............360 ,,
Width of Entrance on Top......66 ,,
,, ,, Bottom 53 ,,
Water on Blocks at Spring Tide 22 ,,

PATENT SLIP (at Kosuge).

Can take vessels up to 1,000 tons gross

THE WORKS are well equipped with the LATEST IMPROVEMENTS, and can execute any kind of work in SHIPBUILDING and MARINE ENGINEERING, as well as in REPAIRING of SHIPS.

The COMPANY'S new powerfu steamer OURA-MARU (712 tons, 700 I.H.P.), specially built for SALVAGE PURPOSES, and equipped with necessary gear, is always READY at SHORT NOTICE.

THE METHODIST PUBLISHING HOUSE,
Little West Gate, Seoul.

JOB PRINTING, TYPEWRITER PAPER
CARBON PAPER, VISITING CARDS
STATIONERY, BOOK BINDING
BOOK PUBLISHERS
AMERICAN SCHOOL BOOKS
SPENCERIAN COPY BOOKS
PEN CARBON LETTER AND BILL BOOKS

S. A. BECK, Manager.

DAI-ICHI GINKO
LIMITED.

(Formerly the First National Bank)

ESTABLISHED 1873

INCORPORATED UNDER PRESENT LAW 1896

Capital - - - - - - - - Yen 5,000,000
Reserve Fund - - - - - 1,500,000

HEAD OFFICE:—TOKIO.

President: Baron SHIBUSAWA.

BRANCHES AND CORRESPONDENTS
In the Principal Cities and Towns of Japan.

Interest Allowed on

Fixed deposits 1 year - - - 6½ per cent
" " 6 months - - - 6 per cent

Special current accounts 1½ sen daily per Y 100
General " " 1 " " " 100

M. TANAKA,
Manager, Chemulpo.

SINGER SEWING MACHINES

씽거조봉침

SOLE AGENTS FOR KOREA

전매쇼

HOLME RINGER & CO.
Chemulpo.

제물포 함릉거양힝

KAMEYA CO.

GENERAL STOREKEEPERS

Chinkokai - - Seoul

(*Established 1895, Tokyo*)

Confectionery, Hams, Canned Goods, Cutlery, Hirano & Tansan Water. Provisions, Gents, Furnishing goods, Toilet Articles, Travelling Bags, Tobacco, Cigars & Cigarettes Kitchen Utensils. Coffee. Biscuits.

Fresh Goods always kept in Stock.
Prices Moderate
☞ *Please come and inspect our goods.*

NIPPON YUSEN KAISHA.

JAPANESE MAIL STEAMSHIP CO.

UNDER MAIL CONTRACT WITH THE IMPERIAL JAPANESE GOVERNMENT.

European Line

Regular Fortnightly Service between Yokohama Kobe, Moji, Shanghai, Hongkong, Singapore, Penang Colombo, Port Said, Marseilles, London and Antwerp

American Line

Regular Fortnightly Service between Hongkong and Seattle, calling at Shanghai, Moji, Kobe, Yokohama and Victoria, B. C.

Australian Line

Regular weekly Service betwen Japan Ports and Australia, calling at Hongkong and Manila.

(Above Three Lines Suspended until further notice).

Shanghai Line

Weekly Service between Shanghai and Japan Ports

Korea Line

Service Kobe, Moji, Nagasaki, Fusan Chemulpo Chefoo, Taku.

S. S. Babelsberg, 2181 tons.

Service Kobe, Moji, Fusan, Chemulpo, Chinnampo

S. S. ARGO, S. S. Ohio.

BORDEN'S CONDENSED MILK CO.

New York, U. S. A.

ALWAYS IN STOCK

Eagle Brand Condensed Milk.

Gold Seal Condensed Milk.

Peerless (Family) Evaporated Cream.

Borden's Malted Milk.

E. MEYER & CO.
Chemulpo Korea,
Sole Agents

ROYAL INSURANCE COMPANY.
Funds exceed £10,000,000
FIRE
AT CURRENT RATES
LIFE
REDUCED PREMIUM.
HOLME RINGER & CO.,
Agents, Chemulpo

HOTEL DU PALAIS.
SEOUL.

The only first class Hotel in Seoul Situated in the centre of the city opposite the palace.

Cuisine under the supervision of an experienced French Chef.

Well ventilated and furnished throughout.

TARIFF UPON APPLICATION

L. MARTIN
Proprietor and Manager.

大韓每日申報
대한미일신보

(뎨이권 이십ᄉᆞ호) (슈요일) 일쳔구빅오년 이월 일일

본사고빅

이신보는영어와한어로셕계리
일출판ᄒᆞᆸ

신문가
한쟝 엽두돈오푼
일삭됴 엽두량닷돈
우표가ᄆᆡ삭닷돈
다ᄉᆞᆺ돈으로밧숨
광고료는
긔한의쟝단과ᄌᆞ힝의다쇼로증
감ᄒᆞ되렴가로밧을터이오며오
리지아니ᄒᆞ야대한사람마다다이신
문을보실터이니광고ᄒᆞ시기를
원ᄒᆞ시는이들은우리신문사에
와서면약ᄒᆞ심을희망ᄒᆞᆸ
○발힝소 박동대한ᄆᆡ일신보
사범어학교압헤젼영국인셜필
림쟝자리오
사쟝 영국인 (빅셜)
평양 디리졈
○평양효동사는권미보씨로우
리신문과미디리인을뎡ᄒᆞ엿
ᄉᆞ오니평양에계신구람코자ᄒᆞ
는 쳠군ᄌᆞ는빙디리졈에왕
림ᄒᆞ와면의ᄒᆞ시옵

사고

○우리대한ᄆᆡ일신보의목뎍은
대한의안녕질서에관한모든뎨
목에ᄃᆡᄒᆞ야는공평한변론을쥬
쟝홈이라우리통신원의담보는
신문보시는쳠군ᄌᆞ의게ᄒᆞ상보
도ᄒᆞ리며편지를긔서ᄒᆞ며주시
는이는셩명과번디를젹어붓치
시기를희망ᄒᆞ오니비거ᄉᆞ신문
샹에긔쟤ᄒᆞ란는거시아니오다
만긔휘신용ᄒᆞ는증거를숨고자
홈이라긔쟈는아모긔서던지긔
쟤홈을되ᄀᆞᆨᄒᆞ는권리가잇ᄉᆞ오
나되쟈ᄒᆞ는리유를말ᄒᆞᆯ터이오
며공중평화를문란케ᄒᆞ는듯ᄒᆞᆫ
긔서는의례히밧지안켓ᄉᆞᆸ나이
다
●본사셜시이래로신문을ᄃᆡ방
우례로분젼ᄒᆞ와례젼부의임의
로젼ᄒᆞ든곳스로면곳에는ᄒᆞᆨ늣게
젼ᄒᆞ기도ᄒᆞ며ᄒᆞᆨ멋첩식ᄭᅥ슴ᄒᆞᆫ겁
에젼ᄒᆞ기도ᄒᆞ며ᄒᆞᆨ아니젼ᄒᆞ는
곳도잇다ᄒᆞ와우리신문을ᄉᆞ랑
ᄒᆞ야구람ᄒᆞ시는 쳠군ᄌᆞ의게
ᄃᆡᄒᆞ야ᄆᆡ우미안ᄒᆞ옵기로지금
은분젼인을두고ᄆᆡ일죠ᄉᆞ게
ᄒᆞ며아니젼ᄒᆞ거나늦게ᄒᆞ거나
폐가업도록ᄒᆞ라ᄒᆞ오니ᄒᆞᆨ아니
젼ᄒᆞ거나ᄒᆞᆨ늣게젼ᄒᆞ거나ᄒᆞᆫ일
이잇스면본사로통긔ᄒᆞ여주심
을희망ᄒᆞᆸ

관보

뎨ᄉᆞ쳔ᄉᆞ빅십구호 광무구
년일월삼십일
서임급ᄉᆞ령
○승셔판임관오등 서흥우톄
사주ᄉᆞ 구자셩
광무팔년십이월삼십일
○승셔판임관삼등 한셩뎐보
사주ᄉᆞ 서상문 한셩뎐보사
주ᄉᆞ 조상순 한셩뎐보사주
ᄉᆞ 안병린
일월삼십일
○임 판임관오등 진위뎐보
사주ᄉᆞ 리죵구
일월삼십일
○임강계우체사주사셔판임관
륙등 홍인희
○임셩진우체ᄉᆞ주ᄉᆞ셔판임관
륙등 리병익
○금셩금봉 강계우체사주사
홍인희 셩진우체사주사 리
병익
이상일월이십오일
○의원면본관 쇼룽참봉 박
봉진 의쥬감리셔쥬사 송셩인
○명궁니부특진관셔칙임관사
등 규장각직학사 남규희
○명니장원경셔칙임관삼등
종이품 구연승
○임규장각직학사셔쥬임관오
등 정삼품 서공슌
○임숭순룽참봉셔판임관팔등
송죵우
○승셔판임관칠등 원구단사
졔셔참봉 남셩희
○임의쥬감리셔쥬사셔판임관
륙등 평양감리셔쥬사 원용
덕
○임평양감리셔쥬ᄉᆞ셔판임관
팔등 무안감리셔쥬ᄉᆞ 홍순
복
○임무안감리셔쥬사셔판임관
팔등 젼주사 송셩인
○임한셩뎐보사주사셔판임
관륙등 은산뎐보사주사 김
셰희
○임은산뎐보사주사셔판임관
륙등 리규오
○면본관 한셩뎐보사주사
김셰희
○정금삼봉 은산뎐보사주사 리
규오
이상일월이십칠일

○구년도예산표 (속)

닉부소관
뎨사관 디방갑부 일만삼쳔
일빅구십사년
뎨일항 봉급 삼쳔륙빅원
뎨이항 쳥비 륙빅원
뎨삼항 쳥사수리비 일빅
원
뎨사항 잡급급잡비 삼빅
륙십원
뎨오항 약품비 팔빅원
뎨구관 디방잡향사비 팔빅
칠십일원
뎨일항 디방잡향사비 팔
빅칠십일원
지화지출차증 칠쳔이빅
닉부소관합계 팔십구만삼
쳔사빅팔십칠원

외부소관
뎨일관 외부본쳥 삼만삼쳔
구빅십사원
뎨일항 봉급 일만팔쳔팔
빅오십원
뎨이항 쳥비 오쳔사빅팔
십원
뎨삼항 쳥사수리비 오빅
원
뎨사항 잡급급잡비 삼쳔
사빅팔십원
뎨오항 려비 륙빅원
뎨륙항 표징비 이쳔원
뎨칠항 연회비 삼쳔원
뎨이관 각기항쟝감리셔 오
만구쳔칠빅사십원(지화)
뎨일항 인쳔감리셔비 오
쳔팔빅이십원
뎨이항 동리감리셔비 오
쳔오빅칠십원
뎨삼항 덕원감리셔비 오
쳔이빅칠십원
뎨사항 경흥감리셔비 오
쳔이십원
뎨오항 무안감리셔비 오
쳔이십원
뎨륙항 삼화감리셔비 오
쳔이십원
뎨칠항 옥구감리셔비 오
쳔이십원
뎨팔항 창원감리셔비 오
쳔이십원
뎨구항 셩진감리셔비 사
쳔칠빅이십원
뎨십항 평양감리셔비 사
쳔삼빅이십원
뎨십일항 의쥬감리셔비
사쳔오빅이십원
뎨십이항 룡쳔감리셔비
사쳔오빅이십원

외부소관
뎨삼관 지외공관 십칠만팔
쳔칠빅이십원 (지화)
뎨일항 주일공관비 일만
팔쳔삼빅이십원
뎨이항 주미공관비 삼만
일쳔이빅팔십원
뎨사항 주영공관비 삼만
륙쳔칠빅팔십원
뎨오항 주법공관비 삼만
칠쳔칠빅팔십원
뎨륙항 주쳥공관비 일만
팔쳔이빅팔십원
지화지출차증 이십삼만팔쳔
사빅륙십원
외부소관합계 오십일만팔
빅삼십사원

탁지부소관
뎨일관 탁지부본쳥 칠만사
빅팔십원
뎨일항 봉급 삼만구쳔일
빅십원
뎨이항 쳥비 사쳔팔빅원
뎨삼항 쳥사수리비 사빅
원
뎨사항 잡급급잡비 일만
이쳔일빅칠십원
뎨오항 려비 삼쳔이빅원
뎨륙항 외국인계급 일만
팔빅원 (지화)
뎨이관 세관 삼십만일쳔륙
빅원 (지화)
뎨일항 인쳔세관 오만륙
쳔삼빅오원
뎨이항 부산세관 삼만일
쳔팔빅삼원
뎨삼항 원산세관 일만구
쳔일빅십오원
뎨사항 무안세관 칠쳔이
빅원
뎨오항 삼화세관 칠쳔이
빅원
뎨륙항 옥구세관 칠쳔이
빅원
뎨칠항 창원세관 칠쳔이
빅원
뎨팔항 셩진세관 칠쳔이
빅원
뎨삼관 국채 일빅구십오만
삼쳔사빅이십오원 (지화)
뎨일항 구미하츄비 사쳔
륙빅원
뎨이항 구미하속비 팔쳔
사빅원

UNION INSURANCE SOCIETY OF CANTON.

Head office Hongkong.
Marine risks underwritten at current rates.
Agents in Chemulpo,
E. MEYER & CO.

COMPAGNIE DES MESSAGERIES MARITIMES.

Fortnightly Direct Service.

for Marseilles
via Ports.
sailing from Yokohama
Calling at Kobe,
Shanghai, Hongkong, Saigon, Singapore,
Colombo, Djibouti, Suez, Port Said
and Marseilles.

For particulars apply to
HOLME RINGER & CO.,
Chemulpo.

HAYASHIDA & CO.,

16 MYENG DONG, CHIN KO KAI, SEOUL.
BRANCH OFFICE AT CHEMULPO.

Money changers, Coal and Wood Merchants, Express Agents.

We are agents for the Pyeng-yang Coal Company and the Karazu Coal Company of Japan. We have the best quality of both anthracite and bituminous coal, and prompt execution of orders is our speciality. Firewood of all kinds kept in stock. Full weight guaranteed. Money of all denominations exchanged at current rates. Parcels received for all parts.

CHINA MUTUAL LIFE INS. OC.

Most favourable terms to policy holders.

Benefit system unsurpassed.

HOLME RINGER & CO.
Agents, Chemulpo.

C. P. R.

CANADIAN PACIFIC RAILWAY COMPANY'S ROYAL MAIL STEAMSHIP LINE.

THE FAST ROUTE BETWEEN CHINA, JAPAN, AND EUROPE VIA CANADA AND THE UNITED STATES.

Route from Hongkong via Shanghai, Nagasaki (Inland Sea of Japan), Kobe, Yokohama, Victoria and Vancouver.

Twin Screw Empress Steamship—6,000 Tons—Speed 19 knots.

PROPOSED SAILING FROM YOKOHAMA.
R. M. S. Empress of India.
R. M. S. Empress of Japan.
R. M. S. Empress of China.
R. M. S. Athenian.
R. M. S. Tartar.

Special reduction (first class only) granted to members of the Military, Naval, Diplomatic and Civil services and to Missionaries.

Passengers have choice of ten routes across the Continent of America and have privilege of travelling by any Atlantic Steamship Line.

Round the World passage tickets in connection with the P. and O. S. N., North German Lloyd and Messageries Co's £125.

All rates payable at current rate of exchange.

For further information, Tickets, Guide Books, etc., apply to

HOLME, RINGER & CO., AGENTS,
Chemulpo.

Grand Hotel,

(Formerly the Station Hotel)

Near the Railway Terminus,
West Gate Seoul.

The Best Hotel in Korea!
Handsome new Building.
Fine Airy Rooms
Excellent Cuisine.
Terms Moderate.
Special terms to Missionaries
and to permanent boarders.

Electric cars within 2 minutes' walk.

W. H. EMBERLEY.
Proprieto

EVERY FACILITY.

In connection with Life Assurance Business is afforded by

The Standard Life Assurance Co.,

One of the largest and wealthiest of the Provident Institutions of the United Kingdom Forms of Application and all information will be promptly afforded on application

10 CENTS A DAY.

Not a very large expenditure is it? But it is sufficient to secure for a man of 30 a policy with the STANDARD LIFE OFFICE for

$1323.

For all particulars of rates, etc., apply to

Holme, Ringer & Co.,
Agents, Chemulpo.

THE NEW YORK LIFE INSURANCE COMPANY.

Have you ever been declined by any Company?

Are you engaged in a specially hazardous occupation?

Have you heard of the New York Life Insurance Company's New Classifications for this class of Risks?

If not, send your date of birth, occupation and particulars of rejection, if any to

E. MEYER & CO.,
Agents, Chemulpo.

MITSUI BUSSAN KAISHA.
(MITSUI & CO.)
MITSUI GINKO.
(MITSUI BANK.)

The Bank is owned by the members of the Mitsui Family, who, as partners, assume an unlimited responsibility for all liabilities of the Bank:—

Capital........................Yen 5,000,000
Reserve Fund.................. " 5,600,000

HEAD OFFICE, TOKYO.
LONDON OFFICE, 34 LIME ST., E. C.

BRANCHES AND AGENCIES:—
New York, San Francisco, Hamburg, Bombay, Singapore, Manila, Hongkong, Amoy, Chefoo, Tientsin.

Kobe, Hakodate, Yokohama, Kure, Yokosuka, Moji, Shimonoseki, Miike, Wakamatsu, Nagasaki, Kuchinotsu, Karatsu, Sasebo, Misume, Taipeh, &c.

Telegraphic Address for all the Offices:
"MITSUI."
A. B. C. AND A. I CODES USED.

Contractors of Coal
To the Imperial Japanese Navy. Arsenals and Railway Bureau, Principal Railway Companies and Industrial Work, Home and Foreign Mail and Freight Steamers.

Sole Proprietors
Of the famous Miike, Tagawa and Yamano Coal Mines.

Sole Agents
For the sale of Fukumo, Hokoku, Ichimura, Kanoda, Mannoura, Onoura, Ostuji, Sonoda, Tsubaruro, Yoshinotani, Yoshio, Yurokibura and other coals.

YANGTSE INSURANCE ASSOCIATION, LTD.

The undersigned, having been appointed agents for the above company, are prepared to issue policies and pay losses on marine risks at regular rates.

E. MEYER & CO.,
Agents, Chemulpo.

AMERICAN KOREAN ELECTRIC CO.

Light and Power.

main Office: Electric Building, Chong No.

RAILWAY DEPARTMENT.

OPERATING CARS BETWEEN EAST AND WEST GATE, EVERY TEN MINUTES:—

First Car leaves East Gate at 7:00 A. M. First Car leaves R. R. Station at 7:25 A. M
Last Car " East Gate at 8.40 P. M. Last " " R. R. Station at 9.05 P.M

OPERATING CARS BETWEEN EAST GATE AND IMPERIAL TOMB TERMINUS, EVERY TWENTY MINUTES:—

CONNECTING WITH EVERY ALTERNATE CAR ARRIVING AT EAST GATE FROM CHONG NO.

First Car leaves East Gate for Tomb at 7:10 A. M
" " " Tomb for East Gate at 7:30 A. M.
Last " " East Gate for Tomb at 7:50 P. M.
" " " Tomb for East Gate at 8:10 P. M.

OPERATING CARS BETWEEN CHONG NO AND YUNG SAN RIVER EVERY TWELVE MINUTES:

First Car leaves Chong No for South Gate at 7:12 A. M.
" " " Chong No for Yung San at 7:36 A. M.
" " " South Gate for Chong No at 7:20 A. M.
" " " Yung San for Chong No at 8:09 A. M.
Last " " South Gate for Chong No 9:00 P. M
" " " Yung San for Chong No at 8.45. p. M.

SPECIAL PRIVATE CARS FURNISHED TO SUIT CONVENIENCE OF PATRONS. PRICES ON APPLICATION AT HEAD OFFICE.

LIGHTING DEPARTMENT

Where less than 250 candle power of light is used, the rate per month will be
Per 16 candle power incandescent lamp,—All night.—Yen 2.50.
32 candle power incandescent lamp:—All night:—Yen 4.00.
50 candle power incandescent lamp:—All night:—Yen 6.00.
150 " " " " " " 10.00.
1200 " " enclosed arc " " " 20.00.

Where more than 250 candle power of light is used, a Meter will be installed, if requested:—Rent of Meter Yen 2.00 per month. Rate of charges by meter reading:—Two Sen per Ampere per hour. (Approximately this is equal to about One Sen per 16 C. P. lamp per hour) Minimum monthly charge where meter is installed, Yen 20.00 per month, which includes rental of meter.

Estimates for installing lights furnished on application

An assortment of chandeliers always on hand.

K. Murakami.

Photograph Studio
Chinkokai, Seoul.

Printing, Developing and Enlargement, of Photographs always Undertaken.

Korean Views and Pictures Illustrating Native Customs always on Sale,

---

THE OSAKA SHOSEN KAISHA

Boats frequently on the berth for Chinnampo.

REGULAR SAILINGS BETWEEN JAPAN AND KOREAN PORTS.

FUSAN AND KOBE VIA SHIMONOSEKI.

OSAKA VIA MOKPO, FUSAN, SHIMONOSEKI AND KOBE.

MOJI DIRECT.

OSAKA VIA KUNSAN, MASANPO, FUSAN, SHIMONOSEKI AND KOBE.

CHEMULPO KUNSAN LINE,
Every three days.

CHEMULPO CHINNAMPO LINE.
Every three days.

For Freight and passage and further particulars apply to
THE OSAKA SHOSEN KAISHA,
Chemulpo.

RONDON, PLAISANT & CO.

General Storekeepers and Merchants, Ships Contractors, Tobacconists, Commission and Forwarding Agents, Coal Merchants

IMPORTERS AND EXPORTERS

Seoul & Chemulpo.

W. D. WENTWORTH.

LANDING
AND
SHIPPING AGENT.
AND
CUSTOMS BROKER.

12 OURA, NAGASAKI.

STEWARD & CO.

Chemulpo.

Shipchandlers and Storekeepers, Naval and Mercantile Contractors, Landing and Shipping Agents.

STEWARD'S HOTEL

Chemulpo.

Best accommodation in the port for travellers. Clean and well-aired rooms, good cuisine and prompt attendance, moderate tariff.

데삼항 데일우항차관 구
십삼만구쳔사빅이십오원
(지화)
데사항 평부편도차관리주
일쳔원 [지화]
데오항 낙쟝원차티 일빅
만원
데사관 공신셰륙 일쳔구빅
오십륙원
데일항 공신셰륙 일쳔구
빅오십륙원
데오관 국고금반운비 이십
만원
데일항 국고금반운비 이
십만원
데륙관 인쇄국 오만칠쳔이
빅팔십오원
데일항 봉급 칠쳔삼빅륙
십원
데이항 쳥비 일만륙쳔칠
빅륙십원
데삼항 쳥사수리비 쳔원
데사항 잡급급잡비 일만
삼쳔이빅사원
데오항 려비 일빅이십원
데륙항 피복비 구빅이십
일원
데칠항 외국인계급 칠쳔
구빅이십원
데팔항 수업원료구매비
일만원
지화지출차총 일빅삼만칠
빅사십오원
데비금 일빅삼십만원
데일 예비금 오십만원
데이 예비금 팔십만원
합계 부쇼관항계 사빅팔십
이만오쳔사빅구십일원
(미완)

론셜

[illegible]

외보

[illegible]

잡보

[illegible]

여보이며무편글ᄉ되이거시용
의필젹이뇨되답ᄒ되그리ᄒ다
문왈비서신을엇던사름쳐에붓
쳐거시뇨답왈본졍에붓쳐거시
라
쟈ᄒᆞᆫ륙지를배여보이며문왈이
거순엇던셔신이뇨답왈이거순
나의글시가아니오또조희품도
다르니확실이작잔ᄒᆞᆫ거슬ᄉᆞ수
로가히변명ᄒᆞᆯ거시오또거즛만
든륙지중에독졍포와밋탐환을
만히비밀히무송ᄒᆞᆫ다ᄂᆞᆫ수외ᄂᆞᆫ
터럭의반만ᄒᆞᆫ부당ᄒᆞ니이글을어
ᄃᆡ셔엇엇ᄂᆞ뇨

[illegible]

뎐보

[illegible]

DAI ICHI BANK.

According to the "Chosen Shimpo" the programme of the Dai Ichi Bank is as follows:—

To handle and control the Government receipts and disbursements throughout Korea.

To withdraw from circulation all its old bank notes and issue a new series.

To collect all the nickel money in circulation and replace it with a new currency.

To establish additional branches at Pyeng Yang, Gensan, Fusan, Mokpo, Chinnampo, Dai Ku and other important centres.

COAL DISCOVERIES IN KOREA.

An investigation conducted by the Japanese has led to the discovery of coal in the following districts:—

Kyeng-chu and Woolsan districts of Kyeng-sang province.

Tong-chin district of Kyeng-ki province.

Sam-chuk and Chŏng-sun districts of Kang-won province.

Pyeng-yang district of Pyeng-an province.

Yeung-heung, Kilchu, Myeng-chŏn and Kyeng-sung districts of Ham-kyeng province.

Although Reuter recently wired that the Baltic fleet was probably returning home, it now seems likely that it has gone to some pre-arranged rendezvous to join forces with the third squadron.

The Empress Dowager of China is reported to have sent a sum of 300,000 taels for the relief of the sufferers in Manchuria, and to have urged General Tseng to spare no effort in their behalf.

Mr. Gibson Bowles, M. P., in his pamphlet on "National Finance," brings out the fact that the total expenditure of Great Britain, imperial and local, amounts to £324,700,000 for this year, against £141,200,000 for 1894.

It is reported that when Mr. Paik Sung Ki was Governor of North Pyeng-an province, he amassed considerable wealth at the expense of the people. Some of the people recently came up to Seoul and compelled him to disgorge.

The Foreign Office has recommended the appointment of Mr. Kim Kio Hun as Kamni of Kunsan, he being well posted in native and foreign affairs, but the people of that place have applied to have Mr. Cheung Hang Cho, the present Kamni retained as his rule has been very satisfactory to them.

According to the Korean law, as it stands at present, it does not seem permissible for the police to arrest the higher officials. Mr. Maruyama, the Japanese police adviser, has applied to have this law amended but the high officials are strenuously opposing the demand. Now that the police is controlled by the Japanese we can quite understand the reluctance of the officials to place themselves entirely at their mercy.

It is a pity that something cannot be done to clear a thoroughfare at Chong No, in the neighbourhood of the Big Bell. At present owing to the large number of oxen laden, with brushwood and firewood, standing about the road is almost impassable. We understand that they were once "moved on" by the police, but as the Japanese hawkers who have preëmpted pitches in this neighbourhood ignored the police orders, the firewood men have returned to the spot.

Robin Hood and his merry men seem to have their counterparts in Korea. The magistrate of Tai-in reports that over 50 robbers armed with rifles invaded his district and "collected" 80 bags of rice from Mr. Kim, 130 bags from Mr. Min, 150 bags from another Mr. Kim, 28 bags from Mr. Choi, $30 from a third Mr. Kim and 150 bags of rice from Mr. Yi. The robbers, after distributing their spoil amongst the poor people of that locality left for fresh fields and pastures news.

THE NORTH SEA INCIDENT.

A correspondent of the "N. Y. Sun" writes:—

How easily war between Great Britain and Russia might have sprung out of the Dogger Bank incident was disclosed by the "Pioneer," an Anglo-Indian paper of Allahabad, India, a few days after it took place. That paper, having unusually good sources of information, learned that at the height of the crisis in London the Imperial Defence Committee there agreed that Lord Kitchener should occupy the plains of Kabul and Kandahar with the consent of the Amir of Afghanistan and should have a free hand regarding the field army, which the committee suggested be 150,000 strong. Details and particulars relating to the appointment of special officers and other matters were also published. The Indian Government at once sent a communication to the press contradicting the fact, but failing to explain the details that were inconsistent with mere rumor.

In India, according to correspondence which I have just received by mail, the circumstance is regarded as a premature disclosure of a plan of operation which was under consideration before the Dogger Bank crisis, and precipitated by its occurrence. By the light of the "Pioneer's" revelation it is now possible to understand the meaning of the preparations for a general mobilization of the Russian army reported in despatches last week, as also the hurrying back and forth of imperial messengers between Vienna and Berlin about the same time. PERA.

NEW YORK, Dec. 2.

SHORT RIFLE FOR THE BRITISH ARMY.

A new short rifle superior in point of lightness, handiness, and rapidity of loading and firing is recommended by the Small Arms Committee as suitable for universal use.

The rifle has undergone a three months' test by sections of cavalry, infantry, Royal Navy, and marines, and the reports received are extremely satisfactory. Its behaviour in sandy, dry climates was tested in Somaliland with good results, and its lightness and convenience gave universal satisfaction.

The features of the rifle are an adjustable sight with open-topped hood lever back sight, long hand-guard, charger system of loading, ten-round magazine, and complete caseing of the barrel in wood.

The new Bulgariam loan for £4,000,000 is to be issued at 82, and will bear five per cent. interest. Nearly a million and a quarter of the amount is required for the purchase of 81 batteries of quick-firing guns—a most unwarrantable extragavance. It may be, but the terms of the loan are still better than any Japan has lately obtained.

It is abundantly clear that the British Government knows the truth about the North Sea affair, and therefore does not stick to the original story, to which no one in the world gave credence. It feels that the matter will be cleared up by the Commission of Enquiry, and that the murder will out. Hence is employed the word "misunderstanding." An excellent word, comprehensive and elastic. Of itself it makes all clear.—Svet, St. Petersburg.

In all probability, says "Export Trade" the present war will remain undecided. Both countries are facing each other in equal strength, neither will be victorious, neither will succumb. Should this lead them to make an early peace neither state will have to bear the financial sacrifices the war has imposed upon her. Should the war last for any great length of time, there is a danger that the financial resources of either state will suffer so severely, that their credit in other countries will be seriously undermined for many years.

MR. DOOLEY REGARDS BANTING WITH DISFAVOR.

"I see th' good woman goin' by here at a gallop to-day," said Mr. Dooley.

"She's thryin' to rayjooce her weight," said Mr. Hennessy.

"What f'r?"

"I don't know. She looks all right," said Mr. Hennessy,

"Well," said Mr. Dooley, "'tis a sthrange thing. Near ivrybody I know is thryin' to rayjooce his weight. Why shud a woman want to be thin onless she is thin? Th' idee iv female beauty that all gr-reat men fr'm Julius Caesar to mesilf has held is much more like a bar'l thin a clothes pole. Hogan tells me that Alexander's wife an' Caesar's missus was no light weights; Martha Wash'nton was short but pleasantly dumpy, an' Audhrew Jackson's good woman weighed two hundred an' smoked a pipe. Hogan says that all th' potes he knows was in love with not to say fat but ample ladies. Th' potes thimsilves was thin but th' ladies was chubby. A pote whin he has wurruked all day at th' typewriter wants to rest his head on a shoulder that won't hurt. Shakespeare's wife was thin an' they quarreled. Th' lady that th' Eyestalian pote Danty made a fool iv himsilf about was no skiliton. All th' pitchers iv beautiful women I've iver see had manny curves an' sivral chins. Th' phottygraft iv Mary Queen iv Scots that I have in me room shows that she took on weight afther she had her dhress made. Th' collar looks to be chokin' her.

"But nowadays 'tis th' fashion to thry to emaciatee y'ersils. I et supper with Carney th' other day. It was th' will iv hiven that Carney shud grow fat, but Carney has a will iv his own an' f'r tin' years he's been thryin' to look like Sinitor Fairbanks whin his thrue model was Grover Cleveland. He used to scald himsilf ivry mornin' with a quart of hot wather on gettin' up. That did him no good. Thin he thried takin' long walks. Th' long walk rayjooced him half a pound and gave him a thirst that made him take on four pounds iv boodweiser. Thin he rented a horse an' thried horseback ridin.' Th' horse liked his weight no more thin Carney did, an' Carney gained tin pounds in th' hospital. He thried starvin' himsilf an' he lost two pounds an' his job f'r bein' cross to th' boss. Thin he raysumed his reg'lar meals an' make up his mind to cut out th' sugar. I see him at breakfast wan mornin.' Nature had been kind to Carney in th' matter iv appytite. I won't tell ye what he consumed. It's too soon afther supper an' th'room is close. But, annyhow, whin his wife had tottered in with th' last flapjack an' fainted, an' whin I begun to wondheo whether it wud be safe to stay, he hauled a little bottle fr'm his pocket an' took a small pill. 'What's that? say I. "Tis what I take in place iv sugar,' says he. 'Sugar is fattenin' an this rayjooces th' weight,' says he. 'An' ar-reye goin' to match that poor little tablet against that breakfast?' says I. 'I am' says he. 'Cow'rd,' says I.

(To be continued.)

We do not know how the erroneous idea has got abroad that we are willing to solve everyone's difficulties, and to "Young Cook," who writes to ask us what is the best method of removing finger-marks from blanc-mange, we can only suggest india-rubber.—Punch

---

Through the recent exposures made by Thomas W. Lawson, of Boston, the stocks of the great trusts of the country have depreciated to the extent of one hundred million dollars. Lawson declares that he will continue his attacks until the material at his command has been exhausted. The principal losers are the Amalgamated Copper company, the Steel Trust and the Standard Oil Company, the first named being the principal loser. It is estimated that the losses of Senator Clark of Montana will aggregate the sum of five million dollars. It is predicted that the inter-state commerce commission will be instructed to investigate the charges that have been made, which, if proved, will lead to the arrest and trial of a number of the great financiers of the country.

AT PORT ARTHUR.

The "China Gazette" had an opportunity of talking with some of General Stoessel's officers when the party passed through Shanghai homeward bound It says:—"Some of the incidents connected with the closing hours of General Stoessel's stay in Port Arthur were extremely curious.

For example, when General Reitz, a Chief of the Staff, went out to confer with our old friend General Idichi, Chief of Baron Nogi's Staff, one of the first questions put to him by the Japanese officer named, was on the delicate subject of the Russian war-chest, its whereabout, dimensions, and general state. In short when they came to business, General Idichi point-blank asked General Reitz "How much money have you got to surrender to us?"

General Reitz replied, "not much. I am afraid very little."

General Idichi asked him again "How much?" and General Reitz said, "Well we have at the moment in our war-chest just exactly 136 roubles, which you can have with great pleasure."

The Japanese officer seemed astonished, and said, "But what of the 3,800,000 roubles that we know you had in cash when the war began?"

General Reitz replied "Oh, that is all right. We may have had it at the beginning, but now the Chinamen have got it all."

General Idichi had no more to say. He knows the Chinaman, having been there before.

Another subject which General Idichi was very anxious about was to know how many standards the Russians had to surrender, the standards being, in the eyes of the Japanese, as in those of the Russians, the most precious emblems of military authority.

General Reitz said in reply to General Idichi with regard to the matter, "I am afraid we have not any. We sent them all away," a reply which apparently astonished the Japanese Chief of Staff considerably.

General Kuropatkin has issued renewed emphasized orders that the effects of the Japanese killed be sent to the prisoner's bureau at St. Petersburg, whence they will be forwarded to the relatives of the killed. This action is in response to similar Japanese courtesy.

The Korea Daily News.

Issued at 5 P. M. daily except Sundays.

Rate of Subscription:—
Per Year,............Yen 25.
Per Quarter,..........Yen 7.
Per Month,...........Yen 2.50.

Postage in Korea not charged extra.
Postage abroad charged extra.

Advertisements, 50 sen per day for 1 inch or less.
5 yen per month per inch.
50 yen per year per inch.

All communications to

E. T. BETHELL,
Editor and Publisher,
Pak-tong, Seoul

THE LOAN.

It really appears as though the Japanese are over reaching themselves in their haste to secure all the good things in Korea, and furthermore it seems nothing short of a scandal that the Korean Government should be compelled to pay a high salary to an official like Mr. Megata whose chief energies are directed to assisting Japan in her schemes.

The loan scheme, the national bank scheme and the control of the customs scheme have all been rolled into one so that for the consideration of $3,000,000 (note the reduction) in Japanese paper money the Korean Government is to part with the Maritime Customs and give the Dai Ichi Bank priveleges which will make it, to all intents and purposes, the National Bank of Korea.

What with the Il-chin-hoi and the police the Japanese have pretty much their own way in Korea and we are afraid that remonstrances will be of little avail, but as we have reason to believe that there is still some opposition to the proposal in high quarters, we will repeat the advice which we have given to Korea on two previous occasions when the talk of loans has been in the air. We have recommended Korea to make sure of two things (1) That she gets the money and (2) that she will be allowed to have the spending of it.

The loan now offered fulfils neither of these conditions; the "money" is to be in paper and the Dai Ichi Bank is to spend it.

The loan is be secured on the Maritime Customs, is to be repayable in ten years and bears interest at the rate of six per cent. Now when Japan borrows money she has to pay nearly 8 per cent for it and there are only two explanations of her anxiety to lend money at a loss of 2 per cent. The first is pure philanthropy and the second is some advantage which is not immediately apparent but is visible enough if looked for.

Mr. Megata has the reputation of being a clever financier and it would not be impossible for him, if he retained control of his Department, to arrange that at the end of the ten years there would be nothing in the Korean exchequer wherewith to repay the loan, when we presume the Japanese would foreclose and the Korean Maritime Customs would be theirs for the consideration of $3 000,000 in paper money.

Then the Dai Ichi Bank is mixed up in the scheme in a way that is far from reassuring. This bank is to establish branches throughout the country for the purpose of collecting the spurious nickels and giving (we presume) paper money in exchange. There seems to be no provision for placing this bank in any way under Korean control and in this respect the Koreans again are at a disadvantage.

The whole programme has so far as we can see not a single redeeming feature for the Koreans and is of such a nature that no country would voluntarily submit to it.

What in the name of all that is mysterious is this new paper money to be like? Is it to be redeemable in gold on demand? If so we advise Korea to cash it in without a moment's delay, as if it once gets into circulation the Government will stand a very small chance of getting it back at the end of ten years and then will to pay back a paper loan in gold!

The whole deal is simply farcical and the funniest thing about it all is the Korean Government paying Mr. Megata Y1,000 a month to prepare these little traps for them.

Presumably the Korean Government is looking forward to the arrival of the Russians, when it can repudiate all these transactions but that is not statesmanship,—poor Korea!

THE ALLIANCE AND NEUTRALITY.

Commenting upon the Japanese complaints against almost every body for breaches of neutrality, "Truth" says:—

"We have a perfect right unofficially to sympathise with the Japanese and wish them the victory. But a considerable number of our journalistic guides do not exactly realise our official position in regard to the Russo-Japanese War. Whether we were right or wrong in making our treaty with Japan is open to difference of opinion. My own impression is that it was a mistake for it might involve us in a war not essential to our own interests. We are not, however, by the terms of that treaty the allies of Japan in a general sense, but only should certain events take place, which have not taken, and I trust never will take place. As it is, we are simply neutrals, looking on regretfully at two friendly nations cutting each other's throats, and bound to act with absolute impartiality in regard to both. The fact, indeed, of our having a contingent treaty with one of the belligerents should make us specially careful in holding the balance even. According to the text writers on international law, it is even held that if one country is bound to afford specific and limited aid to another country in case it be at war with a third, the granting of this aid does not constitute in itself a *casus belli*, although the country thus damnified may make it one if it so please. For instance, if France had agreed by treaty with Russia to allow her ships of war to coal in all French Eastern parts, the coaling by such ships would not have been a violation of neutrality, although the same permission were not accorded to Japanese ships of war.

Where it seems to me that our treaty with Japan might prove useful would be if Japan were to refuse to make peace with Russia on what, in our opinion, were fair and reasonable terms. Under these circumstances we should be justified in telling Japan that if, in consequence of the refusal, she finds some great Power aiding Russia, she must not expect any aid from us. This would probably make for peace."

The 'Standard' says that Gen. Sir William Nicholson is definitely selected as Governor of Gibraltar (in succession to Sir Geoge White, appointed Governor of Chelsea.)

WHAT FAME COST.

An engineer named Knorr, a German who has become a naturalised Russian, built four of the great bridges on the Trans-Siberian Railway, including the big Yenisei and Obi bridges, which cost, respectively, £470,000 and £400,000. They were great engineering feats, and brought him international fame in his profession. But, nevertheless, the price paid was terrible. A writer in "T. A. T." says:—He had five daughters, who were famous in Russia for their beauty, and whom he loved dearly. Just after his first bridge was completed, one of them died; and as each of his three succeeding bridges was built, another died. There seemed to be a fatality in it. He would not build a fifth bridge.

The Japanese Minister is said to have presented a claim against the government for $187,000 being compensation for Japanese killed in some uprising. It is not clear whether or not this is a new edition of the same old claim we have so often heard about.

In the Tokio Chuokoron Mr. Oishi Masami, writing about the war, says that the end is a great way off, and that Japan will require great patience and resolution to see the thing through, and that the last stages of the war and the final settlement will probably be attended with more difficulty than has hitherto been encountered.

William McGee, sole white survivor of Custer's command in the battle of the Little Big Horn, is in jail in New York for stabbing and mortally wounding, Frank Mitchell, a salesman, who died later of his injuries. McGee, who followed border life for forty years, has three holes in his body and a chip over the scalp from Indian bullets and knives. He lay wounded one whole day in the trenches with Reno, standing off the rushes of Sitting Bull's braves. And now he has ended up by getting jailed for a stabbing affray, which started from a dispute with Mitchell over his ability to make kidney stew. McGee has been employed canvassing for Harper's periodicals. He was the neighbour and friend of the man he stabbed.

The following, taken from a "Japan Mail" of some weeks ago, is, in view of the real facts of the case, somewhat amusing. "A report from Shanghai represents a Russian sailor of the 'Askold' as having laid open the head of *jinrikisha* coolie with a cutlass in the sequel of a dispute about a fare. There is a feeling of great uneasiness in Shanghai, especially among the Japanese. At any moment the 'Askold's' men may break out and perpetrate shocking outrages, for their discipline is said to be of the loosest. In truth any ship's crew, lying for months in port under such circumstance would be liable to commit many offenses and Russian men-of-war's men have never been conspicuous for orderly conduct in harbour. The Japanese community of Shanghai deserve commiseration since they live confronted by such a peril. We presume that most of them have taken the precaution of arming themselves."

The Korea Daily News.

VOL. II, TUESDAY, JANUARY 31, 1905. No: 24

大韓每日申報

대한매일신보

(뎨이권이십오호)　　(목요일)　　일쳔구빅오년이월이일

본사고빅

이신보ᄂᆞᆫ영어와한어로셔계티
일츌판ᄒᆞᆷ

신문가

한쟝　엽두돈오룬
일삭표　엽두량닷돈
우표가미삭닷돈
다밧돈으로밧ᄉᆞᆷ

광고료ᄂᆞᆫ

귀한의쟝단과ᄌᆞ형의다쇼로ᄎᆞ등
갑ᄒᆞ되평가로밧을터이오매오
리지아니ᄒᆞᆫ데한사람마다매이신
문을보실터이니광고ᄇᆡ시기를
원ᄒᆞ시ᄂᆞᆫ이들은우리신문사에
와셔편약ᄒᆞ심을희망ᄒᆞᆷ

○빈궁ᄒᆞᆫ소　박동대한매일신보
사법어학교앙릐　젼영국인셜필
립젼자리오
사쟝　영국인 (빅셜)
평양　미리졈

○평양효동계ᄂᆞᆫ권미보씨로우
리신문관리미리인을뎡ᄒᆞ엿
시오니평양에계신구람코져ᄒᆞ
ᄂᆞᆫ　쳠군ᄌᆞᄂᆞᆫ긔ᄒᆞ미리졈에왕
림ᄒᆞ와편의ᄒᆞ시옵

사고

○우리대한매일신보의목뎍은
대한의안녕질서에관ᄒᆞᆫ모든데
목에뒤ᄒᆞ야ᄂᆞᆫ공평ᄒᆞᆫ변론을주
쟝ᄒᆞ이라우리ᄂᆞᆫ신원의탐보ᄂᆞᆫ
신문보시ᄂᆞᆫ쳠군ᄌᆞ의게ᄒᆞᆼ샹보
도ᄒᆞ리며편지들뢰서ᄒᆞ며주시
ᄂᆞᆫ이ᄂᆞᆫ셩명과번디를쳐어봇샤
시기를희망ᄒᆞ오니미기슴신문
샹에긔제ᄒᆞ란ᄂᆞᆫ거시아니오다
반듯히신용ᄒᆞᄂᆞᆫ증거를숭고자
ᄒᆞᆷ이라긔자ᄂᆞᆫ아모긔서던지긔
자ᄒᆞᆷ을뢰ᄀᆞᆨᄒᆞᄂᆞᆫ권리를가젓스
나뢰각ᄒᆞᄂᆞᆫ리유를말ᄒᆞᆯ티이오
며공중평화를문란케ᄒᆞᄂᆞᆫ듯ᄒᆞᆫ
긔셔ᄂᆞᆫ의례히밧지안케ᄉᆞᆸ나이
다

●본사셜시이릭로신문을뎨ᄒᆞᆼ
우례로분젼ᄒᆞ와레젼부의임의
로젼ᄒᆞᄂᆞᆫ듯스로번곳에ᄂᆞᆫ후ᄂᆞᆺ게
젼ᄒᆞ기도ᄒᆞ며혹빗젼키슴ᄒᆞᆫ경
에젼ᄒᆞ기도ᄒᆞ며혹아니젼ᄒᆞᄂᆞᆫ
곳도잇다ᄒᆞ와우리신문을ᄉᆞ랑
ᄒᆞ야구람ᄒᆞ시ᄂᆞᆫ　쳠군ᄌᆞ의계랑
티ᄒᆞ야미우미안ᄒᆞ옵기로지금
은분젼인을두고미일쥬이젼
ᄒᆞ며아니젼ᄒᆞ거나늣게ᄒᆞ거나ᄒᆞᆫ
폐가업도록ᄒᆞ란ᄒᆞ오니혹아니
젼ᄒᆞ거ᄂᆞᆫ혹늣게젼ᄒᆞ거나ᄒᆞᆫ일
이잇스면본사로통긔ᄒᆞ여주심
을희망ᄒᆞᆷ

잡보

○우졍쳘폐　일공사가외부로
죠회ᄒᆞ기를제용사우괴도고일
사ᄂᆞᆫ여러번죠회ᄒᆞ야쳘폐ᄒᆞ기
를쳥ᄒᆞ야도오히려시부ᄒᆞᆷ이업
스니진실로유감ᄒᆞᆫ지라귀국샹
민이일로말미암아빈가를바드
니본방샹민도ᄉᆞᆫᄒᆞᆫ손히가잇스
니이ᄂᆞᆫ통샹됴약의츄지를위빈
ᄒᆞᆷ이라쳥컨ᄃᆡ쳘폐ᄒᆞᆷ이가ᄒᆞ다
ᄒᆞ엿더라

○령평우강　셩동미다지비또
록셩빙에아니텀으로동빙계를
셜힝ᄒᆞ엿다ᄂᆞᆫ데그후로ᄂᆞᆫ일괴
가경쟝ᄒᆞᆫ령ᄒᆞᆫ지라아마ᄎᆞ효형비
잇나보다고들ᄒᆞ더라

○교인금거　평원군에거ᄒᆞᄂᆞᆫ
김동환씨와졍을에수교인에김
영옥씨가ᄉᆞ관ᄒᆞᆫ죡분군슈가김
동환을붓너말ᄒᆞ기를이교을에
예수교가편지법죠치못ᄒᆞ니고
졍은왈지못ᄒᆞ리라ᄒᆞᆷ으로동셰
가팔지아니ᄒᆞ엿ᄂᆞᆫ데지금김영
옥씨가쟝ᄎᆞᆺ호소ᄒᆞ리라더라

○황셜진퇴귀　음력명츈에ᄂᆞᆫ
황셜에셔불가불진퇴가례를셜
힝ᄒᆞ실리이라쟝웰식슴일로퇴
일ᄒᆞ야안동별궁을수리ᄒᆞᆫ다더
라

○츙즁금후ᄉᆞ무송　쳔빈의면담
을유세혁ᄒᆞᆫ집에셔통팔ᄒᆞ더니
리갑셰의면담사ᄂᆞᆫ빈영희셰가
숭반원을도로츙금ᄒᆞ엿거니와
신교ᄒᆞᆫ궁넉때신리경지셰와신
사민영쳘씨와챵쟝빗셩과징에
셔민소의괴교를당ᄒᆞ엿ᄂᆞᆫ데그
면담을도로츙금ᄒᆞᆫ연후라야사
무숭ᄒᆞ리란더라

○강공ᄉᆞ　폐졍　지작일븟터
와각공ᄉᆞ가　폐졍ᄒᆞᄂᆞᆫ데그차례
시간이여좌ᄒᆞ니

삼십일일오후
일공ᄉᆞᄂᆞᆫ삼시반
미공ᄉᆞᄂᆞᆫᄉᆞ시반
삼십일일오후
쳥공사ᄂᆞᆫ삼시반
법공사ᄂᆞᆫ사시반
이월일일오후
영공사ᄂᆞᆫ삼시반
덕공사ᄂᆞᆫ사시반
이월이일오후
비의공사ᄂᆞᆫ삼시반
비공사ᄂᆞᆫ사시반

○차관셩립　지졍과및지계
도ᄅᆞᆯ정리ᄒᆞᆯ샹으로한국졍부에서
일본에차관ᄒᆞᆫ다ᄂᆞᆫ말은젼보에
이긔ᄒᆞ엿거니와지작일브터차
일서지탁지대신민영긔씨와대
일은힝티표자정수티길씨간에
교섭ᄒᆞ야차관게약에됴인ᄒᆞ엿
일본공사가회계약공인ᄒᆞ야이
에그게약비쳥셔ᄒᆞ엿ᄂᆞᆫ데그게
약의젼문은자셰히알기어려우
나그도건에중요ᄒᆞᆫ자ᄂᆞᆫ좌와여
ᄒᆞ니

일　금혜은삼백만원이되지
비　확로쥬고지확로밧을사
　귀한은식개년으로졍ᄒᆞᆯ사
삼　셰쥬ᄂᆞᆫ빅년륙픈으로졍ᄒᆞᆯ사
사　담보ᄂᆞᆫ히관슈입으로졍ᄒᆞᆯ사

미요가이샹과여ᄒᆞᆫ데뎨일은힝
에셔ᄂᆞᆫ중앙은힝을경셩에셜립
ᄒᆞ고각디방에ᄂᆞᆫ동지점을셜치
ᄒᆞ고백동화를환슈ᄒᆞᆯ계획이라
더라

○김씨사졍　영샹김두원이가
거샹이월이십오일에쥬차ᄒᆞᆫ일
본군사령부와공사관과샹중령
사와엄쳔등ᄇᆡ관의게엄가엄졍
이만오쳔구ᄇᆡᆨ구십오환오젼을
빗샹ᄒᆞ야달나고호소ᄒᆞᄂᆞᆫ샹서
를니형일본우체국에젼ᄒᆞ엿ᄂᆞᆫ
ᄃᆡ우금ᄭᆞ지엇지ᄒᆞᆫ말이업다
고여러번일본사와셔통곡셜원
ᄒᆞ엿더니일작에쏘일본군사령부
와공사관과샹중령사와엄쳔등
역관과츄원셔긔광과국분셔긔
와도변경시관쳘쳐에ᄒᆞ소경샹
셔를ᄒᆞ엿ᄂᆞᆫ데저작년에국분셔
긔관이미국창셔관으로졍양ᄒᆞᆫ
기젼에김두원을불너수차담판
ᄒᆞ엿다ᄂᆞᆫ데수년지니되엿던ᄒᆞᆫ
구별이엄다고젼후ᄉᆞ졍을셜명
ᄒᆞ기에다시귀ᄌᆞᆼᄒᆞ노라

○최찬졍하향설　변암최찬졍
은향예로나려간다ᄂᆞᆫ풍셜이잇
다더라

○가등평사의권고　인쳔항평
사가등셰가경위원에권고ᄒᆞ
기를본항경무관은샹봉부쥬인
김모로등별히서잉ᄒᆞ라ᄒᆞ엿다
더라

○죠외쟝의반티　탁지대신민
영긔씨가일본뎨일은힝지점쟝
ᄒᆞ고삼백만원을차관ᄒᆞ기로됴
인셜립ᄒᆞᆫ지라탁지대신이ᄒᆞ한안
건을졍부에졍의ᄒᆞ엿더니죠외
쟝이반ᄃᆡᄒᆞ야결이되이문제로
ᄂᆞᆫ가히회의치못ᄒᆞ겟다ᄒᆞ엿더
라

○귀쟝보고　지평군에사ᄂᆞᆫ밍
일호가로군을모집ᄒᆞ야회민을
탈타ᄒᆞᆫ귀쳐물을탈취ᄒᆞᆫ다ᄒᆞᄂᆞᆫ
고로니부에셔힋군으로면ᄒᆞ야
아밍일호등챠샹ᄒᆞ라ᄒᆞ엿더니
경귀관쟝ᄉᆞ보고니에밍일호가
본부에ᄌᆞ현ᄒᆞ야곧으티작년섯
등에당도ᄒᆞ야방금기샹중에잇
슬ᄯᅢ터리ᄶᅡ츌신병이잇서두문
불츌ᄒᆞᆫ지가아니ᄒᆞᆫ리이라구셜
ᄒᆞ호군을모집ᄒᆞ며회민을구타
ᄒᆞ야취물을탈취ᄒᆞᆫ일이엇다고
구별ᄒᆞᆫ명ᄒᆞ에ᄌᆞ현ᄒᆞ기경ᄒᆞ비엇
두엇다ᄒᆞ엿더라

○ᄒᆞᆼ원군보　ᄒᆞᆼ원군슈죠두환
씨의보고ᄂᆞᆫ이일에방ᄒᆞᆫ보고와
ᄒᆞ오니본년음력십이월오일ᄒᆞ
죠에일병삼십여명이본군동편
셩ᄒᆞ회통상방에셔로군으로
시부리셔로씨화로병이총에마
저당쟝ᄉᆞᄒᆞᆫ자가구명이오몽
린빙읍이오즁샹ᄒᆞᆫ자가샹명인
데불셩은괴제와마필을탈취ᄒᆞ
야가지고ᄒᆞᆼ원군ᄒᆞᆫ관평으로향
ᄒᆞ야도라갓고동으로셤러되
ᄂᆞᆫ쥬호와동은ᄒᆞᆫ문샹포평빅
여명이샹ᄐᆡ에일빙ᄒᆞᆫ의로에샤
분ᄂᆞ가셔ᄌᆞ듯ᄒᆞ엿다ᄒᆞ엿더라

○제취셕　이마디아　엔대ᄒᆞᆫ
구샹거방경실ᄌᆞ니ᄂᆞᆫ쟝야군
약죠ᄒᆞ니헨ᄒᆞᆫ파ᄂᆞᆫ이군대가셔
리고ᄋᆞᆫ의리ᄌᆞ형에ᄂᆞᆫ덤번구ᄉᆞ
ᄒᆞ야지ᄒᆞᆫ붓대에샹대ᄒᆞ되
분들쳐치ᄒᆞ기ᄂᆞᆫ되ᄂᆞᆫ뎌게ᄒᆞ엿
고ᄒᆞ리ᄒᆞ기로사ᄒᆞ엿더라

○뎡젼　아부에서셜명ᄒᆞ오
구약부셔로동구ᄉᆞ가엄회ᄒᆞ엿
더라

○항동쟝사쟈　경무쳥에서ᄂᆞᆫ
뎍샹ᄒᆞ고ᄂᆞᆫ팔미혼

UNION INSURANCE SOCIETY OF CANTON.

Head office Hongkong.
Marine risks underwritten at current rates,
Agents in Chemulpo,
E. MEYER & Co.

COMPAGNIE DES MESSAGERIES MARITIMES.

Fortnightly Direct Service.

For Marseilles via Ports.
Sailing from Yokohama
Calling at Kobe,
Shanghai, Hongkong, Saigon, Singapore,
Colombo. Djibouti, Suez, Port Said
and Marseilles.

For particulars apply to
HOLME, RINGER & Co.,
Chemulpo.

HAYASHIDA & CO.,

16 MYENG DONG, CHIN KO KAI, SEOUL.
BRANCH OFFICE AT CHEMULPO.

Money changers, Coal and Wood Merchants, Express Agents.

We are agents for the Pyeng-yang Coal Company, and the Karazu Coal Company of Japan. We have the best quality of both anthracite and bituminous coal, and prompt execution of orders is our speciality. Firewood of all kinds kept in stock. Full weight guaranteed. Money of all denominations exchanged at current rates. Parcels received for all parts.

CHINA MUTUAL LIFE INS. CO.

Most favourable terms to policy holders.

Benefit system unsurpassed.

HOLME RINGER & Co.
Agents, Chemulpo.

C. P. R.

CANADIAN PACIFIC RAILWAY COMPANY'S ROYAL MAIL STEAMSHIP LINE.

THE FAST ROUTE BETWEEN CHINA, JAPAN, AND EUROPE VIA CANADA AND THE UNITED STATES.

Route from Hongkong via Shanghai, Nagasaki (Inland Sea of Japan) Kobe, Yokohama, Victoria and Vancouver

Twin Screw Empress Steamship—6,000 Tons—Speed 19 knots.

PROPOSED SAILING FROM YOKOHAMA.
R. M. S. Empress of India.
R. M. S. Empress of Japan.
R. M. S. Empress of China.
R. M. S. Athenian.
R. M. S. Tartar.

Special reduction (first class only) granted to members of the Military, Naval, Diplomatic and Civil services and to Missionaries.
Passengers have choice of ten routes across the Continent of America and have privilege of travelling by any Atlantic Steamship Line.
Round the World passage tickets in connection with the P. and O. S. N., North German Lloyd and Messageries Co.'s £125.
All rates payable at current rate of exchange.
For further information, Tickets, Guide Books, etc., apply to
HOLME, RINGER & Co., AGENTS,
Chemulpo.

Grand Hotel,

(Formerly the Station Hotel)

Near the Railway Terminus, West Gate Seoul.

The Best Hotel in Korea.
Handsome new Building.
Fine Airy Rooms
Excellent Cuisine.
Terms Moderate.
Special terms to Missionaries and to permanent boarders.

Electric cars within 2 minutes' walk.

W. H. EMBERLEY.
Proprietor

EVERY FACILITY.

in connection with Life Assurance Business is afforded by

The Standard Life Assurance Co.,

One of the largest and wealthiest of the Provident Institutions of the United Kingdom Forms of Application and all information will be promptly afforded on application.

10 CENTS A DAY.

Not a very large expenditure is it? But it is sufficient to secure for a man of 30 a policy with the STANDARD LIFE OFFICE for

$1323.

For all particulars of rates, etc., apply to

Holme, Ringer & Co.,
Agents, Chemulpo.

THE NEW YORK LIFE INSURANCE COMPANY.

Have you ever been declined by any Company?

Are you engaged in a specially hazardous occupation?

Have you heard of the New York Life Insurance Company's New Classifications for this class of Risks?

If not, send your date of birth, occupation and particulars of rejection, if any to

E. MEYER & Co.,
Agents. Chemulpo.

MITSUI BUSSAN KAISHA.
(MITSUI & Co.)

MITSUI GINKO.
(MITSUI BANK.)

The Bank is owned by the members of the Mitsui Family, who, as partners, assume an unlimited responsibility for all liabilities of the Bank:—

Capital.... ....Yen 5,000,000
Reserve Fund.. .... " 5,600,000

HEAD OFFICE, TOKYO.
LONDON OFFICE, [illegible] LIME ST., E. C.

BRANCHES AND AGENCIES:—
New York, San Francisco, Hamburg, Bombay, Singapore, Manila, Hongkong, Amoy, Chefoo, Tientsin.
Kobe, Hakodate, Yokohama, Kure, Yokosuka, Moji, Shimonoseki, Miike, Wakamatsu, Nagasaki, Kuchinotsu, Karatsu, Sasebo, Misume, Taipeh, &c.

Telegraphic Address for all the Offices:
"MITSUI."

A. B. C. AND A. I CODES USED.

Contractors of Coal
To the Imperial Japanese Navy. Arsenals and Railway Bureau, Principal Railway Companies and Industrial Work, Home and Foreign Mail and Freight Steamers.
Sole Proprietors
Of the famous Miike, Tagawa and Yamano Coal Mines.
Sole Agents
For the sale of Fukumo, Hokoku, Ichimura Kanoda, Mannoura, Onoura, Ostuji, Sonoda, Tsubaruro, Yoshinotani. Yoshio, Yurokibura and other coals.

YANGTSE INSURANCE ASSOCIATION, LTD.

The undersigned, having been appointed agents for the above company, are prepared to issue policies and pay losses on marine risks at regular rates.

E. MEYER & Co.,
Agents, Chemulpo.

AMERICAN KOREAN ELECTRIC CO.

Light and Power.

Main Office: Electric Building, Chong No.

RAILWAY DEPARTMENT.

OPERATING CARS BETWEEN EAST AND WEST GATE, EVERY TEN MINUTES:—

First Car leaves East Gate at 7:00 A. M. First Car leaves R. R. Station at 7:25 A. M
Last Car " East Gate at 8:[illegible] P. M. Last " " R. R. Station at 9.05 P. M

OPERATING CARS BETWEEN EAST GATE AND IMPERIAL TOMB TERMINUS, EVERY TWENTY MINUTES:—
CONNECTING WITH EVERY ALTERNATE CAR ARRIVING AT EAST GATE FROM CHONG NO.

First Car leaves East Gate for Tomb at 7:10 A. M.
" " " Tomb for East Gate at 7:30 A. M.
Last " " East Gate for Tomb at 7:50 P. M.
" " " Tomb for East Gate at 8:10 P. M.

OPERATING CARS BETWEEN CHONG NO AND YUNG SAN RIVER EVERY TWELVE MINUTES:—

First Car leaves Chong No for South Gate at 7:12 A. M.
" " " Chong No for Yung San at 7:36 A. M.
" " " South Gate for Chong No at 7:20 A. M.
" " " Yung San for Chong No at 8:09 A. M.
Last " " South Gate for Chong No 9:00 P. M.
" " " Yung San for Chong No at 8.45. P. M.

SPECIAL PRIVATE CARS FURNISHED TO SUIT CONVENIENCE OF PATRONS. PRICES ON APPLICATION AT HEAD OFFICE.

LIGHTING DEPARTMENT.

Where less than 250 candle power of light is used, the rate per month will be
Per 16 candle power incandescent lamp,—All night.—Yen 2.50.
32 candle power incandescent lamp:—All night:—Yen 4.00.
50 candle power incandescent lamp:—All night,—Yen 6.00.
150 " " " " " " 10.00.
200 " enclosed arc " " " 20.00.

Where more than 250 candle power of light is used, a Meter will be installed, if requested:—Rent of Meter Yen 2.00 per month. Rate of charges by meter reading:—Two Sen per Ampere per hour. (Approximately this is equal to about One Sen per 16 C. P. lamp per hour) Minimum monthly charge where meter is installed, Yen 20.00 per month, which includes rental of meter.

Estimates for installing lights furnished on application
An assortment of Chandeliers always on hand.

K. Murakami.

Photograph Studio
Chinkokai, Seoul.

Printing, Developing and Enlargement, of Photographs always Undertaken.

Korean Views and Pictures Illustrating Native Customs always on Sale.

THE OSAKA SHOSEN KAISHA.

Boats frequently on the berth for Chinnampo.

REGULAR SAILINGS BETWEEN JAPAN AND KOREAN PORTS.

FUSAN AND KOBE VIA SHIMONOSEKI.

OSAKA VIA MOKPO, FUSAN, SHIMONOSEKI AND KOBE.

MOJI DIRECT.

OSAKA VIA KUNSAN, MASANPO, FUSAN, SHIMONOSEKI AND KOBE.

CHEMULPO KUNSAN LINE,
Every three days.

CHEMULPO CHINNAMPO LINE.
Every three days.

For Freight and passage and further particulars apply to
THE OSAKA SHOSEN KAISHA,
Chemulpo.

RONDON, PLAISANT & CO.

General Storekeepers and Merchants, Ships Contractors, Tobacconists, Commission and Forwarding Agents, Coal Merchants

IMPORTERS AND EXPORTERS

Seoul & Chemulpo.

W. D. WENTWORTH.

LANDING
AND
SHIPPING AGENT.
AND
CUSTOMS BROKER.

12 OURA, NAGASAKI.

STEWARD & CO.

Chemulpo.

Shipchandlers and Storekeepers, Naval and Mercantile Contractors, Landing and Shipping Agents

STEWARD'S HOTEL

Chemulpo.

Best accommodation in the port for travellers. Clean and well-aired rooms, good cuisine and prompt attendance, moderate tariff.

션씨의힝동을일본슈가샹여
부로보내고이한진을회지ᄒᆞ야
종ᄉᆞ히됴인케ᄒᆞ라ᄒᆞᆫ고로너부
에셔칙령봉ᄉᆞ빅원을감졍ᄒᆞ야
일본슈와샹의ᄒᆞᆫ즉슈원이ᄂᆞᆫ
가히번경치못ᄒᆞ겟다ᄒᆞ며우리
졍부로쟉졍ᄒᆞᆫ일이오또신쳥졍
졔일시에임의확졍ᄒᆞᆫ일이니추
감치말고일노새협동ᄒᆞᆷ이가ᄒᆞ
다ᄒᆞ엿더라

○옥구항민면 옥구항민이외
부로면보ᄒᆞ기를본항감리졍항
죠씨가도임ᄒᆞᆫ지일주년에방볍
을셜시ᄒᆞ야도적이다블니치고
도망ᄒᆞᆫ고로외쳐를안졉ᄒᆞ야빅셩
이쏘흔퇴안ᄒᆞ더니이리ᄒᆞᆫ쳥후
가기체ᄒᆞᆷ으로대소민졍이젓막
다ᄒᆞ퍼진것ᄀᆞᆺᄒᆞ니 탄폐에젼
달ᄒᆞ야다힝이잉임케ᄒᆞ야빅셩
을편케ᄒᆞ라ᄒᆞ엿더라

○의쥬군보 의쥬군수가외부
로보ᄒᆞ기를련숀함람츅하회
를응ᄒᆞ야본월초오일에일본군디
가보ᄂᆡ리셜연ᄒᆞ고본관과밋각리
가위관을거ᄂᆞ리고회에참예ᄒᆞ
엿더라

○쟝셩도회 숙쳔군수김규형
이가히군민리셩자를탐장ᄒᆞ야
지병ᄒᆞᆫ고로진가의모든일을가도
군슈를힉ᄒᆞ고자ᄒᆞᆷ이군수가도
망ᄒᆞ야평양부에숨엇다더라

지금만일일본이로국을젼승
ᄒᆞ엿드면한국에셔일본인의세
력에간셥말기로약됴ᄒᆞ엿겟지
마ᄂᆞᆫ비록예산과ᄀᆞᆺ치승젼은못
ᄒᆞ엿스나본리쟉졍ᄒᆞᆫ대한졍략
을실시ᄒᆞ기에ᄂᆞᆫ시긔를일치말
고속히ᄒᆞᄂᆞᆫ거시죠흔줄노동경
우에셔ᄉᆡᆼ각ᄒᆞᆫ다ᄒᆞᄂᆞᆫ지라
듯ᄒᆞᆫ거시한국이독립을유지ᄒᆞ
인ᄉᆡᆼ만ᄒᆞᆫ번도ᄐᆡ를졈령아니ᄒᆞ
고도한국의샹업의젼부를가히
반차지ᄒᆞᆯ것을그것은아니ᄒᆞ고그
리ᄐᆡ로이나라에주인된인민의
리익은방히ᄒᆞ고손으로드리온
져의들의사욕만취ᄒᆞ려ᄒᆞ니한
인들이그일을이즐ᄯᅳᆺᄒᆞ지아니
ᄒᆞ도다
한인들의일본인힝위에ᄃᆡᄒᆞ야
ᄉᆡᆼ각ᄒᆞᄂᆞᆫ마음은아모ᄯᅢ라도일
본인의한국에잇ᄂᆞᆫ샹업과고문
관들과국칙와또계반권리들을
다업시ᄒᆞ게될는지나그런시
ᄃᆡ가잇슬는지알수업지마ᄂᆞᆫ한
인들은졍셩스럽게츅수ᄒᆞᄂᆞᆫ지
라
그런셔둙으로우리의ᄉᆡᆼ각에ᄂᆞᆫ
로국이ᄇᆡ를이긔지안코한국에향
ᄒᆞ야힝군ᄒᆞ란ᄒᆞ니한국은지금
괴로옴을밧ᄂᆞᆫ중에셰샹가샹으
로젼쟝이될듯ᄒᆞ다ᄒᆞ노라

론셜

한국의희망

○한국졍부에ᄃᆡᄒᆞ야일본인의
힝위가진실노시졍기션ᄒᆞᄂᆞᆫ목
뎍이잇스면쟝ᄎᆞ라도지톄ᄒᆞ지아
니ᄒᆞᄂᆞᆫ거시올커니와사셜샹으
로보면리쳐병무실이오제반힝동
이쟈긔의욕심만취ᄒᆞ고한국의리
익은ᄉᆡᆼ각도아니ᄒᆞ니만일일본
이한국을졈령ᄒᆞ엿스면그리ᄒᆞᆯ
는거시응당그러ᄒᆞᆯ뜻ᄒᆞ나아죠
은그런쥴아니ᄒᆞ고ᄯᅩ우리의쇼
견에ᄂᆞᆫ비단음에도그런듯십지
아니ᄒᆞ며만일평화됴약이되면세
에만쥬에셔로국의힝동에간셥
아니ᄒᆞᆯ것으로일본이한국졍부
에ᄃᆡᄒᆞ야셜시ᄒᆞᄂᆞᆫ계칙의자유
ᄒᆞᆷ을ᄉᆡᆼ환ᄒᆞ거나ᄒᆞᆷ일이잘못되
면리슌구를로국에돌녀보니고
그ᄃᆡ신일본의대한졍칙에간셥
발나ᄒᆞᆫ면모르거니와그러치도
하나ᄒᆞᆫᄃᆡ지금일본이이나라의
갑둥권을엇으려고발광으로밧
비덤뷔이ᄂᆞᆫ셔둙을셜명ᄒᆞᆯ수업
슨지며일본의범금힝위가ᄂᆞᆫ일
에사긔의번ᄒᆞᆷ을세라셔그리된
것이아님뜻ᄒᆞᆫ거시졍치의시초
ᄒᆞᆫ후에곳쟝ᄎᆞ씨가그럼ᄒᆡ엽ᄂᆞᆫ
쳥구를니노왓스니글로보드리
도한국을사실샹으로졈령ᄒᆞ란
논일본의권ᄒᆞᆫ간모ᄒᆞᆷ게ᄂᆞᆫ졍
알빙졍에한부분이잇셧던것을
졍지ᄒᆞ
다

관보

뎨삼쳔오십호 광무구년
이월삼십일일

셔임급ᄉᆞ령

○임군부대신셔리임관일등
법부대신총군부장 권즁현
○임법부대신셔리임관일등
의졍부찬졍륙군참쟝 박졔슌
○임의졍부찬졍셔임관일등
평무수륙군참쟝 신퇴휴
○임표훈원총재셔임관일등
륙군부장 민병셕
이월이십구일
○임황ᄒᆡ도관찰ᄉᆞ셔임관삼
등 죵일품 셔졍순
이월이십칠일
○조죵이품가션대부비셔원승
교 가션 리도일 교 가션 쟝화
ᄒᆞ규
○조졍삼품통졍대부비셔원승
교 감찰 신ᄐᆡ관
○조구품죵ᄉᆞ랑중학교교관
교 학셩 장창식 교 학셩 김
샹슌
이샹은효힝탁리병시 종진
○의원면본관 됴튼도원쥬수
김힝원 됴튼도원쥬수 리귀식
쥬수 김동현 쳥도원쥬수 졍ᄐᆡ션 쳥도원
종우 후릉참봉 순릉참봉 홍덕쥬
중추원의관 한죵샹 지송
리치경 중추원의관 최한우
중추원의관 김긴희 중추원
의관 함션지 중추원의관
윤명모 중추원의관 려규셕
○임후릉참봉셔판임관팔등
김긔쟝
○임슌릉참봉셔판임관팔등
구품 박봉진
○임중추원의관셔주임관륙등
졍삼품 홍죵우 졍삼품 리
샹익 졍삼품 빅회빈 졍삼
구품 신복균 륙품 안경셕
졍계쇼
이샹은이월이십팔일
○의원면본관 원구단ᄉᆞ졔셔
쟝 평리 병졀 후릉참봉 김긔
○명경위원총관셔칙임관이등
륙군부장 리근퇵
○임비셔원승셔주임관륙등
졍삼품 신셩균
○임원구단ᄉᆞ졔셔겸셔판임관
륙등 시강원시종관 리쇼즁
○임시강원시종관셔주임관륙
등 륙품 리병쳘
○임후릉참봉셔판임관팔등
구품 홍덕쥬
이샹은이월이십구일

○구년도예산표 (속)

군부소관
뎨일관 군부본쳥 칠만이빅
칠원
뎨일항 봉급 ᄉᆞ만륙쳔ᄉᆞ
십원
뎨이항 쳥비 이쳔륙빅이
십원
뎨삼항 쳥ᄉᆞ슈리비 오빅
원
뎨ᄉᆞ항 잡급급쟝비 일만
팔빅ᄉᆞ십칠원
뎨오항 려비 이쳔원
뎨륙항 외국인계급 칠쳔
이빅원
〔지후〕
뎨칠항 교졉비 오빅원
뎨팔항 연회비 오빅원
뎨이관 시위연ᄃᆡ 오쳔팔빅
팔십륙원
뎨일항 봉급 삼쳔구빅십
원
뎨이항 쳥비 삼빅원
뎨삼항 하ᄉᆞ급료 ᄉᆞ빅십
ᄉᆞ원
뎨ᄉᆞ항 량식비 삼빅원
뎨오항 마량비 이빅팔십
팔원
뎨륙항 마쟝비 ᄉᆞ십륙원
뎨칠항 피복비 이빅팔원
뎨팔항 보슈비 ᄉᆞ빅이십
원
뎨삼관 친위연ᄃᆡ 오쳔팔빅
팔십륙원
뎨일항 봉급 삼쳔구빅십
원
뎨이항 쳥비 삼빅원
뎨삼항 하ᄉᆞ급료 ᄉᆞ빅십
ᄉᆞ원
뎨ᄉᆞ항 량식비 삼빅원
뎨오항 마량비 이빅팔십
팔원
뎨륙항 마쟝비 ᄉᆞ십륙원
뎨칠항 피복비 이빅팔원
뎨팔항 보슈비 ᄉᆞ빅이십
원
뎨ᄉᆞ관 진위연ᄃᆡ 오쳔팔빅
팔십륙원
뎨일항 봉급 삼쳔구빅십
원
뎨이항 쳥비 삼빅원
뎨삼항 하ᄉᆞ급료 ᄉᆞ빅십
ᄉᆞ원
뎨ᄉᆞ항 량식비 삼빅원
뎨오항 마량비 이빅팔십
팔원
뎨륙항 마쟝비 ᄉᆞ십륙원
뎨칠항 피복비 이빅팔원
뎨팔항 보슈비 ᄉᆞ빅이십
원
뎨오관 시위ᄃᆡ 칠십륙만오
쳔륙빅삼십구원
뎨일항 봉급 륙만팔쳔칠
빅구십삼원
뎨이항 쳥비 일만오쳔ᄉᆞ
빅팔십원
뎨삼항 쳥ᄉᆞ슈리비 칠빅
오십원
뎨ᄉᆞ항 하ᄉᆞ급료 이십구
만칠쳔칠빅ᄉᆞ십ᄉᆞ원
뎨오항 량식비 이십팔만
오쳔오빅ᄉᆞ십원
뎨륙항 마량비 륙빅륙십
ᄉᆞ원
뎨칠항 피복비 팔만륙쳔
ᄉᆞ십원
뎨구항 보슈비 칠쳔이빅
원
뎨십항 연습비 일쳔팔십
원
뎨십일항 목욕비 일쳔팔
십원
뎨십이항 치료비 일쳔팔
십원
뎨십삼항 뎨쟝비 ᄉᆞ빅오
십원
뎨륙관 친위ᄃᆡ 칠십륙만구
쳔ᄉᆞ빅륙십이원
뎨일항 봉급 륙만팔쳔이
빅칠십일원
뎨이항 쳥비 일만ᄉᆞ쳔ᄉᆞ
빅원
뎨삼항 쳥ᄉᆞ슈리비 칠쳔
오십원
뎨ᄉᆞ항 하ᄉᆞ급료 이십구
만륙쳔오빅륙십팔원
뎨오항 량식비 이십팔만
오쳔오빅ᄉᆞ십원
뎨륙항 마량비 팔빅륙십
ᄉᆞ원
뎨칠항 마쟝비 일빅삼십
팔원
뎨팔항 피복비 팔만륙쳔
ᄉᆞ십원
뎨구항 보슈비 칠쳔이빅
원
뎨십항 연습비 일쳔팔십

THE SHAHO.

Onl-y very meagre reports of the operations up north are to hand. Apparently the battle is still in progress and it may be a week before we get any reliable news.

The Japanese report the capture of some 500 Russian prisoners but give no details of their own losses or of the general movement of the armies.

We appear to be receiving only reports of an isolated engagement which resulted in Japan's favour. The names of places given are un-identifiable and altogether the information so far to hand is of no interest.

THE CHINESE TEACHER.

The employment of a new teacher in the Chinese language school without the sanction of the Japanese Minister is raising quite a hullabaloo.

The Foreign Office has now passed on to the Education Department a letter from the Japanese Minister asking for an explanation.

Some Koreans who have studied police methods in Japan will, it is said, return to Korea and become inspectors.

It is reported that several millions of dollars have been recently received at the Imperial treasury. These are the taxes from the provinces.

On the 30th inst Japanese cruisers made a prize of another Bitish steamer which was bound for Vladivostock with coal. The name is apparently some thing ending in field.

On account of the murder of the Wei-hai-wei Chinaman at Haichu the British Minister has presented a claim against the Korean Government for $2,674 and request that it may be considered.

There is trouble in Djon-Chu. Taxes fell due, and the magistrate (supported by the governor) demanded payment in copper cash. Those who proffered nickels were imprisoned hence the trouble.

We learn that the contract of Mr. Frampton, Head master of the English language school, has been renewed for a further three years dating from January 1st.

The magistrate of Syukchön is in hiding. He punished a man too severely and the man died under the operation and the man's relatives are looking for the magistrate.

The magistrate of Wiju is not, apparently, very busy. He has found time to send the Home Office an account of a Japanese "Port Arthur celebration which he recently attended in his district.

The Japanese consul at Fusan complains that the officials of the Imperial Household Department are demanding excessive taxes on the Japanese exports of cotton, fish, rice and other produce.

A Tokio telegram to a Japanese paper is to the effect that General Kuropatkin is having considerable difficulty with his troops, as, having heard of the fall of Port Arthur, they declare that there is no further object in fighting.

On the 30th ult. at 3 P. M. the Government met to discuss the question of the loan which Japan is so anxious to make to Korea viz $3,000,000, paper money, returnably in ten years and bearing interest at the rate of six per cent per annum.

A rumour is current to the effect that the Emperor of Korea will shortly re-marry. The date of the wedding is said to be fixed for February 17th but the name of the intended consort has not, so far, been announced. Lady Om will probably be raised to the rank of Empress. The wedding of the Crown Prince will take place subsequent to that of the Emperor.

MR. DOOLEY REGARDS BANTING WITH DISFAVOR.

(Continued from yesterday.)

"Th' latest thing that Carney has took up to make th' fight again' Nature is called Fletching. Did ye iver hear iv it? Well, they'se a lad be th' name iv Fletcher who thinks so much iv his stomach that he won't use it an' he tells Carney that if he'll ate on'y wan or two mouthfuls at ivry meal an' thurly chew thim, he will livinchooly be no more thin skin an very handsom to look at. In four weeks a man who Fletchs will lose forty pounds, an' all his frinds. Th' idee is that ye mumble ye'er food f'r tin minyits with a watch in front iv ye. This night Carney was Fletching. It was a fine supper. Th' table groaned beneath all th' indilicacies iv th' season. We tucked our napkins under our chins an' prepared f'r a jaynial avenin.' Not so, Carney. He laid his goold watch on th' table, took a mouthful iv mutton pie an' begun to Fletch. At first Hogan thought he was makin' faces at him, but I explained that he was crazy. I see by th' look in Carney's eye that he didn't like th' explanation, but we wint on with th' supper. Well, 'twas glory-ous. 'Jawn, ye'er health. Pass th' beefsteak, Malachi, Schwartzmeister, ol' boys, can't I help ye to th' part that wint over th' fence last? What's that story? Tell it over here where Carney can't hear. It might make him laugh an' hurt him with his frind Fletcher. No? What? Ye don't say? An' didn't Carney resist it? Haw, haw, haw! This eyesther sauce is th' best I iver see. Michael, this is like ol' times. Look at Schwartzmeister. He's Fletching, too. No, be gorry, he's chokin. I think Carney's watch has stopped. No wondher; he's lookin' at it. Haw, haw, haw, haw, haw. A good joke on Carney. Did ye iver see such a face? Carney, me buck, ye look like a kinetoscop. What is a face without a stomach? Carney, ye make me nervous. If that there idol don't stop f'r a minyit I'll throw something at it. Carney, time's up. win Ye ye'er bet, but' twas a foolish wan. I thought ye were goin' to push Fletcher in a wheelbarrow.'

"I've known Jawn Carney, man and boy, f'r forty year, but I niver knew until that minyit that he was a murdherer at heart. Th' look he give us whin he snapped his watch was tur-rble; but th' look he give th' dinner was even worse. He set there f'r two mortal hours miditatin what form th' assassynations wud take an' Fletchin' each wan iv us in his mind. I walked home with him to see that he came to no harm. Near th' house he wint to a baker's shop an' bought four pies an' a bag iv doughnuts. 'I've promised to take thim home to me wife,' he says. 'I thought she was out iv town,' says I. 'She'll be back in a week,' says he; 'an' anyhow, Misther Dooley, I'll thank ye not to be pryin' into me domestic affairs,' he says.

"An' there ye ar-re. What's th' use iv goin' up again' th' laws iv Nature, says I. If Nature intinded ye to be a little roly-poly, a little roly-poly ye'll be. They ain't aunything to do that ye ought to do that'll make ye thin an' keep ye thin. Th' wan thing in th' wurruld that'll ragjooce ye surely is lack iv sleep, an, who wants to lose his mind with his flesh? I'll guarantee with th' aid iv an alarm clock to make aunny man a livin' skiliton in thirty days. A lady with a young baby won't niver get no chubbier nor th' gintleman, its father. Th' on'y ginooine anti-fat threatment is sickness, worry, throuble an' insomnya. Th' scales ain't aunny judge iv beauty or health. To be beautiful is to be nachral. Ye have gr-reat nachral skinny beauty while my good looks is more buxom. Whin I see an' ol' fool in a sweater an' two coats sprintin' up th' sthreet an' groanin' at ivry step, I want to jine with th' little boys that ar-re throwin' bricks at him. If he takes off th' flesh that Nature has wasted on his ongrateful frame, his skin won't fit him. They'se nawthin' more heejous to look at thin a fat man that has rayjooced his weight. He looks as though he had bought his covern' at an auction. It bags undher th' eyes an' don't fit in th' neck.

"A man is foolish that thries to be too kind to his stomach, anyhow, Fletcher's idee is that th' human stomach is a kind iv little Lord Fauntleroy. If ye give it much to do it will pine away. But Dock Casey tells me 'its a gr-reat, husky, good-natured pugillist that'll take on most aunnything that comes along. It will go to wurruk with grim resolution on a piece iv hard coal. It will get th' worst iv it, but what I mane is that it fears no foe an' dosen't dhraw th' color line. I would put it in th' heavy middle weight class an' it ought to be kept there. It requires plenty iv exercise to be at its best, an' if it dosen't get enough it loses its power, until a chocolate eclair might win against it. It mustn't be allowed to shirk its jooties. It shud be kept in thrainin,' an,' says Dock Casey if its owner is a good matchmaker an' doesn't back it again opponents that ar-re out iv its class, or too manny at wan time, it will still be doin' well whin th' brain is on'y fit f'r light exercise."

"D'ye expict to go on accumylatin' to th' end iv ye'er days?" asked Mr. Hennessy.

"I do that," said Mr. Dooley. "I expict to make me frinds wurruk f'r me to th' last. They'll be no gayety among th' pall bearers at me obsequies. They'll have no sinycure. Before they get through with me they've been to a fun'ral."—The Call.

JAPANESE ENTERPRISE IN CHINA.

We have more than once referred to the undoubted ascendancy of the Japanese at present throughout China says the China Mail. It is not confined to the mere extension of their ever increasing trade, nor is it limited to the metropolitan area. In a Canton paper Japanese opinion on the question of foreign control of the Canton-Hankow railway insists that no foreign power should be allowed to interfere in its control. The writer does not hesitate to affirm that all foreign powers are grasping, and that they are seeking not only legitimate gain but are taking advantage of the decrepitude of China to further their own ends. But Russia comes in, as is not unnatural, for the severest treatment from the right-handed blows of this fighter. If Japan has anything to say in the future in regard to those who shall direct and control the Canton-Hankow railway, it is obvious that foreigners will not have a look in. How far these views represent official opinion in Japan it is, of course, impossible to say, but we suspect we shall be not far wrong in connecting it with the general prevalent ascendancy of Japanese ideas in China, and we may regard it as an index of the future attitude of Japan, when, as is sure to transpire, she and China, become more closely allied.

A RUSSIAN CRITIC ON THE SITUATION.

A Russian correspondent writes in the London "Times" of December 7th as follows:—

The writer of the able and carefully reasoned articles on the military situation, with special reference to the questions of the command of the sea, which still continue to appear daily in the "Novoe Vremya," points out that there is very little foundation for the belief that the Japanese fleet will be found to have suffered seriously from the naval actions of August 10 and 14. He himself witnessed the return of the "Gromoboi" and "Rossia" to Vladivostok after their engagement with Admiral Kamimura, and he asserts that, although at first their injuries appeared to be serious a closer examination proved that they had sustained no really severe damage. In spite of the scanty resources of Vladivostock, they were completely repaired in a month's time, and "there is positively no difference between their present condition and that before the engagement." He argues from this that the injuries inflicted on the vessels of Admiral Kamimura and Admiral Togo are not likely to have been of a vital nature, and that with the superior resources at the command of the Japanese these were probably repaired even more quickly than the Russian ships. He states further that one of the reasons for Admiral Prince Ukhtomsky's return to Port Arthur on August 10 was the dismay caused by the discovery that the Japanese fleet was in far better condition than the Russians had supposed.

In view of the close relations which are known to be maintained by the Russian Admiralty with the "Novoe Vremya," these articles are of exceptional interest. Their author's avowed intention throughout has been to arouse his countrymen to a sense of the extreme gravity of the situation, of the overwhelming importance of regaining the command of the sea, and of the improbability that the Baltic Fleet will prove equal to the task. It is difficult to believe that the leading Russian journal would have been disposed, or, indeed, permitted, to devote upwards of 20 of its columns to an argument of this nature unless there was some important end to be served; and indications are not wanting that these articles are intended to lead to the conclusion that, in view of her pressing necessities, Russia must not hesitate to make use of the Black Sea Fleet, notwithstanding the difficulties that such a step would involve. In an article which appeared in "Novoe Vremya of November 24, the despatch of the Black Sea Fleet was frankly advocated, and, though the writer of the present series has not yet openly expressed the same opinion, his assertion that much more might yet be done to ensure the success of Admiral Rojestvensky, the very idea of whose failure is enough "to make the very hair bristle and the heart contract," can hardly have any other reference.

There are some 3,000 Chinese and Koreans studying in Japan at the present time.

Another belated batch of Il-chin-hoi people arrived in Seoul yesterday. They came from Kangwon province and there were about 50 of them.

The Japanese Minister, acting upon one of the *post bellum* agreements signed by the Korean Government, has negatived the appointment of a teacher to the Chinese language school, because he was not consulted first.

The Korea Daily News.

Issued at 5 P. M. daily except Sundays.

Rate of Subscription:—
Per Year,............Yen 25.
Per Quarter,..........Yen 7.
Per Mouth,..........Yen 2.50.

Postage in Korea not charged extra.
Postage abroad charged extra.

Advertisements, 50 sen per day for 1 inch or less.
5 yen per month per inch.
50 yen per year per inch.

All communications to

E. T. BETHELL,
Editor and Publisher,
Pak-tong, Seoul

SOCIETY NOTES.

THE DOINGS OF THE I. C. H.

When, with the assistance of the Il-chin-hoi agitators, the Japanese had found what they considered to be a good and sufficient excuse to step in and assume control of the of policing of Seoul, the Il-chin-hoi braves from the country were told to retire to their homes and await further orders. We have more than a suspicion that many of the country members of the Il-chin-hoi were led to come to Seoul by mis-representations. Some of them were doubtless of the same "Down with every thing" stamp as their Seoul leaders but it is certain that there were many others who were simple country folk, who, led away by the "electioneering speeches" of the I. C. H. delegates, fancied that they had only to join the gay throng in order to be presented with "3 acres and a cow." These people have now gone back to the land sadder if not wiser, but the Seoul contingent still exists and shows signs of sprouting.

A philosopher once said that "Any fool can set a snowball rolling down a hill." No one will gainsay the philosopher, if there is plenty of snow on the side of the hill, all that is required at the starting place is a neucleus and a push, and it is certain that a nice large snowball will result.

This was the case with the I. C. H. A certain Mr. Komochi organised the neucleus and the "push" came from the Japanese War Fund.

The aforementioned philosopher, continuing his aphorism, said "But it takes a good many clever men to stop it."

And hereby hangs a tale. We forget what the original programme of the Il-chin-hoi exactly was, but speaking roundly, it was a scheme for the reformation of Heaven and Earth succinctly set forth in some half a dozen paragraphs. But how have the mighty fallen! We remember that at the time we said that the dreams of the I. C. H. reformers were somewhat Utopian, and from their latest mainfesto we gather that the reformers themselves have now come to the same conclusion. All the "high fallutin" has been thrown overboard and the Society makes the following declaration:—

"The object of the Society was to reform the Government but since the Society was organized the Japanese have, by placing their gendarmerie in control of the police, assured the welfare of the citizens of Seoul. The Il-chin-hoi Society has also been successful in arranging that anyone in the country who is oppressed may state his case to the nearest Japanese Consul who will report it to the Japanese Minister.

Our reporter adds:—"So everyone said that that Society is the leader of the Japanese."

So far as we can see, the I. C. H. people are at present occupying a very secure and comfortable seat on the fence. The people of Japan are fully persuaded that the Il-chin-hoi is a genuinely patriotic society so that whatever they do will be ascribed to their efforts in the cause of reform.

It can easily be seen, then, that the Japanese here may at any time find themselves in an awkward position. They have invested the I. C. H. with all the *kudos* and glory of a disinterested patriotic society and have given it the benefit of their countenance and support and now stand practically committed to acquiesce in all the society's doings.

From their manifesto we gather that the I. C. H. leaders already consider themselves masters of the situation and we ourselves do not see what the Japanese can have to say if they turn round on their patrons and demand a substantial increase in their emoluments under threat of going over to the other side.

So far as things have gone, the Il-chin-hoi have overtly done nothing worse than disobeying the Imperial orders to disperse—an offence which would be easily forgiven if they announced that they had seen the error of their ways. Or if the worst comes to the worst they can let their hair grow again and return to their ordinary avocations.

A strike for higher wages would therefore have a very fair chance of success. At any rate the I. C. H. people would have much to gain, and little to lose by it.

JAPANESE MISSIONARIES IN CHINA.

"The reply of Governor Neih of Chekiang to the Wai Wu-pu in connection with the transfer of the monasteries of the Province to Japanese, reads: The Hangchow gentry called the abbots to a conference lately to dicuss the establishment of a Buddhist school and to prevent the interference of Japanese monks in the scheme. The expenses of the school are to be borne by the monks, and the balance of money left over will be paid to the support of a preliminary school. These schools will be under official protection. To sum up the matter: Since the monks agree to support a school, their temples will not be confiscated, and since the officials will protect them, these monks do need any protection from the Japanese monks."

These few sentences contain important meanings. The desire of the Chekiang monks to hand over their temples to the Japanese monks was first prompted by the desire to avoid the confiscation of their properties. But now, they have protection and their property will not be confiscated, so that the monks can set their minds at ease with regard to complications. Though the Governor has given them assurances it is not known whether the Chekiang gentry have carried out his recommendation. In the case of Lunshun Temple, the Chekiang men are dissatisfied at the interference of the Japanese monks, and the works of Ting have caused a good deal of comment. We (the Universal Gazette) are of opinion that Ting was not satisfied with Kou, and at the same time could not do anything against him; therefore he transferred his temple to the Japanese. The latter, taking advantage of the opportunity, began to interfere, and have now their segn-boards hung up at the gate of the temple. When the oysters and crabs fight, comes the opportunity for the fishermen. Kou, being unaware of the result, attempted to convert the Lungshun Temple into an industrial institute, and hence arose this important case.

"The works of Kou, are not satisfactory to the people upon three points, namely Ting is of a well-known Hangchow family famous for its charity. All kinds of charitable works are done by him. The establishment of an industrial institute is also a charity. If Ting was trying to protect the Lungshun temple, why did he not secure a suitable building for this purpose instead of appealing to the Japanese monks? He only wanted to defeat Kou's purpose, not knowing that his plan would increase the influence of the Japanese, and cause a great trouble to the country at large. This is the fault of Ting, which cannot be otherwise explained.

People, nowadays, are used to talk of the conversion of temples into schools, in which scheme we (the U. Gazette) cannot concur, Kou quotes at the same time the Imperial decree on the subject, not knowing that the conversion depends on the will of the people. If this were carried out against the will of the people, it would afford the Japanese monks an opportunity to interfere, driving away all the Chinese monks, and making the establishments Japanese. China, in future besides the Roman Catholic and and Protestant religious, will have Buddhism to deal with. Kou was, indeed, very careless. The Japanese monks were in the wrong as well.

"Instead of building temples themselves they are robbing the Chinese temples. They should not avail themselves of the opportunity of a quarrel between the native monks and the gentry, to make the place a Japanese temple, without questioning whether the monks really intened it to be so or not. To remedy the matter the Japanese monks should be made to lower their signboards, and keep from interference in the affairs of the Lung-shun Temple. Secondly, the old monks should be expelled from the temple for having turned it over to foreigners. Thirdly and lastly, the indusitrial instute should be compelled to remove elsewhere. The temple should be returned to the monks to satisfy them, and to avoid foreign intervention in future.

Is it a fact, we wonder, that that in the new Budget Mr. Megata has made sweeping reductions in the estimates for the repair and general upkeep of the Korean Telegraphs. If so we may presently hear of the Japanese taking over this service on account of its inefficiency. As it is, they already control the principal lines on the ground of military neccessity.

Some time ago we noted the fact that the Japanese were following the Russian example in North Korea. After a lot of roundabout correspondence from the magistrate of the affected districts to the Home Office, from the Home Office to the Foreign Office, and thence *via* the Japanese Legation to the Army Headquarters, it transpires that the Japanese officer in Ham Heung had exceeded his authority and that the Japanese only claim to supervise the buying selling and pledging of groun l.

The Korea Daily News.

VOL. II, WEDNESDAY, FEBRUARY 1, 1905. No. 25

大韓每日申報
대한ᄆᆡ일신보

일천구ᄇᆡᆨ오년이월삼일 (금요일) 뎨이권 이십륙호

본사고ᄇᆡᆨ

이신보는영어와한어로셕거ᄆᆡ일츌판ᄒᆞ옵

신문갑

한쟝 엽젼두돈오푼
일삭됴 엽젼두량닷돈
우표가ᄑᆡ삭닷돈
다엽젼으로밧ᄉᆞᆸ

광고료는

귀한의쟝단과ᄌᆞ항의다쇼로죵감ᄒᆞ되뎡가로밧을터이오ᄆᆡ오릭지아니ᄒᆞ되대한사람마다다이신문을보실터이니광고내시기를원ᄒᆞ시는이들은우리신문샤에와셔면약ᄒᆞ심을희망ᄒᆞ옵

○발ᄒᆡᆼ소 박동대한ᄆᆡ일신보사발어학교압흐로쳔영국인셜필림쟝자리오

사쟝 영국인 (ᄇᆡ셜)

평양 ᄃᆡ리졈

○평양초동사는권미보씨로우리신문관ᄃᆡ리인을특뎡ᄒᆞ엿시오니평양에계신구람ᄒᆞ고져ᄒᆞ시는 쳠군ᄌᆞ는ᄃᆡ리졈에왕림ᄒᆞ와면회ᄒᆞ시옵

사고

○우리대한ᄆᆡ일신보의목뎍은대한의안녕질셔에관한모든대목에ᄃᆡᄒᆞ야는공평한변론을주쟝홈이라우리동신원의담보는신문보시는쳠군ᄌᆞ의게ᄒᆞᆼ상보도ᄒᆞ리며편지들과셔ᄒᆞ며주시는이는셩명과번디를적어붓치시기를희망ᄒᆞ오나ᄒᆞ거슨신문샹에과졔ᄒᆞ란는거시아니오다만극히신용ᄒᆞ는증거를숨고자홈이라귀자는아모괴셔던지과쟝ᄒᆞ을되각ᄒᆞ는권리를가젓스나되각ᄒᆞ는리유를말ᄒᆞᆯ터이오며공증평화를문란케ᄒᆞ는듯ᄒᆞᆫ귀셔는의례히밧지안캣ᄉᆞᆸ나이다

●본사셜시이ᄅᆡ로신문을ᄆᆡ양우례로분젼ᄒᆞ와레젼부의일의로젼ᄒᆞᆫ드시스로면곳에는혹늣게젼ᄒᆞ기도ᄒᆞ며혹면쳘거슨ᄒᆞᆫ겹에젼ᄒᆞ기도ᄒᆞ며혹아니젼ᄒᆞ는곳도잇다ᄒᆞ와우리신문을ᄉᆞ랑ᄒᆞ야구람ᄒᆞ시는 쳠군ᄌᆞ의게ᄃᆡᄒᆞ야면우미안ᄒᆞᆷ을기로지금은분젼인을두고ᄆᆡ일즉이젼ᄒᆞ며아니젼ᄒᆞ거나늣게거나ᄒᆞᆫ폐가업도록ᄒᆞ라ᄒᆞ오나혹아니젼ᄒᆞ거나혹늣게젼ᄒᆞ거나ᄒᆞᆫ일이잇스면본사로통긔ᄒᆞ여주심을희망ᄒᆞ옵

논셜

국채문뎨

○한국에셔일본인들이조흔닐을다ᄎᆞ지ᄒᆞ랴고열심ᄒᆞ고한국정부에셔는무한한젼갓흔일본의리익에만진력ᄒᆞ는사름에게져런고등봉급을주는것이우승도ᄒᆞ다국채경영과국민은ᄒᆡᆼ영업과ᄒᆡ관을합동ᄒᆞ는경영을합ᄒᆞ야만한국정부에셔일본지폐샹ᄇᆡᆨ만원의국채로ᄒᆡ관을너노케되고뎨일은ᄒᆡᆼ에권리를주어셔저의므ᄋᆞᆷ되로대한국민은ᄒᆡᆼ을조직ᄒᆞ게된다ᄒᆞ는지라

일본인이한국에셔일진회와경찰권으로만히저의므ᄋᆞᆷ되로ᄒᆞ니국채문뎨에되ᄒᆞ야아모리졍론ᄒᆞ드리도쓸ᄃᆡ업는것갓지마는샹등사회에셔는그리도반ᄃᆡ들이죰잇슬듯우리가젼일에국채문뎨의시작될ᄯᆡ에한국에향ᄒᆞ야두가지로권고ᄒᆞ엿스니

일 한국에셔그돈을ᄎᆞ지ᄒᆞ고

이 한국에셔자유로그돈을쓰게ᄒᆞᆷ이라

지금국채조약에이두가지에ᄒᆞ나도업고돈은지젼이오밋ᄎᆡ쓴자는뎨일은ᄒᆡᆼ이라ᄒᆞ더라

샹국채의담보는ᄒᆡ관이오긔한은년이라ᄒᆞ니지금일본은거의ᄇᆡᆨ가란미팔분변으로국채를쓰면셔ᄇᆡᆨ에잇고분의변리를일코돈을셰여주유니쓰는ᄉᆞ롬은두가지리유

일은 셩샹을보이는것이오

이는 당쟝에는현저치아니ᄒᆞ나자세히ᄉᆡᆼ각ᄒᆞ면보이는게졔가잇슴이라

목ᄒᆞ가젼셰는민칭ᄒᆞᆫ지쟝가로명에가잇는사름이라만일차관가한국탁지부의ᄉᆞ무를십년동안을갑동ᄒᆞ면한국금고에그국채로갑ᄒᆞᆯ것이업슬즁을징쟉ᄒᆞ고그ᄯᆡ에는일본인이지젼샹빗만원셔닭에한국ᄒᆡ관을ᄎᆞ지ᄒᆞ게될지로다

그러ᄒᆞ고뎨일은ᄒᆡᆼ은한국의ᄉᆞ쥬ᄇᆡᆨ동젼을지화로교환ᄒᆞ야슈합ᄒᆞ라고젼국에지졈을셜시ᄒᆞᆯ터인ᄃᆡ한국은그은ᄒᆡᆼ에감독권이엿슬터이나한인의ᄉᆞᆫ히와불편홈이만ᄒᆞ리로다

가령통고계쳥이우리보기에는한ᄂᆡ지도한인을위ᄒᆞ는념은업스나아모나라라도그런념은허락지아니ᄒᆞ겟도다

그지젼의비밀ᄒᆞᆫ리히를누가알리오그것을쳥구ᄒᆞ는ᄃᆡ로금젼으로밧구어쥬겟는가만일그런ᄒᆞᆯᄃᆡ경이면우리는한국에권고ᄒᆞ노니쟝시를지케말고그지폐를금화로밧군지어다만일그지폐가ᄒᆞᆫ번통ᄒᆡᆼ도면한국졍부는지금지젼엇은빗을십년후에금화로갑홀계제가잇슬리ᄒᆞ리노라

한국졍부에서목하젼셰를ᄂᆡᆫ의쳔원의원급을주면서이런달취를예비ᄒᆞ나원통피이ᄒᆞ고계우슈운일이로다

싱각건ᄃᆡ한국졍부는로국사름이와셔지금일본파샹관된수컵이가고들이바이라ᄒᆞ니다본셰이나무효ᄒᆞ게아니ᄒᆞ고효ᄒᆞ니라고셰들가려것은ᄒᆞᆫ졍다ᄒᆞᆫ한국치르

외보

론돈발 일월이십일일

○로국니란의쳐셩 셩피득보곳에셔빈치반란이젹졈치셩ᄒᆞ야은방란반ᄒᆞ고군ᄃᆡ들이무쟝을혜비ᄒᆞ고잇다더라

동더발 동월이십이일

○로국니란의속보 셩피득보예셔비란의샹항이대단ᄒᆞ야쓰에엽는일인ᄃᆡ셩니에면괴와괴ᄒᆞ야셔신문지들도모다정보ᄒᆞ엿스며군괴창에고용ᄒᆞ는문괸들은대권

의빗쳔며ᄒᆞ고쓰아서거민들비록츙을사서가스ᄒᆞ는ᄀᆞ
계중명당에엽합ᄒᆞ야셔ᄒᆞᆫ젼례군쥬
계쳐음민이모아셔청구ᄒᆞ는금속긔

황안을쳥구ᄒᆞ는ᄃᆡ그쳥구ᄒᆞ는밀에ᄒᆞ엿스되로국인민들은복과갓흔ᄃᆡ우를밧고힘에당치로못ᄒᆞᆷ이를답부시이며전졔뎡과관인의압졔혁에못견ᄃᆡ겟고만일그것을견ᄃᆡ라면죽는것시도로셔나ᄒᆞ니국민이쳥심ᄒᆞ야노냐등사회의ᄃᆡ표권을쳥구ᄒᆞ노니이겻시인민의피로온것을면ᄒᆞᆸ유일방칙이라이쳥구를므ᄋᆞᆷᄃᆡ로인ᄒᆞᆯ엇으면로국이깃부고영광스럽게될터이오만일그리

치못ᄒᆞ면우리가ᄎᆞ라리죽어셔즁은이리라ᄒᆞ고소ᄀᆞᄂᆡᄒᆞ니기갓ᄒᆞᆯ수가니회원에ᄒᆞ야난보고가잇셔셔ᄀᆞᆨᄃᆡ방에ᄒᆞᆫ쳥쳬보엉ᄒᆞ엿고모군관들이황뎨를보오고그쳥구를알외고즁회즁에죠항으로우간발숨을ᄒᆞ랴고홈쳬희의로지금황뎨의계신ᄊᆞ쓰고에셴노에ᄒᆞᆫ셰가갓스며각ᄃᆡ방에셔군ᄃᆡ들이급히경셩을향ᄒᆞ야올나간다ᄒᆞ엿더라

론돈발 일월이십일일

○로쟝의셔ᄒᆞᆫ 상히에셔도망ᄒᆞᆫ로국경위ᄒᆡᆷ시ᄒᆞᆫ니뷰씨는로국황뎨께셔그용감ᄒᆞᆷ을칭찬ᄒᆞ기위ᄒᆞ야셩스틘일나우쓰뎨이등훈장을하ᄉᆞᄒᆞ엿다더라

론돈발 일월이십이일

○로국니란의격렬 셩피득보에셔이번오쳔명의창평당이거울에대궐에향ᄒᆞ야가다가곳셕쓰군ᄉᆞ들이막어셔그여러인민의게향ᄒᆞ야총을노코니모는지라그후로는수방에셔전쟁이되엿논ᄃᆡ인민들이니클나쓰다리돌막어셧거는보병들과곳셕쓰군들이미엄습ᄒᆞ랴ᄒᆞᆷ계음에인민홀이죽고군ᄉᆞ들의게항ᄒᆞ야동포형메들은죵들을버리고셜병ᄒᆞ니보병은듯지아니ᄒᆞ고포격ᄒᆞ야곳셕쓰군은중에사ᄃᆡ젼이되야셔교수회들과ᄆᆡ면흔쓰회들이써는간ᄒᆞ고상ᄒᆞ엿스며인민들은면쥬목을ᄶᅢ고면괴첩을일거셔진치고잇다ᄒᆞ엿더라

잡보

○쳥죡숙샹 외부에셔법부에죠회ᄒᆞ기를영용수가죠회ᄒᆞ되힌쥬쳠샹빈샹일수는여러번회동ᄒᆞ야써이쳔칠ᄇᆡᆨ륙십수원으로졍ᄒᆞ엿스즉쳥컨ᄃᆡ곳숙히빈샹케ᄒᆞ라ᄒᆞ엿기이에죠회ᄒᆞ니쳥컨ᄃᆡ죠랑ᄒᆞ라ᄒᆞ엿더라

○습졉피란 ᄎᆡ작일죵로깃젼란에엇던ᄒᆞᆫ사름이와셔빌릴을사고갑슬무른즉그갓쟝수ㅣ쳔량이라ᄒᆞ니그사름이말ᄒᆞ기를어제는넉넉오ᄇᆡᆨ량이오젼에ᄂᆡ는ᄂᆡ가비싸게ᄒᆞ도쳑본이랑오젼에파ᄂᆞᆫ그갓쟝수말ᄒᆞ기를사지아니ᄒᆞᆫ티을

UNION INSURANCE SOCIETY OF CANTON.

Head office Hongkong.
Marine risks underwritten at current rates.

Agents in Chemulpo,
E. MEYER & Co.

COMPAGNIE DES MESSAGERIES MARITIMES.

Fortnightly Direct Service.

For Marseilles
via Ports.
Sailing from Yokohama
Calling at Kobe,
Shanghai, Hongkong, Saigon, Singapore,
Colombo, Djibonti, Suez, Port Said
and Marseilles.

For particulars apply to
HOLME RINGER & Co.,
Chemulpo.

HAYASHIDA & CO.,

16 MYENG DONG, CHIN KO KAI, SEOUL.
BRANCH OFFICE AT CHEMULPO.

Money changers, Coal and Wood Merchants, Express Agents.

We are agents for the Pyeng-yang Coal Company and the Karazu Coal Company of Japan. We have the best quality of both anthracite and bituminous coal, and prompt execution of orders is our speciality. Firewood of all kinds kept in stock. Full weight guaranteed. Money of all denominations exchanged at current rates. Parcels received for all parts.

CHINA MUTUAL LIFE INS. OC.

Most favourable terms to policy holders.

Benefit system unsurpassed.

HOLME RINGER & Co.
Agents, Chemulpo.

C. P. R.

CANADIAN PACIFIC RAILWAY COMPANY'S ROYAL MAIL STEAMSHIP LINE.

THE FAST ROUTE BETWEEN CHINA, JAPAN, AND EUROPE VIA CANADA AND THE UNITED STATES.

Route from Hongkong via Shanghai, Nagasaki (Inland Sea of Japan) Kobe, Yokohama. Victoria and Vancouver.

Twin Screw Empress Steamship—6,000 Tons—Speed 19 knots.

PROPOSED SAILING FROM YOKOHAMA.
R. M. S. Empress of India.
R. M. S. Empress of Japan.
R. M. S. Empress of China.
R. M. S. Athenian.
R. M. S. Tartar.

Special reduction (first class only) granted to members of the Military, Naval, Diplomatic and Civil services and to Missionaries.

Passengers have choice of ten routes across the Continent of America and have privilege of travelling by any Atlantic Steamship Line.

Round the World passage tickets in connection with the P. and O. S. N., North German Lloyd and Messageries Co.'s £125.

All rates payable at current rate of exchange.

For further information, Tickets, Guide Books, etc., apply to

HOLME, RINGER & Co., AGENTS,
Chemulpo.

Grand Hotel,

(Formerly the Station Hotel)

Near the Railway Terminus.
West Gate Seoul.

The Best Hotel in Korea;
Handsome new Building.
Fine Airy Rooms
Excellent Cuisine.
Terms Moderate.
Special terms to Missionaries
and to permanent boarders.

Electric cars within 2 minutes' walk.

W. H. EMBERLEY.
Proprieto

EVERY FACILITY.

In connection with Life Assurance Business is afforded by

The Standard Life Assurance Co.,

One of the largest and wealthiest of the Provident Institutions of the United Kingdom Forms of Application and all information will be promptly afforded on application.

10 CENTS A DAY.

Not a very large expenditure is it? But it is sufficient to secure for a man of 30 a policy with the STANDARD LIFE OFFICE for

$1323.

For all particulars of rates, etc., apply to

Holme, Ringer & Co.,
Agents, Chemulpo.

THE NEW YORK LIFE INSURANCE COMPANY.

Have you ever been declined by any Company?

Are you engaged in a specially hazardous occupation?

Have you heard of the New York Life Insurance Company's New Classifications for this class of Risks?

If not, send your date of birth, occupation and particulars of rejection, if any to

E. MEYER & Co.,
Agents, Chemulpo.

MITSUI BUSSAN KAISHA
(MITSUI & Co.)

MITSUI GINKO.
(MITSUI BANK.)

The Bank is owned by the members of the Mitsui Family, who, as partners, assume an unlimited responsibility for all liabilities of the Bank:—

Capital.............................Yen 5,000,000
Reserve Fund...................... " 5,600,000

HEAD OFFICE, TOKYO.

LONDON OFFICE, 34 LIME ST., E. C.

BRANCHES AND AGENCIES:—
New York, San Francisco, Hamburg, Bombay, Singapore, Manila, Hongkong, Amoy, Chefoo, Tientsin.

Kobe, Hakodate, Yokohama, Kure, Yokosuka, Moji, Shimonoseki, Miike, Wakamatsu, Nagasaki, Kuchinotsu, Karatsu, Sasebo, Misume, Taipeh, &c.

Telegraphic Address for all the Offices:
"MITSUI."

A. B. C. AND A. 1 CODES USED.

Contractors of Coal
To the Imperial Japanese Navy. Arsenals and Railway Bureau, Principal Railway Companies and Industrial Work, Home and Foreign Mail and Freight Steamers.

Sole Proprietors
Of the famous Miike, Tagawa and Yamano Coal Mines.

Sole Agents
For the sale of Fukumo, Hokoku, Ichimura Kanoda, Mannoura, Onoura, Ostuji, Sonoda, Tsubaruro, Yoshinotani, Yoshio, Yurokibura and other coals.

YANGTSE INSURANCE ASSOCIATION, LTD.

The undersigned, having been appointed agents for the above company, are prepared to issue policies and pay losses on marine risks at regular rates.

E. MEYER & Co.,
Agents, Chemulpo.

AMERICAN KOREAN ELECTRIC CO.

Light and Power.

Main Office: Electric Building, Chong No.

RAILWAY DEPARTMENT.

OPERATING CARS BETWEEN EAST AND WEST GATE, EVERY TEN MINUTES:—

First Car leaves East Gate at 7:00 A. M. First Car leaves R. R. Station at 7:25 A. M
Last Car " East Gate at 8.40 P. M. Last " " R. R. Station at 9.05 P. M

OPERATING CARS BETWEEN EAST GATE AND IMPERIAL TOMB TERMINUS, EVERY TWENTY MINUTES:—

CONNECTING WITH EVERY ALTERNATE CAR ARRIVING AT EAST GATE FROM CHONG NO.

First Car leaves East Gate for Tomb at 7:10 A. M.
" " " Tomb for East Gate at 7:30 A. M.
Last " " East Gate for Tomb at 7:50 P. M.
" " " Tomb for East Gate at 8:10 P. M.

OPERATING CARS BETWEEN CHONG NO AND YUNG SAN RIVER EVERY TWELVE MINUTES:—

First Car leaves Chong No for South Gate at 7:12 A. M.
" " " Chong No for Yung San at 7:36 A. M.
" " " South Gate for Chong No at 7:20 A. M.
" " " Yung San for Chong No at 8:09 A. M.
Last " " South Gate for Chong No 9:00 P. M.
" " " Yung San for Chong No at 8.45. P. M.

SPECIAL PRIVATE CARS FURNISHED TO SUIT CONVENIENCE OF PATRONS. PRICES ON APPLICATION AT HEAD OFFICE.

LIGHTING DEPARTMENT.

Where less than 250 candle power of light is used, the rate per month will be
Per 16 candle power incandescent lamp,—All night.—Yen 2.50.
32 candle power incandescent lamp:—All night:—Yen 4.00.
50 candle power incandescent lamp:—All night:—Yen 6.00.
150 " " " " " " " 10.00.
1200 " " enclosed arc " " " " 20.00.

Where more than 250 candle power of light is used, a Meter will be installed, if requested:—Rent of Meter Yen 2.00 per month. Rate of charges by meter reading:—Two Sen per Ampere per hour. (Approximately this is equal to about One Sen per 16 C. P. lamp per hour) Minimum monthly charge where meter is installed, Yen 20.00 per month, which includes rental of meter.

Estimates for installing lights furnished on application
An assortment of chandeliers always on hand.

K. Murakami.
Photograph Studio
Chinkokai, Seoul.

Printing, Developing and Enlargement, of Photographs always Undertaken.

Korean Views and Pictures Illustrating Native Customs always on Sale,

---

THE OSAKA SHOSEN KAISHA.

Boats frequently on the berth for Chinnampo.

REGULAR SAILINGS BETWEEN JAPAN AND KOREAN PORTS.

FUSAN AND KOBE VIA SHIMONOSEKI.

OSAKA VIA MOKPO, FUSAN, SHIMONOSEKI AND KOBE.

MOJI DIRECT.

OSAKA VIA KUNSAN, MASANPO, FUSAN, SHIMONOSEKI AND KOBE.

CHEMULPO KUNSAN LINE,
Every three days.

CHEMULPO CHINNAMPO LINE.
Every three days.

For Freight and passage and further particulars apply to

THE OSAKA SHOSEN KAISHA,
Chemulpo

RONDON, PLAISANT & CO.

General Storekeepers and Merchants, Ships Contractors, Tobacconists, Commission and Forwarding Agents, Coal Merchants

IMPORTERS AND EXPORTERS

Seoul & Chemulpo.

W. D. WENTWORTH

LANDING
AND
SHIPPING AGENT
AND
CUSTOMS BROKER.

12 OURA, NAGASAKI.

STEWARD & CO.

Chemulpo.

Shipchandlers and Storekeepers, Naval and Mercantile Contractors, Landing and Shipping Agents.

STEWARD'S HOTEL

Chemulpo.

Best accommodation in the port for travellers. Clean and well-aired rooms, good cuisine and prompt attendance, moderate tariff.

면고만이지 무ᄉᆞ욕을ᄒᆞ나ᄒᆞ고 잉쌀을세라 피가나ᄂᆞᆫ지라 고영희잇던흙은 갓쟝ᄉᆞ와 어러동ᄒᆞ서 무갓쟝ᄉᆞ 오륙인이 모혀 좌우로 구타ᄒᆞᄂᆞᆫ지라 그사ᄅᆞᆷ이 뎨욱 분ᄒᆞᆷ을 참지못ᄒᆞ야 곳죵로교번소에 가서 말ᄒᆞ기ᄅᆞᆯ 쳠명을 다리고와 아단가 죵취ᄒᆞ라ᄒᆞᄂᆞᆫ 재놈들을 쟝못포박ᄒᆞᆯ 조음에 구ᄒᆞᄂᆞᆫ 고ᄉᆞᆸ검 갓은 도피ᄒᆞᆫ고로 [illegible] 신쟝이 직다ᄒᆞ니 [illegible] 가잇ᄂᆞᆫ 술모로거니와 갓 [illegible] ᄂᆞᆫ사ᄅᆞᆷ은 집으로 평복을 ᄒᆞ엿나보다 더라

○경ᄉᆞ탕진 소안동거ᄒᆞᄂᆞᆫ 쳥쥬ᄉᆞ 한셩호씨ᄂᆞᆫ 비왕에 도외국 인파 교셥도 잇ᄂᆞᆫ ᄉᆞᄅᆞᆷ이라 근일 에서 양인모목ᄉᆞ와 젼도ᄒᆞᄂᆞᆫ 집에서 만나 수인ᄉᆞᄒᆞᆫ후에 서로 초면이나 셜졍으로 상아 샹ᄉᆞ일 단 니디니무사ᄅᆞᆷ 홉ᄒᆞ이 잇던지 흰 고카되ᄂᆞᆫ디 샹인단님사샹원을 쥬민동씨가 말ᄒᆞ기ᄅᆞᆯ 빈가 돈 샹 원을단 ᄀᆞᆫ것이 아님 죵그 만두 라 ᄒᆞ고 져 샹 ᄉᆞ 양ᄒᆞᆫ 즁 그목ᄉᆞ 말 이 돈은 아니 밧으니 내게 면 거 표 가 잇스 니 빗 으 라 ᄒᆞᄂᆞᆫ 지 라 등 씨 가 무숨리 리가 잇던지 차 표 도 수 양 ᄒᆞ엿다더라

○법부훈령 법부에서 십삼도 관찰부로 훈령ᄒᆞ기ᄅᆞᆯ 무론민형 ᄉᆞᄒᆞ고 소송지ᄅᆞᆯ 반다시 인찰지 로쓰ᄂᆞᆫ 것은 쟝졍에 잇ᄂᆞᆫ 바ㅣ 어 란근릐 각디방 민송츄에 인찰지 아니 ᄡᅥ 시 만 흐 니 비 쟝 무 쌍 ᄒᆞ 훈령 이 ᄅᆞᆫ 비 에 각 군 、 야 일반 소송지ᄅᆞᆯ 인찰지로 / ᄒᆞ고 소송지 쓰 ᄂᆞᆫ 법식을 규졍을 츅 차 일 즁 시 ᄒᆡᆼ 케 ᄒᆞ 라 ᄒᆞ 엿 더 라

○협동중지 학부에서 한어교 ᄉᆞ 를 두 방 역 으 로 협 동 ᄒᆞ 엿 더 니 일 공ᄉᆞ 가 외 부 로 조 회 ᄒᆞ 기 ᄅᆞᆯ 뎨 이 국 외 교 셥 을 본 공 ᄉᆞ 의 게 미 리 셩 이 명 ᄒᆞ 지 아 니 ᄒᆞ 엿 다 ᄒᆞ 고 쳥 빅 이 ᄌᆞ 샹 ᄒᆞᆫ 지 라 그 협 동 을 중 지 ᄒᆞ 엿 더 라

○조사셩칙 경무쳥에서 오서 니 거류ᄒᆞᄂᆞᆫ 니외국인의 호구ᄅᆞᆯ 됴ᄉᆞ셩칙ᄒᆞ야 ᄃᆡ니에 붕쟝ᄒᆞ 엿더라

○훈칙사보 국ᄉᆞ범 김쳥직과 샹옥범노 ᄉᆞ ᄉᆞ 를 쳐 교 션 고 ᄒᆞᆫ 지 라 쥭 쳘 년 에 도 모 지 쟉 ᄒᆡᆼ 치 아 니 ᄒᆞ 더 니 헌 금 법 부 에 서 평 리 원 으 로 훈 령 ᄒᆞ 기 ᄅᆞᆯ 그 량 옥 안 을 다 시 사 ᄒᆞ 야 보 리 ᄒᆞ 라 ᄒᆞ 엿 더 라

○쳥구빈샹 일본경부도 번셰 가 한 국 녀 인 사 뵈 명 을 미 명 에 팔 젼 원 에 부 셔 에 민 둑 ᄒᆞ 야 두 엇 더 니 일 신 쟈 지 중 도 리 흔 교 로 등 사 한 인 명 명 을 사 쳐 에 밧 ᄒᆞ 야 삼 십 일 일 빈 에 림 문 교 근 디 에 서 쟉 야 간 죵 헌 벙 이 중 로 에 서 힐 문 ᄒᆞ 야 등 사 ᄅᆞᆷ 무 슈 란 리 ᄒᆞᆯ 지 음 에 그 계 집 을 일 흔 지 라 일 인 이 경 무 쳥 과 헌 병 남 서 에 비 샹 금 일 빅 원 을 쳥 구 ᄒᆞ 엿 더 라

○호위티폐지 호위티ᄂᆞᆫ 폐지 ᄒᆞ야 경위원으로 부쇽ᄒᆞ엿더라

○교사승빙 영어교사 불암돈 씨를 구년일월브터 과ᄒᆞ야 삼개년 을 승빙ᄒᆞ기로 합동ᄒᆞ엿더라

○부왕치사 아오지사 ᄂᆞᆫ 연보 쥬사 정환백은 일젼에 면관이 되 엿더니 티쳐 ᄅᆞᆯ 잡지 못ᄒᆞ니 샬아 서무의 ᄒᆞ다ᄒᆞ고 거이 십구일에 부부가 ᄒᆞᆷ께 복약ᄒᆞ고 치사ᄒᆞ엿 더라

○일사젼죠 쟝곡쳔대쟝이 합 ᄒᆞᆫ병참소에 훈령ᄒᆞ기ᄅᆞᆯ 군용샹 디 쳥구 ᄒᆞ 여 니 에 디 미 ᄒᆞ 거 나 면 당 ᄒᆞᆫ 거 나 기 타 소 유 권 을 이 동 ᄒᆞᄂᆞᆫ 힝 위 ᄂᆞᆫ 졍 지 케 ᄒᆞ 라 ᄒᆞ 엿 다 고 일 본 공 사 가 외 부 로 젼 죠 ᄒᆞ 엿 더 라

○죠쳥쳘폐 일공관에서 외부 에 조회ᄒᆞ기ᄅᆞᆯ 우리 평사가 플충 ᄒᆞ 되 궁니부와 밋 영친왕부에셔 훈령을 발ᄒᆞ야 본방샹민이 슈츌 ᄒᆞᄂᆞᆫ 포빅과 곡물과 어물과 등 물에 티ᄒᆞ야 세ᄅᆞᆯ 빈 나 밧 ᄂᆞᆫ 다 ᄒᆞ니 사실 권디 이 런 한 세 과 가 티 황 실 에 누 가 이 치 쳐 ᄒᆞ 오 니 쳥 컨 되 곳 철 폐 ᄒᆞᆷ 이 가 ᄒᆞ 다 ᄒᆞ 엿 더 라

○쳥의난망 한셩니 빈민을 구 휼차로 대니에서 슈만량을 경 무쳥으로 너하ᄒᆞ신지라 경무쳥 에서 빈민호구ᄅᆞᆯ 됴사ᄒᆞ야 비명 에 셩 량 식 반 급 ᄒᆞ 엿 더 라

○일진회지목 일진회에서 민 국사ᄅᆞᆯ 간셥ᄒᆞ야 각부에 무리히 ᄒᆞᄂᆞᆫ 폐 등 리 귀 쵸 ᄅᆞᆯ 평 고 ᄒᆞᆫ 다 ᄒᆞ 더 니 한 국 광 업 권 등 권 의 교 셥 무 을 명 미 법 비 이 각 국 이 일 본 외 무 성 에 티 ᄒᆞ 야 쳥 구 ᄒᆞ 되 외 부 에 서 도 쳥 이 분 ᄒᆞᆫ 쥰 ᄒᆞ 고 쪼 일 진 회 에 서 진 회 소 위 ᄅᆞᆯ 다 알 교 괴 당 이 라 지 목 ᄒᆞ 고 민 국 사 ᄅᆞᆯ 계 션 ᄒᆞ 다 ᄒᆞ 더 니 일 본 헌 병 사 령 부 에 서 한 셩 니 지 념 젼 서 ᄅᆞᆯ 평 찰 ᄒᆞᆫ 다 ᄒᆞ 고 계 방 셜 안 니 시 ᄒᆞ 고 공 사 ᄂᆞᆫ 쟝 평 사 의 계 훈 령 ᄒᆞ 야 민 원 이 잇 거 든 호 소 ᄅᆞᆯ 받 가 공 관 에 보 명 ᄒᆞ 라 ᄒᆞ 엿 스 니 일 진 회 에 우 금 파 념 에 셩 사 ᄒᆞ 거 ᄂᆞᆫ 이 두 가 지 에 지 아 니 ᄒᆞ 야 일 인 의 당 귀 라 지 목 ᄒᆞᆫ 다 더 라

○죠쳥시명 외부에서 학부에 조회ᄒᆞ기ᄅᆞᆯ 일공ᄉᆞ죠회니 기에 본정부에서 귀국학부샹쇄신ᄒᆞ에 ᄂᆞᆫ 안건에 티ᄒᆞ야 일헌쳥양에 샹 항 을 의 지 ᄒᆞ 야 바 야 흐 로 착 슈 ᄒᆞ 란 ᄒᆞᄂᆞᆫ 티 드 듸 혀 귀 학 부 에 한 어 교 ᄉᆞ ᄅᆞᆯ 고 빙 ᄒᆞ 다 ᄒᆞ 니 쳥 컨 티 곳 시 명 ᄒᆞ 야 가 ᄒᆞ 다 ᄒᆞ 엿 더 라

○만리천쳑병 작샹삼일일일 모에 쳥인이 통쳔에서 ᄂᆞᆫ 이 만 오 쳔 량 을 츄 심 ᄒᆞ 야 만 리 졔 등 디 로 오 드 러 오 ᄂᆞᆫ 티 쟉 당 이 방 포 돌 츌 ᄒᆞ 야 무 론 슈 탈 거 ᄒᆞᆫ 지 라 쳥 순 ᄉᆞ 가 경 무 쳥 에 곳 가 셔 치 셔 ᄒᆞᆫ 일 을 고 ᄒᆞ 며 경 무 쳥 에 서 쳥 원 ᄒᆞ 지 라 경 무 쳥 이 곳 디 교 ᄒᆞ 야 겸 을 ᄉᆞ 쳐 로 발 ᄒᆞ 야 잡 으 라 ᄒᆞ 엿 더 라

○각의미결 거샹십일에 졍부 회의ᄂᆞᆫ 지쟝을 리쟝ᄒᆞᆷ에 관ᄒᆞ야 샹벽만원을 차관ᄒᆞ고 빗ᄂᆞᆫ 회ᄅᆞᆯ 조처ᄒᆞᆯ 사진인디 쳥의가 갓지 아 니ᄒᆞ야 결졍ᄒᆞ지 못ᄒᆞ엿더라

○졍부개회 거샹삼일일하오 두시에 졍부에서 개회의ᄒᆞ엿ᄂᆞᆫ 티 군슈주본샹오파ᄅᆞᆯ 졔츌ᄒᆞ야 의졍ᄒᆞ고 곳주본ᄒᆞ야 셔 임 이 된 다 더 라

○룡기지관 초산군슈 윤셕린 씨가 본군빅셩 샹명을 탐쟝ᄒᆞ야 치폐ᄒᆞᆫ사진으로 일진회에서 평 리원에 겸고ᄒᆞ야 윤군슈ᄅᆞᆯ 착ᄉᆞ원 ᄒᆞ고 샹십일에 공기지관ᄒᆞ야 샹십일일하오세 시에ᄂᆞᆫ 룡기지관ᄒᆞ고 피고 윤군 슈ᄅᆞᆯ 심문ᄒᆞ엿더라

○곡산군보 곡산군슈가 외부로 보고ᄒᆞ기ᄅᆞᆯ 진남포일본령ᄉᆞ의 조회ᄅᆞᆯ 졉ᄒᆞᆫ즉 일진회진보회 인들이 량민을 유인ᄒᆞ야 란민의 계ᄅᆞᆯ 아니 ᄒᆞ게 ᄒᆞᆫ다ᄒᆞ오니 엄금ᄒᆞ 교로 죠 단ᄒᆞ야 금지ᄒᆞᆯ 터 이니 이 ᄉᆞ 의 로 세 포 교 ᄒᆞᆷ 이 가 ᄒᆞ 다 ᄒᆞ 엿 ᄉᆞ 온 즉 엇 지 조 쳐 ᄒᆞᆯ 넌 지 못 희 시 ᄒᆞ 라 ᄒᆞ엿더라

○호샹츄환 일본순ᄉᆞ가 남서 에 리도ᄒᆞ야 교셥ᄒᆞ기ᄅᆞᆯ 근일 젹 한 이 일 인 의 물 긴 은 도 젹 질 ᄒᆞ 면 한 인 뎐 당 포 에 뎐 집 ᄒᆞ 고 한 인 의 물 건 을 도 젹 질 ᄒᆞ 면 일 인 의 뎐 당 포 에 면 집 ᄒᆞ 니 그 손 히 가 불 소 ᄒᆞ 니 지 라 한 일 량 뎐 당 국 을 슈 탐 ᄒᆞ 야 도 젹 질 ᄒᆞ 야 뎐 집 ᄒᆞᆫ 물 건 이 잇 거 든 서 로 츄 환 ᄒᆞ 자 ᄒᆞ 엿 더 라

관보

뎨삼쳔오십일호 광무구 년이월일일

서임급ᄉᆞ령

○의원면본관 한셩부주ᄉᆞ 리계하

○임한셩부주ᄉᆞ서판임관륙등 륙품 노직연

이샹일월이십륙일

○의원면본관 법관양셩소박 ᄉᆞ 박덕환 법관양셩소박ᄉᆞ 권중션 법관양셩소박ᄉᆞ 연 쥰 법관양셩소박ᄉᆞ 권홍슈 법 관양셩소박ᄉᆞ 리연홍 법 관양셩소박ᄉᆞ 김명룡 법관 양셩소박ᄉᆞ 리명용 법관양 셩소박ᄉᆞ 유문규 법관양셩 소박ᄉᆞ 권중환

○임법관양셩소박ᄉᆞ서판임관 륙등 윤일영 공면쥬 윤병 순 최창리 허식 리종우 리용셜 리한길

○임법관양셩소교관서판임관 륙등 김병션

○승서판임관삼등 한셩ᄉᆞ범 학교부교관 리샹익

이샹일월이십팔일

○명서리호위티총관ᄉᆞ무 경위원총관륙군부쟝 리근틱

○종이품가선대부니부협판 교부ᄉᆞ 구샹현

종이품가선대부니쟝원경구연 승외교의방면츄 중

이샹일월이십구일

○명니쟝원경서칙임관삼등 종이품 리병우

○임 지릉참봉서판임관팔등 리인환

○임 희릉령서판임관칠등 룡릉참봉 김명덕

○임 룡릉참봉서판임관팔등 한명셕

○임중추원의관서칙임관ᄉᆞ등 비서원승 리경현

○의원면본관 니부쥬ᄉᆞ 권 중완

○임니부쥬ᄉᆞ서판임관륙등 조풍구

○임외국어학교부교관서판임 관륙등 현헌 유긔멱 쥬영 운 윤붕식 민지호 박광희 리승쥰 조동헌 최학우 함 제원 쟝두샹 현근 전규영 남궁억 고병익 최병옥 권 기옥

이샹일월삼십일

구년도예산표 속

뎨십일항 목욕비 일쳔팔 빅원

뎨십이항 쳐료비 일쳔팔 빅원

뎨십삼항 리쟝비 ᄉᆞ빅오 십원

뎨십ᄉᆞ항 츌쟝비 륙쳔원

뎨칠관 긔병티 십일만이쳔 칠십륙원

뎨일항 봉급 일만칠쳔팔 빅원

뎨이항 쳥비 일쳔삼빅오 십원

뎨삼항 쳥ᄉᆞ슈리비 오십 원

뎨ᄉᆞ항 ᄉᆞ졸급료 이만일 쳔이빅이십오원

뎨오항 량식비 일만구쳔 륙십쳘원

뎨륙항 마료비 구쳔삼빅 원

뎨칠항 마량비 삼만이쳔 오빅삼십륙원

뎨팔항 마쟝비 오쳔삼십 칠원

뎨구항 피복비 일만구십 ᄉᆞ원

뎨십항 보슈비 륙빅원

뎨십일항 연습비 구십원

뎨십이항 목욕비 쳘십이 원

뎨십삼항 쳐료비 일빅팔 십원

뎨십ᄉᆞ항 리쟝비 ᄉᆞ십원

뎨십오항 졔뎐비 쳘빅ᄉᆞ 십원

뎨십륙항 마편급마독비 일쳔삼십원

뎨십칠항 용역비 일쳔원

(미완)

TELEGRAMS.

AFFAIRS IN RUSSIA.

(FROM JAPAN PAPERS.)

Vienna, Jan. 23.

The dockyards and ammunition factories on the Neva have been closed.

The strikers at St. Petersburg are in communication with the labour bodies in various cities in South Russia. A strike has started at the Government workshops on the Baltic and is steadily spreading to those of the other cities.

Vienna, Jan. 23.

Strict vigilance is being maintained at St Petersburg, owing to the rumoured designs to assassinate the Tsar. It is stated that the supporters of the plot are found even in Court and military circles. Arrests of suspects are continually taking place.

London, Jan. 24.

The centre of the city of St. Petersburg was practically deserted on Sunday evening, except by the troops who camped in the snow.

Some of the infantry were withdrawn and replaced by bluejackets.

London, Jan. 24.

Conflicts are constantly occurring between the Cossacks and the workmen in the streets of St. Petersburg.

The strike at Moscow is spreading. The gasworks have ceased business and there is also no electric light.

At Kovno 10,000 of the strikers have commenced to riot, with the result that all the factories have suspended work.

Quietness prevails at Riga, Livonia.

A strike has also been started at Vilna.

The Tsar has agreed to give audience at the Tsarskoe Selo Palace to 12 delegates of the working people.

London Jan. 26.

A rumour is current to the effect that General Trepoff will succeed General Faulon as Governor-General of St. Petersburg and that the latter will proceed to Warsaw. This report tends to confirm the popular suspicion that the Imperial Court is distracted and wavering.

The railway near the Russian capital was destroyed last night to the extent of seven versts.

London, Jan. 26.

The agitation in Russia is spreading with startling rapidity and there are disorders in all the great centres.

Insurrectionary movements have commenced in Poland and Finland.

The people are vowing vengeance for the massacre of Sunday.

St. Petersburg is cowed for the moment, but the storm is gathering.

The situation is paralysing the dispatch of supplies to Kuropatkin, who is making despairing cries for food, men and ammunition.

According to an unconfirmed rumour, twenty miles of the Siberian railway have been destroyed.

M. Trepoff, the Russian Minister of Home Affairs, has been appointed Governor-General of St. Petersburg.

The strikes of workmen are increasing, but collisions with the troops are avoided.

It is rumoured that Maxim Gorki, the well-known novelist, has been arrested and imprisoned.

London, Jan. 26.

Apparently the censorship is being strictly enforced, and news is scanty. But the authorities seem to have gained a complete mastery at St. Petersburg.

London, Jan. 26.

The strike movement in Russia is rapidly spreading in the provinces. The rumour that the novelist Maxim Gorky had been arressed is untrue.

London, Jan. 26.

General Trepoff, the late Chief of the Police at Moscow, has been appointed Governor-General of St. Petersburg, full powers being granted him. Yesterday afternoon he held a conference at the Winter Palace with the chief of police and the officer commanding the troops, and instructed them to adopt rigorous measures in suppressing the disturbances.

London, Jan. 26.

The Cossacks on Tuesday fired on a body of 3,000 demonstrators at Moscow, wounding many of the latter.

General Trepoff, the new Minister of the Interior, has had notices posted at the various works, ordering the workmen to return to work within 24 hours, otherwise they will be deported to the villages. Two of the factories have resumed work. Meanwhile the movement is apparently spreading in the provinces.

By order of the Tsar, General Trepoff and the Minister of Finance have issued a proclamation, explaining to the workers that they are being exploited by self-seeking and evil-disposed persons, who have misled them, thus rendering intervention by armed force inevitable. The Government, the proclamation adds, is now as ever ready to listen to the just desires of the people.

London, Jan. 26.

St. Petersburg has been virtually placed under martial law, administered by a military dictator. The policy of extreme repression and the violent measures adopted prevent any organized demonstration, and the chances are that no immediate revolution will take place. Nevertheless, the whole population is in a state of dangerous unrest, and the strikes are spreading to the provinces

The Moscow police allege that the outbreaks have been provoked by an Anglo-Saxon source in order to prevent the Baltic and Black Sea Fleets from proceeding to the Far East.

The disorders at Libau are hindering the dispatch of the third Pacific squadron.

Danger is feared, owing to the disaffection among the reservists proceeding to the Far East.

Wholesale looting of the supplies for Kuropatkin has occurred at many points on the railway.

Anti-war demonstrations are being organized in Southern Russia, to be held on the anniversary of the outbreak of hostilities.

Berlin, Jan. 27.

The Tsar has published a manifesto exhorting the workmen to remain quiet. The Tsar promises to regulate by law an insurance fund for the working men and to reduce their working hours. In addition, measures are to be taken that will enable the workmen to lay their grievances before the proper authorities.

From Vienna it is reported that the disaffection is increasing amongst the troops in Russian Poland who are about to proceed to the Far East.

London, Jan. 27.

Moscow is quiet. A proclamation issued by the Governor of that town promises that the fullest protection will be given to the men remaining at work.

The police at Moscow have posted notices in the streets, alleging that the strike movement is due to Anglo-Japanese intrigue and that the strikers are supported by British money. Sir Charles Hardinge, the British Ambassador, has protested against this calumny, and has received assurances that measures will be taken to prevent a repetition of the publication of the notices. The British Embassy at St. Petersburg is guarded by sentries. A similar notice to the above was also postedat Odessa.

St. Petersburg is returning to its normal aspect. The Government is confident that the movement has been checked.

VLADIVOSTOCK.

Tokio, Jan. 25.

A German steamer, which arrived at Moji from Vladivostock yesterday, reports that repairs on the "Rossia" have been completed, but those on the "Gromoboi" are still going on. The "Bogatyr" is submerged and wholly covered with water at flood-tide.

THE BALTIC FLEET.

Tokio, Jan. 23.

A telegram received here states that the Baltic Squadron left Madagascar on the 21st for St. Denis, Reunion Island, but this report at present lacks confirmation.

Vienna, Jan. 23.

The Baltic fleet is now on the high sea outside the French territorial waters off Madagascar, the French Government having forbidden the Fleet to remain any longer in French waters. The fleet has despatched several transports to various places in order to obtain supplies and is coaling from the colliers. No orders have yet been received by the Fleet with regard to its recall, but the squadron is apparently awaiting some development.

The section of the Baltic Fleet proceeding via the Mediterranean Sea is continuing its voyage slowly.

ADMIRAL KAMIMURA.

Tokio Jan. 23th.

Vice-Admiral Kamimura and his Staff left Tokyo this afternoon amid loud "Banzais!" The Admiral's family will accompany him as far as Sasebo.

GENERAL NEWS.

Tokio, Jan. 23rd.

The Upper House committee concerned adopted this forenoon, four bills including one in relati[illegible] to the naval arsenal fund. The L[illegible]wer House also dealt with three bills but came to no conclusion regarding them.

London, Jan. 24.

The Peking correspondent of the London "Times," after visiting Port Arthur, says that no more discreditable surrender is recorded in history than of Port Arthur.

Berlin, Jan. 26.

The second son of Kaiser Wilhelm, Prince Eitel Friedrich, has been attacked by pneumonia. All official festivities projected for the Emperor's birthday (January 27) have been concelled.

London, Jan. 21.

"The Times" has reason to believe that Admiral Rozhjestvensky will not attempt to reach the Far East for at least three months.

London, Jan. 24.

M. Rouvier has practically completed the French Cabinet. He has decided to adhere to the programme laid down by M. Combes, the late Premier.

M. Delcasse will continue in office as Minister for Foreign Affairs.

London, Jan. 25.

China has replied to Mr. Hay, U. S. Secretary of State, denying that she has swerved one iota from her neutrality. She, however, considers that Russia has violated her neutrality in a number of instances.

London, Jan. 25.

Viscount Hayashi, Japanese Minister at London, has been invited to Windsor Castle as the guest of the King and Queen. He will stay there three days, returning to London on Saturday.

Berlin, Jan. 25.

The Austro-German Commercial Treaty was signed yesterday.

London, Jan. 36.

The European money markets are firm.

NOTICE.

Mr. T. Ross Reid is no longer connected with the Korea Daily News.

It is requested that all communications on business be addressed to W. C. Fenton, Manager Korea Daily News.

General Hyön and his "lady" are said to be on their way back to Korea.

A Tokio telegram reports the capture, on the 31st ult. of another steamer bound for Vladivostock with cardiff coal.

A rather vague telegram from Tokio seems to indicate that the Japanese police have assumed charge of the Korean Legation there.

By the extremely belated mail which arrived this morning we received exchanges from Japan with dates up to the 28th ult. but many papers prior to that date are missing.

When yesterday, we published a rumour to the effect that His Majesty was contemplating a second marriage, we understood that the news had been brought to us by one of our own reporters. We now find, however, that a Japanese newspaper evolved the story and we regret having given publicity to it.

The Japanese Consul at Chinnampo has written to the magistrate at Koksan that he no longer looks with favour upon the demonstrations of the Il-chin-hoi people as they are liable to make rioters of otherwise peaceable people. He asks the magistrate to publish this information and the magistrate applies to Seoul for instructions.

The Korea Daily News.

Issued at 5 P. M. daily except Sundays.

Rate of Subscription :—
Per Year,............Yen 25.
Per Quarter,..........Yen 7.
Per Month,..........Yen 2.50.

Postage in Korea not charged extra.
Postage abroad charged extra.

Advertisements, 50 sen per day for 1 inch or less
5 yen per month per inch.
50 yen per year per inch.

All communications to

E. T. BETHELL,
Editor and Publisher,
Pak-tong, Seoul.

JAPAN'S ALLIES.

Even if we make considerable allowance for bias in the telegrams which reach Korea from Japan, there is evidently within Russia a party, which by its obstructive policy, is rendering very valuable assistance to Japan.

Several months ago we intimated that there was evidence that this element had not been left out of Japan's calculations, and had all these disturbances occurred six months ago they would very likely have become the determining factor of the war.

As things now stand, however, Russia has safely despatched the Baltic squadron and has had time to mobilise powerful armies at home, and although the drastic measures which are being adopted for the suppression of the agitators are causing indignation in Europe, there is little doubt that they will be effective.

It must be borne in mind that the strikers and political agitators chose their own time for their demonstrations, and chose the time when Russia had her hands full with the war which is now raging in the Far East. Desperate diseases often require desperate remedies and as at this time Russian statesmen have other things to do than parley with political agitators, it is not surprising that sterner measures of repression have been adopted than would have been the case under normal circumstances.

There is undoubtedly a sad lot of injustice and oppression in Russia but the agitators have chosen a time for their demonstrations when they could not expect any other treatment than is now being meted out to them.

There is another point. We in Korea have seen by the reports in Japanese newspapers about the Il-chin-hoi, how easy it is to give the public an absolutely erroneous idea of the true nature and aims of a revolutionist society.

The dock-yard employes are said to be amongst the agitators in Russia and from the point of view of probabilities alone we should say that these men are now probably being better treated than ever they were. Is it likely, at a time when so much depends upon them, that Russian officials would treat them badly? If they have done so they are bigger fools than we take them to be.

A few days ago a Reuter's telegram told us that the revolutionists appeared to be under remarkably sagacious leadership, and it is quite within the bounds of possibility that the professional agitators heading the movement are in the employ of an enemy of Russia. We have been told, by writers with an intimate knowledge of conditions within Russia that the lower classes, constituting the bulk of the population, would never, on their own initiative, take part in any revolutionary movement.

When the vast area of Russia is taken into consideration, these agitations are comparatively insignificant and will not, we think, have any great influence upon the course of the war. Of course, if the measures taken for the suppression of the mal-contents fail, the question would be a grave one, but it hardly seems likely that they will fail.

(*The above was written before the telegrams appearing in todays issue were received.*)

JAPAN'S FINANCES.

The "Nichi Nichi," says that, according to Mr. Sakatani, Vice-Minister of Finance, the Government had spent on the war account something over 400 million yen up to some time in November last, and calculates that as two months have since elapsed, the disbursement must now foot up to fully 500 millions. The Government should have done its best to meet all this expenditure by drawing upon the resources appropriated for the purpose. What has actually taken place is, however, that the Government has, since the commencement of the hostilities, been able to realize so far only 160 million yen from three internal and £10,000,000 from the foreign loans and some 40 millions from taxes and levies, so that is still a deficit of some 200 million yen to make up for the amount of the total disbursement. In order cover the deficit the Government has no doubt accommodated itself to some extent with funds from the surplus and special accounts; but for the rest—which forms the largest portion of the deficit—the Government appears, so says the journal, to have been depending on its borrowings from the Bank of Japan, which now amount to as much as 90 million yen, as the latest report of the bank shows. The journal blames the Government for this poor financing, and thinks the excessive issue of the notes will cause disturbance to the monetary economy of the country.

THE JAPANESE PRESS.

When a future catastrophe of greater magnitude is in view a present calamity should be endured, provided such endurance would result in removing the anticipated dangers from the pale of possibility. The Russo-Japanese war in progress is certainly a calamity; but it is perfectly clear that its cessation, if prematurely obtained, would only hasten the time when Russia would return for a war of revenge. She has by no means exhausted her combative and financial resources yet; on the contrary she has an abundance of energy yet left, and peace now can only give her her a respite which she may take advantage of in reorganizing and rebuilding her army and navy, perhaps in an unexpectedly short space of time. Grant that peace is somehow restored at this moment. On the morrow of the reopening of hostilities Russia will have finished doubling throughout the Siberian railway and augmented the strength of her fleet to be sent out to the Far East to from 300 to 500 thousand tons. Not that this country will find itself unable to cope with the situation then; but certainly it will be that the empire will have to face a campaign of magnitude many times that of the present one, or we will have taxed our energies to such an extent that the exhaustion will retard our national progress for generations. There can be no doubt that the campaign has awakened the Russians to the misconceptions they had entertained about Japan and Japanese; and indeed a section of them, represented by the "Novoe Vremya," is already openly advocating a thorough reconciliation and closer understanding between the present belligerents after the war. But so long as the Anglo-Japanese alliance remains in force and the bureaucracy continues to rule Russia, there can be no hope for such a turn of events, and it is unwise, impossible, for us to think of the termination of the present campaign independent of the idea of a coming war of vengeance. Consequently no terms of peace Russia may concede for the present should be accepted as adequate, unless they are of such nature as would produce in the Russian mind a permanent feeling of the hopelessness of retaliation, or as would distinctly and effectively place Japan in a position of indisputable supremacy in the event of a second conflict. Unfortunately we have not yet brought our blows sufficiently home to the enemy as would compel him to agree to such terms; and for the time being, no matter whether there be a peace party at home, the country must not accept peace. To our great reluctance, as it no doubt will be, we must also decline all overtures for peace from any third Power or Powers for the present. Nor is there any doubt that the Western Powers are exasperated almost beyond patience by the acts of insane lawlessness which in her desperation Russia has been committing everywhere, and are longing for the return of peace, but Russia alone is to be held responsible for the protraction of the war. The question of securing a posion of supremacy is a pregnant matter, which may not be mapped out even in outline at this moment; but one point that must indispensably be included in the conditions will be the placing Vladivostock under the control of our navy. With both Port Arthur and Vladivostock in our hands, Russia will have no naval base in the Far East and her plan of bringing a strong fleet in our neighbourhood will become simply an impossibility. If Russia is not inclined to hand over Vladivostock to us in peace, we will take it by force, and by the time we have captured the port, the operations in the other parts of the field will have made such progress that we may then talk of peace. Such is in substance the "Nippon's" view on the question of peace.—Japan Times.

The "Nichi Nichi" learns that the Korean Government will probably appoint a number of Japanese taxation experts at various important places in Korea, for the purpose of introducing reforms in the present system of collecting taxes.

The Gazette of January 19th contained come edicts relative to currency which we have not yet been able to understand. There are continual references to a gold standard which does not, and is apparently not likely to, exist. We presume that at the time the edict was published it was thought that the Japanese loan would be in gold.

The Korea Daily News.

VOL. II, THURSDAY, FEBRUARY 2, 1905. No. 26

HONGKONG & SHANGHAI BANKING CORPORATION.

Paid-up Capital....	$10,000,000
Reserve Fund:—Sterling Reserve...	10,000,000
Silver Reserve.....	7,000,000
	27,000,000
Reserve Liability of Proprietors...	10,000,000

HEAD OFFICE, HONGKONG.

London Bankers, London and County Banking Company Limited.

Branches and Agencies,
London.

Amoy,	Hankow	Penang,
Bangkok,	Hiogo,	Rangoon,
Batavia,	Iloilo,	Saigon,
Bombay,	Lyons,	San Francisco,
Calcutta,	Manila,	Singapore,
Colombo,	Nagasaki,	Sourabaya,
Foochow,	New York,	Tientsin,
Hamburg,	Peking,	Yokohama,

Credits granted on approved Securities, and every description of Banking and Exchange business transacted.

Drafts granted on London and the chief Commercial places in Europe, India, Australia, America, China and Japan.

HOLME RINGER & CO., AGENTS,
CHEMULPO.

HOKURKU DOBOKU KAISHA.

Branch office in Chong Dong, Seoul.

Japanese telephone No. 165

CONTRACT DEPARTMENT.

We can contract to build any building or construction.

MERCHANDISE DEPARTMENT.

We can provide any building material. We have just contracted to build the new Belgian Legation.

E. MEYER & CO.

Chemulpo.

SOLE AGENTS IN KOREA FOR.

A. T. Morse, Sons & Co.'s

"Fresco" Distemper

In all colours ready for use on walls, Ceilings etc.

and

AVENARIUS CARBOLINEUM

A wood-preserving and antiseptic oil preparation

Against decay, dry-rot, fungus and wood-destroying insects.

A large supply always in stock. Prices upon application.

E. MEYER & Co.,
Chemulpo.

CHARTERED BANK OF INDIA AUSTRALIA & CHINA.

INCORPORATED BY ROYAL CHARTER 1853

HEAD OFFICES.—LONDON.

Paid-up Capital	£800,000
Reserve Liability of Share-holders	800,000
Reserve Fund	800,000

Drafts granted upon all the principal places in the world and every description of Exchange and banking business transacted.

E. MEYER & Co., Agents,
Chemulpo.

MITSU BISHI DOCKYARD & ENGINE WORKS,

NAGASAKI.

CODE WORD, "DOCK."

A 1, A. B. C., and Engineering Codes used.

DOCK No. 1 (at Tategami).

Extreme Length.............	523 feet
Length on blocks	513 ,,
Width of Entrance on Top......	89 ,,
,, ,, Bottom....	77 ,,
Water on Blocks at Spring Tide	26½ ,,

DOCK No. 2 (Mukaijima).

Extreme Length............	371 feet
Length on Blocks.............	360 ,,
Width of Entrance on Top......	66 ,,
,, ,, Bottom	53 ,,
Water on Blocks at Spring Tide	22 ,,

PATENT SLIP (at Kosuge).

Can take vessels up to 1,000 tons gross.

THE WORKS are well equipped with the LATEST IMPROVEMENTS, and can execute any kind of work in SHIPBUILDING and MARINE ENGINEERING, as well as in REPAIRING of SHIPS.

The COMPANY'S new powerfu steamer OURA-MARU (712 tons, 700 I.H.P.), specially built for SALVAGE PURPOSES, and equipped with necessary gear, is always READY at SHORT NOTICE.

THE METHODIST PUBLISHING HOUSE.

Little West Gate, Seoul.

JOB PRINTING, TYPEWRITER PAPER
CARBON PAPER, VISITING CARDS
STATIONERY, BOOK BINDING
BOOK PUBLISHERS
AMERICAN SCHOOL BOOKS
SPENCERIAN COPY BOOKS
PEN CARBON LETTER AND BILL BOOKS

S.A. BECK, Manager.

DAI-ICHI GINKO.

LIMITED.

(Formerly the First National Bank)

ESTABLISHED 1873

INCORPORATED UNDER PRESENT LAW 1896

Capital - - - - - - - - -	Yen 5,000,000
Reserve Fund - . - - -	1,500,000

HEAD OFFICE:—TOKIO.

President: Baron SHIBUSAWA.

BRANCHES AND CORRESPONDENTS

In the Principal Cities and Towns of Japan.

Interest Allowed on

Fixed deposits 1 year - - -	6½ per cent
" " 6 months - - -	6 per cent

Special current accounts 1½ sen daily per	Y 100
General " " 1 " " "	100

M. TANAKA,
Manager, Chemulpo.

SINGER SEWING MACHINES

씽거ᄌᆞ봉침

SOLE AGENTS FOR KOREA

젼매쇼

HOLME RINGER & CO.
Chemulpo.

졔물포 함릉거양힝

KAMEYA & CO.

GENERAL STOREKEEPERS

Chinkokai - - Seoul

(Established 1895, Tokyo)

Confectionery, Hams, Canned Goods, Cutlery, Hirano & Tansan Water. Provisions, Gents, Furnishing goods, Toilet Articles, Travelling Bags, Tobacco, Cigars & Cigarettes Kitchen Utensils. Coffee, Biscuits.

Fresh Goods always kept in Stock.

Prices Moderate

☞ Please come and inspect our goods.

NIPPON YUSEN KAISHA.

JAPANESE MAIL STEAMSHIP CO.

UNDER MAIL CONTRACT WITH THE IMPERIAL JAPANESE GOVERNMENT.

European Line

Regular Fortnightly Service between Yokohama Kobe, Moji, Shanghai, Hongkong, Singapore, Penang Colombo, Port Said, Marseilles, London and Antwerp

American Line

Regular Fortnightly Service between Hongkong and Seattle, calling at Shanghai, Moji, Kobe, Yokohama and Victoria, B. C.

Australian Line

Regular weekly Service betwen Japan Ports and Australia, calling at Hongkong and Manila.

(Above Three Lines Suspended until further notice).

Shanghai Line

Weekly Service between Shanghai and Japan Ports

Korea Line

Service Kobe, Moji, Nagasaki, Fusan Chemulpo Chefoo, Taku.

S. S. Babelsberg, 2181 tons.

Service Kobe, Moji, Fusan, Chemulpo, Chinnampo

S. S. ARGO, S. S. Ohio.

BORDEN'S CONDENSED MILK CO.

New York, U. S. A.

ALWAYS IN STOCK

Eagle Brand Condensed Milk.

Gold Seal Condensed Milk.

Peerless (Family) Evaporated Cream.

Borden's Malted Milk.

E. MEYER & CO.
Chemulpo Korea,
Sole Agents

ROYAL INSURANCE COMPANY,
Funds exceed £10,000,000
FIRE
AT CURRENT RATES
LIFE
REDUCED PREMIUM.
HOLME RINGER & Co.,
Agents, Chemulpo.

HOTEL DU PALAIS.

SEOUL.

The only first class Hotel in Seoul Situated in the centre of the city opposite the palace.

Cuisine under the supervision of an experienced French Chef.

Well ventilated and furnished throughout.

TARIFF UPON APPLICATION

L. MARTIN
Proprietor and Manager.

大韓每日申報
대한ᄆᆡ일신보

(뎨이권이십칠호)　(금요일)　일쳔구ᄇᆡᆨ오년이월수일

본샤고ᄇᆡᆨ

이신보는영어와한국문으로셔계ᄆᆡ
일출판ᄒᆞ옵
신문가
한쟝 엽두돈오푼
일삭도 엽두량닷돈
우표가ᄆᆡ삭닷돈
다맛돈으로밧ᄉᆞᆷ
광고료는
귀한외쟝단과ᄌᆞ힝의다쇼로쥭
량ᄒᆞ되련가로밧을터이오며오
리저하야내대한사람마다다이신
문을보실터이니광고ᄂᆡ시기룰
원ᄒᆞ시는이들은우리신문사에
와셔면약ᄒᆞ심을희망ᄒᆞ옵
○발힝소 박동대한ᄆᆡ일신보
샤 법어학교압헤젼영국인셜필
립집자리오
사쟝 영국인 (빅셜)
평양 ᄃᆡ리졈
○평양효동사는 권미보씨로우
리신문관ᄆᆡᄃᆡ리인을ᄐᆡᆨ졍ᄒᆞ엿
ᄉᆞ오니평양에계신구람코져ᄒᆞ
시는 쳠군ᄌᆞ는히ᄃᆡ리졈에왕
림ᄒᆞ와면의ᄒᆞ시옵

사고

○우리대한ᄆᆡ일신보의목뎍은
대한의안녕질셔에관한모든대
목에ᄃᆡᄒᆞ야는공평한변론을주
쟝ᄒᆞᆷ이라우리통신원의탐보는
신문보시는쳠군ᄌᆞ의계ᄒᆞ샹보
도ᄒᆞ리며편지들긔셔ᄒᆞ며주시
는이는셩명과번디를젹어붓치
시기를희망ᄒᆞ오나히기슨신문
샹에긔ᄌᆡᄒᆞᆯ나는거시아니오다
만극히신용ᄒᆞ는증거를숨고자
ᄒᆞᆷ이라긔ᄌᆞ는아모긔셔던지과
지ᄒᆞᆷ을되ᄌᆞᄒᆞ는권리를가젓소
나되ᄌᆞᄒᆞ는리유를말ᄒᆞᆯ터이오
며공중평화를문란케ᄒᆞ는듯ᄒᆞᆫ
긔셔는이ᄯᆡ히밧지안케ᄉᆞᆸ나이
다
●본샤셜시이리로신문을ᄃᆡ양
우레로분젼ᄒᆞ와레젼부와일의
로젼ᄒᆞ든곳스로면곳에는혹늣게
젼ᄒᆞ기도ᄒᆞ며혹몃칠계숩ᄒᆞᆫ넙
에젼ᄒᆞ기도ᄒᆞ며혹아니젼ᄒᆞ는
곳도잇다ᄒᆞ와우리신문을ᄉᆞ랑
ᄒᆞ야구람ᄒᆞ시는 쳠군ᄌᆞ의게
되ᄒᆞ야미우미안ᄒᆞ옵기로지금
은분젼인을두고ᄆᆡ일존이젼
ᄒᆞ며아니젼ᄒᆞ거나늣게거나ᄒᆞᆫ
폐가업도록ᄒᆞ랴ᄒᆞ오니혹아니
젼ᄒᆞ거는혹늣게젼ᄒᆞ거나ᄒᆞᆫ일
이잇스면본샤로통긔ᄒᆞ여주심
을희망ᄒᆞ옵

외보

○불ᄅᆡᆨ함ᄃᆡ의향지 비록구러
면보에불ᄅᆡᆨ함ᄃᆡ가도라갈듯ᄒᆞ
다ᄒᆞ나그함ᄃᆡ가베쟝훈치소에
셔뎨삼함ᄃᆡ와연합ᄒᆞ랴고간듯
ᄒᆞ다더라
○청후션싱 청국황태후께셔
만쥬에란리겻는ᄇᆡᆨ셩들을구조
ᄒᆞ라고은삼십만량을보내고중
긔쟝군에게신칙ᄒᆞ기를진력보
호ᄒᆞ라ᄒᆞ엿다더라
○영국세출의증가 영국졍부
에셔거년세출은일억사쳔이ᄇᆡᆨ
이십만방이며니금년에는삼억
이쳔사ᄇᆡᆨ칠십만방이라더라
○로쟝의답례 구로팟긴대쟝
이세로히발령ᄒᆞ되셩쾨등보감
옥셔로보고ᄒᆞ는일본군의사망
ᄒᆞᆫ졔파들이다음브리는그친속
에게도알게ᄒᆞ다ᄒᆞ엿스니가
소일본인이로군에ᄃᆡᄒᆞ야그러
ᄒᆞᆫ교로그답례로그런케홈이더
라
○회샹위군함수 회샹위에셔
츌범ᄒᆞᆫ덕국긔션함쟝의답화에
왈회ᄃᆡ샹황을드론즉군함(로
시아)호는이미수리ᄒᆞ야젼투
에빙힘이업는듯ᄒᆞ고(구론보
이)호는수리중이로ᄃᆡ아즉완
셩치못ᄒᆞ고보기젼호는의연히
침몰ᄒᆞ고슈뢰뎡은십이쳑비
고샹션은이십쳑이졍박ᄒᆞ고륙잇
나고에는병졸삼사만명이잇다ᄒᆞ
나고셜수는자셰치못ᄒᆞ다더라
○미국훈쳡 론돈뎐보를거ᄒᆞᆫ즉
미국국무부헤이씨가일아젼쟁
이결국된세에청국강토가분할
됨을방ᄒᆞ고쏘청국본토의기
방과및그쳔샹을유지ᄒᆞ기위ᄒᆞ
야렬국에운칭을발ᄒᆞ엿는ᄃᆡ영
덕법삼국에셔이훈쳡에ᄃᆡᄒᆞ야
열심으로찬셩ᄒᆞ는회답을보냇
다더라
○퇴한령폐지헌단말 한국에
리도ᄒᆞᆫ일인중에불량ᄒᆞᆫ사ᄅᆞᆷ이
잇스면령사가환국ᄒᆞ라ᄒᆞ고명령
ᄒᆞ더니근리에는법률노쳐치ᄒᆞ
는수단이잇슬ᄲᅮᆫ더러한국에잇
셔싱애ᄒᆞ는자와셔로리사ᄒᆞ야
오는자가등랍ᄒᆞ야싱애ᄒᆞ기를
쥬쟈ᄒᆞ는고로일본졍부에셔근
일에그법률을폐지ᄒᆞᆯ터이라더
라

잡보

○죠뎡경찰 일본경찰셔탐보
원이삼십일뵈젼병문교번쇼
에와셔말ᄒᆞ기를죄인을잡을세
에경뎡이부죡ᄒᆞ거든곳경찰셔
에통긔ᄒᆞ면일쳔숲ᄉᆞ가곳가셔조
력ᄒᆞᆯ터이니일로써죠관ᄒᆞ이가
ᄒᆞ다ᄒᆞ엿더라
○영관셜연 거삼십일하오칠
시에영국공관에셔연회를셜힝
ᄒᆞ엿는ᄃᆡ일본청국덕국공ᄉᆞ와
및고문관들이참회ᄒᆞ엿더라
○졔두 쳘폐 쟝단군수가너
부로보고ᄒᆞ기를거이십칠일밤
에 젹한미삼문에방을붓쳐길오
ᄃᆡ 쳘폐를도졔ᄒᆞ여가니돈을
젼ᄒᆞᆫ후에첫ᄶᅢ가란ᄒᆞ엿가로
쳘폐를가셔본즉과연위쾌가뷔
엿는지라이거슨젼에엉든ᄃᆡ번
이오ᄃᆡ방금긔찰ᄒᆞ는중이라ᄒᆞ
엿더라
○림피군보 림피군수ᄇᆡᆨ남규
보고니에본군온련금ᄇᆡᆨ동화는
영교령젼을숩용ᄒᆞ는고로관찰
부훈령을의지ᄒᆞ야빈결두필식
예오식낭은영젼이오삼칙식양
은쉬동이으로숩용ᄒᆞ는ᄃᆡ취회상
등이소등ᄒᆞ고쟝츗지료를ᄒᆞ다
는고로쟝쳑ᄒᆞᆯ흥뷔이미등이군산
항일본령ᄉᆞ의게원쇼ᄒᆞ야일률
수를화송ᄒᆞ는ᄃᆡ셔지이르면법
외에일을힝ᄒᆞ니헝공관에리죠
ᄒᆞ야다시간셥지못ᄒᆞ게ᄒᆞ시기
를보란다ᄒᆞ엿더라
를(찬졍졔씨수직 의졍부관졔
인을두는지라찬졍이일병수
○도졍상소ᄒᆞ고총무국장박의병씨
수직ᄒᆞ고총무국장박의병씨
○이심상군수 상쟉일에졍부
회의에셔니부대신이각군수의
쥬본안건을경의ᄒᆞᆫ후샹쥬군수몽셰
ᄒᆞ엿다는ᄃᆡ그신임군수가여
좌ᄒᆞ니
영괴군수 리헌구 평양군수
리승지 홍괴군수 리지형
리의ᄌᆡᆨ군수 신우균 리원군수
유진셤 강동군수 오영퇴
리홍ᄌᆡ양군수 박남규 리곡산군수
계승 쟝홍군수 리ᄌᆡ용
리쳔군수 리창용 리봉쳔군수
유승동 영월군수 김쳘규
무주군수 조면근 태구군수
김종원 평주군수 한홍수
연풍군수 하리빈 초산군수
문봉오 봉산군수 졍홍퇴
회령군수 김지연 희쳔군수
오학션 부평군수 홍응조
ᄇᆡᆨ쳔군수 죠원규 공쥬군수
민영희 졔씨더라

관보

뎨삼쳔오십이호 광무구
년이월이일
셔임급ᄉᆞ령
○명ᄂᆡ부랑계원림시위원 리
명쳘 리종수 민병규
광무팔년십이월삼십일일
○명ᄂᆡ부랑계원림시위원 김
유희 오인규 졍경수 박돈
수 샹용진 문행섭
광무팔년십이월십이일
○육군감리셔주임관샹등 졍
삼품 김교헌
○승셔주임관오등 공수관참
셔관 리우영
○면본관 인쳔우쳬수쟝 셩
낙호
○승셔주임관샹등 진위면보
수쟝 죠중은
○경힝경무수 의졍부찬졍
신ᄐᆡ후
비샹일월삼십일
○희관졔리졍소의졍관 종일
품 김셩근
○명관계리졍소의졍관 탁지
부대신 민영긔
○민본관 충청남도관찰부총
순 윤영구
○명총무관찬수셔칙임관삼등
종이품 리근하
○의원면본관 숙동평 리응
국 비셔원승 리셔종
○임충청남도관찰부총순셔판
임관은등 경무청총순 홍병
티
○임경무청총순셔판임관일등
경무청주수 홍종익
○의원면경임 시강원시독관
기로소수직관 김중한
○임시강원시독관셔판임관수
등 규쟝각직각 리인규
○임 규쟝각직각셔판임관수
등 봉룸 리의구
○임봉샹수주수셔판임관ᄉᆞ등
외평원참봉 졍연셰
○임 의평원참봉셔판임관팔

UNION INSURANCE SOCIETY OF CANTON

Head office Hongkong.
Marine risks underwritten at current rates.
Agents in Chemulpo,
E. MEYER & Co.

COMPAGNIE DES MESSAGERIES MARITIMES.

Fortnightly Direct Service.

For Marseilles via Ports.

Sailing from Yokohama

Calling at Kobe, Shanghai, Hongkong, Saigon, Singapore, Colombo, Djibouti, Suez, Port Said and Marseilles.

For particulars apply to
HOLME RINGER & Co.,
Chemulpo.

HAYASHIDA & CO.,

16 MYENG DONG, CHIN KO KAI, SEOUL.
BRANCH OFFICE AT CHEMULPO.

Money changers, Coal and Wood Merchants, Express Agents.

We are agents for the Pyeng-yang Coal Company and the Karazu Coal Company of Japan. We have the best quality of both anthracite and bituminous coal, and prompt execution of orders is our speciality. Firewood of all kinds kept in stock. Full weight guaranteed. Money of all denominations exchanged at current rates. Parcels received for all parts.

CHINA MUTUAL LIFE INS. OC.

Most favourable terms to policy holders.

Benefit system unsurpassed.

HOLME RINGER & Co.
Agents, Chemulpo.

C. P. R.

CANADIAN PACIFIC RAILWAY COMPANY'S ROYAL MAIL STEAMSHIP LINE.

THE FAST ROUTE BETWEEN CHINA, JAPAN, AND EUROPE VIA CANADA AND THE UNITED STATES.

Route from Hongkong via Shanghai, Nagasaki (Inland Sea of Japan) Kobe, Yokohama, Victoria and Vancouver.

Twin Screw Empress Steamship—6,000 Tons—Speed 19 knots.

PROPOSED SAILING FROM YOKOHAMA.

R. M. S. Empress of India.
R. M. S. Empress of Japan.
R. M. S. Empress of China.
R. M. S. Athenian.
R. M. S. Tartar.

Special reduction (first class only) granted to members of the Military, Naval, Diplomatic and Civil services and to Missionaries.

Passengers have choice of ten routes across the Continent of America and have privilege of travelling by any Atlantic Steamship Line.

Round the World passage tickets in connection with the P. and O. S. N., North German Lloyd and Messageries Co.'s £125.

All rates payable at current rate of exchange.

For further information, Tickets, Guide Books, etc., apply to

HOLME, RINGER & Co., AGENTS,
Chemulpo.

Grand Hotel,

(Formerly the Station Hotel)

Near the Railway Terminus, West Gate Seoul.

The Best Hotel in Korea
Handsome new Building.
Fine Airy Rooms
Excellent Cuisine.
Terms Moderate.
Special terms to Missionaries and to permanent boarders.

Electric cars within 2 minutes' walk.

W. H. EMBERLEY.
Proprieto

EVERY FACILITY.

In connection with Life Assurance Business is afforded by

The Standard Life Assurance Co.,

One of the largest and wealthiest of the Provident Institutions of the United Kingdom Forms of Application and all information will be promptly afforded on application.

10 CENTS A DAY.

Not a very large expenditure is it? But it is sufficient to secure for a man of 30 a policy with the STANDARD LIFE OFFICE for

$1323.

For all particulars of rates, etc., apply to

Holme, Ringer & Co.,
Agents, Chemulpo.

THE NEW YORK LIFE INSURANCE COMPANY.

Have you ever been declined by any Company?

Are you engaged in a specially hazardous occupation?

Have you heard of the New York Life Insurance Company's New Classifications for this class of Risks?

If not, send your date of birth, occupation and particulars of rejection, if any to

E. MEYER & Co.,
Agents, Chemulpo.

MITSUI BUSSAN KAISHA.
(MITSUI & Co.)

MITSUI GINKO.
(MITSUI BANK.)

The Bank is owned by the members of the Mitsui Family, who, as partners, assume an unlimited responsibility for all liabilities of the Bank:—

Capital........................Yen 5,000,000
Reserve Fund.................. " 5,600,000

HEAD OFFICE, TOKYO.

LONDON OFFICE, 34 LIME ST., E. C

BRANCHES AND AGENCIES:—
New York, San Francisco, Hamburg, Bombay, Singapore, Manila, Hongkong, Amoy, Chefoo, Tientsin.

Kobe, Hakodate, Yokohama, Kure, Yokosuka, Moji, Shimonoseki, Miike, Wakamatsu, Nagasaki, Kuchinotsu, Karatsu, Sasebo, Misume, Taipeh, &c

Telegraphic Address for all the Offices:
"MITSUI."

A. B. C. AND A. I CODES USED.

Contractors of Coal
To the Imperial Japanese Navy. Arsenals and Railway Bureau, Principal Railway Companies and Industrial Work, Home and Foreign Mail and Freight Steamers.

Sole Proprietors
Of the famous Miike, Tagawa and Yamano Coal Mines.

Sole Agents
For the sale of Fukumo, Hokoku, Ichimura Kanoda, Mannoura, Onoura, Ostuji, Sonoda Tsubaruro, Yoshinotani, Yoshio, Yurokibura and other coals.

YANGTSE INSURANCE ASSOCIATION, LTD.

The undersigned, having been appointed agents for the above company, are prepared to issue policies and pay losses on marine risks at regular rates.

E. MEYER & Co.,
Agents, Chemulpo.

AMERICAN KOREAN ELECTRIC CO.

Light and Power.

Main Office: Electric Building, Chong No.

RAILWAY DEPARTMENT.

OPERATING CARS BETWEEN EAST AND WEST GATE, EVERY TEN MINUTES:—

First Car leaves East Gate at 7:00 A. M. First Car leaves R. R. Station at 7:25 A. M
Last Car " East Gate at 8.40 P. M. Last " " R. R. Station at 9.05 P.M

OPERATING CARS BETWEEN EAST GATE AND IMPERIAL TOMB TERMINUS, EVERY TWENTY MINUTES:—

CONNECTING WITH EVERY ALTERNATE CAR ARRIVING AT EAST GATE FROM CHONG NO.

First Car leaves East Gate for Tomb at 7:10 A. M.
" " " Tomb for East Gate at 7:30 A. M.
Last " " East Gate for Tomb at 7:50 P. M.
" " " Tomb for East Gate at 8:10 P. M.

OPERATING CARS BETWEEN CHONG NO AND YUNG SAN RIVER EVERY TWELVE MINUTES:—

First Car leaves Chong No for South Gate at 7:12 A. M.
" " " Chong No for Yung San at 7:36 A. M.
" " " South Gate for Chong No at 7:20 A. M.
" " " Yung San for Chong No at 8:09 A. M.
Last " " South Gate for Chong No 9:00 P. M.
" " " Yung San for Chong No at 8.45 P. M.

SPECIAL PRIVATE CARS FURNISHED TO SUIT CONVENIENCE OF PATRONS. PRICES ON APPLICATION AT HEAD OFFICE.

LIGHTING DEPARTMENT.

Where less than 250 candle power of light is used, the rate per month will be
Per 16 candle power incandescent lamp,—All night.—Yen 2.50.
32 candle power incandescent lamp:—All night:—Yen 4.00.
50 candle power incandescent lamp:—All night:—Yen 6.00.
150 " " " " " " 10.00.
1200 " " enclosed arc " " " 20.00.

Where more than 250 candle power of light is used, a Meter will be installed, if requested:—Rent of Meter Yen 2.00 per month. Rate of charges by meter reading:—Two Sen per Ampere per hour. (Approximately this is equal to about One Sen per 16 C. P. lamp per hour) Minimum monthly charge where meter is installed, Yen 20.00 per month, which includes rental of meter.

Estimates for installing lights furnished on application

An assortment of chandeliers always on hand.

K. Murakami.
Photograph Studio
Chinkokai, Seoul.

Printing, Developing and Enlargement, of Photographs always Undertaken.

Korean Views and Pictures Illustrating Native Customs always on Sale,

THE OSAKA SHOSEN KAISHA.

Boats frequently on the berth for Chinnampo.

REGULAR SAILINGS BETWEEN JAPAN AND KOREAN PORTS

FUSAN AND KOBE VIA SHIMONOSEKI.

OSAKA VIA MOKPO, FUSAN, SHIMONOSEKI AND KOBE.

MOJI DIRECT.

OSAKA VIA KUNSAN, MASANPO, FUSAN, SHIMONOSEKI AND KOBE.

CHEMULPO KUNSAN LINE,
Every three days

CHEMULPO CHINNAMPO LINE.
Every three days

For Freight and passage and further particulars apply to

THE OSAKA SHOSEN KAISHA,
Chemulpo.

RONDON, PLAISANT & CO.

General Storekeepers and Merchants, Ships Contractors, Tobacconists, Commission and Forwarding Agents, Coal Merchants

IMPORTERS AND EXPORTERS

Seoul Chemulpo.

W. D. WENTWORTH.

LANDING AND SHIPPING AGENT.
AND
CUSTOMS BROKER.

12 OURA, NAGASAKI.

STEWARD & CO.

Chemulpo.

Shipchandlers and Storekeepers, Naval and Mercantile Contractors, Landing and Shipping Agents.

STEWARD'S HOTEL

Chemulpo.

Best accommodation in the port for travellers. Clean and well-aired rooms, good cuisine and prompt attendance, moderate tariff.

등 진병근
○임비서원승서주임관륙등 경상룡 김요셥
○중종이품가션대부군부협판 표영쟝 리운화
○중정삼품통정대부비서원승 표등경 김형수 고광찰 김황
비샹호령이탈리ᄒᆞ야병시 중지
○중구품통사랑중학교교관 교학성 김지귀
학령이탈리ᄒᆞ야시이 중지
○중경이품자헌대부내부대신 중참찬 신셩구
○중종이품가션대부의정부참찬 고군수 신언모
○중정삼품통정대부비서원승 야화장례 신광룡
이상중이품가션대부의정부 참정신태휴교조교중조교의 범연츄 중
○임 슈릉령서관임팔졍등 의릉령 노셕삼
○임 의릉령서관임팔졍등 륭릉 리응국
○임 공릉참봉서관임관팔등 홍순삼
이상일월삼십일일

○구별도세산표 [속]

군부소관

뎨신수관 헌병ᄉᆞ령부 오쳔쳘빅륙원
뎨일항 봉급 삼쳔이빅오십원
뎨이항 쳥비 이빅오십원
뎨삼항 수츌급료 륙빅오십원
뎨사항 용인비 일빅팔십원
뎨오항 령사비 삼빅팔십원
뎨륙항 마량비 이빅팔십원
뎨칠항 마장비 수십륙원
뎨팔항 피복비 삼빅팔십원
뎨구항 보슈비 삼빅오십원

뎨빅신오관 헌병ᄃᆡ 십삼만구빅삼십이원
뎨일항 봉급 일만일쳔빅삼십원
뎨이항 쳥비 이쳔칠빅원
뎨삼항 쳥수슈리비 이빅오십원
뎨사항 수츌급료 수만오쳔구빅십팔원
뎨오항 량샤비 삼만팔쳔수빅오십삼원
뎨륙항 마량비 팔쳔삼빅오십이원
뎨칠항 마장비 일쳔이빅뉵십오원
뎨팔항 피복비 일만칠쳔팔빅이십원
뎨구항 보슈비 일쳔팔빅원
뎨십항 근무비 일쳔이빅원
뎨십일항 계쳔비 일빅수십수원
뎨십이항 쳐료비 이빅칠십원
뎨십삼항 미장비 팔십원
뎨십수항 용인비 일쳔이빅원
뎨십오항 려비 일빅오십원
뎨십륙항 긔밀비 이빅원

론셜

일진회의행위

○일본인이일진회의죠직으로 셔울의경찰권을피탈ᄒᆞᄂᆞᆫ광계를엇은후에시골회원들은다도라가셔다시명령ᄒᆞᆷ을기다린다ᄂᆞᆫ되시골회원들은셔울에올나오기ᄂᆞᆫ슈이나셔와셔무슴큰슈나날줄노아랏다가지금랑ᄑᆡᄒᆞ야도라갓거니와셔울에잇ᄂᆞᆫ회원들은여젼이열심ᄒᆞᄂᆞᆫ지라

ᄒᆞᆫ리학자가말ᄒᆞ엿스되아모리도ᄒᆞᆫ얼덕우희셔ᄒᆞᆫ눈덩이들을니기ᄂᆞᆫ용이ᄒᆞ다ᄒᆞ엿스니그말이을튼다말인얼덕에눈이만히ᄒᆞ엿스면그우에셔져운눈덩이로미ᄂᆞᆫ힘만되엿스면큰경은ᄒᆞᆫ큰눈덩이가될지니그것이일본인교모ᄒᆞ라ᄂᆞᆫ자가일진회들자ᄒᆞᆫ것과갓도다

비우에말ᄒᆞᆫ리학자가ᄯᅩ말ᄒᆞ되그눈덩이들굴니기ᄂᆞᆫ쉬우나그거슬졍지ᄒᆞ게ᄒᆞ라면밋칭ᄒᆞᆫ사ᄅᆞᆷ이라ᄒᆞ시드라야ᄒᆞᆫ다ᄒᆞ엿스니일진회들두고죵비ᄒᆞᆫ말이로다일진회의본리목젹ᄋᆞᆫ돈무엇이던지이젼스나그가랑ᄒᆞ구셔ᄂᆞᆫ오륙가지나되지만ᄂᆞᆫ지금ᄋᆞᆫ다흘넛도다일진회원들이샹을사시다가지금ᄋᆞᆫ일이ᄭᅳᆫ너저셔ᄒᆞ고시부젓스되

본회의목젹은졍부를기량ᄒᆞ란홈이더니본회의조직ᄒᆞᆫ후로일본헌병이셔울경찰권을피탈ᄒᆞ야안령질셔를유지ᄒᆞ니시골회원들은만일일본계밧ᄂᆞᆫ날이잇거던근쳐에일본병수의게고소ᄒᆞ야병수가공수의게보ᄒᆞ게ᄒᆞ라ᄒᆞ엿스니모다말ᄒᆞ되그회ᄂᆞᆫ일본인의젼봉이라ᄒᆞ더라더라

우리보기에ᄂᆞᆫ일진회원들이단단히색리를박고일본인들은생각ᄒᆞ되일진회ᄂᆞᆫ에국ᄒᆞᄂᆞᆫ회사인고로무엇시던지그회원들이ᄒᆞᄂᆞᆫ거슨다시졍귀션에열심ᄒᆞᄂᆞᆫ거스로들너보니ᄂᆞᆫ지라

일본인이아모ᄯᅢ라도죵ᄉᆞ쟝ᄒᆞᆯ계계가잇슬거시일진회들에국ᄒᆞᄂᆞᆫ회사라고칭찬ᄒᆞ고찬조ᄒᆞ야지금은그회에셔마음ᄃᆡ로무슴일이던지ᄒᆞ게되엿스니만일그회의주쟝ᄒᆞᄂᆞᆫ사ᄅᆞᆷ들이져의들의찬셩원의게향ᄒᆞ야월급을만히ᄂᆞ리ᄂᆞᆫ딥나ᄒᆞ면셔만일아니ᄂᆞ리주면셔ᄂᆞᆫ편으로간니가졋다ᄒᆞ리경이면그ᄯᅢ가셔ᄂᆞᆫ일본사람이무엇이라ᄒᆞ고말ᄒᆞᆯ티인가이세쳐지날뒤거슬보면일진회에셔

칙명을로횡ᄒᆞ지라ᄒᆞᄂᆞᆫ것도거역ᄒᆞ엿지마ᄂᆞᆫ만일져의들이장못ᄒᆞ엿다고사과ᄒᆞ면용셔ᄒᆞ기ᄂᆞᆫ쉬운일이오그보다더ᄒᆞᆫ일이잇스란변쟈의들의머리를터시기로ᄒᆞ고그젼ᄒᆞᆫ됫쟈업으로도라가기도ᄒᆞᆯ지라

봉급을며ᄂᆞᆯ터닐나고야단치기가되우죠ᄒᆞᆫ계제이니엇더ᄒᆞᆫ지일진회원들은유등무샹이로다

잡보

○연초회사 한동일한연초회사에셔계죠ᄒᆞᄂᆞᆫ권연초죠일표가대일반칭찬ᄒᆞ고수입이츠츠증왕ᄒᆞ더니지금ᄂᆞᆫ츠츠본을더드리라계비관들더사다가놋ᄂᆞᆫ다더라

○광계반포과 광계리경안은경성일일오후두시에반포ᄒᆞ기로일젼각의에취결이되엿더라

○젼교과설치 이젼관계ᄂᆞᆫ일병풍시가되ᄂᆞᆫ고로대광들이모도소직ᄒᆞᆫ다ᄒᆞ매경부에ᄂᆞᆫ원인을뢰용ᄒᆞᆯ츠로젼교과를셜치ᄒᆞᆫ다더라

○공진회폐지 공진회ᄂᆞᆫ지쟉일에일본군ᄉᆞ령부에셔명령ᄒᆞ야폐지식엿더라

○국분셰공홈 일본공ᄉᆞ관셔긔관국분상퇴탁씨가지작일에너부로공함ᄒᆞ기를원금에드ᄂᆞᆫ즉작일에졍부에셔귀회ᄒᆞ엿다ᄒᆞ니과연이면환산경시의항통지수ᄂᆞᆫ결졍이되엿ᄂᆞᆫ지아니되엿ᄂᆞᆫ지그뢰회들회시ᄒᆞᆯ을바란노라ᄒᆞ엿더라

○일ᄉᆞ공함 일본공사기너부로공함ᄒᆞ기를이번에군샤항감리경향쇼가젼임이되엿ᄂᆞᆫ뒤동항귀국상민이일동ᄒᆞ야우리령수뒤리의게쇼거ᄒᆞ야허갑리를잉임케ᄒᆞᄂᆞᆫ운동에조력ᄒᆞ니청컨딕환임케ᄒᆞ라ᄒᆞ엿더라

○일ᄉᆞ우함 일본공ᄉᆞ가ᄯᅩ너부로공함ᄒᆞ기를황히도안악군슈김용악이가부임ᄒᆞᆫ이래로가세를슈렴ᄒᆞ며그부하의항쟝과순교들도산ᄒᆞᆫ군수의ᄆᆞᆺ치벗셩을괴롭게ᄒᆞᄂᆞᆫ고로우리진남포령수가ᄒᆞ는인민의곤경에ᄃᆡᄒᆞ야그구제ᄒᆞᆯ방책을위ᄒᆞ여보낸샹히기세의별지쳥원을부송ᄒᆞ니탕ᄒᆞ게죠치ᄒᆞ라ᄒᆞ엿더라

○졍부회의 지작분월일일에졍부에셔관제리졍안건으로ᄯᅩ회의가되엿다라

○잠ᄃᆡ반송 지금음력셜을당ᄒᆞ엿ᄂᆞᆫ고로각군ᄃᆡ에셔소들장아쟝인의게우금ᄒᆞ엿더라

○비샹샹쳥 향쟈에탁지대신민영긔씨와일본공ᄉᆞ림권죠씨가챠관수진으로상지ᄒᆞ매에일본공ᄉᆞ의말이잠오을미년간에본방인민과병뎡의손히가만흔지라이거슬비샹ᄒᆞ라ᄒᆞᆫ즉탁지가티답ᄒᆞ기를쳥오년에일쳥교젼ᄒᆞᆯ세에일본군ᄉᆞ상에인연ᄒᆞ야광산와샹남의경세의손히가불소ᄒᆞ니이거슬비샹ᄒᆞ라ᄒᆞᆫ즉다시ᄂᆞᆫ경볼거론이라ᄒᆞ엿다라

○쟝씨의운 아라보셩교지사ᄂᆞᆫ쟝보혁씨가금년가을에탕남사ᄂᆞᆫ김대형이라ᄒᆞᄂᆞᆫ사람의게돈몃만량을취급ᄒᆞ엿더니김대현의부친이샹경ᄒᆞ야말ᄒᆞ기를쟝씨가유인주ᄃᆡᄒᆞ야괴인편지라ᄒᆞ고경무청에정ᄒᆞ야쟝씨와ᄌᆡ판ᄒᆞ야김씨가락과ᄒᆞ고쟝씨산한셩부에졍소ᄒᆞ야쟈판파혹ᄒᆞᆫ지라그후에ᄂᆞᆫ엇더케주션ᄒᆞ엿던지일본수령부에졍소ᄒᆞ며일헌병이쟝씨를착거ᄒᆞ야분ᄂᆞᆫ곡직ᄒᆞᆫ고무슈란리ᄒᆞ고팔구일을착슈ᄒᆞ다가돈이젼여원을못밧치라ᄒᆞᄂᆞᆫ고로세부등이ᄒᆞ야져작일에죠수히빗쳔죵ᄒᆞᆫ셩지판소로뤌송ᄒᆞ엿더라

○동리강리면보 동리감리가외부로면보ᄒᆞ기를교셥수안으로발착의게죠회ᄒᆞ엿더니엇지죠쳐ᄒᆞᄂᆞᆫ지회시ᄒᆞ라ᄒᆞ셧더라

○회쥬군수면보 회쥬군수가외부로면보ᄒᆞ기를일인칭수가본회토젹거ᄒᆞᆯ추로징을통당포에긴쥭ᄒᆞᆯ뜻으로쳥원ᄒᆞ오니그허시여부를회시ᄒᆞ라ᄒᆞ엿더라

○죠복발관 외부에셔법공관에죠복ᄒᆞ기를귀국샹민롱등이가인쳔에잇셔일인오가와라로더브러니단을져정ᄒᆞᆫ수ᄂᆞᆫ일이티방에잇고본대신이그경리를아지못ᄒᆞ겟고셜결리가능히일을판단ᄒᆞ야명빅히졍ᄒᆞᆯ것이니쳥컨대귀국령수가ᄌᆡ결리로디브리판관ᄒᆞ이가ᄒᆞ다ᄒᆞ엿더라

○쳔왕탈셜 젼셰를드른즉의쳔왕이미국상항으로브티비락ᄅᆞ코ᄯᅥᄂᆞᆫ지오래되엿다며라

○려관샹쵝 이월일일밤두시량에졍동법국려관에셔실화ᄒᆞ엿ᄂᆞᆫ되그ᄯᅢ에일본병뎡과한국슌검이합력ᄒᆞ야구화ᄒᆞᄂᆞᆫ되블힝즁다힝이바람이업셔ᄂᆞᆫ고로비구에화광을박멸ᄒᆞ엿고ᄯᅩ히리관의ᄌᆞ물을대강운츌ᄒᆞ엿고그로방에셧ᄂᆞᆫ편젼죵와면젼이소화ᄒᆞ엿슴으로동서빈에셔그소화ᄒᆞᆫ면젼을슈리ᄒᆞᄂᆞᆫ중이라ᄒᆞ며라

○평뎡부수 동문밧총동히자뇌에엇더ᄒᆞᆫ병뎡이형티며죽엿논되모자가엿시빌며리로죽엇다더라

○별죵평보 금에은음력원월초칠일고로이회후진ᄒᆞ엿다가음력월초오일브터속간ᄒᆞ겟스오니 에듕쳠군자ᄂᆞᆫ 죠량ᄒᆞ시옵.

THE WAR.

There is a very marked absence of news from the Shaho and Hunho. As a rule, news of Japanese successes reach Seoul very quickly.

JAPANESE IN THE PALACE.

Some time ago we suggested that the Japanese were using the infamous Il-chin-hoi as a means towards getting control of the palace.

We now learn from a Japanese journal, the "Daihan Ilpo" that:—

"Of late the sorcerers in the Palace have disturbed the peace of the Emperor, so from now on the Japanese gendarmerie will assume control of the palace.

THE STRIKES IN RUSSIA.

According to Tokio telegrams published by Japanese papers, 5000 agitators have been arrested and sentenced to exile.

It having been officially stated in Russia that the strikes owed their origin to assistance from England the British Ambassador has lodged a protest with the Foreign Office.

It is also reported that there is considerable indignation in Europe at the drastic measures which are being employed to quell the disturbances.

On Thursday night the Hotel du Palais was destroyed by fire.

Nothing new has transpired in connection with the projected loan. We presume the Japanese are doing as they like.

A proposal is on foot to appoint only Japanese-speaking magistrates to the districts in North and South Ham Kyeng provinces.

A telegram received at the Foreign Office contains a Reuter message dated Penang, January 20, to the effect that four Japanese warships are in the neighbourhood of Pulo Lancava island, north of Penang.

A lively fight is going on in London between the "Daily Mail and Messrs. Chappell & Co., the former having embarked upon the publication of music at cheap prices and the latter having declined to consider manuscripts from composers who issue their copyright music in cheap editions.

Mr. Megata, the adviser to the Financial Department, and General Hasegawa are apparently in the habit of applying for audiences entirely at their own convenience. The Emperor has intimated that they will be informed through the proper channels when His Majesty is willing to receive them.

The Japanese telegraphic reports of the operations on the Shaho which have arrived today are all obscure. From a mass of undecipherable names of places, etc, we gather that the operations involved the whole of the front of both armies and that the Russians in one action lost 1,200 in killed and wounded. No particulars of Japanese casualties are given.

The "Asahi" says, in summarizing the situation in Russia, that if the Tsar yields one point the populace would follow it with ten, and there will be no stopping in popular demands, so that nothing like mutual concession now appears possible between the ruler and the ruled. Unlike the "Kokumin," the "Asahi" does not hesitate to say openly that the Neva strike proved that Russian labour is in revolt, and the gun incident that the revolutionary spirit has taken root in the Army. Russia is to be sympathized with for all this, but, it says, this trend of affairs there is rather to be welcomed for the sake of humanity and the peace of the world.

THE AMERICAN TRUSTS

San Francisco, Dec. 28.—An action has been instituted in the Superior Court of New York City for the dissolution of the paper trust, and the directors and promoters of the corporation have been indicted for fraud and various infractions of the law. The investigation which led to the arrest of the directors of the company is part of a general plan to enquire into the formation and busines methods of all trusts throughout the State. The prosecution of the smaller corporations was inspired by sensational disclosures recently made by Thomas W. Lawson in his crusade against the giant trusts of United States.

It is understood that a certain foreigner from Yokohama is being detained either at Kobe or Moji pending the necessary examination.

Collins who was arrested in Yokohama on suspicion of being a Russian spy, has been tried and sentenced to eleven years penal servitude.

Official statistics show that the number of offences committed in Tokyo Fu during 1903 was 39,557. Of the total, forgery of coin reached 363; robbery, 186, theft from vessels, 1,119; theft from hotels, 640; theft from private dwellings etc., 5,871; fraud, 2,670; incendiarism, 146; and sundries, including those charged with having infringed various regulations, 2,555. The numbers of cases of theft and fraud are gradually increasing.

A Liberal organ at Berlin writes to the following effect:—In addition to the plucky foreign enemy, the Russian Government has now to fight with a domestic enemy. As there exist close relations between the foreign enemy and the revolutionary movement, the Tsar and his Ministers now find themselves between two fires. Japan is evidently pleased with the turn events are taking in Russia, and it will be to Japan's advantage to cause the news of the trouble to be widely scattered among the troops under General Kuropatkin.

As an evidence of how very little "say" Koreans are allowed in their affairs we may cite the case of Mr. Maruyama, the new police adviser. According to the Japanese newspapers Mr. Maruyama was appointed some weeks ago, but according to fact his appointment is not yet *un fait accompli* and the Japanese are exhibiting considerable impatience and anxiety on the subject.

An English paper remarks that all his old characteristics were exhibited by John Roberts on his reappearance in December at the Argyll Hall, London; his apparent carelessness, his jerky style of play, its brilliancy from a spectacular point of view, and his occasional bad missing. The financial difficulties from which he has suffered seem to have impaired his powers very little, although his hair and beard are perceptibly whiter. His reception was, of course, immense and he received it with his customary staid dignity. His play, at the age of fifty-five, is a decisive answer to the dictum that this is the age of infant prodigies and young men.

An hysterical act of feminine unreason has nearly cost the life of one of the highest functionaries of the Paris Law Courts. A Mdme. Moret had acted as housekeeper to a gentleman named Moitiet, who had left her a comfortable provision, of which she was deprived by legal technicalities. These technicalities she did not understand herself, and she seems to have thought that it would be a comfort to shoot somebody who did. She selected the Procureur-General, and went to the Court of Cassation for the purpose. As the Procureur was out she inquired for his substitute, and was introduced to M. Bonnisseau, on whom she fired at sight "on general principles." The bullet only grazed his shoulder lightly, and the lady was handed over for medical examination, after firing two more harmless shots.

DISCOVERY OF A COALFIELD IN KOREA.

The "Chugai Shogyo" learns that a Mr. T. Kida has discovered a coalfield in Kyong-sang-do, Korea, consisting of two strata, the upper being 10 ft. 9 in thickness and the lower 6 ft. 2 in. The coal is stated to be suitable for steam purposes. The coalfield in question is, it is futher stated, situated about one and a half mile from a bay, which can amply accommodate ships of 3,000 tons.

Mr. Kida, who had been at home of late, again started for Korea several days ago, accompanied by an expert to carry out further examinations.—Japan Times.

GENEROUS JAPAN.

The "Osaka Asahi" believes itself reliably informed when it reports that the Japanese Government has decided to grant mining concessions in Korea to foreigners, and would regard the decision an opportuneone. Mining operations necessitate the sinking of large capital, and under the present circumstances foreign concessionaires may with advantage be allowed to undertake them, provided they do not inferfere with the Japanese and Korean interests. The creation of new mining centres in Korea will both directly and indirectly benefit the labour and supply markets of the two countries; besides the granting of the concessions will be in consonance with the Japanese policy of the open door and equality for commercial and industrial opportunities in the Far East.

RUSSIA ALREADY BEATEN.

Berlin, Dec. 21.—General Meckel, formerly military adviser to the Japanese, is quoted as saying that the German general staff concurs in his conviction that the Russians have not the faintest chance of winning the war, the result of which is already irrevocably decided. Admiral Rojestvensky will be as powerless as Gen. Kuropatkin is to turn the scale in Russia's favour. Gen. Meckel does not believe that the present tranquility in Manchuria will continue through the winter, but he says that Field Marshal Oyama is wise to deter attacking, is possible, until the fall of Port Arthur affords him big reinforcements especially of artillery.

The "Krese Zeitung," which is very influential in conservate military circles, is gravely impressed by General Meckel's statements. It preaches the yellow peril, and exhorts the white nations to organize diplomatic opposition to the aspirations of Japan, which it declares, menace Great Britain in India, France in Siam and Tonquin, and the United States in the Philippines.

FINANCIAL TROUBLES IN JAPAN.

The half yearly meeting of the Teikoku Shogyo Gingo (Imperial Commercial Bank), held in Tokio on Wednesday morning, was marked with disorderly scenes. Mr. K. Magoshi presided. The Chairman, in moving the adoption of the business report for the half year just ended, stated that, owing to the inactivity in the Kyushu coal trade last year, the Moji Branch of the bank lost during the term under review 115,000 yen in the form of loans, while the heavy fall in the value of various stocks held by the bank caused a further loss of some 36,000 yen. These losses had all been defrayed from the special reserve fund. On the conclusion of his speech, numerous questions were addressed to Mr. Magoshi by the discontented shareholders, and several proposals, among which was one censuring the Board of Directors, were successively introduced but were eventually abandoned. The report and accounts were finally passed amid a scene of great disorder.

According to a London telegram dated Jan. 26 both Japanese and Russian bonds advanced seven eighths on that day.

THE SIBERIAN RAILWAY.

Reports received in Tokyo, says the "Japan Times," state that traffic on the Siberian railway has been partially suspended owing to the snow. Quantities of munitions of war have now accumulated at Baikal and neighbouring districts, and more than 100 freight cars laden with provisions for the front have also been detained at the trans-Baikal railway. According to another message, there is a great scarcity of provisions at Vladivostock, owing to the suspension of supplies from both land and sea.

In conection with the above, a report received in official quarters states:—

The railway between Slatoust and Samara was blocked on the 21st inst, due to the snowfall of the past few days. The railway employes are engaged in the removal of the snow, but traffic is unusually delayed. At every station between Samara and Belebei there are three to five trains, which are despatched in turn at intervals of eight hours, Under these circumstances the Department of Public Works and Railway, after consulting with the Navy Department, has taken steps to remove the snow by employing those troops who happen to be snow bound during their transportation to the front, the men receiving wages for their labour. Four locomotives, specially constructed for the removal of snow, are now in use on the railway. Owing to this stoppage of military trains, the transportation of cereals recently permitted for certain towns along the line, has now again been prohibited.

Our reporter says:—One of Korean police men who was drunk had been arrested by Japanese police man for that drunken one spoken somethin g impolite, to that Jap police man but he was released.

The Korea Daily News.

Issued at 5 P. M. daily except Sundays.

Rate of Subscription:—

Per Year,............Yen 25.
Per Quarter,..........Yen 7.
Per Month,..........Yen 2.50.

Postage in Korea not charged extra.
Postage abroad charged extra.

Advertisements, 50 sen per day for 1 inch or less.
5 yen per month per inch.
50 yen per year per inch.

All communications to

E. T. BETHELL,
Editor and Publisher,
Pak-tong, Seoul.

NOTICE.

February 4th, 5th and 6th being Korean National Holidays, there will be no issue of the KOREA DAILY NEWS on those dates.

JAPANESE POLICING.

Having assumed control of, and responsibility for, the Seoul Police, the Japanese will find that they have a nice little claim on their hands.

During the fire which occurred on Wednesday night at the Hotel du Palais the premises of Mr. Victor Goldstein, watchmaker and jeweller which are near, but not next, the Hotel du Palais were entered by the Japanese military and the general populace and very completely looted.

Mr. and Mrs. Goldstein were present but helpess; directly the fire started they were turned out of their premises by the Japanese gendarmes who assumed control although there was no immediate danger of the fire spreading to their house.

We do not think there can be any question as to the responsibility of the Japanese for the stolen property, and as the loss is a very serious one to Mr. Goldstein we trust that no time will be lost in affording them satisfaction.

THE CAPTAIN KETTLES OF PORT ARTHUR.

AN EXPLANATION OF THE BLOCKADE RUNNERS' TACTICS.

The following exposition of the wiles and methods of blockake runners of Port Arthur recently appeared in The Times:—

203-Metre Hill, near Port Arthur, stands well back north by a little west of the new twn, which lies on a gentle sloping plain running back about a mile and a-half from western harbour. The new town has hitherto been almost immune from shell fire, and its wide streets, completed and half-built public offices, hotels, and houses of business were all intact until recently. The pleasure park, the acres of Chinese vegetable gardens, once only corn fields, all surrounded by an amphitheatre of hills and facing towarde the western harbour, have all been a source of health and pleasure to the beleaguered inhabitants, and an asylum from their enemy's long-distance fire. Port Arthur New Town (Novoe Gorod) was clean and fresh, owing to which the sick and wounded have done fairly well.

During the past months hundreds of Chinese junks have found their way from Chefoo, Teng-chang-fu, Tientsin, and elsewhere with tons of fresh provisions, vegetables, and fruit, which they landed on the land at the remoter side of the western harbour. The Northern Chinese junks of the medium size make first-class blockade-runners. They are built very low, their waists are almost awash when loaded, the low hatchways are always securely battened down, and only at the stern and bow do these craft seem to rise above the water-line. They are of immense strength, flat-bottomed, and of dirty plain wood, with no bright colour about them. Dodging along near shore, or amongst the numerous islets of brown rock which extend from the Shangtung coast across the mouth of the Gulf of Pechi-li to the Port Arthur promontory, these junks look exactly like low rocks, even when their brown sails are hoisted. Knowing the tides and taking advantage of the familiar and strong currents, these fearless Shantung sailors and fishermen have run many a cargo into Port Arthur. Their craft are often propelled by from ten to twenty oarsmen, like the old Norse galleys, and thus, with no noise or smoke, glide from islet to islet and make across to the Liaoshan Promontory, where they quickly find security by hugging the shore under the brown cliffs, well out of Japanese gunshot and within the belt of Russian mines. At night, with the searchlights playing on the water, all is darkness near the cliffs, while the rocks, well known to the junksmen, cause them no alarm. The frequent and dense fogs of autumn favoured them.

Should these adventurers be caught in crossing by the Japanese they are always "en route for Dalny, Pitszewo, or Kin-chau with supplies for the Japanese." A few have been caught and dealt with but generally the kindhearted Japanese believe their story and simply with, them go on towards some place which they have sworn they were bound for. A few, however, have been confiscated. These northern, lowbuilt, and very heavily-timbered junks will float in a rougher sea than an ordinary torpedo-boat can live in. The pay is good and sure, and these enterprising Shantung men are fond of gambling and games of chance, and enjoy running the blockade of Port Arthur.

THE QUESTION OF NEUTRALITY.

The "Jiji's Peking correspondent wires as follows:—

Commanded by the Empress Dowager and the Emperor, and urged by Viceroy Yuen Shihkai, the Chinese Government on the evening of January 21st forwarded a reply to the American Legation at Peking in connection with the U. S. Government's advice in reference to China's neutrality. The reply states that China has not violated her neutrality nor will she do so in the future. Incidentally the charges preferred by the Russian Government are refuted to the following effect:—

1.—China has never offered the service of the mounted bandits to the Japanese Army. The use, however, of the mounted bandits by a foreign army as initiated by a Russian officer, Lieut.-Colonel Madrinoff, and the Chinese army, whose power does not prevail in Manchuria, cannot prevent the bandits from joining either belligerent.

2.—It is untrue that the Chinese police or army employs Japanese instructors.

3.—China has never given any tacit or explicit permission to export contraband articles to the Japanese forces. Under strict insructions from the Government, the customs houses have never given given clearance to any vessels bound for Dalny or other places occupied by the Japanese.

4.—China has never leased the Miao Islands as a Japanese naval base.

5.—The Taya Iron mine business is governed by a contract between Japanese and Chinese merchants, and not between the Japanese and Chinese Government.

The Chinese Government, while telegraphically communicating the above reply to the Chinese Ministers abroad, alleges that Russia has infringed China's neutrality, first, by attempting to smuggle an enormous quentity of arms and ammunition to Port Arthur via Kalgan and Shanhaikwan; secondly, by sending her troops throughout Mongolia for requisition purposes; and thirdly, by causing the Captain of the "Riesitelini" to escape from detention.

THE JAPANESE POINT OF VIEW.

The "Jiji" says the facts revealed by the capitulation of Port Arthur came as a surprise, in that the enemy there gave up his defence, having so much to fight with left in his hand. But on a second thought—which takes into consideration the friction that existed between the naval and military elements that constituted the enemy; the dissension of views among the officers who could not free their mind from the notion that they were being made victims of the blundering bureaucray; the feeling of dissatisfaction that was general among the rank and file,—it must be admitted that the defence was well maintained, and General Stoessel and the whole garrison should be credited with great gallantry. The fact remains, however, that disunion, and the revolt of men in mind, if not in act, caused the fall of the place. The same logic may be applied to the state of things in Russia at present, and we are therefore masters of the situation in the war. It may be incomprehensible to the Japanese that, however great their grievances may be, and however great their ignorance, the Russian workers should indulge in uprising just when their country is in the throes of a foreign war. But the matter must be looked at from their point of view. The bureaucracy wants them to fight; but what for? In order that the bureaucrats may remain their rulers. What are the masses to gain should Russia win in the struggle? Absolutely nothing; but in the meantime, when called upon, they must go to the front to be shot. No wonder they cry for the cessation of the campaign. Even the educated classes are now in full sympathy with them. The opportunity is most favourable to us, and we should be stronger than ever in our determination to carry the war to the finish. The world recognizes the justice of our cause. Moreover the down-trodden and enslaved millions of Russia cry for help. The peace of the Far East and the cry of humanity demand, says the "Jiji," that we must not stop the war till our noble end is attained.

The Korea Daily News.

VOL. II, FRIDAY, FEBRUARY 3, 1905. No. 27

大韓每日申報
대한매일신보

(뎨이권이십팔호) (슈요일) 일쳔구빅오년이월팔일

본사고빅

이신보는영어와한어로셕거미일츌판ᄒᆞ옵

신문가

한쟝 엽두돈오푼

일삭표 엽두량닷돈

우표가미삭닷돈

다맛돈으로밧숩

광고료는

귀한의쟝단과ᄌᆞ힝의다쇼로중감ᄒᆞ되렴가로밧을터이오며오리지아녀대한사람마다다이신문을보실터이니광고내시기를원ᄒᆞ시는이들은우리신문샤에와셔면약ᄒᆞ심을희망ᄒᆞ옵

○발힝소 박동대한미일신보샤법어학교압헤젼영국인셜필림집자리오

사쟝 영국인 (비셜)

평양 뒤리졈

○평양효동사는권미보씨로우리신문판미뒤리인을뎡ᄒᆞ엿ᄉᆞ오니평양에계신구람코져ᄒᆞ시는쳠군ᄌᆞ는뒤리졈에왕림ᄒᆞ와면의ᄒᆞ시옵

사고

○우리대한미일신보의목뎍은대한의안녕질셔에관한모든뎨목에뒤ᄒᆞ야는공평한변론을쥬쟝ᄒᆞᆷ이라우리동신원의담보는신문보시는쳠군ᄌᆞ의계홍상보도ᄒᆞ리며편지들긔셔ᄒᆞ여주셔는이는셩명과반뒤를젹어붓치서기를희망ᄒᆞ오니이거슬신문샹에긔지ᄒᆞ라는거시아니오다만극히신용ᄒᆞ는증거를숨고쟈ᄒᆞᆷ이라긔쟝ᄒᆞ는아모긔셔던지긔지ᄒᆞᆷ을되각ᄒᆞ는권리를가졋스나되각ᄒᆞ는리유를말ᄒᆞᆯ터이오며공즁평화를문란케ᄒᆞ는듯ᄒᆞᆫ긔셔는의례히밧지안켓숩나이다

●본사셜시이러로신문을미양우례로분젼ᄒᆞ와례젼부의임의로젼ᄒᆞᆫ듯스로면곳에는혹늣게젼ᄒᆞ기도ᄒᆞ며혹몃칠거슬ᄒᆞᆫ겁에젼ᄒᆞ기도ᄒᆞ며혹아니젼ᄒᆞ는곳도잇다ᄒᆞ와우리신문을ᄉᆞ랑ᄒᆞ야구람ᄒᆞ시는 쳠군ᄌᆞ의계뒤ᄒᆞ야미우미안ᄒᆞ옵기로지금온분젼인을두고미일일즉이젼ᄒᆞ며아니젼ᄒᆞ거나늣게거나ᄒᆞᆫ폐가업도록ᄒᆞ라ᄒᆞ오니혹아니젼ᄒᆞ거나혹늣게젼ᄒᆞ거나ᄒᆞᆫ일이잇스면본샤로통긔ᄒᆞ여쥬심을희망ᄒᆞ옵

잡보

○파슈병착거 남촌장동병문온친삼뒤병슌찰긔더인뒤삼작일샹오팔시량의슌찰긔디건너편일샹가에셔숫ᄒᆞᆫ셤을일어버린지라얼마아니잇다가히일인이숫도젹질ᄒᆞᆫ한인일명을잡아가지고파슈ᄒᆞ는병뎡의게압부ᄒᆞ엿더니그파슈병이그도젹놈을일어버린지라일샹삼ᄉᆞ인이리도ᄒᆞ야도젹놈을일어버렷다ᄒᆞ고그파슈병일명을일본병ᄉᆞ관으로잡아갓다더라

○위관통곡 일젼에죵로에셔엇더ᄒᆞᆫ평복ᄒᆞᆫ고머리싹근사름이히방곡슌검파무샹샹일이되엿던지슌검이그평복ᄒᆞᆫ사름을포박ᄒᆞ려ᄒᆞᆫ즉그평복ᄒᆞᆫ사름이말이나는친삼려디훈소뒤쟝고영셕이라ᄒᆞᆫ즉그긔디파슈병뎡들이말ᄒᆞ되이러ᄒᆞᆫ위관은우리도쳐음본다ᄒᆞᆫ뒤슌검이ᄒᆞᆫ손만포박ᄒᆞ엿다가곳노앗는뒤그위관말이몸이군인쥬임관이되야슌검의계포박ᄒᆞᆷ이창피라ᄒᆞ고통곡ᄒᆞ더라

○현씨귀국 일본에시찰로젼왕ᄒᆞᆫ현참장영운씨닉외가이월쵸싱에귀국ᄒᆞᆫ다고모모쳐에편지ᄒᆞ엿다더라

관보

뎨삼쳔오십삼호 광무구년이월삼일

셔임급ᄉᆞ령

○희경임황히도순회지판소판ᄉᆞ 법부참셔관 윤셩보

○면겸임인쳔항지판소판ᄉᆞ 졀인쳔감리 하상긔

○겸임인쳔항지판소판ᄉᆞ 인쳔감리 유 찬

이샹일월이십팔일

면본관 합경북도변계경무관 김병약

합경북도변계경무관 최남륭

○임합경북도변계경무관셔쥬임관륙등 칠픔 최병찬 칠픔빅락헌

이샹일월삼십일

○의원면본관 회령군슈 최병식 곡산군슈 리경직 임피군슈 빅남규 강동군슈 셔샹쥰 연풍군슈 리민제 닉부기ᄉᆞ 리긔영 장흥군슈 리희익 의쥬군슈 구완희 초산군슈 윤셕린 무쥬군슈 김션유 풍긔군슈 신명호

○임법부회계국쟝셔쥬임관일등 졍삼픔 리종셩

○임법부참셔관셔쥬임관삼등 졍삼픔 김긔죠

○임닉부기ᄉᆞ셔쥬임관륙등 륙품 박쥰용

○임경무쳥경무관셔쥬임관륙등 털도원기ᄉᆞ 셔회슌

○의원면본관 비셔원승 김요협 동신ᄉᆞ면화관쥬ᄉᆞ 빅익대 지룡참봉 리인환 법관양셩소박ᄉᆞ 윤일영 법관양셩소박ᄉᆞ 공면쥬 법관양셩소박ᄉᆞ 윤병슌 법관양셩소박ᄉᆞ 최창리 법관양셩소박ᄉᆞ 허 식 법관양셩소박ᄉᆞ 리종우 법관양셩소박ᄉᆞ 리용셜 법관양셩소교관 홍틱한길 법관양셩소교관 김병션형

○명비셔원승셔칙임관삼등 충청남도관찰ᄉᆞ 심건틱

○명닉쟝원경셔칙임관삼등 종이품 김지슌

○겸임태의원소경 비셔원승 신헌균

○임 지룡참봉셔판임관팔등 박용식

○면중계 륙품 신셕린

○중구품종ᄉᆞ랑중학교교관 고학생 죠한규

○명림시셔리참모부총쟝ᄉᆞ무 효힝탁리ᄒᆞ야시이 중직 군부대신 권중현

○임법관양셩쇼박ᄉᆞ셔판임관륙등 윤형중 리힝션 리종악 김문영 리명세

○임법관양셩소교관셔판임관륙등 비동렴 박규슌

○경위원경무관셔쥬임관륙등 경위원총슌 리덕슌

○임경위원총슌셔판임관륙등 김창슈

이샹이월일일

○의원면본관 닉부쥬ᄉᆞ 죠졍희

○임닉부쥬ᄉᆞ셔판임관륙등 죠중탁

○승셔판임관삼등 닉부죵두ᄉᆞ기슈 리공우

이샹이월이일

○구년도예산표 〔속〕

뎨십륙관 륙군법원 팔쳔륙빅칠십ᄉᆞ원

뎨일항 봉급 륙쳔오빅원

뎨이항 청비 구빅륙십원

뎨삼항 쳥ᄉᆞ슈리비 일빅오십원

뎨ᄉᆞ항 잡급급잡비 팔빅

뎨오항 려비 아빅원

뎨십칠관 륙군감옥 삼쳔칠빅륙십ᄉᆞ원

뎨일항 봉급 구빅원

뎨이항 쳥비 ᄉᆞ빅원

뎨삼항 쳥ᄉᆞ슈리비 일빅

뎨ᄉᆞ항 잡급급잡비 칠빅ᄉᆞ십ᄉᆞ원

뎨오항 죄슈비 일쳔륙빅이십원

뎨십팔관 륙군위싱원 일쳔ᄉᆞ빅칠원

뎨일항 청비 일쳔이빅구십일원

뎨이항 쳥ᄉᆞ슈리비 팔십원

뎨삼항 잡급급잡비 삼삼륙원

뎨십구관 무예청 일만삼천칠빅오십일원

뎨일항 잡급급잡비 일만삼쳔칠빅오십일원

뎨이십관 장츙단 이쳔ᄉᆞ빅ᄉᆞ원

뎨일항 청비 일쳔원

뎨이항 쳥ᄉᆞ슈리비 오빅원

뎨삼항 잡급급잡비 오빅

뎨ᄉᆞ항 치제비 ᄉᆞ빅원

뎨이십일관 군긔창 삼십칠만이빅오십칠원

뎨일항 봉급 일만이쳔구빅십이원

뎨이항 쳥비 륙쳔원

뎨삼항 쳥ᄉᆞ슈리비 이쳔원

뎨ᄉᆞ항 잡급급잡비 일만이쳔원

뎨오항 ᄉᆞ업비 삼십삼만칠쳔삼빅ᄉᆞ십오원

뎨이십이관 교육부 삼만이쳔이빅오십오원

UNION INSURANCE SOCIETY OF CANTON.

Head office Hongkong.
Marine risks underwritten at current rates.
Agents in Chemulpo,
E. MEYER & Co.

COMPAGNIE DES MESSAGERIES MARITIMES.

Fortnightly Direct Service.

For Marseilles
via Ports.
Sailing from Yokohama
Calling at Kobe,
Shanghai, Hongkong, Saigon, Singapore,
Colombo, Djibouti, Suez, Port Said
and Marseilles.

For particulars apply to
HOLME RINGER & Co.,
Chemulpo.

HAYASHIDA & CO.,
16 MYENG DONG, CHIN KO KAI, SEOUL.
BRANCH OFFICE AT CHEMULPO.

Money changers, Coal and Wood Merchants, Express Agents.

We are agents for the Pyeng-yang Coal Company and the Karazu Coal Company of Japan. We have the best quality of both anthracite and bituminous coal, and prompt execution of orders is our speciality. Firewood of all kinds kept in stock. Full weight guaranteed. Money of all denominations exchanged at current rates. Parcels received for all parts.

CHINA MUTUAL LIFE INS. OC.

Most favourable terms to policy holders.

Benefit system unsurpassed.

HOLME RINGER & Co.
Agents, Chemulpo.

C. P. R.

CANADIAN PACIFIC RAILWAY COMPANY'S ROYAL MAIL STEAMSHIP LINE.

THE FAST ROUTE BETWEEN CHINA, JAPAN, AND EUROPE VIA CANADA AND THE UNITED STATES.

Route from Hongkong via Shanghai, Nagasaki (Inland Sea of Japan) Kobe, Yokohama, Victoria and Vancouver.

Twin Screw Empress Steamship—6,000 Tons—Speed 19 knots.

PROPOSED SAILING FROM YOKOHAMA.
R. M. S. Empress of India.
R. M. S. Empress of Japan.
R. M. ? Empress of China.
R. M. S. Athenian.
R. M. S. Tartar.

Special reduction (first class only) granted to members of the Military, Naval, Diplomatic and Civil services and to Missionaries.

Passengers have choice of ten routes across the Continent of America and have privilege of travelling by any Atlantic Steamship Line.

Round the World passage tickets in connection with the P. and O. S. N., North German Lloyd and Messageries Co.'s **£125.**

All rates payable at current rate of exchange.

For further information, Tickets, Guide Books, etc., apply to

HOLME, RINGER & Co., AGENTS,
Chemulpo.

Grand Hotel,

(Formerly the Station Hotel)

Near the Railway Terminus, West Gate Seoul.

The Best Hotel in Korea
Handsome new Building.
Fine Airy Rooms
Excellent Cuisine.
Terms Moderate.
Special terms to Missionaries
and to permanent boarders.

Electric cars within 2 minutes' walk.

W. H. EMBERLEY.
Proprieto

EVERY FACILITY.

In connection with Life Assurance Business is afforded by

The Standard Life Assurance Co.,

One of the largest and wealthiest of the Provident Institutions of the United Kingdom Forms of Application and all information will be promptly afforded on application.

10 CENTS A DAY.

Not a very large expenditure is it? But it is sufficient to secure for a man of 30 a policy with the STANDARD LIFE OFFICE for

$1323.

For all particulars of rates, etc., apply to

Holme, Ringer & Co.,
Agents, Chemulpo.

THE NEW YORK LIFE INSURANCE COMPANY.

Have you ever been declined by any Company?

Are you engaged in a specially hazardous occupation?

Have you heard of the New York Life Insurance Company's New Classifications for this class of Risks?

If not, send your date of birth, occupation and particulars of rejection, if any to

E. MEYER & Co.,
Agents, Chemulpo.

MITSUI BUSSAN KAISHA.
(MITSUI & Co.)
MITSUI GINKO.
(MITSUI BANK.)

The Bank is owned by the members of the Mitsui Family, who, as partners, assume an unlimited responsibility for all liabilities of the Bank:—

Capital..........................Yen 5,000,000
Reserve Fund.................. " 5,600,000

HEAD OFFICE, TOKYO.
LONDON OFFICE, 34 LIME ST., E. C.

BRANCHES AND AGENCIES:—
New York, San Francisco, Hamburg, Bombay, Singapore, Manila, Hongkong, Amoy, Chefoo, Tientsin.

Kobe, Hakodate, Yokohama, Kure, Yokosuka, Moji, Shimonoseki, Miike, Wakamatsu, Nagasaki, Kuchinotsu, Karatsu, Sasebo, Misume, Taipeh, &c.

Telegraphic Address for all the Offices:
"MITSUI."
A. B. C. AND A. I CODES USED.

Contractors of Coal
To the Imperial Japanese Navy. Arsenals and Railway Bureau, Principal Railway Companies and Industrial Work, Home and Foreign Mail and Freight Steamers.

Sole Proprietors
Of the famous Miike, Tagawa and Yamano Coal Mines.

Sole Agents
For the sale of Fukumo, Hokoku, Ichimura Kanoda, Mannoura, Onoura, Ostuji, Sonoda Tsubaruro, Yoshinotani, Yoshio, Yurokibura and other coals.

YANGTSE INSURANCE ASSOCIATION, LTD.

The undersigned, having been appointed agents for the above company, are prepared to issue policies and pay losses on marine risks at regular rates.

E. MEYER & Co.,
Agents, Chemulpo.

AMERICAN KOREAN ELECTRIC CO.

Light and Power.

Main Office: Electric Building, Chong No.

RAILWAY DEPARTMENT.

OPERATING CARS BETWEEN EAST AND WEST GATE, EVERY TEN MINUTES:—

First Car leaves East Gate at 7:00 A. M. First Car leaves R. R. Station at 7:25 A. M
Last Car " East Gate at 8.40 P. M. Last " " R. R. Station at 9.05 P.M

OPERATING CARS BETWEEN EAST GATE AND IMPERIAL TOMB TERMINUS, EVERY TWENTY MINUTES:—

CONNECTING WITH EVERY ALTERNATE CAR ARRIVING AT EAST GATE FROM CHONG NO.

First Car leaves East Gate for Tomb at 7:10 A. M.
" " " Tomb for East Gate at 7:30 A. M.
Last " " East Gate for Tomb at 7:50 P. M.
" " " Tomb for East Gate at 8:10 P. M.

OPERATING CARS BETWEEN CHONG NO AND YUNG SAN RIVER EVERY TWELVE MINUTES:—

First Car leaves Chong No for South Gate at 7:12 A. M.
" " " Chong No for Yung San at 7:36 A. M.
" " " South Gate for Chong No at 7:20 A. M.
" " " Yung San for Chong No at 8:09 A. M.
Last " " South Gate for Chong No 9:00 P. M.
" " " Yung San for Chong No at 8.45. P. M.

SPECIAL PRIVATE CARS FURNISHED TO SUIT CONVENIENCE OF PATRONS. PRICES ON APPLICATION AT HEAD OFFICE.

LIGHTING DEPARTMENT

Where less than 250 candle power of light is used, the rate per month will be
Per 16 candle power incandescent lamp,—All night.—Yen 2.50.
32 candle power incandescent lamp:—All night:—Yen 4.00.
50 candle power incandescent lamp:—All night:—Yen 6.00.
150 " " " " " " 10.00.
1200 " " enclosed arc " " " " 20.00.

Where more than 250 candle power of light is used, a Meter will be installed, if requested:—Rent of Meter Yen 2.00 per month. Rate of charges by meter reading:—Two Sen per Ampere per hour. (Approximately this is equal to about One Sen per 16 C. P. lamp per hour) Minimum monthly charge where meter is installed, Yen 20.00 per month, which includes rental of meter.

Estimates for installing lights furnished on application

An assortment of chandeliers always on hand.

K. Murakami.
Photograph Studio
Chinkokai, Seoul.

Printing, Developing and Enlargement, of Photographs always Undertaken.

Korean Views and Pictures Illustrating Native Customs always on Sale,

---

THE OSAKA SHOSEN KAISHA.

Boats frequently on the berth for Chinnampo.

REGULAR SAILINGS BETWEEN JAPAN AND KOREAN PORTS.

FUSAN AND KOBE VIA SHIMONOSEKI.

OSAKA VIA MOKPO, FUSAN, SHIMONOSEKI AND KOBE.

MOJI DIRECT.

OSAKA VIA KUNSAN, MASANPO, FUSAN, SHIMONOSEKI AND KOBE.

CHEMULPO KUNSAN LINE,
Every three days.

CHEMULPO CHINNAMPO LINE.
Every three days.

For Freight and passage and further particulars apply to
THE OSAKA SHOSEN KAISHA,
Cemulpo

RONDON, PLAISANT & CO.

General Storekeepers and Merchants, Ships Contractors Tobacconists, Commission and Forwarding Agents, Coal Merchants

IMPORTERS AND EXPORTERS

Seoul Chemulpo.

W. D. WENTWORTH.

LANDING
AND
SHIPPING AGENT.
AND
CUSTOMS BROKER.

12 OURA, NAGASAKI.

STEWARD & CO.
Chemulpo.

Shipchandlers and Storekeepers, Naval and Mercantile Contractors, Landing and Shipping Agents.

STEWARD'S HOTEL
Chemulpo.

Best accommodation in the port for travellers. Clean and well-aired rooms, good cuisine and prompt attendance, oderate tariff.

[illegible]

론셜

[illegible]

잡보

[illegible]

외보

[illegible]

…의 승젼ᄒᆞ엿다는 소식은 셔울에 빈우승ᄒᆞ게 오는데 웬일인지

○로국에 혁명운동 일본신문지에 게지ᄒᆞᆫ 것을 본즉 오쳥명의 혁명당을 ᄒᆞᆼ포 [illegible] 도ᄒᆞ며 호유비 도ᄒᆞ엿다ᄒᆞ며 그 혁명당들을 장령으로 양제ᄒᆞᆷ으로 구쥬에셔 ᄃᆡ우 불평히 녀인다ᄒᆞ엿더라

○면보의 의미 사하에셔 싸홈 싸운 말을 보ᄒᆞᆫ 일본 면보가 일젼에 왓는데 그 면보는 도모지 알수 업는 것이 ᄃᆡ명도 희미ᄒᆞ거니와 그런데 로샹교ᄒᆞ야 본즉 량군의 젼명은 다 졍젼된 모양인데 ᄒᆞᆫ번 로병 일쳔이 빅명 사샹ᄒᆞᆫ 말만 잇고 일본군의 사샹은 말ᄒᆞ지 아니ᄒᆞ엿더라

○론담정명 셔양인 굴련쓰라는 사ᄅᆞᆷ이 일본횡빈에셔 로국정탐의 혐의로 잡혀셔 심문ᄒᆞᆫ 후에 샹ᄒᆡ로 징역에 처ᄒᆞ엿다더라

○포로샹환 일로 간에셔 로쟝 [illegible]

광고

[illegible]

TELEGRAMS.

AFFAIRS IN RUSSIA.

(FROM JAPAN PAPERS.)

London, Jan. 27.

The policy of repression by Russia has been successful. The Capital is quiet. Despite the riots and conflicts in the provinces, the revolutionary movement has been crushed for the present. The leaders are, however, organising a greater rising in the future.

London, Jan. 27.

The London Daily Chronicle's correspondent at St. Petersburg states that 5,000 persons were arrested in the capital on Wednesday evening. This number included one hundred lawyers who are now en route to Siberia.

London, Jan. 28.

It is stated that Sir Charles Hardinge, the British Ambassador to St. Petersburg, has made a fresh and stronger protest in the matter of the placards posted by the Moscow police saying that the strikes were the result of Anglo-Japanese intrigues and that the strikers were being supplied with English gold. The Chief of Police at Moscow, it seems, has informed the British Consul that he was leaving the posters for two days longer on his own responsibility as an assistance towards tiding over the present troubles and to prevent further difficulties. Thereupon the Consul telegraphed to Sir Charles Hardinge.

London, Jan. 28.

The strikes are extending to the provinces. In several cities of Poland serious collisions have taken place. It is reported that several thousand workmen are advancing from Moscow to St. Petersburg. Socialists say that the Czar will be assassinated by rioters in the end. A number of troops who have arrived at Bovlinsk by train have caused trouble, and blame the Czar for the war.

Berlin, Jan. 28.

Although order has been restored in St. Petersburg, the strike agitation is still in full progress in the provinces. An encounter between the workmen and the troops, which resulted in serious bloodshed, has taken place at Riga. A rumour is in circulation at St. Petersburg to the effect that the Czar, Czarina and the Empress Dowager will leave Russia for abroad, but this report is contradicted by the authorities. The Czar has announced that he is willing to see representatives of the strikers on any date they may desire, provided the number of delegates is not too large.—Mainichi,

London, Jan. 28.

Thirty-five bombs have been exploded at Lodz, Poland, with the result that one hundred and fifty persons was killed on the spot. Street fighting on a serious scale has taken place at Radom, Poland. The disturbances at Warsaw have been resumed and the situation is very grave. The strikes are rapidly spreading all over the Russian provinces. As the result of a Council held at the Czar's Palace last night, the Russian authorities will take up a moderate attitude. The powers of the Military Governor have been restricted. It has been announced that the Government will concede all reasonable demands made by the people, and the factory employes have no resumed work.

Berlin, Jan. 29.

Order has been restored completely at St. Petersburg and to some extent at Moscow, and the newspapers, in the capital have resumed publication. At Warsaw, however, about 100,000 labourers are on strike, and there has been a good deal of bloodshed, and similar conditions prevail at Lodz.—Mainichi.

London, Jan. 30.

A circular has been issued by the Holy Synod to all Orthodox believers in Russia. It says the strikers are being instigated by the enemies of the country both at home and abroad. These, led by a criminal priest (Father Gapon), have broken out in a movement when all should have co-operated to protect the Fatherland. The objects of the enemies of Russia, says the circular, is to produce a state of civil war so as to prevent reinforcements for the Manchurian Army being obtainable. The circular concludes with an appeal for obedience to the Emperor and to the commands of God, and with a warning against listening to the advice of those who are in the pay of Russia's enemies.

Serious riots took place at Warsaw on Saturday, when many of the finest shops in the town were sacked and burned. The cavalry charged the crowds, and the troops fired on the people at several points.

The British Consul-General and Vice-Consul were separately charged by patrols, the Vice-Consul receiving several terrible sword-cuts on the face.

Later.

Sir Charles Hardinge, the British Ambassador at St. Petersburg, has sent a military attaché to investigate the reports of the attack on Mr. Murray, the British Consul-General, and Mr. Mupukain, the pro-Consul, at Warsaw by the soldiery.

The Ambassador has protested against the republication at Libau of the notice alleging that the strike is due to Anglo-Japanese intrigues, pointing out that it will seriously affect the friendly relations now existing between Great Britain and Russia.

The disturbances at Warsaw were renewed yesterday, one hundred and sixty being killed and wounded.

The troops at Libau have been reinforced as the situation has become worse.

London, Jan. 31.

Count Lamsdoff, the Russian Minister for Foreign Affairs, has informed Sir Charles Hardinge, the British Ambassador at St. Petersburg, that he has ordered a searching inquiry into the recent attacks made on British Consular officials at Warsaw, and also the complete effacement of the placards posted in Moscow and Libau alleging that the present disorders are the result of Anglo-Japanese intrigues. Count Lamsdorff has expressed his unqualified disapproval of the conduct of the Prefect of Moscow in allowing the posters to remain after the protest had been made by the British Ambassador.

London, January, 30.

Bombs have been exploded under the walls of the Imperial Palace at Moscow and at the residence of the Grand Duke Serge, the late Governor. The Grand Duke had a narrow escape from death. Very grave riots are still in progress at Warsaw and there are constant severe encounters between the troops and the people. All the factories are closed and the shops are being plundered by the mob. The Russian troops at Warsaw have attacked the British Consul there. The British Government have consequently made strong representations to the Russian authorities. St. Petersburg is outwardly quiet, but is really very far from tranquil. General Trepoff is having police searches made on a huge scale at the houses of suspected people. Many distinguished writers and well-known members of the Liberial Party have been arrested, and a leader of the Poles has been killed at Batoum. The Czar is still at Tsarkoe seloe. Father Gapon has escaped to Switzerland.

Berlin, Jan. 31.

No new disturbances have broken out in Russia during the last few days, and in several places the strikers have resumed work. The Czar has granted audiences to delegates from the labourers, and it is believed that the strikes will shortly end.

THE HULL INCIDENT.

London, Jan. 30.

The International Commission appointed to investigate the circumstances of the sinking of British trawlers in the North Sea has now been sitting a week with open doors. The Commission has examined several of the Hull fishermen, eliciting flat denials of the presence of Japanese torpedo-boats among the trawling fleet on the night of the attack.

London, Jan. 31.

Captain Clado, one of the chief witnesses for Russia at the International Commission now sitting in Paris to investigate the circumstances of the sinking of British trawlers in the North Sea, has given his evidence. He emphatically and circumstantially reiterated the assertion that the Baltic Squadron encountered torpedo-boats.

THE BALTIC SQUADRON.

London, Jap. 28.

It is rumoured in Sevastopol that during a gale the warships under Admiral Rojestvensky sustained severe damage. —Asahi.

London, Jan. 28.

Reuter's agent at Port Said telegraphs that there is reason to believe that at least some of the Baltic Squadron will shortly return by the Suez Canal. Of those that remain some will visit the Persian Gulf.

THE WAR.

London, Jan. 30.

There is anxiety at St. Petersburg with regard to the safety of General Mischenko's Brigade.

Goundjulin, Jan. 25.

Reports are circulating that preparations have been made on the Kiachta Road in Mongolia, for the provisioning of an army of 15,000 men, The Chinese say these preparations have been made by the Russians.

CHINA'S NEUTRALITY.

London, Januery 29th.

The efforts of Mr. John Hay, Amerian Secretary of State, to call a conference of the Powers to discuss the question of China's integrity, is doomed to failure. With the exception of Russia, favourable answers were received by Mr. Hay from the Powers. Russia does not see the necessity for such a conference, therefore it will not be held.

Berlin, Jan. 31.

None of the Powers have expressed approval of the Russian circular regarding the alleged Chinese violations of neutrality.

GENERAL NEWS.

Vienna, Jan. 30

Owing to severe dissensions among the naval authorities, the scheme for a great expansion of the Russian navy under the control of Admiral Avellan, the Naval Minister, has had to be abandoned

Mondon, Jan. 28.

M. Delcassé, Minister of the French Office, has stated in the Chamber of Deputies that the alliance between France and Russia is maintained.—Asahi.

London, Jan. 29.

M. Fouvier's reference to the French alliance with Russia [the new Premier's statement that he intended to adhere to the alliance] was greeted with uproar. M. Jaurés and others protested against a a continuance of an alliance with a government composed of murderers, etc, etc. M. Declassé repeatedly intervened imploring the Deputies to refrain from making such remarks for the sake of France's good name and interest. It must never be fogotten, he said, that the alliance had given France security. A vote of confidence in the new Ministry was passed by 410 to 170.

London, Jan. 31.

A meeting of six thousand persons was was held in Paris last evening for the purpose of denouncing the recent treatment of the strikers by the Russian Government.

Extraordinary precautions were taken by the police against disorder, but as the audience was leaving a bomb was thrown and two of the Republican Guard were wounded. Several arrests were made.

Another bomb was found outside the residence of Prince Trubetmikoi, the Russian attachè in Paris.

Peking, January 29.

The Chinese Government has long been advised by the British and American Ministers to dispense with the Likin Duties but, as the Viceroys are complaining of the difficulty of finding the money for the Boxer indemnity, the authorities have decided that the advice cannot be complied with.

JAPANESE BAR ASSOCIATION AND THE MANCHURIAN QUESTION.

Some time ago the Board of Councillors of the Japanese Bar Association elected a committee of seven, including Mr. Kinozuke Yamada, chairman, Mr. Takuzo Honai, Mr. Shiro Isobe, and others, for the purpose of making inquiries into the subject, "The Manchurian question viewed from the standpoint of International Law." The committee have now completed their task, and Mr. Yamada has submitted to the above Board a resolution which will be discused at an extraordinary meeting of councillors to be held on the 28th inst. The resolution is as follows:—

That, in order to ensure the peace of the East and to guarantee the integrity of China Proper and the opening of Manchuria, China shall unconditionally hand over to the Imperial Japanese Government her sovereignty over Manchuria.

That as the administration in Manchuria grows with the progress of the war, the foregoing resolution shall be effected before the termination of the war.

LIEUTENANT BENCKENDORFF OF THE RUSSIAN NAVY.

The Russian Ambassador at London has formally communicated with the Bureau of Information for the Russian Prisoners in Tokyo, through the British Minister to Japan, asking for information as to the whereabouts of his son, Lieutenant Benckendorff of the Russian Navy, who was at Port Arthur during the siege, but was subsequently reported missing. A reference to the list of the Russian prisoners at Matsuyama revealed the fact that Lieutenant Benckendorff is detained there.

The Korea Daily News.

Issued at 5 P. M. daily except Sundays.

Rate of Subscription:—
Per Year,............Yen 25.
Per Quarter,..........Yen 7.
Per Month,..........Yen 2.50.

Postage in Korea not charged extra.
Postage abroad charged extra.

Advertisements, 50 sen per day for 1 inch or less.
5 yen per month per inch.
50 yen per year per inch.

All communications to

E. T. BETHELL,
Editor and Publisher,
Pak-tong, Seoul.

JAPAN'S PROMISES.

It would be hard to say whether the indications and evidence of deviation from Japan's ante-bellum programme which are now constantly cropping up are symptoms of confidence or desperation.

The theory that this war was thrust upon Japan—that she did not choose her own time and place, having been disposed of as fallacious, there only remain two explanations of her recent change of attitude with regard to Korea and Manchuria. One is that the progress of the war has fallen short of expectations, and the other is that Japan is wantonly disregarding her promises.

Japanese officialdom in Korea has impressed us no better than it has the Koreans and we are quite ready to ascribe to both the above motives, or no to motive at all, the rank breach of faith which Japan has committed in this country.

The "Japan Herald" on January 19th said:—"The fact is that Japan is hampered by her declarations as to the independence of Korea." This is undoubtedly true; but it must not be forgotten that it was by this declaration and similar declarations regarding her disinterestedness in Manchuria that Japan gained all the sympathy which she has received in regard to the war

If Japan had said that her existence was threatened, the world would have laughed. So Japan made herself the champion of Manchuria and Korea and thereby enlisted the sympathies of the world. Japan did not fight for gain. Oh no. Her object in going to war was to hand back Manchuria to China and to protect the independence and integrity of Korea.

And now the "Japan Herald" has put into words what we have all been thinking for months past. Japan is hampered by her promises. So are we all. So perhaps may be Great Britain.

Then there is the other point. It may be that the progress of the war has fallen short of Japan's expectations. This we think is the true explanation of the present state of affairs in this unfortunate country, Japan is even now preparing for disaster. Otherwise she would do something of permanent benefit to Korea. Instead of this we get a succession of attempts to "collar" Korea, beginning with the Nagamori scheme and ending with the $3,000,000 paper loan, all of which belong more properly to the realms of comic opera or burlesque than to practical politics.

We note that a Mr. Komuchi (is this the promoter of the Il-chin-hoi?) has said that "Should we meet with reverses in the war later on, there is no saying what difficulties may occur in Korea. Herein we are heartily in agreement with Mr. Komuchi and we can add that his Il-chin-hoi Society (if it be his) will not be the least of them.

From the first we have endeavored to stay the hands of the Japanese in their work of hopelessly alienating the sympathies of all true Koreans but to no effect; and now, whatever the outcome of the war may be the Japanese must lie on the bed they have made for themselves.

Mr. Komuchi's remarks about Korea are very instructive, and in another column we reproduce an epitome, for which, we believe, the "Japan Mail" is responsible.

JAPAN AND HER INTENTIONS.

The following is from a summary of an article contributed by Mr. Komuchi Tomotsune to the "Taiyo" as translated by the "Japan Mail:"—

We gather from the article that Mr. Komuchi has lately returned from a visit to Korea. We have no space for anything more than a statement of the salient points of his very interesting and instructive essay. (1) The present state of feeling among high officials and the Court. This may be briefly described as sitting on the fence. The leading Koreans are astonished at our success in the war, but they are by no means certain that the tables won't be turned on us later on. It is on this account that the King is advised by the principal statesmen not to proceed too far in the display of sympathy with Japan. The King's own inclinations go this way. He has always had a leaning towards Russia, as was signally shown eight years ago when he took refuge in the Russian Legation. Then the flocking of Japanese to Korea for business purposes is regarded with suspicion by the Korean authorities. They think it indicates that Japan intends to appropriate and govern the country*. Should we meet with reverses in the war later on, there is no saying what difficulties may occur in Korea. It is important then that our actions should be adapted to the prevailing sentiment in the country. (2) We must give Korea adequate protection. There are some who advocate the immediate annexation of the peninsula, arguing that no other course will prove safe or satisfactory, and observing that no Western Powers would interfere. But such an action on Japan's part as the sudden and arbitary annexation of Korea constitutes a departure from her traditional policy of resepecting what is right and just in all her dealings with other countries. Japan must maintain Korean independence. She must guard her against the danger of becoming the prey of other countries, while at the same time instructing her how to grow into a self-protecting State. At present she must be treated as a child whose education Japan does not intend to intrust to any other Power. We must protect her, but not attempt to govern her. (3) How can this Protection be made effectual? It can only be done by our reforming existing abuses in government throughout the country and by our giving the Koreans abundant proof that we are working in their interests as well as in our own in all we do. When Count Inoue was Minister in Seoul he gave it as his opinion that reform in Korea must begin with the creation of a new financial basis for the State, and he proposed that Japan should lend Korea some five or six million yed on the security of the customs and should further advance money towards the development of the promising industries which though started by Koreans are languishing from want of capital. (4) The actual situation of affairs must be explained to the King of Korea. It is said that the King dislikes the idea of our acting as a protector of the country. It seems to us that steps should at once be taken to place the facts of the case before him and to insist on his coming to a decision as to his future action. It should be pointed out that Japan in saving herself from Russian aggression by this war has prevented the annexation of Korea, and saved the Throne of Korea for its present occupant. Under Russian rule the present King would no longer retain even the shadow of independence or authority. If the King of Korea is made to realize this, then he will feel that he and we are in the same boat, that our interests are identical, and he will work in harmony with us in devising measures against further disturbances. If he absolutely refuses to take this view of the situation and shows a determination to go back to his old ways of reaping the benefits to be obtained by encouraging rival plotters in Seoul to the detriment and peril of this country, then he must be told that our interests and safety make it necessary for us to force him into acquiescence. The King is not such a fool as to be unable to perceive wherein his interests lie; so that it is highly probable that when he sees we are really in earnest, he will give in. (5) A last resource in case our wishes are not complied with. This resource is the annexation of the peninsula. In saying this I may seem to be contradicting myself, as above I have protested against annexation as contrary to what is right. But in the first part of this article I was only combating the notion that Japan should annex Korea at once without further parley. I maintain that we should exhaust every resource and try every means of persuasion in order to get Korea to voluntarily cast in her lot with us. But if from one cause or another, she refuses to do this, in that case annexation would be absolutely essentiae to the safety of this empire. To save ourselves from extinction we should be justified in adopting this extreme measure. (6) Our policy towards Korea. There is no denying that hitherto we have afforded the Koreans much reason for suspicion and misgivings as regards our objects in the measures we have taken in the peninsula. Some people imagine that the Koreans must see that the railway which we have built will benefit the country immensely and that they ought to be grateful to us for laying out so much capital on that enterprise. But up to a very recent date they regarded the construction of this railway as a proof that we Japanese had designs on the country, that we contemplated using the railway exclusively for our own benefit. Now it is beginning to dawn on them that our chief object in building the

(To be continued)

* it is said that even today the manner in which the Koreans were treated by Hideyoshi is remembered and resented by leading men in the peninsula and that it contributes a good deal towards the anti-Japanese feeling in the country.—(WRITER OF SUMMARY.)

The Korea Daily News.

VOL. II, TUESDAY, FEBRUARY 7, 1905. No. 28

HONGKONG & SHANGHAI BANKING CORPORATION.

Paid-up Capital....................	$10,000,000
Reserve Fund:—Sterling Reserve...	10,000,000
Silver Reserve.....	7,000,000
	27,000,000
Reserve Liability of Proprietors...	10,000,000

HEAD OFFICE, HONGKONG.

London Bankers, London and County Banking Company Limited.

Branches and Agencies,

London,

	Hankow	Penang,
	Hiogo,	Rangoon,
	Iloilo,	Saigon,
	Lyons,	San Francisco,
Calcutta,	Manila,	Singapore,
Colombo,	Nagasaki,	Sourabaya,
Foochow,	New York,	Tientsin,
Hamburg,	Peking,	Yokohama,

Credits granted on approved Securities, and every description of Banking and Exchange business transacted.

Drafts granted on London and the chief Commercial places in Europe, India, Australia, America, China and Japan.

HOLME RINGER & CO., AGENTS,
CHEMULPO.

HOKURKU DOBOKU KAISHA.

Branch office in Chong Dong, Seoul.

Japanese telephone No. 165

CONTRACT DEPARTMENT.

We can contract to build any building or construction.

MERCHANDISE DEPARTMENT.

We can provide any building material. We have just contracted to build the new Belgian Legation.

E. MEYER & CO.

Chemulpo.

SOLE AGENTS IN KOREA FOR.

A. T. Morse, Sons & Co.'s

"Fresco" Distemper

In all colours ready for use on walls, Ceilings etc.

and

AVENARIUS CARBOLINEUM

A wood-preserving and antiseptic oil preparation

Against decay, dry-rot, fungus and wood-destroying insects.

A large supply always in stock.
Prices upon application.

E. MEYER & Co.,
Chemulpo.

CHARTERED BANK OF INDIA AUSTRALIA & CHINA.

INCORPORATED BY ROYAL CHARTER 1853

HEAD OFFICES.—LONDON.

Paid-up Capital	£800,000
Reserve Liability of Shareholders	800,000
Reserve Fund	800,000

Drafts granted upon all the principal places in the world and every description of Exchange and banking business transacted.

E. MEYER & Co., Agents,
Chemulpo.

MITSU BISHI DOCKYARD & ENGINE WORKS,

NAGASAKI.

CODE WORD, "DOCK."

A 1, A. B. C., and Engineering Codes used.

DOCK No. 1 (at Tategami).

Extreme Length..............	523 feet
Length on blocks	513 ,,
Width of Entrance on Top......	89 ,,
,, ,, Bottom....	77 ,,
Water on Blocks at Spring Tide	26½ ,,

DOCK No. 2 (Mukaijima).

Extreme Length..............	371 feet
Length on Blocks.............	360 ,,
Width of Entrance on Top......	66 ,,
,, ,, Bottom	53 ,,
Water on Blocks at Spring Tide	22 ,,

PATENT SLIP (at Kosuge).

Can take vessels up to 1,000 tons gross

THE WORKS are well equipped with the LATEST IMPROVEMENTS, and can execute any kind of work in SHIPBUILDING and MARINE ENGINEERING, as well as in REPAIRING of SHIPS.

The COMPANY'S new powerful steamer OURA-MARU (712 tons, 700 I.H.P.), specially built for SALVAGE PURPOSES, and equipped with necessary gear, is always READY at SHORT NOTICE.

THE METHODIST PUBLISHING HOUSE,

Little West Gate, Seoul.

JOB PRINTING, TYPEWRITER PAPER
CARBON PAPER, VISITING CARDS
STATIONERY, BOOK BINDING
BOOK PUBLISHERS
AMERICAN SCHOOL BOOKS
SPENCERIAN COPY BOOKS
PEN CARBON LETTER AND BILL BOOKS

S. A. BECK, Manager.

DAI-ICHI GINKO.

LIMITED.

(Formerly the First National Bank)

ESTABLISHED 1873

INCORPORATED UNDER PRESENT LAW 1896

Capital - - - - - - - -	Yen 5,000,000
Reserve Fund - - - - -	1,500,000

HEAD OFFICE:—TOKIO.

President: Baron SHIBUSAWA.

BRANCHES AND CORRESPONDENTS

In the Principal Cities and Towns of Japan.

Interest Allowed on

Fixed deposits 1 year - - -	6½	per cent
" " 6 months - - -	6	per cent

Special current accounts 1½ sen daily per	Y 100
General " " 1 " " "	100

M. TANAKA,
Manager, Chemulpo.

SINGER SEWING

MACHINES

씽거즈봉침

SOLE AGENTS
FOR KOREA

전매쇼

HOLME RINGER & CO.

Chemulpo.

졔믈포 함룽거양힝

KAMEYA CO.

GENERAL STOREKEEPERS

Chinkokai - - Seoul

(*Established 1895, Tokyo*)

Confectionery, Hams, Canned Goods, Cutlery, Hirano & Tansan Water, Provisions, Gents, Furnishing goods, Toilet Articles, Travelling Bags, Tobacco, Cigars & Cigarettes Kitchen Utensils. Coffee, Biscuits.

Fresh Goods always kept in Stock.

Prices Moderate

☞ *Please come and inspect our goods.*

NIPPON YUSEN KAISHA.

JAPANESE MAIL STEAMSHIP CO.

UNDER MAIL CONTRACT WITH THE IMPERIAL JAPANESE GOVERNMENT.

European Line

Regular Fortnightly Service between Yokohama Kobe, Moji, Shanghai, Hongkong, Singapore, Penang Colombo, Port Said, Marseilles, London and Antwerp

American Line

Regular Fortnightly Service between Hongkong and Seattle, calling at Shanghai, Moji, Kobe, Yokohama and Victoria, B. C.

Australian Line

Regular weekly Service betwen Japan Ports and Australia, calling at Hongkong and Manila.

(Above Three Lines Suspended until further notice).

Shanghai Line

Weekly Service between Shanghai and Japan Ports

Korea Line

Service Kobe, Moji, Nagasaki, Fusan Chemulpo Chefoo, Taku.

S. S. Babelsberg, 2181 tons.

Service Kobe, Moji, Fusan, Chemulpo, Chinnampo

S. S. ARGO, S. S. Ohio.

BORDEN'S CONDENSED MILK CO.

New York, U. S. A.

ALWAYS IN STOCK

Eagle Brand Condensed Milk.

Gold Seal Condensed Milk.

Peerless (Family) Evaporated Cream

Borden's Malted Milk.

E. MEYER & CO.
Chemulpo Korea,
Sole Agents

ROYAL INSURANCE COMPANY,

Funds exceed £10,000,000.

FIRE

AT CURRENT RATES

LIFE

REDUCED PREMIUM.

HOLME RINGER & Co.,
Agents, Chemulpo.

廣

KWANG ● CHANG

昌

BENNETT & CO.

Merchants

Chemulpo.

Offices opposite the Imperial Japanese Post and Telegraph Office Chemulpo.

Telephone Number 201.

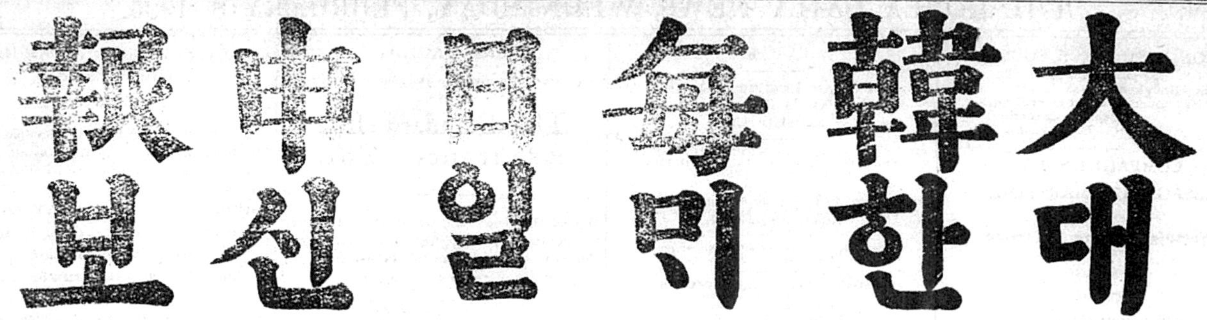

(호구십이권이데)　　(일요목)　　일구월이년오빅구쳔일

본샤고빅

이신보는영어와한국문신계리
일츌판ᄒᆞᆷ
신문가
일쟝한　엿푼도오푼
일삭도　엿푼량닷돈
우표가딕샥닷돈
다맛돈으로밧ᄉᆞᆷ
광고료는
귀한의쟝단과ᄌᆞ힝의다쇼로ᄌᆞ
감ᄒᆞ되렴가로밧을터이오매오
린지아니ᄒᆞ대한사람마다이신
문을보실터이니광고버시기를
원ᄒᆞ시는이들은우리신문사에
와서편약ᄒᆞ심을희망ᄒᆞᆷ
○발힝소　박동대한미일신보
사법어한교양쉐젼영국인셜필
림쟝자리오
사쟝 영국인 (비셜)
평양 디리졈
○평양효동사는권미보씨로우
리신문관디리인을뎡ᄒᆞ엿
시ᄉᆞ오니평양에계신구람코져ᄒᆞ
는 첨군ᄌᆞ는칙디리졈에왕
림ᄒᆞ와면외ᄒᆞ시옵

샤고

○우리대한미일신보의목뎍은
대한의안녕질서에관한모든대
목에디ᄒᆞ야는공평한변론을쥬
쟝ᄒᆞᆷ이라우리동신원의탐보ᄒᆞᆫ
신문보셔는첨군ᄌᆞ의게ᄒᆞᆼ샹보
도ᄒᆞ려며펀지를긔서ᄒᆞ며주ᄉᆡ
는이는셩명과번디를젹어붓치
시기를희망ᄒᆞ오니이거슨신문
샹에긔쥐ᄒᆞ라는거시아니오다
만구히신용ᄒᆞ는증거를솜고자
ᄒᆞᆷ이라긔자는아모긔서던지긔
재ᄒᆞᆷ을뢰착ᄒᆞ는권리난가젓스
나뢰착ᄒᆞ는리유를말ᄒᆞᆯ터이오
며공중평화를문란케ᄒᆞ는듯ᄒᆞᆫ
긔서는의례히밧지안켓ᄉᆞᆸ나ㅣ
다
●본사셜시이리로신문을미ᄉᆞ
우회로분젼ᄒᆞ와회젼부의임의
로젼ᄒᆞᄂᆞᆫ스로면곳에는혹누계
젼ᄒᆞ기도ᄒᆞ며혹면칠계ᄒᆞᄂᆞᆫ법
에젼ᄒᆞ기도ᄒᆞ며혹아니젼ᄒᆞᄂᆞᆫ
곳도잇다ᄒᆞ와우리신문을수람
ᄒᆞ야구람ᄒᆞ시는 첨군ᄌᆞ의게금
디ᄒᆞ야면우미안ᄒᆞ옵기로지금
은분젼인을두고미일일증이젼
ᄒᆞ며아니젼ᄒᆞ거나늦게져나ᄒᆞᆫ
폐가잇도록ᄒᆞ랴ᄒᆞ오니흐회아니

젼ᄒᆞ거나혹늦게젼ᄒᆞ거나ᄒᆞᆫ일
이잇스면본사로통긔ᄒᆞ여주심
을희망ᄒᆞᆷ

뎐보

이심구일평셩발수관착뎐
대샹원슈보고요령
○흑구지방　운하안의젹은이
십오일이리로화녕의샹리를졍
ᄒᆞ엿ᄂᆞᆫ디그수가소불하일키군
단이　쟝한　ᄒᆞᆫ젼우안봉뎐의
서님은로악이심팔리의남방분
오리과흑구디　첨차보　쟝한의남으로악
으로악오리에향ᄒᆞ야젼진ᄒᆞ엿
는디우리군ᄉᆞᄂᆞᆫ공세를취ᄒᆞ야
일부디ᄂᆞᆫ미심흑이른예일수단의
젹을첨차보에서격퇴ᄒᆞ엿고다
른일부디ᄂᆞᆫ동일이리로일키ᄉᆞ
단비샹의젹과흑구디에서샹금
젼투중이라ᄒᆞ엿더라
삼십일발수관착
○포퇴오빅　일월이십구일오
후우태본영에칙ᄒᆞᆫ뎐보를거ᄒᆞᆫ즉
작일유도구부근을졈령ᄒᆞᆫ우리
부디가작야에이회우렬ᄒᆞᆫ젹의
습ᄒᆞᆷ을밧아스나이거슬다격
퇴ᄒᆞ엿스며조다ᄂᆞᆫ일부디ᄂᆞᆫ금
샹명에비차하자흑구디북방약
십리부근의젹을공격ᄒᆞ야동디
를졈령ᄒᆞ엿고흑구디를공격ᄒᆞᆫ
우리부디ᄂᆞᆫ작야에밍렬ᄒᆞᆫ젹의
거역ᄒᆞ야엄습을밧아스나이거
슬다격퇴ᄒᆞ고금조에동디부근
을졈령ᄒᆞ엿고유도구와밋흑구
디방면의젹이다ᄒᆞᆫ하우안으로
퇴격ᄒᆞ야우리군수이진격ᄒᆞᄂᆞᆫ
중이며첨차보와밋리대인둔방
면에도작야에무ᄎᆞ젹의습격을
밧아스나쏘이거슬다퇴격ᄒᆞ엿
고
리대인둔과밋첨차보방면에공
격ᄒᆞ든젹은대팔공대신군단
이오흑구대방면에리도ᄒᆞᆫ젹은
대일군단교밋미시지벤교의지
휘ᄒᆞᄂᆞᆫ긔병수단이오젹의포퇴
ᄂᆞᆫ쟝교이하약오빅명이오기타
퇴각ᄒᆞ야와손히ᄂᆞᆫ불하도사중이라
ᄒᆞ엿더라
부인나발　일월이십삼일
○로국나란의반연　비밧에잇
ᄂᆞᆫ제션소와군물제조소ᄂᆞᆫ다졍
업ᄒᆞ엿고셩파등보에잇ᄂᆞᆫ협명
당들이로국남방에잇ᄂᆞᆫ로동단

톄와과귄띠비샹ᄒᆞ야불칙
에잇ᄂᆞᆫ졍부계조소에셔도졍공
ᄒᆞ고그영향이다른도회들에밋
쳐서만연ᄒᆞ엿더라
동디발　동일
○로황의위험　셩피득보에서
ᄂᆞᆫ황뎨를암살ᄒᆞᆫ다ᄂᆞᆫ풍셜이잇
ᄂᆞᆫ고로엄쳥히계엄ᄒᆞ며졍부와
군인중에도ᄒᆞᆼ계를가진자가잇
서무죄ᄒᆞᆫ자의로박비연숑ᄒᆞ더
다
로돈발　동월이십사일
○로경의계엄　일요일밤에셩
피득보도셩중앙에서ᄂᆞᆫ셩중에
유진ᄒᆞᆫ군디외에신민은모다도
망ᄒᆞ엿ᄂᆞᆫ데계엄병중에보병은더
러첩환ᄒᆞ고슈병을두엇더라
동디발　동일
○로국분요　셩피득보가샹에
서ᄂᆞᆫ항샹코가셰별파로동쟈사
이에싸홈이싱기며모스코에ᄂᆞᆫ
동밍파공비만연ᄒᆞ야세쓰공쟝
도졍지되코면그등도엄스며코
이노지방에서ᄂᆞᆫ일만명의형명
당이티단ᄒᆞᆫᄂᆞᆫᄒᆞ야그결과로모
든제조소들이파공ᄒᆞ엿다ᄒᆞ며
리가와리보니보아방은아종안
졍ᄒᆞ나빌나지방에서도동밍파
공이쏘ᄒᆞᆫ이리나서로대가쟐스
교셀노디켓에서로동자의총티
심이인에게쾌힌을칙ᄒᆞ셧더라
동지발　동월이십륙일
○로팬의동졍　로국드레포표
쟝군이콜논쟝군후잉으로셩피
득보총독을임ᄒᆞ고콜논쟝군은
룩군대신을임ᄒᆞᆫ다ᄒᆞᄂᆞᆫ디이ᄂᆞᆫ
궁중이착란ᄒᆞ고안졍치못ᄒᆞᆫ보
통의와심을젼졍코자ᄒᆞᆷ인듯ᄒᆞ
고작야에아국도셩근처에어느
쳘로ᄂᆞᆫ아국리수로쳘리나파괴
ᄒᆞ엿더라
동디발　동일
○로국나란의속보　로국나에
각소동의반연됨이티단금속ᄒᆞ야
쳐티ᄂᆞᆫ회에젼셔가문란ᄒᆞ고
파란과분란에서ᄂᆞᆫ반란의운동
이봉긔ᄒᆞ야인민이젼일에샬육
당ᄒᆞᆷ을복슈ᄒᆞ기로맹셔ᄒᆞᆫ다ᄒᆞ
며피득보에서ᄂᆞᆫ쟝시경동ᄒᆞ
엿스나소란이중지되고구로
팟기쟝군의젼망ᄒᆞᄂᆞᆫ바군량군
분과군티의파숀ᄒᆞᆷ은경향엽시
되며서빌리쳘도ᄂᆞᆫ이심영리가
파괴세엿다ᄂᆞᆫ풍셜이잇스며아

국나부대신은레포포쟝군으로피
득보총독을임ᄒᆞ엿다ᄒᆞ며로동
자의동밍파공은졈졈더ᄒᆞ나군
티와총돌ᄒᆞᆷ은업고아국유명ᄒᆞᆫ
소셜가맥심고르키씨가포박하
옥되엿다ᄂᆞᆫ젼셜이잇더라
동디발　동일
○로국신문　피득보에서ᄂᆞᆫ신
문검찰이엄즁ᄒᆞ야발힝ᄒᆞᄂᆞᆫ신
문이젹으미졍부쥬권자들이신
분은젼ᄒᆞᆫ위세를잇은듯이넉이
더라

관보

데삼쳔오십ᄉᆞ호　광무구
년이월ᄉᆞ일
서임급ᄉᆞ령
○의원면경임　황태ᄌᆞ비궁대
부　농상공부샹공국쟝　송틱
쳔
일월오일
○임룩군법원쟝셔칙임관샹등
룩군참쟝　원우샹
○임경무청쥬ᄉᆞ서판임관륙등
구품　권봉슈
이월이일
○허비서원승　종이품　심진
틱
○임비서원승서주임관오등
졍삼품　리셕종
○임경무ᄉᆞ서칙임관이등　룩
군참쟝　신틱휴
○임충쳥남도관찰ᄉᆞ서칙임관
삼등　졍이품　조종필
이월이일
○의원면본관　니부쥬ᄉᆞ　조
종탁
○임니부쥬ᄉᆞ서판관륙등　빅
희슈
이월삼일
○임의졍부찬졍서칙임관일등
졍이품　졍쥬영
○임의졍부찬졍서칙임관일등
룩군참쟝　구영조
○허팀시서리표훈원총지ᄉᆞ무
니부대신　조병식
○명서리교육부총감ᄉᆞ무　군
부협판　엄쥬익
이월삼일
데삼쳔오빅오호　광무구
년이월륙일
서임급ᄉᆞ령
○명궁니부특진관서칙임관샹
등　룩군부쟝　리종건

UNION INSURANCE SOCIETY OF CANTON.

Head office Hongkong.
Marine risks underwritten at current rates.
Agents in Chemulpo,
E. MEYER & Co.

COMPAGNIE DES MESSAGERIES MARITIMES.

Fortnightly Direct Service.

For Marseilles
via Ports.
Sailing from Yokohama
Calling at Kobe,
Shanghai, Hongkong, Saigon, Singapore,
Colombo, Djibonti, Suez, Port Said
and Marseilles.

For particulars apply to
HOLME RINGER & Co.,
Chemulpo.

HAYASHIDA & CO.,

16 MYENG DONG, CHIN KO KAI, SEOUL.
BRANCH OFFICE AT CHEMULPO.

Money changers, Coal and Wood Merchants, Express Agents.

We are agents for the Pyeng-yang Coal Company and the Karazu Coal Company of Japan. We have the best quality of both authracite and bituminous coal, and prompt execution of orders is our speciality. Firewood of all kinds kept in stock. Full weight guaranteed. Money of all denominations exchanged at current rates. Parcels received for all parts.

CHINA MUTUAL LIFE INS. OC.

Most favourable terms to policy holders.

Benefit system unsurpassed.

HOLME RINGER & Co.
Agents, Chemulpo.

C. P. R.

CANADIAN PACIFIC RAILWAY COMPANY'S ROYAL MAIL STEAMSHIP LINE.

THE FAST ROUTE BETWEEN CHINA, JAPAN. AND EUROPE VIA CANADA AND THE UNITED STATES.

Route from Hongkong via Shanghai, Nagasaki (Inland Sea of Japan) Kobe, Yokohama Victoria and Vancouver.

Twin Screw Empress Steamship—6,000 Tons—Speed 19 knots.

PROPOSED SAILING FROM YOKOHAMA.
R. M. S. Empress of India.
R. M. S. Empress of Japan.
R. M. S. Empress of China.
R. M. S. Athenian.
R. M. S. Tartar.

Special reduction (first class only) granted to members of the Military, Naval, Diplomatic and Civil services and to Missionaries.

Passengers have choice of ten routes across the Continent of America and have privilege of travelling by any Atlantic Steamship Line.

Round the World passage tickets in connection with the P. and O. S. N., North German Lloyd and Messageries Co.'s **£125.**

All rates payable at current rate of exchange.

For further information, Tickets, Guide Books, etc., apply to

HOLME, RINGER & CO., AGENTS,
Chemulpo.

Grand Hotel

(Formerly the Station Hotel)

Near the Railway Terminus, West Gate Seoul.

The Best Hotel in Korea
Handsome new Building.
Fine Airy Rooms
Excellent Cuisine.
Terms Moderate.
Special terms to Missionaries
and to permanent boarders.

Electric cars within 2 minutes' walk.

W. H. EMBERLEY.

Proprietor

EVERY FACILITY.

In connection with Life Assurance Business is afforded by

The Standard Life Assurance Co.,

One of the largest and wealthiest of the Provident Institutions of the United Kingdom Forms of Application and all information will be promptly afforded on application.

10 CENTS A DAY.

Not a very large expenditure is it? But it is sufficient to secure for a man of 30 a policy with the STANDARD LIFE OFFICE for

$1323.

For all particulars of rates, etc., apply to

Holme, Ringer & Co.,
Agents, Chemulpo.

THE NEW YORK LIFE INSURANCE COMPANY.

Have you ever been declined by any Company?

Are you engaged in a specially hazardous occupation?

Have you heard of the New York Life Insurance Company's New Classifications for this class of Risks?

If not, send your date of birth, occupation and particulars of rejection, if any to

E. MEYER & Co.,
Agents, Chemulpo.

MITSUI BUSSAN KAISHA.
(MITSUI & Co.)
MITSUI GINKO.
(MITSUI BANK.)

The Bank is owned by the members of the Mitsui Family, who, as partners, assume an unlimited responsibility for all liabilities of the Bank:—

Capital........................Yen 5,000,000
Reserve Fund.................. " 5,600,000

HEAD OFFICE, TOKYO.
LONDON OFFICE, 34 LIME ST., E. C.

BRANCHES AND AGENCIES:—

New York, San Francisco, Hamburg, Bombay, Singapore, Manila, Hongkong, Amoy, Chefoo, Tientsin.

Kobe, Hakodate, Yokohama, Kure, Yokosuka, Moji, Shimonoseki, Miike, Wakamatsu, Nagasaki, Kuchinotsu, Karatsu, Sasebo, Misume, Taipeh, &c.

Telegraphic Address for all the Offices:
"MITSUI."

A. B. C. AND A. 1 CODES USED.

Contractors of Coal

To the Imperial Japanese Navy. Arsenals and Railway Bureau, Principal Railway Companies and Industrial Work, Home and Foreign Mail and Freight Steamers.

Sole Proprietors

Of the famous Miike, Tagawa and Yamano Coal Mines.

Sole Agents

For the sale of Fukumo, Hokoku, Ichimura Kanoda, Mannoura, Onoura, Ostuji, Sonoda Tsubaruro, Yoshinotani, Yoshio, Yurokiburu and other coals.

YANGTSE INSURANCE ASSOCIATION, LTD.

The undersigned, having been appointed agents for the above company, are prepared to issue policies and pay losses on marine risks at regular rates.

E. MEYER & Co.,
Agents, Chemulpo.

AMERICAN KOREAN ELECTRIC CO.

Light and Power.

Main Office: Electric Building, Chong No.

RAILWAY DEPARTMENT.

OPERATING CARS BETWEEN EAST AND WEST GATE, EVERY TEN MINUTES:—

First Car leaves East Gate at 7:00 A. M. First Car leaves R. R. Station at 7:25 A. M
Last Car " East Gate at 8.40 P. M. Last " " R. R. Station at 9.05 P. M

OPERATING CARS BETWEEN EAST GATE AND IMPERIAL TOMB TERMINUS, EVERY TWENTY MINUTES:—
CONNECTING WITH EVERY ALTERNATE CAR ARRIVING AT EAST GATE FROM CHONG NO.

First Car leaves East Gate for Tomb at 7:10 A. M.
" " " Tomb for East Gate at 7:30 A. M.
Last " " East Gate for Tomb at 7:50 P. M.
" " " Tomb for East Gate at 8:10 P. M.

OPERATING CARS BETWEEN CHONG NO AND YUNG SAN RIVER EVERY TWELVE MINUTES:—

First Car leaves Chong No for South Gate at 7:12 A. M.
" " " Chong No for Yung San at 7:36 A. M.
" " " South Gate for Chong No at 7:20 A. M.
" " " Yung San for Chong No at 8:09 A. M.
Last " " South Gate for Chong No 9:00 P. M.
" " " Yung San for Chong No at 8.45. p. M.

SPECIAL PRIVATE CARS FURNISHED TO SUIT CONVENIENCE OF PATRONS. PRICES ON APPLICATION AT HEAD OFFICE.

LIGHTING DEPARTMENT.

Where less than 250 candle power of light is used, the rate per month will be
Per 16 candle power incandescent lamp,—All night.—Yen 2.50.
32 candle power incandescent lamp:—All night:—Yen 4.00.
50 candle power incandescent lamp:—All night:—Yen 6.00.
150 " " " " " " " 10.00.
1200 " " enclosed arc " " " " 20.00.

Where more than 250 candle power of light is used, a Meter will be installed, if requested:—Rent of Meter Yen 2.00 per month. Rate of charges by meter reading:—Two Sen per Ampere per hour. (Approximately this is equal to about One Sen per 16 C. P. lamp per hour) Minimum monthly charge where meter is installed, Yen 20.00 per month, which includes rental of meter.

Estimates for installing lights furnished on application

An assortment of chandeliers always on hand.

K. Murakami.

Photograph Studio
Chinkokai, Seoul.

Printing, Developing and Enlargement, of Photographs always Undertaken.

Korean Views and Pictures Illustrating Native Customs always on Sale,

---

THE OSAKA SHOSEN KAISHA.

Boats frequently on the berth for Chinnampo.

REGULAR SAILINGS BETWEEN JAPAN AND KOREAN PORTS.

FUSAN AND KOBE VIA SHIMONOSEKI

OSAKA VIA MOKPO, FUSAN, SHIMONOSEKI AND KOBE.

MOJI DIRECT.

OSAKA VIA KUNSAN, MASANPO, FUSAN, SHIMONOSEKI AND KOBE.

CHEMULPO KUNSAN LINE,
Every three days.

CHEMULPO CHINNAMPO LINE.
Every three days.

For Freight and passage and further particulars apply to
THE OSAKA SHOSEN KAISHA,
Cemulpo

RONDON, PLAISANT & CO.

General Storekeepers and Merchants, Ships Contractors Tobacconists, Commission and Forwarding Agents, Coal Merchants

IMPORTERS AND EXPORTERS

Seoul Chemulpo.

W. D. WENTWORTH.

LANDING
AND
SHIPPING AGENT.
AND
CUSTOMS BROKER.

12 OURA, NAGASAKI.

STEWARD & CO.

Chemulpo.

Shipchandlers and Storekeepers, Naval and Mercantile Contractors, Landing and Shipping Agents.

STEWARD'S HOTEL

Chemulpo.

Best accommodation in the port for travellers. Clean and well-aired rooms, good cuisine and prompt attendance, oderate tariff.

○명홍문관학ᄉᆞ셔칙임관삼등
정삼픔 남뎡쳘
○명니장원경셔칙임관삼등
죵이픔 오영셕
○의원면본관 비셔원승 리
셕죵
○임비셔원승셔쥬임관륙등
정삼픔 김유홍
이상이월삼일
뎨삼쳔오십륙호 광무구
년이월칠일
셔임급ᄉᆞ령
○의원면본겸임외국어학지교
쟝 쥬일공관참셔관 하샹긔
○겸임외국어학교지교쟝 인
쳔감리 유찬
이상이월일일
○임즁츄원부의쟝셔칙임관일
동 졍이픔 리근호
○명 기로소면무관 죵이픔
엄쥬원
이상이월이일
○의원면본관 즁츄원의관
하셩일 즁츄원의관 민의호
○임즁츄원의관셔쥬임관륙등
탁지부쥬ᄉᆞ 리규영
○면즁계 갑산젼군슈 리근
풍 신계젼군슈 윤티션
리원젼군슈, 최우낙 남양젼
군슈 리강년 안쥬젼군슈
강두험 결셩젼군슈 홍죵소
북쳥젼군슈 강홍도 옹진젼
군슈 윤희슌 경흥젼군슈
쟝셕쥬 삼쳑젼군슈 최윤졍
기쳔젼군슈 젼효슌 예안젼
군슈 유호영 풍긔젼군슈
김종인 신령젼군슈 길민익
홍양젼군슈 죠두현 능쥬젼
군슈 송린용 화슌젼군슈
셥운턱
○임즁츄원의관셔칙임관ᄉᆞ등
죵일픔 하셩일 정삼픔 민
의호 정삼픔 박승목 정삼
픔 민츙식
○급이급봉 즁츄원의관 리
규영
○의원면본관 즁학교교관
구일모
○임즁학교교관셔판임관륙등
안죵겸
이상이월ᄉᆞ일
○의원면본관 니부쥬ᄉᆞ 빅
희수 졔쥬목쥬ᄉᆞ 리샹구
○임니부쥬ᄉᆞ셔판임관륙등
민영셕
○임졔쥬목쥬ᄉᆞ셔판임관륙등
함세권
이상이월오일
○구년도예산표 (속)
군부소관
뎨이십ᄉᆞ관 연셩학교 이만
칠쳔팔빅륙십칠원
뎨일항 봉급 일만이쳔팔
빅륙십륙원
뎨이항 쳥비 ᄉᆞ쳔원
뎨삼항 쳥ᄉᆞ슈리비 오빅
원
뎨ᄉᆞ항 잡급급잡비 오쳔
구빅ᄉᆞ십원
뎨오항 피복비 일쳔일빅
칠십구원
뎨륙항 량식비 이쳔삼빅
팔십원
뎨칠항 마필비 일쳔이원
뎨이십오관 유년학교 삼만
삼쳔ᄉᆞ십륙원
뎨일항 봉급 일만구쳔구
빅칠원
뎨이항 쳥비 이쳔팔빅원
뎨삼항 쳥ᄉᆞ슈리비 오빅
원
뎨ᄉᆞ항 잡급급잡비 오쳔
팔빅십팔원
뎨오항 피복비 칠빅륙십
원
뎨륙항 량식비 이쳔칠빅
륙십원
뎨칠항 마필비 오빅일원
뎨이십륙관 참모부 삼만일
쳔팔빅칠원
뎨일항 봉급 일만구쳔이
빅이십ᄉᆞ원
뎨이항 쳥비 이쳔이빅오
십원
뎨삼항 쳥ᄉᆞ슈리비 일쳔
원
뎨ᄉᆞ항 잡급급잡비 삼쳔
일빅이십원
뎨오항 피복비 팔빅ᄉᆞ십
원
뎨륙항 마필비 삼쳔일빅
칠십삼원
뎨칠항 려비 일쳔이원
뎨팔항 긔밀비 일쳔원
뎨이십칠관 시죵무관부 일
만칠쳔팔빅칠원
뎨일항 봉급 칠쳔삼빅삼
십원
뎨이항 쳥비 일쳔이빅원
뎨삼항 쳥ᄉᆞ슈리비 오십
원
뎨ᄉᆞ항 잡급급잡비 오쳔
이빅ᄉᆞ십구원
뎨오항 피복비 일쳔삼빅
팔십칠원
뎨륙항 려비 이빅원
뎨칠항 치료비 이십원
뎨팔항 미쟝비 이십원
뎨구항 마필비 이쳔삼빅
오십일원
뎨이십팔관 비죵무관부 일
만칠쳔ᄉᆞ빅륙십칠원
뎨일항 봉급 륙쳔구빅구
십원
뎨이항 쳥비 일쳔이빅원

론셜

일본인의경찰

○셔울에셔경찰권을디리ᄒᆞ고감독ᄒᆞ눈칙임으로일본인은져의들의계조고파호아름다온쳥구ᄒᆞ눈거슬드럿슬듯일젼밤에대안문압려관에셔불나셔일본병정파또다른사름들이드러가셔그불을쎄눈디그려관쥬인은그근쳐잇눈외국파물젼쥬인골스텐씨라골스텐씨와부인이그불나던밤에그려관에와셔락망ᄒᆞ고셧눈디그불이곳그집에퍼져셔탈렴너눈아즉업슬때에셔울경찰권을디리ᄒᆞ다ᄒᆞ눈일본헌병이드러와셔골스텐스씨의니외를밧게로모라낸지라우리의싱각에눈그날도젹마진물건에티ᄒᆞ야일본인이칙임잇눈거손무를것도업거니와골스텐씨의실물ᄒᆞᆫ거시미우익셕ᄒᆞ니우리눈곳동씨를만족ᄒᆞ게ᄒᆞ기를밋노라

잡보

○부쟈졍호 부즉다욕 대구부닉에사눈부쟈졍호셕씨눈즁경참셔관을지냇고또본도관찰사와친ᄒᆞ더니동씨가샹경ᄒᆞᆫ후에히관찰사가무숨욕심이발ᄒᆞ엿든지무숨셔돍이잇던지동씨의정쳐를착수ᄒᆞ엿다눈가셔를보고동씨가곳발졍ᄒᆞ야집으로내려가면셔그친고의게말ᄒᆞ기를녜로브터부즉다욕이라ᄒᆞ더니참말부쟈일홈엇은거시평싱에위티ᄒᆞᆫ일이로다ᄒᆞ더라

○신셕두젼 탁지부에셔샹납젼의두젼을새법으로작정ᄒᆞ야양력이월브터각디방에엽젼쓰눈곳에눈미쳔량머리에이빅량식가봉ᄒᆞ기로결정ᄒᆞ엿다더라

○황은감샤 일공사가외부로죠회ᄒᆞ기를명치이십구년에본방인손히금을니하ᄒᆞ신고로그유족의게반급ᄒᆞ엿더니 황샹인덕을감사ᄒᆞ다ᄒᆞ엿더라

○고문시무 경무쳥공문관환산씨를임의합동됴인ᄒᆞᆫ지라환산씨가칠일브터사진ᄒᆞ야시무ᄒᆞᆫ다더라

○직합감하 의정부에셔샹쥬ᄒᆞ고각도순찰사를소환ᄒᆞᆯ사로이미지가ᄒᆞ엿눈디현디ᄒᆞᆫ사합을모다감하ᄒᆞ고평안남북합경남북안무사황히도션유사도모다감하ᄒᆞᆫ다더라

○죠례식원 작일외부에셔례식원으로죠회ᄒᆞ기를쳥공사죠회녀기에우리외무부로브터교도ᄒᆞᆫ작년황태후칠슌반수졀에회답국셔의부본을공복ᄒᆞ야비문죠달ᄒᆞ오니쳥본구쥬ᄒᆞ고뎡긔뎡례ᄒᆞ라눈등인을쥰ᄒᆞ야죠회다ᄒᆞ엿더라

●단쳔면보 단쳔군슈김유직이가닉부로면보ᄒᆞ기를음력납월이십ᄉᆞ일에부임ᄒᆞ엿더니로병이일작에쳘귀ᄒᆞ엿스니로병의힐거가이굿치지체ᄒᆞ니황송ᄒᆞ다ᄒᆞ엿더라

○쥬쳥공관보고 쥬쳥공관에셔외부로보고ᄒᆞ기를작년겨울로브터지금ᄭᆞ지공관경비를지발치아니ᄒᆞ야군졸히막심ᄒᆞ니곳지발케ᄒᆞ라ᄒᆞ엿더라

○어젼회의 칠일상오십이시에리졍ᄒᆞᆫ관제를다시정ᄒᆞᆯ추로어젼회의를ᄒᆞ엿더라

○일ᄉᆞ공함 일공사가의정셔리죠병식씨의게공함ᄒᆞ기를학부와농부가아즉쓸디가업스니폐지홈이가ᄒᆞ다ᄒᆞ엿더라

○금광합동 의공사가외부에죠회ᄒᆞ기를금광쥰허를이미어덧고회사티표쟈가리도ᄒᆞ엿슨즉그금광을쟝ᄎᆞᆺ지정ᄒᆞ랴면그합동을불가불체결ᄒᆞᆯ것인디(일)은광산계한 영광합등뎨일됴」(일)은쥰허년긔(영파뎨사됴)(일)은광산닉제광소유권(영광뎨이됴)(일은광세[영광뎨십됴」를의지ᄒᆞ야정긔시명ᄒᆞ야합동작뎡ᄒᆞ엿더라

○민씨곤경 민경호씨가평남관찰사지임시에덕쳔오씨의게엽구쳔량을토식ᄒᆞ엿더니젼의관김셩긔씨가오씨의디프쟈가되야작일에민씨를가보고토색젼을도로닉라홈의민씨가ᄒᆞᆯ말업시곤란즁이라더라

○소긔독촉 리용티씨가락혼훈이후로진신ᄒᆞᆯ계교가업셔빅반운동즁인디그신복소위척샤송진옥을부려리방협의게후이되물ᄒᆞ야일본인이등후작의게소긔ᄒᆞ눈길을도득ᄒᆞᆫ다더라

뎐보

동지발 동일

○로국닉란의소식 셩피득보는군령밋헤두어군졍관으로행졍ᄒᆞ야극진히진압ᄒᆞ고밍렬ᄒᆞᆫ졍칙으로혁명당의죠직파박두ᄒᆞᆫ반관의긔미를금지ᄒᆞ려ᄒᆞ눈일반인민은위협ᄒᆞ고모스코경무부는영국사롬들이불틱합디와흑히합디가극동으로행ᄒᆞ눈것을검지ᄒᆞ려고운동을이르켯다고명언ᄒᆞ엿고로국리보항구에문란홈은뎨삼티평양합티를.파견ᄒᆞ눈디방히가되고에비병들은극동으로행홈을원망ᄒᆞ눈고로위협ᄒᆞᆫ긔샹이잇고구로팟긴쟝군의게공급ᄒᆞᆯ럿식을텰도갓가온여러곳에셔만이강탈ᄒᆞ엿고남방아라사에셔는현금극동젼쟁을정지ᄒᆞᆯ량으로젼쟁반디ᄒᆞ눈혁명당이죠직되엿더라

광고

○본인의셩명도쟝을음력십이월이십칠일에셔실ᄒᆞ왓기로이에광고ᄒᆞ오니수모습득ᄒᆞ와도물시ᄒᆞᆯᄉᆞ
새문밧 냉동 손덕쥰 고빅

TELEGRAMS.

(FROM JAPAN PAPERS)

Berlin, January 29.

The text of the new commercial treaty which has been signed between Germany and Austria has been made public.

Berlin, Jan. 29.

The legislation for ameliorating the condition of the miners has been sanctioned by the Kaiser.

Berlin, Jan. 29.

The German financial estimates for the next fiscal year provide for the construction of a new pier at Tsingtao. Captain Trabtel, Governor of the island of Tsingtao, has been promoted Rear-Admiral.

Berlin, Jan. 31.

Prince Eitel Fridrich's condition is improving, in spite of the fact that he is now suffering from pleurisy, in addition to the previous symptoms of pneumonia.

Berlin, Jan. 28.

A general election has been held in Hungary. The result was unfavourable to the Government.

London, Jan. 14.

The provisional running of trains on the Orenburg-Tashkend railway commences on the 14th inst.

[Orenburg is on the Ural, 727 miles E. S. E. of Moscow. Tashkend is the capital of Russian Turkestan, and is 300 miles N. E. of Samarkand.

London, Jan. 16.

In the Mile End election Mr. Lawson, the Conservative, obtained 2,136 votes against Mr. Strauss, the Liberal Candidate's 2,000. The election was largely fought on the question of the exclusion of undesirable aliens, which Mr. Lawson advocated.

London, Jan. 23.

John Blair Balfour, first Baron Kinross, is dead.

London, Jan. 28.

A diamond of extraordinary size, weighing over 3,000 carats, has been discovered at Johannesburg.

London, Feb. 1.

At St. Petersburg yesterday the police surprised a meeting of strikers held at a tavern, and fired upon them, wounding four men and killing one girl.

Later.

The Czar to-day received a deputation of workmen at Tsarkoe Selo.

With the exception of Warsaw, where there is still considerable ferment, the Russian provinces seem to be generally settling down.

London, Feb. 1.

Prince Sviatopolk Mirsky, the Russian Minister of the Interior, has finally resigned.

London, Feb. 1.

General Sakharoff estimates the number of Japanese prisoners which the Russians captured during the recent fighting to be over three hundred.

Berlin, Jan. 31.

Public opinion is favourable to the new Commercial Treaties entered into between Germany and the Powers. The journals which represent the Conservative and Clerical parties are particularly warm in their approval. On the other hand the Liberal journals are divided in opinion on the subjects, while the Socialists are disposed to oppose the new agreements. The Government intends to present all the seven treaties to the Reichstag at the same time and to ask the latter to either pass the whole of them as they stand or reject them. Most of the treaties come into force a year hence, but some of them will go into operation at an earlier date.

Berlin, Jan. 31.

The German Crown Prince will pay a visit to Italy in the course of February.

Berlin, Jan. 31.

The condition of Prince Eitel Fridrich is still improving.

GENERAL NEWS.

Berlin, Jan. 28.

The Spanish Cabinet has resigned. Senor Villaverde is regarded as the probable successor to the premiership.

London, Jan. 31.

Princess Victoria has been operated upon for appendicitis. The operation was successful, and the Royal patient is progressing satisfactorily.

London, Jan. 31.

Mr. Lawrence Colvile Sackson, K. C., until lately Judicial Commissioner, Federated Malay States, is dead.

THE SHAHO.

Until this morning no further news had been received from the front, so we are in the dark as to the operations for the past six days.

We have received maps of the battlefield and from them we gather that most of the fighting took place in the area enclosed by the rivers Hun, Sha and Taitz, that is to say, on the Japanese left wing.

The Russian objective appears to have been Liaoyang, but having been driven back they retreated in a north westerly direction, crossing the Hun river. A large body of Japanese was reported to be following them up and it is surprising that we have heard no more of this movement.

Mr. Megata unostentatiously departed on a visit to Japan some days ago.

Mr. Nagamori is said to be in Chemulpo and we await developments.

The Japanese are now talking of sending us over a batch of sanitary "advisers."

H. E. Chang Kwang Chuen, the new Chinese Minister, has arrived and presented his credentials at an audience yesterday.

It is reported that the Chinese Government has ordered sixty-six big guns from Germany, to be delivered within ten months' time.

We find that we were correct in our supposition that the Mr. Komuchi, whose article appears in another column is the proud father of the Il-chin-hoi.

It is said that two battleships will shortly be despatched from the Mediterranean Squadron to strengthen the China Squadron, and that the Duncan will probably be one of the two selected for duty.

It is reported that arrangements are nearly complete for the floatation of another Japanese loan in London. The interest is to be 6% and the security again the customs. The issue price has not yet been announced but will probably be higher than the last.

Trouble is expected between the Roman Catholic converts and Japanese Buddhist converts in Fokien province owing to one of the Buddhist converts being murdered by a convert of the Roman Catholic faith. It is reported that the Japanese Consul has taken action in that matter.

The Board of Revenue and the Finance Department in China are busy discussing what steps should be adopted for punishing counterfeiters of Government bank notes. They are in a position to deal with Chinese counterfeiters, but have no law for the punishment of foreign offenders. Owing to this, the Ministers of the Board of Revenue and Finance Department are in communication with the different foreign Ministers with the view to a satisfactory solution of the difficulty.

JAPAN AND HER INTENTIONS.

(Concluded from last issue).

railway was to prepare against a possible Russian invasion of northern Korea. This is only one among many instances of the manner in which our motives are mistaken by the Koreans. What we need to do is to thoroughly convince them that we are working for their benefit. In order to do this the reforms in administration that we insist on must extend to local government. Heretofore our Government has been content to expend all its efforts on the Korean Central Government and to let the terrible corruption of the provincial government alone. In the provinces to day neither life no property is safe. In consequence of the insecurity attached to everything nobody feels like engaging in any great enterprise. Industries languish on this account. Now if we set about transforming this state of things, if we restore order in lawless districts and establish a stable form of government throughout the country, the Koreans as a nation will begin to see that we are real benefactors. There are thoroughout the provinces a large number of progressive Koreans. Some say they exceed 30,000. Their action has hitherto been mistaken by their own Government and Imperial decrees have been issued denouncing them in unmeasured terms as the enemies of their country. But there is reason to believe that most of these would-be reformers are only actuated by a desire to put an end to those abuses which are the curse of Korean local administration. Japan should work in union with these patriots.

Mr. Kömuchi next discusses what should be Japan's policy towards Manchuria at the close of the war. We can only give his conclusions in barest outline. Manchuria must be restored to China, but not unconditionally. Steps must be taken against the possibility of future Russian aggression in this direction. In the first place if it be true that the East China Railway be owned by the Russian Government,† then it will fall into our hands at the close of the war and our government must run it in the interests of all the great trading Powers. At first it would be unsafe to place it in the hands of a private company; though eventually this might be done. Mr. Komuchi next discusses the many openings for Japanese enterprise which Korea and Manchuria will provide at the war. He says that there is a great difference between the Tokyo business men and the Osaka business men as regards readines to utilize the opportunities which recent events have created. The Osaka people are far ahead of the metropolitans in their knowledge of Chinese and Korean business affairs and in their eagerness to open up trade in those countries. A great many Osaka business men have already started branch establishments in Korea and Manchuria. But Tokyo is listless and quite unenterprising in this direction.

† We observe that several Japanese writers have expressed doubts as to the Russian Government's ownership of this railway, owing to the fact that Russia caused reports to be circulated representing the railway to be owned by a syndicate. In that case the Russian Government would not be under any obligation to hand it over to the Japanese, in case it was demanded as one of the conditions of peace. One Japanese writer advocates the purchase of the Railway by the Russian Government for the purpose of placing Japan in control of it. But this is a pretty tall order to send to St. Petersburg.—(WRITER OF SUMMARY.)

There is talk in Tokio of a new foreign loan being projected the security being either the customs, the railways or the camphor and tobacco monopolies, or perhaps all of them. The difficulty seems to be that no foreign capitalists can be found to underwrite the loan, they being only willing to act as Japanese Government agents, assuming no responsibility themselves.

THE MARTEL-ECKERT WEDDING.

The Roman Catholic Cathedral in Seoul was yesterday the scene of a brilliant wedding when M. E. Martel, professor at the French language school, was married to Amalie, the eldest daughter of Here Eckert.

The attendance at the church, and at the subsequent reception at Miss Sontag's residence, was very large and representative.

All the Foreign Ministers were present, and among the assemblage we noticed the following Korean high officials:—

Gen. Min Young Hoan, 1st aide de-camp of His Majesty; Gen. Min Pyong Suk, president of the Board of Decorations; Gen. Cho Dong Yun, aide de camp of the Crown Pricce; Gen. Pak Chai Soun, Minister of Justice; Min Yong Su, brother of the late Crown Princess: H. E. Yi Chai Kok, Minister of Education; H. E. Ko Yong Hei, Vice of Ecucation and all the chiefs of bureau of the Education Department. Mr. Ko Hei Kiong director of the Bureau of Protocol in the Palace.

Amongst other distinguished guests present were: Mr. and Mrs. Koto, Mr. Mrs. and Miss Mimashi, Mesdames, Berteaux Hagiwara, Bostwick, Elliott, McLellan, English, Bethell, Remion, Laporte, Cuvillier, Morgan, Plaissant, Rondon, Martin, Joly, Hulbert, Avison, Beck, Hallifax, Bennett, Rosetsu, Miss Clemencet.

At the church and at the reception practically the whole of the foreign community was present. In the intervals which occurred in the cermony the Imperial Band provided stirring music.

In the evening the happy couple were entertained at dinner at the French Legation by the Minister, H. E. M. Collin de Plancy, when the elite of the French and German community were present.

We are not in a position to report the proceedings but we are safe in saying that the healths of the bride and bridegroom were pledged many times over and we are sure that all in Seoul will join us in wishing "every thing good" to the new couple.

It is reported that the United States Minister has quite recently introduced a wealthy American financier to Prince Ching.

The Korea Daily News.

Issued at 5 P. M. daily except Sundays.

Rate of Subscription:—
Per Year,............Yen 25.
Per Quarter,..........Yen 7.
Per Month,..........Yen 2.50.

Postage in Korea not charged extra.
Postage abroad charged extra.

Advertisements, 50 sen per day for 1 inch or less.
5 yen per month per inch.
50 yen per year per inch.

All communications to

E. T. BETHELL,
Editor and Publisher,
Pak-tong, Seoul.

FREE TELEGRAMS.

We are not surprised to find that the action of the Japanese Government in in supplying sympathetic newspapers with telegrams from Europe has aroused considerable adverse criticism on the part of newspapers who have not placed themselves wholly at the disposal of the Japanese.

The action would be correct enough if the telegrams given out for publication were cut and dried official messages, dealing only with facts, but the sheaves of messages "received at the Tokio Foreign office" which have been published by most of the newspapers in the far east do not answer to this description. They are nearly always grossly partial and sometimes untrue.

We are not subscribers to Reuters' agency so it is not within our province to criticise their service, but we think it will be agreed that in view of the way in which the strikes and demonstrations in Russia are now gradually fizzling out, a great deal more importance has been given to the incidents than was really deserved. Still, Reuter's agency has to cater for its subscribers, and as most of the newspapers in the far east are pro-Japanese in tone,—from the "Singapore Free press" which is so from honest conviction, to the "Japan Mail," which is actuated by other motives,—it is not a matter for wonder that some bias pervades its messages.

But no excuse can be found for the "coloured" messages officially issued by the Japanese Government, and in this connection the "China Review" says:—

"As a clear case in point, we reproduce the following, which appeared in the North China "Daily News" of the 9th instant:—

"We have to thank the Consul General for Japan for the following official telegram:"—

Tokio, Jan. 7th.

"According to Reuter, Prince Trubetskoi, President of the Moscow Zemstvo, addressed to the Minister of Interior on the 5th inst., an open letter, explaining his reasons for allowing his Zemstvo to discuss state affairs. The letter says that Russia is on the brink of anarchy and revolution. It is not the action of the youth of the Empire. but a reflex of the general situation which is dangerous for society, and especially for the person of the Czar. The duty of all loyal subjects compels them to make known to the Czar the thoughts that are oppressing them. The only way of averting revolution is for the Czar to place confidence in the nation. The Prince concludes that it is no moment to be silent when the Fatherland is in danger."

Now, in connection with this specious lie, we are officially authorised to state that Prince Trubetskoy never wrote or issued such a letter to the minister of the interior; and any sensible person would at once perceive the improbability of the whole story; which bears "manufacture" on the face of it.

The "China Gazette" condemns the practise as impertinent and demands to know what England would do did France adopt a similar policy with regard to English internal affairs. The comparison is somewhat far fetched; for the simple reason that Great Britain and France are not at war.

Although we have different reasons, we quite agree with our contemporaries in deploring the establishment of a "news bureau" in the Japanese Government. Most of the news given out has been fairly accurate and our complaint is not that we do not get "the truth" but that we do not get "the whole truth." News of a nature favourable to Japan reaches Korea in very short order from Tokio, but we have to depend upon other sources for adverse news.

So that by this expensive process the Japanese are gradually but surely defeating their own ends, and of late after reading the Japanese version of an incident, the public, grown wary, reserves its judgment until in due course the other side of the question is put before them.

We do not know how it is in China, but there can be no doubt that in Korea, by wide-spread advertising of successes and the careful suppression of adverse news, the Japanese have convinced the Koreans that this war will end in their favour and have thereby been able to assume a much "stronger" attitude in Korea than would otherwise have been the case.

THE FRIEND OF MAN.

Writing in "The Scottish Field" (a well-illustrated magazine devoted to natural history and sport), Mr. G. W. Murdoch relates the following story:—

One of my deerhounds, Luath, became very much attached to the Rev. Mr. Moore, minister of the Shrewsbury Presbyterian Church, a young man of great promise, and very fond of natural history rambles in the beautiful country around that town, often in my company and the dog's, and, if by himself, rarely without Luath. Mr. Moore caught typhus fever, sickened, rapidly and died. For three days and nights before his death and burial that hound lay on the mat outside the door of his lodgings where he had lived. It attended the funeral, a very large one, quietly stationed itself immediately behind the hearse, and sedately marched to the graveyard. It stood over the grave, silently listened to the sublime and solemn Burial Service, watched the coffin lowered, gazed down and then disapeared. Many a time and oft have I and friends seen that hound visit the grave for a few minutes and quietly walk off.

In modern sheep-worrying the object is not food. Reynard kills and carries off a lamb now and, but that is for food. He does not go rampaging among a whole flock, tearing and worrying the helpless brutes, as dogs do, and the reason is this. Primitive hunting man did not train dogs to single out an individual deer, cow, or bull from a head, run it down and kill it. He knew his work too well for that, so he trained his dogs to round the heards, tear at them, maim them, as many as posible, and he with his flint arrows, hatchets, or bludgeons gave them the "coup de grace". And so it is in many things. "We travel in a circle, and as we near the end we approach the being."

In the case of bull dogs tracking deer, that is an impossibility as these brutes are bred now-a-days. But it was was not so formerly. My old King Dick the Third was a powerfully built dog of the old Staffordshire King Dick strain, and he was quite abnormally active and enduring on his feet. But there must have been even more active and powerful bull dogs in Scotland long before his day, for Charles St. John, in his fascinating "Tour in Sutherlandshire" (1848) mentions the use he made of a powerful "bull dog" for tracking a wounded deer for many miles in a wild and "stiff" country, which work it did splendidly! It it possible to breed "back" the bull dog to a condition of shapeliness, intelligence, and stamina as indicated by the facts recorded in even my own personal experience stretching back, say, forty years?

A PERSONAL NARRATIVE OF THE SIEGE OF PORT ARTHUR.

(Specially written for The "China Review" by a Russian Naval Officer.)

Now it is quiet. The strain is over, and I am sitting before a warm fire here in Chefoo. I am surprised to find myself taking a new interest in things. Death seems to have gone in the distance. I feel, in fact, as one who convalesces from a long sickness that brought nigh the hereafter, and I welcome this rush of the new-founded love of life to my heart.

Love of life is the natural attribute of all men, but we of the garrison of Port Arthur learned to do without it. For once we were brought face to face with the inevitable—surrender or death, we welcomed the latter, for we knew the iron wills of Stoessel, Wirenius and others must be broken before the former would be possible. Life was then but a constant nervous, mental and physical strain from which there was no relief nor rest except death or desertion.

In these days when men talked of future action, they spoke in the subjunctive. The use of the phrase "if I am alive to-morrow" was instinctively general with us. It was used unostentatiously, however, without emphasis, quite as a matter of course. We were familiarized with the possibilities of the future. And as little by little our hope of succor dwindled, we became mere automatons impelled by a seeming inertia in the performance of our duty; our sympathies were deadened; even the wounded in the hospitals.—who, under stress of great physical suffering, seemed more human than we in the trenches and the forts,—complained that the sisters of charity and the doctors handled them roughly, not appearing to care whether they lived or died.

I remember once hearing a sister of charity say, at the termination of two days of unceasing labor with the wounded, that she did not think she would ever again experience a feeling of sympathy for human suffering.

(To be continued).

The Korea Daily News.

VOL. II, WEDNESDAY, FEBRUARY 8, 1905. No. 29

HONGKONG & SHANGHAI BANKING CORPORATION.

Paid-up Capital	$10,000,000
Reserve Fund:—Sterling Reserve	10,000,000
Silver Reserve	7,000,000
	27,000,000
Reserve Liability of Proprietors	10,000,000

HEAD OFFICE, HONGKONG.

London Bankers, London and County Banking Company Limited.

Branches and Agencies,

London.

Amoy,	Hankow	Penang,
Bangkok,	Hiogo,	Rangoon,
Batavia,	Iloilo,	Saigon,
Bombay,	Lyons,	San Francisco,
Calcutta,	Manila,	Singapore,
Colombo,	Nagasaki,	Sourabaya,
Foochow,	New York,	Tientsin,
Hamburg,	Peking,	Yokohama,

Credits granted on approved Securities, and every description of Banking and Exchange business transacted.

Drafts granted on London and the chief Commercial places in Europe, India, Australia, America, China and Japan.

HOLME RINGER & CO., AGENTS,
CHEMULPO.

HOKURKU DOBOKU KAISHA.

Branch office in Chong Dong, Seoul.

Japanese telephone No. 165

CONTRACT DEPARTMENT.

We can contract to build any building or construction.

MERCHANDISE DEPARTMENT.

We can provide any building material. We have just contracted to build the new Belgian Legation.

E. MEYER & CO.

Chemulpo.

SOLE AGENTS IN KOREA FOR.

A. T. Morse, Sons & Co.'s

"Fresco" Distemper

In all colours ready for use on walls,

Ceilings etc.

and

AVENARIUS CARBOLINEUM

A wood-preserving and antiseptic oil preparation

Against decay, dry-rot, fungus and wood-destroying insects.

A large supply always in stock.
Prices upon application.

E. MEYER & Co.,
Chemulpo.

CHARTERED BANK OF INDIA AUSTRALIA & CHINA.

INCORPORATED BY ROYAL CHARTER 1853

HEAD OFFICES.—LONDON.

Paid-up Capital	£800,000
Reserve Liability of Shareholders	800,000
Reserve Fund	800,000

Drafts granted upon all the principal places in the world and every description of Exchange and banking business transacted.

E. MEYER & Co., Agents,
Chemulpo.

MITSU BISHI DOCKYARD & ENGINE WORKS,

NAGASAKI.

CODE WORD, "DOCK."

A 1, A. B. C., and Engineering Codes used.

DOCK No. 1 (at Tategami).

Extreme Length	523 feet
Length on blocks	513 ,,
Width of Entrance on Top	89 ,,
,, ,, Bottom	77 ,,
Water on Blocks at Spring Tide	26½ ,,

DOCK No. 2 (Mukaijima).

Extreme Length	371 feet
Length on Blocks	360 ,,
Width of Entrance on Top	66 ,,
,, ,, Bottom	53 ,,
Water on Blocks at Spring Tide	22 ,,

PATENT SLIP (at Kosuge).

Can take vessels up to 1,000 tons gross.

THE WORKS are well equipped with the LATEST IMPROVEMENTS, and can execute any kind of work in SHIPBUILDING and MARINE ENGINEERING, as well as in REPAIRING of SHIPS.

The COMPANY'S new powerful steamer OURA-MARU (712 tons, 700 I.H.P.), specially built for SALVAGE PURPOSES, and equipped with necessary gear, is always READY at SHORT NOTICE.

THE METHODIST PUBLISHING HOUSE,

Little West Gate, Seoul.

JOB PRINTING, TYPEWRITER PAPER
CARBON PAPER, VISITING CARDS
STATIONERY, BOOK BINDING
BOOK PUBLISHERS
AMERICAN SCHOOL BOOKS
SPENCERIAN COPY BOOKS
PEN CARBON LETTER AND BILL BOOKS

S. A. BECK, Manager.

DAI-ICHI GINKO.

LIMITED.

(Formerly the First National Bank)

ESTABLISHED 1873

INCORPORATED UNDER PRESENT LAW 1896

Capital	Yen 5,000,000
Reserve Fund	1,500,000

HEAD OFFICE:—TOKIO.

President: Baron SHIBUSAWA.

BRANCHES AND CORRESPONDENTS

In the Principal Cities and Towns of Japan.

Interest Allowed on

Fixed deposits 1 year	6½	per cent
" " 6 months	6	per cent

Special current accounts 1½ sen daily per Y 100
General " " 1 " " " 100

M. TANAKA,
Manager, Chemulpo.

SINGER SEWING MACHINES

씽거즈봉침

SOLE AGENTS
FOR KOREA
전매쇼

HOLME RINGER & CO.
Chemulpo.

졔물포 함릉거양힝

KAMEYA CO.

GENERAL STOREKEEPERS

Chinkokai - - Seoul

(*Established 1895, Tokyo*)

Confectionery, Hams, Canned Goods, Cutlery, Hirano & Tansan Water. Provisions, Gents, Furnishing goods, Toilet Articles, Travelling Bags, Tobacco, Cigars & Cigarettes Kitchen Utensils. Coffee, Biscuits

Fresh Goods always kept in Stock.

Prices Moderate

Please come and inspect our goods.

NIPPON YUSEN KAISHA.

JAPANESE MAIL STEAMSHIP CO.

UNDER MAIL CONTRACT WITH THE IMPERIAL JAPANESE GOVERNMENT.

European Line

Regular Fortnightly Service between Yokohama Kobe, Moji, Shanghai, Hongkong, Singapore, Penang Colombo, Port Said, Marseilles, London and Antwerp

American Line

Regular Fortnightly Service between Hongkong and Seattle, calling at Shanghai, Moji, Kobe, Yokohama and Victoria, B. C.

Australian Line

Regular weekly Service betwen Japan Ports and Australia, calling at Hongkong and Manila.

(Above Three Lines Suspended until further notice).

Shanghai Line

Weekly Service between Shanghai and Japan Ports

Korea Line

Service Kobe, Moji, Nagasaki, Fusan Chemulpo Chefoo, Taku.

S. S. Babelsberg, 2181 tons.

Service Kobe, Moji, Fusan Chemulpo, Chinnampo

S. S. ARGO, S. S. Ohio.

BORDEN'S CONDENSED MILK CO.

New York, U. S. A.

ALWAYS IN STOCK

Eagle Brand Condensed Milk.

Gold Seal Condensed Milk.

Peerless (Family) Evaporated Cream.

Borden's Malted Milk.

E. MEYER & CO.
Chemulpo Korea,
Sole Agents

ROYAL INSURANCE COMPANY,

Funds exceed £10,000,000

FIRE

AT CURRENT RATES

LIFE

REDUCED PREMIUM.

HOLME RINGER & Co.,
Agents, Chemulpo

廣

KWANG ◉ C'HANG

昌

BENNETT & CO.

Merchants

Chemulpo.

Offices opposite the Imperial Japanese Post and Telegraph Office Chemulpo

Telephone Number [illegible]

大韓每日申報
대한ᄆᆡ일신보

(뎨이쳔삼십호) (금요일) 일쳔구ᄇᆡᆨ오년이월십일

본사고ᄇᆡᆨ

이신보는영어와한어로셕거ᄆᆡ일츌판ᄒᆞᆷ

신문갑

한쟝 엽두돈오푼

일삭표 엽두량엿돈

우표갑대신엿돈

다엿돈으로밧슴

광고료는

긔한의쟝단과ᄌᆞᆼ횡의대쇼로증감ᄒᆞ되렴가로밧을터이오ᄆᆡ오린지아니ᄒᆞᆫ대한사ᄅᆞᆷ마다마다이신문을보실터이니광고ᄒᆞ시기를원ᄒᆞ시는이들은우리신문사에와서면약ᄒᆞ심을희망ᄒᆞᆷ

○발ᄒᆡᆼ소 박동대한ᄆᆡ일신보사 법어학교앏희젼영국인셜필립졍자리오

사쟝 영국인 (비셜)

평양 디리졈

○평양효동사는권미보씨로우리신문판ᄆᆡ대리인을뎡ᄒᆞ엿시ᄉᆞ오니평양에계신구람코쟈ᄒᆞ시는 쳠군ᄌᆞ는히디리졈에왕림ᄒᆞ와면의ᄒᆞ시옵

사고

○우리대한ᄆᆡ일신보의목뎍은대한의안녕질셔에관ᄒᆞᆫ모든대목에ᄃᆡᄒᆞ야는공평ᄒᆞᆫ변론을쥬쟝ᄒᆞᆷ이라우리등신원의담보는신문보시는쳠군ᄌᆞ의계ᄒᆞᆼ샹보도ᄒᆞ리며편지등과셔ᄒᆞ며주시는이는셩명과번디를적어붓치시기를희망ᄒᆞ오니이거슨신문샹에긔재ᄒᆞ란는거시아니오다만극히신용ᄒᆞᄂᆞᆫ증거를숨고자ᄒᆞᆷ이라긔자는아모긔셔던지긔재ᄒᆞᆷ을퇴ᄌᆞᆨᄒᆞ는권리를가졋스나퇴ᄌᆞᆨᄒᆞ는리유는말ᄒᆞᆯ터이오며공중평화를문란케ᄒᆞᄂᆞᆫ듯ᄒᆞᆫ긔셔는의례히밧지안켓ᄉᆞᆸᄂᆞ이다

●본사셜시ᄒᆞᆫ리로신문을대ᄇᆡᆼ우례로분젼ᄒᆞ와례젼부의일의로젼ᄒᆞᄂᆞᆫ듯스로면곳에는ᄒᆞᆨ늣게젼ᄒᆞ기도ᄒᆞ며ᄒᆞᆨ면쳘거슬ᄒᆞᆫ젼에젼ᄒᆞ기도ᄒᆞ며ᄒᆞᆨ아니젼ᄒᆞ는곳도잇다ᄒᆞ와우리신문을수람ᄒᆞ야구람ᄒᆞ시는 쳠군ᄌᆞ의게탕티ᄒᆞ야[illegible]운분젼인을[illegible]교[illegible]등이젼ᄒᆞ며야[illegible]젼ᄒᆞ기난[illegible]게ᄒᆞ나ᄒᆞᆷ폐가업도록ᄒᆞ랴ᄒᆞ오니ᄒᆞᆨ아니젼ᄒᆞ거는ᄒᆞᆨ늣게젼ᄒᆞ거나ᄒᆞᆫ일이잇스면본사로통긔ᄒᆞ여주심을희망ᄒᆞᆷ

론셜

일본의언약

○지금일본이젼에언약ᄒᆞᆫ것과는틀니게일을ᄒᆞ야가는것시인심을엇을쟝본인지일을징죠인지말ᄒᆞ기어렵도다

젼쟁의ᄆᆡ린후로일본이한국과만쥬에ᄃᆡᄒᆞ야졍칙을변ᄒᆞᆫ셔류가두가지가잇스니ᄒᆞ나는젼쟁의진보가에쟝ᄒᆞᆫ것보다속히되엿고두가지는일본이무ᄋᆞᆷ티로젼에언약ᄒᆞᆫ것을저ᄇᆞ린는것이라

한국에셔지금일본인의ᄒᆡᆼ위가우리보기에는한국졍부에셔ᄒᆞ던ᄒᆡᆼ위보다낫지못ᄒᆞ고우리는량편이다그르다고말ᄒᆞ겟스며그중에일본인이아니라에셔셜신ᄒᆞᆷ으로돌넘벗게엿다ᄒᆞ노라일본에잇는ᄌᆡ펀헤렐드라는신문의일월십구일지면에긔재ᄒᆞᆫ것스되일본이한국의독립으로ᄒᆞ야피롭게지번다ᄒᆞ엿스니그것은참말이로다그러ᄒᆞ나일본이한국의독립을보젼ᄒᆞ고만쥬는샹관아니ᄒᆞ겟다고공포ᄒᆞᆫ셔류에이번젼쟁에세계의동졍을엇은지라

만일일본이말ᄒᆞ되져의나라가망ᄒᆞᆯ셔렴려ᄒᆞ야이번싸홈을ᄒᆞᆫ다ᄒᆞ면세상에셔밋지아니ᄒᆞᆯ터이라그럼으로일본이한국과만쥬를위ᄒᆞ야싸운다ᄒᆞ야세계의감졍을엇엇스니일본은무엇을엇으랴고싸우는것이아니오만쥬를쳥국에돌녀보내고한국의독립과강토보젼을위ᄒᆞᆷ이로다지금ᄌᆡ펀헤렐드신문은우리가여러달젼에ᄉᆡᆼ각ᄒᆞ든일을말ᄒᆞ엿도다일본이젼에언약ᄒᆞᆫ것으로ᄒᆞ야피롭게지내고우리도그러ᄒᆞ며아마영국도그러ᄒᆞᆯ듯ᄒᆞᆫ지라

이젼쟁이일본의게샹보다속히진보가되야가니우리의ᄉᆡᆼ각에는그것시이분ᄒᆡᆼᄒᆞᆫ나라의쳥금에엳되야가는근원이로다일본이지금이나라에셔권리을쟈만ᄒᆞᄂᆞᆫ거시그럿치아니ᄒᆞ면한국에ᄃᆡᄒᆞᆫ리익이필요ᄒᆞᆫ여슨이라그러ᄒᆞ기는ᄒᆞ고수ᄒᆞ고쟝샹ᄉᆞ건으로브터샹법만연ᄒᆞᄂᆞᆫ찬ᄉᆞ건ᄭᆞ지모든일이샹ᄃᆡ쟝칙과곳지아니ᄒᆞ고쟝ᄒᆞᆫ곳도다

일본인고무치라는쟈이말ᄒᆞ되만일우리가이다음에젼쟁에불리ᄒᆞ면한국에셔이리남원관이말ᄒᆞᆯ수업게되리라ᄒᆞ엿스니우리는실심으로고무치씨의의견을찬셩ᄒᆞ며ᄯᅩᄒᆞᆫ말을더ᄒᆞᆯ것이그ᄯᅢ에는일진회도져의불진이조곰도못되리라ᄒᆞ노라

처음브터우리는일본이진실ᄒᆞᆫ한인들의감졍을다샹ᄒᆞ게ᄒᆞᄂᆞᆫ수단을말녀지마는효험은업스며지금은젼쟁이엇지든지일본사ᄅᆞᆷ는져의들이보아노흔쟈리에붓가불셔져의들이누을지라ᄒᆞ노라

뎐보

동지발 동일

○로국내란위급 동맹파공의운동이각도에급속만연ᄒᆞ며쇼셜가ᄆᆡ샹고로키씨의포박되엿다는말은진젹지못ᄒᆞ더라

동지발 동일

○진압졍칙 젼모스코졍부쟝드레포프쟝군이피득보총독임ᄒᆞ고젼권을득ᄒᆞ야작일오후에황졔ᄭᅴ셔동ᄒᆞ는궁젼에셔피득보경부쟝과군디를명솔ᄒᆞᆫ관원들노터브러샹의ᄒᆞ고쳥금소관을진압ᄒᆞᄂᆞᆫ티는엄혹ᄒᆞᆫ방침을ᄒᆡᆼᄒᆞ라명령ᄒᆞ엿더라

동지발 동일

○진무졍칙 모스코에셔코가색병이샹젼명의혁명당에게코가격ᄒᆞ야다수의혁명당이샹ᄒᆞ엿스며신임니무ᄃᆡ신드레포프쟝군이로동쟈등이미셔사셔너에각기졍에도라가거나져의촌에으로가라고각공쟝에고시ᄒᆞ야두어졔죠쟝은사무가회복ᄒᆞ엿스나파공의운동은졈연히각도로만연ᄒᆞ며아ᄆᆡ의혁명으로논자뢰포포쟝군과탁지ᄃᆡ신이로동쟈에게포고ᄒᆞ되여등이여등을잘못인도ᄒᆞ는불량ᄒᆞᆫ고사욕을탐ᄒᆞ는쟈들에게이용ᄒᆞᆷ이되여무력으로져항키어려우나셜명ᄒᆞ고졍부가지금인민의공평ᄒᆞᆫ소원을쳥죵ᄒᆞ기를쥰비ᄒᆞᆫ다ᄒᆞ엿더라

로국의경형

론돈발 일월이십칠일

○로국졍부의압졔졍칙이실시가되야서경셩은조용ᄒᆞ야졋스나혁명운동을주쟝ᄒᆞᄂᆞᆫ사ᄅᆞᆷ들이다음에더큰분요를이르키기로조직ᄒᆞᆫ다더라

론돈데일니크로니클신문의셩피득보통신원이보고ᄒᆞ되셩피득보에셔오젼명의혁명당을지낸쇼ᄋᆡᆯ에가두엇더니포박ᄒᆞ엿ᄂᆞᆫ디지금사ᄒᆞ엿는티지고번ᄃᆡ베쥬아브로유빈ᄒᆞ야나간다ᄒᆞ엿더라

동더발 동월이십팔일

○셩피득보에잇는영국대사하되지씨가모스코경무쳥에셔교셥ᄒᆞ되지금혁명운동이영국과일본의츙동ᄒᆞᆫ것과이오영국에셔혁명당의게돈을공급ᄒᆞᆫ다ᄒᆞ는날에ᄃᆡᄒᆞ야셰로이변명ᄒᆞᆫ항의를졔츌ᄒᆞ엿다더라

혁명당들이각디방에면연ᄒᆞ며파란도회에셔도분요를이르키고로동쟈수쳔명이모스코로브터셩피득보로향ᄒᆞ야진칩ᄒᆞᆫ다는말이잇스며샤회당들은말ᄒᆞ되황뎨가필경은혁명당들의게암샬이되리라ᄒᆞ고보블닉스코돌졔에와로도착ᄒᆞᆫ군ᄃᆡ는분란을원으며이번젼졍에ᄃᆡᄒᆞ야황뎨망ᄒᆞᆫ다더라

ᄇᆡᆨ림발 일월이십구일

○셩피득보에셔는혼동취셔가되엿고모스코에셔도ᄎᆞᄎᆞ죵돈경이되야가며셩피득보에신문들은다시발간ᄒᆞ나위쇼에셔는로동쟈십만명이아직나셔셔샹공이니ᄒᆞ며로드쓰에셔도야단이낫다더라

론돈발 동월삼십일

○위쇼에셔지번요요ᄒᆞᆫ에ᄃᆡᄒᆞᆫ비ᄋᆡᆨ라나셔큰샹졈들을깁탈ᄒᆞ고쇼화ᄒᆞ엿는ᄃᆡ긔병이무력으로진압ᄒᆞ야먹번은즁인에향ᄒᆞ야방포ᄒᆞ엿스며

위쇼에잇는영국총령ᄉᆞ무레이씨와쇼계와부령ᄉᆞ무포는ᄉᆞ게인씨는광병의게셔셩젼을당ᄒᆞ엿다더라

ᄒᆞᆫ편위쇼에셔작일에분요가다시일죽엇스며ᄇᆡᆨ여명이샹ᄒᆞ고계엄을더엄즁히ᄒᆞᆫ다더라

론돈발 일월삼십일

○모스코황궁뎐덕과젼래슈셔지대공의집에폭발약을두어셔대공은거의즉을번ᄒᆞ엿스며셔

UNION INSURANCE SOCIETY OF CANTON.

Head office Hongkong.
Marine risks underwritten at current rates.

Agents in Chemulpo,
E. MEYER & Co.

COMPAGNIE DES MESSAGERIES MARITIMES.

Fortnightly Direct Service.

For Marseilles
via Ports.
Sailing from Yokohama.
Calling at Kobe,
Shanghai, Hongkong, Saigon, Singapore,
Colombo, Djibonti, Suez, Port Said
and Marseilles

For particulars apply to
HOLME RINGER & Co.,
Chemulpo.

HAYASHIDA & CO.,

16 MYENG DONG, CHIN KO KAI, SEOUL.
BRANCH OFFICE AT CHEMULPO.

Money changers, Coal and Wood Merchants, Express Agents.

We are agents for the Pyeng-yang Coal Company and the Karazu Coal Company of Japan. We have the best quality of both anthracite and bituminous coal, and prompt execution of orders is our speciality. Firewood of all kinds kept in stock. Full weight guaranteed. Money of all denominations exchanged at current rates. Parcels received for all parts.

CHINA MUTUAL LIFE INS. OC.

Most favourable terms to policy holders.

Benefit system unsurpassed.

HOLME RINGER & Co.
Agents, Chemulpo.

C. P. R.

CANADIAN PACIFIC RAILWAY COMPANY'S ROYAL MAIL STEAMSHIP LINE.

THE FAST ROUTE BETWEEN CHINA, JAPAN, AND EUROPE VIA CANADA AND THE UNITED STATES.

Route from Hongkong via Shanghai, Nagasaki (Inland Sea of Japan) Kobe, Yokohama. Victoria and Vancouver.

Twin Screw Empress Steamship—6,000 Tons—Speed 19 knots.

PROPOSED SAILING FROM YOKOHAMA.
R. M. S. Empress of India.
R. M. S. Empress of Japan.
R. M. S. Empress of China.
R. M. S. Athenian.
R. M. S. Tartar.

Special reduction (first class only) granted to members of the Military, Naval, Diplomatic and Civil services and to Missionaries.

Passengers have choice of ten routes across the Continent of America and have privilege of travelling by any Atlantic Steamship Line.

Round the World passage tickets in connection with the P. and O. S. N., North German Lloyd and Messageries Co.'s £125.

All rates payable at current rate of exchange.

For further information, Tickets, Guide Books, etc., apply to

HOLME, RINGER & Co., AGENTS,
Chemulpo.

Grand Hotel

(Formerly the Station Hotel)

Near the Railway Terminus,
West Gate Seoul.

The Best Hotel in Korea
Handsome new Building.
Fine Airy Rooms
Excellent Cuisine.
Terms Moderate.
Special terms to Missionaries
and to permanent boarders.

Electric cars within 2 minutes' walk.

W. H. EMBERLEY.
Proprie to

EVERY FACILITY.

In connection with Life Assurance Business is afforded by

The Standard Life Assurance Co.,

One of the largest and wealthiest of the Provident Institutions of the United Kingdom Forms of Application and all information will be promptly afforded on application.

10 CENTS A DAY.

Not a very large expenditure is it? But it is sufficient to secure for a man of 30 a policy with the STANDARD LIFE OFFICE for

$1323.

For all particulars of rates, etc., apply to

Holme, Ringer & Co.,
Agents, Chemulpo.

THE NEW YORK LIFE INSURANCE COMPANY.

Have you ever been declined by any Company?

Are you engaged in a specially hazardous occupation?

Have you heard of the New York Life Insurance Company's New Classifications for this class of Risks?

If not, send your date of birth, occupation and particulars of rejection, if any to

E. MEYER & Co.,
Agents, Chemulpo.

MITSUI BUSSAN KAISHA.
(MITSUI & Co.)
MITSUI GINKO.
(MITSUI BANK.)

The Bank is owned by the members of the Mitsui Family, who, as partners, assume an unlimited responsibility for all liabilities of the Bank:—

Capital........................Yen 5,000,000
Reserve Fund.................. " 5,600,000

HEAD OFFICE, TOKYO.
LONDON OFFICE, 34 LIME ST., E. C.

BRANCHES AND AGENCIES:—
New York, San Francisco, Hamburg, Bombay, Singapore, Manila, Hongkong, Amoy, Chefoo, Tientsin.

Kobe, Hakodate, Yokohama, Kure, Yokosuka, Moji, Shimonoseki, Miike, Wakamatsu, Nagasaki, Kuchinotsu, Karatsu, Sasebo, Misume, Taipeh, &c.

Telegraphic Address for all the Offices:
"MITSUI."
A. B. C. AND A. 1 CODES USED.

Contractors of Coal
To the Imperial Japanese Navy. Arsenals and Railway Bureau, Principal Railway Companies and Industrial Work, Home and Foreign Mail and Freight Steamers.

Sole Proprietors
Of the famous Miike, Tagawa and Yamano Coal Mines.

Sole Agents
For the sale of Fukumo, Hokoku, Ichimura Kanoda, Mannoura, Onoura, Ostuji, Sonoda Tsubaruro, Yoshinotani, Yoshio, Yurokibura and other coals.

YANGTSE INSURANCE ASSOCIATION, LTD.

The undersigned, having been appointed agents for the above company, are prepared to issue policies and pay losses on marine risks at regular rates.

E. MEYER & Co.,
Agents, Chemulpo.

AMERICAN KOREAN ELECTRIC CO.

Light and Power.

Main Office: Electric Building, Chong No.

RAILWAY DEPARTMENT.

OPERATING CARS BETWEEN EAST AND WEST GATE, EVERY TEN MINUTES:—

First Car leaves East Gate at 7:00 A. M. First Car leaves R. R. Station at 7:25 A. M
Last Car " East Gate at 8.40 P. M. Last " " R. R. Station at 9.05 P.M

OPERATING CARS BETWEEN EAST GATE AND IMPERIAL TOMB TERMINUS, EVERY TWENTY MINUTES:—

CONNECTING WITH EVERY ALTERNATE CAR ARRIVING AT EAST GATE FROM CHONG NO.

First Car leaves East Gate for Tomb at 7:10 A. M.
" " " Tomb for East Gate at 7:30 A. M.
Last " " East Gate for Tomb at 7:50 P. M.
" " " Tomb for East Gate at 8:10 P. M.

OPERATING CARS BETWEEN CHONG NO AND YUNG SAN RIVER EVERY TWELVE MINUTES:—

First Car leaves Chong No for South Gate at 7:12 A. M.
" " " Chong No for Yung San at 7:36 A. M.
" " " South Gate for Chong No at 7:20 A. M.
" " " Yung San for Chong No at 8:09 A. M.
Last " " South Gate for Chong No 9:00 P. M.
" " " Yung San for Chong No at 8:45. p. M.

SPECIAL PRIVATE CARS FURNISHED TO SUIT CONVENIENCE OF PATRONS. PRICES ON APPLICATION AT HEAD OFFICE.

LIGHTING DEPARTMENT.

Where less than 250 candle power of light is used, the rate per month will be
Per 16 candle power incandescent lamp,—All night.—Yen 2.50.
32 candle power incandescent lamp:—All night:—Yen 4.00.
50 candle power incandescent lamp:—All night:—Yen 6.00.
150 " " " " " " " 10.00.
1200 " " enclosed arc " " " 20.00.

Where more than 250 candle power of light is used, a Meter will be installed, if requested:—Rent of Meter Yen 2.00 per month. Rate of charges by meter reading:—Two Sen per Ampere per hour. (Approximately this is equal to about One Sen per 16 C. P. lamp per hour) Minimum monthly charge where meter is installed, Yen 20.00 per month, which includes rental of meter.

Estimates for installing lights furnished on application

An assortment of chandeliers always on hand.

K. Murakami.

Photograph Studio
Chinkokai, Seoul.

Printing, Developing and Enlargement, of Photographs always Undertaken.

Korean Views and Pictures Illustrating Native Customs always on Sale,

---

THE OSAKA SHOSEN KAISHA.

Boats frequently on the berth for Chinnampo.

REGULAR SAILINGS BETWEEN JAPAN AND KOREAN PORTS.

FUSAN AND KOBE VIA SHIMONOSEKI.

OSAKA VIA MOKPO, FUSAN, SHIMONOSEKI AND KOBE.

MOJI DIRECT.

OSAKA VIA KUNSAN, MASANPO, FUSAN, SHIMONOSEKI AND KOBE.

CHEMULPO KUNSAN LINE,
Every three days.

CHEMULPO CHINNAMPO LINE.
Every three days.

For Freight and passage and further particulars apply to

THE OSAKA SHOSEN KAISHA,
Cemulpo.

RONDON, PLAISANT & CO.

General Storekeepers and Merchants, Ships Contractors Tobacconists, Commission and Forwarding Agents, Coal Merchants

IMPORTERS AND EXPORTERS

Seoul Chemulpo.

W. D. WENTWORTH.

LANDING
AND
SHIPPING AGENT.
AND
CUSTOMS BROKER.

12 OURA, NAGASAKI.

STEWARD & CO.

Chemulpo.

Shipchandlers and Storekeepers, Naval and Mercantile Contractors, Landing and Shipping Agents.

STEWARD'S HOTEL

Chemulpo.

Best accommodation in the port for travellers. Clean and well-aired rooms, good cuisine and prompt attendance, oderate tariff.

피득보는것으로는죠용ᄒᆞ나속으로는미우위험ᄒᆞ고트레포프쟝군은의심잇는사ᄅᆞᆷ의집은순검을보내슈탐ᄒᆞ야유명ᄒᆞᆫ져술가와자유대의유명ᄒᆞᆫ회원들을만히포박ᄒᆞ엿고교사기ᄅᆞᆫ은셔샤국으로도망ᄒᆞ엿다더라

빅림발 동월삼십일일

○지낸수일동안은로국에셔시로이이러는분요는업고몃곳은란민들이다시져의들의직무에도라갓스며황뎨께셔로동쟈의총ᄃᆡ들을친히보시기를허락ᄒᆞ엿다는ᄃᆡ그분요가미구에진졍되리라ᄒᆞ엿더라

볼틱함ᄃᆡ의소식

론돈발 일월이십팔일

○세바스토폴에셔젼ᄒᆞᄂᆞᆫ풍셜을거ᄒᆞᆫ즉로졔스트벤스기대쟝의함ᄃᆡ에ᄯᆞᆯ닌군함들이 자낸풍랑에미우샹ᄒᆞ엿다더라

론돈발 일월이십팔일

○포트세이도에잇는류터통신원이보ᄒᆞ되가신ᄒᆞᆯ만ᄒᆞᆫ말을드론즉볼틱함ᄃᆡ의ᄒᆞᆫ부분은미구에소ᄉᆞ운하로지내셔도라갈터이오그남어지비들은파ᄉᆞ만에향ᄒᆞ야갈터이라ᄒᆞ엿다더라

청국의즁립

빅림발 일월삼십일일

○청국이즁립을위반ᄒᆞᆫ다는로국션고문에ᄃᆡᄒᆞ야각국이하나도승인ᄒᆞᆫ나라가업다더라

각국소식

론돈발 일월이십팔일

○로법동밍의쥬슈 법국외부대신델캇세재가하의원에셔공언ᄒᆞ되로법동밍은여젼히쥬수ᄒᆞᆫ다ᄒᆞ엿다더라

북경발 동월이십구일

○청국세졍과영미 영미량국공ᄉᆞ가청국졍부에리긴세금을업시이라고권고ᄒᆞᆫ지가오ᄅᆡ이나의화단비상을갑ᄒᆞᆯ지졍을변통ᄒᆞ기어렵다고총독이반ᄃᆡᄒᆞ는보고를ᄒᆞᆫ고닭에청국졍부에셔영미권고를능히듯지못ᄒᆞ기로작졍ᄒᆞ엿다더라

빅림발 일월이십칠일

○아뎨죠칙 로뎨께셔로동쟈들에게안졍히잇스라고효유ᄒᆞ는죠칙을반포ᄒᆞ샤법률노로동쟈를위ᄒᆞ야보험쥰비금을졍ᄒᆞ고일ᄒᆞ는시간감ᄒᆞᆷ을언약ᄒᆞ며또로동쟈들이져이의고초를젹당ᄒᆞᆫ쥬권쟈에게신원ᄒᆞᆯ방편을말ᄉᆞᆷᄒᆞ엿스며부인나에셔는말ᄒᆞ되극동젼쟁으로향ᄒᆞᆯ바로국속디파란군ᄃᆡ는원한ᄒᆞᆷ이ᄃᆡ단ᄒᆞ다더라

론돈발 동일

○영소발명 모스코는안졍ᄒᆞ나부윤이로동쟈들을십분보호ᄒᆞᆯ줄노교시ᄒᆞ고경무셔에셔는동맹파공의운동은영일의간계ᄅᆞᆯ인ᄒᆞᆷ이며동밍파공쟈들이영국의돈을밧는다명언ᄒᆞ야힘디가로에고셔ᄒᆞ고로로국에쥬지ᄒᆞᆫ영국ᄃᆡ사는이무망ᄒᆞᆫ교시를반ᄃᆡᄒᆞ야여사ᄒᆞᆫ고시는다시포고치못ᄒᆞᆯ확증을엇어쓰며동ᄃᆡ사는병뎡어보호ᄒᆞ며피득보는이젼형세로회복ᄒᆞ엿는ᄃᆡ졍부는소란이아조졍지된줄확신ᄒᆞ더라

동경발 일월이십오일

○군함수보 작일히삼위로브터문사에도박ᄒᆞᆫ덕국긔션의공보를거ᄒᆞᆫ즉로국군함로시아호는수보를완결ᄒᆞ엿고그로모보이호는수보즁이며ᄲᅥ게터호는아죠침수되엿더라

부인나발 동월이십삼일

○법국금지 법국졍부에셔볼틱함ᄃᆡ가법국이관활ᄒᆞᄂᆞᆫ히샹에머믈기를금지ᄒᆞᆫ고로지금동함ᄃᆡ는마다싸스카를격ᄒᆞᆫ법국소관의히샹밧겻ᄃᆡ양에잇는ᄃᆡ량식과셕탄을시러오라고운송션두어쳑을각쳐로파송ᄒᆞ엿고동함ᄃᆡ의소환에ᄃᆡᄒᆞ야는아즉아모명령이업스며동함ᄃᆡ는젼진되기를발아는듯ᄒᆞ고지즁히로도라오는동함ᄃᆡ의일부는완완히항ᄒᆞ는즁이더라

동경발 동일

○함ᄃᆡ발향 모쳐에달ᄒᆞᆫ뎐보ᄅᆞᆯ거ᄒᆞᆫ즉본월이십일일에볼틱함ᄃᆡ가데니쓰루니언셤을향ᄒᆞ야마다싸스카를ᄯᅥ낫다ᄒᆞ나아즉미샹ᄒᆞ더라

동지발 동일

○의안치용 일본귀족원에셔사긔의안을치용ᄒᆞ엿는ᄃᆡ그즁일죠는히군공창비에관계ᄒᆞᆫ것이며즁의원에셔또삼긔의안을제출ᄒᆞ엿는ᄃᆡ아즉결뎡치못ᄒᆞ엿더라

론돈발 동월이십ᄉᆞ일

○명셩대오 론돈타임스신문의북경통신원이려슌구를유람ᄒᆞᆫ후공보ᄒᆞ되금번려슌투항은력사샹에명셩을ᄃᆡ오ᄒᆞ엿다더라

동지발 동월이십일일

○도달필디 타임스신문은로쓰졔스벤스키제독은아모리ᄒᆞ여도삼긔월동안에극동으로도달ᄒᆞᆫ기를발아지안는다고밋더라

동지발 동원이십오일

○삼일뉴쥬 쥬영일본공사림동씨는영황과황후량폐하ᄭᅴ셔원듯소카슬궁으로청요ᄒᆞᆷ이되여동씨가동궁에셔삼일머믄후논돈으로도라온다ᄒᆞ엿더라

빅림발 동일

○됴약조인 오지리와덕국의상업조약은작일죠인되엿더라

잡보

○청원우사령부 즁셔졍션방거ᄒᆞᆫ는리규후씨가긔션협동회샤설시사로일본헌병사령부에청원ᄒᆞ엿다더라

○소안동실화 소안동거ᄒᆞ는김영준의위첩오소ᄉᆞ가에셔지작야에실화ᄒᆞ엿는ᄃᆡ니외국인이일졔히구화ᄒᆞ야물소는아니ᄒᆞ엿다더라

○총관분로 일젼에경위원슌검일명이가칭군인ᄒᆞ고병뎡을란타ᄒᆞᆫ지라헌병북셔소ᄃᆡ쟝홍쳘뉴씨가착슈ᄒᆞ고헌병사령관의게보고ᄒᆞᆫ지라미구에경위총관이친이면화ᄒᆞ고그슌검을방송ᄒᆞ면니가즁치ᄒᆞ겟다ᄒᆞᆫ즉소ᄃᆡ쟝말이사령부에보고ᄒᆞ엿슨즉가히스스로쳔단못ᄒᆞ겟다ᄒᆞ엿더니경위총관말이나는부쟝이라요마ᄒᆞᆫ소ᄃᆡ쟝이명령을좃지아니ᄒᆞᆫ다고분로ᄒᆞ엿다더라

○일샹착거 작일종로에셔엇던아회가일인샹젼에셔무ᄉᆞᆷ놀건을사랴고만져보고사지안니ᄒᆞᆫ지라일샹이그아회를도적놈이라고무수란타ᄒᆞ미엇던일어ᄒᆞ는사ᄅᆞᆷ삼사인이일본령사관에가셔일본슌사를다리고와셔그일샹을잡아갓다더라

○편젼치사 작일굴ᄶᅢ편싸홈에사ᄅᆞᆷᄒᆞᆫ명이죽엇다더라

○승거견탈 지작일에대ᄒᆞᆫ사ᄅᆞᆷᄒᆞ나히야현둥디로인력거를타고가는ᄃᆡ일인ᄒᆞ나히별안간달녀들어봉자로란타ᄒᆞ고그인력거를ᄲᅢ앗사타고갓다더라

○부지거쳐 젼평양군슈팽한씨는폐임ᄒᆞᆫ후로거쳐를아지못ᄒᆞ는지라셔울셔는평양에잇는줄노알고평양셔는셔울잇는줄노알앗더니팽씨의사돈이일젼에샹경ᄒᆞ야팽씨를사면심방ᄒᆞ야도간곳을알슈업는지라혹은일본갓다고ᄒᆞᆫ다더라

○샹미결뎡 작일관제의뎡회의에셔또결뎡이못되엿다더라

○국셔봉뎡 신임쳥공사즁광젼씨와례임쳥공사허ᄐᆡᆨ신씨가칠일하오삼시반에폐현ᄒᆞ야신임국셔와뎨임국셔와셔태후칠슌경하의회답국셔를병ᄒᆞ야셕쟝을봉뎡ᄒᆞ엿다ᄒᆞ며동일하오사시반에일공사도폐현ᄒᆞ엿다더라

○병뎡나심 신임법원쟝원우샹씨가시무ᄒᆞ는ᄃᆡ대안문밧게셔일진회와샹지ᄒᆞᆫ병뎡사십여명을쟝차포박ᄒᆞ야심문ᄒᆞᆯ터이라더라

○의졍인뎡 의뎡을총졍으로기졍ᄒᆞᆫ다더니의뎡으로인졍ᄒᆞ야됴병호씨가시로임ᄒᆞᆫ다더라

○도로불통 함경북도등디에아병이다북으로향ᄒᆞ야갓다ᄒᆞ나도로는샹금불통이된다더라

○경평렬도 평양리인의젼셜을드른즉경평렬도는평양대동강과파쥬림진강교량외에는미셩ᄒᆞᆫ곳이업다더라

구년도예산포 속

뎨삼항 쳥소슈리비 오십원

뎨ᄉᆞ항 잡급급잡비 오쳔이빅ᄉᆞ십구원

뎨오항 피복비 일쳔삼빅팔십칠원

뎨륙항 려비 이빅원

뎨칠항 치료비 이십원

뎨팔항 미장비 이십원

뎨구항 마필비 이쳔삼빅원

뎨이십구관 쳔왕부 삼쳔ᄉᆞ빅ᄉᆞ십원

뎨일항 봉급 팔빅오십원

뎨이항 쳥비 오빅원

뎨삼항 쳥소슈리비 이십원

뎨ᄉᆞ항 잡급급잡비 일쳔오빅구십륙원

뎨오항 피복비 일빅오십삼원

뎨륙항 려비 칠십원

뎨칠항 치료비 칠원

뎨팔항 미장비 칠원

뎨구항 마필비 삼빅삼십칠원

뎨삼십관 군함비 이십이만일쳔구빅원 지화

뎨일항 양무함비 이십이만일쳔구빅원

지화지출차즁 이십이만구쳔일빅원

군부쇼관합계ᄉᆞ빅팔십오만이쳔일빅칠십오원

법부쇼판

뎨일관 법부본쳥 삼만오쳔칠빅팔십오원

뎨일항 봉급 이만삼쳔륙빅구십오원

뎨이항 쳥비 이쳔오빅원

뎨삼항 쳥소슈리비 삼빅오십원

뎨ᄉᆞ항 잡급급잡비 이쳔ᄉᆞ십원

뎨오항 려비 일쳔이빅원

뎨륙항 외국인제급 륙쳔원 지화

뎨이관 평리원 일만삼쳔륙원

뎨일항 봉급 일만삼빅원

뎨이항 쳥비 오빅원

뎨삼항 쳥소슈리비 일빅원

뎨ᄉᆞ항 잡급급잡비 이쳔일빅륙원

뎨삼관 한셩직판쇼 칠쳔칠빅이십팔원

뎨일항 봉급 ᄉᆞ쳔륙빅십원

뎨이항 쳥비 오빅원

뎨삼항 쳥소슈리비 일빅원

뎨ᄉᆞ항 잡급급잡비 이쳔오빅십팔원

(미완)

THE "STONE FIGHTS."

One killed and a number severely wounded was yesterday's record of the "Stone Fights" which are now taking place outside the South Gate. With a little practice the Koreans could bring the casualty list of their national game up to that of an American Thanksgiving foot ball game.

JAPANESE FINANCES.

The following from the "Japan Herald' gives one a good insight to Japan's present financial condition of Japan: "Of the local financial and commercial disturbances brought on by the war two striking illustrations have lately appeared in the papers in connection with the notorious One Hundred and Thirtieth Bank of Osaka and the Kigyo Ginko of Kyoto. Both banks to make up losses had to make calls upon shares not fully paid up. The shareholders in both cases could not or would not respond. In consequence, after repeated delays, the shares of defaulted shareholders of the first bank were put up to auction last month. The bids on the twenty four thousand old shares, Y35 paid up, ranged from Y2.90 to Y3.80. No offers were made for the new shares, Y17.50 paid up. It is clear Osaka has little money to spare or has absolutely no confidence in the success of Mr. Yasuda's attempt to reorganise the bank, even with a loan of six millions at two per cent. interest. The Kyoto Bank is even in worse plight, for out of 12,000 shares no less than eleven thousand will have to be sold on the 15th, the owners having failed to meet the call of Y15."

AMERICAN IMPERIALISM.

The Government of the United States has announced its assumption of a Pro tectorate in the case of the republic of Santo Domingo.

Mr. Maruyama's contract has at last been signed.

From the 5th inst the wire between Seoul and Wiju was opened to public business.

There is a remarkable cessation of telegrams referring to the "unrest in Russia."

The Japanese Minister has again demanded the abolition of the Departments for Education and Agriculture. This is reform with a vengeance

According to a Tokio telegram dated the 4th inst. it is thought in France that peace between Russia and Japan will be declared within four months.

In our list of those present at the Martel-Eckert wedding yesterday we omitted to mention the names of M. and Madame Vincart and their two daughters.

A German steamer, name unknown, from Singapore consigned to Kiaochow with field guns and ammunition, has been detained at Padang, the capital of Dutch Sumatra.

The revolutionary movements in Russia are subsiding except in Poland where reserve troops are continually deserting availing themselves of the confusion.

"Le Journal says that the Russian authorities are greatly to blame for their lack of coolness and their adoption of unjustifiable measures, in dealing with the present situation. The disturbances may, as for as outward appearances are concerned, be suppressed to some extent, but, asks the paper, will they not grow stronger fundamentally? Order may possibly be restored by force, but the journal fears that the memory of the recent disaster may lead to a great spiritual barrier springing up between the Tsar and his people.

RAISING THE RUSSIAN FLEET.

An officer recently returned from port Arthur has given it as his opinion that though the damage sustained may possibly be heavy, the raising of the Russian vessels is not an impracticable task, and when this has been accomplished, the vessels will, in the opinion of the said officer, be again available after repairs. The full extent of the damage to the Russian vessels can only be ascertained by a thorough examination by divers. Diving operations during the winter are very difficult at Port Arthur, owing to the strong northerly winds that prevail during January and February, and therefore an examination will probably not take place until the advent of warm weather.

Unless they can do better with these ships than they did with the "Varyag" in Chemulpo harbour, we advise the Japanese to let them alone. The only result of six month's operations on this vessel was the death, by drowning of some seven or eight divers.

TO THE POWERS.

A telegram has been received by the Shanghai Taotai to pay over to the authorised parties, the indemnity difference to-day, January 31st at 12 o'clock. China it will be seen from this, says the "Shanghai-Times," always meets her obligations even if these are are not anticipated when the agreements are made. She agreed to pay a certain war indemnity which represented a certain sum in the coin of her country at that time. Subsequently foreigners interested in commerce and finance so jockeyed the exchange that China unwittingly found herself burdened with a debt which she did not anticipate, but which was manipulated for her by the said foreigners. Now we have had a brief period of an improvement in the exchange between gold and silver and we wonder if there will be any rebate towards China in consequence.

A newly-married couple of Wisconsin are spending their honeymoon in the local hospital. They have both got appendicitis. It is so delightful when husband and wife are interested in the same thing.

It is rumoured in St. Petersburg with regard to the insufficient supply of food-stuffs and clothing, that among the Russians at Mukden there has been a revolutionary disturbance and that the news is kept secret by the authorities in the capital.

The German Consul-General at Simla has issued a striking report which shows that Indian differential duties on sugar have practically killed German and Austrian imports into India. Javean and British sugar imports have correspondingly increased.

The Japanese House of Representives has received a pitition signed by Miss Haruko Kawamura and over 500 other women, claiming the right to join in political associations and participate in political meetings—privileges now denied the women of that country.

The "Tōa-kōshi" is the name of a company recently organized in Tokyo for the sale in Korea and China of miscellaneous goods, including drugs, books, etc. The company has a capital of 800,000 yen, represented by 16,000 shares. The subscription list closes on February eight, and up to the present over 13,000 shares have been taken up. The shares are of the value of 50 yen and the first call of 12 yen 50 sen is to paid by the end of February. A general meeting will be held in March next for the purpose of drawing up the rules and appointing the officers. Branches are to be established at Sōul, Shanghai, Dalny and Yingkow. It is the intention of the Company to establish in the near future commercial museums at various important places in China and Korea.

NEW CAPTAIN OF THE "ROSSIA."

It is reported that Commander Chargin, who was for some time naval attaché to the Russian Legation in Tokio has been promoted to the rank of captain and appointed to the command of the Russian cruiser "Rossia," now at Vladivostock.

THE WAR.

There are a number of Japanese telegrams referring to the operations on the Shaho.

They seem to be the work of a diabolically clever genius who is bent on frustrating the inquisitive. We have stories of attacks and counter-attacks. When the Russians retreated they "fled" and when the Japanese retreated they "retired."

We are still without particulars of the Japanese casualties prior to Jan. 28th but we are told that up to Feb. 4th the Russians have lost over 6,000 in killed and wounded.

We are not given any indication as to the trend of the battle, so we presume that, so far, the Japanese have not been successful.

THE NORTH SEA INCIDENT.

Latest telegraphic advices report that at the Commission sitting in Paris to enquire into the trawler incident, Captain Klado has emphatically and circumstantially reiterated his assertion that there were foreign torpeds boats among the fishing fleet. Speaking of the incident, a London paper says:—

"No paper pointed out at the time how one of our own cruisers struck her flag to a fleet of trawlers one foggy morning during our naval manoeuvres, under the impression that she was surrounded by the enemy's torpedo-boats. No paper pointed out—perhaps none know—how our sailors in 1900, between Peking and Tientsin, fired at and killed several Russians, believing them to be Boxers. That case was not on all fours certainly, but the fact remains that Russia accepted Admiral Seymour's apology for that outrage, and demanded no compensation of any kind, thereby admitting the easiness of honest mistake. Nor did the Russian papers raise an outcry against us as our papers lately did against Russia."

THE UNREST IN RUSSIA.

The following statement as to the state of affairs in Russia, appearing in a contemporary from the pen of Roger Pocock will be found of interest at the present juncture:—

"It must not be supposed that Russia is frightened of these conspirators, or sorry for them.

"The students are noisy, talkative, and silly, rather than dangerous. Nearly all are training for the Government service, and once they get an appointment they forget all their liberal opinions.

"The Jews—a nation gets such Jews as it deserves—are not like our magnificent British Jews—able, enlightened, and loyal. Tyranny has made them mean, cowardly, and treacherous, content to cheat the Russians, but afraid to conspire or revolt.

"The Poles never trusted their own leaders, and when they revolt are easily shot down.

"The Finns, the only really civilised nation in the whole Empire, are so rude to Russians that the nation delights in oppressing them. They were free, loyal, highly civilised, the noblest people in the Empire. So the Emperor has broken his Coronation vow—to reduce them to the dead level of Russian misery. But Finland is too small to be dangerous.

"There is discontent in Russia, but as it is not mainly the discontent of Russians there will be no revolution. Only in so far as the aristocracy despises the Grand Ducal party for its incompetence, that party is trying to please with promises of reform. There will be real reform, but until Russia has become a liberal nation she cannot have a liberal Government."

From Japan exchanges we learn that in addition to the Department of Agriculture and Education the Japanese here are pressing for the abolition of the Mining and Civil Engineering Departments.

A Peking special to the "Jiji" says that the new Governor of Shantung Province, regarding whose appointment the German Minister in Peking recently filed a complaint in the Chinese Foreign Office, held a secret meeting with the Minister at a temple outside the wall of Peking on the 29th inst. on his way to Shangtung, though he had formally declined an interview proposed by the latter. There is now strong disfavour manifested in Peking as to the attitude of Germany on the allegation that Germany, by whom the mining railway in Shantung is practically monopolized, has begun to interfere with China's domestic administration, following the example shown by Russia in the three Eastern Provinces.

AFFAIRS IN RUSSIA.

The Korea Daily News.

Issued at 5 P. M. daily except Sundays.

Rate of Subscription:—

Per Year,............Yen 25.
Per Quarter,..........Yen 7.
Per Month,..........Yen 2.50.

Postage in Korea not charged extra.
Postage abroad charged extra.

Advertisements, 50 sen per day for 1 inch or less.
5 yen per month per inch.
50 yen per year per inch.

All communications to

E. T. BETHELL,
Editor and Publisher,
Pak-tong, Seoul.

A YEAR OF REFORM.

It is hardly neccessary to say that there is room for reform in Korea.

The fact that the Korean administration is corrupt has been exploited by the Japanese for all it is worth, and they also seek to convince the world that they are the heaven-chosen people to put things in order. They claim contiguity of domain, community of interests, and no end of other high-sounding things as good and valid reasons why they should impose their uninvited and un-desired "assistance" upon this independent empire.

Yesterday the Japanese in Chemulpo celebrated the anniversary of the "Battle of Chemulpo" and this brings to notice that it is now just one year since the Japanese became paramount in Korea. And what has been done towards ameliorating the lot of the victimized Koreans for whom Japan appointed herself the champion? Nothing. Worse than nothing. Apologists tell us to "wait and see." They told us the same thing six months ago and unless Japan meets with reverses in the war they will be telling us the same thing six months hence.

Every move of the Japanese in Korea has, upon investigation, turned out to have an ulterior motive, and however benignant the proposition may, on the face of it, appear to be, invariably turns out, subsequently, to have for its object the enrichment of Japan at the expense of Korea.

If Japan established her claim to Korea by right of conquest, we should none of us have anything to say, but Japan has, until quite recently, persisted in her Pharisaical cant about the independence of Korea and we therefore have a right to point out any deviations that she may essay to make from the strict letter of her promises.

If we go upon precedent and take experience as our guide we get but scanty consolation. A little over ten years ago Japan fought, as now, uninvited, for Korea's independence, and, after having given it to her, pleaded that Korea, alone, was incapable and commenced to "assist" her in much the same way as she is doing now. There were of course some disgraceful incidents which will not find parallels this time but the "advisory" process now being exploited differs very little from that of ten years ago. On neither occasion has any beneficial reform been inaugurated, the energies of the Japanese being solely directed towards subduing the Koreans, gaining control of the country and finding soft jobs for their nominees.

So far, Mr. Megata has not succeeded in his endeavours to get the gathering of the taxes in to Japanese hands, but we have no doubt that so long as the war pursues a course apparently favourable to Japan no stone will be left unturned to accomplish this and then we expect that Japan will, for the time being, congratulate herself upon the "reform" of Korea.

A PERSONAL NARRATIVE OF THE SIEGE OF PORT ARTHUR.

(Specially written for The "China Review" by a Russian Naval Officer.)

(Continued from last issue).

In a way I think we were all demented. We ate our food without knowing whether it was good or bad; and so long as there was enough to satisfy the cravings of hunger, the quality was of no consequence; that which was not nauseating was good enough to eat. Money lost its value, officers and men leaving their roubles and notes about as if silver were iron and notes waste paper. It was wonderful how quickly the most avaricious among us lost the love of money. It was instructive to see officers, accustomed to rich food and heady wines, chewing tough horse meat with vigor, and savagely eyeing the one who had the largest piece.

But you ask me for the story of Port Arthur, and I shall not tell you in cold dates and hard facts. I am, in fact, unable to do so at the present time; but of what we felt and what we did it is a pleasure to talk. It is also a pleasure to feel that, though we did lose our more human sensibilities, we soon learned how to put duty and love of country before everything else, until the chief himself said it was time to stop.

September was a comparatively easy month. The outpost skirmishes were regarded with little interest. Feeling our position impregnable, we regarded the initial movements of the Japanese on the Liaotung Peninsula as of little consequence. After we had repulsed their first several assaults, undoubtedly the fiercest made by them during the siege, this fancied impregnability grew stronger in our minds. It was during September, however, we first recognized the necessity of economizing the use of ammunition for the heavier guns. And at about the same time, having taken the cue from the Japanese we began to manufacture and use hand grenades, which proved most effective in repelling assaults. The enemy's bombardment during this month did comparatively little damage to the town or fortifications, the guns he used not being of particularly heavy calibre. And so September passed with attacks, counter-attacks; and the bombardment—which usually began at 8.30 in the morning, stopped at 11, that the Japanese artillerymen might eat their noon ration, and reopened at 1 P. M.,—usually continuing until 5 in the evening.

October, however, was ushered into existence by the booming of eleven-inch guns, which the enemy, after weeks of hardest labor, had succeeded in dragging to positions within range of the city. The fire of these monstrous cannon played havoc with the forts and the town, and there was no place within our lines where the shells might not reach; they penetrated through the strongest bombproof, they dug great holes in the streets; and, when they exploded near houses, the latter shook as if there were an earthquake. The introduction of eleven inch guns into the bombardment was a surprise to us, at first, we were totally unprepared to answer their fire. Immediately, however, we began the work of removing some of our heaviest cannon from the seaward forts and the ships to the landward forts, that we might answer it effectually. Then came the time of artillery duels unprecedented in the world's history.

Notwithstanding the severity of the enemy's bombardment, the shops in Port Arthur were open for business. On occasions when one of the big shells would strike and partly demolish a store, the unfortunate proprietor would calmly remove his remaining signs and merchandise to another building, and, in a short time, be ready again to answer the demands of trade.

We knew when the Japanese meditated an assault on a certain part of our line, because it was always preceeded by the concentration of their entire artillery-five against it. It was then the inhabitants of Port Arthur took advantage of the cessation in the bombardment of the town, and walked about the streets, paying calls, etc. The repulse of the assault would be followed by the enemy,—evidently much enraged over his defeat,—directing his shell fire upon the line of march taken by the wounded and their bearers from the scene of the repulse to the hospital. In this manner many of our wounded were either killed or more seriously wounded.

I wish to say here that, previous to the time when we had suitable guns in position to answer the eleven-inch artillery of the enemy, the morale of our men, exposed to its fire, was almost perfect. Only those experienced in modern warfare know how nerve-destroying it is to lie under a terrific shell fire with no means at hand of effectually striking back.

In August I was wounded and sent to the Red Cross hospital. At that time three times as many men as there were beds were being treated there; mattresses littered the floor, and, during the night, doctors and nurses had to walk with care not to step on wounded limbs. The other hospitals I learned were similary crowded, and nearly all the private houses were also being used for the accommodation of wounded. Dysentery and contagious diseases, formerly not uncommon in the town, were during the siege unusually rare; the hospital returns showing the grand total to be only five hundred. Towards the end of the siege, however, scurvy became very common, evidencing itself by producing mouth ulcers that were most painful and disgusting. This disease was the result of our liberal and daily consumption of salt meat. Few of us escaped it entirely, and it caused many deaths among the wounded, so tainting their blood that the slightest abrasions became hideous ulcers. Before the appearance of scurvy, wounds quickly healed, and it was common for slightly wounded men to leave the hospital after two or three weeks confinement. At times we did not know which was the worst—the Japanese or the scurvy.

Our first snow storm occurred on the 14th day of November, and some of the men welcomed it with tears. It reminded all of us of our homes in distant Russia that we never expected to see again. What is Kuropatkin doing? Where is the Baltic Fleet? These questions were no longer on every tongue.

(To be continued).

The Korea Daily News.

VOL. II, THURSDAY, FEBRUARY 9, 1905. No. 30

HONGKONG & SHANGHAI BANKING CORPORATION.

Paid-up Capital..... ....$10,000,000
Reserve Fund:—Sterling Reserve... 10,000,000
Silver Reserve..... 7,000,000

27,000,000

Reserve Liability of Proprietors... 10,000,000

HEAD OFFICE, HONGKONG.

London Bankers, London and County Banking Company Limited.

Branches and Agencies,

London.

Amoy,	Hankow	Penang,
Bangkok,	Hiogo,	Rangoon,
Batavia,	Iloilo,	Saigon,
Bombay,	Lyons,	San Francisco,
Calcutta,	Manila,	Singapore,
Colombo,	Nagasaki,	Sourabaya,
Foochow,	New York,	Tientsin,
Hamburg,	Peking,	Yokohama,

Credits granted on approved Securities, and every description of Banking and Exchange business transacted.

Drafts granted on London and the chief Commercial places in Europe, India, Australia, America, China and Japan.

HOLME RINGER & Co., AGENTS, CHEMULPO.

HOKURKU DOBOKU KAISHA.

Branch office in Chong Dong, Seoul.

Japanese telephone No. 165

CONTRACT DEPARTMENT.

We can contract to build any building or construction.

MERCHANDISE DEPARTMENT.

We can provide any building material. We have just contracted to build the new Belgian Legation.

E. MEYER & CO.

Chemulpo.

SOLE AGENTS IN KOREA FOR.

A. T. Morse, Sons & Co.'s "Fresco" Distemper

In all colours ready for use on walls, Ceilings etc.

and

AVENARIUS CARBOLINEUM

A wood-preserving and antiseptic oil preparation

Against decay, dry-rot, fungus and wood-destroying insects.

A large supply always in stock.
Prices upon application.

E. MEYER & Co.,

Chemulpo.

CHARTERED BANK OF INDIA AUSTRALIA & CHINA.

INCORPORATED BY ROYAL CHARTER 1853

HEAD OFFICES.—LONDON.

Paid-up Capital £800,000
Reserve Liability of Shareholders 800,000
Reserve Fund 800,000

Drafts granted upon all the principal places in the world and every description of Exchange and banking business transacted.

E. MEYER & Co., Agents,
Chemulpo.

MITSU BISHI DOCKYARD & ENGINE WORKS,

NAGASAKI.

CODE WORD, "DOCK."

A 1, A. B. C., and Engineering Codes used.

DOCK No. 1 (at Tategami).

Extreme Length..............523 feet
Length on blocks .... 513 „
Width of Entrance on Top......89 „
„ „ Bottom....77 „
Water on Blocks at Spring Tide 26½ „

DOCK No. 2 (Mukaijima).

Extreme Length..............371 feet
Length on Blocks...........360 „
Width of Entrance on Top.......66 „
„ „ Bottom 53 „
Water on Blocks at Spring Tide 22 „

PATENT SLIP (at Kosuge).

Can take vessels up to 1,000 tons gross.

THE WORKS are well equipped with the LATEST IMPROVEMENTS, and can execute any kind of work in SHIPBUILDING and MARINE ENGINEERING, as well as in REPAIRING of SHIPS.

The COMPANY'S new powerful steamer OURA-MARU (712 tons, 700 I.H.P.), specially built for SALVAGE PURPOSES, and equipped with necessary gear, is always READY at SHORT NOTICE.

THE METHODIST PUBLISHING HOUSE,

Little West Gate, Seoul.

JOB PRINTING, TYPEWRITER PAPER
CARBON PAPER, VISITING CARDS
STATIONERY, BOOK BINDING
BOOK PUBLISHERS
AMERICAN SCHOOL BOOKS
SPENCERIAN COPY BOOKS
PEN CARBON LETTER AND BILL BOOKS

S. A. BECK, Manager.

DAI-ICHI GINKO.

LIMITED.

(Formerly the First National Bank)

ESTABLISHED 1873.

INCORPORATED UNDER PRESENT LAW 1896

Capital - - - - - - - - Yen 5,000,000
Reserve Fund - - - - - 1,500,000

HEAD OFFICE:—TOKIO.

President: Baron SHIBUSAWA.

BRANCHES AND CORRESPONDENTS
In the Principal Cities and Towns of Japan.

Interest Allowed on

Fixed deposits 1 year - - - 6½ per cent
" " 6 months - - - 6 per cent

Special current accounts 1½ sen daily per Y 100
General " " 1 " " " 100

M. TANAKA,
Manager, Chemulpo.

SINGER SEWING MACHINES

씽거조봉침

SOLE AGENTS FOR KOREA

전매쇼

HOLME RINGER & CO.

Chemulpo.

제물포 함룽거양힝

KAMEYA & CO.

GENERAL STOREKEEPERS

Chinkokai - - Seoul

(Established 1895, Tokyo)

Confectionery, Hams, Canned Goods, Cutlery, Hirano & Tansan Water. Provisions, Gents, Furnishing goods, Toilet Articles, Travelling Bags, Tobacco, Cigars & Cigarettes Kitchen Utensils. Coffee, Biscuits

Fresh Goods always kept in Stock.

Prices Moderate

☞ *Please come and inspect our goods.*

NIPPON YUSEN KAISHA.

JAPANESE MAIL STEAMSHIP CO.

UNDER MAIL CONTRACT WITH THE IMPERIAL JAPANESE GOVERNMENT.

European Line

Regular Fortnightly Service between Yokohama Kobe, Moji, Shanghai, Hongkong, Singapore, Penang Colombo, Port Said, Marseilles, London and Antwerp

American Line

Regular Fortnightly Service between Hongkong and Seattle, calling at Shanghai, Moji, Kobe, Yokohama and Victoria, B. C.

Australian Line

Regular weekly Service between Japan Ports and Australia, calling at Hongkong and Manila.

(Above Three Lines Suspended until further notice).

Shanghai Line

Weekly Service between Shanghai and Japan Ports

Korea Line

Service Kobe, Moji, Nagasaki, Fusan Chemulpo Chefoo, Taku.

S. S. Babelsberg, 2181 tons.

Service Kobe, Moji, Fusan, Chemulpo, Chinnampo S. S. ARGO, S. S. Ohio.

BORDEN'S CONDENSED MILK CO.

New York, U. S. A.

ALWAYS IN STOCK

Eagle Brand Condensed Milk.

Gold Seal Condensed Milk.

Peerless (Family) Evaporated Cream.

Borden's Malted Milk.

E. MEYER & CO.
Chemulpo Korea,
Sole Agents.

ROYAL INSURANCE COMPANY,

Funds exceed £10,000,000

FIRE

AT CURRENT RATES

LIFE

REDUCED PREMIUM.

HOLME RINGER & Co.,
Agents, Chemulpo.

廣

KWANG ◎ C'HANG

昌

BENNETT & CO.

Merchants

Chemulpo.

Offices opposite the Imperial Japanese Post and Telegraph Office Chemulpo.

Telephone Number 201.

大韓每日申報
대한미일신보

(뎨이권삼십일호)　(토요일)　일천구빅오년이월십일일

본샤고빅

이신보는영어와한어로셔계리
일출판홈

신문가

한쟝　엽두돈오푼
일삭됴　엽두량닷돈
우표가리샤닷돈
다밧돈으로밧솜

광고료는

귀한의정년과ᄎ횡외디쇼로종
광흥되희가로밧을터이오며오
린저아녀대한사람마다다이신
문을보실터이니광고버시기를
원흥시는이들은우리신문사에
와셔번야흥심을희망흥읍

○발힝소　박동대한미일신보
사벌어학교앙헤전영국인셜펄
발졍자리오

사쟝 영국인 (비셜)

평양 티리경

○평양효동사는권미보씨로우
리신문광미티리인을뒤졍흥엿
시ᄉ오니평양에계신구람코저흥
는　첨군ᄌ는위티리졍에왕
림흥와변희흥시옵

샤고

○우리대한미일신보의목뎍은
대한의안녕질서에관한모든데
목에티흥야는공평한변론을쥬
쟝흉희라우리동신원외탐보는
신문보시는첨군ᄌ의게흥샹보
도흥리며편지들귀셔흥며주시
는이는셩명과번티들쟈어분치
서기들희망흥오니하거슨신문
샹에긔쟈흥란는커시아니오다
만극히신용흥는중거들숨고쟈
흥이라귀자는하모귀서런지귀
지흥올뒤쟉흥는권리들가졋스
나뒤쟉흥는리유들말흘티미오
며공중평화들문란케흥는듯흔
귀서는외례히밧지안켓숩나이
다

●본사셜시이리로신문을티양
우헤로분전흥와레전부의임의
로전흥든ᄉ로면곳에는홍누게
전흥기도흥며흐면쳔거슴흔졉
에전흥기도흥며흥아니전흥는
곳도잇다흥와우리신문을수랑
흥야구람흥시는　첨군ᄌ의계금
티흥야미우미안흥옵기로지금
은분전인을두고미일일주이전
흥며하니전흥거나늣게거나흔
폐가엽도록흥관흥오니흥야넘

일기잇스면본사로동괴흥여주심
을희망흥옵

관보

대샹쳔오십팔호　광무구
년이월구일목료
셔임급사령

○면본관　평안북도관찰부총
쉰쳔샹하
우희원이불고직사흥고샹지기
가운고로면당희부흥야졍기회
보흔증수유뉴로샤에샹불희티라
흥엿기면본관

경무청총쉰김준영

○임평안북도관찰부총쉰셔권
임관륙등

○경무청총쉰셔관임관이등봉
급　김지졍

비샹이월삼일

○임의졍부찬졍서칙임관이등
법부사리국쟝김사준

○명졍원경셔칙임관삼등
륙군부장리지용

○명궁니부특진관서칙임관삼
등종이품　됴동완

○명쟝레원소경서칙임관사등
경효뎐제조민영돈

명경효뎐제조서칙임관사등
봉샹사제조　김대제

○명봉샹사제조서칙임관사등
궁니부특진관　남규회

○의원면본관　범평양셩소교
관　리강연

범관양셩소교
관　비동렴

범관양셩소교
관　박기순

니부주사　민
영셕

니부주사　리
인졍

○임범관양셩소교관서관임관
륙등　서샹영　윤호영　김영
구

○임니부주사서관임관륙등
김종돈　리윤구

○면본관　함경남도　관찰부
총쉰　김명두
우희원이셔임사샤에죵불부임
이기서이로면본관

함경북도변계총쉰　김일
환

○임함경남도관찰부총쉰셔관
임관륙등

○임함경북도변계총쉰셔관임
관륙등구품　김세진

○구년도에산표　슉
군부소관

뎨팔관　포병디　심일만구쳔
칠빅삼십사원
뎨일항　봉급　일만일쳔일
빅구십이원
뎨이항　쳥비　일쳔오빅원
뎨삼항　청사슈리비　일빅
원
뎨사항　사졸급료　삼만일
쳔이빅심팔원
뎨오항　량식비　이만구쳔
사빅심일원
뎨륙항　마필비　일쳔오빅
원
뎨칠항　마량비　일만이쳔
륙빅칠십이원
뎨팔항　마장비　이만이빅
사십원
뎨구항　피복비　구쳔칠빅
삼원
뎨십항　보숙비　오빅원
뎨십일항　연습비　일빅이
십원
뎨십이항　목욕비　일빅이
십원
뎨십삼항　치료비　일빅팔
십원
뎨십ᄉ항　미장비　오십원
뎨십오항　제쳘비　이빅륙
십삼원
뎨십륙항　마편급마륙비
삼빅륙십오원
뎨십칠항　포운슈리비　륙
빅원

뎨구관　헌미도포디　일만칠
빅삼십이원
뎨일항　쳥비　ᄉ빅십ᄉ원
뎨이항　쳥ᄉ슈리비　이십
원
뎨삼항　피비　구쳔구빅십
칠원
뎨ᄉ항　잡급급잡비　삼빅
원
뎨오항　연회비　팔십원

뎨십관　공병디　ᄉ만ᄉ쳔ᄉ
빅삼십원
뎨일항　봉급　삼쳔륙빅팔
십륙원
뎨이항　쳥비　구빅오십원
뎨삼항　쳥ᄉ슈리비　오십
원

뎨ᄉ항　ᄉ졸급료　ᄒ만륙
쳔구빅ᄉ십ᄉ원
뎨오항　량식비　일만륙쳔
이빅쳘십륙원
뎨륙항　마량비　오빅칠십
륙원
뎨칠항　마장비　구십이원
뎨팔항　피복비　ᄉ쳔구빅
ᄉ십일원
뎨구항　보숙비　륙빅원
뎨십항　연습비　구십륙원
뎨십일항　목욕비　구십륙
원
뎨십이항　치료비　구십륙
원
뎨십삼항　미쟝비　삼십원

뎨십일관　치중병디　일만오
쳔삼빅십삼원
뎨일항　쳥비　오빅원
뎨이항　쳥ᄉ슈리비　오십
원
뎨삼항　ᄉ졸급료　일만일
쳔삼빅ᄉ십원
뎨ᄉ항　량식비　오빅칠십
일원
뎨오항　피복비　이쳔팔빅
오십이원

뎨십이관　군악디　삼만ᄉ쳔
칠빅이십원
뎨일항　봉급　이쳔ᄉ빅원
뎨이항　쳥비　사빅팔십오
원

잡보

○교빙협동　경무청고문환
산중준의협동교빙이여좌ᄒ니
대한국니부대신됴병식은칙령
을봉승ᄒ야대일본대국졍부의
츄쳔흔바환산즁준간에좌기됴
항을쳠졍흠
뎨일됴환산즁준은대한국졍부
의경무고문으로경찰사무를
쳥쳔졍리ᄒ고경찰사무샹모
든셜비에관ᄒ야지극히셩실
히심의ᄒ는칙에임ᄒᆷ
뎨이됴대한국졍부는경찰에관
ᄒ는일체사무에대ᄒ야환산
중준의동의를요흔후시힝ᄒᆯ
사
뎨삼됴환산중준은경찰의관ᄒ는
졍부회의에참여ᄒ고또경찰
에관ᄒ는의견을니부대신을
ᄒ야의졍부뎨의ᄒᆷ을득ᄒᆷ
뎨사됴환산중준의봉급은원뎨
금화사빅원으로ᄒ고미월말
일에지급ᄒᆯ사

UNION INSURANCE SOCIETY OF CANTON.

Head office Hongkong.
Marine risks underwritten at current rates.

Agents in Chemulpo,
E. MEYER & Co.

COMPAGNIE DES MESSAGERIES MARITIMES.

Fortnightly Direct Service.

For Marseilles
via Ports.
Sailing from Yokohama
Calling at Kobe,
Shanghai, Hongkong, Saigon, Singapore.
Colombo, Djibonti, Suez, Port Said
and Marseilles.

For particulars apply to
HOLME RINGER & Co.,
Chemulpo.

HAYASHIDA & CO.,

16 MYENG DONG, CHIN KO KAI, SEOUL.
BRANCH OFFICE AT CHEMULPO.

Money changers, Coal and Wood Merchants, Express Agents.

We are agents for the Pyeng-yang Coal Company and the Karazu Coal Company of Japan. We have the best quality of both anthracite and bituminous coal, and prompt execution of orders is our speciality. Firewood of all kinds kept in stock. Full weight guaranteed. Money of all denominations exchanged at current rates. Parcels received for all parts.

CHINA MUTUAL LIFE INS. OC.

Most favourable terms to policy holders.

Benefit system unsurpassed.

HOLME RINGER & Co.
Agents, Chemulpo.

C. P. R.

CANADIAN PACIFIC RAILWAY COMPANY'S ROYAL MAIL STEAMSHIP LINE.

THE FAST ROUTE BETWEEN CHINA, JAPAN, AND EUROPE VIA CANADA AND THE UNITED STATES.

Route from Hongkong via Shanghai, Nagasaki (Inland Sea of Japan) Kobe, Yokohama, Victoria and Vancouver.

Twin Screw Empress Steamship—6,000 Tons—Speed 19 Knots.

PROPOSED SAILING FROM YOKOHAMA.

R. M. S. Empress of India.
R. M. S. Empress of Japan.
R. M. S. Empress of China.
R. M. S. Athenian.
R. M. S. Tartar.

Special reduction (first class only) granted to members of the Military, Naval, Diplomatic and Civil services and to Missionaries.

Passengers have choice of ten routes across the Continent of America and have privilege of travelling by any Atlantic Steamship Line.

Round the World passage tickets in connection with the P. and O. S. N., North German Lloyd and Messageries Co.'s **£125.**

All rates payable at current rate of exchange.

For further information, Tickets, Guide Books, etc., apply to

HOLME, RINGER & Co., AGENTS,
Chemulpo.

Grand Hotel

(Formerly the Station Hotel)

Near the Railway Terminus, West Gate Seoul.

The Best Hotel in Korea
Handsome new Building.
Fine Airy Rooms
Excellent Cuisine.
Terms Moderate.
Special terms to Missionaries
and to permanent boarders.

Electric cars within 2 minutes' walk.

W. H. EMBERLEY.
Proprieto

AMERICAN KOREAN ELECTRIC CO.

Light and Power.

Main Office: Electric Building, Chong No.

RAILWAY DEPARTMENT.

OPERATING CARS BETWEEN EAST AND WEST GATE, EVERY TEN MINUTES:—

First Car leaves East Gate at 7:00 A. M. First Car leaves R. R. Station at 7:25 A. M
Last Car " East Gate at 8.40 P. M. Last " " R. R. Station at 9.05 P.M

OPERATING CARS BETWEEN EAST GATE AND IMPERIAL TOMB TERMINUS, EVERY TWENTY MINUTES:—

CONNECTING WITH EVERY ALTERNATE CAR ARRIVING AT EAST GATE FROM CHONG NO.

First Car leaves East Gate for Tomb at 7:10 A. M.
" " " Tomb for East Gate at 7:30 A. M.
Last " " East Gate for Tomb at 7:50 P. M.
" Tomb for East Gate at 8:10 P. M.

OPERATING CARS BETWEEN CHONG NO AND YUNG SAN RIVER EVERY TWELVE MINUTES:—

First Car leaves Chong No for South Gate at 7:12 A. M.
" " " Chong No for Yung San at 7:36 A. M.
" " " South Gate for Chong No at 7:20 A. M.
" " " Yung San for Chong No at 8:09 A. M.
Last " " South Gate for Chong No 9:00 P. M.
" " Yung San for Chong No at 8.45. P. M.

SPECIAL PRIVATE CARS FURNISHED TO SUIT CONVENIENCE OF PATRONS. PRICES ON APPLICATION AT HEAD OFFICE.

LIGHTING DEPARTMENT.

Where less than 250 candle power of light is used, the rate per month will be
Per 16 candle power incandescent lamp,—All night.—Yen 2.50.
32 candle power incandescent lamp:—All night:—Yen 4.00.
50 candle power incandescent lamp:—All night:—Yen 6.00.
150 " " " " " " " 10.00.
1200 " " enclosed arc " " " " 20.00.

Where more than 250 candle power of light is used, a Meter will be installed, if requested:—Rent of Meter Yen 2.00 per month. Rate of charges by meter reading:—Two Sen per Ampere per hour. (Approximately this is equal to about One Sen per 16 C. P. lamp per hour) Minimum monthly charge where meter is installed, Yen 20.00 per month, which includes rental of meter.

Estimates for installing lights furnished on application

An assortment of chandeliers always on hand.

EVERY FACILITY.

In connection with Life Assurance Business is afforded by

The Standard Life Assurance Co.,

One of the largest and wealthiest of the Provident Institutions of the United Kingdom Forms of Application and all information will be promptly afforded on application.

10 CENTS A DAY.

Not a very large expenditure is it? But it is sufficient to secure for a man of 30 a policy with the STANDARD LIFE OFFICE for

$1323.

For all particulars of rates, etc., apply to

Holme, Ringer & Co.,
Agents, Chemulpo.

THE NEW YORK LIFE INSURANCE COMPANY.

Have you ever been declined by any Company?

Are you engaged in a specially hazardous occupation?

Have you heard of the New York Life Insurance Company's New Classifications for this class of Risks?

If not, send your date of birth, occupation and particulars of rejection, if any to

E. MEYER & Co.,
Agents, Chemulpo.

K. Murakami.

Photograph Studio
Chinkokai, Seoul.

Printing, Developing and Enlargement, of Photographs always Undertaken.

Korean Views and Pictures Illustrating Native Customs always on Sale,

---

THE OSAKA SHOSEN KAISHA.

Boats frequently on the berth for Chinnampo.

REGULAR SAILINGS BETWEEN JAPAN AND KOREAN PORTS.

FUSAN AND KOBE VIA SHIMONOSEKI.

OSAKA VIA MOKPO, FUSAN, SHIMONOSEKI AND KOBE.

MOJI DIRECT.

OSAKA VIA KUNSAN, MASANPO, FUSAN, SHIMONOSEKI AND KOBE.

CHEMULPO KUNSAN LINE,
Every three days.

CHEMULPO CHINNAMPO LINE.
Every three days.

For Freight and passage and further particulars apply to

THE OSAKA SHOSEN KAISHA,
Cemulpo

MITSUI BUSSAN KAISHA.
(MITSUI & Co.)

MITSUI GINKO.
(MITSUI BANK.)

The Bank is owned by the members of the Mitsui Family, who, as partners, assume an unlimited responsibility for all liabilities of the Bank:—

Capital........................Yen 5,000,000
Reserve Fund..................... " 5,600,000

HEAD OFFICE, TOKYO.

LONDON OFFICE, 34 LIME ST., E. C.

BRANCHES AND AGENCIES:—

New York, San Francisco, Hamburg, Bombay, Singapore, Manila, Hongkong, Amoy, Chefoo, Tientsin.

Kobe, Hakodate, Yokohama, Kure, Yokosuka, Moji, Shimonoseki, Miike, Wakamatsu, Nagasaki, Kuchinotsu, Karatsu, Sasebo, Misume, Taipeh, &c.

Telegraphic Address for all the Offices:

"MITSUI."

A. B. C. AND A. 1 CODES USED.

Contractors of Coal

To the Imperial Japanese Navy. Arsenals and Railway Bureau, Principal Railway Companies and Industrial Work, Home and Foreign Mail and Freight Steamers.

Sole Proprietors

Of the famous Miike, Tagawa and Yamano Coal Mines.

Sole Agents

For the sale of Fukumo, Hokoku, Ichimura Kanoda, Mannoura, Onoura, Ostuji, Sonoda Tsubaruro, Yoshinotani, Yoshio, Yurokibura and other coals.

YANGTSE INSURANCE ASSOCIATION, LTD.

The undersigned, having been appointed agents for the above company, are prepared to issue policies and pay losses on marine risks at regular rates.

E. MEYER & Co.,
Agents, Chemulpo.

RONDON, PLAISANT & CO.

General Storekeepers and Merchants, Ships Contractors Tobacconists, Commission and Forwarding Agents, Coal Merchants

IMPORTERS AND EXPORTERS

Seoul Chemulpo.

W. D. WENTWORTH.

LANDING
AND
SHIPPING AGENT.
AND
CUSTOMS BROKER.

12 OURA, NAGASAKI.

STEWARD & CO.

Chemulpo.

Shipchandlers and Storekeepers, Naval and Mercantile Contractors, Landing and Shipping Agents.

STEWARD'S HOTEL

Chemulpo.

Best accommodation in the port for travellers. Clean and well-aired rooms, good cuisine and prompt attendance, moderate tariff.

우봉급외에대ᄒᆞᆫ경부ᄂᆞᆫ샹당
ᄒᆞᆫ관사를환산중쥰의게공급
ᄒᆞᆯ사다만샹당ᄒᆞᆫ관사가무ᄒᆞᆫ
시에ᄂᆞᆫ관사료월ᄒᆡᆨ금화팔십
원으로지급ᄒᆞᆯ사
뎨사됴환산중쥰의내임환국급
휴가환국시에ᄂᆞᆫ션거료실비
외에금이빅원을지급ᄒᆞᆯ사
경찰사무에관ᄒᆞ야대한ᄂᆡ지
에젼왕ᄒᆞᆯ시에ᄂᆞᆫ션거료실비
외에미일금화팔원을지급ᄒᆞᆯ
사
뎨오됴본계약은그긔한을예졍
치아니ᄒᆞ나본계약을ᄒᆡ졔ᄒᆞᆯ
필요가잇ᄂᆞᆫ시에ᄂᆞᆫ호상협의
후에일본대국ᄃᆡ표자의동의
를경ᄒᆞ야본계약을ᄒᆡ졔ᄒᆞᆯ사
우계약을본월삼일샹오십시
에ᄂᆡ부대신외부대신탁지대
신일본공사환산고문이외부
에회동됴인ᄒᆞᆫ지라칠일브터
환산씨가사진시무ᄒᆞᆫ다더라
○티동폐현 팔일하오삼시반
에일공사가일젼에조쳥ᄒᆞᆫ든사
관사인과공관셔긔관의모든
부인과공녕부고문관부인을ᄃᆡ
동폐현ᄒᆞ엿더라
○자연감액 탁지부에서각관
쳥일월도봉급은능히변통인고
로의젼례ᄒᆞ야지급ᄒᆞ엿거니와
이월샤봉급브터ᄂᆞᆫ감셩ᄒᆞᆫ예산
티로지발ᄒᆞᆯ터인즉관계리졍반
포를연ᄅᆡ불반ᄒᆞ여도자연감액
이된다더라
○소계군셜치 쳥결사무소에
셔각셔에오예물소계군십오명
식비치ᄒᆞ야츅일졔거케ᄒᆞ고거
름치ᄂᆞᆫ군민빗호에두명식비치
ᄒᆞ고츅일졔거케ᄒᆞ며민호에셔
빈사에빗동화ᄒᆞᆫ푼식거름장슈
를츌급케ᄒᆞ고거름은소계한바
리에일원이오몰계한바리에팔
십젼으로졍급ᄒᆞ엿다더라
○쳥ᄉᆞ조회 신임쳥공ᄉᆞ가외
부로조회ᄒᆞᆫ니ᄀᆡ에본대신이초
사일에국셔를뎡졔ᄒᆞᆫ지라교셥
ᄉᆞ무를본대신이졉관ᄒᆞᆯ터이니
쳥컨대사조ᄒᆞ라ᄒᆞ엿더라
○조회ᄒᆞ고 ᄂᆡ장원에셔외부
로조회ᄒᆞ엿스되평양민광ᄉᆞ로
광무칠년에비국인귀빈례리슈
씨를기사로고빙ᄒᆞ고ᄯᅩ그후
위슈등삼인을ᄯᅩ고빙ᄒᆞ엿더
니민광에소입비가리익보다도
로혀만ᄒᆞᆫ지라금에뎡지코자ᄒᆞ
니ᄒᆞᆼ기사등의긔한이다만ᄒᆞ엿
스나불가불히고ᄒᆞᆯ터이니이듯
으로면죠ᄒᆞ라ᄒᆞ엿더라
○젼별ᄎᆞ셜연 ᄅᆡ임ᄒᆞᆫ쳥공ᄉᆞ
허티신씨가리초구일에귀죠ᄒᆞᆯ
ᄎᆞ로인티초칠일에외부에셔젼별
로연회ᄒᆞᆫ다더라
○불사도일 주일공관참셔관
하샹긔씨ᄂᆞᆫ 대ᄂᆡ에복십이라
국졔샹에방ᄒᆡ가잇겟다고ᄒᆞ야
일본셔동씨를건너오지못ᄒᆞ도
록ᄒᆞᆫ다더라

○회의미과 칠일오후에어젼
회의를긔ᄒᆞᆫ다더니인원이미비
ᄒᆞ야기회치못ᄒᆞ엿더라
○탄핵졍부 찬졍최익현씨가
졍부각대신을탄핵ᄒᆞ야샹소ᄒᆞᆫ
지라모든대신들이다자인ᄒᆞ야
사직샹소를ᄒᆞᆫ다더라
○직권힝ᄉᆞ 일인고하송지조
씨가경무쳥고문관의보좌원으
로시무ᄒᆞᄂᆞᆫ중인ᄃᆡ히원의직권
도ᄂᆡ부대신과교셥ᄒᆞ야힝ᄒᆞᆯ이
될터이라더라
○민ᄉᆞ샹소 쥬쳥공ᄉᆞ민영쳘
씨ᄂᆞᆫ샹소를샹ᄒᆞ엿더라
○소윤방문 종로빅목젼압회
일인이고시티를셜ᄒᆞᆫ고로한셩
소윤박승조씨가일령ᄉᆞ를방문
ᄒᆞ고쳘거ᄒᆞ라ᄒᆞ고ᄯᅩ종노길에
젼벼려놋ᄂᆞᆫ일본샹민들도쳘거
ᄒᆞ라ᄒᆞ되히령ᄉᆞ가불응ᄒᆞᆫ다더
라
○학대신임 리지용씨ᄂᆞᆫ오릐
한양ᄒᆞ더니일간학부대신을피
명ᄒᆞᆫ다더라
○야학신셜 젼평위원홍필관
종셕씨가셔무에진흥을위ᄒᆞ야
일어야학교를셜립ᄒᆞᆫ다더라
○과녀시원 평양거ᄒᆞᄂᆞᆫ김소
사의신원사로령의분보에긔ᄌᆡ
ᄒᆞ엿거니와다시샹탐ᄒᆞᆫ즉남편
김치오가그편답을탈취ᄒᆞᆯ흉계
로그과슈와십오셰된양ᄌᆞ사이
에멸륜픽샹ᄒᆞᆫ말을쥬츌ᄒᆞ야관
찰부와평리원에지쳥ᄒᆞ야판
결을득ᄒᆞ얏고츅츌ᄒᆞᆫ지라그과
슈가빅빅무하ᄒᆞᆫ놈으로이러ᄒᆞᆫ
셰샹에용납못ᄒᆞᆯ쥬명을쓰고호
소무쳐ᄒᆞ야대안문압헤읍혈복
닙ᄒᆞ엿더니
대황뎨폐하게옵셔둥촉ᄒᆞ시와
신원ᄒᆞ야쥬라신쳐분이법부로
나렷다더라
○손녀연회 칠일샹오십이시
에각국공령ᄉᆞ와한국각대관이
명동손탁부인집에셔연회ᄒᆞ엿
다더라
○교사혼례 법어교사마티을
씨가군악교사덕인의령녀와뎡
혼ᄒᆞ야팔일샹오일시에법공관
에셔셩례ᄒᆞ엿다더라
○군슈징류 고원군슈셔리문
쳔군슈뎡유셥씨보고에ᄂᆞᆫ원산
항에셔히군슈류병훈의게인쟝
을면ᄒᆞ엿더니고원군슈류병훈
보고에ᄂᆞᆫ경셩군사령부인허가
무ᄒᆞ다ᄒᆞ고원산사령부에셔집
류ᄒᆞ야도임치못ᄒᆞ엿다더니즉
금들은즉원산사령부에셔본항
경무관박긔호로셔리군슈를차
졍ᄒᆞ엿다더라
○원류차도 공쥬관찰셔리면
보니에갈닌관찰심건택이발뎡
ᄒᆞᄂᆞᆫ티한일쳥삼국빅셩이길을
막고원류ᄒᆞᆫ다ᄒᆞ엿더라
○가칭일병 시위티결습위관

쟝규형씨가일젼에남대문외등
지로츌왕ᄒᆞ엿더니그ᄯᅢ시위
티병뎡일명이일병모자를쓰고
일인이됴션말ᄒᆞᄂᆞᆫ것쳐럼어를
ᄒᆞᆫ말노ᄒᆞ며그위관을욕ᄒᆞ고
리ᄂᆞᆫ지라그위관이처음에ᄂᆞᆫ일
병인쥴알고두려워피ᄒᆞ엿더니
맛참포티병뎡ᄒᆞᆫ명이그위관다
려말ᄒᆞ기를져놈이됴션병뎡이
라ᄒᆞᄂᆞᆫ고로즉시헌병의게압부
ᄒᆞ엿더라
○리졍하디 군졔와관졔를리
졍ᄒᆞᆫ다ᄂᆞᆫ지가슈삭이되엿스
나오히려연타미결ᄒᆞᄂᆞᆫ지라본
월초십일ᄂᆡ로귀졍이안되면
젼에차관됴약쳐럼한졍에셔ᄂᆞᆫ
착슈도못ᄒᆞ고타인이자긔임의
로편졔ᄒᆞᆫ다ᄂᆞᆫ항셜이분분ᄒᆞ니
이제라도졍ᄉᆞ을졍차리스면됴
켓다고들ᄒᆞᆫ다더라
○ᄒᆞ샹구남 일본사령부에셔
경찰티리ᄒᆞᆫ후로한국관인중에
혹한인의불법ᄒᆡᆼ위를고ᄒᆞᄂᆞᆫ
자도잇스며혹젼협으로구남ᄒᆞᆫ
야교준ᄒᆞᄂᆞᆫ자ㅣ도파다ᄒᆞᆫ지라
려항간에셔말ᄒᆞ기를샹이샹을
먹ᄂᆞᆫ다ᄒᆞ더라
○야외연습 작일오후일시량
에동문외에일병이빅여명이야
외연습ᄒᆞ엿다더라
○심민호원 울산거ᄒᆞᄂᆞᆫ신졍
퇴씨가향쟈에경위원에피슈ᄒᆞ
야슬ᄯᅢ경위원총관권즁셕씨의
게돈몃만량을젼탈ᄒᆞ엿다ᄂᆞᆫ티
신씨가불승원굴ᄒᆞ야일본사령
부에권즁셕씨를걸어뎡ᄒᆞ엿다
더라

뎐보

사일대본영발

○쳘티교젼 작삼일야에근소
ᄒᆞᆫ뎍의보병이왜두산뎍뎍산부
근으로퇴습ᄒᆞ엿스나다격퇴ᄒᆞ
엿고ᄯᅩ동일오후규자듄만보산
사하북보방현셩보동고가ᄌᆞ와
밋셔고가ᄌᆞ심조보북방약십리
부근에셔우리진디각처를포격
ᄒᆞ엿고본일오후삼시경에뎍
의긔병오쳔빅이승티ᄌᆞ(쳘티
ᄌᆞ북방약십리)에셔혼하우안
을면ᄒᆞ고ᄯᅩ뎍의보병약일즁디
와포병약일즁디로편셩ᄒᆞᆫ뎍은
승티ᄌᆞ에셔쳘티ᄌᆞ로향ᄒᆞ야공
격ᄒᆞᄂᆞᆫ티뎍은후속부티가잇ᄂᆞᆫ
것ᄀᆞᆺᄒᆞ며쳘티ᄌᆞ의우리부티ᄂᆞᆫ
차와교젼ᄒᆞᄂᆞᆫ중이라ᄒᆞ엿더라

동경뎐보 팔일발

○아원평화 아국태공년은평
화극복ᄒᆞ기를결의ᄒᆞ고론돈쥬
찰ᄒᆞᄂᆞᆫ아국대사ᄂᆞᆫ평화됴건에
관ᄒᆞ야본국[illegible]쟝을슈ᄒᆞ엿
다더라

동뎐

○아병반란 셔부리아지방의
소요ᄂᆞᆫ거거의심ᄒᆞᆫ모양으로만
연ᄒᆞ야경찰관과밋예비병삼쳔
인은반란을긔ᄒᆞ엿다더라

동뎐

○로병퇴습 오일아참에뎍보
병약일소티가로어라시로엄습
ᄒᆞ엿스나우리부티가차를격퇴
ᄒᆞ엿다더라

동뎐

○로병포격 동일하오오시반
량에삼셩자산의뎍포병이소류
듄부근을포격ᄒᆞ엿스나일군에
ᄂᆞᆫ손ᄒᆡ가업고

동뎐

○뎍병난사 동일하오에고가
ᄌᆞ와소림ᄌᆞ부근에집ᄒᆞᆫ각팔문
의뎍포병이티티부근을사격ᄒᆞ
엿고ᄯᅩ동야십시량에사방티부
근의뎍포병은텰도교부근사격
ᄒᆞ고뎍의소척후ᄂᆞᆫ리대인둔의
동북방으로리ᄒᆞ야난사ᄒᆞᆫ외에
큰변화ᄂᆞᆫ업다더라

북관뎐보

○픽복곤란 북관방면에셔티
ᄒᆞᆫ졍보를거ᄒᆞᆫ즉목하에동방면
에뉴쥬ᄒᆞᄂᆞᆫ로병들은일빅인중
에삼사십인의비례로한복을습
착ᄒᆞᆫ다ᄂᆞᆫ티향ᄌᆞ홍원에셔일로
쳑후충돌시에우에ᄯᅡ로외투를
면용ᄒᆞᆫ소를츄량컨티히지방에
졔ᄒᆞᆫ로병들의픽복공급이심분
치못ᄒᆞ야엇더케곤란ᄒᆞᄂᆞᆫ지그
졍티를가히알니라ᄒᆞ더라

○냥쵸자소 동뎐

셩진에쥬둔ᄒᆞᆫ뎍군이그젹쳐ᄒᆞ
엿든냥쵸에방화ᄒᆞ야자슈로살
ᄂᆞᆫ고임의대부분은북방으로퇴
각ᄒᆞ고잔부ᄂᆞᆫ퇴각ᄒᆞᆯ쥰비중이
라ᄒᆞ고

○뎍병퇴각 경발동

수일오후에뎍병이탑산ᄌᆞ부근
에셔마권ᄌᆞ부근을공격ᄒᆞ고오
일아참에근소ᄒᆞᆫ뎍의보병은각
쳐에리습ᄒᆞ엿스나다차를격퇴
ᄒᆞ엿고수일쳘티ᄌᆞ를공격ᄒᆞᆫ뎍
병은우리수비병으로인ᄒᆞ야막
고승티ᄌᆞ에톄지ᄒᆞ더니오일아
참에자유타방면으로격퇴ᄒᆞ엿
다더라

TELEGRAMS.

(FROM JAPAN PAPERS)

AFFAIRS IN RUSSIA.

London, Feb. 2.

It is officially announced that the Tsar and Tsaritsa and the Empress Dowager sympathising deeply with the families, of those killed and wounded in the disturbances in St. Petersburg on the 22nd ultimo, have placed the sum of five thousand pounds sterling at the disposal Trepoff, Governor of St. Petersburg, to assist those in need of relief.

Berlin, Feb. 2.

The Czar has received representatives of the labourers in audience. His Majesty counselled them to avoid rash courses and apply themselves diligently to their occupations. He promised that their requests should be granted as far as practicable.

London, Feb. 2.

In a speech to a deputation from the strikers yesterday the Czar advised the men to return to work and stated that he would pardon their transgressions. He gave no promises to reforms and made it evident that the autocracy is to be firmly upheld. His Majesty has given fifty thousand roubles to the families of the victims of the massacre by the troops on Jan. 22nd.

London, Feb. 2.

On the afternoon of Feb. 1, the Czar received in audience at Tsarkoe Seloe over thirty representatives of the working classes. The Daily Telegraph correspondent at St. Petersburg states that the deputation was composed of men selected by the employers, two men being chosen out of each thousand employes. This was done in accordance with orders given by the Financial Minister. The Czar addressed the Delegates as follows:—The recent deplorable incidents have been occasioned by the fact that you were deceived by the enemy and by traitors to their country. It was the enemy who persuaded you to give up your work and induced you to oppose us and our Government. But this is a period when all Russians must unite to subdue the obstinate foe.

We are well aware that your condition requires improvement. But you must have patience. By attempting to make your wishes known through strikes and political agitation you offend against the law. As we are solicitious for the happiness and welfare of the labourers, we will take steps to ameliorate your condition and investigate your desires. We will also pardon the offences committed by you in the recent disturbances, as we know well that, at heart, all the working people are faithful and loyal.

Berlin Feb. 2.

The Czar has issued the following Decree:—

1.—We order M. de Witte to carry out the reforms mentioned in the Imperial Decree issued on December 23, and to consult with the representatives of the labourers on the matter.

2.—The liberty of the Press is to be recognised.

3.—Pensions shall be granted to the families of the persons killed or wounded January 22.

London, Feb. 2.

The strike movement is spreading to Siberia and railway traffic is menaced at Irkutsk and Krasnoyarsk. There is consequently danger of Kuropatkin's communications being cut off.

London, Feb. 2.

M. Brignin has been appointed Minister of the Interior by the Czar, in succession to Prince Sviatopolk Mirski. M. Muravieff, formerly Minister of Justice. has been appointed Ambassador at Rome,

London, Jan. 31.

Grand Duke Vladimir justifies all the measures taken by the authorities. arguing that the Russians are unfitted for a Constitution

London, Feb. 1.

Mr. Schwab, representing an American company, is going to St. Petersburg to close negotiations for the construction of ten battleships for the Russian Government. The revolutionary agencies are seizing this opportunity to disseminate statements in order to increase the unpopularity of the war.

JAPANESE INTRIGUES IN RUSSIA.

London, Feb. 2.

The Russian newspaper Rusky Invalid state that, from telegrams received by the Russian Imperial Household and the War Department from several quarters, it is certain that the recent disturbances in Russia were instigated by Japan and Great Britain. It is known that the Japanese Government has distributed 18,000,000 roubles among the members of the revolutionary and liberal parties and the labourers. In return they asked the strikers to destroy the naval Arsenals, in order to prevent the remaining Baltic warships and the Black Sea Fleet from being sent to the Far East, and to hinder the sending of military necessaries to General Kuropatkin. It was hoped that in this way Russia might be compelled to sue for peace. Such action upon the part of Japan is natural, as she urgently needs the termination of the war at the earliest possible date, her financial resources being nearly exhausted. The Japanese in Paris publicly boast of the success of their Government in stirring up riots in Russia.

THE THIRD BALTIC SQUADRON.

London, Feb. 1.

It is reported that the Third Baltic Squadron will sail for the Far East on the 6th instant.

The Squadron will consist of three battleships and two cruisers, and will be under the command of Admiral Willnaytoff.

London, Feb. 2.

The departure of the third Baltic Squadron has been delayed by the strikes. Admiral Rojestvensky has consequently been instructed to proceed immediately to the Far East. He will be joined by Admiral Botrovsky's vessels.

THE SHAHO.

London, Feb. 2.

It is reported from St. Petersburg that a battle has raged along the entire front. The Russians have everywhere been repulsed. General Kuropatkin accuses General Gripenberg of having needlessly sacrificed ten thousand men.

GENERAL NEWS.

Paris, Jan. 28.

In the Chamber the Government appealed to all republicans for a reconciliation and an understanding in order that the Cabinet might pursue the reforms of its predecessor. This declaration was received by applause from the centre. The name of retired Commandant Beynicourt has been erased from the list of the Legion of Honour for acts of espionage. Generals Peigne, Delarbout and Nonancourt have been relieved from their commands, the first for having consulted the Grand Orient Freemason Lodge on the subject of his officers, and the second and third for remarks reflecting on the Government.

Berlin, Feb. 1.

The Dutch troops in Acheen, Sumatra, have killed the Pretender.

Berlin, Feb. 2.

Count von Buelow has submitted the new Commercial Treaties to the Reichstag. The majority of the members greeted them with enthusiasm.

Berlin, Feb. 2.

The employees of the electric light works at Paris have gone on strike.

RECENT ADDITIONS TO THE JAPANESE MERCANTILE MARINE.

Since December last the following eleven foreign steamers have been seized in the Japan Sea and Hokkaido waters on their way to Vladivostock :—

	Tonnage.	Cargo.	Time of capture.
Nigretia (British)	..2,368	Kerosene	Dec. 19
King Arthur ,,	..1,416	None	,,
Rosalie ,,	..4,370	6,500 tons Cardiff coal	Jan. 8
Lethington ,,	..4,421	,,	,, 12
Wilhelmina (Dutch)	.4,395	6,000 tons Cardiff coal	,, 16
Bawtry (British)	...2,407	Provisions machine oil, ship building materials	
Oskley ,,	...2,456	5,900 tons Cardiff coal	,, 18
Barmar (Austrian)	.3,071	4,000 tons Cardiff coal	,, 25
M. S. Dollar (Am'can)	4,216	Forage provisions, coal	,, 27
Wyefield (British)	..3,235	Provisions, etc.	,, 30
Siam (Austrian)	3,160	Coal	,, 13

SPURIOUS NICKELS.

A correspondent, writing to us on the subject of counterfeit money, says:—

"It may not be generally known that there is *no* good money when you get away from Seoul into the country.

Recently a man came with me from Whang Hai do to Chemulpo. At the railway ticket office they refused to take his money and he asked me what he should do. He had heard that Seoul people were particular and had picked out what he thought were good nickels. If the country people were to blame it would be right for them to lose all the counterfeit money in their possession—amounting to thousands of dollars—but it is no fault of theirs. It is not the fault of the Korean Government either (that is, altogether) for it is generally understood that Japanese carried on the work of counterfeiting and it is not always easy for a Korean to arrest a Japanese. It seems to me that it will be a great injustice to the poor people to make them pay for the fault of the government and the Japanese.

AFFAIRS IN RUSSIA.

Reports from Irkutsk, dated Feb. 1, state that over four hundred railway labourers have gone on strike at Grasnoirsk station, and that Irkutsk is to be placed under martial law. Kadom, a city east of Moscow, has become involved in the strikes, as have also also Kakutze, near the German frontier, and Samara, on the Volga. An association of business men at St. Peterburg passed the following resolution on Feb. 1.—"That we petition the Financial Minister to frame laws dealing with the reforms desired by the strikers; that the complaints of the men as to their work in the factories should not be investigated until they have resumed their duties; that those strikers who resume work should not be subjected to any form of punishment."

The Australian Commonwealth has rejected an amended Orient Mail tender of £140,000 sterling.

The following telegram has been received by the Tokio Foreign Department:—A question having been asked in the Austrian Parliament as to whether an agreement existed between Austro-Hungary and Russia, providing for the preservation of order by Austro-Hungarian troops in Russian territory adjacent to the Austrian empire's frontiers, the Prime Minister replied that there was no foundation whatever for such an idea.

A London telegram dated Jan. 25th reports the death, at the age of eighty-four of The Right Rev. Richard Lewis, D. D., Bishop of Llandaff.

Early in January an Army Order was issued in England which adopts with a slight modification Lord Esher's decentralising proposals. There are to be seven commands, each co-extensive with administrative districts.

The Korea Daily News.

Issued at 3 P. M. daily except Sundays.

Rate of Subscription:—
Per Year,............Yen 25.
Per Quarter,..........Yen 7.
Per Month,..........Yen 2.50.

Postage in Korea not charged extra.
Postage abroad charged extra.

Advertisements, 50 sen per day for 1 inch or less
5 yen per month per inch.
50 yen per year per inch.

All communications to

E. T. BETHELL,
Editor and Publisher,
Pak-tong, Seoul.

THE ANGLO—JAPANESE ALLIANCE.

The London Times is already advocating an extension of the Anglo-Japanese Alliance.

In view of the well-known Russophobe proclivities of the Times, it is not to be expected that its efforts in this direction will meet with more appreciation than they deserve, but it is at the same time sad to see a journal, claiming to be responsible, doing its very best to involve Great Britain in a costly war to oblige Allies who have yet to prove their worth.

In spite of the undoubted efficiency of Japan's fighting forces, it must be evident to all that Japan is letting no opportunity slip of encouraging and guiding all other forces likely to be of service. The Anglo-Japanese Alliance and the British press are not least among these and the pro-Japanese portion of the British press advocates an extension of the Alliance.

At present the Alliance is a purely defensive one, and as such has doubtless been of great use to the world in confining the war to the two original belligerents, but it certainly appears that an extension of the scope of the agreement would be equivalent to placing us all on the top of a vast powder magazine. It is only because passive or technical breaches of neutrality do not, under present conditions, constitute a course for England's interference, that we are not at present at war with France. Japan has continually protested against France's non-observance of neutrality and it appears to us that the limited scope of the alliance is a matter upon which Great Britain is to be congratulated.

At the same time, the alliance, even in its present form, has not been without ill-effects. Although Russia has for years been menacing India, there can be no doubt that her recently increased activities on the borders of Afghanistan have been in the nature of a reply to the Anglo-Japanese compact, and it appears to us that any addition to the agreement would only increase Great Britain's dangers and responsibilities without giving anything approaching a corresponding benefit.

The most that those, who, speaking on behalf of the Japanese, advocate on extension of the scope of the alliance, seem able to put forward as an inducement to Great Britain, is the offer of the assistance of the Japanese Army in the defense of India. This appears to be a very inadequate return for Great Britain's sacrifice of her independence and there are several reasons which help to make the offer a far from tempting one.

The very newspapers which have advocated the extension of the alliance have also pointed out that Russia could without difficulty carry on a campaign against India simultaneously with the one in Manchuria, and it is evident that under such circumstances Japan would have no soldiers to spare to assist Great Britain. Even supposing that this war is brought to a conclusion before Russia commences an invasion of India, we do not think it likely that Japan would be able to come to our assistance with a very great force. There can be no doubt that this war has told, and will tell, very heavily on Japan; and however this war may terminate, it will be years before its army can be restored to it previous efficiency.

There is another point which we touch upon with some hesitation; it is that of Japan's trustworthiness. We have frequently pointed out her continuous breaches of faith and general unscrupulousness in Korea and the bill for the imposition of a tax of 10 and 15 per cent upon all cotton and woolen textiles, reads, in the light of the instructions given relative to the collection of the tax on domestic productions, very like an attempt on Japan's part to break the present treaty obligations by the imposition of a protectionist tax on imported textiles.

Such actions as these breed distrust, and lead us to doubt whether, even if all other conditions were favourable, great Baitain would be justified in entering into an agreement such as the Anglo-Japanese press advocates.

A PERSONAL NARRATIVE OF THE SIEGE OF PORT ARTHUR.

(Specially written for The "China Review" by a Russian Naval Officer.)

(Continued from last issue).

It seemed as if the great coggy, white blanket of snow had covered our last hope of succor. With the snow came a reduction in rations. Horse and mule meat became luxuries that money could not buy, and the pangs of hunger seemed to make demons of some of the men, who quarreled over a cup of soup or an ounce of sugar, as you have seen dogs snarling over a bone.

Late in October the old town was practically in ruins, and the Japanese turned their attention to the new town which, by the end of November, had been laid waste by the eleven inch shells; there were great gaping ragged holes in many houses, and roofs of others had caved in. In all the town I do not believe there was sash containing unbroken window glass. The bombardment, however, was intermittent, the enemy every now and then training his big guns against the forts with telling effect. So great was the damage does to the fortifications that our men were at work night and day repairing holes in the walls, but no matter how strenuously they worked there was always something left undone. Hundreds of brave fellows gave up their lives in the work of repair.

Historians and military critics may, in the future, deal harshly with the administrative officers of Port Arthur, and I am free to admit that serious blunders were not unknown among them. But of the conduct of the sailors and soldiers I have only words of praise. They were truly great in their perfect self-abnegation and grim patience. In all the history of the world there is not chronicled a greater heroism than theirs. While the heroes of the past may have performed many brilliant and daring acts, hope was always with them. Not so with the heroes of Port Arthur. They fought on and on, knowing that victory was impossible and death almost certain.

It is the truth that, near the end of October, the majority of officers and men had given up all hope of succor and were prepared in mind to die for the colors when the opportunity offered. It is also the truth that some officers and some men were not sufficiently strong in mind to thus calmly wait for the end, whatever it might be, and preferred to blow out their brains or throw themselves on the bayonets of the enemy. Stoessel knew the character of the men, he knew he could depend upon them, no matter how hopeless the situation, how dangerous the emergency.

Early on the morning of November 19th the Japanese concentrated their artillery fire upon the summit of 203-Metre Hill where we had a fort and a few small guns. On account of the scarcity of ammunition our artillerymen were not permitted to answer the enemy's fire. For three days the Japanese batteries pounded away with varying intensity, and, during lulls in their bombardment, they made eleven consecutive and futile efforts to carry the mountain by assault. Time and time again they retreated pell mell down the declivities, leaving them scattered with thousands of their dead. On December 2nd the mountain was still in our hands, but the forts on its summit had been razed by the enemy's shell fire, and its devoted defenders were forced to take refuge in furrows dug by Japanese shells. Then came the fierce bombardment of December 3rd, when the summit was completely hidden by dense clouds of smoke and dust caused by the explosion of hundreds of projectiles. At ten o'clock in the morning there was a sudden cessation in the enemy's fire, and ten minutes later they were storming up the steep and rugged sides to the assault—climbing, creeping, running all doubled up, and shrieking that hideous battle-cry of theirs—The first to reach our line of defence were met in hand to hand conflict by the defenders who, holding the uphill side, were able to do great execution with the bayonet—a parry, a thrust, a groan or a scream, and in this manner hundreds of the enemy fell. They came on, however, in constantly increasing numbers, and it soon become apparent that our forces on the hill would have to be heavily reinforced. Such a condition, however, had been anticipated, and reserve companies had been drawn up ever since the opening of the fight. The men stood in ranks leaning on their rifles, gazing almost disinterestedly upon the smoke-capped hill all criss-crossed by the flashing of rifles and bursting shells. It was an old story to them. With heavy hearts we watched company after company disappear up the slope, for we knew and they knew death awaited them. These companies, mostly sailors, were a religious lot, and when the order came for them to go, each man uncovered and made the sign of the cross with pathetic earnestness. And in this action he found strength, and he went to his death with a calm, also contented countenance. How we admired them; Thus did the rank and the file prove their mettle; of some of the officers I have nothing to say.

(To be continued).

The Korea Daily News.

VOL. II, FRIDAY, FEBRUARY 10, 1905. No. 31

HONGKONG & SHANGHAI BANKING CORPORATION.

Paid-up Capital..... ....$10,000,000
Reserve Fund:—Sterling Reserve... 10,000,000
Silver Reserve..... 7,000,000

27,000,000
Reserve Liability of Proprietors... 10,000,000

HEAD OFFICE, HONGKONG.

London Bankers, London and County Banking Company Limited.

Branches and Agencies,
London.

Amoy,	Hankow	Penang,
Bangkok	Hiogo,	Rangoon,
Batavia,	Iloilo,	Saigon,
Bombay,	Lyons,	San Francisco,
Calcutta,	Manila,	Singapore,
Colombo,	Nagasak	Sourabaya,
Foochow,	New York,	Tientsin,
Hamburg,	Peking,	Yokohama,

Credits granted on approved Securities, and every description of Banking and Exchange business transacted.

Drafts granted on London and the chief Commercial places in Europe, India, Australia, America, China and Japan.

HOLME RINGER & CO., AGENTS,
CHEMULPO.

HOKURKU DOBOKU KAISHA.

Branch office in Chong Dong, Seoul.
Japanese telephone No. 165

CONTRACT DEPARTMENT.

We can contract to build any building or construction.

MERCHANDISE DEPARTMENT.

We can provide any building material.
We have just contracted to build the new Belgian Legation.

E. MEYER & CO.

Chemulpo.

SOLE AGENTS IN KOREA FOR.

A. T. Morse, Sons & Co.'s

"Fresco" Distemper

In all colours ready for use on walls,

Ceilings etc.

and

AVENARIUS CARBOLINEUM

A wood-preserving and antiseptic oil preparation

Against decay, dry-rot, fungus and wood-destroying insects.

A large supply always in stock.
Prices upon application.

E. MEYER & Co.,
Chemulpo.

CHARTERED BANK OF INDIA AUSTRALIA & CHINA.

INCORPORATED BY ROYAL CHARTER 1853

HEAD OFFICES —LONDON.

Paid-up Capital £800,000
Reserve Liability of Share-
holders 800,000
Reserve Fund 800,000

Drafts granted upon all the principal places in the world and every description of Exchange and banking business transacted.

E. MEYER & Co., Agents,
Chemulpo.

MITSU BISHI DOCKYARD & ENGINE WORKS,

NAGASAKI.

CODE WORD, "DOCK."

A 1, A. B. C., and Engineering Codes used.

DOCK No. 1 (at Tategami).

Extreme Length..............523 feet
Length on blocks .... 513 ,,
Width of Entrance on Top......89 ,,
,, ,, Bottom....77 ,,
Water on Blocks at Spring Tide 26½ ,,

DOCK No. 2 (Mukaijima).

Extreme Length..............371 feet
Length on Blocks..............360 ,,
Width of Entrance on Top......66 ,,
,, ,, Bottom 53 ,,
Water on Blocks at Spring Tide 22 ,,

PATENT SLIP (at Kosuge).

Can take vessels up to 1,000 tons gross.

THE WORKS are well equipped with the LATEST IMPROVEMENTS, and can execute any kind of work in SHIPBUILDING and MARINE ENGINEERING, as well as in REPAIRING of SHIPS.

The COMPANY'S new powerful steamer OURA-MARU (712 tons, 700 I.H.P.), specially built for SALVAGE PURPOSES, and equipped with necessary gear, is always READY at SHORT NOTICE.

THE METHODIST PUBLISHING HOUSE,

Little West Gate, Seoul.

JOB PRINTING, TYPEWRITER PAPER
CARBON PAPER, VISITING CARDS
STATIONERY, BOOK BINDING
BOOK PUBLISHERS
AMERICAN SCHOOL BOOKS
SPENCERIAN COPY BOOKS
PEN CARBON LETTER AND BILL BOOKS

S. A. BECK, Manager.

DAI-ICHI GINKO.

LIMITED.

(Formerly the First National Bank)

ESTABLISHED 1873

INCORPORATED UNDER PRESENT LAW 1896

Capital - - - - - - - - Yen 5,000,000
Reserve Fund - - - - - 1,500,000

HEAD OFFICE:—TOKIO.

President: Baron SHIBUSAWA.

BRANCHES AND CORRESPONDENTS
In the Principal Cities and Towns of Japan.

Interest Allowed on
Fixed deposits 1 year - - - 6½ per cent
" " 6 months - - - 6 per cent

Special current accounts 1½ sen daily per Y 100
General " " 1 " " " 100

M. TANAKA,
Manager, Chemulpo.

SINGER SEWING MACHINES

씽거ᄌᆞ봉침

SOLE AGENTS FOR KOREA

젼매쇼

HOLME RINGER & CO.
Chemulpo.

졔믈포 함릉거양힝

KAMEYA & CO.

GENERAL STOREKEEPERS

Chinkokai - - - Seoul

(*Established 1895, Tokyo*)

Confectionery, Hams, Canned Goods, Cutlery, Hirano & Tansan Water. Provisions, Gents, Furnishing goods, Toilet Articles, Travelling Bags, Tobacco, Cigars & Cigarettes Kitchen Utensils. Coffee, Biscuits.

Fresh Goods always kept in Stock.
Prices Moderate
☞ *Please come and inspect our goods.*

NIPPON YUSEN KAISHA.
JAPANESE MAIL STEAMSHIP CO.

UNDER MAIL CONTRACT WITH THE IMPERIAL JAPANESE GOVERNMENT.

European Line

Regular Fortnightly Service between Yokohama Kobe, Moji, Shanghai, Hongkong, Singapore, Penang Colombo, Port Said, Marseilles, London and Antwerp

American Line

Regular Fortnightly Service between Hongkong and Seattle, calling at Shanghai, Moji, Kobe, Yokohama and Victoria, B. C.

Australian Line

Regular weekly Service betwen Japan Ports and Australia, calling at Hongkong and Manila.
(Above Three Lines Suspended until further notice).

Shanghai Line

Weekly Service between Shanghai and Japan Ports

Korea Line

Service Kobe, Moji, Nagasaki, Fusan Chemulpo Chefoo, Taku.
S. S. Babelsberg, 2181 tons.
Service Kobe, Moji, Fusan, Chemulpo, Chinnampo
S. S. ARGO, S. S. Ohio.

BORDEN'S CONDENSED MILK CO.

New York, U. S. A.

ALWAYS IN STOCK

Eagle Brand Condensed Milk.

Gold Seal Condensed Milk.

Peerless (Family) Evaporated Cream.

Borden's Malted Milk.

E. MEYER & CO.
Chemulpo Korea,
Sole Agents.

ROYAL INSURANCE COMPANY,

Funds exceed £10,000,000

FIRE

AT CURRENT RATES

LIFE

REDUCED PREMIUM.

HOLME RINGER & Co.,
Agents, Chemulpo.

廣
KWANG ◉ C'HANG
昌

BENNETT & CO.
Merchants
Chemulpo.

Offices opposite the Imperial Japanese Post and Telegraph Office Chemulpo.

Telephone Number 201.

大韓每日申報

대한ᄆᆡ일신보

(뎨이권삼십이호) (월요일) 일천구빅오년이월십삼일

본사고ᄇᆡᆨ

이 신보는 영어와 한어로 셔계리 일출판ᄒᆞᆸ

신문가

한장 엽두돈오푼

일삭도 엽두량닷돈

우표가 ᄆᆡ삭닷돈

다 맛돈으로 밧ᄉᆞᆷ

광고료는

귀한의장단과ᄌᆞ힝의다쇼로ᄌᆞ증감ᄒᆞ되평가로밧을터이오ᄆᆡ오틔지아녀ᄃᆡ한사ᄅᆞᆷ마다다이신문을보실터이니광고내시기를원ᄒᆞ시는이들은우리신문사에와셔면의ᄒᆞ심을희망ᄒᆞᆸ

○발힝소 박동ᄃᆡ한ᄆᆡ일신보사 법어학교앞해 젼영국인셜필림집자리오

사장 영국인 (ᄇᆡ셜)

평양 ᄃᆡ리졈

○평양효동사는 권미보씨로우리신문발매ᄃᆡ리인을뎡ᄒᆞ엿시오니평양에계신구람ᄒᆞ고져ᄒᆞ시는 쳠군ᄌᆞ는ᄒᆞᆫ대리졈에왕림ᄒᆞ와면의ᄒᆞ시옵

사고

○우리ᄃᆡ한ᄆᆡ일신보의목뎍은ᄃᆡ한의안녕질셔에관한모든ᄃᆡ목에ᄃᆡᄒᆞ야는공평한변론을쥬장ᄒᆞᆷ이라우리동신원의담보는신문보시는쳠군ᄌᆞ의계ᄒᆞᆼ상보도ᄒᆞ리며편지들귀셔ᄒᆞ며주시는이는셩명과번디를져어붓치시기를희망ᄒᆞ오니이거슨신문샹에게ᄌᆡᄒᆞ란는거시아니오다만극히신용ᄒᆞ는증거를숨고자ᄒᆞᆷ이라귀자는아모리셔던지과쥐ᄒᆞ올곳과ᄎᆞᄒᆞ는권리를가졋소나되가ᄒᆞ는리유를말ᄒᆞᆯ터이오며공증평화를문란케ᄒᆞ는듯ᄒᆞᆫ귀셔는의례히밧지안켓슴니다

●본사셰시이리로신문을미양우례로분젼ᄒᆞ와례젼부의잉의로젼ᄒᆞ든ᄉᆞ로번곳에는후는게젼ᄒᆞ기도ᄒᆞ며후면칠거슬ᄒᆞ는뎝에젼ᄒᆞ기도ᄒᆞ며후ᄒᆞ야니젼ᄒᆞ는곳도잇다ᄒᆞ와우리신문을슈탕ᄒᆞ야구람ᄒᆞ시는 쳠군ᄌᆞ의계ᄃᆡᄒᆞ야미우미안ᄒᆞ옵기로지금은분젼인을두고미일아ᄎᆞᆷ이젼ᄒᆞ며야나젼ᄒᆞ거나늣게거나ᄎᆞᆫ폐가얩도록ᄒᆞ란ᄒᆞ오나혹야너젼ᄒᆞ거나혹늣게젼ᄒᆞ거나ᄒᆞ면일이잇스면본사로통긔ᄒᆞ여주시을희망ᄒᆞᆸ

잡보

평양통신

○교원의수 평양사는김창걸위명인이ᄒᆡ되세수구한에ᄒᆞᆫ부계녀로ᄆᆡᆺ혓탈ᄒᆞ기위ᄒᆞ야ᄇᆡᆨ가지로병이발ᄒᆞ여도불여의ᄒᆞ니ᄒᆞᆫ남은희녀의본부가출타ᄒᆞᆫ새에즉셔녀뎡에돌입ᄒᆞ쥬불힝이맛나지못ᄒᆞ고나아와ᄒᆞ는말이벼가그게집을샹관ᄒᆞ엿다고ᄒᆞ베소문이각쳐에광자ᄒᆞ야ᄒᆞ녀는원통ᄒᆞᆷ을이긔지못ᄒᆞ야ᄃᆡ동강수에세져죽엇는ᄃᆡ김가는젼녀그소실은아지못ᄒᆞ고인졋다가감리셔로피착이되엿스나금년두살된계집아히가ᄯᅥ울불샹ᄒᆞ다ᄒᆞ엿라

○변화회경원 평양은본ᄅᆡ기셩이만하음한풍괴가ᄃᆡ단ᄒᆞ더니향자일로긔젼지초에ᄒᆞᄃᆡ가신분위ᄒᆞ야일병이다수리쥬ᄒᆞ는고로그시는음란음녀가창궁ᄒᆞ야산ᄒᆞ야경나무문ᄒᆞ다더니근일에쏘ᄒᆞ시전파곳치될셰아니라일층ᄒᆞᄂᆞᆫ소위한량계라칭ᄒᆞ고수방란봉긴남들이모집되야는ᄌᆞ와소녀전매돌유인ᄒᆞ여호생례견ᄒᆞ고의면으로는위친계라ᄒᆞ야기섭ᄉᆞ슈렴ᄒᆞ며후시주ᄉᆞ청루에기생을부르고수다외입쟝미들이등탐거리고노는ᄃᆡ거시고쌍의인죵평양금슈강다산이무셕ᄒᆞ며감으로빗출넌다ᄒᆞ며계죵잉참ᄒᆞᆫ자는기셩의화인회들오샹랑으로며ᄒᆞ고그계외ᄒᆞ는ᄇᆡᆨ회에셔죵틔위원들이편찰부학회와감리셔에ᄃᆡ하거치민쟝칭면회소관도에ᄃᆡ단홀티생래국가폐풍뎡슌교후생에는방히가ᄃᆡ샹ᄒᆞᆫᄂᆡ다더라

○남김교활 평양감리신ᄃᆡ씨가지시장니에말과져을파자ᄀᆞᆫ가ᄒᆞᆫ길곳지못ᄒᆞᆷ으로피ᄆᆡ샹에속히ᄒᆞ고분쟝이만ᄒᆞᆫ민샹산엽에ᄐᆡ울파닐을이라ᄒᆞ야금히본감리가져적재분ᄒᆞ엿는ᄃᆡ히거샥조ᄒᆞ야안각에분곱ᄒᆞ엿는ᄃᆡ히ᄃᆡ남문미샹김응샹김말명랑인이ᄌᆞ수로말을곳쳐지어무쌍이숙히다가감리셔로피착이된지수일에방면ᄒᆞ여달나고은근이기쳔량어음을갑리수메로보니ᄆᆡ신갑린가대로ᄒᆞ야김가의다리에다음표를붓치고엄쟝치벌ᄒᆞ엿다더라

○셕젼의약습 평양셔이젼보리음력셩이월경에는무식ᄒᆞᆫ자등이셔문밧용ᄒᆞᆫ싸히셔셔젼ᄒᆞ논유리승광이되여셩명이종종사샹ᄒᆞᆫ다더니금번에도ᄎᆞ습이갱긔ᄒᆞ여시작된지기일에희디감리가인민셩명의관ᄒᆞᆫ악습을엄금ᄒᆞ는고로일반빅셩이이젼관찰사와군수는셰젼에일등자로등미샹급주어미일은권쟝ᄒᆞ엿는ᄃᆡ이신감리는유별ᄒᆞᆫ다ᄒᆞ더라

○간상사출 평양상민의박병쳔최덕순량인은피차동무쟝사로호상잔계ᄒᆞ야옥양목미필에젹슈가분명ᄒᆞ엿마는미양당무필슉셧호로오류쳑식ᄉᆞᆫ히ᄒᆞᆫ두필을파란명는쟈자미가신동ᄒᆞ야이모양으로쳔여필을일향미셔시ᄒᆞ다가히디샹업중의소에셔발각ᄒᆞ여판찰부와감리셔에보고ᄒᆞ고일변도사실ᄒᆞᆫ후각쳐자부를사원을셜명ᄒᆞ야최박순를면케ᄒᆞ기로젼렴ᄒᆞ야의최량인쳐에를녀주케ᄒᆞ엿다ᄒᆞ더라

○교회흥왕 음력신년월이삼일경에평양야소교회당에셔셩경공부를시작ᄒᆞᆯ졔에황평량도의일반교인들이구름ᄀᆞᆺ치모혓는ᄃᆡ그시에참ᄒᆞᆫ사ᄅᆞᆷ에경영이만하히티교회는인이의왕셩ᄒᆞᆫ다ᄒᆞ더라

평쎠피신 젼평양군슈평한주씨의며관된사실은본보에긔ᄌᆡᄒᆞ엿거니와져간평씨가일본인가에셔피신ᄒᆞᆫ다가하쳐로도망ᄒᆞ엿다고풍셜이랑자ᄒᆞ다더라

●아편만면 평양셩니부자소년들이아편연을만히먹는ᄃᆡ그슈효는오륙빅명에달ᄒᆞ되금지ᄒᆞ는방법이업다ᄒᆞ는가보더라

○사샹이종렴 평양외셩등디에셔일진지회원들이쳘로역에엇지실수가되는지죵죵사샹이되는자만타더라

○규축흥리 평안북도각군에셔는일진회민을의병이란동학이라ᄒᆞ야ᄇᆡᆨ반곤란을당ᄒᆞᆫ다는풍셜이잇사나평양일진지회에셔는념려업다ᄒᆞ고근일셔울본회에셔규칙ᄎᆡᆨ이젼권이ᄒᆞᆫ티ᄒᆞᆫ교로일간지회ᄒᆞᆫ다는말이잇다더라

평양통신

○쥬보확장 일본인평상희쟝씨가일본거류디에셔광무칠년브터위시ᄒᆞ야평양쥬보라명ᄒᆞ고쳥소ᄒᆞᆫ지헝에일쥬일ᄎᆞ에식당더시사들귀치ᄒᆞ더니금번에일층더확쟝ᄒᆞ기위ᄒᆞ야신문에소낭ᄒᆞᆫ물품을일본으로주문ᄒᆞ엿다더라

○흉사샹열 평양은일괴가이샹열과갓타셔음력신이월쳘일경에ᄃᆡ동강결빙이히강되셔샹션이다수리빅ᄒᆞ더라

○자살횡인 평양남문밧사는쟝창순이가동중인김모을무삼ᄌᆞ탐긔임지공연미위ᄒᆞ노라고가귀잉으로말ᄒᆞ다가근조에장가들희롱계ᄒᆞ란고야편을먹조셕쳥ᄃᆡ사죽엇다ᄒᆞᆫ니리가로가를차자죽이란교ᄒᆞᆫ다더라

○쳥원고교 히디빅셩쟝지셥씨등이본시감리셔에쳥원ᄒᆞ엿는데그사의인증ᄃᆡ동강에는다수샹젼이리왕ᄒᆞ는ᄃᆡ방금군용질도에다리를노우되그다리구멍이나자셔샹젼에돗ᄃᆡ가통힝치못ᄒᆞ겟다고희디일본쳘도감부에조회ᄒᆞ야다리구멍을놉히ᄒᆞ여달나고ᄒᆞ엿다더라

뎡오

○음력신이월삼십일에본보뎨이권일호잡보중에평양남도관찰부주사리중회씨가ᄒᆞ더니승졔ᄒᆞ부금을모음기로ᄒᆞ야쟝의례문을관다는말은기시오탐이고젼평양군슈평한주씨가방ᄆᆡᄒᆞ엿다ᄒᆞ더라

양력이월일일

양력이월일일위시ᄒᆞ야일자를영쇄ᄒᆞ시오일주일간수문수록ᄒᆞ야일이도식귀송ᄒᆞ오리다이말삼으로사쟝계엽ᄉᆞᆸᄒᆞ시옵

○교문쳥폐 외부에셔례식원으로조회ᄒᆞ기를폐부교문관쉬지븐의공함을졍ᄒᆞᆫ니ᄭᅡ예국제

UNION INSURANCE SOCIETY OF CANTON.

Head office Hongkong.
Marine risks underwritten at current rates.

Agents in Chemulpo,
E. MEYER & Co.

COMPAGNIE DES MESSAGERIES MARITIMES.

Fortnightly Direct Service.

For Marseilles
via Ports.
Sailing from Yokohama
Calling at Kobe,
Shanghai, Hongkong, Saigon, Singapore, Colombo. Djibonti, Suez, Port Said and Marseilles.

For particulars apply to
HOLME RINGER & Co.,
Chemulpo.

HAYASHIDA & CO.,

16 MYENG DONG, CHIN KO KAI, SEOUL.
BRANCH OFFICE AT CHEMULPO.

Money changers, Coal and Wood Merchants, Express Agents.

We are agents for the Pyeng-yang Coal Company and the Karazu Coal Company of Japan. We have the best quality of both anthracite and bituminous coal, and prompt execution of orders is our speciality. Firewood of all kinds kept in stock. Full weight guaranteed. Money of all denominations exchanged at current rates. Parcels received for all parts.

CHINA MUTUAL LIFE INS. OC.

Most favourable terms to policy holders.

Benefit system unsurpassed.

HOLME RINGER & Co.
Agents, Chemulpo.

C. P. R.

CANADIAN PACIFIC RAILWAY COMPANY'S ROYAL MAIL STEAMSHIP LINE.

THE FAST ROUTE BETWEEN CHINA, JAPAN, AND EUROPE VIA CANADA AND THE UNITED STATES.

Route from Hongkong via Shanghai, Nagasaki (Inland Sea of Japan) Kobe, Yokohama, Victoria and Vancouver.

Twin Screw. Empress Steamship—6,000 Tons—Speed 19 knots.

PROPOSED SAILING FROM YOKOHAMA.

R. M. S. Empress of India.
R. M. S. Empress of Japan.
R. M. S. Empress of China.
R. M. S. Athenian.
R. M. S. Tartar.

Special reduction (first class only) granted to members of the Military, Naval, Diplomatic and Civil services and to Missionaries.

Passengers have choice of ten routes across the Continent of America and have privilege of travelling by any Atlantic Steamship Line.

Round the World passage tickets in connection with the P. and O. S. N., North German Lloyd and Messageries Co.'s **£125.**

All rates payable at current rate of exchange.

For further information, Tickets, Guide Books, etc., apply to

HOLME, RINGER & CO., AGENTS,
Chemulpo.

Grand Hotel

(Formerly the Station Hotel)

Near the Railway Terminus, West Gate Seoul.

The Best Hotel in Korea
Handsome new Building.
Fine Airy Rooms
Excellent Cuisine.
Terms Moderate.
Special terms to Missionaries and to permanent boarders.

Electric cars within 2 minutes' walk.

W. H. EMBERLEY.
Proprieto

EVERY FACILITY.

In connection with Life Assurance Business is afforded by

The Standard Life Assurance Co.,

One of the largest and wealthiest of the Provident Institutions of the United Kingdom Forms of Application and all information will be promptly afforded on application.

10 CENTS A DAY.

Not a very large expenditure is it? But it is sufficient to secure for a man of 30 a policy with the STANDARD LIFE OFFICE for

$1323.

For all particulars of rates, etc., apply to

Holme, Ringer & Co.,
Agents, Chemulpo.

THE NEW YORK LIFE INSURANCE COMPANY.

Have you ever been declined by any Company?

Are you engaged in a specially hazardous occupation?

Have you heard of the New York Life Insurance Company's New Classifications for this class of Risks?

If not, send your date of birth, occupation and particulars of rejection, if any to

E. MEYER & Co.,
Agents, Chemulpo.

MITSUI BUSSAN KAISHA.
(MITSUI & Co.)

MITSUI GINKO.
(MITSUI BANK.)

The Bank is owned by the members of the Mitsui Family, who, as partners, assume an unlimited responsibility for all liabilities of the Bank:—

Capital.........................Yen 5,000,000
Reserve Fund.................... " 5,600,000

HEAD OFFICE, TOKYO.
LONDON OFFICE, 34 LIME ST., E. C.

BRANCHES AND AGENCIES:—
New York, San Francisco, Hamburg, Bombay, Singapore, Manila, Hongkong, Amoy, Chefoo, Tientsin.
Kobe, Hakodate, Yokohama, Kure, Yokosuka, Moji, Shimonoseki, Miike, Wakamatsu, Nagasaki, Kuchinotsu, Karatsu, Sasebo Misume, Taipeh, &c.

Telegraphic Address for all the Offices:
"MITSUI."
A. B. C. AND A. I CODES USED.

Contractors of Coal
To the Imperial Japanese Navy. Arsenalr and Railway Bureau, Principal Railway Companies and Industrial Work, Home and Foreign Mail and Freight Steamers.

Sole Proprietors
Of the famous Miike, Tagawa and Yamano Coal Mines.

Sole Agents
For the sale of Fukumo, Hokoku, Ichimura Kanoda, Mannoura, Onoura, Ostuji, Sonoda Tsubaruro, Yoshinotani, Yoshio, Yurokibura and other coals.

YANGTSE INSURANCE ASSOCIATION, LTD.

The undersigned, having been appointed agents for the above company, are prepared to issue policies and pay losses on marine risks at regular rates.

E. MEYER & Co.,
Agents, Chemulpo.

AMERICAN KOREAN ELECTRIC CO.

Light and Power.

Main Office: Electric Building, Chong No.

RAILWAY DEPARTMENT.

OPERATING CARS BETWEEN EAST AND WEST GATE, EVERY TEN MINUTES:—

First Car leaves East Gate at 7:00 A. M. First Car leaves R. R. Station at 7:25 A. M
Last Car " East Gate at 8.40 P. M. Last " " R. R. Station at 9.05 P.M

OPERATING CARS BETWEEN EAST GATE AND IMPERIAL TOMB TERMINUS, EVERY TWENTY MINUTES:—
CONNECTING WITH EVERY ALTERNATE CAR ARRIVING AT EAST GATE FROM CHONG NO.

First Car leaves East Gate for Tomb at 7:10 A. M.
" " " Tomb for East Gate at 7:30 A. M.
Last " " East Gate for Tomb at 7:50 P. M.
" " " Tomb for East Gate at 8:10 P. M.

OPERATING CARS BETWEEN CHONG NO AND YUNG SAN RIVER EVERY TWELVE MINUTES:—

First Car leaves Chong No for South Gate at 7:12 A. M.
" " " Chong No for Yung San at 7:36 A. M.
" " " South Gate for Chong No at 7:20 A. M.
" " " Yung San for Chong No at 8:09 A. M.
Last " " South Gate for Chong No 9:00 P. M.
" " Yung San for Chong No at 8.45. p. M.

SPECIAL PRIVATE CARS FURNISHED TO SUIT CONVENIENCE OF PATRONS. PRICES ON APPLICATION AT HEAD OFFICE.

LIGHTING DEPARTMENT.

Where less than 250 candle power of light is used, the rate per month will be
Per 16 candle power incandescent lamp,—All night.—Yen 2.50.
32 candle power incandescent lamp:—All night:—Yen 4.00.
50 candle power incandescent lamp:—All night:—Yen. 6.00.
150 " " " " " " ,, 10.00.
1200 ,, ,, enclosed arc " " " ,, 20.00.

Where more than 250 candle power of light is used, a Meter will be installed, if requested:—Rent of Meter Yen 2.00 per month. Rate of charges by meter reading:—Two Sen per Ampere per hour. (Approximately this is equal to about One Sen per 16 C. P. lamp per hour) Minimum monthly charge where meter is installed, Yen 20.00 per month, which includes rental of meter.

Estimates for installing lights furnished on application

An assortment of chandeliers always on hand.

K. Murakami.

Photograph Studio
Chinkokai, Seoul.

Printing, Developing and Enlargement, of Photographs always Undertaken.

Korean Views and Pictures Illustrating Native Customs always on Sale,

THE OSAKA SHOSEN KAISHA.

Boats frequently on the berth for Chinnampo.

REGULAR SAILINGS BETWEEN JAPAN AND KOREAN PORTS.

FUSAN AND KOBE VIA SHIMONOSEKI.

OSAKA VIA MOKPO, FUSAN, SHIMONOSEKI AND KOBE.

MOJI DIRECT.

OSAKA VIA KUNSAN, MASANPO, FUSAN, SHIMONOSEKI AND KOBE.

CHEMULPO KUNSAN LINE,
Every three days.

CHEMULPO CHINNAMPO LINE.
Every three days.

For Freight and passage and further particulars apply to
THE OSAKA SHOSEN KAISHA,
Chemulpo.

RONDON, PLAISANT & CO.

General Storekeepers and Merchants, Ships Contractors Tobacconists, Commission and Forwarding Agents, Coal Merchants

IMPORTERS AND EXPORTERS

Seoul Chemulpo.

W. D. WENTWORTH.

LANDING
AND
SHIPPING AGENT.
AND
CUSTOMS BROKER.

12 OURA, NAGASAKI.

STEWARD & CO.

Chemulpo.

Shipchandlers and Storekeepers, Naval and Mercantile Contractors, Landing and Shipping Agents.

STEWARD'S HOTEL

Chemulpo.

Best accommodation in the port for travellers. Clean and well-aired rooms, good cuisine and prompt attendance, oderate tariff.

샹에 져권리챵쥬ᄒᆞᄂᆞᆫ수잇스니졍
권리샹쥬ᄒᆞ야쥬ᄒᆞᆫ소견계ᄒᆞ라
ᄂᆞᆫ등인을죠ᄒᆞ야죠회ᄒᆞ오니졍
권리면쥬ᄒᆞ라ᄒᆞ엿더라

○내부의고빙 궁내부에셔외부로죠회ᄒᆞ기를일본의고교유ᄌᆞ를인부니무셩의면회ᄒᆞᆯ랑ᄒᆞ야폐부에고빙ᄒᆞᄂᆞᆫ고로죠회ᄒᆞᄂᆞ셔를쳠부ᄒᆞ야숑교ᄒᆞ오니졍권리판셔자교ᄒᆞ라ᄒᆞ엿더라

○셩면권리 거쳔일하오쳥졈죵에외부에셔 판쳔회를셜ᄒᆞ고쳥국신구공ᄉᆞ와 및쳥쳔관원들과각부대관들을쳥ᄒᆞ고권리ᄒᆞ엿더라

○군물팔기 유쳔군슈권셕구씨가닉부로보고ᄒᆞ엿ᄂᆞᆫ데가령면쳔진의군긔고가기헐벗에잇ᄂᆞᆫ터음력셧달에이셧샹을ᄂᆡ셔반히일인밀샹에병이들엇ᄒᆞ야하고부면관벼슬팔아ᄒᆞ고잇ᄂᆞᆫ바군물을몰슈히팔거ᄒᆞ엿고동일에이샹판일아츔에화론셜판셔를이젼셩면군긔고의ᄒᆡᆼ도밧ᄒᆞ고군긔고의벽을헐파ᄒᆞ고쇼유군물을일의터로가져가ᄂᆞᆫ고로츈민들이월거ᄒᆞ주이일인밀샹벼명이칼을들에며죵을ᄂᆞ라고엄위ᄂᆞᆫ히랑거져못ᄒᆞ고필경팔거ᄒᆞ엿더라

○됴원로자인 의졍서리됴병식씨가자인ᄒᆞ야샹소ᄒᆞ엿더니비지ᄂᆞᆫ에빈드시거인ᄒᆞᆯ것이업스니못니ᄒᆞ지말나ᄒᆞ셧더라

○냥군슈됴졍 일본공ᄉᆞ가닉부로공함ᄒᆞ엿스되안악군슈김용악과젼쥬군슈김윤ᄐᆞᆨ진을죵쳔ᄒᆞ야민간에폐를끼치ᄂᆞᆫ지라닉부에셔엄쳐ᄒᆞ기를바라ᄂᆞᆫ다사실ᄒᆞ야파면ᄒᆞᆯ젼이잇스면민관에죵쥬ᄒᆞ겟다고ᄒᆞ엿더라

○졍티일졀 찬졍최익현씨가별리변샹소ᄒᆞ야시졍기책의실시ᄒᆞ기를죵간ᄒᆞ엿스나조필도호령이무효지라구애에쳥티ᄒᆞ로못에권ᄒᆞ엿더라

○각부훈됴 탁지부에셔각부부원쳥에훈됴ᄒᆞ기를각셔명용하ᄒᆞᆫ경셩셔들졍셩ᄒᆞ야부원이쳥ᄒᆞ오일안으로송교ᄒᆞ라ᄒᆞ엿더라

○일ᄉᆞ공함 일본공ᄉᆞ가닉부로공함ᄒᆞ기를무관젼군슈와고원군슈을곳쳐졍ᄒᆞ야하송ᄒᆞ되고원군슈ᄂᆞᆫ무병들의터를ᄎᆞ송ᄒᆞ야부진군군ᄉᆞ샹에방휘가무ᄒᆞ도록ᄒᆞ라ᄒᆞ엿더라

○쳥슈무관 작일에일진회원들이경위원ᄎᆞ관리근틔에셔테에왕ᄒᆞ야말ᄒᆞ기를진졍이원ᄎᆞ관젼공셕에가일진회ᄉᆞ무소들들이엄쳔귀ᄒᆞ게시에랑긴졀뎐과지폐쳘뒤원을젼셜ᄒᆞ엿스니곳권세를착슈ᄒᆞ고차자믿니ᄒᆞ죵리근틔셔의터말이경위원에셔ᄂᆞᆫᄌᆞ금브터젼슈ᄒᆞᄂᆞᆫ권원이업ᄉᆞ니항수업노라ᄒᆞᆫ즉회원들이쳥원ᄉᆞᆯ이로경원ᄒᆞ니고ᄒᆞ고갓다더라

○쥬민의문셔 향쟈원쥬부을문시ᄒᆞᄂᆞᆫ데말은각젼문이의계자혼바아니와더시갑으로혼쥬고죵에남보자만물셔원ᄒᆞ엿다더라

○귀지사경 작일대대부가셔문밧등디에셔면관독슈리ᄒᆞ다가가세관계사경에니르럿다더라

○강계구람 대국신문샤쟝리죵일씨가각국인이기탐ᄒᆞ기를위ᄒᆞ야각국쟝에경계신문샤를셜립ᄒᆞ고졍향간에일계히구람계ᄒᆞ기로ᄒᆞ엿다더라

○원로남셜 관계리쟝소에셔샹공부를페지ᄒᆞ라ᄂᆞᆫ말은낭셜이라더라

○다슈인쳥 작일에소문으로시로ᄂᆞᆫ진남은인병이다슈인되엿다더라

○동셩원두럄 관계리쟝소에셔동셩원은두럄의문이으로뎡ᄒᆞ야각국에신며신관리등조회ᄒᆞᆫ다더라

○젼쟁의영향 금번일로젼쟁에일승이각의영향이미쳐이공부ᄒᆞᄂᆞᆫ즈ㅣ젹다니잇다더라

뎐보

뮈령발 일월이십구일

○덕오샹약 덕국파오디리국수이에도일혼신샹약을약의멧지ᄂᆞᆫ동조ᄒᆞ엿다더라

동뎌발 동일

○광산발기광 덕국황뎨계셔광산ᄒᆞᄂᆞᆫ공쟝에티ᄒᆞ야지탐ᄒᆞᆫ한웅지가ᄒᆞ셧다더라

동뎌발 동일

○덕국의셔신수업 덕국금번에샹애쳥도에셔로이부로ᄒᆞᆫ곳을대싸기를준비ᄒᆞ고쳥도예관대위정원은형쟝이로숭으ᄒᆞ엿다더라

동뎌발 동월이십팔일

○홍아리의총리쳔거 홍아리국예셔국회의원이총리천거를대신ᄒᆞ엿ᄂᆞᆫ데그결과ᄂᆞᆫ정부편이마ᄒᆞᆷ다ᄒᆞ엿다더라

론돈발 이월일일

○로국니관의슈보 작일에셔피득보에서령관관리가혁명당의회를규쥰ᄒᆞ고방ᄒᆞ야비사들은샹ᄒᆞ고리어ᄒᆞ나ᄂᆞᆫ죽엿스며오남에셔ᄒᆞ고의셔는노에셔로동자의종리들보샹ᄒᆞ엿스며위소에셔ᄂᆞᆫ아쥬봉요가가라안지아니ᄒᆞ엿스니다른디방에셔ᄂᆞᆫ초초진졍되야가ᄂᆞᆫ모양이라더라

동뎌발 동일

○로관슈직 로국니부대신스바토록ᄂᆞᆫ사기로원관뎡경셩에서수직ᄒᆞ엿다더라

동뎌발 동일

○일군피쟝슈 샤하로부터쟝위요량ᄒᆞᆫ바를기ᄒᆞ주요견쌔ᄒᆞ샹에뎡병의수로쟝을일본부로가연이될병이샹이라ᄒᆞ엿더라

론셜

자야면보

○일본졍부에셔각귀의조아ᄒᆞᄂᆞᆫ신문샤에계구주에셔오ᄂᆞᆫ면보들을긔공급ᄒᆞᄂᆞᆫ뎡위를일본졍부와조아ᄒᆞ니ᄒᆞᄂᆞᆫ신문샤등에시비ᄒᆞᄂᆞᆫ것이뢰이치아니ᄒᆞ도다

만일그면보들이다츙실ᄒᆞᆫ것으면그쳥위가불관ᄒᆞᆯ것이업거니와구주등각신문에발ᄒᆞᆫ면보들은그뎟지셩에셔졍수ᄒᆞᆫ면보들은그뎟지못ᄒᆞ야항샹미편지안이오ᄒᆞ시ᄂᆞ거지잇말이잇ᄂᆞᆫ지라

우리가구리면보를사보ᄂᆞᆫ사름이아니라구리면보의ᄉᆞ무를시비ᄒᆞᆯ수업거니와로국에셔면령을동이지금은츙츙ᄒᆞᆫ야가ᄂᆞᆫ모양인데그사건을일셰ᄒᆞ보다부터셰보ᄒᆞ엿ᄂᆞᆫ지라

그러ᄒᆞ나일본졍부에셔ᄂᆞᆫ번만드리냇면보ᄂᆞᆫ웅셔혹술업ᄂᆞᆫ것이그사건에티ᄒᆞ야졍국에잇ᄂᆞᆫ놈드러가나면바ᄂᆞ게스다ᄂᆞᆫ신문의어렬구일지면에게지ᄒᆞᆫ말을보증이아것ᄒᆞ니그말에ᄒᆞ엿스되우리가이곳에잇ᄂᆞᆫ일본총령샤의됨합사ᄒᆞ니나노니일본총령사가우리의게면보ᄒᆞ나를보인논듸그면보에ᄒᆞ엿스되

로국면을거ᄒᆞᆫ죽로국모스코니방희의소회쟝드루벳스코의친왕이금병오일에티부대신의게공함을보니야자긔의회의소젼리ᄒᆞ야각국ᄉᆞ름이ᄂᆞᆫ도시교셜을ᄒᆞ엿ᄂᆞᆫ데그편지에ᄒᆞ엿스되로국이지금병란을ᄯᅳᆯ과무쟝부흥쟝이잇스니이것은국니소변들을쇠와가아니라사회쟝과핀레의계유권리를닐이잇슬조졍이니허랑스리오에민의직권은을비아셔계ᄒᆞᄂᆞᆫ것이오확쳐계셔ᄒᆡᆼ졍을동본진ᄒᆞᆫ시리면국민의계신ᄒᆞ엿ᄂᆞᆫ데잇스며부모지국이위에돈티향구를절ᄒᆞ엿네가이니라ᄒᆞ엿다ᄒᆞ엿더라ᄒᆞ엿스니

이것은혼경거진쳥일젼이라드루벳스코의친왕이니부대신의계그편지를보닐이업ᄂᆞᆫ것을공포ᄒᆞ엿고그편혼ᄂᆞ니라지가잇ᄂᆞᆫ사름들은아모리도이업다ᄒᆞ리리니빈말를밋지아니ᄒᆞᆯ듯ᄒᆞ도다

삭이나게맛ᄂᆞᆫ다ᄂᆞᆫ신문에닐혼편지되말일법국이영국니평계되ᄒᆞ야그리케서겨졋ᄒᆞᆫ말을곤공거ᄒᆞ면영국이엇지결졍ᄒᆞ엿스니그비교ᄂᆞᆫ카녕자아니ᄒᆞᆫ것이영방으로의금젼칭을ᄒᆞ지아니ᄒᆞᆫ셔운로로다

범률우리ᄂᆞᆫ소견이다르니우리의동무신문은일본졍부에셔로이신문국찻ᄒᆞᆫ것을챵셜ᄒᆞᆫ것을슬퍼아ᄂᆞᆫ모옹에항샹ᄒᆞ노라일본이젼ᄒᆞᄂᆞᆫᄉᆞ분이졍미ᄒᆞ너우리가츙말이하니라고시비ᄒᆞᄂᆞᆫ것이아니라그중에혹셜딕지못ᄒᆞᆫᄉᆞ분이잇스며일본에계조호ᄒᆞᆫᄉᆞ문은동경으로브터한국에숑히나오고그외반티ᄒᆞᆫᄉᆞ문은낭니둣ᄂᆞᆫ외에드들수업ᄂᆞᆫ지라

그러ᄒᆞ기에일본사름은돈을써가며셔졍졍쟈의뒤삯을찬못되게만드ᄂᆞᆫ것이근릭에ᄂᆞᆫ무슘ᄉᆞ건이던지ᄀᆡ본권으로은ᄉᆞ문을들펴이락괘ᄒᆞᆫ지아니ᄒᆞ고다욜본편으로뵈ᄂᆞᆫ소문둣기셔셔죠ᄒᆞ되노국에셔ᄂᆞᆫ엇더ᄒᆞᆫ지알수엄나쳥국에셔일본인이각의를승인ᄒᆞᆫᄉᆞ문이광포ᄒᆞ고그비밀의소식은페지ᄒᆞᄂᆞᆫ것을엇ᄂᆞᆫ것은한인을위하셔이젼쟁에일본의마음되로뒤엿나셔한국에셔일본인이망ᄒᆞᆫ권력이졈졈더ᄒᆞ엿게될줄ᄇᆡ이고피ᄒᆞ이라ᄒᆞ노라

광고

AN IMPROVED COMPASS.

M. Heit, a French inventor, has recently patented a c mpass which automatically registers minute by minute. The compass card is fixed on a steel pivot, which rests on a fixed agate, instead of having at its center an agate resting on a fixed steel point. The fixed agate is immersed in a drop of mercury, which serves as a conductor for the electric current that causes the move ments of registering.

JAPANESE MUST GO.

Residents of the Tonopah and Goldfields mining districts, in Nevada, have given out that the Japanese must go and the subjects of the doughty Mikado have already started to give heed to the unction. For several months the ps have been been flocking to the camps until finally they became so erous that the miners and business thought it best to protect their own interests by ordering them away from the two camps. I thus far the orders have been obeyed and no trouble is anticipated.—"Butte Miner."

THE PROGRESS OF THE BALTIC FLEET.

The "Times" publishes a statement of the movements of the Baltic Fleet from the 26th of November to 30th of December—On the 26th of November 5 battleships, 3 cruisers, 2 steamers flying mercantile flags, 2 flying the naval flag, a water vessel, a hospital ship, a scouting-ship (flying a mercantile flag) and a French provision ship (l'Esperance) arrived ouside the harbour of Gaboon in French Western Africa. Of the above the Roland (scouting vessel) entered the harbour and conveyed instructions to two coaling steamers—one British and one German—which had been waiting there that they should move out to the squadron, which, with several other German coaling steamers, was anchored 4 miles outside. Thereafter the work of coaling continued until 30th, when the colliers, with the exception of those which had discharged their cargo, were ordered to move on to Great Fish Bay (Portuguese West Africa) where they arrived on December 5th. The Squadron followed, reaching Great Fish Bay on the 5th and coaling there until the 7th. Then the colliers were directed to steam for Angra Pequina (German Southwest Africa). There on the 10th of December 3 of the coaling steamers (2 English and 1 German) arrived; while two others, the Kaschira and the Orel, proceeded to Capetown, the Orel being ordered to take off any coal remaining in the Kaschira. On the 12th of December the squadron reached Sheer Water Bay and ordered the colliers to approach, but this was prevented by the state of the sea. Five German colliers from Dakar had already been for a week in Angra Pequina. The work of coaling commenced on Dec. 14th at night and continued till the 15th, when the colliers were ordered to proceed to St. Mary's Island in Madagascar, where 2 English ships and 2 German arrived on the 29th of December. The squadron left Sheer Water on the 17th of December and (including the Orel which had joined it) arrived at St. Mary's Island on the 30th of that month. The place for the squadron to assemble for coaling purposes is Diego Suarez, whither the remaining colliers and detroyers are to come, it is said. The work of coaling has resulted in injuring several of the colliers.

A PERSONAL NARRATIVE OF MISCHENKO'S RAID.

FROM THE CHINA REVIEW.

General Mischenko crossed the Hun River on January the 8th, at the head of a strong Cavalry force, which swept south-ward over the Liao plain, in three columns; extending over a front of five miles.

It was the most magnificent sight of this war; the men and horses being in splendid spirits and condition; with fine warm weather.

The country was searched so thoroughly that hares and foxes fled before our advance. We rested the first night at Sifoutai; and on the second night we reached a village near the confluence of the Hun and Liao Rivers. This evening our scouts first came upon some Japanese and a transport-train; which they captured, the Japanese guards running away.

When our main body came up we found a house in the village burning, and sending up enormous columns of black smoke, An examination of this house showed that it had been previously stored with combustibles.

When the darkness came we saw signal after signal fire lighted up.

On January 10th 8 a. m. we came into contact with a large body of Hunghuzes. The Daghistan Regiment charged them with extraordinary swiftness and fierceness, cuting them all to pieces. The Hunghuzes resisted and fought bravly leaving over 100 dead on the ground. A Japanese flag was captured from them; and there were some Japanese themselves among the Hunghuzes.

Furthur south our right and central columns attacked the walled village of Shoutoze near the confluence of the Taitze River with the Liao. This strong position was held by some 300 Japanese infantry, who resisted stubbornly for a time but were forced to give way.

Another Cossack force had gone out to cut the Railway line north of Haicheng, in order to prevent the dispatch of Japaneses troops as reinforcements.

To the southward was the Caucasian Brigade, a picturesque Mahomedan force specially led by Guards officers.

The village of Shoutoze was taken at night fall by the Verkhnyudinsky Cossacks.

On January 11th we advanced further south unopposed, crossing the Taitze River; just past which 50 Japanese resisted, in a house on the outskirts of old Newchwang; but after killing and capturing some prisoners, we left the rest alone and galloped away. Further on we siezed several valuable transport trains, including provisions, clothing, end hundreds of cattle.

The light of these burning stores illuminated the whole surrounding landscape, when we reached at nightfull the village of Hindyatun, 20 miles from Yingkou.

To-day a Caucasian detachment destroyed 500 metres of the railway; and the dragoons blew up a bridge near Tashicho; and also committed a wholesale destruction of the telegraph and telephone lines.

The Japanese fired the villges all along our route as signals, so that the route was marked even in the daytime by pillars of ascending smoke, and at night time by flaming hamlets on the horizon.

On January 12 we marched to a village near Yingkow; where there were a few hundred Japanese and about nine million roubles' worth of Japanese stores. The attack on the railway station began at 4 P. M. About 500 Japanese were strongly entrenched near the station when we came up; and, before our real attack began, a train, with about another 500 Infantry came in by train via Tashichi, probably from the south; and we therefore found that the Tashicho-Yingkow junction line could not have been properly broken.

Our attacking force consisted of only 1000 dismounted Cossacks, an insufficient number against 1,000 entrenched infantry. All the rest of our force was in reserve, guarding our flanks, or otherwise occupied; and General Mischenko had previously determined to burn only the stores at the station, advance no further and fall back at sunset.

When therefore he found by nightfall that his purpose had not been completely attained, he withdrew his force, in perfect order to a village 17 versts north of Yingkow; and proceeded slowly northwards next day. Breaking camp again on his way at noon.

This raid was, on the whole, a most successful one, owing to the number of transport trains etc., which were destroyed; and the great number of sheep and cattle which were captured and taken back to Moukden. Amongst the prisoners there were three Japanese officers.

THE RUSSIAN NAVY CRITICISED.

In an outspoken article in reply to a recent letter of Admiral Birileff, which appealed to Russians not to openly criticise*the condition of the navy, the "Russ" to day declares the time is passed for silence in view of the fact that the "old system of concealing facts is responsible for the loss of 150,000,000 roubles' worth of war-ships and has covered us with shame and grief. It would be absurd to hide the defects that can still be repaired in the ships which remain at Cronstadt and Libau. We have already criminally wasted enough time."

The "Russ" numerates the defects in the ships still in Russian waters, averring that the "peculiarities of structure of several of the vessels destined for the Far East make the voyage dangerous, and the torpedo-boats are in such a shocking condition that it is a matter of surprise that the authorities accepted their delivery. Torpedo-boats intended to reinforce Vice-Admiral Rohjestvensky must clearly not be dispatched with the numerous defects which have been proved to exist in them."

In conclusion the "Russ" says: "Even if Admiral Rohjestvensky is a clever leader and his 12,000 comrades are heroic sailors, every one knows that we have impossed upon them an almost super-human task in consequence of our not being furnished with a true account of the gravity of the events which have occurred since the fatal night of February 8th."

THE SUNKEN WARSHIPS.

(FROM MANILA CABLENEWS.)

The Japanese are working industriously to salve the Russian warships recently sunk in the inner harbour at Port Arthur. The Japanese divers have reported that the battleships Peresveit, Poltava, and the cruisers Bayan and Pallada are but slightly injured and within three months can be raised and prepared for service.

The divers have reported the injury to the Pobieda, Retvisan. Sevastopol and the other warships, sunk by the Japanese siege guns and topedo-boats, is of a more serious nature and, that the ships are not considered salvabie.

The Peresviet and Poltava will be placed in the drydock at once and when completed will be sent to join the Japanese buttleship squadron.

It is not believed that the Baltic squadron will attempt to reach far Eastern waters during the season in which Vladvistostok is icebound and before the ice breaks up in the Spring. The addition of the salved battleship will give Japan a battleship tonnage greater than that of Russia.

NEW RUSSIAN NAVY.

Paris, January 7th.—Vice-Admiral Doubassoff, who succeded Admiral Kaznakoff as Russian representative on the International North Sea Commissoin, arrived here to-day and was received by Foreign Minister Delcasse. It is known that his service on the North Sea Commission is a mere incident, his chief mission being to preside at the meeting of the Naval Technical Commission which is considering the complete rehabilitation of the Russian navy.

This is not connected with the fall of Port Arthur or with the present war, as the Russians recognize the necessity for recruiting their navy without reference to the contest with Japan. Therefore Dolgeroukoff, Porectkine, Brink and other naval experts have arrived here after visiting the shipyards of Europe for the purpose of learning their capacity for the execution of an extensive programme for naval construction. Admiral Doubassoff will preside at the meeting of experts and go over the reports.

It is understood that the Russian programme contemplates the expenditure of $20,000,000 during the next three years of naval rehabilitation. The meeting of the experts leads to a coincidental gathering of the representatives of the leading shipyards, including the American yards.

According to a telegram to the "Pioneer" it is unofficially reported that England will retain Wei-hai-wei, holding that the fact of the Russians maintaining a claim to Port Arthur constitutes a theoretical occupation sufficient to satisfy the terms of our lease.

The Korea Daily News.

Issued at 5 P. M. daily except Sundays.

Rate of Subscription :—
Per Year,............Yen 25.
Per Quarter,..........Yen 7.
Per Month,..........Yen 2.50.

Postage in Korea not charged extra.
Postage abroad charged extra.

Advertisements, 50 sen per day for 1 inch or less.
5 yen per month per inch.
50 yen per year per inch.

All communications to

E. T. BETHELL,
Editor and Publisher,
Pak-tong, Seoul.

THE WAR.

From the accounts so far to hand of the operations on the Shaho it appears that the results up to Feb. 2nd were practically nil. A large number of lives were lost on both sides, the Japanese estimating the Russian casualties at 10,000 and their own at 7,000. On Feb. 2nd the position of the two armies was apparently the same as before the battle although the Russians seem to have gained some ground in the centre of the Japanese left wing. The position of both centres remains absolutely unchanged, the armies facing each other on the high ground east of the railway and north of the Yentai mines

When a decisive action is fought, it will be a terrible affair, as, according to reports from Mukden, nearly the whole of the ground between the two armies is honeycombed with mines and pitfalls. These pitfalls or wolf-traps are holes about six feet wide and six feet deep lightly covered with brushwood and soil with a stake in the centre upon which the fallen soldier is impaled. The snow has of course rendered the locality of these traps undiscernable.

It is reported that General Grippenberg and 3,500 other wounded officers and men have arrived at Mukden.

The following is the official report issued by the Japanese relative to the action on Feb. 2nd :—

On the 1st, several small Russian detachments made attacks on our right wing, but were repulsed by our outposts. This morning, (the 2nd) at about six o'clock, the Russians at the foot of Tohshan and at a place to the west of Liusiangton began to fire upon Fangshen and a locality two kilometres south of Liusiangton. A little afterwards, about three Russian companies attempted to surround Tangshen, but were all repulsed. Their losses are not yet known, but our troops captured two prisoners, while the enemy left one dead body on the field. In the direction of the centre of the Japanese Army, the Russian Artillery located two kilometres northeast of Shahopao fired to-day (the 2nd) upon the heights south of Shahopao, and the Artillery on the heights west of Baupaoshan bombarded north Changlintze and Yaoton. Occasional encounters between scouts have also taken place. In the direction of the Japanese left wing, the Russian Artillery commenced a severe bombardment of Chinchiepao this morning, and our guns at once responded. According to reliable natives, the Russians have constructed a railway between Suchaton (about two ri north of Lamuton) and Suhopao (about two ri north of Menta, pao) and trains pass over it several times a day. This morning, at about eight o'clock, some Russian heavy and field-guns concentrated their fire on the vicinity of Yatzepao. A little later about one division of the enemy attacked Wanchawopeng, southeast of Chantau, and about one brigade assaulted our position, but was repulsed. The Russians who attacked Luitaokao on the 1st left about one hundred and seventy dead bodies behind when they retreated. Our troops captured many rifles and other articles. The prisoners state that the commanders of the 2nd and 4th Regiments of Sharpshooters were wounded on this occasion. According to trustworthy natives, a Japanese officer and twenty-eight others were surrounded by the Russians at Hwanloatatze, on Jan. 26. They made a brave defence but were eventually taken prisoners, after many had been wounded. All the injured men were killed by the Russians.

A PERSONAL NARRATIVE OF THE SIEGE OF PORT ARTHUR.

(Specially written for The "China Review" by a Russian Naval Officer.)

(Concluded from last issue).

On December 4th the fact that we could not hold the hill dawned on Stoessel, but already we had paid the penalty of bad judgment. For our losses in defence of the position had amounted to four thousand five hundred men, and one hundred and five officers killed and wounded. Had the defence been continued longer, the garrison would surely have been exterminated.

At two o'clock in the morning the order left head quarters for the retirement, and only twenty half dead men came back to us. At six o'clock that morning our telescope revealed the enemy in possession of the mountain. That was a sad day for Port Arthur.

Thus was the most important step in their siege of the city accomplished by the Japanese, as 203 Metre Hill overlooks the harbour and the city. Eleven inch guns placed on its summit would have forced our surrender in a day, but fortunately its declivities were so steep and rugged that the enemy only succeeded in dragging six of their largest mountain guns to the top, and the fire of these, although galling, was not particularly consequential. Nevertheless we welcomed the rare occasions when permission was granted us for the bombardment of the hill. But if the Japanese were unsuccessful in placing heavy artillery on its summit, they soon learned its value as a lookout station, and thus was the fate of the harbour sealed. For the eleven-inch guns on lower positions were fired according to the signals of the lookouts on the mountain, who had a perfect bird's-eye view of the harbor, and were wonderfully proficient in wig-wagging directions for the guns. In three days the greater portion of the fleet had been rendered unfit for service by this devastating fire. It usually began at nine in the morning, continuing, with a short intermission at noon, until five o'clock in the evening. I have known the shells to fall among the the shipping not more than fifty seconds apart, and the enemy frequently sent as many as five hundred in one day against us. Sometime they fired in salvos of three guns each.

Why did not the fleet when thus threatened with extermination, [illegible] for the open sea and engage the Japanese ships? one naturally asks. The question, however, is easily answered. The ships were without guns or men to man them; they were also badly out of repair, and it would have been madness for them to have atempted the blockade; their guns were on the forts, the majority of their crews were dead, their magazines were empty. An exception, the "Sevastopol," having two hundred of an original crew of six hundred men, and without quick-firers, sought refuge in White Wolf Bay between Tiger, Tail and Laotishan. But here she was forced to maintain a constant fight against the constant attacks of the enemy's torpedo boat flotillas.
times she drove them away, and [illegible]
one snowy night of intense darkness [illegible]
of the enemy's picket boats succeeded in gaining a position about one hun[illegible] yards astern of her, and discharging a torpedo into her hull. Thus were the days of the "Sevastopol" numbered. There was no excitement, no panic; somebody said "we are torpedoed," and somebody else fired a rifle at the picket boat skimming away in the darkness, and then the word was given and we took to the boats.

If you had come to Port Arthur after the capture of High Hill and the destruction of our ships, you would have been astonished at the insensibility of officers and men. We were mentally prepared for anything the Japanese might do. The conflagration of the oil store houses, although a most awe inspiring spectacle, we regarded with little interest. The tremendous explosions caused by Japanese shells striking our powder magazines were, to our minds, trifling occurrences, so was the blowing to pieces of a comrade.

To my mind the break of the Gregorian new year of 1906 was marked by the beginning of the end of the siege. On that day the Japanese blew up Sunsushan fort, and bombarded us with great intensity. Now began talk of surrender. It was said General Stoessel had sent an envoy to Nogi bearing a proposal to capitulate. Sadness reigned in the garrison. Several officers committed suicide. The idea of surrender was not welcome, even to the wounded in the hospital, and most of us began to have dismal thoughts concerning many months of incarceration in Japanese prisons. But of the end of Port Arthur I know little, for on the night of January 1st, I stood on the bridge of my ship, the torpedoer "Vlastni" as she crept out between the lines of the blockaders, on her dangerous voyage to Chefoo with dispatches for His Majesty, the Czar.

CHAMPION WEIGHT CARRIERS.

The world[illegible] champion heavyweight carriers said to be the miners of Chile. Probably the greatest weights carried on the backs of men are borne by these South Americans. In a copper mine in a ravine leading from the main range of the Cordilleras all the ore is carried a vertical distance of 450 feet, and the average weight per man is 250 pounds. This load is carried up ladders made of notched trunks of trees, set up almost upright one touching the other.

The Korea Daily News.

VOL. II, SATURDAY, FEBRUARY 11, 1905. No. 32

大韓每日申報

대한매일신보

(뎨이권 삼십삼호) (화요일) 일쳔구뵉오년 이월 십ᄉᆞ일

본샤고빅

이신보는영어와한어로셔계미
일츌판ᄒᆞ옵

신문가

한쟝 엽두돈오푼
일샥토 엽두량닷돈
우표가미샥닷돈
다밋돈으로밧숨

광고료는

귀쳔의쟝단과ᄌᆞ항의다쇼로즁
감ᄒᆞ되렴가로밧을터이오며오
린지아니ᄒᆞ야대한사람마다다이신
문을보실터이니광고내시기를
원ᄒᆞ시는이들은우리신문사에
와셔면약ᄒᆞ심을희망ᄒᆞ옵

○발힝소 박동대한매일신보
사법어학교압헤젼영국인셜필
림졍자리오

사쟝 영국인 (븨셜)

평양 디리졈

○평양흥동사는권미보씨로우
리신문관의디리인을뎡ᄒᆞ엿
시ᄉᆞ오니평양에계신구람코져ᄒᆞ
는 쳠군ᄌᆞ는이디리졈에왕
림ᄒᆞ와면의ᄒᆞ시옵

사고

○우리대한매일신보의목뎍은
대한의안녕질셔에관한모든대
목에디ᄒᆞ야는공평한변론을쥬
쟝ᄒᆞᆷ이라우리동신원의탐보는
신문보시는 쳠군ᄌᆞ의계ᄒᆞ상보
도ᄒᆞ리며편지들긔셔ᄒᆞ며주시
는이는셩명과번디들젹어붓치
시기를희망ᄒᆞ오나이거슨신문
상에긔재ᄒᆞ란는거시아니오다
만구히신용ᄒᆞ는증거를삼고자
ᄒᆞᆷ이라긔재는아모긔셔던지긔
재ᄒᆞᆯ터이나아모쪼록말ᄒᆞ기를깃소
나되각ᄒᆞ는리유를말ᄒᆞᆯ터이오
며공정평화를관리케ᄒᆞ는듯ᄒᆞᆫ
거셔는의례히밧지안켓숨나이
다

●본사셔셔이리로신문을미양
우례로분젼ᄒᆞ와리젼부의일위
로젼ᄒᆞᆫ듯ᄒᆞ오면곳에는홀늣게
젼ᄒᆞ기도ᄒᆞ며혹먹칠거슬ᄒᆞᆫ던
에젼ᄒᆞ기도ᄒᆞ며혹아니젼ᄒᆞ는
곳도잇다ᄒᆞ와우리신문을ᄉᆞ랑
ᄒᆞ야구람ᄒᆞ시는 쳠군ᄌᆞ의계
디ᄒᆞ야미우미안ᄒᆞ오니지금
은분젼ᄒᆞᆫ을두고디원ᄒᆞ는이젼
ᄒᆞ며야니젼ᄒᆞ거나늣게거나ᄒᆞᆫ
폐가잇도록ᄒᆞ란ᄒᆞ오니ᄒᆞ야니
젼ᄒᆞ거나늣게젼ᄒᆞ거나ᄒᆞᆫ일
의잇ᄉᆞ면본사로통긔ᄒᆞ여주심
을희망ᄒᆞ옵

관보

뎨삼쳔오십구호 광무구
년이월십일일

셔임급ᄉᆞ령

○승셔쥬임관ᄉᆞ등 파쳔군수 셔인순
○승셔쥬임관이등 남양군수 쟝호진
○승셔쥬임관일등 련산군수 박항린
○승셔쥬임관ᄉᆞ등 뎨쳔군수 김병황
○승셔쥬임관오등 슌흥군수 박민영
○승셔쥬임관삼등 고셩군수 리명희
○승셔쥬임관오등 자셩군수 구쟝회
○승셔쥬임관오등 죵셩군수 쥬철준
○승셔쥬임관삼등 대졍군수 남만리

우는각히도관찰ᄉᆞ의보고셔
를거ᄒᆞᆫ온즉히원등의치젹이
거최이옵기가ᄉᆞ일등

○승셔관임관오등 한셩면보
지ᄉᆞ쥬ᄉᆞ 황쳥연

이상광무팔년십이월이십구
일

○승셔관임관ᄉᆞ등 부산면보ᄉᆞ과
쥬ᄉᆞ 김상준 안쥬면보ᄉᆞ과
쥬ᄉᆞ 김병건

이상일월이십칠일

○승셔관임관삼등 한셩면보
지ᄉᆞ쥬ᄉᆞ 리죵홍

이상이월이일

○의원면본관 덕원감리셔쥬
ᄉᆞ 리건틔

○임덕원감리셔쥬ᄉᆞ셔관임관
ᄉᆞ등 인쳔감리셔쥬ᄉᆞ 됴남
직

○임인쳔감리셔쥬ᄉᆞ셔관임관
삼등 젼쥬ᄉᆞ 리진틔

○임즁추원의관셔칙임관ᄉᆞ등
종이품 됴병틱

○ᄒᆡᆼ법부법률긔초위원 법부
참셔관 윤셩보

이상이월팔일

궁뎡록ᄉᆞ

즁효해젼뎐뎨읍락쟝월삼오일
의졍부의졍리ᄉᆞ셔리니부대신
조병식자헌소
비지셩소구셜평간기블펠며시
위언이니우블가기블갱계ᄒᆞ고
즁괴시무사라젼부당젼유

이월팔일

구년도예산표 속

뎨삼항 졍ᄉᆞ슈리비 오십
만원
뎨ᄉᆞ항 ᄉᆞ츌금료 일만륙
쳔팔빅십륙원
뎨오항 량식비 구쳔륙빅
십삼원
뎨륙항 피복비 ᄉᆞ쳔륙빅
삼십ᄉᆞ원
뎨칠항 보슈비 삼빅원
뎨팔항 연습비 삼십륙원
뎨구항 목욕비 삼십륙원
뎨십항 치비료 삼십륙원
뎨십일항 미쟝비 이쳔원
뎨십이항 악긔슈리비 삼빅원
뎨십삼항 상여금 칠빅이
십원
뎨십삼관 진위디 일빅륙십
팔만ᄉᆞ빅ᄉᆞ십오원
뎨일항 봉급 십ᄉᆞ만삼쳔
구빅ᄉᆞ원
뎨이항 쳥비 이만이쳔ᄉᆞ
빅ᄉᆞ십원
뎨삼항 졍ᄉᆞ슈리비 미쳔
오빅원
뎨ᄉᆞ항 ᄉᆞ츌금료 ᄉᆞ쳔륙
빅팔십륙원
뎨오항 량식비 칠쳔ᄉᆞ빅
팔십오원
뎨륙항 피복비 이만이쳔
오빅팔십팔원
뎨칠항 마쟝비 ᄉᆞ빅이십
원
뎨팔항 마료비 팔빅구십원
뎨구항 피복비 이십오만
ᄉᆞ쳔이빅원
뎨십항 보슈비 일만삼쳔
륙빅원
뎨십일항 운반비 오쳔이
빅이십오원
뎨십이항 연습비 이쳔여
빅륙십원
뎨십삼항 츌쟝비 이만일
쳔일빅원
뎨십ᄉᆞ항 목욕비 칠빅이
십원
뎨십오항 치료비 이쳔이
빅칠십원
뎨십륙항 미쟝비 일쳔이
빅원

잡보

○과란쳥방 경무쳥의셔외부
로조회ᄒᆞ기를함경북도변계순
검등의등소니에본서경비를탁
지의셔영ᄒᆞ고원월분졍급쳥구
미회됴를츄봉ᄎᆞ로히등군에왕
ᄒᆞ엿더니원샹에ᄌᆞ지ᄒᆞᆫ일본군
디의셔의등을챵거ᄒᆞ야경셩일
등디에압괴ᄒᆞ고밧은바공젼졀
목빅여량은원산일디에빅졍롤ᄒᆞ
엿고경셩이니외셔본쳥으로편
수ᄒᆞ엿ᄉᆞ나수실이어울ᄒᆞ린디
공간에관ᄒᆞᆫ지라본쳥으로니미
로맛당히방환ᄒᆞᆯ터이니일본군
디의셔압괴ᄒᆞᆫ지라괴의샹에자
의방송키난ᄒᆞ니지란쳥컨디일공
관으로면조ᄒᆞ야ᄒᆞ퇴사쳥뷘에
괴셥ᄒᆞ야곳방환케ᄒᆞ고원산일
디에졍류ᄒᆞᆫ공젼도ᄯᅩᄒᆞᆫ곳츌급
ᄒᆞ야금공용케ᄒᆞ라ᄒᆞ엿더라

○녀의계약 궁니부에셔교빙
ᄒᆞᆫ녀의함동이며좌ᄒᆞ뫼켤은
궁니부참셔관김용제와교유
ᄌᆞ의간에청의ᄒᆞ야ᄒᆞ되본년이
월일이노브리일지년을한ᄒᆞ고
월급은일화토륙십원식이오일
은가수비는디월이십원식이옷
일교유ᄌᆞ를다랴교시던ᄒᆞ고구
ᄒᆞᆯ시요ᄒᆞᆫ은시간에사쳑쥬일에
키오인비는경우에ᄒᆞ야진ᄒᆞ고
오ᄒᆞᆫ은한평되아ᄒᆞ고가분이츄
지이ᄒᆞᆫ빅원금여ᄒᆞ며고ᄒᆞ시진쳥
가결ᄒᆞ면면은곳귀ᄒᆞ고ᄒᆞᆯ에쟝
셜잇셔부등이급ᄒᆞᆫ사일은교유ᄌᆞ
긔셔지후가듬즁ᄒᆞ되교유샹
면휘교ᄒᆞᆯᄉᆞ라ᄒᆞ엿더라

○송비우디 의양군리지씨
가한영수씨와면담사로삼샹사
쟁송ᄒᆞᆫ다가의양군이나파ᄒᆞᆫ연
괴는송되평리원판결에송비는
의양군이ᄉᆞᆯ쳥구ᄒᆞᆫ지라한씨는
계산ᄒᆞ야낫과ᄌᆞ사사이번디읫
의비만쳔탈ᄒᆞ리리가그박송ᄒᆞ
을쳔이니과법원이되는지란경
지나니스ᄒᆞ엿더라

○포묵니하 의친왕의리이셩
일에도찬ᄒᆞ는중의화궁을포묵
으로ᄒᆞ시니ᄒᆞ엿더라

UNION INSURANCE SOCIETY OF CANTON.

Head office Hongkong.
Marine risks underwritten at current rates.

Agents in Chemulpo,
E. MEYER & Co.

COMPAGNIE DES MESSAGERIES MARITIMES.

Fortnightly Direct Service.

For Marseilles
via Ports.

Sailing from Yokohama
Calling at Kobe,
Shanghai, Hongkong, Saigon, Singapore,
Colombo, Djibonti, Suez, Port Said
and Marseilles.

For particulars apply to
HOLME RINGER & Co.,
Chemulpo.

HAYASHIDA & CO.,

16 MYENG DONG, CHIN KO KAI, SEOUL.
BRANCH OFFICE AT CHEMULPO.

Money changers, Coal and Wood Merchants, Express Agents.

We are agents for the Pyeng-yang Coal Company and the Karazu Coal Company of Japan. We have the best quality of both anthracite and bituminous coal, and prompt execution of orders is our speciality. Firewood of all kinds kept in stock. Full weight guaranteed. Money of all denominations exchanged at current rates. Parcels received for all parts.

CHINA MUTUAL LIFE INS. OC.

Most favourable terms to policy holders.

Benefit system unsurpassed.

HOLME RINGER & Co.
Agents, Chemulpo.

C. P. R.

CANADIAN PACIFIC RAILWAY COMPANY'S ROYAL MAIL STEAMSHIP LINE.

THE FAST ROUTE BETWEEN CHINA, JAPAN, AND EUROPE VIA CANADA AND THE UNITED STATES.

Route from Hongkong via Shanghai, Nagasaki (Inland Sea of Japan) Kobe, Yokohama, Victoria and Vancouver.

Twin Screw Empress Steamship—6,000 Tons—Speed 19 knots.

PROPOSED SAILING FROM YOKOHAMA.
R. M. S. Empress of India.
R. M. S. Empress of Japan.
R. M. S. Empress of China.
R. M. S. Athenian.
R. M. S. Tartar.

Special reduction (first class only) granted to members of the Military, Naval, Diplomatic and Civil services and to Missionaries.

Passengers have choice of ten routes across the Continent of America and have privilege of travelling by any Atlantic Steamship Line.

Round the World passage tickets in connection with the P. and O. S. N., North German Lloyd and Messageries Co.'s **£125.**

All rates payable at current rate of exchange.

For further information, Tickets, Guide Books, etc., apply to

HOLME, RINGER & Co., AGENTS,
Chemulpo.

Grand Hotel

(Formerly the Station Hotel)

Near the Railway Terminus.
West Gate Seoul.

The Best Hotel in Korea
Handsome new Building.
Fine Airy Rooms
Excellent Cuisine.
Terms Moderate.
Special terms to Missionaries
and to permanent boarders.

Electric cars within 2 minutes' walk.

W. H. EMBERLEY.
Proprieto

AMERICAN KOREAN ELECTRIC CO.

Light and Power.

Main Office: Electric Building, Chong No.

RAILWAY DEPARTMENT.

OPERATING CARS BETWEEN EAST AND WEST GATE, EVERY TEN MINUTES:—

First Car leaves East Gate at 7:00 A. M. First Car leaves R. R. Station at 7:25 A. M
Fast Car " East Gate at 8.40 P. M. Last " " R. R. Station at 9.05 P.M

OPERATING CARS BETWEEN EAST GATE AND IMPERIAL TOMB TERMINUS, EVERY TWENTY MINUTES:—

CONNECTING WITH EVERY ALTERNATE CAR ARRIVING AT EAST GATE FROM CHONG NO,

First Car leaves East Gate for Tomb at 7:10 A. M.
" " " Tomb for East Gate at 7:30 A. M.
Last " " East Gate for Tomb at 7:50 P. M.
" " " Tomb for East Gate at 8:10 P. M.

OPERATING CARS BETWEEN CHONG NO AND YUNG SAN RIVER EVERY TWELVE MINUTES:—

First Car leaves Chong No for South Gate at 7:12 A. M.
" " " Chong No for Yung San at 7:36 A. M.
" " " South Gate for Chong No at 7:20 A. M.
" " " Yung San for Chong No at 8:09 A. M.
Last " " South Gate for Chong No 9:00 P. M.
" " " Yung San for Chong No at 8.45. P. M.

SPECIAL PRIVATE CARS FURNISHED TO SUIT CONVENIENCE OF PATRONS. PRICES ON APPLICATION AT HEAD OFFICE.

LIGHTING DEPARTMENT.

Where less than 250 candle power of light is used, the rate per month will be
Per 16 candle power incandescent lamp,—All night.—Yen 2.50.
32 candle power incandescent lamp:—All night:—Yen 4.00.
50 candle power incandescent lamp:—All night:—Yen 6.00.
150 " " " " " " " 10.00.
1200 " " enclosed arc " " " " 20.00.

Where more than 250 candle power of light is used, a Meter will be installed, if requested:—Rent of Meter Yen 2.00 per month. Rate of charges by meter reading:—Two Sen per Ampere per hour. (Approximately this is equal to about One Sen per 16 C. P. lamp per hour) Minimum monthly charge where meter is installed, Yen 20.00 per month, which includes rental of meter.

Estimates for installing lights furnished on application

An assortment of chandeliers always on hand.

EVERY FACILITY.

in connection with Life Assurance Business is afforded by

The Standard Life Assurance Co.,

One of the largest and wealthiest of the Provident Institutions of the United Kingdom Forms of Application and all information will be promptly afforded on application.

10 CENTS A DAY.

Not a very large expenditure is it? But it is sufficient to secure for a man of 30 a policy with the STANDARD LIFE OFFICE for

$1323.

For all particulars of rates, etc., apply to

Holme, Ringer & Co.,
Agents, Chemulpo.

THE NEW YORK LIFE INSURANCE COMPANY.

Have you ever been declined by any Company?

Are you engaged in a specially hazardous occupation?

Have you heard of the New York Life Insurance Company's New Classifications for this class of Risks?

If not, send your date of birth, occupation and particulars of rejection, if any to

E. MEYER & Co.,
Agents, Chemulpo.

K. Murakami.
Photograph Studio
Chinkokai, Seoul.

Printing, Developing and Enlargement, of Photographs always Undertaken.

Korean Views and Pictures Illustrating Native Customs always on Sale,

---

THE OSAKA SHOSEN KAISHA.

Boats frequently on the berth for Chinnampo.

REGULAR SAILINGS BETWEEN JAPAN AND KOREAN PORTS.

FUSAN AND KOBE VIA SHIMONOSEKI.

OSAKA VIA MOKPO, FUSAN, SHIMONOSEKI AND KOBE.

MOJI DIRECT.

OSAKA VIA KUNSAN, MASANPO, FUSAN, SHIMONOSEKI AND KOBE.

CHEMULPO KUNSAN LINE,
Every three days.

CHEMULPO CHINNAMPO LINE.
Every three days.

For Freight and passage and further particulars apply to
THE OSAKA SHOSEN KAISHA,
Cemulpo.

MITSUI BUSSAN KAISHA.
(MITSUI & Co.)

MITSUI GINKO.
(MITSUI BANK.)

The Bank is owned by the members of the Mitsui Family, who, as partners, assume an unlimited responsibility for all liabilities of the Bank:—

Capital........................Yen 5,000,000
Reserve Fund.................. " 5,600,000

HEAD OFFICE, TOKYO.
LONDON OFFICE, 34 LIME ST., E. C.

BRANCHES AND AGENCIES:—
New York, San Francisco, Hamburg, Bombay, Singapore, Manila, Hongkong, Amoy, Chefoo, Tientsin.
Kobe, Hakodate, Yokohama, Kure, Yokosuka, Moji, Shimonoseki, Miike, Wakamatsu, Nagasaki, Kuchinotsu, Karatsu, Sasebo, Misume, Taipeh, &c.

Telegraphic Address for all the Offices:
"MITSUI."

A. B. C. AND A. 1 CODES USED.

Contractors of Coal
To the Imperial Japanese Navy. Arsenals and Railway Bureau, Principal Railway Companies and Industrial Work, Home and Foreign Mail and Freight Steamers.

Sole Proprietors
Of the famous Miike, Tagawa and Yamano Coal Mines.

Sole Agents
For the sale of Fukumo, Hokoku, Ichimura Kanoda, Mannoura, Onoura, Ostuji, Sonoda, Tsubaruro, Yoshinotani, Yoshio, Yurokiura and other coals.

YANGTSE INSURANCE ASSOCIATION, LTD.

The undersigned, having been appointed agents for the above company, are prepared to issue policies and pay losses on marine risks at regular rates.

E. MEYER & Co.,
Agents, Chemulpo.

LONDON, PLAISANT & CO.

General Storekeepers and Merchants, Ships Contractors Tobacconists, Commission and Forwarding Agents, Coal Merchants

IMPORTERS AND EXPORTERS

Seoul Chemulpo.

W. D. WENTWORTH,

LANDING
AND
SHIPPING AGENT.
AND
CUSTOMS BROKER.

12 OURA, NAGASAKI.

STEWARD & CO.

Chemulpo.

Shipchandlers and Storekeepers, Naval and Mercantile Contractors, Landing and Shipping Agents.

STEWARD'S HOTEL

Chemulpo.

Best accommodation in the port for travellers. Clean and well-aired rooms, good cuisine and prompt attendance, oderate tariff.

론셜

한국의일년기량

○한국에지금기량홀남비만흔것은말홀을기ᄃ릴것이업스나한국의형졍ᄉ무도혼잡ᄒ지마는일본사름이쌍만흔것도모다엇시교셰계에향ᄒ야ᄂ저의들이무승념이번지바로졍기ᄂ던하며일인닷이ᄒ며경계가상졍ᄒ니리의미상동ᄒ니고외에도여러가지져담을말ᄒ야가면서일본사름이이죵립대국에와서쳥ᄒ지아니ᄒ고원ᄒ지아니ᄒ는찬조를ᄒ는지라

지번ᄉ요일에인쳔잇는일본인들이작년제물포항젼의긔념으로논것을보니일본인이한국에와서사무를주장ᄒ미지금약일년이된것이분명ᄒ도다

그러ᄒ나일본이도아준다는한인을위ᄒ야흔일이무엇인고ᄒ면아모념도업스며ᄎ라리아모념도업는것만못ᄒ지라엇던사롬은말ᄒ되더ᄂ러보자ᄒ나오륙삭젼에도그말이오지금일본미만일젼쟁에불힝ᄒ지아니ᄒ면자금이후로는오륙삭뒤에도그말일듯ᄒ도다

한국에서일본인의힝위가사사이상원ᄒ것이무승권고를ᄒ던지목젼에는얼마ᄯᅳᆷ한국을위ᄒ야인후ᄒ듯ᄒ날이라도필경은한국의지경으로일본의케리ᄒ미잇게ᄒ는목젹에로도라가는지라

만일일본이한국을졍복ᄒ것곳ᄒ면우리가다무슴발을ᄒ리가엽지마ᄂ는근일ᄭ지일본이한국독립이라ᄂ말을닉세엿스니그평으로우리가일본이언약ᄒ문자와동니ᄂ권리를젹발ᄒ권리를가진지라

젼ᄉ를징계ᄒᄂ리도무옹에위로될것이업는것이지금브리셩넘젼에일본이지금갓치불쳥갭이자리로한국의독립을위ᄒ야싸운다ᄒ야독립을식인후에한국이홀로무승념이던지ᄒ슈엿다ᄒ야저금과곳치찬조ᄒ다ᄒ엿ᄂ디지금은그버에이러ᄂ대번을엉자ᄂ는십년젼보다별로다를것이엽스며어ᄂ베일ᄂ지한국에리의ᄒ미량ᄒ것이엇고일본인의졍신은한인을굴복식이고국가를겸병ᄒ고저의들을위ᄒ야조흔일자리를찻ᄂ디반셰엿도다

아직저지ᄂ는목하젼쌔가슈세권을일본인쟝중에넘지못ᄒ엿지마ᄂ젼쟁이일본의게조케만되야가ᄂ동안은의심업시그목젹을달ᄒ리라고친력ᄒ것이오그리흔후쎄는일본이졍시라도한국을기량ᄒ엿다고셔로칭하ᄒ흘ᄎ노우리ᄂ예탁ᄒ노라

잡보

○농업확장　참졍됴병호씨가장ᄎ출사ᄒ린인티젼국에농업이쳐발달치못ᄒ흠으로진황ᄒᄂ쳐에만ᄒ지라일인은차ᄯᅢ를하로알고진황지간을칙수ᄒ더논말이죵죵잇고금츈에ᄂ일본사우농업조맛만명이도한ᄒ다ᄒ을ᄉ신려ᄒ야지나간구일밤에경무교농업발달ᄒ기를강구ᄒ엿논티소국니라도빗보이외에ᄂ긔간흥을힘ᄒ고식목케ᄒ야차제로견죵에을너기로결졍ᄒ엿논티참졍이출사ᄒᄂ날에ᄂ차의을션제홀티인티농대ᄂ김죵ᄒᄂ기로써에명ᄒ엿다더라

○낭패　최찬졍의찬힝자명상소ᄒ사에티ᄒ야라지ᄌ재신민가신괴상쇠와법부대신박제슌씨가소ᄒ엿단더라

○관찰사면관　젼라남도관찰사김규셰기씨는슐찬사의쥬본으로면관되엿다더라

○면동시화　면동시위샹대티영문간소화ᄒ엿스나죠사ᄒ시면에는소ᄒ엿다더라

○쥬쳔양구　관제리졍소에서졀도원은영히쳥과ᄒ는고로히원의소속관원들은항ᄒ홀곳이업서사면으로잉구ᄒ기를쥬쳔ᄒ다더라

○노젼쳥귀　일본샹민들의죵노에가ᄂ가를버엿든거순경무사와일본령ᄉ간에교셥ᄒ야작일에브터쳥귀ᄒ엿다더라

○츄후계약　경무청고문관의보좌원ᄂ은본티계약중에업ᄂ바인티일본인으로하송지조로보좌원을차뎡ᄒ고츄후로계약중에다시쳠입ᄒ티너사람을위ᄒ야게약을번경ᄒ이온당치못ᄒ다더라

○고문계약　경무청고문관환산중쥰의중대사항에뎡약ᄒ지권이여좌ᄒ니일은교등경찰에관ᄒ사건이오이ᄂ일은외국인의게관ᄒ사건이오삼은외국인명방의보좌ᄒᄂ사건이요ᄉ은도장찬죄에관ᄒ사건의진퇴상벌에관ᄒ사건이라더라

○경무공문　경무청에서외부로조회ᄒ기를함경남도관찰부경무서총슌신공우김일환이가신임ᄒ야등뎡ᄒ흘티인티근일에일본군티일공관에면조ᄒ야ᄒ사부터의를졍공문을쳥등ᄒ야휘나렁케ᄒ기에편케ᄒ라ᄒ엿더라

○조회퇴급　한어교사두방협을일공사의게불유ᄒ고합동ᄒ흔사에퇴ᄒ야일본사가조쳥ᄒ흠으로외부의서학부로면조ᄒ엿더나학부에서외부로조복ᄒ기를각ᄒ교교사의교빙을합동과안ᄒ후에교셥ᄒ는것시명레인초로금번한어교사의합동을과초ᄒ야졍셔ᄒ야교셥교자홀이오일죵걋안치아ᄒ니ᄒ엿거논이조셔회는샹히ᄒ야ᄒ나히합동파영서교사ᄑ람은의합동을쇄ᄒ졍서ᄒ엿기로각일진을승교ᄒ오니이되로이공관에뎡복ᄒ라ᄒ엿더라

○교사합동　한어교사두방협의합동이년한은삼괴년이오월금은일빅십원이오가세비는티삭교이십원으로작뎡ᄒ엿더라

○고문폐관　외부고문관수제씨는실일하오시에폐관ᄒ엿다더라

○대관면임　학부대신리지용씨는궁내대신으로면임ᄒ고종졍원경리원경은학부대신을피명ᄒ엿다더라

뎐보

동경발 륙일

○공사계속　로일당가두생란조소한티생차보지북방약일리부근의적포병이우리진지각쳐를포격ᄒ엿고쳘일아원자산승룡이부소차근에티ᄒ야격퇴ᄒ엿스나우리가원조ᄒ리ᄂ는졔다고젼투ᄒ여구무ᄒ고나와밋ᄒ야병사의보티에는중이명ᄒ엿다더라

○아병퇴각　북한아병이사퇴ᄒ엿ᄂ티한퇴ᄒ는자와자오히아라ᄉ빅이사ᄌ삼이링이오ᄂ일의ᄎ퇴가ᄒ는자ᄂ의빅명병쳥이한편으로빅퇴를ᄒ야복북쳥에서명이오자ᄂ각ᄒ도도쥬로면보ᄒ고쳥에서퇴각ᄒ여기는졔긔ᄒ고

○북한뎡황　모쳐에단흔보빈정보를거ᄒ즉셩진에서남쵸로북방으로퇴각ᄒ고면선은졀츄ᄒ다ᄒ고저컬거ᄒ엿다ᄒ고

북관면보　사일오후사시반착

○북한방면에주둔ᄒ엿든덕군군이리슌합락의보를졉ᄒ고비상ᄒ히공포ᄒ야단북방으로퇴각ᄒ고목하헙경도셩진이남에는덕병의그림자도업다더라

로국의내란졍형

론돈발 이월일일

○황뎨와황후와황태후계서월이일에섬피득보븐에서요죵게에사샹ᄒ자들의권속을셩괴듀브녀에서홀금오쳔방을볏이너리보부운ᄂ레포파쟝군의게ᄂ러보분금ᄒ라ᄒ셧다더라

빅림발　동일

○황뎨계서로동쟈의총티들을보시고말ᄒ되조금히말고직업ᄒ사ᄂ지리니ᄒ라ᄒ시고그청구ᄒᄂ간들은실형ᄒ만ᄒ것은다ᄒ리라ᄒ셧다더라

론돈발　동일

○이월일일오후에황뎨계셔싸교에셔노예셔로동자의총티삼십인을졉견ᄒ엿ᄂ디그총티들은탁지대신의명령으로젼명에들식ᄒ은거시라황뎨계셔그총사들이에게비련ᄒ신말ᄒ시되너의들이디의국의간계에승ᄒ여되엿도다너의들이너의들을폐ᄒ고졍부에셔ᄂ티의게ᄒ은거시나이세ᄂ우리로반티국인민들이불가불힝셔ᄒ야저희고졉ᄒ는티면을졍복ᄒ야흘베이단너의들의사졍을기탐ᄒ야잇잇흘거슨우리도자세히알고잇ᄂ니너의들은불가불참어티너의들이너의들의상중에잇는발을알게ᄒ랴ᄒ고분요를니르기며졍부를반티ᄒᄂ거시죡ᄒ벌에범ᄒᄂ는거시니라우리가로동자를의향븍과안락을위ᄒ야간졀이바라서너의들의졍형을기랑ᄒ고너의들의소원을셩갑ᄒ리이오로동자들이다마음으로논신실ᄒ고충셩ᄒ존을우리가자세히아는지라너의들이그사이분요즁에범ᄒ죄ᄂ는다용셔ᄒ리라ᄒ셧다더라

빅림발　동일

○황뎨계서조칙을ᄂ리셧ᄂ티그조칙에ᄒ엿스되일졍부ᄂ는거년십이월이십샹일에ᄂ린조칙에발ᄒ기량안을실시ᄒᄂ티로동자의총티들과샹의ᄒ사

이실문의쟈유를인허ᄒ사샹인들샹이일에사샹ᄒ쟈들의권속의게넌금을허급ᄒ사

광고

○본인의셩명도쟝을음력십이월에신쳔일에서실ᄒ엿기로이에광고ᄒ오니수모승득ᄒ와도물시ᄒ홀ᄉ
　　　　　　서문밧　병동　손덕쥰　고빅

차터드은힝
자본금총액은이쳔오빅만원
본졈은영국론돈에잇고지졈은각티도회쳐에잇소
　　인쳔세창양힝티리졈

미국우젼회사와동경동양긔젼회사
미국휘젼과연락ᄒ엿슴
　　인쳔함릉가양힝티리졈

덕국아세아은힝
본졈은덕국빅림에잇고향항
지졈은샹히등지에잇소
　　인쳔세창양힝티리졈

향항샹히은힝
자본금총익슝쳔륙빅오십만원
본졈은향항에잇고
지졈은청국일본기타각국티쳐에잇소
　　인쳔세창양힝티리졈

TELEGRAMS.

(FROM JAPAN PAPERS)

AFFAIRS IN RUSSIA.

London, Feb. 3.

With reference to one section of the Tsar's reform Ukase, the Committee of Ministers have decided to recommend a series of measures, limiting the individual initiative of Ministers with the Tsar, especially with reference to alterations and suspension of laws; increasing the control and initiative of the Senate thereanent; facilitating prosecutions of officials by private individuals for illegalities; and establishing local Courts in connection with the Senate, and educated juries where the loss of civil rights is involved.

London, Feb. 3.

The report that a Magna Charta has been granted to the Russians is incorrect. M. de Witte has merely been empowered to devise a scheme for social legislative reform.

Berlin, Feb. 3.

The Russian novelist Maxim Gorki, who was arrested during the riots, has been released.

Berlin Feb. 3.

During the riots at Warsaw 600 men were killed and 1,000 wounded.

Berlin, Feb. 3.

The Tsar has appointed M. Bulyguine, Vice-Governor of Moscow, to the post of Minister of the Interior.

London, Feb. 6.

Father Gapon, the priest who took a prominent part in the protest made by the strikers in St. Petersburg recently, and who was later reported to have fled to Switzerland, is now stated to be on his way to England.

London, Feb. 6.

The Assembly of the Nobles of Moscow has decided to present two addresses to the Czar. One of the addresses is of a Conservative nature and was adopted by the majority. It says that peace at present is impossible without humiliation, and expresses confidence in ultimate victory, but deprecates internal reform till the war is ended. The other address is Liberal in tone. It rejects the above address and advocates collaboration between the Czar and the people for reform.

London, Feb. 7.

A conference of the Grand Dukes has been held at St. Petersburg, when it is reported a decision was arrived at in favour of opening negotiations for peace. It is stated that as a result of this decision the Russian Ambassador in London has been instructed to approach the British Government with a view to securing its good offices in the discussion of terms.

London, Feb. 8.

The St. Petersburg nobility has adopted, by 158 votes to 20, the text of an address to the Czar urging him to summon an assembly of representatives of the nation.

A LARGE RUSSIAN LOAN

London, Feb. 7.

Negotiations have been completed for the issue of a five per cent. Russian loan at Paris, amounting to nearly a milliard francs.

AN INDISCREET SPEECH.

London, Feb. 7.

With reference to the report of a speech made by Mr. A. H. Lee, Civil Lord of the Admiralty and M.P. for the Fareham Division, in which he stated it was not so much to keep eyes off France in the Mediterranean as that Great Britain had to look with more anxiety, but without fear, towards the North Sea, that was the reason of the redistribution of the fleet. If war was declared the British Navy had to get her blow in first.

Mr. Lee now writes that the speech was incorrectly reported. What he said was that Great Britain must assume all naval powers to be possible enemies, and therefore it is necessary to keep our eyes not only on the Mediterranean but also on the Atlantic and the North Sea.

The German press is very angry and demands that the Marquis of Lansdowne, British Foreign Minister, should repudiate the speech.

London, Feb. 6.

Kuropatkin reports that the Japanese on the 1st inst., after a hot bombardment, attacked Ljantankhenam (Liangtaukan) on the left bank of the Hun-ho and drove out the Russians, who, however, on being reinforced, recaptured the village.

KUROPATKIN'S ARMY.

London, Feb. 3.

A report from General Kuropatkin dated January 31, states that owing to the fierce bombardment of Chentanpao and neighbourhood by the Russian artillery, the Japanese troops there have been compelled the abandon most of their positions.

Berlin, Feb. 3.

Anxiety is felt at St. Petersburg with regard to the provisioning of Kuropatkin's forces in April and may next, owing to the exhaustion of the resources of Manchuria.

THE U. S. AND VENEZUELA.

Berlin Feb, 3.

U. S. warships are making a naval demonstration against Venezuela, owing to the affronts tendered by President Castro to Mr Bowen, the U. S. Minister.

THE FRANCO-RUSSIAN ALLIANCE.

Berlin Feb, 3.

The Paris "Temps declares, in the name of M. Delcasse, the French Minister of Foreign Affairs that France will maintain the Russian alliance.

A CURIOUS ERROR.

The "Shanghai Time now has an exclusive service of telegrams from London, receives "special" telegrams from Tokio, and subscribes to Reuters. Even this multiplicity of sources does not seem to be any protection against mistakes as we find the Russian Casualties given as 40,000 in all three messages.

Exclusive Service.

London, Jan. 31.

The Russian losses in killed, wounded and prisoners at the Shaho approximate 40,000. The Japanese killed exceed 3,000. The wounded not estimated yet. Russian prisoners are believed to be 2,500.

(Special)

Tokyo, Jan. 31.

It is officially stated that the Japanese casualties in the battle of Heikhutai were 2,500 and the Russian losses are estimated at double that number, exclusive of prisoners to the number of 2,500. The total Russian losses in the last six days fighting in killed and wounded are estimated at 40,000.

(Reuter's)

London, Feb. 1.

An official telegram from Tokyo states that the Russian casualties between January 25 and January 29 are now estimated from 36,000 to 41,000, and the Japanese about 7,000.

General Sakharoff estimates the Japanese prisoners at over 300.

According to the "Chefoo Daily News," the rouble is still the favoured currency in Newchwang.

A letter, privately received here from a Russian officer at the Shaho, says that until the end of January the casualties on either side during the recent fighting were about equal.

MOUKDEN NOTES.

FROM THE "CHEFOO DAILY NEWS."

Moukden has come to the front again as the probable base of operations of the Russian army, for the reason that a new railway line has been built which branches off from the main line at the city named, extending in an easterly direction through the Hunho Valley. Communication over this line reaches Fushun, forty kilometres east of Moukden.

The three Russian armies are divided over an extensive front as follows: The third army in the center, the second army on the right and the first army on the left. The leaders are now all with their armies. The first to arrive was General Linievitch, who entered Moukden on November 8th. General Baron Kaulbars, the last to reach the front, telegraphed the Czar on December 27th that he had assumed command of his troops.

The Russian front, taking into account the cavalry outposts to the Liao River, and covers a distancee of 130 kilometres. In spite of the modern means of communication which are at the disposal of the leader, will be a difficult task to keep well in hand the movement of so vast an army.

MISGIVINGS IN JAPAN.

The Nichi Nichi, a Tokio newspaper, says that President Roosevelt's message of the 6th December last is a virtual declaration of imperialism as the United States' foreign policy. The journal gladly welcomes it because, as it says, the President's and the American people's sole aim is to maintain and promote the righteous peace of the world, and be fair and upright in their diplomacy. Yet, it would remind its compatriots that the economic powers America possesses to-day are indeed untold and unprecedented, and that, however well placed their reliance on the personality of President Roosevelt and the rectitude and sincerity of the people he rules over, it does not behoove them to rest content in viewing with too roseate a hue our relations with our frieds across the Pacific. Only suppose that American trusts have begun in earnest to extend their arms to the Far East: great will be the effect on our commercial and industrial interests. Awake and prepare, cries the journal, to face the tremendous war of economic competition soon be forced on us.

An earthquake occurred shortly before 10 P. M. Saturday. There was no oscillation, but very loud rumbling.

We understand that the Cabinet is very strongly opposed to the Japanese Ministers' request for the abolition of the Educational Department.

There is no change in the Tokio telegams. More riots in Russia. It is reported that all the Russian Generals are quarrelling. All the Berlin newspapers congratulate Japan on what she has accomplished in one year. A very powerful party in Russia is agitating for peace.

Stone fights are still of daily occurrence, pitched battles being held every evening outside the East and South gates. The police make half-hearted efforts to stop them but soon yield to superior numbers. The Koreans are very enthusiastic over their extraordinary national pastime.

From the office of the "Eastern World" Yokohama we have received three pamphlets dealing with "The gold question in Japan," "The national wealth of Japan" and "The present financial and monetary condition." The author, Mr. S. Schroeder, is an extremely clear-sighted and able writer and deals with his subjects exhaustively. We recommend all who seek for information on these subjects to send for these pamphlets which are published at the moderate price of 25 cents each.

Mr. Stevens, the adviser to the Foreign Office, was received in audience by the Emperor on Friday.

It has not yet been announced whether the value of the Korean nickel will ascend to that of the Japanese currency or whether the Japanese coin will descend to the level of the Korean.

On the recommendation of the inspectors who have been investigating administration in the provinces, eight magistrates, found guilty of peculation and oppression, have been dismissed.

Mr. Megata need not have gone to Japan for his wonderful $3,000,000 loan. It could have been raised easily in Korea in hard cash and we belive the government has received several offers of the money.

The police adviser, Mr. Maruyama, has introduced an assistant named Furukawa into his department. It has been pointed out that this is not in the contract but Mr. Maruyama airily remarks that it will by-byeand bye.

We regret to have to announce the death of the wife of the Vice Minister for Foreign Affairs. Mrs. Yun Chi Ho succumbed under an operation on Saturday and the funeral took place this morning. The service at the hospital was largely attended. The Diplomatic and Consular corps were represented and many Korean and Foreign officials present. We extend our sincere sympathy to Mr. Yun Chi Ho in his sad bereavement.

The Korea Daily News.

Issued at 5 P. M. daily except Sundays.

Rate of Subscription:—
Per Year,............Yen 25.
Per Quarter,..........Yen 7.
Per Month,...........Yen 2.50.

Postage in Korea not charged extra.
Postage abroad charged extra.

Advertisements, 50 sen per day for 1 inch or less.
5 yen per month per inch.
50 yen per year per inch.

All communications to
E. T. BETHELL,
Editor and Publisher,
Pak-tong, Seoul.

PEACE RUMOURS.

On the principle that where there is smoke there must be some fire we suppose that some importance must be attached to the persistent rumours of impending peace which are in the air.

It is however, difficult to see how a solution satisfactory to all concerned could be reached at the present juncture even if Russia and Japan were willing to cease hostilities and place their fate in the hands of a committee of the powers.

Russia has until now sustained a series of defeats which were due mainly to her unreadiness, and which cannot be ascribed to any inferiority as a fighting power. Many of the defects evident in the earlier stages of the war no longer exist, and even if she is unable to assume the offensive and drive the Japanese back to the sea, it now seems evident that the Japanese will never succeed in reaching their original goal, Harbin, where alone can any important strategic advantage be obtained.

Japan has won Port Arthur and evidently intends to stick to it; she has occupied Korea and all the signs point to her intention of remaining here. Russia's encroachments in Korea and Manchuria were understood to be directed towards the acquisition of an ice-free port for the terminus of the trans-Siberian railway and all the territory containing such ports is now in the hands of the Japanese.

It is to the last degree improbable that Japan will voluntarily hand back any thing which she has already taken and it seems equally improbable that Russia will allow herself to be deprived of what she has been scheming for for years, without a desperate struggle.

Taking all this into consideration, it must be admitted that the possibility of a pacific solution being arrived at while the war is in its present stage is extremely remote. The neutral powers might claim a right to interfere on behalf of their shipping trade should the Baltic Squadron remain in the Malay Archipelago and carry on a commerce-destroying policy, but we have so far had no indication that such is the intention of Admiral Rohdjestvensky. Under any other circumstances the derangement of commerce will not seriously effect anyone but the belligerents and will not constitute a sufficient cause for intervention.

It has been repeatedly said that Russia would be willing to discuss a peaceful settlement after one good victory had been put to her credit. This may of course possibly be true but it must be admitted that present circumstances do not lend any colour to this view. Kuropatkin, after many months of retreating has at last checked the Japanese advance, and seems also to have discovered some of Oyama's weak spots so that it is hard to believe that if, by a signal victory, he should succeed in turning the tide, he would, instead of following up his advantage, be willing to sit down and discuss terms of peace.

Russia's worst enemies will admit that she has played a good uphill game. The miserable inefficiency of her Asiatic Squadron, the vulnerability of the trans-Siberian railway and the attempted revolution in Russia must all of them been heart-breaking to Kuropatkin; and now that Russia is quieter, the railway is safe, and a better fleet is coming it will indeed be surprising if the Czar and his advisers are willing to listen to talk of peace.

Whatever their protestations may have been it is clear that both countries are fighting for the same thing viz: Manuchuria and Korea and the only logical solution seems to, be for them to fight it out. Peace was at least possible before the fall of Port Arthur, but it does not seem to be within the range of practical politics at present.

Those in a position to know tell us that Japan, financially is in a bad way and we are assured that she cannot find the money to continue the war until the end of this year. This is, of course, well known in Russia and constitutes another very good reason why Russia should defer peace negotiations for some time yet.

CHINESE CRITICISM OF FRIEDENTHAL'S PLAYING.

The following comical criticism of a Chinese aesthetic, who had been present at a concert given by Herr Friedenthal at Canton is worthy of reproduction. It appeared originally in the "Ling Nam Yat Pao" of Canton.

"On the 11th instant at 9-15 p. m. the celebrated German Piano-virtuose Friedenthal San gave a concert at the house of the Deputy Commissioner General Mr. Rocher, in which all the rooms were filled with the luxury of the occident. It was a marvellous clear night; the moon sparkled on the sky like a looking-glass Absolute quietude reigned in nature, and the spectators also listened with silence when the charming music began. Now it sounded like the murmuring of water flowing over stones, now like the whispering of the chryptomerias softly moved by the zephyr; and his loud playing resembled the thunder of the waves in the ocean. Now the player was sitting at his instrument as quiet as the tops of the mountains, now he developed a liveliness and vigour of playing like the player in Yung-Len. His soft and sweet playing formed a heavy contrast to the ill-famed music at the borders of the river Fu. Friedenthal San possesses the talent of Chungi, who, as is known, was able to play everything. He plays like Shih Kuang who, on his queer instrument, knew how to call forth the songs of the nightingale. At the concert all the diplomats, consuls, deputies, officials and the merchants of Shamseen, with their families, were present, so that the vast halls were completely filled. All held in their hands a paper, in which they read what Friedenthal San was going the play, just as in the European hotels the guests read a paper to see what they are going to eat. After every piece they beat loudly with their hands, producing a loud noise, and so they gave the celebrated artist to understand what pleasure they enjoyed with his music; but I thought this noise was rather a bitter contrast to the beautiful music which preceded it. I, the humble writer of these lines and editor of the "Ling Nam Yat Pao" was also invited by the Consul of virtuous Germany, and stayed in the saloons until the end of the concert. Just as Chenlein understood how to lead the people in moral ways through his music, so was I also prevented from doing anything wrong that night,"

A LADY'S SPEECH.

Miss Ellis Jefferys, the well known actress, in replying to the toast of her health at recent banquet at the Playgoers Club, said that whatever her faults might be the Playgoers had invited her to be their guest at one of their banquets—those *noctes cenaeque deorum*, to quote the words of Horace, who, as archaeolgists knew, was president of the Ancient Roman Branch of the Playgoers' Club about 12 B. C. (Laughter.) That remarkable organisation did much for the theatrical life of the Romans, and made the Coliseum what it was it is to-day. (Laughter.) She did not allude to the great revival in St. Martin's-lane. The club had accomplished much in the few years of its existence. It had set the seal of its approval on the triumph of virtue and the punishment of villainy and vice; it had curbed the crudities of the comic man and had all but abolished the demon king, it had espoused the cause of the suffering heroine, and rescued her from the slow starvation of the property loaf, it had shown the adventuress how wrong she, was, and had weaned her from the lurid crimson frock and the sinful sables, and by mere power of moral suasion it had shown the men how to lead a better life.. (Laughter.) The Playgoers' Club was about to enter its twenty-first year. So was she (Laughter.) Though she loved playgoers individually she feared them collectively. Their compliment that evening had caused her sleepless nights and anxious days. All through dinner she had been suffering the agonies of a new malady, with symptoms similar to stage fright—a form of the dreaded "tetanus theatricalis," or "Playgoers' paralysis." (Laughter.) She had missed the support of the soup, the exhilaration of the entree, and the joviality of the joint (Laughter.) There was no lack of sympathy between playgoers and artists, and she hoped that there would always be an *entente cordiale* between them that no footlights, no fireproof curtains, nor even orchestras could divide. (Cheers.)

The latest addition to the glad throng of advisers to be thrust upon the Korean Government is Miss Takabashi who is a lady doctor or nurse. Her pay is not much—60 yen a month and a free house —but it is quite certain that she will not earn even that.

We have to acknowledge receipt of the "Korea Review" for January. Although the "Review" is under new management, Mr. Homer B. Hulbert still fills the editorial chair and the contents of this issue are fully up to previous standard. We are promised a series of article on the industries of Korea the first of which, appearing in this issue is on "The Iron Mines of Kang Wun Province," very entertainingly written by the Rev. J. R. Moose.

The Korea Daily News.

VOL. II, MONDAY, FEBRUARY 13, 1905 No. 33

大韓每日申報

대한미일신보

(뎨이권십삼소호) (슈요일) 일천구백오년이월십오일

본샤고빅

이신보는영어와한어로셕거미일출판호옵

신문가

한쟝 엽두돈오푼

일삭됴 엽두량닷돈

우표가미삭닷돈

다맛돈으로밧숩

광고료는

긔한의쟝단과즈힝의다쇼로즁감호되렴가로밧을터이오며오티지아녀대한사람마다다이신문을보실터이니광고내시기를원호시는이들은우리신문샤에와셔면약호심을희망호옵

○발힝소 박동대한미일신보샤법어학교압혜젼영국인셜필림집자리오

사쟝 영국인 (비셜)

평양 디리점

○평양효동사는권미보씨로우리신문관디리인을뎡호엿스오니평양에계신구람코져호시는쳠군즈는히디리점에왕림호와면의호시옵

사고

○우리대한미일신보의목뎍은대한의안녕질서에관한모든대목에디호야논공평한변론을쥬쟝홈이라우리동신원의담보는신문보시는쳠군조의계홍상보도호리며편지를긔셔호여주시는이논셩명과반디를젹어붓처시기를희망호오니이거슨신문상에긔지호라는거시아니오다만극히신용호논즁거를숨고자홈이라긔자는아모긔셔던지긔저홈을되각호논권리를가젓스나되각호는리유를말홀터이오며공즁평화를문란케호는듯호긔셔는의례히밧지안켓습나이다

●본사셜시이리로신문을미양우례로분젼호와례젼부의임의로젼흔듯스로면곳에는혹늣게젼호기도호며혹몃칠거슬호겁에젼호기도호며혹아니젼호는곳도잇다호와우리신문을스랑호야구람호시는 쳠군조의계딕호야디우미안호옵기로지금온분젼인을두고미일일즉이젼호며아다젼호거나늣게거나호폐가업도록호라호오니혹아니젼호거나혹늣게젼호거나호일이잇스면본샤로통긔호여쥬심을희망호옵

잡보

평양통신

○열심미로 일본인대면과빅로견지죠량씨가평양즁셩등디에병원긔지를만히샷다는디지금황히도황쥬등디에서히일본인등이두루호며일심쥬의호는것이한국토디사기를결심호고황쥬삼방이나되는광야를미독코자호야빅가지로운동호는지라황쥬인민등이근일평양감리서에청원호기를군용디외에는외국인이쌍을사지못호는법인디지금일본인태면이가토디를륵미코져호야만단압제가자심호오니즉속히일본령사관으로죠회호야됴약외에토디미민호는거슬금지호게호여달나호엿더라

○반위구타 평양일본거류디니에엇던일본인이한인목슈로목욕탕을만달고일삭이되도록공전을주지안는고로히디감리서에청원하엿스나샹금차자주지안는지라세말에다인의빗은만하할수업서다시ᄉᆞ스로히일본인의게로가서달나한즉무수히난타호여보냇다더라

○부지하고 평양서촌사는.최운오씨등이젼평양군슈평한쥬씨의담쟝사건으로법부에뎡호고향으로나려간지수십일만에무숨사건인지평양일본사령부에셔헌병을보니여최씨의아들를착력호야일본헌병사령부에엄슈호엿다더라

○방불일본 평양셩니셩외의긴요한곳에는일본인이열심으로집을사는지라그런고로히디방집갑이작년에비호면십비나되고종노등디에는일본뎐디와흡사호다더라

○학교홍왕 평양대동학교는광무칠년에히디거호는김셕윤씨가창설훈것인터동씨가쥬야로열심교육호는고로학업이일취월쟝호야금번동긔시험에우등훈학원이십여명이라히교찬셩원들이물픔을샹여호야권쟝호엿다더라

○금명입셩 평안북도태천군슈됴뎡윤씨는평리원에서압샹호라는훈령을맛나금명간입셩훈다더라

○착거젼탈 평양디병뎡한명이무숨불법힝위가잇던지작일에헌병이잡아가는디동셔평양병뎡이다슈히리도호야히피착훈병뎡을탈거호엿다더라

○평리쥬 합경도에출쥬호엿던평양디병뎡이비오기압헤천위일디영문으로리주케훈다더라

○빅일공고 거십이일은슌명비샹후빅일인고로쥬다레공고가되엿다더라

○의효면다려 거십삼일은의효면쥬다레공고라더라

○이죠법부 각도쇼찰사의봉고를당훈진쥬군슈리용교산청군슈죠유승김제군슈경옥홍천군슈유과환서홍군슈리병훈제씨와론보훈거제군슈권즁훈김천군슈김현태를정부에서쥬본호야면관호고녀부로죠회호기를법부로이죠호야죠률감처호고범훈바쟝젼은낫낫치쇄봉호라호엿다더라

○동의연소 찬졍최익현씨의샹소를동의호야김학진윤용구제씨가련소호엿고리셩렬씨도샹소호더라

○됴원로샹경 수교대신죠병세씨도최찬졍과동일한목적으로샹소를차로샹경훈다는대씨는빅관을솔호고뎡청홀터이라더라

○농대신임 리지용씨가학부대신을피임훈다더니농샹공부대신을신임훈다더라

○관사면임 한셩지관소수반관사리샹면임천은학지부출납국쟝으로젼임훈는더그디에는전검사홍종억씨가피임훈다더라

○면임찬졍 평리원지관장민병한씨는찬졍으로젼임훈다더라

○면관난면 즁서서장리용승씨가지작야에쥬호야젼참서관유치셜형대를무수히난타호고중서에착고를치와엄수호여글오더니가비록유괴환의아들이오신티휴의사위라도봉욕을면치못호리라호지라유참서가평리원에지관을청훈다호니서장은면관을면치못호리라더라

○신문우송 일본공사가학부로공함호기를일본대판미일신문사쟝산본언일이가동사신문을본월일일로노브리한쟝일부식우송호니뎡수케호라호지라학부대신리지극씨가각관청으로면포호엿더라

○마씨졸서 외부협관윤치호씨의부인 (청녀뎡부인)마씨가졸서호엿는디작일제즁원에서쟝례식을힝호엿다더라

○샹의쳐분 일공ᄉᆞ가외부로죠회호기를합경남도관찰ᄉᆞ가우리군ᄉᆞ샹에되호야방히가심호니청컨디니부대신파샹의호야샹당훈쳐분을시힝호고속히서리를니여군ᄉᆞ샹에편케호라호엿더라

○평민제진 젼평남관찰ᄉᆞ민영철씨가재임시에서경을영건훈다칭호고향녹비렴시에담장훈돈이여러빅만냥이되는지라작일에평안남북도민인리병히로덕언등십여인이룡산민영철씨의강뎡에제진호야일장질문호엿다더라

○합청승인 일본공ᄉᆞ가니부로공함호기를귀부경무고문관환산즁즁의동역을고하송지조로정호고월급은금화일빅오십원으로작뎡호엿스니승인호시고관사나혹관사비는지급홀것업ᄉᆞ오니량하호기를위요라호엿더라

○방히불소 일본공ᄉᆞ가또외부로죠회호기를표원군슈의관인을교인홀ᄉᆞ로긔월이십일일에신청호엿숩더니오히려교부치아니호야히군에는칙임의디방관이업서군ᄉᆞ힝동에방히불소호오니그절ᄎᆞ를급속히결뇨호기를면훈호시고문천군에도군슈가샹경훈후천환을청탁호고귀임치아니홈으로또훈방히불무호오니급히귀임홀ᄉᆞ로발훈호시고또긱월이십사일에평양군슈의관훈ᄉᆞ건을신청호엿더니동인의태포령을아직철소치아니홈으로히디방관에불안훈디위에처호야군ᄉᆞ힝동에방히가불소호오니또훈결뎡홀ᄉᆞ로군ᄉᆞ샹당국자의간청이잇ᄉᆞ오니회보호옵소서호엿더라

○다수자원 오강부민들이국처자원호ᄉᆞ에디호야다동부민들도또훈자원훈다더라

UNION INSURANCE SOCIETY OF CANTON.

Head office Hongkong.
Marine risks underwritten at current rates.
Agents in Chemulpo,
E. MEYER & Co.

COMPAGNIE DES MESSAGERIES MARITIMES.

Fortnightly Direct Service.

For Marseilles via Ports.

Sailing from Yokohama

Calling at Kobe, Shanghai, Hongkong, Saigon, Singapore, Colombo, Djibouti, Suez, Port Said and Marseilles.

For particulars apply to
HOLME RINGER & Co.,
Chemulpo.

HAYASHIDA & CO.,

16 MYENG DONG, CHIN KO KAI, SEOUL.
BRANCH OFFICE AT CHEMULPO.

Money changers, Coal and Wood Merchants, Express Agents.

We are agents for the Pyeng-yang Coal Company and the Karazu Coal Company of Japan. We have the best quality of both anthracite and bituminous coal, and prompt execution of orders is our speciality. Firewood of all kinds kept in stock. Full weight guaranteed. Money of all denominations exchanged at current rates. Parcels received for all parts.

CHINA MUTUAL LIFE INS. OC.

Most favourable terms to policy holders.

Benefit system unsurpassed.

HOLME RINGER & Co.
Agents, Chemulpo.

C. P. R.

CANADIAN PACIFIC RAILWAY COMPANY'S ROYAL MAIL STEAMSHIP LINE.

THE FAST ROUTE BETWEEN CHINA, JAPAN, AND EUROPE VIA CANADA AND THE UNITED STATES.

Route from Hongkong via Shanghai, Nagasaki (Inland Sea of Japan) Kobe, Yokohama, Victoria and Vancouver.

Twin Screw Empress Steamship—6,000 Tons—Speed 19 knots.

PROPOSED SAILING FROM YOKOHAMA.
R. M. S. Empress of India.
R. M. S. Empress of Japan.
R. M. S. Empress of China.
R. M. S. Athenian.
R. M. S. Taatar.

Special reduction (first class only) granted to members of the Military, Naval, Diplomatic and Civil services and to Missionaries.

Passengers have choice of ten routes across the Continent of America and have privilege of travelling by any Atlantic Steamship Line.

Round the World passage tickets in connection with the P. and O. S. N., North German Lloyd and Messageries Co.'s **£125.**

All rates payable at current rate of exchange.

For further information, Tickets, Guide Books, etc., apply to
HOLME, RINGER & Co., AGENTS,
Chemulpo.

Grand Hotel

(Formerly the Station Hotel)

Near the Railway Terminus, West Gate Seoul.

The Best Hotel in Korea
Handsome new Building.
Fine Airy Rooms
Excellent Cuisine.
Terms Moderate.
Special terms to Missionaries
and to permanent boarders.

Electric cars within 2 minutes' walk.

W. H. EMBERLEY.
Proprieto

EVERY FACILITY.

in connection with Life Assurance Business is afforded by

The Standard Life Assurance Co.,

One of the largest and wealthiest of the Provident Institutions of the United Kingdom Forms of Application and all information will be promptly afforded on application.

10 CENTS A DAY.

Not a very large expenditure is it? But it is sufficient to secure for a man of 30 a policy with the STANDARD LIFE OFFICE for

$1323.

For all particulars of rates, etc., apply to

Holme, Ringer & Co.,
Agents, Chemulpo.

THE NEW YORK LIFE INSURANCE COMPANY.

Have you ever been declined by any Company?

Are you engaged in a specially hazardous occupation?

Have you heard of the New York Life Insurance Company's New Classifications for this class of Risks?

If not, send your date of birth, occupation and particulars of rejection, if any to

E. MEYER & Co.,
Agents, Chemulpo.

MITSUI BUSSAN KAISHA.
(MITSUI & Co.)

MITSUI GINKO.
(MITSUI BANK.)

The Bank is owned by the members of the Mitsui Family, who, as partners, assume an unlimited responsibility for all liabilities of the Bank:—

Capital........................Yen 5,000,000
Reserve Fund.................. " 5,600,000

HEAD OFFICE, TOKYO.

LONDON OFFICE, 34 LIME ST., E. C.

BRANCHES AND AGENCIES:—

New York, San Francisco, Hamburg, Bombay, Singapore, Manila, Hongkong, Amoy, Chefoo, Tientsin.

Kobe, Hakodate, Yokohama, Kure, Yokosuka, Moji, Shimonoseki, Miike, Wakamatsu, Nagasaki, Kuchinotsu, Karatsu, Sasebo, Misume, Taipeh, &c.

Telegraphic Address for all the Offices
"MITSUI."

A. B. C. AND A. I CODES USED.

Contractors of Coal

To the Imperial Japanese Navy. Arsenals and Railway Bureau, Principal Railway Companies and Industrial Work, Home and Foreign Mail and Freight Steamers.

Sole Proprietors

Of the famous Miike, Tagawa and Yamano Coal Mines.

Sole Agents

For the sale of Fukumo, Hokoku, Ichimura Kanoda, Mannoura, Onoura, Ostuji, Sonoda, Tsubaruro, Yoshinotani, Yoshio, Yurokiburu and other coals.

YANGTSE INSURANCE ASSOCIATION, LTD.

The undersigned, having been appointed agents for the above company, are prepared to issue policies and pay losses on marine risks at regular rates.

E. MEYER & Co.,
Agents, Chemulpo.

AMERICAN KOREAN ELECTRIC CO.

Light and Power.

Main Office: Electric Building, Chong No.

RAILWAY DEPARTMENT.

OPERATING CARS BETWEEN EAST AND WEST GATE, EVERY TEN MINUTES:—

First Car leaves East Gate at 7:00 A. M. First Car leaves R. R. Station at 7:25 A. M
Last Car " East Gate at 8.40 P. M. Last " " R. R. Station at 9.05 P.M

OPERATING CARS BETWEEN EAST GATE AND IMPERIAL TOMB TERMINUS, EVERY TWENTY MINUTES:—

CONNECTING WITH EVERY ALTERNATE CAR ARRIVING AT EAST GATE FROM CHONG NO.

First Car leaves East Gate for Tomb at 7:10 A. M.
" " " Tomb for East Gate at 7:30 A. M.
Last " " East Gate for Tomb at 7:50 P. M.
" " " Tomb for East Gate at 8:10 P. M.

OPERATING CARS BETWEEN CHONG NO AND YUNG SAN RIVER EVERY TWELVE MINUTES:—

First Car leaves Chong No for South Gate at 7:12 A. M.
" " " Chong No for Yung San at 7:36 A. M.
" " " South Gate for Chong No at 7:20 A. M.
" " " Yung San for Chong No at 8:09 A. M.
Last " " South Gate for Chong No 9:00 P. M.
" " " Yung San for Chong No at 8.45 P. M.

SPECIAL PRIVATE CARS FURNISHED TO SUIT CONVENIENCE OF PATRONS. PRICES ON APPLICATION AT HEAD OFFICE.

LIGHTING DEPARTMENT.

Where less than 250 candle power of light is used, the rate per month will be
Per 16 candle power incandescent lamp,—All night.—Yen 2.50.
32 candle power incandescent lamp:—All night:—Yen 4.00.
50 candle power incandescent lamp:—All night:—Yen 6.00.
150 " " " " " " " 10.00.
1200 " " enclosed arc " " " " 20.00.

Where more than 250 candle power of light is used, a Meter will be installed, if requested:—Rent of Meter Yen 2.00 per month. Rate of charges by meter reading:—Two Sen per Ampere per hour. (Approximately this is equal to about One Sen per 16 C. P. lamp per hour) Minimum monthly charge where meter is installed, Yen 20.00 per month, which includes rental of meter.

Estimates for installing lights furnished on application

An assortment of chandeliers always on hand.

K. Murakami.

Photograph Studio
Chinkokai, Seoul.

Printing, Developing and Enlargement, of Photographs always Undertaken.

Korean Views and Pictures Illustrating Native Customs always on Sale,

---

THE OSAKA SHOSEN KAISHA.

Boats frequently on the berth for Chinnampo.

REGULAR SAILINGS BETWEEN JAPAN AND KOREAN PORTS.

FUSAN AND KOBE VIA SHIMONOSEKI

OSAKA VIA MOKPO, FUSAN, SHIMONOSEKI AND KOBE.

MOJI DIRECT.

OSAKA VIA KUNSAN, MASANPO, FUSAN, SHIMONOSEKI AND KOBE.

CHEMULPO KUNSAN LINE, Every three days.

CHEMULPO CHINNAMPO LINE. Every three days.

For Freight and passage and further particulars apply to
THE OSAKA SHOSEN KAISHA,
Cemulpo

RONDON, PLAISANT & CO.

General Storekeepers and Merchants, Ships Contractors Tobacconists, Commission and Forwarding Agents, Coal Merchants

IMPORTERS AND EXPORTERS

Seoul Chemulpo.

W. D. WENTWORTH.

LANDING
AND
SHIPPING AGENT,
AND
CUSTOMS BROKER.

12 OURA, NAGASAKI.

STEWARD & CO.

Chemulpo.

Shipchandlers and Storekeepers, Naval and Mercantile Contractors, Landing and Shipping Agents.

STEWARD'S HOTEL

Chemulpo.

Best accommodation in the port for travellers. Clean and well-aired rooms, good cuisine and prompt attendance, oderate tariff.

○잉존학부 림공ᄉ의권고에학부와농부를폐지홈으로졍부에셔주션ᄒᆞ야학부ᄂᆞᆫ잉존ᄒᆞ기로ᄒᆞᆫ다더라

○황궁경찰의풍셜 음력삼월브터일병이우리황궁경찰을ᄒᆞᆫ다ᄂᆞᆫ항셜이잇다더라

○ᄂᆡ탕시지 지나간음력월죵에ᄂᆞᆫᄂᆡ탕시지금이불과사만원가량이라더라

론셜

영일동맹

○론논다임쓰신문이별셔일영동맹의범위를확쟝홈을찬죠ᄒᆞ엿스니다임쓰외로국반ᄃᆡᄒᆞᄂᆞᆫ본색으로그말ᄒᆞᆫ것과ᄀᆞᆺ치될지ᄂᆞᆫ예탁아니ᄒᆞ나그러ᄒᆞ나쳑임잇다ᄂᆞᆫᄒᆞᆫ신문이아직ᄭᅡ지감당ᄒᆞ야가ᄂᆞᆫᄒᆞᆫ동밍국을위ᄒᆞ야영국을ᄒᆞᆫ즁대ᄒᆞᆫ젼쟁에ᄭᅡ지도록진력ᄒᆞᄂᆞᆫ것이불힝ᄒᆞᆫ일이로다 일본이지금싸우ᄂᆞᆫ힘이족족ᄒᆞ며이다음에쓸군ᄉ들도권쟝ᄒᆞ고보호ᄒᆞᄂᆞᆫ계제를일치아니ᄒᆞ거ᄂᆞᆯ영국신문에일본을위ᄒᆞᄂᆞᆫ부분에영일동맹의확쟝을찬셩ᄒᆞᄂᆞᆫ도다

지금은영일동밍의쥬의가보수적이라그것은두교젼국ᄉ이에젼쟁을제한ᄒᆞ야세계에크게유죠ᄒᆞ거니와동밍의범위를확쟝ᄒᆞᄂᆞᆫ것은우리를ᄒᆞᆫ큰화약고우에올녀안친것과ᄀᆞᆺ흠이분명ᄒᆞ며지금졍형으로ᄂᆞᆫ다만즁립위반ᄉ건으로도영국의참셥이업ᄂᆞᆫ것이우리가지금법국과션젼ᄒᆞ지아니ᄒᆞᄂᆞᆫ것을보아도알것이오일본이법국의즁립위반에ᄃᆡᄒᆞ야항샹항의를제출ᄒᆞᄂᆞᆫ것을보면영일동밍의범위가제한잇ᄂᆞᆫ것을ᄭᅢ닷게홀만ᄒᆞᆫ지라

그러ᄒᆞ나영일동밍이지금모양으로도좃치못ᄒᆞᆫ결과가업지아니ᄒᆞᆫ것이비록로국이여러ᄒᆡ를두고인도를위핍ᄒᆞ엿지마ᄂᆞᆫ근일에아부한국경에활동력을더홈은의심업시영일연합에ᄃᆡᄒᆞ야ᄃᆡ답홈이오무ᄉᆞᆷ죠약이던지영일동밍에더홀다경이면아모리의도업시영국에위험과척임만더홀ᄲᅮᆫ이로다

일본을위ᄒᆞ야영일동밍의범위를확쟝홈을찬죠ᄒᆞᄂᆞᆫ쟈들은영국을달니되일본측군으로인도방슈에협죠홈을말ᄒᆞ나글로ᄒᆞ야영국의독립권을침범ᄒᆞᄂᆞᆫᄃᆡᄃᆡᄒᆞ야샹당ᄒᆞᆫ보복이못되고그외에도그럿치아니ᄒᆞᆫᄭᅡ닭이만이잇ᄂᆞᆫ지라

영일동맹의범위를확쟝ᄒᆞ기를찬죠ᄒᆞᄂᆞᆫ각신문들은ᄯᅩᄒᆞᆫ말ᄒᆞ되로국이능히만쥬에셔젼쟁을ᄒᆞ야가면셔ᄒᆞᆫ편으로인도에셔젼쟁을이르킴이무란ᄒᆞ다ᄒᆞ엿스니만일그런계제가되면일본이영국을협죠홀군ᄉ가업게될터이오로국이인도에침범ᄒᆞ기를시쟉ᄒᆞ기젼에이젼징이긋ᄂᆞᆫ다고홀지라도일본이능히큰병력으로우리를협죠홀듯ᄒᆞ지아니ᄒᆞᆫ것이이젼쟁에일본이피폐ᄒᆞ야이젼쟁이긋나드ᄅᆡ도일본륙군이젼일셰력에회복ᄒᆞ랴면여러ᄒᆡ가되여야홀터이로다

우리가좀쥬져ᄒᆞ면셔말홀수단이ᄯᅩ잇ᄂᆞᆫ것이그것은일본을능히신임홀ᄭᅡ못홀ᄭᅡ홈이라한국에셔일본의실신ᄒᆞ고방쟈히ᄒᆞᄂᆞᆫ것을우리가쟈로말ᄒᆞ엿거니와져외너디물산의셰금은경ᄒᆞ게ᄒᆞ면셔양목과모직물품은다ᄇᆡᆨ분지십이나ᄇᆡᆨ분지십오의셰를밧쟈ᄂᆞᆫ법안을ᄂᆡᄂᆞᆫ것이립구ᄒᆞᄂᆞᆫ직물에ᄂᆞᆫ보호셰를밧ᄂᆞᆫ현힝죠약을일본이위반ᄒᆞᄂᆞᆫ것갓도다

이런힝위들이우리들로불신임ᄒᆞ게ᄒᆞ며만일다른닐이다죠케될지라다영국이그일본을위ᄒᆞᄂᆞᆫ각신문들의찬죠ᄒᆞᄂᆞᆫ것갓치영일동맹의범위를확쟝ᄒᆞᄂᆞᆫ것이적당홀ᄂᆞᆫ지우리들로의심이잇게만드ᄂᆞᆫ것이라ᄒᆞ노라

관보

뎨삼쳔륙십호 광무구년
이월십일일토요

셔임급ᄉ령

○면본관 운산면보사쥬사 유뎡대

이월팔일

○승셔판임관ᄉ등 외국어학교교관 진수

한셩공립소학교교원 김교희

이월구일

뎨삼쳔륙십일호 광무구년이월십삼일

셔임급ᄉ령

○면징계 젼덕원감리 유한익

이월구일

○의원면본관 비셔원승 신셩균 영션샤쥬사 홍종환

옥구감리셔쥬ᄉ 명인환

임비셔원승셔쥬임관륙등 졍삼품 김덕진

○임영션사쥬사셔판임관륙등 교방사쥬사 젼달홍

○임교방사쥬사셔판임관륙등 영릉령 황범수

○임영릉령셔판임관칠등 경릉참봉 리지호

○임경릉참봉셔판임관팔등 리수현

○면본관 젼라남도관찰사 김셰괴

○임옥구감리셔쥬ᄉ셔판임관륙등 셔괴면

이샹이월십일

○광무구년도예산표

학부소관 속

뎨구관 관립소학교 일만삼쳔사ᄇᆡᆨ이십이원

뎨일항 봉급 칠쳔구ᄇᆡᆨ이십원

뎨이항 쳥비 삼쳔구ᄇᆡᆨ원

뎨삼항 쳥사슈리비 사ᄇᆡᆨ원

뎨사항 잡급급잡비 일쳔이ᄇᆡᆨ이원

뎨십관 일어학교 칠쳔칠십사원

뎨일항 봉급 일쳔팔ᄇᆡᆨ원

뎨이항 쳥비 륙ᄇᆡᆨ팔십원

뎨삼항 교료칙구미비 이ᄇᆡᆨ원

뎨사항 쳥사슈리비 일ᄇᆡᆨ원

뎨오항 잡급급잡비 일ᄇᆡᆨ구십사원

뎨륙항 외국인제급 사쳔일ᄇᆡᆨ원 지화

뎨십일관 영어학교 일만일쳔일ᄇᆡᆨ십팔원

뎨일항 봉급 일쳔구ᄇᆡᆨ팔십원

뎨이항 쳥비 륙ᄇᆡᆨ팔십원

뎨삼항 교료칙구미비 이ᄇᆡᆨ원

뎨사항 쳥사슈리비 일ᄇᆡᆨ원

뎨오항 잡급과잡비 삼ᄇᆡᆨ삼십팔원

뎨륙항 외국인제급 칠쳔팔ᄇᆡᆨ이십원 지화

뎨십이관 법어학교 칠쳔사ᄇᆡᆨ십사원

뎨일항 봉급 이쳔이ᄇᆡᆨ팔십원

뎨이항 쳥비 륙ᄇᆡᆨ팔십원

뎨삼항 교료칙구미비 이ᄇᆡᆨ원

뎨사항 쳥사슈리비 일ᄇᆡᆨ원

뎨오항 잡급과잡비 일ᄇᆡᆨ구십사원

뎨륙항 외국인제급 삼쳔구ᄇᆡᆨ륙십원 지화

뎨십삼관 한어학교 삼쳔오ᄇᆡᆨ팔십사원

뎨일항 봉급 일쳔삼ᄇᆡᆨ팔십원

뎨이항 쳥비 사ᄇᆡᆨ원

뎨삼항 쳥사슈리비 오십원

뎨사항 잡급과잡비 일ᄇᆡᆨ구십사원

뎨오항 외국인제급 일쳔오ᄇᆡᆨ륙십원 지화

잡보

○부임불호 일공사가외부로공합ᄒᆞ기를주일공관참셔관하상긔씨가일간능뎡ᄒᆞᆫ다ᄒᆞ오니만일씨가부임하면불호의사가잇슬줄노뎨의가잇고ᄯᅩ현지에일공관에주지ᄒᆞᆫ관원들이능히시무홀터이니령지ᄒᆞ라ᄒᆞ엿더라

○녜무황침 영친왕부에셔궁ᄂᆡ부로수본ᄒᆞ기를본궁쟝도가무안항쟝항포에잇ᄂᆞᆫᄃᆡ일본인대ᄂᆡ참삼이가유대현이라ᄒᆞᄂᆞᆫ사람으로삼ᄇᆡᆨ셕작인을차츌ᄒᆞ야다른작인의작농을침쳑ᄒᆞ니일공관에면죠ᄒᆞ야횡침ᄒᆞᄂᆞᆫ뵈가업게ᄒᆞ라ᄒᆞ엿더라

○일제사진 졍부에셔각부에통쳡ᄒᆞ기를근일에졍부대신들이사진을뎡셩히ᄒᆞ야죠무가건졔홈이만호니자금이후로ᄂᆞᆫ실병과실고외에ᄂᆞᆫ일제히사진ᄒᆞ야수소강구ᄒᆞᆫ실의로입직대신이지의를봉승ᄒᆞ왓숩기양포ᄒᆞ노라ᄒᆞ엿더라

○경피사형 철산군슈ᄇᆡᆨ낙형씨가ᄂᆡ부로보고ᄒᆞ기를음력본월십ᄉ일ᄉ시에본군차련관에류주ᄒᆞᄂᆞᆫ일본병참ᄉ령관의조회를접준ᄒᆞᆫ즉본군송산리거ᄒᆞᄂᆞᆫ노학념이가양력십이월이십일일에송산뎡거장에셔철도지료를졀취ᄒᆞᆫ지라임의광고ᄒᆞᆫ즁률에죠ᄒᆞ야력일월이십일일오후ᄒᆞᆫ시에사형에쳐ᄒᆞ니관하인민은다시범치말게ᄒᆞ라ᄒᆞᆫ지라군슈가히병참소에젼왕ᄒᆞ야속사홀ᄉ로쟝황히담화ᄒᆞ엿스나마참ᄂᆡ사형을피ᄒᆞ엿다더라

○면간목발거 북쳥군슈됴길하씨가ᄂᆡ부로보고ᄒᆞ기를음력십이월십오일노브터십칠일ᄭᅡ지본군향쳥파우면사와밋읍남쪽오리허에류쥬ᄒᆞ든아병이몰수히리원으로향ᄒᆞ야철환ᄒᆞᄂᆞᆫᄃᆡ경ᄂᆡ셰운바면간목은낫낫치ᄯᅦ여버리고줄은것어가지고갓다ᄒᆞ엿더라

○사심피상 경긔관찰ᄉ 가외부로보고ᄒᆞ기를인천군보고니ᄅᆡ에본군읍하안산에일인이긔를세운ᄉᆞᄂᆞᆫ입의치보ᄒᆞ엿거니와지작일읍하학산리에ᄯᅩ홍긔를세우고나모를ᄡᅡ가세우고톡셔ᄒᆞ엿스되군용철도더라ᄒᆞᆫ지라일이피상ᄒᆞᆫ기로보고ᄒᆞ옵니다ᄒᆞ엿더라

○속빙션취 외부에셔을공관에죠회ᄒᆞ기를학부죠회니ᄅᆡ에한어교ᄉ와영어교ᄉ의속빙을즉금션취ᄒᆞ엿스니쳥컨대일ᄉ의게죠회ᄒᆞ라ᄒᆞᆫ등인을쥰ᄒᆞ야조회ᄒᆞ노라ᄒᆞ엿더라

광고

TELEGRAMS.

(FROM JAPAN PAPERS.)

AFFAIRS IN RUSSIA.

London, Feb. 6.

M. Saproff, Privy Councillor, has been appointed Chairman of the Administrative Reform Committee in Russia.

London, Feb. 6.

M. de Witte is steadily gaining influence with the Tsar.

London, Feb. 7.

The strike movement is spreading in all direction in Russia. It is increasing in Tiflis and Batoum (Caucasus), and along the Trans-Caucasian Railway sanguinary conflicts are taking place between the Cossacks and the revolutionary mob.

London, Feb. 7.

The agitation of Russian workmen is spreading to Siberia, and the situation is becoming serious. All telegrams to Europe have now been stopped.

The mutiny is reported in which three thousand police and reservists participated.

Berlin, Feb. 7.

Martial law has been proclaimed at Sosnowicz, Russian Poland: In Warsaw fresh collisions have occured between the people and the military.

Berlin, Feb. 7.

The Odessa University has been closed.

GENERAL NEWS.

Berlin, Feb. 7.

The German Crown Prince will shortly proceed on a pleasure tour to Florence, Italy.

Berlin, Feb. 7.

The Prussian Diet has adopted the Canal Bill, namely, the construction of the Rhine Hanover Canal, the first section of the great Middle Land Canal.

Berlin, Feb. 8.

The German Emperor and Empress are to leave Berlin on the 23rd March next for a trip in the Mediterranean.

Berlin, Feb. 5.

The miners in Belgium have now gone on strike

London, Feb. 6.

General Stoessel arrived at Colombo to-day. He emphatically protests against the criticism that the capitulation of Port Arthur was untimely.

Berlin, Eeb. 8.

Austria has rescinded the commercial treaty with Servia.

It really seems necessary to take all Japanese announcements *cum grano salis*. The world has been informed that the Emperor had consented to a considerable reduction of the Korean army. It now transpires that this is not the case and that, with the exception of the dismissal of few undesirables, the army will remain as before.

Says an exchange:—"The snail's sense of smell has been located in the horns by some observers, but authorities quite as good have regarded this conclusion as incorrect. M. Yong, who has been making experiments to settle the matter, now claims to have proven that the snail's nose is distributed over the entire body." Prize-fighting is evident-not unknown in Snail-dom.

THE ROUBLE IN MANCHURIA

FROM THE CHEFOO DAILY NEWS.

Newchwang, January 16th.

As intimated in former letters, the value of the rouble here has remained stable, and is so still, in defiance of the most unfavorable conditions. In spite of Russian reverses here, the rouble is in as great demand as ever, and an extensive rouble business was carried on locally the first month after the Russian evacuation.

The attention of the Japanese was early attracted by the marked predilection which the Chinese had for the rouble, and prohibitive measures were applied to prevent its circulation. This had no effect further than to cause the wide-spread rouble business to be transacted with the greatest secrecy. Through numerous spies, both disguised Japanese and Chinese, who infested the town, this was discovered and a rigorous investigation ensued. This inquiry seriously affected but a very few persons. In these cases all roubles found were confiscated, never to be returned to the owners. At the same time all inns were thoroughly searched every night, and innocent travellers from the north who happened to have stray Russian coins about them were decried as pro-Russians, shamefully maltreated, and subsequently deprived of their effects.

Now-a-days, since the Chinese jeer at the Japanese over the Russian occupation of Mouken, the invaders have become more savage and relentless, and decapitation is often the punishment which follows the discovery of a rouble on the person of a Chinaman. Three were ruthlessly beheaded recently. No one now dares to mention the word "rouble," and the presumption would be that it has fallen into oblivion. The initiated, however, know that under the calm surface, rouble transactions are still in vogue, though on a considerably diminished scale.

THE CASE OF DU SENG TAI.

On the allegation that he had sold vehicles, grain and cattle to the Russians during their *regime* here, all of which was correct enough, the manager of this firm was arrested by the Japanese, cruelly lashed, and subsequently subjected to further torture. He was strung up and his thumbs pulled out of their sockets in order to extort a confession of guilt, upon which his persecutors might fall back as an excuse for their barbarous acts. The firm purchased the liberty of its manager for five thousand taels and went bankrupt on the strength of it. Not content with what had already been done to the unfortunate man, his cue was cut off before he was liberated.

Of late it appears that the Japanese are making a business of accusing merchants in good standing of entertaining pro-Russian sentiments, of having shipped again to Port Arthur, of sending merchandise to Moukden via Hsiumintun, of smelting Japanese yen into syce, of transacting business in roubles, etc., etc.; without the slightest reason they have imprisoned managers of Chinese business houses and overhauled their books, partly for appearance sake and partly to ascertain the nature of their dealings with the Russo-Chinese Bank. Luckily, all clients of that bank have had the prudence to efface all record of their dealings with it, long before this.

The charge is made, and it seems to be a conclusion easily arrived at, that it is one of the ways the Japanese have of extorting money, as they are said to be very susceptible to the attractions of the dollar.

Yu Sheng Chang, Yi Teng Heng, Tien Ho Ying, Ho Sheng Tung, Hui Chuen Heng, and a number of others have all been imprisoned for reasons that the Japanese fail to formulate when interrogated. These men freely give their version of the unfortunate incidents, though perhaps their statements should be accepted with some reservation, their unlimited contempt for the Japanese possibly inclining them to exaggeration.

Yu Sheng Chang was seized twice. The first time eight thousand taels was paid for his liberty. The second time twelve thousand taels was surrendered. The rest of them have paid more or less dearly for their freedom. In merchant circles the Japanese *regime* is a reign of terror. No one is safe for a moment. The consequence is that a number have fled from here, especially merchants having agencies in the north. Those who have done an extensive business with the Russians in the north are pounced upon here and punished for it. It would seem from this that Moukden and the other northern centres must be filled with Japanese spies.

The light in which the Chinese view the dominating influence in southern Manchuria is always interesting, as the Chinese have so much at stake. From my investigations the tide of sympathy for the Japanese, if there was any, has changed long ago. The Chinese now speak in the highest terms of the Russians, particularly the merchant class —and the merchant class in the backbone of Chinese influence. They say that the friendship between the Chinese and the Russians has been and is ideal. Rich and poor apparently long for the day when the Russian flag may again wave over the country, proclaiming a new era and the downfall of the infamous Japanese.

AN EFFECT OF THE WAR.

The following, which we take from the annual report of the usually prosperous Japan Brewery Company, indicates that industries in Japan are already being adversely affected by the war. The greatest slump usually comes *after* the war and this probably accounts for the recommendation of the directors that the reserve be increased by the large sum of Y60,000.

The report says:—

From the 1st January, 1905, the Government has raised the Excise Tax on Beer, and the Income and Business Taxes; the Import Duty on Malt and Hops is doubled, and the Duties on other brewing materials are largely increased.

Competition has become keener than before, probably caused by over-production and the decrease in consumption.

All these factors have had the careful consideration of your Directors, and as the outlook at present is not encouraging, they cannot recommend a Dividend. They think it will be for the best interest of Shareholders to place the sum of yen 60,000 to Reserve Fund, and and carry forward the balance of yen 478,187. If this is done, the Reserve Fund will amount to yen 170,000.

THE SHAHO.

Little of interest has come to hand from this quarter. A Tokio telegram of the 11th instant represents the Russians as being busily engaged in entrenching themselves in front of the Japanese positions at Heikentai Chentanpan and Litajentun—that is to say, South of the Hun River and facing the Japanese left wing.

This corresponds with the Russian version which we publish in another column but does not agree with the previous official statement issued by the Japanese to the effect that the Russians had been driven back over the Hun ho.

In the centre the Russians are reported to be shelling the Japanese positions south of the Shaho and we also hear of infantry attacks, all of which have, according to Japanese reports, been repulsed.

The net result of the operations, so far, seems to be that the Russians have gained a footing on the left bank of the Hun Reiver.

LONG SIEGES.

Among modern sieges that of Sevastopol, 1854-55, is interesting, inasmuch as the besieged were Russians. Sevastopol and Port Arthur are seaports. When the former was invested the Russians blocked the harbor with sunken battleships. When the evacuation took place they sank all of their remaining ships. The siege of Sevastopol lasted 349 days, during which the besteged were heavily reinfored.

The siege of Port Arthur has been one of the longest in modern warfare, but by no means the longest. The longest was that of Richmond in the American Civil war. It lasted for 1,485 davs. General Gordon held out for 300 days in Khartoum. Fifteen thousand men held the fortress of Kars during the Crimean war for 163 days against a force of 50,000, and then only surrendered through hunger. In the Franco-German war Paris was besieged for 131 days, Belfort for 105 days and Metz for 70 days. The sieges of Ladysmith, Kimberly and Mafeking, in the South African war lasted 120, 123 and 261 days, respectively.

A BASIS FOR SETTLEMENT.

Japan can never hope to drive Russia out of Munchuria, or to force her way to the Amur, says a home paper. Russia cannot hope within our generation to recover the Liaotung peninsula or Korea. *Uti possidetis* seems a practicable basis of an ultimate settlement. There is a settlement which is far from improbable, and which would doubtless be the best for human civilisation. It is one which the European Powers would fiercely resent and oppose—which at any rate would rouse the wrath and pride of Germany and of Britain, though it should ultimately coincide with all their true interests. It is a settlement which the parties could make for themselves at once without any foreign interference, which they could themselves force Europe and America to recognise as a fact. That is, a confederation of Russia, Japan and China, with their respective tributaries and dependencies, to treat as their common State system and sphere of influence the whole of North-Eastern Asia—say North of the Tropic of Cancer, or latitude 23 deg. and East of longitude 100 deg.—that is practically, China, Mongolia, Manchuria, Korea, Siberia, Japan, and the parts of the Pacific Ocean adjoining their coasts,

---

The Korea Daily News.

Issued at 5 P. M. daily except Sundays.

Rate of Subscription:—
Per Year,............Yen 25.
Per Quarter,..........Yen 7.
Per Month,..........Yen 2.50.

Postage in Korea not charged extra.
Postage abroad charged extra.

Advertisements, 50 sen per day for 1 inch or less.
5 yen per month per inch.
50 yen per year per inch.

All communications to
E. T. BETHELL,
Editor and Publisher,
Pak-tong, Seoul.

A CANDID JAPANESE.

Mr. Jihei Hashiguchi contributes the following article to the New York "World":—

In an address delivered on the departure of German troops for China during the Boxer war Kaiser Wilhelm said that that was the beginning of a long war between the East and the West. This statement is very suggestive of the possibility of a racial feud.

For a century England fought the Hindoos and occupied India, France fought the Chinese and occupied Cochin-China, and, again, England occupied Hongkong. The world began to think that there was a vast unoccupied territory in Asia which was at the mercy of Europe, regardless of the fact that there are 400,000,000 of Chinese, 200,000,000 of Hindoos and other Asiatics in occupancy who would outnumber the Europeans more than two to one.

Apparently the Asiatics have been powerless, and the Europeans, taking advantage of their weakness, have spat on them as if they were dogs, butchered them as if they were cattle and deprived them of the fatherland as if they were predestined to be disinherited.

But the Asiatics have senses just as the Europeans. If you love them they will reciprocate love; if you hate them they will resent hatred; if you treat them as gentlemen they will treat you as gentlemen; if you "Hello, John!" them they will "Hello, John!" you. The insults inflicted upon them by the Europeans for a hundred years are indelibly printed upon their memory, so that their nature is hardened against all Europeans, good as well as bad. The Boxer war of 1900, while it was an outrageous act on the part of the Boxers, was but an expression of their revengeful spirit.

Do you say that this spirit of revenge is immoral, that it is unchristian? But why should the Asiatics listen to sermons by their enemies who are trying to destroy them?

The Boxer war was a failure because the time was not yet come, not because the Chinese are foredoomed to fall under the blows of the Europeans. The Boxer war has indeed apprised the Chinese that they are in a helpless state. Already there are signs that reform is steadfastly being carried on. The reorganization of the Chinese army under Japanese supervision started some years ago, and the Chinese students graduated from the War College of Tokio will be instrumental in bringing to modernity the land of their fathers.

The contention that the Chinese are different from the Japanese in military prowess is untrue. The history of China abounds in stories of heroism. These very stories, which have been studied by the Japanese youth for years, have inculcated in the minds of the islanders the warrior virtues.

Heroes do not appear in peace. It was the French Revolution that produced Napoleon. China has had many Napoleons in the past: China will have Napoleons in future if she is involved in a universal war.

Japan is fighting Russia, apparently to preserve her own as well as Korea's integrity. But she is bound to protect not only Korea but also China and other Asiatic nations. Nay, without having her neighbors strong Japan cannot look for her own national greatness.

When a king rules a domain, says one,
Shall he guard and defend the neighbors?
Korea and China once without protection.
The land of ours may not be safe.

It is for Japan's interest that she reinvigorate her neighbors. For a half century prominent men of these countries have been planning an alliance. This has led to the formation by the late Hon. Mr. Konoe, ex-Speaker of the Upper House of the Japanese Diet, of "The East Asiatic Association of Those Who Use the Same Letters," or the "Pan-Mongolian Alliance." This alliance has not gained political influence, but its future is promising.

For one from the East to tell Westerners that this protagonists are bound to antagonize them is apparently strange. But truth must be told. I prophesy that this Pan-Mongolian-Pan-Caucasian struggle for supremacy will become certain in the near future, when the former of the two antagonists have gathered up their strength. Woe to them that provoke the ill-feeling of the Mongolians!

Is there, then, no means of arbitrating some of the differences between the two opposing parties whereby the atrocities of wars can be mitigated? I say Yes and No. For any means of arbitration which might be urged, all depend for their practicability upon the disposition of the parties involved.

First of these means is the recognition of the social as well as political equality.

Second, wider knowledge of the affairs of each other through liberal intercourse.

Third, intermarriage between the parties and obliteration of racial distinctions.

ANOTHER CRITIC.

Life is not without its humourous side. One of our greatest joys is when, on the arrival of the mail from Japan we unfold the pages of a certain unmentionable journal and see what a certain unspeakable editor has to say about us. Unexpectedness adds piquancy to pleasure and therefore, after having been told that were were beneath contempt and "Scurrilous," it is with unalloyed joy that we find our unworthy selves from time to time the subject of "boosk" in the newspaper which shall be nameless.

The last one however, does not entirely satisfy us. It is not written by the unspeakable editor but by "Yours obediently, Observer." "Observer" says:—

As far as my experience in Korea goes, there are few or no newspaper writers who have the slightest knowledge of things Korean, and I doubt that anyone who criticises Japanese doings in Korea would even attempt to lay a claim to a shadow of honesty and justice as to what he imparts to the public abroad on the subject. The only source of information, for critics abroad, that I could discover while in Korea, is the *Korea Daily News*, a tiny sheet, whose editor is either absolutely ignorant of conditions in Korea, or wilfully disfigures conditions there, for reasons best known to himself. Any critic of average common sense, who knows anything about the Nagamori scheme could not help but compare it with what British enterprise has actually accomplished in Egypt on a larger scale.

It is not very long ago that we had the pleasure of meeting "Observer," and endeavoured to convert him to saner views and we are sorry to find that our eloquence had no effect on him and that he trotting out the same old fallacies.

England introduced Capital into Egypt and employed, native labour: Japan has no capital and seeks to introduce labor into Korea. There is no parallel at all.

We put this in italics as our conversation to the same effect seems to have slipped "Observer's" memory.

The remaining part of the letter is to the effect that Japan's help would be of immense advantage to Korea. That may be—some day—or it may not. Anyhow we shall all have an opportunity of judging when the Japanese adviser to the Finance Department gets back here with his three millon paper dollar loan. We remember asking "Observer" (at the time it was not known that loan was to be in "paper") how it was that Japan could afford to borrow at eight per cent and lend at six per cent. An answer to this would still help to enlighten our ignorance.

LORDS OF THE MAIN.

Mr. Harold G. Parsons, in a recent number of "Blackwood's," traces the history of the ancient English pretension that the narrow seas were a British possession. When Philip of Spain, he says, came to England to marry Mary, his hundred and sixty ships were met in the Channel by Lord High Admiral Effinghan with his twenty-eight. Effingham fired a shotted gun at the Spaniard, and the Spaniard dutifully struck his topsails and the English returned the salute. Selden took the extreme form of arguing that "Great Britain stands confined by the shores of other lands." But it would seem that there were difficulties in carrying out the Admiralty order of 1731, by which all commanders were to compel foreign ships to "strike their topsails and take in their flag within His Majesties seas, which extend to Cape Finisterre." In 1769 a zealous commander acted on this order with regard to a French frigate, and diplomatic complications ensued. Precedents were looked into, but were found to be few and doubtful. On the advice of Sir Henry Hawke, the zealous captain was sent to the West Indies. The French Government were told that he would be abroad for three years, and that it would not be possible to inquire into the case till his return home. The French did not want a war at the time and so the incident was closed. Apparently the theoretical dominion of the sea in its extremest form was dropped after this incident.

The Korea Daily News.

VOL. II, . TUESDAY, FEBRUARY 14, 1905. No. 34

HONGKONG & SHANGHAI BANKING CORPORATION.

Paid-up Capital..... ....$10,000,000
Reserve Fund:—Sterling Reserve... 10,000,000
Silver Reserve..... 7,000,000

27,000,000
Reserve Liability of Proprietors... 10,000,000

HEAD OFFICE, HONGKONG.

London Bankers, London and County Banking Company Limited.

Branches and Agencies,

London.

Amoy,.	Hankow	Penang,
Bangkok,	Hiogo,	Rangoon,
Batavia,	Iloilo,	Saigon,
Bombay,	Lyons,	San Francisco,
Calcutta,	Manila,	Singapore,
olombo,	Nagasaki,	Sourabaya,
Foochow,	New York,	Tientsin,
Hamburg,	Peking,	Yokohama,

Credits granted on approved Securities, and every description of Banking and Exchange business transacted.

Drafts granted on London and the chief Commercial places in Europe, India, Australia, America, China and Japan.

HOLME RINGER & CO., AGENTS, CHEMULPO.

HOKURKU DOBOKU KAISHA.

Branch office in Chong Dong, Seoul.

Japanese telephone No. 165

CONTRACT DEPARTMENT.

We can contract to build any building or construction.

MERCHANDISE DEPARTMENT.

We can provide any building material. We have just contracted to build the new Belgian Legation.

E. MEYER & CO.

Chemulpo.

SOLE AGENTS IN KOREA FOR.

A. T. Morse, Sons & Co.'s

"Fresco" Distemper

In all colours ready for use on walls, Ceilings etc.

and

AVENARIUS CARBOLINEUM

A wood-preserving and antiseptic oil preparation

Against decay, dry-rot, fungus and wood-destroying insects.

A large supply always in stock.
Prices upon application.

E. MEYER & Co.,
Chemulpo.

CHARTERED BANK OF INDIA AUSTRALIA & CHINA.

INCORPORATED BY ROYAL CHARTER 1853

HEAD OFFICES.—LONDON.

Paid-up Capital £800,000
Reserve Liability of Shareholders 800,000
Reserve Fund 800,000

Drafts granted upon all the principal places in the world and every description of Exchange and banking business transacted.

E. MEYER & Co., Agents,
Chemulpo.

MITSU BISHI DOCKYARD & ENGINE WORKS,

NAGASAKI.

CODE WORD, "DOCK."

A 1, A. B. C., and Engineering Codes used.

DOCK No. 1 (at Tategami).

Extreme Length.............523 feet
Length on blocks .... 513 ,,
Width of Entrance on Top......89 ,,
,, ,, Bottom....77 ,,
Water on Blocks at Spring Tide 26½ ,,

DOCK No. 2 (Mukaijima).

Extreme Length.............371 feet
Length on Blocks...........360 ,,
Width of Entrance on Top......66 ,,
,, ,, Bottom 53 ,,
Water on Blocks at Spring Tide 22 ,,

PATENT SLIP (at Kosuge).

Can take vessels up to 1,000 tons gross.

THE WORKS are well equipped with the LATEST IMPROVEMENTS, and can execute any kind of work in SHIPBUILDING and MARINE ENGINEERING, as well as in REPAIRING of SHIPS.

The COMPANY'S new powerful steamer OURA-MARU (712 tons, 700 I.H.P.), specially built for SALVAGE PURPOSES, and equipped with necessary gear, is always READY at SHORT NOTICE.

THE METHODIST PUBLISHING HOUSE,

Little West Gate, Seoul.

JOB PRINTING, TYPEWRITER PAPER
CARBON PAPER, VISITING-CARDS
STATIONERY, BOOK BINDING
BOOK PUBLISHERS
AMERICAN SCHOOL BOOKS
SPENCERIAN COPY BOOKS
PEN CARBON LETTER AND BILL BOOKS

S. A. BECK, Manager.

DAI-ICHI GINKO.

LIMITED.

(Formerly the First National Bank)

ESTABLISHED 1873

INCORPORATED UNDER PRESENT LAW 1896

Capital - - - - - - - - - Yen 5,000,000
Reserve Fund - . - - - 1,500,000

HEAD OFFICE:—TOKIO.

President: Baron SHIBUSAWA.

BRANCHES AND CORRESPONDENTS

In the Principal Cities and Towns of Japan.

Interest Allowed on

Fixed deposits 1 year - - - 6½ per cent
" " 6 months - - - 6 per cent

Special current accounts 1½ sen daily per Y 100
General " " 1 " " " 100

M. TANAKA,
Manager, Chemulpo.

SINGER SEWING MACHINES

씽거ᄌᆞ봉침

SOLE AGENTS FOR KOREA

젼매쇼

HOLME RINGER & CO.

Chemulpo.

제물포 함릉거양힝

KAMEYA & CO.

GENERAL STOREKEEPERS

Chinkokai - - Seoul

(*Established 1895, Tokyo*)

Confectionery, Hams, Canned Goods, Cutlery, Hirano & Tansan Water. Provisions, Gents, Furnishing goods, Toilet Articles, Travelling Bags, Tobacco, Cigars & Cigarettes Kitchen Utensils. Coffee, Biscuits

Fresh Goods always kept in Stock.

Prices Moderate

Please come and inspect our goods.

NIPPON YUSEN KAISHA.

JAPANESE MAIL STEAMSHIP CO.

UNDER MAIL CONTRACT WITH THE IMPERIAL JAPANESE GOVERNMENT.

European Line

Regular Fortnightly Service between Yokohama Kobe, Moji, Shanghai, Hongkong, Singapore, Penang Colombo, Port Said, Marseilles, London and Antwerp

American Line

Regular Fortnightly Service between Hongkong and Seattle, calling at Shanghai, Moji, Kobe, Yokohama an Victoria, B. C.

Australian Line

Regular weekly Service between Japan Ports and Australia, calling at Hongkong and Manila.

(Above Three Lines Suspended until further notice).

Shanghai Line

Weekly Service between Shanghai and Japan Port

Korea Line

Service Kobe, Moji, Nagasaki, Fusan Chemulpo Chefoo, Taku.

S. S. Babelsberg, 2181 tons.

Service Kobe, Moji, Fusan, Chemulpo, Chinnamp

S. S. ARGO, S. S. Ohio.

BORDEN'S CONDENSED MILK CO.

New York, U. S. A.

ALWAYS IN STOCK

Eagle Brand Condensed Milk.

Gold Seal Condensed Milk.

Peerless (Family) Evaporated Cream.

Borden's Malted Milk.

E. MEYER & CO.
Chemulpo Korea,
Sole Agents.

ROYAL INSURANCE COMPANY,

Funds exceed £10,000,000

FIRF

AT CURRENT RATES

LIFE

REDUCED PREMIUM.

HOLME RINGER & Co.,
Agents, Chemulpo

廣
KWANG ◎ C'HANG
昌

BENNETT & CO.

Merchants

Chemulpo.

Offices opposite the Imperial Japanese Post and Telegraph Office Chemulpo.

Telephone Number 201.

大韓每日申報
대한미일신보

(뎨이권삼십오호)　(목요일)　일쳔구빅오년이월십륙일

본사고빅

이신보는영어와한어로셔거리
일츌판ᄒᆞ옵

신문가
한쟝 엽두돈오푼
일삭표 엽두량닷돈
우표가디삭닷돈
다밧돈으로밧ᄉᆞᆸ

광고료는
귀한의쟝단과ᄌᆞ형의다쇼로즁
강ᄒᆞ퇴렴가로밧을터이오며오
흰지아녀대한사람마다다이신
문을보실터이니광고내시기를
원ᄒᆞ시는이들은우리신문사에
와셔편야ᄒᆞ심을희망ᄒᆞᄋᆞᆸ

○발힝소 박동대한미일신보
사변이하교옵쇄젼영국인셜필
림젼자리오
사쟝 영국인 (빅셜)

평양 디리졈
○평양효동사는권미보씨로우
리신문관미디리인을뤼졍ᄒᆞ엿
시스오니평양에계신구람코져ᄒᆞ
시는 쳠군ᄌᆞ는히디리졈에왕
림ᄒᆞ와편의ᄒᆞ시ᄋᆞᆸ

사고

○우리대한미일신보의목뎍은
대한의안녕질셔에관한모든뎨
목에디ᄒᆞ야논공평ᄒᆞᆫ변론을주
쟝ᄒᆞᆷ이라우리통신원의탐보ᄒᆞᆫ
신문보시논쳠군ᄌᆞ의계ᄒᆞ상보
도ᄒᆞ리며횐지를귀셔ᄒᆞ며주시
논이논셩명과반디를졍이붓치
시기를희망ᄒᆞ오니이거슨신문
샹에긔졔ᄒᆞ란ᄂᆞᆫ거시아니오다
만극히신용ᄒᆞ논즁거를숨고자
ᄒᆞᆷ이라귀자논아모귀셔연지귀
지ᄒᆞᆷ을뫼각ᄒᆞ논권리논가졋스
나뫼각ᄒᆞ논리유를말ᄒᆞᆯ터이오
며공중괭화를문란케ᄒᆞ논듯ᄒᆞᆫ
귀셔논의례히밧지안켓ᄉᆞᆸ나이
다

●본사셜시이리로신문을미양
우례로분젼ᄒᆞ와례젼부의임의
로젼ᄒᆞ논듯스로번곳에논흑늣게
젼ᄒᆞ기도ᄒᆞ며흑편칠게슬혼일
에젼ᄒᆞ기도ᄒᆞ며흑아니젼ᄒᆞ논
곳도잇다ᄒᆞ와우리신문을슈탕
ᄒᆞ야구람ᄒᆞ시논 쳠군ᄌᆞ의게탕
티ᄒᆞ야미우미안ᄒᆞ옵기로지금
은본젼인을두고미일즁이젼
ᄒᆞ며아니젼ᄒᆞ거나늣게거나ᄒᆞᆫ
폐가업도록ᄒᆞ란ᄒᆞ오니혹아니
젼ᄒᆞ거논흑늣게젼ᄒᆞ거나ᄒᆞᆫ일
이잇스면본사로통긔ᄒᆞ여주심
을희망ᄒᆞᄋᆞᆸ

잡보

○디졍계판 일작에동군번원
에셔원쥬디챵평리민회와셔일
진회원사룹명이디졍계관ᄒᆞ엿
논디리씨의말이원쥬에일진회
원이빅며명이쟝회ᄒᆞ야연셜ᄒᆞᆫ다
ᄒᆞ기로병뎡이분티를광복으로
파견ᄒᆞ야방청케ᄒᆞ엿더니회보
ᄒᆞ되회원연셜니에 대황뎨폐
하시나우리회원이나국등지신
은일반이노ᄌᆞ유권도일반이라
ᄒᆞ엿다ᄒᆞ기로너가회원의두령
을초리ᄒᆞ야무ᄉᆞ기를 대황뎨폐
하도국등지신이라ᄒᆞ엿다니무
ᄉᆞᆷ외람ᄒᆞᆫ말이뇨ᄒᆞᆫ즉회쟝의말
이죄를아노라ᄒᆞᄋᆞᆸ기히회쟝의
복죄ᄒᆞᆫ즁거표와방쳥인쟝원일
의즁거표를나쟝ᄒᆞ며밧은후에
힝차맛케본도지관소로월송ᄒᆞ
ᄒᆞ엿고회원의어평지존ᄒᆞᆫ말을
ᄒᆞᆫ것은모든병뎡과관속비가다
즁거라ᄒᆞ고회원젼셩환씨의말
은그바에나가원쥬에하거ᄒᆞ야
목격ᄒᆞ엿스니몽겨ᄒᆞᆫ티로이사
말ᄒᆞ오리다그바원쥬회쟝이ᄒᆞ야
대강평을연셜ᄒᆞᆫ후에연숔ᄒᆞ야
말ᄒᆞ기를우리도 대황뎨폐하
의국등지신이라고ᄒᆞ엿논티원
쥬창평의말은 대황뎨 폐하도
국등지신이라ᄒᆞ엿다니 대황
뎨폐하의ᄒᆞᆫ(의)로도를(도)로번쟉
ᄒᆞ야죄를회원의게돌니논거시
오즁거표로말ᄒᆞ면당시참평으
로다수ᄒᆞᆫ병뎡을징총ᄒᆞ야좌우
에나렬ᄒᆞ고일외라고소리를질
으며익륵으로즁거표를자귀의
손으로쓰고도쟝은병뎡으로ᄒᆞ
여곰몽을슈탐ᄒᆞ야나쟝ᄒᆞ엿손
즉이것을엇지즁거라ᄒᆞ오릿가
샹회원의벌금벌이퓌폼령이
빅며건을륵탈ᄒᆞ엿고당하에모
든관쇽비가즁거라고ᄒᆞ니관쇽
을빈말ᄒᆞ오면회원의방쳥의관
가위로ᄒᆞᆫ지가ᄒᆞ고방쳥평의편
을위ᄒᆞ야소리를ᄒᆞᆫ티방쳥관
가거슈되ᄒᆞ옵고즁가슈즁ᄒᆞᆫ
니잇스니ᄒᆞᆯ슈업ᄂᆞᆫ듯ᄒᆞ외다ᄒᆞ엿
더라

○샹소봉환 한셩졔판소쥬사
리샹쳔씨가사직샹소ᄒᆞ엿더니
봉환이되엿더라

○죵즁강연 시위련디에서
쥬ᄒᆞ고쟈쳐방곽과슈ᄒᆞᆫ도빅영
을볼시ᄒᆞ고쟈쟝관의계과숑ᄒᆞ
는죵즁도강영ᄒᆞ엿다더라

○의계상납 일연이나쟝원과
교셔ᄒᆞ기를각뎨뎨관도등일인이
의계하가ᄒᆞ야경교뎨ᄒᆞ엿면도세논
의레히샹납ᄒᆞ고관관ᄒᆞ야마ᄒᆞ논
지라뎨칙쟝명셰기령영진셰 가
방금샹지ᄒᆞ논즁이라더라

○호소졍평 젼나부대신리용
티세가무ᄉᆞ일을인ᄒᆞ야뎡소를
샹셔오관ᄒᆞ야음을쥬졍ᄒᆞ야교쥬
지아니ᄒᆞ흥이안셰가경무청에져
ᄒᆞ엿더니경무셩에서그반편이
츌금ᄒᆞ엿다더라

○샹여우금 평무청에셔빈렵
ᄒᆞ야변쇼졍중에일심반에계되
이샹명을졍ᄒᆞ논조ᄒᆞ야잇스면젼이
만광을샹여ᄒᆞ논즁이라ᄒᆞ엿더니사
오명잡은주가우등이라경무청
에셔젼수젼량을시샹ᄒᆞ엿더라

○영빅여시 경샹남도관찰스
셩규와운씨는셰샹이다텩빅ᄒᆞ다
칭ᄒᆞ더니금번관찰소로관하잡
류에외칙으로흔칙ᄒᆞ야리도
(뎨가와요젼가계)요샹관량을
득ᄒᆞ엿다더라

○대관원납 셩니지샹들이각
기고자셰를밧아가면셰원납으로
부ᄒᆞ와원납ᄒᆞ기로관리지방노
령ᄒᆞ엿다더라

○뎨약영급 일작에졍부에셔
금번차관ᄒᆞ논금액과국공셰금
을탁지부에져쳐ᄒᆞ논것을낫낫
치계관일은ᄒᆞ얏더니ᄒᆞ기로계약
을셩립ᄒᆞ엿다더라

○셰관의구 즁노에셔일본샹
민이셰관젼ᄒᆞ논물을평무ᄉᆞ신민
츄에셔가일본셔평수와교셩ᄒᆞ야
게ᄒᆞ엿다더니도로어졉ᄒᆞ면
을버ᄒᆞ노흔지라샹민들이실원ᄒᆞ
이논셩문을부에호소ᄒᆞ엿다더라

○청원호소 을샨계ᄒᆞ논삼셰
가뎐핑무면원홈안편중셔셔원들
에일본지관부에셔민ᄒᆞ엿다논말
은이셩과제ᄒᆞ여가니와셰편
탐문ᄒᆞᆫ즉아직ᄒᆞ논지안이ᄒᆞᆫ고쟝
이츈명ᄒᆞ엿다더라

○도로죠셩 남도로오논샤룸
의편의를ᄒᆞ논듯ᄒᆞ고일본셩공지

메젼졍이메져ᄒᆞ야볏쥬데도에
사봉졍히ᄒᆞ고조졍을위탕휴ᄒᆞ논
페가업ᄂᆞ니야셰도론에일힝윈
이죠젼이라ᄒᆞ엿다라

론셜

일로젼징

○일본젼셔가지하젼징의소문을
셧샹의벌로엽ᄂᆞᆫ듯ᄒᆞ나방편에
서셔로젼쟁을만히셜혀ᄒᆞ고지이
일본젼의소문을드른즉로국군
의수샹은일만명이오일본군의
수샹은칠천명이라ᄒᆞ며피로젼이
일셔지광군의터워가셔극진파
ᄒᆞ고비록로군이일본군의젹압ᄒᆞ듯

UNION INSURANCE SOCIETY OF CANTON.

Head office Hongkong.
Marine risks underwritten at current rates

Agents in Chemulpo,
E. MEYER & Co.

COMPAGNIE DES MESSAGERIES MARITIMES.

Fortnightly Direct Service.

For Marseilles
via Ports.
Sailing from Yokohama
Calling at Kobe,
Shanghai, Hongkong, Saigon, Singapore,
Colombo, Djibouti, Suez, Port Said
and Marseilles.

For particulars apply to
HOLME RINGER & CO.,
Chemulpo.

HAYASHIDA & CO.,

16 MYENG DONG, CHIN KO KAI, SEOUL.
BRANCH OFFICE AT CHEMULPO.

Money changers, Coal and Wood Merchants, Express Agents.

We are agents for the Pyeng-yang Coal Company and the Karazu Coal Company of Japan. We have the best quality of both anthracite and bituminous coal, and prompt execution of orders is our speciality. Firewood of all kinds kept in stock. Full weight guaranteed. Money of all denominations exchanged at current rates. Parcels received for all parts.

CHINA MUTUAL LIFE INS. OC.

Most favourable terms to policy holders.

Benefit system unsurpassed.

HOLME RINGER & Co.
Agents, Chemulpo.

C. P. R.

CANADIAN PACIFIC RAILWAY COMPANY'S ROYAL MAIL STEAMSHIP LINE.

THE FAST ROUTE BETWEEN CHINA, JAPAN, AND EUROPE VIA CANADA AND THE UNITED STATES.

Route from Hongkong via Shanghai, Nagasaki (Inland Sea of Japan) Kobe, Yokohama, Victoria and Vancouver.

Twin Screw Empress Steamship—6,000 Tons—Speed 19 knots.

PROPOSED SAILING FROM YOKOHAMA.
R. M. S. Empress of India.
R. M. S. Empress of Japan.
R. M. S. Empress of China.
R. M. S. Athenian.
R. M. S. Tartar.

Special reduction (first class only) granted to members of the Military, Naval, Diplomatic and Civil services and to Missionaries.

Passengers have choice of ten routes across the Continent of America and have privilege of travelling by any Atlantic Steamship Line.

Round the World passage tickets in connection with the P. and O. S. N., North German Lloyd and Messageries Co.'s **£125.**

All rates payable at current rate of exchange.

For further information, Tickets, Guide Books, etc., apply to

HOLME, RINGER & CO., AGENTS,
Chemulpo.

Grand Hotel

(Formerly the Station Hotel)

Near the Railway Terminus, West Gate Seoul.

The Best Hotel in Korea
Handsome new Building.
Fine Airy Rooms
Excellent Cuisine.
Terms Moderate.
Special terms to Missionaries
and to permanent boarders.

Electric cars within 2 minutes' walk.

W. H. EMBERLEY.
Proprieto

EVERY FACILITY.

In connection with Life Assurance Business is afforded by

The Standard Life Assurance Co.,

One of the largest and wealthiest of the Provident Institutions of the United Kingdom. Forms of Application and all information will be promptly afforded on application.

10 CENTS A DAY.

Not a very large expenditure is it? But it is sufficient to secure for a man of 30 a policy with the STANDARD LIFE OFFICE for

$1323.

For all particulars of rates, etc., apply to

Holme, Ringer & Co.,
Agents, Chemulpo.

THE NEW YORK LIFE INSURANCE COMPANY.

Have you ever been declined by any Company?

Are you engaged in a specially hazardous occupation?

Have you heard of the New York Life Insurance Company's New Classifications for this class of Risks?

If not, send your date of birth, occupation and particulars of rejection, if any to

E. MEYER & Co.,
Agents, Chemulpo.

MITSUIBUSSAN KAIS.

(MITSUI & Co.)

MITSUI GINKO.

(MITSUI BANK.)

The Bank is owned by the members of the Mitsui Family, who, as partners, assume an unlimited responsibility for all liabilities of the Bank:—

Capital........................Yen 5,000,000
Reserve Fund................... " 5,600,000

HEAD OFFICE, TOKYO.
LONDON OFFICE, 34 LIME ST., E. C.

BRANCHES AND AGENCIES:—
New York, San Francisco, Hamburg, Bombay, Singapore, Manila, Hongkong, Amoy, Chefoo, Tientsin.

Kobe, Hakodate, Yokohama, Kure, Yokosuka, Moji, Shimonoseki, Miike, Wakamatsu, Nagasaki, Kuchinotsu, Karatsu, Sasebo, Misume, Taipeh, &c.

Telegraphic Address for all the Offices:
"MITSUI."
A. B. C. AND A. 1 CODES USED.

Contractors of Coal

To the Imperial Japanese Navy. Arsenals and Railway Bureau, Principal Railway Companies and Industrial Work, Home and Foreign Mail and Freight Steamers.

Sole Proprietors

Of the famous Miike, Tagawa and Yamano Coal Mines.

Sole Agents

For the sale of Fukumo, Hokoku, Ichimura Kanoda, Mannoura, Onoura, Ostuji, Sonoda Tsubaruro, Yoshinotani, Yoshio, Yurokibura and other coals.

YANGTSE INSURANCE ASSOCIATION, LTD.

The undersigned, having been appointed agents for the above company, are prepared to issue policies and pay losses on marine risks at regular rates.

E. MEYER & Co.,
Agents, Chemulpo.

AMERICAN KOREAN ELECTRIC CO.

Light and Power.

Main Office: Electric Building, Chong No.

RAILWAY DEPARTMENT.

PERATING CARS BETWEEN EAST AND WEST GATE, EVERY TEN MINUTES:—

irst Car leaves East Gate at 7:00 A. M. First Car leaves R. R. Station at 7:25 A. M
ast Car " East Gate at 8.40 P. M. Last " " R. R. Station at 9.05 P. M

OPERATING CARS BETWEEN EAST GATE AND IMPERIAL TOMB TERMINUS, EVERY TWENTY MINUTES:—
CONNECTING WITH EVERY ALTERNATE CAR ARRIVING AT EAST GATE FROM CHONG NO.

First Car leaves East Gate for Tomb at 7:10 A. M.
" " " Tomb for East Gate at 7:30 A. M.
Last " " East Gate for Tomb at 7:50 P. M.
" " Tomb for East Gate at 8:10 P. M.

OPERATING CARS BETWEEN CHONG NO AND YUNG SAN RIVER EVERY TWELVE MINUTES:—

First Car leaves Chong No for South Gate at 7:12 A. M.
" " " Chong No for Yung San at 7:36 A. M.
" " " South Gate for Chong No at 7:20 A. M.
" " " Yung San for Chong No at 8:09 A. M.
Last " " South Gate for Chong No 9:00 P. M.
" " " Yung San for Chong No at 8.45. P. M.

SPECIAL PRIVATE CARS FURNISHED TO SUIT CONVENIENCE OF PATRONS. PRICES ON APPLICATION AT HEAD OFFICE.

LIGHTING DEPARTMENT.

Where less than 250 candle power of light is used, the rate per month will be
Per 16 candle power incandescent lamp,—All night.—Yen 2.50.
32 candle power incandescent lamp:—All night:—Yen 4.00.
50 candle power incandescent lamp:—All night:—Yen 6.00.
150 " " " " " " " 10.00.
1200 " " enclosed arc " " " " 20.00.

Where more than 250 candle power of light is used, a Meter will be installed, if requested:—Rent of Meter Yen 2.00 per month. Rate of charges by meter reading:—Two Sen per Ampere per hour. (Approximately this is equal to about One Sen per 16 C. P. lamp per hour) Minimum monthly charge where meter is installed, Yen 20.00 per month, which includes rental of meter.

Estimates for installing lights furnished on application
An assortment of chandeliers always on hand.

K. Murakami.

Photograph Studio
Chinkokai, Seoul.

Printing, Developing and Enlargement, of Photographs always Undertaken.

Korean Views and Pictures Illustrating Native Customs always on Sale,

---

THE OSAKA SHOSEN KAISHA.

Boats frequently on the berth for Chinnampo.

REGULAR SAILINGS BETWEEN JAPAN AND KOREAN PORTS.

FUSAN AND KOBE VIA SHIMONOSEKI.

OSAKA VIA MOKPO, FUSAN, SHIMONOSEKI AND KOBE.

MOJI DIRECT.

OSAKA VIA KUNSAN, MASANPO, FUSAN, SHIMONOSEKI AND KOBE.

CHEMULPO KUNSAN LINE,
Every three days.

CHEMULPO CHINNAMPO LINE.
Every three days.

For Freight and passage and further particulars apply to

THE OSAKA SHOSEN KAISHA,
Cemulpo

RONDON, PLAISANT & CO.

General Storekeepers and Merchants, Ships Contractors Tobacconists, Commission and Forwarding Agents, Coal Merchants

IMPORTERS AND EXPORTERS

Seoul Chemulpo.

W. D. WENTWORTH.

LANDING
AND
SHIPPING AGENT.
AND
CUSTOMS BROKER.

12 OURA, NAGASAKI.

STEWARD & CO.

Chemulpo.

Shipchandlers and Storekeepers, Naval and Mercantile Contractors, Landing and Shipping Agents.

STEWARD'S HOTEL

Chemulpo.

Best accommodation in the port for travellers. Clean and well-aired rooms, good cuisine and prompt attendance, oderate tariff.

신ᄒᆞᆯ만ᄒᆞᆫ도인의말을드른즉 로병이누자돈과슈하부수이에 텰로를건츅ᄒᆞ고미일슈ᄎᆞ식론쳔 거를등ᄒᆡᆼᄒᆞᆫ다ᄒᆞ고오날(이월 이일) 아총며듦시에로군의회 젼포란ᄒᆞᆫ이야세부근디에향ᄒᆞ 야모아세리지며니쟝시후에젹 군의ᄒᆞᆫ수단이왕자우방을엄습 ᄒᆞ고ᄒᆞ란단가량은우리ᄒᆡ위치 에칭병ᄒᆞ다가문니칭이되엿스 며금월이일에류도고돌엄습ᄒᆞ 텬로군은져의들의문녀갈베에 쥭은신케일빅칠십명을버리고 찻고우리군수는단총들파다른 문포들을만히탈취ᄒᆞ엿스며부 로로잡힌젹군의말을드른즉젹 군의속사병의며이데사연티의 사병관이샹ᄒᆞ엿다ᄒᆞ고가신ᄒᆞᆯ 만ᄒᆞᆫ도인의말을기ᄒᆞᆫ즉일본쟝 츌함비십구인이일월이십륙일 에환로대사에셔로군의게에위 싸엿비되며미우용맹스럽게방 어ᄒᆞ다가필경은만히샹ᄒᆞᆫ후에 사로잡혓ᄂᆞᆫ데샹ᄒᆞᆫ사ᄅᆞᆷ들은이 로병의게꾀앗되엿다ᄒᆞ엿더 라

관보

뎨삼쳔륙십이호 광무구년이월십사일 화요

서임급사령

○승종이품 졍삼품 리쟝직

○승졍삼품 륙품 김종연

○승졍삼품 륙품 리능화

이상광무팔년오월십일일

○임법부사리국쟝서칙임관사등 닉부디방국쟝 리규환

○임닉부디방국쟝서칙임관사등 탁지부출납국쟝 오샹규

이샹이월구일

○면궁닉부특진관서칙임관일등 비서원경 리지용

○명비서원경서칙임관이등 태의원경 박용대

○명태의원경서칙임관삼등 종일품 김셩근

○명규쟝각학사겸임시졍원일강관서칙임관사등 종일품 홍순형

○임중추원의관서칙임관사등 종일품 김종한

○의원면본관 중추원의관 홍종우 림샹익 박희빈 셔진감 리셔주사 리용규 동리항종순 경두현 졍홍항종순 강순규 권양기서 쟝춘순 리진명

○임중추원의관서주임관륙등 졍삼품 리종셩 졍삼품 홍순관 륙품 김주홍

○임동래항종순서판임관륙등 경무원종순 남태환

○임법종흥쟝종순서판임관륙등 경위원종순 고형셕

○임광양계사쟝종순서판임관륙등 경위원종순 리졍헌

이상이월십일일

○의원면본관 비서원승 김택진

○임비서원승서주임관륙등 졍삼품 신셩균

이샹이월십이일

궁내부대신사리

○조원황희도황주군젼도류오년죄인라유셕류삼년죄인리즁윤ᄒᆞᆫ교명방

광무구년이월십이일

○광무구년도예산표

뎨십사관 덕어학교 륙쳔이빅삼십사원

뎨일항 봉급 일쳔삼빅이십원

뎨이항 쳥비 사빅팔십원

뎨삼항 교로칙구비 이빅원

뎨사항 쳥수슈리비 팔십원

뎨오항 잡급급잡비 일빅구십사원

뎨륙항 외국인 삼쳔구빅지화

뎨십오관 한어학교보조비 이만쳔쳘빅팔십이원

뎨일항 공립소학교비 일만구쳔삼빅륙십원

뎨이항 사립소학교비 수쳔삼빅이십이원

뎨삼항 경셩학당비 륙빅원

뎨사항 인부일어학교비 삼쳔오빅원

뎨십륙관 외국류학비 팔쳔원

뎨일항 의쳔왕학자금 팔쳔원지화

지화지출차죵 사만팔쳔칠빅이십원

학부소관합계 이십일만팔쳔칠빅오십륙원

농상공부소관

뎨일관 농상공부소관

뎨일관 농상공부본쳥 사만사쳔오빅팔원

뎨일항 봉급 삼만이쳔륙빅원

뎨이항 쳥비 일쳔팔빅원

뎨삼항 쳥사슈리비 사빅원

뎨사항 잡급급잡비 삼쳔사빅팔원

뎨오항 려비 일쳔원

뎨륙항 외국인계급 쳔쳔이빅원지화

뎨이관 사업비 오쳔사빅원

뎨일항 공졔슈리비 사빅원

뎨이항 잡업비 오쳔원

지쳥지출차죵 칠쳔이빅원

농상공부소관합계 오만칠쳔팔빅원

중추원소관

뎨일관 중추원본쳥 예만쳘쳔팔빅삼십사원

뎐보

동일발 동월이일

○뎨삼함디의출발이너란ᄉᆞ담 장에지케퇴미로케스트벤스기대 명령ᄒᆞ엿다더라 곳극동으로젼진ᄒᆞ라고

심일동경발

○쟝귀셕경령 본월구일샹오 구시에우리일부티가쟝귀셕남 방고디를졈령ᄒᆞ엿ᄂᆞᆫ티칭디에 잇든덕보병약이중티ᄂᆞᆫ즉은주 ㅣᄒᆞ나와샹ᄒᆞᆫ주ㅣ열을운반ᄒᆞ 야쟝귀셕방향으로퇴각ᄒᆞ엿다 더라

○덕병의포격 쏘동일하오에 덕포병이당가둔북방고디와샹 남주와만부산서방고디와한셩 보와밋밍블보부근에서우리진 디쟈처를포격ᄒᆞ엿더라

○사하보포격 십일사하보와 한셩보부근의중포가우리부티 를포격ᄒᆞ엿더라

로국의정형

론돈발 이월십일

○로국에서인민의게헌법을허 락ᄒᆞ엿다ᄂᆞᆫ보고ᄂᆞᆫ셔샹이엄ᄂᆞᆫ 말이오로국졍부에서다만사회 리법권의기량ᄒᆞᆯ방칙만강구ᄒᆞᆫ 다더라

빅림발 동일

○로국소셜가마심골기씨ᄂᆞᆫ젼 분요중에포박되엿더니다시방 면되엿다더라

동디발 동일

○위소에서분요중에쥭은사ᄅᆞᆷ 이륙빅명이오샹ᄒᆞᆫ사ᄅᆞᆷ이일쳔 명이라더라

론돈발 동월륙일

○요젼셩피득보분요에주쟝ᄒᆞ 던고수기폰씨ᄂᆞᆫ셔사국으로망 명ᄒᆞ엿다더니지금영국으로향 ᄒᆞ야오ᄂᆞᆫ중이라더라

동디발 동월칠일

○파리에서로국공채신약ᄇᆡ을 빅분지오에빈리로모집ᄒᆞᆯ조약 이셩립되엿다더라

론돈발 이월륙일

○모스코에서귀족들이회의ᄒᆞ 고황뎨께쳥구서이도를밧치기 로작졍ᄒᆞ엿ᄂᆞᆫ티ᄒᆞ나ᄂᆞᆫ보슈젹 이오다슈로의결ᄒᆞ엿스니그대 지ᄂᆞᆫ지금은평화가굴욕되지안 코ᄂᆞᆫ되지못ᄒᆞᆯ것이니승젼ᄒᆞ기 저지싸우기로결단ᄒᆞ고빈졍 리량도젼쟁의ᄯᅳᆺ나가져지기ᄂᆞᆫ 리셔ᄒᆞᆫ쟈ᄒᆞ엿스며쏘ᄒᆞ나ᄂᆞᆫ다 인른젹과반티ᄒᆞᆫᄯᅳᆺ인디쳥황 을민사이에향샹ᄒᆞ야정치개 셜힝ᄒᆞᆯ쟈ᄒᆞ엿다더라

동디발 동월칠일

○셩피득보에서대공들이회의 ᄒᆞᆫ졀도광화담판을시작ᄒᆞᄂᆞᆫ계 에이조흔로로국대수의견ᄒᆞ엿ᄂᆞᆫ티 영국졍부에교섭ᄒᆞ야셔셰로도 을의논ᄒᆞᆯ때에방히가엽계화조약 ...ᄒᆞ라 ... 진ᄒᆞ라

ᄒᆞ엿다ᄂᆞᆫ말이잇다더라

동디발 동월팔일

○셩피득보귀족들이회의ᄒᆞ야 황뎨께국민의티의수회의들모 졍ᄒᆞ자ᄂᆞᆫ샹쥬안을의결ᄒᆞ엿ᄂᆞᆫ 티오부카란ᄒᆞᆫ표졔ᄂᆞᆫ이빅오십팔이 며반ᄃᆡᄒᆞᆫ표ᄂᆞᆫ이십이표라ᄒᆞ 엿더라

잡보

○경시경의 빅목젼합쾌 노젼 ᄒᆞ든일인이모젼합ᄒᆞ므로진톄ᄒᆞ 미모젼시민등이경무쳥에쳥원 ᄒᆞ야히일인을쳘시케ᄒᆞ엿고고 시비를종노에긔졀ᄒᆞ사로빅목 젼시민등이한셩부에등소ᄒᆞᆫ즉 관문민정식씨가합제로인민을 구즁ᄒᆞ녀결아디잇의도약ᄒᆞ엿 스니빈등ᄒᆞᆯ수업다ᄒᆞᄂᆞᆫ지라롱 쥐비젼시졍이샹의ᄒᆞ야차젼을 일졔히쳘시ᄒᆞ고등소ᄒᆞ기로결 뎡ᄒᆞ엿더라

○망유더디 일용사가서경귀 셔에관ᄒᆞ야졍부에권고ᄒᆞᆫ다ᄒᆞ 되관제리경에티ᄒᆞ야제빈ᄒᆞᆫ일방 홈이여티가무ᄒᆞᆫ지라근일셔샹 챵용사들이무승빈티운동이잇 슴으로리졍안의다소빈경이잇 슴이라ᄒᆞ더라

○퇴복미동 향츌과에복제ᄒᆞ 엿든챤졍최의챵씨ᄂᆞᆫ미동모동 이미젼으로퇴복ᄒᆞ엿더라

○졸연로망 됴병세씨를샹경 ᄒᆞ라고쳥ᄒᆞ야젼인ᄒᆞ엿더니출 지에됴합이로망ᄒᆞ야죠신ᄒᆞᆯ비 를아지못ᄒᆞ더라더라

○림표하다 남셔자너쳥룡뎡 사티를일인이자괴의소유라지 라ᄒᆞ고표목을세웟더라더라

○파병룸시 마포광창에젹치 ᄒᆞ엿든니쟝원쌀일빅셕을쟝흥 고로수입ᄒᆞ고파송ᄒᆞ든병뎡은 분시ᄒᆞ엿더라

○회취묘연 의친왕이부산 니도착ᄒᆞ엿다ᄂᆞᆫ풍셜이낭자ᄒᆞ더 국할금셔지일본에궤류ᄒᆞ고회 괴약은묘무ᄒᆞ다더라

○항졍면세 표훈원에서 쟝광을실신조본서구입ᄒᆞ는 기로반포ᄒᆞ고 ... 수입ᄒᆞᄂᆞᆫ티교로히외부 ... 세합을쳥ᄒᆞ엿더라

광고

TELEGRAMS.

(FROM THE "SHANGHAI TIMES.")

Berlin, Feb. 4.

Admiral Roshdestvensky's fleet has arranged to get the necessary coal on its way to East Asia, until the ships have passed the 24th degree of latitude, from Batavia, and then from Saigon.

London, Feb. 5.

The revolutionary movement is reported to be growing stronger. The Czar and M. de Witte are said fo be in favour of making concessions to quiet the malcontents, while the Empress Dowager and the Grand Dukes insist the movement shall be suppressed by force,

(FROM JAPAN PAPERS.)

London, Feb. 6.

In the course of discusssions in the British Press respecting the renewal of Anglo-Japanese Alliance, it is suggested that the Agreement should be extended to mutual guarantees regarding territorial integrity of Asiatic countries.

London, Feb. 5.

The railway employees at Tomsk are rather refractory, their action threatening to render the provisioning of Kuropatkin's troops more difficult than over.

It is expected that all the supplies in Manchuria will be exhausted in April next. Russia is therefore chartering here a number of vessels for the purpose of carrying provisions to Vladivostock.

London, Jan. 11.

His Holiness the Pope has received in audience the Duke and Duchess of Genoa. This is the first time that a Prince of the House of Savoy has entered the Vatican.

THE PEACE RUMOURS.

London, Feb. 8.

There are persistent rumours in circulation regarding efforts for mediation between Japan and Russia.

Baron Hayashi, the Japanese Minister in London, interviewed as the truth of recent reports, said that Japan would be willing to meet Russia reasonably, but he had no knowledge of any negotiation being in progress.

It is reported that the Russian Government has cancelled orders for stores and new ships, and also that an order for the mobilisation of an Army Corps has been withdrawn.

London, Feb. 8.

In spite of various rumours as to peace overtures by Russia, no reliable information has yet been received to indicate that Russia is likely to accept terms which could be agreed to by Japan.

[It is worthy of remark that the telegrams relating to peace rumours received in Japan have been "special" services to individual newspapers and that so far Reuter has sent no message on the subject. Rumours of peace greatly aid in the flotation of loans by either belligerent.—Ed. K. D. N].

GENERAL KUROPATKIN.

London, Feb. 8.

Strenuous efforts are being made at St. Petersburg in order to secure the recall of General Kuropatkin.

Berlin, Feb. 8.

Reports received here from several quarters confirm the existence of dissensions among the Russian commanders in the Far East.

London, Feb. 9.

General Gripenberg and his staff have arrived at Irtkusk, "en route" to St. Petersburg. Current reports state that Gripenberg is going to St. Petersburg for the purpose of accusing Kuropatkin of leaving him in the lurch, and of general inertia.

RUSSIAN AFFAIRS.

London, Feb. 8.

General Trepoff, the Governor-General of St. Petersburg, has summoned the Curator of the Education and informed him that the Government is determined to put down all academic anarchy. All students and scholars refusing to return to their studies transquilly would be summarily expelled, and if the professors sympathised with the students, education in St. Petersburg would cease.

London, Feb. 8.

General Dantchenko reports to the Russian Government that the transport capacity of the Siberian Railway is inadequate to cope with the requirements of the Russian army.

London, Feb. 9.

Despite an official announcement to the contrary, rumours are rife in St. Petersburg of general resumption of the strike on Sunday next. The whole situation is full of uncertainty.

The hospitals in Warsaw are at present full, the authorities refusing to admit any more patients.

London, Feb. 9.

Reuter's agent at St. Peterburg states that Father Gapon, who led the strikers during the recent riots in St. Petersburg, is known to be in Switerland.

GENERAL NEWS.

Berlin, Feb. 8.

With regard to the speech by Mr. Arthur Lee, Civil Lord of the British Admiralty, which was stated to have given umbrage to the German Government, the British Ambassador at Berlin has tendered an explanation which is regarded as satisfactory.

London, Feb. 9.

King Oscar II. of Sweden and Norway, who is at present in indifferent health, has transferred his functions to the Crown Prince.

Later.

The reason King Oscar is transferring his functions to the Crown Prince is that he is not robust enough to deal with the new crisis arising from the disagreement between Sweden and Norway concerning the question of separate Consular services.

London, Feb. 9,

A Chinese Five-per-cent loan for £1,000,000 is to be issued on Friday in London and Berlin at 97.

South Chulla province seems to be very badly administered. Armed robberies are of daily occurrence there.

According to a Tokio telegram, the arbitration treaty between Japan and the United States was signed on February 11th.

Mr. K. Takahashi, Vice-Governor of the Bank of Japan, will again leave Tokyo for London on the 17th inst., presumably in connection with the loan questions.

It is reported that Mr. Yi Chi Yong will be appointed Minister of Agriculture and Commerce, and Mr. Min Pyeng Han, Chief judge of the Supreme Court will be made a cabinet councillor.

There is much dis-satisfaction in Seoul at the action of the Government in accepting a loan from Japan. As a protest nearly all the high officials have written to the Finance Department offering to lend whatever money may be required, each one contributing according to his means.

The Japanese Minister has sent an official letter to the Foreign Office asking that the newly appointed Secretary to the Korean Legation at Tokio be not allowed to proceed to his post as he will only cause troble. Mr. Hayashi adds that the Legation is doing very well as it is.

A QUESTION OF POLICE.

An incident occurred yesterday afternoon which points to bad management somewhere. The electric cars are run here with what must strike anyone, with any knowledge of the promiscuous way in which Koreans wander about, as a remarkable absence of casualties.

However, yesterday afternoon an accident happened; a small boy was run over and one of his legs was seriously injured.

A crowd gathered and the American Legation Guard was sent for, and it was here that we think a mistake was made. The Japanese have made themselves responsible for the good order of the city and any disturbances should be left to them to deal with. We admit that, so far, they have given no evidence of their efficiency,—rather the reverse,—but if all the Legations take to turning out their guards on such slight provocation, thing will soon be worse than ever.

It is estimated that the cost of Russian prisoners in Japan will be Yen 15,000 per day.

M. de Witte's return to the Cabinet is regarded in St. Petersburg as a manifestation of indirect pressure for the opening of peace negotiations.

It is said that at a recent cabinet council it was decided that all taxes shall be paid into the financial department, while the expected loan from Japan shall be deposited with the Dai Ichi Bank.

The magistrate of Inchun (near Chemulpo) reports that the Japanese are taking more land in his district. They have recently planted a red flag at Haksan li, upon the pole of which is written "This is the railroad land for use of the army."

The magistrate of Pukchong reports that the Russians who occupied the post and Telegraph offices and the deputy-magistrate's office in his district until Jan. 20th have all gone back to Iwon, breaking the telegraph poles and wires as they went.

The Russians are enroling and arming Chinese mounted brigands for the protection of their telegraphic communications. Two brigands are told off to guard each telegraph pole, and each brigand is drawing $30 a month for his service.

Mr. Hayashi has notified the Department of Education that the manager of the "Osaka Mainichi Shimbun" would like to send his journal to all the public offices in Korea and requests that all the offices be instructed to receive them. We do not know whether this a commercial or a benevolent proposition as nothing is said about the price.

Mr. Min Yŏng Chul, until recently Korean Minister to Peking is in trouble. It appears that during his administration as Governor of Pyeng Yang there was a considerable mis-direction of public funds which at the time escaped investigation owing to Mr. Min's departure for China. Hearing of his return to Korea, about a dozen indignant Pyeng Yang-ites have come to town and are worrying Mr. Min.

Many people are asking the question how and why certain firms are so successful in securing orders for arms from the Chinese and can fulfill them at so much lower rates than others. Perhaps the following may be a slight, side-light, says the Tientsin Times. A military correspondent, writing to a home journal from Milan states that the Italian Government have just disposed of their hundred thousand old rifles to a Continental firm. None of the rifles date beyond 1888, and they represent a stock of various patterns which has been kept and accumulated in the Government depots for the last fifteen years. It is said to be the firm's intention to ship them all to China through their agents at an important shipping port on the Continent.

PRESENT CONDITIONS AT PORT ARTHUR.

A Majis telegram to the Mainichi states that Japanese who have just returned from Port Arthur report that the officials of the new Naval Station (the Port Arthur Chinjufu) are very busily engaged in putting everything in order both on land and sea. The Chinese who left the port on account of the war are returning home in crowds, and the gendarmes have plenty of occupation. Over one thousand Russians are still at the Red Cross hospitals at Port Arthur, They will be sent to Japan when convalescent. It will be long before all the arrangements for the administration of the port have been got into working order, Tairen Bay has been frozen to the depth of three inches, causing much inconvenience in the landing and shipping of goods.

T. Kamiya (39) and Y. Kubota residing at Asakusa in Tokyo, were sentenced on Feb. 2nd in the Tokyo District Court to fines of yen 795 and yen 500 respectively on a charge of having clandestinely manufactured sake. The same day Mr. K. Makino, a graduate of the College of Science, was prosecuted on a similar charge.

Wolf hunting is now the popular sport in the Northumbrian dales. Some hundreds of eager sportsmen, many of them on horseback, join in the great drives which have been organised from day to day for the capture of the predatory beast, which escaped from a collection of wild animals at Shotley Bridge, near Newcastle, and whose taste for fresh mutton is costing the farmers of Allenale so dear. The wolf, up to the present, has had the best of it.

The Korea Daily News.

Issued at 5 P. M. daily except Sundays.

Rate of Subscription:—
Per Year,............Yen 25.
Per Quarter,..........Yen 7.
Per Month,..........Yen 2.50.

Postage in Korea not charged extra.
Postage abroad charged extra.

Advertisements, 50 sen per day for 1 inch or less.
5 yen per month per inch.
50 yen per year per inch.

All communications to
E. T. BETHELL,
Editor and Publisher,
Pak-tong, Seoul.

VLADIVOSTOK

It seems that it will not be possible for any more coal or supplies to reach Vladivosk until the arrival of Spring. The Soya or La perouse straits having now frozen up the only routes to Vladivostock are *via* either the Tsushima or the Tsugaru straits. That these routes are being well watched by the Japanese is borne out by the large list of captures which we published recently to which must now be added the British steamer "Eastry," (2998 tons gross,) carrying Welsh coal, which was captured on the 7th instant and the German steamer "Palos" which feel into Japanese hands off the Hokkaido on February 10th.

There seems to be no probability of a coal famine, however, as the captain of a British steamer which reeently reached Moji from Vladivostock says that the coal already in stock amounts to 150,000 tons. He adds, however, that four steamers, which left Cardiff the same time as his own vessel, were captured *en* route to Vladivostock by Japanese war-ships. After this steamer, however, at least one German steamer succeeded in getting through the Soya Straits before the ice made them impassable.

Certainly the fates seem to be conspiring to assist Japan. We are by no means inclined to accept unreservedly the statement made in a London telegram to the effect that the disturbances along the Siberian railway render it imperative that supplies for Kuropatkin's commissariat shall be conveyed through Vladivostok, but it is evident that a big reserve of coal and other supplies at this place would be of material assistance to the Russian army and navy.

It is certain that a large number of steamers are still *en route* for Vladivostok and, according to London messages, there is great uneasiness amongst the owners and insurers lest these vessels should also fall a prey to the Japanese cruisers. Besides many colliers which are on their way, three steamers have been loaded at Seattle and four in Australia, all of them carrying foodsuffs for Vladivostok.

Apprehensions as to their safety are well-founded, as unless conditions alter very much there is only a very remote chance of vessels carrying contraband reaching Vladivostok until Spring comes and the Soya straits are again navigable.

THE SHAHO.

There is again a dearth of interesting incidents but there appears to be no cessation of Russian activity. Having established themselves south of the Hun River, facing the Japanese left wing, the Russians now appear to be turning their attention to the army in the centre.

Field Marshal Oyama reports that on the 9th and 10th instant, all his positions to the southwest of Shahupu were heavily bombarded from the neighbouring heights but he says nothing as to the effect of the bombardment although in a previous message he said that not much damage was being done.

Several infantry and cavalry skirmishes are reported but they were only affairs of outposts and we have no map which indicates their locality.

It is reported that up to the 10th inst. the Japanese had buried 20,000 corpses at Heikeutai and captured 2,000 rifles.

A report from Tokio is to the effect that there will not be another big, general engagement for another two weeks but the increased activity on the Russian side indicates the coutrary.

THE BALTIC SQUADRONS.

According to telegraphic advices received in Japan, Admiral Rohdjestvensky's squadron is at present cruising about north of Madagascar, with it depot at Nossi be, a small island to the north-west of Madagascar. A report received at Lloyds in London states that on Jan. 28th there were 12 colliers at Diego Suarez (a port on the north coast of Madagascar), most of which were Hamburg-Amerika line Steamers, carrying altogether some 100,000 tons of coal.

Botrovski's squadron consisting of the *Oleg*, *Izumrud*, *Petersburg* and *Smolensk*, with three destroyers and eighteen German colliers left Jiboutil on February 2nd, with the apparent object of joining the first squadron.

The third squadron, under the command of Admiral Wilayatoff was to have left Libau on the 8th instant. We are told that it consists of eight warships, of which three are battleships and two are cruisers but the only names that are given are the *Admiral Senyavin*, *Oushokoff Aparaxine* and *Vladmir Monoach*.

A Berlin telegram says that on its way to these waters, the fleet will coal first off Batavia and then off Saigon.

RUSSIAN VERSION OF THE BATTLE OF HEIKEUTAI.

A Mukden telegram, dated February 6, which han been received by Major-General Dessino at Shanghai, is to the following effect:—

"The fighting commenced on the 25th ult. when our detachments advanced one by one. On that day our troops carried the Japanese positions in the neighbourhood of Shwangtaitsz and Tutaitsz on the Hun-ho, at a distance of 23 miles from Mukden, and our cavalry occupied two villages to the south. Our troops still pressed on, and charging the Japanese completely drove them out of Heikeutai. From early on the morning of the 26th, our force attacked the strongly fortified Japanese positions in the neighourhood of Chentanpao, and captured all of them, with the exception of Chentanpao, where the Japanese forces were concentrated. On the same day our cavalry crossed the Hun-ho and defeated at a place 10 versts from Chentaupao the Japanese forces retreating from Heikeutai. From early in the morning on the 28th untill the night of the same day, the Japanese artillery bombarded our positions and the infantry delivered four attacks, which were repulsed with heavy losses each time. The enemy's attack on the north-west of Chentaupao also failed, his columns being mown down by our gunfire. Moreover our forces charged and carried Siaotaitsz' and a portion of Lapatai (east of Chentanpao). The same night the enemy attempted to advance on both sides of the railway, but was repulsed with heavy losses. The enemy twice attacked Peitaitsz, northeast of Chentanpao, but was also repulsed. On the 29th, the enemy concentrated an overwhelming force in the direction of Chentanpao and endeavoured to drive out our troops, but was totally unsuccessful. Toward evening on the 30th, the enemy delivered an attack on Hutsz'chwang, 6 versts east of Chentanpao, but was repulsed. Our artillery bombarded Chentaupao during the day. On the 31st, the Japanese at Chentanpao again made an unsuccessful attack on Peitaitsz. After a series of stubborn engagements at various places of no strategical importance, quiet prevailed along the front of our right wing. As the result of our offensive movements, we now hold all the positions recently captured, with the exception of Chentaupao and a few unimportant positions on the extreme right. The evacuation of these positions was not effected until after the enemy's tactics had been foiled and his strength totally crushed. Our casualties numbered 10,000, while the enemy's losses are unknown, though believed to be great. During the battle, artillery duels took place along the whole front of our Army. We captured a large number of prisoners and a large quantity of arms and ammunition, wagons, and other articles. These spoils of war were all taken at the positions from which the enemy had been driven off.

GOOD FOR TRADE.

There are at present in Shanghai some 2,000 Russian workmen, belonging neither to the Army nor to the Navy, says the Shanghai times. During the siege of Port Arthur a good workman received seven roubles a day, if he worked overtime he could make from 12 to 15 dollars. The least paid to any man was two dollars. So far these men have received in Shanghai from the Russian government no less than $500,000, of which it is estimated at least half will be spent before they leave.

The mininmum wages paid to Chinese workmen was $1 per day. Coolies, 60 cents, if they worked overtime $1 and upwards. To help them, rice was sold at ordinary prices, five cents per lb a single man was allowed two lbs a day, a married man three lbs.

Of the higher class there are some 700 officials in Shanghai, of whom 200 or thereabouts are army and Naval Officers. Besides the cost of their tickets for the voyage, 400 or 600 dollars. each as the case may be, it is probable that the average expenditure here will be about $700 per man, making a neat little total of about $500,000.

Even in Nagasaki, although they were "hard up," the Japanese reckoned they left $20,000 behind them

Britian and Russia have signed an agreement similar to that concluded between Russia and America, enabling British companies to sue Russian companies in Russia.

The Korea Daily News.

VOL. II, WEDNESDAY, FEBRUARY 15, 1905. No. 35

大韓每日申報

대한매일신보

일쳔구빅오년이월십칠일 (금요일) (뎨이권삼십륙호)

본사고빅

이신보는영어와한어로셔거리
일출판ᄒᆞᆸ

신문가

한쟝 엽두돈오푼
일삭됴 엽두량닷돈
우표가미삭닷돈
다밧ᄂᆞᆫ으로밧ᄉᆞᆸ

광고료는

귀한의장단과ᄌᆞ힝의다쇼로즁
감ᄒᆞ되렴가로밧을터이오매오
리지아니ᄒᆞ며대한사람마다다이신
문을보실터이니광고버시기를
원ᄒᆞ시ᄂᆞᆫ이들은우리신문사에
와서면약ᄒᆞ심을희망ᄒᆞᆸ

○발힝소 발동대한매일신보
사법어학교압헤젼영국인셜필
림정자리오
사쟝 영국인 (빅셜)

평양 ᄃᆡ리졈

○평양효동사ᄂᆞᆫ권미보씨로우
리신문관ᄃᆡ리인을뎡ᄒᆞ엿
시ᄉᆞ오니평양에계신구람코져ᄒᆞ
ᄂᆞᆫ 쳠군ᄌᆞᄂᆞᆫ 이ᄃᆡ리졈에와왕
림ᄒᆞ와면의ᄒᆞ시옵

샤고

○우리대한매일신보의목뎍은
대한의안녕질서에관한모든대
목에ᄃᆡᄒᆞ야는공평한변론을주
쟝ᄒᆞᆷ이라우리동신원의긔보는
신문보시ᄂᆞᆫ쳠군ᄌᆞ의게ᄒᆞᆼ상보
도ᄒᆞ리며편지들긔서ᄒᆞ여주시
ᄂᆞᆫ이ᄂᆞᆫ셩명과번디를젹어붓치
시기를희망ᄒᆞ오니이거슨신문
샹에긔재ᄒᆞ랴ᄂᆞᆫ거시아니오다
만극히신용ᄒᆞᄂᆞᆫ증거를삼고자
ᄒᆞᆷ이라긔재ᄂᆞᆫ아모긔서던지긔
재ᄒᆞᆷ을뵈가ᄒᆞᄂᆞᆫ권리를가졋스
나뵈가ᄒᆞᄂᆞᆫ리유ᄂᆞᆫ말ᄒᆞᆯ터이오
며공중평화를문란케ᄒᆞᄂᆞᆫ듯ᄒᆞᆫ
긔서ᄂᆞᆫ의례히밧지안켓ᄉᆞᆸ나이
다

●본사셜시이래로신문을미양
우톄로분젼ᄒᆞ와톄젼부의일힝의
로젼ᄒᆞᄂᆞᆫ듯스로면곳에는혹늣게
젼ᄒᆞ기도ᄒᆞ며혹멋칠거슬ᄒᆞᆫ번
에젼ᄒᆞ기도ᄒᆞ며혹아니젼ᄒᆞᄂᆞᆫ
곳도잇다ᄒᆞ와우리신문을ᄉᆞ랑
ᄒᆞ야구람ᄒᆞ시ᄂᆞᆫ 쳠군ᄌᆞ의게
되ᄒᆞ야미안ᄒᆞ옵기로지금
은분젼인을두고미일일죽이젼
ᄒᆞ며아니젼ᄒᆞ거나늣게거나ᄒᆞ
폐가업도록ᄒᆞ라ᄒᆞ오니혹아니
젼ᄒᆞ거나혹늣게젼ᄒᆞ거나ᄒᆞᆫ일
이잇스면본사로통긔ᄒᆞ여주심
을희망ᄒᆞᆸ

관보

뎨삼쳔륙십삼호 광무구
년이월십오일슈요
서임급사령

○헌서리륙군법원쟝사무륙군
병법원리사륙군보병참령 신졔
영

이월칠일

○승서주임관사등 경무청경
무관 강종우

이월십일일

○명종졍원경서칙임관삼등
의양군 리재각
○의원면본관 비서원승 윤
주셩 쟝례원좌쟝례 김셕룡
ᄒᆞᆼ문관시독 임빅영 경
룡창봉 리수현
중학교교관 안죵겸
○의원면겸임태의원소경 비
서원승 신헌균
○임비서원승서주임관이등
정삼품 리범구
○겸임태의원소경 비서원승
김유홍
○겸임쟝례원쟝례 비서원승
리조영
○임쟝례원좌쟝례서주임관륙
등 쟝례원우쟝례 리범셜
○임쟝례원우쟝례서주임관륙
등사품 김셕룡
○임홍문관 시독서판임관륙
등 륙품고명주
○임경룡창봉서판임관팔등홍
슌창
○승서판임관사등평안남도관
찰부주사 김관션
○임중학교교관서판임관륙등
최힝익
○임농상대신서칙관일등종졍
원경 리지용
○명서리대신사무 궁내부경
관박용화

이상이월십삼일

광무구년도예산표 속

뎨일항 봉급 일만ᄉᆞ쳔구
빅삼십원
뎨이항 쳥비 이쳔일빅ᄉᆞ
십원
뎨삼항 잡급과잡비 일쳔
륙빅륙십ᄉᆞ원
뎨ᄉᆞ항 경ᄉᆞ슈리비 일빅
원
즁추원소관합계 일만칠쳔
팔빅십ᄉᆞ원

호위ᄃᆡ소관

뎨일관 호위ᄃᆡ본쳥 팔만칠
빅십팔원
뎨일항 봉급 칠쳔륙빅구
십이원
뎨이항 쳥비 일쳔ᄉᆞ빅사
십원
뎨삼항 잡급과잡비 오만
륙쳔오빅팔십륙원
뎨ᄉᆞ항 마필비 이쳔ᄉᆞ빅
십삼원
뎨오항 량식비 칠쳔팔원
뎨륙항 피복비 오쳔삼빅
십구원
뎨칠항 병긔졔조비 이빅
오십원
호위ᄃᆡ소관합계 팔만칠빅
십팔원

통신원소관

뎨일관 통신원본쳥 이만구
쳔이빅삼십이원
뎨일항 봉급 일만삼쳔이
빅륙십원
뎨이항 쳥비 일쳔륙빅팔
십원
뎨삼항 경ᄉᆞ슈리비 오빅
원
뎨ᄉᆞ항 려비 일빅오십원
뎨오항 잡급과잡비 일쳔
칠빅이십팔원
뎨륙항 외국인계급 칠쳔
팔빅십삼원 지화
뎨칠항 슈입금운반비 ᄉᆞ
쳔원
뎨이관 우톄사업비 이십사
만일쳔륙빅오십륙원
뎨일항 봉급 사만사쳔원
뎨이항 쳥비 이만팔빅륙
십원
뎨삼항 경ᄉᆞ슈리비 륙쳔
구빅원
뎨ᄉᆞ항 외톄금소포톤비등
비 팔쳔오빅원
뎨오항 우표인쇄비 오쳔원
뎨륙항 잡급과잡비 칠만
칠쳔오빅원
뎨칠항 려비 일쳔구십원
뎨팔항 니계학교비 삼빅
원
뎨구항 외계학교비 삼빅
원
뎨십항 림시우톄경비 칠
만팔쳔이빅사원

잡보

○하이조처 평안북도관찰사
서리가니부로면보ᄒᆞ엿ᄂᆞᆫᄃᆡ일
진지회회쟝김쳘연의룡힙닉응
령을월십이일에기회연셜ᄒᆞᆫ다
ᄒᆞᆺ사오니엇지조치ᄒᆞ을ᄂᆞᆫ지
ᄒᆞ엿더라

○문의시힝 지작셩상일에니
부에서경무고문관환산중쥰씨
의항ᄂᆞᆼ됴관을변ᄂᆞᆼᄒᆞ야경무청
으로공문ᄒᆞ고경찰에관한사항
을문의시힝ᄒᆞ라ᄒᆞ엿더라

○대관면임 종졍원경리지용
씨ᄂᆞᆫ농상공부대신을피임ᄒᆞ고
그ᄃᆡᄂᆞᆫ의양군리재각씨가피명
ᄒᆞ엿다더라

○힝규담판 법국공사가외부
로조복ᄒᆞ엿ᄂᆞᆫᄃᆡ민광기사귀빈
례등의힝규ᄒᆞᄂᆞᆫ사ᄂᆞᆫ힝기사쳐
에알앗거니와쟝원경김명진
씨가힝기사에ᄃᆡᄒᆞ야며하히쳐
관ᄒᆞᄂᆞᆫ거슨시명ᄒᆞ라ᄒᆞ엿더다
닉지작년에하오셔시에외부에서
김명진씨를쳥ᄒᆞ엿ᄂᆞᆫᄃᆡ등씨가
힝사자일인을승리ᄒᆞ야외부에
서힝고사진을담판ᄒᆞᆫ다더라

○탐긔최슈 광쥬부에서본부
츈월면거ᄒᆞᄂᆞᆫ김진사젼답ᄉᆞ로
ᄃᆡ쳔거ᄒᆞᄂᆞᆫ김의셩을착치ᄒᆞ엿
ᄃᆡ니금곡츌쥬ᄒᆞ사일인이병
뎡일명을다리고본ᄃᆡ참령편지
를가지고리도ᄒᆞ야힝리를볼너
김의셩을탈거ᄒᆞ며픠슈ᄒᆞᆫ동안
에쓴부비쳔원과ᄯᅥ의들의고가
힝ᄒᆞ야구원을ᄂᆞᆨ셰ᄒᆞ야가지고
갓다더라

●관찰신임 황히도관찰사서
졍슌씨ᄂᆞᆫ소쳬ᄒᆞ고그ᄃᆡᄂᆞᆫ찬졍
구영조씨가피임ᄒᆞ엿다더라

●학자금납하 의친왕이회국
ᄒᆞᆫ다ᄒᆞᄂᆞᆫᄃᆡ니힝금동경에계ᄒᆞ야
ᄒᆞᆫ학자금오만원을니하ᄒᆞ사면칙
ᄒᆞᆫ사ᄃᆡ미국으로다서가서유학
ᄒᆞ라ᄒᆞ옵셧다더라

○ᄃᆡ표교셥 죵노에일인의셜
젼사와교시ᄃᆡ를건츅ᄒᆞᄂᆞᆫ소로한
셩부와일령사간에누차교셥ᄒᆞ
엿스나효험이업더니섀가셔사일에
외부교문관슈지분씨가교섭ᄒᆞᆫ
표자로일본공관에젼왕ᄒᆞ야담판
귀졍ᄒᆞ엿ᄂᆞᆫᄃᆡ셜젼ᄒᆞᄂᆞᆫ일인은도쟝
십오일에쳘거ᄒᆞ고교시ᄃᆡᄂᆞᆫ
ᄎᆔ졍ᄒᆞᆫ다더라

UNION INSURANCE SOCIETY OF CANTON.

Head office Hongkong.
Marine risks underwritten at current rates.

Agents in Chemulpo,
E. MEYER & Co.

COMPAGNIE DES MESSAGERIES MARITIMES.

Fortnightly Direct Service.

For Marseilles
via Ports.
Sailing from Yokohama
Calling at Kobe,
Shanghai, Hongkong, Saigon, Singapore, Colombo, Djibonti, Suez, Port Said and Marseilles.

For particulars apply to
HOLME, RINGER & Co.,
Chemulpo.

HAYASHIDA & CO.,

16 MYENG DONG, CHIN KO KAI, SEOUL.
BRANCH OFFICE AT CHEMULPO.

Money changers, Coal and Wood Merchants, Express Agents.

We are agents for the Pyeng-yang Coal Company and the Karazu Coal Company of Japan. We have the best quality of both anthracite and bituminous coal, and prompt execution of orders is our speciality. Firewood of all kinds kept in stock. Full weight guaranteed. Money of all denominations exchanged at current rates. Parcels received for all parts.

CHINA MUTUAL LIFE INS. OC.

Most favourable terms to policy holders.

Benefit system unsurpassed.

HOLME RINGER & Co.
Agents, Chemulpo.

C. P. R.

CANADIAN PACIFIC RAILWAY COMPANY'S ROYAL MAIL STEAMSHIP LINE.

THE FAST ROUTE BETWEEN CHINA, JAPAN, AND EUROPE VIA CANADA AND THE UNITED STATES.

Route from Hongkong via Shanghai, Nagasaki (Inland Sea of Japan) Kobe, Yokohama, Victoria and Vancouver.

Twin Screw Empress Steamship—6,000 Tons—Speed 19 knots.

PROPOSED SAILING FROM YOKOHAMA.
R. M. S. Empress of India.
R. M. S. Empress of Japan.
R. M. S. Empress of China.
R. M. S. Athenian.
R. M. S. Tartar.

Special reduction (first class only) granted to members of the Military, Naval, Diplomatic and Civil services and to Missionaries.

Passengers have choice of ten routes across the Continent of America and have privilege of travelling by any Atlantic Steamship Line.

Round the World passage tickets in connection with the P. and O. S. N., North German Lloyd and Messageries Co.'s **£125.**

All rates payable at current rate of exchange.

For further information, Tickets, Guide Books, etc., apply to

HOLME, RINGER & Co., AGENTS,
Chemulpo.

Grand Hotel

(Formerly the Station Hotel)

Near the Railway Terminus, West Gate Seoul.

The Best Hotel in Korea
Handsome new Building.
Fine Airy Rooms
Excellent Cuisine.
Terms Moderate.
Special terms to Missionaries
and to permanent boarders.

Electric cars within 2 minutes' walk.

W. H. EMBERLEY.
Proprieto

EVERY FACILITY.

in connection with Life Assurance Business is afforded by

The Standard Life Assurance Co.,

One of the largest and wealthiest of the Provident Institutions of the United Kingdom Forms of Application and all information will be promptly afforded on application.

10 CENTS A DAY.

Not a very large expenditure is it? But it is sufficient to secure for a man of 30 a policy with the STANDARD LIFE OFFICE for

$1323.

For all particulars of rates, etc., apply to

Holme, Ringer & Co.,
Agents, Chemulpo.

THE NEW YORK LIFE INSURANCE COMPANY.

Have you ever been declined by any Company?

Are you engaged in a specially hazardous occupation?

Have you heard of the New York Life Insurance Company's New Classifications for this class of Risks?

If not, send your date of birth, occupation and particulars of rejection, if any to

E. MEYER & Co.,
Agents, Chemulpo.

MITSUIBUSSAN KAIS.
(MITSUI & Co.)
MITSUI GINKO.
(MITSUI BANK.)

The Bank is owned by the members of the Mitsui Family, who, as partners, assume an unlimited responsibility for all liabilities of the Bank:—

Capital........................Yen 5,000,000
Reserve Fund.................. " 5,600,000

HEAD OFFICE, TOKYO.
LONDON OFFICE, 34 LIME ST., E. C.

BRANCHES AND AGENCIES:—

New York, San Francisco, Hamburg, Bombay, Singapore, Manila, Hongkong, Amoy, Chefoo, Tientsin.

Kobe, Hakodate, Yokohama, Kure, Yokosuka, Moji, Shimonoseki, Miike, Wakamatsu, Nagasaki, Kuchinotsu, Karatsu, Sasebo, Misume, Taipeh, &c.

Telegraphic Address for all the Offices:
"MITSUI."
A. B. C. AND A. I CODES USED.

Contractors of Coal
To the Imperial Japanese Navy. Arsenals and Railway Bureau, Principal Railway Companies and Industrial Work, Home and Foreign Mail and Freight Steamers.

Sole Proprietors
Of the famous Miike, Tagawa and Yamano Coal Mines.

Sole Agents
For the sale of Fukumo, Hokoku, Ichimura Kanoda, Mannoura, Onoura, Ostuji, Sonoda Tsubaruro, Yoshinotani, Yoshio, Yurokibura and other coals.

YANGTSE INSURANCE ASSOCIATION, LTD.

The undersigned, having been appointed agents for the above company, are prepared to issue policies and pay losses on marine risks at regular rates.

E. MEYER & Co.,
Agents, Chemulpo.

AMERICAN KOREAN ELECTRIC CO.

Light and Power.

Main Office: Electric Building, Chong No.

RAILWAY DEPARTMENT.

PERATING CARS BETWEEN EAST AND WEST GATE, EVERY TEN MINUTES:—

First Car leaves East Gate at 7:00 A. M. First Car leaves R. R. Station at 7:25 A. M
Last Car " East Gate at 8.40 P. M. Last " " R. R. Station at 9.05 P.M

OPERATING CARS BETWEEN EAST GATE AND IMPERIAL TOMB TERMINUS, EVERY TWENTY MINUTES:—
CONNECTING WITH EVERY ALTERNATE CAR ARRIVING AT EAST GATE FROM CHONG NO.

First Car leaves East Gate for Tomb at 7:10 A. M.
" " " Tomb for East Gate at 7:30 A. M.
Last " " East Gate for Tomb at 7:50 P. M.
" " " Tomb for East Gate at 8:10 P. M.

OPERATING CARS BETWEEN CHONG NO AND YUNG SAN RIVER EVERY TWELVE MINUTES:—

First Car leaves Chong No for South Gate at 7:12 A. M.
" " " Chong No for Yung San at 7:36 A. M.
" " " South Gate for Chong No at 7:20 A. M.
" " " Yung San for Chong No at 8:09 A. M.
Last " " South Gate for Chong No 9:00 P. M.
" " " Yung San for Chong No at 8.45. p. M.

SPECIAL PRIVATE CARS FURNISHED TO SUIT CONVENIENCE OF PATRONS. PRICES ON APPLICATION AT HEAD OFFICE.

LIGHTING DEPARTMENT.

Where less than 250 candle power of light is used, the rate per month will be
Per 16 candle power incandescent lamp,—All night.—Yen 2.50.
32 candle power incandescent lamp:—All night:—Yen 4.00.
50 candle power incandescent lamp:—All night:—Yen 6.00.
150 " " " " " " 10.00.
1200 " " enclosed arc " " " 20.00.

Where more than 250 candle power of light is used, a Meter will be installed, if requested:—Rent of Meter Yen 2.00 per month. Rate of charges by meter reading:—Two Sen per Ampere per hour. (Approximately this is equal to about One Sen per 16 C. P. lamp per hour) Minimum monthly charge where meter is installed, Yen 20.00 per month, which includes rental of meter.

Estimates for installing lights furnished on application

An assortment of chandeliers always on hand.

K. Murakami.
Photograph Studio
Chinkokai, Seoul.

Printing, Developing and Enlargement, of Photographs always Undertaken.

Korean Views and Pictures Illustrating Native Customs always on Sale,

---

THE OSAKA SHOSEN KAISHA.

Boats frequently on the berth for Chinnampo.

REGULAR SAILINGS BETWEEN JAPAN AND KOREAN PORTS.

FUSAN AND KOBE VIA SHIMONOSEKI.

OSAKA VIA MOKPO, FUSAN, SHIMONOSEKI AND KOBE.

MOJI DIRECT.

OSAKA VIA KUNSAN, MASANPO, FUSAN, SHIMONOSEKI AND KOBE.

CHEMULPO KUNSAN LINE,
Every three days.

CHEMULPO CHINNAMPO LINE.
Every three days.

For Freight and passage and further particulars apply to

THE OSAKA SHOSEN KAISHA,
Cemulpo

RONDON, PLAISANT & CO.

General Storekeepers and Merchants, Ships Contractors Tobacconists, Commission and Forwarding Agents, Coal Merchants

IMPORTERS AND EXPORTERS

Seoul Chemulpo.

W. D. WENTWORTH.

LANDING
AND
SHIPPING AGENT.
AND
CUSTOMS BROKER.

12 OURA, NAGASAKI.

STEWARD & CO.

Chemulpo.

Shipchandlers and Storekeepers, Naval and Mercantile Contractors, Landing and Shipping Agents.

STEWARD'S HOTEL

Chemulpo.

Best accommodation in the port for travellers. Clean and well-aired rooms, good cuisine and prompt attendance, oderate tariff.

론셜

평화소식

○연긔나는곳에는반다시불이잇다는리치로보면향샹젼쟁과흉는평화론셜이반다시무슴ᄉ등이잇는듯ᄒ나그런ᄒ나지금비롤로국과일본이싸홈을정지ᄒ고져의들의날을다렴ᄒ회의에맥기드리도현금사세로는능히강화이디만족ᄒ게졍졍ᄒ기어려울터이로다

로국이지금ᄭ지여러번패ᄒ엿스ᄂ예비가업는ᄉ룸이오젼투력이못ᄒ다고를녀보병슈업스며지금은젼쟁의시초에여러번패ᄒ것과갓지아니ᄒ야비록나아와쳐셔일본군을힘안으로몰니치기는능치못ᄒ드리도일본군이군략샹으로진ᄒ게를엇을본리쟈졍ᄒ목젹디되는할빈에득달ᄒ지는못ᄒ게될것이분명ᄒ도다

일본은려슌구를졈령ᄒ야셜디로명령ᄒ차지ᄒ리들고한국을거유ᄒ야제반항동이다령ᄒ하이나란에잇스란ᄒ고ᄒ며로국은한국과만쥬에졈노ᄒ는것이사이베리아쳘로의극단에일기부동항구를엇자는ᄯᅳᆺ인티그런항구들의잇는로디는지금일본이쟝중에다잇는지라

평졍은일본이벌셔취ᄒ것을차의로를녀보벌리엽고그외갓치로국도ᄯᅩᄒ여러ᄒ를두고경영ᄒ것을ᄒ번사싱을걸단ᄒ는군싸홈도엽시쎗기란고홀ᄯᅳᆺᄒ지아니ᄒ도다

이런것을다싱각ᄒ면나는반드시말ᄒ되젼쟁이쳠금평편티로잇는동안은평화담판의가망이매우며다ᄒ지나만일불리ᄒ티가마리군도에잇서서샹업을방히ᄒ는힝위를ᄒ디경이면중립렬강들이자긔들의히샹샹업을위ᄒ야간셥ᄒ기가쉬울터이나우리는로졔스트벤스기대쟝이어련의사롤가졋다는표젹을못보앗고무슴다른사세로말ᄒ드리도샹업의손히는두고젼국의샹업외에는다른나라의게는잔셥ᄒ를만ᄒᄉ름이업는지라

로국이ᄒ번크게승젼ᄒ야자긔의명예를회복ᄒ후에는평화조약을의논ᄒ기를긍락ᄒ런다고홀만ᄒ말들을ᄒ나그말이그런홀듯ᄒ지만는현금사샹으로논ᄒ고런홀ᄯᅳᆺᄒ지아니ᄒ것이구로팻긴대쟝이여러달을두고패ᄒ야놀너가다가종말은일본의젼진력을제어ᄒ엿고대산원슈의약ᄒ졈을터런일앗스나만일등비ᄒ셩젼을ᄒ터경에빈그대쟝이므옴을를녀ᄊ자긔의조ᄒ게ᄂ약치지ᄒ고를녀안져서평화조약을의론ᄒ기를긴거홀로밋기어렵도다

로국이그시비에란감ᄒ일을지번것이동양함대가부족ᄒ고사베리아쳘도가위령ᄒ고로국의로팟긴의무음놉샹ᄒ엿더니지금은너란도간쟁이되야가고쳘이도무사ᄒ고함대도더나은것나오니만일이세에로국황뎨외대신들이평화지셜을청죵ᄒ깃갓ᄒ면쟝놀보만ᄒ일이라이말저말ᄒ것업시두나라가갓ᄒ목젹으로싸우는티그목젹은한국과만쥬이라런션항락젼에는평화가근사ᄒ다고도흘만ᄒ거니와지금은정치샹실디로보면될듯ᄒ지아니ᄒ지라

아모라도일본의졍쟝이말못된것을알거니와우리도일본이금번말ᄭ지젼쟁을연속ᄒ평비를능히티지못ᄒ것을확실히알고로국에서도그런형편을자세히알고잇스니그런일이또ᄒ아즉ᄭ지는로국이평화담판에반ᄃᆡᄒ런유라ᄒ노라

외보

○너시마젹　항ᄌ아병이료서를웜ᄒ야우가뮨영ᄂ등디로티습ᄒ는배청국관병이ᄒ인ᄒ엿승으로본쟝부에셔죠시ᄒ항의를계츌ᄒ엿는티청국쟝부에셔죠사ᄒ즉우는아군의계ᄉ역ᄒ는마적이오그봉쟝들도피등이착용식긴ᄉ가분명ᄒ고결단코관병은아니라는의로회답ᄒ엿더라

○영ᄉ젼언　빅림쥬찰ᄒ영국대사가동국궁군차관리ㅣ써의연셜에티ᄒ야만쥬ᄒ젼쳔언을며ᄒ엿는티그연셜은덕국에티ᄒ며ᄒ야티며ᄒ의건을불합ᄒ즈로힐흠이라더라

○충독만한　셩피득보총독도레보ㅣ쟝군이학무부쥬사롤볼너다가고유ᄒ되학구생에무쟝부쥬의는반멸흘건싱인죠학교에셔다시더러남을거젼흘것시머싱도는디쟝온히방츙ᄒ되만일다시교슈중에학싱의계동쟝을표ᄒ는자가잇스면피등보교후은젼폐흘이가ᄒ다고ᄒ엿더라

○쟝욕판흰　루리면셩거ᄒ죵로국메이군단사령관삭리광벨구쟝군그막ᄂ외동도ᄒ야로경에귀ᄒ는도차이롤구쏘구예착ᄒ엿다는티동쟝군의샹경ᄒ는목젹은흉구쟝군이며차난국에지ᄒ야조롱도고려흠이무ᄒ교쏘젼군으로ᄒ야곰단티케ᄒ사에티ᄒ야흉구쟝군을핀힉코져ᄒ이라ᄒ엿더라

○강화불원　론돈뎐보에ᄒ엿스되강화셜이아이셩힝ᄒ고로국에셔는군용품파군함제조의쥬문을정지ᄒ고군티동원령을중지ᄒ엿다ᄒ엿더라

○신문평론　론돈뎐보를거ᄒ즉영국각신문에는론평ᄒ야골아ᄃᆡ일로기젼ᄒ지일쥬년에로국이야심은젼혀파ᄒ엿고법국모든신문에는론평ᄒ야골아ᄃᆡ목하로국의젼쟁이무법ᄒ지라고인민의혁명운동을두젼교쟈ᄒ흘진티강화ᄒ는외에죠흔슈가단이업다ᄒ고ᄯᅩ로법동맹이불ᄒ흔자라다ᄒ엿더라

○차관계약　북경뎐을거ᄒ즉북쳥사변의비샹부족익을보충ᄒ기위ᄒ야쳥국졍부에셔향항과및상회은힝과덕국아세아은힝에셔년리오푼으로계약ᄒ고일쳔만방을차관ᄒ는티그담보는산셔셩리금세로뎡ᄒ엿다더라

○덕뎨란힝　덕국황뎨와및황ᄐ후ᄭ셔셔년금사월이십삼일노위디시ᄒ야디중히연안을란힝ᄒ신다더라

잡보

○환퇴북도　함경남도관찰사가너부로뎐보ᄒ엿스되〔십ᄉ일밤에〕아병삼빅여명이남으로나아와함흥ᄭ지도달ᄒ엿다가다시북도로환퇴ᄒ엿다ᄒ엿더라

○빙교셜치　마포탕뎡과지예일인산본씨가빙교를셜치ᄒ는고로순검이금지ᄒ즉일인의말이경무쳥과한셩부에고ᄒ엿라ᄒ는고로다시불쳥ᄒ는지라경무쳥에셔한셩부로조회ᄒ엿다더라

○부등불허　작일하오삼시에너부쟝원경셔리김명진씨가사롤셜명ᄒ야골아ᄃᆡ빅사의소영이소츌의리익이보다희팔ᄒ고로부등불허ᄒ고ᄒᆯ슈밧게엽다ᄒ엿더라

○청화무퇴착　근일각대관의청들이쟝ᄉ롤빙자ᄒ고화투롤소크게너기ᄒ다가경무쳥에퇴착ᄒ엿는ᄃᆡ모대관의소쳥은그본가의셔퇴착된줄은아지못ᄒ고도주ᄒ는줄노안다더라

○가사남뎡　김판셔종헌씨는소안동가사롤공젼쇼부에대ᄒ야대ᄂ니쳥ᄒ에납뎡ᄒ엿더라

○경리쳥츅　평무관엄셕우씨가숭계최병쥬등의리포령을볼시ᄒ야달나고션경무ᄉ의게간쳥ᄒ는지라션씨가ᄃᆡ답ᄒ되이는위벼가쳥ᄒ야도로허쳥ᄒ야안니ᄒ무엄이경리막심ᄒ다ᄒ고곳자퇴ᄒ라ᄒ엿다더라

○조쳥호조　일공ᄉ가외부로조회ᄒ기를우리문부셩시학관이웃고쟝일비가귀국의학무시찰ᄒ기위ᄒ야금번평셩에리도ᄒ야각ᄃᆡ방의교휴시찰을밧ᄂ니편케ᄒ야달나ᄒ엿더라

○면조너부　외부에서너부로조회ᄒ기를일공ᄉ조회니에함

○경남도관찰ᄉ리헌경이가우리군ᄉ샹에뎐당치못ᄒ산가잇스니급히면판ᄒ고함흥군슈리교셩으로관찰사를잉명ᄒ든지혹셔나로차정ᄒ든지ᄒ야주시되만일디연ᄒ면구리군티에셔자힝조쳐홀수로군사령부의통교가잇시니청컨티너부대신으로ᄒ여금속히조쳐ᄒ라ᄒ엿기로조회ᄒ노라ᄒ엿더라

○관게비평　외부에서일공관에조회ᄒ기를농상공부조회너에빅목젼시민등이등소ᄒ엿스되마국이리로본민등이ᄒ티로셔업자싱ᄒ던니불의에일본인이젼앙히목쳐을세워우리샹무샤방히ᄒ니외부로조회ᄒ와일공샤와교셥ᄒ야금히쳘키ᄒ야안업케ᄒ야달나흠을의ᄒ야조회ᄒ오니일공사의게면조ᄒ야조히를쳑을불일휘철ᄒ야샹업에안케ᄒ라ᄒ는ᄉ라히시젼은본리관가로서셜시ᄒ야상민으로ᄒ야금티티로영업ᄒ야뎨국도셩의켸졔를위ᄒ이어늘금에귀국상민의젼ᄀᆞᆫ앙히목쳐을세우는거순우리상민에만히로올쌘아니라지믜도면시의계계에손히가잇는지라청컨티경셩에주ᄒ귀공ᄉ의계훈칙ᄒ야금히철거ᄒ야샹민의졍형을편안케ᄒ고목의물도타올케ᄒ라ᄒ엿더라

○군량소화　셩진감리가외부로뎐보ᄒ엿는티일작에로병이군량수만셕을소화ᄒ고경셩으로퇴거ᄒ엿다더라

○반포젼불급　관제와군제의의뎡반포ᄒ기젼에는월급을지발치안니ᄒᆫ다더라

○사진근무　작일브터는각부대신이사진사퇴ᄒ기를특별히근무ᄒ다더라

○장임천졍　갑빈능내리도지셔는천정을임ᄒ다더라

○디자쳥장　강원도등쳔거ᄒ는빅소수랍ᄒ는너인이빅부인이라자쳥ᄒ며순빈궁에친긴ᄒ다ᄒ고부인가지고시찰노단니면서무세ᄒ인민의계징렴ᄒ야지로밋기교롤을버ᄒ엿다더라

광고

TELEGRAMS.

(FROM JAPAN PAPERS.)

RUSSIAN AFFAIRS.

London, Feb. 9.

The Paris correspondent of the *Times* declares that the prospects of early peace are slender.

The same correspondent also reports that the Russian loan, which is being issued in Paris, is meeting with very little success, only a hundred million francs having been subscribed up to the present.

Berlin, Feb. 9.

The Russian loan in Paris has failed. Russian circles allege that a new attempt will be made again in April. Other parties take the failure as a hope for peace.

Berlin, Feb. 9.

The revolution in Russian Poland is assuming a national Polish character.

London, Feb. 9.

The Tsar has issued an Imperial Ordinance appointing M. Kobeco (?), Privy Councillor, Censor of the Press and also Chairman of the Committee for the amendment of the Press Law.

GENERAL NEWS.

London, Feb. 9.

In spite of the number of vessels captured by the Japanese recently, underwriters at Lloyds are stated to be realising substantial profits on the insurance of ships carrying contraband cargoes to Vladivostok.

Berlin, Feb. 9.

The celebrated German painter Adolf von Menzel is dead.

SEVERE PUNISHMENT FOR BLOCKADE RUNNERS.

Lond, Jan. 4.

The Standard learns from an authoritative source that Japan intends to propose an alteration of the rules of war affecting blockade runners. The fall of Port Arthur has revealed the full extent to which blockade running enabled the garrison to prolong its resistance, resulting in the sacrifice of thousands of Japanese lives. International law inflicts no penalty upon those in charge of blockade runners beyond the confiscation of the vessel and cargo. Japan demands that captains and crews should be treated as belligerents and severely punished. Japan, the "Standard" says, will ask for a conference of jurists-consults to discuss the question.

The magistrate of Chulsan (near Wiju) reports that he received notice from the commandant of the Japanese garrison in that district that a Korean named No Hak Nyom had been found guilty of pilfering railway materials, and would, on January 21st, in accordance with martial law, be publicly shot as a warning to others. The magistrate interceded for the man, but to no effect, and the sentence was duly carried out.

It seems at last to be dawning on some of the higher officials that unless it is wished to furnish the Japanese with pretexts for taking over the country, there is no time to be lost in effecting reforms. Mr. Choi Ik-hyen, a councillor of state, has presented three or four memorials to the throne praying for an improvement in the administration. In his last petition he says that he would sooner die than live with affairs as they are. He is very influentially supported; Messrs. Kim Hak-chin and Yun Yong-kou have presented memorials to the same effect and it is said that a former prime minister, Mr. Cho Pyeng-se will come up to Seoul, and, in company with all the government officials, will attend the court to support Mr. Choi's proposals.

THE CAR ACCIDENT.

With reference to the accident whereby a boy lost his leg the day before yesterday, we have received the following details which prove our view that the company was in no way to blame. "On a crowded car going to East Gate, a boy was standing on the steps and as the car neared the Gate, without giving any sign to the conductor or waiting for the car to stop the boy jumped from the moving car. In doing so he struck a telegraph pole, and was thrown back against the side of the car with his leg under the wheel. Neither conductor nor motorman could be held to blame for such an accident, due entirely to the boy's carelessness in jumping from a moving car. The accident happened almost directly in front of the Powerhouse compound at East Gate, and at the time there were hundreds of people, (probably thousands) in the street and immediate vicinity, en route to the Stone Fight. The fight was taking place only a very short distance away and from past experience we have learned that with the people excited over their national game, it requires but a spark to start a riot. Had one happened the day before yesterday so near the Powerhouse, the consequences might have been most serious and prompt action was necessary."

This is all very true, but in view of the fact that the Japanese have superceded the Korean police on the grounds of inefficiency, they are now responsible for order. So far as we have heard, there were no Japanese present, while they surely should afforded extra protection to the locality of a stone fight.

MORE SQUATTERS.

The Japanese have staked out a piece of ground in a district in the south of the city which is known to expert linguists as Ichŏng-nyong-chŏng. The preempted ground includes Korean archery pavilions and butts.

STILL THEY COME.

A Mr. Noshiri, an inspector of the Japanese Educational Department has arrived in Seoul. He will inspect all the schools in Korea, and the Japanese Minister asks for a passport for him.

The Japanese Minister's policy of abolishing various departments and installing Japanese advisers is not popular with the Koreans. It is said that there are hopes that some of the other Ministers may protest.

According to locally received Tokio telegrams there seems to have been a protest in America against the arbitration treaty with Japan. Another telegram says that the Czar has ordered his ministers to coöperate with popular representives in the formation of a representative Government.

Something akin to the Nagamori scheme seems to be in the air. It seems that the Japanese are negotiating with the Imperial Treasury bureau for permission to cultivate those fields which are set apart by the Government for the maintainence of the army and posting service. They offer to pay fair taxes and divide profits with the present owners. Query. Would the lion and the lamb live together in harmony.

At Chong No, in the centre of the city some enterprising Japanese has errected an immense hoarding immediately in front of some of the corner houses. The people who have thus been deprived of light and air, are naturally enough, strenuously kicking, but so far without result. The governor of Seoul gave the Japanese permission to put the thing there and this in itself is scandalous, but the wanton disregard of ancient Korean rights which the Japanese exhibit when they plant a big advertizing board right in front of some of the most important stores in the city must strike the Koreans as a very unhappy augury of what the future would be should the Japanese succeed in getting hold of the country. We advise the Japanese to take the thing away and erect it in Japan.

JAPAN'S NAVAL TACTICS.

Mr. H. W. Wilson has contributed to the Montly Magazine an instructive technical article on "Naval Lessons of the War." He points out that in this war the material employed has been of the very newest and best; the Japanese fleet was ahead of most of its European competitiors in obtaining the most perfect appliances, while the Russian ships were excellent. Japan scored first, and the blow struck on Feb. 8-9 was stunning, and had it been intantly followed up by the Japanese, Port Arther would have fallen within the first three weeks of war. The unreadiness of the Russians does not appear to have been altogether understood at Tokio, or else there were conditions, of which we know nothing, that intervened to prevent the seizure of Dalny—an event expected after the first blow at Port Arthur—since the opportunity was allowed to pass. One patent fact Mr. Wilson points out is the inefficiency of the torpedo, whilst the mine has played a conspicuous part. The British navy has Captain Ottley's mine, which is of a type similar to those used by the Japanese, but the use of these mines in war does not appear to have been thoroughly worked out as it was in Japan. "Yet mines in the Far East have done what torpedoes have failed do, and there is an enormous list of casualties to their credit." Mr. Wilson thinks the Japanese have not sufficiently used Nelson tactics. Had Admiral Togo struck hard and heavily in August tho Baltic Fleet would never have sailed, and though he might have lost a ship, it is probable that he would have taken at least one of the enemy's in exchange. At the same time, the writer admits, Togo had many difficulties to face. Again, in Kamimura's fight, the Japanese fought with the more fury because of the extreme severity shown by the Vladivostock ships to Japanese and neutral shipping, but when Kamimura may be said to have had the shattered Gromoboi and Rossia at his mercy he let them go, and broke off the pursuit instead of following them at all costs and sinking them. The more the history of this war is studied the more clearly does it appear that it is the first duty of the commander to press the immediate advantage to the umost, and that the ulterior results are, as a rule, best secured by such a course. "Not victory, but annihilation," is the true aim of naval war. "Generally speaking, the lessons of the war confirm predictions, except with regard to the deadliness of the torpedo and mine and the efficacy of modern artillery. The immense value of the large battleship and armoured cruiser has been again and again demonstrated."

The St. Louis World's Fair buildings, which cost £3,000,000 sterling, have been sold, to be taken down and carted away, for something under £80,000.

Several hundred workmen employed at the Uraga Shipbuilding Yard, Japan, struck work on February 7th, asking for an increase in wages by sen 15 per day. The employers refused their request.

According to a Berlin telegram, the Japanese Government, taking cognizance of an impression that Germany has not observed strict neutrality, has sent a formal dispatch of thanks to the German Government. It expresses the conviction that Germany has fulfilled her duties as a neutral throughout the war with exactness, and especially during the recent events in the war zone,

It is now being stated very definitely in well-informed quarters in London that the Japanese Minister will return to Japan in April or May next, the reason alleged being his growing inability to stand the English climate. The Viscountess Hayashi left England some weeks ago, chiefly for the same reason, and as she is not to return this is further cause for believing that the viscount will soon vacate his post. There are two nominees for the vacancy. One is M. Kato, who preceded Viscount Hayashi, the other, Baron Suyematsu who has been in Europe for some months on a special diplomatic mission.

TWEEDLEDUM AND TWEEDLEDEE.

At a court martial yesterday Major Yi of the Korean army was arraigned for maltreating some of the Il-chin-hc patriots at Wonchow.

The Major deposed that he dispersed the meeting because one of the speakers said "His Majesty the Emperor is also a subject of the Nation and we are the same as he, and have equal rights and liberties."

The speaker said that he did not say any such thing. He said "We are also the subjects of His Majesty the Emperor,"

The Major has plenty of evidence in support of his assertion and we should anyhow be disinclined to believe anyone who had fallen so low as to become an Il-chin-hoi-ite. It is exasperating to reflect that such an aggregation of unwashed loafers should be able to annoy responsible people.

In addition to their nasty caps many of these people have suddenly got weak eyes and taken to dark glasses. They most of them want a wash and we suggest that they see whether they will be allowed to spend part of their $18 a month subsidy in some of the Japanese bath houses.

Seoul has always been exempt from taxation and we are willing to wager the majority of these agitators do not know what they are agitating for.

By all means let them lay claim to equality with whomever they like. No one will be misled by them and any fuss only assists them in their object of self-advertisement.

Mr. H. R. Raspe, a partner in the well-known firm of Messrs. Raspe and Co., Kobe, died suddenly on the 9th inst. It is believed that he committed suicide.

The Korea Daily News.

Issued at 5 P. M. daily except Sundays.

Rate of Subscription:—
Per Year,............Yen 25.
Per Quarter,..........Yen 7.
Per Month,..........Yen 2.50.

Postage in Korea not charged extra.
Postage abroad charged extra.

Advertisements, 50 sen per day for 1 inch or less.
5 yen per month per inch.
50 yen per year per inch.

All communications to
E. T. BETHELL,
Editor and Publisher,
Pak-tong, Seoul.

THE PEACE RUMOURS.

Except for several "special service" telegrams which have reached Japan recently there are absolutely no indications that peace is any nearer now than it was a year ago.

Japan would certainly not ask for a cessation of hostilities now, and although what stands for a Government in Russia is at the moment confronted by serious internal troubles, there seems to be no real objection to the continuance of the war. On the contrary, most of those who have memorialized the Czar urge that an amelioration of the condition of the people would enable the Empire to bring this war to a successful finish.

It is said that the Czar is not only willing, but anxious, to grant the reforms asked for by the people, but that his advisers are restraining him. Whether these advisers are acting from a sincere desire to benefit the nation or from motives of self interest we cannot say, but at any rate the spectacle of Father Gapon, who after leading a mob to slaughter, skipped to Switzerland is a far from edifying one and not calculated to impress the Czar or his advisers in favour of the cause which he pretended to champion.

The following telegram, which has been received at the Tokio Foreign Office, seems to indicate, pretty clearly, the attitude which has been assumed by the people in Russia.

According to a Russian news agency the Council of Nobles in St. Petersburg adopted a petition to the Tsar. In it they said that Russia has now to face two foes, foes at home and foes abroad. In this difficult situation their loyalty was unshaken and they relied on the Sovereign to recue the people from their troubles. The petition proceeded as follows:—"This is not the first time that Russia has encountered evil fortune. But since ancient times whenever she has met trials she has emerged from them successfully and even with increased strength. In truth everything depends upon cöoperation between Sovereign and subject. We nobles, firmly believe that none can stand against such a union and that victory must crown it. Your Majesty is wise and all the people pray to see the practical operation of your wisdom. But unhappily the officials of the Government and the statesmen have no intelligence to solve problems that concern the weal of the State. Your Majesty's ancestors sought an expression of popular view through the people's representatives, but the foundations of autocratic government were never weakened by the act. On the contrary there resulted the State as it now is. Therefore, we Your Majesty's subjects, trust that Your Majesty will order the people's representatives to submit their opinions to the Throne, and that Your Majesty will grant them a share in the legislative and administrative power. If Your Majesty will permit cöoperation between ruler and ruled, the domestic troubles of the country will disappear, all the people will become zealous for the glory of Russia and will discharge their loyal duty so as to overthrow the enemy."

This address says nothing about the cessation of the war, on the contrary it urges these reforms as necessary in order that success in the war may be achieved.

The Japanese vernacular papers all discredit the rumours of peace, and one, the "Jiji," apparently looks upon the circulation of them as a Russian *ruse de guerre* and advises Japan not to abate her efforts on the strength of them.

There is, of course, another explanation. Those who are interested in the attempt to float another Japanese loan in London would find their task a far easier one, could the public be persuaded of the probability of an immediate conclusion of the war. The longer this war continues the harder will Japan find it to borrow money. China has just floated a five per cent loan at 97, while, from all we hear, Japan is having great difficulty in getting 85 for a six per cent loan.

Whichever way the subject is looked at, it seems hard to believe that Russia is about to sue for peace. If she is, then the Russians are not the people we took them to be, and the internal condition of Russia must be even worse than it is represented to be by the Tokio telegrams.

THE SHAHO.

There is no news today from the front, although telegrams may arrive before we go to press.

Commenting on the situation the "Kokumin" states that the lowest temperature has now been reached in Manchuria. A great movement on the part of the opposing Armies may therefore be expected to take place between the end of February and the beginning of March, for any delay after that time will greatly impede the movements of troops, owing to the melting of the snow, which usually begins about the 10th March. It is very probable, says our contemporary, that the approaching battle will prove a decisive one. But the Japanese Army is said to be fully prepared for any emergency, and the "Kokumin" assures the nation that the development of the situation may be watched without uneasiness.

Speaking of the battle at the end of January the "Japan Mail" says that there is in Japan, an impression that Kuropatkin hoped to induce a general advance of the Japanese centre and right when he struck at their left. In fact he expected that they would repeat the strategy of the Shaho battle when, as will be remembered, Oyama assumed the offensive with his centre and left so soon as the Russian attack developed on his right. But the Japanese did not move from their lines on the Shaho in response to Gripenberg's stroke on the Hun and thus Kuropatkin did not find his desired opportunity. That may very well be, but to the "Japan Mail" it appears that Kuropatkin looked for his great opportunity in Gripenberg's success against Liaoyang. Had such a success come in sight, the Russian Commander-in-Chief would have struck all along his front without awaiting any Japanese stroke.

VLADIVOSTOK

Telegrams have been received saying that Vladivostok, which has heretofore been a second class fortress, will now rank as a first-class fortress. This will presumably mean promotion for the commandant and his staff. It is also said that non-combatants have received notice that they are liable to be sent away should necessity arise.

The garrison is said to consist of 30,000 troops, and we learn that the repairs to the "Rossia" and "Gromoboi" have been completed, but that the "Bogatyr" is still under repair. The approaches to the harbour are blocked with thick ice, and ice-breakers are incessantly engaged in clearing a passage to the harbour. It is believed that these operations have caused many of the Russian mines to drift away, thus making navigation in those waters extremely dangerous.

Rear Admiral Jessen has succeeded Skrydloff in command of the fleet and has hoisted his flag on the "Rossia".

Two trains leave Vladivostok daily for Harbin, but little appears to be known there, as to the position on the Shaho.

The Japanese Government has issued an official notification to the effect that the lights and buoys and beacons in Tsugaru Strait and neighbouring places may often be extinguished to suit military necessities.

AMENITIES IN CHINA.

Writes "the Saunterer" in the Chefoo "Daily News;—The headline "artist" on the "N. C. Daily News" must be blessed with the type of cranium that is low in the frontal, and runs to a peak in the occipital regions. He is still under the spell of the nightmare that produces that beautiful specimen "The Bund Tragedy and repeats it several times on a single page. Here are some of his efforts in connection with paragaphs referring to the possible arrival at Shanghai of some of the Port Arthur non-combatants: "The Threatened Russian Invasion," and "The Prospective Russian Invasion." The gentlemay has mistaken his calling. He should have been the star boarder in a lunatic asylum. However, he may have had that end in view when he sought his present employment."

A London correspondent has good authority for stating that the Japanese Government, through Viscount Hayashi, has inquired of the British Government whether facilities might be expected to be given for the coaling of Japanese warships in the British East Indies. Coal, it is said, will not be actually wanted, as the Japanese will provide their own fuel; and all that is desired is the advantage of transferring it from colliers to warships in harbour.

The Minister of the Board of Foreign Affairs, Peking, has telegraphed to the Chinese Minister in Japan instructing him to do his utmost to induce the Japanese Government to suppress the publication of seditious and revolutionary publications by Chinese residents. He points out that these publications are exerting a dangerous disturbing influence and that they are undermining the loyalty of the people.

The Korea Daily News.

VOL. II, THURSDAY, FEBRUARY 16 1905 No. 36

大韓每日申報
대한미일신보

(뎨이쳔삼십칠호) (토요일) 일쳔구빅오년이월십팔일

본사고빅

이신보는영어와한어로석거미일츌판ᄒᆞ옵

신문가
한쟝 엽두돈오푼
일삭표 엽두량닷돈
우표가미삭닷돈
다맛돈으로밧숩

광고료는
긔한의쟝단과ᄌᆞ힝의다쇼로중감ᄒᆞ되렴가로밧을터이오며오티지아녀대한사람마다다이신문을보실터이니광고내실기롤원ᄒᆞ시는이들은우리신문샤에와서면약ᄒᆞ심을희망ᄒᆞ옵

○발힝소 박동대한미일신보샤법어학교압헤젼영국인셜필립집자리오
사쟝 영국인 (비셜)

평양 디리졈
○평양효동사는권미보씨로우리신문관의디리인을뎡ᄒᆞ엿스오니평양에계신구람코져ᄒᆞ시는쳠군ᄌᆞ는히디리졈에왕림ᄒᆞ와면의ᄒᆞ시옵

사고

○우리대한미일신보의목뎍은대한의안녕질서에관한모든뎨목에디ᄒᆞ야는공평한변론을쥬쟝홈이라우리동신원의탐보는신문보시는쳠군ᄌᆞ의게ᄒᆞᆼ샹보도ᄒᆞ리며편지를긔셔ᄒᆞ여주시는이는셩명과반디를젹어붓치시기를희망ᄒᆞ오니이거슬신문샹에긔지ᄒᆞ랴는거시아니오다만극히신용ᄒᆞ는증거를ᄉᆞᆷ고자홈이라긔자는아모긔셔던지긔지홈을되각ᄒᆞ논권리를가졋스나되각ᄒᆞ는리유를말홀터이오며공중평화를문란케ᄒᆞ논듯ᄒᆞᆫ긔셔는의례히밧지안켓숩나이다

●본샤셜시이릭로신문을미양우례로분젼ᄒᆞ와례젼부의임의로젼ᄒᆞᆫ듯스로면곳에는혹늦게젼ᄒᆞ기도ᄒᆞ며혹몃칠거슬ᄒᆞᆫ겁에젼ᄒᆞ기도ᄒᆞ며혹아니젼ᄒᆞ는곳도잇다ᄒᆞ와우리신문을ᄉᆞ랑ᄒᆞ야구람ᄒᆞ시는쳠군ᄌᆞ의게되ᄒᆞ야미우미안ᄒᆞ옴기로지금은분젼인을두고미일일즉이젼ᄒᆞ며아니젼ᄒᆞ거나늦게거나ᄒᆞᆫ폐가업도록ᄒᆞ랴ᄒᆞ오니혹아니젼ᄒᆞ거나혹늣게젼ᄒᆞ거나ᄒᆞᆫ일이잇스면본샤로통긔ᄒᆞ여쥬심을희망ᄒᆞ옵

관보

뎨삼쳔륙십ᄉᆞ호
광무구년이월십륙일목요

서임급사령
○히경임충청남도지판소판ᄉᆞ 충청남도젼관찰ᄉᆞ 심건틱
○히경임황히도지판소판ᄉᆞ 황히도젼관찰ᄉᆞ 김학수
○명경임충청남도지판소판ᄉᆞ 충청남도관찰ᄉᆞ 됴죵필
○명경임황히도지판소판ᄉᆞ 황히도관찰ᄉᆞ 서정슌
○면본관 경무청총슌 송지, 슈
○의원면본관 충청남도관찰부쥬ᄉᆞ 리긔필 ᄂᆡ부광제원쥬ᄉᆞ 라치면
○임충청남도관찰부쥬ᄉᆞ셔판임관륙등 박슌연
○임ᄂᆡ부광제원쥬ᄉᆞ셔판임관륙등 김정휘
○히ᄂᆡ부광제원위원곽죵한 셔현쥬
○명ᄂᆡ부광제원위원 ᄂᆡ부광제원쥬ᄉᆞ 허협 ᄂᆡ부광제원쥬ᄉᆞ 강대창
○임ᄂᆡ부광제원쥬ᄉᆞ셔판임관륙등 김현국 송광옥
○히ᄂᆡ부광제원위원 리종원 쟝영근 윤문히 리승화
○명ᄂᆡ부광제원위원 리춘셰 허면 안기호 박경진
이샹이월십삼일
○의원면본관 시강원시종관 리긔용
○임시강원시종관셔판임관륙등 구품 리희츙
○승셔판임관오등 철도원기수 최한됴
이샹이월십ᄉᆞ일

통신원소관
뎨삼관 뎐보ᄉᆞ업비십사만륙쳔팔빅륙십원
뎨일항 봉급일만륙쳔십원
뎨이항 청비 일만팔쳔일빅ᄉᆞ원
뎨삼항 청사수리비 이쳔이빅오십원
뎨사항 뎐료구미비 삼만원 지화
뎨오항 뎐간구미비 이만원
뎨륙항 뎐료운반급비치비 일만원
뎨칠항 잡급과잡비 사만륙쳔오빅팔십원
뎨팔항 려비 일쳔삼빅원
뎨구항 뎐보학교비 이빅사십원
뎨십이항 학도류학비 이쳔삼빅이십원 지화
뎨사관 션사업비 일만사쳔칠빅륙십원
뎨일항 청비 삼쳔십오원
뎨이항 잡급과잡비 일만구빅륙십이원
뎨삼항 려비 칠빅팔십삼원
지화지츌차중 사만일빅삼십삼원
통신원소관합계 사십칠만이쳔오빅사십원
세츌경상부합계 일쳔사빅이십사만칠쳔륙빅이십사원
세츌림시부
궁ᄂᆡ부소관
뎨일관 즁건비 이십만원
뎨일항 경운궁즁건비 이십만원
뎨이관 신축비 일만원
뎨일항 긔항쟝 경무셔신축비 일만원
궁ᄂᆡ부소관합계 이십일만원
의정부소관
뎨일관 관제리정소 삼쳔삼빅원
뎨일항 봉급 일쳔오빅륙십원
뎨이항 청비 일쳔일빅륙십사원
뎨삼항 잡급과잡비 오빅칠십륙원
의정부소관합계 삼쳔삼빅원
ᄂᆡ부소관
뎨일관 토목비 이만구쳔원
뎨일항 준쳔비 오쳔원
뎨이항 치도비 이만원
뎨삼항 셕축비 ᄉᆞ쳔원
뎨사항 각군교션수리비 일쳔원

잡보

○청원미축 미축회샤쟝리쥰영씨가외부에청원ᄒᆞ엿는디인쳔부산삼화삼항니히만에샹업물픔싯교푸는디편리ᄒᆞ기위ᄒᆞ야본샤에서미축코자ᄒᆞ야잔략ᄒᆞᆫ디도두쟝을쳠년ᄒᆞ야앙고ᄒᆞ오니사죠ᄒᆞ신후소유미축권을본샤에특허ᄒᆞ시와긔공에편리를독케ᄒᆞ옵소셔ᄒᆞ엿더라

○훈칙각항 외부에서각항시에훈령ᄒᆞ기를청국공사죠회ᄂᆡ기에본사가임의도임ᄒᆞᆫ지라각항구령사를션틱쥬픠ᄒᆞ야통샹사건을샹관ᄒᆞ야피ᄎᆞ샹민이고르럽게리익을득ᄒᆞ기위ᄒᆞ야금에오이창으로인쳔졍령사를대리ᄒᆞ야군산목포사무를겸관케ᄒᆞ고오기조로부산령사를대리ᄒᆞ야마산사무를겸관케ᄒᆞ고당은샹으로삼화부령사을잉츙ᄒᆞ야평양사무를겸관케ᄒᆞ고녀자샹으로원산부령사를대리케ᄒᆞ노니히관원등이다사리에명달ᄒᆞ기로파왕ᄒᆞ노니청컨대각히관관원의게훈칙ᄒᆞ라ᄒᆞ는등인을쥰ᄒᆞ야훈령ᄒᆞ노라ᄒᆞ엿더라

뎐보

론돈발 동일
○혁명운동 이사이베리아철로근디에만연ᄒᆞ야열구스크와그라스노야스크에는무역이위황ᄒᆞ며그ᄭᆞ닭으로구로팟긴대장의동신과관이단졀홀렴녀가잇다더라

동디발 동일
○부닉넌씨로ᄂᆡ부대신을임명ᄒᆞ엿다더라

볼틱함디의뎨삼회
론돈발 이월일일
○뎨삼볼틱함디가금월륙일에극동으로향ᄒᆞ야츌발ᄒᆞᆫ다는디그함디는젼투함삼쳑과슌양함이쳑으로조직ᄒᆞ엿스며ᄉᆞ령관희군대장월네토푸씨라더라

○구로팟긴의보고 구로팟긴
논돈발 이월륙일
의보고를거ᄒᆞᆫ즉금월일일에일본인이혼하좌안에장탄혜남이라는쎠를포격ᄒᆞ야로국인을모라니스나로군이병력을더ᄒᆞ야다시그동리를쎄아섯다더라

동디발 동월삼일
○구로팟긴의셩젼 일월삼십일일에로국포병이챈탄부와그근디에포격ᄒᆞ야일본군이물너가셔위치를쎄앗겻다더라

빅림발 동월삼일
○구로팟긴의군비 셩피득보에셔구로팟긴의ᄉᆞ월과오월분

UNION INSURANCE SOCIETY OF CANTON.

Head office Hongkong.
Marine risks underwritten at current rates.
Agents in Chemulpo,
E. MEYER & Co.

COMPAGNIE DES MESSAGERIES MARITIMES.

'ortnightly Direct Service.

For Marseilles
via Ports.
Sailing from Yokohama
Calling at Kobe,
Shanghai, Hongkong, Saigon, Singapore,
Colombo, Djibonti, Suez, Port Said
and Marseilles.

For particulars apply to
HOLME RINGER & Co.,
Chemulpo.

HAYASHIDA & CO.,

16 MYENG DONG, CHIN KO KAI, SEOUL.
BRANCH OFFICE AT CHEMULPO.

Money changers, Coal and Wood Merchants, Express Agents.

We are agents for the Pyeng-yang Coal Company and the Karazu Coal Company of Japan. We have the best quality of both anthracite and bituminous coal, and prompt execution of orders is our speciality. Firewood of all kinds kept in stock. Full weight guaranteed. Money of all denominations exchanged at current rates. Parcels received for all parts.

CHINA MUTUAL LIFE INS. OC.

Most favourable terms to policy holders.

Benefit system unsurpassed.

HOLME RINGER & Co.
Agents, Chemulpo.

C. P. R.

CANADIAN PACIFIC RAILWAY COMPANY'S ROYAL MAIL STEAMSHIP LINE.

THE FAST ROUTE BETWEEN CHINA, JAPAN, AND EUROPE VIA CANADA AND THE UNITED STATES.

Route from Hongkong via Shanghai, Nagasaki (Inland Sea of Japan) Kobe, Yokohama, Victoria and Vancouver.

Twin Screw Empress Steamship—6,000 Tons—Speed 19 knots.

PROPOSED SAILING FROM YOKOHAMA.
R. M. S. Empress of India.
R. M. S. Empress of Japan.
R. M. S. Empress of China.
R. M. S. Athenian.
R. M. S. Tastar.

Special reduction (first class only) granted to members of the Military, Naval, Diplomatic and Civil services and to Missionaries.

Passengers have choice of ten routes across the Continent of America and have privilege of travelling by any Atlantic Steamship Line.

Round the World passage tickets in connection with the P. and O. S. N., North German Lloyd and Messageries Co.'s £125.

All rates payable at current rate of exchange.

For further information, Tickets, Guide Books, etc., apply to

HOLME, RINGER & Co., AGENTS,
Chemulpo.

Grand Hotel

(Formerly the Station Hotel)

Near the Railway Terminus,
West Gate Seoul.

The Best Hotel in Korea
Handsome new Building.
Fine Airy Rooms
Excellent Cuisine.
Terms Moderate.
Special terms to Missionaries
and to permanent boarders.

Electric cars within 2 minutes' walk.

W. H. EMBERLEY.
Proprieto

EVERY FACILITY.

In connection with Life Assurance Business is afforded by

The Standard Life Assurance Co.,

One of the largest and wealthiest of the Provident Institutions of the United Kingdom Forms of Application and all information will be promptly afforded on application.

10 CENTS A DAY.

Not a very large expenditure is it? But it is sufficient to secure for a man of 30 a policy with the STANDARD LIFE OFFICE for

$1323.

For all particulars of rates, etc., apply to
Holme, Ringer & Co.,
Agents, Chemulpo.

THE NEW YORK LIFE INSURANCE COMPANY.

Have you ever been declined by any Company?

Are you engaged in a specially hazardous occupation?

Have you heard of the New York Life Insurance Company's New Classifications for this class of Risks?

If not, send your date of birth, occupation and particulars of rejection, if any to

E. MEYER & Co.,
Agents, Chemulpo.

MITSUI BUSSAN KAISHA.
(MITSUI & Co.)

MITSUI GINKO.
(MITSUI BANK.)

The Bank is owned by the members of the Mitsui Family, who, as partners, assume an unlimited responsibility for all liabilities of the Bank:—

Capital........................Yen 5,000,000
Reserve Fund.................. " 5,600,000

HEAD OFFICE, TOKYO.
LONDON OFFICE, 34 LIME ST., E. C.

BRANCHES AND AGENCIES:—
New York, San Francisco, Hamburg, Bombay, Singapore, Manila, Hongkong, Amoy, Chefoo, Tientsin.
Kobe, Hakodate, Yokohama, Kure, Yokosuka, Moji, Shimonoseki, Miike, Wakamatsu, Nagasaki, Kuchinotsu, Karatsu, Sasebo, Misume, Taipeh, &c.

Telegraphic Address for all the Offices:
"MITSUI."
A. B. C. AND A. 1 CODES USED.

Contractors of Coal
To the Imperial Japanese Navy. Arsenals and Railway Bureau, Principal Railway Companies and Industrial Work, Home and Foreign Mail and Freight Steamers.

Sole Proprietors
Of the famous Miike, Tagawa and Yamano Coal Mines.

Sole Agents
For the sale of Fukumo, Hokoku, Ichimura Kanoda, Mannoura, Onoura, Ostuji, Sonoda Tsubarr[illegible], Yoshinotani, Yoshio, Yurokibura and other coals.

YANGTSE INSURANCE ASSOCIATION, LTD.

The undersigned, having been appointed agents for the above company, are prepared to issue policies and pay losses on marine risks at regular rates.

E. MEYER & Co.,
Agents, Chemulpo.

AMERICAN KOREAN ELECTRIC CO.

Light and Power.

Main Office: Electric Building, Chong No.

RAILWAY DEPARTMENT.

OPERATING CARS BETWEEN EAST AND WEST GATE, EVERY TEN MINUTES:—

First Car leaves East Gate at 7:00 A. M. First Car leaves R. R. Station at 7:25 A. M
Last Car " East Gate at 8.40 P. M. Last " " R. R. Station at 9.05 P.M

OPERATING CARS BETWEEN EAST GATE AND IMPERIAL TOMB TERMINUS, EVERY TWENTY MINUTES:—

CONNECTING WITH EVERY ALTERNATE CAR ARRIVING AT EAST GATE FROM CHONG NO.

First Car leaves East Gate for Tomb at 7:10 A. M.
" " " Tomb for East Gate at 7:30 A. M.
Last " " East Gate for Tomb at 7:50 P. M.
" " " Tomb for East Gate at 8:10 P. M.

OPERATING CARS BETWEEN CHONG NO AND YUNG SAN RIVER EVERY TWELVE MINUTES:—

First Car leaves Chong No for South Gate at 7:12 A. M.
" " " Chong No for Yung San at 7:36 A. M.
" " " South Gate for Chong No at 7:20 A. M.
" " " Yung San for Chong No at 8:09 A. M.
Last " " South Gate for Chong No 9:00 P. M.
" " " Yung San for Chong No at 8.45. p. M.

SPECIAL PRIVATE CARS FURNISHED TO SUIT CONVENIENCE OF PATRONS. PRICES ON APPLICATION AT HEAD OFFICE.

LIGHTING DEPARTMENT.

Where less than 250 candle power of light is used, the rate per month will be
Per 16 candle power incandescent lamp,—All night.—Yen 2.50.
32 candle power incandescent lamp:—All night:—Yen 4.00.
50 candle power incandescent lamp:—All night:—Yen 6.00.
150 " " " " " " ,, 10.00.
1200 " " enclosed arc " " " ,, 20.00.

Where more than 250 candle power of light is used, a Meter will be installed, if requested:—Rent of Meter Yen 2.00 per month. Rate of charges by meter reading:—Two Sen per Ampere per hour. (Approximately this is equal to about One Sen per 16 C. P. lamp per hour) Minimum monthly charge where meter is installed, Yen 20.00 per month, which includes rental of meter.

Estimates for installing lights furnished on application

An assortment of chandeliers always on hand.

K. Murakami.

Photograph Studio
Chinkokai, Seoul.

Printing, Developing and Enlargement, of Photographs always Undertaken.

Korean Views and Pictures Illustrating Native Customs always on Sale,

---

THE OSAKA SHOSEN KAISHA.

Boats frequently on the berth for Chinnampo.

REGULAR SAILINGS BETWEEN JAPAN AND KOREAN PORTS.

FUSAN AND KOBE VIA SHIMONOSEKI.

OSAKA VIA MOKPO, FUSAN, SHIMONOSEKI AND KOBE.

MOJI DIRECT.

OSAKA VIA KUNSAN, MASANPO, FUSAN, SHIMONOSEKI AND KOBE.

CHEMULPO KUNSAN LINE,
Every three days.

CHEMULPO CHINNAMPO LINE,
Every three days.

For Freight and passage and further particulars apply to
THE OSAKA SHOSEN KAISHA,
Chemulpo.

RONDON, PLAISANT & CO.

General Storekeepers and Merchants, Ships Contractors Tobacconists, Commission and Forwarding Agents, Coal Merchants

IMPORTERS AND EXPORTERS

Seoul Chemulpo.

W. D. WENTWORTH.

LANDING
AND
SHIPPING AGENT.
AND
CUSTOMS BROKER.

12 OURA, NAGASAKI.

STEWARD & CO.

Chemulpo.

Shipchandlers and Storekeepers, Naval and Mercantile Contractors, Landing and Shipping Agents.

STEWARD'S HOTEL

Chemulpo.

Best accommodation in the port for travellers. Clean and well-aired rooms, good cuisine and prompt attendance,moderatetariff.

군ᄒᆞᆫ군비를거졍ᄒᆞᄂᆞᆫᄃᆡ그것
은만주에셔문표등이결핍된연고
이더라

동뎐발 동월삼일

○북미합즁국과베비숑나
베숑나대통령카스드로씨가그 베
나라에잇ᄂᆞᆫ미국공사색랏운씨
의게무례히ᄒᆞᆫᄉᆞ단으로미국군
함이베비숑나에ᄃᆡᄒᆞ야시위운
동을ᄒᆞ다더라

로국의졍형

론돈발 이월륙일

○로국즁추원참의관사표로표
씨ᄂᆞᆫ형졍기랑위원쟝을명ᄒᆞ엿
다더라

동뎐발 동일

○ᄇᆡ각의쟝원드씨ᄂᆞᆫ황뎨께셔
ᄒᆡᆨ이졍졍ᄃᆡᄒᆞ여간다더라

동뎐발 동일

○혁명운동이로국사면에만연
ᄒᆞ여교가ᄉᆡᆼᄃᆡ방과쳘로연변에
ᄒᆞᆫ셰쓰군과혁명당등사비에챵
ᄒᆞᆫ젼쥐가니러난다더라

동뎐발 동일

○로동자의분요가사이버리아
셔지방연ᄒᆞ여사졍이심난ᄒᆞ게
되엿스며구주에가ᄂᆞᆫ뎐보ᄂᆞᆫ다
졍지되엿고쇼젼과헤비병샹젼
ᄒᆞ며명이그니란에연합ᄒᆞ엿다더
라

빅린발 동일

○오렛사ᄃᆡ학교ᄂᆞᆫ한엉을피ᄒᆞ
고학교를닷쳣다더라

외보

○ᄃᆡ오비평 일아기젼이일주
년이되엿ᄂᆞᆫ지라론돈타임쓰신
평ᄒᆞ엿스되일본국을비교ᄒᆞ야챵
예의ᄒᆞ야비샹히즁ᄃᆡᄒᆞᆫ시졍ᄒᆞ
에렴ᄒᆞᆫᄌᆞㅣ오쏘일본은오히려
싱관활동을계속ᄒᆞ야그압박을
능감ᄒᆞ야화쳔ᄒᆞᆫᄃᆡ위를교ᄃᆡᄒᆞ
엿스니셜노일본에무루ᄒᆞᆫ셰력
은그열셩ᄒᆞᆫ챵셩ᄌᆞ가에괴ᄒᆞᆷ보
다더쟝ᄃᆡᄒᆞᆷ을시ᄒᆞ엿ᄂᆞᆫᄃᆡ우리
ᄂᆞᆫ일본이즁국에ᄂᆞᆫ승리를수ᄒᆞᆷ
을예괴ᄒᆞ야죠곰도의려업고즁
리의소망을괴ᄒᆞᆫ다ᄒᆞ엿더라

○뉴욕통신 뉴욕근신을드른
ᄒᆞᆫ즉근일병혁을공포ᄒᆞ야도란
ᄒᆞᄂᆞᆫ아국평디(혜루화)인비히
디로뎐속리도ᄒᆞᄂᆞᆫ즁인ᄃᆡ최근
오기월간에리챡ᄒᆞᆫ아인수가쳘
만오쳔일빅룩십인에달ᄒᆞ엿ᄂᆞᆫ
ᄃᆡ이민관헌이차를불열ᄒᆞ고각
기숑환ᄒᆞᄂᆞᆫ방법을인츌ᄒᆞ야최ㄷ
싱일간에보조를요구ᄒᆞ야숑환
ᄒᆞᆫᄌᆞ이오빅이십팔명인ᄃᆡ특히
샹무이민에관ᄒᆞᆫ당국ᄌᆞᄂᆞᆫ이것
치랍일홈에관ᄒᆞ야극히비려ᄒᆞ
ᄂᆞᆫ즁이며(예리수)도의관헌은
우보조이민에관ᄒᆞ야하등법령
을셩안ᄒᆞ야금회린방회의에졔
츌ᄒᆞ기를결뎡ᄒᆞ엿다더라

론셜

ᄒᆡ삼위의졍형

○츈졀이도라와셔ᄒᆡ동되기젼
에ᄂᆞᆫᄒᆡ샹위항구에셔란이나셔
믈이드리가기어려운것이쇼야
ᄒᆡ쳥은지금항빙ᄒᆞ엿고ᄒᆡ샹위
에드러가ᄂᆞᆫ항로ᄂᆞᆫ다만쇄시마
나죽삭가루ᄒᆡ협쌘인ᄃᆡ그ᄒᆡ협
은일본사롬이졍밀히경찰ᄒᆞᄂᆞᆫ
것이분명ᄒᆞ도다그ᄒᆡ협에셔일
본이포획ᄒᆞᆫ쥰션슈효를우리가
요젼에반포ᄒᆞ엿거니와그후에
셔이쳔구빅구십팔톤되ᄂᆞᆫ영국륜
션이쓰트리호가쇗웰심ᄐᆡᄅᆞᆫ을싯
고가다가금월칠일에포획되엿
고덕국륜션팔노쓰호ᄂᆞᆫ금월십
일에북ᄒᆡ도에셔포획되엿ᄂᆞᆫ지
라ᄒᆡ샹위에셔셕탄은넉넉ᄒᆞᆫ듯
ᄒᆞᆫ것이ᄒᆞᆫ영국륜션의챵겅이ᄒᆡ
샹위로브터문스에와셔말ᄒᆞ되
ᄒᆡ샹위에잇ᄂᆞᆫ셕탄이심오만톤
가량이나된다ᄒᆞ며쏘말ᄒᆞ되자
괴ᄇᆡ와ᄀᆞᆺ치카듸푸에셔셰난빈
가비젹인ᄃᆡ일본군함의게쟝
ᄒᆡ고그뒤에덕국륜션일쳑이소
야ᄒᆡ쳥을지니셔겔빙ᄒᆞ기젼에
라ᄒᆡ샹위에잡ᄒᆞᆫ듯ᄒᆞ엿다ᄒᆞ엿더
론돈소식을드른즉사이베리아
연로에분요가니러나셔구로팟
셔공급ᄒᆞ게되리라ᄒᆞ엿스니ᄒᆡ
삼위에셕탄과식물의반ᄒᆡ비
가ᄒᆞᆫ것이로국을ᄒᆡ군에진ᄒᆞᆫ쳔됴
되리로다
지금ᄒᆞ야도쳔들이반히ᄒᆡ샹위로
향ᄒᆞ야간다ᄒᆞ나론돈소식을드
른즉빈입자들과보ᄒᆞᆫ자를이
그빈들이일본승양ᄒᆞᆷ에쟝ᄒᆞᆯ셰이
코게ᄒᆞ녀ᄒᆞ다ᄒᆞ며셰란실을빈
가ᄂᆞᆫ즁에만히지금ᄒᆡ샹위로향ᄒᆞ야
분디ᄉᆞ쳑은미국시앗를부터셔낫다
아니ᄒᆞ면춘졀이도라와셔소야지
ᄒᆡ샹위에쳥션ᄒᆞᆯ반ᄒᆞ게되기젼에
기미우어려우리라ᄒᆞ노라

잡보

○봉현봉금 탁지고문관목하
뎐씨가칭금귀국ᄒᆞᆫ즁인ᄃᆡ각부
부원쳥의봉금은ᄒᆡ씨가단녀나
온후에야지발ᄒᆞᆯ터이라더라

○조회청쟝 법공사가외부로
조회ᄒᆞ기를공나부에광학국을
셜치ᄒᆞᆯ시에기사너리를니의자
담ᄒᆞᆫ경비가일만삼쳔여원이라ᄒᆞ
공나부로조회ᄒᆞ야쳥쟝ᄒᆞ라ᄒᆞ
엿더라

○농부잉존 농샹공부가폐지
된다ᄒᆞ더니리지용씨가대신으
로피임ᄒᆞ야만단운동ᄒᆞᄂᆞᆫ고로
잉존ᄒᆞᆫ다더라

○뎐션립표 일인병마뎐씨가
뎐션을가셜ᄒᆞᆯᄎᆞ로현병사령부
로브터져등쟝교쳥을교등디즁
노셔지표목을립ᄒᆞ엿더라

○원조금안건 셩록일오후두
시에졍부에셔회의ᄒᆞ야부민의
원조금안건을졔츌ᄒᆞ야샹의ᄒᆞ
엿더라

○탐보부득 일젼에남셔쟝
ᄃᆡ니에셔포셩이굉발ᄒᆞ엿ᄂᆞᆫᄃᆡ
ᄃᆡ니에셔둥죽ᄒᆞ시고포셩의츌
쳐를곳탐보ᄒᆞ라ᄒᆞ오셧스나죵
금ᄭᆞ지탐득지못ᄒᆞᆫ지라ᄒᆞ셔쟝
셔ᄒᆞ슌쎄ᄂᆞᆫ반기월감봉에쳐ᄒᆞ
고기시엉지층춘숑적수씨ᄂᆞᆫ면
관이되엿더라

○법원심사 경계뎌에셔지휘
관리용관씨명령으로동항에셔
사무ᄒᆞᆫ인민을포샹ᄒᆞ엿다ᄒᆞᆷ으로
사셜ᄒᆞ기위ᄒᆞ야룡군법원에셔
평안북도관찰사리용관씨를압
샹ᄒᆞ엿다더니쟉셩오일에법원
쟝원우샹씨가기명ᄒᆞ고ᄒᆡ수진
을심문ᄒᆞ엿더라

○완거불납 동셔남북즁각셔
에셔우물치ᄂᆞᆫ츄렴을낫낫치봉
납ᄒᆞ되오직북셔니에젼ᄃᆡ신깅
규ᄒᆞᆼ쟝쟝권즁셕쳠평깅명계샹
진현께씨가완거불납ᄒᆞᄂᆞᆫ지라
경무쳥에셔ᄒᆡᆼ령ᄒᆞᆯ수가업다더
라

○궁금슈쳥 근일 황샹폐하
ᄭᅦ옵셔궁금을지칭수쳥ᄒᆞ시와
비수를반다시공수쳥을경유ᄒᆞ
야주풍시ᄒᆡᆼᄒᆞ고지밀에츌입ᄒᆞ
ᄂᆞᆫ거손일졀금ᄒᆞ옵셧ᄂᆞᆫᄃᆡ무
별과감ᄒᆞᆫ명이ᄯᆡ쳥ᄒᆞᆷ으로무랍ᄒᆞ
ᄂᆞᆫ자ᄂᆞᆫ칙명으로엄히진셥ᄒᆞ시리
사굿경쳥으로엄부ᄒᆞ라ᄒᆞ오셧
더라

○리씨구타 젼참셔관유치쥬셜
외일ᄒᆡᆼ을무단히쳥수ᄒᆞ고후주
ᄒᆞᆫᄃᆡ즁셔쟝리용승씨ᄂᆞᆫ평리원
에셔구타ᄒᆞ고법부에셔샹주ᄒᆞ
엿더라

○리씨손ᄒᆡ 경무쳥에셔최가
ᄒᆞ야각젼에쟝명등을셕유로쏘가
든것은불시ᄒᆞ고뎐등을실시ᄒᆞ
기로ᄒᆞᆫ지라일인셕유회사원샹
인이쟉심오일에경무수를방문ᄒᆞ
ᄒᆞ고셕유회사의손ᄒᆡ가불소ᄒᆞ
다고무수히샹지ᄒᆞ엿다더라

○학교일쥬 젼즁쟝엄쥰원씨
가시무에진흥을위ᄒᆞ야모든유
지ᄒᆞᆫ신사로단합ᄒᆞ야경법학교
를야쥬쳥에셜립ᄒᆞᆫ다더라

○로젼쳘거 죵노에셜젼ᄒᆞ엿
던일본샹민들이잉의쳘거ᄒᆞ엿
ᄂᆞᆫᄃᆡ졍부에셔일본샹민의게죵
로외에어ᄃᆡ든지기지를영쳑ᄒᆞ엿
자샤ᄒᆞ금ᄒᆞᆫ다ᄂᆞᆫ챵셜이잇더라

○호유샹민 죵로에모든샹민
들이경무쳥에호소ᄒᆞ기를일의투
계ᄒᆞᆫ바이어니와일젼에신경무
사가ᄒᆡ샹민ᄂᆞᆫ을경무쳥쳥샹으
로불너면유ᄒᆞ야잘아ᄃᆡ군등의
공린ᄒᆞᆷ은다시론난ᄒᆞᆯ거시아니
오너맛당히경무고문관의게간
츅ᄒᆞ야일샹을쳘거ᄒᆞ의로졔간
셜ᄒᆞ엿다더라

○한관면유 한셩관윤민경식
씨가모든죵로샹민을사계로불
너효유ᄒᆞ되군등의졍경이민망
ᄒᆞ니맛당히일본령ᄉᆞ와
교셥ᄒᆞ야쳘거케ᄒᆞ의로셜명ᄒᆞ
엿다더라

○귀구빅셩 한셩소윤박승조
씨가호소ᄒᆞᆫ샹민의게ᄃᆡᄒᆞ야갈
아ᄃᆡ이아만들아이아만들아샹
권ᄌᆞ모든다ᄅᆞᆫ모든권리를잃의
쟝셔심년젼에다일코엿지인졔와
관판란ᄒᆞ나됴곳믈ᄂᆡ가ᄒᆞᆫ졔교
를일ᄒᆞᆫ거슬빅셩의게ᄒᆡ를을돌
녀보니ᄂᆡ아만아만이라ᄒᆞ니아만분
빙자들은아만에셔엇마나나
ᄒᆞᆫ아고ᄒᆡᆼ셜이잇다더라

○넌결명간 금일은ᄃᆡ황샹원
명졀인고로일ᄉᆡᆯ을ᄯᅥᆨ간ᄒᆞ엿다
가져명보티다시츌간ᄒᆞᆯ터이오
니여러쳠군ᄌᆞᄂᆞᆫ죠량ᄒᆞ시옵

○보좌원셜치 일공ᄉᆞ비부로
공함ᄒᆞ기를현샹경무고문의보
좌원을차츌ᄒᆞ야히고문ᄒᆞᆫ에경
부와숑사를귀ᄒᆞ야졍무흠이가
기로경부숑영방쳘파샹승우
응을치용ᄒᆞᆯ수로계란ᄒᆞ오니경
부숑영방쳘은금칠심오원이오
순사샹승우응은금사십팔원식
슌사지금ᄒᆞᆫ시월차츌ᄒᆞ야국경부
에쥰ᄒᆞᆯ이라쏘히인등의직명파
졍그듸우에관ᄒᆞ야ᄂᆞᆫ추후편계
만ᄒᆞ지안케ᄒᆞ오니하량ᄒᆞ시옵소
셔ᄒᆞ엿더라

○졍부회의 졍부에셔샹확ᄒᆞᆯ
ᄉᆞ가유ᄒᆞ야심룩일하오이시에
ᄃᆡ신이졍부에졔회ᄒᆞ엿다더
라

○칙임감시 덕원군수리죵원
씨가니부로보고ᄒᆞ엿스되원산
에주ᄒᆞᆫ일본군졍장평관명평셔
기에본군니일반ᄒᆡᆼ판인민에좌
사건을ᄒᆞᆫ시ᄒᆞᆫ후부하관리를지
위ᄒᆞ고칙임으로감시ᄒᆞᆷ이가ᄒᆞ
과은군ᄉᆞ샹에필요ᄒᆞᆷ을의ᄒᆞ야
남에좌기ᄒᆞᄂᆞᆫ구역ᄂᆡ에소속ᄒᆞᆫ
기토디를미리ᄒᆞᄂᆞᆫ거ᄂᆞᆫ젼당ᄒᆞ거ᄂᆞᆫ
타소유권의이동ᄒᆞᄂᆞᆫ힝위를ᄃᆡ
금ᄒᆞᆷ그리ᄂᆞᆫ군용졀도용디ᄂᆞᆫ
ᄒᆞ야조계신리ᄂᆞᆫ차한구로브터
ᄒᆞᆷ일은숑진강하구로브터명이
혼에지ᄒᆞ기에회서ᄂᆞᆫ과 이
ᄂᆞᆫ영ᄒᆞ고원사졍봉가목뎡로인
쳥회젼이동파 샹은로인쳥안
변압동의최젼이북이녀뎐표
각향을범ᄒᆞᄂᆞᆫ즈ᄂᆞᆫ군률에조ᄒᆞ
야쳐분ᄒᆞᆫ다ᄒᆞ엿기로보고ᄒᆞ오
니다ᄒᆞ엿더라

○쟈ᄒᆡᆼ경영 원산감리가외부
로보고ᄒᆞ엿스되일인강신탕이
가둥쳔쟝젼에경영기지를답사
ᄒᆞ고졍계ᄒᆞ야결으ᄃᆡ차ᄂᆞᆫ아인
의로경기지인ᄃᆡ일ᄀᆡ변세남을
불납ᄒᆞ니회계약은소소로과귀
ᄒᆞ엿다ᄒᆞ고곳경영을쳥ᄒᆞ더라
고ᄒᆞ엿더라

THE CHONG NO SIGNBOARD.

We hear that, through the good offices of Mr. Stevens, adviser to the Foreign Office, the Japanese have been persuaded to remove the objectionable signboard which they placed at Chong-no.

It is also said that the Japanese peddlers who infested that neighbourhood have ordered to quit.

Captain von Semmern, the acting Governor of Kiao Chiao, is expected to arrive at Tsingtau to day.

Telegrams, in cipher, for Vladivostok are no longer accepted at any of the telegraph offices in China.

General Om Chun Won and some others have established a school of law and political economy at Yachoukai.

The day before yesterday Mr. Yi Yong Ik entertained General Hasegawa and a number of Japanese officials at the Hajo Hotel.

The Governor of north Pyeng an province is being tried by court martial for the shooting of some Tong haks in his province.

The Governor of W'bang-ha Privince resigned two days ago and General Kou yöng Cho has been appointed to the vacancy

---

Prince Eui, who is ostensibly studying in America, is still in Tokio. The Emperor has sent him $50,000 and instructed him to return to his studies in America.

The big floating dock at Tsingtau is expected to be finished in about three months. It will accomodate ships up to 150 metres in length and 32 metres in breadth.

An enterprising Korean, Mr. Yi Chun-yöng, has applied for official permission to erect wharves at Chemulpo, Chinnampo and Fusan to facilitate the landing of cargo.

The Governor of South Ham Kyeng province wired to the Home Department that on the 14th some 300 Russian soldisers came south to Ham Heung but subsequently retired.

According to a Tokio exchange, one of the reform proposals before the Korean Government is the substitution of conscription for the present system of military service. We cannot see that this proposal has anything to recommend it at present.

It is reported at Paris that at the time of the North sea incident, the yacht belonging to the King of Greece, whilst on her way from Denmark to France, was fired upon by the Baltic Fleet, this extraordinary news not having been published before. During a conversation at Paris, the King of Greece is reported to have said that if the Russian ships had mistaken a yacht for a torpedo-boat, they were also likely to mistake fishing vessels for similar craft.

According to the "Engineer," plans for a 20,000-ton battleship are being prepared by the United States Navy Department. It is stated that while the tonnage is enormous, the most radical departure from previous practice is that of armament. Instead of having a main battery of 4 heavy guns, backed by a secondary battery ranging from 6-inch guns to 1-pounders, the main battery of the new ship is to consist of ten 12-inch guns, placed in turrets and broadsides, with a secondary battery made up entirely of at least twenty 3-inch Q. F. guns. The speed of this battleship will probably not exceed 16 knots, but following the successful practice laid down by the Japanese Navy, she would be equipped with the heaviest long-range battery afloat, while the great number of Q. F. 3-inch guns would form the best defence possible against torpedo attacks.

MANUFACTURE OF GUNS.

The Peking Throne has been complaining of the unsatisfactory class of work turned out by the different arsenals and has informed the different viceroys and governors that after the return of Tit Liang to the capital, the work and management of the different arsenals will undergo a thorough re-organization to enable guns, etc., of uniform size and pattern to be manufactured. In the event of a change the different viceroys are also instructed to engage temporary foreign instructors, and to send students abroad to study manufacture of ordnance, etc. Foreign employees who introduce improvements will be amply rewarded by the Government, and those who do not faithfully and diligently discharge their duties will be discharged.

JAPANESE PURCHASES OF LAND.

The Japanese are very persistent in their efforts to buy land an operation, which with the exception of the treaty ports, is contrary to law.

Two Japanese, named Ota and Momichi, have bought a large piece of ground outside the South Gate Pyeng Yang, ostensibly for a hospital, and are now bringing pressure upon the natives of Whangchow to sell them a large piece of ground said to equal three wards.

The people have requested the Kamni of Pyeng Yang to ask the Japanese Consul to deal with the unwelcome speculators.

It is said that in Pyeng yang itself, owing to Japanese purchases, property is now ten times the price it was a year ago.

It is announced that King Edward will visit Malta and Alexandria early in February.

A London paper of January 27th says that a Siamese Loan of two million sterling will shortly be issued in London.

An influential Southern Cotton Convention at New Orleans has adopted a scheme to reduce the acreage under cultivation by twenty-five per cent.

Sir Herbert White, K. C. I. E. has been appointed Lieutenant-Governor of Burmah. He was given his tit'e in 1903, is the Chief Judge of the Chief Court of Lower Burmah.

On the ground that the enterprise does not pay a movement is afoot to dispense with the services of the French engineers engaged for the Pyeng Yang coal mines. Considering that these engineers have never had an opportunity of working it is not surprising that the expenses exceed the income.

An enterprising Japanese in Pyeng Yang persuaded a Korean carpenter to build a bath house for him. Then the Japanese would not pay. Then the Korean applied to Kamni but without result. He then went back to the Japanese and begged for payment but got a thrashing instead. Cannot the the Japanese consuls do something to suppress the overbearing practises of their nationals?

The London "Pall Mall Gazette" returns to its statements that the Chancellor of the Exchequer is considering the feasibility of levying an import duty of five per cent on imported goods. Our contemporary points out that the bulk of our imports, which totalled £542.-000.000 last year will escape the duty. Intoxicants and tobacco are excluded, while £173,500,000 represent raw material. Our colonies send us £54,000,-000 worth of non dutiable food and drink and Mr. Chamberlain will give them them his trifling preference of five per cent. Imports from foreign countries which would probably be made subject to the new duties would be grain, flour, meat live stock, other non-dutiable food and drink, finished and partly finished manufactures, the grand total for the new taxes, being about £300.000 which would yield £15,000,009 by way of import duty.

JAPANESE NAVAL CASUALTIES.

Since the first attack on Port Arthur on Feb. 8th 1904, 2912 Japanese were killed or wounded in the various naval engagements up to Dec. 31st—1758 killed and 1,154 wounded. Of the wounded 88 died; 899 recovered and resumed their duties; 23 recovered but were released of their offices; 130 are still in hospital; and 14 are also under treatment on their ships. The killed, whose number is three fifths of the whole casualties, are mostly victims of various disasters, including 1,472 officers and men, who were drowned in the sinking of the *Hatsuse*, *Yoshino*, *Heyen*, *Saiyen*, etc., and also on the occasions of reconnoisance to Port Arthur in force, If these figures are deducted from the whole dead it transpires that only 286 were killed by shells and fragments of missiles on the scenes of the fighting. Eighty-eight wounded who succumbed later, were all severely injured and died on the day of the injury or the following day, except 12 who expired after they had been re-received in hospital. Of the wounded, 462 entered hospitals, namely at the rate of about 2½ per 100. The number of wounded, who returned to their duties, was 899 at the end of last year, as mentioned above, but is now increased to about one thousand. The wound caused by shells is the severest of all the wounds of war, but such good results as those shown are certainly due to the progress in modern surgery.

THE INDEPENDENCE PROGRAMME.

Japan will by-and-bye take charge of the ordinary Korean police in addition to its military police, says a Tokyo paper. She will also undertake Korean national defence as set forth in the Japan-Korea Protocol. These undertakings involve a great sum of money and the Japanese Government has been for some time past negotiating with the Korean Government as to the resources for the necessary funds, the consequence being that there is now a fair prospect that the Korean monopolies of tobacco and salt will be secured by the Japanese in order to appropriate the proceeds for the intended purposes.

The Rt. Hon. Andrew Graham Murray, P. C., K. C., Secretary for Scotland has been made a Peer.

The well-known Russian writer, Nemirovich Danchenko, telegraphed from the front last month that General Kuropatkin was looking as fresh and young as when he was at Plevna. The General said that all he wanted was more men of the class of soldiers recently sent out, and then he would do well.

The Japanese kerosine dealers are exercised over the determination of the principal Korean shopkeepers to use electric light. Believing that this dicision is due to the advice of the police a deputation of oil dealers called on the Commissioner yesterday and protested.

The number of Russian reservists called to the colours in the Varsovie military district is about 110,000 men; 40,000 have already been mobilised, and 13,000 men have been enrolled in the rifle and artillery regiments which are destined to reinforce the Army in the Far East; 3,400 have been called up to fill the ranks of the 48th Infantry Division, which will replace the rifle brigade leaving for the threatre of war.

Some disagreeable features of the transfer of the Port Arthur Fortress from Russian to Japanese authority are coming to light, says the "China Review." While the police surveillance of the town is fairly good, considerable looting has been indulged in, both by the Chinese and a few of the Japanese troops. Strong measures had to be taken to prevent it, and several heads have been lopped off. It is stated that two Japanese soldiers have also been given a sentence of death on account of a too bold exhibition of their convetousness.

BRITISH POLITICS.

Coincident with the rumours that the Government intends to dissolve Parliament early in the coming session says a London paper of Jan. 17, comes another rumour that it is intended to stop further importation of coolies into South Africa. Lord Tyneham, presiding at a meeting of a big Rand Company, publicly announced his fear that such was the case, and the rumour caused depression in Kaffirs on the Stock Exchange. Being interviewed afterwards, Lord Tyneham said he had good reason to believe that the rumour was well founded. He supposed that if it is so, it is in anticipation of a general election, the coolie question having greatly embarrassed the Government candidates at recent by-elections.

In connection with the dissolution rumours, it is a curious fact that as many as 78 Ministerial members of Parliament have already announced their intention to retire at the next General Election. Their names, published to-day, include many prominent men, like Sir Michael Hicks-Beach, Mr. Ritchie, Sir W. H. Walrond and Sir John Colomb. Most of these will quit Parliament. Others like Mr. Winston Churchill, are leaving the Unionist for Liberal ranks on the fiscal controversy.

UNREST IN RUSSIA.

The following telegram, which was received by the Japanese Government in Tokio, appears to be a very lucid statement of affairs in Russia:—The aristocratic class at St. Petersburg has also joined the reform movement. At a recent meeting of the above, a resolution was passed, which was presented to the Tsar, advocating the granting of a franchise to the people. The resolution further states that Russia's enemy is endeavouring to force an ignominious peace on her, to exhaust her strength, to dispossess her of her territories in the Far East, and to overthrow the present regimé in Russia, concludes, by stating that the only way to suppress the internal disturbances, to maintain absolutism, and to enable the Russian army to be finally crowned with success, is to grant the representatives of the people the right to freely participate in the affairs of the State.

The chief of police has drawn the attention of the Governor of Seoul to the action of a certain Japanese named Yamamoto. This gentleman in company with about 20 coolies has taken unto himself a plot of land on the river bank at Mapo and is there erecting a godown for the storage of ice.

The Korea Daily News.

Issued at 5 P. M. daily except Sundays.

Rate of Subscription:—

Per Year,............Yen 25.
Per Quarter,..........Yen 7.
Per Month,..........Yen 2.50.

Postage in Korea not charged extra.
Postage abroad charged extra.

Advertisements, 50 sen per day for 1 inch or less.
5 yen per month per inch.
50 yen per year per inch.

All communications to

E. T. BETHELL,
Editor and Publisher,
Pak-tong, Seoul.

NOTICE.

Saturday, February 18th being a Korean National Holiday. there will be no issue of the KOREA DAILY NEWS on that date.

THE SHAHO.

We are without any news as to what has been going on in this district since the 11th inst. but details of the battle of Heikeutai at the end of January are coming in. The day before yesterday we gave the number of Russian dead found on the field and buried by the Japanese as 20,000. This, of course, was a printers error and should read 2,000, corresponding with the number of rifles "captured."

The Japanese casualty list is gradually mounting up. The latest estimate places the losses at 9,000 while Kuropatkin gives his casualties as 10,000.

It appears that Gripenberg's advance was very nearly successful and it was only the aprival of the Awomori division that saved the Japanese left from disaster. This division had just come from Japan and by forced marches through the snow arrived at the front only just in time. We understand that until now these troops have been held in Japan in readiness to march on Vladivostok so that the Japanese seem for the present to have abandoned all idea of an attack on that fortress.

The rumour that Kuropatkin intends to transfer 30,000 troops from Vladivostok to Mukden explains the recent withdrawal of the outposts in North Korea and indicates that he does not anticipate an attack from that direction.

There is no corroboration of the stories of dissention between Kuropatkin and Gripenberg and the original explanation that Gripenberg is returning on account of sickness seems as likely to be true as any of the other rumours.

The telegraphic message from London that, in spite of the large number of captures by the Japanese, the underwriters of Vladivostok shipments are still making a profit, indicates that the number of ships which safely reach Vladivostok is greater than the number captured by the Japanese. Kuropatkin must therefore be getting, if necessary, large quantities of supplies from this direction.

Some of the Japanese newspapers publish statements that 30,000 colonists will be sent to Manchuria to cultivate the land in the rear of the army. This is probably what the Japanese intend to do ultimately, but the position of their army is certainly not at present secure enough to warrant such a proceeding.

MR. LAWSON—PANIC MAKER.

That a man named Lawson has become the most amazing "bear" of modern times, and has engineered panic after panic on the New York Stock Exchange, with tremendous corresponding effects upon English operators, is about all that is generally known on this side of an astonishing personality, says a London paper.

Mr. Lawson is a man of overflowing energies. The Ticker of the Stock Exchange and the manipulation of Montana copper have demanded only a part of his time, mere incidents filling intervals of his busy days. Dreamwold Hall, his palatial farm-house, is a paradise for blooded stock, with its 300 horses of noble pedigree, its 150 high-bred dogs, the herds of fancy cattle in its meadows, its 3,000 hens of all varieties, and its large flocks of choice ducks, geese, and pigeons. His racing horses have won large purses—which he has given to charity; he has paid $30,000 for the right to cultivate a single flower, named by him after his wife; he has fitted out a steam-yacht at a cost of $250,000, and has built the "Independence," a racing yacht, qualified to defend the "America's" Cup. These are some of the things that have occupied his hours of leisure from dealings in sugar, copper, and oil, and the governing of his millions.

Thomas W. Lawson is of Bostonian birth, the son of a Nova Scotia carpenter. He ran away from school at the age of twelve to take a place as office boy in a State Street brokerage house, and made his way so rapidly that before he was seventeen he was dealing heavily in stocks, and had won and lost $60,000. So he went on, now on the stock board; now in a printing firm that went to pieces and buried his capital under its ruins; now promoting a boom town in Kentucky, from which also he emerged penniless: finally becoming a power in the money market, and closely associated with Rogers and Rockefeller, of Standard Oil fame.

Trouble between him and the Standard Oil magnates broke out in the spring of 1904, and he withdrew from the brokerage firm of Lawson, Arnold, & Co.. that he might speak his mind freely, without detriment to Stock Exchange courtesy.

The articles he has been printing in a magazine have become a literary and social phenomenon of extraordinary interest. They are devoured with avidity in all parts of the country. Go into the backwoods of Michigan, and the first question you will be asked is, "Have you read Lawson's last article?" Look out of the car window when the train stops for water in Arizona, and the inquiry will be fired at you by a native, "What do they think of Lawson in New York?" In sage-brush and mining camp, as well as in brokers' offices and Old Ladies Homes, Lawson is the chief purveyor of matter for reading and infinite gossip. If Macaulay supplanted with his history the latest novel on the boudoir table, Lawson has displaced the sensational prints and the flashy journals in barber-shops and bar-rooms, penetrating to the lowest stratum of readers as well as piquing the curiosity of the highest, and making of himself in a few months a veritable literary prodigy—or terror.

Lawson's tremendous audience so suddenly acquired, his clean sweep of the field, should not lead professional writers to renounce a craft in which any upstart may appear and carry off the laurels. The wonder is explicable. Lawson has taking literary qualities. Leaving out the prime requisite of truth which is neither here nor there in his articles, he has nearly all the elements which the big-wigs declare necessary in a popular style. His frank and pungent slanginess is the precise medium for his tale. It yields a splendid touch of veri-similitude. Then he abounds in minute detail. Defoe did not surpass Lawson in the art of buttressing incredible romances with an amount of apparently veracious incident which makes unbelievers ashamed of themselves. The close observer who noted an angry magnate's eyes pass through all the colours of the spectrum cannot be altogether wrong, one feels, in his exact account of millions stolen. Lawson is also overwhelmingly concrete. Places and dates are set down with the accuracy of extracts from a detective's note-book. A society novelist could not exceed him in faithful description of the surroundings of his criminal millionaries. He is highly dramatic, too. None of the tedious *oratio obliqua* for him. His articles bristle with quotation marks, and racy dialogue fills his pages. Neither Aristotle nor Horace, Quintilian nor Sainte-Beuve, could have laid down more infallible rules for attaining immense literary vogue than those which Lawson has found in his mother-wit.

HIS STORY: FOLLY AND "CRIME."

To so lucky a style Lawson has added the further advantage of a theme which ever lies near the heart of the masses in a democracy. Vast wealth is the subject of his story; and the editors of popular magazines long since discovered that no topic is dearer to the great body of ten-cent readers.

With a subject thus as broad as human folly, Mr. Lawson has also the good fortune of being able to add crime to great wealth. If the very rich are interesting *per se*, the criminal rich are doubly fascinating. And Lawson pitched upon a public predisposed to believe. The sublime fervour of faith is nothing to the credulousness of a loser in Wall Street. *Credo quia impossibile*. Thousands all over the land had been bitten in the financial operations which Lawson professes to describe. They knew that it was through no fault of their own. Every innocent who "takes a flyer" in a blown speculation is certain that his own judgment is exellent, his financial shrewdness beyond dispute, and that nothing but the machinations of wicked men could have parted him from his money. Lawson shows him the millionaire schemers at their nefarious work. The victim pores over the story of the unscrupulous manipulation of stocks and the heartless fleecing of investors, and takes comfort to his soul. Now he sees it all. He was taken in by a set of villains. Thus, besides the agreeable fillip to a morbid imagination which Lawson gives in his narrative of crime in seven figures, he makes his appeal to the multitude which no man can number of luckless investors and ruined speculators, In such circumstances, instantaneous literary fame and circulation above 600,000 are no longer a mystery.

The Korea Daily News.

VOL. II, FRIDAY, FEBRUARY 17, 1905. No. 37

報申日每韓大

보신일ᄆᆡ한대

(호팔십삼쳔이뎨)　(일요화)　일일십이월이년오ᄇᆡᆨ구쳔일

본사고ᄇᆡᆨ

이신보는영어와한어로셔게ᄃᆡ
일츌판ᄒᆞ옴

신문가

한쟝　엽두돈오푼
일삭됴　엽두량닷돈
우표가ᄆᆡ삭닷돈
다엿돈으로밧솜

광고료는

귀한외쟝단과ᄌᆞ힝의디쇼로죵
감ᄒᆞ되량가로밧을터이오ᄆᆡ오
ᄃᆡ지아녀대한사람바다다이신
문을보실터이니광고ᄇᆡ시기를
원ᄒᆞ시는이들은우리신문사에
와셔면약ᄒᆞ시믈희망ᄒᆞᆷ

○발힝소　박동대한ᄆᆡ일신보
사벽이하교향히진영국인셜핍
평졍자리오

사쟝 영국인 (ᄇᆡ셜)

평양 ᄃᆡ리졍

○평양효동사는권미보씨로우
리신문관ᄃᆡ리인을뒤졍ᄒᆞ엿
시스오니평양에계신구람코자ᄒᆞ
는　쳠군ᄌᆞ는뒤ᄃᆡ리졍에왕
림ᄒᆞ와면의ᄒᆞ시옴

사고

○우리대한ᄆᆡ일신보의목뎍은
ᄃᆡ한의인민젼셔에ᄇᆞᆫ한모든ᄃᆡ
목에ᄃᆡᄒᆞ야는공평한변론을ᄌᆞ
쟝ᄒᆞᆷ이라우리등신원의ᄇᆞ람보는
신문보시는쳠군ᄌᆞ의게ᄒᆞᆼ샹보
도ᄒᆞ리며편지들귀셔ᄒᆞ며주시
는이는셩명과번디를쟈이븟치
시기를희망ᄒᆞ오니ᄇᆡ기슴신문
샹에긔ᄌᆡᄒᆞ란는거시아니오다
만극히신용ᄒᆞ는죵거를숨고자
ᄒᆞᆷ이라귀자는아모귀셔던지귀
지ᄒᆞᆷ을되가ᄒᆞ는권리는가졋소
나되쟈ᄒᆞ는리유는말ᄒᆞᆯ터이오
며공중평화를문란케ᄒᆞ는듯ᄒᆞᆫ
귀셔는의례히밧지안켓ᄉᆞᆸ나이
다

●본사셜시이리로신문을ᄃᆡ양
우례로볼젼ᄒᆞ와례졍부의일의
로졍ᄒᆞᆫ듯ᄉᆞ로면ᄀᆞᆺ에는ᄒᆞᆨ늣게
젼ᄒᆞ기도ᄒᆞ며ᄒᆞᆨ벗쳣거ᄉᆞᆯ훈겁
에젼ᄒᆞ기도ᄒᆞ며ᄒᆞ야니젼ᄒᆞ는
ᄀᆞᆺ도잇다ᄒᆞ오니우리신문을슈탕
ᄒᆞ야구람ᄒᆞ시는　쳠군ᄌᆞ의ᄆᆡ
ᄃᆡᄒᆞ야ᄆᆡ우미안ᄒᆞ옵기로지금
은본젼인을두고ᄃᆡ일죵이젼
ᄒᆞ며ᄒᆞ니젼ᄒᆞ거나늣게거나ᄒᆞᆫ
폐가업도록ᄒᆞ랴ᄒᆞ오니ᄒᆞ야니
젼ᄒᆞ거나ᄒᆞᆨ늣게젼ᄒᆞ거나ᄒᆞᆫ일
이잇스면본사로통긔ᄒᆞ며주심
을희망ᄒᆞᆷ

론셜

일본인의평화론

○일본인교구라ᄒᆞ는사ᄅᆞᆷ이미
국뉴욕월드신문에긔셔ᄒᆞ엿
는ᄃᆡ그긔셔에ᄃᆡᆼᄒᆞᆫ것을이아ᄅᆡ
에등ᄌᆡᄒᆞ노라

쳥국의화단란리에덕국군ᄃᆡ가
쳥국에향ᄒᆞ야셔날새에덕국황
뎨게셔말ᄉᆞᆷᄒᆞ시되그것이동양
과셔양ᄉᆞ이에ᄒᆞᆫ지리ᄒᆞᆫ젼쟁의
시초라ᄒᆞ엿스니그말이인죵경
쟁을계셩ᄒᆞᆫ것이로다

ᄇᆡᆨ여년을두고영국이인도와싸
와셔그ᄃᆡ방을차지ᄒᆞ엿고법국
이쳥국과싸워셔안남을졈령ᄒᆞ
엿스며영국이향항을세아섯스
니세계에셔셩쟈ᄒᆞ기를아시아
의졍령아니된곳도ᄃᆡ는구라파의
마옹ᄃᆡ로ᄒᆞᆯ줄로알고스ᄇᆡᆨ만의
쳥인과비어말의인도인과또벋
논아시아ᄇᆡᆨ셩들이구라파와힌
보다ᄋᆡ이번나ᄃᆡ만흔것일셰차
도아니ᄒᆞ는도다

아시아인이현재ᄒᆞ무력ᄒᆞ나구
라파인이그계졔를리셔아시아
인을귀ᄀᆞᆺ치구라ᄒᆞ고우양ᄀᆞᆺ치
샹히ᄒᆞ며져의들의부모지국에
셔빈쫏기를맛당히당ᄒᆞᆯ일ᄀᆞᆺ치
ᄒᆞ엿는지라

그러ᄒᆞ나아시아인도구라파인
과ᄶᆞᆨᄀᆞᆺ치지각이잇스니만일그
ᄃᆡ들이그들을사랑ᄒᆞ면그들도
그ᄃᆡ들을사랑ᄒᆞᆯ터이오만일
그ᄃᆡ들이그들을미워ᄒᆞ면그들도
그ᄃᆡ들을미워ᄒᆞᆯ터이며만일그
ᄃᆡ들이그들을신슈로ᄃᆡ졉ᄒᆞ면
그들도그ᄃᆡ들을신슈로ᄃᆡ졉ᄒᆞᆯ
ᄃᆡ리ᄒᆞ면그들도그ᄃᆡ들을ᄒᆞᄃᆡᄒᆞᆯ
지라ᄇᆡᆨ여년을두고구라파인
아시아인을능욕ᄒᆞᆫ일이과연미
인의셩각에서ᄉᆞ지셔아시아
과힌교수ᄒᆞ고무ᄉᆞᆷ일이더잇는지
셩ᄒᆞ계셔[illegible]구라파로이미ᄒᆞᆫ말은
위ᄒᆞ드리듯ᄒᆞᆫ것은ᄇᆡᆨ년젼에
의ᄒᆞᆫ화단들이[illegible]
그보로다사름들이보복ᄒᆞᄂᆞᆫ
니오ᄉᆡᆼ교에위반ᄒᆞᆫ다ᄒᆞ겟는
[illegible]

가그러ᄒᆞ나아시아인이엿지져
의들을멸망ᄒᆞ랴는원슈의피ᄒᆞᆫ
을도로라고ᄒᆞᆯ리가잇스리오
외화단비망ᄒᆞᆫ것은ᄡᅦ가ᄒᆞᆼ쥬아
니라그러ᄒᆞᆫ것이오쳥국인이비의
궤히구라파인종의게관ᄒᆞᆫ라
교예쟝ᄒᆞᆫ것은아니라의화단
젼쟁이쳥국사름을ᄇᆡᆨ셩ᄒᆞ야
벌셔기랑ᄒᆞ는졍신이환실히잇
서셔벗ᄒᆞ젼에쳥국군계들일본
감동밋ᄒᆞ긔탐ᄒᆞ기를시작ᄒᆞ엿
교동경슈관ᄒᆞᆨ교에쳥국류학싱
들은져의들의본국에신셔을슈
입ᄒᆞᆯ귀관이로다

다쳥인의군ᄉᆞ샹용망이일본인과
그로다는말이ᄒᆡᆼ말인것이쳥국
의사력이엉웅사계비만ᄒᆞᆫ지라
그쟈등을일본소년들이며리
힘들두고공부ᄒᆞ야고사계를이
일본인의젼ᄌᆡᆼ신을가리ᄎᆞᆫ것도
다

영웅이광화시에는현츌ᄒᆞ야
되나니법국창명이나폴네온
츌ᄒᆞ엿는지라쳥국에도이왕에
나폴네온이만히잇셧고이후에는
만일법국젼쟁에쳥국이창셜ᄒᆞ
일면나폴네온이다마이엇스리로다

[illegible]

잡보

○리무웅씨　원산감리가일본
군용디로졈령된디안의조세를
웅납ᄒᆞ라고히병참소로공문ᄒᆞ
엿더니히병참관의조복내에군
용디조세는한일협졍셔를의
ᄒᆞ야응세ᄒᆞᆯ리유가무ᄒᆞ다ᄒᆞ엿
더라

○츙남경셔　쳔란남도관찰ᄉᆞ
김세기를구란ᄎᆞ로법부에셔경
무쳥으로혼령ᄒᆞ엿더라

○ᄃᆡ관면임　평리원재판장민
병한씨는친경으로면임ᄒᆞ고그
ᄃᆡ는한셩관윤민경식씨가승임
ᄒᆞ고발와병세는한셩관윤을임
ᄒᆞ고는상응부협판리근상씨가
소ᄃᆡ에님쟝원검두리준명
ᄒᆞ다ᄒᆞ더라

○ᄡᅥ가ᄒᆞᆫ다더라

○관찰소계　함경남도관찰ᄉᆞ
리현경씨는상소ᄒᆞ야갈녓다더
라

○일수폐현　작샹툭일하오샹
시에일공수와및쟝곡쳔대쟝이
폐현ᄒᆞ엿더라

○단녀계신　근일항셜에말ᄒᆞ
기를금ᄋᆡ대일은항과경부간에
게약ᄒᆞ고국고금액을다히은힝
에잉거ᄒᆞᆫ다ᄒᆞ니인게ᄇᆡ되는한

○버국의남아잇는자는사름의밧가
손들밧게는엉다더라

○오가자등　경무쳥에셔도로
작졍결ᄒᆞ기위ᄒᆞ여ᄆᆡ동에오가
세를ᄒᆞ여도중에오에틀을보이
ᄃᆡ로처리ᄒᆞ되ᄆᆡ호에분과다
샹ᄎᆡ빗동ᄒᆞᆫ푼식증ᄒᆞᆷ이
라

○ᄃᆡ둔으로졍작　일용사가니졍원
열듀도조회ᄒᆞᆫ기를즁금빈ᄃᆡ각ᄒᆞ
ᄃᆡ도리를인ᄒᆞ이경작ᄒᆞ겟다고역ᄒᆞ
라

UNION INSURANCE SOCIETY OF CANTON.

Head office Hongkong.
Marine risks underwritten at current rates.
Agents in Chemulpo,
E. MEYER & Co.

COMPAGNIE DES MESSAGERIES MARITIMES.

Fortnightly Direct Service.

For Marseilles
via Ports.
Sailing from Yokohama
Calling at Kobe,
Shanghai, Hongkong, Saigon, Singapore,
Colombo, Djibonti, Suez, Port Said
and Marseilles.

For particulars apply to
HOLME RINGER & Co.,
Chemulpo.

HAYASHIDA & CO.,

16 MYENG DONG, CHIN KO KAI, SEOUL.
BRANCH OFFICE AT CHEMULPO.

Money changers, Coal and Wood Merchants, Express Agents.

We are agents for the Pyeng-yang Coal Company and the Karazu Coal Company of Japan. We have the best quality of both anthracite and bituminous coal, and prompt execution of orders is our speciality. Firewood of all kinds kept in stock. Full weight guaranteed. Money of all denominations exchanged at current rates. Parcels received for all parts.

CHINA MUTUAL LIFE INS. OC.

Most favourable terms to policy holders.

Benefit system unsurpassed.

HOLME RINGER & Co.
Agents, Chemulpo.

C. P. R.

CANADIAN PACIFIC RAILWAY COMPANY'S ROYAL MAIL STEAMSHIP LINE.

THE FAST ROUTE BETWEEN CHINA, JAPAN, AND EUROPE VIA CANADA AND THE UNITED STATES.

Route from Hongkong via Shanghai, Nagasaki (Inland Sea of Japan) Kobe, Yokohama, Victoria and Vancouver.

Twin Screw Empress Steamship—6,000 Tons—Speed 19 knots.

PROPOSED SAILING FROM YOKOHAMA.

R. M. S. Empress of India.
R. M. S. Empress of Japan.
R. M. S. Empress of China.
R. M. S. Athenian.
R. M. S. Tartar.

Special reduction (first class only) granted to members of the Military, Naval, Diplomatic and Civil services and to Missionaries.
Passengers have choice of ten routes across the Continent of America and have privilege of travelling by any Atlantic Steamship Line.
Round the World passage tickets in connection with the P. and O. S. N., North German Lloyd and Messageries Co.'s £125.
All rates payable at current rate of exchange.
For further information, Tickets, Guide Books, etc., apply to
HOLME, RINGER & CO., AGENTS, Chemulpo.

Grand Hotel

(Formerly the Station Hotel)

Near the Railway Terminus, West Gate Seoul.

The Best Hotel in Korea
Handsome new Building.
Fine Airy Rooms
Excellent Cuisine.
Terms Moderate.
Special terms to Missionaries
and to permanent boarders.

Electric cars within 2 minutes' walk.

W. H. EMBERLEY.
Proprieto

EVERY FACILITY.

In connection with Life Assurance Business is afforded by

The Standard Life Assurance Co.,

One of the largest and wealthiest of the Provident Institutions of the United Kingdom Forms of Application and all information will be promptly afforded on application.

10 CENTS A DAY.

Not a very large expenditure is it? But it is sufficient to secure for a man of 30 a policy with the STANDARD LIFE OFFICE for

$1323.

For all particulars of rates, etc., apply to

Holme, Ringer & Co.,
Agents, Chemulpo.

THE NEW YORK LIFE INSURANCE COMPANY.

Have you ever been declined by any Company?

Are you engaged in a specially hazardous occupation?

Have you heard of the New York Life Insurance Company's New Classifications for this class of Risks?

If not, send your date of birth, occupation and particulars of rejection, if any to

E. MEYER & Co.,
Agents, Chemulpo.

MITSUI BUSSAN KAISHA.
(MITSUI & Co.)
MITSUI GINKO.
(MITSUI BANK.)

The Bank is owned by the members of the Mitsui Family, who, as partners, assume an unlimited responsibility for all liabilities of the Bank:—

Capital........................Yen 5,000,000
Reserve Fund.................. " 5,600,000

HEAD OFFICE, TOKYO.
LONDON OFFICE, 34 LIME ST., E. C.

BRANCHES AND AGENCIES:—
New York, San Francisco, Hamburg, Bombay, Singapore, Manila, Hongkong, Amoy, Chefoo, Tientsin.
Kobe, Hakodate, Yokohama, Kure, Yokosuka, Moji, Shimonoseki, Miike, Wakamatsu, Nagasaki, Kuchinotsu, Karatsu, Sasebo, Misume, Taipeh, &c.

Telegraphic Address for all the Offices:
"MITSUI."
A. B. C. AND A. 1 CODES USED.

Contractors of Coal
To the Imperial Japanese Navy, Arsenal and Railway Bureau, Principal Railway Companies and Industrial Work, Home and Foreign Mail and Freight Steamers.
Sole Proprietors
Of the famous Miike, Tagawa and Yamano Coal Mines.
Sole Agents
For the sale of Fukumo, Hokoku, Ichimura Kanoda, Mannoura, Onoura, Ostuji, Sonoda, Tsubaruro, Yoshinotani, Yoshio, Yurokiburu and other coals.

YANGTSE INSURANCE ASSOCIATION, LTD.

The undersigned, having been appointed agents for the above company, are prepared to issue policies and pay losses on marine risks at regular rates.

E. MEYER & Co.,
Agents, Chemulpo.

AMERICAN KOREAN ELECTRIC CO.

Light and Power.

Main Office: Electric Building, Chong No.

RAILWAY DEPARTMENT.

OPERATING CARS BETWEEN EAST AND WEST GATE, EVERY TEN MINUTES:—

First Car leaves East Gate at 7:00 A. M. First Car leaves R. R. Station at 7:25 A. M
Last Car " East Gate at 8.40 P. M. Last " " R. R. Station at 9.05 P.M

OPERATING CARS BETWEEN EAST GATE AND IMPERIAL TOMB TERMINUS, EVERY TWENTY MINUTES:—

CONNECTING WITH EVERY ALTERNATE CAR ARRIVING AT EAST GATE FROM CHONG NO.

First Car leaves East Gate for Tomb at 7:10 A. M.
" " " Tomb for East Gate at 7:30 A. M.
Last " " East Gate for Tomb at 7:50 P. M.
" " " Tomb for East Gate at 8:10 P. M

OPERATING CARS BETWEEN CHONG NO AND YUNG SAN RIVER EVERY TWELVE MINUTES:—

First Car leaves Chong No for South Gate at 7:12 A. M.
" " " Chong No for Yung San at 7:36 A. M.
" " " South Gate for Chong No at 7:20 A. M.
" " " Yung San for Chong No at 8:09 A. M.
Last " " South Gate for Chong No 9:00 P. M.
" " " Yung San for Chong No at 8.45 P. M.

SPECIAL PRIVATE CARS FURNISHED TO SUIT CONVENIENCE OF PATRONS. PRICES ON APPLICATION AT HEAD OFFICE.

LIGHTING DEPARTMENT.

Where less than 250 candle power of light is used, the rate per month will be
Per 16 candle power incandescent lamp,—All night.—Yen 2.50.
32 candle power incandescent lamp:—All night:—Yen 4.00.
50 candle power incandescent lamp:—All night:—Yen 6.00.
150 " " " " " " " 10.00
1200 " " enclosed arc " " " " 20.00.

Where more than 250 candle power of light is used, a Meter will be installed, if requested:—Rent of Meter Yen 2.00 per month. Rate of charges by meter reading:—Two Sen per Ampere per hour. (Approximately this is equal to about One Sen per 16 c. P. lamp per hour) Minimum monthly charge where meter is installed, Yen 20.00 per month, which includes rental of meter.

Estimates for installing lights furnished on application

An assortment of chandeliers always on hand.

K. Murakami.
Photograph Studio
Chinkokai, Seoul.

Printing, Developing and Enlargement, of Photographs always Undertaken.

Korean Views and Pictures Illustrating Native Customs always on Sale,

---

THE OSAKA SHOSEN KAISHA.

Boats frequently on the berth for Chinnampo.

REGULAR SAILINGS BETWEEN JAPAN AND KOREAN PORTS.

FUSAN AND KOBE VIA SHIMONOSEKI.

OSAKA VIA MOKPO, FUSAN, SHIMONOSEKI AND KOBE.

MOJI DIRECT.

OSAKA VIA KUNSAN, MASANPO FUSAN, SHIMONOSEKI AND KOBE.

CHEMULPO KUNSAN LINE,
Every three days.

CHEMULPO CHINNAMPO LINE.
Every three days.

For Freight and passage and further particulars apply to

THE OSAKA SHOSEN KAISHA,
Chemulpo.

RONDON, PLAISANT & CO.

General Storekeepers and Merchants, Ships Contractors Tobacconists, Commission and Forwarding Agents, Coal Merchants

IMPORTERS AND EXPORTERS

Seoul Chemulpo.

W. D. WENTWORTH.

LANDING
AND
SHIPPING AGENT.
AND
CUSTOMS BROKER.

12 OURA, NAGASAKI.

STEWARD & CO.

Chemulpo.

Shipchandlers and Storekeepers Naval and Mercantile Contractors, Landing and Shipping Agents.

STEWARD'S HOTEL

Chemulpo.

Best accommodation in the port for travellers. Clean and well-aired rooms, good cuisine and prompt attendance, moderate tariff.

관보

뎨삼쳔륙십오호 금요

셔임급사령

○승셔관임관오등 시위뎨일련대뎨이대뎨륙군군의보 림도한

이월팔일

○명휴직 군부부관륙군보병졍위 리셕지 친위뎨일련대장보병졍령 현흥택 진위뎨일련대부륙군보병참위 김인규 진위뎨이련대뎨이대대부륙군보병부위 됴동원 진위뎨륙련대뎨일대대장륙군보병참령 신우균 진위대륙련대뎨이대대 부륙군보병부위 리지윤

○의원면본관 즁츄원의관 리군용 즁츄원의관 박영대 즁츄원의관 셔현보 즁츄원의관 오셩규

○입즁츄원의관셔쥬임관륙등 졍삼품 최인식 졍삼품 빅주현 졍삼품 홍은주 구강덕봉

이상이월십사일

○명효뎡왕후련제시졔주관 졍삼품 리뎡렬

○명효뎡왕후련제시졔주관예차 졍삼품 김연회

○의원면보관 비셔원승 리범구 비셔원승 신헌균 규장각직학ᄉᆞ 셔궁순

○임비셔원승셔쥬임관륙등 졍삼품 민광식 졍삼품 리현의

○임규장각직학ᄉᆞ셔쥬임관륙등 졍삼품 윤주셩

○면본관 군부쥬ᄉᆞ 셔사근

○임군부쥬ᄉᆞ셔판임관륙등 권도진

○면본관 인쥬면보샤쥬ᄉᆞ 김노셕

이상이월십오일

뎐보

평화소식

론돈발 이월팔일

○일로젼쟁을즁지ᄒᆞ야평화된다ᄂᆞᆫ소문이셩ᄒᆡᆼᄒᆞᄂᆞᆫᄃᆡ론돈잇ᄂᆞᆫ일본공ᄉᆞ하야시남쟉이말ᄒᆞ되일본이샹당ᄒᆞ면로국과교섭ᄒᆞ기를죠아ᄒᆞ겟지마ᄂᆞᆫ지금평화죠약이되야간다ᄂᆞᆫ말은모를말이라ᄒᆞ엿고로국졍부ᄂᆞᆫ군ᄃᆡ와군함을시로히맛츄엇던것을물느며동병ᄒᆞᄂᆞᆫ명령도쟉소ᄒᆞ엿다더라

동경뎐 십오일오후사시발

○디방고문 ᄯᅳ금회에한국졍부에디방ᄒᆡᆼ졍고문관을셜치ᄒᆞ기로결뎡ᄒᆞ야니무셩참셔관아도원삼랑씨가피임ᄒᆞ엿ᄂᆞᆫᄃᆡ불일니에동경에셔츌발ᄒᆞ야부임ᄒᆞᆫ다더라

구쥬면보 십륙일착

○흑구공사표 구쥬면보를거ᄒᆞᆫ즉만쥬군총지휘관흑구공은부하의군사령관등과됴화치못ᄒᆞ야금번에사표를졔츌ᄒᆞ엿다ᄂᆞᆫᄃᆡ그말은ᄉᆞ실인듯ᄒᆞ다더라

○아국젼비 법국파리에고ㅣ신문의아도롱신원또루의보고를거ᄒᆞᆫ즉아국이ᄀᆡ젼이리로작년십일월이십삼일ᄭᆞ지국고에셔지발ᄒᆞᆫ젼비의총액은사억칠쳔륙빅만루인ᄃᆡ본년이월십사일에지ᄒᆞᆫ십이ᄀᆡ월간의젼비총액은칠억이쳔팔빅만루가된다더라

동디발 동일

○로국에셔평화ᄒᆞ랴ᄒᆞᆫ다ᄂᆞᆫ풍셜은셩ᄒᆡᆼᄒᆞ나로국에셔일본이졔츌ᄒᆞᆯ조건ᄃᆡ로승락ᄒᆞᆯ듯ᄒᆞᆫ젹실ᄒᆞᆫ소문은업다더라

구로팟긴의소식

론돈발 이월팔일

○셩피득보에셔구로팟긴ᄃᆡ장을소환ᄒᆞ랴고열심운동ᄒᆞᄂᆞᆫ쟈들이만히잇다더라

빅림발 동일

○극동에잇ᄂᆞᆫ로국장군들이셔로불화ᄒᆞ다ᄂᆞᆫ소문이만히잇더라

론돈발 동월구일

○그리펜벅장군은구로팟긴대장을박론ᄒᆞ랴고셩피득보로향ᄒᆞ야ᄯᅥ낫다더라

잡보

○일간실시 찬졍최익현씨의시폐샹소가한두번이아닌거슨세소공디어니와일간실시가된다ᄒᆞ더라

○국장면관 닉부디방국장오샹규씨ᄂᆞᆫ무삼사건이잇ᄂᆞᆫ지면관이되엿다더라

○검ᄉᆞ소체 민영우씨가월미도ᄉᆞ건으로평리원에지수ᄒᆞ엿슬ᄯᅵ에검ᄉᆞ리휘션씨가용형ᄒᆞᆫ지라민경식씨가평리원지판장을피임ᄒᆞᆷ이혐피가되야샹소ᄒᆞ야체임ᄒᆞ엿더라

○초무원ᄃᆡ 셔강부민들이팔빅만원을자원민ᄃᆡ케ᄒᆞᆫ것이수인의운동인지히부민등이작일에탁지대신을방견ᄒᆞ고히자원차관을만일과긔치안으면젼국인민의게대죄를난면이라ᄒᆞ엿고ᄯᅩ몃사ᄅᆞᆷ은황셩신문사에가셔질문ᄒᆞ기를오강부민들이원ᄃᆡᄒᆞᄂᆞᆫ장ᄉᆞ가업셧ᄂᆞᆫᄃᆡ신문상에무ᄉᆞᆷᄶᆞ닭으로게지ᄒᆞ엿ᄂᆞ뇨ᄒᆞ고무수히상지ᄒᆞ엿더라

○조쳥시명 일젼에미국공ᄉᆞ가외부로조회ᄒᆞ기를화셩돈에주지ᄒᆞᆫ귀국공ᄉᆞ가면보ᄒᆞᆫ미금륙빅륙십삼쳔팔십젼을지급ᄒᆞ라ᄂᆞᆫᄉᆞ로회젼ᄒᆞ엿슬ᄯᅵ제언ᄒᆞ엿고ᄯᅩ탁지고문관의게말ᄒᆞ야목하면씨가회국ᄎᆞ로발뎡ᄒᆞᆯᄯᅵ에지발ᄒᆞ랴고ᄒᆞ엿스ᄂᆞ오리려송교치안으니곳지발ᄒᆞ야히문부를쳥장ᄒᆞ라ᄒᆞ엿더라

○병뎡ᄒᆡᆼ픽 제작일오후ᄒᆞᆫ시량에진위ᄃᆡ병뎡ᄒᆞᆫ명이홍제원에셔안력거를타고새문안ᄭᆞ지와셔인력거세를주지안코차부들도로혀구타ᄒᆞᄂᆞᆫ지라헌병이즉시착거ᄒᆞ엿더라

○일진공합 일진회에셔일젼에권고ᄒᆞᆫ신법을반포ᄒᆞ라고법대외게공합ᄒᆞ엿더라

○만란지보 한셩닉에물가ᄂᆞᆫ일이삭젼보다오히려고등ᄒᆞ야졈졈지보ᄒᆞᆯ수업다더라

○방지사경 진쥬관찰사가외부로보고ᄒᆞ엿스되김히군수보고닉에음력십이월초이일에일인송셕등륙십인과밋통사최진구등이요지경을가지고와셔구경을팔더니그날밤에한인들과무ᄉᆞᆷ쟁투가잇셔한인두명은방지사경이옵고사명은즁샹은면ᄒᆞ엿ᄂᆞᆫᄃᆡ일인등은다도타ᄒᆞ엿기동리향경무셔에이조ᄒᆞ옵고몬져졍형을치보ᄒᆞ옵ᄂᆞ니다ᄒᆞ엿더라

○죠쳥시명 외부에셔궁닉부에죠복ᄒᆞ되평양민란기사법인귀빈례등사인의히고사로입의법관에셩명ᄒᆞ엿고히공사의죠복을졉준ᄒᆞᆫ닉기에닉장원경의귀빈례를ᄃᆡ귀결ᄒᆞ야히고안건을여하히관리를귀결ᄒᆞᄂᆞᆫ거슬시명ᄒᆞ라ᄒᆞᆫ지라히기사등의고빙을폐부를불유ᄒᆞ고립약ᄒᆞᆫ바ㅣ라그면말을샹시ᄒᆞ야회답ᄒᆞ기에편케ᄒᆞ라ᄒᆞ엿더라

○민씨소비 민영철씨샹소에ᄃᆡᄒᆞᆫ비지에경을신셜ᄒᆞ며궁간창건ᄒᆞᄂᆞᆫ거슨거창ᄒᆞᆫ사인ᄃᆡ간우ᄒᆞᆫᄯᅢ를당ᄒᆞ야공역의미필ᄒᆞᆫ거슨사셰가진실노그러ᄒᆞ고지졍으로말ᄒᆞ면그소입과소츌이소샹ᄒᆞ니혹부허ᄒᆞᆫ비방이잇스나무어슬미의ᄒᆞ리오소쳥이임의이곳흐니감동의임은외시ᄒᆞ고미필ᄒᆞᆫ공역은졍부로ᄒᆞ여곰품쳐ᄒᆞ라ᄒᆞ옵셧더라

○면화훈칙 일본군ᄉᆞ상에방히자ᄂᆞᆫ군률을의ᄒᆞ야시ᄒᆡᆼᄒᆞᆫ다더니경무쳥에셔ᄂᆞᆫ부언을셔ᄒᆞᄒᆞ야경찰샹에방히ᄒᆞᄂᆞᆫ자ᄂᆞᆫ잡으라고각셔에면화로훈칙ᄒᆞ엿더라

○조쳥연조 미공ᄉᆞ가외부로조회ᄒᆞ기를남문외시병원은곳동현에잇ᄂᆞᆫ졔즁원이라셔비란ᄉᆞ가연조ᄒᆞ야병원을신건ᄒᆞ엿ᄂᆞᆫᄃᆡ남녀인치료가점점만하군인도만흔지라의ᄉᆞ와간호부가시무ᄒᆞᆫ즉부득불발료ᄒᆞᆯ터이며병원보조가외국에도잇ᄂᆞᆫ바라귀졍부에셔미삭일화오륙빅원식연조ᄒᆞ야병원을완셩케ᄒᆞ라ᄒᆞ엿더라

○ᄒᆡᆼ졍이이 탁지에셔졍공수쇄ᄒᆞᄂᆞᆫ규칙을셩립ᄒᆞ야각군장ᄎᆞ츈령ᄒᆞᆯ터인ᄃᆡ대ᄀᆡ를거ᄒᆞᆫ즉운ᄒᆡᆼ지졈을각쳐에셜립ᄒᆞ고즁셰관이수셰ᄒᆞ야운ᄒᆡᆼ소로송부ᄒᆞ고군수난다만ᄒᆡᆼ졍만ᄒᆞᆯᄲᅮᆫ이라더라

○인장탈거 갈닌합경남도관찰사리헌경씨가닉부로면보ᄒᆞ엿스되일본사령부에셔관찰사의인장을탈거ᄒᆞ고올나가기를독쵹ᄒᆞᆫ다ᄒᆞ엿더라

○인장송부 함흥군수리교영씨가닉부로면보ᄒᆞ엿스되일본사령부에셔관찰인장을본군수의게로송부ᄒᆞ야셔리ᄒᆞ라ᄒᆞ엿스니엇지ᄒᆞ올는지ᄒᆞ엿더라

○던훈샹리 닉부에셔합경남도관찰부로면훈ᄒᆞ기를본관찰사ᄂᆞᆫ소체ᄒᆞ엿스니본군수의게인장을곳던ᄒᆞ고샹경ᄒᆞ라ᄒᆞ엿더라

○훈령각셔 경무쳥에셔각셔로훈령ᄒᆞ기를모든관리가시무ᄒᆞᆯ세에평복은일졀금단ᄒᆞ라ᄒᆞ고순검이간무ᄒᆞᆯᄯᅢ본장을단졍히ᄒᆞ며장닉식졍을슈츅ᄒᆞᆯᄯᅢ민원이잇다ᄒᆞ니모삼위졀이잇ᄂᆞᆫ지슈졍츌렴을얼마식민호에슈봉ᄒᆞᆫ것과슈졍ᄒᆞᄂᆞᆫᄃᆡ얼마소일된것을상셰긔록ᄒᆞ야오며금졍를ᄯᅳ에물장슈가밟고올나셔물을ᄯᅳ지못ᄒᆞ게ᄒᆞ라ᄒᆞ엿더라

○쳥원겸임 셩진거ᄒᆞᄂᆞᆫ최창욱씨가외부로쳥원ᄒᆞ엿스되본항감리죠죵환씨를룡쳔감리의히군수를겸ᄒᆞᄂᆞᆫ뎨를의ᄒᆞ야닉부로이죠ᄒᆞ야ᄒᆞ여곰겸임케ᄒᆞ야달나ᄒᆞ엿더라

외보

○소환운동 도국경셩의셔흑구장군을소환코쟈ᄒᆞ야열심으로운동ᄒᆞᄂᆞᆫᄌᆞㅣ잇다더라

○쥬모사형 로국에셔금번에제바스도보루소란에쥬모자삼십명룡사형에쳐ᄒᆞ엿다더라

○오인수뢰 파리에셔던셜이잇셔골으ᄃᆡ로국할ᄃᆡ가북히에셔어선을포격ᄒᆞᆯ당시에회탑황뎨의츈선이뎡말노브러법국을향ᄒᆞᄂᆞᆫ도즁에로국함대의포격을피ᄒᆞᆫ지라기후에회탑황뎨가파리에셔혹조를ᄃᆡᄒᆞ야골으ᄃᆡ로국의합ᄃᆡ가아외우편을수뢰명으로오젼ᄒᆞᆫᄌᆞㅣ라ᄒᆞ물며어선일야ᄒᆞ엿ᄃᆡ라

○갱욕알현 로국도셩의직공등이향일에로뎨ᄭᅦ알젼을득ᄒᆞᆫᄌᆞᄂᆞᆫ다그고쥬의선졈ᄒᆞᆫᄌᆞ요파공ᄌᆞ젼체의ᄃᆡ표ᄌᆞ가아니라금번에다시직공등이기ᄃᆡ표ᄌᆞ를자당선거ᄒᆞ야알젼ᄒᆞ기를쳥원ᄒᆞᆫ다더라

TELEGRAMS.

(FROM JAPAN PAPERS.)

The PEACE RUMOURS.

Washington, February 20th.

President Roosevelt, through the medium of a certain personage, tendered advice to Russia as to the making of overtures for peace, but his efforts were unsuccessful. Count Cassini, Russian Ambassador at Washington, has received instructions from St. Petersburg that no foreign mediation can be accepted. The Count therefore repeats his former statement that no idea of peace can be entertained by Russia until General Kuropatkin has secured a victory that will enable Russia to regain her prestige in the Far East.

Berlin, Feb. 11.

Reports from St. Petersburg declare emphatically that Russia has not requested any Power to enter into negotiations regarding peace on her behalf.

London, Feb. 12.

Rumours as to the conclusion of peace still continue.

In France the opinion prevails that Russia should find a way to opening negotiations for the conclusion of peace on honourable terms.

Baron Hayashi, the Japanese Minister in London, declares, however, his belief in the probability of the continuance of the war.

AFFAIRS IN RUSSIA.

London, Feb. 11th.

It is realiably stated that the Czar promised Tolstoy's son yesterday that he would proclaim the opening of a public meeting next week as a preliminary to organizing a constitutional government.

London, Feb. 11.

The strikes have been renewed in St. Petersburg, and thirty thousand men are at present idle.

The house of M. de Witte (the President of the Council of Ministers appointed to consider the new reforms) has been searched by the police.

London, Febuary 12th,

There is a revival of anxiety at St. Petersburg.

The general strike of artisans at Warsaw has been renewed.

London, Febuary 13th.

Sunday passed quietly at St. Petersburg. The strikers made no demonstration, being overawed by the military. The situasion in Poland is very serious.

THE BALTIC SQUADRONS.

London, Feb. 10.

It is rumoured that seven Argentine battleships and cruisers will join Admiral Roiestvensky's Squadron.

London, Feb. 11.

Reuter's correspondent at Port Louis wires that recent arrivals from Nossi Be (northeast of Madagascar) report that the Baltic Fleet still remains there. A conflict, it is reported, has arisen between Admiral Rohjestvensky and the German companies who are supplying the fleet with coal. The Admiaal wishes the colliers to follow the fleet, but they refuse on account of the too close proximity of the Japanese.

London, Feb. 13.

Five Russian cruisers, anchored in German waters at Dar-es-Salaam, near Zanzibar, received orders to leave, and have complied therewith.

The Third Baltic Squadron has been ordered to be ready to sail from the Baltic immediately.

London, Feb. 13.

A certain amount of insubordination prevails in the Third Baltic Squadron. On Saturday last a sailor was shot for stabbing a Lieutenant.

KUROPATKIN'S ARMY.

London, Feb. 10.

A private report from St. Petersburg states that General Kuropatkin is suffering from neuralgia. As a consequence he is not in a condition to form prompt decisions as to the matters with which he has to deal. It is stated that Grand Duke Nicholas Nicholaivitch is likely to be sent to the front in order to ascertain the true position of affairs.

London, Feb. 10.

It is reported, on good authority, from Europe, that General Kuropatkin has only 300,000 troops under him, and it is believed that, if he attempts aggresive action with this comparatively small force, he will simply suffer another severe defeat.

Berlin, Feb. 11.

The Czar has invited Prince Frederic Leopold of Prussia, a brother-in-law of the Kaiser, to visit the scene of the war in Manchuria. The Prince has already begun to make preparations for his departure.

BRITISH POLITICS.

London, Feb. 10.

Mr. Herbert Gladstone, the Chief Liberal Whip, has warned the Liberal agents throughout the country to complete immediately all arrangements for a General Election, as he expects a dissolution at any moment after the opening of Parliament, which takes place on the 14th inst.

THE LIBERAL MANIFESTO.

London, Feb. 10.

The Liberal Party has published its platform, which includes an anti-Chinese labour proposal.

GENERAL NEWS.

London, Feb. 11.

There has been a great rush at the offices of the Hongkong and Shanghai Bank here of subscribers to the new Chinese Five-per-cent. loan for £1,000,000, issued on Friday at 97. So great was the crowd beseiging the office that it had to be controlled by the police.

The issue was closed immediately instead of on Monday as at first intended, the loan being already largely over-subscribed.

London, Feb. 12.

The new Chinese Five-per-cent. loan for £1,000,000, which was issued at 97 by the Hongkong and Shanghai Bank, was over-subscribed three times within an hour.

London, Feb. 10.

According to the "New York World" the United States Government has practically decided to return to China after the present war the sum of twenty two million dollars, being the amount of indemnity money remaining after the settlement of the American claims.

London, Feb. 14th.

The United States Senate, disregarding strong pressure from President Roosevelt, inserted and amendment in the Arbitration Treaties Bill by fifty votes to nine, securing the right to the Senate to intervene before any question is submitted to arbitration.

In consequence of the Senate's action, President Roosevelt will drop the arbitration treaties which are being arranged with Japan, Great Britain, and other countries.

Public opinion in the United States endorses the action of the Senate.

London, Feb. 9.

A submarine for Russia, described as agricultural implements, has been shipped from America via Antwerp and London, and cleared the British port yesterday. Nine more are coming in a similar manner, and the question of contraband is now under consideration.—Asahi.

London, Feb. 14.

An urgent order has been received at Glasgow from Japan for fifty locomotives.

Bombay, February 10.

Pest has appeared at Rangoon, and there have been many fatal cases. The disease is, as usual, rampant in Bombay.

London, Feb. 12th.

The express train from Scotland collided in a dense fog with the Leeds-Sheffield mail train near Darfield. The express from St. Pancras ran into the wreckage, which became ignited. Six persons were killed and twenty seriously injured.

London, Feb. 10.

A Government Bill providing for the separation of Church and State has deen introducedinto the French Chamber and referred to Committee.

London, Feb. 10.

The steamship "Craftsman," from Calcutta, while entering the harbour at Port Said collided with and sank the collier "Cougal," bound for Hongkong.

NOTES ON THE WAR.

It is now quite clear, says the China Gazette, that the Japanese claims to an important gain on the Hunho put forward last week, not in their own official reports, but by their irresponsible worshipers in the Anglo-Jap press, do not rest upon any more solid foundation than the advantage which the first word always carries with a credulous world.

According to a Russian official report, the Colonels of the Second, Third and Six Regiments of Rifles and the officer who commanded the Second Brigade of Rifles were wounded in the Battle of Heikautai.

Kuropatkin seems determined to retain the ground he gained at the battle of Heikautai. His troops are well entrenched facing the Japanese left and a 24 gun breastwork has been built south of Mentapao opposite the Japanese centre.

A Yinkow telegram says that the Russians have established a base of requisition on the left bank of the East Liao. The place is a prosperous town and offers facilities for Russians to transport their requisitioned articles to the front from Mongolia.

News from St. Petursburg is to the effect that General Kuropatkin is suffering from a disorder of the nerves, and that his indecision in all matters is marked. It is believed that the Grand Duke Nicolaivitch will visit Manchuria to report on the situation.

According to the reports of General Kuropatkin and the military attache's who have been with him the stories of privation among the Russian soldiers are untrue. They are on the contrary said to be well clothed and well fed and it is asserted that there have been very few cases of frostbite.

A train-load of trophies taken from the Japanese, mainly at Putiloff Hill, is expected at Moscow in a few days. The trophies consists of five mountain guns and nine field guns, 11 boxes of ammuition and cartridges, with about 2,000 rifles, swords, and other objects taken from the Japanese soldiers.

A Reuter telegram received in Tokio says that General Kuropatkin reports that on the 8th at 11 P. M. the Japanese assumed the offensive on the front extending two versts on the Russian left but were repulsed at 5 A. M. on the 9th. The Japanese resumed the offensive at 7 A. M. on the 9th, but were repulsed likewise, Russian casualties were 5.

A Tokio telegram announces the appointment of a Mr. Kojima as adviser to the provincial administration of this afflicted government.

CRITICISM.

We commend to the notice of our readers an indictment of Mr. Yi Yong Ik which appears in the Daihan Ilpo and of which we publish a rough translation in another column.

The article differs very little from what is called, in respectable circles "blackmail" and, from a moral standpoint at least, we can congratulate Mr. Yi Yong Ik upon being in the "black books" of a journal resorting to such dirty tactics.

We have neither seen Mr. Yi Yong Ik nor communicated with him, so that in dealing with the Daihan Ilpo's allegations we are simply dealing with the case as set forth by that paper

(1) and (2) Mr. Yi Yong Ik has shown that there was no need for Korea to borrow from Japan. There is no harm done here because there is nothing new in it. All Koreans know that the Emperor simply borrowed the money under pressure, and that this was one of the principal objects of Mr. Megata's trip.

(3) We know nothing about it-Neither does the Daihan Ilpo

(4) Ditto:

(5) If he does made secret plans, why should he not. It is the only comfort left to a Korean in these times.

(6) He says the Il-chin-hoi is a frand. So do we. We have exhausted all our adjectives in speaking of this degenerate society. The members get sixty cents a day for the dirty work they do.

Mr. Pak Ei Pung has been appointed governor Seoul.

More claims are being laid against Mr. Min Yung Chul for extortion during his term of governorship.

A cabinet meeting was held on Thursday to discuss the offer of the people to lend the government what money it wants sooner than allow the country to become indebted to Japan, but the result has, so far, not transpired.

The straits in which the Japanese Government finds itself for gold is rapidly becoming a serious matter. It is now announced that no new railway enterprises will be sanctioned this year as these inevitably involve the sending of gold out of the country.

We have received from Messrs. Holme Ringer & Co., the agents for the Standard Life Assurance Co., a very pretty and useful calendar for 1905. Though somewhat belated it is still welcome as calendars are not so common in Korea as they might be.

Investigations made by the Japanese authorities have led them to the conclusion that the present is a favourable time for the issue of the fourth domestic loans. It is expected that it will be issued at par and will bear interest at the rate of 7 per cent. The Government estimates that between Y200,000,000 and Y300,000,000 can be raised in this way, but this seems to us to be a very optimistic view of the position.

It is reported that the Empress Dowager of China is paying the greatest attention to the politics of the day, and that she has ordered a plan of the Trans-Siberian Railway to be hung up in the drawing-room of Fat Chiu Lau, at Nanhai, where she is at present residing. It is said that this residence of the Empress Dowager is lavishly furnished in foreign style, and that it is lighted with electricity.

The Korea Daily News.

Issued at 5 P. M. daily except Sundays.

Rate of Subscription:—
Per Year,............Yen 25.
Per Quarter,..........Yen 7.
Per Month,..........Yen 2.50.

Postage in Korea not charged extra.
Postage abroad charged extra.

Advertisements, 50 sen per day for 1 inch or less.
5 yen per month per inch.
50 yen per year per inch.

All communications to

E. T. BETHELL,
Editor and Publisher,
Pak-tong, Seoul.

JAPAN AND KOREA.

It is devoutly to be hoped that a record is being kept of what the Japanese have done and are doing in Korea.

The little list would dispel many of the illusions so industriously fostered by those who speak from a blind love of Japan or a blind hatred of Russia or from interested motives.

Japan has not "played the game." From the beginning of February last year, when all the Korean telegraph wires in and around Seoul were cut to prevent the Russian Minister from communicating with the outside world and to prevent the "Koreetz" and "Varyag" from receiving any instructions, until to-day when we receive news of another addition to the already large army of Japanese "advisers" in Korea, Japan has not "played the game."

We received a letter the other day. It was anonymous and so we could not publish it. But it had not what we believe are the usual characteristics of anonymous letters: it was sensible and courteous in tone and its purport was that the KOREA DAILY NEWS, having taken up the cause of Korea, had become very keen-sighted for Japanese defects and blind to all redeeming features of the Japanese *regime* in Korea. The writer went into no details so that his letter was more of a suggestion than an argument. We have thought it over and invite his attention to what we now have to say, and in the meantime we point out, to those who maintain that Japan's policy in Korea, although it produces no immediate good results is for the ultimate benefit of the country, that it is by no means certain that Japan will be in power long enough to give Korea the benefit of such a far-sighted policy. The Koreans or any other observers would be more favourably impressed by immediate or visible results.

To commence with, there was the well known protocol whereby Japan secured a free hand in Korea for "military operations." This protocol was not explicit, but the Japanese have taken the widest possible interpretation of it. By virtue of it they have grabbed ground, forced labour, suppressed all indignation meetings, established martial law in various parts of Korea and assumed control of the Seoul police.

Then followed the extraction of certain fishing concessions, more land grabbing, (including an island in Chemulpo harbour for an observatory!) the establishment of Major Nodzu as military adviser, and the Nagamori Scheme.

Had the Nagamori Scheme gone through, the Japanese would today, without any payment whatever, have been the principal land owners in Korea. Fortunately the proposal collapsed at the very last moment and for this the KOREA DAILY NEWS takes some credit to itself. The scheme could not bear the light of day.

Then came the formation of the Il-chin-hoi Society. It pretended to be a patriotic society, aiming at the reformation of the many abuses which exist in Korea undoubtedly, but its real object was to frighten the Emperor and his Ministers into acquiescence with the Japanese demands. The one fact that that this society made no protest against the iniquitous Japanese loan of Y3.000,-000 on the security of the customs is sufficient indication of whom it is working for. All attempts of the Korean police and military authorities to suppress this society were frustrated by the Japanese and these incidents furnished the Japanese with an excuse to assume control of the police administration of Seoul.

And now we are hearing, almost daily of the appointment of Japanese advisers to this or that Government department. There has so far been nothing to show that these appointments are made for the furtherance of any but Japanese interests and one of them at least, viz: the appointment of a Japanese lady doctor to the Household Department was entirely superfluous and a piece of rank jobbery. Mr. Megata's effors so far have been directed towards obtaining control of the sources of Imperial revenue by forcing on the Koreans loans which they do not want.

By tactics similar to those now being adopted by the "Daihan Ilpo" against Mr. Yi Yong Ik, many Korean officials who stood in the way of the success of Japanese schemes have been frightened out of Seoul, and there are of course many minor incidents of jobbery which we have not noticed.

We now see by Tokio newspapers that the Japanese expect shortly to obtain monopolies of the tobacco and salt businesses in Korea, on the ground that money is required for the furtherance of their reform policy.

For the Japanese, it may be claimed that since they have been paramount in this country, many corrupt officials have been deprived of office. This is probably true, but it is equally true that many equally corrupt officials who have not been in the way of Japanese ambitions have been allowed to retain their offices. It cannot be denied that if the Japanese had a free hand here, Agricultural, Mining and Commercial enterprises would receive a tremendous impetus and the revenue of the country would go up by leaps and bounds. But all this development would be by the Japanese and for the Japanese. The Japanese are far ahead of the Koreans in business knowledge and enterprise and if the two nationals started side by side under the same conditions the Japanese would start with an enormous advantage which he would maintain to the gradual effacement of the Korean. The Japanese feared this very thing themselves when foreigners first came to their own country, and it is only now that they feel, themselves strong enough to grant foreigners equal land owning and mining rights with themselves.

Therefore, although we entirely agree that under Japanese direction the resources of this country would be enormously developed, we are also certain that in view of the Japanese policy of obtaining control of the finances and government of this country, that it is the Japanese and not the Koreans who would receive the benefit of these improvements.

Although it does not justify the Japanese actions there is something to be said for the contention that the Koreans if left to themselves, would do nothing to develope their own country. The history of their stagnation for the past fifteen years while Japan has steadily forged ahead, is used to point the moral, but it must be remembered that while Japan has been free to concentrate all her energies upon progress, Korea has been hampered by being the political Tom Tiddler's ground of the Far East.

MR. YI YONG-IK.

The "Daihan Ilpo" is apparently the mouthpiece for Japanese officialdom in Korea.

It publishes a number of "reports" about Mr. Yi Yong-ik, prefacing them, however, as follows:—

"We expect the following reports about Mr. Yi Yong-ik are not true, they seem to originate from those who hate and backbite him. When he returned to Korea he was enlightened and commenced to devote all his attention to education. There is no reason why he should change his mind so suddenly and behave as his critics say he does, but as all the allegations against him are serious we give them in brief and await his reply."

Then follows the indictment:—

(1) "The rich people living in the vicinity of five rivers" (near Seoul) offered $8,000,000 of their own money to the National treasury. This was planned by Yi Yong-ik.

(2) He is at present interfering by reporting to the Emperor that the merchants of Ham-kyeng province offer their money to the National treasury.

(3) He frequently visits the French Legation to borrow money.

(4) He is in communication with and conspiring with General Hyon, who is now in Japan to arrange for Marquis Ito to come to Korea.

(5) He has at present no official position yet he goes to the palace every night and makes various secret plans.

(6) He says that the Il-chin-hoi protect their country by the mouth only, and asks how it is that they did not protest against the foreign loan, which is directly opposed to the principles upon which the society was formed, and says that the deal with the Japanese Minister and the Dai Ichi Bank was put through with the assistance of the Il-chin-hoi at a time when the money could easily have been raised in Korea.

The Koreans are not the only ones who jump off a tramcar backwards when it is going at full speed and then wonder where the earthquake came from. Says the "Hongkong Telegraph." "Being in too much of a hurry does not always pay as Wu In found to his cost yesterday. He was riding in a tram-car along Praya East when finding the car was passing the corner at which he wanted to alight, he jumped out while the car was in motion at full speed, with the result that he sustained a cracked cranium, some teeth were torn out, and other damage caused to his anatomy necessitating his removal to the Government Civil Hospital for treatment."

The Korea Daily News.

VOL. II, MONDAY, FEBRUARY 20, 1905. No. 38

大韓每日申報
대한미일신보

(뎨이쳔삼십구호) (슈요일) 일쳔구빅오년이월이십이일

본샤고빅

이신보는영어와한어로석거미일츌판ᄒᆞᆸ

신문가

한쟝 엽두돈오푼
일삭표 엽두량닷돈
우표가미삭닷돈
다맛돈으로밧습

광고료는

긔한의쟝단과ᄌᆞ힝의다쇼로쥬감ᄒᆞ되렴가로밧을터이오며오티지아녀대한사람마다다이신문을보실터이니광고내시기들원ᄒᆞ시ᄂᆞᆫ이들은우리신문샤에와셔면약ᄒᆞ심을희망ᄒᆞᆸ

○발힝소 박동대한미일신보샤법어학교압혜젼영국인셜필림집자리오

샤쟝 영국인 (비셜)

평양 디리졈

○평양효동사ᄂᆞᆫ권미보씨로우리신문관미디리인을뎡ᄒᆞ엿ᄉᆞ오니평양에계신구람코져ᄒᆞ시ᄂᆞᆫ쳠군ᄌᆞᄂᆞᆫ허디리졈에왕림ᄒᆞ와면외ᄒᆞ십

사고

○우리대한미일신보의목뎍은대한의안녕질서에관한모든데목에디ᄒᆞ야ᄂᆞᆫ공평한변론을쥬쟝홈이라우리통신원의탐보ᄂᆞᆫ신문보시ᄂᆞᆫ쳠군ᄌᆞ의게홍상보도ᄒᆞ리며편지를긔셔ᄒᆞ여주시ᄂᆞᆫ이ᄂᆞᆫ셩명과반ᄃᆞ시를젹어붓치시기를희망ᄒᆞ오니이거슬신문샹에긔지ᄒᆞ랴ᄂᆞᆫ거시아니오다만극히신용ᄒᆞᄂᆞᆫ증거를삼고쟈홈이라긔자ᄂᆞᆫ아모긔셔던지긔지홈을되각ᄒᆞᄂᆞᆫ권리를가졋스나되각ᄒᆞᄂᆞᆫ리유를말홀터이오며공즁평화를문란케ᄒᆞᄂᆞᆫ듯ᄒᆞᆫ긔셔ᄂᆞᆫ의례히밧지안켓ᄉᆞᆸ나이다

●본샤셜시이릭로신문을미양우례로분젼ᄒᆞ와례젼부의입의로젼ᄒᆞᆫ듯스로먼곳에ᄂᆞᆫ혹늣게젼ᄒᆞ기도ᄒᆞ며혹몃칠거슬ᄒᆞᆫ겁에젼ᄒᆞ기도ᄒᆞ며혹아니젼ᄒᆞᄂᆞᆫ곳도잇다ᄒᆞ와우리신문을ᄉᆞ랑ᄒᆞ야구람ᄒᆞ시ᄂᆞᆫ 쳠군ᄌᆞ의게되ᄒᆞ야미우미안ᄒᆞᆸ기로지금은분젼인을두고미일일즉이젼ᄒᆞ며아니젼ᄒᆞ거나늣게ᄒᆞ거나ᄒᆞᆫ폐가업도록ᄒᆞ랴ᄒᆞ오니혹아니젼ᄒᆞ거나혹늣게젼ᄒᆞ거나ᄒᆞᆫ일이잇스면본샤로통긔ᄒᆞ여쥬심을희망ᄒᆞᆸ

론셜

평화풍셜

○일본에도착ᄒᆞᆫ특별면보면가지외에ᄂᆞᆫ평화에디ᄒᆞ야지금이일년젼보다더긴ᄒᆞᆫ소식이업도다일본은확실히젼쟁을졍지ᄒᆞ기를쳥홀리업고로국도비록지금삼상처아니ᄒᆞᆫ니란이잇스나젼쟁의연속ᄒᆞᄂᆞᆫ되ᄂᆞᆫ확실ᄒᆞᆫ반ᄃᆡ가업슬ᄲᅮᆫ외에로국황뎨셔샹쥬ᄒᆞᄂᆞᆫ사ᄅᆞᆷ들은만히말ᄒᆞ되니디인민의졍형을ᄀᆡ량ᄒᆞᄂᆞᆫ것이대국으로젼쟁의호결과ᄅᆞᆯ엇게ᄒᆞ리라고들ᄒᆞᄂᆞᆫ지라

로국황뎨셔ᄂᆞᆫ인민들이청구ᄒᆞᄂᆞᆫᄀᆡ량안을허락ᄒᆞ기ᄅᆞᆯ청죵ᄒᆞ시나국무대신들이막ᄂᆞᆫ다ᄒᆞ니그대신들이국민의힝복을위ᄒᆞᄂᆞᆫ신실ᄒᆞᆫ모음으로그리ᄒᆞᄂᆞᆫ지사욕을위ᄒᆞ야그리ᄒᆞᄂᆞᆫ지우리ᄂᆞᆫ능히말홀슈업스나엇뎌ᄒᆞᆫ지즁인을령솔ᄒᆞ고솔샹을만히니고셔사국에로도망ᄒᆞᆫ교사ᄶᅥ폰의목젹은아니될것이그사ᄅᆞᆷ의목젹을황뎨와대신들을핍박ᄒᆞ야실시ᄒᆞ지못ᄒᆞ게되엿도다동경외무셩에셔접슈ᄒᆞᆫ뎐보롤보면로국인민의ᄉᆞ샹을분명히알지니그뎐보에ᄒᆞ엿스되로국셩피득보에셔귀족들이회의ᄒᆞ고황뎨ᄶᅥ샹쥬안을의결ᄒᆞ엿ᄂᆞᆫ디그샹쥬안에말ᄒᆞ되로국어지금ᄂᆡ외로디젹이잇스니이러ᄒᆞᆫ어려운ᄯᅢ롤당ᄒᆞ야쟈긔들의츙심은일졍불변ᄒᆞᆫ다ᄒᆞ고ᄯᅩ인민들을그잔고ᄒᆞᆫ디로브러구제홈을황뎨ᄶᅥ의뢰ᄒᆞᆫ다ᄒᆞ엿고ᄯᅩ연ᄒᆞ야말ᄒᆞ되지금이로국이불힝ᄒᆞᆫ닐을당ᄒᆞ기가쳐음이아니오넷젹브터로국은환란이잇슬ᄯᅢ면그일을잘조쳐ᄒᆞ엿슬ᄲᅮᆫ외라도로혀강력을더ᄒᆞ기라도ᄒᆞ엿스니진실노모단일이군민이합심ᄒᆞᄂᆞᆫ디달넛고우리귀족들은밋되군민이샹합ᄒᆞ면항거홀이업슬터이오반다시셩젼ᄒᆞ리라ᄒᆞ며폐하ᄶᅥ셔총명예지ᄒᆞ시니모단인민이폐하의건단ᄒᆞ심을보기롤빌거놀불힝이졍부관인들과졍치가들이국가의안령힝복에관ᄒᆞᆫ문졔롤결졍홀지식이업ᄂᆞᆫ지라폐하의죠종ᄶᅥ셔인민의디표롤소집ᄒᆞ심으로인민의의견을구ᄒᆞ셧스나글로ᄒᆞ야젼제졍치의긔초가약ᄒᆞ야지지아니ᄒᆞ엿슬ᄲᅮᆫ외라국가외지금모양ᄀᆞᆺ치결과가조호오니그럼으로폐하의신민된우리들은ᄇᆞ라고밋되폐하ᄶᅥ셔인민의디표롤소집ᄒᆞ샤져의들의의견을옥탑에올니게ᄒᆞ시며그들의게립법권과힝졍권에참셥ᄒᆞ기롤허락ᄒᆞ시리라ᄒᆞ고만일폐하ᄶᅥ셔군현간협력ᄒᆞ기롤허락ᄒᆞ시면국가의ᄂᆡ란이업셔질터이오모단인민이다로국의영광을위ᄒᆞ야열심ᄒᆞ야디젹을격파ᄒᆞᄂᆞᆫ츙셩스러운직칙을다홀터이라ᄒᆞ엿스니

그샹쥬안에젼쟁을졍지ᄒᆞ쟈ᄂᆞᆫ말은업고ᄀᆡ량홈을권ᄒᆞᆫ고홈은젼쟁의셩공홈에긴요ᄒᆞ다고말ᄒᆞ엿도다

ᄯᅩ다론ᄉᆞ닭이ᄒᆞ나잇ᄂᆞᆫ것이론돈에셔일본공채롤모집ᄒᆞ기에용력ᄒᆞᄂᆞᆫ쟈들은젼쟁이미구에졍지될가망이잇다고셰샹을달ᄂᆡ면져의일이쉬운ᄉᆞ닭이라어젼쟁이오리나갈소록일본은ᄎᆞ관ᄒᆞ기가더어려운지라청국은지금빅에구십칠파빅분의오분변으로ᄎᆞ관이잘되ᄂᆞᆫ디우리ᄂᆞᆫ드론즉일본은빅에팔십오와빅분의륙분번으로도ᄎᆞ관ᄒᆞ기가미우어렵다ᄒᆞᄂᆞᆫ지라

엇더턴지로국이평화롤청ᄒᆞ랴ᄒᆞᆫ다ᄂᆞᆫ것은밋기어려우며만일그럴것갓ᄒᆞ면로국샤ᄅᆞᆷ들은우리가평일에예샹ᄒᆞ던인민이아니오로국의ᄂᆡ디형편도반다시동경뎐보에말ᄒᆞᆫ것보다더못되게라도되리라ᄒᆞ노라

뎐보

빅림발 이월사일

○로합지란의예산 로졔스토벤스기대쟝의합디ᄂᆞᆫ극동으로향ᄒᆞᄂᆞᆫ길에바타비아와사곤에셔슈용홀셕탄을싯게마련ᄒᆞ엿다더라

론돈발 동월오일

○로국ᄂᆡ란의속보 로국에셔혁명운동이졈졈더셩ᄒᆞ야가ᄂᆞᆫ디황뎨와ᄂᆡ각의쟝윗트씨ᄂᆞᆫ진무ᄒᆞᄂᆞᆫ졍칙을쓰랴ᄒᆞ고황태후와에대공들은압제슈단으로진압ᄒᆞ랴ᄒᆞᆫ다더라

동디발 동월륙일

○일영동밍의긔졍셜 일영동밍을긔졍홀다ᄂᆞᆫ사건에대ᄒᆞ야영국신문들이발ᄒᆞᆫ되동밍의범위롤아시아제국의강토보젼을셔로보호ᄒᆞ기로확쟝ᄒᆞᄂᆞᆫ것이젹당ᄒᆞ다고ᄒᆞ엿다더라

빅림발 동월구일

○셔젼왕의젼위 셔젼노위왕오스카이셰ᄶᅥ셔지금병환이잇셔셔황태자로대리를명ᄒᆞ엿다더라

론돈발 동일

○청국의공채 론돈파빅림에셔청국공채일빅만방을모집ᄒᆞᄂᆞᆫ대빅에구십칠오번리ᄂᆞᆫ빅분지오분이라더라

로국의졍형

론돈발 동월구일

○론돈다임쓰신문의파리통신원이보고ᄒᆞ되평화가일즉이될희망이젹다ᄒᆞ며ᄯᅩ말ᄒᆞ되파리에셔모집ᄒᆞᄂᆞᆫ로국공채의결과ᄂᆞᆫ잘못되야셔다만지금ᄭᆞ지일억법ᄯᅳᆷ모집이되엿다ᄒᆞ엿더라

빅림발 동일

○파리에셔로국공채의모집이잘못되야셔로국에셔오ᄂᆞᆫ사월에다시모집ᄒᆞ라ᄒᆞᄂᆞᆫ디혹은그것이평화될긔미라ᄒᆞ더라

동디발 동일

○로국파란에셔혁명운동이이러낫ᄂᆞᆫ디그혁명운동이파란국국민젹졍신으로죠직이된거시더라

잡보

○민김사화 의쥬거ᄒᆞᄂᆞᆫ젼의관김우용씨가일젼에민영철씨가로젼왕ᄒᆞ야힐문ᄒᆞ기를변젼에셔도향녹홀ᄯᅢ본인의일홈을류명ᄒᆞ야소청ᄒᆞᆫ후그돈은그대가혼자먹고죠금셔관인민은나를원망ᄒᆞ야나외고기를먹고자ᄒᆞ니오날우리량인이ᄀᆞᆺ치죽ᄂᆞᆫ것이당연ᄒᆞ다ᄒᆞ고팔독을ᄲᅧᆺ닉고소리를지르ᄆᆡ민씨가황황ᄒᆞ야셔울부조우셩일외어음엽삼십만냥을취ᄒᆞ야쥬고평화ᄒᆞ엿다더라

○쳐쳐립표 일젼에일병이안동으로브터사동ᄭᆞ지표목을세

UNION INSURANCE SOCIETY OF CANTON.

Head office Hongkong.
Marine risks underwritteu at current rates.

Agents in Chemulpo,
E. MEYER & Co.

COMPAGNIE DES MESSAGERIES MARITIMES.

Fortnightly Direct Service.

For Marseilles
via Ports.
Sailing from Yokohama
Calling at Kobe,
Shanghai, Hongkong, Saigon, Singapore,
Colombo, Djibonti, Suez, Port Said
and Marseilles.

For particulars apply to
HOLME RINGER & Co.,
Chemulpo.

HAYASHIDA & CO.,

16 MYENG DONG, CHIN KO KAI, SEOUL.
BRANCH OFFICE AT CHEMULPO.

Money changers, Coal and Wood Merchants, Express Agents.

We are agents for the Pyeng-yang Coa Company and the Karazu Coal Company ot Japan. We have the best quality of both anthracite and bituminous coal, and prompt ex ecution of orders is our speciality. Firewood of all kinds kept in stock. Full weight guaranteed. Money of all denominations exchanged at current rates. Parcels received for all parts.

CHINA MUTUAL LIFE INS. OC.

Most favourable terms to policy holders.

Benefit system unsurpassed.

HOLME RINGER & Co.
Agents, Chemulpo.

C. P. R.

CANADIAN PACIFIC RAILWAY COMPANY'S ROYAL MAIL STEAMSHIP LINE.

THE FAST ROUTE BETWEEN CHINA, JAPAN, AND EUROPE VIA CANADA AND THE UNITED STATES.

Route from Hongkong via Shanghai, Nagasaki (Inland Sea of Japan) Kobe, Yokohama, Victoria and Vancouver.

Twin Screw Empress Steamship—6,000 Tons—Speed 19 knots.

PROPOSED SAILING FROM YOKOHAMA.

R. M. S. Empress of India.
R. M. S. Empress of Japan.
R. M. S. Empress of China.
R. M. S. Athenian.
R. M. S. Taatar.

Special reduction (first class only) granted to mem bers of the Military, Naval, Diplomatic and Civil ser vices and to Missionaries.

Passengers have choice of ten routes across the Continent of America and have privilege of travelling by any Atlantic Steamship Line.

Round the World passage tickets in connection with the P. and O. S. N., North German Lloyd and Messageries Co.'s £125.

All rates payable at current rate of exchange.

For further information, Tickets, Guide Books, etc., apply to

HOLME, RINGER & Co., AGENTS,
Chemulpo.

Grand Hotel

(Formerly the Station Hotel)

Near the Railway Terminus, West Gate Seoul.

The Best Hotel in Korea
Handsome new Building.
Fine Airy Rooms
Excellent Cuisine.
Terms Moderate.
Special terms to Missionaries
and to permanent boarders.

Electric cars within 2 minutes' walk.

W. H. EMBERLEY.
Proprieto

AMERICAN KOREAN ELECTRIC CO.

Light and Power.

Main Office: Electric Building, Chong No.

RAILWAY DEPARTMENT.

OPERATING CARS BETWEEN EAST AND WEST GATE, EVERY TEN MINUTES:—

First Car leaves East Gate at 7:00 A. M. First Car leaves R. R. Station at 7:25 A. M
Last Car " East Gate at 8.40 P. M. Last " " R. R. Station at 9.05 P.M

OPERATING CARS BETWEEN EAST GATE AND IMPERIAL TOMB TERMINUS, EVERY TWENTY MINUTES:—

CONNECTING WITH EVERY ALTERNATE CAR ARRIVING AT EAST GATE FROM CHONG NO.

First Car leaves East Gate for Tomb at 7:10 A. M.
" " " Tomb for East Gate at 7:30 A. M.
Last " " East Gate for Tomb at 7:50 P. M.
" " " Tomb for East Gate at 8:10 P. M.

OPERATING CARS BETWEEN CHONG NO AND YUNG SAN RIVER EVERY TWELVE MINUTES:—

First Car leaves Chong No for South Gate at 7:12 A. M.
" " " Chong No for Yung San at 7:36 A. M.
" " " South Gate for Chong No at 7:20 A. M.
" " " Yung San for Chong No at 8:09 A. M.
Last " " South Gate for Chong No 9:00 P. M.
" " " Yung San for Chong No at 8.45. p. M.

PECIAL PRIVATE CARS FURNISHED TO SUIT CONVENIENCE OF PATRONS. PRICES ON APPLICATION AT HEAD OFFICE.

LIGHTING DEPARTMENT.

Where less than 250 candle power of light is used, the rate per month will be
Per 16 candle power incandescent lamp,—All night.—Yen 2.50.
32 candle power incandescent lamp:—All night:—Yen 4.00.
50 candle power incandescent lamp:—All night:—Yen 6.00.
150 " " " " " " ,, 10.00.
1200 ,, ,, enclosed arc " ,, ,, ,, 20.00.

Where more than 250 candle power of light is used, a Meter will be installed, if requested:—Rent of Meter Yen 2.00 per month. Rate of charges by meter reading:—Two Sen per Ampere per hour. (Approximately this is equal to about One Sen pei 16 C. P. lamp per hour) Minimum monthly charge where meter is installed, Yen 20.00 per month, which includes rental of meter.

Estimates for installing lights furnished on application

An assortment of chandeliers always on hand.

EVERY FACILITY.

In connection with Life Assurance Business is afforded by

The Standard Life Assurance Co.,

One of the largest and wealthiest of the Provident Institutions of the United Kingdom Forms of Application and all information will be promptly afforded on application.

10 CENTS A DAY.

Not a very large expenditure is it? But it is sufficient to secure for a man of 30 a policy with the STANDARD LIFE OFFICE for

$1323.

For all particulars of rates, etc., apply to

Holme, Ringer & Co.,
Agents, Chemulpo.

THE NEW YORK LIFE INSURANCE COMPANY.

Have you ever been declined by any Company?

Are you engaged in a specially hazardous occupation?

Have you heard of the New York Life Insurance Company's New Classifications for this class of Risks?

If not, send your date of birth, occupation and particulars of rejection, if any to

E. MEYER & Co.,
Agents, Chemulpo.

K. Murakami.

Photograph Studio
Chinkokai, Seoul.

Printing, Developing and Enlargement, of Photographs always Undertaken.

Korean Views and Pictures Illustrating Native Customs always on Sale,

---

THE OSAKA SHOSEN KAISHA.

Boats frequently on the berth for Chinnampo.

REGULAR SAILINGS BETWEEN JAPAN AND KOREAN PORTS.

FUSAN AND KOBE VIA SHIMONOSEKI.

OSAKA VIA MOKPO, FUSAN, SHIMONOSEKI AND KOBE.

MOJI DIRECT.

OSAKA VIA KUNSAN, MASANPO, FUSAN, SHIMONOSEKI AND KOBE.

CHEMULPO KUNSAN LINE,
Every three days.

CHEMULPO CHINNAMPO LINE.
Every three days.

For Freight and passage and further particulars apply to

THE OSAKA SHOSEN KAISHA,
Chemulpo

MITSUI BUSSAN KAISHA.
(MITSUI & Co.)

MITSUI GINKO.
(MITSUI BANK.)

The Bank is owned by the members of the Mitsui Family, who, as partners, assume an unlimited responsibility for all liabilities of the Bank:—

Capital..........................Yen 5,000,000
Reserve Fund.................. " 5,600,000

HEAD OFFICE, TOKYO.

LONDON OFFICE, 34 LIME ST., E. C.

BRANCHES AND AGENCIES:—

New York, San Francisco, Hamburg, Bombay, Singapore, Manila, Hongkong, Amoy, Chefoo, Tientsin.

Kobe, Hakodate, Yokohama, Kure, Yokosuka, Moji, Shimonoseki, Miike, Wakamatsu, Nagasaki, Kuchinotsu, Karatsu, Sasebo, Misu me, Taipeh, &c.

Telegraphic Address for all the Offices:

"MITSUI."

A. B. C. AND A. 1 CODES USED.

Contractors of Coal

To the Imperial Japanese Navy. Arsenals and Railway Bureau, Principal Railway Companies and Industrial Work, Home and Foreign Mail and Freight Steamers.

Sole Proprietors

Of the famous Miike, Tagawa and Yamano Coal Mines.

Sole Agents

For the sale of Fukumo, Hokoku, Ichimura Kanoda, Mannoura, Onoura, Ostuji, Sonoda Tsubaruro, Yoshinotani, Yoshio, Yurokibura and other coals.

YANGTSE INSURANCE ASSOCIATION, LTD.

The undersigned, having been appointed agents for the above company, are prepared to issue policies and pay losses on marine risks at regular rates.

E. MEYER & Co.,
Agents, Chemulpo.

RONDON, PLAISANT & CO.

General Storekeepers and Merchants, Ships Contractors Tobacconists, Commission and Forwarding Agents, Coal Merchants

IMPORTERS AND EXPORTERS

Seoul Chemulpo.

W. D. WENTWORTH.

LANDING
AND
SHIPPING AGENT.
AND
CUSTOMS BROKER.

12 OURA, NAGASAKI.

STEWARD & CO.

Chemulpo.

Shipchandlers and Storekeepers, Naval and Mercantile Contractors, Landing and Shipping Agents.

STEWARD'S HOTEL

Chemulpo.

Best accommodation in the port for travellers. Clean and well-aired rooms, good cuisine and prompt attendance,m oderatetariff.

원는뒤목면에쓰기를병마참쥬라ᄒᆞ엿더라

○면거늑사 일전에동대문안에셔사나히일명이면거에늑사ᄒᆞ엿는뒤히샤에셔훌금이십원을쥬엇다더라

○죠쳥디단 일공ᄉᆞ가외부로죠회ᄒᆞ엿스되원산에일어학교를설립코쟈ᄒᆞ니교ᄉᆞ건축ᄒᆞᆯ디단을챠여ᄒᆞ라ᄒᆞ엿더라

●최씨샹셔 전철산군수최뎡헌씨가전평안남도관찰ᄉᆞ민영철씨의탐장ᄒᆞᆫᄉᆞ를탄힉ᄒᆞ야졍부에샹셔ᄒᆞ엿다더라

○불일압샹 갈닌광쥬관찰사김세기씨를경무쳥에셔불일닉로압샹ᄒᆞᆫ다더라

●신씨가련 전부평군수신찬희씨가지임ᄒᆞ엿슬ᄯᅢ에리방의게가하오천이빅여량을썻다가히리가범포ᄒᆞᆫ고도타ᄒᆞ미히군수의게담칙이되여평리원감옥서에루년지수ᄒᆞ엿다가히군으로중역이되미신씨가호구를칙ᄒᆞ더니히군수셔긔림셩학이가교의를싱각ᄒᆞ야됴셕을공급ᄒᆞᄂᆞ동졀을당ᄒᆞ야도착면ᄒᆞᆯ도리언는지라칠십로인의졍경이가긍가련ᄒᆞᆯ섇더러신씨는전일다년포장으로유명ᄒᆞᆫ든신졍희씨의셔제라얻디오늘여차비참ᄒᆞᆫ경우를몽샹인들ᄒᆞ엿스리오미동사는박홍준씨가마춤부평에소잔이잇셔갓다가신씨가련ᄒᆞᆫ졍경을보고비록천분은업스나측은히싱각ᄒᆞ야동사당오십냥을헤급ᄒᆞ야동사를면케ᄒᆞᆫ지라박씨의자비ᄒᆞᆷ을칭션ᄒᆞᄂᆞᆫ조ㅣ다ᄒᆞ더라

○교졉귀졍 종로고시대사건과닥영졍에빙표사건으로경무쳥에셔일본경찰셔와여러날샹지ᄒᆞ더니빙고는금지ᄒᆞ엿고고시대는광교동쳔변으로이셜ᄒᆞ기로작졍ᄒᆞ엿더라

○압부경쳥 륙군법원에셔경무쳥압동으로묘구적의졍교참교병뎡사오명을착독제디ᄒᆞ야경무쳥으로압교ᄒᆞ엿더라

○조쳥실시 경무쳥에셔륙군ᄉᆞ령부로조회ᄒᆞ기를쳥결ᄉᆞ무를부득불실시ᄒᆞᆯ터인디인민의로방방분은경리가엄금ᄒᆞ려니와병뎡의로상방시등힝위헌병이엄금케ᄒᆞ라ᄒᆞ엿더라

○중치티삼 무론모인ᄒᆞ고로방에셔방시ᄒᆞ는ᄌᆞ는경찰셔에셔티삼긔식중치ᄒᆞ야방송ᄒᆞ기로작졍ᄒᆞ엿더라

○잉위허급 명동오예장에일인이회대를설립ᄒᆞ더니한셩부와샹지ᄒᆞ야히디단을인ᄒᆞ야허급ᄒᆞ얏다더라

○죡차쳥결 경무쳥에셔각셔에훈칙ᄒᆞ기를길쌰에생누ᄂᆞᆫ것파창밋헤오줌버리ᄂᆞᆫ것을일졀금단ᄒᆞ고됴뎡을방산ᄒᆞ는자잇스면곳압치ᄒᆞ되주임관은명함을밧아올ᄉᆞ라ᄒᆞ엿더라

○파송보호 경무쳥에셔면거교환ᄒᆞ는각기디에슌검이인식파송ᄒᆞ야승킥의오르고ᄂᆡ리는것을보호ᄒᆞ라ᄒᆞ엿더라

○면쳥슈유 무안감리한영원씨는외부로뎐보ᄒᆞ야슈유를쳥ᄒᆞ엿더라

○쳥원납세 셔쳔룡당진에거ᄒᆞ는인민이외부에쳥원ᄒᆞ기를본진사공김학수가졍세지공이라칭ᄒᆞ고힝인의게션가를람봉ᄒᆞ야폐단이만ᄒᆞ니규측을셩립ᄒᆞ야츈츄등세오빅량을상납케인가ᄒᆞ라ᄒᆞ엿더라

○회원중가 종로면거회샤뒤에쳥년회에셔근일학문샹에실험이만흔고로회원이날노중가ᄒᆞᆫ다더라

○도티무롱 경무쳥에셔경무관파춍순을문필이유여ᄒᆞᆫ자로틱츌ᄒᆞ고무식ᄒᆞ야능히감임못ᄒᆞᆯ자들은도태ᄒᆞᆫ다는항셜이잇더라

○군슈보결 각곤에궐ᄒᆞᆫ군슈는일간쥬본ᄒᆞ려차츌ᄒᆞᆫ다더라

○인쟝츌부 원산항경무관박긔호씨가니부로뎐보ᄒᆞ엿스되본항에쥬재ᄒᆞᆫ일본사령관이고원군슈인쟝을츌부ᄒᆞ오며히군사무를집힝ᄒᆞ라ᄒᆞ오니엇지죠쳐ᄒᆞ올는지ᄒᆞ엿더라

○필득승인 덕원군슈리종원씨가니부로보고ᄒᆞ엿ᄂᆞᆫ디본항에리쥬ᄒᆞᆫ일본군졍집힝관후바보병대사쳘련티쟝죠면만경씨명령니에귀국졍부에셔신임ᄒᆞᄂᆞᆫ디방관은한국쥬찰군사령관의승인쟝을수득ᄒᆞᆫ자아니면취임파직무를실ᄒᆞᆷ을부득ᄒᆞ며또귀국의규칙과풍속을의ᄒᆞ야디방관권리니에셔임명ᄒᆞᄂᆞᆫ관속과향쟝은그디방관이일본군졍집힝관의승인을예수ᄒᆞᆫ후에임명ᄒᆞᆷ이가ᄒᆞ다ᄒᆞ엿더라

○뒤츈홍공 춍세무사빅탁안씨가니부로복합ᄒᆞ엿스되양화진대로를수치ᄒᆞ야니외국인의게편케ᄒᆞᄂᆞᆫ사는진실노긴요ᄒᆞᆫ지라곳홍공수치ᄒᆞᆯ거시나다만금일에동한ᄒᆞ야착수ᄒᆞ기에불편ᄒᆞ니맛당히빙소ᄒᆞ기를기다려판공ᄒᆞᆷ이조타ᄒᆞ엿더라

○호상룡디 경무쳥에셔한셩부로죠회ᄒᆞ기를종금이후로는무론니외국인ᄒᆞ고가사를건축ᄒᆞ거든그디단을영미ᄒᆞᄂᆞᆫ것과권미ᄒᆞᄂᆞᆫ것과완축권축의등절을셔로룡디케ᄒᆞᆷ이가ᄒᆞ다ᄒᆞ엿더라

○취회가민 진쥬관찰사가니부로뎐보ᄒᆞ엿ᄂᆞᆫ디일진회원수빅명이각사에둔취ᄒᆞ야국긔를세우고연속히취회ᄒᆞ오니심히민망ᄒᆞ다ᄒᆞ엿더라

○갱입북도 단천군슈김유직씨가이월소일에니부로보고ᄒᆞ엿스되북쳥등디에류쥬ᄒᆞ든아병쳔여명이음력십이월십구일에본군에리도ᄒᆞ엿다가이십삼일야에다시북도로몰수히입ᄒᆞ엿다더라

○광군운집 평안남도슌안금광에셔근릭로사금의소츌이풍셩ᄒᆞ야한혈에소츌이삼사십량즁에나리지안는지라광군집취자ㅣ사만여명이라더라

○면화우셜 경복궁대궐안에도면화를셜립ᄒᆞᆫ다더라

○농부모집 묵셔가기쳑ᄒᆞᆯ한국인부를십만명가량모집ᄒᆞᆫ다는뒤금번에쳔여명을운송ᄒᆞᆫ다더라

외보

○막사과회의 막사과에셔귀족들이이월사일에회의ᄒᆞᆫ결과로샹쥬안이이건을결뎡ᄒᆞ엿는뒤그일건은보수쥬의니젼쟁이종결되고소란이진졍되기ᄭᆞ지졍부죠직을연긔ᄒᆞᆯ사들창도ᄒᆞ야이빅구명의다수가찬셩ᄒᆞ엿고타일건은자유쥬의를쥬쟝ᄒᆞ야일즉이국민의뒤표자를소집ᄒᆞᆷ을쳥구ᄒᆞ는자ㅣ니일빅오십삼명의소수가찬셩ᄒᆞ엿더라

○군슈품슈송 로국이근자에합즁국태평양연안을경ᄒᆞ야히셥위로향ᄒᆞ야젼시금제품을슈송ᄒᆞ는뒤그왕릭ᄒᆞ는션쳑이젼에비ᄒᆞ면죰만흔지라차는로국졍부가군슈품공급을셔빅리아텰도이외에운반코자ᄒᆞᆫ결과ㅣ라목하히삼위에샹륙ᄒᆞᆫ물화는합이빈으로수송ᄒᆞᆫ다ᄒᆞ더라

○모집국난 아국이파리에셔모집ᄒᆞ는외채는불호ᄒᆞᆫ결과를셩ᄒᆞ야아국인은리사월에채모집ᄒᆞᆷ이라언ᄒᆞ되타공론은금회의불호ᄒᆞᆫ결과로강화ᄒᆞᆯ소망이잇다더라

관보

광무구년이월십팔일

셔임급사령

○임의정부찬정셔칙임관일등 평리원지관장 민병한

이월십오일

○승셔판임관사등 법부주ᄉᆞ 심형틱

○임황히도관찰ᄉᆞ셔칙임관삼등 륙군참쟝 구영조

이샹이월십사일

○임평리원지관장셔칙임관이등 한셩부판윤 민경식

○임즁츄원의관셔칙임관사등 졍삼품 민봉식

이샹이월십오일

○의원면본관 비셔원승 리현의 군부쥬ᄉᆞ 홍열셥

○임비셔원승셔쥬임관오등 졍삼품 리셕종

○명녀쟝원감독셔칙임관사등 법부협판 김규희

○임한셩부판윤셔칙임관삼등 종이품 박의병

○임군부주ᄉᆞ셔판임관륙등 박션양

○면본관 군긔창기수 박셩환 리사셜

○임군긔창기수셔판임관륙등 한룡현 권병쳘 한규영

이샹이월십륙일

○의원면본관 탁지부주ᄉᆞ 홍태뎡

광무팔년십이월삼십일일

○임운산면보ᄉᆞ주ᄉᆞ셔판임관삼등 공주면보ᄉᆞ주ᄉᆞ 박셩호

○임공주면보ᄉᆞ주ᄉᆞ셔판임관삼등 안주면보ᄉᆞ주ᄉᆞ 최종악

○임안주면보ᄉᆞ주ᄉᆞ셔판임관륙등 종셩면보ᄉᆞ주ᄉᆞ 김한규

○면즁계 전주ᄉᆞ 남기훈

○임법부협판셔칙임관삼등종이품 리근샹

○임평리원검ᄉᆞ셔칙임관사등 김허군수 리근홍

이샹이월십륙일

○의원면본관 홍문관시독 허만필 비셔원승 리셕종 즁추원의관 신복균 즁추원의관 명지우 즁추원의관 안경셕 즁추원의관 리종형

○명궁니부특진관셔칙임관삼등 경긔관찰ᄉᆞ 리근교 경샹북도관찰ᄉᆞ 장승원

○명녀쟝원경셔칙임관삼등 종이품 윤쵸영

○임비셔원승셔주임관오등 졍삼품 신헌균

○임홍문관시독셔판임관ᄉᆞ등 졍삼품 표진셜

○임중추원의관셔주임관륙등 졍삼품 박형빈 졍삼품 박종목 륙품 리긔룡 륙품 김병호

○탁지부주ᄉᆞ셔판임관륙등 김종원 박룡턱

○면즁계 젼주ᄉᆞ 리종순

이샹이월십칠일

광고

TELEGRAMS.

(FROM JAPAN PAPERS.)

THE BALTIC FLEET.

London, Feb. 13.

Five Russian cruisers have left Zanzibar for Diego Suarez (on the northeast coast of Madagascar).

VLADIVOSTOK.

London, Feb. 14.

It is announced at St. Petersburg that a state of siege has been proclaimed at Vladivostok by the Russian authorities, and that in consequence a part of the inhabitants are hurriedly leaving the town.

London, Feb. 13.

It is belived that with the advent of mild weather, General Kawamura, with a large force of field artillery, will endeavour to sever the Russian lines of communication, at a point north of Vladivostock.

RUSSIAN AFFAIRS.

London, Feb. 14.

By a Ukase dated the 12th inst., the Tsar orders the formation of a commission to represent the Government, factory-owners and employees, in order to investigate the causes of complaints on the part of workmen in St. Petersburg and the provinces, and to prevent the further fermentation of troubles.

London, Feb. 13.

It is stated in St. Petersburg that the Tsar is consulting his statesmen as to the best means of securing an armistice between the two armies in the field.

London, Feb. 13.

General Gripenberg is lying seriously ill at Irkutsk.

London, Feb. 14.

The situation is Russia is now regarded as somewhat more hopeful (from the Government point of view).

At Lodz the employes in many of the factories have resumed work.

London, Feb. 11.

The strike of the Proffessors and Students of the Russian universities is spreading throughout the country.

GENERAL NEWS

London, Feb. 10.

The German miners have resumed work in Westphalia.

Tientsin, Feb. 8.

Dr. Morrison, the "Times'" correspondent, has returned from Port Arthur. He denies absolutely using the expression "dishonourable" as applicable to the Russian surrender.

SIR HENRY CAMPBELL-BANNERMAN'S CRITICISM.

London, Feb. 15.

Parliament was opened yesterday.

In the House of Commons Sir Henry Campbell-Bannerman, the Liberal leader said the Fiscal question still overshadowed everything. Sir Henry vigorously condemned the Government for clinging to office, despite the fact that the feeling of the country demonstrated indubitably that the prolongation of the present situation was a public danger and usurpation of power.

In reference to the war, Sir Henry said he hoped Lord Lansdowne would embrace the earliest opportunity of using England's influence on the side of peace. The Thibet Expedition Sir Henry characterised as a tragic comedy, and asked why the Government censure of the Agent was not carried higher.

Speaking in the House of Lords, Earl Spencer (Liberal leader) said he trusted the Government would not lose any opportunity that might present itself of endeavouring in conjunction with other Powers to bring about a peaceful solution of the present war.

GENERAL GRIPENBERG'S COMMAND.

The Russians, according to a Shanghai telegram, are claiming that General Gripenberg did not command the troops engaged in the Heikoutai battle. They say that the troops concerned were a mixed corps consising of men from the Kaulbars and Linnevitch forces, and that General Gripenberg left for home five days before the battle and was no longer in command of the Russian right from that day.

General Kaulbars has been appointed Commander of the Second Army in Manchuria.

The Japanese loans, domestic and foreign seem to be hanging fire, so do the reports of casualties at the battle of Heikoutai.

Owing, presumably, to the peace rumours, both Japanese and Russian bonds have risen in price in Europe and America.

According to a London telegram of Feb. 10, it is reported at St. Petersburg that seven Argentine battleships and cruisers have joined Admiral Rojestvensky at Madagascar.

A telegram received in official quarters in Tokio says:—The Baltic squadron will not leave Nossibé till the end of February. Seventeen transports (including the *Esperance*) are accompanying the squadron.

The British steamer *Eastly*, which was seized by a Japanese warship in Hokkaido waters on the 8th inst., was examined at the Sasebo Prize Court on the 13th inst., with the result that the vessel with her whole cargo was released.

There is no war news of interest. Field Marshal Oyama reports several minor Japanese successes and the "Echo de Chine" says that the Japanese have been driven back to Liaoyang. Whatever the truth of these reports, it certainly appears as if the Japanese have gone as far north as they are likely to get.

The Gulf of Pechili is now becoming free from ice, and the Nippon Yusen Kaisha is making arrangements to reopen its services to North China ports. The British steamer "Prometheus" will sail from Kobe on the 23rd inst., on the company's first trip to Taku for the present year.

The "Jiji" Shanghai correspondent wires on reliable authority that the Russian cruiser "Askold," now at that port, has been coaled and is now ready for navigation. The correspondent adds that the electric light on board the vessel is supplied by the Russian gunboat "Mandjur by means of a wire connecting the two warships. But, in view of his evident suspicions it is a pity that the correspondent does not say what will become of the wire when the ships sail.

The Japanese Minister has sent a despatch to the Home Department as follows:—"It is advisable to have one police inspector and one policeman under the control of the police adviser as his assistants so I intend to appoint Messrs Matsunaga and Morinaga to these posts with salaries of 75 and 48 yen respectively, which are to be paid out of the national treasury." Mr. Hayashi further says that these are the salaries which the Japanese pay to their police in Korea. That may be, but in Japan a policeman gets about ten yen a month and it is difficult to account for the enormous difference in this country.

SHANGHAI NEWSPAPER CONTROVERSY.

The following appears in a Shanghai telegram received by the "Jiji" dated the 12th inst.:—

The French paper "Echo de Chine" has accused the British press published at Shanghai of having been "purchased" by Japan, but the statement was subsequently withdrawn at the protest of the "Shanghai Mercury." and the "Shanghai Times." The "Mercury," however, says that there is reason to believe that the "Times" is in the pay of Japan, as it often prints slanderous reports concerning Russia.

The "Echo de Chine" publishes a rumour to the effect that a syndicate, backed by a capital of 60,000 taels, has been organized for the purpose of establishing a Japanese printing office at Shanghai and publishing a Chinese newspaper in co-operation with the "Shanghai Daily Press." The "Echo de Chine" has also printed a telegram originally forwarded from Shanghai to Vladivostock and subsequently retransmitted to Shanghai, stating that the "Mercury," "Times." and "Daily Press" are each receiving a subsidy of 8,000 yen from the Japanese Government

The Marquis of Bath has been appointed Under-Secretary for India.

Marquis Ito is reported to be slightly indisposed.

It is reported that three Osaka banks, namely, the 13oth, 34th and another bank, are about to establish branch offices in Korea.

With reference to the murder of the two Japanese engineers in the employ of the Chaochou Swatow railway, it has transpired that it was committed on account of some personal grievances suffered by the villagers who accordingly gathered in large numbers and caused trouble.

The Tokio Department of Agriculture and Commerce has received samples of 15 American and Japanese varieties of cotton, experimentally cultivated in the neighbourhood of Mokpo, Korea. The quality of the cotton is tolerably good, so that the Department will probably carry out an investigation as to the extent of land available for cotton cultivation in Korea.

Lloyd's being unable to discover any evidence that Russia is arranging to supply the Baltic fleet with coal and provisions beyond Diego Suarez Bay, in the extreme north of Madagascar, has cancelled the insurance on two large shiploads of arms and ammunition bound from Libau, in the Baltic, to the East Indian Archipelago and Saigon, the capital of French Indo-China.

It is reported in Tokio that negotiations are going on between the Japanese Government and the French authorities concerning the Baltic fleet, which has not only been coaled and provisioned at Madagascar but is also remaining there. Similar negotiations between the Japanese Government and two other countries have, it is stated, recently been concluded, but the publication of the result is deferred owing to the noncompletion of the negotiations with the French authorities.

Apparently the Russian Minister to China is getting as tired as we are of the fuss which has been made of the accidental killing of a Chinaman in Shanghai by a sailor from the Askold. We see that the Chinese Minister of the Board of Foreign Affairs has telegraphed to Yuan Taotai, of Shanghai, that he has failed in his negotiations with the Russian Minister for a public trial of the murderer of the Ningpo Chinaman, and that the behaviour of the Russian Minister has been disrespectful and his language unreasonable. He also states that he has telegraphed to the Chinese Minister at St. Petersburg regarding the matter.

NEW GERMAN STEAMER.

THE RHENANIA.

A steamer that inaugurates a new passenger line between Europe and the Far East the Hamburg Amerika Linie s. s. Rhenania (Capt. Behrens, formerly of the Kiaochow). The H. A. L. are building several steamers of this class to compete in the passenger traffic, offering such inducements as cheaper passages and better accommodation.

The Rhenania is a well made vessel of good lines, and can take about 50 passengers in the saloon and 100 in the steerage. There are smoking and ladies' rooms on board, the cabins are very large, lofty and airy, and each contains two bedsteads (not berths), two almeirahs, a table and sofa. Thus, some forty passengers on the steamer will have much the same accommodation at their disposal as about five times the number of passengers have on a mail boat. She is 420 ft. long, with a draught of 25 ft. and is built with bilged keels to prevent her rolling in heavy seas. Her engines are 3,400 h. p. and she has a speed of thirteen knots. The dining room is spacious and comfortable, and like the ladies' saloon and smoking saloon, is lofty and well lighted and ventilated. The furniture in the ladies' saloon is all white, and in keeping with the richly embossed walls, and on the Jugendstile pattern, while the couches are all upholstered with velvet-pile tapestry. A doctor and stewardess are carried on board, while a very neat dispensary is on the overdeck, where also an up-to-date hairdressing saloon is present. A library is well stocked with English, German and French literature, and a glance at the catalogue shows that the works of leading authors have been selected.

The vessel carries a total crew of [illegible]. The sanitary arrangements are perfect and, like the cabin accommodation, are unsurpassed on any steamers coming out East. The boat generally has a fine appearance and is painted black with yellow funnel. The ports of call on the homeward journey are Penang, Colombo, Suez, Port Said, Marseilles, Havre and Hamburg, and the journey will occupy about 28 days, while it is optional for passengers to proceed overland by rail from Marseilles.

The Rhenania has also a cargo carrying capacity of 8,000 tons. Two sister ships will follow shortly, the Rhatia and Rugia.

A telegram has been received in Japan to the effect that, President Roosevelt has addressed a note to the Russian Ambassador saying that notwithstanding the outward tranquillity, the relations between England and Germany had become so strained that there was danger of war.

Dr G. E. Morrison, the Peking correspondent of the Times, after inspecting the actual condition of Port Arthur, has wired to the paper some very sensational and biased reports on Jan 25th, which are, mysteriously remarks the China Review, receiving attention and will be dealt with in the proper quarter.

According to a Paris telegram of Feb. 7th there is a insurrectionary movement in the Argentine Republic, in which several of the revolutionaries have been killed and wounded, in contact with the government troops. The latest telegram from Buenos Ayres states that the Government declares they are complete masters of the situation.

The Korea Daily News.

Issued at 5 P. M. daily except Sundays.

Rate of Subscription:—

Per Year,............Yen 25.
Per Quarter,..........Yen 7.
Per Month,..........Yen 2.50.

Postage in Korea not charged extra.
Postage abroad charged extra.

Advertisements, 50 sen per day for 1 inch or less.
5 yen per month per inch.
50 yen per year per inch.

All communications to

E. T. BETHELL,
Editor and Publisher,
Pak-tong, Seoul.

NEWS.

It must by now have become evident to those whose fate it is to follow the progress of the war and its contingencies in the light of the telegrams which are published by the newspapers in the Far East, that things are by no means what they are represented to be.

Without entering into the question of motive, we can without hesitation affirm that what reaches us as "news" is a very small piece of fact surrounded with a large piece of pro-Japanese and anti-Russian colouring matter. Japan might be excused for evincing partiality, but it is sad to find Reuter and all the London "special services" guilty of the same.

A recent incident will serve to illustrate our meaning. After the battle of Heikoutai a London telegram appeared in a Tokio paper saying that General Kuropatkin had dismissed General Gripenberg, accusing him of having thrown away 10,000 men. Then came a story from somewhere *en route*, to the effect that Gripenberg was returning to Russia in order to accuse Kuropatkin of dilatoriness and general helplessness.

Upon this wonderful foundation were based many reports of dissention among the Russian commanders, all of which have been gleefully disseminated by the press in Japan, the Japanese and pro-Japanese press in Korea and, we expect, by a certain portion of the press in China.

So far, we have found Russian reports much more reliable than Japanese, and we therefore believe the statement issued from Russian headquarters, that General Gripenberg did not participate in the recent battle, (having been invalided some days previously), to be the truth. Later telegraphic advices inform us that General Gripenberg is lying critically ill at Irkutsk, and this, taken in conjunction with the fact that he was unable to take part in the Heikoutai engagement, convinces us that it was a serious illness and nothing else that caused his retirement from the front.

And yet through the Japanese press and telegraphic agencies this unfortunate illness has become "serious dissention among the Russian commanders."

A Japanese general died the other day, through, according to the "Japan Mail," a marked prediliction for alcohol. Had he been a Russian general we should have heard that he committed suicide through fright.

And so on and so on, *ad libitum*.

Nervous friends abjure us to be careful; to criticise the Japanese is to be anti-Japanese; to be anti-Japanese is to be pro-Russian and to be pro-Russian, is at present unwise. We are, however pro-Korean, and share the view of all unbribed Koreans that no greater disaster could befall Korea—either as a nation or a people—than a recognized Japanese ascendancy in this country.

Therefore we advise Koreans to wait for facts before finally giving up their birthright. If the Japanese are so sure of victory as they pretend to be, a few months will make no difference to then and they can absorb this country at their leisure after the war is over.

In the meantime it is advisable to adopt a very conservative attitude when receiving news. All war reports must reach Korea *via* Japan, and Korea only gets such news Japan sends or allows to come through.

HOW THE COSSACK RAID FAILED

SMART WORK OF JAPANESE RAILWAY GANG.

Just before the recent Russian attack on Newchwang, a troop of Cossacks left the main body and made for the railway line between Yinkow and Tashichao. The object was, of course, to isolate Newchwang, since its sole means of communication with the main line of railway is via Tashichao junction. They succeeded in making several breaches in the line, and they concluded that no reinforcements would be able to come to save Newchwang. But, according to the China Times, information very promptly reached the Japanese superintendent engineer at Tashichao, and he sent out a gang of coolies at once to repair the damage. On the heels of the repair train, there came a troop train, crammed as full of soldiers as it could be. The Cossacks still hung about the vicinity, and had just learned of the repair gang's arrival at the first break. The Russians hurried to the place, thinking to chase away a few coolies, but just then up came the trainload of soldiers. Grasping the situation promptly, the Japanese tumbled out of the train and gave the Cossacks "Banzai." Then, soldiers and coolies together, all bundled back into the train, and made full speed ahead to the next break in the line. The Cossacks might return and repeat their work at the first place, but that did not matter; the order was to get to Newchwang somehow. Thus each gap in the line was negotiated. The Russians were chased away whenever seen, and Yinkow was reached in safety. But then came the most exciting part of all. The engine-driver was told to get back to Tashichao for another batch of reinforcements; for it would seem that only one train plies, between Newchwang and Tashichao, about 35 miles. Or perhaps all available cars had been used, as one extra long train, on the first trip. At any rate, a contingent of Port Arthur troops would be due and the engine-driver had to do his best. With an empty train, no soldiers, he had to run the gauntlet through country that might be full of Cossacks; he had no means of knowing what futher damage there might be done along the line. There was no time to worry about such things; he simply threw the lever and dashed on, and, as fortune would have it, he got through and brought the second lot of troops all right, in good time. The Russian official report says, sadly, "Our destruction of the railway proved to be incomplete."

When the reinforcements reached Newchwang, fortune again favoured the Japanese, for the railway line runs just along the flank of the position where the fight was in progress. This greatly helped to complete the discomfiture of the Russians.

GERMAN INTERESTS IN CHINA.

A STATEMENT OF THE POSITIOM.

The following is from a German publication on German interests in China "If we look on the German spheres of interest outside of Shantung, we find in Shanghai, for example, two German stock companies with a working capital $228,000. These companies are engaged in the weaving of silk and cotton goods. There are in addition $2,380,000 of German capital engaged in selling silk, $1,500,000 in flour mills, and large amounts in agricultural companies, banks, wharves, docks, gas houses, &c. In numerous other places in China large sums of German capital have been invested in all kinds of industrial enterprises, although it would be hard to obtain exact figures in regard to them.

Still another picture—the German merchant in China. Shanghai alone has at least 68 large German firms, whose annual turnover amounts of $28,560,000, or 22 per cent. of the total turnover of the city of Shanghai.

After Shanghai, Tientsin is the most Germanised city in China. It has 29 large German firms working with an active capital of $4,552,000. The Germans' part in the business of that city amounts to 60 per cent. of the total imports and 45 per cent. of total exports.

In Canton, 12 German commercial houses are stationed, doing 50 per cent of the total import, and 75 per cent. of the total export business.

Chefoo has 4 German firms with a capital of $357,000; Amoy has 3 German firms, with a capital of $71,400. Of the other treaty ports, Swatow, Foochow, and Hankow are domiciles of large German firms. Germany's share in the imports of Hankow is placed at $2,850,000 and her share in exports at $700,000 to $900,000."

MR. AUSTEN CHAMBERLAIN.

"If Disraeli was born in a library," writes Mr. Herbert Vivian in the new "Pall Mall Magazine," "'Chamberlain the younger' was brought forth in a polling booth and cradled in a political atmosphere. It is scarcely surprising that when Mr. Vivian met him at Cambridge he should describe the future Chancellor of the Exchequer as 'an elderly young man.'

"He could talk well. His opinins were evidently all cut and dried, and he was absolutely inflexible in argument. His sense of humor was rather of the American type.

"His character was curiously complex. He was reserved and rather proud—held himself aloof, and almost repelled acquaintances. He never mentioned his ambitions, but he evidently considered his lightest statement was likely to be criticised by posterity. It is useless to pretend that he was ever very popular."

The writer adds that though he saw young Chamberlain nearly every day for a term of two years he never felt that he knew him well. "Bound about his character there was an outer shell which few were able to penetrate."

The Korea Daily News.

VOL. II, TUESDAY, FEBRUARY 21, 1905. No. 39

HONGKONG & SHANGHAI BANKING CORPORATION.

Paid-up Capital............$10,000,000
Reserve Fund:—Sterling Reserve... 10,000,000
Silver Reserve..... 7,000,000

27,000,000
Reserve Liability of Proprietors... 10,000,000

HEAD OFFICE, HONGKONG.

London Bankers, London and County Banking Company Limited.

Branches and Agencies,

London.

Amoy,	Hankow	Penang,
Bangkok,	Hiogo,	Rangoon,
Batavia,	Iloilo,	Saigon,
Bombay,	Lyons,	San Francisco,
Calcutta,	Manila,	Singapore,
Colombo,	Nagasaki,	Sourabaya,
Foochow,	New York,	Tientsin,
Hamburg,	Peking,	Yokohama,

Credits granted on approved Securities, and every description of Banking and Exchange business transacted.

Drafts granted on London and the chief Commercial places in Europe, India, Australia, America, China and Japan.

HOLME RINGER & Co., AGENTS, CHEMULPO.

HOKURKU DOBOKU KAISHA.

Branch office in Chong Dong. Seoul.

Japanese telephone No. 165

CONTRACT DEPARTMENT.

We can contract to build any building or construction.

MERCHANDISE DEPARTMENT.

We can provide any building material. We have just contracted to build the new Belgian Legation.

E. MEYER & CO.

Chemulpo.

SOLE AGENTS IN KOREA FOR,

A. T. Morse, Sons & Co.'s

"Fresco" Distemper

In all colours ready for use on walls, Ceilings etc.

and

AVENARIUS CARBOLINEUM

A wood-preserving and antiseptic oil preparation

Against decay, dry-rot, fungus and wood-destroying insects.

A large supply always in stock. Prices upon application.

E. MEYER & Co.,
Chemulpo.

CHARTERED BANK OF INDIA AUSTRALIA & CHINA.

INCORPORATED BY ROYAL CHARTER 1853

HEAD OFFICES.—LONDON.

Paid-up Capital £800,000
Reserve Liability of Shareholders 800,000
Reserve Fund 800,000

Drafts granted upon all the principal places in the world and every description of Exchange and banking business transacted.

E. MEYER & Co., Agents,
Chemulpo.

MITSU BISHI DOCKYARD & ENGINE WORKS,

NAGASAKI.

CODE WORD, "DOCK."

A 1, A. B. C., and Engineering Codes used.

DOCK No. 1 (at Tategami).

Extreme Length.............523 feet
Length on blocks ....513 ,,
Width of Entrance on Top......89 ,,
,, ,, Bottom....77 ,,
Water on Blocks at Spring Tide 26½ ,,

DOCK No. 2 (Mukaijima).

Extreme Length.............371 feet
Length on Blocks............360 ,,
Width of Entrance on Top......66 ,,
,, ,, Bottom 53 ,,
Water on Blocks at Spring Tide 22 ,,

PATENT SLIP (at Kosuge).

Can take vessels up to 1,000 tons gross.

THE WORKS are well equipped with the LATEST IMPROVEMENTS, and can execute any kind of work in SHIPBUILDING and MARINE ENGINEERING, as well as in REPAIRING of SHIPS.

The COMPANY'S new powerful steamer OURA-MARU (712 tons, 700 I.H.P.), specially built for SALVAGE PURPOSES, and equipped with necessary gear, is always READY at SHORT NOTICE.

THE METHODIST PUBLISHING HOUSE.

Little West Gate, Seoul.

JOB PRINTING, TYPEWRITER PAPER
CARBON PAPER, VISITING CARDS
STATIONERY, BOOK-BINDING
BOOK PUBLISHERS
AMERICAN SCHOOL BOOKS
SPENCERIAN COPY BOOKS
PEN CARBON LETTER AND BILL BOOKS

S. A BECK, Manager.

DAI-ICHI GINKO.

LIMITED.

(Formerly the First National Bank)

ESTABLISHED 1873

INCORPORATED UNDER PRESENT LAW 1896

Capital - - - - - - - - - Yen 5,000,000
Reserve Fund - - - - - 1,500,000

HEAD OFFICE—TOKIO.

President: Baron SHIBUSAWA.

BRANCHES AND CORRESPONDENTS

In the Principal Cities and Towns of Japan.

Interest Allowed on

Fixed deposits 1 year - - - 6½ per cent
" " 6 months - - - 6 per cent

Special current accounts 1½ sen daily per Y 100
General " " 1 " " " 100

M. TANAKA,
Manager, Chemulpo.

SINGER SEWING MACHINES

씽거ᄌᆞ봉침

SOLE AGENTS FOR KOREA

전매쇼

HOLME RINGER & CO.

Chemulpo.

졔물포 함릉거양힝

KAMEYA & CO.

GENERAL STOREKEEPERS

Chinkokai - - Seoul

(Established 1895, Tokyo)

Confectionery, Hams, Canned Goods, Cutlery, Hirano & Tansan Water. Provisions, Gents, Furnishing goods, Toilet Articles, Travelling Bags, Tobacco, Cigars & Cigarettes Kitchen Utensils. Coffee, Biscuits

Fresh Goods always kept in Stock.

Prices Moderate

☞ *Please come and inspect our goods.*

NIPPON YUSEN KAISHA.

JAPANESE MAIL STEAMSHIP CO.

UNDER MAIL CONTRACT WITH THE IMPERIAL JAPANESE GOVERNMENT.

European Line.

Regular Fortnightly Service between Yokohama Kobe, Moji, Shanghai, Hongkong, Singapore, Penang Colombo, Port Said, Marseilles, London and Antwerp

American Line

Regular Fortnightly Service between Hongkong and Seattle, calling at Shanghai, Moji, Kobe, Yokohama and Victoria, B. C.

Australian Line

Regular weekly Service betwen Japan Ports and Australia, calling at Hongkong and Manila.

(Above Three Lines, Suspended until further notice).

Shanghai Line

Weekly Service between Shanghai and Japan Po

Korea Line

Service Kobe, Moji, Nagasaki, Fusan Chemulpo Chefoo, Taku.

S. S. Babelsberg, 2181 tons.

Service Kobe. Moji, Fusan, Chemulpo, Chinnampo

S. S. ARGO, S. S. Ohio.

BORDEN'S CONDENSED MILK CO.

New York, U. S. A.

ALWAYS IN STOCK

Eagle Brand Condensed Milk.

Gold Seal Condensed Milk.

Peerless (Family) Evaporated Cream.

Borden's Malted Milk.

E. MEYER & CO.
Chemulpo Korea,
Sole Agents.

ROYAL INSURANCE COMPANY,

Funds exceed £10,000,000

FIRE

AT CURRENT RATES

LIFE

REDUCED PREMIUM,

HOLME RINGER & Co.,
Agents, Chemulpo.

廣 KWANG ● CH'ANG 昌

BENNETT & CO.

Merchants

Chemulpo.

Offices opposite the Imperial Japanese Post and Telegraph Office Chemulpo.

Telephone Number 201.

大韓每日申報

대한민일신보

(뎨이쳔ᄉ십호) (목요일) 일쳔구빅오년이월이십삼일

본샤고빅

이신보는영어와한어로셔계리일츌판ᄒᆞ옵

신문가

한쟝 엽두돈오푼

일삭도 엽두량닷돈

우표가리삭닷돈

다맛돈으로밧숩

광고료는

긔한의쟝단과ᄌ칭의다쇼로증감ᄒᆞ되렴가로밧을터이오며오린지아니ᄒᆞ며대한사람마다더이신문을보실터이니광고버셔기를원ᄒᆞ시는이들은우리신문사에와셔편의ᄒᆞ게샹의ᄒᆞ시옵

○발힝소 박동대한민일신보사범어학교앏헤젼영국인셜필립쟝자리오

사쟝 영국인 (빅셜)

평양 디리졈

○평양효동사는권미보씨로우리신문판미디리인을뎡ᄒᆞ엿시ᄉᆞ오니평양에계신구람코져ᄒᆞ시는 쳠군ᄌ는ᄒᆡ디리졈에왕림ᄒᆞ와면회ᄒᆞ시옵

사고

○우리대한민일신보의목뎍은대한의인민ᄭᅴ셔에관ᄒᆞᆫ모든미목에디ᄒᆞ야는공평ᄒᆞᆫ변론을쥬쟝ᄒᆞᆷ이라우리통신원의탐보는신문보시는쳠군ᄌ의게ᄒᆞ샹보도ᄒᆞ리며편지들긔서ᄒᆞ여주시는이는셩명과번디를적어붓치시기를희망ᄒᆞ오니이거슨신문샹에긔재ᄒᆞ랴는거시아니오다만극히신용ᄒᆞ는증거를숨고자홈이라긔자는아모긔서편지과저홈을되쟉ᄒᆞ는권리를가졋ᄉᆞ나편쟉ᄒᆞ는리유를말ᄒᆞᆯ터이오며공중평론을판단케ᄒᆞ는듯ᄒᆞᆫ긔서는의례히밧지안켓습니이다

●본사셜시ᄒᆞᆫ이리로신문을미망우레로분젼ᄒᆞ와레젼부의임의로젼ᄒᆞ는것스로면곳에는추눗계젼ᄒᆞ기도ᄒᆞ며혹면쳡거슬ᄒᆞᆫ텹에젼ᄒᆞ기도ᄒᆞ며혹아니젼ᄒᆞ는곳도잇다ᄒᆞ오니우리신문을ᄉ랑ᄒᆞ야구람ᄒᆞ시는 쳠군ᄌ의계랑터ᄒᆞ야리우미안ᄒᆞ옵기로지금은본젼인을두고미일쥬이젼ᄒᆞ며아니젼ᄒᆞ거나늣게가나혼페가업도록ᄒᆞ랴ᄒᆞ오니쟝하니젼ᄒᆞ거나혹늣게젼ᄒᆞ거나ᄒᆞᆫ일이잇스면본사로통긔ᄒᆞ여주심을희망ᄒᆞ옵

론셜

사하의형편

○사하디방으로브터오는소문은국월십일일이후로는드른것이업스며거월말에싸운헤구태젼쟁의소문이ᄎᆞᄎᆞ들니는디로병의시체를일본인이젼쟁에못은곰이비쳔ᄒᆞᆫ오로국단쳥이쳥병을일병의게피랍ᄒᆞ엿스며일병의ᄉᆞ샹은ᄎᆞᄎᆞ느리가셔최근소문을거ᄒᆞᆫ즉구쳔명이라ᄒᆞ고구로팟긴군ᄉ의ᄉ샹은도합비일만명이라고공포ᄒᆞ엿더라그리펀박대쟝의모든형비민우찬된것이일본쟝군청목의령술ᄒᆞᆫ수단이와서일군의죄익군을구원ᄒᆞ엿는디그ᄉ단은그때에곳일본으로브터와서셜중에쥬야겸힝ᄒᆞ야젼디에거우빠맛츄어왓스며그ᄉ단의군ᄉ들은젼에는희샹위로가랏고예비ᄒᆞ엿던것이라ᄒᆞ니글로보면지금은일본이히승위를숨겨ᄒᆞ랴는싱각을즁지ᄒᆞᆫ듯ᄒᆞ도다

구로팟긴대쟝이히승위로브터봉텬에숨만명의군ᄉ들을거오라ᄒᆞᆫ다ᄒᆞ며한국북방에서츌쥬군을소환ᄒᆞ랴ᄒᆞᆫ다는풍셜을드른즉구로팟긴도히승위나한국북방으로는일군의습격이잇슬줄로예산치아니ᄒᆞ는것이분명ᄒᆞᆫ지라

구로팟긴과그리펀박쟝군사이에불화ᄒᆞ다는말이젹실ᄒᆞᆫ것이아엽스며그리펀박이환국ᄒᆞ는것이이자긔의신병ᄶᅢ문이라는말이란말중에떼일진셜ᄒᆞᆫ듯ᄒᆞ도다

론둔소식을드른즉희승위에흘넌보변사ᄅ들이일본인의게희포되엿자마는그리ᄒᆞ야도만비리의음만히남겻다ᄒᆞ엿스니글로브터면히승위셔지무사ᄒᆞ듯ᄒᆞ다ᄒᆞᆫ셜ᄎ들이일본인의게포획되구라보다면반ᄒᆞᆫ것이나그림으로로팟긴대쟝은히승위로군비를만히갓다쓰켓는디라지

엿더일본신문지에말ᄒᆞ되일본미쥬전진후면에삼만명의식민을보내서만쥬도디를기쳑ᄒᆞᆯ라ᄒᆞ다ᄒᆞ엿스니이것은필경일본의목젹인듯ᄒᆞ나그러ᄒᆞ나일본군의형편이지금은이런일을보호ᄒᆞ기에확실ᄒᆞᆷ이밋치지못ᄒᆞ리라ᄒᆞ노라

외보

○강화최량 법국갈신문에셔아국이디ᄒᆞ야론평ᄒᆞᆷ이젹ᄎᆞ이번긔동밍파공과기타항일ᄉ변티로등수ᄒᆞᆫ티 유ㅣ마니데신문파여ᄒᆞᆫ샤희당신문에도공연ᄒᆞᆫ법아동밍을비방ᄒᆞ엿고단부지바리쟝파여홈은화페의각신문과쳔아ᄒᆞᆫ신문 에교ㅣ도바리셔지종리와여히수수방광ᄒᆞ는티도를보도ᄒᆞ는면문과서신을미일ᄆ그지샹에게지ᄒᆞ엿스되이월오일부지바리쟝신문에게ᄌᆡᄒᆞᆫ이월일일발ᄒᆞᆫ아도통신은동사통신원이아국에현요ᄒᆞᆫ디위를졈득ᄒᆞᆫ모셔와회젼ᄒᆞᆫ요령을보도ᄒᆞᆫ것인ᄃᆡ차에거ᄒᆞᆫ즉모씨는격렬히아국정부의조쳐를공격ᄒᆞ야목하젼쟁으로셜게ᄒᆞ며쏘무모ᄒᆞᆫ사라ᄒᆞ며혁명운동을두젼홈최량ᄎᆡᆨ은일본과강화홈에잇다는의견을담화ᄒᆞ엿다더라

잡보

○죠광정관 경무쳥에셔외부로조회ᄒᆞ기를일본헌병디위져동파및쟝교등디에일인이병쟝마창죤쥬셩오긔를린ᄒᆞ엿는디랑의차면쥬를셜립ᄒᆞ다ᄒᆞ니일이쳐샹ᄒᆞ기로자에죠회ᄒᆞ오니관ᄒᆞ는기를위요라ᄒᆞ엿더니가라조이

○티동폐쳥 궁니부로브터각부에공문ᄒᆞ되폐쟝곡쳥디쟝은부하오사시관폐쇄ᄒᆞ고쟝곡쳥디쟝일ᄒᆞ오사사관이병을티동쳥폐ᄒᆞ엿더라

○조쳥사죠 원산항일본령사ᄃᆡ목안지죠씨가문쳥군으로조회ᄒᆞ엿스되관하송면리반도를쳥금가옥수와면답의문젹과관리유지면젹의디장을조사ᄒᆞ야리이월오일에회시ᄒᆞ라ᄒᆞ엿더라

○동측안샹 일본헌병쟝봉본길씨가광주부항쟝의계공함ᄒᆞ기를본부ᄃᆡ왕면셔츤ᄂᆞᆫᄒᆞᆫ경승의계사가잇기로셔넘권사평부셔ᄒᆞ야아니ᄒᆞ기로경샹에죠회ᄒᆞ오지아니ᄒᆞ야공사등ᄒᆞ야중ᄃᆡᄒᆞᆫ사건이라우인을착리쳥군송명일본면신등

신소로향쟝이동리ᄒᆞ라ᄒᆞ엿스나도티ᄒᆞ야쟝지못ᄒᆞᆫ사유로보향ᄒᆞᆫ엿더니계차용ᄒᆞᆫ빈즉일창등ᄒᆞ야곳경셩사령부로동힝압샹ᄒᆞ라ᄒᆞ엿더라

●쇼무기란 샤평군슈민봉젼씨가너부로보고ᄒᆞ엿스되쇼위일진회라칭ᄒᆞᆫ읍저에취당ᄒᆞ야물범힝위를낫낫치보고ᄒᆞᆯ수업자오나관졍민사에방자히간예ᄒᆞᆯ쎈더러부녀를능간ᄒᆞ며촌쟝에힝ᄒᆞᆷ이망유기극이오며평민을멸시ᄒᆞ야조롱도기탄이업스니능볍히엄ᄒᆞᆫᄒᆞ야히산케ᄒᆞ옵소셔ᄒᆞ엿더라

●민셰셜연 십구일오후두시에동산민영철씨가뎌서긔연ᄒᆞ엿는디일관에모든관원과및경부문에광고ᄒᆞ엿더라

○시샹의젼긔 작이십일에일본인의종로빅목젼에셔의젼히긔ᄒᆞ엿더라

○니하쳠판셜 종로에회동ᄒᆞᆫ지젼을다시진츌ᄒᆞᆯᄎᆞ로삼만원은빈ᄒᆞᆫᄒᆞ신지라쳠금리용익씨가주판ᄒᆞ야히지젼진츌경비를차관ᄒᆞᆫ즉항사반원가량이라더라

○의논불일 일진회에셔일쟉해평의회를기ᄒᆞ고토론ᄒᆞ는디좌우당파가잇셔일당의의론은각군에보좌원일인식을일본사람으로셜치ᄒᆞ야군수의탐학을금지ᄒᆞ자ᄒᆞ고쏘일당에셔는군수일인이어날엇지ᄒᆞ야혈방쳥인을가셜ᄒᆞ며쏘일인은탐학ᄒᆞᆯ자ㅣ업스리오ᄒᆞᆫ즉평의쟝숑병쥰씨가약간시ᄒᆞ깃ᄃᆡ사의권코방쳥이쟝ᄎᆞ가야졍부에권고ᄒᆞ는것이라ᄒᆞᆫ즉시셰등의개를기미시이ᄎᆞ나ᄒᆞᆫ회는지ᄒᆞ야일인의창의평의원을갑셩ᄒᆞ야회ᄒᆞ고일엇던명이되회ᄒᆞ엿더라

○몰수착득 서강부민박여도씨의셜산한물을요구젹이굴이강ᄒᆞ고금젼을도ᄉᆞᄒᆞ더니일쟝경무쳥에셔히젹당을착ᄒᆞ엿더라

○셩기연회 이십일오후칠시에명동손탁부인가에연회를기ᄒᆞ고눈부한부탄지논부대신과일본공ᄉ와장곡쳔대쟝이연회ᄒᆞ엿더라

UNION INSURANCE SOCIETY OF CANTON.

Head office Hongkong.
Marine risks underwritten at current rates.
Agents in Chemulpo,
E. MEYER & Co.

COMPAGNIE DES MESSAGERIES MARITIMES.

Fortnightly Direct Service.

For Marseilles
via Ports.
Sailing from Yokohama
Calling at Kobe,
Shanghai, Hongkong, Saigon, Singapore,
Colombo, Djibouti, Suez, Port Said
and Marseilles.

For particulars apply to
HOLME RINGER & Co.,
Chemulpo

HAYASHIDA & CO.,
16 MYENG DONG, CHIN KO KAI, SEOUL.
BRANCH OFFICE AT CHEMULPO.

Money changers, Coal and Wood Merchants, Express Agents.

We are agents for the Pyeng-yang Coal Company and the Karazu Coal Company of Japan. We have the best quality of both anthracite and bituminous coal, and prompt execution of orders is our speciality. Firewood of all kinds kept in stock. Full weight guaranteed. Money of all denominations exchanged at current rates. Parcels received for all parts.

CHINA MUTUAL LIFE INS. CO.

Most favourable terms to policy holders.

Benefit system unsurpassed.

HOLME RINGER & Co.
Agents, Chemulpo.

C. P. R.

CANADIAN PACIFIC RAILWAY COMPANY'S ROYAL MAIL STEAMSHIP LINE.

THE FAST ROUTE BETWEEN CHINA, JAPAN, AND EUROPE VIA CANADA AND THE UNITED STATES.

Route from Hongkong via Shanghai, Nagasaki (Inland Sea of Japan) Kobe, Yokohama, Victoria and Vancouver.

Twin Screw Empress Steamship—6,000 Tons—Speed 19 knots.

PROPOSED SAILING FROM YOKOHAMA.
R. M. S. Empress of India.
R. M. S. Empress of Japan.
R. M. S. Empress of China.
R. M. S. Athenian.
R. M. S. Tartar.

Special reduction (first class only) granted to members of the Military, Naval, Diplomatic and Civil services and to Missionaries.

Passengers have choice of ten routes across the Continent of America and have privilege of travelling by any Atlantic Steamship Line.

Round the World passage tickets in connection with the P. and O. S. N., North German Lloyd and Messageries Co.'s **£125.**

All rates payable at current rate of exchange.

For further information, Tickets, Guide Books, etc., apply to
HOLME, RINGER & Co., AGENTS,
Chemulpo.

Grand Hotel

(Formerly the Station Hotel)

Near the Railway Terminus,
West Gate Seoul.

The Best Hotel in Korea.
Handsome new Building.
Fine Airy Rooms.
Excellent Cuisine.
Terms Moderate.
Special terms to Missionaries
and to permanent boarders.

Electric cars within 2 minutes' walk.

W. H. EMBERLEY.
Proprietor.

EVERY FACILITY.

in connection with Life Assurance Business is afforded by

The Standard Life Assurance Co.,

One of the largest and wealthiest of the Provident Institutions of the United Kingdom Forms of Application and all information will be promptly afforded on application.

10 CENTS A DAY.

Not a very large expenditure is it? But it is sufficient to secure for a man of 30 a policy with the STANDARD LIFE OFFICE for

$1323.

For all particulars of rates, etc., apply to
Holme, Ringer & Co.,
Agents, Chemulpo.

THE NEW YORK LIFE INSURANCE COMPANY.

Have you ever been declined by any Company?

Are you engaged in a specially hazardous occupation?

Have you heard of the New York Life Insurance Company's New Classifications for this class of Risks?

If not, send your date of birth, occupation and particulars of rejection, if any to

E. MEYER & Co.,
Agents, Chemulpo.

MITSUI BUSSAN KAISHA.
(MITSUI & Co.)

MITSUI GINKO.
(MITSUI BANK.)

The Bank is owned by the members of the Mitsui Family, who, as partners, assume an unlimited responsibility for all liabilities of the Bank:—

Capital........................Yen 5,000,000
Reserve Fund.................. " 5,600,000

HEAD OFFICE, TOKYO.
LONDON OFFICE, 34 LIME ST., E. C.

BRANCHES AND AGENCIES:—
New York, San Francisco, Hamburg, Bombay, Singapore, Manila, Hongkong, Amoy, Chefoo, Tientsin.
Kobe, Hakodate, Yokohama, Kure, Yokosuka, Moji, Shimonoseki, Miike, Wakamatsu, Nagasaki, Kuchinotsu, Karatsu, Sasebo, Misume, Taipeh, &c.

Telegraphic Address for all the Offices:
"MITSUI."
A. B. C. AND A. 1 CODES USED.

Contractors of Coal
To the Imperial Japanese Navy. Arsenals and Railway Bureau, Principal Railway Companies and Industrial Work, Home and Foreign Mail and Freight Steamers.

Sole Proprietors
Of the famous Miike, Tagawa and Yamano Coal Mines.

Sole Agents
For the sale of Fukumo, Hokoku, Ichimura, Kanoda, Mannoura, Onoura, Ostuji, Sonoda, Tsubaruro, Yoshinotani, Yoshio, Yurokibura and other coals.

YANGTSE INSURANCE ASSOCIATION, LTD.

The undersigned, having been appointed agents for the above company, are prepared to issue policies and pay losses on marine risks at regular rates.

E. MEYER & Co.,
Agents, Chemulpo.

AMERICAN KOREAN ELECTRIC CO.

Light and Power.

Main Office: Electric Building, Chong No.

RAILWAY DEPARTMENT.

OPERATING CARS BETWEEN EAST AND WEST GATE, EVERY TEN MINUTES:—

First Car leaves East Gate at 7:00 A. M. First Car leaves R. R. Station at 7:25 A.M.
Last Car " East Gate at 8.40 P. M. Last " " R. R. Station at 9.05 P.M.

OPERATING CARS BETWEEN EAST GATE AND IMPERIAL TOMB TERMINUS, EVERY TWENTY MINUTES:—

CONNECTING WITH EVERY ALTERNATE CAR ARRIVING AT EAST GATE FROM CHONG NO.

First Car leaves East Gate for Tomb at 7:10 A. M.
" " " Tomb for East Gate at 7:30 A. M.
Last " " East Gate for Tomb at 7:50 P. M.
" " " Tomb for East Gate at 8:10 P. M.

OPERATING CARS BETWEEN CHONG NO AND YUNG SAN RIVER EVERY TWELVE MINUTES:—

First Car leaves Chong No for South Gate at 7:12 A. M.
" " " Chong No for Yung San at 7:36 A. M.
" " " South Gate for Chong No at 7:20 A. M.
" " " Yung San for Chong No at 8:09 A. M.
Last " " South Gate for Chong No 9:00 P. M.
" " " Yung San for Chong No at 8,45. P. M.

SPECIAL PRIVATE CARS FURNISHED TO SUIT CONVENIENCE OF PATRONS. PRICES ON APPLICATION AT HEAD OFFICE.

LIGHTING DEPARTMENT.

Where less than 250 candle power of light is used, the rate per month will be
Per 16 candle power incandescent lamp,—All night.—Yen 2.50.
32 candle power incandescent lamp,—All night:—Yen 4.00.
50 candle power incandescent lamp,—All night:—Yen 6.00.
150 " " " " " " 10.00.
1200 " " enclosed arc " " " 20.00.

Where more than 250 candle power of light is used, a Meter will be installed, if requested:—Rent of Meter, Yen 2.00 per month. Rate of charges by meter reading:—Two Sen per Ampere per hour. (Approximately this is equal to about One Sen per 16 C. P. lamp per hour) Minimum monthly charge where meter is installed, Yen 20.00 per month, which includes rental of meter.

Estimates for installing lights furnished on application
An assortment of chandeliers always on hand.

K. Murakami.
Photograph Studio
Chinkokai, Seoul.

Printing, Developing and Enlargement, of Photographs always Undertaken.

Korean Views and Pictures Illustrating Native Customs always on Sale,

---

THE OSAKA SHOSEN KAISHA.

Boats frequently on the berth for Chinnampo.

REGULAR SAILINGS BETWEEN JAPAN AND KOREAN PORTS.

FUSAN AND KOBE VIA SHIMONOSEKI.

OSAKA VIA MOKPO, FUSAN, SHIMONOSEKI AND KOBE.

MOJI DIRECT.

OSAKA VIA KUNSAN, MASANPO, FUSAN, SHIMONOSEKI AND KOBE.

CHEMULPO KUNSAN LINE,
Every three days.

CHEMULPO CHINNAMPO LINE.
Every three days.

For Freight and passage and further particulars apply to
THE OSAKA SHOSEN KAISHA,
Chemulpo.

RONDON, PLAISANT & CO.

General Storekeepers and Merchants, Ships Contractors Tobacconists, Commission and Forwarding Agents, Coal Merchants

IMPORTERS AND EXPORTERS

Seoul, Chemulpo.

W. D. WENTWORTH.

LANDING
AND
SHIPPING AGENT.
AND
CUSTOMS BROKER.

12 OURA, NAGASAKI.

STEWARD & CO.

Chemulpo.

Shipchandlers and Storekeepers, Naval and Mercantile Contractors, Landing and Shipping Agents.

STEWARD'S HOTEL

Chemulpo.

Best accommodation in the port for travellers. Clean and well-aired rooms, good cuisine and prompt attendance, moderate tariff.

관보

데삼천륙십팔호 화료

셔임급사령

○승셔관입관오등 철도원주사 김죵구

광무팔년십이월륙일

○임농상공부협판셔칙임관삼등 니장원감독 리준영

○승셔관임관사등 경위원총슌 김학신

이샹이월십오일

○임젼라남도관찰사셔칙임관삼등 강원도관찰사 주셕면

○임강원도관찰사셔칙임관삼등 츙청남도관찰사 됴종필

○임츙청남도관찰사셔칙임관삼등 죵일픔 리건하

○임경상북도관찰사셔칙임관삼등 륙군참장 리용익

○임경긔관찰사셔칙임관삼등 의졍부찬졍 최익현

이샹이월십칠일

○의원면본관 비셔원승 리죠영 비셔원승 민광식 철도원주사 셔덕슌

○명장례원경셔칙임관삼등 륙군부장 리도지

○명비셔원승셔칙임관사등 봉상사제죠 윤샹학

○명봉상사제죠셔칙임관삼등 궁니부특진관 리근교

○명궁니부특진관셔칙임관삼등 죵이픔 오정근

○명궁니부특진관셔칙임관사등 죵이픔 박영두

○명궁니부특진관셔칙임관삼등 쟝례원소경 민영돈

○명쟝례원소경셔칙임관삼등 시강원첨사 됴한국

○명시강원첨사셔칙임관이등 궁니부특진관 리지현

○임비셔원승셔주임관륙등 졍삼픔 리범세

○겸임쟝례원쟝례 비셔원승 리범세

○임철도원주사셔판임관륙등 구픔 셔상용 김규원 박리홍 리린규 박리학 변즁호

●면본관 경무청총슌 뎡규셕

이샹이월십팔일

○명셔리총관사무 통신원회관 장화식

○명궁니부특진관셔칙임관이등 비셔원경 박용대 죵일픔 김죵한

●명궁니부특진관셔칙임관삼등 졍이픔 박기양 죵이픔 됴병승

○명비셔원경셔칙임관이등 쟝례원소경 됴한국

○명쟝례원소경셔칙임관사등 궁니부특진관 박영두

○의원면본관 비셔원승 신헌균 쟝례원샹례 리병소

○임비셔원승셔주임관륙등 졍삼픔 박필원

○임쟝례원샹례셔주임관륙등 륙품 셔상훈

○의원면겸임시강원시독관 쟝례원샹례 리병소

○임시강원시독관셔판임관사등 륙픔 리병소

명문헌비고속션위원 졍삼픔 졍인표 구픔 리정의

이샹이월십구일

광무구년도 예산표 속

데이관 특별사금 오빅원

데일항 특별사금 오빅원

데삼관 표소츌금 오천원

데일항 표소츌금 오천원

데사관 수민비 삼빅원

데일항 수민비 삼빅원

데오관 소에비 이천사빅팔십팔원

니부소관합계 삼만칠천이빅팔십팔원

탁지부소관

데일관 젼년도세입부족면보액 사빅륙십일만사천이빅륙십삼원

데일항 젼년도세입부족면보액 사빅륙십일만사천이빅륙십삼원

데이관 일본병변가사차입비 일천일빅구십원

데일항 가사차입비 사빅팔십원

데이항 청비 칠빅십원

탁지부소관합계사빅륙십일만오천사빅오십삼원

셰출림시부합계사빅팔십륙만

셰츌총계일천구빅십일만삼천륙빅륙십오원 완

법부소관 속

데사관 법관양셩소 오천이빅삼십륙원

데일항 봉급 삼천일빅이십원

데이항 청비 일천팔빅원

데삼항 청사슈리비 일빅원

데사항 잡급급잡비 이빅십륙원

데오관 디방지관소 구빅십륙원

데일항 봉급 칠빅원

데이항 잡급급잡비 이빅십륙원

지화지츌차즁 륙천원

법부소관합계 륙만팔천륙빅칠십일원

경무청소관

데일관 경무본청 이십칠만사천륙빅삼십오원

데일항 봉급 이만오천일원

데이항 청비 이만오천팔빅오십사원

데삼항 청사슈리비 오천팔빅원

데사항 잡급급잡비 십칠만오천륙빅십사원

데오항 피복비 사만삼천일빅이십원

데륙항 긔밀비 삼빅원

데칠항 려비 이천구빅사십륙원

데이관 감옥셔 삼만오천칠빅사십구원

데일항 봉급 이천오십원

데이항 청비 삼천륙빅사십이원

데삼항 청사슈리비 오빅원

데사항 잡급급잡비 일만이천륙빅이십륙원

데오항 피복비 일천사빅팔십칠원

데륙항 죄슈식비 일만오천사빅사십사원

데삼관 디방각도경무셔 오만일천팔빅삼십삼원

데일항 봉급 사천구빅구십이원

데이항 청비 사천륙빅팔십원

데삼항 잡급급잡비 이만구천팔빅팔원

데사항 죄슈비 오천칠빅사십삼원

데오항 려비 륙천륙빅십원

잡보

○군슈셔임 이십일졍부회의에평하훈군슈이십구명을면관ᄒᆞ고십삼군슈를주본ᄒᆞ야셔임ᄒᆞ엿다더라

○즉위방셕 즁셔경무관리용승씨는휴쥬구인ᄉᆞ로평리원에피고지슈ᄒᆞ엿는ᄃᆡ그당질에일인은법협이오일인은검ᄉᆞ인고로곳방셕ᄒᆞ고여하훈죠쳐가업다더라

○셩최피신 강홍대셩광호최병쥬삼씨를잡술긱으로구라ᄒᆞ려다가즁지가되미삼씨가아울너자멸소를복진훈바우비를봉승훈지라강술객은의젼히예겸ᄒᆞ고셩최량인은영히피신ᄒᆞ엿더라

○선ᄉᆞ셜힝 금번정초에도궐니에셔대신ᄉᆞ를셜힝ᄒᆞ야양옥의쳐쳐에떡죠각이오히려흣터잇다더라

○훈칙금집 니부에셔십삼도에훈령ᄒᆞ기를무뢰비가로인가자와쥬ᄉᆞ참봉첩지를위죠ᄒᆞ야민간에단니며젼량을토색훈다ᄒᆞ니일병금집ᄒᆞ야후폐를막으라ᄒᆞ엿더라

○션원보수샹 경샹북도관찰ᄉᆞ장승원씨가니부로보고ᄒᆞ엿스되션원보이십륙권을수샹훈다ᄒᆞ엿더라

○가례장힝 황태ᄌᆞ뎐하가례는셔병션씨의령양으로퇴정ᄒᆞ엿다운운ᄒᆞ더라

○직접히관 일공ᄉᆞ가외부로죠회ᄒᆞ엿스되군ᄉᆞ샹에소용ᄒᆞ논폭발약등의물픔을슈입혹미입ᄒᆞ는때즁앙관청을유ᄒᆞ야히관에면칙ᄒᆞ야인쥰ᄒᆞ는고로요급훈경우에는불편훈일이만흐니자금위시ᄒᆞ야우리륙군관헌과밋당히령ᄉᆞ가당디히관에직접으로증명ᄒᆞ야수입과미입과루치훌터이니죠량ᄒᆞ라ᄒᆞ엿더라

○민원잉류 경상북도관찰ᄉᆞ가니부로면보ᄒᆞ엿스되상주군에츌주훈병뎡을철환ᄒᆞ는ᄉᆞ에ᄃᆡᄒᆞ야인민수빅명이회집ᄒᆞ야다시류주ᄒᆞ기를호소ᄒᆞ오니청컨ᄃᆡ군부에면죠ᄒᆞ와잉존ᄒᆞ기를바라옵나이다ᄒᆞ엿더라

○종식확장 농상공부에셔식목훌ᄉᆞ로십삼도에훈령ᄒᆞ되례가여좌ᄒᆞ니 일은미년에청명젼후일이일간으로식목일을작뎡ᄒᆞ고과목파쌍나무와닥나무와챠와오동파버들과솔파잣나무와상술이와삼송과빅양목등을종식훌ᄉᆞ 일은종목훌씩젼긔ᄒᆞ야디방관이밀이각동에디위ᄒᆞ야미일호에몃주식심을ᄉᆞ 일은비록사양산이라도고관ᄒᆞ고승인훈후작벌홈을독ᄒᆞ되쟈산을면케훌ᄉᆞ 일은사양산에그작목훈수를게교ᄒᆞ야미일주작벌훈곳에어린나무십주식심을ᄉᆞ 일은각디방관이공용훌지목을빙자ᄒᆞ고사양을는작ᄒᆞ며갑을안이주면본부로보ᄒᆞ야갑을추급훌것이며히군수는론경훌ᄉᆞ 일은근리에면잔목소용으로작벌ᄒᆞ면통신원에셔히군공젼등으로획급ᄒᆞ거놀선로각군에록작ᄒᆞ는ᄌᆞㅣ만히잇며쏘갑을주지앗코아전들이투식ᄒᆞ다ᄒᆞ니히디방관이추급훌ᄉᆞ 일은근일에들은즉외국인이철도소용으로혹사양을륵벌훈다ᄒᆞ니반다시히공ᄉᆞ를담임훈ᄌᆞ들의중간투식이니곳본부와관찰부에호소ᄒᆞ야외부로면조ᄒᆞ야교섭타판훌ᄉᆞ 일은각동에그근잔가감ᄌᆞ일인을틱ᄒᆞ야종식사무를젼판케훌ᄉᆞ 일은만주이상을종식ᄒᆞ야현져이유훈ᄌᆞ는특별표양훌ᄉᆞ 일은각동에반다시면기지가유ᄒᆞ니인민으로ᄒᆞ야곰직식케ᄒᆞ되만일기지가업스면산야유주훈디방에한광훈땅에지식훌ᄉᆞ 일은주인잇는땅에지식ᄒᆞ는경우에는장리리익을디주의게삼분일을획급케ᄒᆞ되히디단립지를관가에셔본주의게셩급ᄒᆞ야후고를삼게훌ᄉᆞ 일은종식권과에근무실젹이잇는군수는그쩌고를좃차사실훈후에니부로조회ᄒᆞ야곳주픔ᄒᆞ야승등케훌ᄉᆞ라ᄒᆞ엿더라

TELEGRAMS.

(FROM JAPAN PAPERS.)

PEACE PROSPECTS.

London, Feb. 12.

Peace rumours are still prevailing here. The French public is of opinion that Russia should seek a means for opening negotiations in order to close the war under honourable conditions. Viscount Hayashi, Japanese Minister at London, is of the opinion that the war will be continued for some time.

London, Feb. 13.

It is stated at St. Petersburg that the Tsar, assisted by his Ministers, is taking measures for the purpose of effecting an armistice.

RUSSIAN AFFAIRS.

London, Feb. 13.

According to the "Times" correspondent at St. Petersburg, Russia has acquired the Hamburg-Amerika Linie's "Hamburg and Deutschland" at the price of a million pounds sterling.

London, Feb. 13.

The owners of iron foundries in Russia have presented a petition to M. de Witte asking him to improve the condition of the workmen, to give them liberty of speech and the right to express their opinions in newspapers, to draft laws giving power to ask for enquiry to all classes of people, and to encourage national primary education.

London, Feb. 14.

Four thousand Reservists at Bologaya (in the province of Tver) who have revolted are being starved into submission by the Russian authorities.

At Kieff the troops have fired on an assembly of twelve thousand disaffected citizens.

Berlin, Feb. 14.

Le Petit Parisien reports that M. De Witte recently stated at a Council held by the Russian Ministers that the Kaiser had prophesied a decisive victory for Russia in the Far East. Berlin officials absolutely contradict this assertion, and they further state that for several months past German military officers have ceased to anticipate any Russian victory.

BRITISH POLITICS.

London, Feb. 15.

Replying to Earl Spencer, who had said that he hoped the Government would not lose any proper opportunity with other Powers in trying to bring the present war to a close, Lord Lansdowne, Secretary of State for Foreign Affairs, said that any ill-considered intervention was likely to be fraught with the worst possible results. It was, however, unnecessary to say that should a favourable opportunity offer, his Majesty's Government would avail itself thereof with alacrity.

London, Feb. 15.

In reply to the Speech from the Throne an amendment has been moved in the House of Commons by Mr. H. Asquith (Liberal), to the effect that Fiscal policy having now been discussed for two years, the time has come for submitting the issue to the country without further delay.

Mr. Balfour, the Premier, in the course of a speech said that with reference to the suggestion made by Sir Henry Campbell-Bannerman, that the present Ministry should resign, he would point out that that was a matter which rested with the House of Commons. Further discussion of the Fiscal policy during the present Parliament would, he said, be irrelevant. Mr. Balfour taunted the Opposition with the confusion which he alleged prevailed among its members as to the future programme of the party.

GENERAL NEWS.

Washington, Feb. 13.

Baron Speck de Sternburg, the German Ambassador at Washington, has assured President Roosevelt that Germany has abandoned the policy of bringing Shangtung Province under her sphere of influence, and has offered her active support towards maintaining the territorial integrity of China as well as the "open door" policy in that country. It is believed that this attitude is due to the recent declaration of Mr. Hay, Secretary of State, who is reported to have said that if Germany does not change her policy, international troubles between Great Britain and Germany are likely to occur.

London, Feb. 14.

In view of the persistent rumours regarding the prospects of peace, the price of Japanese bonds shows a steady rise. The new Five per cents. (? Six per cents). are to-day quoted at £97 15s.

Berlin, Feb. 14.

The Committee appointed by the Reichstag to consider the budget for Kiaochao has approved of the expenditure. The Naval Minister, in replying to an interpellation by Herr Bebel, leader of the Socialists, declared that Germany has no intention of making Tsingtao a second Port Arthur. There was no discussion, however, with regard to the construction of forts at Tsingtao.

Shanghai, Feb. 15.

An official despatch from Hongkong states that the French cruiser Sully (9856 tons) went ashore on the coast of Annam a few days ago.

NEW GOVERNORS.

The following gubernatorial appointments are announced:—

Mr. Choi Ik-hyŭn to Kyŭngki province; Mr. Shin Ki-syŏn to South Hamkyeng; Mr. Yi Kŏu-ha to South Chungchŭng; Major Gen. Yi Young-ik to North Kyŭngsang; Mr. Cho Chong-pil to Kangwon; Mr. Chu Suk-myŭn to South Chulla.

Major G. H. Mockler, Indian Army, has been ordered to join the staff of General Sir Montagu Gerard in Manchuria as military attaché with the Russian Field Force.

The consensus of opinion in Japan is that the Russian raid on the Liao river was principally designed to interrupt the northward transport of General Nogi's army.

A Michigan editor has had a streak of bad luck. He was just about to step into his new £2,000 automobile the other night, when three bed slats gave way and he awoke.—"Auto Era," New York.

The Home Office has protested against the action of Mr. Maruyama, the police adviser, in appointing a lot of Japanese assistants. It is pointed out, quite rightly, that his contract confers no such powers on him.

Song Pyong-chun, who is the "boss" of the Il-chin-hoi was formerly a high official, who for reasons of his own, escaped to Japan some ten years ago. He returned to Korea to establish this society, and as is the sole go-between for the society and the Japanese army headquarters, whence come the "sinews of war," he has, until the recent split, held autocratic powers over his adherents. Let us hope that it will soon be again necessary for him to escape to Japan.

The Japanese do not for a moment relax their efforts to oust all foreigners from the Korean service. There seem to be considerable friction between the French minister and the Korean Government over the proposed dismissal of French mining engineers. Were the Japanese actuated by a sincere desire for the welfare of Korea they would urge the Government to commence work on the mines and give the engineers an opportunity of earning their salaries.

THE CHARITY CONCERT.

On Monday and Tuesday evenings, an entertainment was given in one of the Customs buildings in aid of a local charity. Judging from the attendance on Tuesday, there should be a very substantial sum to be handed over.

The management was in the hands of Captain Phillips R. M. L. I. and the programme was divided into two parts, the first consisting of songs etc, while the second was devoted to a comedietta entitled "An Armed Truce."

The lion's share of the first part fell to our old friends of the R. M. L. I. and they again acquitted themselves well although we really must protest against the K. D. N. being characterized as a regular howler—a cat on the fence. We "howl" perhaps, but are not on the fence. Mr. Frampton and Captain Pillips sang and Bishop Corfe gave an amusing reading. We have placed age before beauty as we have still to mention the song contributed by the ladies, Mrs. Elliott and Miss Scranton; both were in excellent voice and had to respond to encores.

In the comedietta all the performers did themselves justice, the antics of the butler causing much merriment. The Imperial band under the personal direction of Herr Eckert, discoursed sweet music during the various intervals. The programme was as follows:—

CONCERT.

1. Song .... Pvte. Cheatle.
2. Song .... Mr. G. Frampton.
3. Comic Song, ... Pvte. Wareham.
4. Song .... Pvte. McKinley.
5. Song .... Miss Scranton
6. Song .... Capt. Phillips.
7. Comic Duet ...... Pvte Browne & Fairbairn.
8. Song .... Mrs. Elliott.
9. Reading .... Bishop Corfe.

Followed by the small comedietta entitled:—

"AN ARMED TRUCE.

Mrs. Effinghan	Miss Scranton
Mr. Rivers (her father)	Mr. E. Holmes
Wallis (a butler)	Mr. H. Porter
Mr. Effingham	Capt. Phillips

On the 17th instant, the Japanese captured another British steamer of over 4000 tons which was bound for Vladivostok.

According to telegrams received by local Japanese papers there are now 30,000 strikers in St. Petersburg, and at Moscow a strike among railway employees has again stopped traffic.

A Peking telegram of Feb. 2nd says that the Hupeh has borrowed from Austria the sum of Tls. 6,000,000, giving the likin revenue of Hupeh as security. The conditions were signed on the 1st instant.

A Russian newspaper, speaking of a batch of Japanese prisoners which recently passed through Moscow, remarks that they are not only infantry but include cavalry and artillery men. They are said to speak Russian.

As a result of negotiations beteeen the Korean and Japanese authorities, the Japanese who erected a shed for storing ice near the river has been ordered to remove it and it it is also reported that the advertising hoarding a Chongno will be pulled down and erected alse where. We regret to find however that many Japanese hawkers have again pitched their stalls at Chong-no.

According to a Nagasaki despatch of the 13th inst., an official who has just returned from North China states that the Russian warships at Tsingtao are still under repairs, though the damage to most of the hulls has been made good. The vessels were flying the German flag. Owing to the scarcity of labour there, more than 300 Chinese mechanics have been engaged from other ports and are now working on the above warships.

THE IL-CHIN-HOI.

It is with great pleasure that we receive news of a split in the ranks of the Il-chin hoi. It appears that Song Pyong Chun, their ringleader, proposed at a recent session that the Society should urge that a Japanese should be appointed to every district in the country to supervise the magistrate and prevent him from oppressing and plundering the people.

This proposal raised considerable opposition; it was pointed out, with great justice that there was nothing to indicate that the Japanese would not squeeze just as much as the magistrates and the situation would then be worse than ever. The opposition decided that the proper course to recommend was the exercise of more care in the selection of magistrate

Song Pyong Chun then said that a the proposal emanated from the Japanese Minister and as the Japanese proposals were invariably adopted it would be unwise of the Il-chin-hoi not to assist with this one. To this the opposition, led by Mr. Hong Keung Syŏp, reported that "If this be so, is not this Society only the forerunner for the Japanese just the same as the guide devil which runs before the tiger to lead it to its prey?"

Great dissention then arose with the result that many councillors were turned out of office and a number of members resigned or were dismissed.

Mr. Megata has ensured a welcome for himself when he returns from his trip to Japan as it said that no officia salaries will be paid until he gets back.

There is again a rumous that most of the eunuchs are to the turned out of the palace. If they are they should be well indemnified as such men cannot be expected to devote themselves to ordinary pursuits.

Says our Korean reporter:—"There are street rumours that the remainders for Koreans are only the bare bodies a all the rights were deprived by the Japanese as well as the money matt which were contracted between the D Ichi Bank and the Government.

It is reported that the Dalai Lama of Thibet and a party of Lama priests have been in secret conference with the Minister of the Chinese Board of Foreign Affairs regarding Tibetan affairs, and that as a result of this conference a lengthy telegraphic despatch has been sent to Special Commissioner Tong Chiu Yee.

The "Musashiro Maru," which left Moji on the 3rd for Dalny, was caught in a snow storm an rauon a rock near the Miao group of islands on the 5th instant. The troops, of whom she carried some hundreds, were all taken off safely by the "Hiyei, but the horses, about 160, were lost. There is no hope of saving the steamer.

Some very sensational telegrams dated Tokio January 21st appear in the local Japanese paper. It is definitely announced that General Kuropatkin, on account of his non-success has been recalled to St. Petersburg and that General Linnevitch has been appointed to succeed him. We are also told that the total casualties due to the strikes in Poland amount to 1800 killed and 6000 wounded. The story about about the casualties is obviously "fake" because none but the authorities can have these figures and they would hardly be likely to publish them. There is no balance of evidence for or against the report of Kuropatkin's return being true.

The Korea Daily News.

Issued at 5 P. M. daily except Sundays.

Rate of Subscription:—

Per Year,............Yen 25.
Per Quarter,..........Yen 7.
Per Month,..........Yen 2.50.

Postage in Korea not charged extra.
Postage abroad charged extra.

Advertisements, 50 sen per day for 1 inch or less.
5 yen per month per inch.
50 yen per year per inch.

All communications to

E. T. BETHELL,
Editor and Publisher,
Pak-tong, Seoul.

THE SHAHO.

It now transpires that the stories of disaffection among the Russean troops originated with a missionary who recently reached Peking from Mukden. The same authority is responsible for the statement that the Russian losses at the battle of Heikoutai were 7,000 killed and 5,000 wounded. Although there is no doubt that an action fought in heavy weather such as prevailed at Heikoutai would involve a heavier proportion of deaths than usual, these figures are, on the face of them, absurd.

* * *

The Russian front extends over a distance of 75 miles, the various points being connected by light railways. Kuropatkin is reported to have 300,000 men at and around Mukden with a further 40,000 in the extreme east at Hangchang. The Russians continue to strengthen their newly captured positions opposite the Japanese centre and have recently brought a number of 13 c. m. field guns into action.

* * *

A Japanese official report dated the 14th inst. speaks of the Russians as being at Luishengpao, Litajentun and north of Heikoutai. Previously they have been spoken of as being "in front of" all these places so that it appears that Kuropatkin's advance is a steady one. There is, otherwise, no news from the Japanese centre.

Another report dated the 14th inst. says that a Russian cavalry corps some 8,000 or 9,000 strong with artillery, was about to cross the Hun River at a point about 15 miles below the junction of the Hun and Taitz. This point is due W.S.W. of Liaoyang and the movement is probably directed against the Japanese communications between that place and Haicheng As this occurred over a week ago it is rather remarkable that we have had no telegraphic advices of the result of the operation.

The Russians continue to bombard the Japanese right wing and on the 12th instant they followed this up with an infantry attack on Waiteushan (about 12 miles southeast of Shahopao and 3 or 4 miles south of the Shaho) which, however, was, according to Marshal Oyama, repulsed.

It now seems to be the turn of the Japanese to be hampered by the Chinese On the 5th instant a Chinaman attempted to set fire to a quantity of Japanese stores at Niuchiautun and was immediately arrested as a Russian spy.

The Governors (Chinese) of Liaoyang and Haicheng are also said to have been arrested by the Japanese as Russian spies and to have been sent to Dalny. The former official had previously served as Governor of Mukden, and it is supposed that he established very close relations with the Russians when acting in that capacity. If this step has really been taken, it will cause some commotion, though, according to the "Japan Mail" the Russians have acted similarly on more than one occasion.

ADMIRAL ROZHDESTYENSKY.

A comparatively young man, Admiral Rozhdestvensky was born near Moscow in 1848 and after being educated as a Russian Naval officer he suddenly became a hero. For two unexampled feats of bravery in the war of 1877-8 he gained the St. George's Cross. He served in the Black and Baltic Seas, gaining a high reputation as a seaman; and last year abandoned sea-going for the post of Chief of Staff at the Ministry of Marine. In this post he made a great reputation.

Rozhdestvensky is a typical Russian and a typical Naval officer. His men call him "Admiral Moltchalivi," the Silent Admiral, and taciturnity goes well with the reserved expression and manners of the Russian aristocrat. The Naval man shows himself in his tastes, for he is devoted to the sea, not merely as a profession, but also as life-passion. Rozhdestvensky is always at sea. When tied to the Ministry of Marine (says a writer in the "Daily Dispatch") he spent his leisure navigating experimental craft and tiny sailing boats in the Gulf of Finland; he has written of the sea, and it is said that his society friends dreaded him because he insisted on talking of nothing but the sea. In fact, as a sailor and navigator not even Makharoff surpassed him.

"He is a believer in the big battleship. "A fleet gains in mobility by not being hampered with small craft" is one of his dicta. He declared that the Japanese successes at Port Arthur were not gained really by the torpedo-boats and destroyers, but by the battleships behind them. His whole conception of a naval battle is a fight between big ships until the bigger and more powerful destroy the smaller and weaker.

Neatness of person and irreproachable uniforms he regards almost as important as gunnery and seamanship. His own appearance is not distinguished, though his features are regular, and he has a life-long wart over the nose, which is the subject of much joking among irreverent "mitchmen." The Admiral, however, is invariably uniformed like an Emperor, and in this condition he will grub in grimy stokeholds, and pick his way among greasy cases of beef for hours in the hope of discovering something wrong. He is intensely punctilious, and is responsible for the paraphrase of Bacon, "Manners make seamen." Another foible is his love of pretty surroundings. His office under the gilt spire of the St. Petersburg "Admiralteistvo" was adorned with photographs, mirrors, relics of old friendships, and cosy, furniture, and resembled a lady's boudoir rather than a place of work. Apparently these harmless luxuries in no way demoralised his tough character; for his long swims and solitary cruises in single-handed yachts are constantly referred to in the Russian Press.

CHINA'S NEUTRALITY.

Baron Hayashi, the Japanese Minister to great Britain, has been interviewed concerning Russia's cercular to the powers charging China with breaches of neutrality.

Baron Hayashi said:—"The Japanese have not replied to the innumerable allegations of breaches of neutrality and of International law charged by Russia since the beginning of the war, but the Japanese Government will probably reply to this formal charge."

Baron Hayashi thought, however, that it was in line with the with other charges and similar to the "Yellow Peril.' He said that Great Britain, the United States and Germany all have great interests in China and, being well represented there, know from their own agents whether it is necessary to interfere. Incidentally, Baron Hayashi said he was pleased to learn of the intention of the American Government to establish a district court for the Consular service in China and Korea, as it would facilitate Japanese appeals from the Consular courts.

At the German Embassy a discussion of the Russian circular was productive of the opinion that China had too severe a lesson in the Boxer movement to permit of another outbreak against Europeans. It was thought improbable at the Embassy that Russia really intended to withdraw from adherence to the agreement regarding the zone of hostilities in the Far East.

At the Chinese Legation it was asserted that China had maintained a neutrality such as few European Powers could have kept in the face of most trying circumstances. "If China violated neutrality," it was asked, "what have Germany and France done? Why select China for such a formal charge to the Powers? It is not a question of preference with the present Chinese population, for I assure you that the great mass of the Chinese do not favor the Japanese any more than they do the Russians."

BRITISH NAVY.

The battleship "Alexandra," built twenty-nine years ago at a cost of £653,-915, has been struck out of the Royal Navy as non-effective.

The new armoured cruiser "Shannon" was laid down at Chatham on Monday, and on the same day the "Minotaur," a sister ship, was commenced at Devonport.

The battleship "Superb," which cost £556,662, and first hoisted her pennant on October 4, 1889, has been struck off the War Fleet as unfit for effective service.

HONEYCOMBED WITH SECRET SOCIETIES.

It is reported that during an audience with the Empress Dowager a certain Hupeh official informed Her Majesty that although the province of Hupeh is honeycombed with secret society men, the provincial officials are exerting a strict and vigilant watch. All passenger steamers are carefully examined on their arrival and departure, and any suspicious individual found on board is immediately arrested and tried.

The Central News learns that the turbine destroyer "Caroline," which was run out of the Thames to join the Russian fleet, is still lying at Libau. The vessel's machinery has become so deranged that the Russians have been unable to find artificers sufficiently skilled to repair the damage.

The Korea Daily News.

VOL. II, WEDNESDAY, FEBRUARY 22, 1905. No. 40

HONGKONG & SHANGHAI BANKING CORPORATION.

Paid-up Capital..................$10,000,000
Reserve Fund:—Sterling Reserve... 10,000,000
Silver Reserve..... 7,000,000

27,000,000
Reserve Liability of Proprietors... 10,000,000

HEAD OFFICE, HONGKONG.

London Bankers, London and County Banking Company Limited.
Branches and Agencies, London.

Amoy,	Hankow	Penang,
Bangkok,	Hiogo,	Rangoon,
Batavia,	Iloilo,	Saigon,
Bombay,	Lyons,	San Francisco,
Calcutta,	Manila,	Singapore,
Colombo,	Nagasaki,	Sourabaya,
Foochow,	New York,	Tientsin,
Hamburg,	Peking,	Yokohama,

Credits granted on approved Securities, and every description of Banking and Exchange business transacted.

Drafts granted on London and the chief Commercial places in Europe, India, Australia, America, China and Japan.

HOLME RINGER & Co., AGENTS, CHEMULPO.

HOKURKU DOBOKU KAISHA.

Branch office in Chong Dong, Seoul.
Japanese telephone No. 165

CONTRACT DEPARTMENT.

We can contract to build any building or construction.

MERCHANDISE DEPARTMENT.

We can provide any building material. We have just contracted to build the new Belgian Legation.

E. MEYER & CO.

Chemulpo.

SOLE AGENTS IN KOREA FOR.

A. T. Morse, Sons & Co.'s "Fresco" Distemper

In all colours ready for use on walls, Ceilings etc.

and

AVENARIUS CARBOLINEUM

A wood-preserving and antiseptic oil preparation

Against decay, dry-rot, fungus and wood-destroying insects.

A large supply always in stock.
Prices upon application.

E. MEYER & Co.,
Chemulpo.

CHARTERED BANK OF INDIA AUSTRALIA & CHINA.

INCORPORATED BY ROYAL CHARTER 1853

HEAD OFFICES —LONDON.

Paid-up Capital £800,000
Reserve Liability of Shareholders 800,000
Reserve Fund 800,000

Drafts granted upon all the principal places in the world and every description of Exchange and banking business transacted.

E. MEYER & Co., Agents,
Chemulpo.

MITSU BISHI DOCKYARD & ENGINE WORKS,

NAGASAKI.

CODE WORD, "DOCK."

A 1, A. B. C., and Engineering Codes used.

DOCK No. 1 (at Tategami).

Extreme Length..............523 feet
Length on blocks .... 513 ,,
Width of Entrance on Top......89 ,,
,, ,, Bottom....77 ,,
Water on Blocks at Spring Tide 26½ ,,

DOCK No. 2 (Mukaijima).

Extreme Length..............371 feet
Length on Blocks..............360 ,,
Width of Entrance on Top......66 ,,
,, ,, Bottom 53 ,,
Water on Blocks at Spring Tide 22 ,,

PATENT SLIP (at Kosuge).
Can take vessels up to 1,000 tons gross.

THE WORKS are well equipped with the LATEST IMPROVEMENTS, and can execute any kind of work in SHIPBUILDING and MARINE ENGINEERING, as well as in REPAIRING of SHIPS.

The COMPANY'S new powerful steamer OURA-MARU (712 tons, 700 I.H.P.), specially built for SALVAGE PURPOSES, and equipped with necessary gear, is always READY at SHORT NOTICE.

THE METHODIST PUBLISHING HOUSE,

Little West Gate, Seoul.

JOB PRINTING, TYPEWRITER PAPER
CARBON PAPER, VISITING CARDS
STATIONERY, BOOK BINDING
BOOK PUBLISHERS
AMERICAN SCHOOL BOOKS
SPENCERIAN COPY BOOKS
PEN CARBON LETTER AND BILL BOOKS

S. A BECK, Manager.

DAI-ICHI GINKO.

LIMITED.

(Formerly the First National Bank)

ESTABLISHED 1873.

INCORPORATED UNDER PRESENT LAW 1896

Capital - - - - - - - - - - Yen 5,000,000
Reserve Fund - . - - - 1,500,000

HEAD OFFICE —TOKIO.

President: Baron SHIBUSAWA.

BRANCHES AND CORRESPONDENTS
In the Principal Cities and Towns of Japan.

Interest Allowed on
Fixed deposits 1 year - - 6½ per cent
" " 6 months - - - 6 per cent

Special current accounts 1½ sen daily per Y 100
General " " 1 " " " 100

M. TANAKA,
Manager, Chemulpo.

SINGER SEWING MACHINES

씽거즈봉침

SOLE AGENTS FOR KOREA
전매쇼

HOLME RINGER & CO.
Chemulpo.
제물포 함릉거양힝

KAMEYA & CO.

GENERAL STOREKEEPERS
Chinkokai - - Seoul
(*Established 1895, Tokyo*)

Confectionery, Hams, Canned Goods, Cutlery, Hirano & Tansan Water. Provisions, Gents, Furnishing goods, Toilet Articles, Travelling Bags, Tobacco, Cigars & Cigarettes Kitchen Utensils. Coffee, Biscuits

Fresh Goods always kept in Stock.
Prices Moderate
Please come and inspect our goods.

NIPPON YUSEN KAISHA.
JAPANESE MAIL STEAMSHIP CO.

UNDER MAIL CONTRACT WITH THE IMPERIAL JAPANESE GOVERNMENT.

European Line

Regular Fortnightly Service between Yokohama Kobe, Moji, Shanghai, Hongkong, Singapore, Penang Colombo, Port Said, Marseilles, London and Antwerp

American Line

Regular Fortnightly Service between Hongkong and Seattle, calling at Shanghai, Moji, Kobe, Yokohama and Victoria, B. C.

Australian Line

Regular weekly Service betwen Japan Ports and Australia, calling at Hongkong and Manila.
(Above Three Lines Suspended until further notice).

Shanghai Line

Weekly Service between Shanghai and Japan Fo

Korea Line

Service Kobe, Moji, Nagasaki, Fusan Chemulpo Chefoo, Taku.
S. S. Babelsberg, 2181 tons.
Service Kobe. Moji, Fusan, Chemulpo, Chinnampo
S. S. ARGO, S. S. Ohio.

BORDEN'S CONDENSED MILK CO.

New York, U. S. A.

ALWAYS IN STOCK

Eagle Brand Condensed Milk.

Gold Seal Condensed Milk.

Peerless (Family) Evaporated Cream.

Borden's Malted Milk.

E. MEYER & CO.
Chemulpo Korea,
Sole Agents.

ROYAL INSURANCE COMPANY,
Funds exceed £10,000,000

FIRE
AT CURRENT RATES

LIFE,
REDUCED PREMIUM,

HOLME RINGER & Co.,
Agents, Chemulpo.

廣
KWANG C'HANG
昌

BENNETT & CO.
Merchants
Chemulpo.

Offices opposite the Imperial Japanese Post and Telegraph Office Chemulpo.

Telephone Number 201.

大韓每日申報

대한ᄆᆡ일신보

(뎨이권 ᄉᆞ십일호) (금요일) 일쳔구ᄇᆡᆨ오년 이월 이십ᄉᆞ일

본샤고ᄇᆡᆨ

이 신보는 영어와 한어로 셔ᄀᆡ ᄆᆡ일 출판ᄒᆞ옵

신문가

한쟝 엽뎐 두돈오푼

일삭됴 엽뎐 두량닷돈

우표가 ᄆᆡ삭 닷돈

다 엽뎐으로 밧ᄉᆞᆸ

광고료는

귀ᄌᆞ의 쟝단과 ᄌᆞ힝의 다쇼로 ᄎᆞ감ᄒᆞ되 렴가로 밧을터이오며 오ᄅᆡ지 아녀 대한 사ᄅᆞᆷ마다 다 이 신문을 보실터이니 광고ᄒᆞ시기를 원ᄒᆞ시ᄂᆞᆫ 이들은 우리 신문사에 와서 면약ᄒᆞ심을 희망ᄒᆞ옵

○발ᄒᆡᆼ소 ᄇᆡᆨ동 대한ᄆᆡ일신보사 발ᄒᆡᆼ인 겸 편즙인 영국인 셜필림 겸쟈리오

사쟝 영국인 (비셜)

평양 ᄃᆡ리졈

○평양 효동 사ᄂᆞᆫ 권미보 씨로 우리 신문관 ᄃᆡ리인을 뎡ᄒᆞ엿ᄉᆞ오니 평양에 계신 구람코져ᄒᆞ시ᄂᆞᆫ 쳠군ᄌᆞᄂᆞᆫ 그 ᄃᆡ리졈에 왕림ᄒᆞ와 면의ᄒᆞ시옵

샤고

○우리 대한ᄆᆡ일신보의 목뎍은 대한의 안녕질셔에 관ᄒᆞᆫ 모든 ᄃᆡ목에 ᄃᆡᄒᆞ야ᄂᆞᆫ 공평ᄒᆞᆫ 변론을 쥬쟝ᄒᆞᆷ이라 우리 통신원의 탐보ᄂᆞᆫ 신문보시ᄂᆞᆫ 쳠군ᄌᆞ의 계ᄒᆞ샹 보도ᄒᆞ리며 편지를 긔셔ᄒᆞ며 주시ᄂᆞᆫ 이ᄂᆞᆫ 셩명과 번디를 젹어 붓치셔 기를 희망ᄒᆞ오니 이거슨 신문샹에 긔ᄌᆡᄒᆞ라ᄂᆞᆫ 거시 아니오 다만 긔셔신용ᄒᆞᄂᆞᆫ 증거를 ᄉᆞᆷ고쟈 ᄒᆞᆷ이라 긔쟈ᄂᆞᆫ 아모 긔셔던지 과ᄎᆔᄒᆞᆷ을 퇴쟉ᄒᆞᄂᆞᆫ 권리ᄂᆞᆫ 가졋ᄉᆞ나 퇴쟉ᄒᆞᄂᆞᆫ 리유ᄂᆞᆫ 말ᄒᆞᆯ터이오며 공즁평론을 문란케ᄒᆞᄂᆞᆫ 듯ᄒᆞᆫ 긔셔ᄂᆞᆫ 의례히 밧지 안켓ᄉᆞᆸ나이다

●본샤셜시 이ᄅᆡ로 신문을 ᄆᆡ양 우톄로 분젼ᄒᆞ와 톄젼부의 임의로 젼ᄒᆞᄂᆞᆫ 듯ᄉᆞ로 먼 곳에ᄂᆞᆫ 혹 늣게 젼ᄒᆞ기도 ᄒᆞ며 혹 몃쳡 거슬 ᄒᆞᆫ법에 젼ᄒᆞ기도 ᄒᆞ며 혹 아니 젼ᄒᆞᄂᆞᆫ 곳도 잇다ᄒᆞ와 우리 신문을 ᄉᆞ랑ᄒᆞ야 구람ᄒᆞ시ᄂᆞᆫ 쳠군ᄌᆞ의게 당ᄃᆡᄒᆞ야 면우 미안ᄒᆞ올 기로 지금은 분관인을 두고 ᄆᆡ일 일즉이 젼ᄒᆞ며 아니 젼ᄒᆞ거나 늣게 ᄒᆞ거나 혹 폐가 업도록 ᄒᆞ랴ᄒᆞ오니 혹 아니 젼ᄒᆞ거나 혹 늣게 젼ᄒᆞ거나 ᄒᆞᆫ일이 잇스면 본샤로 통긔ᄒᆞ여 주심을 희망ᄒᆞ옵

론셜

일본국과 한국

○일본이 한국에 와서 ᄒᆞᆫ 일과 지금 ᄒᆞᄂᆞᆫ 일을 ᄎᆞ례로 긔록ᄒᆞ야 두기ᄂᆞᆫ 간졀히 바라노니 그 긔록ᄒᆞᆫ 것이 아모것도 모로고 일본을 조아ᄒᆞ고 로국을 미워ᄒᆞ거나 혹 다른 ᄉᆡᆼ각으로 말ᄒᆞᄂᆞᆫ 자들의 회황ᄒᆞᆷ을 ᄉᆞᆯ피기에 일됴가 되리로다 일젼에 우리가 ᄒᆞᆫ 긔셔를 밧엇ᄂᆞᆫᄃᆡ 그것은 익명셔라 우리가 공포ᄒᆞ기 불능이나 그러ᄒᆞ나 그 긔셔에 말ᄒᆞᆫ 것은 예사 익명셔의 힝투가 아니오 지각 잇고 공손ᄒᆞ며 그 말ᄒᆞᆫ 의취ᄂᆞᆫ 우리 대한ᄆᆡ일신보가 한국의 편을 드러셔 일본의 단쳐만 잡히 ᄉᆞᆯ피고 일본이 한국을 구원ᄒᆞᄂᆞᆫ 것은 모른다 ᄒᆞ엿스며 엇지 그런 이야기ᄂᆞᆫ 아니ᄒᆞ엿ᄂᆞ니ᄒᆞ더라 우리가 그것을 ᄉᆡᆼ각ᄒᆞ고 ᄯᅩ ᄉᆡᆼ각ᄒᆞ야 우리가 지금 말ᄒᆞᄂᆞᆫ 것을 그 긔셔 보낸 사ᄅᆞᆷ은 자세히 보기를 쳥ᄒᆞ며 ᄯᅩ 일본의 대한졍ᄎᆡᆨ이 비록 당쟝의 호결과ᄂᆞᆫ 엇ᄉᆞ나 필경은 나라의 리익이 되리라 말ᄒᆞᄂᆞᆫ 사ᄅᆞᆷ들의게 우리ᄂᆞᆫ 넘이로리노니 일본이 한국에 이런 쟝원ᄒᆞᆫ 익을 쥬게 될 권력이 오ᄅᆡ가지 못ᄒᆞᆯ 것이오 ᄯᅩ 한인들이나 다른 방관지인들도 목젼에 조흔 결과를 더 조아ᄒᆞᄂᆞᆫ도다

일본이 의졍셔를 광게ᄒᆞ고 군사샹 힝동의 자유를 엇은지라 그의 졍셔ᄂᆞᆫ 분명치 아니ᄒᆞ나 그러ᄒᆞ나 일본인은 그것을 널게 미련셔 번역ᄒᆞ야 글로ᄒᆞ야 토디를 졈령ᄒᆞ고 공역을 억지로 시이며 반ᄃᆡᄒᆞᄂᆞᆫ 공회들은 다 압졔ᄒᆞ고 한국 각ᄃᆡ방에 군법을 힝ᄒᆞ며 셔울 경찰권을 ᄆᆡ리ᄒᆞ엿ᄂᆞᆫ지라

그 다음에ᄂᆞᆫ 어업권을 엇고 토디를 더 졈령ᄒᆞ며 아진씨를 군부고문관으로 졍ᄒᆞ고 ᄯᅩ 그 다음은 쟝샹씨의 진황디 문졔라 만일 진황디 문졔가 찬되엿더면 오날 일본인이 아모 걸도 아니고 한국의 토디 주인이 되ᄂᆞᆫ 것을 다 ᄒᆡᆼ히 그 문졔가 필경에ᄂᆞᆫ 실패ᄒᆞ야 능셩ᄉᆞ이 못되엿도다

그 다음에ᄂᆞᆫ 일진회의 조직이라 그 회ᄂᆞᆫ 한국의 폐졍을 기혁ᄒᆞᄂᆞᆫ 국회가 되랴고 ᄒᆞ나 그 츙복젹은 대황뎨 폐하와 졍부대신들을ᄂᆞᆫ ᄇᆡ셔 일본인의 쳥구를 잘 듯게 ᄒᆞ자ᄂᆞᆫ 것이니 그 회에셔 이번 일본이 희관을 젼당ᄒᆞ고 삼ᄇᆡᆨ만원의 국채를 쓸ᄃᆡ 업시 주ᄂᆞᆫᄃᆡ ᄃᆡᄒᆞ야 반ᄃᆡ를 아니ᄒᆞᄂᆞᆫ 것으로 보아도 일본인을 위ᄒᆞ야 일ᄒᆞᄂᆞᆫ 회가 분명ᄒᆞ며 한국 경찰관리와 군ᄃᆡ가 그 회를 진압ᄒᆞ랴다가 일본인의게 막음이 되고 그 관계로 일본인이 셔울에셔 경찰권을 ᄆᆡ리ᄒᆞ엿ᄂᆞᆫ지라

지금은 우리가 거의 날마다 참부에 일본 고문관을 고용ᄒᆞᆫ다ᄂᆞᆫ 것을 드르니 그것이 다 일본의 리익을 위ᄒᆞᆷ인ᄃᆡ 그 즁에 궁ᄂᆡ부에 일본녀의 ᄒᆞ나를 고용ᄒᆞᆫ 것을 보면 우ᄉᆞ우며 이ᄇᆡ셔 지목ᄒᆞ 젼ᄒᆡ의 ᄌᆡ졍은 한인이 원ᄒᆞ지 아니ᄒᆞᄂᆞᆫ 권을 억지로 쥬기로 ᄒᆞ야 ᄃᆡ셜리의 근본을 감독ᄒᆞ라 ᄒᆞᄂᆞᆫ도다 셰리용의 쎄에 ᄃᆡᄒᆞ야 대한일보가 반ᄃᆡᄒᆞᄂᆞᆫ 것 곳치 일본 졍최에 반ᄃᆡᄒᆞᄂᆞᆫ 한국관인들은 다 셔울 밧게로 내여 쫏ᄎᆞ 보니고 우리가 리라ᄒᆞ노라 세쇄ᄒᆞᆫ 일이 만히 잇스리라

지금 동경신문을 보니 일본인이 한국에셔 연초와 소금의 젼ᄆᆡ를 미구에 엇어셔 긔량 경ᄎᆡ에 ᄆᆡᄒᆞᆫ 경비를 쓰게 ᄒᆞᆫ다 ᄒᆞ엿더라

일본인은 말ᄒᆞ되 져의들이 이 나라를 감독ᄒᆞᆫ 후로 쳥잡관리들을 만히 쫏ᄎᆞᆺ다ᄒᆞ나 그것은 그런듯ᄒᆞ지마ᄂᆞᆫ 쳥잡관리라도 일본졍최에 반ᄃᆡ만 ᄒᆞ지 아니ᄒᆞ면 가만히 두ᄂᆞᆫ 자들이 만히 잇스며 일본이 곳에셔 마음ᄃᆡ로 ᄒᆞ면ᄂᆞᆫ 어업과 광산과 샹업이 ᄆᆡ우 왕ᄒᆞ야 국가의 셰입이 증가ᄒᆞᆯ 것이의 ᄉᆡᆼ업지마ᄂᆞᆫ 그런 긔량산진은 다 일본인이 져의들을 위ᄒᆞ야 ᄒᆞᆯ 일이며 일본인이 사무에 ᄃᆡᄒᆞ야 한문과 ᄌᆞ흑이 한인보다 나어셔 만일 두 국민이 ᄎᆞᆺ치 일을 시작ᄒᆞ면 일본인이 더 ᄒᆞ와 ᄒᆞ게 되야셔 필경은 한인을 업시ᄒᆞ라 ᄒᆞᆯ터이라 일본인도 져의 나라에 외국인을 미워ᄒᆞᆷ슴 뿐에 그 일을 두려워ᄒᆞ엿더니 지금 미야쟈의 들이강ᄒᆞ여 진즁을 알고 외국인들의게 자의 드ᄂᆞᆫ 곳ᄎᆞᆫ 토디 경유권과 광산권을 ᄒᆞ락ᄒᆞ엿ᄂᆞᆫ지라

그럼으로 비록 우리가 이 나라가 일본의 감독아래 잇서서 ᄌᆡ졍하발달 될 줄은 아나 일본인의 졍ᄎᆡᆨ이 이 나라의 ᄌᆡ졍과 졍부의 감독권을 ᄎᆞ지ᄒᆞ랴 ᄒᆞ니 그 긔량ᄒᆞᄂᆞᆫ 리익을 밧을 자ᄂᆞᆫ 일본인이오 한인은 아니 될 것이 확실ᄒᆞ도다 ᄇᆡ록 일본인의 힝위가 졍당ᄒᆞ지 못ᄒᆞ지마ᄂᆞᆫ 만일 한인을 져의 마음ᄃᆡ로 버려두면 져의 나라 들긔랑ᄒᆞᆯ 일을 못ᄒᆞ리라지 ᄇᆞᆫ ᄉᆡᆼ오년 동안에 일본은 능히 진보ᄒᆞᄂᆞᆫᄃᆡ 한인은 저ᄃᆞᆫ 불변ᄒᆞᄂᆞᆫ 것을 징거로 부망ᄒᆞ나 그러ᄒᆞ나 일본이 진보ᄒᆞᄂᆞᆫ ᄇᆞ름에 한국은 극동에 졍치상 즁심이 되야셔 리롭게 지낸 것을 불가불 ᄉᆡᆼ각ᄒᆞᆯ 일이라 ᄒᆞ노라

잡보

○수형착취 경무쳥에셔 작셔에 지휘ᄒᆞ엿ᄉᆞ되 한국쟝 류빈가 일본 변호사들 부동ᄒᆞ야 비리의 송ᄉᆞ를 조와ᄒᆞᄂᆞᆫ 고ㅣ만ᄒᆞ니 보ᄂᆞᆫᄃᆡ로 착치ᄒᆞ라 ᄒᆞ엿더라

○리졍이결 제쟝이 ᄉᆡᆼ일ᄒᆡ졍부에셔 관계 리쟝안을 거졀ᄒᆞ야 일간 반포ᄒᆞᆯ터인ᄃᆡ 외졍부에ᄂᆞᆫ 쟁대신 참졍대신 찬졍 일인이오 참셔관 쥬ᄉᆞ 과인 셉이라더라

○회동시쟝 광교하와 남문외 련못가에 고시ᄃᆡ를 셜치ᄒᆞᆯ 위치를 ᄐᆡᆨ간ᄒᆞ야 작졍ᄒᆞᆯ ᄎᆞ로 남셔셔 셔경관과 한셩부 관인과 일령사관원들이 이ᄉᆡᆼ이 일상오싱시에 회동 젼왕ᄒᆞ엿더라

○비샹쟉뎡 면거리왕셔에 운수가 도모지 쇼피치 안이ᄒᆞ야 인명이 만히 샹ᄒᆞᄂᆞᆫ지라 각 뎡거쟝에 슌검을 가파ᄒᆞ야 승ᄀᆡᆨ의 타고 나리ᄂᆞᆫ 거슬 보호ᄒᆞᆫ다ᄂᆞᆫᄃᆡ 경쳥에셔 조회ᄒᆞ되 종금이후로ᄂᆞᆫ 뎐거에 인명이 치샹ᄒᆞ면 관등을 분별ᄒᆞ야 비샹을 쟉뎡케ᄒᆞ라ᄒᆞ엿더라

○안동뎍간 경무쳥에셔 한셩부로 조회ᄒᆞ기를 자금이후로ᄂᆞᆫ 가사와 멋ᄃᆡ단의 방민ᄒᆞᄂᆞᆫ 거슬 외국인의게 인허ᄒᆞᄂᆞᆫ 경우에ᄂᆞᆫ 본쳥과 안동뎍간ᄒᆞᆫ 후에 허가케ᄒᆞ라 ᄒᆞ엿더라

UNION INSURANCE SOCIETY OF CANTON.

Head office Hongkong.
Marine risks underwritten at current rates.
Agents in Chemulpo,
E. MEYER & Co.

COMPAGNIE DES MESSAGERIES MARITIMES.

Fortnightly Direct Service.

For Marseilles
via Ports.
Sailing from Yokohama
Calling at Kobe,
Shanghai, Hongkong, Saigon, Singapore, Colombo, Djibouti, Suez, Port Said
and Marseilles.

For particulars apply to
HOLME RINGER & Co.,
Chemulpo

HAYASHIDA & CO.,

16 MYENG DONG, CHIN KO KAI, SEOUL.
BRANCH OFFICE AT CHEMULPO.

Money changers, Coal and Wood Merchants
Express Agents.

We are agents for the Pyeng-yang Coal Company and the Karazu Coal Company of Japan. We have the best quality of both anthracite and bituminous coal, and prompt execution of orders is our speciality. Firewood of all kinds kept in stock. Full weight guaranteed. Money of all denominations exchanged at current rates. Parcels received for all parts.

CHINA MUTUAL LIFE INS. CO.

Most favourable terms to policy holders.

Benefit system unsurpassed.

HOLME RINGER & Co.
Agents, Chemulpo.

C. P. R.

CANADIAN PACIFIC RAILWAY COMPANY'S ROYAL MAIL STEAMSHIP LINE.

THE FAST ROUTE BETWEEN CHINA, JAPAN, AND EUROPE VIA CANADA AND THE UNITED STATES.

Route from Hongkong via Shanghai, Nagasaki (Inland Sea of Japan) Kobe, Yokohama, Victoria and Vancouver.

Twin Screw Empress Steamship—6,000 Tons—Speed 19 knots.

PROPOSED SAILING FROM YOKOHAMA.
R. M. S. Empress of India.
R. M. S. Empress of Japan.
R. M. S. Empress of China.
R. M. S. Athenian.
R. M. S. Tartar.

Special reduction (first class only) granted to members of the Military, Naval, Diplomatic and Civil services and to Missionaries.

Passengers have choice of ten routes across the Continent of America and have privilege of travelling by any Atlantic Steamship Line.

Round the World passage tickets in connection with the P. and O. S. N., North German Lloyd and Messageries Co.'s £125.

All rates payable at current rate of exchange.

For further information, Tickets, Guide Books, etc., apply to
HOLME, RINGER & Co., AGENTS,
Chemulpo.

Grand Hotel

(Formerly the Station Hotel)

Near the Railway Terminus,
West Gate Seoul.

The Best Hotel in Korea.
Handsome new Building.
Fine Airy Rooms.
Excellent Cuisine.
Terms Moderate.
Special terms to Missionaries
and to permanent boarders.

Electric cars within 2 minutes' walk.

W. H. EMBERLEY.
Proprietor

EVERY FACILITY.

In connection with Life Assurance Business is afforded by

The Standard Life Assurance Co.,

One of the largest and wealthiest of the Provident Institutions of the United Kingdom Forms of Application and all information will be promptly afforded on application.

10 CENTS A DAY.

Not a very large expenditure is it? But it is sufficient to secure for a man of 30 a policy with the STANDARD LIFE OFFICE for

$1323.

For all particulars of rates, etc., apply to
Holme, Ringer & Co.,
Agents, Chemulpo.

THE NEW YORK LIFE INSURANCE COMPANY.

Have you ever been declined by any Company?

Are you engaged in a specially hazardous occupation?

Have you heard of the New York Life Insurance Company's New Classifications for this class of Risks?

If not, send your date of birth, occupation and particulars of rejection, if any to

E. MEYER & Co.,
Agents, Chemulpo.

MITSUI BUSSAN KAISHA.
(MITSUI & Co.)
MITSUI GINKO.
(MITSUI BANK.)

The Bank is owned by the members of the Mitsui Family, who, as partners, assume an unlimited responsibility for all liabilities of the Bank:—

Capital.......................Yen 5,000,000
Reserve Fund.................. " 5,600,000

HEAD OFFICE, TOKYO.
LONDON OFFICE, 34 LIME ST., E. C.

BRANCHES AND AGENCIES:—
New York, San Francisco, Hamburg, Bombay, Singapore, Manila, Hongkong, Amoy, Chefoo, Tientsin.
Kobe, Hakodate, Yokohama, Kure, Yokosuka, Moji, Shimonoseki, Miike, Wakamatsu, Nagasaki, Kuchinotsu, Karatsu, Sasebo, Misume, Taipeh, &c.

Telegraphic Address for all the Offices:
"MITSUI."
A. B. C. AND A. 1 CODES USED.

Contractors of Coal
To the Imperial Japanese Navy. Arsenal and Railway Bureau, Principal Railway Companies and Industrial Work, Home and Foreign Mail and Freight Steamers.

Sole Proprietors
Of the famous Miike, Tagawa and Yamano Coal Mines.

Sole Agents
For the sale of Fukumo, Hokoku, Ichimura, Kanoda, Mannoura, Onoura, Ostuji, Sonoda, Tsubaruro, Yoshinotani, Yoshio, Yurokibura and other coals.

YANGTSE INSURANCE ASSOCIATION, LTD.

The undersigned, having been appointed agents for the above company, are prepared to issue policies and pay losses on marine risks at regular rates.

E. MEYER & Co.,
Agents, Chemulpo.

AMERICAN KOREAN ELECTRIC CO.

Light and Power.

Main Office: Electric Building, Chong No.

RAILWAY DEPARTMENT.

OPERATING CARS BETWEEN EAST AND WEST GATE, EVERY TEN MINUTES:—

First Car leaves East Gate at 7:00 A. M. First Car leaves R. R. Station at 7:25 A.M.
Last Car " East Gate at 8.40 P. M. Last " " R. R. Station at 9.05 P.M.

OPERATING CARS BETWEEN EAST GATE AND IMPERIAL TOMB TERMINUS, EVERY TWENTY MINUTES:—
CONNECTING WITH EVERY ALTERNATE CAR ARRIVING AT EAST GATE FROM CHONG NO.

First Car leaves East Gate for Tomb at 7:10 A. M.
" " " Tomb for East Gate at 7:30 A. M.
Last " " East Gate for Tomb at 7:50 P. M.
" " " Tomb for East Gate at 8:10 P. M.

OPERATING CARS BETWEEN CHONG NO AND YUNG SAN RIVER EVERY TWELVE MINUTES:—

First Car leaves Chong No for South Gate at 7:12 A. M.
" " " Chong No for Yung San at 7:36 A. M.
" " " South Gate for Chong No at 7:20 A. M.
" " " Yung San for Chong No at 8:09 A. M.
Last " " South Gate for Chong No 9:00 P. M.
" " " Yung San for Chong No at 8.45. P. M.

SPECIAL PRIVATE CARS FURNISHED TO SUIT CONVENIENCE OF PATRONS. PRICES ON APPLICATION AT HEAD OFFICE.

LIGHTING DEPARTMENT.

Where less than 250 candle power of light is used, the rate per month will be
Per 16 candle power incandescent lamp,—All night.—Yen 2.50.
32 candle power incandescent lamp,—All night:—Yen 4.00.
50 candle power incandescent lamp,—All night:—Yen 6.00.
150 " " " " " " " 10.00.
1200 " " enclosed arc " " " " 20.00.

Where more than 250 candle power of light is used, a Meter will be installed, if requested:—Rent of Meter, Yen 2.00 per month. Rate of charges by meter reading:—Two Sen per Ampere per hour. (Approximately this is equal to about One Sen per 16 C. P. lamp per hour) Minimum monthly charge where meter is installed, Yen 20.00 per month, which includes rental of meter.
Estimates for installing lights furnished on application
An assortment of chandeliers always on hand.

K. Murakami.

Photograph Studio
Chinkokai, Seoul.

Printing, Developing and Enlargement, of Photographs always Undertaken.

Korean Views and Pictures Illustrating Native Customs always on Sale,

THE OSAKA SHOSEN KAISHA.

Boats frequently on the berth for Chinnampo.

REGULAR SAILINGS BETWEEN JAPAN AND KOREAN PORTS.

FUSAN AND KOBE VIA SHIMONOSEKI.

OSAKA VIA MOKPO, FUSAN, SHIMONOSEKI AND KOBE.

MOJI DIRECT.

OSAKA VIA KUNSAN, MASANPO, FUSAN, SHIMONOSEKI AND KOBE.

CHEMULPO KUNSAN LINE,
Every three days.

CHEMULPO CHINNAMPO LINE.
Every three days.

For Freight and passage and further particulars apply to
THE OSAKA SHOSEN KAISHA,
Chemulpo.

RONDON, PLAISANT & CO.

General Storekeepers and Merchants, Ships Contractors Tobacconists, Commission and Forwarding Agents, Coal Merchants

IMPORTERS AND EXPORTERS

Seoul, Chemulpo.

W. D. WENTWORTH.

LANDING
AND
SHIPPING AGENT.
AND
CUSTOMS BROKER.

12 OURA, NAGASAKI.

STEWARD & CO.

Chemulpo.

Shipchandlers and Storekeepers, Naval and Mercantile Contractors, Landing and Shipping Agents.

STEWARD'S HOTEL

Chemulpo.

Best accommodation in the port for travellers. Clean and well-aired rooms, good cuisine and prompt attendance, moderate tariff.

관보

데삼천륙십구호 광무구년이월이십이일

셔임급사령

○의원면본관 수원면보사주ᄉ 신복히 ○임수원면보사주ᄉ셔관임관륙등 츙주면보사주ᄉ 정규동 ○츙임주면보사주ᄉ셔관임관사등 전주ᄉ 신복히

이상이월십사일

○임탁지부출납국장셔주임관사등 탁지부회계국장 리준상 ○임탁지부회계국장셔주임관사등 탁지부참셔관 김철현 ○의원면본관 셩진우톄사주ᄉ 리병익 즁학교교관 최히익 ○임즁학교교관판임관륙등 리완응 ○임셩진우톄시주ᄉ셔판임관륙등 종셩우톄사주ᄉ 전기순

이상이월십륙일

○면본관 창원감리셔주ᄉ 홍순규 ○임창원감리셔주ᄉ셔관임관사등 삼화감리셔주ᄉ 민복훈 ○임삼화감리셔주ᄉ셔관임관사등 동래감리셔주ᄉ 정보셥 ○임동래감리셔주ᄉ셔관임관사등 룡천감리셔주ᄉ 리규동 ○임룡천감리셔주ᄉ셔관임관륙등 리종덕 ○의원면본관 경상북도관찰부주ᄉ 허병 경상북도관찰부주ᄉ 박민하 ○임경상북도관찰부주ᄉ셔관임관륙등 뎡 경 박응주

이상이월십구일

○의원면본관 비셔원승 박필원 군부주ᄉ 권도진 군부주ᄉ 박선양 군기창기수 김기셕 ○명궁니부특진관셔칙임관사등 비셔원승 윤상하 ○임비셔원승셔주임관륙등 정삼품 송정섭 규장각직학ᄉ 윤주셩 ○임 규장각직학ᄉ셔주임관오등 정삼품 셔긍순 ○임시종원시종셔주임관륙등 륙품 리룡호 ○히관제리정소의정관 장례원경 리도지 ○명관제리정소의정관 농상공부대신 리지용 한셩부관윤 박의병 ○임군부주ᄉ셔판임관륙등 낭주훈 엄주은 ○임군기창기수셔판임관륙등 태호선

이상이월이십일

광무구년도예산표 속

데ᄉ관 번계경무셔 이만ᄉ천오빅삼십이원
데일항 봉급 이천삼빅륙십원
데이항 청비 이천오십원
데삼항 청ᄉ슈리비 ᄉ빅원
데ᄉ항 잡급급잡비 일만ᄉ천륙빅십륙원
데오항 피복비 이천삼빅오십원
데륙항 죄슈비 이빅팔십륙원
데칠항 려비 이천ᄉ빅칠십원
경무청소관 합계삼십팔만륙천칠빅ᄉ십구원

학부소관
데일관 학부본청 이만삼천삼빅칠십ᄉ원
데일항 봉급 일만ᄉ천이빅오십원
데이항 청비 이천ᄉ빅삼십원
데삼항 청ᄉ슈리비 이빅오십원
데ᄉ항 교과서인쇄비 오천ᄉ빅원
데오항 잡급급잡비 일천팔빅ᄉ십ᄉ원
데이관 관상소 륙천삼빅ᄉ원
데일항 봉급 오천원
데이항 청비 일빅이십원
데삼항 청ᄉ슈리비 ᄉ십원
데ᄉ항 력셔비 일천원
데오항 잡급과잡비 일빅ᄉ십ᄉ원
데삼관 셩균관 구천오십구원
데일항 봉급 이천구빅팔십원
데이항 청비 륙빅륙십원
데삼항 급여비 삼천팔빅오십ᄉ원
데ᄉ항 청ᄉ슈리비 일빅원
데오항 잡급과잡비 일천ᄉ빅륙십오원
데ᄉ관 ᄉ범학교 오천칠빅오십오원
데일항 봉급 일천삼빅이십원
데이항 청비 팔빅이십원
데삼항 급여비 삼천이빅이십ᄉ원
데ᄉ항 청ᄉ슈리비 일빅오십원
데오항 잡급과잡비 이빅ᄉ십일원
데오관 즁학교 일만이천륙빅이십륙원
데일항 봉급 ᄉ천이빅십원
데이항 청비 구빅원
데삼항 교과칙구미급번역비 오빅원
데ᄉ항 청ᄉ슈리비 일빅오십원
데오항 잡급과잡비 이빅륙십륙원
데륙항 외국인제급 륙천륙빅원 지화

잡보

○수수방관 이십일일관제리정회의에각대신은수수방관홀ᄯᅡ름이오궁니부고문관가등씨가홀노조종ᄒ야가감ᄒ엿다더라

○환산씨셜연 이십이일하오이시에경무청고문관환산씨가파셩관에연회를비셜ᄒ고경무청관원을청료ᄒ엿더라

○경사상쥬 경무국장김사묵씨는희사인이어놀전군슈김종원씨로희사국쟝을숩임훈다홈이경무사가불가천동홀리유를상쥬ᄒ엿다더라

○면훈축출 니부에셔강계군슈의게던훈ᄒ기를군ᄃᆡ와합력ᄒ야회민을축출ᄒ여잔민을지보케ᄒ라ᄒ엿더라

○고디지령 황히도빅천신천등군에일진회원등이방금회집ᄒ야읍니에가소요ᄒ다ᄒ고희군슈들이니부로보고ᄒ엿는ᄃᆡ지령을기다려죠쳐ᄒ겟다ᄒ엿더라

○군슈치젹 양양민인등이히군슈의치젹을니부에리ᄒ고원류ᄒ야삼차에지ᄒ엿다더라

○일사공합 일공사가니부로공합ᄒ기를원산항경무관박기호씨로고원군슈를서리케ᄒ라고공함ᄒ엿더라

○일사보조 수원으로온사람의전셜을문훈즉일전에쟝곡쳔대쟝과림공사와밋제관원이슈원에하거ᄒ엿다가화셩학교에유람ᄒ고보조금을각히수십원식즁여ᄒ엿다더라

○조청회심 일본군사령부에서착상훈곡산민요쟝두를그등안에평리원으로이슈ᄒ엿더니평리원에서외부로조회ᄒ기를리금료일하오이시에심판홀터이니일관에조회ᄒ야일본관원도심관홈을리청케ᄒ라ᄒ엿더라

○함청셔훈 일ᄉ가외부로함청훈니기에륙군즁좌던야와소쪼언관량원이긔전이리로귀국에지ᄒ야전지력을오리넨지라맛당히셔훈을청홀터인ᄃᆡ현금압록강전쟁를보좌홀ᄎ로발뎡ᄒ는고로쟝곡천대쟝이히원등을ᄃᆡ동 폐현홀터인ᄃᆡ이시에훈쟝을사ᄒ면영광이네사ᄒ리라ᄒ엿더라

○사민무의 경무청에셔슈뎡비를피잔에슈렴홀ᄉ는각신문루에게ᄒ엿거니와수렴훈전수와용ᄒ훈전수를신문에반포ᄒ야빅셩으로ᄒ여곰소샹히알고의심이업게ᄒ다ᄂᆞᆫᄃᆡ그수렴견은아직신실훈전당포에임치ᄒ엿다더라

뎐보

론돈발 일동

○로국황뎨셔셔칙령으로고베코씨로신문금찰관겸신문됴례긔정위원장을임명ᄒ엿다더라

동디발 동월팔일

○덴으졔끄대장이로국정부에보고ᄒ되사이베리아철로의운송력량이로국군ᄃᆡ의슈요품을슈응ᄒ기부족ᄒ다ᄒ엿다더라

평화의소식

화셩돈발 이월십이일

●미국대통령루스벨트씨가엇던사름의즁지로로국졍부에평화ᄒ기를권고ᄒ엿는ᄃᆡ결과가잘못되엿는지라화셩돈에잇는로국대ᄉ빅쟉켓시니씨가쟈긔의졍부의훈칙을의지ᄒ야미국졍부에셩언ᄒ되구로팻긴대쟝이승젼ᄒ야극동에로국의위망을회복ᄒ기ᄭᆞ지외국에셔즁지ᄒ는평화소건에합의ᄒ지아니ᄒ겟다ᄒ엿다더라

론돈발 동일

○평화풍셜이지금ᄭᆞ지연속ᄒ며법국에셔는로국이평화죠약을잘시작홀도리가잇스리라고들ᄒ고론돈에잇는일본공ᄉ하야시씨는젼정이연속ᄒ기가쉽다ᄒ고들ᄒ더라더라

빈림발 동월십일일

○셩피득보통신을거ᄒ즉로국이어늬나라에향ᄒ야쟈긔나라를위ᄒ야평화ᄒ기를청ᄒ지아니ᄒ엿다고강경ᄒ션언을ᄒ엿다ᄒ엿더라

로국의졍형

론돈발 이월십일일

○가신홀만ᄒ말을거ᄒ즉작일에로국황뎨셔셔돌스토이의의아들의게립헌졍부를죠직홀예비로다음쥬안에ᄒ공회를열기를허락ᄒ엿다더라

동디발 동일

○셩피득보에셔분요가다시이러나셔지금삼만명이놀고잇스며셰로이ᄀ량안을샹의ᄒ는니각의장윗트씨의집을경찰관리들이슈식ᄒ엿다더라

광고

TELEGRAMS.

(FROM JAPAN PAPERS.)

THE THIRD SQUADRON.

London, February 17th.

The Third Squadron of the Baltic Fleet has left Libau, en route to the Far East.

FROM CHINA PAPERS.

THE WAR.

Berlin, Feb. 17.

On the right bank of the Hunho ten Russian squadrons with artillery advanced, on the 14th inst., to Chenchiawatse, and retired, after the arrival of strong Japanese forces, to Heiyuku.

(We cannot find these places in any map but it is evident that this is the cavalry movement reported by Oyama on the 14th inst.)

Berlin, Feb. 17.

Gen. Stackelberg is reported wounded. Apparently Gen. Kaulbars is preparing an advance on the Russian left towards the Yalu, in order to outflank the Japanese.

BRITISH POLITICS.

London, February 17th.

Mr. Asquith has introduced his amendment, in which the Government is urged to submit the fiscal reform question to the country.

The debate, which is proceeding, is lifeless.

EXPLOSION ON A SUBMARINE.

London, February 17th.

An explosion took place on a British submarine at Queenstown.

A sub-lieutenant and three men were killed and 14 men wounded.

GENERAL NEWS.

Paris, Feb. 17.

The Chamber of Deputies has elected Mons. Doumergue as vice-president by 215 votes, against 142 polled for Mons. Denys-Cochin.

Paris, Feb. 17th.

At London the address from the Throne on the opening of parliament stated that the Russo-Japanese war still unhappily continued; but that Great Britain would contine to observe the strictest neutrality.

Berlin, Feb. 17.

Prince Leopold of Prussia will visit the Czar at Tsarskoe Tselo; and starts by the German mail s. s. "Genoa" for East Asia; probably visiting Peking.

Berlin, Feb. 17.

Admiral Tirpitz announces the new German naval bill for 1906.

It is reported that orders were issued for the arrest of three astrologers Kang Hong-tai, Sung Kwang-ho and Choi Pyong-chou but were subsequently rescinded at, it is believed, the request of the Emperor. Mr. Kang attends at the Palace as usual but the two have gone into hiding.

The magistrate of Sakyung (about 65 miles north of Seoul) has written to the Home Office for special powers to deal severely with the Il-chin-hoi people in his district. He says that they are absolutely lawless and dissolute, are causing great disorder and making the proper administration of his district impossible.

The American Minister has applied to the Korean Government for a contribution towards the new Severance Hospital which is largely availed of by the Korean people, civil and military. He points out that it is customary for hospitals abroad to receive government support and asks that this hospital be endowed to the extent of $500 or $600 monthly.

THE FOREIGN SQUADRONS IN THE FAR EAST.

The British flagships "Glory" and "Albion" and almost all the other vessels of the squadron on the China station are at anchor at Hongkong. The U.S. flagships "Wisconsin," "Rainbow" and "Baltimore" and the remainder of the U. S. Far Eastern Squadron, are at Manila. The French flagship "Montcalm" is at Haiphong, while the "Chateaurenault" and the greater portion of the French squadron are at Saigon. The "Fuerst Bismarck," the German flagship, is at Hongkong, while the other vessels are at Kiaochow, Chefoo, and Shanghai.

It is now reported that the daughter of Mr. Soh Puing Sûn has been selected as a consort for the Crown Prince.

At a meeting of the Council of State held on the 20th inst. 29 magistrates were dismissed and 13 new appointments made.

The Japanese Consul at Wonsan has demanded from the magistrate of Moonchun full particulars of the census and area of ground in the small Song-chun li peninsula.

Mr. McLeavy Brown has notified the Home Department that repairs on the leading to the Foreign Cemetery at Yangwha-chin will be commenced as soon as the winter breaks.

A number of very sensible regulations have been issued by the police with regard to sanitation, committing nuisances etc., which it is to be hoped will not be allowed to become a dead letter.

Mr. Min Yung Chul, who is alleged to have plundered the people of Pyeng An while he was governor there, recently entertained all the officials of the Japanese Legation at his house at Ryong San.

With the object of getting money out of a rich man name Pak Yer To, some thieves recently opened his father's grave and took away the skull. Their arrest has, however, put a stop to their schemes.

The magistrate of Duk-wan has reported to the Home Office that he has been notified by the Colonel commanding the Japanese forces in his district, that no official appointment may be made without the permission of Japanese headquarters.

A report has been received from the magistrate of Kimhai in Kyŏng Sang province that recently during a quarrel with a Japanese named Matsui and five others, two Koreans were mortally stabbed and four others slightly wounded. The Japanese have escaped.

With a view of avoiding a large increase in the American navy, the New York "Sun" recomends an alliance between the United States and Great Britain for self-defence in the event of either Power being attacked by more than one naval Power.—"Australian paper."

The Department of Finance has issued a regulation that as branch banks will be established in all districts throughout the country, the tax gatherers must immediately deposit therein all taxes as soon as they are collected. Magistrates are not to interfere in these matters but are to devote their energies to governing the people well.

Two Japanese colonels, Asano and Futosaki, who have been in Seoul for some time are now ordered to the front. They were to have had an audience yesterday and in applying for it the Japanes Minister informed His Majesty that as these officers had been in Korea for some time, they would esteen it a great honour if some decoration was conferred on them.

RUSSIAN CASUALTIES.

A Siberian paper gives the following list of Russian casualties, excluding Port Arthur, up to the end of the year.

OFFICERS.

Places.	Killed.	Wounded.	Missing.
Yalu	26	38	6
Wafangou	18	85	10
Liaokalin	8	37	2
Taschitschiac	4	30	3
Yanselingpass	11	43	2
Liaoyang	87	419	10
*Mukden	187	854	33
	341	1,506	66

MEN.

Places.	Killed.	Wounded.	Missing.
Yalu	564	1,081	679
Wafangou	559	2,150	754
Liakalin	215	1,069	224
Taschitschiao	141	646	107
Yanseling pass	355	1,192	219
Liaoyang	2,027	12,486	1,461
*Mukden	4,969	31,002	1,641
	8,730	49,626	10,085

Making a grand total of 70,354 namely 9,071 killed, 51,132 wounded and 10,151 missing.

* This includes all the engagements after the battle of Liaoyang and until the end of the year.

The Chief of police has issued instructions that all those who agitate the people by the dissemination of false reports shall be arrested.

The Japanese authorities have issued a further lot of regulations prohibiting the sale or transfer of certain ground on the north east coast.

The Italian Minister has asked the Foreign Office to arrange a meeting so that the recent concessions of a gold mine may be finally settled.

The magistrate of Sersan has reported that a piece of land in his district is enclosed by stakes bearing the legend "occupied by Tanaka."

There seems to be a complaint that Japanese "shyster" lawyers are wasting the time of the court by advocating frivolous and improper cases.

Yesterday a number of police officials accompanied some officers of the Japanese consulate on a trip round the town in search of nice positions for Japanese advertising hoardings.

Mr. Pak Ki Ho, chief of police at Gensan, telegraphs that the Japanese have turned out the magistrate of Kowon and ask him to take his place. He awaits Government sanction.

The occurrence of a demonstration in favour of peace being apprehended at Odessa and Sevastopol, General Stoessel will land at an unknown point in the Black Sea, avoiding the above ports.

Mr. Hayashi has applied that the Customs be authorised to permit the import of dynamite upon a certificate from a Japanese consul or military officer. The present process of obtaining special permission from the government, leads, it is said, to a great waste of valuable time.

The Governor of South Ham Kyŏng province has telegraphed to the Home Office that the Japanese military authorities there have deprived him of his seals and turned him out of office. In this connection, the magistrate of Hamheung also wires that the Japanese have given him the seals and urge him to take the governor's place. He asks for instructions.

The Japanese Minister has been pressing the Cabinet for an announcement of the reforms it is intended to make in the government. A meeting was accordingly held yesterday when some alterations were made to the existing state of things. According to our reporter, Mr. Kato, adviser to the Household Department, did all the talking.

VLADIVOSTOK.

According to the "Chefoo Daily News" passengers arriving on the steamer "Taiping" from Vladivostok tell of great activity reigning at that port. New fortifications are constantly being built or the old ones strengthened. Trains are arriving every day with fresh soldiers. In this way the garrison is reinforced at the rate of about one thousand a day. The soldiers in Vladivostok at the end of January were calculated to number about forty thousand.

The stretch of railway between Vladivostok and Harbin is said to be very strongly guarded, military posts of great strength being scattered all long the line.

Several submarine boats have arrived lately per rail from Russian. On the 10th of January three submarines arrived, but they could not be put into water as the harbor was icecovered. The boats arrived on waggons specially constructed for this purpose. It is stated that fourteen in all are due.

* * *

It is quite interesting to find that Japan is forsaking its policy of secrecy and is now informing Russia and the world, through the medium of a London telegraph agency that General Kawamura will attack Vladivostok in the Spring. This will enable the Vladivostok garrison to get ready, but, in the meantime where is Kawamua? Up north waiting for the mild weather? He left Japan for a "certain place" long ago, according to the Tokio papers.

It is stated, on good authority, that Lord Milner will leave South Africa in August.

Yesterday Mr. Maruyama entained the Korean police officials at the Hajo Hotel.

In one of his last reports, General Stoessel estimated the Japanese casualties before Port Arthur at 93,000.

It is reported that Viscount Hayashi, Japanese Minister, has said that Japan would welcome proposals for peace, provided they came from Russia. This we can quite believe.

Presumably in connection with the approach of the Baltic fleet Viceroy Chowfu has reported to Peking that he has given orders to Admiral Yeh to attend to the defenses of the southern ports, and to provide against any emergency.

The British Minister has sent a despatch to the Foreign Office with reference to the indemnity of Y 2,764 for the murder of a Weihaiwei Chinaman at Haichu. His Excellency says that he hopes the government will find it convenient to pay at once.

The Japanese Army, according to the "Jiji," is now using the "Shimakawa" powder, invented by Colonel Shimakawa of artillery who is now commanding a certain artillery regiment in tho Shaho direction. It is generally known that the "Shimose" powder has already acquired a world-wide reputation, but nothing is yet reported by the "Jiji" of the effects of the new powder.

We note that the Japanese still entertain hopes that most of the men of war submerged at Port Arthur may be floated and added to the Japanese Navy. If is said that the vessels were not completely destroyed by the Russian, only the outer parts being blown up, probably due to the insufficiency of time between the date of the proposal of surrender and the conclusion of capitulation.

The Korea Daily News.

Issued at 5 P. M. daily except Sundays.

Rate of Subscription :—
Per Year,............Yen 25.
Per Quarter,..........Yen 7.
Per Month,..........Yen 2.50.

Postage in Korea not charged extra.
Postage abroad charged extra.

Advertisements, 50 sen per day for 1 inch or less.
5 yen per month per inch.
50 yen per year per inch.

All communications to

E. T. BETHELL,
Editor and Publisher,
Pak-tong, Seoul.

JAPAN'S FINANCES.

The legislators of Japan are evidently awake to the fact something must speedily be done unless this war is to fizzle out through lack of money. We have previously pointed out that under existing conditions it is hard to see how Japan can raise the money to maintain her overgrown navy and the large army which she has in Manchuria. Large sums will also have to be provided for the administration of such territory as she has occupied and for extensive repairs at Port Arthur.

For all these things much money will be required,—a sum probably nearer three than two million yen per day—and it is interesting to speculate upon the action which is being taken to stave off the inevitable bankruptcy.

Having been compelled to mortgage her customs revenue as security for the two loans which were floated abroad in the earlier stages of the war, when the progress of her armies was uninterrupted-ly victorious, it is quite certain, as financiers are not philauthropists in business hours, that Japan will have to submit to much more onerous terms now that the emptiness of her previous victories has become apparent and the prospects of further successes are becoming daily more distant.

There can be no doubt then that Japan will have to put up good security for every penny which she borrows from abroad, and, the customs revenue having already been pledged, there only remain the revenues from internal taxation and various Government monopolies and enterprises.

The first is of course out of the question and, of the monopolies, the only one which has yet stood the test of a year's working is camphor, and the money obtainable on this security would not carry the war much further.

Railways and all enterprises involving the ownership of land cannot be hypothecated as the laws of Japan do not permit of the ownership of land by foreigners, and, apparently, never will. Quite recently a draft of the Revised Mining Law was before the Japanese Diet and a proposal that the clause reading. "The right of mining is restricted to Japanese subjects and legal persons organized in accordance with Japanese law" should be deleted, had to be withdrawn through lack of support.

There is however a Government proposal now before the Diet which might, under certain circumstances, if adopted, lead to the much desired influx of foreign gold. The idea is to form a trust company (or companies) who will act as intermediaries between the foreign investor and the Japanese borrower. It is apparently proposed that the security should be vested in the trust company who would give the foreigner bonds in return for his money.

Such a scheme, of course, depends entirely on its details, but if the investor is properly safeguarded against all untoward contingencies, it is certain that it would succeed in introducing foreign capital, but of course not to an extent approaching the value of the properties hypothecated.

The expedient is, however a desperate one. Short of the actual ownership of land, Japan has nothing more to offer. He who goes a borrowing goes a sorrowing and each time she attempts to borrow money she will find her task increasingly difficult and her securities steadily dropping in the foreign markets.

Russia knows Japan's position, and the war, however it ends, will not provide Japan with a hansome indemnity like the war with China did, and we forsee that at the best it be several decades before the "Land of the Rising Sun" recovers from the effects of its rash enterprise. It may be urged in excuse of those who brought on this war, that, in view of increasing Russian ascendancy in China and Korea in was "Now or Never" for Japan. This we agree with but we think the Japanese statesmen should have resigned themselves to to the inevitable, mustered up all their philosopy and said "Well then—Never."

THE NORTH SEA ENQUIRY.

SOME RUSSIAN EVIDENCE.

The correspondent of the "Patrie" at Marseilles sends an account of an interview which he has had with Lieutenant Pobiesky, of the battleship "Kniaz Suvaroff." The Lieutenant states in effect that the following is the evidence which he intends to give before the Commission of Inquiry. He was on the bridge of the "Kniaz Suvaroff" at the time of the Hull incident. The moon was shining brightly. The sea was calm and the horizon very clear. With his fieldglass he could see a distance of 10 miles. He is absolutely certain that they were in the presence of two Japanese torpedo-boats, one having four funnels, the other three, and both having masked lights. After some minutes' observation he noticed that the torpedo-boats were proceeding towards them at slow speed. The Russians allowed them to approach to within 1,000 metres, and being then certain that they were not mistaken, they opened fire. He thinks that the two torpedo-boats must have sunk, as his ship stopped and remained on the spot at least 10 minutes. He remarks that it is entirely false to say that they fired at the English fishing-boats, but it is possible that the latter may have been struck by some of the shells aimed at the torpedo-boats. Lieut. Pobiesky adds that by order of the Czar he disembarked at Dakar and returned to Russia.

Lieutenant Valrond, of the Russian cruiser "Kamtchatka," with the whole of the recording bands of the wireless telegraph apparatus of the vessels belonging to Admiral Roshjestvensky's Fleet, has arrived in Paris. He says that if he was chosen by Admiral Roshjestvensky for this mission, it was because he was also an eye-witness of the Dogger Bank incident. He was working the search-lights on board the "Kamtchatka," and says that he distinctly saw the attacking torpedo-boats, which were painted a dirty-grey colour and had four funnels. They could not have been Russian torpedo-boats, he added, because their vessels were painted black.

KOREA NOT THE ONLY ONE.

In the outer city, in front of a popular temple of the god of war is a space in which, from time to time, the people gather for worship says the Canton correspondent of the China Mail, and it is not permitted that vendors of wares shall open their stalls on this sacred spot.

This notwithstanding, a few days ago two Japanese came and set up a stall, on which they arranged sponge cakes for sale. The temple keeper ordered them off; but as the Japanese did not understand Cantonese, they refused to obey orders and when the crowd gathered, they turned on the temple keeper and with their fists gave him a sound thrashing. The people then became enraged. They began to knock the Japanese about and they fled, leaving their kettles and frying pans behind to the mercy of the mob.

The Japanese retreated to their consul, and reported the matter to him. He at once took the matter up, and a local minor official was sent to look into it. The result was that the temple keeper was compelled to indemnify the Japanese for the loss of their cooking apparatus. The people are feeling very sore about the affair.

THE DATE OF EASTER.

It seems that the purists are somewhat exercised as to whether we are going to keep Easter on the right day this year or not, and Mr. A. M. W. Dowing has to explain in the current number of "Nature," that the "moon" referred to in the ecclesiastical calendar is not the actual moon in the sky, which is full at a definite instant of time but a fictitious moon, the times of the phases of which are so arranged as not to differ much from those of the actual moon. These phases are held to occur, vaguely, on certain days, and therefore hold good for all longitudes, and so avoid a practical inconvenience that would arise from the use of the actual moon. The necessity for some such ecclesiastical fiction is shown by the present instance, in which, while the actual moon is full at 4.56 A. M. in England by Greenwich mean time, it is full at 11.48 P. M. on the preceding day by Washington mean time. But for the convention the people adopting Greenwich time would, therefore, keep Easter Day on March 26, while those who take their time from Washington would have to wait until April 23. It is obvious, says the "Globe," that such an arrangement would result in hopeless confusion.

In the "North American Review' Lieut. Carlyon Bellairs strongly urges the importance of a naval alliance between the United States and the United Kingdom. His arguments are, of course, primarily addressed to Americans, and he has little difficulty in showing how greatly the United States would gain by the alliance that he advocates. He points out that the existence of the navy has already more than once saved the United States from a combination of European Powers, and at the present moment if France and Germany chose to sink their home quarrel in order to pursue a joint policy of adventure on the South American Continent, the United States by itself would be powerless to resist.

The Korea Daily News.

VOL. II, THURSDAY, FEBRUARY 23, 1905. No. 41

大韓每日申報

대한매일신보

(뎨이권ᄉᆞ십이호)　(토요일)　일쳔구빅오년이월이십오일

본샤고빅

이신보는영어와한어로셕거ᄆᆡ
일츌판ᄒᆞᆸ

신문갑

한쟝　엽젼두돈오푼
일삭됴　엽젼두량닷돈
우표가ᄃᆡ삭닷돈
다밋돈으로밧ᄉᆞᆸ

광고료는
긔한의장단과ᄌᆞ항의다쇼로ᄌᆞᆷ
작ᄒᆞ되뎡가로밧을터이오ᄆᆡ오
린지아녀대한사람마다이신
문을보실터이니광고버시기를
원ᄒᆞ시는이들은우리신문샤에
와셔면약ᄒᆞ심을희망ᄒᆞᆸ

○발힝소　박동대한ᄆᆡ일신보
샤발어학교엽희젼영국인셜필
링집자리오

샤쟝　영국인　(빈셜)

평양　ᄃᆡ리점

○평양효동사는권미보씨로우
리신문광고ᄃᆡ리인을뎡ᄒᆞ엿
시ᄉᆞ오니평양에계신구람코져ᄒᆞ
시는　쳠군ᄌᆞ는허ᄒᆡᄃᆡ리점에왕
림ᄒᆞ와면의ᄒᆞ시옵

샤고

○우리대한ᄆᆡ일신보의목뎍은
대한의안녕질서에관한모든뎨
목에ᄃᆡᄒᆞ야논공평한번론을주
쟝ᄒᆞᆷ이라우리통신원의탐보는
신문보시는쳠군ᄌᆞ의게ᄒᆞᆼ상보
도ᄒᆞ리며편지를긔셔ᄒᆞ여주시
는이는셩명과번ᄃᆡ를쟤어붓치
시기를희망ᄒᆞ오니이거슬신문
샹에긔ᄌᆡᄒᆞ란는거시아니오다
만크히신용ᄒᆞ는증거를ᄉᆞᆷ고자
ᄒᆞᆷ이라긔자는아모긔셔던지긔
ᄌᆡᄒᆞᆷ을퇴각ᄒᆞ는권리를가졋스
나퇴각ᄒᆞ는리유를말ᄒᆞᆯ터이오
며공중평화를문란케ᄒᆞ는듯ᄒᆞᆫ
긔셔는의례히밧지안켓ᄉᆞᆸ나이
다

●본샤셜시이리로신문을ᄆᆡ양
우희로붓쳔ᄒᆞ와희젼부의인의
로젼ᄒᆞ든ᄉᆞ로면곳에는ᄒᆞᆨ붓게
젼ᄒᆞ기도ᄒᆞ며ᄒᆞᆨ멋칠거슬ᄒᆞᆫ법
에젼ᄒᆞ기도ᄒᆞ며ᄒᆞᆨ아니젼ᄒᆞ는
곳도잇다ᄒᆞ와우리신문을ᄉᆞ랑
ᄒᆞ야구람ᄒᆞ시는　쳠군ᄌᆞ의게
ᄃᆡᄒᆞ야면우미안ᄒᆞ옵기로지금
은본젼인을두고ᄆᆡ일일ᄌᆞ이젼
ᄒᆞ며아니젼ᄒᆞ거나늣게ᄀᆞ나ᄒᆞᆫ
폐가업도록ᄒᆞ랴ᄒᆞ오니혹아니
젼ᄒᆞ거나ᄒᆞᆨ늣게젼ᄒᆞ거나ᄒᆞᆫ일
이잇스면본샤로통긔ᄒᆞ여주심
을희망ᄒᆞᆸ

뎐보

동경발　동월십이일

○셩피득보에셔다시일반인심
이ᄀᆞ장ᄒᆞ야졋스며외소에셔는
공장들이다시분요를니르켯다
더라

동경발　동월십삼일

○셩피득보에셔일요일은조용
히지내엿스며군ᄃᆡ의진압ᄒᆞᆷ으로
분요는아죠간졍된모양이라ᄒᆞ
엿다라

분릐협뎌의동쟁

륜돈발　이월십일

○아졔리인국의젼투함과슌양
함쳑쳑을쟝차분릐협뎌계뎌
ᄒᆞᆯ터이라ᄒᆞ엿더라

동경발　동월십삼일

○대삼분릐홈뎌는분릐히에셔
곳ᄯᅥ나기를예비ᄒᆞ라명령ᄒᆞ다
엿더라

로국의쟁형

륜돈발　이월십사일

○금월십이일에로국황뎨계셔
칙령을나리여셔졍부와제조소
쥬인들과로동자들의ᄃᆡ표위원
회를조직ᄒᆞ야셩피득보와각디
방에로동자들의불평ᄒᆞᆫ사샹을
련구ᄒᆞ야분요가ᄯᅥ니러나지아
니ᄒᆞ게ᄒᆞ라ᄒᆞ엿다더라

동경발　동월십삼일

○셩피득보통신을거ᄒᆞᆫ즉로국
황뎨계셔졍치가들과샹의ᄒᆞ야
란호양죠쳐로랑군이후졍ᄒᆞ게ᄒᆞ
ᄒᆞᆫ다더라

동경발　동월십사일

○로국에셔분요가ᄎᆞ차가라안
[illegible]

동경발　동월십삼일

○그리편박쟝군은어굿스코에
셔대단히병드러셔누엇다더라

동경발　동월십일일

○로국대학교들의교사들과학
싱들의분요는젼ᄉᆡᆼ에관련ᄒᆞ야
간다ᄒᆞ엿더라

륜돈발　이월십삼일

○륜돈타임쓰신문의통신을거
ᄒᆞᆫ즉로국이헝벅아미리가로젼
회사외교관이계을ᄒᆡᆼ빅만방에
ᄆᆡ일ᄒᆞ엿다ᄒᆞ엿더라

동경발　동일

○로국졔쳘회사의쥬인들이너
각의쟝위리시의게쳥원ᄒᆞ되로
동자들의쟁형을기랑ᄒᆞ야언권
의자유와지괴의동등을허락ᄒᆞ
고초등교육을권쟝ᄒᆞ라ᄒᆞ엿다
더라

동경발　동월십사일

○로국볼노가아ᄃᆡ방에비병
사쳔명이반ᄒᆞ엿더니랑식이평
졍ᄒᆞ야관군에게항복ᄒᆞ엿다더
라

론셜

소문을불가진신

○젼쟁의형편을살피고구동에
셔발간ᄒᆞ는신문지들의발포ᄒᆞ
는뎐보를보는사람들은그뎐보
에말ᄒᆞᆫ거슬미덧울수업도다
우리들의게오는소문은그실샤
에는조곰잇스면그ᄒᆡ에ᄃᆡᄒᆞ야졍
언부익ᄒᆞ되일본을위ᄒᆞ고로국
을반ᄃᆡᄒᆞ는말로윤ᄉᆡᆨᄒᆞ니ᄒᆡ본치
은져의ᄒᆡ이라그리ᄒᆞᆷ이ᄆᆡ이치
아니ᄒᆞ거니와류리뎐보와ᄯᅩ로
는ᄃᆡ등보에도다그러ᄒᆞᆫ이잇는거
시어셔ᄒᆞᆫ지라
요젼에우리의지금ᄒᆞ는말에징
거될일이잇스니ᄒᆡ구레젼쟁후
에동경ᄒᆞᆫ신문에론ᄒᆞᆫ뎐보들게
지ᄒᆞ엿는ᄃᆡ그뎐보에말ᄒᆞ되구
로팟긴대쟝이그리편박쟝군을
일반병의군사들쓰티엽시니버
린거스로칙망ᄒᆞ야과변ᄒᆞ엿다
ᄒᆞ며ᄯᅩ어ᄂᆞ곳스로도라ᄒᆞ오는소
국에도라가는거시구로팟긴의
[illegible]
ᄒᆞ는지라
아직ᄭᆞ지는우리의ᄉᆡᆼ각에는로
국편으로오는소문들이일본편
으로오는것들보다가히밋을만
ᄒᆞᆷ으로로국편의소문을거ᄒᆞᆫ즉
그리편박쟝군은그젼쟁되기젼
수일에셔나셔그젼쟁에는참셥
ᄒᆞ지아니ᄒᆞ엿다ᄒᆞ니우리는그
거시진실ᄒᆞᆫ다고밋으며그다음
에뎐보는거즛쇼그리편박쟝군
이어굿스코에셔대단히아리샤
누엇다ᄒᆞ엿스니그로보드리도
그쟝군이ᄒᆡ구레젼쟁에참예ᄒᆞ
지못ᄒᆞᆫ징거가되며ᄯᅩ리일이다
우리의ᄉᆡᆼ각에는그쟝군의젼디
로브리릭퇴거ᄒᆞᆫ거시병이ᄃᆡ단ᄒᆞ
샤ᄃᆞᆯ외에는다른일은아니거시
분명ᄒᆞ게되는도다그러ᄒᆞ나일
본신문들과뎐보들을보면그불
ᄒᆡᆼᄒᆞᆫ병이로국쟝군들사이에불
화ᄒᆞᆷ이되엿는지라
젼일에ᄒᆞᆫ일본쟝군이화쥬들과
음ᄒᆞ야죽엇다ᄒᆞ니만일그쟝군과
비로국쟝군이엿다면그쟝군이
는너머셔자결ᄒᆞ엿다는소문이
우리의게왓슬터이로다
ᄯᅩ그리ᄒᆞ고그리ᄒᆞ고그리ᄒᆞᆫ채
라약ᄒᆞᆫ친구들은우리들의게조
샹ᄒᆞ라고권ᄒᆞ는거시일본인을
박ᄃᆡᄒᆞ는거시오일본인을반ᄃᆡᄒᆞ
는거시로국인을위ᄒᆞ는거이오로국
을위ᄒᆞ며한국에는일본인의권
리를이러타는ᄭᆡ닷지못ᄒᆞ는사
ᄅᆞᆷ이엿다는지각잇는한인의소
견과우리도ᄒᆞᆼ상ᄒᆞ노라
그리ᄒᆞᆷ으로우리는한인의게자
긔들의리익과권리를ᄆᆡ셰기자
랑ᄒᆞ며만일그ᄉᆞ실을기논리라고권
ᄒᆞ노라
시나란톤마음노코소문듯는듸로미우리
중ᄒᆞᆫ리도들져ᄒᆡᆼ지니젼쟁의소
문은다반다시일본을지나셔한
국에오는고로한국은다만일본
이보내거나혹통ᄒᆞ기를허락ᄒᆞ
는소문들만듯고잇슴이로다

잡보

○이비불우　샹슈군슈리빈총
씨가너부로보고ᄒᆞ엿스되쳥비
이싱오명이본군월변니시궁예
츌몰ᄒᆞ는고로포군이싱명이주ᄃᆡ
졍티로졍협ᄒᆞ야슈셩방어ᄒᆞᆫ쳥
니작년헤산월변에셔괴ᄒᆞᆫ쳥국
비여당이샹조소취ᄒᆞ는뒤쳥국
병장졍차류명지는쳥명에셔초
환ᄒᆞᆫ다ᄒᆞ나번계이모가더욱민
망ᄒᆞᆫ지라하물며본군춍쥬들폐
지ᄒᆞ야쳘환ᄒᆞ오니번우들랍ᄒᆞ고월
이라산포일빙명을셜잉ᄒᆞ고
금을에산회하ᄒᆞ야새불우들에
비게ᄒᆞ라ᄒᆞ엿더라

UNION INSURANCE SOCIETY OF CANTON.

Head office Hongkong.
Marine risks underwritten at current rates.

Agents in Chemulpo,
E. MEYER & Co.

COMPAGNIE DES MESSAGERIES MARITIMES

Fortnightly Direct Service.

For Marseilles
via Ports.
Sailing from Yokohama
Calling at Kobe,
Shanghai, Hongkong, Saigon, Singapore,
Colombo, Djibonti, Suez, Port Said
and Marseilles.

For particulars apply to
HOLME RINGER & Co.,
Chemulpo.

HAYASHIDA & CO.,

16 MYENG DONG, CHIN KO KAI, SEOUL.
BRANCH OFFICE AT CHEMULPO.

Money changers, Coal and Wood Merchants, Express Agents.

We are agents for the Pyeng-yang Coal Company and the Karazu Coal Company of Japan. We have the best quality of both anthracite and bituminous coal, and prompt execution of orders is our speciality. Firewood of all kinds kept in stock. Full weight guaranteed. Money of all denominations exchanged at current rates. Parcels received for all parts.

CHINA MUTUAL LIFE INS. CO.

Most favourable terms to policy holders.

Benefit system unsurpassed.

HOLME RINGER & Co.
Agents, Chemulpo.

C. P. R.

CANADIAN PACIFIC RAILWAY COMPANY'S ROYAL MAIL STEAMSHIP LINE.

THE FAST ROUTE BETWEEN CHINA, JAPAN, AND EUROPE VIA CANADA AND THE UNITED STATES.

Route from Hongkong via Shanghai, Nagasaki (Inland Sea of Japan) Kobe, Yokohama, Victoria and Vancouver.

Twin Screw Empress Steamship—6,000 Tons—Speed 19 knots.

PROPOSED SAILING FROM YOKOHAMA.
R. M. S. Empress of India.
R. M. S. Empress of Japan.
R. M. S. Empress of China.
R. M. S. Athenian.
R. M. S. Tartar.

Special reduction (first class only) granted to members of the Military, Naval, Diplomatic and Civil services and to Missionaries.

Passengers have choice of ten routes across the Continent of America and have privilege of travelling by any Atlantic Steamship Line.

Round the World passage tickets in connection with the P. and O. S. N., North German Lloyd and Messageries Co.'s **£125**.

All rates payable at current rate of exchange.

For further information, Tickets, Guide Books, etc., apply to

HOLME, RINGER & Co., AGENTS,
Chemulpo.

Grand Hotel

(Formerly the Station Hotel)

Near the Railway Terminus, West Gate Seoul.

The Best Hotel in Korea.
Handsome new Building.
Fine Airy Rooms.
Excellent Cuisine.
Terms Moderate.
Special terms to Missionaries
and to permanent boarders.

Electric cars within 2 minutes' walk.

W. H. EMBERLEY.
Proprietor

EVERY FACILITY.

In connection with Life Assurance Business is afforded by

The Standard Life Assurance Co.,

One of the largest and wealthiest of the Provident Institutions of the United Kingdom Forms of Application and all information will be promptly afforded on application.

10 CENTS A DAY.

Not a very large expenditure is it? But it is ufficient to secure for a man of 30 a policy with he STANDARD LIFE OFFICE for

$1323.

For all particulars of rates, etc., apply to

Holme, Ringer & Co.,
Agents, Chemulpo.

THE NEW YORK LIFE INSURANCE COMPANY.

Have you ever been declined by any Company?

Are you engaged in a specially hazardous occupation?

Have you heard of the New York Life Insurance Company's New Classifications for this class of Risks?

If not, send your date of birth, occupation and particulars of rejection, if any to

E. MEYER & Co.,
Agents, Chemulpo.

MITSUI BUSSAN KAISHA.
(MITSUI & Co.)
MITSUI GINKO.
(MITSUI BANK.)

The Bank is owned by the members of the Mitsui Family, who, as partners, assume an unlimited responsibility for all liabilities of the Bank:—

Capital........................Yen 5,000,000
Reserve Fund.................. " 5,600,000

HEAD OFFICE, TOKYO.
LONDON OFFICE, 34 LIME ST., E. C.

BRANCHES AND AGENCIES:—
New York, San Francisco, Hamburg, Bombay, Singapore, Manila, Hongkong, Amoy, Chefoo, Tientsin.
Kobe, Hakodate, Yokohama, Kure, Yokosuka, Moji, Shimonoseki, Miike, Wakamatsu, Nagasaki, Kuchinotsu, Karatsu, Sasebo, Misume, Taipeh, &c.

Telegraphic Address for all the Offices:
"MITSUI."
A. B. C. AND A. 1 CODES USED.

Contractors of Coal
To the Imperial Japanese Navy, Arsenal and Railway Bureau, Principal Railway Companies and Industrial Work, Home and Foreign Mail and Freight Steamers.

Sole Proprietors
Of the famous Miike, Tagawa and Yamano Coal Mines.

Sole Agents
For the sale of Fukumo, Hokoku, Ichimura, Kanoda, Mannoura, Onoura, Ostuji, Sonoda, Tsubaruro, Yoshinotani, Yoshio, Yurokibura and other coals.

YANGTSE INSURANCE ASSOCIATION, LTD.

The undersigned, having been appointed agents for the above company, are prepared to issue policies and pay losses on marine risks at regular rates.

E. MEYER & Co.,
Agents, Chemulpo.

AMERICAN KOREAN ELECTRIC CO.

Light and Power.

Main Office: Electric Building, Chong No.

RAILWAY DEPARTMENT.

OPERATING CARS BETWEEN EAST AND WEST GATE, EVERY TEN MINUTES:—

First Car leaves East Gate at 7:00 A. M. First Car leaves R. R. Station at 7:25 A.M
Last Car " East Gate at 8.40 P. M. Last " " R. R. Station at 9.05 P.M

OPERATING CARS BETWEEN EAST GATE AND IMPERIAL TOMB TERMINUS, EVERY TWENTY MINUTES:—
CONNECTING WITH EVERY ALTERNATE CAR ARRIVING AT EAST GATE FROM CHONG NO.

First Car leaves East Gate for Tomb at 7:10 A. M.
" " Tomb for East Gate at 7:30 A. M.
Last " " East Gate for Tomb at 7:50 P. M.
" " " Tomb for East Gate at 8:10 P. M.

OPERATING CARS BETWEEN CHONG NO AND YUNG SAN RIVER EVERY TWELVE MINUTES:—

First Car leaves Chong No for South Gate at 7:12 A. M.
" " " Chong No for Yung San at 7:36 A. M.
" " " South Gate for Chong No at 7:20 A. M.
" " " Yung San for Chong No at 8:09 A. M.
Last " " South Gate for Chong No 9:00 P. M.
" " " Yung San for Chong No at 8.45 P. M.

SPECIAL PRIVATE CARS FURNISHED TO SUIT CONVENIENCE OF PATRONS. PRICES ON APPLICATION AT HEAD OFFICE.

LIGHTING DEPARTMENT.

Where less than 250 candle power of light is used, the rate per month will be
Per 16 candle power incandescent lamp,—All night.—Yen 2.50.
32 candle power incandescent lamp,—All night:—Yen 4.00.
50 candle power incandescent lamp,—All night:—Yen 6.00.
150 " " " " " " 10.00.
1200 " " enclosed arc " " " " 20.00.

Where more than 250 candle power of light is used, a Meter will be installed, if requested:—Rent of Meter, Yen 2.00 per month. Rate of charges by meter reading:—Two Sen per Ampere per hour. (Approximately this is equal to about One Sen per 16 C. P. lamp per hour) Minimum monthly charge where meter is installed, Yen 20.00 per month, which includes rental of meter.

Estimates for installing lights furnished on application
An assortment of chandeliers always on hand.

K. Murakami.
Photograph Studio
Chinkokai, Seoul.

Printing, Developing and Enlargement, of Photographs always Undertaken.

Korean Views and Pictures Illustrating Native Customs always on Sale,

---

THE OSAKA SHOSEN KAISHA.

Boats frequently on the berth for Chinnampo.

REGULAR SAILINGS BETWEEN JAPAN AND KOREAN PORTS.

FUSAN AND KOBE VIA SHIMONOSEKI.

OSAKA VIA MOKPO, FUSAN, SHIMONOSEKI AND KOBE.

MOJI DIRECT.

OSAKA VIA KUNSAN, MASANPO, FUSAN, SHIMONOSEKI AND KOBE.

CHEMULPO KUNSAN LINE,
Every three days.

CHEMULPO CHINNAMPO LINE.
Every three days.

For Freight and passage and further particulars apply to
THE OSAKA SHOSEN KAISHA,
Chemulpo.

RONDON, PLAISANT & CO.

General Storekeepers and Merchants, Ships Contractors Tobacconists, Commission and Forwarding Agents, Coal Merchants

IMPORTERS AND EXPORTERS

Seoul, Chemulpo.

W. D. WENTWORTH

LANDING
AND
SHIPPING AGENT.
AND
CUSTOMS BROKER.

12 OURA, NAGASAKI.

STEWARD & CO.

Chemulpo.

Shipchandlers and Storekeepers, Naval and Mercantile Contractors, Landing and Shipping Agents.

STEWARD'S HOTEL

Chemulpo.

Best accommodation in the port for travellers. Clean and well-aired rooms, good cuisine and prompt attendance, moderate tariff.

○회부사판 평리원에셔외부로조회ᄒᆞ기를관산민요사로일본사령부에셔작상ᄒᆞ야본원에송교ᄒᆞᆫ죄인응리금로일하오두시에졔회ᄒᆞᆫ리이니입본공관으로면죄ᄒᆞ야희원으로회등상관케ᄒᆞ라ᄒᆞ엿더라

○죵시박멸 이십일일오후삼시량에슈옥헌후츈방면에셔실화ᄒᆞ엿스나다ᄒᆡᆼ이곳박멸ᄒᆞ엿더라

○졍부기회 이십이일하오삼시에졍부에셔각대신이회동ᄒᆞ야샹긔회ᄒᆞ엿다더라

○우졍츄금 일본ᄉᆞ가ᄂᆡ부로공함ᄒᆞ엿스되젼경쥬군슈김윤관과젼평강군슈됴셩지의탐학쟝젼을취ᄒᆞᆫ등의계츄금홀수로임의함졍ᄒᆞ엿더니오히려머하ᄒᆞᆫ관리가무ᄒᆞᆫ고로ᄒᆞᆫ민이쇼소원ᄒᆞᄂᆞᆫ지라원쟝을졉견ᄒᆞ야보ᄂᆡ오니곳츄금ᄒᆞ라ᄒᆞᆫ지라비부에셔히량군슈를구관ᄒᆞ로법부에이죠ᄒᆞ엿더라

○경위반포 젼참졍신긔션씨의함남관찰수죠칙이환임되엿더니작일에다시반포ᄒᆞ엿다더라

○강창설소 한원관찰수죠죵필씨가ᄉᆞ직상소ᄒᆞ엿다더라

○군부관할 이십일일에리경ᄒᆞᆫ관제를곳반포ᄒᆞᆫ다더니분ᄂᆡ에군부관제를관쟝소에셔임의리정ᄒᆞ엿스니참모교육텽부도군부에셔일졔로관할ᄒᆞ기로신관제에편입ᄒᆞ야분이ᄂᆞᆫ경외ᄒᆞ야 주졔시ᄒᆡᆼᄒᆞ라ᄒᆞ옵셧다더라

○경건셜시 ᄂᆡ부에신에됴목과밋쳥견비가샹반원가량인티됴목과쳥견은경무쳥에셔ᄂᆞᆫ실시ᄒᆞᄂᆞᆫᄂᆡ부에셔ᄂᆞᆫ조금도실시가무ᄒᆞᆫ지라경무고문관환산씨가탁지부와교셥ᄒᆞ이희경비삼만원을경쳥으로지발ᄒᆞ라ᄒᆞ엿더라

○의관찰부리 경무관제를기졍ᄒᆞ야경무쳥에셔ᄂᆞᆫ오셔구역ᄂᆡ만경찰ᄒᆞ고ᄂᆡ부경무국에셔ᄂᆞᆫ각지방경찰을관할ᄒᆞᆫ다ᄒᆞ며각항구에도경무관을두시ᄒᆞ고며관찰부경찰셔를의ᄒᆞ야총순을셜치ᄒᆞᆫ다더라

○나시쳥령 광주부에셔민소를인ᄒᆞ야김의셥을착수ᄒᆞ엿더니참령김원계씨가자긔의친족을착수ᄒᆞ엿다ᄒᆞ고하수금병뎡이명을파송ᄒᆞ야광주부쳥리를무수난타ᄒᆞ며죄친젼사빙여랑을탈취ᄒᆞ고죄인을탈거ᄒᆞᆫ수건으로간샹이탈로ᄒᆞ야룩군법원에셔김참령을나치ᄒᆞᆫ다더라

○부로단속 각국ᄉᆞ가외부와중대ᄉᆞ안을교셥ᄒᆞ면리쳐로쥬셜ᄒᆞ야ᄒᆡᆼ문ᄒᆞᆫ지이ᄂᆞᆫᄂᆡ근비밀문셰계졍ㅣ되ᄂᆞᆫ지라일본ᄉᆞ가신외부를향ᄒᆞ야신민리히못ᄒᆞᆫ깃슬쳡무ᄒᆞ엿고법미남광ᄉᆞ수도교셥교부안ᄒᆞ비밀히ᄒᆞᄂᆞᆫ긔ᄒᆞᆷ의외부아케관과협판이부로를단속ᄒᆞ게엄ᄒᆞᆫ다더라

○국졍잉임 경무국쟝김사묵씨가궁ᄂᆡ긔임ᄒᆞᆫ다ᄒᆞᆷ으로신경무사가상주ᄒᆞ야길ᄋᆞ되국쟝은차인안이면불가ᄒᆞ다ᄒᆞ고또이유ᄒᆞ수지시를당ᄒᆞ야기직을잉임ᄒᆞ야경찰지휘을의면케ᄒᆞ옵소셔ᄒᆞ야쳐분을봉승ᄒᆞ엿더라

○조졍변셔 일본공ᄉᆞ가외부로조회ᄒᆞ엿스되부산에주재ᄒᆞᆫ우리령ᄉᆞ가품ᄒᆞ엿스되젼교주시회사등수년젼에귀졍부의인허를득ᄒᆞ야착챠ᄒᆞ지음에뭇지로셜립ᄒᆞ야착쳥ᄒᆞ니진보ᄒᆞ더니공과의소괴로인ᄒᆞ아다시각쳘주로셜립코자ᄒᆞᄂᆞᆫ바ᄃᆡ목하젼시에빌다ᄒᆞ아희ᄉᆞ셜슈의비용이과ᄃᆡᄒᆞ오니ᄒᆞ얏수입홀세에등변ᄒᆞ후면귀ᄒᆞ켸ᄒᆞ라ᄒᆞ엿고오유ᄒᆞᆫ지라졍부에셔미등권이신시ᄒᆡᆼᄒᆞ라ᄒᆞ엿더라

○합졍민됴 일본공ᄉᆞ가외부로조회ᄒᆞ엿스되원산에주재ᄒᆞᆫ우리령ᄉᆞ가품ᄒᆞ엿스되쇼학교가셜립ᄒᆞ야셔뒤산에잇셔경ᄒᆞ교ᄃᆡ나리ᄃᆡ에관유민유디도와민유ᄃᆡ도잇ᄂᆞᆫ티디ᄂᆞᆫ갑을리셕ᄒᆞ엿미ᄒᆞᆫ티비ᄂᆞᆫ관유티ᄂᆞᆫ귀졍부에셔에ᄂᆞᆫ쳔민이못ᄒᆞ더니쳥권티휘관유티ᄂᆞᆫ우리터규민의소학교에영ᄒᆞ쳥ᄒᆞᆫ다ᄒᆞ기를ᄎᆞ지ᄒᆞ라ᄒᆞ엿더라

○외대부진 외부대신리하영씨ᄂᆞᆫ신병으로연일ᄉᆞ진치못ᄒᆞᆫ다더라

○금리발령 육구참리김교헌씨ᄂᆞᆫ본일ᄉᆞ로작일ᄂᆡ발ᄒᆞ엿더라

○희저면셤 돌산군슈가본군에보고ᄒᆞ엿스되본군삼산면수원면보쳔원에셔일본인이삼산면에셩쳐ᄒᆞ야일본파졔주와인이희에교ᄒᆞ야통신ᄒᆞᆫ다ᄒᆞ기로자에보고ᄒᆞ엿더라

○군제지하 군제의졍은작일시벽에안보ᄒᆞ야졔하ᄒᆞ엿더라

○관제주하 관제리졍은어제밤에주하ᄒᆞ엿다더라

○교쟝피임 유년학교쟝우죵철씨가피임ᄒᆞ엿다더라

○지회찬회 일진회에셔평안도회민의계지회ᄒᆞ되회민셩만명가량이강계로회집ᄒᆞ라ᄒᆞ엿더라

○한위사쳠파 군부에셔평북도관찰수의계훈령ᄒᆞ엿더라 한위사를쳠파ᄒᆞ라ᄒᆞ고평안북도

○일수페현 관제와군제가의졍됨으로졍츙ᄉᆞ졍기쳔에진보에와밋셔긔관이셩취홈이라일본수작일ᄒᆞᆫ관이차를위ᄒᆞ야폐현ᄒᆞ엿다더라

○군제반포 명일군제의졍이됴보에반포될이라더라

○츈찰샹소 츈쳔관찰ᄉᆞ됴죵필씨ᄂᆞᆫ사직소를샹ᄒᆞ엿더라

○노동자구졔 일젼에룩군부쟝관윤웅렬씨가동대문안으로부터면거를타고종로를향ᄒᆞ야리힝ᄒᆞᆯ시ᄒᆞᆫ노동자ㅣ군부쟝의게향ᄒᆞ야걸ᄋᆞ되ᄂᆡ빈을죵을붓지자ᄒᆞ거날군부쟝이ᄃᆡ답ᄒᆞ야걸으ᄃᆡᄂᆡ가년금칠십이어ᄂᆞᆯ비졔지감히무례ᄒᆞᆫ냐ᄒᆞ고인젼에죵로헌에도챡ᄒᆞ야헌병을초치ᄒᆞ야일본헌병샤령부에셔교용ᄒᆞᄂᆞᆫ자ㅣ라ᄒᆞᆫ관압부ᄒᆞ엿더니그놈은일본헌병ᄒᆞᆫ명이헌병티고잇ᄂᆞᆫ남일본헌병ᄒᆞᆫ명이헌병ᄒᆞᆫ관사령부에셔교용ᄒᆞᄂᆞᆫ자ㅣ라ᄒᆞᆫ인은곳우리도ᄒᆞ야골으ᄃᆡ작일착ᄒᆞᄂᆞᆫ사ᄅᆞᆷ인ᄃᆡ엇지감히챡수ᄒᆞ나냐곳방송ᄒᆞ라ᄒᆞ고히헌병이곳헌병사령관남셩환씨가에왕ᄒᆞ야힐졔ᄒᆞ고갓다더라

○조졍지발 영국공ᄉᆞ가외부로조회ᄒᆞ엿스되히주쳥샹외손ᄒᆞ셩빈샹인사ᄂᆞᆫ임의면관료안ᄒᆞ엿거니와힝빈샹금이쳔칠빅룩원을곳지발ᄒᆞ야본샤의게분급ᄒᆞ교부ᄒᆞ야응슈홀사ᄅᆞᆷ의게분급ᄒᆞ케ᄒᆞᄂᆞᆫ티편리케ᄒᆞ라ᄒᆞ엿더라

○조쳥명괴 왜대리공사가외부로조회ᄒᆞ엿스되쯘리로회사의귀광사ᄂᆞᆫ그소수죠관과밋자의경을귀대신의의견을응쥰ᄒᆞᆯ터이니쳥컨티승허ᄒᆞ명괴ᄒᆞ야면ᄒᆞ외라겨ᄒᆞ기에편케ᄒᆞ라ᄒᆞ엿더라

○사셩피샹 셔산군수가외부로보고ᄒᆞ엿스되본군동암면한셩평에음력졍월일에하히ᄒᆞᆫ일인표를세우고갓다ᄒᆞ기로덕간ᄒᆞᆫ즉과연표목총쥬를세웟ᄂᆞᆫ티일인면중의졍형ᄒᆞᆫ티단이라보고쓴져라ᄒᆞ이셩취파샹ᄒᆞ기로ᄒᆞ엿더라

○외부쳥의 외부쳥의셔에젼ᄂᆡ의관양ᄒᆞ믁은외무에등련ᄒᆞ오공사관샹등참셔관을임ᄒᆞᆯ안건을회의에졔출ᄒᆞ라ᄒᆞ엿더라

관보

뎨삼쳔칠십삼호 광무구년
이월이십삼일

셔임급사령

○임함경남도관찰사 셔칙임관삼등 룩군부쟝 신긔션

○임궁ᄂᆡ부특진관 셔주임관룩등 룩품 리병헌

○의원면본관 단양군수 셔상우 음쥭군수 리범하 광양군수 됴례셕 광주군수 권즁은 즁츄원의관 홍승관 즁츄원의관 김쥬룡 즁츄원의관 박쥬헌 최인식 즁츄원의관 심승틱 한셩사범학교교관 영션 농샹공학교셔기 김

○면본관 젹셩군수 리규회 쳥풍군수 리덕상 금산군수 리흥셩 한산군수 리현두 령창군수 김기수 연양군수 명하현 동ᄂᆡ군수 명영표 진희군수 박긍희 강녕군수 리셕원

○임광주군수서주임관일등 종이품 리용션

○임평양군수서주임관일등 종이품 됴동완

○임영쳔군수서주임관이등 서산군수 서명철

○임서산군수서주임관륙등 시강원시종 김영진

○임김히군수서주임관일등 정삼품 리최션

○임진주군수서주임관륙등 정삼품 민병셕

○임금산군수서주임관륙등 륙품 민우호

○임김제군수서주임관일등 정삼품 됴례셕

○임광양군수서주임관사등 금산군수 류제관

○임산청군수서주임관륙등 륙품 리계틱

○임거제군수서주임관륙등 륙품 윤상우

○임금쳔군수서주임관륙등 평양군수 김희수

○임중추원의관서주임관륙등 정삼품 김진우 정삼품 지용 군부주사 리보현 구장룡

○임한성사범학교교관서주임관륙등 강기의

○임한셩사범학교부교관셔판임관륙등 쳔명수

○승서관임관사등 덕원항공립소학교교원 리중은

○의원면본관 군기창기수 한규영 군기창기수 권병철 시종원시종 리룡호 경흥감리서주사 권평철

○임군기창기수서판임관륙등 서승관 쳔셕순 리희승

○임군부주사서판임관륙등 구품 안경렬

○승서판임관륙등 평양기사장 충승 홍병은

○명궁ᄂᆡ부소관사원 사무분부도위원 궁ᄂᆡ부참서관 김용셔제 상흥 궁ᄂᆡ부주사 김진현 ○이상이월이십일일 외부주사 김봉선

○명법부법률기초위원장 부협판 김규희

○명법부법률기초위원장 법부협판 리근상 ○이상이월이십일일

○명경상남도세무감 경상남도관찰사 진주군수 안긴근 평리원 진주소관역 조세관 률규

○임경흥감리서주사서판임관륙등 남정신 외부주사

TELEGRAMS.

FROM THE "JAPAN CHRONICLE."

Note. The messages marked* are those which are described as "special service" or "special telegrams or "received by the Government." The others are from properly authenticated sources.

RUSSIAN AFFAIRS.

London, Feb. 17.

*The Grand Duke Sergius, Governor-General of Moscow and uncle of the Tsar, has been assassinated.

He was driving from the Kremlin when a bomb was thrown under his carriage. The bomb exploded, and the Grand Duke was killed instantly.

London, Feb. 16.

A Cabinet Council has been hastily summoned by the premier and met last night.

While no definite information is obtainable, it is rumoured in parliamentary circles that the Council is connected with peace prospects.

THE BRITISH GOVERNMENT.

London, Feb. 17.

The amendment to the Address, proposed by Mr. Asquith declaring that the time has arrived for submitting the fiscal issue to the electorate, has been rejected by 311 votes to 248.

Mr. Joseph Chamberlain, who took part in the debate, said he himself would welcome a dissolution of Parliament at once, and declared that no difference of opnion existed between the Premier and himself regarding the need for fiscal reform.

Mr. A. J. Balfour, the Premier, replying to the criticisms of the Opposition, repeated his previous arguments in favour of Retaliation, and declared that these threats had already had a good effect on the commercial policy of other nations. If the country at the next election gave the present Government the manadate for which it asked, he believed that without having to make any changes in the matter of taxes, the country would be saved a vast number of commercial outrages from which she now suffered.

Mr. Hayashi left for Fusan to-day in order to meet Mrs. Hayashi who is expected from Japan.

On account of sickness, the Minister for Foreign Affairs has not been at his office for several days.

The adherents of the American Mission in Pyeng Yang are about to establish a school for the blind in that city.

We are told that the Crown Princess elect, the daughter of Mr. Soh Pyengsun, is 16 years of age and of virtuous behaviour.

The Il-chin-hoi people are now pestering the magistrates of Pechon and Shinchon who have written to Seoul for instructions.

There was a slight outbreak of fire in the Ham-perk hall of the palace yesterday but it was, fortunately, immediately extinguished.

An amount of $30,000 appears in the budget as set apart for engineering and scavenging operations to be carried out by the Home Department. Mr. Marayama, the police adviser, has got his eye on this nice little sum and is agitating for its transfer to his department.

The "Kanjo Shimpo" inveighs against the action of Messrs. Chŏng Pyŏng-wan, Yun Ton-kon and 29 other signatories in issuing a circular protesting against the Japanese loan. This action is a contravention of a law laid down by a Mr. Takayama, chief of the Japanese gendarmes, prohibiting the formation of political or other societies, so, according to the "Kanjo," the offenders have been brought to book.

SHOT GUN ACCIDENT IN CHFOO.

A sad accident occurred yesterday, says the "Chefoo Daily News" of Feb. 15, to Dr. Hill who has lately arrived here from Korea. Dr. Hill and two companions, two young gentlemen of this town, were out in the harbor duck-shooting yesterday morning and they had a nice time of it the weather being bright and plenty of ducks about. The company was just discussing the possibility of a gun going off when cocked, without the trigger being touched, when a report was heard and Dr. Hill tumbled over crying out that he was shot. He had the gun standing just beside him the muzzle pointing at his upper left arm when it went off. The shot went through the fleshy part of the arm just below the shoulder happily without injuring the bone. The wound itself, however, was a nasty one causing a considerable loss of blood. Dr. Hill himself assisted at the preliminary dressing of the wound, being conscious the whole time in spite of the intense pain and the loss of blood. After half an hours' pulling the company landed, and the unfortunate gentleman was brought to the General Hospital where he was attended to by the local Doctors. The wound is said to be of a somewhat serious nature but there is good hope that the patient will recover the use of his arm.

The Loochoo islands have been visited by a severe famine and great distress prevails.

The United States Naval Bill provides for the construction of two additional battleships for the navy.

The attention of members of the Seoul Club is called to the Annual General Meeting which takes place on Monday at 5.30 P. M.

Governor Trepoff has warned some of the foreign correspondents in St. Petersburg that they will be deported if they continue to send out sensational telegrams.

The bridge over the Han River on the Seoul-Chemulpo Railway is in a very shaky condition and repairs are necessary. A temporary wooden bridge is being built to accomodate the traffic in the meantime.

The Minister for Foreign affairs hsa petitioned the cabinet that Mr. Yang Hong Muk, who is well qualified, be appointed 3rd Secretary to some Legation abroad. What Korea wants with more than one secretary at any of its Legations we do not know.

A telegram received by the "Osaka Mainichi" from Seoul, dated Feb. 7th states that it is reported that Yi Yong-yik, who has been intriguing against the interests of Japan since his return to Korea from Tokio, will shortly be sent back to Japan, or be given a position in some remote Korean province.

The Tokio "Jiji" although not entirely rejecting the story of the sale of the Argentine navy to Japan, considers that its truth is very doubtful. The Argentine Republic might sell one or two vessels, it says, but that it should dispose of its whole fleet is not credible, in view of its relations with Chile.

The railway work between Fusan and Masampo is, accoring to a Japanese report, progressing satisfactorily, but the construction of tunnels will take at least another three months. The opening to traffic of the branch line of the Seoul-Fusan Railway will therefore not take place before the end of May next.

According to a Peking despatch it is reported there that eight French warships have proceeded to Tonking Bay and over ten torpedo boats to the Hingho (the Red river) on the pretext that they are required as a guard against the insurgents in Kwangsi and Yunnan. The construction of the French railway between Yunnan and Monji will be finished by April next, when it will be connected with the Chinese Yunnan railway,

THE DAI-ICHI BANK.

In response to our request we have very courteously been favoured with the following statement of notes in circulation and reserve funds held by the bank in Korea :—

	Notes in Circulation	Specie Reserve
Seoul	1,924,436.20	1,260,000.00
Chemulpo	255,861.20	200,000.00
Fusan	645,254.20	330,000.00
Mokpo	96,845.20	50,000.00
Chinnampo	174,676.40	100,000.00
Kunsan	107,391.10	60,000.00
Total	3,204,464.30	2,000,000.00

There is also a reserve, in various securities amounting to Y1,826,000.00.

Geneval Mischenko reports that General Kondratovitch's wounds are serious.

According to a London telegram of Jan. 31st Russia is negotiating for the construction of warships in England, Germany and the United States.

Governor von Semmer, the successor of Governor Truppel during the latter's absence in Europe, has arrived at Tsingtau asumed his duties.

Smallpox has broken out in the city of Osaka, several cases being reported. The disease is said to be of a virulent type, and vigorous measures are being taken by the authorities to stamp it out.

We learn from the Chefoo Daily News that the sea at Chinwangtao is frozen for a mile out. This affords some idea of the degree of cold being experienced there.

According to the crew of a German steamer, which left Vladivostok on the 11th instant, that place is now completely fortified and there are over ten warships and torpedo boats in the harbour.

The magistrate of Tolsan (South Chulla province) reports to the Foreign Office that the Japanese have announced that they will lay a cable through his district in order to connect Quelpart with Chemulpo.

The Osaka Iron Work has lately employed about ten Chinese workmen and is in favour of an increase of their number, claiming that the result of their work is better than that of Japanese employees.

According to the Peking correspondent of the "Nichi Nichi," it is stated that M. Leasar, Russian Minister to China, will be recalled shortly. The correspondent of the Kokumin also makes the same assertion.

Mr. Uchida, Japanese Minister in Peking, called on Price Ching on the 9th and gave him several warnings in regard to the neutral question and other affairs, says the "Nichi Nichi's" correspondent in the Chinese capital.

Passengers who arrived at Chefoo by the "Sushun" on her last trip accross from Chemulpo have given the rather disturbing information that the steamer passed within fifty yards of a floating mine at a point about five hours steaming south of Chefoo.

According to a report from Europe the action of Germany in withdrawing her troops from the Russian frontier has released 50,000 Russian soldiers of a very high standard. These men were immediately despatched for the front and should be at Mukden by now.

A report is current that, at his last audience with the Emperor, the Japanese Minister accused the Korean Government with having opened negotiations in order to place themselves under the protection of another foreign power. It is not clear how this has leaked out as Mr. Hayashi always insists on the exclusion of all Koreans when he is receiv-ed in audience but we can readily understand that the Government feels that any *regime* would be preferable to the present one.

AMERICAN CAPITAL IN JAPAN.

It has been recently announced that the General Electric Company of America, whose principal manufacturing plant is located at Schenectady, New York, has become interested in the Tokyo Electric Co. Ltd, of Tokyo, a concern which manufactures incandescent electric lamps.

This amalgamation of Japanese and American capital will no doubt prove to be beneficial to the users of electric light in Japan.

These lamps are now to be made in Japan under the Edison patents owned by the General Electric Co., and the same methods which have produced such high efficiency in this particular class of work in America, are to be used here.

We learned that Mr. George Denny, the correspondent for the "Associated Press" and Mr. Richard H. Little of the "Chicago Daily News" (formerly on the "Tawan") who were both at the front with the Russian Army in Manchuria, have now left for home.

The magistracy of Kyŏng Chow, (north Kyong Sang province) has been vacant for a long time and the reason for this has at last come to light. It appears that this position is a particularly fat one and there are no fewer than sixteen applicants for the job. The bidding for it started at about $50,000, has now reached $200,000 and as it is expected to go higher still our reporter quaintly informs us that no one has yet been recommended to the Emperor for the position.

The "Nichi Nichi" states that Major Ohara, the Chief of the Military Administration Office at Antung, has recently offered several experienced educationists at Tokyo the positions of teachers at a school which is to be shortly established at Antung by the authorities and which will be devoted to the teaching of the Japanese language and general education. In view of China's promise to open Antung to foreign commerce, it is said that measures have also been taken, in co-operation with the Chinese authorities, to prepare for the event, and the town, especially the Japanese settlement, now presents a much improved appearance.

The Korea Daily News.

Issued at 5 P. M. daily except Sundays.

Rate of Subscription:—
Per Year,............Yen 25.
Per Quarter,..........Yen 7.
Per Month,..........Yen 2.50.

Postage in Korea not charged extra.
Postage abroad charged extra.

Advertisements, 50 sen per day for 1 inch or less.
5 yen per month per inch.
50 yen per year per inch.

All communications to

E. T. BETHELL,
Editor and Publisher,
Pak-tong, Seoul.

A FORECAST.

The *sang froid* of the Japanese commands admiration. From Japan's newspapers and from the demeanour of her responsible men none would believe that Japan had staked her all on one throw of the dice—and lost.

And yet such appears to be the case. From the beginning of the war until last mid-summer when successes were falling into Japan's lap like apples, the whole world took her at her own valuation, and Port Arthur, Vladivostok and Harbin were taken for granted as only modest preliminaries to a programme which was to astonish and shake the whole world.

We were portentiously given to understand, by means of vague hints, and "the wink is as good as a nod" process, that another bubble was about to be pricked. Remembering the events of 1894-5 and taking for granted another walk over in 1904-5, simple people even commenced to speculate upon what new country Japan would conquer in 1914-5.

And yet, what has Japan accomplished? It is true that Port Arthur capitulated, but the cost of the reduction was such that it will never again be attempted either there or elsewhere. Instead of attacking Vladivostok the Japanese are taking steps to defend Gensan and the army destined for Harbin is now being driven back after having taken over six months to advance to a point fifteen miles north of Liaoyang.

We are of course now given to understand that the Japanese army never intended to proceed any further north than the point it has now reached, but a glance at the map will dispel this illusion. Mischenko's recent raid demonstrated the vulnerability of Oyama's main communications and the movements of the Russian troops at and near Hangchang, to the east of the Japanese right wing are a constant menace to Kuroki's communications between Motienling and the Yalu.

Apparently it is the efficiency of the trans-Siberian Railway that has upset all Japan's calculations, and the Russians have indeed achieved wonders in this direction. But the failure of Japan's emissaries to wreck the line in the earlier stages of the war is a matter for great surprise. Recently, an expert on Manchuria, who knows the whole railway thoroughly, told us that had the Boers been fighting the Russians the line would have hopelessly wrecked in twenty or thirty places in very short order.

However, the fact remains that Japan has shot her bolt; and yet, on the surface, there is nothing, in Korea to indicate that Japan does not consider herself complete master of the situation. With all the assurance in the world the Japanese representatives continue to make claim after claim on the Korean Government. New advisers are continually coming and the advocacy of "reforms" is so persistent, that in spite of knowledge that the reverse is the case, one is almost persuaded to believe that the Japanese are certain of their continued tenure of the country.

But, the talk of peace having now fizzled out it appears that Russia is only just commencing. By dint of concessions to the reasonable people and the adoption of repressive measures with the revolutionists, Russia will soon set her country in order again and will then, it appears, be able to maintain in Manchuria an army at least half as large again as the Japanese.

It has taken the Japanese a year to advance to where they are now, and unless something unforseen happens we imagine it will take the Russians about a year to reverse the process.

JAPAN AND KOREA.

(WEDNESDAY, FEBRUARY 1ST.)

The "Japan Mail" this morning again recurs to the Nagamori scheme, which it apparently regards as a philanthropic venture which was killed by the foreign critics. Mr. Nagamori's scheme is compared to the work of reclamation being performed in Egypt by the construction of the Nile dams and to the proposals for reclamation work in the valley of the Euphrates. Our contemporary, however, appears to be playing with words, not dealing with facts. We have yet to hear that Mr. Nagamori proposed to construct any large irrigation works, or even that the land was waste because of the lack of irrgation. In fact we have always understood that the term "waste lands" as applied to the said land in Korea meant something quite different to unreclaimed land. Mr. Nagamori did not propose to reclaim the land; he proposed to bring it under cultivation, a very different matter, which at once raises the questions, why has it gone out of cultivation or has it never been cultivated. The answers to these questions, as we can learn, is that the land has been cultivated and that it has gone out of cultivation on account of the high taxes and squeezes by the officials not enabling the farmers to make a profit. Thus Mr. Nagamori's scheme practically amounts to taking advantage of the official corruption in Korea to get a lease of tillable land for a long period of years. No doubt Mr. Nagamori was not entirely actuated by philanthropic motives, just the same as the foreign merchants in Japan, according to the "Mail," are not actuated by philanthropic motives in conducting business in this country. If the question of the supply of rice is such a serious one surely the best way for the Japanese to secure its cultivation in Korea is to make it worth the Korean farmer's while to grow it by forcing the Korean Government to make administrative reforms. Of course if the Japanese secured a lease of the land, with the support of their Government behind them they could successfully fight against any attempts at extortion on the part of the Korean authorities, but surely it is hardly right for them to take advantage of their superior position to oust the Korean farmer. The Japanese is a foreigner in Korea—at present at all events—and the editor of the "Japan Mail," who has a very keen sense for foreign aggression, would do well to appreciate this fact. Mr. Yokoi's scheme for the encouragement of Japanese emigration to Korea, also referred to by the "Mail," is on all fours with Mr. Nagamori's scheme. Surely, under the circumstances, a more extraordinary proposal was never made. Imagine Russia, say, putting forward a proposal for the encouragement of Russian emigration to Japan. Would the "Mail" view this with quite so much equanimity? It is true that the editor wisely refrains from expressing any opinion as to whether any such scheme is feasible or not, but when he goes on to talk of emigration as "an instrument of economical and imperial expansion as approved and practiced by all the Western States," one can guess what his opinion would be if he expressed it. It is true that there have unfortunately been cases where expansion has been carried out by means of emigration, but the "Mail" would find it hard to point to a case where a Government assists its nationals to emigrate to another country, unless it does so in the method of Russia. If the inhabitants of Korea were a savage race, who were unable to get the full value from the soil, then there might be some excuse for taking possession of the land. But we have yet to hear that this is the case. As a matter of fact Mr. Yokoi gives his hand away when he talks of Korea being furnished, through emigration from Japan, with a population which would serve effectively to guard her integrity and independence.—Japan Herald.

MR. MEGATA.

Mr. Megata, interviewed in Tokio by the "Shogye Shimpo," professess to be very optimistic about this country. He says that there is no occasion to be in a hurry about Korean reform. The time has fortunately come when the interference of other countries has ceased to impede Japan's efforts. As to the Koreans themselves, Mr. Megata seems to think that one of their great faults is love of academical formalities and neglect of practical facts.

We certainly agree with Mr. Megata as to the Koreans' neglect of practical facts. Otherwise they would never have allowed him to impose his celebrated $3,000,000 loan on them. How fortunate it was that Mr. Megata left Korea before the agitation against his loan arose.

In a contribution to the report issued by the Director-General of the Navy Department, the staff-surgeon of H. M. ship Thetis draws attention to the dangers of tattooing. He cites a case in which there was every reason to believe that one of the ship's stokers contracted disease from being tattooed at Wei-hai-wei, and recommends anyone who has himself tattooed, whether in the China Seas or elsewhere, to make sure that the operation is performed with properly sterilised needles. The precaution is obviously such an impossible one in many of the cases in which persons of higher social status than stokers subject themselves to the process while on a visit to Chinese or Japanese ports, that it is a great deal wiser to forego the experience altogether. A Japanese Nature-study on the forearm is rather dearly bought at the price of a severe attack of blood-poisoning, and this is no uncommon consequence of its acquisition.

The Korea Daily News.

VOL. II, FRIDAY, FEBRUARY 24, 1905. No. 42

HONGKONG & SHANGHAI BANKING CORPORATION.

Paid-up Capital.....	$10,000,000
Reserve Fund:—Sterling Reserve...	10,000,000
Silver Reserve.....	7,000,000
	27,000,000
Reserve Liability of Proprietors...	10,000,000

HEAD OFFICE, HONGKONG.

London Bankers, London and County Banking Company Limited.

Branches and Agencies,

London.

Amoy,	Hankow	Penang,
Bangkok	Hiogo,	Rangoon,
Batavia,	Iloilo,	Saigon,
Bombay,	Lyons,	San Francisco,
Calcutta,	Manila,	Singapore,
Colombo,	Nagasaki,	Sourabaya,
Foochow,	New York,	Tientsin,
Hamburg,	Peking,	Yokohama,

Credits granted on approved Securities, and every description of Banking and Exchange business transacted.

Drafts granted on London and the chief Commercial places in Europe, India, Australia, America, China and Japan.

HOLME RINGER & CO., AGENTS,
CHEMULPO.

HOKURKU DOBOKU KAISHA.

Branch office in Chong Doug, Seoul.

Japanese telephone No. 165

CONTRACT DEPARTMENT.

We can contract to build any building or construction.

MERCHANDISE DEPARTMENT.

We can provide any building material. We have just contracted to build the new Belgian Legation.

E. MEYER & CO.

Chemulpo.

SOLE AGENTS IN KOREA FOR.

A. T. Morse, Sons & Co.'s

"Fresco" Distemper

In all colours ready for use on walls, Ceilings etc.

and

AVENARIUS CARBOLINEUM

A wood-preserving and antiseptic oil preparation

Against decay, dry-rot, fungus and wood-destroying insects.

A large supply always in stock.
Prices upon application.

E. MEYER & Co.,
Chemulpo.

CHARTERED BANK OF INDIA AUSTRALIA & CHINA.

INCORPORATED BY ROYAL CHARTER 1853

HEAD OFFICES.—LONDON.

Paid-up Capital	£800,000
Reserve Liability of Share-holders	800,000
Reserve Fund	800,000

Drafts granted upon all the principal places in the world and every description of Exchange and banking business transacted.

E. MEYER & Co., Agents,
Chemulpo.

MITSU BISHI DOCKYARD & ENGINE WORKS,

NAGASAKI.

CODE WORD, "DOCK."

A 1, A. B. C., and Engineering Codes used.

DOCK No. 1 (at Tategami).

Extreme Length..............	523 feet
Length on blocks	513 ,,
Width of Entrance on Top......	89 ,,
,, ,, Bottom....	77 ,,
Water on Blocks at Spring Tide	26½ ,,

DOCK No. 2 (Mukaijima).

Extreme Length..............	371 feet
Length on Blocks............	360 ,,
Width of Entrance on Top......	66 ,,
,, ,, Bottom	53 ,,
Water on Blocks at Spring Tide	22 ,,

PATENT SLIP (at Kosuge).

Can take vessels up to 1,000 tons gross

THE WORKS are well equipped with the LATEST IMPROVEMENTS, and can execute any kind of work in SHIPBUILDING and MARINE ENGINEERING, as well as in REPAIRING of SHIPS.

The COMPANY'S new powerful steamer OURA-MARU (712 tons, 700 I.H.P.), specially built for SALVAGE PURPOSES, and equipped with necessary gear, is always READY at SHORT NOTICE.

THE METHODIST PUBLISHING HOUSE,

Little West Gate, Seoul.

JOB PRINTING, TYPEWRITER PAPER
CARBON PAPER, VISITING CARDS
STATIONERY, BOOK BINDING
BOOK PUBLISHERS
AMERICAN SCHOOL BOOKS
SPENCERIAN COPY BOOKS
PEN CARBON LETTER AND BILL BOOKS

S. A. BECK, Manager.

DAI-ICHI GINKO.

LIMITED.

(Formerly the First National Bank)

ESTABLISHED 1873

INCORPORATED UNDER PRESENT LAW 1896

Capital - - - - - - - - -	Yen 5,000,000
Reserve Fund - . - - -	1,500,000

HEAD OFFICE:—TOKIO.

President: Baron SHIBUSAWA.

BRANCHES AND CORRESPONDENTS
In the Principal Cities and Towns of Japan.

Interest Allowed on

Fixed deposits 1 year - - -	6½	per cent
" " 6 months - - -	6	per cent

Special current accounts 1½ sen daily per Y 100
General " " 1 " " " 100

M. TANAKA,
Manager, Chemulpo.

SINGER SEWING

MACHINES

씽거즈봉침

SOLE AGENTS FOR KOREA

젼매쇼

HOLME RINGER & CO.
Chemulpo.

제물포 함릉거양힝

KAMEYA & CO.

GENERAL STOREKEEPERS

Chinkokai - - Seoul

(Established 1895, Tokyo)

Confectionery, Hams, Canned Goods, Cutlery, Hirano & Tansan Water. Provisions, Gents, Furnishing goods, Toilet Articles, Travelling Bags, Tobacco, Cigars & Cigarettes Kitchen Utensils. Coffee, Biscuits

Fresh Goods always kept in Stock.
Prices Moderate
Please come and inspect our goods.

NIPPON YUSEN KAISHA.
JAPANESE MAIL STEAMSHIP CO.

UNDER MAIL CONTRACT WITH THE IMPERIAL JAPANESE GOVERNMENT.

European Line

Regular Fortnightly Service between Yokohama Kobe, Moji, Shanghai, Hongkong, Singapore, Penang Colombo, Port Said, Marseilles, London and Antwerp

American Line

Regular Fortnightly Service between Hongkong and Seattle, calling at Shanghai, Moji, Kobe, Yokohama and Victoria, B. C.

Australian Line

Regular weekly Service betwen Japan Ports and Australia, calling at Hongkong and Manila.

(Above Three Lines Suspended until further noticed)

Shanghai Line

Weekly Service between Shanghai and Japan Po

Korea Line

Service Kobe, Moji, Nagasaki, Fusan Chemulpo, Chefoo, Taku.

S. S. Babelsberg, 2181 tons.

Service Kobe. Moji, Fusan, Chemulpo, Chinnam

S. S. ARGO, S. S. Ohio.

BORDEN'S CONDENSED MILK CO.

New York, U. S. A.

ALWAYS IN STOCK

Eagle Brand Condensed Milk.

Gold Seal Condensed Milk.

Peerless (Family) Evaporated Cream.

Borden's Malted Milk.

E. MEYER & CO.
Chemulpo Korea,
Sole Agents

ROYAL INSURANCE COMPANY,
Funds exceed £10,000,000

FIRE

AT CURRENT RATES

LIFE

REDUCED PREMIUM,
HOLME RINGER & Co.,
Agents, Chemulpo

廣
KWANG ◉ C'HANG
昌

BENNETT & CO.
Merchants
Chemulpo.

Offices opposite the Imperial Japanese Post and Telegraph Office Chemulpo.

Telephone Number 201.

大韓每日申報

대한미일신보

(뎨이쳔ᄉᆞ십삼호)　(월요일)　일쳔구빅오년이월이십칠일

본사고빅

이신보는영어와한어로써겨뎌
일출판ᄒᆞᆸ

신문가
한쟝　엽두돈오푼
일삭표　엽두량닷돈
우표가티삭닷돈
다밧돈으로밧숩
광고료는
귀ᄒᆞᆫ의장단과ᄌᆞᄒᆡᆼ의다쇼로즁
감ᄒᆞ되ᄆᆡᆷ가로밧을터이오매오
린지ᄒᆞ녀대한사람마다다이신
문을보실터이니광고내시기를
원ᄒᆞ시는이들은우리신문사에
와셔면약ᄒᆞ심을희망ᄒᆞᆸ
○발ᄒᆡᆼ소　박동대한미일신보
사발ᄒᆡᆼ겸편집인영국인셜필
림장ᄌᆞ리오
샤쟝 영국인 (빈셜)
평양 뎌리쟝
○평양효동사는권미보씨로우
리신문쳔미뎌리인을뎡ᄒᆞ엿
시ᄉᆞ오니평양에계신구람코져ᄒᆞ
시는　첨군ᄌᆞ는ᄒᆡ뎌리졍에왕
림ᄒᆞ와면회ᄒᆞ시옵

샤고

○우리대한미일신보의목뎍은
대한의안녕질서에관한모든대
목에되ᄒᆞ야는공평한변론을주
쟝홈이라우리들신원의탐보는
신문보시는쳠군ᄌᆞ의게ᄒᆞᆼ상보
도ᄒᆞ리며편지를귀셔ᄒᆞ며주시
는이는셩명과반ᄃᆡ를쳐어붓치
시기를희망ᄒᆞ오니비거슨신문
샹에게졔ᄒᆞ란는거시아니오다
만구히신용ᄒᆞ는증거를숨고자
홈이라귀자는아모귀셔된지과
지ᄒᆞ을퇴ᄎᆞᄒᆞ는권리를가젓소
나퇴ᄎᆞᄒᆞ는리유를말ᄒᆞᆯ터이오
며공증평화를문란케ᄒᆞ는듯ᄒᆞᆫ
말셔는의례히밧지아니ᄒᆞᆯ터이
다귀
●본사셜시이리로신문을리양
우례로본젼ᄒᆞ와례젼부의일의
로젼ᄒᆞ든ᄃᆞᆺ스로면곳에는ᄒᆞᆨ놋게
젼ᄒᆞ기도ᄒᆞ며ᄒᆞᆨ면쳘ᄒᆞ게ᄒᆞᆫ겹
에젼ᄒᆞ기도ᄒᆞ며ᄒᆞ야니젼ᄒᆞᄂᆞᆫ
곳도잇다ᄒᆞ와우리신문을ᄉᆞ랑
ᄒᆞ야구람ᄒᆞ시는　쳠군ᄌᆞ의게
되ᄒᆞ야미우미안ᄒᆞ옵기로지금
은본젼인을두고미일쥬이젼
ᄒᆞ며아니젼ᄒᆞ거나늣게거나ᄒᆞᆫ
폐가엽도록ᄒᆞ랴ᄒᆞ오니ᄒᆞᆨ아니
젼ᄒᆞ거는ᄒᆞᆨ늣게젼ᄒᆞ거나ᄒᆞᆫ일
이잇스면본샤로통긔ᄒᆞ여주심
을희망ᄒᆞ옵

론셜

사하의소식
○지금소식을드른즉로국군중
에불화ᄒᆞ다는말이봉텬으로브
터요젼에북경에온션교ᄉᆞᄒᆞ나
이젼ᄒᆞᆫ것이오또그사룸이희구
태젼쟁에쳥쳔명이죽고오쳔명
이상ᄒᆞ엿ᄂᆞᆫ되젼인ᄒᆞᆫ자비라비
록희구태에서그런엄ᄒᆞᆫ리귀
에싸홈을ᄒᆞᆫ배에ᄉᆞ샹이만히낫
겟지마는그션교ᄉᆞ의젼ᄒᆞᆫ수효
는황당ᄒᆞ도다
로국젼진은쳘싱오영리를연쟝
ᄒᆞ엿는뒤각쳐에경편쳘로로연
락ᄒᆞ고구로팟긴은봉쳔에샹반
명의군ᄉᆞ를가지고잇스며동편
으로히창에수만명이잇고일본
군즁앙의근녀편으로시로이셰
앗은되방에엄쉭히군ᄉᆞ를더ᄒᆞ
며일젼에야젼포식아문을니왓
다더라
금월십수일일본공보에말ᄒᆞ되
로군이류샹부와리타쟝둔과해
구태북방에잇다ᄒᆞ고젼에쏘말
ᄒᆞ되가티방젼면에잇다고ᄒᆞ엿
스나구로팟긴의진군은쳔합불
빈ᄒᆞᆫ것이뵈이는겨이그릿치아
니ᄒᆞ면이를군즁앙으로브터소
문이엽슬지로다
금월십수일에쏘ᄒᆞᆫ일본공보에
말ᄒᆞ되로국과병팔구쳔명이대
포를가지고혼하와리쓰강ᄉᆞ이
에연락ᄒᆞᆫ디방에서십오영리를
니러가서혼하동진녀오리ᄒᆞᆫ디
ᄒᆞ엿스니그디방은료양에서남
강방의라그힝군이그디방파히
창ᄉᆞ이에일본군의동산귀판을
향ᄒᆞᆷ인듯ᄒᆞᆫ되지금브리이를주일
젼지사라고결과에되ᄒᆞ야면보
가업는것이샹ᄒᆞᆫ지라
로병이일군의우익을연속히포
격ᄒᆞ더니금월십이일에그포격
ᄒᆞ는후면에보병이싸흠을나와
린되셔사하부동남으로싱이영
리퇴ᄒᆞ고사하부동서남방으로삼
군의케룰나침이되엿다고대산
원슈의보고가잇더라
저금은일본인이쳥국인의게피
로움을밧는ᄎᆡ레인듯ᄒᆞᆫ경이금
월오일에ᄒᆞᆫ쳥인이우쥬듄에잇
는일본교간에방화ᄒᆞ다가당쟝
에일본인의게로국간쳡으로쟝
히엿다더라
료양과히창에잇는쳥국대슈를
도쏘ᄒᆞᆫ결연의게로국간쳡으로
장히여서쳥나와로보냇는뒤료
양대슈는젼에봉텬대슈로잇던
사롬인뒤그사롬이그세에로국
인과긴ᄒᆞᆫ관계가잇다고징쟉홈
이라만일두대슈의쟝히엿다는
말이참말갓ᄒᆞ면비록젼에로국
인도그런일을힝ᄒᆞᆫ것이일이ᄎᆞ
가아니라고쳐편메일신문에말
ᄒᆞ엿스나글로ᄒᆞ야무숨번동이
잇스리라ᄒᆞ노라

잡보

○에방문시　류ᄒᆡᆼ에에방위원
을각서에파쥬ᄒᆞ야경비만히비
ᄒᆞ고실디가무ᄒᆞᆫ지라위원쟝신
티쥬씨가봄셔ᄎᆞ로샹　츄ᄒᆞ엿
다더라
○츄엽환쟝　경무쳥에셔시종
픔샹환실빙표를셩급ᄒᆞ엿는뒤
히동중에경력이유ᄒᆞᆫ자로ᄉᆞ영
을ᄎᆞ정ᄒᆞ야규칙을조직ᄒᆞ고츄
엽을환쟝ᄒᆞ되차분을수취ᄒᆞ야
회사를셜립ᄒᆞ고관은으로一二
층을진츌ᄒᆞᆫ다더라
○무이덩무　리쟝ᄒᆞᆫ관계를런
방반포ᄒᆞ는지라관원이만히잡
앗ᄒᆞᆫ다홈으로각부부원쳥외사
진이칠평팔탁ᄒᆞ야덩무ᄒᆞᆫ모양
곳다더라
○소학교신셜　탁지부참서관
신히영씨가소학교를셜립ᄒᆞ는
데학교쟝은젼아이학교로졍ᄒᆞᆫ
다고학부로쳥원ᄒᆞ엿더라
○북간도셜교　북간도인민등
이학부에쳥원ᄒᆞ기를본도인민
의지식이젼미ᄒᆞ야진취홀희망
이무ᄒᆞᆫ지라소학교를셜립ᄒᆞ
엿스니인허ᄒᆞ음소셔ᄒᆞ엿더라
○션쳔슈쳥원　션쳔군수리인
셩씨가니부로쳥원ᄒᆞ엿는뒤신
병으로능히시무치못ᄒᆞ겟사오
니본직을쥬면ᄒᆞ라ᄒᆞ엿더라
○위관츄쥬　일젼밤에입직만
ᄒᆞᆫ참위리병교씨가하리ᄒᆞᆫ샹민
으ᄅᆞᆯ브리져동ᄒᆞᆫ다에셔휴쥬ᄒᆡᆼ
핏ᄒᆞᄂᆞᆫ지라헌병이그ᄒᆡᆼ피ᄒᆞᆷ을
보고히위관의명함을바다간즉
히위관이헌병남셔로츄리ᄒᆞ야
바ᄒᆞᆫ힝귀ᄒᆞ는지라궁쥬ᄒᆞ고
디시룰이오지못ᄒᆞ게ᄒᆞᆫ츄히위
관이기구병으로영리ᄒᆞᆫ지라필
경에는남셔헌병이히위관을고
졍사지휴게ᄒᆞ엿다더라
○군인낙샹　군계가의쳥이퇴
엿다홈으로각디군인들이낙샤
ᄒᆞᆯ가두려워ᄒᆞ야외를이불일ᄒᆞ
다더라
○윤동경졔　귀포풍각대퇴를
퇴폐ᄒᆞ고일본중퇴셔만셜치ᄒᆞᆫ다
되각일종퇴시방인ᄒᆞ면되는퇴
장은자연면제비될터인고로쳥
임각대퇴쟝은다세평이잇는과
이ㅣ각중퇴쟝을두지못ᄒᆞ고퇴쟝
이경지케ᄒᆞᆫ다더라
○홀영회소　경셩각대퇴에쥼
영쟝잇는종퇴쟝이팔구인에불
과ᄒᆞᆫ지라군계의경이반포가되
면중퇴쟝과관은반홀미라더라
○쥬사구처　공번관계리경에
남부쥬ᄉᆞ는쟝혜ᄒᆞᆫ바로조한이불
과ᄒᆞᆫ지라슈모든지공셩에쳥ᄒᆞ
ᄒᆞᆫ는자는군슈일과셕셔임ᄒᆞᆫ다
고브부대신이예언ᄒᆞ더라더라
○불쟈홍션　외부에셔법관으
로불ᄒᆡᆼᄒᆞ엿스되방비탐국방ᄒᆞᆨ
박사남쟉뎍긴과빗노이을폐의
폐쳔ᄒᆞᆫ바반국약쟝쳥필ᄒᆞᆫ젼을
며려번기염홍이불잡ᄒᆞᆫ셔ᄒᆞᆯ셰
뎌번죵히탐방사의항문이연셩
홈을알겟다ᄒᆞ엿더라

뎐보

동경발　　동일
○기에쥬에서평군이불평ᄒᆞᆫ산
민일만이쳔명의회집ᄒᆞᆫ뒤되ᄒᆞᆫ
야방츙ᄒᆞ엿다더라
빅림발　　동일
○로국니각회의쟝위례세가니챠
회의에서말ᄒᆞ되뎍국황뎨게서
극동에로국이겨를닷코승젼ᄒᆞ리
라고혜언ᄒᆞ엿다ᄒᆞ엿는뒤빅림
팡리들은말ᄒᆞ되그말이확실치
아니ᄒᆞ다ᄒᆞ며뎌셩덥을두고뎍국
군인들은로국이승젼ᄒᆞ기를바
샹ᄒᆞ지아니ᄒᆞ엿다ᄒᆞ더라더라
론돈발　동월십사일
○평화와일본쳐권　평화를셜
비셩ᄒᆡᆼᄒᆞ면일본은쳐가ᄎᆔᄒᆞ
야시로이모장ᄒᆞ는빅히오분번
리되는쳐권은오남빅에구셜젼
히벼미찻다더라

UNION INSURANCE SOCIETY OF CANTON.

Head office Hongkong.
Marine risks underwritten at current rates.

Agents in Chemulpo,
E. MEYER & Co.

COMPAGNIE DES MESSAGERIES MARITIMES.

Fortnightly Direct Service.

For Marseilles
an Ports.
Sailing from Yokohama
Calling at Kobe,
Shanghai, Hongkong, Saigon, Singapore,
Colombo, Djibonti, Suez, Port Said
and Marseilles.

For particulars apply to
HOLME RINGER & Co.,
Chemulpo.

HAYASHIDA & CO.,

16 MYENG DONG, CHIN KO KAI, SEOUL.
BRANCH OFFICE AT CHEMULPO.

Money changers, Coal and Wood Merchants, Express Agents.

We are agents for the Pyeng-yang Coal Company and the Karazu Coal Company of Japan. We have the best quality of both anthracite and bituminous coal, and prompt execution of orders is our speciality. Firewood of all kinds kept in stock. Full weight guaranteed. Money of all denominations exchanged at current rates. Parcels received for all parts.

CHINA MUTUAL LIFE INS. CO.

Most favourable terms to policy holders.

Benefit system unsurpassed.

HOLME RINGER & Co.
Agents, Chemulpo.

C. P. R.

CANADIAN PACIFIC RAILWAY COMPANY'S ROYAL MAIL STEAMSHIP LINE.

THE FAST ROUTE BETWEEN CHINA, JAPAN, AND EUROPE VIA CANADA AND THE UNITED STATES.

Route from Hongkong via Shanghai, Nagasaki (Inland Sea of Japan) Kobe, Yokohama, Victoria and Vancouver.

Twin Screw Empress Steamship—6,000 Tons—Speed 19 knots.

PROPOSED SAILING FROM YOKOHAMA.

R. M. S. Empress of India.
R. M. S. Empress of Japan.
R. M. S. Empress of China.
R. M. S. Athenian.
R. M. S. Tartar.

Special reduction (first class only) granted to members of the Military, Naval, Diplomatic and Civil services and to Missionaries.

Passengers have choice of ten routes across the Continent of America and have privilege of travelling by any Atlantic Steamship Line.

Round the World passage tickets in connection with the P. and O. S. N., North German Lloyd and Messageries Co.'s £125.

All rates payable at current rate of exchange.

For further information, Tickets, Guide Books, etc., apply to

HOLME, RINGER & Co., AGENTS,
Chemulpo.

Grand Hotel

(Formerly the Station Hotel)

Near the Railway Terminus, West Gate Seoul.

The Best Hotel in Korea.
Handsome new Building.
Fine Airy Rooms.
Excellent Cuisine.
Terms Moderate.
Special terms to Missionaries and to permanent boarders.

Electric cars within 2 minutes' walk.

W. H. EMBERLEY.
Proprietor

AMERICAN KOREAN ELECTRIC CO.

Light and Power.

Main Office: Electric Building, Chong No.

RAILWAY DEPARTMENT.

OPERATING CARS BETWEEN EAST AND WEST GATE, EVERY TEN MINUTES:—

First Car leaves East Gate at 7:00 A. M. First Car leaves R. R. Station at 7:25 A.M
Last Car " East Gate at 8.40 P. M. Last " " R. R. Station at 9.05 P.M

OPERATING CARS BETWEEN EAST GATE AND IMPERIAL TOMB TERMINUS, EVERY TWENTY MINUTES:—

CONNECTING WITH EVERY ALTERNATE CAR ARRIVING AT EAST GATE FROM CHONG NO.

First Car leaves East Gate for Tomb at 7:10 A. M.
" " " Tomb for East Gate at 7:30 A. M.
Last " " East Gate for Tomb at 7:50 P. M.
" " " Tomb for East Gate at 8:10 P. M.

OPERATING CARS BETWEEN CHONG NO AND YUNG SAN RIVER EVERY TWELVE MINUTES:—

First Car leaves Chong No for South Gate at 7:12 A. M.
" " " Chong No for Yung San at 7:36 A. M.
" " " South Gate for Chong No at 7:20 A. M.
" " " Yung San for Chong No at 8:09 A. M.
Last " " South Gate for Chong No 9:00 P. M.
" " " Yung San for Chong No at 8.45. P. M.

SPECIAL PRIVATE CARS FURNISHED TO SUIT CONVENIENCE OF PATRONS. PRICES ON APPLICATION AT HEAD OFFICE.

LIGHTING DEPARTMENT.

Where less than 250 candle power of light is used, the rate per month will be

Per 16 candle power incandescent lamp,—All night.—Yen 2.50.
32 candle power incandescent lamp,—All night:—Yen 4.00.
50 candle power incandescent lamp,—All night:—Yen 6.00.
150 " " " " " " " 10.00.
1200 " " enclosed arc " " " " 20.00.

Where more than 250 candle power of light is used, a Meter will be installed, if requested:—Rent of Meter, Yen 2.00 per month. Rate of charges by meter reading:—Two Sen per Ampere per hour. (Approximately this is equal to about One Sen per 16 C. P. lamp per hour) Minimum monthly charge where meter is installed, Yen 20.00 per month, which includes rental of meter.

Estimates for installing lights furnished on application

An assortment of chandeliers always on hand.

EVERY FACILITY.

In connection with Life Assurance Business is afforded by

The Standard Life Assurance Co.,

One of the largest and wealthiest of the Provident Institutions of the United Kingdom Forms of Application and all information will be promptly afforded on application.

10 CENTS A DAY.

Not a very large expenditure is it? But it is sufficient to secure for a man of 30 a policy with the STANDARD LIFE OFFICE for

$1323.

For all particulars of rates, etc., apply to

Holme, Ringer & Co.,
Agents, Chemulpo.

THE NEW YORK LIFE INSURANCE COMPANY.

Have you ever been declined by any Company?

Are you engaged in a specially hazardous occupation?

Have you heard of the New York Life Insurance Company's New Classifications for this class of Risks?

If not, send your date of birth, occupation and particulars of rejection, if any to

E. MEYER & Co.,
Agents, Chemulpo.

K. Murakami.
Photograph Studio
Chinkokai, Seoul.

Printing, Developing and Enlargement, of Photographs always Undertaken.

Korean Views and Pictures Illustrating Native Customs always on Sale,

---

THE OSAKA SHOSEN KAISHA.

Boats frequently on the berth for Chinnampo.

REGULAR SAILINGS BETWEEN JAPAN AND KOREAN PORTS.

FUSAN AND KOBE VIA SHIMONOSEKI.

OSAKA VIA MOKPO, FUSAN, SHIMONOSEKI AND KOBE.

MOJI DIRECT.

OSAKA VIA KUNSAN, MASANPO, FUSAN, SHIMONOSEKI AND KOBE.

CHEMULPO KUNSAN LINE,
Every three days.

CHEMULPO CHINNAMPO LINE
Every three days.

For Freight and passage and further particulars apply to

THE OSAKA SHOSEN KAISHA,
Chemulpo.

MITSUI BUSSAN KAISHA.
(MITSUI & Co.)

MITSUI GINKO.
(MITSUI BANK.)

The Bank is owned by the members of the Mitsui Family, who, as partners, assume an unsimited responsibility for all liabilities of the Bank:—

Capital.......................... Yen 5,000,000
Reserve Fund................... " 5,600,000

HEAD OFFICE, TOKYO.

LONDON OFFICE, 34 LIME ST., E. C.

BRANCHES AND AGENCIES:—

New York, San Francisco, Hamburg, Bombay, Singapore, Manila, Hongkong, Amoy, Chefoo, Tientsin.

Kobe, Hakodate, Yokohama, Kure, Yokosuka, Moji, Shimonoseki, Miike, Wakamatsu, Nagasaki, Kuchinotsu, Karatsu, Sasebo, Misume, Taipeh, &c.

Telegraphic Address for all the Offices:
"MITSUI."
A. B. C. AND A. 1 CODES USED.

Contractors of Coal

To the Imperial Japanese Navy. Arsenal and Railway Bureau, Principal Railway Companies and Industrial Work, Home and Foreign Mail and Freight Steamers.

Sole Proprietors

Of the famous Miike, Tagawa and Yamano Coal Mines.

Sole Agents

For the sale of Fukumo, Hokoku, Ichimura, Kanoda, Mannoura, Onoura, Ostuji, Sonoda, Tsubaruro, Yoshinotani, Yoshio, Yurokibura and other coals.

YANGTSE INSURANCE ASSOCIATION, LTD.

The undersigned, having been appointed agents for the above company, are prepared to issue policies and pay losses on marine risks at regular rates.

E. MEYER & Co.,
Agents, Chemulpo.

RONDON, PLAISANT & CO.

General Storekeepers and Merchants, Ships Contractors Tobacconists, Commission and Forwarding Agents, Coal Merchants

IMPORTERS AND EXPORTERS

Seoul, Chemulpo.

W. D. WENTWORTH

LANDING
AND
SHIPPING AGENT.
AND
CUSTOMS BROKER.

12 OURA, NAGASAKI.

STEWARD & CO.

Chemulpo.

Shipchandlers and Storekeepers, Naval and Mercantile Contractors, Landing and Shipping Agents.

STEWARD'S HOTEL

Chemulpo.

Best accommodation in the port for travellers. Clean and well-aired rooms, good cuisine and prompt attendance, moderate tariff.

관보

데삼쳔칠십일호 광무구년이월이십사일 금료

셔임급사령

●승셔관임관삼등 한셩뎐보지사쥬사 김상규 광무팔년십월십삼일

○승셔관임관사등 대구뎐보샤쥬사 홍태건 이상광무팔년십일월칠일

○승셔관임관오등 한셩우체사쥬사 홍고수 이월십이일

○승셔관임관사등 탁지부쥬사 김상혁 이월십오일

○승셔관임관오등 군기창소쟝 송경화 이월십륙일

○의원면본관 닉부광제원쥬사 김정휘 닉부광제원쥬사 김현국 닉부광제원쥬사 송광옥

○임닉부광제원쥬사셔관임관륙등 리문규 유치삼 유진억

○히는부광제원위원 셔지명 김사영 장용셩

○명닉부광제원위원 장신달 명만선 오시용 이상이월십칠일

○승셔관임관사등 한셩우체사쥬사 유문상 이상이월십구일

○임외국어학교교관셔쥬임관륙등 즁학교교관 김한규 이월이십일

○히겸임젼라남도지관소관사 젼라남도젼관찰사 김세기

○히겸임옥구항지관소관사 옥구젼감리 뎡항됴

○히겸임강원도지관소판소 강원도젼관찰소 주셕면

○히겸임경긔지관소관소 경긔젼관찰소 리근교

○히겸임경상북도지관소관소 경상북도젼관찰사 장승원

○명겸임젼라남도지관소관소 젼라남도관찰소 주셕면

○명겸임옥구항지판소판소 옥구감리 김교헌

○명겸임강원도지판소관소 경긔관찰소 최익현

○명겸임경상북도지판소관소 경상북도관찰사 리용익

○히겸임법관양성소장 법부젼협판 김규히

○명겸임법관양셩소장 법부협판 리근상

○임법관양셩소박사셔관임관륙등 리봉쥰 홍종쥰 권봉수

○면겸임유년학교장 륙군마관학교장 륙군보병부령 리병무

○명휴직 시위긔병대대부 륙군긔병참위 안영수

진위데일련대데일대대보륙군보병참위 민하소

○면본직 친위데일련딕데이대딕부륙군보병참위 최한구 진위데이련딕데이대딕부륙군보병참위 태영선 진위데이련딕데삼대딕즁딕장륙군보병정위 원세록 진위데오련딕데일대딕즁딕장륙군보병정위 리지한 진위데륙련딕데일대딕부륙군보병참위 림영선

○임륙군긔병참위 륙군보병참위 윤치셩

○보유년학교장륙군보병부령 됴철히

○보시위데일련딕데삼대딕부륙군보병참위 림영선

○보시위긔병대딕부 륙군긔병참위 윤치셩

○보친위데일련딕데이대딕부륙군보병참위 태영선

○보진위데이련딕데이대딕부륙군보병참위 최한구

○보진위데삼련딕데삼대딕즁딕장륙군보병정위 리지한

○보친위데오련딕데일대딕즁딕장륙군보병정위 원세록

○보진위데륙련딕데일대딕부륙군보병참위 박동원

○의원면본관 즁추원의관 흥은주 즁추원의관 강태봉 즁추원의관 박형비 즁추원의관 박종묵 즁추원의관 리긔룡

○임즁추원의관셔주임관륙등 종이픔 리종운 륙픔 김만형 륙픔 박기돈 륙픔 권덕규 구품 리종철

○면본관 유년학교도뎌부 륙군보병참위 강용히

○면본관 농상공부농무국장 리규원 이상이월이십일일

○의원면겸임쟝례원쟝례 봉상사제죠 서병찬

○의원면본관 교방사주소 홍진표 군부주소 양주훈 군부주소 엄주은 즁학교교관 리완응

○명궁닉부특진관셔칙임관일등 종일픔 됴병필 상의사장겸임쟝례원쟝례 심구퇴

○임교방사주소셔판임관칠등 환구단사제셔령 리윤수

○임환구단사제서령셔판임관칠등 사직서령 장길상

○임사직서령셔판입관칠등 현능참봉 셩전영

○임현릉참봉셔관임관팔등 구품 홍순비

○임군부주소셔판임관팔등 구품 윤태욱 김힝범

○임즁학교교관셔관임관륙등 리덕응 이상이월이십이일

광무구년도예산표 속

데륙관 의학교 팔쳔구빅칠십륙원

데일항 봉급 삼쳔일빅이십원

데이항 청비 칠빅오십원

데삼항 교과셔번역비 오빅원

데사항 약료긔계구미비 일쳔원

데오항 청사슈리비 일빅원

데륙항 잡급과잡비 이빅륙십원

데칠항 외국인제급 삼쳔이빅사십원 지화

데칠관 농상공학교 일만륙쳔이빅팔십원

데일항 봉급 오쳔륙빅사십원

데이항 청비 일쳔사빅오십원

데삼항 교과척비 오빅원

데오항 외국인제급 팔쳔이빅팔십원 지화

데팔관 고등소학교 삼쳔삼십사원

데일항 봉급 이쳔일빅륙십원

데이항 청비 오빅팔십원

데삼항 청사슈리비 일빅원

데사항 잡급과잡비 일빅구십사원

뎐보

빅림발 동일

○덕국과청도 덕국의회에셔임명훈위원회에셔 귀쥬에딧혼예산을가결호엿는딕 히군대신이샤회당령슈베벨씨의뭇는딕딕호야말호되덕국이청도에포딕롤건축홀경영이업다고호엿다더라

론돈발 이월십삼일

○볼틱함딕의출발 슌양함오쳑이샌시바에셔써나셔마다가스카의동북방에잇는딕에고쇄렛스디방으로향호엿다더라

화셩돈발 동일

○덕사의청국강토보젼의션언 화셩돈에잇는덕국대사스런벅남작이미국대통령루스벨트씨의게단언호되덕국이청국산동셩을세력범위안에너랴고호던정칙을버리고청국의강토보젼과기방정칙을찬죠호다호엿스니그러케말혼것은요젼에미국국무대신헤이씨가말호되만일덕국이정칙을변호지아니호면영덕사이에국제분란이이러나리라고홈미인연홈이라호더라

잡보

평양통신

○감리셜연 음력정월초사일에평양감리신대균씨가만찬회를셜호고일본사령관이하제씨를청료관딕호엿더라

○멸룬이국 평안남도덕천읍에거호는감시철위명인이일진회에입참호야단니다가회비를닉다호고자긔집에미엿던농우를팔나호즉그동싱이집안사세가만불셩양홀줄노말호고무수히몰니나종닉불텽호는지라그동싱이칼노그형의넙적다리를찔너즉사호엿다더라

○홍씨협잡 평안남도강셔읍에거호는홍룡섭이라호는자가이젼브터가어소로민간에서기인편지훈일이만타는딕근일에궁닉부대신의인장을위죠호야쥬소차함쳡지를미매호다가평양관찰부경무서에피착호엿다더라

○디방하기 평양셩닉는본릭음풍이대단훈중에근일에는더옥심호야년소자의침혹호야겨가파산호는쟈허다훈지라평양인민들의말이경무소신태휴씨가경성의경찰은엄숙히홈으로잡생이잇스나디방경찰은관활간섭이무훈야고훈다더라

○잉즉파산 거음력십이월에평양시닉에무곡상민칠팔인이자긔집에서곡식거간호는한인들과합동호야소위거간계라칭호고일본인집에서거간호는자외에는곡식미매상에상관치못호게훈고로다른상로거간등이차에딕호야심히격분호야관찰부에뎡장호엿더니재지니에부하샹업회의소에서공의결뎡호라홈으로상업회의소에서십분공의호야곳파산케호엿다더라

○교섭불통 창원감리가외부로면보호엿스되본항총슌이일본헌병소에파수호야스나교섭을불통호오니복민호외다호엿더라

○이시담화 이십이일하오이시에법공사가외부협판을방문호고미란기사의히고안에딕호야이시담화호엿더라

○간상탄로 원산감리신힝모씨가그쳐족하리병목씨의게지화일빅오십원을셔찰에동봉호야일본우편국으로부송호엿더니히화는우편국에류치호고서찰은우체사로면송호야당자가츄거케호엿더니기시입직쥬사과인이히찰을기탁호교리씨의도장을위조호야지화를일본우편국에서추거호엿더니간상이탄로호야이십삼일한셩지판소에서히쥬사를나치호야지관호엿더라

○과결역다 닉부에현지훈군수과컬이삼십일과라더라

광고

TELEGRAMS.

Note. The messages marked* are those which are described as "special service" or "special telegrams or "received by the Government." The others are from properly authenticated sources.

THE WAR.

London, February 13th.

The "New York Herald's" Tientsin correspondent wires that the Russian Government has threatened China to the effect that if the authorities do not prevent the transportation of contraband in favour of Japan, Russia will be forced to make a demonstration in Northern China and Chinese Turkestan.

London, Feb. 17.

*It is reported that Russia is now seeking to maintain the Manchurian army at the strength of half a million men with the object of exhausting the Japanese.

Berlin, Feb. 19.

Prince Frederick Leopold of Prussia, who is to proceed to Manchuria to join the Russian staff, has returned to Berlin after visiting the Tsar.

PEACE PROSPECTS.

London, 13th.

The Chinese Minister at St. Petersburg has telegraphed to his government that after careful investigation, he is forced to believe that Russia has not the slightest inclination towards peace, but instead, the Czar has ordered that the Russian troops in Manchuria shall give decisive battle.

Berlin, Feb. 15.

According to a report from London, the Russian Ambassador to the Court of St. James's has received a letter from the Tsar to present to King Edward. The subject dealt with in the letter is stated to be of great importance, and is believed to refer to the question of peace.

London, Feb. 19.

Mysterious rumours regarding peace, which it is impossible to trace to any direct source, have been constantly cropping up during the last few days.

Berlin, Feb. 19.

The Russian papers are publishing numerous articles demanding that peace be concluded as early as possible. The "Birshewiya Viedomosti" is carrying on an energetic crusade in favour of peace.

Berlin, Feb. 19.

According to London dispatches to the "Novoye Vremya," very little sympathy is expressed for the late Grand Duke Sergius. It is generally believed that his death will have very little effect either upon the granting of reforms or upon Russia's attiude in regard to the war.

RUSSIAN AFFAIRS.

London, Feb. 14.

*** At Blagoy, four thousand persons have created disturbances. They were at once quelled by the reservists. Troops have fired upon twelve thousand persons who made a demonstration at Kieff. Russia is threatened with famine.**

Vienna, Feb. 16.

*** The revolutionists of Finland and Poland are about to co-operate in an attempt to make the two provinces independent countries. In Finland the revolutionists are reported to be collecting arms for reprisals against the troops.**

London, Feb. 16.

*** The University students in Russia, who had decided to absent themselves from the colleges until their demand for a Constitution had been granted, are now beginning to reattend the institutions.**

London, Feb. 16.

*** The disturbances in Russia are gradually subsiding. The strikers at Lodz,** St. Petersburg and Moscow are returning to their work.

London, Feb. 18.

The strike in St. Petersburg is again rapidly extending, and already 30,000 persons have rejoined the strikers, whose temper is threatening.

The troops employed to quell the previous riots have been re-drafted to the vicinity of the various works, while the police are renewing domiciliary visits and arresting the leaders of the strike.

Later.

An extraordinary sitting of the Council of the Empire was held yesterday to consider the situation resulting from the assasssination of the Grand Duke Sergius.

St. Petersburg is now being flooded with revolutionary literature.

The employés on the railways running from Moscow have gone on strike, and traffic has had to be suspended.

The leading Russian papers, while denouncing the assassination, declare that the crying necessity for reform is responsible for the tragedy.

London, Feb. 19.

King Edward has ordered the British Court into mourning for one week for the late Grand Duke Sergius.

London, Feb. 18.

*The assassin of the Grand Duke Sergius declares that he is a member of the Workmen's Social Democratic Party, and says that he has accomplished the will of the executive.

The Czar has issued a Manifesto beseeching the populace for its sympathies in the great loss he has sustained.

In St. Petersburg everything is calm at present, but in Warsaw the police are reported to have shot many workmen.

GENERAL NEWS.

London, February 15.

*The German collier Bulgaria and the British collier Sandford (?) have arrived at Hatchphon, a northern point in Sumatra. The Dutch authorities have ordered them to land their cargoes at Batavia.

London, Feb. 16.

*Replying in the House of Commons to the hostile criticisms regarding the Tibetan question, Mr. Balfour, the Premier, stated that no criticism was valuable that did not take into consideration the interests of the Indian Government in connection with Tibet. The people of India had recognized the supreme authority of the Imperial Government in the matter, and had never diverged from this principle in dealing with the question.

London, Feb. 16.

*The Russian naval and military authorities are impeaching each other with reference to the capitulation of Port Arthur.

Shanghai Feb. 17.

*Three Chinese have been arrested at Chefoo on a charge of murdering German and French military officers who left Port Arthur in August last. A later despatch from Chefoo states that two of the above men have been released on account of insufficient evidence.

Berlin, Feb. 15.

Mr. Thomas Barclay, the well-known British journalist, who is endeavouring to cultivate more friendly relations between Great Britain and Germany, has arrived in Berlin, where he was accorded a hearty welcome by the members of the German Commercial Congress, now in session.

London, Feb. 17.

*By the capture of the British steamers "Apollo" and "Scotsman," laden with contraband cargo for Vladivostok, the underwriters suffer a loss of £111,000. The total loss of underwriters as a result of the seizure by the Japanese of twelves vessels since January 13th, amounts to £800,000,

Washington, D.C., Feb. 11.

*Hon. John Goodnow, Consul-General at Shanghai, after a searching investigation by the State Department into the charges of malfeasance in office made by Lawyer Curtis, formerly of Shanghai, has been officially cleared. Mr. Goodnow intends to sail for Shanghai on the 14th inst.

It is understood here that there is a likelihood of Mr. Goodnow being transferred to an important position in Cuba, and that Prof Coolidge, of Harvard University, is slated for Shanghai.

London, Fob. 19.

General Stoessel has arrived at Constantinople "en route" to St. Petersburg.

London, Feb. 20.

*The Chinese Minister at Washington has presented President Roosevelt with a portrait of the Empress Dowager. This unique honour is in recognition of the part played by America toward the preservation of Chinese neutrality and also of her disinterested friendship.

COUNT CASSINI ON THE WAR.

Count Cassini, Russian Ambassador to the United States, recently celebrated the completion of his 50th year of diplomatic service. He was the recipent of congratulations from all over the world and was of course interviewed.

Amongst other things, the count stated that the personally knew that Nicholas II did his utmost to present "the present unhappy struggle in Asia."

"The inventions of civilization have brought the peoples of all countries into a closer understanding. There is no need for the old style of diplomacy. The nations of the world understand, as they did not seem to understand before, that there is no profit in war. Take the present war, for instance; it was not caused by a Russian army of conquest. It was the result of an extension of a useful railway system by a nation whose manifest commercial destiny turned her face to the east.

"Russia was unwilling to engage in as struggle with her European neighbour over an outlet in the Mediterranean. She turned toward undeveloped Asia. She poured out her millions of treasure and sent her people to cultivate the great steppes. She guarded her advance at her own cost, and restored order to brigand-ravaged districts. The war which followed might have been prevented if Japan had only waited. Had Russia abandoned her great and peaceful work in Manchuria it would have been a political crime; it would have confused the whole future'

INVALIDS FOR CHEFOO.

In view of the lack of accomodation there, great indignation has been aroused in Chefoo at the Japanese proposal to land 2,500 Port Arthur invalids there.

The "Chefoo Daily News" says:—

As a climax to the phenomenal red tape attending the exodus of thousands of non-combatants from Port Arthur since the capitulation, the news is wafted in that the Japanese authorities now intend to send to Chefoo the convalescent sick and wounded still remaining in the citadel.

On February 9th the local Russian Vice Consul wrote to the French Consul, requesting the latter to inquire of the Japanese Consul if there was any truth in the rumor embodied in the words of the above paragraph. Almost a week elapsed before a reply was received from that quarter in which are the following words:

"About two thousand five hundred Russian soldiers who have recovered from their sickness or wounds, but are physically unable to take part in the present war (invalid) will be sent over to Chefoo, beginning from the 20th instant, or thereabouts; and under present circumstances of our military transportation, it is impossible to send them direct to Shanghai."

H. I. M. the Kaiser, on his Mediterranean cruise next month, will have an interview with Italy's King Emanuel, at Naples, of a political character.

FIRST IN PEACE AND FIRST IN WAR.

It cannot be said that the Kobe tailors lack enterprise. Witness the following advertisement which appeared in the Kobe Daily News:—

KOBE TAILORS' UNION.

The International Exhibition at St. Louis has awarded the Honourable Diploma upon the exhibits sent by Mr. Otokichi Shibata, member of our Union. It shows certainly that his exhibits were superior than many hundred exhibits sent from other countries where we first learned from, giving them great fame in the trade. This we feel as the Honour of our Union, the Kobe Yofuku Shoko Kumiai. Since the Japan-Russia War was commenced, Japan is getting unique victory upon Russia and Japan has been settled widely as one of the strong empires under the heaven. At this moment we wish, expressing our real energy, that our tailoring arts are superior than others, as in the case of our Army and Navy in their brillant victories. Now We wish, Ladies and Gentleman, will give us their generous support. All orders will be executed carefully and promptly.

Kobe Yofuku Shoko Kumiai.

A Berlin telegram of February 11th states that the St. Petersburg authorities categorically declare that Russia has asked nobody to intervene as regards peace terms.

The repairs to the "Cesarevitch" at Tingtau are proceeding apace. A recent visitor to the port states that temporary patches have been put over the holes pierced by the shells of the enemy. Most of these were apparently caused by the smaller Japanese guns. Her second funnel was pretty well riddled, and a new one has been partially reared in its place, upon which workmen are busily engaged riveting the sections. The forward mast has been entirely removed.

A message from Colombo says that the German collier Dartmonod arrived there from Madagascar on Jan 23rd. She reported that the Baltic Fleet is accompanied by twenty colliers the coaling being effected on the high seas. The stock of coal is about 110,000 tons. The Fleet is waiting for the Third Squadron. The officers have learned of the fall of Port Arthur, but the news has been withheld from the bluejackets. The warships are in good condition. Provisions are obtained from French transports of special construction. The Russian Admiral has been informed that a Japanese squadron is at Penang.

The Korea Daily News.

Issued at 5 P. M. daily except Sundays.

Rate of Subscription :—
Per Year,............Yen 25.
Per Quarter,..........Yen 7.
Per Month,..........Yen 2.50.

Postage in Korea not charged extra
Postage abroad charged extra.

Advertisements, 50 sen per day for 1 inch or less.
5 yen per month per inch.
50 yen per year per inch.

All communications to
E. T. BETHELL,
Editor and Publisher,
Pak-tong, Seoul.

NERVOUS COLLAPSE.

A DISEASE IN MODERN WARFARE.

Unprecedented medical aspects of war have been noted during the progress of the Russio-Japanese conflict, and the "Indian Medical Gazette" quotes from an American medical journal an account of the nervous stories of modern fighting.

"Warfare" they declare, "has lost its personal charactar and is now merely wholesale butchery. This fact is impressively demonstrated by a letter from Dr. Paul Jacoby, of Orel, Russia, whose experience at the seat of war has shown that the battles and mine explosions affect men like great cosmic phenomena in which the personal element is entirely lacking. Danger, death itself, present themselve under new and strange forms altogether different from the ideas of war to which we have been accustomed since the days when knighthood was in flower. Our psychology has not adapted itself to the new aspect of warfare. A cruiser which in less than two minutes sinks with 800 men on board; a skirmish in which 104 out of 107 of the horses are killed; an assault in which every assailant drops to the very last man; an assault over a surface known to be undermined by fifteen hunded mines: these things effect one like a tremendous earthquake or volcanic eruption. Every physician knows that catastrophes of this kind breed psychosis, and the nervous condition of those who escaped from such catastrophes as the blowing up of the Variag, the Petropavlovsk and the Hatsuse, is similar to that of the survivors of some great cosmic upheaval. Nervous disturbances and psycho-physical troubles should be treated at once, and on the spot in condition of absolute repose. Some of the survivors of the battle and explosions at the seat of war were hurried away from the spot and sent home, the interminable railroad journey rendering their curable psychosis probably incurable insanity. Jacoby has urged on the Russian Red Cross, and his suggestions have recently been put in practice, that certain barracks and tents should be set apart for such patients to isolate them and render possible the restoration of their nervous balance. The conditions of warfare all predispose to psychosis under the most favourable surroundings, and the new forms of death—forms to which the mind is not accustomed—and the psychologic conditions which they create must certainly have an influence on the psycho-physical condition and on the pathogenesis of nervous morbidity among troops in active warfare. They may, perhaps, originate new morbid forms akin to the nervous deseases of industrial origin. In the campaign in Manchuria all these causes are co-operating with an unprecedented intensity, and the physicians at the seat of war war have been so preoccupied with their surgical duties that these victims of the war have been neglected or sent home, thirty or forty days of railroad travelling being superadded to the other factors of their psychosis. Jacoby refers to brutal acts and preversions of men in camp life to unrecognised psychoses generated by their environment. The authorities and public opinion, however, are not always able to distinguish between a psychosis and a crime. He refers to the recent suicide of General MacDonald as an instance in point. The two armies now fighting have the sad privilege of in-augurating these new psychologic and psychopathic conditions of modern warfare with its character of industrial butchery by perfected processes."

THE OTHER SIDE.

The following vigorous defense of the Russians appears in the "China Review."

Dear Sir,—Can you inform me (or the enquiring Public) when the Japanese Official Reports and Japanese owned or subsidised papers are ever going to admit even a trifling reverse, for I, as a man at the front, can assure you that they have had plenty since the 25th ult, and that the Russian forces are slowly but nevertheless surely forcing their way Southward. Your report, published in your issue of the 30th January, that the Russian main front had moved southward of the Hunho where they came into collision with the enemy at two points; in both cases being successful and in one capturing six guns, is a perfectly correct one: yet I have not, up to date, seen any admission of this fact in any of the "published." Official Reports. The belittleing of General Metschenko's eminently successful Newchang raid is a true indication of the Oriental habit of perversion of the truth, which the Japanese Official Reports so lucidly illustrate. The report published in the pro-Japanese papers, that General Kuropatkin is greatly hampered by the reluctance on the part of his European regiments to advance against the enemy is so absurd in itself that I am sure that no sane person would ever give credence to such a fabrication, even through it came through Reuter. On the other hand the troops are in excellent spirits at the resumption of hostilities after long spell of inactivity. They also have that which so essential to ultimate victory; every confidence in their able commander-in-chief, which confidence has not been lessened by their recent successes. The reports, even as published in pro-Japanese papers, will convince the public that Gen. Kuropatkin is on the war-path and means business.

The report published by your worthy contemporary, the "China Times" of the 1st inst., that General Kuropatkin, in order to keep well in with the natives offered to contribute ten thousand taels for the relief of sufferers through the war, will not stand the strain of enquiry and must be another Oriental delusion. For it is well-known that the well-fare of all refugees has been well looked after by the Russian Red Cross Society, who have expended, not ten thousand taels, but three quarters of a million roubles in this work of charity.

General Kuropatkin has no need to pay in such a manner for the goodwill of the poorer class of Chinese in Manchuria, for they were never so well-off before in their lives; and they thank the Russians for it. They get good wages for any work they do and No. 1 prices for what they sell, a thing they cannot get from the Japanese. The Chinaman is not such an idiot as not to know on which side his bread is buttered. It is only the lawless class—who are in Japanese pay—who cause the Russian General any trouble, certainly not the working classes. Neither is it true that the Russian authorities have put any taxes whatever on the Chinese of any condition in Manchuria; such as taxing the peasantry $5 to $8 on each of their carts for the purpose of raising a revenue.

This statement is also palpably absurd, for, in the first place the peasantry have no carts to tax; and secondly all the carts at present in Tieling and Mukden and those running backwards and forwards from Hsin-Mun-Tun to those places, all belong to a syndicate of Chinese in Hsin-Mun-Tun, who have monopolised the whole cart trade.

I am, Yours, &c.,

"ON THE SCENE."

Hsin-mun-tun, Feb. 5th.

JAPAN'S MILITARY CAPACITY.

The German official military organ, the Militär Wochenblatt has gone into figures in order to arrive at an estimate of the strength at which Japan will be able to maintain its army in Manchuria and arrives at the conclusion that 350,000 would be a liberal estimate.

It points and that although a much larger number of men could be put into the field at any given moment, Japan in time of war is seriously hampered by the lack of instructors for new troops and has only sufficient officers for the soldiers now at the front.

The Militär Wochenblatt thinks Japan has been remiss in not providing for these contingencies, and concludes its article by saying "Japan's example proves once more that a nation, even if it possesses the greatest military qualities, and is animated by the highest patriotism, is bound to maintain in peace as large an army as it can, and always in proportion to the growth of its population. unless it wishes to expose itself to the gravest dangers if war should find it unable to make the most of its men in its own defence."

When the Japanese entered Port Arthur there was in the Russo-Chinese Bank a considerable amount of postal matter intended for the outside world which had accumulated there. This correspondence was turned over by the postal authorities to the bank for safe keeping during the last days of the siege. The shell fire of the Japanese was very heavy, and the post office people, fearing a possible destruction of a large amount of mail matter which they were awaiting opportunity to send out had placed the same in the Bank Building. This correspondence is mostly of a commercial nature, and concerns foreign firms in all countries, particularly those having property interests in Port Arthur, in the way of merchandise, etc. The Japanese authorities upon entering the town of course seized the bank, and with it the letters mentioned. Protests have been made by the people who are interested in the letters, and though it is stated that promises were made to release the letters promptly, they have not been fulfilled.

The Korea Daily News.

VOL. II, SATURDAY, FEBRUARY 25, 1905. No. 43

報申日每韓大
보신일미한대

(호 ᄉᆞ 십 ᄉᆞ 쳔 이 뎨)　(일 요 화)　일 팔 십 이 월 이 년 오 빅 구 쳔 일

본사고빅

이신보는영어와한어로셔ᄆᆡ
일출판ᄒᆞ옵
신문가
일쟝 한ᄃᆞᆯ 엽두돈오분
일삭표 엽두량닷돈
우표가미삭닷돈
다밧돈으로밧숩
광고료는
귀한의쟝단과ᄌᆞ항의다쇼로쥬
감ᄒᆞ되몬져가로밧을터이오ᄆᆡ오
린지아닌대한사람마다더이신
문을보실터이니광고내시기를
원ᄒᆞ시는이들은우리신문사에
와서편약ᄒᆞ심을희망ᄒᆞ옵
○발형소 박동대한ᄆᆡ일신보
사 발어학교압회 젼영국인셜필
림쟝자리오
사쟝 영국인 (비셜)
평양 ᄃᆡ리졈
○평양종로사는 권미보씨로우
리신문좌ᄃᆡ리인을뎡ᄒᆞ엿
시ᄉᆞ오니평양에계신구람코져ᄒᆞ
는 쳠군ᄌᆞ는ᄒᆞ뎌리졈에왕
림ᄒᆞ와면회ᄒᆞ시옵

사고

○우리대한ᄆᆡ일신보의목뎍은
대한의인민이셰샹에관한모든대
목에ᄃᆡᄒᆞ야는공평한변론을쥬
쟝ᄒᆞᆷ이라우리동신원의탐보는
신문보시는쳠군ᄌᆞ의게ᄒᆞ상보
도ᄒᆞ리며편지들귀셔ᄒᆞ며주시
는이는셩명과번디를ᄌᆡ어붓치
시기를희망ᄒᆞ오나비거슨신문
상에긔ᄌᆡᄒᆞ란는거시아니오단
반드시신용ᄒᆞ는증거를숨고자
ᄒᆞᆷ이라귀자는아모귀셔던지과
격ᄒᆞᆷ을퇴각ᄒᆞ는권리를가졋소
나퇴각ᄒᆞ는리유를말ᄒᆞᆯ터이오
며공중평화를문란케ᄒᆞ는듯ᄒᆞᆫ
다귀셔는의례히밧지안켓숩나이
●본사셜시이리로신문을ᄃᆡ양
우례로불젼ᄒᆞ와례젼부의압의
로졍ᄒᆞᆫ곳스로번곳에는죵늣게
젼ᄒᆞ기도ᄒᆞ며혹면쳘ᄒᆞ거싈ᄒᆞᆫ졉
에젼ᄒᆞ게도ᄒᆞ며혹아니젼ᄒᆞ는
곳도잇다ᄒᆞ와우리신문을수랑
ᄒᆞ야구람ᄒᆞ시는 쳠군ᄌᆞ의게
ᄃᆡᄒᆞ야미우미안ᄒᆞ옵기로지금
은분젼인을두고미일조ᄉᆞ이젼
ᄒᆞ며아니젼ᄒᆞ거나늣게거나ᄒᆞᆫ
폐가업도록ᄒᆞ라ᄒᆞ오니혹아니
젼ᄒᆞ거나늣게젼ᄒᆞ거나ᄒᆞᆫ일
이잇스면본사로통긔ᄒᆞ여주심
을희망ᄒᆞ옵

잡보

○송환월소 외부에서일공사
와교셥ᄒᆞ야한국인민이일본령
사의게월소ᄒᆞ는자ㅣ만ᄒᆞᆫ지라
자금이후로쇼월소ᄒᆞ는자ㅣ잇
거든밧지말고본국지관소로송
교ᄒᆞ란ᄒᆞ엿더라
○이걸감세 영친왕궁에속한
시쟝산군에츅보ᄒᆞ고수도ᄒᆞ는거
시잇는ᄃᆡ궁감이탐봉ᄒᆞ는지라
ᄒᆡ군인민등이일공관에등소ᄒᆞ
야감세신원ᄒᆞ기를이걸ᄒᆞ엿더
라
○환산셔연셜 이상오일하오
이시에경무고문관이각서장을
경무청으로청회ᄒᆞ야경찰사무
상에긴요한사항을연셜ᄒᆞ엿더
라
○대쳐기뎨 전주군수권익상
씨가민요들맛나면관된후에신닙
한탕의뇌물을리근ᄒᆞ씨의게납
ᄒᆞ고갱임ᄒᆞ기를간청ᄒᆞ미졈사
리근ᄒᆞ씨가좌우로주션ᄒᆞ다가
그중형리근틱씨의게송교ᄒᆞ엿
더니리근틱씨가그아오를대쳐
ᄒᆞ엿더라
○민심소요 덕쥬군에옥쟝이
가잇는ᄃᆡ인민이귀찬ᄒᆞ미히도ᄃᆡ
를명례궁에부속ᄒᆞ고도ᄃᆡ뎌젼
을미셰에이샹오랑식자리로뎡
ᄒᆞ야수쇄ᄒᆞᆫ다가쟉추에지ᄒᆞ
야는보셰조로일쳔이빅셕을수
쇄ᄒᆞ미농부들이불응ᄒᆞ는지라
히궁에서평북관찰부로훈령ᄒᆞ
야순검을파송ᄒᆞ야륵봉ᄒᆞ는고
로인민이대단히쇼요ᄒᆞ는중이
라더라
○리정직가 관제리정을이
오일에정부회의를경ᄒᆞ야샹쥬
ᄒᆞ야제가ᄒᆞᆫ다더라
○조량쳐관 경무청에서외부
로조회ᄒᆞ기를남서쟝셔회순보
고내게에본국인뎡병원운돈구
낭인을일헌병이군사령부계시
를위반ᄒᆞ엿다ᄒᆞ고착거ᄒᆞ엿다
ᄒᆞ오니조량쳐관ᄒᆞ옵소셔ᄒᆞ엿
더라
○현금쳥냥 덕원감리가외부
로면보ᄒᆞ엿스되본서쇼부봉수
ᄒᆞ던ᄃᆡ에서군사생수옹
ᄃᆡ라청ᄒᆞ고현금쳥량ᄒᆞ오니하
측ᄒᆞ옵쇼셔ᄒᆞ엿더라
불가양치 숙천군수김규형
씨는평민을남살ᄒᆞ고평양일본
병참소에피신ᄒᆞ엿다더니관찰
사리중하씨가니부로보고ᄒᆞ기
를히민리샹언이가비롤인병쳐
패ᄒᆞ엿다ᄒᆞ드리도공회를좌종
ᄒᆞᆯ차로롱촌친속을티수뇌형ᄒᆞ
는거시법외의일이라가히잉치
ᄒᆞᆯ수업사오니히군수는위션면
본관ᄒᆞ옵소셔ᄒᆞ엿더라
○미위지령 외부에서니부로
조회ᄒᆞ기를이본인이웅쳔가덕
도에서군귀고들파쇄ᄒᆞ고군물
탈취ᄒᆞᆫ사로귀조회를좁사ᄒᆞ온
바본부에서히도관찰사보고를
인ᄒᆞ야부근감리와히국령사의
계면조ᄒᆞ야교섭타결ᄒᆞᆫ사로임
의지령ᄒᆞ엿노라ᄒᆞ엿더라
평양통신
○민항교찬셜 평양야소교중
에유지자들이당디에민인학교
를창셜코자ᄒᆞ야서양인파할동
ᄒᆞ야자본금을모집ᄒᆞᆫ다는ᄃᆡ그
리유인즉좌와여ᄒᆞ니 쥬예수
의은혜아ᄅᆡ잇는평양민인학교
위원들은각쳐에계신 쥬예수
의일홈으로굿치린국사업을누
리평생ᄃᆡ들의케관지ᄒᆞ옴나니우
리나라에구세교가창립된후에
우리들만히밧아남녀소학교와
중학교를세워캄캄ᄒᆞ며렷든눈
을밝히나엇지감사치안으리오
그러하나이는세상빗츨보는소
경이아니와아조눈을감아이세
상빗츨보지못ᄒᆞ는소경들이젹
지안니ᄒᆞᆫᄃᆡ보지못ᄒᆞ는것도불
샹ᄒᆞ거니와소경됨으로인ᄒᆞ야
하나님의명령을어귀는일에의
례히빠지여마귀위ᄒᆞ는일로영
을샹ᄒᆞ야사람을속이는ᄃᆡ망령됨
을하다히지을쌘더러흉ᄒᆞ고중에
참리치를ᄭᆡ닷아회기ᄒᆞ란ᄒᆞ나
용이치못ᄒᆞ니엇지더욱가셕ᄒᆞ
고불샹치안으리오이는대강그
러ᄒᆞ거니와압의교회에드러온
쳥ᄆᆡ와아회들이업마잇ᄉᆞ며쟝
찻ᄎᆞ셩들도잇슬터인ᄃᆡ셰수게
서ᄇᆞᆯ샹ᄒᆞ시기를녀회눈의봉미
누잇삼은불이라ᄒᆞ샹과ᄀᆞᆺ치우리
ᄒᆞ보며산ᄒᆞᆫ듯케기로는일도하
나와소경된쳥ᄆᆡ들은하나님
의말숨을귀가브어주지안이ᄒᆞ
면ᄒᆞᆯ수업스며잉의아는것외에
는ᄒᆞᆫ자ᄒᆞᆯ수업스며쇼한실업쟝
이들면치ᄒᆞ못ᄒᆞᆯ터이니엇지답
답ᄒᆞ고한심치안으리오그럼으
로우리평양교회에서이들위ᄒᆞ
야만히의론ᄒᆞᆫ후에소경들을위
ᄒᆞ야교를세우기로작뎡ᄒᆞ고
셩친한학교인을션뎡ᄒᆞ야학교ᄉᆞ무를위
ᄒᆞ야볼게ᄒᆞ엿스니쳣지로하나님의
보조ᄒᆞᆷ을부신은혜를갑사ᄒᆞ고들
지라ᄒᆞ고소경된형데와ᄌᆞ매들
의헹복을위ᄒᆞᆫ뎡성의로유지ᄒᆞᆯ
ᄒᆞ고사소경들이쳥ᄒᆞ야드러온다ᄒᆞ야
대지못ᄒᆞᆯ지니비록그러ᄒᆞ나
위ᄒᆞ야볼것은ᄃᆡ로하나님의
마련한보조를수합ᄒᆞ야녀디
ᄒᆞᆯ터이니각쳐에게신 ᄌᆞ매
여러분은의보조ᄒᆞᆷ을바라오며
그립고혼례로다소간보조ᄒᆞ심을
그ᄂᆞᆫ혼례로다소간보조ᄒᆞ여주심을
바라ᄂᆞ이다
○오리원군 동강군사ᄂᆞᆫ뎡양
자순가귀와빗수미포사는김창은
처ᄒᆞ여양을다못ᄒᆞ고금년일본인에
게빗보아로고흥박롤나오네서우
부리보교ᄒᆞ다라ᄒᆞ엿더라
○군인불법 평양지위ᄃᆡ보병
참위김셕수씨는자귀의세력박
과면쟝ᄉᆞ로남의집의면주와
작인을자귀ᄒᆞ야빼앗고주는
감리서에졍쟝ᄒᆞ엿더니김씨가
벽로강제ᄒᆞ야빼앗ᄒᆞᄂᆞᆫ엿다
라
○일평기탐 평양인민들이ᄆᆡ
양경쟝을당하면국가를ᄃᆡ기는
ᄃᆡ하나모다쳠치부졔ᄒᆞᆫ지라회
샹업회의쇼에서감리서에쳥원
ᄒᆞ고이를평하게기탐ᄒᆞᆫ다더라
○샹금단취 평북도북청진
위ᄃᆡ병뎡들이오히려파ᄒᆞ엿는ᄃᆡ
ᄃᆡ셜흉경쟝부에서쳥파ᄒᆞ여남으
리도우리는단취ᄒᆞ야하회를ᄀᆡ
다린다ᄒᆞ엿더라
○이주동령판 일진회에서군
일에동령판으로주졍케ᄒᆞᆫ다더
라

론셜

일본의지경

○일본의립법관들이지경이핍졀ᄒᆞ야젼쟁이실패되지아니ᄒᆞ도록급히쥬션ᄒᆞ야ᄒᆞᆯ일을셰드럿도다우리가젼에도말ᄒᆞ엿지마ᄂᆞᆫ현금사셰로ᄂᆞᆫ일본이엇더케돈을만ᄒᆞ야그팽창ᄒᆞᆫ히군과만쥬에잇ᄂᆞᆫ대군을유지ᄒᆞ야갈ᄂᆞᆫ지알슈업스며젼쟁에졈령ᄒᆞᆫ토디를관활ᄒᆞ고려슌구돌핑장히슈츅ᄒᆞᄂᆞᆫ뒤ᄯᅩᄒᆞᆫ큰돈이드러가야될것이로다

이런날에돈이만히드려갈터이니ᄆᆡ일에이삼빅만원이잇서야ᄒᆞᆯ터이니그면ᄒᆞ지못ᄒᆞᆯ국가파산을쇠러가노라고익쓰ᄂᆞᆫ힝동을구경ᄒᆞᆯ만ᄒᆞ도다

일부의히관은젼쟁의시쵸에일본륙군이온젼히셩젼ᄒᆞᆫ셰에두번외채의젼당으로드럿갓고지정가들은션심으로닐ᄒᆞᄂᆞᆫ쟈들이아니라지금은일본이젼일셩젼ᄒᆞᆫ것은귀어허ᄃᆞᄒᆞ고장리셩젼ᄒᆞᆯ희망은ᄆᆡ일머러가니외채돌엇으랴면젼당물과각항죠약이더죵ᄒᆞ야될지라

지금은일본이ᄒᆞᆫ푼이라도외채를엇으랴면젹실ᄒᆞᆫ젼당이잇서야ᄒᆞᆯ것이의심업스나히관셰ᄂᆞᆫ벌셔잡혓고다만너디셰와정부의젼ᄆᆡ와다른ᄉᆞ업만남엇도다

쳐음에말ᄒᆞᆯ것은정부와젼ᄆᆡ물이니그즁에잡힐만ᄒᆞᆫ것은쟝릐젼ᄆᆡ인ᄃᆡ그젼당으로엇을돈으로젼쟁을만히연속ᄒᆞ야가지못ᄒᆞᆯ터이라

철로와ᄯᅩ다른토디권에샹관되ᄂᆞᆫᄉᆞ업은잡힐슈가업ᄂᆞᆫ것이일본법률에외국인의게ᄂᆞᆫ토디쇼유권을허락지아니ᄒᆞ엿스며쟝릭라도허락ᄒᆞᆯ듯ᄒᆞ지아닌것이근일에일본국회에서광산법긔량안을제츌ᄒᆞᆯ셰에광산권은일본인이일본법률을의지ᄒᆞ야죠직ᄒᆞᆷ에만제한ᄒᆞᆫ다ᄂᆞᆫ귀졀을업시이쟈ᄂᆞᆫ돗의가쇼슈로가결이못되엿ᄂᆞᆫ지라

지금일본졍부에서국회와샹의ᄒᆞ야외국금젼을유입ᄒᆞᆯ방칙을강구ᄒᆞᆫ다ᄂᆞᆫᄃᆡ그방칙은연합회샤들을죠직ᄒᆞ야외국쟈본가와일본차권쟈ᄉᆞ이에거간인이되야젼당물은그회샤에쥬고그회샤에서외국쟈본가에게공채징권을쥬게ᄒᆞ랴ᄒᆞᆫ다ᄒᆞᆫ더라

그런방칙은의례히그죠직ᄒᆞᆫ본죠건에달녓스나만일외국쟈본가들을불편ᄒᆞᆫ닐이업게보호ᄒᆞ면외국쟈본을유입ᄒᆞ게될것이확실ᄒᆞᆫ지라그럿치마ᄂᆞᆫ젼당잡힌물건의갑보다더지니게되지ᄂᆞᆫ못ᄒᆞ리라

이계칙이엇더ᄒᆞ던지궁극ᄒᆞᆫ셰라토디의쇼유권이엇슴으로일본이더잡힐것도업고아모라도돈을ᄭᅮ러가ᄂᆞᆫ것은스럼올밧으러간다ᄂᆞᆫ말이잇스니지금일본이빗을내셔마다다졈졈더어려울것이오젼당물은모다다외국시장에ᄯᅥ러지리로다

로국이일본의ᄉᆞ셰를알고ᄯᅩ이젼쟁이엇더케씃치나던지일본의연젼청국파젼징ᄒᆞᆫ때ᄀᆞᆺ치만ᄒᆞᆫ빈샹금은못밧을터이니우리ᄂᆞᆫ미리말ᄒᆞ노니일본이이젼쟁의영향으로손히됨을회복ᄒᆞ랴면잘ᄒᆞ야도여러십년이되여야ᄒᆞᆯ지라이젼쟁을쥬쟝ᄒᆞ던사름을용서ᄒᆞᆯ말은일본이청국파ᄒᆞᆫ국예로국의세력을막으랴면지금ᄒᆞᆫ던지그러치아니ᄒᆞ면영영히못ᄒᆞ리라ᄒᆞᄂᆞᆫ말인ᄃᆡ우리도그리ᄒᆞ다ᄒᆞ나우리의ᄉᆡᆼ각에ᄂᆞᆫ일본정치가들은맛당이ᄒᆞᆯ슈업다ᄒᆞ고ᄉᆡᆼ각ᄒᆞ고ᄯᅩᄉᆡᆼ각ᄒᆞ야영영ᄒᆞᆯ슈업다ᄒᆞ엿더면죠앗슬줄노아노라

관보

뎨삼쳔칠십이호 광무구년이월이십오일 토요

셔임급ᄉᆞ령

○승셔판임관사등 농샹공부쥬사 김교필

이월십이일

○임장흥우체ᄉᆞ쥬ᄉᆞ셔판임관오등 졔쥬우체ᄉᆞ쥬ᄉᆞ 김동철

○임졔쥬우체사쥬ᄉᆞ셔판임관륙등 죵셩우체사쥬ᄉᆞ 김룡한

○히위싱청결소ᄉᆞ무위원 경무쳥경무관 황영쥬 경무쳥경무관 강죵우 경무쳥경무관 리민호

○명위싱청결소ᄉᆞ무위원 경무쳥경무관 셔히쇼

이샹이월이십일일

○의원면본관 군부쥬ᄉᆞ 최지용 군긔창기ᄉᆞ 우준모

○임군부쥬ᄉᆞ셔판임관륙등 권령규

○임군긔창기슈셔판임관륙등 신용구

이샹이월이십이일

○의원면본관 비셔원승 리범세 환구단사제셔령 리소종 숭션면참봉 김종도 긔셩면보사쥬ᄉᆞ 리남구 함경북도변계총슌 김세진

○임비셔원승셔쥬임관륙등 정삼품 리범인

○겸임쟝례원쟝례 비셔원승 리범인

○임환구단사제셔령셔판임관륙등 교방사쥬ᄉᆞ 황범수

○임교방사쥬ᄉᆞ셔판임관칠등 태복사쥬ᄉᆞ 민회식

○임태복사쥬ᄉᆞ셔판임관륙등 시강원시종관 심태셥

○임시강원시종관셔판임관륙등 륙품 리소종

○임숭션면참봉셔판임관팔등 김종학

○승셔판임관이등 외부쥬ᄉᆞ 리원용

○임긔셩면보사쥬ᄉᆞ셔판임관사등 진쥬면보사쥬ᄉᆞ 김동셕

○임진쥬면보사쥬ᄉᆞ셔판임관륙등 젼쥬ᄉᆞ 리남구

○임함경북도변계총슌셔판임관일등 츙청남도관찰부총순 리하진

○임츙청남도관찰부총슌셔판임관ᄉᆞ등 륙품 김세진

이샹이월이십삼일

잡보

○졸업자퇴용 군제의졍에헌병되ᄂᆞᆫ륙군되로편제ᄒᆞ고군긔창에ᄂᆞᆫ졸업ᄒᆞᆫ인원으로기수륙인기ᄉᆞ이인만셜치ᄒᆞᆫ다더라

○지명잔반포 관제리정이의결되엿슴으로지명일에ᄂᆞᆫ반포되리라더라

○칙교긔차 리목포황히도션세위원은일작아에칙교로긔차ᄒᆞ라ᄒᆞ셧다더라

○신칙각셔 경무쳥에셔각셔에신칙ᄒᆞ야갈ᄋᆞ되슌검이셔을단졍이ᄒᆞ고외투구명에손복쟝넛치말며노샹혹쳥ᄂᆡ와뎡샹에대쇼변ᄒᆞᄂᆞᆫ것과코푸ᄂᆞᆫ것을일졀금ᄒᆞ며길에어림에셔슌검이단속을특별이ᄒᆞ야ᄉᆞ무샹에도져히주의ᄒᆞ며현힝ᄒᆞᄂᆞᆫ범을체포ᄒᆞᆯ셰에포동ᄒᆞᄂᆞᆫ외에ᄂᆞᆫ포박ᄒᆞ지말며교번쇼기둥에달아ᄆᆡ지말며차부가곳비를놋코마쇼뒤에셔가지말게ᄒᆞ며시샹우쳑을가로쟝변에렬립ᄒᆞ야왕ᄅᆡ에불편ᄒᆞᆷ이업도록ᄒᆞ며창밧게오좀버리ᄂᆞᆫ것과말타고횡치ᄒᆞᄂᆞᆫ것을금ᄒᆞ고황혼후에ᄂᆞᆫ인력거에등불놀켜게ᄒᆞ라ᄒᆞ엿더라

○법관연회 이십삼일하오칠시에영미일덕비각국공ᄉᆞ가법공관에서연회ᄒᆞ엿더라

○김씨구라 외쥬거ᄒᆞᄂᆞᆫ젼의관김우용씨가민영철씨를밧견ᄒᆞ고발검위협ᄒᆞ야엽샹십만량을ᄲᅢ앗다더니젼쥬ᄉᆞ렴병션씨특가토ᄒᆞ야쟝서ᄒᆞ기를셔경역비ᄂᆞᆫ문부가자지ᄒᆞᆯ이니그츌입을됴사ᄒᆞ며료연ᄒᆞᆯ것이오김우용의발검영악ᄒᆞ야대관을위핍ᄒᆞᆫᄉᆞᄂᆞᆫ무젼ᄒᆞᆫ대변이온ᄃᆡ나라에샹헌이잇ᄉᆞ오니엄히죠쳐ᄒᆞ옵쇼셔ᄒᆞᆫ지라정부에서법부에죠회ᄒᆞ기를샹서원본을의ᄒᆞ야셔경역비ᄂᆞᆫ문부를죠사ᄒᆞ고김우용은각즉형착ᄒᆞ야샹당ᄒᆞᆫ률을시ᄒᆞ라ᄒᆞᆫ지라법부대신이샹쥬ᄒᆞ야김씨를구라ᄒᆞᆫ다더라

○온쳔립표 온양군슈쥬억씨가외부로보고ᄒᆞ기를본군셔면온쳔동에사ᄂᆞᆫ빈셩졍쥰호등의품고ᄒᆞᆫ거슬거ᄒᆞᆫ즉본동은본시멸셩조ᄭᅴ셔거동ᄒᆞ시든ᄯᅡᆼ이라소즁ᄒᆞᆷ이여타ᄌᆞ별ᄒᆞ야힝궁이조지ᄒᆞᆫ온바음력본월일일에일본인삼명이본동에리도ᄒᆞ야ᄉᆞ방수쳔보에립표ᄒᆞ옵고본동사ᄂᆞᆫ리좌형박봉교량인의집을곳쳘폐ᄒᆞ라고독촉이셩화ᄀᆞᆺᄉᆞ오니외부로젼치ᄒᆞ야보고ᄒᆞ야금단케ᄒᆞ여달나ᄒᆞ엿다더라

○둔지미립표 거이십오일에일인ᄉᆞ명이군용측량이라칭ᄒᆞ고동대문밧둔지미신촌에셔졍조동ᄯᅵ립표ᄒᆞ엿더라

○군슈탐쟝 쳘산군민인뎡셕범씨가젼쳘산군슈리두연씨의탐쟝젼이십만량과젼평안도심찰ᄉᆞ리쇼하씨가쳘산셔탐쟝ᄒᆞᆫ젼이삼만여량이라고평리원에뎡ᄒᆞ야지관츄급ᄒᆞ기를쳥ᄒᆞ엿더니지작일에신입지관쟝민경식씨가출사지초에리두연씨에착슈ᄒᆞ엿고리슌하씨ᄂᆞᆫ령젼에출ᄒᆞᆫ지라아직착슈치못ᄒᆞ엿스나필경나치ᄒᆞᆫ다더라

○쇽셜상면 오강민인들이이젼브터셔로면ᄒᆞᄂᆞᆫ말이나라의안위와년ᄉᆞ의풍흉놀강구외결빙ᄒᆞᄂᆞᆫ것이평탄ᄒᆞ고험악ᄒᆞᆫ것을보고중험ᄒᆞᆫ다ᄂᆞᆫᄃᆡ작년에ᄂᆞᆫ히수가역루ᄒᆞ야결빙ᄒᆞ고로흉험박측ᄒᆞ야사ᄅᆞᆷ이감히그우에올나가지못ᄒᆞ게되엿더니사오일젼밤에ᄒᆞᆯ연히강물이뒤집고던디진동ᄒᆞ며어름ᄯᅩ각이다쉬어다라나강ᄭᅥ에산ᄀᆞᆺ치싸인지라사ᄅᆞᆷ이다니르되쟝ᄎᆡᆺ대변이잇스리라고들ᄒᆞ며일인이가셔사진을박혀갓다더라

○주본수샹 군제의뎡의주하와군부의입직주본을지쟈야에수샹ᄒᆞ엿더라

○군슈택임 지작일하오이시에각군슈를틱임ᄒᆞᆯ초로졍부에셔회의ᄒᆞ엿더라

뎐보

론돈발 이월십칠일

○뎨삼합ᄃᆡ츌의발 뎨삼불릭합ᄃᆡᄂᆞᆫ극동으로향ᄒᆞ야리보에셔ᄯᅥ낫다더라

빅림발 동일

○젼쟁의소식 로국골바쓰쟝군은일본군을칙면으로습격ᄒᆞ랴고로국군의좌익에압록디방으로향ᄒᆞ야진군ᄒᆞ기를예비ᄒᆞᆫ다더라

파리발 동일

○영국국회의긔회죠칙 영국회의긔회죠칙에말ᄒᆞ엿스되일본과로국ᄉᆞ이에젼쟁이불힝히지금ᄭᅡ지연속ᄒᆞ나영국은연ᄒᆞ야엄쟝즁립을직힐터이라ᄒᆞ엿다더라

빅림발 동일

○덕국친왕의동리 덕국료폴드친왕은싸스고에셀노에셔로국황뎨를방문ᄒᆞ고그후에덕국션뎨노아를타고국돗을향ᄒᆞ야온다ᄂᆞᆫ대쳥국북경을찻기가십다더라

TELEGRAMS.

(FROM JAPAN PAPERS)

Note. The messages marked* are those which are described as special service" or "special telegrams or "received by the Government." The others are from properly authenticated sources.

KUROPATKIN'S ARMY.

London, Feb. 20.

General Gripenberg, who has just returned from the front, where he vacated his command of the Second Manchurian Army, has been favourably received by the Czar, and says that influences are at work to undermine the position of General Kuropatkin.

London, Feb. 19.

*A Russian military train has been in collision at Hoviara(?). Many of the troops were injured.

THE BALTIC SQUADRON.

London, Feb. 19.

*M. Diedrichsen, the Russian Consul at Kiel, is reported to have purchased two former Castle liners for use as transports with the third Baltic Squadron.

London, Feb. 19.

*It is reported that Admiral Rojestvensky's flagship, the "Kniaz Suvaroff," recently struck a rock and severely damaged her hull. She had difficulty in reaching St. Louis.

AFFAIRS IN RUSSIA.

London, Feb. 20.

The funeral of the Grand Duke Sergius will take place on the 23rd intant, and will be practically private. The Tsar and leading members of the Imperial family will be absent.

King Edward and Prince of Wales have called on Count Benckendorff, the Russian Ambassador in London, to express their condolences with the Imperial family.

It is stated that the death of the Grand Duke has had a crushing effect upon the members of the Russian Imperial family, the Grand Duke Vladimir (brother of the murdered man) being terribly affected.

London, Feb. 20.

The Commission appointed at St. Petersburg to make an investigation into the grievances of workmen has issued a a most elaborate scheme whereby employers and workmen may elect delegates to a Commission which will consider labour disputes.

London, Feb. 20.

The St Petersburg correspondent of the "Daily Telegraph" states that among the highest dignitaries in Russia the conviction is growing that it is in the vital interests of the Government and the dynasty that the war should be ended as soon as possibe

---

The kamni of Masanpo telegraphs that the Japanese gendarmerie have arrested a Korean police inspector and that he cannot get any explantion from them.

As only some 8 or 9 of the captains in the Seoul regiment have properly qualified for their positions by passing examinations, there will be plenty of vacancies when the contemplated reforms come into effect.

The Japanese, American and French Ministers have complained to the Foreign Office that they find all their despatches published in the newspapers on the day following their receipt. As the contents are sometimes of a confidential nature it is requested that the leakage be stopped.

THE POLICE AND THE WELLS.

In view of the accusations against the police of jobbery in connection with the house to house collection of funds for the well crusade which is now going on, we have been requested by the police authorities to publish the following:—

"As pure drinking water is essential to public health, and as there are no Government funds available for the purpose it is neccessary that the people obey the orders of the police and subscribe the cost of cleaning the wells.

"The total sum to be collected was $14,088 and this was divided amongst 22,300 houses at varying rates according to whether the roofs were tile or thatch and the houses large or small, and the sum collected will be expended exactly even to the last farthing.

"But of late false rumours have been circulated. It has been said that there are far more than 100,000 houses and that over $40,000 has been collected. These statements are false and inimical to the welfare of the city and we therefore publish this in order to allay unjust suspicions.

"As soon as possible an exact statement of money collected and spent will be issued."

The death is announced, at the age of 80, of Sir Robert Jardine, head of the firm of Jardine Matheson and Co.

It is rumoured in St. Petersburg that the Grand Duke Vladmir is next on the list for assassination at the hands of the revolutionists.

A subscriber informs us that he has for sale a number of good guns and a large quantity of cartridge shells Nos 12 and 8. Those interested will please apply to this office.

Recently four representatives of the rich people at 5 rivers who have offered to lend the Government $8,000,000 were summoned to meet the members of the Cabinet for the purpose of discussing the proposal. The outcome has not transpired.

The condition of some of the roads in Seoul is a matter which calls for the immediate attention of those responsible. The road between the South Gate and the foot of Chinkokai would be a disgrace to a fishing village, and if something is not soon done to the road which follows the palace wall the Legations will be cut off from the rest of the world.

It is reported in Japan papers that negotiations are now taking place between the Korean Government and the French Minister at Seoul concerning the contract for the supply of material for the Seoul Wiju Railway, which contract was concluded between the Korean authorities and a French subject, prior to the outbreak of the Japan-Russia war.

We learn from the Japan Times that the "Kokumin" taunts Count Okuma with being far behind the times as regards the Korean question. It makes this charge because of a passage that occurs in a collection of the Count's utterances on and about Korea, recently published with his lordship's permission, and which may be construed into implying that, according to the Count, Japan should deal with Korea only as a full-powered independent State. But, says the "Kokumin," when the Japan-Korea Agreement was made public last year, the world at once implicitly recognized that the agreement would make Korea stand toward Japan as Egypt does to England, and ever since then this country has steadly been acting up to this recognized principle. Let Korea be what the Count would have her to be then Japan's Korean policy will become unworkable and the present Russo-Japanese conflict would lose half its meaning. Besides, says the journal, Korea, as a matter of fact, is not and cannot be a fully qualified independent country, and it is astonished that the veteran statesman has so far outlived the age.

THE IL-CHIN-HOI.

The Il chin-hoi people have sent a note to Mr. Yi Yong Ik advising him not to attempt to enter the palace or any of the Legations. Believing that Mr. Yi Yong Ik does not intend to accept their advice the executive have told off ten men to watch his movements and prevent him from entering the palace. They have also advised him to return to his native province North Ham Kyŏng.

The "boss" of the Il-chin-hoi has telegraphed to the chief of the society in North Pyeng An Province ordering all the members in North and South Pyeng An to assemble and attack the soldiers and riflemen of the public guard at Kangkei. The soldiers are to be deprived of their arms and uniforms and dispersed. There are said to be already some 10,000 membere at Kangkei and a fight is impending. The trouble seems to be that the soldiers recently dispersed an Il-chin-hoi meeting and wounded 12 of the agitators.

It is reported that the 19 magistrates recently appointed were men recommended by the Japanese Minister.

According to the latest news from the front the opposing forces on the Shaho have now drawn so near each other that they are separated by only 1,000 metres or so at some points.

The Press Association states that Mr. James Nicol Dun, of the "Morning Post," will be the new editor of the "Manchester Courier," and will have a proprietary interest. Sir Alfred Harmsworth is the principal proprietor of the "Courier."

In view of the extraordinarily mild winter which we have had, there are great apprehensions among the Koreans that diseases and epidemics will arrive with the Spring The Governor of Seoul has accordingly issued a proclamation enjoining the people to exercise great care in sanitary matters.

The official opening of the Seoul-Fusan railway will take place about the middle of May by which time the branch line to Masanpo and the repairs to the bridge over the Han River will be completed. A large number of visitiors are expected from Japan including members of the diet, leading business men, press representatives etc and great preparations are being made for their reception.

It may not be out of place, says a contemporary, to note that Captain Troubridge, who, in the capacity of naval representative of Great Britain, was present on Admiral Togo's flagship, during the torpedo attacks upon the Russian fleet, at Port Arthur, has decided that we have little to learn from his hosts in the way of naval warfare, and the highest praise he can bestow upon them is that they appear to have followed our own methods with remarkable fidelity.

The Japanese Minister has endorsed and forwarded to the Foreign Office a request from the Japanese consul, at Chemulpo that the iron required for the construction of a pier by a Japanese company in that port be permitted to be imported duty free. We perceive no reason why the Korean Government should be expected to accede to this calm request. Then argument used Is that the Korean Government has the option of buying the pier at the expiration of fifteen years, but this does not to our mind, in any way affect the question of duty.

We frequently hear of Japanese desperadoes lending their services to Koreans for debt collecting purposes. An incident of this kind recently happened in Kempo near Pyeng Yang. It appears that a Mr. Kim Sang Lun of that place owed money to a man named Chŏng Yang Chun and according Chŏng, having provided himself with a body guard of ten Japanese set out for Kim's house to collect the debt. Kim was however not at home, so the Japanese, not to be robbed of their fun captured a Mr. O In Sik, who happened to be on the premises, but had nothing to do with Kim's money affairs, tied him up and amused themselves. O In Sik died.

NORTHEAST KOREA.

As the telegraph service in Korea is under Japanese control it naturally follows that we hear only the Japanese side of things at first.

In due course, however, the other side gets heard and in this connection an interview which we had to-day with a Korean from Songchin is interesting.

We asked him if he had seen many Russian soldiers in his district. Yes, plenty until recently when they went away. What kind of soldiers were they? Oh, very good. Well behaved? Yes. Drunken? No. Well, we have been told that they robbed the people, outraged the women and generally behaved badly. Is that so? No. I have seen nothing of the kind neither have I heard I heard any complaints. Of course when there was no fodder in the towns a detachment would go into the surrounding villages and commandeer what there was, but it was always paid for. The people who owned the fodder and wanted it for their own cattle were angry but I heard no other complaints.

Our informant also told us that there were no Russians at Kapsan, although scouts occasionally rode into the place.

NOTICE.

Dr. Harold Slade, Resident Dentist of Kobe, will visit Seoul professionally about the end of February.

The Korea Daily News.

Issued at 5 P. M. daily except Sundays.

Rate of Subscription:—
Per Year,............Yen 25.
Per Quarter,..........Yen 7.
Per Month,..........Yen 2.50.

Postage in Korea not charged extra.
Postage abroad charged extra.

Advertisements, 50 sen per day for 1 inch or less.
5 yen per month per inch.
50 yen per year per inch.

All communications to
E. T. BETHELL,
Editor and Publisher,
Pak-tong, Seoul.

THE WAR AND THE TRUTH.

We imagine the public has long ago ceased to place any confidence in the reports emanating from Tokio regarding the war—rather happily dubbed, by a Shanghai exchange, "Japograms."

We do not for a moment suggest that the reports forwarded to his Government by Field Marshal Marquis Oyama are untrue, or that such of them as are issued to the public in any way differ from the original reports, but it is very evident that many of the reports are suppressed. We are not referring to the suppression of such reports as would lead to the disclosure of military secrets, but we have very good grounds for asserting that for a whole month the Japanese army has been steadily retreating and the news has been withheld from the public.

A little over a month ago we were given to understand that there were no Russians on the left bank of the Hun River, then came the battle of Heikantai which was described as an attempt on the part of Kuropatkin to establish a footing on the left bank of the river, and the result of this engagement was hailed by all the Japanese and pro-Japanese press as a Japanese victory. Slowly but surely the facts of the case are coming to light. Immediately after the engagement, the Tokio correspondent of a London newspaper (the Daily Telegraph we think) wired to London that the Russian casualties were 30,000 and the Japanese, 7,000.

So far, no official list of the Japanese casualties has come to hand, but a medical statement—whatever that may be—published in Tokio on February 20th gives the Japanese losses as 9,382. No explanation to given as to the unusual course of publishing a "medical statement" before the official list and it is therefore obvious that the official returns are being withheld because they show much more damaging results.

In the meantime, apart from the flight of imagination of the Tokio correspondent of the Daily Telegraph—which need not be taken into consideration—there is no evidence that Kuropatkin's original estimate of his losses, viz, 10,000, was at all wide of the mark.

It therefore appears that the losses at the battle of Heikoutai were about the same on both sides; and now we will see what the result was as regards position.

We may premise our remarks on this subject by saying that if it is the duty of whoever is responsible for the issuance of the official bulletins to bewilder the reader he has succeeded admirably, while if it is his duty to impart to the public some intelligent idea of what is going on, he has failed miserably.

Still there are straws which show which way the wind blows, and it is upon these straws which we, in danger of drowning in the torrent of long and unpronouncable names which monopolize the latest official reports, seize. One arrived this morning and we give it in the exact words of the "Japan Mail."

(Received at the Military Head Quarters on the 19th instant.)

Yesterday (18th) the ememy's guns cannonaded our positions from Wanpaoshan, Sanglantsz, Kwantun (about 2 kilo. northwest of Shahopau) Liuchangtum, Hananchingnan and Paohsiangtun.

To day (19th) in the forenoon a column of the enemy numbering at least a division moved westward from Tashan and entered Hangkiataitsz (about 2 kilo. north-west of Wankiayuantsz.)

Now, to the casual reader this portends nothing. "A Division moved westward from Tashan and entered Wangkiayuantz!" Tashan is an elevation immediately fronting the right of the Japanese centre, not more than two or three miles distant, and when a matter of 30,000 men advance from there and take up a new position it means one of two things; either the Japanese have declined to fight and retreated or they have been beaten and retreated.

From the Japanese left we hear little. The Russian cavalry are still hovering about and threaten to attack Liaoyang at any moment. In the centre the Russians appears to be very strong, and although we are not told so in so many words, there can be no doubt that the Japanese are steadily losing ground.

A study of the position leads to the conviction that we shall soon be given an opportunity of seeing in what fashion the Japanese can retreat and whether the Russians will be better in advancing than they were. There can be no doubt that a big engagement——the biggest of the war—is impending and, in spite of all that inspired newspapers say to the contrary we cannot see how it can end in anything but a Japanese reverse.

Kuropatkin has just as good men as the Japanese and more of them, and that is sufficient for us. "Bushido" can inspire nothing more than what an ordinary white man calls courage, and in resourcefulness and tactical and strategic skill we do not think the Russians have anything to learn from the Japanese.

Another thing to be taken into consideration is the "way home." Should the Japanese be compelled to retreat, there is but one road open to them. They dare not split up into their original three armies, and if they retired they would have to fall back, *en bloc*, into the Liao Tung peninsula.

This will contribute toward making the coming battle a particularly desperate one. If the Russians lose they will retreat,—to Mukden: if the Japanese lose they will retreat—South of Liaoyang.

JAPANESE EMIGRANTS.

Both for its own sake and that of its people the Japanese Government should place some restriction upon the indiscriminate irresponsible emigration which is now going on to this country and to Manchuria. An impression prevails among the ignorant classes in Japan that wealth is here waiting to be picked up and the result is that a continuous stream of 'ne'er do weels" and adventurers is pouring into Korea.

Of course the Japanese Government can hardly be blamed for putting no obstacles in the way of worthless people "leaving their country for their country's good" but at the same time it is a process which will inevitably, and in the very near future, lead to great distress.

Skilled artisans are in great demand here and in Manchuria, but then Japan itself has never had a sufficiency of skilled labour so but little of it needs to leave the country. A man with capital can make money here but that is another commodity which is scarce in Japan.

The result is that the Japanese population in Korea consists largely of feckless undersirables: men and women who set stalls in the streets and peddle toffee and cakes and fruit, or gimcrack haberdashery and notions from Osaka, or worse than all, bogus cure-all medicines.

As these people do nothing to develop commerce, antagonize the natives wherever thy go and would be a serious care to their government should reverses happen in the war, we suggest that the placing of-restrictions on such emigration would, in the end, be a wise step.

The Tokio Government has introduced to the House the Bill of Corporation of Japanese Settlement abroad. This Bill proposes to incorporate the Japanese subjects resident in any one settlement into an autonomous entity, to be superintended by the Consul, the Minister and the Foreign Minister. It is believed that this bill, should it become law, will improve the administration of the Japanese settlements abroad.

Preliminary surveys are about to be made with regard to the long-talked of canal which is to connect the White Sea with Lake Onega and the whole system of the river Neva. The distance between the White Sea and Lake Onega is 146 miles, of which 86 miles are already navigable. The remaining waterway of 60 miles will have to be deepened, at an estimated cost of £850,000. The project is favoured very much by the naval authorities, as such a canal could be used by warships, which would then be able to make for the ocean round the North Cape, at least for some months in the year.

With reference to the recent confirmation of the clause in the Japanese mining laws prohibiting foreigners from engaging in mining operations, the "Yorodzu," the leading liberal daily paper in Tokio, vents its feelings in very severe language in a few short paragraphs, with such headings as "Narrow Anti-foreign Spirit," "A Craven and Ignorant Crowd," &c. "For a country which claims the open door abroad, and which talks so much of the necessity of establishing close economic ties with the outer world, to monopolise mining business at home and abroad (presumably in Korea) is inconsistent, disorderly, unreasonable, reactionary. It betrays a narrow antforegn spirit, and is a disgrace to a victorious country." The "Jiji's" report of the debate concludes: "Such a measure, inspired by the "Joi" spirit, was, after all, the only thing to expect from a House composed mainly of bald-pated old man born in the time of *Tempo* (a play upon the slang phrase *temposen*, a fool) and before "Mei-ji" (enlightened era)."

The Korea Daily News.

VOL. II, MONDAY, FEBRUARY 27, 1905. No. 44

HONGKONG & SHANGHAI BANKING CORPORATION.

Paid-up Capital.................$10,000,000
Reserve Fund:—Sterling Reserve... 10,000,000
Silver Reserve..... 7,000,000

27,000,000

Reserve Liability of Proprietors... 10,000,000

HEAD OFFICE, HONGKONG.

London Bankers, London and County Banking Company Limited.

Branches and Agencies,

London.		
Amoy,	Hankow	Penang,
Bangkok,	Hiogo,	Rangoon,
Batavia,	Iloilo,	Saigon,
Bombay,	Lyons,	San Francisco,
Calcutta,	Manila,	Singapore,
Colombo,	Nagasaki,	Sourabaya,
Foochow,	New York,	Tientsin,
Hamburg,	Peking,	Yokohama,

Credits granted on approved Securities, and every description of Banking and Exchange business transacted.

Drafts granted on London and the chief Commercial places in Europe, India, Australia, America, China and Japan.

HOLME RINGER & CO., AGENTS,
CHEMULPO.

HOKURKU DOBOKU KAISHA.

Branch office in Chong Dong, Seoul.

Japanese telephone No. 165

CONTRACT DEPARTMENT.

We can contract to build any building or construction.

MERCHANDISE DEPARTMENT.

We can provide any building material. We have just contracted to build the new Belgian Legation.

E. MEYER & CO.

Chemulpo.

SOLE AGENTS IN KOREA FOR.

A. T. Morse, Sons & Co.'s

"Fresco" Distemper

In all colours ready for use on walls, Ceilings etc.

and

AVENARIUS CARBOLINEUM

A wood-preserving and antiseptic oil preparation

Against decay, dry-rot, fungus and wood-destroying insects.

A large supply always in stock. Prices upon application.

E. MEYER & CO.,
Chemulpo.

CHARTERED BANK OF INDIA AUSTRALIA & CHINA.

INCORPORATED BY ROYAL CHARTER 1853

HEAD OFFICES.—LONDON.

Paid-up Capital £800,000
Reserve Liability of Shareholders 800,000
Reserve Fund 800,000

Drafts granted upon all the principal places in the world and every description of Exchange and banking business transacted.

E. MEYER & Co., Agents,
Chemulpo.

MITSU BISHI DOCKYARD & ENGINE WORKS,

NAGASAKI.

CODE WORD, "DOCK."

A 1, A. B. C., and Engineering Codes used.

DOCK No. 1 (at Tategami).

Extreme Length..............523 feet
Length on blocks .... 513 ,,
Width of Entrance on Top......89 ,,
,, ,, Bottom....77 ,,
Water on Blocks at Spring Tide 26½ ,,

DOCK No. 2 (Mukaijima).

Extreme Length........ ....371 feet
Length on Blocks............360 ,,
Width of Entrance on Top......66 ,,
,, ,, Bottom 53 ,,
Water on Blocks at Spring Tide 22 ,,

PATENT SLIP (at Kosuge).

Can take vessels up to 1,000 tons gross.

THE WORKS are well equipped with the LATEST IMPROVEMENTS, and can execute any kind of work in SHIPBUILDING and MARINE ENGINEERING, as well as in REPAIRING of SHIPS.

The COMPANY'S new powerful steamer OURA-MARU (712 tons, 700 I.H.P.), specially built for SALVAGE PURPOSES, and equipped with necessary gear, is always READY at SHORT NOTICE.

THE METHODIST PUBLISHING HOUSE,

Little West Gate, Seoul.

JOB PRINTING, TYPEWRITER PAPER
CARBON PAPER, VISITING CARDS
STATIONERY, BOOK BINDING
BOOK PUBLISHERS
AMERICAN SCHOOL BOOKS
SPENCERIAN COPY BOOKS
PEN CARBON LETTER AND BILL BOOKS

S. A. BECK, Manager.

DAI-ICHI GINKO

LIMITED.

(Formerly the First National Bank)

ESTABLISHED 1873

INCORPORATED UNDER PRESENT LAW 1896

Capital - - - - - - - - Yen 5,000,000
Reserve Fund - - - - - 1,500,000

HEAD OFFICE:—TOKIO.

President: Baron SHIBUSAWA.

BRANCHES AND CORRESPONDENTS in the Principal Cities and Towns of Japan.

Interest Allowed on

Fixed deposits 1 year - - - 6½ per cent
,, ,, 6 months - - - 6 per cent

Special current accounts 1½ sen daily per Y 100
General ,, ,, 1 ,, ,, ,, 100

M. TANAKA,
Manager, Chemulpo.

SINGER SEWING MACHINES

씽거즈봉침

SOLE AGENTS FOR KOREA

전매쇼

HOLME RINGER & CO.
Chemulpo.

졔물포 함릉거양힝

KAMEYA & CO.

GENERAL STOREKEEPERS

Chinkokai - - Seoul

(*Established 1895, Tokyo*)

Confectionery, Hams, Canned Goods, Cutlery, Hirano & Tansan Water. Provisions, Gents, Furnishing goods, Toilet Articles, Travelling Bags, Tobacco, Cigars & Cigarettes Kitchen Utensils. Coffee, Biscuits

Fresh Goods always kept in Stock.

Prices Moderate

Please come and inspect our goods.

NIPPON YUSEN KAISHA.

JAPANESE MAIL STEAMSHIP CO.

UNDER MAIL CONTRACT WITH THE IMPERIAL JAPANESE GOVERNMENT.

European Line

Regular Fortnightly Service between Yokohama Kobe, Moji, Shanghai, Hongkong, Singapore, Penang Colombo, Port Said, Marseilles, London and Antwerp

American Line

Regular Fortnightly Service between Hongkong and Seattle, calling at Shanghai, Moji, Kobe, Yokohama and Victoria, B. C.

Australian Line

Regular weekly Service between Japan Ports and Australia, calling at Hongkong and Manila.

(Above Three Lines Suspended until further notice)

Shanghai Line

Weekly Service between Shanghai and Japan Po

Korea Line

Service Kobe, Moji, Nagasaki, Fusan Chemulpo Chefoo, Taku.

S. S. Babelsberg, 2181 tons.

Service Kobe. Moji, Fusan, Chemulpo, Chinnampo

S. S. ARGO, S. S. Ohio.

BORDEN'S CONDENSED MILK CO.

New York, U. S. A.

ALWAYS IN STOCK

Eagle Brand Condensed Milk.

Gold Seal Condensed Milk.

Peerless (Family) Evaporated Cream.

Borden's Malted Milk.

E. MEYER & CO.
Chemulpo Korea,
Sole Agents

ROYAL INSURANCE COMPANY,

Funds exceed £10,000,000

FIRE

AT CURRENT RATES

LIFE

REDUCED PREMIUM,

HOLME RINGER & Co.,
Agents, Chemulpo.

廣 KWANG C'HANG 昌

BENNETT & CO.

Merchants

Chemulpo.

Offices opposite the Imperial Japanese Post and Telegraph Office Chemulpo.

Telephone Number 201.

大韓每日申報
대한미일신보

(뎨이권 ᄉᆞ십오호) (슈요일) 일쳔구빅오년이월이십구일

본샤고빅

이신보는영어와한어로셕거ᄆᆡ
일츌판ᄒᆞ옵

신문갑

한쟝 엽젼두돈오푼
일삭료 엽젼두량닷돈
우표가ᄂᆞᆫ ᄉᆞ닷돈
다닷돈으로밧숩

광고료ᄂᆞᆫ

긔한의쟝단과ᄌᆞ힝의다쇼로즁
감ᄒᆞ되한가로밧을터이오ᄆᆡ오
리지아니ᄒᆞᆫ사ᄅᆞᆷ마다다이신
문을보실터이니광고내시기를
원ᄒᆞ시는이들은우리신문사에
와셔면약ᄒᆞ심을희망ᄒᆞ옵

○발힝소 박동대한ᄆᆡ일신보
사법어학교압희젼영국인셜필
림쟈리오

사쟝 영국인 (배셜)

평양 ᄃᆡ리졈

○평양효동사ᄂᆞᆫ 권ᄆᆡ보씨로우
리신문지ᄃᆡ리인을뎡ᄒᆞ엿
ᄉᆞ오니평양에계신구람ᄒᆞ고져ᄒᆞ
시ᄂᆞᆫ 쳠군ᄌᆞᄂᆞᆫ흥히ᄃᆡ리졈에왕
림ᄒᆞ와면의ᄒᆞ시옵

사고

○우리대한ᄆᆡ일신보의목뎍은
대한의안녕질셔에관한모든대
목에ᄃᆡᄒᆞ야ᄂᆞᆫ공평한변론을쥬
장홈이라우리동신원의ᄃᆞᆷ보ᄂᆞᆫ
신문보시ᄂᆞᆫ쳠군ᄌᆞ의게ᄒᆞᆼ상보
도ᄒᆞ려며편지를긔셔ᄒᆞ며주시
ᄂᆞᆫ이ᄂᆞᆫ셩명과번디를ᄌᆞ셰ᄒᆞ붓쳐
셔기를희망ᄒᆞ오니히거슨신문
샹에긔ᄌᆡᄒᆞᆫ논거시아니오다
만귀히신용ᄒᆞᄂᆞᆫ증거를숨고자
홈이라긔자ᄂᆞᆫ아모긔셔던지긔
ᄌᆡᄒᆞᆷ을뢰각ᄒᆞᄂᆞᆫ권리를가졋소
나뢰각ᄒᆞᄂᆞᆫ리유ᄂᆞᆫ말ᄒᆞᆯ터이오
며ᄭᅩᆼ즁평화를문란케ᄒᆞᄂᆞᆫ듯ᄒᆞᆫ
긔셔ᄂᆞᆫ의례히밧지안켓ᄉᆞᆸ나이
다

●본사셜시이ᄅᆡ로신문을ᄃᆡ양
우레로분젼ᄒᆞ와레젼부의임의
로젼ᄒᆞᄂᆞᆫ듯스로벗곳에ᄂᆞᆫ호ᄂᆞᆫ게
젼ᄒᆞ기도ᄒᆞ며호벗쳘거슨ᄒᆞᆫ겁
에젼ᄒᆞ기도ᄒᆞ며호아나젼ᄒᆞᄂᆞᆫ
곳도잇다ᄒᆞ와우리신문을ᄉᆞ랑
ᄒᆞ야구람ᄒᆞ시ᄂᆞᆫ 쳠군ᄌᆞ의게ᄆᆡ
ᄐᆡᄒᆞ야면우미안ᄒᆞ옵기로지금
은분젼인을두고ᄆᆡ일죠이젼
ᄒᆞ며ᄒᆞ나젼ᄒᆞ거나늣게거나ᄒᆞᆫ
폐가잇ᄉᆞᆸ도록ᄒᆞᆫ오나ᄒᆞ야
젼ᄒᆞ거ᄂᆞᆫ혹늣게젼ᄒᆞ거나ᄒᆞᆫ일
이잇스면본사로통긔ᄒᆞ여쥬심
을희망ᄒᆞ옵

잡보

○헌병ᄃᆡ힝 도셩ᄂᆡ각방곡에
잇ᄂᆞᆫᄃᆡ파슈병뎡은이십오일브터
일병참거ᄒᆞ엿슴으로파수신ᄃᆡ
에계반ᄉᆞ무와경찰은헌병으로
ᄃᆡ힝ᄒᆞᆷ의로거이십오일에헌병
ᄃᆡ로쳐교가나겻다더라

○삼분지일 금번군졔의뎡된
후에미참ᄒᆞᆫ군인은휴직이되ᄂᆞᆫ
ᄃᆡ휴직ᄒᆞᆫ령위관의월봉은셜치
월봉의삼분지이ᄂᆞᆫ노마련반급ᄒᆞᆫ
다더라

○셜면문회 셩ᄂᆡ각방곡에경
무쳥에셔괴믈세웟ᄂᆞᆫᄃᆡᄂᆡ외국
인을분론ᄒᆞ고대로법에셜젼ᄒᆞᆷ
을분회ᄒᆞᆯ수라ᄒᆞ엿더라

○불가쳔편 덕원군수리죵원
씨가ᄂᆡ부로보고ᄒᆞ엿스되분향
가에주진ᄒᆞᆫ일본령ᄉᆞᄃᆡ목인지죠
이잇스니군니형금군사상에소용가
ᄒᆞ와면담과환유디를됴사ᄒᆞ야
회시ᄒᆞ란교뎌편법힐난ᄒᆞ나쳔
편히ᄒᆞᆯ수업스니곳쳐분ᄒᆞ라ᄒᆞ
엿더라

○불가면무 강원관찰ᄉᆞ가ᄂᆡ
부로보고ᄒᆞ엿스되관하쳥곡군
슈박계션의치적은입의샹년츄
동에포보ᄒᆞ엿거니와ᄃᆡ져차군
슈가위인이자셔ᄒᆞ고빅셩의게
자혜ᄒᆞ야흉년을당ᄒᆞ야진휼을
셜ᄒᆞ야케ᄒᆞ고쳥송이공결ᄒᆞ미사
경이안도ᄒᆞ며용남은진최가무
ᄒᆞ고아젼이간활홈을힝치못ᄒᆞ
ᄂᆞᆫ지라폐리ᄒᆞᆫ우젹은가히민묵
ᄒᆞᆯ수가업기로자에보고ᄒᆞ오니
특별히포상을나리사ᄯᅥ웅권장
ᄒᆞ시기를바라옵나이다ᄒᆞ엿더
라

○군수샹방ᄒᆡ 일본공ᄉᆞ가ᄂᆡ
부로공함ᄒᆞ엿스되거제도에우
리군ᄉᆞ샹힝동의필요홈을위ᄒᆞ
야디역ᄂᆡ에가셜ᄒᆞᆫ통신과판을
방ᄃᆡ히군슈의게양종ᄒᆞ고보호
ᄒᆞᄂᆞᆫ칙임을담부케ᄒᆞ엿스나ᄒᆡ
군슈권즁ᄒᆞᆫ은차를등한히알고
그보호ᄒᆞ기에용력지안ᄂᆞᆫ결과
로자주뎐화션을졀단ᄒᆞ야졀취
ᄒᆞᄂᆞᆫ자잇ᄂᆞᆫ지라우리군ᄉᆞ샹에
방ᄒᆡ가불소홈으로히군슈를ᄀᆡᆼ
칙ᄒᆞ라고마산포에주진ᄒᆞᆫ우리
령ᄉᆞ가앙진ᄒᆞᆷ이니속히경힝ᄒᆞ
시오ᄯᅩᄒᆞ고ᄒᆞ후임을일본시찰원으
로수힝즁에가감ᄒᆞᆫ자로임용ᄒᆞ
시면피아교셥에편리ᄒᆞᆯ줄노아
옵나이다ᄒᆞ엿더라

○사속부임 ᄂᆡ부대신이봉함
에ᄒᆞ엿스되거제군수권즁ᄒᆞᆫ이
가진무에불근ᄒᆞ야군ᄉᆞ샹에방
ᄒᆡ를귀ᄒᆞ엿다니등기에심히ᄒᆞᆫ
연ᄒᆞᆯ샌더러경ᄒᆞ야불법ᄉᆞ건이
잇기로입의샹쥬ᄒᆞ야면관ᄒᆞ엿
고ᄯᅩᄒᆞᆫ그ᄃᆡ에음샹우등임ᄒᆞ엿
스니맛당히신슈의게편칙ᄒᆞ야
ᄒᆞ여금불일ᄂᆡ로부임ᄒᆞ야ᄉᆞᄉᆞ
준판케ᄒᆞ겟노라ᄒᆞ엿더라

○주본진하 거이십륙일에ᄂᆡ
부에셔군수주본을주하ᄒᆞ엿ᄂᆞᆫ
ᄃᆡ대구에김한뎡쳥풍에리병화
금산에김병욱슌흥에뎡진학군위
에김교헌곽산에셩셥동진에리
보헌교평에셩심셩렬진양쳔안즁식
영동에최쥬긔평에리지틱합창에젼
광복창평에장복규지례에김황
진단셩에김병걸창셩에박반원
강셩에리우영룡쥬에윤규셥진
위에뎡히팔동리에원우샹남ᄒᆡ
에린슌영쳥녕에민병진단양에
박초양인동에셔샹기평창에졍
명식츈쳔에리명긔원쥬에김영규
식흥션쳔에민평기이쳔에박승언
교셩에장운원쳘원에로병직금화
산에쳔셰힝안의에리범환졔샹인
에ᄃᆡ샹향군수ᄂᆞᆫ각부부ᄃᆡ신일인
식쳔임ᄒᆞ고기ᄂᆞᆫ됴니ᄃᆡ와리
라근틱씨가주관ᄒᆞ야조종ᄒᆞ엿더
라

○우위셜힝 거이십칠일ᄂᆡ부
에셔ᄯᅩ군수주본을셜힝ᄒᆞ엿더
라

○향동편셔 학부에셔외부로
조회ᄒᆞ기를폐부소ᄡᅡᆼ즁학교교
사폐원탄은본부참여관으로면
임ᄒᆞᆫ티에일본인교교항으로장
ᄎᆞ연빙ᄒᆞ니향동을변쳐ᄒᆞ라ᄒᆞ
엿ᄂᆞᆫᄃᆡ월급은일빅오십원이오
거졉비ᄂᆞᆫᄆᆡ삭이십원이라더라

○군물수샹 이십륙일에종셩
ᄃᆡ병뎡십명이쳔환사십ᄃᆡ와총
일ᄃᆡ와장셥일ᄃᆡ를령솔ᄒᆞ고입
셩ᄒᆞ엿더라

○혼유히송 케끝ᄃᆡ구판찰ᄉᆞ
리용익씨가에ᄂᆞᆫ일진회회원들
이파수ᄒᆞ고쳘염을게힝ᄒᆞᄂᆞᆫ고
로경무쳥에셔효유ᄒᆞ야히송ᄒᆞ
엿더라

○쟝힝질문 법부대신박졔슌
씨가교관과빅수를존힝으로헤
의지인만임면ᄒᆞ고젼사림법관
양셩소졸업싱은셔임치안ᄂᆞᆫ고
로졸업싱금일진회회원ᄒᆞ긍셩
씨등오륙인이쳥원ᄒᆞ고그불임
ᄒᆞᄂᆞᆫ리유를장ᄎᆞᄃᆡ질문ᄒᆞ리라
ᄒᆞ더라

○협졍긔차 일용사가ᄂᆡ부로
공함ᄒᆞ기를젼라도제주도ᄂᆞᆫ일
한젼박의항ᄒᆡᄒᆞᄂᆞᆫ왕리수면에
져ᄒᆞ야젼박이차항에괴ᄒᆞᄂᆞᆫᄌᆞ
에ㅣ만훈쌘더러우리군ᄉᆞ샹힝동
에요로인고로귀아간에즁요ᄒᆞᆫ
교셥이불소ᄒᆞ거ᄂᆞᆯ쳥임목ᄉᆞ홍
즁우ᄂᆞᆫ그소종리의경력을조ᄒᆞ
드리도뎍당치못ᄒᆞᆫ인믈이오일
본인에ᄃᆡᄒᆞ야감졍이심히맛당
치못ᄒᆞ니ᄎᆞ졔귀졍부에셔뎍당
ᄒᆞᆫ인믈을션틱ᄒᆞ야임명ᄒᆞᆫ쥬조
쳐ᄒᆞ시오며ᄃᆡ신임목ᄉᆞ의부임ᄒᆞ기
젼에ᄒᆞᆫ필요가잇스니분간ᄒᆞ야
오롤귀빙ᄒᆞ게ᄒᆞ야곡속히조쳐
로리방ᄒᆞ게ᄒᆞ기를ᄇᆞ라노라ᄒᆞ
엿더라

론셜

젼쟁에ᄃᆡᄒᆞᆫ쳔견

○일본의신문들을보던지일본
당국자들의힝동을보면아모던
지못ᄒᆞᆫ일본이젼쟁을ᄒᆞᆫ번에
리긴것을알지로라
그러ᄒᆞ나젼쟁의시초브터지금
ᄭᆞ지일본이언ᄒᆞ야승젼ᄒᆞᆫ것을
ᄆᆡ양셰계에쟈랑ᄒᆞ고포로ᄒᆞᆫ것
이며가지고빅셩의게그리ᄒᆞᆫ것
들은ᄯᅩ리ᄒᆞ야보면언다ᄒᆞᆫ사ᄅᆞᆷ
이업지아니ᄒᆞ나일본이청국과
로셔아와젼쟁ᄒᆞᆯᄯᅢ에승젼ᄒᆞᆫ
의리ᄂᆞᆫ일본ᄉᆞ람들이졍복ᄒᆞᆯ가
두려ᄒᆞ니ᄂᆞᆫ것이아니라
무엇시라고ᄒᆞᆯ수업스나우리가
보건ᄃᆡ일본이군ᄉᆞ를니여로
셔아를치ᄂᆞᆫ것은동양의평화
를위ᄒᆞᆷ이라ᄒᆞ엿스니
진실로그러ᄒᆞ면일본이뎌신
문에셔말ᄒᆞᄂᆞᆫ거시보ᄂᆞᆫ이로
ᄒᆞ여곰의심치아니케ᄒᆞᆯ지라

지금은일본군이지금도달ᄒᆞᆫᄃᆡ셔브터더북방으로나아갈ᄉᆡᆼ각도못ᄒᆞᄂᆞᆫ것을우리도아ᄂᆞᆫ것시ᄃᆡ도로보면분명ᄒᆞᆫ지라로국쟝군미쓰쳰코씨의엄습ᄒᆞᆫ것시대산원슈의동신긔관을파피ᄒᆞ엿고일본군우익의동편에희창근ᄃᆡ에잇ᄂᆞᆫ로군의운동이모단령과압록ᄉᆞ이에흑목대쟝의동신긔관을위ᄐᆡᄒᆞ게ᄒᆞᄂᆞᆫ지라로국의사이베리아철로의효험이일본의계칙을다실피ᄒᆞ게만드럿스며로국이진실로그철로ᄉᆞ업은놀낼만ᄒᆞ게진보ᄒᆞ엿고젼쟁의시초에일본의졍탐군이사이베리아철로를ᄭᅳᆫ치못ᄒᆞᆷ이괴이ᄒᆞᆫ일이로다요젼에그철로의형편을자셰히아ᄂᆞᆫᄒᆞᆫ사ᄅᆞᆷ이말ᄒᆞ되만일의화단들이로국과싸울것갓ᄒᆞ면그철로를능히이삼십쳐를쉽게후망업시ᄭᅳᆫ헛스리라ᄒᆞ더라

엇더ᄒᆞᆫ지일본은쟈긔의발등을ᄶᅵ어노코한국에셔ᄂᆞᆫ져의가뎨일인듯이ᄒᆞ야일본ᄃᆡ표쟈들이세계에셔보증ᄒᆞ야가면셔연속히한국졍부에향ᄒᆞ야졔반쳥구를ᄒᆞ며ᄀᆞ문판들은서로이연속히나아오고시졍ᄀᆡ션ᄒᆞ라ᄂᆞᆫ강경ᄒᆞᆫ권고ᄂᆞᆫ그실상은ᄀᆡ션이아니라ᄀᆡ션의반ᄃᆡ이오ᄒᆞᆫ가지확실ᄒᆞᆫ것은일본인이이나라를차죵ᄒᆞ라ᄒᆞᄂᆞᆫ것이라

그러ᄒᆞ나평화소식은머러가고로국은지금젼쟁을시작ᄒᆞᄂᆞᆫ모양이라인민의게허락ᄒᆞᆯ만ᄒᆞᆫ것은허락ᄒᆞ고혁명당의게ᄂᆞᆫ압제졍칙을써셔로국이ᄂᆡ란을진졍ᄒᆞ고그런후에ᄂᆞᆫ만쥬에셔능히지금일본군보다소불하반슈이상은더ᄂᆡ보ᄂᆡ게될터이로다일본군이일년만에져의들의지금잇ᄂᆞᆫ곳에득달ᄒᆞ엿스니무ᄉᆞᆷ의외지ᄉᆞ가이러나지아니ᄒᆞ면우리의료량에ᄂᆞᆫ로국군도일년만에ᄂᆞᆫ일본군의드러간것만콤모라나아오리라ᄒᆞ노라

관보

뎨삼쳔칠십삼호 광무구년이월이십칠일월료

셔임급사령

○승셔판임관사등 운산면보사쥬사 박셩호 은진면보사쥬사 됴태하

이상일월이십칠일

○히관제리졍소위원 의졍부비셔관 윤덕영 셩균관쟝 셔샹훈 탁지부지무관 리도익 졍삼품 남궁억

○회관제리졍소위원 농샹공학교교관 김샹연 구픔 윤돈구 군부쥬사 김죵한 탁지부량지국쥬사 뎡인방

○의원면본관 비셔원승 윤셩 경릉참봉 홍슌찬 향원감리셔쥬사 리지옥 군부쥬사 윤태욱 군부쥬사 김힝범 군기창쥬사 태호션

○임비셔원승셔쥬임관륙등 졍삼품 리윤종

○임경릉참봉셔판임관팔등 환구단사제셔참봉 남셩희

○임환구단사제셔참봉셔판임관팔등 슌창원참봉 남뎡칠

○임슌창원참봉셔판임관팔등 구픔 홍순찬

○임창원감리셔쥬사셔판임관륙등 안죵보

○임군부쥬사셔판임관륙등 홍승록 뎡셩윤

○임군기창기수셔판임관륙등 박두병

○히경샹남도뎨일션셰위원 매경츈

○히경샹남도뎨삼션셰위원 쳔지헌

○히젼라북도뎨일션셰위원 림만식

○명경샹남도뎨일션셰위원 됴룡원

○명경샹남도뎨삼션셰위원 남학수

○명젼라북도뎨일션셰위원 리을규

○승셔판임관삼등경무청기수 강두식

○승셔판임관오등삼화면보사쥬사 됴동철

이상이월이십사일

뎐보

론돈발

○로국친왕의암살 로국황뎨의숙부요모스코관윤셔져쓰대공은크램린으로부터마차를타고올ᄯᅢ에엇던쟈이폭발약을던져셔그약이터져셔그대공이곳피살ᄒᆞ엿다더라

동디발

○로국각의와평화풍셜 간밤에로국ᄂᆡ각의쟝이급히ᄂᆡ각회의를여럿ᄂᆞᆫᄃᆡ그소문은자셰히알슈업스나평화문졔에관ᄒᆞᆫ것이라ᄂᆞᆫ풍셜이잇더라

젼쟁의소식

론돈발 이월십삼일

○미국뉴욕헤랠드신문뎐진ᄒᆞᆫ신원의보고를거ᄒᆞᆫ즉로국졍부에셔쳥국에핍박ᄒᆞ되만일쳥국졍부에셔일본의게편리ᄒᆞ게젼시금물을슈송ᄒᆞᄂᆞᆫ거슬금ᄒᆞ지아니ᄒᆞ면로국이북쳥다방과쳥국토이기ᄉᆞ단에위핍ᄒᆞ리라ᄒᆞ엿다더라

동디발 동월십칠일

○로국이만쥬에군ᄉᆞ를오십만명을두어셔일본을경갈ᄒᆞ게만들목적이라ᄂᆞᆫ말이잇다더라

평화의소식

론돈발 이월십삼일

○셩피득보에잇ᄂᆞᆫ쳥국공ᄉᆞ가자긔의졍부에뎐보ᄒᆞ되자셰ᄒᆞᆫ아려본즉로국은평화의의샹이죠곰도업슬ᄲᅮᆫ외라로국황뎨ᄭᅴ셔명령ᄒᆞ야만쥬에셔승부를결뎡ᄒᆞ라ᄒᆞ엿다ᄒᆞ엿더라

동지발 동월십구일

○어느곳으로낫ᄂᆞᆫ지알슈업ᄂᆞᆫ평화풍셜은슈일ᄂᆡ에젼과갓치셩힝ᄒᆞᆫ다더라

로국의졍형

론돈발 이월십ᄉᆞ일

○불나고이에셔ᄉᆞ쳔명의반란쟈를예비병이진압ᄒᆞ엿고기에푸에셔ᄂᆞᆫ일만이쳔명의반란쟈의게관군이방포ᄒᆞ엿스며로국은금년에흉년이드럿다더라

비엔나발 동월십륙일

○분란과파란에셔반란쟈들이져의디방을다독립국을만들냐고합력운동ᄒᆞᆫ다ᄂᆞᆫᄃᆡ분란에셔ᄂᆞᆫ반란쟈들이관병에향ᄒᆞ야복슈ᄒᆞ랴고군긔를취합ᄒᆞᆫ다더라

론돈발 동일

○로국의대학교학ᄉᆡᆼ들이져의들의청구ᄒᆞᄂᆞᆫᄃᆡ로청죵ᄒᆞ기ᄭᆞ지폐업ᄒᆞ엿더니지금은다시샹학ᄒᆞ기를시작ᄒᆞ엿다더라

동디발 동일

○로국의ᄂᆡ란이점점간졍되야가셔롯쓰와셩피득보와모스코의혁명당들은다시져의들의직업에도라갓다더라

동디발 동월십팔일

○셩피득보에셔분란이다시급속히만연ᄒᆞ야삼만명이다시분란에가입ᄒᆞ고병졍과슌검이혁명당들을포박ᄒᆞ노라고분주ᄒᆞ며셩피득보ᄂᆞᆫ혁명당의츌판ᄒᆞᆫ셔칙들이ᄉᆞ방에유힝ᄒᆞ고모스코에셔셩피득보에오ᄂᆞᆫ철로회샤의고용인들이이러나셔그철로가불통이라더라

론돈발 이월십칠일

○영션의폭발 영국퀸쓰타운에셔히져션이폭발ᄒᆞ야참위일인과군ᄉᆞ삼명이죽ᄉᆞᄒᆞ고군ᄉᆞ십ᄉᆞ명은피샹ᄒᆞ엿다더라

파리발 동일

○법국의회의쟝의피션 법국의회부의쟝은두머씨가피션ᄒᆞ엿더라

론돈발 이월십륙일

○려순함락과로국히륙군 로국히륙군은려슌함락에ᄃᆡᄒᆞ야서로칙망ᄒᆞᆫ다더라

동디발 동월십칠일

○일본의젼시금물의포획 히삼위로젼시금물을싯고가다가일본인의게잡힌영국륜션아폴노와스캇스민에실은물품의가치가십일만일쳔방인ᄃᆡ지ᄂᆡᆫ일월십삼일이후로일본인이포획ᄒᆞᆫᄇᆡ가십이척이라그ᄇᆡ에실은물건의가치가도합팔십만방이라다더라

동디발 동월십구일

○스틋셀장군의일힝 스틋셀쟝군은토이기경셩군ᄉᆞ단졍보에도달ᄒᆞ엿ᄂᆞᆫᄃᆡ도라셔셩피득보에도라간다더라

동디발 동월이십일

○쳥국황ᄐᆡ후의사진특징 화셩돈에잇ᄂᆞᆫ쳥국공ᄉᆞ가대통령루스벨트씨의게쳥국황ᄐᆡ후의사진을보냇ᄂᆞᆫᄃᆡ이특별ᄒᆞᆫ영광스러운징여픔은미국이쳥국의즁립보젼을위ᄒᆞ야쥰것을표졍ᄒᆞᆷ이라더라

잡보

○편젼칙식 삼작일에헌병ᄃᆡ로칙교가나리시기를셔소문밧게셔편쌈이오히려그치지안다ᄒᆞ니헌병ᄃᆡ에셔엇지금지치안ᄂᆞᆫ뇨곳헌병을파견ᄒᆞ야일졀금단ᄒᆞ라ᄒᆞ신고로헌병과슌검이극력ᄒᆞ야금지ᄒᆞᆫ지라작일에편쌈이침식되엿더라

○ᄉᆞ유질문 슌쳔군슈리우규씨의담쟝ᄒᆞᆫᄉᆞ에ᄃᆡᄒᆞ야질문ᄒᆞᆯ일이잇다고일진회에셔총ᄃᆡ삼인이작일ᄂᆡ부에젼왕ᄒᆞ엿다더라

○불가불수리 주미공ᄉᆞ가외부로보고ᄒᆞ엿스되공관의창벽이퇴락ᄒᆞ야불가불수리를ᄒᆞᆯ터이오니수리비이쳔여원을지발ᄒᆞ라ᄒᆞ엿더라

○다일지체 금번군졔를져ᄒᆞᆫ후로군부임원을위션셔임ᄒᆞᆯ터인ᄃᆡ다셔하ᄒᆞ시ᄂᆞᆫ고로다일디체가되겟다더라

○오호일등 오셔ᄂᆡ에다셧집마다면긔등한좌식현셜ᄒᆞᆯ터인ᄃᆡ쉬션죵로근ᄃᆡ에ᄂᆞᆫ작일브터미호에지화일원식수렴ᄒᆞᆫ다더라

광고

덕국아셰아은힝
본졈은덕국빅림에잇고향항지졈은샹히등지에잇소

향항샹히은힝
조본금총익숨쳔륙빅오십만원
본졈은향항에잇고지졈은쳥국일본기타각국ᄃᆡ쳐에잇소
인쳔셰창양힝ᄃᆡ리졈

차터드은힝
자본금총액은이쳔오빅만원
본졈은영국론돈에잇고지졈은각ᄃᆡ도회쳐잇소에
인쳔셰창양힝ᄃᆡ리졈

미국우션회샤와
동경동양긔션회샤
각국히션과연락ᄒᆞ엿숩

셔울우션회샤
속힝ᄒᆞᄂᆞᆫ일등륜션들인ᄃᆡ
쳥국과일본셔영국과각국으로왕ᄅᆡᄒᆞᆷ
인쳔함릉가양힝ᄃᆡ리졈

TELEGRAMS.

(FROM JAPAN PAPERS.)

Note. The messages marked* are those which are described as special service" or "special telegrams or "received by the Government." The others are from properly authenticated sources.

THE RUSSIAN FLEET.

London, Feb. 21.

The 3rd Baltic Fleet passed the Straits of Denmark on fhe 20th inst. It consists of the following vessels:—The battleship Nicholas (9,672 tons), the armoured coast defence vessels Washacoff (4,126 tons) and Seniyawin (4,960 tons), the cruiser Monouracoff (5,193 tons), the auxiliary cruiser Russ (5,383 tons), with balloons on board, the repairing vessel Cosenia (3,700 tons), and the transports Riwania, Coronia, Storsgof, Swire, and Cutchina. The transports are said to have been bought by Russia from a certain country after the commencement of the war.

London, Feb. 21.

According to a Port Louis telegram, dated the 20th, the first two Baltic Squadrons, and their transports, seventy vessels in all, were at Nossi Bé on Feb. 16th. One Russian destroyer and six German colliers arrived at Diego Suarez on Feb. 14th. The Russians are now engaged in buying large quantities of provisions at Mojanga and the vicinity.

London, Feb. 20.

*The Russian Government is attempting to reopen the Dardanelles question. The Black Sea Fleet is rapidly making preparations to pass through the strait in order to join the Baltic Fleet.

London, Feb. 23.

A French steamer has landed a quantity of stores and dynamite for the Russians, principally at Jibutil and Degio Suarez.

PEACE PROSPECTS.

Berlin, Feb. 21.

*In spite of the increasing desire among the nobles for the restoration of peace the Czar still insists on the continuance of the war. His Majesty is not in the least affected by the death of Grand Duke Serge.

London, Feb. 22.

Reuter's correspondent at St. Petersburg states that, despite official denials, according to information received from a source enjoying high patronage, the question of conditions on which Russia is prepared to conclude peace has not only been formally discussed by the Tsar, but has been practically decided. The conditions are given as follows:—The recognition of Japanese suzerainty in Korea; the cession of the Liaotung Peninsula to Japan; the conversion of Vladivostok into an open port; the administration of the Chinese Eastern Railway by a neutral international body; and the restoration to China of territory in Manchuria south of Harbin. The only difficulty in the question of indemnity, on which it is known Japan will insist.

It is thought possible that Russia may still risk another battle before arriving at a decision in regard to peace terms; but in view of difficulties encountered by the military, and in the internal situation in Russia, it is probable peace will be concluded very shortly if the indemnity question can be arranged.

London, Feb. 23.

It now appears certain that Russia has not actually proposed any terms, but those given in yesterday's telegram are regarded as reflecting the views of an increasingly influential peace party in Russia.

Baron Suyematsu (now in London), interviewed as to the reported terms of peace, pronounces them as propsterous, and says that their acceptance by Japan will leave Russia the gainer by the present war.

Upon the publication of the report regarding peace terms the quotation of Japanese bonds rose by one and a quarter.

TROUBLES IN RUSSIA.

London, Feb. 18.

*The Czar has summoned all the Ministers of State and M. de White to attend a conference at the Tsarskoe seloe Palace, to be presided over by himself, in order to discuss the advisability or not of converting the Council of the Committee of Ministers into a responsible advisory body, to sit regularly.

Vienna, Feb. 20.

*Political circles at St. Petersburg are in a state of chaos. The relations between the supporters of the Grand Dukes and the other official elements are strained, and it is not yet clear which faction will gain the upper hand. The Grand Ducal clique has been rendered desperate by its repeated failures and is believed to be ready to adopt reckless measures. Its menacing attitude is occasioning much anxiety among the public.

Vienna, Feb. 20.

*The labourers on the Trans-Caucasus Railway have gone on strike and traffic has almost entirely ceased. The strike is expected to spread to other districts.

Berlin, Feb. 20.

*German official circles are very reticent concerning recent incidents in Russia. The authorities decline to make any statement whatever on the subject.

London, Feb. 20.

*The dissatisfaction ot the Russian populace is increasing. Railway traffic is interrupted at various places. The Government's promises of reforms are derided. It is reported from St. Petersburg that the revolutionary movement is gradually extending to the troops in Manchuria.

London, Feb. 20.

*The assassination of the Grand Duke Sergius has greatly terrified the members of the Imperial Russian family, who have petitioned the Tsar for increased protection. A quantity of bombs, supposed to be destined for members of Anarchist organisations, have been intercepted on the frontier.

London, Feb. 21.

* In Finland a revolution is being openly advocated.

London, Feb. 21.

An Imperial Manifesto has been issued stating that it has been decided to convene the Zemskysoboe, or National Parliament, probably on March 4th.

London, Feb. 21.

Owing to the large number of threatening letters received, and at the direct request of the Czar, Prince Henry of Prussia, who was to have represented the Kaiser at the funeral of the Grand Duke Sergius, will not attend the ceremony as was at first intended.

London, Feb. 21.

Martial law has been proclaimed at Tsarskoe Selo.

London, Feb. 23.

A laconic telegram from Baku, on the Caspian Sea, states that all the offices there are closed, and the streets are filled with corpses.

GENERAL NEWS.

Washington, Feb. 7.

*President Roosevelt signed the Philippine Extradition Bill to-day. The new law extends the extradition laws of the United States to the Phillippine Islands.

Peking, Feb. 20.

*Through the joint efforts of Viceroy Yuan and the French Minister to Peking, Imperial sanction has been obtained for the establishment of a Franco-Chinese Bank. The capital will be four million taels and the head office will be at Tientsin.

Peking, Feb. 20.

Sir Robert Hart, Superintendent of of the Chinese Customs, has called on Prince Ch'ing and discussed with him the present sources of revenue of the Chinese Empire. Sir Robert advocated an increase of the taxes on wines and tobacco and the placing of the control of taxation under the Superintendent of the Customs.

Washington, Feb. 21.

*A deputation appointed by cotton goods manufacturers has waited on the President and recommended the despatch of an investigating committee to the Orient with a view to fostering the cotton goods trade with the United States. The President expressed acquiescence with the Deputation's views and promised that he would endeavour to have their wishes carried into effect.

Vienna, Feb. 21.

*The Balkan eninsula, particularly Bulgaria and SePia, has been greatly affected by the frVl of Port Arthur and the disturbances ial Russia. Anti-Slav feeling is becominn stronger every day. The Turkish Govgrnment also intends to take advantagee f Russia's troubles for the purpose of oincreasing its influence in the Peniusul a. Russia is therefore likely to be conf routed by new difficulties. On the oth er hand, the Hungarian Government is xtremely anxious for peace in the Far East.

London, Feb. 22.

The Earl of Dudley denies the report published by the "Times" that he is resigning the post of Lord-Lieutenant of Ireland.

Mr. A. J. Balfour, the Premier, in a speech said it was evident that Home Rule is still a living and burning question in British politics, and appealed to all Unionists to sink their differences and not let smaller controversies imperil the Unionist cause.

London, Feb. 23.

The International Commission which has been sitting in Paris to investigate the sinking of British trawlers by the Baltic Squadron in the North Sea has completed its report, which will probably be published on Saturday.

A report has been received in Tokio that the Vladivostok fleet is again cruising but it is not credited by the more responsible newspapers.

It is said of a report from Kuropatkin essued in St. Petersburg that it is confused and misleading. Russia is, apparently, taking a leaf out of Japan's book.

The Japanese newspapers here publish another bunch of telegrams relative to the strikes and disturbances in Russia. These strikes must cost the Japanese Government a good deal of money for telegrams alone.

The Department of Education has forwarded to Prince Eui the sum of $4000 towards his expenses and has sent another remittance of $4000 to Japan to cover the expenses for two months of the Korean students in Tokio.

A delegate of the Il-chin hoi has been to the Supreme court and pestered the judge about the trials of various people charged with obstructing this Society in its nefarious work. The judge asked him to call again.

The programme for the reform of the Korean Government has been decided upon by the cabinet. From a hasty inspection we see no signs of any radical changes and therefore suppose that the Japanese Minister and the Il-chin-hoi will soon be heard from on the subject.

From the latest available reports we find that the number of wounded at the battle of Heikoutai were; Russians 7,000, Japanese 8,000.

A Tokio telegram of February 27th to the "Daihan Ilpo" states that an official report has been received in St. Petersburg to the effect that the Russian front has been greatly extended and a fierce battle is now in progress.

A telegram to the Jiji dated Feb. 18th stated that when the Russians left Hamheung their retreat was covered by a torpedo flotilla. Our information is to the effect that no Russian warships have appeared on that coast this year although one or two transports came down with men and supplies.

At a recent sitting of the Tokio House of Peers a recommendation was submitted by Viscount Soga, Chairman of the Committee appointed to consider modifications of the Law regarding the hypothecation of railways. The recommendation, which was in favour of hypothecation being permitted, was adopted unanimously.

NOTICE.

Dr. Harold Slade, Resident Dentist of Kobe, will visit Seoul professionally about the end of February.

The Korea Daily News.

Issued at 5 P. M. daily except Sundays.

Rate of Subscription:—
Per Year,............Yen 25.
Per Quarter,..........Yen 7.
Per Month,..........Yen 2.50.

Postage in Korea not charged extra.
Postage abroad charged extra.

Advertisements, 50 sen per day for 1 inch or less.
5 yen per month per inch.
50 yen per year per inch.

All communications to
E. T. BETHELL,
Editor and Publisher,
Pak-tong, Seoul.

MR. YI YONG IK.

Under Japanese influence in Korea, liberty is just as much a dead letter here as it is in Russia.

We see going on under our noses a steady process of robbing the Korean of all his possessions that are worth having. Under thinly veiled threats of personal violence the Koreans are forced to acquiesce in the proposals of Mr. Haysh and General Hasegawa and only a few days ago three Koreans were arrested by the Japanese and condemned to imprisonment for having dared to publish their opinion, in extremely moderate language, that raising money at home would be preferable to borrowing from Japan.

Mr. Yi Yong Ik has, apparently dared to express the same opinion, and he has therefore, through the machinations of the Japanese, and to the huge delight of the "Japan Mail," been appointed to the governorship of a remote province (We may here remark, in passing that if Mr. Yi Yong Ik is the corrupt man that the Japanese allege him to be, the Japanese are pursuing a very peculiar "reform" policy when they procure his appointment as governor of a province.)

Now it is just as well to see what all this means. Mr. Megata, in his capacity of financial adviser found a way to make the Korean Government accept, against its will, a loan from Japan, and directly he succeeded he hurriedly departed for Japan to escape the storm of protests which he knew would ensue, leaving the Japanese gendarmerie and their allies of the Il-chin-hoi to deal with those who dared to express their opinions on the subject.

As not even the most ardent Japanophil can claim that this loan will ever be of the slightest benefit to Korea and was nothing more or less than a very weak excuse for getting control of the revenue of this country, it is now evident that Japan has definitely embarked upon the exploitation of Korea for her own ends and that any Koreans who dare to protest will be promptly dealt with.

Probably the Koreans are somewhat surprised at the use which is being made of the treaty of friendship which they signed with Japan, and we can well believe that there' is considerable uneasiness as to the future, and all the cant about reform probably only adds to their disgust and hatred. It is certainly calm impudence for Japanese to talk about corruption in Russia and Korea.

CONDITIONS IN RUSSIA.

The following letter written on Dec. 18th is by the special correspondent of the "Pesther Lloyd."

"I have now been for a week in the capital of the Czar's Empire," writes the correspondent in question, "which is now engaged in one of the bloodiest wars of all times And yet there are no evidences of war. This may be due to the present standstill of operations which has calmed the waves of excitement, but it is said that they were not very high during the days of Liaoyang. The seat of war is many thousand miles away from the heart of the Empire, and that fact alone gives to the war and to its Hinterland a stamp different from cases in which the capital is also the object of the military operations of the enemy.

A comparison of St. Petersburg to-day with Vienna in July 1866, or with Paris during the German advance, may serve as basis for forming an opinion upon the political and military situation. In Russia space and time play a different part than is the case in West and Middle Europe. What do the couple of hundred of kilometer from the Yalu signify —of course only considered as a loss of space—in comparison with the gigantic space of the Empire, and what signify one or two years more of war in the slowly rolling history of Russia. The adage "time is money" is unknown to the Russian, but if patience really did bring roses providence would long ago have put a rose into the buttonhole of each orthodox Russian.

Everything goes in its wonted course. Quietly and seriously, and but for the merry jingling of hundreds and hundreds of sleighbells of small sledges—the public conveyances of St. Petersburg in winter—which sound till late into the night through the wide streets and squares, the ear, which is used to the deafening noise of our large cities would scarcely make us believe that we are in a city of millions. But let us look deeper into the soul of the people, let us inquire into what lies behind this almost lazy calm.

On the frontier I had already made an observation. Near the ticket window stands a small collection box, and on it there is a red cross.

Many I saw, who were in very modest attire, throwing their small change of kopeks into the box, gifts for the field-hospitals and lazarette. On the road, as well as here in St. Petersburg, on every table in hotels, and in each shop, I found collection boxes for gifts destined for the orphans of fallen soldiers, pretty little tin houses into whose chimneys sometimes a kopek, sometimes a gold piece, is dropped.

But let us pass on. Let us enter a salon of the high life of St. Petersburg. The cheery voices of girls are heard, and from adjoining rooms the humming of sewing machines. The lady of the house with a pair of scissors in her right hand stands at a long tailor's table. Around her, radiant youth, chatting and laughing—and sewing for the wounded soldiers in the Far East. After the theatres close gentlemen in evening dress appear and are pressed into service as tailors' apprentices, and there is much chatting and flirting. Everything is discussed but the war, and yet the white linen that to-day passes through fair hands will soon be stained with red bloood.

Some of the ladies have already left. During the summer they have taken a course in Red Cross work, and now they assist in the hospitals in the nursing of the reconvalescent wounded, so that punctuality is necessary. The lady of the house says that must be so when the august Empress herself sets such an inspiring example. I am told I must go to the Winter Palace to see what the love of the Empress is doing for the soldiers.

The next day I ascend the broad marble staircase to the Winter Palace. An officer of the guard takes my card. Servants in gold-embroidered liveries carry tea trays to the rooms. Near the the walls lie parcels large and small sewn in coarse linen, addressed to Mukden, Charbin, etc. I am introduced to Countess M. who conducts me, first into a roomy apartment where some hundred of sewing machines are whirring, hemming and stitching all manner of things. In an adjoining room four stately ladies preside at large cutter's tables, cutting and giving out work to the young ladies who look very pretty in their white aprons and sleeve protectors, and wherever I look slim white fingers are busily at work.

(Continued in next issue.)

SIR T. LIPTON AND THE AMERICA CUP.

Sir Thomas Lipton has by no means lost hope of one day bringing home the America Cup. All that he wants to induce him once again to issue a challenge to the New York Yacht Club says a London despatch of Jan 13th is a designer who can produce for him a vessel with a chance of winning. He is searching the country for that designer. Yesterday he sought him on the Clyde, and interviewed a number of experts in that great center of shipuilding.

In an interview with a press representative in the evening Sir Thomas emphatically stated his willingness to challenge again for the Cup.

"My ambition to bring it to this side of the Atlantic, and to justify the claim of Britain to supremacy in nautical sport, has outlived my many disappointments," he said. "It is stronger now than ever, and I am not only willing to challenge again, but most anxious to.

"As soon as I can see any reasonable grounds for hoping that I can carry through a contest with success, I shall go right ahead. My plans are too indefinite as yet, however, to enable me to give you any information regarding them."

Despite Sir Thomas' reticence, however, it was stated in Clyde circles yesterday that the result of his visit to Glasgow is that a yacht will probably be designed by Mr. Willie Fife, Mr. John Ward (who superintended the tank experiments in connection with the last Shamrock), and a leading Clyde amateur, in collaboration.

According to a Tokyo papaer says the "Japan Chronicle," Viscount Okabe, a member of the House of Peers and formerly Vice-Minister for Foreign Affairs has decided to settle in Korea with his family, and has already purchased 30,000 "cho" of land in the peninsula. It is stated that the Vicount is now pulling down even the stone walls of Kishiwada Castle, which formed his patrimony, with the object of investing the money realised by the sale of the stones in Korean land. His plan is to settle a large number of farmers in Korea and establish a model Japanese village there. Viscount Okabe will shortly proceed to Korea, and will send for his family upon the completion of his preparations,

The Korea Daily News.

VOL. II, TUESDAY, FEBRUARY 28, 1905. No. 45

大韓每日申報
대한ᄆᆡ일신보

(뎨이권ᄉᆞ십륙호) (목요일) 일천구빅오년삼월이일

본샤고빅

이신보는영어와한어로셔거미일츌판ᄒᆞᆸ

신문가

한장 엽두돈오푼

일삭됴 엽두량닷돈

우표가미삭닷돈

다맛돈으로밧솝

광고료는

귀한의장단과ᄌᆞ힝의다쇼로중감ᄒᆞ되렴가로밧을터이오며오리지아녀대한사람마다다이신문을보실터이니광고내시기됴원ᄒᆞ시는이들은우리신문샤에와셔면약ᄒᆞ심을희망ᄒᆞᆸ

○발힝소 박동대한미일신보샤법어학교압헤젼영국인설필림집자리오

샤쟝 영국인 (비설)

평양 디리졈

○평양효동사는권미보씨로우리신문관미디리인을뎡ᄒᆞ엿스오니평양에계신구람코져ᄒᆞ시는쳠군ᄌᆞ는히디리졈에왕림ᄒᆞ와면외ᄒᆞ십

사고

○우리대한미일신보의목뎍은대한의안녕질서에관한모든데목에되ᄒᆞ야논공평한변론을쥬쟝홈이라우리동신원의탐보는신문보시논쳠군ᄌᆞ의게홍상보도ᄒᆞ리며편지를괴셔ᄒᆞ여주시는이논셩명과반디들젹어붓치시기를희망ᄒᆞ오니이거슨신문상에괴지ᄒᆞ라는거시아니오다만극히신용ᄒᆞ논증거를솜고쟈홈이라괴쟈는아모괴서던지괴지홈을되각ᄒᆞ논권리를가젓스나되각ᄒᆞ논리유를말홀터이오며공쥼평화를문란케ᄒᆞ논듯훈괴셔는의례히밧지안켓솝나이다

●본사셜시이릭로신문을미양우례로분젼ᄒᆞ와례젼부의임의로젼ᄒᆞᆫ듯스로먼곳에는혹늣게젼ᄒᆞ기도ᄒᆞ도ᄒᆞ며혹몃칠거슬ᄒᆞᆫ겁에젼ᄒᆞ기도ᄒᆞ도ᄒᆞ며혹아니젼ᄒᆞ논곳도잇다ᄒᆞ와우리신문을ᄉᆞ랑ᄒᆞ야구람ᄒᆞ시논 쳠군ᄌᆞ의게덕ᄒᆞ야ᄅᆡ우미안ᄒᆞ옵기로지금온분젼인을두고미일일즉이젼ᄒᆞ며아니젼ᄒᆞ거나늣게거나ᄒᆞᆫ폐가업도록ᄒᆞ라ᄒᆞ오니혹아니젼ᄒᆞ거나혹늣게젼ᄒᆞ거나ᄒᆞᆫ일이잇스면본샤로통긔ᄒᆞ여쥬심을희망ᄒᆞᆸ

론셜

근세젼쟁에졍신병

○이번일로젼쟁에젼에업던병이싱겻는디인도에의약신문에미국의약신문의근세젼쟁에졍신병론을등지ᄒᆞ엿는디그론문에말ᄒᆞ되젼쟁이라는거ᄉᆞᆫ사람의평시힝위를이러버리게ᄒᆞ논거시오다만사람들을빅졍질ᄒᆞ는거시라지금젼쟁에이력잇는로국오랠에잇는의원ᄯᅢ크뵈씨가말ᄒᆞ되싸홈싸우는것과디퇴포의터지는거시ᄒᆞᆫ번던디개벽ᄒᆞ는것과갓ᄒᆞ야셔위틱홈과죽엄이젼에우리가듯고보던것과모다다르며우리의심리학도근리신식젼쟁에는젹합지아니ᄒᆞᆫ거시ᄒᆞᆫ슌양함이이분동안에팔빅명을싯고침몰ᄒᆞ는것도잇고젹은싸홈에일빅칠십필의말이일빅ᄉᆞ필이죽은일도잇스며디하에일빅오십쳐의디뢰를뭇어셔그거시터질ᄯᅢ면큰디동ᄒᆞ거나화산의터지는것과갓ᄒᆞ셔그런지란이졍신병을나게ᄒᆞ고근리의비략과폐트로패불노스크과핫숫셰의폭발ᄒᆞ논디로브러힝면ᄒᆞᆫ쟈들의졍신병도글로ᄒᆞ야난거시니그병을그당디에셔곳곳칠거시어놉그사람들을그젼디로브터밧비고향으로보니서철로로가는동안에그병을난치ᄒᆞᆫ광징이되게만든다ᄒᆞ야ᄶᅢ코비씨가로국젹십쟈사오청원ᄒᆞ야젼디에병막을써로히멀니짓고그런병인들을치료홈을실시ᄒᆞ아결과가ᄆᆡ우됴ᄒᆞᆫ디만쥬에서그병이젼에업시만이잇거놀젼디에잇는의원들이외치에밧버셔그병인들은치료를잘ᄒᆞ지아니ᄒᆞ거나고향으로보니니삼사십일동안을철로로가는것이졍신병을더ᄒᆞ게ᄒᆞ논거시라셰샹에셔그병을자셰히분별ᄒᆞ지못ᄒᆞ며근리에맥도벌드대쟝의쟈살ᄒᆞᆫ것도그ᄭᅡ닭이라ᄒᆞ고지금만쥬에셔싸호는두군ᄃᆡ가인류의살샹ᄒᆞ논방법의ᄯᅡ러근리젼쟁에졍신병을쟈셰히쥬의ᄒᆞ지아니ᄒᆞ는거시이참혹ᄒᆞ다ᄒᆞ엿더라

잡보

○장힝리졍 각디방제도를차뎨로리졍홀터인디증경디신은관찰ᄉᆞ를셔임치안키로작졍ᄒᆞᆫ다더라

○박ᄉᆞ무식 일본모박ᄉᆞ가동양평화론이라ᄒᆞ는칙을저술ᄒᆞ야우리궁닉부로송뎡ᄒᆞ엿는디봉투에써스되대일본뎨국모박ᄉᆞ는한국국왕면하의게들이노라ᄒᆞᆫ지라궁닉부에셔차를주문ᄒᆞ엿다더라

○경민거봉 거이십칠일야에경샹북도인민삼십여명이남산에거봉ᄒᆞ다가경쳥에피착ᄒᆞ엿는디히ᄉᆞ실은관찰ᄉᆞ쟝승원씨가허셩민을착슈ᄒᆞ엿다박송ᄒᆞᆫ후에치폐ᄒᆞᆫ소건에디ᄒᆞ야발명홀ᄉᆞ건이라더라

○장임닉대 민영철씨는쟝ᄎᆞ닉부대신을피임ᄒᆞᆫ다더라

○이유며약 일본공ᄉᆞ가외부로죠회ᄒᆞ기를리젼ᄒᆞᆫ이리로우리군용픔운송ᄒᆞ기민속홈을위ᄒᆞ야귀안의졍셔쥼에도또ᄒᆞᆫ우리군ᄉᆞ힝동에디ᄒᆞ야편ᄋᆡ홈을주기로명약이잇는비라금번에본졍부에셔본ᄉᆞ의게디ᄒᆞ야귀국의당히관헌이다만우리군용픔운송홀목젹으로긔항쟝이나긔항쟝이안이나출입선박을당ᄒᆡ관헌의즁명으로뎍당ᄒᆞᆫ법을심아그국긔의여하ᄒᆞᆫ것을거리기지말고그보통상션의규뎡에되ᄒᆞ야젼연히덕용치안을ᄉᆞ유로귀졍부에신졔홀ᄉᆞ라훈시가리도ᄒᆞᆫ고로자에죠청ᄒᆞ노라ᄒᆞ엿더라

○적송되리 원산감리가외부로보고ᄒᆞ엿스되본월십사일에일본군정집힝관죠면만향은합홍으로젼진ᄒᆞ고그디에젹송ᄉᆞ령관이되리ᄒᆞ오니죠량ᄒᆞ옵소서ᄒᆞ엿더라

○항졍극민 인쳔감리가외부로보고ᄒᆞ엿스되본항응신쳥은곳모군회쳥이온디일본인령목경쟝이노동죠직이라칭ᄒᆞ고ᄒᆞᆫ인과일인쳔여명을합ᄒᆞ야각각목픽을차고응신쳥리익을ᄲᅢ앗는고로본항샹민과히쳥의회소가답지ᄒᆞ는지라일본령ᄉᆞ로더브러글노ᄒᆞ고말노ᄒᆞ야련일교섭ᄒᆞ되맛참닉쳥준치안코일본헌병디에셔헌병을파견ᄒᆞ야즉금아직무ᄉᆞᄒᆞ나항구의졍형을싱각ᄒᆞ면극히민망ᄒᆞ다ᄒᆞ엿더라

○보쳥뎡ᄉᆞ 쥬미공ᄉᆞ가외부로보고ᄒᆞ엿스되포아에우민빅윤셥등의쳥원니에본도닉거류민수가오륙쳔명에지ᄒᆞ오나령솔ᄒᆞ는관원이무ᄒᆞ온지라싱명과지산을보죠홀수업ᄉᆞ오니우리졍부에셔보고ᄒᆞ야외교에련숙ᄒᆞᆫ관원으로파견ᄒᆞ야슈다민인을보호ᄒᆞ기를복망이라ᄒᆞᆫ등졍을보고ᄒᆞ오니속히령ᄉᆞ를파견ᄒᆞ와우리인민을보호ᄒᆞ기를바라노라ᄒᆞ엿더라

○즉위긔송 주법공ᄉᆞ가외부로보고ᄒᆞ엿스되본공관셔긔싱김명수가수토불복으로신병이잇셔귀국ᄒᆞ야치료ᄒᆞ기를쳥원ᄒᆞ나다만보관ᄉᆞ무가젹체ᄒᆞ야송환치못ᄒᆞ겟ᄉᆞ오니본관참셔관을곳긔송ᄒᆞ야히셔긔싱의회국됴병케홈을바라노라ᄒᆞ엿더라

○원사합부 닉부소관광제원급죵두사관제는원샤를합부ᄒᆞ야쟝일인의사십이인제약사이인셔긔이인기슈이인으로뎡ᄒᆞ고죵두사쟝일인기사일인제약사이인주사삼인위원십륙인은감하

○경무셔 닉부관하각긔항시장경무셔관졔에는경무관은병폐지ᄒᆞ고총순각이인식셜치

○경무쳥 경무사일인국쟝일인경무관십이인이닉주사팔인총순삼십사인이닉기사일인

○감옥셔 셔쟝일인주사이인간수장이인에의사이인은즁

○탁지부 대신일인협판등인국쟝사인(사셰사계인셔샹국일동출납국이등) 참셔관이인비셔관일인지무관칠인 참셔로미츙) 기사사인주ᄉᆞ오십칠인기슈이인으로뎡ᄒᆞ고국쟝삼인참셔일인지무관칠인기사이인주ᄉᆞ십륙인기수팔은감하

○군부 대신일인협판일인관방쟝일인부관일인(부쟝으로긔츙) 과원이인(방원으로긔츙) 국쟝사인(참모경리냥국일등(의무군법냥국이등) 과쟝구인과원십륙인리사이인기사일인주사에십인기수이인으로뎡ᄒᆞ고부관일인국쟝일인과원오인주사십인은감하

UNION INSURANCE SOCIETY OF CANTON.

Head office Hongkong.
Marine risks underwritten at current rates.

Agents in Chemulpo,
E. MEYER & Co.

COMPAGNIE DES MESSAGERIES MARITIMES.

Fortnightly Direct Service.

For Marseilles
via Ports.
Sailing from Yokohama
Calling at Kobe,
Shanghai, Hongkong, Saigon, Singapore,
Colombo, Djibonti, Suez, Port Said
and Marseilles.

For particulars apply to
HOLME RINGER & Co.,
Chemulpo.

HAYASHIDA & CO.,

16 MYENG DONG, CHIN KO KAI, SEOUL.
BRANCH OFFICE AT CHEMULPO.

Money changers, Coal and Wood Merchants, Express Agents.

We are agents for the Pyeng-yang Coal Company and the Karazu Coal Company of Japan. We have the best quality of both anthracite and bituminous coal, and prompt execution of orders is our speciality. Firewood of all kinds kept in stock. Full weight guaranteed. Money of all denominations exchanged at current rates. Parcels received for all parts.

CHINA MUTUAL LIFE INS. CO.

Most favourable terms to policy holders.

Benefit system unsurpassed.

HOLME RINGER & Co.
Agents, Chemulpo.

C. P. R.

CANADIAN PACIFIC RAILWAY COMPANY'S ROYAL MAIL STEAMSHIP LINE.

THE FAST ROUTE BETWEEN CHINA, JAPAN, AND EUROPE VIA CANADA AND THE UNITED STATES.

Route from Hongkong via Shanghai, Nagasaki (Inland Sea of Japan) Kobe, Yokohama, Victoria and Vancouver.

Twin Screw Empress Steamship—6,000 Tons—Speed 19 knots.

PROPOSED SAILING FROM YOKOHAMA.

R. M. S. Empress of India.
R. M. S. Empress of Japan.
R. M. S. Empress of China.
R. M. S. Athenian.
R. M. S. Tartar.

Special reduction (first class only) granted to members of the Military, Naval, Diplomatic and Civil services and to Missionaries.

Passengers have choice of ten routes across the Continent of America and have privilege of travelling by any Atlantic Steamship Line.

Round the World passage tickets in connection with the P. and O. S. N., North German Lloyd and Messageries Co.'s £125.

All rates payable at current rate of exchange.

For further information, Tickets, Guide Books, etc., apply to

HOLME, RINGER & Co., AGENTS,
Chemulpo.

Grand Hotel

(Formerly the Station Hotel)

Near the Railway Terminus, West Gate Seoul.

The Best Hotel in Korea.
Handsome new Building.
Fine Airy Rooms.
Excellent Cuisine.
Terms Moderate.
Special terms to Missionaries
and to permanent boarders.

Electric cars within 2 minutes' walk.

W. H. EMBERLEY.
Proprietor

EVERY FACILITY.

In connection with Life Assurance Business is afforded by

The Standard Life Assurance Co.,

One of the largest and wealthiest of the Provident Institutions of the United Kingdom Forms of Application and all information will be promptly afforded on application.

10 CENTS A DAY.

Not a very large expenditure is it? But it is sufficient to secure for a man of 30 a policy with the STANDARD LIFE OFFICE for

$1323.

For all particulars of rates, etc., apply to

Holme, Ringer & Co.,
Agents, Chemulpo.

THE NEW YORK LIFE INSURANCE COMPANY.

Have you ever been declined by any Company?

Are you engaged in a specially hazardous occupation?

Have you heard of the New York Life Insurance Company's New Classifications for this class of Risks?

If not, send your date of birth, occupation and particulars of rejection, if any to

E. MEYER & Co.,
Agents, Chemulpo.

MITSUI BUSSAN KAISHA.
(MITSUI & Co.)

MITSUI GINKO.
(MITSUI BANK.)

The Bank is owned by the members of the Mitsui Family, who, as partners, assume an unlimited responsibility for all liabilities of the Bank:—

Capital........................Yen 5,000,000
Reserve Fund.................. " 5,600,000

HEAD OFFICE, TOKYO.
LONDON OFFICE, 34 LIME ST., E. C.

BRANCHES AND AGENCIES:—
New York, San Francisco, Hamburg, Bombay, Singapore, Manila, Hongkong, Amoy, Chefoo, Tientsin.
Kobe, Hakodate, Yokohama, Kure, Yokosuka, Moji, Shimonoseki, Miike, Wakamatsu Nagasaki, Kuchinotsu, Karatsu, Sasebo, Misume, Taipeh, &c.

Telegraphic Address for all the Offices:
"MITSUI."
A. B. C. AND A. 1 CODES USED.

Contractors of Coal
To the Imperial Japanese Navy. Arsenal and Railway Bureau, Principal Railway Companies and Industrial Work, Home and Foreign Mail and Freight Steamers.

Sole Proprietors
Of the famous Miike, Tagawa and Yamano Coal Mines.

Sole Agents
For the sale of Fukumo, Hokoku, Ichimura, Kanoda, Mannoura, Onoura, Ostuji, Sonoda, Tsubaruro, Yoshinotani, Yoshio, Yurokibura and other coals.

YANGTSE INSURANCE ASSOCIATION, LTD.

The undersigned, having been appointed agents for the above company, are prepared to issue policies and pay losses on marine risks at regular rates.

E. MEYER & Co.,
Agents, Chemulpo.

AMERICAN KOREAN ELECTRIC CO.

Light and Power.

Main Office: Electric Building, Chong No.

RAILWAY DEPARTMENT.

OPERATING CARS BETWEEN EAST AND WEST GATE, EVERY TEN MINUTES:—

First Car leaves East Gate at 7:00 A. M. First Car leaves R. R. Station at 7:25 A.M
Last Car " East Gate at 8.40 P. M. Last " " R. R. Station at 9.05 P.M

OPERATING CARS BETWEEN EAST GATE AND IMPERIAL TOMB TERMINUS, EVERY TWENTY MINUTES:—
CONNECTING WITH EVERY ALTERNATE CAR ARRIVING AT EAST GATE FROM CHONG NO.

First Car leaves East Gate for Tomb at 7:10 A. M.
" " " Tomb for East Gate at 7:30 A. M.
Last " " East Gate for Tomb at 7:50 P. M.
" " " Tomb for East Gate at 8:10 P. M.

OPERATING CARS BETWEEN CHONG NO AND YUNG SAN RIVER EVERY TWELVE MINUTES:—

First Car leaves Chong No for South Gate at 7:12 A. M.
" " " Chong No for Yung San at 7:36 A. M.
" " " South Gate for Chong No at 7:20 A. M.
" " " Yung San for Chong No at 8:09 A. M.
Last " " South Gate for Chong No 9:00 P. M.
" " " Yung San for Chong No at 8.45. p. M.

SPECIAL PRIVATE CARS FURNISHED TO SUIT CONVENIENCE OF PATRONS. PRICES ON APPLICATION AT HEAD OFFICE.

LIGHTING DEPARTMENT.

Where less than 250 candle power of light is used, the rate per month will be
Per 16 candle power incandescent lamp,—All night.—Yen 2.50.
32 candle power incandescent lamp,—All night:—Yen 4.00.
50 candle power incandescent lamp,—All night:—Yen 6.00.
150 " " " " " " " 10.00.
1200 " " enclosed arc " " " " 20.00.

Where more than 250 candle power of light is used, a Meter will be installed, if requested:—Rent of Meter, Yen 2.00 per month. Rate of charges by meter reading:—Two Sen per Ampere per hour. (Approximately this is equal to about One Sen per 16 C. P. lamp per hour) Minimum monthly charge where meter is installed, Yen 20.00 per month, which includes rental of meter.
Estimates for installing lights furnished on application
An assortment of chandeliers always on hand.

K. Murakami.
Photograph Studio
Chinkokai, Seoul.

Printing, Developing and Enlargement, of Photographs always Undertaken.

Korean Views and Pictures Illustrating Native Customs always on Sale,

---

THE OSAKA SHOSEN KAISHA.

Boats frequently on the berth for Chinnampo.

REGULAR SAILINGS BETWEEN JAPAN AND KOREAN PORTS.

FUSAN AND KOBE VIA SHIMONOSEKI

OSAKA VIA MOKPO, FUSAN, SHIMONOSEKI AND KOBE.

MOJI DIRECT.

OSAKA VIA KUNSAN, MASANPO, FUSAN, SHIMONOSEKI AND KOBE.

CHEMULPO KUNSAN LINE,
Every three days.

CHEMULPO CHINNAMPO LINE.
Every three days.

For Freight and passage and further particulars apply to
THE OSAKA SHOSEN KAISHA,
Chemulpo.

RONDON, PLAISANT & CO.

General Storekeepers and Merchants, Ships Contractors Tobacconists, Commission and Forwarding Agents, Coal Merchants

IMPORTERS AND EXPORTERS

Seoul Chemulpo.

W. D. WENTWORTH

LANDING
AND
SHIPPING AGENT.
AND
CUSTOMS BROKER.

12 OURA, NAGASAKI.

STEWARD & CO.

Chemulpo.

Shipchandlers and Storekeepers, Naval and Mercantile Contractors, Landing and Shipping Agents.

STEWARD'S HOTEL

Chemulpo.

Best accommodation in the port for travellers. Clean and well-aired rooms, good cuisine and prompt attendance, moderate tariff.

○각부원뎡관제리졍건 세인의주목ᄒᆞ든관제리뎡건이일간발표될여란말은본보에이계ᄒᆞ엿거니와그리졍결과로금뎡잔반포홀각부원뎡리졍안건이여폐ᄒᆞ엿더라

○표훈원 총직일인의쳥관십오인이닉참셔관일인기사삼인쥬ᄉ이안기수ᄉ인으로뎡ᄒᆞ고졔장국장일인기ᄉ일인은감하

○즁츄원 의장일인부의장일인찬의십오인(칙임관즁경이기변실지ᄌ보써임)참셔관이인쥬ᄉ사인으로뎡ᄒᆞ고의관이십오인은감하

○외부 대신일인협판일인국장이인(교섭국일등통상국이등)참셔관사인비셔관일인쥬ᄉ십구인이니비셔관일인쥬ᄉ삼인이증가ᄒᆞ고참셔관일인번역관이인번역관보오인은감하

○닉부 대신일인협판일인국장삼인(디방국장일등경무회계냥국이등)참셔관사안비셔관일인기사일인쥬사이십구인기수이인이니경무국은증가ᄒᆞ고토목국위싱국에국장이인참셔관이인시찰관ᄉ인기사삼인쥬ᄉ십일인기수이인은감하

○군긔창 관리일인향관일인주사삼인기사삼인기수구인으뎡ᄒᆞ고부관리일인검사관이인향관일인제조소장오인기사오인기수이십이인은감하

륙군법원은여젼

○법부 대신일인협판일인국장이인(사리국일등검사국이등)참셔관삼인비관일인쥬사십오인으로뎡ᄒᆞ고국장일인참셔관삼인주사오인긔초위원이인은감하

○양셩소 장일인(법부참셔관겸임)교관륙인(쥬임일관임오)으로뎡ᄒᆞ고교관십일인은감하

○평리원은여젼

학부 대신일인협판일인국장이인(학무국일등편집국이등)참셔관삼인비셔관일인주사십일인기수일인으로뎡ᄒᆞ고참셔관일인은감하 다만동부소관관상소는여젼ᄒᆞ고셩균관관제즁사업일인이증가ᄒᆞ고각학교관제는여젼

○농부 대신일인협판일인국장삼인 털도국이등농상국광공국삼등(참셔관사인비셔관일인기사사인쥬사이십이인기수팔인으로뎡ᄒᆞ고털도원셔북털도국은일국으로합ᄒᆞ야농부에부속ᄒᆞ고털도원총지일인부총지일인감독사인국장일인참셔관일인과장이인쥬ᄉ십륙인기수사인(셔북털도국)총지일인감독삼인국장일인참셔관이인기사사인기ᄉ십오인수칠쥬ᄉ팔인기인기수륙안쥬ᄉ오인은감하

○통신원 총지일인참셔관삼인기사일인쥬ᄉ십륙인이니쥬ᄉ일인이증가ᄒᆞ고회관일안참셔이인번역관이인은감하

○긔복시무 감옥서장김영션씨가부상을망ᄒᆞᆫ지빅일이임의지낸지라니부로쳐분을하ᄒᆞ샤긔복시무케ᄒᆞ라ᄒᆞ오셧더라

○대신상환 법부대신박졔슌씨와농부대신리지용씨가상환이된다더라

○가쾌뎍졍 근일각동에가쾌가태다ᄒᆞᆫ되긔셔무실무가ᄒᆞ야가권을혹잠미ᄒᆞ고외국인의게면당ᄒᆞ고또타ᄒᆞ야폐단이허다ᄒᆞᆫ지라경무청에셔한셩부와교섭ᄒᆞ야가쾌를다시뎡ᄒᆞ되유실유가ᄒᆞᆫ근실ᄌ로몃빅호에일이명식작뎡ᄒᆞ고그나마는감하ᄒᆞ기로결뎡ᄒᆞ엿다더라

○계속시무 탁지고문관목하면이귀국ᄒᆞᆫ후에기보좌원목씨가지졍ᄉ무를게속시무ᄒᆞᆫ다더라

○청원지관 진주군수리용교씨가담쟝훈ᄉ로쇼찰ᄉ김련식씨의게봉고면관이되엿는되리군수가호무법쟝이라ᄒᆞ고극히발명ᄒᆞ야평리원에지관변명홈을청ᄒᆞ엿더라

○다소변경 일작관제리졍회의에이졍ᄒᆞᆫ관제가다소간변경된다더라

○셔민청원 한셩지관소검소홍종한씨가니취ᄒᆞ야간동셔셩가에돌입ᄒᆞ야힝픠ᄒᆞ는고로셔씨가박되ᄒᆞ엿더니홍검ᄉ가셔민을경무북셔로압부ᄒᆞ니작일에공함ᄒᆞ고지관소로압교ᄒᆞ라ᄒᆞ는지라셔민이히ᄉ실을거ᄒᆞ야평리원에셔청원ᄒᆞ다더라

○조청타관 외부에셔법공관으로조복ᄒᆞ엿는되평양미광기사귀빈레등사인의히고ᄉ는니장원리문의뜻으로임의조명ᄒᆞ엿거니와히광에소입비가태다ᄒᆞ야리익이무ᄒᆞᆯ지라불가리삼월삼십일일간에장ᄎᆞ히고홀러인되일긔년봉급과가옥비와회국비와밋상금은약됴되로지급홀더이니청컨되귀공ᄉ는히안을잘됴뎡ᄒᆞ야다관되기를요훈다ᄒᆞ엿더라

○일ᄉ상경 동리감리가외부로면보ᄒᆞ엿스되일공ᄉ림권조씨가지작일오후에상경ᄎᆞ로탑거ᄒᆞ엿다더라

○련일최착 외교관들의대례복비지화로일만일쳔여원을탁지에셔거절ᄒᆞ고지발치안는지라일인양복상원등복송이련일외부에리도ᄒᆞ야지촉ᄒᆞᆫ다더라

○훈령각도 의정부에셔각도에훈령ᄒᆞ기를민회와보부상등을효휴히산ᄒᆞ엿더라

○조량쳐판 직산군수파찬씨가닉부로보고ᄒᆞ엿스되본군금광이인민의고막이될뿐아니라전군수의피히훈번도차에유홀이라의졍부에셔봉폐ᄉ로상주ᄒᆞ야봉지외주ᄒᆞ라신훈령을승쥰ᄒᆞ야경닉셕토광을일변봉폐ᄒᆞ야빅셩이다안도ᄒᆞ더니현금한인김셩운이가일본인으로더브러체결ᄒᆞ야본군삼곡리에셔기치작변이디단ᄒᆞ기로본군슈가출왕금단ᄒᆞ죡일인젹졍구삼이언닉에광무오년팔월에됴약을이셩ᄒᆞ엿다가즉금비로소기취ᄒᆞ노ᄯᅢᄒᆞ니과연됴약어잇는지죠량죠쳐ᄒᆞ옵소셔ᄒᆞ엿더라

○유셩등소 됴학수등이결세젼을히도에셰엽젼으로수봉ᄒᆞ니공평히쳐분ᄒᆞᆯ라고졍부에등소ᄒᆞ엿더라

○군물쳥거 풍덕군슈박쥰우씨가히군의젹경을금방홀차로양춍이십병파탄환일쳔발을군부에쳥원ᄒᆞ야가져갓다더라

○진위대입셩 이십칠일하오ᄉ시에진위대이대대뎡위관십칠원과병뎡륙빅명이동문으로입셩ᄒᆞ엿더라

○죠쳥지발 학부에셔탁지부로죠회ᄒᆞ기를즁학교교ᄉ일본인폐원단을본부학졍참리관으로본월일일에긔ᄒᆞ야합동됴약ᄒᆞ엿스니본월노십이월ᄉ지미삭신수금삼빅원파가옥셰삼십오원합ᄒᆞ야지화삼쳔륙빅팔십오원을졍부회의에졔출ᄒᆞ야안월지발ᄒᆞ며히원의시무쳐소를부득불신건ᄒᆞ야겟고의자와탁자와보진파일용물픔을또훈신비ᄒᆞ겟스니건축비오쳔팔빅오십삼원륙십사젼과물픔구입비구빅칠십구원[illegible]한화로지발ᄒᆞ라ᄒᆞ엿더라

○경관피상 모화관등디에셔연일평ᄊᆞᆷ이심훈고로순검을파송ᄒᆞ야금지ᄒᆞ는되병뎡이션봉으로나셔돌을던져경찰관리가피상ᄒᆞ엿다더라

○호픽회사 젼교셥국장김익승씨가경향호회사를셜시ᄒᆞ고무론모인ᄒᆞ고각각ᄒᆞ나식가지게ᄒᆞᆫ다더라

○훈장봉뎡 쥬법공ᄉ가또외부로보고ᄒᆞ니[illegible]귀부훈령을봉접ᄒᆞ온바의국대군쥬쳐에될이는바금쳑대수장을본ᄉ로명ᄒᆞ야쳔뎡ᄒᆞ라셧기로광무팔년십월십이일에라마경셩에젼왕ᄒᆞ야훈쟝을봉뎡ᄒᆞ고인ᄒᆞ야ᄒᆞ란국히아젹십자회에가셔참관훈후죠즁셔에각국위원으로더브러훈가지로화압ᄒᆞ고동월이십사일에환임ᄒᆞ야히약셔는번역ᄒᆞ야송뎡ᄒᆞ오니사됴ᄒᆞ시기를바라노라ᄒᆞ엿더라

○훈장교도 쥬법공ᄉ가또외부로보고ᄒᆞ엿는되의국에셔본ᄉ의게이등훈장과참셔관리죵넙의게삼등훈장을도교ᄒᆞ엿다더라

○합부군부 참모부와교육부를합ᄒᆞ야군부에붓치는고로군부관졔리졍안에주ᄉ십팔과가감하ᄒᆞ엿다더라

○옵무시급 평안남도관찰소가닉부로면보ᄒᆞ엿스되숙쳔읍에공무가티단서급ᄒᆞ오니히군수를속히하송ᄒᆞ옵소셔ᄒᆞ엿더라

○군부주본 삼작야에군부관원의임직주본이되엿다더라

○현셥미안 경상북도관찰소장승원씨가닉부로면보ᄒᆞ엿는되도닉빅셩이비록원루ᄒᆞ나도로ᄯᅢ미안ᄒᆞ온지라부하군수로셔리케ᄒᆞ엿스면조흘듯ᄒᆞ오다ᄒᆞ엿더라

○하이조쳐 순쳔군수가닉부로면보ᄒᆞ엿스되일진회회원이본군읍ᄯᅢ에회집ᄒᆞ야회소를청ᄒᆞ오니엇지조쳐ᄒᆞᆯ는지ᄒᆞ엿더라

○청원포양 옥쳔군민뎡환필등이닉부에뎡소ᄒᆞ엿스되본군북상면ᄉ는젼ᄉ리수양의효힝이학어ᄒᆞ야굴읍퓰고디순올구ᄒᆞ는효도로그어머이를셤기니특별히포양ᄒᆞ옵소셔ᄒᆞ엿더라

○덕관셜연 삼작일하오구시에덕공ᄉ사이뎐씨가만찬회를관니에셜ᄒᆞ고각공ᄉ와한뎡대관을청료관되ᄒᆞ엿더라

○지관우긔 일진회원파원주되참령간의지관훈ᄉ는이왕본보에긔저ᄒᆞ엿거니와일간다시지관훈다더라

외보

○황족류학 주미청공ᄉ냥셩씨가근일북경에륙군대학당을셜립ᄒᆞ고각셩에ᄯᅩ륙군사관학교를셜치홀이라ᄒᆞ고ᄯᅩ왕공귀자귀족과밋삼름이상의대관자뎨는각국에유학케홀의로상주ᄒᆞ엿는뒤차로유홀인지항일궁뎡에셔는순귀족을삼년간일본에류학케ᄒᆞ고도귀족은삼년간미국에류학케ᄒᆞ고ᄯᅩ순친왕의아돌론귀조를다시외국에류학케홀이라는면설이잇더라

광고

TELEGRAMS.

(FROM JAPAN PAPERS.)

Note. The messages marked* are those which are described as special service" or "special telegrams or "received by the Government." The others are from properly authenticated sources.

KUROPATKIN.

London, Feb. 21.

Kuropatkin has submitted a confusing report, from which it is gathered that a Russian detachment has been enveloped by the Japanese. He does not mention anything about the loss of guns, though he reports a scheme to recover them. The Russian were pursued 12 miles by the Japanese.

RUSSIAN AFFAIRS.

London, Feb. 21.

*The Tsar in a Ukase expresses his deep regret at the death of Grand Duke Sergius, whose life, he states, has been sacrificed in the service of the Tsar and State.

London, Feb. 21.

*The leading Russian papers condemn the action of assassins. But at the same time, they urge the necessity of the enactment of reforms, lest the assassination lead to the spreading of the revolutionary movement.

Berlin, Jan. 22.

In high Russian circles there is an increasing desire for peace. The Tsar advocates the continuation of the war, and is not at all broken down by the assassination of the Grand Duke Sergius.

GENERAL NEWS.

London, Feb. 20.

The London Police are about to adopt the Japanese system of "Jujutsu."

London, Feb. 21.

*According to a semi-official report emanating from St. Petersburg, the statement that the officers of the "Lena," detained at San Francisco, have escaped is based upon a misunderstanding. As these officers had not given their parole to stay in the United States, the U. S. authorities could not prevent them from leaving that country. Negotiations in this connection will be shortly brought to a successful conclusion.

Chefoo, February 17th.

*Two junk-men, who cashed here some time ago a compradore order, given by Commander von Gillgenheimb in August last for his passage from Port Arthur to Chefoo, and who were arrested in the interior of Shantung, have admitted when on trial before the Taoti, that they threw Commander von Gilgenheimb and Baron de Cuverville overboard.

London, February 15th.

*The London correspondent of the "Birmingham Post" learns that plans have been adopted by the Government for the constraction of new fortifications and a dock capable of admitting the largest British warship afloat, and increased barrack accommodation of Hongkong.

The same journal states that the standing garrison of the Colony will be increased by the addition of five hundred British soldiers and the raising of two Chinese regiments.

The people of On-chun are still making complaints about Japanese land-grabbers in their district.

The Il-chin-hoi seem at last to have a genuine grievance. They complain that although there is a law school the graduates receive no precedence over laymen when positions are vacant. They further alleging that as these positions entail no work, they want some of them themselves. Why not?

JAPAN'S OPPORTUNITY AT SWATOW.

The Universal Gazette says that the Japanese Consul has made the following representations and demands in connection with the recent riot, resulting in the death of two Japanese coolies attached to the Tsao-san Railway.

1.—In spite of the Chinese Government's ordering the Prefect and the District Magistrate, to arrest the perpetrators of the murder, no arrest has been made up to the present. The order must be renewed and the culprits arrested and punished.

2.—The uprising was caused by the District Magistrates not being able to afford effectual protection. The two Magistrates must be deprived of their rank and punished.

3.—An indemnity must be paid on the same basis as in the Hupeh case. An account will be submitted to China in due course.

4.—China must be held responsible for whatever damages are incurred by the corporation.

5.—A certain Chen of Hulu, who had leased his house to the Japanese, has thereby suffered damages. China must, therefore, indemnify him also for his loss.

6.—China must be held responsible for the safety of the Japanese at work on the railway line. An order must be made to the people to his effect.—China Gazette.

The Japanese Minister demands on an average the dismissal of about two magistrates a day. For military purposes.

Some Japanese have staked out some ground in the vicinity of the late Crown Princess' tomb. For military purposes.

The Il-chin-hoi members who were set to watch the house of Mr. Yi Yong Ik have been sent about their business by the Korean police, and marvellous to relate, the Japanese gendarmes did not interfere.

The Japanese Minister has sent a long letter to the Home Department the burden of which is that for "military purposes" the present Governor of Quelpart must be dismissed and someone of whom he approves appointed in his stead.

Our reporter says that:—

A certain professor in Japan wrote a a composition of Eastern peace and sent it to the Imperial Household September. It was addressed in the envelope, "Offering to His highness the King of Korea, from the Professor so and so in Japan." These Japanese professors are real hustlers.

We learn from Japan papers that the work of refloating the Russian cruiser "Varyag," the operations having been suspended in December last owing to the winter season, will be started early in March. According to the authorities, there is reason to belive that the vessel will be floated during the course of that month.

Rear-Admiral Arai, who was some time ago despatched by the Imperial Headquarters to Port Arthur in order to investigate and report on the condition of the sunken Russian war-ships there, has returned to Tokio. As the result of his report. the work of refloating the vessels will, the Japanese papers say, soon be started.

Early in February the Grand Duke Vladimir was interviewed, when he said that the Government could not allow 140,000 men to march to the Winter Palace. They would have sacked it and afterwards the whole city. The workmen were the tools of Anarchist plotters and looters. Unfortunately the innocent suffered with the guilty and 126 were killed and several hundred wounded. The Grand Duke ridiculed the idea of a Cousititution, which would lead to the ruin and disintegration of Russia, but he admitted the necessity of reforms, enabling the people to present their needs and grievances direct to the Czar.

TAKING ADVANTAGE

The Japanese Minister has given notice that he has received the following instructions from his Government;—

"By virtue of the agreement made between Japan and Korea at the outbreak of the war vessels carring materials to be used in military operations shall hence-forth be free to enter or leave any port in Korea. The vessels may be under various flags but a certificate from the Japanese authorities shall make them free from interference.

We have already found that the term "military operations" covers a multitude of sins.

Mr. Megata is being extensively dined and wined in Japan.

The Korean Minister and his secretary at Paris have been decorated by the King of Italy.

It is reported that Mr. Min Yung Chul will be appointed Minister for Home Affairs.

The Kamni of Wonsan reports that the former military administrator has left that town and moved on to Ham-heung.

According to a recent telegram from London, Japanese gunboats are being prepared to enter and operate in the Amur.

We recently announced the appointment of 13 magistrates, 37 were subsequently appointed and the last batch of 20 have been fixed up today.

The S. S. "Brindburn," which was about to proceed to Vladivostock, has received orders from Vancouver to abandon her voyage in consequence of the blockade.

Mr. Masuda and Mr. Hata of the Railway Construction and Traffic Bureau left Tokyo on the 20th inst. for Korea and Manchuria, in order to inspect the railways here.

The Tokio correspondent of the "Daily Telegraph" says that orders for four battleships have been placed in England, as well as contracts for guns to the value of half-a-million pounds sterling.

According to the Tokio "Asahi" it is reported among the Koreans that when Minister Hayashi repaired to the Palace on the 15th instant, he urged the Emperor of Corea to take a trip to Japan.

According to the "Japan Times" H. I. H. Prince of Korea and his suite, who had been in America for some time, arrived at Yokohama a few days ago. The Prince is now residing at Shibahamakan in Tokyo, but for some unknown reason he refuses to receive visitors.

A despatch from Chinchow dated February 15th states that General Kaulbars, formerly commander of the 3rd Army, has been appointed by the St. Petersburg Government, Commander of the 2nd Army. He has 60 guns, and his army is on the right bank of the Hunho, where he is entrenching in the rear of his positions.

It is said that as the committee of officers detached from the various police stations to take measures for the prevention of epidemics have spent all the funds without achieving any result, Mr. Shin Tai Hyu has recommended to the Emperor that the committee be now abolished. This is "locking the stable door after the horse is stolen" with a vengeance.

A Tientsin despatch to the Tokio "Asahi" dated the 19th inst., states that General Kuropatkin has his headquarters between the western gate of Mukden and the railway station, and that there are 10,000 Russian troops at Muden. It is further stated that fears are entertained by the Chinese there that the Russians, should they be compelled to withdraw from that place, will set fire to the greater portion of the houses there before retreating.

Seven Chinese were arrested at Tairen (formerly Dalny) on the 14th inst. as Russian spies and would-be incendiaries. They confessed that they had been ordered by General Kuropatkin to set fire to the Japanese post at Tairen on the line of communications. Each of the seven had received 600 taels and were promised that in the event of success 20,000 taels would be given them per head. They also stated that General Kuropatkin despatched fifty Chinese to the whole Japanese line of communications on this mission of destroying stores. The seven men will shortly be or have been executed.

A Shanghai despatch to the "Nichi Nichi," dated the 14th inst, state that in view of the possibility of troubles arising after the conclusion of the Russo-Japanese war, the Chinese Government has instructed the Tartar Generals and the provincial Viceroys to increase, commensurate with the financial resources, the number of their troops and to co-operate with each other in time of emergency. It is generally believed that this measure has been solely taken for the purpose of providing against possible disturbances in the Yangtse valley.

NOTICE.

Dr. Harold Slade, Resident Dentist of Kobe, will visit Seoul professionally about the end of February.

The Korea Daily News.

Issued at 5 P. M. daily except Sundays.

Rate of Subscription :—
Per Year,............Yen 25.
Per Quarter,..........Yen 7.
Per Month,..........Yen 2.50.

Postage in Korea not charged extra.
Postage abroad charged extra.

Advertisements, 50 sen per day for 1 inch or less.
5 yen per month per inch.
50 yen per year per inch.

All communications to

E. T. BETHELL,
Editor and Publisher,
Pak-tong, Seoul.

THE FIGHTING.

From both Japanese and Russian sources we are told that a fierce battle is now being waged in Manchuria, the centre of the Japanese army being on the railway about 20 miles north of Liaoyang.

Both Kuropatkin and Oyama would appear to have staked very heavily upon the results of this campaign. Many political questions will be decided by this battle. Should Kuropatkin be victorious the tension in Russia will be be relieved and the revolutionists could be got under control and rationally dealt with. Should he lose he will probably retreat a little further north and the situation in Russia will have to be dealt with on its own merits.

Should Oyama win, no time would be lost in floating a big Japanese loan in London or New York and Japan would be assured of the wherewithal to carry on the war for another six months. Should he lose he will probably retire towards Haicheng, as Liaoyang does not lend itself to defense against an attack from the north.

The disposition of the two armies does not lend colour to the view that the result will be a drawn battle, as was the case with the "Shaho" engagement. It is evident that Oyama is concentrating his forces, he has retired before Russian advances and his movements indicate that either he is nervous about his own own communications or is preparing for an advance against the Russian centre.

The Japanese army appears to be arranged in the form of a letter A with its apex at, or near, Lamutun, and the Russian army faces it on both sides. So close are the belligerents' lines to each other that for a long time past amenities have been exchanged, conversations can be plainly overheard, and the neutral strip is the play ground of stray pigs and chickens belonging to either army.

On the west, the Russians threaten to outflank the Japanese at any moment, witness the recent raid on Newchwang; in the centre both forces are confident that they can hold their own; but we cannot find any information which throws much light upon the relative positions on the east. The country here is very hilly and difficult and both armies have taken up very strong artillery positions. Kuropatkin has many six-inch mortars and we are told that the Japanese are using eight-inch siege guns brought up from Port Arthur.

From west to east, from the foot of the letter A on one side to its foot on the other, the front of the two armies extends for a distance of between 50 and 60 miles but there is in addition to this, another movement in progress at an around Sankiatz which is some 45 miles east of the right wing of the Japanese army.

At this point, the Russians are, plainly enough, assuming the offensive and as it is connected with Mukden by a recently-built military railway and threatens an attack on Motienling or an advance down the Yalu, this movent assumes considerable importance, and on account of the facilities afforded by the railway communication with the main Russian base, the strategic advantages would appear to be all on the side of Kuropatkin.

Judging from the mild spell which has set in here—and the climatic conditions in Korea are said to be a fair indication of those prevailing up north—it will only be a few weeks before the country between Liaoyang and Mukden becomes a regular quagmire when it will be almost impossible for either army to move and it will therefore be to the advantage of the losing side to stubbornly hold all positions until the weather comes to the rescue.

In short, everything points to the present battle being a particularly desperate one, and although the contents of the recent telegrams professing to give the terms of peace have pre-disposed us in favour of a continuance of the war, we still hope, in view of the sickening list of casualties that will presently come before us, that some means may be found of putting a stop to what appears to us to be an absolutely useless waste of life.

From our knowledge of the "hand-to mouth" way in which the Japanese live we are quite sure that there is already much privation amongst the families of those conscripts who have been killed in the war, and although efforts are being made to relieve the trouble it is not possible that permanent provision can be made.

With professional soldiers it is another matter, but our sympathy goes out to the conscripts and their families.

CONDITIONS IN RUSSIA.

(Concluded from last issue.)

All linen is washed before it is packed up. In another room all linen is stamped and sorted. What profane activity under goldglittering chandeliers and amongst marble chimneys! We next enter a salon where bedlinen for hospital railway trains is sewn, then into rooms where woollen stuffs and warm footwear are in hand. Now we enter the famous winter garden of the Empress. In the ante-room there is a large machine which cuts bandages automatically, and there I meet ladies of last night's party. Their hands are sticky with paste, they have to pack up bandages and paste labels on the parcels.

Is work done here every day?

Yes, every day from 3 to 7 P. M., excepting Thursdays when the school children come to us.

And who furnishes all the material?

Partly the Czaritza from her private means and partly it is bought from voluntary contributions received here. Princess Galitzin receives contributions and gives receipts for them.

How many ladies might there be who daily work here in the Winter Palace?

At present about one thousand, but in the summer when the Empress was here there may have been twice as many.

On the second floor I find several rooms filled to overflowing with books and journals, old and new, Russian, German, French, just as they are brought in from the street, reading matter for the wounded in the field hospitals. Adjoining is a room full of small parcels packed in coloured stuff of all kinds, and addressed "Dia Soldat," "for the soldier." These are gifts from poor people which are collected and forwarded free of charge. The Christmas presents were dispatched last month (November). Each soldier received a tin with sugar, tea, chocolate, tobacco, a pipe, sewing materials, underwear, smoked beef and a piece of soap. The whole country contributed these gifts, and each giver has enclosed a postal card with his address, requesting the receiver to let him know how and where he spent Christmas Eve.

Next we enter long corridors in which boxes are packed up to the ceiling. These are gifts from abroad, principally from France. Mumm and Roederer are largely represented. To my great surprise I learn that, next to France, England has been the most liberal benefactor. From Miss B. twenty-four large cases arrived this week; besides large quantities of portwine, Germany also has not remained behind. Over a small winding staircase we get into the interior of the Imperial theatre—but it is hardly to be recognized as such. Seats, boxes, the stage, all are filled with cases and bales and goods not yet packed.

It serves as a depot from which the trains are loaded. Two goods-trains a week are occupied with the transport of this collossal mass of goods. The transport takes two months as goods-trains must still give way to trains with troops,

I must say that I have changed many preconceived opinions which I had brought over the frontier."

THE PEACE RUMOURS.

We presume that the rumours of peace will continue to come along until the Japanese loans. They are so contradictory that they are hardly worth printing, but the publication of them does at any rate no harm as they are not likely to mislead anyone.

One message says that it is the Czar who desires peace and that it is the Grand Dukes who are determined to continue the war and other telegrams, say the exact opposite. The riots in Russia only bear upon the war inasmuch as the revolutionists have taken advantage of the chaos to push their claims and objection to the war, as a war, is probably stronger in Japan than in Russia.

With the railway working at high pressure, it would takes six weeks for troops to return from Manchuria to Russia therefore the recall of any of these cannot be contemplated.

Kuropatkin is now better off than ever he was; he has all the troops he wants and supplies are abundant so there is no liklihood of his being in favour of peace.

There is said to be a large party in Russia in favour of ending the war; so there was in England during the Boer war but those who advocated giving in to the enemy were very few and far between.

A Shanghai telegram to the Mainichi states that is is reported there that 2,500 of the Russian wounded at Port Arthur are crippled for life. They will be taken to Chefoo and thence sent to Europe.

The Korea Daily News.

VOL. II, WEDNESDAY, MARCH 1, 1905. No. 46

大韓每日申報
대한ᄆᆡ일신보

(뎨이권ᄉᆞ십칠호) (금요일) 일쳔구ᄇᆡᆨ오년삼월삼일

본샤고ᄇᆡᆨ

이신보는영어와한어로셔거ᄐᆡ
일츌판ᄒᆞᆷ

신문가

한쟝 엽두돈오푼
일삭됴 엽두량닷돈
우표가ᄐᆡ 샤닷돈
다엽돈으로밧숨

광고료는

귀한의쟝단과ᄌᆞ항의다쇼로즁
감ᄒᆞ되ᄒᆞᆫ가로밧을터이오메오
리거아녀대한사ᄅᆞᆷ마다마이신
문을보실터이니광고내시기를
원ᄒᆞ시는이들은우리신문사에
와셔편약ᄒᆞ심을ᄇᆞ라ᄒᆞᆷ

○발ᄒᆡᆼ소 박동대한ᄆᆡ일신보
사발어학교압ᄒᆡ전영국인셜필
립쟈라오
사쟝 영국인 (ᄇᆡ셜)

평양 ᄃᆡ리졈

○평양효동사는권미보씨로우
리신문관ᄃᆡ리인을뎡ᄒᆞ엿
시ᄉᆞ오니평양에계신구람ᄒᆞ저
는 쳠군ᄌᆞ는ᄃᆡ리졈에왕
림ᄒᆞ와면의ᄒᆞ시옵

사고

○우리대한ᄆᆡ일신보의목뎍은
대한의안녕질셔에관한모든뎨
목에ᄃᆡᄒᆞ야는공평한변론을주
장홈이라우리동신원의ᄆᆞᆷ보논
신문보시는쳠군ᄌᆞ의게ᄒᆞ상보
도ᄒᆞ리며편지들귀셔ᄒᆞ며주시
는이논셩명과번디를져어ᄇᆞ치
시기를ᄇᆞ라ᄒᆞ오니ᄒᆞ게슬신문
상에긔ᄌᆡᄒᆞ라는거시아니오다
만구ᄒᆞ신용ᄒᆞ는즁거를숨고자
홈이라귀자는아모리편지가젹소과
ᄎᆔᄒᆞᆷ을되각ᄒᆞ는권리들가젹스오
나되각ᄒᆞ는리유를말ᄒᆞᆯ터이오
며공즁평회들문란케ᄒᆞ는듯ᄒᆞᆫ
타귀셔는의례히밧지안켓슴니이

●본샤셜시이리로신문을미양
우례로분젼ᄒᆞ와례젼부의임의
로젼ᄒᆞ든ᄉᆞ스로면곳에는ᄒᆞᆨ늣게
젼ᄒᆞ기도ᄒᆞ며혹면쳘ᄒᆡ슬혼ᄐᆡᆸ
곳에젼ᄒᆞ기도ᄒᆞ며혹아니젼ᄒᆞ는
뎌ᄒᆞ야구ᄅᆞᆷ시는 쳠군ᄌᆞ의ᄇᆡᆼ
은ᄒᆞ야ᄆᆞ미안ᄒᆞ오ᄂᆞᆫ기로지금
부터는젼인을ᄌᆞ두료ᄆᆡ일슈이젼
폐가엿ᄂᆞ니젼ᄒᆞ커나늣게거나혹아니

젼ᄒᆞ거나혹늣게젼ᄒᆞ거나ᄒᆞᆫ일
이잇스면본샤로통긔ᄒᆞ여주심
을ᄇᆞ라ᄒᆞᆷ

론셜

한국에일본인의압제

○일본셰력밋헤잇는한국에자
유권은조국에자유권찻치싱긔
가업는지라
우리가목젼에한인들의참나가
는쳠빈은모다도젹맛고탐용ᄉᆞ
와쟝곽쳔대쟝의쳥구는압제로
쳥죵ᄒᆞ는것을보거니와슈일젼
에한국사름삼명을일본인이포
박ᄒᆞ야구류ᄒᆞ엿는뒤그ᄌᆞ목은
일본에차권ᄒᆞ는것보다ᄂᆡ디에
셔돈을슈합ᄒᆞ는것이죠타고예
ᄉᆞ말로져의들의의견을공포ᄒᆞᆫ
ᄉᆞ건이라더라
리용익씨도감히그와갓흔차권
에반ᄃᆡᄒᆞ는의견을셜명ᄒᆞ다가
일본인의운동으로원ᄃᆡ의관찰
ᄉᆞ로ᄶᅩᆺ차보냇스니만일일본인
의말과갓치리용익씨가협잡ᄇᆡᆫ
갓ᄒᆞ면지금시졍개션ᄒᆞ는ᄯᅢ에
관찰ᄉᆞ는엇지시엿는지
그의미롤다ᄒᆞᆯ지라목하젼씨가
탁지고문관으로한국졍부의의
향과는반ᄃᆡ되는차권을쓰게ᄒᆞ
야약조가된후에곳일본으로도
망ᄒᆞ야반ᄃᆡ가셩히이러남을알
고일본헌병과일진회에게그차
권ᄉᆞ건에갑히반ᄃᆡᄒᆞ는의견을
셜명ᄒᆞ는ᄉᆞᄅᆞᆷ들과뎌셤ᄒᆞ는ᄉᆞ
무롤맥진지란
아모리일본인을위ᄒᆞ는ᄉᆞᄅᆞᆷ이
라도차권이한국에유익ᄒᆞ다고
는죠곰도말홀슈업스며이나라
의셰입을감독ᄒᆞ란고ᄒᆞ는계ᄎᆡᆨ
이나지금일본인이져의리익을
위ᄒᆞ야한국을리용ᄒᆞ기를시작
ᄒᆞ는거시분명ᄒᆞᆫ뒤아모한인이
라도그계ᄎᆡᆨ을반ᄃᆡᄒᆞ는자는단
단히ᄒᆞ보란홀지라
한인들은일본인이일한의졍셔
들엿본이리용ᄒᆞ는거슬놀별듯
ᄒᆞ고우리도쟝ᄂᆡ에분쾌ᄒᆞᆫ일이
잇슬줄로보앗으며시졍개션ᄒᆞᆫ다
고ᄒᆞ는거슨한인들을심ᄒᆞᆫ란ᄒᆞ고
미워ᄒᆞ는마음을더나게ᄒᆞ는거
시라일본인이조국과한국에졍
계의부패홈을맛는기가ᄌᆞᆷ샹션
ᄒᆞ게라ᄒᆞ노라

외보

○남쳥요항 남쳥에는광동오
문셔비외에경히유망ᄒᆞᆫ휘구는광
젼셔지항히항이니동항은신녕이
든길소항이더니군녕에는현져
ᄒᆞ진보ᄒᆞ야거진ᄒᆞᆫ남항을엄두
셔ᄒᆞ기히지도지란원리광셔셩에
는에남도에남항으로히구들에
뎡ᄒᆞ규셩나에ᄇᆞᆫ광과법령이안남
과밋남양제도에교통ᄒᆞ야기명
이반곽등게에헌로ᄒᆞ엿는데일셕
금반곽등운히남항으로뎨통이아
민근거ᄃᆡ인ᄃᆡ동항은대톄이아
님으로젼진ᄒᆞ히망이무ᄒᆞ되북
휘항은차에금ᄒᆞ야광셔셩일휘
구쟁안니란운남귀쥬이셩도차
휘구에의뢰ᄒᆞ는형셰잇으로목
하법인은젼쳘동ᄃᆡ경영에로력
ᄒᆞ야거진법령과곳ᄒᆞᆫᄃᆡ향일파
라지합ᄃᆡ가리왕ᄒᆞ야남쳥에군
휘가ᄃᆡ에셔구혼다는셜이잇스미
엿다더라

뎐보

로국의쟁형

론돈발 이월이십일

○셩피득보에셔로동자의쟁형
을기량ᄒᆞ는위원회에셔결졍ᄒᆞᆫ
되각회사의쥬인들과로동자들
이그위원회에ᄃᆡ표롤표션ᄒᆞ야
로동자의분요롤의론ᄒᆞ기로ᄒᆞ
엿다더라

동디발 동일

○론돈뎰니텔네그라푸의셩피
득보통신원의보고롤거ᄒᆞᆫ즉로
국샹등샤회안에셔논이번젼쟁
을아모조록속히맛치는것이졍
부와황셜에긴요ᄒᆞᆫ닐이라는의
견이셩ᄒᆡᆼᄒᆞᆫ다ᄒᆞ엿더라

구로파긴의군ᄃᆡ

론돈발 이월이십일

○그리폐는빅대쟝이만쥬뎨이군
의수령관으로잇다가지금피득
보로도라갓는ᄃᆡ황뎨께셔환영
ᄒᆞ신지라그대쟝이구로파긴의
위롤젼복ᄒᆞ란고운동ᄒᆞᆫ다더
라

동디발 동월십구일

○로국의군용쳘도가호바라
셔셔부리쳐서벽쟝이만히샹에
ᄒᆞ엿더라

론돈발 이월십구일

○기엘에잇는로국평ᄉᆞ가귀쏠
샤의군션이격을ᄉᆞ셔대샹봉
회

뎌ᄒᆞᆫ퇴임ᄒᆞ운송션으로쓰란ᄒᆞᆫ다
더라

뎨샹쳔쳘셩사호 광무구
년이월이십팔일 ᄒᆞ포
셔임금사평

○춍관셔ᄒᆞᆫ이등사팔괘쟝 경위원
리근턱
○동군셔ᄒᆞᆫ샹등사태극쟝 일본국
중좌 민야쟝
○동군셔ᄒᆞᆫ샹등사팔괘쟝 일본국
소좌 언관미만
이샹이월이십이일
○희ᄒᆡ도경임황ᄒᆡ도지관소관사쳥
○희ᄒᆡ도경임함경남도 제관소관
○사 함경남도젼관찰ᄉᆞ 리현
○황ᄒᆡ도관찰ᄉᆞ 구영조
○명경임함경남도 제관소관
○사 면본관 함경남도관찰ᄉᆞ 창원항춍슌 신귀 김샹션
이샹이월이십사일
○의원면본관 중추원의관 김진우 중추원의관 쟝지용
○의관 중추원의관 리보형 중추원
의관 김기익 중추원의관
○김병호 리죵운 중추원의관 김만형 중추원
○임중추원의관셔주임관륙등 신흥구
○갑산군수 쟝셩군수 김승표
○평취군수 신영군수 창원군수 디도군수 김쳘구 리긔쟝군수 송샹희 안변군수 창
○지혜군수 임기찬 기수쟝원 셔판임관륙등
○최희원션 함경남도종두사무위원 리
○규용 명함경남도종두사무위원
○김하범 명희경샹남도종두사무위원
○김셩슌 명경샹북도종두사무의원
○용츈 명쳥북도종두사무위원 리셰
○김정규 명츙쳥북도종두사무위원
○승셔구 셔쥬임관사등 외부주사 리
이샹이월이십오일
○명종졍원경셔칙임관사등
○중이프 리인쳘
○의원면본관 중학교교관 리
○덕응 임중학교교관셔판임관륙등
○동화
이샹이월이십칠일 궁ᄂᆡ부

대샹천쳘십오호 광무구
년삼월칠일
서임급ᄉᆞ령
●임찬원칭충순서 판임관칠등
구품 박흰원
이월이십오일
○임용사관생등참서관셔주임
관륙등 륙품 량홍묵
○임 종묘서령셔판임관칠등
교방ᄉᆞ쥬ᄉᆞ 민회식
○임교방ᄉᆞ쥬ᄉᆞ서판임관륙등
영희뎐참봉 허 명
○임영희뎐참봉서판임관팔등
구품 서천수
○임시강원ᄉᆞ종관서판임관팔
등 효릉참봉 김경진
○임효릉참봉서판임관팔등
최영조
○명계신계도경리국위원 중
너부참서관 김용제
○의원면본관 대구군수
종원 광창군수 박용훈 함길
영군수 젼광묵 안의군수
민병길 양성군수 리종철
진보군수 오진규 계주군수
홍우순 은진군수 장홍식
○임동리군수서주임관일등
종이품 원유상
○임남회군수서주임관륙등
정삼품 리순영
○임원주군수서주임관륙등
춘천군수 김영규
○임춘천군수서주임관삼등
고성군수 리명퇴
○임고성군수서주임관륙등
탁지부무계관 민형기
○임인동군수서주임관륙등
륙품 서상규
○임창평군수서주임관륙등
륙품 장봉규
○임강서군수서주임관륙등
륙품 리우영
○임창령군수서주임관륙등
정삼품 민벽건
○임지례군수서주임관륙등
시강원시종관 김황진
○임단성군수서주임관륙등
륙품 김병건
○임평산군수서주임관륙등
륙품 장순원
○임고령군수서주임관륙등
고령군수 신택진
○임함창군수서주임관오등
륙품 전광묵
○임적성군수서주임관사등
이천군수 조병직
○임이천군수서주임관칠등
종이품 박승연
○임곡성군수서주임관륙등
정삼품 심상퇴
○임한산군수서주임관륙등
시종원좌시어 류석주
○임광창군수서주임관오등
젼군수 장홍섭
○임대구군수서주임관삼등
륙군참령 김한영
○임은진군수서주임관륙등
홍덕군수 김상기
○임홍덕군수서주임관륙등
인동군수 민병석
○임김화군수서주임관륙등
영동군수 천세헌
○임영동군수서주임관륙등
륙품 최영근

○임금산군수서주임관륙등
정삼품 김병욱
○임순흥군수서주임관륙등
륙품 명제학
○임창녕군수서주임관륙등
륙품 박승원
○임단양군수서주임관륙등
군부주ᄉᆞ 박초양
○임군위군수서주임관륙등
종묘령 김교헌
○임황간군수서주임관륙등
기평군수 표동선
○임기평군수서주임관륙등
륙품 리제퇴
○임양천군수서주임관오등
통진군수 안동식
○임통진군수서주임관륙등
젼의관 리보현
○임진위군수서주임관륙등
젼군수 명희팔
○임안의군수서주임관륙등
륙품 리범직
○임응주군수서주임관삼등
농상공부참서관 윤규섭
○임청풍군수서주임관륙등
정삼품 리병화
이월이십륙일
○명장례원경서칙임관삼등
궁너부특진관 조병필
○명궁너부특진관서칙임관사
등 장례원소경 박영두
○명장례원소경서칙임관사등
종이품 홍종영
○의원면본관 홍문관시독
조진설 홍문관시독 명헌제
숭덕뎐참봉 박인순 숭령
뎐참봉 조영복 군부주ᄉᆞ
홍승규 군부주
ᄉᆞ 명성윤 군기창기수 박
두병 농상공부주ᄉᆞ 리종
덕 영흥군공립소학교교원
한헌수
○임홍문관시독서판임관사등
륙품 녀인섭 법부주ᄉᆞ 김
남제
○임숭덕뎐참봉서판임관팔등
박준교
○임숭령뎐참봉서판임관팔등
김명제
○임시종원좌시어서판임관팔
등 심종서
○임시종원우시어서판임관팔
등 사품 남익환
○임공능령서판임관칠등 교
방사주ᄉᆞ 리윤수
○임교방사주ᄉᆞ서판임관사등
통신사뎐화과주ᄉᆞ 명광묘
○임홍능령서판임관칠등 홍
능사승 홍우순
○임홍능사승서판임관팔등
경효뎐사승 리원하
○임경효뎐사승서판임관륙등
환구단사제서령 황범수
○임환구단사제서령서판임관
사등 통신사뎐화과주ᄉᆞ 리
승진
○임너부주ᄉᆞ서판임관륙등

륙품 리기훈
○임군부주ᄉᆞ서판임관비등
구품 송영만 구품 원지상
○임군부주ᄉᆞ서판임관륙등
구품 한규명
○임군기창기수서판임관륙등
박용근
○임농상공부주ᄉᆞ서판임관
륙등 추월오
○임탁지부주ᄉᆞ서판임관륙등
문벽규
○임탁지부주ᄉᆞ서판임관륙등
리규승
○임중학교교관서판임관륙등
외국어학교부교관 주영환
○임영흥군공립소학교교원서
판임관삼등 북청군공립소학
교교원 도근하
○임북청군공립소학교교원서
판임관사등 젼교원 한헌수
○임중추원의관서칙임관삼등
평안북도관찰사 리용관
○임중추원의관서칙임관사등
회계원검사과장 홍정섭
이월이십칠일
○의원면본관 군부주ᄉᆞ 권
병규
○임군부주ᄉᆞ서판임관륙등
구품 차진익
이월이십팔일

잡보

○방대상소 법부대신박제순
씨는사직소를샹ᄒᆞ엿다더라
○비오권한 일진회원이너부
지방국쟝을방문ᄒᆞ고면회에종
등에게ᄒᆞᆫ군수를엇지면관치아
니ᄒᆞ나냐ᄒᆞ고샹지ᄒᆞᆫ즉국쟝의
대답이너의권한이아니라다언
홈게시엄다ᄒᆞ엿다더라
○국쟝신임 경무청경무국쟝
윤승엽ᄒᆞ란든젼군수김종원씨
는너부경무국쟝을피임ᄒᆞᆫ다더
라
○무젼대변 봉화군수가외부
로보고ᄒᆞ엿스되순흥거ᄒᆞ는홍
국유가분리부탁ᄒᆞᆫ셩질노번젹ᄒᆞ
홍의유인을너엄일쳬샹만샹젼
광은가칭ᄒᆞ고그종행딕유의
종즁교자ᄒᆞ는고로관찰부에서
국유를본군에이수ᄒᆞ엿더니위
법한등이순ᄒᆞ관부의긴계운쥬
사커회의게흑탐ᄒᆞ고또일인홍
진퇴중첩이인을부동ᄒᆞ야홍사
가를지리고홍덕유카에리도ᄒᆞ야일
타동에칭행ᄒᆞ며사밤을만나면난
거ᄒᆞ오ᄒᆞ고면권과곡포와지물을탈
로사셜를커ᄒᆞ야보고ᄒᆞ오니일
쏘관에교셥ᄒᆞ와휘문을추환ᄒᆞ며
후환방두ᄒᆞ을소서ᄒᆞ엿다더라
○커져공평 일본수가너부로
공함ᄒᆞ기를대구관찰ᄉᆞ쟝승원
의루주건에관ᄒᆞ야휘관하커국
인종에서변지원셔를본ᄉᆞ의케
계홀조유ᄒᆞ나그리ᄒᆞ노휘관
샤사가귀임ᄒᆞᆫ고의후인이계결

정뵈엿스니금일에젼관외투임
은사졍에뢰치못ᄒᆞᆫ바ㅣ라ᄒᆞ엿
스니원셔젼잉광의쳔량ᄒᆞᆫ치졔
을칭예ᄒᆞ엿스니참교하탑ᄒᆞ시
오ᄒᆞ엿는되히치계이민우공평
정직ᄒᆞ다더라
○인쟝조셩 대신계도쟝리국
죵지리지국써가각부부원쳥에
론조ᄒᆞ기를본국을공너부에권
셥ᄒᆞ온바인쟝을일의조셩ᄒᆞ야
갸본을쳥부ᄒᆞ노라ᄒᆞ엿더라
○답샤ᄒᆞ죵 답양군수가너부
로면보ᄒᆞ엿스되희원이맛춤너
휘산귀안교창면에출ᄒᆞ야견
호총셩침을답사ᄒᆞ는고로민정
이되요ᄒᆞ오나엇지ᄒᆞ올는지ᄒᆞ
엿더라
○외패시무 외부대신리하영
씨카신병으로오리사직귀츙ᄒᆞ
니본월일일브터칭공시무ᄒᆞᆫ다
더라
○외서등쳐 외공ᄉᆞ보관 께
카비샹팔일외부에젼왈ᄒᆞᄂᆞᆫ외
부교문관수지분써를방문ᄒᆞ고외
금광합동조약을좀쉬케ᄒᆞ자고
교등쳐ᄒᆞ엿다더라
○교문셜현 외부교문관수지
분씨가퇴오일하오일시에덕동
슌탁앙저에셜연ᄒᆞ고외부대신
미하참서관을쳥ᄒᆞ야연회ᄒᆞ
엿더라
○수칙젼쇄 각부부원쳥관
제리경에는져평을론계계한이
ᄒᆞ엿스나외경부관계에는의경
참경에퇴쳔ᄒᆞ자를카정ᄒᆞ고보
탁칭관경좌관을반다시정입치
안이ᄒᆞ되의경대신참경대신은
다시셔잉ᄒᆞᆫ다는거쾨창경됴병
호씨가창경대신오로다시셔잉
ᄒᆞ엿는되수계전에는너부대신
됴병식씨가의정대신서듸를피
명ᄒᆞ엿더라
○항의불윤 의정대신계군수
를피임ᄒᆞᆫ너부주사김영운씨터
에피잉ᄒᆞᆫ리기ᄒᆞᆫ쎄는증리근텩
쎄외아드이라칭관계를받포ᄒᆞᆫ
면너부주사실내인을캉하ᄒᆞ
인되리써는자괴의세력으로모
ᄒᆞ미셩ᄒᆞᆫ이런아휘를서잉ᄒᆞ엿
다고항의가불일ᄒᆞᆫ다더라

광고

The wedding of the German Crown Prince will be celebrated May 24th.

Lady Curzon has completely recovered, and returns shortly to India with her children.

The German Red Cross Society has sent two of its members to Japan to assist the Japanese society.

We understand that H. M. cruiser "Diadem" is shortly to relieve the "Amphitrite" on this station.

The German Cruiser "Hansa," Admiral Count von Moltke's flagship, is expected at Chemulpo on the 8th inst.

According to the Russian maps about 5,000 mines were sunk in the vicinity of Port Arthur. So far only about half of them have been removed.

The Russian sailor, who stabbed a German Midshipman in Tsingtau some time ago, has been sentenced to four year's imprisonment by a court-martial composed of officers from the "Tsarevitch."

The German Naval authorities at Tsingtau are experimenting with Shantung coal, the "Hansa" having taken that fuel for trial purposes. It will be interesting to learn that this coal is suitable for naval use.

The recent remarkable rescue of the guns as well as so of many human lives of this battery is to be explained by the fact that in the first gunlimber was carried the ikon of the Saviour, handed over to the 43rd Brigade by his Majesty the Czar himself.—"Manchurian Army Messenger" (Russian Official Organ).

One of the foreign Admirals on the North Sea Commission, in an interview with a representative of Reuter, said that while the Commissioners were presently convinced of the Russians' good faith with reference to the torpedo boats, the Commissioners were unable to believe that there were any torpedo craft among the fishing boats. The Admiral said he expected the decision would be such as would enable the Russians to walk out of the affair with their heads erect.

With the object of meeting the demand for alcohol in Manchuria and Korea, which is reported to be very large, Mr. D. Kamiya and some prominent "sake" brewers in Tokyo and Osaka intend to establish an alcohol distillery at Seoul with a capital of two million yen. It is said by the "Nichi Nichi" that the Korean Court has promised to subscribe for shares in the proposed factory.

The following telegram has been received by the Tokio Foreign Department:—On Sunday, Feb. 12, the members of the Supreme Council held a meeting. As a result, on the following day, the Minister for Finance was ordered to draft a bill for establishing measures to improve the condition of the workmen. For this purpose, a special committee has been instructed to examine further the petitions of owners of factories and workmen.

It is reported that great depression has been occasioned in Ministerial circles in Peking through the receipt of a lengthy cypher telegraphic despatch from the Chinese Minister to St. Petersburg. The contents are of so grave a nature that the meetings of the Ministers of the Grand Council have been prolonged, and they were been observed to disperse with dejected countenances. Prince Ching has instructed the two secretaries of the Grand Council to keep the contents of the despatch strictly secret. It is surmised that the despatch deals with the Russian charge of violation of neutrality by China, and the aggressive designs of Russia in North and West China.

On the morning of February 20th a party of insurgents attacked the electric power station at Russeki in Formosa. They killed eight men and four women among the Chinese also two natives, and wounded one (whose nationality is not mentioned). They also burned a storehouse.

The Times' military critic states that it is now beyond doubt that the Russian casualties, resulting from the fight at the Shaho, numbered 60,000 while the Japanese losses were not more than 16,000. All of which is interesting, says the "Shanghai Times," yet we cannot but wonder where he got the information.

A telegram from Mukden says that energetic measures are being taken there to raise the exchange value of the Russian rouble. Bars of silver have been ordered from Hamburg and "yamben," silver coins of the value about 63s. each, are to be struck. Small silver coins have been put into circulation already; the Russo-Chinese Bank has had these coins made.

A "special" telegram to the "Shanghai Times" says:—The war party in St. Petersburg is greatly puzzled at the situation on the Shaho and Hunho, and for the first time since the commencement of the war have begun to doubt the result. They have begun to consider that there is great fear with regard to the safety of General Kuropatkin and his army in face of the methods of attack adopted by Marshal Oyama.

Recent arrivals from Moukden, says the "China Review," deny in toto the statements published in the "China Times" from a "perfectly credible correspondent" and state that there is no sign of relaxing in the efforts of either General Kuropatkin or his subordinates; and that also there is no discontent among either officers or men, except at the inaction. Several low class purveyors of so-called liquors have been severely punished when caught in the act of vending their vile poisons.

The Minister at Peking of a certain foreign Power has warned the Minister of the Board of Foreign Affairs that it is Russia's intention to create a rupture with China by violating her neutrality. He advises the Central Government to communicate with the Governments of the different foreign Powers with a view to the frustration of Russia's evil designs. The Minister also advises the Central Government to warn the administration of her outlying dominions not to allow themselves to become the dupes of Russian intrigues.

A remarkable struggle between the German and French Embassies at Constantinople, to induce the Porte to expend a considerable proportion of the projected new loan of five million from the Ottoman Bank upon guns, in their respective countries, has ended in a victory for Germany. The Port consented to buy Krupp guns, whereupon M. Constans, the French Ambassador at Constantinople notified the Porte that the Paris market was closed against the new loan, and the Ottoman Bank withdrew the whole transaction. The Deutsche Bank is now offering to assist the Turkish Treasury.

It was in Manchester that John Roberts accomplished the finest performance of his career, on May 3 and 4, 1894, when, under spot-barred rules of the Gentleman's Concert Hall, he compiled his wonderful break of 1392. His opponent was Diggle, and hitherto Roberts's highest break had been 867. When he passed that total there was loud cheering, but that was nothing compared with the noise when he reached 1,000, and finished the evening's play with 1,033 unfinished. On the following day he added 358 more points, and put up a performance that is never likely to be beaten, for the spot-barred rules are are almost obsolete.

RUSSIAN SPIES.

We note that the Japanese are providing themselves with another weapon for dealing with such Koreans as venture to differ from them. They are to be treated as Russian spies! The "Kokumin's" Seoul correspondent has wired the following to his journal:—

An association of secret intelligence workers, who are antagonistic to Japan's influence and who are unfavourable to Japan, is exchanging correspondence with Seoul, Shanghai and St. Petersburg. The headquarters of this intelligence office are established at Shanghai where two Koreans, Hyon and Yi, are staying. Some of the French residents are alleged to be supporting them. Communications of the kind are suspected to have also been sent to and from Vladivostock and Hamgyong Province, but correspondence in that direction is now likely to have been suspended owing to the recent withdrawal of Russian troops from North Korea. There being signs that these intelligence workers in Seoul have instigated a demonstration against Japan's influence in order to effect their communications with the north, the Japanese authorities concerned are keeping stringent watch on these people whom they regard as Russian spies. It is said that Russia is still appropriating the expenditure formerly required by the Russian Legation in Seoul, for this purpose.

It is rumoured in ecclesiastical circles that Rev. Stephen Gladstone and Dr. J. W. Birkbeck, the well known authority on Eastern Church questions, both of whom are sojourning in Rome, are about to join the Roman communion.

A telegram from M. Jadot, engineer-in-chief of the Peking-Hankow rail-way, on January 2nd, said that the line is now finished as far as the Yelloy River, the total length being 600 kilometres. The last 300 kilometres, including the laying of the rails, were constructed during 1904.

The British steamer "Sylvian" (4,187 tons, carrying 6,500 tons of Cardiff coal for Vladivostock, was seized by a Japanese warship on the 19th at noon. Another British steamer the "Powderham" (3,019), bound for Vladivostock with 4,000 tons of British coal on board, was also captured in Hokkaido waters on the night of the 19th.

The greatest thickness of ice on the river measured in Tientsin this winter was ten and a half inches on the 10th, 11th and 12th ult. on the 13th the measurement showed one inch less, a considerable decrease for one day, and the ice is now expected to get gradually less day by day. The river will probably be open by the end of the month. When, first the ice breaks up and commences to float away it gets jammed up at the curves, and takes some considerable, time to clear all away. The ice at Tongku is still a little over seven inches thick.

Several Manila speculators are said to have made much money by running the blockade at Port Arthur. The Manila "Times" say: "It is stated by those in this city who keep in touch with affairs in the north, that Louis Spitzel has been highly successful in his blockade running. The steamer "Sishan," chartered by him last fall, made one successful trip into Port Arthur with 300,000 rifles and almost a hundred head of cattle. The trip is said to have netted Spitzel something over $280,-000."

A subscriber has sent the "China Review" the following translation of an advertisement which appeared in the Sporting Supplement, of the Tientsin "Daily Times," a Chinese paper:—

"Mr. E. P. the great Japanese Lawyer. All kinds of foreign and native codes and laws. This great lawyer just knows it all completely. I have permission from the Japanese Consul General to live in Tientsin and practice law. If any Chinese or foreign officials meet with any troubles I pray them to come to me at my office in the Japanese Concession near the hospital and see me. And it will be all right. I know everything, There is no mistake about this."

The Russian battleships "Alexander II" and "Pashanakazoff" did not accompany the third Baltic fleet from Libau.

The French Ottoman Bank has refused to advance any more money to Turkey, so the Deutsche Bank at Berlin has promised assistance. The Porte has ordered sixty batteries of Krupp guns.

A telegram from Washington states that the German Ambassador has informed President Roosevelt that Germany is now ready to strictly carry out the principle of the open door in China and the preservation of China's integrity, quite discarding the view of any sphere of influence in the Shantung Province.

With the marriage of the Earl of Suffolk to Miss Daisy Leiter, the Americans married to peers number twenty-five. As usual, there is a great deal of rather foolish talk of Americanising the peerage, new blood, and other fancies of a similar kind. As a matter of fact, this number includes all the Americans, with one exception, married to peers since 1850, a period of forty-four years. Nor is this all. Ten of these ladies have no sons, so that the peerage is not likely to be Americanised yet awhile.—King.

The Korea Daily News.

Issued at 5 P. M. daily except Sundays.

Rate of Subscription:—
Per Year,............Yen 25.
Per Quarter,..........Yen 7.
Per Month,..........Yen 2.50.

Postage in Korea not charged extra.
Postage abroad charged extra.

Advertisements, 50 sen per day for 1 inch or less.
5 yen per month per inch.
50 yen per year per inch.

All communications to

E. T. BETHELL,
Editor and Publisher.
Pak-tong, Seoul.

THE DARDANELLES.

If the telegram which we published three days ago be correct, the Russian authorities still contemplate the despatch of the Black Sea squadron to reinforce Admiral Rohdjestvensky.

Negotiations to secure Great Britain's noninterference with the passage of the fleet through the Dardanelles are now in progress, and therefore the clause in the Treaty of Paris which it is sought to annul is of interest. It is as follows:—

"His Majesty the Sultan, on the one part, declares that he is firmly resolved to maintain for the future the principle, invariably established as the ancient rule of his empire, and in virtue of which it has all times been prohibited for the ships of war of foreign powers to enter the straits of the Dardanelles and of the Bosphorus and that so long as the Porte is at peace His Majesty will admit no foreign ship of war into the said straits. And their majesties (the sovereigns of the contracting parties), on the other part, engage to respect this determination of the Sultan and to conform themselves to the principle above declared."

The point at issue is of course whether, if Russia obtains the consent of the Turkish Government to the violation of this clause, Great Britain, by virtue of her undertaking to respect the determination and conform herself to the principle will consider herself obliged to actively interfere.

There can be no doubt that Japan has done and will do, all she can to impress upon Great Britian the view that she must interfere but as a previous violation of this treaty by Russia called forth nothing more than a protest it does not seem likely that Japan's representations will meet with much success. In January 1903 Russia sent four torpedo boats though the straits and this led the British Government to address a protest to the Porte, which was, however, allowed to remain unanswered. His Majesty's Government did, however, declare to Parliament that the treaties of 1841, 1856, and 1871, prohibiting the entrance of the Straits by foreign ships of war, were still in force, and that the passage of the torpedo-boats was a contravention of the stipulations of those treaties.

Great Britain also entered protests against the recent passage of the "Smolensk" and "Petersburg" but on the essential point as to her right to pass ships of war through the Dardanelles, Russia has reserved her reply.

The Black Sea fleet is an important one, its vessels aggregating a total of 103,156 tons and it includes ten battle-ships, the oldest of which was built in 1892. According to the famous Captain Klado, the addition of this fleet to Admiral Rohdjestvensky's squadron would render the defeat of the Japanese navy a certainty and it is therefore evident that Japan will use every means in her power to presuade her ally that the strict observance of the Treaty of Paris must be insisted upon.

From the Russian point of view the only objection to the passage of the Black Sea fleet through the Dardanelles seems to be that it would confer a right upon other powers to send their fleets through the straits, thus undermining Russian influence in Asia Minor. The following extract from an article in a leading Russian newspaper seems to represent Russian opinion:—

"Unless therefore a time limit is fixed in the Treaty relating to the passage of Russian warships through the Dardanelles, Russia would have the undoubted right to terminate it by giving six months' notice to the signatory powers. Apart from this fact civil law does not enforce immoral contracts. It would not enforce an agreement, for instance, to the effect that a man in case of an attack by a neighbour, or by some one else, must not call his servants to his assistance from an outhouse, and it would not call upon the forces of the state to prevent the servants from coming to his defence if he did call upon them to do so. Any such agreement the law would consider and declare void as a legally immoral one, for the right of self-defence overrides all other considerations.

"For the same reason an agreement, which, to all practical intents and purposes, binds a state not to use any particular portion of its armed forces for its defence, in case of an attack by a powerful enemy, is and must be void *ab initio*. Any attempt, therefore, to enforce such an agreement by force of arms would be a breach of neutrality equal to a declaration of war, which, so far as Russia is concerned, would at once bring the Franco-Russian alliance into action, and we are firmly convinced that England would not go to war with Russia and France on that acount. The utmost she could do would be to demand that as soon as the emergencies of the present war no longer require the service of the Black Sea Fleet outside of the Black Sea, the fleet shall return to the Black Sea and remain there."

THE BALTIC FLEET.

SPECIAL CORRESPONDENCE.

(From the "Shanghai Times")

St. Petersburg, December, 4th.

A few day days ago I called upon Rear Admiral N......of the Naval Headquarter staff. After considerable reminiscences of past days in St. Petersburg, our conversation naturally turned to the Russo-Japanese war. The question of the war led to the stubborn defence of Port Arthur and the Russian Asiatic Squadron. Admiral Alexeieff received a considerable amount of severe handling from my friend for his waut of foresight in not having the Asiatic fleet mobilized at the time of tension prior to the outbreak of the war. He said it seemed as if Alexeieff had been bought to keep the squadron in the one place where it would be destroyed with impunity. Nothing could have suited the Japanese better than the retention of the fleet at Port Arthur and the continuous gaieties which kept the Russian officers away from their duty at a critical moment.

I remarked that critical moments were not over and gradually the conversation drifted to the Baltic Fleet. Admiral N.'s eye sparkled as he said, "That is a fleet that will not be caught in a trap like Port Arthur. The Baltic Fleet represents the best fleet belonging to Russia both with regard to construction, speed and armament. The crews are picked men and officered by men of unquestionable energy. Vice Admiral Rozhdiestvensky is noted for his bravery throughout the whole of Russia.

"His appointment to the command of the Baltic fleet is a most fitting one. There is not an admiral in the Russian navy who knows more about the Baltic fleet than does this naval strategist. Admiral Rozhdiestvensky stands with regard to the navy in a similar position to that of General Kuropatkin to the army.'

My friend of the Naval Headquarter Staff has had an intimate association with both Admiral Rozhdiestveusky and the Baltic fleet, and he is therefore qualified to speak of both.

His association with the fleet in question has simply been with its fitting out for taking a part in the present war. All preparations of construction, armament, and refitting has been done under his direct supervision and his opinion is therefore worth the having.

Vice-Admiral N. feels convinced that the Baltic fleet as it will arrive in the Far East will be sufficiently powerful to drive the Japanese from the China Seas. He said:—

"You will know the greatest strength of the Russian fleet when it has struck a vital and unexpected blow at the Japanese naval power in Eastern waters. One of my sons goes under the direct charge of Admiral Rozhdiestvensky and he will not return without honour.

"Many critics form their opinions of the fighting strength of the Baltic fleet from what they read in badly informed newspapers. It is not usual for Governments to expound the deficiencies of their naval and military defences to newspapers and thence to the world, and consequently opinions divulged in those quarters were usually unofficial, devoid of all semblance of fact. I can assure you," said Admiral N. "the Baltic Squadron which will reach the east will be a most powerful one. There is undoubtedly room for criticism, but the newspapers of the world have not got at the points for real criticism. Some say that the fleet is such a crocked affair that it will never round the Cape of Good Hope. Well, we shall see. Others, that if it does get there at the end of weary months it will be unfit for fighting, having been damaged on the way. Well, we shall see. I think there is a surprise in store for those critics.

(To be continued)

One of the ways in which wars cost neutrals money was illustrated the other day in the French Foreign Minister's demand for a supplementary vote to pay for telegrams to and from the East. The bill was presented, and the items were as follow: Tokio telegrams £2,752. Peking telegrams £1,920, Shanghai telegrams £555, Chefoo telegrams £212. Seoul telegrams £1,225; Total £6,664. There disbursements cover a period of about six months, and work out at the rate of approximately £40 a day.

The Korea Daily News.

VOL. II, THURSDAY, MARCH 2, 1905. No. 47

HONGKONG & SHANGHAI BANKING CORPORATION.

Paid-up Capital $10,000,000
Reserve Fund:—Sterling Reserve... 10,000,000
Silver Reserve..... 7,000,000

27,000,000
Reserve Liability of Proprietors... 10,000,000

HEAD OFFICE, HONGKONG.

London Bankers, London and County Banking Company Limited.

Branches and Agencies,
London.

Amoy,	Hankow	Penang,
Bangkok,	Hiogo,	Rangoon,
Batavia,	Iloilo,	Saigon,
Bombay,	Lyons,	San Francisco,
Calcutta,	Manila,	Singapore,
Colombo,	Nagasaki,	Sourabaya,
Foochow,	New York,	Tientsin,
Hamburg,	Peking,	Yokohama,

Credits granted on approved Securities, and every description of Banking and Exchange business transacted.

Drafts granted on London and the chief Commercial places in Europe, India, Australia, America, China and Japan.

HOLME RINGER & CO., AGENTS,
CHEMULPO.

HOKURKU DOBOKU KAISHA.

Branch office in Chong Dong, Seoul.
Japanese telephone No. 165

CONTRACT DEPARTMENT.

We can contract to build any building or construction.

MERCHANDISE DEPARTMENT.

We can provide any building material. We have just contracted to build the new Belgian Legation.

E. MEYER & CO.
Chemulpo.

SOLE AGENTS IN KOREA FOR.

A. T. Morse, Sons & Co.'s "Fresco" Distemper

In all colours ready for use on walls, Ceilings etc.

and

AVENARIUS CARBOLINEUM

A wood-preserving and antiseptic oil preparation

Against decay, dry-rot, fungus and wood-destroying insects.

A large supply always in stock.
Prices upon application.

E. MEYER & CO.,
Chemulpo.

CHARTERED BANK OF INDIA AUSTRALIA & CHINA.

INCORPORATED BY ROYAL CHARTER 1853

HEAD OFFICES.—LONDON.

Paid-up Capital £800,000
Reserve Liability of Shareholders 800,000
Reserve Fund 800,000

Drafts granted upon all the principal places in the world and every description of Exchange and banking business transacted.

E. MEYER & Co., Agents,
Chemulpo.

MITSU BISHI DOCKYARD & ENGINE WORKS.

NAGASAKI.

CODE WORD, "DOCK."

A 1, A. B. C., and Engineering Codes used.

DOCK No. 1 (at Tategami).

Extreme Length.............. 523 feet
Length on blocks .... 513 ,,
Width of Entrance on Top...... 89 ,,
,, ,, Bottom.... 77 ,,
Water on Blocks at Spring Tide 26½ ,,

DOCK No. 2 (Mukaijima).

Extreme Length............. 371 feet
Length on Blocks............. 360 ,,
Width of Entrance on Top...... 66 ,,
,, ,, Bottom 53 ,,
Water on Blocks at Spring Tide 22 ,,

PATENT SLIP (at Kosuge).

Can take vessels up to 1,000 tons gross.

THE WORKS are well equipped with the LATEST IMPROVEMENTS, and can execute any kind of work in SHIPBUILDING and MARINE ENGINEERING, as well as in REPAIRING of SHIPS.

The COMPANY'S new powerful steamer OURA-MARU (712 tons, 700 I.H.P.), specially built for SALVAGE PURPOSES, and equipped with necessary gear, is always READY at SHORT NOTICE.

THE METHODIST PUBLISHING HOUSE,

Little West Gate, Seoul.

JOB PRINTING, TYPEWRITER PAPER
CARBON PAPER, VISITING CARDS
STATIONERY, BOOK BINDING
BOOK PUBLISHERS
AMERICAN SCHOOL BOOKS
SPENCERIAN COPY BOOKS
PEN CARBON LETTER AND BILL BOOKS

S. A. BECK, Manager.

DAI-ICHI GINKO.

LIMITED.

(Formerly the First National Bank)

ESTABLISHED 1873

INCORPORATED UNDER PRESENT LAW 1896

Capital - - - - - - - Yen 5,000,000
Reserve Fund - - - - 1,500,000

HEAD OFFICE:—TOKIO.

President: Baron SHIBUSAWA.

BRANCHES AND CORRESPONDENTS In the Principal Cities and Towns of Japan.

Interest Allowed on
Fixed deposits 1 year - - - 6½ per cent
" " 6 months - - - 6 per cent

Special current accounts 1½ sen daily per Y 100
General " " 1 " " " 100

M. TANAKA,
Manager, Chemulpo.

SINGER SEWING MACHINES

생거조봉침

SOLE AGENTS FOR KOREA

전매쇼

HOLME RINGER & CO.
Chemulpo.

제물포 함룽거양힝

KAMEYA & CO.

GENERAL STOREKEEPERS

Chinkokai - - Seoul

(Established 1895, Tokyo)

Confectionery, Hams, Canned Goods, Cutlery, Hirano & Tansan Water. Provisions, Gents, Furnishing goods, Toilet Articles, Travelling Bags, Tobacco, Cigars & Cigarettes Kitchen Utensils. Coffee, Biscuits

Fresh Goods always kept in Stock.
Prices Moderate
☞ *Please come and inspect our goods.*

NIPPON YUSEN KAISHA.

JAPANESE MAIL STEAMSHIP CO.

UNDER MAIL CONTRACT WITH THE IMPERIAL JAPANESE GOVERNMENT.

European Line

Regular Fortnightly Service between Yokohama, Kobe, Moji, Shanghai, Hongkong, Singapore, Penang, Colombo, Port Said, Marseilles, London and Antwerp.

American Line

Regular Fortnightly Service between Hongkong and Seattle, calling at Shanghai, Moji, Kobe, Yokohama an Victoria, B. C.

Regular weekly Service betwen Japan Ports and Australia, calling at Hongkong and Manila.

(Above Three Lines Suspended until further notice

Shanghai Line

Weekly Service between Shanghai and Japan Ports.

Korea Line

Service Kobe, Moji, Nagasaki, Fusan Chemulpo Chefoo, Taku.
S. S. Babelsberg, 2181 tons.
Service Kobe, Moji, Fusan, Chemulpo, Chinnampo
S. S. ARGO, S. S. Ohio.

BORDEN'S CONDENSED MILK CO.

New York, U. S. A.

ALWAYS IN STOCK

Eagle Brand Condensed Milk.

Gold Seal Condensed Milk.

Peerless (Family) Evaporated Cream.

Borden's Malted Milk.

E. MEYER & CO.
Chemulpo Korea,
Sole Agents

ROYAL INSURANCE COMPANY,

Funds exceed £10,000,000

FIRE

AT CURRENT RATES

LIFE

REDUCED PREMIUM,

HOLME RINGER & Co.
Agents, Chemulpo.

廣
KWANG C'HANG
昌

BENNETT & CO.

Merchants
Chemulpo.

Offices opposite the Imperial Japanese Post and Telegraph Office Chemulpo.
Telephone Number 201.

大韓每日申報
대한매일신보

(뎨이쳔ᄉᆞ십팔호) (토요일) 일쳔구ᄇᆡᆨ오년삼월ᄉᆞ일

본샤고ᄇᆡᆨ

이신보ᄂᆞᆫ영어와한어로셔거리
일츌판ᄒᆞᆷ

신문가

한쟝 엽두돈오푼
일샤됴 엽두량닷돈
우표가ᄃᆡ샤닷돈
다맛돈으로밧ᄉᆞᆷ

광고료ᄂᆞᆫ

귀한의쟝단과ᄌᆞ항의ᄃᆡ쇼로종
광ᄒᆞ되ᄒᆞᆫ가로밧을터이오매오
티저아녀ᄆᆡ한사람마다다이신
문을보실터이니광고버시기를
원ᄒᆞ시ᄂᆞᆫ이들은우리신문사에
와셔면약ᄒᆞ심을희망ᄒᆞᆷ

○발ᄒᆡᆼ소 박동대한ᄆᆡ일신보
사빙어학교앞ᄒᆡ젼영국인셜빌
립징자리오

사쟝 영국인 (빅셜)

평양 ᄃᆡ리졈

○평양쵸동사ᄂᆞᆫ권ᄆᆡ보셔로우
리신문ᄃᆡ리졈인을티졍ᄒᆞ엿
시ᄉᆞ오니평양에계신구람코져ᄒᆞ
시ᄂᆞᆫ 쳠군ᄌᆞᄂᆞᆫ편히ᄃᆡ리졈에왕ᄒᆞ
림ᄒᆞ와면의ᄒᆞ시옵

사고

○우리대한ᄆᆡ일신보의목뎍은
ᄆᆡ한의인민졍셔에관한모든ᄃᆡ
목에ᄃᆡᄒᆞ야ᄂᆞᆫ공평한변론을쥬
쟝ᄒᆞᆷ이라우리ᄂᆞᆫ신원의탐보ᄂᆞᆫ
신문보시ᄂᆞᆫ쳠군ᄌᆞ의게ᄒᆞᆼ샹보
도ᄒᆞ리며편지들긔셔ᄒᆞ여주시
ᄂᆞᆫ이ᄂᆞᆫ셩명과반ᄃᆡ를졍어부치
셔기를희망ᄒᆞ오니비거슨신문
샹에긔졔ᄒᆞ라ᄂᆞᆫ거시아니오다
반극히신용ᄒᆞᄂᆞᆫ증거를숨고자
ᄒᆞᆷ이라긔자ᄂᆞᆫ아모긔셔던지긔
재ᄒᆞᆷ을되각ᄒᆞᄂᆞᆫ권리들가졋ᄉᆞ
나되각ᄒᆞᄂᆞᆫ리유를말ᄒᆞᆯ터이오
매공즁광화를관계ᄒᆞᄂᆞᆫ듯ᄒᆞᆫ
다긔셔ᄂᆞᆫ의례히반지안켓ᄉᆞᆸ나이

●본사셜시이래로신문을ᄃᆡ양
우레로분젼ᄒᆞ와레젼부의앙의
로젼ᄒᆞᆫ듯ᄉᆞ로면곳에ᄂᆞᆫ혹ᄂᆞᆺ게
젼ᄒᆞ기도ᄒᆞ며혹번쳔ᄒᆞ기쉽ᄒᆞᆫ경
에젼ᄒᆞ기도ᄒᆞ며혹아니젼ᄒᆞᄂᆞᆫ
곳도잇다ᄒᆞ와우리신문을ᄉᆞ랑
ᄒᆞ야구람ᄒᆞ시ᄂᆞᆫ 쳠군ᄌᆞ의게
ᄃᆡᄒᆞ야면우미안ᄒᆞ옵기로지금
은분젼ᄉᆞᆫ을두고미일죠이젼
ᄒᆞ며ᄒᆞ니젼ᄒᆞ기나늣게거나ᄒᆞ
폐가엽도록ᄒᆞ리ᄒᆞ오니혹아니
젼ᄒᆞ거ᄂᆞᆫ혹늣게젼ᄒᆞ거나ᄒᆞ면일
이잇스면본사로통긔ᄒᆞ여주심
을희망ᄒᆞᆷ

잡보

○대관졍임 헌병ᄃᆡ사령관량
셩환씨ᄂᆞᆫ군부참모국쟝으로창
쟝빅셩귀씨ᄂᆞᆫ군부교휵국쟝으
로창쟝영쥰원씨ᄂᆞᆫ헌병ᄃᆡ사령
관으로피명ᄒᆞ엿더라

○구제관랍 남도로온사름의
면셜을듯ᄒᆞᆫ즉충쳥남도ᄒᆡ미군
수가ᄒᆡ군에잇ᄂᆞᆫ바봉수산을부
민의게쳑ᄆᆡᄒᆞ야양쟝홈을ᄒᆡᄒᆞᆫ
지란
일진회원이두차쳥난ᄒᆞ미그쳑
망을분감ᄒᆞ야교자두상들셔셜
ᄒᆞ야희회원을후티ᄒᆞ엿더니재
간에경신이되엿ᄂᆞᆫ티희산하동
쳑민들이단희ᄒᆞ야일진회원을ᄃᆡ
쳑ᄒᆞ미일진회원과희군수가셜
계로곤란중에잇다더라

○죠쳥란관 너부에서탁지부
로죠회ᄒᆞ엿스되경긔순찰사리
헌구와충쳥순찰사리시지의리
비들각군경세중으로나용ᄒᆞ엿
스니희익을곳티관ᄒᆞ라ᄒᆞ엿더
라

○일간반포 형법교정서ᄂᆞᆫ금
명간반포된다더라

○세력여구 일본사령부에서
쳑수ᄒᆞ엿다방숑ᄒᆞᆫ전영수씨가
근간에쇼번일시로셰력이쟝ᄃᆡ
ᄒᆞ다더라

○쥬사가례교 너부쥬사중에
셔ᄂᆞᆫ엽사만랑을납티ᄒᆞ고실에
직주사들도등ᄒᆞ엿더라

평양통신

○박씨곤란 평양사ᄂᆞᆫ박항면
에셜씨ᄂᆞᆫ희티관찰부주사로
박너ᄂᆞᆫ분에고시광찰사빈영철
씨가쳥쟝을엇지ᄒᆞ엿든지ᄆᆡ무
두광귀면쟝ᄒᆞ고의쳡을삼사인
ᄒᆞ교일ᄇᆡᆫ으로ᄂᆞᆫ가을닷진츅ᄒᆞ
덕니금번일진회에서박씨의젼
후사들사실ᄒᆞ야엇지조쳐ᄒᆞᆫ
ᄂᆞᆫ지박씨가일잔샹경ᄒᆞᆫ다ᄂᆞᆫ티
ᄒᆞ티인민들이말ᄒᆞ티박씨의이
번길은미우불길ᄒᆞ다ᄒᆞ더라

○죠쳥ᄒᆞᆫ령 외부에셔탁지부
로죠회ᄒᆞ엿스되경흥평양의주
삼쳐감리의봉급을다른항구감
리의례들의ᄒᆞ야지화로밧듭ᄒᆞ엿
의로임의귀부에셔평양ᄒᆞ엿
손주일월노분터희삼쳐디방관
희에ᄒᆞᆫ빙샹도를곳쳔숑ᄒᆞ라ᄒᆞ
엿더라

○미사폐졍 작일하오사시에
미국공사가폐졍ᄒᆞ엿다더라

○상블방환 마산포민리종션
등이외부에등소ᄒᆞ엿ᄂᆞᆫ티본항
아거ᄒᆞᄂᆞᆫ손덕우가일인을부동ᄒᆞ
힝ᄒᆞ야도용디라칭ᄒᆞ고일평을분횡
등이희ᄎᆞ유로갑리셔에명ᄒᆞ엿더
니희손한이일본졍도감부에무
오ᄒᆡ려아본인등이안ᄂᆞᆫ고로쳐수ᄒᆞ고
쇼ᄒᆞ오니가사죠ᄒᆞ신후죠ᄎᆡ외에
빈우ᄃᆡ가과연쳘도용티에관계
ᄒᆞ엿숀쥭희ᄒᆞ고가롤죵시셰ᄒᆞ아
츄급ᄒᆞ시고손덕우롤쳐치ᄒᆞ와
ᄀᆞ퀴숨을죵쳐ᄒᆞ야주옵소서ᄒᆞ
엿더라

뎐보

블퇴합ᄃᆡ의동쟝

론돈반 이월이십일

○로국졍부에셔다ᄇᆡᆨ셜쓰무죵
돌다시니르키라고쥬션ᄒᆞ며혹
ᄒᆞᆷ티ᄂᆞᆫ블퇴합ᄃᆡ에합ᄒᆞ라ᄒᆞ고
긔다넨쓰ᄒᆞ졍을통과ᄒᆞᆷ에빈돌
쥼수ᄒᆞᆫ다더라

동ᄃᆡ반 동월이십삼일

○법국츈쳔ᄒᆞ나미지부퇴라ᄒᆞᆫᄃᆡ
표셔러쓰에셔로국을위ᄒᆞ야셔
ᄃᆡ물파쥭밧약을면ᄒᆞ롬ᄒᆞ엿다
라

동ᄃᆡ반 동월이십일일

○작일에ᄃᆡ샹블퇴합ᄃᆡ가덕말
희쳥을저벗ᄂᆞᆫᄃᆡ고합ᄃᆡᄂᆞᆫ젼투
합일쳑과쳘갑희인쳔이쳑과숀
양합비쳑과수리션일쳑과운송
션오쳑으로조직ᄒᆞ엿고그운송
션들은젼쟁의시작된후에엇던
나라로브터산거시라더라

동ᄃᆡ반 동일

○블퇴합ᄃᆡ와그합ᄃᆡ의운송션
들과도합비쳘신쳑이금월십륙
일에놋시배에잇다ᄒᆞ더라

평화의쇼식

빅림반 이월이십일일

○로국귀족들은평화를회복ᄒᆞ
기를졀망ᄒᆞ나황뎨셔셔ᄂᆞᆫ젼쟁
을연속ᄒᆞ란ᄒᆞ고교쥭ᄒᆞᄂᆞᆫᄃᆡ
용셔지의피샹ᄒᆞᆫ일은죠곰도영
향이업다더라

론돈반 동월이십이일

○셩피득보에잇ᄂᆞᆫ루터통신원
의보고를거ᄒᆞᆫ즉평화에관ᄒᆞᆫ사
건은로국관인샤회에셔ᄂᆞᆫ엄단
코거졀ᄒᆞ나가신ᄒᆞᆯ만ᄒᆞᆫ소문을
드르즉로국에셔평화ᄒᆞ라고에
비ᄒᆞᄂᆞᆫ사건에ᄃᆡᄒᆞ야로국황데
셰서샹의ᄒᆞᆫ분외에실샹은쟝경
되엿ᄂᆞᆫᄃᆡ고죠건은ᄃᆡ아ᄒᆞ와등
지ᄒᆞᆫ것과갓ᄒᆞ니

일 한국에셔일본의쥬권을인
허ᄒᆞᆯ사

이 일본의게료동반도를양여
ᄒᆞᆯ사

삼 하샹의항구를기방ᄒᆞᆯ사

사 동쳥쳘로를중립케ᄒᆞ야ᄋᆞ로
죠직ᄒᆞᆯ사

오 항비닌남방에만쥬쟝로ᄂᆞᆫ
쳥국에환귀ᄒᆞᆯ사

다만결졍못된것은비샹금일ᄉᆞ
인ᄃᆡ일본에셔ᄂᆞᆫ비샹금문졔로
상지ᄒᆞ리라ᄒᆞ더라
로국에셔평화를결졍ᄒᆞ기젼에
최후결젼을ᄒᆞᆯ듯ᄒᆞ나군사샹관
란과나ᄃᆡ부요쳐동쳡에만일비샹
금문졔가죠쳐되면평화가미구
에될듯ᄒᆞ다더라

론돈반 이월이십삼일

○로국에셔실샹은평화죠건을
졔츌ᄒᆞ지아니ᄒᆞ엿고쟈일면보
ᄂᆞᆫ로국에평화파들의외쳔이라
더라

론셜

젼쟁과소문의실샹

○우리가졔에도세샹에경표ᄒᆞ
되동경으로브터오ᄂᆞᆫ젼쟁에관
ᄒᆞᆫ소문은밋지말나ᄒᆞ엿더니지
금샹히에잇ᄂᆞᆫ제포그랍쓰라ᄂᆞᆫ
신문에도의샹ᄒᆞ야말ᄒᆞ엿도다
우리ᄂᆞᆫ뎌샹원수가쟈긔의졍부
에보고ᄒᆞᄂᆞᆫ것이진셜치아니ᄒᆞ
다ᄒᆞᄂᆞᆫ것이아니오세샹에공포
ᄒᆞᄂᆞᆫ것이고본보와다르다ᄂᆞᆫ것
이아니라진쟁ᄒᆞᆫ소문을밋지은
익홈을말ᄒᆞᄂᆞᆫ것인ᄃᆡ군사샹비
밀사건은자셰히비밀ᄒᆞ리니와
ᄒᆞᆫ달동안을두고일본군이놀퇴
각ᄒᆞ거늘그일에ᄃᆡᄒᆞ야ᄂᆞᆫ세샹
에소문을숨기ᄂᆞᆫ도다
일샤젼에ᄂᆞᆫ우리가ᄒᆞᆫ하쟉안에
로병이업ᄂᆞᆫ것을알엇ᄂᆞᆫᄃᆡ그후
희구퇴전쟁은구로팟긴ᄃᆡ쟝이
ᄒᆞᆫ하좌안에착수ᄒᆞ란ᄒᆞᆫ젼쟁이
라고젼쟁의결과ᄂᆞᆫ일본인들과
일본인을위ᄒᆞᄂᆞᆫ신문지들은일
본이승젼ᄒᆞ엿다고환영ᄒᆞ더니
차차그사실이발거오ᄂᆞᆫ지라그

UNION INSURANCE SOCIETY OF CANTON.

Head office Hongkong.
Marine risks underwritten at current rates.

Agents in Chemulpo,
E. MEYER & Co.

COMPAGNIE DES MESSAGERIES MARITIMES.

Fortnightly Direct Service.

For Marseilles
via Ports.
Sailing from Yokohama
Calling at Kobe,
Shanghai, Hongkong, Saigon, Singapore
Colombo, Djibonti, Suez, Port Said
and Marseilles.

For particulars apply to
HOLME RINGER & Co.,
Chemulpo.

HAYASHIDA & CO.,

16 MYENG DONG, CHIN KO KAI, SEOUL.
BRANCH OFFICE AT CHEMULPO.

Money changers, Coal and Wood Merchants, Express Agents.

We are agents for the Pyeng-yang Coal Company and the Karazu Coal Company of Japan. We have the best quality of both anthracite and bituminous coal, and prompt execution of orders is our speciality. Firewood of all kinds kept in stock. Full weight guaranteed. Money of all denominations exchanged at current rates. Parcels received for all parts.

CHINA MUTUAL LIFE INS. CO.

Most favourable terms to policy holders.

Benefit system unsurpassed.

HOLME RINGER & Co.
Agents, Chemulpo.

C. P. R.

CANADIAN PACIFIC RAILWAY COMPANY'S ROYAL MAIL STEAMSHIP LINE.

THE FAST ROUTE BETWEEN CHINA, JAPAN, AND EUROPE VIA CANADA AND THE UNITED STATES.

Route from Hongkong via Shanghai, Nagasaki (Inland Sea of Japan) Kobe, Yokohama, Victoria and Vancouver.

Twin Screw Empress Steamship—6,000 Tons—Speed 19 knots.

PROPOSED SAILING FROM YOKOHAMA.
R. M. S. Empress of India.
R. M. S. Empress of Japan.
R. M. S. Empress of China.
R. M. S. Athenian.
R. M. S. Tartar.

Special reduction (first class only) granted to members of the Military, Naval, Diplomatic and Civil services and to Missionaries.

Passengers have choice of ten routes across the Continent of America and have privilege of travelling by any Atlantic Steamship Line.

Round the World passage tickets in connection with the P. and O. S. N., North German Lloyd and Messageries Co.'s £125.

All rates payable at current rate of exchange.

For further information, Tickets, Guide Books, etc., apply to

HOLME, RINGER & Co., AGENTS,
Chemulpo.

Grand Hotel

(Formerly the Station Hotel)

Near the Railway Terminus, West Gate Seoul.

The Best Hotel in Korea.
Handsome new Building.
Fine Airy Rooms.
Excellent Cuisine.
Terms Moderate.
Special terms to Missionaries
and to permanent boarders.

Electric cars within 2 minutes' walk.

W. H. EMBERLEY.
Proprietor

EVERY FACILITY.

In connection with Life Assurance Business is afforded by

The Standard Life Assurance Co.,

One of the largest and wealthiest of the Provident Institutions of the United Kingdom Forms of Application and all information wil be promptly afforded on application.

10 CENTS A DAY.

Not a very large expenditure is it? But it is ufficient to secure for a man of 30 a policy with he STANDARD LIFE OFFICE fo

$1323.

For all particulars of rates, etc., apply to

Holme, Ringer & Co.,
Agents, Chemulpo.

THE NEW YORK LIFE INSURANCE COMPANY.

Have you ever been declined by any Company?

Are you engaged in a specially hazardous occupation?

Have you heard of the New York Life Insurance Company's New Classifications for this class of Risks?

If not, send your date of birth, occupation and particulars of rejection, if any to

E. MEYER & Co.,
Agents, Chemulpo.

MITSUI BUSSAN KAISHA.
(MITSUI & Co.)

MITSUI GINKO.
(MITSUI BANK.)

The Bank is owned by the members of the Mitsui Family, who, as partners, assume an unsimited responsibility for all liabilities of the Bank:—

Capital......................Yen 5,000,000
Reserve Fund.................. " 5,600,000

HEAD OFFICE, TOKYO.
LONDON OFFICE, 34 LIME ST., E. C.

BRANCHES AND AGENCIES:—
New York, San Francisco, Hamburg, Bombay, Singapore, Manila, Hongkong, Amoy, Chefoo, Tientsin.
Kobe, Hakodate, Yokohama, Kure, Yokosuka, Moji, Shimonoseki, Miike, Wakamatsu Nagasaki, Kuchinotsu, Karatsu, Sasebo, Misume, Taipeh, &c.

Telegraphic Address for all the Offices:
"MITSUI."

A. B. C. AND A. I CODES USED.

Contractors of Coal
To the Imperial Japanese Navy. Arsenal and Railway Bureau, Principal Railway Companies and Industrial Work, Home and Foreign Mail and Freight Steamers.

Sole Proprietors
Of the famous Miike, Tagawa and Yamano Coal Mines.

Sole Agents
For the sale of Fukumo, Hokoku, Ichimura, Kanoda, Mannoura, Onoura, Ostuji, Sonoda, Tsubaruro, Yoshinotani, Yoshio, Yurokibura and other coals.

YANGTSE INSURANCE ASSOCIATION, LTD.

The undersigned, having been appointed agents for the above company, are prepared to issue policies and pay losses on marine risks at regular rates.

E. MEYER & Co.,
Agents, Chemulpo.

AMERICAN KOREAN ELECTRIC CO.

Light and Power.

Main Office: Electric Building, Chong No.

RAILWAY DEPARTMENT.

OPERATING CARS BETWEEN EAST AND WEST GATE, EVERY TEN MINUTES:—

First Car leaves East Gate at 7:00 A. M. First Car leaves R. R. Station at 7:25 A.M
Last Car " East Gate at 8.40 P. M. Last " " R. R. Station at 9.05 P.M

OPERATING CARS BETWEEN EAST GATE AND IMPERIAL TOMB TERMINUS, EVERY TWENTY MINUTES:—

CONNECTING WITH EVERY ALTERNATE CAR ARRIVING AT EAST GATE FROM CHONG NO.

First Car leaves East Gate for Tomb at 7:10 A. M.
" " " Tomb for East Gate at 7:30 A. M.
Last " " East Gate for Tomb at 7:50 P. M.
" " " Tomb for East Gate at 8:10 P. M.

OPERATING CARS BETWEEN CHONG NO AND YUNG SAN RIVER EVERY TWELVE MINUTES:—

First Car leaves Chong No for South Gate at 7:12 A. M.
" " " Chong No for Yung San at 7:36 A. M.
" " " South Gate for Chong No at 7:20 A. M.
" " " Yung San for Chong No at 8:09 A. M.
Last " " South Gate for Chong No 9:00 P. M.
" " " Yung San for Chong No at 8.45. p. M.

PECIAL PRIVATE CARS FURNISHED TO SUIT CONVENIENCE OF PATRONS. PRICES ON APPLICATION AT HEAD OFFICE.

LIGHTING DEPARTMENT.

Where less than 250 candle power of light is used, the rate per month will be
Per 16 candle power incandescent lamp,—All night.—Yen 2.50.
32 candle power incandescent lamp,—All night:—Yen 4.00.
50 candle power incandescent lamp,—All night:—Yen 6.00.
150 " " " " " " " 10.00.
1200 " " enclosed arc " " " " 20.00.

Where more than 250 candle power of light is used, a Meter will be installed, if requested:—Rent of Meter, Yen 2.00 per month. Rate of charges by meter reading:—Two Sen per Ampere per hour. (Approximately this is equal to about One Sen per 16 C. P. lamp per hour) Minimum monthly charge where meter is installed, Yen 20.00 per month, which includes rental of meter.

Estimates for installing lights furnished on application
An assortment of chandeliers always on hand.

K. Murakami.
Photograph Studio
Chinkokai, Seoul.

Printing, Developing and Enlargement, of Photographs always Undertaken.

Korean Views and Pictures Illustrating Native Customs always on Sale,

---

THE OSAKA SHOSEN KAISHA.

Boats frequently on the berth for Chinnampo.

REGULAR SAILINGS BETWEEN JAPAN AND KOREAN PORTS.

FUSAN AND KOBE VIA SHIMONOSEKI

OSAKA VIA MOKPO, FUSAN, SHIMONOSEKI AND KOBE.

MOJI DIRECT.

OSAKA VIA KUNSAN, MASANPO, FUSAN, SHIMONOSEKI AND KOBE.

CHEMULPO KUNSAN LINE,
Every three days.

CHEMULPO CHINNAMPO LINE.
Every three days.

For Freight and passage and further particulars apply to

THE OSAKA SHOSEN KAISHA,
Chemulpo.

LONDON, PLAISANT & CO.

General Storekeepers and Merchants, Ships Contractors Tobacconists, Commission and Forwarding Agents, Coal Merchants

IMPORTERS AND EXPORTERS

Seoul Chemulpo.

W. D. WENTWORTH

LANDING
AND
SHIPPING AGENT.
AND
CUSTOMS BROKER.

12 OURA, NAGASAKI.

STEWARD & CO.

Chemulpo.

Shipchandlers and Storekeepers, Naval and Mercantile Contractors, Landing and Shipping Agents.

STEWARD'S HOTEL

Chemulpo.

Best accommodation in the port for travellers. Clean and well-aired rooms, good cuisine and prompt attendance, moderate tariff.

젼정후에론돈에잇는뎨닉텔비
고리포의동경통신원이져의신
문의뎐보ᄒᆞ되로병의사상은심
만명이오일병의사상은칠쳔명
이라ᄒᆞ엿스나아직서지일본군
의사상은우리는자세ᄒᆞᆫ소식은
모르나동경에서치병소에서
공포ᄒᆞᆫ수효는구쳔삼빅팔십이
인이라ᄒᆞ엿는ᄃᆡ그후에공보로
반포ᄒᆞᆫ수효는엿는것이그결과
가대단히손상ᄒᆞᆫ일이분명ᄒᆞ고
뎌닉텔비그리포의동경통신원
의뎐보는싱각ᄒᆞᆯ것도못되며구
로팟긴군의사상실수는다불과
일만명이니골로보면ᄒᆞ구리젼
졍의사상은광편이ᄀᆞᆺᄒᆞ며그젼
졍의결과로광군의지위를상고
ᄒᆞ면젼졍의소식을은이ᄒᆞ란다
가그보고로브터븕게상고ᄒᆞ야
변것을보면탁신ᄒᆞ깃지마는그
뒤도지변공보에희미ᄒᆞᆫ디명이
북잡ᄒᆞᆫ것이잇는ᄃᆡ그뒤로등지
ᄒᆞ야노크보면이와ᄀᆞᆺᄒᆞᆫ니

금월십구일에군사팡부착
작일십팔일에ᄃᆡ적의ᄃᆡ포가왕
부산과상란자와관둔과류청둔
과하남청난과부상둔으로브터
우리진에향ᄒᆞ야사격ᄒᆞ엿고
금일십구일에적병의일시단가
량이다산으로브터셔편으로향
군ᄒᆞ야황계패자에드러왓다ᄒᆞ
엿스니

무싱이보는사ᄅᆞᆷ들은ᄒᆞᆫ사단의
군사가다산으로브터셔편으로
행군ᄒᆞ야황계패자에드러왓다
ᄒᆞᆷ은무싱이뵈이깃지마는다산
비라는ᄯᅦ이일본군중앙에우편
에미심령리쯤되는팡디미라삼
반명의군사가젼진ᄒᆞ야서로이
디졈을졈령ᄒᆞᆷ이일본군이싸우
지아니ᄒᆞ란고퇴각ᄒᆞ엿거나퇴
ᄒᆞ야ᄶᅩᆺ겨갓거나ᄒᆞᆫ것이로다
일본좌익군에는우리가드론소
식이젹으나로국긔병이아직서
지퇴청ᄒᆞ야아모베라도로양을
엄습ᄒᆞ란ᄒᆞ고중앙방면으로는
로병이미우강ᄒᆞ야여러말ᄒᆞᆯ것
업시일본군이디위를늘이려버
린는거시의심업도다

디도를샹고ᄒᆞ면일본군이엇더
케퇴각ᄒᆞ고로국군이엇더케진
군ᄒᆞᆯ는지알거시오젼에엇던데
일ᄃᆡ젼이봉천에잇슬터인ᄃᆡ다
론신문들은엇지말ᄒᆞ던지우리
는일본이패ᄒᆞ리라고밧게말못
ᄒᆞ깃는지라.

구로팟긴도일본군만큼졍병을
가지고수효는ᄃᆡ만ᄒᆞ며각식지
에와용밍이일본인의게젼거시
업도다

젼쟁각ᄒᆞᆫ이래로이일본인의귀국ᄒᆞᆯ
진ᄃᆡ니반일일본군이피주ᄒᆞᆯ베
션교ᄒᆞᆫ으로믈니갈터인ᄃᆡ오는
론젼쟁에로군이피ᄒᆞ면봉텬으
로퇴거ᄒᆞᆯ터이오일군이피ᄒᆞ면
로양남방으로퇴각ᄒᆞ리라ᄒᆞ노
라

관보

례샹쳔칙ᄉᆞ통호 광무구
년삼월이일

셔임급사령

○승셔원임관ᄉᆞ등 청주우톄
사주사 리셕우 한셩뎐보사
주사 권중철 경흥우톄사주
사 한셕원 령변우톄사주사
김준영 평양뎐보사주사 김
용제

이샹일월삼십일일

○임평안북도관찰사셔칙임관
삼등 종이품 리근풍
○임뎡주군림시우톄주사 김
주면
○임창셩군림시우톄주사 강
국봉
○의원면본관 광주부윤 윤
찬 홍원군수 조두환
션쳔군수 녀인셥 평산군수
리용구 양덕군수 젼벽훈
부평군수 홍응조 초계군수
리셕호 위원군수 신우균
○임광주부윤셔주임관이등
남원군수 윤창근
○임오쳔군수셔주임관륙등
영쳔군수 리병묵
○임진안군수셔주임관사등
정삼품 하규일
○임영양군수셔주임관륙등
륙품 리범철
○임룡담군수셔주임관륙등
종이품 윤상덕
○임셔흥군수셔주임관륙등
정삼품 오경조
○임션쳔군수셔주임관륙등
평안북도관찰부주사 빅락삼
○임안변군수셔주임관사등
철산군수 송영티
○임진보군수셔주임관륙등
사쳔군수 윤슈빅
○임양셩군수셔주임관오등
자셩군수 구장회
○임고원군수셔주임관륙등
덕원항경무관 박긔호
○임협쳔군수셔주임관륙등
홍쳔군수 조중익
○임용쳔군수셔주임관륙등
비인군수 윤 종
○임갑산군수셔주임관륙등
셕셩군수 박희셩
○임양덕군수셔주임관이등
젼군수 리용구
○임긔장군수셔주임관륙등
정삼품 림승학
○임제주군수셔주임관륙등
련산군수 리중익
○임덕산군수셔주임관륙등
젼군수 채홍신
○임셕산군수셔주임관륙등
젼군수 박용찬
○임초계군수셔주임관륙등
지평군수 신태철
○임강령군수셔주임관륙등
시종원우시어 민강영

○임남원군수셔주임관륙등
○정삼품 윤관쳔
○임위원군수셔주임관륙등
○젼군수 조두환
○임사쳔군수셔주임관오등
○젼군수 소진규
○임낭산군수셔주임관륙등
○젼군수 권종은
○임지도군수셔주임관오등
○정삼품 홍세영
○임홍원군수셔주임관륙등
○젼군수 신우균
○임련산군수셔주임관륙등
젼군수 리중철
○임평산군수셔주임관삼등
젼군수 홍응조
○임자셩군수셔주임관륙등
○륙품 윤동한
○임부평군수셔주임관륙등
○젼군수 젼병훈
○임영쳔군수셔주임관오등
○닉부주사 김영운
○임지평군수셔주임관사등
○젼군수 리셕호
○임비인군수셔주임관륙등
○륙품 윤병구
○임셕셩군수셔주임관륙등
○정삼품 오근션
○임홍쳔군수셔주임관륙등
홍릉사승 명숙조

이샹이월이십칠일

○명궁닉부특진관셔칙임관삼
등 종정원경 리인철
○명궁닉부특진관셔칙임관사
등 장례원소경 홍종영
○명종정원경셔칙임관삼등
종이품 리병셩
○명장례원소경셔칙임관사등
종이품 김병옥
○의원면본관 홍문관시독
녀인셥 홍문관시독 김남계
환구단사제셔령 리호징 순
릉참봉 박봉진 후릉참봉
홍덕쥬 군긔창기슈 서승교
군긔창기슈 쳥셕순 군긔창
기슈 리희승
○임홍문관시독셔주임관륙등
구품 뉴덩 구품 강원형
○임환구단사제셔령셔주임관
칠등 권중만
○임제릉령셔주임관칠등 공
릉령 리윤수
○임공릉령셔주임관칠등 경
릉령 리긴승
○임경릉령셔주임관칠등 사
직셔령 셩진영
○임사직셔령셔주임관륙등
봉상사주사 명쳘영
○임봉상사주사셔판임관사등
륙품 리호집
○임순릉참봉셔판임관팔등
됴병의
○임후릉참봉셔판임관팔등
셔승필
승셔원임관ᄉᆞ등 외부번역관
보 김셕영
○임군긔창기수셔판임관륙등
리봉용 홍명션 권태휘

이샹이월이십팔일

○의원면본관 군긔창기수
박용근
○임군긔창기수셔판임관륙등
량제훈

이샹삼월일일

뎐보

로국닉란의졍형
론돈발 이월십팔일

○로국황뎨폐하셔국무대신들과
닉각의장위테씨를싸스코에셜
노로불너셔회의ᄒᆞ엿는ᄃᆡ닉각
을츅임니가으로ᄒᆞᆯ거ᄒᆞ야닉ᄒᆞ사
ᄒᆞ는렬을상의ᄒᆞ엿다더라

동ᄃᆡ발 동월이십일

○로국인민의불평싱이더ᄒᆞ야
쳘로의동ᄒᆡᆼ을간셔에셔방히ᄒᆞ
고졍부에셔약조ᄒᆞᆫ귀광인을조
롱ᄒᆞ며셩의특보에셔는혁명운
동이만쥬군에셔지만연ᄒᆞ야간
다는말이잇더라

동ᄃᆡ발 동월이십일일

황뎨폐하셔조칙을니리여셔국
민의회를소집ᄒᆞ엿는ᄃᆡ일주는
오는삼월수일쯤될듯ᄒᆞ다더라

동ᄃᆡ발 동일

○분란서에는혁명운동을폐노
코실ᄒᆡᆼᄒᆞᆫ다더라

잡보

○방알신찰 경상북도관찰수
리용익씨가일월일상오륙광에발
졍ᄒᆞ야긔차로부임ᄒᆞᆫ다더니ᄒᆞᆯ
도일진회원이작일니부로뎐보
ᄒᆞ엿스되셔관찰이도임ᄒᆞ면일
도인민이방알ᄒᆞ야사셰급박ᄒᆞ
리라ᄒᆞ엿더라

○수영수감 리쟝ᄒᆞᆫ판계룡장
쳣반포홍리관원이다수히감하
ᄒᆞ는지라작이일에닉부대신표ᄒᆞ
수감을리관ᄒᆞᆫ셩ᄒᆞ엿다더라

본사광고

○본사신문갑을미양초샹에 면
쳥구ᄒᆞᆫ바기로ᄒᆞᆫ거슨이독ᄒᆞ시는쳠
군ᄌᆞ들의게보내기로시니왕왕히신금
을아직도보내지아니ᄒᆞ신곳시만흔
ᄃᆡ거니와호망ᄒᆞ셔ᄉᆞᆫ는관계가애지못
ᄒᆞ오며신문갑을속히보내주시기
를ᄇᆞ라오며이후로신문을보신닉
는신문갑을수히보ᄂᆡ지안는곳
에는신문을정지ᄒᆞᆯ터이오니
속히보ᄂᆡ시기를ᄇᆞ라옵ᄂᆞ이다

외보

○쳥렬중지 덕국황뎨의이오
헤린친왕은쳥조황뎨우이루헤
ᄃᆡ를폐ᄒᆞ의ᄃᆡ표자로아국졔ᄉᆞ
ᄃᆡ용장의에참렬ᄒᆞᆯ터이ᄃᆡ니아스
되엿더니졍요구를인ᄒᆞ야중지가
되엿다더라

광고

TELEGRAMS.

(FROM JAPAN PAPERS.)

Note. The messages marked* are those which are described as special service" on "special telegrams or "received by the Government." The others are from properly authenticated sources.

THE NORTH SEA ENQUIRY COMMISSION.

Berlin Feb. 23.

In diplomatic circles the opinion exists that the North Sea Conference will deal very leniently with Russia as England, supported by France, is seeking a more cordial understanding with Russia.

London, Feb. 24.

The papers generally express surprise and disappointment at the finding of the North Sea Commission, which does not discuss the question of the presence or absence of torpedoboats among the Hull trawling fleet at the time the attack was made by the Baltic Fleet. The Commission declares that Admiral Rohjestvensky might legitimately have believed his squadron to be in danger, and was entitled in the circumstances to act as he did.

The finding takes note of Russia's undertaking to indemnify the victims.

The papers, in commenting on the finding of the Commission, describe it as a diplomatic victory for Russia.

THE PEACE RUMOURS.

Berlin, Feb. 23.

*The Russian Government have contradicted all the peace reports which have lately been in circulation.

RUSSIAN AFFAIRS.

London, Feb. 23.

The situation at Warsaw is still deplorable. A Russian Prince (the name given in the cable is unintelligible) was today stabbed to death there. It is stated that the crime was committed on account of his action in ordering the troops to fire upon the strikers. The strike is still continually spreading. More than half of the higher employees at the Libau Dockyard are taking part in the movement. Owing to the strike, railway traffic between Warsaw and Vienna has been stopped. Batoum, the centre of the petroleum industry, is in a state of entire anarchy. The shipping agencies of France and Austria have stopped sending their vessels there.

London, Feb. 24.

Owing the railway strikes Poland has been cut off from communication with Germany and Austria.

The terminus of the Vienna-Warsaw railway at Warsaw is occupied by troops.

Later.

Alarming reports as to the condition of affairs in the Caucasus, especially at Batoum and Baku, have reached St. Petersburg.

Communication with the capital has been severed, and no details have been received, but all the reports agree in saying that there has been much bloodshed.

ITALIAN TROOPS IN CHINA.

Shanghai, Feb. 24.

The Italian Government has decided to withdraw all the Italian troops now in China, with the exception of a few bluejackets and Cavalry forming a guard for the Legation at Peking. The Italian troops will leave for home in the course of next May, and the warships, with the exception of one or two cruisers, will also be recalled.

THE FRENCH NAVAL PROGRAMME.

London, Feb. 23

The French Minister of Marine has announced in the Chamber of Deputies a proposed new naval programme, including the construction of twenty-four large warships, the programme involving an annual expenditure of 4 millions sterling till 1917. The minister stated that two bases would be established in Indo-China and that a second dock at Saigon was also essential.

Paris, Feb. 23.

In the Chamber of Deputies, on the discussion about the Marine Budget Mons. Deloncle made a great speech in defence of Indo-Chine. He demanded the augmentation of the fleet in those parts; the urgent necessity of constructing a floating dock; and a second dock, which would permit of repairs to all men-of-war or merchant vessels of the largest size; and the increase of the provision for coal, munition of war, tools, machinery and materials for properly fitting out the Arsenal. He paid a high tribute to the authorities of the port.

Indo-Chine, he continued, contributed to its own expenses a sum of forty millions francs, and should be properly organised as the fixed centre of defence in the Far East; whilst Saint Jaques would become a regular port of refuge, the whole to be made an autonomous naval station under the sole orders of the Governor-general. In conclusion Mons. Deloncle demanded the appointment of a large Marine commission; outside of parliament, to consult and deal with all questions in connection with Indo-Chine; and he made a strong appeal to the Chamber to take rapid measures to fulfil the desired necessities. The speech was received throughout with great applause.

GERMAN POLITICS.

Berlin Feb. 23rd.

The German Commercial Treaties have been passed in the Reichstag by an unexpectedly large majority, 227 against 80 votes. All factions, from the extreme Liberals to the Agrarians, voted for the Treaties. The result serves to strengthen the position of Count von Bülow, the Chancellor.

THE ANNEXATION OF CRETE.

London, Feb. 20.

Great Britain, France, Italy, and Russir have presented to Germany and Austria a note practically replying to Prince George's memorandum of November last. It says that the protecting Powers cannot tolerate annexation without the consent of the inhabitants, but the wording generally appears to defer indefinitely the realisation of the hopes of Greece. The Powers are willing, however, to withdraw their troops from Crete.

THE SHAHO.

Although we have reports of desperate fighting attended with heavy casualties all along the front we have no details of any engagement since the 24th ultimo.

On that date the Japanese report a victory over the Russians at Chengchang which is situated on the upper reaches of the western branch of the Yalu about 20 miles south of Singking (or Yenden). The Russians are said to have retreated in great disorder and to have carried away 1,000 dead. It is almost superfluous to point out that these two reports contradict each other. An army retreating in disorder would hardly carry away 1,000 dead.

The fighting of the main armies is concentrated around the railway almost exactly midway between Liaoyang and Mukden and as Oyama is reported to have assumed the offensive the Japanese are probably attempting to regain "Putiloff" or "Lone tree" hill which seems to be the key to the position for an advance northwards. On the other hand there are indications that the Russians intend to strike a blow at the Japanese communications near Liaoyang so the *denouement* of this engagement, or series of engagements, promises to be a remarkable one and fraught with grave consequences.

ANOTHER RUSSIAN RAID.

Collating reports from Japan and China papers we get the following particulars of a descent of a body of about 300 cossacks to a point due west of Haicheng and on the road from there to Yinkow.

According to the Japanese papers the object of the raid was the destruction of the Japanese railway and telegraphs and from the same source we learn that they arrived on the 21st and were immediately driven off by Japanese troops.

From the "Chefoo Daily News" however, we learn that a number of Chinamen who fled from Yinkow when the fighting commenced and have reached Chefoo that they had left their places of business at that port, either closed up entirely or in possession of subordinates, on account of a heavy engagement between Russian and Japanese troops on February 20th at a point about ten miles from Yinkow. The fight was in progress when they left town on the afternoon of the 20th.

They indicated the position of the fight on the map, but the place they named, which they stated is a small village, does not appear on the maps. The Japanese had established a small base there, and the Russians attacked it in force. The Japanese removed most of their commissary and quartermaster stores to another point a considerable distance south, resisting in the meantime in a spirited fight. The Japanese retreat is assigned by the informants as their reason for leaving Yinkow. They were afraid hostilities might reach Newchwang, so they closed their places of business and left.

Considerable alterations and additions are being made to the battleship King Edward VII. to fit her for liquid fuel as an alternative to coal.

A Kanazawa telegram says that owing to dullness in the "habutaye" silk business and also to the imposition of the heavy tax, many of the factories have closed down.

We note that the Japanese hoarding, formerly on the corner of South Gate and West Gate streets, has been removed to the bridge on South Gate street.

According to a Tokio paper, the Russians are again active in north-east Korea, their scouts having descended as far south as Songjin while their main body is some 30 miles further north.

The funeral of Amos Shrigley Broadhurst, well known as the man with the longest beard, recently took place at Astbury Church, Congleton. At the time of his death his beard measure 14ft., and his moustache at full length was over two yards.

There is a rumour in the Peking Palaces that his Imperial Majesty Kuang Hsü is to be allowed once more to hold the reins of Government, next spring, while his aged Aunt seeks rest and leisure at Eho Park Palace, which has been embellished during the past fifteen months with many new buildings, a foreign-styled one amongst the number.

In view of the celerity which the Japanese telegraph over voluminous reports of the disturbance in Russia it is rather amusing to note that such important news as the Russian denial of the peace rumours and the finding of the North Sea commission was allowed to reach us by post. The telegraphic service to this country is evidently another of those "Special" ones.

The "Asahi's" Shanghai correspondent wires that Germany has purchased a lot of ground at Woosung, in the neighbourhood of the Great Northern Telegraph Office, where the submarine cable she is now laying between Kiaochow and Woosung will be landed. From the latter place, the cable will pass into the hands of the Great Northern and Great Eastern Telegraph Offices.

THE NEW FRENCH GUN.

The "France Militaire" publishes a glowing account of the new French 9.45 in. gun by one of the French members of Parliament who were present with the French Minister of War during the experiments at Havre on December 18. According to this account, the French regulation 10.63 in. mortar is a mere toy in its effects in comparison with the new gun, which weighs ten tons and throws a projectile of 359.35 lb., with a muzzle velocity of 1.610 ft. per second, making it impossible to follow its flight. The energy of the recoil being used for doing all the heavy work, including the loading, the crew of the gun is reduced to three—one to attend to the sighting, a second to duties which may not be revealed, and a third to the loading. The last is protected by a cuirass of padded material and a mask of the same, which closes hermetically his ears and mouth, as the return of the flame from that portion of the powder which ignites only on coming into contact with the air at the muzzle is so considerable as to be dangerous and the noise requires the ears to be protected. The three gunners who fired the 15 rounds at the experiments had worked the gun only three times before These 15 rounds, however, made 480 rounds altogether which had been fired from the gun without it showing signs of serious damage, although 500 rounds represent the average capability of guns of this calibre. The cost of a single gun, including ammunition (the number of rounds is not stated), is estimated at £20,000. The firing of the gun took place from the battery of the Heve, which is so elevated as to be considered out of danger of return fire from the sea. The rate of firing was three rounds a minute directed against a target, towed at a speed of five knots, 5,000 metres (3 miles and 188 yards) out at sea. The French Minister of War expressed himself as highly satisfied with the results of the experiments.

The Russians are said to be fortifying the left bank of the Tumen. They evidently anticipate a Japanese irruption from the direction of north-eastern Korea.

NOTICE.

Dr. Harold Slade, Resident Dentist of Kobe, will visit Seoul professionally about the end of February.

The Korea Daily News.

Issued at 5 P. M. daily except Sundays.

Rate of Subscription:—

Per Year,..............Yen 25.

Per Quarter,..........Yen 7.

Per Month,..........Yen 2.50.

Postage in Korea not charged extra.

Postage abroad charged extra.

Advertisements, 50 sen per day for 1 inch or less.
5 yen per month per inch.
50 yen per year per inch.

All communications to

E. T. BETHELL,
Editor and Publisher,
Pak-tong, Seoul.

THE NORTH SEA INCIDENT.

The finding of the International Commission which sat at Paris to adjudicate upon the North Sea incident is a thoroughly sensible one and nothing more or less than was expected by those who were able to take an unprejudiced view of the unfortunate affair.

In view of the positive assertion by the Russians that there were strange torpedo craft among the fishing boats and the equally emphatic denial of this by the fishermen, it is not surprising that the commission declined to commit itself on the subject, but the decision that Admiral Rohdjestvensky "might legitimately have believed himself to be in danger" indicates that the commission had before it evidence showing that the Russian commander had good reason for acting as he did.

The Commission was solely concerned with the question whether or not Rohdjestvensky was justified in opening fire when he did, and it has decided that he was, without committing itself to an opinion on such a delicate point as the presence or otherwise of Japanese warships in British waters.

The chagrin of the British press over the decision is only natural and their expressions of surprise and disappointment and their description of the finding as a diplomatic victory for Russia are natural sequences to the extremely bellicose utterances they indulged in when the incident took place.

Now that the decision has been given out, it is of interest to give particulars of the commission and the points before it for decision.

The officers who composed the Commission were: Admiral Fournier, (France), Admiral Beaumont (Great Britain), Admiral Davis (U. S. A.,) Admiral Spaun (Austria) and Admiral Kaznakoff, (Russia). Admiral Fournier presided.

The principal charges of the British statement were as follows:—

"On the night in question there were not any warships whatever in the neighbourhood of the fishing fleet, except those of the Russian navy.

"No warships had been seen by the fishing boats since a long time previous.

"None of the boats making up the fishing fleet carried any kind of material of war.

"No Japanese warship of any kind whatever was at that moment in the North Sea.

"There were not any Japanese upon the fishing boats.

"The Russian fire continued after their searchlights clearly showed the vessels were peaceful fishing boats.

"None of the Russian ships gave or even offered assistance.

"The fire killed two men, wounded six, sank one boat and damaged five others."

The statement concludes that the attack was without any provocation upon pacific fishing boats pursuing their usual and rightful vocation.

The following are the principal points of the Russian reply.

"At about midnight the flagship Knaiz Souvaroff saw the outlines of two small boats which approached, with all lights extinguished, directly toward the battleship.

"When the two suspicious boats came within range of the Russian searchlights they were recognized as torpedo-boats. Thereupon the battleship opened fire.

"Thereafter a number of small fishing boats, not showing required lights, were observed. Precautionary measures were adopted nevertheless. There was a strong feeling of danger upon the battleships, and the imperious duty of protecting themselves against the attack of torpedo-boats obliged a continuance of the fire, despite the evident risks of hitting not only the fishing boats but also the ships of the squadron itself, which had arrived within the zone of the fire.

"In the meantime the two torpedo boats drew off and shortly after disappeared. Fearing that some of the fishing boats were damaged, yet being certain that all danger from the two torpedo boats, or possibly others, was not completely removed, Admiral Rodjestvensky considered it indispensable for the entire squadron to continue its route without stopping.

"Admiral Rodjestvensky, while taking into account the damage caused to inoffensive fishermen, subjects of a neutral power, nevertheless was compelled to use all the means in his power to destroy the torpedo boats which attacked his squadron."

THE BALTIC FLEET.

SPECIAL CORRESPONDENCE.

(From the "Shanghai Times")

St. Petersburg, December, 4th
(Concluded from last issue.)

"Critics say the engines of some of our newest vessels are no better than those of our most obsolete coast defenders. My answer to that is the test for engines is sustained speed and in this repect our newest vessels will compare with anything in the world. It is certainly true that much of the work on these latest vessels had to be hastily completed, but it has been most efficiently done under the circumstances. The vessels are capable of a sustained speed of thirteen knots per hour and this makes allowance for the time necessary to slow down and coal at sea. Can you say if the naval critics of the world are capable of estimating the importance of this uniformity of speed. Critics state that if the Russian navy contains good officers and good sailors, it is very deficient in naval engineers. This may or may not be so, it is not my department, but I believe in this branch there is also a surprise in store for our critics. There is absolutely no truth in the statement that the admiralty have engaged the services of the highest class British naval engineers. Russian relations with Great Britain are far too strained for anything like that, and were trouble to arise between the two countries our magnificent fleet would be at the mercy of any engineers so engaged. We have a few men of Swedish birth, but they are naturalized Russian subjects, otherwise there are no foreigners in our fleet.

"The fleet proceeding to the Far East, at present consists of three divisions or squadrons and later another will follow.

"The first squadron under the command of Vice-Admiral Rozhdiestvenky consists of the newly built battleships:—Alexander III, Boloduo, Orel, Kniaz Suaroff, and Oslabya, the newly built armoured cruiser the Aurora, besides the older cruisers, Admiral Nakhimoff and Dimitri Donskoi. They are accompanied by the naval colliers Kamchatka, Anadier, Maraga, and Korea, as well as fresh water supply ships, and the hospital ship Orel.

"All the battleships of this first division are of too deep draught to navigate the Suez Canal, hence the journey via the Cape.

"The second squadron under the command of Rear Admiral Foelkersahm consists of the second class battleships:—Sissoi Veliky, and Navarin, the newly built cruisers Jemchug, Spietarama, Almaz, with seven destroyers. It is accompanied by the naval transports and naval colliers—Gelchakoff, Voloneju, Kitai, Tamboff, Kief Juter, Melker, Vlaineit, Chinstsku, and Valoslav. This squadron is strengthened by two submarines.

"The third Squadron under the command of Rear Admiral Botourovosky, consists of the newly built cruisers Oleg, and Dsmltd, with five destroyers and is accompanied by the naval transports and naval colliers Teletsk, Vral, Lion and Dinepel.

"These latter two squadrons, which are of sufficiently shallow draught to take the short route through the Suez canal, have arranged to concentate at D' Josalez, the French naval base on the northeast coast of Madagascar. From here the fleet is to proceed direct to Singapore. As soon as the combined fleets pass Saigon the Vladivostock squadron will proceed to sea and will harass the Japanese coast and so draw off a portion of the Japanese squadron. Simultaneously General Kuropatkin will initiate his main advance while his cavalry by flanking movements will harass the Japanese lines of communication in Manchuria and Korea. The Japanese have, you will see, by recent moves but run into the trap laid for them by General Kuropatkin."

THE CEREMONIES WERE IMPRESSIVE!

The "Japan Gazette" informs us that a funeral of horses killed at the front for the sake of that country was recently held in Migyagi Prefecture, a well-known horse breeding district in Japan. In the presence of the Governor and other officials each victim was given a religious posthumous name and a post was erected on the burial place of all dead. Further offerings, consisting of beans and wheat, were placed thereon while a large number of Buddhist priests read prayers. The obsequies were practically the same as those of soldiers. The President of the Miyagi military horse-breeding yard delivered an address of condolence. The ceremonies were impressive and came off successfully.

The Korea Daily News.

VOL. II, FRIDAY, MARCH 3, 1905. No. 48

HONGKONG & SHANGHAI BANKING CORPORATION.

Paid-up Capital....................$10,000,000
Reserve Fund:—Sterling Reserve... 10,000,000
Silver Reserve..... 7,000,000

27,000,000
Reserve Liability of Proprietors... 10,000,000

HEAD OFFICE, HONGKONG.

London Bankers, London and County Banking Company Limited.

Branches and Agencies,
London.

Amoy,	Hankow	Penang,
Bangkok,	Hiogo,	Rangoon,
Batavia,	Iloilo,	Saigon,
Bombay,	Lyons,	San Francisco,
Calcutta,	Manila,	Singapore,
Colombo,	Nagasaki,	Sourabaya,
Foochow,	New York,	Tientsin,
Hamburg,	Peking,	Yokohama,

Credits granted on approved Securities, and every description of Banking and Exchange business transacted.

Drafts granted on London and the chief Commercial places in Europe, India, Australia, America, China and Japan.

HOLME RINGER & CO., AGENTS,
CHEMULPO.

HOKURKU DOBOKU KAISHA.

Branch office in Chong Dong, Seoul.

Japanese telephone No. 165

CONTRACT DEPARTMENT.

We can contract to build any building or construction.

MERCHANDISE DEPARTMENT.

We can provide any building material. We have just contracted to build the new Belgian Legation.

E. MEYER & Co.,
Agents,
Chemulpo.

CHARTERED BANK OF INDIA AUSTRALIA & CHINA.

INCORPORATED BY ROYAL CHARTER 1853

HEAD OFFICES.—LONDON.

Paid-up Capital £800,000
Reserve Liability of Shareholders 800,000
Reserve Fund 800,000

Drafts granted upon all the principal places in the world and every description of Exchange and banking business transacted.

E. MEYER & Co., Agents,
Chemulpo.

MITSU BISHI DOCKYARD & ENGINE WORKS,

NAGASAKI.

CODE WORD, "DOCK."

A 1, A. B. C., and Engineering Codes used.

DOCK No. 1 (at Tategami)

Extreme Length.............523 feet
Length on blocks .... 513 ,,
Width of Entrance on Top......89 ,,
,, ,, Bottom....77 ,,
Water on Blocks at Spring Tide 26½ ,,

DOCK No. 2 (Mukaijima).

Extreme Length.............371 feet
Length on Blocks...........360 ,,
Width of Entrance on Top......66 ,,
,, ,, Bottom 53 ,,
Water on Blocks at Spring Tide 22 ,,

PATENT SLIP (at Kosuge).

Can take vessels up to 1,000 tons gross.

THE WORKS are well equipped with the LATEST IMPROVEMENTS, and can execute any kind of work in SHIPBUILDING and MARINE ENGINEERING, as well as in REPAIRING of SHIPS.

The COMPANY'S new powerful steamer OURA-MARU (712 tons, 700 I.H.P.), specially built for SALVAGE PURPOSES, and equipped with necessary gear, is always READY at SHORT NOTICE.

THE METHODIST PUBLISHING HOUSE,

Little West Gate, Seoul.

JOB PRINTING, TYPEWRITER PAPER
CARBON PAPER, VISITING CARDS
STATIONERY, BOOK BINDING
BOOK PUBLISHERS
AMERICAN SCHOOL BOOKS
SPENCERIAN COPY BOOKS
PEN CARBON LETTER AND BILL BOOKS

S. A. BECK, Manager.

DAI-ICHI GINKO.

LIMITED.

(Formerly the First National Bank)

ESTABLISHED 1873

INCORPORATED UNDER PRESENT LAW 1896

Capital - - - - - - - - - Yen 5,000,000
Reserve Fund - - - - - 1,500,000

HEAD OFFICE:—TOKIO.

President: Baron SHIBUSAWA.

BRANCHES AND CORRESPONDENTS
In the Principal Cities and Towns of Japan.

Interest Allowed on
Fixed deposits 1 year - - - 6½ per cent
" " 6 months - - - 6 per cent

Special current accounts 1½ sen daily per Y 100
General " " 1 " " " 100

M. TANAKA,
Manager, Chemulpo.

SINGER SEWING MACHINES

씽거ᄌᆞ봉침

SOLE AGENTS FOR KOREA

전매쇼

HOLME RINGER & CO.
Chemulpo.

졔물포 함릉거양힝

KAMEYA & CO.

GENERAL STOREKEEPERS

Chinkokai - - Seoul

(*Established 1895, Tokyo*)

Confectionery, Hams, Canned Goods, Cutlery, Hirano & Tansan Water. Provisions, Gents, Furnishing goods, Toilet Articles, Travelling Bags, Tobacco, Cigars & Cigarettes Kitchen Utensils. Coffee, Biscuits

Fresh Goods always kept in Stock.

Prices Moderate

☞ *Please come and inspect our goods.*

NIPPON YUSEN KAISHA.

JAPANESE MAIL STEAMSHIP CO.

UNDER MAIL CONTRACT WITH THE IMPERIAL JAPANESE GOVERNMENT.

European Line

Regular Fortnightly Service between Yokohama, Kobe, Moji, Shanghai, Hongkong, Singapore, Penang, Colombo, Port Said, Marseilles, London and Antwerp

American Line

Regular Fortnightly Service between Hongkong and Seattle, calling at Shanghai, Moji, Kobe, Yokohama and Victoria, B. C.

Australian Line

Regular weekly Service betwen Japan Ports and Australia, calling at Hongkong and Manila.

(Above Three Lines Suspended until further notice.

Shanghai Line

Weekly Service between Shanghai and Japan Ports

Korea Line

Service Kobe, Moji, Nagasaki, Fusan Chemulpo Chefoo, Taku.

S. S. Babelsberg, 2181 tons.

Service Kobe. Moji, Fusan, Chemulpo, Chinnampo

S. S. ARGO, S. S. Ohio.

BORDEN'S CONDENSED MILK CO.

New York, U. S. A.

ALWAYS IN STOCK

Eagle Brand Condensed Milk.

Gold Seal Condensed Milk.

Peerless (Family) Evaporated Cream.

Borden's Malted Milk.

E. MEYER & CO.
Chemulpo Korea,
Sole Agents

ROYAL INSURANCE COMPANY,

Funds exceed £10,000,000

FIRE

AT CURRENT RATES

LIFE

REDUCED PREMIUM,
HOLME RINGER & Co.
Agents, Chemulpo

廣
KWANG ◎ C'HANG
昌

BENNETT & CO.
Merchants
Chemulpo.

Offices opposite the Imperial Japanese Post and Telegraph Office Chemulpo.

Telephone Number 201.

大韓每日申報

대한미일신보

(뎨이쳔ᄉ십구호) (월요일) 일쳔구빅오년삼월륙일

본샤고빅

이신보는영어와한어로셕거미
일츌판ᄒ옵

신문가

한장 엽두돈오분

일삭료 엽두량닷돈

우표가미삭닷돈

다닷돈으로밧숩

광고료는

귀한의장단과ᄌ힝의다소로좃
갑ᄒ되졍가로밧을터이오며조오
릭자아녀대한사람마다다이신
문을보실터이니광고내시기를
원ᄒ시는이들은우리신문사에
와셔면약ᄒ심을희망ᄒ옵

○발힝소 박동대한미일신보
사법어학교앏헤젼영국인셜필
립집자리오

사장 영국인 (베셜)

평양 디리졈

○평양효동사는권대보씨로우
리신문판미디리인을뎡ᄒ엿사
오니평양에계신구람ᄒ고져ᄒ
시는쳠군ᄌ는ᄒ디리졈에왕
림ᄒ와면의ᄒ시옵

사고

○우리대한미일신보의목뎍은
대한의안녕질서에관한모든대
문제에대ᄒ야논공평한변론을쥬
장홈이라우리통신원의탐보는
신문보시는쳠군ᄌ의게ᄒ샹보
도ᄒ리며편지들귀셔ᄒ여주시
는이는셩명과번디를젹어붓치
시기를희망ᄒ오니이거슨신문
샹에긔지ᄒ랴는거시아니오다
만그취신용ᄒ는증거를숨고자
홈이라긔자는아모긔셔던지긔
지ᄒ엿던ᄌ긔ᄒ는권리를가졋스
나퇴쟝ᄒ는리유를말ᄒ터이오
며공중평화를문란케ᄒ는듯ᄒᆫ
긔셔는의례히밧지안켓숩니
다

●본샤셜시이리로신문을미양
우톄로브터젼ᄒ와리찬부의잎의
로젼ᄒ든스스로번곳에는ᄒ늣게
젼ᄒ기도ᄒ며혹빠지기도ᄒ야
곳에젼ᄒ기도ᄒ며혹이니젼ᄒ는
ᄒ는도잇다ᄒ와우리신문을슈량
디ᄒ야우미잇ᄒ기로지의계급
은본견인을두고리ᄃᆞᆯ증이젼
ᄒ며이니젼ᄒ거나늣게거나ᄒᆫ
폐가엽ᄉ록ᄒ란ᄒ오니ᄒ아니
젼ᄒ거나혹늣게젼ᄒ거나ᄒᆫ일
이잇스면본샤로통긔ᄒ여주심
을희망ᄒ옵

잡보

○군부주본 삼작야에군부주
본이되엿는ᄃᆡ졍위민대식류뢰
한량세는참령을임ᄒ고참령리
긔ᄒᆼ신졔영량세는부령을임ᄒ
엿더라

○병위혁파 병위원과및호위
ᄃᆡ는작야에혁파가되엿다더라

○위문사쳥연 삼작일하오칠
시에대관뎡에셔쟝곡천대쟝이
연회를기ᄒ고강뎍시종무관장
의일ᄒᆼ을쳥요ᄒ엿고지작
일하오칠시에일본공사가쏘용
관에기연ᄒ고히일ᄒᆼ을쳥요ᄒ
엿다더라

○벽반준비 경부텰도회사에
셔연셩노량흔건과로각사무의
쥰비도되엿고리경도편리케되
야리사월브터는과차간이차셰
등랄거로운뎐케퇴다더라

○츄풍령적경 영동리신을거
흔즉거월이십칠일오후칠시에
황간츄풍령부근에화적오십여
명이각각총검을가지고쳘도공
스와부소쳥간도차랑의정을슬여
ᄒ엿스나기ᄃᆞ란방인이쳥ᄒ야방어ᄒ야
화적에는즉사자이인과중상자
일명을잡흔지라그젼두는지구
에히구렬ᄒ엿다ᄒ며또이삼일
에는츄풍령금천간에화적오
륙십명이습리ᄒ엿다더라

○결불쳥시 외부에서법관으
로조복ᄒ엿스되제조와및류리
사ᄒᆫ아인미이로와밋슈리친의
긔쳐ᄒ녕신금과밋샹사들의도
원등의쥰발ᄒ엿고또희국시
에전듸윈이안인즉을당회리ᄒ야
복무ᄒᆯ리인티자귀의안젼을위
ᄒ야다시오지아니ᄒ니차논자
년가스사로파약ᄒ이리ᄒ일기
걸단고죤비샹은본졍부에서논
과과죤치안는다ᄒ엿더라

○과어사직 경무신리쥬씨는
히사직ᄒ는것로지차상소ᄒ
더라더라

○관난실시 농샹공부에는별
시ᄒᆫ논쳠셔관인과헌광산국

장긔태진냥쎄의세력으로부령
이셔거지못ᄒ야과연셜시가어렵
다더라

○수헌포착 경무쳥에셔각셔
장로기수헌칙ᄒ기를근일ᄃᆡ
문포과ᄒ고셩향ᄒᆫ티니패소관리
로ᄒ란ᄒᆫ보ᄒ엿는ᄃᆡ이거든보니
뎨ᄒ더라

○감리보고 원산감리가외부
에보고ᄒ엿스되일본영ᄉ조회
를밧은즉의경과신일평수ᄂᆞᆫ거
로야파약은ᄀᆞ엽스니에본회돈건
ᄌ가문이의교ᄒ원ᄉᆞᆯ찰ᄒ얏더라
논ᄒ러이틀이ᄒ엿다ᄒ더라

○신소에명 찬정최익현씨가
경과관찰수를평임ᄒ훈후에별노
히동졍이무ᄒ더니장ᄎ샹소를
ᄒ겟다ᄒ기로ᄒ의문ᄒᆫ즉
ᄒ다는뒤그지ᄒ야신문ᄒ시
고하ᄒ엇ᄒ치안니ᄒ시며퇴
그층셧을ᄒ얏신닙ᄒ며퇴고폐

남시ᄒ과ᄒ얏니외라○
군니와란의ᄀᆞ이로ᄒ셩의권을
이ᄂᆞᆫ펄미동경에ᄂᆞᆫ리신을ᄃᆡ왕
신을리로씨관찰ᄒ야권은샹이
롱홈이유찰셔쳐ᄒᆫ지잇ᄂᆞᆫ결벌ᄒᆫ
이것쳐차로ᄒ역ᄒ야ᄒ되ᄒ오
칙이엽되향ᄒ며오ᄒ얏ᄒ고ᄒ
싱ᄒᆞ라ᄒ티출거폐시ᄒᆞᆫ오문

○일간쳥티 원로대신됴병세
씨가입셩ᄒ엿는ᄃᆡ금명간에
권ᄒ야쳥티ᄒᆫ다더라

○일간입셩 협경남도관찰사
리쳔씨가명일조입셩ᄒᆫ다더라

○봉급지출 탁지부에셔진쟝
일본리각군티월급을지발ᄒᆫ다
ᄒ더라더라

○횡피란리 삼작일혜뎡동근
디에셔광양티병뎡과영공관에
셔고용ᄒ논자가서로구타ᄒᆷ에
영용관에서영병이다수히뢰도
ᄒ야맛참그버지나가논시위티
병뎡이일명을무수히란타ᄒ엿다
더라

○위문사폐쳥 충쳥군위문사
일본무관쟝강텬씨일힝이지쟝
일샹오시에입셩ᄒ엿는ᄃᆡ
틱쟈일하오사시에일공사가강
씨의일힝을티동ᄒ엿다더라

○피수착죵 니부에서대구관
찰사의게뎐보ᄒ엿스되일진회
원등을피신임관찰사를밧알ᄒᆫ다
ᄒ니피수를착치ᄒ야엄징ᄒ고
여당은효유ᄒ야히산ᄒ라ᄒ엿
더라

○민졍잉임 함경북도인민황
의현등이니부에뎡소ᄒ엿는ᄃᆡ
본도관찰사리윤졔씨가리임ᄒᆫ
후로쳬막이소셩ᄒ고쟉년곳흔
흉년에찬도곡식을이리ᄒ야빅
셩을구ᄒ홀지라ᄒ과ᄒ히잉임시
키ᄒ신을북방이라ᄒ엿더라

론셜

젼쟁

○일본편과로국편으로다갓치
젼ᄒ는소식을드른즉지금만쥬
에셔대젼이잇는모양인ᄃᆡ일본
군의중앙진은료양북방에셔이
셩영리되는졀로근ᄃᆡ에잇다더
라

구로팟긴과대산원슈가이번싸
홈에는최임이졍즁ᄒ건것이미젼
쟁의결과로여러가지정치샹문
데가결정될것이니만일구로팟
긴대쟝이승젼ᄒ면로국의퇴란
한젼쟁쳐오ᄒ명방등을보진
압ᄒ털이며만일신괴ᄒ면복방
으로퇴거ᄒᆯ터이오로국의졍
형은사세로진무ᄒ야갈터이
며말ᄒ대산원슈가이번로돈이
에나뉴욕에셔일본공ᄎᆡ를엿게
모집ᄒ야글리가게될터이오만
달은며면로양은북방으로브러
실퓌ᄒ면방어ᄒ기어려운청도
영습흉휼방로물너갈뿐ᄒ도다
랑에히참으로뒤위가젼에샤하젼쟁과
논군의디무어엇이때산원슈가자귀의
진군사들이일쳐로모우고로군의젼
괴ᄒ논동신ᄃᆡ티ᄒ야피ᄒ는것은자
논것아니며로국중앙진으로향
ᄒ야진군ᄒ란코예비ᄒ는것이
라

일본군의진형은샹각형으로되
엿서두모소린는리무등근ᄃᆡ로
샹티ᄒ야ᄂᆞᆫ티랑진비에다로군이
엿지적균ᄉ리서로뎍ᄒᆫ즁ᄒ는소리
덕공가는ᄒ녕ᄒ고랑진중에셔와간에
게셔ᄒ편돈블에도ᄂᆞᆫ랑진중의간에
이셔ᄒ편들의에논랑진즁ᄒ셔에논
지적ᄒ란ᄒ나동평에논랑진이쳔에
이ᄒᆞᆫ다ᄒᆫ지로티ᄒ는라
되게이지적ᄒ셔계공가던샹연아일
논건만ᄒ알슈업논지ᄂᆞᆫ랑등편ᄒ
빗출ᄒ야랑균이라동편에논항이
샤ᄒ고로중앙평에논랑편이본이
대포를구로팟긴이포티를편디방은
만히진은가지고여긔에어더이군이
가지고ᄒ셔ᄒᆫ쟝샹ᄒ며산을
일ᄒ킈ᄒ고ᄒ산샹위ᄒ에포티

UNION INSURANCE SOCIETY OF CANTON.

Head office Hongkong.
Marine risks underwritten at current rates,
Agents in Chemulpo,
E. MEYER & Co.

COMPAGNIE DES MESSAGERIES MARITIMES.

Fortnightly Direct Service.

For Marseilles
via Ports.
Sailing from Yokohama
Calling at Kobe,
Shanghai, Hongkong, Saigon, Singapore, Colombo, Djibonti, Suez, Port Said and Marseilles.

For particulars apply to
HOLME RINGER & Co.,
Chemulpo.

HAYASHIDA & CO.

16 MYENG DONG, CHIN KO KAI, SEOUL.
BRANCH OFFICE AT CHEMULPO.

Money changers, Coal and Wood Merchants, Express Agents.

We are agents for the Pyeng-yang Coal Company and the Karazu Coal Company of Japan. We have the best quality of both anthracite and bituminous coal, and prompt execution of orders is our speciality. Firewood of all kinds kept in stock. Full weight guaranteed. Money of all denominations exchanged at current rates. Parcels received for all parts.

CHINA MUTUAL LIFE INS. CO.

Most favourable terms to policy holders.

Benefit system unsurpassed.

HOLME RINGER & Co.
Agents, Chemulpo.

C. P. R.

CANADIAN PACIFIC RAILWAY COMPANY'S ROYAL MAIL STEAMSHIP LINE.

THE FAST ROUTE BETWEEN CHINA, JAPAN, AND EUROPE VIA CANADA AND THE UNITED STATES.

Route from Hongkong via Shanghai, Nagasaki (Inland Sea of Japan) Kobe, Yokohama, Victoria and Vancouver.

Twin Screw Empress Steamship—6,000 Tons—Speed 19 knots.

PROPOSED SAILING FROM YOKOHAMA.
R. M. S. Empress of India.
R. M. S. Empress of Japan.
R. M. S. Empress of China.
R. M. S. Athenian.
R. M. S. Tartar.

Special reduction (first class only) granted to members of the Military, Naval, Diplomatic and Civil services and to Missionaries.

Passengers have choice of ten routes across the Continent of America and have privilege of travelling by any Atlantic Steamship Line.

Round the World passage tickets in connection with the P. and O. S. N., North German Lloyd and Messageries Co.'s £125.

All rates payable at current rate of exchange.

For further information, Tickets, Guide Books, etc., apply to

HOLME, RINGER & Co., AGENTS,
Chemulpo.

Grand Hotel

(Formerly the Station Hotel)

Near the Railway Terminus.
West Gate Seoul.

The Best Hotel in Korea.
Handsome new Building.
Fine Airy Rooms.
Excellent Cuisine.
Terms Moderate.
Special terms to Missionaries and to permanent boarders

Electric cars within 2 minutes' walk.

W. H. EMBERLEY,
Proprietor

EVERY FACILITY.

In connection with Life Assurance Business is afforded by

The Standard Life Assurance Co.,

One of the largest and wealthiest of the Provident Institutions of the United Kingdom Forms of Application and all information will be promptly afforded on application.

10 CENTS A DAY.

Not a very large expenditure is it? But it is sufficient to secure for a man of 30 a policy with the STANDARD LIFE OFFICE for

$1323.

For all particulars of rates, etc., apply to

Holme, Ringer & Co.,
Agents, Chemulpo.

THE NEW YORK LIFE INSURANCE COMPANY.

Have you ever been declined by any Company?

Are you engaged in a specially hazardous occupation?

Have you heard of the New York Life Insurance Company's New Classifications for this class of Risks?

If not, send your date of birth, occupation and particulars of rejection, if any to

E. MEYER & Co.,
Agents, Chemulpo.

MITSUI BUSSAN KAISHA.
(MITSUI & Co.)
MITSUI GINKO.
(MITSUI BANK.)

The Bank is owned by the members of the Mitsui Family, who, as partners, assume an unlimited responsibility for all liabilities of the Bank:—

Capital.............................Yen 5,000,000
Reserve Fund.......................... " 5,600,000

HEAD OFFICE, TOKYO.

LONDON OFFICE, 34 LIME ST., E. C.

BRANCHES AND AGENCIES:—
New York, San Francisco, Hamburg, Bombay, Singapore, Manila, Hongkong, Amoy, Chefoo, Tientsin.
Kobe, Hakodate, Yokohama, Kure, Yokosuka, Moji, Shimonoseki, Miike, Wakamatsu Nagasaki, Kuchinotsu, Karatsu, Sasebo, Misume, Taipeh, &c.

Telegraphic Address for all the Offices:
"MITSUI."

A. B. C. AND A. 1 CODES USED.

Contractors of Coal
To the Imperial Japanese Navy. Arsenal and Railway Bureau, Principal Railway Companies and Industrial Work, Home and Foreign Mail and Freight Steamers.

Sole Proprietors
Of the famous Miike, Tagawa and Yamano Coal Mines.

Sole Agents
For the sale of Fukumo, Hokoku, Ichimura Kanoda, Mannoura, Onoura, Ostuji, Sonoda Tsubaruro, Yoshinotani, Yoshio, Yurokibura and other coals.

YANGTSE INSURANCE ASSOCIATION, LTD.

The undersigned, having been appointed agents for the above company, are prepared to issue policies and pay losses on marine risks at regular rates.

E. MEYER & Co.,
Agents, Chemulpo.

AMERICAN KOREAN ELECTRIC CO.

Light and Power.

Main office: Electric Building, Chong No

RAILWAY DEPARTMENT.

OPERATING CARS BETWEEN EAST AND WEST GATE, EVERY TEN MINUTES:—

First Car leaves East Gate at 7:00 A. M. First Car leaves R. R. Station at 7:25 A. M
Last Car " East Gate at 8.40 P. M. Last " " R. R. Station at 9.05 P. M

OPERATING CARS BETWEEN EAST GATE AND IMPERIAL TOMB TERMINUS, EVERY TWENTY MINUTES:-
CONNECTING WITH EVERY ALTERNATE CAR ARRIVING AT EAST GATE FROM CHONG NO.

First Car leaves East Gate for Tomb at 7:10 A. M.
" " " Tomb for East Gate at 7:30 A. M.
Last " " East Gate for Tomb at 7:50 P. M.
" " " Tomb for East Gate at 8:10 P. M.

OPERATING CARS BETWEEN CHONG NO AND YUNG SAN RIVER EVERY TWELVE MINUTES:—

First Car leaves Chong No for South Gate at 7:12 A. M.
" " " Chong No for Yung San at 7:36 A. M.
" " " South Gate for Chong No at 7:20 A. M.
" " " Yung San for Chong No at 8:09 A. M.
Last " " South Gate for Chong No 9:00 P. M.
" " " Yung San for Chong No at 8.45 P. M.

SPECIAL PRIVATE CARS FURNISHED TO SUIT CONVENIENCE OF PATRONS. PRICES ON APPLICATION AT HEAD OFFICE.

LIGHTING DEPARTMENT.

Where less than 250 candle power of light is used, the rate per month will be
Per 16 candle power incandescent lamp,—All night.—Yen 2.50.
32 candle power incandescent lamp,—All night:—Yen 4.00.
50 candle power incandescent lamp,—All night:—Yen 6.00.
150 " " " " " " " " 10.00.
1200 " " enclosed arc " " " " " 20.00.

Where more than 250 candle power of light is used, a Meter will be installed, if requested:—Rent of Meter, Yen 2.00 per month. Rate of charges by meter reading:—Two Sen per Ampere per hour. (Approximately this is equal to about One Sen per 16 C. P. lamp per hour) Minimum monthly charge where meter is installed, Yen 20.00 per month, which includes rental of meter.

Estimates for installing lights furnished on application
An assortment of chandeliers always on hand.

K. Murakami.
Photograph Studio
Chinkokai, Seoul.

Printing, Developing and Enlargement, of Photographs always Undertaken.

Korean Views and Pictures Illustrating Native Customs always on Sale,

THE OSAKA SHOSEN KAISHA.

Boats frequently on the berth for Chinnampo.

REGULAR SAILINGS BETWEEN JAPAN AND KOREAN PORTS.

FUSAN AND KOBE VIA SHIMONOSEKI.

OSAKA VIA MOKPO, FUSAN, SHIMONOSEKI AND KOBE.

MOJI DIRECT.

OSAKA VIA KUNSAN, MASANPO, FUSAN, SHIMONOSEKI AND KOBE.

CHEMULPO KUNSAN LINE,
Every three days.

CHEMULPO CHINNAMPO LINE.
Every three days.

For Freight and passage and further particulars apply to

THE OSAKA SHOSEN KAISHA,
Chemulpo.

RONDON, PLAISANT & CO.

General Storekeepers and Merchants, Ships Contractors Tobacconists, Commission and Forwarding Agents, Coal Merchants

IMPORTERS AND EXPORTERS

Seoul Chemulpo.

W. D. WENTWORTH

LANDING
AND
SHIPPING AGENT.
AND
CUSTOMS BROKER.

12 OURA, NAGASAKI.

STEWARD & CO.

Chemulpo.

Shipchandlers and Storekeepers, Naval and Mercantile Contractors, Landing and Shipping Agents.

STEWARD'S HOTEL

Chemulpo.

Best accommodation in the port for travellers. Clean and well-aired rooms, good cuisine and prompt attendance, moderate tariff.

본군은란슌구에서가져온며람
취되는때포를쏜다ᄒᆞ며동편으
로셔편쳐지샹감ᄒᆡᆼ의두모소리
의거리의탕군이오륙십명리를
연쟝ᄒᆞ엿고그외에일본군의우
익의동편에사십오명리되는산
계자라셔에로군의운동이잇

TELEGRAMS.

(FROM JAPAN PAPERS.)

THE WAR.

London, February 36th.

A report from St. Petersburg states the Japanese made an attack upon the night of the 23rd inst., but were repulsed. They renewed the attack the following day and the Russians were forced to retire.

There has been desperate fighting along the whole of the front, but the result is, as yet, indecisive.

A railway bridge in the vicinity of Haicheng has been blown up and the Japanese communications interrupted.

AFFAIRS IN RUSSIA.

London, Feb. 25.

The situation at Batoum and Poti is becoming so serious that a portion of the Black Sea Fleet has bombarded Poti, which is a Caucasian port about 40 miles north of Batoum. The stikers there are all Georgians and number about forty thousand.

The Trans-Caucasian railway strike is spreading rapidly.

Fresh strikes are being constantly reported from all parts of Russia

London Feb. 26th.

The whole of Eastern Siberia (Russia ?) is now in a similar ferment to that in the Caucasus.

London, Feb. 26.

The connection between St. Petersburg and Warsaw has been cut.

The city of Warsaw is reeking with every dangerous element. The local police are threatening to strike. The gasworks is occupied by troops.

GENERAL NEWS.

London, Feb. 26.

The Simplon Tunnel has been pierced, thus completing six years work.

Eleven Chinese spies, engaged by the Russians, who recently attempted arson at the Japanese depot at Tairen (Dalny), are reported to have been sentenced to death on the 17th inst.; according to a Moji telegram.

It is reported that the Korean army will be re-organized as follows:—The Seoul garrison will consist of 3 battalions each 800 Imperial guards and 3 battalion each 800 Seoul guards together with artillery, pioneers and gendarmes. In the country 1 battalion of 600 men will be alloted to each of the eight provinces.

A Masampo man named Yi Ci Chong-hün, who dates his petition from the local prison, complains to the foreign office that a man named Sun Dok-woo, working with a number of Japanese, has been surveying the ground everywhere and claiming it by stating that it is for railway use. Yi Chong-hün protested that such ground as is really required for railway use should be paid for at market price and for this he was denounced to the railway authorities. He now prays for his own release and the punishment of Sun.

The "Asahi" reproduces from a German paper the statement that, about the middle of last January, after the arrival in Manchuria of three Brigades of Sharpshooters and the Sixteenth Army Corps, the German Major-General Count Richard von Pfeil made the following estimate as the to the strength of General Kuropatkin's forces:—

Infantry	334,700
Cavalry	33,960
Artillery	35,340
Total	404,000
Guns	1,500

The above figures do not include volunteers and railway guards.

NICE TIMES AT THE FRONT.

With reference to the report of a man being shot at Shinmintun a few days ago, says the "China Gazette," it appears that an American named Kearney, who was up in that district trying to buy cattle, had a dispute with a German on the same errand, named Grippendorf; and the former shot the latter through the arm; and then cleared out. We learn that the Chinese authorities are on the man's track; and it will certainly be difficult for him to get away. The injured man was at once sent down by train to the Tongshan Hospital, where he is reported to be doing well.

THE JAPANESE INTERNAL LOAN.

Although the bonds of the next, which is the fourth, internal Japanese loan have not yet been placed upon the market, the terms, as agreed upon by the Government and the bankers of Japan are as follows:—

The amount is to be 100 million yen; the rate of interest 6 per cent; the selling price 90 and the period 7 years.

There is also a somewhat vague story to the effect that the bankers have engaged themselves to take up a similar loan three months after the flotation of this one. The interest on this loan works out at 8¼ per cent; which is high, even in Japan.

Mr. Yi Yong Ik who was recently appointed Governor of North Kyŏng Sang province, has departed for his post.

Mr. Kil Yung Su until recently a prisoner in the Japanese army headquarters has been released and now attends the palace every day.

Some Il-chin-hoi members applied to the Minister of War for passes into the palace. They were dismissed with a caution.

According to the "China Review" cattle disease is working havoc in Tientsin. One fine herd has been swept away and another bids fair to follow.

The Argentine man-of-war "Uruguay" has returned to Buenos Ayres after a prolonged and fruitless search for the missing French Antaractic expedition under Dr. Chorcot. It is feared that all perished in the great storm in April 1904.

The magistrate of Pong Wha asks the Foreign Office to obtain redress from the Japanese Legation for an outrage which has occurred in his district. It appears that a Korean named Pyon had some grievance against another Korean named Hong Dŏ Yu and accordingly, having obtained the services of two Japanese toughs named Hiroku and Nakagawa, one of whom seems to have been armed with a visiting card of Major Nodzu's, proceeded to Hong's house and looted it. They carred away some title deeds, a quantity of rice and all the furniture and offered violence to those who interfered with them.

A simple device for the discouragement of bores has been introduced to London by a firm of American business men, is in operation frequently in their city office. On the table in front of the principal who interviews visitors is a telephone, and under the table, and out of the visitors' sight, is a little button which connects the business man with his clerks' office. When the city man finds that his caller's conversation is becoming tiresome he surreptitiously presses the button. Then there comes a ring upon the telephone. "Tell him to wait a few seconds," He replies to an apochryphal message through the 'phone, "I am just finishing with this gentleman." The treatment may have to be repeated in obstinate cases, but the caller usually takes the hint promptly and departs,

THE RUSSIAN DISORDERS.

St. Petersburg. January 25.

Sir Charies Hardinge, the British Ambassador, received from Capt Grove, the British Consul at Moscow, confirmation of the press dispatch from Moscow announcing the public posting of a London telegram imputing the disorders to British and Japanese influence, and he will ask explanations from Foreign Minister Lamsdorff to-day. It is not expected, however, that the affair will lead to a serious diplomatic incident, and it is thought the Russian Government will disavow responsibility for the course of Acting Chief of Police Roudneff

Moscow, January 25.

Captain Grove, the British Consul, has called upon M. Roudneff. the Assistant Police Master who is acting in the absence of Chief Volkoff, and requested an explanation of the posted telegram from London alleging that the disturbances at the Russian dock-yards and arsenal were due to Anglo-Japanese instigation; that both Great Britain and Japan are spending vast sums of money to prevent the Russian second Pacific squadron from reaching the Far East, and adding "that all Russians who strike are therefore in connivance with the enemy."

M. Roudneff produced the original telegram in evidence of good faith. Captain Grove stated that he would report the matter to the embassy at St. Petersburg, as he considered that the posting of the alleged telegram imperiled the lives of subjects of Great Britain who are employed in factories here. M. Roudneff assured him that there was absolutely no cause for apprehension, but assumed the responsibility for the publication.

M. Roudneff also offered Captain Grove personal satisfaction in a resort to arms.

King Edward has presented a Korean bull to the Royal Zoological Society of Ireland.

The final replies of the parties in the Japanese House Tax Arbitration were exchanged at The Hague on February 15th.

At the interview of the German Prince Frederick Leopold with the Czar, no questions regarding war or peace were touched on.

Japanese names have been given to the streets in Port Arthur. Thus there is now a Nogi-machi, a Shibai-machi, a Shirasaki-machi and so on.

The Turkish gun order difficulty has been compromised, France receiving a portion of the order. The new Turkish guns will be paid for from a loan issued by the Ottoman Bank, negotiations for which have now been opened. German financiers are to find the money to pay for the part of the order that is to go to Krupp's.

The "Chefoo Daily News" reports that a junk without cargo or passengers arrived there on February 27th from Pigeon Bay. The crew reported that they left Chefoo with the intention of picking up passengers among the numbers of persons leaving Port Arthur via Pigeon Bay. They stated that the Japanese will not allow any further departures from that point, neither will a landing at Pigeon Bay be permitted. A guard is stationed at the latter place to carry out the order.

The "North China Herald" gave publicity to a story to the effect that M. Lessar, the Russian Minister at Peking would shortly be recalled. In view of this, the following, from the "China Gazette," is of interest. The rumours alluded to about the replacement of Mons. Lessar by either Mons. Pokotiloff or General Wogack are purely from native sources; and were distincitly so stated in our columns. As a matter of fact no change is contemplated or would be possible under present circumstances. Mons. Lessar's intimate knowledge of the Far East and all questions in connection with the war being too valuable and varied to be wasted at the present time, however much the Russian Minister may deserve promotion.

PORT ARTHUR.

The China Gazette by way of refuting the statement of Dr. Morrison, the "Times" correspondent, that the surrender of Port Arthur was a discreditable one makes use of a report of a Special Correspondent of the "London Express" who was with the investing army under General Nogi, which he telegraphed to his paper on January the 4th via Tientsin. Extracts from it ran as follows:—"By the courtesy of the Japanese commanders I have been enabled to get at close quarters with the surrendered city of Port Arthur.

"The surprising thing about it is that, so far as the streets are concerned, the town does not seem to have suffered as much from the bombardment as was expected. Port Arthur old town, however, has suffered greatly.

"But if the houses and shops show comparatively little trace of damage, the forts are pictures of desolation. Every trace of defence works has disappeared from some of the positions, which suggest the tumbled bareness of a mining country. The town is completely dominated at close quarters by the Wangtai Fort, which was captured by the Japanese on the Sunday before the surrender. Had the Russians continued to resist, it is difficult to see how a single house could have remained standing.

"I have seen warfare in many lands, but nothing so appalling as this siege has shown. A visit to the ruined fort of Soushu was like a revolting nightmare. A tumbled heap of loose masonry, and beneath it the bodies of soldiers, was all that remained of the battlements; and festering corpses were a loathsome sight in the trenches. General Stoessel need have no fear that his surrender will be blamed by military men. His position was hopeless—no ammunition, hospitals full of wounded men, for whom there were no medical comforts, dwindling rations, and no hope of relief. He had fought as long as man could."

A Tokio newspaper says that the Russian Telegraphic News Agency circulates a "communique" stating that Reuter's report regarding peace terms is based on a misunderstanding and the original decision to continue the war is unshaken.

NOTICE.

Dr. Harold Slade, Resident Dentist of Kobe, will visit Seoul professionally about the end of February.

The Korea Daily News.

Issued at 5 P. M. daily except Sundays.

Rate of Subscription:—
Per Year,............Yen 25.
Per Quarter,..........Yen 7.
Per Month,..........Yen 2.50.

Postage in Korea not charged extra.
Postage abroad charged extra.

Advertisements, 50 sen per day for 1 inch or less.
5 yen per month per inch.
50 yen per year per inch.

All communications to

E. T. BETHELL,
Editor and Publisher,
Pak-tong, Seoul.

KOREA'S ADMINISTRATION.

The last issue of the "Japan Mail" to hand contains a leading article on Korea the peroration of which is as follows:—

Korea is more to Japan, much more, than Egypt is to England, and if Japan limit herself to following in Seoul the example set by Great Britian on the banks of the Nile, she will be showing much moderation.

The "Japan Mail" not alone in its programme of delivering itself of opinions calculated to pave the way for a Japanese annexation of Korea. Most of the Japanese newspapers speak in a similar way and as only one side of the question is heard, the people of Japan probably share their opinions.

It is undoubtedly true that corruption is rife among the official classes in Korea and it is evident that a very large proportion of the population lives in luxury and idleness at the expense of the working classes. These are undeniable facts and it is these facts which have furnished Japan with plausible excuses for getting control of the country and its finance and, should the war terminate in the eviction of Japan from Korea, will serve the same purpose for the next comer.

It should therefore be evident to all enlightened Koreans that however much adventitious circumstances may, *pro-tem*, help their country out of its difficulties, a time is bound to come when Japan or some other adventuring power will again take advantage of Korea's weakness, incapacity, corruption and general policy of *laissez faire* to step in and turn the country topsey turvey with a new policy, a lot of new ideas and lots of other things calculated to raise ructions.

An idea seems to prevail among the Koreans that this country maybe, perhaps, by and bye, become a sort of Buffer Power. The idea is good, and it is feasable if Korea becomes a Power. A Buffer Power without the "power" is a "Buffer," and that is precisely what Korea is at present.

We think we are voicing the opinions of all intelligent observers when we say that the weak spot of Korea lies in its conservatism. Somewhere back in the dim and distant past, a ruler of Korea inaugurated the system of "farming out" provinces and districts which prevails to this day. The system has nothing inherently wrong about it and it probably arose through an Oriental dislike of having to check a lot of beastly accounts. Still, the system invites abuses and in this respect Korean officials need no invitation.

It was only a few days ago that we received reports of the bidding for a certain magistracy. We do not remember the name of the district or the amount of the bid but anyhow they do not matter as it is quite sufficient for the purposes of our argument that a magistrate's job was put up for auction.

It is very easy to see how this can, and does lead to rank abuses. Until he is recalled or kicked out by his exasperated subjects, a magistrate in Korea administers his district for the sole benefit of his own lazy self.

We do not for a moment suggest that things will improve under the Japanese *regime*—quite the reverse, the Japanese are clever in their own way but so are the Koreans and the man is yet to be born who can, by disillusionising the Korean *yangban* class of the idea that they have an inherited right to waste their own and other people's time, establish some sort of order out of the present corrupt state of things.

This is the truth and we cannot expect that our Korean readers will relish it, but it is just as well to swallow a nasty dose now as presently.

We all know that the Japanese "reforms" will leave the country with the Japanese, but real reforms are none the less neccessary and true Korean statesmen should bear this in mind.

FORECASTING JAPAN'S TERMS OF PEACE.

The following article by "Diplomaticus" in the "Westminster," says an exchange, bears quite sufficient internal evidence of inspiration to merit quotation:—

What are the chances of an early restoration of peace in the Far East now that Port Arthur has fallen? Mr. Greenwood's anticipation that Japan would "come down to the footlights" and "throw peace in the air" has not been fulfilled. On the other hand, it is seen that with a well-equipped army of 400,000 men on the Sha-ho, with a new loan just floated in Berlin, and the confidence of the Continental money market unabated, and with the internal problem still showing no sign of becoming unmanageable, Russia is under no compulsion to throw up the sponge. There is another aspect which has not been sufficiently considered, and without which it is impossible to arrive at any clear conclusion of the matter. What would throwing up the sponge mean to Russia? What price would she have to pay for peace? In a word, what are the terms Japan is likely in her present circumstances to demand?

The Japanese demands must be governed by three fundamental requirements. Japan must, of course, secure what she in vain sought to obtain by the ante-bellum negotiations. Then she must possess herself of further concessions to compensate her for the sacrifices she has incurred in waging a great war. Finally, she must see that the terms comprise adequate guarantees for the permanent peace of the Far East. The Japanese side of this bargain would now become the first terms of peace. That is to say, that Russia would be called upon to evacuate Manchuria and to recognise Japan's "preponderating interests" in Korea, together with her right to safeguard them in the terms of the recent treaty with that country. The proposed concessions to Russia would, of course, fall to the ground. In pursuance of the second requirement, Japan would claim to succeed to all the property and privileges enjoyed by Russia in Manchuria, such as the Port Arthur lease, the railway and banking concessions, and the railway itself, and would also demand—though this, I fancy, would not be insisted upon—a money indemnity. Together with the Russian property, Japan would take the obligation to restore Manchuria to Chinese sovereignty, which she would be prepared to execute promptly, subject to an extension of the railway concession to the Korean border and perhaps some other concessions of a similar kind. The third requirement would be adequately met by the dismantling of the fortifications of Vladivostock and an engagement not to use the port as a naval base. Besides this, the retrocession of Saghalien, which the Japanese have always regarded as a sort of Alsace, would be insisted upon.

Now these terms, whether reasonable or not, are clearly impossible to Russia while she still has a great army in the field and believes she has a fair prospect of employing it effectively. They may be summed up in a sentence—the disappearance of the Russian flag from the far East. With the mouth of the Amur commanded by a Japanese Saghalien; with Vladivostock demilitarised, and with Port Arthur and its entire hinterland confiscated, the patient work of a century's ambitions expansion would be completely destroyed. It is true that for commercial purposes the position of Russian would be no worse than it was before she acquired Port Arthur; but Russia is not essentially a commercial Power. Her ambition is chiefly political, and she attaches no importance to commercial facilities of which she is not the military arbiter. There is, moreover, humiliation in this proposed disarmament of her which she must find peculiarly intolerable. Clearly then, peace by direct negotiation between the belligerents is—for the moment at any rate—impossible. But it may be asked, is not this a fair opportunity for mediation or even intervention? It would be if the Japanese terms were flagrantly unreasonable or if the Powers could be brought to see them with the same eyes. As a matter of fact, they are by no means exorbitant. If Russia had triumphed in this war, Japan—barring a generous interpretation of her alliance with Great Britain, upon which it would have been unwise to count—would have been as helpless in the orbit of Russian influence as Persia. It is no secret that Russia has contemplated a peace by which Yezo and Kiushu would be annexed and the Sea of Japan transformed virtually into a Russian lake. In these circumstances Japan cannot make her position too secure, and if she has to wage another great campaign to achieve her end, the sacrifice will be worth it. Nor can we in this country blame her. We certainly cannot desire a peace which whould be a mere truce, and which, besides unsettling the whole trade of the Far East, would bring the risk of war permanently to our own threshold.

We have already heard of Mrs. Hagiwara having entertained a number of Korean ladies and we now learn that when Mr. Yi Chi-yong, the Minister for Agriculture recently entertained the members of the Japanese Legation, his wife was present at the feast. Following upon this we are told that Mrs. Hagiwara intends holding a series of parties for Korean ladies.

The Korea Daily News.

VOL. II, SATURDAY, MARCH 4, 1905. No. 49

HONGKONG & SHANGHAI BANKING CORPORATION.

Paid-up Capital $10,000,000
Reserve Fund:—Sterling Reserve... 10,000,000
Silver Reserve..... 7,000,000

27,000,000

Reserve Liability of Proprietors... 10,000,000

HEAD OFFICE, HONGKONG.

London Bankers, London and County Banking Company Limited.

Branches and Agencies,
London.

Amoy,	Hankow	Penang,
Bangkok	Hiogo,	Rangoon,
Batavia,	Iloilo,	Saigon,
Bombay,	Lyons,	San Francisco,
Calcutta,	Manila,	Singapore,
Colombo,	Nagasaki,	Sourabaya,
Foochow,	New York,	Tientsin,
Hamburg,	Peking,	Yokohama,

Credits granted on approved Securities, and every description of Banking and Exchange business transacted.

Drafts granted on London and the chief Commercial places in Europe, India, Australia, America, China and Japan.

HOLME RINGER & CO., AGENTS,
CHEMULPO.

HOKURKU DOBOKU KAISHA.

Branch office in Chong Dong, Seoul.

Japanese telephone No. 165

CONTRACT DEPARTMENT.

We can contract to build any building or construction.

MERCHANDISE DEPARTMENT.

We can provide any building material. We have just contracted to build the new Belgian Legation.

E. MEYER & Co.,
Agents,
Chemulpo

CHARTERED BANK OF INDIA AUSTRALIA & CHINA.

INCORPORATED BY ROYAL CHARTER 1853

HEAD OFFICES.—LONDON.

Paid-up Capital £800,000
Reserve Liability of Shareholders 800,000
Reserve Fund 800,000

Drafts granted upon all the principal places in the world and every description of Exchange and banking business transacted.

E. MEYER & Co., Agents,
Chemulpo.

MITSU BISHI DOCKYARD & ENGINE WORKS,
NAGASAKI.

CODE WORD, "DOCK."

A 1, A. B. C., and Engineering Codes used.

DOCK No. 1 (at Tategami).

Extreme Length.............. 523 feet
Length on blocks .... 513 ,,
Width of Entrance on Top...... 89 ,,
,, ,, Bottom.... 77 ,,
Water on Blocks at Spring Tide 26½ ,,

DOCK No. 2 (Mukaijima).

Extreme Length.............. 371 feet
Length on Blocks............ 360 ,,
Width of Entrance on Top...... 66 ,,
,, ,, Bottom 53 ,,
Water on Blocks at Spring Tide 22 ,,

PATENT SLIP (at Kosuge).

Can take vessels up to 1,000 tons gross.

THE WORKS are well equipped with the LATEST IMPROVEMENTS, and can execute any kind of work in SHIPBUILDING and MARINE ENGINEERING, as well as in REPAIRING of SHIPS.

The COMPANY'S new powerful steamer OURA-MARU (712 tons, 700 I.H.P.), specially built for SALVAGE PURPOSES, and equipped with necessary gear, is always READY at SHORT NOTICE.

THE METHODIST PUBLISHING HOUSE,
Little West Gate, Seoul.

JOB PRINTING, TYPEWRITER PAPER
CARBON PAPER, VISITING CARDS
STATIONERY, BOOK BINDING
BOOK PUBLISHERS
AMERICAN SCHOOL BOOKS
SPENCERIAN COPY BOOKS
PEN CARBON LETTER AND BILL BOOKS

S. A. BECK, Manager.

DAI-ICHI GINKO.

LIMITED.

(Formerly the First National Bank)

ESTABLISHED 1873

INCORPORATED UNDER PRESENT LAW 1896

Capital - - - - - - - - Yen 5,000,000
Reserve Fund - - - - - 1,500,000

HEAD OFFICE:—TOKIO.

President: Baron SHIBUSAWA.

BRANCHES AND CORRESPONDENTS

In the Principal Cities and Towns of Japan.

Interest Allowed on

Fixed deposits 1 year - - - 6½ per cent
" " 6 months - - - 6 per cent

Special current accounts 1½ sen daily per Y 100
General " " 1 " " " 100

M. TANAKA,
Manager, Chemulpo.

SINGER SEWING MACHINES

씽거ᄌᆞ봉침

SOLE AGENTS FOR KOREA

젼매쇼

HOLME RINGER & CO.
Chemulpo.

졔물포 함릉거양힝

KAMEYA & CO.

GENERAL STOREKEEPERS

Chinkokai - - Seoul

(*Established 1895, Tokyo*)

Confectionery, Hams, Canned Goods, Cutlery, Hirano & Tansan Water. Provisions, Gents, Furnishing goods, Toilet Articles, Travelling Bags, Tobacco, Cigars & Cigarettes Kitchen Utensils. Coffee, Biscuits

Fresh Goods always kept in Stock.

Prices Moderate

☞ *Please come and inspect our goods.*

NIPPON YUSEN KAISHA.
JAPANESE MAIL STEAMSHIP CO.

UNDER MAIL CONTRACT WITH THE IMPERIAL JAPANESE GOVERNMENT.

European Line

Regular Fortnightly Service between Yokohama, Kobe, Moji, Shanghai, Hongkong, Singapore, Penang, Colombo, Port Said, Marseilles, London and Antwerp

American Line

Regular Fortnightly Service between Hongkong and Seattle, calling at Shanghai, Moji, Kobe, Yokohama and Victoria, B. C.

Australian Line

Regular weekly Service betwen Japan Ports and Australia, calling at Hongkong and Manila.

(Above Three Lines Suspended until further notice.

Shanghai Line

Weekly Service between Shanghai and Japan Ports

Korea Line

Service Kobe, Moji, Nagasaki, Fusan Chemulpo Chefoo, Taku.

S. S. Babelsberg, 2181 tons.

Service Kobe. Moji, Fusan, Chemulpo, Chinnampo

S. S. ARGO, S. S. Ohio.

BORDEN'S CONDENSED MILK CO.

New York, U. S. A.

ALWAYS IN STOCK

Eagle Brand Condensed Milk.

Gold Seal Condensed Milk.

Peerless (Family) Evaporated Cream.

Borden's Malted Milk.

E. MEYER & CO.
Chemulpo Korea,
Sole Agents

ROYAL INSURANCE COMPANY,

Funds exceed £10,000,000

FIRE

AT CURRENT RATES

LIFE

REDUCED PREMIUM,

HOLME RINGER & Co.
Agents, Chemulpo

廣
KWANG C'HANG
昌

BENNETT & CO.

Merchants
Chemulpo.

Offices opposite the Imperial Japanese Post and Telegraph Office Chemulpo.

Telephone Number 201.

大韓每日申報
대한ᄆᆡ일신보

(뎨이권오십호) (화요일) 일천구ᄇᆡᆨ오년삼월칠일

본샤고ᄇᆡᆨ

이신보는영어와한어로셔계디
일출판ᄒᆞᆷ을

신문가
한쟝 엽두돈오푼
일삭료 엽두량닷돈
ᄉᆞ 소가미 샤닷돈
ᄃᆡ 맛돈으로밧ᄉᆞᆷ
광고료는

귀한의쟝단과ᄌᆞ항의다쇼로좃
갑ᄒᆞ되뎌가로밧을터이오며오
티지아녀매한사람마다이신
문을보실터이니광고버시기를
원ᄒᆞ시는이들은우리신문샤에
와셔면약ᄒᆞ심을ᄇᆞ라ᄋᆞᆸ

○발힝소 박동대한ᄆᆡ일신보
샤본방에허고 영국인셜필
형젼자리오
사쟝 영국인 (베셜)
평양 디리졈
○평양흠동사는권ᄃᆡ보씨로우
리신문광매디리인을퇴졍ᄒᆞ엿
시스오니평양에계신구람코져ᄒᆞ
는 쳠군ᄌᆞ는희디리졈에왕
림ᄒᆞ와면회ᄒᆞ시옵

사고

ᄒᆞ우리대한ᄆᆡ일신보의목뎍은
ᄃᆡ한의인민쳔셔에관한모든대
목에ᄃᆡᄒᆞ야는공평한변론을쥬
쟝ᄒᆞ이라우리ᄒᆞᆫ신원의담보는
신문보시는쳠군ᄌᆞ의게ᄒᆞ샹보
도ᄒᆞ리며편지론귀셔ᄒᆞ며주시
논이는셩명과빈티론쟈어붓치
시기를희망ᄒᆞ오나비거슬신문
샹에과계ᄒᆞ란는거시아니오다
반극히신용ᄒᆞ논즁거를숨고자
ᄒᆞᆷ이라귀쟈는아모과셔던지과
지ᄒᆞᆷ을퇴각ᄒᆞ논권리를가졋스
나퇴각ᄒᆞ논리유를말ᄒᆞᆯ터이오
며공쥬평화론문란케ᄒᆞ논듯ᄒᆞᆫ
타괴셔논의헤하ᄒᆞ박지한켓ᄉᆞᆸ나이
다

●본사셜시이린로신문을미양
우헤로분젼ᄒᆞ와헤젼부의임의
로젼ᄒᆞᆫ는스스로빈곳에는ᄒᆞ눗게
젼ᄒᆞ기도ᄒᆞ며ᄒᆞ면칠거슬ᄒᆞᆫ졉
에젼ᄒᆞ기도ᄒᆞ며ᄒᆞ야니젼ᄒᆞ논
곳도잇다ᄒᆞ와우리신문을ᄉᆞ랑
ᄒᆞ야구람ᄒᆞ시는 쳠군ᄌᆞ의게
티ᄒᆞ야미우미안ᄒᆞ옵기로지금
은분젼인을두고퇴일ᄒᆞ즉이젼
ᄉᆞ마ᄒᆞ야니젼ᄒᆞ거나늣게거나ᄒᆞᆫ
폐가업도록ᄒᆞ란ᄒᆞ오니ᄒᆞ야나
젼ᄒᆞ거는ᄒᆞ눗게젼ᄒᆞ거나ᄒᆞᆫ일
이잇스면본사로통긔ᄒᆞ여주샴
을희망ᄒᆞᆷ

론셜

디다넌쓰문제

○이ᄂᆞᆫ젼에우리신문에반포ᄒᆞᆫ뎐
보가진셜ᄒᆞ면로국졍부에셔지
금셔지ᄒᆞ히합디를니보니셔로
제스트벤스기대쟝의졍디에가
부ᄒᆞ라ᄒᆞ는것이분명ᄒᆞ도다
로국이영국과다다넌쓰문제에
간셥ᄒᆞ지말나는약됴를지금은
동ᄒᆞᆫ다는티글로ᄒᆞ야과리죠약
즁의ᄒᆞᆫ귀졀을폐ᄒᆞ기를쳥구ᄒᆞ
니그귀졀에말ᄒᆞ엿스되
토이기황뎨폐하께셔는토이
뎨국의젼권ᄒᆞ논규칙을영원히
고슈ᄒᆞ기를션언ᄒᆞ야그젼과로
약스모폐하도다다넌쓰와보쓰포
뤗스ᄒᆞ협에외국군함의드란올
을금ᄒᆞ엿거니와ᄒᆞ며배도로
이두ᄒᆞ뎡부가광화를보젼ᄒᆞ베에
는혀략ᄒᆞ지아니ᄒᆞᆫ리미매이약조
에참셥ᄒᆞᆫ각국황뎨폐하와대군
쥬폐하께셔는토이기황뎨의결
졍ᄒᆞᆫ것을존즁이넉비졍기우에
션언ᄒᆞᆫ쥬의에확실히졍ᄒᆞ키된
다ᄒᆞ엿스니
그귀졀의의미로본즉로국이그
귀졀을폐ᄒᆞ자논티탁을토이기
졍부에엇더린도영국은토이기
황뎨의결졍ᄒᆞᆫ것을존즁히너이
고셔언ᄒᆞᆫ쥬의에확징이된다는
일켸셕ᄃᆞᆯ으로분가불한동이간셥ᄒᆞ
의권으로의쟝영시간쳥ᄒᆞ엿슴
리이오쓰쟝리에도간쳥ᄒᆞ깻지
마는젼에로국이이약됴론손샹
ᄒᆞᆫ디디ᄒᆞ야향의ᄒᆞᆫ일외에다른
일은업셧스니일분외셜명ᄒᆞ논
것이만ᄒᆞᆫ효힘이업스리미라일
쳔구ᄇᆡᆨ삼년일월에로국이그희
쳥을통ᄒᆞ야슈뢰졍수쳑을너보
법으로영국졍부에셔토이기졍
부항ᄒᆞ야항의를졔츌ᄒᆞ엿더니
회답이업게되엿스며영국졍부
에셔외회에통엉ᄒᆞ되그협졍에
외국군함의츌입을금ᄒᆞ논일쳔
팔ᄇᆡᆨ수삼일년약죠와일쳔팔ᄇᆡᆨ칠
오십륙년약죠와일쳔팔ᄇᆡᆨ칠십신
일년약죠가아죵셔지우호ᄒᆞᆫ티
슈뢰졍의통과ᄒᆞᆷ이그약죠를
위반ᄒᆞᆷ이라ᄒᆞ엿더라
요젼에로국군함스몰넨스크와
괴터스빅의그ᄒᆞ칭을통과ᄒᆞᆷ에
디ᄒᆞ야쓴ᄒᆞᆫ영국이항의를제츌
ᄒᆞ엿스나로국이자긔나라의군
함들을그히쳥으로통과ᄒᆞᆷ이긴
요ᄒᆞᆫ처닭으로티답이엇셧더라
티흑히합디논비우긴요ᄒᆞ야젼
티의돈슈가도합상만삼쳔일빅
오십륙돈이오젼투함이신쳔인
티그즁에오리된것이열쳑팔빅
구십이넌에진것이라유명ᄒᆞᆫ졍
외군나도쌔의밧을거ᄒᆞᆫ즉볼
휘합티예이합티돌합ᄒᆞ면일본
함디돌멸ᄒᆞ기가분명ᄒᆞ니그렁
으로일본이진력ᄒᆞ야영국을달
ᄂᆡ셔파리약죠돌갑경ᄒᆞ게보젼
ᄒᆞ게ᄒᆞ리로다
로국에유명ᄒᆞᆫ신문에귀쥐ᄒᆞᆫ말
을요랑ᄒᆞ노니그말에ᄒᆞ엿스되
로아리는졔ᄒᆞ야로국의의견
다다넌쓰히협을통ᄒᆞ야로국군
항의츌립에관ᄒᆞᆫ약죠가졍ᄒᆞᆫ
타히엿스니죠예참셥ᄒᆞᆫ여러나라
가예동지ᄒᆞ고군함을동과ᄒᆞᆫ귀권
젹의군티ᄒᆞ게용ᄒᆞᆫ리나라ᄒᆞᆫ
계ᄒᆞ야병력의홀부분을나누지못ᄒᆞ
계ᄒᆞ야즁립의ᄒᆞᆫ로셔쳥ᄒᆞ논
셜것이즁립의위ᄒᆞᆫ...

외보

○티덕쳐울갓구 북경뎐보를
거ᄒᆞᆫ즉덕국공ᄉᆞ문마씨가산동
에졔ᄒᆞᆫ긔군권화쟝ᄒᆞ논이외에
긴요ᄒᆞᆫ샹문대들졔츌ᄒᆞ야외무
부대신등과교셥ᄒᆞᆫ논즁인티그
에ᄒᆞᆫ나ᄒᆞ란뎡부논교주만부근연안
을지방수ᄒᆞᆫ살력이무흠을가칭ᄒᆞ
고쟝시ᄒᆞ구안일티의지라디방
광지라벙을쳘되ᄒᆞ고덕국빙은
즁과ᄒᆞ야안평졍셔들유지케ᄒᆞ
라ᄒᆞᆫ다운ᄒᆞ떼기이논지라졍부
에셔덕국세렴빙ᄒᆞ호을젼제ᄒᆞ

기시잇논쟝부ᄒᆞ기ᄒᆞ야ᄃᆡ이위
시쟝경영에티ᄒᆞ야덕국리익이
잇논게류티규칙을제뎡케ᄒᆞ야
쳥정부최초의목적을최회ᄒᆞ야으로
귀케ᄒᆞ기를도모ᄒᆞ야수긔죠통
의안진을로뎔ᄒᆞ야젼순무호뎡
간차를단연거졀ᄒᆞ고외무부와
그후임ᄌᆞ된양씨의게티ᄒᆞ야도
주의를며ᄒᆞ엿고기상은덕주게
남부에셔졔뎡을경ᄒᆞ야쟝소셩
연안에달ᄒᆞ논쳘도션로의부셜
권을회득ᄒᆞ기에진ᄒᆞ티원리동
국의소쟝되논화졔가튼경광젹
쥬의논군일에졍졍탄로ᄒᆞ야외
무부에셔논비샹히고셩즁에잇
스며그런임ᄒᆞ논슌무양사도즁
은기졍즁조쳐가극난ᄒᆞᆷ을부임후에
아자붓샹히주저ᄒᆞᆫ논모양인티
목ᄒᆞ히예원츙동과자조티덕졍쳥
을쟝구ᄒᆞᆫ논즁이라더라
○비엿ᄂᆞᆫ협뎍쟈셩ᄒᆞ셔 망덕
호아위퇴ᄒᆞ여국ᄉᆞ박야
리야ᄃᆡ셩 뎐보에의
티로뎐우ᄒᆞ리에가반대ᄒᆞ
뎡ᄒᆞᆫ로우한외국(지마)ᄒᆞ에
용뎐이이론구슈아가곰
셕을샹쥬일(노쳬비)의
운가비게ᄒᆞᆫ바가리
의게통구롱에ᄌᆞ들야
...
○로국협티의손횟 로국신문
을거ᄒᆞᆫ즉ᄌᆞ논쵀ᄉᆞ고
이월노브리스...
...
○청국의왕 범국히군대신이
하의원에셔이신ᄉᆞ쳑대군함을
졔조ᄒᆞᆯ수와지금으로브터일쳔
구빅칠년에지ᄒᆞ도록미년사군
신계획에ᄉᆞ다만방식출ᄒᆞ야히군
비예쳥오빅만방슈를뎌표ᄒᆞ고
쇼지게...

UNION INSURANCE SOCIETY OF CANTON.

Head office Hongkong.
Marine risks underwritten at current rates.

Agents in Chemulpo,
E. MEYER & Co.

COMPAGNIE DES MESSAGERIES MARITIMES.

Fortnightly Direct Service.

For Marseilles
via Ports.
Sailing from Yokohama
Calling at Kobe,
Shanghai, Hongkong, Saigon, Singapore,
Colombo, Djibouti, Suez, Port Said
and Marseilles.

For particulars apply to
HOLME RINGER & Co.,
Chemulpo.

HAYASHIDA & CO.,
16 MYENG DONG, CHIN KO KAI, SEOUL.
BRANCH OFFICE AT CHEMULPO.

Money changers, Coal and Wood Merchants, Express Agents.

We are agents for the Pyeng-yang Coal Company and the Karazu Coal Company ot Japan. We have the best quality of both anthracite and bituminous coal, and prompt execution of orders is our speciality. Firewood of all kinds kept in stock. Full weight guaranteed. Money of all denominations exchanged at current rates. Parcels received for all parts.

CHINA MUTUAL LIFE INS. CO.

Most favourable terms to policy holders.

Benefit system unsurpassed.

HOLME RINGER & Co.
Agents, Chemulpo.

C. P. R.

CANADIAN PACIFIC RAILWAY COMPANY'S ROYAL MAIL STEAMSHIP LINE.

THE FAST ROUTE BETWEEN CHINA, JAPAN, AND EUROPE VIA CANADA AND THE UNITED STATES.

Route from Hongkong via Shanghai, Nagasaki (Inland Sea of Japan) Kobe, Yokohama, Victoria and Vancouver.

Twin Screw Empress Steamship—6,000 Tons—Speed 19 knots.

PROPOSED SAILING FROM YOKOHAMA.
R. M. S. Empress of India.
R. M. S. Empress of Japan.
R. M. S. Empress of China.
R. M. S. Athonian.
R. M. S. Tartar.

Special reduction (first class only) granted to members of the Military, Naval, Diplomatic and Civil services and to Missionaries.

Passengers have choice of ten routes across the Continent of America and have privilege of travelling by any Atlantic Steamship Line.

Round the World passage tickets in connection with the P. and O. S. N., North German Lloyd and Messageries Co.'s £125.

All rates payable at current rate of exchange.

For further information, Tickets, Guide Books, etc., apply to

HOLME, RINGER & Co., AGENTS,
Chemulpo.

Grand Hotel

(Formerly the Station Hotel)

Near the Railway Terminus, West Gate Seoul.

The Best Hotel in Korea.
Handsome new Building.
Fine Airy Rooms.
Excellent Cuisine.
Terms Moderate.
Special terms to Missionaries and to permanent boarders.

Electric cars within 2 minutes' walk.

W. H. EMBERLEY.
Proprietor

EVERY FACILITY.

In connection with Life Assurance Business is afforded by

The Standard Life Assurance Co.,

One of the largest and wealthiest of the Provident Institutions of the United Kingdom Forms of Application and all information wil be promptly afforded on application.

10 CENTS A DAY.

Not a very large expenditure is it? But it is sufficient to secure for a man of 30 a policy with the STANDARD LIFE OFFICE for

$1323.

For all particulars of rates, etc., apply to

Holme, Ringer & Co.,
Agents, Chemulpo.

THE NEW YORK LIFE INSURANCE COMPANY.

Have you ever been declined by any Company?

Are you engaged in a specially hazardous occupation?

Have you heard of the New York Life Insurance Company's New Classifications for this class of Risks?

If not, send your date of birth, occupation and particulars of rejection, if any to

E. MEYER & Co.,
Agents, Chemulpo.

MITSUI BUSSAN KAISHA.
(MITSUI & Co.)
MITSUI GINKO.
(MITSUI BANK.)

The Bank is owned by the members of the Mitsui Family, who, as partners, assume an unsimited responsibility for all liabilities of the Bank:—

Capital........................Yen 5,000,000
Reserve Fund.................. " 5,600,000

HEAD OFFICE, TOKYO.
LONDON OFFICE, 34 LIME ST., E. C.

BRANCHES AND AGENCIES:—
New York, San Francisco, Hamburg, Bombay, Singapore, Manila, Hongkong, Amoy, Chefoo, Tientsin.
Kobe, Hakodate, Yokohama, Kure, Yokosuka, Moji, Shimonoseki, Miike, Wakamatsu Nagasaki, Kuchinotsu, Karatsu, Sasebo, Misu me, Taipeh, &c.

Telegraphic Address for all the Offices:
"MITSUI."
A. B. C. AND A. I CODES USED.

Contractors of Coal
To the Imperial Japanese Navy. Arsena and Railway Bureau, Principal Railway Companies and Industrial Work, Home and Foreign Mail and Freight Steamers.

Sole Proprietors
Of the famous Miike, Tagawa and Yamano Coal Mines.

Sole Agents
For the sale of Fukumo, Hokoku, Ichimura Kanoda, Mannoura, Onoura, Ostuji, Sonoda Tsubaruro, Yoshinotani, Yoshio, Yurokibura and other coals.

YANGTSE INSURANCE ASSOCIATION, LTD.

The undersigned, having been appointed agents for the above company, are prepared to issue policies and pay losses on marine risks at regular rates.

E. MEYER & Co.,
Agents, Chemulpo.

AMERICAN KOREAN ELECTRIC CO.

Light and Power.

Main Office: Electric Building, Chong No.

RAILWAY DEPARTMENT.

OPERATING CARS BETWEEN EAST AND WEST GATE, EVERY TEN MINUTES:—

First Car leaves East Gate at 6:30 A. M. First Car leaves R. R. Station at 6:55 A.M
Last Car " East Gate at 9.50 P. M. Last " " R. R. Station at 10.05 P.M

OPERATING CARS BETWEEN EAST GATE AND IMPERIAL TOMB TERMINUS, EVERY TWENTY MINUTES:—
CONNECTING WITH EVERY ALTERNATE CAR ARRIVING AT EAST GATE FROM CHONG NO.

First Car leaves East Gate for Tomb at 6:50 A. M.
" " " Tomb for East Gate at 7:10 A. M.
Last " " East Gate for Tomb at 7:50 P. M.
" " " Tomb for East Gate at 8:10 P. M.

OPERATING CARS BETWEEN CHONG NO AND YUNG SAN RIVER EVERY TWELVE MINUTES:—

First Car leaves Chong No for South Gate at 6:48 A. M.
" " " Chong No for Yung San at 7:24 A. M.
" " " South Gate for Chong No at 6:56 A. M.
" " " Yung San for Chong No at 7:57 A. M.
Last " " South Gate for Chong No 10:08 P. M.
" " " Yung San for Chong No at 9.09. P. M.

SPECIAL PRIVATE CARS FURNISHED TO SUIT CONVENIENCE OF PATRONS. PRICES ON APPLICATION AT HEAD OFFICE.

LIGHTING DEPARTMENT.

Where less than 250 candle power of light is used, the rate per month will be
Per 16 candle power incandescent lamp,—All night.—Yen 2.50.
32 candle power incandescent lamp,—All night:—Yen 4.00.
50 candle power incandescent lamp,—All night:—Yen 6.00.
150 " " " " " " " 10.00.
1200 " " enclosed arc " " " " 20.00.

Where more than 250 candle power of light is used, a Meter will be installed, if requested:—Rent of Meter, Yen 2.00 per month. Rate of charges by meter reading:—Two Sen per Ampere per hour. (Approximately this is equal to about One Sen per 16 C. P. lamp per hour) Minimum monthly charge where meter is installed Yen 20.00 per month, which includes rental of meter.

Estimates for installing lights furnished on application

An assortment of chandeliers always on hand.

K. Murakami.
Photograph Studio
Chinkokai, Seoul

Printing, Developing and Enlargement, of Photographs always Undertaken.

Korean Views and Pictures Illustrating Native Customs always on Sale,

THE OSAKA SHOSEN KAISHA.

Boats frequently on the berth for Chinnampo.

REGULAR SAILINGS BETWEEN JAPAN AND KOREAN PORTS.

FUSAN AND KOBE VIA SHIMONOSEKI.

OSAKA VIA MOKPO, FUSAN, SHIMONOSEKI AND KOBE.

MOJI DIRECT.

OSAKA VIA KUNSAN, MASANPO, FUSAN, SHIMONOSEKI AND KOBE.

CHEMULPO KUNSAN LINE,
Every three days.

CHEMULPO CHINNAMPO LINE,
Every three days.

For Freight and passage and further particulars apply to

THE OSAKA SHOSEN KAISHA,
Chemulpo.

RONDON, PLAISANT & CO.

General Storekeepers and Merchants, Ships Contractors Tobacconists, Commission and Forwarding Agents, Coal Merchants

IMPORTERS AND EXPORTERS

Seoul Chemulpo.

W. D. WENTWORTH

LANDING
AND
SHIPPING AGENT.
AND
CUSTOMS BROKER.

12. OURA, NAGASAKI.

STEWARD & CO.

Chemulpo.

Shipchandlers and Storekeepers, Naval and Mercantile Contractors, Landing and Shipping Agents.

STEWARD'S HOTEL

Chemulpo.

Best accommodation in the port for travellers. Clean and well-aired rooms, good cuisine and prompt attendance, moderate tariff.

설치ᄒᆞ고 뎨이조션소를 셔공에 건설필요가 잇다ᄒᆞ엿더라

○일본부인회 일본에셔 ᄋᆡ국부인총회를 사월이일에 ᄀᆡ회ᄒᆞ는ᄃᆡ 동회쟝은 신숙식물어원에 뎡ᄒᆞ고 일본황후폐하ᄭᅴ셔 도쳔림ᄒᆞ실예뎡이오 회원부녀의 복쟝은 질박홈으로 위쥬ᄒᆞ야 각각계급부녀로ᄒᆞ야곰 불편홈이 업게ᄒᆞ고 각디방부녀의 출셕을 위ᄒᆞ야 쳘도급긔션회샤에 특별히 션셰를 감ᄒᆞᆯ수로 결뎡되엿다더라

뎐보

빅림발 이월이십삼일

○로국정부와 평화 로국정부에셔 근릭젼파ᄒᆞᆫ 평화젼셜을 다 박론ᄒᆞ엿다더라

샹히발 동월이십ᄉᆞ일

○청국에 의대리의 군ᄉᆞ 의대리정부에셔 청국북경에 잇ᄂᆞᆫ 공ᄉᆞ관보호병히륙군 몃명외에 청국에 잇ᄂᆞᆫ 군ᄉᆞᄂᆞᆫ 다 불너드리ᄂᆞᆫᄃᆡ 너오월쯤 ᄯᅥᄂᆞᆫ다ᄒᆞ고 군함들도 슌양함 일이쳑외에다 소환ᄒᆞᆫ다더라

로국의졍형 론돈발 이월이십ᄉᆞ일

○파란에셔 쳘로가 불통ᄒᆞ야 덕국과 오디리와 통신이 ᄭᅳᆫ쳣다더라

동디발 동일

○워소에 잇ᄂᆞᆫ 부엔나워소쳘로의 정거장에ᄂᆞᆫ 병정이 파슈ᄒᆞᆫ다더라

동디발 동일

○고가석디방에셔 경보가 셩피독보에 리도ᄒᆞ엿ᄂᆞᆫᄃᆡ 고가석파 셩피독보 ᄉᆞ이에 동신이 불편ᄒᆞ야 자셰ᄒᆞᆫ 소문은 업ᄉᆞ나 풍셜에 젼ᄒᆞᄂᆞᆫ 말은 ᄉᆞ샹이 만히 낫다더라

동디발 동월이십ᄉᆞ일

○워소의 형편은 아직ᄭᆞ지 참혹ᄒᆞ야 로국쳔왕ᄒᆞ나이 암살을 당ᄒᆞ엿ᄂᆞᆫᄃᆡ 그 쳔왕의 죽은 ᄭᆞ닭은 병뎡을 명ᄒᆞ야 혁명당들의게 방총ᄒᆞ라 홈이라ᄒᆞ며 연속ᄒᆞ야 분요가 만연ᄒᆞ야 간다더라

관보

뎨삼쳔칠십팔호 광무구년삼월사일 토료

셔임급사령

○셔대훈사리화대수쟝 쳥국군긔대신총리외무부편의사무 화셕경친왕 혁광

○임평안북도관찰부쥬사 셔관임관륙등 문봉의

○의원면본관 평안북도관찰부쥬사 리지찬

○임평안북도관찰부쥬사 셔관임관륙등 송남현

이상이월이십칠일

○의원면본관 경샹북도관찰부쥬사 뎡경

○임경샹북도관찰부쥬사 셔관임관륙등 한뎡셕

이상이월이십팔일

○임군부참모국쟝셔칙임관사등 헌병사령관륙군참쟝 냥셩환

○임군부교육국쟝셔칙임관사등 륙군참쟝 빅셩긔

○임헌병사령관 륙군참쟝 엄쥰원

○임륙군삼등사계 륙군보병참령 빅웅쥰

○명휴직 진위뎨이련ᄃᆡ뎨이대ᄃᆡ부륙군보병참위 민치완

○면본직 진위뎨일련ᄃᆡ뎨일대ᄃᆡ부륙군보병참위 민병의

○보진위뎨이련ᄃᆡ뎨이대ᄃᆡ부 륙군보병참위 리길용

○명휴직 진위뎨이련ᄃᆡ뎨이대ᄃᆡ쟝륙군보병참령 김원계

○명뇌장원경셔칙임관삼등 종이품 신셔영

○의원면본관 시강원시종관 리희츙 시강원시종관 김진숙

○임시강원시종관셔관임관칠등 태능령 리긔종

○임태능령셔관임관칠등 륙품 홍승범

○임시강원시종관셔관임관칠등 홍릉사승 리갑승

○임홍릉사승셔관임관팔등 홍릉참봉 송돈헌

○임헌릉참봉셔관임관팔등 구품 김진숙

이상삼월일일

○의원면본관 지릉참봉 허민 의효뎐충의 리시용

○임지릉참봉셔관임관팔등 구품 윤종헌

○임의효뎐충의셔관임관팔등 리태슌

임의정부쥬사셔관임관삼등 학부쥬사 리호직

○임의정부쥬사셔관임관륙등 륙품 김덕규 구품 리명훈 김인긔

이상삼월삼일

잡보

○공진부흥 츙쳥북도관찰ᄉᆞ 리승우씨가 니부로 보고ᄒᆞ엿스되 리용괴위명인이 공진회도소를 각군에 셜립ᄒᆞ고 히도지회쟝이되야 각군샹민쳐에 샤통샹무쟝뎡을 수거ᄒᆞ라ᄒᆞ고 도총무김한민이가 고시를 샹민쳐에셔송홈이 샹민들이 만단회의ᄒᆞᄂᆞᆫ지라 차공진회가 임의 스스로 샹무에 관계ᄒᆞ야 각군에셔 방쟝힝회ᄒᆞᆫ다ᄒᆞ오니 차회죠직은 됴령이 업ᄂᆞᆫ고로 자에보고ᄒᆞ오며 그 공함을 거ᄒᆞᆫ즉 ᄒᆞ엿스되 팔역샹민이 소리를 가직히 부르질너 스ᄉᆞ로 단례를 셩ᄒᆞ니 공진샹업회라ᄒᆞ고 목젹은 황실위권의 면범소졍이니 에지ᄒᆞᆫ 조를 존즁ᄒᆞᆯᄉᆞ 졍부명령의 법률규측이니 에지ᄒᆞᆫ 자를 복죵ᄒᆞᆯᄉᆞ 인민위권의 고유범한이니 에득ᄒᆞᆫ 조를 ᄌᆞ유ᄒᆞᆯ소 일심단회ᄒᆞ야 본회소를 각군에 셜립ᄒᆞ고 공함ᄒᆞ니 통량ᄒᆞ라ᄒᆞ엿더라

○디무관계 미국녀인민길년이가 신문외디단을 믿득ᄒᆞ고 히령ᄉᆞ를 경유ᄒᆞ야 관계를 맛기를 원ᄒᆞᄂᆞᆫ고로 한셩부에셔 답복ᄒᆞᆫ니에 현금아국은 아직 실시ᄒᆞᄂᆞᆫ 디계가 업ᄉᆞᆫ즉 가히 쥰시치 못ᄒᆞ겟다ᄒᆞ엿더니 미공ᄉᆞ가 외부로 죠회ᄒᆞ엿스되 본국녀인민길년이가 미득ᄒᆞᆫ 신문외소지디단에 장ᄎᆞ 양옥을 건축ᄒᆞᆯ터인ᄃᆡ 신구문긔를 교환ᄒᆞᆯ스로 우리령ᄉᆞ가 한판으로 교섭ᄒᆞᆫ즉 디단에 관계가 업다칭ᄒᆞ고 거졀ᄒᆞ니 디계ᄉᆞ로 귀부와 외ᄉᆞ간에 임의 교섭을 경ᄒᆞᆫ자이 구ᄒᆞᆫᄃᆡ 관계를 불급홈이 졍명을 위비홈이라 들은즉 귀졍부에셔 외타국인에ᄂᆞᆫ 디계를 방익홈이 업서 발급ᄒᆞ고 홀노 미인의게만 이 불공평ᄒᆞᆫ 구별이 잇ᄉᆞ니 심히 아혹ᄒᆞ며 본대신이 본졍부훈령을 인ᄒᆞ야 귀졍부로 더브러 엄졍히 교섭ᄒᆞ야 차불공평ᄒᆞᆫ 구별과 밋 그다른 슈건을 지명ᄒᆞ라홀터이라ᄒᆞ엿스니 차ᄉᆞ를 사실컨ᄃᆡ 불파시 한관외 허물이니 뎨약쟝뎡을 죠준ᄒᆞ야 판리귀졍홈이 가ᄒᆞ다ᄒᆞ고 외부에셔 한셩부로 훈령ᄒᆞ기를 임의 타국에ᄂᆞᆫ 디계를 무익발급ᄒᆞ고 홀노 미인의게 그지ᄒᆞᄂᆞᆫ거슨 미ᄉᆞ의 아혹을 니르킬ᄲᅮᆫ 아니라 일이 심히 불공ᄒᆞ니 곳 발급ᄒᆞ라ᄒᆞᆫ지라 한판이 외부로 보고ᄒᆞ기를 디계를 발급홈이 본리 젼례가 무ᄒᆞᆫ지라 작년삼월경에 미국인고불안과 밋 도하암과 영국사롬히우의 민득ᄒᆞᆫ 바쳐면에 방옥을 구죠ᄒᆞ고 허명ᄉᆞ를 경유ᄒᆞ야 가계를 죠청ᄒᆞᆫ고로 가계만 밧고야 쥬고 디단문권은 발급지 아니ᄒᆞ엿고 ᄯᅩ 우리인민의 가옥가진ᄃᆡ 인의계 미도홀시에 그 디단 디빙거홀 문권이 업ᄂᆞᆫ지라 가옥소유디단외에 억지로 옹거ᄒᆞ며 넙니 쳠령ᄒᆞ야 민소가 분라ᄒᆞ니 엇지 죠쳐ᄒᆞᆯᄂᆞᆫ지 훈령ᄒᆞ옵소셔ᄒᆞ엿더라

●훈장하사 위문ᄉᆞ 강택시종무관쟝과 존목동궁무관쟝과 밋 히수원일힝이 ᄉᆞ일하오칠셔에 폐현ᄒᆞ엿ᄂᆞᆫᄃᆡ 그ᄯᅢ에 강택셔종무관쟝은 니화대수쟝을 수ᄒᆞ엿고 존목무관쟝은 팔괘쟝일등을 하사ᄒᆞ시고 기타 사명에도 각각 셔훈ᄒᆞ신후에 민형환씨가 히일힝을 손택부인집에셔 연ᄃᆡᄒᆞ엿더라

○민원지임 젼라남도인민등이 니부로 면교ᄒᆞ엿스되 리찬쟝근호씨가 본도관찰을 지임ᄒᆞ기를 원ᄒᆞ야 인퇴수빅명이 청원ᄒᆞ오니 죵민원ᄒᆞ와 뎐폐에 상달ᄒᆞ기를 복망이라ᄒᆞ엿더라

○불가쳔허 연기군수가 니부로 보고ᄒᆞ엿스되 일진회쟝리죵필이가 회원칠인으로 졍부긔션 졍치와 관리탐학과 무명잡셰와 인민의지산보젼등ᄉᆞ로 론렬ᄒᆞ고ᄒᆞ고 경니가호와 남녀인구를 뎍간ᄎᆞ로 민간에 츌ᄒᆞ야 실시코자ᄒᆞ오나 빅셩이 다 불청ᄒᆞ야 셰무니ᄒᆞᆫ훈지라 지회쟝 리졀필파 부회쟝 김현게가 회원이인으로ᄒᆞ야곰 군슈의게 합쳥ᄒᆞ엿스나 부부간 공문이 무ᄒᆞ니 군슈가 쳔편히 허ᄒᆞᆯ수 업ᄂᆞᆫ 뜻으로 답함ᄒᆞ엿ᄂᆞ라

○일진됴사 회덕군슈가 니부로 보고ᄒᆞ엿스되 일진회에서 회원을 파송ᄒᆞ야 호구를 됴사ᄒᆞᆫ다ᄒᆞ기로 군슈가 공함ᄒᆞ야 그ᄉᆞ유를 회에 질문ᄒᆞ엿더니 회쟝리현식 답함니에 싱령을 보호ᄒᆞ고 멸강의 문명을 효방ᄒᆞᄂᆞᆫ 목적인ᄃᆡ 가삼인구를 됴ᄒᆞ랴 선조칙을 봉승ᄒᆞ고 회원을 파송ᄒᆞ야 호구를 됴사ᄒᆞᄂᆞᆫ고로 본군에도 일체로 힝사ᄒᆞᆯ러이라ᄒᆞ오나 조처을 오히려 봉승치 못ᄒᆞ엿ᄂᆞᆫᄃᆡ 호구를 됴사ᄒᆞᄂᆞᆫ것이 심히 아혹ᄒᆞ고 ᄯᅩ 히연ᄒᆞᆫ 기ᄯᅢ 보고ᄒᆞ노라ᄒᆞ다ᄒᆞ엿더라

○니장원실화 시일샹오자시량에 니장원에셔 실화ᄒᆞ야 이간만 소신ᄒᆞ고 다힝히 박멸ᄒᆞ엿더라

○정부회의 사일하오이시에 졍부에셔 회의ᄒᆞ야 각관청주임관의 셔임건을 제의ᄒᆞ엿더라

○합동긔정 즁학교교사고교형의 합동에 삼긔년으로 로긔뎡ᄒᆞ엿ᄂᆞᆫᄃᆡ 허교사의 교빙어만현젼이라도 만일 한편에셔 히약코자ᄒᆞ면 삼긔월젼에 면졈셩명ᄒᆞ고 허약ᄒᆞᄂᆞᆫᄃᆡ 학부에셔 면쳠셩명을 ᄒᆞᆯ경우에ᄂᆞᆫ 히약일ᄭᆞ지 응급ᄒᆞᆯ 월봉과 회국려비를 준발ᄒᆞᆫ외에 삼긔월봉급을 가발ᄒᆞ고 허교사가 면쳠쳥원ᄒᆞ면 다만 본합동의 의무의실힝일ᄭᆞ지 응급ᄒᆞᆯ 봉액과 회국려비만 쥰발ᄒᆞᆯᄉᆞ라ᄒᆞ엿ᄂᆞᆫᄃᆡ 이것은 외부고문관이 긔뎡ᄒᆞ엿다더라

광고

TELEGRAMS.

(FROM JAPAN PAPERS.)

Note. The messages marked* are those which are described as special service" or "special telegrams" or "received by the Government." The others are from properly authenticated sources.

THE WAR.

London, Feb. 27.

Accounts to hand of the fighting in Manchuria are very meagre, and still come exclusively from Russian sources. They indicate, however, that the engagement at Beresneff Hill was the beginning of a great battle, and part of a general movement by the Japanese against the left flank of the Russian army. Beresneff Hill is one of the strongest of several fortified heights of the position at Tsinghocheng, and is situated on the south slope of the Taling range, eighteen miles southwest of Shinking. It bars the way to the passes leading to Fushun, where General Kuropatkin has the centre of his Army.

London, Feb. 26.

The "Times'" correspondent at St. Petersburg states that the transport of troops for the front has been greatly delayed all the winter, and that none of the reinforcements dispatched during December will reach General Kuropatkin before April.

THE NORTH SEA COMMISSION.

London, Feb. 24.

*The "Matin," of Paris, states that the North Sea Commission, in its report, blames Admiral Rohjestvensky for continuing to fire on the trawlers after being signalled, and also for not having at the earliest opportunity notified the British Government of what had occurred.

London, Feb. 26.

***The citizens of Hull are delighted with the verdict given by the North Sea Commission. One of the fishermen, who witnessed from the trawler "Avis" the attack made by the Baltic squadron, states that the decision is a complete victory for the fishermen, "The verdict," he says, "is just and honest. All we wanted was a declaration that the firing by the Baltic Squadron was unjustifiable."**

PEACE RUMOURS.

London, Feb. 25.

*King Edward has denied that he has any knowledge of peace negotiations between Russia and Japan.

Berlin, Feb. 26.

*The Russian representatives abroad have declared that Russia has no intention of suing for peace at present.

AFFAIRS IN RUSSA.

Lonkon, Feb. 22.

It is reported that Prince Andlonnikoff has been stabbed to death at Warsaw.

London, Feb. 24.

A state of anarchy continues to prevail throughout Russia. The railway services from Warsaw and Moscow to Kieff have been suspended.

A general insurrection is now being hatched in the Caucasus.

London, Feb. 25

Communication with the Caucasus has been stopped, but reports to hand suggest that a well-organised Armenian insurrection has taken place and that a provisional insurgent government has been constituted.

Batoum is now held by the insurgents.

In St. Petersburg the strikes have been renewed, and at present forty thousand workmen employed by the Government are out.

London, Feb. 25.

The whole of the Caucasus is now in a state of anarchy.

There appears to be a general strike movement of a semi-revolutionary character, which is being directed by a secret committee in St. Petersburg. Added to this are a number of racial feuds of a ferocious nature, producing horrible atrocities.

Later.

The St. Petersburg Press states that the whole of Eastern Siberia is now in the same state as the Caucasus, and is virtually cut off from communication with Russia.

London, Feb. 27.

The workmen employed on the Siberian railway have struck work and demand the cessation of the war.

Reuter's correspondent at St. Petersburg states that in order to ensure a regular railway service the Russian Government has ordered that all railway men throughout the Empire are to be treated as a soldiers and subjected to martial law.

According to a Reuter's message from Warsaw, every policeman is now accompanied by soldiers as the authorites fear a strike by the police.

London, Feb. 27.

The Tsar has directed that steps be taken with a view to summoning a representative Assembly for the purpose of drafting a Constitution and giving to the people a large measure of representative government.

A meeting of Ministers is now discussing the steps to be taken to give the Tsar's decision a practical form.

GENERAL NEWS.

Berlin, Feb. 24.

The Kaiser has sent to Count von Buelow his bust in marble, together with an autographic letter, in appreciation of the Chancellor's services in negotiating the new Commercial Treaties.

Several German Princes have also sent their congratulations to Count Buelow.

London, Feb. 23.

Mr. Tong Shaoji, the Chinese Commissioner to Thibet, has been appointed Minister in London.

London, Feb. 25.

*Their Majesties King Edward and Queen Alexandra held a Court yesterday at which Viscount Hayashi, Japanese Minister at London, his four secretaries, and Mr. Inagaki were present. Viscount Hayashi has been specially invited by their Majesties to dinner at Buckingham Palace this evening.

Berlin, Feb. 26.

During his forthcoming cruise in the Mediterranean the Kaiser will meet the Kings of Spain, Portugal, and Italy. The interviews will take place respectively at Vigo, Lisbon, and Naples.

Peking Feb. 26.

* M. Lessar, Russian Minister at Peking, alleges that Japanese officers have been employing mounted bandits in Manchuria for the purpose of destroying the railway. He also says that he has received a trustworthy report to the effect that the railway bridge at Kunjurin has been destroyed by bandits. He has asked the Chinese Foreign Department how they reconcile these facts with the Chinese note to the Powers as to neutrality. The Chinese Foreign Department thereupon communicsted with Mr. Uchida, Japanese Miniater at Peking, who at once denied the truth of M. Lessar's statements.

London, Feb. 27.

It is officially announced that the Prince and Princess of Wales will visit India in November.

Shanghai, Feb. 27

* A firm of Chinese merchants agents for the Russian Government, have landed 2,600 tons of British coal at Amoy through the influence of a Russian employed at the Custom house.

SPECIAL NEWS.

The "China Gazette" furnishes its readers with the following selection of *canards* issued during the war and published, as news, by its contemporaries :—

No. 1.—The lie that the flagship of Admiral Rodjestvensky had struck a rock and gone down off Madagascar.

2.—That the Baltic fleet had been ordered home again. That Admiral Rodjestvensky had been recalled.

3.—That General Kuropatkin had resigned.

4.—That he was displaying mental affection and unable to cope with the situation. That he had given way to "General Inertia!"

5.—That he was mad! That he had been superseded by General Grippenberg.

6.—That General Grippenberg had attacked Liaoyang and been defeated and driven back across the Hun River.

7.—That he lost 42,000 men and resigned instauter in order to go home with his entire staff to complain that General Kuropatkin had "left him in the lurch."

8.—That Mistchenko's dashing, rail-road-smashing raid was a ghastly failure, and was repulsed everywhere by the Japanese infantry.

9.—That the Russians were falling back on Tiehling and sending their stores to Harbin, after being terribly routed and driven across both the Shaho and Hun.

10.—That Admirals Togo and Kamimura had started on a westward voyage with their fleets to smash up the Baltic Squadron in the Indian Ocean; that Japanese battleships and heavy cruisers were seen west of Singapore.

11.—That the Dutch had sold one of their East Indian Islands to Russia as a coaling station.

12.—That the Russian cruiser Diana had escaped from Saigon to join the Baltic fleet.

13.—That her ammunition was transferred to the British steamer Tungchow and seized at Hongkong.

14. That the Russian warships at Shanghai were attempting to escape.

15.—That the Russian authorities here would not punish the Askold sailor for the accidental killing of a Chinese which accident our "Mad dog" contemporaries for weeks falsely stigmatised as a savage murder.

16.—That there was a terrible revolution in Russia in which the first act was the killing of over 2,700 people by the Czar's orders in front of his palace in St. Petersburg.

17.—That the revolution had put an end to all chance of Russia carrying on the war. That the revolutionists demanded first of all the stoppage of the war. That the government was everywhere staughtering innocent people.

18.—That the railway and telegraph communication with the Manchurian Army was interrupted, and that the strikes prevented either reinforcements or supplies being sent to Kuropatkin; that the revolution was universal in Russia and Poland.

19.—That the third or supplementary Baltic Squadron would not sail.

20.—That Russia was suing for peace.

21.—That the Czar had fled, his whereabouts being unknown, and that the Empress Dowager and other members of the Russian Imperial family were trying to escape from the pandemonium in St. Petersburg caused by the revolution.

22.—That the Czar had been compelled by the revolutionists to surrender his rights as an absolute monarch and grant a Magna Charta.

23.—That Russia had seized and occupied Kashgar and was getting ready to attack China.

According to a Tokio telegram, the last division of the Baltic Squadron consisting of five Russian warships and three transports passed Prawle Point (southern extremity of England) on the evening of the 26th February.

TELEGRAMS RECEIVED BY THE TOKIO GOVERNMENT.

A Reuter depatch dated Chita, east Baikal, February 25, states :—A strike has broken out at the railway factories at Chita. The principal demand of the strikers is the cessation of the war.

Chita despatches published in the Austrian papers of February 27, state that the employees of the railway works in Chita went on strike from early on the morning of the 26th. The main object of the agitation is to stop the war. A strong force of troops has been ordered to guard the railway against possible destruction by the strikers.

RAILWAY STRIKES.

The ordinary traffic on the principal railways at Moscow, Warsaw, and other provinces has been suspended several days. It is reported, however, that military trains are being despatched.

Reuter's telegram is to the following effect :—

All the claims by the Warsaw-Vienna railway employees having been acceded to, the line was re-opened to traffic on February 25.

The railway traffic between Moscow and Kieff was also restored on February 24.

The "London Times'" St. Petersburg correspondent, wiring on February 25, says :—The necessity for Russia to secure the transportation of re-inforcements to Manchuria has induced her Government to adopt urgent measures in order to check the strikes on the railways. While acquiescing in all the demands of the strikers, the Russian Government has applied martial law to all the railways, with the result that the employees will in future be controlled by the military.

The Osaka Life Insurance Co. has been ordered to wind up its business, which is recognized by the authorities to be dangerous for the policy holders. The company has, according to the "Japan Gazette," been suffering from domestic trouble for some time past.

Arrivals from the North, says the Chefoo Daily News of Feb. 26, report a slow but steady advance of the Russian forces. A Russian officer who was present during the fighting at Heikoutai from January 25th to January 30th estimates the losses of the Russians at about ten to twelve thousand, and those of the Japanese at eighteen thousand men.

We believe it was Dan Leno who said that things are *so* different in Japan. We have lately heard that Mr. Hayashi has been urging the Emperor of Korea to visit Japan and now we learn from the "Japan Chronicle" that Messrs. Senoshita and Ishii, members of the House of Representatives, propose to address a Representation to the Emperor asking that his Majesty's headquarters be removed to Korea. The exchange might be beneficial as we believe there are some Koreans in Japan who need a little attention.

In all haste 10 large hospitals are now being built at Irkutsk, where they will form a central point for accommodating for a time the sick and wounded sent from the front until they can be sent on further: but cases of urgency will be dealt with at Irkutsk. The authorities in charges of the medical district of Moscow have been requested to organise a dozen enormous hospital trains, each consisting of about 30 cars. The first of these trains was sent off from Moscow on Dec. 8, and the last of them was to leave Moscow, on January 23rd, new style.

The Korea Daily News.

Issued at 5 P. M. daily except Sundays.

Rate of Subscription:—
Per Year,............Yen 25.
Per Quarter,..........Yen 7.
Per Month,..........Yen 2.50.

Postage in Korea not charged extra.
Postage abroad charged extra.

Advertisements, 50 sen per day for 1 inch or less.
5 yen per month per inch.
50 yen per year per inch.

All communications to
E. T. BETHELL,
Editor and Publisher,
Pak-tong, Seoul.

PEACE TERMS.

Even under the most favourable circumstances there is always a tendency, when a point is at issue, for the main consideration to be lost sight of among a multitude of pettifogging details.

For instance, with regard to the war, which will probably take a very decided turn within the next fortnight, public opinion has been so influenced by a number of petty events that when the unfounded rumours of impending peace first reached Korea they were at once accepted and taken for granted.

But there are after all, very much more important things than Port Arthur, Liaoyang and Mukden at stake in this war. Russia's prestige is at stake, and the peace of the world is at stake, and there can be no peace between the two nations now fighting until these two issues have been decided.

It the light of the present position it is very easy to see that when, single-handed, Japan undertook to "prick the bubble" of Russia's reputation in the far east, she set herself to achieve the impossible. Among the Mikado's counsellors there are many wise old men and there can be no doubt that it was only a quite unexpected and unprovided for miscarriage of their plans which has placed Japan in its present hopeless position. It is not for us to say what Japan's plans really were, but there can be no doubt that the failure of the many expeditions having for their object the wrecking of the trans—Siberian railway must have been a very great disappointment, and the closeness with which events connected with the disturbances in Russia are followed by the Japanese Government and press indicates that these are, or were, expected to have a very important share in the "pricking of the bubble."

However something has evidently gone wrong, and, under the circumstances, the regularity and resoursefulness of the wet nurses to the Japanese and pro-Japanese press commands unstinted admiration. In default of any recent Japanese victories, or other desirable subjects for discussion, our attention has lately been directed to the question of peace.

Now any two nations may go to war with each other and it is always open to one of them to say when it has had enough, but there are now so many conflicting interests in this small world of ours that when, following upon the war, the redistribution of spoils takes place, the exhausted fighters are by no means allowed to settle it between themselves.

Japan went to war to check Russia's expansion in the Far East. There is nothing to show that any other nation shared this desire. Japan's ally, Great Britain, would, we should think, be inclined to look with a very benign eye upon Russian activities in the far east as every fresh responsibility assumed by Russia out here would tend to lessen the pressure in the direction of India. So far as the other powers are concerned, they probably none of them care very much what the outcome of the war may be. It is a moral certainty that they have all got in their pigeon-holes nice little programmes of commercial or territorial concessions arranged to fit all eventualities.

The point that appears to us to stand absolutely in the way of any peaceful ending to this war favourable to Japan, is the fact that her interests are all her own and that among the foreign powers there is none to share them. Commenting upon the alleged peace terms Japanese jurists and newspapers said with one voice that nothing short of the absolute closing of eastern waters to Russian warships could be acceptable to Japan. This is undoubtedly true. Any peace leaving Russia defeated but with a port in these waters could but be an armistice and it would be only a few years before Russia with her immense resources would be able to reopen hostilities and overwhelm Japan.

Unless, however, Japan can, in the engagement which is now in progress, succeed in cutting off and surrounding the whole of Kuropatkin's army, she can never hope to be in a position to dictate terms of peace and the war can then only be ended in two ways; by intervention or by the defeat of Japan.

Leaving the later contingency out of the question, should intervention take place, Japan can, at the most, only demand the objects for which she avowedly went to war, viz:—the return of Manchuria to China, and the independence and integrity (real, not nominal) of Korea, while Russia will probably secure what has always been her ambition—an ice free port in eastern waters.

RUMOURS OF PEACE.

While we have the earnest desire to see peace re-established as early as possible, says the Eastern World, we can attach but little or no credence to the various rumours and reports as to any propositions emanating from Russia at this stage, as to terms and conditions. For Russia the question is not one of simply pocketing her pride for the nonce, but a question of her position in Asia and Europe. We can simply make a forecast therefore of what, in spite of all, and even if Kuropatkin should be beaten again, her political and geographical position will not permit her to do:—

1—She can not and will not allow herself to be cut off from the sea;

2—She can not and will not allow any dictation as to what she is to or is not to do in Vladivostock;

3—She will under no circumstances pay any indemnity to Japan.

What Russia can and may do, is to give her consent to anything Japan may wish to do in Southern Manchuria, even at some sacrifice, because she has got the worst of it in this war so far.

She may also give Japan in the Liaotung peninsula all that she has to give, that is the unexpired term of her lease.

She may consent to any Japanese claim to suzerainty over Korea with the same good grace as to any Japanese claim on the Diego Rocks, because neither are her own, and, besides, in that question England and America will be heard later.

True, Russian sea power is lost for the time being, and it will be quite a number of years before it will have to be taken in account again (of this we are not quite so positive. Ed. K. D. N.) and Russia may have to retire still further upon her bases of supply, but all that will not end the war, unless such terms as Russia may accept are made. Otherwise there are likely to be repetitions of the present situation on the Shaho until Japan is throughly exhausted, and, with all brave words and Reuterized news on this side, we know how hard the shoe pinches.

THE T. P. D.

The Tokio Asahi has apparently got hold of some hitherto unpublished information about torpedo boat destroyers. It goes into rhapsodies over them. The destroyer, it says, is a parent-excelling child born of the torpedo-gunboat as father and the torpedo-boat as mother, and as a late comer in the field she had no opportunity of showing her worth until the present war, which has proved her wonderful capacities. As the Japanese Government has decided to at once build 30 more of these craft (presumably for defensive purposes) they are evidently useful little boats and beyond this the Asahi probably knows no more than we do although it goes on to say "The great service rendered by our torpedo-boat destroyers in the present war is almost incomparable, the successes attained in robbing the enemy of fully half of his moral and material fighting strength in the very first engagement, in taking the principal part in the work of maintaining the blockade, and in making themselves the ears and eyes, hands and feet of the great fleet, in carrying out the reconnoisances, orderly and intelligence services—all these being placed to their credit."

On the morning of February 19th a foreign steamer just entering the Tokio Bay failed to answer to the signal from the Kwannonsaki Fort, and proceeded even after having been fired on four times with blank cartridges. She was finally stopped and taken to Yokosuka under the escort of two torpedo boats. Examinations ensued and it was transpired that the steamer was the French ship "Caledonien", and the mistake was dne, as is declared by her captain, to her ignorance of the affairs in the East. The steamer was released toward the evening of the same day.

Mr. Nagamori, who has lately got a name in connection with the famous Korean waste land reclamation affair, has again come out with a fresh scheme at Chemulpo, says a Tokio paper. In view of the poor accommodation the local Japanese settlement is affording to the ever increasing emigrants from this country that enterprising gentleman has hit upon the happy idea to reclaim the foreshore of Chemulpo at the expense of the hill of the Japanese public garden, from which he intends to take necessary materials for the work proposed. The Japanese residents, however, object to this arrangement, saying that their common property cannot be sacrificed for an individual gain. Thus Mr. Nagamori's plans are once more brought to nought.

The Korea Daily News.

VOL. II, | MONDAY, MARCH 6, 1905. | No. 50

HONGKONG & SHANGHAI BANKING CORPORATION.

Paid-up Capital	$10,000,000
Reserve Fund:—Sterling Reserve...	10,000,000
Silver Reserve.....	7,000,000
	27,000,000
Reserve Liability of Proprietors...	10,000,000

HEAD OFFICE, HONGKONG.

London Bankers, London and County Banking Company Limited.

Branches and Agencies,

London.

Amoy,	Hankow	Penang,
Bangkok,	Hiogo,	Rangoon,
Batavia,	Iloilo,	Saigon,
Bombay,	Lyons,	San Francisco,
Calcutta,	Manila,	Singapore,
Colombo,	Nagasaki,	Sourabaya,
Foochow,	New York,	Tientsin,
Hamburg,	Peking	Yokohama,

Credits granted on approved Securities, and every description of Banking and Exchange business transacted.

Drafts granted on London and the chief Commercial places in Europe, India, Australia, America, China and Japan.

HOLME RINGER & Co., AGENTS,
CHEMULPO.

HOKURKU DOBOKU KAISHA.

Branch office in Chong Dong, Seoul.

Japanese telephone No. 165

CONTRACT DEPARTMENT.

We can contract to build any building or construction.

MERCHANDISE DEPARTMENT.

We can provide any building material. We have just contracted to build the new Belgian Legation.

E. MEYER & CO.,
Agents,
Chemulpo.

CHARTERED BANK OF INDIA AUSTRALIA & CHINA.

INCORPORATED BY ROYAL CHARTER 1853

HEAD OFFICES.—LONDON.

Paid-up Capital	£800,000
Reserve Liability of Shareholders	800,000
Reserve Fund	800,000

Drafts granted upon all the principal places in the world and every description of Exchange and banking business transacted.

E. MEYER & Co., Agents,
Chemulpo.

MITSU BISHI DOCKYARD & ENGINE WORKS,

NAGASAKI.

CODE WORD, "DOCK."

A 1, A. B. C., and Engineering Codes used,

DOCK No. 1 (at Tategami).

Extreme Length	523 feet
Length on blocks	513 ,,
Width of Entrance on Top	89 ,,
,, ,, Bottom	77 ,,
Water on Blocks at Spring Tide	26½ ,,

DOCK No. 2 (Mukaijima).

Extreme Length	371 feet
Length on Blocks	360 ,,
Width of Entrance on Top	66 ,,
,, ,, Bottom	53 ,,
Water on Blocks at Spring Tide	22 ,,

PATENT SLIP (at Kosuge).

Can take vessels up to 1,000 tons gross.

THE WORKS are well equipped with the LATEST IMPROVEMENTS, and can execute any kind of work in SHIPBUILDING and MARINE ENGINEERING, as well as in REPAIRING of SHIPS.

The COMPANY'S new powerful steamer OURA-MARU (712 tons, 700 I.H.P.), specially built for SALVAGE PURPOSES, and equipped with necessary gear, is always READY at SHORT NOTICE.

THE METHODIST PUBLISHING HOUSE,

Little West Gate, Seoul.

JOB PRINTING, TYPEWRITER PAPER
CARBON PAPER, VISITING CARDS
STATIONERY, BOOK BINDING
BOOK PUBLISHERS
AMERICAN SCHOOL BOOKS
SPENCERIAN COPY BOOKS
PEN CARBON LETTER AND BILL BOOKS

S. A, BECK, Manager.

DAI-ICHI GINKO.

LIMITED.

(Formerly the First National Bank)

ESTABLISHED 1873

INCORPORATED UNDER PRESENT LAW 1896

Capital	Yen 5,000,000
Reserve Fund	1,500,000

HEAD OFFICE:—TOKIO.

President: Baron SHIBUSAWA.

BRANCHES AND CORRESPONDENTS

In the Principal Cities and Towns of Japan.

Interest Allowed on

Fixed deposits 1 year	6½ per cent
" " 6 months	6 per cent

Special current accounts 1½ sen daily per Y 100
General " " 1 " " " 100

M. TANAKA,
Manager, Chemulpo.

SINGER SEWING MACHINES

씽거즈봉침

SOLE AGENTS FOR KOREA

젼매쇼

HOLME RINGER & CO.
Chemulpo.

제물포 함릉거양힝

KAMEYA & CO.

GENERAL STOREKEEPERS

Chinkokai - Seoul

(Established 1895, Tokyo)

Confectionery, Hams, Canned Goods, Cutlery, Hirano & Tansan Water. Provisions, Gents, Furnishing goods, Toilet Articles, Travelling Bags, Tobacco, Cigars & Cigarettes Kitchen Utensils. Coffee, Biscuits

Fresh Goods always kept in Stock.

Prices Moderate.

☞ *Please come and inspect our goods.*

NIPPON YUSEN KAISHA.

JAPANESE MAIL STEAMSHIP CO.

UNDER MAIL CONTRACT WITH THE IMPERIAL JAPANESE GOVERNMENT.

European Line

Regular Fortnightly Service between Yokohama Kobe, Moji, Shanghai, Hongkong, Singapore, Penang Colombo, Port Said, Marseilles, London and Antwerp

American Line

Regular Fortnightly Service between Hongkong and Seattle, calling at Shanghai, Moji, Kobe, Yokohama and Victoria, B. C.

Australian Line

Regular weekly Service betwen Japan Ports and Australia, calling at Hongkong and Manila.

(Above Three Lines Suspended until further notice

Shanghai Line

Weekly Service between Shanghai and Japan Po

Korea Line

Service Kobe, Moji. Nagasaki, Fusan Chemulpo Chefoo, Taku.

S. S. Babelsberg, 2181 tons.

Service Kobe. Moji, Fusan, Chemulpo, Chinnampo

S. S. ARGO, S. S. Ohio.

BORDEN'S CONDENSED MILK CO.

New York, U. S. A.

ALWAYS IN STOCK

Eagle Brand Condensed Milk.

Gold Seal Condensed Milk.

Peerless (Family) Evaporated Cream.

Borden's Malted Milk.

E. MEYER & CO.
Chemulpo Korea,
Sole Agents

ROYAL INSURANCE COMPANY,

Funds exceed £10,000,000

FIRE

AT CURRENT RATES

LIFE

REDUCED PREMIUM,

HOLME RINGER & Co.
Agents, Chemulpo

廣 KWANG ◉ C'HANG 昌

BENNETT & CO.

Merchants

Chemulpo.

Offices opposite the Imperial Japanese Post and Telegraph Office Chemulpo.

Telephone Number 201.

大韓每日申報
대한미일신보

일쳔구빅오년삼월팔일 (일요日) (뎨이권오십일호)

본사고빅

이신보는영어와한어로셕거ᄆᆡ일츌판ᄒᆞᆸ

신문가

ᄒᆞᆫ쟝 엽두돈오푼
일삭료 엽두량닷돈
우표가ᄆᆡ삭닷돈
다맛돈으로밧ᄉᆞᆸ

광고료는

긔한의쟝단과ᄌᆞ힝의다쇼로즁감ᄒᆞ되혐가로밧을터이오며오ᄅᆡ지아녀대한사람마다다이신문을보실터이니광고내시기를원ᄒᆞ시ᄂᆞᆫ이들은우리신문샤에와셔면약ᄒᆞ심을희망ᄒᆞᆸ

○발힝소 박동대한미일신보샤법어학교압혜젼영국인셜필림집자리오

샤쟝 영국인 (빈셜)

평양 디리점

○평양효동사ᄂᆞᆫ권미보씨로우리신문관미디리인을뎡ᄒᆞ엿ᄉᆞ오니평양에계신구람코져ᄒᆞ시는쳠군ᄌᆞᄂᆞᆫ히디리점에왕림ᄒᆞ와면의ᄒᆞ시옵

사고

○우리대한미일신보의목뎍은대한의안녕질셔에관한모든데목에디ᄒᆞ야ᄂᆞᆫ공평한변론을쥬쟝홈이라우리동신원의탐보ᄂᆞᆫ신문보시ᄂᆞᆫ쳠군ᄌᆞ의게흥샹보도ᄒᆞ리며편지를긔셔ᄒᆞ여주시ᄂᆞᆫ이ᄂᆞᆫ셩명과반ᄃᆞ시를젹어붓치시기를희망ᄒᆞ오니이거슬신문샹에긔ᄌᆡᄒᆞ라ᄂᆞᆫ거시아니오다만극히신용ᄒᆞᄂᆞᆫ증거를숨고쟈홈이라긔쟈ᄂᆞᆫ아모긔셔던지긔지홈을되각ᄒᆞᄂᆞᆫ권리를가졋스나되각ᄒᆞᆫ리유를말홀터이오며공즁평화를문란케ᄒᆞᄂᆞᆫ듯ᄒᆞᆫ긔셔ᄂᆞᆫ의례히밧지안켓ᄉᆞᆸ나이다

●본사셜시이ᄅᆡ로신문을미양우례로분젼ᄒᆞ와례젼부의임의로젼ᄒᆞᆫ듯ᄉᆞ로면곳에ᄂᆞᆫ혹늣게젼ᄒᆞ기도ᄒᆞ며혹몃칠거슬ᄒᆞᆫ겁에젼ᄒᆞ기도ᄒᆞ며혹아니젼ᄒᆞᄂᆞᆫ곳도잇다ᄒᆞ와우리신문을ᄉᆞ랑ᄒᆞ야구람ᄒᆞ시ᄂᆞᆫ 쳠군ᄌᆞ의계되ᄒᆞ야미우미안ᄒᆞ옵기로지금은분젼인을두고미일일쥭이젼ᄒᆞ며아니젼ᄒᆞ거나늣게거나ᄒᆞᆫ폐가업도록ᄒᆞ랴ᄒᆞ오니혹아니젼ᄒᆞ거나혹늣게젼ᄒᆞ거나ᄒᆞᆫ일이잇스면본샤로통긔ᄒᆞ여쥬심을희망ᄒᆞᆸ

론셜

북히ᄉᆞ건

○북히ᄉᆞ건을됴사ᄒᆞ랴고파리에뫼인만국회의외됴사ᄒᆞᆫ것이공평ᄒᆞ야이불힝ᄒᆞᆫ날에디ᄒᆞ야편견을가지지아니ᄒᆞᆫᄉᆞᄅᆞᆷ의예료와틀니지아니ᄒᆞ며다ᄉᆞ로국은이샹ᄒᆞᆫ슈뢰졍이어션ᄉᆞ이에잇더라고확실히말ᄒᆞ고영국어부들은그런치아니ᄒᆞ엿다고단언홈으로북히ᄉᆞ건됴사위원회에셔그ᄉᆞ건을질졍ᄒᆞ거룰ᄉᆞ양ᄒᆞᄂᆞᆫ것이피이치아니ᄒᆞ나그러ᄒᆞ나그회에셔결졍ᄒᆞ기룰로국히군대쟝로졔스트벤스기씨가쟈긔의위험홈을졍당히밋고그리ᄒᆞ엿스리라고ᄒᆞ엿스니그것이그회에셔로국히군대쟝이쟈긔의훈닐의분명ᄒᆞᆫ리유가잇ᄂᆞᆫᄉᆞ실을본것이로다그회에셔로졔스트벤스기대쟝의방포ᄒᆞᆫ것이젹당ᄒᆞᆫ가아니ᄒᆞᆫ가ᄒᆞᄂᆞᆫ문뎨룰젼일히강구ᄒᆞᄂᆞᆫ디그것은결졍ᄒᆞ기룰로졔스트벤스기대쟝이영국바다에일본군함의드러오ᄂᆞᆫ것을허락ᄒᆞᄂᆞᆫ지아니ᄒᆞᄂᆞᆫ지싱각ᄒᆞᄂᆞᆫ의견을밋쳐못ᄒᆞ엿다ᄒᆞ엿더라그회에셔결졍ᄒᆞᆫ디ᄒᆞ야영국신문지들의분로홈은의례건ᄉᆞ이오그ᄉᆞ건의쳐음니러날ᄯᆡ에젼쟁을이르키기룰츙동ᄒᆞ던신문지들이경동ᄒᆞ고락망ᄒᆞ며그회에셔됴사ᄒᆞᆫ것이로국의외교샹승젼이라ᄒᆞ고ᄒᆞᄂᆞᆫ것이피이치아니ᄒᆞᆫ도다그회의됴사결졍ᄒᆞᆫ말을ᄒᆞᆫ엿스니그회의쟈셰ᄒᆞᆫ이야기와그ᄉᆞ건을결졍ᄒᆞ기젼에긴요ᄒᆞᆫᄉᆞ단을말ᄒᆞᄂᆞᆫ것이불만홀지라그회에참예ᄒᆞᆫ위원들은법국히군대쟝푸루녀와영국히군대쟝부몬드와미국히군대쟝대비쓰와오지리히군대쟝스파운과로국히군대쟝가쓰나고푸졔씨인대푸루녀대쟝이위원쟝이되엿더라

영국의고소쟝은이아리와갓ᄒᆞ니

그ᄉᆞ건의이러나던밤에영국어션들의잇ᄂᆞᆫ근쳐에로국합디외에ᄂᆞᆫ아모다른군함은업셧스며

그어션들이그ᄯᆡ에오리젼에도군함들은보지못ᄒᆞ엿스며

그어션들즁에군물은가진비가업셧스며

그ᄯᆡ에일본군함의엇던종류던지북히안에업셧스며

그어션들안에엇던일본ᄉᆞᄅᆞᆷ이던지잇지아니ᄒᆞ엿스며

로국군함에셔담히등으로그비들이평안무ᄉᆞᄒᆞᆫ어션들인것을분명히안후에도방포ᄒᆞ기를연속ᄒᆞ엿스며

로국비들이ᄒᆞᆫ나도어션들을구원ᄒᆞ지아니ᄒᆞ엿스며

로국군함의포화로두ᄉᆞᄅᆞᆷ이죽고여셧ᄉᆞᄅᆞᆷ이샹ᄒᆞ고비일쳑이침몰ᄒᆞ고오쳑이파샹ᄒᆞ엿다ᄒᆞ엿스니

이말은로국군함이아모죡로얼도업시평안무사ᄒᆞᆫ어션이져의들의직업홈을안ᄒᆞᄂᆞᆫ것에디ᄒᆞ야방포ᄒᆞ엿다홈이라

거긔디ᄒᆞ야로국의셜명셔ᄂᆞᆫ이아리와ᄀᆞᆺᄒᆞ니

슈샹ᄒᆞᆫ비이쳑이로국군함에담히등의빗치ᄂᆞᆫ디경안에온세함에되졍인줄아러보고그젼두함은방포ᄒᆞ기를시작ᄒᆞ엿고그후에불도식원치아니ᄒᆞᆫ젹은어션들을보고예비ᄒᆞ야죠셩ᄒᆞᆫ엿스나젼투합들의위험ᄒᆞᆫ렴려가대단ᄒᆞ고슈뢰졍의공격에디ᄒᆞ야위엄잇게보호ᄒᆞ랴고방포ᄒᆞ기를연속ᄒᆞ야홈빗게홈슈업게되야셔그어션들에만포환이맛질ᄲᅮᆫ아니라그포환에밋칠만ᄒᆞᆫ거리에도착ᄒᆞᄂᆞᆫ쟈긔합디에ᄯᅡᆯ닌비들에도ᄯᅩᄒᆞᆫ맛졋고그동안에그슈뢰졍이쳑은물너가더니잠간뒤에보이지아니ᄒᆞ고어션을이더러파샹ᄒᆞ엿슬가렴려ᄒᆞ엿지마ᄂᆞᆫ그슈뢰졍이쳑이나혹다른것들의위험ᄒᆞᆫ것이패히업셔지지아니ᄒᆞᆫ줄노싱각ᄒᆞ야로졔스트벤스기대쟝이부독이ᄒᆞ야그합디를졍지ᄒᆞ지아니ᄒᆞ고항힝ᄒᆞ기를연속ᄒᆞ엿고로졔스트벤스기대쟝이즁립국에ᄯᅡᆯ닌무히ᄒᆞᆫ어부들의게손히놀나게ᄒᆞᆫ것을싱각ᄒᆞ엿지마ᄂᆞᆫ쟈긔의함디를업슴ᄒᆞᄂᆞᆫ슈뢰졍을파멸ᄒᆞ라고쟈긔의권력디로ᄂᆞᆫ다ᄒᆞ야ᄒᆞ게되엿다ᄒᆞ엿더라

관보

뎨삼쳔칠십구호 광무구년삼월륙일

서임급ᄉᆞ령

○임농샹공부대신셔칙임관일등 법부대신 박제슌
○임법부대신셔칙임관일등 륙군부쟝 리지용
이샹삼월이일
○승셔판임관오등 한셩우체지ᄉᆞ쥬ᄉᆞ 윤회찬
이월십팔일
○승셔판임관ᄉᆞ등 졍쥬우체ᄉᆞ쥬ᄉᆞ 김대경
이샹이월이십이일
○승셔판임관오등 한셩면보ᄉᆞ쥬ᄉᆞ 리봉승
이월이십사일
○히임시셔리참모부총쟝ᄉᆞ무 군부대신륙군부쟝 권즁현
○히셔리교육부총감ᄉᆞ무 군부협판륙군참쟝 엄쥬익
이샹이월이십팔일
○의원면본관 [illegible] 군부쥬ᄉᆞ 신태히
삼월이일
○임군부쥬ᄉᆞ셔판임관륙등 신태즁
○의원면본관 [illegible] 함경남도관찰부총슌 신궁우
○임함경남도관찰부총슌셔판임관칠등 즁청북도관찰부총슌 리근비
○임츙청북도관찰부총슌셔판임관륙등 륙품 신궁우
○면본관 옥구면보ᄉᆞ쥬사 송지헌
○임옥구면보ᄉᆞ쥬ᄉᆞ셔판임관륙등 김희면
이샹삼월삼일
○승종일품 륙군부쟝 민영철
○승졍헌 겸임비셔원경 리재극
○승졍헌 겸임쟝례원경 됴명구
○승졍헌 시강원쳠사 윤헌
○승종이품 시종원시종 리봉로
○승졍삼품 홍문관셔독 뎡용목
○승졍삼품 홍문관시독 안틱진
○승졍삼품 홍문관시독 빅의힝
○승졍삼품 겸시종 됴홍군
○승졍삼품 륙군졍위 셔졍우
○승졍삼품 륙군졍위 빅남혁
○승졍삼품 륙군부위 김종현
○승졍삼품 륙군참위 권린슈
○승졍삼품 륙군참위 리셕응

UNION INSURANCE SOCIETY OF CANTON.

Head office Hongkong.
Marine risks underwritten at current rates.
Agents in Chemulpo,
E. MEYER & Co.

COMPAGNIE DES MESSAGERIES MARITIMES.

Fortnightly Direct Service.

For Marseilles
via Ports.
Sailing from Yokohama
Calling at Kobe,
Shanghai, Hongkong, Saigon, Singapore,
Colombo, Djibonti, Suez, Port Said
and Marseilles

For particulars apply to
HOLME RINGER & Co.,
Chemulpo.

HAYASHIDA & CO.,

16 MYENG DONG, CHIN KO KAI, SEOUL.
BRANCH OFFICE AT CHEMULPO.

Money changers, Coal and Wood Merchants, Express Agents.

We are agents for the Pyeng-yang Coal Company and the Karazu Coal Company of Japan. We have the best quality of both anthracite and bituminous coal, and prompt execution of orders is our speciality. Firewood of all kinds kept in stock. Full weight guaranteed. Money of all denominations exchanged at current rates. Parcels received for all parts.

CHINA MUTUAL LIFE INS. CO.

Most favourable terms to policy holders.

Benefit system unsurpassed.

HOLME RINGER & Co.
Agents, Chemulpo.

C. P. R.

CANADIAN PACIFIC RAILWAY COMPANY'S ROYAL MAIL STEAMSHIP LINE.

THE FAST ROUTE BETWEEN CHINA, JAPAN, AND EUROPE VIA CANADA AND THE UNITED STATES.

Route from Hongkong via Shanghai, Nagasaki (Inland Sea of Japan) Kobe, Yokohama, Victoria and Vancouver.

Twin Screw Empress Steamship—6,000 Tons—Speed 19 knots.

PROPOSED SAILING FROM YOKOHAMA.
R. M. S. Empress of India.
R. M. S. Empress of Japan.
R. M. S. Empress of China.
R. M. S. Athenian.
R. M. S. Tartar.

Special reduction (first class only) granted to members of the Military, Naval, Diplomatic and Civil services and to Missionaries.

Passengers have choice of ten routes across the Continent of America and have privilege of travelling by any Atlantic Steamship Line.

Round the World passage tickets in connection with the P. and O. S. N., North German Lloyd and Messageries Co.'s **£125.**

All rates payable at current rate of exchange.

For further information, Tickets, Guide Books, etc., apply to

HOLME, RINGER & CO., AGENTS,
Chemulpo.

Grand Hotel

(Formerly the Station Hotel)

Near the Railway Terminus,
West Gate Seoul

The Best Hotel in Korea.
Handsome new Building
Fine Airy Rooms.
Excellent Cuisine.
Terms Moderate.
Special terms to Missionaries
and to permanent boarders.

Electric cars within 2 minutes' walk.

W. H. EMBERLEY.

Proprietor

EVERY FACILITY.

In connection with Life Assurance Business is afforded by

The Standard Life Assurance Co.,

One of the largest and wealthiest of the Provident Institutions of the United Kingdom Forms of Application and all information wil be promptly afforded on application.

10 CENTS A DAY.

Not a very large expenditure is it? But it is sufficient to secure for a man of 30 a policy with the STANDARD LIFE OFFICE for

$1323.

For all particulars of rates, etc., apply to

Holme, Ringer & Co.,
Agents, Chemulpo.

THE NEW YORK LIFE INSURANCE COMPANY.

Have you ever been declined by any Company?

Are you engaged in a specially hazardous occupation?

Have you heard of the New York Life Insurance Company's New Classifications for this class of Risks?

If not, send your date of birth, occupation and particulars of rejection, if any to

E. MEYER & Co.,
Agents, Chemulpo.

MITSUI BUSSAN KAISHA.
(MITSUI & Co.)

MITSUI GINKO.
(MITSUI BANK.)

The Bank is owned by the members of the Mitsui Family, who, as partners, assume an unlimited responsibility for all liabilities of the Bank:—

Capital........................Yen 5,000,000
Reserve Fund.................. " 5,600,000

HEAD OFFICE, TOKYO.
LONDON OFFICE, 34 LIME ST., E. C.

BRANCHES AND AGENCIES:—
New York, San Francisco, Hamburg, Bombay, Singapore, Manila, Hongkong, Amoy Chefoo, Tientsin.
Kobe, Hakodate, Yokohama, Kure, Yokosuka, Moji, Shimonoseki, Miike, Wakamatsu Nagasaki, Kuchinotsu, Karatsu, Sasebo, Misume, Taipeh, &c.

Telegraphic Address for all the Offices:
"MITSUI."
A. B. C. AND A. 1 CODES USED.

Contractors of Coal
To the Imperial Japanese Navy. Arsena and Railway Bureau, Principal Railway Companies and Industrial Work, Home and Foreign Mail and Freight Steamers.

Sole Proprietors
Of the famous Miike, Tagawa and Yamano Coal Mines.

Sole Agents
For the sale of Fukumo, Hokoku, Ichimura Kanoda, Mannoura, Onoura, Ostuji, Sonoda Tsubaruro, Yoshinotani, Yoshio, Yurokibura and other coals.

YANGTSE INSURANCE ASSOCIATION, LTD.

The undersigned, having been appointed agents for the above company, are prepared to issue policies and pay losses on marine risks at regular rates.

E. MEYER & Co.,
Agents, Chemulpo.

AMERICAN KOREAN ELECTRIC CO.

Light and Power.

Main. Office: Electric Building, Chong No.

RAILWAY DEPARTMENT.

OPERATING CARS BETWEEN EAST AND WEST GATE, EVERY TEN MINUTES:—

First Car leaves East Gate at 6:30 A. M. First Car leaves R. R. Station at 6:55 A.M
Last Car " East Gate at 9.50 P. M. Last " " R. R. Station at 10.75 P.M

OPERATING CARS BETWEEN EAST GATE AND IMPERIAL TOMB TERMINUS, EVERY TWENTY MINUTES:—
CONNECTING WITH EVERY ALTERNATE CAR ARRIVING AT EAST GATE FROM CHONG NO.

First Car leaves East Gate for Tomb at 6:50 A. M.
" " " Tomb for East Gate at 7:10 A. M.
Last " " East Gate for Tomb at 7:50 P. M.
" " " Tomb for East Gate at 8:10 P. M.

OPERATING CARS BETWEEN CHONG NO AND YUNG SAN RIVER EVERY TWELVE MINUTES:—

First Car leaves Chong No for South Gate at 6:48 A. M.
" " " Chong No for Yung San at 7:24 A. M.
" " " South Gate for Chong No at 6:56 A. M.
" " " Yung San for Chong No at 7:57 A. M.
Last " " South Gate for Chong No 10:08 P. M.
" " " Yung San for Chong No at 9.09 P. M.

SPECIAL PRIVATE CARS FURNISHED TO SUIT CONVENIENCE OF PATRONS. PRICES ON APPLICATION AT HEAD OFFICE.

LIGHTING DEPARTMENT.

Where less than 250 candle power of light is used, the rate per month will be
Per 16 candle power incandescent lamp,—All night.—Yen 2.50.
32 candle power incandescent lamp,—All night:—Yen 4.00.
50 candle power incandescent lamp,—All night:—Yen 6.00.
150 " " " " " " " 10.00.
1200 " " enclosed arc " " " " 20.00.

Where more than 250 candle power of light is used, a Meter will be installed, if requested:—Rent of Meter, Yen 2.00 per month. Rate of charges by meter reading:—Two Sen per Ampere per hour. (Approximately this is equal to about One Sen per 16 C. P. lamp per hour) Minimum monthly charge where meter is installed Yen 20.00 per month, which includes rental of meter.

Estimates for installing lights furnished on application
An assortment of chandeliers always on hand.

K. Murakami.

Photograph Studio
Chinkokai, Seoul.

Printing, Developing and Enlargement, of Photographs always Undertaken.

Korean Views and Pictures Illustrating Native Customs always on Sale.

THE OSAKA SHOSEN KAISHA.

Boats frequently on the berth for Chinnampo

REGULAR SAILINGS BETWEEN JAPAN AND KOREAN PORTS.

FUSAN AND KOBE VIA SHIMONOSEKI.

OSAKA VIA MOKPO, FUSAN, SHIMONOSEKI AND KOBE.

MOJI DIRECT.

OSAKA VIA KUNSAN, MASANPO, FUSAN, SHIMONOSEKI AND KOBE.

CHEMULPO KUNSAN LINE,
Every three days.

CHEMULPO CHINNAMPO LINE.
Every three days.

For Freight and passage and further particulars apply to

THE OSAKA SHOSEN KAISHA,
Chemulpo.

RONDON, PLAISANT & CO.

General Storekeepers and Merchants, Ships Contractors Tobacconists, Commission and Forwarding Agents, Coal Merchants

IMPORTERS AND EXPORTERS

Seoul Chemulpo.

W. D. WENTWORTH

LANDING
AND
SHIPPING AGENT
AND
CUSTOMS BROKER.

12 OURA, NAGASAKI.

STEWARD & CO.

Chemulpo.

Shipchandlers and Storekeepers, Naval and Mercantile Contractors, Landing and Shipping Agents.

STEWARD'S HOTEL

Chemulpo.

Best accommodation in the port for travellers. Clean and well-aired rooms, good cuisine and prompt attendance, moderate tariff.

○승졍삼품 륙군참위 리준셥
○승졍삼품 륙군참위 박운쳔
○승셔주임관삼등 경위원경무관 류영렬
○승셔주임관삼등 경위원경무관 김윤영
○승셔판임관칠등 리규면참봉 황 엽
이샹광무칠년십이월십일
○승종이품 비서원승 권영수
광무팔년십이월십륙일
○승가외 경운군 리졔셩
○승종이품 졍삼품 리졍렬
이샹이월십팔일
○승종일품 졍이품 리헌영
○승가외 봉샹사제조 리재덕
○승졍삼품 륙품 됴한수
○승졍삼품 젼주사 리빈응
○승졍삼품 륙품 리 졔
○승졍삼품 륙품 리용호
○승졍삼품 륙품 리헌완
○승셔판임관이등 궁내부주사 빅만흥
이샹이월이십삼일

잡보

○졍츅명계 샹화감리가외부로보고ᄒ엿스되본항을기셜ᄒᆫ이뤼로아직조계를획졍치못ᄒ야외국인의게류디가빈다시졍리의폐가잇슬터이니사면셩리를졍계ᄒᆯ의로도사ᄒ야샹송ᄒ오니바라컨티쳐판ᄒ라ᄒ엿더라

○권졈셔임 리졍훈관계등일뢰반포ᄒᆫ고로방부주관임관을권졈으로감히ᄒ논티일졈도무ᄒᆫᄎ논주임관중에리과중이오칙임관중에논엄총장의셩질리승연과쳥관리용복의권수인티졍ᄎ례례ᄒᆫ다더라

○경찰사직 경샹남도관찰ᄉ신귀션씨가제작일사직소를샹ᄒ엿더라

○단회화충 향ᄌ에신셜립ᄒᆫ범학교에셔논무슴분힝ᄒᆫᄉ고가잇논지교감과수연씨가쳥원ᄒ엿고강사면사룸도ᄯᅩᄒᆫ쳥원블침ᄒ논고로지작야에제원이단회ᄒ야화충관리ᄒ엿다더라

○시불가실 내부소관광제원의사및주ᄉ를졍ᄎ퇴ᄎ고자ᄒ논티의학교졸업ᄉᆡᆼ들의만이우리논졸업ᄉᆡᆼ인티라힌은다시거우본말나ᄒ고내부주ᄉ도산ᄒᆫ퇴ᄎᄒ논중인티분경이넘지안논날이업논티됴내미의말이우리졍셕구를이러버에구치치못ᄒ면언제쓸야ᄒ더라

○군대왕참 작일은음력이월일일경칭인고로각신사계졔ᄒ엿논티관대도졔항에논군대권중졍씨가ᄎ쳔관으로왕참ᄒ엿더라

○의능실확 약핍샹휜ᄉ잉빔공에의능에서실화ᄒ엿논티농샹엿고히낭대신이젼왕ᄒ야봉ᄒ샹부로론ᄒ야픔조를중관ᄒ라ᄒ셧더라

○조칭금지 인셕부졔양인본의졈마다에동중아히등이돈을봉져사가다작란ᄒ야구싱ᄒ지를회ᄒ야금지ᄒ노인ᄒ엿다ᄒ니외부조미최ᄒ야금지ᄒ라ᄒ엿더라

○차항부폐 향셜에가니기를궁ᄒ녀의관가티폐지ᄒ고류디티기항의관폐지ᄒ고가쟝ᄒ녀부의리차를에관자원은탕명ᄒᆫ쟝쓰지못ᄒ게하ᄒ고하엿다더라

○면편기통 경셩파셔운사이덕에라보가쟉일보터가증이되엿다더라

○불긔자잉임 일쟉룩일에경부쳥에셔회의ᄒ얏논티각부원들이칙임관셔명ᄒ야불잉임ᄒᆫ졔로닛ᄒᆫ지아니ᄒ노니부훈령ᄒ엿더라

○도로조졍 셔관으로브터조졍의면셜을거ᄒ고우ᄒ도로황평ᄒ라ᄒᆫ고로평쟉에셔면케ᄒ엿다더라

●사딕쳔죵 내부에셔리귀ᄒᆫ씨는외주사신임ᄒ고로봉은로져방ᄒ엿다더라

○분수쇼화 동일밤구시량에남문밧이문의수칭에셔실화ᄒ야초가두어간을쇼화ᄒ엿다더라

○승가변쳔 쟝셔우권씨논분뎡으로빌어가져참셔논쳥관리를횡폐ᄒ엿다더라

○비교무위 학부에서각학교의쳐분을무시ᄒ고ᄒ엿더라

○도쥬관임 ᄌ식귀외쟈의단속을보라ᄒ더라

○표목국수팀 남셔문지미의리홍이용홈으로빌오기를수팀ᄒ엿더라

○함경남도관찰사 ᄌ신○작회의의 ᄌ씨가소를샹ᄒ엿더라

○부논견논 즁졍회의부ᄀ와관ᄒ엿더라

○쥬관면원 셜졍리

○빅관잉참 일쟉룩일에빅관이참ᄒ엿논티효면사제와ᄃᆡ신료병세씨가진참ᄒ엿더라

○문사힝공 경무ᄉ신태휴씨가일쟉사지사진ᄒ야경무쳥을브터ᄉᆞᆷ은사진ᄒ엿더라

○거간중치 경무ᄉ신태휴씨가샹조상힝화를셜시ᄒ기위ᄒ야가생을봉치ᄒ고후에ᄂᆞᆷ을시힝ᄒ야무ᄉ가쇼계ᄒᆫ다ᄒ엿더니그제무ᄉ가쇼계ᄒᆫ다ᄒᆫ듯이종로잡ᄒᆫ사ᄅᆞᆷ들이ᄃᆞ시ᄂᆞᆫ지라경무쳥에셔혀과다이ᄒᆫ녀스평이만ᄒ엿더라

○학대샹소 학부대신리재극씨가사직쇼를샹ᄒ엿더라

○하게향폐 젼관셔기종한씨는대쇼가를합ᄒ야츈원향폐ᄒ엿더라

○우착기례 동셔등닉면당포ᄒ눈한식의게젼승지리시계진씨가면향이십ᄀᆡ를오빅량에젼당ᄒ엿더니고면ᄒᆫ라ᄒ고ᄌᆞ젼ᄒ엿더라

○의졍과쳥 ᄒ엿더라

○일졔창셕 일본공ᄉ가외부로조회ᄒ엿스되영미랑공ᄉ를되동ᄒ야폐현코자ᄒ오니쳥귄티부에당국대신을요ᄒᆫ다ᄒ고뎐졔참셕ᄒ기를요ᄒ노라ᄒ엿더라

○윤민호소 평양거윤귀쳥이가외부로소장ᄒ니에평양감리셔젼쥬ᄉ원용덕의불법힝위논인롬ᄒᆫ것이엄ᄒ니와넌젼미쳥인녑셔무가분인데란무가분을경텽ᄒ고로분인이거간에하하ᄒ기를쳥ᄒ논고로부인이ᄀᆞ분을경텽ᄒ엿더니가로감리셔에뎡토ᄒ야쳥국평수의게교셥ᄒ야ᄌ금하여무금ᄒ엿스나셔장ᄒᆫ쳥원ᄒ엿더니ᄌᆞ쇼평안감리가쟝셩ᄒ야용덕의기를쳥원ᄒ엿다ᄒ고류ᄒ야주기를거ᄒ고ᄎᆞᄒ야율ᄒᆫ다ᄒ엿더라

○사안구엽 셔쳔군동당진에사ᄒᆞ는김셩일이가외부로쳥원ᄒ엿ᄂᆞᆫ티본면에ᄯᅥ러진지논문빅넌향을거하ᄒ고이왓셔유리하여ᄒ엿더니본의ᄒ야ᄒ얏구ᄒᆞᆫ다ᄒ엿더라

에거ᄒᆞ논일인이그리잇을별보교억지로졈탈ᄒ고자ᄒ오니셰샹에엇지이런무리의수가잇소오핏가증ᄒᆞᆫ감리의게엄칙ᄒ시와일인의횡탈ᄒᆞ논폐를환쳥ᄒ시고젼민으로ᄒ여금구업에안케ᄒ샤심을복망이라ᄒ엿더라

외보

삼월사일오젼중사관차

○병기경토 홍경방면에셔우리일본부티에티시ᄒᆫ뎍은젹ᄎ중가ᄒ논모양이잇고모계호방면에우리부티논뢰평동방고디금쟝구부근에뎍군더를탈취ᄒ엿고샤하방면에논왜두산부근젼면의뎍은소티로야숨을시힝ᄒ엿고혼하좌안의뎍은침도보부근으로브터혼하에날ᄒ엿논디변에티ᄒ야대역습을힝ᄒ엿스논다격퇴ᄒ엿고장란궁사방디의뎍은ᄯᅩ격퇴ᄒ엿다더라

뎐보

동디발 동월이십일일

○로국신문과대공암살 로국에유명ᄒᆫ신문지들은다셰계쌍대공을암살ᄒᆫ자를칭망ᄒ엿스나ᄒᆫ편으로논말ᄒ되경부에셔맛당히긔광을숙칭ᄒ야졍병운동에앙샹ᄒ논힝위가만연ᄒ지아니ᄒ게ᄒ라ᄒ엿다더라

동디발 동월이십일일

○영국의일본을모방ᄒ논일 론돈경무쳥에셔일본경찰법을 번력모방ᄒᆫ다더라

광고

본사광고

○본사신문쳡을미양초샹에쳠밧기로ᄒᆫ거순이동ᄒ시논쳠군ᄌ들도아시거니와왕왕히금음이지나도록보지안논곳시만ᄒ거니와분명ᄒ셧논지아지못ᄒ오니아모됴록신속히보니주시오며신문쳡을보니지안논곳순자금이후로신문을ᄯᅩ보니지안켓사오니이동ᄒ시논쳠군ᄌ들은더욱본신문을수탐ᄒ셔으로티금을슈히보니시기를ᄇᆞ라옴니다

본인이미국으로셔일본에와연습ᄒ고대한경셩에와쟝시류ᄒ면셔병인들을보기원ᄒ논이다니시구멍에금과류회로베이기도ᄒ오며ᄶᅢ진니셰미에셰니도박되엽ᄂᆞ지안케곳칠터미오니쳠군ᄌ논조량ᄒ시옵쇼셔
수무소논셰문밧졍거쟝위이층양옥엽분니리관이오

셔울우션회사
숙힝ᄒ논이듣은션들인티
쳥국과일본셔영국과각국으로
왕리홍
긴법봄등가 [illegible] 리졍

TELEGRAMS.

(FROM JAPAN PAPERS.)

Note. The messages marked* are those which are described as "special service" or "special telegrams" or "received by the Government." The others are from properly authenticated sources.

A FOURTH SQUADRON.

London, Feb. 27.

*A fourth Baltic Squadron is now taking in its armament at Cronstad. It includes two battleships, six cruisers, and four destroyers,

THE PEACE REPORTS.

London, Feb. 25.

*A rumour that the King of Great Britain if endeavouring to bring about peace is contradicted.

MARTIAL LAW ON RUSSIAN RAILWAYS.

Berlin, Feb. 27.

*Prince Kilkoff, Minister of the Russian Communication Department, has proclaimed martial law along all the Russian railways.

ENGLISH POLITICS.

London, Feb. 22.

Mr. Redmond's amendment to the Address has been rejected by 286 votes to 236.

In the course of the debate, Sir H. Campbell-Bannerman said he still continued to support the policy of a thorough fundamental alteration in the whole system of Irish government.

THE HUNGARIAN CRISIS.

London, Feb. 14.

The Emperor of Austria has had an interview with Kossuth, at Vienna, in connection with the Hungarian crisis. It is a notable historical event, being Kossuth's first entrance into the Palace to pay homage to the Emperor who condemned to death Kossuth's father.

IMMENSE LOSS OF COTTON.

London, Feb. 27.

*There has been a great fire at New Orleans, U. S. A. Immense quantities of cotton were destroyed, the total damage being estimated at a million sterling.

THE WAR

The "Speaker" is of opinion that the battle now raging on the Shaho will mark the beginning of the end of the war.

In a recent issue it says:—

If between this and May the Russians can win a first-class action against their opponents in the neighbourhood of Moukden they will from that time onwards slightly retrieve the fortunes of the campaign. If they lose such a first class action they will not be able to win either this or any future campaign. It is true that a decisive success at sea would put them right at once, and it is equally true that such a decisive success is extremely unlikely, but it must not be argued that because a decisive success at sea would put the Russian straight at once, the lack of it would prevent their ever getting straight. If Orloff's Brigade had not broken at Liaoyang, in spite of the Russian inferiority in artillery, the Japanese would have been smashed, and the process of smashing after one big battle like that would have been very rapid. Similarly if the Japanese had first success on the Shaho, the Russian organization would have gone to pieces and we should have seen the end of the war. If in a third venture either seriously scores, command of the sea or no command of the sea, the party that scores will win, and that rapidly."

JAPANESE AT HANKOW.

The Japanese population at Hankow at present is more than 450, about four times larger than at the beginning of the war. The number of Japanese firms established there is 37.

PROSPECTS OF PEACE.

"In the face of the extravagant estimate placed by public opinion upon the fall of Port Arthur we are almost inclined to apply to it Talleyand's dictum on the death of Napoleon, 'it is no longer an event, it is only a piece of news.' Of course, it is very much more than this as affecting the Asiatic position of Russia, but in the conduct of war in can hardly be much more than an incident and an incident that probably has been long discounted. . . . Russia has never fought for glory but always for some solid and substantial advantage of polity; and she has never had any hesitation in postponing the acquisition of what she desired to a more convenient season if external preasure was too strong for the moment. . . . This being the history of Russian wars, it is little short of incredible that the idea of peace following the loss of Port Arthur should have appeared probable to so many worthy folk. Of course in reality peace is a diminishing probability since that event. . . . Exactly similar reasons to those which forbade England to abandon South Africa without a life-and-death struggle forbid Russia to abandon this war after a defeat which does not paralyse her powers of resistance. The fall of Port Arthur will not be placed in that category of phenomena even by the most sanguine partisans.—Saturday Review.

THE ACCIDENT TO A FRENCH WARSHIP.

Some further details of the stranding of the French armoured cruiser Sully in the Bay of Hailong, are given by "Le Courier de Haiphong." It appears that the Sully was returning from torpedo practice, and was in the course of some evolutions, and not following correctly the usual channel. She struck on a peak, where the chart, dated February 18, 1889, shows a depth of 17 metres. The Sully has turned with her head to the south. Her actual situation suggests that she has ripped open about thirty metres of her plates below, caused by the sudden shock and impetus when striking the peak. It seems an impossibility to turn her round without the possibility of a catastrophe. On the evening of the 10th the Sully had plunged about four degree. Her stability is questionable. On account of her unfavourable position the small arms and guns are being taken off. It is, however, impossible to remove the guns in the turrets and casemates, which necessitate the use of powerful appliances. Admiral Bayle was to be in the Bay of Hailong on Sunday following, 12th February, and would adopt the best measures for saving the Sully, but it appears impossible to save the ship, as the French have apparently not the necessary appliances to effect the salvage of the cruiser. Mr. Jamieson, the well-known salvage expert, has left for Hongay to inspect the Sully and to see if he can save her.

RUSSIAN OFFICIALS.

Ask any man not in official life what he thinks of the Russian bureaucrary, says a writer in the "Washington Post." He will denounce it for its ignorance, its sloth, its redtapeism, and for the effect he will point to the war. Ask him again if it is corrupt.

"The rouble," he will sententiously answer. "will open any office."

But, extensive as is this venality, it does not compare with what it was. There are more refined ways in the bureaucracy to receive compensation for services rendered than by mere gratuities. Yet it must not be believed that all are corrupt. Hundreds of officials are as straightforward, as honest as British or American officials. They see the abuses and wink at them because there is no correction. Few rulers have the vigour and independence which President Roosevelt manifested in the postal scandal, to examine publicly the iniquitious acts of their own administrations. Alexander III evinced these qualities, but he could reach a few men only, not the system.

"Even if an official be prosecuted," one of the honest Russian offcials said, "anoth er will taken his place, who will become also the victim of the system. Do not blame the men in office. They are no better, no worse, than the system, and remember also you have national and municipal vice in America. The Emperor is largely powerless, because, while he is ostensibly the master of the bureaucracy, it is really his master."

The people are aware of the power and evils of the bureaucracy, and therefore differentiate between it and the Czar. Contemptuous of it as they are, they naturally look upon its acts with suspicion. They only know that the Czar is behind an order when force is employed to back it up, as in the recent riot in St. Petersburg.

The danger to the autocracy, all enlightened Russians say, is not that the people will move to overthrow the Czar, but that, inspired by the belief that their ruler desires its destruction, they will attack the bureaucracy system; and, aware of this danger, the Emperor is endeavouring to avert it by practical reforms.

STRANGE CURATIVE PROPERTIES IN STONE.

The mystery of the "miracle stone," which for centuries has been regarded with awe and interest by the inhabitants of a remote mountain region in the Sierra Madres in the western part of the State of Chihuahua, Mexico, has been solved. When the first explorers entered that region many years ago they found that the Indians there wore a small piece of a peculiar stone, which was attached to a thong around their necks. The Indians ascribed miraculous healing powers to the stone. They claimed that it was a cure for rheumatism and all chronic diseases of the body. It had no power in fevers or sicknesses of that character.

As an evidence of the truth of this belief the Indians pointed out that no one who had worn the stone had ever died from the diseases which they claimed it cured. Many Englishmen and other were convinced of the wonderful powers of the stone by the cures which they saw it perform, and there is now hardly a man in the mining camps of that region who does not carry a piece of the stone in his pocket.

Scientific men who were told from time to time of this wonderful stone ridiculed the idea of it possessing any curative properties. They considered that it was a superstitious idea which had been handed down from generation to generation by the Indians. A short time ago several pieces of the stone, which is found in considerable quantities in the mountains, were obtained by a mineralogist, and taken to the City of Mexico, where they were analysed.

They were found to possess radioactive properties of a very high degree. Some of these specimens emitted a brilliant light when placed in contact with a metal substance, and when thus placed under water the light was intense in its brilliancy.

It is now admitted by the scientists who have investigated the matter that the cures alleged to have been performed by this stone were probably genuine, and that its curative properties consist of the rare element which it contains. Further tests and experments are to be made with the stone.

ARCTIC DISCOVERIES.

Captain Low, the leader of the Neptune expedition to Hudson's Bay and the northern waters, tells an interesting story of his discoveries in a lonely place where several members of the Franklin expedition met their fate.

On Beachy Island in Lancaster Sound were found five solitary graves over which are wooden monuments. The inscriptions make it clear that two of the graves were those of Sir John Franklin the and his men and other three those of an Arctic expedition of a later date.

In the vicinity of the graves were the ruins of three huts and two broken boats thrown up on the icy shore. Great quantities of flour, oatmeal, peas, beans and cheese were scattered around in a spoilt condition, also a great quantity of tinned meat.

Sir John Franklin's last expedition was made in the Erebus and Terror, which sailed from Greenhithe on May 19, 1845, and was last seen by a whaler on July 26 in Baffin Bay.

Fifteen expeditions were fitted out in search of the explorers between 1848 and 1854. and many skeletons and articles belonging to the men were found in various parts of North America, also a record discovered in a cairn stating that Sir John Franklin died on July 11, 1847. Over 100 men perished in this ill-fated venture.

A STORY OF DAN LENO.

One of Dan Leno's most striking characteristics was his extravagant generosity, in which connexion many amusing stories are told. Once, for instance, he asked a waiter what was the biggest tip he had ever received. "Two pounds," was the reply. Well, my boy," said Leno, "I'll make that fellow look foolish. Here's a fiver for you. Who was the other chap, by the way?" "Well, Mr. Leno," said the waiter after he had pocketed the note, "it was yourself, sir." It was, indeed, the prodigality with which the late commedian gave away his money to all and sundry that first necessitated his being placed under restraint.

The orders for new artillery for the army which will cost £2,500,000 are the long-delayed result of Sir George Marshall's Committee of 1901. The recommendations of the committee were in favour of an 18½ pounder quickfiring gun for the field artillery and a 12½-pounder quickfiring gun for the horse artillery. The existing guns are 15-pounders in the field artillery and 12-pounders in the horse artillery, both being slow firers. They are not modern guns at all. The only really modern guns we have in the army are the German quick-firing guns, eighteen batteries of which were hurriedly bought during the South African war. These guns are in the Aldershot command, under Sir John French. Such new guns as are being made at this moment are to be sent to India. The Indian army will have eighteen batteries of the new field guns and three batteries of the new horse guns. Those officers who have tried the new guns at Okehampton and elsewhere say, that when we get them we shall have the best guns in the world. The effective range of the new field guns is over 7,000 yards, whereas the present 15-pounders have an effective range of under 4,000, and they will fire about 20 aounds a minute instead of three or four. The £2,500,000 is estimated to provide 90 batteries of field artillery and 17 batteries of horse artillery.

The Korea Daily News.

Issued at 5 P. M. daily except Sundays.

Rate of Subscription :—
Per Year,............Yen 25.
Per Quarter,..........Yen 7.
Per Month,..........Yen 2.50.

Postage in Korea not charged extra.
Postage abroad charged extra.

Advertisements, 50 sen per day for 1 inch or less.
5 yen per month per inch.
50 yen per year per inch.

All communications to

E. T. BETHELL,
Editor and Publisher,
Pak-tong, Seoul.

THE TRANS-SIBERIAN RAILWAY.

The "Kriegstechnische Zeitschrift" publishes a long article on the Trans-Siberian Railway. The best portion of the line is that which passes through Manchuria, to the improvement of which £9,500,000 was devoted in 1898, and since the opening of the Khingan tunnel of two and a half miles in length, in 1903, military trains of 40 wagons each have been able to run on this portion of the line all the year round. West of Lake Baikal the largest number of wagons to a military train has been 24, while in European Russia the number varies from 20 to 40. At the beginning of the war the great distance, as much as 20 miles, between the stations west of Baikal, kept the number of trains run daily very low, but the subsequent building of 68 new stations enabled the number to be increased to 13 daily in June last. The worst constructed section of the line is that which passes through the hilly country directly east of Baikal. The The addition of 11 new stations since the beginning of the war and the construction of a third line at 12 stations, already existing, enabled the daily number of trains on this section to be increased to nine, of which six were military and three for the railway service. It is probable that some improvements carried out last summer have increased the daily number of trains on this section yet more. In Manchuria the gradients never exceed 1 in 66, and the curves have never a radius of less than a quarter of a mile. The bridges, however, are frequent and form altogether slightly under one per cent of the permanent way. There are 14 bridges over an eighth of a mile long, and those over the Sungari at Kharbin are over half a mile in length. The more important bridges are of metal on stone piers. The line in Manchuria is guarded by 55 stonias of cossacks, 55 companies of infantry, and six batteries, in all 25,000 men, and their patrol extends for nearly 40 miles on each side of the railway. The distance from the western boundary of Manchuria to Mukden is 925 miles.

It is calculated that if the military trains travelled at the rate of 12 miles an hour as far as Lake Baikal, and at the rate of nine and a half miles an hour beyond, the time taken from Moscow to Mukden, including four days' stoppage, would be 24 days. As a matter of fact, the time actually taken has usually been about 31 days, and in some cases as much as 10 days longer. There are 21 halting-places between Moscow and Baikal, 15 having been built during the war. One of them between Irkutsk and Baikal, has barrack accommodation for 4,000 men. At some other places the barrack accommodation is for 500 men only. From Baikal to Mukden the halting-places are organized to feed as many as 8,000 men per day, including, therefore, those who are merely passing through.

FAMOUS DESPATCHES.

Every general at some period of his career is called upon to pen despatches, but it is certainly not given to every officer to compose sentences in these historic documents that will never be forgotten. "Great Sovereign, forgive!" These words will not be forgotten. After the almost superhuman efforts made by Stössel during a siege lasting seventeen days longer than that of Mafeking, more than a hundred days longer than the seige of Paris, more than twice the length of the never-to-be-forgotten siege of Belfort, such an appeal does the man who makes it the highest honour.

Stössel's message will rank in Russian archives with Suwarrow's famous despatch when, his rank being only that of a major, he disobeyed orders in order to inflict a signal defeat on the enemy. "As a soldier," he wrote, "I deserve death for disobeying orders; as a Russian, I have done my duty. The enemy is no more." It will be recalled that the Empress Catherine replied to this despatch in the words, "As a soldier, I leave you to the mercy of the Commander-in-Chief; as a Russian, I congratulate you as my lieutenant colonel." Catherine apparently took a delight in paraphrasing this General's despatches, for when after the capture of Prague, he laconically wrote, "Hurrah! Prague! Suwarrow!" she promptly replied, "Bravo! Field Marshal! Catherine!" Her reply to his terse epistle in respect to the capture of Ismali, which he took in three days after it had held out for several months, is not recorded, but his despatch read, "Glory to God and the Empress, Ismaili is ours."

Even since Caesar wrote "Veni, vidi, vici," victorious generals have essayed to record their triumphs in as few words as possible. It has been placed upon record that Lord High Admiral Effingham announced the defeat of the Spanish armada with the single word "Cantharides," a somewhat enigmatical despatch to all but druggists familiar with the name of "the Spanish fly." This despatch, which is almost too good to be true, has, however, been exceeded in brevity by Sir Charles Napier's punning message after the battle of Hyderabad, in Scinde; it read, "Peccavi"—which, being interpreted, signifies "I have sinned."

Sir Harry Johnston on one occasion advanced against a slave trader of the name of Tmosé. He delighted the late Marquis of Salisbury by announcing his victory in the following sentence:—"Advanced against Tmosé; defeated captured, hanged him.—Johnston." This matter-of-fact announcement recalls the business-like brevity of Captain G. Walton when he was successful over a Spanish fleet comprising three line-of-battle ships, five frigates, three bomb vessels, and a storeship in 1718. Writing to Sir George Byng, who had sent him with six vessels to cut off the Spaniards, he said: "Sir, I have taken and burned, as per margin, going for Syracuse, and am, sir, your obedient servant, G. Walton."

One can almost see Turenne yawning so graphic is his notification of the condition in which he was left after his victory at Dunkirk. "The enemy came, was beaten, I am tired, good night," wrote he in a despatch that doubtless provoked as much delight as General Sherman's famous Christmas-card despatch to President Lincoln in December, 1864:—"I beg to present you, as a Christmas gift, the city of Savannah, with 150 guns, plenty of ammunition 825,000 bales of cotton."

THE FINDING OF THE NORTH SEA COMMISSION.

The Tokio Foreign Office has received a telegram to the following effect:—

The International Commission appointed to investigate the Hull Incident, published on February 25 the report of its finding, which is substantially as follows:—

1.—In view of the fact that war exists at the present moment and that Admiral Rojestvensky as Commander of the Russian Squadron was forced to rely upon the warnings furnished by different Russian agents, he was justified under certain contingencies in ordering his subordinate officers to open fire.

2.—All the British trawlers were displaying the regulation lights, and were engaged in fishing according to the laws universally accepted.

3.—No urgent warning whatever from the detachment preceding the main Russian squadron had been received by the Russian Commander.

4.—The Commander should take the responsibility for having opened fire, and the result of such fire on the trawlers.

5.—No hostile action whatever was committed by the trawlers and there were no torpedo-boats present at the scene. The act of opening fire was therefore unjustifiable.

6.—The duration of the firing exceeded the limits of necessity. But it is recognised that the Russian Commander tried his utmost to stop the firing on those boats which he regarded as trawlers.

7.—There is no confirmation of the alleged danger to the Russian warships, such at to cause the Commander to conclude after the firing that he had no choice but to continue his voyage on the pre-arranged route. The Commission regrets that the Commander, while proceeding in the sea off Calais, did not inform the neighbouring countries of the necessity of rescuing the trawlers which had been fired at.

8.—The Commission declares that this report does not embody any criticism of the valour or moral principles of the Commander and crews of the Russian squadron.

GRAND DUKE NICHOLAS.

Grand Duke Nicholas Nicholaivitch, who is said to have been appointed to succeed Kuropatkin in command of the Russian army, is justly famed, not merely in Russia, but also among the military experts in Germany, as one of the most superb horsemen and skillful cavalry leaders in Europe. He is entirely engrossed in his profession, very popular in the army and gave evidence of the possession of much shrewdness in political matters in a moment of acute crisis in Bulgaria some years ago.

The Korea Daily News.

VOL. II, TUESDAY, MARCH 7, 1905. No. 51

HONGKONG & SHANGHAI BANKING CORPORATION.

Paid-up Capital.....................$10,000,000
Reserve Fund:—Sterling Reserve... 10,000,000
Silver Reserve..... 7,000,000
27,000,000
Reserve Liability of Proprietors... 10,000,000

HEAD OFFICE, HONGKONG.

London Bankers, London and County Banking Company Limited.

Branches and Agencies, London.

Amoy,	Hankow	Penang,
Bangkok,	Hiogo,	Rangoon,
Batavia,	Iloilo,	Saigon,
Bombay,	Lyons,	San Francisco,
Calcutta,	Manila,	Singapore,
Colombo,	Nagasaki,	Sourabaya,
Foochow,	New York,	Tientsin,
Hamburg,	Peking,	Yokohama,

Credits granted on approved Securities, and every description of Banking and Exchange business transacted.

Drafts granted on London and the chief Commercial places in Europe, India, Australia, America, China and Japan.

HOLME RINGER & Co., AGENTS, CHEMULPO.

HOKURKU DOBOKU KAISHA.

Branch office in Chong Dong. Seoul.

Japanese telephone No. 165

CONTRACT DEPARTMENT.

We can contract to build any building or construction.

MERCHANDISE DEPARTMENT.

We can provide any building material. We have just contracted to build the new Belgian Legation.

E. MEYER & CO., Agents, Chemulpo.

CHARTERED BANK OF INDIA AUSTRALIA & CHINA.

INCORPORATED BY ROYAL CHARTER 1853

HEAD OFFICES.—LONDON.

Paid-up Capital £800,000
Reserve Liability of Shareholders 800,000
Reserve Fund 800,000

Drafts granted upon all the principal places in the world and every description of Exchange and banking business transacted.

E. MEYER & Co., Agents, Chemulpo.

MITSU BISHI DOCKYARD & ENGINE WORKS,

NAGASAKI.

CODE WORD, "DOCK."

A 1, A. B. C., and Engineering Codes used.

DOCK No. 1 (at Tategami).

Extreme Length	523 feet
Length on blocks	513 ,,
Width of Entrance on Top	89 ,,
,, ,, Bottom	77 ,,
Water on Blocks at Spring Tide	26½ ,,

DOCK No. 2 (Mukaijima).

Extreme Length	371 feet
Length on Blocks	360 ,,
Width of Entrance on Top	66 ,,
,, ,, Bottom	53 ,,
Water on Blocks at Spring Tide	22 ,,

PATENT SLIP (at Kosuge).

Can take vessels up to 1,000 tons gross.

THE WORKS are well equipped with the LATEST IMPROVEMENTS, and can execute any kind of work in SHIPBUILDING and MARINE ENGINEERING, as well as in REPAIRING of SHIPS.

The COMPANY'S new powerful steamer OURA-MARU (712 tons, 700 I.H.P.), specially built for SALVAGE PURPOSES, and equipped with necessary gear, is always READY at SHORT NOTICE.

THE METHODIST PUBLISHING HOUSE,

Little West Gate, Seoul.

JOB PRINTING, TYPEWRITER PAPER
CARBON PAPER, VISITING CARDS
STATIONERY, BOOK BINDING
BOOK PUBLISHERS
AMERICAN SCHOOL BOOKS
SPENCERIAN COPY BOOKS
PEN CARBON LETTER AND BILL BOOKS

S. A. BECK, Manager.

DAI-ICHI GINKO.

LIMITED.

(Formerly the First National Bank)

ESTABLISHED 1873

INCORPORATED UNDER PRESENT LAW 1896

Capital - - - - - - - - Yen 5,000,000
Reserve Fund - - - - - 1,500,000

HEAD OFFICE:—TOKIO.

President: Baron SHIBUSAWA.

BRANCHES AND CORRESPONDENTS In the Principal Cities and Towns of Japan.

Interest Allowed on

Fixed deposits 1 year - - - 6½ per cent
" " 6 months - - - 6 per cent

Special current accounts 1½ sen daily per Y 100
General " " 1 " " " 100

M. TANAKA, Manager, Chemulpo.

SINGER SEWING MACHINES

씽거즈봉침

SOLE AGENTS FOR KOREA

전매쇼

HOLME RINGER & CO. Chemulpo.

졔물포 함룽거양힝

KAMEYA & CO.

GENERAL STOREKEEPERS

Chinkokai - - Seoul

(*Established 1895, Tokyo*)

Confectionery, Hams, Canned Goods, Cutlery, Hirano & Tansan Water. Provisions, Gents, Furnishing goods, Toilet Articles, Travelling Bags, Tobacco, Cigars & Cigarettes Kitchen Utensils. Coffee, Biscuits

Fresh Goods always kept in Stock.

Prices Moderate

Please come and inspect our goods.

NIPPON YUSEN KAISHA.

JAPANESE MAIL STEAMSHIP CO.

UNDER MAIL CONTRACT WITH THE IMPERIAL JAPANESE GOVERNMENT.

European Line

Regular Fortnightly Service between Yokohama Kobe, Moji, Shanghai, Hongkong, Singapore, Penang Colombo, Port Said, Marseilles, London and Antwerp

American Line

Regular Fortnightly Service between Hongkong and Seattle, calling at Shanghai, Moji, Kobe, Yokohama and Victoria, B. C.

Australian Line

Regular weekly Service betwen Japan Ports and Australia, callingjat Hongkong and Manila.

(Above Three Lines Suspended until further noticed

Shanghai Line

Weekly Service between Shanghai and Japan Port

Korea Line

Service Kobe, Moji, Nagasaki, Fusan Chemulpo Chefoo, Taku.

S.-S. Babelsberg, 2181 tons.

Service Kobe. Moji, Fusan, Chemulpo, Chinnampo

S. S. ARGO, S. S. Ohio.

BORDEN'S CONDENSED MILK CO.

New York, U. S. A.

ALWAYS IN STOCK

Eagle Brand Condensed Milk.

Gold Seal Condensed Milk.

Peerless (Family) Evaporated Cream.

Borden's Malted Milk.

E. MEYER & CO. Chemulpo Korea, Sole Agents

ROYAL INSURANCE COMPANY,

Funds exceed £10,000,000

FIRE

AT CURRENT RATES

LIFE

REDUCED PREMIUM,

HOLME RINGER & Co. Agents, Chemulpo

廣 KWANG ◉ CH'ANG 昌

BENNETT & CO.

Merchants

Chemulpo.

Offices opposite the Imperial Japanese Post and Telegraph Office Chemulpo

Telephone Number 201.

大韓每日申報

대한매일신보

(뎨이권 오십이호) (목요일) 일천구백오년삼월구일

본샤고빅

론셜

샤고

뎐보

법국의 히군확쟝

론돈발 이월이십삼일

관보

○임 통신사면회과주사 셔판임
관사등 륙품 박호병
○명 휴직 진위뎨일련ᄃᆡ뎨일
대ᄃᆡ쟝 륙군보병참령 리동휘
○의원면본관 룡쳥뎐참봉
림규명
○임 봉쳥뎐참봉 셔판임관팔등
유계렬
이샹삼월이일
○명 궁내부특진관 셔칙임관일
등 홍문관학사 남뎡쳘
○의원면본관 룡쳥뎐참봉
유계렬
○임 봉쳥뎐참봉 셔판임관팔등
구품 림규명
○면본관 무안우체사주사
셩의형
○임 무안우체사주사 셔판임관
륙등 젼주사 신용우
이샹삼월삼일
○명 홍문관학사 셔칙임관삼등
졍일품 리순익
○명 비셔감경 셔칙임관이등
시종원경 김규홍
○명 시종원경 셔칙임관일등
졍일품 민영휘
○명 시강원부쳠사 셔칙임관삼
등 궁내부특진관 민영돈
○명 례식원례식경 셔칙임관이
등 종일품 민종묵
○명 례식원쟝례경 셔칙임관이
등 종일품 됴병필
○의원면본관 시강원시독관
리인규
○면본관 의릉령 리춍용
○겸임 시강원시독관 기로소
쥬직관 김춘희
○임 의릉령 셔판임관칠등 지
능령 리윤슈
○임 졔릉령 셔판임관칠등 종
신사면회과주사 윤쳘직
○임 외부참셔관 셔주임관삼
등 졍삼품 윤덕영
○임 외부참셔관 셔주임관오
등 외부주사 최동식
○임 셩균관쟝 셔칙임관사등
졍삼품 셔샹훈
○임 외부참셔관 셔주임관삼등
졍삼품 리건춘
○셔주임관이등 춍령사관
홍운표
○셔주임관사등 령사관 김
봉션 평사관 김화규 평사관
관 뎡평리 평사관 박지양
평사관 리원용
○임 외부주사 셔판임관삼등
구품 변표졍 륙품 방대영
○임 외부주사 셔판임관사등
칠품 김셕영
이샹삼월사일
○임 외부주사 셔판임관륙등
구품 리원규
○의원면본관 덕원감리서주
사 됴남직
○임 덕원감리서주사 셔판임관
륙사등 평양감리서주사 홍순
복
○임 평양감리서주사 셔판임관
삼등 인쳔감리서주사 리진틱
○임 인쳔감리서주사 셔판임관
사등 젼주사 됴남직
○임 법부주사 셔판임관일등
륙품 김샹직 륙품 류원셩
륙품 안치윤 륙품 리원국
륙품 리명직
○임 법부주사 셔판임관이등
사품 리인승 륙품 노병슈
○임 법부주사 셔판임관삼등
륙품 유중렬
○임 법부주사 셔판임관사등
륙품 류갑슈 륙품 남길희
륙품 권중민 륙품 신형틱
○임 법부주사 셔판임관륙등
구품 리완종 구품 리용샹
구품 김종대
이샹삼월오일
○탁지부주사 셔판임관륙등
구품 리응세
삼월륙일

잡보

○계씨면임 법부형사국쟝은
젼군슈최셕민씨가피임ᄒ고민
사국쟝은참셔관윤셩보씨가면
임ᄒ고농샹공부농광국쟝은참
셔관셔병슈씨가면임ᄒ고샹공
국쟝은송태헌씨가피임ᄒ엿더
라
○병뎡퇴숨 일젼에ᄒ른번역
관샹촌시일씨가한국병뎡의모
조일계를가지고헌병ᄃᆡ에리소
ᄒ되동ᄃᆡ문밧원ᄒ사방해셔한
병수샹인이나를질으기로ᄒᆡᆼ병
뎡의모조를졍에가지고왓스니
사셜ᄒ야중치ᄒ며덜나고ᄒ며
뽀발ᄒ대니카만원우리군사령
부에호소ᄒ면반다시국졔샹관
계가될터인고로이쳐를한국헌
병ᄃᆡ에보내소ᄒ노라ᄒ거놀헌병
ᄃᆡ오셔그칭되훈병뎡을수탐ᄒ
즉시위샹대ᄃᆡ병뎡인ᄃᆡ죵금헌
병ᄃᆡ종셔에착수ᄒ엿다더라
○군률희이 군계의뎡ᄒ다논
말이반년이나현란ᄒ되죵금쳐
지못ᄒ지라위관이논병졸이
논모도군무에희ᄒ야방희ᄒ가
분소ᄒ논중군인에는자퇴병졸중
에도타ᄒ는자ㅣ며옥반ᄒᄃᆡ또
ᄒ논샹히간과ᄒ다더라
○부득이소환 각국에주졔ᄒ
한국공ᄉ를소환ᄒ다논셜은임
의여러번각신문샹에긔재ᄒ엿
거니와근일향셜에일본공ᄉ가
공ᄉ소환ᄒ기를샹치ᄒ고ᄒ므
로셔부득이ᄒ야일간소환ᄒ수
로각공ᄉ의게훈칙ᄒ엿다더라
○죵편리왕 너쟝원에셔너부
로조회ᄒ기를탁지부에셔남부
공젼을ᄃᆡ용ᄒ고졍ᄒ남도각군
의갑진년도결젼으로보샹ᄒ야
획리ᄒ고임의각히군에훈칙ᄒ
엿더니각군에셔ᄒ는긋ᄎ유고ᄒ고
폐원에는수랍지안이ᄒ는지라
부득이ᄒ야 창규일노둑시판을
차뎡ᄒ야젼왕수시케ᄒ바쳔원
수의쳥임진안군수의온쥭희견
시ᄎ로ᄃᆡ왕ᄒ기에구이흡이젼
못ᄉ니부에셔젼라북도관찰
ᄉ의게훈칙ᄒ야ᄒᆡ원으로ᄒ야유
공죵ᄐᆡ리왕케ᄒ라ᄒ엿더라
○니채소계 참졍대신됴병호
씨가륙일에수칙ᄒ고칠일브터
등연ᄒ논ᄃᆡ의졍셔리도병식씨
는셔로평피가잇논고로됴병식
씨논니부대신도소계ᄒ다ᄒ며됴
ᄐᆡ신의후임은리지극씨가피임
ᄒ다더라
○도로뎡간 근일에파후가졍
추히빙ᄒ고온화ᄒ여지논지라
경무쳥에셔도로를수치ᄒ기위
ᄒ야각셔도로를뎡간ᄒ엿다더
라
○봉슈ᄃᆡ쳑량 일본사령부에
셔군용지졍으로수용ᄒ다ᄒ고
남산봉슈ᄃᆡ를쳑량ᄒ고횡귀를
셰웟존지라경무쳥에셔뎡간ᄒ엿
다더라
○챵회쟝리경 쳘일하오칠시
에남도일진회회쟝리용구씨가
셔셩ᄒ야경셩일진회ᄉ무소에
셔류숙ᄒ엿더라
○셔임문시 쥬일공관참셔관
하샹긔씨의자리에리분용씨가
ᄒ신봉리씨의부임치안으므로리
ᄒ흔힐란ᄒ야엿다논ᄃᆡ무ᄉ소고가잇
논지라미샹ᄒ거니와리분용씨의
셔임은물시ᄒ라더라
○표원로샹쥬 원임의졍됴병
셰씨가쳘일하오수경즁에샹쥬
ᄒ야시국의급혼ᄉ건을샹쥬ᄒ
ᄒ엿다더라
○경위핍차 경무쳥에셔한셩
부로죠회ᄒ기를이왕방곰ᄒ가
쾌차쳥을몬수히환슈ᄒ고유실
가ᄒ고근실ᄒ쟈를차뎡ᄒ야
민오뵈호에뎡식쟉뎡케ᄒ라ᄒ
ᄒ엿더라
○셔구쳐ᄃᆡ 방경찰권은너
부로부속ᄒ엿논ᄃᆡ대신은케임
ᄒ다ᄒ의로종슐을요동ᄒ야자
궈졉셔구로승인ᄒ다더라
○탕셔련소 젼관셔김방진씨
가소ᄒ비지들미슈ᄒ엿논ᄃᆡ쏘
승ᄒ논ᄃᆡ금번에부본ᄒ고최찬졍의헌씨도
ᄉ의셩명을발표ᄒ다더라
○사죨망ᄌ파반 인쳔리인의
젼셜을문ᄒ즉허젼에무셔가
부운송션미츔반ᄒ흔셰에한국병
뎡이ᄂ즁ᄃᆡ가랑이ᄀ셜즁에탐계
ᄒ엿다더라
○일긔가룡 년젼에북송헌커
ᄒ논권동슈씨가일인조쳥쳥범
으로계약ᄒ고샹쳥동져수를공
니로인영ᄒ다흠비한셩뎐리회
사에셔샹지ᄒ야결으ᄃᆡ셩녀면
귀와밋수도등젼은본사에셔담
당ᄒ기로셔약ᄒ엿슨즉슈도등
ᄉ들가히쳔셜치못ᄒ리란ᄒ야
샹ᄒᆡᆼᄒ더니귀ᄉ진이졍차취결
ᄒ지라편들슈씨와죠쳔씨가쥬
관ᄒ야룡일브터긔용ᄒ엿논ᄃᆡ
황도편에셔괴ᄒ야힐젼은샹졍
동으로향ᄒ야슈흥을셜ᄒ고일
쳔은경운궁으로향ᄒ야슈도를
셜치ᄒ다더라

광고

본사광고

○본사신문챰을미앙ᄎ샹에련
쳠받기로ᄒ는거슨이독ᄒ시는쳠
군ᄌ들도아시거니와왕왕히금
음비지나도톡보니지안논곳시
ᄒ반ᄒ니흐망치ᄒ셧는지계가이지못
ᄒ호거니와본사에는관계가업
시오오니신표문을보니지안는곳
슨자금이후로신문을또보니지
안캣사오니이독ᄒ시는쳠군ᄌ
들은더욱본신문을ᄉ랑ᄒ셔으
로ᄃᆡ금을속히보니시기를ᄇ라
옵니다

본인이미국으로셔일본에와셔엿
습ᄒ고대한경셩에와쟝시류ᄒ
면셔병인들을보기원ᄒᄂ이다
기니시히구명에금과류회로셰니
도도ᄒ오며ᄯᅢ진니셔이에셔오
나쳥군ᄌ는조량ᄒ시읍소셔
ᄉ무소는셰문밧졍거쟝위에
중앙옥헌불니려관이오

셔울우젼회사
속칭ᄒ는이등록쳔등인ᄃᆡ
쳥국과일본셔영국과각국으로
왕리홈
인쳔항등가방히ᄃᆡ리졈

미국우젼회사와
동경동양긔션회사
각국ᄒᆡ션화물련락홍셩홍
덕국아셰아은ᄒᆡᆼ
본졈은덕국ᄇᆡᆨ림에잇고향항
지졈은샹ᄒᆡ등지에잇소
차리드은ᄒᆡᆼ
ᄌ본금총헤은이쳔오ᄇᆡᆨ만원
본졈은영국론돈에잇고지졈은
각디도회쳐에잇소
인쳔셰창양ᄒᆡᆼᄃᆡ리졈
대일은ᄒᆡᆼ[대일국립은ᄒᆡᆼ]
본뎜은일본동경에잇고
ᄌ본금총익륙ᄇᆡᆨ이십오만원
리식은ᄆᆡᄇᆡᆨ원에삼젼오리에셔
륙젼오리ᄭ지인ᄃᆡ
명셰ᄒ는ᄃᆡ로계산홈
경셩대일은ᄒᆡᆼᄀ졈쟝 뎐중
항향샹회은ᄒᆡᆼ
ᄌ본금총익삼쳔륙ᄇᆡᆨ오십만원
본졈은항향에잇고
지졈은쳥국일본기타각국디쳐
에잇소
인쳔셰창양ᄒᆡᆼᄃᆡ리졈

TELEGRAMS.

(FROM JAPAN PAPERS)

Note. The messages marked* are those which are described as "special service" or "special telegrams" or "received by the Government." The others are from properly authenticated sources.

THE WAR.

London, Feb. 28.

*A correspondent of Reuter with the Russian Army reports that the Japanese have occupied an advanced post of the Russians and are threatening the latter's main force. Desperate fighting is taking place.

London, Feb. 28.

*The military correspondent of the "Times," in the course of an important article reviewing the events of the war, describes the situation in the Russian army as precarious. "Nothing that human foresight and energy can provide," says the writer, "can radically alter the position except a crushing victory."

Regarding the Baltic Fleet, the writer says; "Whatever may be the fate of the chief battleships, Admiral Rohjestvensky is cursed with an escort of a great unwieldy and vulnerable convoy, rendering free manoevres impossible."

London, Mar. 1.

The Japanese have captured Taling Pass, which is of the same importance in relation to Mukden as Motienling was to Liaoyang.

London, March 1.

Russia, in a circular note to the Powers, declares that the Japanese have violated Chinese neutrality by appearing in the rear of the Russian Army at the west of the railway.

Vienna, March, 1.

***All the European military experts believe that another great battle between the Japanese and Russian troops is now at hand. They estimate that Kuropatkin's forces exceed Marquis Oyama's in number, but much doubt if the Russian troops can stand comparison with the Japanese in valour and energy. Most of them foretell another Russian defeat, leading upto a lengthy truce.**

AFFAIRS IN RUSSIA.

London, Feb. 28.

Reuter's correspondent at Warsaw states that the peasants in Poland, incited by the Socialists, are joining the strike movement. This is considered the most serious development of the siuation, as the peasants form seventenths of the population.

London, Feb. 28.

*The Russian newspapers now openly advocate peace. The Novosti and the Novoe Vremya insist on the folly of prolonging the struggle. Military experts take a gloomy view of the Russian cause, agreeing that, if Japan resumes the struggle, she has solid grounds for expecting a triumphant issue.

Berlin, Feb. 28.

Acting on the advice of M. de Yermoloff, the Russian Minister of Agriculture, the Tsar has ordered a Manifesto to be published promising that a Constitution shall be granted.

Berlin, Feb. 28.

Maxim Gorki, the celebrated Russian novelist, who was arrested during the recent troubles, has been released on bail.

London, Mar. 1.

*A quarter of a million miners have struck work in the Donetz coal district, South Russia. At Lugansk the strikers have obtained possession of quantities of dynamite. The Russian police are threatening to go on strike. There is no improvement in the general situation.

London, Mar. 1.

*On account of the railway strike there have been no trains for Manchuria by the Trans-Baikal railway for nine days. Altogether thirteen railways are affected by the strike, and trains are running only between Irkutsk and Cholyabinsk.

Vienna, Mar. 1.

*The Imperial Bank of Russia has issued an exceptional amount of paper money, with the result that the Moscow public, being compelled to take this form of currency, is expressing much dissatisfaction on the subject, and it is giving rise to frequent disturbances. In Siberia the prices of commodities, which have been steadily rising since the commencement of the war, are now double or thrice what they were at the outbreak of hostilities. Owing to the forced use of new paper money, all the exchanges have been closed, and the region is seriously impoverished.

GENERAL NEWS.

London, Mar. 1.

General Stoessel has reached Moscow, where he is the hero of the hour, his hotel being besieged by crowds.

The General yesterday lunched with the Grand Duchess Sergius, and afterwards received a deputation from the Municipal Council. Replying to an address of welcome from the Council General Stoessel declared that it was his duty to surrender the fortress at Port Arthur in order to avoid a massacre, the Japanese having, at the time of the capitulation, captured all the important forts.

London, Mar. 1.

*General Stoessel has arrived at St. Petersburg. There was no demonstration and only a few military and naval officers were present to receive him.

London, Feb. 27.

*In French official quarters it is thought that as a result of the verdict given by the North Sea Commission, **Admiral Rohjestvensky will probably be recalled.**

London, Feb. 27.

***The tour of the Prince and Princess of Wales, who leave for India in November next, will extend over a period of four months.**

Berlin, Feb. 28.

The inauguration ceremonies in connection with the new cathedral at Berlin were attended by numerous German Princes of the Protestant faith.

Berlin, Mar. 1.

***The European Powers have been exchanging diplomatic notes, with regard to Near Eastern questions.** They have all agreed that they cannot consent to withdraw their troops from Crete. They are still exchanging opinions with respect to the Macedonian qu estion, particularly its financial aspect.

London, March 1.

* Mr. Abe Moritaro, Secretary to the Japanese Legation in London, is leaving for Japan in the S. S. Bayern on April 4.

London, March. 1.

* Lord Milner will leave South Africa on the expiration of his term of office.

The American, British and Japanese Ministers are all to have audiences for the purpose of discussing mining concessions.

A telegram from the north-east states that the Russians are steadily retreating and that the Japanese have now accupied Söng-chin.

Owing to the recent reductions in the *personnel* of the government, the authorities are rather in a quandary as to what officials should be selected for dismissal. The Minister for Agriculture has hit upon the happy idea of drawing lots while in the Law Department the question is to be put to the vote. The simple expedient of dismissing the least competent seems to have occurred to no one.

THE WAR.

According to telegrams received by the Japanese Legation, Kuropatkin is alredy making a movement to withdraw from Fushun and Mukden to Tieling. It appears that on the Japanese right Kuroki's army has succeeding in taking several Russian positions in the hills near Waitenshan, commanding the small road leading to Mukden.

In the centre but little progress appears to have been made but on the west the Japanese left wing is advancing on Mukden between the Hunho and the Railway and the Russian right is being driven in to the centre.

Away in the direction of Singking the Russians still hold several strong positions and were until the 6th instant, resisting the Japanese advance.

THE BATTLE OF CHINGHOCHENG.

Commenting on the battle of Chinghocheng the "Asahi" says that the commencement of Japanese offensive operations in that direction was probably unexpected by the Russians. The Reuter telegram, dated Feb. 26th, reporting the outbreak of operations along the whole line, is thought to have been constructed by Reuter's representative either at Mukden or Fushan, he having seen many Russian dead and wounded brought in from the front. As the Russian strength is reported to be 17,000 and and their casualties to be about 2,000 this battle was not such a small affair but is practically equal to that of the Yalu. Though it is not yet extended to the whole line, the fresh engagement may be regarded as an initiative of the pending big battle of Shaho, which will possibly take place as a necessary sequel of General Kuropatkin having been disturbed by the sudden appearance on his extreme left of such a large Japanese force as to be able to repulse 17,000 Russians in half a day. The "Asahi," which is of the opinion that the party which is able to extend both its wings on the Shaho farther and quicker than the other can secure a victory, concludes that prospects of victory are now in the hands of the Japanese as usual.

Sir Ewen Cameron, K. C. M. G., the London Manager of the Hongkong and Shanghai Banking Corporation, has resigned his post.

H. M. S. Pylades went aground on Peel Reef near Thursday Island, on Feb. 12th. She was not seriously damaged and was successfully floated.

When General Okazawa left here for Japan he took with him a Korean sword and an antique vase dating from over 600 years ago, as present to the Mikado from H. E. Mr. Hayashi, the Japanese Minister.

We note that the governor of Seoul, in the course of some correspondence regarding the transfer of land to foreigners alleges that owing to the lack of definite boundaries, foreigners frequently take in more ground than they are entitled to.

According to Japanese telegrams received locally, things in St. Petersburg and Moscow are in a pretty bad way. Foreign Diplomatic representatives in St. Petersburg are advised not to venture out into the streets and those who can afford to are preparing to leave the larger cities.

A REMARKABLE NAVAL INVENTION.

With the assertion that the exigencies of modern warfare call for an engine more powerful than 16,000-tons battleships and 12-inch guns, Anson Phelps Stokes, ex-Vice-Commodore of the New York Yacht Club, presented to the twelfth general meeting of the Society of Naval Architects in New York, his latest plans for an impregnable floating naval battery for harbour and coast defence. The members of the Society, including naval officers, shipbuilders and naval architects, gave the closest attention to Mr. Stokes' novel scheme, which is a departure from existing designs as radical as was the Monitor. In the discussion which followed the reading of the paper, the naval men present spoke favourably of the idea. Drawings and diagrams of the new fighting monster were examined with the keenest interest The machine described by Mr. Stokes is an improvement of his first invention. The first plan was for a circular battery; the modified form is semi-globular. Mr. Stokes has named his island of steel, with its equipment of guns of awful destructive power, the "Cerberus," and has protected himself with patents at Washington and in Europe. Mr. Stokes said of his invention:

"The late naval battles make it evident that for a leading position in sea power and for the proper protection of our coasts and of our officers and crews in battle, there is need for something more powerful than the present 16,000-ton battleship, with its 12-inch guns and insufficient armour, and that only the very foremost nations will be able to maintain really effective fleets.

"With the increase in size and power of new types of battleships and naval batteries may come the naval supremacy of America alone.

"Nations weak in battleships may hug the idea of commerce destroyers, but that barbarous system of waging war must be destroyed as were privateering and piracy. Commercial vessels are now built much larger than the largest battleships. But more powerful battleships are sure to be built and more powerful guns. Land fortifications cannot now be made sufficient to protect our ports.

"How dangerous will be the position of New York and other large cities when attacked by naval guns having a range of twenty miles or more if we do not provide adequate coast defence ships. What would the capture of all our foreign merchant vessels benefit an enemy or injure us as compared with the capture of one of our great cities by a hostile fleet!"

Mr. Stokes then described his invention in detail.

"One such semi-globular battery," said Mr. Stokes, "could defend or blockade an important strait; could protect the mouth of a transcontinental canal, or dominate almost any large seaport, and could safely resist more than a dozen of the largest battleships, which cost $7,500,000 apiece.

"As the purpose of the Cerberus is defence rather than aggression, it is not necessary that it be able to move rapidly from one place to another. Should the Cerberus need to move quickly to a distance, an armoured cruiser might find useful and safe employment in towing her. The two vessels might sometimes be used together as a small squadron. The roll of the Cerberus in a gale would be very slight.

"The naval Powers know the exact position of the large guns in our coast fortification, but the Cerberus could change its position.

"When the great struggle comes for the control of the Windward Passage, that key to the Caribbean and to the Panama Canal, which we may be called upon to defend, the existing type of battleships may be insufficient, and land fortifications and mines will not suffice, for the Windward Passage is wide and deep, as are also the other entrances to the Caribbean Sea."

Mr. Stokes concluded by saying he was planning a still large battery, with less draught and a larger number of guns.

The Korea Daily News.

Issued at 5 P. M. daily except Sundays.

Rate of Subscription :—
Per Year,............Yen 25.
Per Quarter,..........Yen 7.
Per Month,..........Yen 2.50.

Postage in Korea not charged extra.
Postage abroad charged extra.

Advertisements, 50 sen per day for 1 inch or less.
5 yen per month per inch.
50 yen per year per inch.

All communications to

E. T. BETHELL,
Editor and Publisher,
Pak-tong, Seoul.

RUMOURS.

The atmosphere in Seoul is very heavily charged with rumours of a coming discomfiture of the Japanese. We can only give the story for what it is worth but it is said that H. E. the Chinese Minister Mr. Seng Kwang Chwen has found fault with the Japanese policy in Korea and seems inclined to insist on a reversion to a state of affairs more in accordance with the terms of the Sino-Japanese treaty. Of the truth of this we know nothing but it is quite evident that if the Chinese Minister wishes to make a protest he has plenty of grounds for it.

The "Daito Shimpo," a Japanese organ, pretends, of course, to see Russia at the bottom of all this and further states that the people of Korea propose to presently rise and drive the Japanese out of the country.

In addition of this there are many rumours of heavy Japanese reverses in the north which are, on the face of them local inventions.

The Kong-chin-hoi, which is a society established in opposition to the Il-chin-hoi and which was, apparently, suppressed by the Japanese immediately after its inception, seems to have come to life again in a remarkable way and is very active in some of the provinces, and altogether there seem to be the makings of a very pretty kettle of fish in Korea.

This ebullition of anti-Japanese feeling is regrettable but by no means surprising. The Koreans have had a little over a year of Japanese ascendancy and it has been a year of mortification. To an unsuspicious mind the terms of the protocol signed on February 16th last year gave promise of an era of neighbourly assistance and brotherly love between the two countries, but in Japanese hands it has turned out to be a weapon for the wrecking of Korea. In the names of "reform" and "military necessity" demands followed each other so rapidly that the Koreans were driven to distraction, and besides this the Il-chin-hoi was started to accomplish what could not be done by virtue of the protocol.

If therefore a movement is on foot to destroy the Il-chin-hoi and all its works it has our complete approval and sympathy and our readers must also be aware that any proposal to keep the power of the Japanese within proper bounds will receive our hearty support.

But although the Koreans will be well within their rights in dispersing the Il-chin-hoi and demanding a strict adherence to the letter and spirit of the Protocol, they should stop at this, and bewa[illegible] of going to extremes. To the Japanes[illegible] mind, apparently, every one who is not pro-Japanese must be pro-Russian—that is at any rate what they pretend think. The "Daito Shi[illegible] alone in st[illegible]

movements here originate with some Koreans and the Russian Minister in Shanghai, and various French subjects and the French and Chinese Legations here have been in turn accused of acting in concert with the party in Shaughai.

Therefore, unless the Koreans wish to be treated as Russian spies, it is essential that they should move on strictly constitutional lines. By all means let them demand the dispersal of the Il-chin-hoi, which has been guilty of intimidation and espionage, and let the government yield no more to the Japanese, who have clearly shown that the welfare of the Koreans is not the principal object of their machinations.

Any action outside of these limits will put the Koreans in an entirely false position and the condition of the country would become more chaotic than ever.

FRANCE'S FOREIGN MINISTER.

Few modern statesmen have enjoyed happier moments than M. Delcassé, the French Minister for Foreign Affairs. He had a larger share in concluding the Franco-Russian alliance than anyone else, and that instrument which, five years ago, was the most powerful factor in the preservation of the peace of Europe, is still, as he loves to declare, the pivot of French foreign policy. It was M. Delcassé who was the first French statesman to welcome with outstreched arms King Edward's offer of mutual toleration, trust, and esteem two years ago. It does not require a very lively imagination to picture M. Delcassé's delight on that Sunday afternoon in the spring of 1903, when the sovereign of the British Empire was his guest at the Quai d'Orsai. M. Delcassé's pride could not have been less keen when he found himself presiding at a Foreign Office luncheon given in honor of Vice-Admiral Sir Lewis Beaumont, Admiral Fournier, and Admiral Kaznakoff.

M. Delcassé is the one indispensable Minister his country possesses. A substitute could be found even for M. Rouvier, one of the ablest masters of finance now living. But it is hard to imgine a French administration without the shrewd, silent, and successful statesman who has guided the foreign policy of France since M. Hanotaux left office on the eve of the Fashoda crisis. His rise to fame has been meteoric. A very few years ago he was a lobby journalist, who used to waylay Ministers in the Salle des Pas Perdus. An insignificant figure with penetrating eyes and a demeanour always polite and deferential, he came from the Middle-West if one may thus Americanise south-western France, and was invariably known by the nickname of "Le Pou" (flea). As a matter of fact, he has ever since been ca[illegible] insect in some form [illegible] graphs w[illegible] tion. T[illegible] spirati[illegible] hims[illegible] or[illegible]

To-day no living Foreign Minister can show such a record of triumphant statesmanship. He has raised France from the depths of despair and compelled recognition and respect for her among all the chancelleries of the world. [illegible] heard an English publicist say not lo[illegible] ago that Delcasse was not a great statesman so much as a clever diplomat with [illegible] quick eye for seeing the main chan[illegible]e, and a capacity for surrendering non-essentials. The difference is probably not material.

The most rem[illegible]able of M. Delcasse's achievements is undoubtedly the isolation of Germany. His French critics taunt him with excess of zeal in courting the friendship of Englan[illegible]d and [illegible] to say nothing of the United States. But they studiously ignore the fact that the Franco-Italian entente has virtually broken up the Triple Alliance, which the ardent French Nationalists find it convenient to forget, was aimed against France. The world now talks of th[illegible] isolation not of Great Britain but o[illegible] Germany. That is a feat well calculated to help France to bury in oblivion the tear-stained memories of "Soixante-dix."

THE FRONT.

Fighting is now evidently proceeding on in all directions but it is impossible to gather any clear idea of what is going on from the reports which are telegraphed over here.

On the extreme left the Japanese seem to have made good progress, having driven the Russians from Changtan and Szfangtai, which places are to the west of the Hun river in the same latitude as Shahopao. In the centre there se[illegible] be no change but the right [illegible] reported some progress [illegible] Away on the [illegible] direction [illegible] [illegible]nking, said to b[illegible] steadily retreat [illegible] The Jap[illegible]anese se[illegible] to have taken [illegible] Russians by surpri[illegible] here as not only [illegible]ve they advanced a co[illegible]iderable arm in this direction but they seem to h[illegible] established communication between it and the main army at Penshu. [illegible]sumably a light railway has been [illegible]ilt between these two points as an an[illegible]wer to that which Kuropatkin recentl[illegible] constructed between Fushun and Sinking.

These reports do not however appear appear to carry us any further than the 3rd instant and as they refer more to small detachments than to the main army it would seem that we shall have to wait some time for news of the reall[illegible] decisive engagement.

In the meantime, the weather conditions seem as bad ever again. Snow fell steadily during the last week of February and the ground is covered to a depth of over twelve inches.

We never hear of a war without someone inventing a bullet-proof coat. A Japan[illegible] [illegible]nventor is the latest to go and do

[illegible] seem to hint that [illegible] east, south [illegible] decid[illegible]

The Korea Daily News.

VOL. II, WEDNE[illegible]Y, MA[illegible]H 8, 1905. No. 52

대한매일신보 1

인쇄일: 2023년 06월 15일
발행일: 2023년 06월 25일
지은이: 편집부
발행인: 윤영수
발행처: 한국학자료원
서울시 구로구 개봉본동 170-30
전화: 02-3159-8050 팩스: 02-3159-8051
문의: 010-4799-9729
등록번호: 제312-1999-074호

정가 350,000원